THE NEW
COLLINS
DICTIONARY
AND
THESAURUS
IN ONE VOLUME

THE NEW
COLLINS
DICTIONARY
AND
THESAURUS
IN ONE VOLUME

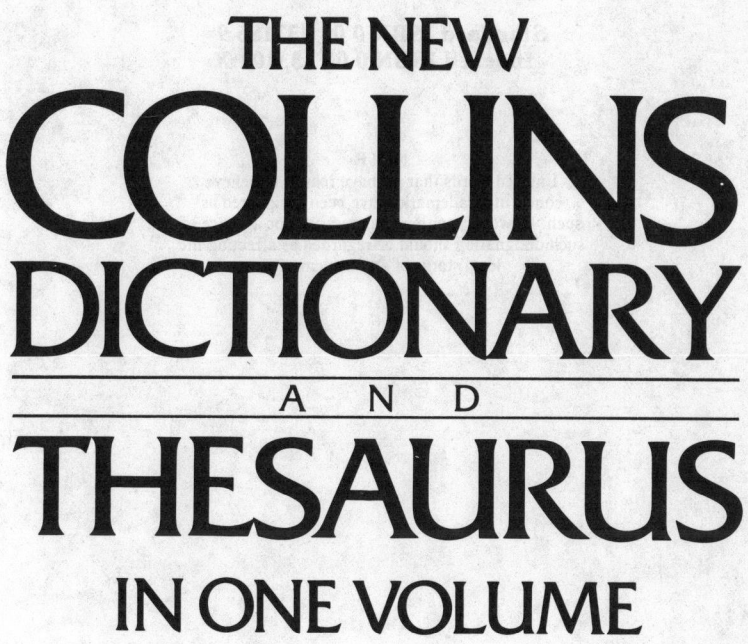

THE NEW
COLLINS
DICTIONARY
AND
THESAURUS
IN ONE VOLUME

MANAGING EDITOR
William T McLeod

COLLINS
LONDON & GLASGOW

First published in this edition 1987
Reprinted 1988 (twice)
© 1986, 1987 William Collins Sons & Co Ltd

Standard ISBN 0 00 433186 9
Indexed ISBN 0 00 433101 X

NOTE
Entered words that we have reason to believe
constitute trademarks have been designated as
such. However, neither the presence nor absence of
such designation should be regarded as affecting the
legal status of any trademarks.

Computer typeset by C R Barber & Partners,
Wrotham, England.

Manufactured for
William Collins Sons & Co Ltd
P O Box, Glasgow G4 0NB

FOREWORD

Here for the first time in one handy volume the reader is offered a general-purpose Dictionary and a Thesaurus in dictionary form, conveniently arranged so that the relevant material from each appears on the same page, an arrangement made possible by modern computer data handling techniques. Meanings, spelling, pronunciation, usage, and a wide range of substitutable words and phrases are instantly available without the need to consult a second volume or indeed to search in other parts of the same volume.

The Dictionary in this volume is derived from the authoritative *Collins English Dictionary* and, with over one million words of text and 71,000 references, is a substantial work that provides a balanced, modern survey of contemporary English, fully related to today's needs.

The Thesaurus element is derived from the successful *New Collins Thesaurus* and gives practical and accessible help to the writer or speaker who wants to find a better word to replace one that is not quite right for his purpose.

Because the two parts march in step from page to page the user can go straight to the word he requires in either case and easily move from Dictionary to Thesaurus and back again.

Nor must the crossword addict be forgotten. Every crossword solver will find this combined volume a unique crossword aid.

The range of information provided and the convenience of the arrangement make this the ideal companion for all who wish to exercise or increase their language skills.

W.T.M.

USING THE DICTIONARY AND THESAURUS

The following Notes are provided to help the reader to use this combined volume more efficiently and to find what he is looking for more quickly.

THE DICTIONARY

1. Order of definitions

As a general rule, when a word has more than one meaning, the one commonest in current use is placed first. Subsequent definitions are arranged so as to give a full and coherent account of the meaning. Technical meanings usually follow general meanings; old and obsolete meanings follow technical meanings; idioms and phrases are generally placed last. But note that fixed noun phrases and certain other invariable idioms like *dark horse, mail order,* and *mind's eye* are given full headword status.

2. Units

In accordance with the recommendations of the International Standards Organization, all scientific measurements are given in SI units (*Système International d'Unités*). Measurements and quantities in more traditional units are often given as well.

3. Abbreviations, etc.

Abbreviations, acronyms, and symbols are treated as entries in their alphabetical order.

4. Parts of speech

In addition to the traditional parts of speech — adjective, adverb, conjunction, interjection, noun, preposition, pronoun, verb — the following less traditional parts of speech have been adopted to give additional precision.

determiner. This denotes such words as *the, a, some, any, that, this,* possessives like *my, his,* and *your,* and the numerals. Many determiners can have a pronoun function without change of meaning, and this is shown thus:

some (sʌm; *unstressed* səm) *determiner.* . . . **2.a.** an unknown or unspecified quantity or amount of: *he owns some horses.* **b.** (*as pronoun; functioning as sing. or pl.*): *we'll buy some.* . . .

sentence connector. This denotes words like *however* and *therefore* which have been traditionally classed as adverbs but which function as conjunctions, linking sentences, without being restricted, as are conjunctions, to the initial position in their clause.

sentence substitute. Sentence substitutes comprise words such as *yes, no, perhaps, definitely,* and *maybe,* which can stand as meaningful utterances by themselves.

5. Additional information

(i) Some adjectives and determiners are restricted by usage to a particular position relative to the nouns they qualify. This is indicated by the following labels:

postpositive (used predicatively or after the noun, but not before the noun):

ablaze (ə'bleɪz) *adj.* (*postpositive*), *adv.* **1.** on fire; burning. . . .

immediately postpositive (always used immediately following the noun qualified and never used predicatively):

galore (gə'lɔː) *determiner.* (*immediately postpositive*) *Inf.* in great numbers or quantity: *there were daffodils galore in the park.* . . .

prenominal (used before the noun, and never used predicatively):

chief (tʃiːf) . . . ~*adj.* **3.** (*prenominal*) **a.** most important; principal. **b.** highest in rank or authority.

(ii) Adjectives and adverbs that perform an exclusively intensifying function, with no addition of meaning, are described as (intensifier) without further explanation.

blooming ('bluːmɪŋ) *adv., adj. Brit. inf.* (intensifier): *a blooming genius; blooming painful.* . . .

(iii) A noun that is commonly used with adjectival force is labelled *modifier.*
If the sense of the modifier is strictly inferable from the sense of the noun, the modifier is shown without further explanation, with an example to illustrate its use; otherwise an account of its meaning and/or usage is given in a separate numbered definition.

key[1] (kiː) *n.* . . . **18.** (*modifier*) of great importance: *a key issue.* . . .

(iv) Verbal constructions consisting of a verb and a preposition or adverb are given as main entries in their alphabetical place if the meaning cannot be deduced from the separate meanings of the component parts. Examples are: *play up, take for, take on, take up.*

(v) *Derog.* (*Derogatory*). This label implies that the connotations of a word are unpleasant with intent on the part of the speaker or writer.

(vi) *Offens.* (*Offensive*). This label indicates that a word may be regarded as offensive by the person described or referred to, even if the speaker uses the word without any malicious intention.

6. Listed entries

In English many words are formed by adding productive prefixes such as *non-*, *over-*, *un-*, etc., to existing words. In most cases, the meanings of these words are obvious. A selection of such words is listed alphabetically, without further explanation at the foot of the page on which the prefix in question is entered as a headword and on following pages if necessary.

7. Usage notes

A brief note introduced by the label **Usage** and the marginal sign ▷ has been added at the end of a number of entries in order to comment on matters of usage. These comments are based on the observed practice or preference of the majority of educated speakers and writers.

THE THESAURUS

1. Under each main entry word, the synonyms are arranged alphabetically. When a word has distinctly separate meanings, separate numbered lists are given for the different senses.

2. Where it is desirable to distinguish between different parts of speech, labels have been added as follows: *n.* (noun), *v.* (verb), *adj.* (adjective), *adv.* (adverb), *pron.* (pronoun), *conj.* (conjunction), *prep.* (preposition), *interj.* (interjection). See entries for *living, loaf, loan, lob, local*.

3. Usually the synonyms for a particular part of speech are grouped together. Thus, in the entry

catch synonyms for all the verb senses are given first, followed by synonyms for all the noun senses. Sometimes, however, noun and verb functions are very closely associated in specific meanings, and where this is the case the synonyms are grouped by meanings, as in the entry for *cover*.

4. When a headword has more than one meaning *and* can function as more than one part of speech, a new part-of-speech function is shown by a large swung dash (∼), as in the entry for *glance* or *grasp*.

5. Much-used phrases appear as main entries; for instance, *act for* comes after *act*. Expressions such as *a priori* or *en route* are also given as main entries within the alphabetical listing. Short idiomatic phrases are entered under their key word and are to be found either at the end of the entry or immediately following the sense with which they are associated. Thus, the phrase *take a dim view* appears as sense 7 of the entry *dim*, since the synonyms in sense 6 most closely approximate to the meaning of the phrase.

6. Plural forms that have a distinctly separate meaning, such as *provisions*, are entered at their own alphabetical position, while those with a less distinct difference, such as *appurtenances*, are given as a separate sense under the singular form, e.g. *appurtenance ... 2. Plural ...*

7. Words formed with a negative prefix (im-, in-, un-, etc.) are not always entered in the section on Antonyms, (pp. 557 ff.) as antonyms for such items can readily be found among the *synonyms* for the positive form; e.g., antonyms for *imperfect* can be found among the synonyms for *perfect*.

8. A label in brackets applies only to the synonym preceding it while one which is not bracketed relates to the whole of that particular sense. Labels have been abbreviated when a readily understandable shortened form exists, such as *Sl.* (Slang), *Inf.* (Informal), and *Fig.* (Figurative).

PRONUNCIATION KEY

The pronunciations shown for the vocabulary of standard English are those common in educated British English speech. The symbols used are those of the International Phonetic Alphabet. The following consonant symbols have their usual English values: *b, d, f, h, k, l, m, n, p, r, s, t, v, w, z*. The remaining symbols and their interpretations are listed below. Though they may appear strange at first, a little practice soon makes their use perfectly familiar. The gain in precision and lack of ambiguity repay the degree of effort involved.

Stress

Three grades of stress are shown in the transcriptions by the presence or absence of marks placed immediately *before* the affected syllable. Primary or strong stress is shown by ', while secondary or weak stress is shown by ˌ. Unstressed syllables are not marked. In *photographic* (ˌfəutəˈgræfɪk), for example, the first syllable carries secondary stress and the third primary stress, while the second and fourth are unstressed.

Notes

(i) Though words like *castle, path, fast* are shown as pronounced with an /ɑː/ sound, many speakers use an /æ/. Such variations are acceptable and are to be assumed by the reader.

(ii) The letter "r" in some positions is not sounded in the speech of Southern England and elsewhere. However, many speakers in other areas do sound the "r" in such positions with varying degrees of distinctness. Again, such variations are to be assumed, and in such words as *fern, fear, arm* the reader will sound or not sound the "r" according to his speech habits.

(iii) Though the widely received pronunciation of words like *which, why* is with a simple /w/ sound and is so shown in the dictionary, many speakers, in Scotland and elsewhere, preserve an aspirated sound: /hw/. Once again this variation is to be assumed.

English Sounds

ɑː as in *father* ('fɑːðə), *alms* (ɑːmz), *clerk* (klɑːk)

æ as in *act* (ækt), *rat* (ræt), *plait* (plæt)

aɪ as in *dive* (daɪv), *aisle* (aɪl), *guy* (gaɪ)

aɪə as in *fire* (faɪə), *buyer* ('baɪə), *liar* ('laɪə), *tyre* (taɪə)

aʊ as in *out* (aʊt), *bough* (baʊ), *crowd* (kraʊd)

aʊə as in *flour* ('flaʊə), *cower* ('kaʊə), *flower* ('flaʊə)

ɛ as in *bet* (bɛt), *ate* (ɛt), *bury* ('bɛrɪ), *heifer* ('hɛfə)

eɪ as in *paid* (peɪd), *day* (deɪ), *gauge* (geɪdʒ)

ɛə as in *bear* (bɛə), *dare* (dɛə), *stairs* (stɛəz)

---

g as in *get* (gɛt), *ghoul* (guːl), *guard* (gɑːd)

ɪ as in *pretty* ('prɪtɪ), *build* (bɪld), *busy* ('bɪzɪ), *nymph* (nɪmf), *pocket* ('pɒkɪt), *seive* (sɪv)

iː as in *see* (siː), *aesthete* ('iːsθiːt), *evil* ('iːvᵊl), *magazine* (ˌmægəˈziːn), *receive* (rɪˈsiːv)

ɪə as in *fear* (fɪə), *beer* (bɪə), *mere* (mɪə), *tier* (tɪə)

j as in *yes* (jɛs), *onion* ('ʌnjən), *vignette* (vɪˈnjɛt)

ɒ as in *pot* (pɒt), *botch* (bɒtʃ), *sorry* ('sɒrɪ)

əʊ as in *note* (nəʊt), *beau* (bəʊ), *dough* (dəʊ)

ɔː as in *thaw* (θɔː), *broad* (brɔːd), *drawer* ('drɔːə)

ɔɪ as in *void* (vɔɪd), *boy* (bɔɪ), *destroy* (dɪˈstrɔɪ)

ʊ as in *pull* (pʊl), *good* (gʊd), *should* (ʃʊd)

uː as in *zoo* (zuː), *do* (duː), *queue* (kjuː), *shoe* (ʃuː)

ʊə as in *poor* (pʊə), *skewer* ('skjʊə), *sure* (ʃʊə)

ə as in *potter* ('pɒtə), *alone* (əˈləʊn), *the* (ðə)

ɜː as in *fern* (fɜːn), *burn* (bɜːn), *fir* (fɜː)

ʌ as in *cut* (kʌt), *flood* (flʌd), *rough* (rʌf), *son* (sʌn)

ʃ as in *ship* (ʃɪp), *election* (ɪˈlɛkʃən), *machine* (məˈʃiːn), *mission* ('mɪʃən), *pressure* ('prɛʃə)

ʒ as in *treasure* ('trɛʒə), *azure* ('æʒə), *closure* ('kləʊʒə), *evasion* (ɪˈveɪʒən)

tʃ as in *chew* (tʃuː), *nature* ('neɪtʃə)

dʒ as in *jaw* (dʒɔː), *adjective* ('ædʒɪktɪv), *lodge* (lɒdʒ), *soldier* ('səʊldʒə), *usage* ('juːsɪdʒ)

θ as in *thin* (θɪn), *strength* (strɛŋθ), *three* (θriː)

ð as in *these* (ðiːz), *bathe* (beɪð), *lather* ('lɑːðə)

ŋ as in *sing* (sɪŋ), *finger* ('fɪŋgə), *sling* (slɪŋ)

x as in Scottish *loch* (lɒx)

ᵊ indicates that the following consonant (*l* or *n*) is syllabic, as in *bundle* ('bʌndᵊl), *button* ('bʌtᵊn)

Foreign Sounds

The preceding symbols are also used to represent foreign sounds where these are similar to English sounds. However, certain common foreign sounds require symbols with markedly different values, as follows:

a *a* in French *ami*, German *Mann*, Italian *pasta:* a sound between English (æ) and (ɑː).

ɑ *a* as in French *bas:* similar to English (ɑː), but shorter.

e *é* in French *été, eh* in German *sehr, e* in Italian *che:* a sound similar to the Scottish vowel in *day*.

i   *i* in French *il,* German *Idee,* Spanish *filo,* Italian *signor:* similar to English (i:), but shorter.

ɔ   *o* in Italian *no,* French *bonne,* German *Sonne:* a vowel resembling English (ɒ), but with a higher tongue position and more rounding of the lips.

o   *o* in French *rose,* German *so,* Italian *voce:* similar to the Scottish vowel in *so.*

u   *ou* in French *genou, u* in German *kulant,* Spanish *puna:* similar to English (u:), but shorter.

y   *u* in French *tu, ü* in German *über:* similar to English (i:) but made with closely rounded lips.

ø   *eu* in French *deux, ö* in German *schön:* similar to (e) but made with closely rounded lips.

œ   *œu* in French *œuf, ö* in German *zwölf:* similar to English (ɛ) but made with open rounded lips.

~   above a vowel indicates nasalization, as in French *un* (œ̃), *bon* (bɔ̃), *vin* (vɛ̃), *blanc* (blã).

x   *ch* in German *Buch, j* in Spanish *Juan.*

ç   *ch* in German *ich:* similar to the first sound in *huge.*

β   *b* in Spanish *Habana:* similar to (v), but made by the two lips.

ʎ   *ll* in Spanish *llamar, gl* in Italian *consiglio:* similar to the (lj) sequence in *million.*

ɥ   *u* in French *lui:* a short (y).

ɲ   *gn* in French *vigne,* Italian *gnocchi, ñ* in Spanish *España:* similar to the (nj) sequence in *onion.*

ɣ   *g* in Spanish *luego:* a weak (g) made with voiced friction.

Length

The symbol : denotes length and is shown together with certain vowel symbols when the vowels are typically long.

ABBREVIATIONS USED

abbrev. abbreviation
adj. adjective
adv. adverb(ial)
Anat. Anatomy
approx. approximate(ly)
Arch. Archaic
Archaeol. Archaeology
Archit. Architecture
Astrol. Astrology
Astron. Astronomy
Austral. Australian

Biol. Biology
Bot. Botany
Brit. Britain; British

°C degrees Celsius
Canad. Canadian
cap. capital
cf. compare
Chem. Chemistry
comp. comparative
conj. conjunction

Derog. Derogatory
dim. diminutive

E east(ern)
Econ. Economics
e.g. for example
esp. especially

fem. feminine
foll. followed

Geog. Geography
Geol. Geology
Geom. Geometry

i.e. that is
imit. of imitative origin
Inf. Informal
interj. interjection
intr. intransitive

lit. literally

masc. masculine
Maths. Mathematics
Med. Medicine
Mil. Military
Myth. Mythology

N north(ern)
n. noun
Naut. Nautical
NE northeast(ern)
no. number
NW northwest(ern)
N.Z. New Zealand

Obs. Obsolete
Offens. Offensive
orig. originally

Photog. Photography
pl. plural
p.p. past participle
prep. preposition(al)
prob. probably
pron. pronoun
Psychol. Psychology
p.t. past tense

rel. related

S south(ern)
S. African South African
Scot. Scottish; Scots
SE southeast(ern)
sing. singular
Sl. Slang
sup. superlative
SW southwest(ern)

Theol. Theology
tr. transitive

U.S. United States

var. variant
vb. verb

W west(ern)
wt. weight

Zool. Zoology

A

a *or* **A** (eɪ) *n., pl.* **a's, A's,** *or* **As. 1.** the first letter and first vowel of the English alphabet. **2.** any of several speech sounds represented by this letter, as in *take, bag,* or *calm.* **3.** Also called: **alpha.** the first in a series, esp. the highest mark. **4. from A to Z.** from start to finish.

a (ə; *emphatic* eɪ) *determiner.* (*indefinite article;* used before an initial consonant. Cf. **an**[1]) **1.** used preceding a singular countable noun, not previously specified: *a dog; a terrible disappointment.* **2.** used preceding a noun or determiner of quantity: *a dozen eggs; a great many; to read a lot.* **3.** (preceded by *once, twice, several times,* etc.) each or every; per: *once a day.* **4.** a certain; one: *a Mr. Jones called.* **5.** (preceded by *not*) any at all: *not a hope.* ~Cf. **the**[1].

A *symbol for:* **1.** *Music.* **a.** the sixth note of the scale of C major. **b.** the major or minor key having this note as its tonic. **2.** a human blood type of the ABO group, containing the A antigen. **3.** (in Britain) a major arterial road. **4.** (in Britain, formerly) a film certified for viewing by anyone, but which contains material that some parents may not wish their children to see. **5.** ampere(s). **6.** absolute (temperature). **7.** area. **8.** (*in combination*) atomic: *an A-bomb; an A-plant.*

a. *abbrev. for:* **1.** acre(s). **2.** Also **A.** alto. **3.** answer. **4.** are(s) (metric measure of land).

A. *abbrev. for:* **1.** acre(s). **2.** America(n). **3.** answer.

a-[1] *or before a vowel* **an-** *prefix.* not; without; opposite to: *atonal; asocial.*

a-[2] *prefix.* **1.** on; in; towards: *aground; aback.* **2.** in the state of: *afloat; asleep.*

A1, A-1, *or* **A-one** ('eɪ'wʌn) *adj.* **1.** physically fit. **2.** *Inf.* first class; excellent. **3.** (of a vessel) in first-class condition.

A4 *n.* a standard paper size, 297 × 210 mm.

AA *abbrev. for:* **1.** Alcoholics Anonymous. **2.** antiaircraft. **3.** (in Britain) Automobile Association.

A.A.A. *abbrev. for:* **1.** *Brit.* Amateur Athletic Association. **2.** *U.S.* Automobile Association of America.

A & R *abbrev. for* artists and repertoire.

AAP *abbrev. for* Australian Associated Press.

aardvark ('ɑːdˌvɑːk) *n.* a nocturnal burrowing African mammal, which has long ears and snout, and feeds on termites. Also called: **ant bear.**

Aaron's beard ('ɛərənz) *n.* another name for **rose of Sharon.**

AB *symbol for* a human blood type of the ABO group, containing both the A antigen and the B antigen.

A.B. *abbrev. for:* **1.** Also: **a.b.** able-bodied seaman. **2.** (in the U.S.) Bachelor of Arts.

ab-[1] *prefix.* away from; opposite to: *abnormal.*

ab-[2] *prefix.* a cgs unit of measurement in the electromagnetic system: *abampere, abwatt, abvolt.*

aba ('æbə) *n.* **1.** a type of cloth from Syria, made of goat or camel hair. **2.** a sleeveless outer garment of such cloth.

aback (ə'bæk) *adv.* **taken aback. a.** startled or disconcerted. **b.** *Naut.* (of a vessel or sail) having the wind against the forward side so as to prevent forward motion.

abacus ('æbəkəs) *n., pl.* **-ci** (-ˌsaɪ) *or* **-cuses. 1.** a counting device that consists of a frame holding rods on which a number of beads are free to move. **2.** *Archit.* the flat upper part of the capital of a column.

abaft (ə'bɑːft) *Naut.* ~*adv., adj.* (*postpositive*) **1.** closer to the stern than to another place on a vessel. ~*prep.* **2.** behind; aft of.

abalone (ˌæbə'ləʊnɪ) *n.* an edible marine mollusc having an ear-shaped shell perforated with a row of respiratory holes and lined with mother-of-pearl. Also called: **ear shell.**

abandon (ə'bændən) *vb.* (*tr.*) **1.** to forsake completely; desert; leave behind. **2.** to give up completely: *to abandon hope.* **3.** to give up (something begun) before completion: *the game was abandoned.* **4.** to surrender (oneself) to emotion without restraint. **5.** to give (insured property that has suffered partial loss or damage) to the insurers in order that a claim for a total loss may be made. ~*n.* **6.** freedom from inhibitions, restraint, or worry: *she danced with abandon.* —a'**bandonment** *n.*

abandoned (ə'bændənd) *adj.* **1.** deserted: *an abandoned windmill.* **2.** forsaken: *an abandoned child.* **3.** uninhibited.

abase (ə'beɪs) *vb.* (*tr.*) **1.** to humble or belittle (oneself, etc.). **2.** to lower or reduce, as in rank. —a'**basement** *n.*

abash (ə'bæʃ) *vb.* (*tr.; usually passive*) to cause to feel ill at ease, embarrassed, or confused. —a'**bashed** *adj.*

abate (ə'beɪt) *vb.* **1.** to make or become less in amount, intensity, degree, etc. **2.** (*tr.*) *Law.* **a.** to suppress, or terminate (a nuisance). **b.** to suspend or extinguish (a claim or action). **c.** to annul (a writ). **3.** (*intr.*) *Law.* (of a writ, etc.) to become null and void. —a'**batement** *n.*

abattoir ('æbəˌtwɑː) *n.* another name for **slaughterhouse.**

abbacy ('æbəsɪ) *n., pl.* **-cies.** the office, term of office, or jurisdiction of an abbot or abbess.

abbé ('æbeɪ) *n.* **1.** a French abbot. **2.** a title used in addressing any other French cleric, such as a priest.

abbess ('æbɪs) *n.* the female superior of a convent.

abbey ('æbɪ) *n.* **1.** a building inhabited by a community of monks or nuns. **2.** a church built in conjunction with such a building. **3.** a community of monks or nuns.

abbot ('æbət) *n.* the superior of an abbey of monks. —'**abbotˌship** *or* '**abbotcy** *n.*

abbr. *or* **abbrev.** *abbrev. for:* **1.** abbreviation. **2.** abbreviated.

abbreviate (ə'briːvɪˌeɪt) *vb.* (*tr.*) **1.** to shorten (a word or phrase) by contraction or omission of some letters or words. **2.** to cut short; curtail. —abˌbrevi'**ation** *n.*

▰ THESAURUS ▰

abaft *Nautical* aft, astern, behind

abandon *v.* **1.** desert, forsake, jilt, leave, leave behind **2.** evacuate, quit, vacate, withdraw from **3.** abdicate, cede, give up, relinquish, renounce, resign, surrender, waive, yield **4.** desist, discontinue, drop, forgo ~*n.* **5.** careless freedom, dash, recklessness, unrestraint, wantonness, wild impulse, wildness

abandoned 1. cast aside, cast away, cast out, derelict, deserted, discarded, dropped, forlorn, forsaken, jilted, left, neglected, outcast, rejected, relinquished, unoccupied, vacant **2.** corrupt, debauched, depraved, dissipated, dissolute, profligate, reprobate, sinful, wanton, wicked **3.** uncontrolled, uninhibited, unrestrained, wild

abandonment 1. dereliction, desertion, forsaking, jilting, leaving **2.** evacuation, quitting, withdrawal from **3.** abdication, cession,

giving up, relinquishment, renunciation, resignation, surrender, waiver **4.** desistance, discontinuation, dropping

abase belittle, bring low, cast down, debase, degrade, demean, demote, depress, disgrace, dishonour, downgrade, humble, humiliate, lower, mortify, reduce

abasement belittlement, debasement, degradation, demotion, depression, disgrace, dishonour, downgrading, humbling, humiliation, lowering, mortification, reduction, shame

abashed affronted, ashamed, astounded, bewildered, chagrined, confounded, confused, discomfited, discomposed, disconcerted, discountenanced, dismayed, embarrassed, humbled, humiliated, mortified, perturbed, shamefaced, taken aback

abate 1. alleviate, appease, attenuate, decline, decrease, diminish, dull, dwindle, ease, ebb, fade, lessen, let up, mitigate, moderate, quell, reduce, relieve, sink, slacken, slake, slow, subside, taper off, wane, weaken **2.** deduct, discount, subtract

abatement 1. alleviation, allowance, attenuation, cessation, decline, decrease, diminution, dulling, dwindling, easing, extenuation, fading, lessening, let-up (*Inf.*), mitigation, moderation, quelling, reduction, relief, remission, slackening, slaking, slowing, tapering off, waning, weakening **2.** deduction, discount, subtraction

abbey cloister, convent, friary, monastery, nunnery, priory

abbreviate abridge, abstract, clip, compress, condense, contract, curtail, cut, digest, epitomize, précis, reduce, shorten, summa-

ABC n. 1. (often pl. in U.S.) the alphabet. 2. (pl. in U.S.) the rudiments of a subject. 3. an alphabetical guide.

abdicate ('æbdɪˌkeɪt) vb. to renounce (a throne, responsibility, rights, etc.), esp. formally. —ˌabdi'cation n. —'abdiˌcator n.

abdomen ('æbdəmən) n. 1. the region of the body of a vertebrate that contains the viscera other than the heart and lungs. 2. the front or surface of this region· belly. 3. (in arthropods) the posterior part of the body behind the thorax. —**abdominal** (æb'dɒmɪnəl) adj.

abduct (æb'dʌkt) vb. (tr.) 1. to remove (a person) by force or cunning; kidnap. 2. (of certain muscles) to pull away (a leg, arm, etc.) from the median axis of the body. —ab'duction n. —ab'ductor n.

abeam (ə'biːm) adv., adj. (postpositive) at right angles to the length of a vessel or aircraft.

abed (ə'bɛd) adv. Arch. in bed.

Aberdeen Angus ('æbədiːn 'æŋgəs) n. a black hornless breed of beef cattle originating in Scotland.

aberration (ˌæbə'reɪʃən) n. 1. deviation from what is normal, expected, or usual. 2. departure from truth, morality, etc. 3. a lapse in control of one's mental faculties. 4. Optics. a defect in a lens or mirror that causes either a distorted image or one with coloured fringes. 5. Astron. the apparent displacement of a celestial body due to the motion of the observer with the earth.

abet (ə'bɛt) vb. abetting, abetted. (tr.) to assist or encourage, esp. in wrongdoing. —a'betment n. —a'bettor or a'better n.

abeyance (ə'beɪəns) n. 1. (usually preceded by in or into) a state of being suspended or put aside temporarily. 2. (usually preceded by in) Law. an indeterminate state of ownership.

abhor (əb'hɔː) vb. -horring, -horred. (tr.) to detest vehemently; find repugnant. —ab'horrence n. —ab'horrer n.

abhorrent (əb'hɒrənt) adj. 1. repugnant; loathsome. 2. (when postpositive, foll. by of) feeling extreme aversion (for): abhorrent of vulgarity. 3. (usually postpositive and foll. by to) conflicting (with): abhorrent to common sense.

abide (ə'baɪd) vb. abiding, abode or abided. 1. (tr.) to tolerate; put up with. 2. (tr.) to accept or submit to. 3. (intr.; foll. by by) a. to comply (with): to abide by the decision. b. to remain faithful (to): to abide by your promise. 4. (intr.) to remain or continue. 5. (intr.) Arch. to dwell. 6. (tr.) Arch. to await in expectation.

—a'bider n.

abiding (ə'baɪdɪŋ) adj. permanent; enduring: an abiding belief.

ability (ə'bɪlɪtɪ) n., pl. -ties. 1. possession of necessary skill, competence, or power. 2. considerable proficiency; natural capability: a man of ability. 3. (pl.) special talents.

abject ('æbdʒɛkt) adj. 1. utterly wretched or hopeless. 2. forlorn; dejected. 3. submissive: an abject apology. 4. contemptible; despicable: an abject liar. —ab'jection n. —'abjectly adv. —'abjectness n.

abjure (əb'dʒʊə) vb. (tr.) 1. to renounce or retract, esp. formally or under oath. 2. to abstain from. —ˌabju'ration n. —ab'jurer n.

ablation (æb'leɪʃən) n. 1. the surgical removal of an organ, structure, or part. 2. the melting or wearing away of a part, such as the heat shield of a space re-entry vehicle on passing through the earth's atmosphere. 3. the wearing away of a rock or glacier. —**ablate** (æb'leɪt) vb. (tr.)

ablative ('æblətɪv) Grammar. ~adj. 1. (in certain inflected languages such as Latin) denoting a case of nouns, pronouns, and adjectives indicating the agent, or the instrument, manner, or place of the action. ~n. 2. the ablative case or a speech element in it.

ablaut ('æblaut) n. Linguistics. vowel gradation, esp. in Indo-European languages. See **gradation** (sense 5).

ablaze (ə'bleɪz) adj. (postpositive), adv. 1. on fire; burning. 2. brightly illuminated. 3. emotionally aroused.

able ('eɪbl) adj. 1. (postpositive) having the necessary power, resources, skill, opportunity, etc., to do something. 2. capable; talented. 3. Law. competent or authorized.

-able suffix forming adjectives. 1. capable of or deserving of (being acted upon as indicated): enjoyable; washable. 2. inclined to; able to; causing: comfortable; variable. —**-ably** suffix forming adverbs. —**-ability** suffix forming nouns.

able-bodied adj. physically strong and healthy; robust.

able-bodied seaman n. a seaman, esp. one in the merchant navy, who has been trained in certain skills. Also: **able seaman**. Abbrev.: **A.B., a.b.**

able rating n. (esp. in the Royal Navy) a rating who is qualified to perform certain duties of seamanship.

ablution (ə'bluːʃən) n. 1. the ritual washing of a priest's hands or of sacred vessels. 2. (often pl.) the act of washing: perform one's ablutions. 3. (pl.) Mil. inf. latrines.

THESAURUS

rize, trim, truncate

abbreviation abridgment, abstract, clipping, compendium, compression, condensation, conspectus, contraction, curtailment, digest, epitome, précis, reduction, résumé, shortening, summary, synopsis, trimming, truncation

abdicate abandon, abjure, abnegate, cede, forgo, give up, quit, relinquish, renounce, resign, retire, surrender, vacate, waive, yield

abdication abandonment, abjuration, abnegation, cession, giving up, quitting, relinquishment, renunciation, resignation, retiral (esp. Scot.), retirement, surrender, waiver, yielding

abdominal gastric, intestinal, stomachic, stomachical, visceral

abduct carry off, kidnap, make off with, run away with, run off with, seize, snatch (Sl.)

abduction carrying off, kidnapping, seizure

aberration 1. aberrancy, abnormality, anomaly, defect, deviation, divergence, eccentricity, irregularity, lapse, oddity, peculiarity, quirk, rambling, straying, wandering 2. delusion, hallucination, illusion, instability, mental disorder, vagary

abet 1. aid, assist, back, condone, connive at, help, promote, sanction, second, succour, support, sustain, uphold 2. egg on, encourage, incite, prompt, spur, urge

abeyance 1. adjournment, deferral, dis-

continuation, inactivity, intermission, postponement, recess, reservation, suspense, suspension, waiting 2. **in abeyance** hanging fire, on ice (Inf.), pending, shelved, suspended

abhor abominate, detest, execrate, hate, loathe, recoil from, regard with repugnance or horror, shrink from, shudder at

abhorrent abominable, detestable, disgusting, distasteful, execrable, hated, hateful, heinous, horrible, horrid, loathsome, obnoxious, odious, offensive, repellent, repugnant, repulsive, revolting

abide 1. accept, bear, brook, endure, put up with, stand, stomach, submit to, suffer, tolerate 2. dwell, linger, live, lodge, reside, rest, sojourn, stay, stop, tarry, wait 3. continue, endure, last, persist, remain, survive

abide by 1. acknowledge, agree to, comply with, conform to, follow, obey, observe, submit to 2. adhere to, carry out, discharge, fulfil, hold to, keep to, persist in, stand by

abiding constant, continuing, durable, enduring, eternal, everlasting, fast, firm, immortal, immutable, indissoluble, lasting, permanent, persistent, persisting, steadfast, surviving, tenacious, unchanging, unending

ability adeptness, aptitude, capability, capacity, competence, competency, dexterity, endowment, energy, expertise, expertness, facility, faculty, flair, force, gift, knack, know-how (Inf.), potentiality, power, proficiency, qualification, skill, talent

abject 1. base, contemptible, cringing, debased, degraded, despicable, dishonourable,

fawning, grovelling, humiliating, ignoble, ignominious, low, mean, servile, slavish, sordid, submissive, vile, worthless 2. deplorable, forlorn, hopeless, miserable, outcast, pitiable, wretched

abjectness 1. abjection, baseness, contemptibleness, debasement, degradation, dishonour, humbleness, humiliation, ignominy, lowness, meanness, servility, slavishness, sordidness, submissiveness, vileness, worthlessness 2. destitution, forlornness, hopelessness, misery, pitiableness, pitifulness, squalor, wretchedness

ablaze 1. afire, aflame, alight, blazing, burning, fiery, flaming, ignited, lighted, on fire 2. aglow, brilliant, flashing, gleaming, glowing, illuminated, incandescent, luminous, radiant, sparkling 3. angry, aroused, enthusiastic, excited, fervent, frenzied, fuming, furious, impassioned, incensed, passionate, raging, stimulated

able accomplished, adept, adequate, adroit, capable, clever, competent, effective, efficient, experienced, expert, fit, fitted, gifted, highly endowed, masterful, masterly, powerful, practised, proficient, qualified, skilful, skilled, strong, talented

able-bodied firm, fit, hale, hardy, healthy, hearty, lusty, powerful, robust, sound, staunch, stout, strapping, strong, sturdy, vigorous

ablution bath, bathing, cleansing, lavation, purification, shower, wash, washing

—**ab'lutionary** adj.

ably ('eıblı) adv. in a competent or skilful manner.

ABM abbrev. for antiballistic missile.

abnegate ('æbnı‚geıt) vb. (tr.) to deny to oneself; renounce. —‚abne'gation n. —'abne‚gator n.

abnormal (æb'nɔːməl) adj. 1. not normal; deviating from the usual or typical. 2. concerned with the abnormal: abnormal psychology. 3. Inf. odd; strange. —ab'normality (‚æbnɔː'mælıtı) n. —ab'normally adv.

Abo ('æbəʊ) n., pl. **Abos**. (sometimes not cap.) Aust. inf., often derog. short for **Aborigine**.

aboard (ə'bɔːd) adv., adj. (postpositive), prep. 1. on, in, onto, or into (a ship, train, etc.). 2. Naut. alongside. 3. **all aboard!** (interj.) a warning to passengers to board a vehicle, ship, etc.

abode¹ (ə'bəʊd) n. a place in which one lives; one's home.

abode² (ə'bəʊd) vb. a past tense and past participle of **abide**.

abolish (ə'bɒlıʃ) vb. (tr.) to do away with (laws, regulations, customs, etc.). —a'bolishable adj. —a'bolisher n. —a'bolishment n.

abolition (‚æbə'lıʃən) n. 1. the act of abolishing or the state of being abolished; annulment. 2. (often cap.) (in British territories) the ending of the slave trade (1807) or of slavery (1833). 3. (often cap.) (in the U.S.) the emancipation of slaves, by the Emancipation Proclamation (1863, ratified 1865). —‚abo'litionary adj. —‚abo'litionism n. —‚abo'litionist n., adj.

A-bomb n. short for **atom bomb**.

abominable (ə'bɒmınəbəl) adj. 1. offensive; loathsome; detestable. 2. Inf. very bad or inferior: abominable workmanship. —a'bominably adv.

abominable snowman n. a large manlike or apelike creature alleged to inhabit the Himalayas. Also called: **yeti**.

abominate (ə'bɒmı‚neıt) vb. (tr.) to dislike intensely; detest. —a‚bomi'nation n. —a'bomi‚nator n.

aboriginal (‚æbə'rıdʒınəl) adj. existing in a place from the earliest known period; indigenous. —‚abo'riginally adv.

Aboriginal (‚æbə'rıdʒınəl) adj. 1. of, relating to, or characteristic of the Aborigines of Australia. ~n. 2. another word for an Australian **Aborigine**.

aborigine (‚æbə'rıdʒını) n. an original inhabitant of a country or region.

Aborigine (‚æbə'rıdʒını) n. 1. Also called: **native Australian**. a member of a dark-skinned hunting and gathering people who were living in Australia when European settlers arrived. Often shortened to **Abo**. 2. any of the languages of this people.

abort (ə'bɔːt) vb. 1. to terminate or cause to terminate pregnancy before the foetus is viable. 2. (intr.) to fail to come to completion. 3. (tr.) to interrupt the development of. 4. (intr.) to give birth to a dead or nonviable foetus. 5. (of a space flight or other undertaking) to fail or terminate prematurely. 6. (intr.) (of an organism or part of an organism) to fail to develop into the mature form.

abortion (ə'bɔːʃən) n. 1. an operation or other procedure to terminate pregnancy before the foetus is viable. 2. the premature termination of pregnancy by spontaneous or induced expulsion of a nonviable foetus from the uterus. 3. an aborted foetus. 4. a failure to develop to completion or maturity. 5. a person or thing that is deformed. —a'bortionist n.

abortive (ə'bɔːtıv) adj. 1. failing to achieve a purpose; fruitless. 2. (of organisms) imperfectly developed. 3. causing abortion.

abound (ə'baʊnd) vb. (intr.) 1. to exist or occur in abundance. 2. (foll. by with or in) to be plentifully supplied (with): the fields abound in corn.

about (ə'baʊt) prep. 1. relating to; concerning. 2. near or close to. 3. carried on: I haven't any money about me. 4. on every side of. 5. active in or engaged in. 6. (foll. by an infinitive) ready to or intending to: he was about to jump. ~adv. 7. near in number, time, degree, etc.: about 50 years old. 8. nearby. 9. here and there: walk about to keep warm. 10. all around; on every side. 11. in or to the opposite direction. 12. in rotation or revolution: turn and turn about. 13. used in informal phrases to indicate understatement: it's about time you stopped. 14. Arch. around. ~adj. 15. (predicative) active; astir after sleep: up and about.

about turn or U.S. **about face** interj. 1. a military command to a formation of men to reverse the direction in which they are facing. ~n. **about-turn** or U.S. **about-face**. 2. a complete change of opinion, direction, etc. ~vb. **about-turn** or U.S. **about-face**. 3. (intr.) to perform an about-turn.

above (ə'bʌv) prep. 1. on top of or higher than; over. 2. greater than in quantity or degree: above average. 3. superior to or prior to: to place honour above wealth. 4. too high-minded for: above petty gossiping. 5. too respected for; beyond: above suspicion. 6. too difficult to be understood by: the talk was above me. 7. louder or higher than (other noise). 8. in preference to. 9. north of. 10. upstream from. 11. **above all**. most of all or most important. 12. **above and beyond**. in addition to. ~adv.

THESAURUS

abnegation abandonment, abjuration, abstinence, continence, disallowance, eschewal, forbearance, giving up, refusal, rejection, relinquishment, renunciation, sacrifice, self-denial, surrender, temperance

abnormal aberrant, anomalous, atypical, curious, deviant, eccentric, erratic, exceptional, extraordinary, irregular, monstrous, odd, peculiar, queer, singular, strange, uncommon, unexpected, unnatural, untypical, unusual, weird

abnormality aberration, anomaly, atypicalness, bizarreness, deformity, deviation, eccentricity, exception, extraordinariness, flaw, irregularity, monstrosity, oddity, peculiarity, queerness, singularity, strangeness, uncommonness, unexpectedness, unnaturalness, untypicalness, unusualness, weirdness

abode domicile, dwelling, dwelling-place, habitat, habitation, home, house, lodging, quarters, residence

abolish abrogate, annihilate, annul, blot out, cancel, destroy, do away with, eliminate, end, eradicate, expunge, exterminate, extinguish, extirpate, invalidate, nullify, obliterate, overthrow, overturn, put an end to, quash, repeal, repudiate, rescind, revoke, stamp out, subvert, suppress, terminate, vitiate, void, wipe out

abolition abrogation, annihilation, annulment, blotting out, cancellation, destruction, elimination, end, ending, eradication, ex-

punction, extermination, extinction, extirpation, invalidation, nullification, obliteration, overthrow, overturning, quashing, repeal, repudiation, rescission, revocation, stamping out, subversion, suppression, termination, vitiation, voiding, wiping out, withdrawal

abominable abhorrent, accursed, atrocious, base, contemptible, despicable, detestable, disgusting, execrable, foul, hateful, heinous, hellish, horrible, horrid, loathsome, nauseous, obnoxious, odious, repellent, reprehensible, repugnant, repulsive, revolting, terrible, vile, villainous, wretched

abomination 1. abhorrence, antipathy, aversion, detestation, disgust, distaste, execration, hate, hatred, horror, loathing, odium, repugnance, revulsion 2. anathema, bête noire, bugbear, curse, disgrace, evil, horror, plague, shame, torment

aboriginal ancient, autochthonous, earliest, first, indigenous, native, original, primary, primeval, primitive, primordial, pristine

abort 1. miscarry, terminate (a pregnancy) 2. arrest, call off, check, end, fail, halt, stop, terminate

abortion 1. aborticide, deliberate miscarriage, foeticide, miscarriage, termination 2. disappointment, failure, fiasco, misadventure, monstrosity, vain effort

abortive adj. 1. bootless, failed, failing, fruitless, futile, idle, ineffectual, miscarried, unavailing, unsuccessful, useless, vain 2. Biol. imperfectly developed, incomplete, rudimentary, stunted ~n. 3. Medical abortifacient

abound be jammed with, be packed with, be plentiful, crowd, flourish, increase, infest, luxuriate, overflow, proliferate, superabound, swarm, swell, teem, thrive

abounding abundant, bountiful, copious, filled, flourishing, flowing, flush, full, lavish, luxuriant, overflowing, plenteous, plentiful, profuse, prolific, rank, replete, rich, superabundant, teeming

about prep. 1. anent (Scot.), as regards, concerned with, concerning, connected with, dealing with, on, re, referring to, regarding, relating to, relative to, respecting, touching, with respect to 2. adjacent, beside, circa (used with dates), close to, near, nearby 3. around, encircling, on all sides, round, surrounding 4. all over, over, through, throughout ~adv. 5. almost, approaching, approximately, around, close to, more or less, nearing, nearly, roughly 6. from place to place, here and there, hither and thither, to and fro ~adj. 7. active, around, astir, in motion, present, stirring

about to intending to, on the point of, on the verge or brink of, ready to

13. in or to a higher place: *the sky above.* **14. a.** in a previous place (in something written). **b.** (*in combination*): *the above-mentioned clause.* **15.** higher in rank or position. **16.** in or concerned with heaven. ~*n.* **17.** the **above.** something previously mentioned. ~*adj.* **18.** appearing in a previous place (in something written).

above board *adj.* (**aboveboard** *when prenominal*), *adv.* in the open; without dishonesty, concealment, or fraud.

abracadabra (ˌæbrəkəˈdæbrə) *interj.* **1.** a spoken formula, used esp. by conjurors. ~*n.* **2.** a word used in incantations, etc., considered to possess magic powers. **3.** gibberish.

abrade (əˈbreɪd) *vb.* (*tr.*) to scrape away or wear down by friction. —**aˈbrader** *n.*

abrasion (əˈbreɪʒən) *n.* **1.** the process of scraping or wearing down by friction. **2.** a scraped area or spot; graze. **3.** *Geog.* the effect of mechanical erosion of rock, esp. a river bed, by rock fragments scratching and scraping it.

abrasive (əˈbreɪsɪv) *n.* **1.** a substance or material such as sandpaper, pumice, or emery, used for cleaning, smoothing, or polishing. ~*adj.* **2.** causing abrasion; rough. **3.** irritating in manner or personality.

abreast (əˈbrɛst) *adj.* (*postpositive*) **1.** alongside each other and facing in the same direction. **2.** (foll. by *of* or *with*) up to date (with).

abridge (əˈbrɪdʒ) *vb.* (*tr.*) **1.** to reduce the length of (a written work) by condensing. **2.** to curtail. —**aˈbridgable** *or* **aˈbridgeable** *adj.* —**aˈbridger** *n.* —**aˈbridgment** *or* **aˈbridgement** *n.*

abroad (əˈbrɔːd) *adv.* **1.** to or in a foreign country or countries. ~*adj.* (*postpositive*) **2.** (of rumours, etc.) in general circulation. **3.** out in the open. **4.** over a wide area.

abrogate (ˈæbrəʊˌɡeɪt) *vb.* (*tr.*) to cancel or revoke formally or officially. —ˌabroˈgation *n.* —ˈabroˌgator *n.*

abrupt (əˈbrʌpt) *adj.* **1.** sudden; unexpected. **2.** brusque or brief in speech, manner, etc. **3.** (of a style of writing or speaking) disconnected. **4.** precipitous; steep. **5.** *Bot.* truncate. **6.** *Geol.* (of strata) cropping out suddenly. —**abˈruptly** *adv.* —**abˈruptness** *n.*

abscess (ˈæbsɛs) *n.* **1.** a localized collection of pus formed as the product of inflammation. ~*vb.* **2.** (*intr.*)

to form such a collection of pus. —ˈabscessed *adj.*

abscissa (æbˈsɪsə) *n., pl.* **-scissas** *or* **-scissae** (-ˈsɪsiː). the horizontal or *x*-coordinate of a point in a two-dimensional system of Cartesian coordinates. It is the distance from the *y*-axis measured parallel to the *x*-axis. Cf. **ordinate** (sense 1).

abscond (əbˈskɒnd) *vb.* (*intr.*) to run away secretly, esp. to avoid prosecution or arrest. —**abˈsconder** *n.*

abseil (ˈæbsaɪl) *vb.* (*intr.*) **1.** *Mountaineering.* to descend a steep slope or vertical drop by a rope secured from above and coiled around one's body. ~*n.* **2.** an instance or the technique of abseiling.

absence (ˈæbsəns) *n.* **1.** the state of being away. **2.** the time during which a person or thing is away. **3.** the fact of being without something; lack.

absent *adj.* (ˈæbsənt). **1.** away or not present. **2.** lacking. **3.** inattentive. ~*vb.* (æbˈsɛnt). **4.** (*tr.*) to remove (oneself) or keep away. —**abˈsenter** *n.*

absentee (ˌæbsənˈtiː) *n.* **a.** a person who is absent. **b.** (*as modifier*): *an absentee landlord.*

absenteeism (ˌæbsənˈtiːɪzəm) *n.* persistent absence from work, school, etc.

absent-minded *adj.* preoccupied; forgetful. —ˌabsent-ˈmindedly *adv.* —ˌabsent-ˈmindedness *n.*

absinthe *or* **absinth** (ˈæbsɪnθ) *n.* **1.** a potent green alcoholic drink, originally having high wormwood content. **2.** another name for **wormwood** (the plant).

absolute (ˈæbsəˌluːt) *adj.* **1.** complete; perfect. **2.** free from limitations, restrictions, or exceptions. **3.** despotic: *an absolute ruler.* **4.** undoubted; certain: *the absolute truth.* **5.** not dependent on, conditioned by, or relative to anything else; independent: *absolute humidity; absolute units.* **6.** pure; unmixed: *absolute alcohol.* **7.** (of a grammatical construction) syntactically independent of the main clause, as for example the construction *Joking apart* in the sentence *Joking apart, we'd better leave now.* **8.** *Grammar.* (of a transitive verb) used without a direct object, as the verb *intimidate* in the sentence *His intentions are good, but his rough manner tends to intimidate.* **9.** *Grammar.* (of an adjective) used as a noun, as for instance *young* and *aged* in the sentence *The young care little for the aged.* ~*n.* **10.** something that is absolute.

Absolute (ˈæbsəˌluːt) *n.* (*sometimes not cap.*) *Philoso-*

THESAURUS

above *prep.* 1. atop, beyond, exceeding, higher than, on top of, over, upon ~*adv.* 2. atop, in heaven, on high, overhead ~*adj.* 3. aforementioned, aforesaid, earlier, foregoing, preceding, previous, prior 4. before, beyond, exceeding, prior to, superior to, surpassing

aboveboard 1. *adv.* candidly, forthrightly, frankly, honestly, honourably, openly, overtly, straightforwardly, truly, truthfully, uprightly, veraciously, without guile 2. *adj.* candid, fair and square, forthright, frank, guileless, honest, honourable, legitimate, open, overt, square, straight, straightforward, true, trustworthy, truthful, upright, veracious

abracadabra 1. chant, charm, conjuration, hocus-pocus, incantation, invocation, magic, mumbo jumbo, sorcery, spell, voodoo, witchcraft 2. babble, balderdash, blather, drivel, gibberish, gobbledegook, jabber, jargon, nonsense, twaddle

abrade erase, erode, file, grind, rub off, scour, scrape away, scrape out, wear away, wear down, wear off

abrasion 1. *Medical* chafe, graze, scrape, scratch, scuff, surface injury 2. abrading, chafing, erosion, friction, grating, rubbing, scouring, scraping, scratching, scuffing, wearing away, wearing down

abrasive *adj.* 1. chafing, erosive, frictional, grating, rough, scraping, scratching, scratchy, scuffing 2. annoying, biting, caustic, cutting, galling, grating, hurtful, irritating, nasty, rough, sharp, unpleasant ~*n.* 3. abradant, burnisher, grinder, scarifier, scourer

abreast 1. alongside, beside, level, shoulder to shoulder, side by side 2. acquainted, au

courant, au fait, conversant, familiar, informed, in touch, knowledgeable, up to date

abridge abbreviate, abstract, clip, compress, concentrate, condense, contract, curtail, cut, cut down, decrease, digest, diminish, epitomize, lessen, précis, reduce, shorten, summarize, synopsize (*U.S.*), trim

abridgment abbreviation, abstract, compendium, condensation, conspectus, contraction, curtailment, cutting, decrease, digest, diminishing, diminution, epitome, lessening, limitation, outline, précis, reduction, restraint, restriction, résumé, shortening, summary, synopsis

abroad 1. beyond the sea, in foreign lands, out of the country, overseas 2. about, at large, away, circulating, current, elsewhere, extensively, far, far and wide, forth, in circulation, out, out-of-doors, outside, publicly, widely, without

abrupt 1. blunt, brisk, brusque, curt, direct, discourteous, gruff, impolite, rough, rude, short, snappish, snappy, terse, unceremonious, uncivil, ungracious 2. precipitous, sharp, sheer, steep, sudden 3. hasty, headlong, hurried, precipitate, quick, sudden, surprising, swift, unanticipated, unexpected, unforeseen 4. broken, disconnected, discontinuous, irregular, jerky, uneven

abscond bolt, clear out, decamp, disappear, do a bunk (*Sl.*), escape, flee, flit (*Inf.*), fly, make off, run off, slip away, sneak away, steal away

absence 1. absenteeism, nonappearance, nonattendance, truancy 2. default, defect, deficiency, lack, need, nonexistence, omission, privation, unavailability, want 3. absent-mindedness, abstraction, distraction, inattention, preoccupation, reverie

absent *adj.* 1. away, elsewhere, gone, lacking, missing, nonattendant, nonexistent, not present, out, truant, unavailable, wanting 2. absent-minded, absorbed, abstracted, bemused, blank, daydreaming, distracted, dreamy, empty, faraway, heedless, inattentive, musing, oblivious, preoccupied, unaware, unconscious, unheeding, unthinking, vacant, vague ~*v.* 3. **absent oneself** abscond, depart, keep away, play truant, remove, stay away, truant, withdraw

absently absent-mindedly, abstractedly, bemusedly, blankly, distractedly, dreamily, emptily, heedlessly, inattentively, obliviously, unconsciously, unheedingly, vacantly, vaguely

absent-minded absent, absorbed, abstracted, bemused, distracted, dreaming, dreamy, engrossed, faraway, forgetful, heedless, in a brown study, inattentive, musing, oblivious, preoccupied, unaware, unconscious, unheeding, unthinking

absolute 1. complete, consummate, downright, entire, out-and-out, outright, perfect, pure, sheer, thorough, total, unadulterated, unalloyed, unmitigated, unmixed, unqualified, utter 2. actual, categorical, certain, conclusive, decided, decisive, definite, exact, genuine, infallible, positive, precise, sure, unambiguous, unequivocal, unquestionable 3. absolutist, arbitrary, autarchical, autocratic, autonomous, despotic, dictatorial, full, peremptory, sovereign, supreme, tyrannical, unbounded, unconditional, unlimited, unqualified, unquestionable, unrestrained, unrestricted

phy. 1. the ultimate basis of reality. **2.** that which is totally unconditioned, unrestricted, pure, perfect, or complete.

absolutely (ˌæbsəˈluːtlɪ) *adv.* **1.** in an absolute manner, esp. completely or perfectly. **2.** (*sentence substitute*) yes; certainly.

absolute majority *n.* a majority of over 50 per cent, such as the total number of votes or seats obtained by a party that beats the combined opposition.

absolute pitch *n.* **1.** Also called: **perfect pitch.** the ability to identify or to reproduce the pitch of a note. **2.** the exact pitch of a note determined by vibration per second.

absolute zero *n.* the lowest temperature theoretically attainable, at which the particles constituting matter would be at rest: equivalent to –273.15°C or –459.67°F.

absolution (ˌæbsəˈluːʃən) *n.* **1.** the act of absolving or the state of being absolved; release from guilt, obligation, or punishment. **2.** *Christianity.* **a.** a formal remission of sin pronounced by a priest in the sacrament of penance. **b.** the form of words granting such a remission.

absolutism (ˈæbsəluːˌtɪzəm) *n.* the principle or practice of a political system in which unrestricted power is vested in a monarch, dictator, etc.; despotism. —ˈabsolutist *n.*

absolve (əbˈzɒlv) *vb.* (*tr.*) **1.** (usually foll. by *from*) to release from blame, sin, obligation, or responsibility. **2.** to pronounce not guilty. —abˈsolver *n.*

absorb (əbˈsɔːb) *vb.* (*tr.*) **1.** to soak or suck up (liquids). **2.** to engage or occupy (the interest or time) of (someone). **3.** to receive or take in (the energy of an impact). **4.** *Physics.* to take in all or part of incident radiated energy and retain it. **5.** to take in or assimilate; incorporate. **6.** to pay for as part of a commercial transaction: *the distributor absorbed the cost of transport.* **7.** *Chem.* to undergo or cause to undergo a process in which one substance permeates into or is dissolved by a liquid or solid: *porous solids absorb water.* —abˌsorbaˈbility *n.* —ˈsorbable *adj.* —abˈsorbent *adj.*

absorption (əbˈsɔːpʃən) *n.* **1.** the process of absorbing or the state of being absorbed. **2.** *Physiol.* **a.** normal assimilation by the tissues of the products of digestion. **b.** the process of taking up various fluids, drugs, etc., through the mucous membranes or skin. —abˈsorptive *adj.*

abstain (əbˈsteɪn) *vb.* (*intr.*; usually foll. by *from*) **1.** to choose to refrain. **2.** to refrain from voting, esp. in a committee, legislature, etc. —abˈstainer *n.*

abstemious (əbˈstiːmɪəs) *adj.* sparing, esp. in the consumption of alcohol or food. —abˈstemiously *adv.* —abˈstemiousness *n.*

abstention (əbˈstɛnʃən) *n.* **1.** the act of refraining or abstaining. **2.** the act of withholding one's vote.

abstinence (ˈæbstɪnəns) *n.* the act or practice of refraining from some action or from the use of something, esp. alcohol. —ˈabstinent *adj.*

abstract *adj.* (ˈæbstrækt). **1.** having no reference to material objects or specific examples. **2.** not applied or practical; theoretical. **3.** hard to understand. **4.** *Fine arts.* characterized by geometric, formalized, or otherwise nonrepresentational qualities. ~*n.* (ˈæbstrækt). **5.** a condensed version of a piece of writing, speech, etc.; summary. **6.** an abstract term or idea. **7.** an abstract painting, sculpture, etc. **8. in the abstract.** without reference to specific circumstances. ~*vb.* (æbˈstrækt). (*tr.*) **9.** to regard theoretically. **10.** (ˈæbstrækt). (*also intr.*) to summarize. **11.** to remove or extract.

abstracted (æbˈstræktɪd) *adj.* **1.** lost in thought; preoccupied. **2.** taken out or separated. —abˈstractedly *adv.*

abstraction (æbˈstrækʃən) *n.* **1.** preoccupation. **2.** the process of formulating generalized concepts by extracting common qualities from specific examples. **3.** a concept formulated in this way: *good and evil are abstractions.* **4.** an abstract painting, sculpture, etc. —abˈstractive *adj.*

abstruse (əbˈstruːs) *adj.* not easy to understand. —abˈstrusely *adv.* —abˈstruseness *n.*

absurd (əbˈsɜːd) *adj.* **1.** incongruous; ridiculous. **2.** ludicrous. —abˈsurdity *or* abˈsurdness *n.* —abˈsurdly *adv.*

abundance (əˈbʌndəns) *n.* **1.** a copious supply; great

THESAURUS

absolutely 1. completely, consummately, entirely, fully, perfectly, purely, thoroughly, totally, unmitigatedly, utterly, wholly **2.** actually, categorically, certainly, conclusively, decidedly, decisively, definitely, exactly, genuinely, infallibly, positively, precisely, surely, truly, unambiguously, unequivocally, unquestionably **3.** arbitrarily, autocratically, autonomously, despotically, dictatorially, fully, peremptorily, sovereignly, supremely, tyrannically, unconditionally, unquestionably, unrestrainedly

absoluteness 1. consummateness, entirety, perfection, purity, thoroughness, totality, unmitigatedness, wholeness **2.** assuredness, certainty, certitude, conclusiveness, correctness, decidedness, decisiveness, definiteness, exactitude, genuineness, infallibility, positiveness, precision, sureness, surety, truth, unambiguousness, unequivocalness **3.** arbitrariness, autonomy, despotism, dictatorialness, fullness, peremptoriness, supremacy, tyranny, unboundedness, unquestionability, unrestrainedness, unrestrictedness

absolution acquittal, amnesty, deliverance, discharge, dispensation, exculpation, exemption, exoneration, forgiveness, freeing, indulgence, liberation, mercy, pardon, release, remission, setting free, shriving, vindication

absolutism absoluteness, arbitrariness, autarchy, authoritarianism, autocracy, despotism, dictatorship, totalitarianism, tyranny

absolutist arbiter, authoritarian, autocrat, despot, dictator, totalitarian, tyrant

absolve acquit, clear, deliver, discharge, exculpate, excuse, exempt, exonerate, forgive, free, let off, liberate, loose, pardon, release, remit, set free, shrive, vindicate

absorb 1. assimilate, consume, devour, digest, drink in, exhaust, imbibe, incorporate, ingest, osmose, receive, soak up, suck up,

take in **2.** captivate, engage, engross, enwrap, fascinate, fill, fill up, fix, hold, immerse, monopolize, occupy, preoccupy, rivet

absorbed 1. captivated, concentrating, engaged, engrossed, fascinated, fixed, held, immersed, involved, lost, occupied, preoccupied, rapt, riveted, wrapped up **2.** assimilated, consumed, devoured, digested, exhausted, imbibed, incorporated, received

absorbing arresting, captivating, engrossing, fascinating, gripping, interesting, intriguing, preoccupying, riveting, spellbinding

absorption 1. assimilation, consumption, digestion, exhaustion, incorporation, osmosis, soaking up, sucking up **2.** captivation, concentration, engagement, fascination, holding, immersion, intentness, involvement, occupation, preoccupation, raptness

abstain avoid, cease, decline, deny (oneself), desist, forbear, forgo, give up, keep from, refrain, refuse, renounce, shun, stop, withhold

abstemious abstinent, ascetic, austere, continent, frugal, moderate, self-denying, sober, sparing, temperate

abstention abstaining, abstinence, avoidance, desistance, eschewal, forbearance, nonindulgence, refraining, refusal, self-control, self-denial, self-restraint

abstinence abstemiousness, asceticism, avoidance, continence, forbearance, moderation, refraining, self-denial, self-restraint, soberness, sobriety, teetotalism, temperance

abstinent abstaining, abstemious, continent, forbearing, moderate, self-controlled, self-denying, self-restraining, sober, temperate

abstract *adj.* **1.** abstruse, arcane, complex, conceptual, deep, general, generalized, hypothetical, indefinite, intellectual, nonconcrete, occult, philosophical, profound,

recondite, separate, subtle, theoretic, theoretical, unpractical, unrealistic ~*n.* **2.** abridgment, compendium, condensation, digest, epitome, essence, outline, précis, recapitulation, résumé, summary, synopsis ~*v.* **3.** abbreviate, abridge, condense, digest, epitomize, outline, précis, shorten, summarize, synopsize (*U.S.*) **4.** detach, dissociate, extract, isolate, remove, separate, steal, take away, take out, withdraw

abstracted 1. absent, absent-minded, bemused, daydreaming, dreamy, faraway, inattentive, preoccupied, remote, withdrawn, woolgathering **2.** abbreviated, abridged, condensed, digested, epitomized, shortened, summarized, synopsized (*U.S.*)

abstraction 1. absence, absentmindedness, bemusedness, dreaminess, inattention, pensiveness, preoccupation, remoteness, woolgathering **2.** concept, formula, generality, generalization, hypothesis, idea, notion, theorem, theory, thought

abstruse abstract, arcane, complex, dark, deep, enigmatic, esoteric, hidden, incomprehensible, mysterious, mystical, obscure, occult, perplexing, profound, puzzling, recondite, subtle, unfathomable, vague

absurd crazy (*Inf.*), daft (*Inf.*), farcical, foolish, idiotic, illogical, incongruous, irrational, laughable, ludicrous, meaningless, nonsensical, preposterous, ridiculous, senseless, silly, stupid, unreasonable

absurdity craziness (*Inf.*), daftness (*Inf.*), farce, farcicality, farcicalness, folly, foolishness, idiocy, illogicality, illogicalness, incongruity, irrationality, joke, ludicrousness, meaninglessness, nonsense, preposterousness, ridiculousness, senselessness, silliness, stupidity, unreasonableness

amount. **2.** fullness or benevolence: *from the abundance of my heart.* **3.** degree of plentifulness: *the abundance of uranium-235 in natural uranium.* **4.** Also: **abondance.** a call in solo whist undertaking to make nine tricks. **5.** affluence. —a'**bundant** *adj.*

abuse *vb.* (ə'bju:z). (*tr.*) **1.** to use incorrectly or improperly; misuse. **2.** to maltreat. **3.** to speak insultingly or cruelly to. ~*n.* (ə'bju:s). **4.** improper, incorrect, or excessive use. **5.** maltreatment of a person; injury. **6.** insulting or coarse speech. **7.** an evil, unjust, or corrupt practice. **8.** *Arch.* a deception. —a'**buser** *n.* —**abusive** (ə'bju:sɪv) *adj.*

abut (ə'bʌt) *vb.* **abutting, abutted.** (usually foll. by *on, upon,* or *against*) to adjoin, touch, or border on (something) at one end.

abutment (ə'bʌtmənt) *or* **abuttal** *n.* **1.** the state or process of abutting. **2. a.** something that abuts. **b.** the thing on which something abuts. **c.** the point of junction between them. **3.** a construction that supports the end of a bridge.

abysmal (ə'bɪzməl) *adj.* **1.** immeasurable; very great. **2.** *Inf.* extremely bad. —a'**bysmally** *adv.*

abyss (ə'bɪs) *n.* **1.** a very deep gorge or chasm. **2.** anything that appears to be endless or immeasurably deep, such as time, despair, or shame. **3.** hell. —a'**byssal** *adj.*

Ac *the chemical symbol for* actinium.

AC *abbrev. for* alternating current. Cf. **DC.**

a/c *Book-keeping. abbrev. for:* **1.** account. **2.** account current.

acacia (ə'keɪʃə) *n.* **1.** a tropical or subtropical shrub or tree, having small yellow or white flowers. In Australia the term is applied esp. to the wattle. **2. false acacia.** another name for **locust** (senses 2, 3). **3. gum acacia.** another name for **gum arabic.**

academic (,ækə'dɛmɪk) *adj.* **1.** belonging or relating to a place of learning, esp. a college, university, or academy. **2.** of purely theoretical or speculative interest. **3.** excessively concerned with intellectual matters. **4.** conforming to set rules and traditions: *an academic painter.* **5.** *Chiefly U.S.* relating to studies such as languages and pure science rather than technical or professional studies. ~*n.* **6.** a member of a college or university. —,**aca'demically** *adv.*

academy (ə'kædəmɪ) *n., pl.* -**mies. 1.** an institution or society for the advancement of literature, art, or science. **2.** a school for training in a particular skill or profession: *a military academy.* **3.** a secondary school, esp. in Scotland. —,**aca'demical** *adj.* —**academician** (ə,kædə'mɪʃən) *n.*

acanthus (ə'kænθəs) *n., pl.* -**thuses** *or* -**thi** (-θaɪ). **1.** a shrub or herbaceous plant, native to the Mediterranean region but widely cultivated as an ornamental plant, having large spiny leaves and spikes of white or purplish flowers. **2.** a carved ornament based on the leaves of the acanthus plant, esp. as used on the capital of a Corinthian column.

ACAS ('eɪkæs) *n.* (in Britain) *acronym for* Advisory Conciliation and Arbitration Service.

acc. *abbrev. for:* **1.** accompanied. **2.** according. **3.** *Book-keeping.* account. **4.** *Grammar.* accusative.

accede (æk'si:d) *vb.* (*intr.;* usually foll. by *to*) **1.** to assent or give one's consent. **2.** to enter upon or attain (to an office, right, etc.): *the prince acceded to the throne.* **3.** *International law.* to become a party (to an agreement between nations, etc.). —ac'**cedence** *n.*

accelerando (æk,sɛlə'rændəʊ) ~*adj., adv. Music.* becoming faster.

accelerate (æk'sɛlə,reɪt) *vb.* **1.** to go, occur, or cause to go or occur more quickly; speed up. **2.** (*tr.*) to cause to happen sooner than expected. **3.** (*tr.*) to increase the velocity of (a body, reaction, etc.). —ac,**cele'ration** *n.* —ac'**celerative** *adj.*

accelerator (æk'sɛlə,reɪtə) *n.* **1.** a device for increasing speed, esp. a pedal for controlling the fuel intake in a motor vehicle; throttle. **2.** *Physics.* a machine for increasing the kinetic energy of subatomic particles or atomic nuclei. **3.** Also: **accelerant.** *Chem.* a substance that increases the speed of a chemical reaction; catalyst.

accent *n.* ('æksənt). **1.** the relative prominence of a spoken or sung syllable, esp. with regard to stress or pitch. **2.** a mark (such as ˈ , ˌ , ´ , or `) used in writing to indicate the stress or prominence of a syllable. **3.** any of various marks or symbols conventionally used in writing certain languages to indicate the quality of a vowel. See **acute** (sense 8), **grave²** (sense 5), **circumflex. 4.** rhythmical stress in verse or prose. **5.** *Music.* **a.** stress placed on certain notes in a piece of music, indicated by a symbol printed over the note concerned. **b.** the rhythmical pulse of a piece or passage, usually represented as the stress on the first beat of each bar. **6.** the characteristic mode of pronunciation of a person or group, esp. one that betrays social or geographical origin. **7.** a distinctive characteristic of anything, such as taste, pattern, style, etc. **8.** particular attention or emphasis: *an accent on learning.* **9.** a strongly contrasting detail. ~*vb.* (æk'sɛnt). (*tr.*) **10.** to mark with an accent in writing, speech, music, etc. **11.** to lay particular emphasis or stress on.

accentor (æk'sɛntə) *n.* a small sparrow-like songbird, which inhabits mainly mountainous regions of Europe and Asia. See also **hedge sparrow.**

accentuate (æk'sɛntʃʊ,eɪt) *vb.* (*tr.*) to stress or emphasize. —ac,**centu'ation** *n.*

accept (ək'sɛpt) *vb.* (mainly *tr.*) **1.** to take or receive (something offered). **2.** to give an affirmative reply to. **3.** to take on the responsibilities, duties, etc., of: *he accepted office.* **4.** to tolerate. **5.** to consider as true or believe in (a philosophy, theory, etc.). **6.** (*may take a clause as object*) to be willing to believe: *you must accept that he lied.* **7.** to receive with approval or admit, as into a community, group, etc. **8.** *Commerce.* to agree to pay (a bill, draft, etc.). **9.** to receive as adequate or valid. —ac'**cepter** *n.*

THESAURUS

abundance 1. affluence, ampleness, bounty, copiousness, exuberance, fullness, heap (*Inf.*), plenitude, plenteousness, plenty, profusion **2.** affluence, fortune, opulence, riches, wealth

abundant ample, bounteous, bountiful, copious, exuberant, filled, full, lavish, luxuriant, overflowing, plenteous, plentiful, profuse, rank, rich, teeming, well-provided, well-supplied

abuse *v.* **1.** damage, exploit, harm, hurt, illtreat, impose upon, injure, maltreat, manhandle, mar, misapply, misuse, oppress, spoil, take advantage of, wrong **2.** calumniate, castigate, curse, defame, disparage, insult, inveigh against, libel, malign, revile, scold, slander, smear, swear at, traduce, upbraid, vilify, vituperate ~*n.* **3.** damage, exploitation, harm, hurt, ill-treatment, imposition, injury, maltreatment, manhandling, misapplication, misuse, oppression, spoiling, wrong **4.** blame, calumniation, castigation, censure, contumely, curses, cursing, defamation, derision, disparagement, insults, invective, libel, opprobrium, reproach, revilement, scolding, slander, swearing, tirade, tra-

ducement, upbraiding, vilification, vituperation **5.** corruption, crime, delinquency, fault, injustice, misconduct, misdeed, offence, sin, wrong, wrongdoing

abusive 1. calumniating, castigating, censorious, contumelious, defamatory, derisive, disparaging, insulting, invective, libellous, maligning, offensive, opprobrious, reproachful, reviling, rude, scathing, scolding, slanderous, traducing, upbraiding, vilifying, vituperative **2.** brutal, cruel, destructive, harmful, hurtful, injurious, rough

abysmal bottomless, boundless, complete, deep, endless, extreme, immeasurable, incalculable, infinite, profound, thorough, unending, unfathomable, vast

abyss abysm, bottomless depth, chasm, crevasse, fissure, gorge, gulf, pit, void

academic *adj.* **1.** bookish, campus, college, collegiate, erudite, highbrow, learned, lettered, literary, scholarly, scholastic, school, studious, university **2.** abstract, conjectural, hypothetical, impractical, notional, speculative, theoretical ~*n.* **3.** academician, don, fellow, lecturer, master, professor, pupil, scholar, scholastic, schoolman,

student, tutor

accede 1. accept, acquiesce, admit, agree, assent, comply, concede, concur, consent, endorse, grant, yield **2.** assume, attain, come to, enter upon, inherit, succeed, succeed to (*as heir*)

accelerate advance, expedite, forward, further, hasten, hurry, pick up speed, precipitate, quicken, speed, speed up, spur, step up (*Inf.*), stimulate

acceleration expedition, hastening, hurrying, quickening, speeding up, spurring, stepping up (*Inf.*), stimulation

accent *n.* **1.** beat, cadence, emphasis, force, pitch, rhythm, stress, timbre, tonality **2.** articulation, enunciation, inflection, intonation, modulation, pronunciation, tone ~*v.* **3.** accentuate, emphasize, stress, underline, underscore

accentuate accent, draw attention to, emphasize, highlight, stress, underline, underscore

accept 1. acquire, gain, get, have, obtain, receive, secure, take **2.** accede, acknowledge, acquiesce, admit, adopt, affirm, agree to, approve, believe, concur with, consent to,

acceptable (ək'sɛptəbəl) *adj.* **1.** satisfactory; adequate. **2.** pleasing; welcome. **3.** tolerable. —**ac,cepta'bility** *or* **ac'ceptableness** *n.* —**ac'ceptably** *adv.*

acceptance (ək'sɛptəns) *n.* **1.** the act of accepting or the state of being accepted or acceptable. **2.** favourable reception. **3.** (often foll. by *of*) belief (in) or assent (to). **4.** *Commerce.* a formal agreement by a debtor to pay a draft, bill, etc.

accepted (ək'sɛptɪd) *adj.* commonly approved or recognized; customary; established.

acceptor (ək'sɛptə) *n.* **1.** *Commerce.* the person or organization on which a draft or bill of exchange is drawn. **2.** *Electronics.* an impurity, such as gallium, added to a semiconductor material to increase its p-type conductivity.

access ('æksɛs) *n.* **1.** the act of approaching or entering. **2.** the state or condition of being approachable. **3.** the right or privilege to approach, enter, or make use of something. **4.** a way or means of approach or entry. **5.** (*modifier*): designating programmes made by the general public: *access television.* **6.** a sudden outburst or attack, as of rage or disease. ~*vb.* **7.** (*tr.*) *Computers.* **a.** to obtain or retrieve (information) from a storage device. **b.** to place (information) in a storage device.

accessary (ək'sɛsərɪ) *n., pl.* **-ries.** *Law.* a less common spelling of **accessory.**

accessible (ək'sɛsəbəl) *adj.* **1.** easy to approach, enter, or use. **2. accessible to.** likely to be affected by. **3.** obtainable; available. —**ac,cessi'bility** *n.*

accession (ək'sɛʃən) *n.* **1.** the act of attaining to an office, right, condition, etc. **2.** an increase due to an addition. **3.** an addition, as to a collection. **4.** *Property law.* an addition to land or property by natural increase or improvement. **5.** *International law.* the formal acceptance of a convention or treaty. ~*vb.* **7.** (*tr.*) to make a record of (additions to a collection). —**ac'cessional** *adj.*

accessory (ək'sɛsərɪ) *n., pl.* **-ries.** **1.** a supplementary part or object, as of a car, appliance, etc. **2.** (*often pl.*) a small accompanying item of dress, esp. of women's dress. **3.** (formerly) a person involved in a crime although absent during its commission. ~*adj.* **4.** supplementary; additional. **5.** assisting in or having knowledge of an act, esp. a crime. —**accessorial** (,æksɛ'sɔːrɪəl) *adj.* —**ac'cessorily** *adv.*

access time *n. Computers.* the time required to re-trieve a piece of stored information.

accident ('æksɪdənt) *n.* **1.** an unforeseen event or one without an apparent cause. **2.** anything that occurs unintentionally or by chance: *I met him by accident.* **3.** a misfortune or mishap, esp. one causing injury or death. **4.** a material quality that is not an essential part of something. **5.** *Geol.* a surface irregularity in a natural formation.

accidental (,æksɪ'dɛntəl) *adj.* **1.** occurring by chance, unexpectedly, or unintentionally. **2.** nonessential; incidental. **3.** *Music.* denoting sharps, flats, or naturals that are not in the key signature of a piece. ~*n.* **4.** an incidental or supplementary circumstance, factor, or attribute. **5.** *Music.* a symbol denoting that the following note is a sharp, flat, or natural that is not a part of the key signature. —**,acci'dentally** *adv.*

accident-prone *adj.* liable to become involved in accidents.

acclaim (ə'kleɪm) *vb.* **1.** (*tr.*) to acknowledge publicly the excellence of (a person, act, etc.). **2.** to applaud. **3.** (*tr.*) to acknowledge publicly: *they acclaimed him king.* ~*n.* **4.** an enthusiastic expression of approval, etc. —**ac'claimer** *n.*

acclamation (,æklə'meɪʃən) *n.* **1.** an enthusiastic reception or exhibition of welcome, approval, etc. **2.** an expression of approval with shouts or applause. **3. by acclamation.** *Canad.* (of an election or electoral victory) without opposition: *he won by acclamation.* —**acclamatory** (ə'klæmətərɪ) *adj.*

acclimatize *or* **-tise** (ə'klaɪmə,taɪz) *vb.* to adapt or become accustomed to a new climate or environment. —**ac'clima,tizable** *or* **-tisable** *adj.* —**ac,climati'zation** *or* **-ti'sation** *n.*

accolade ('ækə,leɪd) *n.* **1.** strong praise or approval. **2.** an award or honour. **3.** the ceremonial gesture used to confer knighthood, a touch on the shoulder with a sword. **4.** a rare word for **brace** (sense 6).

accommodate (ə'kɒmə,deɪt) *vb.* **1.** (*tr.*) to supply or provide, esp. with lodging. **2.** (*tr.*) to oblige or do a favour for. **3.** to adapt. **4.** (*tr.*) to bring into harmony. **5.** (*tr.*) to allow room for. **6.** (*tr.*) to lend money to.

accommodating (ə'kɒmə,deɪtɪŋ) *adj.* willing to help; kind; obliging.

accommodation (ə,kɒmə'deɪʃən) *n.* **1.** adjustment, as of differences or to new circumstances; settlement or reconciliation. **2.** lodging or board and lodging. **3.**

THESAURUS

cooperate with, recognize, swallow (*Inf.*) **3.** bear, bow to, brook, defer to, put up with, stand, submit to, suffer, take, yield to **4.** acknowledge, admit, assume, avow, bear, take on, undertake

acceptable 1. agreeable, delightful, grateful, gratifying, pleasant, pleasing, welcome **2.** adequate, admissible, all right, fair, moderate, passable, satisfactory, so-so (*Inf.*), standard, tolerable

acceptance 1. accepting, acquiring, gaining, getting, having, obtaining, receipt, securing, taking **2.** accedence, accession, acknowledgment, acquiescence, admission, adoption, affirmation, agreement, approbation, approval, assent, belief, compliance, concession, concurrence, consent, cooperation, credence, O.K. (*Inf.*), permission, recognition, stamp *or* seal of approval **3.** deference, standing, submission, taking, yielding **4.** acknowledgment, admission, assumption, avowal, taking on, undertaking

accepted acceptable, acknowledged, admitted, agreed, agreed upon, approved, authorized, common, confirmed, conventional, customary, established, normal, received, recognized, regular, sanctioned, standard, time-honoured, traditional, universal, usual

access 1. admission, admittance, approach, avenue, course, door, entering, entrance, entrée, entry, gateway, key, passage, passageway, path, road **2.** *Medical* attack, fit, onset, outburst, paroxysm

accessibility 1. approachability, attainability, availability, handiness, nearness, obtainability, possibility, readiness **2.** affability, approachability, conversableness, cordiality,

friendliness, informality **3.** exposedness, openness, susceptibility

accessible 1. achievable, at hand, attainable, available, get-at-able (*Inf.*), handy, near, nearby, obtainable, on hand, possible, reachable, ready **2.** affable, approachable, available, conversable, cordial, friendly, informal **3.** exposed, liable, open, subject, susceptible, vulnerable, wide-open

accession 1. addition, augmentation, enlargement, extension, increase **2.** assumption, attaining to, attainment of, entering upon, succession (*to a throne, dignity, or office*), taking on, taking over **3.** accedence, acceptance, acquiescence, agreement, concurrence, consent

accessory *n.* **1.** abettor, accomplice, assistant, associate (*in crime*), colleague, confederate, helper, partner **2.** accent, accompaniment, addition, adjunct, adornment, aid, appendage, attachment, component, convenience, decoration, extension, extra, frill, help, supplement, trim, trimming ~*adj.* **3.** abetting, additional, aiding, ancillary, assisting in, auxiliary, contributory, extra, secondary, subordinate, supplemental, supplementary

accident 1. blow, calamity, casualty, chance, collision, crash, disaster, misadventure, mischance, misfortune, mishap, pile-up **2.** chance, fate, fluke, fortuity, fortune, hazard, luck

accidental adventitious, casual, chance, contingent, fortuitous, haphazard, inadvertent, incidental, inessential, nonessential, random, uncalculated, uncertain, unessential, unexpected, unforeseen, unintended, unin-

tentional, unlooked-for, unplanned, unpremeditated, unwitting

accidentally adventitiously, by accident, by chance, by mistake, casually, fortuitously, haphazardly, inadvertently, incidentally, randomly, unconsciously, undesignedly, unexpectedly, unintentionally, unwittingly

acclaim 1. *v.* applaud, approve, celebrate, cheer, clap, commend, eulogize, exalt, extol, hail, honour, laud, praise, salute, welcome **2.** *n.* acclamation, applause, approbation, approval, celebration, cheering, clapping, commendation, eulogizing, exaltation, honour, laudation, plaudits, praise, welcome

acclamation acclaim, adulation, approbation, cheer, cheering, cheers, enthusiasm, laudation, loud homage, ovation, plaudit, praise, salutation, shouting, tribute

acclimatization acclimation, accommodation, acculturation, adaptation, adjustment, habituation, inurement, naturalization

acclimatize accommodate, acculture, accustom, adapt, adjust, become seasoned to, get used to, habituate, inure, naturalize

accommodate 1. billet, board, cater for, entertain, harbour, house, lodge, put up, quarter, shelter **2.** afford, aid, assist, furnish, help, oblige, provide, serve, supply **3.** accustom, adapt, adjust, comply, compose, conform, fit, harmonize, modify, reconcile, settle

accommodating complaisant, considerate, cooperative, friendly, helpful, hospitable, kind, obliging, polite, unselfish, willing

something fulfilling a need, want, etc. **4.** *Physiol.* the automatic or voluntary adjustment of the thickness of the lens of the eye for far or near vision. **5.** willingness to help or oblige. **6.** *Commerce.* a loan.

accommodation address *n.* an address on letters, etc., to a person or business that does not wish or is not able to receive post at a permanent or actual address.

accompaniment (ə'kʌmpənimənt) *n.* **1.** something that accompanies or is served or used with something else. **2.** *Music.* a subordinate or supporting part for an instrument, voices, or an orchestra.

accompanist (ə'kʌmpənist) *n.* a person who supplies a musical accompaniment.

accompany (ə'kʌmpəni) *vb.* **-nying, -nied.** **1.** (*tr.*) to go along with, so as to be in company with. **2.** (*tr.;* foll. by *with*) to supplement. **3.** (*tr.*) to occur or be associated with. **4.** to provide a musical accompaniment for (a soloist, etc.).

accomplice (ə'kɒmplis, ə'kʌm-) *n.* a person who has helped another in committing a crime.

accomplish (ə'kɒmpliʃ, ə'kʌm-) *vb.* (*tr.*) **1.** to manage to do; achieve. **2.** to complete.

accomplished (ə'kɒmpliʃt, ə'kʌm-) *adj.* **1.** successfully completed; achieved. **2.** expert; proficient.

accomplishment (ə'kɒmpliʃmənt, ə'kʌm-) *n.* **1.** the act of achieving. **2.** something successfully completed. **3.** (*often pl.*) skill or talent. **4.** (*often pl.*) social grace and poise.

accord (ə'kɔːd) *n.* **1.** agreement; accordance (esp. in **in accord with**). **2.** concurrence of opinion. **3. with one accord.** unanimously. **4.** pleasing relationship between sounds, colours, etc. **5. of one's own accord.** voluntarily. ~*vb.* **6.** to be or cause to be in harmony or agreement. **7.** (*tr.*) to grant; bestow. —**ac'cordance** *n.*

according (ə'kɔːdɪŋ) *adj.* **1.** (foll. by *to*) in proportion. **2.** (foll. by *to*) as stated (by). **3.** (foll. by *to*) in conformity (with). **4.** (foll. by *as*) depending (on whether).

accordingly (ə'kɔːdɪŋlɪ) *adv.* **1.** in an appropriate manner; suitably. ~ **2.** (*sentence connector*) consequently.

accordion (ə'kɔːdɪən) *n.* **1.** a portable box-shaped instrument consisting of metallic reeds that are made to vibrate by air from a set of bellows controlled by the player's hands. Notes are produced by means of studlike keys. **2.** short for **piano accordion.** —**ac'cordionist** *n.*

accost (ə'kɒst) *vb.* (*tr.*) to approach, stop, and speak to (a person), as to ask a question, solicit sexually, etc. —**ac'costable** *adj.*

account (ə'kaʊnt) *n.* **1.** a verbal or written report, description, or narration of some occurrence, event, etc. **2.** an explanation of conduct, esp. one made to someone in authority. **3.** basis; consideration: *on this account.* **4.** importance, consequence, or value: *of little account.* **5.** assessment; judgment. **6.** profit or advantage: *to good account.* **7.** part or behalf (only in **on one's** *or* **someone's account**). **8.** *Finance.* **a.** a business relationship between a bank, department store, etc., and a depositor, customer, or client permitting the latter certain banking or credit services. **b.** the sum of money deposited at a bank. **c.** the amount of credit available to the holder of an account. **d.** a record of these. **9.** a statement of monetary transactions with the resulting balance. **10.** (on the London Stock Exchange) the period, ordinarily of a fortnight's duration, at the end of which settlements are made. **11.** *Chiefly U.S.* **a.** a regular client or customer. **b.** an area of business assigned to another: *they transferred their publicity account to a new agent.* **12. call** (*or* **bring**) **to account. a.** to insist on explanation. **b.** to reprimand. **c.** to hold responsible. **13. give a good (bad,** *etc.*) **account of oneself.** to perform well (badly, etc.). **14. on account.** a. on credit. **b.** Also: **to account.** as partial payment. **15. on account of.** (*prep.*) because of. **16. take account of** *or* **take into account.** to take into consideration; allow for. **17. settle** *or* **square accounts with. a.** to pay or receive a balance due. **b.** to get revenge on (someone). **18.** See **bank account.** ~*vb.* **19.** (*tr.*) to consider or reckon: *he accounts himself poor.*

accountable (ə'kaʊntəbəl) *adj.* **1.** responsible to someone or for some action. **2.** able to be explained. —**ac₁counta'bility** *n.* —**ac'countably** *adv.*

accountant (ə'kaʊntənt) *n.* a person concerned with the maintenance and audit of business accounts. —**ac'countancy** *n.*

account for *vb.* (*intr., prep.*) **1.** to give reasons for (an event, act, etc.). **2.** to make or provide a reckoning of (expenditure, etc.). **3.** to be responsible for destroying or putting (people, aircraft, etc.) out of action.

accounting (ə'kaʊntɪŋ) *n.* the skill or practice of maintaining and auditing accounts and preparing reports on the assets, liabilities, etc., of a business.

accoutrement *or U.S.* **accouterment** (ə'kuːtrəmənt, ə'kuːtər-) *n.* **1.** equipment worn by soldiers in addition to their clothing and weapons. **2.** (*usually pl.*) clothing, equipment, etc.; trappings: *the accoutrements of war.*

accredit (ə'krɛdɪt) *vb.* (*tr.*) **1.** to ascribe or attribute. **2.** to give official recognition to. **3.** to certify as meeting required standards. **4.** (often foll. by *at or to*) **a.** to send (an envoy, etc.) with official credentials. **b.** to appoint

---

THESAURUS

accommodation 1. adaptation, adjustment, compliance, composition, compromise, conformity, fitting, harmony, modification, reconciliation, settlement 2. board, digs (*Inf.*), harbouring, house, housing, lodging(s), quartering, quarters, shelter, sheltering 3. aid, assistance, help, provision, service, supply

accompany 1. attend, chaperon, conduct, convoy, escort, go with, squire, usher 2. belong to, coexist with, coincide with, come with, follow, go together with, join with, occur with, supplement

accompanying accessory, added, additional, appended, associate, associated, attached, attendant, complementary, concomitant, concurrent, connected, fellow, joint, related, supplemental, supplementary

accomplice abettor, accessory, ally, assistant, associate, coadjutor, collaborator, colleague, confederate, helper, henchman, partner

accomplish achieve, attain, bring about, bring off (*Inf.*), carry out, complete, conclude, consummate, do, effect, effectuate, execute, finish, fulfil, manage, perform, produce, realize

accomplished 1. achieved, attained, brought about, carried out, completed, concluded, consummated, done, effected, executed, finished, fulfilled, managed, performed, produced, realized 2. adept, consummate, cultivated, expert, gifted, masterly, polished, practised, proficient, skilful, skilled,

talented

accomplishment 1. achievement, attainment, bringing about, carrying out, completion, conclusion, consummation, doing, effecting, execution, finishing, fulfilment, management, performance, production, realization 2. achievement, act, attainment, coup, deed, exploit, feat, stroke, triumph 3. ability, achievement, art, attainment, capability, gift, proficiency, skill, talent

accord v. 1. agree, assent, be in tune (*Inf.*), concur, conform, correspond, fit, harmonize, match, suit, tally 2. allow, bestow, concede, confer, endow, give, grant, present, render, tender, vouchsafe ~*n.* 3. accordance, agreement, concert, concurrence, conformity, congruence, correspondence, harmony, rapport, sympathy, unanimity

accordance 1. accord, agreement, assent, concert, concurrence, conformity, congruence, correspondence, harmony, rapport, sympathy, unanimity 2. according, allowance, bestowal, concession, conferment, conferral, endowment, gift, giving, granting, presentation, rendering, tendering

accordingly 1. appropriately, correspondingly, fitly, properly, suitably 2. as a result, consequently, ergo, hence, in consequence, so, therefore, thus

according to 1. commensurate with, in proportion, in relation 2. as believed by, as maintained by, as stated by, in the light of, on the authority of, on the report of 3. after, after the manner of, consistent with, in ac-

cordance with, in compliance with, in conformity with, in harmony with, in keeping with, in line with, in obedience to, in step with, in the manner of, obedient to

account n. 1. chronicle, description, detail, explanation, history, narration, narrative, recital, record, relation, report, statement, story, tale, version 2. *Commerce* balance, bill, book, books, charge, computation, inventory, invoice, ledger, reckoning, register, score, statement, tally 3. advantage, benefit, consequence, distinction, esteem, honour, import, importance, merit, note, profit, rank, repute, significance, standing, use, value, worth 4. basis, cause, consideration, ground, grounds, interest, motive, reason, regard, sake, score (*Inf.*) ~*v.* 5. appraise, assess, believe, calculate, compute, consider, count, deem, esteem, estimate, explain, gauge, hold, judge, rate, reckon, regard, think, value, weigh

accountability 1. answerability, chargeability, culpability, liability, responsibility 2. comprehensibility, explainability, explicability, intelligibility, understandability

accountable 1. amenable, answerable, charged with, liable, obligated, obliged, responsible 2. comprehensible, explainable, explicable, intelligible, understandable

account for 1. answer for, clarify, clear up, elucidate, explain, illuminate, justify, rationalize 2. destroy, incapacitate, kill, put out of action

(someone) as an envoy, etc. **5.** to believe. **6.** *N.Z.* to pass a candidate for university entrance on school recommendation, without external examination. —**ac,credi'tation** *n.*

accredited (ə'krɛdɪtɪd) *adj.* **1.** officially authorized; recognized. **2.** (of milk, cattle, etc.) certified as free from disease; meeting certain standards. **3.** *N.Z.* accepted for university entrance on school recommendation, without external examination.

accretion (ə'kriːʃən) *n.* **1.** any gradual increase in size, as through growth or external addition. **2.** something added, esp. extraneously, to cause growth or an increase in size. **3.** the growing together of normally separate plant or animal parts. —**ac'cretive** *adj.*

accrue (ə'kruː) *vb.* **-cruing, -crued.** (*intr.*) **1.** to increase by growth or addition, esp. (of capital) to increase by periodic addition of interest. **2.** (often foll. by *to*) to fall naturally (to). —**ac'crual** *n.*

acct. *Book-keeping. abbrev. for* account.

accumulate (ə'kjuːmjuˌleɪt) *vb.* to gather or become gathered together in an increasing quantity; collect. —**ac'cumulable** *adj.* —**ac'cumulative** *adj.*

accumulation (əˌkjuːmjuˈleɪʃən) *n.* **1.** the act or process of collecting together or becoming collected. **2.** something that has been collected, gathered, heaped, etc. **3.** *Finance.* the continuous growth of capital by retention of interest or earnings.

accumulator (ə'kjuːmjuˌleɪtə) *n.* **1.** Also called: **battery, storage battery.** a rechargeable device for storing electrical energy in the form of chemical energy. **2.** *Horse racing, Brit.* a collective bet on successive races, with both stake and winnings being carried forward to accumulate progressively. **3.** a register in a calculator or a location in a computer in which figures are stored and arithmetical operations performed on them.

accuracy ('ækjʊrəsɪ) *n., pl.* **-cies.** faithful measurement or representation of the truth; correctness; precision.

accurate ('ækjərɪt) *adj.* **1.** faithfully representing or describing the truth. **2.** showing a negligible or permissible deviation from a standard: *an accurate ruler.* **3.** without error; precise. —**'accurately** *adv.*

accursed (ə'kɜːsɪd, ə'kɜːst) *or* **accurst** (ə'kɜːst) *adj.* **1.** under or subject to a curse. **2.** (*prenominal*) hateful; detestable. —**accursedly** (ə'kɜːsɪdlɪ) *adv.* —**ac'cursedness** *n.*

accusation (ˌækjʊˈzeɪʃən) *n.* **1.** an allegation that a person is guilty of some fault or crime. **2.** a formal charge brought against a person.

accusative (ə'kjuːzətɪv) *adj.* **1.** *Grammar.* denoting a case of nouns, pronouns, and adjectives in inflected languages that is used to identify the direct object of a finite verb, of certain prepositions, and for certain other purposes. ~*n.* **2.** *Grammar.* the accusative case, or a speech element in it. —**accusatival** (əˌkjuːzəˈtaɪvəl) *adj.* —**ac'cusatively** *adv.*

accuse (ə'kjuːz) *vb.* to charge (a person or persons)

with some fault, offence, crime, etc. —**ac'cused** *n.* —**ac'cuser** *n.* —**ac'cusingly** *adv.*

accustom (ə'kʌstəm) *vb.* (*tr.*; usually foll. by *to*) to make (oneself) familiar (with) or used (to), as by habit or experience.

accustomed (ə'kʌstəmd) *adj.* **1.** usual; customary. **2.** (*postpositive;* foll. by *to*) used (to). **3.** (*postpositive;* foll. by *to*) in the habit (of).

ace (eɪs) *n.* **1.** any die, domino, or any of four playing cards with one spot. **2.** a single spot or pip on a playing card, die, etc. **3.** *Tennis.* **a.** a winning serve that the opponent fails to reach. **b.** any winning serve. **4.** a fighter pilot accredited with destroying many enemy aircraft. **5.** *Inf.* an expert: *an ace at driving.* **6.** **an ace up one's sleeve.** a hidden and powerful advantage. ~*adj.* **7.** *Inf.* superb; excellent.

-aceous *suffix forming adjectives.* relating to, having the nature of, or resembling: *herbaceous.*

acerbate ('æsəˌbeɪt) *vb.* (*tr.*) **1.** to embitter or exasperate. **2.** to make sour or bitter.

acerbity (ə'sɜːbɪtɪ) *n., pl.* **-ties.** **1.** vitriolic or embittered speech, temper, etc. **2.** sourness or bitterness of taste.

acetaldehyde (ˌæsɪ'tældɪˌhaɪd) *n.* a colourless volatile pungent liquid, used in the manufacture of organic compounds and as a solvent. Formula: CH_3CHO.

acetate ('æsɪˌteɪt) *n.* **1.** any salt or ester of acetic acid. **2.** short for **acetate rayon** *or* **cellulose acetate.**

acetate rayon *n.* a synthetic textile fibre made from cellulose acetate.

acetic (ə'siːtɪk) *adj.* of, containing, producing, or derived from acetic acid or vinegar.

acetic acid *n.* a colourless pungent liquid widely used in the manufacture of plastics, pharmaceuticals, dyes, etc. Formula: CH_3COOH. See also **vinegar.**

aceto- *or before a vowel* **acet-** *combining form.* containing an acetyl group or derived from acetic acid: *acetone.*

acetone ('æsɪˌtəʊn) *n.* a colourless volatile pungent liquid used in the manufacture of chemicals and as a solvent for paints, varnishes, and lacquers. Formula: CH_3COCH_3.

acetylene (ə'sɛtɪˌliːn) *n.* a colourless soluble flammable gas used in the manufacture of organic chemicals and in cutting and welding metals. Formula: C_2H_2.

ache (eɪk) *vb.* (*intr.*) **1.** to feel, suffer, or be the source of a continuous dull pain. **2.** to suffer mental anguish. ~*n.* **3.** a continuous dull pain. —'**aching** *adj.*

achieve (ə'tʃiːv) *vb.* **1.** to bring to a successful conclusion. **2.** (*tr.*) to gain as by hard work or effort: *to achieve success.* —**a'chievable** *adj.* —**a'chiever** *n.*

achievement (ə'tʃiːvmənt) *n.* **1.** something that has been accomplished, esp. by hard work, ability, or heroism. **2.** successful completion; accomplishment.

THESAURUS

accredit 1. appoint, authorize, certify, commission, depute, empower, endorse, entrust, guarantee, license, recognize, sanction, vouch for **2.** ascribe, assign, attribute, credit

accredited appointed, authorized, certified, commissioned, deputed, deputized, empowered, endorsed, guaranteed, licensed, official, recognized, sanctioned, vouched for

accrue accumulate, amass, arise, be added, build up, collect, enlarge, ensue, flow, follow, grow, increase, issue, spring up

accumulate accrue, amass, build up, collect, cumulate, gather, grow, hoard, increase, pile up, stockpile, store

accumulation aggregation, augmentation, build-up, collection, conglomeration, gathering, growth, heap, hoard, increase, mass, pile, stack, stock, stockpile, store

accuracy accurateness, authenticity, carefulness, closeness, correctness, exactitude, exactness, faithfulness, faultlessness, fidelity, meticulousness, niceness, nicety, precision, strictness, truth, truthfulness, veracity, verity

accurate authentic, careful, close, correct, exact, faithful, faultless, just, meticulous, nice, precise, proper, regular, right,

scrupulous, spot-on (*Inf.*), strict, true, truthful, unerring, veracious

accurately authentically, carefully, closely, correctly, exactly, faithfully, faultlessly, justly, meticulously, nicely, precisely, properly, regularly, rightly, scrupulously, strictly, truly, truthfully, unerringly, veraciously

accursed 1. bedevilled, bewitched, condemned, cursed, damned, doomed, hopeless, ill-fated, ill-omened, jinxed, luckless, ruined, undone, unfortunate, unlucky, wretched **2.** abominable, despicable, detestable, execrable, hateful, hellish, horrible

accusation allegation, arraignment, attribution, charge, citation, complaint, denunciation, impeachment, imputation, incrimination, indictment, recrimination

accuse allege, arraign, attribute, blame, censure, charge, cite, denounce, impeach, impute, incriminate, indict, recriminate, tax

accustom acclimatize, acquaint, adapt, discipline, exercise, familiarize, habituate, inure, season, train

accustomed 1. acclimatized, acquainted, adapted, disciplined, exercised, familiar, familiarized, given to, habituated, in the hab-

it of, inured, seasoned, trained, used **2.** common, conventional, customary, established, everyday, expected, fixed, general, habitual, normal, ordinary, regular, routine, set, traditional, usual, wonted

ace *n.* **1.** *Cards, dice, etc.* one, single point **2.** *Inf.* adept, champion, dab hand (*Inf.*), expert, genius, master, star, virtuoso, winner, wizard (*Inf.*) ~*adj.* **3.** *Inf.* brilliant, champion, excellent, expert, fine, great, masterly, outstanding, superb, virtuoso

ache *v.* **1.** hurt, pain, pound, smart, suffer, throb, twinge **2.** agonize, grieve, mourn, sorrow, suffer **3.** covet, crave, desire, hanker, hunger, long, need, pine, yearn ~*n.* **4.** hurt, pain, pang, pounding, smart, smarting, soreness, suffering, throb, throbbing **5.** anguish, grief, mourning, sorrow, suffering **6.** craving, desire, hankering, hunger, longing, need, pining, yearning

achievable accessible, accomplishable, acquirable, attainable, feasible, obtainable, possible, practicable, reachable, realizable, winnable, within one's grasp

achieve accomplish, acquire, attain, bring about, carry out, complete, consummate, do, earn, effect, execute, finish, fulfil,

Achilles heel (əˈkɪliːz) n. a small but fatal weakness.
Achilles tendon n. the fibrous cord that connects the muscles of the calf to the heelbone.
achromatic (ˌækrəˈmætɪk) adj. **1.** without colour. **2.** capable of reflecting or refracting light without chromatic aberration. **3.** Music. involving no sharps or flats. —ˌachroˈmatically adv. —**achromatism** (əˈkrəʊməˌtɪzəm) or **achromaticity** (ə,krəʊməˈtɪsɪtɪ) n.
acid (ˈæsɪd) n. **1.** any substance that dissociates in water to yield a sour corrosive solution containing hydrogen ions, and turning litmus red. **2.** a sour-tasting substance. **3.** a slang name for **LSD**. **4. put the acid on** (someone). Austral. inf. to apply pressure to someone, usually when seeking a favour. ~adj. **5.** Chem. **a.** of, derived from, or containing acid. **b.** being or having the properties of an acid. **6.** sharp or sour in taste. **7.** cutting, sharp, or hurtful in speech, manner, etc. —ˈacidly adv. —ˈacidness n.
acidic (əˈsɪdɪk) adj. another word for **acid**.
acidify (əˈsɪdɪ,faɪ) vb. **-fying, -fied.** to convert into or become acid. —aˈcidiˌfiable adj. —a,cidifiˈcation n.
acidity (əˈsɪdɪtɪ) n., pl. **-ties. 1.** the quality or state of being acid. **2.** the amount of acid present in a solution.
acidosis (ˌæsɪˈdəʊsɪs) n. a condition characterized by an abnormal increase in the acidity of the blood. —**acidotic** (ˌæsɪˈdɒtɪk) adj.
acid test n. a rigorous and conclusive test to establish worth or value.
acidulous (əˈsɪdjʊləs) or **acidulent** adj. **1.** rather sour. **2.** sharp or sour in speech, manner, etc.; acid.
ack-ack (ˈæk,æk) n. Mil. **1.** anti-aircraft fire. **2.** (as modifier): ack-ack guns.
acknowledge (əkˈnɒlɪdʒ) vb. (tr.) **1.** (may take a clause as object) to recognize or admit the existence, truth, or reality of. **2.** to indicate recognition or awareness of, as by a greeting, glance, etc. **3.** to express appreciation or thanks for. **4.** to make the receipt of known: to acknowledge a letter. **5.** to recognize, esp. in legal form, the authority, rights, or claims of. —acˈknowledgeable adj.
acknowledgment or **acknowledgement** (əkˈnɒlɪdʒmənt) n. **1.** the act of acknowledging or state of being acknowledged. **2.** something done or given as an expression of thanks. **3.** (pl.) an author's statement acknowledging his use of the works of other authors.
acme (ˈækmɪ) n. the culminating point, as of achievement or excellence.
acne (ˈæknɪ) n. a chronic skin disease common in adolescence, characterized by pustules on the face.
acolyte (ˈækə,laɪt) n. **1.** a follower or attendant. **2.**

Christianity. an officer who assists a priest.
aconite (ˈækə,naɪt) n. **1.** any of a genus of N temperate plants, such as monkshood and wolfsbane, many of which are poisonous. **2.** the dried poisonous root of many of these plants, sometimes used as a narcotic. —**aconitic** (ˌækəˈnɪtɪk) adj.
acorn (ˈeɪkɔːn) n. the fruit of the oak tree, consisting of a smooth thick-walled nut in a woody scaly cuplike base.
acoustic (əˈkuːstɪk) or **acoustical** adj. **1.** of or related to sound, the sense of hearing, or acoustics. **2.** designed to respond to or absorb sound: an acoustic tile. **3.** (of a musical instrument or recording) without electronic amplification: an acoustic guitar. —aˈcoustically adv.
acoustics (əˈkuːstɪks) n. **1.** (functioning as sing.) the scientific study of sound and sound waves. **2.** (functioning as pl.) the characteristics of a room, auditorium, etc., that determine the fidelity with which sound can be heard within it.
acquaint (əˈkweɪnt) vb. (tr.) (foll. by with or of) to make (a person) familiar (with).
acquaintance (əˈkweɪntəns) n. **1.** a person whom one knows but who is not a close friend. **2.** knowledge of a person or thing, esp. when slight. **3. make the acquaintance of.** to come into social contact with. **4.** those persons collectively whom one knows. —acˈquaintance,ship n.
acquainted (əˈkweɪntɪd) adj. (postpositive) **1.** (sometimes foll. by with) on terms of familiarity but not intimacy. **2.** (foll. by with) familiar (with).
acquiesce (ˌækwɪˈɛs) vb. (intr.; often foll. by in or to) to comply (with); assent (to) without protest. —ˌacquiˈescence n. —ˌacquiˈescent adj.
acquire (əˈkwaɪə) vb. (tr.) to get or gain (something, such as an object, trait, or ability). —acˈquirable adj. —acˈquirement n. —**acquisition** (ˌækwɪˈzɪʃən) n.
acquired taste n. **1.** a liking for something at first considered unpleasant. **2.** the thing liked.
acquisitive (əˈkwɪzɪtɪv) adj. inclined or eager to acquire things, esp. material possessions or ideas. —acˈquisitively adv. —acˈquisitiveness n.
acquit (əˈkwɪt) vb. **-quitting, -quitted.** (tr.) **1.** (foll. by of) **a.** to free or release (from a charge of crime). **b.** to pronounce not guilty. **2.** (foll. by of) to free or relieve (from an obligation, duty, etc.). **3.** to repay or settle (a debt or obligation). **4.** to conduct (oneself). —acˈquittal n. —acˈquitter n.
acre (ˈeɪkə) n. **1.** a unit of area used in certain English-speaking countries, equal to 4840 square yards or 4046.86 square metres. **2.** (pl.) **a.** land, esp. a large area. **b.** Inf. a large amount. **3. farm the long acre.** N.Z. to graze

---

THESAURUS

gain, get, obtain, perform, procure, reach, realize, win
achievement 1. accomplishment, acquirement, attainment, completion, execution, fulfilment, performance, production, realization **2.** accomplishment, act, deed, effort, exploit, feat, stroke
acid 1. acerbic, acidulous, acrid, biting, pungent, sharp, sour, tart, vinegarish, vinegary **2.** acerbic, acid, biting, bitter, caustic, cutting, harsh, hurtful, mordant, pungent, sharp, stinging, trenchant, vitriolic
acidity 1. acerbity, acidulousness, acridity, acridness, bitterness, pungency, sharpness, sourness, tartness, vinegariness, vinegarishness **2.** acerbity, acridity, acridness, bitterness, causticity, causticness, harshness, hurtfulness, mordancy, pungency, sharpness, trenchancy
acknowledge 1. accede, accept, acquiesce, admit, allow, concede, confess, declare, grant, own, profess, recognize, yield **2.** address, greet, hail, notice, recognize, salute **3.** answer, notice, react to, recognize, reply to, respond to, return
acknowledged accepted, accredited, admitted, answered, approved, conceded, confessed, declared, professed, recognized, returned
acknowledgment 1. acceptance, accession, acquiescence, admission, allowing, confession, declaration, profession, realiza-

tion, yielding **2.** addressing, greeting, hail, hailing, notice, recognition, salutation, salute **3.** answer, appreciation, credit, gratitude, action, recognition, reply, response, return, thanks
acme apex, climax, crown, culmination, height, high point, optimum, peak, pinnacle, summit, top, vertex, zenith
acquaint advise, announce, apprise, disclose, divulge, enlighten, familiarize, inform, let (someone) know, notify, reveal, tell
acquaintance 1. associate, colleague, contact **2.** association, awareness, cognizance, companionship, conversance, conversancy, experience, familiarity, fellowship, intimacy, knowledge, relationship, social contact, understanding
acquainted alive to, apprised of, au fait, aware of, cognizant of, conscious of, conversant with, experienced in, familiar with, informed of, in on, knowledgeable about, privy to, versed in
acquiesce accede, accept, agree, allow, approve, assent, bow to, comply, concur, conform, consent, give in, go along with, submit, yield
acquiescence acceptance, accession, agreement, approval, assent, compliance, concurrence, conformity, consent, giving in, obedience, submission, yielding
acquiescent acceding, accepting, agreeable, agreeing, approving, assenting,

compliant, concurrent, conforming, consenting, obedient, submissive, yielding
acquire achieve, amass, attain, buy, collect, earn, gain, gather, get, obtain, pick up, procure, realize, receive, secure, win
acquirement accomplishment, achievement, acquisition, attainment, gathering, knowledge, learning, mastery, mental gains, qualification, skill
acquisition 1. buy, gain, possession, prize, property, purchase **2.** achievement, acquirement, attainment, gaining, learning, obtainment, procurement, pursuit
acquisitive avaricious, avid, covetous, grabbing, grasping, greedy, predatory, rapacious
acquisitiveness avarice, avidity, avidness, covetousness, graspingness, greed, predatoriness, rapaciousness, rapacity
acquit 1. absolve, clear, deliver, discharge, exculpate, exonerate, free, fulfil, liberate, release, relieve, vindicate **2.** discharge, pay, pay off, repay, satisfy, settle **3.** bear, behave, comport, conduct, perform
acquittal absolution, clearance, deliverance, discharge, exculpation, exoneration, freeing, liberation, release, relief, vindication
acquittance acknowledgment, discharge, payment, receipt, release, settlement, settling

stock on the grass along a highway.

acreage ('eɪkərɪdʒ) n. land area in acres.

acrid ('ækrɪd) adj. 1. unpleasantly pungent or sharp to the smell or taste. 2. sharp or caustic, esp. in speech or nature. —**acridity** (ə'krɪdɪtɪ) n. —**acridly** adv.

acrimony ('ækrɪmənɪ) n., pl. -nies. bitterness or sharpness of manner, speech, temper, etc. —**acrimonious** (,ækrɪ'məʊnɪəs) adj.

acro- combining form. 1. denoting something at a height, top, beginning, or end: acropolis. 2. denoting an extremity of the human body: acromegaly.

acrobat ('ækrə,bæt) n. 1. an entertainer who performs acts that require skill, agility, and coordination, such as swinging from a trapeze or walking a tightrope. 2. Inf. a person noted for his frequent and rapid changes of position or allegiance. —**acrobatic** adj. —**acrobatically** adv.

acrobatics (,ækrə'bætɪks) n. 1. (functioning as pl.) the skills or feats of an acrobat. 2. (functioning as pl.) any activity requiring agility and skill: mental acrobatics.

acromegaly (,ækrəʊ'mɛgəlɪ) n. a chronic disease characterized by enlargement of the bones of the head, hands, and feet. It is caused by excessive secretion of growth hormone by the pituitary gland. —**acromegalic** (,ækrəʊmɪ'gælɪk) adj., n.

acronym ('ækrənɪm) n. a word formed from the initial letters of a group of words; for example, UNESCO for the United Nations Educational, Scientific, and Cultural Organization.

acrophobia (,ækrə'fəʊbɪə) n. abnormal fear or dread of being at a great height. —**acrophobic** adj.

acropolis (ə'krɒpəlɪs) n. the citadel of an ancient Greek city.

Acropolis n. the citadel of Athens on which the Parthenon stands.

across (ə'krɒs) prep. 1. from one side to the other side of. 2. on or at the other side of. ~adv. 3. from one side to the other. 4. on or to the other side.

across-the-board adj. (of salary increases, taxation cuts, etc.) affecting all ranks or classes equally.

acrostic (ə'krɒstɪk) n. a number of lines of writing, such as a poem, certain letters of which form a word, proverb, etc. A **single acrostic** is formed by the initial letters of the lines, a **double acrostic** by the initial and final letters, and a **triple acrostic** by the initial, middle, and final letters. —**acrostically** adv.

acrylic (ə'krɪlɪk) adj. 1. of, derived from, or concerned with acrylic acid. ~n. 2. short for **acrylic resin**.

acrylic fibre n. a textile fibre, such as Orlon or Acrilan.

acrylic resin n. any of a group of polymers of acrylic acid, its esters, or amides, used as synthetic rubbers, paints, and as plastics such as Perspex.

act (ækt) n. 1. something done or performed. 2. the performance of some physical or mental process; action. 3. (cap. when part of a name) the formally codified result of deliberation by a legislative body. 4. (often pl.) a formal written record of transactions, proceedings, etc., as of a society, committee, or legislative body. 5. a major division of a dramatic work. 6. a. a short performance of skill, a comic sketch, dance, etc. b. those giv-

ing such a performance. 7. an assumed attitude or pose, esp. one intended to impress ~vb. 8. (intr.) to do something. 9. (intr.) to operate; react: his mind acted quickly. 10. to perform (a part or role) in a play, etc. 11. (tr.) to present (a play, etc.) on stage. 12. (intr.; usually foll. by for or as) to be a substitute (for). 13. (intr.; foll. by as) to serve the function or purpose (of). 14. (intr.) to conduct oneself or behave (as if one were): she usually acts like a lady. 15. (intr.) to behave in an unnatural or affected way. 16. (copula) to play the part of: to act the fool. 17. (copula) to behave in a manner appropriate to: to act one's age. ~See also **act up**. —**actable** adj. —**acta'bility** n.

A.C.T. abbrev. for Australian Capital Territory.

acting ('æktɪŋ) adj. (prenominal) 1. taking on duties temporarily, esp. as a substitute for another. 2. performing the duties of though not yet holding the rank of: acting lieutenant. 3. operating or functioning. 4. intended for stage performance; provided with directions for actors: an acting version of "Hedda Gabler". ~n. 5. the art or profession of an actor.

actinide series ('æktɪ,naɪd) n. a series of 15 radioactive elements with increasing atomic numbers from actinium to lawrencium.

actinium (æk'tɪnɪəm) n. a radioactive element of the actinide series, occurring as a decay product of uranium. It is used in neutron production. Symbol: Ac; atomic no.: 89; half-life of most stable isotope,^{227}Ac: 22 years.

action ('ækʃən) n. 1. the state or process of doing something or being active. 2. something done, such as an act or deed. 3. movement or posture during some physical activity. 4. activity, force, or energy: a man of action. 5. (usually pl.) conduct or behaviour. 6. Law. a legal proceeding brought by one party against another; lawsuit. 7. the operating mechanism, esp. in a piano, gun, watch, etc. 8. the force applied to a body. 9. the way in which something operates or works. 10. **out of action**. not functioning. 11. the events that form the plot of a story, play, or other composition. 12. Mil. a. a minor engagement. b. fighting at sea or on land: he saw action in the war. 13. Inf. the profits of an enterprise or transaction (esp. in **a piece of the action**). 14. Sl. the main activity, esp. social activity. ~interj. 15. a command given by a film director to indicate that filming is to begin. ~vb. 16. to put (a proposal or plan) into operation.

actionable ('ækʃənəb⁰l) adj. Law. affording grounds for legal action. —**actionably** adv.

action painting n. a development of abstract expressionism characterized by accidental effects of thrown, smeared, dripped, or spattered paint. Also called: **tachisme**.

action stations pl. n. Mil. 1. the positions taken up by individuals in preparation for or during a battle. ~interj. 2. a command to take up such positions. 3. Inf. a warning to get ready for something.

activate ('æktɪ,veɪt) vb. (tr.) 1. to make active or capable of action. 2. Physics. to make radioactive. 3. Chem. to increase the rate of (a reaction). 4. to purify (sewage) by aeration. 5. U.S. mil. to mobilize or organize (a unit). —**acti'vation** n. —**'acti,vator** n.

THESAURUS

acrid 1. acid, astringent, biting, bitter, burning, caustic, harsh, irritating, pungent, sharp, stinging 2. acrimonious, biting, bitter, caustic, cutting, harsh, mordant, nasty, sarcastic, sharp, trenchant, vitriolic

acrimonious acerbic, astringent, biting, bitter, caustic, censorious, churlish, crabbed, cutting, irascible, mordant, peevish, petulant, pungent, rancorous, sarcastic, severe, sharp, spiteful, splenetic, tart, testy, trenchant

acrimony acerbity, asperity, astringency, bitterness, churlishness, harshness, ill will, irascibility, mordancy, peevishness, rancour, sarcasm, spleen, tartness, trenchancy, virulence

act n. 1. accomplishment, achievement, action, blow, deed, doing, execution, exertion, exploit, feat, move, operation, performance, step, stroke, undertaking 2. bill, decree, edict, enactment, law, measure, ordinance,

resolution, statute 3. affectation, attitude, counterfeit, dissimulation, fake, feigning, front, performance, pose, posture, pretence, sham, show, stance 4. performance, routine, show, sketch, turn ~v. 5. acquit, bear, behave, carry, carry out, comport, conduct, do, enact, execute, exert, function, go about, make, move, operate, perform, react, serve, strike, take effect, undertake, work 6. affect, assume, counterfeit, dissimulate, feign, imitate, perform, pose, posture, pretend, put on, seem, sham 7. act out, characterize, enact, impersonate, mime, mimic, perform, personate, personify, play, play or take the part of, portray, represent

act for cover for, deputize for, fill in for, function in place of, replace, represent, serve, stand in for, substitute for, take the place of

acting adj. 1. interim, pro tem, provisional, substitute, surrogate, temporary ~n. 2. characterization, dramatics, enacting, im-

personation, performance, performing, playing, portrayal, portraying, stagecraft, theatre 3. assuming, counterfeiting, dissimulation, feigning, imitating, imitation, imposture, play-acting, posing, posturing, pretence, pretending, putting on, seeming, shamming

action 1. accomplishment, achievement, act, blow, deed, exercise, exertion, exploit, feat, move, operation, performance, stop, stroke, undertaking 2. activity, energy, force, liveliness, spirit, vigour, vim, vitality 3. activity, effect, effort, exertion, force, functioning, influence, motion, movement, operation, power, process, work, working 4. battle, combat, conflict, fighting, warfare 5. affray, battle, clash, combat, contest, encounter, engagement, fight, fray, skirmish, sortie 6. case, cause, lawsuit, litigation, proceeding, prosecution, suit

actions bearing, behaviour, comportment, conduct, demeanour, deportment, manners, ways

activated carbon *n.* a highly adsorptive form of carbon used to remove colour or impurities from liquids and gases.

activated sludge *n.* a mass of aerated precipitated sewage added to untreated sewage to bring about purification by hastening bacterial decomposition.

active ('æktɪv) *adj.* 1. moving, working, or doing something. 2. busy or involved: *an active life*. 3. physically energetic. 4. effective: *an active ingredient*. 5. *Grammar.* denoting a voice of verbs used to indicate that the subject of a sentence is performing the action or causing the event or process described by the verb, as *kicked* in *The boy kicked the football*. 6. being fully engaged in military service. 7. (of a volcano) erupting periodically; not extinct. 8. *Astron.* (of the sun) exhibiting a large number of sunspots, solar flares, etc., and a marked variation in intensity and frequency of radio emission. ~*n.* 9. *Grammar.* **a.** the active voice. **b.** an active verb. —'**actively** *adv.* —'**activeness** *n.*

active list *n. Mil.* a list of officers available for full duty.

activism ('æktɪˌvɪzəm) *n.* a policy of taking direct and often militant action to achieve an end, esp. a political or social one. —'**activist** *n.*

activity (æk'tɪvɪtɪ) *n., pl.* -**ties.** 1. the state or quality of being active. 2. lively action or movement. 3. any specific action, pursuit, etc.: *recreational activities*. 4. the number of disintegrations of a radioactive substance in a given unit of time.

act of God *n. Law.* a sudden and inevitable occurrence caused by natural forces, such as a flood or earthquake.

actor ('æktə) *or (fem.)* **actress** ('æktrɪs) *n.* a person who acts in a play, film, broadcast, etc.

ACTU *abbrev. for* Australian Council of Trade Unions.

actual ('æktʃʊəl) *adj.* 1. existing in reality or as a matter of fact. 2. real or genuine. 3. existing at the present time; current.

▷ **Usage.** The excessive use of *actual* and *actually* should be avoided. They are unnecessary in sentences such as *in actual fact, he is forty-two,* and *he did actually go to the play but did not enjoy it.*

actuality (ˌæktʃʊ'ælɪtɪ) *n., pl.* -**ties.** 1. true existence; reality. 2. (*sometimes pl.*) a fact or condition that is real.

actually ('æktʃʊəlɪ) *adv.* 1. **a.** as an actual fact; really. **b.** (*as sentence modifier*): *actually, I haven't seen him.* 2. at present.

actuarius ('æktʃʊˌɛərɪəs) *n. S. African history.* an official of the synod of a Dutch Reformed Church.

actuary ('æktʃʊərɪ) *n., pl.* -**aries.** a statistician, esp. one employed by insurance companies to calculate risks,

policy premiums, and dividends. —**actuarial** (ˌæktʃʊ-'ɛərɪəl) *adj.*

actuate ('æktʃʊˌeɪt) *vb.* (*tr.*) 1. to put into action or mechanical motion. 2. to motivate: *actuated by unworthy desires.* —ˌactu'**ation** *n.* —'**actu**ˌ**ator** *n.*

act up *vb.* (*intr., adv.*) *Inf.* to behave in a troublesome way: *the engine began to act up.*

acuity (ə'kjuːɪtɪ) *n.* keenness or acuteness, esp. in vision or thought.

aculeus (ə'kjuːlɪəs) *n.* 1. a prickle, such as the thorn of a rose. 2. a sting. —a'**culeate** *adj.*

acumen ('ækjʊˌmɛn, ə'kjuːmən) *n.* the ability to judge well; insight. —a'**cuminous** *adj.*

acupuncture ('ækjʊˌpʌŋktʃə) *n.* the insertion of the tips of needles into the skin at specific points for the purpose of treating various disorders by stimulating nerve impulses.

acute (ə'kjuːt) *adj.* 1. penetrating in perception or insight. 2. sensitive to details; keen. 3. of extreme importance; crucial. 4. sharp or severe; intense. 5. having a sharp end or point. 6. *Maths.* (of an angle) less than 90°. 7. (of a disease) **a.** arising suddenly and manifesting intense severity. **b.** of relatively short duration. 8. *Phonetics.* of or relating to an accent (´) placed over vowels, denoting that the vowel is pronounced with higher musical pitch (as in ancient Greek) or with certain special quality (as in French). ~*n.* 9. an acute accent. —a'**cutely** *adv.* —a'**cuteness** *n.*

acute accent *n.* the diacritical mark (´), used in some languages to indicate that the vowel over which it is placed has a special quality (as in French été) or that it receives the strongest stress in the word (as in Spanish hablé).

ad (æd) *n. Inf.* short for **advertisement.**

A.D. (indicating years numbered from the supposed year of the birth of Christ) *abbrev. for* anno Domini: *70 A.D.*

▷ **Usage.** In strict usage, A.D. is only employed with specific years: *he died in 1621 A.D.,* but *he died in the 17th century.* Formerly the practice was to write A.D. preceding the date (*A.D. 1621*), and it is also strictly correct to omit *in* when A.D. is used, since this is already contained in the meaning of the Latin *anno Domini* (in the year of Our Lord), but this is no longer general practice. B.C. is used with both specific dates and indications of the period: *Heraclitus was born about 540 B.C.; the battle took place in the 4th century B.C.*

ad- *prefix.* 1. to; towards: *adverb.* 2. near; next to: *adrenal.*

adage ('ædɪdʒ) *n.* a traditional saying that is accepted by many as true; proverb.

THESAURUS

activate actuate, animate, arouse, energize, galvanize, impel, initiate, mobilize, motivate, move, prompt, propel, rouse, set going, set in motion, set off, start, stimulate, stir, switch on, trigger (off), turn on

active 1. acting, astir, at work, doing, effectual, functioning, in action, in force, in operation, live, moving, operative, running, stirring, working 2. bustling, busy, engaged, full, hard-working, involved, occupied, on the go (*Inf.*), on the move, strenuous 3. alert, animated, diligent, energetic, industrious, lively, nimble, on the go (*Inf.*), quick, spirited, sprightly, spry, vibrant, vigorous, vital, vivacious 4. activist, aggressive, ambitious, assertive, committed, devoted, energetic, engaged, enterprising, enthusiastic, forceful, forward, hard-working, industrious, militant, zealous

activity 1. action, activeness, animation, bustle, enterprise, exercise, exertion, hurly-burly, hustle, labour, life, liveliness, motion, movement, stir, work 2. act, avocation, deed, endeavour, enterprise, hobby, interest, job, labour, occupation, pastime, project, pursuit, scheme, task, undertaking, venture, work

act on, act upon 1. act in accordance with, carry out, comply with, conform to, follow, heed, obey, yield to 2. affect, alter, change, influence, modify, sway, transform

actor 1. actress, dramatic artist, leading

man, performer, play-actor, player, Thespian, tragedian, trouper 2. agent, doer, executor, factor, functionary, operative, operator, participant, participator, performer, perpetrator, practitioner, worker

actress actor, dramatic artist, leading lady, performer, play-actor, player, starlet, Thespian, tragedienne, trouper

actual 1. absolute, categorical, certain, concrete, corporeal, definite, factual, indisputable, indubitable, physical, positive, real, substantial, tangible, undeniable, unquestionable 2. authentic, confirmed, genuine, real, realistic, true, truthful, verified 3. current, existent, extant, live, living, present, present-day, prevailing

actually absolutely, as a matter of fact, de facto, essentially, indeed, in fact, in point of fact, in reality, in truth, literally, really, truly, veritably

actuate animate, arouse, cause, dispose, drive, excite, impel, incite, induce, influence, inspire, instigate, motivate, move, prompt, quicken, rouse, spur, stimulate, stir, urge

act up be naughty, carry on, cause trouble, give bother, give trouble, horse around (*Inf.*), malfunction, mess about, misbehave, play up (*Brit. inf.*)

act upon *see* ACT ON

acumen acuteness, astuteness, clever-

ness, discernment, ingenuity, insight, intelligence, judgment, keenness, penetration, perception, perspicacity, perspicuity, sagacity, sharpness, shrewdness, smartness, wisdom, wit

acute 1. astute, canny, clever, discerning, discriminating, incisive, ingenious, insightful, intuitive, keen, observant, penetrating, perceptive, perspicacious, piercing, sensitive, sharp, smart, subtle 2. critical, crucial, dangerous, decisive, essential, grave, important, serious, severe, sudden, urgent, vital 3. cutting, distressing, excruciating, exquisite, fierce, intense, overpowering, overwhelming, piercing, poignant, powerful, racking, severe, sharp, shooting, shrill, stabbing, sudden, violent 4. cuspate, needle-shaped, peaked, pointed, sharp, sharpened

acuteness 1. acuity, astuteness, canniness, cleverness, discernment, discrimination, ingenuity, insight, intuition, intuitiveness, keenness, perception, perceptiveness, perspicacity, sensitivity, sharpness, smartness, subtleness, subtlety, wit 2. criticality, criticalness, cruciality, danger, dangerousness, decisiveness, essentiality, gravity, importance, seriousness, severity, suddenness, urgency, vitalness 3. distressingness, exquisiteness, fierceness, intenseness, intensity, poignancy, powerfulness, severity, sharpness, shrillness, suddenness, violence 4.

adagio (ə'dɑːdʒɪ,əʊ) *Music.* ~*adj., adv.* **1.** slow. ~*n., pl.* **-gios.** **2.** a movement or piece to be performed slowly.

Adam ('ædəm) *n.* **1.** *Bible.* the first man, created by God (Genesis 2–3). **2. not know (someone) from Adam.** to fail to be acquainted with someone. **3. Adam's ale** *or* **wine.** water.

adamant ('ædəmənt) *adj.* **1.** unyielding; inflexible. **2.** unbreakable; impenetrable. ~*n.* **3.** any extremely hard substance. **4.** a legendary stone said to be impenetrable. —ˌada'mantine *adj.*

Adam's apple *n.* the visible projection of the thyroid cartilage of the larynx at the front of the neck.

adapt (ə'dæpt) *vb.* **1.** (often foll. by *to*) to adjust (someone or something) to different conditions. **2.** (*tr.*) to fit, change, or modify to suit a new or different purpose. —a'daptable *adj.* —aˌdapta'bility *n.* —a'daptive *adj.*

adaptation (ˌædəp'teɪʃən) *n.* **1.** the act or process of adapting or the state of being adapted. **2.** something that is produced by adapting something else. **3.** something that is changed or modified to suit new conditions. **4.** *Biol.* a modification in organisms that makes them better suited to survive and reproduce in a particular environment.

adapter *or* **adaptor** (ə'dæptə) *n.* **1.** a person or thing that adapts. **2.** any device for connecting two parts, esp. ones that are of different sizes. **3. a.** a plug used to connect an electrical device to a mains supply when they have different types of terminals. **b.** a device used to connect several electrical appliances to a single socket.

A.D.C. *abbrev. for:* **1.** aide-de-camp. **2.** analog-digital converter.

add (æd) *vb.* **1.** to combine (two or more numbers or quantities) by addition. **2.** (*tr.;* foll. by *to*) to increase (a number or quantity) by another number or quantity using addition. **3.** (*tr.;* often foll. by *to*) to join (something) to something else in order to increase the size, effect, or scope: *to add insult to injury.* **4.** (*intr.;* foll. by *to*) to have an extra and increased effect (on). **5.** (*tr.*) to say or write further. **6.** (*tr.;* foll. by *in*) to include.

addend ('ædɛnd) *n.* any of a set of numbers that form a sum.

addendum (ə'dɛndəm) *n., pl.* **-da** (-də). **1.** something added; an addition. **2.** a supplement or appendix to a book, magazine, etc.

adder ('ædə) *n.* **1.** Also called: **viper.** a common viper that is widely distributed in Europe, including Britain, and Asia and is dark grey with a black zigzag pattern along the back. **2.** any of various similar venomous or nonvenomous snakes. ~See also **puff adder.**

addict *vb.* (ə'dɪkt). **1.** (*tr.;* usually passive; often foll. by *to*) to cause (someone or oneself) to become dependent (on something, esp. a narcotic drug). ~*n.* ('ædɪkt). **2.** a person who is addicted, esp. to narcotic drugs. **3.** *Inf.* a person devoted to something: *a jazz addict.* —ad'diction *n.* —ad'dictive *adj.*

addition (ə'dɪʃən) *n.* **1.** the act, process, or result of adding. **2.** a person or thing that is added or acquired. **3.** a mathematical operation in which the sum of two numbers or quantities is calculated. Usually indicated by the symbol +. **4.** *Obs.* a title. **5. in addition.** (*adv.*) also; as well. **6. in addition to.** (*prep.*) besides; as well as. —ad'ditional *adj.*

additive ('ædɪtɪv) *adj.* **1.** characterized or produced by addition. ~*n.* **2.** any substance added to something to improve it, prevent deterioration, etc.

addle ('æd³l) *vb.* **1.** to make or become confused or muddled. **2.** to make or become rotten. ~*adj.* **3.** (*in combination*) indicating a confused or muddled state: *addle-brained.*

address (ə'drɛs) *n.* **1.** the conventional form by which the location of a building is described. **2.** the written form of this, as on a letter or parcel. **3.** the place at which someone lives. **4.** a speech or written communication, esp. one of a formal nature. **5.** skilfulness or tact. **6.** *Arch.* manner of speaking. **7.** *Computers.* a number giving the location of a piece of stored information. **8.** (usually *pl.*) expressions of affection made by a man in courting a woman. ~*vb.* (*tr.*) **9.** to mark (a letter, parcel, etc.) with an address. **10.** to speak to, refer to in speaking, or deliver a speech to. **11.** (used reflexively; foll. by *to*) **a.** to speak or write to. **b.** apply oneself to: *he addressed himself to the task.* **12.** to direct (a message, warning, etc.) to the attention of. **13.** to adopt a position facing (the ball in golf, etc.). —ad'dresser *or* ad'dressor *n.*

addressee (ˌædrɛ'siː) *n.* a person or organization to whom a letter, etc., is addressed.

adduce (ə'djuːs) *vb.* (*tr.*) to cite (reasons, examples, etc.) as evidence or proof. —ad'ducible *adj.* —ad'ducent *adj.* —**adduction** (ə'dʌkʃən) *n.*

-ade *suffix forming nouns.* a sweetened drink made of various fruits: *lemonade.*

adeno- *or before a vowel* **aden-** *combining form.* gland or glandular: *adenoid; adenology.*

adenoidal (ˌædɪ'nɔɪd³l) *adj.* **1.** having the nasal tones or impaired breathing of one with enlarged adenoids. **2.** of adenoids.

adenoids ('ædɪˌnɔɪdz) *pl. n.* a mass of lymphoid tissue at the back of the throat behind the uvula: when enlarged it often restricts nasal breathing, esp. in young children.

adept *adj.* (ə'dɛpt). **1.** proficient in something requiring skill or manual dexterity. **2.** expert. ~*n.* ('ædɛpt). **3.** a person who is skilled or proficient in something. —a'deptness *n.*

THESAURUS

pointedness, sharpness

adage aphorism, apophthegm, axiom, byword, dictum, maxim, motto, precept, proverb, saw, saying

adamant 1. determined, firm, fixed, immovable, inexorable, inflexible, insistent, intransigent, obdurate, resolute, rigid, set, stiff, stubborn, unbending, uncompromising, unrelenting, unshakable, unyielding 2. adamantine, flinty, hard, impenetrable, indestructible, rock-hard, rocky, steely, stony, tough, unbreakable

adapt acclimatize, accommodate, adjust, alter, apply, change, comply, conform, familiarize, fashion, fit, habituate, harmonize, make, match, modify, prepare, qualify, remodel, shape, suit, tailor

adaptability adaptableness, adjustability, alterability, changeability, compliancy, convertibility, flexibility, malleability, modifiability, plasticity, pliability, pliancy, resilience, variability, versatility

adaptable adjustable, alterable, changeable, compliant, conformable, convertible, easy-going, flexible, malleable, modifiable, plastic, pliant, resilient, variable, versatile

adaptation 1. adjustment, alteration, change, conversion, modification, refitting, remodelling, reworking, shift, transformation, variation, version 2. acclimatization, ac-

customedness, familiarization, habituation, naturalization

add 1. adjoin, affix, amplify, annex, append, attach, augment, enlarge by, include, increase by, supplement 2. add up, compute, count up, reckon, sum up, total, tot up

addendum addition, adjunct, affix, appendage, appendix, attachment, augmentation, codicil, extension, extra, postscript, supplement

addict 1. dope-fiend (*Sl.*), fiend (*Inf.*), freak (*Sl.*), head (*Sl.*), junkie (*Sl.*), user (*Inf.*) 2. adherent, buff (*Sl.*), devotee, enthusiast, fan, follower, freak (*Sl.*), nut (*Sl.*)

addicted absorbed, accustomed, dedicated, dependent, devoted, disposed, fond, habituated, hooked (*Sl.*), inclined, obsessed, prone

addiction craving, dependence, enslavement, habit, obsession

addition 1. accession, adding, adjoining, affixing, amplification, annexation, attachment, augmentation, enlargement, extension, inclusion, increasing 2. addendum, additive, adjunct, affix, appendage, appendix, extension, extra, gain, increase, increment, supplement 3. adding up, computation, counting up, reckoning, summation, summing up, totalling, totting up 4. in addition (to) additionally, also, as well (as), besides,

into the bargain, moreover, over and above, to boot, too, withal

additional added, affixed, appended, extra, fresh, further, increased, more, new, other, over-and-above, spare, supplementary

address *n.* 1. abode, domicile, dwelling, home, house, location, lodging, place, residence, situation, whereabouts 2. direction, inscription, superscription 3. discourse, disquisition, dissertation, harangue, lecture, oration, sermon, speech, talk 4. adroitness, art, dexterity, discretion, expertness, ingenuity, skilfulness, skill, tact ~*v.* 5. accost, apostrophize, approach, greet, hail, invoke, salute, speak to, talk to 6. discourse, give a speech, give a talk, harangue, lecture, orate, sermonize, speak, talk 7. **address (oneself) to** apply (oneself) to, attend to, concentrate on, devote (oneself) to, engage in, focus on, knuckle down to, look to, take care of, take up, turn to, undertake

adduce advance, allege, cite, designate, mention, name, offer, present, quote

add up 1. add, compute, count, count up, reckon, sum up, total, tot up 2. amount, come to, imply, indicate, mean, reveal, signify 3. be plausible, be reasonable, hold water, make sense, ring true, stand to reason

adept 1. *adj.* able, accomplished, adroit, dexterous, expert, masterful, masterly, prac-

adequate ('ædɪkwɪt) *adj.* able to fulfil a need without being abundant, outstanding, etc. —**adequacy** ('ædɪkwəsɪ) *n.* —'**adequately** *adv.*

à deux French. (a 'dø) *adj., adv.* of or for two persons.

adhere (əd'hɪə) *vb.* (*intr.*) **1.** (usually foll. by *to*) to stick or hold fast. **2.** (foll. by *to*) to be devoted (to a political party, religion, etc.). **3.** (foll. by *to*) to follow exactly. —**ad'herence** *n.*

adherent (əd'hɪərənt) *n.* **1.** (usually foll. by *of*) a supporter or follower. ~*adj.* **2.** sticking, holding fast, or attached.

adhesion (əd'hi:ʒən) *n.* **1.** the quality or condition of sticking together or holding fast. **2.** ability to make firm contact without slipping. **3.** attachment, as to a political party, cause, etc. **4.** an attraction or repulsion between the molecules of unlike substances in contact. **5.** *Pathol.* abnormal union of structures or parts.

adhesive (əd'hi:sɪv) *adj.* **1.** able or designed to adhere: *adhesive tape.* **2.** tenacious or clinging. ~*n.* **3.** a substance used for sticking, such as glue or paste. —**ad'hesively** *adv.* —**ad'hesiveness** *n.*

ad hoc (æd 'hɒk) *adj., adv.* for a particular purpose only: *an ad hoc committee.*

adieu (ə'dju:) *interj., n., pl.* **adieus** or **adieux** (ə'dju:z). goodbye.

ad infinitum (æd ˌɪnfɪ'naɪtəm) *adv.* without end; endlessly; to infinity. Abbrev.: **ad inf.**

adipose ('ædɪˌpəʊs) *adj.* **1.** of, resembling, or containing fat; fatty. ~*n.* **2.** animal fat.

adj. *abbrev. for:* **1.** *Maths.* adjacent. **2.** adjective. **3.** adjunct. **4.** Also: **adjt.** adjutant.

adjacent (ə'dʒeɪsənt) *adj.* being near or close, esp. having a common boundary; contiguous. —**ad'jacency** *n.* —**ad'jacently** *adv.*

adjective ('ædʒɪktɪv) *n.* **1. a.** a word imputing a characteristic to a noun or pronoun. **b.** (*as modifier*): *an adjective phrase.* Abbrev.: **adj.** ~*adj.* **2.** additional or dependent. —**adjectival** (ˌædʒɪk'taɪvəl) *adj.*

adjoin (ə'dʒɔɪn) *vb.* **1.** to be next to (an area of land, etc.). **2.** (*tr.;* foll. by *to*) to join; attach. —**ad'joining** *adj.*

adjourn (ə'dʒɜːn) *vb.* **1.** (*intr.*) (of a court, etc.) to close at the end of a session. **2.** to postpone or be postponed, esp. temporarily. **3.** (*tr.*) to put off (a problem, discussion, etc.) for later consideration. **4.** (*intr.*) *Inf.* to move elsewhere: *let's adjourn to the kitchen.* —**ad'journment** *n.*

adjudge (ə'dʒʌdʒ) *vb.* (*tr.; usually passive*) **1.** to pronounce formally; declare. **2. a.** to judge. **b.** to decree: *he was adjudged bankrupt.* **c.** to award (costs, damages, etc.). **3.** *Arch.* to condemn.

adjudicate (ə'dʒuːdɪˌkeɪt) *vb.* **1.** (when *intr.*, usually foll. by *upon*) to decide (an issue) judicially. **2.** (*intr.*) to serve as a judge or arbiter, as in a competition. —**ad,judi'cation** *n.*

adjunct ('ædʒʌŋkt) *n.* **1.** something incidental or not essential that is added to something else. **2.** a person who is subordinate to another. **3.** *Grammar.* **a.** part of a sentence other than the subject or the predicate. **b.** a modifier. ~*adj.* **4.** added or connected in a secondary position. —**adjunctive** (ə'dʒʌŋktɪv) *adj.* —'**adjunctly** *adv.*

adjure (ə'dʒʊə) *vb.* (*tr.*) **1.** to command, often by exacting an oath. **2.** to appeal earnestly to. —**adjuration** (ˌædʒʊə'reɪʃən) *n.* —**ad'juratory** *adj.* —**ad'jurer** or **ad-'juror** *n.*

adjust (ə'dʒʌst) *vb.* **1.** (*tr.*) to alter slightly, esp. to achieve accuracy. **2.** to adapt, as to a new environment, etc. **3.** (*tr.*) to put into order. **4.** (*tr.*) *Insurance.* to determine the amount payable in settlement of (a claim). —**ad'justable** *adj.* —**ad'juster** *n.*

adjustment (ə'dʒʌstmənt) *n.* **1.** the act of adjusting or state of being adjusted. **2.** a control for regulating.

adjutant ('ædʒətənt) *n.* an officer who acts as administrative assistant to a superior officer. —'**adjutancy** *n.*

adjutant general *n., pl.* **adjutants general.** **1.** *Brit. Army.* the head of a department of the general staff. **2.** *U.S. Army.* the adjutant of a military unit with general staff.

ad-lib (æd'lɪb) *vb.* **-libbing, -libbed.** **1.** to improvise and deliver spontaneously (a speech, etc.). ~*adj.* (**ad lib** when predicative) **2.** improvised. ~*adv.* **ad lib.** **3.** spontaneously; freely. ~*n.* **4.** an improvised performance, often humorous.

ad libitum (ˌæd'lɪbɪtəm) *adv., adj. Music.* at the performer's discretion.

Adm. *abbrev. for:* **1.** Admiral. **2.** Admiralty.

adman ('æd,mæn) *n., pl.* **-men.** *Inf.* a person who works in advertising.

admass ('ædmæs) *n.* the section of the public that is susceptible to advertising etc., and the processes involved in influencing them.

admin ('ædmɪn) *n. Inf.* short for **administration.**

administer (əd'mɪnɪstə) *vb.* (*mainly tr.*) **1.** (*also intr.*) to direct or control the affairs of a business, etc.). **2.** to dispense: *administer justice.* **3.** (when *intr.*, foll. by *to*) to give or apply (medicine, etc.). **4.** to supervise the taking of (an oath, etc.). **5.** to manage (an estate, property, etc.).

administrate (əd'mɪnɪˌstreɪt) *vb.* to manage or direct (the affairs of a business, institution, etc.).

THESAURUS

tised, proficient, skilful, skilled, versed **2.** *n.* dab hand (*Inf.*), expert, genius, master

adequacy capability, commensurateness, competence, fairness, requisiteness, satisfactoriness, sufficiency, suitability, tolerability

adequate capable, commensurate, competent, enough, fair, passable, requisite, satisfactory, sufficient, suitable, tolerable

adhere **1.** attach, cement, cleave, cling, cohere, fasten, fix, glue, glue on, hold fast, paste, stick, stick fast, unite **2.** abide by, be attached, be constant, be devoted, be faithful, be loyal, be true, cleave to, cling, follow, fulfil, heed, keep, keep to, maintain, mind, obey, observe, respect, stand by, support

adherent **1.** *n.* admirer, advocate, devotee, disciple, fan, follower, hanger-on, partisan, sectary, supporter, upholder, votary **2.** *adj.* adhering, adhesive, clinging, gluey, glutinous, gummy, holding, mucilaginous, sticking, sticky, tacky, tenacious

adhesive **1.** *adj.* adhering, attaching, clinging, cohesive, gluey, glutinous, gummy, holding, mucilaginous, sticking, sticky, tacky, tenacious **2.** *n.* cement, glue, gum, mucilage, paste

adieu congé, farewell, goodbye, leave-taking, parting, valediction

adipose fat, fatty, greasy, obese, oily, oleaginous, sebaceous

adjacent abutting, adjoining, alongside,

beside, bordering, close, contiguous, near, neighbouring, next door, touching

adjoin abut, add, affix, annex, append, approximate, attach, border, combine, communicate with, connect, couple, impinge, interconnect, join, link, neighbour, touch, unite, verge

adjoining abutting, adjacent, bordering, connecting, contiguous, impinging, interconnecting, joined, joining, near, neighbouring, next door, touching, verging

adjourn defer, delay, discontinue, interrupt, postpone, prorogue, put off, recess, stay, suspend

adjournment deferment, deferral, delay, discontinuation, interruption, postponement, prorogation, putting off, recess, stay, suspension

adjudge adjudicate, allot, apportion, assign, award, decide, declare, decree, determine, distribute, judge, order, pronounce

adjudicate adjudge, arbitrate, decide, determine, judge, referee, settle, umpire

adjudication adjudgment, arbitration, conclusion, decision, determination, finding, judgment, pronouncement, ruling, settlement, verdict

adjunct accessory, addendum, addition, appendage, appurtenance, auxiliary, complement, supplement

adjure **1.** appeal to, beg, beseech, entreat, implore, invoke, pray, supplicate **2.** charge,

command, direct, enjoin, order

adjust acclimatize, accommodate, accustom, adapt, alter, arrange, compose, dispose, fit, fix, harmonize, make conform, measure, modify, order, reconcile, rectify, redress, regulate, remodel, set, settle, suit, tune (up)

adjustable adaptable, alterable, flexible, malleable, modifiable, mouldable, movable, tractable

adjustment **1.** adaptation, alteration, arrangement, arranging, fitting, fixing, modification, ordering, rectification, redress, regulation, remodelling, setting, tuning **2.** acclimatization, harmonization, orientation, reconciliation, settlement, settling in

ad-lib **1.** *v.* extemporize, improvise, make up, speak extemporaneously, speak impromptu, speak off the cuff **2.** *adj.* extemporaneous, extempore, extemporized, impromptu, improvised, made up, off-the-cuff (*Inf.*), unprepared, unrehearsed **3.** *adv.* extemporaneously, extempore, impromptu, off the cuff, off the top of one's head (*Inf.*), without preparation, without rehearsal

administer **1.** conduct, control, direct, govern, manage, oversee, run, superintend, supervise **2.** apply, contribute, dispense, distribute, execute, give, impose, mete out, perform, provide

administration (əd,mɪnɪ'streɪʃən) n. 1. management of the affairs of an organization, such as a business or institution. 2. the duties of an administrator. 3. the body of people who administer an organization. 4. the conduct of the affairs of government. 5. term of office: used of governments, etc. 6. the government as a whole. 7. (often cap.) Chiefly U.S. the political executive, esp. of the U.S. 8. Property law. a. the conduct or disposal of the estate of a deceased person. b. the management by a trustee of an estate. 9. something administered, such as a sacrament or medical treatment. —ad'ministrative adj. —ad'ministratively adv.

administrator (əd'mɪnɪ,streɪtə) n. 1. a person who administers the affairs of an organization, official body, etc. 2. Property law. a person authorized to manage an estate.

admirable ('ædmərəbəl) adj. deserving or inspiring admiration; excellent. —'admirably adv.

admiral ('ædmərəl) n. 1. the supreme commander of a fleet or navy. 2. Also called: **admiral of the fleet, fleet admiral.** a naval officer of the highest rank. 3. a senior naval officer entitled to fly his own flag. See also **rear admiral, vice admiral.** 4. Chiefly Brit. the master of a fishing fleet. 5. any of various butterflies, esp. the red admiral or white admiral. —'admiral,ship n.

admiralty ('ædmərəltɪ) n., pl. **-ties.** 1. the office or jurisdiction of an admiral. 2. jurisdiction over naval affairs.

admire (əd'maɪə) vb. (tr.) 1. to regard with esteem, approval, or pleased surprise. 2. Arch. to wonder at. —admiration (,ædmə'reɪʃən) n. —ad'miringly adv.

admissible (əd'mɪsəbəl) adj. 1. able or deserving to be considered or allowed. 2. deserving to be allowed to enter. 3. Law. (esp. of evidence) capable of being admitted in a court of law. —ad,missi'bility n.

admission (əd'mɪʃən) n. 1. permission to enter or the right to enter. 2. the price charged for entrance. 3. acceptance for a position, etc. 4. a confession, as of a crime, etc. 5. an acknowledgment of the truth of something. —ad'missive adj.

admit (əd'mɪt) vb. **-mitting, -mitted.** (mainly tr.) 1. (may take a clause as object) to confess or acknowledge (a crime, mistake, etc.). 2. (may take a clause as object) to concede (the truth of something). 3. to allow to enter. 4. (foll. by to) to allow participation (in) or the right to be part (of). 5. (when intr., foll. by of) to allow (of).

admittance (əd'mɪt²ns) n. 1. the right or authority to enter. 2. the act of giving entrance. 3. Electricity. the reciprocal of impedance.

admittedly (əd'mɪtɪdlɪ) adv. (sentence modifier) willingly conceded: admittedly I am afraid.

admixture (əd'mɪkstʃə) n. 1. a less common word for **mixture.** 2. an ingredient.

admonish (əd'mɒnɪʃ) vb. (tr.) 1. to reprove firmly but not harshly. 2. to warn; caution. —**admonition** (,ædmə'nɪʃən) n. —ad'monitory adj.

ad nauseam (æd 'nɔːzɪ,æm) adv. to a disgusting extent.

ado (ə'duː) n. bustling activity; fuss; bother; delay (esp. in without more ado, with much ado).

adobe (ə'dəʊbɪ) n. 1. a sun-dried brick used for building. 2. a building constructed of such bricks. 3. the clayey material from which such bricks are made.

adolescence (,ædə'lɛsəns) n. the period in human development that occurs between the beginning of puberty and adulthood.

adolescent (,ædə'lɛsənt) adj. 1. of or relating to adolescence. 2. Inf. behaving in an immature way. ~n. 3. an adolescent person.

Adonis (ə'dəʊnɪs) n. 1. Greek myth. a handsome youth loved by Aphrodite. 2. a handsome young man.

adopt (ə'dɒpt) vb. (tr.) 1. Law. to take (another's child) as one's own child. 2. to choose and follow (a plan, technique, etc.). 3. to take over (an idea, etc.) as if it were one's own. 4. to assume: to adopt a title. 5. to accept (a report, etc.). —a'doption n.

adoptive (ə'dɒptɪv) adj. due to adoption; foster: an adoptive parent.

adorable (ə'dɔːrəbəl) adj. 1. very attractive; lovable. 2. Becoming rare. deserving adoration. —a'dorably adv.

adore (ə'dɔː) vb. 1. (tr.) to love intensely or deeply. 2. to worship (a god) with religious rites. 3. (tr.) Inf. to like very much. —,ado'ration n. —a'dorer n.

adorn (ə'dɔːn) vb. (tr.) 1. to decorate. 2. to increase the beauty, distinction, etc., of. —a'dornment n.

ADP n. Biochem. adenosine diphosphate; a substance derived from ATP with the liberation of energy that is then used in the performance of muscular work.

A.D.P. abbrev. for automatic data processing.

adrenal (ə'driːnəl) adj. 1. on or near the kidneys. 2. of or relating to the adrenal glands or their secretions. ~n. 3. an adrenal gland.

adrenal gland n. an endocrine gland at the anterior end of each kidney. It secretes adrenaline. Also called: **suprarenal gland.**

adrenaline or **adrenalin** (ə'drɛnəlɪn) n. a hormone that is secreted by the adrenal medulla in response to stress and increases heart rate, pulse rate, and blood pressure. It is extracted from animals or synthesized for medical use. U.S. name: **epinephrine.**

THESAURUS

administration 1. administering, application, conduct, control, direction, dispensation, distribution, execution, governing, government, management, overseeing, performance, provision, running, superintendence, supervision 2. executive, governing body, government, management, ministry, term of office

administrative directorial, executive, governmental, gubernatorial (Chiefly U.S.), management, managerial, organizational, regulatory, supervisory

admirable choice, commendable, estimable, excellent, exquisite, fine, laudable, meritorious, praiseworthy, rare, superior, valuable, wonderful, worthy

admiration adoration, affection, amazement, appreciation, approbation, approval, astonishment, delight, esteem, pleasure, praise, regard, respect, surprise, veneration, wonder, wonderment

admire 1. adore, appreciate, approve, esteem, idolize, look up to, praise, prize, respect, think highly of, value, venerate, worship 2. appreciate, delight in, marvel at, take pleasure in, wonder at

admirer 1. beau, boyfriend, lover, suitor, sweetheart, wooer 2. adherent, devotee, disciple, enthusiast, fan, follower, partisan, supporter, votary, worshipper

admissible acceptable, allowable, allowed, passable, permissible, permitted, tolerable, tolerated

admission 1. acceptance, access, admittance, entrance, entrée, entry, ingress, initiation, introduction 2. acknowledgment, admitting, affirmation, allowance, avowal, concession, confession, declaration, disclosure, divulgence, profession, revelation

admit 1. accept, allow, allow to enter, give access, initiate, introduce, let in, receive, take in 2. acknowledge, affirm, avow, concede, confess, declare, disclose, divulge, profess, reveal 3. agree, allow, grant, let, permit, recognize

admittance acceptance, access, admitting, allowing, entrance, entry, letting in, passage, reception

admonish advise, berate, caution, censure, check, chide, counsel, enjoin, exhort, forewarn, rebuke, reprimand, reprove, scold, tell off (Inf.), upbraid, warn

admonition advice, berating, caution, chiding, counsel, rebuke, remonstrance, reprimand, reproach, reproof, scolding, telling off (Inf.), upbraiding, warning

admonitory admonishing, advisory, cautionary, rebuking, reprimanding, reproachful, reproving, scolding, warning

ado agitation, bother, bustle, commotion, confusion, delay, disturbance, excitement, flurry, fuss, pother, stir, to-do, trouble

adolescence 1. boyhood, girlhood, juvenescence, minority, teens, youth 2. boyishness, childishness, girlishness, immaturity, juvenility, puerility, youthfulness

adolescent 1. adj. boyish, girlish, growing, immature, juvenile, puerile, teenage, young, youthful 2. n. juvenile, minor, teenager, youngster, youth

adopt 1. accept, appropriate, approve, assume, choose, embrace, endorse, espouse, follow, maintain, ratify, select, support, take on, take over, take up 2. foster, take in

adoption 1. acceptance, approbation, appropriation, approval, assumption, choice, embracing, endorsement, espousal, following, maintenance, ratification, selection, support, taking on, taking over, taking up 2. adopting, fosterage, fostering, taking in

adorable appealing, attractive, captivating, charming, darling, dear, delightful, fetching, lovable, pleasing, precious

adoration admiration, esteem, estimation, exaltation, glorification, honour, idolatry, idolization, love, reverence, veneration, worship, worshipping

adore admire, bow to, cherish, dote on, esteem, exalt, glorify, honour, idolize, love, revere, reverence, venerate, worship

adorn array, beautify, bedeck, deck, decorate, embellish, emblazon, enhance, enrich, garnish, grace, ornament, trim

adornment 1. accessory, decoration, embellishment, frill, frippery, ornament, trimming 2. beautification, decorating, decoration, embellishment, ornamentation, trimming

adrift (əˈdrɪft) adj. (postpositive), adv. 1. floating without steering or mooring; drifting. 2. without purpose; aimless. 3. Inf. off course.

adroit (əˈdrɔɪt) adj. 1. skilful or dexterous. 2. quick in thought or reaction. —aˈdroitly adv. —aˈdroitness n.

adsorb (adˈsɔːb) vb. to undergo or cause to undergo a process in which a substance, usually a gas, accumulates on the surface of a solid forming a thin film. —adˈsorbable adj. —adˈsorbent adj. —adˈsorption n.

A.D.T. (in the U.S. and Canada) abbrev. for Atlantic Daylight Time.

adulate (ˈædjʊˌleɪt) vb. (tr.) to flatter or praise obsequiously. —ˌaduˈlation n. —ˈaduˌlator n. —adulatory (ˌædjuˈleɪtərɪ) adj.

adult (ˈædʌlt, əˈdʌlt) adj. 1. having reached maturity; fully developed. 2. of or intended for mature people: adult education. ~n. 3. a person who has attained maturity. 4. a mature fully grown animal or plant. 5. Law. a person who has attained the age of legal majority. —aˈdulthood n.

adulterant (əˈdʌltərənt) n. 1. a substance that adulterates. ~adj. 2. adulterating.

adulterate vb. (əˈdʌltəˌreɪt). 1. (tr.) to debase by adding inferior material: to adulterate milk with water. ~adj. (əˈdʌltərɪt). 2. debased or impure. —aˌdulterˈation n. —aˈdulterˌator n.

adulterer (əˈdʌltərə) or (fem.) **adulteress** n. a person who has committed adultery.

adultery (əˈdʌltərɪ) n., pl. -teries. voluntary sexual intercourse between a married man or woman and partner other than the legal spouse. —aˈdulterous adj.

adumbrate (ˈædʌmˌbreɪt) vb. (tr.) 1. to outline; give a faint indication of. 2. to foreshadow. 3. to obscure. —ˌadumˈbration n. —adumbrative (ædˈʌmbrətɪv) adj.

adv. abbrev. for: 1. adverb. 2. adverbial. 3. adversus. 4. advertisement. 5. advocate.

ad valorem (æd vəˈlɔːrəm) adj., adv. (of taxes) in proportion to the estimated value of the goods taxed. Abbrev.: ad val.

advance (ədˈvɑːns) vb. 1. to go or bring forward in position. 2. (foll. by on) to move (towards) in a threatening manner. 3. (tr.) to present for consideration. 4. to improve; further. 5. (tr.) to cause (an event) to occur earlier. 6. (tr.) to supply (money, goods, etc.) beforehand, either for a loan or as an initial payment. 7. to increase (a price, etc.) or (of a price, etc.) to be increased. 8. (intr.) to be promoted. ~n. 9. forward movement; progress in time or space. 10. improvement; progress in development. 11. Commerce. a. the supplying of commodities or funds before receipt of an agreed consideration. b. the commodities or funds supplied in this manner. 12. Also called: advance payment. a money payment made before it is legally due. 13. increase in price, etc. 14. in advance. a. beforehand: payment in advance. b. (foll. by of) ahead in time or development: ideas in advance of the time. 15. (modifier) forward in position or time: advance booking. —adˈvancement n. —adˈvancer n.

advanced (ədˈvɑːnst) adj. 1. being ahead in development, knowledge, progress, etc. 2. having reached a comparatively late stage: a man of advanced age. 3. ahead of the times.

Advanced level n. a formal name for A level.

advances (ədˈvɑːnsɪz) pl. n. (sometimes sing.; often foll. by to or towards) overtures made in an attempt to become friendly, etc.

advantage (ədˈvɑːntɪdʒ) n. 1. (often foll. by over or of) a more favourable position; superiority. 2. benefit or profit (esp. in to one's advantage). 3. Tennis. the point scored after deuce. 4. take advantage of. a. to make good use of. b. to impose upon the weakness, good nature, etc., of. c. to seduce. 5. to advantage. to good effect. ~vb. 6. (tr.) to put in a better position; favour.

advantageous (ˌædvənˈteɪdʒəs) adj. producing advantage. —ˌadvanˈtageously adv.

advection (ədˈvɛkʃən) n. the transference of heat energy in a horizontal stream of gas, esp. of air.

advent (ˈædvɛnt, -vənt) n. an arrival or coming, esp. one which is awaited.

Advent (ˈædvɛnt) n. the season including the four Sundays preceding Christmas.

Adventist (ˈædvɛntɪst) n. a member of a Christian group that holds that the Second Coming of Christ is imminent.

adventitious (ˌædvɛnˈtɪʃəs) adj. 1. added or appearing accidentally. 2. (of a plant or animal part) developing in an abnormal position. —ˌadvenˈtitiously adv.

adventure (ədˈvɛntʃə) n. 1. a risky undertaking of unknown outcome. 2. an exciting or unexpected event or course of events. 3. a hazardous financial operation. ~vb. 4. to take a risk or put at risk. 5. (intr.; foll. by into, on, upon) to dare to enter (into a place, dangerous activity, etc.). 6. to dare to say (something): he adventured his opinion. —adˈventurous adj.

adventure playground n. Brit. a playground for children that contains building materials, etc., used to build with, climb on, etc.

adventurer (ədˈvɛntʃərə) or (fem.) **adventuress** n.

THESAURUS

adrift 1. afloat, drifting, unanchored, unmoored 2. aimless, directionless, goalless, purposeless 3. amiss, astray, off course, wrong

adroit able, adept, apt, artful, clever, cunning, deft, dexterous, expert, ingenious, masterful, neat, nimble, proficient, quick-witted, skilful, skilled

adroitness ability, ableness, address, adeptness, aptness, artfulness, cleverness, cunning, deftness, dexterity, expertise, ingeniousness, ingenuity, masterfulness, mastery, nimbleness, proficiency, quick-wittedness, skilfulness, skill

adulation blandishment, bootlicking (Inf.), extravagant flattery, fawning, fulsome praise, servile flattery, sycophancy, worship

adulatory blandishing, bootlicking (Inf.), fawning, flattering, obsequious, praising, servile, slavish, sycophantic, worshipping

adult 1. adj. full grown, fully developed, fully grown, grown-up, mature, of age, ripe 2. n. grown or grown-up person (man or woman), grown-up, person of mature age

adulterate 1. v. attenuate, bastardize, contaminate, corrupt, debase, depreciate, deteriorate, devalue, make impure, mix with, thin, vitiate, water down, weaken 2. adj. adulterated, attenuated, bastardized, contaminated, corrupt, debased, depreciated, deteriorated, devalued, mixed, thinned, vitiated, watered down, weakened

adumbrate 1. delineate, indicate, outline, silhouette, sketch, suggest 2. augur, forecast, foreshadow, foretell, portend, predict, prefigure, presage, prognosticate, prophesy 3. bedim, darken, eclipse, obfuscate, obscure, overshadow

adumbration 1. delineation, draft, indication, outline, rough, silhouette, sketch, suggestion 2. augury, forecast, foreshadowing, foretelling, omen, portent, prediction, prefiguration, prefigurement, presage, prognostication, prophecy, sign 3. bedimming, cloud, darkening, darkness, eclipse, eclipsing, obfuscation, obscuring, overshadowing, shadow

advance v. 1. accelerate, bring forward, bring up, come forward, elevate, go ahead, go forward, go on, hasten, move onward, move up, press on, proceed, progress, promote, send forward, send up, speed, upgrade 2. benefit, further, grow, improve, multiply, prosper, thrive 3. adduce, allege, cite, offer, present, proffer, put forward, submit, suggest 4. increase (price), lend, pay beforehand, raise (price), supply on credit ~n. 5. advancement, development, forward movement, headway, onward movement, progress 6. advancement, amelioration, betterment, breakthrough, furtherance, gain, growth, improvement, progress, promotion, step 7. appreciation, credit, deposit, down payment, increase (in price), loan, prepayment, retainer, rise (in price) 8. advances approach, approaches, moves, overtures, proposals, proposition ~adj. 9. beforehand, early, foremost, forward, in front, leading, prior 10. in

advance ahead, beforehand, earlier, in the forefront, in the lead, in the van, previously

advanced ahead, avant-garde, extreme, foremost, forward, higher, late, leading, precocious, progressive

advancement 1. advance, forward movement, headway, onward movement, progress 2. advance, amelioration, betterment, gain, growth, improvement, preferment, progress, promotion, rise

advantage aid, ascendancy, asset, assistance, avail, benefit, blessing, boon, convenience, dominance, edge, gain, good, help, interest, lead, precedence, pre-eminence, profit, service, start, superiority, sway, upper hand, use, utility, welfare

advantageous 1. dominant, dominating, favourable, superior 2. beneficial, convenient, helpful, of service, profitable, useful, valuable, worthwhile

advent appearance, approach, arrival, coming, entrance, occurrence, onset, visitation

adventitious accidental, casual, chance, extraneous, foreign, fortuitous, incidental, nonessential, unexpected

adventure 1. n. chance, contingency, enterprise, experience, exploit, hazard, incident, occurrence, risk, speculation, undertaking, venture 2. v. dare, endanger, hazard, imperil, jeopardize, risk, venture

1. a person who seeks adventure, esp. one who seeks success or money through daring exploits. **2.** a person who seeks money or power by unscrupulous means. **3.** a speculator.

adventurism (əd'vɛntʃə,rɪzəm) *n.* recklessness, esp. in politics and finance. —**ad'venturist** *n.*

adverb ('æd,vɜːb) *n.* **a.** a word or group of words that serves to modify a whole sentence, a verb, another adverb, or an adjective; for example, *easily, very,* and *happily* respectively in the sentence *They could easily envy the very happily married couple.* **b.** (*as modifier*): *an adverb marker.* Abbrev.: **adv.** —**ad'verbial** *adj.*

adversary ('ædvəsəri) *n., pl.* **-saries. 1.** a person or group that is hostile to someone. **2.** an opposing contestant in a sport.

adverse ('ædvɜːs) *adj.* **1.** antagonistic; hostile: *adverse criticism.* **2.** unfavourable to one's interests: *adverse circumstances.* **3.** contrary or opposite: *adverse winds.* —**ad'versely** *adv.* —**ad'verseness** *n.*

adversity (əd'vɜːsɪti) *n., pl.* **-ties. 1.** distress; affliction; hardship. **2.** an unfortunate event.

advertise *or U.S.* (*sometimes*) **-tize** ('ædvə,taɪz) *vb.* **1.** to present or praise (goods, a service, etc.) to the public, esp. in order to encourage sales. **2.** to make (a vacancy, article for sale, etc.) publicly known: *to advertise a job.* **3.** (*intr.; foll. by for*) to make a public request (for): *she advertised for a cook.* —**'adver,tiser** *or U.S.* (*sometimes*) **-tizer** *n.* —**'adver,tising** *or U.S.* (*sometimes*) **-tizing** *n.*

advertisement *or U.S.* (*sometimes*) **-tizement** (əd-'vɜːtɪsmənt) *n.* any public notice, as a printed display in a newspaper, short film on television, etc., designed to sell goods, publicize an event, etc.

advice (əd'vaɪs) *n.* **1.** recommendation as to appropriate choice of action. **2.** (*sometimes pl.*) formal notification of facts.

advisable (əd'vaɪzəbəl) *adj.* worthy of recommendation; prudent. —**ad'visably** *adv.*

advise (əd'vaɪz) *vb.* (*when tr., may take a clause as object or an infinitive*) **1.** to offer advice (to a person or persons): *he advised caution.* **2.** (*tr.; sometimes foll. by of*) to inform or notify. **3.** (*intr.; foll. by with*) *Chiefly U.S., obs. in Brit.* to consult. —**ad'viser** *or* **a'dvisor** *n.*
▷ **Usage.** *Advise* is often used in the same sense as *inform: as we advised you in our last communication, the order is being dealt with.* This use is common in business correspondence. Careful users of English prefer *inform, notify,* or *tell* in general English: *the police informed him that his car had been stolen.*

advised (əd'vaɪzd) *adj.* resulting from deliberation. See also **ill-advised.** —**advisedly** (əd'vaɪzɪdlɪ) *adv.*

advisory (əd'vaɪzərɪ) *adj.* empowered to make recommendations: *an advisory body.*

advocaat ('ædvəʊ,kɑː) *n.* a liqueur having a raw egg base.

advocacy ('ædvəkəsɪ) *n., pl.* **-cies.** active support, esp. of a cause.

advocate *vb.* ('ædvə,keɪt). **1.** (*tr.; may take a clause as object*) to support or recommend publicly. ~*n.* ('ædvəkɪt). **2.** a person who upholds or defends a cause. **3.** a person who intercedes on behalf of another. **4.** a person who pleads his client's cause in a court of law. **5.** *Scots Law.* the usual word for **counsel.**

advowson (əd'vauzən) *n. English ecclesiastical law.* the right of presentation to a vacant benefice.

advt. *abbrev. for* advertisement.

adze *or U.S.* **adz** (ædz) *n.* a hand tool with a steel blade attached at right angles to a wooden handle, used for dressing timber.

A.E.A. (in Britain) *abbrev. for* Atomic Energy Authority.

A.E.C. (in the U.S.) *abbrev. for* Atomic Energy Commission.

aegis *or U.S.* (*sometimes*) **egis** ('iːdʒɪs) *n.* **1.** sponsorship or protection (esp. in **under the aegis of**). **2.** *Greek myth.* the shield of Zeus.

aegrotat ('aɪɡrəʊ,tæt, 'iː-) *n.* **1.** (in British and certain other universities) a certificate allowing a candidate to pass an examination although he has missed all or part of it through illness. **2.** a degree obtained in such circumstances.

-aemia, -haemia, *or U.S.* **-emia, -hemia** *n. combining form.* denoting blood, esp. a specified condition of the blood in diseases: *leukaemia.*

aeolian harp (iː'əʊliən) *n.* a stringed instrument that produces a musical sound when wind passes over the strings. Also called: **wind harp.**

aeon *or U.S.* **eon** ('iːən, 'iːɒn) *n.* **1.** an immeasurably long period of time. **2.** *Geol.* the longest division of geological time, comprising two or more eras.

aerate ('ɛəreɪt) *vb.* (*tr.*) **1.** to charge (a liquid) with a gas, as in the manufacture of effervescent drink. **2.** to expose to the action or circulation of the air. —**aer'a-tion** *n.* —**'aerator** *n.*

aeri- *combining form.* a variant of **aero-**.

aerial ('ɛərɪəl) *adj.* **1.** of or resembling air. **2.** existing, moving, or operating in the air: *aerial cable car.* **3.** ethereal; light and delicate. **4.** imaginary. **5.** extending high into the air. **6.** of or relating to aircraft: *aerial combat.* ~*n.* **7.** Also called: **antenna.** the part of a radio or television system by means of which radio waves are transmitted or received.

aerialist ('ɛərɪə,lɪst) *n. Chiefly U.S.* a trapeze artist or tightrope walker.

aerie ('ɛərɪ) *n.* a variant spelling (esp. U.S.) of **eyrie.**

aero ('ɛərəʊ) *n.* (*modifier*) of or relating to aircraft or aeronautics: *an aero engine.*

aero-, aeri-, *or, before a vowel* **aer-** *combining form.* **1.** denoting air, atmosphere, or gas: *aerodynamics.* **2.** denoting aircraft: *aeronautics.*

aerobatics (,ɛərəʊ'bætɪks) *pl. n.* spectacular or dangerous manoeuvres, such as loops or rolls, performed in an aircraft or glider.

aerodrome ('ɛərə,drəʊm) *n. Brit.* a landing area that is

---

adventurer 1. daredevil, hero, heroine, knight-errant, soldier of fortune, swashbuckler, traveller, venturer, voyager, wanderer **2.** charlatan, fortune-hunter, gambler, mercenary, opportunist, rogue, speculator

adventurous adventuresome, audacious, bold, dangerous, daredevil, daring, enterprising, foolhardy, hazardous, headstrong, intrepid, rash, reckless, risky, temerarious (*Rare*), venturesome

adversary antagonist, competitor, contestant, enemy, foe, opponent, opposer, rival

adverse antagonistic, conflicting, contrary, detrimental, disadvantageous, hostile, inexpedient, inimical, injurious, inopportune, negative, opposing, opposite, reluctant, repugnant, unfavourable, unfortunate, unfriendly, unlucky, unpropitious, unwilling

adversity affliction, bad luck, calamity, catastrophe, disaster, distress, hardship, hard times, ill-fortune, ill-luck, misery, misfortune, mishap, reverse, sorrow, suffering, trial, trouble, woe, wretchedness

advertise advise, announce, apprise, blazon, declare, display, flaunt, inform, make

known, notify, plug (*Inf.*), praise, proclaim, promote, promulgate, publicize, publish, puff, push (*Inf.*), tout

advertisement ad (*Inf.*), advert (*Inf.*), announcement, bill, blurb, circular, commercial, display, notice, placard, plug (*Inf.*), poster, promotion, publicity, puff

advice 1. admonition, caution, counsel, guidance, help, injunction, opinion, recommendation, suggestion, view **2.** information, instruction, intelligence, notice, notification, warning, word

advisability appropriateness, aptness, desirability, expediency, fitness, judiciousness, profitability, propriety, prudence, seemliness, soundness, suitability, wisdom

advisable appropriate, apt, desirable, expedient, fit, fitting, judicious, politic, profitable, proper, prudent, recommended, seemly, sensible, sound, suggested, suitable, wise

advise 1. admonish, caution, commend, counsel, enjoin, recommend, suggest, urge **2.** acquaint, apprise, inform, make known, notify, report, tell, warn

adviser aide, authority, coach, confidant,

consultant, counsel, counsellor, guide, helper, lawyer, mentor, right-hand man, solicitor, teacher, tutor

advisory advising, consultative, counselling, helping, recommending

advocacy advancement, argument for, backing, campaigning for, championing, defence, encouragement, justification, pleading for, promotion, promulgation, propagation, proposal, recommendation, spokesmanship, support, upholding, urging

advocate *v.* **1.** advise, argue for, campaign for, champion, countenance, defend, encourage, favour, hold a brief for (*Inf.*), justify, plead for, press for, promote, propose, recommend, speak for, support, uphold, urge ~*n.* **2.** apologist, apostle, backer, campaigner, champion, counsellor, defender, pleader, promoter, proponent, proposer, speaker, spokesman, supporter, upholder **3.** *Law.* attorney, barrister, counsel, lawyer, solicitor

aegis advocacy, auspices, backing, favour, guardianship, patronage, protection, shelter, sponsorship, support, wing

smaller than an airport.

aerodynamics (ˌɛərəʊdaɪˈnæmɪks) n. (functioning as sing.) the study of the dynamics of gases, esp. of the forces acting on a body passing through air. —ˌaerody-ˈnamic adj. —ˌaerodyˈnamically adv.

aero engine n. an engine for powering an aircraft.

aerofoil (ˈɛərəʊˌfɔɪl) n. Brit. a surface, such as an aileron or tailplane, that is designed to produce lift, or to control an aircraft in flight.

aerogram or **aerogramme** (ˈɛərəˌgræm) n. Also called: **air letter**. an air-mail letter written on a single sheet of lightweight paper that folds and is sealed to form an envelope.

aerolite (ˈɛərəˌlaɪt) n. a stony meteorite consisting of silicate minerals.

aeronautics (ˌɛərəˈnɔːtɪks) n. (functioning as sing.) the study or practice of all aspects of flight through the air —ˌaeroˈnautical adj.

aeroplane (ˈɛərəˌpleɪn) or U.S. **airplane** (ˈɛəˌpleɪn) n. a heavier-than-air powered flying vehicle with fixed wings.

aerosol (ˈɛərəˌsɒl) n. 1. a colloidal dispersion of solid or liquid particles in a gas. 2. a substance, such as a paint or insecticide, dispensed from a small metal container by a propellant under pressure. 3. Also called: **air spray**. such a substance together with its container.

aerospace (ˈɛərəˌspeɪs) n. 1. the atmosphere and space beyond. 2. (modifier) of rockets, missiles, space vehicles, etc: the aerospace industry.

aerostatics (ˌɛərəˈstætɪks) n. (functioning as sing.) 1. the study of gases in equilibrium and bodies held in equilibrium in gases. Cf. **aerodynamics**. 2. the study of lighter-than-air craft, such as balloons.

aery (ˈɛərɪ) n., pl. **aeries**. a variant spelling of **eyrie**.

aesthesia or U.S. **esthesia** (iːsˈθiːzɪə) n. the normal ability to experience sensation.

aesthete or U.S. **esthete** (ˈiːsθiːt) n. a person who has or who affects a highly developed appreciation of beauty.

aesthetic (iːsˈθɛtɪk, ɪs-), **aesthetical** or U.S. (sometimes) **esthetic, esthetical** adj. 1. connected with aesthetics. 2. a. relating to pure beauty rather than to other considerations. b. artistic: an aesthetic consideration. —aesˈthetically or U.S. (sometimes) esˈthetically adv. —aesˈtheticism or U.S. (sometimes) esˈtheticism n.

aesthetics or U.S. (sometimes) **esthetics** (iːsˈθɛtɪks) n. (functioning as sing.) 1. the branch of philosophy concerned with the study of such concepts as beauty, taste, etc. 2. the study of the rules and principles of art.

aestival or U.S. **estival** (iːˈstaɪvəl) adj. Rare. of or occurring in summer.

aestivate or U.S. **estivate** (ˈiːstɪˌveɪt) vb. (intr.) 1. to pass the summer. 2. (of animals) to pass the summer or dry season in a dormant condition. —ˌaestiˈvation or U.S. ˌestiˈvation n.

aether (ˈiːθə) n. a variant spelling of **ether** (senses 3, 4).

aetiology or U.S. **etiology** (ˌiːtɪˈɒlədʒɪ) n., pl. **-gies**. 1. the philosophy or study of causation. 2. the study of the causes of diseases. 3. the cause of a disease. —aetiological or U.S. **etiological** (ˌiːtɪəˈlɒdʒɪkəl) adj. —ˌaetiˈologist or U.S. ˌetiˈologist n.

A.E.U. (in Britain) abbrev. for Amalgamated Engineering Union.

a.f. abbrev. for audio frequency.

afar (əˈfɑː) adv. 1. at, from, or to a great distance. ~n. 2. a great distance (esp. in **from afar**).

A.F.C. abbrev. for: 1. Air Force Cross. 2. Association Football Club.

affable (ˈæfəbəl) adj. 1. showing warmth and friendliness. 2. easy to converse with; approachable. —ˌaffaˈbility n.

affair (əˈfɛə) n. 1. a thing to be done or attended to; matter. 2. an event or happening: a strange affair. 3. (qualified by an adjective or descriptive phrase) something previously specified: our house is a tumbledown affair. 4. a sexual relationship between two people who are not married to each other.

affairs (əˈfɛəz) pl. n. 1. personal or business interests. 2. matters of public interest: current affairs.

affect¹ (əˈfɛkt). (tr.) 1. to act upon or influence, esp. in an adverse way. 2. to move or disturb emotionally or mentally. 3. (of pain, disease, etc.) to attack. ~n. (ˈæfɛkt). 4. Psychol. the emotion associated with an idea or set of ideas.

affect² (əˈfɛkt) vb. (mainly tr.) 1. to put on an appearance or show of: to affect ignorance. 2. to imitate or assume, esp. pretentiously. 3. to have or use by preference. 4. to adopt the character, manner, etc., of. 5. to incline habitually towards.

affectation (ˌæfɛkˈteɪʃən) n. 1. an assumed manner of speech, dress, or behaviour, esp. one that is intended to impress others. 2. (often foll. by of) deliberate pretence.

affected¹ (əˈfɛktɪd) adj. (usually postpositive) 1. deeply moved, esp. by sorrow or grief. 2. changed, esp. detrimentally.

affected² (əˈfɛktɪd) adj. 1. behaving, speaking, etc., in an assumed way, esp. in order to impress others. 2. feigned: affected indifference. —afˈfectedly adv.

affecting (əˈfɛktɪŋ) adj. evoking feelings of pity; moving. —afˈfectingly adv.

affection (əˈfɛkʃən) n. 1. a feeling of fondness or tenderness for a person or thing. 2. (often pl.) emotion, feeling, or sentiment: to play on a person's affections. 3. Pathol. any disease or pathological condition. 4. the act of affecting or the state of being affected. —afˈfectional adj. —afˈfectionally adv.

affectionate (əˈfɛkʃənɪt) adj. having or displaying tender feelings, affection, or warmth. —afˈfectionately adv.

afferent (ˈæfərənt) adj. bringing or directing inwards to a part or an organ of the body, esp. towards the brain or spinal cord.

affiance (əˈfaɪəns) vb. (tr.) to bind (a person or oneself) in a promise of marriage; betroth.

affidavit (ˌæfɪˈdeɪvɪt) n. Law. a declaration in writing made upon oath before a person authorized to administer oaths.

affiliate vb. (əˈfɪlɪˌeɪt). 1. (tr.; foll. by to or with) to receive into close connection or association (with a larger body, group, organization, etc.). 2. (foll. by with) to associate (oneself) or be associated, esp. as a subordinate or subsidiary. ~n. (əˈfɪlɪɪt). 3. a. a person or organization that is affiliated with another. b. (as modifier): an affili-

---

THESAURUS

affability amiability, amicability, approachability, benevolence, benignity, civility, congeniality, cordiality, courtesy, friendliness, geniality, good humour, good nature, graciousness, kindliness, mildness, obligingness, pleasantness, sociability, urbanity, warmth

affable amiable, amicable, approachable, benevolent, benign, civil, congenial, cordial, courteous, friendly, genial, good-humoured, good-natured, gracious, kindly, mild, obliging, pleasant, sociable, urbane, warm

affair 1. activity, business, circumstance, concern, episode, event, happening, incident, interest, matter, occurrence, proceeding, project, question, subject, transaction, undertaking 2. amour, intrigue, liaison, relationship, romance

affect 1. act on, alter, bear upon, change, concern, impinge upon, influence, interest,

involve, modify, prevail over, regard, relate to, sway, transform 2. disturb, impress, move, overcome, perturb, stir, touch, upset 3. adopt, aspire to, assume, contrive, counterfeit, feign, imitate, pretend, put on, sham, simulate

affectation act, affectedness, appearance, artificiality, assumed manners, façade, fakery, false display, insincerity, mannerism, pose, pretence, pretension, pretentiousness, sham, show, simulation, unnatural imitation

affected 1. afflicted, altered, changed, concerned, damaged, deeply moved, distressed, hurt, impaired, impressed, influenced, injured, melted, stimulated, stirred, touched, troubled, upset 2. artificial, assumed, conceited, contrived, counterfeit, feigned, insincere, la-di-da (Inf.), mannered, mincing, phoney (Inf.), pompous, precious, pretended, pretentious, put-on, sham, simu-

lated, spurious, stiff, studied, unnatural

affecting moving, pathetic, piteous, pitiable, pitiful, poignant, sad, saddening, touching

affection amity, attachment, care, desire, feeling, fondness, friendliness, good will, inclination, kindness, liking, love, passion, propensity, tenderness, warmth

affectionate attached, caring, devoted, doting, fond, friendly, kind, loving, tender, warm, warm-hearted

affiliate ally, amalgamate, annex, associate, band together, combine, confederate, connect, incorporate, join, unite

affiliation alliance, amalgamation, association, banding together, coalition, combination, confederation, connection, incorporation, joining, league, merging, relationship, union

ate member. —**af,fili'ation** n.

affiliation order n. Law. an order that a man adjudged to be the father of an illegitimate child shall contribute towards the child's maintenance.

affinity (ə'fɪnɪtɪ) n., pl. **-ties.** 1. a natural liking, taste, or inclination for a person or thing. 2. the person or thing so liked. 3. a close similarity in appearance or quality. 4. relationship by marriage. 5. similarity in structure, form, etc., between different animals, plants, or languages. 6. Chem. chemical attraction. —**af'finitive** adj.

affirm (ə'fɜːm) vb. (mainly tr.) 1. (may take a clause as object) to declare to be true. 2. to uphold, confirm, or ratify. 3. (intr.) Law. to make an affirmation. —**ₐaffir-'mation** n. —**af'firmer** or **af'firmant** n.

affirmative (ə'fɜːmətɪv) adj. 1. confirming or asserting something as true or valid. 2. indicating agreement or assent. 3. Logic. (of a proposition) affirming the truth of the predicate, as in the proposition some men are married. ~n. 4. a positive assertion. 5. a word or phrase stating agreement or assent, such as yes: to answer in the affirmative. ~ 6. sentence substitute. Mil., etc. a signal codeword used to express assent or confirmation. —**af'firmatively** adv.

affix vb. (ə'fɪks). (tr.; usually foll. by to or on) 1. to attach, fasten, join, or stick. 2. to add or append: to affix a signature to a document. 3. to attach or attribute (guilt, blame, etc.). ~n. ('æfɪks). 4. a linguistic element added to a word or root to produce a derived or inflected form, as -ment in establishment. See also **prefix, suffix, infix.** 5. something fastened or attached. —**affixture** (ə'fɪkstʃə) n.

afflatus (ə'fleɪtəs) n. an impulse of creative power or inspiration considered to be of divine origin.

afflict (ə'flɪkt) vb. (tr.) to cause suffering or unhappiness to; distress greatly. —**af'flictive** adj.

affliction (ə'flɪkʃən) n. 1. a condition of great distress or suffering. 2. something responsible for physical or mental suffering.

affluence ('æfluəns) n. 1. an abundant supply of money, goods, or property; wealth. 2. Rare. abundance or profusion.

affluent ('æfluənt) adj. 1. rich; wealthy. 2. abundant; copious. 3. flowing freely. ~n. 4. a tributary stream.

affluent society n. a society in which the material benefits of prosperity are widely available.

afford (ə'fɔːd) vb. 1. (preceded by can, could, etc.) to be able to do or spare something, esp. without incurring financial difficulties or without risk of undesirable consequences. 2. to give, yield, or supply.

afforest (ə'fɒrɪst) vb. (tr.) to plant trees on. —**af,for-est'ation** n.

affray (ə'freɪ) n. a fight, noisy quarrel, or disturbance between two or more persons in a public place.

affront (ə'frʌnt) n. 1. a deliberate insult. ~vb. (tr.) 2. to insult openly. 3. to offend the pride or dignity of.

afghan ('æfgæn, -gən) n. 1. a knitted or crocheted wool blanket or shawl, esp. one with a geometric pattern. 2. a

sheepskin coat, often embroidered.

Afghan ('æfgæn) or **Afghani** (æf'gænɪ) n. 1. a native, citizen, or inhabitant of Afghanistan. 2. an official language of Afghanistan. ~adj. 3. denoting Afghanistan, its people, or their language.

aficionado (ə,fɪʃjə'nɑːdəʊ) n., pl. **-dos.** 1. an ardent supporter or devotee: a jazz aficionado. 2. a devotee of bullfighting.

afield (ə'fiːld) adv., adj. (postpositive) 1. away from one's usual surroundings or home (esp. in **far afield**). 2. off the subject (esp. in **far afield**). 3. in or to the field.

aflame (ə'fleɪm) adv., adj. (postpositive) 1. in flames. 2. deeply aroused, as with passion: he was aflame with desire.

afloat (ə'fləʊt) adj. (postpositive), adv. 1. floating. 2. aboard ship; at sea. 3. covered with water. 4. aimlessly drifting. 5. in circulation: nasty rumours were afloat. 6. free of debt.

A.F.M. abbrev. for Air Force Medal.

afoot (ə'fʊt) adj. (postpositive), adv. 1. in operation; astir: mischief was afoot. 2. on or by foot.

afore (ə'fɔː) adv., prep., conj. an archaic or dialect word for **before.**

aforementioned (ə'fɔː,mɛnʃənd) adj. (usually prenominal) (chiefly in legal documents) stated or mentioned before.

aforesaid (ə'fɔː,sɛd) adj. (usually prenominal) (chiefly in legal documents) spoken of or referred to previously.

aforethought (ə'fɔː,θɔːt) adj. (immediately postpositive) premeditated (esp. in **malice aforethought**).

a fortiori (eɪ,fɔːtɪ'ɔːraɪ) adv. for a stronger, or more convincing reason.

Afr. abbrev. for Africa(n).

afraid (ə'freɪd) adj. (postpositive) 1. (often foll. by of) feeling fear or apprehension. 2. reluctant (to do something), as through fear or timidity. 3. (often foll. by that; used to lessen the effect of an unpleasant statement) regretful: I'm afraid that I shall have to tell you to go.

afresh (ə'frɛʃ) adv. once more; again; anew.

African ('æfrɪkən) adj. 1. denoting or relating to Africa or any of its peoples, languages, nations, etc. ~n. 2. a native or inhabitant of any of the countries of Africa. 3. a member or descendant of any of the peoples of Africa, esp. a Negro.

Africana (,æfrɪ'kɑːnə, ,æf-) pl. n. objects of cultural or historical interest of southern African origin.

Africander (,æfrɪ'kændə, ,æf-) n. a breed of humped-back beef cattle originally raised in southern Africa.

African lily n. a plant of southern Africa, having rounded clusters of blue or white funnel-shaped flowers.

African violet n. a tropical African plant cultivated as a house plant, with violet, white, or pink flowers and hairy leaves.

Afrikaans (,æfrɪ'kɑːns, -'kɑːnz, æf-) n. an official language of all the Republic of South Africa, closely related to Dutch and Flemish.

Afrikaner (,æfrɪ'kɑːnə, ,æf-) n. a White native of the Republic of South Africa whose mother tongue is Afrikaans.

THESAURUS

affinity 1. alliance, analogy, closeness, compatibility, connection, correspondence, kinship, likeness, relation, relationship, resemblance, similarity 2. attraction, fondness, inclination, leaning, liking, partiality, rapport, sympathy

affirm assert, asseverate, attest, aver, avouch, avow, certify, confirm, declare, maintain, pronounce, ratify, state, swear, testify

affirmation assertion, asseveration, attestation, averment, avouchment, avowal, certification, confirmation, declaration, oath, pronouncement, ratification, statement, testimony

affirmative agreeing, approving, assenting, concurring, confirming, consenting, corroborative, favourable, positive

affix add, annex, append, attach, bind, fasten, glue, join, paste, put on, stick, subjoin, tack, tag

afflict beset, burden, distress, grieve, harass, hurt, oppress, pain, plague, rack, smite, torment, trouble, try, wound

affliction adversity, calamity, cross, curse, depression, disease, distress, grief, hardship, misery, misfortune, ordeal, pain, plague, scourge, sickness, sorrow, suffering, torment, trial, tribulation, trouble, woe, wretchedness

affluence abundance, exuberance, fortune, opulence, plenty, profusion, prosperity, riches, wealth

affluent 1. loaded (Sl.), moneyed, opulent, prosperous, rich, wealthy, well-heeled (Inf.), well-off, well-to-do 2. abundant, copious, exuberant, plenteous, plentiful

afford 1. bear, spare, stand, sustain 2. bestow, furnish, give, grant, impart, offer, produce, provide, render, supply, yield

affray brawl, contest, disturbance, dogfight, encounter, feud, fight, fracas, free-for-all (Inf.), mêlée, outbreak, quarrel, scrap, scuffle, set-to (Inf.), tumult

affront 1. v. abuse, anger, annoy, displease, insult, offend, outrage, pique, provoke, slight, vex 2. n. abuse, indignity, injury, insult, offence, outrage, provocation, slap in

the face (Inf.), slight, slur, vexation, wrong

afire 1. ablaze, aflame, alight, blazing, burning, fiery, flaming, ignited, lighted, lit, on fire 2. aglow, aroused, excited, fervent, impassioned, passionate, stimulated

aflame 1. ablaze, afire, alight, blazing, burning, fiery, flaming, ignited, lighted, lit, on fire 2. afire, aroused, excited, fervent, impassioned, passionate, stimulated 3. aglow, flushed, inflamed, red, ruddy

afoot about, abroad, afloat, astir, brewing, circulating, current, going on, hatching, in preparation, in progress, in the wind, on the go (Inf.), operating, up (Inf.)

afraid 1. alarmed, anxious, apprehensive, cowardly, faint-hearted, fearful, frightened, intimidated, nervous, reluctant, scared, suspicious, timid, timorous 2. regretful, sorry, unhappy

afresh again, anew, newly, once again, once more, over again

See also **Boer.**

Afro ('æfrəʊ) *n., pl.* **-ros.** a hair style in which the hair is shaped into a wide frizzy bush, popular esp. among Negroes.

Afro- ('æfrəʊ-) *combining form.* indicating Africa or African: *Afro-Asiatic.*

Afro-American *n.* **1.** an American Negro. ~*adj.* **2.** denoting or relating to American Negroes, their history, or their culture.

afrormosia (ˌæfrɔːˈməʊzɪə) *n.* a hard teaklike wood obtained from a genus of tropical African trees.

aft (ɑːft) *adv., adj. Chiefly naut.* towards or at the stern or rear: *the aft deck.*

after ('ɑːftə) *prep.* **1.** following in time; in succession to: *after dinner.* **2.** following in space; behind. **3.** in pursuit or search of: *he's only after money.* **4.** concerning: *to inquire after his health.* **5.** considering: *after what you have done, you shouldn't complain.* **6.** next in excellence or importance to. **7.** in imitation of; in the manner of. **8.** in accordance with or in conformity to: *a man after her own heart.* **9.** with a name derived from. **10.** *U.S.* past (the hour of): *twenty after three.* **11. after all. a.** when everything is considered. **b.** in spite of expectations, efforts, etc. **12. after you.** please go, enter, etc., before me. ~*adv.* **13.** at a later time; afterwards. **14.** coming afterwards. **15.** *Naut.* further aft. ~*conj.* **16.** (*subordinating*) at a time later than that at which. ~*adj.* **17.** *Naut.* further aft: *the after cabin.*

afterbirth ('ɑːftə,bɜːθ) *n.* the placenta and foetal membranes expelled from the uterus after the birth of offspring.

afterburner ('ɑːftə,bɜːnə) *n.* **1.** a device in the exhaust system of an internal-combustion engine for removing dangerous exhaust gases. **2.** a device in an aircraft jet engine to ignite additional fuel.

aftercare ('ɑːftə,kɛə) *n. Med.* the care of a patient after a serious illness or operation.

afterdamp ('ɑːftə,dæmp) *n.* a poisonous gas, consisting mainly of carbon monoxide, formed after the explosion of firedamp in coal mines.

aftereffect ('ɑːftərɪ,fɛkt) *n.* any result occurring some time after its cause.

afterglow ('ɑːftə,gləʊ) *n.* **1.** the glow left after a light has disappeared, such as that sometimes seen after sunset. **2.** the glow of an incandescent metal after the source of heat has been removed.

afterlife ('ɑːftə,laɪf) *n.* life after death or at a later time in a person's lifetime.

aftermath ('ɑːftə,mæθ) *n.* **1.** signs or results of an event or occurrence considered collectively: *the aftermath of war.* **2.** *Agriculture.* a second crop of grass from land that has already yielded one crop earlier in the same year.

aftermost ('ɑːftə,məʊst) *adj.* closer or closest to the rear or (in a vessel) the stern; last.

afternoon (ˌɑːftəˈnuːn) *n.* **1. a.** the period between noon and evening. **b.** (*as modifier*): *afternoon tea.* **2.** a later part: *the afternoon of life.* —**after'noons** *adv.*

afterpains ('ɑːftə,peɪnz) *pl. n.* cramplike pains caused by contraction of the uterus after childbirth.

afters ('ɑːftəz) *n.* (*functioning as sing. or pl.*) *Brit. inf.* dessert; sweet.

aftertaste ('ɑːftə,teɪst) *n.* **1.** a taste that lingers on after eating or drinking. **2.** a lingering impression or sensation.

afterthought ('ɑːftə,θɔːt) *n.* **1.** a comment, reply, etc., that occurs to one after the opportunity to deliver it has passed. **2.** an addition to something already completed.

afterwards ('ɑːftəwədz) *or* **afterward** *adv.* after an earlier event or time.

Ag *the chemical symbol for* silver.

again (əˈgɛn, əˈgeɪn) *adv.* **1.** another or a second time: *he had to start again.* **2.** once more in a previously experienced state or condition: *he is ill again.* **3.** in addition to the original amount, quantity, etc. (esp. in **as much again; half as much again**). **4.** (*sentence modifier*) on the other hand. **5.** besides; also. **6.** *Arch.* in reply; back: *he answered again.* **7. again and again.** continuously; repeatedly. ~ **8.** *sentence connector.* moreover; furthermore.

against (əˈgɛnst, əˈgeɪnst) *prep.* **1.** opposed to; in conflict or disagreement with. **2.** standing or leaning beside: *a ladder against the wall.* **3.** coming in contact with. **4.** in contrast to: *silhouettes are outlines against a light background.* **5.** having an unfavourable effect on: *the system works against small companies.* **6.** as a protection from: *a safeguard against contaminated water.* **7.** in exchange for or in return for. **8.** *Now rare.* in preparation for: *he gave them warm clothing against their journey.* **9. as against.** as opposed to or as compared with.

agape (əˈgeɪp) *adj.* (*postpositive*) **1.** (esp. of the mouth) wide open. **2.** very surprised, expectant, or eager.

Agape ('ægəpɪ) *n.* **1.** Christian love, esp. as contrasted with erotic love; charity. **2.** a communal meal in the early Church in commemoration of the Last Supper.

agaric ('ægərɪk) *n.* a fungus having gills on the underside of the cap. The group includes the edible mushrooms and poisonous forms such as the fly agaric.

agate ('ægɪt) *n.* **1.** an impure form of quartz consisting of a variegated, usually banded chalcedony, used as a gemstone and in making pestles and mortars. **2.** a playing marble of this quartz or resembling it.

agave (əˈgeɪvɪ) *n.* a plant native to tropical America with tall flower stalks rising from thick fleshy leaves. Some species are the source of fibres such as sisal.

age (eɪdʒ) *n.* **1.** the period of time that a person, animal, or plant has lived or is expected to live. **2.** the period of existence of an object, material, group, etc.: *the age of this table is 200 years.* **3. a.** a period or state of human life: *he should know better at his age.* **b.** (*as modifier*): *age group.* **4.** the latter part of life. **5. a.** a period of history marked by some feature or characteristic. **b.** (*cap.* when part of a name): *the Middle Ages.* **6.** generation: *the Edwardian age.* **7.** *Geol., palaeontol.* **a.** a period of the earth's history distinguished by special characteristics: *the age of reptiles.* **b.** a subdivision of an epoch. **8.** (*often pl.*) *Inf.* a relatively long time: *I've been waiting ages.* **9.** *Psychol.* the level in years that a person has reached in any area of development, compared with the normal level for his chronological age. **10. of age.** adult and legally responsible for one's actions (usually at 18 years). ~*vb.* **ageing** *or* **aging, aged.** **11.** to become or cause to become old or aged. **12.** to begin to seem older: *to have aged a lot in the past year.* **13.** *Brewing.* to mature or cause to mature.

-age *suffix forming nouns.* **1.** indicating a collection, set, or group: *baggage.* **2.** indicating a process or action or the result of an action: *breakage.* **3.** indicating a state or relationship: *bondage.* **4.** indicating a house or place: *orphanage.* **5.** indicating a charge or fee: *postage.* **6.** indicating a rate: *dosage.*

aged ('eɪdʒɪd) *adj.* **1. a.** advanced in years; old. **b.** (*as collective n.* preceded by *the*): *the aged.* **2.** of, connected with, or characteristic of old age. **3.** (eɪdʒd). (*postpositive*) having the age of: *a woman aged twenty.*

ageless ('eɪdʒlɪs) *adj.* **1.** apparently never growing old. **2.** timeless; eternal: *an ageless quality.*

agency ('eɪdʒənsɪ) *n., pl.* **-cies.** **1.** a business or other organization providing a specific service: *an employment agency.* **2.** the place where an agent conducts business. **3.** the business, duties, or functions of an agent. **4.** action, power, or operation: *the agency of fate.*

THESAURUS

after afterwards, behind, below, following, later, subsequently, succeeding, thereafter

aftermath after-effects, consequences, effects, end, outcome, results, upshot

again 1. afresh, anew, another time, once more 2. also, besides, furthermore, in addition, moreover, on the contrary, on the other hand

against 1. counter, hostile to, in contrast to, in defiance of, in opposition to, in the face of, opposed to, opposing, resisting, versus 2. abutting, close up to, facing, fronting, in contact with, on, opposite to, touching, upon 3. in anticipation of, in expectation of, in preparation for, in provision for

age *n.* 1. date, day(s), duration, epoch, era, generation, lifetime, period, span, time 2. advancing years, decline (*of life*), majority, maturity, old age, senescence, senility, seniority ~*v.* 3. decline, deteriorate, grow old, mature, mellow, ripen

aged age-old, ancient, antiquated, antique, elderly, getting on, grey, hoary, old, senescent, superannuated

agency 1. action, activity, auspices, efficiency, force, influence, instrumentality, intercession, intervention, means, mechanism, mediation, medium, operation, power, work 2. bureau, business, department, office, organization

agenda (ə'dʒɛndə) n. 1. (functioning as sing.) a schedule or list of items to be attended to. Also: **agendum**. 2.
(functioning as pl.) matters to be attended to, as at a
meeting. Also: **agendas, agendums.**
agent ('eɪdʒənt) n. 1. a person who acts on behalf of another person, group, business, government, etc. 2. a person or thing that acts or has the power to act. 3. a substance or organism that exerts some force or effect: a
chemical agent. 4. the means by which something occurs or is achieved. 5. a person representing a business
concern, esp. a travelling salesman. —**agential**
(eɪ'dʒɛnʃəl) adj.
agent provocateur French. (aˈʒã prɔvɔkaˈtœːr) n., pl.
agents provocateurs (aˈʒã prɔvɔkaˈtœːr). a secret
agent employed to provoke suspected persons to commit
illegal acts and so be discredited or liable to punishment.
age-old or **age-long** adj. very old or of long duration;
ancient.
agglomerate vb. (ə'glɒmə,reɪt). 1. to form or be
formed into a mass or cluster. ~n. (ə'glɒmərɪt, -,reɪt).
2. a confused mass. 3. a volcanic rock consisting of angular fragments within a groundmass of lava. ~adj.
(ə'glɒmərɪt, -,reɪt). 4. formed into a mass. —**ag,glom-
er'ation** n. —**ag'glomerative** adj.
agglutinate (ə'gluːtɪ,neɪt). vb. 1. to cause to adhere,
as with glue. 2. Linguistics. to combine or be combined
by agglutination. 3. (tr.) to cause (bacteria, red blood
cells, etc.) to clump together. —**ag'glutinable** adj.
—**ag'glutinant** adj.
agglutination (ə,gluːtɪ'neɪʃən) n. 1. the act or process
of agglutinating. 2. a united mass of parts. 3. Linguistics. the building up of words from component morphemes in such a way that these undergo little or no
change of form or meaning.
aggrandize or **-dise** (ə'grændaɪz) vb. (tr.) 1. to increase the power, wealth, prestige, scope, etc., of. 2. to
cause (something) to seem greater. —**aggrandizement**
or **-disement** (ə'grændɪzmənt) n. —**'aggran,dizer** or
-,diser n.
aggravate ('ægrə,veɪt) vb. (tr.) 1. to make (a disease,
situation, problem, etc.) worse. 2. Inf. to annoy.
—**,aggra'vation** n.
▷ Usage. The use of aggravate and aggravation for annoy
and annoyance is usually avoided in formal English.
aggregate adj. ('ægrɪgɪt). 1. formed of separate units
collected into a whole. 2. (of fruits and flowers) composed of a dense cluster of florets. ~n. ('ægrɪgɪt, -,geɪt).
3. a sum or assemblage of many separate units. 4. Geol.
a rock, such as granite, consisting of a mixture of minerals. 5. the sand, etc., mixed with cement and water to
make concrete. 6. **in the aggregate.** taken as a whole.
~vb. ('ægrɪ,geɪt). 7. to combine or be combined into a
body, etc. 8. (tr.) to amount to (a number). —**,aggre-**

'gation n. —**aggregative** ('ægrɪ,geɪtɪv) adj.
aggression (ə'grɛʃən) n. 1. an attack or harmful action, esp. an unprovoked attack by one country against
another. 2. any offensive activity, practice, etc. 3.
Psychol. a hostile or destructive mental attitude. —**aggressor** (ə'grɛsə) n.
aggressive (ə'grɛsɪv) adj. 1. quarrelsome or belligerent. 2. assertive; vigorous. —**ag'gressively** adv.
aggrieve (ə'griːv) vb. (tr.) 1. (often impersonal or passive) to grieve; distress; afflict. 2. to injure unjustly, esp.
by infringing a person's legal rights. —**aggrievedly**
(ə'griːvɪdlɪ) adv.
aggro ('ægrəʊ) n. Brit. sl. aggressive behaviour.
aghast (ə'gɑːst) adj. (postpositive) overcome with
amazement or horror.
agile ('ædʒaɪl) adj. 1. quick in movement; nimble. 2.
mentally quick or acute. —**'agilely** adv. —**agility**
(ə'dʒɪlɪtɪ) n.
agin (ə'gɪn) prep. Inf. or dialect. against.
agitate ('ædʒɪ,teɪt) vb. 1. (tr.) to excite, disturb, or trouble (a person, the mind or feelings). 2. (tr.) to shake,
stir, or disturb. 3. (intr.; often foll. by for or against) to
attempt to stir up public opinion for or against
something. —**,agi'tation** n. —**'agi,tator** n.
agitprop ('ædʒɪt,prɒp) n. any promotion of political agitation and propaganda, esp. of a Communist nature.
agley (ə'gleɪ, ə'gliː, ə'glaɪ) adj. Scot. awry.
aglitter (ə'glɪtə) adj. (postpositive) sparkling; glittering.
aglow (ə'gləʊ) adj. (postpositive) glowing.
A.G.M. abbrev. for annual general meeting.
agnail ('æg,neɪl) n. another name for **hangnail.**
agnate ('ægneɪt) adj. 1. related by descent from a common male ancestor. 2. related in any way. ~n. 3. a
male or female descendant by male links from a common male ancestor.
agnostic (æg'nɒstɪk) n. 1. a person who holds that
knowledge of a Supreme Being, ultimate cause, etc., is
impossible. ~adj. 2. of or relating to agnostics. —**ag-
'nosticism** n.
ago (ə'gəʊ) adv. in the past: five years ago; long ago.
▷ Usage. The use of ago with since (it's ten years ago
since he wrote the novel) is redundant and is therefore
avoided in careful English. Ago should be followed by
that: it was ten years ago that he wrote the novel.
agog (ə'gɒg) adj. (postpositive) eager or curious.
agonize or **-nise** ('ægə,naɪz) vb. 1. to suffer or cause
to suffer agony. 2. (intr.) to struggle; strive. —**'ago,niz-
ingly** or **-,nisingly** adv.
agony ('ægənɪ) n., pl. **-nies.** 1. acute physical or mental
pain; anguish. 2. the suffering or struggle preceding
death.
agony column n. 1. a newspaper or magazine fea-

THESAURUS

agenda calendar, diary, list, plan, programme, schedule, timetable
agent 1. advocate, deputy, emissary, envoy, factor, go-between, negotiator, rep
(Inf.), representative, substitute, surrogate 2.
actor, author, doer, executor, mover, officer,
operative, operator, performer, worker 3.
agency, cause, force, instrument, means,
power, vehicle
aggravate 1. exacerbate, exaggerate,
heighten, increase, inflame, intensify, magnify, make worse, worsen 2. Inf. annoy, exasperate, get on one's nerves (Inf.), irk, irritate, needle (Inf.), nettle, pester, provoke,
tease, vex
aggravation 1. exacerbation, exaggeration, heightening, increase, inflaming, intensification, magnification, worsening 2. Inf.
annoyance, exasperation, irksomeness, irritation, provocation, teasing, vexation
aggregate 1. v. accumulate, amass, assemble, collect, combine, heap, mix, pile 2. n.
accumulation, agglomeration, amount, assemblage, body, bulk, collection, combination, heap, lump, mass, mixture, pile, sum,
total, whole 3. adj. accumulated, added, assembled, collected, collective, combined,
composite, corporate, cumulative, mixed, total
aggression 1. assault, attack, encroach-

ment, injury, invasion, offence, offensive, onslaught, raid 2. aggressiveness, antagonism,
belligerence, destructiveness, hostility, pugnacity
aggressive 1. belligerent, destructive,
hostile, offensive, pugnacious, quarrelsome
2. assertive, bold, dynamic, energetic, enterprising, forceful, militant, pushing, pushy
(Inf.), vigorous, zealous
aggressor assailant, assaulter, attacker,
invader
aggrieved afflicted, distressed, disturbed, harmed, hurt, ill-used, injured,
peeved (Inf.), saddened, unhappy, woeful,
wronged
aghast afraid, amazed, appalled, astonished, astounded, awestruck, confounded,
frightened, horrified, horror-struck, shocked,
startled, stunned, thunder-struck
agile active, acute, alert, brisk, clever, limber, lithe, lively, nimble, prompt, quick,
quick-witted, sharp, sprightly, spry, supple,
swift
agility activity, acuteness, alertness,
briskness, cleverness, litheness, liveliness,
nimbleness, promptitude, promptness, quickness, quick-wittedness, sharpness, sprightliness, spryness, suppleness, swiftness
agitate 1. beat, churn, convulse, disturb,
rock, rouse, shake, stir, toss 2. alarm, arouse,

confuse, disconcert, disquiet, distract, disturb, excite, ferment, fluster, incite, inflame,
perturb, rouse, ruffle, stimulate, trouble, upset, work up, worry 3. argue, debate, discuss,
dispute, examine, ventilate
agitation 1. churning, convulsion, disturbance, rocking, shake, shaking, stir, stirring, tossing, turbulence 2. alarm, arousal,
clamour, commotion, confusion, discomposure, disquiet, distraction, disturbance, excitement, ferment, flurry, fluster, incitement, lather (Inf.), outcry, stimulation, trouble, tumult, turmoil, upset, worry 3. argument, controversy, debate, discussion, disputation, dispute, ventilation
agitator agent provocateur, demagogue,
firebrand, inciter, instigator, rabble-rouser,
revolutionary, troublemaker
agog avid, curious, eager, enthralled, enthusiastic, excited, expectant, impatient, in
suspense, keen
agonize afflict, be in agony, be in anguish,
distress, harrow, labour, pain, rack, strain,
strive, struggle, suffer, torment, torture, worry, writhe
agony affliction, anguish, distress, misery,
pain, pangs, suffering, throes, torment, torture, woe

ture offering sympathetic advice to readers on their personal problems. **2.** *Inf.* a newspaper or magazine column devoted to advertisements relating esp. to personal problems.

agoraphobia (ˌægərəˈfəʊbɪə) *n.* an abnormal dread of open spaces. —ˌagoraˈphobic *adj., n.*

agouti (əˈguːtɪ) *n., pl.* **-tis** *or* **-ties.** a rodent of Central and South America and the West Indies. Agoutis are agile and long-legged, with hooflike claws, and are valued for their meat.

agrarian (əˈɡrɛərɪən) *adj.* **1.** of or relating to land or its cultivation. **2.** of or relating to rural or agricultural matters. ~*n.* **3.** a person who favours the redistribution of landed property. —aˈgrarianism *n.*

agree (əˈɡriː) *vb.* **agreeing, agreed.** (*mainly intr.*) **1.** (often foll. by *with*) to be of the same opinion. **2.** (*also tr.;* when *intr.,* often foll. by *to;* when *tr.,* takes a clause as *object or an infinitive*) to give assent; consent. **3.** (*also tr.;* when *intr.,* foll. by *on* or *about;* when *tr.,* may take a clause as *object*) to come to terms (about). **4.** (foll. by *with*) to be similar or consistent; harmonize. **5.** (foll. by *with*) to be agreeable or suitable (to one's health, etc.). **6.** *Grammar.* to undergo agreement. **7.** (*tr.;* takes a clause as *object*) to concede: *they agreed that the price was too high.* —aˈgreed *adj.*

agreeable (əˈɡriːəbəl) *adj.* **1.** pleasing; pleasant. **2.** prepared to consent. **3.** (foll. by *to* or *with*) in keeping. **4.** (foll. by *to*) to one's liking. —aˈgreeableness *n.* —aˈgreeably *adv.*

agreement (əˈɡriːmənt) *n.* **1.** the act of agreeing. **2.** a settlement, esp. one that is legally enforceable. **3.** a contract or document containing such a settlement. **4.** the state of being of the same opinion. **5.** the state of being similar or consistent. **6.** *Grammar.* the determination of the inflectional form of one word by some grammatical feature, such as number or gender, of another word.

agriculture (ˈæɡrɪˌkʌltʃə) *n.* the science or occupation of cultivating land and rearing crops and livestock; farming. —ˌagriˈcultural *adj.* —ˌagriˈculturist *or* ˌagriˈculturalist *n.*

agrimony (ˈæɡrɪmənɪ) *n.* **1.** any of various plants of the rose family, which have compound leaves, long spikes of small yellow flowers, and bristly burlike fruits. **2.** any of several other plants, such as hemp agrimony.

agronomy (əˈɡrɒnəmɪ) *n.* the science of cultivation of land, soil management, and crop production. —aˈgronomist *n.*

aground (əˈɡraʊnd) *adv., adj.* (*postpositive*) on or onto the ground or bottom, as in shallow water.

agterskot (ˈaxtəˌskɒt) *n.* (in South Africa) the final instalment of payment to a farmers' cooperative for a crop or wool clip.

ague (ˈeɪɡjuː) *n.* **1.** malarial fever with successive stages of fever and chills. **2.** a fit of shivering. —ˈaguish *adj.*

ah (ɑː) *interj.* an exclamation expressing pleasure, pain, sympathy, etc., according to the intonation of the speaker.

A.H. (indicating years in the Muslim system of dating, numbered from the Hegira (622 A.D.)) *abbrev. for* anno Hegirae.

aha (ɑːˈhɑː) *interj.* an exclamation expressing triumph, surprise, etc., according to the intonation of the speaker.

ahead (əˈhɛd) *adj.* **1.** (*postpositive*) in front; in advance. ~*adv.* **2.** at or in the front; before. **3.** forwards: *go straight ahead.* **4. ahead of. a.** in front of; at a further advanced position than. **b.** *Stock Exchange.* in anticipation of: *the share price rose ahead of the annual figures.* **5.** *Inf.* **be ahead.** to have an advantage; be winning. **6. get ahead.** to attain success.

ahem (əˈhɛm) *interj.* a clearing of the throat, used to attract attention, express doubt, etc.

ahoy (əˈhɔɪ) *interj. Naut.* a hail used to call a ship or to attract attention.

A.I. *abbrev. for:* **1.** artificial insemination. **2.** artificial intelligence.

aid (eɪd) *vb.* **1.** to give support to (someone to do something); help or assist. **2.** (*tr.*) to assist financially. ~*n.* **3.** assistance; help; support. **4.** a person, device, etc., that helps or assists. **5.** (in medieval Europe) a feudal payment made to the king or any lord by his vassals on certain occasions such as the knighting of an eldest son. —ˈaider *n.*

A.I.D. *abbrev. for:* **1.** artificial insemination (by) donor. **2.** *U.S.* Agency for International Development.

aide (eɪd) *n.* **1.** short for **aide-de-camp. 2.** an assistant.

aide-de-camp *or* **aid-de-camp** (ˈeɪd də ˈkɒŋ) *n., pl.* **aides-de-camp** *or* **aids-de-camp.** a military officer serving as personal assistant to a senior. Abbrev.: **A.D.C., ADC, a.d.c.**

aigrette *or* **aigret** (ˈeɪɡrɛt) *n.* **1.** a long plume worn on hats or as a headdress, esp. one of long egret feathers. **2.** an ornament in imitation of a plume of feathers.

A.I.H. *abbrev. for* artificial insemination (by) husband.

ail (eɪl) *vb.* **1.** (*tr.*) to trouble; afflict. **2.** (*intr.*) to feel unwell.

aileron (ˈeɪləˌrɒn) *n.* a flap hinged to the trailing edge of an aircraft wing to provide lateral control.

ailing (ˈeɪlɪŋ) *adj.* unwell, esp. over a long period.

ailment (ˈeɪlmənt) *n.* a slight but often persistent illness.

aim (eɪm) *vb.* **1.** to point (a weapon, missile, etc.) or direct (a blow) at a particular person or object. **2.** (*tr.*) to direct (satire, criticism, etc.) at a person, object, etc. **3.** (*intr.;* foll. by *at* or an infinitive) to propose or intend. **4.** (*intr.;* often foll. by *at* or *for*) to direct one's efforts or strive (towards). ~*n.* **5.** the action of directing something at an object. **6.** the direction in which something is pointed: *to take aim.* **7.** the object at which something is aimed. **8.** intention; purpose.

aimless (ˈeɪmlɪs) *adj.* having no purpose or direction. —ˈaimlessly *adv.* —ˈaimlessness *n.*

ain't (eɪnt) *Not standard.* contraction of am not, is not, are not, have not, *or* has not: *I ain't seen it.*
▷ **Usage.** Although the interrogative form *ain't I?* would be a natural contraction of *am not I?,* it is generally avoided in spoken English and never used in formal English.

air (ɛə) *n.* **1.** the mixture of gases that forms the earth's atmosphere. It consists chiefly of nitrogen, oxygen, argon, and carbon dioxide. **2.** the space above and around the earth; sky. Related adj.: **aerial. 3.** breeze; slight wind. **4.** public expression; utterance. **5.** a distinctive quality: *an air of mystery.* **6.** a person's distinctive appearance, manner, or bearing. **7.** *Music.* a simple tune for either vocal or instrumental performance. **8.** transportation in aircraft (esp. in **by air**). **9.** an archaic word for *breath* (senses 1-3). **10. clear the air.** to rid a situation of tension by settling misunderstandings, etc. **11. in the air. a.** in circulation; current. **b.** unsettled. **12. into thin air.** leaving no trace behind. **13. on** (*or* **off**) **the air.**

THESAURUS

agree 1. accede, acquiesce, admit, allow, assent, be of the same mind, comply, concede, concur, consent, engage, grant, permit, see eye to eye, settle 2. accord, answer, chime, coincide, conform, correspond, fit, get on (together), harmonize, match, square, suit, tally

agreeable 1. acceptable, delightful, enjoyable, gratifying, pleasant, pleasing, pleasurable, satisfying, to one's liking, to one's taste 2. appropriate, befitting, compatible, consistent, fitting, in keeping, proper, suitable 3. acquiescent, amenable, approving, complying, concurring, consenting, in accord, responsive, sympathetic, well-disposed, willing

agreement 1. accord, accordance, affinity, analogy, compatibility, compliance, concert, concord, concurrence, conformity, congruity, consistency, correspondence, harmony, similarity, suitableness, union 2. arrangement, bargain, compact, contract, covenant, deal (*Inf.*), pact, settlement, treaty, understanding

agriculture agronomics, agronomy, cultivation, culture, farming, husbandry, tillage

aground ashore, beached, foundered, grounded, high and dry, on the rocks, stranded, stuck

ahead along, at an advantage, at the head, before, forwards, in advance, in front, in the foreground, in the lead, in the vanguard, leading, on, onwards, to the fore, winning

aid v. 1. abet, assist, befriend, encourage, favour, help, promote, relieve, second, serve, subsidize, succour, support, sustain ~n. 2. assistance, benefit, encouragement, favour, help, relief, service, succour, support 3. abettor, adjutant, aide, aide-de-camp, assistant, helper, second, supporter

aim 1. v. aspire, attempt, design, direct, draw a bead (on), endeavour, intend, level, mean, plan, point, propose, purpose, resolve, seek, set one's sights on, sight, strive, take aim (at), train, try, want, wish 2. n. ambition, aspiration, course, design, desire, direction, end, goal, intent, intention, mark, object, objective, plan, purpose, scheme, target, wish

aimless chance, directionless, erratic, frivolous, goalless, haphazard, pointless, purposeless, random, stray, undirected, unguided, unpredictable, vagrant, wayward

(not) in the act of broadcasting or (not) being broadcast on radio or television. **14. take the air.** to go out of doors, as for a short walk. **15. up in the air. a.** uncertain. **b.** *Inf.* agitated or excited. **16. walk** (*or* **tread**) **on air.** to feel elated. **17.** (*modifier*) *Astrol.* of or relating to a group of three signs of the zodiac, Gemini, Libra, and Aquarius. ~*vb.* **18.** to expose or be exposed to the air so as to cool or freshen. **19.** to expose or be exposed to warm or heated air so as to dry: *to air linen.* **20.** (*tr.*) to make known publicly: *to air one's opinions.*

air bag *n.* a safety device in a car, consisting of a bag that inflates automatically in an accident and prevents the passengers from being thrown forwards.

air base *n.* a centre from which military aircraft operate.

air bladder *n.* **1.** an air-filled sac, lying above the alimentary canal in bony fishes, that regulates buoyancy at different depths by a variation in the pressure of the air. **2.** any air-filled sac, such as one in seaweeds.

airborne ('εə,bɔːn) *adj.* **1.** conveyed by or through the air. **2.** (of aircraft) flying; in the air.

air brake *n.* **1.** a brake operated by compressed air, esp. in heavy vehicles and trains. **2.** an articulated flap or small parachute for reducing the speed of an aircraft.

airbrick ('εə,brɪk) *n. Chiefly Brit.* a brick with holes in it, put into the wall of a building for ventilation.

airbus ('εə,bʌs) *n.* an airliner operated over short distances.

air chief marshal *n.* a senior officer of the Royal Air Force and certain other air forces, of equivalent rank to admiral in the Royal Navy.

air commodore *n.* a senior officer of the Royal Air Force and certain other air forces, of equivalent rank to brigadier in the Army.

air conditioning *n.* a system or process for controlling the temperature and sometimes the humidity of the air in a house, etc. —'**air-con,dition** *vb.* (*tr.*) —**air con-ditioner** *n.*

aircraft ('εə,krɑːft) *n., pl.* **-craft.** any machine capable of flying by means of buoyancy or aerodynamic forces, such as a glider, helicopter, or aeroplane.

aircraft carrier *n.* a warship with an extensive flat deck for the launch of aircraft.

aircraftman ('εə,krɑːftmən) *n., pl.* **-men.** a serviceman of the most junior rank in the Royal Air Force. —'**aircraft,woman** *fem. n.*

air curtain *n.* an air stream across a doorway to exclude draughts, etc.

air cushion *n.* **1.** an inflatable cushion. **2.** the pocket of air that supports a hovercraft.

Airedale ('εə,deɪl) *n.* a large rough-haired tan-coloured breed of terrier with a black saddle-shaped patch on the back. Also called: **Airedale terrier.**

airfield ('εə,fiːld) *n.* a landing and taking-off area for aircraft.

air force *n.* **a.** the branch of a nation's armed services primarily responsible for military aircraft. **b.** (*as modifier*): *an air-force base.*

air gun *n.* a gun discharged by means of compressed air.

air hole *n.* **1.** a hole that allows the passage of air, esp. for ventilation. **2.** a section of open water in a frozen surface.

air hostess *n.* a stewardess on an airliner.

airily ('εərɪlɪ) *adv.* **1.** in a jaunty or high-spirited manner. **2.** in a light or delicate manner.

airiness ('εərɪnɪs) *n.* **1.** the quality or condition of being fresh, light, or breezy. **2.** gaiety.

airing ('εərɪŋ) *n.* **1. a.** exposure to air or warmth, as for

drying or ventilation. **b.** (*as modifier*): *airing cupboard.* **2.** an excursion in the open air. **3.** exposure to public debate.

airless ('εəlɪs) *adj.* **1.** lacking fresh air; stuffy or sultry. **2.** devoid of air. —'**airlessness** *n.*

air letter *n.* another name for **aerogram.**

airlift ('εə,lɪft) *n.* **1.** the transportation by air of passengers, troops, cargo, etc., esp. when other routes are blocked. ~*vb.* **2.** (*tr.*) to transport by an airlift.

airline ('εə,laɪn) *n.* **1. a.** a system or organization that provides scheduled flights for passengers or cargo. **b.** (*as modifier*): *an airline pilot.* **2.** a hose or tube carrying air under pressure.

airliner ('εə,laɪnə) *n.* a large passenger aircraft.

airlock ('εə,lɒk) *n.* **1.** a bubble in a pipe causing an obstruction. **2.** an airtight chamber with regulated air pressure used to gain access to a space that has air under pressure.

air mail *n.* **1.** the system of conveying mail by aircraft. **2.** mail conveyed by aircraft. ~*adj.* **air-mail. 3.** of or for air mail.

airman ('εəmən) *n., pl.* **-men.** an aviator, esp. one serving in the armed forces.

air marshal *n.* **1.** a senior Royal Air Force officer of equivalent rank to a vice admiral in the Royal Navy. **2.** a Royal Australian Air Force officer of the highest rank.

airplane ('εə,pleɪn) *n.* the U.S. name for **aeroplane.**

air pocket *n.* a localized region of low air density or a descending air current, causing an aircraft to suffer an abrupt decrease in height.

airport ('εə,pɔːt) *n.* a landing and taking-off area for civil aircraft, usually with runways and aircraft maintenance and passenger facilities.

air pump *n.* a device for pumping air into or out of something.

air raid *n.* **a.** an attack by hostile aircraft or missiles. **b.** (*as modifier*): *an air-raid shelter.*

air rifle *n.* a rifle discharged by compressed air.

airs (εəz) *pl. n.* affected manners intended to impress others: *to give oneself airs, put on airs.*

air sac *n.* any of the membranous air-filled extensions of the lungs of birds, which increase the efficiency of respiration.

air-sea rescue *n.* an air rescue at sea.

airship ('εə,ʃɪp) *n.* a lighter-than-air self-propelled craft. Also called: **dirigible.**

airsick ('εə,sɪk) *adj.* nauseated from travelling in an aircraft.

airspace ('εə,speɪs) *n.* the atmosphere above the earth or part of the earth, esp. the atmosphere above a particular country.

airspeed ('εə,spiːd) *n.* the speed of an aircraft relative to the air in which it moves.

airstrip ('εə,strɪp) *n.* a cleared area for the landing and taking-off of aircraft; runway. Also called: **landing strip.**

air terminal *n. Brit.* a building in a city from which air passengers are taken to an airport.

airtight ('εə,taɪt) *adj.* **1.** not permitting the passage of air. **2.** having no weak points; invulnerable.

air-to-air *adj.* operating between aircraft in flight.

air vice-marshal *n.* **1.** a senior Royal Air Force officer of equivalent rank to a rear admiral in the Royal Navy. **2.** a Royal Australian Air Force officer of the second highest rank.

airwaves ('εə,weɪvz) *pl. n. Inf.* radio waves used in radio and television broadcasting.

airy ('εərɪ) *adj.* **airier, airiest. 1.** abounding in fresh air. **2.** spacious or uncluttered. **3.** of or relating to air. **4.**

THESAURUS

air *n.* **1.** atmosphere, heavens, sky **2.** blast, breath, breeze, draught, puff, waft, whiff, wind, zephyr **3.** ambience, appearance, atmosphere, aura, bearing, character, demeanour, effect, feeling, flavour, impression, look, manner, mood, quality, style, tone **4.** circulation, display, dissemination, exposure, expression, publicity, utterance, vent, ventilation **5.** aria, lay, melody, song, tune ~*v.* **6.** aerate, expose, freshen, ventilate **7.** circulate, communicate, declare, disclose, display, disseminate, divulge, exhibit, expose, express, give vent to, make known, make pub-

lic, proclaim, publicize, reveal, tell, utter, ventilate, voice

airily 1. animatedly, blithely, breezily, buoyantly, gaily, happily, high-spiritedly, jauntily, light-heartedly **2.** daintily, delicately, ethereally, gracefully, lightly

airiness 1. breeziness, draughtiness, freshness, gustiness, lightness, openness, windiness **2.** ethereality, immateriality, incorporeality, insubstantiality, lightness, weightlessness **3.** animation, blitheness, breeziness, buoyancy, gaiety, happiness, high spirits, jauntiness, light-heartedness, light-

ness of heart

airing 1. aeration, drying, freshening, ventilation **2.** excursion, jaunt, outing, promenade, stroll, walk **3.** circulation, display, dissemination, exposure, expression, publicity, utterance, vent, ventilation

airless breathless, close, heavy, muggy, oppressive, stale, stifling, stuffy, suffocating, sultry, unventilated

airs affectation, affectedness, arrogance, haughtiness, hauteur, pomposity, pretensions, superciliousness, swank (*Inf.*)

weightless and insubstantial. **5.** light and graceful in movement. **6.** buoyant and gay; lively. **7.** visionary; fanciful: *airy promises.* **8.** high up in the air. **9.** *Inf.* nonchalant.

aisle (ail) *n.* **1.** a passageway separating seating areas in a theatre, church, etc. **2.** a lateral division in a church flanking the nave or chancel. —**aisled** *adj.*

aitch (eitʃ) *n.* the letter *h* or the sound represented by it.

aitchbone ('eitʃ,bəʊn) *n.* **1.** the rump bone in cattle. **2.** a cut of beef from or including the rump bone.

ajar[1] (ə'dʒɑː) *adj.* (*postpositive*), *adv.* (esp. of a door) slightly open.

ajar[2] (ə'dʒɑː) *adj.* (*postpositive*) not in harmony.

akimbo (ə'kimbəʊ) *adj.* (*postpositive*), *adv.* with hands on hips and elbows out.

akin (ə'kin) *adj.* (*postpositive*) **1.** related by blood. **2.** (often foll. by *to*) having similar characteristics, properties, etc.

Al the chemical symbol for aluminium.

-al[1] *suffix forming adjectives.* of; related to: *functional; sectional; tonal.*

-al[2] *suffix forming nouns.* the act or process of doing what is indicated by the verb stem: *renewal.*

-al[3] *suffix forming nouns.* **1.** (*not used systematically*) indicating any aldehyde: *salicylal.* **2.** indicating a pharmaceutical product: *phenobarbital.*

à la (ɑː lɑː) *prep.* **1.** in the manner or style of. **2.** as prepared in (a particular place) or by or for (a particular person).

alabaster ('ælə,bɑːstə) *n.* **1.** a fine-grained usually white, opaque, or translucent variety of gypsum. **2.** a variety of hard semitranslucent calcite. —*adj.* **3.** of or resembling alabaster. —,ala'**bastrine** *adj.*

à la carte (ɑː lɑː 'kɑːt) *adj., adv.* (of a menu) having dishes listed separately and individually priced. Cf. **table d'hôte.**

alack (ə'læk) *or* **alackaday** (ə'lækə,dei) *interj.* an archaic or poetic word for **alas.**

alacrity (ə'lækriti) *n.* liveliness or briskness.

Aladdin's cave (ə'lædinz) *n.* a source of boundless riches.

à la mode (ɑː lɑː 'məʊd) *adj.* **1.** fashionable in style, design, etc. **2.** (of meats) braised with vegetables in wine.

alarm (ə'lɑːm) *vb.* (*tr.*) **1.** to fill with apprehension, anxiety, or fear. **2.** to warn about danger; alert. ~*n.* **3.** fear or terror aroused by awareness of danger. **4.** apprehension or uneasiness. **5.** a noise, signal, etc., warning of danger. **6.** any device that transmits such a warning: *a burglar alarm.* **7. a.** the device in an alarm clock that triggers off the bell or buzzer. **b.** short for **alarm clock. 8.** *Arch.* a call to arms. —**a'larming** *adj.*

alarm clock *n.* a clock with a mechanism that sounds at a set time: used esp. for waking a person up.

alarmist (ə'lɑːmist) *n.* **1.** a person who alarms or attempts to alarm others needlessly. **2.** a person who is easily alarmed. ~*adj.* **3.** characteristic of an alarmist.

alarum (ə'lærəm, -'lɑː-r-) *n.* **1.** *Arch.* an alarm, esp. a call to arms. **2.** (used as a stage direction, esp. in Elizabethan drama) a loud disturbance or conflict (esp. in **alarums and excursions**).

alas (ə'læs) *interj.* an exclamation of grief or alarm.

alate ('eileit) *adj.* having wings or winglike extensions.

alb (ælb) *n. Christianity.* a long white linen vestment with sleeves worn by priests and others.

albacore ('ælbə,kɔː) *n.* a tunny occurring mainly in warm regions of the Atlantic and Pacific. It has very long pectoral fins and is a valued food fish.

albatross ('ælbə,trɒs) *n.* **1.** a large bird of cool south-ern oceans, with long narrow wings and a powerful gliding flight. **2.** *Golf.* a score of three strokes under par for a hole.

albeit (ɔːl'biːit) *conj.* even though.

albert ('ælbət) *n.* a kind of watch chain usually attached to a waistcoat.

Albertan (æl'bɜːtən) *adj.* **1.** of or denoting Alberta, a province of W Canada. ~*n.* **2.** a native or inhabitant of Alberta.

albino (æl'biːnəʊ) *n., pl.* -**nos. 1.** a person with congenital absence of pigmentation in the skin, eyes, and hair. **2.** any animal or plant that is deficient in pigment. —**albinism** ('ælbi,nizəm) *n.* —**albinotic** (,ælbi'nɒtik) *adj.*

Albion ('ælbiən) *n. Arch. or poetic.* Britain or England.

album ('ælbəm) *n.* **1.** a book or binder consisting of blank pages, for keeping photographs, stamps, autographs, etc. **2.** a booklike holder containing sleeves for gramophone records. **3.** one or more long-playing records released as a single item. **4.** *Chiefly Brit.* an anthology.

albumen ('ælbjumin) *n.* **1.** the white of an egg; the nutritive substance that surrounds the yolk. **2.** a variant spelling of **albumin.**

albumin *or* **albumen** ('ælbjumin) *n.* any of a group of simple water-soluble proteins that are found in blood plasma, egg white, etc.

albuminous (æl'bjuːminəs) *adj.* of or containing albumin.

ALCAN *acronym for* Aluminium Company of Canada.

alchemy ('ælkəmi) *n., pl.* -**mies. 1.** the pseudoscientific predecessor of chemistry that sought a method of transmuting base metals into gold, and an elixir to prolong life indefinitely. **2.** a power like that of alchemy: *her beauty had a potent alchemy.* —**alchemic** (æl-'kɛmik) *or* al'**chemical** *adj.* —'**alchemist** *n.*

alcohol ('ælkə,hɒl) *n.* **1.** a colourless flammable liquid, the active principle of intoxicating drinks, produced by the fermentation of sugars. Formula: C_2H_5OH. Also called: **ethanol, ethyl alcohol. 2.** a drink or drinks containing this substance. **3.** *Chem.* any one of a class of organic compounds that contain one or more hydroxyl groups bound to carbon atoms that are not part of an aromatic ring. Cf. **phenol** (sense 2).

alcoholic (,ælkə'hɒlik) *n.* **1.** a person affected by alcoholism. ~*adj.* **2.** of, relating to, containing, or resulting from alcohol.

alcoholism ('ælkəhɒ,lizəm) *n.* **1.** continual heavy consumption of alcoholic drink. **2.** a physiological disorder resulting from this.

alcove ('ælkəʊv) *n.* **1.** a recess or niche in the wall of a room, as for a bed, books, etc. **2.** any recessed usually vaulted area, as in a garden wall. **3.** any covered or secluded spot.

aldehyde ('ældi,haid) *n.* **1.** any organic compound containing the group -CHO. Aldehydes are oxidized to carboxylic acids. **2.** (*modifier*) consisting of, containing, or concerned with the group -CHO. —**aldehydic** (,ældə-'hidik) *adj.*

alder ('ɔːldə) *n.* **1.** a shrub or tree of the birch family, having toothed leaves and conelike fruits. The wood is used for bridges, etc. because it resists underwater rot. **2.** any of several similar trees or shrubs. ~Cf. **elder**[2].

alderman ('ɔːldəmən) *n., pl.* -**men. 1.** (in England and Wales until 1974) one of the senior members of a local council, elected by other councillors. **2.** (in the U.S., Canada, etc.) a member of the governing body of a municipality. —**aldermanic** (,ɔːldə'mænik) *adj.*

ale (eil) *n.* **1.** an alcoholic drink made by fermenting a

---

THESAURUS

airy 1. blowy, breezy, draughty, fresh, gusty, light, lofty, open, spacious, uncluttered, well-ventilated, windy **2.** aerial, delicate, ethereal, fanciful, flimsy, illusory, imaginary, immaterial, incorporeal, insubstantial, light, vaporous, visionary, weightless, wispy **3.** animated, blithe, buoyant, cheerful, cheery, debonair, frolicsome, gay, graceful, happy, high-spirited, jaunty, light, lighthearted, lively, merry, nonchalant, sprightly
aisle corridor, gangway, lane, passage, passageway, path
alacrity alertness, avidity, briskness, cheerfulness, dispatch, eagerness, enthusi-asm, gaiety, hilarity, joyousness, liveliness, promptness, quickness, readiness, speed, sprightliness, willingness, zeal
alarm v. **1.** daunt, dismay, distress, frighten, give (someone) a turn (*Inf.*), panic, put the wind up (someone) (*Inf.*), scare, startle, terrify, unnerve **2.** alert, arouse, signal, warn ~*n.* **3.** anxiety, apprehension, consternation, dismay, distress, fear, fright, nervousness, panic, scare, terror, trepidation, unease, uneasiness **4.** alarm-bell, alert, bell, danger signal, distress signal, siren, tocsin, warning **5.** *Archaic* call to arms
alarming daunting, dismaying, distress-ing, disturbing, dreadful, frightening, scaring, shocking, startling, terrifying, unnerving
alcoholic 1. *adj.* brewed, distilled, fermented, hard, inebriant, inebriating, intoxicating, spirituous, strong, vinous **2.** *n.* bibber, boozer (*Inf.*), dipsomaniac, drunk, drunkard, hard drinker, inebriate, soak (*Inf.*), sot, sponge (*Inf.*), tippler, toper, tosspot (*Inf.*), wino (*Inf.*)
alcove bay, bower, compartment, corner, cubbyhole, cubicle, niche, nook, recess

cereal, esp. barley, originally differing from beer by being unflavoured by hops. **2.** *Chiefly Brit.* another word for **beer.**

aleatory (ˈeɪlɪətərɪ) *or* **aleatoric** (ˌeɪlɪəˈtɒrɪk) *adj.* **1.** dependent on chance. **2.** (esp. of a musical composition) involving elements chosen at random by the performer.

alehouse (ˈeɪlˌhaʊs) *n.* an archaic or dialect name for **pub.**

alembic (əˈlɛmbɪk) *n.* **1.** an obsolete type of retort used for distillation. **2.** anything that distils or purifies.

aleph (ˈɑːlɪf; *Hebrew* ˈa:lɛf) *n.* the first letter in the Hebrew alphabet.

alert (əˈlɜːt) *adj.* (*usually postpositive*) **1.** vigilantly attentive: *alert to the problems.* **2.** brisk, nimble, or lively. ~*n.* **3.** an alarm or warning. **4.** the period during which such a warning remains in effect. **5. on the alert. a.** on guard against danger, attack, etc. **b.** watchful; ready. ~*vb.* (*tr.*) **6.** to warn or signal (troops, police, etc.) to prepare for action. **7.** to warn of danger, an attack, etc. —aˈlertly *adv.* —aˈlertness *n.*

A level *n. Brit.* the advanced level of a subject taken for General Certificate of Education (G.C.E.).

Alexandrine (ˌælɪɡˈzændraɪn) *n.* **1.** a line of verse having six iambic feet, usually with a caesura after the third foot. ~*adj.* **2.** of or written in Alexandrines.

alexandrite (ˌælɪɡˈzændraɪt) *n.* a green variety of chrysoberyl used as a gemstone.

alexia (əˈlɛksɪə) *n.* a disorder of the central nervous system characterized by impaired ability to read.

alfalfa (ælˈfælfə) *n.* a leguminous plant of Europe and Asia, widely cultivated for forage. Also called: **lucerne.**

alfresco (ælˈfrɛskəʊ) *adj., adv.* in the open air.

alg. *abbrev. for* algebra *or* algebraic.

algae (ˈældʒiː) *pl. n., sing.* **alga** (ˈælɡə). unicellular or multicellular plants, occurring in water or moist ground, that have chlorophyll but lack true stems, roots, and leaves. —**algal** (ˈælɡəl) *or* **algoid** (ˈælɡɔɪd) *adj.*

algebra (ˈældʒɪbrə) *n.* **1.** a branch of mathematics in which arithmetical operations and relationships are generalized by using symbols to represent numbers. **2.** a system of logical notation in which variables represent propositions and symbols represent the relations between them. —**algebraic** (ˌældʒɪˈbreɪɪk) *or* ˌalgeˈbraical *adj.* —**algebraist** (ˌældʒɪˈbreɪɪst) *n.*

-algia *n. combining form.* denoting pain in the part specified: *neuralgia; odontalgia.* —**-algic** *adj. combining form.*

algid (ˈældʒɪd) *adj. Med.* chilly or cold. —alˈgidity *n.*

ALGOL (ˈælɡɒl) *n.* a computer programming language designed for mathematical and scientific purposes, in which algorithms can be expressed unambiguously. Cf. FORTRAN, COBOL.

algorism (ˈælɡəˌrɪzəm) *n.* **1.** the Arabic or decimal system of counting. **2.** the skill of computation. **3.** an algorithm.

algorithm (ˈælɡəˌrɪðəm) *n.* any method or procedure of computation, usually involving a series of steps as in long division. Also called: **algorism.** —ˌalgoˈrithmic *adj.*

alias (ˈeɪlɪəs) *adv.* **1.** at another time or place known as or named: *Dylan, alias Zimmerman.* ~*n., pl.* **-ases. 2.** an assumed name.

alibi (ˈælɪˌbaɪ) *n., pl.* **-bis. 1.** *Law.* **a.** a defence by an ac-

cused person that he was elsewhere at the time the crime was committed. **b.** the evidence given to prove this. **2.** *Inf.* an excuse. ~*vb.* **3.** (*tr.*) to provide with an alibi.

▷ **Usage.** The noun *alibi* is often used informally to mean an excuse: *he was late but, as always, had a good alibi.* In formal English, however, only the legal sense is acceptable.

alien (ˈeɪlɪən) *n.* **1.** a person owing allegiance to a country other than that in which he lives. **2.** any being or thing foreign to its environment: *an alien from another planet.* ~*adj.* **3.** unnaturalized; foreign. **4.** having foreign allegiance: *alien territory.* **5.** unfamiliar: *an alien quality.* **6.** (*postpositive* and foll. *by to*) repugnant or opposed (to): *war is alien to his philosophy.*

alienable (ˈeɪlɪənəbəl) *adj. Law.* (of property) transferable to another owner. —ˌalienaˈbility *n.*

alienate (ˈeɪlɪəˌneɪt) *vb.* (*tr.*) **1.** to cause (a friend, etc.) to become unfriendly or hostile. **2.** to turn away: *to alienate the affections of a person.* **3.** *Law.* to transfer the ownership of (property, etc.) to another person. —ˌalienˈation *n.* —ˈalienˌator *n.*

alienist (ˈeɪlɪənɪst) *n. U.S.* a psychiatrist who specializes in the legal aspects of mental illness.

alight¹ (əˈlaɪt) *vb.* **alighting, alighted** *or* **alit.** (*intr.*) **1.** (usually foll. *by from*) to step out (of): *to alight from a taxi.* **2.** to come to rest; land: *a thrush alighted on the wall.*

alight² (əˈlaɪt) *adj.* (*postpositive*), *adv.* **1.** burning; on fire. **2.** illuminated.

align (əˈlaɪn) *vb.* **1.** to place or become placed in a line. **2.** to bring (components or parts) into proper coordination or relation. **3.** (*tr.*; usually foll. *by with*) to bring (a person, country, etc.) into agreement with the policy, etc. of another. —aˈlignment *n.*

alike (əˈlaɪk) *adj.* (*postpositive*) **1.** possessing the same or similar characteristics: *they all look alike.* ~*adv.* **2.** in the same or a similar manner or degree: *they walk alike.*

aliment (ˈælɪmənt) *n.* something that nourishes or sustains the body or mind. —ˌaliˈmental *adj.*

alimentary (ˌælɪˈmɛntərɪ) *adj.* **1.** of or relating to nutrition. **2.** providing sustenance or nourishment.

alimentary canal *n.* the tubular passage extending from the mouth to the anus, through which food is passed and digested.

alimony (ˈælɪmənɪ) *n. Law.* an allowance paid under a court order by one spouse to another when they are separated, either before or after divorce.

aline (əˈlaɪn) *vb.* a rare spelling of **align.** —aˈlinement *n.*

A-line (ˈeɪˌlaɪn) *adj.* (of garments) flaring out slightly from the waist or shoulders.

aliphatic (ˌælɪˈfætɪk) *adj.* (of an organic compound) not aromatic, esp. having an open chain structure.

aliquant (ˈælɪkwənt) *adj. Maths.* of or signifying a quantity or number that is not an exact divisor of a given quantity or number: *5 is an aliquant part of 12.*

aliquot (ˈælɪˌkwɒt) *adj. Maths.* of or signifying an exact divisor of a quantity or number: *3 is an aliquot part of 12.*

alive (əˈlaɪv) *adj.* (*postpositive*) **1.** living; having life. **2.** in existence; active: *they kept hope alive.* **3.** (*immedi-*

THESAURUS

alert 1. *adj.* active, agile, attentive, brisk, careful, circumspect, heedful, lively, nimble, observant, on guard, on one's toes, on the ball (*Inf.*), on the lookout, on the watch, perceptive, quick, ready, spirited, sprightly, vigilant, wary, watchful, wide-awake **2.** *n.* alarm, signal, siren, warning **3.** *v.* alarm, forewarn, inform, notify, signal, warn

alertness activeness, agility, attentiveness, briskness, carefulness, circumspection, heedfulness, liveliness, nimbleness, perceptiveness, promptitude, quickness, readiness, spiritedness, sprightliness, vigilance, wariness, watchfulness

alias 1. *adv.* also called, also known as, otherwise, otherwise known as **2.** *n.* assumed name, *nom de guerre,* nom de plume, pen name, pseudonym, stage name

alibi defence, excuse, explanation, justification, plea, pretext, reason

alien 1. *adj.* adverse, conflicting, contrary, estranged, exotic, foreign, inappropriate, incompatible, incongruous, not native, not naturalized, opposed, outlandish, remote, repugnant, separated, strange, unfamiliar **2.** *n.* foreigner, newcomer, outsider, stranger

alienate 1. break off, disaffect, divert, divorce, estrange, make unfriendly, separate, set against, turn away, withdraw **2.** *Law* abalienate, convey, transfer

alienation 1. breaking off, disaffection, diversion, divorce, estrangement, indifference, remoteness, rupture, separation, setting against, turning away, withdrawal **2.** *Law* abalienation, conveyance, transfer

alight¹ *v.* come down, come to rest, descend, disembark, dismount, get down, get off, land, light, perch, settle, touch down

alight² *adj.* **1.** ablaze, aflame, blazing, burning, fiery, flaming, flaring, ignited, lighted,

lit, on fire **2.** bright, brilliant, illuminated, lit up, shining

align 1. arrange in line, coordinate, even, even up, line up, make parallel, order, range, regulate, straighten **2.** affiliate, agree, ally, associate, cooperate, join, side, sympathize

alignment 1. adjustment, arrangement, coordination, evening, evening up, line, lining up, order, ranging, regulating, sequence, straightening up **2.** affiliation, agreement, alliance, association, cooperation, sympathy, union

alike 1. *adj.* akin, analogous, corresponding, duplicate, equal, equivalent, even, identical, parallel, resembling, similar, the same, uniform **2.** *adv.* analogously, correspondingly, equally, evenly, identically, similarly, uniformly

ately *postpositive*) now living: *the happiest woman alive.*
4. full of life; lively. **5.** (usually foll. by *with*) animated: *a face alive with emotion.* **6.** (foll. by *to*) aware (of); sensitive (to). **7.** (foll. by *with*) teeming (with): *the mattress was alive with fleas.* **8.** *Electronics.* another word for **live²** (sense 10). **9. look alive! a.** hurry up! **b.** pay attention!

alkali ('ælkə,laɪ) *n., pl.* **-lis** *or* **-lies. 1.** *Chem.* a soluble base or a solution of a base. **2.** a soluble mineral salt that occurs in arid soils.

alkaline ('ælkə,laɪn) *adj.* having the properties of or containing an alkali. —**alkalinity** (,ælkə'lɪnɪtɪ) *n.*

alkaloid ('ælkə,lɔɪd) *n.* any of a group of nitrogenous compounds found in plants. Many are poisonous and some are used as drugs.

Alkoran *or* **Alcoran** (,ælkɒ'rɑːn) *n.* a less common name for the **Koran.**

all (ɔːl) *determiner.* **1. a.** the whole quantity or amount of: *all the rice.* **b.** (*as pronoun; functioning as sing. or pl.*): *all of it is nice; all are welcome.* **2.** every one of a class: *all men are mortal.* **3.** the greatest possible: *in all earnestness.* **4.** any whatever: *beyond all doubt.* **5. above all.** most important. **6. after all.** in spite of everything: *it's only a game, after all.* **7. all but.** nearly: *all but dead.* **8. all of.** no less or smaller than: *she's all of thirteen years.* **9. all over. a.** finished. **b.** everywhere (in, on, etc.): *all over England.* **c.** *Inf.* typically (in **that's me** (him, *etc.*) **all over**). **d.** unduly effusive towards. **10. all in all. a.** everything considered: *all in all, it was a great success.* **b.** the object of one's attention: *you are my all in all.* **11. all the.** (foll. by a comp. adj. or adv.) so much (more or less) than otherwise: *we must work all the faster now.* **12. at all. a.** (*used with a negative or in a question*) in any way or to any degree: *I didn't know that at all.* **b.** anyway: *I'm surprised you came at all.* **13. be all for.** *Inf.* to be strongly in favour of. **14. for all. a.** in so far as: *for all anyone knows, he was a baron.* **b.** notwithstanding: *for all my pushing, I still couldn't move it.* **15. for all that.** in spite of that: *he was a nice man for all that.* **16. in all.** altogether: *there were five in all.* ~*adv.* **17.** (in scores of games) apiece; each: *the score was three all.* ~*n.* **18.** (preceded by *my, his,* etc.) (one's) complete effort or interest: *to give your all.* **19.** totality or whole.

all- *combining form.* variant of **allo-** before a vowel, indicating variation, or opposition.

alla breve ('ælə 'breɪvɪ) *Music. adj., adv.* **1.** with two beats to the bar instead of four, i.e. twice as fast as written. ~*n.* **2.** (formerly) a time of two or four minims to the bar. Symbol: ¢.

Allah ('ælə) *n. Islam.* the principal Muslim name for God.

allay (ə'leɪ) *vb.* **1.** to relieve (pain, grief, etc.) or be relieved. **2.** (*tr.*) to reduce (fear, anger, etc.).

all clear *n.* **1.** a signal indicating that some danger, such as an air raid, is over. **2.** permission to proceed.

allegation (,ælɪ'geɪʃən) *n.* **1.** the act of alleging. **2.** an unproved assertion, esp. an accusation.

allege (ə'lɛdʒ) *vb.* (*tr.; may take a clause as object*) **1.** to state without or before proof: *he alleged malpractice.* **2.** to put forward (an argument or plea) for or against an accusation, claim, etc.

alleged (ə'lɛdʒd) *adj.* (*prenominal*) **1.** stated to be such:

the alleged murderer. **2.** dubious: *an alleged miracle.* —**allegedly** (ə'lɛdʒɪdlɪ) *adv.*

allegiance (ə'liːdʒəns) *n.* **1.** loyalty, as of a subject to his sovereign. **2.** (in feudal society) the obligations of a vassal to his liege lord.

allegorize *or* **-ise** ('ælɪgə,raɪz) *vb.* **1.** to transform (a story, fable, etc.) into or compose in the form of allegory. **2.** (*tr.*) to interpret allegorically. —**allegori'zation** *or* **-i'sation** *n.*

allegory ('ælɪgərɪ) *n., pl.* **-ries. 1.** a poem, play, picture, etc., in which the apparent meaning of the characters and events is used to symbolize a moral or spiritual meaning. **2.** use of such symbolism. **3.** anything used as a symbol. —**allegorical** (,ælɪ'gɒrɪkəl) *adj.* —**'allegorist** *n.*

allegretto (,ælɪ'grɛtəʊ) *Music.* ~*adj., adv.* **1.** quickly or briskly. ~*n., pl.* **-tos. 2.** a piece or passage to be performed in this manner.

allegro (ə'leɪgrəʊ, -'lɛg-) *Music.* ~*adj., adv.* **1.** in a brisk lively manner. ~*n., pl.* **-gros. 2.** a piece or passage to be performed in this manner.

alleluia (,ælɪ'luːjə) *interj.* praise the Lord! Used in liturgical contexts in place of *hallelujah.*

allergen ('ælə,dʒɛn) *n.* any substance capable of inducing an allergy. —**,aller'genic** *adj.*

allergic (ə'lɜːdʒɪk) *adj.* **1.** of, having, or caused by an allergy. **2.** (*postpositive*; foll. by *to*) *Inf.* having an aversion (to): *allergic to work.*

allergy ('ælədʒɪ) *n., pl.* **-gies. 1.** a hypersensitivity to a substance that causes the body to react to any contact with it. Hay fever is an allergic reaction to pollen. **2.** *Inf.* an aversion.

alleviate (ə'liːvɪ,eɪt) *vb.* (*tr.*) to make (pain, sorrow, etc.) easier to bear; lessen. —**al,levi'ation** *n.* —**al'leviˌator** *n.*

alley¹ ('ælɪ) *n.* **1.** a narrow passage, esp. one between or behind buildings. **2. a.** a long narrow wooden lane down which the ball is rolled in tenpin bowling **b.** a similar lane or alley for playing skittles. **3.** a building having lanes for tenpin bowling. **4.** *Tennis, chiefly U.S.* the space between the singles and doubles sidelines. **5.** a walk in a garden, esp. one lined with trees. **6. up** (*or* **down**) **one's alley.** *Sl.* suited to one's abilities or interests.

alley² ('ælɪ) *n.* a large playing marble.

alleyway ('ælɪ,weɪ) *n.* a narrow passage; alley.

all found *adj.* (of charges for accommodation) inclusive of meals, heating, etc.

Allhallows (,ɔːl'hæləʊz) *n.* a less common term for **All Saints' Day.**

alliaceous (,ælɪ'eɪʃəs) *adj.* **1.** of or relating to a genus of plants that have a strong smell and often have bulbs. The genus occurs in the N hemisphere and includes onion and garlic. **2.** tasting or smelling like garlic or onions.

alliance (ə'laɪəns) *n.* **1.** the act of allying or state of being allied; union. **2.** a formal agreement, esp. a military one, between two or more countries. **3.** the countries involved. **4.** a union between families through marriage. **5.** affinity or correspondence in characteristics. **6.** *Bot.* a taxonomic category consisting of a group of related families.

allied (ə'laɪd, 'ælaɪd) *adj.* **1.** joined, as by treaty or marriage; united. **2.** of the same type or class.

THESAURUS

alive 1. animate, breathing, having life, in the land of the living (*Inf.*), living, subsisting **2.** active, existent, existing, extant, functioning, in existence, in force, operative, unquenched **3.** active, alert, animated, awake, brisk, cheerful, eager, energetic, full of life, lively, quick, spirited, sprightly, spry, vigorous, vital, vivacious, zestful

alive to alert to, awake to, aware of, cognizant of, eager for, sensible of, sensitive to, susceptible to

alive with abounding in, bristling with, bustling with, buzzing with, crawling with, hopping with, infested with, jumping with, lousy with (*Sl.*), overrun by, packed with, swarming with, teeming with, thronged with

all *adj.* **1.** every bit of, the complete, the entire, the sum of, the totality of, the total of, the whole of **2.** each, each and every, every, every one of, every single **3.** complete, en-

tire, full, greatest, perfect, total, utter ~*n.* **4.** aggregate, entirety, everything, sum, sum total, tal, total, total amount, totality, utmost, whole, whole amount ~*adv.* **5.** altogether, completely, entirely, fully, totally, utterly, wholly

allegation accusation, affirmation, assertion, asseveration, averment, avowal, charge, claim, declaration, deposition, plea, profession, statement

allege advance, affirm, assert, asseverate, aver, avow, charge, claim, declare, depose, maintain, plead, profess, put forward, state

alleged 1. affirmed, asserted, averred, declared, described, designated, stated **2.** doubtful, dubious, ostensible, professed, purported, so-called, supposed, suspect, suspicious

allegiance adherence, constancy, devotion, duty, faithfulness, fealty, fidelity, hom-

age, loyalty, obedience, obligation

allegorical emblematic, figurative, parabolic, symbolic, symbolizing

allegory apologue, emblem, fable, myth, parable, story, symbol, symbolism, tale

allergic 1. affected by, hypersensitive, sensitive, sensitized, susceptible **2.** *Inf.* antipathetic, averse, disinclined, hostile, loath, opposed

allergy 1. antipathy, hypersensitivity, sensitivity, susceptibility **2.** *Inf.* antipathy, aversion, disinclination, dislike, hostility, loathing, opposition

alley alleyway, backstreet, lane, passage, passageway, pathway, walk

alliance affiliation, affinity, agreement, association, coalition, combination, compact, concordat, confederacy, confederation, connection, federation, league, marriage, pact, partnership, treaty, union

Allied ('ælaɪd) *adj.* of or relating to the Allies.

Allies ('ælaɪz) *pl. n.* **1.** (in World War I) the powers of the Triple Entente (France, Russia, and Britain) together with the nations allied with them. **2.** (in World War II) the countries that fought against the Axis and Japan, esp. Britain and the Commonwealth countries, the U.S., the Soviet Union, and France.

alligator ('ælɪ,geɪtə) *n.* **1.** a large crocodilian of the southern U.S., having powerful jaws but differing from the crocodiles in having a shorter and broader snout. **2.** a similar but smaller species occurring in China. **3.** any of various tools or machines having adjustable toothed jaws.

alligator pear *n.* another name for **avocado.**

all in *adj.* **1.** (*postpositive*) *Sl.* completely exhausted. ~*adv., adj.* (**all-in** *when prenominal*). **2.** with all expenses included: *twenty pounds a week all in.* **3.** (of wrestling) in freestyle.

alliterate (ə'lɪtə,reɪt) *vb.* **1.** to contain or cause to contain alliteration. **2.** (*intr.*) to speak or write using alliteration.

alliteration (ə,lɪtə'reɪʃən) *n.* the use of the same consonant (**consonantal alliteration**) or of a vowel (**vocalic alliteration**), at the beginning of each word or stressed syllable in a line of verse, as in *around the rock the ragged rascal ran.* —**al'literative** *adj.*

allocate ('ælə,keɪt) *vb.* (*tr.*) **1.** to assign for a particular purpose. **2.** a less common word for **locate** (sense 2). —**'allo,catable** *adj.* —**,allo'cation** *n.*

allopathy (ə'lopəθɪ) *n.* the usual method of treating disease, by inducing a condition different from the cause of the disease. Cf. **homeopathy.** —**allopathic** (,ælə'pæθɪk) *adj.*

allot (ə'lot) *vb.* **-lotting, -lotted.** (*tr.*) **1.** to assign or distribute (shares, etc.). **2.** to designate for a particular purpose; apportion: *we allotted two hours to the case.*

allotment (ə'lotmənt) *n.* **1.** the act of allotting. **2.** a portion or amount allotted. **3.** *Brit.* a small piece of land rented by an individual for cultivation.

allotrope ('ælə,trəup) *n.* any of two or more physical forms in which an element can exist: *diamond and graphite are allotropes of carbon.*

allotropy (ə'lotrəpɪ) *or* **allotropism** *n.* the existence of an element in two or more physical forms. —**allotropic** (,ælə'tropɪk) *adj.*

all-out *Inf.* ~*adj.* **1.** using one's maximum powers: *an all-out effort.* ~*adv.* **all out. 2.** to one's maximum capacity: *he went all out.*

allow (ə'lau) *vb.* **1.** (*tr.*) to permit (to do something). **2.** (*tr.*) to set aside: *five hours were allowed to do the job.* **3.** (*tr.*) to let enter or stay: *they don't allow dogs.* **4.** (*tr.*) to acknowledge (a point, claim, etc.). **5.** (*tr.*) to let have: *he was allowed few visitors.* **6.** (*intr.; foll. by for*) to take into account. **7.** (*intr.; often foll. by of*) to permit: *a question that allows of only one reply.* **8.** (*tr.; may take a clause as object*) *U.S. dialect.* to assert; maintain. —**al'lowable** *adj.* —**al'lowably** *adv.*

allowance (ə'lauəns) *n.* **1.** an amount of something, esp. money or food, given at regular intervals. **2.** a discount, as in consideration for something given in part exchange; rebate. **3.** a portion set aside to cover special expenses. **4.** admission; concession. **5.** the act of allowing; toleration. **6. make allowances** (*or* **allowance**). (*usually foll. by for*) **a.** to take mitigating circumstances into account. **b.** to allow (for). ~*vb.* (*tr.*) **7.** to supply (something) in limited amounts.

allowedly (ə'lauɪdlɪ) *adv.* (*sentence modifier*) by general admission or agreement; admittedly.

alloy *n.* ('æloɪ, ə'loɪ). **1.** a metallic material, such as steel, consisting of a mixture of two or more metals or of metallic with nonmetallic elements. **2.** something that impairs the quality of the thing to which it is added. ~*vb.* (ə'loɪ). (*tr.*) **3.** to add (one metal or element to another) to obtain a substance with a desired property. **4.** to debase (a pure substance) by mixing with an inferior element. **5.** to diminish or impair.

all-purpose *adj.* useful for many things.

all right *adj.* (*postpositive except in slang use*), *adv.* **1.** adequate; satisfactory. **2.** unharmed; safe. **3. all-right.** *U.S. sl.* acceptable; reliable. ~*adv.* **4.** very well: used to express assent. **5.** satisfactorily: *the car goes all right.* **6.** without doubt. ~Also (not standard): **alright.**

all-round *adj.* **1.** efficient in all respects, esp. in sport: *an all-round player.* **2.** comprehensive; many-sided: *an all-round education.*

all-rounder *n.* a versatile person, esp. in a sport.

All Saints' Day *n.* a Christian festival celebrated on Nov. 1 to honour all the saints.

All Souls' Day *n. R.C. Church.* a day of prayer (Nov. 2) for the dead in purgatory.

allspice ('ɔːl,spaɪs) *n.* **1.** a tropical American tree, having small white flowers and aromatic berries. **2.** the seeds of this berry used as a spice, having a flavour said to resemble a mixture of cinnamon, cloves, and nutmeg. ~Also called: **pimento.**

all-time *adj.* (*prenominal*) *Inf.* unsurpassed.

▷ **Usage.** *All-time* is an imprecise superlative and is avoided by careful writers as being superfluous: *his high jump was a record* (not *an all-time record*).

allude (ə'luːd) *vb.* (*intr.; foll. by to*) to refer indirectly.

allure (ə'ljuə) *vb.* **1.** (*tr.*) to entice or tempt (someone); attract. ~*n.* **2.** attractiveness; appeal. —**al'lurement** *n.* —**al'luring** *adj.*

allusion (ə'luːʒən) *n.* **1.** the act of alluding. **2.** a passing reference. —**al'lusive** *adj.*

alluvial (ə'luːvɪəl) *adj.* **1.** of or relating to alluvium. ~*n.* **2.** another name for **alluvium.**

alluvium (ə'luːvɪəm) *n., pl.* **-viums** *or* **-via** (-vɪə). a fine-grained fertile soil consisting of mud, silt, and sand deposited by flowing water.

ally *vb.* (ə'laɪ). **-lying, -lied.** (*usually foll. by to or with*) **1.** to unite or be united, esp. formally, as by treaty. **2.** (*tr.; usually passive*) to be related, as through being similar. ~*n.* ('ælaɪ), *pl.* **-lies. 3.** a country, person, or group allied with another. **4.** a plant, animal, etc., closely related to another in characteristics or form.

THESAURUS

allied affiliated, amalgamated, associated, bound, combined, confederate, connected, hand in glove (*Inf.*), in cahoots (*U.S. inf.*), in league, joined, joint, kindred, leagued, linked, married, related, unified, united, wed

allocate allot, apportion, appropriate, assign, budget, designate, earmark, mete, set aside, share out

allocation allotment, allowance, apportionment, appropriation, grant, lot, measure, portion, quota, ration, share, stint

allot allocate, apportion, appropriate, assign, budget, designate, earmark, mete, set aside, share out

allotment 1. allocation, allowance, apportionment, appropriation, grant, lot, measure, portion, quota, ration, share, stint 2. kitchen garden, patch, plot, tract

all-out complete, determined, exhaustive, full, full-scale, maximum, optimum, resolute, supreme, thorough, thoroughgoing, total, undivided, unlimited, unremitting, unrestrained, unstinted, utmost

allow 1. acknowledge, acquiesce, admit, concede, confess, grant, own 2. approve, authorize, bear, brook, endure, give leave, let, permit, put up with (*Inf.*), sanction, stand, suffer, tolerate 3. allocate, allot, assign, deduct, give, grant, provide, remit, spare

allowable acceptable, admissible, all right, appropriate, approved, permissible, sanctionable, sufferable, suitable, tolerable

allowance 1. allocation, allotment, amount, annuity, apportionment, grant, lot, measure, pension, portion, quota, ration, remittance, share, stint, stipend, subsidy 2. admission, concession, sanction, sufferance, toleration 3. concession, deduction, discount, rebate, reduction

allow for arrange for, consider, foresee, keep in mind, make allowances for, make concessions for, make provision for, plan for, provide for, set (something) aside for, take into account, take into consideration

alloy *n.* 1. admixture, amalgam, blend, combination, composite, compound, hybrid, mixture ~*v.* 2. admix, amalgamate, blend, combine, compound, fuse, mix 3. adulterate, debase, devalue, diminish, impair

all right *adj.* 1. acceptable, adequate, average, fair, O.K. (*Inf.*), passable, satisfactory, standard, unobjectionable 2. hale, healthy, safe, sound, unharmed, unimpaired, uninjured, well, whole ~*adv.* 3. acceptably, adequately, O.K. (*Inf.*), passably, satisfactorily, unobjectionably, well enough

allure 1. *v.* attract, beguile, cajole, captivate, charm, coax, decoy, enchant, entice, inveigle, lead on, lure, persuade, seduce, tempt, win over 2. *n.* appeal, attraction, charm, enchantment, enticement, glamour, lure, persuasion, seductiveness, temptation

alluring attractive, beguiling, bewitching, captivating, come-hither, enchanting, fascinating, fetching, intriguing, seductive, sexy, tempting

allusion casual remark, glance, hint, implication, indirect reference, innuendo, insinuation, intimation, mention, suggestion

ally 1. *n.* abettor, accessory, accomplice, associate, coadjutor, collaborator, colleague, confederate, co-worker, friend, helper, partner 2. *v.* affiliate, associate, band together,

alma mater (ˈælmə ˈmɑːtə, ˈmeɪtə) n. (often caps.) one's school, college, or university.

almanac (ˈɔːlmə,næk) n. a yearly calendar giving statistical information, such as the phases of the moon, tides, anniversaries, etc. Also (archaic): **almanack.**

almighty (ɔːlˈmaɪtɪ) adj. **1.** all-powerful. **2.** Inf. (intensifier): an almighty row. ~adv. **3.** Inf. (intensifier): an almighty loud bang.

Almighty (ɔːlˈmaɪtɪ) n. the. another name for **God.**

almond (ˈɑːmənd) n. **1.** a small widely cultivated rosaceous tree that is native to W Asia and has pink flowers and an edible nutlike seed. **2.** the seed, which has a yellowish-brown shell. **3.** (modifier) made of or containing almonds: almond cake.

almoner (ˈɑːmənə) n. **1.** Brit. a former name for a trained hospital social worker. **2.** (formerly) a person who distributes charity on behalf of a household or institution.

almost (ˈɔːlməʊst) adv. very nearly.

alms (ɑːmz) pl. n. charitable donations of money or goods to the poor or needy.

almshouse (ˈɑːmz,haʊs) n. Brit. a privately supported house offering accommodation to the aged or needy.

aloe (ˈæləʊ) n., pl. **-oes.** **1.** any plant of the genus Aloe, chiefly native to southern Africa, with fleshy spiny-toothed leaves. **2. American aloe.** a tropical American agave which blooms only once in 10 to 30 years. Also called: **century plant.**

aloft (əˈlɒft) adv., adj. (postpositive) **1.** in or into a high or higher place. **2.** Naut. in or into the rigging of a vessel.

alone (əˈləʊn) adj. (postpositive), adv. **1.** apart from another or others. **2.** without anyone or anything else: one man alone could lift it. **3.** without equal: he stands alone in the field of microbiology. **4.** to the exclusion of others: she alone believed him. **5. leave** or **let alone.** to refrain from annoying or interfering with. **6. leave well alone.** to be content with the state of things. **7. let alone.** even less: he can't afford beer, let alone whisky.

along (əˈlɒŋ) prep. **1.** over or for the length of: along the road. ~adv. **2.** continuing over the length of some specified thing. **3.** together with some specified person or people: he'd like to come along. **4.** forward: the horse trotted along. **5.** to a more advanced state: he got the work moving along. **6. along with.** together with: consider the advantages along with the disadvantages.

▷ Usage. See at **plus.**

alongshore (ə,lɒŋˈʃɔː) adv., adj. (postpositive) close to, by, or along a shore.

alongside (əˈlɒŋˈsaɪd) prep. **1.** (often foll. by of) close beside: alongside the quay. ~adv. **2.** near the side of something: come alongside.

aloof (əˈluːf) adj. distant, unsympathetic, or supercilious in manner. —aˈloofly adv. —aˈloofness n.

alopecia (,æləˈpiːʃɪə) n. baldness.

aloud (əˈlaʊd) adv., adj. (postpositive) **1.** in a normal voice. **2.** in a spoken voice; not silently.

alp (ælp) n. **1.** a high mountain. **2. the Alps.** a high mountain range in S central Europe.

alpaca (ælˈpækə) n. **1.** a domesticated South American mammal related to the llama, with dark shaggy hair. **2.** the wool or cloth obtained from this hair. **3.** a glossy fabric simulating this.

alpenstock (ˈælpən,stɒk) n. a stout stick with an iron tip used by hikers, mountain climbers, etc.

alpha (ˈælfə) n. **1.** the first letter in the Greek alphabet

(Α, α). **2.** Brit. the highest grade or mark, as in an examination. **3.** (modifier) **a.** involving helium nuclei. **b.** denoting an isomeric or allotropic form of a substance.

alpha and omega n. the first and last, a phrase used in Revelation 1:8 to signify God's eternity.

alphabet (ˈælfə,bɛt) n. **1.** a set of letters or other signs used in a writing system, each letter or sign being used to represent one or sometimes more than one phoneme in the language being transcribed. **2.** any set of characters, esp. one representing sounds of speech. **3.** basic principles or rudiments.

alphabetical (,ælfəˈbɛtɪkəl) or **alphabetic** adj. **1.** in the conventional order of the letters of an alphabet. **2.** of or expressed by an alphabet. —,alphaˈbetically adv.

alphabetize or **-ise** (ˈælfəbə,taɪz) vb. (tr.) **1.** to arrange in conventional alphabetical order. **2.** to express by an alphabet. —,alphabetiˈzation or -iˈsation n.

alphanumeric (,ælfənjuːˈmɛrɪk) or **alphameric** adj. (of a character set or file of data) consisting of alphabetical and numerical symbols.

alpha particle n. a helium nucleus, containing two neutrons and two protons, emitted during some radioactive transformations.

alpha ray n. ionizing radiation consisting of a stream of alpha particles.

alpine (ˈælpaɪn) adj. **1.** of or relating to high mountains. **2.** (of plants) growing on mountains above the limit for tree growth. **3.** connected with mountaineering. **4.** Skiing. of events such as the slalom and downhill. ~n. **5.** a plant grown in or native to high altitudes.

already (ɔːlˈrɛdɪ) adv. **1.** by or before a stated or implied time: he is already here. **2.** at a time earlier than expected: is it ten o'clock already?

alright (ɔːlˈraɪt) adv. Not standard. a variant spelling of **all right.**

Alsatian (ælˈseɪʃən) n. **1.** a large wolflike breed of dog often used as a guard dog and by the police. Also called: **German shepherd dog.** **2.** a native or inhabitant of Alsace, a region of NE France. ~adj. **3.** of or relating to Alsace or its inhabitants.

also (ˈɔːlsəʊ) adv. (sentence modifier) **1.** in addition; as well; too. ~ **2.** sentence connector. besides; moreover.

▷ Usage. Since also is not a conjunction, careful writers and speakers consider it poor style to use it alone as a connector in sentences like he bought pens, paper, ink, also notebooks. In such sentences, and or and also would be the appropriate words: he bought pens, paper, ink, and notebooks.

also-ran n. **1.** a contestant, horse, etc., failing to finish among the first three. **2.** Inf. a loser.

alt. abbrev. for: **1.** alternate. **2.** altitude. **3.** alto.

Alta. abbrev. for Alberta.

altar (ˈɔːltə) n. **1.** a raised place or structure where sacrifices are offered and religious rites performed. **2.** (in Christian churches) the communion table. **3.** a step in the wall of a dry dock.

altarpiece (ˈɔːltə,piːs) n. a work of art set above and behind an altar; a reredos.

alter (ˈɔːltə) vb. **1.** to make or become different in some respect; change. **2.** (tr.) Inf., chiefly U.S. a euphemistic word for **castrate** or **spay.** —ˈalterable adj.

alteration (,ɔːltəˈreɪʃən) n. **1.** a change or modification. **2.** the act of altering.

altercate (ˈɔːltə,keɪt) vb. (intr.) to argue, esp. heatedly; dispute. —,alterˈcation n.

alter ego (ˈæltər ˈiːgəʊ, ˈɛgəʊ) n. **1.** a second self. **2.** a

collaborate, combine, confederate, connect, join, join forces, league, marry, unify, unite

almighty 1. absolute, all-powerful, invincible, omnipotent, supreme, unlimited 2. Inf. awful, desperate, enormous, excessive, great, intense, loud, severe, terrible

almost about, all but, approximately, as good as, close to, just about, nearly, not far from, not quite, on the brink of, practically, virtually, well-nigh

alone 1. abandoned, apart, by itself, by oneself, deserted, desolate, detached, forlorn, forsaken, isolated, lonely, lonesome, only, separate, single, single-handed, sole, solitary, unaccompanied, unaided, unassisted, unattended, uncombined, unconnected, unescort-

ed 2. incomparable, matchless, peerless, singular, unequalled, unique, unparalleled, unsurpassed

aloof 1. chilly, cold, cool, detached, distant, forbidding, formal, haughty, indifferent, remote, reserved, standoffish, supercilious, unapproachable, unfriendly, uninterested, unresponsive, unsociable, unsympathetic 2. above, apart, at a distance, away, distanced, distant

aloud 1. audibly, clearly, distinctly, intelligibly, out loud, plainly 2. clamorously, loudly, noisily, vociferously

already as of now, at present, before now, by now, by that time, by then, by this time, even now, heretofore, just now, previously

also additionally, along with, and, as well, as well as, besides, further, furthermore, in addition, including, into the bargain, moreover, on top of that, plus, to boot, too

alter adapt, adjust, amend, change, convert, diversify, metamorphose, modify, recast, reform, remodel, reshape, revise, shift, transform, transmute, turn, vary

alteration adaptation, adjustment, amendment, change, conversion, difference, diversification, metamorphosis, modification, reformation, remodelling, reshaping, revision, shift, transformation, transmutation, variance, variation

very close friend.

alternate vb. ('ɔːltə,neɪt). 1. (often foll. by with) to occur or cause to occur by turns: day and night alternate. 2. (intr.; often foll. by between) to swing repeatedly from one condition, action, etc., to another. 3. (tr.) to interchange regularly or in succession. 4. (intr.) (of an electric current, voltage, etc.) to reverse direction or sign at regular intervals. ~adj. (ɔːl'tɜːnɪt). 5. occurring by turns: alternate feelings of love and hate. 6. every other or second one of a series: he came on alternate days. 7. being a second choice; alternative. 8. Bot. (of leaves, flowers, etc.) arranged singly at different heights on either side of the stem. ~n. ('ɔːltənɪt, ɔːl'tɜːnɪt). 9. U.S. a person who substitutes for another; stand-in. —**al'ternately** adv. —,alter'nation n.

alternate angles pl. n. two angles at opposite ends and on opposite sides of a transversal cutting two lines.

alternating current n. an electric current that reverses direction with a frequency independent of the characteristics of the circuit through which it flows. Abbrev.: **a.c.**

alternative (ɔːl'tɜːnətɪv) n. 1. a possibility of choice, esp. between two things. 2. either of such choices: we took the alternative of walking. ~adj. 3. presenting a choice, esp. between two possibilities only. 4. (of two things) mutually exclusive. 5. denoting a lifestyle, culture, art form, etc. that is regarded as preferable to that of contemporary society because it is less conventional, materialistic, or institutionalized. —**al'ternatively** adv.

alternator ('ɔːltə,neɪtə) n. an electrical machine that generates an alternating current.

althaea or U.S. **althea** (æl'θiːə) n. any Eurasian plant of the genus Althaea, such as the hollyhock, having tall spikes of showy flowers.

althorn ('ælt,hɔːn) n. a valved brass musical instrument belonging to the saxhorn family.

although (ɔːl'ðəʊ) conj. (subordinating) even though: although she was ill, she worked hard.

altimeter (æl'tɪmɪtə, 'æltɪ,miːtə) n. an instrument that indicates height above sea level, esp. one based on an aneroid barometer and fitted to an aircraft.

altitude ('æltɪ,tjuːd) n. 1. the vertical height of an object, esp. above sea level. 2. Maths. the perpendicular distance from the base of a figure to the opposite vertex. 3. Also called: **elevation**. Astron., navigation. the angular distance of a celestial body from the horizon. 4. Surveying. the angle of elevation of a point above the horizontal plane of the observer. 5. (often pl.) a high place or region.

alto ('æltəʊ) n., pl. -**tos**. 1. the lowest female voice. 2. the highest adult male voice; countertenor. 3. a singer with such a voice. Cf. **contralto**. 4. a flute, saxophone, etc., that is the third or fourth highest instrument in its group. ~adj. 5. denoting such an instrument.

alto clef n. the clef that establishes middle C as being on the third line of the staff.

altogether (,ɔːltə'geðə, 'ɔːltə,geðə) adv. 1. with everything included: altogether he owed me sixty pounds. 2. completely; utterly: altogether mad. 3. on the whole: altogether it was very good. ~n. 4. **in the altogether**. Inf. naked.

altruism ('æltruː,ɪzəm) n. unselfish concern for the welfare of others. —**'altruist** n. —,**altru'istic** adj. —,altru'istically adv.

alum ('æləm) n. 1. a colourless soluble hydrated double sulphate of aluminium and potassium used in manufac-

turing and in medicine. 2. any of a group of compounds of a monovalent metal or group and a trivalent metal.

aluminium (,ælju'mɪnɪəm) or U.S. **aluminum** (ə'luːmɪnəm) n. a light malleable silvery-white metallic element that resists corrosion; the third most abundant element in the earth's crust, occurring as a compound, principally in bauxite. Symbol: Al; atomic no.: 13; atomic wt.: 26.981.

aluminize or **-ise** (ə'luːmɪ,naɪz) vb. (tr.) to cover with aluminium or aluminium paint.

alumnus (ə'lʌmnəs) or (fem.) **alumna** (ə'lʌmnə) n., pl. **-ni** (-naɪ) or **-nae** (-niː). Chiefly U.S. a graduate of a school, college, etc.

always ('ɔːlweɪz) adv. 1. without exception; every time: he always arrives on time. 2. continually; repeatedly. 3. in any case: you could always take a day off work. ~Also (archaic): **alway**.

alyssum ('ælɪsəm) n. a widely cultivated herbaceous garden plant, having clusters of small yellow or white flowers.

am (æm; unstressed əm) vb. (used with I) a form of the present tense of **be**.

Am the chemical symbol for americium.

AM or **am** abbrev. for amplitude modulation.

Am. abbrev. for America(n).

a.m. or **A.M.** (indicating the time period from midnight to midday) abbrev. for ante meridiem.

Amadhlozi or **Amadlozi** (,æmæ'hlɒʒiː) pl.n. S. African. the ancestral spirits.

amadoda (,æmæ'dɒdə) pl.n. S. African. men, esp. Black men.

amah ('ɑːmə) n. (in the East, esp. formerly) a nurse or maidservant.

amain (ə'meɪn) adv. Arch. or poetic. with great strength or haste.

amalgam (ə'mælgəm) n. 1. an alloy of mercury with another metal, esp. silver: dental amalgam. 2. a blend or combination.

amalgamate (ə'mælgə,meɪt) vb. 1. to combine or cause to combine; unite. 2. to alloy (a metal) with mercury. —a,malga'mation n.

amanuensis (ə,mænjʊ'ɛnsɪs) n., pl. -**ses** (-siːz). a person employed to take dictation or to copy manuscripts.

amaranth ('æmə,rænθ) n. 1. Poetic. an imaginary flower that never fades. 2. any of numerous plants having tassel-like heads of small green, red, or purple flowers.

amaryllis (,æmə'rɪlɪs) n. 1. a plant native to southern Africa having large lily-like reddish or white flowers. 2. any of several related plants.

amass (ə'mæs) vb. 1. (tr.) to accumulate or collect (esp. riches, etc.). 2. to gather in a heap. —a'masser n.

amateur ('æmətə) n. 1. a person who engages in an activity, esp. a sport, as a pastime rather than for gain. 2. a person unskilled in a subject or activity. 3. a person who is fond of or admires something. 4. (modifier) of or for amateurs: an amateur event. ~adj. 5. not professional or expert: an amateur approach. —'amateurish adj. —'amateurism n.

amatory ('æmətərɪ) or **amatorial** adj. of, relating to, or inciting sexual love or desire.

amaze (ə'meɪz) vb. (tr.) 1. to fill with incredulity or surprise; astonish. ~n. 2. Arch. amazement. —a'mazement n. —a'mazing adj.

THESAURUS

alternate v. 1. act reciprocally, alter, change, follow in turn, follow one another, interchange, intersperse, oscillate, rotate, substitute, take turns, vary ~adj. 2. alternating, every other, every second, interchanging, rotating 3. alternative, another, different, second, substitute

alternative 1. n. choice, option, other (of two), preference, recourse, selection, substitute 2. adj. alternate, another, different, other, second, substitute

alternatively as an alternative, by way of alternative, if not, instead, on the other hand, or, otherwise

although albeit, despite the fact that, even if, even supposing, even though, notwithstanding, though, while

altitude elevation, height, loftiness, peak, summit

altogether 1. absolutely, completely, fully, perfectly, quite, thoroughly, totally, utterly, wholly 2. all in all, all things considered, as a whole, collectively, generally, in general, in toto, on the whole 3. all told, everything included, in all, in sum, in toto, taken together

altruistic benevolent, charitable, considerate, generous, humanitarian, philanthropic, public-spirited, self-sacrificing, unselfish

always consistently, constantly, continually, eternally, ever, everlastingly, evermore, every time, forever, in perpetuum, invariably, perpetually, repeatedly, unceasingly, without exception

amalgamate alloy, ally, blend, coalesce, combine, commingle, compound, fuse, incorporate, integrate, intermix, merge, mingle, unite

amalgamation admixture, alliance, alloy, amalgam, amalgamating, blend, coalition, combination, commingling, composite, compound, fusion, incorporation, integration, joining, merger, mingling, mixing, mixture, union

amass accumulate, aggregate, assemble, collect, compile, garner, gather, heap up, hoard, pile up, rake up, scrape together

amateur dabbler, dilettante, layman, nonprofessional

amateurish amateur, bungling, clumsy, crude, inexpert, unaccomplished, unprofes-

Amazon ('æmɔzən) *n.* **1.** *Greek myth.* one of a race of women warriors of Scythia near the Black Sea. **2.** (*often not cap.*) any tall, strong, or aggressive woman. —**Amazonian** (,æmə'zəʊnɪən) *adj.*

ambassador (æm'bæsədə) *n.* **1.** a diplomat of the highest rank, accredited as permanent representative to another country. **2. ambassador extraordinary.** a diplomat of the highest rank sent on a special mission. **3. ambassador plenipotentiary.** a diplomat of the first rank with treaty-signing powers. **4. ambassador-at-large.** *U.S.* an ambassador with special duties who may be sent to more than one government. **5.** an authorized representative or messenger. —**am'bassadress** *fem. n.* —**ambassadorial** (æm,bæsə'dɔːrɪəl) *adj.* —**am'bassador,ship** *n.*

amber ('æmbə) *n.* **1.** a yellow translucent fossil resin derived from extinct coniferous trees and often containing trapped insects. **2.** a brownish-yellow colour. **3.** an amber traffic light used as a warning between red and green.

ambergris ('æmbə,griːs, -grɪs) *n.* a waxy substance secreted by the intestinal tract of the sperm whale and often found floating in the sea: used in the manufacture of some perfumes.

ambi- *combining form.* indicating both: *ambidextrous; ambivalence.*

ambidextrous (,æmbɪ'dɛkstrəs) *adj.* **1.** equally expert with each hand. **2.** *Inf.* skilled or adept. **3.** underhanded. —**ambidexterity** (,æmbɪdɛk'stɛrɪtɪ) *or* ,**ambi'dexterousness** *n.*

ambience *or* **ambiance** ('æmbɪəns) *n.* the atmosphere of a place.

ambient ('æmbɪənt) *adj.* surrounding.

ambiguity (,æmbɪ'gjuːɪtɪ) *n., pl.* -**ties.** **1.** vagueness or uncertainty of meaning. **2.** an instance or example of this, as in the sentence *they are cooking apples.*

ambiguous (æm'bɪgjʊəs) *adj.* **1.** having more than one possible interpretation. **2.** difficult to understand; obscure. —**am'biguously** *adv.* —**am'biguousness** *n.*

ambit ('æmbɪt) *n.* **1.** scope or extent. **2.** limits or boundary.

ambition (æm'bɪʃən) *n.* **1.** strong desire for success or distinction. **2.** something so desired; goal.

ambitious (æm'bɪʃəs) *adj.* **1.** having a strong desire for success or achievement. **2.** necessitating extraordinary effort or ability: *an ambitious project.* **3.** (often foll. by *of*) having a great desire (for something or to do something). —**am'bitiousness** *n.*

ambivalence (æm'bɪvələns) *or* **ambivalency** *n.* the co-existence of two opposed and conflicting emotions, etc. —**am'bivalent** *adj.*

amble ('æmbəl) *vb.* (*intr.*) **1.** to walk at a leisurely relaxed pace. **2.** (of a horse) to move, lifting both legs on one side together. **3.** to ride a horse at an amble. ~*n.* **4.** a leisurely motion in walking. **5.** a leisurely walk. **6.** the ambling gait of a horse.

ambrosia (æm'brəʊzɪə) *n.* **1.** *Classical myth.* the food of the gods, said to bestow immortality. Cf. **nectar** (sense 2). **2.** anything particularly delightful to taste or smell. **3.** another name for **beebread.** —**am'brosial** *or* **am'brosian** *adj.*

ambry ('æmbrɪ) *or* **aumbry** ('ɔːmbrɪ) *n., pl.* -**bries.** **1.** a recessed cupboard in the wall of a church near the altar, used to store sacred vessels, etc. **2.** *Obs.* a small cupboard.

ambulance ('æmbjʊləns) *n.* a motor vehicle designed to carry sick or injured people.

ambulate ('æmbjʊ,leɪt) *vb.* (*intr.*) to wander about or move from place to place. —'**ambulant** *adj.* —,**ambu'lation** *n.*

ambulatory ('æmbjʊlətərɪ) *adj.* **1.** of or designed for walking. **2.** changing position; not fixed. **3.** Also: **ambulant.** able to walk. ~*n., pl.* -**ries.** **4.** a place for walking, such as an aisle or a cloister.

ambuscade (,æmbə'skeɪd) *n.* **1.** an ambush. ~*vb.* **2.** to ambush or lie in ambush.

ambush ('æmbʊʃ) *n.* **1.** the act of waiting in a concealed position in order to launch a surprise attack. **2.** a surprise attack from such a position. **3.** the concealed position from which such an attack is launched. **4.** the person or persons waiting to launch such an attack. ~*vb.* **5.** to lie in wait (for). **6.** (*tr.*) to attack suddenly from a concealed position.

ameer (ə'mɪə) *n.* a variant spelling of **emir.**

ameliorate (ə'miːljə,reɪt) *vb.* to make or become better. —**a,melio'ration** *n.* —**a'meliorative** *adj.* —**a'melio,rator** *n.*

amen (,eɪ'mɛn, ,ɑː'mɛn) *interj.* **1.** So be it! A term used at the end of a prayer. ~*n.* **2.** the use of the word *amen.*

amenable (ə'miːnəbəl) *adj.* **1.** likely to listen, cooperate, etc. **2.** accountable to some authority; answerable. **3.** capable of being tested, judged, etc. —**a,mena'bility** *or* **a'menableness** *n.* —**a'menably** *adv.*

amend (ə'mɛnd) *vb.* (*tr.*) **1.** to improve; change for the better. **2.** to correct. **3.** to alter or revise (legislation, etc.) by formal procedure. —**a'mendable** *adj.* —**a'mender** *n.*

amendment (ə'mɛndmənt) *n.* **1.** correction. **2.** an addition or alteration to a document, etc.

amends (ə'mɛndz) *n.* recompense or compensation for some injury, insult, etc.: *to make amends.*

amenity (ə'miːnɪtɪ) *n., pl.* -**ties.** **1.** (often *pl.*) a useful or pleasant facility: *a swimming pool was one of the amenities.* **2.** the fact or condition of being agreeable. **3.** (*usually pl.*) a social courtesy.

amenorrhoea *or esp. U.S.* **amenorrhea** (æ,mɛnə'rɪə, eɪ-) *n.* abnormal absence of menstruation.

amerce (ə'mɜːs) *vb.* (*tr.*) *Obs.* **1.** *Law.* to punish by a fine. **2.** to punish with any arbitrary penalty. —**a'mercement** *n.*

American (ə'mɛrɪkən) *adj.* **1.** of or relating to the United States of America, its inhabitants, or their form of English. **2.** of or relating to the American continent.

THESAURUS

sional, unskilful

amaze alarm, astonish, astound, bewilder, bowl over (*Inf.*), confound, daze, dumbfound, electrify, flabbergast, shock, stagger, startle, stun, stupefy, surprise

amazement admiration, astonishment, bewilderment, confusion, marvel, perplexity, shock, stupefaction, surprise, wonder

ambassador agent, consul, deputy, diplomat, emissary, envoy, legate, minister, plenipotentiary, representative

ambiguity doubt, doubtfulness, dubiety, dubiousness, enigma, equivocacy, equivocality, equivocation, inconclusiveness, indefiniteness, indeterminateness, obscurity, puzzle, tergiversation, uncertainty, unclearness, vagueness

ambiguous cryptic, doubtful, dubious, enigmatic, enigmatical, equivocal, inconclusive, indefinite, indeterminate, obscure, puzzling, uncertain, unclear, vague

ambition 1. aspiration, avidity, desire, drive, eagerness, enterprise, get-up-and-go (*Inf.*), hankering, longing, striving, yearning, zeal 2. aim, aspiration, desire, dream, end,

goal, hope, intent, objective, purpose, wish

ambitious 1. aspiring, avid, desirous, driving, eager, enterprising, hopeful, intent, purposeful, striving, zealous 2. arduous, bold, challenging, demanding, difficult, elaborate, energetic, exacting, formidable, grandiose, hard, impressive, industrious, pretentious, severe, strenuous

ambivalence clash, conflict, contradiction, doubt, equivocation, fluctuation, hesitancy, indecision, irresolution, opposition, uncertainty, vacillation, wavering

ambivalent clashing, conflicting, contradictory, debatable, doubtful, equivocal, fluctuating, hesitant, inconclusive, in two minds, irresolute, mixed, opposed, uncertain, undecided, unresolved, unsure, vacillating, warring, wavering

amble dawdle, meander, mosey (*Inf.*), ramble, saunter, stroll, walk, wander

ambush 1. *n.* ambuscade, concealment, cover, hiding, hiding place, lying in wait, retreat, shelter, trap, waylaying 2. *v.* ambuscade, bushwhack (*U.S.*), ensnare, surprise, trap, waylay

amenable 1. able to be influenced, acquiescent, agreeable, open, persuadable, responsive, susceptible, tractable 2. accountable, answerable, chargeable, liable, responsible

amend alter, ameliorate, better, change, correct, enhance, fix, improve, mend, modify, rectify, reform, remedy, repair, revise

amendment 1. alteration, amelioration, betterment, change, correction, enhancement, improvement, mending, modification, rectification, reform, remedy, repair, revision 2. addendum, addition, adjunct, alteration, attachment, clarification

amends apology, atonement, compensation, expiation, indemnity, recompense, redress, reparation, requital, restitution, restoration, satisfaction

amenity 1. advantage, comfort, convenience, facility, service 2. affability, agreeableness, amiability, complaisance, courtesy, mildness, pleasantness (*of situation*), politeness, refinement, suavity

~*n.* **3.** a native or citizen of the U.S. **4.** a native or inhabitant of any country of North, Central, or South America. **5.** the English language as spoken or written in the United States. —**A'merica,nize** *or* **-ise** *vb.*
American Indian *n.* **1.** Also called: **Indian, Red Indian, Amerindian.** a member of any of the indigenous peoples of America, having straight black hair and a yellow to brown skin. ~*adj.* **2.** of or relating to any of these peoples, their languages, or their cultures.
Americanism (ə'mɛrɪkə,nɪzəm) *n.* **1.** a custom, linguistic usage, or other feature peculiar to or characteristic of the United States. **2.** loyalty to the United States.
americium (,æmə'rɪsɪəm) *n.* a white metallic transuranic element artificially produced from plutonium. It is used as an alpha-particle source. Symbol: Am; atomic no.: 95; half-life of most stable isotope, ^{243}Am: 7.4×10^3 years.
amethyst ('æmɪθɪst) *n.* **1.** a purple or violet variety of quartz used as a gemstone. **2.** a purple variety of sapphire. **3.** the purple colour of amethyst. —**amethystine** (,æmɪ'θɪstaɪn) *adj.*
Amharic (æm'hærɪk) *n.* **1.** the official language of Ethiopia. ~*adj.* **2.** denoting this language.
amiable ('eɪmɪəbl) *adj.* having or displaying a pleasant or agreeable nature; friendly. —,amia'bility *or* 'amiableness *n.* —'amiably *adv.*
amicable ('æmɪkəbl) *adj.* characterized by friendliness: *an amicable agreement.* —,amica'bility *or* 'amicableness *n.* —'amicably *adv.*
amice ('æmɪs) *n. Christianity.* a rectangular piece of white linen worn by priests around the neck and shoulders under the alb or, formerly, on the head.
amicus curiae (æ'miːkus 'kjʊərɪ,iː) *n., pl.* **amici curiae** (æ'miːkaɪ) *Law.* a person, not directly engaged in a case, who advises the court.
amid (ə'mɪd) *or* **amidst** *prep.* in the middle of; among.
amide ('æmaɪd) *n.* **1.** any organic compound containing the group -CONH₂. **2.** (*modifier*) containing the group -CONH₂: *amide group or radical.* **3.** an inorganic compound having the general formula $M(NH_2)_x$, where M is a metal atom.
amidships (ə'mɪdʃɪps) *adv., adj.* (*postpositive*) *Naut.* at, near, or towards the centre of a vessel.
amine (ə'miːn, 'æmɪn) *n.* an organic base formed by replacing one or more of the hydrogen atoms of ammonia by organic groups.
amino acid *n.* **1.** any of a group of organic compounds containing one or more amino groups, -NH₂, and one or more carboxyl groups, -COOH. **2.** any of a group of organic nitrogenous compounds that form the component molecules of proteins.
amir (ə'mɪə) *n.* a variant spelling of **emir.** —a'mirate *n.*
amiss (ə'mɪs) *adv.* **1.** in an incorrect or defective manner. **2. take amiss.** to feel offended by. ~*adj.* **3.** (*postpositive*) wrong or faulty.
amity ('æmɪtɪ) *n., pl.* **-ties.** friendship; cordiality.
ammeter ('æm,miːtə) *n.* an instrument for measuring an electric current in amperes.
ammo ('æməʊ) *n. Inf.* short for **ammunition.**
ammonia (ə'məʊnɪə) *n.* a colourless pungent gas used in the manufacture of fertilizers and as a refrigerant and solvent. Formula: NH₃.

ammonite ('æmə,naɪt) *n.* **1.** any extinct marine cephalopod mollusc of the order *Ammonoidea,* which were common in Mesozoic times and had a coiled partitioned shell. **2.** the shell of any of these animals, commonly occurring as a fossil.
ammonium (ə'məʊnɪəm) *n.* (*modifier*) of or containing the monovalent group NH₄- or the ion NH₄⁺ :*ammonium compounds.*
ammunition (,æmju'nɪʃən) *n.* **1.** any projectiles, such as bullets, rockets, etc., that can be discharged from a weapon. **2.** bombs, missiles, chemicals, etc., capable of use as weapons. **3.** any means of defence or attack, as in an argument.
amnesia (æm'niːzɪə) *n.* partial or total loss of memory. —**amnesiac** (æm'niːzɪ,æk) *or* **amnesic** (æm'niːsɪk, -zɪk) *adj., n.*
amnesty ('æmnɪstɪ) *n., pl.* **-ties. 1.** a general pardon, esp. for offences against a government. **2.** a period during which a law is suspended to allow offenders to admit their crime without fear of prosecution. ~*vb.* **-tying, -tied. 3.** (*tr.*) to overlook or forget (an offence).
amniocentesis (,æmnɪəʊsɛn'tiːsɪs) *n., pl.* **-ses** (-siːz). removal of amniotic fluid for diagnostic purposes.
amnion ('æmnɪən) *n., pl.* **-nions** *or* **-nia** (-nɪə). the innermost of two membranes enclosing an embryonic reptile, bird, or mammal. —**amniotic** (,æmnɪ'ɒtɪk) *adj.*
amoeba *or U.S.* **ameba** (ə'miːbə) *n., pl.* **-bae** (-biː) *or* **-bas.** any of an order of protozoans able to change shape because of the movements of cell processes. They live in fresh water or soil or as parasites in man and animals. —a'moebic *or U.S.* a'mebic *adj.*
amok (ə'mʌk, ə'mɒk) *n., adv.* a variant spelling of **amuck.**
among (ə'mʌŋ) *or* **amongst** *prep.* **1.** in the midst of: *he lived among the Indians.* **2.** to each of: *divide the reward among yourselves.* **3.** in the group, class, or number of: *among the greatest writers.* **4.** taken out of (a group): *he is one among many.* **5.** with one another within a group: *decide it among yourselves.* **6.** in the general opinion or practice of: *accepted among experts.*
▷ *Usage.* See at **between.**
amontillado (ə,mɒntɪ'lɑːdəʊ) *n.* a medium dry sherry.
amoral (eɪ'mɒrəl) *adj.* **1.** having no moral quality; nonmoral. **2.** without moral standards or principles. —**amorality** (,eɪmɒ'rælɪtɪ) *n.*
▷ *Usage.* *Amoral* is frequently and incorrectly used where *immoral* is meant. In careful usage, *immoral* is used of that which infringes moral rules and *amoral* only of that to which considerations of morality are irrelevant or of persons who lack any moral code.
amorous ('æmərəs) *adj.* **1.** inclined towards or displaying love or desire. **2.** in love. **3.** of or relating to love. —'amorously *adv.* —'amorousness *n.*
amorphous (ə'mɔːfəs) *adj.* **1.** lacking a definite shape. **2.** of no recognizable character or type. **3.** (of rocks, etc.) not having a crystalline structure. —a'morphism *n.* —a'morphousness *n.*
amortize *or* **-tise** (ə'mɔːtaɪz) *vb.* (*tr.*) **1.** *Finance.* to liquidate (a debt, mortgage, etc.) by payments or by periodic transfers to a sinking fund. **2.** to write off (a wasting asset) by transfers to a sinking fund. **3.** *Property law.* (formerly) to transfer (lands, etc.) in mortmain. —a,morti'zation *or* -ti'sation *n.*
amount (ə'maʊnt) *n.* **1.** extent; quantity. **2.** the total of two or more quantities. **3.** the full value or significance

---

THESAURUS

amiability affability, agreeableness, amiableness, attractiveness, benignity, charm, cheerfulness, delightfulness, engagingness, friendliness, friendship, geniality, good humour, good nature, kindliness, kindness, lovableness, pleasantness, pleasingness, sociability, sweetness, sweetness and light (*Inf.*), sweet temper, winsomeness
amiable affable, agreeable, attractive, benign, charming, cheerful, delightful, engaging, friendly, genial, good-humoured, good-natured, kind, kindly, lovable, obliging, pleasant, pleasing, sociable, sweet-tempered, winning, winsome
amicable amiable, brotherly, civil, cordial, courteous, fraternal, friendly, good-humoured, harmonious, kind, kindly, neighbourly, peaceable, peaceful, polite, sociable

amid amidst, among, amongst, in the middle of, in the midst of, in the thick of, surrounded by
amiss 1. *adj.* awry, confused, defective, erroneous, fallacious, false, faulty, improper, inaccurate, inappropriate, incorrect, mistaken, out of order, unsuitable, untoward, wrong **2.** *adv.* as an insult, as offensive, erroneously, faultily, improperly, inappropriately, incorrectly, mistakenly, out of turn, unsuitably, wrongly
ammunition armaments, cartridges, explosives, materiel, munitions, powder, rounds, shells, shot, shot and shell
amnesty absolution, condonation, dispensation, forgiveness, general pardon, immunity, oblivion, remission (*of penalty*), reprieve

amok see AMUCK
among, amongst 1. amid, in association with, in the middle of, in the midst of, in the thick of, midst, surrounded by, together with, with **2.** between, to each of **3.** in the class of, in the company of, in the group of, in the number of, out of **4.** by all of, by the joint action of, by the whole of, mutually, with one another
amorous affectionate, amatory, ardent, attached, doting, enamoured, erotic, fond, impassioned, in love, lovesick, loving, lustful, passionate, tender
amorphous characterless, formless, inchoate, indeterminate, irregular, nebulous, nondescript, shapeless, unformed, unshaped, unshapen, unstructured, vague

of something. **4.** a principal sum plus the interest on it, as in a loan. ~*vb.* **5.** (*intr.;* usually foll. by *to*) to be equal or add up.

amour (ə'muʊə) *n.* a love affair, esp. a secret or illicit one.

amp. *abbrev. for:* **1.** amperage. **2.** ampere.

ampelopsis (ˌæmpɪ'lɒpsɪs) *n.* any of a genus of woody climbing plants of tropical and subtropical Asia and America.

amperage ('æmpərɪdʒ) *n.* the strength of an electric current measured in amperes.

ampere ('æmpɛə) *n.* **1.** the basic SI unit of electric current; the constant current that, when maintained in two parallel conductors of infinite length and negligible cross section placed 1 metre apart in a vacuum, produces a force of 2×10^{-7} newton per metre between them. **2.** a former unit of electric current (**international ampere**); the current that, when passed through a solution of silver nitrate, deposits silver at the rate of 0.001118 gram per second. ~Abbrev.: **amp.** Symbol: **A**

ampersand ('æmpəˌsænd) *n.* the character (&), meaning *and: John Brown & Co.*

amphetamine (æm'fɛtəˌmiːn) *n.* a synthetic colourless liquid used medicinally, mainly for its stimulant action on the central nervous system.

amphi- *prefix of nouns and adjectives.* **1.** on both sides; at both ends; of both kinds: *amphipod; amphibious.* **2.** around: *amphibole.*

amphibian (æm'fɪbɪən) *n.* **1.** any cold-blooded vertebrate of the class *Amphibia,* typically living on land but breeding in water. The class includes newts, frogs, and toads. **2.** an aircraft able to land and take off from both water and land. **3.** any vehicle able to travel on both water and land. ~*adj.* **4.** another word for **amphibious. 5.** of or belonging to the class *Amphibia.*

amphibious (æm'fɪbɪəs) *adj.* **1.** able to live both on land and in the water, as frogs, etc. **2.** designed for operation on or from both water and land. **3.** relating to military forces and operations launched from the sea against an enemy shore. **4.** having a dual or mixed nature. —**am'phibiousness** *n.*

amphitheatre *or U.S.* **amphitheater** ('æmfɪˌθɪətə) *n.* **1.** a building, usually circular or oval, in which tiers of seats rise from a central open arena. **2.** a place where contests are held. **3.** any level circular area of ground surrounded by higher ground. **4.** a gallery in a theatre. **5.** a lecture room in which seats are tiered away from a central area.

amphora ('æmfərə) *n., pl.* **-phorae** (-fəˌriː) *or* **-phoras.** a Greek or Roman two-handled narrow-necked jar for oil, etc.

ample ('æmpəl) *adj.* **1.** more than sufficient: *an ample helping.* **2.** large: *of ample proportions.* —'**ampleness** *n.*

amplifier ('æmplɪˌfaɪə) *n.* **1.** an electronic device used to increase the strength of the current fed into it, esp. one for the amplification of sound in a radio, record player, etc. **2.** *Photog.* an additional lens for altering focal length. **3.** a person or thing that amplifies.

amplify ('æmplɪˌfaɪ) *vb.* **-fying, -fied. 1.** (*tr.*) to increase in size, extent, effect, etc., as by the addition of extra material. **2.** *Electronics.* to produce amplification of (electrical signals, sound, etc.). **3.** (*intr.*) to expand a

speech, narrative, etc.

amplitude ('æmplɪˌtjuːd) *n.* **1.** greatness of extent; magnitude. **2.** abundance. **3.** breadth or scope, as of the mind. **4.** the maximum displacement from the zero or mean position of a periodic motion. **5.** *Astron.* the angular distance along the horizon measured from true east or west to the point of intersection of the vertical circle passing through a celestial body.

amplitude modulation *n.* one of the principal methods of transmitting information using radio waves, the relevant signal being superimposed onto a radio-frequency carrier wave. The frequency of the carrier wave remains unchanged but its amplitude is varied in accordance with the amplitude of the input signal. Cf. **frequency modulation.**

amply ('æmplɪ) *adv.* fully; generously.

ampoule ('æmpuːl, -pjuːl) *or* (*esp. U.S.*) **ampule** *n. Med.* a small glass vessel in which liquids for injection are hermetically sealed.

ampulla (æm'pʊlə) *n., pl.* **-pullae** (-'pʊliː). **1.** *Anat.* the dilated end part of certain ducts or canals. **2.** *Christianity.* **a.** a vessel for the wine and water used at the Eucharist. **b.** a small flask for consecrated oil. **3.** a Roman two-handled bottle for oil, wine, or perfume.

amputate ('æmpjuˌteɪt) *vb. Surgery.* to remove (all or part of a limb). —ˌ**ampu'tation** *n.*

amuck (ə'mʌk) *or* **amok** *n.* **1.** a state of murderous frenzy. ~*adv.* **2. run amuck.** to run about as with a frenzied desire to kill.

amulet ('æmjulɪt) *n.* a trinket or piece of jewellery worn as a protection against evil; charm.

amuse (ə'mjuːz) *vb.* (*tr.*) **1.** to entertain; divert. **2.** to cause to laugh or smile. —**a'musing** *adj.*

amusement (ə'mjuːzmənt) *n.* **1.** something that amuses, such as a game or pastime. **2.** a mechanical device used for entertainment, as at a fair. **3.** the act of amusing or the state or quality of being amused.

amylase ('æmɪˌleɪz) *n.* any of several enzymes that hydrolyse starch and glycogen to simple sugars, such as glucose.

amylum ('æmɪləm) *n.* another name for **starch** (senses 1,2).

an[1] (æn; *unstressed* ən) *determiner.* (*article*) a form of **a,** used before an initial vowel and sometimes before an initial h: *an old car; an elf; an historic moment.*

an[2] *or* **an'** (æn; *unstressed* ən) *conj.* (*subordinating*) an obsolete word for **if.** See **and** (sense 8).

an. *abbrev. for* anno.

an- *or before a consonant* **a-** *prefix.* not; without: *anaphrodisiac.*

-an, -ean, *or* **-ian** *suffix.* **1.** (*forming adjectives and nouns*) belonging to; coming from; typical of; adhering to: *European; Elizabethan; Christian.* **2.** (*forming nouns*) a person who specializes or is expert in: *dietician.*

Anabaptist (ˌænə'bæptɪst) *n.* **1.** a member of any of various Protestant movements, esp. of the 16th century, that rejected infant baptism, insisted that adults be rebaptized, and sought to establish Christian communism. ~*adj.* **2.** of these sects or their doctrines. —ˌ**Ana'baptism** *n.*

anabolism (ə'næbəˌlɪzəm) *n.* a metabolic process in which complex molecules are synthesized from simpler

---

THESAURUS

amount 1. bulk, expanse, extent, lot, magnitude, mass, measure, number, quantity, supply, volume 2. addition, aggregate, entirety, extent, lot, sum, sum total, total, whole 3. full effect, full value, import, result, significance

amount to add up to, aggregate, become, come, come to, develop into, equal, grow, mean, purport, total

ample abounding, abundant, big, bountiful, broad, capacious, commodious, copious, enough and to spare, expansive, extensive, full, generous, great, large, lavish, liberal, plenteous, plentiful, plenty, profuse, rich, roomy, spacious, substantial, unrestricted, voluminous, wide

amplification augmentation, boosting, deepening, development, dilation, elaboration, enlargement, expansion, expatiation, extension, fleshing out, heightening, in-

crease, intensification, lengthening, magnification, raising, rounding out, strengthening, stretching, supplementing, widening

amplify augment, boost, deepen, develop, dilate, elaborate, enlarge, expand, expatiate, extend, flesh out, go into detail, heighten, increase, intensify, lengthen, magnify, raise, round out, strengthen, stretch, supplement, widen

amply abundantly, bountifully, capaciously, completely, copiously, extensively, fully, generously, greatly, lavishly, liberally, plenteously, plentifully, profusely, richly, substantially, thoroughly, unstintingly, well

amputate curtail, cut off, lop, remove, separate, sever, truncate

amuck, amok berserk, destructively, ferociously, frenziedly, in a frenzy, insanely, madly, maniacally, murderously, savagely, uncontrollably, violently, wildly

amuse beguile, charm, cheer, delight, divert, enliven, entertain, gladden, gratify, interest, occupy, please, recreate, regale, tickle (*Inf.*)

amusement 1. beguilement, cheer, delight, diversion, enjoyment, entertainment, fun, gladdening, gratification, hilarity, interest, laughter, merriment, mirth, pleasing, pleasure, recreation, regalement, sport 2. distraction, diversion, entertainment, game, hobby, joke, lark, pastime, prank, recreation, sport

amusing charming, cheerful, cheering, comical, delightful, diverting, droll, enjoyable, entertaining, facetious, funny, gladdening, gratifying, humorous, interesting, jocular, laughable, lively, merry, pleasant, pleasing, witty

ones with the storage of energy; constructive metabolism. —**anabolic** (ˌænəˈbɒlɪk) adj.

anachronism (əˈnækrəˌnɪzəm) n. 1. the representation of an event, person, or thing in a historical context in which it could not have occurred or existed. 2. a person or thing that belongs or seems to belong to another time. —**aˌnachroˈnistic** adj. —**aˌnachroˈnistically** adv.

anaconda (ˌænəˈkɒndə) n. a very large nonvenomous arboreal and semiaquatic snake of tropical South America, which kills its prey by constriction.

anadromous (əˈnædrəməs) adj. (of fishes such as the salmon) migrating up rivers from the sea in order to breed.

anaemia or U.S. **anemia** (əˈniːmɪə) n. a deficiency in the number of red blood cells or in their haemoglobin content, resulting in pallor and lack of energy.

anaemic or U.S. **anemic** (əˈniːmɪk) adj. 1. relating to or suffering from anaemia. 2. pale and sickly looking; lacking vitality.

anaerobe (ænˈɛərəub) or **anaerobium** (ˌænɛəˈrəubɪəm) n., pl. -**obes** or -**obia** (-ˈəubɪə). an organism that does not require or requires the absence of free oxygen or air. —ˌanaerˈobic adj.

anaesthesia or U.S. **anesthesia** (ˌænɪsˈθiːzɪə) n. 1. loss of bodily sensation, esp. of touch, as the result of nerve damage or other abnormality. 2. loss of sensation, esp. of pain, induced by drugs: called **general anaesthesia** when consciousness is lost and **local anaesthesia** when only a specific area of the body is involved.

anaesthetic or U.S. **anesthetic** (ˌænɪsˈθɛtɪk) n. 1. a substance that causes anaesthesia. ~adj. 2. causing or characterized by anaesthesia.

anaesthetist (əˈniːsθətɪst) n. Brit. a doctor specializing in the administration of anaesthetics. U.S. name: **anesthesiologist**.

anaesthetize, anaesthetise, or U.S. **anesthetize** (əˈniːsθəˌtaɪz) vb. (tr.) to render insensible to pain by administering an anaesthetic. —aˌnaesthetiˈzation, aˌnaestheˈtiˈsation, or U.S. aˌnestheˈtiˈzation n.

anaglypta (ˌænəˈɡlɪptə) n. a type of thick embossed wallpaper designed to be painted.

anagram (ˈænəˌɡræm) n. a word or phrase the letters of which can be rearranged into another word or phrase. —**anagrammatic** (ˌænəɡrəˈmætɪk) or ˌanagramˈmatical adj.

anal (ˈeɪnəl) adj. 1. of or near the anus. 2. Psychoanal. relating to a stage of psychosexual development during which the child's interest is concentrated on the anal region and excremental functions. —ˈanally adv.

analects (ˈænəˌlɛkts) or **analecta** (ˌænəˈlɛktə) pl. n. selected literary passages from one or more works.

analgesia (ˌænəlˈdʒiːzɪə) or **analgia** (ænˈældʒɪə) n. inability to feel pain. —ˌanalˈgesic adj., n.

analogize or -**gise** (əˈnæləˌdʒaɪz) vb. 1. (intr.) to make use of analogy, as in argument. 2. (tr.) to make analogous or reveal analogy in.

analogous (əˈnæləɡəs) adj. 1. similar or corresponding in some respect. 2. Biol. (of organs and parts) having the same function but different evolutionary origin. 3. Linguistics. formed by analogy: an analogous plural.

analogue or U.S. (sometimes) **analog** (ˈænəˌlɒɡ) n. 1. something analogous to something else. 2. Biol. an analogous part or organ.

analogy (əˈnælədʒɪ) n., pl. -**gies**. 1. agreement or similarity, esp. in a limited number of features. 2. a comparison made to show such a similarity: an analogy be-

tween an atom and the solar system. 3. Biol. the relationship between analogous organs or parts. 4. Logic, Maths., Philosophy. a form of reasoning in which a similarity between two or more things is inferred from a known similarity between them in other respects. 5. Linguistics. imitation of existing models or regular patterns in the formation of words, etc.: a child may use "sheeps" as the plural of "sheep" by analogy with "cat," "cats," etc.

analyse or U.S. -**lyze** (ˈænəˌlaɪz) vb. 1. (tr.) to examine in detail in order to discover meaning, essential features, etc. 2. (tr.) to break down into components or essential features. 3. (tr.) to make a mathematical, chemical, grammatical, etc., analysis of. 4. another word for **psychoanalyse**. —ˈanaˌlyser or U.S. -ˌlyzer n.

analysis (əˈnælɪsɪs) n., pl. -**ses** (-ˌsiːz) 1. the division of a physical or abstract whole into its constituent parts to examine or determine their relationship. 2. a statement of the results of this. 3. short for **psychoanalysis**. 4. Chem. **a.** the decomposition of a substance in order to determine the kinds of constituents present (**qualitative analysis**) or the amount of each constituent (**quantitative analysis**). **b.** the result obtained by such a determination. 5. Linguistics. the use of word order together with word function to express syntactic relations in a language, as opposed to the use of inflections. 6. Maths. the branch of mathematics principally concerned with algebra and calculus. 7. **in the last, final,** or **ultimate analysis.** after everything has been given due consideration.

analyst (ˈænəlɪst) n. 1. a person who analyses or is skilled in analysis. 2. a psychoanalyst.

analytic (ˌænəˈlɪtɪk) or **analytical** adj. 1. relating to analysis. 2. capable of or given to analysing: an analytic mind. 3. Linguistics. denoting languages characterized by analysis. 4. Logic. (of a proposition) necessarily true by reference to meaning alone, as in all spinsters are unmarried. —ˌanaˈlytically adv. —**analyticity** (ˌænəlɪˈtɪsɪtɪ) n.

anapaest or **anapest** (ˈænəpɛst, -ˌpiːst) n. Prosody. a metrical foot of three syllables, the first two short, the last long (˘˘—). —ˌanaˈpaestic or ˌanaˈpestic adj.

anaphora (əˈnæfərə) n. 1. Rhetoric. the repetition of a word or phrase at the beginning of successive clauses. 2. Grammar. the use of a word such as a pronoun to avoid repetition, as for example of one in He offered me a drink but I didn't want one.

anarchism (ˈænəˌkɪzəm) n. 1. Political theory. a doctrine advocating the abolition of government. 2. the principles or practice of anarchists.

anarchist (ˈænəkɪst) n. 1. a person who advocates the abolition of government and a social system based on voluntary cooperation. 2. a person who causes disorder or upheaval.

anarchy (ˈænəkɪ) n. 1. general lawlessness and disorder, esp. when thought to result from an absence or failure of government. 2. the absence of government. 3. the absence of any guiding or uniting principle; chaos. 4. political anarchism. —**anarchic** (ænˈɑːkɪk) or **anˈarchical** adj.

anastigmatic (ˌænəstɪɡˈmætɪk) adj. (of a lens or optical device) not astigmatic.

anathema (əˈnæθəmə) n., pl. -**mas**. 1. a detested person or thing: he is anathema to me. 2. a formal ecclesiastical excommunication, or denunciation of a doctrine. 3. the person or thing so cursed. 4. a strong curse.

THESAURUS

anaemic ashen, bloodless, characterless, colourless, dull, enervated, feeble, frail, infirm, pale, pallid, sickly, wan, weak

anaesthetic 1. n. analgesic, anodyne, narcotic, opiate, painkiller, sedative, soporific, stupefacient, stupefactive 2. adj. analgesic, anodyne, deadening, dulling, narcotic, numbing, opiate, pain-killing, sedative, sleep-inducing, soporific, stupefacient, stupefactive

analogous agreeing, akin, alike, comparable, corresponding, equivalent, homologous, like, parallel, related, resembling, similar

analogy agreement, comparison, correla-

tion, correspondence, equivalence, homology, likeness, parallel, relation, resemblance, similarity, similitude

analyse 1. assay, estimate, evaluate, examine, interpret, investigate, judge, test 2. anatomize, break down, consider, dissect, dissolve, divide, resolve, separate, study, think through

analysis 1. anatomization, anatomy, assay, breakdown, dissection, dissolution, division, enquiry, examination, investigation, resolution, scrutiny, separation, sifting, test 2. estimation, evaluation, finding, interpretation, judgment, opinion, reasoning, study

analytic, analytical detailed, diag-

nostic, discrete, dissecting, explanatory, expository, inquiring, inquisitive, interpretative, interpretive, investigative, logical, organized, problem-solving, questioning, rational, searching, studious, systematic, testing

anarchic chaotic, confused, disordered, disorganized, lawless, misgoverned, misruled, rebellious, revolutionary, rioting, riotous, ungoverned

anarchist insurgent, nihilist, rebel, revolutionary, terrorist

anarchy chaos, confusion, disorder, disorganization, lawlessness, misgovernment, misrule, rebellion, revolution, riot

anathematize or **-tise** (ə'næθɪmə,taɪz) vb. to pronounce an anathema (upon a person, etc.); curse.

anatomize or **-mise** (ə'nætə,maɪz) vb. (tr.) 1. to dissect (an animal or plant). 2. to examine in minute detail.

anatomy (ə'nætəmɪ) n., pl. **-mies.** 1. the science concerned with the physical structure of animals and plants. 2. the physical structure of an animal or plant or any of its parts. 3. a book or treatise on this subject. 4. dissection of an animal or plant. 5. any detailed analysis: *the anatomy of a crime.* 6. *Inf.* the human body. —**anatomical** (,ænə'tɒmɪkəl) adj. —**a'natomist** n.

-ance or **-ancy** suffix forming nouns. indicating an action, state or condition, or quality: *utterance; resemblance.*

ancestor ('ænsɛstə) n. 1. a person from whom another is directly descended; forefather. 2. an early type of animal or plant from which a later type has evolved. 3. a person or thing regarded as a forerunner: *the ancestor of the modern camera.* —**'ancestress** fem. n.

ancestral (æn'sɛstrəl) adj. of or inherited from ancestors.

ancestry ('ænsɛstrɪ) n., pl. **-tries.** 1. lineage or descent, esp. when noble or distinguished. 2. ancestors collectively.

anchor ('æŋkə) n. 1. a device attached to a vessel by a cable and dropped overboard so as to grip the bottom and restrict movement. 2. an object used to hold something else firmly in place: *the rock provided an anchor for the rope.* 3. a source of stability or security. 4. *Sport.* short for **anchor man.** 5. **cast, come to,** or **drop anchor.** to anchor a vessel. 6. **weigh anchor.** to haul in an anchor. 7. **ride at anchor.** to be anchored. ~vb. 8. to use an anchor to hold (a vessel) in one place. 9. to fasten or be fastened securely; fix or become fixed firmly.

anchorage ('æŋkərɪdʒ) n. 1. the act of anchoring. 2. any place where a vessel is anchored. 3. a place designated for vessels to anchor. 4. a fee imposed for anchoring. 5. anything used as an anchor. 6. a source of security or strength.

anchorite ('æŋkə,raɪt) n. a person who lives in seclusion, esp. a religious recluse; hermit. —**'anchoress** fem. n.

anchor man n. 1. *Sport.* the last person in a team to compete, esp. in a relay race. 2. (in broadcasting) a person in a central studio who links up and maintains contact with various outside camera units, reporters, etc.

anchovy ('æntʃəvɪ) n., pl. **-vies** or **-vy.** any of various small marine food fishes which have a salty taste and are often tinned or made into a paste or essence.

anchusa (æŋ'kjuːsə) n. any of several Eurasian plants having rough hairy stems and leaves and blue flowers.

ancient ('eɪnʃənt) adj. 1. dating from very long ago: *ancient ruins.* 2. very old. 3. of the far past, esp. before the collapse of the Western Roman Empire (476 A.D.). 4. **ancient light.** a right to the access of light through a window, recognized at law when it has been enjoyed for 20 years or more. ~n. 5. (often pl.) a member of a civilized nation in the ancient world, esp. a Greek or Roman. 6. (often pl.) one of the classical authors of Greek or Roman antiquity. 7. *Arch.* an old man. —**'ancientness** n.

anciently ('eɪnʃəntlɪ) adv. in ancient times.

ancillary (æn'sɪlərɪ) adj. 1. subsidiary. 2. auxiliary; supplementary: *ancillary services.* ~n., pl. **-laries.** 3. a subsidiary or auxiliary thing or person.

-ancy suffix forming nouns. variant of **-ance,** indicating condition or quality: *poignancy.*

and (ænd; unstressed ənd, ən) conj. (coordinating) 1. in

addition to: *boys and girls.* 2. as a consequence: *he fell down and cut his knee.* 3. afterwards: *we pay and go through that door.* 4. plus: *two and two equals four.* 5. used to give emphasis or indicate repetition or continuity: *it rained and rained.* 6. used to express a contrast between instances of what is named: *there are jobs and jobs.* 7. *Inf.* used in place of *to* in infinitives after verbs such as *try, go,* and *come: try and see it my way.* 8. an obsolete word for **if:** *and it please you.*
▷ **Usage.** See at **to.**

-and or **-end** suffix forming nouns. indicating a person or thing that is to be dealt with in a specified way: *dividend; multiplicand.*

andante (æn'dæntɪ) *Music.* ~adj., adv. 1. at a moderately slow tempo. ~n. 2. a passage or piece to be performed in this manner.

andantino (,ændæn'tiːnəʊ) *Music.* ~adj., adv. 1. slightly faster or slower than andante. ~n., pl. **-nos.** 2. a passage or piece to be performed in this manner.

andiron ('ænd,aɪən) n. either of a pair of metal stands for supporting logs in a hearth.

and/or conj. (coordinating). used to join terms when either one or the other or both is indicated: *passports and/or other means of identification.*
▷ **Usage.** *And/or* is not universally accepted as being good usage outside legal and commercial contexts. It is never used by careful writers and speakers where *or* is meant: *he must bring his car or his bicycle* (not *his car and/or his bicycle*).

andro- or before a vowel **andr-** combining form. 1. male; masculine: *androsterone.* 2. (in botany) stamen or anther: *androecium.*

androgen ('ændrədʒən) n. any of several steroids that promote development of male sexual characteristics. —**androgenic** (,ændrə'dʒɛnɪk) adj.

androgynous (æn'drɒdʒɪnəs) adj. 1. *Bot.* having male and female flowers in the same inflorescence. 2. hermaphrodite.

android ('ændrɔɪd) n. 1. (in science fiction) a robot resembling a human being. ~adj. 2. resembling a human being.

anecdote ('ænɪk,dəʊt) n. a short usually amusing account of an incident. —**anec'dotal** or **anec'dotic** adj. —**,anec'dotalist** or **'anec,dotist** n.

anechoic (,ænɪ'kəʊɪk) adj. having a low degree of reverberation: *an anechoic recording studio.*

anemia (ə'niːmɪə) n. the usual U.S. spelling of **anaemia.**

anemometer (,ænɪ'mɒmɪtə) n. Also called: **wind gauge.** an instrument for recording the speed and often the direction of winds. —**,ane'mometry** n. —**anemometric** (,ænɪməʊ'mɛtrɪk) adj.

anemone (ə'nɛmənɪ) n. any woodland plant of the genus *Anemone* of N temperate regions, such as the white-flowered **wood anemone** or **windflower.** Some cultivated anemones have coloured flowers.

anent (ə'nɛnt) prep. *Arch.* or *Scot.* concerning; about.

aneroid barometer ('ænə,rɔɪd) n. a device for measuring atmospheric pressure without the use of fluids. It consists of a partially evacuated chamber, the lid of which is displaced by variations in air pressure. This displacement is magnified by levers and made to operate a pointer.

anesthesia (,ænɪs'θiːzɪə) n. the usual U.S. spelling of **anaesthesia.**

aneurysm or **aneurism** ('ænjə,rɪzəm) n. a sac formed by abnormal dilation of the weakened wall of a blood vessel.

anew (ə'njuː) adv. 1. once more. 2. in a different way; afresh.

THESAURUS

anathema 1. ban, condemnation, curse, damnation, denunciation, excommunication, execration, imprecation, malediction, proscription, taboo 2. abomination, bane, *bête noire,* bugbear, enemy, pariah
anathematize abominate, ban, condemn, curse, damn, denounce, excommunicate, execrate, imprecate, proscribe
anatomize analyse, break down, dissect, dissolve, divide, examine, resolve, scrutinize, separate, study
anatomy 1. analysis, dismemberment, dissection, division, enquiry, examination, in-

vestigation, study 2. build, composition, frame, framework, make-up, structure
ancestor forebear, forefather, forerunner, precursor, predecessor, progenitor
ancestry ancestors, antecedents, blood, derivation, descent, extraction, family, forebears, forefathers, genealogy, house, line, lineage, origin, parentage, pedigree, progenitors, race, stock
ancient aged, age-old, antediluvian, antiquated, antique, archaic, bygone, early, hoary, obsolete, old, olden, old-fashioned, outmoded, out-of-date, primeval, primordial,

superannuated, timeworn
ancillary accessory, additional, auxiliary, contributory, extra, secondary, subordinate, subsidiary, supplementary
and along with, also, as well as, furthermore, in addition to, including, moreover, plus, together with
anecdote reminiscence, short story, sketch, story, tale, yarn
anew afresh, again, another time, from scratch, from the beginning, once again, once more, over again

angel ('eɪndʒəl) n. 1. *Theol.* one of a class of spiritual beings attendant upon God. In medieval angelology they are divided by rank into nine orders. 2. a divine messenger from God. 3. a guardian spirit. 4. a conventional representation of any of these beings, depicted in human form with wings. 5. *Inf.* a person who is kind, pure, or beautiful. 6. *Inf.* an investor esp. in a theatrical production. 7. Also called: **angel-noble.** a former English gold coin with a representation of the archangel Michael on it. 8. *Inf.* an unexplained signal on a radar screen.

angel cake or esp. U.S. **angel food cake** n. a very light sponge cake made without egg yolks.

angelfish ('eɪndʒəl,fɪʃ) n., pl. **-fish** or **-fishes.** 1. any of various small tropical marine fishes which have a deep flattened brightly coloured body. 2. a South American freshwater fish having a compressed body and large dorsal and anal fins: a popular aquarium fish. 3. a shark with flattened pectoral fins.

angelic (æn'dʒelɪk) adj. 1. of or relating to angels. 2. *Inf.* resembling an angel in beauty, etc. —**an'gelical** adj. —**an'gelically** adv.

angelica (æn'dʒelɪkə) n. 1. an umbelliferous plant, the aromatic seeds, leaves, and stems of which are used in medicine and cookery. 2. the candied stems of this plant, used for decorating and flavouring sweet dishes.

Angelus ('ændʒɪləs) n. R.C. Church. 1. a series of prayers recited in the morning, at midday, and in the evening. 2. the bell (**Angelus bell**) signalling the times of these prayers.

anger ('æŋgə) n. 1. a feeling of great annoyance or antagonism as the result of some real or supposed grievance; rage; wrath. ~vb. (tr.) 2. to make angry; enrage.

Angevin ('ændʒɪvɪn) n. 1. a native or inhabitant of Anjou, in France. 2. *History.* a member of the Plantagenet royal line, esp. one of the kings of England from Henry II to Richard II (1154–1216). ~adj. 3. of Anjou or its inhabitants. 4. of the Plantagenet kings of England.

angina (æn'dʒaɪnə) n. 1. any disease marked by painful attacks of spasmodic choking. 2. short for **angina pectoris.**

angina pectoris ('pɛktərɪs) n. a sudden intense pain in the chest, caused by momentary lack of adequate blood supply to the heart muscle. Sometimes shortened to **angina.**

angiosperm ('ændʒɪə,spɜːm) n. any seed-bearing plant in which the ovules are enclosed in an ovary which develops into the fruit after fertilization; any flowering plant. Cf. **gymnosperm.**

angle¹ ('æŋgəl) n. 1. the space between two straight lines or two planes that extend from a common point. 2. the shape formed by two such lines or planes. 3. the extent to which one such line or plane diverges from the other, measured in degrees or radians. 4. a recess; corner. 5. point of view: *look at the question from another angle.* 6. See **angle iron.** ~vb. 7. to move in or bend into angles or an angle. 8. (tr.) to produce (an article, statement, etc.) with a particular point of view. 9. (tr.) to present, or place at an angle. 10. (intr.) to turn in a different direction.

angle² ('æŋgəl) vb. (intr.) 1. to fish with a hook and line. 2. (often foll. by for) to attempt to get: *he angled for a compliment.* ~n. 3. *Obs.* a fishhook.

angle iron n. Also called: **angle, angle bar.** an iron or a steel structural bar that has an L-shaped cross section.

angle of incidence n. 1. the angle that a line or beam of radiation makes with a line perpendicular to the surface at the point of incidence. 2. the angle between the chord line of an aircraft wing or tailplane and the

aircraft's longitudinal axis.

angler ('æŋglə) n. 1. a person who fishes with a rod and line. 2. Also called: **angler fish.** any of various spiny-finned fishes which live at the bottom of the sea and typically have a long movable dorsal fin with which they lure their prey.

Anglican ('æŋglɪkən) adj. 1. denoting or relating to the Church of England or one of the churches in communion with it. ~n. 2. a member of the Anglican Church.

Anglicism ('æŋglɪ,sɪzəm) n. 1. a word, or idiom peculiar to the English language, esp. as spoken in England. 2. an English mannerism, custom, etc. 3. the fact of being English.

anglicize or **-cise** ('æŋglɪ,saɪz) vb. **-cizing, -cized** or **-cising, -cised.** (sometimes cap.) to make or become English in outlook, form, etc.

angling ('æŋglɪŋ) n. the art or sport of catching fish with a baited hook or other lure, such as a fly; fishing.

Anglo ('æŋgləʊ) n., pl. **-glos.** Canad. an English-speaking Canadian, esp. one of Anglo-Celtic origin; an Anglo-Canadian.

Anglo- ('æŋgləʊ-) combining form. denoting English or England: *Anglo-Saxon.*

Anglo-French adj. 1. of England and France. 2. of Anglo-French. ~n. 3. the Norman-French language of medieval England.

Anglo-Indian adj. 1. of England and India. 2. denoting or relating to Anglo-Indians. 3. (of a word) introduced into English from an Indian language. ~n. 4. a person of mixed British and Indian descent. 5. an Englishman who lives or has lived for a long time in India.

Anglo-Norman adj. 1. relating to the Norman conquerors of England, their society, or their language. ~n. 2. a Norman inhabitant of England after 1066. 3. the Anglo-French language.

Anglophile ('æŋgləʊfɪl, -,faɪl) or **Anglophil** n. a person having admiration for England or the English.

Anglo-Saxon n. 1. a member of any of the West Germanic tribes that settled in Britain from the 5th century A.D. 2. the language of these tribes. See **Old English.** 3. any White person whose native language is English. 4. *Inf.* plain blunt English. ~adj. 5. forming part of the Germanic element in Modern English: *"forget" is an Anglo-Saxon word.* 6. of the Anglo-Saxons or the Old English language. 7. of the White Protestant culture of Britain and the U.S.

angora (æŋ'gɔːrə) n. (sometimes cap.) 1. the long soft hair of the Angora goat or the fur of the Angora rabbit. 2. yarn, cloth, or clothing made from this hair. 3. (as modifier): *an angora sweater.* ~See also **mohair.**

angostura bitters (,æŋgə'stjʊərə) pl. n. (often cap.) Trademark. a bitter aromatic tonic, used as a flavouring in alcoholic drinks.

angry ('æŋgrɪ) adj. **-grier, -griest.** 1. feeling or expressing annoyance, animosity, or resentment. 2. suggestive of anger: *angry clouds.* 3. severely inflamed: *an angry sore.* —**'angrily** adv.

angst (æŋst) n. an acute but nonspecific sense of anxiety or remorse.

angstrom ('æŋstrəm) n. a unit of length equal to 10^{-10} metre, used principally to express the wavelengths of electromagnetic radiations. Symbol: Å or A Also called: **angstrom unit.**

anguish ('æŋgwɪʃ) n. 1. extreme pain or misery; mental or physical torture; agony. ~vb. 2. to afflict or be afflicted with anguish.

angular ('æŋgjʊlə) adj. 1. lean or bony. 2. awkward or

THESAURUS

angel 1. archangel, cherub, divine messenger, guardian spirit, seraph, spiritual being 2. *Inf.* beauty, darling, dear, dream, gem, ideal, jewel, paragon, saint, treasure

angelic 1. celestial, cherubic, ethereal, heavenly, seraphic 2. adorable, beatific, beautiful, entrancing, innocent, lovely, pure, saintly, virtuous

anger 1. n. annoyance, antagonism, choler, displeasure, exasperation, fury, ill humour, ill temper, indignation, ire, irritability, irritation, outrage, passion, pique, rage, resentment, spleen, temper, vexation, wrath 2. v. affront, annoy, antagonize, displease, enrage,

exasperate, excite, fret, gall, incense, infuriate, irritate, madden, nettle, offend, outrage, pique, provoke, rile, vex

angle n. 1. bend, corner, crook, crotch, cusp, edge, elbow, intersection, knee, nook, point 2. approach, aspect, outlook, perspective, point of view, position, side, slant, standpoint, viewpoint ~v. 3. cast, fish

angle for aim for, be after (Inf.), cast about for, contrive, fish for, hunt, invite, look for, scheme, seek, solicit, try for

angry annoyed, antagonized, choleric, displeased, enraged, exasperated, furious, heated, hot, hot under the collar (Inf.), ill-

tempered, incensed, indignant, infuriated, irascible, irate, ireful, irritable, irritated, mad (Inf.), nettled, outraged, passionate, piqued, provoked, raging, resentful, riled, splenetic, tumultuous, uptight (Sl.), wrathful

anguish agony, distress, grief, heartache, heartbreak, misery, pain, pang, sorrow, suffering, throe, torment, torture, woe

anguished afflicted, agonized, broken-hearted, distressed, grief-stricken, suffering, tormented, tortured, wounded, wretched

stiff. **3.** having an angle or angles. **4.** placed at an angle. **5.** measured by an angle or by the rate at which an angle changes; *angular momentum; angular velocity.*

angularity (ˌæŋgjuˈlærɪtɪ) *n., pl.* **-ties.** **1.** the condition of being angular. **2.** an angular shape.

anhydrous (ænˈhaɪdrəs) *adj.* containing no water, esp. no water of crystallization.

anil (ˈænɪl) *n.* a leguminous West Indian shrub which is a source of indigo. Also called: **indigo.**

aniline (ˈænɪlɪn, -ˌliːn) *n.* a colourless oily poisonous liquid used in the manufacture of dyes, plastics, and explosives. Formula: $C_6H_5NH_2$.

aniline dye *n.* any synthetic dye originally made from aniline, found in coal tar.

anima (ˈænɪmə) *n.* (in Jungian psychology) **a.** the inner personality. **b.** the feminine principle as present in the male unconscious.

animadversion (ˌænɪmædˈvɜːʃən) *n.* criticism or censure.

animadvert (ˌænɪmædˈvɜːt) *vb.* (*intr.*) **1.** (usually foll. by *on* or *upon*) to comment with strong criticism (upon); make censorious remarks (about). **2.** to make an observation or comment.

animal (ˈænɪməl) *n.* **1.** *Zool.* any living organism characterized by voluntary movement, the possession of specialized sense organs enabling rapid response to stimuli, and the ingestion of complex organic substances. **2.** any mammal, esp. except man. **3.** a brutish person. **4.** *Facetious.* a person or thing (esp. in **no such animal**). ~*adj.* **5.** of or relating to animals. **6.** of or relating to physical needs or desires; carnal; sensual.

animalcule (ˌænɪˈmælkjuːl) *n., pl.* **-cules.** a microscopic animal such as an amoeba or rotifer. —ˌaniˈmalcular *adj.*

animal husbandry *n.* the science of breeding, rearing, and caring for farm animals.

animalism (ˈænɪməˌlɪzəm) *n.* **1.** preoccupation with physical matters; sensuality. **2.** the doctrine that man lacks a spiritual nature. **3.** a mode of behaviour typical of animals.

animality (ˌænɪˈmælɪtɪ) *n.* **1.** the animal side of man, as opposed to the intellectual or spiritual. **2.** the characteristics of an animal.

animalize *or* **-ise** (ˈænɪməˌlaɪz) *vb.* (*tr.*) **1.** to rouse to brutality or sensuality or make brutal or sensual. —ˌaniˈmaliˈzation *or* -ˈisation *n.*

animal magnetism *n.* **1.** the quality of being attractive, esp. to members of the opposite sex. **2.** *Obs.* hypnotism.

animal spirits *pl. n.* boisterous exuberance.

animate *vb.* (ˈænɪˌmeɪt) (*tr.*) **1.** to give life to or cause to come alive. **2.** to make gay or lively. **3.** to encourage or inspire. **4.** to impart motion to. **5.** to record on film so as to give movement to. ~*adj.* (ˈænɪmɪt) **6.** having life. **7.** gay, spirited, or lively. —ˈaniˌmatedly *adv.*

animated cartoon *n.* a film produced by photographing a series of gradually changing drawings, etc., which give the illusion of movement when the series is projected rapidly.

animation (ˌænɪˈmeɪʃən) *n.* **1.** vivacity. **2.** the condition of being alive. **3.** the techniques used in the production of animated cartoons.

animato (ˌænɪˈmɑːtəʊ) *adj., adv. Music.* lively; animated.

animism (ˈænɪˌmɪzəm) *n.* **1.** the belief that natural objects possess souls. **2.** (in the philosophies of Plato and Pythagoras) the hypothesis that there is an immaterial force that animates the universe. —**animistic** (ˌænɪˈmɪstɪk) *adj.*

animosity (ˌænɪˈmɒsɪtɪ) *n., pl.* **-ties.** a powerful and active dislike or hostility.

animus (ˈænɪməs) *n.* **1.** intense dislike; hatred; animosity. **2.** motive or purpose. **3.** (in Jungian psychology) the masculine principle present in the female unconscious.

anion (ˈænˌaɪən) *n.* a negatively charged ion; an ion that is attracted to the anode during electrolysis. —**anionic** (ˌænaɪˈɒnɪk) *adj.*

anise (ˈænɪs) *n.* a Mediterranean umbelliferous plant having clusters of small yellowish-white flowers and liquorice-flavoured seeds.

aniseed (ˈænɪˌsiːd) *n.* the liquorice-flavoured aromatic seeds of the anise plant, used medicinally for expelling intestinal gas and in cookery.

ankh (æŋk) *n.* a tall cross with a loop on the top, symbolizing eternal life: often appearing in Egyptian personal names, such as Tutankhamen.

ankle (ˈæŋkəl) *n.* **1.** the joint connecting the leg and the foot. **2.** the part of the leg just above the foot.

anklet (ˈæŋklɪt) *n.* an ornamental chain worn around the ankle.

ankylosis *or* **anchylosis** (ˌæŋkɪˈləʊsɪs) *n.* abnormal adhesion or immobility of the bones in a joint, as by a fibrous growth of tissues within the joint. —**ankylotic** *or* **anchylotic** (ˌæŋkɪˈlɒtɪk) *adj.*

anna (ˈænə) *n.* a former Indian coin, worth one sixteenth of a rupee.

annals (ˈænəlz) *pl. n.* **1.** yearly records of events. **2.** history in general. **3.** regular reports of the work of a society, learned body, etc. —ˈannalist *n.* —ˌannalˈistic *adj.*

annates (ˈæneɪts, -əts) *pl. n. R.C. Church.* the first year's revenue of a see, etc., paid to the pope.

anneal (əˈniːl) *vb.* **1.** to temper or toughen (something) by heat treatment to remove internal stress, crystal defects, and dislocations. **2.** (*tr.*) to toughen or strengthen (the will, determination, etc.). ~*n.* **3.** an act of annealing. —**anˈnealer** *n.*

annelid (ˈænəlɪd) *n.* **1.** a worm in which the body is divided into segments both externally and internally, as the earthworms. ~*adj.* **2.** of such worms. —**annelidan** (əˈnɛlɪdən) *n., adj.*

annex *vb.* (æˈnɛks). (*tr.*) **1.** to join or add, esp. to something larger. **2.** to add territory by conquest or occupation. **3.** to add or append as a condition, etc. **4.** to appropriate without permission. ~*n.* (ˈænɛks). **5.** a variant spelling (esp. U.S.) of **annexe.** —**anˈnexable** *adj.* —ˌannexˈation *n.*

annexe *or esp. U.S.* **annex** (ˈænɛks) *n.* **1. a.** an extension to a main building. **b.** a nearby building used as an addition to a main one. **2.** something added, esp. a supplement to a document.

annihilate (əˈnaɪəˌleɪt) *vb.* (*tr.*) **1.** to destroy completely; extinguish. **2.** *Inf.* to defeat totally, as in argument. —**anˌnihiˈlation** *n.* —**anˈnihiˌlator** *n.*

anniversary (ˌænɪˈvɜːsərɪ) *n., pl.* **-ries.** **1.** the date on which an event occurred in some previous year: *a wed-*

THESAURUS

angular bony, gaunt, lank, lanky, lean, rangy, rawboned, scrawny, skinny, spare

animal *n.* 1. beast, brute, creature 2. *Applied to a person* barbarian, beast, brute, monster, savage, wild man ~*adj.* 3. bestial, bodily, brutish, carnal, fleshly, gross, physical, sensual

animate *v.* 1. activate, embolden, encourage, energize, enliven, excite, fire, gladden, impel, incite, inspire, inspirit, instigate, invigorate, kindle, move, quicken, revive, rouse, spark, spur, stimulate, stir, urge, vitalize, vivify ~*adj.* 2. alive, breathing, live, living, moving 3. gay, lively, spirited, vivacious

animated active, airy, ardent, brisk, buoyant, dynamic, ebullient, elated, energetic, enthusiastic, excited, fervent, gay, lively, passionate, quick, spirited, sprightly, vibrant,

vigorous, vital, vivacious, vivid, zealous, zestful

animation action, activity, airiness, ardour, briskness, buoyancy, dynamism, ebullience, elation, energy, enthusiasm, excitement, exhilaration, fervour, gaiety, high spirits, life, liveliness, passion, pep, sparkle, spirit, sprightliness, verve, vibrancy, vigour, vitality, vivacity, zeal, zest, zing (*Inf.*)

animosity acrimony, animus, antagonism, antipathy, bad blood, bitterness, enmity, hate, hatred, hostility, ill will, malevolence, malice, malignity, rancour, resentment, virulence

annals accounts, archives, chronicles, history, journals, memorials, records, registers

annex 1. add, adjoin, affix, append, attach, connect, fasten, join, subjoin, tack, unite 2.

acquire, appropriate, arrogate, conquer, expropriate, occupy, seize, take over

annexation annexing, appropriation, arrogation, conquest, expropriation, occupation, seizure, takeover

annexe 1. ell, extension, supplementary building, wing 2. addendum, addition, adjunct, affix, appendix, attachment, supplement

annihilate abolish, destroy, eradicate, erase, exterminate, extinguish, extirpate, liquidate, nullify, obliterate, root out, wipe out

annihilation abolition, destruction, eradication, erasure, extermination, extinction, extinguishing, extirpation, liquidation, nullification, obliteration, rooting out, wiping out

ding anniversary. **2.** the celebration of this. *~adj.* **3.** of or relating to an anniversary.

annotate (ˈænəʊˌteɪt, ˈænə-) *vb.* to supply (a written work) with critical or explanatory notes. —ˌannoˈtation *n.* —ˈannotative *adj.* —ˈannoˌtator *n.*

announce (əˈnaʊns) *vb.* **1.** (*tr.; may take a clause as object*) to make known publicly. **2.** (*tr.*) to declare the arrival of: *to announce a guest.* **3.** (*tr.; may take a clause as object*) to presage: *the dark clouds announced rain.* **4.** (*intr.*) to work as an announcer, as on radio or television. —anˈnouncement *n.*

announcer (əˈnaʊnsə) *n.* a person who announces, esp. one who reads the news, etc., on radio or television.

annoy (əˈnɔɪ) *vb.* **1.** to irritate or displease. **2.** to harass with repeated attacks. —anˈnoyance *n.* —anˈnoyer *n.*

annual (ˈænjʊəl) *adj.* **1.** occurring, done, etc., once a year or every year; yearly: *an annual income.* **2.** lasting for a year: *an annual subscription.* *~n.* **3.** a plant that completes its life cycle in one year. **4.** a book, magazine, etc., published once every year. —ˈannually *adv.*

annuity (əˈnjuːɪtɪ) *n., pl.* **-ties.** a fixed sum payable at specified intervals over a period, such as the recipient's life, or in perpetuity, in return for a premium paid either in instalments or in a single payment.

annul (əˈnʌl) *vb.* **-nulling, -nulled.** (*tr.*) to make (something, esp. a law or marriage) void; abolish. —anˈnullable *adj.*

annular (ˈænjʊlə) *adj.* ring-shaped.

annular eclipse *n.* an eclipse of the sun in which the moon does not cover the entire disc of the sun, so that a ring of sunlight surrounds the darkened moon.

annulate (ˈænjʊlɪt, -ˌleɪt) *adj.* having, composed of, or marked with rings. —ˌannuˈlation *n.*

annulment (əˈnʌlmənt) *n.* **1.** a formal invalidation, as of a marriage, judicial proceeding, etc. **2.** the act of annulling.

annunciate (əˈnʌnsɪˌeɪt, -ʃɪ-) *vb.* (*tr.*) a less common word for **announce.**

Annunciation (əˌnʌnsɪˈeɪʃən) *n.* **1. the.** the announcement of the Incarnation by the angel Gabriel to the Virgin Mary (Luke 1:26–38). **2.** Also called: **Annunciation Day.** the festival commemorating this, on March 25 (Lady Day).

annunciator (əˈnʌnsɪˌeɪtə) *n.* **1.** a device that gives a visual indication as to which of a number of electric circuits has operated, such as an indicator showing in which room a bell has been rung. **2.** a device giving an audible signal indicating the position of a train. **3.** an announcer.

anode (ˈænəʊd) *n.* **1.** the positive electrode in an electrolytic cell or in an electronic valve or tube. **2.** the negative terminal of a primary cell. Cf. **cathode.** —**anodal** (eɪˈnəʊdəl) *or* **anodic** (əˈnɒdɪk) *adj.*

anodize *or* **-dise** (ˈænəˌdaɪz) *vb.* to coat (a metal, such as aluminium) with a protective oxide film by electrolysis.

anodyne (ˈænəˌdaɪn) *n.* **1.** a drug that relieves pain. **2.** anything that alleviates mental distress. *~adj.* **3.** capable of relieving pain or distress.

anoint (əˈnɔɪnt) *vb.* (*tr.*) **1.** to smear or rub over with oil. **2.** to apply oil to as a sign of consecration or sanctification. —aˈnointer *n.* —aˈnointment *n.*

anomalous (əˈnɒmələs) *adj.* deviating from the normal or usual order, type, etc. —aˈnomalousness *n.*

anomaly (əˈnɒməlɪ) *n., pl.* **-lies.** **1.** something anomalous. **2.** deviation from the normal; irregularity. **3.** *Astron.* the angle between a planet, the sun, and the previous perihelion of the planet.

anomie *or* **anomy** (ˈænəʊmɪ) *n. Sociol.* lack of social or moral standards in an individual or society. —**anomic** (əˈnɒmɪk) *adj.*

anon (əˈnɒn) *adv. Arch. or literary.* **1.** soon. **2.** ever and anon. now and then.

anon. *abbrev. for* anonymous.

anonym (ˈænənɪm) *n.* **1.** a less common word for **pseudonym.** **2.** an anonymous person or publication.

anonymous (əˈnɒnɪməs) *adj.* **1.** from or by a person, author, etc., whose name is unknown or withheld. **2.** having no known name. **3.** lacking individual characteristics. —**anonymity** (ˌænəˈnɪmɪtɪ) *n.*

anorak (ˈænəˌræk) *n.* a warm waterproof hip-length jacket usually with a hood.

anorexia (ˌænɒˈrɛksɪə) *n.* loss of appetite.

anorexia nervosa (nɜːˈvəʊsə) *n.* a psychological disorder characterized by fear of becoming fat and refusal of food, leading to debility and even death.

another (əˈnʌðə) *determiner.* **1. a.** one more: *another chance.* **b.** (*as pronoun*): *help yourself to another.* **2. a.** a different: *another era from ours.* **b.** (*as pronoun*): *to try one, then another.* **3. a.** a different example of the same sort. **b.** (*as pronoun*): *we got rid of one, but I think this is another.*

A.N. Other *n. Brit.* an unnamed person: used in team lists, etc., to indicate a place that remains to be filled.

anserine (ˈænsəˌraɪn) *adj.* of or resembling a goose.

answer (ˈɑːnsə) *n.* **1.** a reply, either spoken or written, as to a question, request, letter, or article. **2.** a reaction or response: *drunkenness was his answer to disappointment.* **3.** a solution, esp. of a mathematical problem. *~vb.* **4.** (when *tr., may take a clause as object*) to reply or respond (to) by word or act: *to answer a question; to answer the door.* **5.** (*tr.*) to reply correctly to; solve: *I could answer only three questions.* **6.** (*intr.*; usually foll. by *to*) to respond or react: *the steering answers to the slightest touch.* **7. a.** (when *intr.*, often foll. by *for*) to meet the requirements (of); be satisfactory (for): *this will answer his needs.* **b.** to be responsible (to a person or for a thing). **8.** (when *intr.*, foll. by *to*) to match or corre-

---

THESAURUS

annotate commentate, comment on, elucidate, explain, footnote, gloss, illustrate, interpret, make observations, note

annotation comment, commentary, elucidation, exegesis, explanation, explication, footnote, gloss, illustration, interpretation, note, observation

announce 1. advertise, broadcast, declare, disclose, divulge, give out, intimate, make known, proclaim, promulgate, propound, publish, report, reveal, tell 2. augur, betoken, foretell, harbinger, herald, portend, presage, signal, signify

announcement advertisement, broadcast, bulletin, communiqué, declaration, disclosure, divulgence, intimation, proclamation, promulgation, publication, report, revelation, statement

announcer anchor man, broadcaster, commentator, master of ceremonies, newscaster, news reader, reporter

annoy anger, badger, bedevil, bore, bother, bug (*Inf.*), displease, disturb, exasperate, gall, get (*Inf.*), harass, harry, incommode, irk, irritate, madden, molest, needle (*Inf.*), nettle, peeve, pester, plague, provoke, rile, ruffle, tease, trouble, vex

annoyance 1. aggravation, anger, be-

devilment, bother, displeasure, disturbance, exasperation, harassment, irritation, nuisance, provocation, trouble, vexation 2. bind (*Inf.*), bore, bother, nuisance, pain (*Inf.*), pain in the neck (*Inf.*), pest, plague, tease

annoying aggravating, bedevilling, boring, bothersome, displeasing, disturbing, exasperating, galling, harassing, irksome, irritating, maddening, peeving (*Inf.*), provoking, teasing, troublesome, vexatious

annual once a year, yearlong, yearly

annually by the year, each year, every year, once a year, per annum, per year, year after year, yearly

annul abolish, abrogate, cancel, countermand, declare *or* render null and void, invalidate, negate, nullify, recall, repeal, rescind, retract, reverse, revoke, void

annulment abolition, abrogation, cancellation, countermanding, invalidation, negation, nullification, recall, repeal, rescindment, rescission, retraction, reversal, revocation, voiding

anodyne 1. *n.* analgesic, narcotic, painkiller, painreliever, palliative 2. *adj.* analgesic, deadening, dulling, narcotic, numbing, pain-killing, pain-relieving, palliative

anoint 1. daub, embrocate, grease, oil, rub,

smear, spread over 2. anele (*Archaic*), bless, consecrate, hallow, sanctify

anomalous aberrant, abnormal, atypical, bizarre, deviating, eccentric, exceptional, incongruous, inconsistent, irregular, odd, peculiar, rare, unusual

anomaly aberration, abnormality, departure, deviation, eccentricity, exception, incongruity, inconsistency, irregularity, oddity, peculiarity, rarity

anon before long, betimes (*Archaic*), erelong (*Archaic*), forthwith, presently, promptly, shortly, soon

anonymous 1. incognito, innominate, nameless, unacknowledged, unattested, unauthenticated, uncredited, unidentified, unknown, unnamed, unsigned 2. characterless, nondescript, unexceptional

answer *n.* 1. acknowledgment, comeback, defence, explanation, plea, reaction, refutation, rejoinder, reply, report, resolution, response, retort, return, riposte, solution, vindication *~v.* 2. acknowledge, explain, react, refute, rejoin, reply, resolve, respond, retort, return, solve 3. conform, correlate, correspond, do, fill, fit, fulfil, measure up, meet, pass, qualify, satisfy, serve, suffice, suit, work

spond (esp. in **answer** (or **answer to**) **the description**). **9.** (*tr.*) to give a defence or refutation.

answerable ('ɑːnsərəbəl) *adj.* **1.** (*postpositive;* foll. by *for* or *to*) responsible or accountable: *answerable to one's boss.* **2.** able to be answered.

answer back *vb.* (*adv.*) to reply rudely to (a person, esp. someone in authority) when one is expected to remain silent.

ant (ænt) *n.* **1.** a small social insect of a widely distributed hymenopterous family, typically living in highly organized colonies of winged males, wingless sterile females (workers), and fertile females (queens). Related *adj.*: **formic.** **2.** **white ant.** another name for a **termite.**

-ant *suffix forming adjectives and nouns.* causing or performing an action or existing in a certain condition: *pleasant; deodorant; servant.*

antacid (ænt'æsɪd) *n.* **1.** a substance used to treat acidity, esp. in the stomach. ~*adj.* **2.** having the properties of this substance.

antagonism (æn'tægə‚nɪzəm) *n.* **1.** openly expressed and usually mutual opposition. **2.** the inhibiting or nullifying action of one substance or organism on another.

antagonist (æn'tægənɪst) *n.* **1.** an opponent or adversary. **2.** any muscle that opposes the action of another. **3.** a drug that counteracts the effects of another drug. —**an‚tago'nistic** *adj.* —**an‚tago'nistically** *adv.*

antagonize *or* **-nise** (æn'tægə‚naɪz) *vb.* (*tr.*) **1.** to make hostile; annoy or irritate. **2.** to act in opposition to or counteract. —**an‚tagoni'zation** *or* **-ni'sation** *n.*

antalkali (ænt'ælkə‚laɪ) *n., pl.* **-lis** *or* **-lies.** a substance that neutralizes alkalis.

Antarctic (ænt'ɑːktɪk) *adj.* of or relating to the south polar regions.

Antarctic Circle *n.* the imaginary circle around the earth, parallel to the equator, at latitude 66° 32′ S.

ant bear *n.* another name for **aardvark** or giant **anteater.**

ante ('æntɪ) *n.* **1.** the gaming stake put up before the deal in poker by the players. **2.** *Inf.* a sum of money representing a person's share, as in a syndicate. ~*vb.* **-teing, -ted** *or* **-teed. 3.** to place (one's stake) in poker. **4.** (usually foll. by *up*) *Inf.* to pay.

ante- *prefix.* before in time or position: *antedate; antechamber.*

anteater ('ænt‚iːtə) *n.* any of several toothless mammals having a long tubular snout used for eating termites.

antecede (‚æntɪ'siːd) *vb.* (*tr.*) to go before; precede. —**‚ante'cedence** *n.*

antecedent (‚æntɪ'siːdənt) *n.* **1.** an event, etc., that happens before another. **2.** *Grammar.* a word or phrase to which a pronoun refers. In "People who live in glass houses shouldn't throw stones," *people* is the antecedent of *who.* **3.** *Logic.* the first proposition in a conditional. ~*adj.* **4.** preceding in time or order; prior.

antecedents (‚æntɪ'siːdənts) *pl. n.* **1.** ancestry. **2.** a person's past history.

antechamber ('æntɪ‚tʃeɪmbə) *n.* an anteroom.

antedate ('æntɪ‚deɪt) *vb.* (*tr.*) **1.** to be or occur at an earlier date than. **2.** to affix or assign a date to (a document, event, etc.) that is earlier than the actual date. **3.** to cause to occur sooner. ~*n.* **4.** an earlier date.

antediluvian (‚æntɪdɪ'luːvɪən) *adj.* **1.** belonging to the ages before the biblical Flood. **2.** old-fashioned. ~*n.* **3.** an antediluvian person or thing.

antelope ('æntɪ‚ləup) *n., pl.* **-lopes** *or* **-lope.** any of a group of mammals of Africa and Asia. They are typically graceful, having long legs and horns, and include the gazelles, springbok, impala, and dik-diks.

ante meridiem ('æntɪ mə'rɪdɪəm) the full form of **a.m.**

antenatal (‚æntɪ'neɪtəl) *adj.* occurring or present before birth; during pregnancy.

antenna (æn'tɛnə) *n.* **1.** (*pl.* **-nae** (-niː)). one of a pair of mobile appendages on the heads of insects, crustaceans, etc., that often respond to touch and taste but may be specialized for swimming. **2.** (*pl.* **-nas**) an aerial. —**an'tennal** *or* **an'tennary** *adj.*

antenuptial contract (‚æntɪ'nʌpʃəl) *n.* (in South Africa) a marriage contract effected prior to the wedding giving each partner control over his or her property.

antepenult (‚æntɪpɪ'nʌlt) *n.* the third last syllable in a word.

antepenultimate (‚æntɪpɪ'nʌltɪmɪt) *adj.* **1.** third from last. ~*n.* **2.** anything that is third from last.

anterior (æn'tɪərɪə) *adj.* **1.** at or towards the front. **2.** earlier. **3.** *Zool.* of or near the head end. **4.** *Bot.* (of part of a flower or leaf) farthest away from the main stem.

anteroom ('æntɪ‚ruːm, -‚rum) *n.* a room giving entrance to a larger room, often used as a waiting room.

anthem ('ænθəm) *n.* **1.** a song of loyalty or devotion: *a national anthem.* **2.** a musical composition for a choir, usually set to words from the Bible. **3.** a religious chant sung antiphonally.

anther ('ænθə) *n.* the terminal part of a stamen consisting of two lobes each containing two sacs in which the pollen matures.

ant hill *n.* a mound of soil, leaves, etc., near the entrance of an ants' nest, deposited there by the ants while constructing the nest.

anthology (æn'θolədʒɪ) *n., pl.* **-gies. 1.** a collection of literary passages, esp. poems, by various authors. **2.** any printed collection of literary pieces, songs, etc. —**an'thologist** *n.* —**an'tholo‚gize** *or* **-‚gise** *vb.*

anthracene ('ænθrə‚siːn) *n.* a colourless crystalline solid, used in the manufacture of chemicals and as crystals in scintillation counters.

anthracite ('ænθrə‚saɪt) *n.* a hard coal that burns slowly with a nonluminous flame giving out intense heat. Also called: **hard coal.** —**anthracitic** (‚ænθrə'sɪtɪk) *adj.*

anthrax ('ænθræks) *n., pl.* **-thraces** (-θrə‚siːz). **1.** a highly infectious bacterial disease of animals, esp. cattle and sheep, which can be transmitted to man. **2.** a pustule caused by this disease.

anthropo- *combining form.* indicating man or human: *anthropology.*

anthropocentric (‚ænθrəpəu'sɛntrɪk) *adj.* regarding man as the central factor in the universe.

anthropoid ('ænθrə‚pɔɪd) *adj.* **1.** resembling man. **2.** resembling an ape; apelike. ~*n.* **3.** any primate of the suborder *Anthropoidea,* including monkeys, apes, and man.

anthropology (‚ænθrə'polədʒɪ) *n.* the study of man, his origins, institutions, religious beliefs, social relationships, etc. —**anthropological** (‚ænθrəpə'lodʒɪkəl) *adj.* —**‚anthro'pologist** *n.*

anthropomorphism (‚ænθrəpə'mɔːfɪzəm) *n.* the attribution of human form or behaviour to a deity, animal, etc.

anthropomorphous (‚ænθrəpə'mɔːfəs) *adj.* shaped like a human being.

THESAURUS

answerable 1. accountable, amenable, chargeable, liable, responsible, subject, to blame 2. explainable, refutable, resolvable, solvable

answer back argue, be cheeky, be impertinent, cheek (*Inf.*), contradict, disagree, dispute, rebut, retort, talk back

answer for 1. be accountable for, be answerable for, be chargeable for, be liable for, be responsible for, be to blame for, take the rap for (*Sl.*) 2. atone for, make amends for, pay for, suffer for

answer to 1. be accountable to, be answerable to, be responsible to, be ruled by, obey 2. agree, confirm, correspond, fit, match, meet

antagonism antipathy, competition,

conflict, contention, discord, dissension, friction, hostility, opposition, rivalry

antagonist adversary, competitor, contender, enemy, foe, opponent, opposer, rival

antagonistic adverse, antipathetic, at odds, at variance, averse, conflicting, contentious, hostile, ill-disposed, incompatible, in dispute, inimical, opposed, unfriendly

antagonize 1. alienate, anger, annoy, disaffect, estrange, insult, irritate, offend, repel, rub (someone) up the wrong way (*Inf.*) 2. contend with, counteract, neutralize, oppose, struggle with, work against

antecedent anterior, earlier, foregoing, former, preceding, precursory, preliminary, previous, prior

antecedents 1. ancestors, ancestry,

blood, descent, extraction, family, forebears, forefathers, genealogy, line, progenitors, stock 2. background, history, past

antediluvian 1. prehistoric, primeval, primitive, primordial 2. ancient, antiquated, antique, archaic, obsolete, old-fashioned, out-of-date, out of the ark (*Inf.*), passé

anteroom antechamber, foyer, lobby, outer room, reception room, vestibule, waiting room

anthem 1. canticle, chant, chorale, hymn, psalm 2. paean, song of praise

anthology analects, choice, collection, compendium, compilation, digest, garland, miscellany, selection, treasury

anti ('ænti) *Inf.* ~*adj.* **1.** opposed to a party, policy, attitude, etc.: *he won't join because he is rather anti.* ~*n.* **2.** an opponent.

anti- *prefix.* **1.** against; opposing: *anticlerical.* **2.** opposite to: *anticlimax.* **3.** rival; false: *antipope.* **4.** counteracting or neutralizing: *antifreeze; antihistamine.* **5.** designating the antiparticle of the particle specified: *antineutron.*

anti-aircraft (,ænti'ɛəkrɑːft) *n.* (*modifier*) of or relating to defence against aircraft attack: *anti-aircraft batteries.*

antiballistic missile (,æntibə'listik) *n.* a ballistic missile designed to destroy another ballistic missile in flight.

antibiosis (,æntibai'əusis) *n.* an association between two organisms, esp. microorganisms, that is harmful to one of them.

antibiotic (,æntibai'ɒtik) *n.* **1.** any of various chemical substances, such as penicillin, produced by microorganisms, esp. fungi, or made synthetically, and capable of destroying microorganisms, esp. bacteria. ~*adj.* **2.** of or relating to antibiotics.

antibody ('ænti,bɒdi) *n., pl.* -**bodies.** any of various proteins produced in the blood in response to an antigen. It combines with the antigen, rendering it harmless.

antic ('æntik) *Arch.* ~*n.* **1.** an actor in a ludicrous or grotesque part; clown. ~*adj.* **2.** fantastic; grotesque.

Antichrist ('ænti,kraist) *n.* **1.** *Bible.* the antagonist of Christ, expected by early Christians to appear and reign over the world until overthrown at Christ's Second Coming. **2.** (*sometimes not cap.*) an enemy of Christ or Christianity.

anticipate (æn'tisi,peit) *vb.* (*mainly tr.*) **1.** (*may take a clause as object*) to regard as likely; expect. **2.** (*may take a clause as object*) to foresee and act in advance of; forestall: *I anticipated his punch.* **3.** (*also intr.*) to mention (something) before its proper time: *don't anticipate the climax of the story.* **4.** to make use of in advance of possession: *he anticipated his salary in buying a house.* —**an'tici,pator** *n.* —**an'ticipative** *or* **an'ticipatory** *adj.*

anticipation (æn,tisi'peiʃən) *n.* **1.** the act of anticipating; expectation, premonition, or foresight. **2.** *Music.* an unstressed, usually short note introduced before a downbeat.

anticlerical (,ænti'klerikəl) *adj.* **1.** opposed to the power and influence of the clergy, esp. in politics. ~*n.* **2.** a supporter of an anticlerical party. —,**anti'clericalism** *n.*

anticlimax (,ænti'klaimæks) *n.* **1.** a disappointing or ineffective conclusion to a series of events, etc. **2.** a sudden change from a serious subject to one that is disappointing or ludicrous. —**anticlimactic** (,æntiklai-'mæktik) *adj.*

anticline ('ænti,klain) *n.* a formation of stratified rock raised up, by folding, into a broad arch so that the strata slope down on both sides from a common crest. —,**anti'clinal** *adj.*

anticlockwise (,ænti'klɒk,waiz) *adv., adj.* in the opposite direction to the rotation of the hands of a clock. U.S. equivalent: **counterclockwise.**

anticoagulant (,æntikəu'ægjulənt) *adj.* **1.** acting to prevent or retard coagulation, esp. of blood. ~*n.* **2.** an agent that prevents or retards coagulation.

antics ('æntiks) *pl. n.* absurd acts or postures.

anticyclone (,ænti'saikləun) *n. Meteorol.* a body of moving air of higher pressure than the surrounding air, in which the pressure decreases away from the centre. Also called: **high.** —**anticyclonic** (,æntisai'klɒnik) *adj.*

antidepressant (,æntidi'presənt) *n.* **1.** any of a class of drugs used to alleviate depression. ~*adj.* **2.** of this class of drugs.

antidote ('ænti,dəut) *n.* **1.** *Med.* a drug or agent that counteracts or neutralizes the effects of a poison. **2.**

anything that counteracts or relieves a harmful condition. —,**anti'dotal** *adj.*

antifreeze ('ænti,friːz) *n.* a liquid, usually ethylene glycol (ethanediol), added to water to lower its freezing point, esp. for use in an internal-combustion engine.

antigen ('æntidʒən, -,dʒen) *n.* a substance, such as a toxin produced by a bacteruim, that stimulates antibodies.

antihero ('ænti,hiərəu) *n., pl.* -**roes.** a central character in a novel, play, etc., who lacks the traditional heroic virtues.

antihistamine (,ænti'histə,miːn, -min) *n.* any drug that neutralizes the effects of histamine, used esp. in the treatment of allergies.

antiknock (,ænti'nɒk) *n.* a compound, such as lead tetraethyl, added to petrol to reduce knocking in the engine.

antilogarithm (,ænti'lɒgə,riðəm) *n.* a number whose logarithm is the given number: *100 is the antilogarithm of 2.* Often shortened to **antilog.** —,**anti,loga'rithmic** *adj.*

antimacassar (,æntimə'kæsə) *n.* a cloth covering the back and arms of chairs, etc., to prevent soiling.

antimagnetic (,æntimæg'netik) *adj.* of a material that does not acquire permanent magnetism when exposed to a magnetic field.

antimatter ('ænti,mætə) *n.* a hypothetical form of matter composed of antiparticles.

antimissile (,ænti'misail) *adj.* **1.** relating to defensive measures against missile attack: *an antimissile system.* ~*n.* **2.** a defensive missile used to intercept and destroy attacking missiles.

antimony ('æntiməni) *n.* a toxic metallic element that exists in two allotropic forms and is added to alloys to increase their strength and hardness. Symbol: Sb; atomic no.: 51; atomic wt.: 121.75. —**antimonial** (,ænti'məuniəl) *adj.*

antinomian (,ænti'nəumiən) *adj.* **1.** relating to the doctrine that by faith a Christian is released from the obligation of adhering to any moral law. ~*n.* **2.** a member of a Christian sect holding such a doctrine. —,**anti'nomianism** *n.*

antinomy (æn'tinəmi) *n., pl.* -**mies.** **1.** opposition of one law, principle, or rule to another. **2.** *Philosophy.* contradiction existing between two apparently indubitable propositions. —**antinomic** (,ænti'nɒmik) *adj.*

antinovel ('ænti,nɒvəl) *n.* a type of prose fiction in which conventional or traditional novelistic elements are rejected.

antiparticle ('ænti,pɑːtikəl) *n.* any of a group of elementary particles that have the same mass as their corresponding particle but have a charge of equal magnitude but opposite sign. When a particle collides with its antiparticle mutual annihilation occurs.

antipasto (,ænti'pɑːstəu, -'pæs-) *n., pl.* -**tos.** a course of hors d'oeuvres in an Italian meal.

antipathy (æn'tipəθi) *n., pl.* -**thies.** **1.** a feeling of dislike, or hostility. **2.** the object of such a feeling. —**antipathetic** (æn,tipə'θetik, ,æntipə-) *adj.*

antipersonnel (,ænti,pɜːsə'nel) *adj.* (of weapons, etc.) designed to cause casualties to personnel rather than to destroy equipment.

antiperspirant (,ænti'pɜːspərənt) *n.* **1.** a substance applied to the skin to reduce or prevent perspiration. ~*adj.* **2.** reducing perspiration.

antiphon ('æntifən) *n.* **1.** a short passage, usually from the Bible, recited or sung as a response after certain parts of a liturgical service. **2.** a psalm, hymn, etc., chanted or sung in alternate parts. **3.** any response. —**antiphonal** (æn'tifənəl) *adj.* —**an'tiphony** *n.*

antipodes (æn'tipə,diːz) *pl. n.* **1.** either or both of two places that are situated diametrically opposite one another on the earth's surface. **2.** the people who live

---

THESAURUS

anticipate 1. apprehend, await, count upon, expect, forecast, foresee, foretell, hope for, look for, look forward to, predict, prepare for 2. antedate, beat (someone) to it (*Inf.*), forestall, intercept, prevent
anticipation apprehension, awaiting, expectancy, expectation, foresight, foretaste, forethought, hope, preconception, premonition, prescience, presentiment
anticlimax bathos, comedown (*Inf.*),

disappointment, letdown
antics buffoonery, capers, clowning, escapades, foolishness, frolics, larks, mischief, monkey tricks, playfulness, pranks, silliness, skylarking, stunts, tomfoolery, tricks
antidote antitoxin, antivenin, corrective, counteragent, countermeasure, cure, neutralizer, preventive, remedy, specific
antipathetic abhorrent, antagonistic, averse, disgusting, distasteful, hateful, hos-

tile, incompatible, invidious, loathsome, obnoxious, odious, offensive, repellent, repugnant, repulsive, revolting

antipathy abhorrence, animosity, animus, antagonism, aversion, bad blood, contrariety, disgust, dislike, distaste, enmity, hatred, hostility, ill will, incompatibility, loathing, opposition, rancour, repugnance, repulsion

there. **3.** (*often cap.*) **the.** Australia and New Zealand. —**antipodean** (æn‚tɪpə'diːən) *adj.*

antipope ('æntɪ‚pəʊp) *n.* a rival pope elected in opposition to one who has been canonically chosen.

antipyretic (‚æntɪpaɪ'rɛtɪk) *adj.* **1.** preventing or alleviating fever. ~*n.* **2.** an antipyretic remedy or drug.

antiquarian (‚æntɪ'kwɛərɪən) *adj.* **1.** concerned with the study of antiquities or antiques. ~*n.* **2.** a less common name for **antiquary.** —‚anti'quarianism *n.*

antiquary ('æntɪkwərɪ) *n., pl.* **-quaries.** a person who collects, deals in, or studies antiques or ancient works of art. Also called: **antiquarian.**

antiquate ('æntɪ‚kweɪt) *vb.* (*tr.*) to make obsolete or old-fashioned. —'anti‚quated *adj.*

antique (æn'tiːk) *n.* **1. a.** a decorative object, piece of furniture, or other work of art created in an earlier period, that is valued for its beauty, workmanship, and age. **b.** (*as modifier*): *an antique shop.* **2.** any object made in an earlier period. **3. the.** the style of ancient art, esp. Greek or Roman. ~*adj.* **4.** made in or in the style of an earlier period. **5.** of or belonging to the distant past, esp. of ancient Greece or Rome. **6.** *Inf.* old-fashioned. **7.** *Arch.* aged or venerable. ~*vb.* **8.** (*tr.*) to give an antique appearance to.

antiquities (æn'tɪkwɪtɪz) *pl. n.* remains or relics, such as statues, buildings, or coins, that date from ancient times.

antiquity (æn'tɪkwɪtɪ) *n., pl.* **-ties. 1.** the quality of being ancient: *a vase of great antiquity.* **2.** the far distant past, esp. preceding the Middle Ages. **3.** the people of ancient times collectively.

antirrhinum (‚æntɪ'raɪnəm) *n.* any plant of the genus *Antirrhinum,* esp. the snapdragon, which has two-lipped flowers of various colours.

antiscorbutic (‚æntɪskɔː'bjuːtɪk) *adj.* **1.** preventing or curing scurvy. ~*n.* **2.** an antiscorbutic agent.

anti-Semite *n.* a person who persecutes or discriminates against Jews. —‚anti-Se'mitic *adj.* —‚anti-'Semitism *n.*

antisepsis (‚æntɪ'sɛpsɪs) *n.* **1.** destruction of undesirable microorganisms, such as those that cause disease or putrefaction. **2.** the state of being free from such microorganisms.

antiseptic (‚æntɪ'sɛptɪk) *adj.* **1.** of or producing antisepsis. **2.** entirely free from contamination. **3.** *Inf.* lacking spirit or excitement. ~*n.* **4.** an antiseptic agent. —‚anti'septically *adv.*

antiserum (‚æntɪ'sɪərəm) *n., pl.* **-rums** or **-ra** (-rə). blood serum containing antibodies against a specific antigen, used to treat or provide immunity to a disease.

antisocial (‚æntɪ'səʊʃəl) *adj.* **1.** avoiding the company of other people; unsociable. **2.** contrary or injurious to the interests of society in general.

antispasmodic (‚æntɪspæz'mɒdɪk) *adj.* **1.** preventing or arresting spasms. ~*n.* **2.** an antispasmodic drug.

antistatic (‚æntɪ'stætɪk) *adj.* (of a substance, textile, etc.) retaining sufficient moisture to provide a conducting path, thus avoiding the effects of static electricity.

antitank (‚æntɪ'tæŋk) *adj.* designed to immobilize or destroy armoured vehicles.

antithesis (æn'tɪθɪsɪs) *n., pl.* **-ses** (-‚siːz). **1.** the exact opposite. **2.** contrast or opposition. **3.** *Rhetoric.* the juxtaposition of contrasting ideas or words so as to produce an effect of balance, such as *my words fly up, my thoughts remain below.* —**antithetical** (‚æntɪ'θɛtɪkəl) *adj.*

antitoxin (‚æntɪ'tɒksɪn) *n.* **1.** an antibody that neutralizes a toxin. **2.** blood serum that contains a specific anti-body. —‚anti'toxic *adj.*

antitrades ('æntɪ‚treɪdz) *pl. n.* winds in the upper atmosphere blowing in the opposite direction from and above the trade winds.

antitrust (‚æntɪ'trʌst) *n.* (*modifier*) *Chiefly U.S.* regulating or opposing trusts, monopolies, cartels, or similar organizations.

antitype ('æntɪ‚taɪp) *n.* **1.** a person or thing that is foreshadowed or represented by a type or symbol. **2.** an opposite type. —‚anti'typical *adj.*

antler ('æntlə) *n.* one of a pair of bony outgrowths on the heads of male deer and some related species of either sex. —'antlered *adj.*

antonym ('æntənɪm) *n.* a word that means the opposite of another. —**antonymous** (æn'tɒnɪməs) *adj.*

antrum ('æntrəm) *n., pl.* **-tra** (-trə). *Anat.* a natural cavity, hollow, or sinus, esp. in a bone. —'antral *adj.*

anuresis (‚ænjʊ'riːsɪs) *n.* inability to urinate.

anus ('eɪnəs) *n.* the excretory opening at the end of the alimentary canal.

anvil ('ænvɪl) *n.* **1.** a heavy iron or steel block on which metals are hammered during forging. **2.** any part having a similar shape or function, such as the lower part of a telegraph key.

anxiety (æŋ'zaɪɪtɪ) *n., pl.* **-ties. 1.** a state of uneasiness or tension caused by apprehension of possible misfortune, danger, etc. **2.** intense desire; eagerness. **3.** *Psychol.* an intense state of apprehension occurring in a variety of nervous disorders.

anxious ('æŋkʃəs, 'æŋʃəs) *adj.* **1.** worried and tense because of possible misfortune, danger, etc. **2.** causing anxiety; worrying; distressing: *an anxious time.* **3.** intensely desirous: *anxious for promotion.* —'anxiously *adv.* —'anxiousness *n.*

any ('ɛnɪ) *determiner.* **1. a.** one, some, or several, as specified, no matter how much, what kind, etc.: *you may take any clothes you like.* **b.** (*as pronoun; functioning as sing. or pl.*): *take any you like.* **2.** (*usually used with a negative*) **a.** even the smallest amount or even one: *I can't stand any noise.* **b.** (*as pronoun; functioning as sing. or pl.*): *don't give her any.* **3.** whatever or whichever: *any dictionary will do.* **4.** an indefinite or unlimited: *any number of friends.* ~*adv.* **5.** (*usually used with a negative*) (foll. by a comparative adj.) to even the smallest extent: *it isn't any worse.*

▷ **Usage.** Educated speakers and writers avoid using *any* for *at all* in formal English: *a translation would not help at all* (not *would not help any*.)

anybody ('ɛnɪ‚bɒdɪ) *pron.* **1.** any person; anyone. **2.** (*usually used with a negative or a question*) a person of any importance: *he isn't anybody.* ~*n., pl.* **-bodies. 3.** (often preceded by *just*) any person at random.

anyhow ('ɛnɪ‚haʊ) *adv.* **1.** in any case. **2.** by any means whatever. **3.** carelessly.

any more or esp. *U.S.* **anymore** *adv.* any longer; still; nowadays.

anyone ('ɛnɪ‚wʌn) *pron.* **1.** any person; anybody. **2.** (*used with a negative or a question*) a person of any importance: *is he anyone?* **3.** (often preceded by *just*) any person at random.

anything ('ɛnɪ‚θɪŋ) *pron.* **1.** any object, event, action, etc., whatever: *anything might happen.* ~*n.* **2.** a thing of any kind: *have you anything to declare?* ~*adv.* **3.** in any way: *he wasn't anything like his father.* **4. anything but.** not in the least: *she was anything but happy.* **5. like anything.** (intensifier): *he ran like anything.*

anyway ('ɛnɪ‚weɪ) *adv.* **1.** in any case; at any rate; nevertheless. **2.** in a careless manner. **3.** Usually **any**

THESAURUS

antiquated 1. antediluvian, antique, archaic, dated, obsolete, old-fashioned, old hat, outmoded, out-of-date, outworn, passé **2.** aged, ancient, elderly, hoary, old, superannuated

antique *adj.* **1.** aged, ancient, elderly, old, superannuated **2.** archaic, obsolete, old-fashioned, outdated **3.** antiquarian, classic, olden, vintage ~*n.* **4.** bygone, heirloom, object of virtu, relic

antiquity 1. age, ancientness, elderliness, old age, oldness **2.** ancient times, distant past, olden days, time immemorial **3.** antique, relic, ruin

antiseptic 1. *adj.* aseptic, clean, germ-free, hygienic, pure, sanitary, sterile, uncontaminated, unpolluted **2.** *n.* bactericide, disinfectant, germicide, purifier

antisocial 1. alienated, asocial, misanthropic, reserved, retiring, uncommunicative, unfriendly, unsociable, withdrawn **2.** antagonistic, belligerent, disorderly, disruptive, hostile, menacing, rebellious

antithesis 1. antipode, contrary, contrast, converse, inverse, opposite, reverse **2.** contradiction, contraposition, contrariety, contrast, inversion, opposition, reversal

anxiety angst, apprehension, care, con-

cern, disquiet, disquietude, distress, foreboding, fretfulness, misgiving, nervousness, restlessness, solicitude, suspense, tension, unease, uneasiness, watchfulness, worry

anxious 1. apprehensive, careful, concerned, disquieted, distressed, disturbed, fearful, fretful, in suspense, nervous, overwrought, restless, solicitous, taut, tense, troubled, uneasy, unquiet (*Chiefly literary*), watchful, worried **2.** ardent, avid, desirous, eager, expectant, impatient, intent, itching, keen, yearning

way. in any manner.
anywhere ('ɛnɪ,wɛə) adv. 1. in, at, or to any place. 2. **get anywhere**. to be successful.
anywise ('ɛnɪ,waɪz) adv. Chiefly U.S. in any way.
Anzac ('ænzæk) n. 1. Austral. & N.Z. (in World War I) a soldier serving with the Australian and New Zealand Army Corps. 2. Brit. any Australian or New Zealand soldier. 3. the Anzac landing at Gallipoli in 1915.
a.o.b. or **A.O.B.** abbrev. for any other business.
aorist ('eɪərɪst, 'ɛɔrɪst) n. Grammar. a tense of the verb esp. in classical Greek, indicating past action without reference to whether the action involved was momentary or continuous.
aorta (eɪ'ɔːtə) n., pl. **-tas** or **-tae** (-tiː). the main vessel in the arterial network, which conveys oxygen-rich blood from the heart. —**a'ortic** or **a'ortal** adj.
apace (ə'peɪs) adv. quickly; rapidly.
apache (ə'pæʃ) n. a Parisian gangster or ruffian.
Apache (ə'pætʃi) n. 1. (pl. **Apaches** or **Apache**) a member of a North American Indian people inhabiting the southwestern U.S. and N Mexico. 2. the language of this people.
apart (ə'pɑːt) adj. (postpositive), adv. 1. to or in pieces: he had the television apart. 2. placed or kept separately or for a particular purpose, etc.; aside (esp. in **set** or **put apart**). 3. separate in time, place, or position: he stood apart from the group. 4. not being taken into account: these difficulties apart, the project ran smoothly. 5. individual; distinct: a race apart. 6. separately or independently: considered apart, his reasoning was faulty. 7. **apart from**. (prep.) besides. ~See also **take apart**, **tell apart**.
apartheid (ə'pɑːthaɪt, -heɪt) n. (in South Africa) the official government policy of racial segregation.
apartment (ə'pɑːtmənt) n. 1. (often pl.) any room in a building, usually one of several forming a suite, used as living accommodation, offices, etc. 2. **a.** another name (esp. U.S.) for **flat²** (sense 1). **b.** (as modifier): apartment house.
apathy ('æpəθɪ) n. 1. absence of interest in or enthusiasm for things generally considered interesting or moving. 2. absence of emotion. —**apathetic** (,æpə'θɛtɪk) adj.
apatite ('æpə,taɪt) n. a common naturally occurring mineral consisting basically of calcium fluorophosphate. It is a source of phosphorus and is used in fertilizers.
ape (eɪp) n. 1. any of various primates in which the tail is very short or absent. 2. (not in technical use) any monkey. 3. an imitator; mimic. ~vb. 4. (tr.) to imitate. —**'ape,like** adj.
A.P.E.C. Canad. abbrev. for Atlantic Provinces Economic Council.
apeman n., pl. **-men**. any of various extinct apelike primates thought to have been the forerunners of modern man.
aperient (ə'pɪərɪənt) Med. ~adj. 1. laxative. ~n. 2. a mild laxative.
aperiodic (,eɪpɪərɪ'ɒdɪk) adj. 1. not periodic; not occurring at regular intervals. 2. Physics. **a.** (of a system or instrument) being damped sufficiently to reach equilibrium without oscillation. **b.** (of an oscillation or vibration) not having a regular period. —**aperiodicity** (,eɪpɪərɪə'dɪsɪtɪ) n.
apéritif (ə,pɛrɪ'tiːf) n. an alcoholic drink before a meal to whet the appetite.

aperture ('æpətʃə) n. 1. a hole; opening. 2. Physics. a usually circular and often variable opening in an optical instrument or device that controls the quantity of radiation entering or leaving it.
apex ('eɪpɛks) n., pl. **apexes** or **apices** ('æpɪ,siːz, 'eɪ-). 1. the highest point; vertex. 2. the pointed end or tip of something. 3. a high point, as of a career.
APEX acronym for: 1. Advance Purchase Excursion, a reduced airline fare, paid for at least 30 days before departure. 2. Association of Professional, Executive, Clerical, and Computer Staff.
aphasia (ə'feɪzɪə) n. a disorder of the central nervous system characterized by loss of the ability to communicate, esp. in speech.
aphelion (æp'hiːlɪən, ə'fiː-) n., pl. **-lia** (-lɪə). the point in its orbit when a planet or comet is at its greatest distance from the sun.
aphid ('eɪfɪd) n. any of the small homopterous insects of the family Aphididae, which feed by sucking the juices from plants.
aphis ('eɪfɪs) n., pl. **aphides** ('eɪfɪ,diːz). any of a genus of aphids, such as the blackfly.
aphorism ('æfə,rɪzəm) n. a short pithy saying expressing a general truth; maxim. —**'aphorist** n. —**,apho-'ristic** adj.
aphrodisiac (,æfrə'dɪzɪæk) n. 1. a drug, food, etc., that excites sexual desire. ~adj. 2. exciting sexual desire.
apiary ('eɪpɪərɪ) n., pl. **-aries.** a place where bees are kept.
apical ('æpɪkəl, 'eɪ-) adj. of, at, or being the apex. —**'apically** adv.
apices ('æpɪ,siːz, 'eɪ-) n. a plural of **apex**.
apiculture ('eɪpɪ,kʌltʃə) n. the breeding and care of bees. —,api'cultural adj. —,api'culturist n.
apiece (ə'piːs) adv. for, to, or from each one: they were given two apples apiece.
apish ('eɪpɪʃ) adj. 1. stupid; foolish. 2. resembling an ape. 3. slavishly imitative. —**'apishly** adv. —**'apishness** n.
aplomb (ə'plɒm) n. equanimity, self-confidence, or self-possession.
apo- or **ap-** prefix. 1. away from; off: apogee. 2. separation of: apocarpous.
Apoc. abbrev. for: 1. Apocalypse. 2. Apocrypha or Apocryphal.
apocalypse (ə'pɒkəlɪps) n. 1. a prophetic disclosure or revelation. 2. an event of great importance, violence, etc., like the events described in the Apocalypse. —a,poca'lyptic adj.
Apocalypse (ə'pɒkəlɪps) n. Bible. another name for the Book of Revelation.
Apocrypha (ə'pɒkrɪfə) n. **the.** (functioning as sing. or pl.) the 14 books included as an appendix to the Old Testament in the Septuagint and the Vulgate but not in the Hebrew canon.
apocryphal (ə'pɒkrɪfəl) adj. 1. of questionable authenticity. 2. (sometimes cap.) of or like the Apocrypha. 3. untrue; counterfeit.
apogee ('æpə,dʒiː) n. 1. the point in its orbit around the earth when the moon or an artificial satellite is at its greatest distance from the earth. 2. the highest point. —,apo'gean adj.
apolitical (,eɪpə'lɪtɪkəl) adj. politically neutral; without political attitudes, content, or bias.
apologetic (ə,pɒlə'dʒɛtɪk) adj. 1. expressing or anxious

THESAURUS

apart 1. afar, alone, aloof, aside, away, by itself, by oneself, cut off, distant, distinct, divorced, excluded, independent, independently, isolated, piecemeal, separate, separated, separately, singly, to itself, to oneself, to one side 2. asunder, in bits, in pieces, into parts, to bits, to pieces 3. **apart from** aside from, besides, but, except for, excluding, not counting, other than, save

apartment accommodation, chambers, compartment, flat (U.S.), living quarters, penthouse, quarters, room, rooms, suite

apathetic cold, cool, emotionless, impassive, indifferent, insensible, listless, passive, phlegmatic, sluggish, stoic, stoical, torpid, unconcerned, unemotional, unfeeling, uninterested, unmoved, unresponsive

apathy coldness, coolness, emotionlessness, impassibility, impassivity, indifference, insensibility, listlessness, passiveness, passivity, phlegm, sluggishness, stoicism, torpor, unconcern, unfeelingness, uninterestedness, unresponsiveness

ape affect, caricature, copy, counterfeit, echo, imitate, mimic, mirror, mock, parody, parrot

aperture breach, chink, cleft, crack, eye, eyelet, fissure, gap, hole, interstice, opening, orifice, passage, perforation, rent, rift, slit, slot, space

apex acme, apogee, climax, crest, crown, culmination, height, high point, peak, pinnacle, point, summit, tip, top, vertex, zenith

aphorism adage, apothegm, axiom, dic-

tum, gnome, maxim, precept, proverb, saw, saying

apiece each, for each, from each, individually, respectively, separately, severally, to each

aplomb balance, calmness, composure, confidence, coolness, equanimity, levelheadedness, poise, sang-froid, self-assurance, self-confidence, self-possession, stability

apocryphal doubtful, dubious, equivocal, fictitious, legendary, mythical, questionable, spurious, unauthenticated, uncanonical, unsubstantiated, unverified

apologetic contrite, penitent, regretful, remorseful, rueful, sorry

to make apology; contrite. **2.** defending in speech or writing. —**a,polo'getically** adv.

apologetics (ə,pɒlə'dʒɛtɪks) n. (functioning as sing.) **1.** the branch of theology concerned with the rational justification of Christianity. **2.** a defensive method of argument.

apologia (,æpə'ləʊdʒɪə) n. a formal written defence of a cause or one's beliefs or conduct.

apologist (ə'pɒlədʒɪst) n. a person who offers a defence by argument.

apologize or **-gise** (ə'pɒlə,dʒaɪz) vb. (intr.) **1.** to express or make an apology; acknowledge faults. **2.** to defend formally.

apologue ('æpə,lɒg) n. an allegory or moral fable.

apology (ə'pɒlədʒɪ) n., pl. **-gies.** **1.** a verbal or written expression of regret or contrition for a fault or failing. **2.** a poor substitute. **3.** another word for **apologia.**

apophthegm or **apothegm** ('æpə,θɛm) n. a short remark containing some general or generally accepted truth; maxim.

apoplectic (,æpə'plɛktɪk) adj. **1.** of apoplexy. **2.** Inf. furious. —**,apo'plectically** adv.

apoplexy ('æpə,plɛksɪ) n. sudden loss of consciousness, often followed by paralysis, caused by rupture or occlusion of a blood vessel in the brain.

apostasy (ə'pɒstəsɪ) n., pl. **-sies.** abandonment of one's religious faith, party, a cause, etc.

apostate (ə'pɒsteɪt, -tɪt) n. **1.** a person who abandons his religion, party, etc. ~adj. **2.** guilty of apostasy. —**apostatical** (,æpə'stætɪk*ə*l) adj.

a posteriori (eɪ pɒs,tɛrɪ'ɔːraɪ, -rɪ, ɑː) adj. Logic. **1.** relating to inductive reasoning from particular facts to a general principle. **2.** derived from or requiring evidence for its validation; empirical.

apostle (ə'pɒs*ə*l) n. **1.** (often cap.) one of the 12 disciples chosen by Christ to preach his gospel. **2.** any prominent Christian missionary, esp. one who first converts a people. **3.** an ardent early supporter of a cause, movement, etc.

Apostles' Creed n. a concise statement of Christian beliefs dating from about 500 A.D., traditionally ascribed to the Apostles.

apostolate (ə'pɒstəlɪt, -,leɪt) n. the office, authority, or mission of an apostle.

apostolic (,æpə'stɒlɪk) adj. **1.** of or relating to the Apostles or their teachings or practice. **2.** of or relating to the pope as successor of the Apostles. —**,apos'tolical** adj.

Apostolic See (,æpə'stɒlɪk) n. the see of the pope.

apostrophe[1] (ə'pɒstrəfɪ) n. the punctuation mark ' used to indicate the omission of a letter or number, such as he's for he has or he is, also used in English to form the possessive, as in John's father.

apostrophe[2] (ə'pɒstrəfɪ) n. Rhetoric. a digression from a discourse, esp. an address to an imaginary or absent person or a personification.

apostrophize or **-phise** (ə'pɒstrə,faɪz) vb. to address an apostrophe to.

apothecaries' measure n. a system of liquid volume measure used in pharmacy in which 20 fluid ounces equal 1 pint.

apothecaries' weight n. a system of weights formerly used in pharmacy based on the Troy ounce.

apothecary (ə'pɒθɪkərɪ) n., pl. **-caries.** **1.** an archaic word for **chemist. 2.** Law. a chemist licensed by the Society of Apothecaries of London to prescribe, prepare, and sell drugs.

apothegm ('æpə,θɛm) n. a variant spelling of **apophthegm.**

apothem ('æpə,θɛm) n. the perpendicular from the centre of a regular polygon to any of its sides.

apotheosis (ə,pɒθɪ'əʊsɪs) n., pl. **-ses** (-siːz). **1.** elevation to the rank of a god; deification. **2.** glorification of a person or thing. **3.** a glorified ideal.

apotheosize or **-ise** (ə'pɒθɪə,saɪz) vb. (tr.) **1.** to deify. **2.** to glorify or idealize.

appal or U.S. **appall** (ə'pɔːl) vb. **-palling, -palled.** (tr.) to fill with horror; shock or dismay.

appalling (ə'pɔːlɪŋ) adj. causing dismay, horror, or revulsion. —**ap'pallingly** adv.

appanage or **apanage** ('æpənɪdʒ) n. **1.** land or other provision granted by a king for the support of esp. a younger son. **2.** a customary accompaniment or perquisite, as to a job or position.

apparatus (,æpə'reɪtəs, -'rɑːtəs) n., pl. **-ratus** or **-ratuses.** **1.** a collection of equipment used for a particular purpose. **2.** a machine having a specific function: breathing apparatus. **3.** the means by which something operates; organization. **4.** Anat. any group of organs having a specific function.

apparel (ə'pærəl) n. **1.** garments or clothing. **2.** Naut. a vessel's gear and equipment. ~vb. **-elling, -elled** or U.S. **-eling, -eled. 3.** Arch. (tr.) to clothe, adorn, etc.

apparent (ə'pærənt) adj. **1.** readily seen or understood; obvious. **2.** (usually prenominal) seeming, as opposed to real: his apparent innocence. **3.** Physics. as observed but discounting such factors as the motion of the observer, etc. —**ap'parently** adv.

apparition (,æpə'rɪʃən) n. **1.** an appearance, esp. of a ghost or ghostlike figure. **2.** the figure so appearing; spectre. **3.** the act of appearing.

appeal (ə'piːl) n. **1.** a request for relief, aid, etc. **2.** the power to attract, please, stimulate, or interest. **3.** an application or resort to another authority, esp. a higher one, as for a decision. **4.** Law. **a.** the judicial review by a superior court of the decision of a lower tribunal. **b.** a request for such review. **5.** Cricket. a request to the umpire to declare a batsman out. ~vb. **6.** (intr.) to make an earnest request. **7.** (intr.) to attract, please, stimulate, or interest. **8.** Law. to apply to a superior court to review (a case or issue decided by a lower tribunal). **9.** (intr.) to resort to, as for a decision. **10.** (intr.) Cricket. to ask the umpire to declare a batsman out. **11.** (intr.) to challenge the umpire's or referee's decision. —**ap'pealable** adj. —**ap'pealer** n. —**ap'pealingly** adv.

THESAURUS

apologist advocate, arguer, champion, defender, justifier, maintainer, pleader, spokesman, supporter, vindicator

apologize ask forgiveness, beg pardon, express regret, say one is sorry, say sorry

apology **1.** acknowledgment, confession, defence, excuse, explanation, extenuation, justification, plea, vindication **2.** caricature, excuse, imitation, makeshift, mockery, stopgap, substitute, travesty

apostate **1.** n. backslider, defector, deserter, heretic, recreant (Archaic), renegade, traitor, turncoat **2.** adj. backsliding, disloyal, faithless, false, heretical, perfidious, recreant, traitorous, treacherous, unfaithful, untrue

apostle **1.** evangelist, herald, messenger, missionary, preacher, proselytizer **2.** advocate, champion, pioneer, propagandist, propagator, proponent

apotheosis deification, elevation, exaltation, glorification, idealization, idolization

apotheosize deify, elevate, exalt, glorify, idealize, idolize

appal alarm, astound, daunt, dishearten, dismay, frighten, harrow, horrify, intimidate, outrage, petrify, scare, shock, terrify, unnerve

appalling alarming, astounding, awful, daunting, dire, disheartening, dismaying, dreadful, fearful, frightening, frightful, ghastly, grim, harrowing, hideous, horrible, horrid, horrific, horrifying, intimidating, petrifying, scaring, shocking, terrible, terrifying, unnerving

apparatus **1.** appliance, contraption (Inf.), device, equipment, gear, implements, machine, machinery, materials, means, mechanism, outfit, tackle, tools, utensils **2.** bureaucracy, chain of command, hierarchy, network, organization, setup, structure, system

apparel accoutrements, array (Poetic), attire, clothes, clothing, costume, dress, equipment, garb, garments, gear (Sl.), habiliments, habit, outfit, raiment (Archaic), robes, trappings, vestments

apparent **1.** clear, conspicuous, discernible, distinct, evident, indubitable, manifest, marked, obvious, open, overt, patent, plain, understandable, unmistakable, visible **2.** ostensible, outward, seeming, specious, superficial

apparently it appears that, it seems that, on the face of it, ostensibly, outwardly, seemingly, speciously, superficially

apparition **1.** appearance, manifestation, materialization, presence, vision, visitation **2.** chimera, ghost, phantom, revenant, shade (Literary), spectre, spirit, spook (Inf.), visitant, wraith

appeal n. **1.** adjuration, application, entreaty, invocation, petition, plea, prayer, request, solicitation, suit, supplication **2.** allure, attraction, attractiveness, beauty, charm, engagingness, fascination, interestingness, pleasingness ~v. **3.** adjure, apply, ask, beg, beseech, call, call upon, entreat, implore, petition, plead, pray, refer, request, resort to, solicit, sue, supplicate **4.** allure, attract, charm, engage, entice, fascinate, interest, invite, please, tempt

appear (ə'pɪə) vb. (intr.) **1.** to come into sight. **2.** (copula; may take an infinitive) to seem: the evidence appears to support you. **3.** to be plain or clear, as after further evidence, etc.: it appears you were correct after all. **4.** to develop; occur: faults appeared during testing. **5.** to be published: his biography appeared last month. **6.** to perform: he has appeared in many London productions. **7.** to be present in court before a magistrate or judge: he appeared on two charges of theft.

appearance (ə'pɪərəns) n. **1.** the act or an instance of appearing. **2.** the outward aspect of a person or thing. **3.** an outward show; pretence: he gave an appearance of working hard. **4. keep up appearances.** to maintain the public impression of well-being or normality. **5. put in** or **make an appearance.** to attend briefly, as out of politeness. **6. to all appearances.** apparently.

appease (ə'piːz) vb. (tr.) **1.** to calm or pacify, esp. by acceding to the demands of. **2.** to satisfy or quell (a thirst, etc.). —**ap'peaser** n.

appeasement (ə'piːzmənt) n. **1.** the policy of acceding to the demands of a potentially hostile nation in the hope of maintaining peace. **2.** the act of appeasing.

appellant (ə'pɛlənt) n. **1.** a person who appeals. **2.** Law. the party who appeals to a higher court from the decision of a lower tribunal. ~adj. **3.** Law. another word for **appellate.**

appellate (ə'pɛlɪt) adj. Law. **1.** of appeals. **2.** (of a tribunal) having jurisdiction to review cases on appeal.

appellation (ˌæpɪ'leɪʃən) n. **1.** a name or title. **2.** the act of naming.

appellative (ə'pɛlətɪv) n. **1.** a name or title. **2.** Grammar. another word for **common noun.** ~adj. **3.** of or relating to a name **4.** (of a proper noun) used as a common noun.

append (ə'pɛnd) vb. (tr.) **1.** to add as a supplement: to append a footnote. **2.** to attach; hang on. —**ap'pendage** n.

appendicectomy (ˌæpɛndɪ'sɛktəmɪ) or **appendectomy** (ˌæpən'dɛktəmɪ) n., pl. **-mies.** surgical removal of any appendage, esp. the vermiform appendix.

appendicitis (ˌæpɛndɪ'saɪtɪs) n. inflammation of the vermiform appendix.

appendix (ə'pɛndɪks) n., pl. **-dixes** or **-dices** (-dɪˌsiːz). **1.** a body of separate additional material at the end of a book, etc. **2.** any part that is dependent or supplementary. **3.** Anat. See **vermiform appendix.**

apperception (ˌæpə'sɛpʃən) Psychol. ~n. **1.** conscious awareness of the act and significance of perception. **2.** the act of apperceiving. —**apper'ceptive** adj.

appertain (ˌæpə'teɪn) vb. (intr.; usually foll. by to) to belong (to) as a part, function, right, etc.; relate (to) or be connected (with).

appetence ('æpɪtəns) or **appetency** n., pl. **-tences** or **-tencies. 1.** a craving or desire. **2.** an attraction or affinity.

appetite ('æpɪˌtaɪt) n. **1.** a desire for food or drink. **2.** a desire to satisfy a bodily craving, as for sexual pleasure. **3.** (usually foll. by for) a liking or willingness: a great appetite for work. —**appetitive** (ə'pɛtɪtɪv) adj.

appetizer or **-iser** ('æpɪˌtaɪzə) n. **1.** a small amount of food or drink taken to stimulate the appetite. **2.** any stimulating foretaste.

appetizing or **-ising** ('æpɪˌtaɪzɪŋ) adj. pleasing or stimulating to the appetite; delicious; tasty.

applaud (ə'plɔːd) vb. **1.** to indicate approval of (a person, performance, etc.) by clapping the hands. **2.** (usually tr.) to express approval or praise of: I applaud your decision.

applause (ə'plɔːz) n. appreciation or praise, esp. as shown by clapping the hands.

apple ('æpəl) n. **1.** a rosaceous tree, widely cultivated in temperate regions in many varieties. **2.** the fruit of this tree, having red, yellow, or green skin and crisp whitish flesh. **3.** the wood of this tree. **4.** any of several unrelated trees that have fruit similar to the apple. **5. apple of one's eye.** a person or thing that is very much loved.

apple-pie bed n. Brit. a way of making a bed so as to prevent the person from entering it.

apple-pie order n. Inf. perfect order or condition.

appliance (ə'plaɪəns) n. **1.** a machine or device, esp. an electrical one used domestically. **2.** any piece of equipment having a specific function. **3.** another name for a **fire engine.**

applicable ('æplɪkəbəl, ə'plɪkə-) adj. being appropriate or relevant; able to be applied; fitting. —**applica'bility** n. —**'applicably** adv.

applicant ('æplɪkənt) n. a person who applies, as for a job, grant, support, etc.; candidate.

application (ˌæplɪ'keɪʃən) n. **1.** the act of applying to a particular use. **2.** relevance or value: the practical applications of space technology. **3.** the act of asking for something. **4.** a written request, as for a job, etc. **5.** diligent effort: a job requiring application. **6.** something, such as a lotion, that is applied, esp. to the skin.

applicator ('æplɪˌkeɪtə) n. a device, such as a spatula or

---

rod, for applying a medicine, glue, etc.
applied (ə'plaɪd) *adj.* put to practical use: *applied mathematics.* Cf. **pure** (sense 5).
appliqué (æ'pliːkeɪ) *n.* **1.** a decoration of one material sewn or fixed onto another. **2.** the practice of decorating in this way. ~*vb.* **-quéing, -quéd. 3.** (*tr.*) to sew or fix (a decoration) on as an appliqué.
apply (ə'plaɪ) *vb.* **-plying, -plied. 1.** (*tr.*) to put to practical use; employ. **2.** (*intr.*) to be relevant or appropriate. **3.** (*tr.*) to cause to come into contact with. **4.** (*intr.; often foll. by for*) to put in an application or request. **5.** (*tr.; often foll. by to*) to devote (oneself, one's efforts) with diligence. **6.** (*tr.*) to bring into use: *the police only applied the law to aliens.* —**ap'plier** *n.*
appoint (ə'pɔɪnt) *vb.* (*mainly tr.*) **1.** (*also intr.*) to assign officially, as for a position, responsibility, etc. **2.** to establish by agreement or decree. **3.** to prescribe: *laws appointed by tribunal.* **4.** *Property law.* to nominate (a person) to take an interest in property. **5.** to equip with usual features; furnish: *a well-appointed hotel.* —**appoin'tee** *n.* —**ap'pointer** *n.*
appointment (ə'pɔɪntmənt) *n.* **1.** an arrangement to meet a person or be at a place at a certain time. **2.** the act of placing in a job or position. **3.** the person who receives such a job. **4.** the job or position to which such a person is appointed. **5.** (*usually pl.*) a fixture or fitting.
apportion (ə'pɔːʃən) *vb.* (*tr.*) to divide, distribute, or assign shares of; allot proportionally. —**ap'portionable** *adj.* —**ap'portionment** *n.*
appose (ə'pəʊz) *vb.* (*tr.*) **1.** to place side by side. **2.** (usually foll. by *to*) to place (something) near or against another thing. —**ap'posable** *adj.*
apposite ('æpəzɪt) *adj.* appropriate; apt. —**'appositely** *adv.* —**'appositeness** *n.*
apposition (ˌæpə'zɪʃən) *n.* **1.** a putting into juxtaposition. **2.** a grammatical construction in which a word, esp. a noun, is placed after another to modify its meaning. —ˌ**appo'sitional** *adj.*
appraisal (ə'preɪzəl) *or* **appraisement** *n.* **1.** an assessment of the worth or quality of a person or thing. **2.** a valuation.
appraise (ə'preɪz) *vb.* (*tr.*) **1.** to assess the worth, val-

ue, or quality of. **2.** to make a valuation of, as for taxation. —**ap'praisable** *adj.* —**ap'praiser** *n.*
appreciable (ə'priːʃəbəl) *adj.* sufficient to be easily measured or noticed. —**ap'preciably** *adv.*
appreciate (ə'priːʃɪˌeɪt, -sɪ-) *vb.* (*mainly tr.*) **1.** to feel thankful or grateful for. **2.** (*may take a clause as object*) to take sufficient account of: *to appreciate a problem.* **3.** to value highly. **4.** (*usually intr.*) to increase in value. —**ap'preciˌator** *n.*
appreciation (əˌpriːʃɪ'eɪʃən, -sɪ-) *n.* **1.** thanks or gratitude. **2.** assessment of the true worth of persons or things. **3.** perceptive recognition of qualities, as in art. **4.** an increase in value. **5.** a review of a book, etc., esp. when favourable.
appreciative (ə'priːʃɪətɪv, -ʃə-) *or* **appreciatory** *adj.* feeling or expressing appreciation. —**ap'preciativeness** *n.* —**ap'preciatively** *adv.*
apprehend (ˌæprɪ'hend) *vb.* **1.** (*tr.*) to arrest and escort into custody. **2.** to grasp mentally; understand. **3.** to await with fear or anxiety.
apprehension (ˌæprɪ'henʃən) *n.* **1.** anxiety over what may happen. **2.** the act of arresting. **3.** understanding. **4.** a notion or conception.
apprehensive (ˌæprɪ'hensɪv) *adj.* **1.** fearful or anxious. **2.** able to learn quickly. **3.** (*usually postpositive and foll. by of*) perceptive. —ˌ**appre'hensively** *adv.* —ˌ**appre-'hensiveness** *n.*
apprentice (ə'prentɪs) *n.* **1.** someone who works for a skilled or qualified person in order to learn a trade, esp. for a recognized period. **2.** any beginner or novice. ~*vb.* **3.** (*tr.*) to take, place, or bind as an apprentice. —**ap'prenticeˌship** *n.*
apprise *or* **-ize** (ə'praɪz) *vb.* (*tr.; often foll. by of*) to make aware; inform.
appro ('æprəʊ) *n.* an informal shortening of **approval:** *on appro.*
approach (ə'prəʊtʃ) *vb.* **1.** to come nearer in position, time, quality, character, etc., to (someone or something). **2.** (*tr.*) to make a proposal or suggestion. **3.** (*tr.*) to begin to deal with. ~*n.* **4.** the act of drawing close or closer. **5.** a close approximation. **6.** the way or means of entering or leaving. **7.** (*often pl.*) an overture to a person. **8.**

THESAURUS

apply 1. administer, assign, bring into play, bring to bear, carry out, employ, engage, execute, exercise, implement, practise, put to use, use, utilize **2.** appertain, be applicable, be appropriate, bear upon, be fitting, be relevant, fit, pertain, refer, relate, suit **3.** anoint, bring into contact with, cover with, lay on, paint, place, put on, smear, spread on, touch to **4.** appeal, claim, inquire, make application, petition, put in, request, requisition, solicit, sue **5.** address, be assiduous, be diligent, be industrious, buckle down (*Inf.*), commit, concentrate, dedicate, devote, direct, give, make an effort, pay attention, persevere, study, try, work hard
appoint 1. allot, arrange, assign, choose, decide, designate, determine, establish, fix, set, settle **2.** assign, choose, commission, delegate, elect, install, name, nominate, select **3.** command, decree, direct, enjoin, ordain **4.** equip, fit out, furnish, provide, supply
appointed 1. allotted, arranged, assigned, chosen, decided, designated, determined, established, fixed, set, settled **2.** assigned, chosen, commissioned, delegated, elected, installed, named, nominated, selected **3.** commanded, decreed, directed, enjoined, ordained **4.** equipped, fitted out, furnished, provided, supplied
appointment 1. arrangement, assignation, consultation, date, engagement, interview, meeting, rendezvous, session, tryst (*Archaic*) **2.** allotment, assignment, choice, choosing, commissioning, delegation, designation, election, installation, naming, nomination, selection **3.** assignment, berth (*Inf.*), job, office, place, position, post, situation, station **4.** appointee, candidate, delegate, nominee, office-holder, representative **5.** *Usually plural* accoutrements, appurtenances, equipage, fittings, fixtures, furnishings, gear, out-

fit, paraphernalia, trappings
apportion allocate, allot, assign, deal, dispense, distribute, divide, dole out, measure out, mete out, parcel out, ration out, share
apportionment allocation, allotment, assignment, dealing out, dispensing, distribution, division, doling out, measuring out, meting out, parcelling out, rationing out, sharing
apposite appertaining, applicable, appropriate, apropos, apt, befitting, germane, pertinent, proper, relevant, suitable, suited, to the point, to the purpose
appraisal 1. assessment, estimate, estimation, evaluation, judgment, opinion, sizing up (*Inf.*) **2.** assay, pricing, rating, reckoning, survey, valuation
appraise assay, assess, estimate, evaluate, gauge, inspect, judge, price, rate, review, size up (*Inf.*), survey, value
appreciable ascertainable, clear-cut, considerable, definite, detectable, discernible, distinguishable, evident, marked, material, measurable, noticeable, obvious, perceivable, perceptible, pronounced, recognizable, significant, substantial, visible
appreciate 1. be appreciative, be grateful for, be indebted, be obliged, be thankful for, give thanks for **2.** acknowledge, be alive to, be aware (cognizant, conscious) of, comprehend, estimate, know, perceive, realize, recognize, sympathize with, take account of, understand **3.** admire, cherish, enjoy, esteem, like, prize, rate highly, regard, relish, respect, savour, treasure, value **4.** enhance, gain, grow, improve, increase, inflate, raise the value of, rise
appreciation 1. acknowledgment, gratefulness, gratitude, indebtedness, obligation, thankfulness, thanks **2.** admiration, ap-

praisal, assessment, awareness, cognizance, comprehension, enjoyment, esteem, estimation, knowledge, liking, perception, realization, recognition, regard, relish, respect, responsiveness, sensitivity, sympathy, understanding, valuation **3.** enhancement, gain, growth, improvement, increase, inflation, rise **4.** acclamation, criticism, critique, notice, praise, review, tribute
appreciative 1. beholden, grateful, indebted, obliged, thankful **2.** admiring, aware, cognizant, conscious, enthusiastic, in the know (*Inf.*), knowledgeable, mindful, perceptive, pleased, regardful, respectful, responsive, sensitive, supportive, sympathetic, understanding
apprehend 1. arrest, bust (*Inf.*), capture, catch, collar (*Inf.*), nab (*Inf.*), nick (*Sl.*), pinch (*Inf.*), run in (*Sl.*), seize, take, take prisoner **2.** appreciate, believe, comprehend, conceive, grasp, imagine, know, perceive, realize, recognize, think, understand **3.** be afraid of, dread, fear
apprehension 1. alarm, anxiety, apprehensiveness, concern, disquiet, doubt, dread, fear, foreboding, misgiving, mistrust, premonition, suspicion, unease, uneasiness, worry **2.** arrest, capture, catching, seizure, taking **3.** awareness, comprehension, grasp, intellect, intelligence, ken, knowledge, perception, understanding **4.** belief, concept, conception, conjecture, idea, impression, notion, opinion, sentiment, thought, view
apprehensive afraid, alarmed, anxious, concerned, disquieted, doubtful, fearful, foreboding, mistrustful, suspicious, uneasy, worried
apprentice beginner, learner, neophyte, novice, probationer, pupil, student, tyro

a means adopted in tackling a problem, job of work, etc. **9.** Also called: **approach path.** the course followed by an aircraft preparing for landing. **10.** Also called: **approach shot.** *Golf.* a shot made to or towards the green after a tee shot. **—ap'proachable** *adj.* **—ap₁proacha'bility** *n.*

approbation (₁æprə'beɪʃən) *n.* **1.** commendation; praise. **2.** official recognition. **—'appro,bative** *or* **'appro,batory** *adj.*

appropriate *adj.* (ə'prəʊprɪɪt). **1.** right or suitable; fitting. *—vb.* (ə'prəʊprɪ,eɪt). (*tr.*) **2.** to take for one's own use, esp. illegally. **3.** to put aside (funds, etc.) for a particular purpose or person. **—ap'propriately** *adv.* **—ap'propriateness** *n.* **—ap'propri,ator** *n.*

appropriation (ə,prəʊprɪ'eɪʃən) *n.* **1.** the act of setting apart or taking for one's own use. **2.** a sum of money set apart for a specific purpose.

approval (ə'pruːvəl) *n.* **1.** the act of approving. **2.** formal agreement. **3.** a favourable opinion. **4. on approval.** (of articles for sale) for examination with an option to buy or return.

approve (ə'pruːv) *vb.* **1.** to consider fair, good, or right. **2.** (*tr.*) to authorize or sanction.

approx. *abbrev. for* approximate(ly).

approximate *adj.* (ə'prɒksɪmɪt). **1.** almost accurate or exact. **2.** inexact; rough; loose. **3.** much alike; almost the same. **4.** near; close together. *—vb.* (ə'prɒksɪ,meɪt). **5.** (usually foll. by *to*) to come or bring near or close; be almost the same (as). **—ap'proximately** *adv.* **—ap,proxi'mation** *n.*

appurtenance (ə'pɜːtɪnəns) *n.* **1.** a less significant thing or part. **2.** (*pl.*) accessories. **3.** *Property law.* a minor right, interest, or privilege.

Apr. *abbrev. for* April.

apricot ('eɪprɪ,kɒt) *n.* **1.** a tree native to Africa and W Asia, but widely cultivated for its edible fruit. **2.** the yellow juicy fruit of this tree, which resembles a small peach.

April ('eɪprəl) *n.* the fourth month of the year, consisting of 30 days.

April fool *n.* a victim of a practical joke performed on the first of April (**April Fools' Day** *or* **All Fools' Day**).

a priori (eɪ praɪ'ɔːraɪ, ɑː prɪ'ɔːrɪ) *Logic.* *~adj.* **1.** relating to or involving deductive reasoning from a general principle to the expected facts or effects. **2.** known to be true independently of experience of the subject matter. **—apriority** (₁eɪpraɪ'ɒrɪtɪ) *n.*

apron ('eɪprən) *n.* **1.** a protective or sometimes decorative garment worn over the front of the body and tied around the waist. **2.** the part of a stage extending in front of the curtain. **3.** a hard-surfaced area in front of an aircraft hangar, terminal building, etc. **4.** a continuous conveyor belt composed of metal slats. **5.** a protective plate screening the operator of a machine, artillery piece, etc. **6.** *Geol.* a sheet of sand, gravel, etc., deposited at the front of a moraine. **7.** another name for **skirt** (sense 3). **8. tied to someone's apron strings.** dominated by someone, esp. a mother or wife. *~vb.* **9.** (*tr.*) to protect or provide with an apron.

apropos (₁æprə'pəʊ) *adj.* **1.** appropriate. *~adv.* **2.** appropriately. **3.** by the way; incidentally. **4. apropos of.** (*prep.*) in respect of.

apse (æps) *n.* a domed or vaulted semicircular or polygonal recess, esp. at the east end of a church. Also called: **apsis.** **—apsidal** ('æpsɪdəl) *adj.*

apsis ('æpsɪs) *n., pl.* **apsides** (æp'saɪdiːz). either of two points lying at the extremities of an eccentric orbit of a planet, satellite, etc. Also called: **apse.** **—apsidal** ('æpsɪdəl) *adj.*

apt (æpt) *adj.* **1.** suitable; appropriate. **2.** (*postpositive; foll. by an infinitive*) having a tendency (to behave as specified). **3.** having the ability to learn and understand easily. **—'aptly** *adv.* **—'aptness** *n.*

APT *abbrev. for* Advanced Passenger Train.

apteryx ('æptərɪks) *n.* another name for **kiwi** (the bird).

aptitude ('æptɪ,tjuːd) *n.* **1.** inherent or acquired ability. **2.** ease in learning or understanding. **3.** the quality of being apt.

THESAURUS

approach *v.* **1.** advance, catch up, come close, come near, come to, draw near, gain on, meet, move towards, near, push forward, reach **2.** appeal to, apply to, broach the matter with, make advances to, make a proposal to, make overtures to, sound out **3.** begin, begin work on, commence, embark on, enter upon, make a start, set about, undertake **4.** approximate, be comparable to, be like, come close to, come near to, compare with, resemble *~n.* **5.** access, advance, advent, arrival, avenue, coming, drawing near, entrance, nearing, passage, road, way **6.** approximation, likeness, semblance **7.** *Often plural* advance, appeal, application, invitation, offer, overture, proposal, proposition **8.** attitude, course, manner, means, method, mode, modus operandi, procedure, style, technique, way

approachable **1.** accessible, attainable, come-at-able (*Inf.*), get-at-able (*Inf.*), reachable **2.** affable, congenial, cordial, friendly, open, sociable

appropriate *adj.* **1.** adapted, applicable, apposite, appurtenant, apropos, apt, becoming, befitting, belonging, congruous, correct, felicitous, fit, fitting, germane, meet (*Archaic*), opportune, pertinent, proper, relevant, right, seemly, suitable, to the point, to the purpose, well-suited, well-timed *~v.* **2.** allocate, allot, apportion, assign, devote, earmark, set apart **3.** annex, arrogate, assume, commandeer, confiscate, expropriate, impound, pre-empt, seize, take, take over, take possession of, usurp **4.** embezzle, filch, misappropriate, pilfer, pocket, steal

appropriateness applicability, appositeness, aptness, becomingness, congruousness, correctness, felicitousness, felicity, fitness, fittingness, germaneness, opportuneness, pertinence, properness, relevance, rightness, seemliness, suitability, timeliness, well-suitedness

appropriation **1.** allocation, allotment,

apportionment, assignment, earmarking, setting apart **2.** annexation, arrogation, assumption, commandeering, confiscation, expropriation, impoundment, pre-emption, seizure, takeover, taking, usurpation

approval **1.** acquiescence, agreement, assent, authorization, blessing, compliance, concurrence, confirmation, consent, countenance, endorsement, imprimatur, leave, licence, mandate, O.K. (*Inf.*), permission, ratification, recommendation, sanction, the go-ahead (*Inf.*), the green light (*Inf.*), validation **2.** acclaim, admiration, applause, appreciation, approbation, commendation, esteem, favour, good opinion, liking, praise, regard, respect

approve **1.** acclaim, admire, applaud, appreciate, be pleased with, commend, esteem, favour, have a good opinion of, like, praise, regard highly, respect, think highly of **2.** accede to, accept, advocate, agree to, allow, assent to, authorize, bless, concur in, confirm, consent to, countenance, endorse, give the go-ahead (*Inf.*), give the green light (*Inf.*), go along with, mandate, O.K. (*Inf.*), pass, permit, ratify, recommend, sanction, second, subscribe to, uphold, validate

approximate *adj.* **1.** almost accurate, almost exact, close, near **2.** estimated, inexact, loose, rough **3.** analogous, close, comparable, like, near, relative, similar, verging on **4.** adjacent, bordering, close together, contiguous, near, nearby, neighbouring *~v.* **5.** approach, border on, come close, come near, reach, resemble, touch, verge on

approximately about, almost, around, circa (*used with dates*), close to, generally, in the neighbourhood of, in the region of, in the vicinity of, just about, loosely, more or less, nearly, not far off, relatively, roughly

approximation **1.** conjecture, estimate, estimation, guess, guesswork, rough calculation, rough idea **2.** approach, correspondence, likeness, resemblance, sem-

blance

appurtenance **1.** accessory, accompaniment, adjunct, annexe, appendage, appurtenant, attachment, auxiliary, concomitant, incidental, piece of equipment, subordinate, subsidiary, supplement **2.** *Plural* accessories, accompaniments, accoutrements, appendages, equipment, impedimenta, paraphernalia, trappings

a priori **1.** deduced, deductive, from cause to effect, inferential **2.** conjectural, postulated, postulational, presumptive, self-evident, suppositional, theoretical

apron pinafore, pinny (*Inf.*)

apropos *adj.* **1.** applicable, apposite, appropriate, apt, befitting, belonging, correct, fit, fitting, germane, meet (*Archaic*), opportune, pertinent, proper, related, relevant, right, seemly, suitable, to the point, to the purpose *~adv.* **2.** appropriately, aptly, opportunely, pertinently, relevantly, suitably, timely, to the point, to the purpose **3.** by the bye, by the way, incidentally, in passing, parenthetically, while on the subject

apropos of *prep.* in respect of, on the subject of, re, regarding, respecting, with reference to, with regard to, with respect to

apt **1.** applicable, apposite, appropriate, apropos, befitting, correct, fit, fitting, germane, meet (*Archaic*), pertinent, proper, relevant, seemly, suitable, timely, to the point, to the purpose **2.** disposed, given, inclined, liable, likely, of a mind, prone, ready **3.** astute, bright, clever, expert, gifted, ingenious, intelligent, prompt, quick, sharp, skilful, smart, talented, teachable

aptitude **1.** bent, disposition, inclination, leaning, predilection, proclivity, proneness, propensity, tendency **2.** ability, aptness, capability, capacity, cleverness, faculty, flair, gift, giftedness, intelligence, knack, proficiency, quickness, talent **3.** applicability, appositeness, appropriateness, fitness, relevance, suitability, suitableness

aqua ('ækwə) *n., pl.* **aquae** ('ækwiː) *or* **aquas.** **1.** water: used in compound names of certain liquid substances or solutions of substances in water. **2.** short for **aquamarine** (the colour).

aqua fortis ('fɔːtɪs) *n.* an obsolete name for **nitric acid.**

aqualung ('ækwə,lʌŋ) *n.* breathing apparatus used by divers, etc., consisting of an oxygen mask attached to a cylinder strapped to the back.

aquamarine (,ækwəmə'riːn) *n.* **1.** a pale greenish-blue transparent variety of beryl used as a gemstone. **2.** a pale blue to greenish-blue colour.

aquanaut ('ækwənɔːt) *n.* a person who works, swims, or dives underwater.

aquaplane ('ækwə,pleɪn) *n.* **1.** a board on which a person stands and is towed by a motorboat. ~*vb.* (*intr.*) **2.** to ride on an aquaplane. **3.** (of a motor vehicle travelling at high speeds on wet roads) to rise up onto a thin film of water so that contact with the road is lost.

aqua regia ('riːdʒɪə) *n.* a mixture of nitric acid and hydrochloric acid.

aquarium (ə'kwɛərɪəm) *n., pl.* **aquariums** *or* **aquaria** (ə'kwɛərɪə). **1.** a tank, bowl, or pool in which aquatic animals and plants are kept for pleasure, study, or exhibition. **2.** a building housing a collection of aquatic life, as for exhibition.

Aquarius (ə'kwɛərɪəs) *n., Latin genitive* **Aquarii** (ə'kwɛərɪaɪ). **1.** *Astron.* a S constellation. **2.** *Astrol.* the eleventh sign of the zodiac. The sun is in this sign between about Jan. 20 and Feb. 18.

aquatic (ə'kwætɪk) *adj.* **1.** growing, living, or found in water. **2.** *Sport.* performed in or on water. ~*n.* **3.** a marine animal or plant.

aquatics (ə'kwætɪks) *pl. n.* sports or pastimes performed in or on the water.

aquatint ('ækwə,tɪnt) *n.* **1.** a technique of etching copper with acid to produce an effect resembling watercolour. **2.** an etching made in this way. ~*vb.* **3.** (*tr.*) to etch (a block, etc.) in aquatint.

aqua vitae ('viːtaɪ, 'vaɪtiː) *n.* an archaic name for **brandy.**

aqueduct ('ækwɪ,dʌkt) *n.* **1.** a conduit used to convey water over a long distance. **2.** a structure, often a bridge, that carries such a conduit or a canal across a valley or river. **3.** a channel or conduit in the body.

aqueous ('eɪkwɪəs) *adj.* **1.** of, like, or containing water. **2.** (of rocks, etc.) formed from material laid down in water.

aqueous humour *n. Physiol.* the watery fluid within the eyeball between the cornea and the lens.

aquiline ('ækwɪ,laɪn) *adj.* **1.** (of a nose) having the curved shape of an eagle's beak. **2.** of or like an eagle.

Ar *the chemical symbol for* argon.

ar. *abbrev. for:* **1.** arrival. **2.** arrive(s).

Ar. *abbrev. for:* **1.** Arabia(n). **2.** Also: **Ar** Arabic. **3.** Aramaic.

-ar *suffix forming adjectives.* of; belonging to; like: *linear; polar.*

Arab ('ærəb) *n.* **1.** a member of a Semitic people originally inhabiting Arabia. **2.** a small breed of horse, used for riding. **3.** See **street Arab.** **4.** (*modifier*) of or relating to the Arabs.

arabesque (,ærə'bɛsk) *n.* **1.** *Ballet.* a classical position in which the dancer has one leg raised behind. **2.** *Music.* a piece or movement with a highly ornamented melody. **3.** *Arts.* a type of curvilinear decoration in painting, metalwork, etc., with intricate intertwining designs.

Arabian (ə'reɪbɪən) *adj.* **1.** of or relating to Arabia or the Arabs. ~*n.* **2.** another word for an **Arab.**

Arabic ('ærəbɪk) *n.* **1.** the Semitic language of the Arabs, spoken in Algeria, Egypt, Iraq, Jordan, Saudi Arabia, Syria, Tunisia, etc. ~*adj.* **2.** denoting or relating to this language, any of the peoples that speak it, or the countries in which it is spoken.

Arabic numeral *n.* one of the numbers 1,2,3,4,5,6,7,8,9,0 (opposed to *Roman numerals*).

arable ('ærəbəl) *adj.* **1.** (of land) being or capable of being tilled for the production of crops. **2.** of, relating to, or using such land.

arachnid (ə'ræknɪd) *n.* any of a class of arthropods characterized by simple eyes and four pairs of legs, including the spiders, scorpions, and ticks. —**a'rachnidan** *adj., n.*

arak ('ærək) *n.* a variant spelling of **arrack.**

Araldite ('ærəldaɪt) *n. Trademark.* an epoxy resin used as a glue for mending glass, plastic, and china.

Aram. *abbrev. for* Aramaic.

Aramaic (,ærə'meɪɪk) *n.* **1.** an ancient Semitic language of the Middle East, still spoken in parts of Syria and the Lebanon. ~*adj.* **2.** of, relating to, or using this language.

arbiter ('ɑːbɪtə) *n.* **1.** a person empowered to judge in a dispute; referee. **2.** a person having control of something. —**'arbitress** *fem. n.*

arbitrary ('ɑːbɪtrərɪ) *adj.* **1.** founded on or subject to personal whims, prejudices, etc. **2.** not absolute. **3.** (of a government, ruler, etc.) despotic or dictatorial. **4.** *Law.* (esp. of a penalty) within the court's discretion. —**'arbitrarily** *adv.* —**'arbitrariness** *n.*

arbitrate ('ɑːbɪ,treɪt) *vb.* **1.** to achieve a settlement between parties. **2.** to submit to or settle by arbitration. —**'arbi,trator** *n.*

arbitration (,ɑːbɪ'treɪʃən) *n.* the hearing and determination of a dispute by an impartial referee selected or agreed upon by the parties concerned.

arbor¹ ('ɑːbə) *n.* the U.S. spelling of **arbour.**

arbor² ('ɑːbə) *n.* **1.** a rotating shaft in a machine on which a milling cutter or grinding wheel is fitted. **2.** a rotating shaft.

arboraceous (,ɑːbə'reɪʃəs) *adj. Literary.* **1.** resembling a tree. **2.** wooded.

arboreal (ɑː'bɔːrɪəl) *adj.* **1.** of or resembling a tree. **2.** living in or among trees.

arborescent (,ɑːbə'rɛsənt) *adj.* having the shape or characteristics of a tree. —**,arbo'rescence** *n.*

arboretum (,ɑːbə'riːtəm) *n., pl.* **-ta** (-tə) *or* **-tums.** a place where trees or shrubs are cultivated.

arboriculture ('ɑːbərɪ,kʌltʃə) *n.* the cultivation of trees or shrubs. —**,arbori'culturist** *n.*

arbor vitae ('ɑːbɔː 'viːtaɪ, 'vaɪtiː) *n.* any of several Asian and North American evergreen coniferous trees having tiny scalelike leaves and egglike cones.

arbour ('ɑːbə) *n.* a leafy glade or bower shaded by trees, vines, shrubs, etc.

arbutus (ɑː'bjuːtəs) *n., pl.* **-tuses.** any of a genus of shrubs having clusters of white or pinkish flowers, broad evergreen leaves, and strawberry-like berries.

arc (ɑːk) *n.* **1.** something curved in shape. **2.** part of an unbroken curved line. **3.** a luminous discharge that occurs when an electric current flows between two electrodes separated by a small gap. ~*vb.* **arcing, arced** *or* **arcking, arcked.** **4.** (*intr.*) to form an arc. ~*adj.* **5.** *Maths.* specifying an inverse trigonometric function: *arcsin, arccos, arctan.*

THESAURUS

aptness 1. applicability, appositeness, appropriateness, becomingness, congruousness, correctness, felicitousness, felicity, fitness, fittingness, germaneness, opportuneness, pertinence, properness, relevance, rightness, seemliness, suitability, timeliness, well-suitedness **2.** aptitude, bent, disposition, inclination, leaning, liability, likelihood, likeliness, predilection, proclivity, proneness, propensity, readiness, tendency **3.** ability, capability, capacity, cleverness, faculty, fitness, flair, gift, giftedness, intelligence, knack, proficiency, quickness, suitability, talent

arable cultivable, farmable, fecund, fertile, fruitful, ploughable, productive, tillable

arbiter 1. adjudicator, arbitrator, judge, referee, umpire **2.** authority, controller, dictator, expert, governor, lord, master, pundit, ruler

arbitrariness 1. capriciousness, fancifulness, inconsistency, randomness, subjectivity, unreasonableness, whimsicality, wilfulness **2.** absoluteness, despotism, dictatorialness, dogmatism, domineeringness, highhandedness, imperiousness, magisterialness, overbearingness, peremptoriness, summariness, tyrannicalness, tyrannousness, tyranny, uncontrolledness, unlimitedness, unrestrainedness

arbitrary 1. capricious, chance, discretionary, erratic, fanciful, inconsistent, optional, personal, random, subjective, unreasonable, whimsical, wilful **2.** absolute, autocratic, despotic, dictatorial, dogmatic, domineering, high-handed, imperious, magisterial, overbearing, peremptory, summary, tyrannical, tyrannous, uncontrolled, unlimited, unrestrained

arbitrate adjudge, adjudicate, decide, determine, judge, pass judgment, referee, settle, sit in judgment, umpire

arbitration adjudication, arbitrament, decision, determination, judgment, settlement

arcade (ɑː'keɪd) *n.* 1. a set of arches and their supporting columns. 2. a covered and sometimes arched passageway, usually with shops on one or both sides.

Arcadian (ɑː'keɪdɪən) *adj.* 1. of the idealized Arcadia of pastoral poetry. 2. rustic or bucolic. ~*n.* 3. a person who leads a quiet simple rural life. —**Ar'cadianism** *n.*

arcane (ɑː'keɪn) *adj.* requiring secret knowledge to be understood; esoteric.

arch¹ (ɑːtʃ) *n.* 1. a curved structure that spans an opening. 2. Also called: **archway.** a structure in the form of an arch that serves as a gateway. 3. something curved like an arch. 4. any of various parts or structures of the body having a curved or archlike outline, such as the raised vault formed by the tarsal and metatarsal bones (**arch of the foot**). ~*vb.* 5. (*tr.*) to span (an opening) with an arch. 6. to form or cause to form an arch or a curve resembling that of an arch. 7. (*tr.*) to span or extend over.

arch² (ɑːtʃ) *adj.* 1. (*prenominal*) chief; principal; leading. 2. (*prenominal*) expert: *an arch criminal.* 3. knowing or superior; coyly playful: *an arch look.* —**'archly** *adv.* —**'archness** *n.*

arch- or **archi-** *combining form.* 1. chief; principal: *archangel; archbishop.* 2. eminent above all others of the same kind: *archenemy.*

-arch *n. combining form.* leader; ruler; chief: *patriarch; monarch.*

Archaean or *esp. U.S.* **Archean** (ɑː'kiːən) *adj.* of the metamorphosed rocks formed in the early Precambrian era.

archaeology or **archeology** (ˌɑːkɪ'ɒlədʒɪ) *n.* the study of man's past by scientific analysis of the material remains of his cultures. —**archaeological** or **archeological** (ˌɑːkɪə'lɒdʒɪkəl) *adj.* —**archae'ologist** or **ar'che'ologist** *n.*

archaeopteryx (ˌɑːkɪ'ɒptərɪks) *n.* any of several extinct primitive birds which occurred in Jurassic times and had teeth, a long tail, and well-developed wings.

archaic (ɑː'keɪɪk) *adj.* 1. belonging to or characteristic of a much earlier period. 2. out of date; antiquated. 3. (of vocabulary, etc.) characteristic of an earlier period of a language. —**ar'chaically** *adv.*

archaism ('ɑːkeɪˌɪzəm) *n.* 1. the adoption or imitation of archaic words or style. 2. an archaic word, style, etc. —**'archaist** *n.* —**archa'istic** *adj.*

archangel ('ɑːkˌeɪndʒəl) *n.* a principal angel. —**archangelic** (ˌɑːkæn'dʒɛlɪk) *adj.*

archbishop ('ɑːtʃ'bɪʃəp) *n.* a bishop of the highest rank. Abbrev.: **abp., Abp., Arch., Archbp.**

archbishopric ('ɑːtʃ'bɪʃəprɪk) *n.* the rank, office, or jurisdiction of an archbishop.

archdeacon ('ɑːtʃ'diːkən) *n.* 1. an Anglican clergyman ranking just below a bishop 2. a clergyman of similar rank in other Churches. —**'arch'deaconry** *n.*

archdiocese (ˌɑːtʃ'daɪəˌsiːs) *n.* the diocese of an archbishop. —**archdiocesan** (ˌɑːtʃdaɪ'ɒsɪsən) *adj.*

archduchess ('ɑːtʃ'dʌtʃɪs) *n.* 1. the wife or widow of an archduke. 2. (since 1453) a princess of the Austrian imperial family.

archduchy ('ɑːtʃ'dʌtʃɪ) *n., pl.* **-duchies.** the territory ruled by an archduke or archduchess.

archduke ('ɑːtʃ'djuːk) *n.* a chief duke, esp. (since 1453) a prince of the Austrian imperial dynasty.

archenemy ('ɑːtʃ'ɛnɪmɪ) *n., pl.* **-mies.** 1. a chief enemy. 2. (*often cap.;* preceded by *the*) the devil.

archeology (ˌɑːkɪ'ɒlədʒɪ) *n.* a variant spelling of **archaeology.**

archer ('ɑːtʃə) *n.* a person skilled in the use of a bow and arrow.

Archer ('ɑːtʃə) *n. the.* the constellation Sagittarius.

archery ('ɑːtʃərɪ) *n.* 1. the art or sport of shooting with bows and arrows. 2. archers or their weapons collectively.

archetype ('ɑːkɪˌtaɪp) *n.* 1. a perfect or typical specimen. 2. an original model; prototype. 3. *Psychoanal.* one of the inherited mental images postulated by Jung. 4. a recurring symbol or motif in literature, etc. —**'arche,typal** *adj.*

archfiend (ˌɑːtʃ'fiːnd) *n.* (*often cap.*) *the.* the devil; Satan.

archidiaconal (ˌɑːkɪdaɪ'ækənəl) *adj.* of or relating to an archdeacon or his office. —**,archidi'aconate** *n.*

archiepiscopal (ˌɑːkɪɪ'pɪskəpəl) *adj.* of or associated with an archbishop. —**,archie'piscopate** *n.*

archipelago (ˌɑːkɪ'pɛlɪˌgəʊ) *n., pl.* **-gos** or **-goes.** 1. a group of islands. 2. a sea studded with islands. —**archipelagic** (ˌɑːkɪpə'lædʒɪk) *adj.*

architect ('ɑːkɪˌtɛkt) *n.* 1. a person qualified to design buildings and to supervise their erection. 2. a person similarly qualified in another form of construction: *a naval architect.* 3. any planner or creator.

architecture ('ɑːkɪˌtɛktʃə) *n.* 1. the art and science of designing and supervising the construction of buildings, etc. 2. a style of building or structure. 3. buildings or structures collectively. 4. the structure or design of anything. —**,archi'tectural** *adj.*

architrave ('ɑːkɪˌtreɪv) *n. Archit.* 1. the lowest part of an entablature that bears on the columns. 2. a moulding around a doorway, window opening, etc.

archives ('ɑːkaɪvz) *pl. n.* 1. a collection of records of an institution, family, etc. 2. a place where such records are kept. —**ar'chival** *adj.*

archivist ('ɑːkɪvɪst) *n.* a person in charge of archives.

archpriest ('ɑːtʃ'priːst) *n.* 1. (formerly) a chief assistant to a bishop. 2. a senior priest.

archway ('ɑːtʃˌweɪ) *n.* a passageway or entrance under an arch or arches.

-archy *n. combining form.* government; rule: *anarchy; monarchy.*

arctic ('ɑːktɪk) *adj.* 1. of or relating to the Arctic. 2. *Inf.* cold; freezing. ~*n.* 3. (*modifier*) suitable for conditions of extreme cold: *arctic clothing.*

Arctic ('ɑːktɪk) *adj.* of or relating to the regions north of the Arctic Circle.

Arctic Circle *n.* the imaginary circle round the earth, parallel to the equator, at latitude 66° 32′ N.

Arcturus (ɑːk'tjʊərəs) *n.* the brightest star in the constellation Boötes: a red giant.

arc welding *n.* a technique in which metal is welded by heat generated by an electric arc. —**arc welder** *n.*

-ard or **-art** *suffix forming nouns.* indicating a person who does something, esp. to excess: *braggart; drunkard.*

ardent ('ɑːdənt) *adj.* 1. expressive of or characterized by intense desire or emotion. 2. intensely enthusiastic; eager. 3. glowing or shining: *ardent eyes.* 4. **ardent spirits** alcoholic drink. —**'ardency** *n.* —**'ardently** *adv.*

ardour or *U.S.* **ardor** ('ɑːdə) *n.* 1. feelings of great intensity and warmth. 2. eagerness; zeal.

arduous ('ɑːdjuːəs) *adj.* 1. difficult to accomplish;

THESAURUS

arbitrator adjudicator, arbiter, judge, referee, umpire

arc arch, bend, bow, crescent, curve, half-moon

arcane cabbalistic, esoteric, hidden, mysterious, occult, recondite, secret

arch¹ *n.* 1. archway, curve, dome, span, vault 2. arc, bend, bow, curvature, curve, semicircle ~*v.* 3. arc, bend, bow, bridge, curve, embow, span

arch² 1. accomplished, chief, consummate, expert, finished, first, foremost, greatest, highest, leading, main, major, master, pre-eminent, primary, principal, top 2. artful, frolicsome, knowing, mischievous, pert, playful, roguish, saucy, sly, waggish, wily

archaic ancient, antiquated, antique, behind the times, bygone, obsolete, old, olden (*Archaic*), old-fashioned, old hat, outmoded, out of date, passé, primitive, superannuated

arched curved, domed, embowed, vaulted

archer bowman (*Archaic*), toxophilite (*Formal*)

archetype classic, exemplar, form, ideal, model, original, paradigm, pattern, prime example, prototype, standard

architect 1. designer, master builder, planner 2. author, contriver, creator, deviser, engineer, founder, instigator, inventor, maker, originator, planner, prime mover, shaper

architecture 1. architectonics, building, construction, design, planning 2. construction, design, framework, make-up,

structure, style

archives 1. annals, chronicles, documents, papers, records, registers, rolls 2. museum, record office, registry, repository

arctic 1. far-northern, hyperborean, polar 2. *Inf.* chilly, cold, freezing, frigid, frost-bound, frosty, frozen, gelid, glacial, icy

ardent avid, eager, enthusiastic, fervent, fervid, fierce, fiery, hot, hot-blooded, impassioned, intense, keen, lusty, passionate, spirited, vehement, warm, warm-blooded, zealous

ardour avidity, devotion, eagerness, earnestness, enthusiasm, feeling, fervour, fierceness, fire, heat, intensity, keenness, passion, spirit, vehemence, warmth, zeal

strenuous. **2.** hard to endure; harsh. **3.** steep or difficult: *an arduous track.* —'**arduously** *adv.* —'**arduousness** *n.*

are¹ (ɑː; *unstressed* ɔ) *vb.* the plural form of the present tense of **be** and the singular form used with *you.*

are² (ɑː) *n.* a unit of area equal to 100 sq. metres.

area ('ɛərɪə) *n.* **1.** any flat, curved, or irregular expanse of a surface. **2. a.** the extent of a two-dimensional surface: *the area of a triangle.* **b.** the two-dimensional extent of a plane or surface: *the area of a sphere.* **3.** a section or part. **4.** region; district. **5.** a part or section, as of a building, town, etc., having some specified function: *reception area; commercial area.* **6.** the range or scope of anything. **7.** a subject field or field of study. **8.** Also called: **areaway.** a sunken area, usually enclosed, giving light, air, and sometimes access to a cellar basement. —'**areal** *adj.*

arena (ə'riːnə) *n.* **1.** an enclosure or platform, usually surrounded by seats, in which sports events, entertainments, etc., take place: *a boxing arena.* **2.** the central area of an ancient Roman amphitheatre, in which gladiatorial contests were held. **3.** a sphere of intense activity: *the political arena.*

arenaceous (ˌærɪ'neɪʃəs) *adj.* **1.** (of sedimentary rocks) composed of sand. **2.** (of plants) growing in a sandy soil.

aren't (ɑːnt) **1.** *contraction of* are not. **2.** *Inf., chiefly Brit.* (used in interrogative sentences) *contraction of* am not.

areola (ə'rɪələ) *n., pl.* **-lae** (-ˌliː) *or* **-las.** **1.** *Biol.* a space outlined on a surface, such as an area between veins on a leaf. **2.** *Anat.* any small circular area, such as the pigmented ring around the human nipple. —a'**reolar** *or* **areolate** (ə'rɪəlɪt, -ˌleɪt) *adj.*

arête (ə'reɪt) *n.* a sharp ridge that separates glacial valleys.

argent ('ɑːdʒənt) *n.* **a.** an archaic or poetic word for **silver.** **b.** (*as adj.; often postpositive, esp. in heraldry*): *a bend argent.*

argon ('ɑːgɒn) *n.* an unreactive colourless odourless element of the rare gas series that forms almost 1 per cent of the atmosphere. It is used in electric lights. Symbol: Ar; atomic no.: 18; atomic wt.: 39.95.

argosy ('ɑːgəsɪ) *n., pl.* **-sies.** *Arch. or poetic.* a large abundantly laden merchant ship, or a fleet of such ships.

argot ('ɑːgəʊ) *n.* slang or jargon peculiar to a particular group, esp. (formerly) a group of thieves.

argue ('ɑːgjuː) *vb.* **-guing, -gued. 1.** (*intr.*) to quarrel; wrangle. **2.** (*intr.; often foll.* by *for* or *against*) to present supporting or opposing reasons or cases in a dispute. **3.** (*tr.; may take a clause as object*) to try to prove by presenting reasons. **4.** (*tr.; often passive*) to debate or discuss. **5.** (*tr.*) to persuade. **6.** (*tr.*) to suggest: *her looks argue despair.* —'**arguable** *adj.* —'**arguer** *n.*

argument ('ɑːgjumənt) *n.* **1.** a quarrel; altercation. **2.** a discussion in which reasons are put forward; debate. **3.** (*sometimes pl.*) a point or series of reasons presented to support or oppose a proposition. **4.** a summary of the plot or subject of a book, etc. **5.** *Logic.* **a.** a process of reasoning in which the conclusion can be shown to be true or false. **b.** the middle term of a syllogism.

argumentation (ˌɑːgjumɛn'teɪʃən) *n.* **1.** the process of reasoning methodically. **2.** argument; debate.

argumentative (ˌɑːgju'mɛntətɪv) *adj.* **1.** given to arguing. **2.** characterized by argument; controversial.

Argus ('ɑːgəs) *n.* **1.** *Greek myth.* a giant with a hundred eyes who was made guardian of the heifer Io. **2.** a vigilant person.

argy-bargy ('ɑːdʒɪ'bɑːdʒɪ) *n., pl.* **-bargies.** *Brit. inf.* a wrangling argument or verbal dispute.

aria ('ɑːrɪə) *n.* an elaborate accompanied song for solo voice from a cantata, opera, or oratorio.

Arian ('ɛərɪən) *adj.* **1.** of, or relating to Arius, 3rd-century A.D. Greek Christian theologian, or to Arianism. ~*n.* **2.** an adherent of Arianism.

-arian *suffix forming nouns.* indicating a person or thing that advocates, believes, or is associated with something: *vegetarian; librarian.*

Arianism ('ɛərɪəˌnɪzəm) *n. Christian Theol.* the doctrine of Arius, which asserted that Christ was not of one substance with the Father.

arid ('ærɪd) *adj.* **1.** having little or no rain; dry. **2.** devoid of interest. —**aridity** (ə'rɪdɪtɪ) *or* '**aridness** *n.*

Aries ('ɛəriːz) *n., Latin genitive* **Arietis** (ə'raɪɪtɪs). **1.** *Astron.* a N constellation. **2.** *Astrol.* the first sign of the zodiac. The sun is in this sign between about March 21 and April 19.

aright (ə'raɪt) *adv.* correctly; rightly; properly.

arise (ə'raɪz) *vb.* **arising, arose, arisen.** (*intr.*) **1.** to come into being; originate. **2.** (foll. by *from*) to proceed as a consequence. **3.** to get or stand up, as from a sitting or lying position. **4.** to come into notice. **5.** to ascend.

aristocracy (ˌærɪ'stɒkrəsɪ) *n., pl.* **-cies. 1.** government by the best citizens. **2.** a privileged class of people; the nobility. **3.** government by such a class. **4.** a state governed by such a class. **5.** a class of people considered to be outstanding in a sphere of activity.

aristocrat ('ærɪstəˌkræt) *n.* **1.** a member of the aristocracy. **2.** a person who has the manners or qualities of a member of a privileged class. **3.** a supporter of aristocracy as a form of government.

Aristotelian (ˌærɪstə'tiːlɪən) *adj.* **1.** of or relating to Aristotle, 4th-century B.C. Greek philosopher, or to his philosophy. ~*n.* **2.** a follower of Aristotle.

Aristotelian logic *n.* **1.** traditional logic, esp. relying on the theory of syllogism. **2.** the logical method of Aristotle, esp. as developed in the Middle Ages.

THESAURUS

arduous backbreaking, burdensome, difficult, exhausting, fatiguing, formidable, gruelling, hard, harsh, heavy, laborious, onerous, painful, punishing, rigorous, severe, steep, strenuous, taxing, tiring, toilsome, tough, troublesome, trying

area 1. district, domain, locality, neighbourhood, patch, plot, realm, region, sector, sphere, stretch, territory, tract, zone 2. breadth, compass, expanse, extent, range, scope, size, width 3. arena, department, domain, field, province, realm, sphere, territory 4. part, portion, section, sector 5. sunken space, yard

arena 1. amphitheatre, bowl, coliseum, field, ground, park (*Inf.*), ring, stadium, stage 2. area, battlefield, battleground, domain, field, field of conflict, lists, province, realm, scene, scope, sector, sphere, territory, theatre

argot cant, dialect, idiom, jargon, lingo (*Inf.*), parlance, patois, slang, vernacular

argue 1. altercate, bandy words, bicker, disagree, dispute, fall out (*Inf.*), feud, fight, have an argument, quarrel, squabble, wrangle 2. assert, claim, contend, controvert, debate, discuss, dispute, expostulate, hold, maintain, plead, question, reason, remonstrate 3. convince, persuade, prevail upon,

talk into, talk round 4. demonstrate, denote, display, evince, exhibit, imply, indicate, manifest, point to, show, suggest

argument 1. altercation, barney (*Inf.*), bickering, clash, controversy, difference of opinion, disagreement, dispute, falling out (*Inf.*), feud, fight, quarrel, row, squabble, wrangle 2. assertion, claim, contention, debate, discussion, dispute, expostulation, plea, pleading, questioning, remonstrance, remonstration 3. argumentation, case, defence, dialectic, ground(s), line of reasoning, logic, polemic, reason, reasoning 4. abstract, gist, outline, plot, story, story line, subject, summary, synopsis, theme

argumentative 1. belligerent, combative, contentious, contrary, disputatious, litigious, opinionated, quarrelsome 2. contentious, controversial, disputed

arid 1. barren, desert, dried up, dry, moistureless, parched, sterile, waterless 2. boring, colourless, dreary, dry, dull, flat, jejune, lifeless, spiritless, tedious, uninspired, uninteresting, vapid

aridity, aridness 1. barrenness, dryness, moisturelessness, parchedness, sterility, waterlessness 2. boredom, colourlessness, dreariness, dryness, dullness, flatness, jejuneness, jejunity, lifelessness, spiritless-

ness, tediousness, tedium, uninspiredness, uninterestingness, vapidity, vapidness

aright accurately, appropriately, aptly, correctly, duly, exactly, fitly, in due order, justly, properly, rightly, suitably, truly, without error

arise 1. appear, begin, come into being, come to light, commence, crop up (*Inf.*), emanate, emerge, ensue, follow, happen, issue, occur, originate, proceed, result, set in, spring, start, stem 2. get to one's feet, get up, go up, rise, stand up, wake up 3. ascend, climb, lift, mount, move upward, rise, soar, tower

aristocracy body of nobles, elite, gentry, *haut monde*, nobility, noblesse (*Literary*), patricians, patriciate, peerage, ruling class, upper class, upper crust (*Inf.*)

aristocrat grandee, lady, lord, noble, nobleman, noblewoman, patrician, peer, peeress

aristocratic 1. blue-blooded, elite, gentle (*Archaic*), gentlemanly, highborn, lordly, noble, patrician, titled, upper-class, wellborn 2. courtly, dignified, elegant, fine, haughty, polished, refined, snobbish, stylish, well-bred

arithmetic n. (ɔ'rıθmətɪk). **1.** the branch of mathematics concerned with numerical calculations, such as addition, subtraction, multiplication, and division. **2.** calculations involving numerical operations. **3.** knowledge of or skill in using arithmetic. ~adj. (,ærıθ'mɛtɪk), also **arithmetical. 4.** of, related to, or using arithmetic. —a,rithme'tician n.

arithmetic mean n. the average value of a set of terms or quantities, expressed as their sum divided by their number: the arithmetic mean of 3, 4, and 8 is 5. Also called: **average.**

arithmetic progression n. a sequence, each term of which differs from the succeeding term by a constant amount, such as 3,6,9,12.

-arium suffix forming nouns. indicating a place for or associated with something: aquarium; solarium.

ark (ɑːk) n. **1.** the vessel that Noah built which survived the Flood (Genesis 6–9). **2.** a place or thing offering shelter or protection. **3.** Dialect. a box.

Ark (ɑːk) n. Judaism. **1.** Also called: **Ark of the Covenant.** the most sacred symbol of God's presence among the Hebrew people, carried in their journey from Sinai to the Promised Land (Canaan). **2.** Also called: **Holy Ark.** a receptacle for the scrolls of the Law.

arm[1] (ɑːm) n. **1.** (in man) either of the upper limbs from the shoulder to the wrist. **2.** the part of either of the upper limbs from the elbow to the wrist; forearm. **3. a.** the corresponding limb of any other vertebrate. **b.** an armlike appendage of some invertebrates. **4.** an object that covers or supports the human arm, esp. the sleeve of a garment or the side of a chair, etc. **5.** anything considered to resemble an arm in appearance, position, or function: an arm of the sea; the arm of a record player. **6.** an administrative subdivision of an organization: an arm of the government. **7.** power; authority: the arm of the law. **8. arm in arm.** with arms linked. **9. at arm's length.** at a distance. **10. in the arms of Morpheus.** sleeping. **11. with open arms.** with great warmth and hospitality. —'**armless** adj.

arm[2] (ɑːm) vb. **1.** to equip with weapons as a preparation for war. **2.** (tr.) to provide (a person or thing) with something that strengthens, protects, or increases efficiency. **3.** (tr.) to activate a fuse so that it will explode at the required time. ~n. **4.** (usually pl.) a weapon, esp. a firearm.

armada (ɑː'mɑːdə) n. a large number of ships or aircraft.

Armada (ɑː'mɑːdə) n. (usually preceded by the) See the **Spanish Armada.**

armadillo (,ɑːmə'dɪləʊ) n., pl. **-los.** a burrowing mammal of Central and South America with a covering of strong horny plates over most of the body.

Armageddon (,ɑːmə'gɛdən) n. **1.** New Testament. the place designated in Revelation 16:16 as the scene of the final battle at the end of the world. **2.** a catastrophic and extremely destructive conflict.

armament ('ɑːməmənt) n. **1.** the weapon equipment of a military vehicle, ship, or aircraft. **2.** a military force raised and armed ready for war. **3.** preparation for war.

armature ('ɑːmətjʊə) n. **1.** a revolving structure in an electric motor or generator, wound with the coils that carry the current. **2.** any part of an electric machine or device that vibrates under the influence of a magnetic field or within which an electromotive force is induced. **3.** Also called: **keeper.** a soft iron or steel bar placed across the poles of a magnet to close the magnetic circuit. **4.** Sculpture. a framework to support the clay or other material used in modelling. **5.** the protective outer covering of an animal or plant.

armchair ('ɑːm,tʃɛə) n. **1.** a chair, esp. an upholstered one, that has side supports for the arms or elbows. **2.** (modifier) taking or involving no active part: an armchair strategist.

armed[1] (ɑːmd) adj. **1.** equipped with or supported by arms, armour, etc. **2.** prepared for conflict or any difficulty.

armed[2] (ɑːmd) adj. **a.** having an arm or arms. **b.** (in combination): long-armed; one-armed.

armed forces pl. n. the military forces of a nation or nations, including the army, navy, air force, marines, etc.

armhole ('ɑːm,həʊl) n. the opening in an article of clothing through which the arm passes.

armillary sphere (ɑː'mɪlərɪ) n. a model of the celestial sphere formerly used in fixing the positions of heavenly bodies.

armistice ('ɑːmɪstɪs) n. an agreement between opposing armies to suspend hostilities; truce.

Armistice Day ('ɑːmɪstɪs) n. the anniversary of the signing of the armistice that ended World War I, on Nov. 11, 1918.

armlet ('ɑːmlɪt) n. **1.** a small arm, as of a lake. **2.** a band or bracelet worn round the arm.

armoire (ɑːm'wɑː) n. a large cabinet, originally used for storing weapons.

armor ('ɑːmə) n. the U.S. spelling of **armour.**

armorial (ɑː'mɔːrɪəl) adj. of or relating to heraldry or heraldic arms.

armour or U.S. **armor** ('ɑːmə) n. **1.** any defensive covering, esp. that of metal, chain mail, etc., worn by medieval warriors. **2.** the protective metal plates on a tank, warship, etc. **3.** Mil. armoured fighting vehicles in general. **4.** any protective covering, such as the shell of certain animals. **5.** heraldic insignia; arms. ~vb. **6.** (tr.) to equip or cover with armour.

armoured or U.S. **armored** ('ɑːməd) adj. **1.** having a protective covering. **2.** comprising units making use of armoured vehicles: an armoured brigade.

armourer or U.S. **armorer** ('ɑːmərə) n. **1.** a person who makes or mends arms and armour. **2.** a person employed in the maintenance of small arms and weapons in a military unit.

armour plate n. a tough heavy steel often hardened on the surface, used for protecting warships, tanks, etc.

armoury or U.S. **armory** ('ɑːmərɪ) n., pl. **-mouries** or **-mories. 1.** a secure place for the storage of weapons. **2.** armour generally; military supplies.

armpit ('ɑːm,pɪt) n. the small depression beneath the arm where it joins the shoulder.

armrest ('ɑːm,rɛst) n. the part of a chair, sofa, etc., that supports the arm. Sometimes shortened to **arm.**

arms (ɑːmz) pl. n. **1.** weapons collectively. **2.** military exploits: prowess in arms. **3.** the official heraldic symbols of a family, state, etc. **4. bear arms. a.** to carry weapons. **b.** to serve in the armed forces. **c.** to have a coat of arms. **5. in** or **under arms.** armed and prepared for war. **6. lay down one's arms.** to stop fighting; surrender. **7. take (up) arms.** to prepare to fight. **8. up in arms.** indignant; prepared to protest strongly.

army ('ɑːmɪ) n., pl. **-mies. 1.** the military land forces of a nation. **2.** a military unit usually consisting of two or more corps with supporting arms and services. **3.** (modifier) of or characteristic of an army. **4.** any large body of people united for some specific purpose. **5.** a large number of people, animals, etc.

arm[1] n. **1.** appendage, limb, upper limb **2.** bough, branch, department, detachment, division, extension, offshoot, projection, section, sector **3.** branch, channel, estuary, firth, inlet, sound, strait, tributary **4.** authority, command, force, might, potency, power, strength, sway

arm[2] v. **1.** Esp. with weapons accoutre, array, deck out, equip, furnish, issue with, outfit, provide, rig, supply **2.** mobilize, muster forces, prepare for war, take up arms **3.** brace, equip, forearm, fortify, gird one's loins, guard, make ready, outfit, prepare, prime, protect, strengthen

armada fleet, flotilla, navy, squadron

armaments ammunition, arms, guns, materiel, munitions, ordnance, weaponry, weapons

armed accoutred, arrayed, carrying weapons, equipped, fitted out, forearmed, fortified, furnished, girded, guarded, in arms, prepared, primed, protected, provided, ready, rigged out, strengthened, supplied, under arms

armistice ceasefire, peace, suspension of hostilities, truce

armour armour plate, covering, protection, sheathing, shield

armoured armour-plated, bombproof, bulletproof, ironclad, mailed, protected, steel-plated

armoury ammunition dump, arms depot, arsenal, magazine, ordnance depot

arms 1. armaments, firearms, guns, instruments of war, ordnance, weaponry, weapons **2.** blazonry, crest, escutcheon, heraldry, insignia

army 1. armed force, host (Archaic), land forces, legions, military, military force, soldiers, soldiery, troops **2.** Fig. array, horde, host, multitude, pack, swarm, throng, vast number

arnica ('ɑːnɪkə) n. 1. any of a genus of N temperate or arctic plants having yellow flowers. 2. the tincture of the dried flower heads of any of these plants, used in treating bruises.

aroma (ə'rəumə) n. 1. a distinctive usually pleasant smell, esp. of spices, wines, and plants. 2. a subtle pervasive quality or atmosphere.

aromatic (ˌærə'mætɪk) adj. 1. having a distinctive, usually fragrant smell. 2. (of an organic compound) having an unsaturated ring, esp. containing a benzene ring. Cf. **aliphatic**. ~n. 3. something, such as a plant or drug, giving off a fragrant smell. —ˌaro'matically adv. —a,roma'ticity n.

arose (ə'rəuz) vb. the past tense of **arise**.

around (ə'raund) prep. 1. surrounding, encircling, or enclosing: a band around her head. 2. on all or most sides of: to look around one. 3. on or outside the circumference or perimeter of. 4. situated at various points in: a lot of shelves around the house. 5. from place to place in: driving around Ireland. 6. somewhere in or near. 7. reached by making a partial circuit about something: the shop around the corner. 8. revolving round a centre or axis: the earth's motion around its axis. 9. approximately in: it happened around 1957. ~adv. 10. on all or most sides. 11. on or outside the circumference or perimeter: the racing track is two miles around. 12. in all directions from a point of reference: he owns the land for ten miles around. 13. to all members of a group: pass the food around. 14. in the vicinity, esp. restlessly but idly: to stand around. 15. in no particular place or direction: to sleep around. 16. in rotation or revolution: the wheels turn around. 17. by a circuitous route: the road to the farm goes around by the pond. 18. to a specific place: she came around to see me. 19. Inf. (of people) active and prominent in a particular area or profession. 20. Inf. present in some place (the exact location being inexact). 21. Inf. in circulation; available: that type of phone has been around for some years now. 22. Inf. to many places, so as to have gained considerable experience, often of a worldly or social nature: I've been around.
▷ **Usage**. In adverbial and prepositional senses round is now regarded by most speakers and writers of British English as a less formal variant of around, although historically it is the better established form. In American English, around has almost completely replaced round in these senses, except in a few fixed phrases such as all year round.

arouse (ə'rauz) vb. 1. (tr.) to evoke or elicit (a reaction, emotion, or response). 2. to awaken from sleep. —a'rousal n. —a'rouser n.

arpeggio (ɑː'pɛdʒɪəu) n., pl. **-gios**. a chord whose notes are played or sung in rapid succession rather than simultaneously.

arquebus ('ɑːkwɪbəs) or **harquebus** n. a portable long-barrelled gun dating from the 15th century.

arr. abbrev. for: 1. arranged (by). 2. arrival. 3. arrive(d).

arrack or **arak** ('ærək) n. a coarse spirit distilled in various Eastern countries from grain, rice, sugar cane, etc.

arraign (ə'reɪn) vb. 1. (tr.) to bring (a prisoner) before a court to answer an indictment. 2. (tr.) to call to account; accuse. —ar'raigner n. —ar'raignment n.

arrange (ə'reɪndʒ) vb. 1. (tr.) to put into a proper or systematic order. 2. (tr.; may take a clause as object or an infinitive) to arrive at an agreement about. 3. (when intr., often foll. by for; when tr., may take a clause as object or an infinitive) to make plans or preparations in advance (for something): we arranged for her to be met. 4. (tr.) to adapt (a musical composition) for performance in a different way, esp. on different instruments. 5. (intr.; often foll. by with) to come to an agreement. —ar'rangeable adj. —ar'ranger n.

arrangement (ə'reɪndʒmənt) n. 1. the act of arranging or being arranged. 2. the form in which things are arranged. 3. a thing composed of various ordered parts: a flower arrangement. 4. (often pl.) a preparation. 5. an understanding. 6. an adaptation of a piece of music for performance in a different way, esp. on different instruments.

arrant ('ærənt) adj. utter; out-and-out: an arrant fool. —'arrantly adv.

arras ('ærəs) n. a wall hanging, esp. of tapestry.

array (ə'reɪ) n. 1. an impressive display or collection. 2. an orderly arrangement, esp. of troops in battle order. 3. Poetic. rich clothing. 4. Maths. a set of numbers or symbols arranged in rows and columns, as in a determinant or matrix. 5. Law. a panel of jurors. ~vb. (tr.) 6. to dress in rich attire. 7. to arrange in order, esp. troops for battle. 8. Law. to draw up (a panel of jurors). —ar'rayal n.

arrears (ə'rɪəz) n. 1. (sometimes sing.) Also called: **arrearage**. something outstanding or owed. 2. **in arrears** or **arrear**. late in paying a debt or meeting an obligation.

arrest (ə'rɛst) vb. (tr.) 1. to deprive (a person) of liberty by taking him into custody, esp. under lawful authority. 2. to seize (a ship) under lawful authority. 3. to slow or stop the development of (a disease, growth, etc.). 4. to catch and hold (one's attention, etc.). ~n. 5. the act of taking a person into custody, esp. under lawful authority. 6. the act of seizing and holding a ship under lawful authority. 7. the state of being held: under arrest. 8. the slowing or stopping of something: a cardiac arrest.

arresting (ə'rɛstɪŋ) adj. attracting attention; striking. —ar'restingly adv.

arrival (ə'raɪvəl) n. 1. the act or time of arriving. 2. a person or thing that arrives or has arrived.

arrive (ə'raɪv) vb. (intr.) 1. to come to a certain place during or after a journey. 2. to reach: to arrive at a decision. 3. to occur eventually: the moment arrived when

---

THESAURUS

aroma bouquet, fragrance, odour, perfume, redolence, savour, scent, smell

aromatic balmy, fragrant, odoriferous, perfumed, pungent, redolent, savoury, spicy, sweet-scented, sweet-smelling

around prep. 1. about, encircling, enclosing, encompassing, environing, on all sides of, on every side of, surrounding 2. about, approximately, circa (used with dates), roughly ~adv. 3. about, all over, everywhere, here and there, in all directions, on all sides, throughout, to and fro 4. at hand, close, close at hand, close by, near, nearby, nigh (Archaic or dialect)

arouse agitate, animate, awaken, call forth, enliven, excite, foment, foster, goad, incite, inflame, instigate, kindle, move, provoke, quicken, rouse, sharpen, spark, spur, stimulate, stir up, summon up, waken, wake up, warm, whet, whip up

arrange 1. align, array, class, classify, dispose, file, form, group, line up, marshal, order, organize, position, put in order, range, rank, set out, sort, systematize (Inf.), systematize, tidy 2. adjust, agree to, come to terms, compromise, construct, contrive, determine, devise, fix up (Inf.), organize, plan, prepare,

project, schedule, settle 3. adapt, instrument, orchestrate, score

arrangement 1. alignment, array, classification, design, display, disposition, form, grouping, line-up, marshalling, order, ordering, organization, ranging, rank, setup (Inf.), structure, system 2. Often plural adjustment, agreement, compact, compromise, construction, deal, devising, organization, plan, planning, preparation, provision, schedule, settlement, terms 3. adaptation, instrumentation, interpretation, orchestration, score, version

arrant absolute, atrocious, blatant, complete, downright, egregious, extreme, flagrant, gross, infamous, monstrous, notorious, out-and-out, outright, rank, thorough, thoroughgoing, undisguised, unmitigated, utter, vile

array n. 1. arrangement, collection, display, disposition, exhibition, formation, line-up, marshalling, muster, order, parade, show, supply 2. Poetic apparel, attire, clothes, dress, finery, garb, garments, raiment (Archaic), regalia ~v. 3. align, arrange, display, dispose, draw up, exhibit, form up, group, line up, marshal, muster, order, parade, place in order, range, set in line

(Military), show 4. accoutre, adorn, apparel (Archaic), attire, bedeck, caparison, clothe, deck, decorate, dress, equip, fit out, garb, outfit, robe, supply, wrap

arrest v. 1. apprehend, bust (Inf.), capture, catch, collar (Inf.), detain, lay hold of, nab (Inf.), nick (Sl.), pinch (Inf.), run in (Sl.), seize, take, take into custody, take prisoner 2. block, check, delay, end, halt, hinder, hold, inhibit, interrupt, obstruct, restrain, retard, slow, stall, stay, stop, suppress 3. absorb, catch, engage, engross, fascinate, grip, hold, intrigue, occupy ~n. 4. apprehension, bust (Inf.), capture, cop (Sl.), detention, seizure 5. blockage, check, delay, end, halt, hindrance, inhibition, interruption, obstruction, restraint, stalling, stay, stoppage, suppression

arresting conspicuous, engaging, extraordinary, impressive, noticeable, outstanding, remarkable, striking, stunning, surprising

arrival 1. advent, appearance, arriving, coming, entrance, happening, occurrence, taking place 2. arriver, caller, comer, entrant, incomer, newcomer, visitant, visitor

pretence was useless. **4.** *Inf.* (of a baby) to be born. **5.** *Inf.* to attain success.

arrogant ('ærəgənt) *adj.* having or showing an exaggerated opinion of one's own importance, merit, ability, etc.: *an arrogant assumption.* —'**arrogance** *n.* —'**arrogantly** *adv.*

arrogate ('ærə‚geɪt) *vb.* **1.** (*tr.*) to claim or appropriate for oneself without justification. **2.** (*tr.*) to attribute or assign to another without justification. —‚**arro'gation** *n.* —**arrogative** (ə'rɒgətɪv) *adj.*

arrow ('ærəʊ) *n.* **1.** a long slender pointed weapon, usually having feathers fastened at the end as a balance, that is shot from a bow. **2.** any of various things that resemble an arrow in shape, function, or speed.

arrowhead ('ærəʊ‚hɛd) *n.* **1.** the pointed tip of an arrow, often removable from the shaft. **2.** something that resembles the head of an arrow in shape. **3.** an aquatic herbaceous plant having arrow-shaped leaves.

arrowroot ('ærəʊ‚ruːt) *n.* **1.** a white-flowered West Indian plant, whose rhizomes yield an easily digestible starch. **2.** the starch obtained from this plant.

arse (ɑːs) *or U.S.* **ass** *n. Taboo.* **1.** the buttocks. **2.** the anus. **3.** a stupid person; fool. ~Also called (for senses 2, 3): **arsehole** ('ɑːs‚həʊl).

arsenal ('ɑːsənəl) *n.* **1.** a store for arms, ammunition, and other military items. **2.** a workshop that produces munitions. **3.** a store of anything regarded as weapons.

arsenic *n.* ('ɑːsnɪk). **1.** a toxic metalloid element used in transistors, lead-based alloys, and high-temperature brasses. Symbol: As; atomic no.: 33; atomic wt.: 74.92. **2.** a nontechnical name for **arsenic trioxide**, used as rat poison and an insecticide. ~*adj.* (ɑː'sɛnɪk). **3.** of or containing arsenic, esp. in the pentavalent state.

arsenical (ɑː'sɛnɪkəl) *adj.* **1.** of or containing arsenic. ~*n.* **2.** a drug or insecticide containing arsenic.

arson ('ɑːsən) *n. Criminal law.* the act of intentionally or recklessly setting fire to property for some improper reason. —'**arsonist** *n.*

art¹ (ɑːt) *n.* **1. a.** the creation of works of beauty or other special significance. **b.** (*as modifier*): *an art movement.* **2.** the exercise of human skill (as distinguished from *nature*). **3.** imaginative skill as applied to representations of the natural world or figments of the imagination. **4. a.** works of art collectively, esp. of the visual arts. **b.** (*as modifier*): *an art gallery.* See also **arts, fine art.** **5.** any branch of the visual arts, esp. painting. **6.** any field using the techniques of art. **7.** method, facility, or knack: *the art of threading a needle.* **8.** skill governing a particular human activity: *the art of government.* **9.** cunning. **10. get something down to a fine art.** to become highly proficient at something through practice.

art² (ɑːt) *vb. Arch.* (used with the pronoun *thou*) a singular form of the present tense of **be.**

art. *abbrev. for:* **1.** article. **2.** artificial. **3.** Also: **arty.** artillery.

-art *suffix forming nouns.* variant of **-ard.**

Art Deco ('dɛkəʊ) *n.* a style of interior decoration, architecture, etc., at its height in the 1930s and characterized by geometrical shapes.

artefact *or* **artifact** ('ɑːtɪ‚fækt) *n.* **1.** something made or given shape by man, such as a tool or a work of art, esp. an object of archaeological interest. **2.** *Cytology.* a

structure seen in dead tissue that is not normally present in the living tissue.

arterial (ɑː'tɪərɪəl) *adj.* **1.** of or affecting an artery or arteries. **2.** denoting or relating to the bright red reoxygenated blood that circulates in the arteries. **3.** being a major route, esp. one with many minor branches. —**ar'terially** *adv.*

arteriosclerosis (ɑː‚tɪərɪəʊsklɪ'rəʊsɪs) *n., pl.* **-ses** (-siːz). a thickening and loss of elasticity of the walls of the arteries. Nontechnical name: **hardening of the arteries.** —**arteriosclerotic** (ɑː‚tɪərɪəʊsklɪ'rɒtɪk) *adj.*

artery ('ɑːtərɪ) *n., pl.* **-teries.** **1.** any of the tubular thick-walled muscular vessels that convey oxygenated blood from the heart to various parts of the body. Cf. **vein.** **2.** a major road or means of communication.

artesian well (ɑː'tiːzɪən) *n.* a well sunk through impermeable strata into strata receiving water from an area at a higher altitude than that of the well, so the water is forced to flow upwards.

art form *n.* **1.** an accepted mode of artistic composition, such as the sonnet, symphony, etc. **2.** a recognized medium of artistic expression.

artful ('ɑːtfʊl) *adj.* **1.** cunning or tricky. **2.** skilful in achieving a desired end. —'**artfully** *adv.* —'**artfulness** *n.*

arthritis (ɑː'θraɪtɪs) *n.* inflammation of a joint or joints characterized by pain and stiffness of the affected parts. —**arthritic** (ɑː'θrɪtɪk) *adj., n.*

arthropod ('ɑːθrə‚pɒd) *n.* an invertebrate having jointed limbs, a segmented body, and an exoskeleton made of chitin, as the crustaceans, insects, arachnids, and centipedes.

artic (ɑː'tɪk) *n. Inf.* short for **articulated lorry.**

artichoke ('ɑːtɪ‚tʃəʊk) *n.* **1.** Also called: **globe artichoke.** a thistle-like Eurasian plant, cultivated for its large edible flower head. **2.** the unopened flower head of this plant, which can be cooked and eaten. **3.** See **Jerusalem artichoke.**

article ('ɑːtɪkəl) *n.* **1.** one of a class of objects; item. **2.** an unspecified or previously named thing, esp. a small object. **3.** a written composition on a subject, often being one of several found in a magazine, newspaper, etc. **4.** *Grammar.* a kind of determiner, occurring in many languages including English, that lacks independent meaning. See also **definite article, indefinite article.** **5.** a clause or section in a written document. **6.** (*often cap.*) *Christianity.* See **Thirty-nine Articles.** ~*vb.* (*tr.*) **7.** to bind by a written contract, esp. one that governs a period of training: *an articled clerk.*

articular (ɑː'tɪkjʊlə) *adj.* of or relating to joints or to the structural components in a joint.

articulate *adj.* (ɑː'tɪkjʊlɪt). **1.** able to express oneself fluently and coherently. **2.** having the power of speech. **3.** distinct, clear, or definite: *an articulate document.* **4.** *Zool.* (of arthropods and higher vertebrates) possessing joints or jointed segments. ~*vb.* (ɑː'tɪkjʊ‚leɪt). **5.** to speak or enunciate (words, syllables, etc.) clearly and distinctly. **6.** (*tr.*) to express coherently in words. **7.** (*intr.*) *Zool.* to be jointed or form a joint. —**ar'ticulately** *adv.* —**ar'ticulateness** *n.* —**ar'ticu‚lator** *n.*

articulated lorry *n.* a large lorry made in two separate sections, a tractor and a trailer, connected by a pivoted bar. U.S. name: **trailer truck.**

THESAURUS

arrive 1. appear, attain, befall, come, enter, get to, happen, occur, reach, show up (*Inf.*), take place, turn up **2.** *Inf.* achieve recognition, become famous, make good, make it (*Inf.*), make the grade (*Inf.*), reach the top, succeed

arrogance bluster, conceit, conceitedness, contemptuousness, disdainfulness, haughtiness, hauteur, high-handedness, imperiousness, insolence, loftiness, lordliness, overweeningness, pomposity, pompousness, presumption, pretension, pretentiousness, pride, scornfulness, superciliousness, swagger, uppishness (*Brit. inf.*)

arrogant assuming, blustering, conceited, contemptuous, disdainful, haughty, high and mighty (*Inf.*), high-handed, imperious, insolent, lordly, overbearing, overweening, pompous, presumptuous, pretentious, proud, scornful, supercilious, swaggering, uppish

(*Brit. inf.*)

arrogate appropriate, assume, claim unduly, commandeer, demand, expropriate, presume, seize, usurp

arrogation appropriation, assumption, commandeering, demand, expropriation, presumption, seizure, usurpation

arrow 1. bolt, dart, flight, quarrel, reed (*Archaic*), shaft (*Archaic*) **2.** indicator, pointer

arsenal ammunition dump, armoury, arms depot, magazine, ordnance depot, stock, stockpile, store, storehouse, supply

art 1. adroitness, aptitude, artifice (*Archaic*), artistry, craft, craftsmanship, dexterity, expertise, facility, ingenuity, knack, knowledge, mastery, method, profession, skill, trade, virtuosity **2.** artfulness, artifice, astuteness, craftiness, cunning, deceit, duplicity, guile, trickery, wiliness

artful adept, adroit, clever, crafty, cunning, deceitful, designing, dexterous, foxy, ingenious, intriguing, masterly, politic, proficient, resourceful, scheming, sharp, shrewd, skilful, sly, smart, subtle, tricky, wily

article 1. commodity, item, object, piece, substance, thing, unit **2.** composition, discourse, essay, feature, item, paper, piece, story, treatise **3.** branch, clause, count, detail, division, head, heading, item, matter, paragraph, part, particular, passage, piece, point, portion, section

articulate *adj.* **1.** clear, coherent, comprehensible, eloquent, expressive, fluent, intelligible, lucid, meaningful, understandable, vocal, well-spoken ~*v.* **2.** enounce, enunciate, express, pronounce, say, speak, state, talk, utter, verbalize, vocalize, voice **3.** connect, couple, fit together, hinge, join, joint

articulation (ɑːˌtɪkjʊˈleɪʃən) n. 1. the act or process of speaking or expressing in words. 2. a. the process of articulating a speech sound. b. the sound so produced, esp. a consonant. 3. the act or the state of being jointed together. 4. Zool. a. a joint such as that between bones or arthropod segments. b. the way in which jointed parts are connected. 5. Bot. the part of a plant at which natural separation occurs.

artifact (ˈɑːtɪˌfækt) n. a variant spelling of **artefact**.

artifice (ˈɑːtɪfɪs) n. 1. a clever expedient. 2. crafty or subtle deception. 3. skill; cleverness. 4. a skilfully contrived device.

artificer (ɑːˈtɪfɪsə) n. 1. a skilled craftsman. 2. a clever or inventive designer. 3. a serviceman trained in mechanics.

artificial (ˌɑːtɪˈfɪʃəl) adj. 1. produced by man; not occurring naturally. 2. made in imitation of a natural product: artificial cream. 3. pretended; assumed; insincere. 4. lacking in spontaneity; affected: an artificial laugh. —**artificiality** (ˌɑːtɪˌfɪʃɪˈælɪtɪ) n. —**arti'ficially** adv.

artificial insemination n. introduction of spermatozoa into the vagina or uterus by means other than sexual union.

artificial respiration n. 1. any of various methods of restarting breathing after it has stopped. 2. any method of maintaining respiration, as by use of an iron lung.

artillery (ɑːˈtɪlərɪ) n. 1. cannon or any mounted guns of higher calibre than machine guns. 2. troops or military units specializing in using such guns. 3. the science dealing with the use of guns.

artisan (ˈɑːtɪˌzæn, ˌɑːtɪˈzæn) n. a skilled workman; craftsman.

artist (ˈɑːtɪst) n. 1. a person who practises or is skilled in an art, esp. painting, drawing, or sculpture. 2. a person who displays in his work qualities required in art, such as sensibility and imagination. 3. a person whose profession requires artistic expertise. 4. a person skilled in some task or occupation 5. Sl. a person devoted to or proficient in something: a con artist, a booze artist. —**ar'tistic** adj. —**ar'tistically** adv.

artiste (ɑːˈtiːst) n. 1. an entertainer, such as a singer or dancer. 2. a person who is highly skilled in some occupation: a hair artiste.

artistry (ˈɑːtɪstrɪ) n. 1. artistic workmanship, ability, or quality. 2. artistic pursuits. 3. great skill.

artless (ˈɑːtlɪs) adj. 1. free from deceit: an artless manner. 2. natural or simple. 3. without art or skill. 4. naive: an artless remark. 5. ignorant or uncultured. —**'artlessly** adv.

Art Nouveau (ˈɑː nuːˈvəʊ; French ar nuˈvo) n. a style of art and architecture of the 1890s, characterized by sinuous outlines and stylized natural forms.

arts (ɑːts) pl. n. 1. a. the. imaginative, creative, and non-scientific branches of knowledge considered collectively, esp. as studied academically. b. (as modifier): an arts degree. 2. See **fine art**. 3. cunning actions or schemes.

arty (ˈɑːtɪ) adj. **artier, artiest.** Inf. having an affected

interest in artists or art. —**'artiness** n.

arum (ˈɛərəm) n. 1. a plant of Europe and the Mediterranean region, having arrow-shaped leaves and a typically white spathe, such as the cuckoopint. 2. **arum lily.** a southern African plant which has a white funnel-shaped spathe enclosing a yellow spadix.

-ary suffix. 1. (forming adjectives) of; related to; belonging to: cautionary. 2. (forming nouns) a person or thing connected with: missionary; aviary.

Aryan (ˈɛərɪən) n. 1. (in Nazi ideology) a Caucasian of non-Jewish descent. 2. a member of any of the peoples supposedly descended from the Indo-Europeans. ~adj. 3. of or characteristic of an Aryan or Aryans. ~adj., a. 4. Arch. Indo-European.

as (æz; unstressed əz) conj. (subordinating) 1. (often preceded by just) while; when: he caught me as I was leaving. 2. in the way that: dancing as only she can. 3. that which; what: I did as I was told. 4. (of) which fact, event, etc. (referring to the previous statement): to become wise, as we all know, is not easy. 5. as it were. in a way; as if it were really so. 6. since; seeing that. 7. in the same way that: he died of cancer, as his father had done. 8. for instance: capital cities, as London. ~prep., conj. 9. a. used to indicate identity of extent, amount, etc.: she is as heavy as her sister. b. used with this sense after a noun phrase introduced by the same: the same height as her sister. ~prep. 10. in the role of; being: as his friend, my opinions are probably biased. 11. as for or to. with reference to: as for my past, I'm not telling you anything. 12. as if or though. as it would be if: he talked as if he knew all about it. 13. as (it) is. in the existing state of affairs. 14. as per. See per. 15. as regards. See regard. 16. as such. See such. 17. such as. See such. 18. as was. in a previous state. 19. as well. See well[1]. 20. as yet. so far.

As symbol for: 1. Chem. arsenic. 2. altostratus.

A.S.A. abbrev. for: 1. (in Britain) Amateur Swimming Association. 2. (in the U.S.) American Standards Association.

asafoetida or **asafetida** (ˌæsəˈfɛtɪdə) n. a bitter resin with an unpleasant onion-like smell, obtained from the roots of some umbelliferous plants: formerly used to treat flatulence, etc.

asbestos (æsˈbɛstɒs) n. a. any of the fibrous amphibole minerals that are incombustible and resistant to chemicals. It is widely used in the form of fabric or board as a heat-resistant structural material. b. (as modifier): asbestos matting.

asbestosis (ˌæsbɛsˈtəʊsɪs) n. inflammation of the lungs resulting from chronic inhalation of asbestos particles.

ascend (əˈsɛnd) vb. 1. to go or move up (a ladder, hill, slope, etc.). 2. (intr.) to slope or incline upwards. 3. (intr.) to rise to a higher point, level, etc. 4. to trace (a genealogy, etc.) back in time. 5. to sing or play (a scale, etc.) from the lower to higher notes. 6. **ascend the throne.** to become king or queen.

ascendancy, ascendency (əˈsɛndənsɪ) or **ascendance, ascendence** n. the condition of being dominant.

THESAURUS

articulation 1. delivery, diction, enunciation, expression, pronunciation, saying, speaking, statement, talking, utterance, verbalization, vocalization, voicing 2. connection, coupling, hinge, joint, jointing, juncture

artifice 1. contrivance, device, dodge, expedient, hoax, machination, manoeuvre, ruse, stratagem, subterfuge, tactic, trick, wile 2. artfulness, chicanery, craft, craftiness, cunning, deception, duplicity, guile, scheming, slyness, trickery 3. adroitness, cleverness, deftness, facility, finesse, ingenuity, invention, inventiveness, skill

artificer 1. artisan, craftsman, mechanic 2. architect, builder, contriver, creator, designer, deviser, inventor, maker, originator

artificial 1. man-made, manufactured, non-natural, plastic, synthetic 2. bogus, counterfeit, ersatz, fake, imitation, mock, phoney (Inf.), sham, simulated, specious, spurious 3. affected, assumed, contrived, false, feigned, forced, hollow, insincere, meretricious, phoney (Inf.), pretended, spurious, unnatural

artillery battery, big guns, cannon, cannonry, gunnery, ordnance

artisan artificer, craftsman, handicraftsman, journeyman, mechanic, skilled workman, technician

artistic aesthetic, beautiful, creative, cultivated, cultured, decorative, elegant, exquisite, graceful, imaginative, ornamental, refined, sensitive, stylish, tasteful

artistry accomplishment, art, artistic ability, brilliance, craftsmanship, creativity, finesse, flair, genius, mastery, proficiency, sensibility, skill, style, talent, taste, touch, virtuosity, workmanship

artless 1. candid, direct, fair, frank, genuine, guileless, honest, open, plain, sincere, straightforward, true, undesigning 2. humble, natural, plain, pure, simple, unadorned, unaffected, uncontrived, unpretentious 3. awkward, bungling, clumsy, crude, incompetent, inept, maladroit, primitive, rude, unskilled, untalented 4. childlike, ingenuous, innocent, jejune, naive, trustful, trusting, unsophisticated

as conj. 1. at the time that, during the time that, just as, when, while 2. in the manner that, in the way that, like 3. that which, what 4. because, considering that, seeing that, since 5. in the same manner with, in the same way that, like 6. for instance, like, such as ~prep. 7. being, in the character of, in the role of, under the name of 8. **as for** as regards, in reference to, on the subject of, with reference to, with regard to, with respect to 9. **as it were** in a manner of speaking, in a way, so to say, so to speak

ascend climb, float up, fly up, go up, lift off, mount, move up, rise, scale, slope upwards, soar, take off, tower

ascendancy, ascendency authority, command, control, dominance, domination, dominion, hegemony, influence, mastery, power, predominance, pre-eminence, prevalence, reign, rule, sovereignty, superiority, supremacy, sway, upper hand

ascendant *or* **ascendent** (ə'sɛndənt) *adj.* **1.** proceeding upwards; rising. **2.** dominant or influential. ~*n.* **3.** a position or condition of dominance. **4.** *Astrol.* (*sometimes cap.*) **a.** a point on the ecliptic that rises on the eastern horizon at a particular moment. **b.** the sign of the zodiac containing this point. **5. in the ascendant.** increasing in influence, etc.

ascension (ə'sɛnʃən) *n.* the act of ascending. —**as'censional** *adj.*

Ascension (ə'sɛnʃən) *n. Bible.* the passing of Jesus Christ from earth into heaven (Acts 1:9).

Ascension Day *n.* the 40th day after Easter, when the Ascension of Christ into heaven is celebrated.

ascent (ə'sɛnt) *n.* **1.** the act of ascending; upward movement. **2.** an upward slope. **3.** movement back through time (esp. in **line of ascent**).

ascertain (ˌæsə'teɪn) *vb.* (*tr.*) **1.** to determine definitely. **2.** *Arch.* to make certain. —**ascer'tainable** *adj.* —**ˌascer'tainment** *n.*

ascetic (ə'sɛtɪk) *n.* **1.** a person who practises great self-denial and abstains from worldly comforts and pleasures, esp. for religious reasons. ~*adj. also* **as'cetical. 2.** rigidly abstinent or abstemious. **3.** of or relating to ascetics or asceticism. —**as'cetically** *adv.*

ascorbic acid (ə'skɔːbɪk) *n.* a white crystalline vitamin present in plants, esp. citrus fruits, tomatoes, and green vegetables. A deficiency in the diet of man leads to scurvy. Also called: **vitamin C.**

ascribe (ə'skraɪb) *vb.* (*tr.*) **1.** to credit or assign, as to a particular origin or period. **2.** to consider as belonging to: *to ascribe beauty to youth.* —**as'cribable** *adj.* —**as'cription** (ə'skrɪpʃən) *n.*

-ase *suffix forming nouns.* indicating an enzyme: *oxidase.*

asepsis (ə'sɛpsɪs, eɪ-) *n.* **1.** the state of being free from living pathogenic organisms. **2.** the methods of achieving a germ-free condition. —**a'septic** *adj.*

asexual (eɪ'sɛksjʊəl) *adj.* **1.** having no apparent sex or sex organs. **2.** (of reproduction) not involving the fusion of male and female gametes. —**aˌsexu'ality** *n.* —**a'sexually** *adv.*

ash¹ (æʃ) *n.* **1.** the residue formed when matter is burnt. **2.** fine particles of lava thrown out by an erupting volcano. **3.** a light silvery grey colour.

ash² (æʃ) *n.* **1.** a tree having compound leaves, clusters of small greenish flowers, and winged seeds. **2.** the wood of this tree, used for tool handles, etc. **3.** any of several trees resembling the ash, such as the mountain ash. **4.** *Austral.* any of various eucalypts.

ashamed (ə'ʃeɪmd) *adj.* (*usually postpositive*) **1.** overcome with shame or remorse. **2.** (foll. by *of*) suffering from feelings of shame in relation to (a person or deed). **3.** (foll. by *to*) unwilling through fear of humiliation, shame, etc. —**ashamedly** (ə'ʃeɪmɪdlɪ) *adv.*

ash can *n.* a U.S. word for **dustbin.** Also called: **garbage can, ash bin, trash can.**

ashen ('æʃən) *adj.* **1.** drained of colour. **2.** consisting of or resembling ashes. **3.** of a pale greyish colour.

ashes ('æʃɪz) *pl. n.* **1.** ruins or remains, as after burning.

2. the remains of a human body after cremation.

Ashes ('æʃɪz) *pl. n.* **the.** a cremated cricket stump constituting a trophy competed for by England and Australia in test cricket since 1882.

Ashkenazi (ˌæʃkə'nɑːzɪ) *n., pl.* **-zim** (-zɪm). **1.** (*modifier*) of or relating to the Jews of Germany and E Europe. **2.** a Jew of German or E European descent. Cf. **Sephardi.**

ashlar *or* **ashler** ('æʃlə) *n.* **1.** a square block of hewn stone for use in building. **2.** a thin dressed stone with straight edges, used to face a wall. **3.** masonry made of ashlar.

ashore (ə'ʃɔː) *adv.* **1.** towards or onto land from the water. ~*adj.* (*postpositive*), *adv.* **2.** on land: *a day ashore before sailing.*

ashram ('æʃrəm) *n.* a religious retreat or community where a Hindu holy man lives.

ashtray ('æʃˌtreɪ) *n.* a receptacle for tobacco ash, cigarette butts, etc.

Ash Wednesday *n.* the first day of Lent, named from the former Christian custom of sprinkling ashes on penitents' heads.

ashy ('æʃɪ) *adj.* **ashier, ashiest. 1.** of a pale greyish colour; ashen. **2.** consisting of, covered with, or resembling ash.

Asian ('eɪʃən, 'eɪʒən) *adj.* **1.** of or relating to Asia, the largest of the continents, or to any of its people or languages. ~*n.* **2.** a native or inhabitant of Asia or a descendant of one.

▷ **Usage.** *Asian* is used in formal writing as a noun indicating a person from Asia. The use of the word *Asiatic* in this sense is regarded by some people as offensive.

Asian flu *n.* a type of influenza caused by a virus which apparently originated in China in 1957.

aside (ə'saɪd) *adv.* **1.** on or to one side. **2.** out of hearing; in or into seclusion. **3.** away from oneself: *he threw the book aside.* **4.** out of mind or consideration: *he put aside all fears.* **5.** in or into reserve: *to put aside money for old age.* ~*n.* **6.** something spoken by an actor, intended to be heard by the audience, but not by the others on stage. **7.** any confidential statement spoken in undertones. **8.** an incidental remark, note, etc.

asinine ('æsɪˌnaɪn) *adj.* **1.** obstinate or stupid. **2.** resembling an ass. —**'asiˌninely** *adv.* —**asininity** (ˌæsɪ'nɪnɪtɪ) *n.*

ask (ɑːsk) *vb.* **1.** (often foll. by *about*) to put a question (to); request an answer (from). **2.** (*tr.*) to inquire about: *she asked the way.* **3.** (*tr.*) to direct or put (a question). **4.** (*may take a clause as object or an infinitive*; often foll. by *for*) to make a request or demand: *they asked for a deposit.* **5.** (*tr.*) to demand or expect (esp. in **ask a lot of, ask too much of**). **6.** (*tr.*) Also: **ask out, ask over.** to request (a person) politely to come or go to a place: *he asked her to the party.* ~See also **ask after, ask for.** —**'asker** *n.*

ask after *vb.* (*prep.*) to make enquiries about the health of (someone): *he asked after her mother.*

askance (ə'skæns) *or* **askant** (ə'skænt) *adv., adj.* **1.** with an oblique glance. **2.** with doubt or mistrust.

askew (ə'skjuː) *adv., adj.* at an oblique angle; towards

THESAURUS

ascendant, ascendent *adj.* 1. ascending, climbing, going upwards, mounting, rising 2. authoritative, commanding, controlling, dominant, influential, powerful, predominant, pre-eminent, prevailing, ruling, superior, supreme, uppermost ~*n.* 3. **in the ascendant** ascending, climbing, commanding, dominant, dominating, flourishing, growing, increasing, mounting, on the rise, on the way up, prevailing, rising, supreme, up-and-coming, uppermost, winning

ascent 1. ascending, ascension, clambering, climb, climbing, mounting, rise, rising, scaling, upward movement 2. acclivity, gradient, incline, ramp, rise, rising ground, upward slope

ascertain confirm, determine, discover, establish, ferret out, find out, fix, identify, learn, make certain, settle, verify

ascetic 1. *n.* abstainer, anchorite, hermit, monk, nun, recluse, self-denier 2. *adj.* abstemious, abstinent, austere, celibate, frugal, harsh, plain, puritanical, rigorous, self-denying, self-disciplined, severe, Spartan, stern

asceticism abstemiousness, abstinence, austerity, celibacy, frugality, harshness, mortification of the flesh, plainness, puritanism, rigorousness, rigour, self-abnegation, self-denial, self-discipline, self-mortification

ascribe assign, attribute, charge, credit, impute, put down, refer, set down

ashamed abashed, bashful, blushing, chagrined, conscience-stricken, crestfallen, discomfited, distressed, embarrassed, guilty, humbled, humiliated, mortified, prudish, reluctant, remorseful, shamefaced, sheepish, shy, sorry

ashen anaemic, ashy, colourless, grey, leaden, livid, pale, pallid, pasty, wan, white

ashore aground, landwards, on dry land, on land, on the beach, on the shore, shorewards, to the shore

aside 1. *adv.* alone, alongside, apart, away, beside, in isolation, in reserve, on one side, out of mind, out of the way, privately, separately, to one side, to the side 2. *n.* departure, digression, excursion, excursus, interpolation, interposition, parenthesis, tangent

asinine brainless, daft (*Inf.*), dunderheaded, fatuous, foolish, gormless (*Inf.*), halfwitted, idiotic, imbecile, imbecilic, inane, moronic, obstinate, senseless, silly, stupid, thickheaded, thick-witted

ask 1. inquire, interrogate, query, question, quiz 2. appeal, apply, beg, beseech, claim, crave, demand, entreat, implore, petition, plead, pray, request, seek, solicit, sue, supplicate 3. bid, invite, summon

askance 1. awry, indirectly, obliquely, out of the corner of one's eye, sideways, with a side glance 2. disapprovingly, distrustfully, doubtfully, dubiously, mistrustfully, sceptically, suspiciously

askew *adv./ adj.* aslant, awry, cockeyed (*Inf.*), crooked, crookedly, lopsided, oblique, obliquely, off-centre, to one side

one side; awry.

ask for *vb.* (*prep.*) **1.** to try to obtain by requesting. **2.** (*intr.*) *Inf.* to behave in a provocative manner that is regarded as inviting (trouble, etc.): *you're asking for it.*

asking price *n.* the price suggested by a seller but usually considered to be subject to bargaining.

aslant (əˈslɑːnt) *adv.* **1.** at a slant. ~*prep.* **2.** at a slant across or athwart.

asleep (əˈsliːp) *adj.* (*postpositive*) **1.** in or into a state of sleep. **2.** in or into a dormant or inactive state. **3.** (of limbs) numb; lacking sensation. **4.** *Euphemistic.* dead.

ASLEF (ˈæzlɛf) *n.* (in Britain) *acronym for* Associated Society of Locomotive Engineers and Firemen.

asocial (eɪˈsəʊʃəl) *adj.* **1.** avoiding contact. **2.** unconcerned about the welfare of others. **3.** hostile to society.

asp (æsp) *n.* **1.** the venomous snake that caused the death of Cleopatra. **2.** Also called: **asp viper.** a viper that occurs in S Europe and is very similar to but smaller than the adder.

asparagus (əˈspærəgəs) *n.* **1.** a plant of the lily family, having small scaly or needle-like leaves. **2.** the succulent young shoots, which may be cooked and eaten. **3. asparagus fern.** a fernlike species of asparagus, native to southern Africa.

aspect (ˈæspɛkt) *n.* **1.** appearance to the eye; visual effect. **2.** a distinct feature or element in a problem, situation, etc.; facet. **3.** the way in which a problem, idea, etc., may be considered. **4.** a facial expression: *a severe aspect.* **5.** a position facing a particular direction: *the southern aspect of a house.* **6.** a view in a certain direction. **7.** *Astrol.* any of several specific angular distances between two planets. **8.** *Grammar.* a category of verbal inflections that expresses such features as the continuity, repetition, or completeness of the action described.

aspen (ˈæspən) *n.* a kind of poplar tree in which the leaves are attached to the stem by long flattened stalks so that they quiver in the wind.

asperity (æˈspɛrɪtɪ) *n., pl.* **-ties. 1.** roughness or sharpness of temper. **2.** roughness or harshness of a surface, sound, etc.

asperse (əˈspɜːs) *vb.* (*tr.*) to spread false rumours about; defame. —**asˈperser** *n.* —**asˈpersive** *adj.*

aspersion (əˈspɜːʃən) *n.* **1.** a disparaging or malicious remark (esp. in **cast aspersions (on)**). **2.** the act of defaming.

asphalt (ˈæsfælt) *n.* **1.** any of several black semisolid substances composed of bitumen and inert mineral matter. They occur naturally and as a residue from petroleum distillation. **2.** a mixture of this substance with gravel, used in road-surfacing and roofing materials. **3.** (*modifier*) containing or surfaced with asphalt. ~*vb.* **4.** (*tr.*) to cover with asphalt. —**asˈphaltic** *adj.*

asphodel (ˈæsfəˌdɛl) *n.* **1.** any of various S European plants of the lily family having clusters of white or yellow flowers. **2.** an unidentified flower of Greek legend said to cover the Elysian fields.

asphyxia (æsˈfɪksɪə) *n.* lack of oxygen in the blood due to restricted respiration; suffocation. —**asˈphyxial** *adj.* —**asˈphyxiant** *adj.*

asphyxiate (æsˈfɪksɪˌeɪt) *vb.* to cause asphyxia in or undergo asphyxia; smother; suffocate. —**asˌphyxiˈation** *n.* —**asˈphyxiˌator** *n.*

aspic (ˈæspɪk) *n.* a savoury jelly based on meat or fish stock, used as a relish or as a mould for meat, vegetables, etc.

aspidistra (ˌæspɪˈdɪstrə) *n.* a popular house plant of the lily family with long tough evergreen leaves.

aspirant (ˈæspɪrənt) *n.* **1.** a person who aspires, as to a high position. ~*adj.* **2.** aspiring.

aspirate *vb.* (ˈæspɪˌreɪt). (*tr.*) **1.** *Phonetics.* **a.** to articulate (a stop) with some force, so that breath escapes audibly. **b.** to pronounce (a word or syllable) with an initial *h.* **2.** to remove by inhalation or suction, esp. to suck (air or fluid) from a body cavity. ~*n.* (ˈæspɪrɪt). **3.** *Phonetics.* **a.** a stop pronounced with an audible release of breath. **b.** the glottal fricative represented in English and several other languages as *h.* ~*adj.* (ˈæspɪrɪt). **4.** *Phonetics.* (of a stop) pronounced with a forceful expulsion of breath.

aspiration (ˌæspɪˈreɪʃən) *n.* **1.** strong desire to achieve something, such as success. **2.** the aim of such desire. **3.** the act of breathing. **4.** *Phonetics.* **a.** the pronunciation of an aspirated consonant. **b.** an aspirated consonant. **5.** *Med.* the sucking of fluid or foreign matter into the air passages of the body. —**aspiratory** (əˈspaɪrətərɪ) *adj.*

aspirator (ˈæspɪˌreɪtə) *n.* a device employing suction, such as a jet pump or one for removing fluids from a body cavity.

aspire (əˈspaɪə) *vb.* (*intr.*) **1.** (usually foll. by *to* or *after*) to yearn (for), desire, or hope (to do or be something): *to aspire to be a great leader.* **2.** to rise to a great height. —**asˈpiring** *adj.*

aspirin (ˈæsprɪn) *n., pl.* **-rin** or **-rins. 1.** a white crystalline compound widely used in the form of tablets to relieve pain, fever, and colds. Chemical name: **acetylsalicylic acid. 2.** a tablet of aspirin.

Aspirin *n.* in Canada, a trademark for **aspirin.**

ass¹ (æs) *n.* **1.** a mammal related to the horse. It is hardy and sure-footed, having longer ears than the horse. **2.** (*not in technical use*) the donkey. **3.** a foolish or ridiculously pompous person.

ass² (æs) *n.* the usual U.S. word for **arse.**

assail (əˈseɪl) *vb.* (*tr.*) **1.** to attack violently; assault. **2.** to criticize or ridicule vehemently. **3.** to beset or disturb: *his mind was assailed by doubts.* **4.** to encounter with the intention of mastering. —**asˈsailable** *adj.* —**asˈsailant** *or* **asˈsailer** *n.*

assassin (əˈsæsɪn) *n.* a murderer, esp. one who kills a prominent political figure.

assassinate (əˈsæsɪˌneɪt) *vb.* (*tr.*) **1.** to murder (a political figure). **2.** to ruin or harm (a person's reputation, etc.) by slander. —**asˌsassiˈnation** *n.*

assault (əˈsɔːlt) *n.* **1.** a violent attack, either physical or verbal. **2.** *Law.* an act that causes violence to another. **3. a.** the culmination of a military attack. **b.** (*as modifier*): *assault troops.* **4.** rape. ~*vb.* (*tr.*) **5.** to make an assault upon. **6.** to rape or attempt to rape. —**asˈsaultive** *adj.*

assault and battery *n. Criminal law.* a threat of attack to another person followed by actual attack.

assay *vb.* (əˈseɪ). **1.** to subject (a substance, such as silver or gold) to chemical analysis, as in the determination of the amount of impurity. ~*n.* (əˈseɪ, ˈæseɪ). **2.** (*tr.*) to attempt (something or to do something). **3. a.** an analysis, esp. a determination of the amount of metal in an ore or the amounts of impurities in a precious metal. **b.** (*as modifier*): *an assay office.* **4.** a substance undergoing an analysis. **5.** a written report on the results of an analysis. **6.** a test. —**asˈsayer** *n.*

THESAURUS

asleep crashed out (*Sl.*), dead to the world (*Inf.*), dormant, dozing, fast asleep, napping, sleeping, slumbering, snoozing (*Inf.*), sound asleep

aspect 1. air, appearance, attitude, bearing, condition, countenance, demeanour, expression, look, manner, mien (*Literary*) 2. bearing, direction, exposure, outlook, point of view, position, prospect, scene, situation, view 3. angle, facet, feature, side

asperity acerbity, acrimony, bitterness, churlishness, crabbedness, crossness, harshness, irascibility, irritability, moroseness, peevishness, roughness, ruggedness, severity, sharpness, sourness, sullenness

asphyxiate choke, smother, stifle, strangle, strangulate, suffocate, throttle

aspirant 1. *n.* applicant, aspirer, candidate, hopeful, postulant, seeker, suitor 2. *adj.* ambitious, aspiring, eager, endeavouring, hopeful, longing, striving, wishful

aspiration aim, ambition, craving, desire, dream, eagerness, endeavour, goal, hankering, hope, longing, object, objective, wish, yearning

aspire aim, be ambitious, be eager, crave, desire, dream, hanker, hope, long, pursue, seek, wish, yearn

aspiring *adj.* ambitious, aspirant, eager, endeavouring, hopeful, longing, striving, wishful, would-be

ass 1. donkey, jennet, moke (*Sl.*) 2. blockhead, bonehead (*Sl.*), dolt, dope (*Sl.*), dunce, fool, halfwit, idiot, jackass, nincompoop, nin-

ny, nitwit, numskull, simpleton, twerp (*Inf.*), twit (*Inf.*)

assail 1. assault, attack, beset, charge, encounter, fall upon, invade, lay into, maltreat, set about, set upon 2. abuse, berate, criticize, impugn, malign, revile, vilify

assailant aggressor, assailer, assaulter, attacker, invader

assassin eliminator (*Sl.*), executioner, hatchet man (*Sl.*), hit man (*Sl.*), killer, liquidator, murderer, slayer

assassinate eliminate (*Sl.*), hit (*U.S. sl.*), kill, liquidate, murder, slay

assault 1. *n.* aggression, attack, charge, incursion, invasion, offensive, onset, onslaught, storm, storming, strike 2. *v.* assail, attack, beset, charge, fall upon, invade, lay

assegai *or* **assagai** ('æsə,gaı) *n., pl.* **-gais. 1.** a southern African tree, the wood of which is used for making spears. **2.** a sharp light spear.

assemblage (ə'sɛmblɪdʒ) *n.* **1.** a number of things or persons assembled together. **2.** the act of assembling or the state of being assembled. **3.** (,æsəm'blɑːʒ). a three-dimensional work of art that combines various objects.

assemble (ə'sɛmbəl) *vb.* **1.** to come or bring together; collect or congregate. **2.** to fit or join together (the parts) of (something, such as a machine). —**as'sembler** *n.*

assembler (ə'sɛmblə) *n.* **1.** a computer program that converts a set of low-level symbolic data into machine language. Cf. **compiler. 2.** in full: **assembler language.** a symbolic language that uses an assembler program to convert to machine language.

assembly (ə'sɛmblı) *n., pl.* **-blies. 1.** a number of people gathered together, esp. for a formal meeting held at regular intervals. **2.** the act of assembling or the state of being assembled. **3.** the process of putting together a number of parts to make a machine. **4.** *Mil.* a signal for personnel to assemble.

assembly line *n.* a sequence of machines, tools, operations, workers, etc., in a factory, arranged so that at each stage a further process is carried out.

assent (ə'sɛnt) *n.* **1.** agreement, as to a statement, proposal, etc. **2.** compliance. ~*vb.* (*intr.; usually foll. by to*) **3.** to agree or express agreement.

assert (ə'sɜːt) *vb.* (*tr.*) **1.** to insist upon (rights, etc.). **2.** (*may take a clause as object*) to declare. **3.** to put (oneself) forward in an insistent manner. —**as'serter** *or* **as'sertor** *n.*

assertion (ə'sɜːʃən) *n.* **1.** a positive statement, usually made without evidence. **2.** the act of asserting.

assertive (ə'sɜːtɪv) *adj.* given to making assertions; dogmatic or aggressive. —**as'sertively** *adv.* —**as'sertiveness** *n.*

assess (ə'sɛs) *vb.* (*tr.*) **1.** (foll. by *at*) to estimate the value of (income, property, etc.) for taxation purposes. **2.** to determine the amount of (a fine, tax, etc.). **3.** to impose a tax, fine, etc., on (a person or property). **4.** to evaluate. —**as'sessable** *adj.* —**as'sessment** *n.*

assessor (ə'sɛsə) *n.* **1.** a person who values property for taxation. **2.** a person who estimates the value of damage to property for insurance purposes. **3.** a person with technical expertise called in to advise a court. —**assessorial** (,æsɛ'sɔːrɪəl) *adj.*

asset ('æsɛt) *n.* anything valuable or useful.

asset-stripping *n. Commerce.* the practice of taking over a failing company at a low price and then selling the assets piecemeal. —**'asset-,stripper** *n.*

asseverate (ə'sɛvə,reıt) *vb.* (*tr.*) to declare solemnly. —**as,sever'ation** *n.*

assiduity (,æsı'djuːıtı) *n., pl.* **-ties. 1.** constant and close application. **2.** (*often pl.*) devoted attention.

assiduous (ə'sıdjʊəs) *adj.* **1.** hard-working; persevering. **2.** undertaken with perseverance and care. —**as'siduousness** *n.*

assign (ə'saın) *vb.* (*mainly tr.*) **1.** to select for and appoint to a post, etc. **2.** to give out or allot (a task, problem, etc.). **3.** to set apart (a place, person, time, etc.) for a particular function or event: *to assign a day for the meeting.* **4.** to attribute to a specified cause, origin, or source. **5.** to transfer (one's right, interest, or title to property) to someone else. ~*n.* **6.** *Law.* a person to whom property is assigned; assignee. —**as'signable** *adj.* —**as'signer** *or* **,assign'or** *n.*

assignation (,æsıg'neıʃən) *n.* **1.** a secret or forbidden arrangement to meet, esp. one between lovers. **2.** the act of assigning; assignment.

assignee (,æsaı'niː) *n. Law.* a person to whom some right, interest, or property is transferred.

assignment (ə'saınmənt) *n.* **1.** something that has been assigned, such as a mission or task. **2.** a position or post to which a person is assigned. **3.** the act of assigning or state of being assigned. **4.** *Law.* **a.** the transfer to another of a right, interest, or title to property. **b.** the document effecting such a transfer.

assimilate (ə'sımı,leıt) *vb.* **1.** (*tr.*) to learn (information, etc.) and understand it thoroughly. **2.** (*tr.*) to absorb (food). **3.** (*intr.*) to become absorbed, incorporated, or learned and understood. **4.** (usually foll. by *into* or *with*) to adjust or become adjusted: *the new immigrants assimilated easily.* **5.** (usually foll. by *to* or *with*) to become or cause to become similar. **6.** (usually foll. by *to*) *Phonetics.* to change (a consonant) or (of a consonant) to be changed into another under the influence of one adjacent to it. —**as'similable** *adj.* —**as,simi'lation** *n.* —**as'similative** *or* **as'similatory** *adj.* —**as'simi,lator** *n.*

assist (ə'sıst) *vb.* **1.** to give help or support to (a person, cause, etc.). **2.** to work or act as an assistant or subordinate to (another). ~*n.* **3.** *U.S.* the act of helping. —**as'sister** *n.*

assistance (ə'sıstəns) *n.* **1.** help; support. **2.** the act of assisting. **3.** *Brit. inf.* See **national assistance.**

THESAURUS

into, set about, set upon, storm, strike at

assay *v.* **1.** analyse, appraise, assess, evaluate, examine, inspect, investigate, prove, test, try, weigh ~*n.* **2.** *Archaic* attempt, endeavour, essay, try, venture **3.** analysis, examination, inspection, investigation, test, trial

assemble 1. accumulate, amass, bring together, call together, collect, come together, congregate, convene, convoke, flock, forgather, gather, marshal, meet, muster, rally, round up, summon **2.** build up, connect, construct, erect, fabricate, fit together, join, make, manufacture, piece together, put together, set up

assembly 1. accumulation, aggregation, assemblage, body, collection, company, conclave, conference, congregation, convocation, council, crowd, diet, flock, gathering, group, mass, meeting, multitude, rally, synod, throng **2.** building up, connecting, construction, erection, fabrication, fitting together, joining, manufacture, piecing together, putting together, setting up

assent 1. *v.* accede, accept, acquiesce, agree, allow, approve, comply, concur, consent, fall in with, go along with, grant, permit, sanction, subscribe **2.** acceptance, accession, accord, acquiescence, agreement, approval, compliance, concurrence, consent, permission, sanction

assert 1. affirm, allege, asseverate, attest, aver, avouch (*Archaic*), avow, contend, declare, maintain, predicate, profess, pronounce, state, swear **2.** claim, defend, insist

upon, press, put forward, stand up for, stress, uphold, vindicate **3.** assert oneself exert one's influence, make one's presence felt, put oneself forward

assertion 1. affirmation, allegation, asseveration, attestation, avowal, contention, declaration, predication, profession, pronouncement, statement **2.** defence, insistence, maintenance, stressing, vindication

assertive aggressive, confident, decided, decisive, demanding, dogmatic, domineering, emphatic, firm, forceful, forward, insistent, overbearing, positive, pushy (*Inf.*), self-assured, strong-willed

assess 1. appraise, compute, determine, estimate, evaluate, fix, gauge, judge, rate, size up (*Inf.*), value, weigh **2.** demand, evaluate, fix, impose, levy, rate, tax, value

assessment 1. appraisal, computation, determination, estimate, estimation, evaluation, judgment, rating, valuation **2.** charge, demand, duty, evaluation, fee, impost, levy, rate, rating, tariff, tax, taxation, toll, valuation

asset 1. advantage, aid, benefit, blessing, boon, help, resource, service **2.** *Plural* capital, estate, funds, goods, holdings, means, money, possessions, property, reserves, resources, valuables, wealth

assiduous attentive, constant, diligent, hard-working, indefatigable, industrious, laborious, persevering, persistent, sedulous, steady, studious, unflagging, untiring, unwearied

assign 1. appoint, choose, delegate, desig-

nate, name, nominate, select **2.** allocate, allot, apportion, consign, distribute, give, give out, grant, make over **3.** appoint, appropriate, determine, fix, set apart, stipulate **4.** accredit, ascribe, attribute, put down

assignation 1. clandestine meeting, illicit meeting, rendezvous, secret meeting, tryst (*Archaic*) **2.** allocation, allotment, appointment, apportionment, appropriation, ascription, assignment, attribution, choice, consignment, delegation, designation, determination, distribution, giving, grant, nomination, selection, specification, stipulation

assignment 1. appointment, charge, commission, duty, job, mission, position, post, responsibility, task **2.** allocation, allotment, appointment, apportionment, appropriation, ascription, assignation (*Law, chiefly Scot.*), attribution, choice, consignment, delegation, designation, determination, distribution, giving, grant, nomination, selection, specification, stipulation

assimilate 1. absorb, digest, imbibe (*Literary*), incorporate, ingest, learn, take in **2.** acclimatize, accommodate, acculturate, accustom, adapt, adjust, become like, become similar, blend in, conform, fit, homogenize, intermix, mingle

assist abet, aid, back, benefit, boost, collaborate, cooperate, expedite, facilitate, further, help, reinforce, relieve, second, serve, succour, support, sustain, work for, work with

assistance abetment, aid, backing, benefit, boost, collaboration, cooperation, fur-

assistant (ə'sɪstənt) n. 1. a. a person who assists, esp. in a subordinate position. b. (as modifier): assistant manager. 2. See **shop assistant.**
assize (ə'saɪz) n. Scot. law. a. trial by a jury. b. a jury.
assizes (ə'saɪzɪz) pl. n. (formerly in England and Wales) the sessions of the principal court in each county, exercising civil and criminal jurisdiction: replaced in 1971 by crown courts.
assn. abbrev. for association.
assoc. abbrev. for: 1. associate(d). 2. association.
associate vb. (ə'səʊʃɪ,eɪt, -sɪ-). (usually foll. by with) 1. (tr.) to link or connect in the mind or imagination. 2. (intr.) to mix socially: to associate with writers. 3. (intr.) to form or join an association, group, etc. 4. (tr.; usually passive) to consider in conjunction: rainfall is associated with humidity. 5. (tr.) to bring (a person, esp. oneself) into friendship, partnership, etc. 6. (tr.; often passive) to express agreement (with): Bertrand Russell was associated with the C.N.D. movement. ~n. (ə'səʊʃɪɪt). 7. a person joined with another or others in an enterprise, business, etc. 8. a companion or friend. 9. something that usually accompanies another thing. 10. a person having a subordinate position in or admitted to only partial membership of an institution, association, etc. ~adj. (ə'səʊʃɪɪt). (prenominal) 11. joined with another or others in an enterprise, business, etc.: an associate director. 12. having partial rights or subordinate status: an associate member. 13. accompanying; concomitant. —**as'sociable** adj. —**as'soci,ator** n. —**as'sociate,ship** n.
association (ə,səʊsɪ'eɪʃən, -ʃɪ-) n. 1. a group of people having a common purpose or interest; a society or club. 2. the act of associating or the state of being associated. 3. friendship or companionship: their association will not last. 4. a mental connection of ideas, feelings, or sensations. 5. Chem. the formation of groups of molecules and ions held together by weak chemical bonds. 6. Ecology. a group of similar plants that grow in a uniform environment.
association football n. 1. a more formal name for **soccer.** 2. Austral. Australian Rules played in a football association rather than a league.
associative (ə'səʊʃɪətɪv) adj. 1. of, relating to, or causing association or union. 2. Maths, logic. a. of an operation, such as multiplication or division, in which the answer is the same regardless of the way in which the elements are grouped: $(2 \times 3) \times 4 = 2 \times (3 \times 4)$. b. referring to this property: the associative laws of arithmetic.
assonance ('æsənəns) n. 1. the use of the same vowel sound with different consonants or the same consonant with different vowels, as in a line of verse. Examples are time and light or mystery and mastery. 2. partial correspondence. —**'assonant** adj., n.
assort (ə'sɔːt) vb. 1. (tr.) to arrange or distribute into groups of the same type; classify. 2. (intr.; usually foll. by with) to fit or fall into a class or group. 3. (tr.) to supply with an assortment of merchandise. 4. (tr.) to put in the same category as others. —**as'sortative** adj.
assorted (ə'sɔːtɪd) adj. 1. consisting of various kinds mixed together. 2. classified: assorted categories. 3. matched (esp. in **well-assorted, ill-assorted**).
assortment (ə'sɔːtmənt) n. 1. a collection or group of various things or sorts. 2. the act of assorting.
ASSR abbrev. for Autonomous Soviet Socialist Republic.
asst. abbrev. for assistant.
assuage (ə'sweɪdʒ) vb. (tr.) 1. to soothe, moderate, or relieve (grief, pain, etc.). 2. to give relief to (thirst, etc.). 3. to pacify; calm. —**as'suagement** n. —**as'suager** n.
assume (ə'sjuːm) vb. (tr.) 1. (may take a clause as object) to take for granted; suppose. 2. to undertake or take on or over (a position, responsibility, etc.): to assume office. 3. to pretend to; feign: he assumed indifference. 4. to take or put on; adopt: the problem assumed gigantic proportions. 5. to appropriate or usurp (power, control, etc.). —**as'sumable** adj. —**as'sumer** n.
assuming (ə'sjuːmɪŋ) adj. expecting too much; presumptuous.
assumption (ə'sʌmpʃən) n. 1. the act of taking something for granted or something that is taken for granted. 2. an assuming of power or possession. 3. presumption. 4. Logic. a proposition used as a premiss in a logical argument. —**as'sumptive** adj.
Assumption (ə'sʌmpʃən) n. Christianity. 1. the taking up of the Virgin Mary (body and soul) into heaven when her earthly life was ended. 2. the feast commemorating this.
assurance (ə'ʃʊərəns) n. 1. a statement, assertion, etc., intended to inspire confidence. 2. a promise or pledge of support. 3. freedom from doubt; certainty. 4. forwardness; impudence. 5. Chiefly Brit. insurance providing for certainties such as death as contrasted with fire.
assure (ə'ʃʊə) vb. (tr.; may take a clause as object) 1. to convince: to assure a person of one's love. 2. to promise; guarantee. 3. to state positively. 4. to make (an event) certain. 5. Chiefly Brit. to insure against loss, esp. of life. —**as'surable** adj. —**as'surer** n.

THESAURUS

therance, help, helping hand, reinforcement, relief, service, succour, support, sustenance
assistant abettor, accessory, accomplice, aide, aider, ally, associate, auxiliary, backer, coadjutor (Rare), collaborator, colleague, confederate, cooperator, helper, helpmate, henchman, partner, right-hand man, second, supporter
associate v. 1. affiliate, ally, combine, confederate, conjoin, connect, correlate, couple, identify, join, league, link, lump together, mix, pair, relate, think of together, unite, yoke 2. accompany, befriend, be friends, consort, fraternize, hang about, hang out (Inf.), hobnob, mingle, mix, run around (Inf.) ~n. 3. ally, collaborator, colleague, companion, compeer, comrade, confederate, confrère, co-worker, follower, friend, mate, partner
association 1. affiliation, alliance, band, clique, club, coalition, combine, company, confederacy, confederation, cooperative, corporation, federation, fraternity, group, league, organization, partnership, society, syndicate, union 2. companionship, comradeship, familiarity, fellowship, fraternization, friendship, intimacy, partnership, relations, relationship 3. blend, bond, combination, concomitance, connection, correlation, identification, joining, juxtaposition, linkage, linking, lumping together, mixing, mixture, pairing, relation, tie, union, yoking
assort arrange, array, categorize, classify, dispose, distribute, file, grade, group, range,

rank, sort, type
assorted 1. different, diverse, diversified, heterogeneous, miscellaneous, mixed, motley, sundry, varied, variegated, various 2. arranged, arrayed, categorized, classified, disposed, filed, graded, grouped, ranged, ranked, sorted, typed
assortment 1. array, choice, collection, diversity, farrago, hotchpotch, jumble, medley, mélange, miscellany, mishmash, mixed bag (Inf.), mixture, potpourri, salmagundi, selection, variety 2. arrangement, categorizing, classification, disposition, distribution, filing, grading, grouping, ranging, ranking, sorting, typing
assuage allay, alleviate, appease, calm, ease, lessen, lighten, lull, mitigate, moderate, mollify, pacify, palliate, quench, quiet, relieve, satisfy, soften, soothe, still, temper, tranquillize
assume 1. accept, believe, expect, fancy, guess (Inf., chiefly U.S.), imagine, infer, presume, presuppose, suppose, surmise, suspect, take for granted, think 2. adopt, affect, counterfeit, feign, imitate, impersonate, mimic, pretend to, put on, sham, simulate 3. accept, acquire, attend to, begin, don, embark upon, embrace, enter upon, put on, set about, shoulder, take on, take over, take responsibility for, take up, undertake 4. acquire, appropriate, arrogate, commandeer, expropriate, pre-empt, seize, take, take over, usurp
assumed 1. affected, bogus, counterfeit,

fake, false, feigned, fictitious, imitation, made-up, make-believe, phoney (Inf.), pretended, pseudonymous, sham, simulated, spurious 2. accepted, expected, hypothetical, presumed, presupposed, supposed, surmised, taken for granted 3. appropriated, arrogated, pre-empted, seized, usurped
assuming adj. arrogant, bold, conceited, disdainful, domineering, egotistic, forward, haughty, imperious, overbearing, presumptuous, pushy (Inf.), rude
assumption 1. acceptance, belief, conjecture, expectation, fancy, guess, hypothesis, inference, postulate, postulation, premise, premiss, presumption, presupposition, supposition, surmise, suspicion, theory 2. acceptance, acquisition, adoption, embracing, entering upon, putting on, shouldering, takeover, taking on, taking up, undertaking 3. acquisition, appropriation, arrogation, expropriation, pre-empting, seizure, takeover, taking, usurpation 4. arrogance, conceit, imperiousness, presumption, pride, self-importance
assurance 1. affirmation, assertion, declaration, guarantee, oath, pledge, profession, promise, protestation, vow, word, word of honour 2. aggressiveness, assuredness, boldness, certainty, certitude, confidence, conviction, coolness, courage, faith, firmness, nerve, poise, positiveness, security, self-confidence, self-reliance, sureness 3. arrogance, effrontery, gall (Inf.), impudence, nerve (Inf.), presumption
assure 1. comfort, convince, embolden,

assured (ə'ʃʊəd) *adj.* **1.** sure; guaranteed. **2.** self-assured. **3.** *Chiefly Brit.* insured. ~*n. Chiefly Brit.* **4. a.** the beneficiary under a life assurance policy. **b.** the person whose life is insured. —**assuredly** (ə'ʃʊərɪdlɪ) *adv.*

Assyrian (ə'sɪrɪən) *n.* **1.** an inhabitant of ancient Assyria, a kingdom of Mesopotamia. **2.** the extinct Semitic language of the Assyrians. ~*adj.* **3.** of or characteristic of the ancient Assyrians, their language, or culture.

A.S.T. *abbrev. for* Atlantic Standard Time.

astatine ('æstə,tiːn) *n.* a radioactive element that occurs naturally in minute amounts and is artificially produced by bombarding bismuth with alpha particles. Symbol: At; atomic no.: 85; half-life of most stable isotope, ²¹⁰At: 8.3 hours.

aster ('æstə) *n.* **1.** a plant having white, blue, purple, or pink daisy-like flowers. **2. China aster.** a related Chinese plant widely cultivated for its showy brightly coloured flowers.

asterisk ('æstərɪsk) *n.* **1.** a star-shaped character (*) used in printing or writing to indicate a cross-reference to a footnote, an omission, etc. ~*vb.* **2.** (*tr.*) to mark with an asterisk.

astern (ə'stɜːn) *Naut.* ~*adv., adj.* (*postpositive*) **1.** at or towards the stern. **2.** with the stern first: *full speed astern!* **3.** aft of the stern of a vessel.

asteroid ('æstə,rɔɪd) *n.* **1.** Also called: **minor planet, planetoid.** any of numerous small celestial bodies that move around the sun mainly between the orbits of Mars and Jupiter. **2.** a starfish ~*adj.* also **asteroidal** (,æstə-'rɔɪdəl). **3.** of a starfish. **4.** shaped like a star.

asthma ('æsmə) *n.* a respiratory disorder, often of allergic origin, characterized by difficulty in breathing. —**asth'matic** *adj., n.*

astigmatic (,æstɪg'mætɪk) *adj.* of, having, correcting, or corrected for astigmatism. —**astig'matically** *adv.*

astigmatism (ə'stɪgmə,tɪzəm) *or* **astigmia** (ə'stɪgmɪə) *n.* **1.** a defect of a lens resulting in the formation of distorted images, caused by light rays not meeting at a single focal point. **2.** faulty vision resulting from astigmatism of the lens of the eye.

astir (ə'stɜː) *adj.* (*postpositive*) **1.** awake and out of bed. **2.** in motion; on the move.

A.S.T.M.S. (in Britain) *abbrev. for* Association of Scientific, Technical, and Managerial Staffs.

astonish (ə'stɒnɪʃ) *vb.* (*tr.*) to fill with amazement; surprise greatly. —**a'stonishing** *adj.* —**a'stonishment** *n.*

astound (ə'staʊnd) *vb.* (*tr.*) to overwhelm with amazement; bewilder.

astraddle (ə'strædəl) *adj.* **1.** (*postpositive*) with a leg on either side of something. ~*prep.* **2.** astride.

astrakhan (,æstrə'kæn) *n.* **1.** a fur, usually black or grey, made of the closely curled wool of lambs from Astrakhan, in the S Soviet Union. **2.** a cloth with curled pile resembling this. **3.** (*modifier*) made of such fur or cloth.

astral ('æstrəl) *adj.* **1.** relating to or resembling the stars. **2.** *Theosophy.* relating to a supposed supersensible substance taking the form of an aura discernible to certain gifted individuals.

astray (ə'streɪ) *adj.* (*postpositive*), *adv.* **1.** out of the correct path or direction. **2.** out of the right or expected way.

astride (ə'straɪd) *adj.* (*postpositive*) **1.** with a leg on either side. **2.** with the legs far apart. ~*prep.* **3.** with a leg on either side of. **4.** with a part on both sides of; spanning.

astringent (ə'strɪndʒənt) *adj.* **1.** severe; harsh. **2.** sharp or invigorating. **3.** causing contraction of body tissues, checking blood flow; styptic. ~*n.* **4.** an astringent drug or lotion. —**as'tringency** *n.* —**as'tringently** *adv.*

astro- *combining form.* indicating a star or star-shaped structure.

astrol. *abbrev. for:* **1.** astrologer. **2.** astrological. **3.** astrology.

astrolabe ('æstrə,leɪb) *n.* an instrument used by early astronomers to measure the altitude of stars and planets and also as a navigational aid.

astrology (ə'strɒlədʒɪ) *n.* **1.** the study of the motions and relative positions of the planets, sun, and moon, interpreted in terms of human characteristics and activities. **2.** primitive astronomy. —**as'trologer** *or* **as'trologist** *n.* —**astrological** (,æstrə'lɒdʒɪkəl) *adj.*

astron. *abbrev. for:* **1.** astronomer. **2.** astronomical. **3.** astronomy.

astronaut ('æstrə,nɔːt) *n.* a person trained for travelling in space.

astronautics (,æstrə'nɔːtɪks) *n.* (*functioning as sing.*) the science and technology of space flight. —**,astro'nautical** *adj.*

astronomical (,æstrə'nɒmɪkəl) *or* **astronomic** *adj.* **1.** enormously large. **2.** of or relating to astronomy. —**,astro'nomically** *adv.*

astronomy (ə'strɒnəmɪ) *n.* the scientific study of the individual celestial bodies (excluding the earth) and of the universe as a whole. —**as'tronomer** *n.*

astrophysics (,æstrəʊ'fɪzɪks) *n.* (*functioning as sing.*) the branch of physics concerned with the physical and chemical properties of the celestial bodies. —**,astro-'physicist** *n.*

astute (ə'stjuːt) *adj.* having insight or acumen; perceptive; shrewd. —**as'tutely** *adv.* —**as'tuteness** *n.*

asunder (ə'sʌndə) *adv., adj.* (*postpositive*) in or into parts or pieces; apart: *to tear asunder.*

asylum (ə'saɪləm) *n.* **1.** shelter; refuge; sanctuary. **2.** a safe or inviolable place of refuge, esp. as formerly offered by the Christian Church. **3.** *International law.* refuge afforded to a person whose extradition is sought by a foreign government: *political asylum.* **4.** an institution for the care or confinement of individuals, esp. (formerly) a mental hospital.

asymmetry (æ'sɪmɪtrɪ, eɪ-) *n.* lack or absence of symmetry. —**asymmetric** (,æsɪ'mɛtrɪk, ,eɪ-) *or* **asymmetrical** *adj.*

asymptote ('æsɪm,təʊt) *n.* a straight line that is closely approached by a curve so that the distance between them decreases to zero as the distance from the origin increases to infinity. —**asymptotic** (,æsɪm'tɒtɪk) *or* **,asymp'totical** *adj.*

at (æt) *prep.* **1.** used to indicate location or position: *are they at the table?* **2.** towards; in the direction of: *looking at television.* **3.** used to indicate position in time: *come at three o'clock.* **4.** engaged in; in a state of (being): *children at play.* **5.** (in expressions concerned with habitual activity) during the passing of: *he used to work at night.* **6.** for; in exchange for: *it's selling at four pounds.* **7.** used to indicate the object of an emotion: *shocked at his behaviour.* **8. where it's at.** *Sl.* the real place of action.

At *the chemical symbol for* astatine.

THESAURUS

encourage, hearten, persuade, reassure, soothe **2.** affirm, attest, certify, confirm, declare confidently, give one's word to, guarantee, pledge, promise, swear, vow **3.** clinch, complete, confirm, ensure, guarantee, make certain, make sure, seal, secure

assured 1. beyond doubt, clinched, confirmed, dependable, ensured, fixed, guaranteed, indubitable, irrefutable, made certain, sealed, secure, settled, sure, unquestionable **2.** assertive, audacious, bold, brazen, certain, complacent, confident, overconfident, poised, positive, pushy (*Inf.*), self-assured, self-confident, self-possessed, sure of oneself

astonish amaze, astound, bewilder, confound, daze, dumbfound, flabbergast (*Inf.*), stagger, stun, stupefy, surprise

astonishing amazing, astounding, be-

wildering, breathtaking, impressive, staggering, striking, stunning, stupefying, surprising

astonishment amazement, awe, bewilderment, confusion, consternation, stupefaction, surprise, wonder, wonderment

astound amaze, astonish, bewilder, confound, daze, dumbfound, flabbergast (*Inf.*), overwhelm, stagger, stun, stupefy, surprise

astounding amazing, astonishing, bewildering, breathtaking, impressive, staggering, striking, stunning, stupefying, surprising

astray *adj./adv.* **1.** adrift, afield, amiss, lost, off, off course, off the mark, off the right track, off the subject **2.** into error, into sin, to the bad, wrong

astronaut cosmonaut, spaceman, space pilot, space traveller, spacewoman

astute adroit, artful, bright, calculating, canny, clever, crafty, cunning, discerning, foxy, insightful, intelligent, keen, knowing, penetrating, perceptive, politic, sagacious, sharp, shrewd, sly, subtle, wily

astuteness acumen, adroitness, artfulness, brightness, canniness, cleverness, craftiness, cunning, discernment, foxiness, insight, intelligence, keenness, knowledge, penetration, perceptiveness, sagacity, sharpness, shrewdness, slyness, subtlety, wiliness

asylum 1. harbour, haven, preserve, refuge, retreat, safety, sanctuary, shelter **2.** Old-fashioned funny farm (*Sl.*), hospital, institution, loony bin (*Sl.*), madhouse (*Inf.*), mental hospital, nuthouse (*Sl.*), psychiatric hospital

at. *abbrev. for:* **1.** (unit of pressure) atmosphere. **2.** atomic.

atavism ('ætə,vɪzəm) *n.* **1.** the recurrence in a plant or animal of certain primitive characteristics that were present in an ancestor but have not occurred in intermediate generations. **2.** reversion to a former type. —,ata'vistic *adj.*

ataxia (ə'tæksɪə) *or* **ataxy** (ə'tæksɪ) *n. Pathol.* lack of muscular coordination. —a'taxic *adj.*

A.T.C. *abbrev. for:* **1.** air traffic control. **2.** (in Britain) Air Training Corps.

ate (ɛt, eɪt) *vb.* the past tense of **eat.**

-ate[1] *suffix.* **1.** (*forming adjectives*) having the appearance or characteristics of: *fortunate.* **2.** (*forming nouns*) a chemical compound, esp. a salt or ester of an acid: *carbonate.* **3.** (*forming nouns*) the product of a process: *condensate.* **4.** forming verbs from nouns and adjectives: *hyphenate.*

-ate[2] *suffix forming nouns.* denoting office, rank, or a group having a certain function: *episcopate.*

atelier ('ætəl,jeɪ) *n.* an artist's studio or workshop.

atheism ('eɪθɪ,ɪzəm) *n.* **1.** the doctrine or belief that there is no God. **2.** rejection of belief in God or gods. —'atheist *n.,* adj. —,athe'istic *adj.*

athenaeum *or U.S.* **atheneum** (,æθɪ'niːəm) *n.* **1.** an institution for the promotion of learning. **2.** a building containing a reading room or library.

atherosclerosis (,æθərəʊsklɪə'rəʊsɪs) *n., pl.* **-ses** (-siːz). a degenerative disease of the arteries characterized by thickening of the arterial walls, caused by deposits of fatty material. —**atherosclerotic** (,æθərəʊsklɪə'rɒtɪk) *adj.*

athirst (ə'θɜːst) *adj.* (*postpositive*) **1.** (often foll. by *for*) having an eager desire; longing. **2.** *Arch.* thirsty.

athlete ('æθliːt) *n.* **1.** a person trained to compete in sports or exercises. **2.** a person who has a natural aptitude for physical activities. **3.** *Chiefly Brit.* a competitor in track and field events.

athlete's foot *n.* a fungal infection of the skin of the foot, esp. between the toes and on the soles.

athletic (æθ'lɛtɪk) *adj.* **1.** physically fit or strong. **2.** of, relating to, or suitable for an athlete or for athletics. —**ath'letically** *adv.* —**ath'leticism** *n.*

athletics (æθ'lɛtɪks) *n.* (*functioning as sing.*) **1. a.** track and field events. **b.** (*as modifier*): *an athletics meeting.* **2.** sports or exercises engaged in by athletes.

at-home *n.* a social gathering in a person's home.

athwart (ə'θwɔːt) *adv.* **1.** transversely; from one side to another. ~*prep.* **2.** across the path or line of (esp. a ship). **3.** in opposition to; against.

-atic *suffix forming adjectives.* of the nature of the thing specified: *problematic.*

-ation *suffix forming nouns.* indicating an action, process, state, condition, or result: *arbitration; hibernation.*

-ative *suffix forming adjectives.* of, relating to, or tending to: *authoritative; informative.*

Atlantic (ət'læntɪk) *n.* **1. the.** short for the **Atlantic Ocean,** the world's second largest ocean. ~*adj.* **2.** of, relating to, or bordering the Atlantic Ocean. **3.** of or relating to Atlas or the Atlas Mountains.

Atlantic Provinces *pl. n.* another name for the **Maritime Provinces** of Canada.

Atlantis (ət'læntɪs) *n.* (in ancient legend) a continent said to have sunk beneath the Atlantic west of Gibraltar.

atlas ('ætləs) *n.* **1.** a collection of maps, usually in book form. **2.** a book of charts, graphs, etc.: *an anatomical atlas.* **3.** *Anat.* the first cervical vertebra, supporting the skull in man.

atm. *abbrev. for:* **1.** atmosphere (unit of pressure). **2.** atmospheric.

atmosphere ('ætməs,fɪə) *n.* **1.** the gaseous envelope surrounding the earth or any other celestial body. **2.** the air or climate in a particular place. **3.** a general pervasive feeling or mood. **4.** the prevailing tone or mood of a novel, symphony, painting, etc. **5.** any local gaseous environment or medium: *an inert atmosphere.* **6.** Abbrev: **at.** or **atm.** a unit of pressure; the pressure that will support a column of mercury 760 mm high at 0°C at sea level. —,atmos'pheric (,ætməs'fɛrɪk) *adj.* —,atmos-'pherically *adv.*

atmospherics (,ætməs'fɛrɪks) *pl. n.* radio interference, heard as crackling or hissing in receivers, caused by electrical disturbance.

at. no. *abbrev. for* atomic number.

atoll ('ætɒl) *n.* a circular coral reef or string of coral islands surrounding a lagoon.

atom ('ætəm) *n.* **1. a.** the smallest quantity of an element that can take part in a chemical reaction. **b.** this entity as a source of nuclear energy: *the power of the atom.* **2.** the hypothetical indivisible particle of matter postulated by certain ancient philosophers. **3.** a very small amount or quantity: *to smash something to atoms.*

atom bomb *or* **atomic bomb** *n.* a type of bomb in which the energy is provided by nuclear fission. Also called: **A-bomb, fission bomb.**

atomic (ə'tɒmɪk) *adj.* **1.** of, using or characterized by atomic bombs or atomic energy: *atomic warfare.* **2.** of or comprising atoms: *atomic hydrogen.* —a'tomically *adv.*

atomic energy *n.* another name for **nuclear energy.**

atomic mass unit *n.* a unit of mass used to express atomic and molecular weights that is equal to one twelfth of the mass of an atom of carbon-12. Abbrev.: AMU.

atomic number *n.* the number of protons in the nucleus of an atom of an element. Abbrev.: **at. no.**

atomic theory *n.* **1.** any theory in which matter is regarded as consisting of atoms. **2.** the current concept of the atom as an entity with a definite structure.

atomic weight *n.* the ratio of the average mass per atom of an element to one-twelfth the mass of an atom of carbon-12. Abbrev.: **at. wt.** Also called: **relative atomic mass.**

Usage. Until 1961 *atomic weights* were based on the mass of an atom of oxygen-16. The carbon-12 atom is now the usual basis of calculations and *relative atomic mass* is the preferred term for the new atomic weights.

atomize *or* **-ise** ('ætə,maɪz) *vb.* **1.** to separate or be separated into free atoms. **2.** to reduce (a liquid or solid) to fine particles or spray or (of a liquid or solid) to be reduced in this way. **3.** to destroy by weapons, esp. nuclear weapons.

atomizer *or* **-iser** ('ætə,maɪzə) *n.* a device for reducing a liquid to a fine spray, such as a bottle with a fine outlet used to spray perfumes.

atom smasher *n. Physics.* the nontechnical name for **accelerator** (sense 2).

atonality (,eɪtəʊ'nælɪtɪ) *n.* **1.** absence of or disregard for an established musical key in a composition. **2.** the principles of composition embodying this.

atone (ə'təʊn) *vb.* (*intr.;* foll. by *for*) to make amends or reparation (for a crime, sin, etc.). —a'toner *n.*

atonement (ə'təʊnmənt) *n.* **1.** satisfaction, reparation, or expiation given for an injury or wrong. **2.** (*often cap.*) *Christian theology.* **a.** the reconciliation of man with God through the sacrificial death of Christ. **b.** the sufferings and death of Christ.

atop (ə'tɒp) *adv.* **1.** on top; at the top. ~*prep.* **2.** on top of; at the top of.

-ator *suffix forming nouns.* a person or thing that performs a certain action: *agitator; radiator.*

THESAURUS

atheism disbelief, freethinking, godlessness, heathenism, infidelity, irreligion, nonbelief, paganism, scepticism, unbelief

atheist disbeliever, freethinker, heathen, infidel, irreligionist, nonbeliever, pagan, sceptic, unbeliever

athlete competitor, contender, contestant, games player, gymnast, player, runner, sportsman, sportswoman

athletic 1. *adj.* able-bodied, active, brawny, energetic, fit, herculean, husky (*Inf.*), lusty, muscular, powerful, robust, sinewy, strapping, strong, sturdy, vigorous, well-proportioned 2. *pl. n.* contests, exercises, games of strength, gymnastics, races, sports, track and field events

atmosphere 1. aerosphere, air, heavens, sky 2. air, ambience, aura, character, climate, environment, feel, feeling, flavour, mood, quality, spirit, surroundings, tone

atom bit, crumb, dot, fragment, grain, iota, jot, mite, molecule, morsel, mote, particle, scintilla (*Rare*), scrap, shred, speck, spot, tittle, trace, whit

atone 1. *With* **for** answer for, compensate, do penance for, make amends for, make redress, make reparation for, make up for, pay for, recompense, redress 2. appease, expiate, make expiation for, propitiate, reconcile, redeem

atonement amends, compensation, expiation, payment, penance, propitiation, recompense, redress, reparation, restitution, satisfaction

-atory *suffix forming adjectives.* of, relating to, characterized by, or serving to: *circulatory; explanatory.*

atrium (ˈeɪtrɪəm, ˈɑː-) *n., pl.* **atria** (ˈeɪtrɪə, ˈɑː-). **1.** the open main court of a Roman house. **2.** a court in front of an early Christian or medieval church. **3.** *Anat.* a cavity or chamber in the body, esp. the upper chamber of each half of the heart. —ˈ**atrial** *adj.*

atrocious (əˈtrəʊʃəs) *adj.* **1.** extremely cruel or wicked: *atrocious deeds.* **2.** horrifying or shocking. **3.** *Inf.* very bad: *atrocious writing.* —aˈ**trociousness** *n.*

atrocity (əˈtrɒsɪtɪ) *n., pl.* **-ties.** **1.** behaviour or an action that is wicked or ruthless. **2.** the fact or quality of being atrocious. **3.** (*usually pl.*) acts of extreme cruelty.

atrophy (ˈætrəfɪ) *n., pl.* **-phies.** **1.** a wasting away of an organ or part, or a failure to grow to normal size. **2.** any degeneration or diminution. ~*vb.* **-phying, -phied. 3.** to waste away or cause to waste away. —**atrophic** (əˈtrɒfɪk) *adj.*

atropine (ˈætrəˌpiːn) *n.* a poisonous alkaloid obtained from the deadly nightshade, used to treat peptic ulcers, biliary and renal colic, etc.

att. *abbrev. for:* **1.** attached. **2.** attorney.

attach (əˈtætʃ) *vb.* (*mainly tr.*) **1.** to join, fasten, or connect. **2.** (*reflexive or passive*) to become associated with or join. **3.** (*intr.; foll. by to*) to be connected (with): *responsibility attaches to the job.* **4.** to attribute or ascribe. **5.** to include or append: *a proviso attaches to the contract.* **6.** (*usually passive*) *Mil.* to place on temporary duty with another unit. **7.** to appoint officially. **8.** *Law.* to arrest or take (a person, property, etc.) with lawful authority. —atˈ**tachable** *adj.* —atˈ**tacher** *n.*

attaché (əˈtæʃeɪ) *n.* a specialist attached to a diplomatic mission: *military attaché.*

attaché case *n.* a small flat rectangular briefcase used for carrying documents, papers, etc.

attached (əˈtætʃt) *adj.* **1.** (*foll. by to*) fond (of). **2.** married, engaged, or associated in an exclusive sexual relationship.

attachment (əˈtætʃmənt) *n.* **1.** a fastening. **2.** (often foll. by *to*) affection or regard (for). **3.** an object to be attached: *an attachment for an electric drill.* **4.** the act of attaching or the state of being attached. **5. a.** the lawful seizure of property and placing of it under control of a court. **b.** a writ authorizing such seizure.

attack (əˈtæk) *vb.* **1.** to launch a physical assault (against) with or without weapons. **2.** (*intr.*) to take the initiative in a game, sport, etc. **3.** (*tr.*) to criticize or abuse vehemently. **4.** (*tr.*) to turn one's mind or energies to (a job, problem, etc.). **5.** (*tr.*) to begin to injure or affect adversely: *rust attacked the metal.* ~*n.* **6.** the act or an instance of attacking. **7.** strong criticism or abuse. **8.** an offensive move in a game, sport, etc. **9.** commencement of a task, etc. **10.** any sudden and usually severe manifestation of a disease or disorder: *a heart attack.* **11. the attack.** *Ball games.* the players in a team whose main role is to attack the opponents. **12.** *Music.* decisiveness in beginning a passage, movement, or piece. —atˈ**tacker** *n.*

attain (əˈteɪn) *vb.* **1.** (*tr.*) to achieve or accomplish (a task, aim, etc.). **2.** (*tr.*) to reach in space or time. **3.** (*intr.; often foll. by to*) to arrive (at) with effort or exertion. —atˈ**tainable** *adj.* —at,**taina'bility** *or* atˈ**tainableness** *n.*

attainder (əˈteɪndə) *n.* (formerly) the extinction of a person's civil rights resulting from a sentence of death or outlawry on conviction for treason or felony.

attainment (əˈteɪnmənt) *n.* an achievement or the act of achieving; accomplishment.

attaint (əˈteɪnt) *vb.* (*tr.*) *Arch.* **1.** to pass judgment of death or outlawry upon (a person). **2.** (of sickness) to affect or strike (somebody). ~*n.* **3.** a less common word for **attainder.**

attar (ˈætə), **otto** (ˈɒtəʊ), *or* **ottar** (ˈɒtə) *n.* an essential oil from flowers, esp. the damask rose: *attar of roses.*

attempt (əˈtɛmpt) *vb.* (*tr.*) **1.** to make an effort (to do something) or to achieve (something); try. **2.** to try to surmount (an obstacle). **3.** to try to climb. ~*n.* **4.** an endeavour to achieve something; effort. **5.** a result of an attempt or endeavour. **6.** an attack, esp. with the intention to kill. —atˈ**temptable** *adj.*

attend (əˈtɛnd) *vb.* **1.** to be present at (an event, etc.). **2.** (*when intr.*, foll. by *to*) to give care; minister. **3.** (*when intr.*, foll. by *to*) to pay attention. **4.** (*tr.; often passive*) to accompany or follow: *a high temperature attended by a severe cough.* **5.** (*intr.;* foll. by *on* or *upon*) to follow as a consequence (of). **6.** (*intr.;* foll. by *to*) to apply oneself: *to attend to the garden.* **7.** (*tr.*) to escort or accompany. **8.** (*intr.;* foll. by *on* or *upon*) to provide for the needs (of): *to attend on a guest.*

attendance (əˈtɛndəns) *n.* **1.** the act or state of attending. **2.** the number of persons present.

attendant (əˈtɛndənt) *n.* **1.** a person who accompanies or waits upon another. **2.** a person employed to assist, guide, or provide a service for others. **3.** a person who is

---

THESAURUS

atrocious 1. barbaric, brutal, cruel, diabolical, fiendish, flagrant, heinous, infamous, infernal, inhuman, monstrous, nefarious, ruthless, savage, vicious, villainous, wicked **2.** appalling, detestable, execrable, grievous, horrible, horrifying, shocking, terrible

atrocity 1. abomination, act of savagery, barbarity, brutality, crime, cruelty, enormity, evil, horror, monstrosity, outrage, villainy **2.** atrociousness, barbarity, barbarousness, brutality, cruelty, enormity, fiendishness, grievousness, heinousness, horror, infamy, inhumanity, monstrousness, nefariousness, ruthlessness, savagery, shockingness, viciousness, villainousness, wickedness

attach 1. add, adhere, affix, annex, append, bind, connect, couple, fasten, fix, join, link, make fast, secure, stick, subjoin, tie, unite **2.** accompany, affiliate, associate, become associated with, combine, enlist, join, join forces with, latch on to, sign on with, sign up with, unite with **3.** ascribe, assign, associate, attribute, connect, impute, invest with, lay, place, put **4.** allocate, allot, appoint, assign, consign, designate, detail, earmark, second, send

attached 1. affectionate towards, devoted, fond of, full of regard for, possessive **2.** accompanied, engaged, married, partnered, spoken for

attachment 1. adapter, bond, clamp, connection, connector, coupling, fastener, fastening, joint, junction, link, tie **2.** affection, affinity, attraction, bond, devotion, fidelity, fondness, friendship, liking, love, loyalty, partiality, possessiveness, predilection, regard, tenderness **3.** accessory, accoutrement, adapter, addition, adjunct, appendage, appurtenance, auxiliary, extension, extra, fitting, fixture, supplement, supplementary part

attack *n.* **1.** aggression, assault, charge, foray, incursion, inroad, invasion, offensive, onset, onslaught, raid, rush, strike **2.** abuse, blame, calumny, censure, criticism, denigration, impugnment, vilification **3.** access, bout, convulsion, fit, paroxysm, seizure, spasm, spell, stroke ~*v.* **4.** assail, assault, charge, fall upon, invade, lay into, raid, rush, set about, set upon, storm, strike (at) **5.** abuse, berate, blame, censure, criticize, impugn, malign, revile, vilify

attacker aggressor, assailant, assaulter, intruder, invader, raider

attain accomplish, achieve, acquire, arrive at, bring off, complete, earn, effect, fulfil, gain, get, grasp, obtain, procure, reach, realize, reap, secure, win

attainable accessible, accomplishable, achievable, at hand, feasible, gettable, graspable, likely, obtainable, possible, potential, practicable, probable, procurable, reachable, realizable, within reach

attainment 1. accomplishment, achievement, acquirement, acquisition, arrival at, completion, feat, fulfilment, gaining, getting, obtaining, procurement, reaching, realization, reaping, winning **2.** ability, accomplishment, achievement, art, capability, competence, gift, mastery, proficiency, skill, talent

attempt 1. *n.* assault, attack, bid, crack (*Inf.*), effort, endeavour, essay, experiment, go, shot (*Inf.*), trial, try, undertaking, venture **2.** *v.* endeavour, essay, experiment, have a crack (go, shot) (*Inf.*), seek, strive, tackle, take on, try, try one's hand at, undertake, venture

attend 1. appear, be at, be here, be present, be there, frequent, go to, haunt, make one (*Archaic*), put in an appearance, show oneself, show up (*Inf.*), turn up, visit **2.** care for, look after, mind, minister to, nurse, take care of, tend **3.** follow, hear, hearken (*Archaic*), heed, listen, look on, mark, mind, note, notice, observe, pay attention, pay heed, regard, take to heart, watch **4.** accompany, arise from, be associated with, be connected with, be consequent on, follow, go hand in hand with, issue from, occur with, result from **5.** *With* to apply oneself to, concentrate on, devote oneself to, get to work on, look after, occupy oneself with, see to, take care of **6.** accompany, chaperon, companion, convoy, escort, guard, squire, usher **7.** be in the service of, serve, wait upon, work for

attendance 1. appearance, attending, being there, presence **2.** audience, crowd, gate, house, number present, turnout

attendant 1. *n.* aide, assistant, auxiliary, chaperon, companion, custodian, escort, flunky, follower, guard, guide, helper, lackey, menial, servant, steward, underling, usher, waiter **2.** *adj.* accessory, accompanying, associated, concomitant, consequent, related

present. ~*adj.* **4.** being in attendance. **5.** associated: *attendant problems.*

attention (ə'tɛnʃən) *n.* **1.** concentrated direction of the mind, esp. to a problem or task. **2.** consideration, notice, or observation. **3.** detailed care or special treatment: *to pay attention to one's appearance.* **4.** (*usually pl.*) an act of courtesy or gallantry indicating affection or love. **5.** the motionless position of formal military alertness, an upright position with legs and heels together. ~*interj.* **6.** the order to be alert or to adopt a position of formal military alertness.

attentive (ə'tɛntɪv) *adj.* **1.** paying attention; listening carefully. **2.** (*postpositive; often foll. by to*) careful to fulfil the needs or wants (of). —**at'tentively** *adv.* —**at'tentiveness** *n.*

attenuate (ə'tɛnjʊˌeɪt). **1.** to weaken or become weak. **2.** to make or become thin or fine; extend. ~*adj.* (ə'tɛnjʊɪt, -ˌeɪt). **3.** weakened or reduced. **4.** *Bot.* tapering. —**at,tenu'ation** *n.*

attest (ə'tɛst) *vb.* **1.** (*tr.*) to affirm the correctness or truth of. **2.** (when *intr.*, usually foll. by *to*) to witness (an act, event, etc.) or bear witness (to an act, event, etc.). **3.** (*tr.*) to make evident; demonstrate. **4.** (*tr.*) to provide evidence for. —**at'testable** *adj.* —**at'testant, at'tester** or esp. in legal usage **at'testor** *n.* —**attestation** (ˌætɛ'steɪʃən) *n.*

attested (ə'tɛstɪd) *adj. Brit.* (of cattle, etc.) certified to be free from a disease, esp. from tuberculosis.

attic ('ætɪk) *n.* **1.** a space or room within the roof of a house. **2.** *Archit.* a storey or low wall above the cornice of a classical façade.

Attic ('ætɪk) *adj.* **1.** of or relating to Attica, the area around Athens, its inhabitants, or the dialect of Greek spoken there. **2.** (*often not cap.*) classically elegant, simple, or pure. ~*n.* **3.** the dialect of Ancient Greek spoken and written in Athens.

attire (ə'taɪə) *vb.* **1.** (*tr.*) to dress, esp. in fine elegant clothes; array. ~*n.* **2.** clothes or garments, esp. if fine or decorative.

attitude ('ætɪˌtjuːd) *n.* **1.** a mental view or disposition, esp. as it indicates opinion or allegiance. **2.** a theatrical pose created for effect (esp. in **strike an attitude**). **3.** a position of the body indicating mood or emotion. **4.** the orientation of an aircraft's axes or a spacecraft in relation to some plane or the direction of motion. —ˌatti'tudinal *adj.*

attitudinize or **-nise** (ˌætɪ'tjuːdɪˌnaɪz) *vb.* (*intr.*) to adopt a pose or opinion for effect; strike an attitude.

attorney (ə'tɜːnɪ) *n.* a person, esp. a lawyer, appointed or empowered to act for another. —**at'torneyˌship** *n.*

attorney general *n., pl.* **attorneys general** or **attorney generals.** a chief law officer and senior legal adviser of some national and state governments.

attract (ə'trækt) *vb.* (*mainly tr.*) **1.** to draw (notice, a crowd of observers, etc.) to oneself (esp. in **attract attention**). **2.** (*also intr.*) to exert a force on (a body) that tends to oppose a separation: *the gravitational pull of the earth attracts objects to it.* **3.** to possess some property

that pulls or draws (something) towards itself. **4.** (*also intr.*) to exert a pleasing or fascinating influence (upon). —**at'tractable** *adj.* —**at'tractor** *n.*

attraction (ə'trækʃən) *n.* **1.** the act or quality of attracting. **2.** a person or thing that attracts or is intended to attract. **3.** a force by which one object attracts another: *magnetic attraction.*

attractive (ə'træktɪv) *adj.* **1.** appealing to the senses or mind through beauty, form, character, etc. **2.** arousing interest: *an attractive opportunity.* **3.** possessing the ability to draw or pull: *an attractive force.* —**at'tractively** *adv.*

attribute *vb.* (ə'trɪbjuːt). **1.** (*tr.;* usually foll. by *to*) to regard as belonging (to), produced (by), or resulting (from): *to attribute a painting to Picasso.* ~*n.* ('ætrɪˌbjuːt). **2.** a property, quality, or feature belonging to or representative of a person or thing. **3.** an object accepted as belonging to a particular office or position. **4.** *Grammar.* **a.** an adjective or adjectival phrase. **b.** an attributive adjective. **5.** *Logic.* the property or feature that is affirmed or denied concerning the subject of a proposition. —**at'tributable** *adj.* —**attribution** (ˌætrɪ'bjuːʃən) *n.*

attributive (ə'trɪbjʊtɪv) *adj.* **1.** relating to an attribute. **2.** *Grammar.* (of an adjective or adjectival phrase) preceding the noun modified.

attrition (ə'trɪʃən) *n.* **1.** the act of wearing away or the state of being worn away, as by friction. **2.** constant wearing down to weaken or destroy (often in **war of attrition**). **3.** *Geog.* the grinding down of rock particles by friction. **4.** *Theol.* sorrow for sin arising from fear of damnation, esp. as contrasted with contrition.

attune (ə'tjuːn) *vb.* (*tr.*) to adjust or accustom (a person or thing); acclimatize.

A.T.V. (in Britain) *abbrev. for* Associated Television.

at. wt. *abbrev. for* atomic weight.

atypical (eɪ'tɪpɪkəl) *adj.* not typical; deviating from or not conforming to type. —**a'typically** *adv.*

Au *the chemical symbol for* gold.

aubergine ('əʊbəˌʒiːn) *n.* **1.** a tropical Old World plant widely cultivated for its egg-shaped typically dark purple fruit. U.S. name: **eggplant.** **2.** the fruit of this plant, which is cooked and eaten as a vegetable. **3.** a dark purple colour.

aubrietia or **aubretia** (ɔː'briːʃə) *n.* a trailing purple-flowered plant native to European mountains but widely planted in rock gardens.

auburn ('ɔːbən) *n.* **a.** a moderate reddish-brown colour. **b.** (*as adj.*): *auburn hair.*

auction ('ɔːkʃən) *n.* **1.** a public sale of goods or property in which prospective purchasers bid until the highest price is reached. **2.** the competitive calls made in bridge before play begins. ~*vb.* **3.** (*tr.;* often foll. by *off*) to sell by auction.

auction bridge *n.* a variety of bridge in which all the tricks made score towards game.

auctioneer (ˌɔːkʃə'nɪə) *n.* **1.** a person who conducts an

THESAURUS

attention **1.** concentration, consideration, contemplation, deliberation, heed, heedfulness, intentness, mind, scrutiny, thinking, thought, thoughtfulness **2.** awareness, consciousness, consideration, notice, observation, recognition, regard **3.** care, concern, looking after, ministration, treatment **4.** *Often plural* assiduities, care, civility, compliment, consideration, courtesy, deference, gallantry, mindfulness, politeness, regard, respect, service

attentive **1.** alert, awake, careful, concentrating, heedful, intent, listening, mindful, observant, regardful, studious, watchful **2.** accommodating, civil, conscientious, considerate, courteous, devoted, gallant, gracious, kind, obliging, polite, respectful, thoughtful

attest adjure, affirm, assert, authenticate, aver, bear out, bear witness, certify, confirm, corroborate, declare, demonstrate, display, evince, exhibit, give evidence, invoke, manifest, prove, ratify, seal, show, substantiate, swear, testify, verify, vouch for, warrant, witness

attic *n.* garret, loft

attire **1.** *n.* accoutrements, apparel, array (*Poetic*), clothes, clothing, costume, dress, garb, garments, gear (*Sl.*), habiliments, habit, outfit, raiment (*Archaic*), robes, uniform, vestment, wear **2.** *v.* accoutre, apparel (*Archaic*), array, clothe, costume, deck out, dress, equip, fit out, garb, rig out, robe, turn out

attitude **1.** approach, disposition, frame of mind, mood, opinion, outlook, perspective, point of view, position, posture, stance, standing, view **2.** air, aspect, bearing, carriage, condition, demeanour, manner, mien (*Literary*), pose, position, posture, stance

attract allure, appeal to, bewitch, captivate, charm, decoy, draw, enchant, endear, engage, entice, fascinate, incline, induce, interest, invite, lure, pull (*Inf.*), tempt

attraction allure, appeal, attractiveness, bait, captivation, charm, come-on (*Inf.*), draw, enchantment, endearment, enticement, fascination, inducement, interest, invitation, lure, magnetism, pull (*Inf.*), temptation, temptingness

attractive agreeable, alluring, appeal-

ing, beautiful, captivating, charming, comely, engaging, enticing, fair, fascinating, fetching, good-looking, gorgeous, handsome, interesting, inviting, lovely, magnetic, pleasant, pleasing, prepossessing, pretty, seductive, tempting, winning, winsome

attribute **1.** *v.* apply, ascribe, assign, blame, charge, credit, impute, lay at the door of, put down to, refer, set down to, trace to **2.** *n.* aspect, character, characteristic, facet, feature, idiosyncrasy, indication, mark, note, peculiarity, point, property, quality, quirk, sign, symbol, trait, virtue

attrition **1.** abrasion, chafing, erosion, friction, grinding, rubbing, scraping, wear, wearing away, wearing down **2.** attenuation, debilitation, harassment, harrying, thinning out, weakening, wearing down

attune acclimatize, accord, accustom, adapt, adjust, coordinate, familiarize, harmonize, modulate, regulate, set, tune

auburn chestnut-coloured, copper-coloured, henna, nutbrown, reddish-brown, russet, rust-coloured, tawny, Titian red

auction. ~*vb.* **2.** (*tr.*) to sell by auction.
audacious (ɔːˈdeɪʃəs) *adj.* **1.** recklessly bold or daring. **2.** impudent or presumptuous. —**auˈdaciousness** *or* **audacity** (ɔːˈdæsɪtɪ) *n.*
audible (ˈɔːdɪbəl) *adj.* perceptible to the hearing; loud enough to be heard. —ˌaudiˈbility *or* ˈaudibleness *n.* —ˈaudibly *adv.*
audience (ˈɔːdɪəns) *n.* **1.** a group of spectators or listeners, esp. at a concert or play. **2.** the people reached by a book, film, or radio or television programme. **3.** the devotees or followers of a public entertainer, etc. **4.** a formal interview with a monarch or head of state.
audio (ˈɔːdɪəʊ) *n.* **1.** (*modifier*) of or relating to sound or hearing: *audio frequency*. **2.** (*modifier*) relating to or employed in the transmission or reproduction of sound.
audio frequency *n.* a frequency in the range 50 hertz to 20 000 hertz. A sound wave of this frequency would be audible to the human ear.
audiometer (ˌɔːdɪˈɒmɪtə) *n.* an instrument for testing hearing. —ˌaudiˈometrist *n.* —ˌaudiˈometry *n.*
audiotypist (ˈɔːdɪəʊˌtaɪpɪst) *n.* a typist trained to type from a dictating machine. —ˈaudioˌtyping *n.*
audiovisual (ˌɔːdɪəʊˈvɪzjʊəl) *adj.* (esp. of teaching aids) involving or directed at both hearing and sight. —ˌaudioˈvisually *adv.*
audit (ˈɔːdɪt) *n.* **1. a.** an inspection, correction, and verification of business accounts by a qualified accountant. **b.** (*as modifier*): *audit report.* **2.** *U.S.* an audited account. ~*vb.* **3.** to inspect, correct, and certify (accounts, etc.).
audition (ɔːˈdɪʃən) *n.* **1.** a test at which a performer or musician is asked to demonstrate his ability for a particular rôle, etc. **2.** the act or power of hearing. ~*vb.* **3.** to judge by means of or be tested in an audition.
auditor (ˈɔːdɪtə) *n.* **1.** a person qualified to audit accounts. **2.** a person who hears or listens. —ˌaudiˈtorial *adj.*
Auditor General *n.* in Canada, an officer appointed by the Governor General to audit the accounts of the Federal Government and report to Parliament.
auditorium (ˌɔːdɪˈtɔːrɪəm) *n., pl.* -**toriums** *or* -**toria** (-ˈtɔːrɪə). **1.** the area of a concert hall, theatre, etc., in which the audience sits. **2.** *U.S.* a building for public meetings.
auditory (ˈɔːdɪtərɪ) *adj.* of or relating to hearing or the sense of hearing.
A.U.E.W. (in Britain) *abbrev. for* Amalgamated Union of Engineering Workers.
au fait *French.* (o ˈfɛ) *adj.* fully informed; in touch or expert.
Aug. *abbrev. for* August.
Augean (ɔːˈdʒiːən) *adj.* extremely dirty or corrupt.
auger (ˈɔːgə) *n.* **1.** a hand tool with a bit shaped like a corkscrew, for boring holes in wood. **2.** a larger tool of the same kind for boring holes in the ground.
aught *or* **ought** (ɔːt) (*used with a negative or in conditional or interrogative sentences or clauses*) *Arch. or literary.* ~*pron.* **1.** anything whatever (esp. in **for aught I know**). ~*adv.* **2.** *Brit. dialect.* to any degree.
augment (ɔːgˈmɛnt) *vb.* to make or become greater in number, strength, etc. —**augˈmentable** *adj.*

—ˌaugmenˈtation *n.* —**augˈmenter** *n.*
augmentative (ɔːgˈmɛntətɪv) *adj.* **1.** tending or able to augment. **2.** *Grammar.* denoting an affix that may be added to a word to convey the meaning *large* or *great.*
au gratin (*French* o graˈtɛ̃) *adj.* covered and cooked with browned breadcrumbs and sometimes cheese.
augur (ˈɔːgə) *n.* **1.** (in ancient Rome) a religious official who observed and interpreted omens and signs. **2.** any prophet or soothsayer. ~*vb.* **3.** to predict (some future event), as from signs or omens. **4.** (*tr.; may take a clause as object*) to be an omen (of). **5.** (*intr.*) to foreshadow future events: *this augurs well for us.* —**augural** (ˈɔːgjʊrəl) *adj.*
augury (ˈɔːgjʊrɪ) *n., pl.* -**ries**. **1.** the art of or a rite conducted by an augur. **2.** a sign or portent; omen.
august (ɔːˈgʌst) *adj.* **1.** dignified or imposing. **2.** of noble birth or high rank: *an august lineage.* —**auˈgustness** *n.*
August (ˈɔːgəst) *n.* the eighth month of the year, consisting of 31 days.
Augustan (ɔːˈgʌstən) *adj.* **1.** characteristic of or relating to the Roman emperor Augustus Caesar (63 B.C. - 14 A.D.), his period, or the poets writing during his reign. **2.** of or characteristic of any literary period noted for refinement and classicism, esp. the 18th century in England. ~*n.* **3.** an author in an Augustan Age.
auk (ɔːk) *n.* **1.** a diving bird of northern oceans having a heavy body, short tail, narrow wings, and a black-and-white plumage. See also **great auk, razorbill. 2. little auk.** a small short-billed auk, abundant in Arctic regions.
auld (ɔːld) *adj.* a Scottish word for **old.**
auld lang syne (ˈɔːld læŋ ˈsaɪn) *n.* times past, esp. those remembered with nostalgia.
aunt (ɑːnt) *n.* (*often cap., esp. as a term of address*) **1.** a sister of one's father or mother. **2.** the wife of one's uncle. **3.** a term of address used by children for a female friend of the parents. **4. my (sainted) aunt!** an exclamation of surprise.
auntie *or* **aunty** (ˈɑːntɪ) *n., pl.* -**ies**. a familiar or diminutive word for **aunt.**
Aunt Sally (ˈsælɪ) *n., pl.* -**lies**. *Brit.* **1.** a figure of an old woman used in fairgrounds and fêtes as a target. **2.** any person who is a target for insults or criticism.
au pair (əʊ ˈpɛə) *n.* **a.** a young foreigner, usually a girl, who undertakes housework in exchange for board and lodging, esp. in order to learn the language. **b.** (*as modifier*)*: an au pair girl.*
aura (ˈɔːrə) *n., pl.* **auras** *or* **aurae** (ˈɔːriː). **1.** a distinctive air or quality considered to be characteristic of a person or thing. **2.** any invisible emanation, esp. surrounding a person or object. **3.** *Pathol.* a phenomenon, such as noises in the ears or flashes of light, that immediately precedes an attack, esp. of epilepsy.
aural (ˈɔːrəl) *adj.* of or relating to the sense or organs of hearing; auricular. —ˈaurally *adv.*
aureate (ˈɔːrɪɪt) *adj.* **1.** covered with gold; gilded. **2.** (of a style of writing or speaking) excessively elaborate.
aureole (ˈɔːrɪˌəʊl) *or* **aureola** (ɔːˈriːələ) *n.* **1.** a border of light or radiance enveloping the head of a figure represented as holy. **2.** a less common word for **halo. 3.**

THESAURUS

audacious 1. adventurous, bold, brave, courageous, daredevil, daring, dauntless, death-defying, enterprising, fearless, intrepid, rash, reckless, risky, valiant, venturesome 2. assuming, brazen, cheeky, defiant, disrespectful, forward, impertinent, impudent, insolent, pert, presumptuous, rude, shameless
audacity 1. adventurousness, audaciousness, boldness, bravery, courage, daring, dauntlessness, enterprise, fearlessness, guts (*Sl.*), intrepidity, nerve, rashness, recklessness, valour, venturesomeness 2. audaciousness, brass neck (*Inf.*), cheek, defiance, disrespectfulness, effrontery, forwardness, gall (*Inf.*), impertinence, impudence, insolence, nerve, pertness, presumption, rudeness, shamelessness
audible clear, detectable, discernible, distinct, hearable, perceptible
audience 1. assemblage, assembly, congregation, crowd, gallery, gathering, house, listeners, onlookers, spectators, turnout,

viewers 2. devotees, fans, following, market, public 3. consultation, hearing, interview, meeting, reception
audit *Accounting* 1. *n.* balancing, check, checking, examination, inspection, investigation, review, scrutiny, verification 2. *v.* balance, check, examine, go over, go through, inspect, investigate, review, scrutinize, verify
au fait abreast of, *au courant*, clued up (*Sl.*), conversant, expert, familiar, fully informed, in the know, in touch, knowledgeable, on the ball (*Inf.*), well-acquainted, well up
augment add to, amplify, boost, build up, dilate, enhance, enlarge, expand, extend, grow, heighten, increase, inflate, intensify, magnify, multiply, raise, reinforce, strengthen, swell
augmentation accession, addition, amplification, boost, build-up, dilation, enhancement, enlargement, expansion, extension,

growth, heightening, increase, inflation, intensification, magnification, multiplication, reinforcement, rise, strengthening, swelling
augur 1. *n.* auspex, diviner, haruspex, oracle, prophet, seer, soothsayer 2. *v.* be an omen of, bespeak (*Archaic*), betoken, bode, foreshadow, harbinger, herald, portend, predict, prefigure, presage, promise, prophesy, signify
augury 1. divination, prediction, prophecy, soothsaying 2. auspice, forerunner, forewarning, harbinger, herald, omen, portent, precursor, presage, prognostication, promise, prophecy, sign, token, warning
august dignified, exalted, glorious, grand, high-ranking, imposing, impressive, kingly, lofty, magnificent, majestic, monumental, noble, regal, solemn, stately, superb
aura air, ambience, aroma, atmosphere, emanation, feel, feeling, mood, odour, quality, scent, suggestion, tone, vibes (*Inf.*), vibrations (*Inf.*)

another name for **corona** (sense 2).

au revoir French. (o rə'vwaːr) interj. goodbye.

auric ('ɔːrɪk) adj. of or containing gold, esp. in the trivalent state.

auricle ('ɔːrɪkəl) n. 1. the upper chamber of the heart; atrium. 2. Also called: **pinna**. Anat. the external part of the ear. 3. Biol. an ear-shaped part or appendage. —**'auricled** adj.

auricula (ɔː'rɪkjulə) n., pl. **-lae** (-ˌliː) or **-las**. 1. Also called: **bear's-ear**. a widely cultivated alpine primrose with leaves shaped like a bear's ear. 2. another word for **auricle** (sense 3).

auricular (ɔː'rɪkjulə) adj. 1. of, relating to, or received by the sense or organs of hearing; aural. 2. shaped like an ear. 3. of or relating to an auricle of the heart.

auriferous (ɔː'rɪfərəs) adj. (of rock) containing gold; gold-bearing.

aurochs ('ɔːrɒks) n., pl. **-rochs**. a recently extinct member of the cattle tribe that inhabited forests in N Africa, Europe, and SW Asia. Also called: **urus**.

aurora (ɔː'rɔːrə) n., pl. **-ras** or **-rae** (-riː). 1. an atmospheric phenomenon consisting of bands, curtains, or streamers of light, that move across the sky, esp. in polar regions. 2. Poetic. the dawn. —**au'roral** adj.

aurora australis (ɒ'streɪlɪs) n. (sometimes cap.) the aurora seen around the South Pole. Also called: **southern lights**.

aurora borealis (ˌbɔːrɪ'eɪlɪs) n. (sometimes cap.) the aurora seen around the North Pole. Also called: **northern lights**.

auscultation (ˌɔːskəl'teɪʃən) n. 1. the diagnostic technique in medicine of listening to the various internal sounds made by the body, usually with the aid of a stethoscope. 2. the act of listening. —**'auscultate** vb. —**auscultatory** (ɔː'skʌltətərɪ) adj.

auspice ('ɔːspɪs) n., pl. **-pices** (-pɪsɪz). 1. (usually pl.) patronage (esp. in **under the auspices of**). 2. (often pl.) an omen, esp. one that is favourable.

auspicious (ɔː'spɪʃəs) adj. 1. favourable or propitious. 2. Arch. fortunate. —**aus'piciously** adv. —**aus'piciousness** n.

Aussie ('ɒzɪ) n., adj. Inf. Australian.

austere (ɒ'stɪə) adj. 1. stern or severe in attitude or manner. 2. grave, sober, or serious. 3. self-disciplined, abstemious, or ascetic: an austere life. 4. severely simple or plain: an austere design. —**aus'terely** adv.

austerity (ɒ'stɛrɪtɪ) n., pl. **-ties**. 1. the state or quality of being austere. 2. (often pl.) an austere habit, practice, or act. 3. a. reduced availability of luxuries and consumer goods. b. (as modifier): an austerity budget.

austral ('ɔːstrəl) adj. of or coming from the south: austral winds.

Austral. abbrev. for: 1. Australasia. 2. Australia(n).

Australasian (ˌɒstrə'leɪʒən) adj. 1. of or relating to Australia, New Zealand, and neighbouring islands. 2. (of organizations) having members in Australia and New Zealand.

Australian (ɒ'streɪlɪən) n. 1. a native or inhabitant of Australia, the smallest continent. 2. the form of English spoken in Australia. ~adj. 3. of, relating to, or characteristic of Australia, the Australians, or their form of English.

autarchy ('ɔːtɑːkɪ) n., pl. **-chies**. unlimited rule; autocracy. —**au'tarchic** or **au'tarchical** adj.

autarky ('ɔːtɑːkɪ) n., pl. **-kies** (esp. of a political unit) a system or policy of economic self-sufficiency. —**au'tarkic** adj. —**'autarkist** n.

authentic (ɔː'θɛntɪk) adj. 1. of undisputed origin or authorship; genuine. 2. trustworthy; reliable: an authentic account. 3. (of a deed, etc.) duly executed. 4. Music. commencing on the final and ending an octave higher. —**au'thentically** adv. —**authenticity** (ˌɔːθɛn'tɪsɪtɪ) n.

authenticate (ɔː'θɛntɪˌkeɪt) vb. (tr.) 1. to establish as genuine or valid. 2. to give authority or legal validity to. —**au,thenti'cation** n. —**au'thenti,cator** n.

author ('ɔːθə) or (fem.) **authoress** n. 1. a person who composes a book, article, or other written work. 2. a person who writes books as a profession; writer. 3. an originator or creator: the author of this plan. ~vb. Not standard. 4. to write or originate. —**authorial** (ɔː'θɔːrɪəl) adj.

authoritarian (ɔːˌθɒrɪ'tɛərɪən) adj. 1. favouring or characterized by strict obedience to authority. 2. favouring or relating to government by a small elite. 3. dictatorial; domineering. ~n. 4. a person who favours or practises authoritarian policies.

authoritative (ɔː'θɒrɪtətɪv) adj. 1. recognized or accepted as being true or reliable. 2. commanding: an authoritative manner. 3. possessing or supported by authority; official. —**au'thoritatively** adv. —**au'thoritativeness** n.

authority (ɔː'θɒrɪtɪ) n., pl. **-ties**. 1. the power or right to control, judge, or prohibit the actions of others. 2. (often pl.) a person or group of people having this power, such as a government, police force, etc. 3. a position that commands such a power or right (often in **in authority**). 4. such a power or right delegated: she has his authority. 5. the ability to influence or control others. 6. an expert or an authoritative written work in a particular field. 7. evidence or testimony. 8. confidence resulting from great expertise. 9. (cap. when part of a name) a public board or corporation exercising governmental authority: Independent Broadcasting Authority.

authorize or **-rise** ('ɔːθəˌraɪz) vb. (tr.) 1. to confer authority upon (someone to do something). 2. to permit (someone to do or be something) with official sanction. —**ˌauthori'zation** or **-ri'sation** n.

THESAURUS

auspice n. 1. Usually plural advocacy, aegis, authority, backing, care, championship, charge, control, countenance, guidance, influence, patronage, protection, sponsorship, supervision, support 2. augury, indication, omen, portent, prognostication, prophecy, sign, token, warning

auspicious bright, encouraging, favourable, felicitous, fortunate, happy, hopeful, lucky, opportune, promising, propitious, prosperous, rosy, timely

austere 1. cold, exacting, forbidding, formal, grave, grim, hard, harsh, inflexible, rigorous, serious, severe, solemn, stern, stiff, strict, stringent, unfeeling, unrelenting 2. abstemious, abstinent, ascetic, chaste, continent, economical, exacting, puritanical, rigid, self-denying, self-disciplined, sober, solemn, Spartan, strait-laced, strict, unrelenting 3. bleak, economical, plain, severe, simple, spare, Spartan, stark, subdued, unadorned, unornamented

austerity 1. coldness, exactingness, forbiddingness, formality, gravity, grimness, hardness, harshness, inflexibility, rigour, seriousness, severity, solemnity, sternness, stiffness, strictness 2. abstemiousness, abstinence, asceticism, chasteness, chastity, continence, economy, exactingness, puritanism, rigidity, self-denial, self-discipline, sobriety, solemnity, Spartanism, strictness 3. economy, plainness, severity, simplicity, spareness, Spartanism, starkness

authentic accurate, actual, authoritative, bona fide, certain, dependable, factual, faithful, genuine, legitimate, original, pure, real, reliable, simon-pure (Rare), true, true-to-life, trustworthy, valid, veritable

authenticate attest, authorize, avouch, certify, confirm, endorse, guarantee, validate, verify, vouch for, warrant

authenticity accuracy, actuality, authoritativeness, certainty, dependability, factualness, faithfulness, genuineness, legitimacy, purity, realness, reliability, trustworthiness, truth, truthfulness, validity, veritableness, verity

author architect, composer, creator, designer, doer, fabricator, father, founder, framer, initiator, inventor, maker, mover, originator, parent, planner, prime mover, producer, writer

authoritarian 1. adj. absolute, autocratic, despotic, dictatorial, disciplinarian, doctrinaire, dogmatic, domineering, harsh, imperious, rigid, severe, strict, tyrannical, unyielding 2. n. absolutist, autocrat, despot, dictator, disciplinarian, tyrant

authoritative 1. accurate, authentic, definitive, dependable, factual, faithful, learned, reliable, scholarly, sound, true, trustworthy, truthful, valid, veritable 2. assertive, autocratic, commanding, confident, decisive, dictatorial, dogmatic, dominating, imperative, imperious, imposing, lordly, masterly, peremptory, self-assured 3. approved, authorized, commanding, legitimate, official, sanctioned, sovereign

authority 1. ascendancy, charge, command, control, domination, dominion, force, government, influence, jurisdiction, might, power, prerogative, right, rule, say-so, strength, supremacy, sway, weight 2. the authorities administration, government, management, officialdom, police, powers that be, the establishment 3. authorization, justification, licence, permission, permit, sanction, say-so, warrant 4. arbiter, bible, connoisseur, expert, judge, master, professional, scholar, specialist, textbook 5. attestation, avowal, declaration, evidence, profession, say-so, statement, testimony, word

authorization 1. ability, authority, power, right, say-so, strength 2. approval,

Authorized Version *n.* **the.** an English translation of the Bible published in 1611 under James I. Also called: **King James Version.**

authorship ('ɔːθəˌʃɪp) *n.* **1.** the origin or originator of a written work, plan, etc. **2.** the profession of writing books.

autism ('ɔːtɪzəm) *n. Psychiatry.* abnormal self-absorption, usually affecting children, characterized by lack of response to people and limited ability to communicate. —**au'tistic** *adj.*

auto ('ɔːtəʊ) *n., pl.* **-tos.** *U.S. inf.* **a.** short for **automobile.** **b.** (*as modifier*): *auto parts.*

auto- *or sometimes before a vowel* **aut-** *combining form.* **1.** self; same; of or by the same one: *autobiography.* **2.** self-caused: *autohypnosis.* **3.** self-propelling: *automobile.*

autobahn ('ɔːtəˌbɑːn) *n.* a German motorway.

autobiography (ˌɔːtəʊbaɪˈɒɡrəfɪ) *n., pl.* **-phies.** an account of a person's life written or otherwise recorded by that person. —**autobi'ographer** *n.* —**autobiographical** (ˌɔːtəˌbaɪəˈɡræfɪkəl) *adj.*

autoclave ('ɔːtəˌkleɪv) *n.* **1.** a strong sealed vessel used for chemical reactions at high pressure. **2.** an apparatus for sterilizing objects (esp. surgical instruments) by means of steam under pressure.

autocracy (ɔːˈtɒkrəsɪ) *n., pl.* **-cies.** **1.** government by an individual with unrestricted authority. **2.** a country, society, etc., ruled by an autocrat.

autocrat ('ɔːtəˌkræt) *n.* **1.** a ruler who possesses absolute and unrestricted authority. **2.** a domineering or dictatorial person. —**auto'cratic** *adj.* —**auto'cratically** *adv.*

autocross ('ɔːtəʊˌkrɒs) *n.* a motor sport in which cars race over a half-mile circuit of rough grass.

autocue ('ɔːtəʊˌkjuː) *n.* an electronic television prompting device whereby a script, unseen by the audience, is displayed for the speaker.

auto-da-fé (ˌɔːtəʊdəˈfeɪ) *n., pl.* **autos-da-fé.** **1.** *History.* a ceremony of the Spanish Inquisition including the pronouncement and execution of sentences passed on sinners or heretics. **2.** the burning to death of people condemned as heretics by the Inquisition.

autogiro *or* **autogyro** (ˌɔːtəʊˈdʒaɪrəʊ) *n., pl.* **-ros.** a self-propelled aircraft supported in flight mainly by unpowered rotating horizontal blades.

autograph ('ɔːtəˌɡrɑːf) *n.* **1. a.** a handwritten signature, esp. that of a famous person. **b.** (*as modifier*): *an autograph album.* **2.** a person's handwriting. **3. a.** a book, document, etc., handwritten by its author. **b.** (*as modifier*): *an autograph letter.* ~*vb.* **4.** (*tr.*) to write one's signature on or in; sign. **5.** to write with one's own hand. —**autographic** (ˌɔːtəˈɡræfɪk) *adj.* —**auto'graphically** *adv.*

automat ('ɔːtəˌmæt) *n.* Also called: **vending machine.** a machine that automatically dispenses goods such as cigarettes, when money is inserted.

automate ('ɔːtəˌmeɪt) *vb.* to make (a manufacturing process, factory, etc.) automatic, or (of a manufacturing process, etc.) to be made automatic.

automatic (ˌɔːtəˈmætɪk) *adj.* **1.** performed from force of habit or without conscious thought: *an automatic smile.* **2. a.** (of a device, mechanism, etc.) able to activate, move, or regulate itself. **b.** (of an act or process) performed by such automatic equipment. **3.** (of the action of a muscle, etc.) involuntary or reflex. **4.** occurring as a necessary consequence: *promotion is automatic after a year.* **5.** (of a firearm) utilizing some of the force of each explosion to eject the empty shell, replace it with a new one, and fire continuously until release of the trig-

ger. ~*n.* **6.** an automatic firearm. **7.** a motor vehicle having automatic transmission. **8.** a machine that operates automatically. —**auto'matically** *adv.*

automatic data processing *n.* data processing performed by automatic electromechanical devices. Abbrevs.: **A.D.P., ADP, a.d.p.**

automatic pilot *n.* a device that automatically maintains an aircraft on a preset course. Also called: **autopilot.**

automatic transmission *n.* a transmission system in a motor vehicle in which the gears change automatically.

automation (ˌɔːtəˈmeɪʃən) *n.* **1.** the use of methods for controlling industrial processes automatically, esp. by electronically controlled systems. **2.** the extent to which a process is so controlled.

automatism (ɔːˈtɒməˌtɪzəm) *n.* **1.** the state or quality of being automatic; mechanical or involuntary action. **2.** *Psychol.* the performance of actions, such as sleepwalking, without conscious knowledge or control. —**au'tomatist** *n.*

automaton (ɔːˈtɒmətən) *n., pl.* **-tons** *or* **-ta** (-tə). **1.** a mechanical device operating under its own hidden power. **2.** a person who acts mechanically.

automobile ('ɔːtəməˌbiːl) *n. Formal or U.S.* a car (sense 1). —**automobilist** (ˌɔːtəməˈbiːlɪst) *n.*

automotive (ˌɔːtəˈməʊtɪv) *adj.* **1.** relating to motor vehicles. **2.** self-propelling.

autonomous (ɔːˈtɒnəməs) *adj.* **1.** (of a community, country, etc.) possessing a large degree of self-government. **2.** of or relating to an autonomous community. **3.** independent of others. **4.** *Biol.* existing as an organism independent of other organisms or parts. —**au'tonomously** *adv.*

autonomy (ɔːˈtɒnəmɪ) *n., pl.* **-mies.** **1.** the right or state of self-government, esp. when limited. **2.** a state or individual possessing autonomy. **3.** freedom to determine one's own actions, behaviour, etc. **4.** *Philosophy.* the doctrine that the individual human will is governed only by its own principles and laws.

autopilot (ˌɔːtəˈpaɪlət) *n.* short for **automatic pilot.**

autopsy (ɔːˈtɒpsɪ, 'ɔːtəp-) *n., pl.* **-sies.** **1.** Also called: **postmortem examination.** dissection and examination of a dead body to determine the cause of death. **2.** an eyewitness observation. **3.** any critical analysis.

autoroute ('ɔːtəʊˌruːt) *n.* a French motorway.

autostrada ('ɔːtəʊˌstrɑːdə) *n.* an Italian motorway.

autosuggestion (ˌɔːtəʊsəˈdʒestʃən) *n.* a process of suggestion in which the person unconsciously supplies the means of influencing his own behaviour or beliefs.

auto-teller ('ɔːtəʊˌtelə) *n. Banking.* a computerized dispenser that can provide cash or account information at any time.

autumn ('ɔːtəm) *n.* **1.** (*sometimes cap.*) **a.** Also called (esp. U.S.): **fall.** the season of the year between summer and winter, astronomically from the September equinox to the December solstice in the N hemisphere and from the March equinox to the June solstice in the S hemisphere. **b.** (*as modifier*): *autumn leaves.* **2.** a period of late maturity, esp. one followed by a decline. —**autumnal** (ɔːˈtʌmnəl) *adj.*

autumn crocus *n.* a plant of the lily family having pink or purplish autumn flowers and found in Europe and N Africa.

aux. *abbrev. for* auxiliary.

auxiliaries (ɔːɡˈzɪljərɪz, -ˈzɪlə-) *pl. n.* foreign troops serving another nation; mercenaries.

auxiliary (ɔːɡˈzɪljərɪ, -ˈzɪlə-) *adj.* **1.** secondary or supplementary. **2.** supporting. ~*n., pl.* **-ries.** **3.** a person

---

THESAURUS

credentials, leave, licence, permission, permit, sanction, say-so, warrant

authorize 1. accredit, commission, empower, enable, entitle, give authority **2.** accredit, allow, approve, confirm, countenance, give authority for, give leave, license, permit, ratify, sanction, vouch for, warrant

autocracy absolution, despotism, dictatorship, tyranny

autocrat absolutist, despot, dictator, tyrant

autocratic absolute, all-powerful, despotic, dictatorial, domineering, imperious,

tyrannical, tyrannous, unlimited

automatic 1. automated, mechanical, mechanized, push-button, robot, self-acting, self-activating, self-moving, self-propelling, self-regulating **2.** habitual, mechanical, perfunctory, routine, unconscious **3.** instinctive, instinctual, involuntary, mechanical, natural, reflex, spontaneous, unconscious, unwilled **4.** assured, certain, inescapable, inevitable, necessary, routine, unavoidable

autonomous free, independent, self-determining, self-governing, self-ruling, sovereign

autonomy freedom, home rule, independence, self-determination, self-government, self-rule, sovereignty

autopsy dissection, necropsy, postmortem, postmortem examination

auxiliary 1. *adj.* accessory, aiding, ancillary, assisting, back-up, emergency, helping, reserve, secondary, subsidiary, substitute, supplementary, supporting **2.** *n.* accessory, accomplice, ally, assistant, associate, companion, confederate, helper, partner, reserve, subordinate, supporter

or thing that supports or supplements. **4.** *Naut.* **a.** a sailing vessel with an engine. **b.** the engine of such a vessel.
auxiliary verb *n.* a verb used to indicate the tense, voice, or mood of another verb where this is not indicated by inflection, such as English *will* in *he will go.*
av. *abbrev. for:* **1.** average. **2.** avoirdupois.
Av. *or* **av.** *abbrev. for* avenue.
A.V. *abbrev. for* Authorized Version (of the Bible).
avail (ə'veɪl) *vb.* **1.** to be of use, advantage, profit, or assistance (to). **2. avail oneself of.** to make use of to one's advantage. ~*n.* **3.** use or advantage (esp. in **of no avail, to little avail**).
available (ə'veɪləbᵊl) *adj.* **1.** obtainable or accessible; capable of being made use of. **2.** *Arch.* advantageous. —a₁vaila'bility *or* a'vailableness *n.* —a'vailably *adv.*
avalanche ('ævə₁lɑːntʃ) *n.* **1. a.** a fall of large masses of snow and ice down a mountain. **b.** a fall of rocks, sand, etc. **2.** a sudden or overwhelming appearance of a large quantity of things. ~*vb.* **3.** to come down overwhelmingly (upon).
avant-garde (₁ævɒŋ'gɑːd) *n.* **1.** those artists, writers, musicians, etc., whose techniques and ideas are in advance of those generally accepted. ~*adj.* **2.** of such artists, etc., their ideas, or techniques.
avarice ('ævərɪs) *n.* extreme greed for riches. —₁ava-'ricious *adj.*
avast (ə'vɑːst) *interj. Naut.* stop! cease!
avatar ('ævə₁tɑː) *n.* **1.** *Hinduism.* the manifestation of a deity in human or animal form. **2.** a visible manifestation of an abstract concept.
avaunt (ə'vɔːnt) *interj. Arch.* go away! depart!
avdp. *abbrev. for* avoirdupois.
ave ('ɑːvɪ, 'ɑːveɪ) *interj.* welcome or farewell.
Ave ('ɑːvɪ) *n. R.C. Church.* short for **Ave Maria.**
Ave. *or* **ave.** *abbrev. for* avenue.
Ave Maria (mə'riːə) *n. R.C. Church.* a prayer to the Virgin Mary, based on the salutations of the angel Gabriel (Luke 1:28) and Elisabeth (Luke 1:42) to her.
avenge (ə'vɛndʒ) *vb.* (*usually tr.*) to inflict a punishment in retaliation for (harm, injury, etc.) done to (a person or persons): *to avenge a murdered friend.* —a'venger *n.*
avenue ('ævɪnjuː) *n.* **1. a.** a broad street, often lined with trees. **b.** (*cap. as part of a street name*) a road, esp. in a built-up area. **2.** a main approach road, as to a country house. **3.** a way bordered by two rows of trees. **4.** a line of approach: *explore every avenue.*
aver (ə'vɜː) *vb.* **averring, averred.** (*tr.*) **1.** to state positively. **2.** *Law.* to allege as a fact or prove to be true. —a'verment *n.*
average ('ævərɪdʒ, 'ævrɪdʒ) *n.* **1.** the typical or normal amount, quality, degree, etc.: *above average in intelligence.* **2.** Also called: **arithmetic mean.** the result obtained by adding the numbers or quantities in a set and dividing the total by the number of members in the set: *the average of 3, 4, and 8 is 5.* **3.** a similar mean for continuously variable ratios, such as speed. **4.** *Maritime*

law. **a.** a loss incurred or damage suffered by a ship or its cargo at sea. **b.** the equitable apportionment of such loss among the interested parties. **5. on** (**the** *or* **an**) **average.** usually; typically. ~*adj.* **6.** usual or typical. **7.** mediocre or inferior: *his performance was only average.* **8.** constituting a numerical average: *an average speed.* **9.** approximately typical of a range of values: *the average contents of a matchbox.* ~*vb.* **10.** (*tr.*) to obtain or estimate a numerical average of. **11.** (*tr.*) to assess the general quality of. **12.** (*tr.*) to perform or receive a typical number of: *to average eight hours' work a day.* **13.** (*tr.*) to divide up proportionately. **14.** (*intr.*) to amount to or be on average: *the children averaged 15 years of age.* —'averagely *adv.*
averse (ə'vɜːs) *adj.* (*postpositive;* usually foll. by *to*) opposed, disinclined, or loath. —a'versely *adv.* —a'verseness *n.*
▷ **Usage.** *To* is the preposition now normally used with *averse* (*he was averse to giving any assistance*), although *from* is often used with *averse* and *aversion* and was at one time considered to be grammatically correct.
aversion (ə'vɜːʃən) *n.* **1.** (usually foll. by *to* or *for*) extreme dislike or disinclination. **2.** a person or thing that arouses this: *he is my pet aversion.*
avert (ə'vɜːt) *vb.* (*tr.*) **1.** to turn away or aside: *to avert one's gaze.* **2.** to ward off: *to avert danger.* —a'vertible *or* a'vertable *adj.*
Avesta (ə'vɛstə) *n.* a collection of sacred writings of Zoroastrianism, including the Songs of Zoroaster.
aviary ('eɪvjərɪ) *n., pl.* **aviaries.** a large enclosure in which birds are kept.
aviation (₁eɪvɪ'eɪʃən) *n.* **1.** the art or science of flying aircraft. **2.** the design, production, and maintenance of aircraft.
aviator ('eɪvɪ₁eɪtə) *n. Old-fashioned.* the pilot of an aeroplane or airship; flier. —'avi₁atrix *or* 'avi₁atress *fem. n.*
avid ('ævɪd) *adj.* **1.** very keen; enthusiastic: *an avid reader.* **2.** (*postpositive;* often foll. by *for* or *of*) eager (for): *avid for revenge.* —'avidly *adv.* —**avidity** (ə'vɪdɪtɪ) *n.*
avocado (₁ævə'kɑːdəʊ) *n., pl.* **-dos.** **1.** a tropical American tree cultivated for its fruit. **2.** the pear-shaped fruit of this tree, having a leathery green or blackish skin, a large stony seed, and a greenish-yellow edible pulp. ~Also called: **avocado pear, alligator pear.**
avocation (₁ævə'keɪʃən) *n. Arch.* **1.** a minor occupation undertaken as a diversion. **2.** a person's regular job.
avocet *or* **avoset** ('ævə₁sɛt) *n.* a long-legged shore bird having black-and-white plumage and a long slender upward-curving bill.
avoid (ə'vɔɪd) *vb.* (*tr.*) **1.** to keep out of the way of. **2.** to refrain from doing. **3.** not to allow to happen: *to avoid damage to machinery.* **4.** *Law.* to invalidate; quash. —a'voidable *adj.* —a'voidably *adv.* —a'voidance *n.* —a'voider *n.*

THESAURUS

available accessible, applicable, at hand, at one's disposal, attainable, convenient, free, handy, obtainable, on hand, on tap, ready, ready for use, to hand, vacant

avalanche 1. landslide, landslip, snowslide, snow-slip **2.** barrage, deluge, flood, inundation, torrent

avant-garde *adj.* experimental, far-out (*Sl.*), innovative, innovatory, pioneering, progressive, unconventional, way-out (*Inf.*)

avarice acquisitiveness, close-fistedness, covetousness, cupidity, graspingness, greed, greediness, meanness, miserliness, niggardliness, parsimony, penny-pinching, penuriousness, rapacity, stinginess

avaricious acquisitive, close-fisted, covetous, grasping, greedy, mean, miserable, miserly, niggardly, parsimonious, pennypinching, penurious, rapacious, stingy

avenge even the score for, get even for, punish, repay, requite, retaliate, revenge, take satisfaction for, take vengeance

avenue access, alley, approach, boulevard, channel, course, drive, driveway, entrance, entry, pass, passage, path, pathway, road, route, street, thoroughfare, way

aver affirm, allege, assert, asseverate, avouch, avow, declare, maintain, proclaim, profess, pronounce, protest, say, state, swear

average *n.* **1.** common run, mean, medium, midpoint, norm, normal, par, rule, run, run of the mill, standard **2. on average** as a rule, for the most part, generally, normally, typically, usually ~*adj.* **3.** common, commonplace, fair, general, indifferent, mediocre, middling, moderate, normal, not bad, ordinary, passable, regular, run-of-the-mill, so-so (*Inf.*), standard, tolerable, typical, undistinguished, unexceptional, usual **4.** intermediate, mean, median, medium, middle ~*v.* **5.** balance out to, be on average, do on average, even out to, make on average

averse antipathetic, backward, disinclined, hostile, ill-disposed, indisposed, inimical, loath, opposed, reluctant, unfavourable, unwilling

aversion abhorrence, animosity, antipathy, detestation, disgust, disinclination, dislike, distaste, hate, hatred, horror, hostility, indisposition, loathing, odium, opposition, reluctance, repugnance, repulsion, revulsion, unwillingness

avert 1. turn, turn aside, turn away **2.** avoid, fend off, forestall, frustrate, preclude, prevent, stave off, ward off

aviation aeronautics, flight, flying, powered flight

aviator aeronaut, airman, flier, pilot

avid 1. ardent, devoted, eager, enthusiastic, fanatical, fervent, intense, keen, passionate, zealous **2.** acquisitive, athirst, avaricious, covetous, grasping, greedy, hungry, insatiable, rapacious, ravenous, thirsty, voracious

avidity 1. ardour, devotion, eagerness, enthusiasm, fervour, keenness, zeal **2.** acquisitiveness, avarice, covetousness, cupidity, desire, graspingness, greediness, hankering, hunger, insatiability, longing, rapacity, ravenousness, thirst, voracity

avocation 1. diversion, hobby, occupation, pastime, recreation **2.** business, calling, employment, job, occupation, profession, pursuit, trade, vocation, work

avoid avert, bypass, circumvent, dodge, duck (out of) (*Inf.*), elude, escape, eschew, evade, fight shy of, keep aloof from, keep away from, prevent, refrain from, shirk,

avoirdupois or **avoirdupois weight** (ˌævədə'pɔɪz) n. a system of weights used in many English-speaking countries. It is based on the pound, which contains 16 ounces or 7000 grains.

avouch (ə'vaʊtʃ) vb. (tr.) Arch. 1. to vouch for; guarantee. 2. to acknowledge. 3. to assert. —a'**vouchment** n.

avow (ə'vaʊ) vb. (tr.) 1. to state or affirm. 2. to admit openly. —a'**vowal** n. —**avowed** (ə'vaʊd) adj. —**avowedly** (ə'vaʊɪdlɪ) adv. —a'**vower** n.

avuncular (ə'vʌŋkjʊlə) adj. 1. of or concerned with an uncle. 2. resembling an uncle; friendly.

await (ə'weɪt) vb. 1. (tr.) to wait for. 2. (tr.) to be in store for. 3. (intr.) to wait, esp. with expectation.

awake (ə'weɪk) vb. **awaking; awoke** or **awaked; awoken** or **awaked. 1.** to emerge or rouse from sleep. 2. to become or cause to become alert. 3. (usually foll. by to) to become or make aware (of). 4. Also: **awaken.** (tr.) to arouse (a feeling, etc.) or cause to remember (memories, etc.). ~adj. (postpositive) 5. not sleeping. 6. (sometimes foll. by to) lively or alert.

▷ Usage. See at **wake**[1].

award (ə'wɔːd) vb. (tr.) 1. to give (something due), esp. as a reward for merit: to award prizes. 2. Law. to declare to be entitled, as by decision of a court or an arbitrator. ~n. 3. something awarded, such as a prize or medal. 4. Law. **a.** the decision of an arbitrator. **b.** a grant made by a court of law. —a'**warder** n.

aware (ə'wɛə) adj. 1. (postpositive; foll. by of) having knowledge: aware of his error. 2. informed of current developments: politically aware. —a'**wareness** n.

awash (ə'wɒʃ) adv., adj. (postpositive) Naut. 1. at a level even with the surface of the sea. 2. washed over by the waves.

away (ə'weɪ) adv. 1. from a particular place: to swim away. 2. in or to another, a usual, or a proper place: to put toys away. 3. apart; at a distance: to keep away from strangers. 4. out of existence: the music faded away. 5. indicating motion, displacement, transfer, etc., from a normal or proper place: to turn one's head away. 6. indicating activity that is wasteful or designed to get rid of something: to sleep away the hours. 7. continuously: laughing away. 8. **away with.** a command for a person to go or be removed: away with him to prison! ~adj. (usually postpositive) 9. not present: away from school. 10. distant: he is a good way away. 11. having started; released: he was away before sunrise. 12. (also prenominal) Sport. played on an opponent's ground. ~n. 13. Sport. a game played or won at an opponent's ground. ~interj. 14. an expression of dismissal.

awe (ɔː) n. 1. overwhelming wonder, respect, or dread. 2. Arch. power to inspire fear or reverence. ~vb. 3. (tr.) to inspire with reverence or dread.

aweigh (ə'weɪ) adj. (postpositive) Naut. (of an anchor) no longer hooked into the bottom; hanging by its rope or chain.

awesome ('ɔːsəm) adj. inspiring or displaying awe. —'**awesomely** adv. —'**awesomeness** n.

awful ('ɔːfʊl) adj. 1. very bad; unpleasant. 2. Arch. inspiring reverence or dread. 3. Arch. overcome with awe. ~adv. 4. Not standard. (intensifier): an awful cold day. —'**awfulness** n.

awfully ('ɔːfəlɪ) adv. 1. in an unpleasant, bad, or reprehensible manner. 2. Inf. (intensifier): I'm awfully keen to come. 3. Arch. so as to express or inspire awe.

awhile (ə'waɪl) adv. for a brief period.

awkward ('ɔːkwəd) adj. 1. lacking dexterity, proficiency, or skill; clumsy. 2. ungainly or inelegant in movements or posture. 3. unwieldy; difficult to use. 4. embarrassing: an awkward moment. 5. embarrassed: he felt awkward about leaving. 6. difficult to deal with; requiring tact: an awkward customer. 7. dangerous or difficult. —'**awkwardly** adv. —'**awkwardness** n.

THESAURUS

shun, sidestep, steer clear of

avoidance circumvention, dodging, eluding, escape, eschewal, evasion, keeping away from, prevention, refraining, shirking, shunning, steering clear of

avowed acknowledged, admitted, confessed, declared, open, professed, self-proclaimed, sworn

await 1. abide, anticipate, expect, look for, look forward to, stay for, wait for 2. attend, be in readiness for, be in store for, be prepared for, be ready for, wait for

awake v. 1. awaken, rouse, wake, wake up 2. activate, alert, animate, arouse, awaken, call forth, enliven, excite, fan, incite, kindle, provoke, revive, stimulate, stir up, vivify ~adj. 3. alert, alive, aroused, attentive, awakened, aware, conscious, heedful, not sleeping, observant, on guard, on the alert, on the lookout, vigilant, wakeful, waking, watchful, wide-awake

awaken activate, alert, animate, arouse, awake, call forth, enliven, excite, fan, incite, kindle, provoke, revive, rouse, stimulate, stir up, vivify, wake

awakening n. activation, animating, arousal, awaking, birth, enlivening, incitement, kindling, provocation, revival, rousing, stimulation, stirring up, vivification, waking, waking up

award v. 1. accord, adjudge, allot, apportion, assign, bestow, confer, decree, distribute, endow, gift, give, grant, present, render ~n. 2. adjudication, allotment, bestowal, conferment, conferral, decision, decree, endowment, gift, order, presentation 3. decoration, gift, grant, prize, trophy, verdict

aware acquainted, alive to, appreciative, apprised, attentive, au courant, cognizant, conscious, conversant, enlightened, familiar, hip (Sl.), informed, knowing, knowledgeable, mindful, sensible, sentient, wise (Inf.)

awareness acquaintance, appreciation, attention, cognizance, consciousness, enlightenment, familiarity, knowledge, mindfulness, perception, realization, recognition, sensibility, sentience, understanding

away adv. 1. abroad, elsewhere, from here, from home, hence, off 2. apart, at a distance, far, remote 3. aside, out of the way, to one side 4. continuously, incessantly, interminably, relentlessly, repeatedly, uninterruptedly, unremittingly ~adj. 5. abroad, absent, elsewhere, gone, not at home, not here, not present, not there, out ~interj. 6. beat it (Inf.), begone, be off, get lost (Inf.), get out, go, go away, on your way

awe 1. n. admiration, amazement, astonishment, dread, fear, horror, respect, reverence, terror, veneration, wonder 2. v. amaze, astonish, cow, daunt, frighten, horrify, impress, intimidate, stun, terrify

awe-inspiring amazing, astonishing, awesome, breathtaking, daunting, fearsome, impressive, intimidating, magnificent, stunning (Inf.), wonderful, wondrous

awesome alarming, amazing, astonishing, awe-inspiring, awful, breathtaking, daunting, dreadful, fearful, fearsome, formidable, frightening, horrible, horrifying, imposing, impressive, intimidating, magnificent, majestic, overwhelming, redoubtable, shocking, solemn, stunning, stupefying, terrible, terrifying, wonderful, wondrous

awe-stricken, awe-struck afraid, amazed, astonished, awed, awe-inspired, cowed, daunted, dumbfounded, fearful, frightened, horrified, impressed, intimidated, shocked, struck dumb, stunned, terrified, wonder-stricken, wonder-struck

awful 1. alarming, appalling, deplorable, dire, distressing, dreadful, fearful, frightful, ghastly, gruesome, harrowing, hideous, horrendous, horrible, horrific, horrifying, nasty, shocking, terrible, tremendous, ugly, unpleasant, unsightly 2. Archaic amazing, awe-inspiring, awesome, dread, fearsome, majestic, portentous, solemn

awfully 1. badly, disgracefully, disreputably, dreadfully, inadequately, reprehensibly, shoddily, unforgivably, unpleasantly, wickedly, woefully, wretchedly 2. Inf. badly, dreadfully, exceedingly, exceptionally, excessively, extremely, greatly, immensely, quite, terribly, very, very much

awhile briefly, for a little while, for a moment, for a short time, for a while

awkward 1. all thumbs, artless, blundering, bungling, clownish, clumsy, coarse, gauche, gawky, graceless, ham-fisted, ham-handed, ill-bred, inelegant, inept, inexpert, lumbering, maladroit, oafish, rude, skill-less, stiff, uncoordinated, uncouth, ungainly, ungraceful, unpolished, unrefined, unskilful, unskilled 2. cumbersome, difficult, inconvenient, troublesome, unhandy, unmanageable, unwieldy 3. compromising, delicate, difficult, embarrassed, embarrassing, ill at ease, inconvenient, inopportune, painful, perplexing, sticky (Inf.), thorny, ticklish, troublesome, trying, uncomfortable, unpleasant, untimely 4. annoying, bloody-minded (Inf.), difficult, disobliging, exasperating, hard to handle, intractable, irritable, perverse, prickly, stubborn, touchy, troublesome, trying, uncooperative, unhelpful, unpredictable, vexatious, vexing 5. chancy (Inf.), dangerous, difficult, hazardous, perilous, risky

awkwardness 1. artlessness, clownishness, clumsiness, coarseness, gaucheness, gaucherie, gawkiness, gracelessness, ill-breeding, inelegance, ineptness, inexpertness, maladroitness, oafishness, rudeness, skill-lessness, stiffness, uncoordination, uncouthness, ungainliness, unskilfulness, unskilledness 2. cumbersomeness, difficulty, inconvenience, troublesomeness, unhandiness, unmanageability, unwieldiness 3. delicacy, difficulty, discomfort, embarrassment, inconvenience, inopportuneness, painfulness, perplexingness, stickiness (Inf.), thorniness, ticklishness, unpleasantness, untimeliness 4. bloody-mindedness (Inf.), difficulty, disobligingness, intractability, irritability, perversity, prickliness, stubbornness, touchiness, uncooperativeness, unhelpfulness, unpredictability 5. chanciness (Inf.), danger, difficulty, hazardousness, peril, perilousness, risk, riskiness

awl (ɔːl) *n.* a pointed hand tool with a fluted blade used for piercing wood, leather, etc.

awn (ɔːn) *n.* any of the bristles growing from the flowering parts of certain grasses and cereals. —**awned** *adj.*

awning ('ɔːnɪŋ) *n.* a roof of canvas or other material supported by a frame to provide protection from the weather, esp. one placed over a doorway or part of a deck of a ship.

awoke (ə'wəʊk) *vb.* a past tense or (now rare or dialectal) past participle of **awake.**

A.W.O.L. *or* **AWOL** (*when acronym* 'eɪwɒl) *adj. Mil.* absent without leave but without intending to desert.

awry (ə'raɪ) *adv., adj.* (*postpositive*) **1.** with a slant or twist to one side; askew. **2.** away from the appropriate or right course; amiss.

axe *or U.S.* **ax** (æks) *n., pl.* **axes. 1.** a hand tool with one side of its head forged and sharpened to a cutting edge, used for felling trees, splitting timber, etc. **2. an axe to grind. a.** an ulterior motive. **b.** a grievance. **c.** a pet subject. **3. the axe.** *Inf.* **a.** dismissal, esp. from employment (esp. in **get the axe**). **b.** *Brit.* severe cutting down of expenditure, esp. in a public service. ~*vb.* (*tr.*) **4.** to chop or trim with an axe. **5.** *Inf.* to dismiss (employees), restrict (expenditure or services), or terminate (a project, etc.).

axes[1] ('æksiːz) *n.* the plural of **axis.**

axes[2] ('æksɪz) *n.* the plural of **axe.**

axial ('æksɪəl) *adj.* **1.** forming or characteristic of an axis. **2.** situated in, on, or along an axis. —,**axi'ality** *n.* —'**axially** *adv.*

axil ('æksɪl) *n.* the upper angle between a branch or leaf stalk and the stem from which it grows.

axiom ('æksɪəm) *n.* **1.** a generally accepted proposition or principle, sanctioned by experience. **2.** a universally established principle or law that is not a necessary truth. **3.** *Logic, maths.* a self-consistent self-evident statement that is a universally accepted truth.

axiomatic (,æksɪə'mætɪk) *adj.* **1.** self-evident. **2.** containing maxims; aphoristic. —,**axio'matically** *adv.*

axis ('æksɪs) *n., pl.* **axes** ('æksiːz). **1.** a real or imaginary line about which a body, such as an aircraft, can rotate or about which an object, form, composition, or geometrical construction is symmetrical. **2.** one of two or three reference lines used in coordinate geometry to locate a point in a plane or in space. **3.** *Anat.* the second cervical vertebra. **4.** *Bot.* the main central part of a plant, typically consisting of the stem and root. **5.** an alliance between a number of states to coordinate their foreign policy. **6.** Also called: **principal axis.** *Optics.* the line of symmetry of an optical system, such as the line passing through the centre of a lens.

Axis ('æksɪs) *n.* **a. the.** the alliance (1936) of Nazi Germany and Fascist Italy, later joined by Japan and other countries, and lasting until their defeat in World War II. **b.** (*as modifier*): *the Axis powers.*

axle ('æksəl) *n.* a bar or shaft on which a wheel, pair of wheels, or other rotating member revolves.

axletree ('æksəl,triː) *n.* a bar fixed across the underpart of a wagon or carriage that has rounded ends on which the wheels revolve.

Axminster carpet ('æks,mɪnstə) *n.* a type of patterned carpet with a cut pile. Often shortened to **Axminster.**

axolotl ('æksə,lɒtəl) *n.* an aquatic salamander of N America, such as the **Mexican axolotl,** in which the larval form (including external gills) is retained throughout life under natural conditions.

ayah ('aɪə) *n.* (in parts of the former British Empire) a native maidservant or nursemaid.

ayatollah (,aɪə'tɒlə) *n.* one of class of Shiite religious leaders in Iran.

aye *or* **ay** (aɪ) *sentence substitute.* **1.** yes: archaic or dialectal except in voting by voice. ~*n.* **2. a.** a person who votes in the affirmative. **b.** an affirmative vote. ~Cf. **nay.**

aye-aye ('aɪ,aɪ) *n.* a rare nocturnal arboreal primate of Madagascar related to the lemurs. It has long bony fingers and rodent-like incisor teeth.

Ayrshire ('ɛəʃə) *n.* any one of a hardy breed of brown and white dairy cattle.

azalea (ə'zeɪljə) *n.* an ericaceous plant cultivated for its showy pink or purple flowers.

azimuth ('æzɪməθ) *n.* **1.** *Astron., navigation.* the angular distance usually measured clockwise from the south point of the horizon in astronomy or from the north point in navigation to the intersection with the horizon of the vertical circle passing through a celestial body. **2.** *Surveying.* the horizontal angle of a bearing clockwise from north. —**azimuthal** (,æzɪ'mʌθəl) *adj.*

Aztec ('æztɛk) *n.* **1.** a member of a Mexican Indian people who established a great empire, centred on the valley of Mexico, that was overthrown by Cortés in the early 16th century. **2.** the language of the Aztecs. ~*adj.* also **Aztecan. 3.** of, relating to, or characteristic of the Aztecs, their civilization, or their language.

azure ('æʒə, 'eɪ-) *n.* **1.** a deep blue similar to the colour of a clear blue sky. **2.** *Poetic.* a clear blue sky. ~*adj.* **3.** of the colour azure. **4.** (*usually postpositive*) *Heraldry.* of the colour blue.

THESAURUS

axe *n.* **1.** chopper, hatchet **2. an axe to grind** grievance, personal consideration, pet subject, private ends, private purpose, ulterior motive **3. the axe** *Inf.* cancellation, cutback, discharge, dismissal, termination, the boot (*Sl.*), the chop (*Sl.*), the sack (*Inf.*), wind-up ~*v.* **4.** chop, cut down, fell, hew **5.** *Inf.* cancel, cut back, discharge, dismiss, dispense with, eliminate, fire (*Inf.*), get rid of, remove, sack (*Inf.*), terminate, throw out, turn off

(*Inf.*), wind up

axiom adage, aphorism, apophthegm, dictum, fundamental, gnome, maxim, postulate, precept, principle, truism

axiomatic 1. absolute, accepted, apodictic, assumed, certain, fundamental, given, granted, indubitable, manifest, presupposed, self-evident, understood, unquestioned **2.** aphoristic, apophthegmatic, epigrammatic, gnomic, pithy, terse

axis 1. axle, centre line, pivot, shaft, spindle **2.** alliance, bloc, coalition, compact, entente, league, pact

axle arbor, axis, mandrel, pin, pivot, rod, shaft, spindle

azure blue, cerulean, clear blue, sky-blue, sky-coloured, ultramarine

B

b *or* **B** (biː) *n., pl.* **b's, B's,** *or* **Bs.** **1.** the second letter of the English alphabet. **2.** a speech sound represented by this letter, as in *bell.* **3.** Also: **beta.** the second in a series, class, or rank.

B *symbol for:* **1.** *Music.* **a.** the seventh note of the scale of C major. **b.** the major or minor key having this note as its tonic. **2.** the less important of two things. **3.** a human blood type of the ABO group, containing the B antigen. **4.** (in Britain) a secondary road. **5.** *Chem.* boron. **6.** magnetic flux density. **7.** *Chess.* bishop. **8.** (on Brit. pencils, signifying degree of softness of lead) black. **9.** Also: **b** *Physics.* bel. **10.** *Physics.* baryon number.

b. *or* **B.** *abbrev. for:* **1.** *Music.* bass *or* basso. **2.** (on maps, etc.) bay. **3.** (*cap.*) Bible. **4.** book. **5.** born. **6.** (*not cap.*) *Cricket.* **a.** bowled. **b.** bye. **7.** breadth.

Ba *the chemical symbol for barium.*

B.A. *abbrev. for:* **1.** Bachelor of Arts. **2.** British Academy. **3.** British Association (for the Advancement of Science).

B.A.A. *abbrev. for* British Airports Authority.

baa (bɑː) *vb.* **baaing, baaed.** **1.** (*intr.*) to make the cry of a sheep; bleat. ~*n.* **2.** the cry made by sheep.

baas (bɑːs) *n.* a South African word for **boss:** used by Africans and Coloureds in addressing European managers or overseers.

baaskap *or* **baasskap** ('bɑːsˌkap) *n.* (*sometimes cap.*) (in South Africa) control by Whites of non-Whites.

baba ('bɑːbɑː) *n.* a small cake, usually soaked in rum (**rum baba**).

babalas ('bæbəˌlæs) *n. S. African.* a hangover.

Babbitt metal *n.* any of a number of alloys originally based on tin, antimony, and copper but now often including lead: used esp. in bearings.

babble ('bæbəl) *vb.* **1.** to utter (words, sounds, etc.) in an incoherent jumble. **2.** (*intr.*) to talk foolishly, incessantly, or irrelevantly. **3.** (*tr.*) to disclose (secrets, etc.) carelessly. **4.** (*intr.*) (of streams, birds, etc.) to make a low murmuring sound. ~*n.* **5.** incoherent or foolish speech. **6.** a murmuring sound. —'**babbler** *n.*

babe (beɪb) *n.* **1.** a baby. **2.** *Inf.* a naive or gullible person. **3.** *Sl. chiefly U.S.* a girl.

Babel ('beɪbəl) *n.* **1.** *Old Testament.* Also called: **Tower of Babel.** a tower presumptuously intended to reach from earth to heaven, the building of which was frustrated when Jehovah confused the language of the builders (Genesis 11:1-10). **2.** (*often not cap.*) **a.** a confusion of noises or voices. **b.** a scene of noise and confusion.

baboon (bə'buːn) *n.* any of several medium-sized Old World monkeys. They have an elongated muzzle, large teeth, and a fairly long tail.

baby ('beɪbɪ) *n., pl.* -**bies.** **1. a.** a newborn child; infant. **b.** (*as modifier*): *baby food.* **2.** the youngest or smallest of a family or group. **3.** a newborn or recently born animal. **4.** *Usually derog.* an immature person. **5.** *Sl.* a young woman or sweetheart. **6.** *Sl.* a project of personal concern. **7. be left holding the baby.** to be left with the responsibility. ~*adj.* **8.** (*prenominal*) comparatively small of its type: *a baby grand (piano).* ~*vb.* -**bying,** -**bied.** **9.** (*tr.*) to treat with love and attention. **10.** to treat (someone) like a baby; pamper or overprotect. —'**babyhood** *n.* —'**babyish** *adj.*

baby bonus *n. Canad. inf.* Family Allowance.

baby-sit *vb.* -**sitting,** -**sat.** (*intr.*) to act or work as a baby-sitter.

baby-sitter *n.* a person who takes care of a child or children while the parents are out.

B.A.C. *abbrev. for* British Aircraft Corporation.

baccalaureate (ˌbækə'lɔːrɪɪt) *n.* the university degree of Bachelor of Arts.

baccarat ('bækəˌrɑː, ˌbækə'rɑː) *n.* a card game in which two or more punters gamble against the banker.

bacchanal ('bækənəl) *n.* **1.** a follower of Bacchus, Greek god of wine. **2.** a drunken and riotous celebration. **3.** a participant in such a celebration. ~*adj.* **4.** of or relating to Bacchus.

bacchanalia (ˌbækə'neɪlɪə) *pl. n.* **1.** (*often cap.*) orgiastic rites associated with Bacchus. **2.** any drunken revelry. —ˌbaccha'nalian *adj., n.*

bacchant ('bækənt) *or* (*fem.*) **bacchante** (bə'kæntɪ) *n., pl.* **bacchants, bacchantes** (bə'kæntɪz) **1.** a priest, priestess, or votary of Bacchus. **2.** a drunken reveller.

Bacchic ('bækɪk) *adj.* **1.** of or relating to Bacchus. **2.** (*often not cap.*) riotously drunk.

baccy ('bækɪ) *n.* a Brit. informal name for **tobacco.**

bachelor ('bætʃələ, 'bætʃlə) *n.* **1. a.** an unmarried man. **b.** (*as modifier*): *a bachelor flat.* **2.** a person who holds the degree of Bachelor of Arts, Bachelor of Science, etc. **3.** (in the Middle Ages) a young knight serving a great noble. **4. bachelor seal.** a young male seal that has not yet mated. —'**bachelorhood** *n.*

bachelor girl *n.* a young unmarried woman, esp. one who is self-supporting.

Bachelor of Arts *n.* **1.** a degree conferred on a person who has successfully completed undergraduate studies in the liberal arts or humanities. **2.** a person who holds this degree.

bacillary (bə'sɪlərɪ) *or* **bacillar** (bə'sɪlə) *adj.* **1.** of, relating to, or caused by bacilli. **2.** Also: **bacilliform** (bə-'sɪlɪˌfɔːm). shaped like a short rod.

bacillus (bə'sɪləs) *n., pl.* -**cilli** (-'sɪlaɪ). **1.** any rod-shaped bacterium. **2.** any of various rodlike spore-producing bacteria constituting the family *Bacillaceae.*

back (bæk) *n.* **1.** the posterior part of the human body, from the neck to the pelvis. **2.** the corresponding or upper part of an animal. **3.** the spinal column. **4.** the part or side of an object opposite the front. **5.** the part or side of anything less often seen or used. **6.** the part or side of anything that is furthest from the front or from a spectator: *the back of the stage.* **7.** something that supports, covers, or strengthens the rear of an object. **8.** *Ball games.* **a.** a mainly defensive player behind a forward. **b.** the position of such a player. **9.** the part of a book to which the pages are glued or that joins the covers. **10. at the back of one's mind.** not in one's conscious thoughts. **11. behind one's back.** secretly or deceitfully. **12. break one's back.** to overwork or work very hard. **13. break the back of.** to complete the greatest or hardest part of (a task). **14. get off someone's back.** *Inf.* to stop criticizing or pestering someone. **15. back o'Bourke.** *Austral.* in a remote or backward place. **16. put one's back into.** to devote all one's strength to (a task). **17. put (or get) someone's back up.** to annoy someone. **18. the back of beyond.** a very remote place. **19. turn one's back on. a.** to turn away from in anger or contempt. **b.** to refuse to help; abandon. **20. with one's back to the wall.** in a desperate situation. ~*vb.* (*mainly tr.*) **21.** (*also intr.*) to move or cause to move backwards. **22.** to provide support, money, or encouragement for (a person, enterprise, etc.). **23.** to bet on the success of: *to back a horse.* **24.** to provide with a back, backing, or lining. **25.** to provide with a musical accompaniment. **26.** to countersign or endorse. **27.** (*intr.;* foll. by *on* or *onto*) to have the back facing (towards): *the house backs onto a river.* **28.** (*intr.*) (of the wind) to change direction anti-

THESAURUS

babble **1.** *v.* blab, burble, cackle, chatter, gabble, gibber, gurgle, jabber, mumble, murmur, mutter, prate, prattle **2.** *n.* burble, clamour, drivel, gabble, gibberish, murmur

babe **1.** baby, bairn (*Scot.*), child, infant, nursling, suckling **2.** babe in arms, ingénue, innocent

baby **1.** *n.* babe, bairn (*Scot.*), child, infant, newborn child **2.** *adj.* diminutive, dwarf, little, midget, mini, miniature, minute, pygmy, small, tiny, wee **3.** *v.* coddle, cosset, humour, indulge, mollycoddle, overindulge, pamper, pet, spoil, spoon-feed

babyish baby, childish, foolish, immature, infantile, juvenile, namby-pamby, puerile, silly, sissy, soft (*Inf.*), spoiled

bacchanal **1.** carouser, debauchee, drunkard, reveller, roisterer, winebibber **2.** debauch, debauchery, orgy, revel, revelry

clockwise. Cf. **veer** (sense 3). ~*adj.* (*prenominal*) **29.** situated behind: *a back lane.* **30.** of the past: *back issues of a magazine.* **31.** owing from an earlier date: *back rent.* **32.** remote: *a back road.* **33.** *Phonetics.* of or denoting a vowel articulated with the tongue retracted towards the soft palate, as for the vowels in English *hard, fall, hot, full, fool.* ~*adv.* **34.** at, to, or towards the rear; behind. **35.** in, to, or towards the original starting point, place, or condition: *to go back; put the book back.* **36.** in or into the past: *to look back on one's childhood.* **37.** in reply, repayment, or retaliation: *to hit someone back.* **38.** in check: *the dam holds back the water.* **39.** in concealment; in reserve: *to keep something back.* **40.** **back and forth.** to and fro. **41.** **back to front. a.** in reverse. **b.** in disorder.

backbencher ('bæk'bɛntʃə) *n. Brit., Austral., etc.* a member of Parliament who does not hold office in the government or opposition.

backbite ('bæk,baɪt) *vb.* -biting, bit; bitten *or* bit. to talk spitefully about (an absent person). —'back,biter *n.*

backboard ('bæk,bɔːd) *n.* **1.** a board that is placed behind something to form or support its back. **2.** a board worn to straighten or support the back, as after surgery. **3.** (in basketball) a flat upright surface supported on a high frame, under which the basket is attached.

back boiler *n.* a tank or series of pipes at the back of a fireplace for heating water.

backbone ('bæk,bəʊn) *n.* **1.** a nontechnical name for **spinal column. 2.** something that resembles the spinal column in function, position, or appearance. **3.** strength of character; courage.

backbreaking ('bæk,breɪkɪŋ) *adj.* exhausting.

backchat ('bæk,tʃæt) *n. Inf.* the act of answering back, esp. impudently.

backcloth ('bæk,klɒθ) *or* **backdrop** *n.* a painted curtain at the back of a stage set.

backcomb ('bæk,kəʊm) *vb.* to comb the under layers of (the hair) towards the roots to give more bulk to a hair style. Also: **tease.**

back country *n. Austral. & N.Z.* sparsely populated areas.

backdate (,bæk'deɪt) *vb.* (*tr.*) to make effective from an earlier date.

back door *n.* **1.** a door at the rear or side of a building. **2.** a means of entry to a job, etc., that is secret or obtained through influence.

back down *vb.* **1.** (*intr., adv.*) to withdraw an earlier claim. ~*n.* **backdown. 2.** abandonment of an earlier claim.

backer ('bækə) *n.* **1.** a person who gives financial or other support. **2.** a person who bets on a competitor or contestant.

backfire (,bæk'faɪə) *vb.* (*intr.*) **1.** (of an internal-combustion engine) to emit a loud noise as a result of an explosion in the exhaust system. **2.** to fail to have the desired effect, and, instead, recoil upon the originator. **3.** to start a controlled fire in order to halt an advancing forest or prairie fire by creating a barren area. ~*n.* **4.** (in an internal-combustion engine) an explosion of unburnt gases in the exhaust system. **5.** a controlled fire started to create a barren area that will halt an advancing forest or prairie fire.

back formation *n.* **1.** the unwitting invention of a new word on the assumption that a familiar word is derived from it. The verbs *edit* and *burgle* in English were so created from *editor* and *burglar.* **2.** a word formed by this process.

backgammon ('bæk,gæmən) *n.* **1.** a game for two people played on a board with pieces moved according to throws of the dice. **2.** the most complete form of win in this game.

background ('bæk,graʊnd) *n.* **1.** the part of a scene furthest from the viewer. **2. a.** an inconspicuous or unobtrusive position (esp. in **in the background**). **b.** (*as modifier*): *a background influence.* **3.** the plane or ground in a picture upon which all other planes or forms appear superimposed. **4.** a person's social class, education, or experience. **5. a.** the circumstances that lead up to or help to explain something. **b.** (*as modifier*): *background information.* **6. a.** a low level of sound, lighting, etc., whose purpose is to be an unobtrusive accompaniment to something else. **b.** (*as modifier*): *background music.* **7.** Also called: **background radiation.** *Physics.* low-intensity radiation from small amounts of radio isotopes in soil, air, etc. **8.** *Electronics.* unwanted effects, such as noise, occurring in a measuring instrument, electronic device, etc.

backhand ('bæk,hænd) *n.* **1.** *Tennis, etc.* a stroke made across the body with the back of the hand facing the direction of the stroke. **2.** the side on which backhand strokes are made. **3.** handwriting slanting to the left. ~*adv.* **4.** with a backhand stroke.

backhanded (,bæk'hændɪd) *adj.* **1.** (of a blow, shot, etc.) performed with the arm moving across the body. **2.** double-edged; equivocal: *a backhanded compliment.* **3.** (of handwriting) slanting to the left. ~*adv.* **4.** in a backhanded manner.

backhander ('bæk,hændə) *n.* **1.** a backhanded stroke or blow. **2.** *Inf.* an indirect attack. **3.** *Sl.* a bribe.

backing ('bækɪŋ) *n.* **1.** support. **2.** a body of supporters. **3.** something that forms, protects, or strengthens the back of something. **4.** musical accompaniment, esp. for a pop singer.

backlash ('bæk,læʃ) *n.* **1.** a sudden and adverse reaction. **2.** a reaction or recoil between interacting worn or badly fitting parts in a mechanism. **3.** the excessive play between such parts.

backlog ('bæk,lɒg) *n.* an accumulation of uncompleted work, unsold stock, etc., to be dealt with.

back marker *n.* a competitor who is at the back of a field in a race.

back number *n.* **1.** an issue of a newspaper, magazine, etc., that appeared on a previous date. **2.** *Inf.* a person or thing considered to be old-fashioned.

back out *vb.* (*intr., adv.; often foll. by of*) to withdraw (from an agreement, etc.).

back pack *n.* **1.** a rucksack. **2.** a pack carried on the back of an astronaut, containing oxygen cylinders, etc. ~*vb.* (*intr.*) **back-pack. 3.** to travel about or go hiking with a back pack.

back passage *n.* the rectum.

back-pedal *vb.* -pedalling, -pedalled *or U.S.* -pedaling, -pedaled. (*intr.*) **1.** to turn the pedals of a bicycle

---

THESAURUS

back v. **1.** abet, advocate, assist, champion, countenance, encourage, endorse, favour, finance, sanction, second, side with, sponsor, subsidize, support, sustain, underwrite **2.** backtrack, go back, move back, regress, retire, retreat, reverse, turn tail, withdraw ~n. **3.** backside, end, far end, hind part, hindquarters, posterior, rear, reverse, stern, tail end ~adj. **4.** end, hind, hindmost, posterior, rear, tail **5.** *From an earlier time* delayed, earlier, elapsed, former, overdue, past, previous **6. behind one's back** covertly, deceitfully, secretly, sneakily, surreptitiously

backbiting abuse, aspersion, bitchiness (*Sl.*), calumniation, calumny, cattiness (*Inf.*), defamation, denigration, detraction, disparagement, gossip, malice, scandalmongering, slander, spite, spitefulness, vilification, vituperation

backbone 1. *Medical* spinal column, spine, vertebrae, vertebral column **2.** bottle (*Sl.*), character, courage, determination, firmness, fortitude, grit, hardihood, mettle, moral fibre, nerve, pluck, resolution, resolve, stamina, steadfastness, strength of character, tenacity, toughness, will, willpower **3.** basis, foundation, mainstay, support

backbreaking arduous, crushing, exhausting, gruelling, hard, killing, laborious, punishing, strenuous, toilsome, wearing, wearying

back down accede, admit defeat, backpedal, concede, give in, surrender, withdraw, yield

backer advocate, angel (*Inf.*), benefactor, patron, promoter, second, sponsor, subscriber, supporter, underwriter, well-wisher

backfire boomerang, disappoint, fail, flop, miscarry, rebound, recoil

background breeding, circumstances, credentials, culture, education, environment, experience, grounding, history, milieu, preparation, qualifications, tradition, upbringing

backhanded ambiguous, double-edged, equivocal, indirect, ironic, oblique, sarcastic, sardonic, two-edged

backing abetment, accompaniment, advocacy, aid, assistance, championing, encouragement, endorsement, funds, grant, moral support, patronage, sanction, seconding, sponsorship, subsidy, support

backlash backfire, boomerang, counteraction, counterblast, kickback, reaction, recoil, repercussion, resentment, resistance, response, retaliation, retroaction

backlog accumulation, excess, hoard, reserve, reserves, resources, stock, supply

back out abandon, cancel, chicken out (*Inf.*), give up, go back on, recant, renege, resign, retreat, withdraw

backwards. **2.** to retract or modify a previous opinion, principle, etc.

back room *n.* **a.** a place where important and usually secret research is done. **b.** (*as modifier*): *back-room boys.*

back seat *n.* **1.** a seat at the back, esp. of a vehicle. **2.** *Inf.* a subordinate or inconspicuous position (esp. in **take a back seat**).

back-seat driver *n. Inf.* **1.** a passenger in a car who offers unwanted advice to the driver. **2.** a person who offers advice on or tries to direct matters that are not his concern.

backside (ˌbækˈsaɪd) *n. Inf.* the buttocks.

backslide (ˈbækˌslaɪd) *vb.* **-sliding, -slid.** (*intr.*) to relapse into former bad habits or vices. —ˈback,slider *n.*

backspace (ˈbækˌspeɪs) *vb.* to move a (typewriter carriage, etc.) backwards.

backspin (ˈbækˌspɪn) *n. Sport.* a backward ball spin imparted to a ball to minimize its bounce.

backstage (ˌbækˈsteɪdʒ) *adv.* **1.** behind the part of the theatre in view of the audience. **2.** towards the rear of the stage. ~*adj.* **3.** situated backstage. **4.** *Inf.* away from public view.

backstairs (ˈbækˈstɛəz) *pl. n.* **1.** a secondary staircase in a house, esp. one originally for the use of servants. ~*adj.* also **backstair.** **2.** underhand: *backstairs gossip.*

backstreet (ˈbækˌstriːt) *n.* **1.** a street in a town remote from the main roads. **2.** (*modifier*) denoting illicit activities regarded as likely to take place in such a street: *a backstreet abortion.*

backstroke (ˈbækˌstrəʊk) *n. Swimming.* a stroke performed on the back, using backward circular strokes of each arm and flipper movements of the feet. Also called: **back crawl.**

back-to-back *adj.* (*usually postpositive*) **1.** facing in opposite directions, often with the backs touching. **2.** *Chiefly Brit.* (of urban houses) built so that their backs are adjacent or separated only by a narrow alley.

backtrack (ˈbækˌtræk) *vb.* (*intr.*) **1.** to return by the same route by which one has come. **2.** to retract or reverse one's opinion, policy, etc.

back up *vb.* (*adv.*) **1.** (*tr.*) to support. **2.** (*intr.*) *Cricket.* (of a nonstriking batsman) to move down the wicket in readiness for a run as a ball is bowled. **3.** (of water) to accumulate. **4.** *Computers.* to make a copy of (a data file), esp. as a security copy. **5.** (*intr.,* usually foll. by *on*) *Austral.* to repeat an action immediately. ~*n.* **backup.** *Chiefly U.S.* **6.** a support or reinforcement. **7.** a reserve or substitute. **8.** the overflow from a blocked drain or pipe.

backward (ˈbækwəd) *adj.* **1.** (*usually prenominal*) directed towards the rear: *a backward glance.* **2.** retarded in physical, material, or intellectual development. **3. a.** conservative or reactionary. **b.** (*in combination*): *backward-looking.* **4.** reluctant or bashful: *a backward lover.* ~*adv.* **5.** a variant of **backwards.** —ˈbackwardness *n.*

backwards (ˈbækwədz) *or* **backward** *adv.* **1.** towards the rear. **2.** with the back foremost. **3.** in the reverse of usual order or direction. **4.** to or towards the past. **5.** into a worse state. **6.** towards the point of origin. **7. bend, lean** or **fall over backwards.** *Inf.* to make a special effort, esp. in order to please.

backwash (ˈbækˌwɒʃ) *n.* **1.** water washed backwards by the motion of oars or other propelling devices. **2.** the backward flow of air set up by aircraft engines. **3.** a repercussion.

backwater (ˈbækˌwɔːtə) *n.* **1.** a body of stagnant water connected to a river. **2.** an isolated or backward place or condition. ~*vb.* **back water.** **3.** (*intr.*) to reverse the direction of a boat, esp. to push the oars of a rowing boat.

backwoods (ˈbækwʊdz) *pl. n.* **1.** partially cleared, sparsely populated forests. **2.** any remote sparsely populated place. **3.** (*modifier*) of or like the backwoods. **4.** (*modifier*) uncouth; rustic. —ˈback,woodsman *n.*

back yard *n.* **1.** a yard at the back of a house, etc. **2. in one's own back yard.** close at hand.

baclava (ˈbɑːkləˌvɑː) *n.* a variant spelling of **baklava.**

bacon (ˈbeɪkən) *n.* **1.** meat from the back and sides of a pig, dried, salted, and usually smoked. **2. bring home the bacon.** *Inf.* **a.** to achieve success. **b.** to provide material support. **3. save one's bacon.** *Brit. inf.* to escape from danger.

Baconian (beɪˈkəʊnɪən) *adj.* **1.** of or relating to Francis Bacon (1561-1626), English philosopher, or his inductive method of reasoning. ~*n.* **2.** a follower of Bacon's philosophy. **3.** one who believes that plays attributed to Shakespeare were written by Bacon.

bacteria (bækˈtɪərɪə) *pl. n., sing.* **-rium** (-rɪəm). a large group of typically unicellular microorganisms, many of which cause disease. —**bac'terial** *adj.* —**bac'terially** *adv.*

bacterio-, bacteri-, *or sometimes before a vowel* **bacter-** *combining form.* indicating bacteria or an action or condition relating to bacteria: *bacteriology; bactericide.*

bacteriology (bækˌtɪərɪˈɒlədʒɪ) *n.* the study of bacteria. —**bacteriological** (bækˌtɪərɪəˈlɒdʒɪkəl) *adj.* —**bac,teri'ologist** *n.*

bacterium (bækˈtɪərɪəm) *n.* singular of **bacteria.**

Bactrian camel (ˈbæktrɪən) *n.* a two-humped camel, used in the cold deserts of central Asia.

bad¹ (bæd) *adj.* **worse, worst.** **1.** not good; of poor quality; inadequate. **2.** (often foll. by *at*) lacking skill or talent; incompetent. **3.** (often foll. by *for*) harmful. **4.** immoral; evil. **5.** naughty; mischievous. **6.** rotten; decayed: *a bad egg.* **7.** severe; intense: *a bad headache.* **8.** incorrect; faulty: *bad pronunciation.* **9.** ill or in pain (esp. in **feel bad**). **10.** sorry or upset (esp. in **feel bad about**). **11.** unfavourable; distressing: *bad news.* **12.** offensive; unpleasant: *bad language; bad temper.* **13.** not valid or sound: *a bad cheque.* **14.** not recoverable: *a bad debt.* **15. go from bad to worse.** to deteriorate even more. **16. go bad.** to putrefy; spoil. **17. in a bad way.** *Inf.* **a.** seriously ill. **b.** in trouble. **18. make the best of a bad job.** to manage as well as possible in unfavourable circumstances. **19. not bad** *or* **not so bad.** *Inf.* passable; fairly good. **20. too bad.** *Inf.* (often used dismissively) regrettable. ~*n.* **21.** unfortunate or unpleasant events (often in **take the bad with the good**). **22.** an immoral or degenerate state (often in **go to the bad**). **23.** the debit side of an account: *£200 to the bad.* ~*adv.* **24.** *Not standard.* badly: *to want something bad.* —ˈbaddish *adj.* —ˈbadness *n.*

▷ **Usage.** See at **good.**

bad² (bæd) *vb.* a variant spelling of **bade.**

bad blood *n.* a feeling of intense hatred or hostility; enmity.

bade (bæd, beɪd) *or* **bad** *vb.* the past tense of **bid.**

badge (bædʒ) *n.* **1.** a distinguishing emblem or mark worn to signify membership, employment, achievement, etc. **2.** any revealing feature or mark.

THESAURUS

backslide fall from grace, go astray, go wrong, lapse, regress, relapse, renege, retrogress, revert, sin, slip, stray, weaken

backslider apostate, deserter, recidivist, recreant, renegade, reneger, turncoat

back up aid, assist, bolster, confirm, corroborate, reinforce, second, stand by, substantiate, support

backward *adj.* **1.** bashful, diffident, hesitating, late, reluctant, shy, sluggish, tardy, unwilling, wavering **2.** behind, behindhand, dense, dull, retarded, slow, stupid, subnormal, underdeveloped, undeveloped ~*adv.* **3.** aback, behind, in reverse, rearward

backwoods 1. *adj.* hick (*Inf., chiefly U.S.*), isolated, remote, rustic, uncouth **2.** *n.*

back of beyond, outback, sticks (*Inf.*)

bacteria bacilli, bugs (*Sl.*), germs, microbes, microorganisms, pathogens, viruses

bad 1. defective, deficient, erroneous, fallacious, faulty, imperfect, inadequate, incorrect, inferior, poor, substandard, unsatisfactory **2.** damaging, dangerous, deleterious, detrimental, harmful, hurtful, injurious, ruinous, unhealthy **3.** base, corrupt, criminal, delinquent, evil, immoral, mean, sinful, vile, villainous, wicked, wrong **4.** disobedient, mischievous, naughty, unruly **5.** decayed, mouldy, off, putrid, rancid, rotten, sour, spoiled **6.** disastrous, distressing, grave, harsh, painful, serious, severe, terrible **7.** ailing, diseased, ill, sick, unwell **8.** apologetic,

conscience-stricken, contrite, guilty, regretful, remorseful, sad, sorry, upset **9.** adverse, discouraged, discouraging, distressed, distressing, gloomy, grim, melancholy, troubled, troubling, unfortunate, unpleasant **10. not bad** all right, average, fair, fair to middling (*Inf.*), moderate, O.K. (*Inf.*), passable, respectable, so-so (*Inf.*), tolerable

bad blood acrimony, anger, animosity, antagonism, dislike, enmity, feud, hatred, ill feeling, ill will, malevolence, malice, rancour, resentment

badge brand, device, emblem, identification, insignia, mark, sign, stamp, token

badger ('bædʒə) n. 1. any of various stocky omnivorous mammals occurring in Europe, Asia, and N America. They are large burrowing animals, with strong claws and a thick coat striped black and white on the head. ~vb. 2. (tr.) to pester or harass.

badinage ('bædɪ,nɑːʒ) n. playful or frivolous repartee or banter.

badly ('bædlɪ) adv. worse, worst. 1. poorly; defectively; inadequately. 2. unfavourably; unsuccessfully: our scheme worked out badly. 3. severely; gravely: badly hurt. 4. incorrectly or inaccurately: to speak German badly. 5. improperly; wickedly: to behave badly. 6. cruelly: to treat badly. 7. very much (esp. in need badly, want badly). 8. regretfully: he felt badly about it. 9. badly off. poor; impoverished.

badminton ('bædmɪntən) n. 1. a game played with rackets and a shuttlecock, which is hit back and forth across a high net. 2. Also called: badminton cup. a long drink of claret with soda water and sugar.

baffle ('bæfəl) vb. (tr.) 1. to perplex; bewilder; puzzle. 2. to frustrate (plans, efforts, etc.). 3. to check, restrain, or regulate (the flow of a fluid or the emission of sound or light). ~n. 4. Also called: baffle board, baffle plate. a plate or mechanical device to restrain or regulate the flow of fluid, light, or sound, esp. in a loudspeaker or microphone. —'bafflement n. —'baffler n. —'bafflingly adv.

bag (bæg) n. 1. a flexible container with an opening at one end. 2. Also: bagful. the contents of or amount contained in such a container. 3. a piece of portable luggage. 4. short for handbag. 5. anything that sags, or is shaped like a bag, such as a loose fold of skin under the eyes. 6. any pouch or sac forming part of the body of an animal. 7. the quantity of quarry taken in a single hunting trip or by a single hunter. 8. Derog. sl. an ugly or bad-tempered woman or girl (often in old bag). 9. bag and baggage. Inf. a. with all one's belongings. b. entirely. 10. a bag of bones. a lean creature. 11. in the bag. Sl. almost assured of succeeding or being obtained. 12. rough as bags. Austral. sl. a. uncouth. b. shoddy. ~vb. bagging, bagged. 13. (tr.) to put into a bag. 14. to bulge or cause to bulge. 15. (tr.) to capture or kill, as in hunting. 16. (tr.) to catch, seize, or steal. 17. (intr.) to hang loosely; sag. 18. (tr.) Brit. inf. to secure the right to do or to have something: he bagged the best chair.

bagatelle (,bægə'tɛl) n. 1. something of little value; trifle. 2. a board game in which balls are struck into holes, with pins as obstacles. 3. a short light piece of music.

bagel or **beigel** ('beigəl) n. a hard ring-shaped bread roll.

baggage ('bægɪdʒ) n. 1. suitcases, bags, etc., packed for a journey; luggage. 2. an army's portable equipment. 3. Inf., old-fashioned. a. a pert young woman. b. an immoral woman.

baggy ('bægɪ) adj. -gier, -giest. (of clothes) hanging loosely; puffed out. —'baggily adv. —'bagginess n.

bagnio ('bɑːnjəʊ) n., pl. -ios. 1. a brothel. 2. Obs. an oriental prison for slaves. 3. Obs. an Italian or Turkish bathhouse.

bags (bægz) pl. n. 1. Inf. a lot. 2. Brit. inf. trousers. ~interj. 3. Also: bags I. Children's sl., Brit. an indication of the desire to do, be, or have something.

bah (bɑː, bæ) interj. an expression of contempt or disgust.

Bahaism (bə'hɑːɪzəm) n. a religious system founded in 1863, based on Babism and emphasizing the value of all religions and the spiritual unity of mankind. —Ba'haist or Ba'haite adj., n.

bail¹ (beɪl) Law. ~n. 1. a sum of money by which a person is bound to take responsibility for the appearance in court of another person or himself, forfeited if the person fails to appear. 2. the person or persons so binding themselves; surety. 3. the system permitting release of a person from custody where such security has been taken: he was released on bail. 4. jump bail or (formal) forfeit bail. to fail to appear in court to answer to a charge. 5. stand or go bail. to act as surety (for someone). ~vb. (tr.) 6. (often foll. by out) to release or obtain the release of (a person) from custody, security having been made.

bail² or **bale** (beɪl) vb. (often foll. by out) to remove (water) from (a boat). See also bale out. —'bailer or 'baler n.

bail³ (beɪl) n. 1. Cricket. either of two small wooden bars across the tops of the stumps. 2. a partition between stalls in a stable or barn. 3. Austral. & N.Z. a framework in a cowshed used to secure the head of a cow during milking.

bail⁴ or **bale** (beɪl) n. 1. the semicircular handle of a kettle, bucket, etc. 2. a movable bar on a typewriter that holds the paper against the platen.

bailey ('beɪlɪ) n. the outermost wall or court of a castle.

Bailey bridge ('beɪlɪ) n. a temporary bridge made of prefabricated steel parts that can be rapidly assembled.

bailie ('beɪlɪ) n. (in Scotland) a municipal magistrate.

bailiff ('beɪlɪf) n. 1. Brit. the agent of a landlord or landowner. 2. a sheriff's officer who serves writs and summonses, makes arrests, and ensures that the sentences of the court are carried out. 3. Chiefly Brit. (formerly) a high official having judicial powers. 4. Chiefly U.S. an official having custody of prisoners appearing in court.

bailiwick ('beɪlɪwɪk) n. 1. Law. the area over which a bailiff has jurisdiction. 2. a person's special field of interest.

bain-marie French. (bɛ̃ma'ri) n., pl. bains-marie (bɛ̃ma'ri). a vessel for holding hot water, in which sauces and other dishes are gently cooked or kept warm.

bairn (bɛən) n. Scot. & N English. a child.

bait (beɪt) n. 1. something edible fixed to a hook or in a trap to attract fish or animals. 2. an enticement; temptation. 3. Dialect. food, esp. a packed lunch. 4. Arch. a short stop for refreshment during a journey. ~vb. 5. (tr.) to put a piece of food on or in (a hook or trap). 6. (tr.) to persecute or tease. 7. (tr.) to entice; tempt. 8. (tr.) to set dogs upon (a bear, etc.). 9. (intr.) Arch. to stop for rest and refreshment during a journey.

baize (beɪz) n. a woollen fabric resembling felt, usually green, used mainly for the tops of billiard tables.

bake (beɪk) vb. 1. (tr.) to cook by dry heat as in an oven. 2. (intr.) to cook bread, pastry, etc. 3. to make or become hardened by heat. 4. (intr.) Inf. to be extremely hot. ~n. 5. a batch of things baked at one time. 6. Caribbean. a small flat fried cake.

baked Alaska (ə'læskə) n. a cake covered with ice cream, baked with a meringue topping.

baked beans pl. n. haricot beans, baked and tinned in tomato sauce.

Bakelite ('beɪkə,laɪt) n. Trademark. any one of a class of thermosetting resins used as electric insulators and for making plastic ware, etc.

baker ('beɪkə) n. a person whose business or employment is to make or sell bread, cakes, etc.

baker's dozen n. thirteen.

bakery ('beɪkərɪ) n., pl. -eries. 1. a room or building equipped for baking. 2. a shop in which bread, cakes,

---

THESAURUS

badger bully, chivvy, goad, harass, harry, hound, importune, nag, pester, plague, torment

badinage banter, chaff, drollery, mockery, persiflage, pleasantry, raillery, repartee, teasing, waggery, wordplay

badly 1. carelessly, defectively, erroneously, faultily, imperfectly, inadequately, incorrectly, ineptly, poorly, shoddily, wrong, wrongly 2. unfavourably, unfortunately, unsuccessfully 3. criminally, evilly, immorally, improperly, naughtily, shamefully, unethically, wickedly 4. acutely, deeply, desperately, exceedingly, extremely, gravely, greatly, intensely, painfully, seriously, severely

baffle 1. amaze, astound, bewilder, confound, confuse, daze, disconcert, dumbfound, elude, flummox, mystify, nonplus, perplex, puzzle, stump, stun 2. balk, check, defeat, foil, frustrate, hinder, thwart, upset

bag v. 1. balloon, bulge, droop, sag, swell 2. acquire, capture, catch, gain, get, kill, land, shoot, take, trap

baggage accoutrements, bags, belongings, equipment, gear, impedimenta, luggage, paraphernalia, suitcases, things

baggy billowing, bulging, droopy, floppy, ill-fitting, loose, oversize, roomy, sagging, seated, slack

bail¹ n. bond, guarantee, guaranty, pledge,

security, surety, warranty

bail², **bale** v. dip, drain off, ladle, scoop

bail out, **bale out** 1. aid, help, relieve, rescue 2. escape, quit, retreat, withdraw

bait n. 1. allurement, attraction, bribe, decoy, enticement, inducement, lure, snare, temptation ~v. 2. annoy, gall, harass, hound, irk, irritate, needle (Inf.), persecute, provoke, tease, torment 3. allure, beguile, entice, lure, seduce, tempt

baked arid, desiccated, dry, parched, scorched, seared, sun-baked

etc., are sold.

baking powder *n.* a powdered mixture that contains sodium bicarbonate and one or more acidic compounds, such as cream of tartar: used in baking as a substitute for yeast.

baklava *or* **baclava** ('bɑːklə,vɑː) *n.* a rich cake consisting of thin layers of pastry filled with nuts and honey.

baksheesh *or* **backsheesh** ('bækʃiːʃ) *n.* (in some Eastern countries, esp. formerly) money given as a tip, a present, or alms.

bal. *Book-keeping. abbrev. for* balance.

balalaika (,bælə'laɪkə) *n.* a Russian plucked musical instrument, usually having a triangular body and three strings.

balance ('bæləns) *n.* **1.** a weighing device, generally consisting of a horizontal beam pivoted at its centre, from the ends of which two pans are suspended. The substance to be weighed is placed in one pan and weights are placed in the other until the beam returns to the horizontal. **2.** a state of equilibrium. **3.** something that brings about such a state. **4.** equilibrium of the body; steadiness: *to lose one's balance.* **5.** emotional stability. **6.** harmony in the parts of a whole. **7.** the act of weighing factors, quantities, etc., against each other. **8.** the power to influence or control: *the balance of power.* **9.** something that remains: *the balance of what you owe.* **10.** *Accounting.* **a.** equality of debit and credit totals in an account. **b.** a difference between such totals. **11. in the balance.** in an uncertain or undecided condition. **12. on balance.** after weighing up all the factors. **13. strike a balance.** to make a compromise. ~*vb.* **14.** (*tr.*) to weigh in or as if in a balance. **15.** (*intr.*) to be or come into equilibrium. **16.** (*tr.*) to bring into or hold in equilibrium. **17.** (*tr.*) to compare the relative weight, importance, etc., of. **18.** (*tr.*) to be equal to. **19.** (*tr.*) to arrange so as to create a state of harmony. **20.** (*tr.*) *Accounting.* **a.** to compare the credit and debit totals of (an account). **b.** to equalize the credit and debit totals of (an account) by making certain entries. **c.** to settle or adjust (an account) by paying any money due. **21.** (*intr.*) (of a balance sheet, etc.) to have the debit and credit totals equal. —'**balanceable** *adj.* —'**balancer** *n.*

balance of power *n.* the distribution of power among countries so that no one nation can seriously threaten another.

balance of trade *n.* the difference in value between total exports and total imports of goods.

balance sheet *n.* a statement that shows the financial position of a business by listing the asset balances and the claims on such assets.

balance wheel *n.* a wheel oscillating against the hairspring of a timepiece, regulating its beat.

balata ('bælətə) *n.* **1.** a tropical American tree, yielding a latex-like sap. **2.** a rubber-like gum obtained from this sap: a substitute for gutta-percha.

balcony ('bælkənɪ) *n., pl.* -**nies**. **1.** a platform projecting from a building with a balustrade along its outer edge, often with access from a door or window. **2.** a gallery in a theatre, above the dress circle. **3.** *U.S.* the dress circle in a theatre. —'**balconied** *adj.*

bald (bɔːld) *adj.* **1.** having no hair or fur, esp. (of a man) having no hair on the scalp. **2.** lacking natural growth or covering. **3.** plain or blunt: *a bald statement.* **4.** bare or unadorned. **5.** Also: **baldfaced.** (of birds and animals) having white markings on the head and face. **6.** (of a

tyre) having a worn tread. —'**baldish** *adj.* —'**baldly** *adv.* —'**baldness** *n.*

balderdash ('bɔːldə,dæʃ) *n.* stupid or illogical talk; senseless rubbish.

balding ('bɔːldɪŋ) *adj.* somewhat bald or becoming bald.

baldric ('bɔːldrɪk) *n.* a sash or belt worn over the right shoulder to the left hip for carrying a sword, etc.

bale[1] (beɪl) *n.* **1.** a large bundle, package, or carton of goods bound by ropes, wires, etc., for storage or transportation. **2.** *U.S.* 500 pounds of cotton. ~*vb.* **3.** to make (hay, etc.) or put (goods) into a bale or bales.

bale[2] (beɪl) *n. Arch.* **1.** evil; injury. **2.** woe; suffering; pain.

bale[3] (beɪl) *vb.* a variant spelling of bail[2].

bale[4] (beɪl) *n.* a variant spelling of bail[4].

baleen (bə'liːn) *n.* whalebone.

baleen whale *n.* another name for whalebone whale.

baleful ('beɪlfʊl) *adj.* harmful, menacing, or vindictive. —'**balefully** *adv.* —'**balefulness** *n.*

bale out *or* **bail out** *vb.* (*adv.*) **1.** (*intr.*) to make an emergency parachute jump from an aircraft. **2.** (*tr.*) *Inf.* to help (a person, organization, etc.) out of a predicament.

balk *or* **baulk** (bɔːk, bɔːlk) *vb.* **1.** (*intr.*; usually foll. by *at*) to stop short; jib: *the horse balked at the jump.* **2.** (*intr.*; foll. by *at*) to recoil: *he balked at the idea of murder.* **3.** (*tr.*) to thwart, check, or foil: *he was balked in his plans.* ~*n.* **4.** a roughly squared heavy timber beam. **5.** a timber tie beam of a roof. **6.** an unploughed ridge between furrows. **7.** an obstacle; hindrance; disappointment. **8.** *Baseball.* an illegal motion by a pitcher. ~See also **baulk.** —'**balker** *or* '**baulker** *n.*

Balkan ('bɔːlkən) *adj.* of or denoting a large peninsula in SE Europe, between the Adriatic and Aegean Seas, or its inhabitants, countries, etc.

ball[1] (bɔːl) *n.* **1.** a spherical or nearly spherical body or mass. **2.** a round or roundish body, of a size and composition suitable for any of various games. **3.** a ball propelled in a particular way: *a high ball.* **4.** any rudimentary game with a ball: *to play ball.* **5.** a single delivery of the ball in cricket and other games. **6. a.** a solid nonexplosive projectile for a firearm, cannon, etc. **b.** such projectiles collectively. **7.** any more or less rounded part: *the ball of the foot.* **8. ball of muscle.** *Austral.* a very strong, fit person. **9. have the ball at one's feet.** to have the chance of doing something. **10. keep the ball rolling.** to maintain the progress of a project, plan, etc. **11. on the ball.** *Inf.* alert; informed. **12. play ball.** *Inf.* to cooperate. **13. start** *or* **set the ball rolling.** to set a project, plan, etc., in motion; start. ~*vb.* **14.** to make, form, wind, etc., into a ball or balls.

ball[2] (bɔːl) *n.* **1.** a social function for dancing, esp. one that is lavish or formal. **2.** *Inf., chiefly U.S.* a very enjoyable time (esp. in **have a ball**).

ballad ('bæləd) *n.* **1.** a narrative song with a recurrent refrain. **2.** a narrative poem in short stanzas of popular origin. **3.** a slow sentimental song, esp. a pop song.

ballade (bæ'lɑːd) *n.* **1.** *Prosody.* a verse form consisting of three stanzas and an envoy, all ending with the same line. **2.** *Music.* an instrumental composition based on or intended to evoke a narrative.

ball-and-socket joint *n. Anat.* a joint in which a rounded head fits into a rounded cavity, allowing a wide range of movement.

THESAURUS

balance *v.* **1.** level, match, parallel, poise, stabilize, steady **2.** adjust, compensate for, counteract, counterbalance, counterpoise, equalize, equate, make up for, neutralize, offset **3.** assess, compare, consider, deliberate, estimate, evaluate, weigh **4.** calculate, compute, settle, square, tally, total ~*n.* **5.** correspondence, equilibrium, equipoise, equity, equivalence, evenness, parity, symmetry **6.** composure, equanimity, poise, self-control, self-possession, stability, steadiness **7.** difference, remainder, residue, rest, surplus

balanced disinterested, equitable, evenhanded, fair, impartial, just, unbiased, unprejudiced

balance sheet account, budget, credits and debits, ledger, report, statement

balcony 1. terrace, veranda **2.** gallery,

gods, upper circle

bald 1. baldheaded, baldpated, depilated, glabrous (*Biol.*), hairless **2.** barren, bleak, exposed, naked, stark, treeless, uncovered **3.** bare, blunt, direct, downright, forthright, outright, plain, severe, simple, straight, straightforward, unadorned, unvarnished

balderdash bunk (*Inf.*), bunkum, claptrap (*Inf.*), drivel, gibberish, nonsense, poppycock (*Inf.*), rot, rubbish, tommyrot, trash, twaddle

baldness 1. alopecia (*Pathology*), baldheadedness, baldpatedness, glabrousness (*Biol.*), hairlessness **2.** barrenness, bleakness, nakedness, sparseness, starkness, treelessness **3.** austerity, bluntness, plainness, severity, simplicity, spareness

bale *see* BAIL[2]

baleful calamitous, deadly, evil, harmful, hurtful, injurious, malevolent, malignant, menacing, mournful, noxious, ominous, pernicious, ruinous, sad, sinister, venomous, woeful

bale out *see* BAIL OUT

balk 1. demur, dodge, evade, flinch, hesitate, jib, recoil, refuse, resist, shirk, shrink from **2.** baffle, bar, check, counteract, defeat, disconcert, foil, forestall, frustrate, hinder, obstruct, prevent, thwart

balky intractable, obstinate, stubborn, uncooperative, unmanageable, unpredictable, unruly

ball 1. drop, globe, globule, orb, pellet, sphere, spheroid **2.** ammunition, bullet, grapeshot, pellet, shot, slug

ballast ('bæləst) n. 1. any heavy material used to stabilize a vessel, esp. one that is not carrying cargo. 2. crushed rock, broken stone, etc., used for the foundation of a road or railway track or in making concrete. 3. anything that provides stability or weight. 4. *Electronics.* a device for maintaining the current in a circuit. ~vb. (tr.) 5. to give stability or weight to.

ball bearing n. 1. a bearing consisting of steel balls rolling between a metal sleeve fitted over the rotating shaft and an outer sleeve held in the bearing housing, so reducing friction. 2. a metal ball, esp. one used in such a bearing.

ball boy n. (esp. in tennis) a person who retrieves balls that go out of play.

ball cock n. a device for regulating the flow of a liquid into a tank, cistern, etc., consisting of a floating ball mounted at one end of an arm and a valve on the other end that opens and closes as the ball falls and rises.

ballerina (,bælə'ri:nə) n. a female ballet dancer.

ballet ('bæleɪ, bæ'leɪ) n. 1. a classical style of expressive dancing based on precise conventional steps. 2. a theatrical representation of a story or theme performed by ballet dancers. 3. a troupe of ballet dancers. 4. music written for a ballet. —**balletic** (bæ'lɛtɪk) adj.

ball game n. 1. any game played with a ball. 2. *U.S.* a game of baseball. 3. *U.S. inf.* any activity: *aeronautics is a whole new ball game.*

ballista (bə'lɪstə) n., pl. **-tae** (-tiː). an ancient catapult for hurling stones, etc.

ballistic missile n. a missile that has no wings or fins and that follows a ballistic trajectory when its propulsive power is discontinued.

ballistics (bə'lɪstɪks) n. (functioning as sing.) 1. the study of the flight dynamics of projectiles. 2. the study of the effects of firing on firearms and their projectiles.

ballocks ('bɒləks) pl. n., interj., vb. a variant spelling of **bollocks.**

balloon (bə'lu:n) n. 1. an inflatable rubber bag used as a plaything or party decoration. 2. a large bag inflated with a lighter-than-air gas, designed to rise and float in the atmosphere. It may have a basket or gondola for carrying passengers, etc. 3. an outline containing the words or thoughts of a character in a cartoon. 4. a large rounded brandy glass. 5. **when the balloon goes up.** *Inf.* when the action starts. ~vb. 6. (intr.) to go up or fly in a balloon. 7. to inflate or be inflated: *the wind ballooned the sails.* 8. (tr.) *Brit.* to propel (a ball) high into the air. —**bal'loonist** n. —**bal'loon-,like** adj.

ballot ('bælət) n. 1. the practice of selecting a representative, course of action, etc. by submitting the options to a vote of all qualified persons. 2. an instance of voting, usually in secret. 3. a list of candidates standing for office. 4. the number of votes cast in an election. ~vb. **-loting, -loted.** 5. to vote or elicit a vote from: *we ballotted the members on this issue.* 6. (tr.; usually foll. by *for*) to vote for or decide on by lot or ballot.

ballot box n. a box into which ballot papers are dropped after voting.

ballot paper n. a paper used for voting in a ballot.

ballpoint or **ballpoint pen** ('bɔːl,pɔɪnt) n. a pen having a small ball bearing as a writing point.

ballroom ('bɔːl,ruːm, -,rʊm) n. a large hall for dancing.

ballroom dancing n. social dancing, popular since the beginning of the 20th century, to dances in conventional rhythms (**ballroom dances**).

balls (bɔːlz) *Taboo sl.* ~pl. n. 1. the testicles. 2. nonsense; rubbish. ~interj. 3. an exclamation of disagreement, contempt, etc.

balls-up *Taboo sl.* ~n. 1. something botched or muddled. ~vb. **balls up.** 2. (tr., adv.) to muddle or botch.

bally ('bælɪ) adj., adv. (intensifier) *Brit. sl.* a euphemistic word for **bloody** (sense 5).

ballyhoo ('bælɪ,hu:) n. *Inf.* 1. a noisy, confused, or nonsensical situation. 2. sensational or blatant advertising or publicity. ~vb. **-hooing, -hooed.** 3. (tr.) *Chiefly U.S.* to advertise by sensational or blatant methods.

balm (ba:m) n. 1. any of various oily aromatic substances obtained from certain tropical trees and used for healing and soothing. See also **balsam** (sense 1). 2. any plant yielding such a substance, esp. the balm of Gilead. 3. something comforting or soothing. 4. Also called: **lemon balm.** an aromatic Eurasian plant, having clusters of small fragrant white flowers. 5. a pleasant odour.

balmy ('ba:mɪ) adj. **balmier, balmiest.** 1. (of weather) mild and pleasant. 2. having the qualities of balm; fragrant or soothing. 3. a variant spelling (esp. U.S.) of **barmy.** —'**balmily** adv. —'**balminess** n.

baloney or **boloney** (bə'ləʊnɪ) n. *Inf.* foolish talk; nonsense.

BALPA ('bælpə) n. acronym for British Airline Pilots' Association.

balsa ('bɔːlsə) n. 1. a tree of tropical America. 2. Also called: **balsawood.** the very light wood of this tree, used for making rafts, etc. 3. a light raft.

balsam ('bɔːlsəm) n. 1. any of various fragrant oleoresins, such as balm, obtained from any of several trees and shrubs and used as a base for medicines and perfumes. 2. any of various similar substances used as ointments. 3. any of certain aromatic resinous turpentines. 4. any plant yielding balsam. 5. Also called: **busy Lizzie.** any of several plants of the genus *Impatiens.* 6. anything healing or soothing. —**balsamic** (bɔːl'sæmɪk) adj.

Baltic ('bɔːltɪk) adj. 1. denoting or relating to the Baltic Sea in N Europe, or the states bordering it. 2. of or characteristic of Baltic as a group of languages. ~n. 3. a branch of the Indo-European family of languages consisting of Lithuanian, Latvian, and Old Prussian. 4. Also called: **Baltic Exchange.** a commodities exchange in the City of London.

baluster ('bæləstə) n. any of a set of posts supporting a rail or coping.

balustrade ('bælə,streɪd) n. an ornamental rail or coping with its supporting set of balusters.

bamboo (bæm'bu:) n. 1. a tall treelike tropical or semitropical grass having hollow stems with ringed joints. 2. the stem, used for building, poles, and furniture.

bamboozle (bæm'bu:z°l) vb. (tr.) *Inf.* 1. to cheat; mislead. 2. to confuse. —**bam'boozler** n. —**bam'boozlement** n.

ban (bæn) vb. **banning, banned.** 1. (tr.) to prohibit, esp. officially, from action, display, entrance, sale, etc.; forbid. ~n. 2. an official prohibition or interdiction. 3. a public proclamation, esp. of outlawry. 4. *Arch.* a curse; imprecation.

banal (bə'nɑːl) adj. lacking force or originality; trite; commonplace. —**banality** (bə'nælɪtɪ) n. —**ba'nally** adv.

banana (bə'nɑːnə) n. 1. any of several tropical and subtropical treelike plants, esp. a widely cultivated species having hanging clusters of edible fruit. 2. the crescent-shaped fruit of any of these plants.

banana republic n. *Inf.* a small country, esp. in Central America, that is politically unstable and has an economy dominated by foreign interest, usually dependent on one export.

band[1] (bænd) n. 1. a company of people having a common purpose; group: *a band of outlaws.* 2. a group of musicians playing either brass and percussion instru-

---

THESAURUS

ballast balance, counterbalance, counterweight, equilibrium, sandbag, stability, stabilizer, weight

balloon v. belly, billow, bloat, blow up, dilate, distend, enlarge, expand, inflate, puff out, swell

ballot election, poll, polling, vote, voting

ballyhoo 1. babble, commotion, fuss, hubbub, hue and cry, hullabaloo, noise, racket, to-do 2. advertising, build-up, hype (*Sl.*), promotion, propaganda, publicity

balm 1. balsam, cream, embrocation, emollient, lotion, ointment, salve, unguent 2.

anodyne, comfort, consolation, curative, palliative, restorative, solace

balmy 1. clement, mild, pleasant, summery, temperate 2. *Also* **barmy** crazy, daft, foolish, idiotic, insane, loony (*Sl.*), nuts (*Sl.*), nutty (*Sl.*), odd, silly, stupid

bamboozle 1. cheat, con (*Sl.*), deceive, defraud, delude, dupe, fool, hoax, hoodwink, swindle, trick 2. baffle, befuddle, confound, confuse, mystify, perplex, puzzle, stump

ban 1. v. banish, bar, debar, disallow, exclude, forbid, interdict, outlaw, prohibit, proscribe, restrict, suppress 2. n. boycott, cen-

sorship, embargo, interdiction, prohibition, proscription, restriction, stoppage, suppression, taboo

banal clichéd, cliché-ridden, commonplace, everyday, hackneyed, humdrum, old hat, ordinary, pedestrian, platitudinous, stale, stereotyped, stock, threadbare, tired, trite, unimaginative, unoriginal, vapid

banality bromide (*Inf.*), cliché, commonplace, platitude, triteness, trite phrase, triviality, truism, vapidity

ments only (**brass band**) or brass, woodwind, and percussion instruments (**concert band** or **military band**). **3.** a group of musicians who play popular music, jazz, etc., often for dancing. ~*vb.* **4.** (usually foll. by *together*) to unite; assemble.

band[2] (bænd) *n.* **1.** a thin flat strip of some material, used esp. to encircle objects and hold them together: *a rubber band.* **2. a.** a strip of fabric or other material used as an ornament or to reinforce clothing. **b.** (*in combination*): *waistband; hatband.* **3.** a stripe of contrasting colour or texture. **4.** a driving belt in machinery. **5.** a range of values that are close or related in number, degree, or quality. **6.** *Physics.* a range of frequencies or wavelengths between two limits. **7.** short for **energy band**. **8.** *Computers.* one or more tracks on a magnetic disk or drum. **9.** *Anat.* any structure resembling a ribbon or cord that connects, encircles, or binds different parts. **10.** *Archit.* a strip of flat panelling, such as a fascia, usually attached to a wall. **11.** either of a pair of hanging extensions of the collar, forming part of academic, legal, or (formerly) clerical dress. **12.** (of a gramophone record) another word for **track** (sense 10). ~*vb.* (*tr.*) **13.** to fasten or mark with a band.

bandage ('bændɪdʒ) *n.* **1.** a piece of material used to dress a wound, bind a broken limb, etc. ~*vb.* **2.** to cover or bind with a bandage.

bandanna or **bandana** (bæn'dænə) *n.* a large silk or cotton handkerchief or neckerchief.

b. and b. *abbrev.* for bed and breakfast.

bandbox ('bænd,bɒks) *n.* a lightweight usually cylindrical box for small articles, esp. hats.

bandeau ('bændəʊ) *n., pl.* **-deaux** (-dəʊz). a narrow band of ribbon, velvet, etc., worn round the head.

bandicoot ('bændɪ,kuːt) *n.* **1.** an agile terrestrial marsupial of Australia and New Guinea with a long pointed muzzle and a long tail. **2. bandicoot rat.** Also called: **mole rat.** any of three burrowing rats of S and SE Asia.

bandit ('bændɪt) *n., pl.* **-dits** or **-ditti** (-'dɪtɪ). a robber, esp. a member of an armed gang. —'**banditry** *n.*

bandmaster ('bænd,mɑːstə) *n.* the conductor of a band.

bandoleer or **bandolier** (,bændə'lɪə) *n.* a soldier's broad shoulder belt having small pockets or loops for cartridges.

band saw *n.* a power-operated saw consisting of an endless toothed metal band running over and driven by two wheels.

bandsman ('bændzmən) *n., pl.* **-men.** a player in a musical band, esp. a brass or military band.

bandstand ('bænd,stænd) *n.* a platform for a band, usually out of doors and roofed.

bandwagon ('bænd,wægən) *n.* **1.** *U.S.* a wagon for the band in a parade. **2. climb, jump,** or **get on the bandwagon.** *Inf.* to join or support a party or movement that seems assured of success.

bandy ('bændɪ) *adj.* **-dier, -diest.** **1.** Also: **bandy-legged.** having legs curved outwards at the knees. **2.** (of legs) curved thus. ~*vb.* **-dying, -died.** (*tr.*) **3.** to exchange (words) in a heated or hostile manner. **4.** to give and receive (blows). **5.** *Inf.* (often foll. by *about*) to circulate (a name, rumour, etc.).

bane (beɪn) *n.* **1.** a person or thing that causes misery or distress (esp. in **bane of one's life**). **2.** something that causes death or destruction. **3. a.** a fatal poison. **b.** (*in combination*): *ratsbane.* **4.** *Arch.* ruin or distress. —'**baneful** *adj.*

bang[1] (bæŋ) *n.* **1.** a short loud explosive noise, as of the

report of a gun. **2.** a hard blow or knock, esp. a noisy one. **3.** *Sl.* an injection of heroin or other narcotic. **4.** *Taboo sl.* an act of sexual intercourse. **5. with a bang.** successfully: *the party went with a bang.* ~*vb.* **6.** to hit or knock, esp. with a loud noise. **7.** to move noisily or clumsily: *to bang about the house.* **8.** to close (a door, window, etc.) or (of a door, etc.) be closed noisily; slam. **9.** (*tr.*) to cause to move by hitting vigorously: *he banged the ball over the fence.* **10.** to make or cause to make a loud noise, as of an explosion. **11.** *Taboo sl.* to have sexual intercourse with. **12.** (*intr.*) *Sl.* to inject heroin, etc. **13. bang one's head against a brick wall.** *Inf.* to make no progress. ~*adv.* **14.** with a sudden impact or effect: *the car drove bang into a lamp-post.* **15.** precisely: *bang in the middle.* **16. go bang.** to burst, shut, etc., with a loud noise.

bang[2] (bæŋ) *n.* **1.** a fringe of hair cut straight across the forehead. ~*vb.* (*tr.*) **2.** to cut (the hair) in such a style. **3.** to dock (the tail of a horse, etc.).

banger ('bæŋə) *n. Brit.* **1.** *Sl.* a sausage. **2.** an old decrepit car. **3.** a firework that explodes loudly.

bangle ('bæŋgəl) *n.* a bracelet, usually without a clasp, often worn round the arm or sometimes round the ankle.

banian ('bænjən) *n.* a variant spelling of **banyan.**

banish ('bænɪʃ) *vb.* (*tr.*) **1.** to expel from a place, esp. by an official decree as a punishment. **2.** to drive away: *to banish gloom.* —'**banishment** *n.*

banisters ('bænɪstəz) *pl. n.* the railing and supporting balusters on a staircase; balustrade.

banjo ('bændʒəʊ) *n., pl.* **-jos** or **-joes.** a stringed musical instrument with a long neck and a circular drumlike body overlaid with parchment, plucked with the fingers or a plectrum. —'**banjoist** *n.*

bank[1] (bæŋk) *n.* **1.** an institution offering certain financial services, such as the safekeeping of money and lending of money at interest. **2.** the building used by such an institution. **3.** a small container used at home for keeping money. **4.** the funds held by a banker or dealer in some gambling games. **5.** (in various games) **a.** the stock, as of money, etc., on which players may draw. **b.** the player holding this stock. **6.** any supply, store, or reserve: *a data bank.* ~*vb.* **7.** (*tr.*) to deposit (cash, cheques, etc.) in a bank. **8.** (*intr.*) to transact business with a bank. **9.** (*intr.*) to engage in banking. ~See also: **bank on.**

bank[2] (bæŋk) *n.* **1.** a long raised mass, esp. of earth; ridge. **2.** a slope, as of a hill. **3.** the sloping side of any hollow in the ground, esp. when bordering a river. **4.** the ground beside a river or canal. **5. a.** an elevated section of the bed of a sea, lake, or river. **b.** (*in combination*): *sandbank.* **6.** the face of a body of ore in a mine. **7.** the lateral inclination of an aircraft about its longitudinal axis during a turn. **8.** a bend on a road, athletics track, etc. having the outside built higher than the inside to reduce the effects of centrifugal force on vehicles, runners, etc., rounding it at speed. ~*vb.* **9.** (when *tr.*, often foll. by *up*) to form into a bank or mound. **10.** (*tr.*) to border or enclose (a road, etc.) with a bank. **11.** (*tr.*; sometimes foll. by *up*) to cover (a fire) with ashes, fresh fuel, etc., so that it will burn slowly. **12.** to cause (an aircraft) to tip laterally about its longitudinal axis or (of an aircraft) to tip in this way, esp. while turning.

bank[3] (bæŋk) *n.* **1.** an arrangement of similar objects in a row or in tiers: *a bank of dials.* **2.** a tier of oars in a galley. ~*vb.* **3.** (*tr.*) to arrange in a bank.

THESAURUS

band[1] *n.* bandage, belt, binding, bond, chain, cord, fetter, fillet, ligature, manacle, ribbon, shackle, strap, strip, tie

band[2] *n.* **1.** assembly, association, body, clique, club, company, coterie, crew (*Inf.*), gang, horde, party, society, troop **2.** combo, ensemble, group, orchestra ~*v.* **3.** affiliate, ally, consolidate, federate, gather, group, join, merge, unite

bandage **1.** *n.* compress, dressing, gauze, plaster **2.** *v.* bind, cover, dress, swathe

bandit brigand, crook, desperado, footpad, freebooter, gangster, gunman, highwayman, hijacker, marauder, outlaw, pirate, racketeer, robber, thief

bandy **1.** *v.* barter, exchange, interchange,

pass, shuffle, swap, throw, toss, trade **2.** *adj.* bandy-legged, bent, bowed, bow-legged, crooked, curved

bane affliction, *bête noir*, blight, burden, calamity, curse, despair, destruction, disaster, downfall, misery, nuisance, pest, plague, ruin, scourge, torment, trial, trouble, woe

baneful baleful, calamitous, deadly, deleterious, destructive, disastrous, fatal, harmful, hurtful, injurious, noxious, pernicious, pestilential, ruinous, venomous

bang *n.* **1.** boom, burst, clang, clap, clash, detonation, explosion, peal, pop, report, shot, slam, thud, thump **2.** blow, box, bump, cuff, hit, knock, punch, smack, stroke, wallop (*Inf.*), whack ~*v.* **3.** bash (*Inf.*), beat, bump, clatter, crash, hammer, knock, pound, pum-

mel, rap, slam, strike, thump **4.** boom, burst, clang, detonate, drum, echo, explode, peal, resound, thump, thunder ~*adv.* **5.** abruptly, hard, headlong, noisily, precisely, slap, smack, straight, suddenly

banish **1.** deport, drive away, eject, evict, exclude, excommunicate, exile, expatriate, expel, ostracize, outlaw, shut out, transport **2.** ban, cast out, discard, dislodge, dismiss, dispel, eliminate, eradicate, get rid of, oust, remove, shake off

banishment deportation, exile, expatriation, expulsion, proscription, transportation

banisters balusters, balustrade, handrail, rail, railing

bank[1] **1.** *n.* accumulation, depository, fund,

bank account *n.* **1.** an account created by the deposit of money at a bank by a customer. **2.** the amount credited to a depositor at a bank.

bankbook ('bæŋk,bʊk) *n.* a book held by depositors at certain banks, in which the bank enters a record of deposits, withdrawals, and earned interest. Also called: **passbook.**

bank card *n.* another name for **banker's card.**

banker[1] ('bæŋkə) *n.* **1.** a person who owns or is an executive in a bank. **2.** an official or player in charge of the bank in various games. **3.** a result that has been forecast identically in a series of entries on a football pool coupon.

banker[2] ('bæŋkə) *n. Austral. inf.* a stream almost overflowing its banks (esp. in **run a banker**).

banker's card *n.* a card issued by a bank, guaranteeing payment of the cheques of a customer up to a stated value.

banker's order *n.* another name for **standing order** (sense 1).

bank holiday *n.* (in Britain) any of several weekdays on which banks are closed by law and which are observed as national holidays.

banking ('bæŋkɪŋ) *n.* the business engaged in by a bank.

bank manager *n.* a person who directs the business of a local branch of a bank.

bank note *n.* a promissory note, esp. one issued by a central bank, serving as money.

Bank of England *n.* the central bank of England and Wales, concerned with various aspects of government monetary policy.

bank rate *n.* (*sometimes caps.*) the minimum rate by which a central bank, such as the Bank of England, is obliged to rediscount bills of exchange and to lend money.

bankrupt ('bæŋkrʌpt, -rəpt) *n.* **1.** a person adjudged insolvent by a court, his property being administered for the benefit of his creditors. **2.** any person unable to discharge all his debts. **3.** a person whose resources in a certain field are exhausted: *a spiritual bankrupt.* ~*adj.* **4.** adjudged insolvent. **5.** financially ruined. **6.** depleted in resources: *spiritually bankrupt.* **7.** (foll. by *of*) Brit. lacking: *bankrupt of intelligence.* ~*vb.* **8.** (*tr.*) to make bankrupt. —'**bankruptcy** *n.*

bank statement *n.* a statement of transactions in a bank account, esp. one of a series sent at regular intervals to the depositor.

banner ('bænə) *n.* **1.** a long strip of material displaying a slogan, advertisement, etc. **2.** a placard carried in a procession or demonstration. **3.** something that represents a belief or principle. **4.** the flag of a nation, army, etc. **5.** Also called: **banner headline.** a large headline in a newspaper, etc., extending across the page. —'**bannered** *adj.*

bannock ('bænək) *n.* a round flat cake originating in Scotland, made from wheat or barley.

banns *or* **bans** (bænz) *pl. n.* **1.** the public declaration of an intended marriage, usually on three successive Sundays in the parish churches of the betrothed. **2. forbid the banns.** to raise an objection to a marriage announced in this way.

banquet ('bæŋkwɪt) *n.* **1.** a sumptuous meal; feast. **2.** a ceremonial meal for many people. ~*vb.* **-qeting, -queted. 3.** (*intr.*) to hold or take part in a banquet. **4.** (*tr.*) to entertain (a person) with a banquet. —'**banqueter** *n.*

banshee ('bænʃiː, bæn'ʃiː) *n.* (in Irish folklore) a female spirit whose wailing warns of impending death.

bantam ('bæntəm) *n.* **1.** any of various very small

breeds of domestic fowl. **2.** a small but aggressive person. **3.** *Boxing.* short for **bantamweight.**

bantamweight ('bæntəm,weɪt) *n.* **1. a.** a professional boxer weighing 112–118 pounds (51–53.5 kg). **b.** an amateur boxer weighing 112–119 pounds (51–54 kg). **2.** a wrestler weighing usually 115–126 pounds (52–57 kg).

banter ('bæntə) *vb.* **1.** to speak or tease lightly or jokingly. ~*n.* **2.** teasing or joking language or repartee. —'**banterer** *n.*

Bantu ('bɑːntuː) *n.* **1.** a group of languages of Africa, including most of the principal languages spoken from the equator to the Cape of Good Hope. **2.** (*pl.* **-tu** *or* **-tus**) *Derog.* a Black speaker of a Bantu language. ~*adj.* **3.** of or relating to this group of peoples or their languages.

Bantustan ('bɑːntuː,stɑːn) *n. Derog.* (in South Africa) an area reserved for occupation by a Black African people, with limited self-government. Official name: **homeland.**

banyan *or* **banian** ('bænjən) *n.* **1.** an Indian tree with aerial roots that grow down into the soil forming additional trunks. **2.** a member of the Hindu merchant caste of India. **3.** a loose-fitting shirt, jacket, or robe, worn originally in India.

baobab ('beɪəʊ,bæb) *n.* a tropical African tree that has a very thick trunk, angular branches, and a gourdlike fruit with an edible pulp.

bap (bæp) *n. Brit.* a soft bread roll.

baptism ('bæptɪzəm) *n.* a Christian religious rite consisting of immersion in or sprinkling with water as a sign that the subject is cleansed from sin and constituted a member of the Church. —**bap'tismal** *adj.* —**bap'tismally** *adv.*

baptism of fire *n.* **1.** a soldier's first experience of battle. **2.** any initiating ordeal.

Baptist ('bæptɪst) *n.* **1.** a member of any of various Christian sects that affirm the necessity of baptism (usually of adults and by immersion). **2. the Baptist.** John the Baptist, the cousin and forerunner of Jesus, whom he baptized. ~*adj.* **3.** denoting or characteristic of any Christian sect of Baptists.

baptize *or* **-ise** (bæp'taɪz) *vb.* **1.** *Christianity.* to immerse (a person) in water or sprinkle water on (a person) as part of the rite of baptism. **2.** (*tr.*) to give a name to; christen.

bar[1] (bɑː) *n.* **1.** a rigid usually straight length of metal, wood, etc., used esp. as a barrier or as a structural part: *a bar of a gate.* **2.** a solid usually rectangular block of any material: *a bar of soap.* **3.** anything that obstructs or prevents. **4.** an offshore ridge of sand, mud, or shingle across the mouth of a river, bay, or harbour. **5.** a counter or room where alcoholic drinks are served. **6.** a counter, room, or establishment where a particular range of goods, food, services, etc., are sold: *a coffee bar; a heel bar.* **7.** a narrow band or stripe, as of colour or light. **8.** a heating element in an electric fire. **9.** see **Bar. 10.** the place in a court of law where the accused stands during his trial. **11.** a particular court of law. **12.** *Brit.* (in Parliament) the boundary where nonmembers wishing to address either House appear and where persons are arraigned. **13.** a plea showing that a plaintiff has no cause of action. **14.** anything referred to as an authority or tribunal: *the bar of decency.* **15.** *Music.* a group of beats that is repeated with a consistent rhythm throughout a piece of music. The number of beats in the bar is indicated by the time signature. **16. a.** *Brit.* insignia added to a decoration indicating a second award. **b.** *U.S.* a strip of metal worn with uniform, esp. to signify rank or as an award for service. **17.** *Football, etc.* See **crossbar. 18.** *Heraldry.* a narrow horizontal line across a shield. **19. behind bars.** in prison. **20. won't have a**

THESAURUS

hoard, repository, reserve, reservoir, savings, stock, stockpile, store, storehouse **2.** *v.* deal with, deposit, keep, save, transact business with

bank[2] *n.* **1.** banking, embankment, heap, mass, mound, pile, ridge **2.** brink, edge, margin, shore, side ~*v.* **3.** amass, heap, mass, mound, pile, stack **4.** camber, cant, incline, pitch, slant, slope, tilt, tip

bank[3] *n.* array, file, group, line, rank, row, sequence, series, succession, tier, train

bank on assume, believe in, count on, depend on, lean on, look to, rely on, trust

bankrupt broke (*Inf.*), depleted, destitute, exhausted, failed, impoverished, insolvent, lacking, ruined, spent

bankruptcy disaster, exhaustion, failure, indebtedness, insolvency, lack, liquidation, ruin

banner banderole, burgee, colours, ensign, fanion, flag, gonfalon, pennant, pennon, standard, streamer

banquet dinner, feast, meal, repast, revel, treat

banter 1. *v.* chaff, deride, jeer, jest, joke, kid (*Inf.*), make fun of, rib (*Inf.*), ridicule,

taunt, tease, twit **2.** *n.* badinage, chaff, chaffing, derision, jeering, jesting, joking, kidding (*Inf.*), mockery, persiflage, pleasantry, raillery, repartee, ribbing (*Inf.*), ridicule, wordplay

baptism 1. christening, immersion, purification, sprinkling **2.** beginning, debut, dedication, initiation, introduction, launching, rite of passage

baptize 1. besprinkle, cleanse, immerse, purify **2.** admit, enrol, initiate, recruit **3.** call, christen, dub, name, title

bar of. *Austral. & N.Z. inf.* cannot tolerate; dislike. ~*vb.*

barring, barred. (*tr.*) **21.** to secure with a bar: *to bar the door.* **22.** to shut in or out with or as if with barriers: *to bar the entrances.* **23.** to obstruct: *the fallen tree barred the road.* **24.** (usually foll. by *from*) to prohibit; forbid: *to bar a couple from meeting.* **25.** (usually foll. by *from*) to keep out; exclude: *to bar a person from membership.* **26.** to mark with a bar or bars. **27.** *Law.* to prevent or halt (an action) by showing that the plaintiff has no cause. ~*prep.* **28.** except for. **29. bar none.** without exception.

Bar (baː) *n.* **1.** barristers collectively. **2.** the legal profession.

barathea (ˌbærəˈθiə) *n.* a fabric made of silk and wool or cotton and rayon.

barb (baːb) *n.* **1.** a point facing in the opposite direction to the main point of a fish-hook, harpoon, etc., intended to make extraction difficult. **2.** any of various pointed parts. **3.** a cutting remark. **4.** any of the hairlike filaments that form the vane of a feather. **5.** a beardlike growth, hair, or projection. ~*vb.* **6.** (*tr.*) to provide with a barb or barbs. —**barbed** *adj.*

barbarian (baːˈbɛərɪən) *n.* **1.** a member of a primitive or uncivilized people. **2.** a coarse or uncultured person. **3.** a vicious person. ~*adj.* **4.** of an uncivilized culture. **5.** uncultured or brutal.

barbaric (baːˈbærɪk) *adj.* **1.** of or characteristic of barbarians. **2.** primitive; unrestrained. **3.** brutal. —**bar-ˈbarically** *adv.*

barbarism (ˈbaːbəˌrɪzəm) *n.* **1.** a brutal, coarse, or ignorant act. **2.** the condition of being backward, coarse, or ignorant. **3.** a substandard word or expression; solecism. **4.** any act or object that offends against accepted taste.

barbarity (baːˈbærɪtɪ) *n., pl.* -**ties.** **1.** the state of being barbaric or barbarous. **2.** a vicious act.

barbarous (ˈbaːbərəs) *adj.* **1.** uncivilized; primitive. **2.** brutal or cruel. **3.** lacking refinement. —**ˈbarbarously** *adv.* —**ˈbarbarousness** *n.*

Barbary ape (ˈbaːbərɪ) *n.* a tailless macaque that inhabits NW Africa and Gibraltar.

barbecue (ˈbaːbɪˌkjuː) *n.* **1.** a meal cooked out of doors over an open fire. **2.** a grill or fireplace used in barbecuing. **3.** the food so cooked. **4.** a party or picnic at which barbecued food is served. ~*vb.* -**cuing, -cued.** (*tr.*) **5.** to cook (meat, fish, etc.) on a grill, usually over charcoal and often with a highly seasoned sauce.

barbed wire *n.* strong wire with sharply pointed barbs at close intervals.

barbel (ˈbaːbəl) *n.* **1.** any of several slender tactile spines or bristles that hang from the jaws of certain fishes, such as the carp. **2.** any of several European cyprinid fishes that resemble the carp.

barbell (ˈbaːˌbɛl) *n.* a metal rod to which heavy discs are attached at each end for weightlifting.

barber (ˈbaːbə) *n.* **1.** a person whose business is cutting men's hair and shaving beards. ~*vb.* (*tr.*) **2.** to cut the hair of.

barberry (ˈbaːbərɪ) *n., pl.* -**ries.** **1.** any spiny Asian shrub of the genus *Berberis,* having clusters of yellow flowers and orange or red berries. **2.** the fruit of these plants.

barbershop (ˈbaːbəˌʃɒp) *n.* **1.** *Now chiefly U.S.* the premises of a barber. **2.** (*modifier*) *chiefly U.S.* denoting a type of close four-part harmony for male voices: *a barbershop quartet.*

barber's pole *n.* a barber's sign consisting of a pole painted with red and white spiral stripes.

barbican (ˈbaːbɪkən) *n.* **1.** the outwork of a fortified place, esp. to defend a drawbridge. **2.** a watchtower projecting from a fortification.

barbiturate (baːˈbɪtjʊrɪt, -ˌreɪt) *n.* a derivative of barbituric acid, such as barbitone, used in medicine as a sedative or hypnotic.

barbituric acid (ˌbaːbɪˈtjʊərɪk) *n.* a white crystalline solid used in the preparation of barbiturate drugs.

barcarole *or* **barcarolle** (ˈbaːkəˌrəʊl, -ˌrɒl; ˌbaːkəˈrəʊl) *n.* **1.** a Venetian boat song. **2.** an instrumental composition resembling this.

bard[1] (baːd) *n.* **1. a.** (formerly) one of an ancient Celtic order of poets. **b.** a poet who wins a verse competition at a Welsh Eisteddfod. **2.** *Arch. or literary.* any poet. —**ˈbardic** *adj.*

bard[2] (baːd) *n.* **1.** a piece of bacon or pork fat placed on meat during roasting to prevent drying out. ~*vb.* (*tr.*) **2.** to place a bard on.

bare[1] (bɛə) *adj.* **1.** unclothed: used esp. of a part of the body. **2.** without the natural, conventional, or usual covering. **3.** lacking appropriate furnishings, etc. **4.** unembellished; simple: *the bare facts.* **5.** (*prenominal*) just sufficient: *the bare minimum.* **6. with one's bare hands.** without a weapon or tool. ~*vb.* **7.** (*tr.*) to make bare; uncover. —**ˈbareness** *n.*

bare[2] (bɛə) *vb. Arch.* a past tense of **bear**[1].

bareback (ˈbɛəˌbæk) *or* **barebacked** *adj., adv.* (of horse-riding) without a saddle.

barefaced (ˈbɛəˌfeɪst) *adj.* unconcealed or shameless: *a barefaced lie.* —**barefacedly** (ˈbɛəˌfeɪsɪdlɪ) *adv.* —**ˈbareˌfacedness** *n.*

barefoot (ˈbɛəˌfʊt) *or* **barefooted** *adj., adv.* with the feet uncovered.

bareheaded (ˌbɛəˈhɛdɪd) *adj., adv.* with the head uncovered.

barely (ˈbɛəlɪ) *adv.* **1.** only just: *barely enough.* **2.** *Inf.* not quite: *barely old enough.* **3.** scantily: *barely furnished.* **4.** *Arch.* openly.

bargain (ˈbaːgɪn) *n.* **1.** an agreement establishing what each party will give, receive, or perform in a transaction. **2.** something acquired or received in such an agreement. **3. a.** something bought or offered at a low price. **b.** (*modifier*): *a bargain basement.* **4. into the bargain.** in excess; besides. **5. make** *or* **strike a bargain.** to agree on terms. ~*vb.* **6.** (*intr.*) to negotiate the terms of an agreement, transaction, etc. **7.** (*tr.*) to exchange, as in a bargain. **8.** to arrive at (an agreement or settlement). —**ˈbargainer** *n.*

barge (baːdʒ) *n.* **1.** a vessel, usually flat-bottomed and with or without its own power, used for transporting freight, esp. on canals. **2.** a vessel, often decorated, used

---

bar *n.* **1.** batten, crosspiece, paling, pole, rail, rod, shaft, stake, stick **2.** barricade, barrier, deterrent, hindrance, impediment, obstacle, obstruction, rail, railing, stop **3.** boozer (*Inf.*), canteen, counter, inn, lounge, pub (*Inf.*), public house, saloon, tavern **4.** bench, court, courtroom, dock, law court **5.** *Law* barristers, body of lawyers, counsel, court, judgment, tribunal ~*v.* **6.** barricade, bolt, fasten, latch, lock, secure **7.** ban, exclude, forbid, hinder, keep out, obstruct, prevent, prohibit, restrain

barb **1.** bristle, point, prickle, prong, quill, spike, spur, thorn **2.** affront, cut, dig, gibe, insult, rebuff, sarcasm, scoff, sneer

barbarian *n.* **1.** brute, hooligan, lout, ruffian, savage, vandal, yahoo **2.** bigot, boor, ignoramus, illiterate, lowbrow, philistine ~*adj.* **3.** boorish, crude, lowbrow, philistine, primitive, uncouth, uncultivated, uncultured, unsophisticated, vulgar

barbaric **1.** primitive, rude, uncivilized, wild **2.** barbarous, boorish, brutal, coarse, crude, cruel, fierce, inhuman, savage, uncouth, vulgar

barbarism **1.** coarseness, crudity, savagery, uncivilizedness **2.** atrocity, barbarity, enormity, outrage **3.** corruption, misusage, misuse, solecism, vulgarism

barbarity brutality, cruelty, inhumanity, ruthlessness, savagery, viciousness

barbarous **1.** barbarian, brutish, primitive, rough, rude, savage, uncivilized, uncouth, wild **2.** barbaric, brutal, cruel, ferocious, heartless, inhuman, monstrous, ruthless, vicious **3.** coarse, crude, ignorant, uncultured, unlettered, unrefined, vulgar

bare **1.** denuded, exposed, naked, nude, peeled, shorn, stripped, unclad, unclothed, uncovered, undressed **2.** barren, blank, empty, lacking, mean, open, poor, scanty, scarce, unfurnished, vacant, void, wanting **3.** austere, bald, basic, cold, essential, hard, literal, plain, severe, sheer, simple, spare, stark, unadorned, unembellished, unvarnished

barefaced **1.** audacious, bold, brash, brazen, impudent, insolent, shameless **2.** bald, blatant, flagrant, glaring, manifest, naked, obvious, open, palpable, patent, transparent, unconcealed

barely almost, hardly, just, only just, scarcely

bargain *n.* **1.** agreement, arrangement, business, compact, contract, convention, engagement, negotiation, pact, pledge, promise, stipulation, transaction, treaty, understanding **2.** (cheap) purchase, discount, giveaway, good buy, good deal, good value, reduction, snip (*Inf.*) ~*v.* **3.** agree, contract, covenant, negotiate, promise, stipulate, transact **4.** barter, buy, deal, haggle, sell, trade, traffic

bargain for anticipate, contemplate, expect, foresee, imagine, look for, plan for

bargain on assume, bank on, count on, depend on, plan on, rely on

in pageants, etc. **3.** *Navy.* a boat allocated to a flag officer, used esp. for ceremonial occasions. ~*vb.* **4.** (*intr.;* foll. by *into*) *Inf.* to bump (into). **5.** *Inf.* to push (someone or one's way) violently. **6.** (*intr.;* foll. by *into* or *in*) *Inf.* to interrupt rudely or clumsily: *to barge into a conversation.*

bargee (baː'dʒiː) *n., pl.* **bargees.** a person employed on or in charge of a barge.

bargepole ('baːdʒ,pəʊl) *n.* **1.** a long pole used to propel a barge. **2. not touch with a bargepole.** *Inf.* to refuse to have anything to do with.

bar graph *n.* a graph consisting of vertical or horizontal bars whose lengths are proportional to amounts or quantities.

baritone ('bærɪ,təʊn) *n.* **1.** the second lowest adult male voice. **2.** a singer with such a voice. **3.** the second lowest instrument in the families of the saxophone, horn, oboe, etc. ~*adj.* **4.** relating to or denoting a baritone. **5.** denoting the second lowest instrument in a family.

barium ('bɛərɪəm) *n.* a soft silvery-white metallic element of the alkaline earth group. Symbol: Ba; atomic no.: 56; atomic wt.: 137.34.

barium meal *n.* a preparation of barium sulphate, which is opaque to x-rays, swallowed by a patient before x-ray examination of the upper part of his alimentary canal.

bark[1] (baːk) *n.* **1.** the loud abrupt usually harsh cry of a dog or certain other animals. **2.** a similar sound, such as one made by a person, gun, etc. **3. his bark is worse than his bite.** he is bad-tempered but harmless. ~*vb.* **4.** (*intr.*) (of a dog, etc.) to make its typical cry. **5.** (*intr.*) (of a person, gun, etc.) to make a similar loud harsh sound. **6.** to say or shout in a brusque or angry tone: *he barked an order.* **7. bark up the wrong tree.** *Inf.* to misdirect one's attention, efforts, etc.; be mistaken.

bark[2] (baːk) *n.* **1.** a protective layer of dead corky cells on the outside of the stems of woody plants. **2.** any of several varieties of this, used in tanning, dyeing, or in medicine. ~*vb.* (*tr.*) **3.** to scrape or rub off skin, as in an injury. **4.** to remove the bark or a circle of bark from (a tree). **5.** to tan (leather), principally by the tannins in barks.

bark[3] (baːk) *n.* a variant spelling of **barque.**

barker ('baːkə) *n.* **1.** an animal or person that barks. **2.** *Inf.* a person at a fair booth, etc., who loudly addresses passers-by to attract customers.

barley ('baːlɪ) *n.* **1.** any of various annual temperate grasses that have dense bristly flower spikes and are widely cultivated for grain and forage. **2.** the grain of any of these grasses, used in making beer and whisky and for soups, puddings, etc.

barleycorn ('baːlɪ,kɔːn) *n.* **1.** a grain of barley, or barley itself. **2.** an obsolete unit of length equal to one third of an inch.

barley sugar *n.* a brittle clear amber-coloured sweet.

barley water *n.* a drink made from an infusion of barley.

barm (baːm) *n.* **1.** the yeasty froth on fermenting malt liquors. **2.** an archaic or dialect word for **yeast.**

barmaid ('baː,meɪd) *n.* a woman who serves in a pub.

barman ('baːmən) *n., pl.* **-men.** a man who serves in a pub.

bar mitzvah (baː 'mɪtsvə) *n.* (*sometimes caps.*) *Judaism.* **1.** the ceremony and celebration marking the 13th birthday of a boy, who then assumes his full religious obligations. **2.** the boy himself.

barmy ('baːmɪ) *adj.* **-mier, -miest.** *Sl.* insane.

barn[1] (baːn) *n.* **1.** a large farm outbuilding, chiefly for storing grain, etc., but also for livestock. **2.** *U.S.* a large shed for railroad cars, trucks, etc. **3.** any large building, esp. an unattractive one.

barn[2] (baːn) *n.* a unit of nuclear cross section equal to 10⁻²⁸ square metre. Symbol: b

barnacle ('baːnəkəl) *n.* **1.** any of various marine crusta-

ceans that, as adults, live attached to rocks, ship bottoms, etc. **2.** a person or thing that is difficult to get rid of. —'**barnacled** *adj.*

barnacle goose *n.* a N European goose that has a black-and-white head and body.

barn dance *n.* **1.** *Brit.* a progressive round country dance. **2.** *U.S.* a party with hoedown music and square dancing.

barney ('baːnɪ) *Inf., chiefly Austral. & N.Z.* ~*n.* **1.** a noisy fight or argument. ~*vb.* (*intr.*) **2.** to argue or quarrel.

barn owl *n.* an owl with a pale brown and white plumage, and a heart-shaped face.

barnstorm ('baːn,stɔːm) *vb.* (*intr.*) *Chiefly U.S.* **1.** to tour rural districts putting on shows. **2.** to tour rural districts making speeches in a political campaign. —'**barn,stormer** *n.*

barnyard ('baːn,jaːd) *n.* **1.** a yard adjoining a barn. **2.** (*modifier*) characteristic of a barnyard. **3.** (*modifier*) crude or earthy.

baro- *combining form.* indicating weight or pressure: *barometer.*

barograph ('bærə,graːf, -,græf) *n.* *Meteorol.* a self-recording aneroid barometer. —**barographic** (,bærə'græfɪk) *adj.*

barometer (bə'rɒmɪtə) *n.* **1.** an instrument for measuring atmospheric pressure, usually to determine altitude or weather changes. **2.** anything that shows change. —**barometric** (,bærə'mɛtrɪk) *or* ,baro'metrical *adj.* —ba'rometry *n.*

baron ('bærən) *n.* **1.** a member of a specific rank of nobility, esp. the lowest rank in the British Isles. **2.** (in Europe from the Middle Ages) originally any tenant-in-chief of a king or other overlord. **3.** a powerful businessman or financier: *a press baron.* —'**baroness** *fem. n.* —**baronial** (bə'rəʊnɪəl) *adj.*

baronet ('bærənɪt, -,nɛt) *n.* (in Britain) a commoner who holds the lowest hereditary title of honour, ranking below a baron. Abbrev.: **Bart.** or **Bt.** —'**baronetage** *n.* —'**baronetcy** *n.*

baron of beef *n.* a cut of beef consisting of a double sirloin joined at the backbone.

barony ('bærənɪ) *n., pl.* **-nies.** **1. a.** the domain of a baron. **b.** (in Ireland) a division of a county. **c.** (in Scotland) a large estate or manor. **2.** the rank or dignity of a baron.

baroque (bə'rɒk, bə'rəʊk) *n.* (*often cap.*) **1.** a style of architecture and decorative art in Europe from the late 16th to the early 18th century, characterized by extensive ornamentation. **2.** a 17th-century style of music characterized by extensive use of ornamentation. **3.** any ornate or heavily ornamented style. ~*adj.* **4.** denoting, in, or relating to the baroque. **5.** (of pearls) irregularly shaped.

baroscope ('bærə,skəʊp) *n.* any instrument for measuring atmospheric pressure. —**baroscopic** (,bærə'skɒpɪk) *adj.*

barouche (bə'ruːʃ) *n.* a four-wheeled horse-drawn carriage, popular in the 19th century, having a retractable hood over the rear half.

barque (baːk) *n.* **1.** a sailing ship of three or more masts having the foremasts rigged square and the aftermast rigged fore-and-aft. **2.** *Poetic.* any boat.

barrack[1] ('bærək) *vb.* to house (soldiers, etc.) in barracks.

barrack[2] ('bærək) *vb. Brit. & Austral. inf.* **1.** to criticize loudly or shout against (a team, speaker, etc.); jeer. **2.** (*intr.;* foll. by *for*) to shout support (for).

barracks ('bærəks) *pl. n.* (*sometimes sing.; when pl., sometimes functions as sing.*) **1.** a building or group of buildings used to accommodate military personnel. **2.** any large building used for housing people, esp. temporarily. **3.** a large and bleak building.

barracuda (,bærə'kjuːdə) *n., pl.* **-da** *or* **-das.** a preda-

---

THESAURUS

barge canal boat, flatboat, lighter, narrow boat, scow

barge in break in, burst in, butt in, infringe, interrupt, intrude, muscle in (*Inf.*)

barge into bump into, cannon into, collide with, hit, push, shove

bark[1] **1.** *n.* casing, cortex (*Anat., bot.*), covering, crust, husk, rind, skin **2.** *v.* abrade, flay,

rub, scrape, shave, skin, strip

bark[2] **1.** *n./v.* bay, growl, howl, snarl, woof, yap, yelp **2.** *v. Fig.* bawl, bawl at, berate, bluster, growl, shout, snap, snarl, yell

barmy 1. *Also* balmy crazy, daft, foolish, idiotic, insane, loony (*Sl.*), nuts (*Sl.*), nutty (*Sl.*), odd, silly, stupid **2.** fermenting, foamy, frothy, spumy, yeasty

baroque bizarre, convoluted, elaborate, extravagant, flamboyant, florid, grotesque, ornate, overdecorated

barracks billet, camp, cantonment, casern, encampment, garrison, quarters

tory marine mostly tropical fish, which attacks man.

barrage ('bærɑːʒ) n. 1. Mil. the firing of artillery to saturate an area rather than hit a specific target. 2. an overwhelming and continuous delivery of something, as questions. 3. a construction across a watercourse, esp. one to increase the depth.

barrage balloon n. one of a number of tethered balloons with cables or net suspended from them, used to deter low-flying air attack.

barratry or **barretry** ('bærətrı) n. 1. Criminal law. the vexatious stirring up of quarrels or bringing of lawsuits. 2. Maritime law. a fraudulent practice committed by the master or crew of a ship to the prejudice of the owner. 3. the purchase or sale of public or Church offices. —'**barratrous** or '**barretrous** adj.

barre French. (baːr) n. a rail at hip height used for ballet practice.

barrel ('bærəl) n. 1. a cylindrical container usually bulging outwards in the middle and held together by metal hoops. 2. Also called: **barrelful**. the amount that a barrel can hold. 3. a unit of capacity of varying amount in different industries. 4. a thing shaped like a barrel, esp. a tubular part of a machine. 5. the tube through which the projectile of a firearm is discharged. 6. the trunk of a four-legged animal: the barrel of a horse. 7. **over a barrel**. Inf. powerless. 8. **scrape the barrel**. Inf. to be forced to use one's last and weakest resource. ~vb. -**relling**, -**relled** or U.S. -**reling**, -**reled**. 9. (tr.) to put into a barrel or barrels.

barrel organ n. an instrument consisting of a cylinder turned by a handle and having pins on it that interrupt the air flow to certain pipes or pluck strings, thereby playing tunes.

barrel roll n. a flight manoeuvre in which an aircraft rolls about its longitudinal axis while following a spiral course in line with the direction of flight.

barrel vault n. Archit. a vault in the form of a half cylinder.

barren ('bærən) adj. 1. incapable of producing offspring, seed, or fruit; sterile. 2. unable to support the growth of crops, etc.: barren land. 3. lacking in stimulation; dull. 4. not producing worthwhile results; unprofitable: a barren period. 5. (foll. by of) devoid (of): barren of wit. —'**barrenness** n.

Barren Grounds pl. n. **The**. a sparsely inhabited region of tundras in N Canada, extending westwards from Hudson Bay. Also called: **Barren Lands**.

barricade (ˌbærɪ'keɪd, 'bærɪˌkeɪd) n. 1. a barrier for defence, esp. one erected hastily, as during street fighting. ~vb. (tr.) 2. to erect a barricade across (an entrance, etc.) or at points of access to (a room, district, etc.).

barrier ('bærɪə) n. 1. anything serving to obstruct passage or to maintain separation, such as a fence or gate. 2. anything that prevents progress. 3. anything that separates or hinders union: a language barrier.

barrier cream n. a cream used to protect the skin, esp. the hands.

barrier reef n. a long narrow coral reef near the shore, separated from it by deep water.

barring ('bɑːrɪŋ) prep. unless (something) occurs; except for.

barrister ('bærɪstə) n. 1. Also called: **barrister-at-law**. (in England) a lawyer who has been called to the bar and is qualified to plead in the higher courts. Cf. **solicitor**. 2. U.S. a less common word for **lawyer**.

barrow[1] ('bærəʊ) n. 1. See **wheelbarrow**. 2. Also called: **barrowful**. the amount contained in or on a barrow. 3. Chiefly Brit. a handcart with a canvas roof, used

esp. by street vendors.

barrow[2] ('bærəʊ) n. a heap of earth placed over one or more prehistoric tombs, often surrounded by ditches.

barrow boy n. Brit. a man who sells his wares from a barrow; street vendor.

bar sinister n. 1. (not in heraldic usage) another name for **bend sinister**. 2. the condition or stigma of being of illegitimate birth.

Bart. abbrev. for Baronet.

barter ('bɑːtə) vb. 1. to trade (goods, services, etc.) in exchange for other goods, services, etc., rather than for money. 2. (intr.) to haggle over such an exchange; bargain. ~n. 3. trade by the exchange of goods. —'**barterer** n.

baryon ('bærɪˌɒn) n. any of a class of elementary particles that have a mass greater than or equal to that of the proton. Baryons are either nucleons or hyperons. The **baryon number** is the number of baryons in a system minus the number of antibaryons. —ˌbary'**onic** adj.

baryta (bə'raɪtə) n. another name for barium oxide or barium hydroxide.

barytes (bə'raɪtiːz) n. a colourless or white mineral occurring in sedimentary rocks and with sulphide ores: a source of barium.

basal ('beɪsəl) adj. 1. at, of, or constituting a base. 2. of or constituting a basis; fundamental.

basalt ('bæsɔːlt) n. 1. a dark basic igneous rock: the most common volcanic rock. 2. a form of black unglazed pottery resembling basalt. —ba'**saltic** adj.

base[1] (beɪs) n. 1. the bottom or supporting part of anything. 2. the fundamental principle or part. 3. **a**. a centre of operations, organization, or supply. **b**. (as modifier): base camp. 4. starting point: the new discovery became the base for further research. 5. the main ingredient of a mixture: to use rice as a base in cookery. 6. a chemical compound that combines with an acid to form a salt and water. A solution of a base in water turns litmus paper blue and produces hydroxyl ions. 7. a medium such as oil or water in which the pigment is dispersed in paints, inks, etc. 8. Biol. the point of attachment of an organ or part. 9. the bottommost layer or part of anything. 10. Archit. the part of a column between the pedestal and the shaft. 11. the lower side or face of a geometric construction. 12. Maths. the number of units in a counting system that is equivalent to one in the next higher counting place: 10 is the base of the decimal system. 13. Maths. the number that when raised to a certain power has a logarithm (based on that number) equal to that power: the logarithm to the base 10 of 1000 is 3. 14. Linguistics. a root or stem. 15. Electronics. the region in a transistor between the emitter and collector. 16. a starting or finishing point in any of various games. ~vb. 17. (tr.; foll. by on or upon) to use as a basis (for); found (on). 18. (often foll. by at or in) to station, post, or place (a person or oneself).

base[2] (beɪs) adj. 1. devoid of honour or morality; contemptible. 2. of inferior quality or value. 3. debased; alloyed; counterfeit: base currency. 4. English history. (of land tenure) held by villein or other ignoble service. 5. Arch. born of humble parents. 6. Arch. illegitimate. —'**baseness** n.

baseball ('beɪsˌbɔːl) n. 1. a team game with nine players on each side, played on a field with four bases connected to form a diamond. The object is to score runs by batting the ball and running round the bases. 2. the hard rawhide-covered ball used in this game.

baseborn ('beɪsˌbɔːn) adj. Arch. 1. born of humble parents. 2. illegitimate.

baseless ('beɪslɪs) adj. not based on fact; unfounded.

THESAURUS

barrage 1. battery, bombardment, cannonade, curtain of fire, fusillade, gunfire, salvo, shelling, volley 2. assault, attack, burst, deluge, hail, mass, onslaught, plethora, profusion, rain, storm, stream, torrent

barren 1. childless, infecund, infertile, sterile, unprolific 2. arid, desert, desolate, dry, empty, unfruitful, unproductive, waste 3. boring, dull, flat, fruitless, lacklustre, stale, uninformative, uninspiring, uninstructive, uninteresting, unrewarding, useless, vapid

barricade 1. n. barrier, blockade, bulwark, fence, obstruction, palisade, rampart, stockade 2. v. bar, block, blockade, defend,

fortify, obstruct, protect, shut in

barrier 1. bar, barricade, blockade, boundary, ditch, fence, fortification, obstacle, obstruction, railing, rampart, stop, wall 2. Fig. check, difficulty, drawback, handicap, hindrance, hurdle, impediment, limitation, obstacle, restriction, stumbling block

barter bargain, exchange, haggle, sell, swap, trade, traffic

base[1] n. 1. bed, bottom, foot, foundation, groundwork, pedestal, rest, stand, support 2. basis, core, essence, essential, fundamental, heart, key, origin, principal, root, source 3. camp, centre, headquarters, home, post, set-

tlement, starting point, station ~v. 4. build, construct, depend, derive, establish, found, ground, hinge, locate, station

base[2] 1. abject, contemptible, corrupt, depraved, despicable, dishonourable, disreputable, evil, ignoble, immoral, infamous, scandalous, shameful, sordid, vile, villainous, vulgar, wicked 2. downtrodden, grovelling, low, lowly, mean, menial, miserable, paltry, pitiful, poor, servile, slavish, sorry, subservient, worthless, wretched 3. adulterated, alloyed, counterfeit, debased, fake, forged, fraudulent, impure, inferior, pinchbeck, spurious

—**'baselessness** n.

baseline ('beɪsˌlaɪn) n. **1.** Surveying. a measured line through a survey area from which triangulations are made. **2.** a line at each end of a tennis court that marks the limit of play.

basement ('beɪsmənt) n. **1. a.** a partly or wholly underground storey of a building, esp. one used for habitation rather than storage. **b.** (as modifier): a basement flat. **2.** the foundation of a wall or building.

base metal n. any of certain common metals, such as copper and lead, as distinct from precious metals.

basenji (bə'sɛndʒɪ) n. a small African breed of dog having an inability to bark.

bases¹ ('beɪsiːz) n. the plural of **basis**.

bases² ('beɪsɪz) n. the plural of **base**.

bash (bæʃ) Inf. ~vb. **1.** (tr.) to strike violently or crushingly. **2.** (tr.; often foll. by in, down, etc.) to smash, break, etc., with a crashing blow. **3.** (intr.; foll. by into) to crash (into); collide (with). ~n. **4.** a heavy blow. **5.** a party. **6. have a bash.** Inf. to make an attempt.

bashful ('bæʃful) adj. **1.** shy or modest; diffident. **2.** indicating or characterized by shyness or modesty. —**'bashfulness** n.

-**bashing** n. and adj. combining form. Inf. sl. **a.** indicating a malicious attack on members of a group: union-bashing. **b.** indicating various other activities: Bible-bashing. —-**basher** n. combining form.

basic ('beɪsɪk; Austral. also 'bæsɪk) adj. **1.** of, relating to, or forming a base or basis; fundamental. **2.** elementary or simple: a few basic facts. **3.** without additions or extras: basic pay. **4.** Chem. of, denoting, or containing a base; alkaline. **5.** Metallurgy. of or made by a process in which the furnace or converter is made of a basic material, such as magnesium oxide. **6.** (of such igneous rocks as basalt) containing less than 50 per cent silica. ~n. **7.** (usually pl.) a fundamental principle, fact, etc. —**'basically** adv.

BASIC ('beɪsɪk) n. a computer programming language that uses common English terms.

basic English n. a simplified form of English with a vocabulary of approximately 850 common words, intended as an international language.

basic industry n. an industry which is highly important in a nation's economy.

basic slag n. a slag produced in steel-making, containing calcium phosphate.

basil ('bæzəl) n. a Eurasian plant, having spikes of small white flowers and aromatic leaves used as herbs for seasoning. Also called: **sweet basil**.

basilica (bə'zɪlɪkə) n. **1.** a Roman building, used for public administration, having a large rectangular central nave with an aisle on each side and an apse at the end. **2.** a Christian church of similar design. **3.** a Roman Catholic church having special ceremonial rights. —**ba'silican** or **ba'silic** adj.

basilisk ('bæzɪˌlɪsk) n. **1.** (in classical legend) a serpent that could kill by its breath or glance. **2.** a small semi-aquatic lizard of tropical America. The males have an inflatable head crest, used in display.

basin ('beɪsən) n. **1.** a round container open and wide at the top with sides sloping inwards towards the bottom. **2.** Also called: **basinful.** the amount a basin will hold. **3.** a washbasin or sink. **4.** any partially enclosed or sheltered area where vessels may be moored. **5.** the catchment area of a particular river and its tributaries. **6.** a depression in the earth's surface. **7.** Geol. a part of the earth's surface consisting of rock strata that slope down to a common centre.

basis ('beɪsɪs) n., pl. -**ses** (-siːz). **1.** something that underlies, supports, or is essential to something else, esp. an idea. **2.** a principle on which something depends or from which something has issued.

▷ **Usage.** The phrase on the basis of is inappropriate in contexts where because of can be used: he agreed to come because of your promise to protect him, not he agreed to come on the basis of your promise to protect him. On the basis of is correctly used of a criterion of choice: the players were chosen on the basis of their weight.

bask (bɑːsk) vb. (intr.; usually foll. by in) **1.** to lie in or be exposed to pleasant warmth, esp. that of the sun. **2.** to flourish or feel secure under some benevolent influence or favourable condition.

basket ('bɑːskɪt) n. **1.** a container made of interwoven strips of pliable materials, such as cane, and often carried by a handle. **2.** Also called: **basketful.** the amount a basket will hold. **3.** something resembling such a container, such as the structure suspended from a balloon. **4.** Basketball. **a.** the hoop fixed to the backboard, through which a player must throw the ball to score points. **b.** a point or points scored in this way. **5.** Inf. a euphemism for **bastard** (senses 2, 3). —**'basketry** n.

basketball ('bɑːskɪtˌbɔːl) n. **1.** a game played by two teams of five men (or six women), usually on an indoor court. Points are scored by throwing the ball through an elevated horizontal hoop. **2.** the ball used in this game.

basket chair n. a chair made of wickerwork.

basket weave n. a weave of yarns, resembling that of a basket.

basketwork ('bɑːskɪtˌwɜːk) n. another word for **wickerwork**.

basking shark n. a very large plankton-eating shark, often floating at the sea surface.

basque (bæsk) n. a type of tightfitting bodice for women.

Basque (bæsk, bɑːsk) n. **1.** a member of a people living around the W Pyrenees in France and Spain. **2.** the language of this people, of no known relationship with any other language. ~adj. **3.** of or relating to this people or their language.

bas-relief (ˌbɑːrɪ'liːf, 'bæsrɪˌliːf) n. sculpture in low relief, in which the forms project slightly from the background.

bass¹ (beɪs) n. **1.** the lowest adult male voice. **2.** a singer with such a voice. **3. the bass.** the lowest part in a piece of harmony. **4.** Inf. a bass guitar or double bass. **5. a.** the low-frequency gain of an audio amplifier, esp. in a record player or tape recorder. **b.** the knob controlling this. ~adj. **6.** relating to or denoting the bass. **7.** denoting the lowest and largest instrument in a family: a bass clarinet.

bass² (bæs) n. **1.** any of various sea perches. **2.** a European spiny-finned freshwater fish. **3.** any of various predatory North American freshwater fishes.

bass³ (bæs) n. another name for **bast**.

bass clef (beɪs) n. the clef that establishes F a fifth below middle C on the fourth line of the staff.

bass drum (beɪs) n. a large drum of low pitch.

basset ('bæsɪt) n. a smooth-haired breed of hound with

THESAURUS

baseless groundless, unconfirmed, uncorroborated, unfounded, ungrounded, unjustifiable, unjustified, unsubstantiated, unsupported

baseness 1. contemptibility, degradation, depravation, depravity, despicability, disgrace, ignominy, infamy, notoriety, obloquy, turpitude 2. lowliness, meanness, misery, poverty, servility, slavishness, subservience, vileness, worthlessness, wretchedness 3. adulteration, debasement, fraudulence, phoneyness (Sl.), pretence, speciousness, spuriousness

bash 1. v. biff (Sl.), break, crash, crush, hit, punch, slosh (Sl.), smash, sock (Sl.), strike, wallop (Inf.) 2. n. attempt, crack, go, shot, stab, try

bashful abashed, blushing, confused, constrained, coy, diffident, easily embarrassed, nervous, overmodest, reserved, reticent, retiring, self-conscious, self-effacing, shamefaced, sheepish, shrinking, shy, timid, timorous

bashfulness constraint, coyness, diffidence, embarrassment, hesitation, modesty, reserve, self-consciousness, sheepishness, shyness, timidity, timorousness

basic central, elementary, essential, fundamental, indispensable, inherent, intrinsic, key, necessary, primary, underlying, vital

basically at bottom, at heart, au fond, essentially, firstly, fundamentally, inherently, in substance, intrinsically, mostly, primarily, radically

basics brass tacks (Inf.), core, essentials, facts, fundamentals, hard facts, necessaries, nitty-gritty (Sl.), nuts and bolts (Inf.), practicalities, principles, rudiments

basis 1. base, bottom, footing, foundation, ground, groundwork, support 2. chief ingredient, core, essential, fundamental, heart, premise, principal element, principle, theory

bask 1. laze, lie in, loll, lounge, relax, sunbathe, swim in, toast oneself, warm oneself 2. delight in, enjoy, indulge oneself, luxuriate, relish, revel, savour, take pleasure, wallow

bass deep, deep-toned, grave, low, low-pitched, resonant, sonorous

short legs and long ears. Also: **basset hound.**

basset horn *n.* an obsolete woodwind instrument.

bassinet (ˌbæsɪˈnɛt) *n.* a wickerwork or wooden cradle or pram, usually hooded.

basso ('bæsəʊ) *n., pl.* **-sos** *or* **-si** (-sɪ). (esp. in operatic or solo singing) a singer with a bass voice.

bassoon (bəˈsuːn) *n.* **1.** a woodwind instrument, the tenor of the oboe family. **2.** an orchestral musician who plays a bassoon. —**bas'soonist** *n.*

bass viol (beɪs) *n.* **1.** another name for **viola da gamba**. **2.** *U.S.* a less common name for **double bass** (sense 1).

bast (bæst) *n.* **1.** *Bot.* another name for **phloem. 2.** fibrous material obtained from the phloem of jute, flax, etc., used for making rope, matting, etc.

bastard ('baːstəd, 'bæs-) *n.* **1.** a person born of parents not married to each other. **2.** *Inf., offens.* an obnoxious or despicable person. **3.** *Inf.* a person, esp. a man: *lucky bastard.* **4.** *Inf.* something extremely difficult or unpleasant. **5.** something irregular, abnormal, or inferior. **6.** a hybrid, esp. an accidental or inferior one. ~*adj.* (*prenominal*) **7.** illegitimate by birth. **8.** irregular, abnormal, or inferior. **9.** resembling a specified thing, but not actually being such: *a bastard cedar.* **10.** counterfeit; spurious. **11.** hybrid. —'**bastardy** *n.*

bastardize *or* **-ise** ('baːstəˌdaɪz, 'bæs-) *vb.* (*tr.*) **1.** to debase. **2.** to declare illegitimate.

baste[1] (beɪst) *vb.* (*tr.*) to sew with loose temporary stitches.

baste[2] (beɪst) *vb.* to moisten (meat) during cooking with hot fat and the juices produced.

baste[3] (beɪst) *vb.* (*tr.*) to beat thoroughly; thrash.

Bastille (bæ'stiːl) *n.* a fortress in Paris: a prison until its destruction in 1789, at the beginning of the French Revolution.

bastinado (ˌbæstɪˈneɪdəʊ) *n., pl.* **-does. 1.** punishment or torture in which the soles of the feet are beaten with a stick. ~*vb.* **-doing, -doed. 2.** (*tr.*) to beat (a person) thus.

basting ('beɪstɪŋ) *n.* **1.** loose temporary stitches; tacking. **2.** sewing with such stitches.

bastion ('bæstɪən) *n.* **1.** a projecting part of a fortification, esp. one at the angle of a wall. **2.** any fortified place. **3.** a thing or person regarded as defending a principle, etc.

bat[1] (bæt) *n.* **1.** any of various types of club with a handle, used to hit the ball in certain sports, such as cricket. **2.** a flat round club with a short handle used by a man on the ground to guide the pilot of an aircraft when taxiing. **3.** *Cricket.* short for **batsman. 4.** *Inf.* a blow from a stick. **5.** *Sl.* speed; pace: *they went at a fair bat.* **6. carry one's bat.** *Cricket.* (of a batsman) to reach the end of an innings without being dismissed. **7. off one's own bat.** of one's own accord; without being prompted. ~*vb.* **batting, batted. 8.** (*tr.*) to strike with or as if with a bat. **9.** (*intr.*) *Cricket, etc.* (of a player or a team) to take a turn at batting.

bat[2] (bæt) *n.* **1.** a nocturnal mouselike animal flying with a pair of membranous wings. **2. blind as a bat.** having extremely poor eyesight. **3. have bats in the** (*or* **one's**) **belfry.** *Inf.* to be mad or eccentric. —'**batlike** *adj.*

bat[3] (bæt) *vb.* **batting, batted. 1.** (*tr.*) to wink or flutter (one's eyelids). **2. not bat an eye** (*or* **eyelid**). *Inf.* to show no surprise or concern.

batch (bætʃ) *n.* **1.** a group or set of usually similar objects or people, esp. if sent off, handled, or arriving at the same time. **2.** the bread, cakes, etc., produced at one baking. **3.** the amount of a material needed for an operation. ~*vb.* **4.** to group (items) for efficient processing. **5.** to handle by batch processing.

batch processing *n.* a system by which the computer programs of a number of individual users are submitted as a single batch.

bate (beɪt) *vb.* **1.** another word for **abate. 2. with bated breath.** in suspense or fear.

bath (baːθ) *n., pl.* **baths** (baːðz). **1.** a large container used for washing the body. Related adj.: **balneal. 2.** the act or an instance of washing in such a container. **3.** the amount of liquid contained in a bath. **4.** (*usually pl.*) a place having baths or a swimming pool for public use. **5. a.** a vessel in which something is immersed to maintain it at a constant temperature, to process it photographically, etc., or to lubricate it. **b.** the liquid used in such a vessel. ~*vb.* **6.** *Brit.* to wash in a bath.

Bath bun (baːθ) *n. Brit.* a sweet bun containing spices and dried fruit.

Bath chair *n.* a wheelchair for invalids.

bath cube *n.* a cube of soluble scented material for use in a bath.

bathe (beɪð) *vb.* **1.** (*intr.*) to swim in a body of open water, esp. for pleasure. **2.** (*tr.*) to apply liquid to (skin, a wound, etc.) in order to cleanse or soothe. **3.** to immerse or be immersed in a liquid. **4.** *Chiefly U.S.* to wash in a bath. **5.** (*tr.; often passive*) to suffuse. ~*n.* **6.** *Brit.* a swim in a body of open water. —'**bather** *n.*

bathing cap ('beɪðɪŋ) *n.* a tight rubber cap worn by a swimmer to keep the hair dry.

bathing suit ('beɪðɪŋ) *n.* a garment worn for bathing, esp. an old-fashioned one that covers much of the body.

Bath Oliver *n. Brit.* a kind of unsweetened biscuit.

bathometer (bə'θɒmɪtə) *n.* an instrument for measuring the depth of water. —**bathometric** (ˌbæθə'mɛtrɪk) *adj.* —**bathometry** (bə'θɒmɪtrɪ) *n.*

bathos ('beɪθɒs) *n.* **1.** a sudden ludicrous descent from exalted to ordinary matters or style in speech or writing. **2.** insincere or excessive pathos. —**ba'thetic** *adj.*

bathrobe ('baːθˌrəʊb) *n.* **1.** a loose-fitting garment of towelling, for wear before or after a bath or swimming. **2.** *U.S.* a dressing gown.

bathroom ('baːθˌruːm, -ˌrum) *n.* **1.** a room containing a bath or shower and usually a washbasin and lavatory. **2.** *U.S.* another name for **lavatory.**

bath salts *pl. n.* soluble scented salts for use in a bath.

bathy- *or* **batho-** *combining form.* indicating depth: *bathysphere.*

bathyscaph ('bæθɪˌskæf), **bathyscaphe** ('bæθɪˌskeɪf, -ˌskæf), *or* **bathyscape** *n.* a submersible vessel with an observation capsule underneath, capable of reaching ocean depths of over 10 000 metres.

bathysphere ('bæθɪˌsfɪə) *n.* a strong steel deep-sea diving sphere, lowered by cable.

batik *or* **battik** ('bætɪk) *n.* **a.** a process of printing fabric in which parts not to be dyed are covered by wax. **b.** fabric printed in this way.

batiste (bæ'tiːst) *n.* a fine plain-weave cotton.

batman ('bætmən) *n., pl.* **-men.** an officer's servant in the armed forces.

baton ('bætɒn) *n.* **1.** a thin stick used by the conductor of an orchestra, choir, etc. **2.** *Athletics.* a short bar carried by a competitor in a relay race and transferred to the next runner at the end of each stage. **3.** a long stick with a knob on one end, carried, twirled, and thrown up and down by a drum major or majorette, esp. at the head of a parade. **4.** a police truncheon, esp. in **baton charge. 5.** a staff or club carried as a symbol of authority.

batrachian (bə'treɪkɪən) *n.* **1.** any amphibian, esp. a frog or toad. ~*adj.* **2.** of or relating to the frogs and toads.

bats (bæts) *adj. Inf.* mad or eccentric.

batsman ('bætsmən) *n., pl.* **-men. 1.** *Cricket., etc.* **a.** a person who bats or whose turn it is to bat. **b.** a player who specializes in batting. **2.** a person on the ground who uses bats to guide the pilot of an aircraft when taxiing. —'**batsman,ship** *n.*

battalion (bə'tæljən) *n.* **1.** a military unit comprised of three or more companies or formations of similar size. **2.** (*usually pl.*) any large array.

THESAURUS

bastard 1. *n.* illegitimate (child), love child, natural child 2. *adj.* adulterated, base-born, counterfeit, false, illegitimate, imperfect, impure, inferior, irregular, misbegotten, sham, spurious

bastion bulwark, citadel, defence, fastness, fortress, mainstay, prop, rock, stronghold, support, tower of strength

bat bang, hit, rap, smack, strike, swat, thump, wallop (*Inf.*), whack

batch accumulation, aggregation, amount, assemblage, bunch, collection, crowd, group, lot, pack, quantity, set

bath 1. *n.* ablution, cleansing, douche, douse, scrubbing, shower, soak, soaping, sponging, tub, wash, washing 2. *v.* bathe,

clean, douse, lave (*Archaic*), scrub down, shower, soak, soap, sponge, tub, wash

bathe 1. *v.* cleanse, cover, dunk, flood, immerse, moisten, rinse, soak, steep, suffuse, wash, wet 2. *n.* dip, swim

bathing costume bathing suit, bikini, swimming costume, swimsuit, trunks

bathos anticlimax, false pathos, mawkish-

batten[1] ('bæt∂n) n. 1. a sawn strip of wood used in building to cover joints, support lathing, etc. 2. a long narrow board used for flooring. 3. a lath used for holding a tarpaulin along the side of a hatch on a ship. ~vb. 4. (tr.) to furnish or strengthen with battens. 5. **batten down the hatches. a.** to use battens in securing a tarpaulin over a hatch on a ship. **b.** to prepare for action, a crisis, etc.

batten[2] ('bæt∂n) vb. (intr.) (usually foll. by on) to thrive, esp. at the expense of someone else.

batter[1] ('bæt∂) vb. 1. to hit (someone or something) repeatedly using heavy blows, as with a club. 2. (tr.; often passive) to damage or injure, as by blows, heavy wear, etc. —'**batterer** n.

batter[2] ('bæt∂) n. a mixture of flour, eggs, and milk, used to make cakes, pancakes, etc., and to coat certain foods before frying.

battered baby n. a young child who has sustained serious injuries through violence at the hands of a parent or other adult.

battering ram n. (esp. formerly) a large beam used to break down fortifications.

battery ('bæt∂rı) n., pl. -**teries. 1.** two or more primary cells connected, usually in series, to provide a source of electric current. 2. another name for **accumulator** (sense 1). 3. a number of similar things occurring together: a battery of questions. 4. Criminal law. unlawful beating or wounding of a person or mere touching in a hostile or offensive manner. 5. a fortified structure on which artillery is mounted. 6. a group of guns, missile launchers, etc. operated as a single entity. 7. a small unit of artillery. 8. Chiefly Brit. **a.** a large group of cages for intensive rearing of poultry and other farm animals. **b.** (as modifier): battery hens. 9. Baseball. the pitcher and the catcher considered together.

battle ('bæt∂l) n. 1. a fight between large armed forces; military or naval engagement. 2. conflict; struggle. 3. **do, give,** or **join battle.** to start fighting. ~vb. 4. (intr.; often foll. by against, for, or with) to fight in or as if in military combat. 5. to struggle: he battled through the crowd. 6. (intr.) Austral. to scrape a living.

battle-axe n. 1. (formerly) a large broad-headed axe. 2. Inf. an argumentative domineering woman.

battle cruiser n. a high-speed heavily armed warship of battleship size but with light armour.

battle cry n. 1. a shout uttered by soldiers going into battle. 2. a slogan used to rally the supporters of a campaign, movement, etc.

battledore ('bæt∂l,dɔː) n. 1. Also called: **battledore and shuttlecock.** an ancient racket game. 2. a light racket used in this game. 3. (formerly) a wooden utensil used for beating clothes, in baking, etc.

battle dress n. the ordinary uniform of a soldier.

battlefield ('bæt∂l,fiːld) or **battleground** n. the place where a battle is fought.

battlement ('bæt∂lm∂nt) n. a parapet or wall with indentations or embrasures, originally for shooting through. —'**battle,mented** adj.

battle royal n. 1. a fight, esp. with fists or cudgels, involving more than two combatants; melee. 2. a long violent argument.

battleship ('bæt∂l,ʃıp) n. a heavily armoured warship of the largest type.

batty ('bætı) adj. -**tier, -tiest.** Sl. 1. insane; crazy. 2. odd; eccentric.

bauble ('bɔːb∂l) n. 1. a trinket of little value. 2. (formerly) a mock staff of office carried by a jester.

baulk (bɔːk) n. 1. Also: **balk.** Billiards. the space between the baulk line and the bottom cushion. 2. Archaeol. a strip of earth left between excavation trenches for the study of the complete stratigraphy of a site. ~vb., n. 3. a variant spelling of **balk.**

bauxite ('bɔːksaıt) n. an amorphous claylike substance consisting of hydrated alumina with iron and other impurities: the chief source of alumina and aluminium and also used as an abrasive and catalyst.

bawd (bɔːd) n. Arch. 1. a person who runs a brothel, esp. a woman. 2. a prostitute.

bawdry ('bɔːdrı) n. Arch. obscene talk or language.

bawdyhouse ('bɔːdı,haʊs) n. an archaic word for **brothel.**

bawl (bɔːl) vb. 1. (intr.) to utter long loud cries, as from pain or frustration; wail. 2. to shout loudly, as in anger. ~n. 3. a loud shout or cry. —'**bawler** n.

bay[1] (beı) n. 1. a wide semicircular indentation of a shoreline, esp. between two headlands. 2. an extension of lowland into hills that partly surround it.

bay[2] (beı) n. 1. an alcove or recess in a wall. 2. any partly enclosed compartment. 3. See **bay window.** 4. an area off a road in which vehicles may park or unload. 5. a compartment in an aircraft: the bomb bay. 6. Naut. a compartment in a ship, often used as the ship's hospital. 7. Brit. a tracked recess in the platform of a railway station, esp. one forming the terminus of a branch line.

bay[3] (beı) n. 1. a deep howl, esp. of a hound on the scent. 2. **at bay. a.** forced to turn and face attackers: the dogs held the deer at bay. **b.** at a distance. 3. **bring to bay.** to force into a position from which retreat is impossible. ~vb. 4. (intr.) to howl (at) in deep prolonged tones. 5. (tr.) to utter in a loud prolonged tone. 6. (tr.) to hold at bay.

bay[4] (beı) n. 1. a Mediterranean laurel. See **laurel** (sense 1). 2. any of certain other trees or shrubs, esp. bayberry. 3. (pl.) a wreath of bay leaves.

bay[5] (beı) n., adj. 1. (of) a reddish-brown colour. ~n. 2. an animal of this colour.

bayberry ('beıb∂rı) or **bay** n., pl. -**ries. 1.** any of several North American aromatic shrubs or small trees that bear grey waxy berries. 2. a tropical American tree, that yields an oil used in making bay rum. 3. the fruit of any of these plants.

bay leaf n. the leaf of the laurel dried and used in cooking.

bayonet ('beı∂nıt) n. 1. a blade for stabbing that can be attached to the muzzle of a firearm. 2. a type of fastening in which a cylindrical member is inserted into a socket against spring pressure and turned so that pins on its side engage in slots in the socket. ~vb. -**neting, -neted,** or -**netting, -netted.** 3. (tr.) to stab or kill with a bayonet.

THESAURUS

ness, sentimentality

baton club, mace, rod, staff, stick, truncheon, wand

battalion army, brigade, company, contingent, division, force, horde, host, legion, multitude, regiment, squadron, throng

batten[1] board up, clamp down, cover up, fasten, fasten down, fix, nail down, secure, tighten

batten[2] fatten, flourish, gain, grow, increase, prosper, thrive, wax

batter 1. assault, bash, beat, belabour, break, buffet, dash against, lash, pelt, pound, pummel, smash, smite, thrash, wallop (Inf.) 2. bruise, crush, deface, demolish, destroy, disfigure, hurt, injure, mangle, mar, maul, ruin, shatter, shiver

battered beaten, broken-down, bruised, crushed, damaged, dilapidated, injured, ramshackle, squashed, weather-beaten

battery 1. chain, ring, sequence, series,

set, suite 2. assault, attack, beating, mayhem, onslaught, physical violence, thumping 3. artillery, cannon, cannonry, gun emplacements, guns

battle n. 1. action, attack, combat, encounter, engagement, fight, fray, hostilities, skirmish, war, warfare 2. agitation, campaign, clash, conflict, contest, controversy, crusade, debate, disagreement, dispute, strife, struggle ~v. 3. agitate, argue, clamour, combat, contend, contest, dispute, feud, fight, strive, struggle, war

battle cry catchword, motto, slogan, war cry, war whoop, watchword

battlefield battleground, combat zone, field, field of battle, front

battlement barbican, bartizan, bastion, breastwork, bulwark, crenellation, fortification, parapet, rampart

battleship capital ship, gunboat, man-of-war, ship of the line, warship

batty barmy (Sl.), bats (Sl.), bonkers (Sl.), cracked (Sl.), crackers (Sl.), cranky (Inf.), crazy, daft, dotty (Sl.), eccentric, insane, loony (Sl.), lunatic, mad, nuts (Sl.), nutty (Sl.), odd, peculiar, potty (Inf.), queer, screwy (Inf.), touched

bauble bagatelle, gewgaw, gimcrack, kickshaw, knick-knack, plaything, toy, trifle, trinket

bawd brothel-keeper, madam, pimp, procuress, prostitute, whore

bawdy blue, coarse, dirty, erotic, gross, indecent, indecorous, indelicate, lascivious, lecherous, lewd, libidinous, licentious, lustful, obscene, prurient, ribald, risqué, rude, salacious, suggestive, vulgar

bawl 1. bellow, call, clamour, halloo, howl, roar, shout, vociferate, yell 2. blubber, cry, sob, squall, wail, weep

bay[1] bight, cove, gulf, inlet, natural harbour, sound

bay rum *n.* an aromatic liquid, used in medicines and cosmetics, originally obtained by distilling the leaves of the bayberry tree with rum: now also synthesized.

bay window *n.* a window projecting from a wall and forming an alcove of a room.

bazaar *or* **bazar** (bəˈzɑː) *n.* 1. (esp. in the Orient) a market area, esp. a street of small stalls. 2. a sale in aid of charity, esp. of secondhand or handmade articles. 3. a shop where a variety of goods is sold.

bazooka (bəˈzuːkə) *n.* a portable tubular rocket-launcher, used by infantrymen as a short-range antitank weapon.

B.B.C. *abbrev. for* British Broadcasting Corporation.

bbl. *abbrev. for* barrel (container or measure).

B.C. *abbrev. for:* 1. (indicating years numbered back from the supposed year of the birth of Christ) before Christ. 2. British Columbia.

▷ *Usage.* See at **A.D.**

BCG *abbrev. for* Bacillus Calmette-Guérin (antituberculosis vaccine).

B.D. *abbrev. for* Bachelor of Divinity.

bdellium (ˈdɛliəm) *n.* 1. any of several African or W Asian trees that yield a gum resin. 2. the aromatic gum resin produced by these trees.

B.D.S. *abbrev. for* Bachelor of Dental Surgery.

be (biː; *unstressed* bɪ) *vb. pres. sing. 1st pers.* **am;** *2nd pers.* **are;** *3rd pers.* **is.** *pres. pl.* **are.** *past sing. 1st pers.* **was;** *2nd pers.* **were;** *3rd pers.* **was.** *past pl.* **were.** *pres. part.* **being.** *past part.* **been.** *(intr.)* 1. to have presence in perceived reality; exist; live: *I think, therefore I am.* 2. *(used in the perfect tenses only)* to pay a visit; go: *have you been to Spain?* 3. to take place: *my birthday was last Thursday.* 4. *(copula)* used as a linking verb between the subject of a sentence and its noun or adjective complement. *be* has no intrinsic meaning of its own but rather expresses relationship of equivalence or identity (*John is a man; John is a musician*) or specifies an attribute (*honey is sweet; Susan is angry*). It is also used with an adverbial complement to indicate a relationship in space or time (*Bill is at the office; the dance is on Saturday*). 5. *(takes a present participle)* forms the progressive present tense: *the man is running.* 6. *(takes a past participle)* forms the passive voice of all transitive verbs: *a good film is being shown on television tonight.* 7. *(takes an infinitive)* expresses intention, expectation, or obligation: *the president is to arrive at 9.30.* 8. **be that as it may.** the facts concerning (something) are of no importance.

Be *chemical symbol for* beryllium.

be- *prefix forming transitive verbs.* 1. *(from nouns)* to surround or cover: *befog.* 2. *(from nouns)* to affect completely: *bedazzle.* 3. *(from nouns)* to consider as or cause to be: *befriend.* 4. *(from verbs)* at, for, against, on, or over: *bewail; berate.*

B.E. *abbrev. for:* 1. bill of exchange. 2. Bachelor of Education. 3. Bachelor of Engineering.

beach (biːtʃ) *n.* 1. an area of sand or shingle sloping down to a sea or lake, esp. the area between the high and low water marks on a seacoast. ~*vb.* 2. to run or haul (a boat) onto a beach.

beachcomber (ˈbiːtʃˌkəʊmə) *n.* 1. a person who searches shore debris for anything of worth. 2. a long high wave rolling onto a beach.

beachhead (ˈbiːtʃˌhɛd) *n. Mil.* an area on a beach that has been captured from the enemy and on which troops and equipment are landed.

beacon (ˈbiːkən) *n.* 1. a signal fire or light on a hill, tower, etc., esp. formerly as a warning of invasion. 2. a hill on which such fires were lit. 3. a lighthouse, signalling buoy, etc. 4. a radio or other signal marking a flight course in air navigation. 5. short for **Belisha beacon.** 6. a person or thing that serves as a guide, inspiration, or warning.

bead (biːd) *n.* 1. a small pierced usually spherical piece of glass, wood, plastic, etc., which may be strung with others to form a necklace, etc. 2. a small drop of moisture. 3. a small bubble in or on a liquid. 4. a small metallic knob acting as the sight of a firearm. 5. **to draw** *or* **hold a bead on.** to aim a rifle or pistol at. 6. *Archit., furniture.* a small convex moulding having a semicircular cross section. 7. **tell one's beads.** to pray with a rosary. ~*vb.* 8. *(tr.)* to decorate with beads. 9. to form into beads or drops. —**'beaded** *adj.*

beading (ˈbiːdɪŋ) *n.* 1. another name for **bead** (sense 6). 2. a narrow strip of some material used for edging or ornamentation. Also called: **beadwork** (ˈbiːd,wɜːk).

beadle (ˈbiːdəl) *n.* 1. *Brit.* (formerly) a minor parish official who acted as an usher and kept order. 2. *Judaism.* a synagogue attendant. 3. *Scot.* a church official who attends the minister. 4. an official in certain British institutions. —**'beadleship** *n.*

beadsman *or* **bedesman** (ˈbiːdzmən) *n., pl.* **-men.** *Arch.* 1. a person who prays for another's soul, esp. one paid or fed for doing so. 2. a person kept in an almshouse.

beady (ˈbiːdɪ) *adj.* **-ier, -iest.** 1. small, round, and glittering (esp. in **beady eyes**). 2. resembling or covered with beads. —**'beadiness** *n.*

beagle (ˈbiːgəl) *n.* 1. a small breed of hound, often used for hunting hares. 2. *Arch.* a spy. ~*vb.* 3. *(intr.)* to hunt with beagles.

beak¹ (biːk) *n.* 1. the projecting jaws of a bird, covered with a horny sheath. 2. any beaklike mouthpart in other animals. 3. *Sl.* a person's nose. 4. any projecting part, such as the pouring lip of a bucket. 5. *Naut.* another word for **ram** (sense 5). —**beaked** (biːkt) *adj.* —**'beaky** *adj.*

beak² (biːk) *n.* a Brit. slang word for **judge, magistrate,** or **headmaster.**

beaker (ˈbiːkə) *n.* 1. a cup usually having a wide mouth. 2. a cylindrical flat-bottomed container used in laboratories, usually made of glass and having a pouring lip.

Beaker folk (ˈbiːkə) *n.* a prehistoric people inhabiting Europe and Britain during the second millennium B.C.

beam (biːm) *n.* 1. a long thick piece of wood, metal, etc., esp. one used as a horizontal structural member. 2. the breadth of a ship or boat taken at its widest part. 3. a ray or column of light, as from a beacon. 4. a broad smile. 5. one of two cylindrical rollers on a loom, which hold the warp threads and the finished work. 6. the main stem of a deer's antler. 7. the central shaft of a plough to which all the main parts are attached. 8. a narrow unidirectional flow of electromagnetic radiation or particles: *an electron beam.* 9. the horizontal centrally pivoted bar in a balance. 10. **broad in the beam.** *Inf.* having wide hips. 11. **a beam in one's eye.** a fault or grave error greater in oneself than in another person. 12. **off (the) beam. a.** not following a radio beam to maintain a course. **b.** *Inf.* mistaken or irrelevant. 13. **on the beam. a.** following a radio beam to maintain a course. **b.** *Inf.* correct, relevant, or appropriate. ~*vb.* 14. to send out or radiate. 15. *(tr.)* to divert or aim (a radio signal, light, etc.) in a certain direction: *to beam a programme to Tokyo.* 16. *(intr.)* to smile broadly. —**'beamy** *adj.* —**'beaming** *adj.*

beam-ends *pl. n.* 1. **on her beam-ends.** (of a vessel) heeled over through an angle of 90°. 2. **on one's beam-ends.** out of resources; destitute.

THESAURUS

bay² alcove, compartment, embrasure, niche, nook, opening, recess

bay³ 1. bark, bell, clamour, cry, growl, howl, yelp 2. **at bay** caught, cornered, trapped

bayonet *v.* impale, knife, run through, spear, stab, stick, transfix

bays chaplet, garland, glory, laurel crown, praise, prize, renown, trophy

bazaar 1. exchange, market, marketplace, mart 2. bring-and-buy, fair, fête

be 1. be alive, breathe, exist, inhabit, live 2. befall, come about, come to pass, happen, oc-

cur, take place, transpire (*Inf.*) 3. abide, continue, endure, last, obtain, persist, prevail, remain, stand, stay, survive

beach coast, littoral, margin, sands, seaboard (*Chiefly U.S.*), seashore, seaside, shingle, shore, strand, water's edge

beachcomber forager, loafer, scavenger, scrounger, tramp, vagabond, vagrant, wanderer

beached abandoned, aground, ashore, deserted, grounded, high and dry, marooned, stranded, wrecked

beacon beam, bonfire, flare, lighthouse, pharos, rocket, sign, signal, signal fire, smoke signal, watchtower

bead blob, bubble, dot, drop, droplet, globule, pellet, pill, spherule

beads chaplet, choker, necklace, necklet, pearls, pendant, rosary

beak 1. bill, mandible, neb (*Archaic or dialect*), nib 2. nose, proboscis, snout 3. *Naut.* bow, prow, ram, rostrum, stem

beam *n.* 1. girder, joist, plank, rafter, spar, support, timber 2. bar, emission, gleam,

bean (biːn) *n*. **1.** any of various leguminous plants producing edible seeds in pods. **2.** any of various other plants whose seeds are produced in pods or podlike fruits. **3.** the seed or pod of any of these plants. **4.** any of various beanlike seeds, as coffee. **5.** *U.S. sl.* another word for **head. 6. not have a bean.** *Sl.* to be without money. **7. full of beans.** *Inf.* full of energy and vitality. **8. spill the beans.** *Inf.* to disclose something confidential.

beanbag ('biːn,bæg) *n*. **1.** a small cloth bag filled with dried beans and thrown in games. **2.** a very large cushion filled with foam rubber or polystyrene granules and used as a seat.

beanfeast ('biːn,fiːst) *n*. *Brit. inf.* **1.** an annual dinner given by employers to employees. **2.** any festive or merry occasion.

beano ('biːnəʊ) *n*., *pl*. **beanos.** *Brit. sl.* a celebration, party, or other enjoyable time.

beanpole ('biːn,pəʊl) *n*. **1.** a tall stick used to support bean plants. **2.** *Sl.* a tall thin person.

bean sprout *n*. the sprout of newly germinated mung bean, eaten esp. in Chinese dishes.

bear¹ (bɛə) *vb*. **bearing, bore, borne.** (*mainly tr.*) **1.** to support or hold up. **2.** to bring: *to bear gifts.* **3.** to accept or assume the responsibility of: *to bear an expense.* **4. (born** in passive use except when followed by *by*) to give birth to: *to bear children.* **5.** (*also intr.*) to produce as by natural growth: *to bear fruit.* **6.** to tolerate or endure. **7.** to admit or; sustain: *his story does not bear scrutiny.* **8.** to hold in the mind: *to bear a grudge.* **9.** to show or be marked with: *he still bears the scars.* **10.** to render or supply (esp. in **bear witness**). **11.** to conduct (oneself, the body, etc.). **12.** to have, be, or stand in (relation or comparison): *his account bears no relation to the facts.* **13.** (*intr.*) to move or lie in a specified direction. **14. bear a hand.** to give assistance. **15. bring to bear.** to bring into operation or effect. ~See also **bear down, bear on,** etc.

bear² (bɛə) *n*., *pl*. **bears** or **bear. 1.** a plantigrade mammal typically having a large head, a long shaggy coat, and strong claws. **2.** any of various bearlike animals, such as the koala. **3.** a clumsy, churlish, or ill-mannered person. **4.** a teddy bear. **5.** *Stock Exchange.* **a.** a speculator who sells in anticipation of falling prices to make a profit on repurchase. **b.** (*as modifier*): *a bear market.* Cf. **bull**¹ (sense 4). ~*vb*. **bearing, beared. 6.** (*tr.*) to lower or attempt to lower the price or prices of (a stock market or a security) by speculative selling.

Bear (bɛə) *n*. **the. 1.** the English name for either Ursa Major (Great Bear) or Ursa Minor (Little Bear). **2.** an informal name for Russia.

bearable ('bɛərəbəl) *adj*. endurable; tolerable.

beard (bɪəd) *n*. **1.** the hair growing on the lower parts of a man's face. **2.** any similar growth in animals. **3.** a tuft of long hairs in plants such as barley; awn. **4.** a barb, as on a fish-hook. ~*vb*. (*tr.*) **5.** to oppose boldly or impertinently. —'**bearded** *adj*.

bear down *vb*. (*intr., adv.; often foll. by on* or *upon*) **1.** to press or weigh down. **2.** to approach in a determined or threatening manner.

bearer ('bɛərə) *n*. **1.** a person or thing that bears, presents, or upholds. **2.** a person who presents a note or bill for payment. **3.** (in Africa, India, etc., formerly) a native porter or servant. **4.** (*modifier*) *Finance.* payable to the person in possession: *bearer bonds.*

bear garden *n*. **1.** (formerly) a place where bearbaiting took place. **2.** a scene of tumult.

bear hug *n*. **1.** a wrestling hold in which the arms are locked tightly round an opponent's chest and arms. **2.** any similar tight embrace.

bearing ('bɛərɪŋ) *n*. **1.** a support for a rotating or reciprocating mechanical part. **2.** (foll. by *on* or *upon*) relevance (to): *it has no bearing on this problem.* **3.** a person's general social conduct. **4.** the act, period, or capability of producing fruit or young. **5.** anything that carries weight or acts as a support. **6.** the angular direction of a point or course measured from a known position. **7.** (*usually pl.*) the position, as of a ship, fixed with reference to two or more known points. **8.** (*usually pl.*) a sense of one's relative position; orientation (esp. in **lose, get,** *or* **take one's bearings**). **9.** *Heraldry.* **a.** a device on a heraldic shield. **b.** another name for **coat of arms.**

bear on *vb*. (*intr., prep.*) **1.** to be relevant to; relate to. **2.** to be burdensome to or afflict.

bear out *vb*. (*tr., adv.*) to show to be true or truthful; confirm: *the witness will bear me out.*

bearskin ('bɛə,skɪn) *n*. **1.** the pelt of a bear, esp. when used as a rug. **2.** a tall helmet of black fur worn by certain British Army regiments.

bear up *vb*. (*intr., adv.*) to endure cheerfully.

bear with *vb*. (*intr., prep.*) to be patient with.

beast (biːst) *n*. **1.** any animal other than man, esp. a large wild quadruped. **2.** savage nature or characteristics: *the beast in man.* **3.** a brutal, uncivilized, or filthy person.

beastly ('biːstlɪ) *adj*. **-lier, -liest. 1.** *Inf.* unpleasant; disagreeable. **2.** *Obs.* of or like a beast; bestial. ~*adv*. **3.** *Inf.* (intensifier): *the weather is so beastly hot.* —'**beastliness** *n*.

beat (biːt) *vb*. **beating, beat; beaten** *or* **beat. 1.** (when *intr.*, often foll. by *against, on,* etc.) to strike with or as if with a series of violent blows. **2.** (*tr.*) to punish by striking; flog. **3.** to move up and down; flap: *the bird beat its wings heavily.* **4.** (*intr.*) to throb rhythmically; pulsate. **5.** (*tr.; sometimes foll. by up*) *Cookery.* to stir or whisk vigorously. **6.** (*tr.; sometimes foll. by out*) to shape, thin, or flatten (metal) by repeated blows. **7.** (*tr.*) *Music.* to indicate (time) by one's hand, baton, etc., or by a metronome. **8.** (when *tr.*, sometimes foll. by *out*) to produce (a sound or signal) by or as if by striking a drum. **9.** to overcome; defeat. **10.** (*tr.*) to form (a path, track, etc.) by repeatedly walking or riding over it. **11.** (*tr.*) to arrive, achieve, or finish before (someone or something). **12.** (*tr.; often foll. by back, down, off,* etc.) to drive, push, or thrust. **13.** to scour (woodlands or undergrowth) so as to rouse game for shooting. **14.** (*tr.*) *Sl.* to puzzle or baffle: *it beats me.* **15.** (*intr.*) *Naut.* to steer a sailing vessel as close as possible to the direction from which the wind is blowing. **16. beat about the bush.** *Inf.* to avoid the issue. **17. beat a retreat.** to withdraw in haste. **18. beat it.** *Sl.* (*often imperative*) to go away. **19. beat the**

■■■■■■ **THESAURUS** ■■■■■■

glimmer, glint, glow, radiation, ray, shaft, streak, stream ~v. **3.** broadcast, emit, glare, gleam, glitter, glow, radiate, shine, transmit **4.** grin, laugh, smile

beaming 1. beautiful, bright, brilliant, flashing, gleaming, glistening, glittering, radiant, scintillating, shining, sparkling **2.** cheerful, grinning, happy, joyful, smiling, sunny

bear 1. bring, carry, convey, move, take, tote, transport **2.** cherish, entertain, exhibit, harbour, have, hold, maintain, possess, shoulder, support, sustain, uphold, weigh upon **3.** abide, admit, allow, brook, endure, permit, put up with (*Inf.*), stomach, suffer, tolerate, undergo **4.** beget, breed, bring forth, develop, engender, generate, give birth to, produce, yield

bearable admissible, endurable, manageable, passable, sufferable, supportable, sustainable, tolerable

beard 1. *n*. bristles, five-o'clock shadow, stubble, whiskers **2.** *v*. brave, confront, dare,

defy, face, oppose

bearded bewhiskered, bristly, bushy, hairy, hirsute, shaggy, stubbly, unshaven, whiskered

beardless 1. barefaced, clean-shaven, hairless, smooth, smooth-faced **2.** callow, fresh, green, immature, inexperienced

bear down 1. burden, compress, encumber, press down, push, strain, weigh down **2.** advance on, approach, attack, close in, converge on, move in

bearer 1. agent, carrier, conveyor, messenger, porter, runner, servant **2.** beneficiary, consignee, payee

bearing 1. air, aspect, attitude, behaviour, carriage, demeanour, deportment, manner, mien, posture **2.** *Naut.* course, direction, point of compass **3.** application, connection, import, pertinence, reference, relation, relevance, significance

bearings aim, course, direction, location, orientation, position, situation, track, way, whereabouts

bear on affect, appertain to, belong to, concern, involve, pertain to, refer to, relate to, touch upon

bear out confirm, corroborate, endorse, justify, prove, substantiate, support, uphold, vindicate

bear up bear the brunt, carry on, endure, grin and bear it (*Inf.*), persevere, suffer, withstand

bear with be patient, forbear, make allowances, put up with (*Inf.*), suffer, tolerate, wait

beast 1. animal, brute, creature **2.** barbarian, brute, fiend, monster, ogre, sadist, savage, swine

beastly 1. barbarous, bestial, brutal, brutish, coarse, cruel, depraved, inhuman, monstrous, repulsive, sadistic, savage **2.** awful, disagreeable, foul, mean, nasty, rotten, terrible, unpleasant

bounds. *Brit.* (formerly) to define the boundaries of a parish by making a procession around them and hitting the ground with rods. **20. can you beat it** *or* **that?** *Sl.* an expression of surprise. ~*n.* **21.** a stroke or blow. **22.** the sound made by a stroke or blow. **23.** a regular throb. **24.** an assigned or habitual round or route, as of a policeman. **25.** the basic rhythmic unit in a piece of music. **26. a.** pop or rock music characterized by a heavy rhythmic beat. **b.** (*as modifier*): *a beat group.* **27.** *Physics.* one of the regular pulses produced by combining two sounds or electrical signals that have similar frequencies. **28.** *Prosody.* the accent or stress in a metrical foot. **29.** (*modifier*) (*often cap.*) of, characterized by, or relating to the Beat Generation. ~*adj.* **30.** (*postpositive*) *Sl.* totally exhausted. ~See also **beat down, beat up.** —'**beatable** *adj.*

beat down *vb.* (*adv.*) **1.** (*tr.*) *Inf.* to force or persuade (a seller) to accept a lower price. **2.** (*intr.*) (of the sun) to shine intensely.

beaten ('bi:tən) *adj.* **1.** defeated or baffled. **2.** shaped or made thin by hammering: *beaten gold.* **3.** much travelled; well trodden. **4. off the beaten track. a.** in unfamiliar territory. **b.** out of the ordinary; unusual. **5.** (of food) mixed by beating; whipped. **6.** tired out; exhausted.

beater ('bi:tə) *n.* **1.** a person who beats or hammers: *a panel beater.* **2.** a device used for beating: *a carpet beater.* **3.** a person who rouses wild game.

beatific (ˌbi:ə'tɪfɪk) *adj.* **1.** displaying great happiness, calmness, etc. **2.** of or conferring a state of celestial happiness. —ˌbea'**tifically** *adv.*

beatify (bɪ'ætɪˌfaɪ) *vb.* **-fying, -fied. 1.** (*tr.*) *R.C. Church.* (of the pope) to declare formally that (a deceased person) showed a heroic degree of holiness in life and is worthy of veneration: *the first step towards canonization.* **2.** (*tr.*) to make extremely happy. —**beatification** (bɪˌætɪfɪ'keɪʃən) *n.*

beatitude (bɪ'ætɪˌtjuːd) *n.* **1.** supreme blessedness or happiness. **2.** an honorific title of the Eastern Christian Church, applied to those of patriarchal rank.

Beatitude (bɪ'ætɪˌtjuːd) *n. Christianity.* any of eight sayings of Jesus in the Sermon on the Mount (Matthew 5:1-8) in which he declares that the poor, the meek, etc. will, in various ways, receive the blessings of heaven.

beatnik ('bi:tnɪk) *n.* **1.** a member of the Beat Generation. **2.** *Inf.* any person with long hair and shabby clothes.

beat up *Inf.* ~*vb.* **1.** (*tr., adv.*) to strike or kick repeatedly, so as to inflict severe physical damage. ~*adj.* **beat-up. 2.** worn-out; dilapidated.

beau (bəʊ) *n., pl.* **beaus** (bəʊz) *or* **beaux** (bəʊ, bəʊz). **1.** a man who is greatly concerned with his clothes and appearance; dandy. **2.** *Chiefly U.S.* a boyfriend; sweetheart.

Beaufort scale ('bəʊfət) *n. Meteorol.* an international scale of wind velocities from 0 (calm) to 12 (hurricane) (0 to 17 in the U.S.).

beaujolais ('bəʊʒəˌleɪ) *n.* (*sometimes cap.*) a popular fresh-tasting red or white wine from southern Burgundy

in France.

beaut (bjuːt) *Sl., chiefly Austral. & N.Z.* ~*n.* **1.** an outstanding person or thing. ~*adj., interj.* **2.** good or excellent.

beauteous ('bjuːtɪəs) *adj.* a poetic word for **beautiful.** —'**beauteousness** *n.*

beautician (bjuː'tɪʃən) *n.* a person who works in or manages a beauty salon.

beautiful ('bjuːtɪful) *adj.* **1.** possessing beauty; aesthetically pleasing. **2.** highly enjoyable; very pleasant. —'**beautifully** *adv.*

beautify ('bjuːtɪˌfaɪ) *vb.* **-fying, -fied.** to make or become beautiful. —**beautification** (ˌbjuːtɪfɪ'keɪʃən) *n.* —'**beautiˌfier** *n.*

beauty ('bjuːtɪ) *n., pl.* **-ties. 1.** the combination of all the qualities of a person or thing that delight the senses and mind. **2.** a very attractive woman. **3.** *Inf.* an outstanding example of its kind. **4.** *Inf.* an advantageous feature: *one beauty of the job is the short hours.* ~*interj.* **5.** *Austral. & N.Z. sl.* an expression of approval or agreement. Also: **you beauty.**

beauty queen *n.* an attractive young woman, esp. one who has won a beauty contest.

beauty sleep *n. Inf.* sleep, esp. sleep before midnight.

beauty spot *n.* **1.** a small dark-coloured patch or spot worn on a lady's face as an adornment. **2.** a mole or other similar natural mark on the skin. **3.** a place of outstanding beauty.

beaver[1] ('bi:və) *n.* **1.** a large amphibious rodent of Europe, Asia, and North America. It has soft brown fur, a broad flat hairless tail, and webbed hind feet, and constructs complex dams and houses (lodges) in rivers. **2.** its fur. **3.** a tall hat of beaver fur worn during the 19th century. **4.** a woollen napped cloth resembling beaver fur. **5.** *Obs.* a full beard. **6.** a bearded man. **7.** (*modifier*) made of beaver fur or similar material. ~*vb.* **8.** (*intr.*; usually foll. by *away*) *Brit. inf.* to work industriously or steadily.

beaver[2] ('bi:və) *n.* a movable piece on a medieval helmet used to protect the lower face.

bebop ('bi:bɒp) *n.* the full name for **bop** (sense 1). —'**bebopper** *n.*

becalmed (bɪ'kɑːmd) *adj.* (of a sailing boat or ship) motionless through lack of wind.

became (bɪ'keɪm) *vb.* the past tense of **become.**

because (bɪ'kɒz, -'kəz) *conj.* **1.** (*subordinating*) on account of the fact that; since: *because it's so cold we'll go home.* ~ **2. because of.** (*prep.*) on account of: *I lost my job because of her.*
▷ **Usage.** See at **reason.**

béchamel sauce (ˌbeɪʃə'mɛl) *n.* a thick white sauce flavoured with onion and seasonings.

beck[1] (bɛk) *n.* **1.** a nod, wave, or other gesture. **2. at (someone's) beck and call.** subject to (someone's) slightest whim.

beck[2] (bɛk) *n.* (in N England) a stream.

beckon ('bɛkən) *vb.* **1.** to summon with a gesture of the hand or head. **2.** to entice or lure. ~*n.* **3.** a summoning

---

THESAURUS

beat *v.* **1.** bang, batter, break, bruise, buffet, cane, cudgel, drub, flog, hit, knock, lash, maul, pelt, pound, punch, strike, thrash, thwack, whip **2.** best, conquer, defeat, excel, outdo, outrun, outstrip, overcome, overwhelm, subdue, surpass, vanquish **3.** fashion, forge, form, hammer, model, shape, work **4.** flap, flutter, palpitate, pound, pulsate, pulse, quake, quiver, shake, throb, thump, tremble, vibrate ~*n.* **5.** blow, hit, lash, punch, shake, slap, strike, swing, thump **6.** flutter, palpitation, pulsation, pulse, throb **7.** accent, cadence, measure, metre, rhythm, stress, time **8.** circuit, course, path, rounds, route, way ~*adj.* **9.** *Sl.* exhausted, fatigued, tired, wearied, worn out

beaten 1. baffled, cowed, defeated, disappointed, disheartened, frustrated, overcome, overwhelmed, thwarted, vanquished **2.** forged, formed, hammered, shaped, stamped, worked **3.** much travelled, trampled, trodden, well-trodden, well-used, worn **4.** blended, foamy, frothy, mixed, stirred, whipped, whisked

beating 1. belting (*Inf.*), caning, chastisement, corporal punishment, flogging, slapping, smacking, thrashing, whipping **2.** conquest, defeat, downfall, overthrow, rout, ruin

beatitude beatification, blessedness, bliss, ecstasy, exaltation, felicity, happiness, holy joy, saintliness

beat up assault, attack, batter, do over (*Sl.*), duff up (*Sl.*), fill in (*Sl.*), knock about *or* around, thrash

beau 1. admirer, boyfriend, escort, fiancé, lover, suitor, swain, sweetheart **2.** cavalier, coxcomb, dandy, fop, gallant, ladies' man, popinjay, swell (*Inf.*)

beautiful alluring, appealing, attractive, charming, comely, delightful, exquisite, fair, fine, good-looking, gorgeous, graceful, handsome, lovely, pleasing, radiant, ravishing, stunning (*Inf.*)

beautify adorn, array, bedeck, deck, decorate, embellish, enhance, garnish, gild, glamorize, grace, ornament

beauty 1. allure, attractiveness, bloom, charm, comeliness, elegance, exquisiteness, fairness, glamour, grace, handsomeness, loveliness, pulchritude, seemliness, symmetry **2.** belle, charmer, cracker (*Sl.*), goddess, good-looker, lovely (*Sl.*), stunner (*Inf.*), Venus **3.** advantage, asset, attraction, benefit, blessing, boon, excellence, feature, good thing

beaver away exert oneself, graft (*Inf.*), hammer away, peg away, persevere, persist, plug away (*Inf.*), slog, work

becalmed motionless, settled, still, stranded, stuck

because as, by reason of, in that, on account of, owing to, since, thanks to

beckon 1. bid, gesticulate, gesture, motion, nod, signal, summon, wave at **2.** allure, attract, call, coax, draw, entice, invite, lure, pull, tempt

becloud bedim, befog, complicate, confuse, darken, muddle, obfuscate, obscure, overcast, screen, veil

gesture. —**'beckoner** n.

become (bɪ'kʌm) vb. **-coming, -came, -come.** (mainly intr.) **1.** (copula) to come to be; develop or grow into: he became a monster. **2.** (foll. by of; usually used in a question) to happen (to): what became of him? **3.** (tr.) to suit: that dress becomes you. **4.** (tr.) to be appropriate; to befit: it ill becomes you to complain.

becoming (bɪ'kʌmɪŋ) adj. suitable; appropriate. —**be'comingly** adv. —**be'comingness** n.

becquerel (ˌbɛkə'rɛl) n. the SI unit of activity of a radioactive source.

bed (bɛd) n. **1.** a piece of furniture on which to sleep. **2.** the mattress and bedclothes: an unmade bed. **3.** sleep or rest: time for bed. **4.** any place in which a person or animal sleeps or rests. **5.** Inf. sexual intercourse. **6.** a plot of ground in which plants are grown. **7.** the bottom of a river, lake, or sea. **8.** a part of this used for cultivation of a plant or animal: oyster beds. **9.** any underlying structure or part. **10.** a layer of rock, esp. sedimentary rock. **11. a bed of roses.** a situation of comfort or ease. **12. go to bed. a.** (often foll. by with) to have sexual intercourse (with). **b.** Journalism, printing. (of a newspaper, etc.) to go to press; start printing. **13. put to bed.** Journalism. to finalize work on (a newspaper, etc.) so that it is ready to go to press. **14. take to one's bed.** to remain in bed, esp. because of illness. ~vb. **bedding, bedded. 15.** (usually foll. by down) to go to or put into a place to sleep or rest. **16.** (tr.) to have sexual intercourse with. **17.** (tr.) to place firmly into position; embed. **18.** Geol. to form or be arranged in a distinct layer; stratify. **19.** (tr.; often foll. by out) to plant in a bed of soil.

B.Ed. abbrev. for Bachelor of Education.

bed and breakfast n. Chiefly Brit. (in a hotel, boarding house, etc.) overnight accommodation and breakfast.

bedaub (bɪ'dɔːb) vb. (tr.) **1.** to smear all over with something thick, sticky, or dirty. **2.** to ornament in a gaudy or vulgar fashion.

bedbug ('bɛd,bʌg) n. any of several bloodsucking wingless insects of temperate regions, infesting dirty houses.

bedclothes ('bɛd,kləʊðz) pl. n. sheets, blankets, and other coverings of a bed.

bedding ('bɛdɪŋ) n. **1.** bedclothes, sometimes considered with a mattress. **2.** litter, such as straw, for animals. **3.** a foundation, such as mortar under a brick. **4.** the stratification of rocks.

bedding plant n. an immature plant that may be planted out in a garden bed.

bedeck (bɪ'dɛk) vb. (tr.) to cover with decorations; adorn.

bedevil (bɪ'dɛvəl) vb. **-illing, -illed** or U.S. **-iling, -iled.** (tr.) **1.** to harass or torment. **2.** to throw into confusion. **3.** to possess, as with a devil. —**be'devilment** n.

bedew (bɪ'djuː) vb. (tr.) to wet as with dew.

bedfellow ('bɛd,fɛləʊ) n. **1.** a person with whom one shares a bed. **2.** a temporary ally or associate.

bedizen (bɪ'daɪzən, -'dɪzən) vb. (tr.) Arch. to dress or decorate gaudily or tastelessly. —**be'dizenment** n.

bedjacket n. a woman's short upper garment worn over a nightgown when sitting up in bed.

bedlam ('bɛdləm) n. **1.** a noisy confused situation. **2.** Arch. a madhouse.

bed linen n. sheets, pillowcases, etc. for a bed.

Bedouin or **Beduin** ('bɛduɪn) n. **1.** (pl. **-ins** or **-in**) a nomadic Arab tribesman of the deserts of Arabia, Jordan, and Syria. **2.** a wanderer. ~adj. **3.** of or relating to the Bedouins. **4.** wandering.

bedpan ('bɛd,pæn) n. a vessel used by a bedridden patient to collect his faeces and urine.

bedraggle (bɪ'drægəl) vb. (tr.) to make (hair, clothing, etc.) limp, untidy, or dirty, as with rain or mud. —**be'draggled** adj.

bedridden ('bɛd,rɪdən) adj. confined to bed because of illness, esp. for a long or indefinite period.

bedrock ('bɛd,rɒk) n. **1.** the solid rock beneath the surface soil, etc. **2.** basic principles or facts. **3.** the lowest point, level, or layer.

bedroom ('bɛd,ruːm, -,rʊm) n. **1.** a room used for sleeping. **2.** (modifier) containing references to sex: a bedroom comedy.

Beds. abbrev. for Bedfordshire.

bedside ('bɛd,saɪd) n. **a.** the space beside a bed, esp. a sickbed. **b.** (as modifier): a bedside lamp.

bedsitter ('bɛd'sɪtə) n. a furnished sitting room containing sleeping accommodation. Also called: **bedsitting room, bedsit.**

bedsore ('bɛd,sɔː) n. a chronic ulcer on the skin of a bedridden person, caused by prolonged pressure.

bedspread ('bɛd,sprɛd) n. a top cover on a bed.

bedstead ('bɛd,stɛd, -stɪd) n. the framework of a bed.

bedstraw ('bɛd,strɔː) n. any of numerous plants which have small white or yellow flowers and prickly or hairy fruits: formerly used as straw for beds.

bedwetting ('bɛd,wɛtɪŋ) n. the act of urinating in bed.

bee[1] (biː) n. **1.** any of various four-winged insects that collect nectar and pollen and make honey and wax. **2. busy bee.** a person who is industrious or has many things to do. **3. have a bee in one's bonnet.** to be obsessed with an idea.

bee[2] (biː) n. Chiefly U.S. a social gathering for a specific purpose, as to carry out a communal task: quilting bee.

Beeb (biːb) n. **the.** an informal name for the **B.B.C.**

beebread ('biː,brɛd) n. a mixture of pollen and nectar prepared by worker bees and fed to the larvae. Also called: **ambrosia.**

beech (biːtʃ) n. **1.** a European tree, having smooth greyish bark. **2.** a similar tree of temperate Australasia and South America. **3.** the hard wood of any of these trees. **4. copper beech.** a cultivated variety of European beech that has reddish leaves. —**'beechen** or **'beechy** adj.

beechnut ('biːtʃ,nʌt) n. the small brown triangular edible nut of the beech tree, collectively, often termed **beech mast.**

beef (biːf) n. **1.** the flesh of various bovine animals, esp. the cow, when killed for eating. **2.** (pl. **beeves** (biːvz)) an adult ox, etc., reared for its meat. **3.** Inf. human flesh, esp. when muscular. **4.** (pl. **beefs**) Sl. a complaint. ~vb. **5.** (intr.) Sl. to complain, esp. repeatedly. **6.** (tr.; often foll. by up) Sl. to strengthen; reinforce.

beefburger ('biːf,bɜːgə) n. a flat fried cake of minced beef; hamburger.

beefcake ('biːf,keɪk) n. Sl. men displayed for their muscular bodies, esp. in photographs.

beefeater ('biːf,iːtə) n. a yeoman warder of the Tower of London.

beef tea n. a drink made by boiling pieces of lean beef.

beefy ('biːfɪ) adj. **beefier, beefiest. 1.** like beef. **2.** Inf.

THESAURUS

become 1. alter to, be transformed into, change into, develop into, evolve into, grow into, mature into, metamorphose into, ripen into **2.** embellish, enhance, fit, flatter, grace, harmonize, ornament, set off, suit

becoming 1. attractive, comely, enhancing, flattering, graceful, neat, pretty, tasteful **2.** appropriate, befitting, comme il faut, compatible, congruous, decent, decorous, fit, fitting, in keeping, meet (Archaic), proper, seemly, suitable, worthy

bed n. **1.** bedstead, berth, bunk, cot, couch, divan, pallet **2.** area, border, garden, patch, plot, row, strip **3.** base, bottom, foundation, groundwork, substratum ~v. **4.** base, embed, establish, fix, found, implant, insert, plant, settle, set up

bedaub besmear, smear, smirch, soil, spatter, splash, stain

bedazzle amaze, astound, bewilder, blind, captivate, confuse, daze, dazzle, dumbfound, enchant, overwhelm, stagger, stun

bedclothes bedding, bed linen, blankets, coverlets, covers, eiderdowns, pillowcases, pillows, quilts, sheets

bed down lie, retire, settle down, sleep, turn in (Inf.)

bedeck adorn, array, bedight (Archaic), bedizen (Archaic), decorate, embellish, festoon, garnish, ornament, trim

bedevil afflict, annoy, confound, distress, fret, frustrate, harass, irk, irritate, pester, plague, torment, torture, trouble, vex, worry

bedlam chaos, clamour, commotion, confusion, furore, hubbub, madhouse (Inf.), noise, pandemonium, tumult, turmoil, uproar

bedraggled dirty, dishevelled, disordered, drenched, dripping, messy, muddied, muddy, sodden, soiled, stained, sullied, unkempt, untidy

bedridden confined, confined to bed, flat on one's back, incapacitated, laid up (Inf.)

bedrock 1. bed, bottom, foundation, nadir, rock bottom, substratum, substructure **2.** basics, basis, core, essentials, fundamentals, roots

beef 1. Inf. brawn, flesh, heftiness, muscle, physique, robustness, sinew, strength **2.** Sl. complaint, criticism, dispute, grievance, gripe (Inf.), grouse, grumble, objection, protestation

beefy Inf. **1.** brawny, bulky, burly, hulking, muscular, stalwart, stocky, strapping, sturdy **2.** chubby, corpulent, fat, fleshy, heavy, obese, overweight, paunchy, plump, podgy, portly, pudgy, rotund

muscular; brawny. —'**beefiness** n.

beehive ('biː,haɪv) n. 1. a man-made receptacle used to house a swarm of bees. 2. a dome-shaped structure. 3. a place where busy people are assembled. 4. **The Beehive.** the dome-shaped building which houses Parliament in Wellington, New Zealand.

beekeeper ('biː,kiːpə) n. a person who keeps bees for their honey. —'**bee,keeping** n.

beeline ('biː,laɪn) n. the most direct route between two places (esp. in **make a beeline for**).

Beelzebub (bɪ'elzɪ,bʌb) n. Satan or any devil.

bee moth n. any of various moths whose larvae live in the nests of bees or wasps, feeding on nest materials and host larvae.

been (biːn, bɪn) vb. the past participle of **be**.

beep (biːp) n. 1. a short high-pitched sound, as made by a car horn, or by electronic apparatus. ~vb. 2. to make or cause to make such a noise. —'**beeper** n.

beer (bɪə) n. 1. an alcoholic drink brewed from malt, sugar, hops, and water. 2. a slightly fermented drink made from the roots or leaves of certain plants: *ginger beer*. 3. (*modifier*) relating to beer: *beer glass*. 4. (*modifier*) in which beer is drunk, esp. (of licensed premises) having a licence to sell beer but not spirits: *beer house; beer garden*.

beer and skittles n. *Inf.* enjoyment or pleasure.

beer parlour n. *Canad.* a licensed place in which beer is sold to the public.

beery ('bɪərɪ) adj. **beerier**, **beeriest**. 1. smelling or tasting of beer. 2. given to drinking beer. —'**beerily** adv. —'**beeriness** n.

beestings, biestings or *U.S.* **beastings** ('biːstɪŋz) n. (*functioning as sing.*) the first milk secreted by a cow or similar animal after giving birth; colostrum.

beeswax ('biːz,wæks) n. 1. a wax secreted by honeybees for constructing honeycombs. 2. this wax after refining, used in polishes, etc.

beeswing ('biːz,wɪŋ) n. a light filmy crust of tartar that forms in some wines after long keeping in the bottle.

beet (biːt) n. 1. a plant of a genus widely cultivated in such varieties as the sugar beet, mangel-wurzel, and beetroot. 2. the leaves of any of several varieties of this plant, cooked and eaten as a vegetable. 3. **red beet.** the U.S. name for **beetroot**.

beetle[1] ('biːt°l) n. 1. an insect having biting mouthparts and forewings modified to form shell-like protective casings. 2. a game in which the players draw or assemble a beetle-shaped form. ~vb. (*intr.; foll. by along, off,* etc.) 3. *Inf.* to scuttle or scurry; hurry.

beetle[2] ('biːt°l) n. 1. a heavy hand tool for pounding or beating. 2. a machine used to finish cloth by stamping it with wooden hammers.

beetle[3] ('biːt°l) vb. 1. (*intr.*) to overhang; jut. ~adj. 2. overhanging; prominent.

beetle-browed adj. having bushy or overhanging eyebrows.

beetroot ('biːt,ruːt) n. a variety of the beet plant that has a bulbous dark red root that may be eaten as a vegetable, in salads, or pickled.

beet sugar n. the sucrose obtained from sugar beet,

identical in composition to cane sugar.

befall (bɪ'fɔːl) vb. **-falling, -fell, -fallen.** *Arch.* or *literary.* 1. (*intr.*) to take place. 2. (*tr.*) to happen to. 3. (*intr.; usually foll. by to*) to be due, as by right.

befit (bɪ'fɪt) vb. **-fitting, -fitted.** (*tr.*) to be appropriate to or suitable for. —**be'fitting** adj. —**be'fittingly** adv.

before (bɪ'fɔː) conj. (*subordinating*) 1. earlier than the time when. 2. rather than: *he'll resign before he agrees to it.* ~prep. 3. preceding in space or time; in front of; ahead of: *standing before the altar.* 4. in the presence of: *to be brought before a judge.* 5. in preference to: *to put friendship before money.* ~adv. 6. at an earlier time; previously; beforehand; in front.

beforehand (bɪ'fɔː,hænd) adj. (*postpositive*), adv. early; in advance; in anticipation.

befoul (bɪ'faʊl) vb. (*tr.*) to make dirty or foul.

befriend (bɪ'frɛnd) vb. (*tr.*) to be a friend to; assist; favour.

befuddle (bɪ'fʌd°l) vb. (*tr.*) 1. to confuse. 2. to make stupid with drink. —**be'fuddlement** n.

beg (bɛg) vb. **begging, begged.** 1. (when *intr.*, often foll. by *for*) to solicit (for money, food, etc.), esp. in the street. 2. to ask formally, humbly, or earnestly: *I beg forgiveness; I beg to differ.* 3. (*intr.*) (of a dog) to sit up with forepaws raised expectantly. 4. **beg the question. a.** to evade the issue. **b.** to assume the thing under examination as proved. 5. **go begging.** to be unwanted or unused.

began (bɪ'gæn) vb. the past tense of **begin**.

beget (bɪ'gɛt) vb. **-getting, -got** or **-gat; -gotten** or **-got.** (*tr.*) 1. to father. 2. to cause or create. —**be'getter** n.

beggar ('bɛgə) n. 1. a person who begs, esp. one who lives by begging. 2. a person who has no money or resources; pauper. 3. *Chiefly Brit.* a fellow: *lucky beggar!* ~vb. (*tr.*) 4. to be beyond the resources of (esp. in **beggar description**). 5. to impoverish. —'**beggardom** n.

begin (bɪ'gɪn) vb. **-ginning, -gan, -gun.** 1. to start or cause to start (something or to do something). 2. to bring or come into being; arise or originate. 3. to start to say or speak. 4. (*with a negative*) to have the least capacity (to do something): *he couldn't begin to compete.* 5. **to begin with.** in the first place. —**be'ginner** n.

beginner's luck n. the exceptionally good luck that a novice is supposed to enjoy.

beginning (bɪ'gɪnɪŋ) n. 1. a start; commencement. 2. (*often pl.*) a first or early part or stage. 3. the place where or time when something starts. 4. an origin; source.

begone (bɪ'gɒn) interj. go away!

begonia (bɪ'gəʊnjə) n. a plant of warm and tropical regions, having ornamental leaves and waxy flowers.

begorra (bɪ'gɒrə) interj. an emphatic exclamation, regarded as characteristic of Irishmen.

begot (bɪ'gɒt) vb. a past tense or past participle of **beget**.

begotten (bɪ'gɒt°n) vb. a past participle of **beget**.

begrudge (bɪ'grʌdʒ) vb. (*tr.*) 1. to give, admit, or allow unwillingly or with a bad grace. 2. to envy (someone) the possession of (something). —**be'grudgingly** adv.

THESAURUS

beetle, beetling adj. jutting, leaning over, overhanging, pendent, projecting, protruding, sticking out, swelling over

befall bechance, betide, chance, come to pass, ensue, fall, follow, happen, materialize, occur, supervene, take place, transpire (*Inf.*)

befitting appropriate, becoming, fit, fitting, meet (*Archaic*), proper, right, seemly, suitable

before 1. adv. ahead, earlier, formerly, in advance, in front, previously, sooner 2. prep. earlier than, in advance of, in front of, in the presence of, prior to

beforehand ahead of time, already, before, before now, earlier, in advance, in anticipation, previously, sooner

befriend advise, aid, assist, back, benefit, encourage, favour, help, patronize, side with, stand by, succour, support, sustain, uphold, welcome

befuddle baffle, bewilder, confuse, daze, disorient, intoxicate, muddle, puzzle, stupefy

befuddled confused, dazed, fuddled, groggy (*Inf.*), inebriated, intoxicated, muddled, woozy (*Inf.*)

beg 1. beseech, crave, desire, entreat, implore, importune, petition, plead, pray, request, solicit, supplicate 2. cadge, call for alms, scrounge, seek charity, solicit charity, sponge on 3. *As in* **beg the question** avoid, dodge, duck (*Inf.*), equivocate, eschew, evade, fend off, hedge, parry, shirk, shun, sidestep

beget 1. breed, father, generate, get, procreate, propagate, sire 2. bring, bring about, cause, create, effect, engender, give rise to, occasion, produce, result in

beggar n. 1. cadger, mendicant, scrounger (*Inf.*), sponger (*Inf.*), supplicant, tramp, vagrant 2. bankrupt, down-and-out, pauper, starveling ~v. 3. *As in* **beggar description** baffle, challenge, defy, surpass

beggarly abject, base, contemptible, despicable, destitute, impoverished, inadequate,

indigent, low, meagre, mean, miserly, needy, niggardly, pitiful, poor, poverty-stricken, stingy, vile, wretched

beggary bankruptcy, destitution, indigence, need, pauperism, poverty, vagrancy, wretchedness

begin 1. commence, embark on, inaugurate, initiate, instigate, institute, prepare, set about, set on foot, start 2. appear, arise, be born, come into being, come into existence, commence, crop up (*Inf.*), dawn, emerge, happen, originate, spring, start

beginner amateur, apprentice, fledgling, freshman, greenhorn (*Inf.*), initiate, learner, neophyte, novice, recruit, starter, student, tenderfoot, trainee, tyro

beginning 1. birth, commencement, inauguration, inception, initiation, onset, opening, origin, outset, preface, prelude, rise, rudiments, source, start, starting point 2. embryo, fountainhead, germ, root, seed

begrime besmirch, blacken, dirty, mud-

beguile (bɪˈgaɪl) vb. **-guiling, -guiled.** (tr.) **1.** to charm; fascinate. **2.** to delude; influence by slyness. **3.** (often foll. by *of* or *out of*) to cheat (someone) of. **4.** to pass pleasantly; while away. —**be'guiling** adj.

beguine (bɪˈgiːn) n. **1.** a dance of South American origin in bolero rhythm. **2.** a piece of music in the rhythm of this dance.

begum (ˈbeɪgəm) n. (esp. in India) a Muslim woman of high rank.

begun (bɪˈgʌn) vb. the past participle of **begin**.

behalf (bɪˈhɑːf) n. interest, part, benefit, or respect (only in **on (someone's) behalf, on** or U.S. **in behalf of, in this** (or that) **behalf**).

behave (bɪˈheɪv) vb. **1.** (intr.) to act or function in a specified or usual way. **2.** to conduct (oneself) in a specified way: *he behaved badly.* **3.** to conduct (oneself) properly or as desired.

behaviour or U.S. **behavior** (bɪˈheɪvjə) n. **1.** manner of behaving. **2. on one's best behaviour.** behaving with careful good manners. **3.** *Psychol.* the response of an organism to a stimulus. **4.** the reaction or functioning of a machine, etc., under normal or specified circumstances. —**be'havioural** or U.S. **be'havioral** adj.

behavioural science n. the scientific study of the behaviour of organisms.

behaviourism or U.S. **behaviorism** (bɪˈheɪvjə‚rɪzəm) n. a school of psychology that regards objective observable aspects of the behaviour of organisms as the only valid subject for study. —**be'haviourist** or U.S. **be'haviorist** adj., n.

behaviour therapy n. any of various means of treating psychological disorders, such as aversion therapy, that depend on the patient systematically learning new behaviour.

behead (bɪˈhɛd) vb. (tr.) to remove the head from.

beheld (bɪˈhɛld) vb. the past tense or past participle of **behold**.

behemoth (bɪˈhiːmɒθ) n. **1.** *Bible.* a gigantic beast described in Job 40:15. **2.** a huge or monstrous person or thing.

behest (bɪˈhɛst) n. an order or earnest request.

behind (bɪˈhaɪnd) prep. **1.** in or to a position further back than. **2.** in the past in relation to: *I've got the exams behind me now.* **3.** late according to: *running behind schedule.* **4.** concerning the circumstances surrounding: *the reasons behind his departure.* **5.** supporting: *I'm right behind you in your application.* ~adv. **6.** in or to a position further back; following. **7.** remaining after someone's departure: *he left his books behind.* **8.** in debt; in arrears: *to fall behind with payments.* ~adj. **9.** (postpositive) in a position further back. ~n. **10.** *Inf.* the buttocks.

behindhand (bɪˈhaɪnd‚hænd) adj. (postpositive), adv. **1.** remiss in fulfilling an obligation. **2.** in arrears. **3.** backward. **4.** late.

behold (bɪˈhəʊld) vb. **-holding, -held.** (often imperative) *Arch.* or *literary.* to look (at); observe. —**be'holder** n.

beholden (bɪˈhəʊldən) adj. indebted; obliged.

behove (bɪˈhəʊv) vb. (tr.; impersonal) *Arch.* to be necessary or fitting for: *it behoves me to arrest you.*

beige (beɪʒ) n. **1. a.** a very light brown, sometimes with a yellowish tinge. **b.** (as adj.): *beige gloves.* **2.** a fabric made of undyed or unbleached wool.

being (ˈbiːɪŋ) n. **1.** the state or fact of existing; existence. **2.** essential nature; self. **3.** something that exists or is thought to exist: *a being from outer space.* **4.** a person; human being.

bejewel (bɪˈdʒuːəl) vb. **-elling, -elled** or U.S. **-eling, -eled.** (tr.) to decorate as with jewels.

bel (bɛl) n. a unit for comparing two power levels, equal to the logarithm to the base ten of the ratio of the two powers.

belabour or U.S. **belabor** (bɪˈleɪbə) vb. (tr.) **1.** to beat severely; thrash. **2.** to attack verbally.

belated (bɪˈleɪtɪd) adj. late or too late: *belated greetings.* —**be'latedly** adv. —**be'latedness** n.

belay (bɪˈleɪ) vb. **-laying, -layed. 1.** *Naut.* to secure (a line) to a pin, cleat, or bitt. **2.** (usually imperative) *Naut.* to stop. **3.** *Mountaineering.* to turn (a rope) round an object, etc., to secure (a climber). ~n. (ˈbɪleɪ). **4.** *Mountaineering.* a turn of a rope round an object to secure it.

belch (bɛltʃ) vb. **1.** (usually intr.) to expel wind from the stomach noisily through the mouth. **2.** to expel or be expelled forcefully from inside: *smoke belching from factory chimneys.* ~n. **3.** an act of belching.

beldam or **beldame** (ˈbɛldəm) n. *Arch.* an old woman.

beleaguer (bɪˈliːgə) vb. (tr.) **1.** to lay siege to. **2.** to harass.

belfry (ˈbɛlfrɪ) n., pl. **-fries. 1.** the part of a tower or steeple in which bells are hung. **2.** a tower or steeple.

Belial (ˈbiːlɪəl) n. the devil or Satan.

belie (bɪˈlaɪ) vb. **-lying, -lied.** (tr.) **1.** to show to be untrue; contradict. **2.** to misrepresent; disguise the nature of. **3.** to fail to justify; disappoint.

belief (bɪˈliːf) n. **1.** a principle, etc., accepted as true or real, esp. without proof. **2.** opinion; conviction. **3.** religious faith. **4.** trust or confidence, as in a person's abilities, etc.

believe (bɪˈliːv) vb. **1.** (tr.; may take a clause as object) to accept (a statement or opinion) as true or real: *I believe God exists.* **2.** (tr.) to accept the statement or opinion of (a person) as true. **3.** (intr.; foll. by in) to be convinced of the truth or existence (of): *to believe in fairies.* **4.** (intr.) to have religious faith. **5.** (when tr., takes a clause as object) to think, assume, or suppose. **6.** (tr.) to think that someone is able to do (a particular action): *I wouldn't have believed it of him.* —**be'lievable** adj. —**be'liever** n.

THESAURUS

dy, smear, smirch, soil, spatter, stain, sully, tarnish

begrudge be jealous, be reluctant, be stingy, envy, grudge, resent

beguile 1. befool, cheat, deceive, delude, dupe, fool, hoodwink, impose on, mislead, trick **2.** amuse, charm, cheer, delight, distract, divert, engross, entertain, occupy, solace

beguiling alluring, attractive, bewitching, captivating, charming, diverting, enchanting, entertaining, enthralling, interesting, intriguing

behalf account, advantage, benefit, defence, good, interest, part, profit, sake, side, support

behave 1. act, function, operate, perform, run, work **2.** act correctly, conduct oneself properly, mind one's manners

behaviour 1. actions, bearing, carriage, comportment, conduct, demeanour, deportment, manner, manners, ways **2.** action, functioning, operation, performance

behest bidding, charge, command, commandment, decree, dictate, direction, expressed desire, injunction, instruction, mandate, order, precept, wish

behind prep. **1.** after, at the back of, at the rear of, following, later than **2.** at the bottom of, causing, initiating, instigating, responsible for **3.** backing, for, in agreement, on the side of, supporting ~adv. **4.** after, afterwards, following, in the wake (of), next, subsequently **5.** behindhand, in arrears, in debt, overdue ~n. **6.** bottom, buttocks, posterior, rump, seat

behindhand backward, behind time, dilatory, late, remiss, slow, tardy

behold 1. v. consider, contemplate, discern, eye, look at, observe, perceive, regard, scan, survey, view, watch, witness **2.** interj. lo, look, mark, observe, see, watch

beholden bound, grateful, indebted, obligated, obliged, owing, under obligation

beige biscuit, buff, café au lait, camel, cinnamon, coffee, cream, ecru, fawn, khaki, mushroom, neutral, oatmeal, sand, tan

being 1. actuality, animation, existence, life, living, reality **2.** entity, essence, nature, soul, spirit, substance **3.** animal, beast, body, creature, human being, individual, living thing, mortal, thing

belabour 1. batter, beat, flog, lambaste, thrash, whip **2.** attack, berate, castigate, censure, criticize, flay, lay into

belated behindhand, behind time, delayed, late, overdue, tardy

belch 1. burp (Inf.), eruct, eructate, hiccup **2.** discharge, disgorge, emit, erupt, give off, gush, spew forth, vent, vomit

beleaguered badgered, beset, besieged, bothered, harassed, nagged, persecuted, plagued, put upon, set upon, vexed

belie 1. confute, contradict, deny, disprove, gainsay, give the lie to, negate, repudiate **2.** conceal, deceive, disguise, falsify, gloss over, mislead, misrepresent

belief 1. admission, assent, assurance, confidence, conviction, credit, feeling, impression, judgment, notion, opinion, persuasion, presumption, reliance, theory, trust, view **2.** credence, credo, creed, doctrine, dogma, faith, ideology, principles, tenet

believable acceptable, authentic, credible, creditable, imaginable, likely, plausible, possible, probable, reliable, trustworthy

believe 1. accept, be certain of, be convinced of, count on, credit, depend on, have faith in, hold, place confidence in, presume true, rely on, swear by, trust **2.** assume, conjecture, consider, gather, guess, imagine,

Belisha beacon (bə'liːʃə) n. Brit. a flashing orange globe mounted on a post, indicating a pedestrian crossing on a road.

belittle (bɪ'lɪtᵊl) vb. (tr.) **1.** to consider or speak of (something) as less valuable or important than it really is; disparage. **2.** to make small; dwarf. —**be'littlement** n. —**be'littler** n.

bell¹ (bɛl) n. **1.** a hollow, usually metal, cup-shaped instrument that emits a ringing sound when struck. **2.** the sound made by such an instrument, as for marking the beginning or end of a period of time. **3.** an electrical device that rings or buzzes as a signal. **4.** something shaped like a bell, as the tube of certain musical wind instruments, or the corolla of certain flowers. **5.** Naut. a signal rung on a ship's bell to count the number of half-hour intervals during each of six four-hour watches reckoned from midnight. **6. ring a bell.** to sound familiar; recall something previously experienced. **7. sound as a bell.** in perfect condition. **8. bell, book, and candle.** instruments used formerly in excommunications. ~vb. **9.** to be or cause to be shaped like a bell. **10.** (tr.) to attach a bell or bells to.

bell² (bɛl) n. **1.** a bellowing or baying cry, esp. that of a stag in rut. ~vb. **2.** to utter (such a cry).

belladonna (ˌbɛlə'dɒnə) n. **1.** either of two alkaloid drugs obtained from the leaves and roots of the deadly nightshade. **2.** another name for **deadly nightshade.**

bell-bottoms pl. n. trousers that flare from the knee. —'**bell-ˌbottomed** adj.

belle (bɛl) n. **1.** a beautiful woman. **2.** the most attractive woman at a function, etc. (esp. in **belle of the ball**).

belles-lettres (French bɛl'lɛtr) n. (functioning as sing.) literary works, esp. essays and poetry, valued for their aesthetic content. —**bel'letrist** n.

bellicose ('bɛlɪˌkəʊs, -ˌkəʊz) adj. warlike; aggressive; ready to fight. —**bellicosity** (ˌbɛlɪ'kɒsɪtɪ) n.

belligerence (bɪ'lɪdʒərəns) n. the act or quality of being belligerent or warlike; aggressiveness.

belligerent (bɪ'lɪdʒərənt) adj. **1.** marked by readiness to fight or argue; aggressive. **2.** relating to or engaged in a war. ~n. **3.** a person or country engaged in war.

bell jar n. a bell-shaped glass cover to protect flower arrangements, etc. or to cover apparatus in experiments. Also: **bell glass.**

bell metal n. an alloy of copper and tin, with some zinc and lead, used in casting bells.

bellow ('bɛləʊ) vb. **1.** (intr.) to make a loud deep cry like that of a bull; roar. **2.** to shout (something) unrestrainedly, as in anger or pain. ~n. **3.** the characteristic noise of a bull. **4.** a loud deep sound, as of pain or anger.

bellows ('bɛləʊz) n. (functioning as sing. or pl.) **1.** Also: **pair of bellows.** an instrument consisting of an air chamber with flexible sides that is used to create a stream of air, as for producing a draught for a fire or for sounding organ pipes. **2.** a flexible corrugated part, as that connecting the lens system of some cameras to the body.

bell pull n. a handle, rope, or cord pulled to operate a doorbell or servant's bell.

bell push n. a button pressed to operate an electric bell.

bell-ringer n. a person who rings church bells or musical handbells. —'**bell-ˌringing** n.

bell tent n. a cone-shaped tent having a single central supporting pole.

bellwether ('bɛlˌwɛðə) n. **1.** a sheep that leads the herd, often bearing a bell. **2.** a leader, esp. one followed blindly.

belly ('bɛlɪ) n., pl. **-lies. 1.** the lower or front part of the body of a vertebrate, containing the intestines and other organs; abdomen. **2.** the stomach, esp. when regarded as the seat of gluttony. **3.** a part that bulges deeply: the belly of a sail. **4.** the inside or interior cavity of something. **5.** the front, lower, or inner part of something. **6.** the surface of a stringed musical instrument over which the strings are stretched. **7.** Austral. & N.Z. **a.** the wool from a sheep's belly. **b.** (as modifier): belly wool. **8.** an archaic word for **womb** (sense 4). ~vb. **-lying, -lied. 9.** to swell out or cause to swell out; bulge.

belly ache n. **1.** an informal term for **stomachache.** ~vb. **bellyache. 2.** (intr.) Sl. to complain repeatedly. —'**belly,acher** n.

bellybutton ('bɛlɪˌbʌtᵊn) n. an informal name for the navel. Also called: **tummy button.**

belly dance n. **1.** a sensuous dance of Middle Eastern origin, performed by women, with undulating movements of the abdomen. ~vb. **belly-dance. 2.** (intr.) to dance thus. —**belly dancer** n.

belly flop n. **1.** a dive into water in which the body lands horizontally. ~vb. **belly-flop, -flopping, -flopped. 2.** (intr.) to perform a belly flop.

bellyful ('bɛlɪˌfʊl) n. **1.** as much as one wants or can eat. **2.** Sl. more than one can tolerate.

belly landing n. Inf. the landing of an aircraft on its fuselage without use of its landing gear.

belly laugh n. Inf. a loud deep hearty laugh.

belong (bɪ'lɒŋ) vb. (intr.) **1.** (foll. by to) to be the property or possession (of). **2.** (foll. by to) to be a member (of a club, etc.). **3.** (foll. by to, under, with, etc.) to be classified (with): this plant belongs to the daisy family. **4.** (foll. by to) to be a part or adjunct (of). **5.** to have a proper or usual place. **6.** Inf. to be acceptable, esp. socially.

belonging (bɪ'lɒŋɪŋ) n. secure relationship; affinity (esp. in **a sense of belonging**).

belongings (bɪ'lɒŋɪŋz) pl. n. (sometimes sing.) the things that a person owns or has with him.

beloved (bɪ'lʌvɪd, -'lʌvd) adj. **1.** dearly loved. ~n. **2.** a person who is dearly loved.

below (bɪ'ləʊ) prep. **1.** at or to a position lower than; under. **2.** less than. **3.** south of. **4.** downstream of. **5.** unworthy of; beneath. ~adv. **6.** at or to a lower position. **7.** at a later place (in something written). **8.** Arch. on earth or in hell.

belt (bɛlt) n. **1.** a band of cloth, leather, etc., worn, usually around the waist, to support clothing, carry weapons, etc. or as decoration. **2.** a narrow band, circle, or stripe, as of colour. **3.** an area where a specific thing is found; zone: a belt of high pressure. **4.** See **seat belt. 5.** a band of flexible material between rotating shafts or pulleys to transfer motion or transmit goods: a fan belt; a conveyer belt. **6.** Inf. a sharp blow. **7. below the belt. a.** Boxing. below the waist. **b.** Inf. in an unscrupulous or cowardly way. **8. tighten one's belt.** to take measures to reduce expenditure. **9. under one's belt. a.** in one's stomach. **b.** as part of one's experience: he had a degree under his belt. ~vb. **10.** (tr.) to fasten or attach with or as if with a belt. **11.** (tr.) to hit with a belt. **12.** (tr.) Sl. to give a sharp blow; punch. **13.** (intr.; often foll. by along) Sl. to move very fast, esp. in a car. **14.** (tr.) Rare. to encircle. —'**belted** adj.

Beltane ('bɛlteɪn, -tən) n. an ancient Celtic festival with a sacrificial bonfire on May Day.

belt out vb. (tr., adv.) Inf. to sing or emit sound loudly.

THESAURUS

judge, maintain, postulate, presume, reckon, speculate, suppose, think

believer adherent, convert, devotee, disciple, follower, proselyte, supporter, upholder, zealot

belittle decry, deprecate, depreciate, deride, derogate, detract, diminish, disparage, downgrade, minimize, scoff at, scorn, sneer at, underestimate, underrate, undervalue

bellow bawl, call, clamour, cry, howl, roar, scream, shout, shriek, yell

belly 1. n. abdomen, breadbasket (Sl.), corporation (Inf.), gut, insides (Inf.), paunch, potbelly, stomach, tummy, vitals **2.** v. billow, bulge, fill, spread, swell, swell out

belong 1. With **to** be at the disposal of, be held by, be owned by, be the property of **2.** With **to** be affiliated to, be allied to, be a member of, be associated with, be included in **3.** attach to, be connected with, be fitting, be part of, fit, go with, have as a proper place, pertain to, relate to

belonging acceptance, affinity, association, attachment, fellowship, inclusion, kinship, loyalty, rapport, relationship

belongings accoutrements, chattels, effects, gear, goods, paraphernalia, personal property, possessions, stuff, things

beloved admired, adored, cherished, darling, dear, dearest, loved, pet, precious,

prized, revered, sweet, treasured, worshipped

below adv. **1.** beneath, down, lower, under, underneath ~prep. **2.** inferior, lesser, lesser than, subject, subordinate, unworthy of **3. below par** below average, imperfect, inferior, off colour, off form, poor, second-rate, unfit

belt 1. band, cincture, cummerbund, girdle, girth, sash, waistband **2.** Geog. area, district, layer, region, stretch, strip, tract, zone **3. below the belt** cowardly, foul, not playing the game (Inf.), unfair, unjust, unscrupulous, unsporting, unsportsmanlike

belt up *vb.* (*adv.*) **1.** *Sl.* to stop talking: often imperative. **2.** to fasten with a belt.

beluga (bɪˈluːgə) *n.* **1.** a large white sturgeon of the Black and Caspian Seas: a source of caviar and isinglass. **2.** another name for **white whale.**

belvedere (ˈbɛlvɪˌdɪə, ˌbɛlvɪˈdɪə) *n.* a building, such as a summerhouse, sited to command a fine view.

B.E.M. *abbrev. for* British Empire Medal.

bemoan (bɪˈməʊn) *vb.* to mourn; lament (esp. in **bemoan one's fate**).

bemuse (bɪˈmjuːz) *vb.* (*tr.*) to confuse; bewilder.

bemused (bɪˈmjuːzd) *adj.* preoccupied; lost in thought.

ben[1] (bɛn) *Scot.* ~*n.* **1.** an inner room in a cottage. ~*prep., adv.* **2.** in; within; inside. Cf. **but**[2].

ben[2] (bɛn) *n. Scot., Irish.* a mountain peak: *Ben Lomond.*

bench (bɛntʃ) *n.* **1.** a long seat for more than one person, usually lacking a back. **2.** a plain stout work table. **3. the bench.** (*sometimes cap.*) **a.** a judge or magistrate sitting in court. **b.** judges or magistrates collectively. **4.** a ledge in a mine or quarry from which work is carried out. **5.** a platform on which dogs, etc. are exhibited at shows. **6.** *N.Z.* a hollow formed by sheep on a hillside. ~*vb.* (*tr.*) **7.** to provide with benches. **8.** to exhibit (a dog, etc.) at a show.

bencher (ˈbɛntʃə) *n.* (*often pl.*) *Brit.* **1.** a member of the governing body of one of the Inns of Court. **2.** See **backbencher.**

bench mark *n.* **1.** a mark on a stone post or other permanent feature, used as a reference point in surveying. **2.** a criterion by which to measure something; reference point.

bend[1] (bɛnd) *vb.* **bending, bent. 1.** to form or cause to form a curve. **2.** to turn or cause to turn from a particular direction: *the road bends left.* **3.** (*intr.*; often foll. by *down*, etc.) to incline the body; stoop; bow. **4.** to submit or cause to submit: *to bend before superior force.* **5.** (*tr.*) to turn or direct (one's eyes, steps, attention, etc.). **6.** (*tr.*) *Naut.* to attach or fasten, as a sail to a boom. **7. bend the rules.** *Inf.* to ignore rules or change them to suit one's own convenience. ~*n.* **8.** a curved part. **9.** *Naut.* a knot in a line for joining it to another or to an object. **10.** the act of bending. **11. round the bend.** *Brit. sl.* mad. —ˈbendable *adj.* —ˈbendy *adj.*

bend[2] (bɛnd) *n. Heraldry.* a diagonal line traversing a shield.

bender (ˈbɛndə) *n. Inf.* a drinking bout.

bends (bɛndz) *pl. n.* **the.** a nontechnical name for **decompression sickness.**

bend sinister *n. Heraldry.* a diagonal line bisecting a shield from the top right to the bottom left, typically indicating a bastard line.

beneath (bɪˈniːθ) *prep.* **1.** below, esp. if covered, protected, or obscured by. **2.** not as great or good as would be demanded by: *beneath his dignity.* ~*adv.* **3.** below; underneath.

Benedictine *n.* **1.** (ˌbɛnɪˈdɪktiːn, -taɪn) a monk or nun who is a member of the order of Saint Benedict, founded about 540 A.D. **2.** (ˌbɛnɪˈdɪktiːn) a greenish-yellow liqueur first made at the Benedictine monastery at Fécamp in France in about 1510.

benediction (ˌbɛnɪˈdɪkʃən) *n.* **1.** an invocation of divine blessing. **2.** a Roman Catholic service in which the congregation is blessed with the sacrament. **3.** the state of being blessed.

Benedictus (ˌbɛnɪˈdɪktəs) *n.* (*sometimes not cap.*) *Christianity.* **1.** a canticle beginning *Benedictus qui venit in nomine Domini* in Latin and *Blessed is he that cometh in the name of the Lord* in English. **2.** a canticle beginning *Benedictus Dominus Deus Israel* in Latin and *Blessed be the Lord God of Israel* in English.

benefaction (ˌbɛnɪˈfækʃən) *n.* **1.** the act of doing good, esp. by giving a donation to charity. **2.** the donation or help given.

benefactor (ˈbɛnɪˌfæktə, ˌbɛnɪˈfæk-) *n.* a person who supports or helps a person, institution, etc., esp. by giving money. —ˈbene,factress *fem. n.*

benefice (ˈbɛnɪfɪs) *n.* **1.** *Christianity.* an endowed Church office yielding an income to its holder; a Church living. **2.** the property or revenue attached to such an office. —ˈbeneficed *adj.*

beneficent (bɪˈnɛfɪsənt) *adj.* charitable; generous. —beˈneficence *n.*

beneficial (ˌbɛnɪˈfɪʃəl) *adj.* **1.** (sometimes foll. by *to*) advantageous. **2.** *Law.* entitling a person to receive the profits or proceeds of property.

beneficiary (ˌbɛnɪˈfɪʃərɪ) *n., pl.* **-ciaries. 1.** a person who gains or benefits. **2.** *Law.* a person entitled to receive funds or other property under a trust, will, etc. **3.** the holder of a benefice. **4.** *N.Z.* a person who receives government assistance: *social security beneficiary.* ~*adj.* **5.** of or relating to a benefice.

benefit (ˈbɛnɪfɪt) *n.* **1.** something that improves or promotes. **2.** advantage or sake. **3.** (*sometimes pl.*) a payment or series of payments made by an institution or government to a person who is ill, unemployed, etc. **4.** a theatrical performance, sports event, etc., to raise money for a charity. ~*vb.* **-fiting, -fited** *or U.S.* **-fitting, -fitted. 5.** to do or receive good; profit.

benefit of clergy *n. Christianity.* **1.** sanction by the church: *marriage without benefit of clergy.* **2.** (in the Middle Ages) a privilege that placed the clergy outside the jurisdiction of secular courts.

benefit society *n.* a U.S. term for **friendly society.**

benevolence (bɪˈnɛvələns) *n.* **1.** inclination to do good; charity. **2.** an act of kindness. —beˈnevolent *adj.*

Bengali (bɛnˈgɔːlɪ, bɛŋ-) *n.* **1.** a member of a people living chiefly in Bangladesh (a republic in S Asia) and in West Bengal (in NE India). **2.** their language. ~*adj.* **3.** of or relating to Bengal, the Bengalis, or their language.

Bengal light (bɛnˈgɔːl, bɛŋ-) *n.* a firework or flare that burns with a bright blue light, formerly used as a signal.

benighted (bɪˈnaɪtɪd) *adj.* **1.** lacking cultural, moral, or intellectual enlightenment. **2.** *Arch.* overtaken by night. —beˈnightedness *n.*

benign (bɪˈnaɪn) *adj.* **1.** showing kindliness; genial. **2.** (of soil, climate, etc.) mild; gentle. **3.** favourable; propitious. **4.** *Pathol.* (of a tumour, etc.) not malignant. —**be-**

THESAURUS

bemoan bewail, deplore, express sorrow, grieve for, lament, moan over, mourn, regret, rue, weep for

bemuse amaze, bewilder, confuse, daze, muddle, overwhelm, perplex, puzzle, stun

bemused absent-minded, bewildered, confused, dazed, engrossed, fuddled, half-drunk, muddled, perplexed, preoccupied, stunned, stupefied, tipsy

bench 1. form, pew, seat, settle, stall **2.** board, counter, table, trestle table, workbench, worktable **3.** court, courtroom, judge, judges, judiciary, magistrate, magistrates, tribunal

bend v. **1.** bow, buckle, contort, crouch, curve, deflect, diverge, flex, incline, incurvate, lean, stoop, swerve, turn, twist, veer, warp **2.** compel, direct, influence, mould, persuade, shape, subdue, submit, sway, yield ~n. **3.** angle, arc, bow, corner, crook, curve, hook, loop, turn, twist, zigzag

beneath 1. adv. below, in a lower place, underneath **2.** prep. below, inferior to, less than, lower than, unbefitting, underneath, unworthy of

benediction beatitude, benedictus, benison, blessing, consecration, favour, grace, gratitude, invocation, orison, prayer, thankfulness, thanksgiving

benefactor angel (*Inf.*), backer, contributor, donor, helper, patron, philanthropist, promoter, sponsor, subscriber, subsidizer, supporter, well-wisher

beneficial advantageous, benign, favourable, gainful, healthful, helpful, profitable, salubrious, salutary, serviceable, useful, valuable, wholesome

beneficiary assignee, heir, inheritor, legatee, payee, receiver, recipient, successor

benefit 1. n. advantage, aid, asset, assistance, avail, betterment, blessing, boon, favour, gain, good, help, interest, profit, use **2.** v. advance, advantage, aid, ameliorate, assist, avail, better, enhance, further, improve, profit, promote, serve

benevolence altruism, charity, compassion, fellow feeling, generosity, goodness, good will, humanity, kind-heartedness, kindness, sympathy

benevolent altruistic, beneficent, benign, bounteous, bountiful, caring, charitable, compassionate, considerate, generous, humane, humanitarian, kind, kind-hearted, liberal, philanthropic, tender-hearted, warm-hearted, well-disposed

benighted backward, crude, ignorant, illiterate, primitive, uncivilized, uncultivated, unenlightened

benign 1. amiable, complaisant, friendly, generous, genial, gracious, kind, kindly, liberal, obliging, sympathetic **2.** balmy, gentle, healthful, mild, refreshing, temperate, warm, wholesome **3.** advantageous, auspicious, beneficial, encouraging, favourable, good, lucky, propitious, salutary **4.** *Medical* curable, harmless, limited, remediable, slight, superficial

'**nignly** adv.
benignant (bɪ'nɪgnənt) adj. **1.** kind; gracious. **2.** a less common word for **benign** (senses 3, 4). —**be'nignancy** n.

benignity (bɪ'nɪgnɪtɪ) n., pl. **-ties. 1.** the quality of being benign. **2.** a kind or gracious act.

benison ('bɛnɪzən, -sən) n. Arch. a blessing.

bent[1] (bɛnt) adj. **1.** not straight; curved. **2.** (foll. by on) resolved (to); determined (to). **3.** Sl. **a.** dishonest; corrupt. **b.** (of goods) stolen. **c.** crazy. **d.** sexually deviant. ~n. **4.** personal inclination or aptitude. **5.** capacity of endurance (esp. in **to the top of one's bent**).

bent[2] (bɛnt) n. any of various wiry low-growing grasses. Also called: **bentgrass.**

Benthamism ('bɛnθəmɪzəm) n. the utilitarian philosophy of Jeremy Bentham (1748-1832), English philosopher and jurist, which holds that the ultimate goal of society should be to promote the greatest happiness of the greatest number. —'**Benthamite** n., adj.

bentwood ('bɛnt,wʊd) n. **a.** wood bent in moulds after being heated by steaming, used mainly for furniture. **b.** (as modifier): a bentwood chair.

benumb (bɪ'nʌm) vb. (tr.) **1.** to make numb or powerless; deaden, as by cold. **2.** (usually passive) to stupefy (the mind, senses, will, etc.).

benzene ('bɛnziːn, bɛn'ziːn) n. a colourless flammable poisonous liquid used in the manufacture of styrene, phenol, etc., as a solvent for fats, resins, etc., and as an insecticide.

benzine ('bɛnziːn, bɛn'ziːn) or **benzin** ('bɛnzɪn) n. **1.** a volatile mixture of the lighter hydrocarbon constituents of petroleum. **2.** Austral. & N.Z. a rare name for **petrol.**

benzo- or **benz-** combining form. **1.** indicating a fused benzene ring. **2.** indicating derivation from benzene or benzoic acid or the presence of phenyl groups.

bequeath (bɪ'kwiːð, -'kwiːθ) vb. (tr.) **1.** Law. to dispose of (property) by will. **2.** to hand down; pass on. —**be-'queathal** n. —**be'queather** n.

bequest (bɪ'kwɛst) n. **1.** the act of bequeathing. **2.** something that is bequeathed.

berate (bɪ'reɪt) vb. (tr.) to scold harshly.

Berber ('bɜːbə) n. **1.** a member of a Caucasoid Muslim people of N Africa. **2.** the language of this people. ~adj. **3.** of or relating to this people or their language.

berberis ('bɜːbərɪs) n. any of a genus of mainly N temperate shrubs.

berceuse (French bɛr'søːz) n. **1.** a lullaby. **2.** an instrumental piece suggestive of this.

bereave (bɪ'riːv) vb. (tr.) (usually foll. by of) to deprive (of) something or someone valued, esp. through death. —**be'reavement** n.

bereft (bɪ'rɛft) adj. (usually foll. by of) deprived; parted (from): bereft of hope.

beret ('bɛreɪ) n. a round close-fitting brimless cap.

berg (bɜːg) n. short for **iceberg.**

bergamot ('bɜːgə,mɒt) n. **1.** a small Asian tree having sour pear-shaped fruit. **2. essence of bergamot.** a fragrant essential oil from the fruit rind of this plant, used in perfumery. **3.** a Mediterranean mint that yields a similar oil.

Bergie ('bɜːgiː) n. S. African inf. a vagabond, esp. one living on the slopes of Table Mountain in SW South Africa.

bergwind ('bɜːxvənt) n. a hot dry wind in South Africa blowing from the plateau down to the coast.

beriberi (,bɛrɪ'bɛrɪ) n. a disease, endemic in E and S Asia, caused by dietary deficiency of thiamine (vitamin B₁).

berk (bɜːk) n. Brit. sl. a variant spelling of **burk.**

berkelium (bɜː'kiːlɪəm, 'bɜːklɪəm) n. a radioactive transuranic element produced by bombardment of americium. Symbol: Bk; atomic no.: 97; half-life of most stable isotope, ²⁴⁷Bk: 1400 years.

Berks. (bɑːks) abbrev. for Berkshire.

Bermuda shorts (bə'mjuːdə) pl. n. close-fitting shorts that come down to the knees.

berry ('bɛrɪ) n., pl. **-ries. 1.** any of various small edible fruits such as the blackberry and strawberry. **2.** Bot. a fruit with two or more seeds and a fleshy pericarp, such as the grape or gooseberry. **3.** any of various seeds or dried kernels, such as a coffee bean. **4.** the egg of a lobster, crayfish, or similar animal. ~vb. **-rying, -ried.** (intr.) **5.** to bear or produce berries. **6.** to gather or look for berries.

berserk (bə'zɜːk, -'sɜːk) adj. **1.** frenziedly violent or destructive (esp. in **go berserk**). ~n. **2.** Also called: **berserker.** one of a class of ancient Norse warriors who fought frenziedly.

berth (bɜːθ) n. **1.** a bed or bunk in a vessel or train. **2.** Naut. a place assigned to a ship at a mooring. **3.** Naut. sufficient room for a ship to manoeuvre. **4. give a wide berth to.** to keep clear of. **5.** Inf. a job, esp. as a member of a ship's crew. ~vb. **6.** (tr.) Naut. to assign a berth to (a vessel). **7.** Naut. to dock (a vessel). **8.** (tr.) to provide with a sleeping place. **9.** (intr.) Naut. to pick up a mooring in an anchorage.

beryl ('bɛrɪl) n. a green, blue, yellow, or white hard mineral consisting of beryllium aluminium silicate in hexagonal crystalline form. Emerald and aquamarine are transparent varieties. —'**beryline** adj.

beryllium (bɛ'rɪlɪəm) n. a corrosion-resistant toxic silvery-white metallic element used mainly in x-ray windows and alloys. Symbol: Be; atomic no.: 4; atomic wt.: 9.012.

beseech (bɪ'siːtʃ) vb. **-seeching, -sought** or **-seeched.** (tr.) to ask (someone) earnestly (to do something or for something); beg.

beset (bɪ'sɛt) vb. **-setting, -set.** (tr.) **1.** (esp. of dangers or temptations) to trouble or harass constantly. **2.** to surround or attack from all sides. **3.** Arch. to cover with, esp. with jewels.

besetting (bɪ'sɛtɪŋ) adj. tempting, harassing, or assailing (esp. in **besetting sin**).

beside (bɪ'saɪd) prep. **1.** next to; at, by, or to the side of. **2.** as compared with. **3.** away from; wide of. **4.** Arch. besides. **5. beside oneself.** (postpositive; often foll. by with) overwhelmed; overwrought: beside oneself with grief. ~adv. **6.** at, by, to, or along the side of something or someone.

besides (bɪ'saɪdz) prep. **1.** apart from; even considering. ~ **2.** (sentence connector) anyway; moreover. ~adv. **3.** as well.

besiege (bɪ'siːdʒ) vb. (tr.) **1.** to surround (a fortified area) with military forces to bring about its surrender. **2.** to crowd round; hem in. **3.** to overwhelm, as with requests. —**be'sieger** n.

THESAURUS

bent adj. **1.** angled, arched, bowed, crooked, curved, hunched, stooped, twisted **2.** With **on** determined, disposed, fixed, inclined, insistent, predisposed, resolved, set ~n. **3.** ability, aptitude, facility, faculty, flair, forte, inclination, knack, leaning, penchant, preference, proclivity, propensity, talent, tendency

bequeath bestow, commit, endow, entrust, give, grant, hand down, impart, leave to by will, pass on, transmit, will

bequest bequeathal, bestowal, dower, endowment, estate, gift, heritage, inheritance, legacy, settlement, trust

berate castigate, censure, chide, criticize, rail at, rebuke, reprimand, reproach, reprove, revile, scold, tell off (Inf.), upbraid, vituperate

bereave afflict, deprive of kindred, dispossess, divest, make destitute, strip, take away from, widow

bereavement affliction, death, deprivation, loss, misfortune, tribulation

bereft cut off, deprived, destitute, devoid, lacking, minus, parted from, shorn, wanting

berserk crazy, enraged, frantic, frenzied, insane, mad, maniacal, manic, rabid, raging, uncontrollable, violent, wild

berth n. **1.** bed, billet, bunk, cot (Naut.), hammock **2.** anchorage, dock, harbour, haven, pier, port, quay, slip, wharf **3.** appointment, employment, job, living, position, post, situation ~v. **4.** Naut. anchor, dock, drop anchor, land, moor, tie up

beseech adjure, ask, beg, call upon, crave, entreat, implore, importune, petition, plead, pray, solicit, sue, supplicate

beset 1. assail, attack, besiege, encircle, enclose, encompass, environ, hem in, surround **2.** Fig. badger, bedevil, embarrass, entangle, harass, perplex, pester, plague

besetting habitual, harassing, inveterate, persistent, prevalent, troublesome

beside 1. abreast of, adjacent to, alongside, at the side of, close to, near, nearby, neighbouring, next door to, next to, overlooking **2. beside oneself** apoplectic, berserk, crazed, delirious, demented, deranged, distraught, frantic, frenzied, insane, mad, out of one's mind, unbalanced, uncontrolled, unhinged

besides 1. adv. also, as well, further, furthermore, in addition, moreover, otherwise, too, what's more **2.** prep. apart from, barring, excepting, excluding, in addition to, other than, over and above, without

besiege 1. beleaguer, beset, blockade, confine, encircle, encompass, environ, hedge

besmirch (bɪ'smɜ:tʃ) *vb.* (*tr.*) **1.** to make dirty; soil. **2.** to reduce the brightness of. **3.** to sully (often in **besmirch (a person's) name**).

besom ('bi:zəm) *n.* **1.** a broom, esp. one made of a bundle of twigs tied to a handle. **2.** *Arch.* a derogatory term (chiefly N Brit. dialect) for a **woman**.

besotted (bɪ'sɒtɪd) *adj.* **1.** stupefied with drink. **2.** infatuated; doting. **3.** foolish; muddled.

besought (bɪ'sɔ:t) *vb.* the past tense or past participle of **beseech.**

bespangle (bɪ'spæŋgəl) *vb.* (*tr.*) to cover or adorn with or as if with spangles.

bespatter (bɪ'spætə) *vb.* (*tr.*) **1.** to splash, as with dirty water. **2.** to defile; besmirch.

bespeak (bɪ'spi:k) *vb.* **-speaking, -spoke; -spoken** or **-spoke.** (*tr.*) **1.** to engage or ask for in advance. **2.** to indicate or suggest: *this act bespeaks kindness.* **3.** *Poetic.* to address.

bespectacled (bɪ'spɛktəkəld) *adj.* wearing spectacles.

bespoke (bɪ'spəʊk) *adj. Chiefly Brit.* **1.** (of a suit, jacket, etc.) made to the customer's specifications. **2.** making or selling such suits, jackets, etc.: *a bespoke tailor.*

Bessemer process ('bɛsɪmə) *n.* a process for producing steel by blowing air through molten pig iron in a **Bessemer converter** (a refractory-lined furnace): impurities are removed and the carbon content is controlled.

best (bɛst) *adj.* **1.** the superlative of **good. 2.** most excellent of a particular group, category, etc. **3.** most suitable, desirable, etc. **4. the best part of.** most of. ~*adv.* **5.** the superlative of **well**[1]. **6.** in a manner surpassing all others; most excellently, attractively, etc. ~*n.* **7. the best.** the most outstanding or excellent person, thing, or group in a category. **8.** the utmost effort. **9.** a winning majority. **10.** Also: **all the best.** best wishes. **11.** a person's smartest outfit of clothing. **12. at best. a.** in the most favourable interpretation. **b.** under the most favourable conditions. **13. for the best. a.** for an ultimately good outcome. **b.** with good intentions. **14. get** or **have the best of.** to defeat or outwit. **15. give (someone) the best.** to concede (someone's) superiority. **16. make the best of.** to cope as well as possible. ~*vb.* **17.** (*tr.*) to gain the advantage over or defeat.

bestial ('bɛstɪəl) *adj.* **1.** brutal or savage. **2.** sexually depraved. **3.** lacking in refinement; brutish. **4.** of or relating to a beast. —**bestiality** (ˌbɛstɪ'ælɪtɪ) *n.* —'**bestia-ˌlize** or **-ise** *vb.*

bestiary ('bɛstɪərɪ) *n., pl.* **-aries.** a moralizing medieval collection of descriptions of real and/or mythical animals.

bestir (bɪ'stɜ:) *vb.* **-stirring, -stirred.** (*tr.*) to cause (oneself) to become active; rouse.

best man *n.* the (male) attendant of the bridegroom at a wedding.

bestow (bɪ'stəʊ) *vb.* (*tr.*) **1.** to present (a gift) or confer (an honour). **2.** *Arch.* to apply (energy, resources, etc.). **3.** *Arch.* to house (a person) or store (goods). —**be'stowal** *n.*

bestrew (bɪ'stru:) *vb.* **-strewing, -strewed; -strewn** or **-strewed.** (*tr.*) to scatter or be scattered over (a surface).

bestride (bɪ'straɪd) *vb.* **-striding, -strode** or **-strid; -stridden** or **-strid.** (*tr.*) **1.** to have or put a leg on either side of. **2.** to extend across; span. **3.** to stride over or across.

best seller *n.* **1.** a book or other product that has sold in great numbers. **2.** the author of one or more such books, etc.

bet (bɛt) *n.* **1.** an agreement between two parties that a sum of money or other stake will be paid by the loser to the party who correctly predicts the outcome of an event. **2.** the stake risked. **3.** the predicted result in such an agreement. **4.** a person, event, etc., considered as likely to succeed or occur. **5.** a course of action (esp. in **one's best bet**). **6.** *Inf.* an opinion: *my bet is that you've been up to no good.* ~*vb.* **betting, bet** or **betted. 7.** (when *intr.* foll. by **on** or **against**) to make or place a bet with (a person or persons). **8.** (*tr.*) to stake (money, etc.) in a bet. **9.** (*tr.; may take a clause as object*) *Inf.* to predict (a certain outcome). **10. you bet.** *Inf.* of course; naturally.

beta ('bi:tə) *n.* **1.** the second letter in the Greek alphabet (B or β). **2.** the second in a group or series.

betake (bɪ'teɪk) *vb.* **-taking, -took, -taken.** (*tr.*) **1. betake oneself.** to go; move. **2.** *Arch.* to apply (oneself) to.

beta particle *n.* a high-speed electron or positron emitted by a nucleus during radioactive decay or nuclear fission.

betatron ('bi:tə,trɒn) *n.* a type of particle accelerator for producing high-energy beams of electrons by magnetic induction.

betel ('bi:təl) *n.* an Asian climbing plant, the leaves of which are chewed by the peoples of SE Asia.

betel nut *n.* the seed of the betel palm, chewed with betel leaves and lime by people in S and SE Asia as a digestive stimulant and narcotic.

betel palm *n.* a tropical Asian feather palm.

bête noire *French.* (bɛt 'nwa:r) *n., pl.* **bêtes noires** (bɛt 'nwa:r). a person or thing that one particularly dislikes or dreads.

bethink (bɪ'θɪŋk) *vb.* *Arch.* or *dial.* **-thinking, -thought. 1.** to cause (oneself) to consider or meditate. **2.** (*tr.*; often foll. by *of*) to remind (oneself).

betide (bɪ'taɪd) *vb.* to happen or happen to (often in **woe betide (someone)**).

betimes (bɪ'taɪmz) *adv.* *Arch.* **1.** in good time; early. **2.** soon.

betoken (bɪ'təʊkən) *vb.* (*tr.*) **1.** to indicate; signify. **2.** to portend; augur.

betony ('bɛtənɪ) *n., pl.* **-nies. 1.** a Eurasian plant with a spike of reddish-purple flowers, formerly used in medicine and dyeing. **2.** any of several related plants.

betray (bɪ'treɪ) *vb.* (*tr.*) **1.** to hand over or expose (one's nation, friend, etc.) treacherously to an enemy. **2.** to disclose (a secret, confidence, etc.) treacherously. **3.** to break (a promise) or be disloyal to (a person's trust). **4.** to show signs of; indicate. **5.** to reveal unintentionally: *his grin betrayed his satisfaction.* —**be'trayal** *n.* —**be'trayer** *n.*

THESAURUS

in, hem in, invest (*Rare*), lay siege to, shut in, surround **2.** badger, bother, harass, harry, hound, importune, nag, pester, plague, trouble

besotted 1. befuddled, drunk, intoxicated, stupefied **2.** doting, hypnotized, infatuated, smitten, spellbound **3.** confused, foolish, muddled, witless

bespatter bedaub, befoul, begrime, besmirch, besprinkle, muddy, smear, spatter, splatter, sully

best *adj.* **1.** chief, finest, first, first-class, first-rate, foremost, highest, leading, most excellent, outstanding, perfect, pre-eminent, principal, superlative, supreme, unsurpassed **2.** advantageous, apt, correct, golden, most desirable, most fitting, right **3.** greatest, largest, most ~*adv.* **4.** advantageously, attractively, excellently, most fortunately **5.** extremely, greatly, most deeply, most fully, most highly ~*n.* **6.** choice, cream, elite, favourite, finest, first, flower, pick, prime, top **7.** hardest, highest endeavour, utmost ~*v.* **8.** beat, conquer, defeat, get the better of, lick

(*Inf.*), outclass, outdo, surpass, thrash, triumph over, trounce

bestial animal, barbaric, barbarous, beastlike, beastly, brutal, brutish, carnal, degraded, depraved, gross, inhuman, low, savage, sensual, sordid, vile

bestow accord, allot, apportion, award, commit, confer, donate, entrust, give, grant, honour with, impart, lavish, present, render to

bestride bestraddle, bridge, dominate, extend, mount, span, step over, straddle, tower over

bet 1. *n.* ante, gamble, hazard, long shot, pledge, risk, speculation, stake, venture, wager **2.** *v.* chance, gamble, hazard, pledge, punt (*Brit.*), put money on, risk, speculate, stake, venture, wager

bête noir abomination, anathema, aversion, bugbear, pet hate

betide bechance, befall, chance, come to pass, crop up (*Inf.*), ensue, happen, occur, overtake, supervene, take place, tran-

spire (*Inf.*)

betimes anon, beforehand, before long, early, first thing, in good time, punctually, seasonably, soon

betoken augur, bespeak, bode, declare, denote, evidence, indicate, manifest, mark, portend, presage, prognosticate, promise, represent, signify, suggest, typify

betray 1. be disloyal (treacherous, unfaithful), break one's promise, break with, double-cross (*Inf.*), inform on or against, sell down the river (*Inf.*), sell out (*Inf.*) **2.** blurt out, disclose, divulge, evince, expose, give away, lay bare, let slip, manifest, reveal, show, tell, tell on, uncover, unmask **3.** beguile, corrupt, deceive, delude, dupe, ensnare, entrap, lead astray, mislead, undo **4.** abandon, desert, forsake, jilt, walk out on

betrayal 1. deception, disloyalty, double-cross (*Inf.*), double-dealing, duplicity, falseness, perfidy, sell-out (*Inf.*), treachery, treason, trickery, unfaithfulness **2.** blurting out, disclosure, divulgence, giving away, revela-

betroth (bɪ'trəʊð) vb. (tr.) Arch. to promise to marry or to give in marriage. —**be'trothal** n.

betrothed (bɪ'trəʊðd) adj. **1.** engaged to be married: he was betrothed to her. —n. **2.** the person to whom one is engaged; fiancé or fiancée.

better ('bɛtə) adj. **1.** the comparative of **good. 2.** more excellent than others. **3.** more suitable, advantageous, attractive, etc. **4.** improved or fully recovered in health. **5. better off.** in more favourable circumstances, esp. financially. **6. the better part of.** a large part of. ~adv. **7.** the comparative of **well**[1]. **8.** in a more excellent manner; more advantageously, attractively, etc. **9.** in or to a greater degree or extent; more. **10. had better.** would be wise, sensible, etc. to: I had better be off. **11. think better of. a.** to change one's course of action after reconsideration. **b.** to rate more highly. ~n. **12. the better.** something that is the more excellent, useful, etc., of two such things. **13.** (usually pl.) a person who is superior, esp. in social standing or ability. **14. for the better.** by way of improvement. **15. get the better of.** to defeat, outwit, or surpass. ~vb. **16.** to make or become better. **17.** (tr.) to improve upon; surpass.

better half n. Humorous. one's spouse.

betterment ('bɛtəmənt) n. **1.** a change for the better; improvement. **2.** Property law. an improvement effected on real property that enhances the value of the property.

betting shop n. (in Britain) a licensed bookmaker's premises not on a racecourse.

between (bɪ'twiːn) prep. **1.** at a point or in a region intermediate to two other points in space, times, degrees, etc. **2.** in combination; together: between them, they saved enough money to buy a car. **3.** confined or restricted to: between you and me. **4.** indicating a reciprocal relation or comparison. **5.** indicating two or more alternatives. ~adv. also **in between. 6.** between one specified thing and another.

▷ **Usage.** In careful usage, between is restricted to cases where only two people, objects, possibilities, etc., are concerned. Grammatically, between you and I is incorrect. The proper construction is between you and me.

betweentimes (bɪ'twiːn,taɪmz) or **betweenwhiles** adv. between other activities; during intervals.

betwixt (bɪ'twɪkst) prep., adv. **1.** Arch. another word for **between. 2. betwixt and between.** in an intermediate or indecisive position.

bevel ('bɛvəl) n. **1.** Also called: **cant.** a surface that meets another at an angle other than a right angle. ~vb. **-elling, -elled** or U.S. **-eling, -eled. 2.** (intr.) to be inclined; slope. **3.** (tr.) to cut a bevel on (a piece of timber, etc.).

bevel gear n. a gear having teeth cut into a conical surface. Two such gears mesh together to transmit power between two shafts at an angle.

beverage ('bɛvərɪdʒ, 'bɛvrɪdʒ) n. any drink, usually other than water.

beverage room n. Canad. another name for **beer parlour.**

bevvy ('bɛvɪ) n., pl. **-vies.** Dial. **1.** a drink, esp. an alcoholic one. **2.** a night of drinking.

bevy ('bɛvɪ) n., pl. **bevies. 1.** a flock of quails. **2.** a group, esp. of girls.

bewail (bɪ'weɪl) vb. to express great sorrow over (a person or thing); lament. —**be'wailer** n.

beware (bɪ'wɛə) vb. (usually used in the imperative or infinitive, often foll. by of) to be cautious or wary (of); be on one's guard (against).

bewilder (bɪ'wɪldə) vb. (tr.) to confuse utterly; puzzle. —**be'wilderingly** adv. —**be'wilderment** n.

bewitch (bɪ'wɪtʃ) vb. (tr.) **1.** to attract and fascinate. **2.** to cast a spell over. —**be'witching** adj.

bey (beɪ) n. **1.** (in the Ottoman Empire) a title given to provincial governors. **2.** (in modern Turkey) a title of address, corresponding to Mr. ~Also called: **beg.**

beyond (bɪ'jɒnd) prep. **1.** at or to a point on the other side of; at or to the further side of: beyond those hills. **2.** outside the limits or scope of. ~adv. **3.** at or to the other or far side of something. **4.** outside the limits of something. ~n. **5. the beyond.** the unknown, esp. life after death in certain religious beliefs.

bezel ('bɛzəl) n. **1.** the sloping face adjacent to the working edge of a cutting tool. **2.** the upper oblique faces of a cut gem. **3.** a grooved ring or part holding a gem, watch crystal, etc.

bezique (bɪ'ziːk) n. **1.** a card game for two or more players using two packs with nothing below a seven. **2.** (in this game) the queen of spades and jack of diamonds declared together.

b.f. abbrev. for: **1.** Brit. inf. bloody fool. **2.** Printing. bold face.

B/F or **b/f** Book-keeping. abbrev. for brought forward.

BFPO abbrev. for British Forces Post Office.

bhang or **bang** (bæŋ) n. a preparation of the leaves and flower tops of Indian hemp: a narcotic much used in India.

bhindi ('bɪndɪ) n. the okra as used in Indian cooking.

b.h.p. abbrev. for brake horsepower.

Bi the chemical symbol for bismuth.

bi- or sometimes before a vowel **bin-** combining form. **1.** two; having two: bifocal. **2.** occurring every two; lasting for two: biennial. **3.** on both sides, directions, etc.: bilateral. **4.** occurring twice during: biweekly. **5. a.** denoting a compound containing two identical cyclic hydrocarbon systems: biphenyl. **b.** (rare in technical usage) indicating an acid salt of a dibasic acid: sodium bicarbonate. **c.** (not in technical usage) equivalent of **di-**[1] (sense 2).

▷ **Usage.** In order to avoid ambiguity, care should be taken in observing the distinction between bi- and semi- in biweekly, bimonthly, biyearly (once in two weeks, months, years) and semiweekly, semimonthly, semiyearly (twice during one week, month, year). In strict usage, biennial (lasting or occurring once in two years) is distinguished from biannual (occurring twice in one year).

biannual (baɪ'ænjʊəl) adj. occurring twice a year. Cf. **biennial.** —**bi'annually** adv.

bias ('baɪəs) n. **1.** mental tendency or inclination, esp. irrational preference or prejudice. **2.** a diagonal line or cut across the weave of a fabric. **3.** Electronics. the voltage applied to an electrode of a transistor or valve to establish suitable working conditions. **4.** Bowls. **a.** a bulge or weight inside one side of a bowl. **b.** the curved course of such a bowl. **5.** Statistics. a latent influence that dis-

---

THESAURUS

betrayer apostate, conspirator, deceiver, renegade, traitor

betrothal affiancing, betrothing, engagement, espousal (Archaic), marriage compact, plight, promise, troth, vow

better adj. **1.** bigger, excelling, finer, fitter, greater, higher quality, larger, more appropriate (desirable, expert, fitting, suitable, useful, valuable), preferable, superior, surpassing, worthier **2.** cured, fitter, fully recovered, healthier, improving, less ill, mending, more healthy, on the mend (Inf.), progressing, recovering, stronger, well **3.** bigger, greater, larger, longer ~adv. **4.** in a more excellent manner, in a superior way, more advantageously (attractively, competently, completely, effectively, thoroughly), to a greater degree ~v. **5.** advance, ameliorate, amend, correct, enhance, forward, further, improve, meliorate, mend, promote, raise,

rectify, reform **6.** beat, cap (Inf.), exceed, excel, improve on or upon, outdo, outstrip, surpass, top **7. get the better of** beat, defeat, get the upper hand, outdo, outsmart (Inf.), outwit, prevail over, score off, surpass, triumph over, worst

between amidst, among, betwixt, halfway, in the middle of, mid

beverage draught, drink, libation (Facetious), liquid, liquor, potable, potation, refreshment

bevy **1.** band, bunch (Inf.), collection, company, crowd, gathering, group, pack, troupe **2.** covey, flight, flock

bewail bemoan, cry over, deplore, express sorrow, grieve for, keen, lament, moan, mourn, regret, repent, rue, wail, weep over

beware avoid, be careful (cautious, wary), guard against, heed, look out, mind, refrain from, shun, steer clear of, take heed,

watch out

bewilder baffle, befuddle, bemuse, confound, confuse, daze, mix up, mystify, perplex, puzzle, stupefy

bewildered awed, baffled, confused, disconcerted, dizzy, giddy, mystified, perplexed, puzzled, speechless, startled, stunned, surprised, taken aback, uncertain

bewitch allure, attract, beguile, captivate, charm, enchant, enrapture, entrance, fascinate, hypnotize, spellbind

bewitched charmed, enchanted, entranced, mesmerized, possessed, spellbound, transformed, under a spell, unrecognizable

beyond above, apart from, at a distance, away from, before, farther, out of range, out of reach, over, past, remote, superior to, yonder

turbs an analysis. ~*adv.* **6.** obliquely; diagonally. ~*vb.* **-asing, -ased** *or* **-assing, -assed. 7.** (*tr.: usually passive*) to cause to have a bias; prejudice; influence.

bias binding *n.* a strip of material cut on the bias, used for binding hems or for decoration.

biaxial (bai'æksiəl) *adj.* (esp. of a crystal) having two axes.

bib (bib) *n.* **1.** a piece of cloth or plastic worn, esp. by babies, to protect their clothes while eating. **2.** the upper front part of some aprons, dungarees, etc. **3.** Also called: **pout, whiting pout.** a light-brown European marine gadoid food fish with a barbel on its lower jaw. **4. stick one's bib in.** *Austral. inf.* to interfere. ~*vb.* **bibbing, bibbed. 5.** *Arch.* to drink (something).

Bib. *abbrev. for:* **1.** Bible. **2.** Biblical.

bibcock ('bib,kɒk) *or* **bibb** *n.* a tap with a nozzle bent downwards.

bibelot ('biblou) *n.* an attractive or curious trinket.

bibl. *abbrev. for:* **1.** bibliographical. **2.** bibliography.

Bibl. *abbrev. for* Biblical.

Bible ('baibəl) *n.* **1. a. the.** the sacred writings of the Christian religion, comprising the Old and New Testaments. **b.** (*as modifier*): *a Bible reading.* **2.** (*often not cap.*) the sacred writings of a religion. **3.** (*usually not cap.*) a book regarded as authoritative. —**biblical** ('biblikəl) *adj.*

biblio- *combining form.* indicating book or books: *bibliography.*

bibliography (,bibli'ɒgrəfi) *n., pl.* **-phies. 1.** a list of books on a subject or by a particular author. **2.** a list of sources used in a book, thesis, etc. **3. a.** the study of the history, classification, etc., of literary material. **b.** a work on this subject. —**bibli'ographer** *n.* —**bibliographic** (,bibliou'græfik) *or* **biblio'graphical** *adj.*

bibliomania (,bibliou'meiniə) *n.* extreme fondness for books. —**biblio'maniac** *n., adj.*

bibliophile ('bibliə,fail) *or* **bibliophil** ('bibliəfil) *n.* a person who collects or is fond of books. —**bibliophilism** (,bibli'ɒfilizəm) *n.* —**bibli,ophi'listic** *adj.*

bibulous ('bibjuləs) *adj.* addicted to alcohol. —**'bibulously** *adv.* —**'bibulousness** *n.*

bicameral (bai'kæmərəl) *adj.* (of a legislature) consisting of two chambers. —**bi'cameralism** *n.*

bicarb ('baika:b) *n.* short for **bicarbonate of soda.**

bicarbonate (bai'ka:bənit, -,neit) *n.* a salt of carbonic acid.

bicarbonate of soda *n.* sodium bicarbonate, esp. as medicine or a raising agent in baking.

bicentenary (,baisen'ti:nəri) *or U.S.* **bicentennial** (,baisen'teniəl) *adj.* **1.** marking a 200th anniversary. **2.** occurring every 200 years. **3.** lasting 200 years. ~*n., pl.* **-naries. 4.** a 200th anniversary.

biceps ('baiseps) *n., pl.* **-ceps** *or* **-cepses.** *Anat.* any muscle having two heads or origins, esp. the muscle that flexes the forearm.

bicker ('bikə) *vb.* **1.** (*intr.*) to argue over petty matters; squabble. **2.** (*intr.*) *Poetic.* **a.** (esp. of a stream) to run quickly. **b.** to flicker; glitter. ~*n.* **3.** a squabble. —**'bickerer** *n.*

bicolour ('bai,kʌlə), **bicoloured** *or U.S.* **bicolor, bicolored** *adj.* two-coloured.

bicuspid (bai'kʌspid) *or* **bicuspidate** (bai'kʌspi,deit) *adj.* **1.** having two cusps or points. ~*n.* **2.** a bicuspid tooth; premolar.

bicycle ('baisikəl) *n.* **1.** a vehicle with a tubular metal frame mounted on two spoked wheels, one behind the other. The rider sits on a saddle, propels the vehicle by means of pedals and steers with handlebars on the front wheel. Often shortened to **bike** (informal), **cycle.** ~*vb.*

2. (*intr.*) to ride a bicycle; cycle. —**'bicyclist** *or* **'bicycler** *n.*

bid (bid) *vb.* **bidding; bad, bade,** *or* **bid; bidden** *or* **bid. 1.** (often foll. by *for* or *against*) to offer (an amount) in attempting to buy something. **2.** (*tr.*) to say (a greeting, etc.): *to bid farewell.* **3.** to order; command: *do as you are bid!* **4.** (*intr.; usually foll. by for*) to attempt to attain power, etc. **5.** (*tr.*) to utter; express in words: *to bid defiance.* **6.** *Bridge, etc.* to declare before play how many tricks one expects to make. **7. bid fair.** to seem probable. ~*n.* **8. a.** an offer of a specified amount. **b.** the price offered. **9. a.** the quoting by a seller of a price. **b.** the price quoted. **10.** an attempt, esp. to attain power. **11.** *Bridge, etc.* **a.** the number of tricks a player undertakes to make. **b.** a player's turn to make a bid. —**'bidder** *n.*

▷ **Usage.** *Bid* in journalistic usage has become a noun used to refer to any kind of attempt to achieve something: *bid to climb Everest; doctor makes bid to save life.* This use of *bid* is avoided by careful writers, however, and the word is restricted to the sense of an offer of a price: *the auctioneer accepted a bid of 3000 pounds.*

biddable ('bidəbəl) *adj.* **1.** having sufficient value to be bid on, as a hand at bridge. **2.** docile; obedient. —**'biddableness** *n.*

bidding ('bidiŋ) *n.* **1.** an order; command. **2.** an invitation; summons. **3.** bids or the act of making bids.

biddy¹ ('bidi) *n., pl.* **-dies.** a dialect word for **chicken** or **hen.**

biddy² ('bidi) *n., pl.* **-dies.** *Inf.* a woman, esp. an old gossipy one.

bide (baid) *vb.* **biding, bided** *or* **bode, bided. 1.** (*intr.*) *Arch. or dialect* to continue in a certain place or state; stay. **2.** (*tr.*) *Arch. or dialect* to tolerate; endure. **3. bide one's time.** to wait patiently for an opportunity.

bidet ('bi:dei) *n.* a small low basin for washing the genital area.

biennial (bai'eniəl) *adj.* **1.** occurring every two years. **2.** lasting two years. Cf. **biannual.** ~*n.* **3.** a plant that completes its life cycle in two years. **4.** an event that takes place every two years. —**bi'ennially** *adv.*

bier (biə) *n.* a platform or stand on which a corpse or a coffin containing a corpse rests before burial.

biff (bif) *Sl.* ~*n.* **1.** a blow with the fist. ~*vb.* **2.** (*tr.*) to give (someone) such a blow.

bifid ('baifid) *adj.* divided into two lobes by a median cleft. —**bi'fidity** *n.* —**'bifidly** *adv.*

bifocal (bai'foukəl) *adj.* **1.** *Optics.* having two different focuses. **2.** relating to a compound lens permitting near and distant vision.

bifocals (bai'foukəlz) *pl. n.* a pair of spectacles with bifocal lenses.

bifurcate *vb.* ('baifə,keit). **1.** to fork or divide into two branches. ~*adj.* ('baifə,keit, -kit). **2.** forked or divided into two branches. —**,bifur'cation** *n.*

big (big) *adj.* **bigger, biggest. 1.** of great or considerable size, height, weight, number, power, or capacity. **2.** having great significance; important. **3.** important through having power, influence, wealth, authority, etc. **4.** *Inf.* considerable in extent or intensity (esp. in **in a big way**). **5. a.** elder: *my big brother.* **b.** grown-up. **6. a.** generous; magnanimous: *that's very big of you.* **b.** (in combination): *big-hearted.* **7.** extravagant; boastful: *big talk.* **8. too big for one's boots** *or* **breeches.** conceited; unduly self-confident. **9.** in an advanced stage of pregnancy (esp. in **big with child**). ~*adv. Inf.* **10.** boastfully; pretentiously (esp. in **talk big**). **11.** in an exceptional way; well: *his talk went over big.* **12.** on a grand scale (esp. in **think big**). —**'bigness** *n.*

THESAURUS

bias *n.* **1.** bent, bigotry, favouritism, inclination, intolerance, leaning, narrow-mindedness, one-sidedness, partiality, penchant, predilection, predisposition, prejudice, proclivity, proneness, propensity, tendency, turn, unfairness **2.** angle, cross, diagonal line, slant ~*v.* **3.** distort, influence, predispose, prejudice, slant, sway, twist, warp, weight

biased distorted, embittered, jaundiced, one-sided, partial, predisposed, prejudiced, slanted, swayed, twisted, warped, weighted

bicker argue, disagree, dispute, fight,

quarrel, row (*Inf.*), scrap (*Inf.*), spar, squabble, wrangle

bid *v.* **1.** offer, proffer, propose, submit, tender **2.** call, greet, say, tell, wish **3.** ask, call, charge, command, desire, direct, enjoin, instruct, invite, require, solicit, summon, tell ~*n.* **4.** advance, amount, offer, price, proposal, proposition, submission, sum, tender **5.** attempt, crack (*Inf.*), effort, endeavour, try, venture

biddable amenable, complaisant, co-operative, docile, obedient, teachable

bidding 1. behest, call, charge, command,

demand, direction, injunction, instruction, invitation, order, request, summons **2.** auction, offer, offers, proposal, tender

big 1. bulky, burly, colossal, considerable, enormous, extensive, gigantic, great, huge, hulking, immense, large, mammoth, massive, ponderous, prodigious, sizable, spacious, substantial, vast, voluminous **2.** eminent, important, influential, leading, main, momentous, paramount, powerful, prime, principal, prominent, serious, significant, valuable, weighty **3.** adult, elder, grown, grown-up, mature **4.** altruistic, benevolent, generous, gra-

bigamy ('bɪgəmɪ) n., pl. **-mies.** the crime of marrying a person while still legally married to someone else. —'**bigamist** n. —'**bigamous** adj.

big-bang theory n. a cosmological theory postulating that all the matter of the universe was hurled in all directions by a cataclysmic explosion and that the universe is still expanding.

Big Brother n. a person, organization, etc., that exercises total dictatorial control.

big business n. large commercial organizations collectively, esp. when considered as exploitative or socially harmful.

big deal interj. Sl. an exclamation of scorn, derision, etc., used esp. to belittle a claim or offer.

big end n. Brit. the larger end of a connecting rod in an internal-combustion engine.

big game n. large animals that are hunted or fished for sport.

bight (baɪt) n. **1.** a wide indentation of a shoreline, or the body of water bounded by such a curve. **2.** the slack middle part or loop in a rope.

Bight (baɪt) n. **the.** the major indentation of the S coast of Australia. In full: **the Great Australian Bight.**

bignonia (bɪg'nəʊnɪə) n. a tropical American climbing shrub cultivated for its trumpet-shaped yellow or reddish flowers.

bigot ('bɪgət) n. a person who is intolerant, esp. regarding religion, politics, or race. —'**bigoted** adj. —'**bigotry** n.

big shot n. Sl. an important person.

big stick n. Inf. force or the threat of force.

big time n. Sl. **a. the.** the highest level of a profession, esp. entertainment. **b.** (as modifier): a big-time comedian. —'**big-'timer** n.

big top n. Inf. **1.** the main tent of a circus. **2.** the circus itself.

bigwig ('bɪg,wɪg) n. Sl. an important person.

bijou ('biːʒuː) n., pl. **-joux** (-ʒuːz). **1.** something small and delicately worked. **2.** (modifier) Often ironic. small but tasteful: a bijou residence.

bike (baɪk) n. **1.** Inf. short for **bicycle** or **motorcycle. 2.** Austral. sl. a promiscuous woman. **3. get off one's bike.** Austral. to lose one's self-control. ~vb. **4.** to ride a bike.

bikini (bɪ'kiːnɪ) n. a woman's very brief two-piece swimming costume.

bilateral (baɪ'lætərəl) adj. **1.** having or involving two sides. **2.** affecting or undertaken by two parties; mutual. **3.** having identical sides or parts on each side of an axis; symmetrical.

bilberry ('bɪlbərɪ) n., pl. **-ries. 1.** any of several shrubs, such as the whortleberry, having edible blue or blackish berries. **2.** the fruit of any of these plants.

bile (baɪl) n. **1.** a bitter greenish to golden brown alkaline fluid secreted by the liver and stored in the gall bladder. It aids digestion of fats. **2.** a health disorder due to faulty secretion of bile. **3.** irritability or peevishness.

bilge (bɪldʒ) n. **1.** Naut. the parts of a vessel's hull where the sides curve inwards to form the bottom. **2.** (often pl.) the parts of a vessel between the lowermost floorboards and the bottom. **3.** Also called: **bilge water.** the dirty water that collects in a vessel's bilge. **4.** Inf. silly rubbish; nonsense. **5.** the widest part of a cask. ~vb. **6.** (intr.) Naut. (of a vessel) to take in water at the bilge. **7.** (tr.) Naut. to damage (a vessel) in the bilge.

biliary ('bɪlɪərɪ) adj. of or relating to bile, to the ducts that convey bile, or to the gall bladder.

bilingual (baɪ'lɪŋgwəl) adj. **1.** able to speak two languages, esp. with fluency. **2.** expressed in two languages. ~n. **3.** a bilingual person.

bilingualism (baɪ'lɪŋgwəlɪzəm) n. **1.** the ability to use two languages. **2.** the use of two languages. **3.** Canad. the government's official policy of using both French and English in official documents, etc.

bilious ('bɪlɪəs) adj. **1.** of or relating to bile. **2.** affected with or denoting any disorder related to secretion of bile. **3.** Inf. bad-tempered; irritable. —'**biliousness** n.

bilk (bɪlk) vb. (tr.) **1.** to balk; thwart. **2.** (often foll. by of) to cheat or deceive, esp. to avoid making payment to. **3.** to escape from; elude. ~n. **4.** a swindle or cheat. **5.** a person who swindles or cheats. —'**bilker** n.

bill¹ (bɪl) n. **1.** money owed for goods or services supplied. **2.** a statement of money owed. **3.** Chiefly Brit. such an account for food and drink in a restaurant, hotel, etc. **4.** any list of items, events, etc., such as a theatre programme. **5. fill the bill.** Inf. to be entirely satisfactory. **6.** a statute in draft, before it becomes law. **7.** a printed notice or advertisement. **8.** U.S. a piece of paper money; note. **9.** an obsolete name for **promissory note. 10.** See **bill of exchange, bill of fare.** ~vb. (tr.) **11.** to send or present an account for payment to (a person). **12.** to enter (items, goods, etc.) on an account or statement. **13.** to advertise by posters. **14.** to schedule as a future programme.

bill² (bɪl) n. **1.** the projecting jaws of a bird, covered with a horny sheath; beak. **2.** any beaklike mouthpart in other animals. **3.** a narrow promontory. ~vb. (intr.) (esp. in **bill and coo**). **4.** (of birds, esp. doves) to touch bills together. **5.** (of lovers) to kiss and whisper amorously.

bill³ (bɪl) n. **1.** a hooked weapon with a long handle, such as a halberd. **2.** short for **billhook.**

billabong ('bɪlə,bɒŋ) n. Austral. **1.** a stagnant pool in the bed of an intermittent stream. **2.** a branch of a river running to a dead end.

billboard ('bɪl,bɔːd) n. Chiefly U.S. another name for **hoarding.**

billet¹ ('bɪlɪt) n. **1.** accommodation, esp. for a soldier, in civilian lodgings. **2.** the official requisition for such lodgings. **3.** a space or berth in a ship. **4.** Inf. a job. ~vb. **5.** (tr.) to assign a lodging to (a soldier). **6.** to lodge or be lodged.

billet² ('bɪlɪt) n. **1.** a chunk of wood, esp. for fuel. **2.** a small bar of iron or steel.

billet-doux (,bɪlɪ'duː) n., pl. **billets-doux** (,bɪlɪ'duːz). Old-fashioned or jocular. a love letter.

billhook ('bɪl,hʊk) n. a tool with a curved blade terminating in a hook, used for pruning, chopping, etc. Also called: **bill.**

billiard ('bɪljəd) n. (modifier) of or relating to billiards: a billiard table; a billiard cue.

billiards ('bɪljədz) n. any of various games in which long cues are used to drive balls on a rectangular table covered with a smooth cloth and having raised cushioned edges.

billion ('bɪljən) n., pl. **-lions** or **-lion. 1.** (in Britain) one million million: written as 1 000 000 000 000 or 10¹². U.S. word: **trillion. 2.** (in the U.S. and increasingly in Britain and elsewhere) one thousand million: written as 1 000 000 000 or 10⁹. **3.** (often pl.) any exceptionally large number. ~determiner. **4.** (preceded by a or a cardinal number) amounting to a billion. —'**billionth** adj., n.

billionaire (,bɪljə'nɛə) n. a person whose wealth exceeds a billion monetary units of his country.

---

cious, heroic, magnanimous, noble, princely, unselfish **5.** arrogant, boastful, bragging, conceited, haughty, inflated, pompous, pretentious, proud

bigot dogmatist, fanatic, persecutor, sectarian, zealot

bigoted biased, dogmatic, illiberal, intolerant, narrow-minded, obstinate, opinionated, prejudiced, sectarian, twisted, warped

bigotry bias, discrimination, dogmatism, fanaticism, ignorance, injustice, intolerance, mindlessness, narrow-mindedness, prejudice, provincialism, racialism, racism, sectarianism, sexism, unfairness

bigwig big cheese (Sl.), big gun (Sl.), big noise (Sl.), big shot (Sl., chiefly U.S.), celeb-

rity, dignitary, heavyweight (Inf.), nob (Sl.), notability, notable, panjandrum, personage, somebody, V.I.P.

bile anger, bitterness, churlishness, ill humour, irascibility, irritability, nastiness, peevishness, rancour, spleen

bilious 1. liverish, nauseated, out of sorts, queasy, sick **2.** bad-tempered, crabby, cross, crotchety, grouchy, grumpy, irritable, nasty, peevish, short-tempered, testy, touchy

bilk bamboozle, cheat, con (Sl.), deceive, defraud, do (Sl.), fleece, rook (Sl.), swindle, trick

bill¹ n. **1.** account, charges, invoice, note of charge, reckoning, score, statement, tally **2.** advertisement, broadsheet, bulletin, circular,

handbill, handout, leaflet, notice, placard, playbill, poster **3.** agenda, card, catalogue, inventory, list, listing, programme, roster, schedule, syllabus **4.** measure, piece of legislation, projected law, proposal ~v. **5.** charge, debit, figure, invoice, reckon, record **6.** advertise, announce, give advance notice of, post

bill² beak, mandible, neb (Archaic or dialect), nib

billet 1. n. accommodation, barracks, lodging, quarters **2.** v. accommodate, berth, quarter, station

bill of attainder *n.* (formerly) a legislative act finding a person guilty without trial of treason or felony and declaring him attainted.

bill of exchange *n.* (now chiefly in foreign transactions) a document, usually negotiable, instructing a third party to pay a stated sum at a designated future date or on demand.

bill of fare *n.* another name for **menu**.

bill of health *n.* 1. a certificate that attests to the health of a ship's company. 2. **clean bill of health.** *Inf.* a. a good report of one's physical condition. b. a favourable account of a person's or a company's financial position.

bill of lading *n.* (in foreign trade) a document containing full particulars of goods shipped.

bill of sale *n. Law.* a deed transferring personal property.

billow ('bɪləʊ) *n.* 1. a large sea wave. 2. a swelling or surging mass, as of smoke or sound. ~*vb.* 3. to rise up, swell out, or cause to rise up or swell out. —'**billowy** *adj.* —'**billowiness** *n.*

billy ('bɪlɪ) *or* **billycan** ('bɪlɪ,kæn) *n., pl.* -**lies** *or* -**lycans.** 1. a metal can or pot for boiling water, etc., over a camp fire. 2. *Austral. & N.Z.* (*as modifier*): *billytea.* 3. **boil the billy.** *Austral. inf.* to make tea.

billy goat *n.* a male goat.

biltong ('bɪl,tɒŋ) *n. S. African.* strips of meat dried and cured in the sun.

B.I.M. *abbrev. for* British Institute of Management.

bimetallic (,baɪmɪ'tælɪk) *adj.* 1. consisting of two metals. 2. of or based on bimetallism.

bimetallism (baɪ'mɛtə,lɪzəm) *n.* the use of two metals, esp. gold and silver, in fixed relative values as the standard of value and currency. —**bi'metallist** *n.*

bimonthly (baɪ'mʌnθlɪ) *adj., adv.* 1. every two months. 2. twice a month; semimonthly. ~*n., pl.* -**lies.** 3. a periodical published every two months.

bin (bɪn) *n.* 1. a large container for storing something in bulk, such as coal, grain, or bottled wine. 2. Also called: **bread bin.** a small container for bread. 3. Also called: **dustbin, rubbish bin.** a container for rubbish, etc. ~*vb.* **binning, binned.** 4. (*tr.*) to store in a bin.

binary ('baɪnərɪ) *adj.* 1. composed of or involving two; dual. 2. *Maths., computers.* of or expressed in binary notation or binary code. 3. (of a compound or molecule) containing atoms of two different elements. ~*n., pl.* -**ries.** 4. something composed of two parts. 5. Also called: **binary number.** *Maths.* a number expressed in binary notation. 6. *Astron.* See **binary star.**

binary star *n.* a double star system containing two associated stars revolving around a common centre of gravity in different orbits.

bind (baɪnd) *vb.* **binding, bound.** 1. to make or become fast or secure with or as if with a tie or band. 2. (*tr.;* often foll. by *up*) to encircle or enclose with a band: *to bind the hair.* 3. (*tr.*) to place (someone) under obligation; oblige. 4. (*tr.*) to impose legal obligations or duties upon (a person). 5. (*tr.*) to make (a bargain, agreement, etc.) irrevocable; seal. 6. (*tr.*) to restrain or confine with or as if with ties, as of responsibility or loyalty. 7. (*tr.*) to place under certain constraints; govern. 8. (*tr.;* often foll. by *up*) to bandage. 9. to cohere or cause to cohere: *egg binds fat and flour.* 10. to make or become compact, stiff, or hard: *frost binds the earth.* 11. (*tr.*) to enclose and fasten (the pages of a book) between covers. 12. (*tr.*) to provide (a garment, hem, etc.) with a border or edging. 13. (*tr.;* sometimes foll. by *out or over*) to employ as an apprentice; indenture. 14. (*intr.*) *Sl.* to complain. ~*n.* 15. something that binds. 16. *Inf.* a difficult or annoying situation. ~See also **bind over.**

binder ('baɪndə) *n.* 1. a firm cover or folder for holding loose sheets of paper together. 2. a material used to bind separate particles together. 3. a person who binds books; bookbinder. 4. something used to fasten or tie,

such as rope or twine. 5. Also called: **reaper binder.** *Obs.* a machine for cutting grain and binding it into sheaves. 6. an informal agreement giving insurance coverage pending formal issue of a policy.

bindery ('baɪndərɪ) *n., pl.* -**eries.** a place in which books are bound.

binding ('baɪndɪŋ) *n.* 1. anything that binds or fastens. 2. the covering within which the pages of a book are bound. 3. the tape used for binding hems, etc. ~*adj.* 4. imposing an obligation or duty. 5. causing hindrance; restrictive.

bind over *vb.* (*tr., adv.*) to place (a person) under a legal obligation, such as one to keep the peace.

bindweed ('baɪnd,wiːd) *n.* any of various plants that twine around a support. See also **convolvulus.**

bine (baɪn) *n.* the climbing or twining stem of any of various plants, such as the woodbine or bindweed.

binge (bɪndʒ) *n. Inf.* 1. a bout of excessive drinking. 2. excessive indulgence in anything.

bingo ('bɪŋgəʊ) *n.* a gambling game, usually played with several people, in which random numbers are called out and the players cover the numbers on their individual cards. The first to cover a given arrangement of numbers is the winner.

binnacle ('bɪnəkəl) *n.* a housing for a ship's compass.

binocular (bɪ'nɒkjʊlə, baɪ-) *adj.* involving, relating to, seeing with or intended for both eyes: *binocular vision.*

binoculars (bɪ'nɒkjʊləz, baɪ-) *pl. n.* an optical instrument for use with both eyes, consisting of two small telescopes joined together.

binomial (baɪ'nəʊmɪəl) *n.* 1. a mathematical expression consisting of two terms, such as $3x + 2y$. 2. a two-part taxonomic name for an animal or plant indicating genus and species. ~*adj.* 3. referring to two names or terms. —**bi'nomially** *adv.*

binomial theorem *n.* a general mathematical formula that expresses any power of a binomial without multiplying out, as in $(a+b)^2 = a^2 + 2ab + b^2$.

bint (bɪnt) *n. Sl.* a derogatory term for **girl** or **woman.**

bio- *or before a vowel* **bi-** *combining form.* indicating life or living organisms: *biography; biogenesis.*

bioastronautics (,baɪəʊ,æstrə'nɔːtɪks) *n.* (*functioning as sing.*) the study of the effects of space flight on living organisms.

biochemistry (,baɪəʊ'kɛmɪstrɪ) *n.* the study of the chemical compounds, reactions, etc., occurring in living organisms. —**biochemical** (,baɪəʊ'kɛmɪkəl) *adj.* —,**bio'chemist** *n.*

biocoenosis (,baɪəʊsiː'nəʊsɪs) *n.* the relationships between animals and plants subsisting together.

biodegradable (,baɪəʊdɪ'greɪdəbəl) *adj.* (of sewage, packaging, etc.) capable of being decomposed by bacteria or other biological means.

bioengineering (,baɪəʊ,ɛndʒɪ'nɪərɪŋ) *n.* 1. the design and manufacture of aids, such as artificial limbs, to rectify defective body functions. 2. the design, manufacture, and maintenance of engineering equipment used in biosynthetic processes. —,**bio'engi'neer** *n.*

biofeedback (,baɪəʊ'fiːd,bæk) *n. Physiol., psychol.* a technique for controlling autonomic functions, such as the rate of heartbeat or breathing, by concentrating on the desired effect.

biogenesis (,baɪəʊ'dʒɛnɪsɪs) *n.* the principle that a living organism must originate from a parent organism similar to itself. —,**bioge'netic** *or* ,**bioge'netical** *adj.*

biography (baɪ'ɒgrəfɪ) *n., pl.* -**phies.** 1. an account of a person's life by another. 2. such accounts collectively. —**bi'ographer** *n.* —**biographical** (,baɪə'græfɪkəl) *adj.*

biol. *abbrev. for:* 1. biological. 2. biology.

biological (,baɪə'lɒdʒɪkəl) *adj.* 1. of or relating to biology. ~*n.* 2. (*usually pl.*) a drug derived from a living organism.

biological clock *n.* 1. an inherent periodicity in the physiological processes of living organisms that is inde-

---

THESAURUS

billow *n.* 1. breaker, crest, roller, surge, swell, tide, wave 2. cloud, deluge, flood, outpouring, rush, surge, wave ~*v.* 3. balloon, belly, puff up, rise up, roll, surge, swell

billowy heaving, rippling, rolling, surging, swelling, swirling, undulating, waving, wavy

bind *v.* 1. attach, fasten, glue, hitch, lash, paste, rope, secure, stick, strap, tie, tie up,

truss, wrap 2. compel, constrain, engage, force, necessitate, obligate, oblige, prescribe, require 3. confine, detain, hamper, hinder, restrain, restrict 4. bandage, cover, dress, encase, swathe, wrap 5. border, edge, finish, hem, trim ~*n.* 6. *Inf.* bore, difficulty, dilemma, nuisance, predicament, quandary

binding *adj.* compulsory, conclusive, im-

perative, indissoluble, irrevocable, mandatory, necessary, obligatory, unalterable

binge bender (*Sl.*), blind (*Sl.*), bout, fling, jag (*Sl.*), orgy, spree

biography account, life, life history, life story, memoir, profile

pendent of external periodicity. **2.** the hypothetical mechanism responsible for this. ~See also **circadian.**

biological control *n.* the control of destructive organisms by nonchemical means, such as introducing the natural enemy of a pest.

biological warfare *n.* the use of living organisms or their toxic products to induce death or incapacity in humans.

biology (baɪˈɒlədʒɪ) *n.* **1.** the study of living organisms. **2.** the animal and plant life of a particular region. —**bi-ˈologist** *n.*

biomedicine (ˌbaɪəʊˈmɛdɪsɪn) *n.* the medical and biological study of the effects of unusual environmental stress, esp. in connection with space travel.

bionic (baɪˈɒnɪk) *adj.* **1.** of or relating to bionics. **2.** (in science fiction) having physiological functions augmented by electronic equipment.

bionics (baɪˈɒnɪks) *n.* (*functioning as sing.*) the study of certain biological functions that are applicable to the development of electronic equipment designed to operate similarly.

biophysics (ˌbaɪəʊˈfɪzɪks) *n.* (*functioning as sing.*) the physics of biological processes and the application of methods used in physics to biology. —ˌbio'physical *adj.* —ˌbio'physically *adv.* —**biophysicist** (ˌbaɪəʊˈfɪzɪsɪst) *n.*

biopsy (ˈbaɪɒpsɪ) *n., pl.* **-sies.** examination, esp. under a microscope, of tissue from a living body to determine the cause or extent of a disease.

biorhythm (ˈbaɪəʊˌrɪðəm) *n.* a complex repeated pattern of physiological states, believed to affect a person's physical, emotional, or mental states and behaviour.

bioscope (ˈbaɪəˌskəʊp) *n.* **1.** a kind of early film projector. **2.** a South African word for **cinema.**

bioscopy (baɪˈɒskəpɪ) *n., pl.* **-pies.** examination of a body to determine whether it is alive.

biosphere (ˈbaɪəˌsfɪə) *n.* the part of the earth's surface and atmosphere inhabited by living things.

biosynthesis (ˌbaɪəʊˈsɪnθɪsɪs) *n.* the formation of complex compounds from simple substances by living organisms. —**biosynthetic** (ˌbaɪəʊsɪnˈθɛtɪk) *adj.*

biotin (ˈbaɪətɪn) *n.* a vitamin of the B complex, abundant in egg yolk and liver.

bipartisan (ˌbaɪpɑːtɪˈzæn, baɪˈpɑːtɪˌzæn) *adj.* consisting of or supported by two or more political parties. —ˌbipartiˈsanship *n.*

bipartite (baɪˈpɑːtaɪt) *adj.* **1.** consisting of or having two parts. **2.** affecting or made by two parties. **3.** *Bot.* (esp. of some leaves) divided into two parts almost to the base. —**bi'partitely** *adv.* —**bipartition** (ˌbaɪpɑːˈtɪʃən) *n.*

biped (ˈbaɪpɛd) *n.* **1.** any animal with two feet. ~*adj.* *also* **bipedal** (baɪˈpiːdəl, -ˈpɛdəl). **2.** having two feet.

biplane (ˈbaɪˌpleɪn) *n.* a type of aeroplane having two sets of wings, one above the other.

bipolar (baɪˈpəʊlə) *adj.* **1.** having two poles: *a bipolar dynamo.* **2.** of or relating to the North and South Poles. **3.** having or characterized by two opposed opinions, etc. **4.** (of a transistor) utilizing both majority and minority charge carriers. —ˌbipoˈlarity *n.*

birch (bɜːtʃ) *n.* **1.** any catkin-bearing tree or shrub having thin peeling bark. See also **silver birch. 2.** the hard close-grained wood of any of these trees. **3. the birch.** a bundle of birch twigs or a birch rod used, esp. formerly, for flogging offenders. ~*adj.* **4.** consisting or made of birch. ~*vb.* **5.** (*tr.*) to flog with a birch. —**'birchen** *adj.*

bird (bɜːd) *n.* **1.** any warm-blooded egg-laying vertebrate, characterized by a body covering of feathers and forelimbs modified as wings. **2.** *Inf.* a person, as in **rare bird, odd bird, clever bird. 3.** *Sl., chiefly Brit.* a girl or young woman. **4.** *Sl.* prison or a term in prison (esp. in **do bird**). **5. a bird in the hand.** something definite or certain. **6. birds of a feather.** *Often derog.* people with characteristics, ideas, interests, etc., in common. **7. get the bird.** *Inf.* **a.** to be fired or dismissed. **b.** (esp. of a public performer) to be hissed at. **8. kill two birds with one stone.** to accomplish two things at the same time. **9.** (**strictly**) **for the birds.** *Inf.* deserving of disdain or contempt; not important.

birdbath (ˈbɜːdˌbɑːθ) *n.* a small basin or trough for birds to bathe in, usually in a garden.

bird call *n.* **1.** the characteristic call or song of a bird. **2.** an imitation of this.

birdie (ˈbɜːdɪ) *n.* **1.** *Golf.* a score of one stroke under par for a hole. **2.** *Inf.* a bird, esp. a small bird.

birdlime (ˈbɜːdˌlaɪm) *n.* **1.** a sticky substance smeared on twigs to catch small birds. ~*vb.* **2.** (*tr.*) to smear (twigs) with birdlime to catch (small birds).

bird of paradise *n.* **1.** any of various songbirds of New Guinea and neighbouring regions, the males having brilliantly coloured plumage. **2. bird-of-paradise flower.** any of various plants native to tropical southern Africa and South America that have purple bracts and large orange or yellow flowers resembling birds' heads.

bird of passage *n.* **1.** a bird that migrates seasonally. **2.** a transient person.

bird of prey *n.* a bird, such as a hawk or owl, that hunts other animals for food.

birdseed (ˈbɜːdˌsiːd) *n.* a mixture of various kinds of seeds for feeding cage birds.

bird's-eye *adj.* **1. a.** seen or photographed from high above. **b.** summarizing (esp. in **bird's-eye view**). **2.** having markings resembling birds' eyes. ~*n.* **3.** a pattern in linen and cotton fabrics, made up of small diamond shapes with a dot in the centre of each.

biretta *or* **berretta** (bɪˈrɛtə) *n.* *R.C. Church.* a stiff square clerical cap.

biriani (ˌbɪrɪˈɑːnɪ) *n.* an Indian dish made with rice, highly flavoured and coloured, mixed with meat or fish.

Biro (ˈbaɪrəʊ) *n., pl.* **-ros.** *Trademark, Brit.* a kind of ballpoint.

birth (bɜːθ) *n.* **1.** the process of bearing young; childbirth. **2.** the act or fact of being born; nativity. **3.** the coming into existence of something; origin. **4.** ancestry; lineage: *of high birth.* **5.** natural or inherited talent: *an artist by birth.* **6. give birth (to). a.** to bear or bring forth (offspring). **b.** to produce or create (an idea, plan, etc.). ~*vb.* (*tr.*) *Rare.* **7.** to bear or bring forth (a child).

birth certificate *n.* an official form giving details of the time and place of a person's birth.

birth control *n.* limitation of childbearing by means of contraception.

birthday (ˈbɜːθˌdeɪ) *n.* **1. a.** an anniversary of the day of one's birth. **b.** (*as modifier*): *birthday present.* **2.** the day on which a person was born.

birthmark (ˈbɜːθˌmɑːk) *n.* a blemish on the skin formed before birth; naevus.

birthplace (ˈbɜːθˌpleɪs) *n.* the place where someone was born or where something originated.

birth rate *n.* the ratio of live births in a specified area, group, etc., to population, usually expressed per 1000 population per year.

birthright (ˈbɜːθˌraɪt) *n.* **1.** privileges or possessions that a person has or is believed to be entitled to as soon as he is born. **2.** the privileges or possessions of a first-born son. **3.** inheritance.

birthstone (ˈbɜːθˌstəʊn) *n.* a precious or semiprecious stone associated with a month or sign of the zodiac and thought to bring luck if worn by a person born in that month.

biscuit (ˈbɪskɪt) *n.* **1.** *Brit.* a small flat dry sweet or plain cake of many varieties. U.S. word: **cookie. 2.** a pale brown or yellowish-grey colour. **3.** Also called: **bisque.** earthenware or porcelain that has been fired but not glazed. **4. take the biscuit.** *Brit.* to be regarded (by the speaker) as most surprising.

bisect (baɪˈsɛkt) *vb.* **1.** (*tr.*) *Maths.* to divide into two equal parts. **2.** to cut or split into two. —**bisection** (baɪˈsɛkʃən) *n.*

bisexual (baɪˈsɛksjʊəl) *adj.* **1.** sexually attracted by both men and women. **2.** showing characteristics of both sexes. **3.** of or relating to both sexes. ~*n.* **4.** a bisexual organism; a hermaphrodite. **5.** a bisexual person. —**bi'sexualism** *or* **bisexuality** (baɪˌsɛksjʊˈælɪtɪ) *n.*

bishop (ˈbɪʃəp) *n.* **1.** a clergyman having spiritual and

THESAURUS

birth 1. childbirth, delivery, nativity, parturition, 2. beginning, emergence, fountainhead, genesis, origin, rise, source 3. ancestry, background, blood, breeding, derivation, descent, extraction, forebears, genealogy, line, lineage, nobility, noble extraction, parentage, pedigree, race, stock, strain

bisect bifurcate, cross, cut across, cut in half, cut in two, divide in two, halve, intersect, separate, split, split down the middle

administrative powers over a diocese. See also **suffragan**. Related adj.: **episcopal**. **2.** a chess piece, capable of moving diagonally. **3.** mulled wine, usually port, spiced with oranges, cloves, etc.

bishopric ('bɪʃəprɪk) n. the see, diocese, or office of a bishop.

bismuth ('bɪzməθ) n. a brittle pinkish-white crystalline metallic element. It is widely used in alloys; its compounds are used in medicines. Symbol: Bi; atomic no.: 83; atomic wt.: 208.98.

bison ('baɪsən) n., pl. **-son**. **1.** Also called: **American bison, buffalo.** a member of the cattle tribe, formerly widely distributed over the prairies of W North America, with a massive head, shaggy forequarters, and a humped back. **2.** Also called: **wisent, European bison.** a closely related and similar animal formerly widespread in Europe.

bisque[1] (bɪsk) n. a thick rich soup made from shellfish.

bisque[2] (bɪsk) n. **1.** a pink to yellowish tan colour. **2.** Ceramics. another name for **biscuit** (sense 3).

bisque[3] (bɪsk) n. Tennis, golf, croquet. an extra point, stroke, or turn allowed to an inferior player, usually taken when desired.

bistre or U.S. **bister** ('bɪstə) n. **1.** a transparent water-soluble brownish-yellow pigment made by boiling the soot of wood. **2.** a yellowish-brown to dark brown colour.

bistro ('bi:strəʊ) n., pl. **-tros**. a small restaurant.

bit[1] (bɪt) n. **1.** a small piece, portion, or quantity. **2.** a short time or distance. **3.** U.S. inf. the value of an eighth of a dollar: spoken of only in units of two: two bits. **4.** any small coin. **5.** short for **bit part**. **6. a bit**. rather; somewhat: a bit dreary. **7. a bit of. a.** rather: a bit of a dope. **b.** a considerable amount: that must take quite a bit of courage. **8. bit by bit**. gradually. **9. do one's bit**. to make one's expected contribution. **10. every bit**. (foll. by as) to the same degree: she was every bit as clever as her brother.

bit[2] (bɪt) n. **1.** a metal mouthpiece on a bridle for controlling a horse. **2.** anything that restrains or curbs. **3.** a cutting or drilling tool, part, or head in a brace, drill, etc. **4.** the part of a key that engages the levers of a lock. ~vb. **bitting, bitted**. (tr.) **5.** to put a bit in the mouth of (a horse). **6.** to restrain; curb.

bit[3] (bɪt) vb. the past tense of **bite**.

bit[4] (bɪt) n. **1.** either of the two digits 0 or 1, used in binary notation. **2.** a unit of information representing the physical state of a system having one of two values, such as on or off.

bitch (bɪtʃ) n. **1.** a female dog or other female canine animal, such as a wolf. **2.** Sl., derog. a malicious, spiteful, or coarse woman. **3.** Sl. a difficult situation or problem. ~vb. Sl. **4.** (intr.) to complain; grumble. **5.** to behave (towards) in a spiteful manner. **6.** (tr., often foll. by up) to botch; bungle. —'**bitchy** adj.

bite (baɪt) vb. **biting, bit, bitten**. **1.** to grip, cut off, or tear as with the teeth or jaws. **2.** (of animals, insects, etc.) to injure by puncturing or tearing (the skin or flesh) with the teeth, fangs, etc. **3.** (tr.) to cut or penetrate, as with a knife. **4.** (of corrosive material such as acid) to eat away or into. **5.** to smart or cause to smart; sting. **6.** (intr.) Angling. (of a fish) to take or attempt to take the bait or lure. **7.** (tr.) Sl. to annoy or worry: what's biting her? **9. put the bite on**. Austral. to cadge or borrow from. **10.**

(tr.; often foll. by for) Austral. & N.Z. sl. to ask (for); scrounge from. **11. bite someone's head off**. Inf. to respond harshly and rudely (to). **12. bite the dust**. Sl. **a.** to fall down dead. **b.** to be rejected: another good idea bites the dust. ~n. **13.** the act of biting. **14.** a thing or amount bitten off. **15.** a wound, bruise, or sting inflicted by biting. **16.** Angling. an attempt by a fish to take the bait or lure. **17.** Inf. a light meal; snack. **18.** a cutting, stinging, or smarting sensation. **19.** Dentistry. the angle or manner of contact between the upper and lower teeth. —'**biter** n.

biting ('baɪtɪŋ) adj. **1.** piercing; keen: a biting wind. **2.** sarcastic; incisive. —'**bitingly** adv.

bit part n. a very small acting role with few lines to speak.

bitten ('bɪtən) vb. the past participle of **bite**.

bitter ('bɪtə) adj. **1.** having or denoting an unpalatable harsh taste, as the peel of an orange. **2.** showing or caused by strong unrelenting hostility or resentment. **3.** difficult or unpleasant to accept or admit: a bitter blow. **4.** cutting; sarcastic: bitter words. **5.** bitingly cold: a bitter night. ~adv. **6.** very; extremely (esp. in **bitter cold**). ~n. **7.** a thing that is bitter. **8.** Brit. draught beer with a slightly bitter taste. —'**bitterness** n.

bittern ('bɪtən) n. a wading bird related and similar to the herons but with shorter legs and neck and a booming call.

bitters ('bɪtəz) pl. n. **1.** bitter-tasting spirits of varying alcoholic content flavoured with plant extracts. **2.** a similar liquid containing a bitter-tasting substance, used as a tonic.

bittersweet ('bɪtə,swi:t) n. **1.** any of several North American woody climbing plants having orange capsules that open to expose scarlet-coated seeds. **2.** another name for **woody nightshade**. ~adj. **3.** tasting of or being a mixture of bitterness and sweetness. **4.** pleasant but tinged with sadness.

bitty ('bɪtɪ) adj. **-tier, -tiest**. **1.** lacking unity; disjointed. **2.** containing bits, sediment, etc.

bitumen ('bɪtjʊmɪn) n. **1.** any of various viscous or solid impure mixtures of hydrocarbons that occur naturally in asphalt, tar, mineral waxes, etc.: used as a road surfacing and roofing material. **2. the bitumen**. Austral. inf. any road with a bitumen surface. —**bituminous** (bɪ'tju:mɪnəs) adj.

bituminous coal n. a soft black coal that burns with a smoky yellow flame.

bivalent (baɪ'veɪlənt, 'baɪvə-) adj. **1.** Chem. another word for **divalent**. **2.** (of homologous chromosomes) associated together in pairs. —**bi'valency** n.

bivalve ('baɪ,vælv) n. **1.** Also called: **lamellibranch**. a marine or freshwater mollusc, having a laterally compressed body, a shell consisting of two hinged valves, and gills for respiration. The group includes clams, cockles, oysters, and mussels. ~adj. **2.** Also: **lamellibranch**. of or relating to these molluscs.

bivouac ('bɪvʊˌæk, 'bɪvwæk) n. **1.** a temporary encampment, as used by soldiers, mountaineers, etc. ~vb. **-acking, -acked**. **2.** (intr.) to make such an encampment.

biweekly (baɪ'wi:klɪ) adj., adv. **1.** every two weeks. **2.** twice a week; semiweekly. See **bi-**. ~n., pl. **-lies**. **3.** a periodical published every two weeks.

biz (bɪz) n. Inf. short for **business**.

THESAURUS

bishopric diocese, episcopacy, episcopate, primacy, see

bit[1] **1.** atom, chip, crumb, fragment, grain, iota, jot, mite, morsel, mouthful, part, piece, scrap, segment, slice, small piece, speck, tittle, whit **2.** instant, jiffy (Inf.), little while, minute, moment, period, second, spell, tick (Inf.), time

bit[2] **1.** brake, check, curb, restraint, snaffle **2. take the bit in** or **between one's teeth** defy, disobey, get stuck into (Sl.), get to grips with, rebel, resist, revolt, run amok, rush into, set about

bitchy catty (Inf.), cruel, malicious, mean, nasty, rancorous, snide, spiteful, venomous, vindictive, vixenish

bite v. **1.** champ, chew, clamp, crunch, crush, cut, gnaw, grip, hold, masticate, nib-

ble, nip, pierce, pinch, rend, seize, snap, tear, wound **2.** burn, corrode, eat away, eat into, erode, smart, sting, tingle, wear away ~n. **3.** itch, nip, pinch, prick, smarting, sting, tooth marks, wound **4.** food, light meal, morsel, mouthful, piece, refreshment, snack, taste **5.** edge, kick (Inf.), piquancy, punch (Inf.), pungency, spice

biting 1. bitter, blighting, cold, cutting, freezing, harsh, nipping, penetrating, piercing, sharp **2.** caustic, cutting, incisive, mordant, sarcastic, scathing, severe, stinging, trenchant, withering

bitter 1. acid, acrid, astringent, sharp, sour, tart, unsweetened, vinegary **2.** acrimonious, begrudging, crabbed, embittered, hostile, morose, rancorous, resentful, sore, sour, sullen, with a chip on one's shoulder **3.** ca-

lamitous, cruel, dire, distressing, galling, grievous, harsh, heartbreaking, merciless, painful, poignant, ruthless, savage, vexatious **4.** biting, fierce, freezing, intense, severe, stinging

bitterness 1. acerbity, acidity, sharpness, sourness, tartness, vinegariness **2.** animosity, grudge, hostility, pique, rancour, resentment **3.** acrimoniousness, asperity, sarcasm, venom, virulence

bizarre comical, curious, eccentric, extraordinary, fantastic, freakish, grotesque, ludicrous, odd, off-beat, outlandish, outré, peculiar, queer, ridiculous, strange, unusual, weird

bizarre (bɪˈzɑː) *adj.* odd or unusual, esp. in an interesting or amusing way. —**biˈzarreness** *n.*

Bk *the chemical symbol for* berkelium.

bk. *abbrev. for:* 1. bank. 2. book.

B.L. *abbrev. for:* 1. Bachelor of Law. 2. Bachelor of Letters. 3. Barrister-at-Law. 4. British Library.

B/L, b/l, *or* **b.l.** *pl.* **Bs/L, bs/l,** *or* **bs.l.** *abbrev. for* bill of lading.

blab (blæb) *vb.* **blabbing, blabbed.** 1. to divulge (secrets, etc.) indiscreetly. 2. (*intr.*) to chatter thoughtlessly; prattle. ~*n.* 3. a less common word for **blabber.**

blabber (ˈblæbə) *n.* 1. a person who blabs. 2. idle chatter. ~*vb.* 3. (*intr.*) to talk without thinking; chatter.

black (blæk) *adj.* 1. of the colour of jet or carbon black, having no hue due to the absorption of all or nearly all incident light. 2. without light; completely dark. 3. without hope of alleviation; gloomy: *the future looked black.* 4. very dirty or soiled. 5. angry or resentful: *black looks.* 6. (of a play or other work) dealing with the unpleasant realities of life, esp. in a cynical or macabre manner: *black comedy.* 7. (of coffee or tea) without milk or cream. 8. **a.** wicked or harmful: *a black lie.* **b.** (*in combination*): *black-hearted.* 9. *Brit.* (of goods, jobs, works, etc.) being subject to boycott by trade unionists. ~*n.* 10. a black colour. 11. a dye or pigment of or producing this colour. 12. black clothing, worn esp. as a sign of mourning. 13. *Chess, draughts.* a black or dark-coloured piece or square. 14. complete darkness: *the black of the night.* 15. **in the black.** in credit or without debt. ~*vb.* 16. another word for **blacken.** 17. (*tr.*) to polish (shoes, etc.) with blacking. 18. (*tr.*) *Brit. & N.Z.* (of trade unionists) to organize a boycott of (specified goods, jobs, work, etc.). ~See also **blackout.** —**ˈblackness** *n.*

Black (blæk) *n.* 1. a member of a dark-skinned race, esp. a Negro or an Australian Aborigine. ~*adj.* 2. of or relating to a Black or Blacks.

blackamoor (ˈblækəˌmʊə, -ˌmɔː) *n. Arch.* a Negro or other person with dark skin.

black-and-blue *adj.* 1. (of the skin) discoloured, as from a bruise. 2. feeling pain or soreness, as from a beating.

black-and-white *n.* 1. **a.** a photograph, picture, sketch, etc., in black, white, and shades of grey rather than in colour. **b.** (*as modifier*): *black-and-white film.* 2. **in black and white. a.** in print or writing. **b.** in extremes: *he always saw things in black and white.*

black art *n.* **the.** another name for **black magic.**

black-backed gull *n.* either of two common black-and-white European coastal gulls, **lesser black-backed gull** and **great black-backed gull.**

blackball (ˈblækˌbɔːl) *n.* 1. a negative vote or veto. 2. a black wooden ball used to indicate disapproval or to veto in a vote. ~*vb.* (*tr.*) 3. to vote against. 4. to exclude (someone) from a group, profession, etc.; ostracize.

black bear *n.* 1. **American black bear.** a bear inhabiting forests of North America. It is smaller and less ferocious than the brown bear. 2. **Asiatic black bear.** a bear of central and E Asia, black with a pale V-shaped mark on the chest.

black belt *n. Judo & karate.* **a.** a black belt worn by an instructor or expert. **b.** a person entitled to wear this.

blackberry (ˈblækbərɪ) *n., pl.* **-ries.** 1. Also called: **bramble.** any of several woody rosaceous plants that have thorny stems and black or purple edible berry-like fruits. 2. the fruit of any of these plants. ~*vb.* **-rying, -ried.** 3. (*intr.*) to gather blackberries.

blackbird (ˈblækˌbɜːd) *n.* 1. a common European thrush in which the male has black plumage and a yel-

low bill. 2. any of various American orioles having dark plumage. 3. (formerly) a person, esp. a South Sea islander, who was kidnapped and sold as a slave, esp. in Australia. ~*vb.* 4. (*tr.*) (formerly) to kidnap and sell into slavery.

blackboard (ˈblækˌbɔːd) *n.* a sheet of slate, wood, or any of various other materials, used for writing or drawing on with chalk, esp. in teaching.

black book *n.* 1. a book containing the names of people to be punished, blacklisted, etc. 2. **in someone's black books.** *Inf.* out of favour with someone.

black box *n.* 1. a self-contained unit in an electronic or computer system whose circuitry need not be known to understand its function. 2. an informal name for **flight recorder.**

blackcap (ˈblækˌkæp) *n.* a brownish-grey Old World warbler, the male of which has a black crown.

blackcock (ˈblækˌkɒk) *n.* the male of the black grouse.

Black Country *n.* **the.** the heavily industrialized West Midlands of England.

blackcurrant (ˌblækˈkʌrənt) *n.* 1. a N temperate shrub having red or white flowers and small edible black berries. 2. its fruit.

blackdamp (ˈblækˌdæmp) *n.* air that is low in oxygen content and high in carbon dioxide as a result of an explosion in a mine. Also called: **chokedamp.**

Black Death *n.* **the.** a form of bubonic plague pandemic in Europe and Asia during the 14th century. See **bubonic plague.**

black economy *n.* that portion of the income of a nation that remains illegally undeclared.

blacken (ˈblækən) *vb.* 1. to make or become black or dirty. 2. (*tr.*) to defame; slander (esp. in **blacken someone's name**).

black eye *n. Inf.* bruising round the eye.

black flag *n.* another name for the **Jolly Roger.**

Black Friar *n.* a Dominican friar.

blackguard (ˈblægɑːd, -gəd) *n.* 1. an unprincipled contemptible person; scoundrel. ~*vb.* 2. (*tr.*) to ridicule or denounce with abusive language. 3. (*intr.*) to behave like a blackguard. —**ˈblackguardism** *n.* —**ˈblackguardly** *adj.*

blackhead (ˈblækˌhɛd) *n.* 1. a black-tipped plug of fatty matter clogging a pore of the skin. 2. any of various birds with black plumage on the head.

black hole *n. Astron.* a hypothetical region of space resulting from the gravitational collapse of a star and surrounded by a gravitational field so high that neither matter nor radiation could escape from it.

black ice *n.* a thin transparent layer of new ice on a road or similar surface.

blacking (ˈblækɪŋ) *n.* any preparation for giving a black finish to shoes, metals, etc.

blackjack[1] (ˈblækˌdʒæk) *Chiefly U.S.* ~*n.* 1. a truncheon of leather-covered lead with a flexible shaft. ~*vb.* 2. (*tr.*) to hit as with a blackjack. 3. (*tr.*) to compel (a person) by threats.

blackjack[2] (ˈblækˌdʒæk) *n.* pontoon or any similar card game.

black lead (lɛd) *n.* another name for **graphite.**

blackleg (ˈblækˌlɛg) *n.* 1. Also called (esp. U.S.): **scab.** *Brit.* a person who acts against the interests of a trade union, as by continuing to work during a strike or taking over a striker's job. ~*vb.* **-legging, -legged.** 2. *Brit.* to act against the interests of a trade union, esp. by refusing to join a strike.

blacklist (ˈblækˌlɪst) *n.* 1. a list of persons or organizations under suspicion, or considered untrustworthy, disloyal, etc. ~*vb.* 2. (*tr.*) to put on a blacklist.

black magic *n.* magic used for evil purposes.

▌THESAURUS▐

blab blurt out, disclose, divulge, gossip, let slip, reveal, tattle, tell, tell on

blabber 1. *n.* busybody, gossip, informer, rumour-monger, scandalmonger, talebearer, tattler, telltale 2. *v.* blather, blether (*Scot.*), chatter, gab (*Inf.*), jabber, prattle

black *adj.* 1. coal-black, dark, dusky, ebony, inky, jet, murky, pitchy, raven, sable, starless, stygian, swarthy 2. *Fig.* atrocious, depressing, dismal, distressing, doleful, foreboding, funereal, gloomy, hopeless, horrible,

lugubrious, mournful, ominous, sad, sombre 3. dingy, dirty, filthy, grimy, grubby, soiled, sooty, stained 4. angry, furious, hostile, menacing, resentful, sullen, threatening 5. bad, evil, iniquitous, nefarious, villainous, wicked ~*v.* 6. ban, bar, blacklist, boycott 7. **in the black** in credit, in funds, solvent, without debt

blackball *v.* ban, bar, blacklist, debar, drum out, exclude, expel, ostracize, oust, repudiate, snub, vote against

blacken 1. befoul, begrime, cloud, darken, grow black, make black, smudge, soil 2. calumniate, decry, defame, defile, denigrate, dishonour, malign, slander, smear, smirch, stain, sully, taint, tarnish, traduce, vilify

blackguard bastard (*Offensive*), blighter (*Inf.*), bounder (*Brit. inf.*), miscreant, rascal, rogue, scoundrel, swine, villain, wretch

blacklist *v.* ban, bar, blackball, boycott, debar, exclude, expel, ostracize, preclude, proscribe, reject, repudiate, snub, vote

blackmail ('blæk,meɪl) *n.* **1.** the act of attempting to obtain money by intimidation, as by threats to disclose discreditable information. **2.** the exertion of pressure, esp. unfairly, in an attempt to influence someone. ~*vb.* (*tr.*) **3.** to exact or attempt to exact (money or anything of value) from (a person) by threats or intimidation; extort. **4.** to attempt to influence (a person), esp. by unfair pressure. —'**blackmailer** *n.*

Black Maria (mə'raɪə) *n.* a police van for transporting prisoners.

black mark *n.* an indication of disapproval, failure, etc.

black market *n.* **1.** any system in which goods or currencies are sold and bought illegally, esp. in violation of controls or rationing. **2.** the place where such a system operates. ~*vb.* **black-market. 3.** to sell (goods) on the black market. —**black marketeer** *n.*

black mass *n.* (*sometimes cap.*) a blasphemous travesty of the Christian Mass, performed by practitioners of black magic.

Black Muslim *n.* (esp. in the U.S.) a member of an Islamic political movement of Black people who seek to establish a new Black nation.

blackout ('blækaʊt) *n.* **1.** the extinguishing or hiding of all artificial light, esp. in a city visible to an air attack. **2.** a momentary loss of consciousness, vision, or memory. **3.** a temporary electrical power failure or cut. **4.** the suspension of broadcasting, as by a strike or for political reasons. ~*vb.* **black out.** (*adv.*) **5.** (*tr.*) to obliterate or extinguish (lights). **6.** (*tr.*) to create a blackout in (a city, etc.). **7.** (*intr.*) *Inf.* to lose vision, consciousness, or memory temporarily. **8.** (*tr., adv.*) to stop (news, a television programme) from being broadcast.

black pepper *n.* a pungent condiment made by grinding the dried unripe berries and husks of the pepper plant.

Black Power *n.* a social, economic, and political movement of Black people, esp. in the U.S. and Australia, to obtain equality with Whites.

black pudding *n.* a kind of black sausage made from minced pork fat, pig's blood, and other ingredients. Also called: **blood pudding.**

Black Rod *n.* (in Britain) an officer of the House of Lords and of the Order of the Garter, whose main duty is summoning the Commons at the opening and proroguing of Parliament.

black sheep *n.* a person who is regarded as a disgrace or failure by his family or peer group.

Blackshirt ('blæk,ʃɜːt) *n.* (in Europe) a member of a fascist organization, esp. the Italian Fascist party before and during World War II.

blacksmith ('blæk,smɪθ) *n.* an artisan who works iron with a furnace, anvil, hammer, etc.

black spot *n.* **1.** a place on a road where accidents frequently occur. **2.** any dangerous or difficult place.

black tea *n.* tea made from fermented tea leaves.

blackthorn ('blæk,θɔːn) *n.* a thorny Eurasian shrub with black twigs, white flowers, and small sour plumlike fruits. Also called: **sloe.**

black tie *n.* **1.** a black bow tie worn with a dinner jacket. **2.** (*modifier*) denoting an occasion when a dinner jacket should be worn.

black velvet *n.* a mixture of stout and champagne in equal proportions.

Black Watch *n.* **the.** the Royal Highland Regiment in the British army.

black widow *n.* an American spider, the female of which is highly venomous, and commonly eats its mate.

bladder ('blædə) *n.* **1.** *Anat.* a distensible membranous sac, usually containing liquid or gas, esp. the urinary bladder. **2.** an inflatable part of something. **3.** a hollow saclike part in certain plants, such as the bladderwrack. —'**bladdery** *adj.*

bladderwort ('blædə,wɜːt) *n.* an aquatic plant some of whose leaves are modified as small bladders to trap minute aquatic animals.

bladderwrack ('blædə,ræk) *n.* any of several seaweeds that grow in the intertidal regions of rocky shores and have branched brown fronds with air bladders.

blade (bleɪd) *n.* **1.** the part of a sharp weapon, tool, etc., that forms the cutting edge. **2.** the thin flattish part of various tools, implements, etc., as of a propeller. **3.** the flattened expanded part of a leaf, sepal, or petal. **4.** the long narrow leaf of a grass or related plant. **5.** the striking surface of a bat, club, stick, or oar. **6.** the metal runner on an ice skate. **7.** the upper part of the tongue lying directly behind the tip. **8.** *Arch.* a dashing or swaggering young man. **9.** short for **shoulder blade. 10.** a poetic word for a **sword** or **swordsman.** —'**bladed** *adj.*

blaeberry ('bleɪbərɪ) *n., pl.* **-ries.** *Brit.* another name for **whortleberry** (senses 1, 2).

blah *or* **blah blah** (blɑː) *n. Sl.* worthless or silly talk.

blain (bleɪn) *n.* a blister, blotch, or sore on the skin.

blame (bleɪm) *n.* **1.** responsibility for something that is wrong; culpability. **2.** an expression of condemnation. **3. be to blame.** to be at fault. ~*vb.* (*tr.*) **4.** (usually foll. by *for*) to attribute responsibility to: *I blame him for the failure.* **5.** (usually foll. by *on*) to ascribe responsibility for (something) to: *I blame the failure on him.* **6.** to find fault with. —'**blamable** *or* '**blameable** *adj.* —'**blamably** *or* '**blameably** *adv.* —'**blameless** *adj.*

blameworthy ('bleɪm,wɜːðɪ) *adj.* deserving censure. —'**blame,worthiness** *n.*

blanch (blɑːntʃ) *vb.* (*mainly tr.*) **1.** to remove colour from; whiten. **2.** (*usually intr.*) to become or cause to become pale, as with sickness or fear. **3.** to prepare (meat, green vegetables, nuts, etc.) by plunging them in boiling water. **4.** to cause (celery, chicory, etc.) to grow free of chlorophyll by the exclusion of sunlight.

blancmange (blə'mɒnʒ) *n.* a jelly-like dessert of milk, stiffened usually with cornflour.

bland (blænd) *adj.* **1.** devoid of distinctive or stimulating characteristics; uninteresting. **2.** gentle and agreeable; suave. **3.** mild and soothing. —'**blandness** *n.*

blandish ('blændɪʃ) *vb.* (*tr.*) to seek to persuade or influence by mild flattery; coax.

blandishments ('blændɪʃmənts) *pl. n.* (*rarely sing.*) flattery intended to coax or cajole.

blank (blæŋk) *adj.* **1.** (of a writing surface) bearing no marks; not written on. **2.** (of a form, etc.) with spaces left for details to be filled in. **3.** without ornament or break. **4.** not filled in; empty. **5.** exhibiting no interest or expression: *a blank look.* **6.** lacking understanding; confused: *he looked blank.* **7.** absolute; complete: *blank*

THESAURUS

black magic black art, diabolism, necromancy, sorcery, voodoo, witchcraft, wizardry

blackmail 1. *n.* bribe, exaction, extortion, hush money (*Sl.*), intimidation, milking, pay-off (*Inf.*), protection (*Inf.*), ransom, slush fund (*Inf.*) *v.* bleed (*Inf.*), bribe, coerce, compel, demand, exact, extort, force, hold to ransom, milk, squeeze, threaten

blackness darkness, duskiness, gloom, inkiness, melanism, murkiness, nigrescence, nigritude, swarthiness

blackout *n.* **1.** coma, faint, loss of consciousness, oblivion, swoon, syncope (*Pathology*), unconsciousness **2.** power cut, power failure **3.** censorship, noncommunication, radio silence, secrecy, suppression, withholding news

black out *v.* **1.** conceal, cover, darken,

eclipse, obfuscate, shade **2.** collapse, faint, flake out (*Inf.*), lose consciousness, pass out, swoon

black sheep disgrace, ne'er-do-well, outcast, prodigal, renegade, reprobate, wastrel

blame *n.* **1.** accountability, culpability, fault, guilt, incrimination, liability, onus, rap (*Inf.*), responsibility **2.** accusation, castigation, censure, charge, complaint, condemnation, criticism, recrimination, reproach, reproof ~*v.* **3.** accuse, admonish, censure, charge, chide, condemn, criticize, disapprove, express disapprobation, find fault with, hold responsible, reprehend, reproach, reprove, tax, upbraid

blameless above suspicion, clean, faultless, guiltless, immaculate, impeccable, innocent, in the clear, irreproachable, perfect, stainless, unblemished, unimpeachable, unof-

fending, unspotted, unsullied, untarnished, upright, virtuous

blameworthy discreditable, disreputable, indefensible, inexcusable, iniquitous, reprehensible, reproachable, shameful

bland 1. boring, dull, flat, humdrum, insipid, monotonous, tasteless, tedious, undistinctive, unexciting, uninspiring, uninteresting, unstimulating, vapid, weak **2.** affable, amiable, congenial, courteous, friendly, gentle, gracious, smooth, suave, unemotional, urbane **3.** balmy, calm, mild, mollifying, nonirritant *or* non-irritating (*Medical*), soft, soothing, temperate

blandishments blarney, cajolery, coaxing, compliments, fawning, flattery, ingratiation, inveiglement, soft soap (*Inf.*), soft words, sweet talk (*Inf., chiefly U.S.*), wheedling, winning caresses

rejection. **8.** devoid of ideas or inspiration: _his mind went blank._ ~_n._ **9.** an emptiness; void; blank space. **10.** an empty space for writing in. **11.** a printed form containing such empty spaces. **12.** something characterized by incomprehension or confusion: _my mind went a complete blank._ **13.** a mark, often a dash, in place of a word, esp. a taboo word. **14.** short for **blank cartridge**. **15.** a piece of material prepared for stamping, punching, forging, or some other operation. **16. draw a blank. a.** to choose a lottery ticket that fails to win. **b.** _Inf._ to get no results from something. ~_vb._ (_tr._) **17.** (usually foll. by _out_) to cross out, blot, or obscure. —**'blankness** _n._

blank cartridge _n._ a gun cartridge containing powder but no bullet.

blank cheque _n._ **1.** a cheque that has been signed but on which the amount payable has not been specified. **2.** complete freedom of action.

blanket ('blæŋkɪt) _n._ **1.** a large piece of thick cloth for use as a bed covering, animal covering, etc. **2.** a concealing cover, as of smoke, leaves, or snow. **3.** (_modifier_) applying to or covering a wide group or variety of people, conditions, situations, etc.: _blanket insurance against loss, injury, and theft._ ~_vb._ (_tr._) **4.** to cover as with a blanket; overlie. **5.** (usually foll. by _out_) to obscure or suppress.

blanket stitch _n._ a strong reinforcing stitch for the edges of blankets and other thick material.

blank verse _n._ _Prosody._ unrhymed verse, esp. in iambic pentameters.

blare (blɛə) _vb._ **1.** to sound loudly and harshly. **2.** to proclaim loudly and sensationally. ~_n._ **3.** a loud harsh noise.

blarney ('blɑːnɪ) _n._ **1.** flattering talk. ~_vb._ **2.** to cajole with flattery; wheedle.

blasé ('blɑːzeɪ) _adj._ **1.** indifferent to something because of familiarity. **2.** lacking enthusiasm; bored.

blaspheme (blæs'fiːm) _vb._ **1.** (_tr._) to show contempt or disrespect for (God, or sacred things), esp. in speech. **2.** (_intr._) to utter profanities or curses. —**blas'phemer** _n._ —**'blasphemous** _adj._

blasphemy ('blæsfɪmɪ) _n._, _pl._ **-mies.** blasphemous behaviour or language. —**'blasphemous** _adj._

blast (blɑːst) _n._ **1.** an explosion, as of dynamite. **2.** the rapid movement of air resulting from an explosion; shock wave. **3.** the charge used in a single explosion. **4.** a sudden strong gust of wind or air. **5.** a sudden loud sound, as of a trumpet. **6.** a violent verbal outburst, as of criticism. **7.** a forcible jet of air, esp. one used to intensify the heating effect of a furnace. **8.** any of several diseases of plants and animals. **9. (at) full blast.** at maximum speed, volume, etc. ~_interj._ **10.** an exclamation of annoyance. ~_vb._ **11.** (_tr._) to destroy or blow up with explosives, shells, etc. **12.** to make or cause to make a loud harsh noise. **13.** to wither or cause to wither; blight or be blighted. **14.** (_tr._) to criticize severely.

—**'blaster** _n._

-blast _n._ _combining form._ (in biology) indicating an embryonic cell or formative layer: _mesoblast._

blasted ('blɑːstɪd) _adj._ **1.** blighted or withered. ~_adj._ (_prenominal_), _adv._ **2.** _Sl._ (intensifier): _a blasted idiot._

blast furnace _n._ a vertical cylindrical furnace for smelting into which a blast of preheated air is forced.

blasto- _combining form._ indicating an embryo or bud.

blastoff ('blɑːst,ɒf) _n._ **1.** the launching of a rocket under its own power. **2.** the time at which this occurs. ~_vb._ **blast off. 3.** (_adv.; when tr., usually passive_) to be launched.

blatant ('bleɪtənt) _adj._ **1.** glaringly conspicuous or obvious: _a blatant lie._ **2.** offensively noticeable; obtrusive. **3.** offensively noisy. —**'blatancy** _n._

blather ('blæðə) _vb._ **1.** (_intr._) to speak foolishly. ~_n._ **2.** foolish talk; nonsense.

blaze¹ (bleɪz) _n._ **1.** a strong fire or flame. **2.** a very bright light or glare. **3.** an outburst (of passion, acclaim, patriotism, etc.). **4.** brilliance; brightness. ~_vb._ (_intr._) **5.** to burn fiercely. **6.** to shine brightly. **7.** (often foll. by _up_) to become stirred, as with anger or excitement. **8.** (usually foll. by _away_) to shoot continuously.

blaze² (bleɪz) _n._ **1.** a mark, usually indicating a path, made on a tree. **2.** a light-coloured marking on the face of a domestic animal. ~_vb._ (_tr._) **3.** to indicate or mark (a tree, path, etc.) with a blaze. **4. blaze a trail.** to explore new territories, areas of knowledge, etc., so that others can follow.

blaze³ (bleɪz) _vb._ (_tr;_ often foll. by _abroad_) to make widely known; proclaim.

blazer ('bleɪzə) _n._ a fairly lightweight jacket, often in the colours of a sports club, school, etc.

blazes ('bleɪzɪz) _pl. n._ **1.** _Sl._ a euphemistic word for **hell.** **2.** _Inf._ (intensifier): _to run like blazes._

blazon ('bleɪzən) _vb._ (_tr._) **1.** (often foll. by _abroad_) to proclaim publicly. **2.** _Heraldry._ to describe (heraldic arms) in proper terms. **3.** to draw and colour (heraldic arms) conventionally. ~_n._ **4.** _Heraldry._ a conventional description or depiction of heraldic arms. —**'blazoner** _n._ —**'blazonry** _n._

bldg. _abbrev. for_ building.

bleach (bliːtʃ) _vb._ **1.** to make or become white or colourless, as by exposure to sunlight, by the action of chemical agents, etc. ~_n._ **2.** a bleaching agent. **3.** the act of bleaching. —**'bleacher** _n._

bleaching powder _n._ a white powder consisting of chlorinated calcium hydroxide. Also called: **chloride of lime, chlorinated lime.**

bleak¹ (bliːk) _adj._ **1.** exposed and barren. **2.** cold and raw. **3.** offering little hope; dismal: _a bleak future._ —**'bleakness** _n._

bleak² (bliːk) _n._ any of various European cyprinid fishes occurring in slow-flowing rivers.

T H E S A U R U S

blank _adj._ 1. bare, clean, clear, empty, plain, spotless, uncompleted, unfilled, unmarked, void, white 2. deadpan, dull, empty, expressionless, hollow, impassive, inane, lifeless, poker-faced (_Inf._), vacant, vacuous, vague 3. at a loss, bewildered, confounded, confused, disconcerted, dumbfounded, muddled, nonplussed, uncomprehending 4. absolute, complete, outright, thorough, unqualified, utter ~_n._ 5. emptiness, empty space, gap, nothingness, space, tabula rasa, vacancy, vacuity, vacuum, void

blanket _n._ 1. afghan, cover, coverlet, rug 2. carpet, cloak, coat, coating, covering, envelope, film, layer, mantle, sheet, wrapper, wrapping ~_adj._ 3. across-the-board, all-inclusive, comprehensive, overall, sweeping, wide-ranging ~_v._ 4. cloak, cloud, coat, conceal, cover, eclipse, hide, mask, obscure, suppress, surround

blankness abstraction, fatuity, inanity, indifference, no recollection, obliviousness, vacancy, vacuity

blare blast, boom, clamour, clang, honk, hoot, peal, resound, roar, scream, sound out, toot, trumpet

blarney blandishment, cajolery, coaxing, exaggeration, flattery, honeyed words, over-

praise, soft soap (_Inf._), sweet talk (_Inf._, chiefly U.S._), wheedling

blasé apathetic, bored, cloyed, glutted, indifferent, jaded, lukewarm, nonchalant, offhand, satiated, surfeited, unconcerned, unexcited, uninterested, unmoved, weary, world-weary

blaspheme abuse, anathematize, curse, damn, desecrate, execrate, profane, revile, swear

blasphemous godless, impious, irreligious, irreverent, profane, sacrilegious, ungodly

blasphemy cursing, desecration, execration, impiety, impiousness, indignity (_to God_), irreverence, profanation, profaneness, profanity, sacrilege, swearing

blast _n./v._ 1. blare, blow, clang, honk, peal, scream, toot, wail ~_n._ 2. bang, blow-up, burst, crash, detonation, discharge, eruption, explosion, outburst, salvo, volley 3. gale, gust, squall, storm, strong breeze, tempest ~_v._ 4. blow up, break up, burst, demolish, destroy, explode, ruin, shatter 5. blight, kill, shrivel, wither 6. attack, castigate, criticize, flay, rail at

blasted blighted, desolated, destroyed, devastated, ravaged, ruined, shattered,

spoiled, wasted, withered

blastoff n. discharge, expulsion, firing, launch, launching, lift-off, projection, shot

blatant 1. bald, brazen, conspicuous, flagrant, flaunting, glaring, naked, obtrusive, obvious, ostentatious, outright, overt, prominent, pronounced, sheer, unmitigated 2. clamorous, deafening, ear-splitting, harsh, loud, noisy, piercing

blather claptrap (_Inf._), drivel, gibberish, gobbledegook, jabber, jabbering, moonshine, twaddle

blaze _n._ 1. bonfire, conflagration, fire, flame, flames 2. beam, brilliance, flare, flash, glare, gleam, glitter, glow, light, radiance 3. blast, burst, eruption, flare-up, fury, outbreak, outburst, rush, storm, torrent ~_v._ 4. beam, burn, fire, flame, flare, flash, glare, gleam, glow, shine 5. boil, explode, flare up, fume, seethe

blazon broadcast, celebrate, flourish, make known, proclaim, renown, trumpet

bleach blanch, etiolate, fade, grow pale, lighten, peroxide, wash out, whiten

bleached achromatic, etiolated, faded, lightened, peroxided, stone-washed, washed-out

bleak 1. bare, barren, chilly, cold, desolate,

blear (bliə) ~*vb.*(*tr.*) *Arch.* to make (eyes or sight) dim as with tears; blur. —**'bleary** *adj.*

bleary-eyed *or* **blear-eyed** *adj.* with eyes blurred, as with old age or after waking.

bleat (bli:t) *vb.* 1. (*intr.*) (of a sheep, goat, or calf) to utter its characteristic plaintive cry. 2. (*intr.*) to speak with any similar sound. 3. to whine; whimper. ~*n.* 4. the characteristic cry of sheep, goats, and calves. 5. any sound similar to this. 6. a weak complaint or whine. —**'bleater** *n.* —**'bleatingly** *adv.*

bleed (bli:d) *vb.* **bleeding, bled** (blɛd). 1. (*intr.*) to lose or emit blood. 2. (*tr.*) to remove or draw blood from (a person or animal). 3. (*intr.*) to be injured or die, as for a cause. 4. (of plants) to exude (sap or resin), esp. from a cut. 5. (*tr.*) *Inf.* to obtain money, etc., esp. by extortion. 6. (*tr.*) to draw liquid or gas from (a container or enclosed system): *to bleed the hydraulic brakes.* 7. (*intr.*) (of dye or paint) to run or become mixed, as when wet. 8. to print or be printed so that text, illustrations, etc., run off the trimmed page. 9. **one's heart bleeds.** used to express sympathetic grief, often ironically. —**'bleeder** *n.*

bleeding (ˈbli:dɪŋ) *adj., adv. Brit. sl.* (intensifier): *a bleeding fool.*

bleep (bli:p) *n.* 1. a single short high-pitched signal made by an electronic apparatus; beep. 2. Also called: **bleeper.** *Inf.* a small portable radio receiver that makes a bleeping signal. ~*vb.* 3. (*intr.*) to make such a noise.

blemish (ˈblɛmɪʃ) *n.* 1. a defect; flaw; stain. ~*vb.* 2. (*tr.*) to flaw the perfection of; spoil; tarnish.

blench (blɛntʃ) *vb.* (*intr.*) to shy away, as in fear; quail. —**'blencher** *n.*

blend (blɛnd) *vb.* 1. to mix or mingle (components) together thoroughly. 2. (*tr.*) to mix (different grades or varieties of tea, whisky, etc.). 3. (*intr.*) to look good together; harmonize. 4. (*intr.*) (esp. of colours) to shade imperceptibly into each other. ~*n.* 5. a mixture or type produced by blending. 6. the act of blending. 7. Also called: **portmanteau word.** a word formed by joining together the beginning and the end of two other words: *"brunch" is a blend of "breakfast" and "lunch."* —**'blender** *n.*

blende (blɛnd) *n.* any of several sulphide ores.

blenny (ˈblɛnɪ) *n., pl.* **-nies.** any of various small fishes of coastal waters having a tapering scaleless body, a long dorsal fin, and long raylike pelvic fins.

blesbok *or* **blesbuck** (ˈblɛs,bʌk) *n., pl.* **-boks, -bok** *or* **-bucks, -buck.** an antelope of southern Africa. The coat is reddish-brown with a white blaze between the eyes; the horns are lyre-shaped.

bless (blɛs) *vb.* **blessing, blessed** *or* **blest.** (*tr.*) 1. to consecrate or render holy by means of a religious rite. 2. to give honour or glory to (a person or thing) as holy. 3. to call upon God to protect; give a benediction to. 4. to worship or adore (God). 5. (*often passive*) to grant happiness, health, or prosperity to. 6. (*usually passive*) to endow with a talent, beauty, etc. 7. *Rare.* to protect against evil or harm. 8. **bless you!** (*interj.*). **a.** a traditional phrase said to a person who has just sneezed. **b.** an exclamation of well-wishing or surprise. 9. **bless me!** *or* (**God**) **bless my soul!** (*interj.*) an exclamation of surprise.

blessed (ˈblɛsɪd, blɛst) *adj.* 1. made holy; consecrated. 2. worthy of deep reverence or respect. 3. *R.C. Church.* (of a person) beatified by the pope. 4. characterized by happiness or good fortune. 5. bringing great happiness or good fortune. 6. a euphemistic word for **damned,** used in mild oaths: *I'm blessed if I know.* —**'blessedly** *adv.* —**'blessedness** *n.*

blessing (ˈblɛsɪŋ) *n.* 1. the act of invoking divine protection or aid. 2. the words or ceremony used for this. 3. a short prayer before or after a meal; grace. 4. approval; good wishes. 5. the bestowal of a divine gift or favour. 6. a happy event.

blest (blɛst) *vb.* a past participle of **bless.**

blether (ˈblɛðə) *vb.* a variant spelling of **blather.**

blew (blu:) *vb.* the past tense of **blow.**

blight (blaɪt) *n.* 1. any plant disease characterized by withering and shrivelling without rotting. 2. any factor that causes the symptoms of blight in plants. 3. a person or thing that mars or prevents growth. 4. an ugly urban district. ~*vb.* 5. to cause or suffer a blight. 6. (*tr.*) to frustrate or disappoint. 7. (*tr.*) to spoil; destroy.

blighter (ˈblaɪtə) *n. Brit. inf.* 1. a fellow. 2. a despicable or irritating person or thing.

Blighty (ˈblaɪtɪ) *n.* (*sometimes not cap.*) *Brit. sl.* (used esp. by troops serving abroad) 1. England; home. 2. (esp. in World War I) Also called: **a blighty one.** a wound that causes the recipient to be sent home to England.

blimey (ˈblaɪmɪ) *interj. Brit. sl.* an exclamation of surprise or annoyance.

blimp (blɪmp) *n.* 1. a small nonrigid airship. 2. *Films.* a soundproof cover fixed over a camera during shooting.

blind (blaɪnd) *adj.* 1. **a.** unable to see; sightless. **b.** (*as collective n.* preceded by *the*): *the blind.* 2. (usually foll. by *to*) unable or unwilling to understand or discern. 3. not determined by reason: *blind hatred.* 4. acting or performed without control or preparation. 5. done without being able to see, relying on instruments for information. 6. hidden from sight: *a blind corner.* 7. closed at one end: *a blind alley.* 8. completely lacking awareness or consciousness: *a blind stupor.* 9. *Inf.* very drunk. 10. having no openings or outlets: *a blind wall.* 11. (intensifier): *not a blind bit of notice.* 12. **turn a blind eye** (**to**). to disregard or pretend not to notice. ~*adv.* 13. without being able to see ahead or using only instruments: *to drive blind; flying blind.* 14. without adequate knowledge or information; carelessly: *to buy a house blind.* 15. **bake blind.** to bake (an empty pastry case) by half filling with dried peas, crusts, etc., to keep it in shape. ~*vb.* (*mainly tr.*) 16. to deprive of sight permanently or temporarily. 17. to deprive of good sense, reason, or judgment. 18. to darken; conceal. 19. (foll. by *with*) to overwhelm by showing detailed knowledge: *to blind somebody with science.* ~*n.* 20. (*modifier*) for or intended to help the blind: *a blind school.* 21. a shade for a window, usually on a roller. 22. any obstruction or hindrance to sight, light, or air. 23. a person, action, or thing that serves to deceive or conceal the truth. —**'blindly** *adv.* —**'blindness** *n.*

THESAURUS

exposed, gaunt, open, raw, unsheltered, weather-beaten, windswept, windy 2. cheerless, comfortless, depressing, discouraging, disheartening, dismal, dreary, gloomy, grim, hopeless, joyless, sombre, unpromising

bleary blurred, blurry, dim, fogged, foggy, fuzzy, hazy, indistinct, misty, murky, rheumy, watery

bleed 1. exude, flow, gush, lose blood, ooze, run, seep, shed blood, spurt, trickle, weep 2. deplete, drain, draw *or* take blood, exhaust, extort, extract, fleece, leech, milk, phlebotomize (*Medical*), reduce, sap, squeeze 3. ache, agonize, feel for, grieve, pity, suffer, sympathize

blemish 1. *n.* blot, blotch, blur, defect, disfigurement, mark, smudge, speck, spot, stain, taint 2. *v.* blot, blotch, blur, damage, deface, disfigure, flaw, impair, injure, mar, mark, smirch, smudge, spoil, spot, stain, sully, taint, tarnish

blend *v.* 1. amalgamate, coalesce, combine, compound, fuse, intermix, merge, mingle, mix, synthesize, unite 2. complement, fit, go well, go with, harmonize, suit ~*n.* 3. alloy, amalgam, amalgamation, combination, composite, compound, concoction, fusion, mix, mixture, synthesis, union

bless 1. anoint, consecrate, dedicate, exalt, extol, give thanks to, glorify, hallow, invoke happiness on, magnify, ordain, praise, sanctify, thank 2. bestow, endow, favour, give, grace, grant, provide

blessed 1. adored, beatified, divine, hallowed, holy, revered, sacred, sanctified 2. endowed, favoured, fortunate, granted, lucky 3. blissful, contented, glad, happy, joyful, joyous

blessedness beatitude, bliss, blissfulness, content, felicity, happiness, heavenly joy, pleasure, sanctity, state of grace, *summum bonum*

blessing 1. benediction, benison, commendation, consecration, dedication, grace, invocation, thanksgiving 2. approbation, approval, backing, concurrence, consent, favour, good wishes, leave, permission, regard, sanction, support 3. advantage, benefit, boon, bounty, favour, gain, gift, godsend, good fortune, help, kindness, profit, service, windfall

blight *n.* 1. canker, decay, disease, fungus, infestation, mildew, pest, pestilence, rot 2. affliction, bane, contamination, corruption, curse, evil, plague, pollution, scourge, woe ~*v.* 3. blast, destroy, injure, nip in the bud, ruin, shrivel, taint with mildew, wither 4. *Fig.* annihilate, crush, dash, disappoint, frustrate, mar, nullify, ruin, spoil, wreck

blind *adj.* 1. destitute of vision, eyeless, sightless, stone-blind, unseeing, unsighted, visionless 2. *Fig.* careless, heedless, ignorant, inattentive, inconsiderate, indifferent, indiscriminate, injudicious, insensitive, morally darkened, neglectful, oblivious, prejudiced, thoughtless, unaware of, unconscious of, uncritical, undiscerning, unmindful of, unob-

blind alley *n.* **1.** an alley open at one end only; cul-de-sac. **2.** *Inf.* a situation in which no further progress can be made.

blind date *n. Inf.* a social meeting between a man and a woman who have not met before.

blindfold ('blaɪndˌfəʊld) *vb.* (*tr.*) **1.** to prevent (a person or animal) from seeing by covering (the eyes). ~*n.* **2.** a piece of cloth, bandage, etc., used to cover the eyes. ~*adj., adv.* **3.** having the eyes covered with a cloth or bandage. **4.** rash; inconsiderate.

blind man's buff *n.* a game in which a blindfolded person tries to catch and identify the other players.

blind spot *n.* **1.** a small oval-shaped area of the retina, where the optic nerve enters, in which vision is not experienced. **2.** a place or area where vision is obscured. **3.** a subject about which a person is ignorant or prejudiced.

blindworm ('blaɪndˌwɜːm) *n.* another name for **slow-worm**.

blink (blɪŋk) *vb.* **1.** to close and immediately reopen (the eyes or an eye), usually involuntarily. **2.** (*intr.*) to look with the eyes partially closed. **3.** to shine intermittently or unsteadily. **4.** (*tr.*; foll. by *away, from*, etc.) to clear the eyes of (dust, tears, etc.). **5.** (when *tr.*, usually foll. by *at*) to be surprised or amazed. **6.** (when *intr.*, foll. by *at*) to pretend not to know or see (a fault, injustice, etc.). ~*n.* **7.** the act or an instance of blinking. **8.** a glance; glimpse. **9. on the blink.** *Sl.* not working properly.

blinker[1] ('blɪŋkə) *n.* **1.** a flashing light for sending messages, as a warning device, etc., such as a direction indicator on a road vehicle. **2.** (*often pl.*) a slang word for **eye**.

blinker[2] ('blɪŋkə) *vb.* (*tr.*) **1.** to provide (a horse) with blinkers. **2.** to obscure or be obscured with or as with blinkers. —'**blinkered** *adj.*

blinkers ('blɪŋkəz) *pl. n.* (*sometimes sing.*) *Chiefly Brit.* leather sidepieces attached to a horse's bridle to prevent sideways vision.

blinking ('blɪŋkɪŋ) *adj., adv. Inf.* (intensifier): *a blinking fool; a blinking good film.*

blip (blɪp) *n.* **1.** a repetitive sound, such as that produced by an electronic device. **2.** Also called: **pip.** the spot of light on a radar screen indicating the position of an object. ~*vb.* **blipping, blipped. 3.** (*intr.*) to produce such a noise.

bliss (blɪs) *n.* **1.** perfect happiness; serene joy. **2.** the ecstatic joy of heaven. —'**blissful** *adj.*

blister ('blɪstə) *n.* **1.** a small bubble-like elevation of the skin filled with serum, produced as a reaction to a burn, mechanical irritation, etc. **2.** a swelling containing air or liquid, as on a painted surface. **3. a.** *N.Z. sl.* a rebuke. **b.** *N.Z. & Austral. sl.* a summons to court. ~*vb.* **4.** to have or cause to have blisters. **5.** (*tr.*) to attack verbally with great scorn or sarcasm. —'**blistery** *adj.*

blithe (blaɪð) *adj.* **1.** very happy or cheerful; gay. **2.** heedless; casual and indifferent. —'**blithely** *adv.* —'**blitheness** *n.*

blithering ('blɪðərɪŋ) *adj.* **1.** talking foolishly; jabbering. **2.** *Inf.* stupid; foolish: *you blithering idiot.*

blithesome ('blaɪðsəm) *adj. Literary.* cheery; merry.

B.Litt. *or* **B.Lit.** *abbrev. for:* **1.** Bachelor of Letters.

2. Bachelor of Literature.

blitz (blɪts) *n.* **1.** a violent and sustained attack, esp. with intensive aerial bombardment. **2.** any sudden intensive attack or concerted effort. ~*vb.* **3.** (*tr.*) to attack suddenly and intensively.

Blitz (blɪts) *n.* **the.** the systematic bombing of Britain in 1940–41 by the German Luftwaffe.

blitzkrieg ('blɪtsˌkriːg) *n.* an intensive military attack designed to defeat the opposition quickly.

blizzard ('blɪzəd) *n.* a strong cold wind accompanied by widespread heavy snowfall.

bloat (bləʊt) *vb.* **1.** to swell or cause to swell, as with a liquid or air. **2.** to become or cause to be puffed up, as with conceit. **3.** (*tr.*) to cure (fish, esp. herring) by half-drying in smoke.

bloater ('bləʊtə) *n.* a herring that has been salted in brine, smoked, and cured.

blob (blɒb) *n.* **1.** a soft mass or drop. **2.** a spot, dab, or blotch of colour, ink, etc. **3.** an indistinct or shapeless form or object.

bloc (blɒk) *n.* a group of people or countries combined by a common interest.

block (blɒk) *n.* **1.** a large solid piece of wood, stone, or other material usually having at least one face fairly flat. **2.** such a piece on which particular tasks may be done, as chopping, cutting, or beheading. **3.** Also called: **building block.** one of a set of wooden or plastic cubes as a child's toy. **4.** a form on which things are shaped: *a wig block.* **5.** *Inf.* a person's head. **6. do one's block.** *Austral. sl.* to become angry. **7.** a dull, unemotional, or hard-hearted person. **8.** a large building of offices, flats, etc. **9. a.** a group of buildings in a city bounded by intersecting streets on each side. **b.** the area or distance between such intersecting streets. **10.** *Austral. & N.Z.* an area of land, usually extensive, taken up for farming, settlement, etc. **11.** *N.Z.* an area of bush reserved by licence for a trapper or hunter. **12.** a piece of wood, metal, or other material having a design in relief, used for printing. **13.** *Austral. & N.Z.* a log, usually of willow, fastened to a timber base and used in a wood-chopping competition. **14.** a casing housing one or more freely rotating pulleys. See also **block and tackle. 15.** an obstruction or hindrance. **16.** *Pathol.* interference in the normal physiological functioning of an organ or part. **17.** *Psychol.* a short interruption of perceptual or thought processes. **18.** obstruction of an opponent in a sport. **19. a.** a quantity handled or considered as a single unit. **b.** (*as modifier*): *a block booking; block voting.* **20.** *Athletics.* short for **starting block.** ~*vb.* (*mainly tr.*) **21.** (*often foll. by up*) to obstruct (a passage, channel, etc.) or prevent or impede the motion or flow of (something or someone) by introducing an obstacle: *to block the traffic; to block up a pipe.* **22.** to impede, retard, or prevent (an action, procedure, etc.). **23.** to stamp (a title, design, etc.) on (a book cover, etc.) esp. using gold leaf. **24.** to shape by use of a block: *to block a hat.* **25.** (*also intr.*) *Sports.* to obstruct or impede movement by (an opponent). **26.** to interrupt a physiological function, as by use of an anaesthetic. **27.** (*also intr.*) *Cricket.* to play (a ball) defensively. ~See also **block out.** —'**blockage** *n.* —'**blocker** *n.*

blockade (blɒ'keɪd) *n.* **1.** *Mil.* the interdiction of a nation's sea lines of communications, esp. of an individual

---

THESAURUS

servant, unreasoning **3.** hasty, impetuous, irrational, mindless, rash, reckless, senseless, uncontrollable, uncontrolled, unthinking, violent, wild **4.** closed, concealed, dark, dead-end, dim, hidden, leading nowhere, obscured, obstructed, without exit ~*n.* **5.** camouflage, cloak, cover, façade, feint, front, mask, masquerade, screen, smoke screen

blindly 1. aimlessly, at random, confusedly, frantically, indiscriminately, instinctively, madly, purposelessly, wildly **2.** carelessly, heedlessly, impulsively, inconsiderately, passionately, recklessly, regardlessly, senselessly, thoughtlessly, unreasonably, wilfully

blink 1. bat, flutter, glimpse, nictate, nictitate, peer, squint, wink **2.** flash, flicker, gleam, glimmer, scintillate, shine, sparkle, twinkle, wink **3.** *Fig.* condone, connive at, disregard, ignore, overlook, pass by, turn a blind eye to **4. on the blink** *Inf.* faulty, mal-

functioning, not working (properly), out of action, out of order, playing up

bliss beatitude, blessedness, blissfulness, ecstasy, euphoria, felicity, gladness, happiness, heaven, joy, paradise, rapture

blissful delighted, ecstatic, elated, enchanted, enraptured, euphoric, happy, heavenly (*Inf.*), in ecstasies, joyful, joyous, rapturous

blister abscess, blain, bleb, boil, bubble, canker, carbuncle, cyst, furuncle (*Pathology*), pimple, pustule, sore, swelling, ulcer, welt, wen

blithe 1. animated, buoyant, carefree, cheerful, cheery, debonair, gay, gladsome, happy, jaunty, light-hearted, merry, mirthful, sprightly, sunny, vivacious **2.** careless, casual, heedless, indifferent, nonchalant, thoughtless, unconcerned, untroubled

blitz assault, attack, blitzkrieg, bombard-

ment, offensive, onslaught, raid, strike

blizzard blast, gale, snowstorm, squall, storm, tempest

bloat balloon, blow up, dilate, distend, enlarge, expand, inflate, puff up, swell

blob ball, bead, bubble, dab, dewdrop, drop, droplet, glob, globule, lump, mass, pearl, pellet, pill

bloc alliance, axis, cabal, clique, coalition, combine, entente, faction, group, league, ring, union, wing

block *n.* **1.** bar, brick, cake, chunk, cube, hunk, ingot, lump, mass, piece, square **2.** bar, barrier, blockage, hindrance, impediment, jam, obstacle, obstruction, stoppage ~*v.* **3.** bung up (*Inf.*), choke, clog, close, obstruct, plug, stop up **4.** arrest, bar, check, deter, halt, hinder, impede, obstruct, stop, thwart

port by the use of sea power. **2.** something that prevents access or progress. ~*vb.* (*tr.*) **3.** to impose a blockade on. **4.** to obstruct the way to. —**block'ader** *n.*

block and tackle *n.* a hoisting device in which a rope or chain is passed around a pair of blocks containing one or more pulleys.

blockboard ('blɒk,bɔːd) *n.* a bonded board in which strips of soft wood are sandwiched between two layers of veneer.

blockbuster ('blɒk,bʌstə) *n. Inf.* **1.** a large bomb used to demolish extensive areas. **2.** a very forceful person, thing, etc.

blockhead ('blɒk,hɛd) *n. Derog.* a stupid person. —'**block,headed** *adj.*

blockhouse ('blɒk,haʊs) *n.* **1.** (formerly) a wooden fortification with ports for defensive fire, observation, etc. **2.** a concrete structure strengthened to give protection against enemy fire, with apertures to allow defensive gunfire. **3.** a building constructed of logs or squared timber.

blockish ('blɒkɪʃ) *adj.* lacking vivacity or imagination; stupid. —'**blockishly** *adv.*

block letter *n.* **1.** *Printing.* a less common name for **sans serif.** **2.** Also called: **block capital.** a plain capital letter.

block out *vb.* (*tr., adv.*) **1.** to plan or describe (something) in a general fashion. **2.** to prevent the entry or consideration of (something).

block release *n. Brit.* the release of industrial trainees from work for study at a college for several weeks.

bloke (bləʊk) *n. Brit.* an informal word for **man.**

blond (blɒnd) *adj.* **1.** (of hair) of a light colour; fair. **2.** (of people or a race) having fair hair, a light complexion, and, typically, blue or grey eyes. ~*n.* **3.** a man or boy having light-coloured hair and skin. —'**blondness** *n.*

blonde (blɒnd) *n.* **1.** a woman or girl having light-coloured hair. ~*adj.* **2.** (of a woman's or girl's hair) of a light colour; fair. **3.** (of a woman or girl) having light-coloured hair and skin.

blood (blʌd) *n.* **1.** a reddish fluid in vertebrates that is pumped by the heart through the arteries and veins. **2.** a similar fluid in invertebrates. **3.** bloodshed, esp. when resulting in murder. **4.** life itself; lifeblood. **5.** relationship through being of the same family, race, or kind; kinship. **6.** flesh and blood. **a.** near kindred or kinship, esp. that between a parent and child. **b.** human nature (esp. in **it's more than flesh and blood can stand**). **7.** in one's blood. as a natural or inherited characteristic or talent. **8.** the blood. royal or noble descent: *a prince of the blood.* **9.** temperament; disposition; temper. **10. a.** good or pure breeding; pedigree. **b.** (*as modifier*): *blood horses.* **11.** people viewed as members of a group, esp. as an invigorating force (**new blood, young blood**). **12.** *Chiefly Brit., rare.* a dashing young man. **13. bad blood.** hatred; ill feeling. **14. in cold blood. a.** cruelly and ruthlessly. **b.** deliberately and calmly. **15. make one's blood boil.** to cause to be angry or indignant. **16. make one's blood run cold.** to fill with horror. ~*vb.* (*tr.*) **17.** *Hunting.* to cause (young hounds) to taste the blood of a freshly killed quarry. **18.** to initiate (a person) to war or hunting.

blood-and-thunder *adj.* denoting or relating to a melodramatic adventure story.

blood bath *n.* indiscriminate slaughter; a massacre.

blood brother *n.* **1.** a brother by birth. **2.** a man or boy who has sworn to treat another as his brother, often in a ceremony in which their blood is mingled.

blood count *n.* determination of the number of red

and white blood corpuscles in a specific sample of blood.

bloodcurdling ('blʌd,kɜːdlɪŋ) *adj.* terrifying; horrifying. —'**blood,curdlingly** *adv.*

blood donor *n.* a person who gives his blood to be used for transfusion.

blood group *n.* any one of the various groups into which human blood is classified on the basis of its agglutinogens. Also called: **blood type.**

blood heat *n.* the normal temperature of the human body, 98.4°F. or 37°C.

bloodhound ('blʌd,haʊnd) *n.* a large breed of hound, much used in tracking and police work.

bloodless ('blʌdlɪs) *adj.* **1.** without blood. **2.** conducted without violence (esp. in **bloodless revolution**). **3.** anaemic-looking; pale. **4.** lacking vitality; lifeless. **5.** lacking in emotion; unfeeling. —'**bloodlessly** *adv.* —'**bloodlessness** *n.*

blood-letting ('blʌd,lɛtɪŋ) *n.* **1.** the therapeutic removal of blood. **2.** bloodshed, esp. in a feud.

blood money *n.* **1.** compensation paid to the relatives of a murdered person. **2.** money paid to a hired murderer. **3.** a reward for information about a criminal, esp. a murderer.

blood orange *n.* a variety of orange all or part of the pulp of which is dark red when ripe.

blood poisoning *n.* a nontechnical term for **septicaemia.**

blood pressure *n.* the pressure exerted by the blood on the inner walls of the arteries, being relative to the elasticity and diameter of the vessels and the force of the heart beat.

blood relation *or* **relative** *n.* a person related to another by birth, as distinct from one related by marriage.

bloodshed ('blʌd,ʃɛd) *n.* slaughter; killing.

bloodshot ('blʌd,ʃɒt) *adj.* (of an eye) inflamed.

blood sport *n.* any sport involving the killing of an animal, esp. hunting.

bloodstain ('blʌd,steɪn) *n.* a dark discoloration caused by blood, esp. dried blood. —'**blood,stained** *adj.*

bloodstock ('blʌd,stɒk) *n.* thoroughbred horses.

bloodstone ('blʌd,stəʊn) *n.* a dark-green variety of chalcedony with red spots: used as a gemstone. Also called: **heliotrope.**

blood stream *n.* the flow of blood through the vessels of a living body.

bloodsucker ('blʌd,sʌkə) *n.* **1.** an animal that sucks blood, esp. a leech or mosquito. **2.** *Inf.* a person or thing that preys upon another person, esp. by extorting money.

bloodthirsty ('blʌd,θɜːstɪ) *adj.* **-thirstier, -thirstiest. 1.** murderous; cruel. **2.** taking pleasure in bloodshed or violence. **3.** describing or depicting killing and violence; gruesome. —'**blood,thirstily** *adv.* —'**blood,thirstiness** *n.*

blood vessel *n.* an artery, capillary, or vein.

bloody ('blʌdɪ) *adj.* **bloodier, bloodiest. 1.** covered or stained with blood. **2.** resembling or composed of blood. **3.** marked by much killing and bloodshed: *a bloody war.* **4.** cruel or murderous: *a bloody tyrant.* ~*adv., adj.* **5.** *Sl.* (intensifier): *a bloody fool.* ~*vb.* **bloodying, bloodied. 6.** (*tr.*) to stain with blood. —'**bloodily** *adv.* —'**bloodiness** *n.*

Bloody Mary *n.* a drink consisting of tomato juice and vodka.

bloody-minded *adj. Brit. inf.* deliberately obstructive and unhelpful.

bloom[1] (bluːm) *n.* **1.** a blossom on a flowering plant; a flower. **2.** the state, time, or period when flowers open. **3.** open flowers collectively. **4.** a healthy, vigorous, or

---

THESAURUS

blockade barricade, barrier, closure, encirclement, hindrance, impediment, obstacle, obstruction, restriction, siege, stoppage

blockage block, blocking, impediment, obstruction, occlusion, stoppage, stopping up

blockhead bonehead (*Sl.*), dolt, dullard, dunce, fool, idiot, ignoramus, numskull

block out chart, map out, outline, plan, sketch

blond, blonde fair, fair-haired, fair-skinned, flaxen, golden-haired, light, light-coloured, light-complexioned, tow-headed

blood 1. gore, lifeblood, vital fluid 2. ancestry, birth, consanguinity, descendants, descent, extraction, family, kindred, kinship, lineage, noble extraction, relations 3. *Fig.* anger, disposition, feeling, passion, spirit, temper

bloodcurdling appalling, chilling, dreadful, fearful, frightening, hair-raising, horrendous, horrifying, scaring, spine-chilling, terrifying

bloodless 1. cold, languid, lifeless, listless, passionless, spiritless, torpid, unemotional, unfeeling 2. anaemic, ashen, chalky,

colourless, pale, pallid, pasty, sallow, sickly, wan

bloodshed blood bath, bloodletting, butchery, carnage, gore, killing, massacre, murder, slaughter, slaying

bloodthirsty barbarous, brutal, cruel, ferocious, inhuman, murderous, ruthless, savage, vicious, warlike

bloody 1. bleeding, blood-soaked, blood-spattered, bloodstained, gaping, raw, unstaunched 2. cruel, ferocious, fierce, sanguinary, savage

flourishing condition; prime. **5.** youthful or healthy rosiness in the cheeks or face; glow. **6.** a fine whitish coating on the surface of fruits, leaves, etc. **7.** Also called: **chill.** a dull area on the surface of old gloss paint, lacquer, or varnish. ~*vb.* (*intr.*) **8.** (of flowers) to open; come into flower. **9.** to bear flowers; blossom. **10.** to flourish or grow. **11.** to be in a healthy, glowing, or flourishing condition.

bloom² (bluːm) *n.* a rectangular mass of metal obtained by rolling or forging a cast ingot.

bloomer¹ ('bluːmə) *n.* a plant that flowers, esp. in a specified way: *a night bloomer.*

bloomer² ('bluːmə) *n. Brit. inf.* a stupid mistake; blunder.

bloomers ('bluːməz) *pl. n.* **1.** (formerly) women's loose baggy knickers, usually gathered just above the knee. **2.** close-fitting knickers reaching to just above the knee.

blooming ('bluːmɪŋ) *adv., adj. Brit. inf.* (intensifier): *a blooming genius; blooming painful.*

blossom ('blɒsəm) *n.* **1.** the flower or flowers of a plant, esp. producing edible fruit. **2.** the time or period of flowering. ~*vb.* (*intr.*) **3.** (of plants) to come into flower. **4.** to develop or come to a promising stage. —'**blossomy** *adj.*

blot (blɒt) *n.* **1.** a stain or spot of ink, paint, dirt, etc. **2.** something that spoils. **3.** a blemish or stain on one's character or reputation. **4.** *Austral. vulgar sl.* the backside. ~*vb.* **blotting, blotted.** **5.** (of ink, dye, etc.) to form spots or blobs on (a material) or (of a person) to cause such spots or blobs to form on (a material). **6.** **blot one's copybook.** *Inf.* to spoil one's reputation by a mistake or indiscretion. **7.** (*intr.*) to stain or become stained or spotted. **8.** (*tr.*) to cause a blemish in or on; disgrace. **9.** to soak up (excess ink, etc.) by using blotting paper. **10.** (of blotting paper) to absorb (excess ink, etc.). **11.** (*tr.;* often foll. by *out*) **a.** to darken or hide completely; obscure; obliterate. **b.** to destroy; annihilate.

blotch (blɒtʃ) *n.* **1.** an irregular spot or discoloration, esp. a dark and relatively large one. ~*vb.* **2.** to become or cause to become marked by such discoloration. —'**blotchy** *adj.*

blotter ('blɒtə) *n.* something used to absorb excess ink, esp. a sheet of blotting paper.

blotting paper *n.* a soft absorbent unsized paper, used esp. for soaking up surplus ink.

blotto ('blɒtəʊ) *adj. Sl.* unconscious, esp. through drunkenness.

blouse (blaʊz) *n.* **1.** a woman's shirtlike garment. **2.** a waist-length jacket worn by soldiers. ~*vb.* **3.** to hang or make so as to hang in full loose folds.

blouson ('bluːzɒn) *n.* a tight-waisted jacket or top that blouses out softly.

blow¹ (bləʊ) *vb.* **blowing, blew, blown.** **1.** (of a current of air, the wind, etc.) to be or cause to be in motion. **2.** (*intr.*) to move or be carried by or as if by wind. **3.** to expel (air, cigarette smoke, etc.) through the mouth or nose. **4.** to force or cause (air, dust, etc.) to move (into, in, over, etc.) by using an instrument or by expelling breath. **5.** (*intr.*) to breathe hard; pant. **6.** (sometimes foll. by *up*) to inflate with air or the breath. **7.** (*intr.*) (of wind, a storm, etc.) to make a roaring sound. **8.** to cause (a whistle, siren, etc.) to sound by forcing air into it, or (of a whistle, etc.) to sound thus. **9.** (*tr.*) to force air from the lungs through (the nose) to clear out mucus. **10.** (often foll. by *up, down, in,* etc.) to explode, break, or disintegrate completely. **11.** *Electronics.* to burn out (a fuse, valve, etc.) because of excessive current or (of a fuse, valve, etc.) to burn out. **12.** (*tr.*) to wind (a horse)

by making it run excessively. **13.** to cause (a wind instrument) to sound by forcing one's breath into the mouthpiece, or (of such an instrument) to sound in this way. **14.** (*intr.*) (of flies) to lay eggs (in). **15.** to shape (glass, ornaments, etc.) by forcing air or gas through the material when molten. **16.** (*tr.*) *Sl.* to spend (money) freely. **17.** (*tr.*) *Sl.* to use (an opportunity) ineffectively. **18.** *Sl.* to go suddenly away (from). **19.** (p.p.: **blowed**). *Inf.* another word for **damn.** **20.** **blow hot and cold.** *Inf.* to vacillate. **21.** **blow one's own trumpet.** to boast of one's own skills or good qualities. **22.** **blow someone's mind.** *Sl.* **a.** (of a drug, esp. LSD) to cause hallucinatory experiences in a person. **b.** to produce a pleasant or shocking feeling in someone. **23.** **blow one's top.** *Sl.* to lose one's temper. ~*n.* **24.** the act or an instance of blowing. **25.** the sound produced by blowing. **26.** a blast of air or wind. **27.** *Austral. sl.* a brief rest; a breather. ~See also **blow in, blow out, blow over, blow up.**

blow² (bləʊ) *n.* **1.** a powerful or heavy stroke with the fist, a weapon, etc. **2.** **at one** or **a blow.** by or with only one action. **3.** a sudden setback. **4.** **come to blows. a.** to fight. **b.** to result in a fight. **5.** an attacking action: *a blow for freedom.* **6.** *Austral. & N.Z.* a stroke of the shears in sheep-shearing.

blow-by-blow *adj.* (prenominal) explained in great detail: *a blow-by-blow account.*

blow-dry *vb.* **1.** (*tr.*) to style (the hair) smoothly while drying it with a hair dryer. ~*n.* **2.** this method of styling hair.

blower ('bləʊə) *n.* **1.** a mechanical device, such as a fan, that blows. **2.** a low-pressure compressor, esp. in a furnace or internal-combustion engine. **3.** an informal name for **telephone.**

blowfly ('bləʊˌflaɪ) *n., pl.* **-flies.** any of various flies that lay their eggs in rotting meat, dung, carrion, and open wounds. Also called: **bluebottle.**

blowhole ('bləʊˌhəʊl) *n.* **1.** the nostril of whales, situated far back on the skull. **2.** a hole in ice through which whales, seals, etc., breathe. **3. a.** a vent for air or gas. **b.** *N.Z.* a hole emitting gas or steam in a volcanic region.

blow in *vb.* (*intr., adv.*) *Inf.* to arrive or enter suddenly.

blowlamp ('bləʊˌlæmp) *n.* a small burner that produces a very hot flame, used to remove old paint, melt soft metal, etc. U.S. name: **blowtorch.**

blown (bləʊn) *vb.* the past participle of **blow¹** and **blow¹.**

blow out *vb.* (*adv.*) **1.** to extinguish (a flame, candle, etc.) or (of a flame, etc.) to become extinguished. **2.** (*intr.*) (of a tyre) to puncture suddenly, esp. at high speed. **3.** (*intr.*) (of a fuse) to melt suddenly. **4.** (*tr.; often reflexive*) to diminish or use up the energy of: *the storm blew itself out.* **5.** (*intr.*) (of an oil or gas well) to lose oil or gas in an uncontrolled manner. ~*n.* **blowout.** **6.** the sudden melting of an electrical fuse. **7.** a sudden burst in a tyre. **8.** the uncontrolled escape of oil and gas from an oil or gas well. **9.** *Sl.* a large filling meal or lavish entertainment.

blow over *vb.* (*intr., adv.*) **1.** to cease or be finished: *the storm blew over.* **2.** to be forgotten.

blowpipe ('bləʊˌpaɪp) *n.* **1.** a long tube from which pellets, poisoned darts, etc., are shot by blowing. **2.** Also called: **blow tube.** a tube for blowing air or oxygen into a flame to intensify its heat. **3.** a long narrow iron pipe used to gather molten glass and blow it into shape.

blow up *vb.* (*adv.*) **1.** to explode or cause to explode. **2.** (*tr.*) to increase the importance of (something): *they blew the whole affair up.* **3.** (*intr.*) to come into existence with sudden force: *a storm had blown up.* **4.** *Inf.* to lose one's temper (with a person). **5.** *Inf.* (*tr.*) to enlarge

---

THESAURUS

bloom *n.* **1.** blossom, blossoming, bud, efflorescence, flower, opening (*of flowers*) **2.** *Fig.* beauty, blush, flourishing, flush, freshness, glow, health, heyday, lustre, perfection, prime, radiance, rosiness, vigour ~*v.* **3.** blossom, blow, bud, burgeon, open, sprout **4.** develop, fare well, flourish, grow, prosper, succeed, thrive, wax

blossom *n.* **1.** bloom, bud, floret, flower, flowers ~*v.* **2.** bloom, burgeon, flower **3.** *Fig.* bloom, develop, flourish, grow, mature, progress, prosper, thrive

blot *n.* **1.** blotch, mark, patch, smear, smudge, speck, splodge, spot **2.** blemish, blur, defect, disgrace, fault, flaw, spot, stain, taint

~*v.* **3.** bespatter, disfigure, disgrace, mark, smudge, spoil, spot, stain, sully, tarnish **4.** absorb, dry, soak up, take up **5.** blot out cancel, darken, destroy, efface, erase, expunge, obliterate, obscure, shadow

blotch blemish, blot, mark, patch, smudge, smutch, splash, splodge, spot, stain

blow¹ *v.* **1.** blast, breathe, exhale, fan, pant, puff, waft **2.** flow, rush, stream, whirl **3.** bear, buffet, drive, fling, flutter, sweep, waft, whirl, whisk **4.** blare, mouth, pipe, play, sound, toot, trumpet, vibrate ~*n.* **5.** blast, draught, flurry, gale, gust, puff, strong breeze, tempest, wind

blow² *n.* **1.** bang, bash (*Inf.*), belt (*Inf.*), buffet, clomp (*Sl.*), clout (*Inf.*), clump (*Sl.*),

knock, punch, rap, slosh (*Sl.*), smack, sock (*Sl.*), stroke, thump, wallop (*Inf.*), whack **2.** *Fig.* affliction, bolt from the blue, bombshell, calamity, catastrophe, comedown (*Inf.*), disappointment, disaster, jolt, misfortune, reverse, setback, shock, upset

blowout 1. blast, detonation, eruption, explosion **2.** break, burst, escape, flat, flat tyre, fuse, leak, puncture, rupture, tear **3.** binge, feast, party, spree

blow out 1. extinguish, put out, snuff **2.** burst, erupt, explode, rupture, shatter

blow over be forgotten, cease, die down, disappear, end, finish, pass, pass away, subside, vanish

the size of (a photograph). ~n. **blow-up. 6.** an explosion. **7.** *Inf.* an enlarged photograph or part of a photograph. **8.** *Inf.* a fit of temper.

blowy ('bləʊɪ) *adj.* **blowier, blowiest.** another word for **windy** (sense 1).

blowzy or **blowsy** ('blaʊzɪ) *adj.* **blowzier, blowziest** or **blowsier, blowsiest. 1.** (esp. of a woman) untidy in appearance; slovenly or sluttish. **2.** (of a woman) ruddy in complexion.

blubber ('blʌbə) *vb.* **1.** to sob without restraint. **2.** to utter while sobbing. **3.** (*tr.*) to make (the face) wet and swollen by crying. ~n. **4.** the fatty tissue of aquatic mammals such as the whale. **5.** *Inf.* flabby body fat. **6.** the act or an instance of weeping without restraint. ~*adj.* **7.** (*often in combination*) swollen or fleshy: *blubber-faced.* —'**blubberer** *n.* —'**blubbery** *adj.*

bludgeon ('blʌdʒən) *n.* **1.** a stout heavy club, typically thicker at one end. **2.** a person, line of argument, etc., that is effective but unsubtle. ~*vb.* (*tr.*) **3.** to hit as with a bludgeon. **4.** (*often foll. by* into) to force; bully; coerce.

blue (bluː) *n.* **1.** any of a group of colours, such as that of a clear unclouded sky or the deep sea. **2.** a dye or pigment of any of these colours. **3.** blue cloth or clothing: *dressed in blue.* **4.** a sportsman who represents or has represented Oxford or Cambridge University and has the right to wear the university colour. **5.** *Brit.* an informal name for **Tory. 6.** any of numerous small blue-winged butterflies. **7.** a blue substance used in laundering. **8.** *Austral. sl.* an argument or fight: *he had a blue with a taxi driver.* **9.** Also: **bluey.** *Austral. & N.Z. inf.* a summons. **10.** *Austral. & N.Z. inf.* a mistake; error. **11. out of the blue.** apparently from nowhere; unexpectedly. ~*adj.* **bluer, bluest. 12.** of the colour blue. **13.** (of the flesh) having a purple tinge, as from cold or contusion. **14.** depressed, moody, or unhappy. **15.** indecent, titillating, or pornographic: *blue films.* ~*vb.* **blueing** or **bluing, blued. 16.** to make, dye, or become blue. **17.** (*tr.*) to treat (laundry) with blue. **18.** (*tr.*) *Sl.* to spend extravagantly or wastefully; squander. —'**blueness** *n.*

blue baby *n.* a baby born with a bluish tinge to the skin because of lack of oxygen in the blood.

bluebell ('bluːˌbel) *n.* **1.** Also called: **wild** or **wood hyacinth.** a European woodland plant having a one-sided cluster of blue bell-shaped flowers. **2.** a Scottish name for **harebell. 3.** any of various other plants with blue bell-shaped flowers.

blueberry ('bluːbərɪ, -brɪ) *n., pl.* -ries. **1.** Also called: **huckleberry.** any of several North American ericaceous shrubs that have blue-black edible berries with tiny seeds. See also **bilberry. 2.** the fruit of any of these plants.

bluebird ('bluːˌbɜːd) *n.* **1.** a North American songbird of the thrush family having a blue or partly blue plumage. **2.** any of various other birds having a blue plumage.

blue blood *n.* royal or aristocratic descent. —'**blue-'blooded** *adj.*

bluebook ('bluːˌbʊk) *n.* (in Britain) a government publication bound in a stiff blue paper cover: usually the report of a royal commission or a committee.

bluebottle ('bluːˌbɒtəl) *n.* **1.** another name for the **blowfly. 2.** any of various blue-flowered plants, esp. the cornflower. **3.** *Brit.* an informal word for a **policeman. 4.** *an Australian name for* **Portuguese man-of-war.**

blue cheese *n.* cheese containing a blue mould, esp.

Stilton, Roquefort, or Danish Blue.

blue chip *n.* **1.** a gambling chip with the highest value. **2.** *Finance.* a stock considered reliable with respect to both dividend income and capital value.

blue-collar *adj.* of or designating manual industrial workers. Cf. **white-collar.**

blue-eyed boy *n. Inf., chiefly Brit.* the favourite or darling of a person or group.

blue funk *n. Inf., chiefly Brit.* a state of great terror.

blue pencil *n.* **1.** deletion, alteration, or censorship of the contents of a book or other work. ~*vb.* **blue-pencil, -cilling, -cilled** or *U.S.* **-ciling, -ciled. 2.** (*tr.*) to alter or delete parts of (a book, film, etc.), esp. to censor.

blue peter *n.* a signal flag of blue with a white square at the centre, displayed by a vessel about to leave port.

blueprint ('bluːˌprɪnt) *n.* **1.** Also called: **cyanotype.** a photographic print of plans, technical drawings, etc., consisting of white lines on a blue background. **2.** an original plan or prototype. ~*vb.* **3.** (*tr.*) to make a blueprint of (a plan, etc.).

blue ribbon *n.* **1.** (in Britain) a badge of blue silk worn by members of the Order of the Garter. **2.** a badge awarded as the first prize in a competition.

blues (bluːz) *pl. n.* (*sometimes functioning as sing.*) **the. 1.** a feeling of depression or deep unhappiness. **2.** a type of folk song originating among Black Americans, usually employing a basic 12-bar chorus, and frequent minor intervals.

bluestocking ('bluːˌstɒkɪŋ) *n. Usually disparaging.* a scholarly or intellectual woman.

bluetit ('bluːˌtɪt) *n.* a common European tit having a blue crown, wings, and tail, yellow underparts, and a black and grey head.

blue whale *n.* the largest mammal: a widely distributed bluish-grey whalebone whale, closely related and similar to the rorquals.

bluff[1] (blʌf) *vb.* **1.** to pretend to be confident about an uncertain issue in order to influence (someone). ~*n.* **2.** deliberate deception intended to create the impression of a stronger position than one actually has. **3. call someone's bluff.** to challenge someone to give proof of his claims. —'**bluffer** *n.*

bluff[2] (blʌf) *n.* **1.** a steep promontory, bank, or cliff. **2.** *Canad.* a clump of trees on the prairie; copse. ~*adj.* **3.** good-naturedly frank and hearty. **4.** (of a bank, cliff, etc.) presenting a steep broad face. —'**bluffness** *n.*

bluish or **blueish** ('bluːɪʃ) *adj.* somewhat blue.

blunder ('blʌndə) *n.* **1.** a stupid or clumsy mistake. **2.** a foolish tactless remark. ~*vb.* (*mainly intr.*) **3.** to make stupid or clumsy mistakes. **4.** to make foolish tactless remarks. **5.** (*often foll. by* about, into, etc.) to act clumsily; stumble. **6.** (*tr.*) to mismanage; botch. —'**blunderer** *n.* —'**blunderingly** *adv.*

blunderbuss ('blʌndəˌbʌs) *n.* an obsolete short musket with large bore and flared muzzle.

blunt (blʌnt) *adj.* **1.** (esp. of a knife or blade) lacking sharpness or keenness; dull. **2.** not having a sharp edge or point: *a blunt instrument.* **3.** (of people, manner of speaking, etc.) straightforward and uncomplicated. ~*vb.* (*tr.*) **4.** to make less sharp. **5.** to diminish the sensitivity or perception of; make dull. —'**bluntly** *adv.* —'**bluntness** *n.*

THESAURUS

blow up 1. bloat, distend, enlarge, expand, fill, inflate, puff up, pump up, swell **2.** blast, bomb, burst, detonate, dynamite, explode, go off, rupture, shatter **3.** enlarge, enlarge on, exaggerate, heighten, magnify, overstate **4.** *Inf.* become angry, become enraged, erupt, go off the deep end (*Inf.*), hit the roof (*Inf.*), lose one's temper, rage

blowzy, blowsy 1. bedraggled, dishevelled, frowzy, slatternly, slipshod, sloppy, slovenly, sluttish, tousled, unkempt, untidy **2.** florid, red-faced, ruddy

bludgeon *n.* **1.** club, cudgel, shillelagh, truncheon ~*v.* **2.** beat, beat up, club, cudgel, knock down, strike **3.** browbeat, bulldoze (*Inf.*), bully, coerce, force, hector, steamroller

blue 1. azure, cerulean, cobalt, cyan, navy,

sapphire, sky-coloured, ultramarine **2.** *Fig.* dejected, depressed, despondent, dismal, downcast, down-hearted, down in the dumps (*Inf.*), fed up, gloomy, glum, low, melancholy, sad, unhappy **3.** *Inf.* bawdy, dirty, indecent, lewd, naughty, near the knuckle (*Inf.*), obscene, risqué, smutty, vulgar

blueprint design, draft, layout, outline, pattern, pilot scheme, plan, project, prototype, scheme, sketch

blues dejection, depression, despondency, doldrums, dumps (*Inf.*), gloom, gloominess, glumness, low spirits, melancholy, moodiness

bluff[1] **1.** *v.* deceive, defraud, delude, fake, feign, humbug, lie, mislead, pretend, sham **2.** *n.* bluster, boast, braggadocio, bragging, bravado, deceit, deception, fake, feint, fraud,

humbug, idle boast, lie, mere show, pretence, sham, show, subterfuge

bluff[2] *n.* **1.** bank, cliff, crag, escarpment, headland, peak, precipice, promontory, ridge, scarp ~*adj.* **2.** abrupt, blunt, blustering, downright, frank, genial, good-natured, hearty, open, outspoken, plain-spoken **3.** abrupt, perpendicular, precipitous, sheer, steep, towering

blunder *n.* **1.** error, fault, inaccuracy, mistake, oversight, slip, slip-up (*Inf.*) **2.** boob (*Sl.*), clanger (*Inf.*), faux pas, gaffe, gaucherie, howler (*Inf.*), impropriety, indiscretion, mistake ~*v.* **3.** botch, bungle, err, slip up (*Inf.*) **4.** bumble, confuse, flounder, misjudge, stumble

blunt *adj.* **1.** dull, dulled, edgeless, pointless, rounded, unsharpened **2.** *Fig.* bluff, brusque,

blur (blɜː) vb. **blurring, blurred.** 1. to make or become vague or less distinct. 2. to smear or smudge. 3. (tr.) to make (the judgment, memory, or perception) less clear; dim. ~n. 4. something vague, hazy, or indistinct. 5. a smear or smudge. —'**blurredness** n. —'**blurry** adj.

blurb (blɜːb) n. a promotional description, as on the jackets of books.

blurt (blɜːt) vb. (tr.; often foll. by out) to utter suddenly and involuntarily.

blush (blʌʃ) vb. 1. (intr.) to become suddenly red in the face from embarrassment, shame, modesty, or guilt; redden. 2. to make or become reddish or rosy. ~n. 3. a sudden reddening of the face from embarrassment, shame, modesty, or guilt. 4. a rosy glow. 5. **at first blush.** when first seen; as a first impression.

blusher ('blʌʃə) n. a cosmetic applied to the cheeks to give a rosy colour.

bluster ('blʌstə) vb. 1. to speak or say loudly or boastfully. 2. to act in a bullying way. 3. (tr., foll. by into) to force or attempt to force (a person) into doing something by behaving thus. 4. (intr.) (of the wind) to be noisy or gusty. ~n. 5. boisterous talk or action; swagger. 6. empty threats or protests. 7. a strong wind; gale. —'**blusterer** n. —'**blustery** adj.

Blvd. abbrev. for Boulevard.

B.M. abbrev. for: 1. Bachelor of Medicine. 2. Surveying. bench mark. 3. British Museum.

B.M.A. abbrev. for British Medical Association.

B.Mus. abbrev. for Bachelor of Music.

B.N.O.C. abbrev. for British National Oil Corporation.

B.O. abbrev. for: 1. Inf. body odour. 2. box office.

boa ('bəʊə) n. 1. any of various large nonvenomous snakes of Central and South America and the West Indies. They kill their prey by constriction. 2. a woman's long thin scarf, usually of feathers or fur.

boa constrictor n. a very large snake of tropical America and the West Indies, that kills its prey by constriction.

boar (bɔː) n. an uncastrated male pig.

board (bɔːd) n. 1. a long wide flat piece of sawn timber. 2. **a.** a smaller flat piece of rigid material for a specific purpose: ironing board. **b.** (in combination): breadboard. 3. a person's meals, provided regularly for money. 4. Arch. a table, esp. when laden with food. 5. **a.** (sometimes functioning as pl.) a group of people who officially administer a company, trust, etc. **b.** (as modifier): a board meeting. 6. any other committee or council: a board of interviewers. 7. **the boards.** (pl.) the stage. 8. stiff cardboard or similar material, used for the outside covers of a book. 9. a flat thin rectangular sheet of composite material, such as plasterboard or chipboard. 10. Chiefly U.S. **a.** a list of stock-exchange prices. **b.** Inf. the stock exchange itself. 11. Naut. the side of a ship. 12. Austral. & N.Z. the part of the floor of a sheepshearing shed where the shearers work. 13. any of various portable surfaces specially designed for indoor games such as chess, backgammon, etc. 14. **across the board.** including all groups or classes. 15. **go by the board.** Inf. to be in disuse, neglected, or lost: in these days courtesy goes by the board. 16. **on board.** on or in a ship, boat, aeroplane, or other vehicle. ~vb. 17. to go aboard (a vessel, train, aircraft, or other vehicle). 18. to attack (a ship) by forcing one's way aboard. 19. (tr.; often foll. by up, in, etc.) to cover or shut with boards. 20. (intr.) to receive meals or meals and lodging in return

for money. 21. (sometimes foll. by out) to arrange for (someone, esp. a child) to receive food and lodging away from home. 22. (in ice hockey and box lacrosse) to bodycheck an opponent against the boards.

boarder ('bɔːdə) n. 1. a pupil who lives at school during term time. 2. another word for **lodger.** 3. a person who boards a ship, esp. in an attack.

boarding ('bɔːdɪŋ) n. 1. a structure of boards. 2. timber boards collectively. 3. **a.** the act of embarking on an aircraft, train, ship, etc. **b.** (as modifier): a boarding pass. 4. (in ice hockey and box lacrosse) an act of bodychecking an opponent against the boards.

boarding house n. a private house in which accommodation and meals are provided for paying guests.

boarding school n. a school providing living accommodation for some or all of its pupils.

Board of Trade n. (in the United Kingdom) a ministry responsible for the supervision of commerce and the promotion of export trade.

boardroom ('bɔːdˌruːm, -ˌrʊm) n. a room where the board of directors of a company meets.

boast (bəʊst) vb. 1. (intr.; sometimes foll. by of or about) to speak in excessively proud terms of one's possessions, skills, or superior qualities; brag. 2. (tr.) to possess (something to be proud of): the city boasts a fine cathedral. ~n. 3. a bragging statement. 4. a possession, attribute, etc., that is or may be bragged about. —'**boaster** n. —'**boastingly** adv.

boastful ('bəʊstfʊl) adj. tending to boast; characterized by boasting. —'**boastfully** adv. —'**boastfulness** n.

boat (bəʊt) n. 1. a small vessel propelled by oars, paddle, sails, or motor. 2. (not in technical use) another word for **ship.** 3. a container for gravy, sauce, etc. 4. **in the same boat.** sharing the same problems. 5. **miss the boat.** Inf. to fail to do something at the right time. 6. **rock the boat.** Inf. to cause a disturbance in the existing situation. ~vb. 7. (intr.) to travel or go in a boat, esp. as a form of recreation. 8. (tr.) to transport or carry in a boat.

boater ('bəʊtə) n. a stiff straw hat with a straight brim and flat crown.

boathook ('bəʊtˌhʊk) n. a pole with a hook at one end, used aboard a vessel for fending off other vessels or for catching a mooring buoy.

boathouse ('bəʊtˌhaʊs) n. a shelter by the edge of a river, lake, etc., for housing boats.

boating ('bəʊtɪŋ) n. rowing, sailing, or cruising in boats as a form of recreation.

boatman ('bəʊtmən) n., pl. **-men.** a man who works on, hires out, or repairs a boat or boats.

boatswain, bo's'n, or **bosun** ('bəʊsən) n. a petty officer or a warrant officer who is responsible for the maintenance of a ship and its equipment.

boat train n. a train scheduled to take passengers to or from a particular ship.

bob[1] (bɒb) vb. **bobbing, bobbed.** 1. to move or cause to move up and down repeatedly, as while floating in water. 2. to move or cause to move with a short abrupt movement, as of the head. 3. (intr.; usually foll. by up) to appear or emerge suddenly. 4. (intr.; usually foll. by for) to attempt to get hold (of a floating or hanging object, esp. an apple) in the teeth as a game. ~n. 5. a short abrupt movement, as of the head.

bob[2] (bɒb) n. 1. a hair style for women and children in

THESAURUS

discourteous, explicit, forthright, frank, impolite, outspoken, plain-spoken, rude, straightforward, tactless, trenchant, uncivil, unpolished ~v. 3. dampen, deaden, dull, numb, soften, take the edge off, water down, weaken

blur v. 1. becloud, bedim, befog, cloud, darken, dim, fog, make hazy, make indistinct, make vague, mask, obscure, soften 2. blot, smear, smudge, spot, stain ~n. 3. blear, blurredness, cloudiness, confusion, dimness, fog, haze, indistinctness, obscurity 4. blot, smear, smudge, spot, stain

blurred bleary, blurry, faint, foggy, fuzzy, hazy, ill-defined, indistinct, lacking definition, misty, nebulous, out of focus, unclear, vague

blurt out babble, blab, cry, disclose, ex-

claim, gush, reveal, spill, spout (Inf.), sputter, tattle, utter suddenly

blush 1. v. colour, crimson, flush, redden, turn red, turn scarlet 2. n. colour, flush, glow, pink tinge, reddening, rosiness, rosy tint, ruddiness

bluster 1. v. boast, brag, bulldoze, bully, domineer, hector, rant, roar, roister, storm, swagger, swell, vaunt 2. n. bluff, boasting, boisterousness, bombast, bragging, bravado, crowing, swagger, swaggering

blustery blusterous, boisterous, gusty, squally, stormy, tempestuous, violent, wild

board n. 1. panel, piece of timber, plank, slat, timber 2. daily meals, food, meals, provisions, victuals 3. advisers, advisory group, committee, conclave, council, directorate, directors, panel, trustees ~v. 4. embark, em-

bus, enplane, enter, entrain, mount 5. accommodate, feed, house, lodge, put up, quarter, room

boast v. 1. blow one's own trumpet, bluster, brag, crow, exaggerate, puff, strut, swagger, talk big (Sl.), vaunt 2. be proud of, congratulate oneself on, exhibit, flatter oneself, possess, pride oneself on, show off ~n. 3. avowal, brag, gasconade (Rare), rodomontade (Literary), swank (Inf.), vaunt 4. gem, joy, pride, pride and joy, source of pride, treasure

boastful bragging, cocky, conceited, crowing, egotistical, puffed-up, swaggering, swanky (Inf.), swollen-headed, vainglorious, vaunting

which the hair is cut short evenly all round the head. **2.** a dangling or hanging object, such as the weight on a pendulum or on a plumb line. **3.** short for **bobsleigh. 4.** a docked tail, esp. of a horse. ~*vb.* **bobbing, bobbed. 5.** (*tr.*) to cut (the hair) in a bob. **6.** (*tr.*) to cut short (something, esp. the tail of an animal); dock or crop. **7.** (*intr.*) to ride on a bobsleigh.

bob³ (bɒb) *n.*, *pl.* **bob.** *Brit.* (formerly) an informal word for a shilling.

bobbejaan ('bɒbə,jɑːn) *n. S. African.* a baboon.

bobbejaan spanner *n. S. African.* a monkey wrench.

bobbin ('bɒbɪn) *n.* a spool or reel on which thread or yarn is wound.

bobble ('bɒbəl) *n.* a tufted ball, usually for ornament, as on a knitted hat.

bobby ('bɒbɪ) *n.*, *pl.* **-bies.** *Inf.* a British policeman.

bobby-dazzler *n.* anything outstanding, striking, or showy.

bobcat ('bɒb,kæt) *n.* a North American feline mammal, closely related to but smaller than the lynx, having reddish-brown fur with dark spots or stripes, tufted ears, and a short tail. Also called: **bay lynx.**

bobotie (bu'butɪ) *n.* a South African dish consisting of curried mincemeat with a topping of beaten egg baked to a crust.

bobsleigh ('bɒb,sleɪ) *n.* **1.** a racing sledge for two or more people, with a steering mechanism enabling the driver to direct it down a steeply banked ice-covered run. ~*vb.* **2.** (*intr.*) to ride on a bobsleigh. ~Also called (esp. U.S.): **bobsled** ('bɒb,slɛd).

bobtail ('bɒb,teɪl) *n.* **1.** a docked or diminutive tail. **2.** an animal with such a tail. ~*adj. also* **bobtailed. 3.** having the tail cut short. ~*vb.* (*tr.*) **4.** to dock the tail of. **5.** to cut short; curtail.

Boche (bɒʃ) *n. Derog. sl.* (esp. in World Wars I and II) **1.** a German, esp. a German soldier. **2. the.** (*usually functioning as pl.*) Germans collectively, esp. German soldiers regarded as the enemy.

bod (bɒd) *n. Inf.* a fellow; chap: *he's a queer bod.*

bode¹ (bəud) *vb.* **1.** to be an omen of (good or ill, esp. of ill); portend; presage. **2.** (*tr.*) *Arch.* to predict; foretell. —'**bodement** *n.*

bode² (bəud) *vb.* the past tense of **bide** (senses 1,2).

bodega (bəu'diːgə) *n.* a shop selling wine and sometimes groceries, esp. in a Spanish-speaking country.

bodge (bɒdʒ) *vb. Inf.* to make a mess of; botch.

bodice ('bɒdɪs) *n.* **1.** the upper part of a woman's dress, from the shoulder to the waist. **2.** a tight-fitting corset worn laced over a blouse, or (formerly) as a woman's undergarment.

bodily ('bɒdɪlɪ) *adj.* **1.** relating to or being a part of the human body. ~*adv.* **2.** by taking hold of the body: *he threw him bodily from the platform.* **3.** in person; in the flesh.

bodkin ('bɒdkɪn) *n.* **1.** a blunt large-eyed needle. **2.** *Arch.* a dagger. **3.** *Arch.* a long ornamental hairpin.

body ('bɒdɪ) *n.*, *pl.* **bodies. 1. a.** the entire physical structure of an animal or human being. Related adj.: **corporeal. b.** (*as modifier*): *body odour.* **2.** the trunk or torso. **3.** a dead human or animal; corpse. **4.** the flesh as opposed to the spirit. **5.** the largest or main part of anything: *the body of a vehicle; the body of a plant.* **6.** a separate or distinct mass of water or land. **7.** a number of individuals regarded as a single entity; group. **8.** the characteristic full quality of certain wines. **9.** firmness, esp. of cloth. **10. a.** the pigment contained in or added to paint, dye, etc. **b.** the opacity of a paint. **c.** (*as modifier*): *body colour.* **11.** an informal or dialect word for a

person. **12. keep body and soul together.** to manage to keep alive; survive. ~*vb.* **bodying, bodied.** (*tr.*) **13.** (usually foll. by *forth*) to give a body or shape to.

bodycheck ('bɒdɪ,tʃɛk) *n. Ice hockey, etc.* **1.** obstruction of another player. ~*vb.* **2.** (*tr.*) to deliver a bodycheck to (an opponent).

bodyguard ('bɒdɪ,gɑːd) *n.* a man or group of men who escort and protect someone.

body-line *adj. Cricket.* denoting or relating to fast bowling aimed at the batsman's body.

body politic *n.* **the.** the people of a nation or the nation itself considered as a political entity.

body shop *n.* a repair yard for vehicle bodywork.

body snatcher *n.* (formerly) a person who robbed graves and sold the corpses for dissection.

body stocking *n.* a one-piece undergarment for women, usually of nylon, covering the torso.

bodywork ('bɒdɪ,wɜːk) *n.* the external shell of a motor vehicle.

Boer (buə) *n.* **a.** a descendant of any of the Dutch or Huguenot colonists who settled in South Africa. **b.** (*as modifier*): *a Boer farmer.*

boerbul ('buəbəl) *n. S. African.* a crossbred mastiff used esp. as a watchdog.

boeremusiek ('buərə,mœsik) *n. S. African.* light music associated with the culture of the Afrikaners.

boerperd ('buə,pɜːt) *n.* a S. African breed of rugged horse, often palomino.

boet (but) *or* **boetie** *n. S. African inf.* a friend.

boffin ('bɒfɪn) *n. Brit. inf.* a scientist, esp. one carrying out military research.

Bofors gun ('bəufəz) *n.* an automatic double-barrelled anti-aircraft gun.

bog (bɒg) *n.* **1.** wet spongy ground consisting of decomposing vegetation. **2.** an area of such ground. **3.** a slang word for **lavatory.** ~See also **bog down.** —'**boggy** *adj.* —'**bogginess** *n.*

bogan ('bəugən) *n. Canad.* (esp. in the Maritime Provinces) a sluggish side stream. Also called: **logan, pokelogan.**

bog down *vb.* **bogging, bogged.** (*adv.*; when *tr.*, often *passive*) to impede or be impeded physically or mentally.

bogey *or* **bogy** ('bəugɪ) *n.* **1.** an evil or mischievous spirit. **2.** something that worries or annoys. **3.** *Golf.* **a.** a standard score for a hole or course, regarded as one that a good player should make. **b.** a score of one stroke over par on a hole. Cf. **par** (sense 5). **4.** *Sl.* a piece of dried mucus discharged from the nose.

bogeyman ('bəugɪ,mæn) *n.*, *pl.* **-men.** a person, real or imaginary, used as a threat, esp. to children.

boggle ('bɒgəl) *vb.* (*intr.*; often foll. by *at*) **1.** to be surprised, confused, or alarmed (esp. in **the mind boggles**). **2.** to hesitate or be evasive when confronted with a problem.

bogie *or* **bogy** ('bəugɪ) *n.* **1.** an assembly of four or six wheels forming a pivoted support at either end of a railway coach. **2.** *Chiefly Brit.* a small railway truck of short wheelbase, used for conveying coal, ores, etc.

bog oak *n.* oak preserved in peat bogs.

bogtrotter ('bɒg,trɒtə) *n.* a derogatory term for an Irishman, esp. an Irish peasant.

bogus ('bəugəs) *adj.* spurious or counterfeit; not genuine. —'**bogusly** *adv.* —'**bogusness** *n.*

bogy ('bəugɪ) *n.*, *pl.* **-gies.** a variant spelling of **bogey** or **bogie.**

THESAURUS

bob bounce, duck, hop, jerk, leap, nod, oscillate, quiver, skip, waggle, weave, wobble

bode augur, betoken, forebode, foreshadow, foretell, forewarn, impart, omen, portend, predict, presage, prophesy, signify, threaten

bodiless disembodied, ghostly, immaterial, incorporeal, insubstantial, spectral, spiritual, supernatural

bodily 1. *adj.* actual, carnal, corporal, corporeal, fleshly, material, physical, substantial, tangible 2. *adv.* altogether, as a body, as a group, collectively, completely, en masse, entirely, fully, totally, wholly

body 1. build, figure, form, frame, physique,

shape, torso, trunk 2. cadaver, carcass, corpse, dead body, relics, remains, stiff (*Sl.*) 3. being, creature, human, human being, individual, mortal, person 4. bulk, essence, main part, mass, material, matter, substance 5. association, band, bloc, collection, company, confederation, congress, corporation, society 6. crowd, horde, majority, mass, mob, multitude, throng 7. consistency, density, firmness, richness, solidity, substance

bog fen, marsh, marshland, mire, morass, moss (*Northern Eng. & Scot.*), peat bog, quagmire, slough, swamp, wetlands

bog down delay, halt, impede, sink, slow

down, slow up, stall, stick

bogey 1. apparition, bogeyman, goblin, hobgoblin, imp, spectre, spirit, spook (*Inf.*), sprite 2. bête noire, bugaboo, bugbear, nightmare

boggle 1. be alarmed (confused, surprised, taken aback), shy, stagger, startle, take fright 2. demur, dither, doubt, equivocate, falter, hang back, hesitate, hover, jib, shillyshally (*Inf.*), shrink from, vacillate, waver

boggy fenny, marshy, miry, muddy, oozy, quaggy, soft, spongy, swampy, waterlogged, yielding

bogus artificial, counterfeit, dummy, fake,

Bohemian (bəʊ'hiːmɪən) n. 1. a native or inhabitant of Bohemia, a former kingdom; a Czech. 2. (often not cap.) a person, esp. an artist or writer, who lives an unconventional life. 3. the Czech language. ~adj. 4. of, relating to, or characteristic of Bohemia, its people, or their language. 5. unconventional in appearance, behaviour, etc. —Bo'hemia,nism n.

boil¹ (bɔɪl) vb. 1. to change or cause to change from a liquid to a gas, esp. by the application of heat. 2. to reach or cause to reach boiling point. 3. to cook or be cooked by the process of boiling. 4. (intr.) to bubble and be agitated like something boiling; seethe: the ocean was boiling. 5. (intr.) to be extremely angry or indignant. ~n. 6. the state or action of boiling. ~See also **boil away, boil down,** etc.

boil² (bɔɪl) n. a red painful swelling with a hard pus-filled core caused by bacterial infection of the skin. Technical name: **furuncle**.

boil away vb. (adv.) to cause (liquid) to evaporate completely by boiling or (of liquid) to evaporate completely.

boil down vb. (adv.) 1. to reduce or be reduced in quantity by boiling. 2. **boil down to. a.** (intr.) to be the essential element in something. **b.** (tr.) to summarize; reduce to essentials.

boiled shirt n. a dress shirt with stiff front.

boiler ('bɔɪlə) n. 1. a closed vessel in which water is heated to supply steam or provide heat. 2. a domestic device to provide hot water, esp. for central heating. 3. a large tub for boiling laundry.

boilermaker ('bɔɪlə,meɪkə) n. a person who works with metal in heavy industry; plater or welder.

boiler suit n. Brit. a one-piece overall work garment.

boiling point n. 1. the temperature at which a liquid boils at sea level. 2. Inf. the condition of being angered or highly excited.

boil over vb. (adv.) 1. to overflow or cause to overflow while boiling. 2. (intr.) to burst out in anger or excitement.

boisterous ('bɔɪstərəs, -strəs) adj. 1. noisy and lively; unruly. 2. (of the wind, sea, etc.) turbulent or stormy. —'boisterously adv. —'boisterousness n.

bokmakierie (,bɒkmə'kɪərɪ) n. S. African. a large yellow shrike of southern Africa, known for its melodious song.

bold (bəʊld) adj. 1. courageous, confident, and fearless; ready to take risks. 2. showing or requiring courage: a bold plan. 3. immodest or impudent: she gave him a bold look. 4. standing out distinctly; conspicuous: a figure carved in bold relief. 5. very steep: the bold face of the cliff. 6. imaginative in thought or expression. —'boldly adv. —'boldness n.

bold face n. 1. Printing. a weight of type characterized by thick heavy lines, as the entry words in this dictionary. ~adj. **boldface.** 2. (of type) having this weight.

bole (bəʊl) n. the trunk of a tree.

bolero (bə'lɛərəʊ) n., pl. **-ros.** 1. a Spanish dance, usually in triple time. 2. a piece of music for or in the rhythm of this dance. 3. (also 'bɒlərəʊ) a kind of short jacket not reaching the waist, worn by women.

boll (bəʊl) n. the fruit of such plants as flax and cotton, consisting of a rounded capsule containing the seeds.

bollard ('bɒlɑːd, 'bɒləd) n. 1. a strong wooden or metal post on a wharf, quay, etc., used for securing mooring lines. 2. Brit. a small post placed on a kerb or traffic island to make it conspicuous to motorists.

bollocks ('bɒləks) or **ballocks** Taboo sl. ~pl. n. 1. another word for **testicle.** ~interj. 2. an exclamation of annoyance, disbelief, etc.

Bolshevik ('bɒlʃɪ,vɪk) n., pl. **-viks** or **-viki** (-'viːkɪ). 1. (formerly) a Russian Communist. 2. any Communist. 3. (often not cap.) Inf. & derog. any political radical, esp. a revolutionary. —'Bolshe,vism n. —'Bolshevist adj., n.

bolshie or **bolshy** ('bɒlʃɪ) (sometimes cap.) Brit. inf. ~adj. 1. difficult to manage; rebellious. 2. politically radical or left-wing. ~n., pl. **-shies.** 3. Derog. any political radical.

bolster ('bəʊlstə) vb. (tr.) 1. (often foll. by up) to support or reinforce; strengthen: to bolster morale. 2. to prop up with a pillow or cushion. ~n. 3. a long narrow pillow or cushion. 4. any pad or padded support. 5. a cold chisel used for cutting stone slabs, etc. —'bolsterer n.

bolt¹ (bəʊlt) n. 1. a bar that can be slid into a socket to lock a door, gate, etc. 2. a bar or rod that forms part of a locking mechanism and is moved by a key or a knob. 3. a metal rod or pin that has a head and a screw thread to take a nut. 4. a sliding bar in a breech-loading firearm that ejects the empty cartridge, replaces it with a new one, and closes the breech. 5. a flash of lightning. 6. **a bolt from the blue.** a sudden, unexpected, and usually unwelcome event. 7. a sudden start or movement, esp. in order to escape. 8. a roll of something, such as cloth, wallpaper, etc. 9. an arrow, esp. for a crossbow. 10. **shoot one's bolt.** to exhaust one's efforts. ~vb. 11. (tr.) to secure or lock with or as with a bolt. 12. (tr.) to eat hurriedly. 13. (intr.; usually foll. by from or out) to move or jump suddenly: he bolted from the chair. 14. (intr.) (esp. of a horse) to start hurriedly and run away without warning. 15. (tr.) to roll (cloth, wallpaper, etc.) into bolts. 16. (intr.) (of cultivated plants) to produce flowers and seeds prematurely. ~adv. 17. stiffly, firmly, or rigidly (archaic except in **bolt upright**). —'bolter n.

bolt² or **boult** (bəʊlt) vb. (tr.) 1. to pass (flour, a powder, etc.) through a sieve. 2. to examine and separate. —'bolter n.

bolt hole n. a way of escape from danger.

bomb (bɒm) n. 1. **a.** a hollow projectile containing explosive, incendiary, or other destructive substance. **b.** (as modifier): bomb disposal; a bomb bay. **c.** (in combination): bombproof. 2. an object in which an explosive device has been planted: a car bomb; a letter bomb. 3. **the bomb.** a hydrogen or an atom bomb considered as the ultimate destructive weapon. 4. a round mass of volcanic rock, solidified from molten lava that has been thrown into the air. 5. Med. a container for radioactive material, applied therapeutically to any part of the body: a cobalt bomb. 6. Brit. sl. a large sum of money. 7. U.S. sl. a disastrous failure: the new play was a total bomb. 8. Austral. & N.Z. sl. an old or dilapidated motor car. 9. **like a bomb.** Brit. & N.Z. inf. with great speed or success; very well. ~v. 10. to attack with or as if with a bomb or bombs; drop bombs (on). 11. (intr.; often foll. by off, along, etc.) to move or go very quickly. 12. (intr.) U.S. sl. to fail disastrously.

bombard vb. (bɒm'bɑːd). (tr.) 1. to attack with concentrated artillery fire or bombs. **2.** to attack with vigour and persistence. **3.** to attack verbally, esp. with questions. **4.** *Physics.* to direct high-energy particles or photons against (atoms, nuclei, etc.). ~*n.* ('bombɑːd). **5.** an ancient type of cannon that threw stone balls. —**bom-**'**bardment** *n.*

bombardier (ˌbɒmbə'dɪə) *n.* **1.** the member of a bomber aircrew responsible for aiming and releasing the bombs. **2.** *Brit.* a noncommisioned rank, below the rank of sergeant, in the Royal Artillery. **3.** *Canad. trademark.* a snow tractor, usually having caterpillar tracks at the rear and skis at the front.

bombast ('bɒmbæst) *n.* pompous and grandiloquent language. —**bom**'**bastic** *adj.* —**bom**'**bastically** *adv.*

Bombay duck (bɒm'beɪ) *n.* a fish that is eaten dried with curry dishes as a savoury. Also called: **bummalo.**

bombazine *or* **bombasine** (ˌbɒmbə'ziːn, 'bɒmbəˌziːn) *n.* a twilled fabric, esp. one of silk and worsted, formerly worn dyed black for mourning.

bomber ('bɒmə) *n.* **1.** a military aircraft designed to carry out bombing missions. **2.** a person who plants bombs.

bombshell ('bɒmˌʃɛl) *n.* **1.** (esp. formerly) a bomb or artillery shell. **2.** a shocking or unwelcome surprise.

bona fide ('bəʊnə 'faɪdɪ) *adj.* **1.** real or genuine: *a bona fide manuscript.* **2.** undertaken in good faith: *a bona fide agreement.*

bonanza (bə'nænzə) *n.* **1.** a source, usually sudden and unexpected, of luck or wealth. **2.** *U.S.* a mine or vein rich in ore.

bonbon ('bɒnbɒn) *n.* a sweet.

bond (bɒnd) *n.* **1.** something that binds, fastens, or holds together, such as a chain or rope. **2.** (*often pl.*) something that brings or holds people together; tie: *a bond of friendship.* **3.** (*pl.*) something that restrains or imprisons; captivity or imprisonment. **4.** a written or spoken agreement, esp. a promise. **5.** *Finance.* a certificate of debt issued in order to raise funds. It is repayable with or without security at a specified future date. **6.** *Law.* a written acknowledgment of an obligation to pay a sum or to perform a contract. **7.** any of various arrangements of bricks or stones in a wall in which they overlap so as to provide strength. **8. chemical bond.** a mutual attraction between two atoms resulting from a redistribution of their outer electrons, determining chemical properties; shown in some formulae by a dot (.) or stroke (—). **9.** See **bond paper. 10. in bond.** *Commerce.* deposited in a bonded warehouse. ~*vb.* (*mainly tr.*) **11.** (*also intr.*) to hold or be held together, as by a rope or an adhesive; bind; connect. **12.** to put or hold (goods) in bond. **13.** *Law.* to place under bond. **14.** *Finance.* to issue bonds on; mortgage.

bondage ('bɒndɪdʒ) *n.* **1.** slavery or serfdom; servitude. **2.** subjection to some influence or duty.

bonded ('bɒndɪd) *adj.* **1.** *Finance.* consisting of, secured by, or operating under a bond or bonds. **2.** *Commerce.* deposited in a bonded warehouse.

bond paper *n.* a superior quality of strong white paper, used esp. for writing and typing.

bondservant ('bɒndˌsɜːvənt) *n.* a serf or slave.

bone (bəʊn) *n.* **1.** any of the various structures that make up the skeleton in most vertebrates. **2.** the porous rigid tissue of which these parts are made. **3.** something consisting of bone or a bonelike substance. **4.** (*pl.*) *Inf.* the human skeleton or body. **5.** a thin strip of whalebone, plastic, etc., used to stiffen corsets and brassieres. **6.** (*pl.*) the essentials (esp. in **the bare bones**). **7.** (*pl.*) *Inf.* dice. **8. feel in one's bones.** to have an intuition of. **9. have a bone to pick.** to have grounds for a quarrel. **10. make no bones about. a.** to be direct and candid about. **b.** to have no objections to. **11. near** *or* **close to**

the bone. a. risqué or indecent. **b.** in poverty; destitute. **12. point the bone.** (often foll. by *at*) *Austral.* **a.** to wish bad luck (on). **b.** to cast a spell (on) in order to kill. ~*vb.* (*mainly tr.*) **13.** to remove the bones from (meat for cooking, etc.). **14.** to stiffen (a corset, etc.) by inserting bones. **15.** *Brit.* a slang word for **steal.** ~See also **bone up.** —'**boneless** *adj.*

bone china *n.* porcelain containing bone ash.

bone-dry *adj. Inf.* **a.** completely dry: *a bone-dry well.* **b.** (*postpositive*): *the well was bone dry.*

bone idle *adj.* very idle; extremely lazy.

bone meal *n.* dried and ground animal bones, used as a fertilizer or in stock feeds.

boneshaker ('bəʊnˌʃeɪkə) *n.* **1.** an early type of bicycle having solid tyres and no springs. **2.** *Sl.* any decrepit or rickety vehicle.

bone up *vb.* (*adv.; when intr., usually foll. by on*) *Inf.* to study intensively.

bonfire ('bɒnˌfaɪə) *n.* a large outdoor fire.

bongo[1] ('bɒŋgəʊ) *n., pl.* -**go** *or* -**gos.** a rare spiral-horned antelope inhabiting forests of central Africa. The coat is bright red-brown with narrow vertical stripes.

bongo[2] ('bɒŋgəʊ) *n., pl.* -**gos** *or* -**goes.** a small bucket-shaped drum, usually one of a pair, played by beating with the fingers.

bonhomie ('bɒnəmiː) *n.* exuberant friendliness.

bonkers ('bɒŋkəz) *adj. Sl., chiefly Brit.* mad; crazy.

bon mot (French bɔ̃ 'mo) *n., pl.* **bons mots** (bɔ̃ 'mo). a clever and fitting remark.

bonnet ('bɒnɪt) *n.* **1.** any of various hats worn, esp. formerly, by women and girls, and tied with ribbons under the chin. **2.** (in Scotland) a flat brimless cap worn by men. **3.** the hinged metal part of a motor vehicle body that provides access to the engine. **4.** a cowl on a chimney. **5.** *Naut.* a piece of sail laced to the foot of a foresail to give it greater area in light winds. **6.** *U.S.* a headdress of feathers worn by some tribes of American Indians.

bonny ('bɒnɪ) *adj.* -**nier,** -**niest. 1.** *N Brit. dialect.* beautiful or handsome: *a bonny lass.* **2.** good or fine. **3.** (esp. of babies) plump.

bonsai ('bɒnsaɪ) *n., pl.* -**sai. 1.** the art of growing dwarf ornamental varieties of trees or shrubs in small shallow pots by selective pruning, etc. **2.** a tree or shrub grown by this method.

bonus ('bəʊnəs) *n.* **1.** something given, paid, or received above what is due or expected. **2.** *Chiefly Brit.* an extra dividend allotted to shareholders out of profits. **3.** *Insurance, Brit.* a dividend, esp. a percentage of net profits, distributed to policyholders.

bon voyage (French bɔ̃ vwa'jaːʒ) *interj.* a phrase used to wish a traveller a pleasant journey.

bony ('bəʊnɪ) *adj.* **bonier, boniest. 1.** resembling or consisting of bone. **2.** having many bones. **3.** having prominent bones. **4.** thin or emaciated. **5.** (of fishes) having a skeleton of bone rather than cartilage. —'**boniness** *n.*

bonze (bɒnz) *n.* a Chinese or Japanese Buddhist priest or monk.

boo (buː) *interj.* **1.** an exclamation uttered to startle or surprise someone, esp. a child. **2.** a shout uttered to express disgust, dissatisfaction, or contempt. ~*vb.* **booing, booed. 3.** to shout "boo" at (someone or something), esp. as an expression of disapproval.

boob (buːb) *Sl.* ~*n.* **1.** an ignorant or foolish person. **2.** *Brit.* an embarrassing mistake; blunder. **3.** a female breast. ~*vb.* **4.** (*intr.*) *Brit.* to make a blunder.

booby ('buːbɪ) *n., pl.* -**bies. 1.** an ignorant or foolish person. **2.** *Brit.* the losing player in a game. **3.** any of several tropical marine birds related to the gannet. They have a straight stout bill and the plumage is white with darker markings.

THESAURUS

bombard 1. assault, blast, blitz, bomb, cannonade, fire upon, open fire, pound, shell, strafe **2.** assail, attack, barrage, batter, beset, besiege, harass, hound, pester

bombardment assault, attack, barrage, blitz, bombing, cannonade, fire, flak, fusillade, shelling, strafe

bombast bluster, brag, braggadocio, extravagant boasting, fustian, gasconade (*Rare*), grandiloquence, grandiosity, magniloquence, pomposity, rant, rodomontade (*Literary*)

bombastic declamatory, fustian, grandiloquent, grandiose, high-flown, histrionic, inflated, magniloquent, pompous, ranting, turgid, verbose, windy, wordy

bona fide actual, authentic, genuine, honest, lawful, legal, legitimate, real, true

bond *n.* **1.** band, binding, chain, cord, fastening, fetter, ligature, link, manacle, shackle, tie **2.** affiliation, affinity, attachment, connection, link, relation, tie, union **3.** agreement, compact, contract, covenant, guarantee, obligation, pledge, promise, word ~*v.* **4.**

bind, connect, fasten, fix together, fuse, glue, gum, paste

bonny 1. beautiful, comely, fair, handsome, lovely, pretty, sweet **2.** bouncing, buxom, chubby, fine, plump, rounded, shapely **3.** blithe, cheerful, cheery, gay, joyful, merry, sunny, winsome

bonus benefit, bounty, commission, dividend, extra, gift, gratuity, hand-out, honorarium, plus, premium, prize, reward

bony angular, emaciated, gangling, gaunt, lanky, lean, rawboned, scrawny, skinny, thin

booby prize *n.* a mock prize given to the person having the lowest score.

booby trap *n.* **1.** a hidden explosive device primed in such a way as to be set off by an unsuspecting victim. **2.** a trap for an unsuspecting person, esp. one intended as a practical joke. ~*vb.* **booby-trap, -trapping, -trapped. 3.** (*tr.*) to set a booby trap in or on (a building or object) or for (a person).

boodle ('buːdəl) *n. Sl., chiefly U.S.* money or valuables, esp. when stolen, counterfeit, or used as a bribe.

boogie-woogie ('buːgɪ'wugɪ, 'buːgɪ'wuːgɪ) *n.* a style of piano jazz using a dotted bass pattern, usually with eight notes in a bar and the harmonies of the 12-bar blues.

boohoo (ˌbuː'huː) *vb.* **-hooing, -hooed. 1.** to sob or pretend to sob noisily. ~*n., pl.* **-hoos. 2.** (*sometimes pl.*) distressed or pretended sobbing.

book (buk) *n.* **1.** a number of printed or written pages bound together along one edge and usually protected by covers. **2. a.** a written work or composition, such as a novel, technical manual, or dictionary. **b.** (*as modifier*): *book reviews*. **c.** (*in combination*): *bookseller; bookshop; bookshelf*. **3.** a number of blank or ruled sheets of paper bound together, used to record lessons, keep accounts, etc. **4.** the libretto of an opera, musical, etc. **5.** a major division of a written composition, as of a long novel or of the Bible. **6.** a number of tickets, stamps, etc., fastened together along one edge. **7.** a record of betting transactions. **8.** (in card games) the number of tricks that must be taken by a side or player before any trick has a scoring value. **9.** strict or rigid rules or standards (esp. in **by the book**). **10.** a source of knowledge or authority: *the book of life*. **11. an open book.** a person or subject that is thoroughly understood. **12. a closed book.** a person or subject that is unknown or beyond comprehension: *chemistry is a closed book to him.* **13. bring to book.** to reprimand or require (someone) to give an explanation of his conduct. **14. close the books.** *Book-keeping.* to balance accounts in order to prepare a statement or report. **15. in someone's good** (*or* **bad**) **books.** *Inf.* regarded by someone with favour (or disfavour). **16. keep the books.** to keep written records of the finances of a business. **17. on the books. a.** enrolled as a member. **b.** recorded. **18. throw the book at. a.** to charge with every relevant offence. **b.** to inflict the most severe punishment on. ~*vb.* **19.** to reserve (a place, passage, etc.) or engage the services of (a performer, driver, etc.) in advance. **20.** (*tr.*) to take the name and address of (a person guilty of a minor offence) with a view to bringing a prosecution. **21.** (*tr.*) (of a football referee) to take the name of (a player) who grossly infringes the rules. **22.** (*tr.*) *Arch.* to record in a book. ~See also **book in**.

bookcase ('buk,keɪs) *n.* a piece of furniture containing shelves for books.

book club *n.* a club that sells books at low prices to members.

book end *n.* one of a pair of usually ornamental supports for holding a row of books upright.

bookie ('bukɪ) *n. Inf.* short for **bookmaker.**

book in *vb.* (*adv.*) **1.** to reserve a room at a hotel. **2.** *Chiefly Brit.* to register, esp. one's arrival at a hotel.

booking ('bukɪŋ) *n.* **1.** *Chiefly Brit.* a reservation, as of a table, room, or seat. **2.** *Theatre.* an engagement of an actor or company.

bookish ('bukɪʃ) *adj.* **1.** fond of reading; studious. **2.** consisting of or forming opinions through reading rather than experience; academic. **3.** of or relating to books.

—'**bookishness** *n.*

book-keeping *n.* the skill or occupation of systematically recording business transactions. —'**book,keeper** *n.*

booklet ('buklɪt) *n.* a thin book, esp. one having paper covers; pamphlet.

bookmaker ('buk,meɪkə) *n.* a person who as an occupation accepts bets, esp. on horseraces, and pays out to winning betters. —'**book,making** *n.*

bookmark ('buk,mɑːk) *or* **bookmarker** *n.* a strip of some material put between the pages of a book to mark a place.

bookplate ('buk,pleɪt) *n.* a label bearing the owner's name and a design, pasted into a book.

bookstall ('buk,stɔːl) *n.* a stall or stand where periodicals, newspapers, or books are sold.

book token *n. Brit.* a gift token to be exchanged for books.

book value *n.* **1.** the value of an asset of a business according to its books. **2.** the net capital value of an enterprise as shown by the excess of book assets over book liabilities.

bookworm ('buk,wɜːm) *n.* **1.** any of various small insects that feed on the binding paste of books. **2.** a person devoted to reading.

Boolean algebra ('buːlɪən) *n.* a system of symbolic logic devised to codify nonmathematical logical operations. It is used in computers.

boom[1] (buːm) *vb.* **1.** to make a deep prolonged resonant sound. **2.** to prosper or cause to prosper vigorously and rapidly: *business boomed.* ~*n.* **3.** a deep prolonged resonant sound. **4.** a period of high economic growth.

boom[2] (buːm) *n.* **1.** *Naut.* a spar to which a sail is fastened to control its position relative to the wind. **2.** a pole carrying an overhead microphone and projected over a film or television set. **3.** a barrier across a waterway, usually consisting of a chain of logs, to confine free-floating logs, protect a harbour from attack, etc.

boomslang ('buːm,slæŋ) *n.* a large greenish venomous arboreal snake of southern Africa.

boon (buːn) *n.* **1.** something extremely useful, helpful, or beneficial; a blessing or benefit. **2.** *Arch.* a favour; request.

boor (buə) *n.* an ill-mannered, clumsy, or insensitive person. —'**boorish** *adj.* —'**boorishly** *adv.* —'**boorishness** *n.*

boost (buːst) *n.* **1.** encouragement, improvement, or help: *a boost to morale.* **2.** an upward thrust or push. **3.** an increase or rise. **4.** the amount by which the induction pressure of a supercharged internal-combustion engine is increased. ~*vb.* (*tr.*) **5.** to encourage, assist, or improve: *to boost morale.* **6.** to lift by giving a push from below or behind. **7.** to increase or raise: *to boost the voltage in an electrical circuit.* **8.** to cause to rise; increase: *to boost sales.* **9.** to advertise on a big scale. **10.** to increase the induction pressure of (an internal-combustion engine); supercharge.

▷ **Usage.** Except in the terminology of rocketry, the word *boost* is regarded as slightly informal, esp. in a figurative sense: *a boost to the economy.*

booster ('buːstə) *n.* **1.** a person or thing that supports, assists, or increases power. **2.** Also called: **launching vehicle.** the first stage of a multistage rocket. **3.** a radio-frequency amplifier to strengthen signals. **4.** another name for **supercharger. 5.** short for **booster shot.**

booster shot *n. Inf.* a supplementary injection of a

THESAURUS

book *n.* **1.** manual, publication, roll, scroll, textbook, tome, tract, volume, work **2.** album, diary, exercise book, jotter, notebook, pad ~*v.* **3.** arrange for, bill, charter, engage, line up, make reservations, organize, procure, programme, reserve, schedule **4.** enrol, enter, insert, list, log, mark down, note, post, put down, record, register, write down

bookish academic, donnish, erudite, intellectual, learned, literary, pedantic, scholarly, studious

boom *v.* **1.** bang, blast, crash, explode, resound, reverberate, roar, roll, rumble, thunder **2.** develop, expand, flourish, gain, grow, increase, intensify, prosper, spurt, strengthen, succeed, swell, thrive ~*n.* **3.** bang, blast,

burst, clap, crash, explosion, roar, rumble, thunder **4.** advance, boost, development, expansion, gain, growth, improvement, increase, jump, push, spurt, upsurge, upswing, upturn

boomerang backfire, come back, come home to roost, rebound, recoil, return, reverse, ricochet

boon **1.** *n.* advantage, benefaction, benefit, blessing, donation, favour, gift, godsend, grant, gratuity, present, windfall **2.** *adj.* close, intimate, special

boor barbarian, brute, bumpkin, churl, clodhopper (*Inf.*), clodpole, lout, oaf, peasant, philistine, vulgarian

boorish awkward, barbaric, bearish,

churlish, clownish, coarse, crude, gross, gruff, ill-bred, loutish, lubberly, oafish, rude, rustic, uncivilized, uncouth, uneducated, unrefined, vulgar

boost *n.* **1.** encouragement, help, improvement, praise, promotion **2.** heave, hoist, lift, push, raise, shove, thrust **3.** addition, expansion, improvement, increase, increment, jump, rise ~*v.* **4.** advance, advertise, assist, encourage, foster, further, improve, inspire, plug (*Inf.*), praise, promote, support, sustain **5.** elevate, heave, hoist, lift, push, raise, shove, thrust **6.** add to, amplify, develop, enlarge, expand, heighten, hoick, increase, jack up, magnify, raise

vaccine given to maintain the immunization provided by an earlier dose.

boot[1] (bu:t) n. 1. a strong outer covering for the foot; shoe that extends above the ankle, often to the knee. 2. *Brit.* an enclosed compartment of a car for holding luggage, etc., usually at the rear. *U.S. name:* **trunk.** 3. an instrument of torture used to crush the foot and lower leg. 4. *Inf.* a kick: *he gave the door a boot.* 5. **the boot.** *Sl.* dismissal from employment; the sack. 6. **lick the boots of.** to be servile towards. 7. **die with one's boots on.** to die while still active. 8. **put the boot in.** *Sl.* a. to kick a person, esp. when he is already down. b. to harass someone. 9. **the boot is on the other foot** *or* **leg.** the situation is or has now reversed. 10. **boots and all.** *Austral. inf.* making every effort. ~vb. (tr.) 11. to kick. 12. to equip with boots. 13. *Inf.* a. (often foll. by *out*) to eject forcibly. b. to dismiss from employment.

boot[2] (bu:t) vb. 1. *Arch.* to be of advantage or use to (a person): *what boots it to complain?* ~n. 2. *Obs.* an advantage. 3. **to boot.** as well; in addition.

bootee ('bu:ti:, bu:'ti:) n. 1. a soft shoe for a baby, esp. a knitted one. 2. a boot for women and children, esp. an ankle-length one.

Boötes (bəʊˈəʊti:z) n., *Latin genitive* **Boötis** (bəʊˈəʊtɪs). a constellation in the N hemisphere containing the star Arcturus.

booth (bu:ð, bu:θ) n., pl. **booths** (bu:ðz). 1. a stall, esp. a temporary one at a fair or market. 2. a small partially enclosed cubicle, such as one for telephoning (**telephone booth**) or for voting (**polling booth**). 3. *Chiefly U.S.* two high-backed benches with a table between, used esp. in bars and restaurants. 4. (formerly) a temporary structure for shelter, dwelling, storage, etc.

bootleg ('bu:t,lɛg) vb. **-legging, -legged.** 1. to make, carry, or sell (illicit goods, esp. alcohol). ~n. 2. something made or sold illicitly, such as alcohol. ~adj. 3. produced, distributed, or sold illicitly. —'**boot,legger** n.

bootless ('bu:tlɪs) adj. of little or no use; vain; fruitless.

bootlicker ('bu:t,lɪkə) n. *Inf.* one who seeks favour by servile or ingratiating behaviour towards (someone, esp. in authority); toady.

booty ('bu:tɪ) n., pl. **-ties.** any valuable article or articles, esp. when obtained as plunder.

booze (bu:z) *Inf.* ~n. 1. alcoholic drink. 2. a drinking bout. ~vb. 3. (usually intr.) to drink (alcohol), esp. in excess. —'**boozy** adj.

boozer ('bu:zə) n. *Inf.* 1. a person who is fond of drinking. 2. a bar or pub.

booze-up n. *Sl.* a drinking spree.

bop (bɒp) n. 1. a form of jazz originating in the 1940s, characterized by rhythmic and harmonic complexity and instrumental virtuosity. Originally called: **bebop.** ~vb. **bopping, bopped.** 2. (intr.) *Inf.* to dance to pop music. —'**bopper** n.

boracic (bəˈræsɪk) adj. another word for **boric.**

borage ('bɒrɪdʒ, 'bʌrɪdʒ) n. a Mediterranean plant with star-shaped blue flowers. The young leaves are sometimes used in salads.

borax ('bɔ:ræks) n., pl. **-raxes** *or* **-races** (-rəˌsi:z). a soluble readily fusible white mineral in monoclinic crystalline form, occurring in alkaline soils and salt deposits. Formula: $Na_2B_4O_7.10H_2O$.

Bordeaux (bɔ:ˈdəʊ) n. any of several red, white, or rosé wines produced around Bordeaux in SW France.

Bordeaux mixture n. *Horticulture.* a fungicide consisting of a solution of equal quantities of copper sulphate and quicklime.

border ('bɔ:də) n. 1. a band or margin around or along the edge of something. 2. the dividing line or frontier between political or geographic regions. 3. a region straddling such a boundary. 4. a design around the edge of something. 5. a long narrow strip of ground planted with flowers, shrubs, etc.: *a herbaceous border.* ~vb. 6. (tr.) to provide with a border. 7. (when intr., foll. by *on* or *upon*) a. to be adjacent (to); lie along the boundary (of). b. to be nearly the same (as); verge (on): *his stupidity borders on madness.*

Border ('bɔ:də) n. **the.** (sometimes pl.) the area straddling the border between England and Scotland.

borderland ('bɔ:də,lænd) n. 1. land located on or near a frontier or boundary. 2. an indeterminate state or condition.

borderline ('bɔ:də,laɪn) n. 1. a border; dividing line. 2. an indeterminate position between two conditions: *the borderline between friendship and love.* ~adj. 3. on the edge of one category and verging on another: *a borderline failure in the exam.*

bore[1] (bɔ:) vb. 1. to produce (a hole) in (a material) by use of a drill, auger, or rotary cutting tool. 2. to increase the diameter of (a hole), as by turning. 3. (tr.) to produce (a hole in the ground, tunnel, mine shaft, etc.) by digging, drilling, etc. 4. (intr.) *Inf.* (of a horse or athlete in a race) to push other competitors out of the way. ~n. 5. a hole or tunnel in the ground, esp. one drilled in search of minerals, oil, etc. 6. *Austral.* a hole drilled to give access to an underground water supply. 7. a. the hollow part of a tube or cylinder, esp. of a gun barrel. b. the diameter of such a hollow part; calibre. —'**borer** n.

bore[2] (bɔ:) vb. 1. (tr.) to tire or make weary by being dull, repetitious, or uninteresting. ~n. 2. a dull or repetitious person, activity, or state. —'**boring** adj.

bore[3] (bɔ:) n. a high steep-fronted wave moving up a narrow estuary, caused by the tide.

bore[4] (bɔ:) vb. the past tense of **bear**[1].

boredom ('bɔ:dəm) n. the state of being bored.

boric ('bɔ:rɪk) adj. of or containing boron. Also: **boracic.**

boric acid n. a white soluble weakly acid crystalline solid used in the manufacture of heat-resistant glass and porcelain enamels, as a fireproofing material, and as a mild antiseptic. Formula: H_3BO_3. Also called: **orthoboric acid.**

born (bɔ:n) vb. 1. the past participle (in passive usage) of **bear**[1] (sense 4). 2. **not born yesterday.** not gullible or foolish. ~adj. 3. possessing certain qualities from birth: *a born musician.* 4. a. being at birth in a particular social status or other condition as specified: *ignobly born.* b. (in combination): *lowborn.* 5. **in all one's born days.** *Inf.* so far in one's life.

borne (bɔ:n) vb. 1. the past participle of **bear**[1] (for all active uses of the verb; also for all passive uses except sense 4). 2. **be borne in on** *or* **upon.** (of a fact, etc.) to be realized by (someone).

boron ('bɔ:rɒn) n. a very hard almost colourless crystalline metalloid element that in impure form exists as a brown amorphous powder. It occurs principally in borax and is used in hardening steel. Symbol: B; atomic no.: 5; atomic wt.: 10.81.

borough ('bʌrə) n. 1. a town, esp. (in Britain) one that forms the constituency of an M.P. or that was originally incorporated by royal charter. See also **burgh.** 2. any of the 32 constituent divisions of Greater London. 3. any of the five constituent divisions of New York City. 4. (in the U.S.) a self-governing incorporated municipality.

borrow ('bɒrəʊ) vb. 1. to obtain or receive (something, such as money) on loan for temporary use, intending to

---

THESAURUS

boot v. 1. drive, drop-kick, kick, knock, punt, shove 2. *Inf.* dismiss, eject, expel, kick out, oust, sack (*Inf.*), throw out

bootless fruitless, futile, ineffective, profitless, unavailing, unsuccessful, useless, vain

booty boodle (*Sl., chiefly U.S.*), gains, haul, loot, pillage, plunder, prey, spoil, spoils, swag (*Sl.*), takings, winnings

border n. 1. bound, boundary, bounds, brim, brink, confine, confines, edge, hem, limit, limits, lip, margin, rim, skirt, verge 2. borderline, boundary, frontier, line, march ~v. 3. bind, decorate, edge, fringe, hem, rim, trim

borderline adj. ambivalent, doubtful, equivocal, indecisive, indefinite, indeterminate, inexact, marginal, unclassifiable

border on 1. abut, adjoin, connect, contact, impinge, join, march, neighbour, touch, verge on 2. approach, approximate, be like, be similar to, come close to, come near, echo, match, parallel, resemble

bore[1] 1. v. burrow, drill, gouge out, mine, penetrate, perforate, pierce, sink, tunnel 2. n. borehole, calibre, drill hole, hole, shaft, tunnel

bore[2] 1. v. annoy, be tedious, bother, exhaust, fatigue, jade, pall on, pester, send to sleep, tire, trouble, vex, wear out, weary, worry 2. n. bother, drag (*Sl.*), dull person, headache (*Inf.*), nuisance, pain (*Inf.*), pain in the neck (*Inf.*), pest, tiresome person, wearisome talker

boredom apathy, doldrums, dullness, ennui, flatness, irksomeness, monotony, sameness, tedium, tediousness, weariness, worldweariness

boring dead, dull, flat, humdrum, insipid, monotonous, repetitious, routine, stale, tedious, tiresome, tiring, unexciting, uninteresting, unvaried, wearisome

give it, or something equivalent, back to the lender. **2.** to adopt (ideas, words, etc.) from another source; appropriate. **3.** *Not standard.* to lend. **4.** *Golf.* to putt the ball uphill of the direct path to the hole: *make sure you borrow enough.* —'**borrower** *n.*

▷ **Usage.** See at **lend.**

borsch, borsh (bɔːʃ), **borscht** (bɔːʃt), *or* **borshch** (bɔːʃtʃ) *n.* a Russian and Polish soup based on beetroot.

borstal ('bɔːstəl) *n.* (in England) an establishment in which offenders aged 15 to 21 may be detained for corrective training.

borzoi ('bɔːzɔɪ) *n., pl.* -**zois.** a tall fast-moving breed of dog with a long coat. Also called: **Russian wolfhound.**

bosh (bɒʃ) *n. Inf.* empty or meaningless talk or opinions; nonsense.

bo's'n ('bəʊsən) *n. Naut.* a variant spelling of **boatswain.**

bosom ('bʊzəm) *n.* **1.** the chest or breast of a person, esp. (*pl.*) the female breasts. **2.** the part of a woman's dress, coat, etc., that covers the chest. **3.** a protective centre or part: *the bosom of the family.* **4.** the breast considered as the seat of emotions. **5.** (*modifier*) very dear; intimate: *a bosom friend.* ~*vb.* (*tr.*) **6.** to embrace. **7.** to conceal or carry in the bosom.

boss¹ (bɒs) *Inf.* ~*n.* **1.** a person in charge of or employing others. **2.** *Chiefly U.S.* a professional politician who controls a political organization, often using devious or illegal methods. ~*vb.* **3.** to employ, supervise, or be in charge of. **4.** (usually foll. by *around* or *about*) to be domineering or overbearing towards (others). ~*adj.* **5.** *Sl.* excellent; fine: *a boss hand at carpentry; that's boss!*

boss² (bɒs) *n.* **1.** a knob, stud, or other circular rounded protuberance, esp. an ornamental one on a vault, a ceiling, or a shield. **2.** an area of increased thickness, usually cylindrical, that strengthens or provides room for a locating device on a shaft, hub of a wheel, etc. **3.** a rounded mass of igneous rock. ~*vb.* (*tr.*) **4.** to ornament with bosses; emboss.

bossa nova ('bɒsə 'nəʊvə) *n.* **1.** a dance similar to the samba, originating in Brazil. **2.** a piece of music composed for or in the rhythm of this dance.

bossy ('bɒsɪ) *adj.* **bossier, bossiest.** *Inf.* domineering, overbearing, or authoritarian. —'**bossily** *adv.* —'**bossiness** *n.*

bosun ('bəʊsən) *n. Naut.* a variant spelling of **boatswain.**

bot *or* **bott** (bɒt) *n.* **1.** the larva of a botfly, which typically develops inside the body of a horse, sheep, or man. **2.** any similar larva.

bot. *abbrev. for:* **1.** botanical. **2.** botany. **3.** bottle.

botany ('bɒtənɪ) *n., pl.* -**nies.** **1.** the study of plants, including their classification, structure, physiology, ecology, and economic importance. **2.** the plant life of a particular region or time. **3.** the biological characteristics of a particular group of plants. —**botanical** (bə'tænɪkəl) *adj.* —'**botanist** *n.* —'**bota₁nize** *or* -**ise** *vb.*

Botany wool *n.* fine wool from merino sheep.

botch (bɒtʃ) *vb.* (*tr.; often foll. by up*) **1.** to spoil through clumsiness or ineptitude. **2.** to repair badly or clumsily. ~*n.* **3.** a badly done piece of work or repair (esp. in **make a botch of**). —'**botcher** *n.* —'**botchy** *adj.*

botfly ('bɒt₁flaɪ) *n., pl.* -**flies.** any of various stout-bodied hairy dipterous flies, the larvae of which are parasites of man, sheep, and horses.

both (bəʊθ) *determiner.* **1. a.** the two; two considered together: *both dogs were dirty.* **b.** (*as pronoun*): *both are to blame.* ~*conj.* **2.** (*coordinating*) used preceding words, phrases, or clauses joined by *and*: *both Ellen and Keith enjoyed the play; both new and exciting.*

▷ **Usage.** *Both* is redundant when employed together with *as well as, equal, equally, alike,* or *together.* Sentences like *they are both alike, they are both equal,* however, do occur frequently in informal English.

bother ('bɒðə) *vb.* **1.** (*tr.*) to give annoyance, pain, or trouble to. **2.** (*tr.*) to trouble (a person) by repeatedly disturbing; pester. **3.** (*intr.*) to take the time or trouble; concern oneself: *don't bother to come with me.* **4.** (*tr.*) to make (a person) alarmed or confused. ~*n.* **5.** a state of worry, trouble, or confusion. **6.** a person or thing that causes fuss, trouble, or annoyance. **7.** *Inf.* a disturbance or fight; trouble (esp. in **a spot of bother**). ~*interj.* **8.** *Chiefly Brit.* an exclamation of slight annoyance.

botheration (₁bɒðə'reɪʃən) *n., interj. Inf.* another word for **bother** (senses 5, 8).

bothersome ('bɒðəsəm) *adj.* causing bother; troublesome.

bothy ('bɒθɪ) *n., pl.* **bothies.** *Chiefly Scot.* a small roughly built shelter or outhouse, esp. to house labourers.

bottle ('bɒtəl) *n.* **1. a.** a vessel, often of glass and typically cylindrical with a narrow neck, for containing liquids. **b.** (*as modifier*): *a bottle rack.* **2.** Also called: **bottleful.** the amount such a vessel will hold. **3.** *Brit. sl.* courage; nerve; initiative. **4. the bottle.** *Inf.* drinking of alcohol, esp. to excess. ~*vb.* (*tr.*) **5.** to put or place in a bottle or bottles. **6.** to store (gas) in a portable container under pressure. ~*See also* **bottle up.**

bottle-feed *vb.* -**feeding, -fed.** to feed (a baby) with milk from a bottle.

bottle green *n., adj.* a dark green colour.

bottleneck ('bɒtəl₁nɛk) *n.* **1. a.** a narrow stretch of road or a junction at which traffic is or may be held up. **b.** the hold-up. **2.** something that holds up progress.

bottlenose dolphin ('bɒtəl₁nəʊz) *n.* a type of dolphin with a bottle-shaped snout.

bottle party *n.* a party to which guests bring drink.

bottle store *n. S. African & N.Z.* an off-licence.

bottle up *vb.* (*tr., adv.*) **1.** to restrain (powerful emotion). **2.** *Inf.* to keep (an army or other force) contained or trapped.

bottom ('bɒtəm) *n.* **1.** the lowest, deepest, or farthest removed part of a thing: *the bottom of a hill.* **2.** the least important or successful position: *the bottom of a class.* **3.** the ground underneath a sea, lake, or river. **4.** the inner depths of a person's true feelings (esp. in **from the bottom of one's heart**). **5.** the underneath part of a thing. **6.** *Naut.* the parts of a vessel's hull that are under water. **7.** (in literary or commercial contexts) a boat or ship. **8.** (esp. of horses) staying power; stamina. **9.** *Inf.* the buttocks. **10. at bottom.** in reality; basically. **11. be at the bottom of.** to be the ultimate cause of. **12. get to the bottom of.** to discover the real truth about. ~*adj.* (*prenominal*) **13.** lowest or last. **14. bet** (*or* **put**) **one's bottom dollar on.** to be absolutely sure of. **15.** of, relating to, or situated at the bottom. **16.** fundamental; basic. ~*vb.* **17.** (*tr.*) to provide (a chair, etc.) with a bottom or seat. **18.** (*tr.*) to discover the full facts or truth of; fathom. **19.** (usually foll. by *on* or *upon*) to base or be found-

---

THESAURUS

borrow 1. cadge, scrounge (*Inf.*), take and return, take on loan, use temporarily 2. acquire, adopt, appropriate, copy, filch, imitate, obtain, pilfer, pirate, plagiarize, simulate, steal, take, use, usurp

bosom *n.* 1. breast, bust, chest 2. affections, emotions, feelings, heart, sentiments, soul, spirit, sympathies 3. centre, circle, core, midst, protection, shelter ~*adj.* 4. boon, cherished, close, confidential, intimate, very dear

boss¹ 1. *n.* administrator, chief, director, employer, executive, foreman, gaffer (*Inf.*), governor (*Inf.*), head, leader, manager, master, overseer, owner, superintendent, supervisor 2. *v.* administrate, command, control, direct, employ, manage, oversee, run, superintend, supervise, take charge

boss² knob, nub, nubble, point, protuberance, stud, tip

boss around bully, dominate, domineer, oppress, order, overbear, push around (*Sl.*), put upon, tyrannize

bossy arrogant, authoritarian, despotic, dictatorial, domineering, high-handed, imperious, lordly, overbearing, tyrannical

botch 1. *v.* blunder, bungle, butcher, cobble, fumble, mar, mend, mess, mismanage, muff, patch, spoil 2. *n.* blunder, bungle, bungling, failure, fumble, hash, mess, miscarriage

bother 1. *v.* alarm, annoy, concern, dismay, distress, disturb, harass, inconvenience, irritate, molest, nag, pester, plague, put out, trouble, upset, vex, worry 2. *n.* aggravation, annoyance, bustle, difficulty, flurry, fuss, inconvenience, irritation, molestation, nuisance, perplexity, pest, problem, strain, trouble, vexation, worry

bothersome aggravating, annoying, dis-

tressing, exasperating, inconvenient, irritating, tiresome, troublesome, vexatious, vexing

bottleneck block, blockage, congestion, hold-up, impediment, jam, obstacle, obstruction

bottle up check, contain, curb, keep back, restrict, shut in, suppress, trap

bottom *n.* 1. base, basis, bed, deepest part, depths, floor, foot, foundation, groundwork, lowest part, pedestal, support 2. lower side, sole, underneath, underside 3. backside, behind (*Inf.*), bum (*Sl.*), buttocks, fundament, posterior, rear, rear end, rump, seat, tail (*Inf.*) 4. base, basis, cause, core, essence, ground, heart, mainspring, origin, principle, root, source, substance ~*adj.* 5. base, basement, basic, fundamental, ground, last, lowest, undermost

ed (on an idea, etc.).

bottom drawer *n. Brit.* a young woman's collection of linen, cutlery, etc., made in anticipation of marriage. U.S. equivalent: **hope chest.**

bottomless ('bɒtəmlɪs) *adj.* 1. having no bottom. 2. unlimited; inexhaustible. 3. very deep.

bottom line *n.* 1. the last line of a financial statement that shows the net profit or loss of a company or organization. 2. the conclusion or main point of a process, discussion, etc.

bottom out *vb.* (*intr., adv.*) to reach the lowest point.

botulism ('bɒtjʊˌlɪzəm) *n.* severe, often fatal, poisoning resulting from the potent bacterial toxin, **botulin,** produced in imperfectly preserved food, etc.

bouclé ('buːkleɪ) *n.* 1. a curled or looped yarn or fabric giving a thick knobbly effect. ~*adj.* 2. of or designating such a yarn or fabric.

boudoir ('buːdwɑː, -dwɔː) *n.* a woman's bedroom or private sitting room.

bouffant ('buːfɒŋ) *adj.* 1. (of a hair style) having extra height and width through back-combing; puffed out. 2. (of sleeves, skirts, etc.) puffed out.

bougainvillea (ˌbuːgən'vɪlɪə) *n.* a woody American plant having inconspicuous flowers surrounded by showy red or purple bracts.

bough (baʊ) *n.* any of the main branches of a tree.

bought (bɔːt) *vb.* the past tense and past participle of **buy.**

bouillabaisse (ˌbuːjə'bɛs) *n.* a rich stew or soup of fish and vegetables.

bouillon ('buːjɒn) *n.* a plain unclarified broth or stock.

boulder ('bəʊldə) *n.* a smooth rounded mass of rock that has been shaped by erosion.

boulder clay *n.* an unstratified glacial deposit consisting of fine clay, boulders, and pebbles.

boule[1] ('buːliː) *n.* 1. the senate of an ancient Greek city state. 2. the parliament in modern Greece.

boule[2] (buːl) *n.* an imitation ruby, sapphire, etc., made from synthetic corundum.

boulevard ('buːlvɑː, -vɑːd) *n.* a wide usually tree-lined road in a city.

boult (bəʊlt) *vb.* a variant spelling of **bolt**[2].

bounce (baʊns) *vb.* 1. (*intr.*) (of a ball, etc.) to rebound from an impact. 2. (*tr.*) to cause (a ball, etc.) to hit a solid surface and spring back. 3. to move or cause to move suddenly, excitedly, or violently; spring: *she bounced up from her chair.* 4. *Sl.* (of a bank) to send (a cheque) back or (of a cheque) to be sent back by a bank to a payee unredeemed because of lack of funds in the drawer's account. 5. (*tr.*) *Sl.* to force (a person) to leave (a place or job); throw out; eject. ~*n.* 6. the action of rebounding from an impact. 7. a leap; jump; bound. 8. the quality of being able to rebound; springiness. 9. *Inf.* vitality; vigour; resilience. 10. *Brit.* swagger or impudence. —'**bouncy** *adj.*

bounce back *vb.* (*intr., adv.*) to recover one's health, good spirits, confidence, etc., easily.

bouncer ('baʊnsə) *n. Sl.* a man employed at a club, restaurant, etc., to throw out drunks or troublemakers and stop fights.

bouncing ('baʊnsɪŋ) *adj.* (when *postpositive,* foll. by *with*) vigorous and robust (esp. in a **bouncing baby**).

bound[1] (baʊnd) *vb.* 1. the past tense and past participle of **bind.** ~*adj.* 2. in bonds or chains; tied as with a rope. 3. (*postpositive,* foll. by an infinitive) destined; sure; cer-

tain: *it's bound to happen.* 4. (*postpositive,* often foll. by *by*) compelled or obliged. 5. *Rare.* constipated. 6. (of a book) secured within a cover or binding. 7. *Logic.* denoting an occurrence of a variable within the scope of a quantifier. Cf. **free** (sense 18). 8. **bound up with.** closely or inextricably linked with.

bound[2] (baʊnd) *vb.* 1. to move forwards by leaps or jumps. 2. to bounce; spring away from an impact. ~*n.* 3. a jump upwards or forwards. 4. a bounce, as of a ball.

bound[3] (baʊnd) *vb.* 1. (*tr.*) to place restrictions on; limit. 2. (when *intr.,* foll. by *on*) to form a boundary of. ~*n.* 3. See **bounds.** —'**boundless** *adj.*

bound[4] (baʊnd) *adj.* a. (*postpositive,* often foll. by *for*) going or intending to go towards: *bound for Jamaica; homeward bound.* b. (*in combination*): *northbound traffic.*

boundary ('baʊndərɪ, -drɪ) *n., pl.* **-ries.** 1. something that indicates the farthest limit, as of an area; border. 2. *Cricket.* a. the marked limit of the playing area. b. a stroke that hits the ball beyond this limit. c. the four or six runs scored with such a stroke.

bounden ('baʊndən) *adj.* morally obligatory (arch. except in **bounden duty**).

bounder ('baʊndə) *n. Old-fashioned Brit. sl.* a morally reprehensible person; cad.

bounds (baʊndz) *pl. n.* 1. (*sometimes sing.*) a limit; boundary (esp. in **know no bounds**). 2. something that restrains or confines, esp. the standards of a society: *within the bounds of modesty.*

bountiful ('baʊntɪfʊl) *adj.* 1. plentiful; ample (esp. in a **bountiful supply**). 2. giving freely; generous. —'**bountifully** *adv.*

bounty ('baʊntɪ) *n., pl.* **-ties.** 1. generosity; liberality. 2. a generous gift. 3. a payment made by a government, as, formerly, to a sailor on enlisting or to a soldier after a campaign. 4. any reward or premium. —'**bounteous** *adj.*

bouquet (buː'keɪ) *n.* 1. a bunch of flowers, esp. a large carefully arranged one. 2. the characteristic aroma or fragrance of a wine or liqueur. 3. a compliment or expression of praise.

bouquet garni ('buːkeɪ gɑː'niː) *n., pl.* **bouquets garnis** ('buːkeɪz gɑː'niː). a bunch of herbs tied together and used for flavouring soups, stews, etc.

bourbon ('bɜːbən) *n.* a whiskey distilled chiefly in the U.S., from maize, esp. one containing at least 51 per cent maize.

bourgeois ('bʊəʒwɑː) *Often disparaging.* ~*n., pl.* **-geois.** 1. a member of the middle class, esp. one regarded as being conservative and materialistic or capitalistic. 2. a mediocre, unimaginative, or materialistic person. ~*adj.* 3. characteristic of, relating to, or comprising the middle class. 4. conservative or materialistic in outlook. 5. (in Marxist thought) dominated by capitalists or capitalist interests. —**bourgeoise** ('bʊəʒwɑːz, bʊə'ʒwɑːz) *fem. n.*

bourgeoisie (ˌbʊəʒwɑː'ziː) *n.* **the.** 1. the middle classes. 2. (in Marxist thought) the capitalist ruling class. The bourgeoisie owns the means of production, through which it exploits the working class.

bourn[1] *or* **bourne** (bɔːn) *n. Arch.* 1. a destination; goal. 2. a boundary.

bourn[2] (bɔːn) *n. Chiefly southern Brit.* a stream.

bourrée ('bʊəreɪ) *n.* 1. a traditional French dance in fast duple time. 2. a piece of music in the rhythm

---

THESAURUS

bottomless boundless, deep, fathomless, immeasurable, inexhaustible, infinite, unfathomable, unlimited

bounce v. 1. bob, bound, bump, jounce, jump, leap, rebound, recoil, resile, ricochet, spring, thump 2. *Sl.* boot out (*Inf.*), eject, fire (*Inf.*), kick out (*Inf.*), oust, throw out ~n. 3. bound, elasticity, give, rebound, recoil, resilience, spring, springiness 4. animation, dynamism, energy, go (*Inf.*), life, liveliness, pep, vigour, vitality, vivacity, zip (*Inf.*)

bouncing blooming, bonny, healthy, robust, thriving, vigorous

bound[1] *adj.* 1. cased, fastened, fixed, pinioned, secured, tied, tied up 2. certain, destined, doomed, fated, sure 3. beholden, committed, compelled, constrained, duty-bound,

forced, obligated, obliged, pledged, required

bound[2] *v./n.* bob, bounce, caper, frisk, gambol, hurdle, jump, leap, pounce, prance, skip, spring, vault

bound[3] *n.* 1. *Usually plural* border, boundary, confine, edge, extremity, fringe, limit, line, march, margin, pale, periphery, rim, termination, verge 2. **out of bounds** banned, barred, forbidden, off-limits (*Chiefly U.S. military*), prohibited, taboo ~v. 3. circumscribe, confine, define, delimit, demarcate, encircle, enclose, hem in, limit, restrain, restrict, surround, terminate

boundary barrier, border, borderline, bounds, brink, confines, edge, extremity, fringe, frontier, limits, march, margin, precinct, termination, verge

boundless endless, illimitable, immeasurable, immense, incalculable, inexhaustible, infinite, limitless, measureless, unbounded, unconfined, unending, unlimited, untold, vast

bountiful 1. abundant, ample, bounteous, copious, exuberant, lavish, luxuriant, plenteous,'plentiful, prolific 2. beneficent, bounteous, generous, liberal, magnanimous, munificent, open-handed, princely, unstinting

bouquet 1. boutonniere, bunch of flowers, buttonhole, corsage, garland, nosegay, posy, spray, wreath 2. aroma, fragrance, perfume, redolence, savour, scent

bourgeois conventional, hidebound, materialistic, middle-class, traditional

of this dance.

Bourse (buəs) n. a stock exchange of continental Europe, esp. Paris.

bout (baut) n. **1. a.** a period of time spent doing something, such as drinking. **b.** a period of illness. **2.** a contest or fight, esp. a boxing or wrestling match.

boutique (bu:'ti:k) n. a shop, esp. a small one selling fashionable clothes and other items.

bouzouki (bu:'zu:kɪ) n. a Greek long-necked stringed musical instrument related to the mandolin.

bovine ('bəuvaɪn) adj. **1.** of or relating to cattle. **2.** (of people) dull; sluggish; stolid. —'**bovinely** adv.

bow[1] (bau) vb. **1.** to lower (one's head) or bend (one's knee or body) as a sign of respect, greeting, assent, or shame. **2.** to bend or cause to bend. **3.** (intr.; usually foll. by to or before) to comply or accept: bow to the inevitable. **4.** (tr.; foll. by in, out, to, etc.) to usher (someone) in or out with bows and deference. **5.** (tr.; usually foll. by down) to bring (a person, nation, etc.) to a state of submission. **6. bow and scrape.** to behave in an excessively deferential or obsequious way. ~n. **7.** a lowering or inclination of the head or body as a mark of respect, greeting, or assent. **8. take a bow.** to acknowledge or receive applause or praise. ~See also **bow out.**

bow[2] (bəu) n. **1.** a weapon for shooting arrows, consisting of an arch of elastic wood bent by a string fastened at each end. **2. a.** a long stick across which are stretched strands of horsehair, used for playing the strings of a violin, viola, cello, etc. **b.** a stroke with such a stick. **3. a.** a decorative interlacing of ribbon or other fabrics, usually having two loops and two loose ends. **b.** the knot forming such an interlacing. **4.** something that is curved, bent, or arched. ~vb. **5.** to form or cause to form a curve or curves. **6.** to make strokes of a bow across (violin strings).

bow[3] (bau) n. **1.** Chiefly Naut. **a.** (often pl.) the forward end or part of a vessel. **b.** (as modifier): the bow mooring line. **2.** Rowing. the oarsman at the bow.

bowdlerize or **-ise** ('baudlə,raɪz) vb. (tr.) to remove passages or words regarded as indecent from (a play, novel, etc.); expurgate. —,bowdleri'zation or -i'sation n. —'bowdlerism n.

bowel ('bauəl) n. **1.** an intestine, esp. the large intestine in man. **2.** (pl.) innards; entrails. **3.** (pl.) the deep or innermost part (esp. in **the bowels of the earth**).

bower[1] ('bauə) n. **1.** a shady leafy shelter or recess, as in a wood or garden; arbour. **2.** Literary. a lady's bedroom or apartments; boudoir.

bower[2] ('bauə) n. Naut. a vessel's bow anchor.

bowerbird ('bauə,bɜːd) n. **1.** any of various songbirds of Australia and New Guinea. The males build bower-like display grounds to attract the females. **2.** Inf., chiefly Austral. a collector of unconsidered trifles.

bowhead ('bəu,hɛd) n. a large-mouthed arctic whale.

bowie knife ('bəuɪ) n. a stout hunting knife with a short hilt and a guard for the hand.

bowl[1] (bəul) n. **1.** a round container open at the top, used for holding liquid, serving food, etc. **2.** Also: **bowlful.** the amount a bowl will hold. **3.** the rounded or hollow part of an object, esp. of a spoon or tobacco pipe. **4.** any container shaped like a bowl, such as a sink or lavatory. **5.** a bowl-shaped building or other structure, such as an amphitheatre. **6.** a bowl-shaped depression of the land surface. **7.** Literary. a drinking cup.

bowl[2] (bəul) n. **1.** a wooden ball used in the game of bowls, having one flattened side in order to make it run on a curved course. **2.** a large heavy ball with holes for gripping, used in tenpin bowling. ~vb. **3.** to roll smoothly or cause to roll smoothly along the ground. **4.** (intr.; usually foll. by along) to move easily and rapidly,

as in a car. **5.** Cricket. **a.** to send (a ball) from one's hand towards the batsman. **b.** Also: **bowl out.** to dismiss (a batsman) by delivering a ball that breaks his wicket. **6.** (intr.) to play bowls or tenpin bowling. ~See also **bowl over.**

bow legs (bəu) pl. n. a condition in which the legs curve outwards like a bow between the ankle and the thigh. Also called: **bandy legs.** —**bow-legged** (bəu'lɛgɪd, bəu-'lɛgd) adj.

bowler[1] ('bəulə) n. **1.** one who bowls in cricket. **2.** a player at the game of bowls.

bowler[2] ('bəulə) n. a stiff felt hat with a rounded crown and narrow curved brim. U.S. name: **derby.**

bowline ('bəulɪn) n. Naut. **1.** a line for controlling the weather leech of a square sail when a vessel is close-hauled. **2.** a knot used for securing a loop that will not slip at the end of a piece of rope.

bowling ('bəulɪŋ) n. **1.** any of various games in which a heavy ball is rolled down a special alley at a group of wooden pins. **2.** the game of bowls. **3.** Cricket. the act of delivering the ball to the batsman.

bowl over vb. (tr., adv.) **1.** Inf. to surprise (a person) greatly, esp. in a pleasant way; astound; amaze. **2.** to knock down.

bowls (bəulz) pl. n. (functioning as sing.) **1.** a game played on a bowling green in which a small bowl (the jack) is pitched from a mark and two opponents take turns to roll biased wooden bowls as near the jack as possible. **2.** skittles or tenpin bowling.

bow out (bau) vb. (adv.; usually tr.; often foll. by of) to retire or withdraw gracefully.

bowsprit ('bəusprɪt) n. Naut. a spar projecting from the bow of a vessel, esp. a sailing vessel.

bowstring ('bəu,strɪŋ) n. the string of an archer's bow.

bow tie (bəu) n. a man's tie tied in a bow, now chiefly in plain black for formal evening wear.

bow window (bəu) n. a bay window in the shape of a curve.

bow-wow ('bau,wau, -'wau) n. **1.** a child's word for dog. **2.** an imitation of the bark of a dog. ~vb. **3.** (intr.) to bark or imitate a dog's bark.

box[1] (bɒks) n. **1.** a receptacle or container made of wood, cardboard, etc., usually rectangular and having a removable or hinged lid. **2.** Also called: **boxful.** the contents of such a receptacle. **3.** (often in combination) any of various small cubicles, kiosks, or shelters: a telephone box; a signal box. **4.** a separate compartment in a public place for a small group of people, as in a theatre. **5.** an enclosure within a courtroom: witness box. **6.** a compartment for a horse in a stable or a vehicle. **7.** Brit. a small country house occupied by sportsmen when following a field sport, esp. shooting. **8. a.** a protective housing for machinery or mechanical parts. **b.** (in combination): a gearbox. **9.** a shaped device of light tough material worn by sportsmen to protect the genitals, esp. in cricket. **10.** a section of printed matter on a page, enclosed by lines, a border, etc. **11.** a central agency to which mail is addressed and from which it is collected or redistributed: a post-office box; a box number in a newspaper advertisement. **12.** the penalty area of a soccer pitch. **13.** the raised seat on which the driver sits in a horse-drawn coach. **14.** Austral. & N.Z. an accidental mixing of herds or flocks. **15.** Brit. (esp. formerly) a present, esp. of money, given at Christmas to tradesmen, etc. **16.** Austral. taboo sl. the female genitals. **17. the box.** Brit. inf. television. **18. out of the box.** Austral. inf. outstanding or excellent. ~vb. **19.** (tr.) to put into a box. **20.** (tr.; usually foll. by in or up) to prevent from moving freely; confine. **21.** Austral. & N.Z. to mix (flocks or herds) or (of flocks) to become mixed accidentally. **22. box the compass.** Naut. to name the compass points in

---

THESAURUS

bout 1. course, fit, period, round, run, session, spell, spree, stint, stretch, term, time, turn **2.** battle, boxing match, competition, contest, encounter, engagement, fight, match, set-to, struggle

bovine dense, dull, slow, sluggish, stolid, stupid, thick

bow[1] v. **1.** bend, bob, droop, genuflect, incline, make obeisance, nod, stoop **2.** accept, acquiesce, comply, concede, defer, give in, kowtow, relent, submit, surrender, yield **3.** cast down, conquer, crush, depress, over-

power, subdue, subjugate, vanquish, weigh down ~n. **4.** bending, bob, genuflexion, inclination, kowtow, nod, obeisance, salaam

bow[2] Naut. beak, fore, head, prow, stem

bowdlerize blue-pencil, censor, clean up, expurgate, mutilate

bowels 1. entrails, guts, innards (Inf.), insides (Inf.), intestines, viscera, vitals **2.** belly, core, deep, depths, hold, inside, interior **3.** Archaic compassion, mercifulness, mercy, pity, sympathy, tenderness

bower alcove, arbour, grotto, leafy shelter,

shady recess, summerhouse

bowl 1. n. basin, deep dish, vessel **2.** v. fling, hurl, pitch, revolve, roll, rotate, spin, throw, trundle, whirl

bowl over 1. amaze, astonish, astound, dumbfound, stagger, startle, stun, surprise **2.** bring down, fell, floor, knock down, overthrow, overturn

bow out abandon, back out, get out, give up, pull out, quit, resign, retire, step down, withdraw

box 114 **bract**

order. —'**box**,like *adj.*

box² (bɒks) *vb.* **1.** (*tr.*) to fight (an opponent) in a boxing match. **2.** (*intr.*) to engage in boxing. **3.** (*tr.*) to hit (a person) with the fist. ~*n.* **4.** a punch with the fist, esp. on the ear.

box³ (bɒks) *n.* **1.** a slow-growing evergreen tree or shrub with small shiny leaves: used for hedges. **2.** the wood of this tree. **3.** any of several trees the timber or foliage of which resembles this tree, esp. species of *Eucalyptus.*

boxer ('bɒksə) *n.* **1.** a man who boxes; pugilist. **2.** a large smooth-haired breed of dog with a short nose and a docked tail.

Boxer ('bɒksə) *n.* a member of a nationalistic Chinese secret society that led an unsuccessful rebellion in 1900 against foreign interests in China.

box girder *n.* a girder that is hollow and square or rectangular in shape.

boxing ('bɒksɪŋ) *n.* **a.** the act, art, or profession of fighting with the fists. **b.** (*as modifier*): *a boxing enthusiast.*

Boxing Day *n. Brit.* the first weekday after Christmas, observed as a holiday.

box junction *n.* (in Britain) a road junction having yellow cross-hatching painted on the road surface. Vehicles may only enter the hatched area when their exit is clear.

box lacrosse *n. Canad.* lacrosse played indoors. Also called: **boxla.**

box office *n.* **1.** an office at a theatre, cinema, etc., where tickets are sold. **2. a.** the public appeal of an actor or production. **b.** (*as modifier*): *a box-office success.*

box pleat *n.* a flat double pleat made by folding under the fabric on either side of it.

boxroom ('bɒks,ruːm, -,rum) *n.* a small room or large cupboard in which boxes, cases, etc., may be stored.

box spanner *n.* a spanner consisting of a steel cylinder with a hexagonal end that fits over a nut.

box spring *n.* a coiled spring contained in a boxlike frame, used for mattresses, chairs, etc.

boxwood ('bɒks,wʊd) *n.* **1.** the hard close-grained yellow wood of the box tree, used to make tool handles, etc. **2.** the box tree.

boy (bɔɪ) *n.* **1.** a male child; lad; youth. **2.** a man regarded as immature or inexperienced. **3. the boys.** *Inf.* a group of men, esp. a group of friends. **4.** *S. African derog.* a Black male servant. **5. jobs for the boys.** *Inf.* appointment of one's supporters to posts, without reference to their qualifications or ability. ~*interj.* **6.** an exclamation of surprise, pleasure, contempt, etc. —'**boy**hood *n.* —'**boyish** *adj.*

boycott ('bɔɪkɒt) *vb.* **1.** (*tr.*) to refuse to have dealings with (a person, organization, etc.) or refuse to buy (a product) as a protest or means of coercion. ~*n.* **2.** an instance or the use of boycotting.

boyfriend ('bɔɪ,frɛnd) *n.* a male friend with whom a person is romantically or sexually involved; sweetheart or lover.

Boyle's law (bɔɪlz) *n.* the principle that the pressure of a gas varies inversely with its volume at constant temperature.

boy scout *n.* See **Scout.**

boysenberry ('bɔɪzənbərɪ) *n., pl.* **-ries. 1.** a type of bramble: a hybrid of the loganberry and various blackberries and raspberries. **2.** the large red edible fruit of this plant.

bp. *abbrev. for:* **1.** baptized. **2.** birthplace. **3.** bishop.

B.P. *abbrev. for:* **1.** British Pharmacopoeia. **2.** British Petroleum.

b.p.i. *abbrev. for* bits per inch (used of a computer tape).

Bq *Physics symbol for* becquerel.

Br *the chemical symbol for* bromine.

B.R. *abbrev. for* British Rail (British Railways).

Br. *abbrev. for:* **1.** Breton. **2.** Britain. **3.** British. **4.** (in a religious order) Brother.

bra (brɑː) *n.* short for **brassiere.**

braai (braɪ) *n.* short for **braaivleis.**

braaivleis ('braɪ,fleɪs) *n. S. African.* a barbecue.

brace (breɪs) *n.* **1.** a hand tool for drilling holes, with a socket to hold the drill at one end and a cranked handle by which the tool can be turned. See also **brace and bit.** **2.** something that steadies, binds, or holds up another thing. **3.** a structural member, such as a beam or prop, used to stiffen a framework. **4.** a pair, esp. of game birds. **5.** either of a pair of characters, { }, used for connecting lines of printing or writing. **6.** Also called: **accolade.** a line or bracket connecting two or more staves of music. **7.** (*often pl.*) an appliance of metal bands and wires for correcting uneven alignment of teeth. **8.** *Med.* any of various appliances for supporting the trunk or a limb. **9.** See **braces.** ~*vb.* (*mainly tr.*) **10.** to provide, strengthen, or fit with a brace. **11.** to steady or prepare (oneself or something) as before an impact. **12.** (*also intr.*) to stimulate; freshen; invigorate: *sea air is bracing.*

brace and bit *n.* a hand tool for boring holes, consisting of a cranked handle into which a drilling bit is inserted.

bracelet ('breɪslɪt) *n.* an ornamental chain worn around the arm or wrist.

bracelets ('breɪslɪts) *pl. n.* a slang name for **handcuffs.**

braces ('breɪsɪz) *pl. n. Brit.* a pair of straps worn over the shoulders by men for holding up the trousers. U.S. word: **suspenders.**

brachio- *or before a vowel* **brachi-** *combining form.* indicating a brachium: *brachiopod.*

brachiopod ('breɪkɪə,pɒd, 'bræk-) *n.* any marine invertebrate animal having a ciliated feeding organ and shell consisting of dorsal and ventral valves.

brachium ('breɪkɪəm, 'bræk-) *n., pl.* **-chia** (-kɪə). **1.** *Anat.* the arm, esp. the upper part. **2.** a corresponding part in an animal. **3.** *Biol.* a branching or armlike part.

brachy- *combining form.* indicating something short: *brachycephalic.*

bracing ('breɪsɪŋ) *adj.* **1.** refreshing; stimulating; invigorating. ~*n.* **2.** a system of braces used to strengthen or support.

bracken ('brækən) *n.* **1.** Also called: **brake.** any of various large coarse ferns having large fronds with spore cases along the undersides. **2.** a clump of any of these ferns.

bracket ('brækɪt) *n.* **1.** an L-shaped or other support fixed to a wall to hold a shelf, etc. **2.** one or more wall shelves carried on brackets. **3.** *Archit.* a support projecting from the side of a wall or other structure. **4.** Also called: **square bracket.** either of a pair of characters, used to enclose a section of writing or printing. **5.** a general name for **parenthesis, square bracket,** and **brace** (sense 5). **6.** a group or category falling within certain defined limits: *the lower income bracket.* **7.** the distance between two preliminary shots of artillery fire in range-finding. ~*vb.* (*tr.*) **8.** to fix or support by means of brackets. **9.** to put (written or printed matter) in brackets. **10.** to couple or join (two lines of text, etc.) with a brace. **11.** (*often foll. by with*) to group or class together. **12.** to adjust (artillery fire) until the target is hit.

brackish ('brækɪʃ) *adj.* (of water) slightly briny or salty. —'**brackishness** *n.*

bract (brækt) *n.* a specialized leaf with a single flower or

---

THESAURUS

box¹ 1. *n.* carton, case, chest, container, pack, package, portmanteau, receptacle, trunk **2.** *v.* pack, package, wrap

box² 1. *v.* exchange blows, fight, spar **2.** buffet, butt, clout (*Inf.*), cuff, hit, punch, slap, sock (*Sl.*), strike, thwack, wallop (*Inf.*), whack ~*n.* **3.** blow, buffet, clout (*Inf.*), cuff, punch, slap, stroke, thumping, wallop (*Inf.*)

boxer fighter, prizefighter, pugilist, sparrer, sparring partner

box in cage, confine, contain, coop up, enclose, hem in, isolate, shut in, surround, trap

boxing fisticuffs, prizefighting, pugilism,

sparring, the fight game (*Inf.*), the ring

boy fellow, junior, lad, schoolboy, stripling, youngster, youth

boycott ban, bar, black, blackball, blacklist, embargo, exclude, ostracize, outlaw, prohibit, proscribe, refrain from, refuse, reject, spurn

boyfriend admirer, beau, date, follower, lover, man, steady, suitor, swain, sweetheart, young man

boyish adolescent, childish, immature, innocent, juvenile, puerile, young, youthful

brace 1. *n.* bracer, bracket, buttress, prop,

reinforcement, stanchion, stay, strut, support, truss **2.** *v.* bandage, bind, bolster, buttress, fasten, fortify, hold up, prop, reinforce, shove, shove up, steady, strap, strengthen, support, tie, tighten

bracing brisk, chilly, cool, crisp, energizing, exhilarating, fortifying, fresh, invigorating, lively, refreshing, restorative, reviving, rousing, stimulating, tonic, vigorous

brackish bitter, briny, saline, salt, salty, undrinkable

inflorescence growing in its axil. —'**bracteal** *adj.* —**bracteate** ('bræktɪɪt) *adj.*

brad (bræd) *n.* a small tapered nail with a small head.

bradawl ('bræd,ɔːl) *n.* an awl used to pierce wood, leather, etc.

brae (breɪ) *n. Scot.* a hill or hillside; slope.

brag (bræg) *vb.* **bragging, bragged.** **1.** to speak arrogantly and boastfully. ~*n.* **2.** boastful talk or behaviour. **3.** something boasted of. **4.** a braggart; boaster. **5.** a card game: an old form of poker. —'**bragger** *n.*

braggadocio (,brægə'dəʊtʃɪ,əʊ) *n., pl.* **-os.** **1.** vain empty boasting. **2.** a person who boasts; braggart.

braggart ('brægət) *n.* **1.** a person who boasts loudly or exaggeratedly; bragger. ~*adj.* **2.** boastful.

Brahma ('brɑːmə) *n.* **1.** a Hindu god, the Creator. **2.** another name for **Brahman** (sense 2).

Brahman ('brɑːmən) *n., pl.* **-mans.** **1.** (*sometimes not cap.*) Also (*esp. formerly*): **Brahmin.** a member of the highest or priestly caste in the Hindu caste system. **2.** *Hinduism.* the ultimate and impersonal divine reality of the universe. **3.** another name for **Brahma.** —**Brahmanic** (brɑː'mænɪk) *or* **Brah'manical** *adj.*

braid (breɪd) *vb.* (*tr.*) **1.** to interweave (hair, thread, etc.); plait. **2.** to decorate with an ornamental trim or border. ~*n.* **3.** a length of hair, fabric, etc., that has been braided; plait. **4.** narrow ornamental tape of woven silk, wool, etc. —'**braider** *n.* —'**braiding** *n.*

Braille (breɪl) *n.* **1.** a system of writing for the blind consisting of raised dots interpreted by touch. **2.** any writing produced by this method. ~*vb.* **3.** (*tr.*) to print or write using this method.

brain (breɪn) *n.* **1.** the soft convoluted mass of nervous tissue within the skull of vertebrates that is the controlling and coordinating centre of the nervous system and the seat of thought, memory, and emotion. Related adj.: **cerebral.** **2.** (*often pl.*) *Inf.* intellectual ability: *he's got brains.* **3.** *Inf.* shrewdness or cunning. **4.** *Inf.* an intellectual or intelligent person. **5.** (*usually pl.*) *Inf.* a person who plans and organizes. **6. on the brain.** *Inf.* constantly in mind: *I had that song on the brain.* **7. pick someone's brains.** *Inf.* to obtain information or ideas from someone. ~*vb.* (*tr.*) **8.** to smash the skull of. **9.** *Sl.* to hit hard on the head.

brainchild ('breɪn,tʃaɪld) *n., pl.* **-children.** *Inf.* an idea or plan produced by creative thought.

brain death *n.* irreversible cessation of respiration due to irreparable brain damage: widely considered as the criterion of death. —**brain dead** *adj.*

brain drain *n. Inf.* the emigration of scientists, technologists, academics, etc.

brainless ('breɪnlɪs) *adj.* stupid or foolish.

brainstorm ('breɪn,stɔːm) *n.* **1.** a severe outburst of excitement, often as the result of a transitory disturbance of cerebral activity. **2.** *Brit. inf.* a sudden mental aberration. **3.** *U.S. inf.* another word for **brain wave** (sense 2).

brains trust *n.* a group of knowledgeable people who discuss topics in public or on radio or television.

brain-teaser *or* **brain-twister** *n. Inf.* a difficult problem.

brainwash ('breɪn,wɒʃ) *vb.* (*tr.*) to effect a radical change in the ideas and beliefs of (a person), esp. by methods based on conditioning. —'**brain,washing** *n.*

brain wave *n.* **1.** any of the fluctuations of electrical potential in the brain. **2.** *Inf.* a sudden idea or inspiration.

brainy ('breɪnɪ) *adj.* **brainier, brainiest.** *Inf.* clever; intelligent. —'**braininess** *n.*

braise (breɪz) *vb.* to cook (meat, vegetables, etc.) by lightly browning in fat and then cooking slowly in a closed pan with a small amount of liquid.

brak (bræk) *n. S. African.* a crossbred dog; mongrel.

brake[1] (breɪk) *n.* **1.** (*often pl.*) a device for slowing or stopping a vehicle, wheel, shaft, etc., or for keeping it stationary, esp. by means of friction. **2.** a machine or tool for crushing or breaking flax or hemp to separate the fibres. **3.** Also called: **brake harrow.** a heavy harrow for breaking up clods. **4.** short for **shooting brake.** ~*vb.* **5.** to slow down or cause to slow down, by or as if by using a brake. **6.** (*tr.*) to crush or break up using a brake. —'**brakeless** *adj.*

brake[2] (breɪk) *n.* an area of dense undergrowth, shrubs, brushwood, etc.; thicket.

brake[3] (breɪk) *n.* another name for **bracken.**

brake[4] (breɪk) *vb. Arch., chiefly biblical.* a past tense of **break.**

brake horsepower *n.* the rate at which an engine does work, expressed in horsepower. It is measured by the resistance of an applied brake. Abbrev.: **b.h.p.**

brake light *n.* a red light at the rear of a motor vehicle that lights up when the brakes are applied.

brake lining *n.* a renewable strip of asbestos riveted to a brake shoe.

brake shoe *n.* the curved metal casting to which the brake lining is riveted in a drum brake.

brake van *n. Railways, Brit.* the coach or vehicle from which the guard applies the brakes; guard's van. U.S. equivalent: **caboose.**

bramble ('bræmbəl) *n.* **1.** any of various prickly rosaceous plants or shrubs, esp. the blackberry. **2.** any of several similar and related shrubs, such as the dog rose. **3.** *N Brit.* a blackberry. —'**brambly** *adj.*

brambling ('bræmblɪŋ) *n.* a Eurasian finch with a speckled head and back and, in the male, a reddish brown-breast.

bran (bræn) *n.* **1.** husks of cereal grain separated from the flour. **2.** food prepared from these husks.

branch (brɑːntʃ) *n.* **1.** a secondary woody stem arising from the trunk or bough of a tree or the main stem of a shrub. **2.** an offshoot or secondary part: *a branch of a deer's antlers.* **3. a.** a subdivision or subsidiary section of something larger or more complex: *branches of learning; branch of the family.* **b.** (*as modifier*): *a branch office.* **4.** *U.S.* any small stream. ~*vb.* **5.** (*intr.*) (of a tree or other plant) to produce or possess branches. **6.** (*intr.;* usually foll. *by from*) (of stems, roots, etc.) to grow and diverge (from another part). **7.** to divide or be divided into subsidiaries or offshoots. **8.** (*intr.;* often foll. *by off*) to diverge from the main way, road, topic, etc. ~See also **branch out.** —'**branch,like** *adj.*

branch out *vb.* (*intr., adv.;* often foll. *by into*) *Inf.* to expand or extend one's interests.

brand (brænd) *n.* **1.** a trade name identifying a manufacturer or a product; trademark. **2.** a particular kind or variety. **3.** an identifying mark made, usually by burning, on the skin of animals or (formerly) slaves or criminals, esp. as a proof of ownership. **4.** an iron heated and used for branding animals, etc. **5.** a mark of disgrace or infamy; stigma. **6.** a burning or burnt piece of wood, as in a fire. **7.** *Arch. or poetic.* **a.** a flaming torch. **b.** a sword. **8.** a fungal disease of garden plants characterized by brown spots on the leaves. ~*vb.* (*tr.*) **9.** to label, burn, or mark with or as with a brand. **10.** to place indelibly in the memory: *the scene was branded in their minds.* **11.** to denounce; stigmatize: *they branded him a traitor.* —'**brander** *n.*

THESAURUS

brandish ('brændɪʃ) *vb.* **1.** (*tr.*) to wave or flourish (a weapon, etc.) in a triumphant, threatening, or ostentatious way. ~*n.* **2.** a threatening or defiant flourish. —'**brandisher** *n.*

brand-new *adj.* absolutely new.

brandy ('brændɪ) *n.*, *pl.* **-dies. 1.** an alcoholic spirit distilled from grape wine. **2.** a distillation of wines made from other fruits: *plum brandy.*

brandy snap *n.* a crisp sweet biscuit, rolled into a cylinder and filled with whipped cream.

bran tub *n. Brit.* a tub containing bran in which small wrapped gifts are hidden.

brash[1] (bræʃ) *adj.* **1.** tastelessly or offensively loud, showy, or bold. **2.** hasty; rash. **3.** impudent. —'**brashly** *adv.* —'**brashness** *n.*

brash[2] (bræʃ) *n.* loose rubbish, such as broken rock, hedge clippings, etc. —**brashy** ('bræʃɪ) *adj.*

brass (brɑːs) *n.* **1.** an alloy of copper and zinc containing more than 50 per cent of copper. Cf. **bronze** (sense 1). **2.** an object, ornament, or utensil made of brass. **3. a.** the large family of wind instruments including the trumpet, trombone, French horn, etc., made of brass. **b.** (*sometimes functioning as pl.*) instruments of this family forming a section in an orchestra. **4.** (*functioning as pl.*) *Inf.* important or high-ranking officials, esp. military officers: *the top brass.* See also **brass hat. 5.** *N English dialect.* money. **6.** *Brit.* an engraved brass memorial tablet or plaque in a church. **7.** *Inf.* bold self-confidence; cheek; nerve. **8.** (*modifier*) of, consisting of, or relating to brass or brass instruments: *a brass ornament; a brass band.*

brass band *n.* See **band**[1] (sense 2).

brass hat *n. Brit. inf.* a top-ranking official, esp. a military officer.

brassica ('bræsɪkə) *n.* any plant of the genus *Brassica*, such as cabbage, rape, swede, turnip, and mustard.

brassie *or* **brassy** ('bræsɪ, 'brɑ:-) *n.*, *pl.* **brassies.** *Golf.* a club, a No. 2 wood, originally having a brass-plated sole.

brassiere ('bræsɪə, 'bræz-) *n.* a woman's undergarment for covering and supporting the breasts. Often shortened to **bra.**

brass rubbing *n.* **1.** the taking of an impression of an engraved brass tablet or plaque by rubbing a paper placed over it with heel ball, chalk, etc. **2.** an impression made in this way.

brass tacks *pl. n. Inf.* basic realities; hard facts (esp. in **get down to brass tacks**).

brassy ('brɑːsɪ) *adj.* **brassier, brassiest. 1.** *Inf.* insolent; brazen. **2.** flashy; showy. **3.** (of sound) harsh and strident. **4.** like brass, esp. in colour. **5.** decorated with or made of brass. —'**brassily** *adv.* —'**brassiness** *n.*

brat (bræt) *n.* a child, esp. one who is dirty or unruly.

bravado (brəˈvɑːdəʊ) *n.*, *pl.* **-does** *or* **-dos.** vaunted display of courage or self-confidence; swagger.

brave (breɪv) *adj.* **1. a.** having or displaying courage,

resolution, or daring; not cowardly or timid. **b.** (*as collective n.* preceded by *the*): *the brave.* **2.** fine; splendid: *a brave sight.* ~*n.* **3.** a warrior of a North American Indian tribe. ~*vb.* (*tr.*) **4.** to dare or defy: *to brave the odds.* **5.** to confront with resolution or courage: *to brave the storm.* —'**bravely** *adv.* —'**braveness** *n.* —'**bravery** *n.*

bravo *interj.* **1.** (brɑːˈvəʊ). well done! ~*n.* **2.** (brɑː-ˈvəʊ), *pl.* **-vos.** a cry of "bravo." **3.** ('brɑːvəʊ), *pl.* **-voes** *or* **-vos.** a hired killer or assassin.

bravura (brəˈvjʊərə, -ˈvʊərə) *n.* **1.** a display of boldness or daring. **2.** *Music.* a passage or piece requiring great spirit and technical skill by the performer.

brawl (brɔːl) *n.* **1.** a loud disagreement or fight. **2.** *U.S. sl.* an uproarious party. ~*vb.* (*intr.*) **3.** to quarrel or fight noisily; squabble. **4.** (esp. of water) to flow noisily. —'**brawler** *n.*

brawn (brɔːn) *n.* **1.** strong well-developed muscles. **2.** physical strength, esp. as opposed to intelligence. **3.** *Brit.* a seasoned jellied loaf made from the head of a pig or calf. —'**brawny** *adj.*

bray (breɪ) *vb.* **1.** (*intr.*) (of a donkey) to utter its characteristic loud harsh sound; heehaw. **2.** (*intr.*) to make a similar sound, as in laughing. **3.** (*tr.*) to utter with a loud harsh sound. ~*n.* **4.** the loud harsh sound uttered by a donkey. **5.** a similar loud cry or uproar.

braze[1] (breɪz) *vb.* (*tr.*) **1.** to decorate with or make of brass. **2.** to make like brass, as in hardness.

braze[2] (breɪz) *vb.* (*tr.*) to make a joint between (two metal surfaces) by fusing a layer of brass or high-melting solder between them. —'**brazer** *n.*

brazen ('breɪzən) *adj.* **1.** shameless and bold. **2.** made of or resembling brass. **3.** having a ringing metallic sound. ~*vb.* (*tr.*) **4.** (usually foll. by *out* or *through*) to face and overcome boldly or shamelessly. —'**brazenly** *adv.* —'**brazenness** *n.*

brazier[1] *or* **brasier** ('breɪzɪə) *n.* a person engaged in brass-working or brass-founding. —'**braziery** *n.*

brazier[2] *or* **brasier** ('breɪzɪə) *n.* a portable metal receptacle for burning charcoal or coal.

brazil (brəˈzɪl) *n.* **1.** Also called: **brazil wood.** the red wood obtained from various tropical trees of America: used for cabinetwork. **2.** the red or purple dye extracted from these woods. **3.** short for **brazil nut.**

brazil nut *n.* **1.** a tropical South American tree producing large globular capsules, each containing several closely packed triangular nuts. **2.** the nut, having an edible oily kernel and a woody shell. ~Often shortened to **brazil.**

B.R.C.S. *abbrev. for* British Red Cross Society.

breach (briːtʃ) *n.* **1.** a crack, break, or rupture. **2.** a breaking, infringement, or violation of a promise, obligation, etc. **3.** any severance or separation. ~*vb.* **4.** (*tr.*) to break through or make an opening, hole, or incursion in. **5.** (*tr.*) to break a promise, law, etc.

breach of promise *n. Law.* (formerly) failure to car-

THESAURUS

brandish display, exhibit, flaunt, flourish, parade, raise, shake, swing, wield

brash 1. audacious, foolhardy, hasty, impetuous, impulsive, indiscreet, precipitate, rash, reckless **2.** bold, brazen, cocky, forward, heedless, impertinent, impudent, insolent, rude

brass audacity, cheek, effrontery, gall, impertinence, impudence, insolence, nerve (*Inf.*), presumption, rudeness

brassy 1. barefaced, bold, brash, brazen, forward, impudent, insolent, loud-mouthed, pert, saucy **2.** blatant, flashy, garish, gaudy, hard, jazzy (*Inf.*), loud, obtrusive, showy, vulgar **3.** blaring, cacophonous, dissonant, grating, harsh, jangling, jarring, loud, noisy, piercing, raucous, shrill, strident

bravado bluster, boast, boastfulness, boasting, bombast, brag, braggadocio, fanfaronade (*Rare*), swagger, swaggering, swashbuckling, vaunting

brave 1. *adj.* bold, courageous, daring, dauntless, fearless, gallant, heroic, intrepid, plucky, resolute, undaunted, valiant, valorous **2.** *v.* bear, beard, challenge, confront, dare, defy, endure, face, stand up to, suffer,

withstand

bravery boldness, courage, daring, dauntlessness, doughtiness, fearlessness, fortitude, gallantry, grit, guts (*Inf.*), hardihood, hardiness, heroism, indomitability, intrepidity, mettle, pluck, pluckiness, spirit, spunk (*Inf.*), valour

bravo assassin, bandit, brigand, cutthroat, desperado, hired killer, murderer, villain

bravura animation, audacity, boldness, brilliance, brio, daring, dash, display, élan, energy, exhibitionism, ostentation, panache, punch (*Inf.*), spirit, verve, vigour, virtuosity

brawl 1. *n.* affray (*Law*), altercation, argument, battle, broil, clash, disorder, dispute, donnybrook, fight, fracas, fray, free-for-all (*Inf.*), melee, punch-up (*Sl.*), quarrel, row (*Inf.*), ruckus (*Inf.*), rumpus, scrap (*Inf.*), scuffle, squabble, tumult, uproar, wrangle **2.** *v.* altercate, argue, battle, dispute, fight, quarrel, row (*Inf.*), scrap (*Inf.*), scuffle, tussle, wrangle, wrestle

brawn beef (*Inf.*), beefiness, brawniness, flesh, might, muscle, muscles, muscularity, power, robustness, strength, vigour

brawny athletic, beefy (*Inf.*), bulky, burly,

fleshy, hardy, hefty (*Inf.*), herculean, husky (*Inf.*), muscular, powerful, robust, sinewy, stalwart, strapping, strong, sturdy, thewy, vigorous, well-knit

bray 1. *v.* blare, heehaw, hoot, roar, screech, trumpet **2.** *n.* bawl, bellow, blare, cry, harsh sound, heehaw, hoot, roar, screech, shout

brazen *adj.* **1.** audacious, barefaced, bold, brash, brassy (*Inf.*), defiant, forward, immodest, impudent, insolent, pert, saucy, shameless, unabashed, unashamed **2.** brass, brassy, bronze, metallic ~*v.* **3.** *With* **out** be impenitent, be unashamed, confront, defy, outface, outstare, persevere, stare out

breach 1. aperture, break, chasm, cleft, crack, fissure, gap, hole, opening, rent, rift, rupture, split **2.** contravention, disobedience, infraction, infringement, noncompliance, nonobservance, offence, transgression, trespass, violation **3.** alienation, difference, disaffection, disagreement, dissension, division, estrangement, falling-out (*Inf.*), parting of the ways, quarrel, schism, separation, severance, variance

ry out one's promise to marry.

breach of the peace *n. Law.* an offence against public order causing an unnecessary disturbance of the peace.

bread (brɛd) *n.* **1.** a food made from a dough of flour or meal mixed with water or milk, usually raised with yeast or baking powder and then baked. **2.** necessary food; nourishment. **3.** *Sl.* money. **4. break bread.** See **break**. **5. cast one's bread upon the waters.** to do good without expectation of advantage or return. **6. know which side one's bread is buttered.** *Inf.* to know what to do in order to keep one's advantages or privileges. **7. take the bread out of (someone's) mouth.** to deprive of a livelihood. ~*vb.* **8.** (*tr.*) to cover with bread crumbs before cooking.

bread and butter *Inf.* ~*n.* **1.** a means of support or subsistence; livelihood. ~*modifier* (**bread-and-butter**) **a.** providing a basic means of subsistence. **b.** expressing gratitude, as for hospitality (esp. in **bread-and-butter letter**).

breadboard ('brɛd₁bɔːd) *n.* **1.** a wooden board on which bread is sliced. **2.** an experimental arrangement of electronic circuits.

breadfruit ('brɛd₁fruːt) *n., pl.* **-fruits** *or* **-fruit.** **1.** a tree of the Pacific Islands, having edible round, usually seedless, fruit. **2.** the fruit, which is eaten baked or roasted and has a texture like bread.

breadline ('brɛd₁laɪn) *n.* **1.** a queue of people waiting for free food. **2. on the breadline.** *Inf.* impoverished; living at subsistence level.

breadth (brɛdθ, brɛtθ) *n.* **1.** the linear extent or measurement of something from side to side; width. **2.** a piece of fabric, etc., having a standard or definite width. **3.** distance, extent, size, or dimension. **4.** openness and lack of restriction, esp. of viewpoint or interest; liberality.

breadwinner ('brɛd₁wɪnə) *n.* a person supporting a family with his or her earnings.

break (breɪk) *vb.* **breaking, broke, broken.** **1.** to separate or become separated into two or more pieces. **2.** to damage or become damaged so as to be inoperative: *my radio is broken.* **3.** to crack or become cracked without separating. **4.** to burst or cut the surface of (skin, etc.). **5.** to discontinue or become discontinued: *to break a journey.* **6.** to disperse or become dispersed: *the clouds broke.* **7.** (*tr.*) to fail to observe (an agreement, promise, law, etc.): *to break one's word.* **8.** (foll. by *with*) to discontinue an association (with). **9.** to disclose or be disclosed: *he broke the news gently.* **10.** (*tr.*) to fracture (a bone) in (a limb, etc.). **11.** (*tr.*) to divide (something complete or perfect): *to break a set of books.* **12.** to bring or come to an end: *the summer weather broke at last.* **13.** (*tr.*) to bring to an end by force: *to break a strike.* **14.** (when *intr.*, often foll. by *out*) to escape (from): *he broke out of jail.* **15.** to weaken or overwhelm or be weakened or overwhelmed, as in spirit. **16.** (*tr.*) to cut through or penetrate: *a cry broke the silence.* **17.** (*tr.*) to improve on or surpass: *to break a record.* **18.** (*tr.*; often foll. by *in*) to accustom (a horse) to the bridle and saddle, to being ridden, etc. **19.** (*tr.*; often foll. by *of*) to cause (a person) to give up (a habit): *this cure will break you of smoking.* **20.** (*tr.*) to weaken the impact or force of: *this net will break his fall.* **21.** (*tr.*) to decipher: *to break a code.* **22.** (*tr.*) to lose the order of: *to break ranks.* **23.** (*tr.*) to reduce to poverty or the state of bank-ruptcy. **24.** (when *intr.*, foll. by *into*) to obtain, give, or receive smaller units in exchange for; change: *to break a pound note.* **25.** (*tr.*) *Chiefly mil.* to demote to a lower rank. **26.** (*intr.*; often foll. by *from* or *out of*) to proceed suddenly. **27.** (*intr.*) to come into being: *light broke over the mountains.* **28.** (*intr.*; foll. by *into* or *out into*) **a.** to burst into song, laughter, etc. **b.** to change to a faster pace. **29.** (*tr.*) to open with explosives: *to break a safe.* **30.** (*intr.*) (of waves) **a.** (often foll. by *against*) to strike violently. **b.** to collapse into foam or surf. **31.** (*intr.*) (of prices, esp. stock exchange quotations) to fall sharply. **32.** (*intr.*) to make a sudden effort, as in running, horse racing, etc. **33.** (*intr.*) *Cricket.* (of a ball) to change direction on bouncing. **34.** (*intr.*) *Billiards.* to scatter the balls at the start of a game. **35.** (*intr.*) *Boxing, wrestling.* (of two fighters) to separate from a clinch. **36.** (*intr.*) (of the male voice) to undergo a change in register, quality, and range at puberty. **37.** (*tr.*) to open the breech of (certain firearms) by snapping the barrel away from the butt on its hinge. **38.** (*tr.*) to interrupt the flow of current in (an electrical circuit). **39. break bread. a.** to eat a meal, esp. with others. **b.** *Christianity.* to administer or participate in Holy Communion. **40. break camp.** to pack up and leave a camp. **41. break the back of.** to complete the greatest or hardest part of (a task). **42. break the bank.** to ruin financially or deplete the resources of a bank (as in gambling). **43. break the ice. a.** to relieve shyness, esp. between strangers. **b.** to be the first to do something. **44. break service.** *Tennis.* to win a game in which an opponent is serving. ~*n.* **45.** the act or result of breaking; fracture. **46.** a crack formed as the result of breaking. **47.** a brief respite. **48.** a sudden rush, esp. to escape: *to make a break for freedom.* **49.** a breach in a relationship. **50.** any sudden interruption in a continuous action. **51.** *Brit.* a short period between classes at school. **52.** *Inf.* a fortunate opportunity, esp. to prove oneself. **53.** (esp. in a stock exchange) a sudden and substantial decline in prices. **54.** *Billiards.* a series of successful shots during one turn. **55.** *Billiards.* the opening shot that scatters the placed balls. **56.** Also called: **service break, break of serve.** *Tennis.* the act or instance of breaking an opponent's service. **57.** *Jazz.* a short passage during which a soloist plays unaccompanied: it is usually improvised. **58.** a discontinuity in an electrical circuit. **59.** access to a radio channel by a citizens' band radio operator. **60. break of day.** the dawn. ~*interj.* **61.** *Boxing, wrestling.* a command by a referee for two opponents to separate. ~See also **breakaway**, **break down**, etc. —'**breakable** *adj.*

breakage ('breɪkɪdʒ) *n.* **1.** the act or result of breaking. **2.** the quantity or amount broken. **3.** compensation or allowance for goods damaged while in use, transit, etc.

breakaway ('breɪkə₁weɪ) *n.* **1. a.** loss or withdrawal of a group of members from an association, club, etc. **b.** (as *modifier*): *a breakaway faction.* **2.** *Austral.* a stampede of animals, esp. at the smell of water. ~*vb.* **break away.** (*intr., adv.*) **3.** (often foll. by *from*) to leave hastily or escape. **4.** to withdraw or secede.

break down *vb.* (*adv.*) **1.** (*intr.*) to cease to function; become ineffective. **2.** to yield or cause to yield, esp. to strong emotion or tears. **3.** (*tr.*) to crush or destroy. **4.** (*intr.*) to have a nervous breakdown. **5.** to analyse or be subjected to analysis. **6. break it down.** *Austral. inf.* **a.** stop it. **b.** don't expect me to believe that; come off it. ~*n.* **breakdown.** **7.** an act or instance of breaking down; collapse. **8.** short for **nervous breakdown.** **9.** an analy-

---

THESAURUS

bread 1. aliment, diet, fare, food, necessities, nourishment, nutriment, provisions, subsistence, sustenance, viands, victuals **2.** *Sl.* cash, dough (*Sl.*), finance, funds, money

breadth 1. beam (*of a ship*), broadness, latitude, span, spread, wideness, width **2.** amplitude, area, compass, comprehensiveness, dimension, expanse, extensiveness, extent, magnitude, measure, range, reach, scale, scope, size, space, spread, sweep, vastness **3.** broad-mindedness, freedom, latitude, liberality, open-mindedness, openness, permissiveness

break *v.* **1.** batter, burst, crack, crash, demolish, destroy, disintegrate, divide, fracture, fragment, part, rend, separate, sever, shatter, shiver, smash, snap, splinter, split, tear **2.** breach, contravene, disobey, disre-gard, infract (*Law*), infringe, renege on, transgress, violate **3.** cow, cripple, demoralize, dispirit, enervate, enfeeble, impair, incapacitate, subdue, tame, undermine, weaken **4.** abandon, cut, discontinue, give up, interrupt, pause, rest, stop, suspend **5.** bust (*Inf.*), degrade, demote, discharge, dismiss, humiliate, impoverish, make bankrupt, reduce, ruin **6.** announce, come out, disclose, divulge, impart, inform, let out, make public, proclaim, reveal, tell **7.** *Of a record, etc.* beat, better, cap (*Inf.*), exceed, excel, go beyond,outdo, outstrip, surpass, top **8.** appear, burst out, come forth suddenly, emerge, erupt, happen, occur **9.** cut and run (*Inf.*), dash, escape, flee, fly, get away, run away **10.** cushion, diminish, lessen, lighten, moderate, reduce, soften, weaken ~*n.* **11.** breach, cleft, crack, division, fissure, fracture, gap, gash, hole, opening, rent, rift, rupture, split, tear **12.** breather (*Inf.*), halt, hiatus, interlude, intermission, interruption, interval, let-up (*Inf.*), lull, pause, recess, respite, rest, suspension **13.** alienation, breach, disaffection, dispute, divergence, estrangement, rift, rupture, schism, separation, split **14.** *Inf.* advantage, chance, fortune, opening, opportunity, stroke of luck

breakable brittle, crumbly, delicate, flimsy, fragile, frail, frangible, friable

break away 1. decamp, escape, flee, fly, make a break for it, make a run for it (*Inf.*), make off, run away **2.** break with, detach, part company, secede, separate

sis or classification of something into its component parts: *he prepared a breakdown of the report.*

breaker ('breɪkə) *n.* **1.** a person or thing that breaks something, such as a person or firm that breaks up old cars, etc. **2.** a large wave with a white crest on the open sea or one that breaks into foam on the shore. **3.** a citizens' band radio operator requesting the use of a channel.

break even *vb.* **1.** (*intr., adv.*) to attain a level of activity, as in commerce, or a point of operation, as in gambling, at which there is neither profit nor loss. ~*n.* **breakeven.** **2.** *Accounting.* the level of commercial activity at which the total cost and total revenue of a business enterprise are equal.

breakfast ('brɛkfəst) *n.* **1.** the first meal of the day. **2.** the food at this meal. ~*vb.* **3.** to eat or supply with breakfast. —'**breakfaster** *n.*

break in *vb.* (*adv.*) **1.** (sometimes foll. by *on*) to interrupt. **2.** (*intr.*) to enter a house, etc., illegally, esp. by force. **3.** (*tr.*) to accustom (a person or animal) to normal duties or practice. **4.** (*tr.*) to use or wear (shoes, new equipment, etc.) until comfortable or running smoothly. **5.** *Austral.* to bring new land under cultivation. ~*n.* **break-in.** **6.** the illegal entering of a building, esp. by thieves.

breaking and entering *n.* (formerly) the gaining of unauthorized access to a building with intent to commit a crime.

breaking point *n.* the point at which something or someone gives way under strain.

breakneck ('breɪk,nɛk) *adj.* (*prenominal*) (of speed, pace, etc.) excessive and dangerous.

break out *vb.* (*intr., adv.*) **1.** to begin or arise suddenly. **2.** to make an escape, esp. from prison or confinement. **3.** (foll. by *in*) (of the skin) to erupt (in a rash, pimples, etc.). ~*n.* **break-out.** **4.** an escape, esp. from prison or confinement.

break through *vb.* **1.** (*intr.*) to penetrate. **2.** (*intr., adv.*) to achieve success, make a discovery, etc., esp. after lengthy efforts. ~*n.* **breakthrough.** **3.** a significant development or discovery, esp. in science. **4.** the penetration of an enemy's defensive position.

break up *vb.* (*adv.*) **1.** to separate or cause to separate. **2.** to put an end to (a relationship) or (of a relationship) to come to an end. **3.** to dissolve or cause to dissolve; disrupt or be disrupted: *the meeting broke up at noon.* **4.** *Sl.* to lose or cause to lose control of the emotions. **5.** *Sl.* to be or cause to be overcome with laughter. ~*n.* **break-up.** **6.** a separation or disintegration. **7. a.** in the Canadian north, the breaking up of the ice on a body of water that marks the beginning of spring. **b.** this season.

breakwater ('breɪk,wɔːtə) *n.* **1.** Also called: **mole.** a massive wall built out into the sea to protect a shore or harbour from the force of waves. **2.** another name for **groyne.**

bream (briːm; *Austral.* brɪm) *or Austral.* **brim** (brɪm) *n., pl.* **bream** *or* **brim.** **1.** any of several Eurasian freshwater cyprinid fishes having a deep compressed body covered with silvery scales. **2.** *Austral.* any of various marine fishes.

breast (brɛst) *n.* **1.** the front part of the body from the neck to the abdomen; chest. **2.** either of the two soft fleshy milk-secreting glands on the chest in sexually mature human females. **3.** a similar organ in certain other mammals. **4.** anything that resembles a breast in shape or position: *the breast of the hill.* **5.** a source of nourishment. **6.** the source of human emotions. **7.** the part of a garment that covers the breast. **8.** a projection from the side of a wall, esp. that formed by a chimney. **9. beat one's breast. a.** to display guilt and remorse publicly or ostentatiously. **b.** to make a show of victory or success. **10. make a clean breast of.** to make a confession of. ~*vb.* (*tr.*) **11.** to confront boldly; face: *breast the storm.* **12.** to oppose with the breast or meet at breast level: *breasting the waves.* **13.** to reach the summit of: *breasting the mountain top.*

breastbone ('brɛst,bəʊn) *n.* the nontechnical name for **sternum.**

breast-feed *vb.* **-feeding, -fed.** to feed (a baby) with milk from the breast; suckle.

breastplate ('brɛst,pleɪt) *n.* a piece of armour covering the chest.

breaststroke ('brɛst,strəʊk) *n.* a swimming stroke in which the arms are extended in front of the head and swept back on either side while the legs are drawn up beneath the body and thrust back together.

breastwork ('brɛst,wɜːk) *n. Fortifications.* a temporary defensive work, usually breast-high.

breath (brɛθ) *n.* **1.** the intake and expulsion of air during respiration. **2.** the air inhaled or exhaled during respiration. **3.** a single respiration or inhalation of air, etc. **4.** the vapour, heat, or odour of exhaled air. **5.** a slight gust of air. **6.** a short pause or rest. **7.** a brief time. **8.** a suggestion or slight evidence; suspicion: *a breath of scandal.* **9.** a whisper or soft sound. **10.** life, energy, or vitality: *the breath of new industry.* **11.** *Phonetics.* the exhalation of air without vibration of the vocal cords, as in pronouncing fricatives such as (f) or (h) or stops such as (p) or (k). **12. catch one's breath. a.** to rest until breathing is normal, esp. after exertion. **b.** to stop breathing momentarily from excitement, fear, etc. **13. in the same breath.** done or said at the same time. **14. out of breath.** gasping for air after exertion. **15. save one's breath.** to refrain from useless talk. **16. take one's breath away.** to overwhelm with surprise, etc. **17. under or below one's breath.** in a quiet voice or whisper.

Breathalyser *or* **-lyzer** ('brɛθə,laɪzə) *n. Brit., trademark.* a device for estimating the amount of alcohol in the breath: used in testing people suspected of driving under the influence of alcohol. —'**breatha,lyse** *or* -,**lyze** *vb.* (*tr.*)

breathe (briːð) *vb.* **1.** to take in oxygen and give out carbon dioxide; respire. **2.** (*intr.*) to exist; be alive. **3.** (*intr.*) to rest to regain breath, composure, etc. **4.** (*intr.*) (esp. of air) to blow lightly. **5.** (*intr.*) *Machinery.* to take in air, esp. for combustion. **6.** (*tr.*) *Phonetics.* to articulate (a speech sound) without vibration of the vocal cords. **7.** to exhale or emit: *the dragon breathed fire.* **8.** (*tr.*) to impart; instil: *to breathe confidence into the actors.* **9.** (*tr.*) to speak softly; whisper. **10.** (*tr.*) to permit to rest: *to breathe a horse.* **11. breathe again, freely, or**

THESAURUS

breakdown 1. collapse, crackup (*Inf.*), disintegration, disruption, failure, mishap, stoppage **2.** analysis, categorization, classification, detailed list, diagnosis, dissection, itemization

break down be overcome, collapse, conk out (*Sl.*), crack up (*Inf.*), fail, give way, go kaput (*Sl.*), go to pieces, seize up, stop, stop working

breaker billow, comber, roller, wave, whitecap, white horse

break-in breaking and entering, burglary, invasion, robbery

break in 1. barge in, burst in, butt in, interfere, interject, interpose, interrupt, intervene, intrude **2.** break and enter, burgle, invade, rob **3.** accustom, condition, get used to, habituate, initiate, prepare, tame, train

break into begin, burst into, burst out, commence, dissolve into, give way to, launch into

break off 1. detach, divide, part, pull off,

separate, sever, snap off, splinter **2.** cease, desist, discontinue, end, finish, halt, pause, stop, suspend, terminate

break out 1. appear, arise, begin, commence, emerge, happen, occur, set in, spring up, start **2.** abscond, bolt, break loose, burst out, escape, flee, get free **3.** burst out, erupt

break through advance, development, discovery, find, gain, improvement, invention, leap, progress, quantum leap, step forward

break-up breakdown, breaking, crackup (*Inf.*), disintegration, dispersal, dissolution, divorce, ending, parting, rift, separation, split, splitting, termination, wind-up (*Inf., chiefly U.S.*)

break up adjourn, disband, dismantle, disperse, disrupt, dissolve, divide, divorce, end, part, scatter, separate, sever, split, stop, suspend, terminate

breakwater groyne, jetty, mole, sea wall, spur

breast 1. boob (*Sl.*), bosom, bust, chest, front, teat, thorax, udder **2.** being, conscience, core, emotions, feelings, heart, seat of the affections, sentiments, soul, thoughts

breath 1. air, animation, breathing, exhalation, gasp, gulp, inhalation, pant, respiration, wheeze **2.** aroma, odour, smell, vapour, whiff **3.** break, breather, breathing-space, instant, moment, pause, respite, rest, second **4.** faint breeze, flutter, gust, puff, sigh, slight movement, waft, zephyr **5.** hint, murmur, suggestion, suspicion, undertone, whisper **6.** animation, energy, existence, life, lifeblood, life force, vitality

breathe 1. draw in, gasp, gulp, inhale and exhale, pant, puff, respire, wheeze **2.** imbue, impart, infuse, inject, inspire, instil, transfuse **3.** articulate, express, murmur, say, sigh, utter, voice, whisper

easily. to feel relief. **12. breathe one's last.** to die or be finished or defeated.

breather ('briːðə) n. **1.** Inf. a short pause for rest. **2.** a person who breathes in a specified way: a deep breather. **3.** a vent in a container to equalize internal and external pressure.

breathing ('briːðɪŋ) n. **1.** the passage of air into and out of the lungs to supply the body with oxygen. **2.** a single breath: a breathing between words. **3.** Phonetics. **a.** expulsion of breath (**rough breathing**) or absence of such expulsion (**smooth breathing**) preceding the pronunciation of an initial vowel or rho in ancient Greek. **b.** either of two symbols indicating this.

breathless ('brɛθlɪs) adj. **1.** out of breath; gasping, etc. **2.** holding one's breath or having it taken away by excitement, etc. **3.** (esp. of the atmosphere) motionless and stifling. **4.** Rare. lifeless; dead. —'**breathlessly** adv. —'**breathlessness** n.

breathtaking ('brɛθ,teɪkɪŋ) adj. causing awe or excitement. —'**breath,takingly** adv.

breath test n. Brit. a chemical test of a driver's breath to determine the amount of alcohol he has consumed.

breathy ('brɛθɪ) adj. **breathier, breathiest. 1.** (of the speaking voice) accompanied by an audible emission of breath. **2.** (of the singing voice) lacking resonance. —'**breathily** adv. —'**breathiness** n.

bred (brɛd) vb. the past tense or past participle of **breed.**

breech n. (briːtʃ). **1.** the buttocks; rump. **2.** the lower part or bottom of something. **3.** the part of a firearm behind the barrel or bore. ~vb. (briːtʃ, brɪtʃ). (tr.) **4.** to fit (a gun) with a breech. **5.** Arch. to clothe in breeches or any other clothing.

breech delivery n. birth of a baby with the feet or buttocks appearing first.

breeches ('brɪtʃɪz, 'briː-) pl. n. **1.** trousers extending to the knee or just below, worn for riding. **2.** Inf. or dialect. any trousers or pants, esp. extending to the knee.

breeches buoy n. a ring-shaped life buoy with a support in the form of a pair of short breeches, in which a person is suspended for safe transfer from a ship.

breechloader ('briːtʃ,ləʊdə) n. a firearm that is loaded at the breech. —'**breech-,loading** adj.

breed (briːd) vb. **breeding, bred. 1.** to bear (offspring). **2.** (tr.) to bring up; raise. **3.** to produce or cause to produce by mating; propagate. **4.** to produce new or improved strains of (domestic animals and plants). **5.** to produce or be produced; generate: to breed trouble. ~n. **6.** a group of organisms within a species, esp. domestic animals, having clearly defined characteristics. **7.** a lineage or race. **8.** a kind, sort, or group. —'**breeder** n.

breeder reactor n. a type of nuclear reactor that produces more fissionable material than it consumes.

breeding ('briːdɪŋ) n. **1.** the process of bearing offspring; reproduction. **2.** the process of producing plants or animals by hybridization, inbreeding, or other methods of reproduction. **3.** the result of good training, esp. the knowledge of correct social behaviour; refinement.

breeze¹ (briːz) n. **1.** a gentle or light wind. **2.** Meteorol. a wind of force two to six (4–31 m.p.h) inclusive on the Beaufort scale. **3.** Inf. an easy task or state of ease. **4.** Inf., chiefly Brit. a disturbance, esp. a lively quarrel. ~vb. (intr.) **5.** to move quickly or casually: he breezed into the room.

breeze² (briːz) n. ashes of coal, coke, or charcoal used to make breeze blocks.

breeze block n. a light building brick made from the ashes of coal, coke, etc., bonded together by cement.

breezy ('briːzɪ) adj. **breezier, breeziest. 1.** fresh; windy. **2.** casual or carefree; lively; light-hearted. —'**breezily** adv. —'**breeziness** n.

Bren gun (brɛn) n. an air-cooled gas-operated submachine gun: used by the British in World War II.

brent (brɛnt) or esp. U.S. **brant** n., pl. **brents, brants** or **brent, brant.** a small goose that has a dark grey plumage and short neck and occurs in most northern coastal regions. Also called: **brent goose.**

brethren ('brɛðrɪn) pl. n. Arch. except in religious contexts. a plural of **brother.**

Breton ('brɛtⁿn) adj. **1.** of, relating to, or characteristic of Brittany, its people, or their language. ~n. **2.** a native or inhabitant of Brittany.

breve (briːv) n. **1.** an accent, ˘, placed over a vowel to indicate that it is short or is pronounced in a specified way. **2.** Music. a note, now rarely used, equivalent to two semibreves. **3.** R.C. Church. a less common word for **brief** (papal letter).

brevet ('brɛvɪt) n. **1.** a document entitling a commissioned officer to hold temporarily a higher military rank without the appropriate pay and allowances. ~vb. -**vetting, -vetted** or -**veting, -veted. 2.** (tr.) to promote by brevet. —'**brevetcy** n.

breviary ('briːvjərɪ, 'brɛv-) n., pl. -**ries.** R.C. Church. a book of psalms, hymns, prayers, etc., to be recited daily by clerics and certain members of religious orders as part of the divine office.

brevity ('brɛvɪtɪ) n., pl. -**ties. 1.** conciseness of expression; lack of verbosity. **2.** a short duration; brief time.

brew (bruː) vb. **1.** to make (beer, ale, etc.) from malt and other ingredients by steeping, boiling, and fermentation. **2.** to prepare (a drink, such as tea) by boiling or infusing. **3.** (tr.) to devise or plan: to brew a plot. **4.** (intr.) to be in the process of being brewed. **5.** (intr.) to be impending or forming: there's a storm brewing. ~n. **6.** a beverage produced by brewing, esp. tea or beer. **7.** an instance or time of brewing: last year's brew. —'**brewer** n.

brewery ('bruərɪ) n., pl. -**eries.** a place where beer, ale, etc., is brewed.

briar¹ or **brier** ('braɪə) n. **1.** Also called: **tree heath.** a shrub of S Europe, having a hard woody root (briarroot). **2.** a tobacco pipe made from the root of this plant. —'**briary** or '**briery** adj.

briar² ('braɪə) n. a variant spelling of **brier¹.**

bribe (braɪb) vb. **1.** to promise, offer, or give something, often illegally, to (a person) to procure services or gain influence. ~n. **2.** a reward, such as money or favour, given or offered for this purpose. **3.** any persuasion or lure. —'**bribable** or '**bribeable** adj. —'**briber** n. —'**bribery** n.

THESAURUS

breather break, breathing space, breath of air, halt, pause, recess, respite, rest

breathless 1. choking, exhausted, gasping, gulping, out of breath, panting, short-winded, spent, wheezing, winded **2.** agog, anxious, astounded, avid, eager, excited, flabbergasted (Inf.), on tenterhooks, open-mouthed, thunderstruck, with bated breath

breathtaking amazing, astonishing, awe-inspiring, awesome, exciting, heart-stirring, impressive, magnificent, moving, overwhelming, stunning (Inf.), thrilling

breed v. **1.** bear, beget, bring forth, engender, generate, hatch, multiply, originate, procreate, produce, propagate, reproduce **2.** bring up, cultivate, develop, discipline, educate, foster, instruct, nourish, nurture, raise, rear **3.** arouse, bring about, cause, create, generate, give rise to, induce, make, occasion, originate, produce, stir up ~n. **4.** brand, class, extraction, family, ilk, kind, line, lineage, pedigree, progeny, race, sort, species, stamp, stock, strain, type, variety

breeding 1. ancestry, cultivation, development, lineage, nurture, raising, rearing, reproduction, training, upbringing **2.** civility, conduct, courtesy, cultivation, culture, gentility, manners, polish, refinement, urbanity

breeze 1. n. air, breath of wind, capful of wind, current of air, draught, flurry, gust, light wind, puff of air, waft, whiff, zephyr **2.** v. flit, glide, hurry, move briskly, pass, sail, sally, sweep, trip

breezy 1. airy, blowing, blowy, blusterous, blustery, fresh, gusty, squally, windy **2.** airy, animated, blithe, buoyant, carefree, casual, cheerful, debonair, easy-going, free and easy, informal, jaunty, light, light-hearted, lively, sparkling, spirited, sprightly, sunny, vivacious

brevity 1. conciseness, concision, condensation, crispness, curtness, economy, pithiness, succinctness, terseness **2.** briefness, ephemerality, impermanence, shortness, transience, transitoriness

brew v. **1.** boil, ferment, infuse (tea), make (beer), prepare by fermentation, seethe, soak, steep, stew **2.** breed, concoct, contrive, develop, devise, excite, ferment, form, gather, hatch, plan, plot, project, scheme, start, stir up ~n. **3.** beverage, blend, concoction, distillation, drink, fermentation, infusion, liquor, mixture, preparation

bribe 1. n. allurement, backhander (Sl.), boodle (Sl., chiefly U.S.), corrupting gift, enticement, graft, hush money (Sl.), incentive, inducement, kickback (U.S.), pay-off (Inf.), payola (Inf.), reward for treachery **2.** v. buy off, corrupt, get at, grease the palm or hand of (Sl.), influence by gifts, lure, oil the palm of (Inf.), pay off (Inf.), reward, square, suborn

bribery buying off, corruption, graft, inducement, palm-greasing (Sl.), payola (Inf.), protection, subornation

bric-a-brac ('brɪkə,bræk) *n*. miscellaneous small objects, esp. furniture and curios, kept because they are ornamental or rare.

brick (brɪk) *n*. **1. a.** a rectangular block of clay mixed with sand and fired in a kiln or baked by the sun, used in building construction. **b.** (*as modifier*): *a brick house*. **2.** the material used to make such blocks. **3.** any rectangular block: *a brick of ice*. **4.** bricks collectively. **5.** *Inf*. a reliable, trustworthy, or helpful person. **6.** *Brit*. a child's building block. **7. drop a brick.** *Brit. inf*. to make a tactless or indiscreet remark. **8. like a ton of bricks.** *Inf*. with great force; heavily. ~*vb*. **9.** (*tr.; usually foll. by in, up, or over*) to construct, line, pave, fill, or wall up with bricks: *to brick up a window*. —'**bricky** *adj*.

brickbat ('brɪk,bæt) *n*. **1.** a piece of brick or similar material, esp. one used as a weapon. **2.** *Inf*. blunt criticism.

brick red *n., adj*. (of) a reddish-brown colour.

bridal ('braɪdᵊl) *adj*. of or relating to a bride or a wedding; nuptial.

bride (braɪd) *n*. a woman who has just been or is about to be married.

bridegroom ('braɪd,gruːm, -,grom) *n*. a man who has just been or is about to be married.

bridesmaid ('braɪdz,meɪd) *n*. a girl or young unmarried woman who attends a bride at her wedding.

bridge[1] (brɪdʒ) *n*. **1.** a structure that spans and provides a passage over a road, railway, river, or some other obstacle. **2.** something that resembles this in shape or function. **3.** the hard ridge at the upper part of the nose, formed by the underlying nasal bones. **4.** the part of a pair of glasses that rests on the nose. **5.** Also called: **bridgework.** a dental plate containing one or more artificial teeth that is secured to the surrounding natural teeth. **6.** a platform from which a ship is piloted and navigated. **7.** a piece of wood, usually fixed, supporting the strings of a violin, guitar, etc., and transmitting their vibrations to the sounding board. **8.** Also called: **bridge passage.** a passage in a musical, literary, or dramatic work linking two or more important sections. **9.** Also called: **bridge circuit.** *Electronics*. any of several networks across which a device is connected for measuring resistance, capacitance, etc. **10.** *Billiards*. a support for a cue. **11. burn one's bridges.** See **burn**[1]. **12. cross a bridge when (one) comes to it.** to deal with a problem only when it arises. ~*vb*. (*tr.*) **13.** to build or provide a bridge over something; span: *to bridge a river*. **14.** to connect or reduce the distance between: *let us bridge our differences*. —'**bridgeable** *adj*.

bridge[2] (brɪdʒ) *n*. a card game for four players, based on whist, in which one hand (the dummy) is exposed and the trump suit decided by bidding between the players. See also **contract bridge, auction bridge.**

bridgehead ('brɪdʒ,hɛd) *n*. *Mil*. **1.** an area of ground secured or to be taken on the enemy's side of an obstacle. **2.** a fortified or defensive position at the end of a bridge nearest to the enemy.

bridgework ('brɪdʒ,wɜːk) *n*. a partial denture attached to the surrounding teeth.

bridging loan *n*. a loan made to cover the period between two transactions, such as the buying of another house before the sale of the first is completed.

bridle ('braɪdᵊl) *n*. **1.** a headgear for a horse, etc., consisting of a series of buckled straps and a metal mouthpiece (bit) by which the animal is controlled through the reins. **2.** something that curbs or restrains; check. **3.** a Y-shaped cable, rope, or chain, used for holding, towing, etc. ~*vb*. **4.** (*tr.*) to put a bridle on (a horse, mule, etc.). **5.** (*tr.*) to restrain; curb: *he bridled his rage*. **6.** (*intr.*; often foll. by *at*) to show anger, scorn, or indignation.

bridle path *n*. a path suitable for riding or leading horses.

Brie (briː) *n*. a soft creamy white cheese.

brief (briːf) *adj*. **1.** short in duration. **2.** short in length or extent; scanty: *a brief bikini*. **3.** abrupt in manner; brusque: *the professor was brief with me*. **4.** terse or concise. ~*n*. **5.** a condensed statement or written synopsis; abstract. **6.** *Law*. a document containing all the facts and points of law of a case by which a solicitor instructs a barrister to represent a client. **7.** *R.C. Church*. a letter issuing from the Roman court written in modern characters, as contrasted with a papal bull; papal brief. **8.** Also called: **briefing.** instructions. **9. hold a brief for.** to argue for; champion. **10. in brief.** in short; to sum up. ~*vb*. (*tr.*) **11.** to prepare or instruct by giving a summary of relevant facts. **12.** to make a summary or synopsis of. **13.** *English law*. **a.** to instruct (a barrister) by brief. **b.** to retain (a barrister) as counsel. —'**briefly** *adv*. —'**briefness** *n*.

briefcase ('briːf,keɪs) *n*. a flat portable case, often of leather, for carrying papers, books, etc.

briefs (briːfs) *pl. n*. men's underpants or women's pants without legs.

brier[1] *or* **briar** ('braɪə) *n*. any of various thorny shrubs or other plants, such as the sweetbrier. —'**briery** *or* '**briary** *adj*.

brier[2] ('braɪə) *n*. a variant spelling of **briar**[1].

brig[1] (brɪg) *n*. **1.** *Naut*. a two-masted square-rigger. **2.** *Chiefly U.S.* a prison, esp. in a navy ship.

brig[2] (brɪg) *n*. a northern Brit. word for a **bridge**[1].

Brig. *abbrev. for*: **1.** Brigade. **2.** Brigadier.

brigade (brɪ'geɪd) *n*. **1.** a military formation smaller than a division and usually commanded by a brigadier. **2.** a group of people organized for a certain task: *a rescue brigade*. ~*vb*. (*tr.*) **3.** to organize into a brigade.

brigadier (,brɪgə'dɪə) *n*. **1.** an officer of the British Army or Royal Marines junior to a major general but senior to a colonel, usually commanding a brigade. **2.** an equivalent rank in other armed forces.

brigand ('brɪgənd) *n*. a bandit, esp. a member of a gang operating in mountainous areas. —'**brigandage** *or* '**brigandry** *n*.

brigantine ('brɪgən,tiːn, -,taɪn) *n*. a two-masted sailing ship, rigged square on the foremast and fore-and-aft on the mainmast.

bright (braɪt) *adj*. **1.** emitting or reflecting much light; shining. **2.** (of colours) intense or vivid. **3.** full of promise: *a bright future*. **4.** full of animation; cheerful: *a bright face*. **5.** *Inf*. quick-witted or clever: *a bright child*. **6.** magnificent; glorious. **7.** polished; glistening. **8.** (of a liquid) translucent and clear. **9. bright and early.** very early in the morning. ~*adv*. **10.** brightly: *the fire was burning bright*. —'**brightly** *adv*. —'**brightness** *n*.

THESAURUS

bric-a-brac baubles, bibelots, curios, gewgaws, kickshaws, knick-knacks, objects of virtu, *objets d'art*, ornaments, trinkets

bridal bride's, conjugal, connubial, hymeneal, marital, marriage, matrimonial, nuptial, spousal, wedding

bridge *n*. **1.** arch, flyover, overpass, span, viaduct **2.** band, bond, connection, link, tie ~*v*. **3.** arch over, attach, bind, connect, couple, cross, cross over, extend across, go over, join, link, reach across, span, traverse, unite

bridle *v*. **1.** check, constrain, control, curb, govern, keep in check, master, moderate, repress, restrain, subdue **2.** be indignant, bristle, draw (oneself) up, get angry, get one's back up, raise one's hackles, rear up ~*n*. **3.** check, control, curb, restraint, trammels

brief *adj*. **1.** compendious, compressed, concise, crisp, curt, laconic, limited, pithy, short, succint, terse, thumbnail, to the point **2.** ephemeral, fast, fleeting, hasty, little, momentary, quick, short, short-lived, swift, temporary, transitory **3.** abrupt, blunt, brusque, curt, sharp, short, surly ~*n*. **4.** abridgment, abstract, digest, epitome, outline, précis, sketch, summary, synopsis **5.** argument, case, contention, data, defence, demonstration ~*v*. **6.** advise, explain, fill in (*Inf*.), gen up (*Brit. inf*.), give (someone) a rundown, give (someone) the gen (*Brit. inf*.), inform, instruct, prepare, prime, put (someone) in the picture (*Inf*.)

briefing conference, directions, guidance, information, instruction, instructions, meeting, preamble, preparation, priming, rundown

briefly abruptly, briskly, casually, concisely, cursorily, curtly, fleetingly, hastily, hurriedly, in a few words, in a nutshell, in brief, in outline, in passing, momentarily, precisely, quickly, shortly, temporarily

brigade band, body, company, contingent, corps, crew, force, group, organization, outfit, party, squad, team, troop, unit

brigand bandit, desperado, footpad (*Archaic*), freebooter, gangster, highwayman, marauder, outlaw, plunderer, robber, ruffian

bright **1.** beaming, blazing, brilliant, dazzling, effulgent, flashing, gleaming, glistening, glittering, glowing, illuminated, intense, lambent, luminous, lustrous, radiant, resplendent, scintillating, shimmering, shining, sparkling, twinkling, vivid **2.** clear, clement, cloudless, fair, limpid, lucid, pellucid, pleasant, sunny, translucent, transparent, unclouded **3.** acute, astute, aware, brainy, brilliant, clear-headed, clever, ingenious, intelligent, inventive, keen, quick, quick-witted, sharp, smart, wide-awake **4.** auspicious, encouraging, excellent, favourable, golden, good, hopeful, optimistic, palmy, promising, propitious, prosperous, rosy **5.** cheerful, gay, genial, glad, happy, jolly, joyful, joyous, light-

brighten ('braɪtən) vb. **1.** to make or become bright or brighter. **2.** to make or become cheerful.

Bright's disease (braɪts) n. chronic inflammation of the kidneys; chronic nephritis.

brill (brɪl) n., pl. **brill** or **brills.** a European flatfish similar to the turbot.

brilliance ('brɪljəns) or **brilliancy** n. **1.** great brightness; radiance. **2.** excellence or distinction in physical or mental ability; exceptional talent. **3.** splendour; magnificence.

brilliant ('brɪljənt) adj. **1.** shining with light; sparkling. **2.** (of a colour) reflecting a considerable amount of light; vivid. **3.** outstanding; exceptional: a brilliant success. **4.** splendid; magnificent: a brilliant show. **5.** of outstanding intelligence or intellect: a brilliant mind. ~n. **6.** Also called: **brilliant cut. a.** a cut for diamonds and other gemstones in the form of two many-faceted pyramids joined at their bases. **b.** a diamond of this cut. —'**brilliantly** adv.

brilliantine ('brɪljən,tiːn) n. a perfumed oil used to make the hair smooth and shiny.

brim (brɪm) n. **1.** the upper rim of a vessel: the brim of a cup. **2.** a projecting rim or edge: the brim of a hat. **3.** the brink or edge of something. ~vb. **brimming, brimmed. 4.** to fill or be full to the brim: eyes brimming with tears. —,**brim'ful** adj. —'**brimless** adj.

brimstone ('brɪm,stəʊn) n. **1.** an obsolete name for **sulphur. 2.** a common yellow butterfly of N temperate regions of the Old World.

brindled ('brɪndəld) adj. brown or grey streaked or patched with a darker colour: a brindled dog.

brine (braɪn) n. **1.** a strong solution of salt and water, used for salting and pickling meats, etc. **2.** the sea or its water. ~vb. **3.** (tr.) to soak in or treat with brine. —'**brinish** adj.

bring (brɪŋ) vb. **bringing, brought.** (tr.) **1.** to carry, convey, or take (something or someone) to a designated place or person: bring that book to me. **2.** to cause to happen or occur to (oneself or another): to bring disrespect on oneself. **3.** to cause to happen as a consequence: responsibility brings maturity. **4.** to cause to come to mind: it brought back memories. **5.** to cause to be in a certain state, position, etc.: the punch brought him to his knees. **6.** to force, persuade, or make (oneself): I couldn't bring myself to do it. **7.** to sell for; fetch: the painting brought 20 pounds. **8.** Law. **a.** to institute (proceedings, charges, etc.). **b.** to put (evidence, etc.) before a tribunal. **9. bring forth.** to give birth to. **10. bring home to.** to convince of. **11. bring to bear.** See **bear¹.** ~See also **bring about, bring down,** etc. —'**bringer** n.

bring about vb. (tr., adv.) **1.** to cause to happen. **2.** to turn (a ship) around.

bring-and-buy sale n. Brit. an informal sale, often for charity, to which people bring items for sale and buy those that others have brought.

bring down vb. (tr., adv.) to cause to fall.

bring forward vb. (tr., adv.) **1.** to present or introduce (a subject) for discussion. **2.** Book-keeping. to transfer (a sum) to the top of the next page or column.

bring in vb. (tr., adv.) **1.** to yield (income, profit, or cash). **2.** to produce or return (a verdict). **3.** to introduce (a legislative bill, etc.).

bring off vb. (tr., adv.) to succeed in achieving (something), esp. with difficulty.

bring out vb. (tr., adv.) **1.** to produce or publish or have published. **2.** to expose, reveal, or cause to be seen: she brought out the best in me. **3.** (foll. by in) to cause (a person) to become covered (with spots, a rash, etc.). **4.** Brit. to introduce (a girl) formally into society as a debutante.

bring over vb. (tr., adv.) to cause (a person) to change allegiances.

bring round or **around** vb. (tr., adv.) **1.** to restore (a person) to consciousness, esp. after a faint. **2.** Inf. to convince (another person, usually an opponent) of an opinion or point of view.

bring to vb. (tr., adv.) **1.** to restore (a person) to consciousness. **2.** to cause (a ship) to turn into the wind and reduce her headway.

bring up vb. (tr., adv.) **1.** to care for and train (a child); rear. **2.** to raise (a subject) for discussion; mention. **3.** to vomit (food).

brinjal ('brɪndʒəl) n. (in India and Africa) another name for the **aubergine.**

brink (brɪŋk) n. **1.** the edge, border, or verge of a steep place. **2.** the land at the edge of a body of water. **3.** the verge of an event or state: the brink of disaster.

brinkmanship ('brɪŋkmən,ʃɪp) n. the art or practice of pressing a dangerous situation, esp. in international affairs, to the limit of safety and peace in order to win an advantage.

briny ('braɪnɪ) adj. **brinier, briniest. 1.** of or resembling brine; salty. ~n. **2.** (preceded by the) Inf. the sea. —'**brininess** n.

briquette or **briquet** (brɪ'kɛt) n. a small brick made of compressed coal dust, sawdust, charcoal, etc., used for fuel.

brisk (brɪsk) adj. **1.** lively and quick; vigorous: a brisk walk. **2.** invigorating or sharp: brisk weather. ~vb. **3.** (often foll. by up) to enliven; make or become brisk. —'**briskly** adv. —'**briskness** n.

brisket ('brɪskɪt) n. **1.** the breast of a four-legged animal. **2.** the meat from this part, esp. of beef.

brisling ('brɪslɪŋ) n. another name for a **sprat.**

bristle ('brɪsəl) n. **1.** any short stiff hair of an animal or plant, such as on a pig's back. **2.** something resembling these hairs: toothbrush bristle. ~vb. **3.** (when intr., often foll. by up) to stand up or cause to stand up like bristles. **4.** (intr.; sometimes foll. by up) to show anger, indignation, etc.: she bristled at the suggestion. **5.** (intr.) to be thickly covered or set: the target bristled with arrows. —'**bristly** adj.

THESAURUS

hearted, lively, merry, vivacious **6.** distinguished, famous, glorious, illustrious, magnificent, outstanding, remarkable, splendid

brighten 1. clear up, enliven, gleam, glow, illuminate, lighten, light up, make brighter, shine **2.** become cheerful, buck up (Inf.), buoy up, cheer, encourage, enliven, gladden, hearten, make happy, perk up

brilliance, brilliancy 1. blaze, brightness, dazzle, effulgence, gleam, glitter, intensity, luminosity, lustre, radiance, refulgence, resplendence, sheen, sparkle, vividness **2.** acuity, aptitude, braininess, cleverness, distinction, excellence, genius, giftedness, greatness, inventiveness, talent, wisdom **3.** éclat, glamour, gorgeousness, grandeur, illustriousness, magnificence, splendour

brilliant 1. ablaze, bright, coruscating, dazzling, glittering, glossy, intense, luminous, lustrous, radiant, refulgent, resplendent, scintillating, shining, sparkling, vivid **2.** celebrated, eminent, exceptional, famous, glorious, illustrious, magnificent, outstanding, splendid, superb **3.** accomplished, acute, astute, brainy, clever, discerning, expert, gift-

ed, intellectual, intelligent, inventive, masterly, penetrating, profound, quick, talented

brim 1. n. border, brink, circumference, edge, lip, margin, rim, skirt, verge **2.** v. fill, fill up, hold no more, overflow, run over, spill, well over

brimful brimming, filled, flush, full, level with, overflowing, overfull, packed, running over

bring 1. accompany, bear, carry, conduct, convey, deliver, escort, fetch, gather, guide, import, lead, take, transfer, transport, usher **2.** cause, contribute to, create, effect, engender, inflict, occasion, produce, result in, wreak **3.** compel, convince, dispose, force, induce, influence, make, move, persuade, prevail on or upon, prompt, sway **4.** command, earn, fetch, gross, net, produce, return, sell for, yield

bring about accomplish, achieve, bring to pass, cause, compass, create, effect, effectuate, generate, give rise to, make happen, manage, occasion, produce, realize

bring down abase, cut down, drop, fell, floor, lay low, level, lower, overthrow, overturn, pull down, reduce, shoot down, under-

mine, upset

bring in accrue, bear, be worth, fetch, gross, produce, profit, realize, return, yield

bring off accomplish, achieve, bring home the bacon (Inf.), bring to pass, carry off, carry out, discharge, execute, perform, pull off, succeed

bring up 1. breed, develop, educate, form, nurture, raise, rear, support, teach, train **2.** advance, allude to, broach, introduce, mention, move, propose, put forward, submit

brink border, boundary, brim, edge, fringe, frontier, limit, lip, margin, point, rim, skirt, threshold, verge

brisk 1. active, agile, alert, animated, bustling, busy, energetic, lively, nimble, no-nonsense, quick, speedy, sprightly, spry, vigorous, vivacious **2.** biting, bracing, crisp, exhilarating, fresh, invigorating, keen, nippy, refreshing, sharp, snappy, stimulating

briskly actively, brusquely, coolly, decisively, efficiently, energetically, firmly, incisively, nimbly, promptly, quickly, rapidly, readily, smartly, vigorously

bristle n. **1.** barb, hair, prickle, spine, stub-

Brit (brɪt) *n. Inf.* a British person.

Brit. *abbrev. for:* **1.** Britain. **2.** British.

Britannia (brɪ'tænɪə) *n.* **1.** a female warrior carrying a trident and wearing a helmet, personifying Great Britain or the British Empire. **2.** (in the ancient Roman Empire) the S part of Great Britain.

Britannia metal *n.* an alloy of tin with antimony and copper: used for decorative purposes and for bearings.

Britannic (brɪ'tænɪk) *adj.* of Britain; British (esp. in **His** *or* **Her Britannic Majesty**).

britches ('brɪtʃɪz) *pl. n.* **1.** a variant spelling of **breeches**. **2. too big for one's britches.** *Inf.* overconfident; arrogant.

British ('brɪtɪʃ) *adj.* **1.** of or denoting Britain, a country of W Europe, consisting of the island of Great Britain (comprising England, Scotland, and Wales) and part of the island of Ireland (Northern Ireland). **2.** relating to, denoting, or characteristic of the inhabitants of Britain. **3.** relating to or denoting the English language as spoken and written in Britain. **4.** of or relating to the Commonwealth: *British subjects.* ~*n.* **5.** (preceded by *the;* functioning as *pl.*) the natives or inhabitants of Britain. —'**Britishness** *n.*

Briton ('brɪtən) *n.* **1.** a native or inhabitant of Britain. **2.** *History.* any of the early Celtic inhabitants of S Britain.

brittle ('brɪtəl) *adj.* **1.** easily cracked, snapped, or broken; fragile. **2.** curt or irritable. **3.** hard or sharp in quality. ~*n.* **4.** a crunchy sweet made with treacle and nuts: *peanut brittle.* —'**brittleness** *n.*

bro. (brəʊ) *abbrev. for* brother.

broach (brəʊtʃ) *vb.* **1.** (*tr.*) to initiate (a topic) for discussion. **2.** (*tr.*) to tap or pierce (a container) to draw off (a liquid): *to broach a cask.* **3.** (*tr.*) to open in order to begin to use. ~*n.* **4.** a long tapered toothed cutting tool for enlarging holes. **5.** a spit for roasting meat, etc. —'**broacher** *n.*

B-road *n.* a secondary road in Britain.

broad (brɔːd) *adj.* **1.** having relatively great breadth or width. **2.** of vast extent; spacious: *a broad plain.* **3.** (*postpositive*) from one side to the other: *four miles broad.* **4.** of great scope or potential: *that invention had broad applications.* **5.** not detailed; general: *broad plans.* **6.** clear and open; full (esp. in **broad daylight**). **7.** obvious or plain: *broad hints.* **8.** liberal; tolerant: *a broad political stance.* **9.** widely spread; extensive: *broad support.* **10.** vulgar; coarse; indecent: *a broad joke.* **11.** (of a dialect or pronunciation) consisting of a large number of speech sounds characteristic of a particular geographical area: *a broad Yorkshire accent.* **12.** *Phonetics.* the long vowel in English words such as *father, half,* as represented in Received Pronunciation. ~*n.* **13.** the broad part of something. **14.** *Sl., chiefly U.S.* a girl or woman. —'**broadly** *adv.*

broad arrow *n.* **1.** a mark shaped like a broad arrowhead designating British government property and formerly used on prison clothing. **2.** an arrow with a broad head.

broad bean *n.* **1.** an erect annual Eurasian bean plant cultivated for its large edible flattened seeds. **2.** the seed of this plant.

broadcast ('brɔːd,kɑːst) *vb.* **-casting, -cast** *or* **-casted.** **1.** to transmit (announcements or programmes) on radio or television. **2.** (*intr.*) to take part in a radio or television programme. **3.** (*tr.*) to make widely known throughout an area: *to broadcast news.* **4.** (*tr.*) to scatter (seed, etc.) over an area, esp. by hand. ~*n.* **5. a.** a transmission or programme on radio or television. **b.** (*as modifier*): *a broadcast signal.* **6.** the act of scattering seeds. ~*adj.* **7.** dispersed over a wide area. ~*adv.* **8.** far and wide. —'**broad,caster** *n.*

broadcloth ('brɔːd,klɒθ) *n.* **1.** fabric woven on a wide loom. **2.** a closely woven fabric of wool, worsted, cotton, or rayon with lustrous finish, used for clothing.

broaden ('brɔːdən) *vb.* to make or become broad or broader; widen.

broad gauge *n.* **1.** a railway track with a greater distance between the lines than the standard gauge of 56½ inches. ~*adj.* **broad-gauge. 2.** of or denoting a railway having this track.

broad-leaved *adj.* denoting trees other than conifers; having broad rather than needleshaped leaves.

broadloom ('brɔːd,luːm) *n.* (*modifier*) of or designating carpets woven on a wide loom.

broad-minded *adj.* **1.** tolerant of opposing viewpoints; not prejudiced; liberal. **2.** not easily shocked by permissive sexual habits, pornography, etc. —,**broad-'mindedly** *adv.* —,**broad-'mindedness** *n.*

broadsheet ('brɔːd,ʃiːt) *n.* **1.** a newspaper having a large format, approximately 15 by 24 inches (38 by 61 centimetres). **2.** another word for **broadside** (sense 4).

broadside ('brɔːd,saɪd) *n.* **1.** *Naut.* the entire side of a vessel. **2.** *Naval.* **a.** all the armament fired from one side of a warship. **b.** the simultaneous discharge of such armament. **3.** a strong or abusive verbal or written attack. **4.** Also called: **broadside ballad.** a ballad or popular song printed on one side of a sheet of paper, esp. in 16th-century England. ~*adv.* **5.** with a broader side facing an object; sideways.

broadsword ('brɔːd,sɔːd) *n.* a broad-bladed sword used for cutting rather than stabbing.

brocade (brəʊ'keɪd) *n.* **1.** a rich fabric woven with a raised design, often using gold or silver threads. ~*vb.* **2.** (*tr.*) to weave with such a design.

broccoli ('brɒkəlɪ) *n.* **1.** a cultivated variety of cabbage having branched greenish flower heads. **2.** the flower head, eaten as a vegetable before the buds have opened.

broch (brɒk, brɒx) *n.* (in Scotland) a prehistoric circular dry-stone tower large enough to serve as a fortified home.

brochette (brɒ'ʃɛt) *n.* a skewer or small spit, used for holding pieces of meat, etc., while roasting or grilling.

brochure ('brəʊʃjʊə, -ʃə) *n.* a pamphlet or stitched booklet, esp. one containing summarized or introductory information or advertising.

broderie anglaise ('brəʊdərɪ ɑːŋ'glɛz) *n.* open embroidery on white cotton, fine linen, etc.

Broederbond ('brʊdə,bɒnt, 'bruːdə,bɒnt) *n.* (in South Africa) a secret society of Afrikaner Nationalists.

brogue[1] (brəʊg) *n.* a broad gentle-sounding dialectal accent, esp. that used by the Irish in speaking English.

brogue[2] (brəʊg) *n.* **1.** a sturdy walking shoe, often with ornamental perforations. **2.** an untanned shoe worn formerly in Ireland and Scotland.

broil[1] (brɔɪl) *vb.* **1.** the usual U.S. word for **grill** (sense 1). **2.** to become or cause to become extremely hot. **3.** (*intr.*) to be furious.

broil[2] (brɔɪl) *n.* **1.** a loud quarrel or disturbance; brawl. ~*vb.* **2.** (*intr.*) to brawl; quarrel.

broiler ('brɔɪlə) *n.* **1.** a young tender chicken suitable for roasting. **2.** a pan, grate, etc. for broiling food. **3.** a very hot day.

---

ble, thorn, whisker ~*v.* **2.** horripilate, prickle, rise, stand on end, stand up **3.** be angry, be infuriated, be maddened, bridle, flare up, get one's dander up (*Sl.*), rage, see red, seethe, spit (*Inf.*) **4.** *With* **with** abound, be alive, be thick, crawl, hum, swarm, teem

bristly bearded, bewhiskered, hairy, prickly, rough, stubbly, unshaven, whiskered

brittle 1. breakable, crisp, crumbling, crumbly, delicate, fragile, frail, frangible, friable, shatterable, shivery **2.** curt, edgy, irritable, nervous, prim, stiff, stilted, tense

broach 1. approach, bring up, hint at, introduce, mention, open up, propose, raise the subject, speak of, suggest, talk of, touch on **2.** crack, draw off, open, pierce, puncture, start, tap, uncork

broad 1. ample, beamy (*of a ship*), capacious, expansive, extensive, generous, large, roomy, spacious, vast, voluminous, wide, widespread **2.** all-embracing, comprehensive, encyclopedic, far-reaching, general, inclusive, nonspecific, sweeping, undetailed, universal, unlimited, wide, wide-ranging **3.** *As in* **broad daylight** clear, full, obvious, open, plain, straightforward, undisguised **4.** broad-minded, liberal, open, permissive, progressive, tolerant, unbiased **5.** blue, coarse, gross, improper, indecent, indelicate, near the knuckle (*Inf.*), unrefined, vulgar

broadcast *v.* **1.** air, beam, cable, put on the air, radio, relay, show, televise, transmit **2.** advertise, announce, circulate, disseminate, make public, proclaim, promulgate, publish, report, spread ~*n.* **3.** programme, show, telecast, transmission

broaden augment, develop, enlarge, expand, extend, fatten, increase, open up, spread, stretch, supplement, swell, widen

broad-minded catholic, cosmopolitan, dispassionate, flexible, free-thinking, indulgent, liberal, open-minded, permissive, responsive, tolerant, unbiased, unbigoted, undogmatic, unprejudiced

broadside abuse, assault, attack, battering, bombardment, censure, criticism, denunciation, diatribe, philippic

brochure advertisement, booklet, circular, folder, handbill, hand-out, leaflet, pamphlet

broke (brəʊk) vb. **1.** the past tense of **break.** ~adj. Inf. **2.** having no money; bankrupt. **3. go for broke.** to risk everything in a gambling or other venture.

broken ('brəʊkən) vb. **1.** the past participle of **break.** ~adj. **2.** fractured, smashed, or splintered: a broken vase. **3.** interrupted; disturbed; disconnected: broken sleep. **4.** intermittent or discontinuous: broken sunshine. **5.** not functioning. **6.** spoilt or ruined by divorce (esp. in **broken home, broken marriage**). **7.** (of a trust, promise, contract, etc.) violated; infringed. **8.** (of the speech of a foreigner) imperfect in grammar, vocabulary, and pronunciation: broken English. **9.** Also: **broken-in.** made tame or disciplined by training. **10.** exhausted or weakened, as through ill-health or misfortune. **11.** irregular or rough; uneven: broken ground. **12.** bankrupt. —'brokenly adv.

broken chord n. another term for **arpeggio.**

broken-down adj. **1.** worn out, as by age or long use; dilapidated. **2.** not in working order.

brokenhearted (,brəʊkən'hɑːtɪd) adj. overwhelmed by grief or disappointment. —,broken'heartedly adv.

broker ('brəʊkə) n. **1.** an agent who, acting on behalf of a principal, buys or sells goods, securities, etc.: insurance broker. **2.** short for **stockbroker. 3.** a person who deals in second-hand goods.

brokerage ('brəʊkərɪdʒ) n. **1.** commission charged by a broker. **2.** a broker's business or office.

brolly ('brɒlɪ) n., pl. **-lies.** an informal Brit. name for **umbrella** (sense 1).

bromide ('brəʊmaɪd) n. **1.** any salt of hydrobromic acid. **2.** any compound containing a bromine atom. **3.** a dose of sodium or potassium bromide given as a sedative. **4.** Inf. **a.** a platitude. **b.** a boring person.

bromide paper n. a type of photographic paper coated with an emulsion of silver bromide.

bromine ('brəʊmiːn, -mɪn) n. a pungent dark red volatile liquid element that occurs in brine and is used in the production of chemicals. Symbol: Br; atomic no.: 35; atomic wt.: 79.91.

bronchi ('brɒŋkaɪ) n. the plural of **bronchus.**

bronchial ('brɒŋkɪəl) adj. of or relating to the bronchi or the bronchial tubes. —'bronchially adv.

bronchitis (brɒŋ'kaɪtɪs) n. inflammation of the bronchial tubes, characterized by coughing, difficulty in breathing, etc. —**bronchitic** (brɒŋ'kɪtɪk) adj., n.

bronchus ('brɒŋkəs) n., pl. **-chi** (-kaɪ). either of the two main branches of the trachea.

bronco or **broncho** ('brɒŋkəʊ) n., pl. **-cos** or **-chos.** U.S. a wild or partially tamed pony or mustang of the western plains.

brontosaurus (,brɒntə'sɔːrəs) or **brontosaur** ('brɒntə,sɔː) n. a very large herbivorous quadrupedal dinosaur, common in the U.S. in late Jurassic times, having a long neck and long tail.

bronze (brɒnz) n. **1.** any hard water-resistant alloy consisting of copper and smaller proportions of tin and sometimes zinc and lead. **2.** a yellowish-brown colour or pigment. **3.** a statue, medal, or other object made of bronze. ~adj. **4.** made of or resembling bronze. **5.** of a yellowish-brown colour. ~vb. **6.** (esp. of the skin) to make or become brown; tan. **7.** (tr.) to give the appearance of bronze to. —'bronzy adj.

Bronze Age n. **a.** a technological stage between the Stone and Iron Ages, beginning in the Middle East about 4500 B.C. and lasting in Britain from about 2000 to 500 B.C., during which weapons and tools were made of bronze. **b.** (as modifier): a Bronze-Age tool.

bronze medal n. a medal awarded to a competitor who comes third in a contest or race.

brooch (brəʊtʃ) n. an ornament with a hinged pin and catch, worn fastened to clothing.

brood (bruːd) n. **1.** a number of young animals, esp. birds, produced at one hatching. **2.** all the offspring in one family: often used jokingly or contemptuously. **3.** a group of a particular kind; breed. **4.** (as modifier) kept for breeding: a brood mare. ~vb. **5.** (of a bird) **a.** to sit on or hatch (eggs). **b.** (tr.) to cover (young birds) protectively with the wings. **6.** (when intr., often foll. by on, over, or upon) to ponder morbidly or persistently.

brooder ('bruːdə) n. **1.** a structure, usually heated, used for rearing young chickens or other fowl. **2.** a person or thing that broods.

broody ('bruːdɪ) adj. **-ier, -iest. 1.** moody; introspective. **2.** (of poultry) wishing to sit on or hatch eggs. **3.** Inf. (of a woman) wishing to have a baby. —'broodiness n.

brook[1] (brʊk) n. a natural freshwater stream smaller than a river.

brook[2] (brʊk) vb. (tr.) (usually used with a negative) to bear; tolerate.

broom (bruːm, brʊm) n. **1.** an implement for sweeping consisting of a brush of straw, bristles, or twigs, attached to a long handle. **2.** any of various yellow-flowered Eurasian leguminous shrubs. **3. new broom.** a newly appointed official, etc., eager to make radical changes. ~vb. **4.** (tr.) to sweep with a broom.

broomstick ('bruːm,stɪk, 'brʊm-) n. the long handle of a broom.

bros. or **Bros.** abbrev. for brothers.

brose (brəʊz) n. Scot. a porridge made by adding a boiling liquid to meal, esp. oatmeal.

broth (brɒθ) n. **1.** a soup made by boiling meat, fish, vegetables, etc., in water. **2.** another name for **stock** (sense 19).

brothel ('brɒθəl) n. **1.** a house where men pay to have sexual intercourse with prostitutes. **2.** Austral. inf. any untidy or messy place.

brother ('brʌðə) n. **1.** a male person having the same parents as another person. **2. a.** a male person belonging to the same group, profession, nationality, trade union, etc., as another or others; fellow member. **b.** (as modifier): brother workers. **3.** Inf. comrade; friend: used as a form of address. **4.** Christianity. a member of a male religious order. ~Related adj.: **fraternal.**

brotherhood ('brʌðə,hʊd) n. **1.** the state of being related as a brother or brothers. **2.** an association or fellowship, such as a trade union. **3.** all persons engaged in a particular profession, trade, etc. **4.** the belief, feeling, or hope that all men should treat one another as brothers.

brother-in-law n., pl. **brothers-in-law. 1.** the brother of one's wife or husband. **2.** the husband of one's sister. **3.** the husband of the sister of one's husband or wife.

brotherly ('brʌðəlɪ) adj. of, resembling, or suitable to a brother, esp. in showing loyalty and affection; fraternal. —'brotherliness n.

THESAURUS

broke bankrupt, bust (Inf.), cleaned out (Sl.), flat broke (Sl.), impoverished, insolvent, on one's uppers, penniless, penurious, ruined, skint (Brit. inf.), stony-broke (Sl.)

broken 1. burst, demolished, destroyed, fractured, fragmented, rent, ruptured, separated, severed, shattered, shivered **2.** defective, exhausted, feeble, imperfect, kaput (Inf.), not functioning, out of order, ruined, run-down, spent, weak **3.** disconnected, discontinuous, disturbed, erratic, fragmentary, incomplete, intermittent, interrupted, spasmodic **4.** beaten, browbeaten, crippled, crushed, defeated, demoralized, humbled, oppressed, overpowered, subdued, tamed, vanquished **5.** dishonoured, disobeyed, disregarded, forgotten, ignored, infringed, isolated, retracted, traduced, transgressed **6.** disjointed, halting, hesitating, imperfect, stammering

broken-down collapsed, dilapidated, in disrepair, inoperative, kaput (Sl.), not functioning, not in working order, old, on the blink (Inf.), out of commission, out of order, worn out

brokenhearted crestfallen, desolate, despairing, devastated, disappointed, disconsolate, grief-stricken, heartbroken, heartsick, inconsolable, miserable, mournful, prostrated, sorrowful, wretched

broker agent, dealer, factor, go-between, intermediary, middleman, negotiator

bronze brownish, chestnut, copper, copper-coloured, metallic brown, reddish-brown, reddish-tan, rust, tan

brood v. **1.** agonize, dwell upon, fret, meditate, mope, mull over, muse, ponder, repine, ruminate, think upon **2.** cover, hatch, incubate, set, sit upon ~n. **3.** breed, chicks, children, clutch, family, hatch, infants, issue, lit-ter, offspring, progeny, young

brook beck, burn, gill (Dialect), rill, rivulet, runnel (Literary), stream, streamlet, watercourse

brothel bagnio, bawdy house (Archaic), bordello, house of ill fame, house of ill repute, house of prostitution, knocking shop (Sl.), red-light district, stews (Archaic), whorehouse

brother 1. blood brother, kin, kinsman, relation, relative, sibling **2.** associate, chum (Inf.), colleague, companion, compeer, comrade, confrère, fellow member, mate, pal (Inf.), partner **3.** cleric, friar, monk, regular, religious

brotherhood 1. brotherliness, camaraderie, companionship, comradeship, fellowship, friendliness, kinship **2.** alliance, association, clan, clique, community, coterie, fraternity, guild, league, society, union

brougham ('bru:əm, bru:m) *n.* **1.** a four-wheeled horse-drawn closed carriage having a raised open driver's seat in front. **2.** *Obs.* a large car with an open compartment at the front for the driver. **3.** *Obs.* an early electric car.

brought (brɔːt) *vb.* the past tense or past participle of **bring.**

brouhaha (bru:'hɑːhɑː) *n.* a loud confused noise; commotion; uproar.

brow (brau) *n.* **1.** the part of the face from the eyes to the hairline; forehead. **2.** short for **eyebrow. 3.** the expression of the face; countenance: *a troubled brow.* **4.** the jutting top of a hill, etc.

browbeat ('brau‚biːt) *vb.* **-beating, -beat, -beaten.** (*tr.*) to discourage or frighten with threats or a domineering manner; intimidate. —'**brow‚beater** *n.*

brown (braun) *n.* **1.** any of various colours, such as those of wood or earth. **2.** a dye or pigment producing these colours. ~*adj.* **3.** of the colour brown. **4.** (of bread) made from a dark flour, such as wheatmeal or wholemeal flour. **5.** deeply tanned or sunburnt. ~*vb.* **6.** to make (esp. food as a result of cooking) brown or (esp. of food) to become brown. —'**brownish** *or* 'browny *adj.* —'**brownness** *n.*

brown bear *n.* a large ferocious brownish bear inhabiting temperate forests of North America, Europe, and Asia.

brown coal *n.* another name for **lignite.**

browned-off *adj. Inf., chiefly Brit.* thoroughly discouraged or disheartened; fed-up.

brownie ('brauni) *n.* **1.** (in folklore) an elf said to do helpful work at night, esp. household chores. **2.** *Chiefly U.S.* a flat nutty chocolate cake.

Brownie Guide *or* **Brownie** ('brauni) *n.* a member of the junior branch of the Guides.

browning ('brauniŋ) *n. Brit.* a substance used to darken soups, gravies, etc.

brown paper *n.* a kind of coarse unbleached paper used for wrapping.

brown rice *n.* unpolished rice, in which the grains retain the outer yellowish-brown layer (bran).

Brown Shirt *n.* **1.** (in Nazi Germany) a storm trooper. **2.** a member of any fascist party or group.

brown study *n.* a mood of deep absorption or thoughtfulness; reverie.

brown sugar *n.* sugar that is unrefined or only partially refined.

brown trout *n.* a common brownish variety of the trout that occurs in the rivers of N Europe.

browse (brauz) *vb.* **1.** to look through (a book, articles for sale in a shop, etc.) in a casual leisurely manner. **2.** (of deer, goats, etc.) to feed upon (vegetation) by continual nibbling. ~*n.* **3.** the act or an instance of browsing. **4.** the young twigs, shoots, leaves, etc., on which certain animals feed. —'**browser** *n.*

BRS *abbrev. for* British Road Services.

brucellosis (‚bru:sɪ'ləusɪs) *n.* an infectious disease of cattle, goats, and pigs, caused by bacteria and transmittable to man. Also called: **undulant fever.**

bruin ('bru:ɪn) *n.* a name for a bear, used in children's tales, etc.

bruise (bru:z) *vb.* (*mainly tr.*) **1.** (*also intr.*) to injure (tissues) without breaking the skin, usually with discoloration, or (of tissues) to be injured in this way. **2.** to offend or injure (someone's feelings). **3.** to damage the surface of (something). **4.** to crush (food, etc.) by pounding. ~*n.* **5.** a bodily injury without a break in the skin, usually with discoloration; contusion.

bruiser ('bru:zə) *n. Inf.* a strong tough person, esp. a boxer or a bully.

bruit (bru:t) *vb.* **1.** *Arch. or U.S.* (*tr.; often passive;* usually foll. by *about*) to report; rumour. ~*n.* **2.** *Arch.* **a.** a rumour. **b.** a loud outcry; clamour.

brumby ('brʌmbi) *n., pl.* **-bies.** *Austral.* **1.** a wild horse, esp. one descended from runaway stock. **2.** a disorderly person.

brunch (brʌntʃ) *n. Chiefly U.S.* a meal eaten late in the morning, combining breakfast with lunch.

brunette (bru:'nɛt) *n.* **1.** a girl or woman with dark brown hair. ~*adj.* **2.** dark brown: *brunette hair.*

brunt (brʌnt) *n.* the main force or shock of a blow, attack, etc. (esp. in **bear the brunt of**).

brush[1] (brʌʃ) *n.* **1.** a device made of bristles, hairs, wires, etc., set into a firm back or handle: used to apply paint, clean or polish surfaces, groom the hair, etc. **2.** the act or an instance of brushing. **3.** a light stroke made in passing; graze. **4.** a brief encounter or contact, esp. an unfriendly one; skirmish. **5.** the bushy tail of a fox. **6.** an electric conductor, esp. one made of carbon, that conveys current between stationary and rotating parts of a generator, motor, etc. ~*vb.* **7.** (*tr.*) to clean, polish, scrub, paint, etc., with a brush. **8.** (*tr.*) to apply or remove with a brush or brushing movement. **9.** (*tr.*) to touch lightly and briefly. **10.** (*intr.*) to move so as to graze or touch something lightly. ~See also **brush aside, brush off,** etc. —'**brusher** *n.* —'**brush‚like** *or* 'brushy *adj.*

brush[2] (brʌʃ) *n.* **1.** a thick growth of shrubs and small trees; scrub. **2.** land covered with scrub. **3.** broken or cut branches or twigs; brushwood. **4.** wooded sparsely populated country; backwoods. —'**brushy** *adj.*

brush aside *or* **away** *vb.* (*tr., adv.*) to dismiss without consideration; disregard.

brushed (brʌʃt) *adj. Textiles.* treated with a brushing process to raise the nap and give a softer and warmer finish: *brushed nylon.*

brush off *Sl.* ~*vb.* (*tr., adv.*) **1.** to dismiss and ignore (a person), esp. curtly. ~*n.* **brushoff** ('brʌ‚ʃɒf). **2.** an abrupt dismissal or rejection.

brush up *vb.* (*adv.*) *Inf.* **1.** (*tr.*; often foll. by *on*) to refresh one's knowledge, skill, or memory of (a subject). **2.** to make (a person or oneself) clean or neat as after a journey. ~*n.* **brush-up. 3.** *Brit.* the act or an instance of tidying one's appearance (esp. in **wash and brush-up**).

brushwood ('brʌʃ‚wud) *n.* **1.** cut or broken-off tree branches, twigs, etc. **2.** another word for **brush**[2] (sense 1).

brushwork ('brʌʃ‚wɜːk) *n.* **1.** a characteristic manner of applying paint with a brush: *Rembrandt's brushwork.* **2.** work done with a brush.

THESAURUS

brotherly affectionate, altruistic, amicable, benevolent, cordial, fraternal, friendly, kind, neighbourly, philanthropic, sympathetic

brow 1. air, appearance, aspect, bearing, countenance, eyebrow, face, forehead, front, mien, temple 2. brim, brink, crown, edge, peak, rim, summit, tip, top, verge

browbeat badger, bulldoze (*Inf.*), bully, coerce, cow, domineer, dragoon, hector, intimidate, lord it over, oppress, overawe, overbear, threaten, tyrannize

brown 1. *adj.* auburn, bay, brick, bronze, bronzed, browned, brunette, chestnut, chocolate, coffee, dark, donkey brown, dun, dusky, fuscous, ginger, hazel, nigger brown, rust, sunburnt, tan, tanned, tawny, toasted, umber 2. *v.* cook, fry, grill, sauté, seal, sear

browned off cheesed off (*Brit. sl.*), discontented, discouraged, disgruntled, disheartened, fed up, weary

brown study absorption, abstractedness, abstraction, contemplation, meditation, musing, preoccupation, reflection, reverie, rumination

browse 1. dip into, examine cursorily, flip through, glance at, leaf through, look round, look through, peruse, scan, skim, survey 2. crop, eat, feed, graze, nibble, pasture

bruise *v.* 1. blacken, blemish, contuse, crush, damage, deface, discolour, injure, mar, mark, pound, pulverize 2. displease, grieve, hurt, injure, insult, offend, pain, sting, wound ~*n.* 3. black-and-blue mark, black mark, blemish, contusion, discoloration, injury, mark, swelling

brunt burden, force, full force, impact, pressure, shock, strain, stress, thrust, violence

brush[1] *n.* 1. besom, broom, sweeper 2. clash, conflict, confrontation, encounter, fight, fracas, scrap (*Inf.*), set-to (*Inf.*), skirmish, slight engagement, spot of bother (*Inf.*), tussle ~*v.* 3. buff, clean, paint, polish,

sweep, wash 4. caress, contact, flick, glance, graze, kiss, scrape, stroke, sweep, touch

brush[2] *n.* brushwood, bushes, copse, scrub, shrubs, thicket, undergrowth, underwood

brush aside dismiss, disregard, have no time for, ignore, override, sweep aside

brush-off *n.* cold shoulder, cut, dismissal, go-by (*Sl.*), rebuff, refusal, repudiation, repulse, slight, snub

brush off *v.* cold-shoulder, cut, deny, disdain, dismiss, disown, disregard, ignore, rebuff, refuse, reject, repudiate, scorn, slight, snub, spurn

brush up cram, go over, polish up, read up, refresh one's memory, relearn, revise, study

brusque abrupt, blunt, curt, discourteous, gruff, hasty, impolite, sharp, short, surly, tart, terse, unmannerly

brusque (bruːsk, brʊsk) *adj.* blunt or curt in manner or speech. —**'brusquely** *adv.* —**'brusqueness** *n.*

Brussels carpet ('brʌsəlz) *n.* a worsted carpet with a heavy pile formed by uncut loops of wool on a linen warp.

Brussels lace *n.* a fine lace with a raised or appliqué design.

Brussels sprout *n.* **1.** a variety of cabbage, having a stout stem studded with budlike heads resembling tiny cabbages. **2.** the head of this plant, eaten as a vegetable.

brutal ('bruːtəl) *adj.* **1.** cruel; vicious; savage. **2.** extremely honest or coarse in speech or manner. **3.** harsh; severe; extreme: *brutal cold.* —**bru'tality** *n.* —**'brutally** *adv.*

brutalize *or* **-ise** ('bruːtəˌlaɪz) *vb.* **1.** to make or become brutal. **2.** (*tr.*) to treat brutally. —ˌbrutali'zation *or* -i'sation *n.*

brute (bruːt) *n.* **1. a.** any animal except man; beast; lower animal. **b.** (*as modifier*): *brute nature.* **2.** a brutal person. ~*adj.* (*prenominal*) **3.** wholly instinctive or physical (esp. in **brute strength, brute force**). **4.** without reason or intelligence. **5.** coarse and grossly sensual.

brutish ('bruːtɪʃ) *adj.* **1.** of, relating to, or resembling a brute; animal. **2.** coarse; cruel; stupid. —**'brutishly** *adv.* —**'brutishness** *n.*

bryony *or* **briony** ('braɪənɪ) *n., pl.* **-nies.** any of several herbaceous climbing plants of Europe and N Africa.

bryophyte ('braɪəˌfaɪt) *n.* any plant of the division *Bryophyta*, esp. mosses and liverworts. —**bryophytic** (ˌbraɪə'fɪtɪk) *adj.*

Brythonic (brɪ'θɒnɪk) *n.* **1.** the S group of Celtic languages, consisting of Welsh, Cornish, and Breton. ~*adj.* **2.** of or relating to this group of languages.

B.Sc. *abbrev. for* Bachelor of Science.

BSI *abbrev. for* British Standards Institution.

B.S.T. *abbrev. for:* **1.** British Standard Time. **2.** British Summer Time.

Bt. *abbrev. for* Baronet.

btu *or* **B.Th.U.** *abbrev. for* British thermal unit. U.S. abbrev.: BTU

bubble ('bʌbəl) *n.* **1.** a thin film of liquid forming a hollow globule around air or a gas: *a soap bubble.* **2.** a small globule of air or a gas in a liquid or a solid. **3.** the sound made by a bubbling liquid. **4.** something lacking substance, stability, or seriousness. **5.** a dome, esp. a transparent glass or plastic one. ~*vb.* **6.** to form or cause to form bubbles. **7.** (*intr.*) to move or flow with a gurgling sound. **8.** (*intr.*; often foll. by *over*) to overflow (with excitement, anger, etc.).

bubble and squeak *n. Brit.* a dish of leftover boiled cabbage and potatoes fried together.

bubble bath *n.* **1.** a powder, liquid, or crystals used to scent, soften, and foam in bath water. **2.** a bath to which such a substance has been added.

bubble car *n. Brit.* a small car with a transparent bubble-shaped top.

bubble gum *n.* a type of chewing gum that can be blown into large bubbles.

bubbly ('bʌblɪ) *adj.* **-blier, -bliest. 1.** full of or resembling bubbles. **2.** lively; animated; excited. ~*n.* **3.** *Inf.* champagne.

bubo ('bjuːbəʊ) *n., pl.* **-boes.** *Pathol.* inflammation and swelling of a lymph node, esp. in the armpit or groin. —**bubonic** (bju:'bɒnɪk) *adj.*

bubonic plague *n.* an acute infectious febrile disease characterized by chills, prostration, delirium, and formation of buboes: caused by the bite of an infected rat flea.

buccaneer (ˌbʌkə'nɪə) *n.* **1.** a pirate, esp. one who preyed on Spanish shipping in the Caribbean in the 17th and 18th centuries. ~*vb.* (*intr.*) **2.** to be or act like a buccaneer.

buck[1] (bʌk) *n.* **1. a.** the male of various animals including the goat, hare, kangaroo, rabbit, and reindeer. **b.** (*as modifier*): *a buck antelope.* **2.** *Inf.* a robust spirited young man. **3.** *S. African.* an antelope or deer of either sex. **4.** the act of bucking. ~*vb.* **5.** (*intr.*) (of a horse or other animal) to jump vertically, with legs stiff and back arched. **6.** (*tr.*) (of a horse, etc.) to throw (its rider) by bucking. **7.** (when *intr.*, often foll. by *against* or *at*) *U.S. & Austral. inf.* to resist or oppose obstinately. **8.** (*tr.*; usually *passive*) *Inf.* to cheer or encourage: *I was very bucked at passing the exam.* ~See also **buck up.** —**'bucker** *n.*

buck[2] (bʌk) *n. U.S. & Austral. sl.* a dollar.

buck[3] (bʌk) *n.* **1.** *Poker.* a marker in the jackpot to remind the winner of some obligation when his turn comes to deal. **2. pass the buck.** *Inf.* to shift blame or responsibility onto another.

buckboard ('bʌkˌbɔːd) *n. U.S.* an open four-wheeled horse-drawn carriage with the seat attached to a flexible board between the front and rear axles.

bucket ('bʌkɪt) *n.* **1.** an open-topped roughly cylindrical container; pail. **2.** Also called: **bucketful.** the amount a bucket will hold. **3.** any of various bucket-like parts of a machine, such as the scoop on a mechanical shovel. **4.** *Austral.* a small container for ice cream. **5. kick the bucket.** *Inf.* to die. ~*vb.* **6.** (*tr.*) to carry in or put into a bucket. **7.** (*intr.*; often foll. by *along*) *Inf., chiefly Brit.* to travel or drive fast. **8.** (*tr.*) *Austral. sl.* to criticize or denigrate.

bucket down *vb.* (*intr.*) (of rain) to fall very heavily.

bucket seat *n.* a seat in a car, aircraft, etc., having curved sides.

bucket shop *n. Sl.* **1.** an unregistered firm of stockbrokers that engages in fraudulent speculation. **2.** *Chiefly Brit.* a firm specializing in cheap airline tickets.

buckle ('bʌkəl) *n.* **1.** a clasp for fastening together two loose ends, esp. of a belt or strap, usually consisting of a frame with an attached movable prong. **2.** an ornamental representation of a buckle, as on a shoe. **3.** a kink, bulge, or other distortion. ~*vb.* **4.** to fasten or be fastened with a buckle. **5.** to bend or cause to bend out of shape, esp. as a result of pressure or heat.

buckle down *vb.* (*intr., adv.*) *Inf.* to apply oneself with determination.

buckler ('bʌklə) *n.* **1.** a small round shield worn on the forearm. **2.** a means of protection; defence.

buckram ('bʌkrəm) *n.* **a.** cotton or linen cloth stiffened with size, etc., used in lining or stiffening clothes, bookbinding, etc. **b.** (*as modifier*): *a buckram cover.*

Bucks. (bʌks) *abbrev. for* Buckinghamshire.

buckshee (ˌbʌk'ʃiː) *adj. Brit. sl.* without charge; free.

buckshot ('bʌkˌʃɒt) *n.* lead shot of large size used in shotgun shells, esp. for hunting game.

buckskin ('bʌkˌskɪn) *n.* **1.** the skin of a male deer. **2. a.** a strong greyish-yellow suede leather, originally made from deerskin but now usually made from sheepskin. **b.** (*as modifier*): *buckskin boots.* **3.** a stiffly starched cotton cloth. **4.** a strong and heavy satin-woven woollen fabric.

buckthorn ('bʌkˌθɔːn) *n.* any of several thorny small-flowered shrubs whose berries were formerly used as a purgative.

bucktooth ('bʌkˌtuːθ) *n., pl.* **-teeth.** *Derog.* a projecting upper front tooth.

THESAURUS

brutal 1. barbarous, bloodthirsty, cruel, ferocious, heartless, inhuman, merciless, pitiless, remorseless, ruthless, savage, uncivilized, vicious **2.** beastly, bestial, brute, brutish, carnal, coarse, crude, sensual **3.** bearish, callous, gruff, harsh, impolite, insensitive, rough, rude, severe, uncivil, unfeeling, unmannerly

brutally barbarically, barbarously, brutishly, callously, cruelly, ferociously, fiercely, hardheartedly, heartlessly, in cold blood, inhumanly, meanly, mercilessly, murderously, pitilessly, remorselessly, ruthlessly, savagely, unkindly, viciously

brute *n.* **1.** animal, beast, creature, wild animal **2.** barbarian, beast, devil, fiend, monster, ogre, sadist, savage, swine ~*adj.* **3.** bodily, carnal, fleshly, instinctive, mindless, physical, senseless, unthinking **4.** bestial, coarse, depraved, gross, sensual

bubble *n.* **1.** air ball, bead, blister, blob, drop, droplet, globule, vesicle **2.** bagatelle, delusion, fantasy, illusion, toy, trifle, vanity ~*v.* **3.** boil, effervesce, fizz, foam, froth, percolate, seethe, sparkle **4.** babble, burble, gurgle, murmur, purl, ripple, trickle, trill

bubbly 1. carbonated, curly, effervescent, fizzy, foamy, frothy, lathery, sparkling, sudsy **2.** animated, bouncy, elated, excited, happy, lively, merry

buccaneer corsair, freebooter, pirate, privateer, sea-rover

buckle *n.* **1.** catch, clasp, clip, fastener, hasp **2.** bulge, contortion, distortion, kink, warp ~*v.* **3.** catch, clasp, close, fasten, hook, secure **4.** bend, bulge, cave in, collapse, contort, crumple, distort, fold, twist, warp

buckle down apply oneself, exert oneself, launch into, pitch in, put one's shoulder to the wheel, set to

buck up vb. (adv.) Inf. **1.** to make or cause to make haste. **2.** to make or become more cheerful, confident, etc.

buckwheat ('bʌk₁wiːt) n. **1.** a cereal plant with fragrant white flowers, cultivated, esp. in the U.S., for its seeds. **2.** the edible seeds of this plant, ground into flour or used as animal fodder. **3.** the flour obtained from these seeds.

bucolic (bjuː'kɒlɪk) adj. also **bucolical.** **1.** of the countryside or country life; rustic. **2.** of or relating to shepherds; pastoral. ~n. **3.** (sometimes pl.) a pastoral poem. —**bu'colically** adv.

bud (bʌd) n. **1.** a swelling on a plant stem consisting of overlapping immature leaves or petals. **2. a.** a partially opened flower. **b.** (in combination): rosebud. **3.** any small budlike outgrowth: taste buds. **4.** something small or immature. **5.** an asexually produced outgrowth in simple organisms such as yeasts that develops into a new individual. **6. nip in the bud.** to put an end to (an idea, movement, etc.) in its initial stages. ~vb. **budding, budded. 7.** (intr.) (of plants and some animals) to produce buds. **8.** (intr.) to begin to develop or grow. **9.** (tr.) Horticulture. to graft (a bud) from one plant onto another.

Buddhism ('budɪzəm) n. a religious teaching propagated by the Buddha and his followers, which declares that by destroying greed, hatred, and delusion, which are the causes of all suffering, man can attain perfect enlightenment. —'**Buddhist** n., adj.

buddleia ('bʌdlɪə) n. an ornamental shrub which has long spikes of mauve flowers. Also called: **butterfly bush.**

buddy ('bʌdɪ) n., pl. -**dies.** Chiefly U.S. an informal word for **friend.** Also (as a term of address): **bud.**

budge (bʌdʒ) vb. (usually used with a negative) **1.** to move, however slightly. **2.** to change or cause to change opinions, etc.

budgerigar ('bʌdʒərɪ₁gɑː) n. a small green Australian parrot: a popular cage bird bred in many different coloured varieties.

budget ('bʌdʒɪt) n. **1.** a summary of probable financial outlays and incomes over a specified period. **2.** the total amount of money allocated for a specific purpose during a specified period. **3.** a stock, quantity, or supply. ~vb. **4.** (tr.) to enter or provide for in a budget. **5.** to plan the expenditure of (money, time, etc.). **6.** (intr.) to make a budget.

Budget ('bʌdʒɪt) n. **the.** an estimate of British government expenditures and revenues for the ensuing fiscal year presented annually to the House of Commons by the Chancellor of the Exchequer.

budget account n. an account with a department store, etc., enabling a customer to make monthly payments to cover his past and future purchases.

budgie ('bʌdʒɪ) n. Inf. short for **budgerigar.**

buff¹ (bʌf) n. **1. a.** a soft thick flexible undyed leather made chiefly from the skins of buffalo, oxen, and elk. **b.** (as modifier): a buff coat. **2. a.** a dull yellow or yellowish-brown colour. **b.** (as adj.): buff paint. **3.** Also called: **buffer. a.** a cloth or pad of material used for polishing an object. **b.** a disc or wheel impregnated with a fine abrasive for polishing metals, etc. **4.** Inf. one's bare skin (esp. in **in the buff**). ~vb. **5.** to clean or polish (a

metal, floor, shoes, etc.) with a buff. **6.** to remove the grain surface of (a leather).

buff² (bʌf) n. Arch. a blow or buffet (now only in **blind man's buff**).

buff³ (bʌf) n. Inf. an expert on or devotee of a given subject.

buffalo ('bʌfə₁ləʊ) n., pl. -**loes, -los,** or -**lo. 1.** a type of cattle, mostly found in game reserves in southern and eastern Africa and having upward-curving horns. **2.** short for **water buffalo. 3.** a U.S. name for **bison** (sense 1).

buffer¹ ('bʌfə) n. **1.** one of a pair of spring-loaded steel pads attached at both ends of railway vehicles and at the end of a railway track to reduce shock due to contact. **2.** a person or thing that lessens shock or protects from damaging impact, circumstances, etc. **3.** Chem. **a.** an ionic compound added to a solution to resist changes in its acidity or alkalinity and thus stabilize its pH. **b.** Also called: **buffer solution.** a solution containing such a compound. **4.** Computers. a memory device for temporarily storing data.

buffer² ('bʌfə) n. Brit. inf. a stupid or bumbling man (esp. in **old buffer**).

buffer state n. a small and usually neutral state between two rival powers.

buffet¹ n. **1.** ('bʌfɪt). a counter where light refreshments are served. **2.** ('bufeɪ). **a.** a meal at which guests help themselves from a number of dishes. **b.** (as modifier): a buffet lunch. **3.** ('bʌfɪt, 'bufeɪ). a sideboard, esp. of the 16th or 17th century.

buffet² ('bʌfɪt) vb. -**feting, -feted. 1.** (tr.) to knock against or about; batter. **2.** (tr.) to hit, esp. with the fist; cuff. **3.** to force (one's way), as through a crowd. **4.** (intr.) to struggle; battle. ~n. **5.** a blow, esp. with a fist or hand. —'**buffeter** n.

buffet car ('bufeɪ) n. Brit. a railway coach where light refreshments are served.

buffoon (bə'fuːn) n. **1.** a person who amuses others by ridiculous or odd behaviour, jokes, etc. **2.** a foolish person. —**buf'foonery** n.

bug (bʌg) n. **1.** an insect having piercing and sucking mouthparts specialized as a beak. **2.** Chiefly U.S. any insect. **3.** Inf. **a.** a microorganism, esp. a bacterium, that produces disease. **b.** a disease, esp. a stomach infection, caused by a microorganism. **4.** Inf. an obsessive idea, hobby, etc.; craze. **5.** (often pl.) Inf. a fault, as in a machine. **6.** Inf. a concealed microphone used for recording conversations, as in spying. ~vb. **bugging, bugged.** Inf. **7.** (tr.) to irritate; bother. **8.** (tr.) to conceal a microphone in (a room, etc.). **9.** (intr.) U.S. (of eyes) to protrude.

bugbear ('bʌg₁bɛə) n. **1.** a thing that causes obsessive anxiety. **2.** (in English folklore) a goblin in the form of a bear.

bugger ('bʌgə) n. **1.** a person who practises buggery. **2.** Taboo sl. a person or thing considered to be contemptible, unpleasant, or difficult. **3.** Sl. a humorous or affectionate term for a man or child: a friendly little bugger. **4. bugger all.** Sl. nothing. ~vb. **5.** to practise buggery (with). **6.** (tr.) Sl., chiefly Brit. to ruin, complicate, or frustrate. **7.** Sl. to tire; weary. ~interj. **8.** Taboo sl. an exclamation of annoyance or disappointment..

bugger about or **around** vb. (adv.) Sl. **1.** (intr.) to

THESAURUS

buck up 1. get a move on, hasten, hurry up, shake a leg, speed up 2. brighten, cheer up, encourage, hearten, inspirit, perk up, rally, take heart

bucolic agrarian, agricultural, country, pastoral, rural, rustic

bud 1. n. embryo, germ, shoot, sprout 2. v. burgeon, burst forth, develop, grow, pullulate, shoot, sprout

budding beginning, burgeoning, developing, embryonic, fledgling, flowering, germinal, growing, incipient, nascent, potential, promising

budge 1. dislodge, give way, inch, move, propel, push, remove, roll, shift, slide, stir 2. bend, change, convince, give way, influence, persuade, sway, yield

budget 1. n. allocation, allowance, cost, finances, financial statement, fiscal estimate, funds, means, resources 2. v. allocate, appor-

tion, cost, cost out, estimate, plan, ration

buff¹ 1. adj. sandy, straw, tan, yellowish, yellowish-brown 2. n. **in the buff** bare, in one's birthday suit (Inf.), in the altogether (Inf.), in the raw (Inf.), naked, nude, unclad, unclothed, with bare skin 3. v. brush, burnish, polish, rub, shine, smooth

buff² addict, admirer, aficionado, connoisseur, devotee, enthusiast, expert, fan, fiend (Inf.), freak (Sl.)

buffer bulwark, bumper, cushion, fender, intermediary, safeguard, screen, shield, shock absorber

buffet¹ n. café, cafeteria, cold table, counter, cupboard, refreshment-counter, salad bar, sideboard, snack bar

buffet² 1. v. bang, batter, beat, box, bump, clobber (Sl.), cuff, flail, knock, pound, pummel, push, rap, shove, slap, strike, thump, wallop (Inf.) 2. n. bang, blow, box, bump,

cuff, jolt, knock, push, rap, shove, slap, smack, thump, wallop (Inf.)

buffoon clown, comedian, comic, droll, fool, harlequin, jester, joker, merry-andrew, silly billy (Inf.), wag

bug n. Inf. bacterium, disease, germ, infection, microorganism, virus 2. craze, fad, mania, obsession, rage 3. blemish, catch, defect, error, failing, fault, flaw, gremlin, imperfection, snarl-up (Inf.) ~v. 4. Inf. annoy, badger, bother, disturb, get on (someone's) wick (Sl.), harass, irk, irritate, needle (Inf.), nettle, pester, plague, vex 5. eavesdrop, listen in, spy, tap, wiretap

bugbear anathema, bane, bête noire, bogey, bugaboo, devil, dread, fiend, horror, nightmare, pet hate

fool about and waste time. **2.** (*tr.*) to create difficulties or complications for (a person).

bugger off *vb. Taboo sl.* (*intr., adv.*) to go away; depart.

buggery ('bʌgərɪ) *n.* anal intercourse between a man and another man, a woman, or an animal.

buggy[1] ('bʌgɪ) *n., pl.* **-gies. 1.** a light horse-drawn carriage having either four wheels (esp. in the U.S.) or two wheels (esp. in Britain and India). **2.** any small light cart or vehicle, such as a baby buggy, golf buggy, or beach buggy.

buggy[2] ('bʌgɪ) *adj.* **-gier, -giest.** infested with bugs.

bugle ('bju:gəl) *n.* **1.** *Music.* a brass instrument similar to the cornet but usually without valves: used for military fanfares, signal calls, etc. ~*vb.* **2.** (*intr.*) to play or sound (on) a bugle. —'**bugler** *n.*

build (bɪld) *vb.* **building, built. 1.** to make, construct, or form by joining parts or materials: *to build a house.* **2.** (*tr.*) to order the building of: *the government builds most of our hospitals.* **3.** (foll. by *on* or *upon*) to base; found: *his theory was not built on facts.* **4.** (*tr.*) to establish and develop: *it took ten years to build a business.* **5.** (*tr.*) to make in a particular way or for a particular purpose: *the car was not built for speed.* **6.** (*intr.*; often foll. by *up*) to increase in intensity. ~*n.* **7.** physical form, figure, or proportions: *a man with an athletic build.* ~See also **build up.**

builder ('bɪldə) *n.* a person who builds, esp. one who contracts for and supervises the construction or repair of buildings.

building ('bɪldɪŋ) *n.* **1.** something built with a roof and walls. **2.** the act, business, occupation, or art of building houses, boats, etc.

building society *n.* a cooperative banking enterprise financed by deposits on which interest is paid and from which mortgage loans are advanced on homes and real estate.

build up *vb.* (*adv.*) **1.** (*tr.*) to construct gradually, systematically, and in stages. **2.** to increase or strengthen, esp. by degrees: *the murmur built up to a roar.* **3.** (*tr.*) to improve the health or physique of (a person). **4.** to prepare for or gradually approach a climax, as in a story. ~*n.* **5.** progressive increase in number, size, etc.: *the build-up of industry.* **6.** extravagant publicity or praise, esp. in the form of a campaign. **7.** *Mil.* the process of attaining the required strength of forces and equipment.

built (bɪlt) *vb.* the past tense or past participle of **build.**

built-in *adj.* **1.** made or incorporated as an integral part: *a built-in cupboard.* **2.** essential; inherent. ~*n.* **3.** *Austral.* a built-in cupboard.

built-up *adj.* **1.** having many buildings (esp. in **built-up area**). **2.** increased by the addition of parts: *built-up heels.*

bulb (bʌlb) *n.* **1.** a rounded organ of vegetative reproduction in plants such as the tulip and onion: a flattened stem bearing a central shoot surrounded by fleshy nutritive inner leaves and thin brown outer leaves. **2.** a plant, such as a hyacinth or daffodil, that grows from a bulb. **3.** any bulb-shaped thing. —**bulbous** ('bʌlbəs) *or* **bulbaceous** (bʌl'beɪʃəs) *adj.*

bulge (bʌldʒ) *n.* **1.** a swelling or an outward curve. **2.** a sudden increase in number, esp. of population. ~*vb.* **3.** to swell outwards. —'**bulgingly** *adv.* —'**bulgy** *adj.*

bulk (bʌlk) *n.* **1.** volume, size, or magnitude, esp. when great. **2.** the main part: *the bulk of the work is repeti-* *tious.* **3.** a large body, esp. of a person. **4.** the part of food which passes unabsorbed through the digestive system. **5. in bulk. a.** in large quantities. **b.** (of a cargo, etc.) unpackaged. ~*vb.* **6.** to cohere or cause to cohere in a mass. **7. bulk large.** to be or seem important or prominent.

bulk buying *n.* the purchase of goods in large amounts, often at reduced prices.

bulkhead ('bʌlk,hɛd) *n. Naut.* any upright wall-like partition in a vessel.

bulky ('bʌlkɪ) *adj.* **bulkier, bulkiest.** very large and massive, esp. so as to be unwieldy. —'**bulkily** *adv.* —'**bulkiness** *n.*

bull[1] (bʊl) *n.* **1.** any male bovine animal, esp. one that is sexually mature. **2.** the male of various other animals including the elephant and whale. **3.** a very large, strong, or aggressive person. **4.** *Stock Exchange.* **a.** a speculator who buys in anticipation of rising prices in order to make a profit on resale. **b.** (*as modifier*): *a bull market.* Cf. **bear**[2] (sense 5). **5.** *Chiefly Brit.* short for **bull's-eye** (senses 1, 2). **6.** *Sl.* short for **bullshit. 7. a bull in a china shop.** a clumsy person. **8. take the bull by the horns.** to face and tackle a difficulty without shirking. ~*adj.* **9.** male; masculine: *a bull elephant.* **10.** large; strong. —'**bullish** *adj.*

bull[2] (bʊl) *n.* a ludicrously self-contradictory or inconsistent statement.

bull[3] (bʊl) *n.* a formal document issued by the pope.

Bull (bʊl) *n.* **the.** the constellation Taurus, the second sign of the zodiac.

bulldog ('bʊl,dɒg) *n.* a sturdy thickset breed of dog with an undershot jaw, broad head, and a muscular body.

bulldog clip *n.* a clip for holding papers together, consisting of two T-shaped metal clamps held in place by a cylindrical spring.

bulldoze ('bʊl,dəʊz) *vb.* (*tr.*) **1.** to move, demolish, flatten, etc., with a bulldozer. **2.** *Inf.* to force; push. **3.** *Inf.* to intimidate or coerce.

bulldozer ('bʊl,dəʊzə) *n.* **1.** a powerful tractor fitted with caterpillar tracks and a blade at the front, used for moving earth, rocks, etc. **2.** *Inf.* a person who bulldozes.

bullet ('bʊlɪt) *n.* **1. a.** a small metallic missile enclosed in a cartridge, used as the projectile of a gun, rifle, etc. **b.** the entire cartridge. **2.** something resembling a bullet, esp. in shape or effect. —'**bullet-,like** *adj.*

bulletin ('bʊlɪtɪn) *n.* **1.** an official statement on a matter of public interest. **2.** a broadcast summary of the news. **3.** a periodical publication of an association, etc. ~*vb.* **4.** (*tr.*) to make known by bulletin.

bullfight ('bʊl,faɪt) *n.* a traditional Spanish, Portuguese, and Latin American spectacle in which a matador baits and usually kills a bull in an arena. —'**bull,fighter** *n.* —'**bull,fighting** *n.*

bullfinch ('bʊl,fɪntʃ) *n.* **1.** a common European finch: the male has a bright red throat and breast. **2.** any of various similar finches.

bullfrog ('bʊl,frɒg) *n.* any of various large American frogs having a loud deep croak.

bull-headed *adj.* blindly obstinate; stupid. —,**bull-'headedly** *adv.* —,**bull-'headedness** *n.*

bullion ('bʊljən) *n.* **1.** gold or silver in mass. **2.** gold or silver in the form of bars and ingots, suitable for further processing.

bull-necked *adj.* having a short thick neck.

---

build *v.* **1.** assemble, construct, erect, fabricate, form, make, put up, raise **2.** base, begin, constitute, establish, formulate, found, inaugurate, initiate, institute, originate, set up, start **3.** accelerate, amplify, augment, develop, enlarge, escalate, extend, improve, increase, intensify, strengthen ~*n.* **4.** body, figure, form, frame, physique, shape, structure

building **1.** domicile, dwelling, edifice, fabric, house, pile, structure **2.** architecture, construction, erection, fabricating, raising

build-up **1.** accumulation, development, enlargement, escalation, expansion, gain, growth, increase **2.** ballyhoo (*Inf.*), hype (*Sl.*), plug (*Inf.*), promotion, publicity, puff **3.** accretion, accumulation, heap, load, mass, stack, stockpile, store

built-in essential, implicit, in-built, included, incorporated, inherent, inseparable, integral, part and parcel of

bulge *n.* **1.** bump, lump, projection, protrusion, protuberance, swelling **2.** boost, increase, intensification, rise, surge ~*v.* **3.** bag, dilate, distend, enlarge, expand, project, protrude, puff out, sag, stand out, stick out, swell, swell out

bulk **1.** amplitude, bigness, dimensions, immensity, largeness, magnitude, massiveness, size, substance, volume, weight **2.** better part, body, generality, lion's share, main part, majority, major part, mass, most, nearly all, plurality, preponderance **3. bulk large** be important, carry weight, dominate, loom, loom large, preponderate, stand out,

threaten

bulky big, colossal, cumbersome, enormous, heavy, huge, hulking, immense, mammoth, massive, massy, ponderous, substantial, unmanageable, unwieldy, very large, voluminous, weighty

bulldoze **1.** demolish, flatten, level, raze **2.** drive, force, propel, push, shove, thrust **3.** browbeat, bully, coerce, cow, hector, intimidate

bullet ball, missile, pellet, projectile, shot, slug

bulletin account, announcement, communication, communiqué, dispatch, message, news flash, notification, report, statement

bull-headed headstrong, inflexible, mul-

bullock ('bulǝk) n. 1. a gelded bull; steer. ~vb. 2. (intr.) Austral. inf. to work hard and long.

bullring ('bul͵rɪŋ) n. an arena for bullfighting.

bullroarer ('bul͵rɔːrǝ) n. a wooden slat attached to a thong that makes a roaring sound when the thong is whirled: used esp. by Australian Aborigines in religious rites.

bull's-eye n. 1. the small central disc of a target, usually the highest valued area. 2. a shot hitting this. 3. Inf. something that exactly achieves its aim. 4. a small circular or oval window or opening. 5. a thick disc of glass set into a ship's deck, etc., to admit light. 6. the glass boss at the centre of a sheet of blown glass. 7. a. a small thick plano-convex lens used as a condenser. b. a lamp or lantern containing such a lens. 8. a peppermint-flavoured boiled sweet.

bullshit ('bul͵ʃɪt) Taboo sl. ~n. 1. exaggerated or foolish talk; nonsense. 2. deceitful or pretentious talk. 3. (in the British Army) exaggerated zeal, esp. for ceremonial drill, cleaning, polishing, etc. Usually shortened to **bull.** ~vb. **-shitting, -shitted.** 4. (intr.) to talk in an exaggerated or foolish manner. 5. (tr.) to talk bullshit to.

bull terrier n. a breed of terrier having a short smooth coat, developed by crossing a bulldog with the original English terrier.

bully ('bulɪ) n., pl. **-lies.** 1. a person who hurts, persecutes, or intimidates weaker people. 2. a small New Zealand freshwater fish. ~vb. **-lying, -lied.** 3. (when tr., often foll. by into) to hurt, intimidate, or persecute (a weaker or smaller person), esp. to make him do something. ~adj. 4. dashing; jolly: my bully boy. 5. Inf. very good; fine. ~interj. 6. Also: **bully for you, him,** etc. Inf. well done! bravo!

bully beef n. canned corned beef. Often shortened to **bully.**

bully-off Hockey. ~n. 1. the method by which a game is started. Two opposing players stand with the ball between them and alternately strike their sticks together and against the ground three times before trying to hit the ball. ~vb. **bully off.** 2. (intr., adv.) to start play with a bully-off. ~Often shortened to **bully.**

bulrush ('bul͵rʌʃ) n. 1. Also called: **cat's-tail.** any tall reedlike marsh plant having thick straplike leaves and flowers in long dense brown cylindrical spikes. 2. a grasslike marsh plant used for making mats, chair seats, etc. 3. a biblical word for **papyrus** (the plant).

bulwark ('bulwǝk) n. 1. a wall or similar structure used as a fortification; rampart. 2. a person or thing acting as a defence. 3. (often pl.) Naut. a solid vertical fencelike structure along the outward sides of a deck. 4. a breakwater or mole. ~vb. 5. (tr.) to defend or fortify with or as if with a bulwark.

bum¹ (bʌm) n. Brit. sl. the buttocks or anus.

bum² (bʌm) Inf., chiefly U.S. ~n. 1. a disreputable loafer or idler. 2. a tramp; hobo. ~vb. **bumming, bummed.** 3. (tr.) to get by begging; cadge: to bum a lift. 4. (intr.; often foll. by around) to live by begging or as a vagrant or loafer. 5. (intr.; usually foll. by around) to spend time to no good purpose; loaf; idle. ~adj. 6. (prenominal) of poor quality; useless.

bumbailiff (͵bʌm'beɪlɪf) n. Brit. derog. (formerly) an of-

ficer employed to collect debts and arrest debtors.

bumble ('bʌmbǝl) vb. 1. to speak or do in a clumsy, muddled, or inefficient way. 2. (intr.) to proceed unsteadily. —'**bumbler** n. —'**bumbling** adj.

bumblebee ('bʌmbǝl͵biː) or **humblebee** n. any large hairy social bee of temperate regions.

bumf (bʌmf) n. a variant spelling of **bumph.**

bump (bʌmp) vb. 1. (when intr., usually foll. by against or into) to knock or strike with a jolt. 2. (intr.; often foll. by along) to travel or proceed in jerks and jolts. 3. (tr.) to hurt by knocking. 4. Cricket. to bowl (a ball) so that it bounces high on pitching or (of a ball) to bounce high when bowled. ~n. 5. an impact; knock; jolt; collision. 6. a dull thud or other noise from an impact or collision. 7. the shock of a blow or collision. 8. a lump on the body caused by a blow. 9. a protuberance, as on a road surface. 10. any of the natural protuberances of the human skull, said by phrenologists to indicate underlying faculties and character. ~See also **bump into, bump off** etc. —'**bumpy** adj.

bumper¹ ('bʌmpǝ) n. 1. a horizontal usually metal bar attached to the front or rear end of a car, lorry, etc., to protect against damage from impact. 2. Cricket. a ball bowled so that it bounces high on pitching; bouncer.

bumper² ('bʌmpǝ) n. 1. a glass, tankard, etc., filled to the brim, esp. as a toast. 2. an unusually large or fine example of something. ~adj. 3. unusually large, fine, or abundant: a bumper crop.

bumph or **bumf** (bʌmf) n. Brit. 1. Inf., derog. official documents, forms, etc. 2. Sl. toilet paper.

bump into vb. (intr., prep.) to meet by chance; encounter unexpectedly.

bumpkin ('bʌmpkɪn) n. an awkward simple rustic person (esp. in **country bumpkin**).

bump off vb. (tr., adv.) Sl. to murder; kill.

bumptious ('bʌmpʃǝs) adj. offensively self-assertive or conceited. —'**bumptiously** adv. —'**bumptiousness** n.

bump up vb. (tr., adv.) Inf. to raise or increase.

bun (bʌn) n. 1. a small roll, similar to bread but usually containing sweetening, currants, etc. 2. a hair style in which long hair is gathered into a bun shape at the back of the head.

bunch (bʌntʃ) n. 1. a number of things growing, fastened, or grouped together: a bunch of grapes; a bunch of keys. 2. a collection; group: a bunch of queries. 3. Inf. a group or company: a bunch of boys. ~vb. 4. (sometimes foll. by up) to group or be grouped into a bunch.

buncombe ('bʌŋkǝm) n. a variant spelling (esp. U.S.) of **bunkum.**

bundle ('bʌndǝl) n. 1. a number of things or a quantity of material gathered or loosely bound together: a bundle of sticks. Related adj.: **fascicular.** 2. something wrapped or tied for carrying; package. 3. Sl. a large sum of money. 4. **go a bundle on.** Sl. to be extremely fond of. 5. Biol. a collection of strands of specialized tissue such as nerve fibres. 6. **drop one's bundle.** Austral. sl. to panic or give up hope. ~vb. 7. (tr.; often foll. by up) to make into a bundle. 8. (foll. by out, off, into, etc.) to go or cause to go, esp. roughly or unceremoniously. 9.

THESAURUS

ish, obstinate, pig-headed, stiff-necked, stubborn, stupid, tenacious, uncompromising, unyielding, wilful

bullish assured, bold, confident, expectant, improving, positive, rising

bully 1. n. big bully, browbeater, bully boy, coercer, intimidator, oppressor, persecutor, ruffian, tormentor, tough 2. v. bluster, browbeat, bulldoze (Inf.), bullyrag, coerce, cow, domineer, hector, intimidate, oppress, overbear, persecute, push around (Sl.), ride roughshod over, swagger, terrorize, tyrannize 3. adj. admirable, excellent, fine, nifty (Inf.), very good 4. interj. bravo, capital, good, grand, great, well done

bulwark 1. bastion, buttress, defence, embankment, fortification, outwork, partition, rampart, redoubt 2. buffer, guard, mainstay, safeguard, security, support

bumbling awkward, blundering, botching, bungling, clumsy, incompetent, inefficient, inept, lumbering, maladroit, muddled,

stumbling

bump v. 1. bang, collide (with), crash, hit, knock, slam, smash into, strike 2. bounce, jar, jerk, jolt, jostle, jounce, rattle, shake 3. budge, dislodge, displace, move, remove, shift ~n. 4. bang, blow, collision, crash, hit, impact, jar, jolt, knock, rap, shock, smash, thud, thump 5. bulge, contusion, hump, knob, knot, lump, node, nodule, protuberance, swelling

bumper adj. abundant, bountiful, excellent, exceptional, jumbo (Inf.), massive, prodigal, spanking (Inf.), teeming, unusual, whacking (Inf.), whopping (Inf.)

bump into chance upon, come across, encounter, happen upon, light upon, meet, meet up with, run across, run into

bumpkin boor, clodhopper, clown, country bumpkin, hick (U.S. inf.), hillbilly, lout, lubber, oaf, peasant, rustic, yokel

bump off assassinate, dispatch, do away with, do in (Sl.), eliminate, finish off, kill,

knock off (Sl.), liquidate, murder, remove, wipe out (Inf.)

bumptious arrogant, boastful, brash, cocky, conceited, egotistic, forward, full of oneself, impudent, overbearing, overconfident, presumptuous, pushy (Inf.), self-assertive, showy, swaggering, vainglorious, vaunting

bumpy bone-breaking, bouncy, choppy, irregular, jarring, jerky, jolting, jolty, knobby, lumpy, pitted, potholed, rough, rutted, uneven

bunch n. 1. assortment, batch, bouquet, bundle, clump, cluster, collection, heap, lot, mass, number, parcel, pile, quantity, sheaf, spray, stack, tuft 2. band, crew (Inf.), crowd, flock, gang, gathering, group, knot, mob, multitude, party, swarm, team, troop ~v. 3. assemble, bundle, cluster, collect, congregate, cram together, crowd, flock, group, herd, huddle, mass, pack

(tr.; usually foll. by *into)* to push or throw, esp. quickly and untidily. **10.** *(intr.)* to sleep or lie in one's clothes on the same bed as one's betrothed: formerly a custom in New England, Wales, and elsewhere. —'**bundler** *n.*

bundle up *vb. (adv.)* **1.** to dress (somebody) warmly and snugly. **2.** *(tr.)* to make (something) into a bundle or bundles, esp. by tying.

bundu ('bundu) *n. S. African sl.* a largely uninhabited wild region far from towns.

bun fight *n. Brit. sl.* a tea party.

bung (bʌŋ) *n.* **1.** a stopper, esp. of cork or rubber, for a cask, etc. **2.** short for **bunghole**. ~*vb. (tr.)* **3.** (often foll. by *up) Inf.* to close or seal with or as with a bung. **4.** *Brit. sl.* to throw; sling. **5. bung (it) on.** *Austral. sl.* to behave in a pretentious manner.

bungalow ('bʌŋgə,ləʊ) *n.* a one-storey house, sometimes with an attic.

bunghole ('bʌŋ,həʊl) *n.* a hole in a cask, barrel, etc., through which liquid can be drained.

bungle ('bʌŋgəl) *vb.* **1.** *(tr.)* to spoil (an operation) through clumsiness, incompetence, etc.; botch. ~*n.* **2.** a clumsy or unsuccessful performance; mistake; botch. —'**bungler** *n.* —'**bungling** *adj., n.*

bunion ('bʌnjən) *n.* an inflamed swelling of the first joint of the big toe.

bunk[1] (bʌŋk) *n.* **1.** a narrow shelflike bed fixed along a wall. **2.** short for **bunk bed**. **3.** *Inf.* any place where one sleeps. ~*vb.* **4.** *(intr.;* often foll. by *down)* to prepare to sleep: *he bunked down on the floor.* **5.** *(intr.)* to occupy a bunk or bed.

bunk[2] (bʌŋk) *n. Inf.* short for **bunkum** (sense 1).

bunk[3] (bʌŋk) *n. Brit. sl.* a hurried departure, usually under suspicious circumstances (esp. in **do a bunk).**

bunk bed *n.* one of a pair of beds constructed one above the other to save space.

bunker ('bʌŋkə) *n.* **1.** a large storage container or tank, as for coal. **2.** Also called (esp. U.S.): **sand trap.** an obstacle on a golf course, usually a sand-filled hollow bordered by a ridge. **3.** an underground shelter with a bank and embrasures for guns above ground. ~*vb.* **4.** *(tr.) Golf.* **a.** to drive (the ball) into a bunker. **b.** *(passive)* to have one's ball trapped in a bunker.

bunkum *or* **buncombe** ('bʌŋkəm) *n.* **1.** empty talk; nonsense. **2.** *Chiefly U.S.* empty or insincere speech-making by a politician.

bunny ('bʌni) *n., pl.* **-nies. 1.** Also called: **bunny rabbit.** a child's word for **rabbit** (sense 1). **2.** Also called: **bunny girl.** a night-club hostess whose costume includes rabbit-like tail and ears. **3.** *Austral. sl.* a mug; dupe.

Bunsen burner ('bʌnsən) *n.* a gas burner consisting of a metal tube with an adjustable air valve at the base.

bunting[1] ('bʌntɪŋ) *n.* **1.** a coarse, loosely woven cotton fabric used for flags, etc. **2.** decorative flags, pennants, and streamers.

bunting[2] ('bʌntɪŋ) *n.* any of numerous seed-eating songbirds of the Old World and North America. They all have short stout bills.

buoy (bɔɪ; *U.S.* 'buːɪ) *n.* **1.** a distinctively shaped and coloured float, anchored to the bottom, for designating moorings, navigable channels, or obstructions in a body of water. See also **life buoy.** ~*vb.* **2.** *(tr.;* usually foll. by *up)* to prevent from sinking: *the life belt buoyed him*

up. **3.** *(tr.;* usually foll. by *up)* to raise the spirits of; hearten. **4.** *(tr.) Naut.* to mark (a channel or obstruction) with a buoy or buoys. **5.** *(intr.)* to rise to the surface; float.

buoyancy ('bɔɪənsɪ) *n.* **1.** the ability to float in a liquid or to rise in liquid, air, or other gas. **2.** the tendency of a fluid to keep a body afloat. **3.** the ability to recover quickly after setbacks; resilience. **4.** cheerfulness. —'**buoyant** *adj.*

BUPA ('bjuːp) *n. acronym for* British United Provident Association, a private health insurance scheme.

bur (bɜː) *n.* **1.** a seed vessel or flower head having hooks or prickles. **2.** any plant that produces burs. **3.** a person or thing that clings like a bur. **4.** a small surgical or dental drill. ~*vb.* **burring, burred. 5.** *(tr.)* to remove burs from. ~Also: **burr.**

burble ('bɜːbəl) *vb.* **1.** to make or utter with a bubbling sound; gurgle. **2.** *(intr.;* often foll. by *away* or *on)* to talk quickly and excitedly. ~*n.* **3.** a bubbling or gurgling sound. **4.** a flow of excited speech. —'**burbler** *n.*

burbot ('bɜːbət) *n., pl.* **-bots** *or* **-bot.** a freshwater gadoid food fish that has barbels around its mouth and occurs in Europe, Asia, and North America.

burden[1] ('bɜːdən) *n.* **1.** something that is carried; load. **2.** something that is exacting, oppressive, or difficult to bear. Related adj.: **onerous. 3.** *Naut.* **a.** the cargo capacity of a ship. **b.** the weight of a ship's cargo. ~*vb. (tr.)* **4.** (sometimes foll. by *up)* to put or impose a burden on; load. **5.** to weigh down; oppress. —'**burdensome** *adj.*

burden[2] ('bɜːdən) *n.* **1.** a line of words recurring at the end of each verse of a song; chorus or refrain. **2.** the theme of a speech, book, etc. **3.** another word for **bourdon.**

burdock ('bɜː,dɒk) *n.* a coarse weedy Eurasian plant having large heart-shaped leaves, tiny purple flowers surrounded by hooked bristles, and burlike fruits.

bureau ('bjʊərəʊ) *n., pl.* **-reaus** *or* **-reaux** (-rəʊz). **1.** *Chiefly Brit.* a writing desk with pigeonholes, drawers, etc., against which the writing surface can be closed when not in use. **2.** *U.S.* a chest of drawers. **3.** an office or agency, esp. one providing services for the public. **4.** a government department.

bureaucracy (bjʊə'rɒkrəsɪ) *n., pl.* **-cies. 1.** a system of administration based upon organization into bureaus, division of labour, a hierarchy of authority, etc. **2.** government by such a system. **3.** government or other officials collectively. **4.** any administration in which action is impeded by unnecessary official procedures.

bureaucrat ('bjʊərə,kræt) *n.* **1.** an official in a bureaucracy. **2.** an official who adheres to bureaucracy, esp. rigidly. —,**bureau'cratic** *adj.* —,**bureau'cratically** *adv.*

bureaux *n.* a plural of **bureau.**

burette *or* **buret** (bjʊ'rɛt) *n.* a graduated glass tube with a stopcock on one end for dispensing and transferring known volumes of fluids, esp. liquids.

burgeon *or* **bourgeon** ('bɜːdʒən) *vb.* **1.** (often foll. by *forth* or *out)* (of a plant) to sprout (buds). **2.** *(intr.;* often foll. by *forth* or *out)* to develop or grow rapidly; flourish.

burgess ('bɜːdʒɪs) *n.* **1.** (in England) a citizen, freeman, or inhabitant of a borough. **2.** *English history.* a Member of Parliament from a borough, corporate town, or university.

burgh ('bʌrə) *n.* **1.** (in Scotland) a town with a degree of

---

THESAURUS

bundle *n.* **1.** accumulation, assortment, batch, bunch, collection, group, heap, mass, pile, quantity, stack **2.** bag, bale, box, carton, crate, pack, package, packet, pallet, parcel, roll ~*v.* **3.** bale, bind, fasten, pack, package, palletize, tie, tie together, tie up, truss, wrap **4.** *With* out, off, into, *etc.* hurry, hustle, push, rush, shove, throw, thrust **5.** *With* up clothe warmly, muffle up, swathe, wrap up

bungle blunder, bodge *(Inf.)*, botch, butcher, cock up *(Sl.)*, foul up, fudge, louse up *(Sl.)*, make a mess of, mar, mess up, miscalculate, mismanage, muff, ruin, screw up *(Inf.)*, spoil

bungling awkward, blundering, botching, cack-handed *(Inf.)*, clumsy, ham-fisted *(Inf.)*, ham-handed *(Inf.)*, incompetent, inept, maladroit, unskilful

bunk, bunkum balderdash, baloney *(Inf.)*, bilge *(Inf.)*, bosh *(Inf.)*, garbage, havers *(Scot.)*, hooey *(Sl.)*, horsefeathers *(U.S.*

inf.), nonsense, piffle *(Inf.)*, poppycock *(Inf.)*, rot, rubbish, stuff and nonsense, tarradiddle, tomfoolery, tommyrot, tosh *(Inf.)*, trash, truck *(Inf.)*, twaddle

buoy **1.** *n.* beacon, float, guide, marker, signal **2.** *v. With* upboost, cheer, cheer up, encourage, hearten, keep afloat, lift, raise, support, sustain

buoyancy **1.** floatability, lightness, weightlessness **2.** animation, bounce *(Inf.)*, cheerfulness, cheeriness, good humour, high spirits, liveliness, pep, spiritedness, sunniness, zing *(Inf.)*

buoyant 1. afloat, floatable, floating, light, weightless **2.** animated, blithe, bouncy, breezy, bright, carefree, cheerful, debonair, happy, jaunty, joyful, light-hearted, lively, peppy *(Inf.)*, sunny, vivacious

burden *n.* **1.** affliction, anxiety, care, clog, encumbrance, grievance, load, millstone, ob-

struction, onus, responsibility, sorrow, strain, stress, trial, trouble, weight, worry **2.** *Naut.* cargo, freight, lading, tonnage ~*v.* **3.** bother, encumber, handicap, load, oppress, overload, overwhelm, saddle with, strain, tax, weigh down, worry

bureau 1. desk, writing desk **2.** agency, branch, department, division, office, service

bureaucracy 1. administration, authorities, civil service, corridors of power, directorate, government, ministry, officials, officialdom, the system **2.** bumbledom, officialdom, officialese, red tape, regulations

bureaucrat administrator, apparatchik, civil servant, functionary, mandarin, minister, office-holder, officer, official, public servant

self-government: incorporated by charter. **2.** an archaic form of **borough.** —**burghal** (ˈbɜːɡəl) *adj.*

burgher (ˈbɜːɡə) *n.* **1.** a member of the trading or mercantile class of a medieval city. **2.** a respectable citizen; bourgeois. **3.** *Arch.* a citizen or inhabitant of a corporate town, esp on the Continent. **4.** *S. African history.* a citizen of the Cape not employed by the Dutch East India Company.

burglar (ˈbɜːɡlə) *n.* a person who commits burglary; housebreaker.

burglary (ˈbɜːɡlərɪ) *n., pl.* -**ries.** the crime of entering a building as a trespasser to commit theft or another offence. —**burglarious** (bɜːˈɡlɛərɪəs) *adj.* —**ˈburglaˌrize** *or* -**ise** *vb.*

burgle (ˈbɜːɡəl) *vb.* to commit burglary upon (a house, etc.).

burgomaster (ˈbɜːɡəˌmɑːstə) *n.* the chief magistrate of a town in Austria, Belgium, Germany, or the Netherlands; mayor.

burial (ˈbɛrɪəl) *n.* the act of burying, esp. the interment of a dead body.

burin (ˈbjʊərɪn) *n.* **1.** a chisel of tempered steel used for engraving metal, wood, or marble. **2.** *Archaeol.* a prehistoric flint tool.

burk *or* **berk** (bɜːk) *n. Brit. sl.* a stupid person; fool.

burlesque (bɜːˈlɛsk) *n.* **1.** an artistic work, esp. literary or dramatic, satirizing a subject by caricaturing it. **2.** a ludicrous imitation or caricature. **3.** *U.S. theatre.* a bawdy comedy show of the late 19th and early 20th centuries: the striptease eventually became one of its chief elements. ~*adj.* **4.** of, relating to, or characteristic of a burlesque. ~*vb.* -**lesquing,** -**lesqued. 5.** to represent or imitate (a person or thing) in a ludicrous way; caricature. —**burˈlesquer** *n.*

burly (ˈbɜːlɪ) *adj.* -**lier,** -**liest.** large and thick of build; sturdy. —**ˈburliness** *n.*

burn[1] (bɜːn) *vb.* **burning, burnt** *or* **burned. 1.** to undergo or cause to undergo combustion. **2.** to destroy or be destroyed by fire. **3.** (*tr.*) to damage, injure, or mark by heat: *he burnt his hand; she was burnt by the sun.* **4.** to die or put to death by fire. **5.** (*intr.*) to be or feel hot: *my forehead burns.* **6.** to smart or cause to smart: *brandy burns one's throat.* **7.** (*intr.*) to feel strong emotion, esp. anger or passion. **8.** (*tr.*) to use for the purposes of light, heat, or power: *to burn coal.* **9.** (*tr.*) to form by or as if by fire: *to burn a hole.* **10.** to char or become charred: *the potatoes are burning.* **11.** (*tr.*) to brand or cauterize. **12.** to produce by or subject to heat as part of a process: *to burn charcoal.* **13. burn one's boats** *or* **bridges.** *Inf.* to proceed in such a way as to eliminate all alternative courses of action. **14. burn one's fingers.** *Inf.* to suffer from having meddled or interfered. ~*n.* **15.** an injury caused by exposure to heat, electrical, chemical, or radioactive agents. **16.** a mark, e.g. on wood, caused by burning. **17.** a controlled use of rocket propellant, esp. for a course correction. **18.** *Sl.* tobacco or a cigarette. ~See also **burn out.**

burn[2] (bɜːn) *n. N Brit.* a small stream; brook.

burner (ˈbɜːnə) *n.* **1.** the part of a stove, lamp, etc., that produces flame or heat. **2.** an apparatus for burning something, as fuel or refuse.

burning (ˈbɜːnɪŋ) *adj.* **1.** intense; passionate. **2.** urgent; crucial: *a burning problem.*

burning glass *n.* a convex lens for concentrating the sun's rays to produce fire.

burnish (ˈbɜːnɪʃ) *vb.* **1.** to make or become shiny or smooth by friction; polish. ~*n.* **2.** a shiny finish; lustre. —**ˈburnisher** *n.*

burnoose, burnous, *or* **burnouse** (bɜːˈnuːs, -ˈnuːz) *n.* a long circular cloak with a hood attached, worn esp. by Arabs.

burn out *vb.* (*adv.*) **1.** to become or cause to become inoperative as a result of heat or friction: *the clutch burnt out.* **2.** (*intr.*) (of a rocket, jet engine, etc.) to cease functioning as a result of exhaustion of the fuel supply. **3.** (*tr.; usually passive*) to destroy by fire. **4.** to become or cause to become exhausted through overwork or dissipation.

burnt (bɜːnt) *vb.* **1.** a past tense or past participle of **burn**[1]. ~*adj.* **2.** affected by or as if by burning; charred.

burnt sienna *n.* **1.** a reddish-brown pigment obtained by roasting raw sienna. **2.** a reddish-brown colour.

burnt umber *n.* **1.** a brown pigment obtained by heating umber. **2.** a dark brown colour.

burp (bɜːp) *n.* **1.** *Inf.* a belch. ~*vb.* **2.** (*intr.*) *Inf.* to belch. **3.** (*tr.*) to cause (a baby) to burp.

burr (bɜː) *n.* **1.** an articulation of (r) characteristic of certain English dialects, esp. the uvular fricative trill of Northumberland or the retroflex *r* of the West of England. **2.** a whirring sound. ~*vb.* **3.** to pronounce (words) with a burr. **4.** to make a whirring sound.

burrow (ˈbʌrəʊ) *n.* **1.** a hole dug in the ground by a rabbit or other small animal. **2.** a small snug place affording shelter or retreat. ~*vb.* **3.** to dig (a burrow) in, through, or under (ground). **4.** (*intr.; often foll. by through*) to move through by or as by digging. **5.** (*intr.*) to hide or live in a burrow. **6.** (*intr.*) to delve deeply: *he burrowed into his pockets.* **7.** to hide (oneself). —**ˈburrower** *n.*

bursa (ˈbɜːsə) *n., pl.* -**sae** (-siː) *or* -**sas.** *Anat.* a small fluid-filled sac that reduces friction, esp. at joints. —**ˈbursal** *adj.*

bursar (ˈbɜːsə) *n.* **1.** a treasurer of a school, college, or university. **2.** *Scot.* a student holding a bursary.

bursary (ˈbɜːsərɪ) *n., pl.* -**ries. 1.** Also called: **ˈbursarˌship.** a scholarship awarded in Scottish schools and universities. **2.** *Brit.* the treasury of a college, etc. —**bursarial** (bɜːˈsɛərɪəl) *adj.*

bursitis (bɜːˈsaɪtɪs) *n.* inflammation of a bursa.

burst (bɜːst) *vb.* **bursting, burst. 1.** to break or cause to break open or apart suddenly and noisily; explode. **2.** (*intr.*) to come, go, etc., suddenly and forcibly: *he burst into the room.* **3.** (*intr.*) to be full to the point of breaking open. **4.** (*intr.*) to give vent (to) suddenly or loudly: *to burst into song.* **5.** to cause or suffer the rupture of: *to burst a blood vessel.* ~*n.* **6.** a sudden breaking open; explosion. **7.** a break; breach; rupture. **8.** a sudden display or increase of effort; spurt: *a burst of speed.* **9.** a sudden and violent emission, occurrence, or outbreak: *a burst of applause.* **10.** a volley of fire from a weapon.

burglar cat burglar, filcher, housebreaker, picklock, pilferer, robber, sneak thief, thief

burglary break-in, breaking and entering, filching, housebreaking, larceny, pilferage, robbery, stealing, theft, thieving

burial burying, entombment, exequies, funeral, inhumation, interment, obsequies, sepulture

buried 1. coffined, consigned to the grave, entombed, interred, laid to rest **2.** dead and buried, dead and gone, in the grave, long gone, pushing up the daisies, six feet under **3.** covered, forgotten, hidden, repressed, sunk in oblivion, suppressed **4.** cloistered, concealed, hidden, private, sequestered, tucked away **5.** caught up, committed, concentrating, devoted, engrossed, immersed, intent, lost, occupied, preoccupied, rapt

burlesque 1. *n.* caricature, mock, mockery, parody, satire, send-up (*Brit. inf.*), spoof (*Inf.*), takeoff (*Inf.*), travesty **2.** *adj.* caricatur-al, comic, farcical, hudibrastic, ironical, ludicrous, mock, mock-heroic, mocking, parodic, satirical, travestying **3.** *v.* ape, caricature, exaggerate, imitate, lampoon, make fun of, mock, parody, ridicule, satirize, send up (*Brit. inf.*), spoof, (*Inf.*), take off (*Inf.*), travesty

burly beefy, big, brawny, bulky, hefty, hulking, muscular, powerful, stocky, stout, strapping, strong, sturdy, thickset, well-built

burn 1. be ablaze, be on fire, blaze, flame, flare, flash, flicker, glow, smoke **2.** brand, calcine, char, ignite, incinerate, kindle, light, parch, reduce to ashes, scorch, set on fire, shrivel, singe, toast, wither **3.** bite, hurt, pain, smart, sting, tingle **4.** be excited (angry, aroused, inflamed, passionate), blaze, desire, fume, seethe, simmer, smoulder, yearn **5.** consume, eat up, expend, use

burning 1. blazing, fiery, flaming, flashing, gleaming, glowing, hot, illuminated, scorching, smouldering **2.** all-consuming, ardent, eager, earnest, fervent, fervid, frantic, frenzied, impassioned, intense, passionate, vehement, zealous **3.** acrid, biting, caustic, irritating, painful, piercing, prickling, pungent, reeking, smarting, stinging, tingling **4.** acute, compelling, critical, crucial, essential, important, pressing, significant, urgent, vital

burnish 1. *v.* brighten, buff, furbish, glaze, polish, rub up, shine, smooth **2.** *n.* gloss, lustre, patina, polish, sheen, shine

burrow 1. *n.* den, hole, lair, retreat, shelter, tunnel **2.** *v.* delve, dig, excavate, hollow out, scoop out, tunnel

burst *v.* **1.** blow up, break, crack, disintegrate, explode, fly open, fragment, puncture, rend asunder, rupture, shatter, shiver, split, tear apart **2.** barge, break, break out, erupt, gush forth, run, rush, spout ~*n.* **3.** bang, blast, blasting, blowout, blow-up, breach, break, crack, discharge, explosion, rupture, split **4.** eruption, fit, gush, gust, outbreak, outburst, outpouring, rush, spate, spurt, surge,

burton ('bɜːtən) n. **1.** Naut. a kind of light hoisting tackle. **2. go for a burton.** Brit. sl. **a.** to be broken, useless, or lost. **b.** to die.

bury ('bɛrɪ) vb. **burying, buried.** (tr.) **1.** to place (a corpse) in a grave; inter. **2.** to place in the earth and cover with soil. **3.** to cover from sight; hide. **4.** to embed; sink: to bury a nail in plaster. **5.** to occupy (oneself) with deep concentration; engross: to be buried in a book. **6.** to dismiss from the mind; abandon: to bury old hatreds. **7. bury the hatchet.** to cease hostilities and become reconciled.

bus (bʌs) n., pl. **buses** or **busses. 1.** a large motor vehicle designed to carry passengers between stopping places along a regular route. More formal name: **omnibus. 2.** (modifier) of or relating to a bus or buses: a bus driver; a bus station. **3.** Inf. a car or aircraft, esp. one that is old and shaky. **4. miss the bus.** to miss an opportunity. ~vb. **busing, bused** or **bussing, bussed. 5.** to travel or transport by bus. **6.** Chiefly U.S. to transport (children) by bus from one area to another in order to create racially integrated schools.

bus. abbrev. for business.

busby ('bʌzbɪ) n., pl. **-bies. 1.** a tall fur helmet worn by hussars. **2.** another name for **bearskin** (the hat).

bush[1] (bʊʃ) n. **1.** a dense woody plant, smaller than a tree, with many branches arising from the lower part of the stem; shrub. **2.** a dense cluster of such shrubs; thicket. **3.** something resembling a bush, esp. in density: a bush of hair. **4.** (often preceded by the) an uncultivated or sparsely settled area, covered with trees or shrubs, which can vary from open, shrubby country to dense rain-forest. **5.** a forested area; woodland. **6.** (often preceded by the) Inf. the countryside, as opposed to the city: out in the bush. **7.** Obs. a bunch of ivy hung as a vintner's sign in front of a tavern. **8. beat about the bush.** to avoid the point at issue; prevaricate. ~adj. **9.** Austral. & N.Z. Inf. rough and ready. **10. go bush.** Inf., chiefly Austral. **a.** to go off into the bush. **b.** to go into hiding. **c.** to run wild. ~vb. **11.** (intr.) to grow thick and bushy. **12.** (tr.) to cover, decorate, support, etc., with bushes. **13. bush it.** Austral. to camp out in the bush.

bush[2] (bʊʃ) n. **1.** a thin metal sleeve or tubular lining serving as a bearing. ~vb. **2.** to fit a bush to (a casing, bearing, etc.).

bushbaby ('bʊʃ,beɪbɪ) n., pl. **-babies.** an agile nocturnal arboreal primate occurring in Africa south of the Sahara. They have large eyes and ears and a long tail. Also called: **galago.**

bushel ('bʊʃəl) n. **1.** a British unit of dry or liquid measure equal to 8 Imperial gallons. 1 Imperial bushel is equivalent to 0.036 37 cubic metres. **2.** a U.S. unit of dry measure equal to 64 U.S. pints. 1 U.S. bushel is equivalent to 0.035 24 cubic metres. **3.** a container with a capacity equal to either of these quantities. **4.** Inf. a large amount. **5. hide one's light under a bushel.** to conceal one's abilities or good qualities.

bush jacket or **shirt** n. a casual jacket or shirt having four patch pockets and a belt.

bush line n. an airline operating in the bush country of Canada's northern regions.

bush lot n. Canad. a tract of woodland.

bushman ('bʊʃmən) n., pl. **-men.** Austral. & N.Z. a person who lives or travels in the bush, esp. one versed in bush lore.

Bushman ('bʊʃmən) n., pl. **-man** or **-men.** a member of a hunting and gathering people of southern Africa.

bush pilot n. Canad. a pilot who operates in the bush country.

bushranger ('bʊʃ,reɪndʒə) n. **1.** Austral. (formerly), an outlaw living in the bush. **2.** U.S. a person who lives away from civilization.

bush tea n. **1.** a leguminous shrub of southern Africa. **2.** a beverage prepared from the dried leaves of such a plant.

bush telegraph n. Inf. a means of spreading rumour, gossip, etc.

bushveld ('bʊʃ,fɛlt) n. S. African. bushy countryside.

bushy[1] ('bʊʃɪ) adj. **bushier, bushiest. 1.** covered or overgrown with bushes. **2.** thick and shaggy. —**'bushily** adv. —**'bushiness** n.

bushy[2] or **bushie** ('bʊʃɪ) n., pl. **bushies.** Austral. inf. **1.** a person who lives in the bush. **2.** an unsophisticated uncouth person.

busily ('bɪzɪlɪ) adv. in a busy manner.

business ('bɪznɪs) n. **1.** a trade or profession. **2.** the purchase and sale of goods and services. **3.** a commercial or industrial establishment. **4.** volume of commercial activity: business is poor today. **5.** commercial policy: overcharging is bad business. **6.** proper or rightful concern or responsibility (often in **mind one's own business). 7.** a special task; assignment. **8.** an affair; matter. **9.** serious work or activity: get down to business. **10.** Theatre. an incidental action performed by an actor for dramatic effect. **11. mean business.** to be in earnest.

businesslike ('bɪznɪs,laɪk) adj. efficient and methodical.

businessman ('bɪznɪs,mæn, -mən) or (fem.) **businesswoman** n., pl. **-men** or **-women.** a person engaged in commercial or industrial business, esp. as an owner or executive.

busker ('bʌskə) n. a person who entertains for money in public places, as in front of theatre queues. —**busk** vb. (intr.).

buskin ('bʌskɪn) n. **1.** (formerly) a sandal-like covering for the foot and leg, reaching the calf. **2.** a thick-soled laced half boot worn esp. by actors of ancient Greece. **3.** (usually preceded by the) Chiefly literary. tragic drama.

busman's holiday ('bʌsmənz) n. Inf. a holiday spent doing the same as one does at work.

buss (bʌs) n., vb. an archaic or dialect word for **kiss.**

bust[1] (bʌst) n. **1.** the chest of a human being, esp. a woman's bosom. **2.** a sculpture of the head, shoulders, and upper chest of a person.

bust[2] (bʌst) Inf. ~vb. **busting, busted** or **bust. 1.** to burst or break. **2.** to make or become bankrupt. **3.** (tr.) (of the police) to raid, search, or arrest. **4.** (tr.) U.S. to demote, esp. in military rank. ~n. **5.** a raid, search, or arrest by the police. **6.** Chiefly U.S. a punch. **7.** U.S. a failure, esp. bankruptcy. **8.** a drunken party. ~adj. **9.** broken. **10.** bankrupt. **11. go bust.** to become bankrupt.

bustard ('bʌstəd) n. a large terrestrial bird inhabiting open regions of the Old World. It has long strong legs, a heavy body, a long neck, and speckled plumage.

bustle[1] ('bʌsəl) vb. **1.** (when intr., often foll. by about) to hurry or cause to hurry with a great show of energy or activity. ~n. **2.** energetic and noisy activity. —**'bustler** n.

bustle[2] ('bʌsəl) n. a cushion or framework worn by women in the late 19th century at the back in order to expand the skirt.

bust-up Inf. n. **1.** a quarrel, esp. a serious one ending a friendship, etc. **2.** Brit. a disturbance or brawl. ~vb. **bust up** (adv.). **3.** (intr.) to quarrel and part. **4.** (tr.) to disrupt (a meeting), esp. violently.

THESAURUS

torrent ~adj. **5.** flat, punctured, rent, ruptured, split

bury 1. consign to the grave, entomb, inearth, inhume, inter, lay to rest, sepulchre **2.** conceal, cover, cover up, enshroud, hide, secrete, shroud, stow away **3.** drive in, embed, engulf, implant, sink, submerge **4.** absorb, engage, engross, immerse, interest, occupy

bush 1. hedge, plant, shrub, shrubbery, thicket **2.** backwoods, brush, scrub, scrubland, the wild, woodland

bushy bristling, bristly, fluffy, fuzzy, luxuriant, rough, shaggy, spreading, stiff, thick, unruly, wiry

busily actively, assiduously, briskly, care-

fully, diligently, earnestly, energetically, industriously, intently, purposefully, speedily, strenuously

business 1. calling, career, craft, employment, function, job, line, métier, occupation, profession, pursuit, trade, vocation, work **2.** company, concern, corporation, enterprise, establishment, firm, organization, venture **3.** bargaining, commerce, dealings, industry, manufacturing, merchandising, selling, trade, trading, transaction **4.** affair, assignment, concern, duty, function, issue, matter, point, problem, question, responsibility, subject, task, topic

businesslike correct, efficient, matter-

of-fact, methodical, orderly, organized, practical, professional, regular, routine, systematic, thorough, well-ordered, workaday

businessman, businesswoman capitalist, employer, entrepreneur, executive, financier, industrialist, merchant, tradesman, tycoon

bust[1] bosom, breast, chest, torso

bust[2] v. **1.** break, burst, fracture, rupture **2.** bankrupt, break, crash, fail, impoverish, ruin **3.** arrest, catch, collar (Inf.), cop (Sl.), nab (Inf.), raid, search **4. go bust** become insolvent, be ruined, break, fail, go bankrupt ~n. **5.** arrest, capture, cop (Sl.), raid, search, seizure

busy (¹bɪzɪ) *adj.* **busier, busiest. 1.** actively or fully engaged; occupied. **2.** crowded with or characterized by activity. **3.** *Chiefly U.S.* (of a room, telephone line, etc.) in use; engaged. **4.** overcrowded with detail: *a busy painting.* **5.** meddlesome; inquisitive. *~vb.* **busying, busied. 6.** (*tr.*) to make or keep (someone, esp. oneself) busy; occupy. —¹**busily** *adv.* —¹**busyness** *n.*

busybody (¹bɪzɪˌbɒdɪ) *n., pl.* **-bodies.** a meddlesome, prying, or officious person.

busy Lizzie (¹lɪzɪ) *n.* a flowering plant that has fast-growing drooping stems and is often grown as a pot plant.

but¹ (bʌt; *unstressed* bət) *conj.* (*coordinating*) **1.** contrary to expectation: *he cut his knee but didn't cry.* **2.** in contrast; on the contrary: *I like opera but my husband doesn't.* **3.** (*usually used after a negative*) other than: *we can't do anything but wait.* **4.** only: *I can but try.* *~conj.* (*subordinating*) **5.** (*usually used after a negative*) without it happening: *we never go out but it rains.* **6.** (foll. by *that*) except that: *nothing is impossible but that we live forever.* **7.** *Arch.* if not; unless. *~prep.* **8.** except; save: *they saved all but one.* **9. but for.** were it not for: *but for you, we couldn't have managed.* *~adv.* **10.** just; merely: *he was but a child.* **11.** *Austral.* though; however: *it's a rainy day; warm, but.* *~n.* **12.** an objection (esp. in **ifs and buts**).

but² (bʌt) *n. Scot.* the outer room of a two-roomed cottage. Cf. **ben¹**.

butane (¹bjuːteɪn, bjuːˈteɪn) *n.* a colourless flammable gaseous alkane used mainly in the manufacture of rubber and fuels. Formula: C_4H_{10}.

butch (bʊtʃ) *Sl.* *~adj.* **1.** (of a woman or man) markedly or aggressively masculine. *~n.* **2.** a lesbian who is noticeably masculine. **3.** a strong rugged man.

butcher (¹bʊtʃə) *n.* **1.** a retailer of meat. **2.** a person who slaughters or dresses meat. **3.** an indiscriminate or brutal murderer. *~vb.* (*tr.*) **4.** to slaughter or dress (animals) for meat. **5.** to kill indiscriminately or brutally. **6.** to make a mess of; botch.

butcherbird (¹bʊtʃəˌbɜːd) *n.* **1.** a shrike, esp. of the genus *Lanius.* **2.** any of several Australian magpies that impale their prey on thorns.

butchery (¹bʊtʃərɪ) *n., pl.* **-eries. 1.** the business of a butcher. **2.** wanton and indiscriminate slaughter. **3.** a slaughterhouse.

butler (¹bʌtlə) *n.* the male servant of a household in charge of the wines, table, etc.: usually the head servant.

butt¹ (bʌt) *n.* **1.** the thicker or blunt end of something, such as the end of the stock of a rifle. **2.** the unused end of something, esp. of a cigarette; stub. **3.** *U.S.* a slang word for **cigarette.**

butt² (bʌt) *n.* **1.** a person or thing that is the target of ridicule, wit, etc. **2.** *Shooting, archery.* **a.** a mound of earth behind the target that stops bullets or wide shots. **b.** the target itself. **c.** (*pl.*) the target range. **3.** a low barrier behind which sportsmen shoot game birds, esp. grouse. *~vb.* **4.** (usually foll. by *on* or *against*) to lie or be placed end on to; abut.

butt³ (bʌt) *vb.* **1.** to strike or push (something) with the head or horns. **2.** (*intr.*) to project; jut. **3.** (*intr.;* foll. by *in* or *into*) to intrude, esp. into a conversation; interfere. *~n.* **4.** a blow with the head or horns.

butt⁴ (bʌt) *n.* a large cask for storing wine or beer.

butter (¹bʌtə) *n.* **1.** an edible fatty whitish-yellow solid made from cream by churning. **2.** any substance with a

butter-like consistency, such as peanut butter. **3. look as if butter wouldn't melt in one's mouth.** to look innocent, although probably not so. *~vb.* (*tr.*) **4.** to put butter on or in. **5.** to flatter. *~See also* **butter up.**

butter bean *n.* a variety of lima bean that has large pale flat edible seeds.

buttercup (¹bʌtəˌkʌp) *n.* any of various yellow-flowered plants of the genus *Ranunculus* of Europe, Asia, and North America.

butterfingers (¹bʌtəˌfɪŋgəz) *n. Inf.* a person who drops things inadvertently or fails to catch things. —¹**butter-ˌfingered** *adj.*

butterflies (¹bʌtəˌflaɪz) *pl. n. Inf.* tremors in the stomach region due to nervousness.

butterfly (¹bʌtəˌflaɪ) *n., pl.* **-flies. 1.** any diurnal insect that has a slender body with clubbed antennae and typically rests with the wings (often brightly coloured) closed over the back. **2.** a person who never settles with one interest or occupation for long. **3.** a swimming stroke in which the arms are plunged forward together in large circular movements.

butterfly nut *n.* another name for **wing nut.**

buttermilk (¹bʌtəˌmɪlk) *n.* the sourish liquid remaining after the butter has been separated from milk.

butter muslin *n.* a fine loosely woven cotton material originally used for wrapping butter.

butterscotch (¹bʌtəˌskɒtʃ) *n.* **1.** a kind of hard brittle toffee made with butter, brown sugar, etc. **2.** a flavouring made from these ingredients.

butter up *vb.* (*tr., adv.*) *Inf.* to flatter.

butterwort (¹bʌtəˌwɜːt) *n.* a plant that grows in wet places and has violet-blue spurred flowers and fleshy greasy glandular leaves on which insects are trapped and digested.

buttery¹ (¹bʌtərɪ) *adj.* containing, like, or coated with butter. —¹**butteriness** *n.*

buttery² (¹bʌtərɪ) *n., pl.* **-teries. 1.** a room for storing foods or wines. **2.** *Brit.* (in some universities) a room in which food and drink are supplied or sold to students.

buttock (¹bʌtək) *n.* **1.** either of the two large fleshy masses of thick muscular tissue that form the human rump. **2.** the analogous part in some mammals.

button (¹bʌtən) *n.* **1.** a disc or knob of plastic, wood, etc., attached to a garment, etc., usually for fastening two surfaces together by passing it through a buttonhole or loop. **2.** a small round object, such as any of various sweets, decorations, or badges. **3.** a small disc that completes an electric circuit when pushed, as one that operates a doorbell or machine. **4.** *Biol.* any rounded knoblike part or organ, such as an unripe mushroom. **5.** *Fencing.* the protective knob fixed to the point of a foil. **6.** *Brit.* an object of no value (esp. in **not worth a button**). *~vb.* **7.** to fasten with a button or buttons. **8.** (*tr.*) to provide with buttons. *~See also* **button up.** —¹**buttoner** *n.* —¹**buttonless** *adj.*

buttonhole (¹bʌtənˌhəʊl) *n.* **1.** a slit in a garment, etc., through which a button is passed to fasten two surfaces together. **2.** a flower or small bunch of flowers worn pinned to the lapel or in the buttonhole, esp. at weddings. U.S. name: **boutonniere.** *~vb.* (*tr.*) **3.** to detain (a person) in conversation. **4.** to make buttonholes in.

button up *vb.* (*tr., adv.*) **1.** to fasten (a garment) with a button or buttons. **2.** *Inf.* to conclude (business) satisfactorily. **3. button up one's lip** *or* **mouth.** *Sl.* to be silent.

THESAURUS

bustle 1. *v.* bestir, dash, flutter, fuss, hasten, hurry, rush, scamper, scramble, scurry, scuttle, stir, tear **2.** *n.* activity, ado, agitation, commotion, excitement, flurry, fuss, haste, hurly-burly, hurry, pother, stir, to-do, tumult

busy *adj.* **1.** active, assiduous, brisk, diligent, employed, engaged, engrossed, hard at work, industrious, in harness, occupied, on duty, persevering, slaving, working **2.** active, energetic, exacting, full, hectic, hustling, lively, on the go (*Inf.*), restless, strenuous, tireless, tiring **3.** fussy, inquisitive, interfering, meddlesome, meddling, nosy, officious, prying, snoopy, stirring, troublesome *~v.* **4.** absorb, employ, engage, engross, immerse, interest, occupy

busybody eavesdropper, gossip, intriguer, intruder, meddler, nosy parker (*Inf.*),

pry, scandalmonger, snoop, snooper, troublemaker

but 1. *sentence connector* further, however, moreover, nevertheless, on the contrary, on the other hand, still, yet **2.** *conj.* bar, barring, except, excepting, excluding, notwithstanding, save, with the exception of **3.** *adv.* just, merely, only, simply, singly, solely

butcher *n.* **1.** destroyer, killer, murderer, slaughterer, slayer *~v.* **2.** carve, clean, cut, cut up, dress, joint, prepare, slaughter **3.** assassinate, cut down, destroy, exterminate, kill, liquidate, massacre, put to the sword, slaughter, slay **4.** bodge (*Inf.*), botch, destroy, mess up, mutilate, ruin, spoil, wreck

butchery blood bath, blood-letting, bloodshed, carnage, killing, massacre, mass murder, murder, slaughter

butt¹ 1. haft, handle, hilt, shaft, shank, stock **2.** base, end, fag end (*Inf.*), foot, leftover, stub, tail, tip

butt² Aunt Sally, dupe, laughing stock, mark, object, point, subject, target, victim

butt³ *v./n.* **1.** *With or of the head or horns* ram, buck, buffet, bump, bunt, jab, knock, poke, prod, punch, push, ram, shove, thrust *~v.* **2.** abut, join, jut, meet, project, protrude **3.** *With in or into* chip in (*Inf.*), cut in, interfere, interrupt, intrude, meddle, put one's oar in, stick one's nose in

butt⁴ barrel, cask, pipe

buttonhole *v. Fig.* accost, bore, catch, detain in talk, grab, importune, persuade importunately, take aside, waylay

buttress ('bʌtrɪs) n. 1. Also called: **pier**. a construction, usually of brick or stone, built to support a wall. 2. any support or prop. 3. something shaped like a buttress, such as a projection from a mountainside. ~vb. (tr.) 4. to support (a wall) with a buttress. 5. to support or sustain.

butty ('bʌtɪ) n., pl. **-ties**. Chiefly N English dialect. a sandwich: a jam butty.

butyl ('bjuː,taɪl, -tɪl) n. (modifier) of or containing any of four isomeric forms of the group C_4H_9 — : butyl rubber.

buxom ('bʌksəm) adj. 1. (esp. of a woman) healthily plump, attractive, and vigorous. 2. (of a woman) full-bosomed. —'**buxomly** adv. —'**buxomness** n.

buy (baɪ) vb. **buying, bought**. (mainly tr.) 1. to acquire by paying or promising to pay a sum of money; purchase. 2. to be capable of purchasing: money can't buy love. 3. to acquire by any exchange or sacrifice: to buy time by equivocation. 4. to bribe or corrupt; hire by or as by bribery. 5. Inf. to accept as true, practical, etc. 6. (intr.; foll. by into) to purchase shares of (a company). ~n. 7. Inf. a purchase (often in **good** or **bad buy**). ~See also **buy in, buy off**, etc.

buyer ('baɪə) n. 1. a person who buys; customer. 2. a person employed to buy merchandise, materials, etc., as for a shop or factory.

buy in vb. (adv.) 1. (tr.) to buy back for the owner (an item in an auction) at or below the reserve price. 2. (intr.) to purchase shares in a company. 3. (tr.) Also: **buy into**. Inf. to pay money to secure a position or place for (someone, esp. oneself) in some organization, esp. a business or club. 4. (intr.) Also: **buy into**. Austral. to get involved in (an argument or fight). 5. to purchase (goods, etc.) in large quantities.

buy off vb. (tr., adv.) to pay (a person or group) to drop a charge, end opposition, etc.

buy out vb. (tr., adv.) 1. to purchase the ownership, controlling interest, shares, etc., of (a company, etc.). 2. to gain the release of (a person) from the armed forces by payment.

buy up vb. (tr., adv.) 1. to purchase all, or all that is available, of (something). 2. to purchase a controlling interest in (a company, etc.).

buzz (bʌz) n. 1. a rapidly vibrating humming sound, as of a bee. 2. a low sound, as of many voices in conversation. 3. a rumour; report; gossip. 4. Inf. a telephone call. 5. U.S. sl. a pleasant sensation. ~vb. 6. (intr.) to make a vibrating sound like that of a prolonged z. 7. (intr.) to talk or gossip with an air of excitement: the town buzzed with the news. 8. (tr.) to utter or spread (a rumour). 9. (intr.; often foll. by about) to move around quickly and busily. 10. (tr.) to signal or summon with a buzzer. 11. (tr.) Inf. to call by telephone. 12. (tr.) Inf. to fly an aircraft very low over (an object). 13. (tr.) (esp. of insects) to make a buzzing sound with (wings, etc.).

buzzard ('bʌzəd) n. a diurnal bird of prey of the hawk family, typically having broad wings and tail and a soaring flight.

buzzer ('bʌzə) n. 1. a device that produces a buzzing sound, esp. one similar to an electric bell. 2. N.Z. a wood planing machine.

buzz off vb. (intr., adv.; often imperative) Inf., chiefly Brit. to go away; leave; depart.

buzz word n. Inf. a word, originally from a particular jargon, which becomes a popular vogue word.

B.V.M. abbrev. for Beata Virgo Maria.

bwana ('bwɑːnə) n. (in E Africa) a master, often used as a form of address corresponding to sir.

by (baɪ) prep. 1. used to indicate the agent after a passive verb: seeds eaten by the birds. 2. used to indicate the person responsible for a creative work: this song is by Schubert. 3. via; through: enter by the back door. 4. foll. by a gerund to indicate a means used: he frightened her by hiding behind the door. 5. beside; next to; near: a tree by the house. 6. passing the position of; past: he drove by the old cottage. 7. not later than; before: return the books by Tuesday. 8. used to indicate extent, after a comparative: it is hotter by five degrees. 9. (esp. in oaths) invoking the name of: I swear by all the gods. 10. multiplied or divided by: four by three equals twelve. 11. during the passing of (esp. in **by day, by night**). 12. placed between measurements of the various dimensions of something: a plank fourteen inches by seven. ~adv. 13. near: the house is close by. 14. away; aside: he put some money by each week. 15. passing a point near something; past: he drove by. ~n., pl. **byes**. 16. a variant spelling of **bye**.

by- or **bye-** prefix. 1. near: bystander. 2. secondary or incidental: by-election; by-product.

by and by adv. presently or eventually.

bye (baɪ) n. 1. Sport. the situation in which a player or team wins a preliminary round by virtue of having no opponent. 2. Golf. one or more holes that are left unplayed after the match has been decided. 3. Cricket. a run scored off a ball not struck by the batsman. 4. something incidental or secondary. 5. **by the bye**. incidentally; by the way.

bye-bye interj. Brit. inf. goodbye.

by-election or **bye-election** n. (in Great Britain and other countries of the Commonwealth) an election held during the life of a parliament to fill a vacant seat.

bygone ('baɪ,gɒn) adj. 1. (usually prenominal) past; former. ~n. 2. (often pl.) a past occurrence. 3. **let bygones be bygones**. to agree to forget past quarrels.

bylaw or **bye-law** ('baɪ,lɔː) n. 1. a rule made by a local authority. 2. a regulation of a company, society, etc.

by-line n. 1. a line under the title of a newspaper or magazine article giving the author's name. 2. Soccer. another word for **touchline**.

bypass ('baɪ,pɑːs) n. 1. a main road built to avoid a city or other congested area. 2. a means of redirecting the flow of a substance around an appliance through which it would otherwise pass. 3. Electronics. an electrical circuit connected in parallel around one or more components, providing an alternative path for certain frequencies. ~vb. **-passing, -passed** or **-past**. (tr.) 4. to go around or avoid (a city, obstruction, problem, etc.). 5. to cause (traffic, fluid, etc.) to go through a bypass. 6. to proceed without reference to (regulations, a superior, etc.); get round; avoid.

by-play n. Chiefly U.S. secondary action or talking carried on apart while the main action proceeds, esp. in a play.

by-product n. 1. a secondary or incidental product of a manufacturing process. 2. a side effect.

byre (baɪə) n. Brit. a shelter for cows.

byroad ('baɪ,rəud) or **bylane** n. a secondary or side road.

Byronic (baɪ'rɒnɪk) adj. of, like, or characteristic of Byron, his poetry, or his style.

bystander ('baɪ,stændə) n. a person present but not involved; onlooker; spectator.

byte (baɪt) n. Computers. 1. a sequence of bits processed as one unit of information. 2. the storage space allocated to one character. 3. a subdivision of a word.

byway ('baɪ,weɪ) n. 1. a secondary or side road, esp. in the country. 2. an area, field of study, etc., that is very obscure or of secondary importance.

byword ('baɪ,wɜːd) n. 1. a person or thing regarded as

THESAURUS

buttress 1. n. abutment, brace, mainstay, pier, prop, reinforcement, shore, stanchion, stay, strut, support 2. v. back up, bolster, brace, prop, prop up, reinforce, shore, shore up, strengthen, support, sustain, uphold

buy v. 1. acquire, get, invest in, obtain, pay for, procure, purchase, shop for 2. Often with **off** bribe, corrupt, fix (Inf.), grease someone's palm (Inf.), square, suborn ~n. 3. acquisition, bargain, deal, purchase

buzz n. 1. bombilation or bombination (Literary), buzzing, drone, hiss, hum, murmur, purr, ring, ringing, sibilation, susurration or

susurrus (Literary), whir, whisper 2. gossip, hearsay, news, report, rumour, scandal, whisper ~v. 3. bombilate or bombinate (Literary), drone, fizzle, hum, murmur, reverberate, ring, sibilate, susurrate (Literary), whir, whisper, whizz 4. chatter, gossip, natter, rumour, tattle

by prep. 1. along, beside, by way of, close to, near, next to, over, past, via 2. through, through the agency of, under the aegis of ~adv. 3. aside, at hand, away, beyond, close, handy, in reach, near, past, to one side

by and by before long, eventually, in a

while, in the course of time, one day, presently, soon

bygone ancient, antiquated, departed, erstwhile, extinct, forgotten, former, gone by, lost, of old, of yore, olden, one-time, past, past recall, previous, sunk in oblivion

bypass avoid, circumvent, depart from, detour round, deviate from, get round, go round, ignore, neglect, outflank, pass round

bystander eyewitness, looker-on, observer, onlooker, passer-by, spectator, viewer, watcher, witness

a perfect or proverbial example of something: *their name is a byword for good service.* **2.** an object of scorn or derision. **3.** a common saying; proverb.

Byzantine (bɪˈzæn₁taɪn, -₁tiːn, baɪ-; ˈbɪzən₁tiːn, -₁taɪn) *adj.* **1.** of or relating to Byzantium, an ancient Greek city on the Bosphorus. **2.** of or relating to the Byzantine Empire, the continuation of the Roman Empire in the East. **3.** of, relating to, or characterizing the Orthodox Church.

4. of or relating to the highly coloured stylized form of religious art developed in the Byzantine Empire. **5.** of or relating to the style of architecture developed in the Byzantine Empire, characterized by massive domes, rounded arches, spires and minarets, and mosaics. **6.** (of attitudes, etc.) inflexible or complicated. ~*n.* **7.** an inhabitant of Byzantium.

C

c *or* **C** (si:) *n., pl.* **c's, C's,** *or* **Cs. 1.** the third letter of the English alphabet. **2.** a speech sound represented by this letter, usually either as in *cigar*, or as in *case*. **3.** the third in a series, esp. the third highest grade in an examination. **4.** something shaped like a C.

c *symbol for:* **1.** centi-. **2.** cubic. **3.** cycle. **4.** *Maths.* constant. **5.** specific heat capacity. **6.** the velocity of electromagnetic radiation.

C *symbol for:* **1.** *Music.* **a.** the first degree of a major scale containing no sharps or flats (**C major**). **b.** the major or minor key having this note as its tonic. **c.** a time signature denoting four crotchet beats to the bar. See also **alla breve** (sense 2), **common time. 2.** *Chem.* carbon. **3.** capacitance. **4.** heat capacity. **5.** cold (water). **6.** *Physics.* compliance. **7.** Celsius. **8.** centigrade. **9.** century: C20. **~ 10.** *the Roman numeral for* 100.

c. *abbrev. for:* **1.** carat. **2.** carbon (paper). **3.** *Cricket.* caught. **4.** cent(s). **5.** century or centuries. **6.** (*pl.* **cc.**) chapter. **7.** (used esp. preceding a date) circa: *c. 1800.* **8.** colt. **9.** contralto. **10.** copyright. **11.** coulomb.

C. *abbrev. for:* **1.** (on maps as part of name) Cape. **2.** Catholic. **3.** Celtic. **4.** Conservative. **5.** Corps.

Ca *the chemical symbol for* calcium.

ca. *abbrev. for* circa.

C.A. *abbrev. for:* **1.** Central America. **2.** chartered accountant. **3.** Civil Aviation. **4.** (in Britain) Consumers' Association.

C.A.A. (in Britain) *abbrev. for* Civil Aviation Authority.

cab (kæb) *n.* **1. a.** a taxi. **b.** (*as modifier*): *a cab rank.* **2.** the enclosed compartment of a lorry, crane, etc., from which it is driven. **3.** (formerly) a horse-drawn vehicle used for public hire.

cabal (kə'bæl) *n.* **1.** a small group of intriguers, esp. one formed for political purposes. **2.** a secret plot; conspiracy. **3.** a clique. *~vb.* **-balling, -balled. 4.** (*intr.*) to form a cabal; plot.

cabaret ('kæbə,reɪ) *n.* **1.** a floor show of dancing, singing, etc. at a nightclub or restaurant. **2.** *Chiefly U.S.* a nightclub or restaurant providing such entertainment.

cabbage ('kæbɪdʒ) *n.* **1.** Also called: **cole.** any of various cultivated varieties of a cruciferous plant having a short thick stalk and a large head of green or reddish edible leaves. See also **brassica. 2. a.** the head of a cabbage. **b.** the edible leaf bud of the cabbage palm. **3.** *Inf.* a dull or unimaginative person. **4.** *Inf.* a person who has no mental faculties and is dependent on others.

cabbage white *n.* a large white butterfly, the larvae of which feed on the leaves of cabbages and related vegetables.

cabby *or* **cabbie** ('kæbɪ) *n., pl.* **-bies.** *Inf.* a cab driver.

caber ('keɪbə) *n. Scot.* a heavy wooden pole, esp. one thrown in the air in the Highland sport of **tossing the caber.**

cabin ('kæbɪn) *n.* **1.** a small simple dwelling; hut. **2.** a simple house providing accommodation for travellers or holiday-makers. **3.** a room used as an office or living quarters in a ship. **4.** a covered compartment used for shelter in a small boat. **5.** *Brit.* another name for **signal box. 6. a.** the enclosed part of a light aircraft in which the pilot and passengers sit. **b.** the part of an aircraft for passengers or cargo. *~vb.* **7.** to confine in a small space.

cabin boy *n.* a boy who waits on the officers and passengers of a ship.

cabin cruiser *n.* a power boat fitted with a cabin for pleasure cruising or racing.

cabinet ('kæbɪnt) *n.* **1.** a piece of furniture containing shelves, cupboards, or drawers for storage or display. **2.** the outer case of a television, radio, etc. **3. a.** (*often cap.*) the executive and policy-making body of a country, consisting of senior government ministers. **b.** (*sometimes cap.*) an advisory council to a president, governor, etc. **c.** (*as modifier*): *a cabinet reshuffle.* **4. a.** a standard size of paper, 6 × 4 inches (15 × 10 cm), for mounted photographs. **b.** (*as modifier*): *a cabinet photograph.* **5.** *Arch.* a private room.

cabinet-maker *n.* a craftsman specializing in the making of fine furniture. **—'cabinet-,making** *n.*

cable ('keɪbəl) *n.* **1.** a strong thick rope, usually of twisted hemp or steel wire. **2.** *Naut.* an anchor chain or rope. **3.** Also called: **cable length, cable's length.** a unit of length in nautical use that has various values. It is most commonly taken as 120 fathoms (720 feet) in the U.S. and one tenth of a nautical mile (608 feet) in Britain. **4. a.** a wire or bundle of wires that conducts electricity: *a submarine cable.* **5.** Also called: **cablegram.** a telegram sent abroad by submarine cable, telephone line, etc. **6.** Also called: **cable stitch.** a knitting pattern resembling a twisted rope. *~vb.* **7.** to send (a message) to (someone) by cable. **8.** (*tr.*) to fasten or provide with a cable or cables.

cable car *n.* the passenger car on a **cable railway,** drawn along by a strong cable operated by a motor.

cablegram ('keɪbəl,græm) *n.* a more formal name for **cable** (sense 5).

cable television *n.* a television service in which the subscriber's television is connected to the supplier by cable, providing greater choice of channels.

caboodle (kə'bu:dəl) *n. Inf.* a lot, bunch, or group (esp. in **the whole caboodle).**

caboose (kə'bu:s) *n.* **1.** *Railways. U.S.* a guard's van. **2.** *Naut.* a deckhouse for a galley aboard ship. **b.** *Chiefly Brit.* the galley itself. **3.** *Canad.* **a.** a mobile bunkhouse used by lumbermen, etc. **b.** an insulated cabin on runners, equipped with a stove.

cabriolet (,kæbrɪəʊ'leɪ) *n.* **1.** a small two-wheeled horse-drawn carriage with two seats and a folding hood. **2.** a type of motor car with a folding top; drophead coupé.

cacao (kə'kɑ:əʊ, -'keɪəʊ) *n.* **1.** a small tropical American evergreen tree having reddish-brown seed pods from which cocoa and chocolate are prepared. **2. cacao bean.** the dried seed pod; cocoa bean. **3. cacao butter.** another name for **cocoa butter.**

cachalot ('kæʃə,lɒt) *n.* another name for **sperm whale.**

cache (kæʃ) *n.* **1.** a hidden store of provisions, weapons, treasure, etc. **2.** the place where such a store is hidden. *~vb.* **3.** (*tr.*) to store in a cache.

cachet ('kæʃeɪ) *n.* **1.** an official seal on a document, letter, etc. **2.** a distinguishing mark. **3.** prestige; distinction. **4.** *Philately.* a mark stamped by hand on mail for commemorative purposes. **5.** a hollow wafer, formerly used for enclosing an unpleasant-tasting medicine.

cachinnate ('kæki,neɪt) *vb.* (*intr.*) to laugh loudly. **—,cachin'nation** *n.* **—,cachin'natory** *adj.*

cachou ('kæʃu:, kæ'ʃu:) *n.* **1.** a lozenge eaten to sweeten the breath. **2.** another name for **catechu.**

cacique (kə'si:k) *or* **cazique** (kə'zi:k) *n.* **1.** an American Indian chief in a Spanish-speaking region. **2.** (esp. in Spanish America) a local political boss.

cack-handed (,kæk'hændɪd) *adj. Inf.* **1.** left-handed. **2.** clumsy.

cackle ('kækəl) *vb.* **1.** (*intr.*) (esp. of a hen) to squawk with shrill broken notes. **2.** (*intr.*) to laugh or chatter raucously. **3.** (*tr.*) to utter in a cackling manner. *~n.* **4.** the noise or act of cackling. **5.** noisy chatter. **6. cut the cackle.** *Inf.* to be quiet.

caco- *combining form.* bad, unpleasant, or incorrect:

THESAURUS

cab hackney, hackney carriage, minicab, taxi, taxicab

cabin 1. berth, bothy, chalet, cot, cottage, crib, hovel, hut, lodge, shack, shanty, shed **2.** berth, compartment, deckhouse,

quarters, room

cabinet 1. case, chiffonier, closet, commode, cupboard, dresser, escritoire, locker **2.** administration, assembly, council, counsellors, ministry **3.** apartment, boudoir, chamber (*Archaic*)

cackle babble, blather, chatter, chuckle, cluck, crow, gabble, gibber, giggle, jabber, prattle, snicker, snigger, titter

cacophony.

cacoethes (ˌkækəʊˈiːθiːz) n. an uncontrollable urge or desire: *a cacoethes for smoking.*

cacography (kæˈkɒɡrəfɪ) n. **1.** bad handwriting. **2.** incorrect spelling. —**cacographic** (ˌkækəˈɡræfɪk) adj.

cacophony (kəˈkɒfənɪ) n., pl. **-nies.** harsh discordant sound; dissonance. —**caˈcophonous** adj.

cactus (ˈkæktəs) n., pl. **-tuses** or **-ti** (-taɪ). **1.** any of a family of spiny succulent plants of the arid regions of America with swollen tough stems and leaves reduced to spines. **2. cactus dahlia.** a double-flowered variety of dahlia. —**cactaceous** (kækˈteɪʃəs) adj.

cad (kæd) n. *Brit. inf. old-fashioned.* a man who does not behave in a gentlemanly manner towards others. —ˈ**caddish** adj.

cadaver (kəˈdeɪvə, -ˈdɑːv-) n. *Med.* a corpse. —ca**ˈdaveric** adj.

cadaverous (kəˈdævərəs) adj. **1.** of or like a corpse, esp. in being deathly pale. **2.** thin and haggard. —ca**ˈdaverousness** n.

caddie or **caddy** (ˈkædɪ) n., pl. **-dies. 1.** *Golf.* an attendant who carries clubs, etc., for a player. ~vb. **-dying, -died. 2.** (*intr.*) to act as a caddie.

caddis worm or **caddis** (ˈkædɪs) n. the aquatic larva of a caddis fly, which constructs a protective case around itself made of silk, sand, stones, etc. Also called: **caseworm, strawworm.**

caddy[1] (ˈkædɪ) n., pl. **-dies.** *Chiefly Brit.* a small container, esp. for tea.

caddy[2] (ˈkædɪ) n., pl. **-dies,** vb. **-dying, -died.** a variant spelling of **caddie.**

-cade n. *combining form.* indicating a procession of a specified kind: *motorcade.*

cadence (ˈkeɪdəns) or **cadency** n., pl. **-dences** or **-dencies. 1.** the beat or measure of something rhythmic. **2.** a fall in the pitch of the voice, as at the end of a sentence. **3.** intonation. **4.** rhythm in verse or prose. **5.** the close of a musical phrase.

cadenza (kəˈdɛnzə) n. a virtuoso solo passage occurring near the end of a piece of music, formerly improvised by the soloist.

cadet (kəˈdɛt) n. **1.** a young person undergoing preliminary training, usually before full entry to the uniformed services, police, etc. **2.** (in England and in France before 1789) a gentleman who entered the army to prepare for a commission. **3.** a younger son. **4. cadet branch.** the family of a younger son. **5.** (in New Zealand, formerly) a person learning sheep farming on a sheep station. —ca**ˈdetship** n.

cadge (kædʒ) vb. **1.** to get (food, money, etc.) by sponging or begging. ~n. **2.** *Brit.* a person who cadges. —ˈ**cadger** n.

cadi or **kadi** (ˈkɑːdɪ, ˈkeɪdɪ) n., pl. **-dis.** a judge in a Muslim community.

cadmium (ˈkædmɪəm) n. a malleable bluish-white metallic element that occurs in association with zinc ores. It is used in electroplating and alloys. Symbol: Cd; atomic no.: 48; atomic wt.: 112.4.

cadre (ˈkɑːdə) n. **1.** the nucleus of trained professional servicemen forming the basis for military expansion. **2.** a basic unit or structure; nucleus. **3.** a member of a cadre.

caduceus (kəˈdjuːsɪəs) n., pl. **-cei** (-sɪˌaɪ). **1.** *Classical myth.* a winged staff entwined with two serpents carried by Hermes (Mercury) as messenger of the gods. **2.** an insignia resembling this staff used as an emblem of the medical profession.

caecum or U.S. **cecum** (ˈsiːkəm) n., pl. **-ca** (-kə). *Anat.* any structure that ends in a blind sac or pouch, esp. that at the beginning of the large intestine. —ˈ**caecal** or U.S. ˈ**cecal** adj.

Caenozoic (ˌsiːnəˈzəʊɪk) adj. a variant spelling of **Cenozoic.**

Caerphilly (kɛəˈfɪlɪ) n. a creamy white mild-flavoured cheese, orig. made in Caerphilly in SE Wales.

Caesar (ˈsiːzə) n. **1.** any Roman emperor. **2.** (*sometimes not cap.*) any emperor, autocrat, or dictator. **3.** a title of the Roman emperors from Augustus to Hadrian. **4.** *Inf.* in medicine, a Caesarean section.

Caesarean, Caesarian, or U.S. **Cesarean, Cesarian** (sɪˈzɛərɪən) adj. **1.** of or relating to any of the Caesars, esp. Julius Caesar. ~n. **2.** (*sometimes not cap.*) *Surgery.* **a.** a Caesarean section. **b.** (*as modifier*): *Caesarean operation.*

Caesarean section n. surgical incision through the abdominal and uterine walls in order to deliver a baby.

caesium or U.S. **cesium** (ˈsiːzɪəm) n. a ductile silvery-white element of the alkali metal group. It is used in photocells and in an atomic clock (**caesium clock**) that uses the frequency of radiation from changing the spin of electrons. The radioisotope **caesium-137,** with a half-life of 30.2 years, is used in radiotherapy. Symbol: Cs; atomic no.: 55; atomic wt.: 132.905.

caesura (sɪˈzjʊərə) n., pl. **-ras** or **-rae** (-riː). **1.** (in modern prosody) a pause, esp. for sense, usually near the middle of a verse line. **2.** (in classical prosody) a break between words within a metrical foot. —cae**ˈsural** adj.

café (ˈkæfeɪ, ˈkæfɪ) n. a small or inexpensive restaurant serving light or easily prepared meals and refreshments.

cafeteria (ˌkæfɪˈtɪərɪə) n. a self-service restaurant.

caff (kæf) n. a slang word for **café.**

caffeine or **caffein** (ˈkæfiːn) n. a white crystalline bitter alkaloid responsible for the stimulant action of tea, coffee, and cocoa.

caftan (ˈkæfˌtæn, -ˌtɑːn) n. a variant spelling of **kaftan.**

cage (keɪdʒ) n. **1. a.** an enclosure, usually made with bars or wire, for keeping birds, monkeys, etc. **b.** (*as modifier*): *cagebird.* **2.** a thing or place that confines. **3.** something resembling a cage in function or structure: *the rib cage.* **4.** the enclosed platform of a lift, esp. as used in a mine. ~vb. **5.** (*tr.*) to confine in or as in a cage.

cagey or **cagy** (ˈkeɪdʒɪ) adj. **-ier, -iest.** *Inf.* not frank; wary. —ˈ**caginess** n.

cagoule (kəˈɡuːl) n. a lightweight usually knee-length type of anorak.

cahoots (kəˈhuːts) pl. n. (*sometimes sing.*) *Inf.* **1.** U.S. partnership; league. **2. in cahoots.** in collusion.

caiman (ˈkeɪmən) n., pl. **-mans.** a variant spelling of **cayman.**

Cain (keɪn) n. **1.** the first son of Adam and Eve, who killed his brother Abel (Genesis 4:1-16). **2. raise Cain.** *Sl.* to cause a commotion.

Cainozoic (ˌkaɪnəʊˈzəʊɪk, ˌkeɪ-) adj. a variant spelling of **Cenozoic.**

cairn (kɛən) n. **1.** a mound of stones erected as a memorial or marker. **2.** Also called: **cairn terrier.** a small rough-haired breed of terrier originally from Scotland.

cairngorm (ˈkɛənˌɡɔːm) n. a smoky yellow or brown variety of quartz, used as a gemstone. Also called: **smoky quartz.**

caisson (kəˈsuːn, ˈkeɪsən) n. **1.** a watertight chamber open at the bottom and containing air under pressure, used to carry out construction work under water. **2.** a watertight float filled with air, used to raise sunken ships. **3.** a watertight structure placed across the entrance of a dry dock, etc., to exclude water. **4. a.** a box containing explosives formerly used as a mine. **b.** an ammunition chest.

caisson disease n. another name for **decompression sickness.**

cajole (kəˈdʒəʊl) vb. to persuade (someone) by flattery to do what one wants; wheedle; coax. —ca**ˈjolement** n. —ca**ˈjoler** n. —ca**ˈjolery** n.

cake (keɪk) n. **1.** a baked food, usually in loaf or layer form, made from a mixture of flour, sugar, and eggs. **2.**

THESAURUS

cad bounder (*Brit. inf.*), churl, cur, dastard (*Archaic*), heel (*Sl.*), knave, rat (*Sl.*), rotter (*Sl.*)

cadaverous ashen, blanched, bloodless, corpselike, deathlike, deathly, emaciated, exsanguinous, gaunt, ghastly, haggard, hollow-eyed, pale, pallid, wan

caddish despicable, ill-bred, low, ungentlemanly, unmannerly

cadence 1. beat, lilt, measure, metre, pulse, rhythm, swing, tempo, throb 2. accent, inflection, intonation, modulation

café cafeteria, coffee bar, coffee shop, lunchroom, restaurant, snack bar, tearoom

cage 1. v. confine, coop up, fence in, immure, impound, imprison, incarcerate, lock up, mew, restrain, shut up 2. n. corral (*U.S.*), enclosure, pen, pound

cagey, cagy careful, cautious, chary, discreet, guarded, noncommittal, shrewd, wary, wily

cajole beguile, coax, decoy, dupe, entice, entrap, flatter, inveigle, lure, manoeuvre, mislead, seduce, sweet-talk (*U.S. inf.*), tempt, wheedle

a flat thin mass of bread, esp. unleavened bread. **3.** a shaped mass of dough or other food: *a fish cake.* **4.** a mass, slab, or crust of a solidified substance, as of soap. **5. have one's cake and eat it.** to enjoy both of two desirable but incompatible alternatives. **6. go** *or* **sell like hot cakes.** *Inf.* to be sold very quickly. **7. piece of cake.** *Inf.* something that is easily achieved. **8. take the cake.** *Inf.* to surpass all others, esp. in stupidity, folly, etc. **9.** *Inf.* the whole of something that is to be shared or divided: *a larger slice of the cake.* ~*vb.* **10.** (*tr.*) to encrust: *the hull was caked with salt.* **11.** to form or be formed into a hardened mass.

cakewalk ('keɪk,wɔːk) *n.* **1.** a dance based on a march with intricate steps, originally performed by American Negroes with the prize of a cake. **2.** a piece of music for this dance.

cal. *abbrev. for:* **1.** calendar. **2.** calibre. **3.** calorie (small).

Cal. *abbrev. for* Calorie (large).

calabash ('kælə,bæʃ) *n.* **1.** Also called: **calabash tree.** a tropical American evergreen tree that produces large round gourds. **2.** the gourd. **3.** the dried hollow shell of a gourd used as the bowl of a tobacco pipe, a bottle, etc. **4. calabash nutmeg.** a tropical African shrub whose seeds can be used as nutmegs.

calamine ('kælə,maɪn) *n.* a pink powder consisting of zinc oxide and ferric oxide, used medicinally in the form of soothing lotions or ointments.

calamitous (kə'læmɪtəs) *adj.* causing, involving, or resulting in a calamity; disastrous.

calamity (kə'læmɪtɪ) *n., pl.* **-ties. 1.** a disaster or misfortune, esp. one causing distress or misery. **2.** a state or feeling of deep distress or misery.

calandria (kə'lændrɪə) *n.* a cylindrical vessel through which vertical tubes pass, esp. one forming part of a heat exchanger or nuclear reactor.

calcareous (kæl'kɛərɪəs) *adj.* of, containing, or resembling calcium carbonate; chalky.

calceolaria (,kælsɪə'lɛərɪə) *n.* a tropical American plant cultivated for its speckled slipper-shaped flowers. Also called: **slipperwort.**

calces ('kælsiːz) *n.* a plural of **calx.**

calciferol (kæl'sɪfərɒl) *n.* a fat-soluble steroid, found esp. in fish-liver oils and used in the treatment of rickets. Also called: **vitamin D₂.**

calciferous (kæl'sɪfərəs) *adj.* producing salts of calcium, esp. calcium carbonate.

calcify ('kælsɪ,faɪ) *vb.* **-fying, -fied. 1.** to convert or be converted into lime. **2.** to harden or become hardened by impregnation with calcium salts. —**calcifi'cation** *n.*

calcine ('kælsaɪn, -sɪn) *vb.* **1.** (*tr.*) to heat (a substance) so that it is oxidized, is reduced, or loses water. **2.** (*intr.*) to oxidize as a result of heating. —**calcination** (,kælsɪ-'neɪʃən) *n.*

calcite ('kælsaɪt) *n.* a colourless or white mineral consisting of crystalline calcium carbonate: the transparent variety is Iceland spar. Formula: $CaCO_3$.

calcium ('kælsɪəm) *n.* a malleable silvery-white metallic element of the alkaline earth group, occurring esp. as forms of calcium carbonate. It is an essential constituent of bones and teeth. Symbol: Ca; atomic no.: 20; atomic wt.: 40.08.

calcium carbonate *n.* a white crystalline salt occurring in limestone, chalk, and pearl: used in the production of lime. Formula: $CaCO_3$.

calcium hydroxide *n.* a white crystalline slightly soluble alkali with many uses, esp. in cement, water softening, and the neutralization of acid soils. Formula: $Ca(OH)_2$. Also called: **lime, slaked lime, caustic lime.**

calcspar ('kælk,spɑː) *n.* another name for **calcite.**

calculable ('kælkjʊləbəl) *adj.* **1.** that may be computed

or estimated. **2.** predictable. —**calcula'bility** *n.* —**'calculably** *adv.*

calculate ('kælkjʊ,leɪt) *vb.* **1.** to solve (one or more problems) by a mathematical procedure. **2.** (*tr.; may take a clause as object*) to determine beforehand by judgment, etc.; estimate. **3.** (*tr.; usually passive*) to aim: *the car was calculated to appeal to women.* **4.** (*intr.;* foll. by *on* or *upon*) to rely. **5.** (*tr.; may take a clause as object*) *U.S. dialect.* to suppose. —**calculative** ('kælkjʊlətɪv) *adj.*

calculated ('kælkjʊ,leɪtɪd) *adj.* (*usually prenominal*) **1.** undertaken after considering the likelihood of success or failure. **2.** premeditated: *a calculated insult.*

calculating ('kælkjʊ,leɪtɪŋ) *adj.* **1.** selfishly scheming. **2.** shrewd. —**'calcu,latingly** *adv.*

calculation (,kælkjʊ'leɪʃən) *n.* **1.** the act, process, or result of calculating. **2.** a forecast. **3.** careful planning, esp. for selfish motives.

calculator ('kælkjʊ,leɪtə) *n.* **1.** a device for performing mathematical calculations, esp. an electronic device that can be held in the hand. **2.** a person or thing that calculates. **3.** a set of tables used as an aid to calculations.

calculus ('kælkjʊləs) *n., pl.* **-luses. 1.** a branch of mathematics, developed independently by Newton and Leibnitz. Both **differential calculus** and **integral calculus** are concerned with the effect on a function of an infinitesimal change in the independent variable. **2.** *pl.* **-li** (-,laɪ). *Pathol.* a stonelike concretion of minerals found in organs of the body. **3.** any mathematical system of calculation involving the use of symbols.

caldron ('kɔːldrən) *n.* a variant spelling of **cauldron.**

calèche (*French* ka'lɛʃ) *n. Canad.* a horse-drawn carriage used for taking tourists around in cities such as Montreal and Quebec.

Caledonian (,kælɪ'dəʊnɪən) *adj.* **1.** relating to Scotland. **2.** of a period of mountain building in NW Europe in the Palaeozoic era. ~*n.* **3.** *Literary.* a native or inhabitant of Scotland.

calendar ('kælɪndə) *n.* **1.** a system for determining the beginning, length, and order of years and their divisions. **2.** a table showing any such arrangement, esp. as applied to one or more successive years. **3.** a list or schedule of pending court cases, appointments, etc. ~*vb.* **4.** (*tr.*) to enter in a calendar; schedule. —**calendrical** (kæ'lɛn drɪk əl) *or* **ca'lendric** *adj.*

calender ('kælɪndə) *n.* **1.** a machine in which paper or cloth is smoothed by passing between rollers. ~*vb.* **2.** (*tr.*) to subject (material) to such a process.

calends *or* **kalends** ('kælɪndz) *pl. n.* the first day of each month in the ancient Roman calendar.

calendula (kæ'lɛndjʊlə) *n.* any of a genus of Eurasian plants, esp. the pot marigold, having orange-and-yellow rayed flowers.

calf¹ (kɑːf) *n., pl.* **calves. 1.** the young of cattle, esp. domestic cattle. **2.** the young of certain other mammals, such as the buffalo and whale. **3.** a large piece of ice detached from an iceberg, etc. **4. kill the fatted calf.** to celebrate lavishly, esp. as a welcome.

calf² (kɑːf) *n., pl.* **calves.** the thick fleshy part of the back of the leg between the ankle and the knee.

calf love *n.* temporary infatuation of an adolescent for a member of the opposite sex.

calf's-foot jelly *n.* a jelly made from the stock of boiled calves' feet and flavourings.

calfskin ('kɑːf,skɪn) *n.* **1.** the skin or hide of a calf. **2.** Also called: **calf. a.** fine leather made from this skin. **b.** (*as modifier*): *calfskin boots.*

calibrate ('kælɪ,breɪt) *vb.* (*tr.*) **1.** to measure the calibre of (a gun, etc.). **2.** to mark (the scale of a measuring instrument) so that readings can be made in appropriate

---

THESAURUS

cake 1. *v.* bake, cement, coagulate, congeal, consolidate, dry, encrust, harden, inspissate (*Archaic*), ossify, solidify, thicken **2.** *n.* bar, block, cube, loaf, lump, mass, slab

calamitous blighting, cataclysmic, catastrophic, deadly, devastating, dire, disastrous, fatal, pernicious, ruinous, tragic, woeful

calamity adversity, affliction, cataclysm, catastrophe, disaster, distress, downfall, hardship, misadventure, mischance, misfor-

tune, mishap, reverse, ruin, scourge, tragedy, trial, tribulation, woe, wretchedness

calculate 1. adjust, compute, consider, count, determine, enumerate, estimate, figure, gauge, judge, rate, reckon, value, weigh, work out **2.** aim, design, intend, plan

calculated considered, deliberate, intended, intentional, planned, premeditated, purposeful

calculating canny, cautious, contriving, crafty, cunning, designing, devious, Machia-

vellian, manipulative, politic, scheming, sharp, shrewd, sly

calculation 1. answer, computation, estimate, estimation, figuring, forecast, judgment, reckoning, result **2.** caution, circumspection, contrivance, deliberation, discretion, foresight, forethought, planning, precaution

units. **3.** to determine the accuracy of (a measuring instrument, etc.). —,**cali'bration** n. —'**cali,brator** n.

calibre or U.S. **caliber** ('kælɪbə) n. **1.** the diameter of a cylindrical body, esp. the internal diameter of a tube or the bore of a firearm. **2.** the diameter of a shell or bullet. **3.** ability; distinction. **4.** personal character: *a man of high calibre.* —'**calibred** or U.S. '**calibered** adj.

calices ('kælɪ,siːz) n. the plural of **calix.**

calico ('kælɪ,kəʊ) n., pl. **-coes** or **-cos.** **1.** a white or unbleached cotton fabric. **2.** Chiefly U.S. a coarse printed cotton fabric.

californium (,kælɪ'fɔːnɪəm) n. a transuranic element artificially produced from curium. Symbol: Cf; atomic no.: 98; half-life of most stable isotope, ^{251}Cf: 800 years (approx.).

caliper ('kælɪpə) n. the usual U.S. spelling of **calliper.**

caliph, calif, or **khalif** ('keɪlɪf, 'kæl-) n. Islam. the title of the successors of Mohammed as rulers of the Islamic world.

caliphate, califate, or **khalifate** ('keɪlɪ,feɪt) n. the office, jurisdiction, or reign of a caliph.

calisthenics (,kælɪs'θɛnɪks) n. a variant spelling (esp. U.S.) of **callisthenics.**

calix ('keɪlɪks, 'kæ-) n., pl. **calices** ('kælɪ,siːz). a cup; chalice.

calk (kɔːk) vb. a variant spelling of **caulk.**

call (kɔːl) vb. **1.** (often foll. by *out*) to speak or utter (words, sounds, etc.) loudly so as to attract attention: *he called out her name.* **2.** (tr.) to ask or order to come: *to call a policeman.* **3.** (intr.; sometimes foll. by *on*) to make a visit (to): *she called on him.* **4.** (often foll. by *up*) to telephone (a person). **5.** (tr.) to summon to a specific office, profession, etc. **6.** (of animals or birds) to utter (a characteristic sound or cry). **7.** (tr.) to summon (a bird or animal), as by imitating its cry. **8.** (tr.) to name or style: *they called the dog Rover.* **9.** (tr.) to designate: *they called him a coward.* **10.** (tr.) to regard in a specific way: *I call it a foolish waste of time.* **11.** (tr.) to attract (attention). **12.** (tr.) to read (a list, etc.) aloud to check for omissions or absentees. **13.** (when tr., usually foll. by *for*) to give an order (for): *to call a strike.* **14.** (intr.) to try to predict the result of tossing a coin. **15.** (tr.) to awaken: *I was called early this morning.* **16.** (tr.) to cause to assemble. **17.** (tr.) Sport. (of an umpire, etc.) to pass judgment upon (a shot, etc.) with a call. **18.** Austral. to broadcast a commentary on a race, esp. a horse race. **19.** (tr.) to demand repayment of (a loan, security, etc.). **20.** Brit. to award (a student at an Inn of Court) the degree of barrister (esp. in **call to the bar**). **21.** (tr.) Poker. to demand that (a player) expose his hand, after equalling his bet. **22.** (intr.) Bridge. to make a bid. **23.** (tr.) to expose (a person's misleading statements, etc.): *I called his bluff.* **24.** (in square dancing) to call out (instructions) to the dancers. **25.** (intr.; foll by *for*) **a.** to require: *this problem calls for study.* **b.** to come or go (for) in order to fetch. **26.** (intr.; foll. by *on* or *upon*) to make an appeal or request (to): *they called upon him to reply.* **27. call into being.** to create. **28. call into play.** to begin to operate. **29. call into question.** See **question.** **30. call to mind.** to cause to be remembered. ~n. **31.** a cry or shout. **32.** the characteristic cry of a bird or animal. **33.** a device, such as a whistle, intended to imitate the cry of a bird or animal. **34.** a summons or invitation. **35.** a summons or signal sounded on a horn, bugle, etc. **36.** a short visit: *the doctor made six calls this morning.* **37.** an inner urge to some task or profession; vocation. **38.** allure or fascination, esp. of a place: *the call of the forest.* **39.** need, demand, or occasion: *there is no call to shout.* **40.** demand or claim (esp. in **the call of duty**). **41.** Theatre. a notice to actors informing them of times of rehearsals. **42.** a conversation or a request for a connection by telephone. **43.** Commerce. **a.** a demand for repayment of a loan. **b.** (as modifier): call money. **44.** Finance. a demand for redeemable bonds or shares to be presented for repayment. **45.** Poker. a demand for a hand or hands to be exposed. **46.** Bridge. a bid, or a player's turn to bid. **47.** Sport. a decision of an umpire or referee regarding a shot, pitch, etc. **48.** Austral. a broadcast commentary on a race, esp. a horse race. **49.** Also called: **call option.** Stock Exchange. an option to buy a stated amount of securities at a specified price during a specified period. **50. call of nature.** See **nature. 51.** on **call. a.** (of a loan, etc.) repayable on demand. **b.** (of a doctor, etc.) available for duty. **52. within call.** accessible. ~See also **call down, call in,** etc.

call box n. a soundproof enclosure for a public telephone. Also called: **telephone kiosk.**

call down vb. (tr., adv.) to request or invoke: *to call down God's anger.*

caller ('kɔːlə) n. **1.** a person or thing that calls, esp. a person who makes a brief visit. **2.** Austral. a racing commentator.

call girl n. a prostitute with whom appointments are made by telephone.

calligraphy (kə'lɪgrəfɪ) n. handwriting, esp. beautiful handwriting. —**cal'ligrapher** or **cal'ligraphist** n. —**calligraphic** (,kælɪ'græfɪk) adj.

call in vb. (adv.) **1.** (intr.; often foll. by *on*) to pay a visit, esp. a brief one: *call in if you are in the neighbourhood.* **2.** (tr.) to demand payment of: *to call in a loan.* **3.** (tr.) to take (something) out of circulation, because it is defective.

calling ('kɔːlɪŋ) n. **1.** a strong inner urge to follow an occupation, etc.; vocation. **2.** an occupation, profession, or trade.

calliper or U.S. **caliper** ('kælɪpə) n. **1.** (often pl.) Also called: **calliper compasses.** an instrument for measuring internal or external dimensions, consisting of two steel legs hinged together. **2.** Also called: **calliper splint.** Med. a metal splint for supporting the leg. ~vb. **3.** (tr.) to measure with callipers.

calliper rule n. a measuring instrument having two parallel jaws, one fixed and the other sliding.

callisthenics or **calisthenics** (,kælɪs'θɛnɪks) n. **1.** (functioning as pl.) light exercises designed to promote general fitness. **2.** (functioning as sing.) the practice of callisthenic exercises. —,**callis'thenic** or ,**calis'thenic** adj.

call off vb. (tr., adv.) **1.** to cancel or abandon: *the game was called off.* **2.** to order (an animal or person) to desist: *the man called off his dog.* **3.** to stop (something).

callosity (kə'lɒsɪtɪ) n., pl. **-ties. 1.** hard-heartedness. **2.** a callus.

callous ('kæləs) adj. **1.** insensitive. **2.** (of skin) hardened and thickened. ~vb. **3.** Pathol. to make or become callous. —'**callously** adv. —'**callousness** n.

call out vb. (adv.) **1.** to utter aloud, esp. loudly. **2.** (tr.) to summon: *call out the troops.* **3.** (tr.) to order (workers) to strike. **4.** to challenge to a duel.

callow ('kæləʊ) adj. lacking experience of life; immature. —'**callowness** n.

call up vb. (adv.) **1.** to summon to report for active military service, as in time of war. **2.** (tr.) to recall (something); evoke. **3.** (tr.) to bring or summon (people, etc.) into action. **4.** (tr.) to telephone. ~n. **call-up. 5. a.** a general order to report for military service. **b.** the number of men so summoned.

callus ('kæləs) n., pl. **-luses. 1.** Also called: **callosity.** an area of skin that is hard or thick, esp. on the sole of the

---

THESAURUS

calibre 1. bore, diameter, gauge, measure **2.** Fig. ability, capacity, distinction, endowment, faculty, force, gifts, merit, parts, quality, scope, stature, strength, talent, worth

call v. **1.** announce, arouse, awaken, cry, cry out, hail, halloo, proclaim, rouse, shout, waken, yell **2.** assemble, bid, collect, contact, convene, convoke, gather, invite, muster, phone, rally, ring up, summon, telephone **3.** christen, denominate, describe as, designate, dub, entitle, label, name, style, term **4.** announce, appoint, declare, decree, elect, ordain, order, proclaim, set apart **5.** consider,

estimate, judge, regard, think ~n. **6.** cry, hail, scream, shout, signal, whoop, yell **7.** announcement, appeal, command, demand, invitation, notice, order, plea, request, ring (Brit. inf.), summons, supplication, visit **8.** cause, claim, excuse, grounds, justification, need, occasion, reason, right, urge

call for 1. demand, entail, involve, necessitate, need, occasion, require, suggest **2.** collect, fetch, pick up, uplift (Scot.)

calling business, career, employment, life's work, line, métier, mission, occupation, profession, province, pursuit, trade, voca-

tion, walk of life, work

call on 1. drop in on, look in on, look up, see, visit **2.** appeal to, ask, bid, call upon, entreat, invite, invoke, request, summon, supplicate

callous apathetic, case-hardened, cold, hard-bitten, hard-boiled (Inf.), hardened, hardhearted, heartless, indifferent, indurated (Rare), insensate, insensible, insensitive, inured, obdurate, soulless, thick-skinned, torpid, uncaring, unfeeling, unresponsive, unsusceptible, unsympathetic

foot. **2.** an area of bony tissue formed during the healing of a fractured bone. **3.** *Bot.* a mass of hard protective tissue produced in woody plants at the site of an injury.

calm (kɑːm) *adj.* **1.** still: *a calm sea.* **2.** *Meteorol.* without wind, or with wind of less than 1 m.p.h. **3.** not disturbed, agitated, or excited: *he stayed calm.* **4.** tranquil; serene: *a calm voice.* ~*n.* **5.** an absence of disturbance or rough motion. **6.** absence of wind. **7.** tranquillity. ~*vb.* **8.** (often foll. by *down*) to make or become calm. —'**calmly** *adv.* —'**calmness** *n.*

calomel ('kæləˌmɛl, -məl) *n.* a colourless tasteless powder consisting chiefly of mercurous chloride, used medicinally, esp. as a cathartic.

Calor Gas ('kælə) *n. Trademark.* butane gas liquefied under pressure in portable containers for domestic use.

caloric (kə'lɒrɪk) *adj.* **1.** of or concerned with heat or calories. ~*n.* **2.** *Obs.* a hypothetical elastic fluid, the embodiment of heat.

calorie *or* **calory** ('kælərɪ) *n., pl.* -**ries.** a unit of heat, equal to 4.1868 joules (**International Table calorie**): formerly defined as the quantity of heat required to raise the temperature of 1 gram of water by 1°C. Abbrev.: **cal.** Also called: **small calorie.**

Calorie ('kælərɪ) *n.* **1.** Also called: **kilogram calorie, large calorie.** a unit of heat, equal to one thousand calories. Abbrev.: **Cal. 2.** the amount of a specific food capable of producing one thousand calories of energy.

calorific (ˌkælə'rɪfɪk) *adj.* of, concerning, or generating heat. —ˌ**calo'rifically** *adv.*

calorimeter (ˌkælə'rɪmɪtə) *n.* an apparatus for measuring amounts of heat, esp. to find calorific values, etc. —**calorimetric** (ˌkælərɪ'mɛtrɪk) *adj.* —ˌ**calo'rimetry** *n.*

calque (kælk) *n.* another word for **loan translation.**

calumet ('kæljuˌmɛt) *n.* the peace pipe.

calumniate (kə'lʌmnɪˌeɪt) *vb.* (*tr.*) to slander. —ca,lumni'ation *n.* —ca'lumni,ator *n.*

calumny ('kæləmnɪ) *n., pl.* -**nies. 1.** the malicious utterance of false charges or misrepresentation. **2.** such a false charge or misrepresentation. —**calumnious** (kə'lʌmnɪəs) *or* ca'lumniatory *adj.*

Calvary ('kælvərɪ) *n.* the place just outside the walls of Jerusalem where Jesus was crucified. Also called: **Golgotha.**

calve (kɑːv) *vb.* **1.** to give birth to (a calf). **2.** (of a glacier or iceberg) to release (masses of ice) in breaking up.

calves (kɑːvz) *n.* the plural of **calf.**

Calvinism ('kælvɪˌnɪzəm) *n.* the theological system of Calvin, 16th-century French theologian, and his followers, characterized by emphasis on predestination and justification by faith. —'**Calvinist** *n., adj.* —ˌ**Calvin'istic** *or* ˌ**Calvin'istical** *adj.*

calx (kælks) *n., pl.* **calxes** *or* **calces** ('kælsiːz). **1.** the powdery metallic oxide formed when an ore or mineral is roasted. **2.** calcium oxide.

calypso (kə'lɪpsəʊ) *n., pl.* -**sos.** a popular type of satirical West Indian ballad, esp. from Trinidad, usually extemporized to a syncopated accompaniment.

calyx ('keɪlɪks, 'kælɪks) *n., pl.* **calyxes** *or* **calyces** ('keɪlɪˌsiːz, 'kælɪ-). **1.** the sepals of a flower collectively that protect the developing flower bud. **2.** any cup-shaped cavity or structure.

cam (kæm) *n.* a rotating cylinder attached to a revolving shaft to give a reciprocating motion to a part in contact with it.

camaraderie (ˌkæmə'rɑːdərɪ) *n.* a spirit of familiarity and trust existing between friends.

camber ('kæmbə) *n.* **1.** a slight upward curve to the centre of the surface of a road, ship's deck, etc. **2.** another name for **bank²** (sense 8). **3.** an outward inclination of the front wheels of a road vehicle so that they are slight-

ly closer together at the bottom. **4.** the curvature of an aerofoil section from the leading edge. ~*vb.* **5.** to form or be formed with a surface that curves upwards to its centre.

Cambrian ('kæmbrɪən) *adj.* **1.** of or formed in the first 100 million years of the Palaeozoic era. **2.** of or relating to Wales. ~*n.* **3. the.** the Cambrian period or rock system. **4.** a Welshman.

cambric ('keɪmbrɪk) *n.* a fine white linen fabric.

Cambs. *abbrev. for* Cambridgeshire.

came (keɪm) *vb.* the past tense of **come.**

camel ('kæməl) *n.* **1.** either of two cud-chewing, humped mammals (see **Arabian camel, Bactrian camel**) that are adapted for surviving long periods without food or water in desert regions. **2.** a float attached to a vessel to increase its buoyancy. **3.** a fawn colour.

cameleer (ˌkæmɪ'lɪə) *n.* a camel-driver.

camellia (kə'miːlɪə) *n.* any of a genus of ornamental shrubs having glossy evergreen leaves and showy white, pink, or red flowers. Also called: **japonica.**

camelopard ('kæmɪləˌpɑːd, kə'mɛl-) *n.* an obsolete word for **giraffe.**

camel's hair *or* **camelhair** *n.* **1.** the hair of a camel, used in rugs, etc. **2.** soft cloth made of this hair, usually tan in colour. **3.** (*modifier*) (of a painter's brush) made from the tail hairs of squirrels.

Camembert ('kæməmˌbɛə) *n.* a soft creamy cheese.

cameo ('kæmɪˌəʊ) *n., pl.* **cameos. 1.** a medallion, as on a brooch or ring, with a profile head carved in relief. **2.** an engraving upon a gem or other stone so that the background is of a different colour from the raised design. **3.** a stone with such an engraving. **4. a.** a brief dramatic scene played by a well-known actor or actress in a film or television play. **b.** (*as modifier*): *a cameo performance.* **5.** a short literary work.

camera ('kæmərə) *n.* **1.** an optical device consisting of a lens system set in a light-proof construction inside which a light-sensitive film or plate can be positioned. **2.** *Television.* the equipment used to convert the optical image of a scene into the corresponding electrical signals. **3.** *pl.* -**erae** (-əˌriː): a judge's private room. **4. in camera. a.** *Law.* relating to a hearing from which members of the public are excluded. **b.** in private.

camiknickers ('kæmɪˌnɪkəz) *pl. n.* (formerly) women's knickers attached to a camisole top.

camisole ('kæmɪˌsəʊl) *n.* **1.** a woman's underbodice with shoulder straps, originally designed as a cover for a corset. **2.** a woman's short negligee.

camomile *or* **chamomile** ('kæməˌmaɪl) *n.* **1.** any of a genus of aromatic plants whose finely dissected leaves and daisy-like flowers are used medicinally. **2.** any plant of a related genus as **German** *or* **wild camomile. 3. camomile tea.** a medicinal beverage made from the fragrant leaves and flowers of any of these plants.

camouflage ('kæməˌflɑːʒ) *n.* **1.** the exploitation of natural surroundings or artificial aids to conceal or disguise the presence of military units, etc. **2.** the means by which animals escape the notice of predators. **3.** a device or expedient designed to conceal or deceive. ~*vb.* **4.** (*tr.*) to conceal by camouflage.

camp¹ (kæmp) *n.* **1. a.** a place where tents, cabins, etc., are erected for the use of military troops, etc. **b.** (*as modifier*): *a camp fire.* **2.** tents, cabins, etc., used as temporary lodgings by holidaymakers, Scouts, gypsies, etc. **3.** the group of people living in such lodgings. **4.** a group supporting a given doctrine: *the socialist camp.* **5.** (*modifier*) suitable for use in temporary quarters, on holiday, etc.: *a camp bed; a camp chair.* **6.** *S. African.* a field or pasture. **7.** *Austral.* a place where sheep or cattle gather to rest. ~*vb.* **8.** (*intr.*; often foll. by *down*) to establish or set up a camp. **9.** (*intr.*; often foll. by *out*) to live temporarily in or as if in a tent. —'**camper** *n.*

THESAURUS

calm *adj.* **1.** balmy, halcyon, mild, pacific, peaceful, placid, quiet, restful, serene, smooth, still, tranquil, windless **2.** collected, composed, cool, dispassionate, equable, impassive, imperturbable, relaxed, sedate, self-possessed, undisturbed, unemotional, unexcitable, unmoved, unflappable (*Inf.*), unmoved, unruffled ~*v.* **3.** hush, mollify, placate, quieten, relax, soothe ~*n.* **4.** calmness, hush, peace, peacefulness, quiet, repose, serenity, stillness

calmness 1. calm, composure, equability, hush, motionlessness, peace, peacefulness, placidity, quiet, repose, restfulness, serenity, smoothness, stillness, tranquillity **2.** composure, cool (*Sl.*), coolness, dispassion, equanimity, impassivity, imperturbability, poise, sang-froid, self-possession

calumny abuse, aspersion, backbiting, calumniation, defamation, denigration, derogation, detraction, evil-speaking, insult, libel, lying, misrepresentation, obloquy, revile-

ment, slander, smear, stigma, vilification, vituperation

camouflage 1. *n.* blind, cloak, concealment, cover, deceptive markings, disguise, false appearance, front, guise, mask, masquerade, mimicry, protective colouring, screen, subterfuge **2.** *v.* cloak, conceal, cover, disguise, hide, mask, obfuscate, obscure, screen, veil

—**'camping** n.

camp² (kæmp) *Inf.* ~*adj.* **1.** effeminate; affected. **2.** homosexual. **3.** consciously artificial, vulgar, or mannered. ~*vb.* **4.** (*tr.*) to perform or invest with a camp quality. **5. camp it up. a.** to overact. **b.** to flaunt one's homosexuality.

campaign (kæm'peɪn) n. **1.** a series of coordinated activities, such as public speaking, designed to achieve a social, political, or commercial goal: *a presidential campaign.* **2.** *Mil.* a number of operations aimed at achieving a single objective. ~*vb.* **3.** (*intr.*; often foll. by *for*) to conduct, serve in, or go on a campaign. —**cam'paigner** n.

campanile (ˌkæmpə'niːlɪ) n. (esp. in Italy) a bell tower, not usually attached to another building.

campanology (ˌkæmpə'nɒlədʒɪ) n. the art or skill of ringing bells. —**campanological** (ˌkæmpənə'lɒdʒɪkəl) adj. —ˌcampa'nologist or ˌcampa'nologer n.

campanula (kæm'pænjʊlə) n. any of a genus of N temperate plants having blue or white bell-shaped flowers. Also called: **bellflower.**

camp follower n. **1.** any civilian, esp. a prostitute, who unofficially provides services to military personnel. **2.** a nonmember who is sympathetic to a particular group, theory, etc.

camphor ('kæmfə) n. a whitish crystalline aromatic ketone obtained from the wood of an Asian and Australian laurel (**camphor tree**): used in medicine as a liniment. —**camphoric** (kæm'fɒrɪk) adj.

camphorate ('kæmfəˌreɪt) vb. (*tr.*) to apply, treat with, or impregnate with camphor.

campion ('kæmpɪən) n. any of various plants related to the pink, having red, pink, or white flowers.

camp site n. an area on which holiday-makers may pitch a tent, etc. Also called: **camping site.**

campus ('kæmpəs) n., pl. -**puses. 1.** the grounds and buildings of a university. **2.** *Chiefly U.S.* the outside area of a college, etc.

camshaft ('kæmˌʃɑːft) n. a shaft having one or more cams attached to it.

can¹ (kæn; unstressed kən) vb. past **could.** (takes an infinitive without *to* or an implied infinitive) used as an auxiliary: **1.** to indicate ability, skill, or fitness to perform a task: *I can run.* **2.** to indicate permission or the right to something: *can I have a drink?* **3.** to indicate knowledge of how to do something: *he can speak three languages.* **4.** to indicate the possibility, opportunity, or likelihood: *my trainer says I can win the race.*
▷ **Usage.** See at **may¹.**

can² (kæn) n. **1.** a container, esp. for liquids, usually of thin metal: *a petrol can.* **2.** a tin (metal container): *a beer can.* **3.** Also **canful.** the contents of a can or the amount a can will hold. **4.** a slang word for **prison. 5.** *U.S.* a slang word for **toilet. 6.** a shallow cylindrical metal container used for storing and handling film. **7. can of worms.** *Inf.* a complicated problem. **8. in the can. a.** (of a film, piece of music, etc.) having been recorded, edited, etc. **b.** *Inf.* agreed: *the contract is in the can.* **9. carry the can.** *Inf.* to take responsibility for some misdemeanour, etc. ~*vb.* **canning, canned. 10.** to put (food, etc.) into a can or cans. —**'canner** n.

Can. abbrev. for: **1.** Canada. **2.** Canadian.

Canaan ('keɪnən) n. an ancient region between the River Jordan and the Mediterranean: the Promised Land of the Israelites.

Canad. abbrev. for Canadian.

Canada Day ('kænədə) n. (in Canada) July 1, the anniversary of the day in 1867 when Canada received dominion status: a public holiday.

Canada goose n. a large common greyish-brown North American goose with a black neck and head and a white throat patch.

Canada jay n. a grey crestless jay, notorious in northern parts of N America for its stealing. Also called: **camp**

robber, **whisky-jack.**

Canadian (kə'neɪdɪən) adj. **1.** of or relating to Canada or its people. ~n. **2.** a native, citizen, or inhabitant of Canada.

Canadiana (kəˌneɪdɪ'ɑːnə; Canad. -'ænə) n. objects, such as books, furniture, and antiques, relating to Canadian history and culture.

Canadianism (kə'neɪdɪəˌnɪzəm) n. **1.** the Canadian national character or spirit. **2.** a linguistic usage, custom, or other feature peculiar to Canada, its people, or their culture.

Canadianize or -**ise** (kə'neɪdɪəˌnaɪz) vb. to make or become Canadian by changing customs, ownership, character, content, etc.

Canadian Shield n. (in Canada) the wide area of Precambrian rock extending over most of E and C Canada: rich in minerals. Also called: **Laurentian Shield.**

Canadien (ˌkanaˈdjɛ̃; -dɪ'ɛn) or (*fem.*) **Canadienne** (-ˈdjɛn; -dɪ'ɛn) n. a French Canadian.

canaille French. (ka'nɑːj) n. the masses; mob; rabble.

canal (kə'næl) n. **1.** an artificial waterway constructed for navigation, irrigation, etc. **2.** any of various passages or ducts: *the alimentary canal.* **3.** any of various intercellular spaces in plants. **4.** *Astron.* any of the indistinct surface features of Mars originally thought to be a network of channels. ~*vb.* -**nalling, -nalled** or *U.S.* -**naling, -naled.** (*tr.*) **5.** to dig a canal through. **6.** to provide with a canal or canals.

canalize or -**lise** ('kænəˌlaɪz) vb. (*tr.*) **1.** to provide with or convert into a canal or canals. **2.** to give a particular direction to or provide an outlet for. —ˌcanali'zation or -li'sation n.

canapé ('kænəpɪ, -ˌpeɪ) n. a small piece of bread, toast, etc., spread with a savoury topping.

canard (kæ'nɑːd) n. **1.** a false report; rumour or hoax. **2.** an aircraft in which the tailplane is mounted in front of the wing.

canary (kə'nɛərɪ) n., pl. -**naries. 1.** a small finch of the Canary Islands and Azores: a popular cage bird noted for its singing. **2. canary yellow.** a light yellow. **3.** a sweet wine similar to madeira.

canasta (kə'næstə) n. **1.** a card game for two to six players who seek to amass points by declaring sets of cards. **2.** Also called: **meld.** a declared set in this game, containing seven or more like cards.

cancan ('kænˌkæn) n. a high-kicking dance performed by a female chorus, originating in the music halls of 19th-century Paris.

cancel ('kænsəl) vb. -**celling, -celled** or *U.S.* -**celing, -celed.** (*mainly tr.*) **1.** to order (something already arranged, such as a meeting or event) to be postponed indefinitely; call off. **2.** to revoke or annul: *the order was cancelled.* **3.** to delete (writing, numbers, etc.); cross out. **4.** to mark (a cheque, stamp, etc.) with an official stamp to prevent further use. **5.** (*also intr.*; usually foll. by *out*) to counterbalance: *his generosity cancelled out his past unkindness.* **6.** *Maths.* to eliminate (numbers or terms) as common factors from both the numerator and denominator of a fraction or as equal terms from opposite sides of an equation. ~n. **7.** a new leaf or section of a book replacing one containing errors, or one that has been omitted. **8.** a cancellation. **9.** *Music.* a U.S. word for **natural** (sense **15.**). —**'canceller** or *U.S.* **'canceler** n.

cancellation (ˌkænsɪ'leɪʃən) n. **1.** the fact or an instance of cancelling. **2.** something that has been cancelled, such as a theatre ticket: *we have a cancellation in the balcony.* **3.** the marks made by cancelling.

cancer ('kænsə) n. **1.** any type of malignant growth or tumour, caused by abnormal and uncontrolled cell division. **2.** the condition resulting from this. **3.** an evil influence that spreads dangerously. —**'cancerous** adj.

Cancer ('kænsə) n. Latin genitive **Cancri** ('kæŋkriː). **1.** *Astron.* a small N constellation. **2.** *Astrol.* the fourth sign

---

camp¹ bivouac, camping ground, camp site, cantonment (*Mil.*), encampment, tents

camp² affected, artificial, camped up, campy (*Inf.*), effeminate, mannered, ostentatious, poncy (*Sl.*), posturing

campaign attack, crusade, drive, expedition, jihad (*Rare*), movement, offensive, operation, push

cancel 1. abolish, abort, abrogate, annul, blot out, call off, countermand, cross out, delete, do away with, efface, eliminate, erase, expunge, obliterate, quash, repeal, repudiate, rescind, revoke **2.** balance out, compensate for, counterbalance, make up for, neutralize, nullify, offset, redeem

cancellation abandoning, abandon-

ment, abolition, annulment, deletion, elimination, quashing, repeal, revocation

cancer blight, canker, carcinoma (*Pathol.*), corruption, evil, growth, malignancy, pestilence, rot, sickness, tumour

of the zodiac. The sun is in this sign between about June 21 and July 22. **3.** See **tropic of Cancer.** See **tropic** (sense 1).

cancroid ('kæŋkrɔɪd) *adj.* **1.** resembling a cancerous growth. **2.** resembling a crab. ~*n.* **3.** a skin cancer.

candela (kæn'diːlə, -'deɪlə) *n.* the basic SI unit of luminous intensity; the luminous intensity, in a perpendicular direction, of a surface of 1/600 000 square metre of a black body at the temperature of freezing platinum under a pressure of 101 325 newtons per square metre. Symbol: cd

candelabrum (ˌkændɪ'lɑːbrəm) *or* **candelabra** *n.*, *pl.* **-bra** (-brə), **-brums,** *or* **-bras.** a large, branched table candle holder.

candid ('kændɪd) *adj.* **1.** frank and outspoken. **2.** without partiality; unbiased. **3.** unposed or informal: *a candid photograph.* —'**candidly** *adv.* —'**candidness** *n.*

candidate ('kændɪˌdeɪt) *n.* **1.** a person seeking or nominated for election to a position of authority or selection for a job, etc. **2.** a person taking an examination or test. **3.** a person or thing regarded as suitable or likely for a particular fate or position. —**candidacy** ('kændɪdəsɪ) *or* **candidature** ('kændɪdətʃə) *n.*

candid camera *n.* a small camera that may be used to take informal photographs of people.

candied ('kændɪd) *adj.* impregnated or encrusted with or as if with sugar: *candied peel.*

candle ('kændəl) *n.* **1.** a cylindrical piece of wax, tallow, or other fatty substance surrounding a wick, which is burned to produce light. **2.** *Physics.* another name for **candela. 3. burn the candle at both ends.** *Inf.* to exhaust oneself, esp. by being up late enjoying oneself and getting up early to work. **4. not hold a candle to.** *Inf.* to be inferior or contemptible in comparison with. **5. not worth the candle.** *Inf.* not worth the price or trouble entailed. ~*vb.* **6.** (*tr.*) to examine (eggs) for freshness or the likelihood of being hatched by viewing them against a bright light. —'**candler** *n.*

candlelight ('kændəlˌlaɪt) *n.* **1. a.** the light from a candle or candles. **b.** (*as modifier*): *a candlelight dinner.* **2.** dusk; evening.

Candlemas ('kændəlməs) *n. Christianity.* Feb. 2, the Feast of the Purification of the Virgin Mary and the presentation of Christ in the Temple.

candlepower ('kændəlˌpaʊə) *n.* the luminous intensity of a source of light in a given direction: now expressed in candelas.

candlestick ('kændəlˌstɪk) *or* **candleholder** ('kændəlˌhəʊldə) *n.* a holder, usually ornamental, with a spike or socket for a candle.

candlewick ('kændəlˌwɪk) *n.* **1.** unbleached cotton or muslin into which loops of yarn are hooked and then cut to give a tufted pattern. **2.** (*modifier*) being or made of candlewick fabric.

candour *or U.S.* **candor** ('kændə) *n.* **1.** the quality of being open and honest; frankness. **2.** fairness; impartiality.

candy ('kændɪ) *n.*, *pl.* **-dies. 1.** *Chiefly U.S.* sweets, chocolate, etc. ~*vb.* **-dying, -died. 1.** to cause (sugar, etc.) to become crystalline or (of sugar) to become crystalline. **3.** to preserve (fruit peel, ginger, etc.) by boiling in sugar. **4.** to cover with any crystalline substance, such as ice or sugar.

candyfloss ('kændɪˌflɒs) *n. Brit.* a very light fluffy confection made from coloured spun sugar, usually held on a stick. **U.S. name: cotton candy.**

candy-striped *adj.* (esp. of clothing fabric) having narrow coloured stripes on a white background. —**candy stripe** *n.*

cane (keɪn) *n.* **1. a.** the long jointed pithy or hollow flexible stem of the bamboo, rattan, or any similar plant. **b.** any plant having such a stem. **2. a.** strips of such stems, woven or interlaced to make wickerwork, etc. **b.** (*as modifier*): *a cane chair.* **3.** the woody stem of a reed, blackberry, or loganberry. **4.** a flexible rod with which to administer a beating. **5.** a slender rod used as a walking-stick. **6.** see **sugar cane.** ~*vb.* (*tr.*) **7.** to whip or beat with or as if with a cane. **8.** to make or repair with cane. **9.** *Inf.* to defeat: *we got well caned in the match.* —'**caner** *n.* —'**caning** *n.*

cane sugar *n.* **1.** the sucrose obtained from sugar cane. **2.** another name for **sucrose.**

canine ('keɪnaɪn, 'kæn-) *adj.* **1.** of or resembling a dog. **2.** of or belonging to the *Canidae,* a family of mammals, including dogs, wolves, and foxes, typically having a bushy tail, erect ears, and a long muzzle. **3.** of or relating to any of the four teeth, two in each jaw, situated between the incisors and the premolars. ~*n.* **4.** any animal of the family *Canidae.* **5.** a canine tooth.

canister ('kænɪstə) *n.* **1.** a container, usually made of metal, in which dry food, such as tea or coffee, is stored. **2.** (*formerly*) **a.** a type of shrapnel shell for firing from a cannon. **b.** Also called: **canister shot.** the shot or shrapnel packed inside this.

canker ('kæŋkə) *n.* **1.** an ulceration, esp. of the lips. **2.** *Vet. science.* **a.** a disease of horses in which the horn of the hoofs becomes spongy. **b.** an ulcerative disease of the lining of the external ear, esp. in dogs and cats. **3.** an open wound in the stem of a tree or shrub. **4.** something evil that spreads and corrupts. ~*vb.* **5.** to infect or become infected with or as if with canker. —'**cankerous** *adj.*

cankerworm ('kæŋkəˌwɜːm) *n.* the larva of either of two moths, which feed on and destroy fruit and shade trees in North America.

cannabis ('kænəbɪs) *n.* **1.** another name for **hemp** (the plant), esp. Indian hemp. **2.** the dried tops of the female flowers of the hemp plant, which are chewed or smoked for their euphoric effect. See also **hashish, marijuana. 3. cannabis resin.** a poisonous resin obtained from the hemp plant.

canned (kænd) *adj.* **1.** preserved and stored in airtight cans or tins. **2.** *Inf.* prepared or recorded in advance: *canned music.* **3.** *Sl.* drunk.

cannelloni *or* **canneloni** (ˌkænɪ'ləʊnɪ) *pl. n.* tubular pieces of pasta filled with meat or cheese.

cannery ('kænərɪ) *n.*, *pl.* **-neries.** a place where foods are canned.

cannibal ('kænɪbəl) *n.* **1.** a person who eats the flesh of other human beings. **2.** an animal that feeds on the flesh of others of its kind. —'**canniba,lism** *n.*

cannibalize *or* **-lise** ('kænɪbəˌlaɪz) *vb.* (*tr.*) to use (serviceable parts from one machine or vehicle) to repair another. —ˌcannibali'zation *or* -li'sation *n.*

canning ('kænɪŋ) *n.* the process or business of sealing food in cans or tins to preserve it.

cannon ('kænən) *n.*, *pl.* **-nons** *or* **-non. 1.** a heavy artillery piece consisting of a metal tube mounted on a carriage. **2.** an automatic aircraft gun. **3.** a heavy tube or drum, esp. one that can rotate freely. **4.** See **cannon bone. 5.** *Billiards.* a shot in which the cue ball is caused to contact one object ball after another. Usual U.S. word: **carom.** ~*vb.* **6.** (*intr.*) to rebound; collide (*with* into). **7.** (*intr.*) *Billiards.* to make a cannon.

cannonade (ˌkænə'neɪd) *n.* **1.** an intense and continuous gunnery bombardment. ~*vb.* **2.** to attack (a target) with cannon.

cannonball ('kænənˌbɔːl) *n.* **1.** a projectile fired from a cannon: usually a solid round metal shot. ~*vb.* (*intr.*) **2.** (often foll. by *along,* etc.) to rush along. ~*adj.* **3.** very fast or powerful.

cannon bone *n.* a bone in the legs of horses and other hoofed animals consisting of greatly elongated fused metatarsals or metacarpals.

cannon fodder *n.* men regarded as expendable in war because they are part of a huge army.

cannot ('kænɒt, kæ'nɒt) *vb.* an auxiliary verb expressing incapacity, inability, withholding permission, etc.;

THESAURUS

candid 1. blunt, fair, forthright, frank, free, guileless, impartial, ingenuous, just, open, outspoken, plain, sincere, straightforward, truthful, unbiased, unequivocal, unprejudiced **2.** impromptu, informal, uncontrived, unposed

candidate applicant, aspirant, claimant, competitor, contender, contestant, entrant, nominee, possibility, runner, solicitant, suitor

candour artlessness, directness, fairness, forthrightness, frankness, guilelessness, honesty, impartiality, ingenuousness, naïveté, openness, outspokenness, simplicity, sincerity, straightforwardness, truthfulness, unequivocalness

canker 1. *v.* blight, consume, corrode, corrupt, embitter, envenom, inflict, poison, pollute, rot, rust, waste away **2.** *n.* bane, blight, blister, cancer, corrosion, corruption, infection, lesion, rot, scourge, sore, ulcer

cannon 1. artillery piece, big gun (*Inf.*), field gun, gun, mortar **2.** *Plural* artillery, battery, big guns, cannonry, field guns, guns, ordnance

cannonade barrage, battery, bombardment, broadside, pounding, salvo, shelling, volley

can not.

canny ('kænı) *adj.* **-nier, -niest. 1.** shrewd, esp. in business. **2.** *Scot. & NE English dialect* good or nice: used as a general term of approval. **3.** *Scot.* lucky or fortunate. —'**cannily** *adv.* —'**canniness** *n.*

canoe (kə'nuː) *n.* **1.** a light narrow open boat, propelled by one or more paddles. ~*vb.* **-noeing, -noed. 2.** to go in or transport by canoe. —**ca'noeist** *n.*

canon¹ ('kænən) *n.* **1.** *Christianity.* a Church decree enacted to regulate morals or religious practices. **2.** (*often pl.*) a general rule or standard, as of judgment, morals, etc. **3.** (*often pl.*) a principle or criterion applied in a branch of learning or art. **4.** *R.C. Church.* the list of the canonized saints. **5.** *R.C. Church.* Also called: **Eucharistic Prayer.** the prayer in the Mass in which the Host is consecrated. **6.** *Ecclesiast.* a list of sacred books, etc., recognized as genuine. **7.** a piece of music in which an extended melody in one part is imitated successively in one or more other parts. **8.** a list of the works of an author that are accepted as authentic.

canon² ('kænən) *n.* **1.** a priest who is a member of a cathedral chapter. **2.** *R.C. Church.* a member of any of several religious orders (**canons regular**).

canonical (kə'nɒnɪkəl) *or* **canonic** *adj.* **1.** included in the canon of Scripture. **2.** in conformity with canon law. **3.** accepted; authoritative. **4.** *Music.* in the form of a canon. **5.** of or relating to a cathedral chapter. **6.** of a canon (clergyman). —**ca'nonically** *adv.*

canonical hour *n.* **1.** *R.C. Church.* one of the seven prayer times appointed for each day by canon law. **2.** *Church of England.* any time at which marriages may lawfully be celebrated.

canonicals (kə'nɒnɪkəlz) *pl. n.* the vestments worn by clergy when officiating.

canonist ('kænənɪst) *n.* a specialist in canon law.

canonize *or* **-ise** ('kænə,naɪz) *vb.* (*tr.*) **1.** *R.C. Church.* to declare (a person) to be a saint. **2.** to regard as a saint. **3.** to sanction by canon law. —,**canoni'zation** *or* **-i'sation** *n.*

canon law *n.* the codified body of laws enacted by the supreme authorities of a Christian Church.

canoodle (kə'nuːdəl) *vb.* (*intr.; often foll. by with*) *Sl.* to kiss and cuddle.

canopy ('kænəpɪ) *n., pl.* **-pies. 1.** an ornamental awning above a throne, bed or person, etc. **2.** a rooflike covering over an altar, niche, etc. **3.** a roofed structure serving as a sheltered passageway. **4.** a large or wide covering: *the sky was a grey canopy.* **5.** the hemisphere that forms the supporting surface of a parachute. **6.** the transparent cover of an aircraft cockpit. ~*vb.* **-pying, -pied. 7.** (*tr.*) to cover with or as with a canopy.

canst (kænst) *vb. Arch.* the form of **can¹** used with the pronoun *thou* or its relative form.

can't (kɑːnt) *vb.* a contraction of cannot.

cant¹ (kænt) *n.* **1.** insincere talk, esp. concerning religion or morals. **2.** phrases that have become meaningless through repetition. **3.** specialized vocabulary of a particular group, such as thieves, journalists, or lawyers. ~*vb.* **4.** (*intr.*) to speak in or use cant. —'**cantingly** *adv.*

cant² (kænt) *n.* **1.** inclination from a vertical or horizontal plane. **2.** a sudden movement that tilts or turns something. **3.** the angle or tilt thus caused. **4.** a corner or outer angle. **5.** an oblique or slanting surface, edge, or line. ~*vb.* (*tr.*) **6.** to tip, tilt, or overturn. **7.** to set in an oblique position. **8.** another word for **bevel** (sense 1). ~*adj.* **9.** oblique; slanting. **10.** having flat surfaces.

Cantab. (kæn'tæb) *abbrev. for* Cantabrigiensis.

cantabile (kæn'tɑːbɪlɪ) *Music.* ~*adj., adv.* **1.** as if sung ~*n.* **2.** a piece or passage performed in this way.

Cantabrigian (,kæntə'brɪdʒɪən) *adj.* **1.** of or characteristic of Cambridge or Cambridge University. ~*n.* **2.** a member or graduate of Cambridge University. **3.** an inhabitant or native of Cambridge.

cantaloupe *or* **cantaloup** ('kæntə,luːp) *n.* **1.** a cultivated variety of muskmelon with ribbed warty rind and orange flesh. **2.** any of several other muskmelons.

cantankerous (kæn'tæŋkərəs) *adj.* quarrelsome; irascible. —**can'tankerously** *adv.* —**can'tankerousness** *n.*

cantata (kæn'tɑːtə) *n.* a musical setting of a text, esp. a religious text, consisting of arias, duets, and choruses.

canteen (kæn'tiːn) *n.* **1.** a restaurant attached to a factory, school, etc., providing meals for large numbers. **2. a.** a small shop that provides a limited range of items to a military unit. **b.** a recreation centre for military personnel. **3.** a temporary or mobile stand at which food is provided. **4. a.** a box in which a set of cutlery is laid out. **b.** the cutlery itself. **5.** a flask for carrying water or other liquids.

canter ('kæntə) *n.* **1.** a gait of horses, etc., between a trot and a gallop in speed. **2. at a canter.** easily; without effort. ~*vb.* **3.** to move or cause to move at a canter.

cantharides (kæn'θærɪ,diːz) *pl. n., sing.* **cantharis** ('kænθərɪs). a diuretic and urogenital stimulant prepared from the dried bodies of Spanish fly. Also called: **Spanish fly.**

canticle ('kæntɪkəl) *n.* a nonmetrical hymn, derived from the Bible and used in the liturgy of certain Christian churches.

cantilever ('kæntɪ,liːvə) *n.* **1.** a beam, girder, or structural framework that is fixed at one end only. **2.** a part of a beam or a structure projecting outwards beyond its support.

cantilever bridge *n.* a bridge having spans that are constructed as cantilevers.

canto ('kæntəʊ) *n., pl.* **-tos.** a main division of a long poem.

canton ('kæntɒn, kæn'tɒn) *n.* **1.** a political division of Switzerland. **2.** ('kæntɒn). *Heraldry.* a small square charge on a shield, usually in the top left corner. ~*vb.* **3.** (kæn'tɒn). (*tr.*) to divide into cantons. **4.** (kən'tuːn). (*esp. formerly*) to allocate accommodation to (military personnel, etc.). —**cantonal** *adj.*

Cantonese (,kæntə'niːz) *n.* **1.** the Chinese language spoken in Canton, and elsewhere inside and outside China. **2.** (*pl.* **-ese**) a native or inhabitant of Canton. ~*adj.* **3.** of or relating to Canton or the Chinese language spoken there.

cantonment (kən'tuːnmənt) *n. Mil.* (*esp. formerly*) **1.** a large training camp. **2.** the winter quarters of a campaigning army. **3.** *History.* a permanent military camp in British India.

cantor ('kæntɔː) *n.* **1.** *Judaism.* the leading singer in the synagogue liturgy. **2.** *Christianity.* the leader of the singing in a church choir.

Canuck (kə'nʌk) *n., adj. Inf.* Canadian.

canvas ('kænvəs) *n.* **1. a.** a heavy cloth made of cotton, hemp, or jute, used for sails, tents, etc. **b.** (*as modifier*): *a canvas bag.* **2. a.** a piece of canvas, etc. on which a painting is done, usually in oils. **b.** an oil painting. **3.** a tent or tents collectively. **4.** *Naut.* the sails of a vessel collectively. **5.** any coarse loosely woven cloth on which tapestry, etc., is done. **6.** (preceded by *the*) the floor of a boxing or wrestling ring. **7.** *Rowing.* the covered part at either end of a racing boat: *to win by a canvas.* **8. under canvas. a.** in tents. **b.** *Naut.* with sails unfurled.

canvass ('kænvəs) *vb.* **1.** to solicit votes, orders, etc., from. **2.** to determine the opinions of (voters before an election, etc.), esp. by conducting a survey. **3.** to investigate (something) thoroughly, esp. by discussion. **4.** *Chiefly U.S.* to inspect (votes) to determine their validity.

THESAURUS

canny acute, artful, astute, careful, cautious, circumspect, clever, judicious, knowing, perspicacious, prudent, sagacious, sharp, shrewd, subtle, wise, worldly-wise

canon catalogue, criterion, dictate, formula, list, precept, principle, regulation, roll, rule, standard, statute, yardstick

canopy awning, baldachin, covering, shade, sunshade, tester

cant *n.* **1.** affected piety, humbug, hypocrisy, insincerity, lip service, pious platitudes, pretence, pretentiousness, sanctimoniousness, sham holiness **2.** argot, jargon, lingo, slang, vernacular ~*v.* **3.** angle, bevel, incline, rise, slant, slope, tilt

cantankerous bad-tempered, captious, choleric, contrary, crabby, cranky (*U.S. inf.*), crotchety (*Inf.*), crusty, difficult, disagreeable, grouchy (*Inf.*), grumpy, ill-humoured, irascible, irritable, peevish, perverse, quarrelsome, testy

canter *n.* amble, dogtrot, easy gait, jog, lope

canting hypocritical, insincere, Janus-faced, sanctimonious, two-faced

canvass *v.* **1.** analyse, campaign, electioneer, examine, inspect, investigate, poll, scan, scrutinize, sift, solicit, solicit votes, study, ventilate **2.** agitate, debate, discuss, dispute ~*n.* **3.** examination, investigation, poll, scrutiny, survey, tally

~*n.* **5.** a solicitation of opinions, votes, etc. —'**canvass-er** *n.*

canyon *or* **cañon** ('kænjən) *n.* a gorge or ravine, esp. in North America, usually formed by a river.

caoutchouc ('kautʃuk) *n.* another name for **rubber**[1] (sense 1).

cap (kæp) *n.* **1.** a covering for the head, esp. a small close-fitting one. **2.** such a covering serving to identify the wearer's rank, occupation, etc.: *a nurse's cap.* **3.** something that protects or covers: *lens cap.* **4.** an uppermost surface or part: *the cap of a wave.* **5. a.** See **percussion cap. b.** a small amount of explosive enclosed in paper and used in a toy gun. **6.** *Sport, chiefly Brit.* **a.** an emblematic hat or beret given to someone chosen for a representative team. **b.** a player chosen for such a team. **7.** any part like a cap in shape. **8.** *Bot.* the pileus of a mushroom or toadstool. **9.** *Hunting.* money contributed to the funds of a hunt by a follower who is neither a subscriber nor a farmer, in return for a day's hunting. **10.** *Anat.* **a.** the natural enamel covering a tooth. **b.** an artificial protective covering for a tooth. **11.** Also **Dutch cap.** same as **diaphragm** (sense 2). **12.** a mortarboard worn at an academic ceremony (esp. in **cap and gown**). **13. set one's cap for** *or* **at.** (of a woman) to be determined to win as a husband or lover. **14. cap in hand.** humbly, as when asking a favour. ~*vb.* **capping, capped.** (*tr.*) **15.** to cover, as with a cap: *snow capped the mountain tops.* **16.** *Inf.* to outdo; excel. **17. cap it all.** to provide the finishing touch. **18.** *Sport, Brit.* to select (a player) for a representative team. **19.** *Chiefly Scot. & N.Z.* to award a degree to.

cap. *abbrev. for:* **1.** capacity. **2.** capital. **3.** capitalize. **4.** capital letter.

capability (,keɪpə'bɪlɪtɪ) *n., pl.* **-ties. 1.** the quality of being capable; ability. **2.** the quality of being susceptible to the use or treatment indicated: *the capability of a metal to be fused.* **3.** (*usually pl.*) potential aptitude.

capable ('keɪpəbəl) *adj.* **1.** having ability; competent. **2.** (*postpositive; foll. by of*) able or having the skill (to do something): *she is capable of hard work.* **3.** (*postpositive; foll. by of*) having the temperament or inclination (to do something): *he seemed capable of murder.* —'**capableness** *n.* —'**capably** *adv.*

capacious (kə'peɪʃəs) *adj.* capable of holding much; roomy. —**ca'paciously** *adv.* —**ca'paciousness** *n.*

capacitance (kə'pæsɪtəns) *n.* **1.** the property of a system that enables it to store electric charge. **2.** a measure of this, equal to the charge that must be added to such a system to raise its electrical potential by one unit. Former name: **capacity.** —**ca'pacitive** *adj.*

capacitor (kə'pæsɪtə) *n.* a device for accumulating electric charge, usually consisting of two conducting surfaces separated by a dielectric. Former name: **condenser.**

capacity (kə'pæsɪtɪ) *n., pl.* **-ties. 1.** the ability or power to contain, absorb, or hold. **2.** the amount that can be contained: *a capacity of six gallons.* **3. a.** the maximum amount something can contain or absorb (esp. in **filled to capacity**). **b.** (*as modifier*): *a capacity crowd.* **4.** the ability to understand or learn: *he has a great capacity for Greek.* **5.** the ability to do or produce: *the factory's output was not at capacity.* **6.** a specified position or function. **7.** a measure of the electrical output of a piece of apparatus such as a generator or accumulator. **8.** *Electronics.* a former name for **capacitance. 9.** *Computers.* **a.** the number of words or characters that can be stored in a storage device. **b.** the range of numbers that

can be processed in a register. **10.** legal competence: *the capacity to make a will.*

cap-a-pie (,kæpə'piː) *adv.* (dressed, armed, etc.) from head to foot.

caparison (kə'pærɪsən) *n.* **1.** a decorated covering for a horse. **2.** rich or elaborate clothing and ornaments. ~*vb.* **3.** (*tr.*) to put a caparison on.

cape[1] (keɪp) *n.* a sleeveless garment like a cloak but usually shorter.

cape[2] (keɪp) *n.* a headland or promontory.

Cape (keɪp) *n.* **the. 1.** the Cape of Good Hope. **2.** the SW region of the Cape Province of South Africa.

Cape Coloured *n.* (in South Africa) another name for a **Coloured** (sense 2).

Cape doctor *n.* *S. African inf.* a strong fresh SE wind blowing in the vicinity of Cape Town, esp. in the summer.

Cape Dutch *n.* **1.** (in South Africa) a distinctive style in furniture or buildings. **2.** an obsolete name for **Afrikaans.**

caper[1] ('keɪpə) *n.* **1.** a playful skip or leap. **2.** a high-spirited escapade. **3. cut a caper.** to leap or dance about. **4.** *U.S. sl.* a crime. ~*vb.* **5.** (*intr.*) to leap or dance about in a light-hearted manner.

caper[2] ('keɪpə) *n.* **1.** a spiny trailing Mediterranean shrub with edible flower buds. **2.** its pickled flower buds, used in sauces.

capercaillie *or* **capercailzie** (,kæpə'keɪljɪ) *n.* a large European woodland grouse having a black plumage.

Cape salmon *n.* *S. African.* same as **geelbek.**

Cape sparrow *n.* a sparrow very common in southern Africa. Also called (esp. in South Africa): **mossie.**

capillarity (,kæpɪ'lærɪtɪ) *n.* a phenomenon caused by surface tension and resulting in the elevation or depression of the surface of a liquid in contact with a solid. Also called: **capillary action.**

capillary (kə'pɪlərɪ) *adj.* **1.** resembling a hair; slender. **2.** (of tubes) having a fine bore. **3.** *Anat.* of the delicate thin-walled blood vessels that interconnect between the arterioles and the venules. **4.** *Physics.* of or relating to capillarity. ~*n., pl.* **-laries. 5.** *Anat.* any of the capillary blood vessels.

capital[1] ('kæpɪtəl) *n.* **1. a.** the seat of government of a country. **b.** (*as modifier*): *a capital city.* **2.** material wealth owned by an individual or business enterprise. **3.** wealth available for or capable of use in the production of further wealth, as by industrial investment. **4. make capital (out) of.** to get advantage from. **5.** (*sometimes cap.*) the capitalist class or their interests: *capital versus labour.* **6.** *Accounting.* **a.** the ownership interests of a business as represented by the excess of assets over liabilities. **b.** the nominal value of the issued shares. **7.** any assets or resources. **8. a.** a capital letter. Abbrev.: **cap** *or* **cap. b.** (*as modifier*): *capital B.* ~*adj.* **9.** (*prenominal*) *Law.* involving or punishable by death: *a capital offence.* **10.** very serious: *a capital error.* **11.** primary, chief, or principal: *our capital concern.* **12.** of, relating to, or designating the large letter used chiefly as the initial letter in personal names and place names and often for abbreviations and acronyms. See also **upper case. 13.** *Chiefly Brit.* excellent; first-rate: *a capital idea.*

capital[2] ('kæpɪtəl) *n.* the upper part of a column or pier that supports the entablature.

capital expenditure *n.* expenditure to increase fixed assets.

THESAURUS

canyon coulee (*U.S.*), gorge, gulch (*U.S.*), gulf, gully, ravine

cap *v.* beat, better, complete, cover, crown, eclipse, exceed, excel, finish, outdo, outstrip, overtop, surpass, top, transcend

capability ability, capacity, competence, facility, faculty, means, potential, potentiality, power, proficiency, qualification(s), wherewithal

capable able, accomplished, adapted, adept, adequate, apt, clever, competent, efficient, experienced, fitted, gifted, intelligent, masterly, proficient, qualified, skilful, suited, susceptible, talented

capacious ample, broad, comfortable, commodious, comprehensive, expansive, extended, extensive, generous, liberal, roomy, sizable, spacious, substantial, vast, voluminous, wide

capacity 1. amplitude, compass, dimensions, extent, magnitude, range, room, scope, size, space, volume 2. ability, aptitude, aptness, brains, capability, cleverness, competence, competency, efficiency, facility, faculty, forte, genius, gift, intelligence, power, readiness, strength 3. appointment, function, office, position, post, province, role, service, sphere

cape chersonese (*Poetic*), head, headland, ness (*Archaic*), peninsula, point, promontory

caper 1. *v.* bounce, bound, cavort, dance, frisk, frolic, gambol, hop, jump, leap, romp, skip, spring 2. *n.* antic, dido (*Inf.*), escapade, gambol, high jinks, hop, jape, jest, jump, lark (*Inf.*), leap, mischief, practical joke, prank, revel, shenanigan (*Inf.*), sport, stunt

capital *adj.* 1. cardinal, central, chief, controlling, essential, foremost, important, leading, main, major, overruling, paramount, pre-eminent, primary, prime, principal, prominent, vital 2. excellent, fine, first, first-rate, prime, splendid, superb ~*n.* 3. assets, cash, finance, finances, financing, funds, investment(s), means, money, principal, property, resources, stock, wealth, wherewithal

capital gain *n.* the amount by which the selling price of a financial asset exceeds its cost.

capital gains tax *n.* a tax on the profit made from sale of an asset.

capital goods *pl. n. Econ.* goods that are themselves utilized in the production of other goods.

capitalism ('kæpɪtə,lɪzəm) *n.* an economic system based on the private ownership of the means of production, distribution, and exchange. Also called: **free enterprise, private enterprise.** Cf. **socialism** (sense 1).

capitalist ('kæpɪtəlɪst) *n.* **1.** a person who owns capital, esp. capital invested in a business. **2.** *Politics.* a supporter of capitalism. ~*adj.* **3.** relating to capital, capitalists, or capitalism. —,**capital'istic** *adj.*

capitalization *or* **-isation** (,kæpɪtəlaɪ'zeɪʃən) *n.* **1. a.** the act of capitalizing. **b.** the sum so derived. **2.** *Accounting.* the par value of the total share capital issued by a company. **3.** the act of estimating the present value of future payments, etc.

capitalize *or* **-ise** ('kæpɪtə,laɪz) *vb.* (*mainly tr.*) **1.** (*intr.; foll. by on*) to take advantage (of). **2.** to write or print (text) in capital letters. **3.** to convert (debt or earnings) into capital stock. **4.** to authorize (a business enterprise) to issue a specified amount of capital stock. **5.** *Accounting.* to treat (expenditures) as assets. **6. a.** to estimate the present value of (a periodical income). **b.** to compute the present value of (a business) from actual or potential earnings.

capital levy *n.* a tax on capital or property as contrasted with a tax on income.

capitally ('kæpɪtəlɪ) *adv. Chiefly Brit.* in an excellent manner; admirably.

capital punishment *n.* the punishment of death for a crime; death penalty.

capital stock *n.* **1.** the par value of the total share capital that a company is authorized to issue. **2.** the total physical capital existing in an economy at any moment of time.

capital transfer tax *n.* (in Britain) a tax payable on the cumulative total of gifts of money or property made during the donor's lifetime or after his death.

capitation (,kæpɪ'teɪʃən) *n.* **1.** a tax levied on the basis of a fixed amount per head. **2. capitation grant.** a grant of money given to every person who qualifies under certain conditions.

capitulate (kə'pɪtjʊ,leɪt) *vb.* (*intr.*) to surrender, esp. under agreed conditions. —ca'pitu,lator *n.*

capitulation (kə,pɪtjʊ'leɪʃən) *n.* **1.** the act of capitulating. **2.** a document containing terms of surrender. **3.** a statement summarizing the main divisions of a subject. —ca'pitulatory *adj.*

capo ('kæpəʊ) *n., pl.* **-pos.** a device fitted across all the strings of a guitar, lute, etc., so as to raise the pitch of each string simultaneously. Also called: **capo tasto** ('tæstəʊ).

capon ('keɪpən) *n.* a castrated cock fowl fattened for eating. —'capon,ize *or* -,ise *vb.*

cappuccino (,kæpʊ'tʃiːnəʊ) *n., pl.* **-nos.** coffee with steamed milk, sometimes served with whipped cream.

capriccio (kə'prɪtʃɪ,əʊ) *or* **caprice** *n., pl.* **-priccios, -pricci** (-'priːtʃɪ), *or* **-prices.** *Music.* a lively piece of irregular musical form.

caprice (kə'priːs) *n.* **1.** a sudden change of attitude, behaviour, etc. **2.** a tendency to such changes. **3.** another word for **capriccio.**

capricious (kə'prɪʃəs) *adj.* characterized by or liable to sudden unpredictable changes in attitude or behaviour. —ca'priciously *adv.*

Capricorn ('kæprɪ,kɔːn) *n.* **1.** *Astrol.* the tenth sign of the zodiac. The sun is in this sign between about Dec. 22 and Jan. 19. **2.** *Astron.* a S constellation. **3.** See **tropic of Capricorn.** See **tropic** (sense 1).

caprine ('kæpraɪn) *adj.* of or resembling a goat.

capriole ('kæprɪ,əʊl) *n.* **1.** *Dressage.* a high upward but not forward leap made by a horse with all four feet off the ground. ~*vb.* **2.** (*intr.*) to perform a capriole.

caps. *abbrev. for:* **1.** capital letters. **2.** capsule.

capsicum ('kæpsɪkəm) *n.* **1.** any of a genus of tropical American plants related to the potato, having mild or pungent seeds enclosed in a bell-shaped fruit. **2.** the fruit of any of these plants, used as a vegetable or ground to produce a condiment. ~See also **pepper** (sense 4).

capsize (kæp'saɪz) *vb.* to overturn accidentally; upset. —cap'sizal *n.*

capstan ('kæpstən) *n.* **1.** a windlass with a drum equipped with a ratchet, used on ships for hauling in ropes, etc. **2.** the rotating shaft in a tape recorder that pulls the tape past the head.

capstone ('kæp,stəʊn) *or* **copestone** ('kəʊp,stəʊn) *n.* one of a set of slabs on the top of a wall, etc.

capsule ('kæpsjuːl) *n.* **1.** a soluble case of gelatin enclosing a dose of medicine. **2.** a thin metal cap, seal, or cover. **3.** *Bot.* **a.** a dry fruit that liberates its seeds by splitting, as in the violet, or through pores, as in the poppy. **b.** the spore-producing organ of mosses and liverworts. **4.** *Anat.* a membranous envelope surrounding any of certain organs or parts. **5.** See **space capsule. 6.** an aeroplane cockpit that can be ejected in a flight emergency, complete with crew, instruments, etc. **7.** (*modifier*) in a highly concise form: *a capsule summary.* —'capsu,late *adj.*

capsulize *or* **-ise** ('kæpsjʊ,laɪz) *vb.* (*tr.*) **1.** to state (information, etc.) in a highly condensed form. **2.** to enclose in a capsule.

Capt. *abbrev. for* Captain.

captain ('kæptɪn) *n.* **1.** the person in charge of a vessel. **2.** an officer of the navy who holds a rank junior to a rear admiral. **3.** an officer of the army, certain air forces, and the marines who holds a rank junior to a major. **4.** the officer in command of a civil aircraft. **5.** the leader of a team in games. **6.** a person in command over a group, organization, etc.: *a captain of industry.* **7.** *U.S.* a policeman in charge of a precinct. **8.** *U.S.* a head waiter. ~*vb.* **9.** (*tr.*) to be captain of. —'captaincy *or* 'captain,ship *n.*

caption ('kæpʃən) *n.* **1.** a title, brief explanation, or comment accompanying an illustration. **2.** a heading or title of a chapter, article, etc. **3.** graphic material used in television presentation. **4.** another name for **subtitle** (sense 2). **5.** the formal heading of a legal document. ~*vb.* **6.** to provide with a caption or captions.

captious ('kæpʃəs) *adj.* apt to make trivial criticisms. —'captiously *adv.* —'captiousness *n.*

captivate ('kæptɪ,veɪt) *vb.* (*tr.*) to hold the attention of by fascinating; enchant. —'capti,vating *adj.* —,capti'vation *n.*

captive ('kæptɪv) *n.* **1.** a person or animal that is confined or restrained. **2.** a person whose behaviour is dominated by some emotion: *a captive of love.* ~*adj.* **3.** held as prisoner. **4.** held under restriction or control; confined. **5.** captivated. **6.** unable to avoid speeches, advertisements, etc.: *a captive audience.*

captivity (kæp'tɪvɪtɪ) *n., pl.* **-ties. 1.** imprisonment. **2.** the period of imprisonment.

captor ('kæptə) *n.* a person or animal that holds another captive.

THESAURUS

capitalism free enterprise, *laissez faire*, private enterprise, private ownership

capitulate come to terms, give in, give up, relent, submit, succumb, surrender, yield

capitulation accedence, submission, surrender, yielding

caprice changeableness, fad, fancy, fickleness, fitfulness, freak, humour, impulse, inconstancy, notion, quirk, vagary, whim, whimsy

capricious changeful, crotchety (*Inf.*), erratic, fanciful, fickle, fitful, freakish, impulsive, inconstant, mercurial, odd, queer, quirky, unpredictable, variable, wayward, whimsical

capsize invert, keel over, overturn, tip over, turn over, turn turtle, upset

capsule 1. bolus, lozenge, pill, tablet, troche (*Medical*) 2. case, pericarp (*Bot.*), pod, receptacle, seed vessel, sheath, shell, vessel

captain boss, chief, chieftain, commander, head, leader, master, number one (*Inf.*), officer, (senior) pilot, skipper

captivate allure, attract, beguile, bewitch, charm, dazzle, enamour, enchant, enrapture, enslave, ensnare, enthral, entrance, fascinate, hypnotize, infatuate, lure, mesmerize, seduce, win

captive 1. *n.* bondservant, convict, detainee, hostage, internee, prisoner, prisoner of war, slave 2. *adj.* caged, confined, enslaved, ensnared, imprisoned, incarcerated, locked up, penned, restricted, subjugated

captivity bondage, confinement, custody, detention, durance (*Archaic*), duress, enthralment, imprisonment, incarceration, internment, restraint, servitude, slavery, thraldom, vassalage

capture ('kæptʃə) vb. (tr.) **1.** to take prisoner or gain control over: to capture a town. **2.** (in a game) to win possession of: to capture a pawn in chess. **3.** to succeed in representing (something elusive): the artist captured her likeness. **4.** Physics. (of an atom, etc.) to acquire (an additional particle). ~n. **5.** the act of taking by force. **6.** the person or thing captured. **7.** Physics. a process by which an atom, etc. acquires an additional particle. **8.** Geog. the process by which the headwaters of one river are diverted into another. —'**capturer** n.

capuchin ('kæpjutʃin, -ʃin) n. **1.** an agile intelligent S American monkey having a cowl of thick hair on the top of the head. **2.** a woman's hooded cloak. **3.** (sometimes cap.) a variety of domestic fancy pigeon.

Capuchin ('kæpjutʃin, -ʃin) n. a friar belonging to a branch of the Franciscan Order founded in 1528.

car (kɑː) n. **1. a.** Also called: **motorcar, automobile.** a self-propelled road vehicle designed to carry passengers, that is powered by an internal-combustion engine. **b.** (as modifier): car coat. **2.** a conveyance for passengers, freight, etc., such as a cable car or the carrier of an airship or balloon. **3.** Brit. a railway vehicle for passengers only. **4.** Chiefly U.S. a railway carriage or van. **5.** a poetic word for **chariot**.

carabineer or **carabinier** (,kærəbɪ'nɪə) n. variants of **carbineer.**

carabiner (,kærə'biːnə) n. variant of **karabiner.**

caracal ('kærə,kæl) n. **1.** a lynxlike feline mammal inhabiting deserts of N Africa and S Asia, having a smooth coat of reddish fur. **2.** this fur.

caracole ('kærə,kəʊl) or **caracol** ('kærə,kɒl) n. **1.** Dressage. a half turn to the right or left. ~vb. (intr.) **2.** Dressage. to execute a half turn.

carafe (kə'ræf, -'rɑːf) n. a glass bottle for table use, for water or wine.

caramel ('kærəməl) n. **1.** burnt sugar, used for colouring and flavouring food. **2.** a chewy sweet made from sugar, milk, etc.

caramelize or **-ise** ('kærəmə,laɪz) vb. to convert or be converted into caramel.

carapace ('kærə,peɪs) n. the thick hard shield that covers part of the body of crabs, tortoises, etc.

carat ('kærət) n. **1.** a measure of the weight of precious stones, esp. diamonds, now standardized as 0.20 grams. **2.** Usual U.S. spelling: **karat.** a measure of the gold in an alloy, expressed as the number of parts of gold in 24 parts of the alloy.

caravan ('kærə,væn) n. **1. a.** a large enclosed vehicle capable of being pulled by a car and equipped to be lived in. U.S. name: **trailer. b.** (as modifier): a caravan site. **2.** (esp. in some parts of Asia and Africa) a company of traders or other travellers journeying together. **3.** a large covered vehicle, esp. a gaily coloured one used by Gypsies, circuses, etc. ~vb. **-vanning, -vanned. 4.** (intr.) Brit. to travel or have a holiday in a caravan.

caravanserai (,kærə'vænsə,raɪ) or **caravansary** (,kærə'vænsərɪ) n., pl. **-rais** or **-ries.** (in some Eastern countries) a large inn enclosing a courtyard, providing accommodation for caravans.

caravel ('kærə,vɛl) or **carvel** n. a two- or three-masted sailing ship used by the Spanish and Portuguese in the 15th and 16th centuries.

caraway ('kærə,weɪ) n. **1.** an umbelliferous Eurasian plant having finely divided leaves and clusters of small whitish flowers. **2. caraway seed.** the pungent aromatic fruit of this plant, used in cooking.

carbide ('kɑːbaɪd) n. an inorganic compound of carbon with a more electropositive element.

carbine ('kɑːbaɪn) n. **1.** a light automatic or semiautomatic rifle. **2.** a light short-barrelled rifle formerly used by cavalry.

carbineer (,kɑːbɪ'nɪə), **carabineer,** or **carabinier** (,kærəbɪ'nɪə) n. (formerly) a soldier equipped with a carbine.

carbo- or before a vowel **carb-** combining form. carbon: carbohydrate; carbonate.

carbohydrate (,kɑːbəʊ'haɪdreɪt) n. any of a large group of organic compounds, including sugars and starch, that contain carbon, hydrogen, and oxygen, with the general formula $C_m(H_2O)_n$: a source of food and energy for animals.

carbolated ('kɑːbə,leɪtɪd) adj. containing carbolic acid.

carbolic acid (kɑː'bɒlɪk) n. another name for **phenol,** esp. when it is used as a disinfectant.

carbon ('kɑːbən) n. **1. a.** a nonmetallic element existing in the three allotropic forms: amorphous carbon, graphite, and diamond: occurring in all organic compounds. The isotope **carbon-12** is the standard for atomic wt.; **carbon-14** is used in radiocarbon dating and as a tracer. Symbol: C; atomic no.: 6; atomic wt.: 12.011 15. **b.** (as modifier): a carbon compound. **2.** short for **carbon paper** or **carbon copy. 3.** a carbon electrode used in a carbon-arc light. **4.** a rod or plate, made of carbon, used in some types of battery.

carbonaceous (,kɑːbə'neɪʃəs) adj. of, resembling, or containing carbon.

carbonate n. ('kɑːbə,neɪt, -nɪt). **1.** a salt or ester of carbonic acid. ~vb. ('kɑːbə,neɪt). **2.** to turn into a carbonate. **3.** (tr.) to treat with carbon dioxide, as in the manufacture of soft drinks.

carbon black n. a finely divided form of carbon produced by incomplete combustion of natural gas or petroleum: used in pigments and ink.

carbon copy n. **1.** a duplicate copy of writing, typewriting, or drawing obtained by using carbon paper. **2.** Inf. a person or thing that is identical to another.

carbon dating n. a technique for determining the age of organic materials, such as wood, based on their content of the radioisotope ^{14}C acquired from the atmosphere when they formed part of a living plant.

carbon dioxide n. a colourless odourless incombustible gas present in the atmosphere and formed during respiration, etc.: used in fire extinguishers, and as dry ice for refrigeration. Formula: CO_2. Also called: **carbonic-acid gas.**

carbon-14 dating n. another name for **carbon dating.**

carbonic (kɑː'bɒnɪk) adj. (of a compound) containing carbon, esp. tetravalent carbon.

carbonic acid n. a weak acid formed when carbon dioxide combines with water. Formula: H_2CO_3.

carboniferous (,kɑːbə'nɪfərəs) adj. yielding coal or carbon.

Carboniferous (,kɑːbə'nɪfərəs) adj. **1.** of, denoting, or formed in the fifth period of the Palaeozoic era during which coal measures were formed. ~n. **2. the.** the Carboniferous period or rock system divided into the **Upper Carboniferous** period and the **Lower Carboniferous** period.

carbonize or **-ise** ('kɑːbə,naɪz) vb. **1.** to turn into carbon as a result of heating. **2.** (tr.) to coat (a substance) with carbon. —,**carboni'zation** or **-i'sation** n.

carbon monoxide n. a colourless odourless poisonous gas formed when carbon compounds burn in insufficient air. Formula: CO.

carbon paper n. a thin sheet of paper coated on one side with a dark waxy pigment, often containing carbon, that is transferred by pressure onto the copying surface below.

carbon tetrachloride n. a colourless volatile nonflammable liquid made from chlorine and used as a solvent, cleaning fluid, and insecticide. Formula: CCl_4.

Carborundum (,kɑːbə'rʌndəm) n. Trademark. any of various abrasive materials, esp. one consisting of silicon carbide.

carboxyl group or **radical** (kɑː'bɒksaɪl) n. the monovalent group -COOH: the functional group in organic acids.

carboy ('kɑː,bɔɪ) n. a large bottle, usually protected by a basket or box, used for containing corrosive liquids.

carbuncle ('kɑː,bʌŋkəl) n. **1.** an extensive skin eruption, similar to a boil, with several openings. **2.** a rounded gemstone, esp. a garnet cut without facets. —**carbuncular** (kɑː'bʌŋkjʊlə) adj.

carburettor, carburetter (,kɑːbjʊ'rɛtə, 'kɑːbjʊ,rɛtə) or U.S. **carburetor** ('kɑːbjʊ,rɛtə) n. a device used in

---

THESAURUS

capture 1. v. apprehend, arrest, bag, catch, collar (Inf.), lift (Sl.), nab (Inf.), secure, seize, take, take into custody, take prisoner **2.** n. apprehension, arrest, catch, imprisonment, seizure, taking, taking captive, trapping

car 1. auto (U.S.), automobile, jalopy (Inf.), machine, motor, motorcar, vehicle **2.** buffet car, cable car, coach, dining car, (railway) carriage, sleeping car, van

carafe decanter, flagon, flask, jug, pitcher

petrol engines for mixing atomized petrol with air, and regulating the intake of the mixture into the engine.

carcinogen (kɑːˈsɪnədʒən) *n. Pathol.* any substance that produces cancer. —ˌ**carcinoˈgenic** *adj.*

carcinoma (ˌkɑːsɪˈnəumə) *n., pl.* **-mas** *or* **-mata** (-mətə). *Pathol.* any malignant tumour derived from epithelial tissue, esp. a cancer.

card[1] (kɑːd) *n.* **1.** a piece of stiff paper or thin cardboard, usually rectangular, with varied uses, as for bearing a written notice for display, etc. **2.** such a card used for identification, reference, proof of membership, etc.: *identity card.* **3.** such a card used for sending greetings, messages, or invitations: *birthday card.* **4. a.** one of a set of small pieces of cardboard, marked with figures, symbols, etc., used for playing games or for fortune-telling. **b.** (*as modifier*): *a card game.* **5.** *Inf.* a witty or eccentric person. **6.** Also called: **race card.** *Horse racing.* a daily programme of all the races at a meeting. **7. a card up one's sleeve.** a thing or action used in order to gain an advantage, esp. one kept in reserve until needed. ~See also **cards.**

card[2] (kɑːd) *n.* **1.** a machine for combing fibres of cotton, wool, etc., to remove small unwanted fibres before spinning. **2.** a comblike tool for raising the nap on cloth. ~*vb.* **3.** (*tr.*) to process with such a machine or tool. —ˈ**carder** *n.*

cardamom *or* **cardamum** (ˈkɑːdəməm) *n.* **1.** a tropical Asian plant that has large hairy leaves. **2.** the seeds of this plant, used esp. as a spice or condiment.

cardboard (ˈkɑːdˌbɔːd) *n.* **1. a.** a thin stiff board made from paper pulp. **b.** (*as modifier*): *cardboard boxes.* ~*adj.* (*prenominal*) **2.** without substance.

card-carrying *adj.* being an official member of an organization: *a card-carrying Communist.*

cardiac (ˈkɑːdɪˌæk) *adj.* **1.** of or relating to the heart. **2.** of or relating to the portion of the stomach connected to the oesophagus. ~*n.* **3.** a person with a heart disorder.

cardigan (ˈkɑːdɪgən) *n.* a knitted jacket or sweater with buttons up the front.

cardinal (ˈkɑːdɪnəl) *n.* **1.** *R.C. Church.* any of the members of the Sacred College who elect the pope and act as his chief counsellors. **2.** Also called: **cardinal red.** a deep red colour. **3.** See **cardinal number.** **4.** Also called: (U.S.) **redbird.** a crested North American bunting, the male of which has a bright red plumage. **5.** a woman's hooded shoulder cape worn in the 17th and 18th centuries. ~*adj.* **6.** (*usually prenominal*) fundamentally important; principal. **7.** of a deep red. —ˈ**cardinally** *adv.*

cardinalate (ˈkɑːdɪnəˌleɪt) *or* **cardinalship** *n.* **1.** the rank, office, or term of office of a cardinal. **2.** the cardinals collectively.

cardinal number *or* **numeral** *n.* a number denoting quantity but not order in a group. Sometimes shortened to **cardinal.** Cf. **ordinal number.**

cardinal points *pl. n.* the four main points of the compass: north, south, east, and west.

cardinal virtues *pl. n.* the most important moral qualities, traditionally justice, prudence, temperance, and fortitude.

card index *or* **file** *n.* **1.** an index in which each item is separately listed on systematically arranged cards. ~*vb.* **card-index.** (*tr.*) **2.** to make such an index of (a book, etc.).

cardio- *or before a vowel* **cardi-** *combining form.*

heart: *cardiogram.*

cardiogram (ˈkɑːdɪəuˌgræm) *n.* short for **electrocardiogram.** See **electrocardiograph.**

cardiology (ˌkɑːdɪˈɒlədʒɪ) *n.* the branch of medical science concerned with the heart and its diseases. —ˌ**cardiˈologist** *n.*

cardiovascular (ˌkɑːdɪəuˈvæskjulə) *adj.* of or relating to the heart and the blood vessels.

cards (kɑːdz) *n.* **1.** (*usually functioning as sing.*) **a.** any game played with cards. **b.** the playing of such a game. **2.** an employee's tax and national insurance documents or information held by the employer. **3. ask for** *or* **get one's cards.** to ask or be told to terminate one's employment. **4. on the cards.** possible. **5. play one's cards (right).** to manoeuvre (cleverly). **6. put** *or* **lay one's cards on the table.** to declare one's intentions, etc.

cardsharp (ˈkɑːdˌʃɑːp) *or* **cardsharper** *n.* a professional card player who cheats.

card vote *n. Brit.* a vote by delegates, esp. at a trade-union conference, in which each delegate's vote counts as a vote by all his constituents.

care (kɛə) *vb.* **1.** (when *tr., may take a clause as object*) to be troubled or concerned: *he is dying, and she doesn't care.* **2.** (*intr.; foll. by* for *or* about) to have regard or consideration (for): *he cares more for his hobby than his job.* **3.** (*intr.; foll. by* for) to have a desire or taste (for): *would you care for tea?* **4.** (*intr.; foll. by* for) to provide physical needs, help, or comfort (for). **5.** (*tr.*) to agree or like (to do something): *would you care to sit down?* **6. for all I care** *or* **I couldn't care less.** I am completely indifferent. ~*n.* **7.** careful or serious attention: *he does his work with care.* **8.** protective or supervisory control: *in the care of a doctor.* **9.** Also called: **child care.** *Brit.* the provision of a home, etc. for a disturbed or neglected child by a local authority. **10.** (*often pl.*) trouble; worry. **11.** an object of or cause for concern. **12.** caution: *handle with care.* **13. care of.** at the address of: written on envelopes. Usual abbrev.: **c/o.**

CARE (kɛə) *n.* acronym for: **1.** Cooperative for American Relief Everywhere. **2.** *N.Z.* Citizens' Association for Racial Equality.

careen (kəˈriːn) *vb.* **1.** to sway or cause to sway over to one side. **2.** (*tr.*) *Naut.* to cause (a vessel) to keel over to one side, esp. in order to clean its bottom. **3.** (*intr.*) *Naut.* (of a vessel) to keel over to one side. —ca**ˈreenage** *n.*

career (kəˈrɪə) *n.* **1.** a path through life or history. **2.** a profession or occupation chosen as one's life's work. **3.** (*as modifier*): *a career diplomat.* **4.** a course or path, esp. a headlong one. ~*vb.* **5.** (*intr.*) to rush in an uncontrolled way.

careerist (kəˈrɪərɪst) *n.* a person who seeks to advance his career by any possible means.

carefree (ˈkɛəˌfriː) *adj.* without worry or responsibility. —ˈ**careˌfreeness** *n.*

careful (ˈkɛəful) *adj.* **1.** cautious in attitude or action. **2.** painstaking in one's work; exact and thorough. **3.** (*usually postpositive; foll. by* of, in, *or* about) solicitous; protective. **4.** *Brit.* mean or miserly. —ˈ**carefully** *adv.* —ˈ**carefulness** *n.*

careless (ˈkɛəlɪs) *adj.* **1.** done with or acting with insufficient attention. **2.** (*often foll. by* in, of, *or* about) unconcerned in attitude or action. **3.** (*usually prenominal*) carefree. **4.** (*usually prenominal*) unstudied: *careless elegance.* —ˈ**carelessly** *adv.* —ˈ**carelessness** *n.*

THESAURUS

carcass body, cadaver (*Medical*), corpse, corse (*Archaic*), dead body, framework, hulk, remains, shell, skeleton

cardinal capital, central, chief, essential, first, foremost, fundamental, greatest, highest, important, key, leading, main, paramount, pre-eminent, primary, prime, principal

care 1. affliction, anxiety, burden, concern, disquiet, hardship, interest, perplexity, pressure, responsibility, solicitude, stress, tribulation, trouble, vexation, woe, worry 2. attention, carefulness, caution, circumspection, consideration, direction, forethought, heed, management, meticulousness, pains, prudence, regard, vigilance, watchfulness 3. charge, control, custody, guardianship, keep-

ing, management, ministration, protection, supervision, ward

career *n.* 1. calling, employment, life work, livelihood, occupation, pursuit, vocation 2. course, passage, path, procedure, progress, race, walk ~*v.* 3. bolt, dash, hurtle, race, rush, speed, tear

care for 1. attend, foster, look after, mind, minister to, nurse, protect, provide for, tend, watch over 2. be fond of, desire, enjoy, find congenial, like, love, prize, take to, want

carefree airy, blithe, breezy, buoyant, careless, cheerful, cheery, easy-going, happy, happy-go-lucky, insouciant, jaunty, light-hearted, lightsome (*Archaic*), radiant, sunny, untroubled

careful 1. accurate, attentive, cautious,

chary, circumspect, conscientious, discreet, fastidious, heedful, painstaking, precise, prudent, punctilious, scrupulous, thoughtful, thrifty 2. alert, concerned, judicious, mindful, particular, protective, solicitous, vigilant, wary, watchful

careless 1. absent-minded, cursory, forgetful, hasty, heedless, incautious, inconsiderate, indiscreet, negligent, perfunctory, regardless, remiss, thoughtless, unconcerned, unguarded, unmindful, unthinking 2. inaccurate, irresponsible, lackadaisical, neglectful, offhand, slapdash, slipshod, sloppy (*Inf.*) 3. artless, casual, nonchalant, unstudied

carelessness inaccuracy, inattention, inconsiderateness, indiscretion, irresponsibility, neglect, negligence, omission, re-

caress (kə'rɛs) n. 1. a gentle touch or embrace, esp. one given to show affection. ~vb. 2. (tr.) to touch or stroke gently with or as with affection.

caret ('kærɪt) n. a symbol (‸) used to indicate the place in written or printed matter at which something is to be inserted.

caretaker ('kɛə,teɪkə) n. 1. a person who is in charge of a place or thing, esp. in the owner's absence. 2. (modifier) interim: a caretaker government.

careworn ('kɛə,wɔːn) adj. showing signs of care, stress, worry, etc.: a careworn face.

cargo ('kɑːgəʊ) n., pl. **-goes** or **-gos**. 1. a. goods carried by a ship, aircraft, or other vehicle; freight. b. (as modifier): a cargo vessel. 2. any load: a cargo of new arrivals.

Carib ('kærɪb) n. 1. (pl. **-ibs** or **-ib**) a member of a group of American Indian peoples of NE South America and the Lesser Antilles. 2. the family of languages spoken by these peoples.

Caribbean (,kærɪ'bɪən) adj. 1. of the Caribbean Sea and its islands. 2. of the Carib or any of their languages. ~n. 3. the Caribbean Sea. 4. a member of any of the peoples inhabiting the islands of the Caribbean Sea, such as a West Indian or a Carib.

caribou ('kærɪ,buː) n., pl. **-bous** or **-bou**. a large North American reindeer.

caricature ('kærɪkə,tjʊə) n. 1. a pictorial, written, or acted representation of a person, which exaggerates his characteristic traits for comic effect. 2. an inadequate or inaccurate imitation. ~vb. 3. (tr.) to represent in or produce a caricature of. —'carica,turist n.

caries ('kɛəriːz) n., pl. **-ies**. progressive decay of a bone or a tooth. —**carious** ('kɛərɪəs) adj.

carillon (kə'rɪljən) n. Music. 1. a set of bells usually hung in a tower. 2. a tune played on such bells. 3. a mixture stop on an organ giving the effect of a bell.

carinate ('kærɪ,neɪt) or **carinated** adj. Biol. having a keel or ridge.

cariole or **carriole** ('kærɪ,əʊl) n. 1. a small open two-wheeled horse-drawn vehicle. 2. a covered cart.

carl or **carle** (kɑːl) n. Arch. or Scot. another word for **churl**.

Carlovingian (,kɑːləʊ'vɪndʒɪən) adj., n. History. a variant of **Carolingian**.

Carmelite ('kɑːmə,laɪt) n. R.C. Church. 1. a member of an order of mendicant friars founded about 1154. 2. a member of a corresponding order of nuns founded in 1452.

carminative ('kɑːmɪnətɪv) adj. 1. able to relieve flatulence. ~n. 2. a carminative drug.

carmine ('kɑːmaɪn) n. 1. a. a vivid red colour. b. (as adj.): carmine paint. 2. a pigment of this colour obtained from cochineal.

carnage ('kɑːnɪdʒ) n. extensive slaughter.

carnal ('kɑːnəl) adj. relating to the appetites and passions of the body. —**car'nality** n. —**carnally** adv.

carnation (kɑː'neɪʃən) n. 1. Also called: **clove pink**. a Eurasian plant cultivated in many varieties for its white, pink, or red flowers, which have a fragrant scent of cloves. 2. the flower of this plant. 3. a. a pink or reddish-pink colour. b. (as adj.): a carnation dress.

carnelian (kɑː'niːljən) n. a reddish-yellow translucent variety of chalcedony, used as a gemstone.

carnet ('kɑːneɪ) n. 1. a customs licence authorizing the temporary importation of a motor vehicle. 2. an official document permitting motorists to cross certain frontiers.

carnival ('kɑːnɪvəl) n. 1. a. a festive period marked by merrymaking, etc.: esp. in some Roman Catholic countries, the period just before Lent. b. (as modifier): a carnival atmosphere. 2. a travelling fair having side shows, merry-go-rounds, etc. 3. a show or display arranged as an amusement. 4. Austral. a sports meeting.

carnivore ('kɑːnɪ,vɔː) n. 1. any of an order of mammals having large pointed canine teeth specialized for eating flesh. The order includes cats, dogs, bears, and weasels. 2. any other animal or any plant that feeds on animals.

carnivorous (kɑː'nɪvərəs) adj. 1. (esp. of animals) feeding on flesh. 2. (of plants such as the pitcher plant and sundew) able to trap and digest insects. 3. of or relating to the carnivores. —**car'nivorousness** n.

carob ('kærəb) n. 1. an evergreen Mediterranean tree with compound leaves and edible pods. 2. the long blackish sugary pod of this tree, used for animal fodder and sometimes for human food.

carol ('kærəl) n. 1. a joyful hymn or religious song, esp. one (a **Christmas carol**) celebrating the birth of Christ. ~vb. **-olling**, **-olled** or U.S. **-oling**, **-oled**. 2. (intr.) to sing carols at Christmas. 3. to sing (something) in a joyful manner.

Carolingian (,kærə'lɪndʒɪən) adj. 1. of or relating to the Frankish dynasty founded by Pepin the Short which ruled in France from 751–987 A.D. and in Germany until 911 A.D. ~n. 2. a member of the dynasty of the Carolingian Franks. —Also: **Carlovingian, Carolinian**.

carotid (kə'rɒtɪd) n. 1. either of the two principal arteries that supply blood to the head and neck. ~adj. 2. of either of these arteries.

carousal (kə'raʊzəl) n. a merry drinking party.

carouse (kə'raʊz) vb. 1. (intr.) to have a merry drinking spree. ~n. 2. another word for **carousal**. —**ca'rouser** n.

carousel (,kærə'sɛl, -'zɛl) n. 1. U.S. a merry-go-round. 2. a circular tray in which slides for a projector are held in slots from which they can be released in turn. 3. History. a tournament in which horsemen took part in races.

carp[1] (kɑːp) n., pl. **carp** or **carps**. 1. a freshwater food fish having one long dorsal fin, and two barbels on each side of the mouth. 2. a cyprinid.

carp[2] (kɑːp) vb. (intr.) to complain or find fault. —**carper** n.

-carp n. combining form. (in botany) fruit or a reproductive structure that develops into a particular part of the fruit: epicarp.

carpal ('kɑːpəl) n. a. any bone of the wrist. b. (as modifier): carpal bones.

car park n. an area or building reserved for parking cars. Usual U.S. term: **parking lot**.

carpel ('kɑːpəl) n. the female reproductive organ of flowering plants, consisting of an ovary, style, and stigma. —**carpellary** adj.

carpenter ('kɑːpɪntə) n. 1. a person skilled in woodwork, esp. in buildings, ships, etc. 2. (intr.) to do the work of a carpenter. 3. (tr.) to make or fit together by or as if by carpentry.

carpentry ('kɑːpɪntrɪ) n. 1. the art or technique of working wood. 2. the work produced by a carpenter; woodwork.

carpet ('kɑːpɪt) n. 1. a heavy fabric for covering floors. 2. a covering like a carpet: a carpet of leaves. 3. **on the carpet**. Inf. a. before authority to be reproved. b. under consideration. ~vb. (tr.) 4. to cover with or as if with a carpet. 5. Inf. to reprimand.

carpetbag ('kɑːpɪt,bæg) n. a travelling bag originally made of carpeting.

carpetbagger ('kɑːpɪt,bægə) n. U.S. a politician who seeks public office in a locality where he has no real connections.

THESAURUS

missness, slackness, sloppiness (Inf.), thoughtlessness

caress 1. v. cuddle, embrace, fondle, hug, kiss, nuzzle, pet, stroke 2. n. cuddle, embrace, fondling, hug, kiss, pat, stroke

caretaker 1. n. concierge, curator, custodian, janitor, keeper, porter, superintendent, warden, watchman 2. adj. holding, interim, short-term, temporary

cargo baggage, consignment, contents, freight, goods, lading, load, merchandise, shipment, tonnage, ware

caricature 1. n. burlesque, cartoon, distortion, farce, lampoon, mimicry, parody, pasquinade, satire, send-up (Brit. inf.), take-off (Inf.), travesty 2. v. burlesque, distort, lampoon, mimic, mock, parody, ridicule, satirize, send up (Brit. inf.), take off (Inf.)

carnage blood bath, bloodshed, butchery, havoc, holocaust, massacre, mass murder, murder, shambles, slaughter

carnival celebration, fair, festival, fête, fiesta, gala, holiday, jamboree, jubilee, Mardi Gras, merrymaking, revelry

carol canticle, canzonet, chorus, ditty, hymn, lay, noel, song, strain

carouse booze (Inf.), drink, imbibe, make merry, quaff, roister, wassail

carp cavil, censure, complain, criticize, find fault, hypercriticize, knock (Inf.), nag, pick holes (Inf.), quibble, reproach

carpenter cabinet-maker, joiner, woodworker

carpeting ('kɑːpɪtɪŋ) n. carpet material or carpets in general.

carpet snake or **python** n. a large nonvenomous Australian snake having a carpetlike pattern on its back.

carport ('kɑːˌpɔːt) n. a shelter for a car usually consisting of a roof built out from the side of a building and supported by posts.

-carpous or **-carpic** adj. combining form. (in botany) indicating a certain kind or number of fruit: apocarpous.

carpus ('kɑːpəs) n., pl. **-pi** (-paɪ). 1. the technical name for **wrist**. 2. the eight small bones of the human wrist.

carrack ('kærək) n. a galleon sailed in the Mediterranean as a merchantman in the 15th and 16th centuries.

carrageen, carragheen, or **carageen** ('kærəˌgiːn) n. an edible red seaweed, of rocky shores of North America and N Europe, used to make a beverage, medicine, and jelly. Also called: **Irish moss.**

carrel or **carrell** ('kærəl) n. a small individual study room, often in a library.

carriage ('kærɪdʒ) n. 1. Brit. a railway coach for passengers. 2. the manner in which a person holds and moves his head and body. 3. a four-wheeled horse-drawn vehicle for persons. 4. the moving part of a machine that bears another part: a typewriter carriage. 5. ('kærɪdʒ, 'kærɪdʒ). a. the act of conveying. b. the charge made for conveying (esp. in **carriage forward**, when the charge is to be paid by the receiver, and **carriage paid**).

carriage clock n. a portable clock, usually in a rectangular case, originally used by travellers.

carriageway ('kærɪdʒˌweɪ) n. Brit. the part of a road along which traffic passes in a single line moving in one direction only: a dual carriageway.

carrier ('kærɪə) n. 1. a person, thing, or organization employed to carry goods, etc. 2. a mechanism by which something is carried or moved, such as a device for transmitting rotation from the faceplate of a lathe to the workpiece. 3. Pathol. another name for **vector** (sense 2). 4. Pathol. a person or animal that, without having any symptoms of a disease, is capable of transmitting it to others. 5. Also called: **charge carrier.** Physics. an electron or hole that carries the charge in a conductor or semiconductor. 6. Also called: **carrier wave.** Radio. a wave of fixed amplitude and frequency that is modulated in order to carry a signal in radio transmission, etc. 7. Chem. **a.** an inert substance used to absorb a dyestuff, transport a sample through a gas chromatography column, contain a radioisotope for radioactive tracing, etc. **b.** a catalyst or substance used to support a catalyst. 8. See **aircraft carrier.**

carrier bag n. Brit. a large paper or plastic bag for carrying shopping, etc.

carrier pigeon n. any homing pigeon, esp. one used for carrying messages.

carrion ('kærɪən) n. 1. dead and rotting flesh. 2. (modifier) eating carrion. 3. something rotten.

carrion crow n. a common predatory and scavenging European crow similar to the rook but having a pure black bill.

carrot ('kærət) n. 1. an umbelliferous plant, with finely divided leaves. 2. the long tapering orange root of this plant, eaten as a vegetable. 3. something offered as a lure or incentive.

carroty ('kærətɪ) adj. 1. of a reddish or yellowish-orange colour. 2. having red hair.

carrousel (ˌkærəˈsɛl, -ˈzɛl) n. a variant spelling of **carousel.**

carry ('kærɪ) vb. **-rying, -ried.** (mainly tr.) 1. (also intr.) to take or bear (something) from one place to another. 2. to transfer for consideration: he carried his complaints to her superior. 3. to have on one's person: he carries a watch. 4. (also intr.) to be transmitted or serve as a medium for transmitting: sound carries over water. 5. to bear or be able to bear the weight, pressure, or responsibility of: her efforts carry the whole production. 6. to have as an attribute or result: this crime carries a heavy penalty. 7. to bring or communicate: to carry news. 8. (also intr.) to be pregnant with (young). 9. to bear (the head, body, etc.) in a specified manner: she carried her head high. 10. to conduct or bear (oneself) in a specified manner: she carried herself well. 11. to continue or extend: the war was carried into enemy territory. 12. to cause to move or go: desire for riches carried him to the city. 13. to influence, esp. by emotional appeal: his words carried the crowd. 14. to secure the passage of (a bill, motion, etc.). 15. to win (an election). 16. to obtain victory for (a candidate). 17. Chiefly U.S. to win a majority of votes in (a district, etc.): the candidate carried 40 states. 18. to capture: our troops carried the town. 19. (of communications media) to include as the content: this newspaper carries no book reviews. 20. Also (esp. U.S.): **carry over.** Book-keeping. to transfer (an item) to another account, esp. to transfer to the following year's account: to carry a loss. 21. Maths. to transfer (a number) from one column of figures to the next. 22. (of a shop, trader, etc.) to keep in stock: to carry confectionery. 23. to support (a musical part or melody) against the other parts. 24. (intr.) (of a ball, projectile, etc.) to travel through the air or reach a specified point: his first drive carried to the green. 25. Inf. to imbibe (alcoholic drink) without showing ill effects. 26. **carry all before (one).** to win unanimous support or approval for (oneself). 27. **carry a tune.** to be able to sing in tune. 28. **carry the day.** to win a contest; succeed. ~n., pl. **-ries.** 29. the act of carrying. 30. U.S. a portion of land over which a boat must be portaged. 31. the range of a firearm or its projectile. 32. Golf. the distance from where the ball is struck to where it first touches the ground.

carry away vb. (tr., adv.) 1. to remove forcefully. 2. (usually passive) to cause (a person) to lose self-control. 3. (usually passive) to delight: he was carried away by the music.

carrycot ('kærɪˌkɒt) n. a light cot with handles, similar to but smaller than the body of a pram.

carry forward vb. (tr., adv.) 1. Book-keeping. to transfer (a balance) to the next column, etc. 2. Tax accounting. to apply (a legally permitted credit, esp. an operating loss) to the taxable income of following years. ~Also: **carry over.**

carry off vb. (tr., adv.) 1. to remove forcefully. 2. to win. 3. to handle (a situation) successfully: he carried off the introductions well. 4. to cause to die: he was carried off by pneumonia.

carry on vb. (adv.) 1. (intr.) to continue or persevere. 2. (tr.) to conduct: to carry on a business. 3. (intr.; often foll. by with) Inf. to have an affair. 4. (intr.) Inf. to cause a fuss or commotion. ~n. **carry-on.** 5. Inf., chiefly Brit. a fuss.

carry out vb. (tr., adv.) 1. to perform or cause to be implemented: I wish he could afford to carry out his plan. 2. to accomplish. ~n. **carry-out.** Chiefly Scot. 3. alcohol bought at an off-licence, etc. for consumption elsewhere. 4. **a.** a shop which sells hot, cooked food for consumption away from the premises. **b.** (as modifier): a carry-out shop.

carry over vb. (tr., adv.) 1. to postpone or defer. 2. Book-keeping, tax accounting. another term for **carry forward.** ~n. **carry-over.** 3. something left over for future use, esp. goods to be sold. 4. Book-keeping. a sum or balance carried forward.

carry through vb. (tr., adv.) 1. to bring to completion. 2. to enable to endure (hardship, trouble, etc.); support.

carsick ('kɑːˌsɪk) adj. nauseated from riding in a car or other vehicle. —**'car,sickness** n.

THESAURUS

carping captious, cavilling, critical, fault-finding, grouchy (Inf.), hard to please, hyper-critical, nagging, nit-picking (Inf.), picky (Inf.), reproachful

carriage 1. carrying, conveyance, conveying, delivery, freight, transport, transportation 2. cab, coach, conveyance, vehicle 3. Fig. air, bearing, behaviour, comportment, conduct, demeanour, deportment, gait, manner, mien, posture, presence

carry 1. bear, bring, conduct, convey, fetch, haul, lift, lug, move, relay, take, transfer, transmit, transport 2. accomplish, capture, effect, gain, secure, win 3. drive, impel, influence, motivate, spur, urge 4. bear, hold up, maintain, shoulder, stand, suffer, support, sustain, underpin, uphold 5. broadcast, communicate, display, disseminate, give, offer, publish, release, stock

carry on 1. continue, endure, keep going, last, maintain, perpetuate, persevere, persist 2. administer, manage, operate, run 3. Inf. create (Sl.), make a fuss, misbehave

carry out accomplish, achieve, carry through, consummate, discharge, effect, execute, fulfil, implement, perform, realize

cart (kɑːt) *n.* **1.** a heavy open vehicle, usually having two wheels and drawn by horses. **2.** a light open horse-drawn vehicle for business or pleasure. **3.** any small vehicle drawn or pushed by hand, such as a trolley. **4. in the cart. a.** in an awkward situation. **b.** in the lurch. **5. put the cart before the horse.** to reverse the usual order of things. ~*vb.* **6.** (*usually tr.*) to use or draw a cart to convey (goods, etc.). **7.** (*tr.*) to carry with effort: *to cart wood home.* —'**carter** *n.*

carte blanche (ˈkɑːt ˈblɑːntʃ) *n., pl.* **cartes blanches** (ˈkɑːts ˈblɑːntʃ). complete discretion or authority: *the government gave their negotiator carte blanche.*

cartel (kɑːˈtɛl) *n.* **1.** Also called: **trust.** a collusive association of independent enterprises formed to monopolize production and distribution of a product or service. **2.** *Politics.* an alliance of parties to further common aims.

Cartesian (kɑːˈtiːzɪən) *adj.* **1.** of or relating to the works of Descartes, 17th-century French philosopher and mathematician. **2.** of or used in Descartes' mathematical system. —**Car'tesianism** *n.*

Cartesian coordinates *pl. n.* a system of coordinates that defines the location of a point in space in terms of its perpendicular distance from each of a set of mutually perpendicular axes.

carthorse (ˈkɑːtˌhɔːs) *n.* a large heavily built horse kept for pulling carts or carriages.

Carthusian (kɑːˈθjuːzɪən) *n. R.C. Church.* a member of a monastic order founded by Saint Bruno in 1084 near Grenoble, France.

cartilage (ˈkɑːtɪlɪdʒ) *n.* a tough elastic tissue composing most of the embryonic skeleton of vertebrates. In the adults of higher vertebrates it is mostly converted into bone. Nontechnical name: **gristle.** —**cartilaginous** (ˌkɑːtɪˈlædʒɪnəs) *adj.*

cartogram (ˈkɑːtəˌɡræm) *n.* a map showing statistical information in diagrammatic form.

cartography (kɑːˈtɒɡrəfɪ) *n.* the art, technique, or practice of compiling or drawing maps or charts. —**car'tographer** *n.* —**cartographic** (ˌkɑːtəˈɡræfɪk) *or* ˌcarto-'**graphical** *adj.*

carton (ˈkɑːtən) *n.* **1.** a cardboard box for containing goods. **2.** a container of waxed paper in which liquids, such as milk, are sold.

cartoon (kɑːˈtuːn) *n.* **1.** a humorous or satirical drawing, esp. one in a newspaper or magazine. **2.** a sequence of drawings in a newspaper, magazine, etc. U.S. name: **comic strip. 3.** See **animated cartoon. 4.** a full-size preparatory sketch for a fresco, tapestry, mosaic, etc. —**car'toonist** *n.*

cartouche *or* **cartouch** (kɑːˈtuːʃ) *n.* **1.** a carved or cast ornamental tablet or panel in the form of a scroll. **2.** an oblong figure enclosing characters expressing royal or divine names in Egyptian hieroglyphics.

cartridge (ˈkɑːtrɪdʒ) *n.* **1.** a metal casing containing an explosive charge and often a bullet, for a rifle or other small arms. **2.** a stylus unit in the pickup of a gramophone, either containing a piezoelectric crystal (**crystal cartridge**) or an electromagnet (**magnetic cartridge**). **3.** an enclosed container of magnetic tape, photographic film, ink, etc. for insertion into a tape deck, camera, pen, etc.

cartridge belt *n.* a belt with pockets for cartridge clips or loops for cartridges.

cartridge clip *n.* a metallic container holding cartridges for an automatic firearm.

cartridge paper *n.* **1.** an uncoated type of drawing or printing paper. **2.** a heavy paper used in making cartridges or as drawing or printing paper.

cartwheel (ˈkɑːtˌwiːl) *n.* **1.** the wheel of a cart, usually having wooden spokes. **2.** an acrobatic movement in which the body makes a revolution supported on the hands with legs outstretched.

carve (kɑːv) *vb.* **1.** (*tr.*) to cut or chip in order to form something: *to carve wood.* **2.** to form (something) by cutting or chipping: *to carve statues.* **3.** to slice (meat) into pieces. —'**carver** *n.*

carvel (ˈkɑːvəl) *n.* another word for **caravel.**

carve out *vb.* (*tr., adv.*) *Inf.* to make or create (a career): *he carved out his own future.*

carve up *vb.* (*tr., adv.*) **1.** to cut (something) into pieces. **2.** to divide (land, etc.). ~*n.* **carve-up. 3.** *Sl.* the distribution of something.

carving (ˈkɑːvɪŋ) *n.* a figure or design produced by carving stone, wood, etc.

carving knife *n.* a long-bladed knife for carving cooked meat for serving.

carwash (ˈkɑːˌwɒʃ) *n.* an installation for the automatic washing and polishing of cars.

caryatid (ˌkærɪˈætɪd) *n., pl.* **-ids** *or* **-ides** (-ˌdiːz). a column, used to support an entablature, in the form of a draped female figure.

Casanova (ˌkæsəˈnəʊvə) *n.* any man noted for his amorous adventures.

casbah (ˈkæzbɑː) *n.* (*sometimes cap.*) a variant spelling of **kasbah.**

cascade (kæsˈkeɪd) *n.* **1.** a waterfall or series of waterfalls over rocks. **2.** something resembling this, such as folds of lace. **3.** a consecutive sequence of chemical or physical processes. **4.** a set of electrical components connected in series. ~*vb.* **5.** (*intr.*) to flow or fall in or like a cascade.

cascara (kæsˈkɑːrə) *n.* **1.** Also called: **cascara sagrada.** the dried bark of the cascara buckthorn, used as a laxative and stimulant. **2.** Also called: **cascara buckthorn.** a shrub or small tree of NW North America.

case[1] (keɪs) *n.* **1.** a single instance, or example of something. **2.** an instance of disease, injury, etc. **3.** a question or matter for discussion. **4.** a specific condition or state of affairs; situation. **5.** a set of arguments supporting a particular action, cause, etc. **6. a.** a person attended or served by a doctor, social worker, solicitor, etc. **b.** (*as modifier*): *a case study.* **7. a.** an action or suit at law: *he has a good case.* **b.** the evidence offered in court to support a claim. **8.** *Grammar.* **a.** a set of grammatical categories of nouns, pronouns, and adjectives indicating the relation of the noun, adjective, or pronoun to other words in the sentence. **b.** any one of these categories: *the nominative case.* **9.** *Inf.* an eccentric. **10. in any case.** (*adv.*) no matter what. **11. in case.** (*adv.*) **a.** in order to allow for eventualities. **b.** (*as conj.*) in order to allow for the possibility that: *take your coat in case it rains.* **12. in case of.** (*prep.*) in the event of. **13. in no case.** (*adv.*) under no circumstances.

case[2] (keɪs) *n.* **1. a.** a container, such as a box or chest. **b.** (*in combination*): *suitcase.* **2.** an outer cover, esp. for a watch. **3.** a receptacle and its contents: *a case of ammunition.* **4.** *Archit.* another word for **casing** (sense 3). **5.** a cover ready to be fastened to a book to form its binding. **6.** *Printing.* a tray in which a compositor keeps individual metal types of a particular size and style. Cases were originally used in pairs, one (the **upper case**) for capitals, the other (the **lower case**) for small letters. ~*vb.* **7.** to put into or cover with a case. **8.** *U.S. sl.* to inspect carefully (esp. a place to be robbed).

case-harden *vb.* (*tr.*) **1.** *Metallurgy.* to form a hard surface layer of high carbon content on (a steel component). **2.** to make callous: *experience had case-hardened the judge.*

case history *n.* a record of a person's background, medical history, etc.

casein (ˈkeɪsiɪn, -siːn) *n.* a protein, precipitated from milk by the action of rennin, forming the basis of cheese.

case law *n.* law established by following judicial decisions given in earlier cases. Cf. **statute law.**

THESAURUS

carton box, case, container, pack, package, packet

cartoon animated cartoon, animated film, animation, caricature, comic strip, lampoon, parody, satire, sketch, takeoff

cartridge 1. capsule, case, cassette, container, cylinder, magazine 2. charge, round, shell

carve chip, chisel, cut, divide, engrave, etch, fashion, form, grave, hack, hew, incise, indent, mould, sculpt, sculpture, slash, slice, whittle

cascade 1. *n.* avalanche, cataract, deluge, falls, flood, fountain, outpouring, shower, torrent, waterfall 2. *v.* descend, flood, gush, overflow, pitch, plunge, pour, spill, surge, tumble

case 1. box, cabinet, canister, capsule, carton, cartridge, casket, chest, compact, container, crate, holder, receptacle, shell, suit-case, tray, trunk 2. capsule, casing, cover, covering, envelope, folder, integument, jacket, sheath, wrapper, wrapping 3. circumstance(s), condition, context, contingency, dilemma, event, plight, position, predicament, situation, state 4. example, illustration, instance, occasion, occurrence, specimen 5. *Law* action, cause, dispute, lawsuit, proceedings, process, suit, trial

casement ('keɪsmənt) *n.* **1.** a window frame that is hinged on one side. **2.** a window containing frames hinged at the side. **3.** a poetic word for **window**.

casework ('keɪs,wɜːk) *n.* social work based on close study of the personal histories and circumstances of individuals and families. —'**case,worker** *n.*

cash (kæʃ) *n.* **1.** banknotes and coins, esp. in hand or readily available. **2.** immediate payment for goods or services (esp. in **cash down**). **3.** (*modifier*) of, for, or paid by cash: *a cash transaction.* ~*vb.* **4.** (*tr.*) to obtain or pay ready money for. ~See also **cash in.** —'**cashable** *adj.*

cash-and-carry *adj., adv.* sold or operated on a basis of cash payment for merchandise that is not delivered but removed by the purchaser.

cash-book *n. Book-keeping.* a journal in which all receipts and disbursements are recorded.

cash crop *n.* a crop grown for sale rather than for subsistence.

cash desk *n.* a counter or till in a shop where purchases are paid for.

cash discount *n.* a discount granted to a purchaser who pays before a stipulated date.

cashew ('kæʃuː, kæ'ʃuː) *n.* **1.** a tropical American evergreen tree, bearing kidney-shaped nuts. **2.** Also called: **cashew nut.** the nut of this tree, edible only when roasted.

cash flow *n.* the movement of money into and out of a business.

cashier[1] (kæ'ʃɪə) *n.* **1.** a person responsible for receiving payments for goods, services, etc., as in a shop. **2.** an employee of a bank responsible for receiving deposits, cashing cheques, etc.: bank clerk. **3.** any person responsible for handling cash in a business.

cashier[2] (kæ'ʃɪə) *vb.* (*tr.*) to dismiss with dishonour, esp. from the armed forces.

cash in *vb.* (*adv.*) **1.** (*tr.*) to give (something) in exchange. **2.** (*intr.;* often foll. by *on*) *Sl.* **a.** to profit (from). **b.** to take advantage (of).

cashmere ('kæʃmɪə) *n.* **1.** a fine soft wool from goats of the Kashmir area. **2. a.** cloth or knitted material made from this or similar wool. **b.** (*as modifier*): *a cashmere sweater.*

cash on delivery *n.* a service entailing cash payment to the carrier on delivery of merchandise.

cash register *n.* a till with a keyboard that operates a mechanism for displaying and adding the amounts of cash received in individual sales.

casing ('keɪsɪŋ) *n.* **1.** a protective case or cover. **2.** material for a case or cover. **3.** Also called: **case.** a frame containing a door or window.

casino (kə'siːnəʊ) *n., pl.* **-nos.** **1.** a public building or room in which gaming takes place. **2.** a variant spelling of **cassino.**

cask (kɑːsk) *n.* **1.** a strong wooden barrel used mainly to hold alcoholic drink: *a wine cask.* **2.** any barrel. **3.** the quantity contained in a cask.

casket ('kɑːskɪt) *n.* **1.** a small box or chest for valuables, esp. jewels. **2.** another word for **coffin.** (sense 1).

casque (kæsk) *n. Zool.* a helmet or a helmet-like structure, as on the bill of most hornbills. —**casqued** *adj.*

Cassandra (kə'sændrə) *n.* **1.** *Greek myth.* a daughter of Priam and Hecuba, endowed with the gift of prophecy but fated never to be believed. **2.** anyone whose prophecies of doom are unheeded.

cassava (kə'sɑːvə) *n.* **1.** Also called: **manioc.** any of various tropical plants, esp. the widely cultivated American species (**bitter cassava, sweet cassava**). **2.** a starch derived from the root of this plant: a source of tapioca.

casserole ('kæsə,rəʊl) *n.* **1.** a covered dish of earthenware, glass, etc., in which food is cooked and served. **2.** any food cooked and served in such a dish: *chicken casserole.* ~*vb.* **3.** to cook or be cooked in a casserole.

cassette (kæ'sɛt) *n.* **1. a.** a plastic container for magnetic tape, inserted into a tape deck to be played or used. **b.** (*as modifier*): *a cassette recorder.* **2.** *Photog.* another term for **cartridge** (sense 3).

cassia ('kæsɪə) *n.* **1.** any of a genus of tropical plants whose pods yield **cassia pulp,** a mild laxative. See also **senna.** **2.** a lauraceous tree of tropical Asia. **3. cassia bark.** the cinnamon-like bark of this tree, used as a spice.

cassimere *or* **casimere** ('kæsɪ,mɪə) *n.* a woollen suiting cloth of plain or twill weave.

cassino *or* **casino** (kə'siːnəʊ) *n.* a card game for two to four players in which players pair cards with those exposed on the table.

Cassiopeia (,kæsɪə'piːə) *n. Latin genitive* **Cassiopeiae** (,kæsɪə'piːiː). a very conspicuous W-shaped constellation near the Pole Star.

cassock ('kæsək) *n. Ecclesiast.* an ankle-length garment, usually black, worn by priests.

cassowary ('kæsə,wɛərɪ) *n., pl.* **-waries.** a large flightless bird inhabiting forests in NE Australia, New Guinea, and adjacent islands, having a horny head crest, black plumage, and brightly coloured neck.

cast (kɑːst) *vb.* **casting, cast.** (*mainly tr.*) **1.** to throw or expel with force. **2.** to throw off or away: *she cast her clothes to the ground.* **3.** to reject: *he cast the idea from his mind.* **4.** to shed or drop: *the horse cast a shoe.* **5.** to be cast. *N.Z.* (of sheep) to have fallen and been unable to rise. **6.** to cause to appear: *to cast a shadow.* **7.** to express (doubts, etc.) or cause (them) to be felt. **8.** to direct (a glance, etc.): *cast your eye over this.* **9.** to place, esp. violently: *he was cast into prison.* **10.** (*also intr.*) *Angling.* to throw (a baited line) into the water. **11.** to draw or choose (lots). **12.** to give or deposit (a vote). **13.** to select (actors) to play parts in (a play, etc.). **14. a.** to shape (molten metal, glass, etc.) by pouring into a mould. **b.** to make (an object) by such a process. **15.** (*also intr.;* often foll. by *up*) to compute (figures or a total). **16.** *Astrol.* to draw on (a horoscope) details concerning the positions of the planets in the signs of the zodiac at a particular time for interpretation. **17.** to contrive (esp. in **cast a spell**). **18.** to formulate: *he cast his work in the form of a chart.* **19.** (*also intr.*) to twist or cause to twist. **20.** (*intr.*) (of birds of prey) to eject from the crop and bill a pellet consisting of the indigestible parts of birds or animals previously eaten. **21.** *Printing.* to stereotype or electrotype. **22. cast in one's lot with.** to share in the activities of (someone else). ~*n.* **23.** the act of casting or throwing. **24. a.** Also called: **casting.** something that is shed, dropped, or egested, such as the coil of earth left by an earthworm. **b.** another name for **pellet** (sense 4). **25.** the distance an object is or may be thrown. **26. a.** a throw at dice. **b.** the resulting number shown. **27.** *Angling.* the act or an instance of casting a line. **28.** the wide sweep made by a sheepdog to get behind a flock of sheep or by a hunting dog in search of a scent. **29. a.** the actors in a play collectively. **b.** (*as modifier*): *a cast list.* **30. a.** an object made of metal, glass, etc., that has been shaped in a molten state by being poured or pressed into a mould. **b.** the mould used to shape such an object. **31.** form or appearance. **32.** sort, kind, or style. **33.** a fixed twist or defect, esp. in the eye. **34.** a distortion of shape. **35.** *Surgery.* a rigid encircling casing, often made of plaster of Paris, **plaster cast,** for immobilizing broken bones while they heal. **36.** a slight tinge or trace, as of colour. **37.** fortune or stroke of fate. ~See also **cast about, castaway,** etc.

cast about *vb.* (*intr., adv.*) to make a mental or visual search: *to cast about for a plot.*

castanets (,kæstə'nɛts) *pl. n.* curved pieces of hollow wood, usually held between the fingers and thumb and made to click together: used esp. by Spanish dancers.

castaway ('kɑːstə,weɪ) *n.* **1.** a person who has been shipwrecked. ~*adj.* (*prenominal*) **2.** shipwrecked. **3.** thrown away or rejected. ~*vb.* **cast away. 4.** (*tr., adv.;*

THESAURUS

cash banknotes, bread (*Sl.*), bullion, charge, coin, coinage, currency, dough (*Sl.*), funds, money, notes, payment, ready (*Inf.*), ready money, resources, specie, wherewithal

cashier 1. *n.* accountant, bank clerk, banker, bursar, clerk, purser, teller, treasurer 2. *v.* break, cast off, discard, discharge, dismiss, drum out, expel

casket box, case, chest, coffer, jewel box, kist (*Scot.*)

cast *v.* 1. chuck, drive, drop, fling, hurl, impel, launch, lob, pitch, project, shed, shy, sling, throw, thrust, toss 2. bestow, deposit, diffuse, distribute, emit, give, radiate, scatter, shed, spread 3. allot, appoint, assign, choose, name, pick, select 4. add, calculate, compute, figure, forecast, reckon, total 5.

form, found, model, mould, set, shape ~*n.* 6. fling, lob, throw, thrust, toss 7. air, appearance, complexion, demeanour, look, manner, mien, semblance, shade, stamp, style, tinge, tone, turn 8. actors, characters, company, dramatis personae, players, troupe

often passive) to cause (a ship, person, etc.) to be ship-wrecked.

cast back   *vb.* (*adv.*) to turn (the mind) to the past.

cast down   *vb.* (*tr., adv.*) to make (a person) discouraged or dejected.

caste (kɑːst) *n.* **1. a.** any of the four major hereditary classes, namely the **Brahman, Kshatriya, Vaisya,** and **Sudra,** into which Hindu society is divided. **b.** Also called: **caste system.** the system or basis of such classes. **2.** any social class or system based on such distinctions as heredity, rank, wealth, etc. **3.** the position conferred by such a system. **4. lose caste.** *Inf.* to lose one's social position. **5.** *Entomol.* any of various types of individual, such as the worker, in social insects.

castellated ('kæstɪˌleɪtɪd) *adj.* **1.** having turrets and battlements, like a castle. **2.** having indentations similar to battlements: *a castellated nut.* — ,castel'lation *n.*

caster ('kɑːstə) *n.* **1.** a person or thing that casts. **2.** a bottle with a perforated top for sprinkling sugar, etc. **3.** a small swivelling wheel attached to each leg or bottom corner of a piece of furniture to facilitate movement. Also called (for senses 2, 3): **castor.**

caster sugar ('kɑːstə) *n.* finely ground white sugar.

castigate ('kæstɪˌgeɪt) *vb.* (*tr.*) to rebuke or criticize in a severe manner. — ,casti'gation *n.* — 'casti,gator *n.*

casting ('kɑːstɪŋ) *n.* **1.** an object that has been cast, esp. in metal from a mould. **2.** the process of transferring molten steel to a mould. **3.** the choosing of actors for a production. **4.** *Zool.* another word for **cast** (sense 24) or **pellet** (sense 4).

casting vote   *n.* the deciding vote used by the presiding officer of an assembly when votes cast on both sides are equal in number.

cast iron   *n.* **1.** iron containing so much carbon that it cannot be wrought and must be cast into shape. ~*adj.* **cast-iron. 2.** made of cast iron. **3.** rigid or unyielding: *a cast-iron decision.*

castle ('kɑːsəl) *n.* **1.** a fortified building or set of buildings as in medieval Europe. **2.** any fortified place or structure. **3.** a large magnificent house, esp. when the present or former home of a nobleman or prince. **4.** *Chess.* another name for **rook**[2]. ~*vb.* **5.** *Chess.* to move (the king) two squares laterally on the first rank and place the nearest rook on the square passed over by the king.

castle in the air *or* **in Spain** *n.* a hope or desire unlikely to be realized; daydream.

cast-off *adj.* **1.** (*prenominal*) abandoned: *cast-off shoes.* ~*n.* **castoff. 2.** a person or thing that has been discarded or abandoned. **3.** *Printing.* an estimate of the amount of space that a piece of copy will occupy. ~*vb.* **cast off.** (*adv.*) **4.** to loosen (mooring lines) that hold (a vessel) to a dock. **5.** to knot (a row of stitches, esp. the final row) in finishing off knitted or woven material. **6.** *Printing.* to estimate the amount of space that will be taken up by (a book, piece of copy, etc.).

castor[1] ('kɑːstə) *n.* **1.** the aromatic secretion of a beaver, used in perfumery and medicine. **2.** the fur of the beaver. **3.** a hat made of beaver or similar fur.

castor[2] ('kɑːstə) *n.* a variant spelling of **caster** (senses 2, 3).

castor oil   *n.* an oil obtained from the seeds of the castor-oil plant and used as a lubricant and cathartic.

castor-oil plant   *n.* a tall Indian plant cultivated for its poisonous seeds, from which castor oil is extracted.

castrate (kæ'streɪt) *vb.* (*tr.*) **1.** to remove the testicles of. **2.** to deprive of vigour, masculinity, etc. **3.** to remove the ovaries of; spay. — **cas'tration** *n.* — **cas'trator** *n.*

castrato (kæ'strɑːtəʊ) *n., pl.* **-ti** (-tɪ) *or* **-tos.** (in 17th- and 18th-century opera, etc.) a male singer whose testi-

cles were removed before puberty, allowing the retention of a soprano or alto voice.

cast steel   *n.* steel containing varying amounts of carbon, manganese, etc. that is cast into shape rather than wrought.

casual ('kæʒjʊəl) *adj.* **1.** happening by accident or chance. **2.** offhand: *a casual remark.* **3.** shallow or superficial: *a casual affair.* **4.** being or seeming unconcerned or apathetic: *he assumed a casual attitude.* **5.** (esp. of dress) for informal wear: *a casual coat.* **6.** occasional or irregular; part-time: *a casual labourer.* ~*n.* **7.** (*usually pl.*) an informal article of clothing or footwear. **8.** a part-time or occasional worker. — **'casually** *adv.* — **'casualness** *n.*

casualty ('kæʒjʊəltɪ) *n., pl.* **-ties. 1.** a serviceman who is killed, wounded, captured, or missing as a result of enemy action. **2.** a person who is injured or killed in an accident. **3.** the hospital department treating victims of accidents. **4.** anything that is lost, damaged, or destroyed as the result of an accident, etc.

casuarina (ˌkæsjʊəˈraɪnə) *n.* any of a genus of trees of Australia and the East Indies, having jointed leafless branches.

casuistry ('kæzjʊɪstrɪ) *n., pl.* **-ries. 1.** *Philosophy.* the application of general ethical principles to particular moral problems. **2.** reasoning that is specious or over-subtle.

cat (kæt) *n.* **1.** Also called: **domestic cat.** a small domesticated feline mammal having thick soft fur and occurring in many breeds in which the colour of the fur varies greatly: kept as a pet or to catch rats and mice. **2.** Also called: **big cat.** any of the larger felines, such as a lion or tiger. **3.** any wild feline mammal such as the lynx or serval, resembling the domestic cat. **4.** *Inf.* a woman who gossips maliciously. **5.** *Sl.* a man. **6.** *Naut.* a heavy tackle for hoisting an anchor to the cathead. **7.** *Inf.* short for **caterpillar** (the vehicle). **8.** short for **cat-o'-nine-tails. 9. fight like Kilkenny cats.** to fight until both parties are destroyed. **10. let the cat out of the bag.** to disclose a secret, often by mistake. **11. like a cat on a hot tin roof** or **on hot bricks.** in an uneasy or agitated state. **12. put, set,** etc., **the cat among the pigeons.** to introduce some violently disturbing new element. **13. rain cats and dogs.** to rain very heavily. ~*vb.* **catting, catted. 14.** (*tr.*) *Naut.* to hoist (an anchor) to the cathead. **15.** (*intr.*) *Sl.* to vomit. — **'cat,like** *adj.* — **'cattish** *adj.*

C.A.T.   (in Britain) *abbrev. for* College of Advanced Technology.

cat.   *abbrev. for:* **1.** catalogue. **2.** catamaran.

cata-, kata-, *before an aspirate* **cath-,** *or before a vowel* **cat-** *prefix.* **1.** down; downwards; lower in position: *catadromous.* **2.** indicating reversal, opposition, degeneration, etc.: *catatonia.*

catabolism *or* **katabolism** (kəˈtæbəˌlɪzəm) *n.* a metabolic process in which complex molecules are broken down into simple ones with the release of energy; destructive metabolism. — **catabolic** *or* **katabolic** (ˌkætəˈbɒlɪk) *adj.*

cataclysm ('kætəˌklɪzəm) *n.* **1.** a violent upheaval, esp. of a political, military, or social nature. **2.** a disastrous flood. — ,cata'clysmic *or* ,cata'clysmal *adj.* — ,cata-'clysmically *adv.*

catacomb ('kætəˌkuːm) *n.* **1.** (*usually pl.*) an underground burial place, esp. in Rome, consisting of tunnels with niches leading off them for tombs. **2.** a series of underground tunnels or caves.

catafalque ('kætəˌfælk) *n.* a temporary raised platform on which a body lies in state before or during a funeral.

Catalan ('kætəˌlæn) *n.* **1.** a language of Catalonia, closely related to Spanish and Provençal. **2.** a native or inhabitant of Catalonia. ~*adj.* **3.** denoting or charac-

---

THESAURUS

cast down deject, depress, desolate, discourage, dishearten, dispirit

caste class, estate, grade, lineage, order, race, rank, social order, species, station, status, stratum

castigate beat, berate, cane, censure, chasten, chastise, correct, criticize, discipline, dress down (*Inf.*), flail, flay, flog, haul over the coals (*Inf.*), lash, rebuke, reprimand, scold, scourge, whip

castle chateau, citadel, donjon, fastness,

fortress, keep, mansion, palace, peel, stronghold, tower

casual 1. accidental, chance, contingent, fortuitous, incidental, irregular, occasional, random, serendipitous, uncertain, unexpected, unforeseen, unintentional, unpremeditated **2.** apathetic, blasé, cursory, indifferent, informal, insouciant, lackadaisical, nonchalant, offhand, perfunctory, relaxed, unconcerned

casualties dead, fatalities, losses, mis-

sing, wounded

casualty 1. loss, sufferer, victim **2.** accident, calamity, catastrophe, chance, contingency, disaster, misadventure, misfortune, mishap

cat feline, grimalkin, malkin (*Archaic*), moggy (*Sl.*), mouser, puss (*Inf.*), pussy (*Inf.*), tabby

teristic of Catalonia, its inhabitants, or their language.

catalepsy ('kætə,lɛpsɪ) n. a disturbance of consciousness, occurring esp. in schizophrenia, characterized by prolonged maintenance of rigid postures. —,cata'leptic adj.

catalogue or U.S. **catalog** ('kætə,lɒg) n. 1. a complete, usually alphabetical list of items. 2. a list of all the books of a library. 3. U.S. a list of courses offered by a university, etc. ~vb. 4. to compile a catalogue of (a library, etc.). 5. to add (books, items, etc.) to an existing catalogue. —'cata,loguer n.

catalpa (kə'tælpə) n. any of a genus of trees of North America and Asia, having large leaves, bell-shaped whitish flowers, and long slender pods.

catalyse or U.S. **catalyze** ('kætə,laɪz) vb. (tr.) to influence (a chemical reaction) by catalysis.

catalysis (kə'tælɪsɪs) n., pl. **-ses** (-,siːz). acceleration of a chemical reaction by the action of a catalyst. —catalytic (,kætə'lɪtɪk) adj.

catalyst ('kætəlɪst) n. 1. a substance that increases the rate of a chemical reaction without itself suffering any permanent chemical change. 2. a person or thing that causes a change.

catamaran (,kætəmə'ræn) n. 1. a sailing vessel with twin hulls held parallel by a rigid framework. 2. a primitive raft made of logs lashed together. 3. Inf. a quarrelsome woman.

catamite ('kætə,maɪt) n. a boy kept for homosexual purposes.

cataplexy ('kætə,plɛksɪ) n. 1. sudden temporary paralysis, brought on by intense emotion, etc. 2. a state assumed by animals while shamming death. —,cata'plectic adj.

catapult ('kætə,pʌlt) n. 1. a Y-shaped implement with a loop of elastic fastened to the ends of the prongs, used mainly by children for shooting stones, etc. U.S. name: **slingshot.** 2. a war engine used formerly for hurling stones, etc. 3. a device installed in warships to launch aircraft. ~vb. 4. (tr.) to shoot forth from or as if from a catapult. 5. (foll. by over, into, etc.) to move precipitately.

cataract ('kætə,rækt) n. 1. a large waterfall or rapids. 2. a downpour. 3. Pathol. a. partial or total opacity of the lens of the eye. b. the opaque area.

catarrh (kə'tɑː) n. inflammation of a mucous membrane with increased production of mucus, esp. affecting the nose and throat. —ca'tarrhal adj.

catastrophe (kə'tæstrəfɪ) n. 1. a sudden, extensive disaster or misfortune. 2. the dénouement of a play. 3. a final decisive event, usually causing a disastrous end. —catastrophic (,kætə'strɒfɪk) adj. —,cata'strophically adv.

catatonia (,kætə'təʊnɪə) n. a form of schizophrenia characterized by stupor, with outbreaks of excitement. —catatonic (,kætə'tɒnɪk) adj., n.

cat burglar n. a burglar who enters buildings by climbing through upper windows, etc.

catcall ('kæt,kɔːl) n. 1. a shrill whistle or cry expressing disapproval, as at a public meeting, etc. ~vb. 2. to utter such a call (at).

catch (kætʃ) vb. **catching, caught.** 1. (tr.) to take hold of so as to retain or restrain. 2. (tr.) to take or capture, esp. after pursuit. 3. (tr.) to ensnare or deceive. 4. (tr.) to surprise or detect in an act: he caught the dog rifling the larder. 5. (tr.) to reach with a blow: the stone caught him on the side of the head. 6. (tr.) to overtake

or reach in time to board. 7. (tr.) to see or hear; attend. 8. (tr.) to be infected with: to catch a cold. 9. to hook or entangle or become hooked or entangled. 10. to fasten or be fastened with or as if with a latch or other device. 11. (tr.) to attract: she tried to catch his eye. 12. (tr.) to comprehend: I didn't catch his meaning. 13. (tr.) to hear accurately: I didn't catch what you said. 14. (tr.) to captivate or charm. 15. (tr.) to reproduce accurately: the painter managed to catch his model's beauty. 16. (tr.) to hold back or restrain: he caught his breath in surprise. 17. (intr.) to become alight: the fire won't catch. 18. (tr.) Cricket. to dismiss (a batsman) by intercepting and holding a ball struck by him before it touches the ground. 19. (intr.; often foll. by at) a. to grasp or attempt to grasp. b. to take advantage (of): he caught at the chance. 20. **catch it.** Inf. to be scolded or reprimanded. ~n. 21. the act of catching or grasping. 22. a device that catches and fastens, such as a latch. 23. anything that is caught. 24. the amount or number caught. 25. Inf. an eligible matrimonial prospect. 26. a check or break in the voice. 27. Inf. a. a concealed, unexpected, or unforeseen drawback. b. (as modifier): a catch question. 28. Cricket. the catching of a ball struck by a batsman before it touches the ground, resulting in him being out. 29. Music. a type of round having a humorous text that is often indecent or bawdy and hard to articulate. ~See also **catch on, catch out, catch up.** —'catchable adj.

catching ('kætʃɪŋ) adj. 1. infectious. 2. attractive; captivating.

catchment ('kætʃmənt) n. 1. the act of catching or collecting water. 2. a structure in which water is collected. 3. the water so collected. 4. Brit. the intake of a school from one catchment area.

catchment area n. 1. the area of land bounded by watersheds draining into a river, basin, or reservoir. 2. the area from which people are allocated to a particular school, hospital, etc.

catch on vb. (intr., adv.) Inf. 1. to become popular or fashionable. 2. to understand.

catch out vb. (tr., adv.) Inf., chiefly Brit. to trap (a person), esp. in an error.

catchpenny ('kætʃ,pɛnɪ) adj. (prenominal) designed to have instant appeal, esp. in order to sell quickly: catchpenny ornaments.

catch phrase n. a well-known frequently used phrase, esp. one associated with a particular group, etc.

catch-22 n. a situation characterized by obstacles that defeat all attempts of the victim to escape from it.

catch up vb. (adv.) 1. (tr.) to seize and take up (something) quickly. 2. (when intr., often foll. by with) to reach or pass (someone or something): he caught him up. 3. (intr.; usually foll. by on or with) to make up for lost ground or deal with a backlog. 4. (tr.; often passive) to absorb or involve: she was caught up in her reading. 5. (tr.) to raise by or as if by fastening.

catchword ('kætʃ,wɜːd) n. 1. a word or phrase made temporarily popular; slogan. 2. a word printed as a running head in a book. 3. Theatre. an actor's cue to speak or enter. 4. the first word of a page repeated at the bottom of the page preceding.

catchy ('kætʃɪ) adj. **catchier, catchiest.** 1. (of a tune, etc.) pleasant and easily remembered. 2. deceptive: a catchy question. 3. irregular: a catchy breeze.

catechism ('kætɪ,kɪzəm) n. instruction by a series of questions and answers, esp. a book containing such instruction on the religious doctrine of a Christian Church. —,cate'chismal adj.

THESAURUS

catalogue 1. n. directory, gazetteer, index, inventory, list, record, register, roll, roster, schedule 2. v. accession, alphabetize, classify, file, index, inventory, list, register

catapult 1. n. ballista, sling, slingshot (U.S.), trebuchet 2. v. heave, hurl, hurtle, pitch, plunge, propel, shoot, toss

cataract 1. cascade, deluge, downpour, falls, Niagara, rapids, torrent, waterfall 2. Medical opacity (of the eye)

catastrophe 1. adversity, affliction, blow, calamity, cataclysm, devastation, disaster, failure, fiasco, ill, mischance, misfortune, mishap, reverse, tragedy, trial, trouble 2. conclusion, culmination, curtain, debacle, dénouement, end, finale, termination, up-

shot, winding-up

catcall 1. v. boo, deride, gibe, give the bird to (Inf.), hiss, jeer, whistle 2. n. boo, gibe, hiss, jeer, raspberry, whistle

catch v. 1. apprehend, arrest, capture, clutch, ensnare, entangle, entrap, grab, grasp, grip, lay hold of, nab (Inf.), seize, snare, snatch, take 2. detect, discover, expose, find out, surprise, take unawares, unmask 3. bewitch, captivate, charm, delight, enchant, enrapture, fascinate 4. contract, develop, go down with, incur, succumb to, suffer from 5. apprehend, discern, feel, follow, grasp, hear, perceive, recognize, sense, take in, twig (Inf.) ~n. 6. bolt, clasp, clip, fastener, hasp, hook, hook and eye, latch, sneck,

snib (Scot.) 7. disadvantage, drawback, fly in the ointment, hitch, snag, stumbling block, trap, trick

catching 1. communicable, contagious, infectious, infective, transferable, transmittable 2. attractive, captivating, charming, enchanting, fascinating, fetching, taking, winning

catch on comprehend, find out, grasp, see, see through, twig (Inf.), understand

catchword byword, motto, password, refrain, slogan, watchword

catchy captivating, haunting, memorable, popular

catechize or **-ise** ('kætɪ,kaɪz) vb. (tr.) **1.** to teach or examine by means of questions and answers. **2.** Ecclesiast. to give oral instruction in Christianity, esp. by using a catechism. **3.** to put questions to (someone). —'**catechist**, '**cate,chizer** or **-iser** n.

catechu ('kætɪ,tʃuː), **cachou**, or **cutch** n. an astringent resinous substance obtained from any of certain tropical plants, and used in medicine, tanning, and dyeing.

categorical (,kætɪ'gɒrɪkəl) or **categoric** adj. **1.** unqualified; unconditional: a categorical statement. **2.** relating to or included in a category. **3.** (of a statement in logic) consisting of a subject (X) and an attribute (Y) linked by a copula; subject-predicate proposition, as in: all X are Y. —,cate'gorically adv.

categorize or **-ise** ('kætɪgə,raɪz) vb. (tr.) to place in a category. —,categori'zation or **-i'sation** n.

category ('kætɪgərɪ) n., pl. **-ries. 1.** a class or group of things, people, etc., possessing some quality or qualities in common. **2.** Metaphysics. the most basic class into which objects and concepts can be analysed. **3. a.** (in the philosophy of Aristotle) one of ten fundamental modes of being, such as quantity, quality, and substance. **b.** (in the philosophy of Kant) one of twelve concepts required by human beings to interpret the empirical world. —**categorial** (,kætɪ'gɔːrɪəl) adj.

catena (kə'tiːnə) n., pl. **-nae** (-niː). a connected series, esp. of patristic comments on the Bible.

cater ('keɪtə) vb. **1.** (intr.; foll. by for or to) to provide what is required or desired (for). **2.** (when intr., foll. by for) to provide food, services, etc. (for): we cater for parties. —'**catering** n.

caterer ('keɪtərə) n. one who as a profession provides food for large social events, etc.

caterpillar ('kætə,pɪlə) n. **1.** the wormlike larva of butterflies and moths, having numerous pairs of legs and powerful biting jaws. **2.** an endless track, driven by sprockets or wheels, used to propel a heavy vehicle. **3.** a vehicle, such as a tractor, tank, etc., driven by such tracks.

caterwaul ('kætə,wɔːl) vb. (intr.) **1.** to make a yowling noise, as a cat on heat. ~n. **2.** a yell made by or sounding like a cat on heat.

catfish ('kæt,fɪʃ) n., pl. **-fish** or **-fishes.** any of numerous mainly freshwater fishes having whisker-like barbels around the mouth.

catgut ('kæt,gʌt) n. a strong cord made from the dried intestines of sheep and other animals that is used for stringing certain musical instruments and sports rackets.

Cath. abbrev. for: **1.** Cathedral. **2.** Catholic.

cath- prefix. variant of **cata-** before an aspirate: cathode.

catharsis or **katharsis** (kə'θɑːsɪs) n. **1.** the purging or purification of the emotions through the evocation of pity and fear, as in tragedy. **2.** Psychoanal. a method of bringing repressed ideas or experiences to consciousness, by means of free association, etc. **3.** purgation, esp. of the bowels.

cathartic (kə'θɑːtɪk) adj. **1.** purgative. **2.** effecting catharsis. ~n. **3.** a purgative drug or agent. —**ca'thartically** adv.

Cathay (kæ'θeɪ) n. a literary or archaic name for China.

cathedral (kə'θiːdrəl) n. **a.** the principal church of a diocese, containing the bishop's official throne. **b.** (as modifier): a cathedral city.

Catherine wheel ('kæθrɪn) n. **1.** a firework which rotates, producing sparks and coloured flame. **2.** a circular window having ribs radiating from the centre.

catheter ('kæθɪtə) n. Med. a long slender flexible tube for inserting into a bodily cavity for introducing or withdrawing fluid. —'**catheter,ize** or **-,ise** vb.

cathode ('kæθəʊd) n. **1.** the negative electrode in an electrolytic cell. **2.** the negatively charged electron

source in an electronic valve. **3.** the positive terminal of a primary cell. ~Cf. **anode.** —**cathodal** (kæ'θəʊdəl) or **cathodic** (kæ'θɒdɪk, -'θəʊ-) adj.

cathode rays pl. n. a stream of electrons emitted from the surface of a cathode in a vacuum tube.

cathode-ray tube n. a vacuum tube in which a beam of electrons is focused onto a fluorescent screen to give a visible spot of light. The device is used in television tubes, oscilloscopes, etc.

catholic ('kæθəlɪk, 'kæθlɪk) adj. **1.** universal; relating to all men. **2.** broad-minded; liberal. —**catholically** or **catholicly** (kə'θɒlɪklɪ) adv.

Catholic ('kæθəlɪk, 'kæθlɪk) adj. Christianity. **1.** denoting or relating to the entire body of Christians, esp. to the Church before separation into the Eastern and Western Churches. **2.** denoting or relating to the Latin or Western Church after this separation. **3.** denoting or relating to the Roman Catholic Church. ~n. **4.** a member of the Roman Catholic Church.

Catholicism (kə'θɒlɪ,sɪzəm) n. **1.** short for **Roman Catholicism. 2.** the beliefs, practices, etc., of any Catholic Church.

catholicity (,kæθə'lɪsɪtɪ) n. **1.** a wide range of interests, tastes, etc. **2.** comprehensiveness.

cation ('kætaɪən) n. a positively charged ion; an ion that is attracted to the cathode during electrolysis. Cf. **anion.** —**cationic** (,kætaɪ'ɒnɪk) adj.

catkin ('kætkɪn) n. an inflorescence consisting of a hanging spike of much reduced flowers of either sex: occurs in birch, hazel, etc.

catmint ('kæt,mɪnt) n. a Eurasian plant having spikes of purple-spotted white flowers and scented leaves of which cats are fond. Also called: **catnip.**

catnap ('kæt,næp) n. **1.** a short sleep or doze. ~vb. **-napping, -napped. 2.** (intr.) to sleep or doze for a short time or intermittently.

cat-o'-nine-tails n., pl. **-tails.** a rope whip consisting of nine knotted thongs, used formerly to flog prisoners. Often shortened to **cat.**

cat's cradle n. a game played by making patterns with a loop of string between the fingers.

cat's-eye n. **1.** Brit. a glass reflector set into a small fixture, placed at intervals along roads to indicate traffic lanes at night. **2.** any of a group of gemstones that reflect a streak of light when cut in a rounded unfaceted shape.

cat's-paw n. **1.** a person used by another as a tool; dupe. **2.** a pattern of ripples on the surface of water caused by a light wind.

cattle ('kætəl) n. (functioning as pl.) **1.** bovid mammals of the tribe Bovini (bovines). **2.** Also called: **domestic cattle.** any domesticated bovine mammals.

cattle-grid n. a ditch in a roadway covered by a grid, intended to prevent the passage of livestock while allowing vehicles, etc., to pass unhindered.

catty ('kætɪ) or **cattish** adj. **-tier, -tiest. 1.** Inf. spiteful: a catty remark. **2.** of or resembling a cat. —'**cattily** or '**cattishly** adv. —'**cattiness** or '**cattishness** n.

catwalk ('kæt,wɔːk) n. a narrow pathway over the stage of a theatre, along a bridge, etc.

Caucasian (kɔː'keɪzɪən) adj. **1.** another word for **Caucasoid. 2.** of or relating to the Caucasus in the SW Soviet Union. ~n. **3.** a member of the Caucasoid race; a white man. **4.** a native or inhabitant of the Caucasus.

Caucasoid ('kɔːkə,zɔɪd) adj. **1.** denoting or belonging to the light-complexioned racial group of mankind, which includes the peoples indigenous to Europe, N Africa, SW Asia, and the Indian subcontinent. ~n. **2.** a member of this racial group.

caucus ('kɔːkəs) n., pl. **-cuses. 1.** Chiefly U.S. a closed meeting of the members of one party in a legislative chamber, etc., to coordinate policy, choose candidates, etc. **2.** Chiefly U.S. a local meeting of party members. **3.** Brit. a party organization, esp. on a local level. **4.** N.Z.

catechize cross-examine, drill, examine, grill (Inf.), interrogate, question

categorical absolute, direct, downright, emphatic, explicit, express, positive, unambiguous, unconditional, unequivocal, unqualified, unreserved

category class, classification, department, division, grade, grouping, head, head-

ing, list, order, rank, section, sort, type

cater furnish, outfit, provide, provision, purvey, supply, victual

catharsis abreaction, cleansing, lustration, purgation, purging, purification, release

catholic all-embracing, all-inclusive, broad-minded, charitable, comprehensive, eclectic, ecumenical, general, global, liberal,

tolerant, unbigoted, universal, unsectarian, whole, wide, world-wide

cattle beasts, bovines, cows, kine (Archaic), livestock, neat (Archaic), stock

catty backbiting, bitchy (Sl.), ill-natured, malevolent, malicious, mean, rancorous, spiteful, venomous

a formal meeting of all M.P.s of one party. **5.** *Austral.* a group of members of parliament from one party who meet to discuss tactics, etc. ~*vb.* **6.** (*intr.*) to hold a caucus.

caudal ('kɔːdəl) *adj.* **1.** *Anat.* of the posterior part of the body. **2.** *Zool.* resembling or in the position of the tail. —'**caudally** *adv.*

caudle ('kɔːdəl) *n.* a hot spiced wine drink made with gruel, formerly used medicinally.

caught (kɔːt) *vb.* the past tense and past participle of **catch**.

caul (kɔːl) *n. Anat.* a portion of the amniotic sac sometimes covering a child's head at birth.

cauldron *or* **caldron** ('kɔːldrən) *n.* a large pot used for boiling, esp. one with handles.

cauliflower ('kɒlɪ,flaʊə) *n.* **1.** a variety of cabbage having a large edible head of crowded white flowers on a very short thick stem. **2.** the flower head of this plant, used as a vegetable.

cauliflower ear *n.* permanent swelling and distortion of the external ear as the result of ruptures of the blood vessels: usually caused by blows received in boxing.

caulk *or* **calk** (kɔːk) *vb.* **1.** to stop up (cracks, crevices, etc.) with a filler. **2.** *Naut.* to pack (the seams) between the planks of the bottom of (a vessel) with waterproof material to prevent leakage.

causal ('kɔːzəl) *adj.* **1.** acting as or being a cause. **2.** stating, involving, or implying a cause: *the causal part of the argument.* **3.** *Grammar.* (of a word, phrase, or clause) indicating cause or reason: *"because" is a causal conjunction.* —'**causally** *adv.*

causality (kɔːˈzælɪtɪ) *n., pl.* **-ties. 1. a.** the relationship of cause and effect. **b.** the principle that nothing can happen without being caused. **2.** causal agency or quality.

causation (kɔːˈzeɪʃən) *n.* **1.** the production of an effect by a cause. **2.** the relationship of cause and effect. —**cauˈsational** *adj.*

causative ('kɔːzətɪv) *adj.* **1.** *Grammar.* relating to a form or class of verbs that express causation. **2.** (*often postpositive* and foll. by *of*) producing an effect. ~*n.* **3.** the causative form or class of verbs. —'**causatively** *adv.*

cause (kɔːz) *n.* **1.** a person, thing, event, state, or action that produces an effect. **2.** a basis or the grounds for action: *her rudeness was a cause for complaint.* **3.** reason: *she had good cause to shout like that.* **4.** the ideals, etc., of a group or movement: *the Communist cause.* **5.** the welfare or interests of a person or group in a dispute: *they fought for the miners' cause.* **6. a.** a ground for legal action; matter giving rise to a lawsuit. **b.** the lawsuit itself. **7.** *Arch.* a subject of debate or discussion. **8. make common cause with.** to join with (a person, group, etc.) for a common objective. ~*vb.* **9.** (*tr.*) to be the cause of; bring about. —'**causable** *adj.* —'**causeless** *adj.*

cause célèbre ('kɔːz sə'lɛbrə) *n., pl.* **causes célèbres** ('kɔːz sə'lɛbrəz). a famous lawsuit, trial, or controversy.

causerie ('kəʊzərɪ) *n.* an informal talk or conversational piece of writing.

causeway ('kɔːz,weɪ) *n.* **1.** a raised path or road crossing water, marshland, etc. **2.** a paved footpath.

caustic ('kɔːstɪk) *adj.* **1.** capable of burning or corroding by chemical action: *caustic soda.* **2.** sarcastic; cutting: *a caustic reply.* ~*n.* **3.** Also called: **caustic sur-**

face. a surface that envelops the light rays reflected or refracted by a curved surface. **4.** Also called: **caustic curve.** a curve formed by the intersection of a caustic surface with a plane. **5.** *Chem.* a caustic substance, esp. an alkali. —'**caustically** *adv.* —**causticity** (kɔːˈstɪsɪtɪ) *n.*

cauterize *or* **-ise** ('kɔːtə,raɪz) *vb.* (*tr.*) (esp. in the treatment of a wound) to burn or sear (body tissue) with a hot iron or caustic agent. —,**cauteri'zation** *or* **-i'sation** *n.*

caution ('kɔːʃən) *n.* **1.** care, forethought, or prudence, esp. in the face of danger. **2.** something intended or serving as a warning. **3.** *Law, chiefly Brit.* a formal warning given to a person suspected of an offence that his words will be taken down and may be used in evidence. **4.** *Inf.* an amusing or surprising person or thing. ~*vb.* **5.** (*tr.*) to warn (a person) to be careful. **6.** (*tr.*) *Law, chiefly Brit.* to give a caution to (a person). **7.** (*intr.*) to warn, urge, or advise: *he cautioned against optimism.* —'**cautionary** *adj.*

cautious ('kɔːʃəs) *adj.* showing or having caution. —'**cautiously** *adv.* —'**cautiousness** *n.*

cavalcade (,kævəl'keɪd) *n.* **1.** a procession of people on horseback, in cars, etc. **2.** any procession.

cavalier (,kævə'lɪə) *adj.* **1.** supercilious; offhand. ~*n.* **2.** a courtly gentleman, esp. one acting as a lady's escort. **3.** *Arch.* a horseman, esp. one who is armed. —,**cava-'lierly** *adv.*

Cavalier (,kævə'lɪə) *n.* a supporter of Charles I during the English Civil War.

cavalry ('kævəlrɪ) *n., pl.* **-ries. 1.** (esp. formerly) the part of an army composed of mounted troops. **2.** the motorized armoured element of a modern army. **3.** (*as modifier*): *a cavalry unit.* —'**cavalryman** *n.*

cave (keɪv) *n.* **1.** an underground hollow with access from the ground surface or from the sea. **2.** *Brit. history.* a secession or a group seceding from a political party on some issue. **3.** (*modifier*) living in caves. ~*vb.* **4.** (*tr.*) to hollow out.

cave ('keɪvɪ) *Brit. school sl.* ~*n.* **1.** lookout: *keep cave.* ~*interj.* **2.** watch out!

caveat ('keɪvɪ,æt, 'kæv-) *n.* **1.** *Law.* a formal notice requesting the court not to take a certain action without warning the person lodging the caveat. **2.** a caution.

cave in *vb.* (*intr., adv.*) **1.** to collapse; subside. **2.** *Inf.* to yield completely, esp. under pressure. ~*n.* **cave-in. 3.** the sudden collapse of a roof, piece of ground, etc. **4.** the site of such a collapse, as at a mine or tunnel.

cavel ('keɪvəl) *n. N.Z.* a drawing of lots among miners for an easy and profitable place at the coalface.

caveman ('keɪv,mæn) *n., pl.* **-men. 1.** a man of the Palaeolithic age; cave dweller. **2.** *Inf.* a man who is primitive or brutal in behaviour, etc.

cavern ('kævən) *n.* **1.** a cave, esp. when large. ~*vb.* (*tr.*) **2.** to shut in or as if in a cavern. **3.** to hollow out.

cavernous ('kævənəs) *adj.* **1.** suggestive of a cavern in vastness, etc.: *cavernous eyes.* **2.** filled with small cavities. **3.** (of rocks) containing caverns.

caviar *or* **caviare** ('kævɪ,ɑː, ,kævɪ'ɑː) *n.* the salted roe of sturgeon, usually served as an hors d'oeuvre.

cavil ('kævɪl) *vb.* **-illing, -illed** *or U.S.* **-iling, -iled. 1.** (*intr.;* foll. by *at* or *about*) to raise annoying petty objections. ~*n.* **2.** a trifling objection. —'**caviller** *n.*

caving ('keɪvɪŋ) *n.* the sport of climbing in and exploring caves. —'**caver** *n.*

cavity ('kævɪtɪ) *n., pl.* **-ties. 1.** a hollow space. **2.** *Dentistry.* a decayed area on a tooth. **3.** any empty or hollow space within the body.

caucus assembly, conclave, convention, get-together (*Inf.*), meeting, parley, session

cause *n.* **1.** agent, beginning, creator, genesis, mainspring, maker, origin, originator, prime mover, producer, root, source, spring **2.** account, agency, aim, basis, consideration, end, grounds, incentive, inducement, motivation, motive, object, purpose, reason **3.** attempt, belief, conviction, enterprise, ideal, movement, purpose, undertaking ~*v.* **4.** begin, bring about, compel, create, effect, engender, generate, give rise to, incite, induce, lead to, motivate, occasion, precipitate, produce, provoke, result in

caustic 1. acrid, astringent, biting, burning, corroding, corrosive, keen, mordant **2.**

acrimonious, cutting, pungent, sarcastic, scathing, severe, stinging, trenchant, virulent

caution *n.* **1.** alertness, care, carefulness, circumspection, deliberation, discretion, forethought, heed, heedfulness, prudence, vigilance, watchfulness **2.** admonition, advice, counsel, injunction, warning ~*v.* **3.** admonish, advise, tip off, urge, warn

cautious alert, cagey (*Inf.*), careful, chary, circumspect, discreet, guarded, heedful, judicious, prudent, tentative, vigilant, wary, watchful

cavalcade array, march-past, parade, procession, spectacle, train

cavalier *n.* **1.** chevalier, equestrian,

horseman, knight, royalist **2.** beau, blade (*Archaic*), escort, gallant, gentleman ~*adj.* **3.** arrogant, condescending, curt, disdainful, haughty, insolent, lofty, lordly, offhand, scornful, supercilious

cavalry horse, horsemen, mounted troops

cave cavern, cavity, den, grotto, hollow

caveat admonition, caution, warning

cavern cave, hollow, pothole

cavernous 1. concave, deep-set, hollow, sunken, yawning **2.** echoing, resonant, reverberant, sepulchral

cavil carp, censure, complain, find fault, hypercriticize, object, quibble

cavity crater, dent, gap, hole, hollow, pit

cavort (kə'vɔːt) vb. (intr.) to prance; caper. —**ca'vort-er** n.

caw (kɔː) n. 1. the cry of a crow, rook, or raven. ~vb. 2. (intr.) to make this cry.

cay (keı, kiː) n. a small low island or bank composed of sand and coral fragments.

cayenne pepper (keı'ɛn) n. a very hot red condiment made from the dried seeds of various capsicums. Often shortened to **cayenne.** Also called: **red pepper.**

cayman or **caiman** ('keımən) n., pl. **-mans.** a tropical American crocodilian similar to alligators but with a more heavily armoured belly.

Cb the chemical symbol for columbium.

CB abbrev. for Citizens' Band.

C.B. abbrev. for: 1. Companion of the (Order of the) Bath (a Brit. title). 2. County Borough.

CBC abbrev. for Canadian Broadcasting Corporation.

C.B.E. abbrev. for Commander of the (Order of the) British Empire.

C.B.I. abbrev. for: 1. Confederation of British Industry. 2. U.S. Central Bureau of Investigation.

cc or **c.c.** abbrev. for: 1. carbon copy or copies. 2. cubic centimetre(s).

cc. abbrev. for chapters.

C.C. abbrev. for: 1. City Council. 2. County Council. 3. Cricket Club.

cd abbrev. for candela.

Cd the chemical symbol for cadmium.

C.D. abbrev. for: 1. Civil Defence (Corps). 2. Corps Diplomatique (Diplomatic Corps).

Cdr. Mil. abbrev. for Commander.

CDT (in the U.S. & Canada) abbrev. for Central Daylight Time.

Ce the chemical symbol for cerium.

C.E. abbrev. for: 1. Church of England. 2. civil engineer. 3. Common Era.

cease (siːs) vb. 1. (when tr., may take a gerund or an infinitive as object) to bring or come to an end. ~n. 2. **without cease.** without stopping.

cease-fire Chiefly mil. ~n. 1. a period of truce, esp. one that is temporary. ~interj., n. 2. the order to stop firing.

ceaseless ('siːslıs) adj. without stop or pause; incessant. —'**ceaselessly** adv.

cedar ('siːdə) n. 1. any of a genus of Old World coniferous trees having needle-like evergreen leaves, and erect barrel-shaped cones. See also **cedar of Lebanon, deodar.** 2. any of various other conifers, such as the red cedars and white cedars. 3. the wood of any of these trees. ~adj. 4. made of the wood of a cedar tree.

cedar of Lebanon ('lɛbənən) n. a cedar of SW Asia with level spreading branches and fragrant wood.

cede (siːd) vb. 1. (when intr., often foll. by to) to transfer, make over, or surrender (something, esp. territory or legal rights). 2. (tr.) to allow or concede (a point in an argument, etc.). —'**ceder** n.

cedilla (sı'dılə) n. a character (‚) placed underneath a c before a, o, or u, esp. in French, Spanish, or Portuguese, denoting that it is to be pronounced (s), not (k).

Ceefax ('siːfæks) n. Trademark. the B.B.C. teletext service.

ceilidh ('keılı) n. (esp. in Scotland and Ireland) an informal social gathering with singing, dancing, and storytelling.

ceiling ('siːlıŋ) n. 1. the inner upper surface of a room.

2. an upper limit, such as one set by regulation on prices or wages. 3. the upper altitude to which an aircraft can climb measured under specified conditions. 4. Meteorol. the highest level in the atmosphere from which the earth's surface is visible at a particular time, usually the base of a cloud layer.

celandine ('sɛlən‚daın) n. either of two unrelated plants, **greater celandine** or **lesser celandine,** with yellow flowers.

-cele n. combining form. tumour or hernia: hydrocele.

celebrant ('sɛlıbrənt) n. a person participating in a religious ceremony, esp. at the Eucharist.

celebrate ('sɛlı‚breıt) vb. 1. to rejoice in or have special festivities to mark (a happy day, event, etc.). 2. (tr.) to observe (a birthday, anniversary, etc.). 3. (tr.) to perform (a solemn or religious ceremony), esp. to officiate at (Mass). 4. (tr.) to praise publicly; proclaim. —‚**cele'bration** n. —'**cele‚brator** n. —'**cele‚bratory** adj.

celebrated ('sɛlı‚breıtıd) adj. (usually prenominal) famous: a celebrated pianist.

celebrity (sı'lɛbrıtı) n., pl. **-ties.** 1. a famous person. 2. fame or notoriety.

celeriac (sı'lɛrı‚æk) n. a variety of celery with a large turnip-like root, used as a vegetable.

celerity (sı'lɛrıtı) n. rapidity; swiftness; speed.

celery ('sɛlərı) n. 1. an umbelliferous Eurasian plant whose blanched leafstalks are used in salads or cooked as a vegetable. 2. **wild celery.** a related and similar plant.

celesta (sı'lɛstə) or **celeste** (sı'lɛst) n. Music. a keyboard percussion instrument consisting of a set of steel plates of graduated length that are struck with key-operated hammers.

celestial (sı'lɛstıəl) adj. 1. heavenly; divine: celestial peace. 2. of or relating to the sky: celestial bodies. 3. of or connected with the celestial sphere: celestial pole. —ce'lestially adv.

celestial equator n. the great circle lying on the celestial sphere the plane of which is perpendicular to the line joining the north and south celestial poles. Also called: **equinoctial, equinoctial circle.**

celestial sphere n. an imaginary sphere of infinitely large radius enclosing the universe so that all celestial bodies appear to be projected onto its surface.

celibate ('sɛlıbıt) n. 1. a person who is unmarried, esp. one who has taken a religious vow of chastity. ~adj. 2. unmarried. —'**celibacy** n.

cell (sɛl) n. 1. a small simple room, as in a prison, convent, etc. 2. any small compartment: the cells of a honeycomb. 3. Biol. the smallest unit of an organism that is able to function independently. It consists of a nucleus, containing the genetic material, surrounded by the cytoplasm. 4. Biol. any small cavity, such as the cavity containing pollen in an anther. 5. a device for converting chemical energy into electrical energy, usually consisting of a container with two electrodes immersed in an electrolyte. See also **dry cell, fuel cell.** 6. in full **electrolytic cell.** a device in which electrolysis occurs. 7. a small religious house dependent upon a larger one. 8. a small group of persons operating as a nucleus of a larger organization: Communist cell.

cellar ('sɛlə) n. 1. an underground room, or storey of a building, usually used for storage. 2. a place where wine is stored. 3. a stock of bottled wines. ~vb. 4. (tr.) to store in a cellar.

cellarage ('sɛlərıdʒ) n. 1. an area of a cellar. 2. a

THESAURUS

cease break off, bring or come to an end, conclude, culminate, desist, die away, discontinue, end, fail, finish, halt, leave off, refrain, stay, stop, terminate

ceaseless constant, continual, continuous, endless, eternal, everlasting, incessant, indefatigable, interminable, never-ending, nonstop, perennial, perpetual, unending, unremitting, untiring

cede abandon, abdicate, allow, concede, convey, grant, hand over, make over, relinquish, renounce, resign, surrender, transfer, yield

celebrate bless, commemorate, commend, drink to, eulogize, exalt, extol, glorify, honour, keep, laud, observe, perform, praise,

proclaim, publicize, rejoice, reverence, solemnize, toast

celebrated acclaimed, distinguished, eminent, famed, famous, glorious, illustrious, lionized, notable, outstanding, popular, preeminent, prominent, renowned, revered, well-known

celebration 1. carousal, festival, festivity, gala, jollification, jubilee, junketing, merrymaking, party, revelry 2. anniversary, commemoration, honouring, observance, performance, remembrance, solemnization

celebrity 1. big name, big shot (Sl.), bigwig (Sl.), dignitary, lion (Inf.), luminary, name, personage, personality, star, superstar, V.I.P. 2. distinction, éclat, eminence,

fame, glory, honour, notability, popularity, pre-eminence, prestige, prominence, renown, reputation, repute, stardom

celerity dispatch, expedition, fleetness, haste, promptness, quickness, rapidity, speed, swiftness, velocity, vivacity

celestial angelic, astral, divine, elysian, empyrean, eternal, ethereal, godlike, heavenly, immortal, seraphic, spiritual, sublime, supernatural

celibacy chastity, continence, purity, singleness, virginity

cell 1. cavity, chamber, compartment, cubicle, dungeon, stall 2. caucus, coterie, group, nucleus, unit

charge for storing goods in a cellar, etc.

cellaret (ˌsɛlə'rɛt) *n.* a cabinet or sideboard with compartments for holding wine bottles.

cello ('tʃɛləʊ) *n., pl.* **-los.** *Music.* a bowed stringed instrument of the violin family. It has four strings, is held between the knees, and has a metal spike at the lower end, which acts as a support. Full name: **violoncello.** —'**cellist** *n.*

cellophane ('sɛləˌfeɪn) *n.* a flexible thin transparent sheeting made from wood pulp and used as a moisture-proof wrapping.

cellular ('sɛljʊlə) *adj.* **1.** of, relating to, or resembling a cell. **2.** consisting of or having cells or small cavities; porous. **3.** *Textiles.* woven with an open texture: *a cellular blanket.*

cellule ('sɛljuːl) *n.* a very small cell.

cellulite ('sɛljʊˌlaɪt) *n.* a name sometimes given to subcutaneous fat alleged to resist dieting.

Celluloid ('sɛljʊˌlɔɪd) *n.* **1.** *Trademark.* a flammable material consisting of cellulose nitrate and camphor: used in sheets, rods, etc. **2.** (*usually not cap.*) **a.** a cellulose derivative used for coating film. **b.** cinema film.

cellulose ('sɛljʊˌləʊz, -ˌləʊs) *n.* a substance which is the main constituent of plant cell walls and used in making paper, rayon, and film.

cellulose acetate *n.* nonflammable material used in the manufacture of film, dopes, lacquers, and artificial fibres.

Celsius ('sɛlsɪəs) *adj.* denoting a measurement on the Celsius scale. Symbol: C

Celsius scale *n.* a scale of temperature in which 0° represents the melting point of ice and 100° represents the boiling point of water. Also called: **centigrade scale.** Cf. **Fahrenheit scale.**

Celt (kɛlt, sɛlt) *or* **Kelt** *n.* **1.** a person who speaks a Celtic language. **2.** a member of an Indo-European people who in pre-Roman times inhabited Britain, Gaul, and Spain.

Celtic ('kɛltɪk, 'sɛl-) *or* **Keltic** *n.* **1.** a branch of the Indo-European family of languages that includes Gaelic, Welsh, and Breton. Modern Celtic is divided into the Brythonic (southern) and Goidelic (northern) groups. ~*adj.* **2.** of, relating to, or characteristic of the Celts or the Celtic languages. —**Celticism** ('kɛltɪˌsɪzəm, 'sɛl-) *or* '**Kelti,cism** *n.*

cement (sɪ'mɛnt) *n.* **1.** a fine grey powder made of a mixture of limestone and clay, used with water and sand to make mortar, or with water, sand, and aggregate, to make concrete. **2.** a binder, glue, or adhesive. **3.** something that unites or joins. **4.** *Dentistry.* any of various materials used in filling teeth. **5.** to join, bind, or glue together with or as if with cement. **6.** to coat or cover with cement. —**ce'menter** *n.*

cemetery ('sɛmɪtrɪ) *n., pl.* **-teries.** a place where the dead are buried, esp. one not attached to a church.

-cene *n. and adj. combining form.* denoting a recent geological period.

cenobite ('siːnəʊˌbaɪt) *n.* a variant spelling of **coenobite.**

cenotaph ('sɛnəˌtɑːf) *n.* a monument honouring a dead person or persons buried elsewhere.

Cenozoic (ˌsiːnəʊ'zəʊɪk) *or* **Cainozoic** *adj.* **1.** of, denoting, or relating to the most recent geological era characterized by the development and increase of the mammals. ~*n.* **2. the.** the Cenozoic era.

censer ('sɛnsə) *n.* a container for burning incense. Also called: **thurible.**

censor ('sɛnsə) *n.* **1.** a person authorized to examine publications, films, letters, etc., in order to suppress in whole or part those considered obscene, politically unacceptable, etc. **2.** any person who controls or suppresses the behaviour of others, usually on moral grounds. **3.** (in republican Rome) either of two senior magistrates elected to keep the list of citizens up to date, and supervise

public morals. **4.** *Psychoanal.* the postulated factor responsible for regulating the translation of ideas and desires from the unconscious to the conscious mind. ~*vb.* (*tr.*) **5.** to ban or cut portions of (a film, letter, etc.). **6.** to act as a censor of (behaviour, etc.). —**censorial** (sɛn'sɔːrɪəl) *adj.*

censorious (sɛn'sɔːrɪəs) *adj.* harshly critical; fault-finding. —**cen'soriously** *adv.*

censorship ('sɛnsəˌʃɪp) *n.* **1.** a policy or programme of censoring. **2.** the act or system of censoring.

censure ('sɛnʃə) *n.* **1.** severe disapproval. ~*vb.* **2.** to criticize (someone or something) severely. —'**censurable** *adj.*

census ('sɛnsəs) *n., pl.* **-suses.** **1.** an official periodic count of a population including such information as sex, age, occupation, etc. **2.** any official count: *a traffic census.* **3.** (in ancient Rome) a registration of the population and a property evaluation for taxation.

cent (sɛnt) *n.* a monetary unit of Australia, Barbados, Botswana, Canada, Hong Kong, Kenya, Malaysia, New Zealand, Singapore, South Africa, Tanzania, Trinidad and Tobago, Uganda, the United States, etc. It is worth one hundredth of their respective standard units.

cent. *abbrev. for:* **1.** centigrade. **2.** central. **3.** century.

centaur ('sɛntɔː) *n. Greek myth.* one of a race of creatures with the head, arms, and torso of a man, and the lower body and legs of a horse.

centenarian (ˌsɛntɪ'nɛərɪən) *n.* **1.** a person who is at least 100 years old. ~*adj.* **2.** being at least 100 years old. **3.** of or relating to a centenarian.

centenary (sɛn'tiːnərɪ) *adj.* **1.** of or relating to a period of 100 years. **2.** occurring once every 100 years. ~*n., pl.* **-naries.** **3.** a 100th anniversary or its celebration.

centennial (sɛn'tɛnɪəl) *adj.* **1.** relating to or completing a period of 100 years. **2.** occurring every 100 years. ~*n.* **3.** *U.S.* another name for **centenary** (sense 3).

center ('sɛntə) *n., vb.* the U.S. spelling of **centre.**

centesimal (sɛn'tɛsɪməl) *n.* **1.** hundredth. ~*adj.* **2.** relating to division into hundredths. —**cen'tesimally** *adv.*

centi- *or before a vowel* **cent-** *prefix.* **1.** denoting one hundredth: *centimetre.* Symbol: c **2.** *Rare.* denoting a hundred: *centipede.*

centigrade ('sɛntɪˌgreɪd) *adj.* **1.** another name for **Celsius.** ~*n.* **2.** a unit of angle equal to one hundredth of a grade.

▷ **Usage.** *Centigrade,* when indicating the Celsius scale of temperature, is now usually avoided in scientific contexts because of possible confusion with the hundredth part of a grade.

centigram *or* **centigramme** ('sɛntɪˌgræm) *n.* one hundredth of a gram.

centilitre *or U.S.* **centiliter** ('sɛntɪˌliːtə) *n.* one hundredth of a litre.

centime ('sɒnˌtiːm; *French* sã'tim) *n.* a monetary unit of Algeria, Belgium, the Central African Republic, France, Guinea, Haiti, Liechtenstein, Luxembourg, Mali, Mauritania, Switzerland, Tahiti, Togo, etc. It is worth one hundredth of their respective standard units.

centimetre *or U.S.* **centimeter** ('sɛntɪˌmiːtə) *n.* one hundredth of a metre.

centipede ('sɛntɪˌpiːd) *n.* a carnivorous arthropod having a body of between 15 and 190 segments, each bearing one pair of legs.

cento ('sɛntəʊ) *n., pl.* **-tos.** a piece of writing, esp. a poem, composed of quotations from other authors.

CENTO ('sɛntəʊ) *n.* acronym for Central Treaty Organization; an organization for military and economic cooperation formed in 1959 by the U.K., Iran, Pakistan, and Turkey.

central ('sɛntrəl) *adj.* **1.** in, at, of, from, containing, or forming the centre of something: *the central street in a city.* **2.** main, principal, or chief: *the central cause of a*

THESAURUS

cement 1. *v.* attach, bind, bond, cohere, combine, glue, gum, join, plaster, seal, solder, stick together, unite, weld **2.** *n.* adhesive, binder, glue, gum, paste, plaster, sealant

cemetery burial ground, churchyard, God's acre, graveyard, necropolis

censor blue-pencil, bowdlerize, cut, expurgate

censorious captious, carping, cavilling, condemnatory, disapproving, disparaging, fault-finding, hypercritical, severe

censure 1. *v.* abuse, berate, blame, castigate, chide, condemn, criticize, denounce, rebuke, reprehend, reprimand, reproach, reprove, scold, upbraid **2.** *n.* blame, castigation, condemnation, criticism, disapproval, dress-

ing down (*Inf.*), obloquy, rebuke, remonstrance, reprehension, reprimand, reproach, reproof, stricture

central chief, essential, focal, fundamental, inner, interior, key, main, mean, median, mid, middle, primary, principal

problem. —**centrality** (sɛn'trælɪtɪ) *n.* —**'centrally** *adv.*

Central America *n.* an isthmus joining the continents of North and South America, extending from the S border of Mexico to the NW border of Colombia. —**Central American** *adj.*

central bank *n.* a national bank that does business mainly with a government and with other banks: it regulates the volume of credit.

central heating *n.* a system for heating the rooms of a building by means of radiators or air vents connected to a central source of heat.

centralism ('sɛntrə,lɪzəm) *n.* the principle or act of bringing something under central control. —**'centralist** *n., adj.*

centralize *or* **-lise** ('sɛntrə,laɪz) *vb.* 1. to draw or move (something) to or towards a centre. 2. to bring or come under central, esp. governmental control. —**,centrali'zation** *or* **-li'sation** *n.*

central nervous system *n.* the mass of nerve tissue that controls and coordinates the activities of an animal. In vertebrates it consists of the brain and spinal cord.

central processing unit *n.* the part of a computer that performs logical and arithmetical operations on the data. Abbrev.: **CPU**

centre *or U.S.* **center** ('sɛntə) *n.* 1. *Geom.* **a.** the midpoint of any line or figure, esp. the point within a circle or sphere that is equidistant from any point on the circumference or surface. **b.** the point within a body through which a specified force may be considered to act, such as the centre of gravity. 2. the point, axis, or pivot about which a body rotates. 3. a point, area, or part that is approximately in the middle of a larger area or volume. 4. a place at which some specified activity is concentrated: *a shopping centre.* 5. a person or thing that is a focus of interest. 6. a place of activity or influence: *a centre of power.* 7. a person, group, or thing in the middle. 8. (*usually cap.*) *Politics.* a political party or group favouring moderation. 9. a bar with a conical point upon which a workpiece or part may be turned or ground. 10. *Football, hockey, etc.* **a.** a player who plays in the middle of the forward line. **b.** an instance of passing the ball from a wing to the middle of the field, etc. ~*vb.* 11. to move towards, mark, put, or be at a centre. 12. (*tr.*) to focus or bring together: *to centre one's thoughts.* 13. (*intr.*; often foll. by *on*) to have as a main theme: *the novel centred on crime.* 14. (*intr.*; foll. by *on* or *round*) to have as a centre. 15. (*tr.*) *Football, hockey, etc.* to pass (the ball) into the middle of the field or court. ▷ **Usage.** *To centre round* is considered illogical by many writers and speakers, who prefer the more precise phrase *to centre on.*

Centre ('sɛntə) *n.* **the.** Also called: **Centralia** (archaic), **the Red Centre.** the sparsely inhabited central region of Australia.

centreboard ('sɛntə,bɔːd) *n.* a supplementary keel for a sailing vessel.

centrefold *or U.S.* **centerfold** ('sɛntə,fəʊld) *n.* a large coloured illustration folded so that it forms the central spread of a magazine.

centre forward *n. Soccer, hockey, etc.* the central forward in the attack.

centre half *n. Soccer.* a defender who plays in the middle of the defence.

centre of gravity *n.* the point through which the resultant of the gravitational forces on a body always acts.

centrepiece ('sɛntə,piːs) *n.* an object used as the centre of something, esp. for decoration.

centri- *combining form.* variant of **centro-**.

centric ('sɛntrɪk) *or* **centrical** *adj.* 1. being central or having a centre. 2. relating to a nerve centre. —**centricity** (sɛn'trɪsɪtɪ) *n.*

-centric *suffix forming adjectives.* having a centre as specified: *heliocentric.*

centrifugal (sɛn'trɪfjʊgəl, 'sɛntrɪ,fjuːgəl) *adj.* 1. acting, moving, or tending to move away from a centre. Cf. **centripetal.** 2. of, concerned with, or operated by centrifugal force: *centrifugal pump.* —**cen'trifugally** *adv.*

centrifuge ('sɛntrɪ,fjuːdʒ) *n.* 1. any of various rotating machines that separate liquids from solids or other liquids by the action of centrifugal force. 2. any of various rotating devices for subjecting human beings or animals to varying accelerations. ~*vb.* 3. (*tr.*) to subject to the action of a centrifuge. —**centrifugation** (,sɛntrɪfjuː'geɪʃən) *n.*

centring ('sɛntrɪŋ) *or U.S.* **centering** ('sɛntərɪŋ) *n.* a temporary structure, esp. one made of timber, used to support an arch during construction.

centripetal (sɛn'trɪpɪtəl, 'sɛntrɪ,piːtəl) *adj.* 1. acting, moving, or tending to move towards a centre. Cf. **centrifugal.** 2. of, concerned with, or operated by centripetal force. —**cen'tripetally** *adv.*

centrist ('sɛntrɪst) *n.* a person holding moderate political views. —**'centrism** *n.*

centro-, centri-, *or before a vowel* **centr-** *combining form.* denoting a centre: *centrosome; centrist.*

centurion (sɛn'tjʊərɪən) *n.* the officer commanding a Roman century.

century ('sɛntʃərɪ) *n., pl.* **-ries.** 1. a period of 100 years. 2. one of the successive periods of 100 years dated before or after an epoch or event, esp. the birth of Christ. 3. a score or grouping of 100: *to score a century in cricket.* 4. (in ancient Rome) a unit of foot soldiers, originally consisting of 100 men. 5. (in ancient Rome) a division of the people for purposes of voting.

cep (sɛp) *n.* an edible woodland fungus with a brown shining cap and a rich nutty flavour.

cephalic (sɪ'fælɪk) *adj.* 1. of or relating to the head. 2. situated in, on, or near the head.

-cephalic *or* **-cephalous** *adj. combining form.* indicating skull or head; -headed: *brachycephalic.* —**-cephaly** *or* **-cephalism** *n. combining form.*

cephalo- *or before a vowel* **cephal-** *combining form.* indicating the head: *cephalopod.*

cephalopod ('sɛfələ,pɒd) *n.* any of various marine molluscs, characterized by well-developed head and eyes and a ring of sucker-bearing tentacles, including the octopuses, squids, and cuttlefish. —**,cepha'lopodan** *adj., n.*

ceramic (sɪ'ræmɪk) *n.* 1. a hard brittle material made by firing clay and similar substances. 2. an object made from such a material. ~*adj.* 3. of or made from a ceramic. 4. of or relating to ceramics: *ceramic arts.*

ceramics (sɪ'ræmɪks) *n.* (*functioning as sing.*) the art and techniques of producing articles of clay, porcelain, etc. —**ceramist** ('sɛrəmɪst) *n.*

cere (sɪə) *n.* a soft waxy swelling, containing the nostrils, at the base of the upper beak, as in the parrot.

cereal ('sɪərɪəl) *n.* 1. any grass that produces an edible grain, such as oat, wheat, rice, maize, and millet. 2. the grain produced by such a plant. 3. any food made from this grain, esp. breakfast food. 4. (*modifier*) of or relating to any of these plants or their products.

cerebellum (,sɛrɪ'bɛləm) *n., pl.* **-lums** *or* **-la** (-lə). one of the major divisions of the vertebrate brain whose function is coordination of voluntary movements.

cerebral ('sɛrɪbrəl; *U.S. also* sə'riːbrəl) *adj.* 1. of or relating to the cerebrum or to the entire brain. 2. involving intelligence rather than emotions or instinct. —**'cerebrally** *adv.*

cerebral palsy *n.* an impairment of muscular function and weakness of the limbs, caused by damage to the brain before or during birth.

cerebrate ('sɛrɪ,breɪt) *vb.* (*intr.*) *Usually facetious.* to use the mind; think; ponder; consider. —**,cere'bration** *n.*

cerebro- *or before a vowel* **cerebr-** *combining form.* indicating the brain: *cerebrospinal.*

cerebrospinal (,sɛrɪbrəʊ'spaɪnəl) *adj.* of or relating to the brain and spinal cord: *cerebrospinal fluid.*

cerebrovascular (,sɛrɪbrəʊ'væskjʊlə) *adj.* of or relating to the blood vessels and the blood supply of the brain.

cerebrum ('sɛrɪbrəm) *n., pl.* **-brums** *or* **-bra** (-brə). 1. the anterior portion of the brain of vertebrates, consisting of two lateral hemispheres: the dominant part of the brain in man, associated with intellectual function, emotion, and personality. 2. the brain considered as a whole. —**cerebric** ('sɛrɪbrɪk) *adj.*

THESAURUS

centralize amalgamate, compact, concentrate, concentre, condense, converge, incorporate, rationalize, streamline, unify

centre 1. *n.* bull's-eye, core, crux, focus, heart, hub, mid, middle, midpoint, nucleus, pivot 2. *v.* cluster, concentrate, converge, focus, revolve

centrepiece cynosure, epergne, focus, highlight, hub, star

cerecloth (ˈsɪəˌklɒθ) n. waxed waterproof cloth of a kind formerly used as a shroud.

ceremonial (ˌsɛrɪˈməʊnɪəl) adj. 1. involving or relating to ceremony or ritual. ~n. 2. the observance of formality, esp. in etiquette. 3. a plan for formal observances; ritual. 4. Christianity. a. the prescribed order of rites and ceremonies. b. a book containing this. —ˌcereˈmonialism n. —ˌcereˈmonialist n. —ˌcereˈmonially adv.

ceremonious (ˌsɛrɪˈməʊnɪəs) adj. 1. especially or excessively polite or formal. 2. involving formalities. —ˌcereˈmoniously adv.

ceremony (ˈsɛrɪmənɪ) n., pl. **-nies.** 1. a formal act or ritual, often set by custom or tradition, performed in observation of an event or anniversary. 2. a religious rite or series of rites. 3. a courteous gesture or act: *the ceremony of toasting the Queen.* 4. ceremonial observances or gestures collectively. 5. **stand on ceremony.** to insist on or act with excessive formality.

cerise (səˈriːz, -ˈriːs) n. a moderate to dark red colour.

cerium (ˈsɪərɪəm) n. a malleable ductile steel-grey element of the lanthanide series of metals, used in lighter flints. Symbol: Ce; atomic no.: 58; atomic wt.: 140.12.

CERN (sɜːn) n. acronym for Conseil Européen pour la Recherche Nucléaire; an organization of European states with a centre in Geneva, for research in high-energy particle physics.

cert (sɜːt) n. Inf. something that is a certainty, esp. a horse that is certain to win a race.

cert. abbrev. for: 1. certificate. 2. certification. 3. certified.

certain (ˈsɜːtən) adj. 1. (postpositive) positive and confident about the truth of something; convinced: *I am certain that he wrote a book.* 2. (usually postpositive) definitely known: *it is certain that they were on the bus.* 3. (usually postpositive) sure; bound: *he was certain to fail.* 4. fixed: *the date is already certain for the invasion.* 5. reliable: *his judgment is certain.* 6. moderate or minimum: *to a certain extent.* ~adv. 7. **for certain.** without a doubt. ~determiner. 8. a. known but not specified or named: *certain people.* b. (as pronoun; functioning as pl.): *certain of the members have not paid.* 9. named but not known: *he had written to a certain Mrs. Smith.*

certainly (ˈsɜːtənlɪ) adv. 1. without doubt: *he certainly rides very well.* 2. sentence substitute. by all means; definitely.

certainty (ˈsɜːtəntɪ) n., pl. **-ties.** 1. the condition of being certain. 2. something established as inevitable. 3. **for a certainty.** without doubt.

certes (ˈsɜːtɪz) adv. Arch. with certainty; truly.

certificate n. (səˈtɪfɪkɪt). 1. an official document attesting the truth of the facts stated, as of birth, death, completion of an academic course, etc. 2. short for **share certificate.** ~vb. (səˈtɪfɪˌkeɪt). 3. (tr.) to authorize by or present with an official document. —**ˈcerˈtificatory** adj.

Certificate of Secondary Education n. the full name for CSE

certification (ˌsɜːtɪfɪˈkeɪʃən) n. 1. the act of certifying or state of being certified. 2. Law. a document attesting the truth of a fact or statement.

certified (ˈsɜːtɪˌfaɪd) adj. 1. holding or guaranteed by a certificate. 2. endorsed or guaranteed: *a certified cheque.* 3. (of a person) declared legally insane.

certify (ˈsɜːtɪˌfaɪ) vb. **-fying, -fied.** 1. to confirm or attest (to), usually in writing. 2. (tr.) to endorse or guaran-

tee that certain required standards have been met. 3. to give reliable information or assurances: *he certified that it was Walter's handwriting.* 4. (tr.) to declare legally insane. —ˈcertiˌfiable adj.

certitude (ˈsɜːtɪˌtjuːd) n. confidence; certainty.

cerulean (sɪˈruːlɪən) n. a deep blue colour.

cervical smear n. Med. a smear taken from the neck (cervix) of the uterus for detection of cancer. See also **Pap test.**

cervine (ˈsɜːvaɪn) adj. resembling or relating to a deer.

cervix (ˈsɜːvɪks) n., pl. **cervixes** or **cervices** (səˈvaɪsiːz). 1. the technical name for neck. 2. any necklike part, esp. the lower part of the uterus that extends into the vagina. —**cervical** (səˈvaɪkəl, ˈsɜːvɪkəl) adj.

cesium (ˈsiːzɪəm) n. the usual U.S. spelling of **caesium.**

cessation (sɛˈseɪʃən) n. a ceasing or stopping; pause: *temporary cessation of hostilities.*

cession (ˈsɛʃən) n. 1. the act of ceding. 2. something that is ceded, esp. land or territory.

cesspool (ˈsɛsˌpuːl) n. 1. Also called: **cesspit, sink, sump.** a covered cistern, well, or pit, for collecting and storing sewage or waste water. 2. a filthy or corrupt place: *a cesspool of iniquity.*

cestus or **caestus** (ˈsɛstəs) n., pl. **-tus** or **-tuses.** (in classical Roman boxing) a pugilist's gauntlet of bull's hide studded with metal.

cesura (sɪˈzjʊərə) n., pl. **-ras** or **-rae** (-riː). Prosody. a variant spelling of **caesura.**

cetacean (sɪˈteɪʃən) adj. also **cetaceous.** 1. of or belonging to an order of aquatic placental mammals having no hind limbs and a blowhole for breathing: includes toothed whales (dolphins, porpoises, etc.) and whalebone whales (rorquals, etc.). ~n. 2. a whale.

cetane (ˈsiːteɪn) n. a colourless insoluble liquid hydrocarbon used in the determination of the cetane number of diesel fuel. Also called: **hexadecane.**

cetane number n. a measure of the quality of a diesel fuel expressed as the percentage of cetane. Also called: **cetane rating.** Cf. **octane number.**

Cf the chemical symbol for californium.

CF abbrev. for Canadian Forces.

cf. abbrev. for: 1. (in bookbinding, etc.) calfskin. 2. confer.

CFB abbrev. for Canadian Forces Base.

CFL abbrev. for Canadian Football League.

cg abbrev. for centigram.

ch. abbrev. for: 1. chain (unit of measure). 2. chapter. 3. Chess. check. 4. chief. 5. church.

C.H. abbrev. for Companion of Honour (a Brit. title).

chablis (ˈʃæblɪ) n. (sometimes cap.) a dry white wine made around Chablis, France.

chafe (tʃeɪf) vb. 1. to make or become sore or worn by rubbing. 2. (tr.) to warm (the hands, etc.) by rubbing. 3. to irritate or be irritated or impatient. 4. (intr.; often foll. by on, against, etc.) to rub. ~n. 5. a soreness or irritation caused by friction.

chafer (ˈtʃeɪfə) n. any of various beetles, such as the cockchafer.

chaff[1] (tʃɑːf) n. 1. the mass of husks, etc., separated from the seeds during threshing. 2. finely cut straw and hay used to feed cattle. 3. something of little worth; rubbish: *to separate the wheat from the chaff.* 4. thin strips of metallic foil released into the earth's atmosphere to deflect radar signals and prevent detection. —**ˈchaffy** adj.

chaff[2] (tʃɑːf) n. 1. light-hearted teasing or joking; ban-

THESAURUS

ceremonial 1. adj. formal, liturgical, ritual, ritualistic, solemn, stately 2. n. ceremony, formality, rite, ritual, solemnity

ceremonious civil, courteous, courtly, deferential, dignified, exact, formal, precise, punctilious, ritual, solemn, starchy (Inf.), stately, stiff

ceremony 1. commemoration, function, observance, parade, rite, ritual, service, show, solemnities 2. ceremonial, decorum, etiquette, form, formal courtesy, formality, niceties, pomp, propriety, protocol

certain 1. assured, confident, convinced, positive, satisfied, sure 2. ascertained, conclusive, incontrovertible, indubitable, irrefutable, known, plain, true, undeniable, un-

doubted, unequivocal, unmistakable, valid 3. bound, definite, destined, fated, ineluctable, inescapable, inevitable, inexorable, sure 4. decided, definite, established, fixed, settled 5. assured, constant, dependable, reliable, stable, steady, trustworthy, unfailing, unquestionable 6. express, individual, particular, precise, special, specific

certainty 1. assurance, authoritativeness, certitude, confidence, conviction, faith, indubitableness, inevitability, positiveness, sureness, trust, validity 2. fact, reality, sure thing (Inf.), surety, truth

certificate authorization, credential(s), diploma, document, licence, testimonial, voucher, warrant

certify ascertain, assure, attest, authenticate, aver, avow, confirm, corroborate, declare, endorse, guarantee, notify, show, testify, validate, verify, vouch, witness

chafe abrade, anger, annoy, exasperate, fret, fume, gall, grate, incense, inflame, irritate, offend, provoke, rage, rasp, rub, ruffle, scrape, scratch, vex, worry

chaff n. 1. dregs, glumes, hulls, husks, refuse, remains, rubbish, trash, waste 2. badinage, banter, joking, persiflage, raillery, teasing ~v. 3. banter, deride, jeer, mock, rib (Inf.), ridicule, scoff, taunt, tease

ter. ~vb. 2. to tease good-naturedly. —'chaffer n.

chaffer ('tʃæfə) vb. 1. (intr.) to haggle or bargain. 2. to chatter, talk, or say idly. ~n. 3. haggling or bargaining. —'chafferer n.

chaffinch ('tʃæfintʃ) n. a common European finch with black and white wings and, in the male, a reddish body and blue-grey head.

chafing dish ('tʃeifiŋ) n. a vessel with a heating apparatus beneath it, for cooking or keeping food warm at the table.

chagrin ('ʃægrin) n. 1. a feeling of annoyance or mortification. ~vb. 2. to embarrass and annoy.

chain (tʃein) n. 1. a flexible length of metal links, used for confining, connecting, etc., or in jewellery. 2. (usually pl.) anything that confines or restrains: the chains of poverty. 3. (usually pl.) a set of metal links that fit over the tyre of a motor vehicle to reduce skidding on an icy surface. 4. a series of related or connected facts, events, etc. 5. a. a number of establishments such as hotels, shops, etc., having the same owner or management. b. (as modifier): a chain store. 6. Also called: **Gunter's chain**. a unit of length equal to 22 yards. 7. Also called: **engineer's chain**. a unit of length equal to 100 feet. 8. Also called: **nautical chain**. a unit of length equal to 15 feet. 9. Austral. & N.Z. a. the rail along which carcasses are moved in a slaughterhouse. b. the team of workers who slaughter, skin, and otherwise process carcasses in a slaughterhouse. 10. Chem. two or more atoms or groups bonded together so that the resulting molecule, ion, or radical resembles a chain. 11. Geog. a series of natural features, esp. mountain ranges. ~vb. 12. (tr.; often foll. by up) to confine, tie, or make fast with or as if with a chain.

chain gang n. U.S. a group of convicted prisoners chained together.

chain letter n. a letter, often with a request for and promise of money, that is sent to many people who add to or recopy it and send it on.

chain mail n. another term for **mail**² (sense 1).

chain reaction n. 1. a process in which a neutron colliding with an atomic nucleus causes fission and the ejection of one or more other neutrons. 2. a chemical reaction in which the product of one step is a reactant in the following step. 3. a series of events, each of which precipitates the next. —'chain-re,act vb. (intr.)

chain saw n. a motor-driven saw in which the cutting teeth form links in a continuous chain.

chain-smoke vb. to smoke (cigarettes, etc.) continually, esp. lighting one from the preceding one. —**chain smoker** n.

chain stitch n. 1. a looped embroidery stitch resembling the links of a chain. ~vb. **chain-stitch**. 2. to sew (something) with this stitch.

chair (tʃeə) n. 1. a seat with a back on which one person sits, typically having four legs and often having arms. 2. an official position of authority. 3. a person holding an office of authority: questions are to be addressed to the chair. 4. a professorship. 5. Railways. an iron or steel socket designed to take the rail and secure it to the sleeper. 6. short for **sedan chair**. 7. **take the chair**. to preside as chairman for a meeting, etc. 8. **the chair**. Inf. the electric chair. ~vb. (tr.) 9. to preside over (a meeting). 10. Brit. to carry aloft in a sitting position after a triumph. 11. to provide with a chair of office. 12. to install in a chair.

chair lift n. a series of chairs suspended from a power-driven cable for conveying people, esp. skiers, up a mountain.

chairman ('tʃeəmən) n., pl. **-men**. a person who presides over a company's board of directors, a committee, a debate, etc. Also: **chairperson** or (fem.) **chairwoman**.

chaise (ʃeiz) n. 1. a light open horse-drawn carriage,

esp. one with two wheels. 2. short for **post chaise** and **chaise longue**.

chaise longue ('ʃeiz 'lɒŋ) n., pl. **chaise longues** or **chaises longues** ('ʃeiz 'lɒŋ). a long low chair with a back and single armrest.

chalcedony (kæl'sedəni) n., pl. **-nies**. a form of quartz with crystals arranged in parallel fibres: a gemstone. —**chalcedonic** (,kælsi'dɒnik) adj.

chalet ('ʃælei) n. 1. a type of wooden house of Swiss origin, with wide projecting eaves. 2. a similar house used as a ski lodge, etc.

chalice ('tʃælis) n. 1. Poetic. a drinking cup; goblet. 2. Christianity. a gold or silver cup containing the wine at Mass. 3. a cup-shaped flower.

chalk (tʃɔ:k) n. 1. a soft fine-grained white sedimentary rock consisting of nearly pure calcium carbonate, containing minute fossil fragments of marine organisms. 2. a piece of chalk, or substance like chalk, often coloured, used for writing and drawing on blackboards. 3. **as alike (or different) as chalk and cheese**. Inf. totally different in essentials. 4. **by a long chalk**. Brit. inf. by far. 5. **not by a long chalk**. Brit. inf. by no means. 6. (modifier) made of chalk. ~vb. 7. to draw or mark (something) with chalk. 8. (tr.) to mark, rub, or whiten with or as with chalk. —'chalk,like adj. —'chalky adj. —'chalkiness n.

chalk up vb. (tr., adv.) Inf. 1. to score or register (something). 2. to credit (money) to an account etc. (esp. in **chalk it up**).

challenge ('tʃælindʒ) vb. (mainly tr.) 1. to invite or summon (someone to do something, esp. to take part in a contest). 2. (also intr.) to call (something) into question. 3. to make demands on; stimulate: the job challenges his ingenuity. 4. to order (a person) to halt and be identified. 5. Law. to make formal objection to (a juror or jury). 6. to lay claim to (attention, etc.). 7. to inject (an experimental animal immunized with a test substance) with disease microorganisms to test for immunity to the disease. ~n. 8. a call to engage in a fight, argument, or contest. 9. a questioning of a statement or fact. 10. a demanding or stimulating situation, career, etc. 11. a demand by a sentry, etc., for identification or a password. 12. Law. a formal objection to a person selected to serve on a jury or to the whole body of jurors. —'challengeable adj. —'challenger n.

chalybeate (kə'libiit) adj. containing or impregnated with iron salts.

chamber ('tʃeimbə) n. 1. a meeting hall, esp. one used for a legislative or judicial assembly. 2. a reception room in an official residence, palace, etc. 3. Arch. or poetic. a room in a private house, esp. a bedroom. 4. a. a legislative, judicial, or administrative assembly. b. any of the houses of a legislature. 5. an enclosed space; compartment; cavity. 6. an enclosure for a cartridge in the cylinder of a revolver or for a shell in the breech of a cannon. 7. short for **chamber pot**. 8. (modifier) of, relating to, or suitable for chamber music: a chamber concert.

chamberlain ('tʃeimbəlin) n. 1. an officer who manages the household of a king. 2. the steward of a nobleman or land owner. 3. the treasurer of a municipal corporation.

chambermaid ('tʃeimbə,meid) n. a woman employed to clean bedrooms, esp. in hotels.

chamber music n. music for performance by a small group of instrumentalists.

chamber of commerce n. (sometimes cap.) an organization composed mainly of local businessmen to promote, regulate, and protect their interests.

chamber pot n. a vessel for urine, used in bedrooms.

chambers ('tʃeimbəz) pl. n. 1. a judge's room for hearing private cases not taken in open court. 2. (in Eng-

---

THESAURUS

chagrin 1. n. annoyance, discomfiture, discompose, displeasure, disquiet, dissatisfaction, embarrassment, fretfulness, humiliation, ill-humour, irritation, mortification, peevishness, spleen, vexation 2. v. annoy, discomfit, discompose, displease, disquiet, dissatisfy, embarrass, humiliate, irk, irritate, mortify, peeve, vex

chain v. 1. bind, confine, enslave, fetter, gyve (Archaic), handcuff, manacle, restrain, shackle, tether, trammel, unite ~n. 2. bond,

coupling, fetter, link, manacle, shackle, union 3. concatenation, progression, sequence, series, set, string, succession, train

chairman chairperson, chairwoman, director, master of ceremonies, president, presider, speaker, spokesman, toastmaster

chalk up accumulate, achieve, attain, credit, enter, gain, log, mark, record, register, score, tally, win

challenge 1. v. accost, arouse, beard, brave, call out, claim, confront, dare, defy,

demand, dispute, impugn, investigate, object to, provoke, question, require, stimulate, summon, tax, test, throw down the gauntlet, try 2. n. confrontation, dare, defiance, interrogation, provocation, question, summons to contest, test, trial, ultimatum

chamber 1. apartment, bedroom, cavity, compartment, cubicle, enclosure, hall, hollow, room 2. assembly, council, legislative body, legislature

land) the set of rooms occupied by barristers where clients are interviewed.

chameleon (kə'mi:lɪən) n. 1. a lizard of Africa and Madagascar, having long slender legs, a prehensile tail and tongue, and the ability to change colour. 2. a changeable or fickle person. —**chameleonic** (kə,mi:lɪ'ɒnɪk) adj.

chamfer ('tʃæmfə) n. 1. a narrow flat surface at the corner of a beam, post, etc. ~vb. (tr.) 2. to cut such a surface on (a beam, etc.). —**chamferer** n.

chamois ('ʃæmɪ) n., pl. **-ois**. 1. ('ʃæmwɑː). a sure-footed goat antelope of Europe and SW Asia, having vertical horns with backward-pointing tips. 2. a soft suede leather formerly made from this animal, now obtained from the skins of sheep and goats. 3. Also called: **chamois leather, shammy (leather), chammy (leather)**. a piece of such leather or similar material used for polishing, etc. 4. ('ʃæmwɑː). a greyish-yellow colour. ~vb. (tr.) 5. to dress (leather or skin) like chamois. 6. to polish with a chamois.

champ¹ (tʃæmp) vb. 1. to munch (food) noisily like a horse. 2. (when intr., often foll. by on, at, etc.) to bite (something) nervously or impatiently. 3. **champ (or chafe) at the bit.** Inf. to be impatient to start work, a journey, etc. ~n. 4. the act or noise of champing.

champ² (tʃæmp) n. Inf. short for **champion** (sense 1a).

champagne (ʃæm'peɪn) n. 1. (sometimes cap.) a white sparkling wine produced around Reims and Epernay, France. 2. any effervescent white wine. 3. a pale tawny colour.

champers ('ʃæmpəz) n. Sl. champagne.

champion ('tʃæmpɪən) n. 1. a. a person, plant, or animal who has defeated all others in a competition: a chess champion. b. (as modifier): a champion team; a champion marrow. 2. a person who defends a person or cause: champion of the underprivileged. 3. (formerly) a knight who did battle for another, esp. a king or queen. ~adj. 4. N Brit. dialect. excellent. ~adv. 5. N Brit. dialect. very well. ~vb. (tr.) 6. to support: we champion the cause of liberty. —'**champion,ship** n.

chance (tʃɑːns) n. 1. a. the unknown and unpredictable element that causes an event to result in a certain way rather than another, spoken of as a real force. b. (as modifier): a chance meeting. Related adj.: **fortuitous.** 2. fortune; luck; fate. 3. an opportunity or occasion. 4. a risk; gamble. 5. the extent to which an event is likely to occur; probability. 6. an unpredicted event, esp. a fortunate one. 7. **by chance.** accidentally: he slipped by chance. 8. **on the (off) chance.** acting on the (remote) possibility. ~vb. 9. (tr.) to risk; hazard. 10. to happen by chance: I chanced to catch sight of her. 11. **chance on (or upon).** to come upon by accident. 12. **chance one's arm.** to attempt to do something although the chance of success may be slight. —'**chanceful** adj.

chancel ('tʃɑːnsəl) n. the part of a church containing the altar, sanctuary, and choir.

chancellery or **chancellory** ('tʃɑːnsələrɪ) n., pl. **-leries** or **-lories.** 1. the building or room occupied by a chancellor's office. 2. the position or office of a chancellor. 3. U.S. the office of an embassy or legation.

chancellor ('tʃɑːnsələ) n. 1. the head of the government in several European countries. 2. U.S. the president of a university. 3. Brit. the honorary head of a university. Cf. **vice chancellor.** 4. Christianity. a clergyman acting as the law officer of a bishop. —'**chancellor,ship** n.

Chancellor of the Exchequer n. Brit. the cabinet minister responsible for finance.

chancery ('tʃɑːnsərɪ) n., pl. **-ceries.** 1. Also called: **Chancery Division.** (in England) the Lord Chancellor's court, now a division of the High Court of Justice. 2. Also called: **court of chancery.** (in the U.S.) a court of equity. 3. Brit. the political section or offices of an embassy or legation. 4. another name for **chancellery.** 5. a court of public records. 6. Christianity. a diocesan office under the supervision of a bishop's chancellor. 7. **in chancery. a.** Law. (of a suit) pending in a court of equity. **b.** in an awkward situation.

chancre ('ʃæŋkə) n. Pathol. a small hard growth, which is the first sign of syphilis. —'**chancrous** adj.

chancy or **chancey** ('tʃɑːnsɪ) adj. **chancier, chanciest.** Inf. uncertain; risky.

chandelier (,ʃændɪ'lɪə) n. an ornamental hanging light with branches and holders for several candles or bulbs.

chandler ('tʃɑːndlə) n. 1. a dealer in a specified trade or merchandise: ship's chandler. 2. a person who makes or sells candles. —'**chandlery** n.

change (tʃeɪndʒ) vb. 1. to make or become different; alter. 2. (tr.) to replace with or exchange for another: to change one's name. 3. (sometimes foll. by to or into) to transform or convert or be transformed or converted. 4. to give and receive (something) in return: to change places. 5. (tr.) to give or receive (money) in exchange for the equivalent sum in a smaller denomination or different currency. 6. (tr.) to remove or replace the coverings of: to change a baby. 7. (when intr., may be foll. by into or out of) to put on other clothes. 8. to operate (the gear lever of a motor vehicle): to change gear. 9. to alight from (one bus, train, etc.) and board another. 10. **change hands.** to pass from one owner to another. 11. **change one's mind.** to alter one's decision or opinion. 12. **change one's tune.** to alter one's attitude or tone of speech. ~n. 13. the act or fact of changing or being changed. 14. a variation or modification. 15. the substitution of one thing for another. 16. anything that is or may be substituted for something else. 17. variety or novelty (esp. in for a change). 18. a different set, esp. of clothes. 19. money given or received in return for its equivalent in a larger denomination or in a different currency. 20. the balance of money when the amount tendered is larger than the amount due. 21. coins of a small denomination. 22. (often cap.) Arch. a place where merchants meet to transact business. 23. the act of passing from one state or phase to another. 24. the transition from one phase of the moon to the next. 25. the order in which a peal of bells may be rung. 26. **change of heart.** a profound change of outlook, etc. 27. **get no change out of (someone).** Sl. not to be successful in attempts to exploit (someone). 28. **ring the changes.** to vary the manner or performance of an action that is often repeated. ~See also **change down, changeover, change up.** —'**changeful** adj. —'**changeless** adj. —'**changer** n.

changeable ('tʃeɪndʒəbəl) adj. 1. able to change or be changed: changeable weather. 2. varying in colour as when viewed from different angles. —,**changea'bility** n. —'**changeably** adv.

change down vb. (intr., adv.) to select a lower gear when driving.

changeling ('tʃeɪndʒlɪŋ) n. a child believed to have been exchanged by fairies for the parents' true child.

change of life n. a nontechnical name for **menopause.**

THESAURUS

champion 1. n. backer, challenger, conqueror, defender, guardian, hero, nonpareil, patron, protector, title holder, upholder, victor, vindicator, warrior, winner 2. v. advocate, back, defend, espouse, fight for, promote, support, uphold

chance n. 1. liability, likelihood, occasion, odds, opening, opportunity, possibility, probability, prospect, scope, time 2. accident, casualty, coincidence, contingency, destiny, fate, fortuity, fortune, luck, misfortune, peril, providence 3. gamble, hazard, jeopardy, risk, speculation, uncertainty ~v. 4. befall, betide, come about, come to pass, fall out, happen, occur 5. endanger, gamble, go out on a limb (Inf.), hazard, jeopardize, risk, stake, try, venture, wager ~adj. 6. accidental, casual,

contingent, fortuitous, inadvertent, incidental, random, serendipitous, unforeseeable, unforeseen, unintentional, unlooked-for

chancy dangerous, dicey (Sl.), dodgy (Inf.), hazardous, problematical, risky, speculative, uncertain

change v. 1. alter, convert, diversify, fluctuate, metamorphose, moderate, modify, mutate, reform, remodel, reorganize, restyle, shift, transform, transmute, vacillate, vary, veer 2. alternate, barter, convert, displace, exchange, interchange, remove, replace, substitute, swap (Inf.), trade, transmit ~n. 3. alteration, difference, innovation, metamorphosis, modification, mutation, permutation, revolution, transformation, transition, transmutation, vicissitude 4. conversion, ex-

change, interchange, substitution, trade 5. break (Inf.), diversion, novelty, variation, variety

changeable capricious, changeful, chequered, erratic, fickle, fitful, fluid, inconstant, irregular, kaleidoscopic, labile (Chem.), mercurial, mobile, mutable, protean, shifting, uncertain, unpredictable, unreliable, unsettled, unstable, unsteady, vacillating, variable, versatile, volatile, wavering

changeless abiding, consistent, constant, everlasting, fixed, immutable, permanent, perpetual, regular, reliable, resolute, settled, stationary, steadfast, steady, unalterable, unchanging, uniform, unvarying

changeover ('tʃeɪndʒ,əʊvə) *n.* **1.** an alteration or complete reversal from one method, system, or product to another. **2.** a reversal of a situation, attitude, etc. **3.** *Sport.* the act of transferring to or being relieved by a teammate in a relay race, as by handing over a baton, etc. ~*vb.* **change over.** (*adv.*) **4.** to adopt (a different position or attitude): *the driver and navigator changed over.*

change up *vb.* (*intr., adv.*) to select a higher gear when driving.

channel ('tʃænəl) *n.* **1.** a broad strait connecting two areas of sea. **2.** the bed or course of a river, stream, or canal. **3.** a navigable course through a body of water. **4.** (*often pl.*) a means or agency of access, communication, etc.: *through official channels.* **5.** a course into which something can be directed or moved. **6.** *Electronics.* **a.** a band of radio frequencies assigned for a particular purpose, esp. the broadcasting of a television signal. **b.** a path for an electrical signal: *a stereo set has two channels.* **7.** a tubular passage for fluids. **8.** a groove, as in the shaft of a column. **9.** *Computers.* **a.** a path along which data can be transmitted. **b.** one of the lines along the length of a paper tape on which information can be stored in the form of punched holes. ~*vb.* **-nelling, -nelled** *or U.S.* **-neling, -neled. 10.** to make or cut channels in (something). **11.** (*tr.*) to guide into or convey through a channel or channels: *information was channelled through to them.*

Channel ('tʃænəl) *n.* **the.** the English Channel, between England and France.

chant (tʃɑːnt) *n.* **1.** a simple song. **2.** a short simple melody in which several words or syllables are assigned to one note. **3.** a psalm or canticle performed by using such a melody. **4.** a rhythmic or repetitious slogan, usually spoken or sung, as by sports supporters, etc. ~*vb.* **5.** to sing or recite (a psalm, etc.) as a chant. **6.** to intone (a slogan). —'**chanting** *n., adj.*

chanter ('tʃɑːntə) *n.* the pipe on a set of bagpipes on which the melody is played.

chanticleer (,tʃæntɪˈklɪə) *or* **chantecler** (,tʃæntɪˈkleə) *n.* a name for a cock, used esp. in fables.

chantry ('tʃɑːntrɪ) *n., pl.* **-tries.** *Christianity.* **1.** an endowment for the singing of Masses for the soul of the founder. **2.** a chapel or altar so endowed.

chanty ('ʃæntɪ, 'tʃæn-) *n., pl.* **-ties.** a variant spelling of **shanty²**.

chaos ('keɪɒs) *n.* **1.** (*usually cap.*) the disordered formless matter supposed to have existed before the ordered universe. **2.** complete disorder; utter confusion. —**chaotic** (keɪˈɒtɪk) *adj.* —**cha'otically** *adv.*

chap¹ (tʃæp) *vb.* **chapping, chapped. 1.** (of the skin) to make or become raw and cracked, esp. by exposure to cold. ~*n.* **2.** (*usually pl.*) a cracked patch on the skin.

chap² (tʃæp) *n. Inf.* a man or boy; fellow.

chapatti *or* **chapati** (tʃəˈpætɪ, -ˈpɑːtɪ) *n., pl.* **-ti, -tis,** *or* **-ties.** (in Indian cookery) a flat unleavened bread resembling a pancake.

chapel ('tʃæpəl) *n.* **1.** a place of Christian worship, esp. with a separate altar, in a church or cathedral. **2.** a similar place of worship in a large house or institution, such as a college. **3.** a church subordinate to a parish church. **4.** (in Britain) **a.** a Nonconformist place of worship. **b.** Nonconformist religious practices or doctrine. **5. a.** the members of a trade union in a particular newspaper office, printing house, etc. **b.** a meeting of these members.

chaperon *or* **chaperone** ('ʃæpə,rəʊn) *n.* **1.** (esp. formerly) an older or married woman who accompanies or supervises a young unmarried woman on social occasions. ~*vb.* **2.** to act as a chaperon to. —**chaperonage** ('ʃæpərənɪdʒ) *n.*

chaplain ('tʃæplɪn) *n.* a Christian clergyman attached to a chapel of an institution or ministering to a military body, etc. —'**chaplaincy** *or* '**chaplainry** *n.*

chaplet ('tʃæplɪt) *n.* **1.** an ornamental wreath of flowers worn on the head. **2.** a string of beads. **3.** *R.C. Church.* **a.** a string of prayer beads constituting one third of the rosary. **b.** the prayers counted on this string. **4.** a narrow moulding in the form of a string of beads; astragal. —'**chapleted** *adj.*

chapman ('tʃæpmən) *n., pl.* **-men.** *Arch.* a trader, esp. an itinerant pedlar.

chappie ('tʃæpɪ) *n. Inf.* another word for **chap²**.

chaps (tʃæps, ʃæps) *pl. n.* leather overleggings without a seat, worn by cowboys. Also called: **chaparajos, chaparejos.**

chapter ('tʃæptə) *n.* **1.** a division of a written work. **2.** a sequence of events: *a chapter of disasters.* **3.** a period in a life, history, etc. **4.** a numbered reference to that part of a Parliamentary session which relates to a specified Act of Parliament. **5.** a branch of some societies, clubs, etc. **6.** the collective body or a meeting of the canons of a cathedral or of the members of a monastic or knightly order. **7. chapter and verse.** exact authority for an action or statement. ~*vb.* **8.** (*tr.*) to divide into chapters.

char¹ (tʃɑː) *vb.* **charring, charred. 1.** to burn or be burned partially; scorch. **2.** (*tr.*) to reduce (wood) to charcoal by partial combustion.

char² *or* **charr** (tʃɑː) *n., pl.* **char, chars** *or* **charr, charrs.** any of various troutlike fishes occurring in cold lakes and northern seas.

char³ (tʃɑː) *n.* **1.** *Inf.* short for **charwoman.** ~*vb.* **charring, charred. 2.** *Brit. inf.* to do cleaning as a job.

char⁴ (tʃɑː) *n. Brit.* a slang word for **tea.**

charabanc ('ʃærə,bæŋ) *n. Brit.* a coach, esp. for sightseeing.

character ('kærɪktə) *n.* **1.** the combination of traits and qualities distinguishing the individual nature of a person or thing. **2.** one such distinguishing quality; characteristic. **3.** moral force: *a man of character.* **4. a.** reputation, esp. a good reputation. **b.** (*as modifier*): *character assassination.* **5.** a person represented in a play, film, story, etc.; role. **6.** an outstanding person: *one of the great characters of the century.* **7.** *Inf.* an odd, eccentric, or unusual person: *he's quite a character.* **8.** an informal word for **person:** *a shady character.* **9.** a symbol used in a writing system, such as a letter of the alphabet. **10.** Also called: **sort.** *Printing.* any single letter, numeral, etc., cast as a type. **11.** *Computers.* any such letter, numeral, etc., each of which can be represented uniquely by binary code. **12.** a style of writing or printing. **13.** *Genetics.* any structure, function, attribute, etc., in an organism that is determined by a gene or group of genes. **14.** a short prose sketch of a distinctive type of person. **15. in** (*or* **out of**) **character.** typical (or not typical) of the apparent character of a person. —'**characterful** *adj.* —'**characterless** *adj.*

characteristic (,kærɪktəˈrɪstɪk) *n.* **1.** a distinguishing quality, attribute, or trait. **2.** *Maths.* **a.** the integral part of a common logarithm: *the characteristic of 2.4771 is 2.* **b.** another name for **exponent** (sense 4). ~*adj.* **3.** indicative of a distinctive quality, etc.; typical. —,**characteristically** *adv.*

THESAURUS

channel *n.* **1.** canal, chamber, conduit, duct, fluting, furrow, groove, gutter, main, passage, route, strait **2.** *Fig.* approach, artery, avenue, course, means, medium, path, route, way ~*v.* **3.** conduct, convey, direct, guide, transmit

chant **1.** *n.* carol, chorus, melody, psalm, song **2.** *v.* carol, chorus, croon, descant, intone, recite, sing, warble

chaos anarchy, bedlam, confusion, disorder, disorganization, entropy, lawlessness, pandemonium, tumult

chaotic anarchic, confused, deranged, disordered, disorganized, lawless, purposeless, rampageous, riotous, topsy-turvy, tumultuous, uncontrolled

chap bloke (*Inf.*), character, cove (*Sl.*), customer, fellow, guy (*Inf.*), individual, person, sort, type

chaperon **1.** *n.* companion, duenna, escort, governess **2.** *v.* accompany, attend, escort, protect, safeguard, shepherd, watch over

chapter clause, division, episode, part, period, phase, section, stage, topic

char carbonize, cauterize, scorch, sear, singe

character 1. attributes, bent, calibre, cast, complexion, constitution, disposition, individuality, kidney, make-up, marked traits, nature, personality, quality, reputation, temper, temperament, type **2.** honour,

integrity, rectitude, strength, uprightness **3.** card (*Inf.*), eccentric, oddball (*Inf.*), oddity, original, queer fish (*Inf.*) **4.** cipher, device, emblem, figure, hieroglyph, letter, logo, mark, rune, sign, symbol, type **5.** part, persona, portrayal, role **6.** fellow, guy (*Inf.*), individual, person, sort, type

characteristic 1. *adj.* distinctive, distinguishing, idiosyncratic, individual, peculiar, representative, singular, special, specific, symbolic, symptomatic, typical **2.** *n.* attribute, faculty, feature, idiosyncrasy, mark, peculiarity, property, quality, trait

characterize or **-ise** ('kærɪktə,raɪz) vb. (tr.) **1.** to be a characteristic of. **2.** to distinguish or mark as a characteristic. **3.** to describe or portray the character of. —,characteri'zation or -i'sation n.

charade (ʃə'rɑːd) n. **1.** an act in the game of charades. **2.** Chiefly Brit. an absurd act; travesty.

charades (ʃə'rɑːdz) n. a parlour game in which one team acts out each syllable of a word, the other team having to guess the word.

charcoal ('tʃɑː,kəʊl) n. **1.** a black amorphous form of carbon made by heating wood or other organic matter in the absence of air. **2.** a stick of this for drawing. **3.** a drawing done in charcoal. ~vb. **4.** (tr.) to write, draw, or blacken with charcoal.

chard (tʃɑːd) n. a variety of beet with large succulent leaves and thick stalks, used as a vegetable. Also called: **Swiss chard.**

charge (tʃɑːdʒ) vb. **1.** to set or demand (a price). **2.** (tr.) to enter a debit against a person or his account. **3.** (tr.) to accuse or impute a fault to (a person, etc.), as formally in a court of law. **4.** (tr.) to command; place a burden upon or assign responsibility to: I was charged to take the message to headquarters. **5.** to make a rush at or sudden attack upon (a person or thing). **6.** (tr.) to fill (a receptacle) with the proper quantity. **7.** (often foll. by up) to cause (an accumulator, capacitor, etc.) to take or store electricity or (of an accumulator) to have electricity fed into it. **8.** to fill or be filled with matter by dispersion, solution, or absorption: to charge water with carbon dioxide. **9.** (tr.) to fill or suffuse with feeling, emotion, etc.: the atmosphere was charged with excitement. **10.** (tr.) Law. (of a judge) to address (a jury) authoritatively. **11.** (tr.) to load (a firearm). **12.** (tr.) Heraldry. to paint (a shield, banner, etc.) with a charge. ~n. **13.** a price charged for some article or service; cost. **14.** a financial liability, such as a tax. **15.** a debt or a book entry recording it. **16.** an accusation or allegation, such as a formal accusation of a crime in law. **17. a.** an onrush, attack, or assault. **b.** the call to such an attack in battle. **18.** custody or guardianship. **19.** a person or thing committed to someone's care. **20. a.** a cartridge or shell. **b.** the explosive required to discharge a firearm. **c.** an amount of explosive to be detonated at any one time. **21.** the quantity of anything that a receptacle is intended to hold. **22.** Physics. **a.** the attribute of matter responsible for all electrical phenomena, existing in two forms: negative charge; positive charge. **b.** an excess or deficiency of electrons in a system. **c.** a quantity of electricity determined by the product of an electric current and the time for which it flows, measured in coulombs. **d.** the total amount of electricity stored in a capacitor or an accumulator. **23.** a load or burden. **24.** a duty or responsibility; control. **25.** a command, injunction, or order. **26.** Heraldry. a design depicted on heraldic arms. **27. in charge.** in command. **28. in charge of. a.** having responsibility for. **b.** U.S. under the care of.

chargeable ('tʃɑːdʒəbəl) adj. **1.** liable to be charged. **2.** liable to result in a legal charge.

chargé d'affaires ('ʃɑːʒeɪ dæ'feə) n., pl. **chargés d'affaires** ('ʃɑːʒeɪ, -ʒeɪz). **1.** the temporary head of a diplomatic mission in the absence of the ambassador or minister. **2.** the head of a diplomatic mission of the lowest level.

charge hand n. Brit. a workman whose grade of responsibility is just below that of a foreman.

charger[1] ('tʃɑːdʒə) n. **1.** a person or thing that charges. **2.** a horse formerly ridden into battle. **3.** a device for charging an accumulator.

charger[2] ('tʃɑːdʒə) n. Antiques. a large dish.

chariot ('tʃærɪət) n. **1.** a two-wheeled horse-drawn vehicle used in ancient wars, races, etc. **2.** a light four-wheeled horse-drawn ceremonial carriage. **3.** Poetic. any stately vehicle.

charioteer (,tʃærɪə'tɪə) n. the driver of a chariot.

charisma (kə'rɪzmə) or **charism** ('kærɪzəm) n. **1.** a special personal quality or power of an individual making him capable of influencing or inspiring large numbers of people. **2.** a quality inherent in a thing, such as a particular type of car, which inspires great enthusiasm and devotion. **3.** Christianity. a divinely bestowed power or talent. —**charismatic** (,kærɪz'mætɪk) adj.

charismatic movement n. Christianity. any of various groups, within existing denominations, emphasizing the charismatic gifts of speaking in tongues, healing, etc.

charitable ('tʃærɪtəbəl) adj. **1.** generous in giving to the needy. **2.** kind or lenient in one's attitude towards others. **3.** of or for charity. —'**charitableness** n. —'**charitably** adv.

charity ('tʃærɪtɪ) n., pl. -ties. **1. a.** the giving of help, money, food, etc., to those in need. **b.** (as modifier): a charity show. **2.** an institution or organization set up to provide help, money, etc., to those in need. **3.** the help, money, etc., given to the needy; alms. **4.** a kindly attitude towards people. **5.** love of one's fellow men.

charlatan ('ʃɑːlətən) n. someone who professes expertise, esp. in medicine, that he does not have; quack. —'**charlatanism** or '**charlatanry** n.

Charles's Wain ('tʃɑːlzɪz weɪn) n. another name for the **Plough.**

charleston ('tʃɑːlstən) n. a fast rhythmic dance of the 1920s, characterized by kicking and by twisting of the legs from the knee down.

charley horse ('tʃɑːlɪ) n. U.S. inf. cramp following strenuous athletic exercise.

charlie ('tʃɑːlɪ) n. Inf. Brit. a silly person; fool.

charlock ('tʃɑːlɒk) n. a weedy Eurasian plant with hairy stems and foliage and yellow flowers. Also called: **wild mustard.**

charlotte ('ʃɑːlət) n. a dessert made with fruit and layers or a casing of bread or cake crumbs, sponge cake, etc.: apple charlotte.

charm (tʃɑːm) n. **1.** the quality of pleasing, fascinating, or attracting people. **2.** a pleasing or attractive feature. **3.** a small object worn for supposed magical powers; amulet. **4.** a trinket worn on a bracelet. **5.** a magic spell. **6.** a formula used in casting such a spell. **7.** Physics. a property of certain elementary particles, used to explain some scattering experiments. **8. like a charm.** perfectly; successfully. ~vb. **9.** to attract or fascinate; delight greatly. **10.** to cast a magic spell on. **11.** to protect, influence, or heal, supposedly by magic. **12.** (tr.) to influence or obtain by personal charm. —'**charmer** n.

charming ('tʃɑːmɪŋ) adj. delightful; pleasant; attractive. —'**charmingly** adv.

charnel ('tʃɑːnəl) n. **1.** short for **charnel house.** ~adj. **2.** ghastly; sepulchral; deathly.

charnel house n. (esp. formerly) a building or vault where corpses or bones are deposited.

Charon ('kɛərən) n. Greek myth. the ferryman who

THESAURUS

characterize brand, distinguish, identify, indicate, inform, mark, represent, stamp, typify

charade fake, farce, pantomime, parody, pretence, travesty

charge v. **1.** accuse, arraign, blame, impeach, incriminate, indict, involve ~n. **2.** accusation, allegation, imputation, indictment ~v. **3.** assail, assault, attack, rush, storm ~n. **4.** assault, attack, onset, onslaught, rush, sortie ~v. **5.** afflict, burden, commit, entrust, tax ~n. **6.** burden, care, concern, custody, duty, office, responsibility, safekeeping, trust, ward **7.** amount, cost, damage (Inf.), expenditure, expense, outlay, payment, price, rate ~v. **8.** fill, instil, lade, load, suffuse **9.** bid, command, enjoin, exhort, instruct, order, require ~n. **10.** command, dictate, direction, exhortation, injunction, instruction, mandate, order, precept

charitable 1. beneficent, benevolent, bountiful, eleemosynary, generous, kind, lavish, liberal, philanthropic **2.** broad-minded, considerate, favourable, forgiving, gracious, humane, indulgent, kindly, lenient, magnanimous, sympathetic, tolerant, understanding

charity 1. alms-giving, assistance, benefaction, contributions, donations, endowment, fund, gift, hand-out, philanthropy, relief **2.** affection, agape, altruism, benevolence, benignity, bountifulness, bounty, compassion, fellow feeling, generosity, goodness, good will, humanity, indulgence, love, tenderheartedness

charlatan cheat, con man (Inf.), fake, fraud, impostor, mountebank, phoney (Sl.),

pretender, quack, sham, swindler

charm v. **1.** allure, attract, beguile, bewitch, cajole, captivate, delight, enamour, enchant, enrapture, entrance, fascinate, mesmerize, please, win, win over ~n. **2.** allure, allurement, appeal, attraction, desirability, enchantment, fascination, magic, magnetism, sorcery, spell **3.** amulet, fetish, good-luck piece, lucky piece, periapt (Rare), talisman, trinket

charming appealing, attractive, bewitching, captivating, delectable, delightful, engaging, eye-catching, fetching, irresistible, lovely, pleasant, pleasing, seductive, winning, winsome

chart 163 **chauffeur**

brought the dead across the rivers Styx or Acheron to Hades.

chart (tʃɑːt) n. **1.** a map designed to aid navigation by sea or air. **2.** an outline map, esp. one on which weather information is plotted. **3.** a sheet giving graphical, tabular, or diagrammatical information. **4. the charts.** Inf. the lists produced weekly of the best-selling pop singles and albums. ~vb. (tr.) **5.** to make a chart of. **6.** to plot or outline the course of. —'**chartless** adj.

charter ('tʃɑːtə) n. **1.** a formal document from the sovereign or state incorporating a city, bank, college, etc., and specifying its purposes and rights. **2.** (sometimes cap.) a formal document granting or demanding certain rights or liberties. **3.** a document issued by a society or an organization authorizing the establishment of a local branch or chapter. **4.** a special privilege or exemption. **5.** (often cap.) the fundamental principles of an organization; constitution. **6. a.** the hire or lease of transportation. **b.** (as modifier): a charter flight. ~vb. (tr.) **7.** to lease or hire by charter. **8.** to hire (a vehicle, etc.). **9.** to grant a charter to (a group or person). —'**charterer** n.

chartered accountant n. Brit. an accountant who has passed the examinations of the Institute of Chartered Accountants.

chartered bank n. Canad. a privately owned bank that has been incorporated by Parliament to operate in the commercial banking system.

Chartism ('tʃɑːtɪzəm) n. English history. a movement (1838-48) to achieve certain political reforms, demand for which was embodied in charters presented to Parliament. —'**Chartist** n., adj.

chartreuse (ʃɑːˈtrɜːz; French ʃarˈtrøːz) n. **1.** either of two liqueurs, green or yellow, made from herbs. **2.** a yellowish-green colour.

charwoman ('tʃɑːˌwʊmən) n., pl. -**women**. Brit. a woman who is hired to clean a house.

chary ('tʃɛərɪ) adj. **charier, chariest. 1.** wary; careful. **2.** choosy; finicky. **3.** shy. **4.** sparing; mean. —'**charily** adv. —'**chariness** n.

Charybdis (kəˈrɪbdɪs) n. a ship-devouring monster in classical mythology, identified with a whirlpool off the coast of Sicily. Cf. **Scylla.**

chase[1] (tʃeɪs) vb. **1.** to follow or run after (a person, animal, or goal) persistently or quickly. **2.** (tr.; often foll. by out, away, or off) to force to run (away); drive (out). **3.** (tr.) Inf. to court (a member of the opposite sex) in an unsubtle manner. **4.** (tr.; often foll. by up) Inf. to pursue persistently and energetically in order to obtain results, information, etc. **5.** (intr.) Inf. to hurry; rush. ~n. **6.** the act of chasing; pursuit. **7.** any quarry that is pursued. **8.** Brit. an unenclosed area of land where wild animals are preserved to be hunted. **9.** Brit. the right to hunt a particular quarry over the land of others. **10. the chase.** the act or sport of hunting. **11.** short for **steeplechase. 12. give chase.** to pursue (a person, animal, or thing) actively.

chase[2] (tʃeɪs) n. **1.** Letterpress printing. a rectangular steel frame into which metal type and blocks are locked for printing. **2.** the part of a cannon enclosing the bore. **3.** a groove or channel, esp. to take a pipe, cable, etc. ~vb. (tr.) **4.** Also: **chamfer.** to cut a groove, furrow, or flute in (a surface, column, etc.).

chase[3] (tʃeɪs) vb. (tr.) Also: **enchase.** to ornament (metal) by engraving or embossing.

chaser ('tʃeɪsə) n. **1.** a person or thing that chases. **2.** a drink drunk after another of a different kind, as beer after spirits.

chasm ('kæzəm) n. **1.** a deep cleft in the ground; abyss. **2.** a break in continuity; gap. **3.** a wide difference in interests, feelings, etc. —'**chasmal** ('kæzməl) or '**chasmic** adj.

chassis ('ʃæsɪ) n., pl. -**sis** (-sɪz). **1.** the steel frame, wheels, and mechanical parts of a motor vehicle. **2.** Electronics. a mounting for the circuit components of an electrical or electronic device, such as a radio or television. **3.** the landing gear of an aircraft. **4.** the frame on which a cannon carriage moves.

chaste (tʃeɪst) adj. **1.** not having experienced sexual intercourse; virginal. **2.** abstaining from unlawful sexual intercourse. **3.** (of conduct, speech, etc.) pure; decent; modest. **4.** (of style) simple; restrained. —'**chastely** adv. —'**chasteness** n.

chasten ('tʃeɪsən) vb. (tr.) **1.** to bring to submission; subdue. **2.** to discipline or correct by punishment. **3.** to moderate; restrain. —'**chastener** n.

chastise (tʃæsˈtaɪz) vb. (tr.) **1.** to punish, esp. by beating. **2.** to scold severely. —**chastisement** (tʃæs-ˈtaɪzmənt, 'tʃæstɪz-) n. —**chas'tiser** n.

chastity ('tʃæstɪtɪ) n. **1.** the state of being chaste; purity. **2.** abstention from sexual intercourse; virginity or celibacy.

chasuble ('tʃæzjʊbəl) n. Christianity. a long sleeveless outer vestment worn by a priest when celebrating Mass.

chat (tʃæt) n. **1.** informal conversation or talk in an easy familiar manner. **2.** an Old World songbird of the thrush family, having a harsh chattering cry. **3.** any of various North American warblers. **4.** any of various Australian wrens. ~vb. **chatting, chatted. 5.** (intr.) to talk in an easy familiar way. ~See also **chat up.**

chateau or **château** ('ʃætəʊ) n., pl. -**teaux** (-təʊ, -təʊz) or -**teaus. 1.** a country house or castle, esp. in France. **2.** (in the name of a wine) estate or vineyard.

chatelaine ('ʃætəˌleɪn; French ʃatˈlɛn) n. **1.** (esp. formerly) the mistress of a castle or large household. **2.** a chain or clasp worn at the waist by women in the 16th to the 19th centuries, with handkerchief, keys, etc., attached.

chat show n. Brit. a television or radio show in which guests are interviewed informally.

chattel ('tʃætəl) n. **1.** (often pl.) Property law. **a. chattel personal.** an item of movable personal property, such as furniture, etc. **b. chattel real.** an interest in land less than a freehold. **2. goods and chattels.** personal property.

chatter ('tʃætə) vb. **1.** to speak (about unimportant matters) rapidly and incessantly. **2.** (intr.) (of birds, monkeys, etc.) to make rapid repetitive high-pitched noises. **3.** (intr.) (of the teeth) to click together rapidly through cold or fear. **4.** (intr.) to make rapid intermittent contact with a component, as in machining. ~n. **5.** idle or foolish talk; gossip. **6.** the high-pitched repetitive noise made by a bird, monkey, etc. **7.** the rattling of objects, such as parts of a machine. —'**chatterer** n.

chatterbox ('tʃætəˌbɒks) n. Inf. a person who talks constantly, esp. about trivial matters.

chatty ('tʃætɪ) adj. -**tier, -tiest. 1.** full of trivial conversation; talkative. **2.** informal and friendly; gossipy. —'**chattily** adv. —'**chattiness** n.

chat up vb. (tr., adv.) Brit. inf. **1.** to talk persuasively to (a person), esp. with an ulterior motive. **2.** to talk flirtatiously to (a person of the opposite sex).

chauffeur ('ʃəʊfə, ʃəʊˈfɜː) n. **1.** a person employed to drive a car. ~vb. **2.** to act as driver for (a person, etc.): he chauffeured me to the stadium. —**chauffeuse** (ʃəʊ-

---

THESAURUS

chart 1. n. blueprint, diagram, graph, map, plan, table, tabulation **2.** v. delineate, draft, graph, map out, outline, plot, shape, sketch

charter 1. n. bond, concession, contract, deed, document, franchise, indenture, licence, permit, prerogative, privilege, right **2.** v. authorize, commission, employ, hire, lease, rent, sanction

chase 1. v. course, drive, drive away, expel, follow, hound, hunt, pursue, put to flight, run after, track **2.** n. hunt, hunting, pursuit, race, venery (Archaic)

chasm abyss, alienation, breach, cavity, cleft, crater, crevasse, fissure, gap, gorge, gulf, hiatus, hollow, opening, ravine, rent,

rift, split, void

chassis anatomy, bodywork, frame, framework, fuselage, skeleton, substructure

chaste austere, decent, decorous, elegant, immaculate, incorrupt, innocent, modest, moral, neat, pure, quiet, refined, restrained, simple, unaffected, uncontaminated, undefiled, unsullied, vestal, virginal, virtuous, wholesome

chasten afflict, castigate, chastise, correct, cow, curb, discipline, humble, humiliate, repress, soften, subdue, tame

chastise beat, berate, castigate, censure, correct, discipline, flog, lash, punish, scold, scourge, upbraid, whip

chastity celibacy, continence, innocence, maidenhood, modesty, purity, virginity, virtue

chat 1. n. chatter, chinwag (Brit. inf.), confab (Inf.), gossip, heart-to-heart, natter, talk, tête-à-tête **2.** v. chatter, chew the rag or fat (Sl.), gossip, jaw (Sl.), natter, rabbit (on) (Brit. sl.), talk

chatter n./v. babble, blather, chat, gab (Inf.), gossip, jabber, natter, prate, prattle, tattle, twaddle

chatty colloquial, familiar, friendly, gossipy, informal, newsy (Inf.), talkative

'fɜːz) *fem. n.*

chauvinism ('ʃəʊvɪˌnɪzəm) *n.* **1.** aggressive or fanatical patriotism; jingoism. **2.** enthusiastic devotion to a cause. **3.** smug irrational belief in the superiority of one's own race, party, sex, etc.: *male chauvinism.* —'**chauvinist** *n.* —ˌchauvin'istic *adj.* —ˌchauvin'istically *adv.*

cheap (tʃiːp) *adj.* **1.** costing relatively little; inexpensive; good value. **2.** charging low prices: *a cheap hairdresser.* **3.** of poor quality; shoddy: *cheap furniture.* **4.** worth relatively little: *promises are cheap.* **5.** not worthy of respect; vulgar. **6.** ashamed; embarrassed: *to feel cheap.* **7.** stingy; miserly. **8.** *Inf.* mean; despicable: *a cheap liar.* **9. dirt cheap.** *Inf.* extremely inexpensive. ~*n.* **10. on the cheap.** *Brit. inf.* at a low cost. ~*adv.* **11.** at very little cost. —'**cheaply** *adv.* —'**cheapness** *n.*

cheapen ('tʃiːpən) *vb.* **1.** to make or become lower in reputation, quality, etc. **2.** to make or become cheap or cheaper. —'**cheapener** *n.*

cheap-jack *Inf.* ~*n.* **1.** a person who sells cheap and shoddy goods. ~*adj.* **2.** shoddy or inferior.

cheapskate ('tʃiːpˌskeɪt) *n. Inf.* a miserly person.

cheat (tʃiːt) *vb.* **1.** to deceive or practise deceit, esp. for one's own gain; trick or swindle (someone). **2.** (*intr.*) to obtain unfair advantage by trickery, as in a game of cards. **3.** (*tr.*) to escape or avoid (something unpleasant) by luck or cunning: *to cheat death.* **4.** (when *intr.*, usually foll. by *on*) *Inf.* to be sexually unfaithful to (one's wife, husband, or lover). ~*n.* **5.** a person who cheats. **6.** a deliberately dishonest transaction, esp. for gain; fraud. **7.** *Inf.* sham. **8.** *Law.* the obtaining of another's property by fraudulent means. —'**cheater** *n.* —'**cheatingly** *adv.*

check (tʃɛk) *vb.* **1.** to pause or cause to pause, esp. abruptly. **2.** (*tr.*) to restrain or control: *to check one's tears.* **3.** (*tr.*) to slow the growth or progress of; retard. **4.** (*tr.*) to rebuke or rebuff. **5.** (when *intr.*, often foll. by *on* or *up on*) to examine, investigate, or make an inquiry into (facts, a product, etc.) for accuracy, quality, or progress. **6.** (*tr.*) *Chiefly U.S.* to mark off so as to indicate approval, correctness, or preference. **7.** (*intr.*; often foll. by *with*) *Chiefly U.S.* to correspond or agree: *this report checks with the other.* **8.** (*tr.*) *Chiefly U.S.* to leave in or accept for temporary custody. **9.** *Chess.* to place (an opponent's king) in check. **10.** (*tr.*) to mark with a pattern of squares or crossed lines. **11.** to crack or cause to crack. **12.** (*tr.*) *Ice hockey.* to impede (an opponent). **13.** (*intr.*) *Hunting.* (of hounds) to pause while relocating a lost scent. ~*n.* **14.** a break in progress; stoppage. **15.** a restraint or rebuff. **16.** a person or thing that restrains, halts, etc. **17.** a control, esp. a rapid or informal one, to ensure accuracy, progress, etc. **18.** a means or standard to ensure against fraud or error. **19.** the U.S. word for **tick**[1]. **20.** the U.S. spelling of **cheque**. **21.** *U.S.* the bill in a restaurant. **22.** *Chiefly U.S.* a tag used to identify property deposited for custody. **23.** a pattern of squares or crossed lines. **24.** a single square in such a pattern. **25.** fabric with a pattern of squares or crossed lines. **26.** *Chess.* the state or position of a king under direct attack. **27.** a small crack, as one that occurs in timber during seasoning. **28.** a chip or counter used in some card and gambling games. **29.** *Hunting.* a pause by the hounds owing to loss of the scent. **30.** *Ice hockey.* the act of impeding an opponent with one's body or stick. **31. in check.** under control or restraint. ~*interj.* **32.** *Chess.* a call made to an opponent indicating that his king is in check. **33.** *Chiefly U.S.* an expression of agreement.

~See also **check in, check out, checkup.** —'**checkable** *adj.*

checked (tʃɛkt) *adj.* having a pattern of squares.

checker[1] ('tʃɛkə) *n., vb.* **1.** the usual U.S. spelling of **chequer.** ~*n.* **2.** *Textiles.* a variant spelling of **chequer** (sense 2). **3.** the U.S. name for **draughtsman** (sense 3).

checker[2] ('tʃɛkə) *n. Chiefly U.S.* **1.** a cashier, esp. in a supermarket. **2.** an attendant in a cloakroom, left-luggage office, etc.

checkers ('tʃɛkəz) *n.* (*functioning as sing.*) the U.S. name for **draughts.**

check in *vb.* (*adv.*) **1.** (*intr.*) to record one's arrival, as at a hotel or for work; sign in or report. **2.** (*tr.*) to register the arrival of (passengers, etc.). ~*n.* **check-in. 3.** the formal registration of arrival, as at an airport or a hotel. **4.** the place where one registers arrival at an airport, etc.

check list *n.* a list of items, names, etc., to be referred to for identification or verification.

checkmate ('tʃɛkˌmeɪt) *n.* **1.** *Chess.* **a.** the winning position in which an opponent's king is under attack and unable to escape. **b.** the move by which this position is achieved. **2.** utter defeat. ~*vb.* (*tr.*) **3.** *Chess.* to place (an opponent's king) in checkmate. **4.** to thwart or render powerless. ~*interj.* **5.** *Chess.* a call made when placing an opponent's king in checkmate.

check out *vb.* (*adv.*) **1.** (*intr.*) to pay the bill and depart, esp. from a hotel. **2.** (*intr.*) to depart from a place; record one's departure from work. **3.** to investigate or prove to be in order after investigation: *the police checked out all the statements.* ~*n.* **checkout. 4.** the latest time for vacating a room in a hotel, etc. **5.** a counter, esp. in a supermarket, where customers pay.

checkpoint ('tʃɛkˌpɔɪnt) *n.* a place, as at a frontier, where vehicles or travellers are stopped for official identification, inspection, etc.

checkup ('tʃɛkˌʌp) *n.* **1.** an examination to see if something is in order. **2.** *Med.* a medical examination, esp. one taken at regular intervals. ~*vb.* **check up. 3.** (*intr.*, *adv.* sometimes foll. by *on*) to investigate or make an inquiry into (a person's character, evidence, etc.).

Cheddar ('tʃɛdə) *n.* (*sometimes not cap.*) any of several types of smooth hard yellow or whitish cheese.

cheek (tʃiːk) *n.* **1.** either side of the face, esp. that part below the eye. **2.** *Inf.* impudence; effrontery. **3.** (*often pl.*) *Inf.* either side of the buttocks. **4.** (*often pl.*) a side of a door jamb. **5.** one of the jaws of a vice. **6. cheek by jowl.** close together; intimately linked. **7. turn the other cheek.** to be submissive and refuse to retaliate. **8. with one's tongue in one's cheek.** See **tongue** (sense 18). ~*vb.* **9.** (*tr.*) *Inf.* to speak or behave disrespectfully to.

cheeky ('tʃiːkɪ) *adj.* **cheekier, cheekiest.** disrespectful in speech or behaviour; impudent. —'**cheekily** *adv.* —'**cheekiness** *n.*

cheep (tʃiːp) *n.* **1.** the short weak high-pitched cry of a young bird; chirp. ~*vb.* **2.** (*intr.*) (of young birds) to utter such sounds. —'**cheeper** *n.*

cheer (tʃɪə) *vb.* **1.** (usually foll. by *up*) to make or become happy or hopeful; comfort or be comforted. **2.** to applaud with shouts. **3.** (when *tr.*, sometimes foll. by *on*) to encourage (a team, etc.) with shouts. ~*n.* **4.** a shout or cry of approval, encouragement, etc., often using **hurrah! 5.** happiness; good spirits. **6.** state of mind; spirits (archaic, except in **be of good cheer, with good cheer**). **7.** *Arch.* provisions for a feast; fare.

THESAURUS

cheap 1. bargain, cut-price, economical, economy, inexpensive, keen, low-cost, low-priced, reasonable, reduced, sale **2.** common, inferior, paltry, poor, second-rate, shoddy, tatty, tawdry, worthless **3.** base, contemptible, despicable, low, mean, scurvy, sordid, vulgar

cheapen belittle, debase, degrade, demean, denigrate, depreciate, derogate, devalue, discredit, disparage, lower

cheat *v.* **1.** bamboozle (*Inf.*), beguile, bilk, con (*Sl.*), deceive, defraud, diddle (*Inf.*), do (*Sl.*), double-cross (*Inf.*), dupe, finagle (*Inf.*), fleece, fool, gull (*Archaic*), hoax, hoodwink, mislead, rip off (*Sl.*), swindle, take for a ride (*Inf.*), take in (*Inf.*), thwart, trick, victimize **2.** baffle, check, defeat, deprive, foil, frustrate,

prevent, thwart ~*n.* **3.** artifice, deceit, deception, fraud, imposture, rip-off (*Sl.*), swindle, trickery **4.** charlatan, cheater, con man (*Inf.*), deceiver, dodger, double-crosser (*Inf.*), impostor, knave (*Archaic*), rogue, shark, sharper, swindler, trickster

check *v.* **1.** compare, confirm, enquire into, examine, inspect, investigate, look at, look over, make sure, monitor, note, probe, scrutinize, study, test, tick, verify **2.** arrest, bar, bridle, control, curb, delay, halt, hinder, impede, inhibit, limit, nip in the bud, obstruct, pause, repress, restrain, retard, stop, thwart **3.** blame, chide, give (someone) a row (*Inf.*), rate, rebuff, rebuke, reprimand, reprove, scold, tell off (*Inf.*) ~*n.* **4.** examination, inspection, investigation, research,

scrutiny, test **5.** constraint, control, curb, damper, hindrance, impediment, inhibition, limitation, obstruction, restraint, stoppage **6.** blow, disappointment, frustration, rejection, reverse, setback

cheek audacity, brass neck (*Inf.*), brazenness, disrespect, effrontery, gall (*Inf.*), impertinence, impudence, insolence, lip (*Sl.*), nerve, sauce (*Inf.*), temerity

cheeky audacious, disrespectful, forward, impertinent, impudent, insolent, insulting, pert, saucy

cheer *v.* **1.** animate, brighten, buoy up, cheer up, comfort, console, elate, elevate, encourage, enliven, exhilarate, gladden, hearten, incite, inspirit, solace, uplift, warm **2.** acclaim, applaud, clap, hail, hurrah ~*n.* **3.**

cheerful ('tʃɪəful) *adj.* **1.** having a happy disposition; in good spirits. **2.** pleasantly bright: *a cheerful room.* **3.** ungrudging: *cheerful help.* —'**cheerfully** *adv.* —'**cheerfulness** *n.*

cheerio (,tʃɪərɪ'əʊ) *Inf.* ~*interj.* **1.** *Chiefly Brit.* a farewell greeting. **2.** *Chiefly Brit.* a drinking toast. ~*n.* **3.** *N.Z.* a type of small sausage.

cheerleader ('tʃɪə,liːdə) *n. U.S.* a person who leads a crowd in cheers, esp. at sports events.

cheerless ('tʃɪəlɪs) *adj.* dreary or gloomy. —'**cheerlessly** *adv.* —'**cheerlessness** *n.*

cheers (tʃɪəz) *interj. Inf. chiefly Brit.* **1.** a drinking toast. **2.** goodbye! cheerio! **3.** thanks! **4. three cheers.** three shouts of hurrah given in unison to honour someone or celebrate something.

cheery ('tʃɪərɪ) *adj.* **cheerier, cheeriest.** showing or inspiring cheerfulness; gay. —'**cheerily** *adv.* —'**cheeriness** *n.*

cheese (tʃiːz) *n.* **1.** the curd of milk separated from the whey and variously prepared as a food. **2.** a mass or cake of this substance. **3.** any of various substances of similar consistency, etc.: *lemon cheese.* **4.** *Sl.* an important person (esp. in **big cheese**).

cheeseburger ('tʃiːz,bɜːgə) *n.* a hamburger cooked with a slice of cheese on top of it.

cheesecake ('tʃiːz,keɪk) *n.* **1.** a rich tart filled with cheese, esp. cream cheese, cream, sugar, etc. **2.** *Sl.* women displayed for their sex appeal, as in photographs in magazines or films.

cheesecloth ('tʃiːz,klɒθ) *n.* a loosely woven cotton cloth formerly used for wrapping cheese.

cheesed off *adj.* (*usually postpositive*) *Brit. sl.* bored, disgusted, or angry.

cheeseparing ('tʃiːz,pɛərɪŋ) *adj.* **1.** penny-pinching. ~*n.* **2. a.** a paring of cheese rind. **b.** anything similarly worthless. **3.** stinginess.

cheesy ('tʃiːzɪ) *adj.* **cheesier, cheesiest.** like cheese in flavour, smell, or consistency. —'**cheesiness** *n.*

cheetah *or* **chetah** ('tʃiːtə) *n.* a large feline of Africa and SW Asia: the swiftest mammal, having very long legs, and a black-spotted coat.

chef (ʃɛf) *n.* a cook, esp. the principal cook in a restaurant.

Chelsea Pensioner ('tʃɛlsɪ) *n.* an inhabitant of the Chelsea Royal Hospital in SW London, a home for old and infirm soldiers.

chem. *abbrev. for:* **1.** chemical. **2.** chemist. **3.** chemistry.

chem- *combining form.* variant of **chemo-** before a vowel.

chemical ('kɛmɪkəl) *n.* **1.** any substance used in or resulting from a reaction involving changes to atoms or molecules. ~*adj.* **2.** of or used in chemistry. **3.** of, made from, or using chemicals: *chemical fertilizer.* —'**chemically** *adv.*

chemical engineering *n.* the branch of engineering concerned with the design and manufacture of the plant used in industrial chemical processes. —**chemical engineer** *n.*

chemical warfare *n.* warfare using asphyxiating gases, poisons, defoliants, incendiaries, etc.

chemin de fer (ʃə'mæn də 'fɛə) *n.* a gambling game, a variation of baccarat.

chemise (ʃə'miːz) *n.* Also called: **shift. a.** an unwaisted loose-fitting dress hanging straight from the shoulders. **b.** a loose shirtlike undergarment.

chemist ('kɛmɪst) *n.* **1.** *Brit.* a shop selling medicines, cosmetics, etc. **2.** *Brit.* a qualified dispenser of prescribed medicines. **3.** a person studying, trained in, or engaged in chemistry.

chemistry ('kɛmɪstrɪ) *n., pl.* **-tries.** **1.** the branch of physical science concerned with the composition, properties, and reactions of substances. **2.** the composition, properties, and reactions of a particular substance. **3.** the nature and effects of any complex phenomenon: *the chemistry of humour.*

chemo-, chemi-, *or before a vowel* **chem-** *combining form.* indicating that chemicals or chemical reactions are involved: *chemotherapy.*

chemotherapy (,kɛməʊ'θɛrəpɪ) *n.* treatment of disease by means of chemical agents. —,**chemo'therapist** *n.*

chemurgy ('kɛmɜːdʒɪ) *n.* the branch of chemistry concerned with the industrial use of organic raw materials, esp. of agricultural origin. —**chem'urgic** *or* **chem'urgical** *adj.*

chenille (ʃə'niːl) *n.* **1.** a thick soft tufty silk or worsted velvet cord or yarn used in embroidery and for trimmings, etc. **2.** a fabric of such yarn. **3.** a carpet of such fabric.

cheque *or U.S.* **check** (tʃɛk) *n.* **1.** a bill of exchange drawn on a bank by the holder of a current account. **2.** *Austral. & N.Z.* the total sum of money received for contract work or a crop.

cheque card *n.* another name for **banker's card.**

chequer *or U.S.* **checker** ('tʃɛkə) *n.* **1.** any of the marbles, pegs, or other pieces used in the game of Chinese chequers. **2. a.** a pattern of squares. **b.** one of the squares in such a pattern. ~*vb.* (*tr.*) **3.** to make irregular in colour or character; variegate. **4.** to mark off with alternating squares of colour.

chequered *or esp. U.S.* **checkered** ('tʃɛkəd) *adj.* marked by fluctuations of fortune (esp. in **a chequered career**).

chequers ('tʃɛkəz) *n.* (*functioning as sing.*) another name for draughts.

cherish ('tʃɛrɪʃ) *vb.* (*tr.*) **1.** to feel or show great tenderness or care for. **2.** to cling fondly to (a hope, idea, etc.); nurse: *to cherish ambitions.*

cheroot (ʃə'ruːt) *n.* a cigar with both ends cut off squarely.

cherry ('tʃɛrɪ) *n., pl.* **-ries.** **1.** any of several trees of the genus *Prunus,* having a small fleshy rounded fruit containing a hard stone. **2.** the fruit or wood of any of these trees. **3.** any of various unrelated plants, such as the ground cherry and Jerusalem cherry. **4.** a bright red colour; cerise. **5.** *Taboo sl.* virginity or the hymen as its symbol.

cherub ('tʃɛrəb) *n., pl.* **cherubs** *or* **cherubim** ('tʃɛrəbɪm, -ʊbɪm). **1.** *Theol.* a member of the second order of angels, often represented as a winged child. **2.** an innocent or sweet child. —**cherubic** (tʃə'ruːbɪk) *or* **che'rubical** *adj.* —**che'rubically** *adv.*

chervil ('tʃɜːvɪl) *n.* an aromatic umbelliferous Eurasian plant with small white flowers and aniseed-flavoured leaves used as herbs in soups and salads.

chess (tʃɛs) *n.* a game of skill for two players using a chessboard on which chessmen are moved. The object is to checkmate the opponent's king.

chessboard ('tʃɛs,bɔːd) *n.* a square board divided into 64 squares of two alternating colours, used for playing chess or draughts.

chessman ('tʃɛs,mæn, -mən) *or* **chess piece** *n., pl.* **-men** *or* **pieces.** any of the pieces and pawns used in a game of chess.

chest (tʃɛst) *n.* **1. a.** the front part of the trunk from the neck to the belly. Related adj.: **pectoral. b.** (*as modifi-*

THESAURUS

animation, buoyancy, cheerfulness, comfort, gaiety, gladness, glee, hopefulness, joy, liveliness, merriment, merry-making, mirth, optimism, solace **4.** acclamation, applause, ovation, plaudits

cheerful animated, blithe, bright, bucked (*Inf.*), buoyant, cheery, contented, enlivening, enthusiastic, gay, glad, gladsome, happy, hearty, jaunty, jolly, joyful, light-hearted, lightsome (*Archaic*), merry, optimistic, pleasant, sparkling, sprightly, sunny

cheerfulness buoyancy, exuberance, gaiety, geniality, gladness, good cheer, good humour, high spirits, jauntiness, joyousness,

light-heartedness

cheering auspicious, bright, comforting, encouraging, heartening, promising, propitious

cheerless austere, bleak, comfortless, dark, dejected, depressed, desolate, despondent, disconsolate, dismal, dolorous, drab, dreary, dull, forlorn, gloomy, grim, joyless, melancholy, miserable, mournful, sad, sombre, sorrowful, sullen, unhappy, woebegone, woeful

cheer up brighten, buck up (*Inf.*), comfort, encourage, enliven, gladden, hearten, jolly along, perk up, rally, take heart

cheery breezy, carefree, cheerful, good-humoured, happy, jovial, lively, pleasant, sunny

chemical compound, drug, potion, synthetic

cherish care for, cleave to, cling to, comfort, cosset, encourage, entertain, foster, harbour, hold dear, nourish, nurse, nurture, prize, shelter, support, sustain, treasure

cherubic adorable, angelic, heavenly, innocent, lovable, seraphic, sweet

er): *a chest cold.* **2. get (something) off one's chest.** *Inf.* to unburden oneself of troubles, worries, etc., by talking about them. **3.** a box used for storage or shipping: *a tea chest.* —**'chested** *adj.*

chesterfield ('tʃɛstə,fiːld) *n.* **1.** a man's overcoat, usually with a velvet collar. **2.** a large tightly stuffed sofa, with straight upholstered arms of the same height as the back.

chestnut ('tʃɛs,nʌt) *n.* **1.** a N temperate tree such as the **sweet** or **Spanish chestnut**, which produces flowers in long catkins and nuts in a prickly bur. Cf. **horse chestnut. 2.** the edible nut of any of these trees. **3.** the hard wood of any of these trees, used in making furniture, etc. **4. a.** a reddish-brown colour. **b.** (*as adj.*): *chestnut hair.* **5.** a horse of a golden-brown colour. **6.** *Inf.* an old or stale joke.

chest of drawers *n.* a piece of furniture consisting of a set of drawers in a frame.

chesty ('tʃɛstɪ) *adj.* **chestier, chestiest.** *Inf.* **1.** *Brit.* suffering from or symptomatic of chest disease: *a chesty cough.* **2.** having a large well-developed chest or bosom. —**'chestiness** *n.*

cheval glass (ʃə'væl) *n.* a full-length mirror mounted so as to swivel within a frame.

chevalier (,ʃɛvə'lɪə) *n.* **1.** a member of certain orders of merit, such as the French Legion of Honour. **2.** the lowest title of rank in the old French nobility. **3.** an archaic word for **knight. 4.** a chivalrous man; gallant.

Cheviot ('tʃiːvɪət, 'tʃɛv-) *n.* **1.** a large British breed of sheep reared for its wool. **2.** (*often not cap.*) a rough twill-weave woollen suiting fabric.

chevron ('ʃɛvrən) *n.* **1.** *Mil.* a badge or insignia consisting of one or more V-shaped stripes to indicate a non-commissioned rank or length of service. **2.** *Heraldry.* an inverted V-shaped charge on a shield. **3.** any V-shaped pattern or device.

chew (tʃuː) *vb.* **1.** to work the jaws and teeth in order to grind (food); masticate. **2.** to bite repeatedly: *she chewed her nails anxiously.* **3.** (*intr.*) to use chewing tobacco. **4. chew the fat** or **rag.** *Sl.* **a.** to argue over a point. **b.** to talk idly; gossip. ~*n.* **5.** the act of chewing. **6.** something that is chewed. —**'chewable** *adj.* —**'chewer** *n.*

chewing gum *n.* a preparation for chewing, usually made of flavoured and sweetened chicle.

chewy ('tʃuːɪ) *adj.* **chewier, chewiest.** of a consistency requiring chewing.

chez *French.* (ʃe) *prep.* **1.** at the home of. **2.** with, among, or in the manner of.

chg. *Commerce, etc. abbrev. for* charge.

chi (kaɪ) *n.* the 22nd letter of the Greek alphabet (χ, Χ).

chianti (kɪ'æntɪ) *n.* (*sometimes cap.*) a dry red or white wine produced in Tuscany, Italy.

chiaroscuro (kɪ,ɑːrə'skʊərəʊ) *n.,* *pl.* **-ros. 1.** the artistic distribution of light and dark masses in a picture. **2.** monochrome painting using light and dark only.

chic (ʃiːk, ʃɪk) *adj.* **1.** (esp. of fashionable clothes, women, etc.) stylish or elegant. ~*n.* **2.** stylishness, esp. in dress; modishness; fashionable good taste. —**'chicly** *adv.*

chicane (ʃɪ'keɪn) *n.* **1.** a bridge or whist hand without trumps. **2.** *Motor racing.* a barrier placed before a dangerous corner to reduce speeds by allowing drivers through in single file only. **3.** a less common word for **chicanery.** ~*vb.* **4.** (*tr.*) to deceive or trick by chicanery. **5.** (*intr.*) to use tricks or chicanery. —**chi'caner** *n.*

chicanery (ʃɪ'keɪnərɪ) *n.,* *pl.* **-eries. 1.** verbal deception or trickery; dishonest or sharp practice. **2.** a trick, deception, or quibble.

chick (tʃɪk) *n.* **1.** the young of a bird, esp. of a domestic fowl. **2.** *Sl.* a girl or young woman, esp. an attractive one. **3.** a young child: used as a term of endearment.

chicken ('tʃɪkɪn) *n.* **1.** a domestic fowl bred for its flesh

or eggs. **2.** the flesh of such a bird used for food. **3.** any of various similar birds, such as a prairie chicken. **4.** *Sl.* a cowardly person. **5.** *Sl.* a young inexperienced person. **6. count one's chickens before they are hatched.** to be over-optimistic in acting on expectations which are not yet fulfilled. ~*adj.* **7.** *Sl.* easily scared; cowardly; timid.

chicken feed *n. Sl.* a trifling amount of money.

chicken-hearted or **chicken-livered** *adj.* easily frightened; cowardly.

chicken out *vb.* (*intr., adv.*) *Inf.* to fail to do something through fear or lack of conviction.

chickenpox ('tʃɪkɪn,pɒks) *n.* a highly communicable viral disease most commonly affecting children, characterized by slight fever and the eruption of a rash.

chicken wire *n.* wire netting with a hexagonal mesh.

chickpea ('tʃɪk,piː) *n.* **1.** a bushy leguminous plant, cultivated for its edible pealike seeds. **2.** the seed of this plant.

chickweed ('tʃɪk,wiːd) *n.* any of various plants of the pink family, esp. a common garden weed with small white flowers.

chicle ('tʃɪkəl) *n.* a gumlike substance obtained from the sapodilla; the main ingredient of chewing gum.

chicory ('tʃɪkərɪ) *n.,* *pl.* **-ries. 1.** a blue-flowered plant, cultivated for its leaves, which are used in salads, and for its roots. **2.** the root of this plant, roasted, dried, and used as a coffee substitute. ~Cf. **endive.**

chide (tʃaɪd) *vb.* **chiding, chided** or **chid; chided, chid** or **chidden. 1.** to rebuke or scold. **2.** (*tr.*) to goad into action. —**'chider** *n.* —**'chidingly** *adv.*

chief (tʃiːf) *n.* **1.** the head or leader of a group or body of people. **2.** *Heraldry.* the upper third of a shield. ~*adj.* **3.** (*prenominal*) **a.** most important; principal. **b.** highest in rank or authority. ~*adv.* **4. in chief.** primarily; especially. **5.** *Arch.* principally.

chiefly ('tʃiːflɪ) *adv.* **1.** especially or essentially; above all. **2.** in general; mainly; mostly. ~*adj.* **3.** of or relating to a chief or chieftain.

chief petty officer *n.* the senior naval rank for personnel without commissioned or warrant rank.

chieftain ('tʃiːftən, -tɪn) *n.* the head or leader of a tribe or clan. —**'chieftaincy** or **'chieftain,ship** *n.*

chief technician *n.* a noncommissioned officer in the Royal Air Force, junior to a flight sergeant.

chiffchaff ('tʃɪf,tʃæf) *n.* a common European warbler with a yellowish-brown plumage.

chiffon (ʃɪ'fɒn, 'ʃɪfɒn) *n.* **1.** a fine almost transparent fabric of silk, nylon, etc. **2.** (*often pl.*) *Now rare.* feminine finery. ~*adj.* **3.** made of chiffon. **4.** (of soufflés, pies, cakes, etc.) having a very light fluffy texture.

chiffonier or **chiffonnier** (,ʃɪfə'nɪə) *n.* **1.** a tall, elegant chest of drawers. **2.** a wide low open-fronted cabinet.

chignon ('ʃiːnjɒn) *n.* an arrangement of long hair in a roll or knot at the back of the head.

chigoe ('tʃɪgəʊ) *n.* a tropical flea, the female of which burrows into the skin of its host, which includes man.

Chihuahua (tʃɪ'wɑːwɑː, -wə) *n.* a breed of tiny dog originally from Mexico, having short hair and protruding eyes.

chilblain ('tʃɪl,bleɪn) *n.* (*usually pl.*) an inflammation of the fingers or toes, caused by exposure to cold. —**'chil,blained** *adj.*

child (tʃaɪld) *n.,* *pl.* **children. 1. a.** a boy or girl between birth and puberty. **b.** (*as modifier*): *child labour.* **2.** a baby or infant. **3.** an unborn baby. **4. with child.** another term for **pregnant. 5.** a human offspring; a son or daughter. Related adj.: **filial. 6.** a childish or immature person. **7.** a member of a family or tribe; descendant: *a child of Israel.* **8.** a person or thing regarded as the product of an influence or environment: *a child of nature.* —**'childless** *adj.* —**'childlessness** *n.*

THESAURUS

chest box, case, casket, coffer, crate, strongbox, trunk

chew 1. bite, champ, crunch, gnaw, grind, masticate, munch **2.** *Fig. Usually with* **over** consider, deliberate upon, meditate, mull (over), muse on, ponder, reflect upon, ruminate, weigh

chic elegant, fashionable, modish, smart, stylish, trendy (*Brit. inf.*)

chide admonish, berate, blame, censure, check, criticize, find fault, give (someone) a row (*Inf.*), lecture, rebuke, reprehend, reprimand, reproach, reprove, scold, tell off (*Inf.*), upbraid

chief 1. *adj.* capital, cardinal, central, especial, essential, foremost, grand, highest, key, leading, main, most important, outstanding, paramount, predominant, pre-eminent,

premier, prevailing, primary, prime, principal, superior, supreme, uppermost, vital **2.** *n.* boss (*Inf.*), captain, chieftain, commander, director, governor, head, leader, lord, manager, master, principal, ringleader, ruler, superintendent, suzerain

chiefly above all, especially, essentially, in general, in the main, mainly, mostly, on the whole, predominantly, primarily, princi-

child benefit n. (in Britain) a regular government payment to parents of children up to a certain age. Australian equivalent: **child endowment**.

childbirth ('tʃaɪld,bɜːθ) n. the act of giving birth to a child.

childhood ('tʃaɪldhʊd) n. the condition of being a child; the period of life before puberty.

childish ('tʃaɪldɪʃ) adj. 1. in the manner of or suitable to a child. 2. foolish or petty: *childish fears.* —'**childishly** adv. —'**childishness** n.

childlike ('tʃaɪld,laɪk) adj. like or befitting a child, as in being innocent, trustful, etc.

child minder n. a person who looks after children, esp. those whose parents are working.

children ('tʃɪldrən) n. the plural of **child**.

child's play n. Inf. something easy to do.

chiliad ('kɪlɪ,æd) n. 1. a group of one thousand. 2. one thousand years.

chill (tʃɪl) n. 1. a moderate coldness. 2. a sensation of coldness resulting from a cold or damp environment, or from a sudden emotional reaction. 3. a feverish cold. 4. a check on enthusiasm or joy. ~adj. 5. another word for **chilly**. ~vb. 6. (tr.) to make or become cold. 7. (tr.) to cool or freeze (food, drinks, etc.). 8. (tr.) **a.** to depress (enthusiasm, etc.). **b.** to discourage. —'**chiller** n. —'**chillingly** adv. —'**chillness** n.

chilli ('tʃɪlɪ) n., pl. **chillies.** the small red hot-tasting pod of a type of capsicum used for flavouring sauces, etc.

chilli con carne ('tʃɪlɪ kon 'kɑːnɪ) n. a highly seasoned Mexican dish of meat, onions, beans, and chilli powder.

chilly ('tʃɪlɪ) adj. **-lier, -liest.** 1. causing or feeling cool or moderately cold. 2. without warmth; unfriendly. 3. (of people) sensitive to cold. —'**chilliness** n.

Chiltern Hundreds ('tʃɪltən) n. Brit. short for **Stewardship of the Chiltern Hundreds;** a nominal office that an M.P. applies for in order to resign his seat.

chimaera (kaɪ'mɪərə, kɪ-) n. a variant spelling of **chimera**.

chime (tʃaɪm) n. 1. an individual bell or the sound it makes when struck. 2. (often pl.) the machinery employed to sound a bell in this way. 3. Also called: **bell.** a percussion instrument consisting of a set of vertical metal tubes of graduated length, suspended in a frame and struck with a hammer. 4. agreement; concord. ~vb. 5. **a.** to sound (a bell) or (of a bell) to be sounded by a clapper or hammer. **b.** to produce (music or sounds) by chiming. 6. (tr.) to indicate or show (time or the hours) by chiming. 7. (intr.; foll. by with) to agree or harmonize. —'**chimer** n.

chimera or **chimaera** (kaɪ'mɪərə, kɪ-) n. 1. (often cap.) Greek myth. a fire-breathing monster with the head of a lion, body of a goat, and tail of a serpent. 2. a fabulous beast made up of parts taken from various animals. 3. a grotesque product of the imagination. 4. Biol. an organism consisting of at least two genetically different kinds of tissue as a result of mutation, grafting, etc.

chimerical (kaɪ'mɛrɪkəl, kɪ-) or **chimeric** adj. 1. wildly fanciful; imaginary. 2. given to or indulging in fantasies. —chi'**merically** adv.

chimney ('tʃɪmnɪ) n. 1. a vertical structure of brick, masonry, or steel that carries smoke or steam away from a fire, engine, etc. 2. another name for **flue**[1] (sense 1). 3. an open-ended glass tube fitting around the flame of an oil or gas lamp in order to exclude draughts. 4. Brit. a fireplace, esp. an old and large one. 5. the vent of a volcano. 6. Mountaineering. a fissure large enough for a person's body to enter.

chimney sweep or **sweeper** n. a person who cleans soot from chimneys.

chimp (tʃɪmp) n. Inf. short for **chimpanzee.**

chimpanzee (,tʃɪmpæn'ziː) n. a gregarious and intelligent anthropoid ape, inhabiting forests in central W Africa.

chin (tʃɪn) n. 1. the protruding part of the lower jaw. 2. the front part of the face below the lips. 3. **keep one's chin up.** Inf. to keep cheerful under difficult circumstances. 4. **take it on the chin.** Inf. to face squarely up to a defeat, adversity, etc. ~vb. **chinning, chinned.** 5. Gymnastics. to raise one's chin to (a horizontal bar, etc.) when hanging by the arms.

Chin. abbrev. for: 1. China. 2. Chinese.

china ('tʃaɪnə) n. 1. ceramic ware of a type originally from China. 2. any porcelain or similar ware. 3. cups, saucers, etc., collectively. 4. (modifier) made of china.

china clay n. another name for **kaolin.**

Chinaman ('tʃaɪnəmən) n., pl. **-men.** 1. a native or inhabitant of China. 2. Cricket. a ball bowled by a left-handed bowler to a right-handed batsman that spins from off to leg.

Chinatown ('tʃaɪnə,taʊn) n. a quarter of any city or town outside China with a predominantly Chinese population.

chincherinchee (,tʃɪntʃərɪn'tʃiː, -'rɪntʃɪ) n. a bulbous South African liliaceous plant, having long spikes of white or yellow long-lasting flowers.

chinchilla (tʃɪn'tʃɪlə) n. 1. a small gregarious rodent, inhabiting mountainous regions of South America. It is bred in captivity for its soft silvery grey fur. 2. the highly valued fur of this animal. 3. a thick napped woollen cloth used for coats.

chine[1] (tʃaɪn) n. 1. the backbone. 2. the backbone of an animal with adjoining meat, cut for cooking. 3. a ridge or crest of land. ~vb. 4. (tr.) to cut (meat) along or across the backbone.

chine[2] (tʃaɪn) n. Southern Brit. dialect. a deep fissure in the wall of a cliff.

Chinese (tʃaɪ'niːz) adj. 1. of, relating to, or characteristic of China, its people, or their languages. ~n. 2. (pl. **-nese**) a native or inhabitant of China or a descendant of one. 3. any of the languages of China.

Chinese lantern n. 1. a collapsible lantern made of thin coloured paper. 2. an Asian plant, cultivated for its attractive orange-red inflated calyx.

Chinese puzzle n. 1. an intricate puzzle, esp. one consisting of boxes within boxes. 2. a complicated problem.

chink[1] (tʃɪŋk) n. 1. a small narrow opening, such as a fissure or crack. 2. **chink in one's armour.** a small but fatal weakness.

chink[2] (tʃɪŋk) vb. 1. to make or cause to make a light ringing sound, as by the striking of glasses or coins. ~n. 2. such a sound.

chinless wonder ('tʃɪnlɪs) n. Brit. inf. a person, esp. upper-class, lacking strength of character.

chinoiserie (ʃiːn,wɑːzə'riː, -'zɔːrɪ) n. 1. a style of decorative or fine art based on imitations of Chinese motifs. 2. an object or objects in this style.

chinook (tʃɪ'nuːk, -'nʊk) n. 1. a warm dry southwesterly wind blowing down the eastern slopes of the Rocky Mountains. 2. a warm moist wind blowing onto the Washington and Oregon coasts from the sea.

Chinook (tʃɪ'nuːk, -'nʊk) n. 1. (pl. **-nook** or **-nooks**) a North American Indian people of the Pacific coast near the Columbia River. 2. the Chinookan language of this people.

Chinook salmon n. a Pacific salmon valued as a food fish.

chintz (tʃɪnts) n. a printed, patterned cotton fabric, with

THESAURUS

pally, usually

child babe, baby, bairn (Scot.), brat, chit, descendant, infant, issue, juvenile, kid (Inf.), little one, minor, nipper (Inf.), nursling, offspring, progeny, suckling, toddler, tot, wean (Scot.), youngster (Inf.)

childbirth accouchement, child-bearing, confinement, delivery, labour, lying-in, parturition, travail

childhood boyhood, girlhood, immaturity, infancy, minority, schooldays, youth

childish boyish, foolish, frivolous, girlish, immature, infantile, juvenile, puerile, silly,

simple, trifling, weak, young

childlike artless, credulous, guileless, ingenuous, innocent, naive, simple, trustful, trusting, unfeigned

chill adj. 1. biting, bleak, chilly, cold, freezing, frigid, raw, sharp, wintry 2. Fig. aloof, cool, depressing, distant, frigid, hostile, stony, unfriendly, ungenial, unresponsive, unwelcoming ~v. 3. congeal, cool, freeze, refrigerate 4. Fig. dampen, deject, depress, dishearten, dismay ~n. 5. bite, cold, coldness, coolness, crispness, frigidity, nip, rawness, sharpness

chilly 1. blowy, breezy, brisk, cool, crisp, draughty, fresh, nippy, penetrating, sharp 2. frigid, hostile, unfriendly, unresponsive, unsympathetic, unwelcoming

chime boom, clang, dong, jingle, peal, ring, sound, strike, tinkle, tintinnabulate, toll

china ceramics, crockery, porcelain, pottery, service, tableware, ware

chink aperture, cleft, crack, cranny, crevice, cut, fissure, flaw, gap, opening, rift

glazed finish.

chintzy ('tʃɪntsɪ) *adj.* **chintzier, chintziest. 1.** of, resembling, or covered with chintz. **2.** *Brit. inf.* typical of the decor associated with the use of chintz soft furnishings.

chinwag ('tʃɪn,wæg) *n. Brit. inf.* a chat.

chip (tʃɪp) *n.* **1.** a small piece removed by chopping, cutting, or breaking. **2.** a mark left after a small piece has been broken off something. **3.** (in some games) a counter used to represent money. **4.** a thin strip of potato fried in deep fat. **5.** the U.S. name for **crisp** (sense 10). **6.** *Sport.* a shot, kick, etc., lofted into the air, and travelling only a short distance. **7.** *Electronics.* a tiny wafer of semiconductor material, such as silicon, processed to form a type of integrated circuit or component such as a transistor. **8.** a thin strip of wood or straw used for making woven hats, baskets, etc. **9.** *N.Z.* a container for soft fruit, made of thin sheets of wood; punnet. **10. chip off the old block.** *Inf.* a person who resembles one of his or her parents in behaviour. **11. have a chip on one's shoulder.** *Inf.* to be aggressive or bear a grudge. **12. have had one's chips.** *Brit. inf.* to be defeated, condemned to die, killed, etc. **13. when the chips are down.** *Inf.* at a time of crisis. ~*vb.* **chipping, chipped. 14.** to break small pieces from or become broken off in small pieces: *will the paint chip?* **15.** (*tr.*) to break or cut into small pieces: *to chip ice.* **16.** (*tr.*) to shape by chipping. **17.** *Austral.* to dig or weed (a crop) with a hoe. **18.** *Sport.* to strike or kick (a ball) in a high arc.

chip-based ('tʃɪp,beɪst) *adj.* using or incorporating microchips in electronic equipment.

chipboard ('tʃɪp,bɔːd) *n.* a thin rigid sheet made of compressed wood particles.

chip in *vb.* (*adv.*) *Inf.* **1.** to contribute (money, time, etc.) to a cause or fund. **2.** (*intr.*) interpose a remark or interrupt with a remark.

chipmunk ('tʃɪp,mʌŋk) *n.* a burrowing rodent of North America and Asia, typically having black-striped yellowish fur and cheek pouches for storing food.

chipolata (,tʃɪpə'lɑːtə) *n. Chiefly Brit.* a small sausage.

Chippendale ('tʃɪpən,deɪl) *adj.* (of furniture) designed, made by, or in the style of Thomas Chippendale (?1718-79), characterized by the use of Chinese and Gothic motifs, cabriole legs, and massive carving.

chirography (kaɪ'rogrəfɪ) *n.* another name for **calligraphy.** —**chi'rographer** (,kaɪrə-'græfɪk) *or* ,**chiro'graphical** *adj.*

chiromancy ('kaɪrə,mænsɪ) *n.* another word for **palmistry.** —'**chiro,mancer** *n.*

chiropody (kɪ'rɒpədɪ) *n.* the treatment of the feet, esp. corns, verrucas, etc. —**chi'ropodist** *n.*

chiropractic (,kaɪrə'præktɪk) *n.* a system of treating bodily disorders by manipulation of the spine and other parts. —'**chiro,practor** *n.*

chirp (tʃɜːp) *vb.* **1.** (*intr.*) (esp. of some birds and insects) to make a short high-pitched sound. **2.** to speak in a lively fashion. ~*n.* **3.** a chirping sound. —'**chirper** *n.* —'**chirpy** *adj.* —'**chirpily** *adv.* —'**chirpiness** *n.*

chirrup ('tʃɪrəp) *vb.* **1.** (*intr.*) (esp. of some birds) to chirp repeatedly. **2.** to make clucking sounds with the lips. ~*n.* **3.** such a sound. —'**chirruper** *n.* —'**chirrupy** *adj.*

chisel ('tʃɪzəl) *n.* **1. a.** a hand tool for working wood, consisting of a flat steel blade with a handle. **b.** a similar tool without a handle for working stone or metal. ~*vb.* **-elling, -elled** *or U.S.* **-eling, -eled. 2.** to carve (wood, stone, metal, etc.) or form (an engraving, statue, etc.) with or as with a chisel. **3.** *Sl.* to cheat or obtain by cheating. —'**chiseller** *n.*

chit¹ (tʃɪt) *n.* **1.** a voucher for a sum of money owed, esp. for food or drink. **2.** Also called: **chitty.** *Chiefly Brit.* **a.** a note or memorandum. **b.** a requisition or receipt.

chit² (tʃɪt) *n. Facetious or derog.* a pert, impudent, or self-confident girl or child.

chitchat ('tʃɪt,tʃæt) *n.* **1.** gossip. ~*vb.* **-chatting, -chatted. 2.** (*intr.*) to gossip.

chitin ('kaɪtɪn) *n.* a polysaccharide that is the principal component of the exoskeletons of arthropods and of the bodies of fungi. —'**chitinous** *adj.*

chitterlings ('tʃɪtəlɪŋz) *or* **chitlings** ('tʃɪtlɪŋz) *pl. n.* (*sometimes sing.*) the intestines of a pig or other animal prepared as a dish.

chivalrous ('ʃɪvəlrəs) *adj.* **1.** gallant; courteous. **2.** involving chivalry. —'**chivalrously** *adv.* —'**chivalrousness** *n.*

chivalry ('ʃɪvəlrɪ) *n., pl.* **-ries. 1.** the combination of qualities expected of an ideal knight, esp. courage, honour, justice, and a readiness to help the weak. **2.** courteous behaviour, esp. towards women. **3.** the medieval system and principles of knighthood. **4.** knights, noblemen, etc., collectively. —'**chivalric** *adj.*

chive (tʃaɪv) *n.* a small Eurasian purple-flowered alliaceous plant, whose long slender hollow leaves are used in cooking. Also called: **chives.**

chivy, chivvy ('tʃɪvɪ), *or* **chevy** ('tʃɛvɪ) *vb.* **chivying, chivied, chivvying, chivvied,** *or* **chevying, chevied.** *Brit.* **1.** (*tr.*) to harass or nag. **2.** (*tr.*) to hunt. **3.** (*intr.*) to run about. ~*n., pl.* **chivies, chivvies,** *or* **chevies. 4.** *Brit.* a hunt. **5.** *Brit. obsolete.* a hunting cry.

chloral ('klɔːrəl) *n.* **1.** a colourless oily liquid with a pungent odour, made from chlorine and acetaldehyde and used in preparing chloral hydrate and DDT. **2.** short for **chloral hydrate.**

chloral hydrate *n.* a colourless crystalline soluble solid produced by the reaction of chloral with water and used as a sedative and hypnotic.

chlorate ('klɔːreɪt, -rɪt) *n.* any salt of chloric acid, containing the monovalent ion ClO_3^-.

chloric ('klɔːrɪk) *adj.* of or containing chlorine in the pentavalent state.

chloride ('klɔːraɪd) *n.* **1.** any salt of hydrochloric acid, containing the chloride ion Cl^-. **2.** any compound containing a chlorine atom, such as methyl chloride, CH_3Cl.

chlorinate ('klɔːrɪ,neɪt) *vb.* (*tr.*) **1.** to combine or treat (a substance) with chlorine. **2.** to disinfect (water) with chlorine. —,**chlorin'ation** *n.* —'**chlorin,ator** *n.*

chlorine ('klɔːriːn) *or* **chlorin** ('klɔːrɪn) *n.* a toxic pungent greenish-yellow gas of the halogen group; occurring only in the combined state, mainly in common salt: used in the manufacture of many organic chemicals, in water purification, and as a disinfectant and bleaching agent. Symbol: Cl; atomic no.: 17; atomic wt.: 35.453.

chloro- *or before a vowel* **chlor-** *combining form.* **1.** indicating the colour green: *chlorophyll.* **2.** chlorine: *chloroform.*

chloroform ('klɔːrə,fɔːm) *n.* a heavy volatile liquid with a sweet taste and odour, used as a solvent and cleansing agent and in refrigerants: formerly used as an inhalation anaesthetic. Formula: $CHCl_3$.

chlorophyll *or U.S.* **chlorophyl** ('klɔːrəfɪl) *n.* the green pigment of plants, occurring in chloroplasts, that traps the energy of sunlight for photosynthesis. —'**chloro,phylloid** *adj.* —**chlorophyllous** (,klɔːrəʊ'fɪləs) *adj.*

chlorosis (klə'rəʊsɪs) *n.* a once-common iron-deficiency disease of adolescent girls, characterized by greenish-yellow skin colour, weakness, and palpitation. Also called: **greensickness.**

chock (tʃɒk) *n.* **1.** a block or wedge of wood used to prevent the sliding or rolling of a heavy object. **2.** *Naut.* **a.** a ringlike device with an opening at the top through which a rope is placed. **b.** a cradle-like support for a boat, barrel, etc. ~*vb.* (*tr.*) **3.** (usually foll. by *up*) *Brit.* to cram full. **4.** to fit with or secure by a chock. **5.** to support (a boat, barrel, etc.) on chocks. ~*adv.* **6.** as closely or tightly as possible: *chock against the wall.*

chock-a-block *adj., adv.* **1.** filled to capacity; in a crammed state. **2.** *Naut.* with the blocks brought close together, as when a tackle is pulled as tight as possible.

chock-full *or* **choke-full** *adj.* (*postpositive*) completely full.

chocolate ('tʃɒkəlɪt, 'tʃɒklɪt, -lət) *n.* **1.** a food preparation made from roasted ground cacao seeds, usually

---

THESAURUS

chip 1. *n.* dent, flake, flaw, fragment, nick, notch, paring, scrap, scratch, shard, shaving, sliver, wafer **2.** *v.* chisel, damage, gash, nick, whittle
chip in contribute, donate, go Dutch (*Inf.*), interpose, interrupt, pay, subscribe

chivalrous bold, brave, courageous, courteous, courtly, gallant, gentlemanly, heroic, high-minded, honourable, intrepid, knightly, magnanimous, true, valiant
chivalry courage, courtesy, courtliness, gallantry, gentlemanliness, knight-errantry, knighthood, politeness

chivvy annoy, badger, harass, hassle (*Inf.*), hound, nag, pester, plague, pressure (*Inf.*), prod, torment

sweetened and flavoured. **2.** a drink or sweetmeat made from this. **3.** a deep brown colour. —'**chocolaty** adj.

choice (tʃɔɪs) n. **1.** the act or an instance of choosing or selecting. **2.** the opportunity or power of choosing. **3.** a person or thing chosen or that may be chosen: *he was a possible choice.* **4.** an alternative action or possibility: *what choice did I have?* **5.** a supply from which to select. ~adj. **6.** of superior quality; excellent: *choice wine.* —'**choicely** adv. —'**choiceness** n.

choir (kwaɪə) n. **1.** an organized group of singers, esp. for singing in church services. **2.** the part of a cathedral, abbey, or church in front of the altar and used by the choir and clergy. **3.** a number of instruments of the same family playing together: *a brass choir.* **4.** Also called: **choir organ.** one of the manuals on an organ controlling a set of soft sweet-toned pipes.

choirboy ('kwaɪəˌbɔɪ) n. a young boy who sings the treble part in a church choir.

choke (tʃəʊk) vb. **1.** (tr.) to hinder or stop the breathing of (a person or animal), esp. by constricting the windpipe or by asphyxiation. **2.** (intr.) to have trouble or fail in breathing, swallowing, or speaking. **3.** (tr.) to block or clog up (a passage, pipe, street, etc.). **4.** (tr.) to retard the growth or action of: *the weeds are choking my plants.* **5.** (tr.) to enrich the petrol-air mixture by reducing the air supply to (a carburettor, petrol engine, etc.) ~n. **6.** the act or sound of choking. **7.** a device in the carburettor of a petrol engine that enriches the petrol-air mixture by reducing the air supply. **8.** any mechanism for reducing the flow of a fluid in a pipe, tube, etc. **9.** Also called: **choke coil.** Electronics. an inductor having a relatively high impedance, used to prevent the passage of high frequencies or to smooth the output of a rectifier. —'**choky** or '**chokey** adj.

choke back or **down** vb. (tr., adv.) to suppress (anger, tears, etc.).

choke up vb. (tr., adv.) **1.** to block (a drain, pipe, etc.) completely. **2.** Inf. (usually passive) to overcome (a person) with emotion.

cholera ('kɒlərə) n. an acute intestinal infection characterized by severe diarrhoea, cramp, etc.: caused by ingestion of water or food contaminated with the bacterium *Vibrio comma.* —**choleraic** (ˌkɒlə'reɪɪk) adj.

cholesterol (kə'lɛstəˌrɒl) or **cholesterin** (kə'lɛstərɪn) n. a white or pale yellow almost insoluble sterol found in all animal tissues, blood, bile, and animal fats.

choline ('kəʊliːn, -ɪn, 'kɒl-) n. a colourless viscous soluble alkaline substance present in animal tissues, esp. as a constituent of lecithin.

chomp (tʃɒmp) or **chump** vb. **1.** to chew (food) noisily; champ. ~n. **2.** the act or sound of chewing in this manner.

choose (tʃuːz) vb. **choosing, chose, chosen.** **1.** to select (a person, thing, course of action, etc.) from a number of alternatives. **2.** (tr.; takes a clause as object or an infinitive) to consider it desirable or proper: *I don't choose to read that book.* **3.** (intr.) to like; please: *you may stand if you choose.* —'**chooser** n.

choosy ('tʃuːzɪ) adj. **choosier, choosiest.** Inf. particular in making a choice; difficult to please.

chop¹ (tʃɒp) vb. **chopping, chopped.** **1.** (often foll. by *down* or *off*) to cut (something) with a blow from an axe or other sharp tool. **2.** (tr.; often foll. by *up*) to cut into pieces. **3.** (tr.) Brit. inf. to dispense with or reduce. **4.** (intr.) to move quickly or violently. **5.** Tennis, cricket, etc. to hit (a ball) sharply downwards. **6.** Boxing, karate, etc. to punch or strike (an opponent) with a short sharp blow. ~n. **7.** a cutting blow. **8.** the act or an instance of chopping. **9.** a piece chopped off. **10.** a slice of mutton, lamb, or pork, generally including a rib. **11.** Austral. sl. a share (esp. in **get** or **hop in for one's chop**). **12.** Austral & N.Z. a competition of skill and speed in chopping logs.

13. Sport. a sharp downward blow or stroke. **14. not much chop.** Austral. inf. not much good; poor. **15. the chop.** Sl., chiefly Brit. dismissal from employment.

chop² (tʃɒp) vb. **chopping, chopped.** **1.** (intr.) to change direction suddenly; vacillate (esp. in **chop and change**). **2. chop logic.** to argue over small points.

chop chop adv. pidgin English for **quickly.**

chophouse ('tʃɒpˌhaʊs) n. a restaurant specializing in steaks, grills, chops, etc.

chopper ('tʃɒpə) n. **1.** Chiefly Brit. a small hand axe. **2.** a butcher's cleaver. **3.** a person or thing that cuts or chops. **4.** an informal name for a **helicopter. 5.** a device for periodically interrupting an electric current or beam of radiation to produce a pulsed current or beam. **6.** a type of bicycle or motorcycle with very high handlebars. **7.** N.Z. a child's bicycle. **8.** Sl., chiefly U.S. a sub-machine-gun.

choppy ('tʃɒpɪ) adj. **-pier, -piest.** (of the sea, weather, etc.) fairly rough. —'**choppily** adv. —'**choppiness** n.

chops (tʃɒps) pl. n. **1.** the jaws or cheeks; jowls. **2.** the mouth. **3. lick one's chops.** Inf. to anticipate with pleasure.

chopsticks ('tʃɒpstɪks) pl. n. a pair of thin sticks, of ivory, wood, etc., used as eating utensils by the Chinese, Japanese, etc.

chop suey ('suːɪ) n. a Chinese-style dish originating in the U.S., consisting of meat, bean sprouts, etc., stewed and served with rice.

choral ('kɔːrəl) adj. relating to, sung by, or designed for a chorus or choir. —'**chorally** adv.

chorale or **choral** (kɒ'rɑːl) n. **1.** a slow stately hymn tune. **2.** Chiefly U.S. a choir or chorus.

chord¹ (kɔːd) n. **1.** Maths. a straight line connecting two points on a curve or curved surface. **2.** Engineering. one of the principal members of a truss, esp. one that lies along the top or the bottom. **3.** Anat. a variant spelling of **cord. 4.** an emotional response, esp. one of sympathy: *the story struck the right chord.*

chord² (kɔːd) n. **1.** the simultaneous sounding of a group of musical notes, usually three or more in number. ~vb. **2.** (tr.) to provide (a melodic line) with chords. —'**chordal** adj.

chore (tʃɔː) n. **1.** a small routine task, esp. a domestic one. **2.** an unpleasant task.

-chore n. combining form. (in botany) indicating a plant that is distributed by a certain means: *anemochore.* —**-chorous** or **-choric** adj. combining form.

chorea (kɒ'rɪə) n. a disorder of the central nervous system characterized by uncontrollable irregular brief jerky movements. Nontechnical name: **Saint Vitus's dance.**

choreography (ˌkɒrɪ'ɒɡrəfɪ) or **choregraphy** (kɒ'rɛɡrəfɪ) n. **1.** the composition of dance steps and sequences for ballet and stage dancing. **2.** the steps and sequences of a ballet or dance. **3.** the notation representing such steps. **4.** the art of dancing. —ˌchoreˈographer or choˈregrapher n. —choreographic (ˌkɒrɪə'ɡræfɪk) or choregraphic (ˌkɒrɛ'ɡræfɪk) adj. —ˌchoreoˈgraphically or ˌchoreˈgraphically adv.

chorister ('kɒrɪstə) n. a singer in a choir, esp. a choirboy.

chortle ('tʃɔːtəl) vb. **1.** (intr.) Inf. to chuckle gleefully. ~n. **2.** Inf. a gleeful chuckle. —'**chortler** n.

chorus ('kɔːrəs) n., pl. **-ruses. 1.** a large choir of singers or a piece of music composed for such a choir. **2.** a body of singers or dancers who perform together. **3.** a section of a song in which a soloist is joined by a group of singers, esp. in a recurring refrain. **4.** an intermediate section of a pop song, blues, etc., as distinct from the verse. **5.** Jazz. any of a series of variations on a theme. **6.** (in ancient Greece) **a.** a lyric poem sung by a group of danc-

choice 1. n. alternative, discrimination, election, option, pick, preference, say, selection, variety **2.** adj. best, dainty, elect, elite, excellent, exclusive, exquisite, hand-picked, nice, precious, prime, prize, rare, select, special, superior, uncommon, unusual, valuable

choke asphyxiate, bar, block, clog, close, congest, constrict, dam, obstruct, occlude, overpower, smother, stifle, stop, strangle, suffocate, suppress, throttle

choleric angry, bad-tempered, fiery, has-

ty, hot, hot-tempered, ill-tempered, irascible, irritable, passionate, petulant, quick-tempered, testy, touchy

choose adopt, cull, designate, desire, elect, espouse, fix on, opt for, pick, predestine, prefer, see fit, select, settle upon, single out, take, wish

choosy discriminating, exacting, faddy, fastidious, finicky, fussy, particular, selective

chop 1. v. axe, cleave, cut, fell, hack, hew, lop, sever, shear, slash, truncate **2.** n. the

chop Sl. dismissal, one's cards, sacking (Inf.), termination, the axe (Inf.), the boot (Sl.), the sack (Inf.)

choppy blustery, broken, rough, ruffled, squally, tempestuous

chop up cube, dice, divide, fragment, mince

chore burden, duty, errand, fag (Inf.), job, task

chortle cackle, chuckle, crow, guffaw

ers, originally as a religious rite. **b.** an ode or series of odes sung by a group of actors. **c.** the actors who sang the chorus and commented on the action of the play. **7. a.** (esp. in Elizabethan drama) the actor who spoke the prologue, etc. **b.** the part spoken by this actor. **8.** a group of people or animals producing words or sounds simultaneously. **9.** any speech, song, or utterance produced by a group of people or animals simultaneously: *the dawn chorus.* **10. in chorus.** in unison. ~*vb.* **11.** to speak, sing, or utter (words, sounds, etc.) in unison.

chorus girl   *n.* a girl who dances or sings in the chorus of a musical comedy, revue, etc.

chose (tʃəʊz) *vb.* the past tense of **choose.**

chosen ('tʃəʊzən) *vb.* **1.** the past participle of **choose.** ~*adj.* **2.** selected or picked out, esp. for some special quality.

chough (tʃʌf) *n.* a large black passerine bird of parts of Europe, Asia, and Africa, with a long downward-curving red bill: family *Corvidae* (crows).

choux pastry (ʃuː) *n.* a very light pastry made with eggs, used for eclairs, etc.

chow (tʃaʊ) *n.* **1.** *Inf.* food. **2.** short for **chow-chow** (sense 1). **3.** *Austral. & N.Z. obs.* a derogatory term for **Chinese.**

chow-chow   *n.* **1.** a thick-coated breed of dog with a curled tail, originally from China. Often shortened to **chow. 2.** a Chinese preserve of ginger, orange peel, etc. in syrup. **3.** a mixed vegetable pickle.

chowder ('tʃaʊdə) *n. Chiefly U.S.* a thick soup or stew containing clams or fish.

chow mein (meɪn) *n.* a Chinese-American dish, consisting of mushrooms, meat, shrimps, etc., served with fried noodles.

Chr.   *abbrev. for:* **1.** Christ. **2.** Christian.

chrism *or* **chrisom** ('krɪzəm) *n.* a mixture of olive oil and balsam used for sacramental anointing in the Greek Orthodox and Roman Catholic Churches. —**chrismal** ('krɪzməl) *adj.*

Christ (kraɪst) *n.* **1.** Jesus of Nazareth (Jesus Christ), regarded by Christians as fulfilling Old Testament prophecies of the Messiah. **2.** the Messiah or anointed one of God as the subject of Old Testament prophecies. **3.** an image or picture of Christ. ~*interj.* **4.** *Taboo sl.* an oath expressing annoyance, surprise, etc. ~See also **Jesus.** —**'Christly** *adj.*

christen ('krɪsən) *vb.* (*tr.*) **1.** to give a Christian name to in baptism as a sign of incorporation into a Christian Church. **2.** another word for **baptize. 3.** to give a name to anything, esp. with some ceremony. **4.** *Inf.* to use for the first time. —**'christener** *n.* —**'christening** *n.*

Christendom ('krɪsəndəm) *n.* the collective body of Christians throughout the world.

Christian ('krɪstʃən) *n.* **1. a.** a person who believes in and follows Jesus Christ. **b.** a member of a Christian Church or denomination. **2.** *Inf.* a person who possesses Christian virtues. ~*adj.* **3.** of, relating to, or derived from Jesus Christ, his teachings, example, or his followers. **4.** (*sometimes not cap.*) exhibiting kindness or goodness. —**'christianly** *adj., adv.*

Christian Era   *n.* the period beginning with the year of Christ's birth.

Christianity (ˌkrɪstɪ'ænɪtɪ) *n.* **1.** the Christian religion. **2.** Christian beliefs or practices. **3.** a less common word for **Christendom.**

Christianize *or* **-ise** ('krɪstʃəˌnaɪz) *vb.* **1.** (*tr.*) to make Christian or convert to Christianity. **2.** (*tr.*) to imbue with Christian principles, spirit, or outlook. —ˌChristiani'zation *or* -i'sation *n.* —'Christian,izer *or* -ˌiser *n.*

Christian name   *n. Brit.* a personal or given name. It is formally given to Christians at christening.

Christian Science   *n.* the religious system of the Church of Christ, Scientist, founded by Mary Baker Eddy (1866), and emphasizing spiritual healing. —**'Christian 'Scientist** *n.*

Christlike ('kraɪst,laɪk) *adj.* resembling the spirit of Jesus Christ. —**'Christ,likeness** *n.*

Christmas ('krɪsməs) *n.* **a.** the annual commemoration by Christians of the birth of Jesus Christ, on Dec. 25.

b. Also called: **Christmas Day.** Dec. 25, observed as a day of secular celebrations when gifts and greetings are exchanged. **c.** (*as modifier*): *Christmas celebrations.*

Christmas box   *n.* a tip or present given at Christmas, esp. to postmen, tradesmen, etc.

Christmas Eve   *n.* the evening or the whole day before Christmas Day.

Christmas pudding   *n. Brit.* a rich steamed pudding containing suet, dried fruit, spices, etc. Also called: **plum pudding.**

Christmas rose   *n.* an evergreen plant of S Europe and W Asia, with white or pinkish winter-blooming flowers. Also called: **hellebore, winter rose.**

Christmas tree   *n.* **1.** an evergreen tree or an imitation of one, decorated as part of Christmas celebrations. **2.** Also called (Austral.): **Christmas bush.** any of various trees or shrubs flowering at Christmas and used for decoration.

chromate ('krəʊmeɪt) *n.* any salt or ester of chromic acid.

chromatic (krə'mætɪk) *adj.* **1.** of, relating to, or characterized by a colour or colours. **2.** *Music.* **a.** involving the sharpening or flattening of notes or the use of such notes in chords and harmonic progressions. **b.** of or relating to the chromatic scale or an instrument capable of producing it. —**chro'matically** *adv.* —**chro'maticism** *n.* —**chromaticity** (ˌkrəʊmə'tɪsɪtɪ) *n.*

chromatics (krəʊ'mætɪks) *n.* (*functioning as sing.*) the science of colour.

chromatic scale   *n.* a twelve-note scale including all the semitones of the octave.

chromatin ('krəʊmətɪn) *n.* the part of the nucleus that consists of DNA, RNA, and proteins, forms the chromosomes, and stains with basic dyes.

chromato- *or before a vowel* **chromat-**   *combining form.* **1.** indicating colour or coloured: *chromatophore.* **2.** indicating chromatin: *chromatolysis.*

chromatography (ˌkrəʊmə'tɒɡrəfɪ) *n.* the technique of separating and analysing the components of a mixture of liquids or gases by selective adsorption in a column of powder (**column chromatography**) or on a strip of paper (**paper chromatography**).

chrome (krəʊm) *n.* **1. a.** another word for **chromium,** esp. when present in a pigment or dye. **b.** (*as modifier*): *a chrome dye.* **2.** anything plated with chromium. **3.** a pigment or dye that contains chromium. ~*vb.* **4.** to plate or be plated with chromium. **5.** to treat or be treated with a chromium compound, as in dyeing or tanning.

-chrome   *n. and adj. combining form.* colour, coloured, or pigment: *monochrome.*

chromic ('krəʊmɪk) *adj.* **1.** of or containing chromium in the trivalent state. **2.** of or derived from chromic acid.

chromite ('krəʊmaɪt) *n.* a brownish-black mineral consisting of a ferrous chromic oxide in crystalline form: the only commercial source of chromium. Formula: $FeCr_2O_4$.

chromium ('krəʊmɪəm) *n.* a hard grey metallic element, used in steel alloys and electroplating to increase hardness and corrosion-resistance. Symbol: Cr; atomic no.: 24; atomic wt.: 51.996.

chromo- *or before a vowel* **chrom-**   *combining form.* **1.** indicating colour, coloured, or pigment: *chromogen.* **2.** indicating chromium: *chromyl.*

chromosome ('krəʊmə,səʊm) *n.* any of the microscopic rod-shaped structures that appear in a cell nucleus during cell division, consisting of nucleoprotein arranged into units (genes) that are responsible for the transmission of hereditary characteristics. —ˌchromo'somal *adj.*

chromosphere ('krəʊmə,sfɪə) *n.* a gaseous layer of the sun's atmosphere extending from the photosphere to the corona. —**chromospheric** (ˌkrəʊmə'sfɛrɪk) *adj.*

chromous ('krəʊməs) *adj.* of or containing chromium in the divalent state.

chron. *or* **chronol.**   *abbrev. for:* **1.** chronological. **2.** chronology.

Chron.   *Bible. abbrev. for* Chronicles.

THESAURUS

chorus 1. choir, choristers, ensemble, singers, vocalists **2.** burden, refrain, response, strain **3.** accord, concert, harmony,

unison

christen baptize, call, designate, dub, name, style, term, title

chronic ('krɒnɪk) adj. 1. continuing for a long time; constantly recurring. 2. (of a disease) developing slowly, or of long duration. Cf. **acute** (sense 7). 3. inveterate; habitual: a chronic smoker. 4. Inf. a. very bad: the play was chronic. b. very serious: he left her in a chronic condition. —'**chronically** adv. —**chronicity** (krɒ'nɪsɪtɪ) n.

chronicle ('krɒnɪkəl) n. 1. a record or register of events in chronological order. ~vb. 2. (tr.) to record in or as if in a chronicle. —'**chronicler** n.

chrono- or before a vowel **chron-** combining form. time: chronology.

chronological (,krɒnə'lɒdʒɪkəl, ,krəʊ-) or **chronologic** adj. 1. (esp. of a sequence of events) arranged in order of occurrence. 2. relating to or in accordance with chronology. —,**chrono'logically** adv.

chronology (krə'nɒlədʒɪ) n., pl. **-gies.** 1. the determination of the proper sequence of past events. 2. the arrangement of dates, events, etc., in order of occurrence. 3. a table of events arranged in order of occurrence. —**chro'nologist** n.

chronometer (krə'nɒmɪtə) n. a timepiece designed to be accurate in all conditions of temperature, pressure, etc., used esp. at sea. —**chronometric** (,krɒnə'mɛtrɪk) or ,**chrono'metrical** adj. —,**chrono'metrically** adv.

chrysalis ('krɪsəlɪs) n., pl. **chrysalises** or **chrysalides** (krɪ'sælɪ,diːz). 1. the pupa of a moth or butterfly, in a case or cocoon. 2. anything in the process of developing.

chrysanthemum (krɪ'sænθəməm) n. 1. any of various widely cultivated plants of the composite family, having brightly coloured showy flower heads in autumn. 2. any other plant of the genus Chrysanthemum, such as the ox-eye daisy.

chrysoberyl ('krɪsə,bɛrɪl) n. a rare very hard greenish-yellow mineral consisting of beryllium aluminate: used as a gemstone. Formula: $BeAl_2O_4$.

chrysolite ('krɪsə,laɪt) n. a brown or yellowish-green olivine: used as a gemstone.

chrysoprase ('krɪsə,preɪz) n. an apple-green variety of chalcedony: a gemstone.

chub (tʃʌb) n., pl. **chub** or **chubs.** 1. a common European freshwater cyprinid game fish, having a cylindrical dark-greenish body. 2. any of various North American fishes, esp. certain whitefishes and minnows.

chubby ('tʃʌbɪ) adj. **-bier, -biest.** (esp. of the human form) plump and round. —'**chubbiness** n.

chuck[1] (tʃʌk) vb. (mainly tr.) 1. Inf. to throw. 2. to pat affectionately, esp. under the chin. 3. Inf. (sometimes foll. by in or up) to give up; reject: he chucked up his job. ~n. 4. a throw or toss. 5. a pat under the chin. 6. the **chuck.** Inf. dismissal.

chuck[2] (tʃʌk) n. 1. Also called: **chuck steak.** a cut of beef from the neck to the shoulder blade. 2. a device that holds a workpiece in a lathe or tool in a drill.

chuckle ('tʃʌkəl) vb. (intr.) 1. to laugh softly or to oneself. 2. (of animals, esp. hens) to make a clucking sound. ~n. 3. a partly suppressed laugh. —'**chuckler** n.

chucklehead ('tʃʌkəl,hɛd) n. Inf. a stupid person; blockhead; dolt.

chuff[1] (tʃʌf) n. 1. a puffing sound as of a steam engine. ~vb. 2. (intr.) to move while emitting such sounds.

chuff[2] (tʃʌf) vb. (tr.; usually passive) Brit. sl. to please or delight: he was chuffed by his pay rise.

chug (tʃʌg) n. 1. a short dull sound, such as that made by an engine. ~vb. **chugging, chugged.** 2. (intr.) (of an engine, etc.) to operate while making such sounds.

chukker or **chukka** ('tʃʌkə) n. Polo. a period of continuous play, generally lasting 7½ minutes.

chum (tʃʌm) n. 1. Inf. a close friend. ~vb. **chumming, chummed.** 2. (intr.; usually foll. by up with) to be or become an intimate friend (of).

chummy ('tʃʌmɪ) adj. **-mier, -est.** Inf. friendly. —'**chummily** adv. —'**chumminess** n.

chump (tʃʌmp) n. 1. Inf. a stupid person. 2. a thick heavy block of wood. 3. the thick blunt end of anything, esp. of a piece of meat. 4. Brit. sl. the head (esp. in **off one's chump**).

chunk (tʃʌŋk) n. 1. a thick solid piece, as of meat, wood, etc. 2. a considerable amount.

chunky ('tʃʌŋkɪ) adj. **chunkier, chunkiest.** 1. thick and short. 2. containing thick pieces. 3. Chiefly Brit. (of clothes, esp. knitwear) made of thick bulky material. —'**chunkiness** n.

church (tʃɜːtʃ) n. 1. a building for public worship, esp. Christian worship. 2. an occasion of public worship. 3. the clergy as distinguished from the laity. 4. (usually cap.) institutionalized forms of religion as a political or social force: conflict between Church and State. 5. (usually cap.) the collective body of all Christians. 6. (often cap.) a particular Christian denomination or group. 7. (often cap.) the Christian religion. ~Related adj.: **ecclesiastical.** ~vb. (tr.) 8. Church of England. to bring (someone, esp. a woman after childbirth) to church for special ceremonies.

Church Commissioners pl. n. Brit. a group of representatives of Church and State that administers the property of the Church of England.

churchgoer ('tʃɜːtʃ,gəʊə) n. a person who attends church regularly. —'**church,going** n.

churchly ('tʃɜːtʃlɪ) adj. appropriate to or associated with the church. —'**churchliness** n.

Church of England n. the reformed established state Church in England, with the Sovereign as its temporal head.

churchwarden (,tʃɜːtʃ'wɔːdən) n. 1. Church of England, Episcopal Church. one of two assistants of a parish priest who administer the secular affairs of the church. 2. a long-stemmed tobacco pipe made of clay.

churchyard ('tʃɜːtʃ,jɑːd) n. the grounds round a church, used as a graveyard.

churl (tʃɜːl) n. 1. a surly ill-bred person. 2. a farm labourer. 3. a miserly person. —'**churlish** adj.

churn (tʃɜːn) n. 1. Brit. a large container for milk. 2. a vessel or machine in which cream or whole milk is vigorously agitated to produce butter. ~vb. 3. a. to agitate (milk or cream) to make butter. b. to make (butter) by this process. 4. (sometimes foll. by up) to move or cause to move with agitation.

chute[1] (ʃuːt) n. 1. an inclined channel or vertical passage down which water, parcels, coal, etc., may be dropped. 2. a steep slope, used as a slide as for toboggans. 3. a slide into a swimming pool. 4. a rapid or waterfall.

chute[2] (ʃuːt) n., vb. Inf. short for **parachute.** —'**chutist** n.

chutney ('tʃʌtnɪ) n. a pickle of Indian origin, made from fruit, vinegar, spices, sugar, etc.: mango chutney.

chyle (kaɪl) n. a milky fluid composed of lymph and emulsified fat globules, formed in the small intestine during digestion. —**chylaceous** (kaɪ'leɪʃəs) or '**chylous** adj.

chyme (kaɪm) n. the thick fluid mass of partially digested food that leaves the stomach. —'**chymous** adj.

chypre French. ('ʃiːpr) n. a perfume made from sandalwood.

Ci abbrev. for curie.

THESAURUS

chronic 1. confirmed, deep-rooted, deep-seated, habitual, incessant, incurable, ineradicable, ingrained, inveterate, persistent 2. Inf. appalling, atrocious, awful, dreadful

chronicle 1. n. account, annals, diary, history, journal, narrative, record, register, story 2. v. enter, narrate, put on record, record, recount, register, relate, report, set down, tell

chronicler annalist, diarist, historian, historiographer, narrator, recorder, reporter, scribe

chronological consecutive, historical, in sequence, ordered, progressive, sequential

chubby buxom, flabby, fleshy, plump, podgy, portly, rotund, round, stout, tubby

chuck cast, discard, fling, heave, hurl, pitch, shy, sling, throw, toss

chuckle chortle, crow, exult, giggle, laugh, snigger, titter

chum companion, comrade, crony, friend, mate (Inf.), pal (Inf.)

chunk block, dollop (Inf.), hunk, lump, mass, piece, portion, slab, wad, wodge (Inf.)

chunky beefy (Inf.), dumpy, stocky, stubby, thickset

churl 1. boor, lout, oaf 2. bumpkin, clodhopper (Inf.), clown, hillbilly, peasant, rustic,

yokel 3. curmudgeon, miser, niggard, skinflint

churlish 1. boorish, brusque, crabbed, harsh, ill-tempered, impolite, loutish, morose, oafish, rude, sullen, surly, uncivil, unmannerly, vulgar 2. close-fisted, illiberal, inhospitable, mean, miserly, niggardly, unneighbourly, unsociable

churlishness boorishness, crassness, crudeness, loutishness, oafishness, rudeness, surliness, uncouthness

churn agitate, beat, boil, convulse, foam, froth, seethe, stir up, swirl, toss

C.I. *abbrev. for* Channel Islands.

C.I.A. *abbrev. for* Central Intelligence Agency; a federal U.S. bureau created in 1947 to coordinate and conduct espionage and intelligence activities.

cicada (sɪ'kɑːdə) *or* **cicala** *n., pl.* **-das, -dae** (-diː) *or* **-las, -le** (-lɛ). any large broad insect, most common in warm regions, having membranous wings: the males produce a high-pitched drone by vibration of a pair of drumlike abdominal organs.

cicatrix ('sɪkətrɪks) *n., pl.* **cicatrices** (ˌsɪkə'traɪsiːz). 1. the tissue that forms in a wound during healing; scar. 2. a scar on a plant indicating the former point of attachment of a part, esp. a leaf. —**cicatricial** (ˌsɪkə'trɪʃəl) *adj.*

cicerone (ˌsɪsə'rəʊnɪ, ˌtʃɪtʃ-) *n., pl.* **-nes** *or* **-ni** (-nɪ). a person who conducts and informs sightseers.

C.I.D. (in Britain) *abbrev. for* Criminal Investigation Department; the detective division of a police force.

-cide *n. combining form.* 1. indicating a person or thing that kills: *insecticide.* 2. indicating a killing; murder: *homicide.* —**-cidal** *adj. combining form.*

cider *or* **cyder** ('saɪdə) *n.* 1. an alcoholic drink made from the fermented juice of apples. 2. Also called: **sweet cider.** *U.S.* an unfermented drink made from apple juice.

c.i.f. *or* **C.I.F.** *abbrev. for* cost, insurance, and freight (included in the price quoted).

cigar (sɪ'gɑː) *n.* a cylindrical roll of cured tobacco leaves, for smoking.

cigarette *or U.S.* (*sometimes*) **cigaret** (ˌsɪgə'rɛt) *n.* a short tightly rolled cylinder of tobacco, wrapped in thin paper for smoking.

cigarette card *n.* a small picture card, formerly given away with cigarettes, now collected as a hobby.

C in C *or* **C.-in-C.** *Mil. abbrev. for* Commander in Chief.

cinch (sɪntʃ) *n.* 1. *Sl.* an easy task. 2. *Sl.* a certainty. 3. a U.S. name for **girth** (sense 2). 4. *U.S. inf.* a firm grip. ~*vb.* 5. (often foll. by *up*) *U.S.* to fasten a girth around (a horse). 6. (*tr.*) *Inf.* to make sure of. 7. (*tr.*) *Inf., chiefly U.S.* to get a firm grip on.

cinchona (sɪŋ'kəʊnə) *n.* 1. any tree or shrub of the South American genus *Cinchona,* having medicinal bark. 2. the dried bark of any of these trees, which yields quinine. 3. any of the drugs derived from cinchona bark. —**cinchonic** (sɪŋ'kɒnɪk) *adj.*

cincture ('sɪŋktʃə) *n.* something that encircles, esp. a belt or girdle.

cinder ('sɪndə) *n.* 1. a piece of incombustible material left after the combustion of coal, coke, etc.; clinker. 2. a piece of charred material that burns without flames; ember. 3. any solid waste from smelting or refining. 4. (*pl.*) fragments of volcanic lava; scoriae. —**'cindery** *adj.*

Cinderella (ˌsɪndə'rɛlə) *n.* 1. a girl who achieves fame after being obscure. 2. a poor, neglected, or unsuccessful person or thing.

cine- *combining form.* indicating motion picture or cinema: *cinecamera; cinephotography.*

cinema ('sɪnɪmə) *n.* 1. *Chiefly Brit.* a place designed for the exhibition of films. 2. **the cinema. a.** the art or business of making films. **b.** films collectively. —**cinematic** (ˌsɪnɪ'mætɪk) *adj.* —**cine'matically** *adv.*

cinematograph (ˌsɪnɪ'mætəˌgrɑːf, -ˌgræf) *Chiefly Brit.* ~*n.* 1. a combined camera, printer, and projector. ~*vb.* 2. to take (pictures) with a film camera. —**cinematographer** (ˌsɪnɪmə'tɒgrəfə) *n.* —**cinematographic** (ˌsɪnɪˌmætə'græfɪk) *adj.* —**cineˌmato'graphically** *adv.* —ˌ**cinema'tography** *n.*

cineraria (ˌsɪnə'rɛərɪə) *n.* a plant of the Canary Islands, widely cultivated for its blue, purple, red, or variegated daisy-like flowers.

cinerarium (ˌsɪnə'rɛərɪəm) *n., pl.* **-raria** (-'rɛərɪə). a place for keeping the ashes of the dead after cremation. —**cinerary** ('sɪnərərɪ) *adj.*

cinnabar ('sɪnəˌbɑː) *n.* 1. a heavy red mineral consisting of mercuric sulphide: the chief ore of mercury. Formula: HgS. 2. the red form of mercuric sulphide, esp. when used as a pigment. 3. a bright red; vermilion. 4. a large red-and-black European moth.

cinnamon ('sɪnəmən) *n.* 1. a tropical Asian tree, having aromatic yellowish-brown bark. 2. the spice obtained from the bark of this tree, used for flavouring food and drink. 3. a light yellowish-brown.

cinque (sɪŋk) *n.* the number five in cards, dice, etc.

cinquefoil ('sɪŋkˌfɔɪl) *n.* 1. any plant of the N temperate rosaceous genus *Potentilla,* typically having five-lobed compound leaves. 2. an ornamental carving in the form of five arcs arranged in a circle and separated by cusps.

Cinque Ports (sɪŋk) *pl. n.* an association of ports on the SE coast of England, which from late Anglo-Saxon times until 1685 provided ships for the king's service in return for the profits of justice in their courts.

cipher *or* **cypher** ('saɪfə) *n.* 1. a method of secret writing using substitution of letters according to a key. 2. a secret message. 3. the key to a secret message. 4. an obsolete name for **zero** (sense 1). 5. any of the Arabic numerals or the Arabic system of numbering 6. a person or thing of no importance; nonentity. 7. a design consisting of interwoven letters; monogram. ~*vb.* 8. to put (a message) into secret writing. 9. *Rare.* to perform (a calculation) arithmetically.

circa ('sɜːkə) *prep.* (used with a date) at the approximate time of: *circa 1182* B.C. Abbrev: *c*

circadian (sɜː'keɪdɪən) *adj.* of or relating to biological processes that occur regularly at 24-hour intervals. See also **biological clock.**

circle ('sɜːkəl) *n.* 1. a closed plane curve every point of which is equidistant from a given fixed point, the centre. 2. the figure enclosed by such a curve. 3. *Theatre.* the section of seats above the main level of the auditorium, usually comprising the dress circle and the upper circle. 4. something formed or arranged in the shape of a circle. 5. a group of people sharing an interest, activity, upbringing, etc.; set: *golf circles; a family circle.* 6. a domain or area of activity, interest, or influence. 7. a circuit. 8. a process or chain of events or parts that forms a connected whole; cycle. 9. a parallel of latitude. See also **great circle.** 10. one of a number of Neolithic or Bronze Age rings of standing stones, such as Stonehenge. 11. **come full circle.** to arrive back at one's starting point. See also **vicious circle.** ~*vb.* 12. to move in a circle (around). 13. to enclose in a circle; encircle. —**'circler** *n.*

circlet ('sɜːklɪt) *n.* a small circle or ring, esp. a circular ornament worn on the head.

circuit ('sɜːkɪt) *n.* 1. **a.** a complete route or course, esp. one that is curved or circular or that lies around an object. **b.** the area enclosed within such a route. 2. the act of following such a route: *we made three circuits of the course.* 3. **a.** a complete path through which an electric current can flow. **b.** (*as modifier*): *a circuit diagram.* 4. **a.** a periodical journey around an area, as made by judges, salesmen, etc. **b.** the places visited on such a journey. **c.** the persons making such a journey. 5. a number of theatres, cinemas, etc., under one management. 6. *Sport.* **a.** a series of tournaments in which the same players regularly take part: *the international tennis circuit.* **b.** (usually preceded by *the*) the contestants who take part in such a series. 7. *Chiefly Brit.* a motor racing track, usually of irregular shape. ~*vb.* 8. to make or travel in a circuit around (something). —**'circuital** *adj.*

circuit breaker *n.* a device that under abnormal conditions, such as a short circuit, stops the flow of current in an electrical circuit.

circuitous (sə'kjuːɪtəs) *adj.* indirect and lengthy; roundabout: *a circuitous route.* —**cir'cuitously** *adv.* —**cir'cuitousness** *n.*

THESAURUS

cigarette cancer stick (*Sl.*), ciggy (*Inf.*), coffin nail (*Sl.*), fag (*Sl.*), gasper (*Sl.*), smoke

cinema big screen (*Inf.*), films, flicks (*Sl.*), motion pictures, movies, pictures

cipher 1. nil, nothing, nought, zero 2. nobody, nonentity 3. character, digit, figure, number, numeral, symbol 4. code, cryptograph 5. device, logo, mark, monogram

circle *n.* 1. band, circumference, coil, cordon, cycle, disc, globe, lap, loop, orb, perimeter, periphery, revolution, ring, round, sphere, turn 2. area, bounds, circuit, compass, domain, enclosure, field, orbit, province, range, realm, region, scene, sphere 3. assembly, class, clique, club, company, coterie, crowd, fellowship, fraternity, group, school, set, society ~*v.* 4. belt, circumnavigate, circumscribe, coil, compass, curve, encircle, enclose, encompass, envelop, gird, hem in, pivot, revolve, ring, rotate, surround, tour, whirl

circuit 1. area, compass, course, journey, orbit, perambulation, revolution, round, route, tour, track 2. boundary, bounding line,

circuitry ('sɜːkɪtrɪ) n. 1. the design of an electrical circuit. 2. the system of circuits used in an electronic device.

circular ('sɜːkjulə) adj. 1. of, involving, resembling, or shaped like a circle. 2. circuitous. 3. (of arguments, etc.) assuming as one of the premises the conclusion that is to be proved: the fallacy of begging the question. 4. travelling or occurring in a cycle. 5. (of letters, announcements, etc.) intended for general distribution. ~n. 6. a printed advertisement or notice for mass distribution. —**circularity** (ˌsɜːkjuˈlærɪtɪ) n. —**ˈcircularly** adv.

circularize or **-ise** ('sɜːkjuləˌraɪz) vb. (tr.) 1. to distribute circulars to. 2. to canvass or petition (people), as for support, votes, etc., by distributing letters, etc. 3. to make circular. —ˌcirculariˈzation or -iˈsation n.

circular saw n. a power-driven saw in which a circular disc with a toothed edge is rotated at high speed.

circulate ('sɜːkjuˌleɪt) vb. 1. to send, go, or pass from place to place or person to person: don't circulate the news. 2. to distribute or be distributed over a wide area. 3. to move or cause to move through a circuit, system, etc., returning to the starting point: blood circulates through the body. 4. to move in a circle. —ˈcircuˌlative adj. —ˈcircuˌlator n. —ˈcirculatory adj.

circulating library n. 1. another word (esp. U.S.) for **lending library**. 2. a small library circulated in turn to a group of institutions.

circulation (ˌsɜːkjuˈleɪʃən) n. 1. the transport of oxygenated blood through the arteries, and the return of oxygen-depleted blood through the veins to the heart, where the cycle is renewed. 2. the flow of sap through a plant. 3. any movement through a closed circuit. 4. the spreading or transmission of something to a wider group of people or area. 5. (of air and water) free movement within an area or volume. 6. a. the distribution of newspapers, magazines, etc. b. the number of copies of an issue that are distributed. 7. in circulation. a. (of currency) serving as a medium of exchange. b. (of people) active in a social or business context.

circum- prefix. around; surrounding; on all sides: circumlocution; circumpolar.

circumambient (ˌsɜːkəmˈæmbɪənt) adj. surrounding. —ˌcircumˈambience or ˌcircumˈambiency n.

circumcise ('sɜːkəmˌsaɪz) vb. (tr.) 1. to remove the foreskin of (a male). 2. to incise surgically the skin over the clitoris (of a female). 3. to perform this operation as a religious rite on (someone). —ˌcircumˈcision n.

circumference (səˈkʌmfərəns) n. 1. the boundary of a specific area or figure, esp. of a circle. 2. the length of a closed geometric curve, esp. of a circle. —**circumferential** (səˌkʌmfəˈrenʃəl) adj. —ˌcirˌcumferˈentially adv.

circumflex ('sɜːkəmˌfleks) n. 1. a mark (ˆ) placed over a vowel to show that it is pronounced with rising and falling pitch, as in ancient Greek, or as a long vowel, as in French. ~adj. 2. (of nerves, arteries, etc.) bending or curving around. —ˌcircumˈflexion n.

circumlocution (ˌsɜːkəmləˈkjuːʃən) n. 1. an indirect way of expressing something. 2. an indirect expression. —circumlocutory (ˌsɜːkəmˈlɒkjətərɪ, -trɪ) adj.

circumnavigate (ˌsɜːkəmˈnævɪˌgeɪt) vb. (tr.) to sail or fly completely around. —ˌcircumˌnaviˈgation n. —ˌcircumˈnaviˌgator n.

circumscribe (ˌsɜːkəmˈskraɪb, 'sɜːkəmˌskraɪb) vb. (tr.) 1. to restrict within limits. 2. to mark or set the bounds of. 3. to draw a geometric construction around (another construction) so that the two are in contact but do not intersect. 4. to draw a line round. —ˌcircumˈscribable adj. —ˌcircumˈscriber n. —**circumscription** (ˌsɜːkəm-

ˈskrɪpʃən) n.

circumspect ('sɜːkəmˌspekt) adj. cautious, prudent, or discreet. —ˌcircumˈspection n. —ˈcircumˌspectly adv.

circumstance ('sɜːkəmstəns) n. 1. (usually pl.) a condition of time, place, etc., that accompanies or influences an event or condition. 2. an incident or occurrence, esp. a chance one. 3. accessory information or detail. 4. formal display or ceremony (archaic except in **pomp and circumstance**). 5. **under** or **in no circumstances**. in no case; never. 6. **under the circumstances**. because of conditions; this being the case. ~vb. (tr.) 7. to place in a particular condition or situation.

circumstantial (ˌsɜːkəmˈstænʃəl) adj. 1. of or dependent on circumstances. 2. fully detailed. 3. incidental. —**circumstantiality** (ˌsɜːkəmˌstænʃɪˈælɪtɪ) n. —ˌcircum-ˈstantially adv.

circumstantial evidence n. indirect evidence that tends to establish a conclusion by inference.

circumstantiate (ˌsɜːkəmˈstænʃɪˌeɪt) vb. (tr.) to support by giving particulars. —ˌcircumˌstantiˈation n.

circumvent (ˌsɜːkəmˈvent) vb. (tr.) 1. to evade or go around. 2. to outwit. 3. to encircle (an enemy) so as to intercept or capture. —ˌcircumˈvention n.

circus ('sɜːkəs) n., pl. **-cuses**. 1. a travelling company of entertainers such as acrobats, clowns, trapeze artists, and trained animals. 2. a public performance given by such a company. 3. an arena, usually tented, in which such a performance is held. 4. (in ancient Rome) a. an open-air stadium, usually oval or oblong, for chariot races or public games. b. the games themselves. 5. Brit. a. an open place, usually circular, where several streets converge. b. (cap. when part of a name): Piccadilly Circus. 6. Inf. noisy or rowdy behaviour. 7. Inf. a group of people travelling together and putting on a display.

cirrhosis (sɪˈrəʊsɪs) n. any of various chronic progressive diseases of the liver, characterized by death of liver cells, irreversible fibrosis, etc. —**cirrhotic** (sɪˈrɒtɪk) adj.

cirrocumulus (ˌsɪrəʊˈkjuːmjʊləs) n., pl. **-li** (-ˌlaɪ). a high cloud of ice crystals grouped into small separate globular masses.

cirrostratus (ˌsɪrəʊˈstrɑːtəs) n., pl. **-ti** (-taɪ). a uniform layer of cloud above about 6000 metres.

cirrus ('sɪrəs) n., pl. **-ri** (-raɪ). 1. a thin wispy fibrous cloud at high altitudes, composed of ice particles. 2. a plant tendril or similar part. 3. a slender tentacle or filament in barnacles and other marine invertebrates.

cisalpine (sɪsˈælpaɪn) adj. on this (the southern) side of the Alps, as viewed from Rome.

cisco ('sɪskəʊ) n., pl. **-coes** or **-cos**. any of various whitefish, esp. the lake herring of cold deep lakes of North America.

cist¹ (sɪst) n. a wooden box for holding ritual objects used in ancient Rome and Greece.

cist² (sɪst) or **kist** n. a box-shaped burial chamber made from stone slabs or a hollowed tree-trunk.

Cistercian (sɪˈstɜːʃən) n. a member of a Christian order of monks and nuns founded in 1098, which follows an especially strict form of the Benedictine rule. Also called: **White Monk**.

cistern ('sɪstən) n. 1. a tank for the storage of water, esp. on or within the roof of a house or connected to a W.C. 2. an underground reservoir for the storage of a liquid, esp. rainwater. 3. Also called: **cisterna**. Anat. a sac or partially enclosed space containing body fluid.

citadel ('sɪtədəl, -ˌdel) n. 1. a stronghold within or close

bounds, circumference, compass, district, limit, range, region, tract

circuitous ambagious (Archaic), devious, indirect, labyrinthine, meandering, oblique, rambling, roundabout, tortuous, winding

circulate 1. broadcast, diffuse, disseminate, distribute, issue, make known, promulgate, propagate, publicize, publish, spread 2. flow, gyrate, radiate, revolve, rotate

circulation 1. currency, dissemination, distribution, spread, transmission, vogue 2. circling, flow, motion, rotation

circumference border, boundary,

bounds, circuit, edge, extremity, fringe, limits, outline, perimeter, periphery, rim, verge

circumscribe bound, confine, define, delimit, delineate, demarcate, encircle, enclose, encompass, environ, hem in, limit, mark off, restrain, restrict, surround

circumspect attentive, canny, careful, cautious, deliberate, discreet, discriminating, guarded, heedful, judicious, observant, politic, prudent, sagacious, sage, vigilant, wary, watchful

circumstance accident, condition, contingency, detail, element, event, fact, factor, happening, incident, item, occurrence,

particular, position, respect, situation

circumstances life style, means, position, resources, situation, state, state of affairs, station, status, times

circumstantial conjectural, contingent, detailed, founded on circumstances, hearsay, incidental, indirect, inferential, particular, presumptive, provisional, specific

cistern basin, reservoir, sink, tank, vat

citadel bastion, fastness, fortification, fortress, keep, stronghold, tower

to a city. **2.** any strongly fortified building or place of safety; refuge.

citation (saɪ'teɪʃən) *n.* **1.** the quoting of a book or author. **2.** a passage or source cited. **3. a.** an official commendation or award, esp. for bravery or outstanding service. **b.** a formal public statement of this. **4.** *Law.* **a.** an official summons to appear in court. **b.** the document containing such a summons. —**citatory** ('saɪtətərɪ) *adj.*

cite (saɪt) *vb.* (*tr.*) **1.** to quote or refer to (a passage, book, or author). **2.** to mention or commend (a soldier, etc.) for outstanding bravery or meritorious action. **3.** to summon to appear before a court of law. **4.** to enumerate: *he cited the king's virtues.* —**'citable** *or* **'citeable** *adj.*

cithara ('sɪθərə) *or* **kithara** *n.* a stringed musical instrument of ancient Greece, similar to the lyre.

citified *or* **cityfied** ('sɪtɪˌfaɪd) *adj. Often derog.* having the customs, manners, or dress of city people.

citizen ('sɪtɪzən) *n.* **1.** a native or naturalized member of a state, nation, or other political community. **2.** an inhabitant of a city or town. **3.** a civilian, as opposed to a soldier, public official, etc.

citizenry ('sɪtɪzənrɪ) *n., pl.* **-ries.** citizens collectively.

Citizens' Band *n.* a range of radio frequencies assigned officially for use by the public for private communication.

citizenship ('sɪtɪzənˌʃɪp) *n.* **1.** the condition or status of a citizen, with its rights and duties. **2.** a person's conduct as a citizen.

citrate ('sɪtreɪt, -rɪt; 'saɪtreɪt) *n.* any salt or ester of citric acid.

citric ('sɪtrɪk) *adj.* of or derived from citrus fruits or citric acid.

citric acid *n.* a water-soluble weak tribasic acid found in many fruits, esp. citrus fruits, and used in pharmaceuticals and as a flavouring. Formula: $CH_2(COOH)C(OH)(COOH)CH_2COOH$.

citriculture ('sɪtrɪˌkʌltʃə) *n.* the cultivation of citrus fruits.

citron ('sɪtrən) *n.* **1.** a small Asian tree, having lemon-like fruit with a thick aromatic rind. **2.** the fruit of this tree. **3.** the rind of this fruit candied and used for decoration and flavouring of foods.

citronella (ˌsɪtrə'nɛlə) *n.* **1.** a tropical Asian grass, with bluish-green lemon-scented leaves. **2.** Also called: **citronella oil.** the yellow aromatic oil obtained from this grass, used in insect repellents, soaps, perfumes, etc.

citrus ('sɪtrəs) *n., pl.* **-ruses.** **1.** any tree or shrub of the tropical and subtropical genus *Citrus*, which includes the orange, lemon, and lime. ~*adj. also* **citrous.** **2.** of or relating to the genus *Citrus* or to the fruits of plants of this genus.

cittern ('sɪtɜːn), **cither** ('sɪθə) *or* **cithern** ('sɪθən) *n.* a medieval stringed instrument resembling a lute but having wire strings and a flat back.

city ('sɪtɪ) *n., pl.* **cities.** **1.** any large town or populous place. **2.** (in Britain) a large town that has received this title from the Crown: usually the seat of a bishop. **3.** (in the U.S.) an incorporated urban centre with its own government and administration established by state charter. **4.** the people of a city collectively. **5.** (*modifier*) in or characteristic of a city: *city habits.* ~Related adjs.: **civic, urban, municipal.**

City ('sɪtɪ) *n.* **the.** **1.** the area in central London in which the United Kingdom's major financial business is transacted. **2.** the various financial institutions located in this area.

city editor *n.* (on a newspaper) **1.** *Brit.* the editor in charge of financial and commercial news. **2.** *U.S.* the editor in charge of local news.

city-state *n. Ancient history.* a state consisting of a sovereign city and its dependencies.

civet ('sɪvɪt) *n.* **1.** a catlike mammal of Africa and S Asia, typically having spotted fur and secreting a powerfully smelling fluid from anal glands. **2.** the yellowish fatty secretion of such an animal, used as a fixative in the manufacture of perfumes. **3.** the fur of such an animal.

civic ('sɪvɪk) *adj.* of or relating to a city, citizens, or citizenship. —**'civically** *adv.*

civic centre *n. Brit.* the public buildings of a town, including recreational facilities and offices of local administration.

civics ('sɪvɪks) *n.* (*functioning as sing.*) the study of the rights and responsibilities of citizenship.

civil ('sɪvəl) *adj.* **1.** of the ordinary life of citizens as distinguished from military, legal, or ecclesiastical affairs. **2.** of or relating to the citizen as an individual: *civil rights.* **3.** of or occurring within the state or between citizens: *civil strife.* **4.** polite or courteous: *a civil manner.* **5.** of or in accordance with Roman law. —**'civilly** *adv.*

civil defence *n.* the organizing of civilians to deal with enemy attacks.

civil disobedience *n.* a refusal to obey laws, pay taxes, etc.: a nonviolent means of protesting.

civil engineer *n.* a person qualified to design and construct public works, such as roads, bridges, harbours, etc. —**civil engineering** *n.*

civilian (sɪ'vɪljən) *n.* **a.** a person whose occupation is civil or nonmilitary. **b.** (*as modifier*): *civilian life.*

civility (sɪ'vɪlɪtɪ) *n., pl.* **-ties.** **1.** politeness or courtesy. **2.** (*often pl.*) an act of politeness.

civilization *or* **-isation** (ˌsɪvɪlaɪ'zeɪʃən) *n.* **1.** a human society that has a complex cultural, political, and legal organization; an advanced state in social development. **2.** the peoples or nations collectively who have achieved such a state. **3.** the total culture and way of life of a particular people, nation, region, or period. **4.** the process of bringing or achieving civilization. **5.** intellectual, cultural, and moral refinement. **6.** cities or populated areas, as contrasted with sparsely inhabited areas, deserts, etc.

civilize *or* **-ise** ('sɪvɪˌlaɪz) *vb.* (*tr.*) **1.** to bring out of savagery or barbarism into a state characteristic of civilization. **2.** to refine, educate, or enlighten. —**'civiˌlizable** *or* **'civiˌlised** *or* **-ised** *adj.*

civil law *n.* **1.** the law of a state relating to private and civilian affairs. **2.** the body of law in ancient Rome, esp. as applicable to private citizens. **3.** law based on the Roman system as distinguished from common law and canon law.

civil list *n.* (in Britain) the annuities voted by Parliament for the support of the royal household and the royal family.

civil marriage *n. Law.* a marriage performed by an official other than a clergyman.

civil rights *pl. n.* **1.** the personal rights of the individual citizen. **2.** (*modifier*) of, relating to, or promoting equality in social, economic, and political rights.

civil servant *n.* a member of the civil service.

civil service *n.* **1.** the service responsible for the public administration of the government of a country. It excludes the legislative, judicial, and military branches. **2.** the members of the civil service collectively.

civil war *n.* war between parties or factions within the same nation.

civvy ('sɪvɪ) *n., pl.* **civvies** *or* **civies.** *Sl.* **1.** a civilian. **2.** (*pl.*) civilian dress as opposed to uniform. **3.** **civvy**

THESAURUS

citation 1. commendation, excerpt, illustration, passage, quotation, quote, reference, source **2.** award, commendation, mention

cite 1. adduce, advance, allude to, enumerate, evidence, extract, mention, name, quote, specify **2.** *Law* call, subpoena, summon

citizen burgess, burgher, denizen, dweller, freeman, inhabitant, ratepayer, resident, subject, townsman

city 1. *n.* conurbation, megalopolis, metropolis, municipality **2.** *adj.* civic, metropolitan, municipal, urban

civic borough, communal, community, local, municipal, public

civil 1. civic, domestic, home, interior, municipal, political **2.** accommodating, affable, civilized, complaisant, courteous, courtly, obliging, polished, polite, refined, urbane, well-bred, well-mannered

civility affability, amiability, breeding, complaisance, cordiality, courteousness, courtesy, good manners, graciousness, politeness, politesse, tact, urbanity

civilization 1. advancement, cultiva-

tion, culture, development, education, enlightenment, progress, refinement, sophistication **2.** community, nation, people, polity, society **3.** customs, mores, way of life

civilize cultivate, educate, enlighten, humanize, improve, polish, refine, sophisticate, tame

civilized cultured, educated, enlightened, humane, polite, sophisticated, tolerant, urbane

street. civilian life.

Cl *the chemical symbol for* chlorine.

clack (klæk) *vb.* **1.** to make or cause to make a sound like that of two pieces of wood hitting each other. **2.** to jabber. ~*n.* **3.** a short sharp sound. **4.** chatter. **5.** Also called: **clack valve.** a simple nonreturn valve using a hinged flap or a ball. —'**clacker** *n.*

clad[1] (klæd) *vb.* a past participle of **clothe.**

clad[2] (klæd) *vb.* **cladding, clad.** (*tr.*) to bond a metal to (another metal), esp. to form a protective coating.

cladding ('klædɪŋ) *n.* **1.** the process of protecting one metal by bonding a second metal to its surface. **2.** the protective coating so bonded to metal. **3.** the material used for the outside facing of a building, etc.

claim (kleɪm) *vb.* (*mainly tr.*) **1.** to demand as being due or as one's property; assert one's title or right to: *he claimed the record.* **2.** (*takes a clause as object or an infinitive*) to assert as a fact; maintain against denial: *he claimed to be telling the truth.* **3.** to call for or need; deserve: *this problem claims our attention.* **4.** to take: *the accident claimed four lives.* ~*n.* **5.** an assertion of a right; a demand for something as due. **6.** an assertion of something as true, real, or factual. **7.** a right or just title to something; basis for demand: *a claim to fame.* **8.** anything that is claimed, such as a piece of land staked out by a miner. **9. a.** a demand for payment in connection with an insurance policy, etc. **b.** the sum of money demanded. —'**claimable** *adj.* —'**claimant** *or* '**claimer** *n.*

clairvoyance (klɛə'vɔɪəns) *n.* **1.** the alleged power of perceiving things beyond the natural range of the senses. **2.** keen intuitive understanding.

clairvoyant (klɛə'vɔɪənt) *adj.* **1.** of or possessing clairvoyance. **2.** having great insight. ~*n.* **3.** a person claiming to have the power to foretell future events. —clair'**voyantly** *adv.*

clam (klæm) *n.* **1.** any of various burrowing bivalve molluscs. **2.** the edible flesh of such a mollusc. **3.** *Inf.* a reticent person. ~*vb.* **clamming, clammed.** **4.** (*intr.*) *Chiefly U.S.* to gather clams.

clamber ('klæmbə) *vb.* **1.** (usually foll. by *up, over,* etc.) to climb (something) awkwardly, esp. by using both hands and feet. ~*n.* **2.** a climb performed in this manner. —'**clamberer** *n.*

clammy ('klæmɪ) *adj.* -**mier,** -**miest.** **1.** unpleasantly sticky; moist. **2.** (of the weather) close; humid. —'**clammily** *adv.* —'**clamminess** *n.*

clamour *or U.S.* **clamor** ('klæmə) *n.* **1.** a loud persistent outcry. **2.** a vehement expression of collective feeling or outrage: *a clamour against higher prices.* **3.** a loud and persistent noise: *the clamour of traffic.* ~*vb.* **4.** (*intr.;* often foll. by *for* or *against*) to make a loud noise or outcry; make a public demand. **5.** (*tr.*) to move or force by outcry. —'**clamorous** *adj.* —'**clamorously** *adv.* —'**clamorousness** *n.*

clamp[1] (klæmp) *n.* **1.** a mechanical device with movable jaws with which an object can be secured to a bench or with which two objects may be secured together. ~*vb.* (*tr.*) **2.** to fix or fasten with or as if with a clamp. **3.** to inflict or impose forcefully: *they clamped a curfew on the town.*

clamp[2] (klæmp) *n.* **1.** a mound of a harvested root crop, covered with straw and earth to protect it from winter weather. ~*vb.* **2.** (*tr.*) to enclose (a harvested root crop) in a mound.

clan (klæn) *n.* **1.** a group of people interrelated by ancestry or marriage. **2.** a group of families with a common surname and a common ancestor, esp. among the Scots and the Irish. **3.** a group of people united by common characteristics, aims, or interests.

clandestine (klæn'dɛstɪn) *adj.* secret and concealed, often for illicit reasons; furtive. —clan'**destinely** *adv.*

clang (klæŋ) *vb.* **1.** to make or cause to make a loud resounding noise, as metal when struck. **2.** (*intr.*) to move or operate making such a sound. ~*n.* **3.** a resounding metallic noise. **4.** the harsh cry of certain birds.

clanger ('klæŋə) *n.* **1.** *Inf.* a conspicuous mistake (esp. in **drop a clanger**). **2.** something that clangs or causes a clang.

clank (klæŋk) *n.* **1.** an abrupt harsh metallic sound. ~*vb.* **2.** to make or cause to make such a sound. **3.** (*intr.*) to move or operate making such a sound. —'**clankingly** *adv.*

clannish ('klænɪʃ) *adj.* **1.** of or characteristic of a clan. **2.** tending to associate closely within a group to the exclusion of outsiders; cliquish. —'**clannishly** *adv.* —'**clannishness** *n.*

clap[1] (klæp) *vb.* **clapping, clapped.** **1.** to make or cause to make a sharp abrupt sound, as of two nonmetallic objects struck together. **2.** to applaud (someone or something) by striking the palms of the hands together sharply. **3.** (*tr.*) to strike (a person) lightly with an open hand, in greeting, etc. **4.** (*tr.*) to place or put quickly or forcibly: *they clapped him into jail.* **5.** (of certain birds) to flap (the wings) noisily. **6.** (*intr.;* foll. by *up* or *together*) to contrive or put together hastily. **7. clap eyes on.** *Inf.* to catch sight of. **8. clap hold of.** *Inf.* to grasp suddenly or forcibly. ~*n.* **9.** the sharp abrupt sound produced by striking the hands together. **10.** the act of clapping, esp. in applause. **11.** a sudden sharp sound, esp. of thunder. **12.** a light blow. **13.** *Arch.* a sudden action or mishap.

clap[2] (klæp) *n.* (usually preceded by *the*) a slang word for **gonorrhoea.**

clapper ('klæpə) *n.* **1.** a person or thing that claps. **2.** Also called: **tongue.** a small piece of metal suspended within a bell that causes it to sound when made to strike against its side. **3. go (run, move) like the clappers.** *Brit. inf.* to move extremely fast.

claptrap ('klæp,træp) *n.* *Inf.* **1.** contrived but foolish talk. **2.** insincere and pretentious talk: *politicians' claptrap.*

claque (klæk) *n.* **1.** a group of people hired to applaud. **2.** a group of fawning admirers.

claret ('klærət) *n.* **1.** a red wine, esp. one from the Bordeaux district of France. **2.** a purplish-red colour.

clarify ('klærɪ,faɪ) *vb.* -**fying,** -**fied.** **1.** to make or become clear or easy to understand. **2.** to make or become free of impurities. **3.** to make (fat, butter, etc.) clear by heating, etc., or (of fat, etc.) to become clear as a result of such a process. —,**clarifi'cation** *n.* —'**clarifier** *n.*

clarinet (,klærɪ'nɛt) *n.* *Music.* **1.** a keyed woodwind instrument with a cylindrical bore and a single reed. **2.** an orchestral musician who plays the clarinet. —,**clarinetist** *or* ,**clari'nettist** *n.*

clarion ('klærɪən) *n.* **1.** a stop of trumpet quality on an organ. **2.** an obsolete, high-pitched, small-bore trumpet. **3.** the sound of such an instrument or any similar sound. ~*adj.* **4.** (*prenominal*) clear and ringing; inspiring: *a clarion call to action.* ~*vb.* **5.** to proclaim loudly.

clarity ('klærɪtɪ) *n.* **1.** clearness, as of expression. **2.** clearness, as of water.

-**clase** *n. combining form.* (in mineralogy) indicating a particular type of cleavage: *plagioclase.*

clash (klæʃ) *vb.* **1.** to make or cause to make a loud harsh sound, esp. by striking together. **2.** (*intr.*) to be incompatible. **3.** (*intr.*) to engage together in conflict. **4.**

THESAURUS

claim 1. *v.* allege, ask, assert, call for, challenge, collect, demand, exact, hold, insist, maintain, need, pick up, profess, require, take, uphold 2. *n.* affirmation, allegation, application, assertion, call, demand, petition, pretension, privilege, protestation, request, requirement, right, title

clamber claw, climb, scale, scrabble, scramble, shin

clamorous blaring, deafening, insistent, lusty, noisy, riotous, tumultuous, uproarious, vehement, vociferous

clamour agitation, babel, blare, brouha-ha, commotion, din, exclamation, hubbub,

hullabaloo, noise, outcry, racket, shout, shouting, uproar, vociferation

clamp 1. *n.* bracket, fastener, grip, press, vice 2. *v.* brace, clinch, fasten, fix, impose, make fast, secure

clan band, brotherhood, clique, coterie, faction, family, fraternity, gens, group, house, race, sect, sept, set, society, sodality, tribe

clang 1. *v.* bong, chime, clank, clash, jangle, resound, reverberate, ring, toll 2. *n.* clangour, ding-dong, knell, reverberation

clap 1. acclaim, applaud, cheer 2. bang, pat, slap, strike gently, thrust, thwack, wallop (*Inf.*), whack

claptrap affectation, blarney, bombast, bunk (*Inf.*), drivel, flannel (*Inf.*), guff (*Sl.*), hot air (*Inf.*), humbug, insincerity, nonsense, rodomontade, rubbish

clarification elucidation, explanation, exposition, illumination, interpretation, simplification

clarify 1. clear up, elucidate, explain, illuminate, make plain, resolve, simplify, throw *or* shed light on 2. cleanse, purify, refine

clarity clearness, comprehensibility, definition, explicitness, intelligibility, limpidity, lucidity, obviousness, precision, simplicity, transparency

(intr.) (of dates or events) to coincide. **5.** (of colours) to look inharmonious together. ~n. **6.** a loud harsh noise. **7.** a collision or conflict. —'**clasher** n.

clasp (klɑːsp) n. **1.** a fastening, such as a catch or hook, for holding things together. **2.** a firm grasp or embrace. **3.** Mil. a bar on a medal ribbon, to indicate either a second award or the battle, campaign, or reason for its award. ~vb. (tr.) **4.** to hold in a firm grasp. **5.** to grasp firmly with the hand. **6.** to fasten together with or as if with a clasp. —'**clasper** n.

clasp knife n. a large knife with one or more blades or other devices folding into the handle.

class (klɑːs) n. **1.** a collection or division of people or things sharing a common characteristic. **2.** a group of persons sharing a similar social and economic position. **3. a.** the pattern of divisions that exist within a society on the basis of rank, economic status, etc. **b.** (as modifier): the class struggle; class distinctions. **4. a.** a group of pupils or students who are taught together. **b.** a meeting of a group of students for tuition. **5.** U.S. a group of students who graduated in a specified year: the class of '53. **6.** (in combination and as modifier) Brit. a grade of attainment in a university honours degree: second-class honours. **7.** one of several standards of accommodation in public transport. **8.** Inf. excellence or elegance, esp. in dress, design, or behaviour. **9.** Biol. any of the taxonomic groups into which a phylum is divided and which contains one or more orders. **10.** Maths. another name for set[2] (sense 3). **11. in a class by oneself** or **in a class of its own.** unequalled; unparalleled. ~vb. **12.** to have or assign a place within a group, grade, or class.

class. abbrev. for: **1.** classic(al). **2.** classification. **3.** classified.

classic ('klæsɪk) adj. **1.** of the highest class, esp. in art or literature. **2.** serving as a standard or model of its kind. **3.** adhering to an established set of principles in the arts or sciences: a classic proof. **4.** characterized by simplicity, balance, regularity, and purity of form; classical. **5.** of lasting interest or significance. **6.** continuously in fashion because of its simple style: a classic dress. ~n. **7.** an author, artist, or work of art of the highest excellence. **8.** a creation or work considered as definitive. **9.** Horse racing. any of the five principal races for three-year-old horses in Britain, namely the One Thousand Guineas, Two Thousand Guineas, Derby, Oaks, and Saint Leger.

▷ **Usage.** The adjectives classic and classical can often be treated as synonyms, but there are two contexts in which they should be carefully distinguished. Classic is applied to that which is of the first rank, esp. in art and literature, as in: Lewis Carroll's classic works for children. Classical is used to refer to Greek and Roman culture.

classical ('klæsɪkəl) adj. **1.** of, relating to, or characteristic of the ancient Greeks and Romans or their civilization. **2.** designating, following, or influenced by the art or culture of ancient Greece or Rome: classical architecture. **3.** Music. **a.** of, relating to, or denoting any music or its period of composition marked by stability of form, intellectualism, and restraint. Cf. **romantic** (sense 5). **b.** accepted as a standard: the classical suite. **c.** denoting serious art music in general. Cf. **pop**[2]. **4.** denoting or relating to a style in any of the arts characterized by emotional restraint and conservatism: a classical style of painting. **5.** (of an education) based on the humanities and the study of Latin and Greek. **6.** Physics. not involving the quantum theory or the theory of relativity: classi-

cal mechanics. —,**classi'cality** or '**classicalness** n. —'**classically** adv.
▷ **Usage.** See at classic.

classicism ('klæsɪˌsɪzəm) or **classicalism** ('klæsɪkə-ˌlɪzəm) n. **1.** a style based on the study of Greek and Roman models, characterized by emotional restraint and regularity of form; the antithesis of romanticism. **2.** knowledge of the culture of ancient Greece and Rome. **3. a.** a Greek or Latin expression. **b.** an expression in a modern language that is modelled on a Greek or Latin form. —'**classicist** n.

classics ('klæsɪks) n. the. **1.** a body of literature regarded as great or lasting, esp. that of ancient Greece or Rome. **2.** the ancient Greek and Latin languages.

classification (ˌklæsɪfɪ'keɪʃən) n. **1.** systematic placement in categories. **2.** one of the divisions in a system of classifying. **3.** Biol. **a.** the placing of animals and plants in a series of increasingly specialized groups because of similarities in structure, origin, etc., that indicate a common relationship. **b.** the study of the principles and practice of this process; taxonomy. —,**classifi'catory** adj.

classify ('klæsɪˌfaɪ) vb. **-fying, -fied.** (tr.) **1.** to arrange or order by classes; categorize. **2.** Government. to declare (information, documents, etc.) of possible aid to an enemy and therefore not available to people outside a restricted group. —'**classiˌfiable** adj. —'**classiˌfier** n.

classmate ('klɑːsˌmeɪt) n. a friend or contemporary of the same class in a school.

classroom ('klɑːsˌruːm, -ˌrum) n. a room in which classes are conducted, esp. in a school.

classy ('klɑːsɪ) adj. **classier, classiest.** Sl. elegant; stylish. —'**classiness** n.

clatter ('klætə) vb. **1.** to make or cause to make a rattling noise, esp. as a result of movement. **2.** (intr.) to chatter. ~n. **3.** a rattling sound or noise. **4.** a noisy commotion, such as loud chatter. —'**clatterer** n. —'**clatteringly** adv.

clause (klɔːz) n. **1.** Grammar. a group of words, consisting of a subject and a predicate including a finite verb, that does not necessarily constitute a sentence. See also **main clause, subordinate clause. 2.** a section of a legal document such as a contract, will, or statute. —'**clausal** adj.

claustrophobia (ˌklɔːstrə'fəʊbɪə, ˌklɒs-) n. an abnormal fear of being in a confined space. —'**claustroˌphobe** n. —,**claustro'phobic** adj.

clavichord ('klævɪˌkɔːd) n. a keyboard instrument consisting of a number of thin wire strings struck from below by brass tangents.

clavicle ('klævɪkəl) n. **1.** either of the two bones connecting the shoulder blades with the upper part of the breastbone. Nontechnical name: **collarbone. 2.** the corresponding structure in other vertebrates. —**clavicular** (klə'vɪkjʊlə) adj.

clavier (klə'vɪə, 'klævɪə) n. **a.** any keyboard instrument. **b.** the keyboard itself.

claw (klɔː) n. **1.** a curved pointed horny process on the end of each digit in birds, some reptiles, and certain mammals. **2.** a corresponding structure in some invertebrates, such as the pincer of a crab. **3.** a part or member like a claw in function or appearance. ~vb. **4.** to scrape, tear, or dig (something or someone) with claws, etc. **5.** (tr.) to create by scratching as with claws: to claw an opening. —'**clawer** n.

claw back vb. (tr., adv.) **1.** to get back (something) with difficulty. **2.** to recover (a part of a tax, duty, etc.)

THESAURUS

in the form of an allowance. ~n. **clawback**. **3.** the recovery of part of a tax, etc., in the form of an allowance. **4.** the sum so recovered.

clay (kleɪ) n. **1.** a very fine-grained material that occurs as sedimentary rocks, soils, and other deposits. It becomes plastic when moist but hardens on heating and is used in the manufacture of bricks, ceramics, etc. **2.** earth or mud. **3.** Poetic. the material of the human body. —'**clayey**, '**clayish**, or '**clay,like** adj.

claymore ('kleɪ,mɔː) n. a large two-edged broadsword used formerly by Scottish Highlanders.

clay pigeon n. a disc of baked clay hurled into the air from a machine as a target to be shot at.

CLC abbrev. for Canadian Labour Congress.

-cle suffix forming nouns. indicating smallness: cubicle; particle.

clean (kliːn) adj. **1.** without dirt or other impurities; unsoiled. **2.** without anything in it or on it: a clean page. **3.** recently washed; fresh. **4.** without extraneous or foreign materials. **5.** without defect, difficulties, or problems. **6.** (of a nuclear weapon) producing little or no radioactive fall-out or contamination. **7.** (of a wound, etc.) having no pus or other sign of infection. **8.** pure; morally sound. **9.** without objectionable language or obscenity. **10.** thorough or complete: a clean break. **11.** dexterous or adroit: a clean throw. **12.** Sport. played fairly and without fouls. **13.** simple in design: a ship's clean lines. **14.** Aeronautics. causing little turbulence; streamlined. **15.** honourable or respectable. **16.** habitually neat. **17.** (esp. of a driving licence) showing or having no record of offences. **18.** Sl. **a.** innocent; not guilty. **b.** not carrying illegal drugs, weapons, etc. ~vb. **19.** to make or become free of dirt, filth, etc.: the stove cleans easily. **20.** to remove in making clean: to clean marks off the wall. **21.** (tr.) to prepare (fish, poultry, etc.) for cooking: to clean a chicken. ~adv. **22.** in a clean way; cleanly. **23.** Not standard. (intensifier): clean forgotten. **24. come clean.** Inf. to make a revelation or confession. ~n. **25.** the act or an instance of cleaning: he gave his shoes a clean. —'**cleanable** adj. —'**cleanness** n.

clean-cut adj. **1.** clearly outlined; neat: clean-cut lines of a ship. **2.** definite.

cleaner ('kliːnə) n. **1.** a person, device, chemical agent, etc., that removes dirt, as from clothes or carpets. **2.** (usually pl.) a shop, etc. that provides a dry-cleaning service.

cleanly adv. ('kliːnlɪ). **1.** in a fair manner. **2.** easily or smoothly. ~adj. ('klɛnlɪ), **-lier**, **-liest**. **3.** habitually clean or neat. —**cleanlily** ('klɛnlɪlɪ) adv. —**cleanliness** ('klɛnlɪnɪs) n.

cleanse (klɛnz) vb. (tr.) **1.** to remove dirt, filth, etc., from. **2.** to remove guilt from. **3.** Arch. to cure. —'**cleanser** n.

clean-shaven adj. (of men) having the facial hair shaved off.

clean up vb. (adv.) **1.** to rid (something) of dirt, filth, or other impurities. **2.** to make (someone or something) orderly or presentable. **3.** (tr.) to rid (a place) of undesirable people or conditions. **4.** Inf., chiefly U.S. to make (a great profit). ~n. **cleanup**. **5.** the process of cleaning up. **6.** Inf., chiefly U.S. a great profit.

clear (klɪə) adj. **1.** free from darkness or obscurity; bright. **2.** (of weather) free from dullness or clouds. **3.** transparent: clear water. **4.** even and pure in tone or colour. **5.** without blemish, or defect: a clear skin. **6.** easy to see or hear; distinct. **7.** free from doubt or confusion. **8.** (postpositive) certain in the mind; sure: are you clear? **9.** (in combination) perceptive, alert: clear-eyed; clear-headed; clear-sighted. **10.** evident or obvious: it is clear that he won't come now. **11.** (of sounds or the voice) not harsh or hoarse. **12.** serene; calm. **13.** without qualification or limitation; complete: a clear victory. **14.** free of suspicion, guilt, or blame: a clear conscience. **15.** free of obstruction; open: a clear passage. **16.** free from debt or obligation. **17.** (of money, profits, etc.) without deduction; net. **18.** emptied of freight or cargo. **19.** Showjumping. (of a round) ridden without any points being lost. ~adv. **20.** in a clear or distinct manner. **21.** completely or utterly. **22.** (postpositive) often foll. by of) not in contact (with); free: stand clear of the gates. ~n. **23.** a clear space. **24. in the clear. a.** free of suspicion, guilt, or blame. **b.** Sport. able to receive a pass without being tackled. ~vb. **25.** to make or become free from darkness, obscurity, etc. **26.** (intr.) **a.** (of the weather) to become free from dullness, fog, rain, etc. **b.** (of mist, fog, etc.) to disappear. **27.** (tr.) to free from impurity or blemish. **28.** (tr.) to free from doubt or confusion. **29.** (tr.) to rid of objects, obstructions, etc. **30.** (tr.) to make or form (a path, way, etc.) by removing obstructions. **31.** (tr.) to free or remove (a person or thing) from something, as of suspicion, blame, or guilt. **32.** (tr.) to move or pass by or over without contact: he cleared the wall easily. **33.** (tr.) to rid (the throat) of phlegm. **34.** (tr.) to make or gain (money) as profit. **35.** (tr., often foll. by off) to discharge or settle (a debt). **36.** (tr.) to free (a debtor) from obligation. **37.** (intr.) (of a cheque) to pass through one's bank and be charged against one's account. **38.** Banking. to settle accounts by exchanging (commercial documents) in a clearing house. **39.** to permit (ships, aircraft, cargo, passengers, etc.) to unload, disembark, depart, etc., or (of ships, etc.) to be permitted to unload, etc. **40.** to obtain or give (clearance). **41.** (tr.) to obtain clearance from. **42.** (tr.) to permit (a person, company, etc.) to see or handle classified information. **43.** (tr.) Mil., etc. to decode (a message, etc.). **44.** Computers. to remove data from a storage device and revert to zero. **45. clear the air.** to dispel tension, confusion, etc. ~See also **clear away, clear off,** etc. —'**clearable** adj. —'**clearer**. —'**clearly** adv. —'**clearness** n.

clearance ('klɪərəns) n. **1. a.** the process or an instance of clearing: slum clearance. **b.** (as modifier): a clearance order. **2.** space between two parts in motion or in relative motion. **3.** permission for an aircraft, ship, passengers, etc., to proceed. **4.** official permission to have access to secret information, projects, areas, etc. **5.** Banking. the exchange of commercial documents drawn on the members of a clearing house. **6. a.** the disposal of merchandise at reduced prices. **b.** (as modifier): a clearance sale.

clear away vb. (adv.) to remove (objects) from (the table) after a meal.

clear-cut adj. (**clear cut** when postpositive). **1.** definite; not vague: a clear-cut proposal. **2.** clearly outlined.

clearing ('klɪərɪŋ) n. an area with few or no trees or shrubs in wooded or overgrown land.

clearing bank n. Brit. any bank that makes use of the

THESAURUS

clean adj. **1.** faultless, flawless, fresh, hygienic, immaculate, laundered, pure, sanitary, spotless, unblemished, unsoiled, unspotted, unstained, unsullied, washed **2.** antiseptic, clarified, decontaminated, natural, purified, sterile, sterilized, unadulterated, uncontaminated, unpolluted **3.** chaste, decent, exemplary, good, honourable, innocent, moral, pure, respectable, undefiled, upright, virtuous **4.** delicate, elegant, graceful, neat, simple, tidy, trim, uncluttered **5.** complete, conclusive, decisive, entire, final, perfect, thorough, total, unimpaired, whole ~v. **6.** bath, cleanse, deodorize, disinfect, do up, dust, launder, lave, mop, purge, purify, rinse, sanitize, scour, scrub, sponge, swab, sweep, vacuum, wash, wipe

clean-cut chiselled, clear, definite, etched, neat, outlined, sharp, trim, well-defined

cleanse absolve, clean, clear, lustrate, purge, purify, rinse, scour, scrub, wash

cleanser detergent, disinfectant, purifier, scourer, soap, soap powder, solvent

clear[1] adj. **1.** bright, cloudless, fair, fine, halcyon, light, luminous, shining, sunny, unclouded, undimmed **2.** apparent, audible, coherent, comprehensible, conspicuous, definite, distinct, evident, explicit, express, incontrovertible, intelligible, lucid, manifest, obvious, palpable, patent, perceptible, plain, pronounced, recognizable, unambiguous, unequivocal, unmistakable, unquestionable **3.** empty, free, open, smooth, unhampered, unhindered, unimpeded, unlimited, unobstructed **4.** crystalline, glassy, limpid, pellucid, see-through, transparent **5.** certain, convinced, decided, definite, positive, resolved, satisfied, sure **6.** clean, guiltless, immaculate, innocent, pure, sinless, stainless, unblemished,

undefiled, untarnished, untroubled

clear[2] v. **1.** clean, cleanse, erase, purify, refine, sweep away, tidy (up), wipe **2.** break up, brighten, clarify, lighten **3.** absolve, acquit, excuse, exonerate, justify, vindicate **4.** emancipate, free, liberate, set free **5.** disengage, disentangle, extricate, free, loosen, open, rid, unblock, unclog, unload, unpack **6.** jump, leap, miss, pass over, vault **7.** acquire, earn, gain, make, reap, secure

clearance **1.** authorization, consent, endorsement, go-ahead, green light, leave, O.K. (Inf.), permission, sanction **2.** allowance, gap, headroom, margin **3.** depopulation, emptying, evacuation, eviction, removal, unpeopling, withdrawal

clear-cut definite, explicit, plain, precise, specific, straightforward, unambiguous, unequivocal

central clearing house in London.

clearing house *n.* **1.** *Banking.* an institution where cheques and other commercial papers drawn on member banks are cancelled against each other so that only net balances are payable. **2.** a central agency for the collection and distribution of information or materials.

clear off *vb.* (*intr., adv.*) *Inf.* to go away: often used imperatively.

clear out *vb.* (*adv.*) **1.** (*intr.*) *Inf.* to go away: often used imperatively. **2.** (*tr.*) to remove and sort the contents of (a room, container, etc.). **3.** (*tr.*) *Sl.* to leave (someone) with no money. **4.** (*tr.*) *Sl.* to exhaust (stocks, goods, etc.) completely.

clearstory ('klıə,stɔːrı) *n.* a variant spelling of **clerestory.** —'**clear,storied** *adj.*

clear up *vb.* (*adv.*) **1.** (*tr.*) to explain or solve (a mystery, misunderstanding, etc.). **2.** to put (a place or thing that is disordered) in order. **3.** (*intr.*) (of the weather) to become brighter.

clearway ('klıə,weı) *n. Brit.* a stretch of road on which motorists may stop only in an emergency.

cleat (kliːt) *n.* **1.** a wedge-shaped block attached to a structure to act as a support. **2.** a device consisting of two hornlike prongs projecting horizontally in opposite directions from a central base, used for securing lines on vessels, wharves, etc. ~*vb.* (*tr.*) **3.** to supply or support with a cleat or cleats. **4.** to secure (a line) on a cleat.

cleavage ('kliːvıdʒ) *n.* **1.** *Inf.* the separation between a woman's breasts, esp. as revealed by a low-cut dress. **2.** a division or split. **3.** (of crystals) the act of splitting or the tendency to split along definite planes so as to yield smooth surfaces. **4.** (in animals) the repeated division of a fertilized ovum into a solid ball of cells. **5.** the breaking of a chemical bond in a molecule to give smaller molecules or radicals.

cleave[1] (kliːv) *vb.* **cleaving; cleft, cleaved,** *or* **clove; cleft, cleaved,** *or* **cloven. 1.** to split or cause to split, esp. along a natural weakness. **2.** (*tr.*) to make by or as if by cutting: *to cleave a path.* **3.** (when *intr.,* foll. by *through*) to penetrate or traverse. —'**cleavable** *adj.*

cleave[2] (kliːv) *vb.* (*intr.;* foll. by *to*) to cling or adhere.

cleaver ('kliːvə) *n.* a heavy knife or long-bladed hatchet, esp. one used by butchers.

cleavers ('kliːvəz) *n.* (*functioning as sing.*) a Eurasian plant, having small white flowers and prickly stems and fruits. Also called: **goosegrass, hairif.**

clef (klɛf) *n.* one of several symbols placed on the left-hand side beginning of each stave indicating the pitch of the music written after it.

cleft (klɛft) *vb.* **1.** the past tense or a past participle of **cleave**[1]. ~*n.* **2.** a fissure or crevice. **3.** an indentation or split in something, such as the chin, palate, etc. ~*adj.* **4.** split; divided.

cleft palate *n.* a congenital crack or fissure in the midline of the hard palate, often associated with a harelip.

cleg (klɛg) *n.* another name for a **horsefly.**

clematis ('klɛmətıs) *n.* any N temperate climbing plant of the genus *Clematis.* Many species are cultivated for their large colourful flowers.

clement ('klɛmənt) *adj.* **1.** merciful. **2.** (of the weather) mild. —'**clemency** *n.* —'**clemently** *adv.*

clementine ('klɛmən,tiːn, -,taın) *n.* a citrus fruit

thought to be either a variety of tangerine or a hybrid between a tangerine and sweet orange.

clench (klɛntʃ) *vb.* (*tr.*) **1.** to close or squeeze together (the teeth, a fist, etc.) tightly. **2.** to grasp or grip firmly. ~*n.* **3.** a firm grasp or grip. **4.** a device that grasps or grips. ~*n., vb.* **5.** another word for **clinch.**

clerestory *or* **clearstory** ('klıə,stɔːrı) *n., pl.* -**ries. 1.** a row of windows in the upper part of the wall of a church that divides the nave from the aisle. **2.** the part of the wall in which these windows are set. —'**clere,storied** *or* '**clear,storied** *adj.*

clergy ('klɜːdʒı) *n., pl.* -**gies.** the collective body of men and women ordained as ministers of the Christian Church.

clergyman ('klɜːdʒımən) *n., pl.* -**men.** a member of the clergy.

cleric ('klɛrık) *n.* a member of the clergy.

clerical ('klɛrıkəl) *adj.* **1.** relating to or associated with the clergy: *clerical dress.* **2.** of or relating to office clerks or their work: *a clerical error.* **3.** supporting or advocating clericalism. —'**clerically** *adv.*

clerical collar *n.* a stiff white collar with no opening at the front that buttons at the back of the neck; the distinctive mark of the clergy in certain Churches. Informal name: **dog collar.**

clerihew ('klɛrı,hjuː) *n.* a form of comic or satiric verse, consisting of two couplets of metrically irregular lines, containing the name of a well-known person.

clerk (klɑːk; *U.S.* klɜːrk) *n.* **1.** a worker, esp. in an office, who keeps records, files, etc. **2.** an employee of a court, legislature, board, corporation, etc., who keeps records and accounts, etc.: *a town clerk.* **3.** Also called: **clerk in holy orders.** a cleric. **4.** Also called: **desk clerk.** *U.S.* a hotel receptionist. **5.** *Arch.* a scholar. ~*vb.* **6.** (*intr.*) to serve as a clerk. —'**clerkess** *n.* (*chiefly Scot.*) —'**clerkish** *adj.* —'**clerkship** *n.*

clever ('klɛvə) *adj.* **1.** displaying sharp intelligence or mental alertness. **2.** adroit or dexterous, esp. with the hands. **3.** smart in a superficial way. **4.** *Brit. inf.* sly; cunning. —'**cleverly** *adv.* —'**cleverness** *n.*

clew (kluː) *n.* **1.** a ball of thread, yarn, or twine. **2.** *Naut.* either of the lower corners of a square sail or the after lower corner of a fore-and-aft sail. ~*vb.* **3.** (*tr.*) to coil into a ball.

cliché ('kliːʃeı) *n.* **1.** a word or expression that has lost much of its force through overexposure. **2.** an idea, action, or habit that has become trite from overuse. **3.** *Printing, chiefly Brit.* a stereotype or electrotype plate. —'**cliché'd** *or* '**clichéd** *adj.*

click (klık) *n.* **1.** a short light often metallic sound. **2.** the locking member of a ratchet mechanism, such as a pawl or detent. **3.** *Phonetics.* any of various stop consonants that are produced by the suction of air into the mouth. ~*vb.* **4.** to make or cause to make a clicking sound: *to click one's heels.* **5.** (*intr.*) *Sl.* to be a great success: *that idea really clicked.* **6.** (*intr.*) *Inf.* to become suddenly clear: *it finally clicked when her name was mentioned.* **7.** (*intr.*) *Sl.* to go or fit together with ease: *they clicked from their first meeting.* —'**clicker** *n.*

client ('klaıənt) *n.* **1.** a person, company, etc., that seeks the advice of a professional man or woman. **2.** a customer. **3.** a person for whom a social worker, etc., is responsible. —**cliental** (klaı'ɛntəl) *adj.*

THESAURUS

clearly beyond doubt, distinctly, evidently, incontestably, incontrovertibly, markedly, obviously, openly, seemingly, undeniably, undoubtedly

clear out 1. empty, exhaust, get rid of, sort, tidy up **2.** beat it (*Sl.*), decamp, depart, leave, make oneself scarce, retire, take oneself off, withdraw

clear up 1. answer, clarify, elucidate, explain, resolve, solve, straighten out, unravel **2.** order, rearrange, tidy (up)

cleave[1] abide by, adhere, agree, attach, be devoted to, be true, cling, cohere, hold, remain, stand by, stick

cleave[2] crack, dissever, disunite, divide, hew, open, part, rend, rive, sever, slice, split, sunder, tear asunder

clergy churchmen, clergymen, clerics, ecclesiastics, first estate, holy orders, ministry,

priesthood, the cloth

clergyman chaplain, cleric, curate, divine, father, man of God, man of the cloth, minister, padre, parson, pastor, priest, rabbi, rector, reverend (*Inf.*), vicar

clerical 1. ecclesiastical, pastoral, priestly, sacerdotal **2.** book-keeping, clerkish, clerkly, office, secretarial, stenographic

clever able, adroit, apt, astute, brainy (*Inf.*), bright, canny, capable, cunning, deep, dexterous, discerning, expert, gifted, ingenious, intelligent, inventive, keen, knowing, knowledgeable, quick, quick-witted, rational, resourceful, sagacious, sensible, shrewd, skilful, smart, talented, witty

cleverness ability, adroitness, astuteness, brains, brightness, canniness, dexterity, flair, gift, gumption (*Inf.*), ingenuity, intelligence, nous (*Sl.*), quickness, quick wits, re-

sourcefulness, sagacity, sense, sharpness, shrewdness, smartness, talent, wit

cliché banality, bromide, chestnut (*Inf.*), commonplace, hackneyed phrase, old saw, platitude, stereotype, truism

click *n./v.* **1.** beat, clack, snap, tick ~*v.* **2.** *Inf.* become clear, come home (to), fall into place, make sense **3.** *Sl.* be compatible, be on the same wavelength, feel a rapport, get on, go over (*Inf.*), hit it off (*Inf.*), make a hit, succeed, take to each other

client applicant, buyer, consumer, customer, dependant, habitué, patient, protégé, shopper

clientele business, clients, customers, following, market, patronage, regulars, trade

clientele (ˌkliːɒnˈtɛl) *or* **clientage** ('klaɪəntɪdʒ) *n*. customers or clients collectively.

cliff (klɪf) *n*. a steep high rock face, esp. one that runs along the seashore. —'**cliffy** *adj*.

cliffhanger ('klɪf,hæŋə) *n*. **1. a.** a situation of imminent disaster usually occurring at the end of each episode of a serialized film. **b.** the serialized film itself. **2.** a situation that is dramatic or uncertain. —'**cliff,hanging** *adj*.

climacteric (klaɪ'mæktərɪk, ˌklaɪmæk'tɛrɪk) *n*. **1.** a critical event or period. **2.** another name for **menopause**. **3.** the period in the life of a man corresponding to the menopause, chiefly characterized by diminished sexual activity. ~*adj.* also **climacterical** (ˌklaɪmæk-'tɛrɪkəl). **4.** involving a crucial event or period.

climate ('klaɪmɪt) *n*. **1.** the long-term prevalent weather conditions of an area, determined by latitude, altitude, etc. **2.** an area having a particular kind of climate. **3.** a prevailing trend: *the political climate.* —**climatic** (klaɪ-'mætɪk), **cli'matical,** *or* '**climatal** *adj*. —**cli'matically** *adv*.

climax ('klaɪmæks) *n*. **1.** the most intense or highest point of an experience or of a series of events: *the party was the climax of the week.* **2.** a decisive moment in a dramatic or other work. **3.** a rhetorical device by which a series of sentences, clauses, or phrases are arranged in order of increasing intensity. **4.** *Ecology.* the stage in the development of a community during which it remains stable under the prevailing environmental conditions. **5.** another word for **orgasm**. ~*vb.* **6.** to reach or bring to a climax. —**cli'mactic** *adj*.

▷ **Usage.** In formal English careful writers avoid the use of *climax* as a verb. The phrase *reach a climax* is preferred.

climb (klaɪm) *vb.* (*mainly intr.*) **1.** (*also tr.; often foll. by up*) to go up or ascend (stairs, a mountain, etc.). **2.** (often foll. by *along*) to progress with difficulty: *to climb along a ledge.* **3.** to rise to a higher point or intensity: *the temperature climbed.* **4.** to incline or slope upwards: *the road began to climb.* **5.** to ascend in social position. **6.** (of plants) to grow upwards by twining, using tendrils or suckers, etc. **7.** *Inf.* (foll. by *into*) to put (on) or get (into). **8.** to be a climber or mountaineer. ~*n.* **9.** the act of climbing. **10.** a place or thing to be climbed, esp. a route in mountaineering. —'**climbable** *adj*. —'**climber** *n*.

climb down *vb.* (*intr., adv.*) **1.** to descend. **2.** (often foll. by *from*) to retreat (from an opinion, position, etc.). ~*n.* **climb-down. 3.** a retreat from an opinion, etc.

clime (klaɪm) *n*. *Poetic.* a region or its climate.

clinch (klɪntʃ) *vb.* **1.** (*tr.*) to secure a driven nail, by bending the protruding point over. **2.** (*tr.*) to hold together in such a manner. **3.** (*tr.*) to settle something, such as an argument, bargain, etc., in a definite way. **4.** (*tr.*) *Naut.* to fasten by means of a clinch. **5.** (*intr.*) to engage in a clinch, as in boxing or wrestling. ~*n.* **6.** the act of clinching. **7. a.** a nail with its point bent over. **b.** the part of such a nail, etc., that has been bent over. **8.** *Boxing, wrestling, etc.* an act or an instance in which one or both competitors hold on to the other to avoid punches, regain wind, etc. **9.** *Sl.* a lovers' embrace. **10.** *Naut.* a loop or eye formed in a line. ~Also (for senses 1, 2, 4, 7, 8, 10): **clench.**

clincher ('klɪntʃə) *n*. **1.** *Inf.* something decisive, such as fact, score, etc. **2.** a person or thing that clinches.

-cline *n.* combining form. indicating a slope: *anticline.* —**-clinal** *combining form of adjectives.*

cling (klɪŋ) *vb.* **clinging, clung.** (*intr.*) **1.** (often foll. by *to*) to hold fast or adhere closely (to something), as by gripping or sticking. **2.** (foll. by *together*) to remain in contact (with each other). **3.** to be or remain physically

or emotionally close. —'**clinger** *n.* —'**clingingly** *adv.* —'**clingy** *adj.* —'**clinginess** *or* '**clingingness** *n.*

Clingfilm ('klɪŋ,fɪlm) *n. Trademark.* a thin polythene material having the power to adhere closely: used for wrapping food.

clinic ('klɪnɪk) *n*. **1.** a place in which outpatients are given medical treatment or advice. **2.** a similar place staffed by specialist physicians or surgeons: *eye clinic.* **3.** *Brit.* a private hospital or nursing home. **4.** the teaching of medicine to students at the bedside. **5.** *Chiefly U.S.* a group or centre that offers advice or instruction.

clinical ('klɪnɪkəl) *adj*. **1.** of or relating to a clinic. **2.** of or relating to the observation and treatment of patients directly: *clinical medicine.* **3.** scientifically detached; strictly objective: *a clinical attitude to life.* **4.** plain, simple, and usually unattractive. —'**clinically** *adv.*

clinical thermometer *n.* a thermometer for determining the temperature of the body.

clink¹ (klɪŋk) *vb.* **1.** to make or cause to make a light and sharply ringing sound. ~*n.* **2.** such a sound.

clink² (klɪŋk) *n.* a slang word for **prison.**

clinker ('klɪŋkə) *n*. **1.** the ash and partially fused residues from a coal-fired furnace or fire. **2.** a partially vitrified brick or mass of brick. **3.** *U.S. sl.* a mistake or fault, esp. a wrong note in music. ~*vb.* **4.** (*intr.*) to form clinker during burning.

clinker-built *or* **clincher-built** *adj.* (of a boat or ship) having a hull constructed with each plank overlapping that below.

clinometer (klaɪ'nɒmɪtə) *n.* an instrument used in surveying for measuring an angle of inclination. —**clinometric** (ˌklaɪnə'mɛtrɪk) *or* ˌ**clino'metrical** *adj.* —**cli'nometry** *n.*

clip¹ (klɪp) *vb.* **clipping, clipped.** (*mainly tr.*) **1.** (*also intr.*) to cut, snip, or trim with or as if with scissors or shears, esp. in order to shorten or remove a part. **2.** *Brit.* to punch (a hole) in something, esp. a ticket. **3.** to curtail or cut short. **4.** to move a short section from (a film, etc.). **5.** to shorten (a word). **6.** *Inf.* to strike with a sharp, often slanting, blow. **7.** *Sl.* to defraud or swindle, esp. by overcharging. ~*n.* **8.** the act or process of clipping. **9.** something clipped off. **10.** a short extract from a film, newspaper, etc. **11.** *Inf.* a sharp, often slanting, blow. **12.** *Inf.* speed: *a rapid clip.* **13.** *Austral.* the total quantity of wool shorn, as in one place, season, etc. **14.** another word for **clipped form.** —'**clippable** *adj.*

clip² (klɪp) *n.* **1.** any of various small implements used to hold loose articles together or to attach one article to another. **2.** an article of jewellery that can be clipped onto a dress, hat, etc. **3.** short for **paperclip** or **cartridge clip.** ~*vb.* **clipping, clipped.** (*tr.*) **4.** to hold together tightly, as with a clip.

clipboard ('klɪp,bɔːd) *n.* a portable writing board with a clip at the top for holding paper.

clip joint *n. Sl.* a place, such as a nightclub or restaurant, in which customers are overcharged.

clipped form *n.* a shortened form of a word.

clipper ('klɪpə) *n*. **1.** any fast sailing ship. **2.** a person or thing that cuts or clips.

clippers ('klɪpəz) *or* **clips** *pl. n*. **1.** a hand tool for clipping fingernails, veneers, etc. **2.** a hairdresser's tool for cutting short hair.

clippie ('klɪpɪ) *n. Brit. inf.* a bus conductress.

clipping ('klɪpɪŋ) *n.* something cut out, esp. an article from a newspaper; cutting.

clique (kliːk, klɪk) *n.* a small, exclusive group of friends or associates. —'**cliquey** *or* '**cliquy** *adj.* —'**cliquish** *adj.* —'**cliquishly** *adv.* —'**cliquishness** *n.*

clitoris ('klɪtərɪs, 'klaɪ-) *n.* a part of the female genitalia consisting of a small elongated highly sensitive erectile

---

THESAURUS

cliff bluff, crag, escarpment, face, overhang, precipice, rock face, scar, scarp

climactic climactic, critical, crucial, decisive, paramount, peak

climate 1. clime, country, region, temperature, weather **2.** ambience, disposition, feeling, mood, temper, tendency, trend

climax 1. *n.* acme, apogee, culmination, head, height, highlight, high spot (*Inf.*), ne plus ultra, pay-off (*Inf.*), peak, summit, top, zenith **2.** *v.* come to a head, culminate, peak

climb ascend, clamber, mount, rise, scale,

shin up, soar, top

climb down 1. descend, dismount **2.** back down, eat crow (*U.S. inf.*), eat one's words, retract, retreat

clinch 1. assure, cap, conclude, confirm, decide, determine, seal, secure, set the seal on, settle, sew up (*Inf.*), verify **2.** bolt, clamp, fasten, fix, make fast, nail, rivet, secure **3.** clutch, cuddle, embrace, grasp, hug, squeeze

cling adhere, attach to, be true to, clasp, cleave to, clutch, embrace, fasten, grasp, grip, hug, stick, twine round

clip¹ 1. *v.* crop, curtail, cut, cut short, pare, prune, shear, shorten, snip, trim **2.** *n./v. Inf.* blow, box, clout (*Inf.*), cuff, knock, punch, skelp (*Dialect*), smack, thump, wallop (*Inf.*), whack **3.** *n. Inf.* gallop, lick (*Inf.*), rate, speed, velocity

clip² *v.* attach, fasten, fix, hold, pin, staple

clique circle, clan, coterie, crew (*Inf.*), crowd, faction, gang, group, mob, pack, set

organ at the front of the vulva: homologous with the penis. —'**clitoral** adj.

cloak (kləʊk) n. **1.** a wraplike outer garment fastened at the throat and falling straight from the shoulders. **2.** something that covers or conceals. ~vb. (tr.) **3.** to cover with or as if with a cloak. **4.** to hide or disguise.

cloak-and-dagger n. (modifier) characteristic of or concerned with intrigue and espionage.

cloakroom ('kləʊk,ruːm) n. **1.** a room in which hats, coats, etc., may be temporarily deposited. **2.** Brit. a euphemistic word for **lavatory.**

clobber[1] ('klɒbə) vb. (tr.) Sl. **1.** to batter. **2.** to defeat utterly. **3.** to criticize severely.

clobber[2] ('klɒbə) n. Brit. sl. personal belongings, such as clothes.

cloche (klɒʃ) n. **1.** a bell-shaped cover used to protect young plants. **2.** a woman's close-fitting hat.

clock[1] (klɒk) n. **1.** a timepiece having mechanically or electrically driven pointers that move constantly over a dial showing the numbers of the hours. Cf. **watch** (sense 7). **2.** any clocklike device for recording or measuring, such as a taximeter or pressure gauge. **3.** the downy head of a dandelion that has gone to seed. **4.** short for **time clock. 5. around** or **round the clock.** all day and all night. **6.** (usually preceded by the) an informal word for **speedometer** or **mileometer. 7.** Brit. a slang word for **face.** ~vb. **8.** (tr.) Brit. & Austral. sl. to strike, esp. on the face or head. **9.** (tr.) to record time as with a stopwatch, esp. in the calculation of speed.

clock[2] (klɒk) n. an ornamental design on the side of a stocking.

clock off or **out** vb. (intr., adv.) to depart from work, esp. when it involves registering the time of departure on a card.

clock on or **in** vb. (intr., adv.) to arrive at work, esp. when it involves registering the time of arrival on a card.

clock up vb. (tr., adv.) to record or register: this car has clocked up 80 000 miles.

clock-watcher n. an employee who frequently checks the time in anticipation of a break or of the end of the working day.

clockwise ('klɒk,waɪz) adv., adj. in the direction that the hands of a clock rotate; from top to bottom towards the right when seen from the front.

clockwork ('klɒk,wɜːk) n. **1.** the mechanism of a clock. **2.** any similar mechanism, as in a wind-up toy. **3. like clockwork.** with complete regularity and precision; smoothly.

clod (klɒd) n. **1.** a lump of earth or clay. **2.** earth, esp. when heavy or in hard lumps. **3.** Also called: **clod poll, clodpate.** a dull or stupid person. —'**cloddy** adj. —'**cloddish** adj. —'**cloddishly** adv. —'**cloddishness** n.

clodhopper ('klɒd,hɒpə) n. Inf. **1.** a clumsy person; lout. **2.** (usually pl.) a large heavy shoe.

clog (klɒg) vb. **clogging, clogged. 1.** to obstruct or become obstructed with thick or sticky matter. **2.** (tr.) to encumber; hinder; impede. **3.** (intr.) to adhere or stick in a mass. ~n. **4. a.** any of various wooden or woodensoled shoes. **b.** (as modifier): clog dance. **5.** a heavy block, esp. of wood, fastened to the leg of a person or animal to impede motion. **6.** something that impedes motion or action; hindrance. —'**cloggy** adj. —'**clogginess** n.

cloisonné (klwɑː'zɒneɪ) n. **1. a.** a design made by filling in with coloured enamel an outline of flattened wire put on edge. **b.** the method of doing this. ~adj. **2.** of or made by cloisonné.

cloister ('klɔɪstə) n. **1.** a covered walk, usually around a quadrangle in a religious institution, having an open colonnade on the inside. **2.** (sometimes pl.) a place of religious seclusion, such as a monastery. **3.** life in a monastery or convent. ~vb. **4.** (tr.) to confine or seclude in or as if in a monastery. —'**cloistered** adj. —'**cloistral** adj.

clomp (klɒmp) n., vb. a less common word for **clump** (senses 2, 7).

clone (kləʊn) n. also **clon** (klɒn, kləʊn). **1.** a group of organisms or cells of the same genetic constitution that are descended from a common ancestor by asexual reproduction, as by cuttings, grafting, etc. ~vb. **2.** to produce or cause to produce a clone. —'**cloning** n.

clonk (klɒŋk) vb. (intr.) **1.** to make a loud dull thud. **2.** (tr.) Inf. to hit. ~n. **3.** a loud thud.

close vb. (kləʊz). **1.** to put or be put in such a position as to cover an opening; shut: the door closed behind him. **2.** (tr.) to bar, obstruct, or fill up (an entrance, a hole, etc.): to close a road. **3.** to bring the parts or edges of (a wound, etc.) together or (of a wound, etc.) to be brought together. **4.** (intr.; foll. by on, over, etc.) to take hold: his hand closed over the money. **5.** to bring or be brought to an end; terminate. **6.** (of agreements, deals, etc.) to complete or be completed successfully. **7.** to cease or cause to cease to render service: the shop closed at six. **8.** (intr.) Stock Exchange. to have a value at the end of a day's trading, as specified: steels closed two points down. **9.** (tr.) Arch. to enclose or shut in. ~adj. **10.** near in space or time; in proximity. **11.** having the parts near together; dense: a close formation. **12.** near to the surface; short: a close hair-cut. **13.** near in relationship: a close relative. **14.** intimate: a close friend. **15.** almost equal: a close contest. **16.** close call. Inf. a narrow escape. **17.** not deviating or varying greatly from a model or standard: a close resemblance; a close translation. **18.** careful, strict, or searching: a close study. **19.** confined or enclosed. **20.** shut or shut tight. **21.** oppressive, heavy, or airless: a close atmosphere. **22.** strictly guarded: a close prisoner. **23.** neat or tight in fit. **24.** secretive or reticent. **25.** miserly; not generous, esp. with money. **26.** (of money or credit) hard to obtain; scarce. **27.** restricted as to public admission or membership. **28.** hidden or secluded. **29.** Also: **closed.** restricted or prohibited as to the type of game or fish able to be taken. ~adv. (kləʊs). **30. close to the wind.** Naut. sailing as nearly as possible towards the direction from which the wind is blowing. **31.** closely; tightly. **32.** near or in proximity. ~n. (kləʊz). **33.** the act of closing. **34.** the end or conclusion: the close of the day. **35.** (kləʊs). Brit. a courtyard or quadrangle enclosed by buildings or an entry leading to such a courtyard. **36.** (kləʊs). Brit. (cap. when part of a street name) a small quiet residential road: Hillside Close. **37.** (kləʊs). the precincts of a cathedral or similar building. ~See also **close down, close in,** etc. —**closely** ('kləʊslɪ) adv. —**closeness** ('kləʊsnɪs) n. —**closer** ('kləʊzə) n.

closed (kləʊzd) adj. **1.** blocked against entry; shut. **2.** restricted; exclusive. **3.** not open to question or debate. **4.** (of a hunting season, etc.) close. **5.** Maths. **a.** (of a curve or surface) completely enclosing an area or volume. **b.** (of a set) having members that can be produced by a specific operation on other members of the same set. **6.** Phonetics. denoting a syllable that ends in a consonant. **7.** not open to public entry or membership: a closed society.

THESAURUS

cloak 1. v. camouflage, conceal, cover, disguise, hide, mask, obscure, screen, veil 2. n. blind, cape, coat, cover, front, mantle, mask, pretext, shield, wrap

clodhopper booby, boor, bumpkin, clown, galoot (Sl., chiefly U.S.), loon (Inf.), lout, oaf, yokel

clog 1. v. block, burden, congest, dam up, hamper, hinder, impede, jam, obstruct, occlude, shackle, stop up 2. n. burden, dead weight, drag, encumbrance, hindrance, impediment, obstruction

cloistered cloistral, confined, hermitic, insulated, reclusive, restricted, secluded, sequestered, sheltered, shielded, shut off,

withdrawn

close[1] v. 1. bar, block, choke, clog, confine, cork, fill, lock, obstruct, plug, seal, secure, shut, shut up, stop up 2. cease, complete, conclude, culminate, discontinue, end, finish, mothball, shut down, terminate, wind up (Inf.) 3. come together, connect, couple, fuse, grapple, join, unite

close[2] 1. adjacent, adjoining, approaching, at hand, handy, hard by, imminent, impending, near, nearby, neighbouring, nigh 2. compact, congested, cramped, cropped, crowded, dense, impenetrable, jam-packed, packed, short, solid, thick, tight 3. accurate, conscientious, exact, faithful, literal, precise, strict 4. alert, assiduous, attentive, careful,

concentrated, detailed, dogged, earnest, fixed, intense, intent, keen, minute, painstaking, rigorous, searching, thorough 5. attached, confidential, dear, devoted, familiar, inseparable, intimate, loving 6. airless, confined, frowsty, fuggy, heavy, humid, muggy, oppressive, stale, stifling, stuffy, suffocating, sweltering, thick, unventilated 7. hidden, private, reticent, retired, secluded, secret, secretive, taciturn, uncommunicative, unforthcoming 8. illiberal, mean, mingy (Inf.), miserly, near, niggardly, parsimonious, penurious, stingy, tight-fisted, ungenerous

close[3] cessation, completion, conclusion, culmination, denouement, end, ending, finale, finish, termination

closed circuit *n.* a complete electrical circuit through which current can flow.

closed-circuit television *n.* a television system in which signals are transmitted from the television camera to the receivers by cables or telephone links.

close down (kləʊz) *vb.* (*adv.*) 1. to cease or cause to cease operations. ~*n.* **close-down** ('kləʊz,daʊn). 2. a closure or stoppage, esp. in a factory. 3. *Brit. radio, television.* the end of a period of broadcasting, esp. late at night.

closed shop *n.* an industrial establishment in which there exists a contract between a trade union and the employer permitting the employment of the union's members only.

close in (kləʊz) *vb.* (*intr., adv.*) 1. (of days) to become shorter with the approach of winter. 2. (foll. by *on* or *upon*) to advance (on) so as to encircle or surround.

close out (kləʊz) *vb.* (*adv.*) to terminate (a client's or other account) usually by sale of securities to realize cash.

close quarters (kləʊs) *pl. n.* 1. a narrow cramped space or position. 2. **at close quarters. a.** engaged in hand-to-hand combat. **b.** in close proximity; very near together.

close season (kləʊs) *or* **closed season** *n.* the period of the year when it is prohibited to kill certain game or fish.

close shave (kləʊs) *n. Inf.* a narrow escape.

closet ('klɒzɪt) *n.* 1. a small cupboard or recess. 2. a small private room. 3. short for **water closet.** 4. (*modifier*) *U.S.* private or secret. ~*vb.* 5. (*tr.*) to shut up or confine in a small private room, esp. for conference or meditation.

close-up ('kləʊs,ʌp) *n.* 1. a photograph, film, or television shot, taken at close range. 2. a detailed or intimate view or examination. ~*vb.* **close up** (kləʊz). (*adv.*) 3. to shut entirely. 4. (*intr.*) to draw together: *the ranks closed up.* 5. (*intr.*) (of wounds) to heal completely.

close with (kləʊz) *vb.* (*intr., prep.*) to engage in battle with (an enemy).

closure ('kləʊʒə) *n.* 1. the act of closing or the state of being closed. 2. an end or conclusion. 3. something that closes or shuts, such as a cap or seal for a container. 4. (in a deliberative body) a procedure by which debate may be halted and an immediate vote taken. ~*vb.* 5. (*tr.*) (in a deliberative body) to end (debate) by closure.

clot (klɒt) *n.* 1. a soft thick lump or mass. 2. *Brit. sl.* a stupid person; fool. ~*vb.* **clotting, clotted.** 3. to form or cause to form into a soft thick lump or lumps.

cloth (klɒθ) *n., pl.* **cloths** (klɒðs, klɒðz). 1. **a.** a fabric formed by weaving, felting or knitting wool, cotton, etc. **b.** (*as modifier*): *a cloth bag.* 2. a piece of such fabric used for a particular purpose, as for a dishcloth. 3. (usually preceded by *the*) the clergy.

clothe (kləʊð) *vb.* **clothing, clothed** *or* **clad.** (*tr.*) 1. to dress or attire (a person). 2. to provide with clothing. 3. to conceal or disguise. 4. to endow or invest.

clothes (kləʊðz) *pl. n.* 1. articles of dress. 2. *Chiefly Brit.* short for **bedclothes.**

clotheshorse ('kləʊðz,hɔːs) *n.* 1. a frame on which to hang laundry for drying or airing. 2. *Inf.* an excessively fashionable person.

clothes peg *n.* a small wooden or plastic clip for attaching washing to a clothesline.

clothier ('kləʊðɪə) *n.* a person who makes, sells, or deals in clothes or cloth.

clothing ('kləʊðɪŋ) *n.* 1. garments collectively. 2. something that covers or clothes.

clotted cream *n. Brit.* a thick cream made from scalded milk, esp. in SW England.

cloud (klaʊd) *n.* 1. a mass of water or ice particles visible in the sky. 2. any collection of particles visible in the air, esp. of smoke or dust. 3. a large number of insects or other small animals in flight. 4. something that darkens, threatens, or carries gloom. 5. *Jewellery.* a cloudlike blemish in a transparent stone. 6. **in the clouds.** not in contact with reality. 7. **under a cloud. a.** under reproach or suspicion. **b.** in a state of gloom or bad temper. 8. **on cloud nine.** *Inf.* elated; very happy. ~*vb.* 9. (when *intr.*, often foll. by *over* or *up*) to make or become cloudy, overcast, or indistinct. 10. (*tr.*) to make obscure; darken. 11. to make or become gloomy or depressed. 12. (*tr.*) to place under or render liable to suspicion or disgrace. 13. to render (liquids) milky or dull or (of liquids) to become milky or dull. — '**cloudless** *adj.* — '**cloudlessly** *adv.* — '**cloudlessness** *n.*

cloudburst ('klaʊd,bɜːst) *n.* a heavy downpour.

cloud chamber *n. Physics.* an apparatus for detecting high-energy particles by observing their tracks through a chamber containing a supersaturated vapour.

cloudy ('klaʊdɪ) *adj.* **cloudier, cloudiest.** 1. covered with cloud or clouds. 2. of or like clouds. 3. streaked or mottled like a cloud. 4. opaque or muddy. 5. obscure or unclear. 6. troubled or gloomy. — '**cloudily** *adv.* — '**cloudiness** *n.*

clough (klʌf) *n. Brit. dialect.* a ravine.

clout (klaʊt) *n.* 1. *Inf.* a blow with the hand or a hard object. 2. power or influence, esp. political. 3. Also called: **clout nail.** a short, flat-headed nail. 4. *Brit. dialect.* **a.** a piece of cloth: *a dish clout.* **b.** a garment. ~*vb.* (*tr.*) 5. *Inf.* to give a hard blow to, esp. with the hand.

clove[1] (kləʊv) *n.* 1. a tropical evergreen tree of the myrtle family. 2. the dried unopened flower buds of this tree, used as a pungent fragrant spice.

clove[2] (kləʊv) *n.* any of the segments of a compound bulb that arise from the axils of the scales of a large bulb.

clove[3] (kləʊv) *vb.* a past tense of **cleave**[1].

clove hitch *n.* a knot or hitch used for securing a rope to a spar, post, or larger rope.

cloven ('kləʊvən) *vb.* 1. a past participle of **cleave**[1]. ~*adj.* 2. split; cleft; divided.

cloven hoof *or* **foot** *n.* 1. the divided hoof of a pig, goat, cow, deer, or related animal. 2. the mark or symbol of Satan. — ,**cloven-'hoofed** *or* ,**cloven-'footed** *adj.*

clover ('kləʊvə) *n.* 1. a leguminous fodder plant having trifoliate leaves and dense flower heads. 2. any of various similar or related plants. 3. **in clover.** *Inf.* in a state of ease or luxury.

cloverleaf ('kləʊvə,liːf) *n., pl.* **-leaves.** 1. an arrangement of connecting roads, resembling a four-leaf clover in form, that joins two intersecting main roads. 2. (*modifier*) in the shape or pattern of a leaf of clover.

clown (klaʊn) *n.* 1. a comic entertainer, usually grotesquely costumed and made up, appearing in the circus. 2. a person who acts in a comic or buffoon-like manner. 3. a clumsy rude person; boor. 4. *Arch.* a countryman or rustic. ~*vb.* (*intr.*) 5. to perform as a clown. 6. to play jokes or tricks. 7. to act foolishly. — '**clownery** *n.* — '**clownish** *adj.* — '**clownishly** *adv.* — '**clownishness** *n.*

cloy (klɔɪ) *vb.* to make weary or cause weariness through an excess of something initially pleasurable or sweet. — '**cloyingly** *adv.*

club (klʌb) *n.* 1. a stout stick, usually with one end thicker than the other, esp. one used as a weapon. 2. a stick or bat used to strike the ball in various sports, esp. golf.

THESAURUS

closed 1. fastened, locked, out of business, out of service, sealed, shut 2. concluded, decided, ended, finished, over, resolved, settled, terminated 3. exclusive, restricted

cloth dry goods, fabric, material, stuff, textiles

clothe accoutre, apparel, array, attire, bedizen (*Archaic*), caparison, cover, deck, doll up (*Sl.*), drape, dress, endow, enwrap, equip, fit out, garb, habit, invest, outfit, rig, robe, swathe

clothes, clothing apparel, attire, clobber (*Brit. sl.*), costume, dress, duds (*Inf.*), ensemble, garb, garments, gear (*Inf.*), get-up

(*Inf.*), habits, outfit, raiment, rigout (*Inf.*), togs (*Inf.*), vestments, vesture, wardrobe, wear

cloud *n.* 1. billow, darkness, fog, gloom, haze, mist, murk, nebula, nebulosity, obscurity, vapour 2. crowd, dense mass, flock, horde, host, multitude, shower, swarm, throng ~*v.* 3. becloud, darken, dim, eclipse, obfuscate, obscure, overcast, overshadow, shade, shadow, veil 4. confuse, disorient, distort, impair, muddle

cloudy blurred, confused, dark, dim, dismal, dull, dusky, emulsified, gloomy, hazy, indistinct, leaden, lowering, muddy, murky,

nebulous, obscure, opaque, overcast, sombre, sullen, sunless

clout 1. *v.* box, clobber (*Sl.*), cuff, hit, skelp (*Dialect*), sock (*Sl.*), strike, thump, wallop (*Inf.*), wham 2. *n.* authority, influence, power, prestige, pull, standing, weight

clown *n.* 1. buffoon, comedian, dolt, fool, harlequin, jester, joker, merry-andrew, mountebank, pierrot, prankster, punchinello 2. boor, clodhopper (*Inf.*), hind, peasant, swain (*Archaic*), yahoo, yokel ~*v.* 3. act the fool, act the goat, jest, mess about

See **golf club. 3.** short for **Indian club. 4.** a group or association of people with common aims or interests. **5.** the room, building, or facilities used by such a group. **6.** a building in which elected, fee-paying members go to meet, dine, read, etc. **7.** a commercial establishment providing drinks, food, etc. See also **nightclub. 8.** *Chiefly Brit.* an organization, esp. in a shop, set up as a means of saving. **9.** *Brit.* an informal word for **friendly society. 10. a.** the black trefoil symbol on a playing card. **b.** a card with one or more of these symbols or (*when pl.*) the suit of cards so marked. **11. in the club.** *Brit. sl.* pregnant. *~vb.* **clubbing, clubbed. 12.** (*tr.*) to beat with or as if with a club. **13.** (often foll. by *together*) to gather or become gathered into a group. **14.** (often foll. by *together*) to unite or combine (resources, efforts, etc.) for a common purpose. —**'clubber** *n.*

club foot *n.* **1.** a congenital deformity of the foot, esp. one in which the foot is twisted so that most of the weight rests on the heel. Technical name: **talipes. 2.** a foot so deformed. —**club-'footed** *adj.*

clubhouse ('klʌb,haʊs) *n.* the premises of a sports or other club, esp. a golf club.

club root *n.* a fungal disease of cabbages and related plants, in which the roots become thickened and distorted.

cluck (klʌk) *n.* **1.** the low clicking sound made by a hen or any similar sound. *~vb.* **2.** (*intr.*) (of a hen) to make a clicking sound. **3.** (*tr.*) to call or express (a feeling) by making a similar sound.

clue (kluː) *n.* **1.** something that helps to solve a problem or unravel a mystery. **2. not to have a clue. a.** to be completely baffled. **b.** to be ignorant or incompetent. *~vb.* **cluing, clued. 3.** (*tr.; usually foll. by *in* or *up*) to provide with helpful information.

clueless ('kluːlɪs) *adj. Sl.* helpless; stupid.

clump (klʌmp) *n.* **1.** a cluster, as of trees or plants. **2.** a dull heavy tread or any similar sound. **3.** an irregular mass. **4.** an inactive mass of microorganisms, esp. a mass of bacteria produced as a result of agglutination. **5.** an extra sole on a shoe. **6.** *Sl.* a blow. *~vb.* **7.** (*intr.*) to walk or tread heavily. **8.** to gather or be gathered into clumps, clusters, clots, etc. **9.** to cause (bacteria, blood cells, etc.) to collect together or (of bacteria, etc.) to collect together. See also **agglutination** (sense 3). **10.** (*tr.*) *Sl.* to punch (someone). —**'clumpy** or **'clump-ish** *adj.*

clumsy ('klʌmzɪ) *adj.* **-sier, -siest. 1.** lacking in skill or physical coordination. **2.** awkwardly constructed or contrived. —**'clumsily** *adv.* —**'clumsiness** *n.*

clung (klʌŋ) *vb.* the past tense or past participle of **cling.**

clunk (klʌŋk) *n.* **1.** a blow or the sound of a blow. **2.** a dull metallic sound. *~vb.* **3.** to make or cause to make such a sound.

cluster ('klʌstə) *n.* **1.** a number of things growing, fastened, or occurring close together. **2.** a number of persons or things grouped together. *~vb.* **3.** to gather or be gathered in clusters. —**'clustered** *adj.* —**'clustery** *adj.*

clutch[1] (klʌtʃ) *vb.* **1.** (*tr.*) to seize with or as if with hands or claws. **2.** (*tr.*) to grasp or hold firmly. **3.** (*intr.; usually foll. by *at*) to attempt to get hold or possession (of). *~n.* **4.** a device that enables two revolving shafts to be joined or disconnected, esp. one that transmits the drive from the engine to the gearbox in a vehicle. **5.** a device for holding fast. **6.** a firm grasp. **7.** a hand, claw, or talon in the act of clutching: *in the clutches of a bear.* **8.** (often *pl.*) power or control: *in the clutches of the Mafia.*

clutch[2] (klʌtʃ) *n.* **1.** a hatch of eggs laid by a particular bird or laid in a single nest. **2.** a brood of chickens. **3.** *Inf.* a group or cluster. *~vb.* **4.** (*tr.*) to hatch (chickens).

clutter ('klʌtə) *vb.* **1.** (usually *tr.; often foll. by *up*) to strew or amass (objects) in a disorderly manner. **2.** (*intr.*) to move about in a bustling manner. *~n.* **3.** a disordered heap or mass of objects. **4.** a state of disorder. **5.** unwanted echoes that confuse the observation of signals on a radar screen.

Clydesdale ('klaɪdz,deɪl) *n.* a heavy powerful breed of carthorse, originally from Scotland.

cm *or* **cm.** *abbrev. for* centimetre.

Cm *the chemical symbol for* curium.

Cmdr. *Mil. abbrev. for* Commander.

C.M.G. *abbrev. for* Companion of St. Michael and St. George (a Brit. title).

cml. *abbrev. for* commercial.

C.N.D. (in Britain) *abbrev. for* Campaign for Nuclear Disarmament.

Co *the chemical symbol for* cobalt.

Co. *or* **co.** *abbrev. for:* **1.** (esp. in names of business organizations) Company. **2. and co.** (kəʊ) *Inf.* and the rest of them: *Harold and co.*

Co. *abbrev. for* County.

C.O. *abbrev. for:* **1.** Commanding Officer. **2.** conscientious objector.

co- *prefix.* **1.** together; joint or jointly; mutual or mutually: *coproduction.* **2.** indicating partnership or equality: *costar; copilot.* **3.** to the same or a similar degree: *coextend.* **4.** (in mathematics and astronomy) of the complement of an angle: *cosecant.*

c/o *abbrev. for:* **1.** care of. **2.** *Book-keeping.* carried over.

coach (kəʊtʃ) *n.* **1.** a vehicle for several passengers, used for transport over long distances, sightseeing, etc. **2.** a large four-wheeled enclosed carriage, usually horse-drawn. **3.** a railway carriage. **4.** a trainer or instructor: *a drama coach.* **5.** a tutor who prepares students for examinations. *~vb.* **6.** to give tuition or instruction to (a pupil). **7.** (*tr.*) to transport in a bus or coach. —**'coach-er** *n.*

coachman ('kəʊtʃmən) *n., pl.* **-men.** the driver of a coach or carriage.

coachwork ('kəʊtʃ,wɜːk) *n.* **1.** the design and manufacture of car bodies. **2.** the body of a car.

coadjutor (kəʊ'ædʒʊtə) *n.* **1.** a bishop appointed as assistant to a diocesan bishop. **2.** *Rare.* an assistant.

coagulate *vb.* (kəʊ'ægjʊ,leɪt). **1.** to cause (a fluid, such as blood) to change into a soft semisolid mass or (of such a fluid) to change into such a mass; clot; curdle. *~n.* (kəʊ'ægjʊlɪt, -,leɪt). **2.** the solid or semisolid substance produced by coagulation. —**coagulant** (kəʊ-'ægjʊlənt) *or* **co'agu,lator** *n.* —**co,agu'lation** *n.* —**co-agulative** (kəʊ'ægjʊlətɪv) *adj.*

coal (kəʊl) *n.* **1. a.** a compact black or dark brown carbonaceous rock consisting of layers of partially decomposed vegetation deposited in the Carboniferous period: a fuel and a source of coke, coal gas, and coal tar. **b.** (as modifier): *coal cellar; coal mine; coal dust.* **2.** one or more lumps of coal. **3.** short for **charcoal. 4. coals to Newcastle.** something supplied where it already exists. *~vb.* **5.** to take in, provide with, or turn into coal. —**'coaly** *adj.*

coalesce (,kəʊə'lɛs) *vb.* (*intr.*) to unite or come together in one body or mass; merge; fuse; blend. —**,coa'les-cence** *n.* —**,coa'lescent** *adj.*

coalface ('kəʊl,feɪs) *n.* the exposed seam of coal in a mine.

coalfield ('kəʊl,fiːld) *n.* an area rich in deposits of coal.

THESAURUS

club 1. *n.* bat, bludgeon, cosh, cudgel, stick, truncheon **2.** *v.* bash, baste, batter, beat, bludgeon, clobber (*Sl.*), clout (*Inf.*), cosh, hammer, pommel (*Rare*), pummel, strike **3.** *n.* association, circle, clique, company, fraternity, group, guild, lodge, order, set, society, sodality, union

clue evidence, hint, indication, inkling, intimation, lead, pointer, sign, suggestion, suspicion, tip, tip-off, trace

clump 1. *n.* bunch, bundle, cluster, mass, shock **2.** *v.* bumble, clomp, lumber, plod, stamp, stomp, stump, thud, thump, tramp

clumsy awkward, blundering, bumbling, bungling, cack-handed (*Inf.*), gauche, gawky, ham-fisted (*Inf.*), ham-handed (*Inf.*), heavy, ill-shaped, inept, inexpert, lumbering, maladroit, ponderous, uncoordinated, uncouth, ungainly, unhandy, unskilful, unwieldy

cluster 1. *n.* assemblage, batch, bunch, clump, collection, gathering, group, knot **2.** *v.* assemble, bunch, collect, flock, gather, group

clutch catch, clasp, cling to, embrace, fasten, grab, grapple, grasp, grip, seize, snatch

clutches claws, control, custody, grasp, grip, hands, keeping, possession, power,

sway

clutter 1. *n.* confusion, disarray, disorder, hotchpotch, jumble, litter, mess, muddle, untidiness **2.** *v.* litter, scatter, strew

coach *n.* **1.** bus, car, carriage, charabanc, vehicle **2.** instructor, teacher, trainer, tutor *~v.* **3.** cram, drill, instruct, prepare, train, tutor

coalesce amalgamate, blend, cohere, combine, come together, commingle, commix, consolidate, fraternize, fuse, incorporate, integrate, merge, mix, unite

coalfish ('kəulˌfɪʃ) n., pl. **-fish** or **-fishes**. a dark-coloured gadoid food fish occurring in northern seas. Also called (Brit.): **saithe, coley.**

coal gas n. a mixture of gases produced by the distillation of bituminous coal and used for heating and lighting.

coalition (ˌkəuə'lɪʃən) n. 1. a. an alliance between groups or parties, esp. for some temporary and specific reason. b. (as modifier): a coalition government. 2. a fusion or merging into one body or mass. —ˌcoa'litionist n.

coal scuttle n. a domestic metal container for coal.

coal tar n. a black tar, produced by the distillation of bituminous coal, that can be further distilled to yield benzene, toluene, etc.

coal tit n. a small European songbird having a black head with a white patch on the nape.

coaming ('kəumɪŋ) n. a raised frame round a ship's hatchway for keeping out water.

coarse (kɔːs) adj. 1. rough in texture, structure, etc.; not fine: coarse sand. 2. lacking refinement or taste; indelicate; vulgar: coarse jokes. 3. of inferior quality. 4. (of a metal) not refined. —'coarsely adv. —'coarseness n.

coarse fish n. a freshwater fish that is not of the salmon family. —**coarse fishing** n.

coarsen ('kɔːsən) vb. to make or become coarse.

coast (kəust) n. 1. the line or zone where the land meets the sea. Related adj.: **littoral.** 2. Brit. the seaside. 3. U.S. a. a slope down which a sledge may slide. b. the act or an instance of sliding down a slope. 4. **the coast is clear.** Inf. the obstacles or dangers are gone. ~vb. 5. to move or cause to move by momentum or force of gravity. 6. (intr.) to proceed without great effort: to coast to victory. 7. to sail along (a coast). —'coastal adj.

coaster ('kəustə) n. 1. Brit. a vessel engaged in coastal commerce. 2. a small tray for holding a decanter, wine bottle, etc. 3. a person or thing that coasts. 4. Chiefly U.S. a protective mat for glasses. 5. U.S. short for **roller coaster.**

Coaster ('kəustə) n. N.Z. a person from the West Coast of the South Island, New Zealand.

coastguard ('kəustˌɡɑːd) n. 1. a maritime force which aids shipping, saves lives at sea, prevents smuggling, etc. 2. Also called: **coastguardsman.** a member of such a force.

coastline ('kəustˌlaɪn) n. the outline of a coast.

coat (kəut) n. 1. an outdoor garment with sleeves, covering the body from the shoulders to waist, knee, or foot. 2. any similar garment, esp. one forming the top to a suit. 3. a layer that covers or conceals a surface: a coat of dust. 4. the hair, wool, or fur of an animal. ~vb. 5. (tr.; often foll. by with) to cover (with) a layer or covering. 6. (tr.) to provide with a coat.

coating ('kəutɪŋ) n. 1. a layer or film spread over a surface. 2. fabric suitable for coats.

coat of arms n. the heraldic bearings of a person, family, or corporation.

coat of mail n. a protective garment made of linked metal rings or overlapping metal plates.

coat-tail n. the long tapering tails at the back of a man's tailed coat.

coax (kəuks) vb. 1. to seek to manipulate or persuade (someone) by tenderness, flattery, pleading, etc. 2. (tr.) to obtain by persistent coaxing. —**coaxer** n. —**coaxingly** adv.

coaxial (kəu'æksɪəl) or **coaxal** (kəu'æksəl) adj. 1. having or mounted on a common axis. 2. Geom. (of a set of circles) having the same radical axis. 3. Electronics. formed from, using, or connected to a coaxial cable.

cob (kɒb) n. 1. a male swan. 2. a thickset type of riding and draught horse. 3. short for **corncob.** 4. Brit. another name for **hazel** (sense 1). 5. a small rounded lump or heap of coal, ore, etc. 6. a building material consisting of a mixture of clay and chopped straw. 7. Brit. a round loaf of bread.

cobalt ('kəubɔːlt) n. a brittle hard silvery-white element that is a ferromagnetic metal: used in alloys. The radio-isotope **cobalt-60** is used in radiotherapy and as a tracer. Symbol: Co; atomic no.: 27; atomic wt.: 58.933.

cobalt blue n. 1. any greenish-blue pigment containing cobalt aluminate. 2. a. a deep blue colour. b. (as adj.): a cobalt-blue car.

cobalt bomb n. 1. a cobalt-60 device used in radiotherapy. 2. a nuclear weapon consisting of a hydrogen bomb encased in cobalt, which releases large quantities of radioactive cobalt-60 into the atmosphere.

cobber ('kɒbə) n. Austral. arch. & N.Z. a friend; mate: used as a term of address to males.

cobble[1] ('kɒbəl) n. 1. short for **cobblestone.** ~vb. 2. (tr.) to pave (a road, etc.) with cobblestones.

cobble[2] ('kɒbəl) vb. (tr.) 1. to make or mend shoes. 2. to put together clumsily.

cobbler[1] ('kɒblə) n. a person who makes or mends shoes.

cobbler[2] ('kɒblə) n. 1. a sweetened iced drink, usually made from fruit and wine. 2. Chiefly U.S. a hot dessert made of fruit covered with a rich cakelike crust.

cobblers ('kɒbləz) Brit. taboo sl. ~pl. n. 1. testicles. 2. (a load of old) cobblers. rubbish; nonsense.

cobblestone ('kɒbəlˌstəun) n. a rounded stone used for paving. Sometimes shortened to **cobble.**

COBOL ('kəuˌbɒl) n. a high-level computer programming language designed for general commercial use.

cobra ('kəubrə) n. 1. any highly venomous snake such as the **Indian cobra**, of tropical Africa and Asia. When alarmed they spread the skin of the neck region into a hood. 2. any related snake, such as the king cobra.

cobweb ('kɒbˌweb) n. 1. a web spun by certain spiders. 2. a single thread of such a web. 3. something like a cobweb, as in its flimsiness or ability to trap. —'cobˌwebbed adj. —'cobˌwebby adj.

cobwebs ('kɒbˌwebz) pl. n. 1. mustiness, confusion, or obscurity. 2. Inf. stickiness of the eyelids experienced upon first awakening.

coca ('kəukə) n. either of two shrubs, native to the Andes, the dried leaves of which contain cocaine and are chewed for their stimulating effects.

Coca-Cola (ˌkəukə'kəulə) n. Trademark. a carbonated soft drink flavoured with coca leaves, cola nuts, caramel, etc.

cocaine or **cocain** (kə'keɪn) n. an addictive narcotic drug derived from coca leaves or synthesized, used medicinally as a topical anaesthetic.

coccus ('kɒkəs) n., pl. **-ci** (-saɪ). any spherical or nearly spherical bacterium, such as a staphylococcus. —'coccoid or 'coccal adj.

coccyx ('kɒksɪks) n., pl. **coccyges** (kɒk'saɪdʒiːz). a small triangular bone at the end of the spinal column in man and some apes. —**coccygeal** (kɒk'sɪdʒɪəl) adj.

cochineal (ˌkɒtʃɪ'niːl, 'kɒtʃɪˌniːl) n. 1. a Mexican insect that feeds on cacti. 2. a crimson substance obtained from the crushed bodies of these insects, used for colouring food and for dyeing. 3. the colour of this dye.

cochlea ('kɒklɪə) n., pl. **-leae** (-lɪˌiː). the spiral tube that forms part of the internal ear, converting sound vibrations into nerve impulses. —'cochlear adj.

cock[1] (kɒk) n. 1. the male of the domestic fowl. 2. a. any other male bird. b. the male of certain other animals, such as the lobster. c. (as modifier): a cock sparrow. 3. short for **stopcock** or **weathercock.** 4. a taboo slang word for **penis.** 5. a. the hammer of a firearm. b.

---

coalition affiliation, alliance, amalgam, amalgamation, association, bloc, combination, compact, confederacy, confederation, conjunction, fusion, integration, league, merger, union

coarse 1. boorish, brutish, coarse-grained, foul-mouthed, gruff, loutish, rough, rude, uncivil 2. bawdy, earthy, immodest, impolite, improper, impure, indelicate, inelegant, mean, offensive, ribald, rude, smutty, vulgar 3. coarse-grained, crude, homespun, impure, rough-hewn, unfinished, unpolished, unprocessed, unpurified, unrefined

coarsen anaesthetize, blunt, callous, deaden, desensitize, dull, harden, indurate, roughen

coarseness bawdiness, boorishness, crudity, earthiness, indelicacy, offensiveness, poor taste, ribaldry, roughness, smut, smuttiness, uncouthness, unevenness

coast 1. n. beach, border, coastline, littoral, seaboard, seaside, shore, strand 2. v. cruise, drift, freewheel, get by, glide, sail, taxi

coat n. 1. fleece, fur, hair, hide, pelt, skin, wool 2. coating, covering, layer, overlay ~v. 3. apply, cover, plaster, smear, spread

coating blanket, coat, covering, dusting, film, finish, glaze, lamination, layer, membrane, patina, sheet, skin, varnish, veneer

coax allure, beguile, cajole, decoy, entice, flatter, inveigle, persuade, prevail upon, soft-soap (Inf.), soothe, talk into, wheedle

its position when the firearm is ready to be discharged. **6.** *Brit. inf.* a friend, mate, or fellow. **7.** a jaunty or significant tilting upwards: *a cock of the head.* ~*vb.* **8.** (*tr.*) to set or pull the hammer of (a firearm) into firing position. **9.** (*tr.; sometimes foll. by up*) to raise in an alert or jaunty manner. **10.** (*intr.*) to stick or stand up conspicuously. ~See also **cockup.**

cock² (kɒk) *n.* **1.** a small, cone-shaped heap of hay, straw, etc. ~*vb.* **2.** (*tr.*) to stack (hay, etc.) in such heaps.

cockade (kɒˈkeɪd) *n.* a feather or ribbon worn on military headwear. —**cockˈaded** *adj.*

cock-a-hoop *adj.* (*usually postpositive*) **1.** in very high spirits. **2.** boastful. **3.** askew; confused.

cock-a-leekie *or* **cocky-leeky** (ˌkɒkəˈliːkɪ) *n.* a soup made from a fowl boiled with leeks, etc.

cock-and-bull story *n. Inf.* an obviously improbable story, esp. one used as an excuse.

cockatoo (ˌkɒkəˈtuː, ˈkɒkəˌtuː) *n., pl.* **-toos.** **1.** any of a genus of parrots having an erectile crest and light-coloured plumage. **2.** *Austral. & N.Z.* a small farmer or settler. **3.** *Austral. inf.* a lookout during some illegal activity.

cockatrice (ˈkɒkətrɪs, -ˌtraɪs) *n.* **1.** a legendary monster, part snake and part cock, that could kill with a glance. **2.** another name for **basilisk.**

cockchafer (ˈkɒkˌtʃeɪfə) *n.* any of various Old World beetles, whose larvae feed on crops and grasses. Also called: **May beetle, May bug.**

cockcrow (ˈkɒkˌkrəʊ) *or* **cockcrowing** *n.* daybreak.

cocked hat *n.* **1.** a hat with brims turned up and caught together in order to give two points (bicorn) or three points (tricorn). **2. knock into a cocked hat.** *Sl.* to outdo or defeat someone.

cockerel (ˈkɒkərəl, ˈkɒkrəl) *n.* a young domestic cock, less than a year old.

cocker spaniel (ˈkɒkə) *n.* a small compact breed of spaniel.

cockeyed (ˈkɒkˌaɪd) *adj. Inf.* **1.** afflicted with crosseye or squint. **2.** physically or logically abnormal, absurd, etc.; askew: *cockeyed ideas.* **3.** drunk.

cockfight (ˈkɒkˌfaɪt) *n.* a fight between two gamecocks fitted with sharp metal spurs. —**ˈcockˌfighting** *n.*

cockle¹ (ˈkɒkəl) *n.* **1.** any edible sand-burrowing bivalve mollusc of Europe, typically having a rounded shell with radiating ribs. **2.** any of certain similar or related molluscs. **3.** short for **cockleshell** (sense 1). **4.** a wrinkle or puckering. **5.** one's deepest feelings (esp. in **warm the cockles of one's heart**). ~*vb.* **6.** to contract or cause to contract into wrinkles.

cockle² (ˈkɒkəl) *n.* any of several plants, esp. the corn cockle, that grow as weeds in cornfields.

cockleshell (ˈkɒkəlˌʃel) *n.* **1.** the shell of the cockle. **2.** any of the shells of certain other molluscs. **3.** any small light boat.

cockney (ˈkɒknɪ) *n.* **1.** (*often cap.*) a native of London, esp. of the East End, speaking a characteristic dialect of English. Traditionally defined as someone born within the sound of the bells of St. Mary-le-Bow church. **2.** the urban dialect of London or its East End. ~*adj.* **3.** characteristic of cockneys or their dialect of English. —**ˈcockneyish** *adj.* —**ˈcockneyˌism** *n.*

cockpit (ˈkɒkˌpɪt) *n.* **1.** the compartment in a small aircraft in which the pilot, crew, and sometimes the passengers sit. Cf. **flight deck** (sense 1). **2.** the driver's compartment in a racing car. **3.** *Naut.* an enclosed area towards the stern of a small vessel containing the wheel and tiller. **4.** the site of numerous battles or campaigns. **5.** an enclosure used for cockfights.

cockroach (ˈkɒkˌrəʊtʃ) *n.* an insect having an oval flattened body with long antennae and biting mouthparts: a household pest.

cockscomb *or* **coxcomb** (ˈkɒksˌkəʊm) *n.* **1.** the comb of a domestic cock. **2.** a garden plant with yellow, crimson, or purple flowers in a broad spike resembling the comb of a cock. **3.** *Inf.* a conceited dandy.

cockshy (ˈkɒkˌʃaɪ) *n., pl.* **-shies.** *Brit.* **1.** a target aimed at in throwing games. **2.** the throw itself. ~Often shortened to **shy.**

cocksure (ˌkɒkˈʃʊə, -ˈʃɔː) *adj.* overconfident; arrogant. —**ˌcockˈsureness** *n.*

cocktail (ˈkɒkˌteɪl) *n.* **1. a.** any mixed drink with a spirit base. **b.** (*as modifier*): *the cocktail hour.* **2.** an appetizer of seafood, mixed fruits, etc. **3.** (*modifier*) appropriate for formal occasions: *a cocktail dress.*

cockup (ˈkɒkˌʌp) *n.* **1.** *Brit. sl.* something done badly. ~*vb.* **cock up.** (*tr., adv.*). **2.** (of an animal) to raise (ears, etc.), esp. in an alert manner. **3.** (*tr.*) *Brit. sl.* to botch.

cocky¹ (ˈkɒkɪ) *adj.* **cockier, cockiest.** excessively proud of oneself. —**ˈcockily** *adv.* —**ˈcockiness** *n.*

cocky² (ˈkɒkɪ) *n. Austral. & N.Z. inf.* short for **cockatoo** (sense 2).

coco (ˈkəʊkəʊ) *n., pl.* **-cos.** short for **coconut.**

cocoa (ˈkəʊkəʊ) *or* **cacao** *n.* **1.** a powder made from cocoa beans after they have been roasted and ground. **2.** a hot or cold drink made from cocoa and milk or water. **3.** a light to moderate brown colour.

cocoa butter *n.* a yellowish-white waxy solid that is obtained from cocoa beans and used for confectionery, soap, etc.

coconut *or* **cocoanut** (ˈkəʊkəˌnʌt) *n.* **1.** the fruit of a tall tropical tree, the coconut palm, consisting of a thick fibrous oval husk inside which is a thin hard shell enclosing edible white meat. The hollow centre is filled with a milky fluid (**coconut milk**). **2.** the meat of the coconut, often shredded and used in cakes, curries, etc.

coconut matting *n.* a form of coarse matting made from the fibrous husk of the coconut.

cocoon (kəˈkuːn) *n.* **1.** a silky protective envelope secreted by silkworms and certain other insect larvae, in which the pupae develop. **2.** a protective spray covering used as a seal on machinery. **3.** a cosy warm covering. ~*vb.* **4.** (*tr.*) to wrap in a cocoon.

cocopan (ˈkəʊkəʊˌpæn) *n.* (in South Africa) a small wagon running on narrow-gauge railway lines used in mines. Also called: **hopper.**

cocotte (kəʊˈkɒt, kə-) *n.* **1.** a small fireproof dish in which individual portions of food are cooked and served. **2.** a prostitute or promiscuous woman.

cod¹ (kɒd) *n., pl.* **cod** *or* **cods.** **1.** any of the gadoid food fishes which occur in the North Atlantic and have a long body with three rounded dorsal fins. **2.** any of various Australian fishes of fresh or salt water, such as the Murray cod or the red cod.

cod² (kɒd) *n.* **1.** *Brit. & U.S. dialect.* a pod or husk. **2.** *Taboo.* an obsolete word for **scrotum.**

cod³ (kɒd) *Brit. sl.* ~*vb.* **codding, codded.** (*tr.*) **1.** to make fun of; tease. **2.** to play a trick on; befool. ~*n.* **3.** a hoax or trick.

C.O.D. *abbrev. for:* **1.** cash on delivery. **2.** (in the U.S.) collect on delivery.

coda (ˈkəʊdə) *n. Music.* the final part of a musical structure.

coddle (ˈkɒdəl) *vb.* (*tr.*) **1.** to treat with indulgence. **2.** to cook (something, esp. eggs) in water just below the boiling point. —**ˈcoddler** *n.*

code (kəʊd) *n.* **1.** a system of letters or symbols, by which information can be communicated secretly, briefly, etc.: *binary code; Morse code.* See also **genetic code.** **2.** a message in code. **3.** a symbol used in a code. **4.** a conventionalized set of principles or rules: *a code of behaviour.* **5.** a system of letters or digits used for identification purposes. ~*vb.* (*tr.*) **6.** to translate or arrange into a code. —**ˈcoder** *n.*

codeine (ˈkəʊdiːn) *n.* a white crystalline alkaloid prepared mainly from morphine. It is used as an analgesic, a sedative, and to relieve coughing.

codex (ˈkəʊdeks) *n., pl.* **codices** (ˈkəʊdɪˌsiːz, ˈkɒdɪ-). **1.** a volume of manuscripts of an ancient text. **2.** *Obs.* a legal code.

codfish (ˈkɒdˌfɪʃ) *n., pl.* **-fish** *or* **-fishes.** a cod.

codger (ˈkɒdʒə) *n. Inf.* a man, esp. an old or eccentric one: often in **old codger.**

THESAURUS

cock 1. *n.* chanticleer, cockerel, rooster **2.** *v.* perk up, prick, raise, stand up

cockeyed absurd, askew, asymmetrical, awry, crazy, crooked, lopsided, ludicrous, nonsensical, preposterous, skewwhiff (*Brit.*

inf.), squint (*Inf.*)

cocky arrogant, brash, cocksure, conceited, egotistical, lordly, swaggering, swollen-headed, vain

coddle baby, cosset, humour, indulge,

mollycoddle, nurse, pamper, pet, spoil

code 1. cipher, cryptograph **2.** canon, convention, custom, ethics, etiquette, manners, maxim, regulations, rules, system

codicil ('kɒdɪsɪl) *n.* **1.** *Law.* a supplement modifying a will or revoking some provision of it. **2.** an additional provision; appendix. —**codicillary** (ˌkɒdɪ'sɪlərɪ) *adj.*

codify ('kəʊdɪˌfaɪ, 'kɒ-) *vb.* **-fying, -fied.** (*tr.*) to organize or collect together (laws, rules, procedures, etc.) into a system or code. —'**codiˌfier** *n.* —ˌcodifi'**cation** *n.*

codling[1] ('kɒdlɪŋ) *or* **codlin** ('kɒdlɪn) *n.* **1.** any of several varieties of long tapering apples. **2.** any unripe apple.

codling[2] ('kɒdlɪŋ) *n.* a codfish, esp. a young one.

cod-liver oil *n.* an oil extracted from the livers of cod and related fish, rich in vitamins A and D.

codpiece ('kɒdˌpiːs) *n.* a bag covering the male genitals, attached to breeches: worn in the 15th and 16th centuries.

coeducation (ˌkəʊɛdjʊ'keɪʃən) *n.* instruction in schools, colleges, etc., attended by both sexes. —ˌcoedu'**cational** *adj.* —ˌcoedu'**cationally** *adv.*

coefficient (ˌkəʊɪ'fɪʃənt) *n.* **1.** *Maths.* a numerical or constant factor in an algebraic term: *the coefficient of the term 3xyz is 3.* **2.** *Physics.* a number that is the value of a given substance under specified conditions.

coelacanth ('siːləˌkænθ) *n.* a primitive marine bony fish, having fleshy limblike pectoral fins: thought to be extinct until a living specimen was discovered in 1938.

coelenterate (sɪ'lɛntəˌreɪt, -rɪt) *n.* any of various invertebrates having a saclike body with a single opening (mouth), such as jellyfishes, sea anemones, and corals.

coeliac *or U.S.* **celiac** ('siːlɪˌæk) *adj.* of the abdomen.

coeliac disease *n.* a wasting intestinal disease of childhood caused by failure to absorb fats and calcium properly.

coeno- *or (before a vowel)* **coen-** *combining form.* common: *coenobite.*

coenobite *or* **cenobite** ('siːnəʊˌbaɪt) *n.* a member of a religious order following a communal rule of life. —**coenobitic** (ˌsiːnəʊ'bɪtɪk), ˌcoeno'**bitical** *or* ˌceno'**bitic**, ˌceno'**bitical** *adj.*

coequal (kəʊ'iːkwəl) *adj.* **1.** of the same size, rank, etc. ~*n.* **2.** a person or thing equal with another. —**coequality** (ˌkəʊɪ'kwɒlɪtɪ) *n.*

coerce (kəʊ'ɜːs) *vb.* (*tr.*) to compel or restrain by force or authority without regard to individual wishes or desires. —co'**ercer** *n.* —co'**ercible** *adj.* —co'**ercion** *n.*

coeval (kəʊ'iːvəl) *adj.* **1.** of or belonging to the same age or generation. ~*n.* **2.** a contemporary. —**coevality** (ˌkəʊɪ'vælɪtɪ) *n.* —co'**evally** *adv.*

coexist (ˌkəʊɪɡ'zɪst) *vb.* (*intr.*) **1.** to exist together at the same time or in the same place. **2.** to exist together in peace. —ˌcoex'**istence** *n.* —ˌcoex'**istent** *adj.*

coextend (ˌkəʊɪk'stɛnd) *vb.* to extend or cause to extend equally in space or time. —ˌcoex'**tension** *n.* —ˌcoex'**tensive** *adj.*

C. of E. *abbrev. for* Church of England.

coffee ('kɒfɪ) *n.* **1. a.** a drink consisting of an infusion of the roasted and ground seeds of the coffee tree. **b.** (*as modifier*): *coffee grounds.* **2.** Also called: **coffee beans.** the beanlike seeds of the coffee tree, used to make this beverage. **3.** the tree yielding these seeds. **4.** a light brown colour.

coffee bar *n.* a café; snack bar.

coffee house *n.* a place where coffee is served, esp. one that was a fashionable meeting place in 18th-century London.

coffee mill *n.* a machine for grinding roasted coffee beans.

coffee table *n.* a low table, on which coffee may be served.

coffer ('kɒfə) *n.* **1.** a chest, esp. for storing valuables. **2.** (*usually pl.*) a store of money. **3.** an ornamental sunken panel in a ceiling, dome, etc. **4.** a watertight box or chamber. **5.** short for **cofferdam.** ~*vb.* (*tr.*) **6.** to store, as in a coffer. **7.** to decorate (a ceiling, dome, etc.) with coffers.

cofferdam ('kɒfəˌdæm) *n.* a watertight structure that encloses an area under water, pumped dry to enable construction work to be carried out. Often shortened to **coffer.**

coffin ('kɒfɪn) *n.* **1.** a box in which a corpse is buried or cremated. **2.** the bony part of a horse's foot. ~*vb.* **3.** (*tr.*) to place in or as in a coffin.

cog[1] (kɒg) *n.* **1.** any of the teeth or projections on the rim of a gearwheel. **2.** a gearwheel, esp. a small one. **3.** a person or thing playing a small part in a large organization or process.

cog[2] (kɒg) *n.* **1.** a tenon that projects from the end of a timber beam for fitting into a mortise. ~*vb.* **cogging, cogged.** **2.** (*tr.*) to join (pieces of wood) with cogs.

cogent ('kəʊdʒənt) *adj.* compelling belief or assent; forcefully convincing. —'**cogency** *n.* —'**cogently** *adv.*

cogitate ('kɒdʒɪˌteɪt) *vb.* to think deeply about (a problem, possibility, etc.); ponder. —ˌcogi'**tation** *n.* —'**cogitative** *adj.* —'**cogiˌtator** *n.*

Cognac ('kɒnjæk) *n.* (*sometimes not cap.*) a high-quality grape brandy, distilled near Cognac in SW France.

cognate ('kɒgneɪt) *adj.* **1.** akin; related: *cognate languages.* **2.** related by blood or descended from a common maternal ancestor. ~*n.* **3.** something that is cognate with something else. —'**cognately** *adv.* —'**cognateness** *n.* —**cog'nation** *n.*

cognition (kɒg'nɪʃən) *n.* **1.** the mental act or process by which knowledge is acquired, including perception, intuition, and reasoning. **2.** the knowledge that results from such an act or process. —**cog'nitional** *adj.* —**cognitive** ('kɒgnɪtɪv) *adj.*

cognizance *or* **cognisance** ('kɒgnɪzəns, 'kɒnɪ-) *n.* **1.** knowledge; acknowledgment. **2. take cognizance of.** to take notice of; acknowledge, esp. officially. **3.** the range or scope of knowledge or perception. **4.** *Law.* the right of a court to hear and determine a cause or matter. **5.** *Heraldry.* a distinguishing badge or bearing.

cognomen (kɒg'nəʊmɛn) *n., pl.* **-nomens** *or* **-nomina** (-'nɒmɪnə, -'nəʊ-). (*originally*) an ancient Roman's third name or nickname, which later became his family name. —**cognominal** (kɒg'nɒmɪnəl, -'nəʊ-) *adj.*

cognoscenti (ˌkɒnjəʊ'ʃɛntɪ, ˌkɒgnə-) *or* **conoscenti** *pl. n., sing.* **-te** (-tiː). (*sometimes sing.*) people with informed appreciation of a particular field, esp. in the fine arts; connoisseurs.

cogwheel ('kɒgˌwiːl) *n.* another name for **gear** (sense 1).

cohabit (kəʊ'hæbɪt) *vb.* (*intr.*) to live together as husband and wife, esp. without being married. —co'**habitant** *or* co'**habiter** *n.* —coˌhabi'**tation** *n.*

coheir (kəʊ'ɛə) *n.* a person who inherits jointly with others. —co'**heiress** *fem. n.*

cohere (kəʊ'hɪə) *vb.* (*intr.*) **1.** to hold or stick firmly together. **2.** to connect or be connected logically; be consistent. **3.** *Physics.* to be held together by the action of molecular forces.

coherent (kəʊ'hɪərənt) *adj.* **1.** capable of intelligible speech. **2.** logical; consistent and orderly. **3.** cohering or sticking together. **4.** *Physics.* (of two or more waves) having the same frequency and the same phase or a fixed phase difference: *coherent light.* —co'**herence** *n.* —co'**herently** *adv.*

cohesion (kəʊ'hiːʒən) *n.* **1.** the act or state of cohering; tendency to unite. **2.** *Physics.* the force that holds together the atoms or molecules in a solid or liquid, as distinguished from adhesion. **3.** *Bot.* the fusion in some plants of flower parts, such as petals, that are usually separate. —co'**hesive** *adj.*

cohort ('kəʊhɔːt) *n.* **1.** one of the ten units of an ancient Roman Legion. **2.** any band of warriors or associates: *the cohorts of Satan.*

COHSE ('kəʊzɪ) (*in Britain*) *acronym for* Confederation of Health Service Employees.

THESAURUS

cogency conviction, force, potency, power, strength

cogent compelling, conclusive, convincing, effective, forceful, forcible, influential, irresistible, potent, powerful, strong, urgent, weighty

cogitate consider, contemplate, deliberate, meditate, mull over, muse, ponder, reflect, ruminate, think

cogitation consideration, contemplation, deliberation, meditation, reflection, rumination, thought

cognate affiliated, akin, alike, allied, analogous, associated, connected, kindred, related, similar

cognition apprehension, awareness, comprehension, discernment, insight, intelligence, perception, reasoning, understanding

coherent articulate, comprehensible, consistent, intelligible, logical, lucid, meaningful, orderly, organized, rational, reasoned, systematic

C.O.I. (in Britain) *abbrev. for* Central Office of Information.

coif (kɔif) *n.* **1.** a close-fitting cap worn under a veil in the Middle Ages. **2.** a leather cap worn under a chainmail hood. **3.** (kwɑːf) a less common word for **coiffure** (sense 1). ~*vb.* **coiffing, coiffed.** (*tr.*) **4.** to cover with or as if with a coif. **5.** (kwɑːf). to arrange (the hair).

coiffeur (kwɑːˈfɜː) *n.* a hairdresser. —**coiffeuse** (kwɑːˈfɜːz) *fem. n.*

coiffure (kwɑːˈfjuə) *n.* **1.** a hairstyle. **2.** an obsolete word for **headdress.** ~*vb.* **3.** (*tr.*) to dress or arrange (the hair).

coign of vantage (kɔin) *n.* an advantageous position for observation or action.

coil[1] (kɔil) *vb.* **1.** to wind or gather (ropes, hair, etc.) into loops or (of rope, hair, etc.) to be formed in such loops. **2.** (*intr.*) to move in a winding course. ~*n.* **3.** something wound in a connected series of loops. **4.** a single loop of such a series. **5.** an arrangement of pipes in a spiral or loop, as in a condenser. **6.** an electrical conductor wound into the form of a spiral, to provide inductance or a magnetic field. **7.** an intrauterine contraceptive device in the shape of a coil. **8.** the transformer in a petrol engine that supplies the high voltage to the sparking plugs.

coil[2] (kɔil) *n.* the troubles of the world (in Shakespeare's phrase **this mortal coil**).

coin (kɔin) *n.* **1.** a metal disc or piece used as money. **2.** metal currency, as opposed to paper currency, etc. **3.** *Archit.* a variant spelling of **quoin. 4. pay (a person) back in (his) own coin.** to treat (a person) in the way that he has treated others. ~*vb.* **5.** (*tr.*) to make or stamp (coins). **6.** (*tr.*) to make into a coin. **7.** (*tr.*) to fabricate or invent (words, etc.). **8.** (*tr.*) *Inf.* to make (money) rapidly (esp. in **coin it in**).

coinage (ˈkɔinidʒ) *n.* **1.** coins collectively. **2.** the act of striking coins. **3.** the currency of a country. **4.** the act of inventing something, esp. a word or phrase. **5.** a newly invented word, phrase, usage, etc.

coincide (ˌkəuinˈsaid) *vb.* (*intr.*) **1.** to occur or exist simultaneously. **2.** to be identical in nature, character, etc. **3.** to agree.

coincidence (kəuˈinsidəns) *n.* **1.** a chance occurrence of events remarkable either for being simultaneous or for apparently being connected. **2.** the fact, condition, or state of coinciding. **3.** (*modifier*) *Electronics.* of or relating to a circuit that produces an output pulse only when both its input terminals receive pulses within a specified interval: *coincidence gate.*

coincident (kəuˈinsidənt) *adj.* **1.** having the same position in space or time. **2.** (usually *postpositive* and foll. by *with*) in exact agreement. —**coˌinciˈdental** *adj.* —**coˌinciˈdentally** *adv.*

Cointreau (ˈkwɑːntrəu) *n. Trademark.* a colourless liqueur with orange flavouring.

coir (ˈkɔiə) *n.* the fibre from the husk of the coconut, used in making rope and matting.

coitus (ˈkɔuitəs) *or* **coition** (kəuˈiʃən) *n.* a technical term for **sexual intercourse.** —**ˈcoital** *adj.*

coke[1] (kəuk) *n.* **1.** a solid-fuel product produced by distillation of coal to drive off its volatile constituents: used as a fuel. **2.** the layer formed in the cylinders of a car engine by incomplete combustion of the fuel. ~*vb.* **3.** to become or convert into coke.

coke[2] (kəuk) *n. Sl.* short for **cocaine.**

Coke (kəuk) *n. Trademark.* short for **Coca-Cola.**

col (kɒl) *n.* **1.** a strip of land or a ridge connecting two mountain peaks. **2.** *Meteorol.* a low-pressure region between two anticyclones.

Col. *abbrev. for:* **1.** Colombia(n). **2.** Colonel. **3.** *Bible.* Colossians.

col- *prefix.* variant of **com-** before *l*: *collateral.*

cola *or* **kola** (ˈkəulə) *n.* **1.** either of two trees widely cultivated in tropical regions for their seeds (**cola nut**). **2.** a sweet carbonated drink flavoured with cola nuts.

colander (ˈkɒləndə, ˈkʌl-) *or* **cullender** *n.* a pan with a perforated bottom for straining or rinsing foods.

cold (kəuld) *adj.* **1.** having relatively little warmth; of a rather low temperature: *cold weather; cold hands.* **2.** without proper warmth: *this meal is cold.* **3.** lacking in affection or enthusiasm: *a cold manner.* **4.** not affected by emotion: *cold logic.* **5.** dead. **6.** sexually unresponsive or frigid. **7.** lacking in freshness: *a cold scent; cold news.* **8.** chilling to the spirit; depressing. **9.** (of a colour) having violet, blue, or green predominating; giving no sensation of warmth. **10.** *Sl.* unconscious. **11.** *Inf.* (of a seeker) far from the object of a search. **12. cold comfort.** little or no comfort. **13. in cold blood.** without feeling pity or remorse; ruthlessly. **14. leave (someone) cold.** *Inf.* to fail to excite: *the performance left me cold.* **15. throw cold water on.** *Inf.* to be unenthusiastic about or discourage. ~*n.* **16.** the absence of heat regarded as a positive force: *the cold took away our breath.* **17.** the sensation caused by loss or lack of heat. **18. (out) in the cold.** *Inf.* neglected; ignored. **19.** an acute viral infection of the upper respiratory passages characterized by discharge of watery mucus from the nose, sneezing, etc. ~*adv.* **20.** *Inf.* without preparation: *he played his part cold.* —**ˈcoldish** *adj.* —**ˈcoldly** *adv.* —**ˈcoldness** *n.*

cold-blooded *adj.* **1.** having or showing a lack of feeling or pity. **2.** *Inf.* particularly sensitive to cold. **3.** (of all animals except birds and mammals) having a body temperature that varies with that of the surroundings. —ˌcold-ˈbloodedly *adv.* —ˌcold-ˈbloodedness *n.*

cold chisel *n.* a toughened steel chisel.

cold cream *n.* an emulsion of water and fat used for softening and cleansing the skin.

cold feet *n. Inf.* loss or lack of confidence.

cold frame *n.* an unheated wooden frame with a glass top, used to protect young plants.

cold front *n. Meteorol.* the boundary line between a warm air mass and the cold air pushing it from beneath and behind as it moves.

cold-hearted *adj.* lacking in feeling or warmth; unkind. —ˌcold-ˈheartedly *adv.* —ˌcold-ˈheartedness *n.*

cold shoulder *n. Inf.* **1.** (often preceded by *the*) a show of indifference; a slight. ~*vb.* **cold-shoulder.** (*tr.*) **2.** to treat with indifference.

cold sore *n.* a cluster of blisters at the margin of the lips, caused by a viral infection. Technical name: **herpes labialis.**

cold storage *n.* **1.** the storage of things in an artificially cooled place for preservation. **2.** *Inf.* a state of temporary suspension: *to put an idea into cold storage.*

cold sweat *n. Inf.* a bodily reaction to fear or nervousness, characterized by chill and moist skin.

cold war *n.* a state of political hostility and military tension between two countries or power blocs, involving propaganda, threats, etc.

cole (kəul) *n.* any of various plants such as the cabbage and rape. Also called: **colewort.**

coleslaw (ˈkəulˌslɔː) *n.* a salad of shredded cabbage, mayonnaise, carrots, onions, etc.

coletit (ˈkəultit) *n.* another name for **coal tit.**

THESAURUS

coil convolute, curl, entwine, loop, snake, spiral, twine, twist, wind, wreathe, writhe

coin 1. *v.* conceive, create, fabricate, forge, formulate, frame, invent, make up, mint, mould, originate, think up 2. *n.* cash, change, copper, money, silver, specie

coincide 1. be concurrent, coexist, occur simultaneously, synchronize 2. accord, harmonize, match, quadrate, square, tally 3. acquiesce, agree, concur, correspond

coincidence 1. accident, chance, eventuality, fluke, fortuity, happy accident, luck, stroke of luck 2. concomitance, concurrence, conjunction, correlation, correspondence, synchronism

coincident coinciding, concomitant, concurring, consonant, contemporaneous, coordinate, correspondent, synchronous

coincidental 1. accidental, casual, chance, fluky (*Inf.*), fortuitous, unintentional, unplanned 2. coincident, concomitant, concurrent, simultaneous, synchronous

cold *adj.* 1. arctic, biting, bitter, bleak, brumal, chill, chilly, cool, freezing, frigid, frosty, frozen, gelid, icy, inclement, raw, wintry 2. benumbed, chilled, chilly, freezing, frozen to the marrow, numbed, shivery 3. aloof, apathetic, cold-blooded, dead, distant, frigid, glacial, indifferent, inhospitable, lukewarm, passionless, phlegmatic, reserved, spiritless, standoffish, stony, undemonstrative, unfeeling, unmoved, unresponsive, unsympathetic ~*n.* 4. chill, chilliness, coldness, frigidity, frostiness, iciness, inclemency

cold-blooded barbarous, brutal, callous, cruel, dispassionate, heartless, inhuman, merciless, pitiless, ruthless, savage, steely, stony-hearted, unemotional, unfeeling, unmoved

cold-hearted callous, detached, frigid, heartless, indifferent, inhuman, insensitive, stony-hearted, uncaring, unfeeling, unkind, unsympathetic

coleus (ˈkəʊlɪəs) n., pl. **-uses.** any plant of the Old World genus *Coleus:* cultivated for their variegated leaves.

coley (ˈkəʊlɪ, ˈkɒlɪ) n. *Brit.* any of various edible fishes, esp. the coalfish.

colic (ˈkɒlɪk) n. a condition characterized by acute spasmodic abdominal pain, esp. that caused by inflammation, distention, etc., of the gastrointestinal tract. —ˈ**colicky** *adj.*

coliseum (ˌkɒlɪˈsɪəm) or **colosseum** (ˌkɒləˈsɪəm) n. a large building, such as a stadium, used for entertainments, sports, etc.

colitis (kɒˈlaɪtɪs) n. inflammation of the colon.

collaborate (kəˈlæbəˌreɪt) vb. (intr.) **1.** (often foll. by *on, with,* etc.) to work with another or others on a joint project. **2.** to cooperate as a traitor, esp. with an enemy occupying one's own country. —col,laboˈration n. —colˈlaborative adj. —colˈlabo,rator or col,laboˈrationist n.

collage (kəˈlɑːʒ, kɒ-) n. **1.** an art form in which compositions are made out of pieces of paper, cloth, photographs, etc. pasted on a dry ground. **2.** a composition made in this way. **3.** any collection of unrelated things. —colˈlagist n.

collagen (ˈkɒlədʒən) n. a fibrous protein of connective tissue and bones that yields gelatin on boiling.

collapse (kəˈlæps) vb. **1.** (intr.) to fall down or cave in suddenly: *the whole building collapsed.* **2.** (intr.) to fail completely. **3.** (intr.) to break down or fall down from lack of strength. **4.** to fold (furniture, etc.) compactly or (of furniture, etc.) to be designed to fold compactly. ~n. **5.** the act or instance of suddenly falling down, caving in, or crumbling. **6.** a sudden failure or breakdown. —colˈlapsible or colˈlapsable adj. —col,lapsiˈbility n.

collar (ˈkɒlə) n. **1.** the part of a garment around the neck and shoulders, often detachable or folded over. **2.** any band, necklace, garland, etc., encircling the neck. **3.** a band or chain of leather, rope, or metal placed around an animal's neck. **4.** *Biol.* a marking resembling a collar, such as that found around the necks of some birds. **5.** a section of a shaft or rod having a locally increased diameter to provide a bearing seat or a locating ring. **6.** a cut of meat, esp. bacon, taken from around the neck of an animal. **7. hot under the collar.** *Inf.* angry; excited. ~vb. (tr.) **8.** to put a collar on; furnish with a collar. **9.** to seize by the collar. **10.** *Inf.* to seize; arrest; detain.

collarbone (ˈkɒləˌbəʊn) n. the nontechnical name for **clavicle.**

collate (kɒˈleɪt, kə-) vb. (tr.) **1.** to examine and compare (texts, statements, etc.) in order to note points of agreement and disagreement. **2.** to check the number and order of (the pages of a book). **3.** *Bookbinding.* **a.** to check the sequence of (the sections of a book) after gathering. **b.** a nontechnical word for **gather** (sense 8). **4.** (often foll. by *to*) *Christianity.* to appoint (an incumbent) to a benefice. —colˈlator n.

collateral (kɒˈlætərəl, kə-) n. **1. a.** security pledged for the repayment of a loan. **b.** (as modifier): *a collateral loan.* **2.** a person, animal, or plant descended from the same ancestor as another but through a different line. ~adj. **3.** situated or running side by side. **4.** descended from a common ancestor but through different lines. **5.** serving to support or corroborate. —colˈlaterally adv.

collation (kɒˈleɪʃən, kə-) n. **1.** the act or process of collating. **2.** a description of the technical features of a book. **3.** *R.C. Church.* a light meal permitted on fast days. **4.** any light informal meal.

colleague (ˈkɒliːg) n. a fellow worker or member of a staff, department, profession etc.

collect[1] (kəˈlɛkt) vb. **1.** to gather together or be gathered together. **2.** to accumulate (stamps, books, etc.) as a hobby or for study. **3.** (tr.) to call for or receive payment of (taxes, dues, etc.). **4.** (tr.) to regain control of (oneself, one's emotions, etc.) as after a shock or surprise: *he collected his wits.* **5.** (tr.) to fetch: *collect your own post.* **6.** (intr.; sometimes foll. by on) *Sl.* to receive large sums of money. **7.** *Austral. & N.Z. inf.* to collide with; be hit by. ~adv., adj. **8.** *U.S.* (of telephone calls, etc.) on a transferred-charge basis. —colˈlectable or colˈlectible adj.

collect[2] (ˈkɒlɛkt) n. *Christianity.* a short Church prayer in Communion and other services.

collected (kəˈlɛktɪd) adj. **1.** in full control of one's faculties; composed. **2.** assembled in totality or brought together into one volume or a set of volumes: *the collected works of Dickens.* —colˈlectedly adv. —colˈlectedness n.

collection (kəˈlɛkʃən) n. **1.** the act or process of collecting. **2.** a number of things collected or assembled together. **3.** something gathered into a mass or pile; accumulation: *a collection of rubbish.* **4.** a sum of money collected or solicited, as in church. **5.** removal, esp. regular removal of letters from a postbox. **6.** (often pl.) (at Oxford University) a college examination or an oral report by a tutor.

collective (kəˈlɛktɪv) adj. **1.** formed or assembled by collection. **2.** forming a whole or aggregate. **3.** of, done by, or characteristic of individuals acting in cooperation. ~n. **4. a.** a cooperative enterprise or unit, such as a collective farm. **b.** the members of such a cooperative. —colˈlectively adv. —colˈlectiveness n. —ˌcollecˈtivity n.

collective bargaining n. negotiation between a trade union and an employer or an employers' organization on the incomes and working conditions of the employees.

collectivism (kəˈlɛktɪˌvɪzəm) n. the principle of ownership of the means of production, by the state or the people. —colˈlectivist n. —col,lectivˈistic adj.

collectivize or **-vise** (kəˈlɛktɪˌvaɪz) vb. (tr.) to organize according to the principles of collectivism. —col,lectiviˈzation or -viˈsation n.

collector (kəˈlɛktə) n. **1.** a person or thing that collects. **2.** a person employed to collect debts, rents, etc. **3.** a person who collects objects as a hobby. **4.** (formerly, in India) the head of a district administration. **5.** *Electronics.* the region in a transistor into which charge carriers flow from the base.

colleen (ˈkɒliːn, kɒˈliːn) n. an Irish word for **girl.**

college (ˈkɒlɪdʒ) n. **1.** an institution of higher education; part of a university. **2.** a school or an institution providing specialized courses: *a college of music.* **3.** the buildings in which a college is housed. **4.** the staff and students of a college. **5.** an organized body of persons with specific rights and duties: *an electoral college.* **6.** a body organized within a particular profession, concerned with regulating standards. **7.** *Brit.* a name given to some secondary schools.

college pudding n. *Brit.* a baked or steamed suet pudding containing dried fruit and spice.

collegian (kəˈliːdʒən) n. a member of a college.

collegiate (kəˈliːdʒɪt) adj. **1.** Also: **collegial** (kəˈliːdʒɪəl). of or relating to a college or college students. **2.** (of a university) composed of various colleges of equal standing.

collide (kəˈlaɪd) vb. (intr.) **1.** to crash together with a violent impact. **2.** to conflict; clash; disagree.

THESAURUS

collaborate 1. cooperate, coproduce, join forces, participate, team up, work together 2. collude, conspire, cooperate, fraternize

collaboration alliance, association, concert, cooperation, partnership, teamwork

collaborator 1. associate, colleague, confederate, co-worker, partner, team-mate 2. collaborationist, fraternizer, quisling, traitor, turncoat

collapse 1. v. break down, cave in, come to nothing, crack up (*Inf.*), crumple, fail, faint, fall, fold, founder, give way, subside 2. n. breakdown, cave-in, disintegration, down-

fall, exhaustion, failure, faint, flop (*Sl.*), prostration, subsidence

collar v. apprehend, appropriate, capture, catch, grab, lay hands on, seize

colleague aider, ally, assistant, associate, auxiliary, coadjutor (*Rare*), collaborator, companion, comrade, confederate, confrère, fellow worker, helper, partner, team-mate, workmate

collect 1. accumulate, aggregate, amass, assemble, gather, heap, hoard, save, stockpile 2. assemble, cluster, congregate, convene, converge, flock together, rally 3. acquire, muster, obtain, raise, secure, solicit

collected calm, composed, confident, cool, placid, poised, self-possessed, serene, together (*Sl.*), unperturbable, unperturbed, unruffled

collection 1. accumulation, anthology, compilation, congeries, heap, hoard, mass, pile, set, stockpile, store 2. assemblage, assembly, assortment, cluster, company, congregation, convocation, crowd, gathering, group 3. alms, contribution, offering, offertory

collective aggregate, combined, common, composite, concerted, cooperative, corporate, cumulative, joint, shared, unified,

collie ('kɒlɪ) n. a silky-coated breed of sheepdog with a long narrow head.

collier ('kɒlɪə) n. Chiefly Brit. 1. a coal miner. 2. a. a ship designed to transport coal. b. a member of its crew.

colliery ('kɒljərɪ) n., pl. **-lieries**. Chiefly Brit. a coal mine.

collimate ('kɒlɪ‚meɪt) vb. (tr.) 1. to adjust the line of sight of (an optical instrument). 2. to use a collimator on (a beam of radiation). 3. to make parallel or bring into line. —‚colli'mation n.

collision (kə'lɪʒən) n. 1. a violent impact of moving objects; crash. 2. the conflict of opposed ideas, wishes, attitudes, etc.

collocate ('kɒlə‚keɪt) vb. (tr.) to group or place together in some system or order. —‚collo'cation n.

colloid ('kɒlɔɪd) n. 1. a mixture having particles of one component suspended in a continuous phase of another component. The mixture has properties between those of a solution and a fine suspension. 2. Physiol. a gelatinous substance of the thyroid follicles that holds the hormonal secretions of the thyroid gland. —col'loidal adj.

collop ('kɒləp) n. Dialect, chiefly northern Brit. 1. a slice of meat. 2. a small piece of anything.

colloq. abbrev. for colloquial(ly).

colloquial (kə'ləʊkwɪəl) adj. 1. of or relating to conversation. 2. denoting or characterized by informal or conversational idiom or vocabulary. —col'loquially adv. —col'loquialness n.

colloquialism (kə'ləʊkwɪə‚lɪzəm) n. 1. a word or phrase appropriate to conversation and other informal situations. 2. the use of colloquial words and phrases.

colloquium (kə'ləʊkwɪəm) n., pl. **-quiums** or **-quia** (-kwɪə). 1. a gathering for discussion. 2. an academic seminar.

colloquy ('kɒləkwɪ) n., pl. **-quies**. 1. a formal conversation or conference. 2. an informal conference on religious or theological matters. —'colloquist n.

collusion (kə'luːʒən) n. 1. secret agreement for a fraudulent purpose; conspiracy. 2. a secret agreement between opponents at law for some improper purpose. —col'lusive adj.

collywobbles ('kɒlɪ‚wɒbəlz) pl. n. (usually preceded by the) Sl. 1. an upset stomach. 2. an intense feeling of nervousness.

cologne (kə'ləʊn) n. a perfumed liquid or solid made of fragrant essential oils and alcohol. Also called: **Cologne water, eau de cologne**.

colon[1] ('kəʊlən) n., pl. **-lons**. 1. the punctuation mark : , usually preceding an explanation or an example, a list, or an extended quotation. 2. this mark used for certain other purposes, such as when a ratio is given in figures, as in 5:3.

colon[2] ('kəʊlən) n., pl. **-lons** or **-la** (-lə). the part of the large intestine between the caecum and the rectum. —**colonic** (kə'lɒnɪk) adj.

colonel ('kɜːnəl) n. an officer of land or air forces junior to a brigadier but senior to a lieutenant colonel. —'**colonelcy** or '**colonel‚ship** n.

colonial (kə'ləʊnɪəl) adj. 1. of, characteristic of, relating to, possessing, or inhabiting a colony or colonies. 2. (often cap.) characteristic of or relating to the 13 British colonies that became the United States of America (1776). 3. (often cap.) of or relating to the colonies of the British Empire. 4. denoting or having the style of Neoclassical architecture used in the British colonies in America in the 17th and 18th centuries. 5. (of animals and plants) having become established in a community in a new environment. ~n. 6. a native of a colony. —co'lonially adv.

colonialism (kə'ləʊnɪə‚lɪzəm) n. the policy and practice of a power in extending control over weaker peoples or areas. Also called: **imperialism**. —co'lonialist n., adj.

colonist ('kɒlənɪst) n. 1. a person who settles or colonizes an area. 2. an inhabitant of a colony.

colonize or **-ise** ('kɒlə‚naɪz) vb. 1. to send colonists to or establish a colony in (an area). 2. to settle in (an area) as colonists. 3. (tr.) to transform (a community, etc.) into a colony. 4. (of plants and animals) to become established in (a new environment). —‚coloni'zation or **-i'sation** n. —'**colo‚nizer** or **-iser** n.

colonnade (‚kɒlə'neɪd) n. 1. a set of evenly-spaced columns. 2. a row of regularly spaced trees. —‚colon'naded adj.

colony ('kɒlənɪ) n., pl. **-nies**. 1. a body of people who settle in a country distant from their homeland but maintain ties with it. 2. the community formed by such settlers. 3. a subject territory occupied by a settlement from the ruling state. 4. a. a community of people who form a national, racial, or cultural minority concentrated in a particular place: an artists' colony. b. the area itself. 5. Zool. a group of the same type of animal or plant living or growing together. 6. Bacteriol. a group of bacteria, fungi, etc., derived from one or a few spores, esp. when grown on a culture medium.

colophon ('kɒlə‚fon, -fən) n. 1. a publisher's emblem on a book. 2. (formerly) an inscription at the end of a book showing the title, printer, date, etc.

color ('kʌlə) n. the U.S. spelling of **colour**.

Colorado beetle (‚kɒlə'rɑːdəʊ) n. a black-and-yellow beetle that is a serious pest of potatoes, feeding on the leaves.

coloratura (‚kɒlərə'tʊərə) n. Music. 1. (in 18th- and 19th-century arias) a florid virtuoso passage. 2. Also called: **coloratura soprano**. a soprano who specializes in such music.

colossal (kə'lɒsəl) adj. 1. of immense size; huge; gigantic. 2. (in figure sculpture) approximately twice life-size. 3. Archit. of the order of columns that extend more than one storey in a facade. —co'lossally adv.

colossus (kə'lɒsəs) n., pl. **-si** (-saɪ) or **-suses**. something very large, esp. a statue.

colostomy (kə'lɒstəmɪ) n., pl. **-mies**. the surgical formation of an opening from the colon onto the surface of the body, which functions as an anus.

colostrum (kə'lɒstrəm) n. the thin milky secretion from the nipples that precedes and follows true lactation.

colour or U.S. **color** ('kʌlə) n. 1. a. an attribute of things that results from the light they reflect or emit in so far as this causes a visual sensation that depends on its wavelengths. b. the aspect of visual perception by which an observer recognizes this attribute. c. the quality of the light producing this visual perception. 2. Also called: **chromatic colour. a.** a colour, such as red or green, that possesses hue, as opposed to achromatic colours such as white or black. b. (as modifier): colour television. 3. a substance, such as a dye or paint, that imparts colour. 4. a. the skin complexion of a person, esp. as determined by his race. b. (as modifier): colour prejudice. 5. the use of all the hues in painting as distinct from composition, form, and light and shade. 6. the quantity and quality of ink used in a printing process. 7. the distinctive tone of a musical sound. 8. vividness or authenticity: period colour. 9. semblance or pretext: under colour of. 10. off colour. a. not well; ill. b. in bad taste. ~vb. 11. (tr.) to apply colour to (something). 12. (tr.) to give a convincing appearance to: to colour an alibi. 13. (tr.) to influence or distort: anger coloured her judgment. 14. (intr.; often foll. by up) to become red in the face, esp. when embarrassed or annoyed. ~See also **colours**.

THESAURUS

united

collide clash, come into collision, conflict, crash, meet head-on

collision 1. accident, bump, crash, impact, pile-up, prang (Inf.), smash 2. clash, clashing, conflict, confrontation, encounter, opposition, skirmish

colloquial conversational, demotic, everyday, familiar, idiomatic, informal, vernacular

collusion cahoots (Inf.), complicity, connivance, conspiracy, craft, deceit, fraudulent artifice, intrigue, secret understanding

colonist colonial, colonizer, frontiersman, homesteader (U.S.), immigrant, pioneer, planter, settler

colonize open up, people, pioneer, populate, settle

colonnade arcade, cloisters, covered walk, peristyle, portico

colony community, dependency, dominion, outpost, possession, province, satellite state, settlement, territory

colossal Brobdingnagian, elephantine, enormous, gargantuan, gigantic, herculean, huge, immense, mammoth, massive, monstrous, monumental, mountainous, prodigious, titanic, vast

colour n. 1. colorant, coloration, complexion, dye, hue, paint, pigment, pigmentation, shade, tincture, tinge, tint 2. animation, bloom, blush, brilliance, flush, glow, liveliness, rosiness, ruddiness, vividness 3. Fig. ap-

colourable ('kʌlərəbəl) adj. 1. capable of being coloured. 2. appearing to be true; plausible. 3. pretended; feigned.

colour bar n. discrimination against people of a different race, esp. as practised by Whites against Blacks.

colour-blind adj. of or relating to any defect in the normal ability to distinguish certain colours. —**colour blindness** n.

coloured ('kʌləd) adj. 1. possessing colour. 2. having a strong element of fiction or fantasy; distorted (esp. in **highly coloured**).

Coloured ('kʌləd) n. 1. an individual who is not a White, esp. a Negro. 2. Also called: **Cape Coloured.** (in South Africa) a person of racially mixed parentage or descent. ~adj. 3. designating or relating to a Coloured or Coloureds.

colourful ('kʌləful) adj. 1. having intense colour or richly varied colours. 2. vivid, rich, or distinctive in character. —**'colourfully** adv.

colouring ('kʌlərɪŋ) n. 1. the process or art of applying colour. 2. anything used to give colour, such as paint. 3. appearance with regard to shade and colour. 4. arrangements of colours, as in the markings of birds. 5. the colour of a person's complexion. 6. a false or misleading appearance.

colourless ('kʌləlɪs) adj. 1. without colour. 2. lacking in interest: a colourless individual. 3. grey or pallid in tone or hue. 4. without prejudice; neutral. —**'colourlessly** adv.

colours ('kʌləz) pl. n. 1. a. the flag that indicates nationality. b. Mil. the ceremony of hoisting or lowering the colours. 2. true nature or character (esp. in **show one's colours**). 3. a distinguishing badge or flag. 4. Sport, Brit. a badge or other symbol denoting membership of a team, esp. at a school or college. 5. **nail one's colours to the mast.** to refuse to admit defeat. 6. **with flying colours.** very successfully.

colour sergeant n. a sergeant who carries the regimental, battalion, or national colours.

colour supplement n. Brit. an illustrated magazine accompanying a newspaper.

colt (kəʊlt) n. 1. a male horse or pony under the age of four. 2. Sport. a. a young and inexperienced player. b. a member of a junior team.

coltish ('kəʊltɪʃ) adj. 1. inexperienced; unruly. 2. playful and lively. —**'coltishness** n.

coltsfoot ('kəʊlts,fʊt) n., pl. -**foots.** a European plant with yellow daisy-like flowers and heart-shaped leaves: a common weed.

columbine ('kɒləm,baɪn) n. any plant of the genus Aquilegia, having flowers with five spurred petals. Also called: **aquilegia.**

Columbine ('kɒləm,baɪn) n. the sweetheart of Harlequin in English pantomime.

column ('kɒləm) n. 1. an upright pillar usually having a cylindrical shaft, a base, and a capital. 2. a. a form or structure in the shape of a column: a column of air. b. a monument. 3. a line, as of people in a queue. 4. Mil. a formation in which units follow one behind the other. 5. Journalism. a. a single row of type on a newspaper. b. a

regular feature in a paper: the fashion column. 6. a vertical array of numbers. —**columnar** (kə'lʌmnə) adj. —**'columned** adj.

columnist ('kɒləmɪst, -əmnɪst) n. a journalist who writes a regular feature in a newspaper.

COM (kɒm) n. direct conversion of computer output to microfiche or film.

Com. abbrev. for: 1. Commander. 2. Committee. 3. Commodore. 4. Communist.

com- or **con-** prefix. together; with; jointly: commingle.

coma ('kəʊmə) n., pl. -**mas.** a state of unconsciousness from which a person cannot be aroused, caused by injury, narcotics, poisons, etc.

comatose ('kəʊmə,təʊs) adj. 1. in a state of coma. 2. torpid; lethargic.

comb (kəʊm) n. 1. a toothed device for disentangling or arranging hair. 2. a tool or machine that cleans and straightens wool, cotton, etc. 3. Austral. & N.Z. the fixed cutter on a sheep-shearing machine. 4. anything resembling a comb in form or function. 5. the fleshy serrated outgrowth on the heads of certain birds, esp. the domestic fowl. 6. a honeycomb. 7. **go over with a fine-tooth comb.** to search or revise thoroughly. ~vb. 8. to use a comb on. 9. (when tr., often foll. by through) to search with great care: the police combed the woods.

combat n. ('kɒmbæt, -bət, 'kʌm-). 1. a fight, conflict, or struggle. 2. a. an action fought between two military forces. b. (as modifier): a combat jacket. 3. **single combat.** a duel. ~vb. (also kəm'bæt) 4. (tr.) to fight. 5. (intr.; often foll. by with or against) to struggle or strive (against): to combat against disease.

combatant ('kɒmbətənt, 'kʌm-) n. 1. a person or group engaged in or prepared for a fight. ~adj. 2. engaged in or ready for combat.

combe or **comb** (ku:m) n. variant spellings of **coomb.**

comber ('kəʊmə) n. 1. a person, tool, or machine that combs wool, flax, etc. 2. a long curling wave; roller.

combination (,kɒmbɪ'neɪʃən) n. 1. the act of combining or state of being combined. 2. a union of separate parts, qualities, etc. 3. an alliance of people or parties. 4. the set of numbers that opens a combination lock. 5. Brit. a motorcycle with a sidecar attached. 6. Maths. an arrangement of the numbers, terms, etc., of a set into specified groups without regard to order in the group. 7. the chemical reaction of two or more compounds, usually to form one other compound. 8. a coordinated sequence of chess moves. —**combi'national** adj.

combination lock n. a type of lock that can only be opened when a set of dials is turned to show a specific sequence of numbers.

combinations (,kɒmbɪ'neɪʃənz) pl. n. Brit. a one-piece undergarment with long sleeves and legs. Often shortened to **combs** or **coms.**

combine vb. (kəm'baɪn). 1. to join together. 2. to unite or cause to unite to form a chemical compound. ~n. ('kɒmbaɪn). 3. Also called: **combine harvester.** a machine that simultaneously cuts, threshes, and clears a standing crop of grain. 4. an association of enterprises, esp. in order to gain a monopoly of a market. 5. U.S. inf.

THESAURUS

pearance, disguise, excuse, façade, false show, guise, plea, pretence, pretext, semblance ~v. 4. colourwash, dye, paint, stain, tinge, tint 5. Fig. disguise, distort, embroider, exaggerate, falsify, garble, gloss over, misrepresent, pervert, prejudice, slant, taint 6. blush, burn, crimson, flush, go crimson, redden

colourful 1. bright, brilliant, intense, jazzy (Sl.), kaleidoscopic, motley, multicoloured, psychedelic, rich, variegated, vibrant, vivid 2. characterful, distinctive, graphic, interesting, lively, picturesque, rich, stimulating, unusual, vivid

colourless 1. achromatic, achromic, anaemic, ashen, bleached, drab, faded, neutral, sickly, wan, washed out 2. characterless, dreary, insipid, lacklustre, tame, uninteresting, unmemorable, vacuous, vapid

colours 1. banner, emblem, ensign, flag, standard 2. Fig. aspect, breed, character, identity, nature, stamp, strain

column 1. cavalcade, file, line, list, procession, queue, rank, row, string, train 2. caryatid, obelisk, pilaster, pillar, post, shaft, support, upright

columnist correspondent, critic, editor, gossip columnist, reporter, reviewer

coma drowsiness, insensibility, lethargy, oblivion, somnolence, stupor, torpor, trance, unconsciousness

comatose drowsy, drugged, insensible, lethargic, sleepy, sluggish, somnolent, soporose (Medical), stupefied, torpid, unconscious

comb v. 1. arrange, curry, dress, groom, untangle 2. Of flax, wool, etc. card, hackle, hatchel, heckle, tease, teasel, teazle 3. Fig. go through with a fine-tooth comb, hunt, rake, ransack, rummage, scour, screen, search, sift, sweep

combat 1. n. action, battle, conflict, contest, encounter, engagement, fight, skirmish, struggle, war, warfare 2. v. battle, contend,

contest, cope, defy, do battle with, engage, fight, oppose, resist, strive, struggle, withstand

combatant 1. n. adversary, antagonist, belligerent, contender, enemy, fighter, fighting man, opponent, serviceman, soldier, warrior 2. adj. battling, belligerent, combating, conflicting, contending, fighting, opposing, warring

combative aggressive, antagonistic, bellicose, belligerent, contentious, militant, pugnacious, quarrelsome, truculent, warlike

combination 1. amalgam, amalgamation, blend, coalescence, composite, connection, mix, mixture 2. alliance, association, cabal, cartel, coalition, combine, compound, confederacy, confederation, consortium, conspiracy, federation, merger, syndicate, unification, union

an association for the promotion of commercial or other interests, esp. by doubtful means. —**com'binable** *adj.* —**com,bina'bility** *n.* —'**combi,native** *or* '**combi,natory** *adj.*

combings ('kəʊmɪŋz) *pl. n.* **1.** the loose hair removed by combing. **2.** the unwanted fibres removed in combing cotton, etc.

combining form *n.* a linguistic element that occurs only as part of a compound word, such as *anthropo-* in *anthropology* and *anthropomorph.*

combustible (kəm'bʌstəbəl) *adj.* **1.** capable of igniting and burning. **2.** easily annoyed; excitable. ~*n.* **3.** a combustible substance. —**com,busti'bility** *or* **com'bustibleness** *n.*

combustion (kəm'bʌstʃən) *n.* **1.** the process of burning. **2.** any process in which a substance reacts to produce a significant rise in temperature and the emission of light. **3.** a process in which a compound reacts slowly with oxygen to produce little heat and no light. —**com'bustive** *n., adj.*

come (kʌm) *vb.* **coming, came, come.** (*mainly intr.*) **1.** to move towards a specified person or place. **2.** to arrive by movement or by making progress. **3.** to become perceptible: *light came into the sky.* **4.** to occur: *Christmas comes but once a year.* **5.** to happen as a result: *no good will come of this.* **6.** to be derived: *good may come of evil.* **7.** to occur to the mind: *the truth suddenly came to me.* **8.** to reach: *she comes up to my shoulder.* **9.** to be produced: *that dress comes in red.* **10.** to arrive at or be brought into a particular state: *you will soon come to grief.* **11.** (foll. by *from*) to be or have been a resident or native (of): *I come from London.* **12.** to become: *your wishes will come true.* **13.** (*tr.; takes an infinitive*) to be given awareness: *I came to realize its value.* **14.** *Taboo sl.* to have an orgasm. **15.** (*tr.*) *Brit. inf.* to play the part of: *don't come the fine gentleman with me.* **16.** (*tr.*) *Brit. inf.* to cause or produce: *don't come that nonsense.* **17.** (*subjunctive use*): *come next August, he will be fifty years old:* when next August arrives. **18. as...as they come.** the most characteristic example of a type. **19. come again?** *Inf.* what did you say? **20. come clean.** *Inf.* to make a confession. **21. come good.** *Austral. & N.Z. inf.* to recover after a setback; succeed. **22. come to light.** to be revealed. **23. come to light with.** *Austral. & N.Z. inf.* to find or produce. **24. come to pass.** to take place. ~*interj.* **25.** an exclamation expressing annoyance, etc.: *come now!* ~See also **come about, come across,** etc.

come about *vb.* (*intr., adv.*) **1.** to take place; happen. **2.** *Naut.* to change tacks.

come across *vb.* (*intr.*) **1.** (*prep.*) to meet or find by accident. **2.** (*adv.*) to communicate the intended meaning or impression. **3.** (often foll. by *with*) to provide what is expected.

come at *vb.* (*intr., prep.*) **1.** to discover (facts, the truth, etc.). **2.** to attack: *he came at me with an axe.* **3.** (*usually used with a negative*) *Austral. sl.* to agree to do (something).

comeback ('kʌm,bæk) *n. Inf.* **1.** a return to a former position, status, etc. **2.** a response, esp. recriminatory. **3.** a quick retort. ~*vb.* **come back.** (*intr., adv.*) **4.** to return, esp. to the memory. **5.** to become fashionable again.

come between *vb.* (*intr., prep.*) to cause the estrangement or separation of (two people).

come by *vb.* (*intr., prep.*) to find or obtain, esp. accidentally: *do you ever come by any old books?*

Comecon ('kɒmɪ,kɒn) *n.* an association of Soviet-oriented Communist nations, founded in 1949 to coordinate economic development, etc.

comedian (kə'miːdɪən) *n.* **1.** an entertainer who specializes in jokes, comic skits, etc. **2.** an actor in comedy.

comedown ('kʌm,daʊn) *n.* **1.** a decline in status or prosperity. **2.** *Inf.* a disappointment. ~*vb.* **come down.** (*intr., adv.*) **3.** to come to a place regarded as lower. **4.** to lose status, etc. (esp. in **come down in the world**). **5.** (of prices) to become lower. **6.** to reach a decision: *the report came down in favour of a pay increase.* **7.** (often foll. by *to*) to be handed down by tradition or inheritance. **8.** *Brit.* to leave university. **9.** (foll. by *with*) to succumb (to illness). **10.** (foll. by *on*) to rebuke harshly. **11.** (foll. by *to*) to amount in essence (to): *it comes down to two choices.*

comedy ('kɒmɪdɪ) *n., pl.* **-dies. 1.** a dramatic or other work of light and amusing character. **2.** the genre of drama represented by works of this type. **3.** (in classical literature) a play in which the main characters triumph over adversity. **4.** the humorous aspect of life or of events. **5.** an amusing event or sequence of events. **6.** humour: *the comedy of Chaplin.* —**comedic** (kə'miːdɪk) *adj.*

come forward *vb.* (*intr., adv.*) **1.** to offer one's services; volunteer. **2.** to present oneself.

come-hither *adj.* (*usually prenominal*) *Inf.* alluring; seductive: *a come-hither look.*

come in *vb.* (*intr., mainly adv.*) **1.** to enter. **2.** to prove to be: *it came in useful.* **3.** to become fashionable or seasonable. **4.** *Cricket.* to begin an innings. **5.** to finish a race (in a certain position). **6.** to be received: *news is coming in of a big fire in Glasgow.* **7.** (of money) to be received as income. **8.** to play a role: *where do I come in?* **9.** (foll. by *for*) to be the object of: *the Chancellor came in for a lot of criticism*

come into *vb.* (*intr., prep.*) **1.** to enter. **2.** to inherit. **3. come into one's own.** to become fulfilled.

comely ('kʌmlɪ) *adj.* **-lier, -liest. 1.** good-looking; attractive. **2.** *Arch.* suitable; fitting. —'**comeliness** *n.*

come of *vb.* (*intr., prep.*) **1.** to be descended from. **2.** to result from: *nothing came of it.*

come off *vb.* (*intr., mainly adv.*) **1.** (*also prep.*) to fall (from). **2.** to become detached. **3.** (*prep.*) to be removed from (a price, tax, etc.): *will anything come off*

combine amalgamate, associate, bind, blend, bond, compound, connect, cooperate, fuse, incorporate, integrate, join (together), link, marry, merge, mix, pool, put (together), synthesize, unify, unite

combustible explosive, flammable, incendiary, inflammable

come 1. advance, appear, approach, arrive, become, draw near, enter, happen, materialize, move, move towards, near, occur, originate, show up (*Inf.*), turn out, turn up (*Inf.*) **2.** appear, arrive, attain, enter, materialize, reach, show up (*Inf.*), turn up (*Inf.*) **3.** fall, happen, occur, take place **4.** arise, emanate, emerge, end up, flow, issue, originate, result, turn out **5.** extend, reach **6.** be available (made, offered, on offer, produced)

come about arise, befall, come to pass, happen, occur, result, take place, transpire (*Inf.*)

come across bump into (*Inf.*), chance upon, discover, encounter, find, happen upon, hit upon, light upon, meet, notice, stumble upon, unearth

come along develop, improve, mend, perk up, pick up, progress, rally, recover, recuperate

come apart break, come unstuck, crumble, disintegrate, fall to pieces, give way, separate, split, tear

come at 1. attain, discover, find, grasp, reach **2.** assail, assault, attack, charge, fall upon, fly at, go for (*Inf.*), light into, rush, rush at

comeback 1. rally, rebound, recovery, resurgence, return, revival, triumph **2.** rejoinder, reply, response, retaliation, retort, riposte

come back reappear, recur, re-enter, return

come between alienate, divide, estrange, interfere, meddle, part, separate, set at odds

come by acquire, get, lay hold of, obtain, procure, secure, take possession of, win

come clean acknowledge, admit, confess, make a clean breast, own up, reveal

comedian card (*Inf.*), clown, comic, funny man, humorist, jester, joker, laugh (*Inf.*), wag, wit

comedown anticlimax, blow, decline, deflation, demotion, disappointment, humiliation, letdown, reverse

come down 1. decline, degenerate, descend, deteriorate, fall, go downhill, reduce, worsen **2.** choose, decide, favour, recommend

come down on criticize, dress down (*Inf.*), jump on (*Inf.*), rebuke, reprimand

come down to amount to, boil down to, end up as, result in

come down with be stricken with, catch, contract, fall ill, fall victim to, sicken, take, take sick

comedy chaffing, drollery, facetiousness, farce, fun, hilarity, humour, jesting, joking, light entertainment, sitcom (*Inf.*), slapstick, wisecracking, witticisms

come forward offer one's services, present *or* proffer oneself, volunteer

come in appear, arrive, cross the threshold, enter, finish, reach, show up (*Inf.*)

come in for acquire, bear the brunt of, endure, get, receive, suffer

comely 1. attractive, beautiful, becoming, blooming, bonny, buxom, fair, good-looking, graceful, handsome, lovely, pleasing, pretty, wholesome, winsome **2.** *Archaic* decent, decorous, fit, fitting, proper, seemly, suitable

income tax in the budget? **4.** (*copula*) to emerge from or as if from a contest: *he came off the winner.* **5.** *Inf.* to happen. **6.** *Inf.* to have the intended effect: *his jokes did not come off.* **7.** *Taboo sl.* to have an orgasm.

come-on *n. Inf.* **1.** anything that serves as a lure. ~*vb.* **come on** (*intr., mainly adv.*) **2.** (of power, water, etc.) to start running or functioning. **3.** to progress: *my plants are coming on nicely.* **4.** to advance, esp. in battle. **5.** to begin: *a new bowler has come on.* **6.** to make an entrance on stage. **7. come on strong.** to make a forceful or exaggerated impression.

come out *vb.* (*intr., adv.*) **1.** to be made public or revealed: *the news of her death came out last week.* **2.** to make a debut in society. **3.** to declare openly that one is a homosexual. **4.** *Chiefly Brit.* to go on strike. **5.** to declare oneself: *the government came out in favour of scrapping the project.* **6.** to be shown clearly: *you came out very well in the photos.* **7.** to yield a satisfactory solution: *these sums just won't come out.* **8.** to be published: *the paper comes out on Fridays.* **9.** (foll. by *in*) to become covered with. **10.** (foll. by *with*) to declare openly: *you can rely on him to come out with the facts.*

come over *vb.* (*intr.*) **1.** (*adv.*) to communicate the intended meaning or impression: *he came over very well.* **2.** (*adv.*) to change allegiances. **3.** *Inf.* to feel a particular sensation: *I came over funny.*

come round *vb.* (*intr., adv.*) **1.** to be restored to consciousness. **2.** to modify one's opinion.

comestible (kəˈmɛstɪbəl) *n.* (*usually pl.*) food.

comet (ˈkɒmɪt) *n.* a celestial body that travels around the sun, usually in a highly elliptical orbit: thought to consist of a frozen nucleus, part of which vaporizes on approaching the sun to form a long luminous tail. —ˈ**cometary** or **cometic** (kɒˈmɛtɪk) *adj.*

come through *vb.* (*intr.*) **1.** (*adv.*) to emerge successfully. **2.** (*prep.*) to survive (an illness, etc.).

come to *vb.* (*intr.*) **1.** (when *prep.*, used reflexively) to regain consciousness. **2.** (*adv.*) *Naut.* to slow a vessel or bring her to a stop. **3.** (*prep.*) to amount to (a sum of money). **4.** (*prep.*) to arrive at: *what is the world coming to?*

come up *vb.* (*intr., adv.*) **1.** to come to a place regarded as higher. **2.** (of the sun) to rise. **3.** to present itself: *that question will come up again.* **4.** *Brit.* to begin a term at a university. **5.** to appear from out of the ground: *my beans have come up early.* **6.** *Inf.* to win: *have your premium bonds ever come up?* **7. come up against.** to come into conflict with. **8. come up to.** to meet a standard. **9. come up with.** to produce.

come upon *vb.* (*intr., prep.*) to meet or encounter unexpectedly.

comeuppance (ˌkʌmˈʌpəns) *n. Sl.* just retribution.

comfit (ˈkʌmfɪt, ˈkɒm-) *n.* a sugar-coated sweet containing a nut or seed.

comfort (ˈkʌmfət) *n.* **1.** a state of ease or well-being. **2.** relief from affliction, grief, etc. **3.** a person, thing, or event that brings solace or ease. **4.** (*usually pl.*) something that affords physical ease and relaxation. ~*vb.* (*tr.*) **5.** to soothe; cheer. **6.** to bring physical ease to. —ˈ**comforting** *adj.* —ˈ**comfortless** *adj.*

comfortable (ˈkʌmftəbəl) *adj.* **1.** giving comfort. **2.** at ease. **3.** free from affliction or pain. **4.** (of a person or situation) relaxing. **5.** *Inf.* having adequate income. **6.** *Inf.* (of income, etc.) adequate to provide comfort. —ˈ**comfortably** *adv.*

comforter (ˈkʌmfətə) *n.* **1.** a person or thing that comforts. **2.** *Chiefly Brit.* a woollen scarf. **3.** a baby's dummy.

Comforter (ˈkʌmfətə) *n. Christianity.* an epithet of the Holy Spirit.

comfrey (ˈkʌmfrɪ) *n.* a hairy Eurasian plant having blue, purplish-pink, or white flowers.

comfy (ˈkʌmfɪ) *adj.* **-fier, -fiest.** *Inf.* short for **comfortable.**

comic (ˈkɒmɪk) *adj.* **1.** of, characterized by, or characteristic of comedy. **2.** (*prenominal*) acting in or composing comedy: *a comic writer.* **3.** humorous; funny. ~*n.* **4.** a person who is comic; comedian. **5.** a book or magazine containing comic strips.

comical (ˈkɒmɪkəl) *adj.* **1.** causing laughter. **2.** ludicrous; laughable. —ˈ**comically** *adv.*

comic opera *n.* a play largely set to music, employing comic effects or situations.

comic strip *n.* a sequence of drawings in a newspaper, magazine, etc., relating a comic or adventurous situation.

coming (ˈkʌmɪŋ) *adj.* **1.** (*prenominal*) (of time, events, etc.) approaching or next. **2.** promising (esp. in **up and coming**). **3. have it coming to one.** *Inf.* to deserve what one is about to suffer. ~*n.* **4.** arrival or approach.

comity (ˈkɒmɪtɪ) *n., pl.* **-ties.** mutual civility; courtesy.

comm. *abbrev. for:* **1.** commerce. **2.** commercial. **3.** committee. **4.** commonwealth.

comma (ˈkɒmə) *n.* **1.** the punctuation mark , indicating a slight pause and used where there is a listing of items or to separate a nonrestrictive clause from a main clause. **2.** *Music.* a minute interval.

command (kəˈmɑːnd) *vb.* **1.** (when *tr.*, may take a clause as object or an infinitive) to order or compel. **2.** to have or be in control or authority over. **3.** (*tr.*) to receive as due: *his nature commands respect.* **4.** to dominate (a view, etc.) as from a height. ~*n.* **5.** an order. **6.** the act of commanding. **7.** the right to command. **8.** the exercise of the power to command. **9.** knowledge; control: *a command of French.* **10.** *Chiefly mil.* the jurisdiction of a commander. **11.** a military unit or units commanding a specific function, as in the R.A.F. **12.** *Brit.* **a.** an invitation from the monarch. **b.** (*as modifi-*

═══ **THESAURUS** ═══

come off go off, happen, occur, succeed, take place, transpire

come on **1.** advance, develop, improve, make headway, proceed, progress **2.** appear, begin, take place

come out **1.** appear, be published (announced, divulged, issued, released, reported, revealed) **2.** conclude, end, result, terminate

come out with acknowledge, come clean, declare, disclose, divulge, lay open, own, own up, say

come round **1.** accede, acquiesce, allow, concede, grant, mellow, relent, yield **2.** come to, recover, regain consciousness, revive **3.** call, drop in, pop in, stop by, visit

come through **1.** accomplish, achieve, prevail, succeed, triumph **2.** endure, survive, weather the storm, withstand

come up arise, crop up, happen, occur, rise, spring up, turn up

comeuppance chastening, deserts, due reward, dues, merit, punishment, recompense, requital, retribution

come up to admit of comparison with, approach, compare with, equal, match, measure up to, meet, resemble, rival, stand or bear comparison with

come up with advance, create, discover, furnish, offer, present, produce, propose, provide, submit, suggest

comfort *v.* **1.** alleviate, assuage, cheer, commiserate with, compassionate (*Archaic*), console, ease, encourage, enliven, gladden, hearten, inspirit, invigorate, reassure, refresh, relieve, solace, soothe, strengthen ~*n.* **2.** aid, alleviation, cheer, compensation, consolation, ease, encouragement, enjoyment, help, relief, satisfaction, succour, support **3.** cosiness, creature comforts, ease, luxury, opulence, snugness, wellbeing

comfortable **1.** adequate, agreeable, ample, commodious, convenient, cosy, delightful, easy, enjoyable, homely, loose, loose-fitting, pleasant, relaxing, restful, roomy, snug **2.** at ease, contented, gratified, happy, relaxed, serene **3.** affluent, prosperous, well-off, well-to-do

comforting cheering, consolatory, consoling, encouraging, heart-warming, inspiriting, reassuring, soothing

comfortless **1.** bleak, cheerless, cold, desolate, dismal, dreary **2.** disconsolate, forlorn, inconsolable, miserable, sick at heart, woebegone, wretched

comic **1.** *adj.* amusing, comical, droll, facetious, farcical, funny, humorous, jocular, joking, light, rich, waggish, witty **2.** *n.* buffoon, clown, comedian, funny man, humorist, jester, wag, wit

comical absurd, amusing, comic, diverting, droll, entertaining, farcical, funny, hilarious, humorous, laughable, ludicrous, priceless, ridiculous, risible, side-splitting, silly, whimsical

coming *adj.* **1.** approaching, at hand, due, en route, forthcoming, future, imminent, impending, in store, in the wind, near, next, nigh **2.** aspiring, future, promising, up-and-coming ~*n.* **3.** accession, advent, approach, arrival

command *v.* **1.** bid, charge, compel, demand, direct, enjoin, order, require **2.** control, dominate, govern, head, lead, manage, reign over, rule, supervise, sway ~*n.* **3.** behest, bidding, commandment, decree, direction, directive, edict, fiat, injunction, instruction, mandate, order, precept, requirement, ultimatum **4.** authority, charge, control, domination, dominion, government, grasp, management, mastery, power, rule, supervision, sway, upper hand

er): *a command performance.* **13.** *Computers.* another name for **instruction** (sense 3).

commandant ('kɒmən,dænt, -,dɑːnt) *n.* an officer commanding a group or establishment.

commandeer (,kɒmən'dɪə) *vb.* (*tr.*) **1.** to seize for public or military use. **2.** to seize arbitrarily.

commander (kə'mɑːndə) *n.* **1.** an officer in command of a military formation or operation. **2.** a naval commissioned rank junior to captain but senior to lieutenant commander. **3.** the second in command of larger British warships. **4.** someone who holds authority. **5.** a high-ranking member of some knightly orders. **6.** an officer responsible for a district of the Metropolitan Police in London. —**com'mander,ship** *n.*

commander in chief *n., pl.* **commanders in chief.** the officer holding supreme command of the forces in an area or operation.

commanding (kə'mɑːndɪŋ) *adj.* (*usually prenominal*) **1.** being in command. **2.** having the air of authority: *a commanding voice.* **3.** (of a situation) exerting control. **4.** (of a viewpoint, etc.) overlooking; advantageous. —**com'mandingly** *adv.*

commandment (kə'mɑːndmənt) *n.* **1.** a divine command, esp. one of the Ten Commandments of the Old Testament. **2.** *Literary.* any command.

command module *n.* the module used as the living quarters in an Apollo spacecraft and functioning as the splashdown vehicle.

commando (kə'mɑːndəʊ) *n., pl.* **-dos** *or* **-does. 1. a.** an amphibious military unit trained for raiding. **b.** a member of such a unit. **2.** the basic unit of the Royal Marine Corps. **3.** (originally) an armed force raised by Boers during the Boer War. **4.** (*modifier*) denoting or relating to commandos: *a commando unit.*

command paper *n.* (in Britain) a government document that is presented to Parliament, in theory by royal command.

commedia dell'arte (*Italian* kɔm'mɛdja del'larte) *n.* a form of popular improvised comedy in Italy during the 16th to 18th centuries, with stock characters such as Punchinello, Harlequin, and Columbine.

commemorate (kə'mɛmə,reɪt) *vb.* (*tr.*) to honour or keep alive the memory of. —**com,memo'ration** *n.* —**com'memorative** *adj.* —**com'memo,rator** *n.*

commence (kə'mɛns) *vb.* to begin; come or cause to come into being, operation, etc.

commencement (kə'mɛnsmənt) *n.* **1.** the beginning; start. **2.** *U.S.* a ceremony for the conferment of academic degrees.

commend (kə'mɛnd) *vb.* **1.** to represent as being worthy of regard, confidence, etc.; recommend. **2.** to give in charge; entrust. **3.** to praise. **4.** to give the regards of: *commend me to your aunt.* —**com'mendable** *adj.* —**com'mendably** *adv.* —**,commen'dation** *n.* —**com'mendatory** *adj.*

commensurable (kə'mɛnsərəbəl, -ʃə-) *adj.* **1.** *Maths.* **a.** having a common factor. **b.** having units of the same dimensions and being related by whole numbers. **2.** proportionate. —**com,mensura'bility** *n.* —**com'mensurably** *adv.*

commensurate (kə'mɛnsərɪt, -ʃə-) *adj.* **1.** having the same extent or duration. **2.** corresponding in degree, amount, or size; proportionate. **3.** commensurable. —**com'mensurately** *adv.*

comment ('kɒmɛnt) *n.* **1.** a remark, criticism, or observation. **2.** talk or gossip. **3.** a note explaining or criticizing a passage in a text. **4.** explanatory or critical matter added to a text. ~*vb.* **5.** (when *intr.,* often foll. by *on*; when *tr.,* takes a clause as object) to remark or express an opinion. **6.** (*intr.*) to write notes explaining or criticizing a text. —**'commenter** *n.*

commentary ('kɒməntərɪ) *n., pl.* **-taries. 1.** an explanatory series of notes. **2.** a spoken accompaniment to a broadcast, film, etc. **3.** an explanatory treatise on a text. **4.** (*usually pl.*) a personal record of events: *the commentaries of Caesar.*

commentate ('kɒmən,teɪt) *vb.* **1.** to serve as a commentator. **2.** (*tr.*) to make a commentary on.

▷ **Usage.** The verb *commentate,* derived from *commentator,* is sometimes used as a synonym for *comment on* or *provide a commentary for.* It is not yet fully accepted as standard, though widespread in sports reporting and journalism.

commentator ('kɒmən,teɪtə) *n.* **1.** a person who provides a spoken commentary for a broadcast, film, etc., esp. of a sporting event. **2.** a person who writes notes on a text, etc.

commerce ('kɒmɜːs) *n.* **1.** the activity embracing all forms of the purchase and sale of goods and services. **2.** social relations. **3.** *Arch.* sexual intercourse.

commercial (kə'mɜːʃəl) *adj.* **1.** of or engaged in commerce. **2.** sponsored or paid for by an advertiser: *commercial television.* **3.** having profit as the main aim: *commercial music.* **4.** (of chemicals, etc.) unrefined and produced in bulk for use in industry. ~*n.* **5.** a commercially sponsored advertisement on radio or television. —**commerciality** (kə,mɜːʃɪ'ælɪtɪ) *n.* —**com'mercially** *adv.*

commercialism (kə'mɜːʃə,lɪzəm) *n.* **1.** the spirit, principles, or procedure of commerce. **2.** exclusive or inappropriate emphasis on profit.

commercialize *or* **-lise** (kə'mɜːʃə,laɪz) *vb.* (*tr.*) **1.** to make commercial. **2.** to exploit for profit, esp. at the expense of quality. —**com,merciali'zation** *or* **-li'sation** *n.*

commercial traveller *n.* another name for a **travelling salesman.**

commie *or* **commy** ('kɒmɪ) *n., pl.* **-mies,** *adj. Inf. & derog.* short for **communist.**

commination (,kɒmɪ'neɪʃən) *n.* **1.** the act of threatening punishment or vengeance. **2.** *Church of England.* a recital of prayers, including a list of God's judgments against sinners, in the office for Ash Wednesday. —**comminatory** ('kɒmɪnətərɪ) *adj.*

commingle (kɒ'mɪŋgəl) *vb.* to mix or be mixed.

commis ('kɒmɪs, 'kɒmɪ) *n., pl.* **-mis. 1.** an agent or deputy. **2.** an apprentice waiter or chef.

commiserate (kə'mɪzə,reɪt) *vb.* (when *intr.,* usually foll. by *with*) to feel or express sympathy or compassion (for). —**com,miser'ation** *n.* —**com'miser,ator** *n.*

commissar ('kɒmɪ,sɑː, ,kɒmɪ'sɑː) *n.* (in the Soviet Un-

THESAURUS

commandeer appropriate, confiscate, expropriate, hijack, requisition, seize, sequester, sequestrate, usurp

commander boss, captain, chief, C in C, C.O., commander-in-chief, commanding officer, director, head, leader, officer, ruler

commanding 1. advantageous, controlling, decisive, dominant, dominating, superior **2.** assertive, authoritative, autocratic, compelling, forceful, imposing, impressive, peremptory

commemorate celebrate, honour, immortalize, keep, memorialize, observe, pay tribute to, remember, salute, solemnize

commemoration ceremony, honouring, memorial service, observance, remembrance, tribute

commemorative celebratory, dedicatory, in honour, in memory, in remembrance, memorial

commence begin, embark on, enter upon, inaugurate, initiate, open, originate, start

commend 1. acclaim, applaud, approve, compliment, eulogize, extol, praise, recommend, speak highly of **2.** commit, confide, consign, deliver, entrust, hand over, yield

commendable admirable, creditable, deserving, estimable, exemplary, laudable, meritorious, praiseworthy, worthy

commendation acclaim, acclamation, approbation, approval, credit, encomium, encouragement, good opinion, panegyric, praise, recommendation

commensurate adequate, appropriate, coextensive, comparable, compatible, consistent, corresponding, due, equivalent, fit, fitting, in accord, proportionate, sufficient

comment *v.* **1.** animadvert, interpose, mention, note, observe, opine, point out, remark, say **2.** annotate, criticize, elucidate, explain, interpret ~*n.* **3.** animadversion, observation, remark, statement **4.** annotation, commentary, criticism, elucidation, explana-

tion, exposition, illustration, note

commentary analysis, critique, description, exegesis, explanation, narration, notes, review, treatise, voice-over

commentator 1. commenter, reporter, special correspondent, sportscaster **2.** annotator, critic, expositor, interpreter, scholiast

commerce 1. business, dealing, exchange, merchandising, trade, traffic **2.** communication, dealings, intercourse, relations, socializing

commercial 1. business, mercantile, profit-making, sales, trade, trading **2.** in demand, marketable, popular, profitable, saleable **3.** exploited, materialistic, mercenary, monetary, pecuniary, profit-making, venal

commingle amalgamate, blend, combine, commix, intermingle, intermix, join, mingle, unite

ion) **1.** an official of the Communist Party responsible for political education. **2.** (before 1946) the head of a government department.

commissariat (ˌkɒmɪˈsɛərɪət) n. **1.** (in the Soviet Union) a government department before 1946. **2.** a military department in charge of food supplies, etc.

commissary (ˈkɒmɪsərɪ) n., pl. **-saries. 1.** U.S. a shop supplying food or equipment, as in a military camp. **2.** U.S. army. an officer responsible for supplies. **3.** U.S. a restaurant in a film studio. **4.** a representative or deputy, esp. of a bishop. —**commissarial** (ˌkɒmɪˈsɛərɪəl) adj.

commission (kəˈmɪʃən) n. **1.** a duty committed to a person or group to perform. **2.** authority to perform certain duties. **3.** a document granting such authority. **4.** Mil. **a.** a document conferring a rank on an officer. **b.** the rank granted. **5.** a group charged with certain duties: a commission of inquiry. **6.** a government board empowered to exercise administrative, judicial, or legislative authority. **7. a.** the authority given to a person or organization to act as an agent to a principal in commercial transactions. **b.** the fee allotted to an agent for services rendered. **8.** the state of being charged with specific responsibilities. **9.** the act of committing a sin, crime, etc. **10.** good working condition or (esp. of a ship) active service (esp. in **in commission, out of commission**). ~vb. (mainly tr.) **11.** to grant authority to. **12.** Mil. to confer a rank. **13.** to equip and test (a ship) for active service. **14.** to place an order for (something): to commission a portrait. **15.** to make or become operative or operable: the plant is due to commission next year.

commissionaire (kəˌmɪʃəˈnɛə) n. Chiefly Brit. a uniformed doorman at a hotel, theatre, etc.

commissioned officer n. a military officer holding a commission, such as Second Lieutenant in the British Army, Acting Sub-Lieutenant in the Royal Navy, Pilot Officer in the Royal Air Force, and officers of all ranks senior to these.

commissioner (kəˈmɪʃənə) n. **1.** a person endowed with certain powers. **2.** any of several types of civil servant. **3.** a member of a commission. —**com'missioner-ship** n.

commit (kəˈmɪt) vb. **-mitting, -mitted.** (tr.) **1.** to hand over, as for safekeeping; entrust. **2. commit to memory.** to memorize. **3.** to take into custody: to commit someone to prison. **4.** (usually passive) to pledge or align (oneself), as to a particular cause: a committed radical. **5.** to order (forces) into action. **6.** to perform (a crime, error, etc.). **7.** to surrender, esp. for destruction: she committed the letter to the fire. **8.** to refer (a bill, etc.) to a committee. —**com'mittable** adj. —**com'mitter** n.

commitment (kəˈmɪtmənt) n. **1.** the act of committing or pledging. **2.** the state of being committed or pledged. **3.** an obligation, promise, etc. that restricts freedom of action. **4.** Also called (esp. formerly): **mittimus.** Law. a written order of a court directing that a person be imprisoned. **5.** a future financial obligation or contingent liability. ~Also called (esp. for sense 4): **committal** (kəˈmɪtəl).

committee n. **1.** (kəˈmɪtɪ). a group of people appointed to perform a specified service or function. **2.** (ˌkɒmɪˈtiː). (formerly) a person to whom the care of a mentally incompetent person or his property was entrusted by a court.

commode (kəˈməʊd) n. **1.** a piece of furniture, usually highly ornamented, containing drawers or shelves. **2.** a bedside table with a cabinet for a chamber pot or washbasin. **3.** a chair with a hinged flap concealing a chamber pot.

commodious (kəˈməʊdɪəs) adj. **1.** roomy; spacious. **2.**

Arch. convenient. —**com'modiousness** n.

commodity (kəˈmɒdɪtɪ) n., pl. **-ties. 1.** an article of commerce. **2.** something of use or profit. **3.** Econ. an exchangeable unit of economic wealth, such as a primary product.

commodore (ˈkɒməˌdɔː) n. **1.** Brit. a naval rank junior to rear admiral and senior to captain. **2.** the captain of a shipping line. **3.** the officer in command of a merchant convoy. **4.** the titular head of a yacht club.

common (ˈkɒmən) adj. **1.** belonging to two or more people: common property. **2.** belonging to members of one or more communities; public: a common culture. **3.** of ordinary standard; average. **4.** prevailing; widespread: common opinion. **5.** frequently encountered; ordinary: a common brand of soap. **6.** notorious: a common nuisance. **7.** Derog. considered by the speaker to be low-class, vulgar, or coarse. **8.** (prenominal) having no special distinction: the common man. **9.** Maths. having a specified relationship with a group of numbers or quantities: common denominator. **10.** Prosody. (of a syllable) able to be long or short. **11.** Grammar. (in certain languages) denoting or belonging to a gender of nouns that includes both masculine and feminine referents. **12. common or garden.** Inf. ordinary. ~n. **13.** a tract of open public land. **14.** Law. the right to go onto someone else's property and remove natural products, as by pasturing cattle (esp. in **right of common**). **15.** Christianity. **a.** a form of the proper of the Mass used on festivals that have no special proper of their own. **b.** the ordinary of the Mass. **16. in common.** mutually held or used. —**'commonly** adv. —**'commonness** n.

commonality (ˌkɒməˈnælɪtɪ) n., pl. **-ties. 1.** the fact of being common. **2.** another word for **commonalty** (sense 1).

commonalty (ˈkɒmənəltɪ) n., pl. **-ties. 1.** the ordinary people as distinct from those with rank or title. **2.** the members of an incorporated society.

commoner (ˈkɒmənə) n. **1.** a person who does not belong to the nobility. **2.** a person who has a right in or over common land. **3.** Brit. a student at a university who is not on a scholarship.

common fraction n. another name for **simple fraction.**

common law n. the body of law based on judicial decisions and custom, as distinct from statute law.

common-law marriage n. a state of marriage deemed to exist between a man and a woman after a number of years of cohabitation.

Common Market n. **the.** a European economic association, originally composed (1958) of Belgium, France, West Germany, Italy, Luxembourg, and the Netherlands, joined in 1973 by the United Kingdom, the Irish Republic, and Denmark, and in 1981 by Greece. Officially called: **European Economic Community.**

commonplace (ˈkɒmənˌpleɪs) adj. **1.** ordinary; everyday. **2.** dull; trite: commonplace prose. ~n. **3.** a platitude; truism. **4.** a passage in a book marked for inclusion in a commonplace book, etc. **5.** an ordinary thing. —**'common,placeness** n.

common room n. Chiefly Brit. a sitting room in schools, colleges, etc.

commons (ˈkɒmənz) n. **1.** (functioning as pl.) the lower classes as contrasted with the ruling or noble classes of society. **2.** (functioning as sing.) Brit. a hall for dining, recreation, etc., usually attached to a college, etc. **3.** (usually functioning as pl.) Brit. food or rations (esp. in **short commons**).

Commons (ˈkɒmənz) n. **the.** See House of Commons.

common sense n. **1.** sound practical sense. ~adj.

THESAURUS

commission n. **1.** appointment, authority, charge, duty, employment, errand, function, mandate, mission, task, trust, warrant **2.** allowance, brokerage, compensation, cut, fee, percentage, rake-off (Sl.) **3.** board, body of commissioners, commissioners, committee, delegation, deputation, representative ~v. **4.** appoint, authorize, contract, delegate, depute, empower, engage, nominate, order, select, send
commit 1. carry out, do, enact, execute, perform, perpetrate **2.** commend, confide, consign, deliver, deposit, engage, entrust, give, hand over **3.** align, bind, compromise,

endanger, make liable, obligate, pledge, rank **4.** confine, imprison, put in custody
commitment 1. duty, engagement, liability, obligation, responsibility, tie **2.** adherence, dedication, devotion, involvement, loyalty **3.** assurance, guarantee, pledge, promise, undertaking, vow, word
common 1. average, commonplace, conventional, customary, daily, everyday, familiar, frequent, general, habitual, humdrum, obscure, ordinary, plain, regular, routine, run-of-the-mill, simple, standard, stock, usual, workaday **2.** accepted, general, popular, prevailing, prevalent, universal, widespread **3.**

collective, communal, community, popular, public, social **4.** coarse, hackneyed, inferior, low, pedestrian, plebeian, stale, trite, undistinguished, vulgar
commonplace 1. adj. common, customary, everyday, humdrum, obvious, ordinary, pedestrian, stale, threadbare, trite, uninteresting, widespread, worn out **2.** n. banality, cliché, platitude, truism
common-sense, **commonsensical** adj. astute, down-to-earth, hard-headed, judicious, level-headed, matter-of-fact, practical, realistic, reasonable, sane, sensible, shrewd, sound

common-sense; *also* **common-sensical. 2.** inspired by or displaying this.

common time *n. Music.* a time signature indicating four crotchet beats to the bar; four-four time. Symbol: **C**

commonwealth (ˈkɒmənˌwɛlθ) *n.* **1.** the people of a state or nation viewed politically; body politic. **2.** a state in which the people possess sovereignty; republic. **3.** a group of persons united by some common interest.

Commonwealth (ˈkɒmənˌwɛlθ) *n.* **the. 1.** Official name: **the Commonwealth of Nations.** an association of sovereign states that are or at some time have been ruled by Britain. **2.** the republic that existed in Britain from 1649 to 1660. **3.** the official designation of Australia, four states of the U.S., and Puerto Rico.

commotion (kəˈməʊʃən) *n.* **1.** violent disturbance; upheaval. **2.** political insurrection. **3.** a confused noise; din.

communal (ˈkɒmjunəl) *adj.* **1.** belonging to a community as a whole. **2.** of a commune or a religious community. —**communality** (ˌkɒmjuˈnælɪtɪ) *n.* —ˈ**communally** *adv.*

commune[1] *vb.* (kəˈmjuːn). (*intr.;* usually foll. by *with*) **1.** to talk intimately. **2.** to experience strong emotion (for): *to commune with nature.* ~*n.* (ˈkɒmjuːn). **3.** intimate conversation; communion.

commune[2] (ˈkɒmjuːn) *n.* **1.** a group of families or individuals living together and sharing possessions and responsibilities. **2.** any small group of people having common interests or responsibilities. **3.** the smallest administrative unit in Belgium, France, Italy, and Switzerland. **4.** a medieval town enjoying a large degree of autonomy.

Commune (ˈkɒmjuːn) *n. French history.* a committee that governed Paris during the French Revolution: suppressed 1794.

communicable (kəˈmjuːnɪkəbəl) *adj.* **1.** capable of being communicated. **2.** (of a disease) capable of being passed on readily. —**comˌmunicaˈbility** *n.* —**comˈmunicably** *adv.*

communicant (kəˈmjuːnɪkənt) *n.* **1.** *Christianity.* a person who receives Communion. **2.** a person who communicates or informs.

communicate (kəˈmjuːnɪˌkeɪt) *vb.* **1.** to impart (knowledge) or exchange (thoughts) by speech, writing, gestures, etc. **2.** (*tr.;* usually foll. by *to*) to transmit (to): *the dog communicated his fear to the other animals.* **3.** (*intr.*) to have a sympathetic mutual understanding. **4.** (*intr.;* usually foll. by *with*) to make or have a connecting passage: *the kitchen communicates with the dining room.* **5.** (*tr.*) to transmit (a disease). **6.** *Christianity.* to receive Communion. —**comˈmuniˌcator** *n.* —**comˈmunicatory** *adj.*

communication (kəˌmjuːnɪˈkeɪʃən) *n.* **1.** the imparting or exchange of information, ideas, or feelings. **2.** something communicated, such as a message. **3.** (*usually pl.; sometimes functioning as sing.*) the study of ways in which human beings communicate. **4.** a connecting route or link. **5.** (*pl.*) *Mil.* the system by which forces, supplies, etc., are moved within an area of operations.

communication cord *n. Brit.* a cord or chain in a train which may be pulled by a passenger to stop the train in an emergency.

communion (kəˈmjuːnjən) *n.* **1.** an exchange of thoughts, emotions, etc. **2.** sharing in common; participation. **3.** (foll. by *with*) strong feelings (for): *communion with nature.* **4.** a religious group or denomination having common beliefs and practices. **5.** spiritual union.

Communion (kəˈmjuːnjən) *n. Christianity.* **1.** the act of participating in the Eucharist. **2.** the celebration of the Eucharist. **3.** the consecrated elements of the Eucharist. ~Also called: **Holy Communion.**

communiqué (kəˈmjuːnɪˌkeɪ) *n.* an official communication or announcement, esp. to the press or public.

communism (ˈkɒmjuˌnɪzəm) *n.* **1.** advocacy of a classless society in which private ownership has been abolished and the means of production belong to the community. **2.** any movement or doctrine aimed at achieving such a society. **3.** (*usually cap.*) a political movement based upon the writings of Marx that considers history in terms of class conflict and revolutionary struggle. **4.** (*usually cap.*) a system of government established by a ruling Communist Party, esp. in the Soviet Union. **5.** communal living.

communist (ˈkɒmjunɪst) *n.* **1.** a supporter of communism. **2.** (*often cap.*) a supporter of a Communist movement or state. **3.** (*often cap.*) a member of a Communist party. **4.** (*often cap.*) *Chiefly U.S.* any person holding left-wing views, esp. when considered subversive. **5.** a person who practises communal living. ~*adj.* **6.** of, favouring, or relating to communism. —ˌ**commuˈnistic** *adj.*

community (kəˈmjuːnɪtɪ) *n., pl.* **-ties. 1. a.** the people living in one locality. **b.** the locality in which they live. **c.** (*as modifier*): *community spirit.* **2.** a group of people having cultural, religious, or other characteristics in common: *the Protestant community.* **3.** a group of nations having certain interests in common. **4.** the public; society. **5.** common ownership. **6.** similarity or agreement: *community of interests.* **7.** (in Wales and Scotland) the smallest unit of local government. **8.** *Ecology.* a group of interdependent plants and animals inhabiting the same region.

community centre *n.* a building used by a community for social gatherings, etc.

commutation (ˌkɒmjuˈteɪʃən) *n.* **1.** a substitution or exchange. **2.** the replacement of one method of payment by another. **3.** the reduction in severity of a penalty imposed by law. **4.** the process of commutating an electric current.

commutative (kəˈmjuːtətɪv, ˈkɒmjuˌteɪtɪv) *adj.* relating to or involving substitution.

commutator (ˈkɒmjuˌteɪtə) *n.* **1.** a device used to reverse the direction of flow of an electric current. **2.** the segmented metal cylinder or disc of an electric motor, generator, etc., used to make electrical contact with the rotating coils.

commute (kəˈmjuːt) *vb.* **1.** (*intr.*) to travel some distance regularly between one's home and one's place of work. **2.** (*tr.*) to substitute. **3.** (*tr.*) *Law.* to reduce (a sentence) to one less severe. **4.** to pay (an annuity, etc.) at one time, instead of in instalments. **5.** to change: *to commute base metal into gold.* —**comˈmutable** *adj.* —**comˌmutaˈbility** *n.*

THESAURUS

common sense good sense, gumption (*Inf.*), horse sense, level-headedness, mother wit, native intelligence, nous (*Sl.*), practicality, prudence, reasonableness, sound judgment, soundness, wit

commotion ado, agitation, brouhaha, bustle, disorder, disturbance, excitement, ferment, furore, fuss, hubbub, hullabaloo, hurly-burly, perturbation, racket, riot, rumpus, to-do, tumult, turmoil, uproar

communal collective, communistic, community, general, joint, neighbourhood, public, shared

commune[1] *v.* **1.** communicate, confer, confide in, converse, discourse, discuss, parley **2.** contemplate, meditate, muse, ponder, reflect

commune[2] *n.* collective, community, co-operative, kibbutz

communicable catching, contagious, infectious, taking, transferable, transmittable

communicate acquaint, announce, be in contact, be in touch, connect, convey, correspond, declare, disclose, disseminate, divulge, impart, inform, make known, pass on, phone, proclaim, publish, report, reveal, ring up, signify, spread, transmit, unfold

communication 1. connection, contact, conversation, correspondence, dissemination, intercourse, link, transmission **2.** announcement, disclosure, dispatch, information, intelligence, message, news, report, statement, word

communications 1. routes, transport, travel **2.** information technology, media, publicity, public relations, telecommunications

communicative candid, chatty, conversable, expansive, forthcoming, frank, informative, loquacious, open, outgoing, talkative, unreserved, voluble

communion 1. accord, affinity, agreement, closeness, communing, concord, converse, fellowship, harmony, intercourse, participation, rapport, sympathy, togetherness, unity **2.** *Church* Eucharist, Lord's Supper, Mass, Sacrament

communiqué announcement, bulletin, dispatch, news flash, official communication, report

communism Bolshevism, collectivism, Marxism, socialism, state socialism

communist Bolshevik, collectivist, Marxist, Red (*Inf.*), socialist

community 1. association, body politic, brotherhood, commonwealth, company, district, general public, locality, people, populace, population, public, residents, society, state **2.** affinity, agreement, identity, likeness, sameness, similarity

commute 1. barter, exchange, interchange, substitute, switch, trade **2.** *Law: of penalties, etc.* alleviate, curtail, mitigate, modify, reduce, remit, shorten, soften

commuter (kə'mju:tə) n. a person who travels to work over an appreciable distance, usually from the suburbs to the centre of a city.

comp (kɒmp) Inf. ~n. 1. a compositor. 2. an accompaniment. 3. a competition. ~vb. 4. (intr.) to work as a compositor in the printing industry. 5. to play an accompaniment (to).

comp. abbrev. for: 1. companion. 2. comparative. 3. compare. 4. compiled. 5. composer. 6. composition. 7. compositor. 8. compound. 9. comprehensive. 10. comprising.

compact¹ adj. (kəm'pækt). 1. closely packed together. 2. neatly fitted into a restricted space. 3. concise; brief. 4. well constructed; solid; firm. 5. (foll. by of) composed (of). ~vb. (kəm'pækt). (tr.) 6. to pack closely together; compress. 7. (foll. by of) to form by pressing together: sediment compacted of three types of clay. 8. Metallurgy. to compress (a metal powder) to form a stable product suitable for sintering. ~n. ('kɒmpækt). 9. a small flat case containing a mirror, face powder, etc., designed to be carried in a woman's handbag. 10. U.S. a small and economical car. —com'pactly adv. —com'pactness n.

compact² ('kɒmpækt) n. an official contract or agreement.

compact disc ('kɒmpækt) n. 1. a small PVC-covered metal audio disc read by an optical laser system. 2. a similar disc carrying material for display on a VDU or television screen.

companion¹ (kəm'pænjən) n. 1. a person who is an associate of another or others; comrade. 2. (esp. formerly) an employee, usually a woman, who provides company for an employer. 3. a. one of a pair. b. (as modifier): a companion volume. 4. a guidebook or handbook. 5. a member of the lowest rank of certain orders of knighthood. 6. Astron. the fainter of the two components of a double star. ~vb. 7. (tr.) to accompany. —com'panion,ship n.

companion² (kəm'pænjən) n. Naut. a raised frame on an upper deck with windows to give light to the deck below.

companionable (kəm'pænjənəb°l) adj. sociable. —com'panionableness n. —com'panionably adv.

companionway (kəm'pænjən,weɪ) n. a ladder from one deck to another in a ship.

company ('kʌmpənɪ) n., pl. -nies. 1. a number of people gathered together; assembly. 2. the fact of being with someone; companionship: I enjoy her company. 3. a guest or guests. 4. a business enterprise. 5. the members of an enterprise not specifically mentioned in the enterprise's title. Abbrev.: Co., co. 6. a group of actors. 7. a small unit of troops. 8. the officers and crew of a ship. 9. a unit of Girl Guides. 10. English history. a medieval guild. 11. keep company. a. to accompany (someone). b. (esp. of lovers) to spend time together. ~vb. -nying, -nied. 12. Arch. to associate (with someone).

company sergeant-major n. Mil. the senior non-commissioned officer in a company.

comparable ('kɒmpərəb°l) adj. 1. worthy of comparison. 2. able to be compared (with). —,compara'bility or 'comparableness n.

comparative (kəm'pærətɪv) adj. 1. denoting or involving comparison: comparative literature. 2. relative: a comparative loss of prestige. 3. Grammar. denoting the form of an adjective that indicates that the quality denoted is possessed to a greater extent. In English the comparative is marked by the suffix -er or the word more. ~n. 4. the comparative form of an adjective. —com'paratively adv. —com'parativeness n.

compare (kəm'pɛə) vb. 1. (tr.; foll. by to) to regard as similar; liken: the general has been compared to Napoleon. 2. (tr.) to examine in order to observe resemblances or differences: to compare rum and gin. 3. (intr.; usually foll. by with) to be the same or similar: gin compares with rum in alcoholic content. 4. (intr.) to bear a specified relation when examined: this car compares badly with the other. 5. (tr.) Grammar. to give the positive, comparative, and superlative forms of (an adjective). 6. compare notes. to exchange opinions. ~n. 7. comparison (esp. in beyond compare).

comparison (kəm'pærɪs°n) n. 1. the act of comparing. 2. the state of being compared. 3. likeness: there was no comparison between them. 4. a rhetorical device involving comparison, such as a simile. 5. Also called: degrees of comparison. Grammar. the listing of the positive, comparative, and superlative forms of an adjective or adverb. 6. bear or stand comparison (with). to be sufficiently similar to be compared with (something else), esp. favourably.

compartment (kəm'pɑ:tmənt) n. 1. one of the sections into which an area, esp. an enclosed space, is partitioned. 2. any separate section: a compartment of the mind. 3. a small storage space. —compartmental (,kɒmpɑ:t'mɛnt°l) adj. —,compart'mentally adv.

compartmentalize or **-lise** (,kɒmpɑ:t'mɛntə,laɪz) vb. (usually tr.) to put into categories, etc., esp. to an excessive degree. —,compart,mentali'zation or -li'sation n.

compass ('kʌmpəs) n. 1. Also called: magnetic compass. an instrument for finding direction, having a magnetized needle which points to magnetic north. 2. (often pl.) Also called: pair of compasses. an instrument used for drawing circles, measuring distances, etc., that consists of two arms, joined at one end. 3. limits or range: within the compass of education. 4. Music. the interval between the lowest and highest note attainable. ~vb. (tr.) 5. to surround; hem in. 6. to grasp mentally. 7. to achieve; accomplish. 8. Obs. to plot. —'compassable adj.

compassion (kəm'pæʃən) n. a feeling of distress and pity for the suffering or misfortune of another.

compassionate (kəm'pæʃənət) adj. 1. showing or having compassion. 2. compassionate leave. leave granted on the grounds of bereavement, family illness, etc. —com'passionately adv.

THESAURUS

commuter 1. n. daily traveller, straphanger, suburbanite 2. adj. suburban

compact¹ adj. 1. close, compressed, condensed, dense, firm, impenetrable, impermeable, pressed together, solid, thick 2. brief, compendious, concise, epigrammatic, laconic, pithy, pointed, succinct, terse, to the point ~v. 3. compress, condense, cram, pack down, stuff, tamp

compact² n. agreement, alliance, arrangement, bargain, bond, concordat, contract, covenant, deal, entente, pact, stipulation, treaty, understanding

companion 1. accomplice, ally, associate, buddy (Inf.), colleague, comrade, confederate, consort, crony, friend, mate (Inf.), partner 2. aide, assistant, attendant, chaperon, duenna, escort, squire 3. complement, counterpart, fellow, match, mate, twin

companionable affable, congenial, conversable, convivial, cordial, familiar, friendly, genial, gregarious, neighbourly, outgoing, sociable

companionship amity, camaraderie, company, comradeship, conviviality, esprit de corps, fellowship, fraternity, friendship,

rapport, togetherness

company 1. assemblage, assembly, band, body, circle, collection, community, concourse, convention, coterie, crew, crowd, ensemble, gathering, group, league, party, set, throng, troop, troupe, turnout 2. association, business, concern, corporation, establishment, firm, house, partnership, syndicate 3. callers, companionship, fellowship, guests, party, presence, society, visitors

comparable 1. a match for, as good as, commensurate, equal, equivalent, in a class with, on a par, proportionate, tantamount 2. akin, alike, analogous, cognate, corresponding, related, similar

comparative approximate, by comparison, qualified, relative

compare 1. With with balance, collate, contrast, juxtapose, set against, weigh 2. With to correlate, equate, identify with, liken, parallel, resemble 3. Be the equal of approach, approximate to, bear comparison, be in the same class as, be on a par with, come up to, compete with, equal, hold a candle to, match, vie

comparison 1. collation, contrast, dis-

tinction, juxtaposition 2. analogy, comparability, correlation, likeness, resemblance, similarity

compartment 1. alcove, bay, berth, booth, carrel, carriage, cell, chamber, cubbyhole, cubicle, locker, niche, pigeonhole, section 2. area, category, department, division, section, subdivision

compass n. 1. area, bound, boundary, circle, circuit, circumference, enclosure, extent, field, limit, range, reach, realm, round, scope, sphere, stretch, zone ~v. 2. beset, besiege, blockade, circumscribe, encircle, enclose, encompass, environ, hem in, invest (Rare), surround 3. accomplish, achieve, attain, bring about, effect, execute, fulfil, perform, procure, realize

compassion charity, clemency, commiseration, compunction, condolence, fellow feeling, heart, humanity, kindness, mercy, ruth (Archaic), soft-heartedness, sorrow, sympathy, tender-heartedness, tenderness

compassionate benevolent, charitable, humane, humanitarian, indulgent, kind-hearted, kindly, lenient, merciful, pitying, sympathetic, tender, tender-hearted,

compatible (kəm'pætəbəl) *adj.* **1.** (usually foll. by *with*) able to exist together harmoniously. **2.** (usually foll. by *with*) consistent: *her deeds were not compatible with her ideology.* **3.** (of pieces of machinery, etc.) capable of being used together without modification or adaptation. —**com,pati'bility** *n.* —**com'patibly** *adv.*

compatriot (kəm'pætrɪət) *n.* a fellow countryman. —**com,patri'otic** *adj.*

compeer ('kɒmpɪə) *n.* **1.** a person of equal rank, status, or ability. **2.** a comrade.

compel (kəm'pɛl) *vb.* **-pelling, -pelled.** (*tr.*) **1.** to cause (someone) by force (to be or do something). **2.** to obtain by force; exact: *to compel obedience.* —**com'pellable** *adj.* —**com'peller** *n.*

compendious (kəm'pɛndɪəs) *adj.* stating the essentials of a subject in a concise form. —**com'pendiously** *adv.* —**com'pendiousness** *n.*

compendium (kəm'pɛndɪəm) *n., pl.* **-diums** *or* **-dia** (-dɪə). **1.** *Brit.* a book containing a collection of useful hints. **2.** *Brit.* a selection, esp. of different games in one container. **3.** a summary.

compensate ('kɒmpɛn,seɪt) *vb.* **1.** to make amends to (someone), esp. for loss or injury. **2.** (*tr.*) to serve as compensation or damages for (injury, loss, etc.). **3.** to counterbalance the effects of (a force, weight, etc.) so as to produce equilibrium. **4.** (*intr.*) to attempt to conceal one's shortcomings by the exaggerated exhibition of qualities regarded as desirable. —**compensative** ('kɒmpən,seɪtɪv, kəm'pɛnsə-) *or* **compensatory** ('kɒmpɛn,seɪtərɪ, kəm'pɛnsətərɪ) *adj.* —**'compen,sator** *n.*

compensation (,kɒmpɛn'seɪʃən) *n.* **1.** the act of making amends for something. **2.** something given as reparation for loss, injury, etc. **3.** the attempt to conceal one's shortcomings by the exaggerated exhibition of qualities regarded as desirable. —**,compen'sational** *adj.*

compere ('kɒmpɛə) *Brit.* ~*n.* **1.** a master of ceremonies who introduces cabaret, television acts, etc. ~*vb.* **2.** to act as a compere (for).

compete (kəm'piːt) *vb.* (*intr.; often foll. by with*) to contend (against) for profit, an award, etc.

competence ('kɒmpɪtəns) *or* **competency** *n.* **1.** the condition of being capable; ability. **2.** a sufficient income to live on. **3.** the state of being legally competent or qualified.

competent ('kɒmpɪtənt) *adj.* **1.** having sufficient skill, knowledge, etc.; capable. **2.** suitable or sufficient for the purpose: *a competent answer.* **3.** *Law.* (of a witness, etc.) qualified to testify, etc. —**'competently** *adv.* —**'competentness** *n.*

competition (,kɒmpɪ'tɪʃən) *n.* **1.** the act of competing. **2.** a contest in which a winner is selected from among

two or more entrants. **3.** a series of games, sports events, etc. **4.** the opposition offered by competitors. **5.** competitors offering opposition.

competitive (kəm'pɛtɪtɪv) *adj.* **1.** involving rivalry: *competitive sports.* **2.** sufficiently low in price or high in quality to be successful against commercial rivals. **3.** characterized by an urge to compete: *a competitive personality.* —**com'petitiveness** *n.*

competitor (kəm'pɛtɪtə) *n.* a person, group, team, firm, etc., that vies or competes; rival.

compile (kəm'paɪl) *vb.* (*tr.*) **1.** to make or compose from other sources: *to compile a list of names.* **2.** to collect for a book, hobby, etc. **3.** *Computers.* to create a set of machine instructions) from a high-level programming language, using a compiler. —**compilation** (,kɒmpɪ'leɪʃən) *n.*

compiler (kəm'paɪlə) *n.* **1.** a person who compiles something. **2.** a computer program by which a high-level programming language is converted into machine language that can be acted upon by a computer. Cf. **assembler.**

complacency (kəm'pleɪsənsɪ) *or* **complacence** *n.* extreme self-satisfaction; smugness. —**com'placent** *adj.*

complain (kəm'pleɪn) *vb.* (*intr.*) **1.** to express resentment, displeasure, etc.; grumble. **2.** (foll. by *of*) to state the presence of pain, illness, etc.: *she complained of a headache.* —**com'plainer** *n.* —**com'plainingly** *adv.*

complainant (kəm'pleɪnənt) *n. Law.* a plaintiff.

complaint (kəm'pleɪnt) *n.* **1.** the act of complaining. **2.** a cause for complaining; grievance. **3.** a mild ailment.

complaisant (kəm'pleɪzənt) *adj.* showing a desire to comply or oblige; polite. —**com'plaisance** *n.*

complement *n.* ('kɒmplɪmənt). **1.** a person or thing that completes something. **2.** a complete amount, number, etc. (often in **full complement**). **3.** the officers and crew needed to man a ship. **4.** *Grammar.* a word, phrase, or clause that completes the meaning of the predicate, as *an idiot* in *He is an idiot* or *that he would be early* in *I hoped that he would be early.* **5.** *Maths.* the angle that when added to a specified angle produces a right angle. **6.** *Logic.* the class of all the things that are not members of a given class. **7.** a heat-sensitive component of blood serum that destroys pathogenic substances, esp. bacteria. ~*vb.* ('kɒmplɪ,mɛnt). **8.** (*tr.*) to complete or form a complement to.

complementary (,kɒmplɪ'mɛntərɪ) *adj.* **1.** forming a complement. **2.** forming a satisfactory or balanced whole. —**,comple'mentarily** *adv.* —**,comple'mentariness** *n.*

complete (kəm'pliːt) *adj.* **1.** having every necessary part; entire. **2.** finished. **3.** (*prenominal*) thorough: *he is a complete rogue.* **4.** perfect in quality or kind: *he is a complete scholar.* **5.** (of a logical system) constituted

---

THESAURUS

understanding

compatibility affinity, agreement, amity, congeniality, empathy, harmony, likemindedness, rapport, single-mindedness, sympathy

compatible accordant, adaptable, agreeable, congenial, congruent, congruous, consistent, consonant, harmonious, in harmony, in keeping, like-minded, reconcilable, suitable

compatriot countryman, fellow citizen, fellow countryman

compel bulldoze (*Inf.*), coerce, constrain, dragoon, drive, enforce, exact, force, hustle (*Sl.*), impel, make, necessitate, oblige, restrain, squeeze, urge

compelling **1.** cogent, conclusive, convincing, forceful, irrefutable, powerful, telling, weighty **2.** enchanting, enthralling, gripping, hypnotic, irresistible, mesmeric, spellbinding **3.** binding, coercive, imperative, overriding, peremptory, pressing, unavoidable, urgent

compensate **1.** atone, indemnify, make good, make restitution, recompense, refund, reimburse, remunerate, repay, requite, reward, satisfy **2.** balance, cancel (out), counteract, counterbalance, countervail, make amends, make up for, offset, redress

compensation amends, atonement,

damages, indemnification, indemnity, payment, recompense, reimbursement, remuneration, reparation, requital, restitution, reward, satisfaction

compete be in the running, challenge, contend, contest, emulate, fight, pit oneself against, rival, strive, struggle, vie

competence ability, adequacy, appropriateness, capability, capacity, competency, expertise, fitness, proficiency, skill, suitability

competent able, adapted, adequate, appropriate, capable, clever, endowed, equal, fit, pertinent, proficient, qualified, sufficient, suitable

competition **1.** contention, contest, emulation, one-upmanship (*Inf.*), opposition, rivalry, strife, struggle **2.** championship, contest, event, puzzle, quiz, tournament **3.** challengers, field, opposition, rivals

competitive aggressive, ambitious, antagonistic, at odds, combative, cutthroat, dog-eat-dog, emulous, opposing, rival, vying

competitor adversary, antagonist, challenger, competition, contestant, emulator, opponent, opposition, rival

compile accumulate, amass, anthologize, collect, cull, garner, gather, marshal, organize, put together

complacency contentment, gratifica-

tion, pleasure, satisfaction, self-satisfaction, smugness

complacent contented, gratified, pleased, pleased with oneself, satisfied, self-assured, self-contented, self-righteous, self-satisfied, serene, smug, unconcerned

complain beef (*Sl.*), bellyache (*Sl.*), bemoan, bewail, bitch (*Sl.*), carp, deplore, find fault, fuss, grieve, gripe (*Inf.*), groan, grouse, growl, grumble, kick up a fuss (*Inf.*), lament, moan, whine

complaint **1.** accusation, annoyance, beef (*Sl.*), bitch (*Sl.*), charge, criticism, dissatisfaction, fault-finding, grievance, gripe (*Inf.*), grouse, grumble, lament, moan, plaint, remonstrance, trouble, wail **2.** affliction, ailment, disease, disorder, illness, indisposition, malady, sickness, upset

complement *n.* **1.** companion, completion, consummation, correlative, counterpart, finishing touch, rounding-off, supplement **2.** aggregate, capacity, entirety, quota, total, totality, wholeness ~*v.* **3.** cap (*Inf.*), complete, crown, round off, set off

complementary companion, completing, correlative, corresponding, fellow, interdependent, interrelating, matched, reciprocal

such that a contradiction or inconsistency arises on the addition of an axiom that cannot be deduced from the axioms of the system. **6.** *Arch.* skilled; accomplished. ~*vb.* (*tr.*) **7.** to make perfect. **8.** to finish. —**com¬ 'pletely** *adv.* —**com'pleteness** *n.* —**com'pletion** *n.*

complex ('kɒmplɛks) *adj.* **1.** made up of interconnect¬ ed parts. **2.** (of thoughts, writing, etc.) intricate. **3.** *Maths.* **a.** of or involving complex numbers. **b.** consist¬ ing of a real and an imaginary part, either of which can be zero. ~*n.* **4.** a whole made up of related parts: *a building complex.* **5.** *Psychoanal.* a group of emotional impulses that have been banished from the conscious mind but continue to influence a person's behaviour. **6.** *Inf.* an obsession: *he's got a complex about cats.* **7.** any chemical compound in which one molecule is linked to another by a coordinate bond. —**'complexness** *n.*

complex fraction *n. Maths.* a fraction in which the numerator or denominator or both contain fractions. Also called: **compound fraction.**

complexion (kəm'plɛkʃən) *n.* **1.** the colour and gener¬ al appearance of a person's skin, esp. of the face. **2.** as¬ pect or nature: *the general complexion of a nation's fi¬ nances.* **3.** *Obs.* temperament. —**com'plexional** *adj.*

complexity (kəm'plɛksɪtɪ) *n., pl.* **-ties. 1.** the state or quality of being intricate or complex. **2.** something intri¬ cate or complex; complication.

complex number *n.* any number of the form $a + bi$, where a and b are real numbers and $i = \sqrt{-1}$.

compliance (kəm'plaɪəns) *or* **compliancy** *n.* **1.** ac¬ quiescence. **2.** a disposition to yield to others. **3.** a measure of the ability of a mechanical system to re¬ spond to an applied vibrating force. —**com'pliant** *adj.*

complicate *vb.* ('kɒmplɪˌkeɪt). **1.** to make or become complex, etc. ~*adj.* ('kɒmplɪkɪt). **2.** *Biol.* folded on it¬ self: *a complicate leaf.*

complicated ('kɒmplɪˌkeɪtɪd) *adj.* made up of intricate parts or aspects that are difficult to understand or ana¬ lyse. —**'compliˌcatedly** *adv.*

complication (ˌkɒmplɪ'keɪʃən) *n.* **1.** a condition, event, etc., that is complex or confused. **2.** the act of complicating. **3.** an event or condition that complicates or frustrates: *her coming was a serious complication.* **4.** a disease arising as a consequence of another.

complicity (kəm'plɪsɪtɪ) *n., pl.* **-ties. 1.** the fact of being an accomplice, esp. in a criminal act. **2.** a less common word for **complexity.**

compliment *n.* ('kɒmplɪmənt). **1.** a remark or act ex¬ pressing respect, admiration, etc. **2.** (*usually pl.*) a greeting of respect or regard. ~*vb.* ('kɒmplɪˌmɛnt). (*tr.*) **3.** to express admiration for; congratulate. **4.** to

express or show regard for, esp. by a gift.

complimentary (ˌkɒmplɪ'mɛntərɪ) *adj.* **1.** conveying a compliment. **2.** flattering. **3.** given free, esp. as a courtesy or for publicity purposes. —ˌcompli'mentarily *adv.*

compline ('kɒmplɪn, -plaɪn) *or* **complin** ('kɒmplɪn) *n. R.C. Church.* the last of the seven canonical hours of the divine office.

comply (kəm'plaɪ) *vb.* **-plying, -plied.** (*intr.*) (usually foll. by *with*) to act in accordance with rules, wishes, etc.; be obedient (to).

component (kəm'pəunənt) *n.* **1.** a constituent part or aspect of something more complex. **2.** any electrical de¬ vice that has distinct electrical characteristics and may be connected to other devices to form a circuit. **3.** *Maths.* one of a set of two or more vectors whose result¬ ant is a given vector. ~*adj.* **4.** forming or functioning as a part or aspect; constituent. —**componential** (ˌkɒmpə'nɛnʃəl) *adj.*

comport (kəm'pɔːt) *vb.* **1.** (*tr.*) to conduct or bear (one¬ self) in a specified way. **2.** (*intr.*; foll. by *with*) to agree (with). —**com'portment** *n.*

compose (kəm'pəuz) *vb.* (*mainly tr.*) **1.** to put together or make up. **2.** to be the component elements of. **3.** to create (a musical or literary work). **4.** (*intr.*) to write music. **5.** to calm (someone, esp. oneself); make quiet. **6.** to adjust or settle (a quarrel, etc.). **7.** to order the el¬ ements of (a painting, sculpture, etc.); design. **8.** *Print¬ ing.* to set up (type). —**com'poser** *n.*

composed (kəm'pəuzd) *adj.* (of people) calm; tranquil. —**composedly** (kəm'pəuzɪdlɪ) *adv.*

composite ('kɒmpəzɪt) *adj.* **1.** composed of separate parts; compound. **2.** of or belonging to the plant family *Compositae.* **3.** *Maths.* capable of being factorized: *a composite function.* **4.** (*sometimes cap.*) denoting one of the five classical orders of architecture: characterized by a combination of the Ionic and Corinthian styles. ~*n.* **5.** something composed of separate parts; compound. **6.** any plant of the family *Compositae*, having flower heads composed of many small flowers (e.g. dandelion, daisy). **7.** a material, such as reinforced concrete, made of two or more distinct materials. ~*vb.* (*tr.*) (kəm'pɒzɪt). **8.** to merge related motions from local branches (of a politi¬ cal party, trade union, etc.) so as to produce a manage¬ able number of proposals for discussion at national level. —**'compositely** *adv.* —**'compositeness** *n.*

composite school *n. Canad.* a secondary school of¬ fering both academic and nonacademic courses.

composition (ˌkɒmpə'zɪʃən) *n.* **1.** the act of putting to¬ gether or making up by combining parts. **2.** something

---

THESAURUS

complete *adj.* **1.** all, entire, faultless, full, intact, integral, plenary, unabridged, unbro¬ ken, undivided, unimpaired, whole **2.** accom¬ plished, achieved, concluded, ended, finished **3.** absolute, consummate, dyed-in-the-wool, perfect, thorough, thoroughgoing, total, utter ~*v.* **4.** accomplish, achieve, cap, close, con¬ clude, crown, discharge, do, end, execute, fill in, finalize, finish, fulfil, perfect, perform, re¬ alize, round off, settle, terminate, wrap up (*Inf.*)

completely absolutely, altogether, down to the ground, en masse, entirely, from A to Z, from beginning to end, fully, heart and soul, hook, line and sinker, in full, *in toto*, perfectly, quite, root and branch, solidly, thoroughly, totally, utterly, wholly

completion accomplishment, attain¬ ment, close, conclusion, consummation, cul¬ mination, end, expiration, finalization, frui¬ tion, fulfilment, realization

complex *adj.* **1.** circuitous, complicated, convoluted, Daedalian (*Literary*), intricate, involved, knotty, labyrinthine, mingled, mixed, tangled, tortuous **2.** composite, com¬ pound, compounded, heterogeneous, mani¬ fold, multifarious, multiple ~*n.* **3.** aggregate, composite, network, organization, scheme, structure, synthesis, system **4.** fixation, fixed idea, *idée fixe*, obsession, phobia, preoccupa¬ tion

complexion **1.** colour, colouring, hue, pigmentation, skin, skin tone **2.** appearance,

aspect, cast, character, countenance, dispo¬ sition, guise, light, look, make-up, nature, stamp

complexity complication, convolution, elaboration, entanglement, intricacy, in¬ volvement, multiplicity, ramification

compliance acquiescence, agreement, assent, complaisance, concession, concur¬ rence, conformity, consent, deference, obedience, observance, passivity, submis¬ sion, submissiveness, yielding

complicate confuse, entangle, inter¬ weave, involve, make intricate, muddle, snarl up

complicated **1.** Byzantine (*of attitudes, etc.*), complex, convoluted, elaborate, inter¬ laced, intricate, involved, labyrinthine **2.** dif¬ ficult, involved, perplexing, problematic, puzzling, troublesome

complication **1.** combination, complex¬ ity, confusion, entanglement, intricacy, mix¬ ture, web **2.** aggravation, difficulty, draw¬ back, embarrassment, factor, obstacle, prob¬ lem, snag

complicity abetment, collaboration, col¬ lusion, concurrence, connivance

compliment **1.** admiration, bouquet, commendation, congratulations, courtesy, eulogy, favour, flattery, honour, praise, trib¬ ute **2.** *v.* commend, congratulate, extol, felici¬ tate, flatter, laud, pay tribute to, praise, sa¬ lute, sing the praises of, speak highly of, wish joy to

complimentary **1.** appreciative, ap¬ proving, commendatory, congratulatory, eulogistic, flattering, laudatory, panegyrical **2.** courtesy, donated, free, free of charge, gratis, gratuitous, honorary, on the house

compliments good wishes, greetings, regards, remembrances, respects, salutation

comply abide by, accede, accord, acqui¬ esce, adhere to, agree to, conform to, con¬ sent to, defer, discharge, follow, fulfil, obey, observe, perform, respect, satisfy, submit, yield

component **1.** *n.* constituent, element, ingredient, item, part, piece, unit **2.** *adj.* com¬ posing, constituent, inherent, intrinsic

compose **1.** build, compound, comprise, constitute, construct, fashion, form, make, make up, put together **2.** contrive, create, de¬ vise, frame, imagine, indite, invent, produce, write **3.** adjust, arrange, reconcile, regulate, resolve, settle **4.** appease, assuage, calm, col¬ lect, control, pacify, placate, quell, quiet, soothe, still, tranquillize

composed at ease, calm, collected, con¬ fident, cool, imperturbable, level-headed, poised, relaxed, self-possessed, serene, to¬ gether (*Sl.*), tranquil, unflappable, unruffled, unworried

composite **1.** *adj.* blended, combined, complex, compound, conglomerate, mixed, synthesized **2.** *n.* amalgam, blend, compound, conglomerate, fusion, synthesis

formed in this manner; a mixture. **3.** the parts of which something is composed; constitution. **4.** a work of music, art, or literature. **5.** the harmonious arrangement of the parts of a work of art in relation to each other. **6.** a piece of writing undertaken as an academic exercise; an essay. **7.** *Printing.* the act or technique of setting up type. **8.** a settlement by mutual consent, esp. a legal agreement whereby the creditors agree to accept partial payment of a debt in full settlement.

compositor (kəm'pɒzɪtə) *n. Printing.* a person who sets and corrects type.

compos mentis *Latin.* ('kɒmpɒs 'mɛntɪs) *adj. (postpositive)* of sound mind; sane.

compost ('kɒmpɒst) *n.* **1.** a mixture of organic residues such as decomposed vegetation, manure, etc., used as a fertilizer. **2.** *Rare.* a mixture. ~*vb. (tr.)* **3.** to make (vegetable matter) into compost. **4.** to fertilize with compost.

composure (kəm'pəʊʒə) *n.* calmness, esp. of the mind; tranquillity; serenity.

compote ('kɒmpəʊt) *n.* a dish of fruit stewed with sugar or in a syrup.

compound[1] *n.* ('kɒmpaʊnd). **1.** a substance that contains atoms of two or more chemical elements held together by chemical bonds. **2.** any combination of two or more parts, aspects, etc. **3.** a word formed from two existing words or combining forms. ~*vb.* (kəm'paʊnd). *(mainly tr.)* **4.** to combine so as to create a compound. **5.** to make by combining parts, aspects, etc.: *to compound a new plastic.* **6.** to intensify by an added element: *his anxiety was compounded by her crying.* **7.** *(also intr.)* to come to an agreement in (a dispute, etc.) or to settle (a debt, etc.) for less than what is owed; compromise. **8.** *Law.* to agree not to prosecute in return for a consideration: *to compound a crime.* ~*adj.* ('kɒmpaʊnd). **9.** composed of two or more parts, elements, etc. **10.** (of a word) consisting of elements that are also words or combining forms. **11.** *Grammar.* (of tense, mood, etc.) formed by using an auxiliary verb in addition to the main verb. **12.** *Music.* **a.** denoting a time in which the number of beats per bar is a multiple of three: *six-four is an example of compound time.* **b.** (of an interval) greater than an octave. **13.** (of a steam engine, etc.) having multiple stages in which the steam or working fluid from one stage is used in a subsequent stage. **14.** (of a piston engine) having a supercharger powered by a turbine in the exhaust stream. —**com'poundable** *adj.*

compound[2] ('kɒmpaʊnd) *n.* **1.** (esp. in South Africa) an enclosure in which native workers are housed. **2.** any similar enclosure, such as a camp for prisoners of war.

compound eye *n.* the convex eye of insects and some crustaceans, consisting of numerous separate light-sensitive units (ommatidia).

compound fracture *n.* a fracture in which the broken bone pierces the skin.

compound interest *n.* interest calculated on both the principal and its accrued interest.

compound sentence *n.* a sentence containing at least two coordinate clauses.

compound time *n.* see **compound** (sense 12).

comprehend (ˌkɒmprɪ'hɛnd) *vb.* **1.** to understand. **2.** *(tr.)* to comprise; include. —ˌcompre'hensible *adj.*

comprehension (ˌkɒmprɪ'hɛnʃən) *n.* **1.** the act or capacity of understanding. **2.** the state of including; comprehensiveness.

comprehensive (ˌkɒmprɪ'hɛnsɪv) *adj.* **1.** of broad scope or content. **2.** (of a car insurance policy) providing protection against most risks, including third-party liability, fire, theft, and damage. **3.** of or being a comprehensive school. ~*n.* **4.** short for **comprehensive school.** —ˌcompre'hensively *adv.* —ˌcompre'hensiveness *n.*

comprehensive school *n. Chiefly Brit.* a large secondary school for children of all abilities from the same district.

compress *vb.* (kəm'prɛs). **1.** *(tr.)* to squeeze together; condense. ~*n.* ('kɒmprɛs). **2.** a cloth or gauze pad applied firmly to some part of the body to relieve discomfort, reduce fever, etc. —**com'pressible** *adj.* —com,pressi'bility *n.* —**com'pressive** *adj.*

compression (kəm'prɛʃən) *n.* **1.** the act of compressing or the condition of being compressed. **2.** an increase in pressure of the charge in an engine or compressor obtained by reducing its volume.

compressor (kəm'prɛsə) *n.* **1.** any device that compresses a gas. **2.** the part of a gas turbine that compresses the air before it enters the combustion chambers. **3.** any muscle that causes compression. **4.** an electronic device for reducing the variation in signal amplitude in a transmission system.

comprise (kəm'praɪz) *vb. (tr.)* **1.** to include; contain. **2.** to constitute the whole of; consist of: *her singing comprised the entertainment.* —**com'prisable** *adj.*

compromise ('kɒmprə,maɪz) *n.* **1.** settlement of a dispute by concessions on both or all sides. **2.** the terms of such a settlement. **3.** something midway between different things. ~*vb.* **4.** to settle (a dispute) by making concessions. **5.** *(tr.)* to expose (oneself or another) to disrepute. —'compro,miser *n.* —'compro,misingly *adv.*

Comptometer (kɒmp'tɒmɪtə) *n. Trademark.* a high-speed calculating machine.

comptroller (kən'trəʊlə) *n.* a variant spelling of **controller** (sense 2), esp. as a title of any of various financial executives.

compulsion (kəm'pʌlʃən) *n.* **1.** the act of compelling or the state of being compelled. **2.** something that compels. **3.** *Psychiatry.* an inner drive that causes a person to perform actions, often repetitive, against his will. See also **obsession.**

compulsive (kəm'pʌlsɪv) *adj.* relating to or involving compulsion. —**com'pulsively** *adv.*

compulsory (kəm'pʌlsərɪ) *adj.* **1.** required by regulations or laws; obligatory. **2.** involving or employing compulsion; compelling; essential. —**com'pulsorily** *adv.* —**com'pulsoriness** *n.*

THESAURUS

composition 1. arrangement, configuration, constitution, design, form, formation, layout, make-up, organization, structure **2.** compilation, creation, fashioning, formation, formulation, invention, making, mixture, production **3.** creation, essay, exercise, literary work, opus, piece, study, work, writing **4.** arrangement, balance, concord, consonance, harmony, placing, proportion, symmetry

compost humus, mulch, organic fertilizer

composure aplomb, calm, calmness, collectedness, cool *(Sl.)*, coolness, dignity, ease, equanimity, imperturbability, placidity, poise, sang-froid, sedateness, self-assurance, self-possession, serenity, tranquillity

compound *v.* **1.** amalgamate, blend, coalesce, combine, concoct, fuse, intermingle, mingle, mix, synthesize, unite **2.** add to, aggravate, augment, complicate, exacerbate, heighten, intensify, magnify, worsen **3.** *Used of a dispute, difference, etc.* adjust, arrange, compose, settle ~*n.* **4.** alloy, amalgam, blend, combination, composite, composition, conglomerate, fusion, medley, mixture, syn-

thesis ~*adj.* **5.** complex, composite, conglomerate, intricate, multiple, not simple

comprehend 1. apprehend, assimilate, conceive, discern, fathom, grasp, know, make out, perceive, see, take in, understand **2.** comprise, contain, embody, embrace, enclose, encompass, include, involve, take in

comprehensible clear, coherent, conceivable, explicit, graspable, intelligible, plain, understandable

comprehension 1. conception, discernment, grasp, intelligence, judgment, knowledge, perception, realization, sense, understanding **2.** compass, domain, field, limits, province, range, reach, scope

comprehensive all-embracing, all-inclusive, blanket, broad, catholic, complete, encyclopedic, exhaustive, extensive, full, inclusive, sweeping, thorough, umbrella, wide

compress abbreviate, compact, concentrate, condense, constrict, contract, cram, crowd, crush, press, shorten, squash, squeeze, summarize, wedge

compressed abridged, compact, com-

pacted, concentrated, concise, consolidated, constricted, flattened, reduced, shortened, squashed, squeezed

compression condensation, consolidation, constriction, crushing, pressure, squeezing, wedging

comprise 1. be composed of, comprehend, consist of, contain, embrace, encompass, include, take in **2.** compose, constitute, form, make up

compromise *v.* **1.** adjust, agree, arbitrate, compose, compound, concede, give and take, go fifty-fifty *(Inf.)*, meet halfway, settle, strike a balance ~*n.* **2.** accommodation, accord, adjustment, agreement, concession, give-and-take, half measures, middle ground, settlement, trade-off ~*v.* **3.** discredit, dishonour, embarrass, expose, hazard, imperil, implicate, jeopardize, prejudice, weaken

compulsion 1. coercion, constraint, demand, duress, force, obligation, pressure, urgency **2.** drive, necessity, need, obsession, preoccupation, urge

compulsory purchase *n.* purchase of a property by a local authority or government department for public use or development, regardless of whether or not the owner wishes to sell.

compunction (kəm'pʌŋkʃən) *n.* a feeling of remorse, guilt, or regret. **—com'punctious** *adj.* **—com'punctiously** *adv.*

computation (ˌkɒmpjuˈteɪʃən) *n.* a calculation involving numbers or quantities. **—ˌcompu'tational** *adj.*

compute (kəm'pju:t) *vb.* to calculate (an answer, result, etc.), often with the aid of a computer. **—com'putable** *adj.* **—com,puta'bility** *n.*

computer (kəm'pju:tə) *n.* **1. a.** a device, usually electronic, that processes data according to a set of instructions. The **digital computer** stores data in discrete units and performs operations at very high speed. The **analog computer** has no memory and is slower than the digital computer but has a continuous rather than a discrete input. **b.** (*as modifier*): *computer technology.* **2.** a person who computes or calculates.

computerize *or* **-ise** (kəm'pju:tə,raɪz) *vb.* **1.** (*tr.*) to cause (certain operations) to be performed by a computer, esp. as a replacement for human labour. **2.** (*intr.*) to install a computer. **3.** (*tr.*) to control or perform (operations) by means of a computer. **4.** (*tr.*) to process or store (information) by or in a computer. **—com,puteri'zation** *or* **-i'sation** *n.*

comrade ('kɒmreɪd, -rɪd) *n.* **1.** a companion. **2.** a fellow member of a political party, esp. a fellow Communist. **—'comradely** *adj.* **—'comrade,ship** *n.*

con¹ (kɒn) *Sl.* **—n. 1. a.** short for **confidence trick. b.** (*as modifier*): *con man.* **~vb. conning, conned. 2.** (*tr.*) to swindle or defraud.

con² (kɒn) *n.* (*usually pl.*) an argument or vote against a proposal, motion, etc.

con³ *or* (*esp. U.S.*) **conn** (kɒn) *vb.* **conning, conned.** (*tr.*) *Naut.* to direct the steering of (a vessel).

con⁴ (kɒn) *vb.* **conning, conned.** (*tr.*) *Arch.* to study attentively or learn.

con⁵ *prep. Music.* with.

con. *abbrev. for:* **1.** concerto. **2.** conclusion. **3.** connection. **4.** consolidated. **5.** continued.

con- *prefix.* variant of **com-.**

concatenate (kɒn'kætɪ,neɪt) *vb.* (*tr.*) to link or join together, esp. in a chain or series. **—,concate'nation** *n.*

concave ('kɒnkeɪv, kɒn'keɪv) *adj.* **1.** curving inwards; having the shape of a section of the interior of a sphere, paraboloid, etc.: *a concave lens.* **~vb. 2.** (*tr.*) to make concave. **—'concavely** *adv.* **—'concaveness** *n.*

conceal (kən'si:l) *vb.* (*tr.*) **1.** to keep from discovery; hide. **2.** to keep secret. **—con'cealer** *n.* **—con'cealment** *n.*

concede (kən'si:d) *vb.* **1.** (*when tr., may take a clause as object*) to admit or acknowledge (something) as true or correct. **2.** to yield or allow (something, such as a right). **3.** (*tr.*) to admit that defeat is certain: *to concede*

an election. **—con'ceder** *n.*

conceit (kən'si:t) *n.* **1.** a high, often exaggerated, opinion of oneself or one's accomplishments. **2.** *Literary.* an elaborate image or far-fetched comparison. **3.** *Arch.* **a.** a witty expression. **b.** fancy; imagination. **c.** an idea. **~vb.** (*tr.*) **4.** *Obs.* to think.

conceited (kən'si:tɪd) *adj.* having an exaggerated opinion of oneself or one's accomplishments. **—con'ceitedly** *adv.* **—con'ceitedness** *n.*

conceivable (kən'si:vəbəl) *adj.* capable of being understood, believed, or imagined; possible. **—con,ceiva'bility** *n.* **—con'ceivably** *adv.*

conceive (kən'si:v) *vb.* **1.** (when *intr.*, foll. by *of*; when *tr.*, often *takes a clause as object*) to have an idea (of); imagine; think. **2.** (*tr.*; *takes a clause as object or an infinitive*) to believe. **3.** (*tr.*) to develop: *she conceived a passion for music.* **4.** to become pregnant with (a child). **5.** (*tr.*) *Rare.* to express in words.

concentrate ('kɒnsən,treɪt) *vb.* **1.** (*tr.*) to come or cause to come to a single purpose or aim: *to concentrate one's hopes on winning.* **2.** to make or become denser or purer by the removal of certain elements. **3.** (*intr.*; often foll. by *on*) to think intensely (about). **~n.** **4.** a concentrated material or solution. **—'concen,trative** *adj.* **—'concen,trator** *n.*

concentration (ˌkɒnsən'treɪʃən) *n.* **1.** intense mental application. **2.** the act of concentrating. **3.** something that is concentrated. **4.** the strength of a solution, esp. the amount of dissolved substance in a given volume of solvent. **5.** *Mil.* **a.** the act of bringing together military forces. **b.** the application of fire from a number of weapons against a target.

concentration camp *n.* a guarded prison camp, esp. one in Nazi Germany.

concentric (kən'sɛntrɪk) *adj.* having a common centre: *concentric circles.* **—con'centrically** *adv.*

concept ('kɒnsɛpt) *n.* something formed in the mind; thought; general idea.

conception (kən'sɛpʃən) *n.* **1.** something conceived; notion, idea, or plan. **2.** the state of an ovum being fertilized by a sperm in the womb. **3.** origin or beginning. **—con'ceptional** *or* **con'ceptive** *adj.*

conceptual (kən'sɛptjuəl) *adj.* of or characterized by concepts. **—con'ceptually** *adv.*

conceptualize *or* **-lise** (kən'sɛptjuə,laɪz) *vb.* to form (a concept or concepts) out of observations, experience, data, etc. **—con,ceptuali'zation** *or* **-li'sation** *n.*

concern (kən'sɜ:n) *vb.* (*tr.*) **1.** to relate to; affect. **2.** (usually foll. by *with* or *in*) to involve or interest (oneself): *he concerns himself with other people's affairs.* **~n.** **3.** something that affects a person; affair; business. **4.** regard or interest: *he felt a strong concern for her.* **5.** anxiety or solicitude. **6.** important relation: *his news has great concern for us.* **7.** a commercial company. **8.** *Inf.* a material thing, esp. one of which one has a low opinion.

compulsive besetting, compelling, driving, irresistible, obsessive, overwhelming, uncontrollable, urgent

compulsory binding, *de rigueur*, forced, imperative, mandatory, obligatory, required, requisite

compute add up, calculate, cast up, cipher, count, enumerate, estimate, figure, figure out, measure, rate, reckon, sum, tally, total

comrade ally, associate, buddy (*Inf.*), colleague, companion, compatriot, compeer, confederate, co-worker, crony, fellow, friend, mate (*Inf.*), pal (*Inf.*), partner

concave cupped, depressed, excavated, hollow, hollowed, incurved, indented, scooped, sunken

conceal bury, camouflage, cover, disguise, dissemble, hide, keep dark, keep secret, mask, obscure, screen, secrete, shelter

concealed covered, hidden, inconspicuous, masked, obscured, screened, secret, secreted, tucked away, unseen

concealment camouflage, cover, disguise, hideaway, hide-out, hiding, secrecy

concede 1. accept, acknowledge, admit,

allow, confess, grant, own **2.** cede, give up, hand over, relinquish, surrender, yield

conceit 1. amour-propre, arrogance, complacency, egotism, narcissism, pride, self-importance, self-love, swagger, vainglory, vanity **2.** *Archaic* belief, fancy, fantasy, idea, image, imagination, judgment, notion, opinion, quip, thought, vagary, whim, whimsy

conceited arrogant, bigheaded (*Inf.*), cocky, egotistical, immodest, narcissistic, overweening, puffed up, self-important, stuck up (*Inf.*), swollen-headed, vain, vainglorious

conceivable believable, credible, imaginable, possible, thinkable

conceive 1. appreciate, apprehend, believe, comprehend, envisage, fancy, grasp, imagine, realize, suppose, understand **2.** contrive, create, design, develop, devise, form, formulate, produce, project, purpose, think up **3.** become impregnated, become pregnant

concentrate 1. be engrossed in, consider closely, focus attention on, give all one's attention to, put one's mind to, rack one's brains **2.** bring to bear, centre, cluster, converge, focus **3.** accumulate, cluster, collect,

congregate, gather, huddle

concentrated 1. all-out (*Inf.*), deep, hard, intense, intensive **2.** boiled down, condensed, evaporated, reduced, rich, thickened, undiluted

concentration 1. absorption, application, heed, single-mindedness **2.** bringing to bear, centralization, centring, combination, compression, consolidation, convergence, focusing, intensification **3.** accumulation, aggregation, cluster, collection, convergence, horde, mass

concept abstraction, conception, conceptualization, hypothesis, idea, image, impression, notion, theory, view

conception 1. concept, design, idea, image, notion, plan **2.** beginning, birth, formation, inception, initiation, invention, launching, origin, outset **3.** appreciation, clue, comprehension, impression, inkling, perception, picture, understanding **4.** fertilization, germination, impregnation, insemination

concern *v.* **1.** affect, apply to, bear on, be relevant to, interest, involve, pertain to, regard, touch **~n. 2.** affair, business, charge, department, field, interest, involvement, job,

concerned (kən'sɜːnd) *adj.* **1.** (*postpositive*) interested, guilty or involved: *I shall find the boy concerned and punish him.* **2.** worried or solicitous. —**concernedly** (kən'sɜːnɪdlɪ) *adv.*

concerning (kən'sɜːnɪŋ) *prep.* **1.** about; regarding. ~*adj.* **2.** worrying or troublesome.

concert *n.* ('kɒnsɜːt). **1. a.** a performance of music by players or singers that does not involve theatrical staging. **b.** (*as modifier*): *a concert version of an opera.* **2.** agreement in design, plan, or action. **3. in concert. a.** acting with a common purpose. **b.** (of musicians, etc.) performing live. ~*vb.* (kən'sɜːt). **4.** to arrange or contrive (a plan) by mutual agreement.

concerted (kən'sɜːtɪd) *adj.* **1.** mutually contrived, planned, or arranged; combined: *a concerted effort.* **2.** *Music.* arranged in parts for a group of singers or players.

concertina (ˌkɒnsə'tiːnə) *n.* **1.** a hexagonal musical instrument similar to the accordion. ~*vb.* -**naing**, -**naed**. **2.** (*intr.*) to collapse or fold up like a concertina. —ˌ**concer'tinist** *n.*

concerto (kən'tʃɛətəʊ) *n., pl.* -**tos** *or* -**ti** (-tɪ). a composition for an orchestra and one or more soloists.

concert pitch *n.* **1.** the frequency of 440 hertz assigned to the A above middle C. **2.** *Inf.* a state of extreme readiness.

concession (kən'sɛʃən) *n.* **1.** the act of yielding or conceding. **2.** something conceded. **3.** any grant of rights, land, or property by a government, local authority, corporation, or individual. **4.** the right, esp. an exclusive right, to market a particular product in a given area. **5.** *Canad.* **a.** a land subdivision in a township survey. **b.** another name for a **concession road**. —**con'cessible** *adj.* —**con'cessive** *adj.*

concessionaire (kənˌsɛʃə'nɛə), **concessioner** (kən-'sɛʃənə), *or* **concessionary** *n.* someone who holds or operates a concession.

concession road *n. Canad.* any of a number of roughly parallel roads forming a grid pattern along township survey lines.

conch (kɒŋk, kɒntʃ) *n., pl.* **conchs** (kɒŋks) *or* **conches** ('kɒntʃɪz). **1.** any of various tropical marine gastropod molluscs characterized by a large brightly coloured spiral shell. **2.** the shell of such a mollusc, used as a trumpet.

conciliate (kən'sɪlɪˌeɪt) *vb.* (*tr.*) **1.** to overcome the hostility of; win over. **2.** to gain (favour, regard, etc.), esp. by making friendly overtures. —**con'ciliable** *adj.* —**con,cili'ation** *n.* —**con'cili,ator** *n.*

conciliatory (kən'sɪljətərɪ) *or* **conciliative** (kən-'sɪljətɪv) *adj.* intended to placate or reconcile. —**con'ciliatorily** *adv.*

concise (kən'saɪs) *adj.* brief and to the point. —**con'cisely** *adv.* —**con'ciseness** *or* **concision** (kən'sɪʒən) *n.*

conclave ('kɒnkleɪv) *n.* **1.** a secret meeting. **2.** *R.C.* Church. **a.** the closed apartments where the college of cardinals elects a new pope. **b.** a meeting of the college of cardinals for this purpose.

conclude (kən'kluːd) *vb.* (*mainly tr.*) **1.** (*also intr.*) to come or cause to come to an end. **2.** (*takes a clause as object*) to decide by reasoning; deduce: *the judge concluded that the witness had told the truth.* **3.** to settle: *to conclude a treaty.* **4.** *Obs.* to confine.

conclusion (kən'kluːʒən) *n.* **1.** end or termination. **2.** the last main division of a speech, essay, etc. **3.** outcome or result (esp. in **a foregone conclusion**). **4.** an intuitive rather than well-reasoned deduction: *to jump to conclusions.* **5.** a final decision or judgment (esp. in **come to a conclusion**). **6.** *Logic.* a proposition inferred from a set of premisses, that can be shown, on logical grounds, to be true if the premisses are true. **7.** *Law.* **a.** an admission or statement binding on the party making it; estoppel. **b.** the close of a pleading or of a conveyance. **8. in conclusion.** lastly; to sum up.

conclusive (kən'kluːsɪv) *adj.* **1.** putting an end to doubt; decisive; final. **2.** approaching or involving an end. —**con'clusively** *adv.*

concoct (kən'kɒkt) *vb.* (*tr.*) **1.** to make by combining different ingredients. **2.** to invent; make up; contrive. —**con'cocter** *or* **con'coctor** *n.* —**con'coction** *n.*

concomitant (kən'kɒmɪtənt) *adj.* **1.** existing or occurring together. ~*n.* **2.** a concomitant act, person, etc.

concord ('kɒnkɔːd) *n.* **1.** agreement or harmony. **2.** a treaty establishing peaceful relations between nations. **3.** *Music.* a combination of musical notes, esp. one containing a series of consonant intervals. **4.** *Grammar.* another word for **agreement** (sense 6).

concordance (kən'kɔːdəns) *n.* **1.** a state of harmony. **2.** a book that indexes the principal words in a literary work, often with the immediate context and an account of the meaning. **3.** an index produced by computer or machine.

concordat (kɒn'kɔːdæt) *n.* a pact or treaty, esp. one between the Vatican and another state concerning the interests of religion in that state.

concourse ('kɒnkɔːs) *n.* **1.** a crowd; throng. **2.** a coming together; confluence. **3.** a large open space for the gathering of people in a public place.

concrete ('kɒnkriːt) *n.* **1.** a building material made of cement, sand, aggregate, and water that hardens as it dries. ~*adj.* **2.** relating to a particular instance; specific as opposed to general. **3.** relating to things capable of being perceived by the senses, as opposed to abstractions. **4.** formed by the coalescence of particles; condensed; solid. ~*vb.* **5.** (*tr.*) to construct in or cover with concrete. **6.** (kən'kriːt). to become or cause to become solid; coalesce. —**'concretely** *adv.* —**'concreteness** *n.*

concretion (kən'kriːʃən) *n.* **1.** the act of growing together; coalescence. **2.** a solidified mass. **3.** something made real, tangible, or specific. **4.** a rounded or irregular mineral mass different in composition from the sedi-

---

THESAURUS

matter, mission, occupation, responsibility, task, transaction **3.** bearing, importance, interest, reference, relation, relevance ~*v.* **4.** bother, disquiet, distress, disturb, make anxious, make uneasy, perturb, trouble, worry ~*n.* **5.** anxiety, apprehension, attention, burden, care, consideration, disquiet, disquietude, distress, heed, responsibility, solicitude, worry **6.** business, company, corporation, enterprise, establishment, firm, house, organization

concerned 1. active, implicated, interested, involved, mixed up, privy to **2.** anxious, bothered, distressed, disturbed, exercised, troubled, uneasy, upset, worried **3.** attentive, caring, interested, solicitous

concerning about, anent (*Scot.*), apropos of, as regards, as to, in the matter of, on the subject of, re, regarding, relating to, respecting, touching, with reference to

concert *n.* **1.** accord, agreement, concord, concordance, harmony, unanimity, union, unison **2. in concert** concertedly, in collaboration, in league, in unison, jointly, shoulder to shoulder, together, unanimously

concerted agreed upon, collaborative, combined, coordinated, joint, planned, prear-

ranged, united

concession 1. acknowledgment, admission, assent, confession, surrender, yielding **2.** adjustment, allowance, boon, compromise, grant, indulgence, permit, privilege

conciliate appease, disarm, mediate, mollify, pacify, placate, propitiate, reconcile, restore harmony, soothe, win over

conciliation appeasement, disarming, mollification, pacification, placation, propitiation, reconciliation, soothing

conciliatory appeasing, disarming, irenic, mollifying, pacific, peaceable, placatory, propitiative

concise brief, compact, compendious, compressed, condensed, epigrammatic, laconic, pithy, short, succinct, summary, synoptic, terse, to the point

conclave assembly, cabinet, conference, council, parley, secret *or* private meeting, session

conclude 1. bring down the curtain, cease, close, come to an end, complete, draw to a close, end, finish, round off, terminate, wind up (*Inf.*) **2.** assume, decide, deduce, gather, infer, judge, reckon (*Inf.*), sum up, suppose, surmise **3.** accomplish, bring about,

carry out, clinch (*Inf.*), decide, determine, effect, establish, fix, pull off, resolve, settle, work out

conclusion 1. close, completion, end, finale, finish, result, termination **2.** consequence, culmination, issue, outcome, result, upshot **3.** agreement, conviction, decision, deduction, inference, judgment, opinion, resolution, settlement, verdict **4. in conclusion** finally, in closing, lastly, to sum up

conclusive clinching, convincing, decisive, definite, definitive, final, irrefutable, ultimate, unanswerable, unarguable

concoct brew, contrive, cook up (*Inf.*), design, devise, fabricate, formulate, hatch, invent, make up, mature, plot, prepare, project, think up

concoction blend, brew, combination, compound, contrivance, creation, mixture, preparation

concrete *adj.* **1.** actual, definite, explicit, factual, material, real, sensible, specific, substantial, tangible **2.** calcified, compact, compressed, conglomerated, consolidated, firm, petrified, solid, solidified ~*n.* **3.** cement (*Not in technical usage*), concretion

mentary rock that surrounds it. **5.** *Pathol.* another word for **calculus.** —**con'cretionary** *adj.*

concubine ('kɒŋkjʊ,baɪn, 'kɒn-) *n.* **1.** (in polygamous societies) a secondary wife. **2.** a woman who cohabits with a man, esp. (formerly) the mistress of a king, nobleman, etc. —**con'cubinage** *n.* —**con'cubinary** *n., adj.*

concupiscence (kən'kjuːpɪsəns) *n.* strong desire, esp. sexual desire. —**con'cupiscent** *adj.*

concur (kən'kɜː) *vb.* -**curring,** -**red.** (*intr.*) **1.** to agree; be in accord. **2.** to combine or cooperate. **3.** to occur simultaneously; coincide.

concurrence (kən'kʌrəns) *n.* **1.** the act of concurring. **2.** agreement; accord. **3.** cooperation or combination. **4.** simultaneous occurrence.

concurrent (kən'kʌrənt) *adj.* **1.** taking place at the same time or in the same location. **2.** cooperating. **3.** meeting at, approaching, or having a common point: *concurrent lines.* **4.** in agreement; harmonious. —**con'currently** *adv.*

concuss (kən'kʌs) *vb.* (*tr.*) **1.** to injure (the brain) by a violent blow, fall, etc. **2.** to shake violently.

concussion (kən'kʌʃən) *n.* **1.** a jarring of the brain, caused by a blow or a fall, usually resulting in loss of consciousness. **2.** any violent shaking.

condemn (kən'dɛm) *vb.* (*tr.*) **1.** to express strong disapproval of. **2.** to pronounce judicial sentence on. **3.** to demonstrate the guilt of: *his secretive behaviour condemned him.* **4.** to judge or pronounce unfit for use. **5.** to force into a particular state: *his disposition condemned him to boredom.* —**con'demnable** *adj.* —,condem'nation *n.* —con'demnatory *adj.*

condensation (,kɒndɛn'seɪʃən) *n.* **1.** the act or process of condensing, or the state of being condensed. **2.** anything that has condensed from a vapour on a window. **3.** *Chem.* a type of reaction in which two organic molecules combine to form a larger molecule as well as a simple molecule such as water, etc. **4.** an abridged version of a book. —,conden'sational *adj.*

condense (kən'dɛns) *vb.* **1.** (*tr.*) to increase the density of; compress. **2.** to reduce or be reduced in volume or size. **3.** to change or cause to change from a gaseous to a liquid or solid state. **4.** *Chem.* to undergo or cause to undergo condensation. —**con'densable** *or* **con'densible** *adj.*

condensed milk *n.* milk reduced by evaporation to a thick concentration, with sugar added.

condenser (kən'dɛnsə) *n.* **1. a.** an apparatus for reducing gases to their liquid or solid form by the abstraction of heat. **b.** a device for abstracting heat, as in a refrigeration unit. **2.** a lens that concentrates light. **3.** another name for **capacitor.** **4.** a person or device that condenses.

condescend (,kɒndɪ'sɛnd) *vb.* (*intr.*) **1.** to act graciously towards another or others regarded as being on a lower level; behave patronizingly. **2.** to do something that one regards as below one's dignity. —,conde'scending *adj.* —,conde'scension *n.*

condign (kən'daɪn) *adj.* (esp. of a punishment) fitting; deserved. —**con'dignly** *adv.*

condiment ('kɒndɪmənt) *n.* any spice or sauce such as salt, pepper, mustard, etc.

condition (kən'dɪʃən) *n.* **1.** a particular state of being or existence: *the human condition.* **2.** something that limits or restricts; a qualification. **3.** (*pl.*) circumstances: *conditions were right for a takeover.* **4.** an assumption in logical or inductive reasoning that should or must be fulfilled. See **sufficient** (sense 2), **necessary** (sense 3b.). **5.** something required as part of an agreement; terms: *the conditions of the lease are set out.* **6.** *Law.* **a.** a provision in a will, contract, etc., that makes some right or liability contingent upon the happening of some event. **b.** the event itself. **7.** something indispensable: *your happiness is a condition of mine.* **8.** state of physical fitness, esp. good health: *out of condition.* **9.** an ailment: *a heart condition.* **10.** rank, status, or position. **11. on condition that.** (*conj.*) provided that. ~*vb.* (mainly *tr.*) **12.** *Psychol.* **a.** to alter the response of (a person or animal) to a particular stimulus or situation. **b.** to establish a conditioned response in. **13.** to put into a fit condition. **14.** to accustom or inure. **15.** to subject to a condition. —**con'ditioner** *n.* —**con'ditioning** *n.*

conditional (kən'dɪʃənəl) *adj.* **1.** depending on other factors. **2.** *Grammar.* expressing a condition on which something else is contingent: *"If he comes"* is a *conditional clause in the sentence "If he comes I shall go".* **3.** *Logic.* (of a proposition) consisting of two component propositions associated by the words *if...then* so that the proposition is false only when the antecedent is true and the consequent false. ~*n.* **4.** a conditional verb form, clause, sentence, etc. —**con,dition'ality** *n.* —**con'ditionally** *adv.*

condole (kən'dəʊl) *vb.* (*intr.*; foll. by *with*) to express sympathy with someone in grief, pain, etc. —**con'dolence** *n.*

condom ('kɒndəm) *n.* a rubber sheath worn on the penis during sexual intercourse to prevent conception or infection.

condominium (,kɒndə'mɪnɪəm) *n., pl.* -**ums.** **1.** joint rule or sovereignty. **2.** a country ruled by two or more foreign powers. **3.** *U.S.* an apartment building in which each apartment is individually owned and the common areas are jointly owned.

condone (kən'dəʊn) *vb.* (*tr.*) **1.** to overlook or forgive an offence, etc. **2.** *Law.* (esp. of a spouse) to pardon or overlook (an offence, usually adultery). —**condonation** (,kɒndəʊ'neɪʃən) *n.* —**con'doner** *n.*

condor ('kɒndɔː) *n.* either of two very large rare New

THESAURUS

concubine courtesan, kept woman, leman (*Archaic*), mistress, odalisque, paramour

concupiscence appetite, desire, horniness (*Sl.*), lasciviousness, lechery, libidinousness, libido, lickerishness (*Archaic*), lust, lustfulness, randiness (*Sl.*)

concur accede, accord, acquiesce, agree, approve, assent, coincide, combine, consent, cooperate, harmonize, join

concurrent 1. coexisting, coincident, concerted, concomitant, contemporaneous, simultaneous, synchronous **2.** confluent, convergent, converging, uniting **3.** agreeing, at one, compatible, consentient, consistent, cooperating, harmonious, in agreement, in rapport, like-minded, of the same mind

concussion clash, collision, crash, impact, jarring, jolt, jolting, shaking, shock

condemn 1. blame, censure, damn, denounce, disapprove, reprehend, reproach, reprobate, reprove, upbraid **2.** convict, damn, doom, pass sentence on, proscribe, sentence

condemnation 1. blame, censure, denouncement, denunciation, disapproval, reproach, reprobation, reproof, stricture **2.** conviction, damnation, doom, judgment, proscription, sentence

condensation 1. abridgment, contrac-

tion, digest, précis, synopsis **2.** condensate, deliquescence, distillation, liquefaction, precipitate, precipitation **3.** compression, concentration, consolidation, crystallization, curtailment, reduction

condense 1. abbreviate, abridge, compact, compress, concentrate, contract, curtail, encapsulate, epitomize, précis, shorten, summarize **2.** boil down, coagulate, concentrate, decoct, precipitate (*Chem.*), reduce, solidify, thicken

condensed 1. abridged, compressed, concentrated, curtailed, shortened, shrunken, slimmed down, summarized **2.** boiled down, clotted, coagulated, concentrated, precipitated (*Chem.*), reduced, thickened

condescend 1. be courteous, bend, come down off one's high horse (*Inf.*), deign, humble *or* demean oneself, lower oneself, see fit, stoop, submit, unbend (*Inf.*), vouchsafe **2.** patronize, talk down to

condescending disdainful, lofty, lordly, patronizing, snobbish, snooty (*Inf.*), supercilious, superior, toffee-nosed (*Sl.*)

condition *n.* **1.** case, circumstances, plight, position, predicament, shape, situation, state, state of affairs, *status quo* **2.** arrangement, article, demand, limitation, modification, prerequisite, provision, provi-

so, qualification, requirement, requisite, restriction, rule, stipulation, terms **3.** fettle, fitness, health, kilter, order, shape, state of health, trim **4.** ailment, complaint, infirmity, malady, problem, weakness **5.** caste, class, estate, grade, order, position, rank, status, stratum ~*v.* **6.** accustom, adapt, educate, equip, habituate, inure, make ready, prepare, ready, tone up, train, work out

conditional contingent, dependent, limited, provisional, qualified, subject to, with reservations

conditioned acclimatized, accustomed, adapted, adjusted, familiarized, habituated, inured, made ready, prepared, seasoned, trained, used

conditioning *n.* **1.** grooming, preparation, readying, training **2.** accustoming, familiarization, hardening, inurement, reorientation, seasoning ~*adj.* **3.** astringent, toning

conditions circumstances, environment, milieu, situation, surroundings, way of life

condone disregard, excuse, forgive, let pass, look the other way, make allowance for, overlook, pardon, turn a blind eye to, wink at

World vultures, the **Andean condor**, which has black plumage with white around the neck, and the **California condor**, which is nearly extinct.

conduce (kən'dju:s) vb. (intr.; foll. by to) to lead or contribute (to a result). —**con'ducive** adj.

conduct n. ('kɒndʌkt) **1.** behaviour. **2.** the way of managing a business, affair, etc.; handling. **3.** Rare. the act of leading. ~vb. (kən'dʌkt). **4.** (tr.) to accompany and guide (people, a party, etc.) (esp. in **conducted tour**). **5.** (tr.) to direct (affairs, business, etc.); control. **6.** (tr.) to behave (oneself). **7.** to control (an orchestra, etc.) by the movements of the hands or a baton. **8.** to transmit (heat, electricity, etc.). —**con'ductible** adj. —**con,ducti'bility** n.

conductance (kən'dʌktəns) n. the ability of a system to conduct electricity, measured by the ratio of the current flowing through the system to the potential difference across it. Symbol: G

conduction (kən'dʌkʃən) n. **1.** the transfer of heat or electricity through a medium. **2.** the transmission of an impulse along a nerve fibre. **3.** the act of conveying or conducting, as through a pipe. **4.** Physics. another name for **conductivity** (sense 1). —**con'ductional** adj.

conductivity (ˌkɒndʌk'tɪvɪtɪ) n., pl. -**ties.** **1.** the property of transmitting heat, electricity, or sound. **2.** a measure of the ability of a substance to conduct electricity, as determined by the current flowing between opposite faces of a unit cube of the substance when there is unit potential difference between them. Symbol: κ.

conductor (kən'dʌktə) n. **1.** an official on a bus who collects fares. **2.** a person who conducts an orchestra, choir, etc. **3.** a person who leads or guides. **4.** U.S. a railway official in charge of a train. **5.** a substance, body, or system that conducts electricity, heat, etc. **6.** See **lightning conductor.** —**con'ductor,ship** n. —**conductress** (kən'dʌktrɪs) fem. n.

conduit ('kɒndɪt, -djʊɪt) n. **1.** a pipe or channel for carrying a fluid. **2.** a rigid tube for carrying electrical cables.

cone (kəun) n. **1.** a geometric solid consisting of a plane base bounded by a closed curve, usually a circle or an ellipse, every point of which is joined to a fixed point lying outside the plane of the base. **2.** anything that tapers from a circular section to a point, such as a wafer shell used to contain ice cream. **3. a.** the reproductive body of conifers and related plants, made up of overlapping scales. **b.** a similar structure in horsetails, club mosses, etc. **4.** a small cone used as a temporary traffic marker on roads. **5.** any one of the cone-shaped cells in the retina of the eye, sensitive to colour and bright light. ~vb. **6.** (tr.) to shape like a cone.

confab ('kɒnfæb) Inf. ~n. **1.** a conversation. ~vb. -fabbing, -fabbed. **2.** (intr.) to converse.

confabulate (kən'fæbju,leɪt) vb. (intr.) **1.** to talk together; chat. **2.** Psychiatry. to replace the gaps left by a disorder of the memory with imaginary remembered experiences consistently believed to be true. —**con,fabu-'lation** n.

confection (kən'fɛkʃən) n. **1.** the act of compounding or mixing. **2.** any sweet preparation, such as a preserve or a sweet. **3.** Old-fashioned. an elaborate article of clothing, esp. for women.

confectioner (kən'fɛkʃənə) n. a person who makes or sells sweets or confections.

confectionery (kən'fɛkʃənərɪ) n., pl. -eries. **1.** sweets and other confections collectively. **2.** the art or business of a confectioner.

confederacy (kən'fɛdərəsɪ) n., pl. -cies. **1.** a union of states, etc.; alliance; league. **2.** a combination of groups or individuals for unlawful purposes.

confederate n. (kən'fɛdərɪt) **1.** a nation, state, or individual that is part of a confederacy. **2.** someone who is part of a conspiracy. ~adj. (kən'fɛdərɪt) **3.** united; allied. ~vb. (kən'fɛdə,reɪt) **4.** to form into or become part of a confederacy.

Confederate (kən'fɛdərɪt) adj. **1.** of or supporting the **Confederate States of America,** that seceded from the Union in 1861. ~n. **2.** a supporter of the Confederate States.

confederation (kən,fɛdə'reɪʃən) n. **1.** the act of confederating or the state of being confederated. **2.** a loose alliance of political units. **3.** (esp. in Canada) another name for a **federation.** —**con,feder'ationist** n.

confer (kən'fɜː) vb. -ferring, -ferred. **1.** (tr.; foll. by on or upon) to grant or bestow (an honour, gift, etc.). **2.** (intr.) to consult together. —**con'ferment** or **con'ferral** n. —**con'ferrable** adj.

conference ('kɒnfərəns) n. **1.** a meeting for consultation or discussion, esp. one with a formal agenda. **2.** an assembly of the clergy or of clergy and laity of any of certain Protestant Churches acting as representatives of their denomination. **3.** Sport, U.S. a league of clubs or teams. —**conferential** (ˌkɒnfə'rɛnʃəl) adj.

confess (kən'fɛs) vb. (when tr., may take a clause as object) **1.** (when intr., often foll. by to) to make an admission (of faults, crimes, etc.). **2.** (tr.) to admit to be true; concede. **3.** Christianity. to declare (one's sins) to God or to a priest as his representative, so as to obtain pardon and absolution. —**confessedly** (kən'fɛsɪdlɪ) adv.

confession (kən'fɛʃən) n. **1.** the act of confessing. **2.** something confessed. **3.** an acknowledgment, esp. of one's faults or crimes. **4.** Christianity. the act of a penitent accusing himself of his sins. **5. confession of faith.** a formal public avowal of religious beliefs. **6.** a religious sect united by common beliefs. —**con'fessionary** adj.

confessional (kən'fɛʃənəl) adj. **1.** of or suited to a confession. ~n. **2.** Christianity. a small stall where a priest hears confessions.

confessor (kən'fɛsə) n. **1.** Christianity. a priest who hears confessions and sometimes acts as a spiritual counsellor. **2.** History. a person who bears witness to his Christian religious faith by the holiness of his life, but does not suffer martyrdom. **3.** a person who makes a confession.

confetti (kən'fɛtɪ) n. small pieces of coloured paper thrown on festive occasions, esp. at weddings.

confidant or (fem.) **confidante** (ˌkɒnfɪ'dænt, 'kɒnfɪ,dænt) n. a person to whom private matters are confided.

confide (kən'faɪd) vb. **1.** (usually foll. by in; when tr., may take a clause as object) to disclose (secret or personal matters) in confidence (to). **2.** (intr.; foll. by in) to have complete trust. **3.** (tr.) to entrust into another's keeping. —**con'fider** n.

confidence ('kɒnfɪdəns) n. **1.** trust in a person or thing. **2.** belief in one's own abilities; self-assurance. **3.** trust or a trustful relationship: take me into your confidence. **4.** something confided; secret. **5. in confidence.** as a secret.

confidence trick or U.S. **confidence game** n. a swindle involving money in which the victim's trust is won by the swindler.

THESAURUS

conduct n. **1.** administration, control, direction, guidance, leadership, management, organization, running, supervision ~v. **2.** administer, carry on, control, direct, govern, handle, lead, manage, organize, preside over, regulate, run, supervise **3.** accompany, attend, chair, convey, escort, guide, pilot, preside over, steer, usher ~n. **4.** attitude, bearing, behaviour, carriage, comportment, demeanour, deportment, manners, mien (Literary), ways ~v. **5.** acquit, act, behave, carry, comport, deport

confederacy alliance, bund, coalition, compact, confederation, conspiracy, covenant, federation, league, union

confederate 1. adj. allied, associated, combined, federal, federated, in alliance **2.** n.

abettor, accessory, accomplice, ally, associate, colleague, partner **3.** v. ally, amalgamate, associate, band together, combine, federate, merge, unite

confer 1. accord, award, bestow, give, grant, present, vouchsafe **2.** consult, converse, deliberate, discourse, parley, talk

conference colloquium, congress, consultation, convention, convocation, discussion, forum, meeting, seminar, symposium, teach-in

confess 1. acknowledge, admit, allow, blurt out, come clean (Inf.), concede, confide, disclose, divulge, grant, make a clean breast of, own, own up, recognize **2.** affirm, assert, attest, aver, confirm, declare, evince, manifest, profess, prove, reveal

confession acknowledgment, admission, avowal, disclosure, divulgence, exposure, revelation, unbosoming

confidant, confidante alter ego, bosom friend, close friend, crony, familiar, intimate

confide 1. admit, breathe, confess, disclose, divulge, impart, reveal, whisper **2.** commend, commit, consign, entrust

confidence 1. belief, credence, dependence, faith, reliance, trust **2.** aplomb, assurance, boldness, courage, firmness, nerve, self-possession, self-reliance **3. in confidence** between you and me (and the gatepost), confidentially, in secrecy, privately

confident (ˈkɒnfɪdənt) *adj.* **1.** (*postpositive; foll. by of*) having or showing certainty; sure: *confident of success.* **2.** sure of oneself. **3.** presumptuous. —ˈ**confidently** *adv.*

confidential (ˌkɒnfɪˈdɛnʃəl) *adj.* **1.** spoken or given in confidence; private. **2.** entrusted with another's secret affairs: *a confidential secretary.* **3.** suggestive of intimacy: *a confidential approach.* —ˌ**confiˈdentiality** *n.* —ˌ**confiˈdentially** *adv.*

confiding (kənˈfaɪdɪŋ) *adj.* unsuspicious; trustful. —con**ˈfidingly** *adv.* —con**ˈfidingness** *n.*

configuration (kənˌfɪgjʊˈreɪʃən) *n.* **1.** the arrangement of the parts of something. **2.** the external form or outline achieved by such an arrangement. **3.** *Psychol.* the unit or pattern in perception studied by Gestalt psychologists. —con**ˌfiguˈrational** *or* con**ˈfigurative** *adj.*

confine *vb.* (kənˈfaɪn). (*tr.*) **1.** to keep within bounds; limit; restrict. **2.** to restrict the free movement of: *arthritis confined him to bed.* ~*n.* (ˈkɒnfaɪn). **3.** (*often pl.*) a limit; boundary. —con**ˈfiner** *n.*

confinement (kənˈfaɪnmənt) *n.* **1.** the act of confining or the state of being confined. **2.** the period of the birth of a child.

confirm (kənˈfɜːm) *vb.* (*tr.*) **1.** (*may take a clause as object*) to prove to be true or valid; corroborate. **2.** (*may take a clause as object*) to assert for a further time, so as to make more definite: *he confirmed that he would appear in court.* **3.** to strengthen: *his story confirmed my doubts.* **4.** to make valid by a formal act; ratify. **5.** to administer the rite of confirmation to. —con**ˈfirmatory** *or* con**ˈfirmative** *adj.*

confirmation (ˌkɒnfəˈmeɪʃən) *n.* **1.** the act of confirming. **2.** something that confirms. **3.** a rite in several Christian churches that confirms a baptized person in his faith and admits him to full participation in the church.

confirmed (kənˈfɜːmd) *adj.* **1.** (*prenominal*) long-established in a habit, way of life, etc. **2.** having received the rite of confirmation.

confiscate (ˈkɒnfɪˌskeɪt) *vb.* (*tr.*) **1.** to seize (property), esp. for public use and esp. by way of a penalty. ~*adj.* **2.** confiscated; forfeit. —ˌ**confisˈcation** *n.* —ˈ**confisˌcator** *n.* —**confiscatory** (kənˈfɪskətərɪ) *adj.*

conflagration (ˌkɒnfləˈgreɪʃən) *n.* a large destructive fire.

conflate (kənˈfleɪt) *vb.* (*tr.*) to combine or blend (two things, esp. two versions of a text) so as to form a whole. —con**ˈflation** *n.*

conflict *n.* (ˈkɒnflɪkt). **1.** a struggle between opposing forces; battle. **2.** opposition between ideas, interests, etc.; controversy. **3.** *Psychol.* opposition between two simultaneous but incompatible wishes or impulses, sometimes leading to emotional tension. ~*vb.* (kənˈflɪkt).

(*intr.*) **4.** to come into opposition; clash. **5.** to fight. —con**ˈflictingly** *adv.* —con**ˈfliction** *n.*

confluence (ˈkɒnflʊəns) *or* **conflux** (ˈkɒnflʌks) *n.* **1.** a flowing together, esp. of rivers. **2.** a gathering. —ˈ**confluent** *adj.*

conform (kənˈfɔːm) *vb.* **1.** (*intr.; usually foll. by to*) to comply in actions, behaviour, etc., with accepted standards. **2.** (*intr.;* usually foll. by *with*) to be in accordance: *he conforms with my idea of a teacher.* **3.** to make or become similar. **4.** (*intr.*) to comply with the practices of an established church, esp. the Church of England. —con**ˈformer** *n.* —con**ˈformist** *n., adj.*

conformal (kənˈfɔːməl) *adj.* (of a map projection) maintaining true shape over a small area and scale in every direction.

conformation (ˌkɒnfɔːˈmeɪʃən) *n.* **1.** the general shape of an object; configuration. **2.** the arrangement of the parts of an object.

conformity (kənˈfɔːmɪtɪ) *or* **conformance** *n., pl.* **-ities** *or* **-ances. 1.** compliance in actions, behaviour, etc., with certain accepted standards. **2.** likeness; congruity; agreement. **3.** compliance with the practices of an established church.

confound (kənˈfaʊnd) *vb.* (*tr.*) **1.** to astound; bewilder. **2.** to confuse. **3.** to treat mistakenly as similar to or identical with. **4.** (kɒnˈfaʊnd). to curse (usually in **confound it!**). **5.** to contradict or refute (an argument, etc.). **6.** to rout or defeat (an enemy). —con**ˈfounder** *n.*

confounded (kənˈfaʊndɪd) *adj.* **1.** bewildered; confused. **2.** (*prenominal*) *Inf.* execrable; damned. —con**ˈfoundedly** *adv.*

confrère (ˈkɒnfrɛə) *n.* a fellow member of a profession, etc.

confront (kənˈfrʌnt) *vb.* (*tr.*) **1.** (usually foll. by *with*) to present (with something), esp. in order to accuse or criticize. **2.** to face boldly; oppose in hostility. **3.** to be face to face with. —**confrontation** (ˌkɒnfrʌnˈteɪʃən) *n.*

Confucian (kənˈfjuːʃən) *adj.* **1.** of or relating to the doctrines of Confucius. ~*n.* **2.** a follower of Confucius.

Confucianism (kənˈfjuːʃəˌnɪzəm) *n.* the ethical system of Confucius (551–479 B.C.), Chinese philosopher, emphasizing devotion to family (including ancestral spirits), peace, and justice. —Con**ˈfucianist** *n.*

confuse (kənˈfjuːz) *vb.* (*tr.*) **1.** to bewilder; perplex. **2.** to mix up (things, ideas, etc.). **3.** to make unclear: *he confused his talk with irrelevant details.* **4.** to mistake (one thing) for another. **5.** to disconcert; embarrass. **6.** to cause to become disordered: *the enemy ranks were confused by gas.* —con**ˈfusable** *adj.* —**confusedly** (kənˈfjuːzɪdlɪ, -ˈfjuːzd-) *adv.* —con**ˈfusingly** *adv.*

THESAURUS

confident 1. certain, convinced, counting on, positive, satisfied, secure, sure **2.** assured, bold, dauntless, fearless, self-assured, self-reliant

confidential 1. classified, hush-hush (*Inf.*), intimate, off the record, private, privy, secret **2.** faithful, familiar, trusted, trustworthy, trusty

confidentially behind closed doors, between ourselves, in camera, in confidence, in secret, personally, privately, sub rosa

confine 1. *v.* bind, bound, cage, circumscribe, enclose, hem in, hold back, immure, imprison, incarcerate, intern, keep, limit, repress, restrain, restrict, shut up **2.** *n.* border, boundary, frontier, limit, precinct

confined 1. enclosed, limited, restricted **2.** in childbed, in childbirth, lying-in

confinement 1. custody, detention, imprisonment, incarceration, internment **2.** *accouchement*, childbed, childbirth, labour, lying-in, parturition, time, travail

confines boundaries, bounds, circumference, edge, limits, precincts

confirm 1. assure, buttress, clinch, establish, fix, fortify, reinforce, settle, strengthen **2.** approve, authenticate, bear out, corroborate, endorse, ratify, sanction, substantiate, validate, verify

confirmation 1. authentication, corroboration, evidence, proof, substantiation, testimony, validation, verification **2.** acceptance, agreement, approval, assent, endorsement, ratification, sanction

confirmed chronic, dyed-in-the-wool, habitual, hardened, ingrained, inured, inveterate, long-established, rooted, seasoned

confiscate appropriate, commandeer, expropriate, impound, seize, sequester, sequestrate

confiscation appropriation, expropriation, forfeiture, impounding, seizure, sequestration, takeover

conflict *n.* **1.** battle, clash, collision, combat, contention, contest, encounter, engagement, fight, fracas, set-to (*Inf.*), strife, war, warfare **2.** antagonism, bad blood, difference, disagreement, discord, dissension, divided loyalties, friction, hostility, interference, opposition, strife, variance ~*v.* **3.** be at variance, clash, collide, combat, contend, contest, differ, disagree, fight, interfere, strive, struggle

conflicting antagonistic, clashing, contradictory, contrary, discordant, inconsistent, opposed, opposing, paradoxical

conform 1. adapt, adjust, comply, fall in with, follow, follow the crowd, obey, run with the pack, yield **2.** accord, agree, assimilate, correspond, harmonize, match, square, suit, tally

conformation anatomy, arrangement, build, configuration, form, framework, outline, shape, structure

conformist *n.* Babbitt (*U.S.*), conventionalist, stick-in-the-mud (*Inf.*), traditionalist, yes man

conformity 1. allegiance, Babbittry (*U.S.*), compliance, conventionality, observance, orthodoxy **2.** affinity, agreement, conformance, congruity, consonance, correspondence, harmony, likeness, resemblance, similarity

confound 1. amaze, astonish, astound, baffle, bewilder, confuse, dumbfound, flabbergast (*Inf.*), mix up, mystify, nonplus, perplex, startle, surprise **2.** annihilate, contradict, demolish, destroy, explode, overthrow, overwhelm, refute, ruin

confront accost, beard, brave, bring face to face with, challenge, defy, encounter, face, face up to, oppose, stand up to

confrontation conflict, contest, crisis, encounter, set-to (*Inf.*), showdown (*Inf.*)

confuse 1. baffle, bemuse, bewilder, darken, mystify, obscure, perplex, puzzle **2.** blend, confound, disarrange, disorder, intermingle, involve, jumble, mingle, mistake, mix up, muddle, snarl up (*Inf.*), tangle **3.** abash, addle, demoralize, discomfit, discompose, disconcert, discountenance, disorient, embarrass, fluster, mortify, nonplus, rattle (*Inf.*),

confusion (kən'fjuːʒən) n. 1. the act of confusing or the state of being confused. 2. disorder. 3. bewilderment; perplexity. 4. lack of clarity. 5. embarrassment; abashment.

confute (kən'fjuːt) vb. (tr.) to prove (a person or thing) wrong, invalid, or mistaken; disprove. —**con'futable** adj. —**confutation** (ˌkɒnfjuˈteɪʃən) n.

conga ('kɒŋɡə) n. 1. a Latin American dance of three steps and a kick to each bar, performed by a number of people in single file. 2. Also called: **conga drum**. a large tubular bass drum, usually played with the hands. ~vb. -**gaing, -gaed**. 3. (intr.) to perform this dance.

congé ('kɒnʒeɪ) n. 1. permission to depart or dismissal, esp. when formal. 2. a farewell.

congeal (kən'dʒiːl) vb. 1. to change or cause to change from a soft or fluid state to a firm state. 2. to form or cause to form into a coagulated mass; jell. —**con'gealable** adj. —**con'gealment** n.

congener (kən'dʒiːnə, 'kɒndʒɪnə) n. a member of a class, group, or other category, esp. any animal of a specified genus.

congenial (kən'dʒiːnjəl) adj. 1. friendly, pleasant, or agreeable: a congenial atmosphere to work in. 2. having a similar disposition, tastes, etc.; compatible. —**congeniality** (kənˌdʒiːnɪˈælɪtɪ) n.

congenital (kən'dʒɛnɪtəl) adj. 1. denoting any nonhereditary condition, esp. an abnormal condition, existing at birth: congenital blindness. 2. Inf. complete, as if from birth: a congenital idiot. —**con'genitally** adv.

conger ('kɒŋɡə) n. a large marine eel occurring in temperate and tropical coastal waters.

congest (kən'dʒɛst) vb. 1. to crowd or become crowded to excess; overfill. 2. to clog (an organ) with blood or (of an organ) to become clogged with blood. 3. (tr.; usually passive) to block (the nose) with mucus. —**con'gestion** n.

conglomerate n. (kən'ɡlɒmərɪt) 1. a thing composed of heterogeneous elements. 2. any coarse-grained sedimentary rock consisting of rounded fragments of rock embedded in a finer matrix. 3. a large corporation consisting of a group of companies dealing in widely diversified goods, services, etc. ~vb. (kən'ɡlɒmə,reɪt). 4. to form into a mass. ~adj. (kən'ɡlɒmərɪt). 5. made up of heterogeneous elements. 6. (of sedimentary rocks) consisting of rounded fragments within a finer matrix. —**con,glomer'ation** n.

congratulate (kən'ɡrætjʊˌleɪt) vb. (tr.) 1. (usually foll. by on) to communicate pleasure, approval, or praise to; compliment. 2. (often foll. by on) to consider (oneself) clever or fortunate (as a result of): she congratulated herself on her tact. 3. Obs. to greet; salute. —**con,gratu-'lation** n. —**con'gratulatory** or **con'gratulative** adj.

congratulations (kənˌɡrætjʊˈleɪʃənz) pl. n., interj. expressions of pleasure or joy on another's success, good fortune, etc.

congregate ('kɒŋɡrɪˌɡeɪt) vb. to collect together in a body or crowd; assemble. —**'congre,gator** n.

congregation (ˌkɒŋɡrɪˈɡeɪʃən) n. 1. a group of persons gathered for worship, prayer, etc., esp. in a church. 2. the act of congregating together. 3. a group collected together; assemblage. 4. the group of persons habitually attending a given church, chapel, etc. 5. R.C. Church. a. a society of persons who follow a common rule of life but who are bound only by simple vows. b. an administrative subdivision of the papal curia. 6. Chiefly Brit. an assembly of senior members of a university. —**,congre-'gational** adj.

Congregationalism (ˌkɒŋɡrɪˈɡeɪʃənəˌlɪzəm) n. a system of Christian doctrines and ecclesiastical government in which each congregation is self-governing. —**,Congre'gationalist** adj., n.

congress ('kɒŋɡrɛs) n. 1. a meeting or conference, esp. of representatives of sovereign states. 2. a national legislative assembly. 3. a society or association. —**con'gressional** (kən'ɡrɛʃənəl) adj.

Congress ('kɒŋɡrɛs) n. 1. the bicameral federal legislature of the U.S., consisting of the House of Representatives and the Senate. 2. Also called: **Congress Party**. (in India) a major political party. —**Con'gressional** adj.

congruence ('kɒŋɡrʊəns) or **congruency** n. 1. the quality or state of corresponding, agreeing, or being congruent. 2. the relationship between two integers, x and y, such that their difference, with respect to another integer called the modulus, n, is a multiple of the modulus.

congruent ('kɒŋɡrʊənt) adj. 1. agreeing; corresponding. 2. having identical shapes so that all parts correspond: congruent triangles. 3. of or concerning two integers related by a congruence.

congruous ('kɒŋɡrʊəs) adj. 1. corresponding or agreeing. 2. appropriate. —**congruity** (kən'ɡruːɪtɪ) n.

conic ('kɒnɪk) adj. also **conical**. 1. a. having the shape of a cone. b. of a cone. ~n. 2. another name for **conic section**. —**'conically** adv.

conic section n. one of a group of curves formed by the intersection of a plane and a right circular cone. It is either a circle, ellipse, parabola, or hyperbola.

conifer ('kəʊnɪfə, 'kɒn-) n. any tree or shrub of the group Coniferae, typically bearing cones and evergreen leaves. The group includes the pines, spruces, firs, larches, etc. —**co'niferous** adj.

conjectural (kən'dʒɛktʃərəl) adj. involving or inclined to conjecture. —**con'jecturally** adv.

conjecture (kən'dʒɛktʃə) n. 1. the formation of conclusions from incomplete evidence; guess. 2. the conclusion so formed. ~vb. 3. to infer or arrive at (an opinion, conclusion, etc.) from incomplete evidence. —**con-'jecturable** adj.

conjoin (kən'dʒɔɪn) vb. to join or become joined. —**con'joiner** n.

conjoint (kən'dʒɔɪnt) adj. united, joint, or associated. —**con'jointly** adv.

conjugal ('kɒndʒʊɡəl) adj. of or relating to marriage or the relationship between husband and wife: conjugal rights. —**conjugality** (ˌkɒndʒʊˈɡælɪtɪ) n. —**'conjugally** adv.

shame, throw off balance, upset

confused 1. at a loss, at sea, at sixes and sevens, baffled, bewildered, dazed, discombobulated (Inf., chiefly U.S.), disorganized, disorientated, flummoxed, muddled, muzzy (U.S. inf.), nonplussed, not with it (Inf.), perplexed, puzzled, taken aback, thrown off balance, upset 2. at sixes and sevens, chaotic, disarranged, disordered, disorderly, disorganized, higgledy-piggledy (Inf.), huggermugger (Archaic), in disarray, jumbled, mistaken, misunderstood, mixed up, out of order, topsy-turvy, untidy

confusing ambiguous, baffling, complicated, contradictory, disconcerting, inconsistent, misleading, muddling, perplexing, puzzling, unclear

confusion 1. befuddlement, bemusement, bewilderment, disorientation, mystification, perplexity, puzzlement 2. bustle, chaos, clutter, commotion, disarrangement, disorder, disorganization, hotchpotch, jumble, mess, muddle, shambles, tangle, turmoil, untidiness, upheaval 3. abashment, chagrin, demoralization, discomfiture, distraction, em-

barrassment, fluster, perturbation

congenial adapted, agreeable, companionable, compatible, complaisant, favourable, fit, friendly, genial, kindly, kindred, like-minded, pleasant, pleasing, suitable, sympathetic, well-suited

congenital 1. constitutional, inborn, inbred, inherent, innate, natural 2. Inf. complete, inveterate, thorough, utter

congested blocked-up, clogged, crammed, crowded, jammed, overcrowded, overfilled, overflowing, packed, stuffed, stuffed-up, teeming

congestion bottleneck, clogging, crowding, jam, mass, overcrowding, snarl-up (Inf.), surfeit

conglomerate 1. adj. amassed, clustered, composite, heterogeneous, massed 2. v. accumulate, agglomerate, aggregate, cluster, coalesce, snowball 3. n. agglomerate, aggregate, multinational

conglomeration accumulation, aggregation, assortment, combination, composite, hotchpotch, mass, medley, miscellany,

mishmash, potpourri

congratulate compliment, felicitate, wish joy to

congratulations best wishes, compliments, felicitations, good wishes, greetings

congregate assemble, collect, come together, concentrate, convene, converge, convoke, flock, forgather, gather, mass, meet, muster, rally, rendezvous, throng

congregation assembly, brethren, crowd, fellowship, flock, host, laity, multitude, parish, parishioners, throng

congress assembly, chamber of deputies, conclave, conference, convention, convocation, council, delegates, diet, legislative assembly, legislature, meeting, parliament, representatives

conic, conical cone-shaped, conoid, funnel-shaped, pointed, pyramidal, tapered, tapering

conjecture 1. v. assume, fancy, guess, hypothesize, imagine, infer, suppose, surmise, suspect, theorize 2. n. assumption, conclusion, fancy, guess, guesstimate (Inf.),

conjugate vb. ('kɒndʒʊˌgeɪt). 1. (tr.) Grammar. to state or set out the conjugation of (a verb). 2. (intr.) (of a verb) to undergo inflection according to a specific set of rules. 3. (intr.) Biol. to undergo conjugation. 4. (tr.) Obs. to join together, esp. in marriage. ~adj. ('kɒndʒʊgɪt, -ˌgeɪt). 5. joined together in pairs. 6. Maths. **a.** (of two angles) having a sum of 360°. **b.** (of two complex numbers) differing only in the sign of the imaginary part as 4 + 3i and 4 - 3i. 7. Chem. of the state of equilibrium in which two liquids can exist as separate phases that are both solutions. 8. Chem. (of acids and bases) related by loss or gain of a proton. 9. (of a compound leaf) having one pair of leaflets. 10. (of words) cognate; related in origin. ~n. ('kɒndʒʊgɪt). 11. one of a pair or set of conjugate substances, values, quantities, words, etc. —'conjuˌgative adj. —'conjuˌgator n.

conjugation (ˌkɒndʒʊ'geɪʃən) n. 1. Grammar. **a.** inflection of a verb for person, number, tense, voice, mood, etc. **b.** the complete set of the inflections of a given verb. 2. a joining. 3. a type of sexual reproduction in ciliate protozoans involving the temporary union of two individuals and the subsequent migration and fusion of the gametic nuclei. 4. the union of gametes, as in some fungi. 5. the pairing of chromosomes in the early phase of a meiotic division. —ˌconju'gational adj.

conjunction (kən'dʒʌŋkʃən) n. 1. the act of joining together; union. 2. simultaneous occurrence of events; coincidence. 3. any word or group of words, other than a relative pronoun, that connects words, phrases, or clauses; for example and and while. 4. Astron. **a.** the position of a planet when it is in line with the sun as seen from the earth. **b.** the apparent proximity or coincidence of two celestial bodies on the celestial sphere. 5. Logic. **a.** a compound proposition in which the component propositions are joined by and, which is true only if the component propositions are true. **b.** the relation between the terms of such a proposition. —con'junctional adj.

conjunctiva (ˌkɒndʒʌŋk'taɪvə) n., pl. -vas or -vae (-viː). the delicate mucous membrane that covers the eyeball and the under surface of the eyelid. —ˌconjunc'tival adj.

conjunctive (kən'dʒʌŋktɪv) adj. 1. joining; connective. 2. joined. 3. of or relating to conjunctions. ~n. 4. a less common word for **conjunction** (sense 3).

conjunctivitis (kənˌdʒʌŋktɪ'vaɪtɪs) n. inflammation of the conjunctiva.

conjuncture (kən'dʒʌŋktʃə) n. a combination of events, esp. a critical one.

conjuration (ˌkɒndʒʊ'reɪʃən) n. 1. a magic spell; incantation. 2. a less common word for **conjuring**. 3. Arch. supplication; entreaty.

conjure ('kʌndʒə) vb. 1. (intr.) to practise conjuring. 2. (intr.) to call upon supposed supernatural forces by spells and incantations. 3. (tr.) (kən'dʒʊə). to appeal earnestly to: I conjure you to help me. **4. a name to conjure with. a.** a person thought to have great power or influence. **b.** any name that excites the imagination. ~See also **conjure up**.

conjurer or **conjuror** ('kʌndʒərə) n. 1. a person who practises conjuring, esp. for people's entertainment. 2. a sorcerer.

conjure up vb. (tr., adv.) 1. to present to the mind; evoke or imagine: he conjured up a picture of his childhood. 2. to call up or command (a spirit or devil) by an incantation.

conjuring ('kʌndʒərɪŋ) n. 1. the performance of tricks that appear to defy natural laws. ~adj. 2. denoting or of such tricks or entertainment.

conk (kɒŋk) Sl. ~vb. 1. to strike (someone) a blow, esp. on the head or nose. ~n. 2. a punch or blow, esp. on the head or nose. 3. the head or nose.

conker ('kɒŋkə) n. an informal name for the **horse chestnut**.

conkers ('kɒŋkəz) n. (functioning as sing.) Brit. a game in which a player swings a horse chestnut (conker), threaded onto a string, against that of another player to try to break it.

conk out vb. (intr.) Inf. 1. (of machines, cars, etc.) to fail suddenly. 2. to tire suddenly or collapse.

con man n. Inf. a person who swindles another by means of a confidence trick. More formal term: **confidence man.**

connect (kə'nɛkt) vb. 1. to link or be linked. 2. (tr.) to associate: I connect him with my childhood. 3. (tr.) to establish telephone communications with or between. 4. (intr.) (of two public vehicles, such as trains or buses) to have the arrival of one timed to occur just before the departure of the other, for the convenient transfer of passengers. 5. (intr.) Inf. to hit, punch, kick, etc., solidly. —con'nectible or con'nectable adj. —con'nector or con'necter n.

connection or **connexion** (kə'nɛkʃən) n. 1. the act of connecting; union. 2. something that connects or relates; link or bond. 3. a relationship or association. 4. logical sequence in thought or expression; coherence. 5. the relation of a word or phrase to its context: in this connection the word has no political significance. 6. (often pl.) an acquaintance, esp. one who is influential. 7. a relative, esp. if distant and related by marriage. 8. **a.** an opportunity to transfer from one train, bus, etc., to another. **b.** the vehicle scheduled to provide such an opportunity. 9. a link, usually a wire or metallic strip, between two components in an electric circuit. 10. a communications link, esp. by telephone. 11. Sl. a supplier of illegal drugs, such as heroin. 12. Rare. sexual intercourse. —con'nectional or con'nexional adj.

connective (kə'nɛktɪv) adj. 1. connecting. ~n. 2. a thing that connects. 3. Grammar. any word that connects phrases, clauses, or individual words. 4. Bot. the tissue of a stamen that connects the two lobes of the anther. 5. Logic. a symbol used in a formal language in the construction of compound sentences, corresponding to terms such as or, and, etc., in ordinary speech.

connective tissue n. an animal tissue that supports organs, fills the spaces between them, and forms tendons and ligaments.

conning tower ('kɒnɪŋ) n. 1. a superstructure of a submarine, used as the bridge when the vessel is on the surface. 2. the armoured pilot house of a warship.

connivance (kə'naɪvəns) n. 1. the act or fact of conniving. 2. Law. the tacit encouragement of or assent to another's wrongdoing.

connive (kə'naɪv) vb. (intr.) 1. to plot together; conspire. 2. Law. (foll. by at) to give assent or encouragement (to the commission of a wrong). —con'niver n.

connoisseur (ˌkɒnɪ'sɜː) n. a person with special knowledge or appreciation of a field, esp. in the arts. —ˌconnois'seurship n.

connote (kɒ'nəʊt) vb. (tr.; often takes a clause as object) 1. (of a word, phrase, etc.) to imply or suggest (associations or ideas) other than the literal meaning: the

---

THESAURUS

guesswork, hypothesis, inference, notion, presumption, shot in the dark, speculation, supposition, surmise, theorizing, theory

conjugal bridal, connubial, hymeneal, marital, married, matrimonial, nuptial, spousal, wedded

conjunction association, coincidence, combination, concurrence, juxtaposition, union

conjure 1. juggle, play tricks 2. bewitch, call upon, cast a spell, charm, enchant, fascinate, invoke, raise, rouse, summon up 3. adjure, appeal to, beg, beseech, crave, entreat, implore, importune, pray, supplicate

conjurer, conjuror magician, miracle-worker, sorcerer, thaumaturge (Rare), wizard

conjure up bring to mind, contrive, create, evoke, produce as by magic, recall, recollect

connect affix, ally, associate, cohere, combine, couple, fasten, join, link, relate, unite

connected 1. affiliated, akin, allied, associated, banded together, bracketed, combined, coupled, joined, linked, related, united 2. Of speech coherent, comprehensible, consecutive, intelligible

connection 1. alliance, association, attachment, coupling, fastening, junction, link, tie, union 2. affinity, association, bond, commerce, communication, correlation, correspondence, intercourse, interrelation, link, marriage, relation, relationship, relevance,

tie-in 3. context, frame of reference, reference 4. acquaintance, ally, associate, contact, friend, sponsor 5. kin, kindred, kinsman, kith, relation, relative

connivance abetment, abetting, collusion, complicity, conspiring, tacit consent

connive 1. cabal, collude, conspire, cook up (Inf.), intrigue, plot, scheme 2. With at abet, aid, be an accessory to, be a party to, be in collusion with, blink at, disregard, lend oneself to, let pass, look the other way, overlook, pass by, shut one's eyes to, turn a blind eye to, wink at

connoisseur aficionado, appreciator, arbiter, authority, buff (Inf.), cognoscente, devotee, expert, judge, savant, specialist

word "*maiden*" *connotes modesty.* **2.** to involve as a consequence or condition. —**,conno'tation** n.

connubial (kə'njuːbɪəl) *adj.* of or relating to marriage: *connubial bliss.* —**con,nubi'ality** n.

conquer ('kɒŋkə) *vb.* **1.** to overcome (an enemy, army, etc.); defeat. **2.** to overcome (an obstacle, desire, etc.); surmount. **3.** (*tr.*) to gain possession or control of as by force or war; win. —**'conquerable** *adj.* —**'conqueror** n.

conquest ('kɒŋkwɛst) n. **1.** the act of conquering or the state of having been conquered; victory. **2.** a person, thing, etc., that has been conquered. **3.** a person whose compliance, love, etc., has been won.

conquistador (kɒn'kwɪstə,dɔː) n., *pl.* **-dors** or **-dores** (-dɔːrɛs). an adventurer or conqueror, esp. one of the Spanish conquerors of the New World in the 16th century.

cons. *abbrev. for:* **1.** consecrated. **2.** consigned. **3.** consignment. **4.** consolidated. **5.** consonant. **6.** constitutional. **7.** construction.

Cons. *abbrev. for* Conservative.

conscience ('kɒnʃəns) n. **1.** the sense of right and wrong that governs a person's thoughts and actions. **2.** conscientiousness; diligence. **3.** a feeling of guilt or anxiety: *he has a conscience about his unkind action.* **4.** **in (all) conscience. a.** with regard to truth and justice. **b.** certainly. **5.** **on one's conscience.** causing feelings of guilt or remorse.

conscience money n. money paid voluntarily to compensate for dishonesty, esp. for taxes formerly evaded.

conscience-stricken *adj.* feeling anxious or guilty. Also: **conscience-smitten.**

conscientious (,kɒnʃɪ'ɛnʃəs) *adj.* **1.** involving or taking great care; painstaking. **2.** governed by or done according to conscience. —**,consci'entiously** *adv.* —**,consci'entiousness** n.

conscientious objector n. a person who refuses to serve in the armed forces on the grounds of conscience.

conscious ('kɒnʃəs) *adj.* **1. a.** denoting a part of the human mind that is aware of a person's self, environment, and mental activity and that to a certain extent determines his choices of action. **b.** (*as n.*): *the conscious is only a small part of the mind.* **2.** alert and awake. **3. a.** aware of a particular fact: *I am conscious of your great kindness to me.* **b.** (*in combination*): *clothes-conscious.* **4.** deliberate or intended: *he spoke with conscious rudeness.* —**'consciously** *adv.* —**'consciousness** n.

conscript n. ('kɒnskrɪpt). **1. a.** a person who is enrolled for compulsory military service. **b.** (*as modifier*): *a conscript army.* ~*vb.* (kən'skrɪpt). **2.** (*tr.*) to enrol (youths, civilians, etc.) for compulsory military service.

conscription (kən'skrɪpʃən) n. compulsory military service.

consecrate ('kɒnsɪ,kreɪt) *vb.* (*tr.*) **1.** to make or declare sacred or holy. **2.** to dedicate (one's life, time, etc.) to a specific purpose. **3.** to cause to be respected or revered: *time has consecrated this custom.* —**,conse'cration** n. —**'conse,crator** n. —**consecratory** (,kɒnsɪ'kreɪtərɪ) *adj.*

Consecration (,kɒnsɪ'kreɪʃən) n. R.C. Church. the part

of the Mass after the sermon in which the bread and wine to be used in the Mass are ritually offered to God.

consecutive (kən'sɛkjutɪv) *adj.* **1.** (of a narrative, account, etc.) following chronological sequence. **2.** following one another without interruption; successive. **3.** characterized by logical sequence. **4.** *Music.* another word for **parallel** (sense 3). —**con'secutively** *adv.* —**con'secutiveness** n.

consensus (kən'sɛnsəs) n. general or widespread agreement (esp. in **consensus of opinion**).
▷ **Usage.** Since *consensus* refers to a collective opinion, the words *of opinion* in the phrase *consensus of opinion* are redundant and are therefore avoided in careful usage.

consent (kən'sɛnt) *vb.* **1.** to give assent or permission; agree. ~n. **2.** acquiescence to or acceptance of something done or planned by another. **3.** harmony in opinion; agreement (esp. in **with one consent**). **4. age of consent.** the lowest age at which the law recognizes the right of a person, esp. a girl, to consent to sexual intercourse. —**con'sentingly** *adv.*

consequence ('kɒnsɪkwəns) n. **1.** a result or effect. **2.** an unpleasant result (esp. in **take the consequences**). **3.** an inference reached by reasoning; conclusion. **4.** significance or importance (esp. in **man of consequence**). **5. in consequence.** as a result.

consequent ('kɒnsɪkwənt) *adj.* **1.** following as an effect. **2.** following as a logical conclusion. **3.** (of a river) flowing in the direction of the original slope of the land. ~n. **4.** something that follows something else, esp. as a result. **5.** *Logic.* the second proposition in a conditional, such as *he is British* in *if Ian was born in Scotland then he is British.*
▷ **Usage.** See at **consequential.**

consequently ('kɒnsɪkwəntlɪ) *adv., sentence connector.* as a result or effect; therefore; hence.

consequential (,kɒnsɪ'kwɛnʃəl) *adj.* **1.** important or significant. **2.** self-important. **3.** following as a consequence, esp. indirectly: *consequential loss.* —**,conse,quenti'ality** n. —**,conse'quentially** *adv.*
▷ **Usage.** Although both *consequential* and *consequent* can refer to that which follows as a result, *consequent* is more frequently used in this sense in general contexts, while *consequential* is often used in commercial or legal contexts.

consequently ('kɒnsɪkwəntlɪ) *adv. sentence connector.* as a result or effect; therefore; hence.

conservancy (kən'sɜːvənsɪ) n., *pl.* **-cies.** **1.** (in Britain) a court or commission with jurisdiction over a river, port, area of countryside, etc. **2.** another word for **conservation** (sense 2).

conservation (,kɒnsə'veɪʃən) n. **1.** the act of conserving or keeping from change, loss, injury, etc. **2. a.** protection, preservation, and careful management of natural resources. **b.** (*as modifier*): *a conservation area.* **3.** *Physics, etc.* the preservation of a specified aspect or value of a system, as in **conservation of charge, conservation of momentum, conservation of parity.** —**,conser'vational** *adj.* —**,conser'vationist** n.

THESAURUS

conquer 1. beat, checkmate, crush, defeat, discomfit, get the better of, humble, master, overcome, overpower, overthrow, prevail, quell, rout, subdue, subjugate, succeed, surmount, triumph, vanquish **2.** acquire, annex, obtain, occupy, overrun, seize, win

conqueror 1. champion, conquistador, defeater, hero, lord, master, subjugator, vanquisher, victor, winner

conquest 1. defeat, discomfiture, mastery, overthrow, rout, triumph, vanquishment, victory **2.** acquisition, annexation, appropriation, coup, invasion, occupation, subjection, subjugation, takeover **3.** captivation, enchantment, enthralment, enticement, seduction **4.** acquisition, adherent, admirer, catch, fan, feather in one's cap, follower, prize, supporter, worshipper

conscience 1. moral sense, principles, scruples, sense of right and wrong, still small voice **2. in all conscience** assuredly, certainly, fairly, honestly, in truth, rightly, truly

conscience-stricken ashamed, compunctious, contrite, disturbed, guilty, penitent, remorseful, repentant, sorry, troubled

conscientious 1. careful, diligent, exact, faithful, meticulous, painstaking, particular, punctilious, thorough **2.** high-minded, high-principled, honest, honourable, incorruptible, just, moral, responsible, scrupulous, straightforward, strict, upright

conscious 1. alert, alive to, awake, aware, cognizant, percipient, responsive, sensible, sentient, wise to (*Sl.*) **2.** calculated, deliberate, intentional, knowing, premeditated, rational, reasoning, reflective, responsible, self-conscious, studied, wilful

consciousness apprehension, awareness, knowledge, realization, recognition, sensibility

consecrate dedicate, devote, exalt, hallow, ordain, sanctify, set apart, venerate

consecutive chronological, following,

in sequence, in turn, running, sequential, seriatim, succeeding, successive, uninterrupted

consensus agreement, common consent, concord, concurrence, general agreement, harmony, unanimity, unity

consent 1. *v.* accede, acquiesce, agree, allow, approve, assent, comply, concede, concur, permit, yield **2.** *n.* acquiescence, agreement, approval, assent, compliance, concession, concurrence, go-ahead (*Inf.*), O.K. (*Inf.*), permission, sanction

consequence 1. effect, end, event, issue, outcome, repercussion, result, upshot **2.** account, concern, import, importance, interest, moment, note, portent, significance, value, weight **3.** distinction, eminence, notability, rank, repute, standing, status **4. in consequence** as a result, because, following

consequent ensuing, following, resultant, resulting, sequential, subsequent, successive

conservative (kən'sɜːvətɪv) adj. 1. favouring the preservation of established customs, values, etc., and opposing innovation. 2. of conservatism. 3. moderate or cautious: a conservative estimate. 4. conventional in style: a conservative suit. ~n. 5. a person who is reluctant to change or consider new ideas; conformist. 6. a supporter of conservatism. —con'serva,tism n. —con'servatively adv. —con'servativeness n.

Conservative (kən'sɜːvətɪv) (in Britain and elsewhere) ~adj. 1. of, supporting, or relating to a Conservative Party. 2. (in Canada) of, supporting, or relating to the Progressive Conservative Party. 3. of, relating to, or characterizing **Conservative Judaism**, a movement favouring certain moderate relaxations of Jewish law and tradition. ~n. 4. a supporter or member of a Conservative Party, or, (in Canada) of the Progressive Conservative Party.

conservatoire (kən'sɜːvə,twɑː) n. an institution or school for instruction in music. Also called: **conservatory**.

conservatory (kən'sɜːvətrɪ) n., pl. **-tories**. 1. a greenhouse, esp. one attached to a house. 2. another word for **conservatoire**.

conserve vb. (kən'sɜːv). (tr.) 1. to keep or protect from harm, decay, loss, etc. 2. to preserve (a foodstuff, esp. fruit) with sugar. ~n. ('kɒnsɜːv, kən'sɜːv). 3. a preparation similar to jam but containing whole pieces of fruit.

consider (kən'sɪdə) vb. (mainly tr.) 1. (also intr.) to think carefully about (a problem, decision, etc.). 2. (may take a clause as object) to judge; deem: I consider him a fool. 3. to have regard for: consider your mother's feelings. 4. to look at: he considered her face. 5. (may take a clause as object) to bear in mind: when buying a car consider this make. 6. to describe or discuss. —con'siderer n.

considerable (kən'sɪdərəb'l) adj. 1. large enough to reckon with: a considerable quantity. 2. a lot of; much: he had considerable courage. 3. worthy of respect: a considerable man in the scientific world. —con'siderably adv.

considerate (kən'sɪdərɪt) adj. 1. thoughtful towards other people; kind. 2. Rare. carefully thought out; considered. —con'siderately adv.

consideration (kən,sɪdə'reɪʃən) n. 1. deliberation; contemplation. 2. **take into consideration.** to bear in mind; consider. 3. **under consideration.** being currently discussed. 4. a fact to be taken into account when making a judgment or decision. 5. thoughtfulness for other people; kindness. 6. payment for a service. 7. thought resulting from deliberation; opinion. 8. Law. the promise, object, etc., given by one party to persuade another to enter into a contract. 9. esteem. 10. **in consideration of. a.** because of. **b.** in return for.

considered (kən'sɪdəd) adj. 1. presented or thought out with care: a considered opinion. 2. (qualified by a preceding adverb) esteemed: highly considered.

considering (kən'sɪdərɪŋ) prep. 1. in view of. ~adv. 2. Inf. all in all; taking into account the circumstances: it's not bad considering. ~conj. 3. (subordinating) in view of the fact that.

consign (kən'saɪn) vb. (mainly tr.) 1. to give into the care or charge of; entrust. 2. to commit irrevocably: he consigned the papers to the flames. 3. to commit: to consign someone to jail. 4. to address or deliver (goods): it was consigned to his London address. —con'signable adj. —,consign'ee n. —con'signor or con'signer n.

consignment (kən'saɪnmənt) n. 1. the act of consigning; commitment. 2. a shipment of goods consigned. 3. **on consignment.** for payment by the consignee after sale.

consist (kən'sɪst) vb. (intr.) 1. (foll. by of or in) to be composed (of). 2. (foll. by in or of) to have its existence (in): his religion consists only in going to church. 3. to be consistent; accord.

consistency (kən'sɪstənsɪ) or **consistence** n., pl. **-encies** or **-ences**. 1. agreement or accordance. 2. degree of viscosity or firmness. 3. the state or quality of holding or sticking together and retaining shape. 4. conformity with previous attitudes, behaviour, practice, etc.

consistent (kən'sɪstənt) adj. 1. (usually foll. by with) showing consistency or harmony. 2. Logic. (of a logical system) constituted so that the propositions deduced from different axioms of the system do not contradict each other. —con'sistently adv.

consolation (,kɒnsə'leɪʃən) n. 1. the act of consoling or state of being consoled. 2. a person or thing that is a comfort in a time of grief, disappointment, etc. —con'solatory (kən'sɒlətərɪ) adj.

console[1] (kən'səʊl) vb. to serve as a comfort to (someone) in disappointment, sadness, etc. —con'solable adj. —con'soler n. —con'solingly adv.

console[2] ('kɒnsəʊl) n. 1. an ornamental bracket used to support a wall fixture, etc. 2. the part of an organ comprising the manuals, pedals, stops, etc. 3. a desk or table on which the controls of an electronic system are mounted. 4. a cabinet for a television, etc., designed to stand on the floor.

consolidate (kən'sɒlɪ,deɪt) vb. 1. to form or cause to form into a whole. 2. to make or become stronger or more stable. 3. Mil. to strengthen one's control over (a situation, area, etc.). —con'soli,dator n.

consols ('kɒnsɒlz, kən'sɒlz) pl. n. irredeemable British government securities carrying annual interest.

consommé (kən'sɒmeɪ) n. a clear soup made from meat stock.

consonance ('kɒnsənəns) or **consonancy** n., pl.

THESAURUS

consequently accordingly, ergo, hence, necessarily, subsequently, therefore, thus

conservation custody, economy, guardianship, husbandry, maintenance, preservation, protection, safeguarding, safekeeping, saving, upkeep

conservative 1. adj. cautious, conventional, die-hard, guarded, hidebound, middle-of-the-road, moderate, quiet, reactionary, right-wing, sober, tory, traditional 2. n. middle-of-the-roader, moderate, reactionary, right-winger, stick-in-the-mud (Inf.), tory, traditionalist

conservatory glasshouse, greenhouse, hothouse

conserve go easy on (Inf.), hoard, husband, keep, nurse, preserve, protect, save, store up, take care of, use sparingly

consider 1. chew over, cogitate, consult, contemplate, deliberate, discuss, examine, meditate, mull over, muse, ponder, reflect, revolve, ruminate, study, turn over in one's mind, weigh 2. believe, deem, hold to be, judge, rate, regard as, think 3. bear in mind, care for, keep in view, make allowance for, reckon with, regard, remember, respect, take into account

considerable 1. abundant, ample, appreciable, comfortable, goodly, great, large, lavish, marked, much, noticeable, plentiful, reasonable, sizable, tidy, tolerable 2. distinguished, important, influential, noteworthy, renowned, significant, venerable

considerably appreciably, greatly, markedly, noticeably, remarkably, significantly, substantially, very much

considerate attentive, charitable, circumspect, concerned, discreet, forbearing, kind, kindly, mindful, obliging, patient, tactful, thoughtful, unselfish

consideration 1. analysis, attention, cogitation, contemplation, deliberation, discussion, examination, reflection, regard, review, scrutiny, study, thought 2. concern, factor, issue, point 3. concern, considerateness, friendliness, kindliness, kindness, respect, solicitude, tact, thoughtfulness 4. fee, payment, perquisite, recompense, remuneration, reward, tip 5. **take into consideration** bear in mind, make allowance for, take into account, weigh

considering all in all, all things considered, insomuch as, in the light of, in view of

consignment 1. Act of consigning assignment, committal, dispatch, distribution, entrusting, handing over, relegation, sending, shipment, transmittal 2. Something consigned batch, delivery, goods, shipment

consist 1. With of be composed of, be made up of, amount to, comprise, contain, embody, include, incorporate, involve 2. With in be expressed by, be found or contained in, inhere, lie, reside

consistent 1. constant, dependable, persistent, regular, steady, true to type, unchanging, undeviating 2. accordant, agreeing, all of a piece, coherent, compatible, congruous, consonant, harmonious, logical

consolation alleviation, assuagement, cheer, comfort, ease, easement, encouragement, help, relief, solace, succour, support

console assuage, calm, cheer, comfort, encourage, express sympathy for, relieve, solace, soothe

consolidate 1. amalgamate, cement, combine, compact, condense, conjoin, federate, fuse, harden, join, solidify, thicken, unite 2. fortify, reinforce, secure, stabilize, strengthen

consolidation alliance, amalgamation, association, compression, condensation, federation, fortification, fusion, reinforcement, strengthening

-nances *or* **-nancies. 1.** agreement, harmony, or accord. **2.** *Prosody.* similarity between consonants, but not between vowels, as between the *s* and *t* sounds in *sweet silent thought.* **3.** *Music.* a combination of notes which can sound together without harshness.

consonant ('kɒnsənənt) *n.* **1.** a speech sound or letter of the alphabet other than a vowel. ~*adj.* **2.** *(postpositive;* foll. by *with* or *to)* consistent; in agreement. **3.** harmonious. **4.** *Music.* characterized by the presence of a consonance. —,conso'nantal *adj.* —'consonantly *adv.*

consort *vb.* (kən'sɔːt). **1.** *(intr.;* usually foll. by *with)* to keep company (with undesirable people); associate. **2.** *(intr.)* to harmonize. ~*n.* ('kɒnsɔːt). **3.** (esp. formerly) a small group of instruments, either of the same type **(a whole consort)** or of different types **(a broken consort). 4.** the husband or wife of a reigning monarch. **5.** a husband or wife. **6.** a ship that escorts another.

consortium (kən'sɔːtɪəm) *n., pl.* **-tia** (-tɪə). **1.** an association of financiers, companies, etc., esp. for a particular purpose. **2.** *Law.* the right of husband or wife to the company and affection of the other.

conspectus (kən'spɛktəs) *n.* **1.** an overall view; survey. **2.** a summary; resumé.

conspicuous (kən'spɪkjʊəs) *adj.* **1.** clearly visible. **2.** attracting attention because of a striking feature: *conspicuous stupidity.* —con'spicuously *adv.* —con'spicuousness *n.*

conspiracy (kən'spɪrəsɪ) *n., pl.* **-cies. 1.** a secret plan to carry out an illegal or harmful act, esp. with political motivation; plot. **2.** the act of making such plans in secret. —con'spirator *n.* —conspiratorial (kən,spɪrə'tɔːrɪəl) *adj.*

conspire (kən'spaɪə) *vb.* (when *intr.,* sometimes foll. by *against*) **1.** to plan (a crime) together in secret. **2.** *(intr.)* to act together as if by design: *the elements conspired to spoil our picnic.*

constable ('kʌnstəbəl, 'kɒn-) *n.* **1.** (in Britain, Australia, Canada, etc.) a police officer of the lowest rank. **2.** any of various officers of the peace, esp. one who arrests offenders, serves writs, etc. **3.** the keeper of a royal castle. **4.** (in medieval Europe) the chief military officer and functionary of a royal household. **5.** an officer of a hundred in medieval England. —'constable,ship *n.*

constabulary (kən'stæbjʊlərɪ) *Chiefly Brit.* ~*n., pl.* **-laries. 1.** the police force of a town or district. ~*adj.* **2.** of or relating to constables.

constant ('kɒnstənt) *adj.* **1.** unchanging. **2.** incessant: *constant interruptions.* **3.** resolute; loyal. ~*n.* **4.** something that is unchanging. **5.** a specific quantity that is invariable: *the velocity of light is a constant.* **6. a.** *Maths.* a symbol representing an unspecified number that remains invariable throughout a particular series of operations. **b.** *Physics.* a quantity or property that is considered invariable throughout a particular series of experiments. —'constancy *n.* —'constantly *adv.*

constellation (,kɒnstɪ'leɪʃən) *n.* **1.** any of the 88 groups of stars as seen from the earth, many of which were named by the ancient Greeks after animals, objects, or mythological persons. **2.** a gathering of brilliant people or things. **3.** *Psychoanal.* a group of ideas felt to be related. —**constellatory** (kən'stɛlətərɪ) *adj.*

consternation (,kɒnstə'neɪʃən) *n.* a feeling of anxiety, dismay, dread, or confusion.

constipate ('kɒnstɪ,peɪt) *vb.* *(tr.)* to cause constipation in. —'consti,pated *adj.*

constipation (,kɒnstɪ'peɪʃən) *n.* infrequent or difficult evacuation of the bowels.

constituency (kən'stɪtjʊənsɪ) *n., pl.* **-cies. 1.** the whole body of voters who elect one representative to a legislature or all the residents represented by one deputy. **2.** a district that sends one representative to a legislature.

constituent (kən'stɪtjʊənt) *adj. (prenominal)* **1.** forming part of a whole; component. **2.** having the power to frame a constitution or to constitute a government: *constituent assembly.* ~*n.* **3.** a component part; ingredient. **4.** a resident of a constituency, esp. one entitled to vote. **5.** *Chiefly law.* a person who appoints another to act for him. —con'stituently *adv.*

constitute ('kɒnstɪ,tjuːt) *vb.* *(tr.)* **1.** to form; compose: *the people who constitute a jury.* **2.** to appoint to an office: *a legally constituted officer.* **3.** to set up (an institution) formally; found. **4.** *Law.* to give legal form to (a court, assembly, etc.). —'consti,tuter *or* 'consti,tutor *n.*

constitution (,kɒnstɪ'tjuːʃən) *n.* **1.** the act of constituting or state of being constituted. **2.** physical make-up; structure. **3.** the fundamental principles on which a state is governed, esp. when considered as embodying the rights of the subjects. **4.** *(often cap.)* (in certain countries, esp. the U.S.) a statute embodying such principles. **5.** a person's state of health. **6.** a person's temperament.

constitutional (,kɒnstɪ'tjuːʃənəl) *adj.* **1.** of a constitution. **2.** authorized by or subject to a constitution: *constitutional monarchy.* **3.** inherent in the nature of a person or thing: *a constitutional weakness.* **4.** beneficial to one's physical well-being. ~*n.* **5.** a regular walk taken for the benefit of one's health. —,consti,tution'ality *n.* —,consti'tutionally *adv.*

constitutive ('kɒnstɪ,tjuːtɪv) *adj.* **1.** having power to enact or establish. **2.** another word for **constituent** (sense 1). —'consti,tutively *adv.*

constrain (kən'streɪn) *vb.* *(tr.)* **1.** to compel, esp. by circumstances, etc. **2.** to restrain as by force. —con'strainer *n.*

constrained (kən'streɪnd) *adj.* embarrassed, unnatural, or forced: *a constrained smile.*

constraint (kən'streɪnt) *n.* **1.** compulsion or restraint. **2.** repression of natural feelings. **3.** a forced unnatural manner. **4.** something that serves to constrain; restric-

---

THESAURUS

consort *n.* **1.** associate, companion, fellow, husband, partner, spouse *(of a reigning monarch),* wife ~*v.* **2.** associate, fraternize, go around with, hang about *or* around with, keep company, mingle, mix **3.** accord, agree, correspond, harmonize, square, tally

conspicuous 1. apparent, clear, discernible, easily seen, evident, manifest, noticeable, obvious, patent, perceptible, visible **2.** celebrated, distinguished, eminent, famous, illustrious, notable, outstanding, prominent, remarkable, signal, striking **3.** blatant, flagrant, flashy, garish, glaring, showy

conspiracy cabal, collusion, confederacy, frame-up *(Sl.),* intrigue, league, machination, plot, scheme, treason

conspirator cabalist, conspirer, intriguer, plotter, schemer, traitor

conspire 1. cabal, confederate, contrive, devise, hatch treason, intrigue, machinate, manoeuvre, plot, scheme **2.** combine, concur, conduce, contribute, cooperate, tend, work together

constancy decision, determination, devotion, fidelity, firmness, fixedness, permanence, perseverance, regularity, resolution, stability, steadfastness, steadiness, tenacity,

uniformity

constant 1. continual, even, firm, fixed, habitual, immutable, invariable, permanent, perpetual, regular, stable, steadfast, steady, unalterable, unbroken, uniform, unvarying **2.** ceaseless, continual, continuous, endless, eternal, everlasting, incessant, interminable, never-ending, nonstop, perpetual, persistent, relentless, sustained, uninterrupted, unrelenting, unremitting **3.** determined, dogged, persevering, resolute, unflagging, unshaken, unwavering **4.** attached, dependable, devoted, faithful, loyal, staunch, tried-and-true, true, trustworthy, trusty, unfailing

constantly all the time, always, continually, continuously, endlessly, everlastingly, incessantly, interminably, invariably, morning, noon and night, night and day, nonstop, perpetually, relentlessly

consternation alarm, amazement, anxiety, awe, bewilderment, confusion, dismay, distress, dread, fear, fright, horror, panic, shock, terror, trepidation

constituent *adj.* **1.** basic, component, elemental, essential, integral ~*n.* **2.** component, element, essential, factor, ingredient, part, principle, unit **3.** elector, voter

constitute 1. compose, comprise, create,

enact, establish, fix, form, found, make, make up, set up **2.** appoint, authorize, commission, delegate, depute, empower, name, nominate, ordain

constitution 1. composition, establishment, formation, organization **2.** build, character, composition, disposition, form, habit, health, make-up, nature, physique, structure, temper, temperament

constitutional *adj.* **1.** congenital, inborn, inherent, intrinsic, organic **2.** chartered, statutory, vested ~*n.* **3.** airing, stroll, turn, walk

constrain 1. bind, coerce, compel, drive, force, impel, necessitate, oblige, pressure, pressurize, urge **2.** chain, check, confine, constrict, curb, hem in, restrain

constrained embarrassed, forced, guarded, inhibited, reserved, reticent, subdued, unnatural

constraint 1. coercion, compulsion, force, necessity, pressure, restraint **2.** bashfulness, diffidence, embarrassment, inhibition, repression, reservation, restraint, timidity **3.** check, curb, damper, deterrent, hindrance, limitation, restriction

tive condition.

constrict (kən'strɪkt) *vb.* (*tr.*) **1.** to make smaller or narrower, esp. by contracting at one place. **2.** to hold in or inhibit; limit.

constriction (kən'strɪkʃən) *n.* **1.** a feeling of tightness in some part of the body, such as the chest. **2.** the act of constricting or condition of being constricted. **3.** something that is constricted. —**con'strictive** *adj.*

constrictor (kən'strɪktə) *n.* **1.** any of various very large nonvenomous snakes, such as the boas, that coil around and squeeze their prey to kill it. **2.** any muscle that constricts; sphincter.

construct *vb.* (kən'strʌkt). (*tr.*) **1.** to put together substances or parts systematically; build; assemble. **2.** to frame mentally (an argument, sentence, etc.). **3.** *Geom.* to draw (a line, angle, or figure) so that certain requirements are satisfied. ~*n.* ('kɒnstrʌkt). **4.** something formulated or built systematically. **5.** a complex idea resulting from a synthesis of simpler ideas. —**con'structor** or **con'structer** *n.*

construction (kən'strʌkʃən) *n.* **1.** the act of constructing or manner in which a thing is constructed. **2.** a structure. **3. a.** the business or work of building dwellings, offices, etc. **b.** (*as modifier*): *a construction site.* **4.** an interpretation: *they put a sympathetic construction on her behaviour.* **5.** *Grammar.* a group of words that make up one of the constituents into which a sentence may be analysed; a phrase or clause. **6.** an abstract work of art in three dimensions. —**con'structional** *adj.* —**con'structionally** *adv.*

constructive (kən'strʌktɪv) *adj.* **1.** serving to improve; positive: *constructive criticism.* **2.** *Law.* deduced by inference; not expressed. **3.** another word for **structural.** —**con'structively** *adv.*

construe (kən'stru:) *vb.* -**struing, -strued.** (*mainly tr.*) **1.** to interpret the meaning of (something): *you can construe that in different ways.* **2.** (*may take a clause as object*) to infer; deduce. **3.** to analyse the grammatical structure of; parse (esp. a Latin or Greek text as a preliminary to translation). **4.** to combine words syntactically. **5.** (*also intr.*) *Old-fashioned.* to translate literally, esp. aloud. —**con'struable** *adj.*

consul ('kɒnsəl) *n.* **1.** an official appointed by a sovereign state to protect its commercial interests and aid its citizens in a foreign city. **2.** (in ancient Rome) either of two annually elected magistrates who jointly exercised the highest authority in the republic. **3.** (in France from 1799 to 1804) any of the three chief magistrates of the First Republic. —**consular** ('kɒnsjʊlə) *adj.* —**'consul-,ship** *n.*

consulate ('kɒnsjʊlɪt) *n.* **1.** the premises of a consul. **2.** government by consuls. **3.** the office or period of office of a consul. **4.** (*often cap.*) **a.** the government of France by the three consuls from 1799 to 1804. **b.** this period. **5.** (*often cap.*) the consular government of the Roman republic.

consult (kən'sʌlt) *vb.* **1.** (when *intr.*, often foll. by *with*) to ask advice from (someone). **2.** (*tr.*) to refer to for information: *to consult a map.* **3.** (*tr.*) to have regard for (a person's feelings, interests, etc.); consider.

consultant (kən'sʌltənt) *n.* **1. a.** a specialist physician who is asked to confirm a diagnosis. **b.** a physician or surgeon holding the highest appointment in a particular

branch of medicine or surgery in a hospital. **2.** a specialist who gives expert advice or information. **3.** a person who asks advice in a consultation. —**con'sultancy** *n.*

consultation (,kɒnsəl'teɪʃən) *n.* **1.** the act of consulting. **2.** a conference for discussion or the seeking of advice. —**consultative** (kən'sʌltətɪv) *adj.*

consulting (kən'sʌltɪŋ) *adj.* (*prenominal*) acting in an advisory capacity on professional matters: *a consulting engineer.*

consulting room *n.* a room in which a doctor sees his patients.

consume (kən'sju:m) *vb.* **1.** (*tr.*) to eat or drink. **2.** (*tr.; often passive*) to obsess. **3.** (*tr.*) to use up; expend. **4.** to destroy or be destroyed by: *fire consumed the forest.* **5.** (*tr.*) to waste. **6.** (*intr.; passive*) to waste away. —**con'sumable** *adj.* —**con'sumingly** *adv.*

consumer (kən'sju:mə) *n.* **1.** a person who purchases goods and services for his own personal needs. Cf. **producer** (sense 4). **2.** a person or thing that consumes.

consumer goods *pl. n.* goods that satisfy personal needs rather than those required for the production of other goods or services.

consumerism (kən'sju:mə,rɪzəm) *n.* **1.** protection of the interests of consumers. **2.** advocacy of a high rate of consumption as a basis for a sound economy. —**con'sumerist** *n., adj.*

consummate *vb.* ('kɒnsə,meɪt). **1.** (*tr.*) to bring to completion; fulfil. **2.** (*tr.*) to complete (a marriage) legally by sexual intercourse. ~*adj.* (kən'sʌmɪt, 'kɒnsəmɪt). **3.** supremely skilled: *a consummate artist.* **4.** (*prenominal*) (intensifier): *a consummate fool.* —**con-'summately** *adv.* —,**consum'mation** *n.*

consumption (kən'sʌmpʃən) *n.* **1.** the act of consuming or the state of being consumed, esp. by eating, burning, etc. **2.** *Econ.* expenditure on goods and services for final personal use. **3.** the quantity consumed. **4.** a wasting away of the tissues of the body, esp. in tuberculosis of the lungs.

consumptive (kən'sʌmptɪv) *adj.* **1.** causing consumption; wasteful; destructive. **2.** relating to or affected with tuberculosis of the lungs. ~*n.* **3.** *Pathol.* a person who suffers from consumption. —**con'sumptively** *adv.* —**con'sumptiveness** *n.*

cont. *abbrev. for:* **1.** contents. **2.** continued.

contact *n.* ('kɒntækt). **1.** the act or state of touching. **2.** the state or fact of communication (esp. in **in contact, make contact**). **3. a.** a junction of electrical conductors. **b.** the part of the conductors that make the junction. **c.** the part of an electrical device to which such connections are made. **4.** an acquaintance, esp. one who might be useful in business, etc. **5.** any person who has been exposed to a contagious disease. **6.** (*modifier*) caused by touching the causative agent: *contact dermatitis.* **7.** (*modifier*) of or maintaining contact. ~*vb.* ('kɒntækt, kən'tækt). **8.** (when *intr.*, often foll. by *with*) to put, come, or be in association, touch, or communication. —**contactual** (kɒn'tæktjʊəl) *adj.*

contact lens *n.* a lens placed directly on the surface of the eye to correct defects of vision.

contagion (kən'teɪdʒən) *n.* **1.** the transmission of disease from one person to another by contact. **2.** a contagious disease. **3.** a corrupting influence that tends to spread. **4.** the spreading of an emotional or mental state

---

THESAURUS

construct assemble, build, compose, create, design, elevate, engineer, erect, establish, fabricate, fashion, form, formulate, found, frame, make, manufacture, organize, put up, raise, set up, shape
construction **1.** assembly, building, composition, creation, edifice, erection, fabric, fabrication, figure, form, formation, shape, structure **2.** explanation, inference, interpretation, reading, rendering
constructive helpful, positive, practical, productive, useful, valuable
consult **1.** ask, ask advice of, commune, compare notes, confer, consider, debate, deliberate, interrogate, question, refer to, take counsel, turn to **2.** consider, have regard for, regard, respect, take account of, take into consideration
consultant adviser, authority, specialist
consultation appointment, conference,

council, deliberation, dialogue, discussion, examination, hearing, interview, meeting, session
consume **1.** absorb, deplete, dissipate, drain, eat up, employ, exhaust, expend, finish up, fritter away, lavish, lessen, spend, squander, use, use up, utilize, vanish, waste, wear out **2.** devour, eat, eat up, gobble (up), guzzle, polish off (*Inf.*), put away, swallow **3.** annihilate, decay, demolish, destroy, devastate, lay waste, ravage **4.** *Often passive* absorb, devour, dominate, eat up, engross, monopolize, obsess, preoccupy
consumer buyer, customer, purchaser, shopper, user
consuming absorbing, compelling, devouring, engrossing, excruciating, gripping, immoderate, overwhelming, tormenting
consummate **1.** *v.* accomplish, achieve, carry out, compass, complete, conclude,

crown, effectuate, end, finish, perfect, perform **2.** *adj.* absolute, accomplished, complete, conspicuous, finished, matchless, perfect, polished, practised, skilled, superb, supreme, total, transcendent, ultimate, unqualified, utter

consumption **1.** consuming, decay, decrease, depletion, destruction, diminution, dissipation, exhaustion, expenditure, loss, use, using up, utilization, waste **2.** *Medical* atrophy, emaciation, phthisis, T.B., tuberculosis

contact *n.* **1.** association, communication, connection **2.** approximation, contiguity, junction, juxtaposition, touch, union **3.** acquaintance, connection ~*v.* **4.** approach, call, communicate with, get *or* be in touch with, get hold of, phone, reach, ring (up), speak to, write to

among a number of people: *the contagion of mirth.*

contagious (kən'teɪdʒəs) *adj.* **1.** (of a disease) capable of being passed on by direct contact with a diseased individual or by handling his clothing, etc. **2.** (of an organism) harbouring the causative agent of a transmissible disease. **3.** causing or likely to cause the same reaction in several people: *her laughter was contagious.*

contain (kən'teɪn) *vb.* (*tr.*) **1.** to hold or be capable of holding: *this contains five pints.* **2.** to restrain (feelings, behaviour, etc.). **3.** to consist of: *the book contains three sections.* **4.** *Mil.* to prevent (enemy forces) from operating beyond a certain area. **5.** to be a multiple of, leaving no remainder: *6 contains 2 and 3.* —**con'tainable** *adj.*

container (kən'teɪnə) *n.* **1.** an object used for or capable of holding, esp. for transport or storage. **2. a.** a large cargo-carrying standard-sized container that can be loaded from one mode of transport to another. **b.** (*as modifier*): *a container ship.*

containerize *or* **-ise** (kən'teɪnə,raɪz) *vb.* (*tr.*) **1.** to convey (cargo) in standard-sized containers. **2.** to adapt (a port or transportation system) to the use of standard-sized containers. —**con,taineri'zation** *or* **-i'sation** *n.*

containment (kən'teɪnmənt) *n.* the act of containing, esp. of restraining the power of a hostile country or the operations of a hostile military force.

contaminate (kən'tæmɪ,neɪt) *vb.* (*tr.*) **1.** to make impure; pollute. **2.** to make radioactive by the addition of radioactive material. —**con'taminable** *adj.* —**con'taminant** *n.* —**con,tami'nation** *n.* —**con'tami,nator** *n.*

contemn (kən'tɛm) *vb.* (*tr.*) to regard with contempt; scorn. —**contemner** (kən'tɛmnə, -'tɛmə) *n.*

contemplate ('kɒntɛm,pleɪt) *vb.* (*mainly tr.*) **1.** to think about intently and at length. **2.** (*intr.*) to think intently and at length, esp. for spiritual reasons; meditate. **3.** to look at thoughtfully. **4.** to have in mind as a possibility. —,**contem'plation** *n.* —'**contem,plator** *n.*

contemplative ('kɒntɛm,pleɪtɪv, -təm-; kən'tɛmplə-) *adj.* **1.** denoting, concerned with, or inclined to contemplation; meditative. ~*n.* **2.** a person dedicated to religious contemplation.

contemporaneous (kən,tɛmpə'reɪnɪəs) *adj.* existing, beginning, or occurring in the same period of time. —**contemporaneity** (kən,tɛmpərə'niːɪtɪ) *or* **con,tempo-'raneousness** *n.*

contemporary (kən'tɛmprərɪ) *adj.* **1.** living or occurring in the same period. **2.** existing or occurring at the present time. **3.** conforming to modern ideas in style, fashion, etc. **4.** having approximately the same age as one another. ~*n., pl.* **-raries.** **5.** a person living at the same time or of approximately the same age as another.

6. something that is contemporary. —**con'temporarily** *adv.* —**con'temporariness** *n.*

▷ **Usage.** *Contemporary* is most acceptable when used to mean of the same period, in a sentence like *it is useful to compare Shakespeare's plays with those of contemporary* (that is, other Elizabethan) *playwrights.* The word is, however, often used to mean modern or up-to-date in contexts such as *the furniture was of a contemporary design.* The second use should be avoided where ambiguity is likely to arise, as in *a production of* Othello *in contemporary dress.*

contempt (kən'tɛmpt) *n.* **1.** the feeling of a person towards a person or thing that he considers despicable; scorn. **2.** the state of being scorned; disgrace (esp. in **hold in contempt**). **3.** wilful disregard of the authority of a court of law or legislative body: *contempt of court.*

contemptible (kən'tɛmptəb'l) *adj.* deserving or worthy of contempt. —**con,tempti'bility** *or* **con'temptibleness** *n.* —**con'temptibly** *adv.*

contemptuous (kən'tɛmptjʊəs) *adj.* (when *predicative,* often foll. by *of*) showing or feeling contempt; disdainful. —**con'temptuously** *adv.*

contend (kən'tɛnd) *vb.* **1.** (*intr.*; often foll. by *with*) to struggle in rivalry, battle, etc.; vie. **2.** to argue earnestly. **3.** (*tr.*; *may take a clause as object*) to assert. —**con-'tender** *n.*

content[1] ('kɒntɛnt) *n.* **1.** (*often pl.*) everything inside a container. **2.** (*usually pl.*) **a.** the chapters or divisions of a book. **b.** a list of these printed at the front of a book. **3.** the meaning or significance of a work of art, as distinguished from its style or form. **4.** all that is contained or dealt with in a piece of writing, etc.; substance. **5.** the capacity or size of a thing. **6.** the proportion of a substance contained in an alloy, mixture, etc.: *the lead content of petrol.*

content[2] (kən'tɛnt) *adj.* (*postpositive*) **1.** satisfied with things as they are. **2.** assenting to or willing to accept circumstances, a proposed course of action, etc. ~*vb.* **3.** (*tr.*) to make (oneself or another person) satisfied. ~*n.* **4.** peace of mind. —**con'tentment** *n.*

contented (kən'tɛntɪd) *adj.* accepting one's situation or life with equanimity and satisfaction. —**con'tentedly** *adv.* —**con'tentedness** *n.*

contention (kən'tɛnʃən) *n.* **1.** a struggling between opponents; competition. **2.** a point of dispute (esp. in **bone of contention**). **3.** a point asserted in argument.

contentious (kən'tɛnʃəs) *adj.* **1.** tending to quarrel. **2.** causing or characterized by dispute; controversial. —**con'tentiousness** *n.*

conterminous (kən'tɜːmɪnəs) *or* **coterminous** (kəʊ-

THESAURUS

contagious catching, communicable, epidemic, epizootic (*Veterinary medicine*), infectious, pestiferous, pestilential, spreading, taking (*Inf.*), transmissible

contain 1. accommodate, enclose, have capacity for, hold, incorporate, seat 2. comprehend, comprise, embody, embrace, include, involve 3. control, curb, hold back, hold in, repress, restrain, stifle

container holder, receptacle, repository, vessel

contaminate adulterate, befoul, corrupt, defile, deprave, infect, pollute, radioactivate, soil, stain, sully, taint, tarnish, vitiate

contamination adulteration, contagion, corruption, decay, defilement, dirtying, filth, foulness, impurity, infection, poisoning, pollution, radioactivation, rottenness, taint

contemplate 1. brood over, consider, deliberate, meditate, meditate on, mull over, muse over, observe, ponder, reflect upon, revolve or turn over in one's mind, ruminate (upon), study 2. behold, examine, eye, gaze at, inspect, regard, scrutinize, stare at, survey, view 3. aspire to, consider, design, envisage, expect, foresee, have in view or in mind, intend, mean, plan, propose, think of

contemplation 1. cogitation, consideration, deliberation, meditation, musing, pondering, reflection, reverie, rumination, thought 2. examination, gazing at, inspection, looking at, observation, scrutiny, survey, viewing

contemplative deep or lost in thought, in a brown study, intent, introspective, meditative, musing, pensive, rapt, reflective, ruminative, thoughtful

contemporary *adj.* 1. coetaneous (*Rare*), coeval, coexistent, coexisting, concurrent, contemporaneous, synchronous 2. à la mode, current, in fashion, latest, modern, newfangled, present, present-day, recent, ultramodern, up-to-date, up-to-the-minute, with it (*Inf.*) ~*n.* 3. compeer, fellow, peer

contempt 1. condescension, contumely, derision, despite (*Archaic*), disdain, disregard, disrespect, mockery, neglect, scorn, slight 2. *A state of contempt* disgrace, dishonour, humiliation, shame

contemptible abject, base, cheap, degenerate, despicable, detestable, ignominious, low, low-down (*Inf.*), mean, paltry, pitiful, scurvy, shabby, shameful, vile, worthless

contemptuous arrogant, cavalier, condescending, contumelious, derisive, disdainful, haughty, high and mighty, insolent, insulting, scornful, sneering, supercilious

contend 1. clash, compete, contest, cope, emulate, grapple, jostle, litigate, skirmish, strive, struggle, vie 2. affirm, allege, argue, assert, aver, avow, debate, dispute, hold, maintain

content[1] 1. *v.* appease, delight, gladden, gratify, humour, indulge, mollify, placate, please, reconcile, satisfy, suffice 2. *n.* comfort, contentment, ease, gratification, peace,

peace of mind, pleasure, satisfaction 3. *adj.* agreeable, at ease, comfortable, contented, fulfilled, satisfied, willing to accept

content[2] 1. burden, essence, gist, ideas, matter, meaning, significance, substance, text, thoughts 2. capacity, load, measure, size, volume

contented at ease, at peace, cheerful, comfortable, complacent, content, glad, gratified, happy, pleased, satisfied, serene, thankful

contention 1. competition, contest, discord, dispute, dissension, enmity, feuding, hostility, rivalry, strife, struggle, wrangling 2. affirmation, allegation, argument, assertion, asseveration, belief, claim, declaration, ground, idea, maintaining, opinion, position, profession, stand, thesis, view

contentious argumentative, bickering, captious, cavilling, combative, controversial, cross, disputatious, factious, litigious, peevish, perverse, pugnacious, quarrelsome, querulous, wrangling

contentment comfort, complacency, content, contentedness, ease, equanimity, fulfilment, gladness, gratification, happiness, peace, pleasure, repletion, satisfaction, serenity

contents 1. constituents, elements, ingredients, load 2. chapters, divisions, subject matter, subjects, themes, topics

'tɜːmɪnəs) *adj.* **1.** enclosed within a common boundary. **2.** without a break or interruption.

contest *n.* ('kɒntɛst). **1.** a formal game or match in which people, teams, etc., compete. **2.** a struggle for victory between opposing forces. ~*vb.* (kən'tɛst). **3.** (*tr.*) to try to disprove; call in question. **4.** (when *intr.*, foll. by *with* or *against*) to dispute or contend (with): *a contested election.* —**con'testable** *adj.* —**con'tester** *n.*

contestant (kən'tɛstənt) *n.* a person who takes part in a contest; competitor.

context ('kɒntɛkst) *n.* **1.** the parts of a piece of writing, speech, etc., that precede and follow a word or passage and contribute to its full meaning: *it is unfair to quote out of context.* **2.** the circumstances that are relevant to an event, fact, etc. —**con'textual** *adj.*

contiguous (kən'tɪɡjʊəs) *adj.* **1.** touching along the side or boundary; in contact. **2.** neighbouring. **3.** preceding or following in time. —**con'tiguously** *adv.*

continent[1] ('kɒntɪnənt) *n.* **1.** one of the earth's large land masses (Asia, Australia, Africa, Europe, North and South America, and Antarctica). **2.** *Obs.* **a.** mainland. **b.** a continuous extent of land. —**continental** (ˌkɒntɪ-'nɛntəl) *adj.*

continent[2] ('kɒntɪnənt) *adj.* **1.** able to control urination and defecation. **2.** exercising self-restraint, esp. from sexual activity; chaste. —**'continence** *n.*

Continent ('kɒntɪnənt) *n.* **the.** the mainland of Europe as distinguished from the British Isles.

Continental (ˌkɒntɪ'nɛntəl) *adj.* **1.** of or characteristic of Europe, excluding the British Isles. **2.** of or relating to the 13 original British North American colonies during the War of American Independence. ~*n.* **3.** (*sometimes not cap.*) an inhabitant of Europe, excluding the British Isles. **4.** a regular soldier of the rebel army during the War of American Independence.

continental breakfast *n.* a light breakfast of coffee and rolls.

continental climate *n.* a climate characterized by hot summers, cold winters, and little rainfall, typical of the interior of a continent.

continental drift *n. Geol.* the theory that the earth's continents move gradually over the surface of the planet on a substratum of magma.

continental quilt *n. Brit.* a quilt, stuffed with down, used as a bed cover in place of the top sheet and blankets. Also called: **duvet.**

continental shelf *n.* the sea bed surrounding a continent at depths of up to about 200 metres (100 fathoms), at the edge of which the **continental slope** drops steeply.

contingency (kən'tɪndʒənsɪ) *or* **contingence** (kən-'tɪndʒəns) *n., pl.* **-cies** *or* **-ces.** **1. a.** a possible but not very likely future event or condition. **b.** (*as modifier*): *a contingency plan.* **2.** something dependent on a possible future event. **3.** a fact, event, etc., incidental to something else. **4.** *Logic.* the state of being contingent. **5.** uncertainty. **6.** *Statistics.* **a.** the degree of association between theoretical and observed common frequencies of two graded or classified variables. **b.** (*as modifier*): *a contingency table.*

contingent (kən'tɪndʒənt) *adj.* **1.** (when *postpositive,* often foll. by *on* or *upon*) dependent on events, conditions, etc., not yet known; conditional. **2.** *Logic.* (of a

proposition) true under certain conditions, false under others; not logically necessary. **3.** happening by chance; accidental. **4.** uncertain. ~*n.* **5.** a part of a military force, parade, etc. **6.** a group distinguished by common interests, etc., that is part of a larger group. **7.** a chance occurrence.

continual (kən'tɪnjʊəl) *adj.* **1.** recurring frequently, esp. at regular intervals. **2.** occurring without interruption; continuous in time. —**con'tinually** *adv.*

continuance (kən'tɪnjʊəns) *n.* **1.** the act of continuing. **2.** the duration of an action, etc. **3.** *U.S.* the adjournment of a legal proceeding.

continuation (kənˌtɪnjʊ'eɪʃən) *n.* **1.** a part or thing added, esp. to a book or play; sequel. **2.** a renewal of an interrupted action, process, etc.; resumption. **3.** the act of continuing; prolongation.

continue (kən'tɪnjuː) *vb.* **-uing, -ued.** **1.** (when *tr., may take an infinitive*) to remain or cause to remain in a particular condition or place. **2.** (when *tr., may take an infinitive*) to carry on uninterruptedly (a course of action): *he continued running.* **3.** (when *tr., may take an infinitive*) to resume after an interruption: *we'll continue after lunch.* **4.** to prolong or be prolonged: *continue the chord until it meets the tangent.* **5.** (*tr.*) *Law, chiefly Scot.* to adjourn (legal proceedings). —**con'tinuer** *n.*

continuity (ˌkɒntɪ'njuːɪtɪ) *n., pl.* **-ties.** **1.** logical sequence. **2.** a continuous or connected whole. **3.** the comprehensive script or scenario of detail in a film or broadcast. **4.** the continuous projection of a film.

continuo (kən'tɪnjʊəʊ) *n., pl.* **-os.** **1.** *Music.* **a.** Also called: **basso continuo.** a continuous bass accompaniment played on a harpsichord or organ. **b.** (*as modifier*): *a continuo accompaniment.* **2.** the bass part as played on a keyboard instrument.

continuous (kən'tɪnjʊəs) *adj.* **1.** unceasing: *a continuous noise.* **2.** in an unbroken series or pattern. **3.** *Statistics.* (of a variable) having consecutive values that are infinitesimally close, so that its analysis requires integration rather than summation. **4.** *Grammar.* another word for **progressive** (sense 7). —**con'tinuously** *adv.* —**con'tinuousness** *n.*

continuum (kən'tɪnjʊəm) *n., pl.* **-tinua** (-'tɪnjʊə) *or* **-tinuums.** a continuous series or whole, no part of which is perceptibly different from the adjacent parts.

contort (kən'tɔːt) *vb.* to twist or bend out of place or shape. —**con'tortion** *n.* —**con'tortive** *adj.*

contortionist (kən'tɔːʃənɪst) *n.* **1.** a performer who contorts his body for the entertainment of others. **2.** a person who twists or warps meaning.

contour ('kɒntʊə) *n.* **1.** the outline of a mass of land, figure, or body; a defining line. **2. a.** See **contour line. b.** (*as modifier*): *a contour map.* **3.** (*often pl.*) the shape of a curving form: *the contours of her body were full and round.* ~*vb.* (*tr.*) **4.** to shape so as to form the contour of something. **5.** to mark contour lines on. **6.** to construct (a road, railway, etc.) to follow the outline of the land.

contour line *n.* a line on a map or chart joining points of equal height or depth.

contra- *prefix.* **1.** against; contrary; opposing; contrasting: *contraceptive.* **2.** (in music) pitched below: *contrabass.*

THESAURUS

contest *n.* **1.** competition, game, match, tournament, trial **2.** affray, altercation, battle, combat, conflict, controversy, debate, discord, dispute, encounter, fight, shock, struggle ~*v.* **3.** compete, contend, fight, fight over, strive, vie **4.** argue, call in *or* into question, challenge, debate, dispute, doubt, litigate, object to, oppose, question

contestant aspirant, candidate, competitor, contender, entrant, participant, player

context **1.** background, connection, frame of reference, framework, relation **2.** ambience, circumstances, conditions, situation

continent abstemious, abstinent, ascetic, austere, celibate, chaste, self-restrained, sober

contingency accident, chance, emergency, event, eventuality, fortuity, happening, incident, juncture, possibility, uncertainty

contingent *adj.* **1.** With **on** *or* **upon** conditional, controlled by, dependent, subject to **2.** accidental, casual, fortuitous, haphazard, random, uncertain ~*n.* **3.** batch, body, bunch (*Inf.*), deputation, detachment, group, mission, quota, section, set

continual constant, continuous, endless, eternal, everlasting, frequent, incessant, interminable, oft-repeated, perpetual, recurrent, regular, repeated, repetitive, unceasing, uninterrupted, unremitting

continually all the time, always, constantly, endlessly, eternally, everlastingly, forever, incessantly, interminably, nonstop, persistently, repeatedly

continuance continuation, duration, period, protraction, term

continuation **1.** addition, extension, furtherance, postscript, sequel, supplement **2.** maintenance, perpetuation, prolongation, resumption

continue **1.** abide, carry on, endure, last, live on, persist, remain, rest, stay, stay on, survive **2.** go on, keep at, keep on, keep the ball rolling, keep up, maintain, persevere, persist in, prolong, pursue, stick at, stick to, sustain **3.** draw out, extend, lengthen, project, prolong, reach **4.** carry on, pick up where one left off, proceed, recommence, resume, return to, take up

continuing enduring, in progress, lasting, ongoing, sustained

continuity cohesion, connection, flow, interrelationship, progression, sequence, succession, whole

continuous connected, constant, continued, extended, prolonged, unbroken, unceasing, undivided, uninterrupted

contour curve, figure, form, lines, outline, profile, relief, shape, silhouette

contraband ('kɒntrə,bænd) n. **1. a.** goods that are prohibited by law from being exported or imported. **b.** illegally imported or exported goods. **2.** illegal traffic in such goods; smuggling. **3.** Also called: **contraband of war.** goods that a neutral country may not supply to a belligerent. ~adj. **4.** (of goods) **a.** forbidden by law from being imported or exported. **b.** illegally imported or exported. —'**contra,bandist** n.

contraception (,kɒntrə'sɛpʃən) n. the intentional prevention of conception by artificial or natural means. —,**contra'ceptive** adj., n.

contract vb. (kən'trækt). **1.** to make or become smaller, narrower, shorter, etc. **2.** ('kɒntrækt). (when intr., sometimes foll. by for; when tr., may take an infinitive) to enter into an agreement with (a person, company, etc.) to deliver (goods or services) or to do (something) on mutually agreed terms. **3.** to draw or be drawn together. **4.** (tr.) to incur or become affected by (a disease, debt, etc.). **5.** (tr.) to shorten (a word or phrase) by the omission of letters or syllables, usually indicated in writing by an apostrophe. **6.** (tr.) (of the brow) to wrinkle. **7.** (tr.) to arrange (a marriage) for; betroth. ~n. ('kɒntrækt). **8.** a formal agreement between two or more parties. **9.** a document that states the terms of such an agreement. **10.** the branch of law treating of contracts. **11.** marriage considered as a formal agreement. **12.** See **contract bridge. 13.** Bridge. **a.** the highest bid, which determines trumps and the number of tricks one side must make. **b.** the number and suit of these tricks. —**con'tractible** adj.

contract bridge ('kɒntrækt) n. the most common variety of bridge, in which the declarer receives points counting towards game and rubber only for tricks he bids as well as makes. Cf. **auction bridge.**

contractile (kən'træktaɪl) adj. having the power to contract or to cause contraction.

contraction (kən'trækʃən) n. **1.** an instance of contracting or the state of being contracted. **2.** a shortening of a word or group of words, often marked by an apostrophe: I've come for I have come. —**con'tractive** adj.

contractor (kən'træktə) n. **1.** a person or firm that contracts to supply materials or labour, esp. for building. **2.** something that contracts.

contract out vb. (intr., adv.) Brit. to agree not to participate in something, esp. the state pension scheme.

contractual (kən'træktjʊəl) adj. of the nature of or assured by a contract.

contradict (,kɒntrə'dɪkt) vb. **1.** (tr.) to affirm the opposite of (a statement, etc.). **2.** (tr.) to declare (a statement, etc.) to be false or incorrect; deny. **3.** (tr.) to be inconsistent with: the facts contradicted his theory. **4.** (intr.) to be at variance; be in contradiction. —,**contra'dicter** or ,**contra'dictor** n. —,**contra'diction** n.

contradictory (,kɒntrə'dɪktərɪ) adj. **1.** inconsistent; incompatible. **2.** given to argument and contention: a contradictory person. **3.** Logic. (of a pair of propositions) unable to be both true or both false at once; mutually exclusive. —,**contra'dictorily** adv. —,**contra'dictoriness** n.

contradistinction (,kɒntrədɪ'stɪŋkʃən) n. a distinction

made by contrasting different qualities. —,**contradis'tinctive** adj.

contralto (kən'træltəʊ) n., pl. **-tos** or **-ti** (-tɪ). **1.** the alto voice of a female singer. **2.** a singer with such a voice. Cf. **alto.** ~adj. **3.** of or denoting a contralto: the contralto part.

contraption (kən'træpʃən) n. Inf., often facetious or derog. a device or contrivance, esp. one considered strange, unnecessarily intricate, or improvised.

contrapuntal (,kɒntrə'pʌntəl) adj. Music. characterized by counterpoint. —,**contra'puntally** adv. —,**contra'puntist** or ,**contra'puntalist** n.

contrariwise ('kɒntrərɪ,waɪz) adv. **1.** from a contrasting point of view. **2.** in the reverse way. **3.** (kən'trɛərɪ,waɪz). in a contrary manner.

contrary ('kɒntrərɪ) adj. **1.** opposed in nature, position, etc.: contrary ideas. **2.** (kən'trɛərɪ). perverse; obstinate. **3.** (esp. of wind) adverse; unfavourable. **4.** (of plant parts) situated at right angles to each other. **5.** Logic. (of a pair of propositions) related so they cannot both be true, although they may both be false. ~n., pl. **-ries. 6.** the exact opposite (esp. in **to the contrary**). **7. on the contrary.** quite the reverse. **8.** either of two exactly opposite objects, facts, or qualities. ~adv. (usually foll. by to) **9.** in an opposite or unexpected way: contrary to usual belief. **10.** in conflict (with): contrary to nature. —**con'trarily** adv. —**con'trariness** n.

contrast vb. (kən'trɑːst). **1.** (often foll. by with) to distinguish or be distinguished by comparison of unlike or opposite qualities. ~n. ('kɒntrɑːst). **2.** distinction by comparison of opposite or dissimilar things, qualities, etc. (esp. in **by contrast, in contrast to** or **with**). **3.** a person or thing showing differences when compared with another. **4.** the effect of the juxtaposition of different colours, tones, etc. **5.** the extent to which adjacent areas on a television screen differ in brightness. —**con'trastingly** adv. —**con'trastive** adj. —**con'trasty** adj.

contravene (,kɒntrə'viːn) vb. (tr.) **1.** to infringe (rules, laws, etc.). **2.** to dispute or contradict (a statement, proposition, etc.). —,**contra'vener** n. —**contravention** (,kɒntrə'vɛnʃən) n.

contretemps ('kɒntrə,tɑːn) n., pl. **-temps.** an awkward or difficult situation or mishap.

contribute (kən'trɪbjuːt) vb. (often foll. by to) **1.** to give (support, money, etc.) for a common purpose or fund. **2.** to supply (ideas, opinions, etc.). **3.** (intr.) to be partly responsible (for): drink contributed to the accident. **4.** to write (articles, etc.) for a publication. —,**contri'bution** n. —**con'tributive** adj. —**con'tributor** n. —**con'tributory** adj.

contrite (kən'traɪt, 'kɒntraɪt) adj. **1.** full of guilt or regret; remorseful. **2.** arising from a sense of shame or guilt: contrite promises. —**con'tritely** adv. —**con'triteness** or **contrition** (kən'trɪʃən) n.

contrivance (kən'traɪvəns) n. **1.** something contrived, esp. an ingenious device; contraption. **2.** inventive skill or ability. **3.** an artificial rather than natural arrangement of details, parts, etc. **4.** an elaborate or deceitful plan; stratagem.

THESAURUS

contraband 1. n. black-marketing, bootlegging, moonshine (U.S.), rum-running, smuggling, trafficking **2.** adj. banned, blackmarket, bootleg, bootlegged, forbidden, hot (Inf.), illegal, illicit, interdicted, prohibited, smuggled, unlawful

contract v. **1.** abbreviate, abridge, compress, condense, confine, constrict, curtail, dwindle, epitomize, lessen, narrow, purse, reduce, shrink, shrivel, tighten, wither, wrinkle **2.** agree, arrange, bargain, clinch, close, come to terms, commit oneself, covenant, engage, enter into, negotiate, pledge, stipulate **3.** acquire, be afflicted with, catch, develop, go down with (Inf.), incur ~n. **4.** agreement, arrangement, bargain, bond, commission, commitment, compact, concordat, convention, covenant, deal (Inf.), engagement, pact, settlement, stipulation, treaty, understanding

contraction abbreviation, compression, constriction, diminution, drawing in, elision, narrowing, reduction, shortening, shrinkage,

shrivelling, tensing, tightening

contradict be at variance with, belie, challenge, contravene, controvert, counter, counteract, deny, dispute, gainsay (Archaic), impugn, negate, oppose

contradiction conflict, confutation, contravention, denial, incongruity, inconsistency, negation, opposite

contradictory antagonistic, antithetical, conflicting, contrary, discrepant, incompatible, inconsistent, irreconcilable, opposed, opposite, paradoxical, repugnant

contraption apparatus, contrivance, device, gadget, mechanism, rig

contrary adj. **1.** adverse, antagonistic, clashing, contradictory, counter, discordant, hostile, inconsistent, inimical, opposed, opposite, paradoxical **2.** awkward, balky, cantankerous, cussed (Inf.), difficult, disobliging, froward, intractable, obstinate, perverse, stroppy (Brit. sl.), thrawn (Northern dialect), unaccommodating, wayward, wilful ~v. **3.** antithesis, converse, opposite, reverse **4.** on

the contrary conversely, in contrast, not at all, on the other hand, quite the opposite or reverse

contrast 1. n. comparison, contrariety, difference, differentiation, disparity, dissimilarity, distinction, divergence, foil, opposition **2.** v. compare, differ, differentiate, distinguish, oppose, set in opposition, set off

contribute 1. add, afford, bestow, chip in, donate, furnish, give, provide, subscribe, supply **2.** be conducive, be instrumental, be partly responsible for, conduce, help, lead, tend

contribution addition, bestowal, donation, gift, grant, input, offering, subscription

contributor 1. backer, bestower, conferrer, donor, giver, patron, subscriber, supporter **2.** correspondent, freelance, freelancer, journalist, reporter

contrite chastened, conscience-stricken, humble, in sackcloth and ashes, penitent, regretful, remorseful, repentant, sorrowful, sorry

contrive (kən'traɪv) vb. 1. (tr.) to manage (something or to do something), esp. by a trick: *he contrived to make them meet*. 2. (tr.) to think up or adapt ingeniously: *he contrived a new mast for the boat*. 3. to plot or scheme. —**con'triver** n.

control (kən'trəʊl) vb. **-trolling, -trolled.** (tr.) 1. to command, direct, or rule. 2. to check, limit, or restrain: *to control one's emotions*. 3. to regulate or operate (a machine). 4. to verify (a scientific experiment) by conducting a parallel experiment in which the variable being investigated is held constant or is compared with a standard. 5. a. to regulate (financial affairs). b. to examine (financial accounts). ~n. 6. power to direct: *under control*. 7. a curb; check: *a frontier control*. 8. (*often pl.*) a mechanism for operating a car, aircraft, etc. 9. a. a standard of comparison used in a statistical analysis, etc. b. (*as modifier*) *a control group*. 10. a. a device that regulates the operation of a machine. b. (*as modifier*): *control room*. —**con'trollable** adj. —**con,trolla'bility** n. —**con'trollably** adv.

controller (kən'trəʊlə) n. 1. a person who directs. 2. Also called: **comptroller.** a business executive or government officer responsible for financial planning, control, etc. 3. the equipment concerned with controlling the operation of an electrical device. —**con'troller,ship** n.

control tower n. a tower at an airport from which air traffic is controlled.

controversy ('kɒntrə,vɜːsɪ, kən'trɒv-) n., pl. **-sies.** dispute, argument, or debate, esp. one concerning a matter about which there is strong disagreement and esp. one carried on in public or in the press. —**controversial** (,kɒntrə'vɜːʃəl) adj. —,**contro'versial,ism** n. —,**contro'versialist** n. —**controvert** ('kɒntrə,vɜːt, ,kɒntrə'vɜːt) vb.

contumacy ('kɒntjʊməsɪ) n., pl. **-cies.** obstinate and wilful resistance to authority, esp. refusal to comply with a court order. —,**contu'macious** adj.

contumely ('kɒntjʊmɪlɪ) n., pl. **-lies.** 1. scornful or insulting language or behaviour. 2. a humiliating insult. —**contumelious** (,kɒntjʊ'miːlɪəs) adj. —,**contu'meliously** adv.

contuse (kən'tjuːz) vb. (tr.) to injure (the body) without breaking the skin; bruise. —**con'tusion** n.

conundrum (kə'nʌndrəm) n. 1. a riddle, esp. one whose answer makes a play on words. 2. a puzzling question or problem.

conurbation (,kɒnɜː'beɪʃən) n. a large densely populated urban sprawl formed by the growth and coalescence of individual towns or cities.

convalesce (,kɒnvə'lɛs) vb. (intr.) to recover from illness, injury, or the aftereffects of a surgical operation.

convalescence (,kɒnvə'lɛsəns) n. 1. gradual return to health after illness, injury, or an operation. 2. the period during which such recovery occurs. —,**conva'lescent** n., adj.

convection (kən'vɛkʃən) n. 1. the process of heat transfer caused by movement of molecules from cool regions to warmer regions of lower density. 2. *Meteorol.* the process by which masses of relatively warm air are raised into the atmosphere, often cooling and forming clouds, with compensatory downward movements of cooler air. —**con'vectional** adj. —**con'vective** adj.

convector (kən'vɛktə) n. a space-heating device from which heat is transferred to the surrounding air by convection.

convene (kən'viːn) vb. 1. to gather, call together or summon, esp. for a formal meeting. 2. (tr.) to order to appear before a court of law, judge, tribunal, etc. —**con'venable** adj.

convener or **convenor** (kən'viːnə) n. a person who convenes or chairs a meeting, committee, etc., esp. one who is specifically elected to do so: *a convener of shop stewards*.

convenience (kən'viːnɪəns) n. 1. the quality of being suitable or opportune. 2. a convenient time or situation. 3. **at your convenience.** at a time suitable to you. 4. usefulness, comfort, or facility. 5. an object that is useful, esp. a labour-saving device. 6. *Euphemistic, chiefly Brit.* a lavatory, esp. a public one. 7. **make a convenience of.** to take advantage of; impose upon.

convenient (kən'viːnɪənt) adj. 1. suitable; opportune. 2. easy to use. 3. close by; handy. —**con'veniently** adv.

convent ('kɒnvənt) n. 1. a building inhabited by a religious community, usually of nuns. 2. the religious community inhabiting such a building. 3. Also called: **convent school.** a school in which the teachers are nuns.

conventicle (kən'vɛntɪkəl) n. 1. a secret or unauthorized assembly for worship. 2. a small meeting house or chapel, esp. of Dissenters.

convention (kən'vɛnʃən) n. 1. a large formal assembly of a group with common interests, such as a trade union. 2. *U.S. politics.* an assembly of delegates of one party to select candidates for office. 3. an international agreement second only to a treaty in formality. 4. any agreement or contract. 5. the established view of what is thought to be proper behaviour, good taste, etc. 6. an accepted rule, usage, etc.: *a convention used by printers*. 7. *Bridge.* a bid or play not to be taken at its face value, which one's partner can interpret according to a prearranged bidding system.

conventional (kən'vɛnʃənəl) adj. 1. following the accepted customs and proprieties, esp. in a way that lacks originality. 2. established by accepted usage or general agreement. 3. of a convention or assembly. 4. *Visual arts.* conventionalized. 5. (of weapons, warfare, etc.) not nuclear. —**con'ventionalism** n. —**con'ventionally** adv.

conventionality (kən,vɛnʃə'nælɪtɪ) n., pl. **-ties.** 1. the quality of being conventional. 2. (*often pl.*) something conventional.

conventionalize or **-lise** (kən'vɛnʃənə,laɪz) vb. (tr.)

THESAURUS

contrivance 1. artifice, design, dodge, expedient, fabrication, formation, intrigue, inventiveness, machination, measure, plan, plot, project, ruse, scheme, stratagem, trick 2. apparatus, appliance, contraption, device, equipment, gadget, gear, implement, invention, machine, mechanism

contrive 1. concoct, construct, create, design, devise, engineer, fabricate, frame, improvise, invent, wangle (*Inf.*) 2. arrange, bring about, effect, hit upon, manage, manoeuvre, plan, plot, scheme, succeed

contrived artificial, elaborate, forced, laboured, overdone, planned, recherché, strained, unnatural

control v. 1. boss (*Inf.*), call the tune, command, conduct, direct, dominate, govern, have charge of, hold the purse strings, lead, manage, manipulate, oversee, pilot, reign over, rule, steer, superintend, supervise 2. bridle, check, constrain, contain, curb, hold back, limit, master, rein in, repress, restrain, subdue 3. *Used of a machine, an experiment, etc.* counteract, determine, monitor, regulate, verify ~n. 4. authority, charge, command, direction, discipline, government, guidance, jurisdiction, management, mastery, oversight, rule, superintendence, super-

vision, supremacy 5. brake, check, curb, limitation, regulation, restraint

controls console, control panel, dashboard, dials, instruments

controversial at issue, contended, contentious, controvertible, debatable, disputable, disputed, open to question, under discussion

controversy altercation, argument, contention, debate, discussion, dispute, dissension, polemic, quarrel, squabble, strife, wrangle, wrangling

convalescence improvement, recovery, recuperation, rehabilitation, return to health

convalescent adj. getting better, improving, mending, on the mend, recovering, recuperating

convene assemble, bring together, call, come together, congregate, convoke, gather, meet, muster, rally, summon

convenience 1. accessibility, appropriateness, availability, fitness, handiness, opportuneness, serviceability, suitability, usefulness, utility 2. *A convenient time or situation* chance, leisure, opportunity, spare moment, spare time 3. accommodation, advantage, benefit, comfort, ease, enjoyment, satis-

faction, service, use 4. *A useful device* amenity, appliance, comfort, facility, help, labour-saving device

convenient 1. adapted, appropriate, beneficial, commodious, fit, fitted, handy, helpful, labour-saving, opportune, seasonable, serviceable, suitable, suited, timely, useful, well-timed 2. accessible, at hand, available, close at hand, handy, just round the corner, nearby, within reach

convent convent school, nunnery, religious community

convention 1. assembly, conference, congress, convocation, council, delegates, meeting, representatives 2. code, custom, etiquette, formality, practice, propriety, protocol, tradition, usage 3. agreement, bargain, compact, concordat, contract, pact, protocol, stipulation, treaty

conventional 1. accepted, common, correct, customary, decorous, expected, formal, habitual, normal, ordinary, orthodox, prevailing, prevalent, proper, regular, ritual, standard, traditional, usual, wonted 2. bourgeois, commonplace, hackneyed, hidebound, pedestrian, prosaic, routine, run-of-the-mill, stereotyped, unoriginal

1. to make conventional. 2. to simplify or stylize (a design, decorative device, etc.). **—con,ventionali'zation** or **-li'sation** n.

converge (kən'vɜːdʒ) vb. 1. to move or cause to move towards the same point. 2. to meet or join. 3. (intr.) (of opinions, effects, etc.) to tend towards a common conclusion or result. 4. (intr.) Maths. (of an infinite series) to approach a finite limit as the number of terms increases. 5. (intr.) (of animals and plants) to undergo convergence. **—con'vergent** adj.

convergence (kən'vɜːdʒəns) n. 1. Also: **convergency.** the act, degree, or a point of converging. 2. Also called: **convergent evolution.** the evolutionary development of a superficial resemblance between unrelated animals that occupy a similar environment, as in the evolution of wings in birds and bats.

conversable (kən'vɜːsəbəl) adj. 1. easy or pleasant to talk to. 2. able or inclined to talk.

conversant (kən'vɜːsənt) adj. (usually postpositive and foll. by with) experienced (in), familiar (with), or acquainted (with). **—con'versance** or **con'versancy** n. **—con'versantly** adv.

conversation (,kɒnvə'seɪʃən) n. the interchange through speech of information, ideas, etc.; spoken communication.

conversational (,kɒnvə'seɪʃənəl) adj. 1. of, using, or in the manner of conversation. 2. inclined to conversation; conversable. **—,conver'sationalist** n. **—,conver'sationally** adv.

conversation piece n. 1. something, esp. an unusual object, that provokes conversation. 2. (esp. in 18th-century Britain) a group portrait in a landscape or domestic setting.

converse[1] vb. (kən'vɜːs). (intr.; often foll. by with) 1. to engage in conversation (with). 2. to commune spiritually (with). ~n. ('kɒnvɜːs). 3. conversation (often in **hold converse with**). **—con'verser** n.

converse[2] ('kɒnvɜːs) adj. 1. (prenominal) reversed; opposite; contrary. ~n. 2. something that is opposite or contrary. 3. Logic. a proposition inferred from another proposition by the transposition of the subject and predicate: "all bad men are bald" is the converse of "all bald men are bad". In the syllogism this can only be done non-accidentally with universal negative (no x's are y's) and particular affirmative (some x's are y's) propositions. **—con'versely** adv.

conversion (kən'vɜːʃən) n. 1. a. a change or adaptation in form, character, or function. b. something changed in one of these respects. 2. a change to another belief, as in a change of religion. 3. Maths. a change in the units or form of a number or expression: the conversion of miles to kilometres. 4. Rugby. a score made after a try by kicking the ball over the crossbar from a place kick. 5. Physics. a change of fertile material to fissile material in a reactor. 6. an alteration to a car engine to improve its performance.

convert vb. (kən'vɜːt). (mainly tr.) 1. to change or adapt the form, character, or function of. 2. to cause (someone) to change in opinion, belief, etc. 3. (intr.) to admit of being changed (into): the table converts into a tray. 4. (also intr.) to change or be changed into another state: to convert water into ice. 5. Law. to assume un-

lawful proprietary rights over (personal property). 6. (also intr.) Rugby. to make a conversion after (a try). 7. Logic. to transpose the subject and predicate of (a proposition). 8. to change (a value or measurement) from one system of units to another. 9. to exchange (a security or bond) for something of equivalent value. ~n. ('kɒnvɜːt). 10. a person who has been converted to another belief, religion, etc.

converter or **convertor** (kən'vɜːtə) n. 1. a person or thing that converts. 2. Physics. a. a device for converting alternating current to direct current or vice versa. b. a device for converting a signal from one frequency to another. 3. a vessel in which molten metal is refined, using a blast of air or oxygen.

convertible (kən'vɜːtəbəl) adj. 1. capable of being converted. 2. (of a car) having a folding or removable roof. 3. Finance. a. (of a currency) freely exchangeable into other currencies. b. (of a paper currency) exchangeable on demand for precious metal to an equivalent value. ~n. 4. a car with a folding or removable roof. **—con,verti'bility** n. **—con'vertibly** adv.

convex ('kɒnvɛks, kɒn'vɛks) adj. 1. curving outwards. 2. having one or two surfaces curved or ground in the shape of a section of the exterior of a sphere, ellipsoid, etc.: a convex lens. **—con'vexity** n. **—'convexly** adv.

convey (kən'veɪ) vb. (tr.) 1. to take, carry, or transport from one place to another. 2. to communicate (a message, information, etc.). 3. (of a channel, path, etc.) to conduct or transfer. 4. Law. to transfer (the title to property). **—con'veyable** adj.

conveyance (kən'veɪəns) n. 1. the act of conveying. 2. a means of transport. 3. Law. a. a transfer of the legal title to property. b. the document effecting such a transfer. **—con'veyancer** n. **—con'veyancing** n.

conveyor or **conveyer** (kən'veɪə) n. 1. a person or thing that conveys. 2. short for **conveyor belt.**

conveyor belt n. a flexible endless strip of fabric or linked plates driven by rollers and used to transport objects, esp. in a factory.

convict vb. (kən'vɪkt). (tr.) 1. to pronounce (someone) guilty of an offence. ~n. ('kɒnvɪkt). 2. a person found guilty of an offence against the law. 3. a person serving a prison sentence.

conviction (kən'vɪkʃən) n. 1. the state of being convinced. 2. a firmly held belief, opinion, etc. 3. the act of convincing. 4. the act of convicting or the state of being convicted. 5. **carry conviction.** to be convincing. **—con'victional** adj. **—con'victive** adj.

convince (kən'vɪns) vb. (tr.) (may take a clause as object) to make (someone) agree, understand, or realize the truth or validity of something; persuade. **—con'vincer** n. **—con'vincible** adj. **—con'vincing** adj.

convivial (kən'vɪvɪəl) adj. sociable; jovial or festive: a convivial atmosphere. **—con,vivi'ality** n.

convocation (,kɒnvə'keɪʃən) n. 1. a large formal assembly. 2. the act of convoking or state of being convoked. 3. Church of England. either of the synods of the provinces of Canterbury or York. 4. Episcopal Church. an assembly of the clergy and part of the laity of a diocese. 5. (sometimes cap.) (in some British universities) a legislative assembly. **—,convo'cational** adj.

convoke (kən'vəʊk) vb. (tr.) to call (a meeting, assem-

THESAURUS

converge coincide, combine, come together, concentrate, focus, gather, join, meet, merge, mingle

conversant Usually with **with** acquainted, au fait, experienced, familiar, knowledgeable, practised, proficient, skilled, versed, well-informed, well up in (Inf.)

conversation chat, chinwag (Brit. inf.), colloquy, communication, communion, confab (Inf.), confabulation, conference, converse, dialogue, discourse, discussion, exchange, gossip, intercourse, powwow, talk, tête-à-tête

conversational chatty, colloquial, communicative, informal

converse 1. n. antithesis, contrary, obverse, opposite, other side of the coin, reverse 2. adj. contrary, counter, opposite, reverse, reversed, transposed

conversion 1. change, metamorphosis, transfiguration, transformation, transmogri-

fication (Jocular), transmutation 2. adaptation, alteration, modification, reconstruction, remodelling, reorganization 3. change of heart, proselytization, rebirth, reformation, regeneration

convert[1] v. 1. alter, change, interchange, metamorphose, transform, transmogrify (Jocular), transmute, transpose, turn 2. adapt, apply, appropriate, modify, remodel, reorganize, restyle, revise 3. baptize, bring to God, convince, proselytize, reform, regenerate, save

convert[2] n. catechumen, disciple, neophyte, proselyte

convex bulging, gibbous, outcurved, protuberant, rounded

convey 1. bear, bring, carry, conduct, fetch, forward, grant, guide, move, send, support, transmit, transport 2. communicate, disclose, impart, make known, relate, reveal, tell 3. Law bequeath, cede, deliver, demise,

devolve, grant, lease, transfer, will

conveyance 1. carriage, movement, transfer, transference, transmission, transport, transportation 2. transport, vehicle

convict 1. v. condemn, find guilty, imprison, pronounce guilty, sentence 2. n. con (Sl.), criminal, culprit, felon, jailbird, malefactor, old lag (Sl.), prisoner

conviction 1. assurance, certainty, certitude, confidence, earnestness, fervour, firmness, reliance 2. belief, creed, faith, opinion, persuasion, principle, tenet, view

convince assure, bring round, gain the confidence of, persuade, prevail upon, prove to, satisfy, sway, win over

convincing cogent, conclusive, credible, impressive, incontrovertible, likely, persuasive, plausible, powerful, probable, telling

bly, etc.) together; summon. **—con'voker** n.

convolute ('kɒnvə,luːt) vb. (tr.) 1. to form into a twisted, coiled, or rolled shape. ~adj. 2. Bot. rolled longitudinally upon itself: a convolute petal.

convoluted ('kɒnvə,luːtɪd) adj. 1. (esp. of meaning, style, etc.) difficult to comprehend; involved. 2. coiled. —'convo,lutedly adv.

convolution (,kɒnvə'luːʃən) n. 1. a turn, twist, or coil. 2. an intricate or confused matter or condition. 3. any of the numerous convex folds of the surface of the brain. —,convo'lutional or ,convo'lutionary adj.

convolve (kən'vɒlv) vb. to wind or roll together; coil; twist.

convolvulus (kən'vɒlvjuləs) n., pl. -luses or -li (-,laɪ). a twining herbaceous plant having funnel-shaped flowers and triangular leaves.

convoy ('kɒnvɔɪ) n. 1. a group of merchant ships with an escort of warships. 2. a group of land vehicles assembled to travel together. 3. the act of travelling or escorting by convoy (esp. in **in convoy**). ~vb. 4. (tr.) to escort while in transit.

convulse (kən'vʌls) vb. 1. (tr.) to shake or agitate violently. 2. (tr.) to cause (muscles) to undergo violent spasms or contractions. 3. (intr.; often foll. by with) Inf. to shake or be overcome (with violent emotion, esp. laughter). —con'vulsive adj.

convulsion (kən'vʌlʃən) n. 1. a violent involuntary muscular contraction. 2. a violent upheaval, esp. a social one. 3. (usually pl.) Inf. uncontrollable laughter: I was in convulsions.

cony or **coney** ('kəʊnɪ) n., pl. -nies or -neys. a rabbit or fur made from the skin of a rabbit.

coo (kuː) vb. **cooing, cooed.** 1. (intr.) (of doves, pigeons, etc.) to make a characteristic soft throaty call. 2. (tr.) to speak in a soft murmur. 3. (intr.) to murmur lovingly (esp. in **bill and coo**). ~n. 4. the sound of cooing. ~interj. 5. Brit. sl. an exclamation of surprise, awe, etc. —'cooingly adv.

cooee or **cooey** ('kuːiː) interj. 1. a call used to attract attention, esp. a long loud high-pitched call on two notes. ~n. 2. Austral. & N.Z. inf. calling distance (esp. in **within (a) cooee (of)**). ~vb. **cooeeing, cooeed** or **cooeying, cooeyed.** 3. (intr.) to utter this call.

cook (kuk) vb. 1. to prepare (food) by the action of heat, or (of food) to become ready for eating through such a process. Related adj.: **culinary.** 2. to subject or be subjected to intense heat: the town cooked in the sun. 3. (tr.) Sl. to alter or falsify (figures, accounts, etc.): to cook the books. 4. (tr.) Sl. to spoil (something). 5. (intr.) Sl. to happen (esp. in **what's cooking?**). 6. Inf. **cook someone's goose. a.** to spoil a person's plans. **b.** to bring about someone's downfall. ~n. 7. a person who prepares food for eating. ~See also **cook up.** —'cookable adj.

cooker ('kukə) n. 1. an apparatus heated by gas, electricity, oil, or solid fuel, for cooking food. 2. Brit. any large sour apple used in cooking.

cookery ('kukərɪ) n. 1. the art, study, or practice of cooking. 2. U.S. a place for cooking.

cookery book or (esp. U.S.) **cookbook** ('kuk,buk) n. a book containing recipes.

cookie or **cooky** ('kukɪ) n., pl. -ies. 1. the U.S. word for biscuit. 2. Inf., chiefly U.S. a person: smart cookie. 3. **that's the way the cookie crumbles.** Inf., chiefly U.S. matters are inevitably so.

cook up vb. (tr., adv.) 1. Inf. to concoct or invent (a story, alibi, etc.). 2. to prepare (a meal), esp. quickly. 3. Sl. to prepare (a drug) for use by heating, as by dissolving heroin in a spoon.

cool (kuːl) adj. 1. moderately cold: a cool day. 2. comfortably free of heat: a cool room. 3. calm: a cool head. 4. lacking in enthusiasm, cordiality, etc.: a cool welcome. 5. calmly impudent. 6. Inf. (of sums of money, etc.) without exaggeration; actual: a cool ten thousand. 7. (of a colour) having violet, blue, or green predominating; cold. 8. (of jazz) economical and rhythmically relaxed. 9. Inf. sophisticated or elegant; unruffled. 10. Inf., chiefly U.S. marvellous. ~n. 11. coolness: the cool of the evening. 12. Sl. calmness; composure (esp. in **keep one's cool**). 13. Sl. unruffled elegance or sophistication. ~vb. 14. (usually foll. by down or off) to make or become cooler. 15. (usually foll. by down or off) to lessen the intensity of (anger or excitement) or (of anger or excitement) to become less intense; calm down. 16. **cool it.** (usually imperative) Sl., chiefly U.S. to calm down. 17. **cool one's heels.** to be kept waiting. —'coolly adv. —'coolness n.

coolant ('kuːlənt) n. 1. a fluid used to cool a system or to transfer heat from one part of it to another. 2. a liquid used to lubricate and cool the workpiece and cutting tool during machining.

cool drink n. S. African. a soft drink.

cooler ('kuːlə) n. 1. a container, vessel, or apparatus for cooling, such as a heat exchanger. 2. a slang word for **prison.**

coolie or **cooly** ('kuːlɪ) n., pl. -ies. an unskilled Oriental labourer.

cooling tower n. a tall, hollow structure, designed to permit free passage of air, inside which hot water trickles down, becoming cool as it does so: the water is normally reused as part of an industrial process.

coomb, combe, coombe, or **comb** (kuːm) n. Chiefly southeastern Brit. a short valley or deep hollow.

coon (kuːn) n. 1. Inf. short for **raccoon.** 2. Derog. sl. a Negro or Australian Aborigine.

coop[1] (kuːp) n. 1. a cage or small enclosure for poultry or small animals. 2. a small narrow place of confinement, esp. a prison cell. 3. a wicker basket for catching fish. ~vb. 4. (tr.; often foll. by up or in) to confine in a restricted area.

coop[2] or **co-op** ('kəʊ,ɒp) n. a cooperative society or a shop run by a cooperative society.

cooper ('kuːpə) n. 1. a person skilled in making and repairing barrels, casks, etc. ~vb. 2. (tr.) to make or mend (barrels, casks, etc.). —'cooperage n.

cooperate or **co-operate** (kəʊ'ɒpə,reɪt) vb. (intr.) 1. to work or act together. 2. to be of assistance or be willing to assist. 3. Econ. to engage in economic cooperation. —co'oper,ator or co-'oper,ator n. —co-,ope'ration or co-,ope'ration n.

cooperative or **co-operative** (kəʊ'ɒpərətɪv, -'ɒprə-) adj. 1. willing to cooperate; helpful. 2. acting in conjunction with others; cooperating. 3. **a.** (of an enterprise, farm, etc.) owned collectively and managed for joint economic benefit. **b.** (of an economy) based on collective ownership and cooperative use of the means of production and distribution. ~n. 4. a cooperative organization, such as a farm.

cooperative society n. a commercial enterprise owned and managed by and for the benefit of customers or workers.

THESAURUS

convoy 1. n. armed guard, attendance, attendant, escort, guard, protection 2. v. accompany, attend, escort, guard, pilot, protect, shepherd, usher

convulse agitate, churn up, derange, disorder, disturb, shake, shatter, twist, work

convulsion 1. agitation, commotion, disturbance, furore, shaking, tumult, turbulence, upheaval 2. contortion, contraction, cramp, fit, paroxysm, seizure, spasm, throe (Rare), tremor

cook up concoct, contrive, devise, fabricate, improvise, invent, plot, prepare, scheme

cool adj. 1. chilled, chilling, chilly, coldish, nippy, refreshing 2. calm, collected, composed, deliberate, dispassionate, imperturb-

able, level-headed, placid, quiet, relaxed, self-controlled, self-possessed, serene, together (Sl.), unemotional, unexcited, unruffled 3. aloof, apathetic, distant, frigid, incurious, indifferent, lukewarm, offhand, reserved, standoffish, uncommunicative, unconcerned, unenthusiastic, unfriendly, uninterested, unresponsive, unwelcoming 4. audacious, bold, brazen, cheeky, impertinent, impudent, presumptuous, shameless 5. Inf. cosmopolitan, elegant, sophisticated, urbane ~v. 6. chill, cool off, freeze, lose heat, refrigerate 7. abate, allay, assuage, calm (down), dampen, lessen, moderate, quiet, temper ~n. 8. Sl. calmness, composure, control, poise, self-control, self-discipline, self-possession, temper

coop 1. n. box, cage, enclosure, hutch, pen 2. v. cage, confine, immure, imprison, pen, shut up

cooperate abet, aid, assist, collaborate, combine, concur, conduce, conspire, contribute, coordinate, go along with, help, join forces, pitch in, play ball (Inf.), pool resources, pull together, work together

cooperation assistance, collaboration, combined effort, concert, concurrence, esprit de corps, give-and-take, helpfulness, participation, responsiveness, teamwork, unity

cooperative 1. accommodating, helpful, obliging, responsive, supportive 2. coactive, collective, combined, concerted, coordinated, joint, shared, unified, united

coopt or **co-opt** (kəʊˈɒpt) vb. (tr.) to add (someone) to a committee, board, etc., by the agreement of the existing members. —**coˈoption, coˈoption** or ˌ**coopˈtation,** ˌ**co-opˈtation** n.

coordinate or **co-ordinate** vb. (kəʊˈɔːdɪˌneɪt). 1. (tr.) to integrate diverse elements in a harmonious operation. 2. to place (things) in the same class, or (of things) to be placed in the same class, etc. 3. (intr.) to work together harmoniously. 4. (intr.) to take or be in the form of a harmonious order. ~n. (kəʊˈɔːdɪnɪt). 5. Maths. any of a set of numbers that defines the location of a point with reference to a system of axes. 6. a person or thing equal in rank, type, etc. ~adj. (kəʊˈɔːdɪnɪt). 7. of or involving coordination. 8. of the same rank, type, etc. 9. of or involving the use of coordinates: coordinate geometry. 10. Chem. denoting a type of covalent bond in which both the shared electrons are provided by one of the atoms. —**coˈordinative** or **co-ˈordinative** adj. —**coˈordiˌnator** or **co-ˈordiˌnator** n. —**coˌordiˈnation** or **co-ˌordiˈnation** n.

coordinates (kəʊˈɔːdɪnɪts) pl. n. clothes of matching or harmonious colours and design, suitable for wearing together.

coot (kuːt) n. 1. an aquatic bird of Europe and Asia, having dark plumage, and a white bill with a frontal shield: family Rallidae (rails, etc.). 2. a foolish person, esp. an old man.

cop[1] (kɒp) Sl. ~n. 1. another name for **policeman.** 2. Brit. an arrest (esp. in **a fair cop).** ~vb. **copping, copped.** (tr.) 3. to catch. 4. to steal. 5. to suffer (a punishment, etc.): you'll cop a clout if you do that! 6. Sl. **cop this!** just look at this! ~See also **cop out.**

cop[2] (kɒp) n. Brit. sl. (usually used with a negative) value: not much cop.

copal (ˈkəʊpəl, -pæl) n. a hard aromatic resin obtained from various tropical trees and used in making varnishes and lacquers.

copartner (kəʊˈpɑːtnə) n. a partner or associate, esp. an equal partner in business.

cope[1] (kəʊp) vb. 1. (intr.; foll. by with) to contend (against). 2. (intr.) to deal successfully with; manage: she coped well with the problem.

cope[2] (kəʊp) n. 1. a large ceremonial cloak worn at liturgical functions by priests of certain Christian sects. 2. any covering shaped like a cope. ~vb. 3. (tr.) to dress (someone) in a cope.

cope[3] (kəʊp) vb. (tr.) 1. to provide (a wall, etc.) with a coping. ~n. 2. another name for **coping.**

copeck (ˈkəʊpɛk) n. a variant spelling of **kopeck.**

Copernican system (kəˈpɜːnɪkən) n. the theory published in 1543 by Copernicus which stated that the earth and the planets rotated around the sun.

copestone (ˈkəʊpˌstəʊn) n. 1. Also called: **coping stone.** a stone used to form a coping. 2. the stone at the top of a building, wall, etc.

copier (ˈkɒpɪə) n. a person or device that copies.

copilot (ˈkəʊˌpaɪlət) n. a second or relief pilot of an aircraft.

coping (ˈkəʊpɪŋ) n. the sloping top course of a wall, usually made of masonry or brick.

coping saw n. a handsaw with a U-shaped frame used for cutting curves in a material too thick for a fret saw.

copious (ˈkəʊpɪəs) adj. 1. abundant; extensive. 2. having an abundant supply. 3. full of words, ideas, etc.; profuse. —**ˈcopiously** adv. —**ˈcopiousness** n.

cop out U.S. & N.Z. sl. vb. (intr., adv.) to fail to assume responsibility or to fail to perform.

copper[1] (ˈkɒpə) n. 1. a malleable reddish metallic element occurring as the free metal, copper glance, and copper pyrites: used in such alloys as brass and bronze. Symbol: Cu; atomic no.: 29; atomic wt.: 63.54. Related adjs.: **cupric, cuprous.** 2. the reddish-brown colour of copper. 3. Inf. any copper or bronze coin. 4. Chiefly Brit. a large vessel, formerly of copper, used for boiling or washing. 5. any of various small widely distributed butterflies having reddish-brown wings. ~vb. 6. (tr.) to coat or cover with copper.

copper[2] (ˈkɒpə) n. a slang word for **policeman.** Often shortened to **cop.**

copper-bottomed adj. reliable, esp. financially reliable.

copperhead (ˈkɒpəˌhɛd) n. 1. a venomous pit viper of the U.S., with a reddish-brown head. 2. a venomous marsh snake of Australia, with a reddish band behind the head.

copperplate (ˈkɒpəˌpleɪt) n. 1. a polished copper plate on which a design has been etched or engraved. 2. a print taken from such a plate. 3. a fine handwriting based upon that used on copperplate engravings.

coppersmith (ˈkɒpəˌsmɪθ) n. a person who works in copper.

copper sulphate n. a copper salt found naturally and made by the action of sulphuric acid on copper oxide: used as a mordant, in electroplating, and in plant sprays. Formula: $CuSO_4$.

coppice (ˈkɒpɪs) n. another word (esp. Brit.) for **copse.** —**ˈcoppiced** adj.

copra (ˈkɒprə) n. the dried, oil-yielding kernel of the coconut.

copro- or before a vowel **copr-** combining form. indicating dung or obscenity, as in **copˈrology** n. preoccupation with excrement, **copˈrophagous** adj. feeding on dung.

copse (kɒps) n. a thicket or dense growth of small trees or bushes.

Copt (kɒpt) n. 1. a member of the Coptic Church. 2. an Egyptian descended from the ancient Egyptians.

Coptic (ˈkɒptɪk) n. 1. an Afro-Asiatic language, written in the Greek alphabet but descended from ancient Egyptian. Extinct as a spoken language, it survives in the Coptic Church. ~adj. 2. of this language. 3. of the Copts.

copula (ˈkɒpjʊlə) n., pl. **-las** or **-lae** (-ˌliː). 1. a verb, such as be, seem, or taste, that is used to identify or link the subject with the complement of a sentence, as in he became king, sugar tastes sweet. 2. anything that serves as a link. —**ˈcopular** adj.

copulate (ˈkɒpjʊˌleɪt) vb. (intr.) to perform sexual intercourse. —ˌ**copuˈlation** n. —**ˈcopulatory** adj.

copy (ˈkɒpɪ) n., pl. **copies.** 1. an imitation or reproduction of an original. 2. a single specimen of something that occurs in a multiple edition, such as a book. 3. a. matter to be reproduced in print. b. written matter or text as distinct from graphic material in books, etc. 4. Journalism, inf. suitable material for an article: disasters are always good copy. 5. Arch. a model to be copied, esp. an example of penmanship. ~vb. **copying, copied.** 6. (when tr., often foll. by out) to make a copy of. 7. to imitate as a model. 8. (intr.) to imitate unfairly.

copybook (ˈkɒpɪˌbʊk) n. 1. a book of specimens, esp. of penmanship, for imitation. 2. Chiefly U.S. a book for or containing documents. 3. **blot one's copybook.** Inf. to sully one's reputation. 4. (modifier) trite or unoriginal.

copycat (ˈkɒpɪˌkæt) n. Inf. a person, esp. a child, who imitates or copies another.

copyhold (ˈkɒpɪˌhəʊld) n. Law. (formerly) a tenure less than freehold of land in England evidenced by a copy of the Court roll.

copyist (ˈkɒpɪɪst) n. 1. a person who makes written copies. 2. a person who imitates.

copyright (ˈkɒpɪˌraɪt) n. 1. the exclusive right to produce copies and to control an original literary, musical, or artistic work, granted by law for a specified number of years. ~adj. 2. (of a work, etc.) subject to copyright. ~vb. 3. (tr.) to take out a copyright on.

THESAURUS

coordinate 1. v. correlate, harmonize, integrate, match, mesh, organize, relate, synchronize, systematize 2. adj. coequal, correlative, correspondent, equal, equivalent, parallel, tantamount

cope 1. carry on, get by (Inf.), hold one's own, make out (Inf.), make the grade, manage, rise to the occasion, struggle through, survive 2. **cope with** contend, deal, dispatch, encounter, grapple, handle, struggle, tangle, tussle, weather, wrestle

copious abundant, ample, bounteous, bountiful, extensive, exuberant, full, generous, lavish, liberal, luxuriant, overflowing, plenteous, plentiful, profuse, rich, superabundant

copy n. 1. archetype, carbon copy, counterfeit, duplicate, facsimile, forgery, image, imitation, likeness, model, pattern, photocopy, Photostat (Trademark), print, replica, replication, representation, reproduction, transcription, Xerox (Trademark) ~v. 2. counterfeit, duplicate, photocopy, Photostat (Trademark), replicate, reproduce, transcribe, Xerox (Trademark) 3. ape, echo, emulate, follow, follow suit, follow the example of, imitate, mimic, mirror, parrot, repeat, simulate

copy typist *n.* a typist whose job is to type from written or typed drafts rather than dictation.

copywriter ('kɒpɪˌraɪtə) *n.* a person employed to write advertising copy. —'**copy,writing** *n.*

coquette (kəʊ'kɛt, kɒ'kɛt) *n.* 1. a woman who flirts. 2. any humming bird of the genus *Lophornis*. —co'**quettish** *adj.* —co'**quettishness** *n.*

Cor. *Bible. abbrev. for* Corinthians.

coracle ('kɒrəkəl) *n.* a small roundish boat made of waterproofed hides stretched over a wicker frame.

coral ('kɒrəl) *n.* 1. any of a class of marine colonial coelenterates having a calcareous, horny, or soft skeleton. 2. a. the calcareous or horny material forming the skeleton of certain of these animals. b. (*as modifier*): *a coral necklace.* 3. a rocklike aggregation of certain of these animals or their skeletons, forming an island or reef. 4. a yellowish-pink colour. 5. the roe of a lobster or crab, which becomes pink when cooked.

cor anglais ('kɔːr 'ɑːŋgleɪ) *n., pl.* **cors anglais** ('kɔːz 'ɑːŋgleɪ). *Music.* a woodwind instrument, the alto of the oboe family. Also called: **English horn.**

corbel ('kɔːbəl) *Archit.* ~*n.* 1. a bracket, usually of stone or brick. ~*vb.* -**belling**, -**belled** *or U.S.* -**beling**, -**beled**. 2. (*tr.*) to lay (a stone) so that it forms a corbel.

corbie ('kɔːbɪ) *n.* a Scot. name for **raven** or **crow**[1].

cord (kɔːd) *n.* 1. string or thin rope made of twisted strands. 2. a length of woven or twisted strands of silk, etc., used as a belt, etc. 3. a ribbed fabric, esp. corduroy. 4. the U.S. name for **flex** (sense 1). 5. *Anat.* any part resembling a rope: *the spinal cord.* 6. a unit for measuring cut wood, equal to 128 cubic feet. ~*vb.* (*tr.*) 7. to bind or furnish with a cord or cords. —'**cord,like** *adj.*

cordate ('kɔːdeɪt) *adj.* heart-shaped.

corded ('kɔːdɪd) *adj.* 1. bound or fastened with cord. 2. (of a fabric) ribbed. 3. (of muscles) standing out like cords.

cordial ('kɔːdɪəl) *adj.* 1. warm and friendly: *a cordial greeting.* 2. stimulating. ~*n.* 3. a nonalcoholic drink with a fruit base: *lime cordial.* 4. another word for **liqueur.** —'**cordially** *adv.*

cordiality (ˌkɔːdɪ'ælɪtɪ) *n., pl.* -**ties.** warmth of feeling.

cordite ('kɔːdaɪt) *n.* any of various explosive materials containing cellulose nitrate, sometimes mixed with nitroglycerin.

cordon ('kɔːdən) *n.* 1. a chain of police, soldiers, ships, etc., stationed around an area. 2. a ribbon worn as insignia of honour. 3. a cord or ribbon worn as an ornament. 4. *Archit.* another name for **string course.** 5. *Horticulture.* a fruit tree consisting of a single stem bearing fruiting spurs, produced by cutting back all lateral branches. ~*vb.* 6. (*tr.; often foll. by off*) to put or form a cordon (around); close (off).

cordon bleu (*French* kɔrdɔ̃ 'blø) *n.* 1. *French history.* the sky-blue ribbon worn by members of the highest order of knighthood under the Bourbon monarchy. 2. any very high distinction. ~*adj.* 3. of or denoting food prepared to a very high standard.

cordon sanitaire *French.* (kɔrdɔ̃ saniˈtɛːr) *n.* 1. a guarded line isolating an infected area. 2. a line of buffer states shielding a country.

cordovan ('kɔːdəvən) *n.* a fine leather now made principally from horsehide.

cords (kɔːdz) *pl. n.* trousers, esp. jeans, made of corduroy.

corduroy ('kɔːdəˌrɔɪ, ˌkɔːdə'rɔɪ) *n.* a heavy cotton pile fabric with lengthways ribs.

corduroys (ˌkɔːdə'rɔɪz, 'kɔːdəˌrɔɪz) *pl. n.* trousers or breeches of corduroy.

cordwainer ('kɔːdˌweɪnə) *n. Arch.* a shoemaker or worker in leather.

core (kɔː) *n.* 1. the central part of certain fleshy fruits, such as the apple, consisting of the seeds. 2. the central or essential part of something: *the core of the argument.* 3. a piece of magnetic material, such as soft iron, inside an electromagnet or transformer. 4. *Geol.* the central part of the earth. 5. a cylindrical sample of rock, soil, etc., obtained by the use of a hollow drill. 6. *Physics.* the

region of a nuclear reactor in which the reaction takes place. 7. *Computers.* a. a ferrite ring used in a computer memory to store one bit of information. b. the whole memory of a computer when made up of such rings. c. (*as modifier*): *core memory.* 8. *Archaeol.* a stone or flint from which flakes have been removed. ~*vb.* 9. (*tr.*) to remove the core from (fruit).

co-respondent (ˌkəʊrɪ'spɒndənt) *n. Law.* a person cited in divorce proceedings, alleged to have committed adultery with the respondent.

corgi ('kɔːgɪ) *n.* either of two short-legged sturdy breeds of dog, the Cardigan and the Pembroke.

coriander (ˌkɒrɪ'ændə) *n.* 1. a European umbelliferous plant, cultivated for its aromatic seeds. 2. the dried seeds of this plant used in flavouring food, etc.

Corinthian (kə'rɪnθɪən) *adj.* 1. of Corinth. 2. denoting one of the five classical orders of architecture: characterized by a bell-shaped capital having carved ornaments based on acanthus leaves. 3. *Obs.* given to luxury; dissolute. ~*n.* 4. a native or inhabitant of Corinth.

cork (kɔːk) *n.* 1. the thick light porous outer bark of the cork oak. 2. a piece of cork used as a stopper. 3. an angling float. 4. Also called: **phellem.** *Bot.* a protective layer of dead impermeable cells on the outside of the stems and roots of woody plants. ~*vb.* (*tr.*) 5. to stop up (a bottle, etc.) with or as with a cork. 6. (often foll. by *up*) to restrain. 7. to black (the face, hands, etc.) with burnt cork. —'**cork,like** *adj.*

corkage ('kɔːkɪdʒ) *n.* a charge made at a restaurant for serving wine, etc., bought off the premises.

corked (kɔːkt) *adj.* tainted through having a cork containing excess tannin.

corker ('kɔːkə) *n. Old-fashioned sl.* 1. something or somebody striking or outstanding. 2. an irrefutable remark that puts an end to discussion.

corkscrew ('kɔːkˌskruː) *n.* 1. a device for drawing corks from bottles, typically consisting of a pointed metal spiral attached to a handle or screw mechanism. 2. (*modifier*) resembling a corkscrew in shape. ~*vb.* 3. to move or cause to move in a spiral or zigzag course.

corm (kɔːm) *n.* an organ of vegetative reproduction in plants such as the crocus, consisting of a globular stem base swollen with food and surrounded by papery scale leaves.

cormorant ('kɔːmərənt) *n.* an aquatic bird having a dark plumage, a long neck and body, and a slender hooked beak.

corn[1] (kɔːn) *n.* 1. *Brit.* a. any of various cereal plants, esp. the predominant crop of a region, such as wheat in England and oats in Scotland. b. the seeds of such plants, esp. after harvesting. c. a single seed of such plants; a grain. 2. the usual U.S., Austral, & N.Z. name for **maize.** 3. *Sl.* an idea, song, etc., regarded as banal or sentimental. ~*vb.* (*tr.*) 4. a. to preserve in brine. b. to salt.

corn[2] (kɔːn) *n.* 1. a hardening of the skin, esp. of the toes, caused by pressure. 2. **tread on (someone's) corns.** *Brit. inf.* to hurt someone's feelings.

corncob ('kɔːnˌkɒb) *n.* the core of an ear of maize, to which kernels are attached.

corncrake ('kɔːnˌkreɪk) *n.* a common Eurasian rail with a buff speckled plumage and reddish wings.

cornea ('kɔːnɪə) *n., pl.* -**neas** (-nɪəz) *or* -**neae** (-nɪˌiː). the convex transparent membrane that forms the anterior covering of the eyeball. —'**corneal** *adj.*

corned (kɔːnd) *adj.* (esp. of beef) cooked and then preserved or pickled in salt or brine.

cornel ('kɔːnəl) *n.* any plant of the genus *Cornus*, such as the dogwood.

cornelian (kɔː'niːlɪən) *n.* a variant spelling of **carnelian.**

corner ('kɔːnə) *n.* 1. the place or angle formed by the meeting of two converging lines or surfaces. 2. a projecting angle of a solid object. 3. the place where two streets meet. 4. any small, secluded, or private place. 5. a dangerous position from which escape is difficult: *a tight corner.* 6. any region, esp. a remote place. 7. something used to protect or mark a corner, as of the

---

cordial affable, affectionate, agreeable, cheerful, earnest, friendly, genial, heartfelt, hearty, invigorating, sociable, warm, warmhearted, welcoming, wholehearted
cordiality affability, amiability, friendli-

ness, geniality, heartiness, sincerity, warmth, wholeheartedness
cordon 1. *n.* barrier, chain, line, ring 2. *v.* **cordon off** close off, encircle, enclose, fence off, isolate, picket, separate, surround

core centre, crux, essence, gist, heart, kernel, nub, nucleus, pith

hard cover of a book. **8.** *Commerce.* a monopoly over the supply of a commodity so that its market price can be controlled. **9.** *Soccer, hockey, etc.* a free kick or shot from the corner of the field, taken against a defending team when the ball goes out of play over their goal line after last touching one of their players. **10.** either of two opposite angles of a boxing ring in which the opponents take their rests. **11. cut corners.** to take short cuts. **12. turn the corner.** to pass the critical point (in an illness, etc.). **13.** (*modifier*) on a corner: *a corner shop.* ~*vb.* **14.** (*tr.*) to manoeuvre (a person or animal) into a position from which escape is difficult or impossible. **15.** (*tr.*) **a.** to acquire enough of (a commodity) to attain control of the market. **b.** Also: **engross.** to attain control of (a market) in such a manner. **16.** (*intr.*) (of vehicles, etc.) to turn a corner. **17.** (*intr.*) (in soccer, etc.) to take a corner.

cornerstone ('kɔːnəˌstəʊn) *n.* **1.** a stone at the corner of a wall, uniting two intersecting walls. **2.** a stone placed at the corner of a building during a ceremony to mark the start of construction. **3.** a person or thing of prime importance: *the cornerstone of the whole argument.*

cornet ('kɔːnɪt) *n.* **1.** a three-valved brass instrument of the trumpet family. **2.** a person who plays the cornet. **3.** a cone-shaped paper container for sweets, etc. **4.** *Brit.* a cone-shaped wafer container for ice cream. **5.** (formerly) the lowest rank of commissioned cavalry officer in the British army. **6.** the large white headdress of some nuns. —**cor'netist** *n.*

corn exchange *n.* a building where corn is bought and sold.

cornflakes ('kɔːnˌfleɪks) *pl. n.* a breakfast cereal made from toasted maize.

cornflour ('kɔːnˌflaʊə) *n.* a fine maize flour, used for thickening sauces. U.S. name: **cornstarch.**

cornflower ('kɔːnˌflaʊə) *n.* a herbaceous plant, with blue, purple, pink, or white flowers, formerly a common weed in cornfields.

cornice ('kɔːnɪs) *n.* **1.** *Archit.* **a.** the top projecting mouldings of an entablature. **b.** a continuous horizontal projecting course or moulding at the top of a wall, building, etc. **2.** an overhanging ledge of snow.

Cornish ('kɔːnɪʃ) *adj.* **1.** of Cornwall or its inhabitants. ~*n.* **2.** a former language of Cornwall: extinct by 1800. **3. the.** (*functioning as pl.*) the natives or inhabitants of Cornwall. —**'Cornishman** *n.*

Cornish pasty *n. Cookery.* a pastry case with a filling of meat and vegetables.

cornucopia (ˌkɔːnjʊˈkəʊpɪə) *n.* **1.** a representation of a horn in painting, sculpture, etc., overflowing with fruit, vegetables, etc.; horn of plenty. **2.** a great abundance. **3.** a horn-shaped container. —ˌcornu'copian *adj.*

corny ('kɔːnɪ) *adj.* **cornier, corniest.** *Sl.* **1.** trite or banal. **2.** sentimental or mawkish. **3.** abounding in corn.

corolla (kəˈrɒlə) *n.* the petals of a flower collectively, forming an inner floral envelope.

corollary (kəˈrɒlərɪ) *n., pl.* **-laries. 1.** a proposition that follows directly from the proof of another proposition. **2.** an obvious deduction. **3.** a natural consequence.

corona (kəˈrəʊnə) *n., pl.* **-nas** or **-nae** (-niː). **1.** a circle of light around a luminous body, usually the moon. **2.** Also called: **aureole.** the outermost region of the sun's atmosphere, visible as a faint halo during a solar eclipse. **3.** *Archit.* the flat vertical face of a cornice. **4.** a circular chandelier. **5.** *Bot.* **a.** the trumpet-shaped part of the corolla of daffodils and similar plants. **b.** a crown of leafy outgrowths from inside the petals of some flowers. **6.** *Anat.* a crownlike structure. **7.** a long cigar with blunt ends. **8.** *Physics.* an electrical discharge appearing around the surface of a charged conductor.

coronary ('kɒrənərɪ) *adj.* **1.** *Anat.* designating blood

vessels, nerves, ligaments, etc., that encircle a part or structure. ~*n., pl.* **-naries. 2.** short for **coronary thrombosis.**

coronary thrombosis *n.* a condition of interrupted blood flow to the heart due to a blood clot in a coronary artery.

coronation (ˌkɒrəˈneɪʃən) *n.* the act or ceremony of crowning a monarch.

coroner ('kɒrənə) *n.* a public official responsible for the investigation of violent, sudden, or suspicious deaths. —**'coronerˌship** *n.*

coronet ('kɒrənɪt) *n.* **1.** any small crown, esp. one worn by princes or peers. **2.** a woman's jewelled circlet for the head. **3.** the margin between the skin of a horse's pastern and the horn of the hoof.

corporal[1] ('kɔːpərəl, 'kɔːprəl) *adj.* of or relating to the body; bodily. —ˌcorpo'rality *n.* —'corporally *adv.*

corporal[2] ('kɔːpərəl) *n.* **1.** a noncommissioned officer junior to a sergeant in the army, air force, or marines. **2.** (in the Royal Navy) a petty officer who assists the master-at-arms.

corporal punishment *n.* punishment of a physical nature, such as caning.

corporate ('kɔːpərɪt) *adj.* **1.** forming a corporation; incorporated. **2.** of a corporation. **3.** of or belonging to a united group; joint. —**'corporatism** *n.*

corporation (ˌkɔːpəˈreɪʃən) *n.* **1.** an association of persons having separate powers, duties, and liabilities. **2.** Also called: **municipal corporation.** the municipal authorities of a city or town. **3.** a group of people acting as one body. **4.** *Brit. inf.* a large paunch. —**'corporative** *adj.*

corporeal (kɔːˈpɔːrɪəl) *adj.* **1.** of the nature of the physical body; not spiritual. **2.** of a material nature; physical. —cor,pore'ality or **corporeity** (ˌkɔːpəˈriːɪtɪ) *n.* —**cor'poreally** *adv.*

corps (kɔː) *n., pl.* **corps** (kɔːz). **1.** a military formation that comprises two or more divisions. **2.** a body of people associated together: *the diplomatic corps.*

corps de ballet ('kɔː də 'bæleɪ) *n.* the members of a ballet company who dance together in a group.

corpse (kɔːps) *n.* a dead body, esp. of a human being.

corpulent ('kɔːpjʊlənt) *adj.* physically bulky; fat. —**'corpulence** *n.*

corpus ('kɔːpəs) *n., pl.* **-pora** (-pərə). **1.** a body of writings, esp. by a single author or on a specific topic: *the corpus of Dickens' works.* **2.** the main body or substance of something. **3.** *Anat.* **a.** any distinct mass or body. **b.** the main part of an organ or structure. **4.** *Obs.* a corpse.

corpuscle ('kɔːpʌsəl) *n.* **1.** any cell or similar minute body that is suspended in a fluid, esp. any of the **red blood corpuscles** (see **erythrocyte**) or **white blood corpuscles** (see **leucocyte**). **2.** Also: **corpuscule.** any minute particle. —**corpuscular** (kɔːˈpʌskjʊlə) *adj.*

corral (kɒˈrɑːl) *n.* **1.** *Chiefly U.S.* an enclosure for cattle or horses. **2.** *Chiefly U.S.* (formerly) a defensive enclosure formed by a ring of covered wagons. ~*vb.* **-ralling, -ralled.** (*tr.*) *U.S.* **3.** to drive into a corral. **4.** *Inf.* to capture.

corrasion (kəˈreɪʒən) *n.* erosion of a rock surface by rock fragments transported over it by water, wind, or ice.

correct (kəˈrɛkt) *vb.* (*tr.*) **1.** to make free from errors. **2.** to indicate the errors in. **3.** to rebuke or punish in order to improve: *to stand corrected.* **4.** to rectify (a malfunction, ailment, etc.). **5.** to adjust or make conform, esp. to a standard. ~*adj.* **6.** true; accurate: *the correct version.* **7.** in conformity with accepted standards: *correct behaviour.* —**cor'rective** *adj.* —**cor'rectly** *adv.* —**cor'rectness** *n.*

THESAURUS

corner *n.* **1.** angle, bend, crook, joint **2.** cavity, cranny, hideaway, hide-out, hidey-hole (*Inf.*), hole, niche, nook, recess, retreat **3.** hole (*Inf.*), pickle (*Inf.*), predicament, tight spot (*Inf.*) ~*v.* **4.** bring to bay, run to earth, trap **5.** *As in corner the market* engross, hog (*Sl.*), monopolize

cornerstone 1. quoin **2.** basis, bedrock, key, premise, starting point

corny banal, commonplace, dull, feeble, hackneyed, maudlin, mawkish, old-fashioned, old hat, sentimental, stale, stereotyped, trite

corporal anatomical, bodily, carnal, corporeal (*Archaic*), fleshly, material, physical, somatic

corporate allied, collaborative, collective, combined, communal, joint, merged, pooled, shared, united

corporation 1. association, corporate body, society **2.** civic authorities, council, municipal authorities, town council **3.** *Inf.* beer belly, paunch, pod, pot, potbelly, spare tyre

corps band, body, company, contingent, crew, detachment, division, regiment, squad, squadron, team, troop, unit

corpse body, cadaver, carcass, remains, stiff (*Sl.*)

corpulent beefy (*Inf.*), bulky, burly, fat, fattish, fleshy, large, lusty, obese, overweight, plump, portly, roly-poly, rotund, stout, tubby, well-padded

correction (kəˈrɛkʃən) n. **1.** the act of correcting. **2.** something substituted for an error; an improvement. **3.** a reproof. **4.** a quantity added to or subtracted from a scientific calculation or observation to increase its accuracy. —**corˈrectional** adj.

correlate (ˈkɒrɪˌleɪt) vb. **1.** to place or be placed in a complementary or reciprocal relationship. **2.** (tr.) to establish or show a correlation. ~n. **3.** either of two things mutually related. —ˌcorreˈlation n.

correlative (kɒˈrɛlətɪv) adj. **1.** in complementary or reciprocal relationship; corresponding. **2.** denoting words, usually conjunctions, occurring together though not adjacently in certain grammatical constructions, as neither and nor. ~n. **3.** either of two things that are correlative. **4.** a correlative word. —**corˈrelatively** adv. —**corˌrelaˈtivity** n.

correspond (ˌkɒrɪˈspɒnd) vb. (intr.) **1.** (usually foll. by with or to) to be consistent or compatible (with); tally (with). **2.** (usually foll. by to) to be similar in character or function. **3.** (usually foll. by with) to communicate by letter. —ˌcorreˈspondingly adv.
▷ **Usage.** See at **similar**.

correspondence (ˌkɒrɪˈspɒndəns) n. **1.** the condition of agreeing or corresponding. **2.** similarity. **3.** agreement or conformity. **4. a.** communication by letters. **b.** the letters so exchanged.

correspondence school n. an educational institution that offers tuition (**correspondence courses**) by post.

correspondent (ˌkɒrɪˈspɒndənt) n. **1.** a person who communicates by letter. **2.** a person employed by a newspaper, etc., to report on a special subject or from a foreign country. **3.** a person or firm that has regular business relations with another, esp. one abroad. ~adj. **4.** similar or analogous.

corridor (ˈkɒrɪˌdɔː) n. **1.** a passage connecting parts of a building. **2.** a strip of land or air space that affords access, either from a landlocked country to the sea or from a state to an exclave. **3.** a passageway connecting the compartments of a railway coach. **4. corridors of power.** the higher echelons of government, the Civil Service, etc., considered as the location of power and influence.

corrie (ˈkɒrɪ) n. **1.** (in Scotland) a circular hollow on a hillside. **2.** Geol. another name for **cirque**.

corrigendum (ˌkɒrɪˈdʒɛndəm) n., pl. **-da** (-də). **1.** an error to be corrected. **2.** (sometimes pl.) Also called: **erratum**. a slip of paper inserted into a book after printing, listing corrections.

corrigible (ˈkɒrɪdʒɪbəl) adj. **1.** capable of being corrected. **2.** submissive.

corroborate (kəˈrɒbəˌreɪt) vb. (tr.) to confirm or support (facts, opinions, etc.), esp. by providing fresh evidence. —**corˌroboˈration** n. —**corroborative** (kəˈrɒbərətɪv) adj. —**corˈroboˌrator** n.

corroboree (kəˈrɒbərɪ) n. Austral. **1.** a native assembly of sacred, festive, or warlike character. **2.** any noisy gathering.

corrode (kəˈrəʊd) vb. **1.** to eat away or be eaten away, esp. as in the oxidation or rusting of a metal. **2.** (tr.) to destroy gradually: his jealousy corroded his happiness. —**corˈrodible** adj.

corrosion (kəˈrəʊʒən) n. **1.** a process in which a solid, esp. a metal, is eaten away and changed by a chemical action, as in the oxidation of iron. **2.** slow deterioration by being eaten or worn away. **3.** the product of corrosion. —**corrosive** (kəˈrəʊsɪv) adj.

corrugate (ˈkɒrʊˌgeɪt) vb. (usually tr.) to fold or be folded into alternate furrows and ridges. —ˌcorruˈgation n.

corrugated iron n. a thin sheet of iron or steel, formed with alternating ridges and troughs.

corrupt (kəˈrʌpt) adj. **1.** open to or involving bribery or other dishonest practices: a corrupt official; corrupt practices. **2.** morally depraved. **3.** putrid or rotten. **4.** (of a text or manuscript) made meaningless or different in meaning by scribal errors or alterations. ~vb. **5.** to become or cause to become dishonest or disloyal. **6.** to deprave. **7.** (tr.) to infect or contaminate. **8.** (tr.) to cause to become rotten. **9.** (tr.) to alter (a text, etc.) from the original. —**corˈrupter** or **corˈruptor** n. —**corˈruptly** adv. —**corˈruptness** n.

corruptible (kəˈrʌptəbəl) adj. capable of being corrupted. —**corˈruptibly** adv.

corruption (kəˈrʌpʃən) n. **1.** the act of corrupting or state of being corrupt. **2.** depravity. **3.** dishonesty, esp. bribery. **4.** decay. **5.** alteration, as of a manuscript. **6.** an altered form of a word.

corsage (kɔːˈsɑːʒ) n. **1.** a small bunch of flowers worn pinned to the lapel, bosom, etc. **2.** the bodice of a dress.

corsair (ˈkɔːsɛə) n. **1.** a pirate. **2.** a privateer, esp. of the Barbary Coast.

corse (kɔːs) n. an archaic word for **corpse**.

corselet (ˈkɔːslɪt) n. **1.** Also spelt: **corslet**. a piece of armour for the top part of the body. **2.** a one-piece foundation garment.

corset (ˈkɔːsɪt) n. **1. a.** a stiffened, elasticated, or laced foundation garment, worn esp. by women. **b.** a similar garment worn because of injury, weakness, etc., by either sex. **2.** Inf. a restriction or limitation, esp. government control of bank lending. ~vb. **3.** (tr.) to dress or enclose in, or as in, a corset. —**corsetière** (ˌkɔːsɛtɪˈɛə) n. —**corsetry** n.

THESAURUS

correct v. **1.** adjust, amend, cure, emend, improve, rectify, redress, reform, regulate, remedy, right **2.** admonish, chasten, chastise, chide, discipline, punish, reprimand, reprove ~adj. **3.** accurate, equitable, exact, faultless, flawless, just, O.K. (Inf.), precise, regular, right, strict, true **4.** acceptable, appropriate, diplomatic, fitting, O.K. (Inf.), proper, seemly, standard

correction **1.** adjustment, alteration, amendment, improvement, modification, rectification, righting **2.** admonition, castigation, chastisement, discipline, punishment, reformation, reproof

corrective adj. **1.** palliative, rehabilitative, remedial, restorative, therapeutic **2.** disciplinary, penal, punitive, reformatory

correctly accurately, aright, perfectly, precisely, properly, right, rightly

correctness **1.** accuracy, exactitude, exactness, faultlessness, fidelity, preciseness, precision, regularity, truth **2.** bon ton, civility, decorum, good breeding, propriety, seemliness

correlate associate, compare, connect, coordinate, correspond, equate, interact, parallel, tie in

correlation alternation, correspondence, equivalence, interaction, interchange, interdependence, interrelationship, reciprocity

correspond **1.** accord, agree, be consistent, coincide, complement, conform, correlate, dovetail, fit, harmonize, match, square, tally **2.** communicate, exchange letters, keep in touch, write

correspondence **1.** agreement, analogy, coincidence, comparability, comparison, concurrence, conformity, congruity, correlation, fitness, harmony, match, relation, similarity **2.** communication, letters, mail, post, writing

correspondent n. **1.** letter writer, pen friend or pal **2.** contributor, gazetteer (Archaic), journalist, reporter, special correspondent ~adj. **3.** analogous, comparable, like, parallel, reciprocal, similar

corresponding analogous, answering, complementary, correlative, correspondent, equivalent, identical, interrelated, matching, reciprocal, similar, synonymous

corridor aisle, hallway, passage, passageway

corroborate authenticate, back up, bear out, confirm, document, endorse, establish, ratify, substantiate, support, sustain, validate

corrode canker, consume, corrupt, deteriorate, eat away, erode, gnaw, impair, oxidize, rust, waste, wear away

corrosive **1.** acrid, biting, caustic, consuming, corroding, erosive, virulent, wasting, wearing **2.** caustic, cutting, incisive, mordant, sarcastic, trenchant, venomous

corrugated channelled, creased, crinkled, fluted, furrowed, grooved, puckered, ridged, rumpled, wrinkled

corrupt adj. **1.** bent (Sl.), bribable, crooked (Inf.), dishonest, fraudulent, rotten, shady (Inf.), unethical, unprincipled, unscrupulous, venal **2.** abandoned, debased, defiled, degenerate, demoralized, depraved, dishonoured, dissolute, profligate, vicious ~v. **3.** bribe, debauch, demoralize, deprave, entice, fix (Inf.), grease (someone's) palm (Sl.), lure, pervert, square (Inf.), suborn, subvert ~adj. **4.** adulterated, altered, contaminated, decayed, defiled, distorted, doctored, falsified, infected, polluted, putrescent, putrid, rotten, tainted ~v. **5.** adulterate, contaminate, debase, defile, doctor, infect, putrefy, spoil, taint, tamper with, vitiate

corruption **1.** breach of trust, bribery, bribing, crookedness (Inf.), demoralization, dishonesty, extortion, fiddling (Inf.), fraud, fraudulency, graft, jobbery, profiteering, shadiness, shady dealings (Inf.), unscrupulousness, venality **2.** baseness, decadence, degeneration, degradation, depravity, evil, immorality, impurity, iniquity, perversion, profligacy, sinfulness, turpitude, vice, viciousness, wickedness **3.** adulteration, debasement, decay, defilement, distortion, doctor-

cortege or **cortège** (kɔːˈteɪʒ) n. 1. a formal procession, esp. a funeral procession. 2. a train of attendants; retinue.

cortex (ˈkɔːtɛks) n., pl. **-tices** (-tɪˌsiːz). 1. Anat. the outer layer of any organ or part, such as the grey matter in the brain that covers the cerebrum (**cerebral cortex**). 2. Bot. **a.** the tissue in plant stems and roots between the vascular bundles and the epidermis. **b.** the outer layer of a part such as the bark of a stem. —**cortical** (ˈkɔːtɪkəl) adj.

corticate (ˈkɔːtɪkɪt, -ˌkeɪt) or **corticated** adj. (of plants, seeds, etc.) having a bark, husk, or rind.

cortisone (ˈkɔːtɪˌzəʊn) n. a steroid hormone, the synthetic form of which has been used in treating rheumatoid arthritis, allergic and skin diseases, leukaemia, etc.

corundum (kəˈrʌndəm) n. a hard mineral consisting of aluminium oxide: used as an abrasive. Precious varieties include ruby and sapphire. Formula: Al_2O_3.

coruscate (ˈkɒrəˌskeɪt) vb. (intr.) to emit flashes of light; sparkle. —**corusˈcation** n.

corvette (kɔːˈvɛt) n. a lightly armed escort warship.

corymb (ˈkɒrɪmb, -rɪm) n. an inflorescence in the form of a flat-topped flower cluster with the oldest flowers at the periphery.

coryza (kəˈraɪzə) n. acute inflammation of the mucous membrane of the nose, with discharge of mucus; a head cold.

cos¹ or **cos lettuce** (kɒs) n. a variety of lettuce with a long slender head and crisp leaves. Usual U.S. name: **romaine**.

cos² (kɒz) abbrev. for cosine.

Cos. or **cos.** abbrev. for: 1. Companies. 2. Counties.

cosec (ˈkəʊsɛk) abbrev. for cosecant.

cosecant (kəʊˈsiːkənt) n. (of an angle) a trigonometric function that in a right-angled triangle is the ratio of the length of the hypotenuse to that of the opposite side.

cosh¹ (kɒʃ) Brit. ~n. 1. a blunt weapon, often made of hard rubber; bludgeon. 2. an attack with such a weapon. ~vb. 3. to hit with such a weapon, esp. on the head.

cosh² (kɒʃ, ˈkɒsˈeɪtʃ) n. hyperbolic cosine.

cosignatory (kəʊˈsɪgnətərɪ, -trɪ) n., pl. **-ries.** 1. a person, country, etc., that signs a document jointly with others. ~adj. 2. signing jointly.

cosine (ˈkəʊˌsaɪn) n. (of an angle) a trigonometric function that in a right-angled triangle is the ratio of the length of the adjacent side to that of the hypotenuse.

cosmetic (kɒzˈmɛtɪk) n. 1. any preparation applied to the body, esp. the face, with the intention of beautifying it. ~adj. 2. serving or designed to beautify the body, esp. the face. 3. having no other function than to beautify: cosmetic illustrations in a book. —**cosˈmetically** adv.

cosmic (ˈkɒzmɪk) adj. 1. of or relating to the whole universe: cosmic laws. 2. occurring or originating in outer space, esp. as opposed to the vicinity of the earth: cosmic rays. 3. immeasurably extended; vast. —**ˈcosmically** adv.

cosmo- or before a vowel **cosm-** combining form. indicating the world or universe: cosmology; cosmonaut.

cosmogony (kɒzˈmɒgənɪ) n., pl. **-nies.** the study of the origin and development of the universe or of a particular system in the universe, such as the solar system. —**cosmogonic** (ˌkɒzməˈgɒnɪk) or **ˌcosmoˈgonical** adj. —**cosˈmogonist** n.

cosmology (kɒzˈmɒlədʒɪ) n. the study of the origin and nature of the universe. —**cosmological** (ˌkɒzmə-ˈlɒdʒɪkəl) or **ˌcosmoˈlogic** adj. —**cosˈmologist** n.

cosmonaut (ˈkɒzməˌnɔːt) n. a Soviet astronaut.

cosmopolitan (ˌkɒzməˈpɒlɪtən) n. 1. a person who has lived and travelled in many countries, esp. one who is free of national prejudices. ~adj. 2. familiar with many parts of the world. 3. sophisticated or urbane. 4. composed of people or elements from all parts of the world or from many different spheres. —ˌcosmoˈpolitanism n.

cosmos (ˈkɒzmɒs) n. 1. the universe considered as an ordered system. 2. any ordered system. 3. (pl. -mos or -moses) any tropical American plant of the genus Cosmos, cultivated as garden plants for their brightly coloured flowers.

Cossack (ˈkɒsæk) n. 1. (formerly) any of the free warrior-peasants of chiefly East Slavonic descent who served as cavalry under the tsars. ~adj. 2. of, relating to, or characteristic of the Cossacks: a Cossack dance.

cosset (ˈkɒsɪt) vb. 1. (tr.) to pamper; coddle; pet. ~n. 2. any pet animal, esp. a lamb.

cost (kɒst) n. 1. the price paid or required for acquiring, producing, or maintaining something, measured in money, time, or energy; outlay. 2. suffering or sacrifice: I know to my cost. 3. **a.** the amount paid for a commodity by its seller: to sell at cost. **b.** (as modifier): the cost price. 4. (pl.) Law. the expenses of judicial proceedings. 5. **at all costs.** regardless of sacrifice involved. 6. **at the cost of.** at the expense of losing. ~vb. **costing, cost.** 7. (tr.) to be obtained or obtainable in exchange for: a ride cost one pound. 8. to cause or require the loss or sacrifice (of): the accident cost him dearly. 9. to estimate the cost of (a product, process, etc.) for the purposes of pricing, budgeting, control, etc.

cost accounting n. the recording and controlling of all the expenditures of an enterprise in order to facilitate control of separate activities. Also called: **management accounting.** —**cost accountant** n.

costermonger (ˈkɒstəˌmʌŋgə) or **coster** n. Brit., rare. a person who sells fruit, vegetables, etc., from a barrow.

costive (ˈkɒstɪv) adj. 1. constipated. 2. niggardly. —**ˈcostiveness** n.

costly (ˈkɒstlɪ) adj. **-lier, -liest.** 1. expensive. 2. entailing great loss or sacrifice: a costly victory. 3. splendid; lavish. —**ˈcostliness** n.

cost of living n. 1. the basic cost of the food, clothing, shelter, and fuel necessary to maintain life, esp. at a standard of living regarded as basic. 2. (as modifier): the cost-of-living index.

costume (ˈkɒstjuːm) n. 1. a style of dressing, including all the clothes, accessories, etc., worn at one time, as in a particular country or period. 2. Old-fashioned. a woman's suit. 3. a set of clothes, esp. unusual or period clothes: a jester's costume. 4. short for **swimming costume.** ~vb. (tr.) 5. to furnish the costumes for (a show, film, etc.). 6. to dress (someone) in a costume.

costumier (kɒˈstjuːmɪə) or **costumer** n. a person or firm that makes or supplies theatrical or fancy costumes.

cosy or U.S. **cozy** (ˈkəʊzɪ) adj. **-sier, -siest** or U.S. **-zier, -ziest.** 1. warm and snug. 2. intimate; friendly. ~n., pl. **-sies** or U.S. **-zies.** 3. a cover for keeping things warm: egg cosy. —**ˈcosily** or U.S. **ˈcozily** adv. —**ˈcosiness** or U.S. **ˈcoziness** n.

cot¹ (kɒt) n. 1. a child's boxlike bed, usually incorporating vertical bars. 2. a portable bed. 3. a light bedstead. 4. Naut. a hammock-like bed.

cot² (kɒt) n. 1. Literary or arch. a small cottage. 2. Also called: **cote. a.** a small shelter, esp. one for pigeons, sheep, etc. **b.** (in combination): dovecot.

THESAURUS

ing, falsification, foulness, infection, pollution, putrefaction, putrescence, rot, rottenness

corset 1. belt, bodice, corselet, foundation garment, girdle, panty girdle, stays (Rare) 2. Fig. check, curb, limitation, restriction

cosmetic adj. beautifying, nonessential, superficial, surface, touching-up

cosmic grandiose, huge, immense, infinite, limitless, measureless, universal, vast

cosmonaut astronaut, spaceman, space pilot

cosmopolitan 1. adj. catholic, sophisticated, universal, urbane, well-travelled, worldly, worldly-wise 2. n. cosmopolite, jet-setter, man or woman of the world, sophisticate

cost n. 1. amount, charge, damage (Inf.), expenditure, expense, figure, outlay, payment, price, rate, worth 2. damage, deprivation, detriment, expense, harm, hurt, injury, loss, penalty, sacrifice, suffering ~v. 3. come to, command a price of, sell at, set (someone) back (Inf.) 4. Fig. do disservice to, harm, hurt, injure, lose, necessitate

costly 1. dear, excessive, exorbitant, expensive, extortionate, highly-priced, steep (Inf.), valuable 2. gorgeous, lavish, luxurious, opulent, precious, priceless, rich, splendid, sumptuous 3. Entailing loss or sacrifice catastrophic, damaging, deleterious, disastrous, harmful, loss-making, ruinous, sacrificial

costs 1. budget, expenses, outgoings 2. **at all costs** at any price, no matter what, regardless, without fail

costume apparel, attire, clothing, dress, ensemble, garb, get-up (Inf.), livery, national dress, outfit, robes, uniform

cosy comfortable, comfy (Inf.), cuddled up, homely, intimate, secure, sheltered, snug, snuggled down, tucked up, warm

cot³ (kɒt) *abbrev. for* cotangent.

cotangent (kəʊˈtændʒənt) *n.* (of an angle) a trigonometric function that in a right-angled triangle is the ratio of the length of the adjacent side to that of the opposite side.

C.O.T.C. *abbrev. for* Canadian Officers Training Corps.

cot death *n.* the unexplained sudden death of an infant during sleep.

cote (kəʊt) *or* **cot** *n.* **1.** a small shelter for pigeons, sheep, etc. **2.** (*in combination*): *dovecote.*

coterie (ˈkəʊtərɪ) *n.* a small exclusive group of friends or people with common interests; clique.

cotoneaster (kəˌtəʊnɪˈæstə) *n.* any Old World shrub of the rosaceous genus *Cotoneaster:* cultivated for their ornamental flowers and red or black berries.

cottage (ˈkɒtɪdʒ) *n.* a small simple house, esp. in a rural area. —ˈcottager *n.*

cottage cheese *n.* a mild loose soft white cheese made from skimmed milk curds.

cottage industry *n.* an industry in which employees work in their own homes, often using their own equipment.

cotter¹ (ˈkɒtə) *Machinery. n.* **1.** any part, such as a pin, wedge, key, etc., that is used to secure two other parts so that relative motion between them is prevented. **2.** short for **cotter pin.**

cotter² (ˈkɒtə) *n.* **1.** *English history.* a villein in late Anglo-Saxon and early Norman times occupying a cottage and land in return for labour. **2.** Also called: **cottar.** a peasant occupying a cottage and land in the Scottish Highlands.

cotter pin *n. Machinery.* a split pin secured, after passing through holes in the parts to be attached, by spreading the ends.

cotton (ˈkɒtən) *n.* **1.** any of various herbaceous plants and shrubs cultivated in warm climates for the fibre surrounding the seeds and the oil within the seeds. **2.** the soft white downy fibre of these plants, used to manufacture textiles. **3.** cotton plants collectively, as a cultivated crop. **4.** a cloth or thread made from cotton fibres. ~See also **cotton on.** —ˈcottony *adj.*

cotton on *vb.* (*intr., adv.;* often foll. by *to*) *Inf.* to perceive the meaning (of).

cotton wool *n.* **1.** *Chiefly Brit.* bleached and sterilized cotton from which the impurities, such as the seeds, have been removed. Usual U.S. term: **absorbent cotton.** **2.** cotton in the natural state. **3.** *Brit. inf.* a state of pampered comfort and protection.

cotyledon (ˌkɒtɪˈliːdən) *n.* a simple embryonic leaf in seed-bearing plants, which, in some species, forms the first green leaf after germination. —ˌcotyˈledonous *adj.*

couch (kaʊtʃ) *n.* **1.** a piece of upholstered furniture, usually having a back and armrests, for seating more than one person. **2.** a bed, esp. one used in the daytime by the patients of a doctor or a psychoanalyst. ~*vb.* **3.** (*tr.*) to express in a particular style of language: *couched in an archaic style.* **4.** (when *tr., usually reflexive or passive*) to lie down or cause to lie down for or as for sleep. **5.** (*intr.*) *Arch.* to crouch. **6.** (*intr.*) *Arch.* to lie in ambush; lurk. **7.** (*tr.*) *Surgery.* to remove (a cataract) by downward displacement of the lens of the eye. **8.** (*tr.*) *Arch.* to lower (a lance) into a horizontal position. —ˈcoucher *n.*

couchette (kuːˈʃɛt) *n.* a bed or berth in a railway carriage, esp. one converted from seats.

couch grass (kaʊtʃ, kuːtʃ) *n.* a grass with a yellowish-white creeping underground stem by which it spreads quickly: a troublesome weed. Also called: **twitch grass, quitch grass.**

cougar (ˈkuːgə) *n.* another name for **puma.**

cough (kɒf) *vb.* **1.** (*intr.*) to expel air abruptly and explosively through the partially closed vocal chords. **2.**

(*intr.*) to make a sound similar to this. **3.** (*tr.*) to utter or express with a cough or coughs. ~*n.* **4.** an act or sound of coughing. **5.** a condition of the lungs or throat which causes frequent coughing. —ˈcougher *n.*

cough mixture *n.* any medicine that relieves coughing.

cough up *vb.* (*adv.*) **1.** *Inf.* to surrender (money, information, etc.), esp. reluctantly. **2.** (*tr.*) to bring into the mouth or eject (phlegm, food, etc.) by coughing.

could (kʊd) *vb.* (takes an infinitive without *to* or an implied infinitive) used as an auxiliary: **1.** to make the past tense of **can**¹. **2.** to make the subjunctive mood of **can**¹, esp. used in polite requests or in conditional sentences: *could I see you tonight?* **3.** to indicate suggestion of a course of action: *you could take the car if it's raining.* **4.** (often foll. by *well*) to indicate a possibility: *he could well be a spy.*

coulomb (ˈkuːlɒm) *n.* the derived SI unit of electric charge; the quantity of electricity transported in one second by a current of 1 ampere. Symbol: C

coulter (ˈkəʊltə) *n.* a blade or sharp-edged disc attached to a plough so that it cuts through the soil vertically in advance of the ploughshare. Also (esp. U.S.): **colter.**

council (ˈkaʊnsəl) *n.* **1.** an assembly of people meeting for discussion, consultation, etc. **2. a.** a body of people elected or appointed to serve in an administrative, legislative, or advisory capacity: *a student council.* **b.** short for **legislative council. 3.** *Brit.* (*sometimes cap.;* often preceded by *the*) the local governing authority of a town, county, etc. **4.** a meeting of a council. **5.** (*modifier*) of, provided for, or used by a local council: *a council chamber; council offices.* **6.** (*modifier*) *Brit.* provided by a local council, esp. (of housing) at a subsidized rent: *a council house; a council estate; a council school.* **7.** *Christianity.* an assembly of bishops, etc., convened for regulating matters of doctrine or discipline.

councillor *or U.S.* **councilor** (ˈkaʊnsələ) *n.* a member of a council.

counsel (ˈkaʊnsəl) *n.* **1.** advice or guidance on conduct, behaviour, etc. **2.** discussion; consultation: *to take counsel with a friend.* **3.** a person whose advice is sought. **4.** a barrister or group of barristers engaged in conducting cases in court and advising on legal matters. **5.** *Christianity.* any of the **counsels of perfection,** namely poverty, chastity, and obedience. **6. counsel of perfection.** excellent but unrealizable advice. **7.** private opinions (esp. in **keep one's own counsel**). **8.** *Arch.* wisdom; prudence. ~*vb.* **-selling, -selled** *or U.S.* **-seling, -seled. 9.** (*tr.*) to give advice or guidance to. **10.** (*tr.; often takes a clause as object*) to recommend; urge. **11.** (*intr.*) *Arch.* to take counsel; consult.

counsellor *or U.S.* **counselor** (ˈkaʊnsələ) *n.* **1.** a person who gives counsel; adviser. **2.** Also called: **counselor-at-law.** *U.S.* a lawyer, esp. one who conducts cases in court. **3.** a senior diplomatic officer.

count¹ (kaʊnt) *vb.* **1.** to add up or check (each unit in a collection) in order to ascertain the sum: *count your change.* **2.** (*tr.*) to recite numbers in ascending order up to and including. **3.** (*tr.; often foll. by in*) to take into account or include: *we must count him in.* **4. not counting.** excluding. **5.** (*tr.*) to consider; deem: *count yourself lucky.* **6.** (*intr.*) to have importance: *this picture counts as a rarity.* **7.** (*intr.*) *Music.* to keep time by counting beats. ~*n.* **8.** the act of counting. **9.** the number reached by counting; sum: *a blood count.* **10.** *Law.* a paragraph in an indictment containing a separate charge. **11. keep** *or* **lose count.** to keep or fail to keep an accurate record of items, events, etc. **12.** *Boxing, wrestling.* the act of telling off a number of seconds by the referee, as when a boxer has been knocked down by his opponent. **13. out for the count.** *Boxing.* knocked out and unable to continue after a count of ten by the referee. ~See also **count against, countdown,** etc. —ˈcountable *adj.*

THESAURUS

cottage but-and-ben (*Scot.*), cabin, chalet, cot, hut, lodge, shack

couch **1.** *v.* express, frame, phrase, set forth, utter, word **2.** *n.* bed, chaise longue, chesterfield, daybed, divan, ottoman, settee, sofa

cough **1.** *n.* bark, frog *or* tickle in one's throat, hack **2.** *v.* bark, clear one's throat, hack, hawk, hem

cough up ante up (*Inf.*), come across, deliver, fork out (*Sl.*), give up, hand over, shell out (*Inf.*), surrender

council assembly, board, cabinet, chamber, committee, conclave, conference, congress, convention, convocation, diet, governing body, ministry, panel, parliament, synod

counsel *n.* **1.** admonition, advice, caution, consideration, consultation, deliberation, di-

rection, forethought, guidance, information, recommendation, suggestion, warning **2.** advocate, attorney, barrister, legal adviser, solicitor ~*v.* **3.** admonish, advise, advocate, caution, exhort, instruct, recommend, urge, warn

count² (kaʊnt) *n.* **1.** a nobleman in any of various European countries having a rank corresponding to that of a British earl. **2.** any of various officials in the late Roman Empire and in the early Middle Ages.
count against *vb.* (*intr., prep.*) to have influence to the disadvantage of.
countdown ('kaʊnt,daʊn) *n.* **1.** the act of counting backwards to time a critical operation exactly, such as the launching of a rocket. ∼*vb.* **count down.** (*intr., adv.*) **2.** to count thus.
countenance ('kaʊntɪnəns) *n.* **1.** the face, esp. when considered as expressing a person's character or mood. **2.** support or encouragement; sanction. **3.** composure; self-control (esp. in **keep** *or* **lose one's countenance**). ∼*vb.* (*tr.*) **4.** to support or encourage; sanction. **5.** to tolerate; endure.
counter¹ ('kaʊntə) *n.* **1.** a horizontal surface, as in a shop or bank, over which business is transacted. **2.** (in some cafeterias) a long table on which food is served. **3. a.** a small flat disc of wood, metal, or plastic, used in various board games. **b.** a similar disc or token used as an imitation coin. **4.** a person or thing that may be used or manipulated. **5. under the counter.** (**under-the-counter** when prenominal) (of the sale of goods) clandestine, or illegal. **6. over the counter.** (**over-the-counter** when prenominal) (of security transactions) through a broker rather than on a stock exchange.
counter² ('kaʊntə) *n.* **1.** a person who counts. **2.** an apparatus that records the number of occurrences of events.
counter³ ('kaʊntə) *adv.* **1.** in a contrary direction or manner. **2.** in a wrong or reverse direction. **3. run counter to.** to have a contrary effect or action to. ∼*adj.* **4.** opposing; opposite; contrary. ∼*n.* **5.** something that is contrary or opposite to some other thing. **6.** an act, effect, or force that opposes another. **7.** a return attack, such as a blow in boxing. **8.** *Fencing.* a parry in which the foils move in a circular fashion. **9.** the portion of the stern of a boat or ship that overhangs the water aft of the rudder. **10.** a piece of leather forming the back of a shoe. ∼*vb.* **11.** to say or do (something) in retaliation or response. **12.** (*tr.*) to move, act, or perform in a manner or direction opposite to (a person or thing). **13.** to return the attack of (an opponent).
counter- *prefix.* **1.** against; opposite; contrary: *counterattack.* **2.** complementary; corresponding: *counterfoil.* **3.** duplicate or substitute: *counterfeit.*
counteract (,kaʊntər'ækt) *vb.* (*tr.*) to oppose or neutralize by contrary action; check. —,**counter'action** *n.* —,**counter'active** *adj.*
counterattack ('kaʊntərə,tæk) *n.* **1.** an attack in response to an attack. ∼*vb.* **2.** to make a counterattack (against).
counterbalance *n.* ('kaʊntə,bæləns). **1.** a weight or force that balances or offsets another. ∼*vb.* (,kaʊntə'bæləns). (*tr.*) **2.** to act as a counterbalance. ∼Also: **counterpoise.**
counterblast ('kaʊntə,blɑːst) *n.* an aggressive response to a verbal attack.
counterclockwise (,kaʊntə'klɒk,waɪz) *adv., adj.* the U.S. equivalent of **anticlockwise.**
counterespionage (,kaʊntər'ɛspɪə,nɑːʒ) *n.* activities to counteract enemy espionage.
counterfeit ('kaʊntəfɪt) *adj.* **1.** made in imitation of something genuine with the intent to deceive or defraud; forged. **2.** simulated; sham: *counterfeit affection.* ∼*n.* **3.** an imitation designed to deceive or defraud. ∼*vb.* **4.**

(*tr.*) to make a fraudulent imitation of. **5.** (*intr.*) to make counterfeits. **6.** to feign; simulate. —'**counter,feiter** *n.*
counterfoil ('kaʊntə,fɔɪl) *n. Brit.* the part of a cheque, receipt, etc., retained as a record. Also called (esp. in the U.S.): **stub.**
counterintelligence (,kaʊntərɪn'tɛlɪdʒəns) *n.* activities designed to frustrate enemy espionage.
countermand *vb.* (,kaʊntə'mɑːnd). (*tr.*) **1.** to revoke or cancel (a command, order, etc.). **2.** to order (forces, etc.) to retreat; recall. ∼*n.* ('kaʊntə,mɑːnd). **3.** a command revoking another.
countermarch ('kaʊntə,mɑːtʃ) *vb.* **1.** *Chiefly mil.* to march back or in the opposite direction. ∼*n.* **2.** the act or instance of countermarching.
countermeasure (,kaʊntə'mɛʒə) *n.* action taken to oppose, neutralize, or retaliate against some other action.
counterpane ('kaʊntə,peɪn) *n.* another word for **bedspread.**
counterpart ('kaʊntə,pɑːt) *n.* **1.** a person or thing identical to or closely resembling another. **2.** one of two parts that complement or correspond to each other. **3.** a duplicate, esp. of a legal document; copy.
counterpoint ('kaʊntə,pɔɪnt) *n.* **1.** the technique involving the simultaneous sounding of two or more parts or melodies. **2.** a melody or part combined with another melody or part. **3.** the musical texture resulting from the simultaneous sounding of two or more melodies or parts. ∼*vb.* **4.** (*tr.*) to set in contrast. ∼Related adj.: **contrapuntal.**
counterpoise ('kaʊntə,pɔɪz) *n.* **1.** a force, influence, etc., that counterbalances another. **2.** a state of balance; equilibrium. **3.** a weight that balances another. ∼*vb.* **4.** to oppose with something of equal effect, weight, or force; offset. **5.** to bring into equilibrium.
counterproductive (,kaʊntəprə'dʌktɪv) *adj.* tending to hinder the achievement of an aim; having effects contrary to those intended.
countersign *vb.* ('kaʊntə,saɪn, ,kaʊntə'saɪn). **1.** (*tr.*) to sign (a document already signed by another). ∼*n.* ('kaʊntə,saɪn). **2.** Also called: **countersignature.** the signature so written. **3.** a secret sign given in response to another sign. **4.** *Chiefly mil.* a password.
countersink ('kaʊntə,sɪŋk) *vb.* **-sinking, -sank, -sunk.** (*tr.*) **1.** to enlarge the upper part of (a hole) in timber, metal, etc., so that the head of a bolt or screw can be sunk below the surface. **2.** to drive (a screw) or sink (a bolt) into such a hole. ∼*n.* **3.** Also called: **countersink bit.** a tool for countersinking. **4.** a countersunk hole.
countertenor (,kaʊntə'tɛnə) *n.* **1.** an adult male voice with an alto range. **2.** a singer with such a voice.
countervail (,kaʊntə'veɪl, 'kaʊntə,veɪl) *vb.* **1.** (when *intr.*, usually foll. by *against*) to act or act against with equal power or force. **2.** (*tr.*) to make up for; compensate; offset.
counterweigh (,kaʊntə'weɪ) *vb.* another word for **counterbalance.**
countess ('kaʊntɪs) *n.* **1.** the wife or widow of a count or earl. **2.** a woman of the rank of count or earl.
countless ('kaʊntlɪs) *adj.* innumerable; myriad.
count noun *n.* a noun that denotes an object that can exist in the plural without change of meaning and that can be preceded by *a* or *an*, such as *telephone* or *cup*, as contrasted with *honesty.* Cf. **mass noun.**
count on *vb.* (*intr., prep.*) to rely or depend on.

THESAURUS

count *v.* **1.** add (up), calculate, cast up, check, compute, enumerate, estimate, number, reckon, score, tally, tot up **2.** consider, deem, esteem, impute, judge, look upon, rate, regard, think **3.** carry weight, cut any ice (*Inf.*), enter into consideration, matter, rate, signify, tell, weigh **4.** include, number among, take into account *or* consideration ∼*n.* **5.** calculation, computation, enumeration, numbering, poll, reckoning, sum, tally

countenance *n.* **1.** appearance, aspect, expression, face, features, look, mien, physiognomy, visage **2.** aid, approval, assistance, backing, endorsement, favour, sanction, support ∼*v.* **3.** abet, aid, approve, back, champion, condone, encourage, endorse, help, sanc-

tion, support **4.** brook, endure, put up with (*Inf.*), stand for (*Inf.*), tolerate

counter **1.** *adv.* against, at variance with, contrarily, contrariwise, conversely, in defiance of, versus **2.** *adj.* adverse, against, conflicting, contradictory, contrary, contrasting, obverse, opposed, opposing, opposite **3.** *v.* answer, hit back, meet, offset, parry, resist, respond, retaliate, return, ward off

counteract annul, check, contravene, counterbalance, countervail, cross, defeat, foil, frustrate, hinder, invalidate, negate, neutralize, offset, oppose, resist, thwart

counterbalance balance, compensate, counterpoise, countervail, make up for, offset, set off

counterfeit **1.** *v.* copy, fabricate, fake, feign, forge, imitate, impersonate, pretend, sham, simulate **2.** *adj.* bogus, copied, ersatz, faked, false, feigned, forged, fraudulent, imitation, phoney (*Sl.*), pseud (*Inf.*), pseudo (*Inf.*), sham, simulated, spurious, suppositious **3.** *n.* copy, fake, forgery, fraud, imitation, phoney (*Sl.*), reproduction, sham

countermand annul, cancel, override, repeal, rescind, retract, reverse, revoke

counterpart complement, copy, correlative, duplicate, equal, fellow, match, mate, opposite number, supplement, tally, twin

countless endless, immeasurable, incalculable, infinite, innumerable, legion, limit-

count out vb. (tr., adv.) **1.** Inf. to leave out; exclude. **2.** (of a boxing referee) to judge (a floored boxer) to have failed to recover within the specified time.

countrified or **countryfied** ('kʌntrɪ,faɪd) adj. in the style, manners, etc., of the country; rural.

country ('kʌntrɪ) n., pl. **-tries. 1.** a territory distinguished by its people, culture, geography, etc. **2.** an area of land distinguished by its political autonomy; state. **3.** the people of a territory or state. **4. a.** the part of the land that is away from cities or industrial areas; rural districts. **b.** (as modifier): country house. Related adj.: **pastoral, rural. 5. up country.** away from the coast or the capital. **6.** one's native land or nation of citizenship. **7. across country.** not keeping to roads, etc. **8. go** or **appeal to the country.** Chiefly Brit. to dissolve Parliament and hold an election.

country-and-western n. **a.** a type of urban 20th-century White folk music of the southeastern U.S. **b.** (as modifier): country-and-western music.

country club n. a club in the country, having sporting and social facilities.

country dance n. a type of folk dance in which couples face one another in a line.

countryman ('kʌntrɪmən) n., pl. **-men. 1.** a person who lives in the country. **2.** a person from a particular country or from one's own country. **—'country,woman** fem. n.

countryside ('kʌntrɪ,saɪd) n. a rural area or its population.

county ('kauntɪ) n., pl. **-ties. 1. a.** any of various administrative, political, or judicial subdivisions of certain English-speaking countries or states. **b.** (as modifier): county cricket. ~adj. **2.** Brit. inf. upper class; of or like the landed gentry.

coup (kuː) n. **1.** a brilliant and successful stroke or action. **2.** short for **coup d'état.**

coup de grâce French. (ku də 'grɑs) n., pl. **coups de grâce** (ku də 'grɑs). **1.** a mortal or finishing blow, esp. one delivered as an act of mercy to a sufferer. **2.** a final or decisive stroke.

coup d'état ('kuː deɪ'tɑː) n., pl. **coups d'état** ('kuːz deɪ-'tɑː). a sudden violent or illegal seizure of government.

coupe (kuːp) n. **1.** a dessert of fruit and ice cream. **2.** a dish or stemmed glass bowl designed for this dessert.

coupé ('kuːpeɪ) n. **1.** a four-seater car with a sloping back, and usually two doors. **2.** a four-wheeled horse-drawn carriage with two seats inside and one outside for the driver.

couple ('kʌpl) n. **1.** two people who regularly associate with each other or live together: an engaged couple. **2.** (functioning as sing. or pl.) two people considered as a pair, for or as if for dancing, games, etc. **3.** a pair of equal and opposite parallel forces that have a tendency to produce rotation. **4.** a connector or link between two members, such as a tie connecting a pair of rafters in a roof. **5. a couple of.** (functioning as sing. or pl.) **a.** a combination of two; a pair of: a couple of men. **b.** Inf. a small number of; a few: a couple of days. ~pron. **6.** (usually preceded by a; functioning as sing. or pl.) two; a pair: give him a couple. ~vb. **7.** (tr.) to connect (two things) together or to connect (one thing) to (another):

to couple railway carriages. **8.** to form or be formed into a pair or pairs. **9.** to associate, put, or connect together. **10.** (intr.) to have sexual intercourse.

couplet ('kʌplɪt) n. two successive lines of verse, usually rhymed and of the same metre.

coupling ('kʌplɪŋ) n. **1.** a mechanical device that connects two things. **2.** a device for connecting railway cars or trucks together.

coupon ('kuːpɒn) n. **1. a.** a detachable part of a ticket or advertisement entitling the holder to a discount, free gift, etc. **b.** a detachable slip usable as a commercial order form. **c.** a voucher given away with certain goods, a certain number of which are exchangeable for goods offered by the manufacturers. **2.** one of a number of detachable certificates attached to a bond, the surrender of which entitles the bearer to receive interest payments. **3.** Brit. a detachable entry form for any of certain competitions, esp. football pools.

courage ('kʌrɪdʒ) n. **1.** the power or quality of dealing with or facing danger, fear, pain, etc. **2. the courage of one's convictions.** the confidence to act in accordance with one's beliefs.

courageous (kə'reɪdʒəs) adj. possessing or expressing courage. **—cou'rageously** adv. **—cou'rageousness** n.

coureur de bois (French kurœːr də 'bwa) n., pl. **coureurs de bois** (kurœːr də 'bwa). Canad. history. a French Canadian woodsman who traded with Indians for furs.

courgette (kuə'ʒɛt) n. a small variety of vegetable marrow. U.S. name: **zucchini.**

courier ('kuərɪə) n. **1.** a special messenger, esp. one carrying diplomatic correspondence. **2.** a person who makes arrangements for or accompanies a group of travellers on a journey or tour.

course (kɔːs) n. **1.** a continuous progression in time or space; onward movement. **2.** a route or direction followed. **3.** the path or channel along which something moves: the course of a river. **4.** an area or stretch of land or water on which a sport is played or a race is run: a golf course. **5.** a period of time; duration: in the course of the next hour. **6.** the usual order of and time required for a sequence of events; regular procedure: the illness ran its course. **7.** a mode of conduct or action: if you follow that course, you will fail. **8.** a connected series of events, actions, etc. **9. a.** a prescribed number of lessons, lectures, etc., in an educational curriculum. **b.** the material covered in such a curriculum. **10.** a regimen prescribed for a specific period of time: a course of treatment. **11.** a part of a meal served at one time. **12.** a continuous, usually horizontal, layer of building material, such as a row of bricks, tiles, etc. **13. as a matter of course.** as a natural or normal consequence, mode of action, or event. **14. the course of nature.** the ordinary course of events. **15. in course of.** in the process of. **16. in due course.** at some future time, esp. the natural or appropriate time. **17. of course. a.** (adv.) as expected; naturally. **b.** (sentence substitute) certainly; definitely. ~vb. **18.** (intr.) to run, race, or flow. **19.** to cause (hounds) to hunt by sight rather than scent or (of hounds) to hunt (a quarry) thus.

▰THESAURUS▰

less, measureless, multitudinous, myriad, numberless, uncounted, untold

count on or **upon** bank on, believe (in), depend on, lean on, pin one's faith on, reckon on, rely on, take for granted, take on trust, trust

count out disregard, except, exclude, leave out, leave out of account, pass over

country n. **1.** commonwealth, kingdom, nation, people, realm, sovereign state, state **2.** fatherland, homeland, motherland, nationality, native land, patria **3.** land, part, region, terrain, territory **4.** citizenry, citizens, community, electors, grass roots, inhabitants, nation, people, populace, public, society, voters **5.** backwoods, boondocks (U.S. sl.), countryside, farmland, green belt, outback (Australian & New Zealand), outdoors, provinces, rural areas, sticks (Inf.), the back of beyond, the middle of nowhere, wide open spaces (Inf.) ~adj. **6.** agrarian, Arcadian, bucolic, georgic (Literary), landed, pastoral, provin-

cial, rural, rustic

countryman 1. bumpkin, country dweller, farmer, hayseed (U.S. inf.), hind, husbandman, peasant, provincial, rustic, swain, yokel **2.** compatriot, fellow citizen

countryside country, farmland, green belt, outback (Australian & New Zealand), outdoors, panorama, sticks (Inf.), view, wide open spaces (Inf.)

count up add, reckon up, sum, tally, total

county 1. n. province, shire **2.** adj. huntin', shootin', and fishin' (Inf.), plummy (Inf.), tweedy, upper-class, upper-crust (Inf.)

coup accomplishment, action, deed, exploit, feat, manoeuvre, masterstroke, stratagem, stroke, stroke of genius, stunt, tour de force

couple 1. n. brace, duo, pair, span (of horses or oxen), twain (Archaic), twosome **2.** v. buckle, clasp, conjoin, connect, hitch, join, link, marry, pair, unite, wed, yoke

coupon card, certificate, detachable portion, slip, ticket, token, voucher

courage boldness, bottle (Sl.), bravery, daring, dauntlessness, fearlessness, firmness, fortitude, gallantry, grit, guts (Inf.), hardihood, heroism, intrepidity, lion-heartedness, mettle, nerve, pluck, resolution, spunk (Inf.), valour

courageous audacious, bold, brave, daring, dauntless, fearless, gallant, hardy, heroic, indomitable, intrepid, lion-hearted, plucky, resolute, stouthearted, valiant, valorous

course n. **1.** advance, advancement, continuity, development, flow, furtherance, march, movement, order, progress, progression, sequence, succession, unfolding **2.** channel, direction, line, orbit, passage, path, road, route, tack, track, trail, trajectory, way **3.** duration, lapse, passage, passing, sweep, term, time **4.** behaviour, conduct, manner, method, mode, plan, policy, procedure, programme,

courser¹ ('kɔːsə) n. 1. a person who courses hounds or dogs, esp. greyhounds. 2. a hound or dog trained for coursing.

courser² ('kɔːsə) n. Literary. a swift horse; steed.

coursing ('kɔːsɪŋ) n. 1. (of hounds or dogs) hunting by sight. 2. a sport in which hounds are matched against one another in pairs for the hunting of hares by sight.

court (kɔːt) n. 1. an area of ground wholly or partly surrounded by walls or buildings. 2. Brit. a. a block of flats. b. a mansion or country house. c. a short street, sometimes closed at one end. 3. a. the residence, retinues, or household of a sovereign or nobleman. b. (as modifier): a court ball. 4. a sovereign or prince and his retinue, advisers, etc. 5. any formal assembly held by a sovereign or nobleman. 6. homage, flattering attention, or amorous approaches (esp. in **pay court to someone**). 7. Law. a tribunal having power to adjudicate in civil, criminal, military, or ecclesiastical matters. 8. Law. the regular sitting of such a judicial tribunal. 9. a. a marked outdoor or enclosed area used for any of various ball games, such as tennis, squash, etc. b. a marked section of such an area. 10. **go to court.** to take legal action. 11. **hold court.** to preside over admirers, attendants, etc. 12. **out of court.** without a trial or legal case. 13. **the ball is in your court.** you are obliged to make the next move. ~vb. 14. to attempt to gain the love of; woo. 15. (tr.) to pay attention to (someone) in order to gain favour. 16. (tr.) to try to obtain (fame, honour, etc.). 17. (tr.) to invite, usually foolishly, as by taking risks.

court card n. (in a pack of playing cards) a king, queen, or jack of any suit.

Courtelle (kɔː'tɛl) n. Trademark. a synthetic acrylic fibre resembling wool.

courteous ('kɜːtɪəs) adj. polite and considerate in manner. —**'courteously** adv. —**'courteousness** n.

courtesan or **courtezan** (ˌkɔːtɪ'zæn) n. (esp. formerly) a prostitute, or the mistress of a man of rank.

courtesy ('kɜːtɪsɪ) n., pl. -sies. 1. politeness; good manners. 2. a courteous gesture or remark. 3. favour or consent (esp. in **by courtesy of**). 4. common consent as opposed to right (esp. in **by courtesy**).

courthouse ('kɔːt,haʊs) n. a public building in which courts of law are held.

courtier ('kɔːtɪə) n. 1. an attendant at a court. 2. a person who seeks favour in an ingratiating manner.

courtly ('kɔːtlɪ) adj. -lier, -liest. 1. of or suitable for a royal court. 2. refined in manner. 3. ingratiating. —**'courtliness** n.

court martial n., pl. **court martials** or **courts martial.** 1. a military court that tries charges of serious breaches of martial law. ~vb. **court-martial, -tialling, -tialled** or U.S. **-tialing, -tialed.** 2. (tr.) to try by court martial.

court plaster n. a plaster, composed of isinglass on silk, formerly used to cover superficial wounds.

courtship ('kɔːtʃɪp) n. 1. the act, period, or art of seeking the love of someone with intent to marry. 2. the seeking or soliciting of favours.

court shoe n. a low-cut shoe for women, without any laces or straps.

courtyard ('kɔːt,jɑːd) n. an open area of ground surrounded by walls or buildings; court.

couscous ('kuːskuːs) n. a spicy dish, originating in

North Africa, consisting of steamed semolina served with a meat stew.

cousin ('kʌzən) n. 1. Also called: **first cousin, cousin-german, full cousin.** the child of one's aunt or uncle. 2. a relative descended from one of one's common ancestors. 3. a title used by a sovereign when addressing another sovereign or a nobleman. —**'cousin,hood** or **'cousin,ship** n. —**'cousinly** adj., adv.

couture (kuː'tʊə) n. high fashion designing and dressmaking.

couturier (kuː'tʊərɪ,eɪ) n. a person who designs, makes, and sells fashion clothes for women. —**couturière** (kuː-ˌtuːrɪ'ɛə) fem. n.

cove¹ (kəʊv) n. 1. a small bay or inlet. 2. a narrow cavern in the side of a cliff, mountain, etc. 3. Also called: **coving.** Archit. a concave curved surface between the wall and ceiling of a room.

cove² (kəʊv) n. Sl., Brit. old-fashioned & Austral. a fellow; chap.

coven ('kʌvən) n. a meeting of witches.

covenant ('kʌvənənt) n. 1. a binding agreement; contract. 2. Law. an agreement in writing under seal, as to pay a stated annual sum to a charity. 3. Bible. God's promise to the Israelites and their commitment to worship him alone. ~vb. 4. to agree to a covenant (concerning). —**covenantal** (ˌkʌvə'næntəl) adj. —**covenantor** or **covenanter** ('kʌvənəntə) n.

Covenanter ('kʌvənəntə, ˌkʌvə'næntə) n. Scot. history. a person upholding either of two 17th-century covenants to establish and defend Presbyterianism.

Coventry ('kɒvəntrɪ) n. **send to Coventry.** to ostracize or ignore.

cover ('kʌvə) vb. (mainly tr.) 1. to place or spread something over so as to protect or conceal. 2. to provide with a covering; clothe. 3. to put a garment, esp. a hat, on (the body or head). 4. to extend over or lie thickly on the surface of: snow covered the fields. 5. to bring upon (oneself); invest (oneself) as if with a covering: covered with shame. 6. (sometimes foll. by up) to act as a screen or concealment for; hide from view. 7. Mil. to protect (an individual, formation, or place) by taking up a position from which fire may be returned if those being protected are fired upon. 8. (also intr., sometimes foll. by for) to assume responsibility for (a person or thing). 9. (intr.; foll. by for or up for) to provide an alibi (for). 10. to have as one's territory: this salesman covers your area. 11. to travel over. 12. (tr.) to have or place in the aim and within the range of (a firearm). 13. to include or deal with. 14. (of an asset or income) to be sufficient to meet (a liability or expense). 15. a. to insure against loss, risk, etc. b. to provide for (loss, risk, etc.) by insurance. 16. to deposit (an equivalent stake) in a bet. 17. to act as reporter or photographer on (a news event, etc.) for a newspaper or magazine: to cover sports events. 18. Sport. to guard or protect (an opponent, teammate, or area). 19. (of a male animal, esp. a horse) to copulate with (a female animal). ~n. 20. anything that covers, spreads over, protects, or conceals. 21. a. a blanket used on a bed for warmth. b. another word for **bedspread.** 22. a pretext, disguise, or false identity: the thief sold brushes as a cover. 23. an envelope or package for sending through the post: under plain cover. 24. Philately. an entire envelope that has been postmarked. 25. a. an individual table setting, esp. in a restaurant. b.

regimen 5. cinder track, circuit, lap, race, racecourse, round 6. classes, course of study, curriculum, lectures, programme, schedule, studies ~v. 7. dash, flow, gush, move apace, race, run, scud, scurry, speed, stream, surge, tumble 8. chase, follow, hunt, pursue 9. in **due course** eventually, finally, in the course of time, in the end, in time, sooner or later 10. **of course** certainly, definitely, indubitably, naturally, obviously, undoubtedly, without a doubt

court n. 1. cloister, courtyard, piazza, plaza, quad (Inf.), quadrangle, square, yard 2. hall, manor, palace 3. attendants, cortege, entourage, retinue, royal household, suite, train 4. bar, bench, court of justice, lawcourt, seat of judgment, tribunal 5. addresses, attention, homage, respects, suit ~v. 6. chase, date, go (out) with, go steady with (Inf.),

keep company with, make love to, pay court to, pay one's addresses to, pursue, run after, serenade, set one's cap at, sue (Archaic), take out, walk out with, woo 7. cultivate, curry favour with, fawn upon, flatter, pander to, seek, solicit 8. attract, bring about, incite, invite, prompt, provoke, seek

courteous affable, attentive, ceremonious, civil, courtly, elegant, gallant, gracious, mannerly, polished, polite, refined, respectful, urbane, well-bred, well-mannered

courtesy 1. affability, civility, courteousness, courtliness, elegance, gallantness, gallantry, good breeding, good manners, graciousness, polish, politeness, urbanity 2. benevolence, consent, consideration, favour, generosity, indulgence, kindness

courtier attendant, follower, henchman, liegeman, pursuivant (Historical), squire,

train-bearer

courtly affable, aristocratic, ceremonious, chivalrous, civil, decorous, dignified, elegant, flattering, formal, gallant, highbred, lordly, obliging, polished, refined, stately, urbane

courtship courting, engagement, keeping company, pursuit, romance, suit, wooing

courtyard area, enclosure, peristyle, playground, quad, quadrangle, yard

cove anchorage, bay, creek, firth or frith (Scot.), inlet, sound

covenant n. 1. arrangement, bargain, commitment, compact, concordat, contract, convention, pact, promise, stipulation, treaty, trust 2. bond, deed ~v. 3. agree, bargain, contract, engage, pledge, stipulate, undertake

(as modifier): *a cover charge.* **26.** *Cricket.* **a.** (often pl.) the area more or less at right angles to the pitch on the off side and usually about halfway to the boundary. **b.** (as modifier): *a cover drive.* **27. break cover.** to come out from a shelter or hiding place. **28. take cover.** to make for a place of safety or shelter. **29. under cover.** protected, concealed, or in secret. —'**coverable** adj. —'**coverer** n.

coverage ('kʌvərɪdʒ) n. **1.** the amount or extent to which something is covered. **2.** *Journalism.* the amount and quality of reporting or analysis given to a particular subject or event. **3.** the extent of the protection provided by insurance.

cover girl n. a glamorous girl whose picture appears on the cover of a magazine.

covering letter n. an accompanying letter sent as an explanation, introduction, or record.

coverlet ('kʌvəlɪt) n. another word for **bedspread.**

cover note n. *Brit.* a certificate providing temporary insurance.

cover point n. *Cricket.* **a.** a fielding position in the covers. **b.** a fielder in this position.

covert ('kʌvət) adj. **1.** concealed or secret. ~n. **2.** a shelter or disguise. **3.** a thicket or woodland providing shelter for game. **4.** *Ornithol.* any of the small feathers on the wings and tail of a bird that surround the bases of the larger feathers. —'**covertly** adv. —'**covertness** n.

cover-up n. **1.** concealment or attempted concealment of a mistake, crime, etc. ~vb. **cover up.** (adv.). **2.** (tr.) to cover completely. **3.** (when intr., often foll. by for) to attempt to conceal (a mistake or crime).

covet ('kʌvɪt) vb. (tr.) to wish, long, or crave for (something, esp. the property of another person). —'**covetable** adj.

covetous ('kʌvɪtəs) adj. (usually postpositive and foll. by of) jealously eager for the possession of something (esp. the property of another person). —'**covetously** adv. —'**covetousness** n.

covey ('kʌvɪ) n. **1.** a small flock of grouse or partridge. **2.** a small group, as of people.

cow[1] (kau) n. **1.** the mature female of any species of cattle, esp. domesticated cattle. **2.** the mature female of various other mammals, such as the elephant, whale, and seal. **3.** (not in technical use) any domestic species of cattle. **4.** *Inf.* a disagreeable woman. **5.** *Austral. sl.* something objectionable (esp. in **a fair cow**).

cow[2] (kau) vb. (tr.) to frighten or overawe, as with threats.

coward ('kauəd) n. a person who shrinks from or avoids danger, pain, or difficulty. —'**cowardly** adj.

cowardice ('kauədɪs) n. lack of courage in facing danger, pain, or difficulty.

cowbell ('kau,bɛl) n. a bell hung around a cow's neck so that the cow can be easily located.

cowboy ('kau,bɔɪ) n. **1.** Also called: **cowhand.** a hired

man who herds and tends cattle, usually on horseback, esp. in the western U.S. **2.** a conventional character of Wild West folklore, films, etc., esp. one involved in fighting Indians. **3.** *Inf.* an irresponsible or unscrupulous operator in business, etc. —'**cow,girl** fem. n.

cowcatcher ('kau,kætʃə) n. *U.S.* a metal frame on the front of a locomotive to clear the track of obstructions.

cower ('kauə) vb. (intr.) to crouch or cringe, as in fear.

cowhide ('kau,haɪd) n. **1.** the hide of a cow. **2.** the leather made from such a hide.

cowl (kaul) n. **1.** a hood, esp. a loose one. **2.** the hooded habit of a monk. **3.** a cover fitted to a chimney to increase ventilation and prevent draughts. **4.** the part of a car body that supports the windscreen and the bonnet. ~vb. (tr.) **5.** to cover or provide with a cowl.

cowlick ('kau,lɪk) n. *U.S.* a tuft of hair over the forehead.

cowling ('kaulɪŋ) n. a streamlined metal covering, esp. around an aircraft engine.

co-worker n. a fellow worker; associate.

cow parsley n. a common Eurasian umbelliferous hedgerow plant having umbrella-shaped clusters of white flowers.

cowpat ('kau,pæt) n. a single dropping of cow dung.

cowpox ('kau,pɒks) n. a contagious viral disease of cows characterized by vesicles, esp. on the teats and udder. Inoculation of humans with this virus provides temporary immunity to smallpox.

cowry or **cowrie** ('kaurɪ) n., pl. -**ries.** **1.** any marine gastropod mollusc of a mostly tropical family having a glossy brightly marked shell. **2.** the shell of any of these molluscs, esp. the money cowrie, used as money in parts of Africa and S Asia.

cowslip ('kau,slɪp) n. **1.** a primrose native to temperate regions of the Old World, having yellow flowers. **2.** *U.S.* another name for **marsh marigold.**

cox (kɒks) n. **1.** a coxswain. ~vb. **2.** to act as coxswain of (a boat). —'**coxless** adj.

coxcomb ('kɒks,kəum) n. **1.** a variant spelling of **cockscomb. 2.** *Obs.* the cap, resembling a cock's comb, worn by a jester. —'**cox,combry** n.

coxswain ('kɒksən, -,sweɪn) n. the helmsman of a lifeboat, racing shell, etc. Also called: **cockswain.**

coy (kɔɪ) adj. **1.** affectedly demure, esp. in a playful or provocative manner. **2.** shy; modest. **3.** evasive, esp. in an annoying way. —'**coyly** adv. —'**coyness** n.

Coy. *Mil. abbrev. for* company.

coyote ('kɔɪəut, kɔɪ'əuti; esp. U.S. 'kaɪəut, kaɪ'əuti) n., pl. -**otes** or -**ote.** a predatory canine mammal of the deserts and prairies of North America. Also called: **prairie wolf.**

coypu ('kɔɪpu:) n., pl. -**pus** or -**pu.** **1.** an aquatic South American rodent, introduced into Europe. It resembles a small beaver and is bred for its fur. **2.** the fur of this animal. ~Also called: **nutria.**

cozen ('kʌzən) vb. to cheat or trick (someone). —'**coz-**

---

cover v. **1.** camouflage, cloak, conceal, cover up, curtain, disguise, eclipse, enshroud, hide, hood, house, mask, obscure, screen, secrete, shade, shroud, veil ~n. **2.** cloak, cover-up, disguise, façade, front, mask, pretence, screen, smoke screen, veil, window-dressing ~v. **3.** defend, guard, protect, reinforce, shelter, shield, watch over ~n. **4.** camouflage, concealment, defence, guard, hiding place, protection, refuge, sanctuary, shelter, shield, undergrowth, woods ~v. **5.** canopy, clothe, coat, daub, dress, encase, envelop, invest, layer, mantle, overlay, overspread, put on, wrap ~n. **6.** binding, canopy, cap, case, clothing, coating, covering, dress, envelope, jacket, lid, sheath, top, wrapper ~v. **7.** comprehend, comprise, consider, contain, deal with, embody, embrace, encompass, examine, include, incorporate, involve, provide for, refer to, survey, take account of **8.** double for, fill in for, relieve, stand in for, substitute, take over, take the rap for (Sl.) **9.** describe, detail, investigate, narrate, recount, relate, report, tell of, write up **10.** balance, compensate, counterbalance, insure, make good, make up for, offset ~n. **11.** compensation, indemnity, insurance, payment, protec-

tion, reimbursement ~v. **12.** cross, pass through or over, range, travel over, traverse **13.** engulf, flood, overrun, submerge, wash over

covering **1.** n. blanket, casing, clothing, coating, cover, housing, layer, overlay, protection, shelter, top, wrap, wrapper, wrapping **2.** adj. accompanying, descriptive, explanatory, introductory

cover-up complicity, concealment, conspiracy, front, smoke screen, whitewash (Inf.)

cover up **1.** conceal, cover one's tracks, feign ignorance, hide, hush up, keep dark, keep secret, keep silent about, keep under one's hat (Inf.), repress, stonewall, suppress, whitewash (Inf.) **2.** coat, cover, encrust, envelop, hide, plaster, slather (U.S. sl.), swathe

covet aspire to, begrudge, crave, desire, envy, fancy (Inf.), hanker after, have one's eye on, long for, lust after, thirst for, yearn for

covetous acquisitive, avaricious, closefisted, envious, grasping, greedy, jealous, mercenary, rapacious, yearning

cow awe, browbeat, bully, daunt, dishearten, dismay, frighten, intimidate, overawe,

scare, subdue, terrorize, unnerve

coward caitiff (Archaic), craven, dastard (Archaic), faint-heart, funk (Inf.), poltroon, recreant (Archaic), renegade, scaredy-cat (Inf.), skulker, sneak, yellow-belly (Sl.)

cowardly base, caitiff (Archaic), chicken (Sl.), chicken-hearted, craven, dastardly, faint-hearted, fearful, gutless (Inf.), lily-livered, pusillanimous, recreant (Archaic), scared, shrinking, soft, spineless, timorous, weak, weak-kneed (Inf.), white-livered, yellow (Inf.)

cowboy broncobuster (U.S.), cattleman, cowhand, cowpuncher (U.S. inf.), drover, gaucho (S American), herder, herdsman, rancher, ranchero (U.S.), stockman, wrangler (U.S.)

cower cringe, crouch, draw back, fawn, flinch, grovel, quail, shrink, skulk, sneak, tremble, truckle

coy arch, backward, bashful, coquettish, demure, evasive, flirtatious, kittenish, modest, overmodest, prudish, reserved, retiring, self-effacing, shrinking, shy, skittish, timid

enage n.

cp. abbrev. for compare.

c.p. abbrev. for candle power.

C.P. abbrev. for: **1.** Common Prayer. **2.** Communist Party. **3.** (in Australia) Country Party. **4.** Canadian Pacific Ltd.

Cpl. abbrev. for Corporal.

C.P.O. abbrev. for Chief Petty Officer.

c.p.s. Physics. abbrev. for cycles per second.

Cr the chemical symbol for chromium.

cr. abbrev. for: **1.** credit. **2.** creditor.

crab[1] (kræb) n. **1.** any chiefly marine decapod crustacean having a broad flattened carapace covering the cephalothorax, beneath which is folded the abdomen. The first pair of limbs are pincers. **2.** any of various similar or related arthropods. **3.** short for **crab louse. 4.** a mechanical lifting device, esp. the travelling hoist of a gantry crane. **5. catch a crab.** Rowing. to make a stroke in which the oar either misses the water or digs too deeply, causing the rower to fall backwards. ~vb. **crabbing, crabbed. 6.** (intr.) to hunt or catch crabs.

crab[2] (kræb) Inf. vb. **crabbing, crabbed. 1.** (intr.) to find fault; grumble. ~n. **2.** an irritable person.

crab[3] (kræb) n. short for **crab apple.**

Crab (kræb) n. **the.** the constellation Cancer, the fourth sign of the zodiac.

crab apple n. **1.** any of several rosaceous trees that have white, pink, or red flowers and small sour applelike fruits. **2.** the fruit of any of these trees, used to make jam.

crabbed ('kræbid) adj. **1.** surly; irritable; perverse. **2.** (esp. of handwriting) cramped and hard to decipher. **3.** Rare. abstruse. —'**crabbedly** adv. —'**crabbedness** n.

crabby ('kræbɪ) adj. **-bier, -biest.** bad-tempered.

crab louse n. a parasitic louse that infests the pubic region in man.

crack (kræk) vb. **1.** to break or cause to break without complete separation of the parts. **2.** to break or cause to break with a sudden sharp sound; snap. **3.** to make or cause to make a sudden sharp sound: to crack a whip. **4.** to cause (the voice) to change tone or become harsh or (of the voice) to change tone, esp. to a higher register; break. **5.** Inf. to fail or cause to fail. **6.** to yield or cause to yield. **7.** (tr.) to hit with a forceful or resounding blow. **8.** (tr.) to break into or force open: to crack a safe. **9.** (tr.) to solve or decipher (a code, problem, etc.). **10.** (tr.) Inf. to tell (a joke, etc.). **11.** to break (a molecule) into smaller molecules or radicals by the action of heat, as in the distillation of petroleum. **12.** (intr.) Scot. & N English dialect. to chat; gossip. **13.** (tr.) Austral. inf. to achieve (esp. in **crack it**). **14. crack a smile.** Inf. to break into a smile. **15. crack hardy.** Austral. inf. to disguise one's discomfort, etc.; put on a bold front. ~n. **16.** a sudden sharp noise. **17.** a break or fracture without complete separation of the two parts. **18.** a narrow opening or fissure. **19.** Inf. a resounding blow. **20.** a physical or mental defect; flaw. **21.** a moment or specific instant: the crack of day. **22.** a broken or cracked tone of voice, as a boy's during puberty. **23.** (often foll. by at) Inf. an attempt; opportunity to try. **24.** Sl. a gibe; wisecrack; joke. **25.** Sl. a person that excels. **26.** Scot. & N English dialect. a talk; chat. **27. a fair crack of the whip.** Inf. a fair chance or opportunity. **28. crack of doom.** doomsday; the end of the world; the Day of Judgment. ~adj. **29.** (prenominal) Sl. first-class; excellent: a crack shot. ~See also **crack down, crack up.**

crackbrained ('kræk,breɪnd) adj. insane, idiotic, or crazy.

crack down vb. (intr., adv.; often foll. by on) **1.** to take severe measures (against); become stricter (with). ~n. **crackdown. 2.** severe or repressive measures.

cracked (krækt) adj. **1.** damaged by cracking. **2.** Sl. crazy.

cracker ('krækə) n. **1.** a decorated cardboard tube that emits a bang when pulled apart, releasing a toy, a joke, or a paper hat. **2.** short for **firecracker. 3.** a thin crisp biscuit, usually unsweetened. **4.** a person or thing that cracks. **5.** Brit. sl. a person of notable qualities or abilities, esp. an attractive girl.

crackers ('krækəz) adj. (postpositive) Brit. a slang word for **insane.**

cracking ('krækɪŋ) adj. **1.** (prenominal) Inf. fast; vigorous (esp. in **a cracking pace**). **2. get cracking.** Inf. to start doing something quickly or with increased speed. ~adv., adj. **3.** Brit. inf. first-class; excellent. ~n. **4.** the process in which molecules are cracked, esp. the oil-refining process in which heavy oils are broken down into hydrocarbons of lower molecular weight by heat or catalysis.

crackle ('krækəl) vb. **1.** to make or cause to make a series of slight sharp noises, as of paper being crushed. **2.** (tr.) to decorate (porcelain or pottery) by causing fine cracks to appear in the glaze. **3.** (intr.) to abound in vivacity or energy. ~n. **4.** the act or sound of crackling. **5.** intentional crazing in the glaze of porcelain or pottery. **6.** Also called: **crackleware.** porcelain or pottery so decorated. —'**crackly** adj.

crackling ('kræklɪŋ) n. the crisp browned skin of roast pork.

crackpot ('kræk,pɒt) Inf. ~n. **1.** an eccentric person; crank. ~adj. **2.** eccentric; crazy.

crack up vb. (adv.) **1.** (intr.) to break into pieces. **2.** (intr.) Inf. to undergo a physical or mental breakdown. **3.** (tr.) Inf. to present or report, esp. in glowing terms: it's not all it's cracked up to be. ~n. **crackup. 4.** Inf. a physical or mental breakdown.

-cracy n. combining form. indicating a type of government or rule: plutocracy; mobocracy. See also **-crat.**

cradle ('kreɪdəl) n. **1.** a baby's bed, often with rockers. **2.** a place where something originates. **3.** a frame, rest, or trolley made to support a piece of equipment, aircraft, ship, etc. **4.** a platform or trolley in which workmen are suspended on the side of a building or ship. **5.** Agriculture. **a.** a framework of several wooden fingers attached to a scythe to gather the grain into bunches as it is cut. **b.** a scythe with such a cradle. **6.** Also called: **rocker.** a boxlike apparatus for washing rocks, sand, etc., containing gold or gem stones. **7. rob the cradle.** Inf. to take for a lover, husband, or wife a person much younger than oneself. ~vb. **8.** (tr.) to rock or place in or as if in a cradle; hold tenderly. **9.** (tr.) to nurture in or bring up from infancy. **10.** (tr.) to wash (soil bearing gold, etc.) in a cradle. —'**cradler** n.

craft (krɑːft) n. **1.** skill or ability. **2.** skill in deception and trickery. **3.** an occupation or trade requiring special skill, esp. manual dexterity. **4. a.** the members of such a trade, regarded collectively. **b.** (as modifier): a craft union. **5.** a single vessel, aircraft, or spacecraft. **6.** (functioning as pl.) ships, boats, aircraft, or spacecraft collectively. ~vb. **7.** (tr.) to make or fashion with skill, esp. by hand.

---

crabbed 1. acrid, acrimonious, captious, churlish, cross, cynical, difficult, fretful, harsh, ill-tempered, irritable, morose, perverse, petulant, prickly, sour, splenetic, surly, tart, testy, tough, trying **2.** Of handwriting awkward, cramped, hieroglyphical, illegible, indecipherable, laboured, squeezed, unreadable

crack v. **1.** break, burst, chip, chop, cleave, crackle, craze, fracture, rive, snap, splinter, split ~n. **2.** breach, break, chink, chip, cleft, cranny, crevice, fracture, gap, interstice, rift ~v. **3.** burst, crash, detonate, explode, pop, ring, snap ~n. **4.** burst, clap, crash, explosion, pop, report, snap ~v. **5.** break down, give way, go to pieces, lose control, succumb, yield ~v./n. **6.** Inf.

buffet, clip (Inf.), clout (Inf.), cuff, slap, thump, wallop (Inf.), whack ~v. **7.** decipher, fathom, get the answer to, solve, work out ~n. **8.** Inf. attempt, go, opportunity, stab, try **9.** Sl. dig, funny remark, gag, insult, jibe, joke, quip, smart-alecky remark, wisecrack, witticism ~adj. **10.** Sl. ace, choice, elite, excellent, first-class, first-rate, hand-picked, superior

cracked 1. broken, chipped, crazed, damaged, defective, faulty, fissured, flawed, imperfect, split **2.** Sl. bats (Sl.), batty (Sl.), crackbrained, crackpot (Inf.), crazy (Inf.), daft (Sl.), eccentric, insane, loony (Sl.), nuts (Sl.), nutty (Sl.), off one's head or nut (Sl.), out of one's mind, round the bend (Sl.), touched

cracked up blown up, exaggerated,

hyped up (Sl.), overpraised, overrated, puffed up

crack up break down, collapse, come apart at the seams (Inf.), freak out (Inf.), go crazy (Inf.), go off one's rocker (Sl.), go out of one's mind, go to pieces, have a breakdown

cradle n. **1.** bassinet, cot, crib, Moses basket **2.** Fig. beginning, birthplace, fount, fountainhead, origin, source, spring, wellspring ~v. **3.** hold, lull, nestle, nurse, rock, support **4.** nourish, nurture, tend, watch over

craft 1. ability, aptitude, art, artistry, cleverness, dexterity, expertise, expertness, ingenuity, knack, know-how (Inf.), skill, technique, workmanship **2.** artfulness, artifice, contrivance, craftiness, cunning, deceit, du-

craftsman ('krɑːftsmən) *n., pl.* **-men.** **1.** a member of a skilled trade; someone who practises a craft; artisan. **2.** an artist skilled in an art or craft. —'**craftsman,ship** *n.*

crafty ('krɑːftɪ) *adj.* **-tier, -tiest.** **1.** skilled in deception; shrewd; cunning. **2.** *Arch.* skilful. —'**craftily** *adv.* —'**craftiness** *n.*

crag (kræg) *n.* a steep rugged rock or peak. —**craggy** *adj.*

crake (kreɪk) *n. Zool.* any of several rails of the Old World, such as the corncrake.

cram (kræm) *vb.* **cramming, crammed.** **1.** (*tr.*) to force more (people, material, etc.) into (a room, container, etc.) than it can hold; stuff. **2.** to eat or cause to eat more than necessary. **3.** *Inf.* to study or cause to study (facts, etc.), esp. for an examination, by hastily memorizing. ~*n.* **4.** the act or condition of cramming. **5.** a crush.

crammer ('kræmə) *n.* a person or school that prepares pupils for an examination.

cramp[1] (kræmp) *n.* **1.** a painful involuntary contraction of a muscle, typically caused by overexertion, heat, or chill. **2.** temporary partial paralysis of a muscle group: *writer's cramp.* **3.** (*usually pl. in the U.S.*) severe abdominal pain. ~*vb.* **4.** (*tr.*) to affect with or as if with a cramp.

cramp[2] (kræmp) *n.* **1.** Also called: **cramp iron.** a strip of metal with its ends bent at right angles, used to bind masonry. **2.** a device for holding pieces of wood while they are glued; clamp. **3.** something that confines or restricts. ~*vb.* (*tr.*) **4.** to hold with a cramp. **5.** to confine or restrict. **6. cramp (someone's) style.** *Inf.* to prevent (a person) from using his abilities or acting freely and confidently.

cramped (kræmpt) *adj.* **1.** closed in; restricted. **2.** (esp. of handwriting) small and irregular.

crampon ('kræmpən) *or* **crampoon** (kræm'puːn) *n.* **1.** one of a pair of pivoted steel levers used to lift heavy objects; grappling iron. **2.** (*often pl.*) a metal spike fitted to boots for climbing, walking on ice, etc.

cranberry ('krænbərɪ, -brɪ) *n., pl.* **-ries.** **1.** any of several trailing shrubs that bear sour edible red berries. **2.** the berry of this plant.

crane (kreɪn) *n.* **1.** a large long-necked long-legged wading bird inhabiting marshes and plains in most parts of the world. **2.** (*not in ornithological use*) any similar bird, such as a heron. **3.** a device for lifting and moving heavy objects, typically consisting of a pivoted boom rotating about a vertical axis with lifting gear suspended from the end of the boom. ~*vb.* **4.** (*tr.*) to lift or move (an object) by or as if by a crane. **5.** to stretch out (esp. the neck), as to see over other people's heads.

crane fly *n.* a dipterous fly having long legs, slender wings, and a narrow body. Also called (*Brit.*): **daddy-longlegs.**

cranial ('kreɪnɪəl) *adj.* of or relating to the skull. —'**cranially** *adv.*

cranio- *or before a vowel* **crani-** *combining form.* indicating the cranium or cranial.

craniology (,kreɪnɪ'ɒlədʒɪ) *n.* the branch of science concerned with the shape and size of the human skull. —**craniological** (,kreɪnɪə'lɒdʒɪkəl) *adj.* —,**cranio'logical-ly** *adv.* —,**crani'ologist** *n.*

cranium ('kreɪnɪəm) *n., pl.* **-niums** *or* **-nia** (-nɪə). **1.** the skull of a vertebrate. **2.** the part of the skull that encloses the brain.

crank (kræŋk) *n.* **1.** a device for communicating or converting motion, consisting of an arm projecting from a shaft, often with a second member attached to it parallel to the shaft. **2.** Also called: **crank handle, starting handle.** a handle incorporating a crank, used to start an engine or motor. **3.** *Inf.* **a.** an eccentric or odd person. **b.** *U.S.* a bad-tempered person. ~*vb.* **4.** (*tr.*) to rotate (a shaft) by means of a crank. **5.** (*tr.*) to start (an engine, motor, etc.) by means of a crank handle.

crankcase ('kræŋk,keɪs) *n.* the metal housing that encloses the crankshaft, connecting rods, etc., in an internal-combustion engine.

crankpin ('kræŋk,pɪn) *n.* a short cylindrical surface fitted between two arms of a crank parallel to the main shaft of the crankshaft.

crankshaft ('kræŋk,ʃɑːft) *n.* a shaft having one or more cranks, to which the connecting rods are attached.

crank up *vb.* (*tr., adv.*) **1.** to start (an engine, motor, etc.) with a crank handle. **2.** *Sl.* to speed up.

cranky ('kræŋkɪ) *adj.* **crankier, crankiest.** **1.** *Inf.* eccentric. **2.** *U.S. inf.* fussy and bad-tempered. **3.** shaky; out of order. —'**crankily** *adv.* —'**crankiness** *n.*

crannog ('krænəg) *n.* an ancient Celtic lake or bog dwelling.

cranny ('krænɪ) *n., pl.* **-nies.** a narrow opening, as in a wall or rock face; chink; crevice (esp. in **every nook and cranny**). —'**crannied** *adj.*

crap[1] (kræp) *n.* **1.** a losing throw in the game of craps. **2.** another name for **craps.**

crap[2] (kræp) *n. Sl.* **1.** nonsense. **2.** rubbish. **3.** a taboo word for **faeces.** ~*vb.* **crapping, crapped.** **4.** (*intr.*) a taboo word for **defecate.**

crape (kreɪp) *n.* **1.** a variant spelling of **crepe. 2.** crepe, esp. when used for mourning clothes. **3.** a band of black crepe worn in mourning.

craps (kræps) *n.* (*usually functioning as sing.*) **1.** a gambling game using two dice. **2. shoot craps.** to play this game. —'**crap,shooter** *n.*

crapulent ('kræpjʊlənt) *or* **crapulous** ('kræpjʊləs) *adj.* **1.** given to or resulting from intemperance. **2.** suffering from intemperance; drunken. —'**crapulence** *n.*

crash[1] (kræʃ) *vb.* **1.** to make or cause to make a loud noise as of solid objects smashing or clattering. **2.** to fall or cause to fall with force, breaking in pieces with a loud noise. **3.** (*intr.*) to break or smash in pieces with a loud noise. **4.** (*intr.*) to collapse or fail suddenly. **5.** to cause (an aircraft) to land violently resulting in severe damage or (of an aircraft) to land in this way. **6.** to cause (a car, etc.) to collide with another car or other object or (of two or more cars) to be involved in a collision. **7.** to move or cause to move violently or noisily. ~*n.* **8.** an act or instance of breaking and falling to pieces. **9.** a sudden loud noise. **10.** a collision, as between vehicles. **11.** a sudden descent of an aircraft as a result of which it hits land or water. **12.** the sudden collapse of a business, stock exchange, etc. **13.** (*modifier*) requiring or using intensive effort and all possible resources in order to accomplish something quickly: *a crash programme.*

crash[2] (kræʃ) *n.* a coarse cotton or linen cloth.

THESAURUS

plicity, guile, ruse, scheme, shrewdness, stratagem, subterfuge, subtlety, trickery, wiles **3.** business, calling, employment, handicraft, handiwork, line, occupation, pursuit, trade, vocation, work **4.** aircraft, barque, boat, plane, ship, spacecraft, vessel

craftsmanship artfulness, astuteness, canniness, cunning, deviousness, duplicity, foxiness, guile, shrewdness, slyness, subtlety, trickiness, wiliness

craftsman artificer, artisan, maker, master, skilled worker, smith, technician, wright

craftsmanship artistry, expertise, mastery, technique, workmanship

crafty artful, astute, calculating, canny, cunning, deceitful, designing, devious, duplicitous, foxy, fraudulent, guileful, insidious, knowing, scheming, sharp, shrewd, sly, subtle, tricksy, tricky, wily

crag aiguille, bluff, peak, pinnacle, rock, tor

cram 1. compact, compress, crowd, crush, fill to overflowing, force, jam, overcrowd, overfill, pack, pack in, press, ram, shove, squeeze, stuff **2.** glut, gorge, gormandize, guzzle, overeat, overfeed, put *or* pack away, satiate, stuff **3.** *Inf.* con, grind, mug up (*Sl.*), revise, study, swot, swot up

cramp[1] *v.* check, circumscribe, clog, confine, constrain, encumber, hamper, hamstring, handicap, hinder, impede, inhibit, obstruct, restrict, shackle, stymie, thwart

cramp[2] *n.* ache, contraction, convulsion, crick, pain, pang, shooting pain, spasm, stiffness, stitch, twinge

cramped 1. awkward, circumscribed, closed in, confined, congested, crowded, hemmed in, jammed in, narrow, overcrowded, packed, restricted, squeezed, uncomfort-

able **2.** *Esp. of handwriting* crabbed, indecipherable, irregular, small

cranky bizarre, capricious, eccentric, erratic, freakish, freaky (*Sl.*), funny (*Inf.*), idiosyncratic, odd, peculiar, queer, quirky, strange, wacky (*Sl.*)

cranny breach, chink, cleft, crack, crevice, fissure, gap, hole, interstice, nook, opening

crash *n.* **1.** bang, boom, clang, clash, clatter, clattering, din, racket, smash, smashing, thunder ~*v.* **2.** break, break up, dash to pieces, disintegrate, fracture, fragment, shatter, shiver, smash, splinter **3.** come a cropper (*Inf.*), dash, fall, fall headlong, give way, hurtle, lurch, overbalance, pitch, plunge, precipitate oneself, sprawl, topple **4.** bang (into), collide, crash-land (*an aircraft*), drive into, have an accident, hit, hurtle into, plough into, run together, wreck ~*n.* **5.** accident, bump, collision, jar, jolt, pile-up (*Inf.*),

crash barrier _n._ a barrier erected along the centre of a motorway, around a racetrack, etc., for safety purposes.

crash dive _n._ **1.** a sudden steep dive from the surface by a submarine. ~_vb._ **crash-dive. 2.** (usually of an aircraft) to descend steeply and rapidly, before hitting the ground. **3.** to perform or cause to perform a crash dive.

crash helmet _n._ a padded helmet worn for motorcycling, flying, etc., to protect the head.

crashing ('kræʃɪŋ) _adj._ (_prenominal_) _Inf._ (intensifier) (esp. in **a crashing bore**).

crash-land _vb._ to land (an aircraft) causing some damage to it or (of an aircraft) to land in this way. —'crash-,landing _n._

crass (kræs) _adj._ **1.** stupid; gross. **2.** _Rare._ thick or coarse. —'crassly _adv._ —'crassness or 'crassi,tude _n._

-crat _n. combining form._ indicating a person who takes part in or is a member of a form of government or class. —-cratic _or_ -cratical _adj. combining form._

crate (kreɪt) _n._ **1.** a fairly large container, usually made of wooden slats or wickerwork, used for packing, storing, or transporting goods. **2.** _Sl._ an old car, aeroplane, etc. ~_vb._ **3.** (_tr._) to pack or place in a crate. —'crater _n._ —'crateful _n._

crater ('kreɪtə) _n._ **1.** the bowl-shaped opening in a volcano or a geyser. **2.** a similar depression formed by the impact of a meteorite or exploding bomb. **3.** any of the roughly circular or polygonal walled formations on the moon and some other planets. **4.** a large open bowl with two handles, used for mixing wines, esp. in ancient Greece. ~_vb._ **5.** to make or form craters in (a surface, such as the ground). —'crater-,like _adj._ —'craterous _adj._

cravat (krə'væt) _n._ a scarf worn round the neck instead of a tie, esp. by men.

crave (kreɪv) _vb._ **1.** (when _intr._, foll. by _for_ or _after_) to desire intensely; long (for). **2.** (_tr._) to need greatly or urgently. **3.** (_tr._) to beg or plead for. —'craver _n._ —'craving _n._

craven ('kreɪvən) _adj._ **1.** cowardly. ~_n._ **2.** a coward. —'cravenly _adv._ —'cravenness _n._

craw (krɔː) _n._ **1.** a less common word for **crop** (sense 6). **2.** the stomach of an animal. ~_vb._ **3. stick in someone's craw.** _Sl._ to be unacceptable or irritating to someone.

crawfish ('krɔː,fɪʃ) _n._, _pl._ **-fish** _or_ **-fishes.** a variant spelling of **crayfish** (esp. sense 2).

crawl (krɔːl) _vb._ (_intr._) **1.** to move slowly, either by dragging the body along the ground or on the hands and knees. **2.** to proceed very slowly or laboriously. **3.** to act in a servile manner; fawn. **4.** to be or feel as if overrun by crawling creatures: _the pile of refuse crawled with insects._ **5.** (_intr._) (of insects, worms, snakes, etc.) to move with the body close to the ground. **6.** (_intr._) to swim the crawl. ~_n._ **7.** a slow creeping pace or motion. **8.** _Swimming._ a stroke in which the feet are kicked like paddles while the arms reach forward and pull back through the water. —'crawlingly _adv._

crayfish ('kreɪ,fɪʃ) _or esp. U.S._ **crawfish** _n._, _pl._ **-fish** _or_ **-fishes. 1.** a freshwater decapod crustacean resembling a small lobster. **2.** any of various similar crustaceans, esp. the spiny lobster.

crayon ('kreɪən, -ɒn) _n._ **1.** a small stick or pencil of charcoal, wax, clay, or chalk mixed with coloured pigment. **2.** a drawing made with crayons. ~_vb._ **3.** to draw or colour with crayons. —'crayonist _n._

craze (kreɪz) _n._ **1.** a short-lived fashion. **2.** a wild or exaggerated enthusiasm. ~_vb._ **3.** to make or become mad. **4.** _Ceramics, metallurgy._ to develop or cause to develop fine cracks.

crazy ('kreɪzɪ) _adj._ **-zier, -ziest. 1.** _Inf._ insane. **2.** fantastic; strange; ridiculous. **3.** (_postpositive; foll._ by _about_ or _over_) _Inf._ extremely fond (of). —'crazily _adv._ —'craziness _n._

crazy paving _n._ _Brit._ a form of paving, as for a path, made of irregular slabs of stone.

creak (kriːk) _vb._ **1.** to make or cause to make a harsh squeaking sound. **2.** (_intr._) to make such sounds while moving: _the old car creaked along._ ~_n._ **3.** a harsh squeaking sound. —'creaky _adj._ —'creakily _adv._ —'creakiness _n._ —'creakingly _adv._

cream (kriːm) _n._ **1. a.** the fatty part of milk, which rises to the top. **b.** (_as modifier_): _cream buns._ **2.** anything resembling cream in consistency. **3.** the best one or most essential part of something; pick. **4.** a soup containing cream or milk: _cream of chicken soup._ **5.** any of various foods resembling or containing cream. **6. a.** a yellowish-white colour. **b.** (_as adj._): _cream wallpaper._ ~_vb._ **7.** (_tr._) to skim or otherwise separate the cream from (milk). **8.** (_tr._) to beat (foodstuffs) to a light creamy consistency. **9.** (_tr._) to add or apply cream or any creamlike substance to. **10.** (_tr.; sometimes foll._ by _off_) to take away the best part of. **11.** (_tr._) to prepare or cook (vegetables, chicken, etc.) with cream or milk. —'cream-,like _adj._ —'creamy _adj._

cream cheese _n._ a smooth soft white cheese made from soured cream or milk.

creamery ('kriːmərɪ) _n._, _pl._ **-eries. 1.** an establishment where milk and cream are made into butter and cheese. **2.** a place where dairy products are sold.

cream of tartar _n._ potassium hydrogen tartrate, esp. when used in baking powders.

crease (kriːs) _n._ **1.** a line or mark produced by folding, pressing, or wrinkling. **2.** a wrinkle or furrow, esp. on the face. **3.** _Cricket._ any three lines near each wicket marking positions for the bowler or batsman. ~_vb._ **4.** to make or become wrinkled or furrowed. **5.** (_tr._) to

---

THESAURUS

prang (_Inf._), smash, smash-up, thud, thump, wreck **6.** bankruptcy, collapse, debacle, depression, downfall, failure, ruin, smash ~_v._ **7.** be ruined, collapse, fail, fold, fold up, go broke (_Inf._), go bust (_Inf._), go under, smash ~_adj._ **8.** _Of a course of studies, etc._ emergency, intensive, immediate, round-the-clock, speeded-up, telescoped, urgent

crass asinine, blundering, boorish, bovine, coarse, dense, doltish, gross, indelicate, insensitive, lumpish, oafish, obtuse, stupid, unrefined, witless

crate 1. _n._ box, case, container, packing case, tea chest **2.** _v._ box, case, encase, enclose, pack, pack up

crater depression, dip, hollow, shell hole

crave 1. be dying for, cry out for (_Inf._), desire, fancy (_Inf._), hanker after, hunger after, long for, lust after, need, pant for, pine for, require, sigh for, thirst for, want, yearn for **2.** ask, beg, beseech, entreat, implore, petition, plead for, pray for, seek, solicit, supplicate

craven 1. _adj._ caitiff (_Archaic_), chicken-hearted, cowardly, dastardly, fearful, lily-livered, mean-spirited, niddering (_Archaic_), pusillanimous, scared, timorous, weak, yellow (_Inf._) **2.** _n._ base fellow (_Archaic_), caitiff (_Archaic_), coward, dastard (_Archaic_), niddering (_Archaic_), poltroon, recreant (_Archa-_

_ic_), renegade, wheyface, yellow-belly (_Sl._)

craving appetite, cacoethes, desire, hankering, hunger, longing, lust, thirst, urge, yearning, yen (_Inf._)

crawl 1. advance slowly, creep, drag, go on all fours, inch, move at a snail's pace, move on hands and knees, pull _or_ drag oneself along, slither, worm one's way, wriggle, writhe **2.** be overrun (alive, full of, lousy), swarm, teem **3.** abase oneself, cringe, fawn, grovel, humble oneself, toady, truckle

craze 1. _n._ enthusiasm, fad, fashion, infatuation, mania, mode, novelty, passion, preoccupation, rage, the latest (_Inf._), thing, trend, vogue **2.** _v._ bewilder, confuse, dement, derange, distemper, drive mad, enrage, infatuate, inflame, madden, make insane, send crazy _or_ berserk, unbalance, unhinge

crazy 1. _Inf._ a bit lacking upstairs (_Inf._), barmy (_Sl._), batty (_Sl._), berserk, bonkers (_Sl._), cracked (_Sl._), crazed, cuckoo (_Inf._), daft (_Sl._), delirious, demented, deranged, idiotic, insane, lunatic (_Inf. or archaic_), mad, mad as a hatter, mad as a March hare, maniacal, mental (_Sl._), not all there (_Inf._), nuts (_Sl._), nutty (_Sl._), nutty as a fruitcake (_Inf._), off one's head (_Sl._), of unsound mind, potty (_Inf._), round the bend (_Sl._), touched, unbalanced, unhinged **2.** bizarre, eccentric, fantastic, odd,

outrageous, peculiar, ridiculous, silly, strange, weird **3.** absurd, bird-brained (_Inf._), cockeyed (_Inf._), derisory, fatuous, foolhardy, foolish, half-baked (_Inf._), idiotic, ill-conceived, impracticable, imprudent, inane, inappropriate, irresponsible, ludicrous, nonsensical, potty (_Inf._), preposterous, puerile, quixotic, senseless, short-sighted, unrealistic, unwise, unworkable, wild **4.** _Inf._ ardent, beside oneself, devoted, eager, enamoured, enthusiastic, fanatical, hysterical, infatuated, mad, passionate, smitten, very keen, wild (_Inf._), zealous

creak _v._ grate, grind, groan, rasp, scrape, scratch, screech, squeak, squeal

cream _n._ **1.** cosmetic, emulsion, essence, liniment, lotion, oil, ointment, paste, salve, unguent **2.** best, _crème de la crème_, elite, flower, pick, prime ~_adj._ **3.** off-white, yellowish-white

creamy buttery, creamed, lush, milky, oily, rich, smooth, soft, velvety

crease 1. _v._ corrugate, crimp, crinkle, crumple, double up, fold, pucker, ridge, ruck up, rumple, screw up, wrinkle **2.** _n._ bulge, corrugation, fold, groove, line, overlap, pucker, ridge, ruck, tuck, wrinkle

graze with a bullet. —'**creaser** n. —'**creasy** adj.

create (kri:'eit) vb. **1.** (tr.) to cause to come into existence. **2.** (tr.) to invest with a new honour, office, or title; appoint. **3.** (tr.) to be the cause of. **4.** (tr.) to act (a role) in the first production of a play. **5.** (intr.) Brit. sl. to make a fuss or uproar.

creation (kri:'eiʃən) n. **1.** the act or process of creating. **2.** the fact of being created or produced. **3.** something brought into existence or created. **4.** the whole universe

Creation (kri:'eiʃən) n. Christianity. **1.** (often preceded by the) God's act of bringing the universe into being. **2.** the universe as thus brought into being by God.

creative (kri:'eitiv) adj. **1.** having the ability to create. **2.** characterized by originality of thought; having or showing imagination. **3.** designed to or tending to stimulate the imagination. —cre'**atively** adv. —cre'**ativeness** n. —,crea'**tivity** n.

creator (kri:'eitə) n. a person or thing that creates; originator. —cre'**ator,ship** n.

Creator (kri:'eitə) n. (usually preceded by the) an epithet of God.

creature ('kri:tʃə) n. **1.** a living being, esp. an animal. **2.** something that has been created, whether animate or inanimate. **3.** a human being; person: used as a term of scorn, pity, or endearment. **4.** a person who is dependent upon another; tool. —'**creatural** or '**creaturely** adj.

crèche (krɛʃ, kreiʃ) n. **1.** Chiefly Brit. a day nursery for very young children. **2.** a tableau of Christ's Nativity.

credence ('kri:dəns) n. **1.** acceptance or belief, esp. with regard to the evidence of others. **2.** something supporting a claim to belief; credential (esp. in **letters of credence**)

credential (kri'dɛnʃəl) n. **1.** something that entitles a person to confidence, authority, etc. **2.** (pl.) a letter or certificate giving evidence of the bearer's identity or competence.

credibility gap n. a disparity between claims or statements made and the evident facts of the situation or circumstances to which they relate.

credible ('krɛdɪbəl) adj. **1.** capable of being believed. **2.** trustworthy. —'**credibleness** or ,credi'**bility** n. —'**credibly** adv.

credit ('krɛdɪt) n. **1.** commendation or approval, as for an act or quality. **2.** a person or thing serving as a source of good influence, repute, etc. **3.** influence or reputation coming from the good opinion of others. **4.** belief in the truth, reliability, quality, etc., of someone or something. **5.** a sum of money or equivalent purchasing power, available for a person's use. **6. a.** the positive balance in a person's bank account. **b.** the sum of money that a bank makes available to a client in excess of any deposit. **7. a.** the practice of permitting a buyer to receive goods or services before payment. **b.** the time

permitted for paying for such goods or services. **8.** reputation for solvency and probity, inducing confidence among creditors. **9.** Accounting. **a.** acknowledgment of an income, liability, or capital item by entry on the righthand side of an account. **b.** the right-hand side of an account. **c.** an entry on this side. **d.** the total of such entries. **e.** (as modifier): credit entries. **10.** Education. **a.** a distinction awarded to an examination candidate obtaining good marks. **b.** a section of an examination syllabus satisfactorily completed. **11. on credit.** with payment to be made at a future date. ~vb. (tr.) **12.** (foll. by with) to ascribe (to); give credit (for). **13.** to accept as true; believe. **14.** to do credit to. **15.** Accounting. **a.** to enter (an item) as a credit in an account. **b.** to acknowledge (a payer) by making such an entry.

creditable ('krɛdɪtəbəl) adj. deserving credit, honour, etc.; praiseworthy. —'**creditableness** or ,credita'**bility** n. —'**creditably** adv.

credit card n. a card issued by banks, businesses, etc., enabling the holder to obtain goods and services on credit.

Creditiste (,krɛdi'ti:st) Canad. ~adj. **1.** of, supporting, or relating to the Social Credit Rally of Quebec. ~n. **2.** a supporter or member of this organization.

creditor ('krɛdɪtə) n. a person or commercial enterprise to whom money is owed.

credit rating n. an evaluation of the creditworthiness of an individual or business enterprise, based on earning power, previous record of debt repayment, etc.

credits ('krɛdɪts) pl. n. a list of those responsible for the production of a film.

credo ('kri:dəu, 'krei-) n., pl. **-dos.** any formal statement of beliefs, principles, or opinions.

Credo ('kri:dəu, 'krei-) n., pl. **-dos. 1.** the Apostles' or Nicene Creed. **2.** a musical setting of the Creed.

credulity (kri'dju:liti) n. disposition to believe something on little evidence; gullibility.

credulous ('krɛdjuləs) adj. **1.** tending to believe something on little evidence. **2.** arising from or characterized by credulity: credulous beliefs. —'**credulously** adv. —'**credulousness** n.

creed (kri:d) n. **1.** a concise, formal statement of the essential articles of Christian belief, such as the Apostles' Creed or the Nicene Creed. **2.** any statement or system of beliefs or principles. —'**creedal** or '**credal** adj.

creek (kri:k) n. **1.** Chiefly Brit. a narrow inlet or bay, esp. of the sea. **2.** U.S., Canad., Austral. & N.Z. a small stream or tributary. **3. up the creek.** Sl. in trouble; in a difficult position.

Creek (kri:k) n. **1.** (pl. **Creek** or **Creeks**) a member of a confederacy of N American Indian tribes formerly living in Georgia and Alabama. **2.** any of their languages.

creel (kri:l) n. **1.** a wickerwork basket, esp. one used to hold fish. **2.** a wickerwork trap for catching lob-

---

THESAURUS

create 1. beget, bring into being or existence, coin, compose, concoct, design, develop, devise, dream up (Inf.), form, formulate, generate, give birth to, give life to, hatch, initiate, invent, make, originate, produce, spawn **3.** appoint, constitute, establish, found, install, invest, make, set up **3.** bring about, cause, lead to, occasion

creation 1. conception, formation, generation, genesis, making, procreation, siring **2.** constitution, development, establishment, formation, foundation, inception, institution, laying down, origination, production, setting up **3.** achievement, brainchild (Inf.), chef-d'oeuvre, concept, concoction, handiwork, invention, magnum opus, pièce de résistance, production **4.** all living things, cosmos, life, living world, natural world, nature, universe, world

creative artistic, clever, fertile, gifted, imaginative, ingenious, inspired, inventive, original, productive, stimulating, visionary

creativity cleverness, fecundity, fertility, imagination, imaginativeness, ingenuity, inspiration, inventiveness, originality, productivity, talent

creator architect, author, begetter, designer, father, framer, God, initiator, inventor, maker, originator, prime mover

creature 1. animal, beast, being, brute, critter (U.S. dialect), dumb animal, living thing, lower animal, quadruped **2.** body, character, fellow, human being, individual, man, mortal, person, soul, wight (Archaic), woman **3.** dependant, hanger-on, hireling, instrument (Inf.), lackey, minion, puppet, retainer, tool, wretch

credentials attestation, authorization, card, certificate, deed, diploma, docket, letter of recommendation or introduction, letters of credence, licence, missive, passport, recommendation, reference(s), testament, testimonial, title, voucher, warrant

credibility believability, believableness, integrity, plausibility, reliability, tenability, trustworthiness

credible 1. believable, conceivable, imaginable, likely, plausible, possible, probable, reasonable, supposable, tenable, thinkable **2.** dependable, honest, reliable, sincere, trustworthy, trusty

credit n. **1.** acclaim, acknowledgment, approval, commendation, fame, glory, honour, kudos, merit, praise, recognition, thanks, tribute **2.** character, clout (Inf.), esteem, estimation, good name, influence, position, prestige, regard, reputation, repute, standing, status **3.** belief, confidence, credence, faith, reli

ance, trust **4.** As in be a credit to feather in one's cap, honour, source of satisfaction or pride **5. on credit** by deferred payment, by instalments, on account, on hire-purchase, on (the) H.P., on the slate (Inf.), on tick (Inf.) ~v. **6.** With with accredit, ascribe to, assign to, attribute to, chalk up to (Inf.), impute to, refer to **7.** accept, bank on, believe, buy (Inf.), depend on, fall for, have faith in, rely on, swallow (Inf.), trust

creditable admirable, commendable, deserving, estimable, exemplary, honourable, laudable, meritorious, praiseworthy, reputable, respectable, worthy

credulity blind faith, credulousness, gullibility, naiveté, silliness, simplicity, stupidity

credulous born yesterday (Inf.), dupable, green, gullible, naive, overtrusting, trustful, uncritical, unsuspecting, unsuspicious

creed articles of faith, belief, canon, catechism, confession, credo, doctrine, dogma, persuasion, principles, profession (of faith), tenet

creek 1. bay, bight, cove, firth or frith (Scot.), inlet **2.** U.S., Canadian, & Australian brook, rivulet, runnel, stream, streamlet, tributary, watercourse

sters, etc.

creep (kriːp) *vb.* **creeping, crept.** (*intr.*) **1.** to crawl with the body near to or touching the ground. **2.** to move slowly, quietly, or cautiously. **3.** to act in a servile way; fawn; cringe. **4.** to move or slip out of place, as from pressure or wear. **5.** (of plants) to grow along the ground or over rocks. **6.** to develop gradually: *creeping unrest.* **7.** to have the sensation of something crawling over the skin. ~*n.* **8.** the act of creeping or a creeping movement. **9.** *Sl.* a person considered to be obnoxious or servile. **10.** *Geol.* the gradual downward movement of loose rock material, soil, etc., on a slope.

creeper ('kriːpə) *n.* **1.** a person or animal that creeps. **2.** a plant, such as the ivy, that grows by creeping. **3.** the U.S. name for the **tree creeper. 4.** a hooked instrument for dragging deep water. **5.** *Inf.* a shoe with a soft sole.

creeps (kriːps) *pl. n.* (preceded by *the*) *Sl.* a feeling of fear, repulsion, disgust, etc.

creepy ('kriːpɪ) *adj.* **-ier, -iest. 1.** *Inf.* having or causing a sensation of repulsion or fear, as of creatures crawling on the skin. **2.** creeping; slow-moving. —'**creepily** *adv.* —'**creepiness** *n.*

creepy-crawly *Brit. inf.* ~*n., pl.* **-crawlies. 1.** a small crawling creature. ~*adj.* **2.** feeling or causing a sensation as of creatures crawling on one's skin.

cremate (krɪ'meɪt) *vb.* (*tr.*) to burn up (something, esp. a corpse) and reduce to ash. —**cre'mation** *n.* —**cre'mator** *n.* —**crematory** ('krɛmətərɪ, -trɪ) *adj.*

crematorium (ˌkrɛmə'tɔːrɪəm) *n., pl.* **-riums** *or* **-ria** (-rɪə). *Brit.* a building in which corpses are cremated. Also called (esp. U.S.): **crematory.**

crème (krɛm, kriːm, kreɪm; *French* krɛm) *n.* **1.** cream. **2.** any of various sweet liqueurs: *crème de moka.* ~*adj.* **3.** (of a liqueur) rich and sweet.

crème de menthe ('krɛm də 'mɛnθ, 'mɪnt, 'kriːm, 'kreɪm) *n.* a liqueur flavoured with peppermint.

crenate ('kriːneɪt) *or* **crenated** *adj.* having a scalloped margin, as certain leaves. —'**crenately** *adv.* —'**crenation** *n.*

crenellate *or U.S.* **crenelate** ('krɛnɪˌleɪt) *vb.* (*tr.*) to supply with battlements. —'**crenel,lated** *or U.S.* '**crenel,ated** *adj.* —ˌ**crenel'lation** *or U.S.* ˌ**crenel'ation** *n.*

creole ('kriːəʊl) *n.* **1.** a language that has its origin in extended contact between two language communities, one of which is European. ~*adj.* **2.** of or relating to creole. **3.** (of a sauce or dish) containing or cooked with tomatoes, green peppers, onions, etc.

Creole ('kriːəʊl) *n.* **1.** (*sometimes not cap.*) (in the West Indies and Latin America) **a.** a native-born person of European ancestry. **b.** a native-born person of mixed European and Negro ancestry who speaks a creole. **2.** (in Louisiana and other Gulf States) a native-born person of French ancestry. **3.** the French Creole spoken in Louisiana. ~*adj.* **4.** of or relating to any of these peoples.

creosote ('krɪəˌsəʊt) *n.* **1.** a colourless or pale yellow liquid with a burning taste and penetrating odour distilled from wood tar. It is used as an antiseptic. **2.** a thick dark liquid mixture prepared from coal tar: used as a preservative for wood. ~*vb.* **3.** to treat (wood) with creosote. —**creosotic** (ˌkrɪə'sɒtɪk) *adj.*

crepe *or* **crape** (kreɪp) *n.* **1. a.** a light cotton, silk, or other fabric with a fine ridged or crinkled surface. **b.** (*as modifier*): *a crepe dress.* **2.** a black armband originally made of this, worn as a sign of mourning. **3.** a very thin pancake, often folded around a filling. **4.** short for **crepe paper** or **crepe rubber.**

crepe paper *n.* thin crinkled coloured paper, resembling crepe and used for decorations.

crepe rubber *n.* a type of rubber in crinkled sheets : used for the soles of shoes.

crepitate ('krɛpɪˌteɪt) *vb.* (*intr.*) to make a rattling or crackling sound. —'**crepitant** *adj.* —ˌ**crepi'tation** *n.*

crept (krɛpt) *vb.* the past tense or past participle of **creep.**

crepuscular (krɪ'pʌskjʊlə) *adj.* **1.** of or like twilight; dim. **2.** (of certain creatures) active at twilight or just before dawn.

Cres. *abbrev. for* Crescent.

crescendo (krɪ'ʃɛndəʊ) *n., pl.* **-dos** *or* **-di** (-dɪ). **1.** *Music.* **a.** a gradual increase in loudness or the musical direction or symbol indicating this. Abbrev.: **cresc. b.** (*as modifier*): *a crescendo passage.* **2.** any similar gradual increase in loudness. ~*vb.* **-doing, -doed. 3.** (*intr.*) to increase in loudness or force. ~*adv.* **4.** with a crescendo.

crescent ('krɛsənt, -zənt) *n.* **1.** the biconcave shape of the moon in its first or last quarter. **2.** any shape or object resembling this. **3.** *Chiefly Brit.* a crescent-shaped street. **4.** (*often cap.* and preceded by *the*) **a.** the emblem of Islam or Turkey. **b.** Islamic or Turkish power. ~*adj.* **5.** *Arch. or poetic.* increasing or growing. —**crescentic** (krə'sɛntɪk) *adj.*

cress (krɛs) *n.* any of various plants having pungent-tasting leaves often used in salads and as a garnish.

crest (krɛst) *n.* **1.** a tuft or growth of feathers, fur, or skin along the top of the heads of some birds, reptiles, and other animals. **2.** something resembling or suggesting this. **3.** the top, highest point, or highest stage of something. **4.** an ornamental piece, such as a plume, on top of a helmet. **5.** *Heraldry.* a symbol of a family or office, borne in addition to a coat of arms and used in medieval times to decorate the helmet. ~*vb.* **6.** (*intr.*) to come or rise to a high point. **7.** (*tr.*) to lie at the top of; cap. **8.** (*tr.*) to reach the top of (a hill, wave, etc.). —'**crested** *adj.* —'**crestless** *adj.*

crestfallen ('krɛstˌfɔːlən) *adj.* dejected or disheartened. —'**crest,fallenly** *adv.*

cretaceous (krɪ'teɪʃəs) *adj.* consisting of or resembling chalk.

Cretaceous (krɪ'teɪʃəs) *adj.* **1.** of, denoting, or formed in the last period of the Mesozoic era, during which chalk deposits were formed. ~*n.* **2. the.** the Cretaceous period or rock system.

cretin ('krɛtɪn) *n.* **1.** a person afflicted with cretinism. **2.** a person considered to be extremely stupid. —'**cretinous** *adj.*

cretinism ('krɛtɪˌnɪzəm) *n.* a condition arising from a deficiency of thyroid hormone, present from birth, characterized by dwarfism and mental retardation. See also **myxoedema.**

cretonne (krɛ'tɒn, 'krɛtɒn) *n.* a heavy cotton or linen fabric with a printed design, used for furnishing.

crevasse (krɪ'væs) *n.* **1.** a deep crack or fissure, esp. in the ice of a glacier. **2.** *U.S.* a break in a river embankment. ~*vb.* **3.** (*tr.*) *U.S.* to make a break or fissure in (a dyke, wall, etc.).

crevice ('krɛvɪs) *n.* a narrow fissure or crack; split; cleft.

crew¹ (kruː) *n.* (*sometimes functioning as pl.*) **1.** the men who man a ship, boat, aircraft, etc. **2.** *Naut.* a group of people assigned to a particular job or type of work. **3.** *Inf.* a gang, company, or crowd. ~*vb.* **4.** to serve on (a ship) as a member of the crew.

THESAURUS

creep *v.* **1.** crawl, crawl on all fours, glide, insinuate, slither, squirm, worm, wriggle, writhe **2.** approach unnoticed, skulk, slink, sneak, steal, tiptoe **3.** crawl, dawdle, drag, edge, inch, proceed at a snail's pace **4.** bootlick (*Inf.*), cower, cringe, fawn, grovel, kowtow, scrape, suck up to (*Inf.*), toady, truckle ~*n.* **5.** *Sl.* bootlicker (*Inf.*), sneak, sycophant, toady **6. give one the creeps** *or* **make one's flesh creep** disgust, frighten, horrify, make one flinch (quail, shrink, squirm, wince), make one's hair stand on end (*Inf.*), repel, repulse, scare, terrify, terrorize

creeper climber, climbing plant, rambler, runner, trailing plant, vine (*Chiefly U.S.*)

creepy awful, direful, disgusting, disturbing, eerie, frightening, ghoulish, goose-pimply (*Inf.*), gruesome, hair-raising, horrible, macabre, menacing, nightmarish, ominous, scary (*Inf.*), sinister, terrifying, threatening, unpleasant, weird

crescent *n.* **1.** half-moon, meniscus, new moon, old moon, sickle, sickle-shape ~*adj.* **2.** bow-shaped, curved, falcate, semicircular, sickle-shaped **3.** *Archaic* growing, increasing, waxing

crest **1.** apex, crown, head, height, highest point, peak, pinnacle, ridge, summit, top **2.** aigrette, caruncle (*Zoology*), cockscomb, comb, crown, mane, panache, plume, tassel, topknot, tuft **3.** *Heraldry* badge, bearings,

charge, device, emblem, insignia, symbol

crestfallen chapfallen, dejected, depressed, despondent, disappointed, disconsolate, discouraged, disheartened, downcast, downhearted

crevice chink, cleft, crack, cranny, fissure, fracture, gap, hole, interstice, opening, rent, rift, slit, split

crew **1.** hands, (ship's) company, (ship's) complement **2.** company, corps, gang, party, posse, squad, team, working party **3.** *Inf.* assemblage, band, bunch (*Inf.*), company, crowd, gang, herd, horde, lot, mob, pack, set, swarm, troop

crew[2] (kruː) vb. Arch. a past tense of **crow**[2].

crew cut n. a closely cropped haircut for men.

crewel ('kruːɪl) n. a loosely twisted worsted yarn, used in fancy work and embroidery. —'**crewelist** n. —'**crewel,work** n.

crew neck n. a plain round neckline in sweaters. —'**crew-,neck** or '**crew-,necked** adj.

crib (krɪb) n. **1.** a child's bed with slatted wooden sides; cot. **2.** a cattle stall or pen. **3.** a fodder rack or manger. **4.** a small crude cottage or room. **5.** N.Z. a weekend cottage: term is South Island usage only. **6.** any small confined space. **7.** a representation of the manger in which the infant Jesus was laid at birth. **8.** Inf. a theft, esp. of another's writing or thoughts. **9.** Inf., chiefly Brit. a translation of a foreign text or a list of answers used by students, often illicitly, as an aid in lessons, examinations, etc. **10.** short for **cribbage**. **11.** Cribbage. the discard pile. **12.** Also called: **cribwork**. a framework of heavy timbers used in the construction of foundations, mines, etc. ~vb. **cribbing, cribbed**. **13.** (tr.) to put or enclose in or as if in a crib; furnish with a crib. **14.** (tr.) Inf. to steal another's writings or thoughts. **15.** (intr.) Inf. to copy either from a crib or from someone else during a lesson or examination. **16.** Inf. to grumble. —'**cribber** n.

cribbage ('krɪbɪdʒ) n. a game of cards for two to four, in which players try to win a set number of points before their opponents.

crick (krɪk) Inf. ~n. **1.** a painful muscle spasm or cramp, esp. in the neck or back. ~vb. **2.** (tr.) to cause a crick in.

cricket[1] ('krɪkɪt) n. an insect having long antennae and, in the males, the ability to produce a chirping sound by rubbing together the leathery forewings.

cricket[2] ('krɪkɪt) n. **1. a.** a game played by two teams of eleven players on a field with a wicket at either end of a 22-yard pitch, the object being for one side to score runs by hitting a hard leather-covered ball with a bat while the other side tries to dismiss them by bowling, catching, running them out, etc. **b.** (as modifier): a cricket bat. **2. not cricket**. Inf. not fair play. ~vb. (intr.) **3.** to play cricket. —'**cricketer** n.

crier ('kraɪə) n. **1.** a person or animal that cries. **2.** (formerly) an official who made public announcements, esp. in a town or court.

crime (kraɪm) n. **1.** an act or omission prohibited and punished by law. **2.** unlawful acts in general. **3.** an evil act. **4.** Inf. something to be regretted.

criminal ('krɪmɪnəl) n. **1.** a person charged with and convicted of crime. **2.** a person who commits crimes for a living. ~adj. **3.** of, involving, or guilty of crime. **4.** (prenominal) of or relating to crime or its punishment. **5.** Inf. senseless or deplorable. —'**criminally** adv. —,crimi'nality n.

criminology (,krɪmɪ'nɒlədʒɪ) n. the scientific study of crime. —**criminological** (,krɪmɪnə'lɒdʒɪkəl) or ,crimi-no'logic adj. —,crimino'logically adv. —,crimi'nologist n.

crimp (krɪmp) vb. (tr.) **1.** to fold or press into ridges. **2.** to fold and pinch together (something, such as two pieces of metal). **3.** to curl or wave (the hair) tightly,

esp. with curling tongs. **4.** U.S. inf. to hinder. ~n. **5.** the act or result of folding or pressing together into ridges. **6.** a tight wave or curl in the hair. —'**crimper** n. —'**crimpy** adj.

Crimplene ('krɪmpliːn) n. Trademark. a synthetic material similar to Terylene, characterized by its crease-resistance.

crimson ('krɪmzən) n. **1. a.** a deep or vivid red colour. **b.** (as adj.): a crimson rose. ~vb. **2.** to make or become crimson. **3.** (intr.) to blush. —'**crimsonness** n.

cringe (krɪndʒ) vb. (intr.) **1.** to shrink or flinch, esp. in fear or servility. **2.** to behave in a servile or timid way. ~n. **3.** the act of cringing. —'**cringer** n.

crinkle ('krɪŋkəl) vb. **1.** to form or cause to form wrinkles, twists, or folds. **2.** to make or cause to make a rustling noise. ~n. **3.** a wrinkle, twist, or fold. **4.** a rustling noise. —'**crinkly** adj.

crinoline ('krɪnəlɪn) n. **1.** a stiff fabric, originally of horsehair and linen used in lining garments. **2.** a petticoat stiffened with this, worn to distend skirts, esp. in the mid-19th century. **3.** a framework of steel hoops worn for the same purpose.

cripple ('krɪpəl) n. **1.** a person who is lame. **2.** a person who is or seems disabled or deficient in some way: a mental cripple. ~vb. **3.** (tr.) to make a cripple of; disable. —'**crippler** n.

crisis ('kraɪsɪs) n., pl. **-ses** (-siːz). **1.** a crucial stage or turning point, esp. in a sequence of events or a disease. **2.** an unstable period, esp. one of extreme trouble or danger. **3.** Pathol. a sudden change in the course of a disease.

crisp (krɪsp) adj. **1.** dry and brittle. **2.** fresh and firm. **3.** invigorating or bracing: a crisp breeze. **4.** clear; sharp: crisp reasoning. **5.** lively or stimulating. **6.** clean and orderly. **7.** concise and pithy. **8.** wrinkled or curly: crisp hair. ~vb. **9.** to make or become crisp. ~n. **10.** Brit. a very thin slice of potato fried and eaten cold as a snack. **11.** something that is crisp. —'**crisply** adv. —'**crispness** n.

crispbread ('krɪsp,brɛd) n. a thin dry biscuit made of wheat or rye.

crispy ('krɪspɪ) adj. **crispier, crispiest. 1.** crisp. **2.** having waves or curls. —'**crispiness** n.

crisscross ('krɪs,krɒs) vb. **1.** to move or cause to move in a crosswise pattern. **2.** to mark with or consist of a pattern of crossing lines. ~adj. **3.** (esp. of lines) crossing one another in different directions. ~n. **4.** a pattern made of crossing lines. ~adv. **5.** in a crosswise manner or pattern.

criterion (kraɪ'tɪərɪən) n., pl. **-ria** (-rɪə) or **-rions**. a standard by which something can be judged or decided.
▷ **Usage.** Criteria, the plural of criterion, is not acceptable as a singular noun in careful English.

critic ('krɪtɪk) n. **1.** a person who judges something. **2.** a professional judge of art, music, literature, etc. **3.** a person who often finds fault and criticizes.

critical ('krɪtɪkəl) adj. **1.** containing or making severe or negative judgments. **2.** containing analytical evaluations. **3.** of a critic or criticism. **4.** of or forming a crisis; crucial. **5.** urgently needed. **6.** Physics. of, denoting, or concerned with a state in which the properties of a

---

THESAURUS

crib n. **1.** bassinet, bed, cot **2.** bin, box, bunker, manger, rack, stall **3.** Inf. key, translation, trot (U.S. sl.) ~v. **4.** Inf. cheat, pass off as one's own work, pilfer, pirate, plagiarize, purloin, steal **5.** box up, cage, confine, coop, coop up, enclose, fence, imprison, limit, pen, rail, restrict, shut in

crime 1. atrocity, fault, felony, malfeasance, misdeed, misdemeanour, offence, outrage, transgression, trespass, unlawful act, violation, wrong **2.** corruption, delinquency, guilt, illegality, iniquity, lawbreaking, malefaction, misconduct, sin, unrighteousness, vice, villainy, wickedness, wrong, wrongdoing

criminal n. **1.** con (Sl.), convict, crook (Inf.), culprit, delinquent, evildoer, felon, jailbird, lawbreaker, malefactor, offender, sinner, transgressor ~adj. **2.** bent (Sl.), corrupt, crooked (Inf.), culpable, felonious, illegal, illicit, immoral, indictable, iniquitous, lawless, nefarious, peccant (Rare), unlawful, unright-

eous, vicious, villainous, wicked, wrong **3.** Inf. deplorable, foolish, preposterous, ridiculous, scandalous, senseless

criminality corruption, culpability, delinquency, depravity, guiltiness, illegality, sinfulness, turpitude, villainy, wickedness

cringe 1. blench, cower, dodge, draw back, duck, flinch, quail, quiver, recoil, shrink, shy, start, tremble, wince **2.** bend, bootlick (Inf.), bow, crawl, creep, crouch, fawn, grovel, kneel, kowtow, sneak, stoop, toady, truckle

cripple v. **1.** debilitate, disable, enfeeble, hamstring, incapacitate, lame, maim, mutilate, paralyse, weaken **2.** bring to a standstill, cramp, damage, destroy, halt, impair, put out of action, ruin, spoil, vitiate

crippled bedridden, deformed, disabled, enfeebled, handicapped, housebound, incapacitated, laid up (Inf.), lame, paralysed

crisis 1. climacteric, climax, confrontation, critical point, crunch (Inf.), crux, culmi-

nation, height, moment of truth, point of no return, turning point **2.** catastrophe, critical situation, dilemma, dire straits, disaster, emergency, exigency, extremity, mess, plight, predicament, quandary, strait, trouble

crisp 1. brittle, crispy, crumbly, crunchy, firm, fresh, unwilted **2.** bracing, brisk, fresh, invigorating, refreshing **3.** brief, brusque, clear, incisive, pithy, short, succinct, tart, terse **4.** clean-cut, neat, orderly, smart, snappy, spruce, tidy, trig (Dialect), well-groomed, well-pressed

criterion bench mark, canon, gauge, measure, norm, principle, proof, rule, standard, test, touchstone, yardstick

critic 1. analyst, arbiter, authority, commentator, connoisseur, expert, expositor, judge, pundit, reviewer **2.** attacker, carper, caviller, censor, censurer, detractor, faultfinder, knocker (Inf.), Momus, reviler, vilifier

system undergo an abrupt change. **7. go critical.** (of a nuclear power station or reactor) to reach a state in which a nuclear-fission chain reaction becomes self-sustaining. —ˌcriti'cality n. —'critically adv. —'criticalness n.

critical path analysis n. a technique for planning projects with reference to the critical path, which is the sequence of stages requiring the longest time.

criticism ('krɪtɪˌsɪzəm) n. **1.** the act or an instance of making an unfavourable or severe judgment, comment, etc. **2.** the analysis or evaluation of a work of art, literature, etc. **3.** the occupation of a critic. **4.** a work that sets out to evaluate or analyse.

criticize or **-ise** ('krɪtɪˌsaɪz) vb. **1.** to judge (something) with disapproval; censure. **2.** to evaluate or analyse (something). —'criti,cizable or -,cisable adj. —'criti,cizer or -,ciser n.

critique (krɪ'tiːk) n. **1.** a critical essay or commentary. **2.** the act or art of criticizing.

croak (krəʊk) vb. **1.** (intr.) (of frogs, crows, etc.) to make a low, hoarse cry. **2.** to utter (something) in this manner. **3.** (intr.) to grumble or be pessimistic. **4.** Sl. **a.** (intr.) to die. **b.** (tr.) to kill. ~n. **5.** a low hoarse utterance or sound. —'croaky adj. —'croakiness n.

Croatian (krəʊ'eɪʃən) adj. **1.** of or relating to Croatia, its people, or their dialect of Serbo-Croatian. ~n. **2.** the dialect of Croatia. **3. a.** a native or inhabitant of Croatia. **b.** a speaker of Croatian.

crochet ('krəʊʃeɪ, -ʃɪ) vb. **-cheting** (-ʃeɪɪŋ, -ʃɪɪŋ), **-cheted** (-ʃeɪd, -ʃɪd). **1.** to make (a piece of needlework, a garment, etc.) by looping and intertwining thread with a hooked needle (**crochet hook**). ~n. **2.** work made by crocheting. —'crocheter n.

crock¹ (krɒk) n. **1.** an earthen pot, jar, etc. **2.** a piece of broken earthenware.

crock² (krɒk) n. Sl., chiefly Brit. a person or thing that is old or decrepit (esp. in **old crock**).

crockery ('krɒkərɪ) n. china dishes, earthen vessels, etc., collectively.

crocodile ('krɒkəˌdaɪl) n. **1.** a large tropical reptile having a broad head, tapering snout, massive jaws, and a thick outer covering of bony plates. **2. a.** leather made from the skin of any of these animals. **b.** (as modifier): crocodile shoes.

crocodile tears pl. n. an insincere show of grief; false tears.

crocus ('krəʊkəs) n., pl. **-cuses.** any plant of the iridaceous genus Crocus, having white, yellow, or purple flowers.

Croesus ('kriːsəs) n. any very rich man.

croft (krɒft) n. Brit. a small enclosed plot of land, adjoining a house, worked by the occupier and his family, esp. in Scotland. —'crofter n.

croissant ('krwʌsɒŋ) n. a flaky crescent-shaped bread roll.

cromlech ('krɒmlɛk) n. **1.** a megalithic chamber tomb or dolmen. **2.** a circle of prehistoric standing stones or a single one.

crone (krəʊn) n. a witchlike old woman.

crony ('krəʊnɪ) n., pl. **-nies.** a friend or companion.

crook (krʊk) n. **1.** a curved or hooked thing. **2.** a staff with a hooked end, such as a bishop's crosier or shepherd's staff. **3.** a turn or curve; bend. **4.** Inf. a dishonest person, esp. a swindler or thief. ~vb. **5.** to bend or curve or cause to bend or curve. ~adj. **6.** Austral. sl. **a.** ill. **b.** of poor quality. **c.** unpleasant; bad. **7. go (off) crook.** Austral. sl. to lose one's temper. **8. go crook at** or **on.** Austral. sl. to rebuke or upbraid.

crooked ('krʊkɪd) adj. **1.** bent, angled or winding. **2.** set at an angle; not straight. **3.** deformed or contorted. **4.** Inf. dishonest or illegal. **5. crooked on.** (also krʊkt) Austral. inf. hostile or averse to. —'crookedly adv. —'crookedness n.

croon (kruːn) vb. **1.** to sing or speak in a soft low tone. ~n. **2.** a soft low singing or humming. —'crooner n.

crop (krɒp) n. **1.** the produce of cultivated plants, esp. cereals, vegetables, and fruit. **2. a.** the amount of such produce in any particular season. **b.** the yield of some other farm produce: the lamb crop. **3.** a group of products, thoughts, people, etc., appearing at one time or in one season. **4.** the stock of a thonged whip. **5.** short for **riding crop. 6.** a pouchlike part of the oesophagus of birds, in which food is stored or partially digested before passing on to the gizzard. **7.** a short cropped hair style. **8.** a notch in or a piece cut out of the ear of an animal. **9.** the act of cropping. ~vb. **cropping, cropped.** (mainly tr.) **10.** to cut (hair, grass, etc.) very short. **11.** to cut and collect (mature produce) from the land or plant on which it has been grown. **12.** to clip part of (the ear or ears) of (an animal), esp. as a means of identification. **13.** (of herbivorous animals) to graze on (grass or similar vegetation).

crop-eared adj. having the ears or hair cut short.

cropper ('krɒpə) n. **1.** a person who cultivates or harvests a crop. **2. come a cropper.** Inf. **a.** to fall heavily. **b.** to fail completely.

crop up vb. (intr., adv.) Inf. to occur or appear unexpectedly.

croquet ('krəʊkeɪ, -kɪ) n. a game for two to four players who hit a wooden ball through iron hoops with mallets in order to hit a peg.

croquette (krəʊ'kɛt, krɒ-) n. a savoury cake of minced meat, fish, etc., fried in breadcrumbs.

crosier or **crozier** ('krəʊʒə) n. a staff surmounted by a crook or cross, carried by bishops as a symbol of pastoral office.

cross (krɒs) n. **1.** a structure or symbol consisting of two intersecting lines or pieces at right angles to one another. **2.** a wooden structure used as a means of execution, consisting of an upright post with a transverse piece to which people were nailed or tied. **3.** a representation of the Cross used as an emblem of Christianity or as a reminder of Christ's death. **4.** any mark or shape consisting of two intersecting lines, esp. such a symbol (×) used as a signature, error mark, etc. **5.** a sign representing the Cross made either by tracing a figure in the air or by touching the forehead, breast, and either shoulder in turn. **6.** any variation of the Christian symbol, such as a Maltese or Greek cross. **7.** a cruciform emblem awarded to indicate membership of an order or as a decoration for distinguished service. **8.** (sometimes cap.) Christian

---

THESAURUS

critical 1. captious, carping, cavilling, censorious, derogatory, disapproving, disparaging, fault-finding, nagging, niggling, nitpicking (Inf.) **2.** accurate, analytical, diagnostic, discerning, discriminating, fastidious, judicious, penetrating, perceptive, precise **3.** all-important, crucial, dangerous, deciding, decisive, grave, hairy (Sl.), high-priority, momentous, perilous, pivotal, precarious, pressing, psychological, risky, serious, urgent, vital

criticism 1. animadversion, bad press, brickbats (Inf.), censure, critical remarks, disapproval, disparagement, fault-finding, flak (Inf.), knocking (Inf.), panning (Inf.), slam (Sl.), slating (Inf.), stricture **2.** analysis, appraisal, appreciation, assessment, comment, commentary, critique, elucidation, evaluation, judgment, notice, review

criticize 1. animadvert on or upon, carp, censure, condemn, disapprove of, disparage, excoriate, find fault with, give (someone or

something) a bad press, knock (Inf.), nag at, pan (Inf.), pass strictures upon, pick to pieces, slam (Sl.), slate (Inf.) **2.** analyse, appraise, assess, comment upon, evaluate, give an opinion, judge, pass judgment on, review

critique analysis, appraisal, assessment, commentary, essay, examination, review

croak v. **1.** caw, gasp, grunt, squawk, utter or speak harshly (huskily, throatily), wheeze **2.** Inf. complain, groan, grouse, grumble, moan, murmur, mutter, repine **3.** Sl. die, expire, hop the twig (Inf.), kick the bucket (Inf.), pass away, perish

crook 1. n. Inf. cheat, criminal, knave (Archaic), racketeer, robber, rogue, shark, swindler, thief, villain **2.** v. angle, bend, bow, curve, flex, hook

crooked 1. anfractuous, bent, bowed, crippled, curved, deformed, deviating, disfigured, distorted, hooked, irregular, meandering, misshapen, out of shape, tortuous, twisted, twisting, warped, winding, zigzag **2.** an

gled, askew, asymmetric, at an angle, awry, lopsided, off-centre, slanted, slanting, squint, tilted, to one side, uneven, unsymmetrical **3.** Inf. bent (Sl.), corrupt, crafty, criminal, deceitful, dishonest, dishonourable, dubious, fraudulent, illegal, knavish, nefarious, questionable, shady (Inf.), shifty, treacherous, underhand, unlawful, unprincipled, unscrupulous

croon breathe, hum, purr, sing, warble

crop n. **1.** fruits, gathering, harvest, produce, reaping, season's growth, vintage, yield ~v. **2.** clip, curtail, cut, lop, mow, pare, prune, reduce, shear, shorten, snip, top, trim **3.** bring home, bring in, collect, garner, gather, harvest, mow, pick, reap **4.** browse, graze, nibble

crop up appear, arise, emerge, happen, occur, spring up, turn up

ity or Christendom, esp. as contrasted with non-Christian religions. **9.** the place in a town or village where a cross has been set up. **10.** *Biol.* **a.** the process of crossing; hybridization. **b.** an individual produced as a result of this process. **11.** a mixture of two qualities or types. **12.** an opposition, hindrance, or misfortune; affliction (esp. in **bear one's cross**). **13.** *Boxing.* a straight punch delivered from the side, esp. with the right hand. ~*vb.* **14.** (sometimes foll. by *over*) to move or go across (something); traverse or intersect. **15. a.** to meet and pass. **b.** (of each of two letters in the post) to be dispatched before receipt of the other. **16.** (*tr.; usually foll. by *out, off, or *through*) to cancel with a cross or with lines; delete. **17.** (*tr.*) to place or put in a form resembling a cross: *to cross one's legs.* **18.** (*tr.*) to mark with a cross or crosses. **19.** (*tr.*) *Brit.* to draw two parallel lines across the face of (a cheque) and so make it payable only into a bank account. **20.** (*tr.*) **a.** to trace the form of the Cross upon (someone or something) in token of blessing. **b.** to make the sign of the Cross upon (oneself). **21.** (*intr.*) (of telephone lines) to interfere with each other so that several callers are connected together at one time. **22.** to cause fertilization between (plants or animals of different breeds, races, varieties, etc.). **23.** (*tr.*) to oppose the wishes or plans of; thwart. **24. cross one's fingers.** to fold one finger across another in the hope of bringing good luck. **25. cross one's heart.** to promise or pledge, esp. by making the sign of a cross over one's heart. **26. cross one's mind.** to occur to one briefly or suddenly. **27. cross the path (of).** to meet or thwart (someone). **28. cross swords.** to enter into an argument or contest. ~*adj.* **29.** angry; ill-humoured; vexed. **30.** lying or placed across; transverse: *a cross timber.* **31.** involving interchange; reciprocal. **32.** contrary or unfavourable. —'**crossly** *adv.* —'**crossness** *n.*

Cross (krɒs) *n.* **the. 1.** the cross on which Jesus Christ was crucified. **2.** the Crucifixion of Jesus.

cross- *combining form.* **1.** indicating action from one individual, group, etc., to another: *cross-cultural; crossfertilize; cross-refer.* **2.** indicating movement, position, etc., across something: *crosscurrent; crosstalk.* **3.** indicating a crosslike figure or intersection: *crossbones.*

crossbar ('krɒs,baː) *n.* **1.** a horizontal bar, line, stripe, etc. **2.** a horizontal beam across a pair of goal posts. **3.** the horizontal bar on a man's bicycle.

cross-bench *n.* (*usually pl.*) *Brit.* a seat in Parliament occupied by a neutral or independent member. —'**cross-,bencher** *n.*

crossbill ('krɒs,bɪl) *n.* any of various widely distributed finches that occur in coniferous woods and have a bill with crossed tips.

crossbow ('krɒs,bəʊ) *n.* a type of medieval bow fixed transversely on a stock grooved to direct a square-headed arrow. —'**cross,bowman** *n.*

crossbreed ('krɒs,briːd) *vb.* **-breeding, -bred. 1.** Also: **interbreed.** to breed (animals or plants) using parents of different races, varieties, breeds, etc. ~*n.* **2.** the offspring produced by such a breeding.

crosscheck (,krɒs'tʃek) *vb.* **1.** to verify (a fact, report, etc.) by considering conflicting opinions or consulting other sources. ~*n.* **2.** the act or an instance of cross-checking.

cross-country *adj., adv.* **1.** by way of fields, etc., as opposed to roads. **2.** across a country. ~*n.* **3.** a long race held over open ground.

crosscut ('krɒs,kʌt) *adj.* **1.** cut at right angles or obliquely to the major axis. ~*n.* **2.** a transverse cut or course. **3.** *Mining.* a tunnel through a vein of ore or from the shaft to a vein. ~*vb.* **-cutting, -cut. 4.** to cut across.

cross-examine *vb.* (*tr.*) *Law.* to examine (a wit-

ness for the opposing side), as in attempting to discredit his testimony. **2.** to examine closely or relentlessly. —'**cross-ex,ami'nation** *n.* —'**cross-ex'aminer** *n.*

cross-eye *n.* a turning inwards towards the nose of one or both eyes, caused by abnormal alignment. —'**cross-,eyed** *adj.*

cross-fertilize *vb.* to fertilize by fusion of male and female gametes from different individuals of the same species. —,**cross-fertili'zation** *n.*

crossfire ('krɒs,faɪə) *n.* **1.** *Mil., etc.* converging fire from one or more positions. **2.** a lively exchange of ideas, opinions, etc.

crosshatch ('krɒs,hætʃ) *vb. Drawing.* to shade or hatch with two or more sets of parallel lines that cross one another.

crossing ('krɒsɪŋ) *n.* **1.** the place where one thing crosses another. **2.** a place where a street, railway, etc., may be crossed. **3.** the act or process of crossbreeding.

cross-legged ('krɒs'legɪd, -'legd) *adj.* standing or sitting with one leg crossed over the other.

crosspatch ('krɒs,pætʃ) *n. Inf.* a bad-tempered person.

cross-ply *adj.* (of a motor tyre) having the fabric cords in the outer casing running diagonally to stiffen the sidewalls.

cross-purpose *n.* **1.** a contrary aim or purpose. **2. at cross-purposes.** conflicting; opposed; disagreeing.

cross-question *vb.* **1.** to cross-examine. ~*n.* **2.** a question asked in cross-examination.

cross-refer *vb.* to refer from one part of something, esp. a book, to another.

cross-reference *n.* **1.** a reference within a text to another part of the text. ~*vb.* **2.** to cross-refer.

crossroad ('krɒs,rəʊd) *n. U.S.* **1.** a road that crosses another road. **2.** Also called: **crossway.** a road that crosses from one main road to another.

crossroads ('krɒs,rəʊdz) *n.* (*construed as sing.*) **1.** the point at which two or more roads cross each other. **2.** the point at which an important choice has to be made (esp. in **at the crossroads**).

cross section *n.* **1.** *Maths.* a plane surface formed by cutting across a solid, esp. perpendicular to its longest axis. **2.** a section cut off in this way. **3.** the act of cutting anything in this way. **4.** a random sample, esp. one regarded as representative. —'**cross-'sectional** *adj.*

cross-stitch *n.* **1.** an embroidery stitch made by two stitches forming a cross. **2.** embroidery worked with this stitch. ~*vb.* **3.** to embroider (a piece of needlework) with cross-stitch.

crosstalk ('krɒs,tɔːk) *n.* **1.** *Radio, telephony.* unwanted sounds picked up in one receiving channel from other channels. **2.** *Brit.* rapid or witty talk.

crosswise ('krɒs,waɪz) *or* **crossways** ('krɒs,weɪz) *adj., adv.* **1.** across; transversely. **2.** in the shape of a cross.

crossword puzzle ('krɒs,wɜːd) *n.* a puzzle in which the solver guesses words suggested by numbered clues and writes them into a grid to form a vertical and horizontal pattern.

crotch (krɒtʃ) *n.* **1.** Also called (Brit.): **crutch. a.** the angle formed by the legs where they join the human trunk. **b.** the human genital area. **c.** the corresponding part of a pair of trousers, pants, etc. **2.** a forked region formed by the junction of two members. **3.** a forked pole or stick. —**crotched** (krɒtʃt) *adj.*

crotchet ('krɒtʃɪt) *n.* **1.** *Music.* a note having the time value of a quarter of a semibreve. **2.** a perverse notion.

crotchety ('krɒtʃɪtɪ) *adj.* **1.** *Inf.* irritable; contrary. **2.** full of crotchets. —'**crotchetiness** *n.*

crouch (krautʃ) *vb.* **1.** (*intr.*) to bend low with the limbs

---

THESAURUS

cross *adj.* **1.** angry, annoyed, cantankerous, captious, churlish, crotchety (*Inf.*), crusty, disagreeable, fractious, fretful, grouchy (*Inf.*), grumpy, ill-humoured, ill-tempered, impatient, in a bad mood, irascible, irritable, out of humour, peeved (*Inf.*), peevish, pettish, petulant, put out, querulous, shirty (*Sl.*), short, snappish, snappy, splenetic, sullen, surly, testy, vexed, waspish ~*v.* **2.** bridge, cut across, extend over, ford, meet, pass over, ply, span, traverse, zigzag **3.** crisscross, intersect, intertwine, lace, lie athwart of **4.** blend, crossbreed, cross-fertilize, cross-

pollinate, hybridize, interbreed, intercross, mix, mongrelize **5.** block, deny, foil, frustrate, hinder, impede, interfere, obstruct, oppose, resist, thwart ~*n.* **6.** affliction, burden, grief, load, misery, misfortune, trial, tribulation, trouble, woe, worry **7.** crucifix, rood **8.** crossing, crossroads, intersection, junction **9.** amalgam, blend, combination, crossbreed, cur, hybrid, hybridization, mixture, mongrel, mutt (*Sl.*) ~*adj.* **10.** crosswise, intersecting, oblique, transverse **11.** adverse, contrary, opposed, opposing, unfavourable **12.** *Involving an interchange* opposite, reciprocal

cross-examine catechize, grill (*Inf.*), interrogate, pump, question, quiz

cross out *or* **off** blue-pencil, cancel, delete, eliminate, strike off *or* out

crotch crutch, groin

crotchet caprice, fad, fancy, quirk, vagary, whim, whimsy

crotchety awkward, bad-tempered, cantankerous, contrary, crabby, cross, crusty, curmudgeonly, difficult, disagreeable, fractious, grumpy, irritable, obstreperous, peevish, surly, testy

pulled up close together. **2.** (*intr.*) to cringe, as in humility or fear. ~*n.* **3.** the act of stooping or bending.

croup[1] (kru:p) *n.* a throat condition, occurring usually in children, characterized by a hoarse cough and laboured breathing, resulting from inflammation of the larynx. —'**croupous** *or* '**croupy** *adj.*

croup[2] (kru:p) *n.* the hindquarters, esp. of a horse.

croupier ('kru:pɪə) *n.* a person who deals cards, collects bets, etc., at a gaming table.

crouton ('kru:tɒn) *n.* a small piece of fried or toasted bread, usually served in soup.

crow[1] (krəʊ) *n.* **1.** any large gregarious songbird of the genus *Corvus* of Europe and Asia, such as the raven, rook, and jackdaw. All have a heavy bill, glossy black plumage, and rounded wings. **2.** any of various similar birds. **3.** *Sl.* an old or ugly woman. **4. as the crow flies.** as directly as possible. **5. eat crow.** *U.S. inf.* to be forced to do something humiliating. **6. stone the crows.** (*interj.*) *Brit. & Austral. sl.* an expression of surprise, horror, etc.

crow[2] (krəʊ) *vb.* (*intr.*) **1.** (past tense **crowed** *or* **crew**) to utter a shrill squawking sound, as a cock. **2.** (often foll. by *over*) to boast one's superiority. **3.** (esp. of babies) to utter cries of pleasure. ~*n.* **4.** an act or instance of crowing. —'**crower** *n.* —'**crowingly** *adv.*

crowbar ('krəʊ,bɑ:) *n.* a heavy iron lever with one end forged into a wedge shape.

crowd (kraʊd) *n.* **1.** a large number of things or people gathered or considered together. **2.** a particular group of people, esp. considered as a set: *the crowd from the office.* **3.** (preceded by *the*) the common people; the masses. ~*vb.* **4.** (*intr.*) to gather together in large numbers; throng. **5.** (*tr.*) to press together into a confined space. **6.** (*tr.*) to fill to excess; fill by pushing into. **7.** (*tr.*) *Sl.* to urge or harass by urging. —'**crowded** *adj.* —'**crowdedness** *n.*

crowfoot ('krəʊ,fʊt) *n., pl.* **-foots.** any of several plants that have yellow or white flowers and divided leaves resembling the foot of a crow.

crown (kraʊn) *n.* **1.** an ornamental headdress denoting sovereignty, usually made of gold embedded with precious stones. **2.** a wreath or garland for the head, awarded as a sign of victory, success, honour, etc. **3.** (*sometimes cap.*) monarchy or kingship. **4.** an award, distinction, or title, given as an honour to reward merit, victory, etc. **5.** anything resembling or symbolizing a crown. **6. a.** a coin worth 25 pence (five shillings). **b.** any of several continental coins, such as the krona or krone, with a name meaning crown. **7.** the top or summit of something: *crown of a hill.* **8.** the centre part of a road, esp. when it is cambered. **9.** the outstanding quality, achievement, state, etc.: *the crown of his achievements.* **10. a.** the enamel-covered part of a tooth above the gum. **b. artificial crown.** a substitute crown, usually of gold, porcelain, or acrylic resin, fitted over a decayed or broken tooth. **11.** the part of an anchor where the arms are joined to the shank. ~*vb.* (*tr.*) **12.** to put a crown on the head of, symbolically vesting with royal title, powers, etc. **13.** to place a crown, wreath, garland, etc., on someone's head. **14.** to place something on or over the head or top of. **15.** to confer a title, dignity, or reward upon.

16. to form the summit or topmost part of. **17.** to occur as the culminating event in a series: *to crown it all it rained, too.* **18.** *Draughts.* to promote (a draught) to a king by placing another draught on top of it. **19.** to attach a crown to (a tooth). **20.** *Sl.* to hit over the head.

Crown (kraʊn) *n.* (*sometimes not cap;* usually preceded by *the*) **1.** the sovereignty or realm of a monarch. **2. a.** the government of a monarchy. **b.** (*as modifier*): *Crown property.*

crown colony *n.* a British colony whose administration is controlled by the Crown.

crown court *n. English law.* a court of criminal jurisdiction holding sessions in towns throughout England and Wales.

Crown Derby *n.* a type of porcelain manufactured at Derby from 1784–1848.

crown jewels *pl. n.* the jewellery, including the regalia, used by a sovereign on a state occasion.

crown prince *n.* the male heir to a sovereign throne.

crow's-foot *n., pl.* **-feet.** (*often pl.*) a wrinkle at the outer corner of the eye.

crow's-nest *n.* a lookout platform high up on a ship's mast.

crozier ('krəʊʒə) *n.* a variant spelling of **crosier.**

CRTC *abbrev. for* Canadian Radio-television and Telecommunications Commission.

crucial ('kru:ʃəl) *adj.* **1.** involving a final or supremely important decision or event; decisive; critical. **2.** *Inf.* very important. —'**crucially** *adv.*

crucible ('kru:sɪb'l) *n.* **1.** a vessel in which substances are heated to high temperatures. **2.** the hearth at the bottom of a metallurgical furnace in which the metal collects. **3.** a severe trial or test.

crucifix ('kru:sɪfɪks) *n.* a cross or image of a cross with a figure of Christ upon it.

crucifixion (,kru:sɪ'fɪkʃən) *n.* a method of putting to death by nailing or binding to a cross, normally by the hands and feet.

Crucifixion (,kru:sɪ'fɪkʃən) *n.* **1.** (usually preceded by *the*) the crucifying of Christ. **2.** a picture or representation of this.

cruciform ('kru:sɪ,fɔ:m) *adj.* shaped like a cross. —'**cruci,formly** *adv.*

crucify ('kru:sɪ,faɪ) *vb.* **-fying, -fied.** (*tr.*) **1.** to put to death by crucifixion. **2.** *Sl.* to defeat, ridicule, etc., totally. **3.** to treat very cruelly; torment. —'**cruci,fier** *n.*

crud (krʌd) *n.* **1.** *Sl.*, chiefly *U.S.* **a.** a sticky substance, esp. when dirty and encrusted. **b.** a despicable person. **2.** an undesirable residue, esp. one inside a nuclear reactor. —'**cruddy** *adj.*

crude (kru:d) *adj.* **1.** lacking taste, tact, or refinement; vulgar. **2.** in a natural or unrefined state. **3.** lacking care, knowledge, or skill. **4.** (*prenominal*) stark; blunt. ~*n.* **5.** short for **crude oil.** —'**crudely** *adv.* —'**crudity** *or* '**crudeness** *n.*

crude oil *n.* unrefined petroleum.

cruel ('kru:əl) *adj.* **1.** causing or inflicting pain without pity. **2.** causing pain or suffering. ~*vb.* (*tr.*) **3.** *Austral. sl.* to ruin the chances of: *to cruel his pitch.* —'**cruelly** *adv.* —'**cruelness** *n.* —'**cruelty** *n.*

THESAURUS

crouch 1. bend down, bow, duck, hunch, kneel, squat, stoop **2.** abase oneself, cower, cringe, fawn, grovel, truckle

crow bluster, boast, brag, exult, flourish, gloat, glory in, strut, swagger, triumph, vaunt

crowd *n.* **1.** army, assembly, company, concourse, flock, herd, horde, host, mass, mob, multitude, pack, press, rabble, swarm, throng, troupe **2.** bunch (*Inf.*), circle, clique, group, lot, set **3.** attendance, audience, gate, house, spectators ~*v.* **4.** cluster, congregate, cram, flock, forgather, gather, huddle, mass, muster, press, push, stream, surge, swarm, throng **5.** bundle, congest, cram, pack, pile, squeeze **6.** batter, butt, elbow, jostle, shove **7. the crowd** hoi polloi, masses, mob, people, populace, proletariat, public, rabble, rank and file, riffraff, vulgar herd

crowded busy, congested, cramped, crushed, full, huddled, jam-packed, mobbed, overflowing, packed, populous, swarming, teeming, thronged

crown *n.* **1.** chaplet, circlet, coronal (*Poetic*), coronet, diadem, tiara **2.** bays, distinction, garland, honour, kudos, laurels, laurel wreath, prize, trophy **3.** emperor, empress, king, monarch, monarchy, queen, *rex,* royalty, ruler, sovereign, sovereignty **4.** acme, apex, crest, head, perfection, pinnacle, summit, tip, top, ultimate, zenith ~*v.* **5.** adorn, dignify, festoon, honour, invest, reward **6.** be the climax *or* culmination of, cap, complete, consummate, finish, fulfil, perfect, put the finishing touch to, round off, surmount, terminate, top **7.** *Sl.* biff (*Sl.*), box, cuff, hit over the head, punch

crowning *adj.* climactic, consummate, culminating, final, paramount, sovereign, supreme, ultimate

crucial 1. central, critical, decisive, pivotal, psychological, searching, testing, trying **2.** *Inf.* essential, high-priority, important, momentous, pressing, urgent, vital

crucify 1. execute, harrow, persecute,

rack, torment, torture **2.** *Sl.* lampoon, pan (*Inf.*), ridicule, tear to pieces, wipe the floor with (*Inf.*)

crude 1. boorish, coarse, crass, dirty, gross, indecent, lewd, obscene, smutty, tactless, tasteless, uncouth, vulgar **2.** natural, raw, unmilled, unpolished, unprepared, unprocessed, unrefined **3.** clumsy, makeshift, outline, primitive, rough, rough-hewn, rude, rudimentary, sketchy, undeveloped, unfinished, unformed, unpolished

crudely bluntly, clumsily, coarsely, impolitely, indecently, pulling no punches (*Inf.*), roughly, rudely, sketchily, tastelessly, vulgarly

crudity 1. coarseness, crudeness, impropriety, indecency, indelicacy, lewdness, loudness, lowness, obscenity, obtrusiveness, smuttiness, vulgarity **2.** clumsiness, crudeness, primitiveness, roughness, rudeness

cruel 1. atrocious, barbarous, bitter, bloodthirsty, brutal, brutish, callous, cold-blooded,

cruet ('kru:ɪt) n. **1.** a small container for holding pepper, salt, vinegar, oil, etc., at table. **2.** a set of such containers, esp. on a stand.

cruise (kru:z) vb. **1.** (intr.) to make a trip by sea for pleasure, usually calling at a number of ports. **2.** to sail or travel over (a body of water) for pleasure. **3.** to search for enemy vessels in a warship. **4.** (intr.) (of a vehicle, aircraft, or vessel) to travel at a moderate and efficient speed. ~n. **5.** an act or instance of cruising, esp. a trip by sea.

cruise missile n. a subsonic missile that is guided throughout its flight.

cruiser ('kru:zə) n. **1.** a high-speed, long-range warship armed with medium-calibre weapons. **2.** Also called: **cabin cruiser.** a pleasure boat, esp. one that is power-driven and has a cabin. **3.** any person or thing that cruises.

cruiserweight ('kru:zə,weɪt) n. Boxing. another term (esp. Brit.) for **light heavyweight.**

crumb (krʌm) n. **1.** a small fragment of bread, cake, or other baked foods. **2.** a small piece or bit. **3.** the soft inner part of bread. **4.** Sl. a contemptible person. ~vb. **5.** (tr.) to prepare or cover (food) with breadcrumbs. **6.** to break into small fragments.

crumble ('krʌmbəl) vb. **1.** to break or be broken into crumbs or fragments. **2.** (intr.) to fall apart or away. ~n. **3.** Brit. a baked pudding consisting of a crumbly mixture of flour, fat, and sugar over stewed fruit: apple crumble.

crumbly ('krʌmblɪ) adj. **-blier, -bliest.** easily crumbled or crumbling. —**'crumbliness** n.

crumby ('krʌmɪ) adj. **-bier, -biest. 1.** full of or littered with crumbs. **2.** soft, like the inside of bread. **3.** a variant spelling of **crummy.**

crummy ('krʌmɪ) adj. **-mier, -miest.** Sl. **1.** of little value; contemptible. **2.** unwell or depressed: to feel crummy.

crumpet ('krʌmpɪt) n. Chiefly Brit. **1.** a light soft yeast cake, eaten toasted and buttered. **2.** Sl. women collectively.

crumple ('krʌmpəl) vb. **1.** (when intr., often foll. by up) to collapse or cause to collapse. **2.** (when tr., often foll. by up) to crush or cause to be crushed so as to form wrinkles or creases. ~n. **3.** a loose crease or wrinkle. —**'crumply** adj.

crunch (krʌntʃ) vb. **1.** to bite or chew with a crushing or crackling sound. **2.** to make or cause to make a crisp or brittle sound. ~n. **3.** the sound or act of crunching. **4. the crunch.** Inf. the critical moment or situation. —**'crunchy** adj. —**'crunchily** adv. —**'crunchiness** n.

crupper ('krʌpə) n. **1.** a strap from the back of a saddle that passes under a horse's tail. **2.** the horse's rump.

crusade (kru:'seɪd) n. **1.** (often cap.) any of the military expeditions undertaken in the 11th, 12th, and 13th centuries by the Christian powers of Europe to recapture the Holy Land from the Muslims. **2.** (formerly) any holy war. **3.** a vigorous and dedicated action or movement in favour of a cause. ~vb. (intr.) **4.** to campaign vigorously for something. **5.** to go on a crusade. —**cru-'sader** n.

cruse (kru:z) n. a small earthenware container used,

esp. formerly, for liquids.

crush (krʌʃ) vb. (mainly tr.) **1.** to press, mash, or squeeze so as to injure, break, crease, etc. **2.** to break or grind into small particles. **3.** to put down or subdue, esp. by force. **4.** to extract (juice, water, etc.) by pressing. **5.** to oppress harshly. **6.** to hug or clasp tightly. **7.** to defeat or humiliate utterly, as in an argument or by a cruel remark. **8.** (intr.) to crowd; throng. **9.** (intr.) to become injured, broken, or distorted by pressure. ~n. **10.** a dense crowd, esp. at a social occasion. **11.** the act of crushing; pressure. **12.** a drink or pulp prepared by or as if by crushing fruit: orange crush. **13.** Inf. **a.** an infatuation: she had a crush on him. **b.** the person with whom one is infatuated. —**'crushable** adj. —**'crusher** n.

crush barrier n. a barrier erected to separate sections of large crowds.

crust (krʌst) n. **1. a.** the hard outer part of bread. **b.** a piece of bread consisting mainly of this. **2.** the baked shell of a pie, tart, etc. **3.** any hard or stiff outer covering or surface: a crust of ice. **4.** the outer layer of the earth. **5.** the dry covering of a skin sore or lesion; scab. **6.** Sl. impertinence. **7.** Austral. sl. a living (esp. in **earn a crust**). ~vb. **8.** to cover with or acquire a crust. **9.** to form or be formed into a crust.

crustacean (krʌ'steɪʃən) n. **1.** any arthropod of the mainly aquatic class Crustacea, typically having a carapace and including the lobsters, crabs, woodlice, and water fleas. ~adj. also **crustaceous. 2.** of, relating to, or belonging to the Crustacea.

crusty ('krʌstɪ) adj. **-ier, -iest. 1.** having or characterized by a crust. **2.** having a rude or harsh character or exterior. —**'crustily** adv. —**'crustiness** n.

crutch (krʌtʃ) n. **1.** a long staff having a rest for the armpit, for supporting the weight of the body. **2.** something that supports, helps, or sustains. **3.** Brit. another word for **crotch** (sense 1). ~vb. **4.** (tr.) to support or sustain (a person or thing) as with a crutch. **5.** Austral. & N.Z. to clip (wool) from the hindquarters of a sheep.

crux (krʌks) n., pl. **cruxes** or **cruces** ('kru:si:z). **1.** a vital or decisive stage, point, etc. (often in **the crux of the matter**). **2.** a baffling problem or difficulty.

cry (kraɪ) vb. **cries, crying, cried. 1.** (intr.) to utter inarticulate sounds, esp. when weeping; sob. **2.** (intr.) to shed tears; weep. **3.** (intr.; usually foll. by out) to scream or shout in pain, terror, etc. **4.** (tr.; often foll. by out) to utter or shout (words of appeal, exclamation, fear, etc.). **5.** (intr.; often foll. by out) (of animals, birds, etc.) to utter loud characteristic sounds. **6.** (tr.) to hawk or sell by public announcement: to cry newspapers. **7.** to announce (something) publicly or in the streets. **8.** (intr.; foll. by for) to clamour or beg. **9. cry for the moon.** to desire the unattainable. **10. cry one's eyes out** or **heart out.** to weep bitterly. ~n., pl. **cries. 11.** the act or sound of crying; a shout, scream, or wail. **12.** the characteristic utterance of an animal or bird. **13.** a fit of weeping. **14.** Hunting. the baying of a pack of hounds hunting their quarry by scent. **15. a far cry. a.** a long way. **b.** something very different. **16. in full cry. a.** hotly pursuing. **b.** the baying of a pack of hounds hunting together.

◾ THESAURUS ◾

depraved, excruciating, fell (Archaic), ferocious, fierce, flinty, grim, hard, hard-hearted, harsh, heartless, hellish, implacable, inclement, inexorable, inhuman, inhumane, malevolent, painful, poignant, ravening, raw, relentless, remorseless, sadistic, sanguinary, savage, severe, spiteful, stony-hearted, unfeeling, unkind, unnatural, vengeful, vicious **2.** merciless, pitiless, ruthless, unrelenting

cruelly 1. barbarously, brutally, brutishly, callously, ferociously, fiercely, heartlessly, in cold blood, mercilessly, pitilessly, sadistically, savagely, spitefully, unmercifully, viciously **2.** bitterly, deeply, fearfully, grievously, monstrously, mortally, severely

cruelty barbarity, bestiality, bloodthirstiness, brutality, brutishness, callousness, depravity, ferocity, fiendishness, hardheartedness, harshness, heartlessness, inhumanity, mercilessness, murderousness, ruthlessness, sadism, savagery, severity, spite, spitefulness, venom, viciousness

cruise v. **1.** coast, sail, voyage **2.** coast, drift, keep a steady pace, travel along ~n. **3.** boat trip, sail, sea trip, voyage

crumb atom, bit, grain, mite, morsel, particle, scrap, shred, sliver, snippet, soupçon, speck

crumble 1. bruise, crumb, crush, fragment, granulate, grind, pound, powder, pulverize, triturate **2.** break up, collapse, come to dust, decay, decompose, degenerate, deteriorate, disintegrate, fall apart, go to pieces (Inf.), go to wrack and ruin, moulder, perish, tumble down

crumple 1. crease, crush, pucker, rumple, screw up, wrinkle **2.** break down, cave in, collapse, fall, give way, go to pieces

crunch 1. v. champ, chew noisily, chomp, grind, masticate, munch **2.** n. Inf. crisis, critical point, crux, emergency, hour of decision, moment of truth, test

crusade campaign, cause, drive, holy

war, jihad, movement, push

crusader advocate, campaigner, champion, reformer

crush v. **1.** bray, break, bruise, comminute, compress, contuse, crease, crumble, crumple, crunch, mash, pound, pulverize, rumple, smash, squeeze, wrinkle **2.** conquer, extinguish, overcome, overpower, overwhelm, put down, quell, stamp out, subdue, vanquish **3.** abash, browbeat, chagrin, dispose of, humiliate, mortify, put down (Sl.), quash, shame **4.** embrace, enfold, hug, press, squeeze ~n. **5.** crowd, huddle, jam, party

crust caking, coat, coating, concretion, covering, film, incrustation, layer, outside, scab, shell, skin, surface

crusty 1. brittle, crisp, crispy, friable, hard, short, well-baked, well-done **2.** brusque, cantankerous, captious, choleric, crabby, cross, curt, gruff, ill-humoured, irritable, peevish, prickly, short, short-tempered, snappish, snarling, splenetic, surly, testy,

crying ('kraɪɪŋ) *adj. (prenominal)* notorious; lamentable (esp. in **crying shame**).

cry off *vb. (intr.) Inf.* to withdraw from or cancel (an agreement or arrangement).

cryogenics (ˌkraɪə'dʒɛnɪks) *n. (functioning as sing.)* the branch of physics concerned with very low temperatures and the phenomena occurring at these temperatures. —ˌcryo'genic *adj.*

crypt (krɪpt) *n.* a vault or underground chamber, esp. beneath a church, often used as a chapel, burial place, etc.

cryptic ('krɪptɪk) *or* **cryptical** *adj.* **1.** hidden; secret. **2.** esoteric or obscure in meaning. **3.** (of coloration) effecting camouflage or concealment. —'cryptically *adv.*

crypto- *or before a vowel* **crypt-** *combining form.* secret, hidden, or concealed.

cryptogam ('krɪptəʊˌgæm) *n.* (in former classification schemes) any plant that does not produce seeds, including algae, fungi, mosses, and ferns. —ˌcrypto'gamic *or* **cryptogamous** (krɪp'tɒgəməs) *adj.*

cryptography (krɪp'tɒgrəfɪ) *n.* the science or study of analysing and deciphering codes, ciphers, etc. Also called: **cryptanalysis.** —cryp'tographer, cryp'tographist *n.* —cryptographic (ˌkrɪptə'græfɪk) *or* ˌcrypto'graphical *adj.* —ˌcrypto'graphically *adv.*

crystal ('krɪstəl) *n.* **1.** a solid, such as quartz, with a regular shape in which plane faces intersect at definite angles. **2.** a single grain of a crystalline substance. **3.** anything resembling a crystal, such as a piece of cut glass. **4. a.** a highly transparent and brilliant type of glass. **b.** (*as modifier*): *a crystal chandelier.* **5.** something made of or resembling crystal. **6.** crystal glass articles collectively. **7.** *Electronics.* **a.** a crystalline element used in certain electronic devices as a detector, oscillator, etc. **b.** (*as modifier*): *crystal pickup.* **8.** a transparent cover for the face of a watch. **9.** (*modifier*) of or relating to a crystal or the regular atomic arrangement of crystals: *crystal structure.* ~*adj.* **10.** resembling crystal; transparent: *crystal water.*

crystal ball *n.* the glass globe used in crystal gazing.

crystal gazing *n.* **1.** the act of staring into a crystal ball supposedly in order to arouse visual perceptions of the future, etc. **2.** the act of trying to foresee or predict. —**crystal gazer** *n.*

crystalline ('krɪstəˌlaɪn) *adj.* **1.** having the characteristics or structure of crystals. **2.** consisting of or containing crystals. **3.** made of or like crystal; transparent; clear.

crystallize *or* **-ise** ('krɪstəˌlaɪz) *vb.* **1.** to form or cause to form crystals; assume or cause to assume a crystalline form or structure. **2.** to coat or become coated with sugar. **3.** to give a definite form or expression to (an idea, argument, etc.) or (of an idea, argument, etc.) to assume a definite form. —'crystal,lizable *or* **-isable** *adj.* —ˌcrystalli'zation *or* **-i'sation** *n.*

crystallography (ˌkrɪstə'lɒgrəfɪ) *n.* the science of crystals. —ˌcrystal'lographer *n.* —crystallographic (ˌkrɪstələʊ'græfɪk) *adj.*

crystalloid ('krɪstəˌlɔɪd) *adj.* **1.** resembling or having the properties of a crystal. ~*n.* **2.** a substance that in solution can pass through a semipermeable membrane. —ˌcrystal'loidal *adj.*

Cs *the chemical symbol for* caesium.

cs. *abbrev. for* case.

C.S. *abbrev. for:* **1.** Also: **c.s.** Capital Stock. **2.** chartered surveyor. **3.** Christian Science. **4.** Civil Service. **5.** Also: **c.s.** Court of Session.

csc *abbrev. for* cosecant.

CSC *abbrev. for* Canadian Services College.

C.S.C. *abbrev. for* Civil Service Commission.

CSE *n.* (in Britain) *abbrev. for* Certificate of Secondary Education; an examination the first grade pass of which is an equivalent to a GCE O level.

CS gas *n.* a gas causing tears, salivation, and painful breathing, used in chemical warfare and civil disturbances.

C.S.I.R.O. (in Australia) *abbrev. for* Commonwealth Scientific and Industrial Research Organization.

ct. *abbrev. for:* **1.** cent. **2.** carat. **3.** court.

CTV *abbrev. for* Canadian Television (Network Ltd.)

cu *or* **cu.** *abbrev. for* cubic.

Cu *the chemical symbol for* copper.

cub (kʌb) *n.* **1.** the young of certain animals, such as the lion, bear, etc. **2.** a young or inexperienced person. ~*vb.* **cubbing, cubbed.** **3.** to give birth to (cubs). —'cubbish *adj.*

Cub (kʌb) *n.* short for **Cub scout.**

cubbyhole ('kʌbɪˌhəʊl) *n.* a small enclosed space or room.

cube (kjuːb) *n.* **1.** a solid having six plane square faces in which the angle between two adjacent sides is a right angle. **2.** the product of three equal factors. **3.** something in the form of a cube. ~*vb.* **4.** to raise (a number or quantity) to the third power. **5.** (*tr.*) to make, shape, or cut (something) into cubes. —'cuber *n.*

cube root *n.* the number or quantity whose cube is a given number or quantity: 2 is the cube root of 8 (usually written $^3\sqrt{8}$).

cubic ('kjuːbɪk) *adj.* **1.** having the shape of a cube. **2. a.** having three dimensions. **b.** denoting or relating to a linear measure that is raised to the third power: *a cubic metre.* **3.** *Maths.* of, relating to, or containing a variable to the third power or a term in which the sum of the exponents of the variables is three. —'cubical *adj.*

cubicle ('kjuːbɪkəl) *n.* a partially or totally enclosed section of a room, as in a dormitory.

cubic measure *n.* a system of units for the measurement of volumes.

cubism ('kjuːbɪzəm) *n. (often cap.)* a French school of art, initiated in 1907 by Picasso and Braque, which amalgamated viewpoints of natural forms into a multifaceted surface of geometrical planes. —'cubist *adj., n.* —cu'bistic *adj.*

cubit ('kjuːbɪt) *n.* an ancient measure of length based on the length of the forearm.

cuboid ('kjuːbɔɪd) *adj. also* **cuboidal** (kjuː'bɔɪdəl). **1.** shaped like a cube; cubic. **2.** of or denoting the cuboid bone. ~*n.* **3.** the cubelike bone of the foot. **4.** *Maths.* a geometric solid whose six faces are rectangles.

Cub Scout *or* **Cub** *n.* a member of the junior branch of the Scout Association.

cuckold ('kʌkəld) *n.* **1.** a man whose wife has committed adultery. ~*vb.* **2.** (*tr.*) to make a cuckold of. —'cuckoldry *n.*

cuckoo ('kuːkuː) *n., pl.* **-oos. 1.** any bird of the family Cuculidae, having pointed wings and a long tail. Many species, including the **European cuckoo,** lay their eggs in the nests of other birds and have a two-note call. **2.** *Inf.* an insane or foolish person. ~*adj.* **3.** *Inf.* insane or foolish. ~*interj.* **4.** an imitation or representation of the call of a cuckoo. ~*vb.* **-ooing, -ooed. 5.** (*intr.*) to make the sound imitated by the word cuckoo.

cuckoopint ('kuːkuːˌpaɪnt) *n.* a European plant with arrow-shaped leaves, a spathe marked with purple, a pale purple spadix, and scarlet berries. Also called: **lords-and-ladies.**

cuckoo spit *n.* a white frothy mass on the stems and

THESAURUS

touchy

cry *v.* **1.** bawl, bewail, blubber, boohoo, greet (*Scot.*), howl one's eyes out, keen, lament, mewl, pule, shed tears, snivel, sob, wail, weep, whimper, whine, whinge (*Inf.*), yowl ~*n.* **2.** bawling, blubbering, crying, greet (*Scot.*), howl, keening, lament, lamentation, plaint (*Archaic*), snivel, snivelling, sob, sobbing, sorrowing, wailing, weep, weeping ~*v.* **3.** bawl, bellow, call, call out, ejaculate, exclaim, hail, halloo, holler (*Inf.*), howl, roar, scream, screech, shout, shriek, sing out, vociferate, whoop, yell ~*n.* **4.** bawl,

bellow, call, ejaculation, exclamation, holler (*Inf.*), hoot, howl, outcry, roar, scream, screech, shriek, squawk, whoop, yell, yelp, yoo-hoo ~*v.* **5.** advertise, announce, bark (*Inf.*), broadcast, bruit, hawk, noise, proclaim, promulgate, publish, trumpet ~*n.* **6.** announcement, barking (*Inf.*), noising, proclamation, publication ~*v.* **7.** beg, beseech, clamour, entreat, implore, plead, pray ~*n.* **8.** appeal, entreaty, petition, plea, prayer, supplication

cry down belittle, decry, denigrate, disparage, run down

cry off back out, beg off, excuse oneself, quit, withdraw, withdraw from

crypt catacomb, tomb, undercroft, vault

cub 1. offspring, whelp, young **2.** babe (*Inf.*), beginner, fledgling, greenhorn (*Inf.*), lad, learner, puppy, recruit, tenderfoot, trainee, whippersnapper, youngster

cubbyhole 1. den, hideaway, hole, snug **2.** compartment, niche, pigeonhole, recess, slot

leaves of many plants, produced by froghopper larvae.

cucumber ('kju:ˌkʌmbə) n. 1. a creeping plant cultivated in many forms for its edible fruit. 2. the cylindrical fruit of this plant, which has hard thin green rind and white crisp flesh.

cud (kʌd) n. 1. partially digested food regurgitated from the first stomach of ruminants to the mouth for a second chewing. 2. **chew the cud.** to reflect or think over something.

cuddle ('kʌdᵊl) vb. 1. to hold close or (of two people, etc.) to hold each other close, as for affection or warmth; hug. 2. (intr.; foll. by up) to curl or snuggle up into a comfortable or warm position. ~n. 3. a close embrace, esp. when prolonged. —'**cuddlesome** adj. —'**cuddly** adj.

cuddy ('kʌdɪ) n., pl. **-dies.** a small cabin in a boat.

cudgel ('kʌdʒəl) n. 1. a short stout stick used as a weapon. 2. **take up the cudgels.** (often foll. by for or on behalf of) to join in a dispute, esp. to defend oneself or another. ~vb. **-elling, -elled** or U.S. **-eling, -eled.** 3. (tr.) to strike with a cudgel. 4. **cudgel one's brains.** to think hard. —'**cudgeller** n.

cue[1] (kju:) n. 1. a. (in the theatre, films, music, etc.) anything that serves as a signal to an actor, musician, etc., to follow with specific lines or action. b. **on cue.** at the right moment. 2. a signal or reminder to do something. ~vb. **cueing, cued.** 3. (tr.) to give a cue or cues to (an actor). 4. (usually foll. by in or into) to signal (to something or somebody) at a specific moment in a musical or dramatic performance.

cue[2] (kju:) n. 1. Billiards, etc. a long tapered shaft used to drive the balls. 2. hair caught at the back forming a tail or braid. ~vb. **cueing, cued.** 3. to drive (a ball) with a cue.

cuff[1] (kʌf) n. 1. the end of a sleeve, sometimes turned back. 2. the part of a glove that extends past the wrist. 3. the U.S. and Australian name for **turn-up** (sense 5). 4. **off the cuff.** Inf. improvised; extemporary.

cuff[2] (kʌf) vb. 1. (tr.) to strike with an open hand. ~n. 2. a blow of this kind.

cuirass (kwɪ'ræs) n. 1. a piece of armour covering the chest and back. ~vb. 2. (tr.) to equip with a cuirass.

Cuisenaire rod (ˌkwiːzə'nɛə) n. Trademark. one of a set of rods of various colours and lengths representing different numbers, used to teach arithmetic to young children.

cuisine (kwɪ'ziːn) n. 1. a style or manner of cooking: French cuisine. 2. the food prepared by a restaurant, household, etc.

cul-de-sac ('kʌldəˌsæk, 'kʊl-) n., pl. **culs-de-sac** or **cul-de-sacs.** 1. a road with one end blocked off; dead end. 2. an inescapable position.

-cule suffix forming nouns. indicating smallness.

culinary ('kʌlɪnərɪ) adj. of, relating to, or used in the kitchen or in cookery. —'**culinarily** adv.

cull (kʌl) vb. (tr.) 1. to choose or gather the best or required examples. 2. to take out (an animal, esp. an inferior one) from a herd. 3. to gather (flowers, fruit, etc.). ~n. 4. the act or product of culling. 5. an inferior animal taken from a herd. —'**culler** n.

culminate ('kʌlmɪˌneɪt) vb. 1. (when intr., usually foll. by in) to reach or bring to a final or climactic stage. 2. (intr.) (of a celestial body) to cross the meridian. —**culminant** ('kʌlmɪnənt) adj. —ˌculmi'nation n.

culottes (kju:'lɒts) pl. n. women's flared knee-length or ankle-length trousers cut to look like a skirt.

culpable ('kʌlpəbᵊl) adj. deserving censure; blameworthy. —ˌculpa'bility n. —'**culpably** adv.

culprit ('kʌlprɪt) n. 1. Law. a person awaiting trial. 2. the person responsible for a particular offence, misdeed, etc.

cult (kʌlt) n. 1. a specific system of religious worship. 2. a sect devoted to the beliefs of a cult. 3. intense interest in and devotion to a person, idea, or activity. 4. the person, idea, etc., arousing such devotion. 5. any popular fashion; craze. 6. (modifier) of, relating to, or characteristic of a cult or cults: a cult figure. —'**cultic** adj. —'**cultism** n. —'**cultist** n.

cultivable ('kʌltɪvəbᵊl) or **cultivatable** ('kʌltɪˌveɪtəbᵊl) adj. (of land) capable of being cultivated. —ˌcultiva'bility n.

cultivate ('kʌltɪˌveɪt) vb. (tr.) 1. to prepare (land or soil) for the growth of crops. 2. to plant, tend, harvest, or improve (plants). 3. to break up (land or soil) with a cultivator or hoe. 4. to improve (the mind, body, etc.) as by study, education, or labour. 5. to give special attention to: to cultivate a friendship. —'**culti,vated** adj.

cultivation (ˌkʌltɪ'veɪʃən) n. 1. Agriculture. a. the cultivating of crops or plants. b. the preparation of ground to promote their growth. 2. development, esp. through education, training, etc. 3. culture or sophistication.

cultivator ('kʌltɪˌveɪtə) n. 1. a farm implement used to break up soil and remove weeds. 2. a person or thing that cultivates.

culture ('kʌltʃə) n. 1. the total of the inherited ideas, beliefs, values, and knowledge, which constitute the shared bases of social action. 2. the total range of activities and ideas of a people. 3. a particular civilization at a particular period. 4. the artistic and social pursuits, expression, and tastes valued by a society or class. 5. the enlightenment or refinement resulting from these pursuits. 6. the cultivation of plants to improve stock or to produce new ones. 7. the rearing and breeding of animals, esp. with a view to improving the strain. 8. the act or practice of tilling or cultivating the soil. 9. Biol. a. the experimental growth of microorganisms in a nutrient substance. b. a group of microorganisms grown in this way. ~vb. (tr.) 10. to cultivate (plants or animals). 11. to grow (microorganisms) in a culture medium. —'**cultural** adj. —'**culturist** n.

cultured ('kʌltʃəd) adj. 1. showing or having good taste, manners, and education. 2. artificially grown or synthesized: cultured pearls. 3. treated by a culture of

---

THESAURUS

microorganisms.

cultured pearl *n.* a pearl induced to grow in the shell of an oyster or clam, by the insertion of a small object.

culvert ('kʌlvət) *n.* 1. a drain or covered channel that crosses under a road, railway, etc. 2. a channel for an electric cable.

cum (kʌm) *prep.* used between nouns to designate a combined nature: *a kitchen-cum-dining room.*

cumber ('kʌmbə) *vb.* (*tr.*) 1. to obstruct or hinder. 2. *Obs.* to inconvenience.

cumbersome ('kʌmbəsəm) *or* **cumbrous** ('kʌmbrəs) *adj.* 1. awkward because of size, weight, or shape. 2. difficult because of extent or complexity: *cumbersome accounts.* —'**cumbersomeness** *or* '**cumbrousness** *n.*

cumbrance ('kʌmbrəns) *n.* 1. a burden, obstacle, or hindrance. 2. trouble or bother.

cumin *or* **cummin** ('kʌmɪn) *n.* 1. an umbelliferous Mediterranean plant with small white or pink flowers. 2. the aromatic seeds (collectively) of this plant, used as a condiment and a flavouring.

cummerbund *or* **kummerbund** ('kʌmə,bʌnd) *n.* a wide sash, worn with a dinner jacket.

cumquat ('kʌmkwɒt) *n.* a variant spelling of **kumquat**.

cumulate *vb.* ('kju:mju,leɪt). 1. to accumulate. ~*adj.* ('kju:mjulɪt). 2. heaped up. —,**cumu'lation** *n.*

cumulative ('kju:mjulətɪv) *adj.* 1. growing in quantity, strength, or effect by successive additions. 2. (of dividends or interest) intended to be accumulated. 3. *Statistics.* **a.** (of a frequency) including all values of a variable either below or above a specified value. **b.** (of error) tending to increase as the sample size is increased. —'**cumulatively** *adv.* —'**cumulativeness** *n.*

cumulus ('kju:mjuləs) *n., pl.* **-li** (-,laɪ). a bulbous or billowing white or dark grey cloud. —'**cumulous** *adj.*

cuneiform ('kju:nɪ,fɔːm) *adj.* 1. Also: **cuneal**. wedge-shaped. 2. of, relating to, or denoting the wedge-shaped characters in several ancient languages of Mesopotamia and Persia. 3. of or relating to a tablet in which this script is employed. ~*n.* 4. cuneiform characters.

cunnilingus (,kʌnɪ'lɪŋgəs) *or* **cunnilinctus** (,kʌnɪ-'lɪŋktəs) *n.* a sexual activity in which the female genitalia are stimulated by the partner's lips and tongue. Cf. **fellatio**.

cunning ('kʌnɪŋ) *adj.* 1. crafty and shrewd, esp. in deception. 2. made with or showing skill; ingenious. ~*n.* 3. craftiness, esp. in deceiving. 4. skill or ingenuity. —'**cunningly** *adv.* —'**cunningness** *n.*

cunt (kʌnt) *n. Taboo sl.* 1. the female genitals. 2. *Offens.* a woman considered sexually. 3. *Offens.* a mean or obnoxious person.

cup (kʌp) *n.* 1. a small open container, usually having one handle, used for drinking from. 2. the contents of such a container. 3. Also called: **teacup; cupful.** a unit of capacity used in cooking. 4. something resembling a cup. 5. either of two cup-shaped parts of a brassiere. 6. a cup-shaped trophy awarded as a prize. 7. *Brit.* **a.** a sporting contest in which a cup is awarded to the winner. **b.** (*as modifier*): *a cup competition.* 8. a mixed drink with one ingredient as a base: *claret cup.* 9. *Golf.* the hole or metal container in the hole on a green. 10. the chalice or the consecrated wine used in the Eucharist. 11. one's lot in life. 12. **one's cup of tea.** *Inf.* one's chosen or preferred thing, task, company, etc. 13. **in one's cups.** drunk. ~*vb.* **cupping, cupped.** (*tr.*) 14. to form (something, such as the hands) into the shape of a cup. 15. to put into or as if into a cup. 16. to draw blood to the surface of the body by cupping.

cupboard ('kʌbəd) *n.* a piece of furniture or a recessed area of a room, with a door concealing storage space.

cupboard love *n.* a show of love inspired only by some selfish or greedy motive.

Cup Final *n.* 1. (often preceded by *the*) the annual final of the F.A. Cup soccer competition. 2. (*often not cap.*) the final of any cup competition.

Cupid ('kju:pɪd) *n.* 1. the Roman god of love, represented as a winged boy with a bow and arrow. Greek counterpart: **Eros**. 2. (*not cap.*) any similar figure.

cupidity (kju:'pɪdɪtɪ) *n.* strong desire, esp. for wealth; greed.

cupola ('kju:pələ) *n.* 1. a roof or ceiling in the form of a dome. 2. a small structure, usually domed, on the top of a roof or dome. 3. a protective dome for a gun on a warship. 4. a furnace in which metals are remelted. —'**cupolated** ('kju:pə,leɪtɪd) *adj.*

cupping ('kʌpɪŋ) *n. Med.* formerly, the use of an evacuated glass cup to draw blood to the surface of the skin for bloodletting.

cupreous ('kju:prɪəs) *adj.* 1. of, containing, or resembling copper. 2. of the colour of copper.

cupric ('kju:prɪk) *adj.* of or containing copper in the divalent state.

cupriferous (kju:'prɪfərəs) *adj.* (of a substance such as an ore) containing or yielding copper.

cupro-, cupri-, *or before a vowel* **cupr-** *combining form.* indicating copper.

cupronickel (,kju:prəʊ'nɪkəl) *n.* any copper alloy containing up to 40 per cent nickel.

cuprous ('kju:prəs) *adj.* of or containing copper in the monovalent state.

cup tie *n. Sport.* an eliminating match or round between two teams in a cup competition.

cur (kɜː) *n.* 1. any vicious dog, esp. a mongrel. 2. a despicable or cowardly person.

cur. *abbrev. for* currency.

curable ('kjʊərəbəl) *adj.* capable of being cured. —,**cura'bility** *or* '**curableness** *n.*

curaçao (,kjʊərə'səʊ) *n.* an orange-flavoured liqueur originally made in Curaçao, a Caribbean island.

curacy ('kjʊərəsɪ) *n., pl.* **-cies.** the office or position of curate.

curare *or* **curari** (kjʊ'rɑːrɪ) *n.* 1. black resin obtained from certain tropical South American trees, which causes muscular paralysis: used medicinally as a muscle relaxant and by South American Indians as an arrow poison. 2. any of various trees from which this resin is obtained.

curate ('kjʊərɪt) *n.* a clergyman appointed to assist a parish priest.

curative ('kjʊərətɪv) *adj.* 1. able or tending to cure. ~*n.* 2. anything able to heal or cure. —'**curatively** *adv.* —'**curativeness** *n.*

curator (kjʊə'reɪtə) *n.* the administrative head of a museum, art gallery, etc. —**curatorial** (,kjʊərə'tɔːrɪəl) *adj.* —**cu'rator,ship** *n.*

curb (kɜːb) *n.* 1. something that restrains or holds back. 2. any enclosing framework, such as a wall around the top of a well. 3. Also called: **curb bit.** a horse's bit with an attached chain or strap, which checks the horse. ~*vb.* 4. to control with or as if with a curb; restrain. ~See also **kerb**.

curd (kɜːd) *n.* 1. (*often pl.*) a substance formed from the coagulation of milk, used in making cheese or eaten as a food. 2. something similar in consistency. ~*vb.* 3. to turn into or become curd. —'**curdy** *adj.*

curdle ('kɜːdəl) *vb.* 1. to turn or cause to turn into curd. 2. **curdle someone's blood.** to fill someone with fear. —'**curdler** *n.*

cure (kjʊə) *vb.* 1. (*tr.*) to get rid of (an ailment or problem); heal. 2. (*tr.*) to restore to health or good condition. 3. (*intr.*) to bring about a cure. 4. (*tr.*) to preserve

---

THESAURUS

culvert channel, conduit, drain, gutter, watercourse

cumbersome awkward, bulky, burdensome, clumsy, cumbrous, embarrassing, heavy, hefty (*Inf.*), incommodious, inconvenient, oppressive, unmanageable, unwieldy, weighty

cumulative accruing, accumulative, aggregate, amassed, collective, heaped, increasing, snowballing

cunning *adj.* 1. artful, astute, canny, crafty, devious, foxy, guileful, knowing,

Machiavellian, sharp, shifty, shrewd, subtle, tricky, wily ~*n.* 2. artfulness, astuteness, craftiness, deceitfulness, deviousness, foxiness, guile, shrewdness, slyness, trickery, wiliness ~*adj.* 3. adroit, deft, dexterous, imaginative, ingenious, skilful ~*n.* 4. ability, adroitness, art, artifice, cleverness, deftness, dexterity, finesse, ingenuity, skill, subtlety

cup beaker, cannikin, chalice, cupful, demitasse, draught, drink, goblet, potion, teacup, trophy

cupboard ambry (*Obsolete*), cabinet,

closet, locker, press

Cupid amoretto, Eros, god of love, love

curb 1. *v.* bite back, bridle, check, constrain, contain, control, hinder, impede, inhibit, moderate, muzzle, repress, restrain, restrict, retard, subdue, suppress 2. *n.* brake, bridle, check, control, deterrent, limitation, rein, restraint

curdle clot, coagulate, condense, congeal, curd, thicken, turn sour

(meat, fish, etc.) by salting, smoking, etc. **5.** (*tr.*) **a.** to treat or finish (a substance) by chemical or physical means. **b.** to vulcanize (rubber). **6.** (*tr.*) to assist the hardening of (concrete, mortar, etc.) by keeping it moist. ~*n.* **7.** a return to health. **8.** any course of medical therapy, esp. one proved effective. **9.** a means of restoring health or improving a situation, etc. **10.** the spiritual and pastoral charge of a parish. **11.** a process or method of preserving meat, fish, etc. —**'cureless** *adj.* —**'curer** *n.*

cure-all *n.* something reputed to cure anything.

curet *or* **curette** (kjʊə'rɛt) *n.* **1.** a surgical instrument for removing dead tissue, growths, etc., from the walls of body cavities. ~*vb.* **-retting, -retted. 2.** (*tr.*) to scrape or clean with such an instrument. —**curettage** (ˌkjʊərɪ'tɑːʒ, kjʊə'rɛtɪdʒ) *n.*

curfew ('kɜːfjuː) *n.* **1.** an official regulation setting restrictions on movement, esp. after a specific time at night. **2.** the time set as a deadline by such a regulation. **3.** (in medieval Europe) **a.** the ringing of a bell to prompt people to extinguish fires and lights. **b.** the time at which the curfew bell was rung. **c.** the bell itself.

curia ('kjʊərɪə) *n., pl.* **-riae** (-rɪˌiː). **1.** (*sometimes cap.*) the papal court and government of the Roman Catholic Church. **2.** (in the Middle Ages) a court held in the king's name. —**'curial** *adj.*

curie ('kjʊərɪ, -riː) *n.* a unit of radioactivity equal to 3.7 × 10¹⁰ disintegrations per second.

curio ('kjʊərɪˌəʊ) *n., pl.* **-rios.** a small article valued as a collector's item, esp. something unusual.

curiosity (ˌkjʊərɪ'ɒsɪtɪ) *n., pl.* **-ties. 1.** an eager desire to know; inquisitiveness. **2.** the quality of being curious; strangeness. **3.** something strange or fascinating.

curious ('kjʊərɪəs) *adj.* **1.** eager to learn; inquisitive. **2.** overinquisitive; prying. **3.** interesting because of oddness or novelty. —**'curiously** *adv.* —**'curiousness** *n.*

curium ('kjʊərɪəm) *n.* a silvery-white metallic transuranic element artificially produced from plutonium. Symbol: Cm; at. no.: 96; half-life of most stable isotope, ²⁴⁷Cm: 1.6 x 10⁷ years.

curl (kɜːl) *vb.* **1.** (*intr.*) (esp. of hair) to grow into curves or ringlets. **2.** (*tr.*; sometimes foll. by *up*) to twist or roll (esp. hair) into coils or ringlets. **3.** (often foll. by *up*) to become or cause to become spiral-shaped or curved. **4.** (*intr.*) to move in a curving or twisting manner. **5.** (*intr.*) to play the game of curling. **6.** (*tr.*) **curl one's lip.** to show contempt, as by raising a corner of the lip. ~*n.* **7.** a curve or coil of hair. **8.** a curved or spiral shape or mark. **9.** the act of curling or state of being curled. —**'curly** *adj.*

curler ('kɜːlə) *n.* **1.** any of various pins, clasps, or rollers used to curl or wave hair. **2.** a person or thing that curls. **3.** a person who plays curling.

curlew ('kɜːljuː) *n.* any of certain large shore birds of Europe and Asia. They have a long downward-curving bill and occur in northern and arctic regions.

curlicue *or* **curlycue** ('kɜːlɪˌkjuː) *n.* an intricate ornamental curl or twist.

curling ('kɜːlɪŋ) *n.* a game played on ice, esp. in Scotland, in which heavy stones with handles (**curling stones**) are slid towards a target (**tee**).

curmudgeon (kɜː'mʌdʒən) *n.* a surly or miserly

person. —**cur'mudgeonly** *adj.*

currant ('kʌrənt) *n.* **1.** a small dried seedless grape of the Mediterranean region. **2.** any of several mainly N temperate shrubs, esp. redcurrant and blackcurrant. **3.** the small acid fruit of any of these plants.

currency ('kʌrənsɪ) *n., pl.* **-cies. 1.** a metal or paper medium of exchange that is in current use. **2.** general acceptance or circulation; prevalence. **3.** the period of time during which something is valid, accepted, or in force. ~*adj.* **4.** *Austral. inf.* native-born as distinct from immigrant: *a currency lad.*

current ('kʌrənt) *adj.* **1.** of the immediate present; in progress. **2.** most recent; up-to-date. **3.** commonly known, practised, or accepted. **4.** circulating and valid at present: *current coins.* ~*n.* **5.** (esp. of water or air) a steady, usually natural, flow. **6.** a mass of air, body of water, etc., that has a steady flow in a particular direction. **7.** the rate of flow of such a mass. **8.** *Physics.* **a.** a flow of electric charge through a conductor. **b.** the rate of flow of this charge. **9.** a general trend or drift: *currents of opinion.* —**'currently** *adv.* —**'currentness** *n.*

current account *n.* a bank account that usually carries no interest and against which cheques may be drawn at any time.

curricle ('kʌrɪkəl) *n.* a two-wheeled open carriage drawn by two horses side by side.

curriculum (kə'rɪkjʊləm) *n., pl.* **-la** (-lə) *or* **-lums. 1.** a course of study in one subject at a school or college. **2.** a list of all the courses of study offered by a school or college. **3.** any programme or plan of activities. —**cur'ricular** *adj.*

curriculum vitae (kə'rɪkjʊləm 'viːtaɪ, 'vaɪtiː) *n., pl.* **curricula vitae** (kə'rɪkjʊlə). an outline of a person's educational and professional history, usually prepared for job applications.

curry¹ ('kʌrɪ) *n., pl.* **-ries. 1.** a spicy dish of oriental, esp. Indian, origin that usually consists of meat or fish prepared in a hot piquant sauce. **2.** curry seasoning or sauce. **3. give someone curry.** *Austral. sl.* to assault (a person) verbally or physically. ~*vb.* **-ries, -rying, -ried. 4.** (*tr.*) to prepare (food) with curry powder or sauce.

curry² ('kʌrɪ) *vb.* **-ries, -rying, -ried. 1.** to beat vigorously, as in order to clean. **2.** to dress and finish (leather) after it has been tanned. **3.** *Arch.* to groom (a horse). **4. curry favour.** to ingratiate oneself, esp. with superiors.

currycomb ('kʌrɪˌkəʊm) *n.* a square comb used for grooming horses.

curse (kɜːs) *n.* **1.** a profane or obscene expression of anger, disgust, surprise, etc.; oath. **2.** an appeal to a supernatural power for harm to come to a specific person, group, etc. **3.** harm resulting from an appeal to a supernatural power. **4.** something that brings or causes great trouble or harm. **5.** (preceded by *the*) *Inf.* menstruation or a menstrual period. ~*vb.* **cursing, cursed** *or* (*Arch.*) **curst. 6.** (*intr.*) to utter obscenities or oaths. **7.** (*tr.*) to abuse (someone) with obscenities or oaths. **8.** (*tr.*) to invoke supernatural powers to bring harm to (someone or something). **9.** (*tr.*) to bring harm upon. —**'curser** *n.*

cursed ('kɜːsɪd, kɜːst) *or* **curst** *adj.* **1.** under a curse. **2.** deserving to be cursed; detestable; hateful. —**'cursedly** *adv.* —**'cursedness** *n.*

THESAURUS

cure *v.* **1.** alleviate, correct, ease, heal, help, make better, mend, rehabilitate, relieve, remedy, restore, restore to health ~*n.* **2.** alleviation, antidote, corrective, healing, medicine, panacea, recovery, remedy, restorative, specific, treatment ~*v.* **3.** dry, kipper, pickle, preserve, salt, smoke

cure-all catholicon, elixir, *elixir vitae*, nostrum, panacea

curiosity 1. inquisitiveness, interest, nosiness (*Inf.*), prying, snooping (*Inf.*) **2.** celebrity, freak, marvel, novelty, oddity, phenomenon, rarity, sight, spectacle, wonder **3.** bibelot, bygone, curio, knickknack, *objet d'art*, trinket

curious 1. inquiring, inquisitive, interested, puzzled, questioning, searching **2.** inquisitive, meddling, nosy (*Inf.*), peeping, peering, prying, snoopy (*Inf.*) **3.** bizarre, exotic, extraordinary, marvellous, mysterious, novel, odd, peculiar, puzzling, quaint, queer,

rare, singular, strange, unconventional, unexpected, unique, unorthodox, unusual, wonderful

curl 1. *v.* bend, coil, convolute, corkscrew, crimp, crinkle, crisp, curve, entwine, frizz, loop, meander, ripple, spiral, turn, twine, twirl, twist, wind, wreathe, writhe **2.** *n.* coil, curlicue, kink, ringlet, spiral, twist, whorl

curly corkscrew, crimped, crimpy, crinkly, crisp, curled, curling, frizzy, fuzzy, kinky, permed, spiralled, waved, wavy, winding

currency 1. bills, coinage, coins, medium of exchange, money, notes **2.** acceptance, circulation, exposure, popularity, prevalence, publicity, transmission, vogue

current *adj.* **1.** accepted, circulating, common, common knowledge, customary, general, going around, in circulation, in progress, in the air, in the news, ongoing, popular, present, prevailing, prevalent, rife, widespread **2.** contemporary, fashionable, in, in

fashion, in vogue, now (*Inf.*), present-day, trendy (*Inf.*), up-to-date, up-to-the-minute ~*n.* **3.** course, draught, flow, jet, progression, river, stream, tide **4.** atmosphere, drift, feeling, inclination, mood, tendency, trend, undercurrent

curse *n.* **1.** blasphemy, expletive, oath, obscenity, swearing, swearword **2.** anathema, ban, denunciation, evil eye, excommunication, execration, imprecation, jinx, malediction, malison (*Archaic*) **3.** affliction, bane, burden, calamity, cross, disaster, evil, misfortune, ordeal, plague, scourge, torment, tribulation, trouble, vexation ~*v.* **4.** be foulmouthed, blaspheme, cuss (*Inf.*), swear, take the Lord's name in vain, turn the air blue (*Inf.*), use bad language **5.** accurse, anathematize, damn, excommunicate, execrate, fulminate, imprecate **6.** afflict, blight, burden, destroy, doom, plague, scourge, torment, trouble, vex

cursive ('kɜːsɪv) *adj.* **1.** of or relating to handwriting in which letters are joined in a flowing style. **2.** *Printing.* of or relating to typefaces that resemble handwriting. ~*n.* **3.** a cursive letter or printing type. —'**cursively** *adv.*

cursor ('kɜːsə) *n.* **1.** the sliding part of a measuring instrument, esp. on a slide rule. **2.** a movable point of light, etc., that identifies a specific position on a visual display unit.

cursory ('kɜːsərɪ) *adj.* hasty and usually superficial; quick. —'**cursorily** *adv.* —'**cursoriness** *n.*

curt (kɜːt) *adj.* **1.** rudely blunt and brief. **2.** short or concise. —'**curtly** *adv.* —'**curtness** *n.*

curtail (kɜːˈteɪl) *vb.* (*tr.*) to cut short; abridge. —**cur'tailer** *n.* —**cur'tailment** *n.*

curtain ('kɜːtən) *n.* **1.** a piece of material that can be drawn across an opening or window, to shut out light or to provide privacy. **2.** a barrier to vision, access, or communication. **3.** a hanging cloth or similar barrier for concealing all or part of a theatre stage from the audience. **4.** (often preceded by *the*) the end of a scene of a play, opera, etc., marked by the fall or closing of the curtain. **5.** the rise or opening of the curtain at the start of a performance. ~*vb.* **6.** (*tr.;* sometimes foll. by *off*) to shut off or conceal as with a curtain. **7.** (*tr.*) to provide (a window, etc.) with curtains.

curtain-raiser *n.* **1.** *Theatre.* a short dramatic piece presented before the main play. **2.** any preliminary event.

curtains *pl. n. Inf.* death or ruin: the end.

curtain wall *n.* a non-load-bearing external wall attached to a framed structure.

curtsy *or* **curtsey** ('kɜːtsɪ) *n., pl.* **-sies** *or* **-seys.** **1.** a formal gesture of greeting and respect made by women, in which the knees are bent and the head slightly bowed. ~*vb.* **-sying, -sied** *or* **-seying, -seyed.** **2.** (*intr.*) to make a curtsy.

curvaceous (kɜːˈveɪʃəs) *adj. Inf.* (of a woman) having a well-rounded body.

curvature ('kɜːvətʃə) *n.* **1.** something curved or a curved part of a thing. **2.** any curving of a bodily part. **3.** the act of curving or the state or degree of being curved or bent.

curve (kɜːv) *n.* **1.** a continuously bending line that has no straight parts. **2.** something that curves or is curved. **3.** the act or extent of curving; curvature. **4.** *Maths.* a system of points whose coordinates satisfy a given equation. **5.** a line representing data on a graph. ~*vb.* **6.** to take or cause to take the shape or path of a curve; bend. —'**curvedness** *n.* —'**curvy** *adj.*

curvet (kɜːˈvɛt) *n.* **1.** *Dressage.* a low leap with all four feet off the ground. ~*vb.* **-vetting, -vetted** *or* **-veting, -veted.** **2.** *Dressage.* to make or cause to make such a leap. **3.** (*intr.*) to prance or frisk about.

curvilinear (ˌkɜːvɪˈlɪnɪə) *or* **curvilineal** *adj.* consisting of, bounded by, or characterized by a curved line.

cushion ('kʊʃən) *n.* **1.** a bag filled with a yielding substance, used for sitting on, leaning against, etc. **2.** something resembling a cushion in function or appearance, esp. one to support or pad or to absorb shock. **3.** the resilient felt-covered rim of a billiard table. ~*vb.* (*tr.*) **4.** to place on or as on a cushion. **5.** to provide with cush-

ions. **6.** to protect. **7.** to lessen or suppress the effects of. **8.** to provide with a means of absorbing shock. —'**cushiony** *adj.*

cushy ('kʊʃɪ) *adj. Sl.* easy; comfortable.

CUSO *or* **C.U.S.O.** ('kjuːsəʊ) *n.* Canadian University Services Overseas; an organization that sends students to work as volunteers in developing countries.

cusp (kʌsp) *n.* **1.** any of the small elevations on the grinding or chewing surface of a tooth. **2.** any of the triangular flaps of a heart valve. **3.** a point or pointed end. **4.** *Geom.* a point at which two arcs of a curve intersect and at which the two tangents are coincident. **5.** *Archit.* a carving at the meeting place of two arcs. **6.** *Astron.* either of the points of a crescent moon. **7.** *Astrol.* any division between houses or signs of the zodiac. —'**cuspate** *adj.*

cuspid ('kʌspɪd) *n.* a tooth having one point; canine tooth.

cuspidate ('kʌspɪˌdeɪt), **cuspidated,** *or* **cuspidal** ('kʌspɪdᵊl) *adj.* **1.** having a cusp or cusps. **2.** (esp. of leaves) narrowing to a point.

cuspidor ('kʌspɪˌdɔː) *n.* another name (esp. U.S.) for **spittoon.**

cuss (kʌs) *Inf.* ~*n.* **1.** a curse; an oath. **2.** a person or animal, esp. an annoying one. ~*vb.* **3.** another word for **curse** (senses 6, 7).

cussed ('kʌsɪd) *adj. Inf.* **1.** another word for **cursed.** **2.** obstinate. **3.** annoying: *a cussed nuisance.* —'**cussedly** *adv.* —'**cussedness** *n.*

custard ('kʌstəd) *n.* **1.** a baked sweetened mixture of eggs and milk. **2.** a sauce made of milk and sugar thickened with cornflour.

custodian (kʌˈstəʊdɪən) *n.* **1.** a person who has custody, as of a prisoner, ward, etc. **2.** a keeper of an art collection, etc. —**cus'todian,ship** *n.*

custody ('kʌstədɪ) *n., pl.* **-dies.** **1.** the act of keeping safe or guarding. **2.** the state of being held by the police; arrest. —**custodial** (kʌˈstəʊdɪəl) *adj.*

custom ('kʌstəm) *n.* **1.** a usual or habitual practice; typical mode of behaviour. **2.** the long-established habits or traditions of a society collectively; convention. **3. a.** a practice which by long-established usage has come to have the force of law. **b.** such practices collectively (esp. in **custom and practice**). **4.** habitual patronage, esp. of a shop or business. **5.** the customers of a shop or business collectively. ~*adj.* **6.** *Chiefly U.S.* made to the specifications of an individual customer.

customary ('kʌstəmərɪ, -təmrɪ) *adj.* **1.** in accordance with custom or habitual practice; usual. **2.** *Law.* **a.** founded upon long-continued practices and usage. **b.** (of land) held by custom. ~*n., pl.* **-aries.** **3.** a statement in writing of customary laws and practices. —'**customarily** *adv.* —'**customariness** *n.*

custom-built *adj. Chiefly U.S.* (of cars, houses, etc.) made according to the specifications of an individual buyer.

customer ('kʌstəmə) *n.* **1.** a person who buys. **2.** *Inf.* a person with whom one has dealings.

custom house *n.* a government office, esp. at a port, where customs are collected and ships cleared for entry.

customs ('kʌstəmz) *n.* (*functioning as sing. or pl.*) **1.**

THESAURUS

cursed **1.** accursed, bedevilled, blighted, cast out, confounded, damned, doomed, excommunicate, execrable, fey (*Scot.*), foredoomed, ill-fated, star-crossed, unholy, unsanctified, villainous **2.** abominable, damnable, detestable, devilish, fell (*Archaic*), fiendish, hateful, infamous, infernal, loathsome, odious, pernicious, pestilential, vile

curt abrupt, blunt, brief, brusque, concise, gruff, offhand, pithy, rude, sharp, short, snappish, succinct, summary, tart, terse, unceremonious, uncivil, ungracious

curtail abbreviate, abridge, contract, cut, cut back, cut short, decrease, dock, lessen, lop, pare down, reduce, retrench, shorten, trim, truncate

curtailment abbreviation, abridgment, contraction, cutback, cutting, cutting short, docking, retrenchment, truncation

curtain **1.** *n.* drape (*Chiefly U.S.*), hanging **2.** *v.* conceal, drape, hide, screen, shroud,

shut off, shutter, veil

curve **1.** *v.* arc, arch, bend, bow, coil, hook, inflect, spiral, swerve, turn, twist, wind **2.** *n.* arc, bend, camber, curvature, half-moon, loop, trajectory, turn

curved arced, arched, bent, bowed, crooked, humped, rounded, serpentine, sinuous, sweeping, turned, twisted

cushion **1.** *n.* beanbag, bolster, hassock, headrest, pad, pillow, scatter cushion, squab **2.** *v.* bolster, buttress, cradle, dampen, deaden, muffle, pillow, protect, soften, stifle, support, suppress

custody **1.** aegis, auspices, care, charge, custodianship, guardianship, keeping, observation, preservation, protection, safekeeping, supervision, trusteeship, tutelage, ward, watch **2.** arrest, confinement, detention, durance (*Archaic*), duress, imprisonment, incarceration

custom **1.** habit, habitude (*Rare*), manner,

mode, procedure, routine, way, wont **2.** convention, etiquette, fashion, form, formality, matter of course, observance, observation, policy, practice, praxis, ritual, rule, style, unwritten law, usage, use **3.** customers, patronage, trade

customarily as a rule, commonly, generally, habitually, in the ordinary way, normally, ordinarily, regularly, traditionally, usually

customary accepted, accustomed, acknowledged, common, confirmed, conventional, established, everyday, familiar, fashionable, general, habitual, normal, ordinary, popular, regular, routine, traditional, usual, wonted

customer buyer, client, consumer, habitué, patron, prospect, purchaser, regular (*Inf.*), shopper

duty on imports or exports. **2.** the government department responsible for the collection of these duties. **3.** the part of a port, airport, etc., where baggage and freight are examined for dutiable goods and contraband.

cut (kʌt) *vb.* **cutting, cut. 1.** to open up or incise (a person or thing) with a sharp edge or instrument. **2.** (of a sharp instrument) to penetrate or incise (a person or thing). **3.** to divide or be divided with or as if with a sharp instrument. **4.** (*intr.*) to use an instrument that cuts. **5.** (*tr.*) to trim or prune by or as if by clipping. **6.** (*tr.*) to reap or mow (a crop, grass, etc.). **7.** (*tr.*; sometimes foll. by *out*) to make, form, or shape by cutting. **8.** (*tr.*) to hollow or dig out; excavate. **9.** to strike (an object) sharply. **10.** *Cricket.* to hit (the ball) to the off side with a roughly horizontal bat. **11.** to hurt the feelings of (a person). **12.** (*tr.*) *Inf.* to refuse to recognize; snub. **13.** (*tr.*) *Inf.* to absent oneself from, esp. without permission or in haste: *to cut a class.* **14.** (*tr.*) to abridge or shorten. **15.** (*tr.*; often foll. by *down*) to lower, reduce, or curtail. **16.** (*tr.*) to dilute or weaken: *to cut whisky with water.* **17.** (*tr.*) to dissolve or break up: *to cut fat.* **18.** (when *intr.*, foll. by *across* or *through*) to cross or traverse. **19.** (*intr.*) to make a sharp or sudden change in direction; veer. **20.** to grow (teeth) through the gums or (of teeth) to appear through the gums. **21.** (*intr.*) *Films.* **a.** to call a halt to a shooting sequence. **b.** (foll. by *to*) to move quickly to another scene. **22.** *Films.* to edit film. **23.** to switch off a light, car engine, etc. **24.** (*tr.*) to make (a record or tape of a song, performance, etc.). **25.** *Cards.* **a.** to divide (the pack) at random into two parts after shuffling. **b.** (*intr.*) to pick cards from a spread pack to decide dealer, partners, etc. **26.** (*tr.*) (of a tool) to bite into (an object). **27. cut a caper** *or* **capers. a.** to skip or jump playfully. **b.** to act or behave playfully. **28. cut both ways. a.** to have both good and bad effects. **b.** to affect both sides, as two parties in an argument, etc. **29. cut a dash.** to behave or dress showily. **30. cut (a person) dead.** *Inf.* to ignore (a person) completely. **31. cut a (good, poor,** etc.**) figure.** to appear or behave in a specified manner. **32. cut and run.** *Inf.* to make a rapid escape. **33. cut it fine.** *Inf.* to leave little or no margin for error. **34. cut corners.** to take the easiest or shortest way, esp. at the expense of high standards. **35. cut loose.** to free or become freed from restraint, custody, anchorage, etc. **36. cut no ice.** *Inf.* to fail to make an impression. **37. cut one's teeth on.** *Inf.* **a.** to use at an early age or stage. **b.** to practise on. ~*adj.* **38.** detached, divided, or separated by cutting. **39.** made, shaped, or fashioned by cutting. **40.** reduced or diminished as by cutting: *cut prices.* **41.** weakened or diluted. **42.** *Brit.* a slang word for **drunk:** *half cut.* **43. cut and dried.** *Inf.* settled or arranged in advance. ~*n.* **44.** the act of cutting. **45.** a stroke or incision made by cutting; gash. **46.** a piece or part cut off: *a cut of meat.* **47.** the edge of anything cut or sliced. **48.** a passage, channel, path, etc., cut or hollowed out. **49.** an omission or deletion, esp. in a text, film, or play. **50.** a reduction in price, salary, etc. **51.** *Inf.* a portion or share. **52.** *Inf.* a straw, slip of paper, etc., used in drawing lots. **53.** the manner or style in which a thing, esp. a garment, is cut. **54.** a direct route; short cut. **55.** the U.S. name for **block** (sense 13). **56.** *Cricket.* a stroke made with the bat in a roughly horizontal position. **57.** *Films.* an immediate transition from one shot to the next. **58.** words or an action that hurt another person's feelings. **59.** a refusal to recognize an acquaintance; snub. **60.** *Brit.* a stretch of water, esp. a ca-

nal. **61. a cut above.** *Inf.* superior to; better than. **62. cold cuts.** cooked meats. ~See also **cut across, cutback, cut down,** etc.

cut across *vb.* (*intr., prep.*) **1.** to be contrary to ordinary procedure or limitations. **2.** to cross or traverse, making a shorter route.

cutaneous (kjuːˈteɪnɪəs) *adj.* of or relating to the skin.

cutaway (ˈkʌtəˌweɪ) *n.* **1.** a man's coat cut diagonally from the front waist to the back of the knees. **2. a.** a drawing or model of a machine, engine, etc., in which part of the casing is omitted to reveal the workings. **b.** (*as modifier*): *a cutaway model.*

cutback (ˈkʌtˌbæk) *n.* **1.** a decrease or reduction. ~*vb.* **cut back** (*adv.*). **2.** (*tr.*) to shorten by cutting off the end; prune. **3.** (when *intr.*, foll. by *on*) to reduce or make a reduction (in).

cut down *vb.* (*adv.*) **1.** (*tr.*) to fell. **2.** (when *intr.*, often foll. by *on*) to reduce or make a reduction (in). **3.** (*tr.*) to remake (an old garment) in order to make a smaller one. **4.** (*tr.*) to kill. **5. cut (a person) down to size.** to reduce in importance or decrease the conceit of.

cute (kjuːt) *adj.* **1.** appealing or attractive, esp. in a pretty way. **2.** *Inf., chiefly U.S.* affecting cleverness or prettiness. **3.** clever; shrewd. —'**cutely** *adv.* —'**cuteness** *n.*

cut glass *n.* **1.** glass, esp. bowls, vases, etc., decorated by facet-cutting or grinding. **2.** (*modifier*): *a cut-glass vase.*

cuticle (ˈkjuːtɪkəl) *n.* **1.** dead skin, esp. round the base of a fingernail or toenail. **2.** another name for **epidermis. 3.** the protective layer that covers the epidermis of higher plants. **4.** the protective layer covering the epidermis of many invertebrates. —**cuticular** (kjuːˈtɪkjʊlə) *adj.*

cutis (ˈkjuːtɪs) *n., pl.* **-tes** (-tiːz) *or* **-tises.** *Anat.* a technical name for the **skin.**

cutlass (ˈkʌtləs) *n.* a curved, one-edged sword formerly used by sailors.

cutler (ˈkʌtlə) *n.* a person who makes or sells cutlery.

cutlery (ˈkʌtlərɪ) *n.* **1.** implements used for eating, such as knives, forks, and spoons. **2.** instruments used for cutting. **3.** the art or business of a cutler.

cutlet (ˈkʌtlɪt) *n.* **1.** a piece of meat taken esp. from the best end of neck of lamb, pork, etc. **2.** a flat croquette of minced chicken, lobster, etc.

cut off *vb.* (*tr., adv.*) **1.** to remove by cutting. **2.** to intercept or interrupt something, esp. a telephone conversation. **3.** to discontinue the supply of. **4.** to bring to an end. **5.** to deprive of rights; disinherit: *cut off without a penny.* **6.** to sever or separate. **7.** to occupy a position so as to prevent or obstruct (a retreat or escape). ~*n.* **cutoff. 8. a.** the act of cutting off; limit or termination. **b.** (*as modifier*): *the cutoff point.* **9.** *Chiefly U.S.* a short cut. **10.** a device to terminate the flow of a fluid in a pipe or duct.

cut out *vb.* (*adv.*) **1.** (*tr.*) to delete or remove. **2.** (*tr.*) to shape or form by cutting. **3.** (*tr.; usually passive*) to suit or equip for: *you're not cut out for this job.* **4.** (*intr.*) (of an engine, etc.) to cease to operate suddenly. **5.** (*intr.*) (of an electrical device) to switch off, usually automatically. **6.** (*tr.*) *Inf.* to oust and supplant (a rival). **7.** (*intr.*) (of a person) to be excluded from a card game. **8.** (*tr.*) *Inf.* to cease doing something, esp. something undesirable (esp. in **cut it out**). **9.** (*tr.*) *Soccer.* to intercept (a pass). **10.** (*tr.*) *Austral.* to separate (cattle) from a herd. **11.** (*intr.*) *Austral.* to end or finish: *the road cuts out at*

THESAURUS

customs duty, import charges, tariff, taxes, toll

cut *v.* **1.** chop, cleave, divide, gash, incise, lacerate, nick, notch, penetrate, pierce, score, sever, slash, slice, slit, wound **2.** carve, chip, chisel, chop, engrave, fashion, form, saw, sculpt, sculpture, shape, whittle **3.** clip, dock, fell, gather, hack, harvest, hew, lop, mow, pare, prune, reap, saw down, shave, trim **4.** contract, cut back, decrease, ease up on, lower, rationalize, reduce, slash, slim (down) **5.** abbreviate, abridge, condense, curtail, delete, edit out, excise, precis, shorten **6.** *Often with* **through, off,** *or* **across** bisect, carve, cleave, cross, dissect, divide, interrupt, intersect, part, segment, sever, slice, split, sunder **7.** avoid, cold-shoulder, freeze (someone) out (*Inf., chiefly U.S.*), grieve,

hurt, ignore, insult, look straight through (someone), pain, send to Coventry, slight, snub, spurn, sting, turn one's back on, wound ~*n.* **8.** gash, graze, groove, incision, laceration, nick, rent, rip, slash, slit, stroke, wound **9.** cutback, decrease, decrement, diminution, economy, fall, lowering, reduction, saving **10.** *Inf.* chop (*Sl.*), division, kickback (*Chiefly U.S.*), percentage, piece, portion, rake-off (*Sl.*), section, share, slice **11.** configuration, fashion, form, look, mode, shape, style **12. a cut above** *Inf.* better than, higher than, more efficient (capable, competent, reliable, trustworthy, useful) than, superior to **13. cut and dried** *Inf.* automatic, fixed, organized, prearranged, predetermined, settled, sorted out (*Inf.*)

cutback cut, decrease, economy, lessen-

ing, reduction, retrenchment

cut back check, curb, decrease, economize, lessen, lower, prune, reduce, retrench, slash, trim

cut down 1. fell, hew, level, lop, raze **2.** *Sometimes with* **on** decrease, lessen, lower, reduce **3.** dispatch, kill, massacre, mow down, slaughter, slay (*Archaic*) **4. cut (someone) down to size** abash, humiliate, make (someone) look small, take the wind out of (someone's) sails

cut in break in, butt in, interpose, interrupt, intervene, intrude, move in

cut off 1. disconnect, intercept, interrupt, intersect **2.** bring to an end, discontinue, halt, obstruct, suspend **3.** isolate, separate, sever **4.** disinherit, disown, renounce

the creek. **12. have one's work cut out.** to have as much work as one can manage. ~*n.* **cutout. 13.** something that has been or is intended to be cut out from something else. **14.** a device that switches off or interrupts an electric circuit, esp. as a safety device. **15.** *Austral. sl.* the end of shearing.

cut-price *or esp. U.S.* **cut-rate** *adj.* **1.** available at prices or rates below the standard price or rate. **2.** (*prenominal*) offering goods or services at prices below the standard price.

cutter ('kʌtə) *n.* **1.** a person or thing that cuts, esp. a person who cuts cloth for clothing. **2.** a sailing boat with its mast stepped further aft than that of a sloop. **3.** a ship's boat, powered by oars or sail, for carrying passengers or light cargo. **4.** a small lightly armed boat, as used in the enforcement of customs regulations.

cutthroat ('kʌt,θrəʊt) *n.* **1.** a person who cuts throats; murderer. **2.** Also called: **cutthroat razor.** *Brit.* a razor with a long blade that usually folds into the handle. ~*adj.* **3.** bloodthirsty or murderous; cruel. **4.** fierce or relentless in competition: *cutthroat prices.* **5.** (of some games) played by three people: *cutthroat poker.*

cutting ('kʌtɪŋ) *n.* **1.** a piece cut off from something. **2.** *Horticulture.* **a.** a method of propagation in which a part of a plant is induced to form its own roots. **b.** a part separated for this purpose. **3.** Also called (esp. U.S.): **clipping.** an article, photograph, etc., cut from a publication. **4.** the editing process of a film. **5.** an excavation in a piece of high land for a road, railway, etc. **6.** (*modifier*) designed for or adapted to cutting; sharp: *a cutting tool.* ~*adj.* **7.** keen; piercing. **8.** tending to hurt the feelings: *a cutting remark.* —'**cuttingly** *adv.*

cuttlefish ('kʌt²l,fɪʃ) *n., pl.* **-fish** *or* **-fishes.** a cephalopod mollusc which occurs near the bottom of inshore waters and has a broad flattened body. Sometimes shortened to **cuttle.**

cut up *vb.* (*tr., adv.*) **1.** to cut into pieces. **2.** to inflict injuries on. **3.** (*usually passive*) *Inf.* to affect the feelings of deeply. **4.** *Inf.* to subject to severe criticism. **5. cut up rough.** *Brit. inf.* to become angry or bad-tempered.

Cwlth. *abbrev. for* Commonwealth.

cwm (kuːm) *n.* **1.** (in Wales) a valley. **2.** *Geol.* another name for **cirque.**

cwt. *abbrev. for* hundredweight.

-cy *suffix.* **1.** indicating state, quality, or condition: *plutocracy; lunacy.* **2.** rank or office: *captaincy.*

cyanic (saɪ'ænɪk) *adj.* **1.** of or containing cyanogen. **2.** blue.

cyanic acid *n.* a colourless poisonous volatile liquid acid.

cyanide ('saɪə,naɪd) *or* **cyanid** ('saɪənɪd) *n.* any salt of hydrocyanic acid. Cyanides are extremely poisonous. —,cyani'dation *n.*

cyano- *or before a vowel* **cyan-** *combining form.* **1.** blue or dark blue. **2.** indicating cyanogen. **3.** indicating cyanide.

cyanogen (saɪ'ænədʒɪn) *n.* an extremely poisonous colourless flammable gas.

cyanosis (,saɪə'nəʊsɪs) *n. Pathol.* a bluish-purple discoloration of skin and mucous membranes usually resulting from a deficiency of oxygen in the blood. —**cyanotic** (,saɪə'nɒtɪk) *adj.*

cybernetics (,saɪbə'nɛtɪks) *n.* (*functioning as sing.*) the branch of science concerned with control systems and comparisons between man-made and biological systems. —,cyber'netic *adj.* —,cyber'neticist *n.*

cyclamate ('saɪklə,meɪt, 'sɪkləmeɪt) *n.* any of certain compounds formerly used as food additives and sugar substitutes.

cyclamen ('sɪkləmən, -,mɛn) *n.* any Old World plant of the genus *Cyclamen,* having white, pink, or red flowers, with reflexed petals.

cycle ('saɪk²l) *n.* **1.** a recurring period of time in which certain events or phenomena occur and reach completion. **2.** a completed series of events that follows or is followed by another series of similar events occurring in the same sequence. **3.** the time taken or needed for one such series. **4.** a vast period of time; age; aeon. **5.** a group of poems or prose narratives about a central figure or event: *the Arthurian cycle.* **6.** short for **bicycle, motorcycle,** etc. **7.** a recurrent series of events or processes in plants and animals: *a life cycle.* **8.** one of a series of repeated changes in the magnitude of a periodically varying quantity, such as current or voltage. ~*vb.* **9.** (*tr.*) to process through a cycle or system. **10.** (*intr.*) to move in or pass through cycles. **11.** to travel by or ride a bicycle or tricycle.

cyclic ('saɪklɪk, 'sɪklɪk) *or* **cyclical** *adj.* **1.** recurring or revolving in cycles. **2.** (of an organic compound) containing a closed saturated or unsaturated ring of atoms. **3.** *Bot.* **a.** arranged in whorls: *cyclic petals.* **b.** having parts arranged in this way: *cyclic flowers.* —'**cyclically** *adv.*

cyclist ('saɪklɪst) *or U.S.* **cycler** *n.* a person who rides or travels by bicycle, motorcycle, etc.

cyclo- *or before a vowel* **cycl-** *combining form.* **1.** indicating a circle or ring: *cyclotron.* **2.** denoting a cyclic compound: *cyclopropane.*

cyclometer (saɪ'klɒmɪtə) *n.* a device that records the number of revolutions made by a wheel and hence the distance travelled.

cyclone ('saɪkləʊn) *n.* **1.** another name for **depression** (sense 6). **2.** a violent tropical storm; hurricane. ~*adj.* **3.** *Austral. Trademark.* (of fencing) made of interlaced wire and metal. —**cyclonic** (saɪ'klɒnɪk) *adj.* —**cy'clonically** *adv.*

cyclopedia *or* **cyclopaedia** (,saɪkləʊ'piːdɪə) *n.* a less common word for **encyclopedia.**

Cyclops ('saɪklɒps) *n., pl.* **Cyclopes** (saɪ'kləʊpiːz) *or* **Cyclopses.** *Classical myth.* one of a race of giants having a single eye in the middle of the forehead.

cyclostyle ('saɪklə,staɪl) *n.* **1.** a kind of pen with a small toothed wheel, used for cutting holes in a specially prepared stencil. **2.** an office duplicator using such a stencil. ~*vb.* **3.** (*tr.*) to print using such a stencil. —'**cyclo,styled** *adj.*

cyclotron ('saɪklə,trɒn) *n.* a type of particle accelerator in which the particles spiral under the effect of a strong vertical magnetic field.

cyder ('saɪdə) *n.* a variant spelling of **cider.**

cygnet ('sɪgnɪt) *n.* a young swan.

cylinder ('sɪlɪndə) *n.* **1.** a solid consisting of two parallel planes bounded by identical closed curves, usually circles, that are interconnected at every point by a set of parallel lines, usually perpendicular to the planes. **2.** a surface formed by a line moving round a closed plane curve at a fixed angle to it. **3.** any object shaped like a cylinder. **4.** the chamber in a reciprocating internal-combustion engine, pump, or compressor within which the piston moves. The cylinders are housed in the metal **cylinder block,** which is topped by the **cylinder head. 5.** the rotating mechanism of a revolver, containing cartridge chambers. **6.** *Printing.* any of the rotating drums on a printing press. **7.** Also called: **cylinder seal.** an ancient cylindrical seal found in the Middle East and Balkans. —'**cylinder-,like** *adj.* —**cy'lindrical** *adj.*

cymbal ('sɪmb²l) *n.* a percussion instrument consisting of a thin circular piece of brass, which vibrates when clashed together with another cymbal or struck with a

---

THESAURUS

cut out 1. cease, delete, extract, give up, refrain from, remove, sever, stop **2.** *Inf.* displace, eliminate, exclude, oust, supersede, supplant

cut out for adapted, adequate, competent, designed, equipped, fitted, qualified, suitable, suited

cut-price bargain, cheap, cut-rate (*Chiefly U.S.*), reduced, sale

cut short abort, break off, bring to an end, check, halt, interrupt, leave unfinished, postpone, stop, terminate

cutthroat *n.* **1.** assassin, bravo, butcher, executioner, hit man (*Sl.*), homicide, killer, liquidator, murderer, slayer (*Archaic*), thug ~*adj.* **2.** barbarous, bloodthirsty, bloody, cruel, death-dealing, ferocious, homicidal, murderous, savage, thuggish, violent **3.** competitive, dog-eat-dog, fierce, relentless, ruthless, unprincipled

cutting *adj.* **1.** biting, bitter, chill, keen, numbing, penetrating, piercing, raw, sharp, stinging **2.** acid, acrimonious, barbed, bitter, caustic, hurtful, malicious, pointed, sarcastic, sardonic, scathing, severe, trenchant, wounding

cut up *v.* **1.** carve, chop, dice, divide, mince, slice **2.** injure, knife, lacerate, slash, wound **3.** *Inf.* criticize, crucify (*Sl.*), give (someone or something) a rough ride, pan (*Inf.*), ridicule, slate (*Inf.*), vilify ~*adj.* **4.** *Inf.* agitated, dejected, desolated, distressed, disturbed, heartbroken, stricken, upset, wretched

cycle aeon, age, circle, era, period, phase, revolution, rotation, round (*of years*)

stick. —'**cymbalist** n.

cyme (saɪm) n. an inflorescence in which the first flower is the terminal bud of the main stem and subsequent flowers develop as terminal buds of lateral stems. —**cymiferous** (saɪ'mɪfərəs) adj. —**cymose** ('saɪməʊs, -məʊz, saɪ'məʊs) adj.

Cymric or **Kymric** ('kɪmrɪk) n. 1. the Welsh language. 2. the Brythonic group of Celtic languages. ~adj. 3. of or relating to the Cymry, any of their languages, Wales, or the Welsh.

cynic ('sɪnɪk) n. 1. a person who believes the worst about people or the outcome of events. ~adj. 2. a less common word for **cynical**.

Cynic ('sɪnɪk) n. a member of an ancient Greek sect that scorned worldly things.

cynical ('sɪnɪkəl) adj. 1. believing the worst of others, esp. that all acts are selfish. 2. sarcastic; mocking. 3. showing contempt for accepted standards, esp. of honesty or morality. —'**cynically** adv. —'**cynicalness** n.

cynicism ('sɪnɪˌsɪzəm) n. 1. the attitude or beliefs of a cynic. 2. a cynical action, idea, etc.

Cynicism ('sɪnɪˌsɪzəm) n. the doctrines of the Cynics.

cynosure ('sɪnəˌzjʊə, -ˌʃʊə) n. 1. a person or thing that attracts notice. 2. something that serves as a guide.

cypher ('saɪfə) n., vb. a variant spelling of **cipher**.

cypress ('saɪprəs) n. 1. any coniferous tree of a N temperate genus having dark green scalelike leaves and rounded cones. 2. any of several similar and related trees. 3. the wood of any of these trees. 4. cypress branches used as a symbol of mourning.

Cypriot ('sɪprɪət) or **Cypriote** ('sɪprɪˌəʊt) n. 1. a native or inhabitant of Cyprus, an island in the E Mediterranean. 2. the dialect of Greek spoken in Cyprus. ~adj. 3. denoting or relating to Cyprus, its inhabitants, or dialects.

Cyrillic (sɪ'rɪlɪk) adj. 1. denoting or relating to the alphabet devised supposedly by Saint Cyril, for Slavonic languages: now used primarily for Russian and Bulgarian. ~n. 2. this alphabet.

cyst (sɪst) n. 1. Pathol. any abnormal membranous sac or blisterlike pouch containing fluid or semisolid material. 2. Anat. any normal sac in the body. 3. a protective membrane enclosing a cell, larva, or organism. —'**cystic** adj.

-**cyst** n. combining form. indicating a bladder or sac: otocyst.

cystic fibrosis n. a congenital disease of the exocrine glands, usually affecting young children, characterized by chronic infection of the respiratory tract and by pancreatic insufficiency.

cystitis (sɪ'staɪtɪs) n. inflammation of the urinary bladder.

cysto- or before a vowel **cyst-** combining form. indicating a cyst or bladder: cystoscope.

cystoscope ('sɪstəˌskəʊp) n. a slender tubular medical instrument for examining the interior of the urethra and urinary bladder. —**cystoscopic** (ˌsɪstə'skɒpɪk) adj. —**cystoscopy** (sɪs'tɒskəpɪ) n.

-**cyte** n. combining form. indicating a cell.

cyto- combining form. indicating a cell: cytoplasm.

cytology (saɪ'tɒlədʒɪ) n. the study of plant and animal cells. —**cytological** (ˌsaɪtə'lɒdʒɪkəl) adj. —ˌ**cyto'logically** adv. —cy'**tologist** n.

cytoplasm ('saɪtəʊˌplæzəm) n. the protoplasm of a cell excluding the nucleus. —ˌ**cyto'plasmic** adj.

czar (zɑː) n. a variant spelling (esp. U.S.) of **tsar**. —'**czardom** n. —'**Czarevitch**, **cza'revna**, **cza'rina**, '**czarism**, '**czarist**: see **ts-** spellings.

Czech (tʃɛk) adj. 1. of, relating to, or characteristic of Bohemia, Moravia, and, loosely, of Czechoslovakia, a republic of central Europe, of which Bohemia and Moravia (with Slovakia) are constituent parts, or their people or language. ~n. 2. one of the two official languages of Czechoslovakia. Czech and Slovak are closely related and mutually intelligible. 3. a. a native or inhabitant of Bohemia or Moravia. b. (loosely) a native or inhabitant of Czechoslovakia.

Czech. abbrev. for: 1. Czechoslovak. 2. Czechoslovakian. 3. Czechoslovakia.

Czechoslovak (ˌtʃɛkəʊ'sləʊvæk) or **Czechoslovakian** (ˌtʃɛkəʊsləʊ'vækɪən) adj. 1. of or relating to Czechoslovakia, its peoples, or languages. ~n. 2. (loosely) either of the two languages of Czechoslovakia: Czech or Slovak.

THESAURUS

cynic doubter, misanthrope, misanthropist, pessimist, sceptic, scoffer

cynical contemptuous, derisive, distrustful, ironic, misanthropic, misanthropical, mocking, pessimistic, sarcastic, sardonic, sceptical, scoffing, scornful, sneering, unbelieving

cynicism disbelief, doubt, misanthropy, pessimism, sarcasm, sardonicism, scepticism

D

d *or* **D** (di:) *n., pl.* **d's, D's,** *or* **Ds. 1.** the fourth letter of the modern English alphabet. **2.** a speech sound represented by this letter.
D *symbol for:* **1.** *Music.* **a.** the second note of the scale of C major. **b.** the major or minor key having this note as its tonic. **2.** *Chem.* deuterium. ~ **3.** *the Roman numeral for* 500.
d. *abbrev. for:* **1.** date. **2.** daughter. **3.** degree. **4.** delete. **5.** *Brit. currency before decimalization.* penny *or* pennies. **6.** depart(s). **7.** diameter. **8.** died.
D. *abbrev. for:* **1.** *U.S.* Democrat(ic). **2.** Department. **3.** Deus. **4.** *Optics.* diopter. **5.** Director. **6.** Dominus. **7.** Dutch.
dab¹ (dæb) *vb.* **dabbing, dabbed. 1.** to touch or pat lightly and quickly. **2.** (*tr.*) to daub with short tapping strokes: *to dab the wall with paint.* **3.** (*tr.*) to apply (paint, cream, etc.) with short tapping strokes. ~*n.* **4.** a small amount, esp. of something soft or moist. **5.** a light stroke or tap, as with the hand. **6.** (*often pl.*) *Chiefly Brit.* a slang word for **fingerprint.** —**'dabber** *n.*
dab² (dæb) *n.* **1.** a small common European flatfish covered with rough toothed scales. **2.** any of various other small flatfish.
dab³ (dæb) *n. Brit. inf.* See **dab hand.**
dabble ('dæbəl) *vb.* **1.** to dip, move, or splash (the fingers, feet, etc.) in a liquid. **2.** (*intr.; usually foll. by in, with,* or *at*) to deal (with) or work (at) frivolously or superficially. **3.** (*tr.*) to splash or smear. —**'dabbler** *n.*
dabchick ('dæb,tʃɪk) *n.* any of several small grebes.
dab hand *n. Brit. inf.* a person who is particularly skilled at something: *a dab hand at chess.*
da capo (dɑː 'kɑːpəʊ) *adj., adv. Music.* to be repeated from the beginning.
dace (deɪs) *n., pl.* **dace** *or* **daces. 1.** a European freshwater fish of the carp family. **2.** any of various similar fishes.
dachshund ('dæks,hʊnd) *n.* a long-bodied short-legged breed of dog.
Dacron ('deɪkrɒn, 'dæk-) *n.* the U.S. name (trademark) for **Terylene.**
dactyl ('dæktɪl) *n. Prosody.* a metrical foot of three syllables, one long followed by two short (−◡◡).
dad (dæd) *n.* an informal word for **father.** —**'daddy** *n.*
Dada ('dɑːdɑː) *or* **Dadaism** ('dɑːdɑː,ɪzəm) *n.* a nihilistic artistic movement of the early 20th century, founded on principles of irrationality, incongruity, and irreverence towards accepted aesthetic criteria. —**'Dadaist** *n., adj.* —**Dada'istic** *adj.*
daddy-longlegs *n. Brit.* an informal name for a **crane fly.**
dado ('deɪdəʊ) *n., pl.* **-does** *or* **-dos. 1.** the lower part of an interior wall that is decorated differently from the upper part. **2.** *Archit.* the part of a pedestal between the base and the cornice. ~*vb.* **3.** (*tr.*) to provide with a dado.
daemon ('diːmən) *or* **daimon** *n.* **1.** a demigod. **2.** the guardian spirit of a place or person. **3.** a variant spelling of **demon** (sense 3). —**daemonic** (diː'mɒnɪk) *adj.*
daff (dæf) *n. Inf.* short for **daffodil.**
daffodil ('dæfədɪl) *n.* **1.** Also called: **Lent lily.** a widely cultivated Eurasian plant, *Narcissus pseudonarcissus,* having spring-blooming yellow nodding flowers. **2.** any other plant of the genus *Narcissus.* **3.** a brilliant yellow colour.
daft (dɑːft) *adj. Chiefly Brit.* **1.** *Inf.* foolish, simple, or stupid. **2.** a slang word for **insane. 3.** *Inf.* (*postpositive; foll. by about*) extremely fond (of). **4.** *Sl.* frivolous; giddy.
dagga ('daxə, 'dɑːgə) *n.* hemp smoked as a narcotic.
dagger ('dægə) *n.* **1.** a short stabbing weapon with a pointed blade. **2.** Also called: **obelisk.** a character (†) used in printing to indicate a cross-reference. **3. at daggers drawn.** in a state of open hostility. **4. look daggers.** to glare with hostility; scowl.
dago ('deɪgəʊ) *n., pl.* **-gos** *or* **-goes.** *Derog.* a foreigner, esp. a Spaniard or Portuguese.
daguerreotype (də'gɛrəʊ,taɪp) *n.* **1.** one of the earliest photographic processes, in which the image was produced on iodine-sensitized silver and developed in mercury vapour. **2.** a photograph formed by this process. —**da'guerreo,typy** *n.*
dahlia ('deɪljə) *n.* **1.** any herbaceous perennial plant of the Mexican genus *Dahlia,* having showy flowers and tuberous roots. **2.** the flower or root of any of these plants.
Dáil Eireann ('dɔɪl 'ɛərən) *or* **Dáil** *n.* (in the Republic of Ireland) the lower chamber of parliament.
daily ('deɪlɪ) *adj.* **1.** of or occurring every day or every weekday. ~*n., pl.* **-lies. 2.** a daily newspaper. **3.** *Brit.* a charwoman. ~*adv.* **4.** every day. **5.** constantly; often.
dainty ('deɪntɪ) *adj.* **-tier, -tiest. 1.** delicate or elegant. **2.** choice; delicious: *a dainty morsel.* **3.** excessively genteel; fastidious. ~*n., pl.* **-ties. 4.** a choice piece of food; delicacy. —**'daintily** *adv.*
daiquiri ('daɪkɪrɪ, 'dæk-) *n., pl.* **-ris.** an iced drink containing rum, lime juice, and sugar.
dairy ('dɛərɪ) *n., pl.* **dairies. 1.** a shop or company that supplies milk and milk products. **2.** a room or building where milk and cream are stored or made into butter and cheese. **3. a.** (*modifier*) of milk and milk products. **b.** (*in combination*): *a dairymaid.* **4.** *N.Z.* a general shop, selling provisions, cigarettes, etc., and open seven days a week.
dairyman ('dɛərɪmən) *n., pl.* **-men.** a male dairy worker.
dais ('deɪɪs, deɪs) *n.* a raised platform, usually at one end of a hall, used by speakers, etc.
daisy ('deɪzɪ) *n., pl.* **-sies. 1.** a small low-growing European plant having flower heads with a yellow centre and pinkish-white outer rays. **2.** any of various other composite plants having conspicuous ray flowers. **3.** *Sl.* an excellent person or thing. **4. pushing up the daisies.** dead and buried. —**'daisied** *adj.*
Dalai Lama ('dælaɪ 'lɑːmə) *n.* **1.** (until 1959) the chief lama and ruler of Tibet. **2.** the 14th holder of this office (1940), who fled to India (1959).
dale (deɪl) *n.* an open valley.
dalles (dælz) *pl. n. Canad.* the rapids of a river flowing in a narrow channel between high rock walls.
dally ('dælɪ) *vb.* **-lying, -lied.** (*intr.*) **1.** to waste time idly; dawdle. **2.** (*usually foll. by with*) to deal frivolously: *to dally with someone's affections.* —**'dalliance** *n.*

THESAURUS

dabble 1. dip, guddle (*Scot.*), moisten, paddle, spatter, splash, sprinkle, wet **2.** dally, dip into, play at, potter, tinker, trifle (with)
dabbler amateur, dilettante, potterer, tinkerer, trifler
dab hand ace (*Inf.*), adept, dabster (*Dialect*), expert, past master, wizard
daft 1. absurd, asinine, crazy, dopey (*Sl.*), foolish, giddy, idiotic, inane, scatty (*Inf.*), silly, simple, stupid, witless **2.** crackers (*Sl.*), crazy, demented, deranged, insane, lunatic, mental (*Inf.*), nuts (*Sl.*), nutty (*Sl.*), touched, unhinged **3.** *With* **about** besotted by, crazy

(*Inf.*), doting, dotty (*Sl.*), infatuated by, mad, nuts (*Sl.*), nutty (*Inf.*), potty (*Inf.*), sweet on
dagger 1. bayonet, dirk, poniard, skean, stiletto **2. at daggers drawn** at enmity, at loggerheads, at odds, at war, on bad terms, up in arms **3. look daggers** frown, glare, glower, look black, scowl
daily *adj.* **1.** circadian, diurnal, everyday, quotidian **2.** common, commonplace, day-to-day, everyday, ordinary, quotidian, regular, routine ~*adv.* **3.** constantly, day after day, day by day, every day, often, once a day, per diem, regularly

dainty *adj.* **1.** charming, delicate, elegant, exquisite, fine, graceful, neat, petite, pretty **2.** choice, delectable, delicious, palatable, savoury, tasty, tender, toothsome **3.** choosy, fastidious, finical, finicky, fussy, mincing, nice, particular, refined, scrupulous ~*n.* **4.** *bonne bouche,* delicacy, fancy, sweetmeat, titbit
dale bottom, coomb, dell, dingle, glen, strath (*Scot.*), vale, valley

Dalmatian (dælˈmeɪʃən) n. **1.** a large breed of dog having a short smooth white coat with black or brown spots. **2.** a native or inhabitant of Dalmatia. ~adj. **3.** of Dalmatia or its inhabitants.

dal segno ('dæl 'sɛnjəʊ) adv. Music. to be repeated from the point marked with a sign to the word fine.

dam[1] (dæm) n. **1.** a barrier of concrete, earth, etc., built across a river to create a body of water. **2.** a reservoir of water created by such a barrier. **3.** something that resembles or functions as a dam. ~vb. **damming, dammed. 4.** (tr.; often foll. by up) to restrict by a dam.

dam[2] (dæm) n. the female parent of an animal, esp. of domestic livestock.

damage ('dæmɪdʒ) n. **1.** injury or harm impairing the function or condition of a person or thing. **2.** loss of something desirable. **3.** Inf. cost; expense. ~vb. **4.** (tr.) to cause damage to. **5.** (intr.) to suffer damage. —'damagingly adv.

damages ('dæmɪdʒɪz) pl. n. Law. money to be paid as compensation for injury, loss, etc.

damask ('dæməsk) n. **1. a.** a reversible fabric, usually silk or linen, with a pattern woven into it. It is used for table linen, curtains, etc. **b.** table linen made from this. **c.** (as modifier): a damask tablecloth. **2.** the wavy markings on such steel. **3. a.** the greyish-pink colour of the damask rose. **b.** (as adj.): damask wallpaper.

damask rose n. a rose with fragrant flowers, which are used to make the perfume attar.

dame (deɪm) n. **1.** (formerly) a woman of rank or dignity; lady. **2.** Arch., chiefly Brit. an elderly woman. **3.** Sl., chiefly U.S. a woman. **4.** Brit. the role of a comic old woman in a pantomime, usually played by a man.

Dame (deɪm) n. (in Britain) **1.** the title of a woman who has been awarded the Order of the British Empire or any of certain other orders of chivalry. **2.** the title of the wife of a knight or baronet.

damn (dæm) interj. **1.** Sl. an exclamation of annoyance. **2.** Inf. an exclamation of surprise or pleasure. ~adj. **3.** (prenominal) Sl. deserving damnation. ~adv., adj. (prenominal) **4.** Sl. (intensifier): a damn good pianist. ~adv. **5. damn all.** Sl. absolutely nothing. ~vb. (mainly tr.) **6.** to condemn as bad, worthless, etc. **7.** to curse. **8.** to condemn to eternal damnation. **9.** (often passive) to doom to ruin. **10.** (also intr.) to prove (someone) guilty: damning evidence. **11. damn with faint praise.** to praise so unenthusiastically that the effect is condemnation. ~n. **12.** Sl. something of negligible value (esp. in **not worth a damn**). **13. not give a damn.** Inf. not care.

damnable ('dæmnəbəl) adj. **1.** execrable; detestable. **2.** liable to or deserving damnation. —'damnableness or ,damna'bility n.

damnation (dæmˈneɪʃən) n. **1.** the act of damning or state of being damned. ~interj. **2.** an exclamation of anger, disappointment, etc. —'damnatory adj.

damned (dæmd) adj. **1. a.** condemned to hell. **b.** (as n.): the damned. ~adv., adj. Sl. **2.** (intensifier): a damned good try. **3.** used to indicate amazement, disavowal, or refusal (as in **damned if I care**).

damp (dæmp) adj. **1.** slightly wet. ~n. **2.** slight wetness; moisture. **3.** rank air or poisonous gas, esp. in a mine. **4.** a discouragement; damper. ~vb. (tr.) **5.** to

make slightly wet. **6.** (often foll. by down) to stifle or deaden: to damp one's ardour. **7.** (often foll. by down) to reduce the flow of air to (a fire) to make it burn more slowly. **8.** Physics. to reduce the amplitude of (an oscillation or wave). **9.** Music. to muffle (a vibrating string). —'dampness n.

dampcourse ('dæmp,kɔːs) n. a layer of impervious material in a wall, to stop moisture rising. Also called: **damp-proof course.**

dampen ('dæmpən) vb. **1.** to make or become damp. **2.** (tr.) to stifle; deaden. —'dampener n.

damper ('dæmpə) n. **1.** a person, event, or circumstance that depresses or discourages. **2.** a movable plate to regulate the draught in a stove or furnace flue. **3.** a device to reduce electronic, mechanical, acoustical, or aerodynamic oscillations in a system. **4.** the pad in a piano or harpsichord that deadens the vibration of each string as its key is released. **5.** Chiefly Austral. & N.Z. any of various unleavened loaves and scones, typically cooked on an open fire.

damsel ('dæmzəl) n. Arch. or poetic. a young unmarried woman; maiden.

damson ('dæmzən) n. **1.** a small tree cultivated for its blue-black edible plumlike fruit. **2.** the fruit of this tree.

dan (dæn) n. Judo. **1.** any one of the 12 black-belt grades of proficiency. **2.** a competitor entitled to dan grading.

Dan. abbrev. for: **1.** Bible. Daniel. **2.** Danish.

dance (dɑːns) vb. **1.** (intr.) to move the feet and body rhythmically, esp. in time to music. **2.** (tr.) to perform (a particular dance). **3.** (intr.) to skip or leap. **4.** to move or cause to move in a rhythmical way. **5. dance attendance (on someone).** to attend (someone) solicitously or obsequiously. ~n. **6.** a series of rhythmical steps and movements, usually in time to music. **7.** an act of dancing. **8. a.** a social meeting arranged for dancing. **b.** (as modifier): a dance hall. **9.** a piece of music in the rhythm of a particular dance form. **10.** dancelike movements. **11. lead (someone) a dance.** Brit. inf. to cause (someone) continued worry and exasperation. —'dancer n.

D and C n. Med. dilation (of the cervix) and curettage (of the uterus).

dandelion ('dændɪ,laɪən) n. **1.** a plant native to Europe and Asia and naturalized as a weed in North America, having yellow rayed flowers and deeply notched leaves. **2.** any of several similar plants.

dander ('dændə) n. **1.** small particles of hair or feathers. **2. get one's (or someone's) dander up.** Sl., chiefly U.S. to become or cause to become annoyed or angry.

dandify ('dændɪ,faɪ) vb. **-fying, -fied.** (tr.) to dress like or cause to resemble a dandy.

dandle ('dændəl) vb. (tr.) **1.** to move (a young child) up and down (on the knee or in the arms). **2.** to pet; fondle. —'dandler n.

dandruff ('dændrəf) or **dandriff** ('dændrɪf) n. loose scales of dry dead skin shed from the scalp.

dandy ('dændɪ) n., pl. **-dies. 1.** a man greatly concerned with smartness of dress. ~adj. **-dier, -diest. 2.** Inf. very good or fine. —'dandyish adj.

dandy-brush n. a stiff brush used for grooming

THESAURUS

dam 1. n. barrage, barrier, embankment, hindrance, obstruction, wall **2.** v. barricade, block, block up, check, choke, confine, hold back, hold in, obstruct, restrict

damage n. **1.** destruction, detriment, devastation, harm, hurt, impairment, injury, loss, mischief, mutilation, suffering **2.** Inf. bill, charge, cost, expense, total **3.** Plural compensation, fine, indemnity, reimbursement, reparation, satisfaction ~v. **4.** deface, harm, hurt, impair, incapacitate, injure, mar, mutilate, ruin, spoil, tamper with, weaken, wreck

damaging deleterious, detrimental, disadvantageous, harmful, hurtful, injurious, prejudicial, ruinous

dame baroness, dowager, grande dame, lady, matron (Archaic), noblewoman, peeress

damn v. **1.** blast, castigate, censure, condemn, criticize, denounce, denunciate, excoriate, inveigh against, pan (Inf.), slam (Sl.),

slate (Inf.) **2.** abuse, anathematize, blaspheme, curse, execrate, imprecate, revile, swear **3.** condemn, doom, sentence ~n. **4.** brass farthing, hoot, iota, jot, tinker's damn (Sl.), two hoots, whit **5. not give a damn** indifferent, not care, not mind

damnable abominable, accursed, atrocious, culpable, cursed, despicable, detestable, execrable, hateful, horrible, offensive, wicked

damnation anathema, ban, condemnation, consigning to perdition, damning, denunciation, doom, excommunication, objurgation, proscription, sending to hell

damned 1. accursed, anathematized, condemned, doomed, infernal, lost, reprobate, unhappy **2.** Sl. confounded, despicable, detestable, hateful, infamous, infernal, loathsome, revolting

damning accusatorial, condemnatory, damnatory, dooming, implicating, implicative, incriminating

damp n. **1.** clamminess, dampness, darkness, dew, drizzle, fog, humidity, mist, moisture, muzziness, vapour ~adj. **2.** clammy, dank, dewy, dripping, drizzly, humid, misty, moist, muggy, sodden, soggy, sopping, vaporous, wet ~v. **3.** dampen, moisten, wet **4.** Fig. allay, check, chill, cool, curb, dash, deaden, deject, depress, diminish, discourage, dispirit, dull, inhibit, moderate, restrain, stifle ~n. **5.** Fig. check, chill, cold water, curb, damper, discouragement, gloom, restraint, wet blanket

damper chill, cloud, cold water, curb, discouragement, gloom, hindrance, kill-joy, pall, restraint, wet blanket

dance 1. v. bob up and down, caper, frolic, gambol, hop, jig, prance, rock, skip, spin, sway, swing, whirl **2.** n. ball, dancing party, hop (Inf.), social

a horse.

Dane (deɪn) *n.* **1.** a native, citizen, or inhabitant of Denmark. **2.** any of the Vikings who invaded England from the late 8th to the 11th century A.D..

danger ('deɪndʒə) *n.* **1.** the state of being vulnerable to injury, loss, or evil; risk. **2.** a person or thing, that may cause injury, pain, etc. **3. in danger of.** liable to. **4. on the danger list.** critically ill in hospital. —'**dangerless** *adj.*

danger money *n.* extra money paid to compensate for the risks involved in certain dangerous jobs.

dangerous ('deɪndʒərəs) *adj.* causing danger; perilous. —'**dangerously** *adv.*

dangle ('dæŋɡəl) *vb.* **1.** to hang or cause to hang freely: *his legs dangled over the wall.* **2.** (*tr.*) to display as an enticement. —'**dangler** *n.*

Danish ('deɪnɪʃ) *adj.* **1.** of Denmark, its people, or their language. ~*n.* **2.** the official language of Denmark. **3. the Danish.** (*functioning as pl.*) the people of Denmark collectively.

Danish blue *n.* a strong-tasting white cheese with blue veins.

Danish pastry *n.* a rich flaky pastry filled with apple, almond paste, icing, etc.

dank (dæŋk) *adj.* (esp. of cellars, caves, etc.) unpleasantly damp and chilly. —'**dankly** *adv.* —'**dankness** *n.*

dankie ('dæŋkiː) *interj. S. African.* thank you.

daphne ('dæfnɪ) *n.* any of various Eurasian ornamental shrubs with shiny evergreen leaves and clusters of small bell-shaped flowers.

dapper ('dæpə) *adj.* **1.** neat in dress and bearing. **2.** small and nimble. —'**dapperly** *adv.* —'**dapperness** *n.*

dapple ('dæpəl) *vb.* **1.** to mark or become marked with spots of a different colour; mottle. ~*n.* **2.** mottled or spotted markings. **3.** a dappled horse, etc. ~*adj.* **4.** marked with dapples or spots.

dapple-grey *n.* a horse with a grey coat having spots of darker colour.

darbies ('dɑːbɪz) *pl. n. Brit.* a slang term for **handcuffs.**

Darby and Joan ('dɑːbɪ) *n.* **1.** an ideal elderly married couple living in domestic harmony. **2. Darby and Joan Club.** a club for elderly people.

dare (dɛə) *vb.* **1.** (*tr.*) to challenge (a person to do something) as proof of courage. **2.** (can take an infinitive with or without *to*) to be courageous enough to try (to do something). **3.** (*tr.*) *Rare.* to oppose without fear; defy. **4. I dare say. a.** (it is) quite possible (that). **b.** probably. ~*n.* **5.** a challenge to do something as proof of courage. **6.** something done in response to such a challenge. —'**darer** *n.*

▷ **Usage.** When used negatively or interrogatively and

not followed by an infinitive with *to, dare* does not add *-s: he dare not; dare she come?*

daredevil ('dɛə,devəl) *n.* **1.** a recklessly bold person. ~*adj.* **2.** reckless; daring; bold. —'**dare,devilry** or '**dare,deviltry** *n.*

daring ('dɛərɪŋ) *adj.* **1.** bold or adventurous. ~*n.* **2.** courage in taking risks; boldness.

dark (dɑːk) *adj.* **1.** having little or no light. **2.** (of a colour) reflecting or transmitting little light: *dark brown.* **3.** (of complexion, hair colour, etc.) not fair; swarthy; brunette. **4.** gloomy or dismal. **5.** sinister; evil: *a dark purpose.* **6.** sullen or angry. **7.** ignorant or unenlightened: *a dark period in our history.* **8.** secret or mysterious. ~*n.* **9.** absence of light; darkness. **10.** night or nightfall. **11.** a dark place. **12.** a state of ignorance (esp. in **in the dark).** —'**darkish** *adj.* —'**darkly** *adv.* —'**darkness** *n.*

Dark Continent *n.* **the.** a term for Africa when it was relatively unexplored.

darken ('dɑːkən) *vb.* **1.** to make or become dark or darker. **2.** to make or become gloomy, angry, or sad. **3. darken (someone's) door.** (*usually used with a negative*) to visit someone: *never darken my door again!* —'**darkener** *n.*

dark horse *n.* **1.** a competitor in a race or contest about whom little is known. **2.** a person who reveals little about himself, esp. one who has unexpected talents. **3.** *U.S. politics.* a candidate who is unexpectedly nominated or elected.

darkroom ('dɑːk,ruːm) *n.* a room in which photographs are processed in darkness or safe light.

darling ('dɑːlɪŋ) *n.* **1.** a person very much loved. **2.** a favourite. ~*adj.* (*prenominal*) **3.** beloved. **4.** much admired; pleasing: *a darling hat.*

darn[1] (dɑːn) *vb.* **1.** to mend (a hole or a garment) with a series of crossing or interwoven stitches. ~*n.* **2.** a patch of darned work on a garment. —'**darner** *n.*

darn[2] (dɑːn) *interj., adj., adv., n.* a euphemistic word for **damn** (senses 1–4).

darnel ('dɑːnəl) *n.* any of several grasses that grow as weeds in grain fields in Europe and Asia.

darning ('dɑːnɪŋ) *n.* **1.** the act of mending a hole using interwoven stitches. **2.** garments needing to be darned. **3.** (*as modifier*) : *darning needle, darning wool.*

dart (dɑːt) *n.* **1.** a small narrow pointed missile that is thrown or shot, as in the game of darts. **2.** a sudden quick movement. **3.** *Zool.* a slender pointed structure, as in snails for aiding copulation. **4.** a tapered tuck made in dressmaking. ~*vb.* **5.** to move or throw swiftly and suddenly; shoot.

dartboard ('dɑːt,bɔːd) *n.* a circular piece of wood, cork,

THESAURUS

danger endangerment, hazard, insecurity, jeopardy, menace, peril, precariousness, risk, threat, venture, vulnerability

dangerous alarming, breakneck, chancy (*Inf.*), exposed, hairy (*Sl.*), hazardous, insecure, menacing, nasty, parlous (*Archaic*), perilous, precarious, risky, threatening, treacherous, ugly, unchancy (*Scot.*), unsafe, vulnerable

dangerously **1.** alarmingly, carelessly, daringly, desperately, harmfully, hazardously, perilously, precariously, recklessly, riskily, unsafely, unsecurely **2.** critically, gravely, seriously, severely

dangle *v.* **1.** depend, flap, hang, hang down, sway, swing, trail **2.** brandish, entice, flaunt, flourish, lure, tantalize, tempt, wave

dangling disconnected, drooping, hanging, loose, swaying, swinging, trailing, unconnected

dapper active, brisk, chic, dainty, natty (*Inf.*), neat, nice, nimble, smart, spruce, spry, stylish, trig (*Archaic*), trim, well-groomed, well turned out

dapple *v.* bespeckle, dot, fleck, freckle, mottle, spot, stipple

dappled brindled, checkered, flecked, freckled, mottled, piebald, pied, speckled, spotted, stippled, variegated

dare *v.* **1.** challenge, defy, goad, provoke, taunt, throw down the gauntlet **2.** adventure,

brave, endanger, gamble, hazard, make bold, presume, risk, stake, venture ~*n.* **3.** challenge, defiance, provocation, taunt

daredevil 1. *n.* adventurer, desperado, exhibitionist, madcap, show-off (*Inf.*), stunt man **2.** *adj.* adventurous, audacious, bold, daring, death-defying, madcap, reckless

daring 1. *adj.* adventurous, audacious, bold, brave, fearless, game (*Inf.*), impulsive, intrepid, plucky, rash, reckless, valiant, venturesome **2.** *n.* audacity, boldness, bottle (*Sl.*), bravery, courage, derring-do (*Archaic*), fearlessness, grit, guts (*Inf.*), intrepidity, nerve (*Inf.*), pluck, rashness, spirit, spunk (*Inf.*), temerity

dark *adj.* **1.** black, brunette, dark-skinned, dusky, ebony, sable, swarthy **2.** cloudy, darksome (*Literary*), dim, dingy, indistinct, murky, overcast, pitch-black, pitchy, shadowy, shady, sunless, unlit **3.** abstruse, arcane, concealed, cryptic, deep, enigmatic, hidden, mysterious, mystic, obscure, occult, puzzling, recondite, secret **4.** bleak, cheerless, dismal, doleful, drab, gloomy, grim, joyless, morbid, morose, mournful, sombre **5.** benighted, ignorant, uncultivated, unenlightened, unlettered **6.** atrocious, damnable, evil, foul, hellish, horrible, infamous, infernal, nefarious, satanic, sinful, sinister, vile, wicked **7.** angry, dour, forbidding, frowning, glowering, glum, ominous, scowling, sulky, sullen, threatening ~*n.* **8.** darkness, dimness, dusk, gloom,

murk, murkiness, obscurity, semi-darkness **9.** evening, night, nightfall, night-time, twilight **10.** *Fig.* concealment, ignorance, secrecy

darken 1. becloud, blacken, cloud up or over, deepen, dim, eclipse, make dark, make darker, make dim, obscure, overshadow, shade, shadow **2.** become angry, become gloomy, blacken, cast a pall over, cloud, deject, depress, dispirit, grow troubled, look black, sadden

darkness 1. blackness, dark, dimness, dusk, duskiness, gloom, murk, murkiness, nightfall, obscurity, shade, shadiness, shadows **2.** *Fig.* blindness, concealment, ignorance, mystery, privacy, secrecy, unawareness

darling *n.* **1.** beloved, dear, dearest, love, sweetheart, truelove **2.** apple of one's eye, blue-eyed boy, fair-haired boy (*U.S.*), favourite, pet, spoiled child ~*adj.* **3.** adored, beloved, cherished, dear, precious, treasured **4.** adorable, attractive, captivating, charming, enchanting, lovely, sweet

darn 1. *v.* cobble up, mend, patch, repair, sew up, stitch **2.** *n.* invisible repair, mend, patch, reinforcement

dart 1. bound, dash, flash, flit, fly, race, run, rush, scoot, shoot, spring, sprint, start, tear, whistle (*Inf.*), whiz **2.** cast, fling, hurl, launch, propel, send, shoot, sling, throw

etc., used as the target in the game of darts.

darts (dɑːts) *n.* any of various competitive games in which darts are thrown at a dartboard.

Darwinism ('dɑːwɪˌnɪzəm) *or* **Darwinian theory** *n.* the theory of the origin of animal and plant species by evolution through a process of natural selection. —'**Darwinist** *n., adj.*

dash¹ (dæʃ) *vb.* (*mainly tr.*) **1.** to hurl; crash: *he dashed the cup to the floor.* **2.** to mix: *white paint dashed with blue.* **3.** (*intr.*) to move hastily or recklessly; rush. **4.** (usually foll. by *off* or *down*) to write (down) or finish (off) hastily. **5.** to frustrate: *his hopes were dashed.* **6.** to daunt (someone); discourage. ~*n.* **7.** a sudden quick movement. **8.** a small admixture: *coffee with a dash of cream.* **9.** a violent stroke or blow. **10.** the sound of splashing or smashing. **11.** panache; style: *he rides with dash.* **12.** the punctuation mark —, used to indicate a sudden change of subject or to enclose a parenthetical remark. **13.** the symbol (-) used, in combination with the symbol *dot* (.), in the written representation of Morse and other telegraphic codes. **14.** *Athletics.* another word (esp. U.S.) for *sprint*.

dash² (dæʃ) *interj., adj., adv., vb. Inf.* a euphemistic word for **damn** (senses 1, 3, 4).

dashboard ('dæʃˌbɔːd) *n.* **1.** Also called (Brit.): **fascia.** the instrument panel in a car, boat, or aircraft. **2.** *Obs.* a board at the side of a carriage or boat to protect against splashing.

dasher ('dæʃə) *n.* **1.** one that dashes. **2.** *Canad.* the ledge along the top of the boards of an ice hockey rink.

dashing ('dæʃɪŋ) *adj.* **1.** spirited; lively: *a dashing young man.* **2.** stylish; showy.

dassie ('dæsɪ) *n.* another name for a **hyrax,** esp. the rock hyrax.

dastard ('dæstəd) *n. Arch.* a contemptible sneaking coward. —'**dastardly** *adj.*

dat. *abbrev. for* dative.

data ('deɪtə, 'dɑːtə) *n.* **1.** a series of observations, measurements, or facts; information. **2.** Also called: **information.** *Computers* the information operated on by a computer program.
▷ **Usage.** Although now generally used as a singular noun, *data* is properly a plural.

data bank *or* **data base** *n.* a store of a large amount of information, esp. in a form that can be handled by a computer.

data capture *n.* any process for converting information into a form that can be handled by a computer.

data processing *n.* **a.** a sequence of operations performed on data, esp. by a computer, in order to extract information, reorder files, etc. **b.** (*as modifier*): *a data-processing centre.*

date¹ (deɪt) *n.* **1.** a specified day of the month. **2.** the particular day or year of an event. **3.** an inscription on a coin, letter, etc., stating when it was made or written. **4. a.** an appointment for a particular time, esp. with a person of the opposite sex. **b.** the person with whom the appointment is made. **5.** the present moment; now (esp. in **to date, up to date**). ~*vb* **6.** (*tr.*) to mark (a letter, coin, etc.) with the day, month, or year. **7.** (*tr.*) to assign a date of occurrence or creation to. **8.** (*intr.;* foll. by *from* or *back to*) to have originated (at a specified time). **9.** (*tr.*) to reveal the age of: *that dress dates her.* **10.** to become old-fashioned: *some good films hardly date at all.*

11. *Inf., chiefly U.S.* **a.** to be a boyfriend or girlfriend of (someone of the opposite sex). **b.** to accompany (a member of the opposite sex) on a date. —'**datable** *or* '**dateable** *adj.*
▷ **Usage.** See at **day, decade, year.**

date² (deɪt) *n.* **1.** the fruit of the date palm, having sweet edible flesh and a single large woody seed. **2.** short for **date palm.**

dateless ('deɪtlɪs) *adj.* likely to remain fashionable, good or interesting regardless of age.

date line *n.* (*often caps.*) the line approximately following the 180° meridian from Greenwich on the east side of which the date is one day earlier than on the west.

dateline ('deɪtˌlaɪn) *n. Journalism.* the date and location of a story, placed at the top of an article.

date palm *n.* a tall feather palm grown in tropical regions for its sweet edible fruit.

date stamp *n.* **1.** an adjustable rubber stamp for recording the date. **2.** an inked impression made by this.

dative ('deɪtɪv) *Grammar.* ~*adj.* **1.** denoting a case of nouns, pronouns, and adjectives used to express the indirect object, to identify the recipients, and for other purposes. ~*n.* **2. a.** the dative case. **b.** a word or speech element in this case. —'**datival** (deɪ'taɪvəl) *adj.* —'**datively** *adv.*

datum ('deɪtəm, 'dɑːtəm) *n., pl.* -**ta** (-tə). **1.** a single piece of information; fact. **2.** a fact or proposition, known or assumed, from which inferences can be drawn. See also **sense datum.**

daub (dɔːb) *vb.* **1.** (*tr.*) to smear or spread (paint, mud, etc.), esp. carelessly. **2.** (*tr.*) to cover or coat (with paint, plaster, etc.) carelessly. **3.** to paint (a picture) clumsily or badly. ~*n.* **4.** an unskilful or crude painting. **5.** something daubed on, esp. as a wall covering. **6.** a smear (of paint, mud, etc.) —'**dauber** *n.*

daughter ('dɔːtə) *n.* **1.** a female offspring; a girl or woman in relation to her parents. **2.** a female descendant. **3.** a female from a certain country, etc., or one closely connected with a certain environment, etc.: *a daughter of the church.* ~(*modifier*) **4.** *Biol.* denoting a cell or unicellular organism produced by the division of one of its own kind. **5.** *Physics.* (of a nuclide) formed from another nuclide by radioactive decay. —'**daughterhood** *n.* —'**daughterless** *adj.* —'**daughterly** *adj.*

daughter-in-law *n., pl.* **daughters-in-law.** the wife of one's son.

daunt (dɔːnt) *vb.* (*tr.; often passive*) **1.** to intimidate. **2.** to dishearten. —'**daunter** *n.* —'**dauntingly** *adv.*

dauntless ('dɔːntlɪs) *adj.* bold; fearless; intrepid. —'**dauntlessly** *adv.* —'**dauntlessness** *n.*

dauphin ('dɔːfɪn) *n.* (from 1349–1830) the title of the eldest son of the king of France.

davenport ('dævənˌpɔːt) *n.* **1.** *Chiefly Brit.* a small decorative writing desk with drawers. **2.** *U.S.* a large sofa, esp. one convertible into a bed.

davit ('dævɪt, 'deɪ-) *n.* a cranelike device, usually one of a pair, fitted with a tackle for suspending or lowering equipment, esp. a lifeboat.

Davy Jones ('deɪvɪ dʒəʊnz) *n.* **1.** Also called: **Davy Jones's locker.** the ocean's bottom, esp. when regarded as the grave of those lost or buried at sea. **2.** the spirit of the sea.

THESAURUS

dash *v.* **1.** break, crash, destroy, shatter, shiver, smash, splinter **2.** cast, fling, hurl, slam, sling, throw **3.** bolt, bound, dart, fly, haste, hasten, hurry, race, run, rush, speed, spring, sprint, tear **4.** abash, chagrin, confound, dampen, disappoint, discomfort, discourage **5.** blight, foil, frustrate, ruin, spoil, thwart ~*n.* **6.** bolt, dart, haste, onset, race, run, rush, sortie, sprint, spurt **7.** brio, élan, flair, flourish, panache, spirit, style, verve, vigour, vivacity **8.** bit, drop, flavour, hint, little, pinch, smack, soupçon, sprinkling, suggestion, tinge, touch

dashing 1. bold, daring, debonair, exuberant, gallant, lively, plucky, spirited, swashbuckling **2.** dapper, dazzling, elegant, flamboyant, jaunty, showy, smart, sporty, stylish, swish (*Inf.*)

data details, documents, facts, figures, in-

formation, input, materials, statistics

date *n.* **1.** age, epoch, era, period, stage, time **2.** appointment, assignation, engagement, meeting, rendezvous, tryst **3.** escort, friend, partner, steady (*Inf.*) **4. out of date** antiquated, archaic, dated, obsolete, old, old-fashioned, passé **5. to date** now, so far, up to now, up to the present, up to this point, yet **6. up-to-date** à la mode, contemporary, current, fashionable, modern, trendy (*Inf.*), up-to-the-minute ~*v.* **7.** assign a date to, determine the date of, fix the period of, put a date on **8.** bear a date, belong to, come from, exist from, originate in **9.** become obsolete, be dated, obsolesce, show one's age

dated antiquated, archaic, démodé, obsolete, old-fashioned, old hat, out, outdated, outmoded, out of date, passé, unfashionable

daub *v.* **1.** coat, cover, paint, plaster, slap

on (*Inf.*), smear **2.** bedaub, begrime, besmear, blur, deface, dirty, grime, smirch, smudge, spatter, splatter, stain, sully ~*n.* **3.** blot, blotch, smear, splodge, splotch, spot, stain

daunt 1. alarm, appal, cow, dismay, frighten, frighten off, intimidate, overawe, scare, subdue, terrify **2.** deter, discourage, dishearten, dispirit, put off, shake

daunted *adj.* alarmed, cowed, demoralized, deterred, discouraged, disillusioned, dismayed, dispirited, downcast, frightened, hesitant, intimidated, overcome, put off, unnerved

dauntless bold, brave, courageous, daring, doughty, fearless, gallant, heroic, indomitable, intrepid, lion-hearted, resolute, stouthearted, undaunted, unflinching, valiant, valorous

Davy lamp *n.* See **safety lamp.**

dawdle ('dɔːdəl) *vb.* 1. (*intr.*) to be slow or lag behind. 2. (when *tr.*, often foll. by *away*) to waste (time); trifle. —'**dawdler** *n.*

dawn (dɔːn) *n.* 1. daybreak. Related adj.: **auroral.** 2. the sky when light first appears in the morning. 3. the beginning of something. ~*vb.* (*intr.*) 4. to begin to grow light after the night. 5. to begin to develop or appear. 6. (usually foll. by *on* or *upon*) to begin to become apparent (to). —'**dawn,like** *adj.*

dawn chorus *n.* the singing of large numbers of birds at dawn.

day (deɪ) *n.* 1. Also called: **civil day.** the period of time, the **calendar day,** of 24 hours duration reckoned from one midnight to the next. 2. the period of light between sunrise and sunset. 3. the part of a day occupied with regular activity, esp. work. 4. (*sometimes pl.*) a period or point in time: *in days gone by; any day now.* 5. the period of time, the **sidereal day,** during which the earth makes one complete revolution on its axis relative to a particular star. 6. the period of time, the **solar day,** during which the earth makes one complete revolution on its axis relative to the sun. 7. the period of time taken by a specified planet to make one complete rotation on its axis: *the Martian day.* 8. (*often cap.*) a day designated for a special observance: *Christmas Day.* 9. **all in a day's work.** part of one's normal activity. 10. **at the end of the day.** in the final reckoning. 11. **day of rest.** the Sabbath; Sunday. 12. **every dog has his day.** one's luck will come. 13. **in this day and age.** nowadays. 14. **late in the day.** very late (in a particular situation). 15. **that will be the day. a.** that is most unlikely to happen. **b.** I look forward to that. 16. a time of success, recognition, etc.: *his day will come.* 17. a struggle or issue at hand: *the day is lost.* 18. **call it a day.** *Inf.* to stop work or other activity. 19. **day after day.** without respite; relentlessly. 20. **day by day.** gradually or progressively. 21. **day in, day out.** every day and all day long. 22. (*as modifier*): *the day shift.* ~Related adj.: **diurnal.**

▷ **Usage.** Numerals are used for the day of the month: in formal written English, either cardinal or ordinal numbers may be used either preceding or following the month. In this dictionary the date is given in this manner: *May 15. 1974.*

day bed *n.* an armless couch intended for use as a seat and as a bed.

dayboy ('deɪ,bɔɪ) *n. Brit.* a boy who attends a boarding school daily, but returns home each evening. —'**day,girl** *fem. n.*

daybreak ('deɪ,breɪk) *n.* the time in the morning when light first appears; dawn; sunrise.

daydream ('deɪ,driːm) *n.* 1. a pleasant dreamlike fantasy indulged in while awake. 2. a pleasant scheme or wish that is unlikely to be fulfilled. ~*vb.* 3. (*intr.*) to indulge in idle fantasy. —'**day,dreamer** *n.* —'**day,dreamy** *adj.*

daylight ('deɪ,laɪt) *n.* 1. light from the sun. 2. daytime. 3. daybreak. 4. **see daylight. a.** to understand something previously obscure. **b.** to realize that the end of a difficult task is approaching.

daylight robbery *n. Inf.* blatant overcharging.

daylights ('deɪ,laɪts) *pl. n.* consciousness or wits (esp. in **scare, knock,** or **beat the (living) daylights out of someone).**

day release *n. Brit.* a system whereby workers are released for part-time education without loss of pay.

day return *n.* a reduced fare for a journey (by train, etc.) travelling both ways in one day.

day room *n.* a communal living room in a residential institution such as a hospital.

days (deɪz) *adv. Inf.* during the day, esp. regularly: *he works days.*

day school *n.* 1. a private school taking day students only. 2. a school giving instruction during the daytime.

day-to-day *adj.* routine; everyday.

daze (deɪz) *vb.* (*tr.*) 1. to stun, esp. by a blow or shock. 2. to bewilder or amaze. ~*n.* 3. a state of stunned confusion or shock (esp. in **in a daze).**

dazzle ('dæzəl) *vb.* 1. (*usually tr.*) to blind or be blinded partially and temporarily by sudden excessive light. 2. (*tr.*) to amaze, as with brilliance. ~*n.* 3. bright light that dazzles. 4. bewilderment caused by glamour, brilliance, etc.: *the dazzle of fame.* —'**dazzler** *n.* —'**dazzlingly** *adv.*

dB *or* **db** *symbol for* decibel or decibels.

D.B.E. *abbrev. for* Dame Commander of the Order of the British Empire (a Brit. title).

DC *abbrev. for* direct current. Cf. **AC.**

D.C. *abbrev. for:* 1. *Music.* da capo. 2. *U.S.* District of Columbia.

D.C.B. *abbrev. for* Dame Commander of the Order of the Bath (a Brit. title).

D.C.M. *Brit. mil. abbrev. for* Distinguished Conduct Medal.

DD *abbrev. for:* 1. Doctor of Divinity. 2. direct debit.

D-day *n.* the day selected for the start of some operation, esp. of the Allied invasion of Europe on June 6, 1944.

DDR *abbrev. for* Deutsche Demokratische Republik (East Germany; G.D.R.).

D.D.S. *or* **D.D.Sc.** *abbrev. for* Doctor of Dental Surgery or Science.

DDT *n.* dichlorodiphenyltrichloroethane; a colourless odourless substance used as an insecticide.

de- *prefix forming verbs and verbal derivatives.* 1. removal of or from something: *deforest; dethrone.* 2. reversal of something: *decode; desegregate.* 3. departure from: *decamp.*

deacon ('diːkən) *n. Christianity.* 1. (in the Roman Catholic and other episcopal churches) an ordained minister ranking immediately below a priest. 2. (in Protestant churches) a lay official who assists the minister, esp. in secular affairs. —'**deacon,ate** *n.* —'**deacon,ship** *n.*

deaconess ('diːkənɪs) *n. Christianity.* (in the early church and in some modern Churches) a female member of the laity with duties similar to those of a deacon.

deactivate (diːˈæktɪ,veɪt) *vb.* 1. (*tr.*) to make (a bomb, etc.) harmless or inoperative. 2. to make less radioactive. —de'**acti,vator** *n.*

dead (dɛd) *adj.* 1. **a.** no longer alive. **b.** (*as n.*): *the*

THESAURUS

dawdle dally, delay, dilly-dally (*Inf.*), fritter away, hang about, idle, lag, loaf, loiter, potter, trail, waste time

dawn *n.* 1. aurora (*Literary*), cockcrow, crack of dawn, dawning, daybreak, daylight, dayspring (*Poetic*), morning, sunrise, sunup ~*v.* 2. break, brighten, gleam, glimmer, grow light, lighten ~*n.* 3. advent, beginning, birth, dawning, emergence, genesis, inception, onset, origin, outset, rise, start, unfolding ~*v.* 4. appear, begin, develop, emerge, initiate, open, originate, rise, unfold 5. come into one's head, come to mind, cross one's mind, flash across one's mind, hit, occur, register (*Inf.*), strike

day 1. daylight, daylight hours, daytime, twenty-four hours, working day 2. age, ascendancy, cycle, epoch, era, generation, height, heyday, period, prime, time, zenith 3. date, particular day, point in time, set time, time 4. **call it a day** *Inf.* end, finish, knock off (*Inf.*), leave off, pack it in (*Sl.*), pack up (*Inf.*), shut up shop, stop 5. **day after day** continual-

ly, monotonously, persistently, regularly, relentlessly 6. **day by day** daily, gradually, progressively, steadily

daybreak break of day, cockcrow, crack of dawn, dawn, dayspring (*Poetic*), first light, morning, sunrise, sunup

daydream *n.* 1. dream, imagining, musing, reverie, stargazing, vision, woolgathering 2. castle in the air *or* in Spain, dream, fancy, fantasy, figment of the imagination, fond hope, pipe dream, wish ~*v.* 3. dream, envision, fancy, fantasize, hallucinate, imagine, muse, stargaze

daydreamer castle-builder, dreamer, fantast, pipe dreamer, visionary, Walter Mitty, wishful thinker, woolgatherer

daylight 1. light of day, sunlight, sunshine 2. broad day, daylight hours, daytime 3. full view, light of day, openness, public attention

daze *v.* 1. benumb, numb, paralyse, shock, stun, stupefy 2. amaze, astonish, astound, befog, bewilder, blind, confuse, dazzle, dumbfound, flabbergast (*Inf.*), perplex, stagger,

startle, surprise ~*n.* 3. bewilderment, confusion, distraction, shock, stupor, trance, trancelike state

dazed baffled, bemused, bewildered, confused, disorientated, dizzy, dopey (*Sl.*), flabbergasted (*Inf.*), fuddled, groggy (*Inf.*), light-headed, muddled, nonplussed, numbed, perplexed, punch-drunk, shocked, staggered, stunned, stupefied, woozy (*Inf.*)

dazzle *v.* 1. bedazzle, blind, blur, confuse, daze 2. amaze, astonish, awe, bowl over (*Inf.*), fascinate, hypnotize, impress, overawe, overpower, overwhelm, strike dumb, stupefy ~*n.* 3. brilliance, flash, glitter, magnificence, razzle-dazzle (*Sl.*), razzmatazz (*Sl.*), sparkle, splendour

dazzling brilliant, glittering, glorious, radiant, ravishing, scintillating, sensational, shining, sparkling, splendid, stunning, sublime, superb, virtuoso

dead. **2.** not endowed with life; inanimate. **3.** no longer in use, effective, or relevant: *a dead issue; a dead language.* **4.** unresponsive or unaware. **5.** lacking in freshness or vitality. **6.** devoid of physical sensation; numb. **7.** resembling death: *a dead sleep.* **8.** no longer burning or hot: *dead coals.* **9.** (*prenominal*) (intensifier): *a dead stop.* **10.** Also: **dead beat.** *Inf.* very tired. **11.** *Electronics.* **a.** drained of electric charge. **b.** not connected to a source of potential difference or electric charge. **12.** lacking acoustic resonance: *a dead sound.* **13.** *Sport.* (of a ball, etc.) out of play. **14.** accurate; precise (esp. in a **dead shot**). **15.** lacking resilience or bounce: *a dead ball.* **16.** not yielding a return: *dead capital.* **17.** (of colours) not glossy or bright. **18.** stagnant: *dead air.* **19.** *Mil.* shielded from view, as by a geographic feature. **20. dead from the neck up.** *Inf.* stupid. **21. dead to the world.** *Inf.* fast asleep. ~*n.* **22.** a period during which coldness, darkness, etc. is at its most intense: *the dead of winter.* ~*adv.* **23.** (intensifier): *dead easy; stop dead.* **24. dead on.** exactly right. —'**deadness** *n.*

deadbeat ('dɛd,biːt) *n.* **1.** *Inf., chiefly U.S.* a lazy or socially undesirable person. **2.** a high grade escapement used in pendulum clocks. **3.** (*modifier*) without recoil.

dead duck *n. Sl.* a person or thing doomed to death, failure, etc., esp. because of a mistake.

deaden ('dɛdən) *vb.* **1.** to make or become less sensitive, intense, lively, etc. **2.** (*tr.*) to make acoustically less resonant. —'**deadener** *n.*

dead end *n.* **1.** a cul-de-sac. **2.** a situation in which further progress is impossible.

deadhead ('dɛd,hɛd) *n. U.S. inf.* **1.** a person who uses a free ticket, as for the theatre, etc. **2.** a train, etc., travelling empty. **3.** a dull person. **4.** *U.S. & Canad.* a log sticking out of the water as a snag to navigation. ~*vb.* **5.** *U.S. inf.* (*intr.*) to drive an empty bus, train, etc. **6.** (*tr.*) to remove dead flower heads.

dead heat *n.* **a.** a race or contest in which two or more participants tie for first place. **b.** a tie between two or more contestants in any position.

dead letter *n.* a law or ordinance that is no longer enforced.

deadlight ('dɛd,laɪt) *n.* **1.** *Naut.* **a.** a bull's-eye to admit light to a cabin. **b.** a shutter for sealing off a porthole or cabin window. **2.** a skylight designed not to be opened.

deadline ('dɛd,laɪn) *n.* a time limit for any activity.

deadlock ('dɛd,lɒk) *n.* **1.** a state of affairs in which further action between two opposing forces is impossible. **2.** a tie between opponents. **3.** a lock having a full unchamfered bolt. ~*vb.* **4.** to bring or come to a deadlock.

dead loss *n.* **1.** a complete loss for which no compensation is paid. **2.** *Inf.* a useless person or thing.

deadly ('dɛdlɪ) *adj.* **-lier, -liest. 1.** likely to cause death. **2.** *Inf.* extremely boring. ~*adv., adj.* **3.** like death in appearance or certainty.

deadly nightshade *n.* a poisonous Eurasian plant having purple bell-shaped flowers and black berries. Also called: **belladonna, dwale.**

dead man's handle *or* **pedal** *n.* a safety-switch on a piece of machinery that allows operation only while depressed by the operator.

dead march *n.* a piece of solemn funeral music

played to accompany a procession.

dead-nettle *n.* any of several Eurasian plants having leaves resembling nettles but lacking stinging hairs.

deadpan ('dɛd,pæn) *adj., adv.* with a deliberately emotionless face or manner.

dead reckoning *n.* a method of establishing one's position using the distance and direction travelled rather than astronomical observations.

dead set *adv.* **1.** absolutely: *he is dead set against going to Spain.* ~*n.* **2.** the motionless position of a dog when pointing towards game. ~*adj.* **3.** (of a hunting dog) in this position.

dead weight *n.* **1.** a heavy weight or load. **2.** an oppressive burden. **3.** the difference between the loaded and the unloaded weights of a ship. **4.** the intrinsic invariable weight of a structure, such as a bridge.

deadwood ('dɛd,wʊd) *n.* **1.** dead trees or branches. **2.** *Inf.* a useless person; encumbrance.

deaf (dɛf) *adj.* **1. a.** partially or totally unable to hear. **b.** (*as n.*): *the deaf.* **2.** refusing to heed. —'**deafness** *n.*

deaf-and-dumb *adj.* **1.** unable to hear or speak. **2.** for the use of those unable to hear or speak.

deafen ('dɛfən) *vb.* (*tr.*) to make deaf, esp. momentarily, as by a loud noise. —'**deafeningly** *adv.*

deaf-mute *n.* **1.** a person who is unable to hear or speak. ~*adj.* **2.** unable to hear or speak.

deal[1] (diːl) *vb.* **dealing, dealt.** (*mainly intr.*). **1.** (foll. by *with*) to take action on: *to deal with a problem.* **2.** (foll. by *with* or *in*) to treat (some subject matter): *his manuscript deals with art.* **3.** (foll. by *with*) to conduct oneself (towards others), esp. with regard to fairness. **4. a.** (foll. by *with*) to do business. **b.** (foll. by *in*) to engage in commercially: *to deal in upholstery.* **5.** (often foll. by *out*) to apportion or distribute. **6.** (*tr.*) to give·(a blow, etc.) to (someone); inflict. **7.** *Sl.* to sell narcotics. ~*n.* **8.** *Inf.* a bargain, transaction, or agreement. **9.** a particular type of treatment received, esp. as the result of an agreement: *a fair deal.* **10.** an indefinite amount (esp. in **good** or **great deal**). **11.** *Cards.* **a.** the process of distributing the cards. **b.** a player's turn to do this. **c.** a single round in a card game. **12. big deal.** *Inf.* an important person, event, or matter: often used sarcastically. —'**dealer** *n.*

deal[2] (diːl) *n.* **1.** a plank of softwood timber, such as fir or pine, or such planks collectively. **2.** the sawn wood of various coniferous trees. ~*adj.* **3.** of fir or pine.

dealings ('diːlɪŋz) *pl. n.* (*sometimes sing.*) transactions or business relations.

dealt (dɛlt) *vb.* the past tense or past participle of **deal**[1].

dean (diːn) *n.* **1.** the chief administrative official of a college or university faculty. **2.** (at Oxford and Cambridge universities) a college fellow with responsibility for undergraduate discipline. **3.** *Chiefly Church of England.* the head of a chapter of canons and administrator of a cathedral or collegiate church. **4.** *R.C. Church.* the cardinal bishop senior by consecration and head of the college of cardinals. Related adj.: **decanal.** See also: **rural dean.**

deanery ('diːnərɪ) *n., pl.* **-eries. 1.** the office or residence of a dean. **2.** the group of parishes presided over by a rural dean.

dear (dɪə) *adj.* **1.** beloved; precious. **2.** used in conven-

---

THESAURUS

dead *adj.* **1.** deceased, defunct, departed, extinct, gone, inanimate, late, lifeless, passed away, perished **2.** apathetic, callous, cold, dull, frigid, glassy, glazed, indifferent, inert, lukewarm, numb, paralysed, spiritless, torpid, unresponsive, wooden **3.** barren, inactive, inoperative, not working, obsolete, stagnant, sterile, still, unemployed, unprofitable, useless **4.** boring, dead-and-alive, dull, flat, insipid, stale, tasteless, uninteresting, vapid **5.** *Fig.* absolute, complete, downright, entire, outright, thorough, total, unqualified, utter **6.** *Inf.* dead beat (*Inf.*), exhausted, spent, tired, worn out ~*n.* **7.** depth, middle, midst ~*adv.* **8.** absolutely, completely, directly, entirely, exactly, **8.** totally

deaden abate, alleviate, anaesthetize, benumb, blunt, check, cushion, damp, dampen, diminish, dull, hush, impair, lessen, muffle, mute, numb, paralyse, quieten, reduce, smother, stifle, suppress, weaken

deadlock cessation, dead heat, draw, full stop, halt, impasse, stalemate, standoff, standstill, tie

deadly **1.** baleful, baneful, dangerous, death-dealing, deathly, destructive, fatal, lethal, malignant, mortal, noxious, pernicious, poisonous, venomous **2.** cruel, grim, implacable, mortal, ruthless, savage, unrelenting **3.** ashen, deathlike, deathly, ghastly, ghostly, pallid, wan, white **4.** accurate, effective, exact, on target, precise, sure, true, unerring, unfailing **5.** *Inf.* boring, dull, monotonous, tedious, uninteresting, wearisome

deaf *adj.* **1.** hard of hearing, stone deaf, without hearing **2.** indifferent, oblivious, unconcerned, unhearing, unmoved

deafen din, drown out, make deaf, split or burst the eardrums

deafening booming, dinning, ear-piercing, ear-splitting, intense, overpowering, piercing, resounding, ringing,

thunderous

deal *v.* **1.** *With* **with** attend to, cope with, handle, manage, oversee, see to, take care of, treat **2.** *With* **with** concern, consider, treat (of) **3.** *With* **with** act, behave, conduct oneself **4.** bargain, buy and sell, do business, negotiate, sell, stock, trade, traffic, treat (with) ~*n.* **5.** *Inf.* agreement, arrangement, bargain, buy (*Inf.*), contract, pact, transaction, understanding ~*v.* **6.** allot, apportion, assign, bestow, dispense, distribute, divide, dole out, give, mete out, reward, share ~*n.* **7.** amount, degree, distribution, extent, portion, quantity, share, transaction **8.** cut and shuffle, distribution, hand, round, single game

dealer chandler, marketer, merchandiser, merchant, trader, tradesman, wholesaler

dealings business, business relations, commerce, trade, traffic, transactions, truck

tional forms of address, as in *Dear Sir.* **3.** (*postpositive; foll. by to*) important; close. **4. a.** highly priced. **b.** charging high prices. **5.** appealing. **6. for dear life.** as though life were in danger. ~*interj.* **7.** used in exclamations of surprise or dismay, such as *Oh dear!* ~*n.* **8.** Also: **dearest.** (*often used in direct address*) someone regarded with affection and tenderness. ~*adv.* **9.** dearly. —'**dearly** *adv.* —'**dearness** *n.*

dearth (dɜːθ) *n.* an inadequate amount, esp. of food; scarcity.

deary or **dearie** ('dɪərɪ) *n.* **1.** (*pl.* **dearies**) *Inf.* a term of affection: now often sarcastic or facetious. **2. deary** or **dearie me!** an exclamation of surprise or dismay.

death (dɛθ) *n.* **1.** the permanent end of all functions of life in an organism. **2.** an instance of this: *his death ended an era.* **3.** a murder or killing. **4.** termination or destruction. **5.** a state of affairs or an experience considered as terrible as death. **6.** a cause or source of death. **7.** (*usually cap.*) a personification of death, usually a skeleton or an old man holding a scythe. **8. to death. a.** until dead. **b.** very much. **9. at death's door.** likely to die soon. **10. catch one's death (of cold).** *Inf.* to contract a severe cold. **11. do to death. a.** to kill. **b.** to overuse. **12. in at the death. a.** present when a hunted animal is killed. **b.** present at the finish or climax. **13. like death warmed up.** *Inf.* very ill. **14. like grim death.** as if afraid of one's life. **15. put to death.** to kill deliberately or execute. ~Related adjs.: **fatal, lethal, mortal.**

deathbed ('dɛθ,bɛd) *n.* the bed in which a person is about to die.

deathblow ('dɛθ,bləʊ) *n.* a thing or event that destroys life or hope, esp. suddenly.

death certificate *n.* a legal document issued by a qualified medical practitioner certifying the death of a person and stating the cause if known.

death duty *n.* a tax on property inheritances.

deathless ('dɛθlɪs) *adj.* immortal, esp. because of greatness; everlasting. —'**deathlessness** *n.*

deathly ('dɛθlɪ) *adj.* **1.** deadly. **2.** resembling death: *a deathly quiet.*

death rate *n.* the ratio of deaths in a specified area, group, etc., to the population of that area, group, etc. Also called: **mortality rate.**

death rattle *n.* a low-pitched gurgling sound sometimes made by a dying person.

death's-head *n.* a human skull or a representation of one.

deathtrap ('dɛθ,træp) *n.* a building, vehicle, etc., that is considered very unsafe.

death warrant *n.* **1.** the official authorization for carrying out a sentence of death. **2. sign one's (own) death warrant.** to cause one's own destruction.

deathwatch ('dɛθ,wɒtʃ) *n.* **1.** a vigil held beside a dying or dead person. **2. deathwatch beetle.** any of several beetles that bore into wood and produce a tapping sound.

deb (dɛb) *n. Inf.* short for **debutante.**

debacle (deɪ'bɑːkəl, dɪ-) *n.* **1.** a sudden disastrous collapse or defeat; rout. **2.** the breaking up of ice in a river,

often causing flooding. **3.** a violent rush of water carrying along debris.

debag (diː'bæg) *vb.* **-bagging, -bagged.** (*tr.*) *Brit. sl.* to remove the trousers from (someone) by force.

debar (dɪ'bɑː) *vb.* **-barring, -barred.** (*tr.; usually foll. by from*) to exclude from a place, a right, etc.; bar. —de-'**barment** *n.*

debase (dɪ'beɪs) *vb.* (*tr.*) to lower in quality, character, or value; adulterate. —de'**basement** *n.* —de'**baser** *n.*

debate (dɪ'beɪt) *n.* **1.** a formal discussion, as in a legislative body, in which opposing arguments are put forward. **2.** discussion or dispute. **3.** the formal presentation and opposition of a specific motion, followed by a vote. ~*vb.* **4.** to discuss (a motion, etc.), esp. in a formal assembly. **5.** to deliberate upon (something). —de'**batable** *adj.* —de'**bater** *n.*

debauch (dɪ'bɔːtʃ) *vb.* **1.** (when *tr., usually passive*) to lead into a life of depraved self-indulgence. **2.** (*tr.*) to seduce (a woman). ~*n.* **3.** an instance or period of extreme dissipation. —de'**baucher** *n.* —de'**bauchery** *n.*

debauchee (,dɛbɔː'tʃiː) *n.* a man who leads a life of promiscuity, and self-indulgence.

debenture (dɪ'bɛntʃə) *n.* **1.** a long-term bond, bearing fixed interest and usually unsecured, issued by a company or governmental agency. **2.** a certificate acknowledging a debt. **3.** a customs certificate providing for a refund of excise or import duty. —de'**bentured** *adj.*

debenture stock *pl. n.* shares issued by a company, which guarantee a fixed return at regular intervals.

debilitate (dɪ'bɪlɪ,teɪt) *vb.* (*tr.*) to make feeble; weaken. —de,bili'**tation** *n.* —de'**bilitative** *adj.*

debility (dɪ'bɪlɪtɪ) *n., pl.* **-ties.** weakness or infirmity.

debit ('dɛbɪt) *n.* **1. a.** acknowledgment of a sum owing by entry on the left side of an account. **b.** the left side of an account. **c.** an entry on this side. **d.** the total of such entries. **e.** (*as modifier*): *a debit balance.* ~*vb.* **2.** (*tr.*) **a.** to record (an item) as a debit in an account. **b.** to charge (a person or his account) with a debt.

debonair or **debonnaire** (,dɛbə'nɛə) *adj.* **1.** suave and refined. **2.** carefree; gay. **3.** courteous and cheerful. —,**debo'nairly** *adv.* —,**debo'nairness** *n.*

debouch (dɪ'baʊtʃ) *vb.* **1.** (*intr.*) (esp. of troops) to move into a more open space. **2.** (*intr.*) (of a river, glacier, etc.) to flow into a larger area or body. —de'**bouchment** *n.*

debrief (diː'briːf) *vb.* (of a soldier, diplomat, etc.) to make or (of his superiors) to elicit a report after a mission or event. —de'**briefing** *n.*

debris or **débris** ('deɪbrɪ, 'dɛbrɪ) *n.* **1.** fragments of something destroyed or broken; rubble. **2.** a collection of loose material derived from rocks, or an accumulation of animal or vegetable matter.

debt (dɛt) *n.* **1.** something owed, such as money, goods, or services. **2. bad debt.** a debt that has little prospect of being paid. **3.** an obligation to pay or perform something. **4.** the state of owing something, or of being under an obligation (esp. in **in debt, in (someone's) debt**).

THESAURUS

dear *adj.* **1.** beloved, cherished, close, darling, esteemed, familiar, favourite, intimate, precious, prized, respected, treasured **2.** at a premium, costly, expensive, high-priced, overpriced, pricey (*Inf.*) ~*n.* **3.** angel, beloved, darling, loved one, precious, treasure ~*adv.* **4.** at a heavy cost, at a high price, at great cost, dearly

dearly **1.** extremely, greatly, profoundly, very much **2.** affectionately, devotedly, fondly, lovingly, tenderly **3.** at a heavy cost, at a high price, at great cost, dear

death 1. bereavement, cessation, curtains (*Inf.*), decease, demise, departure, dissolution, dying, end, exit, expiration, loss, passing, quietus, release **2.** annihilation, destruction, downfall, eradication, extermination, extinction, finish, grave, obliteration, ruin, ruination, undoing

deathless eternal, everlasting, immortal, imperishable, incorruptible, timeless, undying

deathly 1. cadaverous, deathlike, gaunt,

ghastly, grim, haggard, pale, pallid, wan **2.** deadly, extreme, fatal, intense, mortal, terrible

debacle catastrophe, collapse, defeat, devastation, disaster, downfall, fiasco, havoc, overthrow, reversal, rout, ruin, ruination

debase 1. abase, cheapen, degrade, demean, devalue, disgrace, dishonour, drag down, humble, humiliate, lower, reduce, shame **2.** adulterate, bastardize, contaminate, corrupt, defile, depreciate, impair, pollute, taint, vitiate

debased 1. adulterated, depreciated, devalued, impure, lowered, mixed, polluted, reduced **2.** abandoned, base, corrupt, debauched, degraded, depraved, fallen, low, perverted, sordid, vile

debasement 1. adulteration, contamination, depreciation, devaluation, pollution, reduction **2.** abasement, baseness, corruption, degradation, depravation, perversion

debatable arguable, borderline, controversial, disputable, doubtful, dubious, in dis-

pute, moot, open to question, problematical, questionable, uncertain, undecided, unsettled

debate *v.* **1.** argue, contend, contest, controvert, discuss, dispute, question, wrangle ~*n.* **2.** altercation, argument, contention, controversy, discussion, disputation, dispute, polemic ~*v.* **3.** cogitate, consider, deliberate, meditate upon, mull over, ponder, reflect, revolve, ruminate, weigh ~*n.* **4.** cogitation, consideration, deliberation, meditation, reflection

debilitate devitalize, enervate, enfeeble, exhaust, incapacitate, prostrate, relax, sap, undermine, weaken, wear out

debility decrepitude, enervation, enfeeblement, exhaustion, faintness, feebleness, frailty, incapacity, infirmity, languor, malaise, sickliness, weakness

debonair affable, buoyant, charming, cheerful, courteous, dashing, elegant, jaunty, light-hearted, refined, smooth (*Inf.*), sprightly, suave, urbane, well-bred

debris bits, brash, detritus, dross, frag-

debt of honour *n.* a debt that is morally but not legally binding.

debtor ('dɛtə) *n.* a person or commercial enterprise that owes a financial obligation.

debug (diː'bʌg) *Inf. vb.* **-bugging, -bugged.** (*tr.*) **1.** to locate and remove concealed microphones from (a room, etc.). **2.** to locate and remove defects in (a device, system, plan, etc.). **3.** to remove insects from.

debunk (diː'bʌŋk) *vb.* (*tr.*) *Inf.* to expose the pretensions or falseness of, esp. by ridicule. —**de'bunker** *n.*

debut ('deibjuː, 'dɛbjuː) *n.* **1.** the first public appearance of an actor, musician, etc. **2.** the presentation of a debutante.

debutante ('dɛbjuːtɑːnt, -ˌtænt) *n.* **1.** a young upperclass woman who is formally presented to society. **2.** a young woman regarded as being upper-class, wealthy, and frivolous.

Dec. *abbrev. for* December.

deca-, deka- *or before a vowel* **dec-, dek-** *prefix.* denoting ten: *decagon.* In conjunction with scientific units the symbol **da** is used.

decade ('dɛkeid, di'keid) *n.* **1.** a period of ten years. **2.** a group of ten. —**de'cadal** *adj.*

▷ *Usage.* Specific decades are referred to as follows: *the 1660s: the 1970s.* Where ambiguity does not arise contractions are allowable though it is preferable to write out the contracted forms in words rather than numerals: *the sixties* rather than *the 60s* or *the '60s.*

decadence ('dɛkədəns) *or* **decadency** *n.* **1.** deterioration, esp. of morality or culture. **2.** the state reached through such a process. —**'decadent** *adj.*

decaffeinate (di'kæfiˌneit) *vb.* (*tr.*) to remove all or part of the caffeine from (coffee).

decagon ('dɛkəˌgon) *n.* a polygon having ten sides. —**decagonal** (di'kægənəl) *adj.*

decahedron (ˌdɛkə'hiːdrən) *n.* a solid figure having ten plane faces. —ˌ**deca'hedral** *adj.*

decalitre *or U.S.* **decaliter** ('dɛkəˌliːtə) *n.* a metric measure of volume equivalent to 10 litres.

Decalogue ('dɛkəˌlog) *n.* another name for the **Ten Commandments.**

decametre *or U.S.* **decameter** ('dɛkəˌmiːtə) *n.* a metric measure of length equivalent to 10 metres.

decamp (di'kæmp) *vb.* (*intr.*) **1.** to leave a camp; break camp. **2.** to depart secretly or suddenly; abscond. —**de'campment** *n.*

decant (di'kænt) *vb.* to pour a (liquid, such as wine) from one container to another, esp. without disturbing any sediment.

decanter (di'kæntə) *n.* a stoppered bottle, into which a drink is poured for serving.

decapitate (di'kæpiˌteit) *vb.* (*tr.*) to behead. —de-ˌ**capi'tation** *n.* —de'**capiˌtator** *n.*

decapod ('dɛkəˌpod) *n.* **1.** any crustacean having five pairs of walking limbs, as a crab, lobster, shrimp, etc. **2.** any cephalopod mollusc having eight short tentacles and

two longer ones, as a squid or cuttlefish. —**decapodal** (di'kæpədˀl), **de'capodan,** *or* **de'capodous** *adj.*

decarbonize *or* **-ise** (diː'kɑːbəˌnaiz) *vb.* (*tr.*) to remove carbon from (an internal-combustion engine, etc.). Also: **decoke, decarburize.** —deˌ**carboni'zation** *or* -i'**sation** *n.* —de'**carbonˌizer** *or* -ˌ**iser** *n.*

decathlon (di'kæθlon) *n.* an athletic contest in which each athlete competes in ten different events.

decay (di'kei) *vb.* **1.** to decline or cause to decline gradually in health, prosperity, excellence, etc.; deteriorate. **2.** to rot or cause to rot; decompose. **3.** (*intr.*) Also: **disintegrate.** *Physics.* **a.** (of an atomic nucleus) to undergo radioactive disintegration. **b.** (of an elementary particle) to transform into two or more different elementary particles. **4.** *Physics.* (of a stored charge, magnetic flux, etc.) to decrease gradually when the source of energy has been removed. ~*n.* **5.** the process of decline, as in health, mentality, etc. **6.** the state brought about by this process. **7.** decomposition. **8.** rotten or decayed matter. **9.** *Physics.* **a.** disintegration of a nucleus that occurs spontaneously or as a result of electron capture. Also called: **disintegration. b.** a spontaneous transformation of an elementary particle into two or more different particles. **10.** *Physics.* a gradual decrease of a stored charge, current, etc., when the source of energy has been removed. —de'**cayable** *adj.*

decease (di'siːs) *n.* **1.** a more formal word for **death.** ~*vb.* **2.** (*intr.*) a more formal word for **die**[1].

deceased (di'siːst) *adj.* **a.** a more formal word for **dead** (sense 1). **b.** (*as n.*): *the deceased.*

deceit (di'siːt) *n.* **1.** the act or practice of deceiving. **2.** a statement, act, or device intended to mislead; fraud; trick. **3.** a tendency to deceive.

deceitful (di'siːtful) *adj.* full of deceit.

deceive (di'siːv) *vb.* (*tr.*) **1.** to mislead by deliberate misrepresentation or lies. **2.** to delude (oneself). **3.** *Arch.* to disappoint. —de'**ceivable** *adj.* —de'**ceiver** *n.*

decelerate (diː'sɛləˌreit) *vb.* to slow down or cause to slow down. —deˌ**celer'ation** *n.* —de'**celerˌator** *n.*

December (di'sɛmbə) *n.* the twelfth month of the year, consisting of 31 days.

decencies ('diːsənsiz) *pl. n.* **1. the.** those things that are considered necessary for a decent life. **2.** the proprieties.

decency ('diːsənsi) *n., pl.* **-cies. 1.** conformity to the prevailing standards of propriety, morality, modesty, etc. **2.** the quality of being decent.

decennial (di'sɛniəl) *adj.* **1.** lasting for ten years. **2.** occurring every ten years. ~*n.* **3.** a tenth anniversary. —de'**cennially** *adv.*

decent ('diːsənt) *adj.* **1.** polite or respectable. **2.** proper and suitable; fitting. **3.** conforming to conventions of sexual behaviour; not indecent. **4.** free of oaths, blasphemy, etc. **5.** good or adequate: *a decent wage.* **6.** *Inf.* kind; generous. **7.** *Inf.* sufficiently clothed to be seen by other people: *are you decent?* —'**decently** *adv.*

THESAURUS

ments, litter, pieces, remains, rubbish, rubble, ruins, waste, wreck, wreckage

debt 1. arrears, bill, claim, commitment, debit, due, duty, liability, obligation, score **2. in debt** accountable, beholden, in arrears, in hock (*Inf., chiefly U.S.*), in the red (*Inf.*), liable, owing, responsible

debtor borrower, defaulter, insolvent, mortgagor

debunk cut down to size, deflate, disparage, expose, lampoon, mock, puncture, ridicule, show up

debut beginning, bow, coming out, entrance, first appearance, inauguration, initiation, introduction, launching, presentation

decadence corruption, debasement, decay, decline, degeneration, deterioration, dissipation, dissolution, fall, perversion, retrogression

decadent corrupt, debased, debauched, decaying, declining, degenerate, degraded, depraved, dissolute, immoral, self-indulgent

decant drain, draw off, pour out, tap

decapitate behead, execute, guillotine

decay *v.* **1.** atrophy, crumble, decline, degenerate, deteriorate, disintegrate, dissolve,

dwindle, moulder, shrivel, sink, spoil, wane, waste away, wear away, wither **2.** corrode, decompose, mortify, perish, putrefy, rot ~*n.* **3.** atrophy, collapse, decadence, decline, degeneracy, degeneration, deterioration, dying, fading, failing, wasting, withering **4.** caries, cariosity, decomposition, gangrene, mortification, perishing, putrefaction, putrescence, putridity, rot, rotting

decayed bad, carious, carrion, corroded, decomposed, perished, putrefied, putrid, rank, rotten, spoiled, wasted, withered

decaying crumbling, deteriorating, disintegrating, gangrenous, perishing, putrefacient, rotting, wasting away, wearing away

decease 1. *n.* death, demise, departure, dissolution, dying, release **2.** *v.* cease, die, expire, pass away *or* on *or* over, perish

deceased *adj.* dead, defunct, departed, expired, finished, former, late, lifeless, lost

deceit 1. artifice, cheating, chicanery, craftiness, cunning, deceitfulness, deception, dissimulation, double-dealing, duplicity, fraud, fraudulence, guile, hypocrisy, imposition, pretence, slyness, treachery, trickery,

underhandedness **2.** artifice, blind, cheat, chicanery, deception, duplicity, fake, feint, fraud, imposture, misrepresentation, pretence, ruse, sham, shift, stratagem, subterfuge, swindle, trick, wile

deceitful counterfeit, crafty, deceiving, deceptive, designing, dishonest, disingenuous, double-dealing, duplicitous, fallacious, false, fraudulent, guileful, hypocritical, illusory, insincere, knavish (*Archaic*), sneaky, treacherous, tricky, two-faced, underhand, untrustworthy

deceive 1. bamboozle (*Inf.*), beguile, betray, cheat, con (*Sl.*), cozen, delude, disappoint, double-cross (*Inf.*), dupe, ensnare, entrap, fool, hoax, hoodwink, impose upon, lead (someone) on (*Inf.*), mislead, outwit, pull a fast one (*Sl.*), pull the wool over (someone's) eyes, swindle, take for a ride (*Inf.*), take in (*Inf.*), trick **2. be deceived by** be made a fool of, be taken in (by), be the dupe of, bite, fall for, fall into a trap, swallow, swallow hook, line, and sinker (*Inf.*), take the bait

decency appropriateness, civility, correctness, courtesy, decorum, etiquette, fitness, good form, good manners, modesty,

decentralize *or* **-ise** (diːˈsɛntrəˌlaɪz) *vb.* **1.** to reorganize into smaller more autonomous units. **2.** to disperse (a concentration, as of industry or population). —**deˈcentralist** *n.*, *adj.* —**deˌcentraliˈzation** *or* **-iˈsation** *n.*

deception (dɪˈsɛpʃən) *n.* **1.** the act of deceiving or the state of being deceived. **2.** something that deceives; trick.

deceptive (dɪˈsɛptɪv) *adj.* likely or designed to deceive; misleading. —**deˈceptively** *adv.* —**deˈceptiveness** *n.*

deci- *prefix.* denoting one tenth: *decimetre.* Symbol: d

decibel (ˈdɛsɪˌbɛl) *n.* **1.** a unit for comparing two currents, voltages, or power levels, equal to one tenth of a bel. **2.** a similar unit for measuring the intensity of a sound. Abbrev.: **dB**

decide (dɪˈsaɪd) *vb.* **1.** (*may take a clause or an infinitive as object;* when *intr.,* sometimes foll. by *on* or *about*) to reach a decision: *decide what you want; he decided to go.* **2.** (*tr.*) to cause to reach a decision. **3.** (*tr.*) to determine or settle (a contest or question). **4.** (*tr.*) to influence decisively the outcome of (a contest or question). **5.** (*intr.;* foll. by *for* or *against*) to pronounce a formal verdict. —**deˈcidable** *adj.* —**deˈcider** *n.*

decided (dɪˈsaɪdɪd) *adj.* (*prenominal*) **1.** unmistakable. **2.** determined; resolute: *a decided effort.* —**deˈcidedly** *adv.* —**deˈcidedness** *n.*

deciduous (dɪˈsɪdjʊəs) *adj.* **1.** (of trees and shrubs) shedding all leaves annually at the end of the growing season. Cf. **evergreen.** **2.** (of antlers, teeth, etc.) being shed at the end of a period of growth. —**deˈciduousness** *n.*

decilitre *or U.S.* **deciliter** (ˈdɛsɪˌliːtə) *n.* a metric measure of volume equivalent to one tenth of a litre.

decimal (ˈdɛsɪməl) *n.* **1.** Also called: **decimal fraction.** a fraction that has an unwritten denominator of a power of ten. It is indicated by a decimal point to the left of the numerator: *.2=2/10.* **2.** any number used in the decimal system. ~*adj.* **3. a.** relating to or using powers of ten. **b.** of the base ten. **4.** (*prenominal*) expressed as a decimal. —**ˈdecimally** *adv.*

decimal currency *n.* a system of currency in which the monetary units are parts or powers of ten.

decimalize *or* **-ise** (ˈdɛsɪməˌlaɪz) *vb.* to change (a system, number, etc.) to the decimal system. —**ˌdecimaliˈzation** *or* **-iˈsation** *n.*

decimal point *n.* a full stop or a raised full stop placed between the integral and fractional parts of a number in the decimal system.

▷ **Usage.** Conventions relating to the use of the decimal point are confused. The IX General Conference on Weights and Measures resolved in 1948 that the decimal point should be a point on the line or a comma, but not a centre dot. It also resolved that figures could be grouped in threes about the decimal point, but that no point or comma should be used for this purpose. These conventions are adopted in this dictionary. However, the Decimal Currency Board recommended that for sums of money the centre dot should be used as the decimal point and that the comma should be used as the thousand

marker. Moreover, in some countries the position is reversed, the comma being used as the decimal point and the dot as the thousand marker.

decimal system *n.* **1.** the number system in general use, having a base of ten, in which numbers are expressed by combinations of the ten digits 0 to 9. **2.** a system of measurement in which the multiple and submultiple units are related to a basic unit by powers of ten.

decimate (ˈdɛsɪˌmeɪt) *vb.* (*tr.*) **1.** to destroy or kill a large proportion of. **2.** (esp. in the ancient Roman army) to kill every tenth man of (a mutinous section). —ˌdeciˈmation *n.* —ˈdeciˌmator *n.*

decimetre *or U.S.* **decimeter** (ˈdɛsɪˌmiːtə) *n.* one tenth of a metre. Symbol: **dm**

decipher (dɪˈsaɪfə) *vb.* (*tr.*) **1.** to determine the meaning of (something obscure or illegible). **2.** to convert from code into plain text; decode. —**deˈcipherable** *adj.* —**deˈcipherment** *n.*

decision (dɪˈsɪʒən) *n.* **1.** a judgment, conclusion, or resolution reached or given; verdict. **2.** the act of making up one's mind. **3.** firmness of purpose or character; determination.

decisive (dɪˈsaɪsɪv) *adj.* **1.** influential; conclusive. **2.** characterized by the ability to make decisions, esp. quickly; resolute. —**deˈcisively** *adv.* —**deˈcisiveness** *n.*

deck (dɛk) *n.* **1.** *Naut.* any of various platforms built into a vessel. **2.** a similar platform, as in a bus. **3. a.** the horizontal platform that supports the turntable and pick-up of a gramophone. **b.** See **tape deck.** **4.** a pack of playing cards. **5.** *Computers.* a collection of punched cards relevant to a particular program. **6.** *Sl.* a packet of a narcotic drug. **7.** the flat top part of a skateboard. **8. clear the decks.** *Inf.* to prepare for action, as by removing obstacles. **9. hit the deck.** *Inf.* **a.** to fall to the ground, esp. to avoid injury. **b.** to prepare for action. **c.** to get out of bed. ~*vb.* (*tr.*) **10.** (often foll. by *out*) to dress or decorate. **11.** to build a deck on (a vessel).

deck chair *n.* a folding chair consisting of a wooden frame suspending a length of canvas.

-decker *adj.* (*in combination*): having a certain specified number of levels or layers: *a double-decker bus.*

deck hand *n.* **1.** a seaman assigned duties on the deck of a ship. **2.** (in Britain) a seaman who has seen sea duty for at least one year. **3.** a helper aboard a yacht.

deckle edge *n.* **1.** the rough edge of paper made in a deckle, often left as ornamentation. **2.** an imitation of this. —**ˈdeckle-ˈedged** *adj.*

declaim (dɪˈkleɪm) *vb.* **1.** to make (a speech, statement, etc.) loudly and in a rhetorical manner. **2.** to speak lines from (a play, poem, etc.) with studied eloquence. **3.** (*intr.;* foll. by *against*) to protest (against) loudly and publicly. —**deˈclaimer** *n.* —ˌdeclaˈmation *n.* —**declamatory** (dɪˈklæmətərɪ) *adj.*

declaration (ˌdɛkləˈreɪʃən) *n.* **1.** an explicit or emphatic statement. **2.** a formal statement or announcement. **3.** the act of declaring. **4.** the ruling of a judge or court on a question of law. **5.** *Law.* an unsworn statement of a witness admissible in evidence under certain conditions.

THESAURUS

propriety, respectability, seemliness

decent 1. appropriate, becoming, befitting, chaste, comely, *comme il faut*, decorous, delicate, fit, fitting, modest, nice, polite, presentable, proper, pure, respectable, seemly, suitable 2. acceptable, adequate, ample, average, competent, fair, passable, reasonable, satisfactory, sufficient, tolerable 3. accommodating, courteous, friendly, generous, gracious, helpful, kind, obliging, thoughtful

deception 1. craftiness, cunning, deceit, deceitfulness, deceptiveness, dissimulation, duplicity, fraud, fraudulence, guile, hypocrisy, imposition, insincerity, legerdemain, treachery, trickery 2. artifice, bluff, cheat, decoy, feint, fraud, hoax, illusion, imposture, leg-pull (*Brit. inf.*), lie, ruse, sham, snare, stratagem, subterfuge, trick, wile

deceptive ambiguous, deceitful, delusive, dishonest, fake, fallacious, false, fraudulent, illusory, misleading, mock, specious, spurious, unreliable

decide adjudge, adjudicate, choose, come

to a conclusion, commit oneself, conclude, decree, determine, elect, end, make a decision, make up one's mind, purpose, reach *or* come to a decision, resolve, settle

decided 1. absolute, categorical, certain, clear-cut, definite, distinct, express, indisputable, positive, pronounced, unambiguous, undeniable, undisputed, unequivocal, unquestionable 2. assertive, decisive, deliberate, determined, emphatic, firm, resolute, strong-willed, unfaltering, unhesitating

decidedly absolutely, certainly, clearly, decisively, distinctly, downright, positively, unequivocally, unmistakably

deciding chief, conclusive, critical, crucial, decisive, determining, influential, prime, principal, significant

decipher construe, crack, decode, deduce, explain, figure out (*Inf.*), interpret, make out, read, reveal, solve, understand, unfold, unravel

decision 1. arbitration, conclusion, finding, judgment, outcome, resolution, result, ruling, sentence, settlement, verdict 2. deci-

siveness, determination, firmness, purpose, purposefulness, resoluteness, resolution, resolve, strength of mind *or* will

decisive 1. absolute, conclusive, critical, crucial, definite, definitive, fateful, final, influential, momentous, positive, significant 2. decided, determined, firm, forceful, incisive, resolute, strong-minded, trenchant

deck *v.* 1. adorn, apparel (*Archaic*), array, attire, beautify, bedeck, bedight (*Archaic*), bedizen (*Archaic*), clothe, decorate, dress, embellish, festoon, garland, grace, ornament, trim 2. **deck up** *or* **out** doll up (*Sl.*), prettify, pretty up, prink, rig out, tog up *or* out, trick out

declaim 1. harangue, hold forth, lecture, orate, perorate, proclaim, rant, recite, speak, spiel (*Inf.*) 2. **declaim against** attack, decry, denounce, inveigh, rail

declamation address, harangue, lecture, oration, rant, recitation, speech, tirade

6. *Cricket.* the voluntary closure of an innings before all ten wickets have fallen. **7.** *Contract bridge.* the final contract. **8.** a statement or inventory of goods, etc., submitted for tax assessment.

declare (dɪˈklɛə) *vb.* (*mainly tr.*) **1.** (*may take a clause as object*) to make clearly known or announce officially: *war was declared.* **2.** to state officially that (a person, fact, etc.) is as specified: *he declared him fit.* **3.** (*may take a clause as object*) to state emphatically; assert. **4.** to show, reveal, or manifest. **5.** (*intr.; often foll. by for or against*) to make known one's choice or opinion. **6.** to make a statement of (dutiable goods, etc.). **7.** (*also intr.*) *Cards.* **a.** to display (cards) on the table so as to add to one's score. **b.** to decide (the trump suit) by making the winning bid. **8.** (*intr.*) *Cricket.* to close an innings voluntarily before all ten wickets have fallen. **9.** to authorize payment of (a dividend). —**deˈclarable** *adj.* —**declarative** (dɪˈklærətɪv) *adj.* —**deˈclarer** *n.*

declassify (diːˈklæsɪˌfaɪ) *vb.* -**fying**, -**fied**. (*tr.*) to release (a document or information) from the security list. —**deˌclassifiˈcation** *n.*

declension (dɪˈklɛnʃən) *n.* **1.** *Grammar.* **a.** inflection of nouns, pronouns, or adjectives for case, number, and gender. **b.** the complete set of the inflections of such a word. **2.** a decline or deviation. **3.** a downward slope. —**deˈclensional** *adj.*

declination (ˌdɛklɪˈneɪʃən) *n.* **1.** *Astron.* the angular distance of a star, planet, etc., north or south from the celestial equator. Symbol: δ. **2.** the angle made by a compass needle with the direction of the geographical north pole. **3.** a refusal, esp. a courteous or formal one. —ˌdecliˈnational *adj.*

decline (dɪˈklaɪn) *vb.* **1.** to refuse to do or accept (something), esp. politely. **2.** (*intr.*) to grow smaller; diminish. **3.** to slope or cause to slope downwards. **4.** (*intr.*) to deteriorate gradually. **5.** *Grammar.* to list the inflections of (a noun, adjective, or pronoun), or (of a noun, adjective, or pronoun) to be inflected for number, case, or gender. ~*n.* **6.** gradual deterioration or loss. **7.** a movement downward; diminution. **8.** a downward slope. **9.** *Arch.* any slowly progressive disease, such as tuberculosis. —**deˈclinable** *adj.* —**deˈcliner** *n.*

declivity (dɪˈklɪvɪtɪ) *n.*, *pl.* -**ties.** a downward slope, esp. of the ground. —**deˈclivitous** *adj.*

declutch (diːˈklʌtʃ) *vb.* (*intr.*) to disengage the clutch of a motor vehicle.

decoct (dɪˈkɒkt) *vb.* to extract (the essence or active principle) from (a medicinal or similar substance) by boiling. —**deˈcoction** *n.*

decode (diːˈkəʊd) *vb.* to convert from code into ordinary language. —**deˈcoder** *n.*

decoke (diːˈkəʊk) *vb.* (*tr.*) another word for **decarbonize.**

décolletage (ˌdeɪkɒlˈtɑːʒ) *n.* a low-cut dress or neckline.

décolleté (deɪˈkɒlteɪ) *adj.* **1.** (of a woman's garment) low-cut. **2.** wearing a low-cut garment.

decolonize or -**ise** (diːˈkɒləˌnaɪz) *vb.* (*tr.*) to grant independence to (a colony). —**deˌcoloniˈzation** or -**isˈation** *n.*

decompose (ˌdiːkəmˈpəʊz) *vb.* **1.** to break down or be broken down into constituent elements by bacterial or fungal action; rot. **2.** *Chem.* to break down or cause to break down into simpler chemical compounds. **3.** to break up or separate into constituent parts. —**decomposition** (ˌdiːkɒmpəˈzɪʃən) *n.*

decompress (ˌdiːkəmˈprɛs) *vb.* **1.** to relieve or be relieved of pressure. **2.** to return (a diver, etc.) to a condition of normal atmospheric pressure or to be returned to such a condition. —ˌdecomˈpression *n.*

decompression sickness or **illness** *n.* a disorder characterized by severe pain, cramp, and difficulty in breathing, caused by a sudden and substantial change in atmospheric pressure.

decongestant (ˌdiːkənˈdʒɛstənt) *adj.* **1.** relieving congestion, esp. nasal congestion. ~*n.* **2.** a decongestant drug.

decontaminate (ˌdiːkənˈtæmɪˌneɪt) *vb.* (*tr.*) to render harmless by the removal or neutralization of poisons, radioactivity, etc. —ˌdeconˌtamiˈnation *n.*

décor or **decor** (ˈdeɪkɔː) *n.* **1.** a style or scheme of interior decoration, furnishings, etc., as in a room or house. **2.** stage decoration; scenery.

decorate (ˈdɛkəˌreɪt) *vb.* **1.** (*tr.*) to ornament; adorn. **2.** to paint or wallpaper. **3.** (*tr.*) to confer a mark of distinction, esp. a medal, upon. —**decorative** *adj.* —**ˈdecoˌrator** *n.*

Decorated style *n.* a 14th-century style of English architecture characterized by geometrical tracery and floral decoration.

decoration (ˌdɛkəˈreɪʃən) *n.* **1.** an addition that renders something more attractive or ornate. **2.** the act or art of decorating. **3.** a medal, etc., conferred as a mark of honour.

decorous (ˈdɛkərəs) *adj.* characterized by propriety in manners, conduct, etc. —**ˈdecorously** *adv.* —**ˈdecorousness** *n.*

decorum (dɪˈkɔːrəm) *n.* **1.** propriety, esp. in behaviour or conduct. **2.** a requirement of correct behaviour in polite society.

decoy *n.* (ˈdiːkɔɪ, dɪˈkɔɪ). **1.** a person or thing used to lure someone into danger. **2.** *Mil.* something designed to deceive an enemy. **3.** a bird or animal, or an image of one, used to lure game into a trap or within shooting range. **4.** a place into which game can be lured for capture. ~*vb.* (dɪˈkɔɪ). **5.** to lure or be lured by or as if by means of a decoy. **6.** (*tr.*) *Canad.* another word for **deke.**

decrease *vb.* (dɪˈkriːs). **1.** to diminish or cause to diminish in size, strength, etc. ~*n.* (ˈdiːkriːs, dɪˈkriːs). **2.** a

---

THESAURUS

declaration 1. acknowledgment, affirmation, assertion, attestation, averment, avowal, deposition, disclosure, protestation, revelation, statement, testimony **2.** announcement, edict, manifesto, notification, proclamation, profession, promulgation, pronouncement, pronunciamento

declarative, declaratory affirmative, definite, demonstrative, enunciatory, explanatory, expository, expressive, positive

declare 1. affirm, announce, assert, attest, aver, avow, certify, claim, confirm, maintain, proclaim, profess, pronounce, state, swear, testify, validate **2.** confess, convey, disclose, make known, manifest, reveal, show

decline v. **1.** avoid, deny, forgo, refuse, reject, say 'no', send one's regrets, turn down **2.** decrease, diminish, dwindle, ebb, fade, fail, fall, fall off, flag, lessen, shrink, sink, wane ~n. **3.** abatement, diminution, downturn, dwindling, falling off, lessening, recession, slump ~v. **4.** decay, degenerate, deteriorate, droop, languish, pine, weaken, worsen ~n. **5.** decay, decrepitude, degeneration, deterioration, enfeeblement, failing, senility, weakening, worsening **6.** *Archaic* consumption,

phthisis, tuberculosis ~v. **7.** descend, dip, sink, slant, slope ~n. **8.** declivity, hill, incline, slope

decompose 1. break up, crumble, decay, fall apart, fester, putrefy, rot, spoil **2.** analyse, atomize, break down, break up, decompound, disintegrate, dissect, dissolve, distil, separate

decomposition atomization, breakdown, corruption, decay, disintegration, dissolution, division, putrefaction, putrescence, putridity, rot

décor colour scheme, decoration, furnishing style, ornamentation

decorate 1. adorn, beautify, bedeck, deck, embellish, enrich, grace, ornament, trim **2.** colour, do up (*Inf.*), furbish, paint, paper, renovate, wallpaper **3.** cite, honour, pin a medal on

decoration 1. adornment, beautification, elaboration, embellishment, enrichment, garnishing, ornamentation, trimming **2.** arabesque, bauble, curlicue, falderal, flounce, flourish, frill, furbelow, garnish, ornament, scroll, spangle, trimmings, trinket **3.** award, badge, colours, emblem, garter, medal, order, ribbon, star

decorative adorning, arty-crafty, beauti-

fying, enhancing, fancy, nonfunctional, ornamental, pretty

decorous appropriate, becoming, befitting, comely, *comme il faut*, correct, decent, dignified, fit, mannerly, polite, proper, refined, sedate, seemly, staid, suitable, well-behaved

decorum behaviour, breeding, courtliness, decency, deportment, dignity, etiquette, gentility, good grace, good manners, gravity, politeness, politesse, propriety, protocol, punctilio, respectability, seemliness

decoy 1. *n.* attraction, bait, ensnarement, enticement, inducement, lure, pretence, trap **2.** *v.* allure, bait, deceive, ensnare, entice, entrap, inveigle, lure, seduce, tempt

decrease 1. *v.* abate, contract, curtail, cut down, decline, diminish, drop, dwindle, ease, fall off, lessen, lower, peter out, reduce, shrink, slacken, subside, wane **2.** *n.* abatement, contraction, cutback, decline, diminution, downturn, dwindling, ebb, falling off, lessening, loss, reduction, shrinkage, subsidence

diminution; reduction. **3.** the amount by which something has been diminished. **—de'creasingly** *adv.*

decree (dɪ'kriː) *n.* **1.** an edict, law, etc., made by someone in authority. **2.** an order or judgment of a court. ~*vb.* **decreeing, decreed. 3.** to order, adjudge, or ordain by decree.

decree absolute *n.* the final decree in divorce proceedings, which leaves the parties free to remarry. Cf. **decree nisi.**

decree nisi ('naɪsaɪ) *n.* a provisional decree, esp. in divorce proceedings, which will later be made absolute unless cause is shown why it should not. Cf. **decree absolute.**

decrepit (dɪ'krɛpɪt) *adj.* **1.** enfeebled by old age; infirm. **2.** broken down or worn out by hard or long use; dilapidated. **—de'crepi₁tude** *n.*

decrescendo (ˌdiːkrɪ'ʃɛndəu) *n.* another word for **diminuendo.**

decretal (dɪ'kriːtəl) *n.* **1.** *R.C. Church.* a papal decree; edict on doctrine or church law. ~*adj.* **2.** of or relating to a decree.

decry (dɪ'kraɪ) *vb.* **-crying, -cried.** (*tr.*) **1.** to express open disapproval of; disparage. **2.** to depreciate by proclamation: *to decry obsolete coinage.*

dedicate ('dɛdɪˌkeɪt) *vb.* (*tr.*) **1.** (often foll. by *to*) to devote (oneself, one's time, etc.) wholly to a special purpose or cause. **2.** (foll. by *to*) to address (a book, performance, etc.) to (a person, cause, etc.) as a token of affection or respect. **3.** to set apart for a deity or for sacred uses. **—'dedi₁cator** *n.* **—dedicatory** ('dɛdɪˌkeɪtərɪ, 'dɛdɪkətərɪ) *or* **'dedi₁cative** *adj.*

dedicated ('dɛdɪˌkeɪtɪd) *adj.* **1.** devoted to a particular purpose or cause. **2.** *Computers.* designed to fulfil one function.

dedication (ˌdɛdɪ'keɪʃən) *n.* **1.** the act of dedicating or being dedicated. **2.** an inscription prefixed to a book, etc., dedicating it to a person or thing. **3.** wholehearted devotion, esp. to a career, ideal, etc. **—ˌdedi'cational** *adj.*

deduce (dɪ'djuːs) *vb.* (*tr.*) **1.** (*may take a clause as object*) to reach (a conclusion) by reasoning; conclude (that); infer. **2.** *Arch.* to trace the origin or derivation of. **—de'ducible** *adj.*

deduct (dɪ'dʌkt) *vb.* (*tr.*) to take away or subtract (a number, quantity, part, etc.).

deductible (dɪ'dʌktɪbəl) *adj.* **1.** capable of being deducted. **2.** *U.S.* short for **tax-deductible.** ~*n.* **3.** *Insurance.* the U.S. name for **excess** (sense 5).

deduction (dɪ'dʌkʃən) *n.* **1.** the act or process of deducting or subtracting. **2.** something that is or may be deducted. **3.** *Logic.* **a.** a process of reasoning by which a specific conclusion necessarily follows from a set of general premisses. **b.** a logical conclusion reached by this process. **—de'ductive** *adj.*

deed (diːd) *n.* **1.** something that is done or performed; act. **2.** a notable achievement. **3.** action as opposed to words. **4.** *Law.* a legal document signed, sealed, and delivered to effect a conveyance or transfer of property or to create a legal contract. ~*vb.* **5.** (*tr.*) *U.S.* to convey or transfer (property) by deed.

deed box *n.* a strong box in which deeds and other documents are kept.

deed poll *n. Law.* a deed made by one party only, esp. one by which a person changes his name.

deejay ('diːˌdʒeɪ) *n.* an informal name for **disc jockey.**

deem (diːm) *vb.* (*tr.*) to judge or consider.

deemster ('diːmstə) *n.* the title of one of the two justices in the Isle of Man. Also called: **dempster.**

deep (diːp) *adj.* **1.** extending or situated far down from a surface: *a deep pool.* **2.** extending or situated far inwards, backwards, or sideways. **3.** *Cricket.* far from the pitch: *the deep field.* **4.** (*postpositive*) of a specified dimension downwards, inwards, or backwards: *six feet deep.* **5.** coming from or penetrating to a great depth. **6.** difficult to understand; abstruse. **7.** intellectually demanding: *a deep discussion.* **8.** of great intensity: *deep trouble.* **9.** (*postpositive;* foll. by *in*) absorbed (by); immersed (in): *deep in study.* **10.** very cunning; devious. **11.** mysterious: *a deep secret.* **12.** (of a colour) having an intense or dark hue. **13.** low in pitch: *a deep voice.* **14. deep down.** *Inf.* in reality, esp. as opposed to appearance. **15. go off the deep end.** *Inf.* **a.** to become hysterical; lose one's temper. **b.** *Chiefly U.S.* to act rashly. **16. in deep water.** *Inf.* in a tricky position or in trouble. ~*n.* **17.** any deep place on land or under water. **18. the deep. a.** a poetic term for the **ocean. b.** *Cricket.* the area of the field relatively far from the pitch. **19.** the most profound, intense, or central part: *the deep of winter.* **20.** a vast extent, as of space or time. ~*adv.* **21.** far on in time; late: *they worked deep into the night.* **22.** profoundly or intensely. **—'deeply** *adv.* **—'deepness** *n.*

deepen ('diːpən) *vb.* to make or become deep, deeper, or more intense. **—'deepener** *n.*

deepfreeze (ˌdiːp'friːz) *n.* **1.** a refrigerator in which food, etc., is stored for long periods at temperatures below freezing. **2.** storage in a deepfreeze. **3.** *Inf.* a state of suspended activity. ~*vb.* **deep-freeze, -froze** *or* **-freezed, -frozen** *or* **-freezed. 4.** (*tr.*) to freeze or keep in a deepfreeze.

deep-laid *adj.* (of a plot or plan) carefully worked out and kept secret.

deep-rooted *or* **deep-seated** *adj.* (of ideas, beliefs, etc.) firmly fixed or held; ingrained.

deer (dɪə) *n., pl.* **deer** *or* **deers.** any of a family of hoofed, ruminant mammals including reindeer, elk, and roe deer, typically having antlers in the male. Related adj.: **cervine.**

deerskin ('dɪəˌskɪn) *n.* **a.** the hide of a deer. **b.** (*as modifier*): *a deerskin jacket.*

deerstalker ('dɪəˌstɔːkə) *n.* **1.** a person who stalks deer, esp. in order to shoot them. **2.** a hat, peaked in front and behind, with earflaps usually tied together on the top. **—'deer₁stalking** *adj., n.*

THESAURUS

decree 1. *n.* act, command, dictum, edict, enactment, law, mandate, order, ordinance, precept, proclamation, regulation, ruling, statute 2. *v.* command, decide, determine, dictate, enact, lay down, ordain, order, prescribe, proclaim, pronounce, rule

decrepit 1. aged, crippled, debilitated, doddering, effete, feeble, frail, incapacitated, infirm, superannuated, wasted, weak 2. antiquated, battered, broken-down, deteriorated, dilapidated, ramshackle, rickety, run-down, tumble-down, weather-beaten, worn-out

decry abuse, belittle, blame, censure, condemn, criticize, cry down, denounce, depreciate, derogate, detract, devalue, discredit, disparage, rail against, run down, traduce, underestimate, underrate, undervalue

dedicate 1. commit, devote, give over to, pledge, surrender 2. address, assign, inscribe, offer 3. bless, consecrate, hallow, sanctify, set apart

dedicated committed, devoted, enthusiastic, given over to, purposeful, single-minded, sworn, wholehearted, zealous

dedication 1. adherence, allegiance, commitment, devotedness, devotion, faithfulness, loyalty, single-mindedness, wholeheartedness 2. address, inscription, message 3. consecration, hallowing, sanctification

deduce conclude, derive, draw, gather, glean, infer, reason, take to mean, understand

deduct decrease by, knock off (*Inf.*), reduce by, remove, subtract, take away, take from, take off, take out, withdraw

deduction 1. assumption, conclusion, consequence, corollary, finding, inference, reasoning, result 2. abatement, allowance, decrease, diminution, discount, reduction, subtraction, withdrawal

deed 1. achievement, act, action, exploit, fact, feat, performance, reality, truth 2. *Law* contract, document, indenture, instrument, title, title deed, transaction

deem account, believe, conceive, consider, esteem, estimate, hold, imagine, judge, reckon, regard, suppose, think

deep *adj.* 1. abyssal, bottomless, broad, far, profound, unfathomable, wide, yawning 2. abstract, abstruse, arcane, esoteric, hidden, mysterious, obscure, recondite, secret 3. acute, discerning, learned, penetrating, sagacious, wise 4. artful, astute, canny, cunning, designing, devious, insidious, knowing, scheming, shrewd 5. extreme, grave, great, intense, profound 6. absorbed, engrossed, immersed, lost, preoccupied, rapt 7. *Of a colour* dark, intense, rich, strong, vivid 8. *Of a sound* bass, booming, full-toned, low, low-pitched, resonant, sonorous ~*n.* 9. *Usually preceded by* **the** briny (*Inf.*), high seas, main, ocean, sea 10. culmination, dead, middle, mid point ~*adv.* 11. deeply, far down, far into, late

deepen 1. dig out, dredge, excavate, hollow, scoop out, scrape out 2. grow, increase, intensify, magnify, reinforce, strengthen

deeply 1. completely, gravely, profoundly, seriously, severely, thoroughly, to the heart, to the quick 2. acutely, affectingly, distressingly, feelingly, intensely, mournfully, movingly, passionately, sadly

deep-rooted *or* **deep-seated** confirmed, entrenched, fixed, ineradicable, ingrained, inveterate, rooted, settled, subconscious, unconscious

de-escalate (diːˈɛskəˌleɪt) *vb.* to reduce the level or intensity of. —**de-ˌescaˈlation** *n.*

deface (dɪˈfeɪs) *vb.* (*tr.*) to spoil or mar the surface or appearance of; disfigure. —**deˈfaceable** *adj.* —**deˈfacement** *n.* —**deˈfacer** *n.*

de facto (deɪ ˈfæktəʊ) *adv.* 1. in fact. ~*adj.* 2. existing in fact, whether legally recognized or not: *a de facto regime.* Cf. **de jure.** ~*n.* 3. *N.Z. & Austral.* a de facto wife or husband.

defalcate (ˈdiːfælˌkeɪt) *vb.* (*intr.*) *Law.* to misuse or misappropriate property or funds entrusted to one. —**ˈdefalˌcator** *n.*

defame (dɪˈfeɪm) *vb.* (*tr.*) to attack the good name or reputation of; slander; libel. —**defamation** (ˌdɛfəˈmeɪʃən) *n.* —**defamatory** (dɪˈfæmətərɪ) *adj.*

default (dɪˈfɔːlt) *n.* 1. a failure to act, esp. a failure to meet a financial obligation or to appear in a court of law at a time specified. 2. absence. 3. **in default of.** through or in the lack or absence of. 4. **judgment by default.** *Law.* a judgment in the plaintiff's favour when the defendant fails to plead or to appear. 5. lack, want, or need. ~*vb.* 6. (*intr.; often foll. by* **on** *or* **in**) to fail to make payment when due. 7. (*intr.*) to fail to fulfil an obligation. 8. *Law.* to lose (a case) by failure to appear in court.

defeat (dɪˈfiːt) *vb.* (*tr.*) 1. to overcome; win a victory over. 2. to thwart or frustrate. 3. *Law.* to render null and void. ~*n.* 4. a defeating or being defeated. —**deˈfeatism** *n.*

defecate (ˈdɛfɪˌkeɪt) *vb.* 1. (*intr.*) to discharge waste from the body through the anus. 2. (*tr.*) to remove impurities from. —**defeˈcation** *n.* —**ˈdefeˌcator** *n.*

defect *n.* (dɪˈfɛkt, ˈdiːfɛkt). 1. a lack of something necessary for completeness; deficiency. 2. an imperfection or blemish. ~*vb.* (dɪˈfɛkt). 3. (*intr.*) to desert one's country, cause, etc., esp. in order to join the opposing forces. —**deˈfection** *n.* —**deˈfector** *n.*

defective (dɪˈfɛktɪv) *adj.* 1. having a defect or flaw; imperfect. 2. (of a person) below the usual standard or level, esp. in intelligence. 3. *Grammar.* lacking the full range of inflections characteristic of its form class.

—**deˈfectiveness** *n.*

defence *or U.S.* **defense** (dɪˈfɛns) *n.* 1. resistance against danger or attack. 2. a person or thing that provides such resistance. 3. a plea, essay, etc., in support of something. 4. military measures or resources protecting a country against an opponent. 5. *Law.* a defendant's denial of the truth of the allegations or charge against him. 6. *Law.* the defendant and his legal advisers collectively. 7. *Sport.* **a.** the action of protecting oneself or part of the playing area against an opponent's attacks. **b.** (*usually preceded by* the) the players in a team whose function is to do this. 8. (*pl.*) fortifications. —**deˈfenceless** *or U.S.* **deˈfenseless** *adj.*

defend (dɪˈfɛnd) *vb.* 1. to protect from harm or danger. 2. (*tr.*) to support in the face of criticism, esp. by argument. 3. to represent (a defendant) in court. 4. *Sport.* to guard (one's goal, etc.) against attack. 5. (*tr.*) to protect (a title, etc.) against a challenge. —**deˈfender** *n.*

defendant (dɪˈfɛndənt) *n.* 1. a person against whom an action or claim is brought in a court of law. Cf. **plaintiff.** ~*adj.* 2. defending.

defensible (dɪˈfɛnsɪbəl) *adj.* capable of being defended, as in war, an argument, etc. —**deˌfensiˈbility** *or* **deˈfensibleness** *n.*

defensive (dɪˈfɛnsɪv) *adj.* 1. intended for defence. 2. rejecting criticisms of oneself. ~*n.* 3. a position of defence. 4. **on the defensive.** in a position of defence, as in being ready to reject criticism. —**deˈfensively** *adv.*

defer¹ (dɪˈfɜː) *vb.* **-ferring, -ferred.** to delay until a future time; postpone. —**deˈferment** *or* **deˈferral** *n.* —**deˈferrer** *n.*

defer² (dɪˈfɜː) *vb.* **-ferring, -ferred.** (*intr.; foll. by* **to**) to yield (to) or comply (with) the wishes or judgments of another.

deference (ˈdɛfərəns) *n.* 1. compliance with the wishes of another. 2. courteous regard; respect.

deferential (ˌdɛfəˈrɛnʃəl) *adj.* showing deference; respectful. —**ˌdeferˈentially** *adv.*

defiance (dɪˈfaɪəns) *n.* 1. open or bold resistance to authority, opposition, or power. 2. a challenge. —**deˈfiant** *adj.*

THESAURUS

deface blemish, deform, destroy, disfigure, impair, injure, mar, mutilate, obliterate, spoil, sully, tarnish, vandalize

defacement blemish, damage, destruction, disfigurement, distortion, impairment, injury, mutilation, vandalism

de facto 1. *adv.* actually, in effect, in fact, in reality, really 2. *adj.* actual, existing, real

defamation aspersion, calumny, character assassination, denigration, disparagement, libel, obloquy, opprobrium, scandal, slander, slur, smear, traducement, vilification

defamatory abusive, calumnious, contumelious, denigrating, derogatory, disparaging, injurious, insulting, libellous, slanderous, vilifying, vituperative

defame asperse, belie, besmirch, blacken, calumniate, cast a slur on, cast aspersions on, denigrate, detract, discredit, disgrace, dishonour, disparage, libel, malign, slander, smear, speak evil of, stigmatize, traduce, vilify, vituperate

default 1. *n.* absence, defect, deficiency, dereliction, failure, fault, lack, lapse, neglect, nonpayment, omission, want 2. *v.* bilk, defraud, dodge, evade, fail, levant (*Brit.*), neglect, rat, swindle, welsh (*Sl.*)

defaulter delinquent, embezzler, levanter (*Brit.*), nonpayer, offender, peculator, welsher (*Sl.*)

defeat *v.* 1. beat, conquer, crush, overpower, overthrow, overwhelm, quell, repulse, rout, subdue, subjugate, vanquish 2. baffle, balk, confound, disappoint, discomfit, foil, frustrate, get the better of, ruin, thwart ~*n.* 3. beating, conquest, debacle, overthrow, repulse, rout, trouncing, vanquishment 4. disappointment, discomfiture, failure, frustration, rebuff, repulse, reverse, setback, thwarting

defeated balked, beaten, bested, check-

mated, conquered, crushed, licked (*Inf.*), overcome, overpowered, overwhelmed, routed, thrashed, thwarted, trounced, vanquished, worsted

defeatist 1. *n.* pessimist, prophet of doom, quitter, submitter, yielder 2. *adj.* pessimistic

defect *n.* 1. blemish, blotch, error, failing, fault, flaw, foible, imperfection, mistake, spot, taint, want 2. absence, default, deficiency, frailty, inadequacy, lack, shortcoming, weakness ~*v.* 3. abandon, apostatize, break faith, change sides, desert, go over, rebel, revolt, tergiversate, walk out on (*Inf.*)

defection abandonment, apostasy, backsliding, dereliction, desertion, rebellion, revolt

defective 1. broken, deficient, faulty, flawed, imperfect, inadequate, incomplete, insufficient, not working, out of order, scant, short 2. abnormal, mentally deficient, retarded, subnormal

defector apostate, deserter, rat (*Inf.*), recreant (*Archaic*), renegade, runagate (*Archaic*), tergiversator, turncoat

defence 1. armament, cover, deterrence, guard, immunity, protection, resistance, safeguard, security, shelter 2. barricade, bastion, buckler, bulwark, buttress, fastness, fortification, rampart, shield 3. apologia, apology, argument, excuse, exoneration, explanation, extenuation, justification, plea, vindication 4. *Law* alibi, case, declaration, denial, plea, pleading, rebuttal, testimony

defenceless endangered, exposed, helpless, naked, powerless, unarmed, unguarded, unprotected, vulnerable, wide open

defend 1. cover, fortify, guard, keep safe, preserve, protect, safeguard, screen, secure, shelter, shield, ward off, watch over 2. assert, champion, endorse, espouse, justify, maintain, plead, speak up for, stand by, stand up

for, support, sustain, uphold, vindicate

defendant appellant, defence, litigant, offender, prisoner at the bar, respondent, the accused

defender 1. bodyguard, escort, guard, protector 2. advocate, champion, patron, sponsor, supporter, vindicator

defensible 1. holdable, impregnable, safe, secure, unassailable 2. justifiable, pardonable, permissible, plausible, tenable, valid, vindicable

defensive averting, defending, on the defensive, opposing, protective, safeguarding, uptight (*Sl.*), watchful, withstanding

defensively at bay, in defence, in self-defence, on guard, on the defensive, suspiciously

defer¹ adjourn, delay, hold over, postpone, procrastinate, prorogue, protract, put off, put on ice, set aside, shelve, suspend, table

defer² accede, bow, capitulate, comply, give in, give way to, respect, submit, yield

deference 1. acquiescence, capitulation, complaisance, compliance, obedience, obeisance, submission, yielding 2. attention, civility, consideration, courtesy, esteem, homage, honour, obeisance, politeness, regard, respect, reverence, thoughtfulness, veneration

deferential civil, complaisant, considerate, courteous, dutiful, ingratiating, obedient, obeisant, obsequious, polite, regardful, respectful, reverential, submissive

deferment, deferral adjournment, delay, moratorium, postponement, putting off, stay, suspension

defiance challenge, confrontation, contempt, contumacy, disobedience, disregard, insolence, insubordination, opposition, provocation, rebelliousness, recalcitrance, spite

defiant aggressive, audacious, bold, chal-

deficiency (dɪ'fɪʃənsɪ) *n., pl.* **-cies.** **1.** the state or quality of being deficient. **2.** a lack or insufficiency; shortage. **3.** a deficit.

deficiency disease *n.* any condition, such as pellagra, beriberi, or scurvy, produced by a lack of vitamins or other essential substances.

deficient (dɪ'fɪʃənt) *adj.* **1.** lacking some essential; incomplete; defective. **2.** inadequate in quantity or supply; insufficient. —**de'ficiently** *adv.*

deficit ('defɪsɪt, dɪ'fɪsɪt) *n.* **1.** the amount by which an actual sum is lower than that expected or required. **2. a.** an excess of liabilities over assets. **b.** an excess of expenditures over revenues.

defile¹ (dɪ'faɪl) *vb.* (*tr.*) **1.** to make foul or dirty; pollute. **2.** to taint; corrupt. **3.** to damage or sully (someone's reputation, etc.). **4.** to make unfit for ceremonial use. **5.** to violate the chastity of. —**de'filement** *n.*

defile² ('diːfaɪl, dɪ'faɪl) *n.* **1.** a narrow pass or gorge. **2.** a single file of soldiers, etc. ~*vb.* **3.** to march in single file.

define (dɪ'faɪn) *vb.* (*tr.*) **1.** to state precisely the meaning of (words, etc.). **2.** to describe the nature of. **3.** to determine the boundary or extent of. **4.** (*often passive*) to delineate the form or outline of. **5.** to fix with precision; specify. —**de'finable** *adj.* —**de'finer** *n.*

definite ('defɪnɪt) *adj.* **1.** clearly defined; exact. **2.** having precise limits or boundaries. **3.** known for certain. —**'definitely** *adv.* —**'definiteness** *n.*

▷ **Usage.** *Definite* and *definitive* should be carefully distinguished. *Definite* indicates precision and firmness, as in *a definite decision. Definitive* includes these senses but also indicates conclusiveness. *A definite answer* indicates a clear and firm answer to a particular question; *a definitive answer* implies an authoritative resolution of a complex question.

definite article *n. Grammar.* a determiner that expresses specificity of reference, such as *the* in English. Cf. **indefinite article.**

definition (ˌdefɪ'nɪʃən) *n.* **1.** a formal and concise statement of the meaning of a word, phrase, etc. **2.** the act of defining. **3.** the act of making clear or definite. **4.** the state of being clearly defined. **5.** a measure of the clarity of an optical, photographic, or television image as characterized by its sharpness and contrast.

definitive (dɪ'fɪnɪtɪv) *adj.* **1.** serving to decide or settle finally. **2.** most reliable or authoritative. **3.** serving to define or outline. **4.** *Zool.* fully developed. **5.** (of postage stamps) permanently on sale. ~*n.* **6.** *Grammar.* a word indicating specificity of reference. —**de'finitively** *adv.*

▷ **Usage.** See at **definite.**

deflate (diː'fleɪt) *vb.* **1.** to collapse through the release of gas. **2.** (*tr.*) to take away the self-esteem or conceit from. **3.** *Econ.* to cause deflation of (an economy, the money supply, etc.). —**de'flator** *n.*

deflation (diː'fleɪʃən) *n.* **1.** a deflating or being deflated. **2.** *Econ.* a reduction in economic activity resulting in lower levels of output, employment, investment, trade, profits, and prices. **3.** the removal of loose rock material, etc., by wind. —**de'flationary** *adj.* —**de'flationist** *n., adj.*

deflect (dɪ'flekt) *vb.* to turn or cause to turn aside from a course; swerve. —**de'flection** *n.* —**de'flector** *n.*

deflower (diː'flaʊə) *vb.* (*tr.*) **1.** to deprive (esp. a woman) of virginity. **2.** to despoil of beauty, innocence, etc. **3.** to rob or despoil of flowers. —ˌ**deflo'ration** *n.*

defoliate (diː'fəʊlɪˌeɪt) *vb.* (*tr.*) to deprive (a plant) of its leaves. —deˌ**foli'ation** *n.*

deform (dɪ'fɔːm) *vb.* **1.** to make or become misshapen or distorted. **2.** (*tr.*) to mar the beauty of; disfigure. **3.** (*tr.*) to subject or be subjected to a stress that causes a change of dimensions. —**de'formable** *adj.* —ˌ**defor'mation** *n.*

deformed (dɪ'fɔːmd) *adj.* **1.** disfigured or misshapen. **2.** morally perverted; warped.

deformity (dɪ'fɔːmɪtɪ) *n., pl.* **-ties.** **1.** a deformed condition. **2.** *Pathol.* a distortion of an organ or part. **3.** a deformed person or thing. **4.** a defect, esp. of the mind or morals; depravity.

defraud (dɪ'frɔːd) *vb.* (*tr.*) to take away or withhold money, rights, property, etc., from (a person) by fraud; swindle. —**de'frauder** *n.*

defray (dɪ'freɪ) *vb.* (*tr.*) to provide money for (costs, expenses, etc.); pay. —**de'frayable** *adj.* —**de'frayal** *or* de'**frayment** *n.*

defrock (diː'frɒk) *vb.* (*tr.*) to deprive (a person in holy orders) of ecclesiastical status; unfrock.

defrost (diː'frɒst) *vb.* **1.** to make or become free of frost or ice. **2.** to thaw, esp. through removal from a refrigerator.

deft (deft) *adj.* quick and neat in movement; nimble; dexterous. —**'deftly** *adv.* —**'deftness** *n.*

defunct (dɪ'fʌŋkt) *adj.* **1.** no longer living; dead or extinct. **2.** no longer operative or valid. —**de'functness** *n.*

defuse *or U.S.* (*sometimes*) **defuze** (diː'fjuːz) *vb.* (*tr.*) **1.** to remove the triggering device of (a bomb, etc.). **2.** to remove the cause of tension from (a crisis, etc.).

defy (dɪ'faɪ) *vb.* **-fying, -fied.** (*tr.*) **1.** to resist openly and boldly. **2.** to elude, esp. in a baffling way. **3.** *Formal.* to challenge (someone to do something); dare. **4.** *Arch.* to invite to do battle or combat. —**de'fier** *n.*

degenerate *vb.* (dɪ'dʒenəˌreɪt). (*intr.*) **1.** to become degenerate. **2.** *Biol.* (of organisms or their parts) to become less specialized or functionally useless. ~*adj.* (dɪ'dʒenərɪt). **3.** having declined or deteriorated to a lower mental, moral, or physical level; degraded; cor-

lenging, contumacious, daring, disobedient, insolent, insubordinate, mutinous, provocative, rebellious, recalcitrant, refractory, truculent

deficiency 1. defect, demerit, failing, fault, flaw, frailty, imperfection, shortcoming, weakness 2. absence, dearth, deficit, inadequacy, insufficiency, lack, scantiness, scarcity, shortage

deficient 1. defective, faulty, flawed, impaired, imperfect, incomplete, inferior, unsatisfactory, weak 2. exiguous, inadequate, insufficient, lacking, meagre, scanty, scarce, short, skimpy, wanting

deficit arrears, default, deficiency, loss, shortage, shortfall

defiled besmirched, desecrated, dishonoured, impure, polluted, profaned, ravished, spoilt, tainted, unclean

define 1. characterize, describe, designate, detail, determine, explain, expound, interpret, specify, spell out 2. bound, circumscribe, delimit, delineate, demarcate, limit, mark out, outline

definite 1. clear, clear-cut, clearly defined, determined, exact, explicit, express, fixed, marked, obvious, particular, precise, specific 2. assured, certain, decided, guaranteed, positive, settled, sure

definitely absolutely, beyond any doubt,

categorically, certainly, clearly, decidedly, easily, far and away, finally, indubitably, obviously, plainly, positively, surely, undeniably, unequivocally, unmistakably, unquestionably, without doubt, without fail, without question

definition 1. clarification, description, elucidation, explanation, exposition, statement of meaning 2. delimitation, delineation, demarcation, determination, fixing, outlining, settling 3. clarity, contrast, distinctness, focus, precision, sharpness

definitive absolute, authoritative, complete, conclusive, decisive, exhaustive, final, perfect, reliable, ultimate

deflate 1. collapse, contract, empty, exhaust, flatten, puncture, shrink, void 2. chasten, dash, debunk (*Inf.*), disconcert, dispirit, humble, humiliate, mortify, put down (*Sl.*), squash, take the wind out of (someone's) sails 3. *Economics* decrease, depreciate, depress, devalue, diminish, reduce

deflect bend, deviate, diverge, glance off, ricochet, shy, sidetrack, slew, swerve, turn, turn aside, twist, veer, wind

deflection aberration, bend, declination, deviation, divergence, drift, refraction, swerve, veer

deform 1. buckle, contort, distort, gnarl, malform, mangle, misshape, twist, warp 2.

cripple, deface, disfigure, injure, maim, mar, mutilate, ruin, spoil

deformed 1. bent, blemished, crippled, crooked, disfigured, distorted, maimed, malformed, mangled, marred, misbegotten, misshapen 2. depraved, gross, offensive, perverted, twisted, warped

deformity 1. abnormality, defect, disfigurement, distortion, irregularity, malformation, misproportion, misshapenness, ugliness 2. corruption, depravity, grossness, hatefulness, vileness

defraud beguile, bilk, cheat, con (*Sl.*), cozen, delude, diddle (*Inf.*), do (*Sl.*), dupe, embezzle, fleece, gull (*Archaic*), gyp (*Sl.*), outwit, pilfer, pull a fast one on (*Inf.*), rip off (*Sl.*), rob, rook (*Sl.*), swindle, trick

deft able, adept, adroit, agile, clever, dexterous, expert, handy, neat, nimble, proficient, skilful

defunct 1. dead, deceased, departed, extinct, gone 2. a dead letter, bygone, expired, inoperative, invalid, nonexistent, not functioning, obsolete, out of commission

defy 1. beard, brave, challenge, confront, contemn, dare, despise, disregard, face, flout, hurl defiance at, provoke, scorn, slight, spurn 2. baffle, defeat, elude, foil, frustrate, repel, repulse, resist, thwart, withstand

rupt. ~*n*. (dɪˈdʒɛnərɪt). **4.** a degenerate person. —**de-ˈgeneracy** *or* **deˈgenerateness** *n.* —**deˈgenerately** *adv.* —**deˈgenerative** *adj.*

degeneration (dɪˌdʒɛnəˈreɪʃən) *n.* **1.** the process of degenerating. **2.** the state of being degenerate. **3.** *Biol.* the loss of specialization, function, or structure by organisms and their parts. **4.** impairment or loss of the function and structure of cells or tissues, as by disease or injury. **5.** *Electronics.* negative feedback of a signal.

degrade (dɪˈgreɪd) *vb.* **1.** (*tr.*) to reduce in worth, character, etc.; disgrace. **2.** (dɪːˈgreɪd) (*tr.*) to reduce in rank or status; demote. **3.** (*tr.*) to reduce in strength, quality, etc. **4.** to reduce or be reduced by erosion or down-cutting, as a land surface or bed of a river. **5.** *Chem.* to decompose into atoms or smaller molecules. —ˌdegraˈdation *n.* —deˈgrader *n.* —deˈgrading *adj.*

degree (dɪˈgriː) *n.* **1.** a stage in a scale of relative amount or intensity: *a high degree of competence.* **2.** an academic award conferred by a university or college on successful completion of a course or as an honorary distinction (**honorary degree**). **3.** any of three categories of seriousness of a burn. **4.** (in the U.S.) any of the categories into which a crime is divided according to its seriousness. **5.** *Genealogy.* a step in a line of descent. **6.** *Grammar.* any of the forms of an adjective used to indicate relative amount or intensity: in English they are *positive*, *comparative*, and *superlative.* **7.** *Music.* any note of a diatonic scale relative to the other notes in that scale. **8.** a unit of temperature on a specified scale. Symbol: °. See also **Celsius scale, Fahrenheit scale.** **9.** a measure of angle equal to one three-hundred-and-sixtieth of the angle traced by one complete revolution of a line about one of its ends. Symbol: °. **10.** a unit of latitude or longitude used to define points on the earth's surface. Symbol: °. **11.** a unit on any of several scales of measurement, as for specific gravity. Symbol: °. **12.** *Maths.* **a.** the highest power or the sum of the powers of any term in a polynomial or by itself: $x^4 + x + 3$ and xyz^2 are of the fourth degree. **b.** the greatest power of the highest order derivative in a differential equation. **13.** *Obs.* a step; rung. **14.** *Arch.* a stage in social status or rank. **15. by degrees.** little by little; gradually. **16. to a degree.** somewhat; rather.

dehisce (dɪˈhɪs) *vb.* (*intr.*) (of fruits, anthers, etc.) to burst open spontaneously, releasing seeds, pollen, etc. —deˈhiscent *adj.*

dehumanize *or* **-ise** (diːˈhjuːməˌnaɪz) *vb.* (*tr.*) **1.** to deprive of human qualities. **2.** to render mechanical, artificial, or routine. —deˌhumaniˈzation *or* **-iˈsation** *n.*

dehydrate (diːˈhaɪdreɪt) *vb.* **1.** to lose or cause to lose water. **2.** to lose or deprive of water, as the body or tissues. —ˌdehyˈdration *n.* —deˈhydrator *n.*

de-ice (diːˈaɪs) *vb.* to free or be freed of ice. —**de-icer** *n.*

deify (ˈdiːɪˌfaɪ, ˈdeɪ-) *vb.* **-fying, -fied.** (*tr.*) **1.** to exalt to the position of a god or personify as a god. **2.** to accord divine honour or worship to. —ˌdeifiˈcation *n.* —ˈdeiˌfier *n.*

deign (deɪn) *vb.* (*tr.*) **1.** to think it fit or worthy of oneself (to do something); condescend. **2.** *Arch.* to vouchsafe.

deism (ˈdiːɪzəm, ˈdeɪ-) *n.* belief in the existence of God based solely on natural reason, without reference to revelation. Cf. **theism.** —ˈdeist *n., adj.* —deˈistic *or* deˈistical *adj.* —deˈistically *adv.*

deity (ˈdiːɪtɪ, ˈdeɪ-) *n., pl.* **-ties.** **1.** a god or goddess. **2.** the state of being divine; godhead. **3.** the rank of a god. **4.** the nature or character of God.

Deity (ˈdiːɪtɪ, ˈdeɪ-) *n.* **the.** God.

déjà vu (ˈdeɪʒæ ˈvuː) *n.* the experience of perceiving a new situation as if it had occurred before.

deject (dɪˈdʒɛkt) *vb.* (*tr.*) to have a depressing effect on; dispirit; dishearten. —deˈjection *n.*

dejected (dɪˈdʒɛktɪd) *adj.* miserable; despondent; downhearted. —deˈjectedly *adv.*

de jure (deɪˈdʒuəreɪ) *adj.* according to law; by right; legally. Cf. **de facto.**

deke (diːk) *Canad. sl. vb.* **1.** (*tr.*) (in ice hockey or box lacrosse) to draw a defending player out of position by faking a shot or movement. ~*n.* **2.** such a shot or movement.

dekko (ˈdɛkəʊ) *n., pl.* **-kos.** *Brit. sl.* a look; glance.

delay (dɪˈleɪ) *vb.* **1.** (*tr.*) to put off to a later time; defer. **2.** (*tr.*) to slow up or cause to be late. **3.** (*intr.*) to be irresolute or put off doing something. **4.** (*intr.*) to linger; dawdle. ~*n.* **5.** a delaying or being delayed. **6.** the interval between one event and another. —deˈlayer *n.*

delectable (dɪˈlɛktəbəl) *adj.* highly enjoyable, esp. pleasing to the taste; delightful. —deˈlectableness *or* deˌlectaˈbility *n.*

delectation (ˌdiːlɛkˈteɪʃən) *n.* pleasure; enjoyment.

delegate *n.* (ˈdɛlɪˌgeɪt, -gɪt). **1.** a person chosen to act for another or others, esp. at a conference or meeting. ~*vb.* (ˈdɛlɪˌgeɪt). **2.** to give (duties, powers, etc.) to another as representative; depute. **3.** (*tr.*) to authorize (a person) as representative. —**delegable** (ˈdɛlɪgəbəl) *adj.*

delegation (ˌdɛlɪˈgeɪʃən) *n.* **1.** a person or group chosen to represent another or others. **2.** a delegating or being delegated.

delete (dɪˈliːt) *vb.* (*tr.*) to remove (something printed or

---

THESAURUS

degenerate 1. *adj.* base, corrupt, debased, debauched, decadent, degenerated, degraded, depraved, deteriorated, dissolute, fallen, immoral, low, mean, perverted 2. *v.* decay, decline, decrease, deteriorate, fall off, lapse, regress, retrogress, rot, sink, slip, worsen

degeneration debasement, decline, degeneracy, descent, deterioration, dissipation, dissolution, regression

degradation 1. abasement, debasement, decadence, decline, degeneracy, degeneration, demotion, derogation, deterioration, downgrading, perversion 2. discredit, disgrace, dishonour, humiliation, ignominy, mortification, shame

degrade 1. cheapen, corrupt, debase, demean, deteriorate, discredit, disgrace, dishonour, humble, humiliate, impair, injure, pervert, shame, vitiate 2. break, cashier, demote, depose, downgrade, lower, reduce to inferior rank 3. adulterate, dilute, doctor, mix, thin, water, water down, weaken

degraded abandoned, base, corrupt, debased, debauched, decadent, depraved, despicable, disgraced, disreputable, dissolute, low, mean, profligate, sordid, vicious, vile

degrading cheapening, contemptible, debasing, demeaning, disgraceful, dishonourable, humiliating, infra dig (*Inf.*), lowering, shameful, undignified, unworthy

degree 1. class, grade, level, order, position, rank, standing, station, status 2. division,

extent, gradation, grade, interval, limit, mark, measure, notch, point, rung, scale, stage, step, unit 3. calibre, extent, intensity, level, measure, proportion, quality, quantity, range, rate, ratio, scale, scope, severity, standard 4. **by degrees** bit by bit, gently, gradually, imperceptibly, inch by inch, little by little, slowly, step by step

deign condescend, consent, deem worthy, lower oneself, see fit, stoop, think fit

deity celestial being, divine being, divinity, god, goddess, godhead, idol, immortal, supreme being

dejected blue, cast down, crestfallen, depressed, despondent, disconsolate, disheartened, dismal, doleful, down, downcast, downhearted, gloomy, glum, low, low-spirited, melancholy, miserable, morose, sad, woebegone, wretched

dejection blues, depression, despair, despondency, doldrums, downheartedness, dumps (*Inf.*), gloom, gloominess, heavy-heartedness, low spirits, melancholy, sadness, sorrow, unhappiness

de jure according to the law, by right, legally, rightfully

delay *v.* 1. defer, hold over, postpone, procrastinate, prolong, protract, put off, shelve, stall, suspend, table, temporize ~*n.* 2. deferment, postponement, procrastination, stay, suspension ~*v.* 3. arrest, bog down, check, detain, halt, hinder, hold back, hold up, impede, obstruct, retard, set back, slow up, stop

~*n.* 4. check, detention, hindrance, hold-up, impediment, interruption, interval, obstruction, setback, stoppage, wait ~*v.* 5. dawdle, dilly-dally (*Inf.*), drag, lag, linger, loiter, tarry ~*n.* 6. dawdling, dilly-dallying (*Inf.*), lingering, loitering, tarrying

delectable adorable, agreeable, appetizing, charming, dainty, delicious, delightful, enjoyable, enticing, gratifying, inviting, luscious, lush, pleasant, pleasurable, satisfying, scrumptious (*Inf.*), tasty, toothsome, yummy (*Sl.*)

delectation amusement, delight, diversion, enjoyment, entertainment, gratification, happiness, pleasure, refreshment, relish, satisfaction

delegate *n.* 1. agent, ambassador, commissioner, deputy, envoy, legate, representative, vicar ~*v.* 2. accredit, appoint, authorize, commission, depute, designate, empower, mandate 3. assign, consign, devolve, entrust, give, hand over, pass on, relegate, transfer

delegation 1. commission, contingent, deputation, embassy, envoys, legation, mission 2. assignment, commissioning, committal, deputizing, devolution, entrustment, relegation

delete blot out, blue-pencil, cancel, cross out, cut out, dele, edit, edit out, efface, erase, expunge, obliterate, remove, rub out, strike out

written); erase; strike out. **—de'letion** n.
deleterious (ˌdɛlɪ'tɪərɪəs) adj. harmful; injurious; hurtful. **—ˌdele'teriousness** n.
Delft (dɛlft) n. **1.** a town in the SW Netherlands. **2.** Also called: **delftware.** tin-glazed earthenware which originated in Delft, typically having blue decoration on a white ground.
deliberate adj. (dɪ'lɪbərɪt). **1.** carefully thought out in advance; intentional. **2.** careful or unhurried: *a deliberate pace.* ~vb. (dɪ'lɪbəˌreɪt). **3.** to consider (something) deeply; think over. **—de'liberately** adv. **—de'liberateness** n. **—de'liberative** adj. **—de'liberˌator** n.
deliberation (dɪˌlɪbə'reɪʃən) n. **1.** careful consideration. **2.** (often pl.) formal discussion, as of a committee. **3.** care or absence of hurry.
delicacy ('dɛlɪkəsɪ) n., pl. **-cies.** **1.** fine or subtle quality, character, construction, etc. **2.** fragile or graceful beauty. **3.** something that is considered choice to eat, such as caviar. **4.** fragile construction or constitution. **5.** refinement of feeling, manner, or appreciation. **6.** fussy or squeamish refinement, esp. in matters of taste, propriety, etc. **7.** need for tactful or sensitive handling. **8.** sensitivity of response, as of an instrument.
delicate ('dɛlɪkɪt) adj. **1.** fine or subtle in quality, character, construction, etc. **2.** having a soft or fragile beauty. **3.** (of colour, tone, taste, etc.) pleasantly subtle. **4.** easily damaged or injured; fragile. **5.** precise or sensitive in action: *a delicate mechanism.* **6.** requiring tact. **7.** showing regard for the feelings of others. **8.** excessively refined; squeamish. **—'delicately** adv. **—'delicateness** n.
delicatessen (ˌdɛlɪkə'tɛsən) n. **1.** various foods, esp. unusual or imported foods, already cooked or prepared. **2.** a shop selling these foods.
delicious (dɪ'lɪʃəs) adj. **1.** very appealing, esp. to taste or smell. **2.** extremely enjoyable. **—de'liciously** adv. **—de'liciousness** n.
delight (dɪ'laɪt) vb. **1.** (tr.) to please greatly. **2.** (intr.; foll. by in) to take great pleasure (in). ~n. **3.** extreme pleasure. **4.** something that causes this. **—de'lighted** adj. **—de'lightedly** adv.
delightful (dɪ'laɪtfʊl) adj. giving great delight; very pleasing, beautiful, charming, etc. **—de'lightfully** adv. **—de'lightfulness** n.
delimit (diː'lɪmɪt) or **delimitate** vb. (tr.) to mark or prescribe the limits or boundaries of. **—deˌlimi'tation** n. **—de'limitative** adj.
delineate (dɪ'lɪnɪˌeɪt) vb. (tr.) **1.** to trace the outline of.

2. to represent pictorially; depict. **3.** to portray in words; describe. **—deˌline'ation** n. **—de'lineative** adj.
delinquent (dɪ'lɪŋkwənt) n. **1.** someone, esp. a young person, guilty of delinquency. ~adj. **2.** guilty of an offence or misdeed. **3.** failing in or neglectful of duty or obligation. **—de'linquency** n.
deliquesce (ˌdɛlɪ'kwɛs) vb. (intr.) (esp. of certain salts) to dissolve gradually in water absorbed from the air. **—ˌdeli'quescence** n.
delirious (dɪ'lɪrɪəs) adj. **1.** affected with delirium. **2.** wildly excited, esp. with joy or enthusiasm. **—de'liriously** adv.
delirium (dɪ'lɪrɪəm) n., pl. **-liriums, -liria** (-'lɪrɪə). a state of excitement and mental confusion, often accompanied by hallucinations, caused by high fever, poisoning, brain injury, etc. **2.** violent excitement or emotion; frenzy.
delirium tremens ('trɛmɛnz, 'triː-) n. a severe psychotic condition occurring in some persons with chronic alcoholism, characterized by delirium, tremor, anxiety, and vivid hallucinations. Abbrevs.: **D.T.'s** (informal), **d.t.**
deliver (dɪ'lɪvə) vb. (mainly tr.) **1.** to carry to a destination, esp. to distribute (goods, mail, etc.) to several places. **2.** (often foll. by over or up) to hand over or transfer. **3.** (often foll. by from) to release or rescue (from captivity, harm, etc.). **4.** (also intr.) **a.** to aid in the birth of (offspring). **b.** to give birth to (offspring). **c.** (usually foll. by of) to aid (a female) in the birth (of offspring). **d.** (passive; foll. by of) to give birth to (offspring). **5.** to present (a speech, idea, etc.). **6.** to utter: *to deliver a cry of exultation.* **7.** to discharge or release (something, such as a blow or shot) suddenly. **8.** Chiefly U.S. to cause (voters, etc.) to support a given candidate, cause, etc. **9. deliver oneself of.** to speak with deliberation or at length. **10. deliver the goods.** Inf. to produce something promised or expected. **—de'liverable** adj. **—de'liverance** n. **—de'liverer** n.
delivery (dɪ'lɪvərɪ) n., pl. **-eries.** **1. a.** the act of delivering or distributing goods, mail, etc. **b.** something that is delivered. **2.** the act of giving birth to a child. **3.** manner or style of utterance, esp. in public speaking: *the chairman had a clear delivery.* **4.** the act of giving or transferring or the state of being given or transferred. **5.** a rescuing or being rescued; liberation. **6.** Sport. the act or manner of bowling or throwing a ball. **7.** the handing over of property, a deed, etc.
dell (dɛl) n. a small, esp. wooded hollow.

THESAURUS

deliberate v. **1.** cogitate, consider, consult, debate, discuss, meditate, mull over, ponder, reflect, think, weigh ~adj. **2.** calculated, conscious, considered, designed, intentional, planned, prearranged, premeditated, purposeful, studied, thoughtful, wilful **3.** careful, cautious, circumspect, heedful, measured, methodical, ponderous, prudent, slow, thoughtful, unhurried, wary
deliberately by design, calculatingly, consciously, determinedly, emphatically, in cold blood, intentionally, knowingly, on purpose, pointedly, resolutely, studiously, wilfully, wittingly
deliberation **1.** calculation, care, carefulness, caution, circumspection, cogitation, consideration, coolness, forethought, meditation, prudence, purpose, reflection, speculation, study, thought, wariness **2.** conference, consultation, debate, discussion
delicacy **1.** accuracy, daintiness, elegance, exquisiteness, fineness, lightness, nicety, precision, subtlety **2.** debility, flimsiness, fragility, frailness, frailty, infirmity, slenderness, tenderness, weakness **3.** discrimination, fastidiousness, finesse, purity, refinement, sensibility, sensitiveness, sensitivity, tact, taste **4.** *bonne bouche,* dainty, luxury, relish, savoury, titbit, treat
delicate **1.** ailing, debilitated, flimsy, fragile, frail, sickly, slender, slight, tender, weak **2.** choice, dainty, delicious, elegant, exquisite, fine, graceful, savoury, tender **3.** faint, muted, pastel, soft, subdued, subtle **4.** accurate, deft, detailed, minute, precise, skilled **5.**

considerate, diplomatic, discreet, sensitive, tactful **6.** critical, difficult, precarious, sensitive, sticky (Inf.), ticklish, touchy **7.** careful, critical, discriminating, fastidious, prudish, pure, refined, scrupulous, squeamish
delicately carefully, daintily, deftly, elegantly, exquisitely, fastidiously, finely, gracefully, lightly, precisely, sensitively, skilfully, softly, subtly, tactfully
delicious **1.** ambrosial, appetizing, choice, dainty, delectable, luscious, mouthwatering, nectareous, palatable, savoury, scrumptious (Inf.), tasty, toothsome, yummy (Sl.) **2.** agreeable, charming, delightful, enjoyable, entertaining, exquisite, pleasant, pleasing
delight n. **1.** ecstasy, enjoyment, felicity, gladness, gratification, happiness, joy, pleasure, rapture, transport ~v. **2.** amuse, charm, cheer, divert, enchant, gratify, please, ravish, rejoice, satisfy, thrill **3.** With in appreciate, enjoy, feast on, glory in, indulge in, like, love, luxuriate in, relish, revel in, savour
delighted captivated, charmed, ecstatic, elated, enchanted, gladdened, happy, joyous, jubilant, overjoyed, pleased, thrilled
delightful agreeable, amusing, captivating, charming, congenial, delectable, enchanting, engaging, enjoyable, entertaining, fascinating, gratifying, heavenly, pleasant, pleasing, pleasurable, rapturous, ravishing, thrilling
delinquency crime, fault, misbehaviour, misconduct, misdeed, misdemeanour, offence, wrongdoing

delinquent criminal, culprit, defaulter, juvenile delinquent, lawbreaker, malefactor, miscreant, offender, wrongdoer, young offender
delirious **1.** crazy, demented, deranged, incoherent, insane, light-headed, mad, raving, unhinged **2.** beside oneself, carried away, corybantic, ecstatic, excited, frantic, frenzied, hysterical, wild
delirium **1.** aberration, derangement, hallucination, insanity, lunacy, madness, raving **2.** ecstasy, fever, frenzy, fury, hysteria, passion, rage
deliver **1.** bear, bring, carry, cart, convey, distribute, transport **2.** cede, commit, give up, grant, hand over, make over, relinquish, resign, surrender, transfer, turn over, yield **3.** acquit, discharge, emancipate, free, liberate, loose, ransom, redeem, release, rescue, save **4.** announce, declare, give, give forth, present, proclaim, pronounce, publish, read, utter **5.** administer, aim, deal, direct, give, inflict, launch, strike, throw **6.** discharge, dispense, feed, give forth, provide, release, supply
deliverance emancipation, escape, liberation, ransom, redemption, release, rescue, salvation
delivery **1.** consignment, conveyance, dispatch, distribution, handing over, surrender, transfer, transmission, transmittal **2.** articulation, elocution, enunciation, intonation, speech, utterance **3.** Medical childbirth, confinement, labour, parturition **4.** deliverance, escape, liberation, release, rescue

delouse (diːˈlaʊs, -ˈlaʊz) vb. (tr.) to rid (a person or animal) of lice as a sanitary measure.
Delphic (ˈdɛlfɪk) or **Delphian** adj. 1. of or relating to the ancient Greek city of Delphi or its oracle or temple. 2. obscure or ambiguous.
delphinium (dɛlˈfɪnɪəm) n., pl. **-iums** or **-ia** (-ɪə). a plant with spikes of blue, pink, or white spurred flowers. See also **larkspur**.
delta (ˈdɛltə) n. 1. the fourth letter in the Greek alphabet (Δ or δ). 2. (cap. when part of name) the flat alluvial area at the mouth of some rivers where the mainstream splits up into several distributaries. 3. Maths. a finite increment in a variable. **—deltaic** (dɛlˈteɪɪk) or **'deltic** adj.
delta wing n. a triangular swept-back aircraft wing.
delude (dɪˈluːd) vb. (tr.) to deceive; mislead; beguile. **—de'ludable** adj. **—de'luder** n. **—delusive** (dɪˈluːsɪv) adj.
deluge (ˈdɛljuːdʒ) n. 1. a great flood of water. 2. torrential rain. 3. an overwhelming rush or number. ~vb. (tr.) 4. to flood. 5. to overwhelm; inundate.
Deluge (ˈdɛljuːdʒ) n. **the**. another name for the **Flood**.
delusion (dɪˈluːʒən) n. 1. a mistaken idea, belief, etc. 2. Psychiatry. a belief held in the face of evidence to the contrary, that is resistant to all reason. 3. a deluding or being deluded. **—de'lusional** adj. **—de'lusive** adj. **—delusory** (dɪˈluːsərɪ) adj.
de luxe (də ˈlʌks, ˈlʊks) adj. 1. rich or sumptuous; superior in quality: the de luxe model of a car. ~adv. 2. Chiefly U.S. in a luxurious manner.
delve (dɛlv) vb. (mainly intr.; often foll. by in or into) 1. to research deeply or intensively (for information, etc.). 2. to search or rummage. 3. to dig or burrow deeply. 4. (also tr.) Arch. or Brit. dialect. to dig. **—'delver** n.
demagnetize or **-ise** (diːˈmægnə‚taɪz) vb. to remove or lose magnetic properties. Also: **degauss**. **—de‚magneti'zation** or **-i'sation** n. **—de'magnet‚izer** or **-‚iser** n.
demagogue or U.S. (sometimes) **demagog** (ˈdɛmə‚gɒg) n. 1. a political agitator who appeals with crude oratory to the prejudice and passions of the mob. 2. (esp. in the ancient world) any popular political leader or orator. **—demagogic** (‚dɛmə'gɒgɪk) adj. **—‚dema'goguery** n. **—demagogy** (ˈdɛmə‚gɒgɪ) n.
demand (dɪˈmɑːnd) vb. (tr.; may take a clause as object or an infinitive) 1. to request peremptorily or urgently. 2. to require as just, urgent, etc.: the situation demands attention. 3. to claim as a right; exact. 4. Law. to make a formal legal claim to (property). ~n. 5. an urgent or peremptory requirement or request. 6. something that requires special effort or sacrifice. 7. the act of demanding something or the thing demanded. 8. an insistent question. 9. Econ. a. willingness and ability to purchase goods and services. b. the amount of a commodity that consumers are willing and able to purchase at a specified price. Cf. **supply**¹. 10. Law. a formal legal claim, esp. to real property. 11. **in demand**. sought after. 12. **on demand**. as soon as requested. **—de'mandable** adj. **—de'mander** n.
demanding (dɪˈmɑːndɪŋ) adj. requiring great patience, skill, etc.: a demanding job.

demarcation or **demarkation** (‚diːmɑːˈkeɪʃən) n. 1. the act of establishing limits or boundaries. 2. a limit or boundary. 3. a. a strict separation of the kinds of work performed by members of different trade unions. b. (as modifier): demarcation dispute. 4. separation or distinction (as in **line of demarcation**).
demean (dɪˈmiːn) vb. (tr.) to lower (oneself) in dignity, status, or character; humble; debase.
demeanour or U.S. **demeanor** (dɪˈmiːnə) n. 1. the way a person behaves towards others. 2. bearing or mien.
demented (dɪˈmɛntɪd) adj. mad; insane. **—de'mentedly** adv. **—de'mentedness** n.
dementia (dɪˈmɛnʃə, -ʃɪə) n. a state of serious mental deterioration, of organic or functional origin.
demerara (‚dɛmə'rɛərə, -'rɑːrə) n. brown crystallized cane sugar from the West Indies.
demerit (diːˈmɛrɪt) n. 1. something that deserves censure. 2. U.S. a mark given against a student, etc. for failure or misconduct. 3. a fault. **—de‚meri'torious** adj.
demesne (dɪˈmeɪn, -ˈmiːn) n. 1. land surrounding a house or manor. 2. Property law. the possession and use of one's own property or land. 3. realm; domain. 4. a region or district.
demi- prefix. 1. half: demirelief. 2. of less than full size, status, or rank: demigod.
demigod (ˈdɛmɪ‚gɒd) n. 1. a. a being who is part mortal, part god. b. a lesser deity. 2. a person with godlike attributes. **—'demi‚goddess** fem. n.
demijohn (ˈdɛmɪ‚dʒɒn) n. a large bottle with a short narrow neck, often encased in wickerwork.
demilitarize or **-ise** (diːˈmɪlɪtə‚raɪz) vb. (tr.) 1. to remove and prohibit any military presence or function in (an area): demilitarized zone. 2. to free of military character, purpose, etc. **—de‚militari'zation** or **-i'sation** n.
demimonde (‚dɛmɪ'mɒnd) n. 1. (esp. in the 19th century) those women considered to be outside respectable society, esp. on account of sexual promiscuity. 2. any group considered to be not wholly respectable.
demise (dɪˈmaɪz) n. 1. failure or termination. 2. a euphemistic or formal word for **death**. 3. Property law. a transfer of an estate by lease or on the death of the owner. 4. the transfer of sovereignty to a successor upon the death, abdication, etc., of a ruler (esp. in **demise of the crown**). ~vb. 5. to transfer or be transferred by inheritance, will, or succession. 6. (tr.) Property law. to transfer for a limited period; lease. 7. (tr.) to transfer (sovereignty, a title, etc.) **—de'misable** adj.
demisemiquaver (ˈdɛmɪ‚sɛmɪ‚kweɪvə) n. Music. a note having the time value of one thirty-second of a semibreve. Usual U.S. name: **thirty-second note**.
demo (ˈdɛməʊ) n., pl. **-os**. short for **demonstration**.
demo- or before a vowel **dem-** combining form. indicating people or population: demography.
demob (diːˈmɒb) Brit. inf. ~vb. **-mobbing, -mobbed**. 1. to demobilize. ~n. 2. demobilization.
demobilize or **-ise** (diːˈməʊbɪ‚laɪz) vb. to disband, as troops, etc. **—de‚mobili'zation** or **-i'sation** n.
democracy (dɪˈmɒkrəsɪ) n., pl. **-cies**. 1. government by the people or their elected representatives. 2. control of any organization by its members: industrial democracy.

THESAURUS

delude bamboozle (Inf.), beguile, cheat, con (Sl.), cozen, deceive, dupe, fool, gull (Archaic), hoax, hoodwink, impose on, lead up the garden path (Inf.), misguide, mislead, take in (Inf.), trick
deluge n. 1. cataclysm, downpour, flood, inundation, overflowing, spate, torrent 2. Fig. avalanche, barrage, flood, rush, spate, torrent ~v. 3. douse, drench, drown, flood, inundate, soak, submerge, swamp 4. Fig. engulf, inundate, overload, overrun, overwhelm, swamp
delusion deception, error, fallacy, false impression, fancy, hallucination, illusion, misapprehension, misbelief, misconception, mistake, phantasm, self-deception
de luxe choice, costly, elegant, exclusive, expensive, grand, luxurious, opulent, palatial, plush (Inf.), rich, select, special, splendid, sumptuous, superior
delve burrow, dig into, examine, explore,

ferret out, investigate, look into, probe, ransack, research, rummage, search, unearth
demagogue agitator, firebrand, haranguer, rabble-rouser, soapbox orator
demand v. 1. ask, challenge, inquire, interrogate, question, request 2. call for, cry out for, involve, necessitate, need, require, take, want 3. claim, exact, expect, insist on, order ~n. 4. bidding, charge, inquiry, interrogation, order, question, request, requisition 5. call, claim, necessity, need, requirement, want 6. **in demand** fashionable, in vogue, needed, popular, requested, sought after
demanding 1. challenging, difficult, exacting, exhausting, exigent, hard, taxing, tough, trying, wearing 2. clamorous, imperious, importunate, insistent, nagging, pressing, urgent
demarcate define, delimit, determine, differentiate, distinguish between, fix, mark,

separate
demarcation 1. bound, boundary, confine, enclosure, limit, margin 2. delimitation, differentiation, distinction, division, separation
demean abase, debase, degrade, descend, humble, lower, stoop
demeanour air, bearing, behaviour, carriage, comportment, conduct, deportment, manner, mien
demented crackbrained, crazed, crazy, daft (Sl.), deranged, distraught, dotty (Sl.), foolish, frenzied, idiotic, insane, lunatic, mad, maniacal, manic, non compos mentis, unbalanced, unhinged
democracy commonwealth, government by the people, representative government, republic

3. a political or social unit governed ultimately by all its members. **4.** the practice or spirit of social equality. **5.** a social condition of classlessness and equality.

democrat ('dɛmə,kræt) *n.* **1.** an advocate of democracy. **2.** a member or supporter of a democratic party or movement.

Democrat ('dɛmə,kræt) *n. U.S. politics.* a member or supporter of the Democratic Party. —,**Demo'cratic** *adj.*

democratic (,dɛmə'krætɪk) *adj.* **1.** of or relating to the principles of democracy. **2.** upholding democracy or the interests of the common people. **3.** popular with or for the benefit of all. —,**demo'cratically** *adv.*

demodulation (,di:mɒdjʊ'leɪʃən) *n. Electronics.* the act or process by which an output wave or signal is obtained having the characteristics of the original modulating wave or signal; the reverse of modulation.

demography (dɪ'mɒgrəfɪ) *n.* the science of population statistics. —**de'mographer** *n.* —**demographic** (,di:mə'græfɪk, ,dɛmə-) *adj.*

demolish (dɪ'mɒlɪʃ) *vb.* (*tr.*) **1.** to tear down or break up (buildings, etc.). **2.** to put an end to (an argument, etc.). **3.** *Facetious.* to eat up. —**de'molisher** *n.* —,**demo'lition** *n.*

demon ('di:mən) *n.* **1.** an evil spirit or devil. **2.** a person, obsession, etc., thought of as evil or cruel. **3.** Also called: **daemon.** an attendant or ministering spirit; genius: *the demon of inspiration.* **4. a.** a person extremely skilful in or devoted to a given activity, esp. a sport: *a demon at cycling.* **b.** (*as modifier*): *a demon cyclist.* **5.** a variant spelling of **daemon** (sense 1). **6.** *Austral. sl.* a detective or policeman, esp. one in plain clothes. —**demonic** (dɪ'mɒnɪk) *adj.*

demonetize *or* **-ise** (di:'mʌnɪ,taɪz) *vb.* (*tr.*) **1.** to deprive (a metal) of its capacity as a monetary standard. **2.** to withdraw from use as currency. —**de,moneti'zation** *or* **-i'sation** *n.*

demoniac (dɪ'məʊnɪ,æk) *adj. also* **demoniacal** (,di:mə-'naɪəkəl). **1.** of or like a demon. **2.** suggesting inner possession or inspiration: *the demoniac fire of genius.* **3.** frantic; frenzied. ~*n.* **4.** a person possessed by a demon. —,**demo'niacally** *adv.*

demonolatry (,di:mə'nɒlətrɪ) *n.* the worship of demons.

demonology (,di:mə'nɒlədʒɪ) *n.* the study of demons or demonic beliefs. Also called: **demonism.** —,**demon'ologist** *n.*

demonstrable ('dɛmənstrəbəl) *adj.* able to be demonstrated or proved. —**de,monstra'bility** *n.* —**de'monstrably** *adv.*

demonstrate ('dɛmən,streɪt) *vb.* **1.** (*tr.*) to show or prove, esp. by reasoning, evidence, etc. **2.** (*tr.*) to explain by experiment, example, etc. **3.** (*tr.*) to display and explain the workings of (a machine, product, etc.). **4.** (*intr.*) to manifest support, protest, etc., by public parades or rallies. **5.** (*intr.*) to be employed as a demonstrator of machinery, etc. **6.** (*intr.*) *Mil.* to make a show of force.

demonstration (,dɛmən'streɪʃən) *n.* **1.** the act of demonstrating. **2.** proof or evidence leading to proof. **3.** an explanation, illustration, or experiment showing how something works. **4.** a manifestation of support or protest by public rallies, parades, etc. **5.** a manifestation of emotion. **6.** a show of military force. —**demon'strational** *adj.* —,**demon'strationist** *n.*

demonstrative (dɪ'mɒnstrətɪv) *adj.* **1.** tending to express one's feelings easily or unreservedly. **2.** (*postpositive;* foll. by *of*) serving as proof; indicative. **3.** involving or characterized by demonstration. **4.** conclusive. **5.** *Grammar.* denoting or belonging to a class of determiners used to point out the individual referent or referents intended, such as *this* and *those.* Cf. **interrogative, relative.** ~*n.* **6.** *Grammar.* a demonstrative word. —**de'monstratively** *adv.* —**de'monstrativeness** *n.*

demonstrator ('dɛmən,streɪtə) *n.* **1.** a person who demonstrates equipment, machines, products, etc. **2.** a person who takes part in a public demonstration.

demoralize *or* **-ise** (dɪ'mɒrə,laɪz) *vb.* (*tr.*) **1.** to undermine the morale of; dishearten. **2.** to corrupt. **3.** to throw into confusion. —**de,morali'zation** *or* **-i'sation** *n.*

demote (dɪ'məʊt) *vb.* (*tr.*) to lower in rank or position; relegate. —**de'motion** *n.*

demotic (dɪ'mɒtɪk) *adj.* **1.** of or relating to the common people; popular. **2.** of or relating to a simplified form of hieroglyphics used in ancient Egypt. Cf. **hieratic.** ~*n.* **3.** the demotic script of ancient Egypt. —**de'motist** *n.*

demur (dɪ'mɜː) *vb.* **-murring, -murred.** (*intr.*) **1.** to show reluctance; object. **2.** *Law.* to raise an objection by entering a demurrer. ~*n. also* **demurral** (dɪ'mʌrəl). **3.** the act of demurring. **4.** an objection raised. —**de'murrable** *adj.*

demure (dɪ'mjʊə) *adj.* **1.** sedate; decorous; reserved. **2.** affectedly modest or prim; coy. —**de'murely** *adv.* —**de'mureness** *n.*

demurrer (dɪ'mʌrə) *n.* **1.** *Law.* a pleading that admits an opponent's point but denies that it is relevant or valid. **2.** any objection raised.

demystify (di:'mɪstɪ,faɪ) *vb.* **-fying, -fied.** (*tr.*) to remove the mystery from; make clear. —**de,mystifi'cation** *n.*

den (dɛn) *n.* **1.** the habitat or retreat of a wild animal; lair. **2.** a small or secluded room in a home, often used for carrying on a hobby. **3.** a squalid room or retreat. **4.** a site or haunt: *a den of vice.* **5.** *Scot.* a small wooded valley. ~*vb.* **denning, denned.** **6.** (*intr.*) to live in or as if in a den.

Den. *abbrev. for* Denmark.

denarius (dɪ'nɛərɪəs) *n., pl.* **-narii** (-'nɛərɪ,aɪ). **1.** a silver coin of ancient Rome, often called a penny in translation. **2.** a gold coin worth 25 silver denarii.

denary ('di:nərɪ) *adj.* **1.** calculated by tens; decimal. **2.** containing ten parts; tenfold.

denationalize *or* **-ise** (di:'næʃənə,laɪz) *vb.* **1.** to transfer (an industry, etc.) from public to private ownership. **2.** to deprive of national character or nationality. —**de,nationali'zation** *or* **-i'sation** *n.*

denature (di:'neɪtʃə) *or* **denaturize, -ise** (di:'neɪtʃə-

THESAURUS

democratic autonomous, egalitarian, popular, populist, representative, republican, self-governing

demolish 1. bulldoze, destroy, dismantle, flatten, knock down, level, overthrow, pulverize, raze, ruin, tear down 2. *Fig.* annihilate, defeat, destroy, overthrow, overturn, undo, wreck 3. consume, devour, eat, gobble up, put away

demolition bulldozing, destruction, explosion, knocking down, levelling, razing, wrecking

demon 1. devil, evil spirit, fiend, goblin, malignant spirit 2. *Fig.* devil, fiend, monster, rogue, villain 3. ace (*Inf.*), addict, fanatic, fiend, go-getter (*Inf.*), master, wizard 4. daemon, daimon, genius, guardian spirit, ministering angel, numen

demonic, demoniac, demoniacal 1. devilish, diabolic, diabolical, fiendish, hellish, infernal, satanic 2. crazed, frantic, frenetic, frenzied, furious, hectic, like one possessed, mad, maniacal, manic

demonstrable attestable, axiomatic, certain, evident, evincible, incontrovertible, indubitable, irrefutable, obvious, palpable, positive, provable, self-evident, undeniable, unmistakable, verifiable

demonstrate 1. display, establish, evidence, evince, exhibit, indicate, manifest, prove, show, testify to 2. describe, explain, illustrate, make clear, show how, teach 3. march, parade, picket, protest, rally

demonstration 1. affirmation, confirmation, display, evidence, exhibition, expression, illustration, manifestation, proof, substantiation, testimony, validation 2. description, explanation, exposition, presentation, test, trial 3. march, mass lobby, parade, picket, protest, rally, sit-in

demonstrative 1. affectionate, effusive, emotional, expansive, expressive, gushing, loving, open, unreserved, unrestrained 2. evincive, explanatory, expository, illustrative, indicative, symptomatic

demoralize 1. cripple, daunt, deject, depress, disconcert, discourage, dishearten, dispirit, enfeeble, rattle (*Inf.*), sap, shake, undermine, unnerve, weaken 2. corrupt, debase, debauch, deprave, lower, pervert, vitiate

demoralized 1. broken, crushed, depressed, discouraged, disheartened, dispirited, downcast, subdued, unmanned, unnerved, weakened 2. bad, base, corrupt, degenerate, depraved, dissolute, immoral, low, reprobate, sinful, wicked

demur 1. *v.* balk, cavil, disagree, dispute, doubt, hesitate, object, pause, protest, refuse, take exception, waver 2. *n.* compunction, demurral, demurrer, dissent, hesitation, misgiving, objection, protest, qualm, scruple

demure 1. decorous, diffident, grave, modest, reserved, reticent, retiring, sedate, shy, sober, staid, unassuming 2. affected, bashful, coy, priggish, prim, prissy (*Inf.*), prudish, strait-laced

den 1. cave, cavern, haunt, hide-out, hole, lair, shelter 2. cloister, cubbyhole, hideaway, retreat, sanctuary, sanctum, snuggery, study

ˌraɪz) *vb.* (*tr.*) **1.** to change the nature of. **2.** to change the properties of (a protein), as by the action of acid or heat. **3.** to render (alcohol) unfit for drinking by adding other substances. **4.** to render (fissile material) unfit for use in nuclear weapons by addition of an isotope. —**de-ˈnaturant** *n.* —**deˌnaturˈation** *n.*

dendro-, dendri-, *or before a vowel* **dendr-** *combining form.* tree: *dendrochronology.*

dendrology (dɛnˈdrɒlədʒɪ) *n.* the branch of botany that is concerned with the natural history of trees. —**dendrological** (ˌdɛndrəˈlɒdʒɪkəl) *or* ˌ**dendroˈlogic** *adj.* —**denˈdrologist** *n.*

dene *or* **dean** (diːn) *n. Brit.* a narrow wooded valley.

dengue (ˈdɛŋɡɪ) *or* **dandy** (ˈdændɪ) *n.* an acute viral disease transmitted by mosquitoes, characterized by headache, fever, pains in the joints, and skin rash.

denial (dɪˈnaɪəl) *n.* **1.** a refusal to agree or comply with a statement. **2.** the rejection of the truth of a proposition, doctrine, etc. **3.** a rejection of a request. **4.** a refusal to acknowledge; disavowal. **5.** abstinence; self-denial.

denier *n.* **1.** (ˈdɛnɪˌeɪ, ˈdɛnjə). a unit of weight used to measure the fineness of silk and man-made fibres, esp. when woven into women's tights, etc. **2.** (dəˈnjeɪ, -ˈnɪə). any of several former European coins of various denominations.

denigrate (ˈdɛnɪˌɡreɪt) *vb.* to belittle or disparage the character of; defame. —ˌ**deniˈgration** *n.* —ˈ**deniˌgrator** *n.*

denim (ˈdɛnɪm) *n.* **1.** a hard-wearing twill-weave cotton fabric used for trousers, work clothes, etc. **2.** a similar lighter fabric used in upholstery.

denims (ˈdɛnɪmz) *pl. n.* jeans or overalls made of denim.

denizen (ˈdɛnɪzən) *n.* **1.** an inhabitant; resident. **2.** *Brit.* an individual permanently resident in a foreign country where he enjoys certain rights of citizenship. **3.** a plant or animal established in a place to which it is not native. **4.** a naturalized foreign word.

denominate *vb.* (dɪˈnɒmɪˌneɪt). **1.** (*tr.*) to give a specific name to; designate. ~*adj.* (dɪˈnɒmɪˌnɪt, -ˌneɪt). **2.** *Maths.* (of a number) representing a multiple of a unit of measurement: *4 is the denominate number in 4 miles.*

denomination (dɪˌnɒmɪˈneɪʃən) *n.* **1.** a group having a distinctive interpretation of a religious faith and usually its own organization. **2.** a grade or unit in a series of designations of value, weight, measure, etc. **3.** a name given to a class or group; classification. **4.** the act of giving a name. **5.** a name; designation. —**deˌnomiˈnational** *adj.*

denominator (dɪˈnɒmɪˌneɪtə) *n.* the divisor of a fraction, as 8 in ⅞. Cf. **numerator.**

denotation (ˌdiːnəʊˈteɪʃən) *n.* **1.** a denoting; indication. **2.** a sign, term, etc., that denotes. **3.** a particular meaning given by a sign or symbol. **4.** specific meaning as distinguished from suggestive meaning and associations. **5.** *Logic.* Also called: **extension.** the class of entities to which a given word correctly applies.

denote (dɪˈnəʊt) *vb.* (*tr.; may take a clause as object*) **1.** to be a sign of; designate. **2.** (of words, phrases, etc.) to have as a literal or obvious meaning. —ˌ**denoˈtation** *n.* —**deˈnotative** *adj.*

denouement (deɪˈnuːmɒn) *or* **dénouement** (*French* denuˈmã) *n.* **1.** the clarification or resolution of a plot in a play or other work. **2.** final outcome; solution.

denounce (dɪˈnaʊns) *vb.* (*tr.*) **1.** to condemn openly or vehemently. **2.** to give information against; accuse. **3.** to announce formally the termination of (a treaty, etc.). —**deˈnouncement** *n.* —**deˈnouncer** *n.*

dense (dɛns) *adj.* **1.** thickly crowded or closely set. **2.** thick; impenetrable. **3.** *Physics.* having a high density. **4.** stupid; dull. **5.** (of a photographic negative) having many dark or exposed areas. —ˈ**densely** *adv.* —ˈ**denseness** *n.*

density (ˈdɛnsɪtɪ) *n., pl.* **-ties. 1.** the degree to which something is filled or occupied: *high density of building in towns.* **2.** stupidity. **3.** a measure of the compactness of a substance, expressed as its mass per unit volume. Symbol: ρ **4.** a measure of a physical quantity per unit of length, area, or volume. **5.** *Physics, photog.* a measure of the extent to which a substance or surface transmits or reflects light.

dent (dɛnt) *n.* **1.** a hollow in a surface, as one made by pressure or a blow. **2.** an appreciable effect, esp. of lessening: *a dent in our resources.* ~*vb.* **3.** to make a dent in.

dental (ˈdɛntəl) *adj.* **1.** of or relating to the teeth or dentistry. **2.** *Phonetics.* pronounced with the tip of the tongue touching the backs of the upper teeth, as for *t* in French *tout.* ~*n.* **3.** *Phonetics.* a dental consonant.

dental floss *n.* a soft thread for cleaning the teeth and the spaces between them.

dental surgeon *n.* another name for dentist.

dentate (ˈdɛnteɪt) *adj.* **1.** having teeth or toothlike processes. **2.** (of leaves) having a toothed margin. —ˈ**dentately** *adv.*

denti- *or before a vowel* **dent-** *combining form.* indicating a tooth: *dentine.*

dentifrice (ˈdɛntɪfrɪs) *n.* any substance, esp. paste or powder, for use in cleaning the teeth.

dentine (ˈdɛntiːn) *or* **dentin** (ˈdɛntɪn) *n.* the calcified tissue comprising the bulk of a tooth. —ˈ**dentinal** *adj.*

dentist (ˈdɛntɪst) *n.* a person qualified to practise dentistry.

dentistry (ˈdɛntɪstrɪ) *n.* the branch of medical science concerned with the diagnosis and treatment of disorders of the teeth and gums.

dentition (dɛnˈtɪʃən) *n.* **1.** the arrangement, type, and number of the teeth in a particular species. **2.** the time or process of teething.

denture (ˈdɛntʃə) *n.* (*usually pl.*) **1.** a partial or full set of artificial teeth. **2.** *Rare.* a set of natural teeth.

denude (dɪˈnjuːd) *vb.* (*tr.*) **1.** to make bare; strip. **2.** to expose (rock) by the erosion of the layers above. —**denudation** (ˌdɛnjuˈdeɪʃən) *n.*

denumerable (dɪˈnjuːmərəbəl) *adj. Maths.* capable of being put into a one-to-one correspondence with the positive integers; countable. —**deˈnumerably** *adv.*

denunciate (dɪˈnʌnsɪˌeɪt) *vb.* (*tr.*) to condemn; denounce. —**deˈnunciˌator** *n.* —**deˈnunciatory** *adj.*

denunciation (dɪˌnʌnsɪˈeɪʃən) *n.* **1.** open condemnation; denouncing. **2.** *Law, obsolete.* a charge or accusation of crime made before a public prosecutor or tribunal. **3.** a formal announcement of the termination of a treaty.

deny (dɪˈnaɪ) *vb.* **-nying, -nied.** (*tr.*) **1.** to declare (a statement, etc.) to be untrue. **2.** to reject as false. **3.** to withhold. **4.** to refuse to fulfil the expectations of: *it is hard to deny a child.* **5.** to refuse to acknowledge; disown. **6.** to refuse (oneself) things desired.

deodar (ˈdiːəʊˌdɑː) *n.* **1.** a Himalayan cedar with droop-

---

THESAURUS

denial adjuration, contradiction, disavowal, disclaimer, dismissal, dissent, negation, prohibition, rebuff, refusal, rejection, renunciation, repudiation, repulse, retraction, veto

denigrate belittle, besmirch, blacken, calumniate, decry, defame, disparage, impugn, malign, revile, run down, slander, vilify

denigration aspersion, backbiting, defamation, detraction, disparagement, obloquy, scandal, scurrility, slander, vilification

denominate call, christen, designate, dub, entitle, name, phrase, style, term

denomination 1. belief, communion, creed, persuasion, religious group, school, sect **2.** grade, size, unit, value **3.** body, category, class, classification, group **4.** appellation,

designation, label, name, style, term, title

denote betoken, designate, express, imply, import, indicate, mark, mean, show, signify, typify

denounce accuse, arraign, attack, brand, castigate, censure, condemn, declaim against, decry, denunciate, impugn, proscribe, revile, stigmatize, vilify

dense 1. close, close-knit, compact, compressed, condensed, heavy, impenetrable, opaque, solid, substantial, thick, thickset **2.** blockish, crass, dull, obtuse, slow, slow-witted, stolid, stupid, thick, thick-witted

density 1. body, bulk, closeness, compactness, consistency, crowdedness, denseness, impenetrability, mass, solidity, thickness, tightness **2.** crassness, dullness, obtuseness,

slowness, stolidity, stupidity, thickness

dent 1. *n.* chip, concavity, crater, depression, dimple, dip, hollow, impression, indentation, pit **2.** *v.* depress, dint, gouge, hollow, imprint, make a dent in, make concave, press in, push in

denude bare, divest, expose, lay bare, strip, uncover

deny 1. contradict, disagree with, disprove, gainsay, oppose, rebuff, refute **2.** abjure, disavow, discard, disclaim, disown, recant, renounce, repudiate, revoke **3.** begrudge, decline, disallow, forbid, negative, refuse, reject, turn down, veto, withhold

ing branches. **2.** the durable fragrant highly valued wood of this tree.

deodorant (diːˈəudərənt) n. **1.** a substance applied to the body to suppress or mask the odour of perspiration. **2.** any substance for destroying or masking odours.

deodorize or **-ise** (diːˈəudəˌraɪz) vb. (tr.) to remove, disguise, or absorb the odour of, esp. when unpleasant. —de‚odoriˈzation or -iˈsation n. —deˈodorˌizer or -ˌiser n.

dep. abbrev. for: **1.** department. **2.** departure. **3.** deposed. **4.** deposit. **5.** depot. **6.** deputy.

depart (dɪˈpɑːt) vb. (mainly intr.) **1.** to leave. **2.** to set forth. **3.** (usually foll. by from) to differ; vary: to depart from normal procedure. **4.** (tr.) to quit (arch., except in depart this life).

departed (dɪˈpɑːtɪd) adj. Euphemistic. **a.** dead; deceased. **b.** (as collective n.): the departed.

department (dɪˈpɑːtmənt) n. **1.** a specialized division of a large concern, such as a business, store, or university. **2.** a major subdivision of the administration of a government. **3.** a branch of learning. **4.** an administrative division in several countries, such as France. **5.** Inf. a specialized sphere of skill or activity: wine-making is my wife's department. —departmental (ˌdiːpɑːˈtmentəl) adj.

department store n. a large shop divided into departments selling a great many kinds of goods.

departure (dɪˈpɑːtʃə) n. **1.** the act or an instance of departing. **2.** a variation from previous custom. **3.** a course of action, venture, etc.: selling is a new departure for him. **4.** Naut. the net distance travelled due east or west by a vessel. **5.** a euphemistic word for death.

depend (dɪˈpɛnd) vb. (intr.) **1.** (foll. by on or upon) to put trust (in); rely (on). **2.** (usually foll. by on or upon) to be influenced or determined (by): it all depends on you. **3.** (foll. by on or upon) to rely (on) for income, support, etc. **4.** (foll. by from) Rare. to hang down. **5.** to be undecided.

dependable (dɪˈpɛndəbəl) adj. able to be depended on; reliable. —de‚pendaˈbility or deˈpendableness n. —deˈpendably adv.

dependant (dɪˈpɛndənt) n. a person who depends on another person, organization, etc., for support, aid, or sustenance, esp. financial support.

dependence or U.S. (sometimes) **dependance** (dɪˈpɛndəns) n. **1.** the state or fact of being dependent, esp. for support or help. **2.** reliance; trust; confidence.

dependency or U.S. (sometimes) **dependancy** (dɪˈpɛndənsɪ) n., pl. **-cies. 1.** a territory subject to a state on which it does not border. **2.** a dependent or subordinate person or thing. **3.** another word for **dependence.**

dependent or U.S. (sometimes) **dependant** (dɪˈpɛndənt) adj. **1.** depending on a person or thing for aid, support, etc. **2.** (postpositive; foll. by on or upon) influenced or conditioned (by). **3.** subordinate; subject. **4.** Obs. hanging down. ~n. **5.** a variant spelling (esp. U.S.)

of **dependant.** —deˈpendently adv.

depict (dɪˈpɪkt) vb. (tr.) **1.** to represent by drawing, sculpture, painting, etc. **2.** to represent in words; describe. —deˈpicter or deˈpictor n. —deˈpiction n. —deˈpictive adj.

depilatory (dɪˈpɪlətərɪ, -trɪ) adj. **1.** able or serving to remove hair. ~n., pl. **-ries. 2.** a chemical used to remove hair from the body.

deplete (dɪˈpliːt) vb. (tr.) **1.** to use up (supplies, money, etc.); exhaust. **2.** to empty entirely or partially. —deˈpletion n.

deplorable (dɪˈplɔːrəbəl) adj. **1.** lamentable. **2.** worthy of censure or reproach; very bad. —deˈplorably adv.

deplore (dɪˈplɔː) vb. (tr.) **1.** to express or feel sorrow about. **2.** to express or feel strong disapproval of; censure. —deˈploringly adv.

deploy (dɪˈplɔɪ) vb. Chiefly mil. **1.** to adopt or cause to adopt a battle formation. **2.** (tr.) to redistribute (forces) to or within a given area. —deˈployment n.

depolarize or **-ise** (diːˈpəuləˌraɪz) vb. to undergo or cause to undergo a loss of polarity or polarization. —deˌpolariˈzation or -iˈsation n.

deponent (dɪˈpəunənt) adj. **1.** Grammar. (of a verb, esp. in Latin) having the inflectional endings of a passive verb but the meaning of an active verb. ~n. **2.** Grammar. a deponent verb. **3.** Law. a person who makes an affidavit or a deposition.

depopulate (dɪˈpɒpjuˌleɪt) vb. to be or cause to be reduced in population. —deˌpopuˈlation n.

deport (dɪˈpɔːt) vb. (tr.) **1.** to remove forcibly from a country; expel. **2.** to conduct, hold, or behave (oneself) in a specified manner. —deˈportable adj.

deportation (ˌdiːpɔːˈteɪʃən) n. the act of expelling someone from a country.

deportee (ˌdiːpɔːˈtiː) n. a person deported or awaiting deportation.

deportment (dɪˈpɔːtmənt) n. the manner in which a person behaves, esp. in physical bearing: military deportment.

depose (dɪˈpəuz) vb. **1.** (tr.) to remove from an office or position of power. **2.** Law. to testify or give (evidence, etc.) on oath.

deposit (dɪˈpɒzɪt) vb. (tr.) **1.** to put or set down, esp. carefully; place. **2.** to entrust for safekeeping. **3.** to place (money) in a bank or similar institution to earn interest or for safekeeping. **4.** to give (money) in part payment or as security. **5.** to lay down naturally: the river deposits silt. ~n. **6. a.** an instance of entrusting money or valuables to a bank or similar institution. **b.** the money or valuables so entrusted. **7.** money given in part payment or as security. **8.** an accumulation of sediments, mineral ores, coal, etc. **9.** any deposited material, such as a sediment. **10.** a depository or storehouse. **11. on deposit.** payable as the first instalment, as when buying on hire-purchase.

deodorant air freshener, antiperspirant, deodorizer, disinfectant, fumigant

depart 1. absent (oneself), decamp, disappear, escape, exit, go, go away, leave, migrate, quit, remove, retire, retreat, set forth, start out, take (one's) leave, vanish, withdraw **2.** deviate, differ, digress, diverge, stray, swerve, turn aside, vary, veer

departed dead, deceased, expired, late

department 1. district, division, province, region, sector **2.** branch, bureau, division, office, section, station, subdivision, unit **3.** area, domain, function, line, province, realm, responsibility, speciality, sphere

departure 1. exit, exodus, going, going away, leave-taking, leaving, removal, retirement, withdrawal **2.** abandonment, branching off, deviation, digression, divergence, variation, veering **3.** branching out, change, difference, innovation, novelty, shift

depend 1. bank on, build upon, calculate on, confide in, count on, lean on, reckon on, rely upon, trust in, turn to **2.** be based on, be contingent on, be determined by, be subject to, be subordinate to, hang on, hinge on, rest on, revolve around

dependable faithful, reliable, responsible, steady, sure, trustworthy, trusty, unfailing

dependant n. child, client, hanger-on, henchman, minion, minor, protégé, relative, retainer, subordinate, vassal

dependent adj. **1.** counting on, defenceless, helpless, immature, reliant, relying on, vulnerable, weak **2.** conditional, contingent, depending, determined by, liable to, relative, subject to **3.** feudal, subject, subordinate, tributary

depict 1. delineate, draw, illustrate, limn, outline, paint, picture, portray, render, reproduce, sculpt, sketch **2.** characterize, describe, detail, narrate, outline, sketch

deplete bankrupt, consume, decrease, drain, empty, evacuate, exhaust, expend, impoverish, lessen, milk, reduce, use up

depleted consumed, decreased, depreciated, devoid of, drained, emptied, exhausted, lessened, out of, reduced, short of, spent, used (up), wasted, weakened, worn out

depletion attenuation, consumption, decrease, deficiency, diminution, dwindling, exhaustion, expenditure, lessening, lowering,

reduction, using up

deplorable 1. calamitous, dire, disastrous, distressing, grievous, heartbreaking, lamentable, melancholy, miserable, pitiable, regrettable, sad, unfortunate, wretched **2.** blameworthy, disgraceful, dishonourable, disreputable, execrable, opprobrious, reprehensible, scandalous, shameful

deplore 1. bemoan, bewail, grieve for, lament, mourn, regret, rue, sorrow over **2.** abhor, censure, condemn, denounce, deprecate, disapprove of, object to

deploy arrange, dispose, extend, position, redistribute, set out, set up, spread out, station, use, utilize

deport 1. banish, exile, expatriate, expel, extradite, oust **2.** Used reflexively acquit, act, bear, behave, carry, comport, conduct, hold

deportation banishment, eviction, exile, expatriation, expulsion, extradition, transportation

deportment air, appearance, aspect, bearing, behaviour, carriage, cast, comportment, conduct, demeanour, manner, mien, posture, stance

depose 1. break, cashier, degrade, de-

deposit account *n. Brit.* a bank account that earns interest and usually requires notice of withdrawal.

depositary (dɪˈpɒzɪtərɪ, -trɪ) *n., pl.* **-taries.** 1. a person or group to whom something is entrusted for safety. 2. a variant spelling of **depository.**

deposition (ˌdɛpəˈzɪʃən) *n.* 1. *Law.* **a.** the giving of testimony on oath. **b.** the testimony given. **c.** the sworn statement of a witness used in court in his absence. 2. the act or instance of deposing. 3. the act or an instance of depositing. 4. something deposited.

depositor (dɪˈpɒzɪtə) *n.* a person who places or has money on deposit, esp. in a bank.

depository (dɪˈpɒzɪtərɪ, -trɪ) *n., pl.* **-ries.** 1. a store for furniture, valuables, etc.; repository. 2. a variant spelling of **depositary.**

depot (ˈdɛpəʊ) *n.* 1. a storehouse or warehouse. 2. *Mil.* **a.** a store for supplies. **b.** a training and holding centre for recruits and replacements. 3. *Chiefly Brit.* a building used for the storage and servicing of buses or railway engines. 4. *U.S.* a railway station.

deprave (dɪˈpreɪv) *vb.* (*tr.*) to make morally bad; corrupt. **—depravation** (ˌdɛprəˈveɪʃən) *n.* **—deˈpraved** *adj.*

depravity (dɪˈprævɪtɪ) *n., pl.* **-ties.** the state or an instance of moral corruption.

deprecate (ˈdɛprɪˌkeɪt) *vb.* (*tr.*) 1. to express disapproval of; protest against. 2. to depreciate; belittle. **—ˈdepreˌcatingly** *adv.* **—ˌdepreˈcation** *n.* **—ˈdeprecative** *adj.* **—ˈdepreˌcator** *n.* **—ˌdepreˈcatory** *adj.*

depreciate (dɪˈpriːʃɪˌeɪt) *vb.* 1. to reduce or decline in value or price. 2. (*tr.*) to lessen the value of by derision, criticism, etc. **—deˈpreciˌatingly** *adv.* **—depreciatory** (dɪˈpriːʃɪətərɪ) *or* **deˈpreciative** *adj.*

depreciation (dɪˌpriːʃɪˈeɪʃən) *n.* 1. *Accounting.* **a.** the reduction in value of a fixed asset due to use, obsolescence, etc. **b.** the amount deducted from gross profit to allow for this. 2. the act or an instance of depreciating or belittling. 3. a decrease in the exchange value of a currency brought about by excess supply of that currency under conditions of fluctuating exchange rates.

depredation (ˌdɛprɪˈdeɪʃən) *n.* the act or an instance of plundering; robbery; pillage.

depress (dɪˈprɛs) *vb.* (*tr.*) 1. to lower in spirits; make gloomy. 2. to weaken the force, or energy of. 3. to lower prices of. 4. to press or push down. **—deˈpressingly** *adv.* **—deˈpressive** *adj.*

depressant (dɪˈprɛsənt) *adj.* 1. *Med.* able to reduce

nervous or functional activity. 2. causing gloom; depressing. ~*n.* 3. a depressant drug.

depressed (dɪˈprɛst) *adj.* 1. low in spirits; downcast. 2. lower than the surrounding surface. 3. pressed down or flattened. 4. Also: **distressed.** characterized by economic hardship, such as unemployment: *a depressed area.* 5. lowered in force, intensity, or amount. 6. *Bot., zool.* flattened.

depression (dɪˈprɛʃən) *n.* 1. a depressing or being depressed. 2. a depressed or sunken place. 3. *Psychol.* an emotional state characterized by feelings of gloom and inadequacy. 4. *Pathol.* an abnormal lowering of the rate of any physiological activity or function. 5. an economic condition characterized by substantial unemployment, falling prices and security values, and low levels of investment, trade, etc.; slump. 6. Also called: **cyclone, low.** *Meteorol.* a body of moving air below normal atmospheric pressure, which often brings rain. 7. (esp. in surveying and astronomy) the angular distance of an object below the horizontal plane.

Depression (dɪˈprɛʃən) *n.* (usually preceded by *the*) the worldwide economic depression of the early 1930s, when there was mass unemployment.

deprive (dɪˈpraɪv) *vb.* (*tr.*) 1. (foll. by *of*) to prevent from possessing or enjoying; dispossess (of). 2. *Arch.* to depose; demote. **—deˈprival** *n.* **—deprivation** (ˌdɛprɪˈveɪʃən) *n.*

deprived (dɪˈpraɪvd) *adj.* lacking adequate food, shelter, education, etc.: *deprived inner-city areas.*

dept. *abbrev. for* department.

depth (dɛpθ) *n.* 1. the distance downwards, backwards, or inwards. 2. the quality of being deep; deepness. 3. intensity of emotion. 4. profundity of moral character; sagacity; integrity. 5. complexity or abstruseness, as of thought. 6. intensity, as of silence, colour, etc. 7. lowness of pitch. 8. (*often pl.*) a deep, inner, or remote part, such as an inaccessible region of a country. 9. (*often pl.*) the most intense or severe part: *the depths of winter.* 10. (*usually pl.*) a low moral state. 11. (*often pl.*) a vast space or abyss. 12. **beyond** *or* **out of one's depth. a.** in water deeper than one is tall. **b.** beyond the range of one's competence or understanding. 13. **in depth. a.** thoroughly or comprehensively. **b.** (*as modifier*): *an in-depth study.*

depth charge *or* **bomb** *n.* a bomb used to attack submarines that explodes at a pre-set depth of water.

deputation (ˌdɛpjʊˈteɪʃən) *n.* 1. the act of appointing a person or body of people to represent others. 2. a per-

---

THESAURUS

deposit *v.* 1. drop, lay, locate, place, precipitate, put, settle, sit down 2. amass, bank, consign, entrust, hoard, lodge, save, store ~*n.* 3. down payment, instalment, money (*in bank*), part payment, pledge, retainer, security, stake, warranty 4. accumulation, alluvium, deposition, dregs, lees, precipitate, sediment, silt

deposition 1. dethronement, dismissal, displacement, ousting, removal 2. *Law* affidavit, declaration, evidence, sworn statement, testimony

depository depot, repository, safe-deposit box, store, storehouse, warehouse

depot 1. depository, repository, storehouse, warehouse 2. *Military* arsenal, dump 3. bus station, garage, terminus

deprave brutalize, corrupt, debase, debauch, degrade, demoralize, lead astray, pervert, seduce, subvert, vitiate

depraved abandoned, corrupt, debased, debauched, degenerate, degraded, dissolute, evil, immoral, lascivious, lewd, licentious, perverted, profligate, shameless, sinful, vicious, vile, wicked

depravity baseness, contamination, corruption, criminality, debasement, debauchery, degeneracy, depravation, evil, immorality, iniquity, profligacy, sinfulness, vice, viciousness, vitiation, wickedness

depreciate 1. decrease, deflate, devaluate, devalue, lessen, lose value, lower, re-

duce 2. belittle, decry, denigrate, deride, detract, disparage, look down on, ridicule, run down, scorn, sneer at, traduce, underestimate, underrate, undervalue

depreciation 1. deflation, depression, devaluation, drop, fall, slump 2. belittlement, deprecation, derogation, detraction, disparagement, pejoration

depress 1. cast down, chill, damp, daunt, deject, desolate, discourage, dishearten, dispirit, make despondent, oppress, sadden, weigh down 2. debilitate, devitalize, drain, enervate, exhaust, lower, sap, slow up, weaken 3. cheapen, depreciate, devaluate, devalue, diminish, downgrade, impair, lessen, lower, reduce 4. flatten, level, lower, press down, push down

depressed 1. blue, crestfallen, dejected, despondent, discouraged, dispirited, down, downcast, downhearted, fed up, glum, low, low-spirited, melancholy, moody, morose, pessimistic, sad, unhappy 2. concave, hollow, indented, recessed, set back, sunken 3. *Of an area, circumstances* deprived, destitute, disadvantaged, distressed, grey, needy, poor, poverty-stricken, run-down 4. cheapened, depreciated, devalued, impaired, weakened

depressing black, bleak, daunting, dejecting, depressive, discouraging, disheartening, dismal, dispiriting, distressing, dreary, gloomy, heartbreaking, hopeless, melancholy, sad, saddening, sombre

depression 1. dejection, despair, despondency, dolefulness, downheartedness, dumps (*Inf.*), gloominess, hopelessness, low

spirits, melancholia, melancholy, sadness, the blues 2. *Commerce* dullness, economic decline, hard *or* bad times, inactivity, lowness, recession, slump, stagnation 3. bowl, cavity, concavity, dent, dimple, dip, excavation, hollow, impression, indentation, pit, sag, sink, valley

deprivation 1. denial, deprival, dispossession, divestment, expropriation, removal, withdrawal, withholding 2. destitution, detriment, disadvantage, distress, hardship, need, privation, want

deprive bereave, despoil, dispossess, divest, expropriate, rob, strip, wrest

deprived bereft, denuded, destitute, disadvantaged, forlorn, in need, in want, lacking, necessitous, needy, poor

depth 1. abyss, deepness, drop, extent, measure, profoundness, profundity 2. *Fig.* astuteness, discernment, insight, penetration, profoundness, profundity, sagacity, wisdom 3. abstruseness, complexity, obscurity, reconditeness 4. intensity, richness, strength 5. *Often plural* abyss, bowels of the earth, deepest (furthest, innermost, most intense, remotest) part, middle, midst, slough of despond 6. **in depth** comprehensively, extensively, intensively, thoroughly

deputation 1. commission, delegates, delegation, deputies, embassy, envoys, legation 2. appointment, assignment, commission, designation, nomination

mote, dethrone, dismiss, displace, downgrade, oust, remove from office 2. *Law* avouch, declare, make a deposition, testify

son or body of people so appointed; delegation.

depute (dɪ'pjuːt) vb. (tr.) **1.** to appoint as an agent. **2.** to assign (authority, duties, etc.) to a deputy. ~n. **3.** ('dɛpjuːt) Scot. **a.** a deputy. **b.** (as modifier, usually postpositive): a sheriff-depute.

deputize or **-ise** ('dɛpjuˌtaɪz) vb. to appoint or act as deputy.

deputy ('dɛpjutɪ) n., pl. **-ties. 1.** a person appointed to act on behalf of or represent another. **2.** a member of a legislative assembly in various countries, such as France. **3.** (as modifier): the deputy chairman.

derail (dɪ'reɪl) vb. to go or cause to go off the rails, as a train, tram, etc. —**de'railment** n.

derange (dɪ'reɪndʒ) vb. (tr.) **1.** to throw into disorder; disarrange. **2.** to disturb the action of. **3.** to make insane. —**de'rangement** n.

derby ('dɜːbɪ) n., pl. **-bies.** the U.S. name for **bowler**[2].

Derby ('dɑːbɪ; U.S. 'dɜːbɪ) n. **1. the.** an annual horse race run at Epsom Downs, Surrey, since 1780. **2.** any of various other horse races. **3. local Derby.** a football match between two teams from the same area.

derelict ('dɛrɪlɪkt) adj. **1.** deserted or abandoned, as by an owner, occupant, etc. **2.** falling into ruins. **3.** neglectful of duty; remiss. ~n. **4.** a social outcast or vagrant. **5.** property deserted or abandoned by an owner, occupant, etc. **6.** a vessel abandoned at sea. **7.** a person who is neglectful of duty.

dereliction (ˌdɛrɪ'lɪkʃən) n. **1.** conscious or wilful neglect (esp. in **dereliction of duty**). **2.** an abandoning or being abandoned. **3.** Law. accretion of dry land gained by the gradual receding of the sea.

derestrict (ˌdiːrɪ'strɪkt) vb. (tr.) to render or leave free from restriction, esp. a road from speed limits. —ˌdere'striction n.

deride (dɪ'raɪd) vb. (tr.) to speak of or treat with contempt or ridicule; scoff at. —**de'rider** n. —**de'ridingly** adv.

de rigueur French. (də ri'gœːr) adj. required by etiquette or fashion.

derisive (dɪ'raɪsɪv) or **derisory** (dɪ'raɪsərɪ) adj. **1.** characterized by derision; mocking; scornful. **2.** worthy of derision; ridiculous. —**derision** (dɪ'rɪʒən) n. —**de'risively** adv. —**de'risiveness** n.

derivation (ˌdɛrɪ'veɪʃən) n. **1.** a deriving or being derived. **2.** the origin or descent of something, such as a word. **3.** something derived; a derivative. **4. a.** the process of deducing a mathematical theorem, formula, etc., as a necessary consequence of a set of accepted statements. **b.** this sequence of statements. —ˌderi'vational adj.

derivative (dɪ'rɪvətɪv) adj. **1.** derived. **2.** based on other sources; not original. ~n. **3.** a term, idea, etc., that is based on or derived from another in the same class. **4.** a word derived from another word. **5.** Chem. a compound that is formed from, or can be regarded as formed from, a structurally related compound. **6.** Maths. **a.** Also called: **differential coefficient, first derivative.** the change of a function, f(x), with respect to an infinitesimally small change in the independent variable, x. **b.** the rate of change of one quantity with respect to another. —**de'rivatively** adv.

derive (dɪ'raɪv) vb. **1.** (usually foll. by from) to draw or be drawn (from) in source or origin. **2.** (tr.) to obtain by reasoning; deduce; infer. **3.** (tr.) to trace the source or development of. **4.** (usually foll. by from) to produce or be produced (from) by a chemical reaction. —**de'rivable** adj. —**de'river** n.

-derm n. combining form. indicating skin: endoderm.

dermatitis (ˌdɜːmə'taɪtɪs) n. inflammation of the skin.

dermato-, derma- or before a vowel **dermat-, derm-** combining form. indicating skin: dermatitis.

dermatology (ˌdɜːmə'tɒlədʒɪ) n. the branch of medicine concerned with the skin and its diseases. —**dermatological** (ˌdɜːmətə'lɒdʒɪkəl) adj. —ˌderma'tologist n.

derogate ('dɛrəˌgeɪt) vb. **1.** (intr.; foll. by from) to cause to seem inferior; detract. **2.** (intr.; foll. by from) to deviate in standard or quality. **3.** (tr.) to cause to seem inferior, etc.; disparage. —ˌdero'gation n. —**derogative** (dɪ'rɒgətɪv) adj.

derogatory (dɪ'rɒgətərɪ) adj. tending or intended to detract, disparage, or belittle; intentionally offensive. —**de'rogatorily** adv.

derrick ('dɛrɪk) n. **1.** a simple crane having lifting tackle slung from a boom. **2.** the framework erected over an oil well to enable drill tubes to be raised and lowered.

derring-do ('dɛrɪŋ'duː) n. Arch. or literary. boldness or bold action.

derv (dɜːv) n. a Brit. name for **diesel oil** when used for road transport.

dervish ('dɜːvɪʃ) n. a member of any of various Muslim orders of ascetics, some of which (**whirling dervishes**) are noted for a frenzied, ecstatic, whirling dance.

desalination (diːˌsælɪ'neɪʃən) or **desalinization, -isation** n. the process of removing salt, esp. from sea water.

descant ('dɛskænt) n. **1.** Also called: **discant.** a decorative counterpoint added above a basic melody. **2.** a comment or discourse. ~adj. **3.** Also: **discant.** of the highest member in a family of musical instruments: a descant recorder. ~vb. (intr.) **4.** Also: **discant.** (often foll. by on or upon) to perform a descant. **5.** (often foll. by on or upon) to discourse or make comments. **6.** Arch. to sing sweetly. —**des'canter** n.

descend (dɪ'sɛnd) vb. (mainly intr.) **1.** (also tr.) to move down (a slope, staircase, etc.) **2.** to lead or extend down; slope. **3.** to move to a lower level, pitch, etc.; fall. **4.** (often foll. by from) to be connected by a blood relationship (to a dead or extinct individual, species, etc.). **5.** to be inherited. **6.** to sink or come down in morals or behaviour. **7.** (often foll. by on or upon) to arrive or attack in a sudden or overwhelming way. **8.** (of the sun, moon, etc.) to move towards the horizon. —**des'cendable** or **des'cendible** adj.

descendant (dɪ'sɛndənt) n. **1.** a person, animal, or plant when described as descended from an individual, race, species, etc. **2.** something that derives from an earlier form. ~adj. **3.** a variant spelling of **descendent.**

descendent (dɪ'sɛndənt) adj. **1.** descending. ~n. **2.** a variant spelling of **descendant.**

descent (dɪ'sɛnt) n. **1.** the act of descending. **2.** a

THESAURUS

deputize 1. commission, delegate, depute **2.** act for, stand in for, take the place of, understudy

deputy 1. n. agent, ambassador, commissioner, delegate, legate, lieutenant, nuncio, proxy, representative, second-in-command, substitute, surrogate, vicegerent **2.** adj. assistant, depute (Scot.), subordinate

derange 1. confound, confuse, disarrange, disarray, discompose, disconcert, disorder, displace, disturb, ruffle, unsettle, upset **2.** craze, dement (Rare), drive mad, madden, make insane, unbalance, unhinge

deranged berserk, crazed, crazy, delirious, demented, distracted, frantic, frenzied, insane, irrational, lunatic, mad, maddened, unbalanced, unhinged

derelict adj. **1.** abandoned, deserted, dilapidated, discarded, forsaken, neglected, ruined **2.** careless, irresponsible, lax, negligent, remiss, slack ~n. **3.** down-and-out, good-for-nothing, ne'er-do-well, outcast,

tramp, vagrant, wastrel

dereliction 1. delinquency, evasion, failure, faithlessness, fault, neglect, negligence, nonperformance, remissness **2.** abandonment, abdication, desertion, forsaking, relinquishment, renunciation

deride chaff, contemn, detract, disdain, disparage, flout, gibe, insult, jeer, knock (Inf.), mock, pooh-pooh, ridicule, scoff, scorn, sneer, taunt

derisory contemptible, insulting, laughable, ludicrous, outrageous, preposterous, ridiculous

derivation 1. acquiring, deriving, extraction, getting, obtaining **2.** ancestry, basis, beginning, descent, etymology, foundation, genealogy, origin, root, source

derivative adj. **1.** acquired, borrowed, derived, inferred, obtained, procured, transmitted **2.** copied, imitative, plagiaristic, plagiarized, rehashed, secondary, second-hand, uninventive, unoriginal ~n. **3.** by-product,

derivation, descendant, off-shoot, outgrowth, spin-off

derive 1. collect, deduce, draw, elicit, extract, follow, gain, gather, get, glean, infer, obtain, procure, receive, trace **2.** With **from** arise, descend, emanate, flow, issue, originate, proceed, spring from, stem from

derogatory belittling, damaging, defamatory, depreciative, detracting, discreditable, dishonouring, disparaging, injurious, offensive, slighting, uncomplimentary, unfavourable, unflattering

descend 1. alight, dismount, drop, fall, go down, move down, plummet, plunge, sink, subside, tumble **2.** dip, gravitate, incline, slant, slope **3.** be handed down, be passed down, derive, issue, originate, proceed, spring **4.** abase oneself, condescend, degenerate, deteriorate, lower oneself, stoop **5.** Often with **on** arrive, assail, assault, attack, come in force, invade, pounce, raid, swoop

downward slope. **3.** a path or way leading downwards. **4.** derivation from an ancestor; lineage. **5.** a generation in a particular lineage. **6.** a decline or degeneration. **7.** a movement or passage in degree or state from higher to lower. **8.** (often foll. by *on*) a sudden and overwhelming arrival or attack. **9.** *Property law.* (formerly) the transmission of real property to the heir.

describe (dɪˈskraɪb) *vb.* (*tr.*) **1.** to give an account or representation of in words. **2.** to pronounce or label. **3.** to draw a line or figure, such as a circle. —**de'scribable** *adj.* —**de'scriber** *n.*

description (dɪˈskrɪpʃən) *n.* **1.** a statement or account that describes. **2.** the act, process, or technique of describing. **3.** sort or variety: *reptiles of every description.*

descriptive (dɪˈskrɪptɪv) *adj.* **1.** characterized by or containing description. **2.** *Grammar.* (of an adjective) serving to describe the referent of the noun modified, as for example the adjective *brown* as contrasted with *my.* **3.** relating to description or classification rather than explanation or prescription. —**de'scriptively** *adv.* —**de'scriptiveness** *n.*

descry (dɪˈskraɪ) *vb.* **-scrying, -scried.** (*tr.*) **1.** to catch sight of. **2.** to discover by looking carefully.

desecrate (ˈdɛsɪˌkreɪt) *vb.* (*tr.*) **1.** to violate the sacred character of (an object or place) by destructive, blasphemous, or sacrilegious action. **2.** to deconsecrate. —**dese·cration** *n.* —**ˈdeseˌcrator** or **ˈdeseˌcrater** *n.*

desegregate (diːˈsɛgrɪˌgeɪt) *vb.* to end racial segregation in (a school or other public institution). —**ˌdesegreˈgation** *n.*

desert¹ (ˈdɛzət) *n.* **1.** a region that is devoid or almost devoid of vegetation, esp. because of low rainfall. **2.** an uncultivated uninhabited region. **3.** a place which lacks some desirable feature or quality: *a cultural desert.* **4.** (*modifier*) of, relating to, or like a desert.

desert² (dɪˈzɜːt) *vb.* **1.** (*tr.*) to abandon (a person, place, etc.) without intending to return, esp. in violation of a promise or obligation. **2.** *Mil.* to abscond from (a post or duty) with no intention of returning. **3.** (*tr.*) to fail (someone) in time of need. —**de'serter** *n.* —**de'sertion** *n.*

desert³ (dɪˈzɜːt) *n.* **1.** (*often pl.*) just reward or punishment. **2.** the state of deserving a reward or punishment.

deserve (dɪˈzɜːv) *vb.* **1.** (*tr.*) to be entitled to or worthy of; merit. **2.** (*intr.*; foll. by *of*) *Obs.* to be worthy. —**de'server** *n.*

deserved (dɪˈzɜːvd) *adj.* rightfully earned; justified; war-

ranted. —**deservedly** (dɪˈzɜːvɪdlɪ) *adv.* —**deservedness** (dɪˈzɜːvɪdnɪs) *n.*

deserving (dɪˈzɜːvɪŋ) *adj.* (often *postpositive* and foll. by *of*) worthy, esp. of praise or reward. —**de'servingly** *adv.* —**de'servingness** *n.*

deshabille (ˌdeɪzæˈbiːl) *n.* a variant of **dishabille.**

desiccate (ˈdɛsɪˌkeɪt) *vb.* (*tr.*) **1.** to remove most of the water from; dehydrate. **2.** to preserve (food) by removing moisture; dry. —**ˈdesicˌcated** *adj.* —**ˌdesicˈcation** *n.*

design (dɪˈzaɪn) *vb.* **1.** to work out the structure or form of (something), as by making a sketch or plans. **2.** to plan and make (something) artistically or skilfully. **3.** (*tr.*) to invent. **4.** (*tr.*) to intend, as for a specific purpose; plan. ~*n.* **5.** a plan or preliminary drawing. **6.** the arrangement, elements, or features of an artistic or decorative work: *the design of the desk is Chippendale.* **7.** a finished artistic or decorative creation. **8.** the art of designing. **9.** a plan or project. **10.** an intention; purpose. **11.** (*often pl.*; often foll. by *on* or *against*) a plot, often to gain possession of (something) by illegitimate means. —**de'signable** *adj.*

designate (ˈdɛzɪgˌneɪt) *vb.* (*tr.*) **1.** to indicate or specify. **2.** to give a name to; style; entitle. **3.** to select or name for an office or duty; appoint. ~*adj.* (ˈdɛzɪgnɪt, -ˌneɪt). **4.** (*immediately postpositive*) appointed, but not yet in office: *a minister designate.* —**ˈdesigˌnator** *n.*

designation (ˌdɛzɪgˈneɪʃən) *n.* **1.** something that designates, such as a name. **2.** the act of designating or the fact of being designated.

designedly (dɪˈzaɪnɪdlɪ) *adv.* by intention or design; on purpose.

designer (dɪˈzaɪnə) *n.* **1.** a person who devises and executes designs, as for clothes, machines, etc. **2.** a person who devises plots; intriguer.

designing (dɪˈzaɪnɪŋ) *adj.* artful and scheming.

desirable (dɪˈzaɪərəbəl) *adj.* **1.** worthy of desire: *a desirable residence.* **2.** arousing desire, esp. sexual desire; attractive. —**deˌsiraˈbility** or **de'sirableness** *n.* —**de'sirably** *adv.*

desire (dɪˈzaɪə) *vb.* (*tr.*) **1.** to wish or long for; crave. **2.** to request; ask for. ~*n.* **3.** a wish or longing. **4.** an expressed wish; request. **5.** sexual appetite. **6.** a person or thing that is desired. —**de'sirer** *n.*

desirous (dɪˈzaɪərəs) *adj.* (usually *postpositive* and foll. by *of*) having or expressing desire (for).

THESAURUS

descent **1.** coming down, drop, fall, plunge, swoop **2.** declination, declivity, dip, drop, incline, slant, slope **3.** ancestry, extraction, family tree, genealogy, heredity, lineage, origin, parentage **4.** debasement, decadence, decline, degradation, deterioration **5.** assault, attack, foray, incursion, invasion, pounce, raid, swoop

describe **1.** characterize, define, depict, detail, explain, express, illustrate, narrate, portray, recount, relate, report, specify, tell **2.** delineate, draw, mark out, outline, trace

description **1.** account, characterization, delineation, depiction, detail, explanation, narration, narrative, portrayal, report, representation, sketch **2.** brand, breed, category, class, genre, genus, ilk, kidney, kind, order, sort, species, type, variety

descriptive circumstantial, depictive, detailed, explanatory, expressive, graphic, illustrative, pictorial, picturesque, vivid

desert¹ **1.** *n.* solitude, waste, wasteland, wilderness, wilds **2.** *adj.* arid, bare, barren, desolate, infertile, lonely, solitary, uncultivated, uninhabited, unproductive, untilled, waste, wild

desert² *v.* abandon, abscond, betray, decamp, defect, forsake, give up, go over the hill (*Military sl.*), jilt, leave, leave high and dry, leave (someone) in the lurch, leave stranded, maroon, quit, rat (on), relinquish, renounce, resign, run out on (*Inf.*), strand, throw over, vacate, walk out on (*Inf.*)

deserted abandoned, bereft, cast off, derelict, desolate, empty, forlorn, forsaken, godforsaken, isolated, left in the lurch, left

stranded, lonely, neglected, solitary, unfriended, unoccupied, vacant

deserter absconder, apostate, defector, escapee, fugitive, rat (*Inf.*), renegade, runaway, traitor, truant

desertion abandonment, absconding, apostasy, betrayal, defection, departure, dereliction, escape, evasion, flight, forsaking, relinquishment, truancy

deserve be entitled to, be worthy of, earn, gain, justify, merit, procure, rate, warrant, win

deserved appropriate, condign, due, earned, fair, fitting, just, justifiable, justified, meet (*Archaic*), merited, proper, right, rightful, suitable, warranted, well-earned

deserving commendable, estimable, laudable, meritorious, praiseworthy, righteous, worthy

design *v.* **1.** delineate, describe, draft, draw, outline, plan, sketch, trace ~*n.* **2.** blueprint, delineation, draft, drawing, model, outline, plan, scheme, sketch ~*v.* **3.** conceive, create, fabricate, fashion, invent, originate, think up ~*n.* **4.** arrangement, configuration, construction, figure, form, motif, organization, pattern, shape, style ~*v.* **5.** aim, contrive, destine, devise, intend, make, mean, plan, project, propose, purpose, scheme, tailor ~*n.* **6.** enterprise, plan, project, schema, scheme, undertaking **7.** aim, end, goal, intent, intention, meaning, object, objective, point, purport, purpose, target, view **8.** *Often plural* conspiracy, evil intentions, intrigue, machination, plot, scheme

designate **1.** call, christen, dub, entitle,

label, name, nominate, style, term **2.** allot, appoint, assign, choose, delegate, depute, nominate, select **3.** characterize, define, denote, describe, earmark, indicate, pinpoint, show, specify, stipulate

designation **1.** denomination, description, epithet, label, mark, name, title **2.** appointment, classification, delegation, indication, selection, specification

designer **1.** architect, artificer, couturier, creator, deviser, inventor, originator, stylist **2.** conniver, conspirator, intriguer, plotter, schemer

designing artful, astute, conniving, conspiring, crafty, crooked (*Inf.*), cunning, deceitful, devious, intriguing, Machiavellian, plotting, scheming, sharp, shrewd, sly, treacherous, tricky, unscrupulous, wily

desirability advantage, benefit, merit, profit, usefulness, value, worth

desirable **1.** advantageous, advisable, agreeable, beneficial, covetable, eligible, enviable, good, pleasing, preferable, profitable, worthwhile **2.** adorable, alluring, attractive, fascinating, fetching, seductive, sexy (*Inf.*)

desire *v.* **1.** aspire to, covet, crave, desiderate, fancy, hanker after, long for, set one's heart on, want, wish for, yearn for ~*n.* **2.** appetite, aspiration, craving, hankering, longing, need, want, wish, yearning, yen (*Inf.*) ~*v.* **3.** ask, entreat, importune, petition, request, solicit ~*n.* **4.** appeal, entreaty, importunity, petition, request, solicitation, supplication **5.** appetite, concupiscence, lasciviousness, lechery, libido, lust, lustfulness, passion

desired accurate, appropriate, correct,

desist (dɪ'zɪst) *vb.* (*intr.; often foll. by from*) to cease, as from an action; stop or abstain.

desk (dɛsk) *n.* **1.** a piece of furniture with a writing surface and usually drawers or other compartments. **2.** a service counter or table in a public building, such as a hotel. **3.** a support for the book from which services are read in a church. **4.** the editorial section of a newspaper, etc., responsible for a particular subject: *the news desk.* **5.** a music stand shared by two orchestral players.

desolate *adj.* ('dɛsəlɪt). **1.** uninhabited; deserted. **2.** made uninhabitable; laid waste; devastated. **3.** without friends, hope, or encouragement. **4.** dismal; depressing. ~*vb.* ('dɛsə,leɪt). (*tr.*) **5.** to deprive of inhabitants; depopulate. **6.** to lay waste; devastate. **7.** to make wretched or forlorn. **8.** to forsake or abandon. —'**desolately** *adv.* —'**desolateness** *n.* —'**deso,later** *or* '**deso,lator** *n.*

desolation (,dɛsə'leɪʃən) *n.* **1.** a desolating or being desolated; ruin or devastation. **2.** solitary misery; wretchedness. **3.** a desolate region.

despair (dɪ'spɛə) *vb.* **1.** (*intr.; often foll. by of*) to lose or give up hope: *I despair of his coming.* ~*n.* **2.** total loss of hope. **3.** a person or thing that causes hopelessness or for which there is no hope.

despatch (dɪ'spætʃ) *vb.* (*tr.*) a less common spelling of **dispatch.** —**des'patcher** *n.*

desperado (,dɛspə'rɑːdəʊ) *n., pl.* -**does** *or* -**dos.** a reckless or desperate person, esp. one ready to commit any violent illegal act.

desperate ('dɛspərɪt, -prɪt) *adj.* **1.** careless of danger, as from despair. **2.** (of an act) reckless; risky. **3.** used or undertaken as a last resort. **4.** critical; very grave: *in desperate need.* **5.** (*often postpositive and foll. by for*) in distress and having a great need or desire. **6.** moved by or showing despair. —'**desperately** *adv.* —'**desperateness** *n.*

desperation (,dɛspə'reɪʃən) *n.* **1.** desperate recklessness. **2.** the state of being desperate.

despicable ('dɛspɪkəbəl, dɪ'spɪk-) *adj.* worthy of being

despised; contemptible; mean. —**des'picably** *adv.*

despise (dɪ'spaɪz) *vb.* (*tr.*) to look down on with contempt; scorn: *he despises flattery.* —**de'spiser** *n.*

despite (dɪ'spaɪt) *prep.* **1.** in spite of; undeterred by. ~*n.* **2.** *Arch.* contempt; insult. **3. in despite of.** (*prep.*) *Rare.* in spite of.

despoil (dɪ'spɔɪl) *vb.* (*tr.*) to deprive by force; plunder; loot. —**de'spoiler** *n.* —**de'spoilment** *n.*

despond *vb.* **1.** (*intr.*) (dɪ'spɒnd). to become disheartened; despair. ~*n.* **2.** ('dɛspɒnd, dɪ'spɒnd). *Arch.* despondency. —**de'spondingly** *adv.*

despondent (dɪspɒndənt) *adj.* downcast or disheartened; dejected. —**de'spondency** *or* **de'spondence** *n.* —**de'spondently** *adv.*

despot ('dɛspɒt) *n.* **1.** an absolute or tyrannical ruler. **2.** any person in power who acts tyrannically. —**despotic** (dɛs'pɒtɪk) *or* **des'potical** *adj.* —**des'potically** *adv.*

despotism ('dɛspə,tɪzəm) *n.* **1.** the rule of a despot; absolute or tyrannical government. **2.** arbitrary or tyrannical authority or behaviour.

dessert (dɪ'zɜːt) *n.* **1.** the sweet, usually last course of a meal. **2.** *Chiefly Brit.* (esp. formerly) fruit, dates, nuts, etc., served at the end of a meal.

dessertspoon (dɪ'zɜːt,spuːn) *n.* a spoon intermediate in size between a tablespoon and a teaspoon.

destination (,dɛstɪ'neɪʃən) *n.* **1.** the predetermined end of a journey. **2.** the end or purpose for which something is created or a person is destined.

destine ('dɛstɪn) *vb.* (*tr.*) to set apart (for a certain purpose or person); intend; design.

destiny ('dɛstɪnɪ) *n., pl.* -**nies.** **1.** the future destined for a person or thing. **2.** the predetermined or inevitable course of events. **3.** the power that predetermines the course of events.

destitute ('dɛstɪ,tjuːt) *adj.* **1.** lacking the means of subsistence; totally impoverished. **2.** (*postpositive; foll. by of*) completely lacking: *destitute of words.* —,**desti'tu-**

exact, expected, express, fitting, necessary, particular, proper, required, right

desirous ambitious, anxious, aspiring, avid, craving, desiring, eager, hopeful, hoping, keen, longing, ready, willing, wishing, yearning

desist abstain, break off, cease, discontinue, end, forbear, give over (*Inf.*), give up, have done with, leave off, pause, refrain from, stop, suspend

desolate *adj.* **1.** bare, barren, bleak, desert, dreary, ruined, solitary, unfrequented, uninhabited, waste, wild ~*v.* **2.** depopulate, despoil, destroy, devastate, lay low, lay waste, pillage, plunder, ravage, ruin ~*adj.* **3.** abandoned, bereft, cheerless, comfortless, companionless, dejected, depressing, despondent, disconsolate, dismal, downcast, forlorn, forsaken, gloomy, lonely, melancholy, miserable, wretched ~*v.* **4.** daunt, deject, depress, discourage, dishearten, dismay, distress, grieve

desolation **1.** destruction, devastation, havoc, ravages, ruin, ruination **2.** barrenness, bleakness, desolateness, forlornness, isolation, loneliness, solitariness, solitude, wildness **3.** anguish, dejection, despair, distress, gloom, gloominess, melancholy, misery, sadness, unhappiness, woe, wretchedness

despair *v.* **1.** despond, give up, lose heart, lose hope ~*n.* **2.** anguish, dejection, depression, desperation, despondency, disheartenment, gloom, hopelessness, melancholy, misery, wretchedness **3.** burden, cross, ordeal, pain, trial, tribulation

despairing anxious, broken-hearted, dejected, depressed, desperate, despondent, disconsolate, downcast, frantic, griefstricken, hopeless, inconsolable, melancholy, miserable, suicidal, wretched

desperado bandit, criminal, cutthroat, gangster, gunman, hoodlum (*Chiefly U.S.*), lawbreaker, mugger, outlaw, ruffian, thug

desperate **1.** audacious, dangerous, daring, death-defying, determined, foolhardy,

frantic, furious, hasty, hazardous, headstrong, impetuous, madcap, precipitate, rash, reckless, risky, violent, wild **2.** acute, critical, dire, drastic, extreme, great, urgent, very grave **3.** despairing, despondent, forlorn, hopeless, inconsolable, irrecoverable, irremediable, irretrievable, wretched

desperately **1.** badly, dangerously, gravely, perilously, seriously, severely **2.** appallingly, fearfully, frightfully, hopelessly, shockingly

desperation **1.** defiance, foolhardiness, frenzy, heedlessness, impetuosity, madness, rashness, recklessness **2.** agony, anguish, anxiety, despair, despondency, distraction, heartache, hopelessness, misery, pain, sorrow, torture, trouble, unhappiness, worry

despicable abject, base, beyond contempt, cheap, contemptible, degrading, detestable, disgraceful, disreputable, hateful, ignominious, infamous, low, mean, pitiful, reprehensible, scurvy, shameful, sordid, vile, worthless, wretched

despise abhor, contemn, deride, detest, disdain, disregard, flout, loathe, look down on, neglect, revile, scorn, slight, spurn, undervalue

despite *prep.* against, even with, in contempt of, in defiance of, in spite of, in the face of, in the teeth of, notwithstanding, regardless of, undeterred by

despoil denude, deprive, destroy, devastate, dispossess, divest, loot, pillage, plunder, ravage, rifle, rob, strip, vandalize, wreak havoc upon, wreck

despond be cast down, be depressed, despair, give up, lose heart, lose hope, mourn, sorrow

despondency dejection, depression, despair, desperation, disconsolateness, discouragement, dispiritedness, downheartedness, gloom, hopelessness, low spirits, melancholy, misery, sadness, wretchedness

despondent blue, dejected, depressed, despairing, disconsolate, discouraged, dis-

heartened, dispirited, doleful, down, downcast, downhearted, gloomy, glum, hopeless, in despair, low, low-spirited, melancholy, miserable, morose, sad, sorrowful, woebegone, wretched

despot autocrat, dictator, monocrat, oppressor, tyrant

despotic absolute, arbitrary, arrogant, authoritarian, autocratic, dictatorial, domineering, imperious, monocratic, oppressive, tyrannical, unconstitutional

despotism absolutism, autarchy, autocracy, dictatorship, monocracy, oppression, totalitarianism, tyranny

destination **1.** harbour, haven, journey's end, landing-place, resting-place, station, stop, terminus **2.** aim, ambition, design, end, goal, intention, object, objective, purpose, target

destine allot, appoint, assign, consecrate, decree, design, devote, doom, earmark, fate, intend, mark out, ordain, predetermine, purpose, reserve

destined **1.** bound, certain, designed, doomed, fated, foreordained, ineluctable, inescapable, inevitable, intended, meant, ordained, predestined, unavoidable **2.** assigned, booked, bound for, directed, en route, heading, on the road to, routed, scheduled

destiny cup, divine decree, doom, fate, fortune, karma, kismet, lot, portion

destitute **1.** distressed, down and out, impecunious, impoverished, indigent, insolvent, moneyless, necessitous, needy, on one's uppers, on the breadline (*Inf.*), penniless, penurious, poor, poverty-stricken **2.** bereft of, deficient in, depleted, deprived of, devoid of, drained, empty of, in need of, lacking, wanting, without

destitution beggary, dire straits, distress, impecuniousness, indigence, neediness, pauperism, pennilessness, penury, privation, utter poverty, want

tion n.

destroy (dɪ'strɔɪ) vb. (mainly tr.) **1.** to ruin; spoil. **2.** to tear down or demolish. **3.** to put an end to. **4.** to kill or annihilate. **5.** to crush or defeat. **6.** (intr.) to be destructive or cause destruction.

destroyer (dɪ'strɔɪə) n. **1.** a small fast lightly armoured but heavily armed warship. **2.** a person or thing that destroys.

destruct (dɪ'strʌkt) vb. **1.** to destroy (one's own missile, etc.) for safety. **2.** (intr.) (of a missile, etc.) to be destroyed, for safety, by those controlling it. ~n. **3.** the act of destructing.

destructible (dɪ'strʌktəbəl) adj. capable of being or liable to be destroyed.

destruction (dɪ'strʌkʃən) n. **1.** the act of destroying or state of being destroyed; demolition. **2.** a cause of ruin or means of destroying.

destructive (dɪ'strʌktɪv) adj. **1.** (often postpositive and foll. by of or to) causing or tending to cause the destruction (of). **2.** intended to discredit, esp. without positive suggestions or help; negative: destructive criticism. ·—de'structively adv. —de'structiveness n.

destructor (dɪ'strʌktə) n. **1.** a furnace or incinerator for the disposal of refuse. **2.** a device used to blow up a defective missile.

desuetude (dɪ'sjuːɪˌtjuːd, ˈdɛswɪtjuːd) n. the condition of not being in use or practice; disuse.

desultory (ˈdɛsəltərɪ, -trɪ) adj. **1.** passing from one thing to another, esp. in a fitful way; unmethodical; disconnected. **2.** random or incidental: a desultory thought. —'desultorily adv. —'desultoriness n.

detach (dɪ'tætʃ) vb. (tr.) **1.** to disengage and separate or remove; unfasten; disconnect. **2.** Mil. to separate (a small unit) from a larger, esp. for a special assignment. —de,tacha'bility n. —de'tachable adj.

detached (dɪ'tætʃt) adj. **1.** disconnected or standing apart; not attached: a detached house. **2.** showing no bias or emotional involvement.

detachment (dɪ'tætʃmənt) n. **1.** indifference; aloofness. **2.** freedom from self-interest or bias; disinterest. **3.** the act of detaching something. **4.** the condition of being detached; disconnection. **5.** Mil. **a.** the separation of a small unit from its main body. **b.** the unit so detached.

detail (ˈdiːteɪl) n. **1.** an item that is considered separately; particular. **2.** an item that is unimportant: passengers' comfort was regarded as a detail. **3.** treatment of particulars: this essay includes too much detail. **4.** items collectively; particulars. **5.** a small section or element in a painting, building, statue, etc., esp. when considered in isolation. **6.** Mil. **a.** the act of assigning personnel for a specific duty. **b.** the personnel selected. **c.** the duty. **7. in detail.** including all or most particulars or items thoroughly. ~vb. (tr.) **8.** to list or relate fully. **9.** Mil. to select (personnel) for a specific duty.

detailed (ˈdiːteɪld) adj. having many details or giving careful attention to details.

detain (dɪ'teɪn) vb. (tr.) **1.** to delay; hold back. **2.** to confine or hold in custody. —de'tainable adj. —detainee (ˌdiːteɪ'niː) n. —de'tainment n.

detect (dɪ'tɛkt) vb. (tr.) **1.** to discover or notice. **2.** to discover, or reveal (a crime, criminal, etc.). **3.** to extract information from (an electromagnetic wave). —de'tectable or de'tectible adj. —de'tector n.

detection (dɪ'tɛkʃən) n. **1.** the act of discovering or the fact of being discovered. **2.** the act or process of extracting information, esp. at audio or video frequencies, from an electromagnetic wave; demodulation.

detective (dɪ'tɛktɪv) n. **1. a.** a police officer who investigates crimes. **b.** private detective. an individual privately employed to investigate a crime or make other inquiries. **c.** (as modifier): a detective story. ~adj. **2.** of or for detection.

détente (deɪ'tɑːnt; French de'tãt) n. the relaxing or easing of tension, esp. between nations.

detention (dɪ'tɛnʃən) n. **1.** a detaining or being detained. **2. a.** custody or confinement, esp. of a suspect awaiting trial. **b.** (as modifier): a detention order. **3.** a form of punishment in which a pupil is detained after school.

detention centre n. a place where young persons may be detained for short periods by order of a court.

deter (dɪ'tɜː) vb. **-terring, -terred.** (tr.) to discourage (from acting) or prevent (from occurring), usually by instilling fear, doubt, or anxiety. —de'terment n.

detergent (dɪ'tɜːdʒənt) n. **1.** a cleansing agent, esp. a chemical such as an alkyl sulphonate, widely used in industry, laundering, etc. ~adj. **2.** having cleansing power.

deteriorate (dɪ'tɪərɪəˌreɪt) vb. **1.** to make or become worse; depreciate. **2.** (intr.) to wear away or disintegrate. —de,terio'ration n. —de'teriorative adj.

determinant (dɪ'tɜːmɪnənt) adj. **1.** serving to determine. ~n. **2.** a factor that influences or determines. **3.** Maths. a square array of elements that represents the sum of certain products of these elements, used to solve simultaneous equations, in vector studies, etc.

determinate (dɪ'tɜːmɪnɪt) adj. **1.** definitely limited, defined, or fixed. **2.** determined. **3.** able to be predicted or deduced. **4.** Bot. having the main and branch stems ending in flowers. —de'terminateness n.

THESAURUS

destroy annihilate, blow to bits, break down, crush, demolish, desolate, devastate, dismantle, dispatch, eradicate, extinguish, extirpate, gut, kill, ravage, raze, ruin, shatter, slay, smash, torpedo, waste, wipe out, wreck

destruction annihilation, crushing, demolition, devastation, downfall, end, eradication, extermination, extinction, havoc, liquidation, massacre, overthrow, overwhelming, ruin, ruination, shattering, slaughter, undoing, wreckage, wrecking

destructive 1. baleful, baneful, calamitous, cataclysmic, catastrophic, damaging, deadly, deleterious, detrimental, devastating, fatal, harmful, hurtful, injurious, lethal, noxious, pernicious, ruinous **2.** adverse, antagonistic, contrary, derogatory, discouraging, discrediting, disparaging, hostile, invalidating, negative, opposed, undermining, vicious

detach cut off, disconnect, disengage, disentangle, disjoin, disunite, divide, free, isolate, loosen, remove, segregate, separate, sever, tear off, uncouple, unfasten, unhitch

detached 1. disconnected, discrete, disjoined, divided, free, loosened, separate, severed, unconnected **2.** aloof, disinterested, dispassionate, impartial, impersonal, neutral, objective, reserved, unbiased, uncommitted, uninvolved, unprejudiced

detachment 1. aloofness, coolness, indifference, remoteness, unconcern **2.** disinterestedness, fairness, impartiality, neutral-

ity, nonpartisanship, objectivity **3.** disconnection, disengagement, disjoining, separation, severing **4.** Military body, detail, force, party, patrol, squad, task force, unit

detail n. **1.** aspect, component, count, element, fact, factor, feature, item, particular, point, respect, specific, technicality **2.** Plural fine points, minutiae, niceties, particulars, parts, trivia, trivialities **3. in detail** comprehensively, exhaustively, inside out, item by item, point by point, thoroughly **4.** Military assignment, body, detachment, duty, fatigue, force, party, squad ~v. **5.** catalogue, delineate, depict, describe, enumerate, individualize, itemize, narrate, particularize, portray, recite, recount, rehearse, relate, specify **6.** allocate, appoint, assign, charge, commission, delegate, detach, send

detailed blow-by-blow, circumstantial, comprehensive, elaborate, exact, exhaustive, full, intricate, itemized, meticulous, minute, particular, particularized, specific, thorough

detain 1. check, delay, hinder, hold up, impede, keep, keep back, retard, slow up (or down), stay, stop **2.** arrest, confine, hold, intern, restrain

detect 1. ascertain, catch, descry, distinguish, identify, note, notice, observe, recognize, scent, spot **2.** catch, disclose, discover, expose, reveal, track down, uncover, unmask

detection discovery, exposé, exposure,

ferreting out, revelation, tracking down, uncovering, unearthing, unmasking

detective C.I.D. man, constable, cop (Sl.), copper (Sl.), dick (Sl., chiefly U.S.), gumshoe (U.S. sl.), investigator, private eye, private investigator, sleuth (Inf.)

detention confinement, custody, delay, hindrance, holding back, imprisonment, incarceration, keeping in, quarantine, restraint, withholding

deter caution, check, damp, daunt, debar, discourage, dissuade, frighten, hinder, inhibit from, intimidate, prevent, prohibit, put off, restrain, stop, talk out of

detergent 1. n. cleaner, cleanser **2.** adj. abstergent, cleaning, cleansing, detersive, purifying

deteriorate 1. corrupt, debase, decline, degenerate, degrade, deprave, depreciate, go downhill (Inf.), go to pot, go to the dogs (Inf.), impair, injure, lower, spoil, worsen **2.** be the worse for wear (Inf.), crumble, decay, decline, decompose, disintegrate, ebb, fade, fall apart, lapse, weaken, wear away

deterioration atrophy, corrosion, debasement, decline, degeneration, degradation, dégringolade, depreciation, descent, dilapidation, disintegration, downturn, drop, fall, lapse, retrogression, slump, vitiation, worsening

determination (dɪˌtɜːmɪˈneɪʃən) n. 1. the act of making a decision. 2. the condition of being determined; resoluteness. 3. an ending of an argument by the decision of an authority. 4. the act of fixing the quality, limit, position, etc., of something. 5. a decision or opinion reached. 6. a resolute movement towards some object or end. 7. Law. the termination of an estate or interest. 8. Law. the decision reached by a court of justice on a disputed matter.

determine (dɪˈtɜːmɪn) vb. 1. to settle or decide (an argument, question, etc.) conclusively. 2. (tr.) to conclude, esp. after observation or consideration. 3. (tr.) to influence; give direction to. 4. (tr.) to fix in scope, variety, etc.: the river determined the edge of the property. 5. to make or cause to make a decision. 6. (tr.) Logic. to define or limit (a notion) by adding or requiring certain features or characteristics. 7. (tr.) Geom. to fix or specify the position or form of. 8. Chiefly law. to come or bring to an end, as an estate. —deˈterminable adj.

determined (dɪˈtɜːmɪnd) adj. of unwavering mind; resolute; firm. —deˈterminedly adv.

determiner (dɪˈtɜːmɪnə) n. 1. a word, such as a number, an article, or all, that determines the referent or referents of a noun phrase. 2. a person or thing that determines.

determinism (dɪˈtɜːmɪˌnɪzəm) n. the philosophical doctrine that all acts, choices, and events are the inevitable consequence of antecedent sufficient causes. Cf. free will. —deˈterminist n., adj. —deˌterminˈistic adj.

deterrent (dɪˈtɛrənt) n. 1. something that deters. 2. a weapon, esp. nuclear, held by one state, etc., to deter attack by another. ~adj. 3. tending or used to deter. —deˈterrence n.

detest (dɪˈtɛst) vb. (tr.) to dislike intensely; loathe. —deˈtestable adj. —deˈtester n.

detestation (ˌdiːtɛsˈteɪʃən) n. 1. intense hatred; abhorrence. 2. a person or thing that is detested.

dethrone (dɪˈθrəʊn) vb. (tr.) to remove from a throne or deprive of any high position or title. —deˈthronement n. —deˈthroner n.

detonate (ˈdɛtəˌneɪt) vb. to cause (a bomb, mine, etc.) to explode or (of a bomb, mine, etc.) to explode. —ˌdetoˈnation n.

detonator (ˈdɛtəˌneɪtə) n. 1. a small amount of explosive, as in a percussion cap, used to initiate a larger explosion. 2. a device, such as an electrical generator, used to set off an explosion from a distance. 3. an explosive.

detour (ˈdiːtʊə) n. 1. a deviation from a direct route or course of action. ~vb. 2. to deviate or cause to deviate from a direct route or course of action.

detoxify (diːˈtɒksɪˌfaɪ) vb. -fying, -fied. (tr.) to remove poison from. —deˌtoxifiˈcation n.

detract (dɪˈtrækt) vb. 1. (when intr., usually foll. by from) to take away a part (of); diminish: her anger detracts from her beauty. 2. (tr.) to distract or divert. —deˈtraction n. —deˈtractive adj. —deˈtractor n.

detriment (ˈdɛtrɪmənt) n. 1. disadvantage or damage. 2. a cause of disadvantage or damage. —ˌdetriˈmental adj.

detritus (dɪˈtraɪtəs) n. 1. a loose mass of stones, silt, etc., worn away from rocks. 2. debris. —deˈtrital adj.

detumescence (ˌdiːtjuˈmɛsəns) n. the subsidence of a swelling.

deuce[1] (djuːs) n. 1. a. a playing card or dice with two spots. b. a throw of two in dice. 2. Tennis, etc. a tied score that requires one player to gain two successive points to win the game.

deuce[2] (djuːs) Inf. ~interj. 1. an expression of annoyance or frustration. ~n. 2. the deuce. (intensifier): used in such phrases as what the deuce, where the deuce, etc.

Deut. Bible. abbrev. for Deuteronomy.

deuterium (djuːˈtɪərɪəm) n. a stable isotope of hydrogen, occurring in natural hydrogen and in heavy water. Symbol: D or ^{2}H; atomic no.: 1; atomic wt.: 2.014.

deutero-, deuto- or before a vowel **deuter-, deut-** combining form. second or secondary: deuterium.

Deutsche Mark (ˈdɔɪtʃə) or **Deutschmark** n. the standard monetary unit of West Germany.

devalue (diːˈvæljuː) or **devaluate** (diːˈvæljuˌeɪt) vb. -valuing, -valued or -valuating, -valuated. 1. to reduce (a currency) or (of a currency) be reduced in exchange value. 2. (tr.) to reduce the value of. —deˌvaluˈation n.

devastate (ˈdɛvəˌsteɪt) vb. (tr.) 1. to lay waste or make desolate; ravage; destroy. 2. Inf. to confound or overwhelm. —ˌdevasˈtation n. —ˈdevasˌtator n.

develop (dɪˈvɛləp) vb. 1. to come or bring to a later or more advanced or expanded stage; grow or cause to grow gradually. 2. (tr.) to work out in detail. 3. to disclose or unfold (thoughts, a plot, etc.) gradually or (of thoughts, etc.) to be gradually disclosed or unfolded. 4. to come or bring into existence: he developed a new faith in God. 5. (tr.) to improve the value or change the use of (land). 6. (tr.) Photog. to treat (exposed film, plate, or paper) with chemical solutions in order to produce a visible image. 7. Biol. to progress or cause to progress from simple to complex stages in the growth of an individual or the evolution of a species. 8. (tr.) to elaborate upon (a musical theme) by varying the melody, key, etc. 9. (tr.) Maths. to expand (a function or expression) in the form of a series. 10. (tr.) Geom. to project or roll out (a surface) onto a plane without stretching or shrinking any element. 11. Chess. to bring (a piece) into play from its initial position on the back rank. 12. (tr.) to contract (a disease or illness). —deˈvelopable adj.

developer (dɪˈvɛləpə) n. 1. a person or thing that de-

THESAURUS

determination 1. backbone, constancy, conviction, dedication, doggedness, drive, firmness, fortitude, indomitability, perseverance, persistence, resoluteness, resolution, resolve, single-mindedness, steadfastness, tenacity, willpower 2. conclusion, decision, judgment, purpose, resolve, result, settlement, solution, verdict

determine 1. arbitrate, conclude, decide, end, finish, fix upon, ordain, regulate, settle, terminate 2. ascertain, certify, check, detect, discover, find out, learn, verify, work out 3. choose, decide, elect, establish, fix, make up one's mind, purpose, resolve 4. affect, condition, control, decide, dictate, direct, govern, impel, impose, incline, induce, influence, lead, modify, regulate, rule, shape

determined bent on, constant, dogged, firm, fixed, intent, persevering, persistent, purposeful, resolute, set on, single-minded, steadfast, strong-minded, strong-willed, tenacious, unflinching, unwavering

determining conclusive, critical, crucial, deciding, decisive, definitive, essential, final, important, settling

deterrent n. check, curb, defensive measures, determent, discouragement, disincentive, hindrance, impediment, obstacle, restraint

detest abhor, abominate, despise, dislike intensely, execrate, feel aversion (disgust, hostility, repugnance) towards, hate, loathe, recoil from

detonate blast, blow up, discharge, explode, fulminate, set off, touch off

detonation bang, blast, blow-up, boom, discharge, explosion, fulmination, report

detour bypass, byway, circuitous route, deviation, diversion, indirect course, roundabout way

detract 1. devaluate, diminish, lessen, lower, reduce, take away from 2. deflect, distract, divert, shift

detraction abuse, aspersion, belittlement, calumny, defamation, denigration, deprecation, disparagement, innuendo, insinuation, misrepresentation, muckraking, running down, scandalmongering, scurrility, slander, traducement, vituperation

detractor backbiter, belittler, defamer, denigrator, derogator (Rare), disparager, muckraker, scandalmonger, slanderer, traducer

detriment damage, disadvantage, disservice, harm, hurt, impairment, injury, loss, mischief, prejudice

detrimental adverse, baleful, damaging, deleterious, destructive, disadvantageous, harmful, inimical, injurious, mischievous, pernicious, prejudicial, unfavourable

devastate 1. demolish, desolate, despoil, destroy, lay waste, level, pillage, plunder, ravage, raze, ruin, sack, spoil, waste, wreck 2. Inf. chagrin, confound, discomfit, discompose, disconcert, floor (Inf.), nonplus, overpower, overwhelm, take aback

devastating caustic, cutting, deadly, destructive, effective, incisive, keen, mordant, overpowering, overwhelming, ravishing, sardonic, satirical, savage, stunning, trenchant, withering

devastation demolition, depredation, desolation, destruction, havoc, pillage, plunder, ravages, ruin, ruination, spoliation

develop 1. advance, cultivate, evolve, flourish, foster, grow, mature, progress, promote, prosper, ripen 2. amplify, augment, broaden, dilate upon, elaborate, enlarge, expand, unfold, work out 3. acquire, begin, breed, commence, contract, establish, form, generate, invent, originate, pick up, start 4. be a direct result of, break out, come about, ensue, follow, happen, result

velops something, esp. a person who develops property. **2.** *Photog.* a chemical used to convert the latent image recorded in the emulsion of a film or paper into a visible image.

developing country *n.* a poor or non-industrial country that is seeking to develop its resources by industrialization.

development (dɪ'vɛləpmənt) *n.* **1.** the act or process of growing or developing. **2.** the product of developing. **3.** a fact or event, esp. one that changes a situation. **4.** an area of land that has been developed. **5.** the section of a movement, usually in sonata form, in which the basic musical themes are developed. **6.** *Chess.* the process of developing pieces. —**de₁velop'mental** *adj.*

development area *n.* (in Britain) an area which has experienced economic depression because of the decline of its main industry or industries, and which is given government assistance to establish new industry.

deviant ('di:vɪənt) *adj.* **1.** deviating, as from what is considered acceptable behaviour. ~*n.* **2.** a person whose behaviour, esp. sexual behaviour, deviates from what is considered to be acceptable. —**'deviance** *n.*

deviate ('di:vɪˌeɪt) *vb.* **1.** (*usually intr.*) to differ or cause to differ, as in belief or thought. **2.** (*usually intr.*) to turn aside or cause to turn aside. **3.** (*intr.*) *Psychol.* to depart from an accepted standard. ~*n., adj.* ('di:vɪɪt). **4.** another word for **deviant.** —**'devi₁ator** *n.* —**'deviatory** *adj.*

deviation (ˌdi:vɪ'eɪʃən) *n.* **1.** an act or result of deviating. **2.** *Statistics.* the difference between an observed value in a series of such values and their arithmetic mean. **3.** the error of a compass due to local magnetic disturbances.

device (dɪ'vaɪs) *n.* **1.** a machine or tool used for a specific task. **2.** a plan, esp. a clever or evil one; trick. **3.** any ornamental pattern or picture, as in embroidery. **4.** a design or figure, used as a heraldic sign, emblem, etc. **5.** a particular pattern of words, figures of speech, etc., used in literature to produce an effect on the reader. **6. leave (someone) to his own devices.** to leave (someone) alone to do as he wishes.

devil ('dɛvəl) *n.* **1.** *Theol.* (*often cap.*) the chief spirit of evil and enemy of God, often depicted as a human figure with horns, cloven hoofs, and tail. **2.** *Theol.* any subordinate evil spirit. **3.** a person or animal regarded as wicked or ill-natured. **4.** a person or animal regarded as unfortunate or wretched. **5.** a person or animal regarded as daring, mischievous, or energetic. **6.** *Inf.* something difficult or annoying. **7.** *Christian Science.* an error, lie, or false belief. **8.** (in Malaysia) a ghost. **9.** a portable furnace or brazier. **10.** any of various mechanical devices, such as a machine for making wooden screws or a rag-tearing machine. **11.** See **printer's devil. 12.** *Law.* (in England) a junior barrister who does work for another in order to gain experience, usually for a half fee. **13. between the devil and the deep blue sea.** between equally undesirable alternatives. **14. devil of a.** *Inf.* (intensifier): *a devil of a fine horse.* **15. give the devil his due.** to acknowledge the talent or success of an unpleas-

ant person. **16. go to the devil. a.** to fail or become dissipated. **b.** (*interj.*) used to express annoyance with the person causing it. **17. raise the devil. a.** to cause a commotion. **b.** to make a great protest. **18. talk** (*or* **speak**) **of the devil!** (*interj.*) used when an absent person who has been the subject of conversation appears. **19. the devil!** (intensifier): **a.** used in **what the devil, where the devil,** etc. **b.** an exclamation of anger, surprise, disgust, etc. **20.** (let) **the devil take the hindmost.** look after oneself and leave others to their fate. **21. the devil to pay.** trouble to be faced as a consequence of an action. ~*vb.* -**illing,** -**illed** *or U.S.* -**illing,** -**iled. 22.** (*tr.*) *Inf.* to harass, vex, etc. **23.** (*tr.*) to prepare (food) by coating with a highly flavoured spiced paste or mixture of condiments before cooking. **24.** (*tr.*) to tear (rags) with a devil. **25.** (*intr.*) to serve as a printer's devil. **26.** (*intr.*) *Chiefly Brit.* to do hackwork, esp. for a lawyer or author.

devilish ('dɛvɪlɪʃ) *adj.* **1.** of, resembling, or befitting a devil; diabolic; fiendish. ~*adv., adj. Inf.* **2.** (intensifier): *devilish good food.* —**'devilishly** *adv.* —**'devilishness** *n.*

devil-may-care *adj.* careless or reckless; happy-go-lucky: *a devil-may-care attitude.*

devilment ('dɛvəlmənt) *n.* devilish or mischievous conduct.

devilry ('dɛvəlrɪ) *or* **deviltry** *n., pl.* -**ries** *or* -**tries. 1.** reckless or malicious fun or mischief. **2.** wickedness. **3.** black magic or other forms of diabolism.

devil's advocate *n.* **1.** a person who advocates an opposing or unpopular view, often for the sake of argument. **2.** *R.C. Church.* the official appointed to put the case against the beatification or canonization of a candidate.

devious ('di:vɪəs) *adj.* **1.** not sincere or candid; deceitful. **2.** (of a route or course of action) rambling; indirect. **3.** going astray; erring. —**'deviously** *adv.* —**'deviousness** *n.*

devise (dɪ'vaɪz) *vb.* **1.** to work out or plan (something) in one's mind. **2.** (*tr.*) *Law.* to dispose of (real property) by will. ~*n. Law.* **3.** a disposition of property by will. **4.** a will or clause in a will disposing of real property. —**de'viser** *n.*

devoid (dɪ'vɔɪd) *adj.* (*postpositive;* foll. by *of*) destitute or void (of); free (from).

devolution (ˌdi:və'lu:ʃən) *n.* **1.** a devolving. **2.** a passing onwards or downwards from one stage to another. **3.** a transfer of authority from a central government to regional governments. —**ˌdevo'lutionary** *adj.* —**ˌdevo'lutionist** *n., adj.*

devolve (dɪ'vɒlv) *vb.* **1.** (foll. by *on, upon, to,* etc.) to pass or cause to pass to a successor or substitute, as duties, power, etc. **2.** (*intr.* foll. by *on* or *upon*) *Law.* (of an estate, etc.) to pass to another by operation of law. —**de'volvement** *n.*

Devonian (də'vəʊnɪən) *adj.* **1.** of, denoting, or formed in the fourth period of the Palaeozoic era, between the Silurian and Carboniferous periods. **2.** of or relating to Devon. ~*n.* **3. the.** the Devonian period or rock system.

devote (dɪ'vəʊt) *vb.* (*tr.*) to apply or dedicate (oneself,

---

▬THESAURUS▬

development 1. advance, advancement, evolution, expansion, growth, improvement, increase, maturity, progress, progression, spread, unfolding, unravelling **2.** change, circumstance, event, happening, incident, issue, occurrence, outcome, phenomenon, result, situation, turn of events, upshot

deviant 1. *adj.* aberrant, abnormal, bent (*Sl.*), deviate, devious, freaky (*Sl.*), heretical, kinky (*Sl.*), perverse, perverted, queer (*Inf.*), twisted, wayward **2.** *n.* deviate, freak, misfit, odd type, pervert, queer (*Inf.*)

deviate avert, bend, deflect, depart, differ, digress, diverge, drift, err, part, stray, swerve, turn, turn aside, vary, veer, wander

deviation aberration, alteration, change, deflection, departure, digression, discrepancy, disparity, divergence, fluctuation, inconsistency, irregularity, shift, variance, variation

device 1. apparatus, appliance, contraption, contrivance, gadget, gimmick, implement, instrument, invention, tool, utensil **2.** artifice, design, dodge, expedient, gambit,

improvisation, manoeuvre, plan, ploy, project, purpose, ruse, scheme, shift, stratagem, strategy, stunt, trick, wile **3.** badge, colophon, crest, design, emblem, figure, insignia, logo, motif, motto, symbol, token

devil 1. *Sometimes cap.* Apollyon, archfiend, Beelzebub, Belial, Clootie (*Scot.*), demon, fiend, Lucifer, Old Harry (*Inf.*), Old Nick (*Inf.*), Prince of Darkness, Satan **2.** beast, brute, demon, monster, ogre, rogue, savage, terror, villain **3.** imp, monkey (*Inf.*), rascal, rogue, scamp, scoundrel **4.** beggar, creature, thing, unfortunate, wretch **5.** demon, enthusiast, fiend, go-getter (*Inf.*)

devilish accursed, atrocious, damnable, detestable, diabolic, diabolical, execrable, fiendish, hellish, infernal, satanic, wicked

devilry, deviltry 1. devilment, knavery, mischief, mischievousness, rascality, roguery **2.** cruelty, evil, malevolence, malice, vice, viciousness, villainy, wickedness **3.** black magic, diablerie, diabolism

devious 1. calculating, crooked (*Inf.*), deceitful, dishonest, double-dealing, evasive, in-

direct, insidious, insincere, not straightforward, scheming, sly, surreptitious, treacherous, tricky, underhand, wily **2.** circuitous, confusing, crooked, deviating, erratic, excursive, indirect, misleading, rambling, roundabout, tortuous, wandering

devise arrange, conceive, concoct, construct, contrive, design, dream up, form, formulate, frame, imagine, invent, plan, plot, prepare, project, scheme, think up, work out

devoid barren, bereft, deficient, denuded, destitute, empty, free from, lacking, sans (*Archaic*), unprovided with, vacant, void, wanting, without

devolution decentralization, delegation

devolve 1. be transferred, commission, consign, delegate, depute, entrust, fall upon *or* to, rest with, transfer **2.** *Law* alienate, be handed down, convey

devote allot, apply, appropriate, assign, commit, concern oneself, consecrate, dedicate, enshrine, give, occupy oneself, pledge, reserve, set apart money, etc.) to some pursuit, cause, etc.

devoted (dɪˈvəʊtɪd) *adj.* **1.** feeling or demonstrating loyalty or devotion; devout. **2.** (*postpositive;* foll. by *to*) dedicated or consecrated. —**deˈvotedly** *adv.* —**deˈvotedness** *n.*

devotee (ˌdɛvəˈtiː) *n.* **1.** a person ardently enthusiastic about something, such as a sport or pastime. **2.** a zealous follower of a religion.

devotion (dɪˈvəʊʃən) *n.* **1.** (often foll. by *to*) strong attachment (to) or affection (for a cause, person, etc.) marked by dedicated loyalty. **2.** religious zeal; piety. **3.** (*often pl.*) religious observance or prayers. —**deˈvotional** *adj.*

devour (dɪˈvaʊə) *vb.* (*tr.*) **1.** to eat up greedily or voraciously. **2.** to waste or destroy; consume. **3.** to consume greedily or avidly with the senses or mind. **4.** to engulf or absorb. —**deˈvourer** *n.*

devout (dɪˈvaʊt) *adj.* **1.** deeply religious; reverent. **2.** sincere; earnest; heartfelt. —**deˈvoutly** *adv.* —**deˈvoutness** *n.*

dew (djuː) *n.* **1.** drops of water condensed on a cool surface, esp. at night, from vapour in the air. **2.** something like this, esp. in freshness: *the dew of youth.* **3.** small drops of moisture, such as tears. ~*vb.* **4.** (*tr.*) to moisten with or as with dew. —**ˈdewy** *adj.*

dewclaw (ˈdjuːˌklɔː) *n.* **1.** a nonfunctional claw in dogs. **2.** an analogous rudimentary hoof in deer, goats, etc. —**ˈdewˌclawed** *adj.*

Dewey Decimal System (ˈdjuːɪ) *n.* a system of library book classification with ten main subject classes. Also called: **decimal classification.**

dewlap (ˈdjuːˌlæp) *n.* **1.** a loose fold of skin hanging from beneath the throat in cattle, dogs, etc. **2.** loose skin on an elderly person's throat.

dew point *n.* the temperature at which dew begins to form.

dew pond *n.* a small natural pond.

dexter (ˈdɛkstə) *adj.* **1.** *Arch.* of or located on the right side. **2.** (*usually postpositive*) *Heraldry.* of, on, or starting from the right side of a shield from the bearer's point of view and therefore on the spectator's left. ~Cf. sinister.

dexterity (dɛkˈstɛrɪtɪ) *n.* **1.** physical, esp. manual, skill or nimbleness. **2.** mental skill or adroitness.

dexterous (ˈdɛkstrəs) *adj.* possessing or done with dexterity. —**ˈdexterously** *adv.* —**ˈdexterousness** *n.*

dextrin (ˈdɛkstrɪn) *or* **dextrine** (ˈdɛkstrɪn, -triːn) *n.* any of a group of sticky substances obtained from starch: used as thickening agents in foods and as gums.

dextrose (ˈdɛkstrəʊz, -trəʊs) *n.* a glucose occurring widely in fruit, honey, and in the blood and tissue of animals. Formula: $C_6H_{12}O_6$. Also called: **grape sugar, dextroglucose.**

D.F. *abbrev. for* Defender of the Faith.

D.F.C. *abbrev. for* Distinguished Flying Cross.

D.F.M. *abbrev. for* Distinguished Flying Medal.

dg *or* **dg.** *abbrev. for* decigram.

dhal, dal, *or* **dholl** (dɑːl) *n.* **1.** a tropical African and Asian shrub cultivated for its nutritious pealike seeds. **2.** the seed of this shrub.

dharma (ˈdɑːmə) *n.* **1.** *Hinduism.* social custom regarded as a religious and moral duty. **2.** *Hinduism.* **a.** the essential principle of the cosmos; natural law. **b.** conduct that conforms with this. **3.** *Buddhism.* ideal truth.

dhoti (ˈdəʊtɪ), **dhooti, dhootie,** *or* **dhuti** (ˈduːtɪ) *n.* a long loincloth worn by men in India.

dhow (daʊ) *n.* a lateen-rigged coastal Arab sailing vessel.

DHSS (in Britain) *abbrev. for* Department of Health and Social Security.

di-[1] *prefix.* **1.** twice; two; double: *dicotyledon.* **2.** **a.** containing two specified atoms or groups of atoms: *carbon dioxide.* **b.** a nontechnical equivalent of **bi-** (sense 5).

di-[2] *combining form.* variant of **dia-** before a vowel: *diopter.*

dia- *or* **di-** *prefix.* **1.** through or during: *diachronic.* **2.** across: *diactinic.* **3.** apart: *diacritic.*

diabetes (ˌdaɪəˈbiːtɪs, -tiːz) *n.* any of various disorders, esp. diabetes mellitus, characterized by excretion of an abnormally large amount of urine.

diabetes mellitus (məˈlaɪtəs) *n.* a disorder of carbohydrate metabolism characterized by excessive thirst and excretion of abnormally large quantities of urine containing an excess of sugar, caused by a deficiency of insulin.

diabetic (ˌdaɪəˈbɛtɪk) *adj.* **1.** of, relating to, or having diabetes. **2.** for the use of diabetics. ~*n.* **3.** a person who has diabetes.

diabolic (ˌdaɪəˈbɒlɪk) *adj.* **1.** of the devil; satanic. **2.** extremely cruel or wicked; fiendish. **3.** very difficult or unpleasant. —**ˌdiaˈbolically** *adv.* —**ˌdiaˈbolicalness** *n.*

diabolical (ˌdaɪəˈbɒlɪkəl) *adj. Inf.* **1.** excruciatingly bad. **2.** (intensifier): *a diabolical liberty.* —**ˌdiaˈbolically** *adv.* —**ˌdiaˈbolicalness** *n.*

diabolism (daɪˈæbəˌlɪzəm) *n.* **1. a.** witchcraft or sorcery. **b.** worship of devils or beliefs concerning them. **2.** character or conduct that is devilish. —**diˈabolist** *n.*

diaconate (daɪˈækənɪt, -ˌneɪt) *n.* the office, sacramental status, or period of office of a deacon.

diacritic (ˌdaɪəˈkrɪtɪk) *n.* **1.** a sign placed above or below a character or letter to indicate that it has a different phonetic value, is stressed, or for some other reason. ~*adj.* **2.** another word for **diacritical.**

diacritical (ˌdaɪəˈkrɪtɪkəl) *adj.* **1.** of or relating to a diacritic. **2.** showing up a distinction.

diadem (ˈdaɪəˌdɛm) *n.* **1.** a royal crown, esp. a light jewelled circlet. **2.** royal dignity or power.

diaeresis *or, esp. U.S.,* **dieresis** (daɪˈɛrɪsɪs) *n., pl.* **-ses** (-ˌsiːz). **1.** the mark ¨ placed over the second of two adjacent vowels to indicate that it is to be pronounced separately, as in some spellings of *coöperate, naïve,* etc. **2.** this mark used for any other purpose, such as to indicate a special pronunciation for a particular vowel. **3.** a pause in a line of verse when the end of a foot coincides with the end of a word. —**diaeˈretic** *or* **dieretic** (ˌdaɪəˈrɛtɪk) *adj.*

diagnose (ˈdaɪəgˌnəʊz) *vb.* **1.** to determine by diagnosis. **2.** (*tr.*) to examine (a person or thing), as for a disease. —**ˌdiagˈnosable** *adj.*

diagnosis (ˌdaɪəgˈnəʊsɪs) *n., pl.* **-ses** (-siːz). **1. a.** the identification of diseases from the examination of symptoms. **b.** an opinion so reached. **2. a.** thorough analysis of facts or problems in order to gain understanding. **b.** an opinion reached through such analysis. —**diagnostic** (ˌdaɪəgˈnɒstɪk) *adj.*

diagonal (daɪˈægənəl) *adj.* **1.** *Maths.* connecting any two vertices that in a polygon are not adjacent and in a

---

THESAURUS

devoted ardent, caring, committed, concerned, constant, dedicated, devout, faithful, fond, loving, loyal, staunch, steadfast, true

devotee addict, adherent, admirer, aficionado, disciple, enthusiast, fan, fanatic, follower, supporter, votary

devotion 1. adherence, allegiance, commitment, consecration, constancy, dedication, faithfulness, fidelity, loyalty 2. adoration, devoutness, godliness, holiness, piety, prayer, religiousness, reverence, sanctity, spirituality, worship 3. affection, ardour, attachment, earnestness, fervour, fondness, intensity, love, passion, zeal 4. *Plural* church service, divine office, prayers, religious observance

devour 1. bolt, consume, cram, dispatch, eat, gobble, gorge, gulp, guzzle, polish off

(*Inf.*), stuff, swallow, wolf 2. annihilate, consume, destroy, ravage, spend, waste, wipe out 3. absorb, appreciate, be engrossed by, be preoccupied, delight in, drink in, enjoy, feast on, go through, read compulsively *or* voraciously, relish, revel in, take in

devouring consuming, excessive, insatiable, intense, overwhelming, passionate, powerful

devout 1. godly, holy, orthodox, pious, prayerful, pure, religious, reverent, saintly 2. ardent, deep, devoted, earnest, fervent, genuine, heartfelt, intense, passionate, profound, serious, sincere, zealous

devoutly fervently, heart and soul, profoundly, sincerely, with all one's heart

dexterity 1. adroitness, artistry, deftness, effortlessness, expertise, facility, finesse,

handiness, knack, mastery, neatness, nimbleness, proficiency, skill, smoothness, touch 2. ability, address, adroitness, aptitude, aptness, art, cleverness, expertness, ingenuity, readiness, skilfulness, tact

diabolical appalling, atrocious, damnable, difficult, disastrous, dreadful, excruciating, fiendish, hellish, nasty, outrageous, shocking, tricky, unpleasant, vile

diagnose analyse, determine, distinguish, identify, interpret, investigate, pinpoint, pronounce, recognize

diagnosis 1. analysis, examination, investigation, scrutiny 2. conclusion, interpretation, opinion, pronouncement

diagram 271 **diatonic**

polyhedron are not in the same face. **2.** slanting; oblique. **3.** marked with slanting lines or patterns. *~n.* **4.** a diagonal line, plane, or pattern. **5.** something put, set, or drawn obliquely. **—di'agonally** *adv.*

diagram ('daɪəˌgræm) *n.* **1.** a sketch or plan demonstrating the form or workings of something. **2.** *Maths.* a pictorial representation of a quantity or of a relationship. *~vb.* **-gramming, -grammed** *or U.S.* **-graming, -gramed. 3.** to show in or as if in a diagram. **—diagrammatic** (ˌdaɪəgrə'mætɪk) *adj.*

dial ('daɪəl) *n.* **1.** the face of a watch, clock, etc., marked with divisions representing units of time. **2.** the graduated disc of various measuring instruments. **3. a.** the control on a radio or television set used to change the station or channel. **b.** the panel on a radio on which the frequency, wavelength, or station is indicated. **4.** a numbered disc on a telephone that is rotated a set distance for each digit of a number being called. **5.** *Brit.* a slang word for **face** *~vb.* **dialling, dialled** *or U.S.* **dialing, dialed. 6.** to try to establish a telephone connection with (a subscriber) by operating the dial on a telephone. **7.** *(tr.)* to indicate, measure, or operate with a dial. **—'dialler** *n.*

dial. *abbrev. for* dialect(al).

dialect ('daɪəˌlɛkt) *n.* **a.** a form of a language spoken in a particular geographical area or by members of a particular social class or occupational group, distinguished by its vocabulary, grammar, and pronunciation. **b.** a form of a language that is considered inferior. **—ˌdia-'lectal** *adj.*

dialectic (ˌdaɪə'lɛktɪk) *n.* **1.** the art or practice of assessing the truth of a theory by discussion and logical disputation. **2.** logical argumentation. **3.** a variant of **dialectics** (sense 1). **4.** *Philosophy.* an interpretive method used by Hegel in which contradictions are resolved at a higher level of truth (synthesis). *~adj.* **5.** of or relating to logical disputation. **—ˌdialec'tician** *n.*

dialectical (ˌdaɪə'lɛktɪkəl) *adj.* of or relating to dialectic or dialectics. **—ˌdia'lectically** *adv.*

dialectics (ˌdaɪə'lɛktɪks) *n.* **1.** Also: **dialectic.** *Philosophy.* **a.** logic or a branch of logic. **b.** any formal system of reasoning. **2.** the rationale of dialectical materialism.

dialling tone *or U.S.* **dial tone** *n.* a continuous purring heard over a telephone indicating that a number can be dialled.

dialogue *or U.S. (often)* **dialog** ('daɪəˌlɒg) *n.* **1.** conversation between two or more people. **2.** an exchange of opinions; discussion. **3.** the lines spoken by characters in drama or fiction. **4.** a passage of conversation in a literary or dramatic work. **5.** a literary composition in the form of a dialogue. **6.** a political discussion between representatives of two nations or groups.

dialysis (daɪ'ælɪsɪs) *n., pl.* **-ses** (-ˌsiːz). **1.** the separation of the crystalloids from a solution containing crystalloids and colloids by osmosis of the crystalloids. **2.** *Med.* the filtering of blood through a semipermeable membrane to remove waste products. **—dialytic** (ˌdaɪə'lɪtɪk) *adj.*

diamagnetism (ˌdaɪə'mægnɪˌtɪzəm) *n.* the phenomenon exhibited by substances that are repelled by both poles of a magnet and thus lie across the magnet's line of influence.

diamanté (ˌdaɪə'mæntɪ) *adj.* **1.** decorated with glittering ornaments, such as sequins. *~n.* **2.** a fabric so covered.

diameter (daɪ'æmɪtə) *n.* **1. a.** a straight line connecting the centre of a circle, sphere, etc. with two points on the perimeter or surface. **b.** the length of such a line. **2.** the thickness of something, esp. with circular cross section. **—diametric** (ˌdaɪə'mɛtrɪk) *or* **ˌdia'metrical** *adj.* **—ˌdia-'metrically** *adv.*

diamond ('daɪəmənd) *n.* **1. a.** a usually colourless exceptionally hard form of carbon in cubic crystalline form. It is used as a precious stone and for industrial cutting or abrading. **b.** *(as modifier): a diamond ring.* **2.** *Geom.* a figure having four sides of equal length forming two acute angles and two obtuse angles; rhombus. **3. a.** a red lozenge-shaped symbol on a playing card. **b.** a card with one or more of these symbols or *(when pl.)* the suit of cards so marked. **4.** *Baseball.* **a.** the whole playing field. **b.** the square formed by the four bases. **5.** **rough diamond.** a person of fine character who lacks refinement and polish. *~vb.* **6.** *(tr.)* to decorate with or as with diamonds. **—diamantine** (ˌdaɪə'mæntaɪn) *adj.*

diamond wedding *n.* the 60th, or occasionally the 75th, anniversary of a marriage.

dianthus (daɪ'ænθʊs) *n., pl.* **-thuses.** any Eurasian plant of the widely cultivated genus *Dianthus*, such as the carnation, pink, and sweet william.

diapason (ˌdaɪə'peɪzən) *n. Music.* **1.** either of two stops **(open** and **stopped diapason)** found throughout the compass of a pipe organ that give it its characteristic tone colour. **2.** the compass of an instrument or voice. **3. a.** a standard pitch used for tuning. **b.** a tuning fork or pitch pipe. **4.** (in classical Greece) an octave.

diaper ('daɪəpə) *n.* **1.** the U.S. word for **nappy'. 2. a.** a fabric having a pattern of a small repeating design, esp. diamonds. **b.** such a pattern, used as decoration. *~vb.* **3.** *(tr.)* to decorate with such a pattern.

diaphanous (daɪ'æfənəs) *adj.* (usually of fabrics) fine and translucent. **—di'aphanously** *adv.*

diaphragm ('daɪəˌfræm) *n.* **1.** *Anat.* any separating membrane, esp. the muscular partition that separates the abdominal and thoracic cavities in mammals. **2.** a contraceptive membrane placed over the mouth of the cervix. **3.** any thin dividing membrane. **4.** Also called: **stop.** a device to control the amount of light entering an optical instrument, such as a camera. **5.** a thin vibrating disc used to convert sound signals to electrical signals or vice versa in telephones, etc. **—diaphragmatic** (ˌdaɪəfræg'mætɪk) *adj.*

diapositive (ˌdaɪə'pɒzɪtɪv) *n.* a positive transparency; slide.

diarist ('daɪərɪst) *n.* a person who writes a diary, esp. one that is subsequently published.

diarrhoea *or esp. U.S.* **diarrhea** (ˌdaɪə'rɪə) *n.* frequent and copious discharge of abnormally liquid faeces. **—ˌdiar'rhoeal, ˌdiar'rhoeic** *or esp. U.S.* **ˌdiar'rheal, ˌdiar'rheic** *adj.*

diary ('daɪərɪ) *n., pl.* **-ries. 1.** a personal record of daily events, appointments, observations, etc. **2.** a book for this.

Diaspora (daɪ'æspərə) *n.* **1. a.** the dispersion of the Jews from Palestine after the Babylonian captivity. **b.** the Jewish communities that arose after this dispersion. **2.** *(often not cap.)* a dispersion, as of people originally belonging to one nation.

diastase (ˈdaɪəˌsteɪs, -ˌsteɪz) *n.* any of a group of enzymes that hydrolyse starch to maltose. They are present in germinated barley and in the pancreas. **—ˌdia-'stasic** *adj.*

diatom ('daɪətəm) *n.* a microscopic unicellular alga having a cell wall impregnated with silica.

diatomic (ˌdaɪə'tɒmɪk) *adj.* (of a compound or molecule) **a.** containing two atoms. **b.** containing two characteristic groups or atoms.

diatonic (ˌdaɪə'tɒnɪk) *adj.* **1.** of, relating to, or based upon any scale of five tones and two semitones produced by playing the white keys of a keyboard instrument. **2.** not involving the sharpening or flattening of the notes of the major or minor scale nor the use of such notes as modified by accidentals.

THESAURUS

diagonal *adj.* angled, cater-cornered (*U.S. inf.*), cornerways, cross, crossways, crosswise, oblique, slanting

diagonally aslant, at an angle, cornerwise, crosswise, obliquely, on the bias, on the cross

diagram chart, drawing, figure, layout, outline, plan, representation, sketch

dialect accent, idiom, jargon, language, lingo (*Inf.*), localism, patois, pronunciation, provincialism, speech, tongue, vernacular

dialectic 1. *adj.* analytic, argumentative, dialectical, logical, polemical, rational, rationalistic 2. *n. Often plural* argumentation, contention, discussion, disputation, logic, polemics, ratiocination, reasoning

dialogue 1. colloquy, communication, confabulation, conference, conversation, converse, discourse, discussion, duologue, interlocution 2. conversation, lines, script, spoken part

diametric, diametrical antipodal, antithetical, conflicting, contrary, contrasting, counter, opposed, opposite

diametrically absolutely, completely, entirely, utterly

diary appointment book, chronicle, daily record, day-to-day account, engagement book, journal

diatribe abuse, castigation, criticism, denunciation, disputation, harangue, invective, philippic, reviling, stream of abuse, stricture, tirade, verbal onslaught, vituperation

diatribe ('daɪəˌtraɪb) *n.* a bitter or violent criticism or attack.

dibble ('dɪbəl) *n.* **1.** Also: **dibber** ('dɪbə). a small hand tool used to make holes in the ground for bulbs, seeds, or roots. ~*vb.* **2.** to make a hole in (the ground) with a dibble. **3.** to plant (seeds, etc.) with a dibble.

dice (daɪs) *pl. n.* **1.** cubes of wood, plastic, etc., each of whose sides has a different number of spots (1 to 6), used in games of chance. **2.** (*functioning as sing.*) Also called: **die.** one of these cubes. **3.** small cubes as of vegetables, meat, etc. **4. no dice.** *Sl., chiefly U.S.* an expression of refusal. ~*vb.* **5.** to cut (food, etc.) into small cubes. **6.** (*intr.*) to gamble or play with dice. **7.** (*intr.*) to take a chance or risk (esp. in **dice with death**). **8.** (*tr.*) *Austral. inf.* to abandon or reject (someone or something). —'**dicer** *n.*

dicey ('daɪsɪ) *adj.* **dicier, diciest.** *Sl., chiefly Brit.* difficult or dangerous; risky; tricky.

dichotomy (daɪ'kɒtəmɪ) *n., pl.* -**mies. 1.** division into two parts or classifications, esp. when they are sharply distinguished or opposed. **2.** *Bot.* a simple method of branching by repeated division into two equal parts. —di'**chotomous** *adj.*

dichromatic (ˌdaɪkrəʊ'mætɪk) *adj.* **1.** Also: **dichroic.** having two colours. **2.** (of animal species) having two different colour varieties. **3.** able to perceive only two colours. —**dichromatism** (daɪ'krəʊməˌtɪzəm) *n.*

dick (dɪk) *n. Sl.* **1.** *Brit.* a fellow or person. **2. clever dick.** *Brit.* an opinionated person; know-all. **3.** a taboo word for penis.

dickens ('dɪkɪnz) *n. Inf.* a euphemistic word for devil (used as intensifier in **what the dickens**).

Dickensian (dɪ'kɛnzɪən) *adj.* **1.** of Charles Dickens, (1812–70), English novelist, or his novels. **2. a.** denoting poverty, distress, and exploitation as depicted in the novels of Dickens. **b.** grotesquely comic, as some of the characters of Dickens.

dicker ('dɪkə) *Chiefly U.S.* ~*vb.* **1.** to trade (goods) by bargaining; barter. ~*n.* **2.** a petty bargain or barter.

dicky[1] *or* **dickey** ('dɪkɪ) *n., pl.* **dickies** *or* **dickeys. 1.** a false blouse or shirt front. **2.** Also called: **dicky bow.** *Brit.* a bow tie. **3.** Also called: **dicky-bird, dickeybird.** a child's word for a bird. **4.** a folding outside seat at the rear of some early cars.

dicky[2] *or* **dickey** ('dɪkɪ) *adj.* **dickier, dickiest.** *Brit. sl.* shaky, unsteady, or unreliable: *I feel a bit dicky today.*

dicotyledon (daɪˌkɒtɪ'liːdən) *n.* a flowering plant having two embryonic seed leaves. —ˌdicoty'**ledonous** *adj.*

Dictaphone ('dɪktəˌfəʊn) *n. Trademark.* a tape recorder designed esp. for dictation and subsequent typing.

dictate *vb.* (dɪk'teɪt). **1.** to say (letters, speeches, etc.) aloud for mechanical recording or verbatim transcription by another person. **2.** (*tr.*) to prescribe (commands, etc.) authoritatively. **3.** (*intr.*) to seek to impose one's will on others. ~*n.* ('dɪkteɪt). **4.** an authoritative command. **5.** a guiding principle: *the dictates of reason.*

dictation (dɪk'teɪʃən) *n.* **1.** the act of dictating material to be recorded or taken down in writing. **2.** the material dictated. **3.** authoritative commands or the act of giving them.

dictator (dɪk'teɪtə) *n.* **1. a.** a ruler who is not effectively restricted by a constitution, laws, etc. **b.** an absolute, esp. tyrannical, ruler. **2.** (in ancient Rome) a person appointed during a crisis to exercise supreme authority. **3.** a person who makes pronouncements, which are regarded as authoritative. **4.** a person who behaves in an authoritarian or tyrannical manner. —**dic'tatorˌship** *n.*

dictatorial (ˌdɪktə'tɔːrɪəl) *adj.* **1.** of or characteristic of a dictator. **2.** tending to dictate; tyrannical; overbearing. —ˌdicta'**torially** *adv.*

diction ('dɪkʃən) *n.* **1.** the choice of words in writing or speech. **2.** the manner of enunciating words and sounds.

dictionary ('dɪkʃənərɪ) *n., pl.* -**aries. 1. a.** a book that consists of an alphabetical list of words with their meanings, parts of speech, pronunciations, etymologies, etc. **b.** a similar book giving equivalent words in two or more languages. **2.** a reference book listing words or terms and giving information about a particular subject or activity. **3.** a collection of information or examples with the entries alphabetically arranged: *a dictionary of quotations.*

dictum ('dɪktəm) *n., pl.* -**tums** *or* -**ta** (-tə). **1.** a formal or authoritative statement; pronouncement. **2.** a popular saying or maxim.

did (dɪd) *vb.* the past tense of **do[1]**.

didactic (dɪ'dæktɪk) *adj.* **1.** intended to instruct, esp. excessively. **2.** morally instructive. **3.** (of works of art or literature) containing a political or moral message to which aesthetic considerations are subordinated. —di'**dactically** *adv.* —di'**dacticism** *n.*

diddle ('dɪdəl) *vb.* (*tr.*) *Inf.* to cheat or swindle. —'**diddler** *n.*

didgeridoo ('dɪdʒərɪˌduː) *n. Music.* a native Australian wind instrument.

die[1] (daɪ) *vb.* **dying, died.** (*mainly intr.*) **1.** (of an organism, organs, etc.) to cease all biological activity permanently. **2.** (of something inanimate) to cease to exist. **3.** (often foll. by *away, down,* or *out*) to lose strength, power, or energy, esp. by degrees. **4.** (often foll. by *away* or *down*) to become calm; subside. **5.** to stop functioning: *the engine died.* **6.** to languish, as with love, longing, etc. **7.** (usually foll. by *of*) *Inf.* to be nearly overcome (with laughter, boredom, etc.). **8.** *Theol.* to lack spiritual life within the soul. **9.** (*tr.*) to suffer (a death of a specified kind): *he died a saintly death.* **10. never say die.** *Inf.* never give up. **11. die hard.** to cease to exist after a struggle: *old habits die hard.* **12. die in harness.** to die while still working or active. **13. be dying.** (foll. by *for* or an infinitive) to be eager or desperate (for something or to do something). ~*See also* **die down, die out.**

die[2] (daɪ) *n.* **1. a.** a shaped block used to cut or form metal in a drop forge, press, etc. **b.** a tool with a conical hole through which wires, etc. are drawn to reduce their diameter. **2.** an internally-threaded tool for cutting external threads. **3.** a casting mould. **4.** *Archit.* the dado of a pedestal, usually cubic. **5.** another name for **dice** (sense 2). **6. the die is cast.** the irrevocable decision has been taken.

die down *vb.* (*intr., adv.*) **1.** (of plants) to wither above ground, leaving only the root alive during the winter. **2.** to lose strength or power, esp. by degrees. **3.** to become calm.

die-hard *n.* **1.** a person who resists change or who holds onto an untenable position. **2.** (*modifier*) obstinately resistant to change.

dieldrin ('diːldrɪn) *n.* a crystalline substance, consisting of a chlorinated derivative of naphthalene: a contact insecticide.

dielectric (ˌdaɪɪ'lɛktrɪk) *n.* **1.** a substance that can sustain an electric field. **2.** a substance of very low electrical conductivity; insulator. ~*adj.* **3.** concerned with or

dicey chancy (*Inf.*), dangerous, difficult, risky, ticklish, tricky

dicky *adj.* fluttery, queer, shaky, unreliable, unsound, unsteady, weak

dictate *v.* **1.** read out, say, speak, transmit, utter **2.** command, decree, direct, enjoin, impose, lay down, ordain, order, prescribe, pronounce ~*n.* **3.** behest, bidding, command, decree, direction, edict, fiat, injunction, mandate, order, ordinance, requirement, statute, ultimatum, word **4.** code, dictum, law, precept, principle, rule

dictator absolute ruler, autocrat, despot, oppressor, tyrant

dictatorial 1. absolute, arbitrary, autocratic, despotic, totalitarian, tyrannical, unlimited, unrestricted **2.** authoritarian, bossy

(*Inf.*), dogmatical, domineering, imperious, iron-handed, magisterial, oppressive, overbearing

dictatorship absolute rule, absolutism, authoritarianism, autocracy, despotism, reign of terror, totalitarianism, tyranny

diction 1. expression, language, phraseology, phrasing, style, usage, vocabulary, wording **2.** articulation, delivery, elocution, enunciation, fluency, inflection, intonation, pronunciation, speech

dictionary concordance, encyclopedia, glossary, lexicon, vocabulary, wordbook

didactic edifying, educational, enlightening, homiletic, instructive, moral, moralizing, pedagogic, pedantic, preceptive

die 1. breathe one's last, decease, depart, expire, finish, give up the ghost, hop the twig (*Sl.*), kick the bucket (*Sl.*), pass away, perish, snuff it (*Sl.*) **2.** decay, decline, disappear, dwindle, ebb, end, fade, lapse, pass, sink, subside, vanish, wane, wilt, wither **3.** break down, fade out or away, fail, fizzle out, halt, lose power, peter out, run down, stop **4.** ache, be eager, desire, hunger, languish, long, pine for, swoon, yearn **5.** *Usually with* **of** be overcome, collapse, succumb to

die-hard 1. *n.* fanatic, intransigent, old fogy, reactionary, stick-in-the-mud (*Inf.*), ultraconservative, zealot **2.** *adj.* dyed-in-the-wool, immovable, inflexible, intransigent, reactionary, ultraconservative, uncompromising, unreconstructed (*Chiefly U.S.*)

having the properties of a dielectric. —¸die'lectrically adv.

-diene n. combining form. denoting an organic compound containing two double bonds between carbon atoms: butadiene.

die out or **off** vb. (intr., adv.) **1.** to die one after another until few or none are left. **2.** to become extinct, esp. after a period of gradual decline.

diesel ('diːzəl) n. **1.** See **diesel engine. 2.** a ship, locomotive, lorry, etc., driven by a diesel engine. **3.** Inf. short for **diesel oil** (or **fuel**).

diesel-electric n. **1.** a locomotive fitted with a diesel engine driving an electric generator that feeds electric traction motors. ~adj. **2.** of or relating to such a locomotive or system.

diesel engine or **motor** n. a type of internal-combustion engine in which atomized fuel oil is ignited by compression alone.

diesel oil or **fuel** n. a fuel obtained from petroleum distillation that is used in diesel engines. Also called: **derv.**

Dies Irae Latin. ('diːeɪz 'ɪəraɪ) n. **1.** a Latin hymn of the 13th century, describing the Last Judgment. It is used in the Mass for the dead. **2.** a musical setting of this.

diet¹ ('daɪət) n. **1.** a specific allowance or selection of food, esp. prescribed to control weight or for health reasons: a salt-free diet. **2.** the food and drink that a person or animal regularly consumes. **3.** regular activities or occupations. ~vb. **4.** (usually intr.) to follow or cause to follow a dietary regimen. —'**dietary** adj. —'**dieter** n.

diet² ('daɪət) n. **1.** (sometimes cap.) a legislative assembly in various countries. **2.** (sometimes cap.) the assembly of the estates of the Holy Roman Empire. **3.** Scot. law. a single session of a court.

dietetic (¸daɪɪ'tɛtɪk) or **dietetical** adj. **1.** denoting or relating to diet. **2.** prepared for special dietary requirements. —¸die'tetically adv.

dietetics (¸daɪɪ'tɛtɪks) n. (functioning as sing.) the scientific study and regulation of food intake and preparation.

dietitian or **dietician** (¸daɪɪ'tɪʃən) n. a person who specializes in dietetics.

differ ('dɪfə) vb. (intr.) **1.** (often foll. by from) to be dissimilar in quality, nature, or degree (to); vary (from). **2.** (often foll. by from or with) to disagree (with). **3.** Dialect. to quarrel or dispute.

difference ('dɪfərəns) n. **1.** the state or quality of being unlike. **2.** a specific instance of being unlike. **3.** a distinguishing mark or feature. **4.** a significant change. **5.** a disagreement or argument. **6.** a degree of distinctness, as between two people or things. **7.** the result of the subtraction of one number, quantity, etc., from another. **8.** Heraldry. an addition to the arms of a family to repre-

sent a younger branch. **9. make a difference. a.** to have an effect. **b.** to treat differently. **10. split the difference. a.** to compromise. **b.** to divide a remainder equally. **11. with a difference.** with some distinguishing quality, good or bad.

different ('dɪfərənt) adj. **1.** partly or completely unlike. **2.** not identical or the same; other. **3.** unusual. —'**differently** adv. —'**differentness** n.

differentia (¸dɪfə'rɛnʃɪə) n., pl. **-tiae** (-ʃɪˌiː). Logic. a feature by which two subclasses of the same class of named objects can be distinguished.

differential (¸dɪfə'rɛnʃəl) adj. **1.** of, relating to, or using a difference. **2.** constituting a difference; distinguishing. **3.** Maths. involving one or more derivatives or differentials. **4.** Physics, engineering. relating to, operating on, or based on the difference between two opposing effects, motions, forces, etc. ~n. **5.** a factor that differentiates between two comparable things. **6.** Maths. **a.** an increment in a given function, expressed as the product of the derivative of that function and the corresponding increment in the independent variable. **b.** an increment in a given function of two or more variables, $f(x_1, x_2, ... x_n)$, expressed as the sum of the products of each partial derivative and the increment in the corresponding variable. **7.** See **differential gear. 8.** Chiefly Brit. the difference between rates of pay for different types of labour, esp. when forming a pay structure within an industry. **9.** (in commerce) a difference in rates, esp. between comparable services. —¸differ'entially adv.

differential calculus n. the branch of calculus concerned with the study, evaluation, and use of derivatives and differentials.

differential gear n. the epicyclic gear mounted in the driving axle of a road vehicle that permits one driving wheel to rotate faster than the other, as when cornering.

differentiate (¸dɪfə'rɛnʃɪˌeɪt) vb. **1.** (tr.) to serve to distinguish between. **2.** (when intr., often foll. by between) to perceive, show, or make a difference (in or between); discriminate. **3.** (intr.) to become dissimilar or distinct. **4.** Maths. to perform a differentiation on (a quantity, expression, etc.). **5.** (intr.) (of unspecialized cells, etc.) to change during development to more specialized forms. —¸differ¸enti'ation n. —¸differ'enti¸ator n.

difficult ('dɪfɪkəlt) adj. **1.** not easy to do; requiring effort. **2.** not easy to understand or solve. **3.** troublesome: a difficult child. **4.** not easily convinced, pleased, or satisfied. **5.** full of hardships or trials. —'**difficultly** adv.

difficulty ('dɪfɪkəltɪ) n., pl. **-ties. 1.** the state or quality of being difficult. **2.** a task, problem, etc., that is hard to deal with. **3.** (often pl.) a troublesome or embarrassing situation, esp. a financial one. **4.** a disagreement. **5.** (often pl.) an objection or obstacle. **6.** a trouble or source of trouble; worry. **7.** lack of ease; awkwardness.

THESAURUS

diet¹ n. **1.** abstinence, dietary, fast, regime, regimen **2.** aliment, comestibles, commons, edibles, fare, food, nourishment, nutriment, provisions, rations, subsistence, sustenance, viands, victuals ~v. **3.** abstain, eat sparingly, fast, lose weight, reduce, slim

diet² chamber, congress, convention, council, legislative assembly, legislature, meeting, parliament, sitting

differ 1. be dissimilar, be distinct, contradict, contrast, depart from, diverge, run counter to, stand apart, vary **2.** clash, contend, debate, demur, disagree, dispute, dissent, oppose, take issue

difference 1. alteration, change, contrast, deviation, differentiation, discrepancy, disparity, dissimilarity, distinction, distinctness, divergence, diversity, unlikeness, variation, variety **2.** distinction, exception, idiosyncrasy, particularity, peculiarity, singularity **3.** argument, clash, conflict, contention, contrariety, contretemps, controversy, debate, disagreement, discordance, dispute, quarrel, set-to (Inf.), strife, tiff, wrangle **4.** balance, remainder, rest, result

different 1. altered, at odds, at variance, changed, clashing, contrasting, deviating, discrepant, disparate, dissimilar, divergent, diverse, inconsistent, opposed, unlike **2.** an-

other, discrete, distinct, individual, other, separate **3.** assorted, divers (Archaic), diverse, manifold, many, miscellaneous, multifarious, numerous, several, some, sundry, varied, various **4.** another story, atypical, bizarre, distinctive, extraordinary, out of the ordinary, peculiar, rare, singular, something else, special, strange, uncommon, unconventional, unique, unusual

differential 1. adj. diacritical, discriminative, distinctive, distinguishing **2.** n. amount of difference, difference, discrepancy, disparity

differentiate 1. contrast, discern, discriminate, distinguish, make a distinction, mark off, separate, set off or apart, tell apart **2.** adapt, alter, change, convert, make different, modify, transform

difficult 1. arduous, burdensome, demanding, formidable, hard, laborious, no picnic (Inf.), onerous, painful, strenuous, toilsome, uphill, wearisome **2.** abstract, abstruse, baffling, complex, complicated, delicate, enigmatical, intricate, involved, knotty, obscure, perplexing, problematical, thorny, ticklish **3.** demanding, fastidious, fractious, fussy, hard to please, intractable, obstreperous, perverse, refractory, rigid, tiresome, troublesome, trying, unaccommodating, un-

amenable, unmanageable **4.** dark, full of hardship, grim, hard, straitened, tough, trying

difficulty 1. arduousness, awkwardness, hardship, laboriousness, labour, pain, painfulness, strain, strenuousness, tribulation **2.** deep water, dilemma, distress, embarrassment, fix (Inf.), hot water, jam (Inf.), mess, perplexity, pickle (Inf.), plight, predicament, quandary, spot (Inf.), straits, trial, trouble **3.** Often plural complication, hindrance, hurdle, impediment, objection, obstacle, opposition, pitfall, problem, protest

diffidence backwardness, bashfulness, constraint, doubt, fear, hesitancy, hesitation, humility, insecurity, lack of self-confidence, meekness, modesty, reluctance, reserve, self-consciousness, sheepishness, shyness, timidity, timidness, timorousness, unassertiveness

diffident backward, bashful, constrained, distrustful, doubtful, hesitant, insecure, meek, modest, reluctant, reserved, self-conscious, self-effacing, sheepish, shrinking, shy, suspicious, timid, timorous, unassertive, unassuming, unobtrusive, unsure, withdrawn

diffident ('dɪfɪdənt) *adj*. lacking self-confidence; timid; shy. —'**diffidence** *n*. —'**diffidently** *adv*.

diffract (dɪ'frækt) *vb*. to undergo or cause to undergo diffraction. —**dif'fractive** *adj*. —**dif'fractively** *adv*. —**dif'fractiveness** *n*.

diffraction (dɪ'frækʃən) *n*. **1.** *Physics*. a deviation in the direction of a wave at the edge of an obstacle in its path. **2.** any phenomenon caused by diffraction, such as the formation of light and dark fringes by the passage of light through a small aperture.

diffuse *vb*. (dɪ'fjuːz). **1.** to spread in all directions. **2.** to undergo or cause diffusion. **3.** to scatter; disperse. ~*adj*. (dɪ'fjuːs). **4.** spread out over a wide area. **5.** lacking conciseness. **6.** characterized by diffusion. —**diffusely** (dɪ'fjuːslɪ) *adv*. —**dif'fuseness** *n*. —**diffusible** (dɪ'fjuːzəbəl) *adj*.

diffusion (dɪ'fjuːʒən) *n*. **1.** a diffusing or being diffused; dispersion. **2.** verbosity. **3.** *Physics*. **a.** the random thermal motion of atoms, molecules, etc., in gases, liquids, and some solids. **b.** the transfer of atoms or molecules by their random motion from one part of a medium to another. **4.** *Physics*. the transmission or reflection of electromagnetic radiation, esp. light, in which the radiation is scattered in many directions. **5.** *Anthropol*. the transmission of social institutions, skills, and myths from one culture to another.

dig (dɪg) *vb*. **digging, dug. 1.** (when *tr*., often foll. by *up*) to cut into, break up, and turn over or remove (earth, etc.), esp. with a spade. **2.** to excavate (a hole, tunnel, etc.) by digging, usually with an implement or (of animals) with claws, etc. **3.** (often foll. by *through*) to make or force (one's way): *he dug his way through the crowd*. **4.** (*tr*.; often foll. by *out* or *up*) to obtain by digging. **5.** (*tr*.; often foll. by *out* or *up*) to find by effort or searching: *to dig out facts*. **6.** (*tr*.; foll. by *in* or *into*) to thrust or jab. **7.** (*tr*.; foll. by *in* or *into*) to mix (compost, etc.) with soil by digging. **8.** (*intr*.; foll. by *in* or *into*) *Inf*. to begin vigorously to do something. **9.** *Inf*. to like, understand, or appreciate. **10.** (*intr*.) *U.S. sl*. to work hard, esp. for an examination. ~*n*. **11.** the act of digging. **12.** a thrust or poke. **13.** a cutting remark. **14.** *Inf*. an archaeological excavation. **15.** *Austral. & N.Z. inf*. short for **digger.**

digest *vb*. (dɪ'dʒɛst, daɪ-). **1.** to subject (food) to a process of digestion. **2.** (*tr*.) to assimilate mentally. **3.** *Chem*. to soften or disintegrate by the action of heat, moisture, or chemicals. **4.** (*tr*.) to arrange in a methodical order; classify. **5.** (*tr*.) to reduce to a summary. ~*n*. ('daɪdʒɛst). **6.** a comprehensive and systematic compilation of information or material, often condensed. **7.** a magazine, periodical, etc., that summarizes news. **8.** a compilation of rules of law. —**di'gestible** *adj*.

digestion (dɪ'dʒɛstʃən, daɪ-) *n*. **1.** the act or process in living organisms of breaking down food into easily absorbed substances by the action of enzymes, etc. **2.** mental assimilation, esp. of ideas. **3.** the decomposition of sewage by bacteria. **4.** *Chem*. the treatment of material with heat, solvents, etc., to cause decomposition. —**di'gestional** *adj*.

digestive (dɪ'dʒɛstɪv, daɪ-) *or* **digestant** (daɪ'dʒɛstənt) *adj*. **1.** relating to, aiding, or subjecting to digestion. ~*n*. **2.** any substance that aids digestion. —**di'gestively** *adv*.

digestive biscuit *n*. a round semisweet biscuit made from wholemeal flour.

digger ('dɪgə) *n*. **1.** a person, animal, or machine that digs. **2.** a miner. **3.** a tool or machine used for excavation. **4.** *Austral. & N.Z. inf*. (*sometimes cap*.) an Australian or New Zealander, esp. a soldier: often used as a friendly term of address.

diggings ('dɪgɪŋz) *pl. n*. **1.** (*pl*.) material that has been dug out. **2.** (*sing. or pl*.) a place where mining has taken place. **3.** (*pl*.) *Brit. inf*. a less common name for **digs.**

dig in *vb*. (*adv*.) **1.** *Mil*. to dig foxholes, trenches, etc. **2.** *Inf*. to entrench (oneself). **3.** (*intr*.) *Inf*. to defend a position firmly, as in an argument. **4. dig one's heels in.** *Inf*. to refuse to move or be persuaded.

digit ('dɪdʒɪt) *n*. **1.** a finger or toe. **2.** any of the ten Arabic numerals from 0 to 9.

digital ('dɪdʒɪtəl) *adj*. **1.** of, resembling, or possessing a digit or digits. **2.** performed with the fingers. **3.** *Computers, recording engineer*. operating by the use of discrete signals to represent data in the form of numbers or other characters. **4.** displaying information as numbers rather than by a pointer moving over a dial. ~*n*. **5.** *Music*. a key on a piano, harpsichord, etc. —'**digitally** *adv*.

digital clock *or* **watch** *n*. a clock or watch in which the time is indicated by digits rather than by hands on a dial.

digital computer *n*. an electronic computer in which the input is discrete, consisting of numbers, letters, etc. that are represented internally in binary notation.

digitalis (ˌdɪdʒɪ'teɪlɪs) *n*. **1.** any of a genus of Eurasian plants such as the foxglove, having long spikes of bell-shaped flowers. **2.** a drug prepared from the dried leaves of the foxglove: used medicinally as a heart stimulant.

digitate ('dɪdʒɪ,teɪt) *or* **digitated** *adj*. **1.** (of leaves) having the leaflets in the form of a spread hand. **2.** (of animals) having digits. —'**digi,tately** *adv*. —,**digi'tation** *n*.

digitize *or* **-tise** ('dɪdʒɪ,taɪz) *vb*. (*tr*.) to transcribe (data) into a digital form for processing by a computer. —,**digiti'zation** *or* -**i'sation** *n*.

dignified ('dɪgnɪ,faɪd) *adj*. characterized by dignity of manner or appearance; stately; noble. —'**digni,fiedly** *adv*. —'**digni,fiedness** *n*.

dignify ('dɪgnɪ,faɪ) *vb*. **-fying, -fied.** (*tr*.) **1.** to invest with honour or dignity. **2.** to add distinction to. **3.** to add a semblance of dignity to, esp. by the use of a pretentious name or title.

dignitary ('dɪgnɪtərɪ) *n., pl*. **-taries.** a person of high official position or rank.

dignity ('dɪgnɪtɪ) *n., pl*. **-ties. 1.** a formal, stately, or grave bearing. **2.** the state or quality of being worthy of honour. **3.** relative importance; rank. **4.** sense of self-importance (often in **stand** (*or* **be**) **on one's dignity, beneath one's dignity**). **5.** high rank, esp. in government or the church.

digraph ('daɪgrɑːf) *n*. a combination of two letters used to represent a single sound such as *gh* in *tough*. —**digraphic** (daɪ'græfɪk) *adj*.

digress (daɪ'grɛs) *vb*. (*intr*.) **1.** to depart from the main subject in speech or writing. **2.** to wander from one's path. —**di'gresser** *n*. —**di'gression** *n*.

THESAURUS

diffuse *adj*. **1.** circumlocutory, copious, diffusive, digressive, discursive, long-winded, loose, maundering, meandering, prolix, rambling, vague, verbose, waffling (*Inf*.), wordy **2.** dispersed, scattered, spread out, unconcentrated ~*v*. **3.** circulate, dispel, dispense, disperse, disseminate, dissipate, distribute, propagate, scatter, spread

diffusion 1. circulation, dispersal, dispersion, dissemination, dissipation, distribution, expansion, propaganda, propagation, scattering, spread **2.** circuitousness, diffuseness, digressiveness, discursiveness, longwindedness, prolixity, rambling, verbiage, verbosity, wandering, wordiness

dig *v*. **1.** break up, burrow, delve, excavate, gouge, grub, hoe, hollow out, mine, penetrate, pierce, quarry, scoop, till, tunnel, turn over **2.** drive, jab, poke, prod, punch, thrust **3.** delve, dig down, go into, investigate, probe, research, search **4.** *With* **out** *or* **up** bring to light, come across, come up with, discover, expose, extricate, find, retrieve, root (*Inf*.), rootle, uncover, unearth **5.** *Inf*. appreciate, enjoy, follow, groove (*Sl*.), like, understand ~*n*. **6.** jab, poke, prod, punch, thrust **7.** crack (*Sl*.), cutting remark, gibe, insult, jeer, quip, sneer, taunt, wisecrack (*Inf*.)

digest *v*. **1.** absorb, assimilate, concoct, dissolve, incorporate, macerate **2.** absorb, assimilate, con, consider, contemplate, grasp, master, meditate, ponder, study, take in, understand **3.** arrange, classify, codify, dispose, methodize, systematize, tabulate **4.** abridge, compress, condense, reduce, shorten, summarize ~*n*. **5.** abridgment, abstract, compendium, condensation, epitome, précis, résumé, summary, synopsis

digestion absorption, assimilation, conversion, incorporation, ingestion, transformation

dig in 1. defend, entrench, establish, fortify, maintain **2.** *Inf*. begin, set about, start eating, tuck in (*Inf*.)

dignified august, decorous, distinguished, exalted, formal, grave, honourable, imposing, lofty, lordly, noble, reserved, solemn, stately, upright

dignify adorn, advance, aggrandize, distinguish, elevate, ennoble, exalt, glorify, grace, honour, promote, raise

dignitary *n*. high-up (*Inf*.), notability, notable, personage, pillar of society (the church, the state), public figure, V.I.P., worthy

dignity 1. courtliness, decorum, grandeur, gravity, hauteur, loftiness, majesty, nobility, propriety, solemnity, stateliness **2.** elevation, eminence, excellence, glory, greatness, honour, importance, nobleness, rank, respect

digs (dɪgz) *pl. n. Brit. inf.* lodgings.

dihedral (daɪ'hiːdrəl) *adj.* 1. having or formed by two intersecting planes. ~*n.* 2. Also called: **dihedron, dihedral angle.** the figure formed by two intersecting planes. 3. the upward or downward inclination of an aircraft wing in relation to the lateral axis.

dike (daɪk) *n.* 1. *Inf., chiefly Austral.* a lavatory. ~*n.,vb.* 2. the usual U.S. spelling of **dyke**[1].

dilapidate (dɪ'læpɪˌdeɪt) *vb.* to fall or cause to fall into ruin. —**diˌlapiˈdation** *n.* —**diˈlapiˌdated** *adj.*

dilate (daɪ'leɪt, dɪ-) *vb.* 1. to make or become wider or larger. 2. (*intr.; often foll. by on or upon*) to speak or write at length. —**diˌlataˈbility** *n.* —**diˈlatable** *adj.* —**diˈlation** *or* **dilatation** (ˌdaɪlə'teɪʃən) *n.* —**dilative** (daɪ'leɪtɪv) *adj.*

dilatory ('dɪlətərɪ) *adj.* 1. tending to delay or waste time. 2. intended to waste time or defer action. —**'dilatorily** *adv.* —**'dilatoriness** *n.*

dildo *or* **dildoe** ('dɪldəʊ) *n., pl.* **-dos** *or* **-does.** an object used as a substitute for an erect penis.

dilemma (dɪ'lɛmə, daɪ-) *n.* 1. a situation necessitating a choice between two equally undesirable alternatives. 2. a problem that seems incapable of a solution. 3. **on the horns of a dilemma. a.** faced with the choice between two equal alternatives. **b.** in an awkward situation. —**dilemmatic** (ˌdɪlɪ'mætɪk) *adj.*

dilettante (ˌdɪlɪ'tɑːntɪ) *n., pl.* **-tantes** *or* **-tanti** (-'tɑːntɪ). 1. a person whose interest in a subject is superficial rather than professional. 2. a person who loves the arts. ~*adj.* 3. of or characteristic of a dilettante. —**ˌdilet'tantish** *or* **ˌdilet'tanteish** *adj.* —**ˌdilet'tantism** *or* **ˌdilet-'tanteism** *n.*

diligent ('dɪlɪdʒənt) *adj.* 1. careful and persevering in carrying out tasks or duties. 2. carried out with care and perseverance: *diligent work.* —**'diligence** *n.* —**'diligently** *adv.*

dill (dɪl) *n.* 1. an aromatic Eurasian plant with umbrella-shaped clusters of yellow flowers. 2. the leaves or fruits of this plant, used for flavouring and in medicine.

dilly-dally ('dɪlɪˌdælɪ) *vb.* **-lying, -lied.** (*intr.*) *Inf.* to loiter or vacillate.

dilute (daɪ'luːt) *vb.* 1. to make or become less concentrated, esp. by adding water or a thinner. 2. to make or become weaker in force, effect, etc. ~*adj.* 3. *Chem.* **a.** (of a solution, etc.) having a low concentration. **b.** (of a substance) present in solution, esp. a weak solution in water: *dilute acetic acid.* —**di'luter** *n.* —**di'lution** *n.*

diluvial (daɪ'luːvɪəl, dɪ-) *or* **diluvian** *adj.* of or connected with a deluge, esp. with the great Flood described in Genesis.

dim (dɪm) *adj.* **dimmer, dimmest.** 1. badly illuminated. 2. not clearly seen; faint. 3. having weak or indistinct vision. 4. mentally dull. 5. not clear in the mind; obscure: *a dim memory.* 6. lacking in brightness or lustre. 7. unfavourable; gloomy (esp. in **take a dim view**). ~*vb.* **dimming, dimmed.** 8. to become or cause to become dim. 9. (*tr.*) to cause to seem less bright. 10. the U.S. word for **dip** (sense 5). —**'dimly** *adv.* —**'dimness** *n.*

dim. *abbrev. for:* 1. dimension. 2. Also: **dimin.** *Music.* diminuendo. 3. Also: **dimin.** diminutive.

dime (daɪm) *n.* 1. a coin of the U.S. and Canada, worth one tenth of a dollar or ten cents. 2. **a dime a dozen.** very cheap or common.

dimension (dɪ'mɛnʃən) *n.* 1. (*often pl.*) a measurement of the size of something in a particular direction, such as the length, width, height, or diameter. 2. (*often pl.*) scope; size; extent. 3. aspect: *a new dimension to politics.* 4. *Maths.* the number of coordinates required to locate a point in space. ~*vb.* 5. (*tr.*) *Chiefly U.S.* to cut to or mark with specified dimensions. —**di'mensional** *adj.* —**di'mensionless** *adj.*

diminish (dɪ'mɪnɪʃ) *vb.* 1. to make or become smaller, fewer, or less. 2. (*tr.*) *Archit.* to cause to taper. 3. *Music.* (*tr.*) to decrease (a minor or perfect interval) by a semitone. 4. to reduce in authority, status, etc. —**di-'minishable** *adj.*

diminished responsibility *n. Law.* a plea under which mental derangement is submitted as demonstrating lack of criminal responsibility.

diminuendo (dɪˌmɪnjʊ'ɛndəʊ) *n., pl.* **-dos.** 1. *Music.* **a.** a gradual decrease in loudness. Symbol: > . **b.** a musical passage affected by a diminuendo. ~*adj.* 2. gradually decreasing in loudness. 3. with a diminuendo.

diminution (ˌdɪmɪ'njuːʃən) *n.* 1. reduction; decrease. 2. *Music.* the presentation of the subject of a fugue, etc., in which the note values are reduced in length.

diminutive (dɪ'mɪnjʊtɪv) *adj.* 1. very small; tiny. 2. *Grammar.* **a.** denoting an affix added to a word to convey the meaning *small* or *unimportant* or to express affection. **b.** denoting a word formed by the addition of a diminutive affix. ~*n.* 3. *Grammar.* a diminutive word or affix. 4. a tiny person or thing. —**di'minutively** *adv.* —**di'minutiveness** *n.*

dimity ('dɪmɪtɪ) *n., pl.* **-ties.** a light strong cotton fabric with woven stripes or squares.

dimmer ('dɪmə) *n.* 1. a device for dimming an electric light. 2. (*often pl.*) *U.S.* **a.** a dipped headlight on a road vehicle. **b.** a parking light on a car.

dimple ('dɪmp!) *n.* 1. a small natural dent, esp. on the cheeks or chin. 2. any slight depression in a surface. ~*vb.* 3. to make or become dimpled. 4. (*intr.*) to pro-

---

THESAURUS

ability, standing, station, status 3. *amour-propre*, pride, self-esteem, self-importance, self-possession, self-regard, self-respect

digress be diffuse, depart, deviate, diverge, drift, expatiate, get off the point *or* subject, go off at a tangent, ramble, stray, turn aside, wander

digression apostrophe, aside, departure, detour, deviation, divergence, diversion, footnote, obiter dictum, parenthesis, straying, wandering

dilapidated battered, broken-down, crumbling, decayed, decaying, decrepit, fallen in, falling apart, gone to wrack and ruin, in ruins, neglected, ramshackle, rickety, ruined, ruinous, run-down, shabby, shaky, tumble-down, uncared for, worn-out

dilate 1. broaden, distend, enlarge, expand, extend, puff out, stretch, swell, widen 2. amplify, be profuse, be prolix, descant, detail, develop, dwell on, enlarge, expand, expatiate, expound, spin out

dilation broadening, dilatation, distention, enlargement, expansion, extension, increase, spread

dilatory backward, behindhand, dallying, delaying, laggard, lingering, loitering, procrastinating, putting off, slack, slow, sluggish, snail-like, tardy, tarrying, time-wasting

dilemma 1. difficulty, embarrassment, fix (*Inf.*), jam (*Inf.*), mess, perplexity, pickle (*Inf.*), plight, predicament, problem, puzzle,

quandary, spot (*Inf.*), strait, tight corner 2. **on the horns of a dilemma** between Scylla and Charybdis, between the devil and the deep blue sea

dilettante aesthete, amateur, dabbler, nonprofessional, trifler

diligence activity, application, assiduity, assiduousness, attention, attentiveness, care, constancy, earnestness, heedfulness, industry, intentness, laboriousness, perseverance, sedulousness

diligent active, assiduous, attentive, busy, careful, conscientious, constant, earnest, hard-working, indefatigable, industrious, laborious, painstaking, persevering, persistent, sedulous, studious, tireless

dilly-dally dally, dawdle, delay, dither, falter, fluctuate, hesitate, hover, linger, loiter, potter, procrastinate, shillyshally (*Inf.*), trifle, vacillate, waver

dilute *v.* 1. adulterate, cut, make thinner, thin (out), water down, weaken 2. *Fig.* attenuate, decrease, diffuse, diminish, lessen, mitigate, reduce, temper, weaken

dim *adj.* 1. caliginous (*Archaic*), cloudy, dark, darkish, dusky, grey, overcast, poorly lit, shadowy, tenebrous, unilluminated 2. bleary, blurred, faint, fuzzy, ill-defined, indistinct, obscured, shadowy, unclear 3. dense, doltish, dull, dumb (*Inf.*), obtuse, slow, slow on the uptake (*Inf.*), stupid, thick 4. confused, hazy, imperfect, indistinct, intangible, ob-

scure, remote, shadowy, vague 5. dingy, dull, feeble, lacklustre, muted, opaque, pale, sullied, tarnished, weak 6. dashing, depressing, discouraging, gloomy, sombre, unfavourable, unpromising 7. **take a dim view** be displeased, be sceptical, disapprove, look askance, reject, suspect, take exception, view with disfavour ~*v.* 8. bedim, blur, cloud, darken, dull, fade, lower, obscure, tarnish, turn down

dimension *Often plural* 1. amplitude, bulk, capacity, extent, measurement, proportions, size, volume 2. bigness, extent, greatness, importance, largeness, magnitude, measure, range, scale, scope

diminish 1. abate, contract, curtail, cut, decrease, lessen, lower, reduce, retrench, shrink, weaken 2. decline, die out, dwindle, ebb, fade away, peter out, recede, shrivel, slacken, subside, wane 3. belittle, cheapen, demean, depreciate, devalue

diminution abatement, contraction, curtailment, cut, cutback, decay, decline, decrease, deduction, lessening, reduction, retrenchment, weakening

diminutive *adj.* bantam, Lilliputian, little, midget, mini, miniature, minute, petite, pocket(-sized), pygmy, small, tiny, undersized, wee

duce dimples by smiling. —**'dimply** *adj.*

dimwit ('dɪmˌwɪt) *n. Inf.* a stupid or silly person. —ˌdim-'witted *adj.* —ˌdim-'wittedness *n.*

din (dɪn) *n.* **1.** a loud discordant confused noise. ~*vb.* **dinning, dinned.** **2.** (*tr.;* usually foll. by *into*) to instil by constant repetition. **3.** (*tr.*) to subject to a din. **4.** (*tr.*) to make a din.

dinar ('diːnɑː) *n.* **1.** the standard monetary unit of Algeria, Iraq, Jordan, Kuwait, Libya, Southern Yemen, Tunisia, and Yugoslavia. **2.** an Iranian monetary unit.

dine (daɪn) *vb.* **1.** (*intr.*) to eat dinner. **2.** (*intr.;* often foll. by *on, off,* or *upon*) to make one's meal (of): *the guests dined upon roast beef.* **3.** (*tr.*) *Inf.* to entertain to dinner; (esp. in **to wine and dine someone**).

diner ('daɪnə) *n.* **1.** a person eating a meal, esp. in a restaurant. **2.** *Chiefly U.S.* a small cheap restaurant. **3.** short for **dining car.**

dinette (daɪ'nɛt) *n.* an alcove or small area for use as a dining room.

ding (dɪŋ) *vb.* **1.** to ring, esp. with tedious repetition. **2.** (*tr.*) another word for **din** (sense 2). ~*n.* **3.** an imitation of the sound of a bell.

ding-dong *n.* **1.** the sound of a bell or bells. **2.** an imitation of the sound of a bell. **3. a.** a violent exchange of blows or words. **b.** (*as modifier*): *a ding-dong battle.* ~*adj.* **4.** sounding or ringing repeatedly.

dinges ('dɪŋz) *n. S. African inf.* a jocular word for something whose name is unknown or forgotten; thingumabob.

dinghy, dingy, or **dingey** ('dɪŋɪ) *n., pl.* **-ghies, -gies,** or **-geys.** any small boat, powered by sail, oars, or outboard motor.

dingle ('dɪŋgəl) *n.* a small wooded dell.

dingo ('dɪŋgəʊ) *n., pl.* **-goes.** a wild dog of Australia, having a yellowish-brown coat and resembling a wolf.

dingy ('dɪndʒɪ) *adj.* **-gier, -giest.** **1.** lacking light or brightness; drab. **2.** dirty; discoloured. —**'dingily** *adv.* —**'dinginess** *n.*

dining car *n.* a railway coach in which meals are served at tables. Also called: **restaurant car.**

dining room *n.* a room where meals are eaten.

dinkum ('dɪŋkəm) *adj. Austral. inf.* **1.** genuine or right: *a fair dinkum offer.* **2. dinkum oil.** the truth.

dinky ('dɪŋkɪ) *adj.* **dinkier, dinkiest.** *Inf.* **1.** *Brit.* small and neat; dainty. **2.** *U.S.* inconsequential; insignificant.

dinner ('dɪnə) *n.* **1.** a meal taken in the evening. **2.** a meal taken at midday, esp. when it is the main meal of the day; lunch. **3.** a formal meal or banquet in honour of someone or something. **4.** (*as modifier*): *dinner table; dinner hour.*

dinner-dance *n.* a formal dinner followed by dancing.

dinner jacket *n.* a man's semiformal evening jacket without tails, usually black. U.S. name: **tuxedo.**

dinner service *n.* a set of matching plates, dishes, etc., suitable for serving a meal.

dinosaur ('daɪnəˌsɔː) *n.* any of a large order of extinct reptiles many of which were of gigantic size and abundant in the Mesozoic era. —ˌdino'saurian *adj.*

dint (dɪnt) *n.* **1. by dint of.** by means or use of: *by dint of hard work.* **2.** *Arch.* a blow or a mark made by a blow. ~*vb.* **3.** (*tr.*) to mark with dints.

diocesan (daɪ'ɒsɪsən) *adj.* **1.** of or relating to a diocese. ~*n.* **2.** the bishop of a diocese.

diocese ('daɪəsɪs) *n.* the district under the jurisdiction of a bishop.

diode ('daɪəʊd) *n.* **1.** a semiconductor device used in circuits for converting alternating current to direct current. **2.** the earliest type of electronic valve having two electrodes between which a current can flow only in one direction.

dioecious (daɪ'iːʃəs) *adj.* (of plants) having the male and female reproductive organs on separate plants.

Dionysian (ˌdaɪə'nɪzɪən) *adj.* **1.** of or relating to Dionysus, the Greek god of wine and revelry. **2.** (*often not cap.*) wild or orgiastic.

dioptre or *U.S.* **diopter** (daɪ'ɒptə) *n.* a unit for measuring the refractive power of a lens: the reciprocal of the focal length of the lens expressed in metres. —**di'optral** *adj.*

diorama (ˌdaɪə'rɑːmə) *n.* **1.** a miniature three-dimensional scene, in which models of figures are seen against a background. **2.** a picture made up of illuminated translucent curtains, viewed through an aperture. **3.** a museum display, as of an animal, of a specimen in its natural setting. —**dioramic** (ˌdaɪə'ræmɪk) *adj.*

dioxide (daɪ'ɒksaɪd) *n.* any oxide containing two oxygen atoms per molecule, both of which are bonded to an atom of another element.

dip (dɪp) *vb.* **dipping, dipped.** **1.** to plunge or be plunged quickly or briefly into a liquid, esp. to wet or coat. **2.** (*intr.*) to undergo a slight decline, esp. temporarily: *sales dipped in November.* **3.** (*tr.*) to slope downwards. **4.** to sink quickly. **5.** (*tr.*) to switch (car headlights) from the main to the lower beam. U.S. word: **dim.** **6.** (*tr.*) **a.** to immerse (sheep, etc.) briefly in a chemical to rid them of or prevent infestation by insects, etc. **b.** to immerse (grain, vegetables, or wood) in a preservative liquid. **7.** (*tr.*) to dye by immersing in a liquid. **8.** (*tr.*) to baptize (someone) by immersion. **9.** (*tr.*) to plate or galvanize (a metal, etc.) by immersion in an electrolyte or electrolytic cell. **10.** (*tr.*) to scoop up a liquid or something from a liquid in the hands or in a container. **11.** to lower or be lowered briefly. **12.** (*tr.*) to make (a candle) by plunging the wick into melted wax. **13.** (*intr.*) to plunge a container, the hands, etc., into something, esp. to obtain an object. **14.** (*intr.;* foll. by *in* or *into*) to draw (upon): *he dipped into his savings.* **15.** (*intr.;* foll. by *in* or *into*) to dabble (in); play (at). **16.** (*intr.;* foll. by *in* or *into*) to select passages to read at random (from a book, newspaper, etc.). **17.** (*intr.*) (of an aircraft) to drop suddenly and then regain height. ~*n.* **18.** the act of dipping or state of being dipped. **19.** a brief swim in water. **20. a.** any liquid chemical in which sheep, etc. are dipped. **b.** any liquid preservative into which objects are dipped. **21.** a dye into which fabric is immersed. **22.** a depression, esp. in a landscape. **23.** something taken up by dipping. **24.** a container used for dipping; dipper. **25.** a momentary sinking down. **26.** the angle of slope of rock strata, etc., from the horizontal plane. **27.** the angle between the direction of the earth's magnetic field and the plane of the horizon; the angle that a magnetic needle free to swing in a vertical plane makes with the horizontal. **28.** a creamy savoury mixture into which potato crisps, etc., are dipped before being eaten. **29.** *Surveying.* the angular distance of the horizon below the plane of observation. **30.** a candle made by plunging a wick into wax. **31.** a momentary loss of altitude when flying.

Dip. A. D. *abbrev. for* Diploma in Art and Design.

Dip. Ed. (in Britain) *abbrev. for* Diploma in Education.

diphtheria (dɪp'θɪərɪə) *n.* an acute contagious disease caused by a bacillus, producing fever, severe prostration, and difficulty in breathing and swallowing as the result of swelling of the throat and formation of a false membrane. —**diph'therial, diphtheritic** (ˌdɪpθə'rɪtɪk), or **diphtheric** (dɪp'θɛrɪk) *adj.*

diphthong ('dɪfθɒŋ) *n.* **1.** a vowel sound, occupying a single syllable, during the articulation of which the tongue moves continuously from one position to another, as in the pronunciation of *a* in *late.* **2.** a digraph or ligature representing a composite vowel such as this, as *ae* in *Caesar.* —**diph'thongal** *adj.*

diploma (dɪ'pləʊmə) *n.* **1.** a document conferring a qualification, recording success in examinations or suc-

---

THESAURUS

din 1. *n.* babel, clamour, clangour, clash, clatter, commotion, crash, hubbub, hullabaloo, noise, outcry, pandemonium, racket, row, shout, uproar **2.** *v. Usually with* **into** drum into, go on at, hammer into, inculcate, instil, instruct, teach

dine 1. banquet, eat, feast, lunch, sup **2.** *Often with* **on, off** *or* **upon** consume, eat, feed on

dingy bedimmed, colourless, dark, dim, dirty, discoloured, drab, dreary, dull, dusky, faded, gloomy, grimy, murky, obscure, seedy, shabby, soiled, sombre, tacky

dinner banquet, beanfeast (*Inf.*), blowout (*Sl.*), collation, feast, main meal, meal, refection, repast, spread

dip *v.* **1.** bathe, douse, duck, dunk, immerse, plunge, rinse, souse **2.** decline, descend, disappear, droop, drop (down), fade, fall, lower, sag, set, sink, slope, slump, subside, tilt **3.** ladle, scoop, spoon **4.** *With* **in** *or* **into** browse, dabble, glance at, peruse, play at, run over, sample, skim, try **5.** *With* **in** *or* **into** draw upon, reach into ~*n.* **6.** douche, drenching, ducking, immersion, plunge, soaking **7.** bathe, dive, plunge, swim **8.** concoction, dilution, infusion, mixture, preparation, solution, suspension **9.** basin, concavity, depression, hole, hollow, incline, slope **10.** decline, fall, lowering, sag, slip, slump

cessful completion of a course of study. **2.** an official document that confers an honour or privilege.

diplomacy (dɪ'pləʊməsɪ) n., pl. **-cies. 1.** the conduct of the relations of one state with another by peaceful means. **2.** skill in the management of international relations. **3.** tact, skill, or cunning in dealing with people.

diplomat ('dɪplə,mæt) n. ~Also called: **diplomatist** (dɪ'pləʊmətɪst). **1.** an official such as an ambassador, engaged in diplomacy. **2.** a person who deals with people tactfully or skilfully.

diplomatic (,dɪplə'mætɪk) or **diplomatical** adj. **1.** of or relating to diplomacy or diplomats. **2.** skilled in negotiating, esp. between states or people. **3.** tactful in dealing with people. —,**diplo'matically** adv.

diplomatic immunity n. the immunity from local jurisdiction and exemption from taxation in the country to which they are accredited afforded to diplomats.

dipole ('daɪ,pəʊl) n. **1.** two equal but opposite electric charges or magnetic poles separated by a small distance. **2.** a molecule in which the centre of positive charge does not coincide with the centre of negative charge. **3.** an aerial consisting of a single metal rod with the connecting wire fixed to its midpoint. —**di'polar** adj.

dipper ('dɪpə) n. **1.** a ladle used for dipping. **2.** Also called: **water ouzel.** any of a genus of aquatic songbirds that inhabit fast-flowing streams. **3.** a person or thing that dips. **4.** Arch. an Anabaptist.

dippy ('dɪpɪ) adj. **-pier, -piest.** Sl. odd, eccentric, or crazy.

dipso ('dɪpsəʊ) n., pl. **dipsos** Inf. a dipsomaniac.

dipsomania (,dɪpsəʊ'meɪnɪə) n. a compulsive desire to drink alcoholic beverages. —,**dipso'maniac** n., adj.

dipstick ('dɪp,stɪk) n. a graduated rod or strip dipped into a container to indicate the fluid level.

dip switch n. a device for dipping car headlights.

dipterous ('dɪptərəs) adj. **1.** Also: **dipteran.** of a large order of insects having a single pair of wings and sucking or piercing mouthparts. The group includes flies, mosquitoes, and midges. **2.** Bot. having two winglike parts.

diptych ('dɪptɪk) n. **1.** a pair of hinged wooden tablets with waxed surfaces for writing. **2.** a painting or carving on two hinged panels.

dire (daɪə) adj. (usually prenominal) **1.** Also: **direful.** disastrous; fearful. **2.** desperate; urgent: a dire need. —'**direly** adv. —'**direness** n.

direct (dɪ'rɛkt, daɪ-) vb. (mainly tr.) **1.** to conduct or control the affairs of. **2.** (also intr.) to give commands or orders with authority to (a person or group). **3.** to tell or show (someone) the way to a place. **4.** to aim, point, or cause to move towards a goal. **5.** to address (a letter, etc.). **6.** to address (remarks, etc.). **7.** (also intr.) to provide guidance to (actors, cameramen, etc.) in a play or film. **8.** (also intr.) to conduct (a piece of music or musicians), usually while performing oneself. ~adj. **9.** without delay or evasion; straightforward. **10.** without turning aside; shortest; straight: a direct route. **11.** without intervening persons or agencies: a direct link. **12.** honest; frank. **13.** (usually prenominal) precise; exact: a di-

rect quotation. **14.** diametrical: the direct opposite. **15.** in an unbroken line of descent: a direct descendant. **16.** (of government, decisions, etc.) by or from the electorate rather than through representatives. **17.** Maths. (of a relationship) containing two variables such that an increase (or decrease) in one results in an increase (or decrease) in the other. Cf. **inverse. 18.** Astron. moving from west to east. Cf. **retrograde. 19.** of or relating to direct current. **20.** Music. (of an interval or chord) in root position; not inverted. ~adv. **21.** directly; straight. —**di'rectness** n.

direct access n. a method of reading data from a computer file without reading through the file from the beginning.

direct current n. a continuous electric current that flows in one direction only.

direct-grant school n. (in Britain, formerly) a school financed by endowment, fees, and a state grant conditional upon admittance of a percentage of nonpaying pupils.

direction (dɪ'rɛkʃən, daɪ-) n. **1.** the act of directing or the state of being directed. **2.** management, control, or guidance. **3.** the work of a stage or film director. **4.** the course or line along which a person or thing moves, points, or lies. **5.** the place towards which a person or thing is directed. **6.** a line of action; course. **7.** the name and address on a letter, parcel, etc. **8.** Music. the process of conducting an orchestra, choir, etc. **9.** Music. an instruction to indicate tempo, dynamics, mood, etc.

directional (dɪ'rɛkʃənəl, daɪ-) adj. **1.** of or relating to a spatial direction. **2.** Electronics. **a.** having or relating to an increased sensitivity to radio waves, nuclear particles, etc., coming from a particular direction. **b.** (of an aerial) transmitting or receiving radio waves more effectively in some directions than in others. **3.** Physics, electronics. concentrated in, following, or producing motion in a particular direction. —**di,rection'ality** n.

direction finder n. a device to determine the direction of incoming radio signals, used esp. as a navigation aid.

directions (dɪ'rɛkʃənz, daɪ-) pl. n. (sometimes sing.) instructions for doing something or for reaching a place.

directive (dɪ'rɛktɪv, daɪ-) n. **1.** an instruction; order. ~adj. **2.** tending to direct; directing. **3.** indicating direction.

directly (dɪ'rɛktlɪ, daɪ-) adv. **1.** in a direct manner. **2.** at once; without delay. **3.** (foll. by before or after) immediately; just. ~conj. **4.** (subordinating) as soon as.

direct object n. Grammar. a noun, pronoun, or noun phrase whose referent receives the direct action of a verb. For example, the man in They shot the man with a rifle.

director (dɪ'rɛktə, daɪ-) n. **1.** a person or thing that directs, controls, or regulates. **2.** a member of the governing board of a business concern. **3.** a person who directs the affairs of an institution, trust, etc. **4.** the person responsible for the staging of a play or the making of a film. **5.** Music. another word (esp. U.S.) for **conductor.** —**direc'torial** adj. —**di'rector,ship** n. —**di'rectress** fem. n.

THESAURUS

diplomacy 1. international negotiation, statecraft, statesmanship **2.** artfulness, craft, delicacy, discretion, finesse, savoir faire, skill, subtlety, tact

diplomat conciliator, go-between, mediator, moderator, negotiator, politician, public relations expert, tactician

diplomatic adept, discreet, polite, politic, prudent, sensitive, subtle, tactful

dire 1. alarming, appalling, awful, calamitous, cataclysmic, catastrophic, cruel, disastrous, horrible, horrid, ruinous, terrible, woeful **2.** dismal, dreadful, fearful, gloomy, grim, ominous, portentous **3.** critical, crucial, crying, desperate, drastic, exigent, extreme, pressing, urgent

direct¹ v. **1.** administer, advise, conduct, control, dispose, govern, guide, handle, lead, manage, mastermind, oversee, preside over, regulate, rule, run, superintend, supervise **2.** bid, charge, command, dictate, enjoin, instruct, order **3.** guide, indicate, lead, point in the direction of, point the way, show **4.** ad-

dress, aim, cast, fix, focus, intend, level, mean, point, train, turn **5.** address, label, mail, route, send, superscribe

direct² adj. **1.** candid, frank, honest, man-to-man, matter-of-fact, open, outspoken, plain-spoken, sincere, straight, straightforward **2.** absolute, blunt, categorical, downright, explicit, express, plain, point-blank, unambiguous, unequivocal **3.** nonstop, not crooked, shortest, straight, through, unbroken, undeviating, uninterrupted **4.** face-to-face, first-hand, head-on, immediate, personal

direction 1. administration, charge, command, control, government, guidance, leadership, management, order, oversight, superintendence, supervision **2.** aim, bearing, course, line, path, road, route, track, way **3.** bent, bias, current, drift, end, orientation, proclivity, tack, tendency, tenor, trend **4.** address, label, mark, superscription

directions briefing, guidance, guidelines, indication, instructions, plan, recom-

mendation, regulations

directive n. charge, command, decree, dictate, edict, injunction, instruction, mandate, notice, order, ordinance, regulation, ruling

directly 1. by the shortest route, exactly, in a beeline, precisely, straight, unswervingly, without deviation **2.** as soon as possible, at once, dead, due, forthwith, immediately, in a second, instantaneously, instantly, presently, promptly, pronto (Inf.), quickly, right away, soon, speedily, straightaway **3.** candidly, face-to-face, honestly, in person, openly, personally, plainly, point-blank, straightforwardly, truthfully, unequivocally, without prevarication

director administrator, boss (Inf.), chairman, chief, controller, executive, governor, head, leader, manager, organizer, principal, producer, supervisor

directorate (dı'rɛktərıt, daı-) n. 1. a board of directors. 2. Also: **directorship**. the position of director.

directory (dı'rɛktərı, -trı, daı-) n., pl. **-ries**. 1. a book listing names, addresses, telephone numbers, etc., of individuals or firms. 2. a book giving directions. 3. a book containing the rules to be observed in the forms of worship used in churches. 4. a directorate. ~adj. 5. directing.

direct speech or esp. U.S. **direct discourse** n. the reporting of what someone has said or written by quoting his exact words.

direct tax n. a tax paid by the person or organization on which it is levied.

dirge (dɜːdʒ) n. 1. a chant of lamentation for the dead. 2. the funeral service in its solemn or sung forms. 3. any mourning song or melody. —'**dirgeful** adj.

dirigible ('dırıdʒıbəl) adj. 1. able to be steered or directed. ~n. 2. another name for **airship**. —**dirigi'bility** n.

dirk (dɜːk) n. 1. a dagger, esp. as formerly worn by Scottish Highlanders. ~vb. 2. (tr.) to stab with a dirk.

dirndl ('dɜːndəl) n. 1. a woman's dress with a full gathered skirt and fitted bodice; originating from Tyrolean peasant wear. 2. a gathered skirt of this kind.

dirt (dɜːt) n. 1. any unclean substance, such as mud, etc.; filth. 2. loose earth; soil. 3. a. a packed earth, gravel, cinders, etc., used to make a racetrack. b. (as modifier): a dirt track. 4. Mining. the gravel or soil from which minerals are extracted. 5. a person or thing regarded as worthless. 6. obscene or indecent speech or writing. 7. moral corruption. 8. do (someone) dirt. Sl. to do something vicious to (someone). 9. eat dirt. Sl. to accept insult without complaining.

dirt-cheap adj., adv. Inf. at an extremely low price.

dirty ('dɜːtı) adj. **dirtier**, **dirtiest**. 1. covered or marked with dirt; filthy. 2. obscene: dirty books. 3. causing one to become grimy: a dirty job. 4. (of a colour) not clear and bright. 5. unfair; dishonest. 6. mean; nasty: a dirty cheat. 7. scandalous; unkind. 8. revealing dislike or anger. 9. (of weather) rainy or squally; stormy. 10. (of a nuclear weapon) producing a large quantity of radioactive fall-out. 11. **dirty linen**. Inf. intimate secrets, esp. those that might give rise to gossip. 12. **dirty work**. unpleasant or illicit activity. 13. **do the dirty on**. Inf. to behave meanly towards. ~vb. **dirtying**, **dirtied**. 14. to make or become dirty; stain; soil. —'**dirtily** adv. —'**dirtiness** n.

dis- prefix. 1. indicating reversal: disconnect. 2. indicating negation, lack, or deprivation: dissimilar; disgrace. 3. indicating removal or release: disembowel. 4. expressing intensive force: dissever.

disability (ˌdısə'bılıtı) n., pl. **-ties**. 1. the condition of being physically or mentally impaired. 2. something that disables; handicap. 3. lack of necessary intelligence, strength, etc. 4. an incapacity in the eyes of the law to enter into certain transactions.

disable (dıs'eıbəl) vb. (tr.) 1. to make ineffective, unfit, or incapable, as by crippling. 2. to make or pronounce legally incapable. —**dis'ablement** n.

disabuse (ˌdısə'bjuːz) vb. (tr.; usually foll. by of) to rid of a mistaken idea; set right.

disadvantage (ˌdısəd'vɑːntıdʒ) n. 1. an unfavourable circumstance, thing, person, etc. 2. injury, loss, or detriment. 3. an unfavourable situation (esp. in **at a disadvantage**). ~vb. 4. (tr.) to put at a disadvantage; handicap. —**dis,advan'tageous** adj.

disadvantaged (ˌdısəd'vɑːntıdʒd) adj. socially or economically deprived or discriminated against.

disaffect (ˌdısə'fɛkt) vb. (tr.; often passive) to cause to lose loyalty or affection; alienate. —**disaf'fectedly** adv. —ˌdisaf'fection n.

disagree (ˌdısə'griː) vb. **-greeing**, **-greed**. (intr.; often foll. by with) 1. to dissent in opinion or dispute (about an idea, fact, etc.). 2. to fail to correspond; conflict. 3. to be unacceptable (to) or unfavourable (for): curry disagrees with me. 4. to be opposed (to).

disagreeable (ˌdısə'grıəbəl) adj. 1. not likable; bad-tempered. 2. unpleasant; offensive. —**disa'greeableness** n. —**disa'greeably** adv.

disagreement (ˌdısə'griːmənt) n. 1. refusal or failure to agree. 2. a failure to correspond. 3. an argument or dispute.

disallow (ˌdısə'lau) vb. (tr.) 1. to reject as untrue or invalid. 2. to cancel. —ˌdisal'lowable adj. —ˌdisal'lowance n.

disappear (ˌdısə'pıə) vb. (intr.) 1. to cease to be visible; vanish. 2. to go away or become lost, esp. without explanation. 3. to cease to exist; become extinct or lost. —ˌdisap'pearance n.

disappoint (ˌdısə'pɔınt) vb. (tr.) 1. to fail to meet the expectations, hopes, etc. of; let down. 2. to prevent the fulfilment of (a plan, etc.); frustrate. —ˌdisap'pointed adj. —ˌdisap'pointingly adv.

THESAURUS

dirge coronach (Scot. & Irish), dead march, elegy, funeral song, lament, requiem, threnody

dirt 1. dust, excrement, filth, grime, impurity, mire, muck, mud, slime, smudge, stain, tarnish 2. clay, earth, loam, soil 3. indecency, obscenity, pornography, smut

dirty adj. 1. begrimed, filthy, foul, grimy, grubby, messy, mucky, muddy, nasty, polluted, soiled, sullied, unclean 2. blue, indecent, obscene, off-colour, pornographic, risqué, salacious, smutty, vulgar 3. clouded, dark, dull, miry, muddy, not clear 4. corrupt, crooked, dishonest, fraudulent, illegal, treacherous, unfair, unscrupulous, unsporting 5. base, beggarly, contemptible, cowardly, despicable, ignominious, low, low-down (Inf.), mean, nasty, scurvy, shabby, sordid, squalid, vile 6. angry, annoyed, bitter, indignant, offended, resentful, scorching 7. Of weather gusty, lowering, rainy, squally, stormy ~v. 8. begrime, blacken, defile, foul, mess up, muddy, pollute, smear, smudge, soil, spoil, stain, sully

disability 1. affliction, ailment, complaint, defect, disablement, disorder, handicap, impairment, infirmity, malady 2. disqualification, impotency, inability, incapacity, incompetency, unfitness, weakness

disable 1. cripple, damage, debilitate, enfeeble, hamstring, handicap, immobilize, impair, incapacitate, paralyse, prostrate, put out of action, render hors de combat, render inoperative, unfit, unman, weaken 2. disenable, disqualify, invalidate, render or declare incapable

disabled bedridden, crippled, handi-capped, incapacitated, infirm, lame, maimed, mangled, mutilated, paralysed, weak, weakened, wrecked

disadvantage 1. damage, detriment, disservice, harm, hurt, injury, loss, prejudice 2. Often plural burden, drawback, flaw, fly in the ointment (Inf.), handicap, hardship, hindrance, impediment, inconvenience, liability, minus (Inf.), nuisance, privation, snag, trouble, weakness, weak point 3. **at a disadvantage** boxed in, cornered, handicapped, in a corner, vulnerable

disadvantageous adverse, damaging, deleterious, detrimental, harmful, hurtful, ill-timed, inconvenient, inexpedient, injurious, inopportune, prejudicial, unfavourable

disaffected alienated, antagonistic, discontented, disloyal, dissatisfied, estranged, hostile, mutinous, rebellious, seditious, uncompliant, unsubmissive

disaffection alienation, animosity, antagonism, antipathy, aversion, breach, disagreement, discontent, dislike, disloyalty, dissatisfaction, estrangement, hostility, ill will, repugnance, resentment, unfriendliness

disagree 1. be discordant, be dissimilar, conflict, contradict, counter, depart, deviate, differ, diverge, run counter to, vary 2. argue, bicker, clash, contend, contest, debate, differ (in opinion), dispute, dissent, fall out (Inf.), have words (Inf.), object, oppose, quarrel, take issue with, wrangle 3. be injurious, bother, discomfort, distress, hurt, make ill, nauseate, sicken, trouble, upset

disagreeable 1. bad-tempered, brusque, churlish, contrary, cross, difficult, disobliging, ill-natured, irritable, nasty, peevish, rude, surly, unfriendly, ungracious, unlikable, unpleasant 2. disgusting, displeasing, distasteful, nasty, objectionable, obnoxious, offensive, repellent, repugnant, repulsive, uninviting, unpalatable, unpleasant, unsavoury

disagreement 1. difference, discrepancy, disparity, dissimilarity, dissimilitude, divergence, diversity, incompatibility, incongruity, unlikeness, variance 2. altercation, argument, clash, conflict, debate, difference, discord, dispute, dissent, division, falling out, misunderstanding, quarrel, squabble, strife, wrangle 3. **in disagreement** at daggers drawn, at loggerheads, at odds, at variance, disunited, in conflict

disallow 1. abjure, disavow, disclaim, dismiss, disown, rebuff, refuse, reject, repudiate 2. ban, cancel, embargo, forbid, prohibit, proscribe, veto

disappear 1. be lost to view, depart, drop out of sight, ebb, escape, evanesce, fade away, flee, fly, go, pass, recede, retire, vanish from sight, wane, withdraw 2. cease, cease to be known, die out, dissolve, end, evaporate, expire, fade, leave no trace, melt away, pass away, perish, vanish

disappearance departure, desertion, disappearing, disappearing trick, eclipse, evanescence, evaporation, fading, flight, going, loss, melting, passing, vanishing, vanishing point

disappoint 1. chagrin, dash, deceive, delude, disenchant, disgruntle, dishearten, disillusion, dismay, dissatisfy, fail, let down, sad-

disappointment (ˌdɪsəˈpɔɪntmənt) n. 1. a disappointing or being disappointed. 2. a person or thing that disappoints.

disapprove (ˌdɪsəˈpruːv) vb. 1. (intr.; often foll. by of) to consider wrong, bad, etc. 2. (tr.) to withhold approval from. —ˌdisapˈproval n. —ˌdisapˈprover n. —ˌdisapˈprovingly adv.

disarm (dɪsˈɑːm) vb. 1. (tr.) to remove defensive or offensive capability from (a country, army, etc.). 2. (tr.) to deprive of weapons. 3. (tr.) to win the confidence or affection of. 4. (intr.) (of a nation, etc.) to decrease the size and capability of one's armed forces. 5. (intr.) to lay down weapons. —disˈarmer n.

disarmament (dɪsˈɑːməmənt) n. 1. the reduction of fighting capability, as by a nation. 2. a disarming or being disarmed.

disarming (dɪsˈɑːmɪŋ) adj. tending to neutralize hostility, suspicion, etc. —disˈarmingly adv.

disarrange (ˌdɪsəˈreɪndʒ) vb. (tr.) to throw into disorder. —ˌdisarˈrangement n.

disarray (ˌdɪsəˈreɪ) n. 1. confusion, dismay, and lack of discipline. 2. (esp. of clothing) disorderliness; untidiness. ~vb. (tr.) 3. to throw into confusion. 4. Arch. to undress.

disassociate (ˌdɪsəˈsəʊʃɪˌeɪt) vb. a less common word for **dissociate**. —ˌdisasˌsociˈation n.

disaster (dɪˈzɑːstə) n. 1. an occurrence that causes great distress or destruction. 2. a thing, project, etc., that fails or has been ruined. —disˈastrous adj.

disavow (ˌdɪsəˈvaʊ) vb. (tr.) to deny knowledge of, connection with, or responsibility for. —ˌdisaˈvowal n. —disavowedly (ˌdɪsəˈvaʊɪdlɪ) adv.

disband (dɪsˈbænd) vb. to cease to function or cause to stop functioning, as a unit, group, etc. —disˈbandment n.

disbar (dɪsˈbɑː) vb. -barring, -barred. (tr.) Law. to deprive of the status of barrister; expel from the Bar. —disˈbarment n.

disbelieve (ˌdɪsbɪˈliːv) vb. 1. (tr.) to reject as false or lying. 2. (intr.; usually foll. by in) to have no faith (in). —ˌdisbeˈlief n. —ˌdisbeˈliever n.

disbud (dɪsˈbʌd) vb. -budding, -budded. to remove superfluous buds from (a plant).

disburden (dɪsˈbɜːdən) vb. 1. to remove (a load) from. 2. (tr.) to relieve (one's mind, etc.) of a distressing worry.

disburse (dɪsˈbɜːs) vb. (tr.) to pay out. —disˈbursable

adj. —disˈbursement n. —disˈburser n.

disc (dɪsk) n. 1. a flat circular plate. 2. something resembling this. 3. a gramophone record. 4. Anat. any approximately circular flat structure in the body, esp. an intervertebral disc. 5. the flat receptacle of composite flowers, such as the daisy. 6. a. Also called: **parking disc**. a marker or device for display in a parked vehicle showing the time of arrival or the latest permitted time of departure or both. b. (as modifier): disc parking. 7. Computers. a variant spelling of **disk**.

discard vb. (dɪsˈkɑːd). 1. (tr.) to get rid of as useless or undesirable. 2. Cards. to throw out (a card or cards) from one's hand. 3. Cards. to play (a card not of the suit led nor a trump) when unable to follow suit. ~n. (ˈdɪskɑːd). 4. a person or thing that has been cast aside. 5. Cards. a discarded card. 6. the act of discarding.

disc brake n. a type of brake in which two pads rub against a flat disc attached to the wheel hub when the brake is applied.

discern (dɪˈsɜːn) vb. 1. (tr.) to recognize or perceive clearly. 2. to recognize or perceive (differences). —disˈcerner n. —disˈcernible adj. —disˈcerning adj. —disˈcernment n.

discharge vb. (dɪsˈtʃɑːdʒ). 1. (tr.) to release or allow to go. 2. (tr.) to dismiss from or relieve of duty, employment, etc. 3. to fire or be fired, as a gun. 4. to pour forth or cause to pour forth: the boil discharges pus. 5. (tr.) to remove (the cargo) from (a boat, etc.); unload. 6. (tr.) to perform the duties of or meet the demands of (an office, obligation, etc.). 7. (tr.) to relieve (oneself) of (a responsibility, debt, etc.). 8. Physics. a. to lose or remove electric charge. b. to form an arc, spark, or corona in a gas. c. to take or supply electrical current from a cell or battery. 9. (tr.) Law. to release (a prisoner from custody, etc.). ~n. (ˈdɪstʃɑːdʒ, dɪsˈtʃɑːdʒ). 10. a person or thing that is discharged. 11. a. dismissal or release from an office, job, institution, etc. b. the document certifying such release. 12. the fulfilment of an obligation or release from a responsibility or liability. 13. the act of removing a load, as of cargo. 14. a pouring forth of a fluid; emission. 15. a. the act of firing a projectile. b. the volley, bullet, etc., fired. 16. Law. a. a release, as of a person held under legal restraint. b. an annulment, as of a court order. 17. Physics. a. the act or process of removing or losing charge. b. a conduction of electricity through a gas by the formation and movement of electrons and ions in an applied electric field.

THESAURUS

den, vex 2. baffle, balk, defeat, disconcert, foil, frustrate, hamper, hinder, thwart

disappointed balked, cast down, depressed, despondent, discontented, discouraged, disenchanted, disgruntled, disillusioned, dissatisfied, distressed, downhearted, foiled, frustrated, let down, saddened, thwarted, upset

disappointing depressing, disagreeable, disconcerting, discouraging, failing, inadequate, inferior, insufficient, lame, pathetic, sad, second-rate, sorry, unexpected, unhappy, unsatisfactory, unworthy, upsetting

disappointment 1. chagrin, discontent, discouragement, disenchantment, disillusionment, displeasure, dissatisfaction, distress, failure, frustration, ill-success, mortification, regret, unfulfilment 2. blow, calamity, disaster, failure, fiasco, letdown, miscarriage, misfortune, setback, washout (Inf.)

disapproval censure, condemnation, criticism, denunciation, deprecation, disapprobation, displeasure, dissatisfaction, objection, reproach

disapprove 1. Often with of blame, censure, condemn, deplore, deprecate, discountenance, dislike, find unacceptable, frown on, look down one's nose at (Inf.), object to, reject, take exception to 2. disallow, set aside, spurn, turn down, veto

disarmament arms limitation, arms reduction, de-escalation, demilitarization, demobilization

disarming charming, irresistible, likable, persuasive, winning

disarrange confuse, derange, discom-

pose, disorder, disorganize, disturb, jumble (up), mess (up), scatter, shake (up), shuffle, unsettle, untidy

disarray 1. confusion, discomposure, disharmony, dismay, disorder, disorderliness, disorganization, disunity, indiscipline, unruliness, upset 2. chaos, clutter, dishevelment, jumble, mess, mix-up, muddle, shambles, tangle, untidiness

disaster accident, act of God, adversity, blow, calamity, cataclysm, catastrophe, misadventure, mischance, misfortune, mishap, reverse, ruin, ruination, stroke, tragedy, trouble

disastrous adverse, calamitous, cataclysmal, cataclysmic, catastrophic, destructive, detrimental, devastating, dire, dreadful, fatal, hapless, harmful, ill-fated, ill-starred, ruinous, terrible, tragic, unfortunate, unlucky, unpropitious, untoward

disbelief distrust, doubt, dubiety, incredulity, mistrust, scepticism, unbelief

disbelieve discount, discredit, give no credence to, mistrust, not accept, not buy (Inf.), not credit, not swallow (Inf.), reject, repudiate, scoff at, suspect

disbeliever agnostic, atheist, doubter, doubting Thomas, questioner, sceptic, scoffer

disbelievingly askance, cynically, doubtingly, incredulously, mistrustfully, quizzically, sceptically, suspiciously, with a pinch of salt

discard abandon, cast aside, dispense with, dispose of, ditch (Sl.), drop, dump (Inf.), get rid of, jettison, reject, relinquish, remove,

repudiate, scrap, shed, throw away or out

discerning acute, astute, clear-sighted, critical, discriminating, ingenious, intelligent, judicious, knowing, penetrating, perceptive, percipient, perspicacious, piercing, sagacious, sensitive, sharp, shrewd, subtle, wise

discharge v. 1. absolve, acquit, allow to go, clear, exonerate, free, liberate, pardon, release, set free ~n. 2. acquittal, clearance, exoneration, liberation, pardon, release, remittance ~v. 3. cashier, discard, dismiss, eject, expel, fire (Inf.), give (someone) the sack (Inf.), oust, remove, sack (Inf.) ~n. 4. congé, demobilization, dismissal, ejection, the boot (Sl.), the sack (Inf.) ~v. 5. detonate, explode, fire, let off, set off, shoot ~n. 6. blast, burst, detonation, discharging, explosion, firing, fusillade, report, salvo, shot, volley ~v. 7. disembogue, dispense, emit, empty, excrete, exude, give off, gush, leak, ooze, pour forth, release, void ~n. 8. emission, emptying, excretion, flow, ooze, pus, secretion, seepage, suppuration, vent, voiding ~v. 9. disburden, off-load, remove, unburden, unload ~n. 10. disburdening, emptying, unburdening, unloading ~v. 11. accomplish, carry out, do, execute, fulfil, observe, perform ~n. 12. accomplishment, achievement, execution, fulfilment, observance, performance ~v. 13. clear, honour, meet, pay, relieve, satisfy, settle, square up ~n. 14. payment, satisfaction, settlement

—**dis'chargeable** adj. —**dis'charger** n.
disciple (dɪˈsaɪpəl) n. **1.** a follower of the doctrines of a teacher or a school of thought. **2.** one of the personal followers of Christ (including his 12 apostles) during his earthly life. —**dis'ciple,ship** n. —**discipular** (dɪˈsɪpjulə) adj.
disciplinarian (ˌdɪsɪplɪˈnɛərɪən) n. a person who imposes or advocates strict discipline.
disciplinary (ˈdɪsɪˌplɪnərɪ) adj. of, promoting, or used for discipline; corrective.
discipline (ˈdɪsɪplɪn) n. **1.** training or conditions imposed for the improvement of physical powers, self-control, etc. **2.** systematic training in obedience. **3.** the state of improved behaviour, etc., resulting from such training. **4.** punishment or chastisement. **5.** a system of rules for behaviour, etc. **6.** a branch of learning or instruction. **7.** the laws governing members of a Church. ~vb. (tr.) **8.** to improve or attempt to improve the behaviour, orderliness, etc., of by training, conditions, or rules. **9.** to punish or correct. —**'disci,plinable** adj. —**disciplinal** (ˌdɪsɪˈplaɪnəl) adj. —**'disci,pliner** n.
disc jockey n. a person who announces and plays recorded music, esp. pop music, on a radio programme, etc.
disclaim (dɪsˈkleɪm) vb. **1.** (tr.) to deny or renounce (any claim, connection, etc.). **2.** (tr.) to deny the validity or authority of. **3.** Law. to renounce or repudiate (a legal claim or right).
disclaimer (dɪsˈkleɪmə) n. a repudiation or denial.
disclose (dɪsˈkləuz) vb. (tr.) **1.** to make known. **2.** to allow to be seen. —**dis'closer** n. —**dis'closure** n.
disco (ˈdɪskəu) n., pl. **-cos.** Inf. short for **discotheque.**
discolour or U.S. **discolor** (dɪsˈkʌlə) vb. to change in colour; fade or stain. —**dis,color'ation, dis'colourment,** or U.S. **dis'colorment** n.
discomfit (dɪsˈkʌmfɪt) vb. (tr.) **1.** to make uneasy or confused. **2.** to frustrate the plans or purpose of. **3.** Arch. to defeat. —**dis'comfiture** n.
discomfort (dɪsˈkʌmfət) n. **1.** an inconvenience, distress, or mild pain. **2.** something that disturbs or deprives of ease. ~vb. **3.** (tr.) to make uncomfortable or uneasy.
discommode (ˌdɪskəˈməud) vb. (tr.) to cause inconvenience to; disturb. —**discom'modious** adj.

discompose (ˌdɪskəmˈpəuz) vb. (tr.) **1.** to disturb the composure of; disconcert. **2.** Now rare. to disarrange. —**discom'posure** n.
disconcert (ˌdɪskənˈsɜːt) vb. (tr.) **1.** to disturb the composure of. **2.** to frustrate or upset. —**discon'certed** adj. —**discon'certion** n.
disconnect (ˌdɪskəˈnɛkt) vb. (tr.) to undo or break the connection of or between (something, as a plug and a socket). —**discon'nection** n.
disconnected (ˌdɪskəˈnɛktɪd) adj. **1.** not rationally connected; confused or incoherent. **2.** not connected or joined.
disconsolate (dɪsˈkɒnsəlɪt) adj. sad beyond comfort; dejected. —**dis'consolately** adv. —**dis,conso'lation** or **dis'consolateness** n.
discontent (ˌdɪskənˈtɛnt) n. **1.** Also called: **discontentment.** lack of contentment, as with one's condition or lot in life. ~vb. **2.** (tr.) to make dissatisfied. —**discon-'tented** adj. —**discon'tentedness** n.
discontinue (ˌdɪskənˈtɪnjuː) vb. **-uing, -ued. 1.** to come or bring to an end; interrupt or be interrupted; stop. **2.** (tr.) Law. to terminate or abandon (an action, suit, etc.). —**discon'tinuance** n. —**discon,tinu'ation** n. —**dis,conti'nuity** n.
discontinuous (ˌdɪskənˈtɪnjuəs) adj. characterized by interruptions or breaks; intermittent. —**discon'tinuously** adv. —**discon'tinuousness** n.
discord n. (ˈdɪskɔːd). **1.** lack of agreement or harmony. **2.** harsh confused mingling of sounds. **3.** a combination of musical notes, esp. one containing one or more dissonant intervals. ~vb. (dɪsˈkɔːd). **4.** (intr.) to disagree; clash.
discordant (dɪsˈkɔːdənt) adj. **1.** at variance; disagreeing. **2.** harsh in sound; inharmonious. —**dis'cordance** n. —**dis'cordantly** adv.
discotheque (ˈdɪskəˌtɛk) n. **1.** a club or other public place for dancing to recorded pop music. **2.** mobile equipment for providing amplified pop music for dancing.
discount vb. (dɪsˈkaunt, ˈdɪskaunt). (mainly tr.) **1.** to leave out of account as being unreliable, prejudiced, or irrelevant. **2.** to anticipate and make allowance for. **3. a.** to deduct (an amount or percentage) from the price, cost, etc. **b.** to reduce (the regular price, etc.) by a percentage or amount. **4.** to sell or offer for sale at a re-

---

THESAURUS

disciple adherent, apostle, believer, catechumen, convert, devotee, follower, learner, partisan, proselyte, pupil, student, supporter, votary
disciplinarian authoritarian, despot, drill sergeant, hard master, martinet, stickler, strict teacher, taskmaster, tyrant
discipline n. **1.** drill, exercise, method, practice, regimen, regulation, training **2.** conduct, control, orderliness, regulation, restraint, self-control, strictness **3.** castigation, chastisement, correction, punishment **4.** area, branch of knowledge, course, curriculum, field of study, specialty, subject ~v. **5.** break in, bring up, check, control, drill, educate, exercise, form, govern, instruct, inure, prepare, regulate, restrain, train **6.** castigate, chasten, chastise, correct, penalize, punish, reprimand, reprove
disclaim abandon, abjure, abnegate, decline, deny, disaffirm, disallow, disavow, disown, forswear, reject, renounce, repudiate
disclose **1.** broadcast, communicate, confess, divulge, impart, leak, let slip, make known, make public, publish, relate, reveal, spill the beans about (Inf.), tell, unveil, utter **2.** bring to light, discover, exhibit, expose, lay bare, reveal, show, uncover, unveil
disclosure acknowledgment, admission, announcement, broadcast, confession, declaration, discovery, divulgence, exposé, exposure, leak, publication, revelation, uncovering
discolour fade, mar, mark, rust, soil, stain, streak, tarnish, tinge
discomfort **1.** n. ache, annoyance, disquiet, distress, hardship, hurt, inquietude, irritation, malaise, nuisance, pain, soreness,

trouble, uneasiness, unpleasantness, vexation **2.** v. discomfit, discompose, disquiet, distress, disturb, embarrass, make uncomfortable
discomposure agitation, anxiety, confusion, discomfiture, disquiet, disquietude, distraction, disturbance, embarrassment, fluster, inquietude, malaise, nervousness, perturbation, uneasiness
disconcert **1.** abash, agitate, bewilder, discompose, disturb, flurry, fluster, nonplus, perplex, perturb, put out of countenance, rattle (Inf.), ruffle, shake up (Inf.), take aback, throw off balance, trouble, unbalance, unsettle, upset, worry **2.** baffle, balk, confuse, defeat, disarrange, frustrate, hinder, put off, thwart, undo
disconcerted annoyed, bewildered, caught off balance, confused, distracted, disturbed, embarrassed, fazed (U.S. inf.), flurried, flustered, mixed-up, nonplussed, out of countenance, perturbed, rattled (Inf.), ruffled, shook up (Inf.), taken aback, thrown (Inf.), troubled, unsettled, upset
disconcerting alarming, awkward, baffling, bewildering, bothersome, confusing, dismaying, distracting, disturbing, embarrassing, off-putting (Brit. inf.), perplexing, upsetting
disconnect cut off, detach, disengage, divide, part, separate, sever, take apart, uncouple
disconnected confused, disjointed, garbled, illogical, incoherent, irrational, jumbled, mixed-up, rambling, uncoordinated, unintelligible, wandering
disconnection cessation, cut-off, cutting off, discontinuation, discontinuity, inter-

ruption, separation, severance, stoppage, suspension
disconsolate crushed, dejected, desolate, despairing, forlorn, gloomy, grief-stricken, heartbroken, hopeless, inconsolable, melancholy, miserable, sad, unhappy, woeful, wretched
discontent n. discontentment, displeasure, dissatisfaction, envy, fretfulness, regret, restlessness, uneasiness, unhappiness, vexation
discontented brassed off (Sl.), cheesed off (Brit. sl.), complaining, disaffected, disgruntled, displeased, dissatisfied, exasperated, fed up, fretful, miserable, unhappy, vexed, with a chip on one's shoulder (Inf.)
discontinue abandon, break off, cease, drop, end, finish, give up, halt, interrupt, leave off, pause, put an end to, quit, refrain from, stop, suspend, terminate
discontinued abandoned, ended, finished, given up or over, halted, no longer made, terminated
discord **1.** clashing, conflict, contention, difference, disagreement, discordance, dispute, dissension, disunity, division, friction, incompatibility, lack of concord, opposition, rupture, strife, variance, wrangling **2.** cacophony, din, disharmony, dissonance, harshness, jangle, jarring, racket, tumult
discordant **1.** at odds, clashing, conflicting, contradictory, contrary, different, disagreeing, divergent, incompatible, incongruous, inconsistent, opposite **2.** cacophonous, dissonant, grating, harsh, inharmonious, jangling, jarring, shrill, strident, unmelodious

duced price. **5.** to buy or sell (a bill of exchange, etc.) before maturity, with a deduction for interest. **6.** (*also intr.*) to loan money on (a negotiable instrument) with a deduction for interest. ~*n.* ('dɪskaʊnt). **7.** short for **cash discount. 8.** Also called: **discount rate. a.** the amount of interest deducted in the purchase or sale of or the loan of money on unmatured negotiable instruments. **b.** the rate of interest deducted. **9.** (in the issue of shares) a percentage deducted from the par value to give a reduced amount payable by subscribers. **10.** a discounting. **11. at a discount. a.** below the regular price. **b.** in low regard. **12.** (*modifier*) offering or selling at reduced prices: *a discount shop.* —**dis'countable** *adj.* —'**discounter** *n.*

discountenance (dɪs'kaʊntɪnəns) *vb.* (*tr.*) **1.** to make ashamed or confused. **2.** to disapprove of. ~*n.* **3.** disapproval.

discourage (dɪs'kʌrɪdʒ) *vb.* (*tr.*) **1.** to deprive of the will to persist in something. **2.** to inhibit; prevent: *this solution discourages rust.* **3.** to oppose by expressing disapproval. —**dis'couragement** *n.* —**dis'couragingly** *adv.*

discourse *n.* ('dɪskɔ:s; dɪs'kɔ:s). **1.** verbal communication; talk; conversation. **2.** a formal treatment of a subject in speech or writing. **3.** a unit of text used by linguists for the analysis of linguistic phenomena that range over more than one sentence. **4.** *Arch.* the ability to reason. ~*vb.* (dɪs'kɔ:s). **5.** (*intr.*; often foll. by *on* or *upon*) to speak or write (about) formally. **6.** (*intr.*) to hold a discussion. **7.** (*tr.*) *Arch.* to give forth (music).

discourteous (dɪs'kɜ:tɪəs) *adj.* showing bad manners; impolite; rude. —**dis'courteously** *adv.* —**dis'courteousness** *n.* —**dis'courtesy** *n.*

discover (dɪ'skʌvə) *vb.* (*tr.*; *may take a clause as object*) **1.** to be the first to find or find out about. **2.** to learn about for the first time; realize. **3.** to find after study or search. **4.** to reveal or make known. —**dis'coverable** *adj.* —**dis'coverer** *n.*

discovery (dɪ'skʌvərɪ) *n.*, *pl.* -**eries.** '1. the act, process, or an instance of discovering. **2.** a person, place, or thing that has been discovered. **3.** *Law.* the compulsory

disclosure by a party to an action of relevant documents in his possession.

discredit (dɪs'krɛdɪt) *vb.* (*tr.*) **1.** to damage the reputation of. **2.** to cause to be disbelieved or distrusted. **3.** to reject as untrue. ~*n.* **4.** something that causes disgrace. **5.** damage to a reputation. **6.** lack of belief or confidence. —**dis'creditable** *adj.*

discreet (dɪ'skri:t) *adj.* **1.** careful to avoid embarrassment, esp. by keeping confidences secret; tactful. **2.** unobtrusive. —**dis'creetly** *adv.* —**dis'creetness** *n.*

discrepancy (dɪ'skrɛpənsɪ) *n.*, *pl.* -**cies.** a conflict or variation, as between facts, figures, or claims. —**dis'crepant** *adj.*

discrete (dɪ'skri:t) *adj.* **1.** separate or distinct. **2.** consisting of distinct or separate parts. —**dis'cretely** *adv.* —**dis'creteness** *n.*

discretion (dɪ'skrɛʃən) *n.* **1.** the quality of behaving so as to avoid social embarrassment or distress. **2.** freedom or authority to make judgments and to act as one sees fit (esp. in **at one's own discretion, at the discretion of**). **3. age** or **years of discretion.** the age at which a person is able to manage his own affairs. —**dis'cretionary** *adj.*

discriminate *vb.* (dɪ'skrɪmɪˌneɪt). **1.** (*intr.*) to single out a particular person, group, etc., for special favour or disfavour. **2.** (when *intr.*, foll. by *between* or *among*) to recognize or understand the difference (between); distinguish. **3.** (*tr.*) to constitute or mark a difference. **4.** (*intr.*) to be discerning in matters of taste. ~*adj.* (dɪ'skrɪmɪnɪt). **5.** showing or marked by discrimination. —**dis'criminately** *adv.* —**dis'crimiˌnating** *adj.*

discrimination (dɪˌskrɪmɪ'neɪʃən) *n.* **1.** unfair treatment of a person, racial group, minority, etc.; action based on prejudice. **2.** subtle appreciation in matters of taste. **3.** the ability to see fine distinctions and differences.

discriminatory (dɪ'skrɪmɪnətərɪ, -trɪ) or **discriminative** (dɪ'skrɪmɪnətɪv) *adj.* **1.** based on or showing prejudice; biased. **2.** capable of making fine distinctions.

THESAURUS

discount *v.* **1.** brush off, disbelieve, disregard, ignore, leave out of account, overlook, pass over **2.** deduct, lower, mark down, rebate, reduce, take off ~*n.* **3.** abatement, allowance, concession, cut, cut price, deduction, drawback, percentage (*Inf.*), rebate, reduction

discountenance *v.* **1.** abash, chagrin, confuse, discompose, disconcert, embarrass, humiliate, put down (*Sl.*), shame **2.** condemn, disapprove, discourage, disfavour, frown on, object to, oppose, resist, take exception to, veto

discourage **1.** abash, awe, cast down, cow, damp, dampen, dash, daunt, deject, demoralize, depress, dishearten, dismay, dispirit, frighten, intimidate, overawe, put a damper on, scare, unman, unnerve **2.** check, curb, deprecate, deter, discountenance, disfavour, dissuade, divert from, hinder, inhibit, prevent, put off, restrain, talk out of, throw cold water on (*Inf.*)

discouraged crestfallen, dashed, daunted, deterred, disheartened, dismayed, dispirited, downcast, down in the mouth, glum, pessimistic, put off

discouragement **1.** cold feet (*Inf.*), dejection, depression, despair, despondency, disappointment, discomfiture, dismay, downheartedness, hopelessness, loss of confidence, low spirits, pessimism **2.** constraint, curb, damper, deterrent, disincentive, hindrance, impediment, obstacle, opposition, rebuff, restraint, setback

discouraging dampening, daunting, depressing, disappointing, disheartening, dispiriting, off-putting (*Brit. inf.*), unfavourable, unpropitious

discourse *n.* **1.** chat, communication, conversation, converse, dialogue, discussion, speech, talk **2.** address, disquisition, dissertation, essay, homily, lecture, oration, sermon,

speech, talk, treatise ~*v.* **3.** confer, converse, debate, declaim, discuss, expatiate, hold forth, speak, talk

discourteous abrupt, bad-mannered, boorish, brusque, curt, disrespectful, ill-bred, ill-mannered, impolite, insolent, offhand, rude, uncivil, uncourteous, ungentlemanly, ungracious, unmannerly

discourtesy **1.** bad manners, disrespectfulness, ill-breeding, impertinence, impoliteness, incivility, insolence, rudeness, ungraciousness, unmannerliness **2.** affront, cold shoulder, insult, rebuff, slight, snub

discover **1.** bring to light, come across, come upon, dig up, find, light upon, locate, turn up, uncover, unearth **2.** ascertain, descry, detect, determine, discern, disclose, espy, find out, get wise to (*Inf.*), learn, notice, perceive, realize, recognize, reveal, see, spot, uncover **3.** conceive, contrive, design, devise, invent, originate, pioneer

discoverer author, explorer, founder, initiator, inventor, originator, pioneer

discovery **1.** ascertainment, detection, disclosure, espial, exploration, finding, introduction, locating, location, origination, revelation, uncovering **2.** bonanza, breakthrough, coup, find, findings, godsend, innovation, invention, secret

discredit *v.* **1.** blame, bring into disrepute, censure, defame, degrade, detract from, disgrace, dishonour, disparage, reproach, slander, slur, smear, vilify ~*n.* **2.** aspersion, censure, disgrace, dishonour, disrepute, ignominy, ill-repute, imputation, odium, reproach, scandal, shame, slur, smear, stigma ~*v.* **3.** challenge, deny, disbelieve, discount, dispute, distrust, doubt, mistrust, question ~*n.* **4.** distrust, doubt, mistrust, question, scepticism, suspicion

discreditable blameworthy, degrading, disgraceful, dishonourable, humiliating,

ignominious, improper, infamous, reprehensible, scandalous, shameful, unprincipled, unworthy

discredited brought into disrepute, debunked, discarded, exploded, exposed, obsolete, outworn, refuted, rejected

discreet careful, cautious, circumspect, considerate, diplomatic, discerning, guarded, judicious, politic, prudent, reserved, sagacious, sensible, tactful, wary

discrepancy conflict, contrariety, difference, disagreement, discordance, disparity, dissimilarity, dissonance, divergence, incongruity, inconsistency, variance, variation

discretion **1.** acumen, care, carefulness, caution, circumspection, consideration, diplomacy, discernment, good sense, heedfulness, judgment, judiciousness, maturity, prudence, sagacity, tact, wariness **2.** choice, disposition, inclination, liking, mind, option, pleasure, predilection, preference, responsibility, volition, will, wish

discretionary arbitrary (*Law*), elective, nonmandatory, open, open to choice, optional, unrestricted

discriminate **1.** disfavour, favour, show bias, show prejudice, single out, treat as inferior, treat differently, victimize **2.** assess, differentiate, discern, distinguish, draw a distinction, evaluate, segregate, separate, sift, tell the difference

discriminating acute, astute, critical, cultivated, discerning, fastidious, keen, particular, refined, selective, sensitive, tasteful

discrimination **1.** bias, bigotry, favouritism, inequity, intolerance, prejudice, unfairness **2.** acumen, acuteness, clearness, discernment, insight, judgment, keenness, penetration, perception, refinement, sagacity, subtlety, taste

discriminatory, discriminative 1. biased, favouring, inequitable, one-

discursive (dɪˈskɜːsɪv) *adj.* **1.** rambling; digressive. **2.** *Philosophy.* of or relating to knowledge obtained by reason and argument rather than intuition. —**disˈcursively** *adv.* —**disˈcursiveness** *n.*

discus (ˈdɪskəs) *n., pl.* **discuses** *or* **disci** (ˈdɪskaɪ). **1.** (originally) a circular stone or plate used in throwing competitions by the ancient Greeks. **2.** *Field sports.* a similar disc-shaped object with a heavy middle, thrown by athletes. **3.** (preceded by *the*) the event or sport of throwing the discus.

discuss (dɪˈskʌs) *vb.* (*tr.*) **1.** to have a conversation about; consider by talking over. **2.** to treat (a subject) in speech or writing. —**disˈcussant** *or* **disˈcusser** *n.* —**disˈcussible** *or* **disˈcussable** *adj.*

discussion (dɪˈskʌʃən) *n.* the examination or consideration of a matter in speech or writing.

disdain (dɪsˈdeɪn) *n.* **1.** a feeling or show of superiority and dislike; contempt; scorn. ~*vb.* **2.** (*tr.; may take an infinitive*) to refuse or reject with disdain. —**disˈdainful** *adj.*

disease (dɪˈziːz) *n.* **1.** any impairment of normal physiological function affecting an organism, esp. a change caused by infection, stress, etc., producing characteristic symptoms; illness or sickness in general. **2.** a corresponding condition in plants. **3.** any condition likened to this. —**disˈeased** *adj.*

disembark (ˌdɪsɪmˈbɑːk) *vb.* to land or cause to land from a ship, aircraft, etc. —**disembarkation** (dɪsˌɛmbɑːˈkeɪʃən) *n.*

disembody (ˌdɪsɪmˈbɒdɪ) *vb.* **-bodying, -bodied.** (*tr.*) to free from the body or from physical form. —**disemˈbodied** *adj.* —**disemˈbodiment** *n.*

disembowel (ˌdɪsɪmˈbaʊəl) *vb.* **-elling, -elled** *or U.S.* **-eling, -eled.** (*tr.*) to remove the entrails of. —**disemˈbowelment** *n.*

disenchant (ˌdɪsɪnˈtʃɑːnt) *vb.* (*tr.*) to free from or as if from an enchantment; disillusion. —**disenˈchantingly** *adv.* —**disenˈchantment** *n.*

disengage (ˌdɪsɪnˈɡeɪdʒ) *vb.* **1.** to release or become released from a connection, obligation, etc. **2.** *Mil.* to withdraw (forces) from close action. **3.** *Fencing.* to move (one's blade) from one side of an opponent's blade to another in a circular motion. —**disenˈgaged** *adj.* —**disenˈgagement** *n.*

disentangle (ˌdɪsɪnˈtæŋɡəl) *vb.* **1.** to release or become free from entanglement or confusion. **2.** (*tr.*) to unravel or work out. —**disenˈtanglement** *n.*

disequilibrium (ˌdɪsiːkwɪˈlɪbrɪəm) *n.* a loss or absence of equilibrium, esp. in an economy.

disestablish (ˌdɪsɪˈstæblɪʃ) *vb.* (*tr.*) to deprive (a church, custom, institution, etc.) of established status. —**disesˈtablishment** *n.*

disfavour *or U.S.* **disfavor** (dɪsˈfeɪvə) *n.* **1.** disapproval or dislike. **2.** the state of being disapproved of or disliked. **3.** an unkind act. ~*vb.* **4.** (*tr.*) to treat with disapproval or dislike.

disfigure (dɪsˈfɪɡə) *vb.* (*tr.*) **1.** to spoil the appearance or shape of; deface. **2.** to mar the effect or quality of. —**disˈfigurement** *n.*

disfranchise (dɪsˈfræntʃaɪz) *or* **disenfranchise** *vb.* (*tr.*) **1.** to deprive (a person) of the right to vote or other rights of citizenship. **2.** to deprive (a place) of the right to send representatives to an elected body. **3.** to deprive (a person, place, etc.) of any franchise or right. —**disfranchisement** (dɪsˈfræntʃɪzmənt) *or* ˌdisenˈfranchisement *n.*

disgorge (dɪsˈɡɔːdʒ) *vb.* **1.** to throw out (food, etc.) from the throat or stomach; vomit. **2.** to discharge or empty of (contents). **3.** (*tr.*) to yield up unwillingly. —**disˈgorgement** *n.*

disgrace (dɪsˈɡreɪs) *n.* **1.** a condition of shame, loss of reputation, or dishonour. **2.** a shameful person or thing. **3.** exclusion from confidence or trust: *he is in disgrace with his father.* ~*vb.* (*tr.*) **4.** to bring shame upon. **5.** to treat or cause to be treated with disfavour. —**disˈgraceful** *adj.*

disgruntle (dɪsˈɡrʌntəl) *vb.* (*tr.*) to make sulky or discontented. —**disˈgruntlement** *n.*

disguise (dɪsˈɡaɪz) *vb.* **1.** to modify the appearance or manner in order to conceal the identity of (someone or something). **2.** (*tr.*) to misrepresent in order to obscure the actual nature or meaning. ~*n.* **3.** a mask, costume, or manner that disguises. **4.** a disguising or being disguised.

THESAURUS

sided, partial, partisan, preferential, prejudiced, prejudicial, unjust, weighted **2.** analytical, astute, differentiating, discerning, discriminating, perceptive, perspicacious

discuss argue, confer, consider, consult with, converse, debate, deliberate, examine, exchange views on, get together (*Inf.*), go into, reason about, review, sift, talk about, thrash out, ventilate, weigh up the pros and cons

discussion analysis, argument, colloquy, confabulation, conference, consideration, consultation, conversation, debate, deliberation, dialogue, discourse, examination, exchange, review, scrutiny, symposium

disdain 1. *v.* belittle, contemn, deride, despise, disregard, look down on, look down one's nose at (*Inf.*), misprize, pooh-pooh, reject, scorn, slight, sneer at, spurn, undervalue **2.** *n.* arrogance, contempt, contumely, derision, dislike, haughtiness, hauteur, indifference, scorn, sneering, snobbishness, superciliousness

disdainful aloof, arrogant, contemptuous, derisive, haughty, high and mighty (*Inf.*), hoity-toity (*Inf.*), insolent, proud, scornful, sneering, supercilious, superior

disease 1. affliction, ailment, complaint, condition, disorder, ill health, illness, indisposition, infection, infirmity, malady, sickness, upset **2.** *Fig.* blight, cancer, canker, contagion, contamination, disorder, malady, plague

diseased ailing, infected, rotten, sick, sickly, tainted, unhealthy, unsound, unwell, unwholesome

disembark alight, arrive, get off, go ashore, land, step out of

disembodied bodiless, ghostly, immaterial, incorporeal, intangible, phantom, spectral, spiritual, unbodied

disembowel draw, eviscerate, gut, paunch

disenchanted blasé, cynical, disappointed, disillusioned, indifferent, jaundiced, let down, out of love, sick of, soured, undeceived

disenchantment disappointment, disillusion, disillusionment, revulsion, rude awakening

disengage 1. disentangle, ease, extricate, free, liberate, loosen, release, set free, unloose, untie **2.** detach, disconnect, disjoin, disunite, divide, separate, undo, withdraw

disengaged 1. apart, detached, free, loose, out of gear, released, separate, unattached, unconnected, uncoupled **2.** at ease, at leisure, free, not busy, uncommitted, unoccupied, vacant

disengagement detachment, disconnection, disentanglement, division, separation, withdrawal

disentangle 1. detach, disconnect, disengage, extricate, free, loose, separate, sever, unfold, unravel, unsnarl, untangle, untwist **2.** clarify, clear (up), resolve, simplify, sort out, work out

disfavour 1. disapprobation, disapproval, dislike, displeasure **2.** *As in* fall into disfavour bad books (*Inf.*), discredit, disesteem, disgrace, doghouse (*Inf.*), shame, unpopularity **3.** bad turn, discourtesy, disservice

disfigure blemish, damage, deface, deform, disfeature, distort, injure, maim, make ugly, mar, mutilate, scar

disfigurement blemish, defacement, defect, deformity, distortion, impairment, injury, mutilation, scar, spot, stain

disgorge 1. belch, discharge, eject, empty, expel, regurgitate, spew, spit up, spout,

throw up, vomit **2.** cede, give up, relinquish, renounce, resign, surrender, yield

disgrace *n.* 1. baseness, degradation, dishonour, disrepute, ignominy, infamy, odium, opprobrium, shame **2.** aspersion, blemish, blot, defamation, reproach, scandal, slur, stain, stigma **3.** contempt, discredit, disesteem, disfavour, obloquy ~*v.* **4.** abase, bring shame upon, defame, degrade, discredit, disfavour, dishonour, disparage, humiliate, reproach, shame, slur, stain, stigmatize, sully, taint

disgraced branded, degraded, discredited, dishonoured, humiliated, in disgrace, in the doghouse (*Inf.*), mortified, shamed, stigmatized

disgraceful blameworthy, contemptible, degrading, detestable, discreditable, dishonourable, disreputable, ignominious, infamous, low, mean, opprobrious, scandalous, shameful, shocking, unworthy

disgruntled annoyed, cheesed off (*Brit. sl.*), discontented, displeased, dissatisfied, grumpy, irritated, malcontent, peeved, peevish, petulant, put out, sulky, sullen, testy, vexed

disguise *v.* 1. camouflage, cloak, conceal, cover, hide, mask, screen, secrete, shroud, veil **2.** deceive, dissemble, dissimulate, fake, falsify, fudge, gloss over, misrepresent ~*n.* **3.** camouflage, cloak, costume, cover, get-up (*Inf.*), mask, screen, veil **4.** deception, dissimulation, façade, front, pretence, semblance, trickery, veneer

disguised camouflaged, cloaked, covert, fake, false, feigned, incognito, in disguise, masked, pretend, undercover, unrecognizable

disgust (dɪs'gʌst) vb. (tr.) **1.** to sicken or fill with loathing. **2.** to offend the moral sense of. ~n. **3.** a great loathing or distaste. **4. in disgust.** as a result of disgust. —**dis'gusted** adj. —**dis'gustedly** adv. —**dis'gustedness** n.

dish (dɪʃ) n. **1.** a container used for holding or serving food, esp. an open shallow container. **2.** the food in a dish. **3.** a particular kind of food. **4.** Also called: **'dishful.** the amount contained in a dish. **5.** something resembling a dish. **6.** a concavity. **7.** an informal name for a parabolic aerial. **8.** Sl. an attractive person. **9.** Inf. something that one particularly enjoys or excels in. ~vb. (tr.) **10.** to put into a dish. **11.** to make concave. **12.** Brit. sl. to ruin or spoil. ~See also: **dish out, dish up.** —'dish,like adj.

dishabille (,dɪsæ'biːl) or **deshabille** n. the state of being partly or carelessly dressed.

disharmony (dɪs'hɑːmənɪ) n., pl. **-nies. 1.** lack of accord or harmony. **2.** a situation, circumstance, etc., that is inharmonious. —**disharmonious** (,dɪshɑː'məunɪəs) adj.

dishcloth ('dɪʃ,klɒθ) n. a cloth or rag for washing or drying dishes.

dishearten (dɪs'hɑːt°n) vb. (tr.) to weaken or destroy the hope, courage, enthusiasm, etc., of. —**dis'hearteningly** adv. —**dis'heartenment** n.

dished (dɪʃt) adj. **1.** shaped like a dish. **2.** (of wheels) closer to one another at the bottom than at the top. **3.** Sl. exhausted or defeated.

dishevel (dɪ'ʃɛv°l) vb. **-elling, -elled** or U.S. **-eling, -eled.** to disarrange (the hair or clothes) of (someone). —**di'shevelled** adj. —**di'shevelment** n.

dishonest (dɪs'ɒnɪst) adj. not honest or fair; deceiving or fraudulent. —**dis'honestly** adv. —**dis'honesty** n.

dishonour or U.S. **dishonor** (dɪs'ɒnə) vb. (tr.) **1.** to treat with disrespect. **2.** to fail or refuse to pay (a cheque, etc.). **3.** to cause the disgrace of (a woman) by seduction or rape. ~n. **4.** a lack of honour or respect. **5.** a state of shame or disgrace. **6.** a person or thing that causes a loss of honour. **7.** an insult; affront. **8.** refusal or failure to accept or pay a commercial paper. —**dis'honourable** or U.S. **dis'honorable** adj.

dish out vb. Inf. **1.** (tr., adv.) to distribute. **2. dish it out.** to inflict punishment.

dishtowel ('dɪʃ,tauəl) n. another name (esp. U.S.) for a **tea towel**.

dish up vb. (adv.) **1.** to serve (a meal, food, etc.). **2.** (tr.) Inf. to prepare or present, esp. in an attractive manner.

dishwasher ('dɪʃ,wɒʃə) n. **1.** a machine for washing dishes, etc. **2.** a person who washes dishes, etc.

dishwater ('dɪʃ,wɔːtə) n. **1.** water in which dishes have been washed. **2.** something resembling this.

dishy ('dɪʃɪ) adj. **dishier, dishiest.** Sl., chiefly Brit. good-looking or attractive.

disillusion (,dɪsɪ'luːʒən) vb. **1.** (tr.) to destroy the ideals, illusions, or false ideas of. ~n. also **disillusionment. 2.** the act of disillusioning or the state of being disillusioned.

disincentive (,dɪsɪn'sɛntɪv) n. **1.** something that acts as a deterrent. ~adj. **2.** acting as a deterrent: a disincentive effect on productivity.

disincline (,dɪsɪn'klaɪn) vb. to make or be unwilling, reluctant, or averse. —**disinclination** (,dɪsɪnklɪ'neɪʃən) n.

disinfect (,dɪsɪn'fɛkt) vb. (tr.) to rid of microorganisms potentially harmful to man, esp. by chemical means. —,**disin'fectant** n. —,**disin'fection** n.

disingenuous (,dɪsɪn'dʒɛnjuəs) adj. not sincere; lacking candour. —,**disin'genuously** adv. —,**disin'genuousness** n.

disinherit (,dɪsɪn'hɛrɪt) vb. (tr.) **1.** Law. to deprive (an heir or next of kin) of inheritance or right to inherit. **2.** to deprive of a right or heritage. —,**disin'heritance** n.

disintegrate (dɪs'ɪntɪ,greɪt) vb. **1.** to break or be broken into fragments or parts; shatter. **2.** to lose or cause to lose cohesion. **3.** (intr.) to lose judgment or control. **4.** Physics. **a.** to induce or undergo nuclear fission. **b.** another word for **decay** (sense 3). —**dis,inte'gration** n. —**dis'inte,grator** n.

disinterest (dɪs'ɪntrɪst) n. **1.** freedom from bias or involvement. **2.** lack of interest.

disinterested (dɪs'ɪntrɪstɪd, -tərɪs-) adj. free from bias or partiality; objective. —**dis'interestedly** adv. —**dis'interestedness** n.

▷ **Usage.** In spoken and sometimes written English, disinterested (impartial) is used where uninterested (showing or feeling lack of interest) is meant. Careful writers and speakers avoid this confusion: a disinterested judge; he was uninterested in public reaction.

disjoint (dɪs'dʒɔɪnt) vb. **1.** to take apart or come apart at the joints. **2.** (tr.) to disunite or disjoin. **3.** to dislocate or become dislocated. **4.** (tr.; usually passive) to end the unity, sequence, or coherence of.

disjointed (dɪs'dʒɔɪntɪd) adj. **1.** having no coherence; disconnected. **2.** separated at the joint. **3.** dislocated. —**dis'jointedly** adv.

THESAURUS

disgust 1. v. cause aversion, displease, fill with loathing, nauseate, offend, outrage, put off, repel, revolt, sicken, turn one's stomach **2.** n. abhorrence, abomination, antipathy, aversion, detestation, dislike, distaste, hatefulness, hatred, loathing, nausea, repugnance, repulsion, revulsion

disgusted appalled, nauseated, offended, outraged, repelled, repulsed, scandalized, sick and tired of (Inf.), sickened, sick of (Inf.)

disgusting abominable, detestable, distasteful, foul, gross, hateful, loathsome, nasty, nauseating, nauseous, objectionable, obnoxious, odious, offensive, repellent, repugnant, revolting, shameless, sickening, stinking, vile, vulgar

dish n. **1.** bowl, plate, platter, salver **2.** fare, food, recipe ~v. **3.** Sl. finish, muck up (Sl.), ruin, spoil, torpedo, wreck

dishearten cast down, crush, damp, dampen, dash, daunt, deject, depress, deter, discourage, dismay, dispirit, put a damper on

disheartened crestfallen, crushed, daunted, dejected, depressed, disappointed, discouraged, dismayed, dispirited, downcast, downhearted

dishevelled bedraggled, blowzy, disarranged, disordered, frowzy, hanging loose, messy, ruffled, rumpled, tousled, uncombed, unkempt, untidy

dishonest bent (Sl.), cheating, corrupt, crafty, crooked (Inf.), deceitful, deceiving, deceptive, designing, disreputable, double-dealing, false, fraudulent, guileful, knavish (Archaic), lying, mendacious, perfidious, shady (Inf.), swindling, treacherous, unfair, unprincipled, unscrupulous, untrustworthy, untruthful

dishonesty cheating, chicanery, corruption, craft, criminality, crookedness, deceit, duplicity, falsehood, falsity, fraud, fraudulence, graft, improbity, mendacity, perfidy, sharp practice, stealing, treachery, trickery, unscrupulousness, wiliness

dishonour v. **1.** abase, blacken, corrupt, debase, debauch, defame, degrade, discredit, disgrace, shame, sully **2.** defile, deflower, pollute, rape, ravish, seduce ~n. **3.** abasement, degradation, discredit, disfavour, disgrace, disrepute, ignominy, infamy, obloquy, odium, opprobrium, reproach, scandal, shame **4.** abuse, affront, discourtesy, indignity, insult, offence, outrage, slight

dishonourable 1. base, contemptible, despicable, discreditable, disgraceful, ignoble, ignominious, infamous, scandalous, shameful **2.** blackguardly, corrupt, disreputable, shameless, treacherous, unprincipled, unscrupulous, untrustworthy

dish out allocate, distribute, dole out, hand out, inflict, mete out

dish up ladle, prepare, present, produce, scoop, serve, spoon

disillusion v. break the spell, bring down to earth, disabuse, disenchant, open the eyes of, shatter one's illusions, undeceive

disillusioned disabused enlightened, disappointed, disenchanted, indifferent, out of love, sadder and wiser, undeceived

disincentive damper, determent, deterrent, discouragement, dissuasion, impediment

disinclination alienation, antipathy, aversion, demur, dislike, hesitance, lack of desire, lack of enthusiasm, loathness, objection, opposition, reluctance, repugnance, resistance, unwillingness

disinclined antipathetic, averse, balking, hesitating, indisposed, loath, not in the mood, opposed, reluctant, resistant, unwilling

disinfect clean, cleanse, decontaminate, deodorize, fumigate, purify, sanitize, sterilize

disinfectant antiseptic, germicide, sanitizer, sterilizer

disingenuous artful, cunning, deceitful, designing, dishonest, duplicitous, feigned, guileful, insidious, insincere, shifty, two-faced, uncandid, underhanded, unfair, wily

disinherit cut off, cut off without a penny, disown, dispossess, oust, repudiate

disintegrate break apart, break up, crumble, disunite, fall apart, fall to pieces, reduce to fragments, separate, shatter, splinter

disinterest candidness, detachment, disinterestedness, dispassionateness, equity, fairness, impartiality, justice, neutrality, unbiasedness

disinterested candid, detached, dispas-

disjunctive (dɪsˈdʒʌŋktɪv) adj. 1. serving to disconnect or separate. 2. Grammar. denoting a word, esp. a conjunction, that serves to express opposition or contrast: but in She was poor but she was honest. 3. Logic. characterizing, containing, or included in a disjunction. —n. 4. Grammar. a disjunctive word, esp. a conjunction. 5. Logic. a disjunctive proposition. —dis'junctively adv.

disk (dɪsk) n. 1. a variant spelling (esp. U.S.) of disc. 2. Also called: disk pack, magnetic disk. Computers. a direct-access storage device consisting of a stack of plates coated with a magnetic layer, the whole assembly rotating rapidly as a single unit.

dislike (dɪsˈlaɪk) vb. 1. (tr.) to consider unpleasant or disagreeable. ~n. 2. a feeling of aversion or antipathy. —dis'likable or dis'likeable adj.

dislocate ('dɪsləˌkeɪt) vb. (tr.) 1. to disrupt or shift out of place. 2. to displace from its normal position, esp. a bone from its joint. —ˌdislo'cation n.

dislodge (dɪsˈlɒdʒ) vb. to remove from or leave a lodging place, hiding place, or previously fixed position. —dis'lodgment or dis'lodgement n.

disloyal (dɪsˈlɔɪəl) adj. not loyal or faithful; deserting one's allegiance. —dis'loyally adv. —dis'loyalty n.

dismal ('dɪzməl) adj. 1. causing gloom or depression. 2. causing dismay or terror. —'dismally adv. —'dismalness n.

dismantle (dɪsˈmæntəl) vb. (tr.) 1. to take apart. 2. to demolish or raze. 3. to strip off covering. —dis'mantlement n.

dismay (dɪsˈmeɪ) vb. (tr.) 1. to fill with apprehension or alarm. 2. to fill with depression or discouragement. ~n. 3. consternation or agitation.

dismember (dɪsˈmɛmbə) vb. (tr.) 1. to remove the limbs or members of. 2. to cut to pieces. 3. to divide or partition (something, such as an empire). —dis'memberment n.

dismiss (dɪsˈmɪs) vb. (tr.) 1. to remove or discharge from employment or service. 2. to send away or allow to go. 3. to dispel from one's mind; discard. 4. to cease to consider (a subject). 5. to decline further hearing to (a claim or action). 6. Cricket. to bowl out a side for a particular number of runs. —dis'missal n. —dis'missible adj. —dis'missive adj.

dismount (dɪsˈmaʊnt) vb. 1. to get off a horse, bicycle, etc. 2. (tr.) to disassemble or remove from a mounting. ~n. 3. the act of dismounting.

disobedient (ˌdɪsəˈbiːdɪənt) adj. not obedient; neglecting or refusing to obey. —ˌdiso'bedience n. —ˌdiso'bediently adv.

disobey (ˌdɪsəˈbeɪ) vb. to neglect or refuse to obey (someone, an order, etc.). —ˌdiso'beyer n.

disorder (dɪsˈɔːdə) n. 1. a lack of order; confusion. 2. a disturbance of public order. 3. an upset of health; ailment. 4. a deviation from the normal system or order. ~vb. (tr.) 5. to upset the order of. 6. to disturb the health or mind of.

disorderly (dɪsˈɔːdəlɪ) adj. 1. untidy; irregular. 2. uncontrolled; unruly. 3. Law. violating public peace or order. —dis'orderliness n.

disorganize or **-ise** (dɪsˈɔːgəˌnaɪz) vb. (tr.) to disrupt the arrangement, system, or unity of. —dis,organi'zation or -i'sation n.

disorientate (dɪsˈɔːrɪɛnˌteɪt) or **disorient** vb. (tr.) 1. to cause (someone) to lose his bearings. 2. to perplex; confuse.

disown (dɪsˈəʊn) vb. (tr.) to deny any connection with; refuse to acknowledge. —dis'owner n.

disparage (dɪˈspærɪdʒ) vb. (tr.) 1. to speak contemptuously of; belittle. 2. to damage the reputation of. —dis'paragement n. —dis'paraging adj. —dis'paragingly adv.

disparate ('dɪspərɪt) adj. 1. utterly different or distinct in kind. ~n. 2. (pl.) unlike things or people. —'disparately adv. —'disparateness n. —dis'parity n.

dispassionate (dɪsˈpæʃənɪt) adj. devoid of or uninfluenced by emotion or prejudice; objective; impartial. —dis'passionately adv.

dispatch or **despatch** (dɪˈspætʃ) vb. (tr.) 1. to send off promptly, as to a destination or to perform a task. 2. to discharge or complete (a duty, etc.) promptly. 3. Inf. to eat up quickly. 4. to murder or execute. ~n. 5. the act of sending off a letter, messenger, etc. 6. prompt action or speed (often in with dispatch). 7. an official communication or report, sent in haste. 8. a report sent to a newspaper, etc., by a correspondent. 9. murder or execution. —dis'patcher n.

sionate, equitable, even-handed, free from self-interest, impartial, impersonal, neutral, outside, unbiased, uninvolved, unprejudiced, unselfish

disjointed 1. aimless, confused, disconnected, disordered, fitful, incoherent, loose, rambling, spasmodic, unconnected 2. disconnected, dislocated, displaced, disunited, divided, separated, split

dislike 1. n. animosity, animus, antagonism, antipathy, aversion, detestation, disapprobation, disapproval, disgust, disinclination, displeasure, distaste, enmity, hatred, hostility, loathing, repugnance 2. v. abhor, abominate, be averse to, despise, detest, disapprove, disfavour, disrelish, hate, have no taste or stomach for, loathe, not be able to bear or abide, object to, scorn, shun

dislocate 1. disorder, displace, disrupt, disturb, misplace, shift 2. disarticulate, disconnect, disengage, disjoint, disunite, luxate (Medical), put out of joint, unhinge

dislocation 1. disarray, disorder, disorganization, disruption, disturbance, misplacement 2. disarticulation, disconnection, disengagement, luxation (Medical), unhinging

disloyal apostate, disaffected, faithless, false, perfidious, seditious, subversive, traitorous, treacherous, treasonable, two-faced, unfaithful, unpatriotic, untrustworthy

disloyalty betrayal of trust, breach of trust, breaking of faith, deceitfulness, double-dealing, falseness, falsity, inconstancy, infidelity, perfidy, Punic faith, treachery, treason, unfaithfulness

dismal black, bleak, cheerless, dark, depressing, despondent, discouraging, dolorous, dreary, forlorn, funereal, gloomy, gruesome, lonesome, lowering, lugubrious, melancholy, sad, sombre, sorrowful

dismay v. 1. affright, alarm, appal, distress, fill with consternation, frighten, horrify, paralyse, scare, terrify, unnerve 2. daunt, disappoint, discourage, dishearten, disillusion, dispirit, put off ~n. 3. agitation, alarm, anxiety, apprehension, consternation, distress, dread, fear, fright, horror, panic, terror, trepidation 4. chagrin, disappointment, discouragement, disillusionment, upset

dismember amputate, anatomize, cut into pieces, disjoint, dislimb, dislocate, dissect, divide, mutilate, rend, sever

dismiss 1. axe (Inf.), cashier, discharge, fire (Inf.), give notice to, lay off, oust, remove, sack (Inf.), send packing (Inf.) 2. disband, disperse, dissolve, free, let go, release, send away 3. banish, discard, dispel, disregard, drop, lay aside, pooh-pooh, put out of one's mind, reject, relegate, repudiate, set aside, shelve, spurn

dismissal 1. adjournment, congé, end, freedom to depart, permission to go, release 2. discharge, expulsion, marching orders (Inf.), notice, one's cards, removal, the boot (Sl.), the push (Sl.), the sack (Inf.)

disobedience indiscipline, infraction, insubordination, mutiny, noncompliance, nonobservance, recalcitrance, revolt, unruliness, waywardness

disobedient contrary, contumacious, defiant, disorderly, froward, insubordinate, intractable, mischievous, naughty, noncompliant, nonobservant, obstreperous, refractory, undisciplined, unruly, wayward, wilful

disobey contravene, defy, disregard, flout, go counter to, ignore, infringe, overstep, rebel, refuse to obey, resist, trans-gress, violate

disorderly 1. chaotic, confused, disorganized, higgledy-piggledy (Inf.), indiscriminate, irregular, jumbled, messy, shambolic (Inf.), unsystematic, untidy 2. boisterous, disruptive, indisciplined, lawless, obstreperous, rebellious, refractory, riotous, rowdy, stormy, tumultuous, turbulent, ungovernable, unlawful, unmanageable, unruly

disorganize break up, confuse, derange, destroy, disarrange, discompose, disorder, disrupt, disturb, jumble, make a shambles of, muddle, turn topsy-turvy, unsettle, upset

disorganized chaotic, confused, disordered, haphazard, jumbled, muddled, shuffled, unmethodical, unorganized, unsystematic

disown abandon, abnegate, cast off, deny, disallow, disavow, disclaim, refuse to acknowledge or recognize, reject, renounce, repudiate

disparage belittle, criticize, decry, defame, degrade, denigrate, deprecate, depreciate, deride, derogate, detract from, discredit, disdain, dismiss, malign, minimize, ridicule, run down, scorn, slander, traduce, underestimate, underrate, undervalue, vilify

disparagement aspersion, belittlement, condemnation, contempt, contumely, criticism, debasement, degradation, denunciation, depreciation, derision, derogation, detraction, discredit, disdain, impairment, lessening, prejudice, reproach, ridicule, scorn, slander, underestimation

dispassionate 1. calm, collected, composed, cool, imperturbable, moderate, quiet, serene, sober, temperate, unemotional, unexcitable, unexcited, unmoved, unruffled 2.

dispatch rider *n.* a horseman or motorcyclist who carries dispatches.

dispel (dɪ'spɛl) *vb.* **-pelling, -pelled.** (*tr.*) to disperse or drive away. —**dis'peller** *n.*

dispensable (dɪ'spɛnsəbəl) *adj.* **1.** not essential; expendable. **2.** (of a law, vow, etc.) able to be relaxed. —**dis,pensa'bility** *n.*

dispensary (dɪ'spɛnsərɪ) *n., pl.* **-ries.** a place where medicine, etc. is dispensed.

dispensation (,dɪspɛn'seɪʃən) *n.* **1.** the act of distributing or dispensing. **2.** something distributed or dispensed. **3.** a system or plan of administering or dispensing. **4.** *Chiefly R.C. Church.* permission to dispense with an obligation of church law. **5.** any exemption from an obligation. **6.** *Theol.* **a.** the ordering of life and events by God. **b.** a religious system or code of prescriptions for life and conduct regarded as of divine origin. —**,dispen'sational** *adj.*

dispense (dɪ'spɛns) *vb.* **1.** (*tr.*) to give out or distribute in portions. **2.** (*tr.*) to prepare and distribute (medicine), esp. on prescription. **3.** (*tr.*) to administer (the law, etc.). **4.** (*intr.; foll. by* *with*) to do away (with) or manage (without). **5.** to grant a dispensation to. **6.** to exempt or excuse from a rule or obligation. —**dis'penser** *n.*

disperse (dɪ'spɜːs) *vb.* **1.** to scatter; distribute over a wide area. **2.** to dissipate. **3.** to leave or cause to leave a gathering. **4.** to separate or be separated by dispersion. **5.** (*tr.*) to spread (news, etc.). **6.** to separate (particles) throughout a solid, liquid, or gas. ~*adj.* **7.** of or consisting of the particles in a colloid or suspension: *disperse phase.* —**dis'persal** *n.* —**dis'perser** *n.* —**dis'persion** *n.*

dispirit (dɪ'spɪrɪt) *vb.* (*tr.*) to lower the spirit of; make downhearted; discourage. —**dis'pirited** *adj.* —**dis'piritedness** *n.* —**dis'piriting** *adj.*

displace (dɪs'pleɪs) *vb.* (*tr.*) **1.** to move from the usual or correct location. **2.** to remove from office or employment. **3.** to occupy the place of; replace; supplant.

displaced person *n.* a person forced from his home or country, esp. by war or revolution.

displacement (dɪs'pleɪsmənt) *n.* **1.** a displacing or being displaced. **2.** the weight or volume displaced by a body in a fluid. **3.** *Psychoanal.* the transferring of emotional feelings from their original object to one that disguises their real nature.

display (dɪ'spleɪ) *vb.* (*tr.*) **1.** to show or make visible. **2.** to put out to be seen; exhibit. **3.** to disclose; reveal. **4.** to flaunt in an ostentatious way. **5.** to spread out; unfold. **6.** to give prominence to. ~*n.* **7.** an exhibiting or displaying; show. **8.** something exhibited or displayed. **9.** an ostentatious exhibition. **10.** an arrangement of certain typefaces to give prominence to headings, etc. **11.** *Electronics.* **a.** a device capable of representing information visually, as on a cathode-ray tube screen. **b.** the information so presented. **12.** *Zool.* a pattern of behaviour by which the animal attracts attention while it is courting the female, defending its territory, etc. **13.** (*modifier*) designating typefaces that give prominence to the words they are used to set. —**dis'player** *n.*

displease (dɪs'pliːz) *vb.* to annoy, offend, or cause displeasure to (someone). —**dis'pleasingly** *adv.* —**displeasure** (-'plɛʒə) *n.*

disport (dɪ'spɔːt) *vb.* **1.** (*tr.*) to indulge (oneself) in pleasure. **2.** (*intr.*) to frolic or gambol. ~*n.* **3.** *Arch.* amusement.

disposal (dɪ'spəʊzəl) *n.* **1.** the act or means of getting rid of something. **2.** arrangement in a particular order. **3.** a specific method of tending to matters, as in business. **4.** the act or process of transferring something to or providing something to or providing something for another. **5.** the power or opportunity to make use of someone or something (esp. in **at one's disposal**).

dispose (dɪ'spəʊz) *vb.* **1.** (*intr.; foll. by* *of*) **a.** to deal with or settle. **b.** to give, sell, or transfer to another. **c.** to throw out or away. **d.** to consume, esp. hurriedly. **2.** to arrange or settle (matters). **3.** (*tr.*) to make willing or receptive. **4.** (*tr.*) to place in a certain order. **5.** (*tr.; often foll. by* *to*) to accustom or condition. —**dis'poser** *n.*

disposition (,dɪspə'zɪʃən) *n.* **1.** a person's usual temperament or frame of mind. **2.** a tendency, inclination, or habit. **3.** another word for **disposal** (senses 2-5). **4.** *Arch.* manner of placing or arranging.

dispossess (,dɪspə'zɛs) *vb.* (*tr.*) to take away possession of something, esp. property; expel. —**,dispos'session** *n.*

candid, detached, disinterested, fair, impartial, impersonal, indifferent, neutral, objective, unbiased, uninvolved, unprejudiced

dispatch, despatch *v.* **1.** accelerate, consign, dismiss, express, forward, hasten, hurry, quicken, remit, send, transmit **2.** conclude, discharge, dispose of, expedite, finish, make short work of (*Inf.*), perform, settle **3.** assassinate, bump off (*Sl.*), butcher, eliminate (*Sl.*), execute, finish off, kill, murder, put an end to, slaughter, slay ~*n.* **4.** alacrity, celerity, expedition, haste, precipitateness, promptitude, promptness, quickness, rapidity, speed, swiftness **5.** account, bulletin, communication, communiqué, document, instruction, item, letter, message, missive, news, piece, report, story

dispel allay, banish, chase away, dismiss, disperse, dissipate, drive away, eliminate, expel, resolve, rout, scatter

dispensable disposable, expendable, inessential, needless, nonessential, superfluous, unnecessary, unrequired, useless

dispensation **1.** allotment, appointment, apportionment, bestowal, conferment, consignment, dealing out, disbursement, distribution, endowment, supplying **2.** award, dole, part, portion, quota, share **3.** administration, direction, economy, management, plan, regulation, scheme, stewardship, system **4.** exception, exemption, immunity, indulgence, licence, permission, privilege, relaxation, relief, remission, reprieve

dispense **1.** allocate, allot, apportion, assign, deal out, disburse, distribute, dole out, mete out, share **2.** measure, mix, prepare, supply **3.** administer, apply, carry out, direct, discharge, enforce, execute, implement, operate, undertake **4.** except, excuse, exempt, exonerate, let off (*Inf.*), release, relieve, reprieve **5.** *With* **with** abstain from, do without,

forgo, give up, omit, relinquish, waive **6.** *With* **with** abolish, brush aside, cancel, dispose of, disregard, do away with, get rid of, ignore, pass over, render needless, shake off

disperse **1.** broadcast, circulate, diffuse, disseminate, dissipate, distribute, scatter, spread, strew **2.** break up, disappear, disband, dismiss, dispel, dissolve, rout, scatter, send off, separate, vanish

dispirited crestfallen, dejected, depressed, despondent, discouraged, disheartened, down, downcast, gloomy, glum, in the doldrums, low, morose, sad

displace **1.** derange, disarrange, disturb, misplace, move, shift, transpose **2.** cashier, depose, discard, discharge, dismiss, fire (*Inf.*), remove, sack (*Inf.*) **3.** crowd out, oust, replace, succeed, supersede, supplant, take the place of **4.** dislocate, dislodge, dispossess, eject, evict, force out, unsettle

display *v.* **1.** betray, demonstrate, disclose, evidence, evince, exhibit, expose, manifest, open, open to view, present, reveal, show, unveil **2.** expand, extend, model, open out, spread out, stretch out, unfold, unfurl **3.** boast, flash (*Inf.*), flaunt, flourish, parade, show off, vaunt ~*n.* **4.** array, demonstration, exhibition, exposition, exposure, manifestation, presentation, revelation, show **5.** flourish, ostentation, pageant, parade, pomp, show, spectacle

displease aggravate (*Inf.*), anger, annoy, disgust, dissatisfy, exasperate, gall, incense, irk, irritate, nettle, offend, pique, provoke, put out, rile, upset, vex

displeasure anger, annoyance, disapprobation, disapproval, disfavour, disgruntlement, dislike, dissatisfaction, distaste, indignation, irritation, offence, pique, resentment, vexation, wrath

disposable **1.** biodegradable, compost-

able, decomposable, nonreturnable, paper, throwaway **2.** at one's service, available, consumable, expendable, free for use, spendable

disposal **1.** clearance, discarding, dumping (*Inf.*), ejection, jettisoning, parting with, relinquishment, removal, riddance, scrapping, throwing away **2.** arrangement, array, dispensation, disposition, distribution, grouping, placing, position **3.** assignment, bequest, bestowal, consignment, conveyance, dispensation, gift, settlement, transfer **4.** *As in* **at one's disposal** authority, conduct, control, determination, direction, discretion, government, management, ordering, regulation, responsibility

dispose **1.** adjust, arrange, array, determine, distribute, fix, group, marshal, order, place, put, range, rank, regulate, set, settle, stand **2.** actuate, adapt, bias, condition, incline, induce, influence, lead, motivate, move, predispose, prompt, tempt

disposed apt, given, inclined, liable, likely, minded, of a mind to, predisposed, prone, ready, subject, tending towards

dispose of **1.** deal with, decide, determine, end, finish with, settle **2.** bestow, give, make over, part with, sell, transfer **3.** destroy, discard, dump (*Inf.*), get rid of, jettison, scrap, throw out *or* away, unload

disposition **1.** character, constitution, make-up, nature, spirit, temper, temperament **2.** bent, bias, habit, inclination, leaning, predisposition, proclivity, proneness, propensity, readiness, tendency **3.** adjustment, arrangement, classification, disposal, distribution, grouping, ordering, organization, placement **4.** control, direction, disposal, management, regulation

—ˌdispos'sessor n.
disproportion (ˌdɪsprə'pɔːʃən) n. 1. lack of proportion or equality. 2. an instance of disparity or inequality. ~vb. 3. (tr.) to cause to become exaggerated or unequal. —ˌdispro'portional adj.
disproportionate (ˌdɪsprə'pɔːʃənɪt) adj. out of proportion; unequal. —ˌdispro'portionately adv. —ˌdispro'portionateness n.
disprove (dɪs'pruːv) vb. (tr.) to show (an assertion, claim, etc.) to be incorrect. —dis'provable adj. —dis'proval n.
dispute (dɪ'spjuːt) vb. 1. to argue, debate, or quarrel about (something). 2. (tr.; may take a clause as object) to doubt the validity, etc., of. 3. (tr.) to seek to win; contest for. 4. (tr.) to struggle against; resist. ~n. 5. an argument or quarrel. 6. Rare. a fight. —disputable (dɪ'spjuːtəbəl, 'dɪspjutə-) adj. —disputant (dɪ'spjuːtant; 'dɪspjutənt) n. —ˌdispu'tation n. —ˌdispu'tatious adj. —dis'puter n.
disqualify (dɪs'kwɒlɪˌfaɪ) vb. -fying, -fied. (tr.) 1. to make unfit or unqualified. 2. to make ineligible, as for entry to an examination. 3. to debar from a contest. 4. to deprive of rights, powers, or privileges. —disˌqualifi'cation n.
disquiet (dɪs'kwaɪət) n. 1. a feeling or condition of anxiety or uneasiness. ~vb. 2. (tr.) to make anxious or upset. —dis'quieting adj. —dis'quieˌtude n.
disregard (ˌdɪsrɪ'gɑːd) vb. (tr.) 1. to give little or no attention to; ignore. 2. to treat as unworthy of consideration or respect. ~n. 3. lack of attention or respect. —ˌdisre'gardful adj.
disrepair (ˌdɪsrɪ'pɛə) n. the condition of being worn out or in poor working order; a condition requiring repairs.
disreputable (dɪs'rɛpjutəbəl) adj. 1. having or causing a lack of repute. 2. disordered in appearance. —dis'reputably adv.
disrepute (ˌdɪsrɪ'pjuːt) n. a loss or lack of credit or repute.
disrespect (ˌdɪsrɪ'spɛkt) n. contempt; rudeness; lack of respect. —ˌdisre'spectful adj.

disrobe (dɪs'rəub) vb. 1. to undress. 2. (tr.) to divest of authority, etc. —dis'robement n.
disrupt (dɪs'rʌpt) vb. 1. (tr.) to throw into turmoil or disorder. 2. (tr.) to interrupt the progress of. 3. to break or split apart. —dis'rupter or dis'ruptor n. —dis'ruption n. —dis'ruptive adj.
dissatisfy (dɪs'sætɪsˌfaɪ) vb. -fying, -fied. (tr.) to fail to satisfy; disappoint. —ˌdissatis'faction n. —ˌdissatis'factory adj.
dissect (dɪ'sɛkt, daɪ-) vb. 1. to cut open and examine the structure of (a dead animal or plant). 2. (tr.) to examine critically and minutely. —dis'section n. —dis'sector n.
disselboom ('dɪsəlˌbuːm) n. S. African. the single shaft of a wagon, esp. an ox wagon.
dissemble (dɪ'sɛmbəl) vb. 1. to conceal (one's real motives, emotions, etc.) by pretence. 2. (tr.) to pretend; simulate. —dis'semblance n. —dis'sembler n.
disseminate (dɪ'sɛmɪˌneɪt) vb. (tr.) to distribute or scatter about; diffuse. —disˌsemi'nation n. —dis'semiˌnator n.
disseminated sclerosis n. another name for **multiple sclerosis**.
dissension (dɪ'sɛnʃən) n. disagreement, esp. when leading to a quarrel.
dissent (dɪ'sɛnt) vb. (intr.) 1. to have a disagreement or withhold assent. 2. Christianity. to reject the doctrines, beliefs, or practices of an established church, and to adhere to a different system of beliefs. ~n. 3. a difference of opinion. 4. Christianity. separation from an established church; Nonconformism. 5. the voicing of a minority opinion in the decision on a case at law. —dis'senter n. —dis'senting adj.
Dissenter (dɪ'sɛntə) n. Christianity, chiefly Brit. a Nonconformist or a person who refuses to conform to the established church.
dissentient (dɪ'sɛnʃənt) adj. 1. dissenting, esp. from the opinion of the majority. ~n. 2. a dissenter. —dis'sentience or dis'sentiency n.

THESAURUS

disproportion asymmetry, discrepancy, disparity, imbalance, inadequacy, inequality, insufficiency, lopsidedness, unevenness, unsuitableness
disproportionate excessive, incommensurate, inordinate, out of proportion, too much, unbalanced, unequal, uneven, unreasonable
disprove confute, contradict, controvert, discredit, expose, give the lie to, invalidate, negate, prove false, rebut, refute
disputation argumentation, controversy, debate, dispute, dissension, polemics
dispute v. 1. altercate, argue, brawl, clash, contend, debate, discuss, quarrel, squabble, wrangle 2. challenge, contest, contradict, controvert, deny, doubt, impugn, question ~n. 3. altercation, argument, brawl, conflict, disagreement, discord, disturbance, feud, friction, quarrel, strife, wrangle 4. argument, contention, controversy, debate, discussion, dissension
disqualification 1. disability, disablement, incapacitation, incapacity, unfitness 2. debarment, disenablement, disentitlement, elimination, exclusion, incompetence, ineligibility, rejection
disqualified debarred, eliminated, ineligible, knocked out, out of the running
disqualify 1. disable, incapacitate, invalidate, unfit (Rare) 2. debar, declare ineligible, disentitle, preclude, prohibit, rule out
disquiet 1. n. alarm, angst, anxiety, concern, disquietude, distress, disturbance, fear, foreboding, fretfulness, nervousness, restlessness, trouble, uneasiness, unrest, worry 2. v. agitate, annoy, bother, concern, discompose, distress, disturb, fret, harass, incommode, make uneasy, perturb, pester, plague, trouble, unsettle, upset, vex, worry
disquieting annoying, bothersome, disconcerting, distressing, disturbing, irritating,

perturbing, troubling, unnerving, unsettling, upsetting, vexing, worrying
disregard v. 1. brush aside or away, discount, disobey, ignore, laugh off, leave out of account, make light of, neglect, overlook, pass over, pay no attention to, pay no heed to, take no notice of, turn a blind eye to 2. brush off (Sl.), cold-shoulder, contemn, despise, disdain, disparage, slight, snub ~n. 3. brushoff (Sl.), contempt, disdain, disrespect, heedlessness, ignoring, inattention, indifference, neglect, negligence, oversight, slight, the cold shoulder
disrepair 1. collapse, decay, deterioration, dilapidation, ruination 2. in disrepair broken, bust (Inf.), decayed, decrepit, kaput (Inf.), not functioning, on the blink (Sl.), out of commission, out of order, worn out
disreputable 1. base, contemptible, derogatory, discreditable, disgraceful, dishonourable, disorderly, ignominious, infamous, louche, low, mean, notorious, opprobrious, scandalous, shady (Inf.), shameful, shocking, unprincipled, vicious, vile 2. bedraggled, dilapidated, dingy, dishevelled, down at heel, scruffy, seedy, shabby, threadbare, worn
disrepute discredit, disesteem, disfavour, disgrace, dishonour, ignominy, ill favour, ill repute, infamy, obloquy, shame, unpopularity
disrespect contempt, discourtesy, dishonour, disregard, impertinence, impoliteness, impudence, incivility, insolence, irreverence, lack of respect, lese-majesty, rudeness, unmannerliness
disrespectful bad-mannered, cheeky, contemptuous, discourteous, ill-bred, impertinent, impolite, impudent, insolent, insulting, irreverent, misbehaved, rude, uncivil
disrupt 1. agitate, confuse, disorder, disorganize, disturb, spoil, throw into disorder, upset 2. break up or into, interfere with, interrupt, intrude, obstruct, unsettle, upset

disruption confusion, disarray, disorder, disorderliness, disturbance, interference, interruption, stoppage
disruptive confusing, disorderly, distracting, disturbing, obstreperous, troublemaking, troublesome, unruly, unsettling, upsetting
dissatisfaction annoyance, chagrin, disappointment, discomfort, discontent, dislike, dismay, displeasure, distress, exasperation, frustration, irritation, regret, resentment, unhappiness
dissatisfied disappointed, discontented, disgruntled, displeased, fed up, frustrated, not satisfied, unfulfilled, ungratified, unhappy, unsatisfied
dissect 1. anatomize, cut up or apart, dismember, lay open 2. analyse, break down, explore, inspect, investigate, scrutinize, study
dissection 1. anatomization, anatomy, autopsy, dismemberment, necropsy, post-mortem (examination) 2. analysis, breakdown, examination, inspection, investigation, scrutiny
disseminate broadcast, circulate, diffuse, disperse, dissipate, distribute, proclaim, promulgate, propagate, publicize, publish, scatter, sow, spread
dissemination broadcasting, circulation, diffusion, distribution, promulgation, propagation, publication, publishing, spread
dissension conflict, conflict of opinion, contention, difference, disagreement, discord, discordance, dispute, dissent, friction, quarrel, strife, variance
dissent 1. v. decline, differ, disagree, object, protest, refuse, withhold assent or approval 2. n. difference, disagreement, discord, dissension, dissidence, nonconformity, objection, opposition, refusal, resistance
dissenter disputant, dissident, noncon-

dissertation (ˌdɪsəˈteɪʃən) n. 1. a written thesis, often based on original research, usually required for a higher degree. 2. a formal discourse. —ˌdisserˈtational adj.

disservice (dɪsˈsɜːvɪs) n. an ill turn; wrong; injury, esp. when trying to help.

dissident (ˈdɪsɪdənt) adj. 1. disagreeing; dissenting. ~n. 2. a person who disagrees, esp. one who disagrees with the government. —ˈdissidence n. —ˈdissidently adv.

dissimilar (dɪˈsɪmɪlə) adj. not alike; not similar; different. —ˌdissimiˈlarity n. —disˈsimilarly adv.

dissimulate (dɪˈsɪmjʊˌleɪt) vb. to conceal (one's real feelings, etc.) by pretence. —disˌsimuˈlation n. —disˈsimuˌlator n.

dissipate (ˈdɪsɪˌpeɪt) vb. 1. to exhaust or be exhausted by dispersion. 2. (tr.) to scatter or break up. 3. (intr.) to indulge in the pursuit of pleasure. —ˈdissiˌpater or ˈdissiˌpator n. —ˈdissiˌpative adj.

dissipated (ˈdɪsɪˌpeɪtɪd) adj. 1. indulging without restraint in the pursuit of pleasure; debauched. 2. wasted, scattered, or exhausted.

dissipation (ˌdɪsɪˈpeɪʃən) n. 1. a dissipating or being dissipated. 2. unrestrained indulgence in physical pleasures. 3. excessive expenditure; wastefulness.

dissociate (dɪˈsəʊʃɪˌeɪt, -sɪ-) vb. 1. to break or cause to break the association between (people, organizations, etc.). 2. (tr.) to regard or treat as separate or unconnected. 3. to undergo or subject to dissociation. —disˈsociative adj.

dissoluble (dɪˈsɒljʊbəl) adj. a less common word for **soluble**. —disˌsoluˈbility n.

dissolute (ˈdɪsəˌluːt) adj. given to dissipation; debauched. —ˈdissoˌlutely adv. —ˈdissoˌluteness n.

dissolution (ˌdɪsəˈluːʃən) n. 1. separation into component parts; disintegration. 2. destruction by breaking up and dispersing. 3. the termination of a meeting or assembly, such as Parliament. 4. the termination of a formal or legal relationship, such as a business, marriage, etc. 5. the act or process of dissolving.

dissolve (dɪˈzɒlv) vb. 1. to go or cause to go into solution. 2. to become or cause to become liquid; melt. 3. to disintegrate or disperse. 4. to come or bring to an end. 5. to dismiss (a meeting, parliament, etc.) or (of a meeting, etc.) to be dismissed. 6. to collapse or cause to collapse emotionally: to dissolve into tears. 7. to lose or cause to lose distinctness. 8. (tr.) to terminate legally, as a marriage, etc. 9. (intr.) Films, television. to fade out one scene and replace with another to make two scenes merge imperceptibly or slowly overlap. ~n. 10. Films, television. a scene filmed or televised by dissolving. —disˈsolvable adj.

dissonance (ˈdɪsənəns) or **dissonancy** n. 1. a discordant combination of sounds. 2. lack of agreement or consistency. 3. Music. a. a sensation of harshness and incompleteness associated with certain intervals and chords. b. an interval or chord of this kind. —ˈdissonant adj.

dissuade (dɪˈsweɪd) vb. (tr.) 1. (often foll. by from) to deter (someone) by persuasion from a course of action, policy, etc. 2. to advise against (an action, etc.). —disˈsuader n. —disˈsuasion n. —disˈsuasive adj.

dissyllable (dɪˈsɪləbəl) or **disyllable** (ˈdaɪˌsɪləbəl) n. a word of two syllables. —dissyllabic (ˌdɪsɪˈlæbɪk) or disyllabic (ˌdaɪsɪˈlæbɪk) adj.

distaff (ˈdɪstɑːf) n. 1. the rod on which wool, flax, etc., is wound preparatory to spinning. 2. Figurative. women's work.

distaff side n. the female side of a family.

distal (ˈdɪstəl) adj. Anat. situated farthest from the centre or point of attachment or origin. —ˈdistally adv.

distance (ˈdɪstəns) n. 1. the space between two points. 2. the length of this gap. 3. the state of being apart in space; remoteness. 4. an interval between two points in time. 5. the extent of progress. 6. a distant place or time. 7. a separation or remoteness in relationship. 8. **keep one's distance.** to maintain a reserve in respect of another person. 9. (preceded by the) the most distant or a faraway part of the visible scene. 10. Horse racing. a. Brit. a point on a racecourse 240 yards from the winning post. b. U.S. the part of a racecourse that a horse must reach before the winner passes the finishing line in order to qualify for later heats. 11. **go the distance.** to be able to complete an assigned task or responsibility. 12. **middle distance.** halfway between the foreground or the observer and the horizon. ~vb. (tr.) 13. to hold or place at a distance. 14. to separate (oneself) mentally from something. 15. to outdo; outstrip.

distant (ˈdɪstənt) adj. 1. far apart in space or time. 2. (postpositive) separated in space or time by a specified distance. 3. apart in relationship: a distant cousin. 4. coming from or going to a faraway place. 5. remote in manner; aloof. 6. abstracted; absent: a distant look. —ˈdistantly adv. —ˈdistantness n.

distaste (dɪsˈteɪst) n. (often foll. by for) a dislike (of); aversion (to).

distasteful (dɪsˈteɪstfʊl) adj. unpleasant or offensive.

THESAURUS

formist, objector, protestant
dissentient adj. conflicting, differing, disagreeing, dissenting, dissident, opposing, protesting
dissertation critique, discourse, disquisition, essay, exposition, thesis, treatise
disservice bad turn, disfavour, harm, ill turn, injury, injustice, unkindness, wrong
dissident 1. adj. differing, disagreeing, discordant, dissentient, dissenting, heterodox, nonconformist, schismatic 2. n. agitator, dissenter, protestor, rebel, recusant
dissimilar different, disparate, divergent, diverse, heterogeneous, mismatched, not alike, not capable of comparison, not similar, unlike, unrelated, various
dissimilarity difference, discrepancy, disparity, dissimilitude, distinction, divergence, heterogeneity, incomparability, nonuniformity, unlikeness, unrelatedness
dissipate 1. burn up, consume, deplete, expend, fritter away, indulge oneself, lavish, misspend, run through, spend, squander, waste 2. disappear, dispel, disperse, dissolve, drive away, evaporate, scatter, vanish
dissipated 1. abandoned, debauched, dissolute, intemperate, profligate, rakish, self-indulgent 2. consumed, destroyed, exhausted, scattered, squandered, wasted
dissipation 1. abandonment, debauchery, dissoluteness, drunkenness, excess, extravagance, indulgence, intemperance, lavishness, prodigality, profligacy, squandering, wantonness, waste 2. amusement, distrac-

tion, diversion, entertainment, gratification 3. disappearance, disintegration, dispersion, dissemination, dissolution, scattering, vanishing
dissociate 1. break off, disband, disrupt, part company, quit 2. detach, disconnect, distance, divorce, isolate, segregate, separate, set apart
dissolute abandoned, corrupt, debauched, degenerate, depraved, dissipated, immoral, lax, lewd, libertine, licentious, loose, profligate, rakish, unrestrained, vicious, wanton, wild
dissolution 1. breaking up, disintegration, division, divorce, parting, resolution, separation 2. death, decay, decomposition, demise, destruction, dispersal, extinction, overthrow, ruin 3. adjournment, conclusion, disbandment, discontinuation, dismissal, end, ending, finish, suspension, termination 4. corruption, debauchery, dissipation, intemperance, wantonness 5. disappearance, evaporation, liquefaction, melting, solution
dissolve 1. deliquesce, flux, fuse, liquefy, melt, soften, thaw 2. crumble, decompose, diffuse, disappear, disintegrate, disperse, dissipate, dwindle, evanesce, evaporate, fade, melt away, perish, vanish, waste away 3. break up, destroy, discontinue, dismiss, end, overthrow, ruin, suspend, terminate, wind up 4. break into or up, collapse, disorganize, disunite, divorce, loose, resolve into, separate, sever
dissuade advise against, deter, discourage, disincline, divert, expostulate, persuade

not to, put off, remonstrate, talk out of, urge not to, warn
distance n. 1. absence, extent, gap, interval, lapse, length, range, reach, remoteness, remove, separation, space, span, stretch, width 2. aloofness, coldness, coolness, frigidity, reserve, restraint, stiffness 3. **go the distance** bring to an end, complete, finish, see through, stay the course 4. **keep one's distance** avoid, be aloof (indifferent, reserved), keep (someone) at arm's length, shun 5. **in the distance** afar, far away, far off, on the horizon, yonder ~v. 6. dissociate oneself, put in proportion, separate oneself 7. leave behind, outdistance, outdo, outrun, outstrip, pass
distant 1. abroad, afar, far, faraway, far-flung, far-off, outlying, out-of-the-way, remote, removed 2. apart, disparate, dispersed, distinct, scattered, separate 3. aloof, ceremonious, cold, cool, formal, haughty, reserved, restrained, reticent, standoffish, stiff, unapproachable, unfriendly, withdrawn 4. faint, indirect, indistinct, obscure, slight, uncertain
distaste abhorrence, antipathy, aversion, detestation, disfavour, disgust, disinclination, dislike, displeasure, disrelish, dissatisfaction, horror, loathing, repugnance, revulsion
distasteful abhorrent, disagreeable, displeasing, loathsome, nauseous, objectionable, obnoxious, offensive, repugnant, repulsive, undesirable, uninviting, unpalatable, unpleasant, unsavoury

—**dis'tastefulness** n.

distemper[1] (dɪs'tɛmpə) n. **1.** any of various infectious diseases of animals, esp. **canine distemper,** a highly contagious viral disease of young dogs. **2.** Arch. **a.** a disorder. **b.** disturbance. **c.** discontent.

distemper[2] (dɪs'tɛmpə) n. **1.** a technique of painting in which the pigments are mixed with water, glue, size, etc., used for poster, mural, and scene painting. **2.** the paint used in this technique or any of various water-based paints. ~vb. **3.** to paint (something) with distemper.

distend (dɪ'stɛnd) vb. **1.** to expand by or as if by pressure from within; swell; inflate. **2.** (tr.) to stretch out or extend. —**dis'tensible** adj. —**dis'tension** or **dis'tention** n.

distich ('dɪstɪk) n. Prosody. a unit of two verse lines, usually a couplet.

distil or U.S. **distill** (dɪs'tɪl) vb. **-tilling, -tilled. 1.** to subject to or undergo distillation. **2.** (sometimes foll. by out or off) to purify, separate, or concentrate, or be purified, separated, or concentrated by distillation. **3.** to obtain or be obtained by distillation. **4.** to exude or give off (a substance) in drops. **5.** (tr.) to extract the essence of.

distillate ('dɪstɪlɪt) n. **1.** the product of distillation. **2.** a concentrated essence.

distillation (ˌdɪstɪ'leɪʃən) n. **1.** a distilling. **2.** the process of evaporating or boiling a liquid and condensing its vapour. **3.** purification or separation of mixtures by using different evaporation rates or boiling points of their components. **4.** the process of obtaining the essence or an extract of a substance, usually by heating it in a solvent. **5.** a distillate. **6.** a concentrated essence. —**dis'tillatory** adj.

distiller (dɪ'stɪlə) n. a person or organization that distils, esp. a company that makes spirits.

distillery (dɪ'stɪlərɪ) n., pl. **-eries.** a place where alcoholic drinks, etc., are made by distillation.

distinct (dɪ'stɪŋkt) adj. **1.** easily sensed or understood; clear. **2.** (when postpositive, foll. by from) not the same (as); separate (from). **3.** not alike; different. **4.** sharp; clear. **5.** recognizable; definite. **6.** explicit; unequivocal. —**dis'tinctly** adv. —**dis'tinctness** n.

distinction (dɪ'stɪŋkʃən) n. **1.** the act or an instance of distinguishing or differentiating. **2.** a distinguishing feature. **3.** the state of being different or distinguishable. **4.** special honour, recognition, or fame. **5.** excellence of character; distinctive qualities. **6.** distinguished appear-

ance. **7.** a symbol of honour or rank.

distinctive (dɪ'stɪŋktɪv) adj. serving or tending to distinguish; characteristic. —**dis'tinctively** adv. —**dis'tinctiveness** n.

distingué French. (distɛ̃'ge) adj. distinguished or noble.

distinguish (dɪ'stɪŋgwɪʃ) vb. (mainly tr.) **1.** (when intr., foll. by between or among) to make, show, or recognize a difference (between or among); differentiate (between). **2.** to be a distinctive feature of; characterize. **3.** to make out; perceive. **4.** to mark for a special honour. **5.** to make (oneself) noteworthy. **6.** to classify. —**dis'tinguishable** adj.

distinguished (dɪ'stɪŋgwɪʃt) adj. **1.** noble or dignified in appearance or behaviour. **2.** eminent; famous; celebrated.

distort (dɪ'stɔːt) vb. (tr.) **1.** (often passive) to twist or pull out of shape; contort; deform. **2.** to alter or misrepresent (facts, etc.). **3.** Electronics. to reproduce or amplify (a signal) inaccurately. —**dis'torted** adj. —**dis'tortion** n.

distract (dɪ'strækt) vb. (tr.) **1.** (often passive) to draw the attention of (a person) away from something. **2.** to divide or confuse the attention of (a person). **3.** to amuse or entertain. **4.** to trouble greatly. **5.** to make mad. —**dis'tracted** adj.

distraction (dɪ'strækʃən) n. **1.** a distracting or being distracted. **2.** something that serves as a diversion or entertainment. **3.** an interruption; obstacle to concentration. **4.** mental turmoil or madness.

distrain (dɪ'streɪn) vb. Law. to seize (personal property) as security or indemnity for a debt. —**dis'trainment** n. —**dis'trainor** or **dis'trainer** n. —**dis'traint** n.

distrait (dɪ'streɪ; French di'strɛ) adj. absent-minded; abstracted.

distraught (dɪ'strɔːt) adj. **1.** distracted or agitated. **2.** Rare. mad.

distress (dɪ'strɛs) vb. (tr.) **1.** to cause mental pain to; upset badly. **2.** (usually passive) to subject to financial or other trouble. **3.** Law. a less common word for **distrain.** ~n. **4.** mental pain; anguish. **5.** a distressing or being distressed. **6.** physical or financial trouble. **7. in distress.** (of a ship, etc.) in dire need of help. **8.** Law. **a.** the seizure of property as security for or in satisfaction of a debt, claim, etc.; distraint. **b.** the property thus seized. **c.** U.S. (as modifier): distress merchandise. —**dis'tressful** adj. —**dis'tressing** adj. —**dis'tressingly** adv.

THESAURUS

distend balloon, bloat, bulge, dilate, enlarge, expand, increase, inflate, puff, stretch, swell, widen

distended bloated, dilated, enlarged, expanded, inflated, puffy, stretched, swollen, tumescent

distil condense, draw out, evaporate, express, extract, press out, purify, rectify, refine, sublimate, vaporize

distillation elixir, essence, extract, quintessence, spirit

distinct 1. apparent, clear, clear-cut, decided, definite, evident, lucid, manifest, marked, noticeable, obvious, palpable, patent, plain, recognizable, sharp, unambiguous, unmistakable, well-defined **2.** detached, different, discrete, dissimilar, individual, separate, unconnected

distinction 1. differentiation, discernment, discrimination, penetration, perception, separation **2.** contrast, difference, differential, division, separation **3.** characteristic, distinctiveness, feature, individuality, mark, particularity, peculiarity, quality **4.** account, celebrity, consequence, credit, eminence, excellence, fame, greatness, honour, importance, merit, name, note, prominence, quality, rank, renown, reputation, repute, superiority, worth

distinctive characteristic, different, distinguishing, extraordinary, idiosyncratic, individual, original, peculiar, singular, special, typical, uncommon, unique

distinctly clearly, decidedly, definitely, evidently, manifestly, markedly, noticeably, obviously, palpably, patently, plainly, pre-

cisely, sharply

distinctness 1. clarity, lucidity, obviousness, plainness, sharpness, vividness **2.** detachment, difference, discreteness, disparateness, dissimilarity, dissociation, distinctiveness, individuality, separation

distinguish 1. ascertain, decide, determine, differentiate, discriminate, judge, tell apart, tell between, tell the difference **2.** categorize, characterize, classify, individualize, make distinctive, mark, separate, set apart, single out **3.** discern, know, make out, perceive, pick out, recognize, see, tell **4.** celebrate, dignify, honour, immortalize, make famous, signalize

distinguishable clear, conspicuous, discernible, evident, manifest, noticeable, obvious, perceptible, plain, recognizable, well-marked

distinguished 1. acclaimed, celebrated, conspicuous, eminent, famed, famous, illustrious, notable, noted, renowned, well-known **2.** conspicuous, extraordinary, marked, outstanding, signal, striking

distinguishing characteristic, different, differentiating, distinctive, individualistic, marked, peculiar, typical

distort 1. bend, buckle, contort, deform, disfigure, misshape, twist, warp, wrench, wrest **2.** bias, colour, falsify, garble, misrepresent, pervert, slant, twist

distortion 1. bend, buckle, contortion, crookedness, deformity, malformation, twist, twistedness, warp **2.** bias, colouring, falsification, misrepresentation, perversion, slant

distract 1. divert, draw away, sidetrack,

turn aside **2.** amuse, beguile, engross, entertain, occupy **3.** agitate, bewilder, confound, confuse, derange, discompose, disconcert, disturb, harass, madden, perplex, puzzle, torment, trouble

distracted 1. agitated, bemused, bewildered, confounded, confused, flustered, harassed, in a flap (Inf.), perplexed, puzzled, troubled **2.** crazy, deranged, distraught, frantic, frenzied, grief-stricken, insane, mad, overwrought, raving, wild

distracting bewildering, bothering, confusing, disconcerting, dismaying, disturbing, off-putting (Brit. inf.), perturbing

distraction 1. abstraction, agitation, bewilderment, commotion, confusion, discord, disorder, disturbance **2.** amusement, beguilement, diversion, divertissement, entertainment, pastime, recreation **3.** disturbance, diversion, interference, interruption **4.** aberration, alienation, delirium, derangement, desperation, frenzy, hallucination, incoherence, insanity, mania

distress n. **1.** affliction, agony, anguish, anxiety, desolation, discomfort, grief, heartache, misery, pain, sadness, sorrow, suffering, torment, torture, woe, worry, wretchedness **2.** adversity, calamity, destitution, difficulties, hardship, indigence, misfortune, need, poverty, privation, straits, trial, trouble ~v. **3.** afflict, agonize, bother, disturb, grieve, harass, harrow, pain, perplex, sadden, torment, trouble, upset, worry, wound

distressed (dɪ'strɛst) *adj*. 1. much troubled; upset; afflicted. 2. in financial straits; poor. 3. *Econ*. another word for **depressed**.

distribute (dɪ'strɪbjuːt) *vb*. (*tr*.) 1. to give out in shares; dispense. 2. to hand out or deliver. 3. (*often passive*) to spread throughout an area. 4. (*often passive*) to divide into classes or categories. 5. *Printing*. to return (used type) to the correct positions in the type case. 6. *Logic*. to use (a term) so that it refers to all members of the class it designates. —**dis'tributable** *adj*.

distribution (,dɪstrɪ'bjuːʃən) *n*. 1. the act of distributing or the state or manner of being distributed. 2. a thing or portion distributed. 3. arrangement or location. 4. the transporting, merchandising, and marketing of goods from producer to consumer. 5. *Econ*. the division of the total income of a community among its members. 6. *Statistics*. a set of values with reference to their theoretical or observed frequency. 7. *Law*. the apportioning of the estate of a deceased intestate. —,distri'butional *adj*.

distributive (dɪ'strɪbjutɪv) *adj*. 1. characterized by or relating to distribution. 2. *Grammar*. referring separately to the individual people or items in a group, as the words *each* and *every*. 3. *Maths*., *logic*. (of an operation) leading to the same result whether performed before or after a second specified operation. ~*n*. 4. *Grammar*. a distributive word. —**dis'tributively** *adv*. —**dis'tributiveness** *n*.

distributor (dɪ'strɪbjutə) *n*. 1. a person or thing that distributes. 2. a wholesaler or middleman engaged in the distribution of a category of goods, esp. to retailers in a specific area. 3. the device in a petrol engine that distributes the high-tension voltage to the sparking plugs.

district ('dɪstrɪkt) *n*. 1. a. an area of land marked off for administrative or other purposes. b. (*as modifier*): *district nurse*. 2. a locality separated by geographical attributes; region. 3. any subdivision of a territory, region, etc. 4. a political subdivision of a county, region, etc., that elects a council responsible for certain local services. ~*vb*. 5. (*tr*.) to divide into districts.

district nurse *n*. *Brit*. a nurse appointed to attend patients within a particular district, usually in the patients' homes.

distrust (dɪs'trʌst) *vb*. 1. to regard as untrustworthy or dishonest. ~*n*. 2. suspicion; doubt. —**dis'truster** *n*. —**dis'trustful** *adj*.

disturb (dɪ'stɜːb) *vb*. (*tr*.) 1. to intrude on; interrupt. 2. to destroy the quietness or peace of. 3. to disarrange; muddle. 4. (*often passive*) to upset; trouble. 5. to inconvenience; put out. —**dis'turber** *n*. —**dis'turbing** *adj*. —**dis'turbingly** *adv*.

disturbance (dɪ'stɜːbəns) *n*. 1. a disturbing or being disturbed. 2. an interruption or intrusion. 3. an unruly outburst or tumult. 4. *Law*. an interference with another's rights. 5. *Geol*. a minor movement of the earth causing a small earthquake. 6. *Meteorol*. a small depression. 7. *Psychiatry*. a mental or emotional disorder.

disturbed (dɪ'stɜːbd) *adj*. *Psychiatry*. emotionally upset,

troubled, or maladjusted.

disunite (,dɪsju'naɪt) *vb*. 1. to separate; disrupt. 2. (*tr*.) to set at variance; estrange. —**dis'union** *n*. —**dis'unity** *n*.

disuse (dɪs'juːs) *n*. the condition of being unused; neglect (often in **in** *or* **into disuse**).

disyllable ('daɪ,sɪləbəl) *n*. a variant spelling of **dissyllable**.

ditch (dɪtʃ) *n*. 1. a narrow channel dug in the earth, usually used for drainage, irrigation, or as a boundary marker. 2. **last ditch**. a last resort or place of last defence. ~*vb*. 3. to make a ditch in. 4. (*intr*.) to edge with a ditch. 5. *Sl*. to crash, esp. deliberately, as to avoid more unpleasant circumstances: *he had to ditch the car*. 6. (*tr*.) *Sl*. to abandon. 7. *Sl*. to land (an aircraft) on water in an emergency. 8. (*tr*.) *U.S. sl*. to evade. —**'ditcher** *n*.

dither ('dɪðə) *vb*. (*intr*.) 1. *Chiefly Brit*. to be uncertain or indecisive. 2. *Chiefly U.S.* to be in an agitated state. 3. to tremble, as with cold. ~*n*. 4. *Chiefly Brit*. a state of indecision. 5. a state of agitation. —**'ditherer** *n*.

dithyramb ('dɪθɪ,ræm, -,ræmb) *n*. 1. (in ancient Greece) a passionate choral hymn in honour of Dionysus. 2. any utterance or a piece of writing that resembles this. —,dithy'rambic *adj*.

dittany ('dɪtənɪ) *n*., *pl*. **-nies**. 1. an aromatic Cretan plant with pink flowers: formerly credited with medicinal properties. 2. a North American plant with purplish flowers.

ditto ('dɪtəʊ) *n*., *pl*. **-tos**. 1. the aforementioned; the above; the same. Used in accounts, lists, etc., to avoid repetition, and symbolized by two small marks („) known as **ditto marks**, placed under the thing repeated. 2. *Inf*. a duplicate. ~*adv*. 3. in the same way. ~ 4. *sentence substitute*. *Inf*. used to avoid repeating or to confirm agreement with an immediately preceding sentence. ~*vb*. **-toing, -toed**. 5. (*tr*.) to copy; repeat.

ditty ('dɪtɪ) *n*., *pl*. **-ties**. a short simple song or poem.

diuretic (,daɪju'rɛtɪk) *adj*. 1. acting to increase the flow of urine. ~*n*. 2. a drug or agent that increases the flow of urine. —**diuresis** (,daɪju'riːsɪs) *n*.

diurnal (daɪ'ɜːnəl) *adj*. 1. happening during the day or daily. 2. (of flowers) open during the day and closed at night. 3. (of animals) active during the day. ~Cf. **nocturnal**. —**di'urnally** *adv*.

diva ('diːvə) *n*., *pl*. **-vas** *or* **-ve** (-vɪ). a highly distinguished female singer; prima donna.

divalent (daɪ'veɪlənt, 'daɪ,veɪ-) *adj*. *Chem*. 1. having a valency of two. 2. having two valencies. ~Also: **bivalent**. —**di'valency** *n*.

divan (dɪ'væn) *n*. 1. a. a backless sofa or couch. b. a bed resembling such a couch. 2. (esp. formerly) a smoking room. 3. a. a Muslim law court, council chamber, or counting house. b. a Muslim council of state.

dive (daɪv) *vb*. **diving, dived** *or* *U.S.* **dove, dived**. (*mainly intr*.) 1. to plunge headfirst into water. 2. (of a submarine, etc.) to submerge under water. 3. (*also tr*.) to fly in a steep nose-down descending path. 4. to rush, go, or reach quickly, as in a headlong plunge: *he dived for*

distressed 1. afflicted, agitated, anxious, distracted, distraught, saddened, tormented, troubled, upset, worried, wretched 2. destitute, indigent, needy, poor, poverty-stricken, straitened

distressing affecting, afflicting, distressful, disturbing, grievous, heart-breaking, hurtful, lamentable, nerve-racking, painful, sad, upsetting, worrying

distribute 1. administer, allocate, allot, apportion, assign, deal, dispense, dispose, divide, dole out, give, measure out, mete, share 2. circulate, convey, deliver, hand out, pass round 3. diffuse, disperse, disseminate, scatter, spread, strew 4. arrange, assort, categorize, class, classify, file, group

distribution 1. allocation, allotment, apportionment, dispensation, division, dole, partition, sharing 2. circulation, diffusion, dispersal, dispersion, dissemination, propagation, scattering, spreading 3. arrangement, assortment, classification, disposition, grouping, location, organization, placement 4. *Commerce* dealing, delivery, handling, mailing, marketing, trading, transport, trans-

portation

district area, community, locale, locality, neighbourhood, parish, quarter, region, sector, vicinity, ward

distrust 1. *v*. be sceptical of, be suspicious of, be wary of, disbelieve, discredit, doubt, misbelieve, mistrust, question, smell a rat (*Inf*.), suspect, wonder about 2. *n*. disbelief, doubt, lack of faith, misgiving, mistrust, qualm, question, scepticism, suspicion, wariness

disturb 1. bother, butt in on, disrupt, interfere with, interrupt, intrude on, pester, rouse, startle 2. confuse, derange, disarrange, disorder, disorganize, muddle, unsettle 3. agitate, alarm, annoy, confound, discompose, distract, distress, excite, fluster, harass, perturb, ruffle, shake, trouble, unsettle, upset, worry

disturbance 1. agitation, annoyance, bother, confusion, derangement, disorder, distraction, hindrance, interruption, intrusion, molestation, perturbation, upset 2. bother (*Inf*.), brawl, commotion, disorder, fracas, fray, hubbub, riot, ruckus (*Inf*.), ruction

(*Inf*.), tumult, turmoil, uproar

disturbed 1. *Psychiatry* disordered, maladjusted, neurotic, troubled, unbalanced, upset 2. agitated, anxious, apprehensive, bothered, concerned, disquieted, troubled, uneasy, upset, worried

disturbing agitating, alarming, disconcerting, discouraging, dismaying, disquieting, distressing, frightening, perturbing, startling, threatening, troubling, unsettling, upsetting, worrying

disuse abandonment, decay, desuetude, discontinuance, idleness, neglect, nonemployment, nonuse

ditch *n*. 1. channel, drain, dyke, furrow, gully, moat, trench, watercourse ~*v*. 2. dig, drain, excavate, gouge, trench 3. *Sl*. abandon, discard, dispose of, drop, dump (*Inf*.), get rid of, jettison, scrap, throw out *or* overboard

dither 1. *v*. faff about (*Brit. inf*.), falter, haver, hesitate, oscillate, shillyshally (*Inf*.), swither (*Scot*.), teeter, vacillate, waver 2. *n*. bother, flap (*Inf*.), fluster, flutter, pother, stew (*Inf*.), tiz-woz (*Inf*.), tizzy (*Inf*.), twitter

the ball. **5.** (*also tr.;* foll. by *in* or *into*) to dip or put (one's hand) quickly or forcefully (into). **6.** (usually foll. by *in* or *into*) to involve oneself (in something), as in eating food. *~n.* **7.** a headlong plunge into water. **8.** an act or instance of diving. **9.** a steep nose-down descent of an aircraft. **10.** *Sl.* a disreputable bar or club. **11.** *Boxing sl.* the act of a boxer pretending to be knocked down or out.

dive bomber *n.* a military aircraft designed to release its bombs on a target during a steep dive. —'**dive-bomb** *vb.*

diver ('daɪvə) *n.* **1.** a person or thing that dives. **2.** a person who works or explores underwater. **3.** any of various aquatic birds of northern oceans: noted for skill in diving. U.S. name: **loon.** **4.** any of various other diving birds.

diverge (daɪ'vɜːdʒ) *vb.* **1.** to separate or cause to separate and go in different directions from a point. **2.** (*intr.*) to be at variance; differ. **3.** (*intr.*) to deviate from a prescribed course. **4.** (*intr.*) *Maths.* (of a series) to have no limit. —**di'vergence** *or* **di'vergency** *n.* —**di'vergent** *adj.* —**di'vergently** *adv.*

divers ('daɪvəz) *determiner. Arch. or literary.* various; sundry; some.

▷ **Usage.** In spite of the frequency with which *divers* (several) and *diverse* (disparate, set apart by marked differences) are treated as synonyms, and although they were originally the same word, careful writers and speakers always distinguish between these two words: *there were divers persons in the room; the personalities of those present were extremely diverse.*

diverse (daɪ'vɜːs, 'daɪvɜːs) *adj.* **1.** having variety; assorted. **2.** distinct in kind. —**di'versely** *adv.*

diversify (daɪ'vɜːsɪˌfaɪ) *vb.* **-fying, -fied.** **1.** (*tr.*) to create different forms of; variegate; vary. **2.** (of an enterprise) to vary (products, operations, etc.) in order to spread risk, expand, etc. **3.** to distribute (investments) among several securities in order to spread risk. —di,versifi'cation *n.*

diversion (daɪ'vɜːʃən) *n.* **1.** the act of diverting from a specified course. **2.** *Chiefly Brit.* an official detour used by traffic when a main route is closed. **3.** something that distracts from business, etc.; amusement. **4.** *Mil.* a feint attack designed to draw an enemy away from the main attack. —**di'versional** *or* **di'versionary** *adj.*

diversity (daɪ'vɜːsɪtɪ) *n.* **1.** the state or quality of being different or varied. **2.** a point of difference.

divert (daɪ'vɜːt) *vb.* **1.** to turn aside; deflect. **2.** (*tr.*) to entertain; amuse. **3.** (*tr.*) to distract the attention of. —**di'verting** *adj.* —**di'vertingly** *adv.*

diverticulitis (ˌdaɪvəˌtɪkjʊ'laɪtɪs) *n.* inflammation of one or more diverticula, esp. of the colon.

diverticulum (ˌdaɪvə'tɪkjʊləm) *n., pl.* **-la** (-lə). any sac or pouch formed by herniation of the wall of a tubular organ or part, esp. the intestines.

divertimento (dɪˌvɜːtɪ'mɛntəʊ) *n., pl.* **-ti** (-tɪ). **1.** a piece of entertaining music, often scored for a mixed ensemble and having no fixed form. **2.** an episode in a fugue.

divertissement (dɪ'vɜːtɪsmənt) *n.* a brief entertainment or diversion, usually between the acts of a play.

divest (daɪ'vɛst) *vb.* (*tr.;* usually foll. by *of*) **1.** to strip (of clothes). **2.** to deprive or dispossess. —**divestiture** (daɪ'vɛstɪtʃə), **divesture** (daɪ'vɛstʃə), *or* **di'vestment** *n.*

divide (dɪ'vaɪd) *vb.* **1.** to separate into parts; split up. **2.** to share or be shared out in parts; distribute. **3.** to diverge or cause to diverge in opinion or aim. **4.** (*tr.*) to keep apart or be a boundary between. **5.** (*intr.*) to vote by separating into two groups. **6.** to categorize; classify. **7.** to calculate the quotient of (one number or quantity) and (another number or quantity) by division. **8.** (*intr.*) to diverge: *the roads divide.* **9.** (*tr.*) to mark increments of (length, angle, etc.). *~n.* **10.** *Chiefly U.S.* an area of relatively high ground separating drainage basins; watershed. **11.** a division; split.

dividend ('dɪvɪˌdɛnd) *n.* **1. a.** a distribution from the net profits of a company to its shareholders. **b.** a portion of this distribution received by a shareholder. **2.** the share of a cooperative society's surplus allocated to members. **3.** *Insurance.* a sum of money distributed from a company's net profits to the holders of certain policies. **4.** something extra; a bonus. **5.** a number or quantity to be divided by another number or quantity. **6.** *Law.* the proportion of an insolvent estate payable to the creditors.

divider (dɪ'vaɪdə) *n.* **1.** Also called: **room divider.** an object placed to divide a room into separate areas. **2.** a person or thing that divides.

dividers (dɪ'vaɪdəz) *pl. n.* a type of compass with two pointed arms, used for measuring lines or dividing them.

divination (ˌdɪvɪ'neɪʃən) *n.* **1.** the art or practice of discovering future events or unknown things, as though by supernatural powers. **2.** a prophecy. **3.** a guess. —**divinatory** (dɪ'vɪnətərɪ) *adj.*

divine (dɪ'vaɪn) *adj.* **1.** of God or a deity. **2.** godlike. **3.** of or associated with religion or worship. **4.** of supreme excellence or worth. **5.** *Inf.* splendid; perfect. *~n.* **6.** (*often cap.;* preceded by *the*) another term for God. **7.** a priest, esp. one learned in theology. *~vb.* **8.** to perceive (something) by intuition. **9.** to conjecture (something); guess. **10.** to discern (a hidden or future reality) as though by supernatural power. **11.** (*tr.*) to search for (water, metal, etc.) using a divining rod. —**di'vinely** *adv.* —**di'viner** *n.*

diving bell *n.* an early diving submersible having an open bottom and being supplied with compressed air.

diving board *n.* a platform or springboard from which swimmers may dive.

diving suit *or* **dress** *n.* a waterproof suit used by divers, having a heavy detachable helmet and an air supply.

divining rod *n.* a forked twig said to move when held

THESAURUS

dive *v.* **1.** descend, dip, disappear, drop, duck, fall, go underwater, jump, leap, nosedive, pitch, plummet, plunge, submerge, swoop *~n.* **2.** dash, header (*Inf.*), jump, leap, lunge, nose dive, plunge, spring **3.** *Sl.* honkytonk (*U.S. sl.*), joint (*Sl.*), sleazy bar

diverge 1. bifurcate, branch, divaricate, divide, fork, part, radiate, separate, split, spread **2.** be at odds, be at variance, conflict, differ, disagree, dissent **3.** depart, deviate, digress, stray, turn aside, wander

divergence branching out, departure, deviation, difference, digression, disparity, divagation, ramification, separation deflection, varying

divergent conflicting, deviating, different, differing, disagreeing, dissimilar, diverging, diverse, separate, variant

divers different, manifold, many, multifarious, numerous, several, some, sundry, varied, various

diverse 1. assorted, diversified, miscellaneous, of every description, several, sundry, varied, various **2.** different, differing, discrete, disparate, dissimilar, distinct, divergent, separate, unlike, varying

diversify alter, assort, branch out, change, expand, mix, modify, spread out, transform, variegate, vary

diversion 1. alteration, change, deflection, departure, detour, deviation, digression, variation **2.** amusement, beguilement, delight, distraction, divertissement, enjoyment, entertainment, game, gratification, pastime, play, pleasure, recreation, relaxation, sport

diversity assortment, difference, dissimilarity, distinctiveness, divergence, diverseness, diversification, heterogeneity, medley, multiplicity, range, unlikeness, variance, variegation, variety

divert 1. avert, deflect, redirect, switch, turn aside **2.** amuse, beguile, delight, entertain, gratify, recreate, regale **3.** detract, distract, draw *or* lead away from, lead astray, sidetrack

diverting amusing, beguiling, enjoyable, entertaining, fun, humorous, pleasant

divest 1. denude, disrobe, doff, remove, strip, take off, unclothe, undress **2.** deprive, despoil, dispossess, strip

divide 1. bisect, cleave, cut (up), detach, disconnect, part, partition, segregate, separate, sever, shear, split, subdivide, sunder **2.** allocate, allot, apportion, deal out, dispense,

distribute, divvy (up) (*Inf.*), dole out, measure out, portion, share **3.** alienate, break up, cause to disagree, come between, disunite, estrange, set *or* pit against one another, set at variance *or* odds, sow dissension, split **4.** arrange, categorize, classify, grade, group, put in order, separate, sort

dividend bonus, cut (*Inf.*), divvy (*Inf.*), extra, gain, plus, portion, share, surplus

divine *adj.* **1.** angelic, celestial, godlike, heavenly, holy, spiritual, superhuman, supernatural **2.** consecrated, holy, religious, sacred, sanctified, spiritual **3.** beatific, blissful, exalted, mystical, rapturous, supreme, transcendent, transcendental, transmundane **4.** *Inf.* beautiful, excellent, glorious, marvellous, perfect, splendid, superlative, wonderful *~n.* **5.** churchman, clergyman, cleric, ecclesiastic, minister, pastor, priest, reverend *~v.* **6.** apprehend, conjecture, deduce, discern, foretell, guess, infer, intuit, perceive, prognosticate, suppose, surmise, suspect, understand **7.** *Of water or minerals* dowse

diviner 1. astrologer, augur, oracle, prophet, seer, sibyl, soothsayer **2.** *Of water or minerals* dowser

over ground in which water, metal, etc., is to be found. Also called: **dowsing rod.**

divinity (dɪ'vɪnɪtɪ) n., pl. **-ties.** 1. the nature of a deity or the state of being divine. 2. a god. 3. (often cap.; preceded by the) another term for God. 4. another word for **theology.**

divisible (dɪ'vɪzəbəl) adj. capable of being divided, usually with no remainder. —**di,visi'bility** or —**di'visibleness** n. —**di'visibly** adv.

division (dɪ'vɪʒən) n. 1. a dividing or being divided. 2. the act of sharing out; distribution. 3. something that divides; boundary. 4. one of the parts, groups, etc., into which something is divided. 5. a part of a government, business, etc., that has been made into a unit for administrative or other reasons. 6. a formal vote in Parliament or a similar legislative body. 7. a difference of opinion. 8. (in sports) a section or class organized according to age, weight, skill, etc. 9. a mathematical operation in which the quotient of two numbers or quantities is calculated. Usually written: $a \div b$, a/b, $\frac{a}{b}$. 10. Army. a major formation, larger than a regiment but smaller than a corps, containing the necessary arms to sustain combat. 11. Biol. a major taxonomic division that corresponds to a phylum. —**di'visional** or **di'visionary** adj. —**di'visionally** adv.

division sign n. the symbol $\div$, placed between the dividend and the divisor to indicate division, as in $12 \div 6 = 2$.

divisive (dɪ'vaɪsɪv) adj. tending to cause disagreement or dissension. —**di'visively** adv. —**di'visiveness** n.

divisor (dɪ'vaɪzə) n. 1. a number or quantity to be divided into another number or quantity (the dividend). 2. a number that is a factor of another number.

divorce (dɪ'vɔːs) n. 1. the legal dissolution of a marriage. 2. a judicial decree declaring a marriage to be dissolved. 3. a separation, esp. one that is total or complete. ~vb. 4. to separate or be separated by divorce; give or obtain a divorce. 5. (tr.) to remove or separate, esp. completely. —**di'vorceable** adj.

divorcée (dɪvɔː'siː) or (masc.) **divorcé** (dɪ'vɔːseɪ) n. a person who has been divorced.

divot ('dɪvət) n. a piece of turf dug out of a grass surface, esp. by a golf club or by horses' hooves.

divulge (daɪ'vʌldʒ) vb. (tr.; may take a clause as object) to make known; disclose. —**di'vulgence** or **di'vulgement** n. —**di'vulger** n.

divvy ('dɪvɪ) Inf. ~n., pl. **-vies.** 1. Brit. short for **dividend,** esp. (formerly) one paid by a cooperative society. 2. U.S. a share; portion. ~vb. **-vying, -vied.** 3. (tr.; usually foll. by up) U.S. to divide and share.

dixie ('dɪksɪ) n. 1. Chiefly mil. a large metal pot for cooking, brewing tea, etc. 2. a mess tin.

Dixie ('dɪksɪ) n. 1. Also called: **Dixieland.** the southern states of the U.S. ~adj. 2. of the southern states of the U.S.

D.I.Y. or **d.i.y.** (in Britain) abbrev. for do-it-yourself.

dizzy ('dɪzɪ) adj. **-zier, -ziest.** 1. affected with a whirling or reeling sensation; giddy. 2. mentally confused or bewildered. 3. causing or tending to cause vertigo or bewilderment. 4. Inf. foolish or flighty. ~vb. **-zies, -zying,**

-zied. 5. (tr.) to make dizzy. —**'dizzily** adv. —**'dizziness** n.

D.J. or **d.j.** abbrev. for: 1. dinner jacket. 2. disc jockey.

djinni or **djinny** (dʒɪ'niː, 'dʒɪnɪ) n., pl. **djinn** (dʒɪn). variant spellings of **jinni.**

dl abbrev. for decilitre.

dm abbrev. for decimetre.

DM abbrev. for Deutsche Mark.

D.Mus. or **DMus** abbrev. for Doctor of Music.

DNA n. deoxyribonucleic acid, the main constituent of the chromosomes of all organisms in the form of a double helix. DNA is self-replicating and is responsible for the transmission of hereditary characteristics.

D-notice n. Brit. an official notice sent to newspapers, etc., prohibiting the publication of certain security information.

do[1] (duː; unstressed dʊ, də) vb. **does, doing, did, done.** 1. to perform or complete (a deed or action): to do a portrait. 2. (often intr.; foll. by for) to serve the needs of; be suitable for; suffice. 3. (tr.) to arrange or fix. 4. (tr.) to prepare or provide; serve: this restaurant doesn't do lunch on Sundays. 5. (tr.) to make tidy, elegant, ready, etc.: to do one's hair. 6. (tr.) to improve (esp. in do something to or for). 7. (tr.) to find an answer to (a problem or puzzle). 8. (tr.) to translate or adapt the form or language of: the book was done into a play. 9. (intr.) to conduct oneself: do as you please. 10. (intr.) to fare or manage. 11. (tr.) to cause or produce: complaints do nothing to help. 12. (tr.) to give or render: do me a favour. 13. (tr.) to work at, esp. as a course of study or a profession. 14. (tr.) to perform (a play, etc.); act. 15. (tr.) to travel at a specified speed, esp. as a maximum. 16. (tr.) to travel or traverse (a distance). 17. (takes an infinitive without to) used as an auxiliary **a.** before the subject of an interrogative sentence as a way of forming a question: do you agree? **b.** to intensify positive statements and commands: I do like your new house; do hurry! **c.** before a negative adverb to form negative statements or commands: do not leave me here alone! **d.** in inverted constructions: little did he realize that. 18. used as an auxiliary to replace an earlier verb or verb phrase: he likes you as much as I do. 19. (tr.) Inf. to visit as a sightseer or tourist. 20. (tr.) to wear out; exhaust. 21. (intr.) to happen (esp. in nothing doing). 22. (tr.) Sl. to serve (a specified period) as a prison sentence. 23. (tr.) Sl. to cheat or swindle. 24. (tr.) Sl. to rob. 25. (tr.) Austral. sl. to spend (money). 26. (tr.) Sl., chiefly Brit. to treat violently; assault. 27. (tr.) Taboo sl. (of a male) to have sexual intercourse with. 28. **do or die.** to make a final or supreme effort. 29. **make do.** to manage with whatever is available. ~n., pl. **dos** or **do's.** 30. Sl. an act or instance of cheating or swindling. 31. Inf., chiefly Brit. a formal or festive gathering; party. 32. **do's and don'ts.** Inf. rules. ~See also **do away with, do by, do down, do for,** etc.

do[2] (dəʊ) n., pl. **dos.** a variant spelling of **doh.**

do. abbrev. for ditto.

doable ('duːəbəl) adj. capable of being done.

do away with vb. (intr., adv. + prep.) 1. to kill or de-

THESAURUS

divinity 1. deity, divine nature, godhead, godhood, godliness, holiness, sanctity 2. daemon, deity, genius, god, goddess, guardian spirit, spirit 3. religion, religious studies, theology

divisible dividable, fractional, separable, splittable

division 1. bisection, cutting up, detaching, dividing, partition, separation, splitting up 2. allotment, apportionment, distribution, sharing 3. border, boundary, demarcation, divide, divider, dividing line, partition 4. branch, category, class, compartment, department, group, head, part, portion, section, sector, segment 5. breach, difference of opinion, disagreement, discord, disunion, estrangement, feud, rupture, split, variance

divisive alienating, damaging, detrimental, discordant, disruptive, estranging, inharmonious, pernicious, troublesome, unsettling

divorce 1. n. annulment, breach, break, decree nisi, dissolution, disunion, rupture, separation, severance, split-up 2. v. annul,

disconnect, dissociate, dissolve (marriage), disunite, divide, part, separate, sever, split up, sunder

divulge betray, communicate, confess, declare, disclose, exhibit, expose, impart, leak, let slip, make known, proclaim, promulgate, publish, reveal, spill (Inf.), tell, uncover

dizzy 1. faint, giddy, light-headed, off balance, reeling, shaky, staggering, swimming, vertiginous, weak at the knees, wobbly, woozy (Inf.) 2. befuddled, bemused, bewildered, confused, dazed, dazzled, muddled 3. lofty, steep, vertiginous 4. Inf. capricious, fickle, flighty, foolish, frivolous, giddy, light-headed, scatterbrained, silly

do v. 1. accomplish, achieve, act, carry out, complete, conclude, discharge, end, execute, perform, produce, transact, undertake, work 2. answer, be adequate, be enough, be of use, be sufficient, pass muster, satisfy, serve, suffice, suit 3. arrange, be responsible for, fix, get ready, look after, make, make ready, or-

ganize, prepare, see to, take on 4. decipher, decode, figure out, puzzle out, resolve, solve, work out 5. adapt, render, translate, transpose 6. bear oneself, behave, carry oneself, comport oneself, conduct oneself 7. fare, get along, get on, make out, manage, proceed 8. bring about, cause, create, effect, produce 9. Of a play, etc. act, give, perform, present, produce, put on 10. Inf. cover, explore, journey through or around, look at, stop in, tour, travel, visit 11. Sl. cheat, con (Sl.), cozen, deceive, defraud, dupe, fleece, hoax, swindle, take (someone) for a ride (Inf.), trick ~n. 12. Inf. affair, event, function, gathering, occasion, party 13. **do's and don'ts** Inf. code, customs, etiquette, instructions, regulations, rules, standards

do away with 1. bump off (Sl.), destroy, do in (Sl.), exterminate, kill, liquidate, murder, slay 2. abolish, discard, discontinue, eliminate, get rid of, put an end to, remove

stroy. **2.** to discard or abolish.

dobbin ('dɒbɪn) *n.* a name for a horse, esp. a workhorse.

Doberman pinscher ('dəʊbəmən 'pɪnʃə) *n.* a breed of large dog with a glossy black-and-tan coat.

do by *vb.* (*intr., prep.*) to treat in the manner specified.

doc (dɒk) *n. Inf.* short for doctor.

docile ('dəʊsaɪl) *adj.* **1.** easy to manage or discipline; submissive. **2.** *Rare.* easy to teach. —'**docilely** *adv.* —**docility** (dəʊ'sɪlɪtɪ) *n.*

dock[1] (dɒk) *n.* **1.** a wharf or pier. **2.** a space between two wharves or piers for the mooring of ships. **3.** an area of water that can accommodate a ship and can be closed off to allow regulation of the water level. **4.** short for **dry dock. 5. in** *or* **into dock.** *Brit. inf.* **a.** (of people) in hospital. **b.** (of cars, etc.) in a repair shop. **6.** *Chiefly U.S.* a platform from which lorries, goods trains, etc., are loaded and unloaded. ~*vb.* **7.** to moor or be moored at a dock. **8.** to put (a vessel) into, or (of a vessel) to come into a dry dock. **9.** (of two spacecraft) to link together in space or link together (two spacecraft) in space.

dock[2] (dɒk) *n.* **1.** the bony part of the tail of an animal. **2.** the part of an animal's tail left after the major part of it has been cut off. ~*vb.* (*tr.*) **3.** to remove (the tail or part of the tail) of (an animal) by cutting through the bone. **4.** to deduct (an amount) from (a person's wages, pension, etc.).

dock[3] (dɒk) *n.* an enclosed space in a court of law where the accused sits or stands during his trial.

dock[4] (dɒk) *n.* any of various weedy plants having greenish or reddish flowers and broad leaves.

docker ('dɒkə) *n. Brit.* a man employed in the loading or unloading of ships. *U.S.* equivalent: **longshoreman.** See also **stevedore.**

docket ('dɒkɪt) *n.* **1.** *Chiefly Brit.* a piece of paper accompanying or referring to a package or other delivery, stating contents, delivery instructions, etc., sometimes serving as a receipt. **2.** *Law.* **a.** a summary of the proceedings in a court. **b.** a register containing this. **3.** *Brit.* **a.** a customs certificate declaring that duty has been paid. **b.** a certificate giving particulars of a shipment. **4.** a summary of contents, as in a document. **5.** *U.S.* a list of things to be done. **6.** *U.S. law.* a list of cases awaiting trial. ~*vb.* (*tr.*) **7.** to fix a docket to (a package, etc.). **8.** *Law.* **a.** to make a summary of (a judgment, etc.). **b.** to abstract and enter in a register. **9.** to endorse (a document, etc.) with a summary.

dockyard ('dɒk,jɑːd) *n.* a naval establishment with docks, workshops, etc., for the building, fitting out, and repair of vessels.

doctor ('dɒktə) *n.* **1.** a person licensed to practise medicine. **2.** a person who has been awarded a higher academic degree in any field of knowledge. **3.** *Chiefly U.S.* a person licensed to practise dentistry or veterinary medicine. **4.** (*often cap.*) Also called: **Doctor of the Church.** a title given to any of several of the early Fathers of the Christian Church. **5.** *Angling.* any of various artificial flies. **6.** *Inf.* a person who mends or repairs things. **7.** *Sl.* a cook on a ship or at a camp. **8.** *Arch.* a man, esp. a teacher, of learning. **9. go for the doctor.** *Austral. sl.* to make a great effort or move very fast. **10. what the doctor ordered.** something needed or desired. ~*vb.* **11.** (*tr.*) to give medical treatment to. **12.** (*intr.*) *Inf.* to practise medicine. **13.** (*tr.*) to repair or mend. **14.** (*tr.*) to make different in order to deceive. **15.** (*tr.*) to adapt. **16.** (*tr.*) *Inf.* to castrate (a cat, dog, etc.). —'**doctoral** *or* **doctorial** (dɒk'tɔːrɪəl) *adj.*

doctorate ('dɒktərɪt, -trɪt) *n.* the highest academic degree in any field of knowledge.

doctrinaire (,dɒktrɪ'nɛə) *adj.* **1.** stubbornly insistent on the observation of the niceties of a theory, esp. without regard to practicality, suitability, etc. **2.** theoretical; impractical. ~*n.* **3.** a person who stubbornly attempts to apply a theory without regard to practical difficulties. —,**doctri'nairism** *n.* —,**doctri'narian** *n.*

doctrine ('dɒktrɪn) *n.* **1.** a creed or body of teachings of a religious, political, or philosophical group presented for acceptance or belief; dogma. **2.** a principle or body of principles that is taught or advocated. —**doctrinal** (dɒk'traɪnəl) *adj.* —**doc'trinally** *adv.*

document *n.* ('dɒkjumənt). **1.** a piece of paper, booklet, etc., providing information, esp. of an official nature. **2.** *Arch.* proof. ~*vb.* ('dɒkju,mɛnt). (*tr.*) **3.** to record or report in detail, as in the press, on television, etc. **4.** to support (statements in a book) with references, etc. **5.** to support (a claim, etc.) with evidence. **6.** to furnish (a vessel) with documents specifying its registration, dimensions, etc.

documentary (,dɒkju'mɛntərɪ) *adj.* **1.** Also: **documental.** consisting of or relating to documents. **2.** presenting factual material with few or no fictional additions. ~*n., pl.* **-ries.** **3.** a factual film or television programme about an event, person, etc., presenting the facts with little or no fiction. —,**docu'mentarily** *adv.*

documentation (,dɒkjumɛn'teɪʃən) *n.* **1.** the act of supplying with or using documents or references. **2.** the documents or references supplied.

dodder[1] ('dɒdə) *vb.* (*intr.*) **1.** to move unsteadily; totter. **2.** to shake or tremble, as from age. —'**dodderer** *n.* —'**doddery** *adj.*

doddle ('dɒdəl) *n. Brit. sl.* something easily accomplished.

dodeca- *combining form.* indicating twelve: *dodecaphonic.*

dodecagon (dəʊ'dɛkə,gɒn) *n.* a polygon having twelve sides.

dodecahedron (,dəʊdɛkə'hiːdrən) *n.* a solid figure having twelve plane faces. —,**dodeca'hedral** *adj.*

dodge (dɒdʒ) *vb.* **1.** to avoid or attempt to avoid (a blow, discovery, etc.), as by moving suddenly. **2.** to evade by cleverness or trickery. **3.** (*intr.*) *Change-ringing.* to make a bell change places with its neighbour when sounding in successive changes. **4.** (*tr.*) *Photog.* to lighten or darken (selected areas on a print). ~*n.* **5.** a plan contrived to deceive. **6.** a sudden evasive movement. **7.** a clever contrivance. **8.** *Change-ringing.* the act of dodging.

Dodgem ('dɒdʒəm) *n. Trademark.* another name for bumper car.

dodger ('dɒdʒə) *n.* **1.** a person who evades or shirks. **2.** a shifty dishonest person. **3.** a canvas shelter on a ship's bridge, etc., to protect the helmsman from bad weather. **4.** *Dialect.* food, esp. bread.

dodgy ('dɒdʒɪ) *adj.* **dodgier, dodgiest.** *Brit. inf.* **1.** risky, difficult, or dangerous. **2.** uncertain or unreliable; tricky.

dodo ('dəʊdəʊ) *n., pl.* **dodos** *or* **dodoes.** **1.** any of a now extinct family of flightless birds formerly found on Mauritius. They had a hooked bill and short stout legs. **2.** *Inf.* an intensely conservative person who is unaware of changing fashions, ideas, etc. **3. (as) dead as a dodo.** irretrievably dead or defunct.

THESAURUS

docile amenable, biddable, compliant, ductile, manageable, obedient, pliant, submissive, teachable (*Rare*), tractable

docility amenability, biddableness, compliance, ductility, manageability, meekness, obedience, pliancy, submissiveness, tractability

dock *n.* 1. harbour, pier, quay, waterfront, wharf ~*v.* 2. anchor, berth, drop anchor, land, moor, put in, tie up 3. *Of spacecraft* couple, hook up, join, link up, rendezvous, unite

docket 1. *n.* bill, certificate, chit, chitty, counterfoil, label, receipt, tab, tag, tally, ticket 2. *v.* catalogue, file, index, label, mark, register, tab, tag, ticket

doctor *n.* 1. general practitioner, G.P.,

medic (*Inf.*), medical practitioner, physician ~*v.* 2. apply medication to, give medical treatment to, treat 3. botch, cobble, do up (*Inf.*), fix, mend, patch up, repair 4. alter, change, disguise, falsify, fudge, misrepresent, pervert, tamper with 5. add to, adulterate, cut, dilute, mix with, spike, water down

doctrinaire *adj.* 1. biased, dogmatic, fanatical, inflexible, insistent, opinionated, rigid 2. hypothetical, ideological, impractical, speculative, theoretical, unpragmatic, unrealistic

doctrine article, article of faith, belief, canon, concept, conviction, creed, dogma, opinion, precept, principle, teaching, tenet

document 1. *n.* certificate, instrument, legal form, paper, record, report 2. *v.* authen-

ticate, back up, certify, cite, corroborate, detail, give weight to, instance, particularize, substantiate, support, validate, verify

doddering aged, decrepit, doddery, faltering, feeble, floundering, infirm, senile, shaky, shambling, tottery, trembly, unsteady, weak

dodge *v.* 1. dart, duck, shift, sidestep, swerve, turn aside 2. avoid, deceive, elude, equivocate, evade, fend off, fudge, get out of, hedge, parry, shirk, shuffle, trick ~*n.* 3. contrivance, device, feint, machination, ploy, ruse, scheme, stratagem, subterfuge, trick, wheeze (*Sl.*), wile

dodger evader, shifty so-and-so, shirker, slacker, slippery one, slyboots, trickster

do down vb. (tr., adv.) **1.** to belittle or humiliate. **2.** to deceive or cheat.

doe (dəʊ) n., pl. **does** or **doe.** the female of the deer, hare, rabbit, and certain other animals.

D.O.E. (in Britain) abbrev. for Department of the Environment.

doek (dʊk) n. S. African inf. a square of cloth worn mainly by African women to cover the head.

doer ('duːə) n. **1.** a person or thing that does something. **2.** an active or energetic person. **3.** N.Z. a thriving farm animal.

does (dʌz) vb. (used with a singular noun or the pronouns he, she, or it) a form of the present tense (indicative mood) of **do**[1].

doeskin ('dəʊˌskɪn) n. **1.** the skin of a deer, lamb, or sheep. **2.** a very supple leather made from this. **3.** a heavy smooth cloth.

doff (dɒf) vb. (tr.) **1.** to take off or lift (one's hat) in salutation. **2.** to remove (clothing). —**'doffer** n.

do for vb. (prep.) Inf. **1.** (tr.) to convict of a crime or offence. **2.** (intr.) to cause the ruin, death, or defeat of. **3.** (intr.) to do housework for. **4. do well for oneself.** to thrive or succeed.

dog (dɒg) n. **1.** a domesticated canine mammal occurring in many breeds that show a great variety in size and form. **2.** any other carnivore of the dog family, such as the dingo and coyote. **3.** the male of animals of the dog family. **4.** a mechanical device for gripping or holding. **5.** Inf. a fellow; chap. **6.** Inf. a man or boy regarded as unpleasant or wretched. **7.** U.S. sl. an unattractive girl or woman. **8.** U.S. inf. something unsatisfactory or inferior. **9.** short for **firedog.** **10. a dog's chance.** no chance at all. **11. a dog's life.** a wretched existence. **12. dog eat dog.** ruthless competition. **13. like a dog's dinner.** dressed smartly or ostentatiously. **14. put on the dog.** U.S. inf. to behave pretentiously. ~vb. **dogging, dogged.** (tr.) **15.** to pursue or follow after like a dog. **16.** to trouble; plague. **17.** to chase with a dog. **18.** to grip or secure by a mechanical device. ~See also **dogs.**

dog biscuit n. a hard biscuit for dogs.

dogcart ('dɒgˌkɑːt) n. a light horse-drawn two-wheeled vehicle.

dog collar n. **1.** a collar for a dog. **2.** Inf. a clerical collar. **3.** Inf. a tight-fitting necklace.

dog days pl. n. the hot period of the summer reckoned in ancient times from the heliacal rising of Sirius (the Dog Star).

doge (dəʊdʒ) n. (formerly) the chief magistrate in the republics of Venice and Genoa.

dog-ear vb. **1.** (tr.) to fold down the corner of (a page). ~n. also **dog's-ear.** **2.** a folded-down corner of a page.

dog-eared adj. **1.** having dog-ears. **2.** shabby or worn.

dog-end n. an informal name for a cigarette end.

dogfight ('dɒgˌfaɪt) n. **1.** close-quarters combat between fighter aircraft. **2.** any rough fight.

dogfish ('dɒgˌfɪʃ) n., pl. **-fish** or **-fishes.** any of several small sharks.

dogged ('dɒgɪd) adj. obstinately determined; wilful or tenacious. —**'doggedly** adv. —**'doggedness** n.

doggerel ('dɒgərəl) or **dogrel** ('dɒgrəl) n. **1. a.** comic verse, usually irregular in measure. **b.** (as modifier): a doggerel rhythm. **2.** nonsense.

doggo ('dɒgəʊ) adv. Brit. inf. out of sight; in hiding (esp. in **lie doggo**).

doggy or **doggie** ('dɒgɪ) n., pl. **-gies.** **1.** a children's word for a dog. ~adj. **2.** of, like, or relating to a dog. **3.** fond of dogs.

doghouse ('dɒgˌhaʊs) n. **1.** the U.S. name for **kennel.** **2.** Inf. disfavour (**in in the doghouse**).

dogie, dogy, or **dogey** ('dəʊgɪ) n., pl. **-gies** or **-geys.** U.S. & Canad. a motherless calf.

dogleg ('dɒgˌlɛg) n. **1.** a sharp bend or angle. ~vb. **-legging, -legged.** **2.** (intr.) to go off at an angle. ~adj. **3.** of or with the shape of a dogleg. —**doglegged** (ˌdɒg-'lɛgɪd, 'dɒgˌlɛgd) adj.

dogma ('dɒgmə) n., pl. **-mas** or **-mata** (-mətə). **1.** a religious doctrine or system of doctrines proclaimed by ecclesiastical authority as true. **2.** a belief, principle, or doctrine or a code of beliefs, principles, or doctrines.

dogmatic (dɒg'mætɪk) or **dogmatical** adj. **1.** characterized by making authoritative or arrogant assertions, opinions, etc. **2.** of or constituting dogma. **3.** based on assumption rather than observation. —**dog'matically** adv.

do-gooder n. Inf. a well-intentioned person, esp. a naive or impractical one.

dog paddle n. **1.** a swimming stroke in which the swimmer paddles his hands in imitation of a swimming dog. ~vb. **dog-paddle.** **2.** (intr.) to swim using the dog paddle.

dog rose n. a prickly wild European rose that has pink or white scentless flowers.

dogs (dɒgz) pl. n. **1. the.** Brit. inf. greyhound racing. **2.** Sl. the feet. **3. go to the dogs.** Inf. to go to ruin physically or morally. **4. let sleeping dogs lie.** to leave things undisturbed.

dogsbody ('dɒgzˌbɒdɪ) n., pl. **-bodies.** Inf. a person who carries out menial tasks for others.

Dog Star n. **the.** another name for **Sirius.**

dog-tired adj. (usually postpositive) Inf. exhausted.

dogtooth violet ('dɒgˌtuːθ) n. any of a genus of plants, esp. a North American plant with yellow flowers, or a European plant with purple flowers.

dogtrot ('dɒgˌtrɒt) n. a gently paced trot.

dogwatch ('dɒgˌwɒtʃ) n. either of two two-hour watches aboard ship, from four to six p.m. or from six to eight p.m.

dogwood ('dɒgˌwʊd) n. any of various trees or shrubs, esp. a European shrub with small white flowers and black berries.

doh (dəʊ) n., pl. **dohs.** Music. (tonic sol-fa) the first degree of any major scale.

doily or **doyley** ('dɔɪlɪ) n., pl. **-lies** or **-leys.** a decorative mat of lace or lacelike paper, etc., laid on plates.

do in vb. (tr., adv.) Sl. **1.** to kill. **2.** to exhaust.

doings ('duːɪŋz) pl. n. **1.** deeds, actions, or events. **2.** Inf. anything of which the name is not known, or euphemistically left unsaid, etc.

do-it-yourself n. **a.** the hobby or process of constructing and repairing things oneself. **b.** (as modifier): a do-it-yourself kit.

doldrums ('dɒldrəmz) n. **the.** **1.** a depressed or bored state of mind. **2.** a state of inactivity or stagnation. **3.** a belt of light winds or calms along the equator.

THESAURUS

doer achiever, active person, activist, bustler, dynamo, go-getter (Inf.), live wire (Sl.), organizer, powerhouse (Sl.), wheeler-dealer (Inf.)

doff **1.** Of a hat lift, raise, remove, take off, tip, touch **2.** Of clothing cast off, discard, remove, shed, slip off, slip out of, take off, throw off, undress

dog n. **1.** bitch, canine, cur, hound, man's best friend, mongrel, mutt (Sl.), pooch (Sl.), pup, puppy, tyke **2.** Inf. beast, blackguard, cur, heel (Sl.), knave (Archaic), scoundrel, villain **3. dog-eat-dog** cutthroat, ferocious, fierce, ruthless, vicious, with no holds barred **4. go to the dogs** Inf. degenerate, deteriorate, go down the drain, go to pot, go to ruin ~v. **5.** haunt, hound, plague, pursue, shadow, tail (Inf.), track, trail, trouble

dogged determined, firm, indefatigable, obstinate, persevering, persistent, pertinacious, resolute, single-minded, staunch, steadfast, steady, stubborn, tenacious, unflagging, unshakable, unyielding

doggedness bulldog tenacity, determination, endurance, obstinacy, perseverance, persistence, pertinacity, relentlessness, resolution, single-mindedness, steadfastness, steadiness, stubbornness, tenaciousness, tenacity

dogma article, article of faith, belief, credo, creed, doctrine, opinion, precept, principle, teachings, tenet

dogmatic **1.** arbitrary, arrogant, assertive, categorical, dictatorial, doctrinaire, downright, emphatic, imperious, magisterial, obdurate, opinionated, overbearing, peremp-

tory **2.** authoritative, canonical, categorical, doctrinal, ex cathedra, oracular, positive

dogmatism arbitrariness, arrogance, dictatorialness, imperiousness, opinionatedness, peremptoriness, positiveness, presumption

dogsbody drudge, general factotum, man or maid of all work, menial, skivvy, slave

do in **1.** butcher, dispatch, eliminate (Sl.), execute, kill, liquidate, murder, slaughter, slay **2.** exhaust, fag (Inf.), fatigue, shatter (Inf.), tire, wear out, weary

doing achievement, act, action, carrying out or through, deed, execution, exploit, handiwork, implementation, performance

doings actions, affairs, concerns, dealings, deeds, events, exploits, goings-on (Inf.), handiwork, happenings, proceedings, trans-

dole ('dǝʊl) *n.* **1.** a small portion of money or food given to a poor person. **2.** the act of distributing such portions. **3.** (usually preceded by *the*) *Brit. inf.* money received from the state while out of work. **4. on the dole.** *Brit. inf.* receiving such money. **5.** *Arch.* fate. ~*vb.* **6.** (*tr.;* usually foll. by *out*) to distribute, esp. in small portions.

doleful ('dǝʊlfʊl) *adj.* dreary; mournful. —'**dolefully** *adv.* —'**dolefulness** *n.*

doll (dɒl) *n.* **1.** a small model or dummy of a human being, used as a toy. **2.** *Sl.* a pretty girl or woman of little intelligence.

dollar ('dɒlǝ) *n.* **1.** the standard monetary unit of the U.S., divided into 100 cents. **2.** the standard monetary unit, comprising 100 cents, of various other countries including: Australia, the Bahamas, Barbados, Bermuda, Canada, Guyana, Hong Kong, Jamaica, Malaysia, Singapore, and New Zealand. **3.** *Brit inf.* (formerly) five shillings.

dollop ('dɒlǝp) *n. Inf.* **1.** a semi-solid lump. **2.** a measure or serving. ~*vb.* **3.** (*tr.;* foll. by *out*) to serve out (food).

doll up *vb.* (*tr., adv.*) *Sl.* to dress in a stylish or showy manner.

dolly ('dɒlɪ) *n., pl.* **-lies. 1.** a child's word for a doll. **2.** *Films, etc.* a wheeled support on which a camera may be mounted. **3.** a cup-shaped anvil used to hold a rivet. **4.** *Cricket.* **a.** a simple catch. **b.** a full toss bowled in a slow high arc. **5.** Also called: **dolly bird.** *Sl., chiefly Brit.* an attractive and fashionable girl. ~*vb.* **-lying, -lied. 6.** *Films, etc.* to wheel (a camera) backwards or forwards on a dolly.

dolman sleeve ('dɒlmǝn) *n.* a sleeve that is very wide at the armhole and tapers to a tight wrist.

dolmen ('dɒlmɛn) *n.* a Neolithic stone formation, consisting of a horizontal stone supported by several vertical stones, and thought to be a tomb.

dolomite ('dɒlǝˌmaɪt) *n.* **1.** a mineral consisting of calcium magnesium carbonate. **2.** a rock resembling limestone but consisting principally of the mineral dolomite. —**dolomitic** (ˌdɒlǝ'mɪtɪk) *adj.*

dolos ('dɒlɒs) *n., pl.* **dolosse.** *S. African.* a knucklebone of a sheep, buck, etc., used esp. by diviners.

dolour *or U.S.* **dolor** ('dɒlǝ) *n. Poetic.* grief or sorrow.

dolphin ('dɒlfɪn) *n.* **1.** any of various marine mammals that are typically smaller than whales and larger than porpoises and have a beaklike snout. **2. river dolphin.** any of various freshwater mammals inhabiting rivers of North and South America and S Asia. **3.** either of two large marine fishes that have an iridescent coloration. **4.** *Naut.* a post or buoy for mooring a vessel.

dolphinarium (ˌdɒlfɪ'nɛǝrɪǝm) *n.* a pool or aquarium for dolphins, esp. one in which they give public displays.

dolt (dǝʊlt) *n.* a slow-witted or stupid person. —**doltish** *adj.* —'**doltishness** *n.*

-dom *suffix forming nouns.* **1.** state or condition: *freedom.* **2.** rank, office, or domain of: *earldom.* **3.** a collection of persons: *officialdom.*

domain (dǝ'meɪn) *n.* **1.** land governed by a ruler or government. **2.** land owned by one person or family. **3.** a field or scope of knowledge or activity. **4.** a region having specific characteristics. **5.** *N.Z. & Austral.* a park or recreation reserve maintained by a public authority, often the government. **6.** *Law.* the absolute ownership and right to dispose of land. **7.** *Maths.* the set of values of the independent variable of a function for which the functional value exists. **8.** *Physics.* one of the regions in a ferromagnetic solid in which all the atoms have their magnetic moments aligned in the same direction.

dome (dǝʊm) *n.* **1.** a hemispherical roof or vault. **2.** something shaped like this. **3.** a slang word for the head. ~*vb.* (*tr.*) **4.** to cover with or as if with a dome. **5.** to shape like a dome. —'**dome,like** *adj.* —**domical** ('dǝʊmɪkǝl, 'dɒm-) *adj.*

Domesday Book *or* **Doomsday Book** ('du:mz,deɪ) *n. History.* the record of a survey of the land of England carried out by the commissioners of William I in 1086.

domestic (dǝ'mɛstɪk) *adj.* **1.** of the home or family. **2.** enjoying or accustomed to home or family life. **3.** (of an animal) bred or kept by man as a pet or for purposes such as the supply of food. **4.** of one's own country or a specific country: *domestic and foreign affairs.* ~*n.* **5.** a household servant. —**do'mestically** *adv.*

domesticate (dǝ'mɛstɪˌkeɪt) *or U.S.* (*sometimes*) **domesticize** *vb.* **1.** (*tr.*) to bring or keep (wild animals or plants) under control or cultivation. **2.** (*tr.*) to accustom to home life. **3.** (*tr.*) to adapt to an environment. —**do'mesticable** *adj.* —**do,mesti'cation** *n.*

domesticity (ˌdǝʊmɛ'stɪsɪtɪ) *n., pl.* **-ties. 1.** home life. **2.** devotion to or familiarity with home life. **3.** (*usually pl.*) a domestic duty or matter.

domestic science *n.* the study of cooking, needlework, and other subjects concerned with household skills.

domicile ('dɒmɪˌsaɪl) *or* **domicil** ('dɒmɪsɪl) *n.* **1.** a dwelling place. **2.** a permanent legal residence. **3.** *Commerce, Brit.* the place where a bill of exchange is to be paid. ~*vb. also* **domiciliate** (ˌdɒmɪ'sɪlɪˌeɪt). **4.** to establish or be established in a dwelling place. —**domiciliary** (ˌdɒmɪ'sɪlɪǝrɪ) *adj.*

dominant ('dɒmɪnǝnt) *adj.* **1.** having primary authority or influence; governing; ruling. **2.** predominant or primary: *the dominant topic of the day.* **3.** occupying a commanding position. **4.** *Genetics.* (of a gene) producing the same phenotype in the organism whether its allele is identical or dissimilar. Cf. **recessive. 5.** *Music.* of or relating to the fifth degree of a scale. **6.** *Ecology.* (of a plant or animal species) more prevalent than any other species and determining the appearance and composition of the community. ~*n.* **7.** *Genetics.* a dominant gene. **8.** *Music.* **a.** the fifth degree of a scale. **b.** a key or chord based on this. **9.** *Ecology.* a dominant plant or animal in a community. —'**dominance** *n.* —'**dominantly** *adv.*

dominate ('dɒmɪˌneɪt) *vb.* **1.** to control, rule, or govern. **2.** to tower above (surroundings, etc.). **3.** (*tr.;* usually *passive*) to predominate in. —,**domi'nation** *n.*

dominee ('du:mɪnɪ, 'dʊǝ-) *n.* (in South Africa) a minister in any of the Afrikaner Churches.

domineer (ˌdɒmɪ'nɪǝ) *vb.* (*intr.,* often foll. by *over*) to act with arrogance or tyranny; behave imperiously. —,**domi'neering** *adj.* —,**domi'neeringly** *adv.*

THESAURUS

actions

doldrums apathy, blues, boredom, depression, dullness, dumps (*Inf.*), ennui, gloom, inertia, lassitude, listlessness, malaise, stagnation, tedium, torpor

dole *n.* **1.** allowance, alms, benefit, donation, gift, grant, gratuity, modicum, parcel, pittance, portion, quota, share **2.** allocation, allotment, apportionment, dispensation, distribution, division ~*v.* **3.** *Usually with* **out** administer, allocate, allot, apportion, assign, deal, dispense, distribute, divide, give, hand out, mete, share

dolt ass, blockhead, booby, chump (*Inf.*), clot (*Sl.*), dimwit (*Inf.*), dope (*Sl.*), dullard, dunce, fool, idiot, ignoramus, nitwit, simpleton, thickhead

domestic *adj.* **1.** domiciliary, family, home, household, private **2.** domesticated, home-loving, homely, housewifely, stay-at-home **3.** domesticated, house, house-trained, pet, tame, trained **4.** indigenous, internal, native, not foreign ~*n.* **5.** char (*Inf.*), charwoman, daily, daily help, help, maid, servant, woman (*Inf.*)

domesticate **1.** break, gentle, housetrain, tame, train **2.** acclimatize, accustom, familiarize, habituate, naturalize

domesticated 1. *Of plants or animals* broken (in), naturalized, tame, tamed **2.** *Of people* domestic, home-loving, homely, house-trained (*Jocular*), housewifely

dominant 1. ascendant, assertive, authoritative, commanding, controlling, governing, leading, presiding, ruling, superior, supreme **2.** chief, influential, main, outstanding, paramount, predominant, pre-eminent, prevailing, prevalent, primary, principal, prominent

dominate 1. control, direct, domineer, govern, have the upper hand over, have the whip hand over, keep under one's thumb, lead, lead by the nose (*Inf.*), master, monopolize, overbear, rule, tyrannize **2.** be-

stride, loom over, overlook, stand head and shoulders above, stand over, survey, tower above **3.** detract from, eclipse, outshine, overrule, overshadow, predominate, prevail over

domination 1. ascendancy, authority, command, control, influence, mastery, power, rule, superiority, supremacy, sway **2.** despotism, dictatorship, oppression, repression, subjection, subordination, suppression, tyranny

domineer bluster, boss around *or* about (*Inf.*), browbeat, bully, hector, intimidate, lord (it) over, menace, overbear, ride roughshod over, swagger, threaten, tyrannize

domineering arrogant, authoritarian, autocratic, bossy (*Inf.*), coercive, despotic, dictatorial, high-handed, imperious, ironhanded, magisterial, masterful, oppressive, overbearing, tyrannical

Dominican[1] (dəˈmɪnɪkən) n. **1. a.** a member of an order of preaching friars founded by Saint Dominic in 1215; a Blackfriar. **b.** a nun of one of the orders founded under his patronage. ~adj. **2.** of Saint Dominic or the Dominican order.

Dominican[2] (dəˈmɪnɪkən) adj. **1.** of or relating to the Dominican Republic. ~n. **2.** a native or inhabitant of the Dominican Republic.

dominion (dəˈmɪnjən) n. **1.** rule; authority. **2.** the land governed by one ruler or government. **3.** sphere of influence; area of control. **4.** a name formerly applied to self-governing divisions of the British Empire.

Dominion Day n. another name for **Canada Day.**

domino[1] (ˈdɒmɪˌnəʊ) n., pl. **-noes.** a small rectangular block marked with dots, used in dominoes.

domino[2] (ˈdɒmɪˌnəʊ) n., pl. **-noes** or **-nos.** **1.** a large hooded cloak worn with an eye mask at a masquerade. **2.** the eye mask worn with such a cloak.

dominoes (ˈdɒmɪˌnəʊz) n. (functioning as sing.) any of several games in which dominoes with matching halves are laid together.

domino theory n. the theory that an event in one place will influence the occurrence of similar events elsewhere, esp. that a Communist takeover of one country will lead to Communist takeovers in all the neighbouring states.

don[1] (dɒn) vb. **donning, donned.** (tr.) to put on (clothing).

don[2] (dɒn) n. **1.** Brit. a member of the teaching staff at a university or college, esp. at Oxford or Cambridge. **2.** the head of a student dormitory at certain Canadian universities and colleges. **3.** a Spanish gentleman or nobleman. **4.** Arch. a person of rank. **5.** Austral. inf. an expert.

Don (dɒn) n. a Spanish title equivalent to Mr.

Doña (ˈdɒnja) n. a Spanish title of address equivalent to Mrs. or Madam.

donate (dəʊˈneɪt) vb. to give (money, time, etc.), esp. to a charity. —**doˈnator** n.

donation (dəʊˈneɪʃən) n. **1.** the act of donating. **2.** a contribution.

donder (ˈdɒndə) S. African sl. ~vb. **1.** (tr.) to beat someone up. ~n. **2.** a wretch; swine.

done (dʌn) vb. **1.** the past participle of **do**[1]. **2. be or have done with.** to end relations with. **3. have done.** to be completely finished: have you done? ~interj. **4.** an expression of agreement, as on the settlement of a bargain. ~adj. **5.** completed. **6.** cooked enough. **7.** used up. **8.** socially acceptable. **9.** Inf. cheated; tricked. **10. done for. a.** dead or almost dead. **b.** in serious difficulty. **11. done in** or **up.** Inf. exhausted.

dong (dɒŋ) n. **1.** an imitation of the sound of a bell. ~vb. **2.** (intr.) to make such a sound.

donga (ˈdɒŋgə) n. S. African & Austral. a steep-sided gully created by soil erosion.

donjon (ˈdʌndʒən, ˈdɒn-) n. the heavily fortified central tower or keep of a medieval castle. Also: **dungeon.**

Don Juan (dɒn ˈdʒuːən) n. **1.** a legendary Spanish nobleman and philanderer: hero of many poems, plays, and operas. **2.** a successful seducer of women.

donkey (ˈdɒŋkɪ) n. **1.** a long-eared member of the horse family. **2.** a person who is considered to be stupid or stubborn. **3.** (modifier) auxiliary: a donkey engine. **4. talk the hind leg(s) off a donkey.** to talk endlessly.

donkey jacket n. a short thick jacket, often worn by workmen.

donkey's years n. Inf. a long time.

donkey-work n. **a.** groundwork. **b.** drudgery.

Donna (ˈdɒnə) n. an Italian title of address equivalent to Madam.

donnish (ˈdɒnɪʃ) adj. of or resembling a university don, esp. denoting pedantry or fussiness. —**ˈdonnishness** n.

donor (ˈdəʊnə) n. **1.** a person who makes a donation. **2.** Med. any person who gives blood, organs, etc., for use in the treatment of another person. **3.** the atom supplying both electrons in a coordinate bond.

Don Quixote (ˈdɒn kiːˈhəʊtiː, ˈkwɪksət) n. an impractical idealist.

doodah (ˈduːdɑː) or U.S. **doodad** (ˈduːdæd) n. Inf. an unnamed thing, esp. an object the name of which is unknown or forgotten.

doodle (ˈduːdəl) Inf. ~vb. **1.** to scribble or draw aimlessly. **2.** to play or improvise idly. **3.** (intr.; often foll. by away) U.S. to dawdle or waste time. ~n. **4.** a shape, picture, etc., drawn aimlessly. —**ˈdoodler** n.

doodlebug (ˈduːdəlˌbʌg) n. **1.** a robot bomb invented by the Germans in World War II: used esp. to bombard London. Also called: **V-1, buzzbomb. 2.** a diviner's rod.

doom (duːm) n. **1.** death or a terrible fate. **2.** a judgment. **3.** (sometimes cap.) another term for the **Last Judgment.** ~vb. **4.** (tr.) to destine or condemn to death or a terrible fate.

doomsday or **domesday** (ˈduːmzˌdeɪ) n. **1.** (sometimes cap.) the day on which the Last Judgment will occur. **2.** any day of reckoning.

door (dɔː) n. **1.** a hinged or sliding panel for closing the entrance to a room, cupboard, etc. **2.** a doorway or entrance. **3.** a means of access or escape: a door to success. **4. lay at someone's door.** to lay (the blame or responsibility) on someone. **5. out of doors.** in or into the open air. **6. show someone the door.** to order someone to leave.

doorjamb (ˈdɔːˌdʒæm) n. one of the two vertical members forming the sides of a doorframe. Also called: **doorpost.**

doorman (ˈdɔːˌmæn, -mən) n., pl. **-men.** a man employed to attend the doors of certain buildings.

doormat (ˈdɔːˌmæt) n. **1.** a mat, placed at an entrance, for wiping dirt from shoes. **2.** Sl. a person who offers little resistance to ill-treatment.

doorstep (ˈdɔːˌstɛp) n. **1.** a step in front of a door. **2.** Sl. a thick slice of bread.

doorstop (ˈdɔːˌstɒp) n. any device which prevents an open door from moving.

door to door adj. (door-to-door when prenominal), adv. **1.** (of selling, etc.) from one house to the next. **2.** (of journeys, etc.) direct.

doorway (ˈdɔːˌweɪ) n. **1.** an opening into a building, room, etc., esp. one that has a door. **2.** a means of access or escape: a doorway to freedom.

dop (dɒp) n. S. African sl. **1.** Cape brandy. **2.** a tot of this.

THESAURUS

dominion 1. ascendancy, authority, command, control, domination, government, jurisdiction, mastery, power, rule, sovereignty, supremacy, sway **2.** country, domain, empire, kingdom, province, realm, region, territory

don clothe oneself in, dress in, get into, pull on, put on, slip on or into

donate bequeath, bestow, chip in (Inf.), contribute, gift, give, make a gift of, present, subscribe

donation alms, benefaction, boon, contribution, gift, grant, gratuity, largess, offering, present, subscription

done adj. **1.** accomplished, completed, concluded, consummated, ended, executed, finished, over, perfected, realized, terminated, through **2.** cooked, cooked enough, cooked sufficiently, cooked to a turn, ready **3.** depleted, exhausted, finished, spent, used up **4.** acceptable, conventional, de rigueur, proper **5.**

Inf. cheated, conned (Sl.), duped, taken for a ride (Inf.), tricked ~interj. **6.** agreed, it's a bargain, O.K. (Inf.), settled, you're on (Inf.) **7.** done for Inf. beaten, broken, dashed, defeated, destroyed, doomed, finished, foiled, lost, ruined, undone, wrecked **8.** done in or up Inf. all in (Sl.), bushed (Inf.), dead (Inf.), dead beat (Inf.), dog-tired (Inf.), exhausted, fagged out (Inf.), knackered (Sl.), on one's last legs, ready to drop, tired out, worn out, worn to a frazzle (Inf.) **9.** have done with be through with, desist, end relations with, finish with, give up, throw over, wash one's hands of

donnish bookish, erudite, formalistic, pedagogic, pedantic, precise, scholarly, scholastic

donor almsgiver, benefactor, contributor, donator, giver, grantor (Law), philanthropist

doom n. **1.** catastrophe, death, destiny, destruction, downfall, fate, fortune, lot, portion, ruin **2.** condemnation, decision, decree, judg-

ment, sentence, verdict **3.** Armageddon, Doomsday, end of the world, Judgment Day, the Last Day, the Last Judgment, the last trump ~v. **4.** condemn, consign, damn, decree, destine, foreordain, judge, predestine, sentence, threaten

doomed bedevilled, bewitched, condemned, cursed, fated, hopeless, ill-fated, ill-omened, luckless, star-crossed

door 1. doorway, egress, entrance, entry, exit, ingress, opening **2. lay at the door of** blame, censure, charge, hold responsible, impute to **3. out of doors** alfresco, in the air, out, outdoors, outside **4. show someone the door** ask to leave, boot out (Inf.), bounce (Sl.), eject, oust, show out

do out of balk, bilk, cheat, con (Sl.), deprive, diddle (Inf.), swindle, trick

dope (dəup) n. **1.** any of a number of preparations applied to fabric in order to improve strength, tautness, etc. **2.** an additive, such as an antiknock compound added to petrol. **3.** a thick liquid, such as a lubricant, applied to a surface. **4.** a combustible absorbent material used to hold the nitroglycerine in dynamite. **5.** Sl. any illegal drug. **6.** a drug administered to a racehorse or greyhound to affect its performance. **7.** Sl. a stupid or slow-witted person. **8.** Sl. news or facts, esp. confidential information. ~vb. (tr.) **9.** Electronics. to add impurities to (a semiconductor) in order to produce or modify its properties. **10.** to apply or add dope to. **11.** Sl. to administer a drug to (oneself or another).

dopey or **dopy** ('dəupɪ) adj. **dopier, dopiest.** Sl. **1.** silly. **2.** under the influence of a drug.

doppelgänger ('dɒpl,gɛŋə) n. Legend. a ghostly duplicate of a living person.

Doppler effect ('dɒplə) n. a change in the apparent frequency of a sound or light wave, etc., as a result of relative motion between the observer and the source. Also called: **Doppler shift.**

Doric ('dɒrɪk) adj. **1.** of the inhabitants of Doris in ancient Greece or their dialect. **2.** of or denoting one of the five classical orders of architecture: characterized by a heavy fluted column and a simple capital. **3.** (sometimes not cap.) rustic. ~n. **4.** one of four chief dialects of Ancient Greek.

dormant ('dɔːmənt) adj. **1.** quiet and inactive, as during sleep. **2.** latent or inoperative. **3.** (of a volcano) neither extinct nor erupting. **4.** Biol. alive but in a resting condition with reduced metabolism. **5.** (usually postpositive) Heraldry. (of a beast) in a sleeping position. —'dormancy n.

dormer ('dɔːmə) n. a construction with a gable roof and a window that projects from a sloping roof. Also called: **dormer window.**

dormitory ('dɔːmɪtərɪ, -trɪ) n., pl. **-ries. 1.** a large room, esp. at a school, containing several beds. **2.** U.S. a building, esp. at a college or camp, providing living and sleeping accommodation. **3.** (modifier) Brit. denoting or relating to an area from which most of the residents commute to work (esp. in **dormitory suburb**).

Dormobile ('dɔːməu,biːl) n. Trademark. a vanlike vehicle specially equipped for living in while travelling.

dormouse ('dɔː,maus) n., pl. **-mice.** a small Eurasian rodent resembling a mouse with a furry tail.

dorp (dɔːp) n. S. African. a small town or village.

dorsal ('dɔːsəl) adj. Anat., zool. relating to the back or spinal part of the body. —'dorsally adv.

dory ('dɔːrɪ) n., pl. **-ries.** any of various spiny-finned food fishes, esp. the John Dory.

dose (dəus) n. **1.** Med. a specific quantity of a therapeutic drug or agent taken at any one time or at specified intervals. **2.** Inf. something unpleasant to experience: a dose of influenza. **3.** Also called: **dosage.** the total energy of ionizing radiation absorbed by unit mass of material, esp. of living tissue; usually measured in rads. **4.** Also called: **dosage.** a small amount of syrup added to wine during bottling. **5.** Sl. a venereal infection. **6. like a dose of salts.** very quickly. ~vb. (tr.) **7.** to administer a dose to (someone). **8.** Med. to prescribe (a drug) in appropriate quantities. **9.** to add syrup to (wine) during bottling. —'dosage n.

doss (dɒs) Brit. sl. ~vb. **1.** (intr.; often foll. by down) to sleep, esp. in a dosshouse. ~n. **2.** a bed, esp. in a dosshouse. **3.** a slang word for sleep. **4.** short for dosshouse. —'dosser n.

dosshouse ('dɒs,haus) n. Brit. sl. a cheap lodging house, esp. one used by tramps. U.S. name: **flophouse.**

dossier ('dɒsɪ,eɪ) n. a collection of papers about a subject or person.

dot (dɒt) n. **1.** a small round mark; spot; point. **2.** anything resembling a dot; a small amount. **3.** the mark (˙) above the letters i, j. **4.** Music. **a.** the symbol (.) placed after a note or rest to increase its time value by half. **b.** this symbol written above or below a note indicating staccato. **5.** Maths., logic. **a.** the symbol (.) indicating multiplication or logical conjunction. **b.** a decimal point. **6.** the symbol (·) used, in combination with the symbol for dash (—), in Morse and other codes. **7. the year dot.** Inf. as long ago as can be remembered. **8. on the dot.** at exactly the arranged time. ~vb. **dotting, dotted. 9.** (tr.) to mark or form with a dot. **10.** (tr.) to scatter or intersperse (as with dots): bushes dotting the plain. **11.** (intr.) to make a dot or dots. **12. dot one's i's and cross one's t's.** Inf. to be meticulous. —'dotter n.

dotage ('dəutɪdʒ) n. **1.** feebleness of mind, esp. as a result of old age. **2.** foolish infatuation.

dotard ('dəutəd) n. a person who is weak-minded, esp. through senility. —'dotardly adv.

dote (dəut) vb. (intr.) **1.** (foll. by on or upon) to love to an excessive or foolish degree. **2.** to be foolish or weak-minded, esp. as a result of old age. —'doter n.

dotterel or **dottrel** ('dɒtrəl) n. **1.** a rare Eurasian plover with white bands around the head and neck. **2.** Brit. dialect. a person who is foolish or easily duped.

dottle ('dɒtl) n. the plug of tobacco left in a pipe after smoking.

dotty ('dɒtɪ) adj. **-tier, tiest. 1.** Sl., chiefly Brit. feebleminded; slightly crazy. **2.** Brit. sl. (foll. by about) extremely fond (of) **3.** marked with dots. —'dottily adv. —'dottiness n.

double ('dʌbl) adj. (usually prenominal) **1.** as much again in size, strength, number, etc.: a double portion. **2.** composed of two equal or similar parts. **3.** designed for two users: a double room. **4.** folded in two; composed of two layers. **5.** stooping; bent over. **6.** having two aspects; ambiguous: a double meaning. **7.** false, deceitful, or hypocritical: a double life. **8.** (of flowers) having more than the normal number of petals. **9.** Music. **a.** (of an instrument) sounding an octave lower: a double bass. **b.** (of time) duple. ~adv. **10.** twice over; twofold. **11.** two together; two at a time (esp. in **see double**). ~n. **12.** twice the number, amount, size, etc. **13.** Inf. a double measure of spirits. **14.** a duplicate or counterpart, esp. a person who closely resembles another; understudy. **15.** a ghostly apparition of a living person; Doppelgänger. **16.** a sharp turn, esp. a return on one's own tracks. **17.** Bridge. a call that increases certain scoring points if the last preceding bid becomes the contract. **18.** Billiards, etc. a strike in which the object ball is struck so as to make it rebound against the cushion to an opposite pocket. **19.** a bet on two horses in different races in which any winnings from the first race are placed on the horse in the later race. **20. a.** the narrow outermost ring on a dartboard. **b.** a hit on this ring. **21. at or on the double. a.** at twice normal marching speed. **b.** quickly or immediately. ~vb. **22.** to make or become twice as much. **23.** to bend or fold (material, etc.). **24.** (tr.; sometimes foll. by up) to clench (a fist). **25.** (tr.; often foll. by together or up) to join or couple. **26.** (tr.) to repeat exactly; copy. **27.** (intr.) to play two parts or serve two roles. **28.** (intr.) to turn sharply; follow a winding course. **29.** Naut. to sail around (a headland or other point). **30.** Music. **a.** to duplicate (a part) either in unison or at the octave above or below it. **b.** (intr.; usually foll. by on) to be capable of performing (upon an additional instrument). **31.** Bridge. to make a call that will double certain scoring points if the preceding bid becomes the contract. **32.** Billiards, etc. to cause (a ball) to rebound or (of a ball) to rebound. **33.** (intr.; foll. by for) to act as substitute. **34.** (intr.) to go or march at twice the normal speed. ~See also **doubles.** —'doubler n.

THESAURUS

dope n. **1.** drugs, narcotic, opiate **2.** blockhead, dimwit (Inf.), dolt, dunce, fool, idiot, simpleton **3.** details, facts, gen (Inf.), info (Inf.), information, inside information, lowdown (Inf.), news, tip ~v. **4.** anaesthetize, doctor, drug, inject, knock out, narcotize, sedate, stupefy

dormant asleep, comatose, fallow, hibernating, inactive, inert, inoperative, latent, quiescent, sleeping, sluggish, slumbering, suspended, torpid

dose dosage, draught, drench, measure, portion, potion, prescription, quantity

dot n. **1.** atom, circle, dab, fleck, full stop, iota, jot, mark, mite, mote, point, speck, spot **2. on the dot** exactly, on time, precisely, promptly, punctually, to the minute ~v. **3.** dab, dabble, fleck, spot, sprinkle, stipple, stud

dotage 1. decrepitude, feebleness, imbecility, old age, second childhood, senility, weakness **2.** doting, foolish fondness, infatuation

dote on or **upon** admire, adore, hold dear, idolize, lavish affection on, prize, treasure

doting adoring, devoted, fond, foolish, indulgent, lovesick

double adj. **1.** binate (Botany), coupled, doubled, dual, duplicate, in pairs, paired, twice, twin, twofold **2.** deceitful, dishonest, false, hypocritical, insincere, Janus-faced, knavish (Archaic), perfidious, treacherous,

double agent *n.* a spy employed by two mutually antagonistic countries, companies, etc.

double-barrelled *or U.S.* **-barreled** *adj.* **1.** (of a gun) having two barrels. **2.** extremely forceful. **3.** *Brit.* (of surnames) having two or more hyphenated parts. **4.** serving two purposes; ambiguous: *a double-barrelled remark.*

double bass (beɪs) *n.* **1.** Also called (U.S.): **bass viol.** a stringed instrument, the largest and lowest member of the violin family with a range of almost three octaves. Informal name: **bass fiddle.** ~*adj.* **double-bass. 2.** of an instrument whose pitch lies below the bass; contrabass.

double-breasted *adj.* (of a garment) having overlapping fronts.

double-check *vb.* **1.** to check again; verify. ~*n.* **double check. 2.** a second examination or verification. **3.** *Chess.* a simultaneous check from two pieces.

double chin *n.* a fold of fat under the chin. —ˌdouble-ˈchinned *adj.*

double cream *n.* thick cream with a high fat content.

double-cross *Inf.* ~*vb.* **1.** (*tr.*) to cheat or betray. ~*n.* **2.** the act or an instance of double-crossing; betrayal. —ˈdouble-ˈcrosser *n.*

double-dealing *n.* **a.** action characterized by treachery or deceit. **b.** (*as modifier*): *double-dealing treachery.* —ˈdouble-ˈdealer *n.*

double-decker *n.* **1.** *Chiefly Brit.* a bus with two passenger decks. **2.** *Inf., chiefly U.S.* **a.** a thing or structure having two decks, layers, etc. **b.** (*as modifier*): *a double-decker sandwich.*

double Dutch *n. Brit. inf.* incomprehensible talk; gibberish.

double-edged *adj.* **1.** acting in two ways. **2.** (of a remark, etc.) having two possible interpretations, esp. applicable both for and against. **3.** (of a knife, etc.) having a cutting edge on either side of the blade.

double entendre (ˈdʌbəl ɑːnˈtɑːndrə) *n.* **1.** a word, phrase, etc., that can be interpreted in two ways, esp. one having one meaning that is indelicate. **2.** the type of humour that depends upon this.

double entry *n.* **a.** a book-keeping system in which any commercial transaction is entered as a debit in one account and as a credit in another. **b.** (*as modifier*): *double-entry book-keeping.*

double glazing *n.* **1.** two panes of glass in a window, fitted to reduce heat loss, etc. **2.** the fitting of glass in such a manner.

double-jointed *adj.* having unusually flexible joints permitting an abnormal degree of motion.

double knitting *n.* knitting wool of medium thickness.

double pneumonia *n.* pneumonia affecting both lungs.

double-quick *adj.* **1.** very quick; rapid. ~*adv.* **2.** in a very quick or rapid manner.

doubles (ˈdʌbəlz) *n.* **a.** a game between two pairs of players. **b.** (*as modifier*): *a doubles match.*

double standard *n.* a set of principles that allows greater freedom to one person or group than to another.

doublet (ˈdʌblɪt) *n.* **1.** (formerly) a man's close-fitting jacket, with or without sleeves (esp. in **doublet and hose**). **2. a.** a pair of similar things, esp. two words deriving ultimately from the same source. **b.** one of such a pair. **3.** *Jewellery.* a false gem made by welding or fusing stones together. **4.** *Physics.* a closely spaced pair of related spectral lines. **5.** (*in pl.*) two dice each showing the same number of spots on one throw.

double take *n.* (esp. in comedy) a delayed reaction by a person to a remark, situation, etc.

double talk *n.* **1.** rapid speech with a mixture of nonsense syllables and real words; gibberish. **2.** empty, deceptive, or ambiguous talk.

doublethink (ˈdʌbəlˌθɪŋk) *n.* deliberate, perverse, or unconscious acceptance or promulgation of conflicting facts, principles, etc.

double time *n.* **1.** a doubled wage rate, paid for working on public holidays, etc. **2.** *Music.* two beats per bar. **3.** *U.S. Army.* **a.** a fast march. **b.** a slow running pace, keeping in step.

doubloon (dʌˈbluːn) *n.* **1.** a former Spanish gold coin. **2.** (*pl.*) *Sl.* money.

doubly (ˈdʌblɪ) *adv.* **1.** to or in a double degree, quantity, or measure. **2.** in two ways.

doubt (daʊt) *n.* **1.** uncertainty about the truth, fact, or existence of something (esp. in **in doubt, without doubt,** etc.). **2.** (*often pl.*) lack of belief in or conviction about something. **3.** an unresolved difficulty, point, etc. **4.** *Obs.* fear. **5. give (someone) the benefit of the doubt.** to presume (someone suspected of guilt) innocent. **6. no doubt.** almost certainly. ~*vb.* **7.** (*tr.; may take a clause as object*) to be inclined to disbelieve. **8.** (*tr.*) to distrust or be suspicious of. **9.** (*intr.*) to feel uncertainty or be undecided. **10.** (*tr.*) *Arch.* to fear. —ˈdoubtable *adj.* —ˈdoubter *n.* —ˈdoubtingly *adv.*

▷ **Usage.** Where a clause follows *doubt* in a positive statement, the conjunction may be *whether, that,* or *if.* *Whether* (I doubt whether he is there) is universally accepted; *that* (I doubt that he is there) is less widely accepted and *if* (I doubt if he is there) is usually restricted to informal contexts. In negative statements, *doubt* is followed by *that: I do not doubt that he is telling the truth.* In such sentences, *but* (I do not doubt but that he is telling the truth) is redundant.

doubtful (ˈdaʊtful) *adj.* **1.** unlikely; improbable. **2.** uncertain: *a doubtful answer.* **3.** unsettled; unresolved. **4.** of questionable reputation or morality. **5.** having reservations or misgivings. —ˈdoubtfully *adv.* —ˈdoubtfulness *n.*

doubtless (ˈdaʊtlɪs) *adv. also* **doubtlessly.** *sentence substitute or sentence modifier.* **1.** certainly. **2.** probably. ~*adj.* **3.** certain; assured. —ˈdoubtlessness *n.*

douche (duːʃ) *n.* **1.** a stream of water directed onto or into the body for cleansing or medical purposes. **2.** the application of such a stream of water. **3.** an instrument for applying a douche. ~*vb.* **4.** to cleanse or treat or be cleansed or treated by means of a douche.

dough (dəʊ) *n.* **1.** a thick mixture of flour or meal and water or milk, used for making bread, pastry, etc. **2.** any similar pasty mass. **3.** *Chiefly U.S.* a slang word for money. —ˈdoughy *adj.*

doughnut (ˈdəʊnʌt) *n.* **1.** a small cake of sweetened dough, often ring-shaped, cooked in hot fat. **2.** anything shaped like a ring, such as the reaction vessel of a ther-

---

THESAURUS

two-faced, vacillating ~*v.* **3.** duplicate, enlarge, fold, grow, increase, magnify, multiply, plait, repeat ~*n.* **4.** clone, copy, counterpart, dead ringer (*Sl.*), Doppelgänger, duplicate, fellow, impersonator, lookalike, mate, replica, ringer (*Sl.*), spitting image (*Inf.*), twin **5. at** *or* **on the double** at full speed, briskly, immediately, in double-quick time, p.d.q. (*Sl.*), posthaste, quickly, without delay

double-cross betray, cheat, defraud, hoodwink, mislead, swindle, trick, two-time (*Inf.*)

double-dealer betrayer, cheat, con man (*Inf.*), deceiver, dissembler, double-crosser (*Inf.*), fraud, hypocrite, rogue, swindler, traitor, two-timer (*Inf.*)

double-dealing 1. *n.* bad faith, betrayal, cheating, deceit, deception, dishonesty, duplicity, foul play, hypocrisy, mendacity, perfidy, treachery, trickery, two-timing (*Inf.*) **2.** *adj.* cheating, crooked (*Inf.*), deceit-

ful, dishonest, duplicitous, fraudulent, hypocritical, lying, perfidious, sneaky, swindling, treacherous, tricky, two-faced, two-timing (*Inf.*), underhanded, untrustworthy, wily

double entendre ambiguity, double meaning, innuendo, play on words, pun

doubt *v.* **1.** discredit, distrust, fear, lack confidence in, misgive, mistrust, query, question, suspect ~*n.* **2.** apprehension, disquiet, distrust, fear, incredulity, lack of faith, misgiving, mistrust, qualm, scepticism, suspicion ~*v.* **3.** be dubious, be uncertain, demur, fluctuate, hesitate, scruple, vacillate, waver ~*n.* **4.** dubiety, hesitancy, hesitation, indecision, irresolution, lack of conviction, suspense, uncertainty, vacillation **5.** ambiguity, confusion, difficulty, dilemma, perplexity, problem, quandary **6. no doubt** admittedly, assuredly, certainly, doubtless, doubtlessly, probably, surely

doubter agnostic, disbeliever, doubting

Thomas, questioner, sceptic, unbeliever

doubtful 1. ambiguous, debatable, dubious, equivocal, hazardous, inconclusive, indefinite, indeterminate, obscure, precarious, problematic, questionable, unclear, unconfirmed, unsettled, vague **2.** distrustful, hesitating, in two minds (*Inf.*), irresolute, perplexed, sceptical, suspicious, tentative, uncertain, unconvinced, undecided, unresolved, unsettled, unsure, vacillating, wavering **3.** disreputable, dubious, questionable, shady (*Inf.*), suspect, suspicious

doubtless 1. assuredly, certainly, clearly, indisputably, of course, precisely, surely, truly, undoubtedly, unquestionably, without doubt **2.** apparently, most likely, ostensibly, presumably, probably, seemingly, supposedly

monuclear reactor.

doughty ('daʊtɪ) *adj.* **-tier, -tiest.** hardy; resolute. —'**doughtily** *adv.* —'**doughtiness** *n.*

Douglas fir, spruce, *or* **hemlock** ('dʌɡləs) *n.* a North American pyramidal coniferous tree, widely planted for ornament and for timber.

do up *vb.* (*adv.; mainly tr.*) **1.** to wrap and make into a bundle: *to do up a parcel.* **2.** to cause the downfall of (a person). **3.** to beautify or adorn. **4.** (*also intr.*) to fasten or be fastened. **5.** *Inf.* to renovate or redecorate. **6.** *Sl.* to assault.

dour (dʊə) *adj.* **1.** sullen. **2.** hard or obstinate. —'**dourly** *adv.* —'**dourness** *n.*

douse *or* **dowse** (daʊs) *vb.* **1.** to plunge or be plunged into liquid; duck. **2.** (*tr.*) to drench with water. **3.** (*tr.*) to put out (a light, candle, etc.). ∼*n.* **4.** an immersion.

dove (dʌv) *n.* **1.** any of a family of birds having a heavy body, small head, short legs, and long pointed wings. **2.** a gentle or innocent person: used as a term of endearment. **3.** *Politics.* a person opposed to war. **4.** a greyish-brown colour. —'**dove,like** *adj.*

Dove (dʌv) *n. Christianity.* **the.** a manifestation of the Holy Ghost (John 1:32).

dovecote ('dʌv,kəʊt) *or* **dovecot** ('dʌv,kɒt) *n.* a structure for housing pigeons.

dovetail ('dʌv,teɪl) *n.* **1.** a wedge-shaped tenon. **2.** Also called: **dovetail joint.** a joint containing such tenons. ∼*vb.* **3.** (*tr.*) to join by means of dovetails. **4.** to fit or cause to fit together closely or neatly.

dowager ('daʊədʒə) *n.* **1. a.** a widow possessing property or a title obtained from her husband. **b.** (*as modifier*): *the dowager duchess.* **2.** a wealthy or dignified elderly woman.

dowdy ('daʊdɪ) *adj.* **-dier, -diest. 1.** (*esp.* of a woman or a woman's dress) shabby or old-fashioned. ∼*n., pl.* **-dies. 2.** a dowdy woman. —'**dowdily** *adv.* —'**dowdiness** *n.* —'**dowdyish** *adj.*

dowel ('daʊəl) *n.* a wooden or metal peg that fits into two corresponding holes to join two adjacent parts.

dower ('daʊə) *n.* **1.** the life interest in a part of her husband's estate allotted to a widow by law. **2.** an archaic word for **dowry** (sense 1). **3.** a natural gift. ∼*vb.* **4.** (*tr.*) to endow.

dower house *n.* a house for the use of a widow, often on her deceased husband's estate.

do with *vb.* **1. could** *or* **can do with.** to find useful; benefit from. **2. have to do with.** to be involved in or connected with. **3. to do with.** concerning; related to. **4. what...do with. a.** to put or place: *what did you do with my coat?* **b.** to handle or treat. **c.** to fill one's time usefully: *she didn't know what to do with herself when the project was finished.*

do without *vb.* (*intr.*) **1.** to forgo; manage without. **2.** (*prep.*) not to require (uncalled-for comments): *we can do without your criticisms.*

down¹ (daʊn) *prep.* **1.** used to indicate movement from a higher to a lower position. **2.** at a lower or further level or position on, in, or along: *he ran down the street.* ∼*adv.* **3.** downwards; at or to a lower level or position. **4.** (*particle*) used with many verbs when the result of the verb's action is to lower or destroy its object: *knock down.* **5.** (*particle*) used with several verbs to indicate intensity or completion: *calm down.* **6.** immediate: *a*

down payment. **7.** on paper: *write this down.* **8.** arranged; scheduled. **9.** in a helpless position. **10. a.** away from a more important place. **b.** away from a more northerly place. **c.** (of a member of some British universities) away from the university. **d.** in a particular part of a country: *down south.* **11.** *Naut.* (of a helm) having the rudder to windward. **12.** reduced to a state of lack or want: *down to the last pound.* **13.** lacking a specified amount. **14.** lower in price. **15.** including all intermediate grades. **16.** from an earlier to a later time. **17.** to a finer or more concentrated state: *to grind down.* **18.** *Sport.* being a specified number of points, goals, etc. behind another competitor, team, etc. **19.** (of a person) being inactive, owing to illness: *down with flu.* **20.** (*functioning as imperative*) (to dogs, etc.): *down, Rover!* **21.** (*functioning as imperative*) **down with.** wanting the end of somebody or something: *down with the king!* ∼*adj.* **22.** (*postpositive*) depressed. **23.** (*prenominal*) of or relating to a train or trains from a more important place or one regarded as higher: *the down line.* ∼*vb.* **24.** (*tr.*) to knock, push, or pull down. **25.** (*intr.*) to go or come down. **26.** (*tr.*) *Inf.* to drink, esp. quickly. **27.** (*tr.*) to bring (someone) down, esp. by tackling. ∼*n.* **28.** a descent; downward movement. **29.** a lowering or a poor period (esp. in **ups and downs**). **30.** in Canadian football, any of a series of three attempts to advance the ball ten yards. **31. have a down on.** *Inf.* to bear ill will towards.

down² (daʊn) *n.* **1.** soft fine feathers. **2.** another name for **eiderdown** (sense 1). **3.** *Bot.* a fine coating of soft hairs, as on certain leaves, fruits, and seeds. **4.** any growth or coating of soft fine hair. —'**downy** *adj.*

down³ (daʊn) *n. Arch.* a hill, esp. a sand dune. ∼See also **downs.**

downbeat ('daʊn,biːt) *n.* **1.** *Music.* the first beat of a bar or the downward gesture of a conductor's baton indicating this. ∼*adj.* **2.** *Inf.* depressed; gloomy. **3.** *Inf.* relaxed.

downcast ('daʊn,kɑːst) *adj.* **1.** dejected. **2.** (esp. of the eyes) directed downwards. ∼*n.* **3.** *Mining.* a ventilation shaft.

downer ('daʊnə) *n. Sl.* **1.** a barbiturate or tranquillizer pill which reverses the effect of a stimulant. **2.** a depressing experience.

downfall ('daʊn,fɔːl) *n.* **1.** a sudden loss of position, health, or reputation. **2.** a fall of rain, snow, etc., esp. a sudden heavy one.

downgrade ('daʊn,ɡreɪd) *vb.* (*tr.*) **1.** to reduce in importance or value, esp. to demote (a person) to a poorer job. **2.** to speak of disparagingly. ∼*n.* **3.** *Chiefly U.S.* a downward slope. **4. on the downgrade.** waning in importance, health, etc.

downhearted (,daʊn'hɑːtɪd) *adj.* discouraged; dejected. —,**down'heartedly** *adv.*

downhill ('daʊn'hɪl) *adj.* **1.** going or sloping down. ∼*adv.* **2.** towards the bottom of a hill; downwards. **3. go downhill.** *Inf.* to decline; deteriorate. ∼*n.* **4.** the downward slope of a hill; a descent. **5.** a skiing race downhill.

Downing Street ('daʊnɪŋ) *n.* **1.** a street in W central London: official residences of the prime minister of Great Britain and the chancellor of the exchequer. **2.** *Inf.* the prime minister or the British Government.

down-market *adj.* relating to commercial products, services, etc., that are cheap, have little prestige, or are poor in quality.

THESAURUS

dour **1.** dismal, dreary, forbidding, gloomy, grim, morose, sour, sullen, unfriendly **2.** austere, hard, inflexible, obstinate, rigid, rigorous, severe, strict, uncompromising, unyielding

dovetail *v.* **1.** fit, fit together, interlock, join, link, mortise, tenon, unite **2.** accord, agree, coincide, conform, correspond, harmonize, match, tally

dowdy dingy, drab, frowzy, frumpish, frumpy, ill-dressed, old-fashioned, scrubby (*Inf.*), shabby, slovenly, tacky (*U.S. inf.*), unfashionable

dower **1.** dowry, inheritance, legacy, portion, provision, share **2.** endowment, faculty, gift, talent

do without abstain from, dispense with, forgo, get along without, give up, manage without

down *adj.* **1.** blue, dejected, depressed, disheartened, downcast, low, miserable, sad, unhappy ∼*v.* **2.** bring down, fell, floor, knock down, overthrow, prostrate, subdue, tackle, throw, trip **3.** *Inf.* drain, drink (down), gulp, put away, swallow, toss off ∼*n.* **4.** decline, descent, drop, dropping, fall, falling, reverse **5. have a down on** *Inf.* be antagonistic *or* hostile to, bear a grudge towards, be prejudiced against, be set against, feel ill will towards, have it in for (*Sl.*) **6. down with** away with, get rid of, kick out (*Inf.*), oust, push out

down and out **1.** *adj.* derelict, destitute, impoverished, penniless, ruined **2. down-and-out** *n.* beggar, derelict, dosser (*Sl.*), loser, outcast, pauper, tramp, vagabond, vagrant

downcast cheerless, crestfallen, daunted, dejected, depressed, despondent, disap-

pointed, disconsolate, discouraged, disheartened, dismayed, dispirited, miserable, sad, unhappy

downfall **1.** breakdown, collapse, comedown, comeuppance (*Sl.*), debacle, descent, destruction, disgrace, fall, overthrow, ruin, undoing **2.** cloudburst, deluge, downpour, rainstorm

downgrade **1.** degrade, demote, humble, lower *or* reduce in rank, take down a peg (*Inf.*) **2.** decry, denigrate, detract from, disparage, run down

downhearted blue, chapfallen, crestfallen, dejected, depressed, despondent, discouraged, disheartened, dismayed, dispirited, downcast, low-spirited, sad, sorrowful, unhappy

down payment *n.* the deposit paid on an item purchased on hire-purchase, mortgage, etc.

downpour ('daun‚pɔː) *n.* a heavy continuous fall of rain.

downright ('daun‚raɪt) *adj.* 1. frank or straightforward; blunt. ~*adv., adj.* (*prenominal*) 2. (intensifier): *downright rude.* —'**down,rightly** *adv.* —'**down,right-ness** *n.*

downs (daunz) *pl. n.* 1. rolling upland, esp. in the chalk areas of S Britain, characterized by lack of trees and used mainly as pasture. 2. *N.Z.* a flat grassy area, not necessarily of uplands.

Down's syndrome *n. Pathol.* another term for **mongolism.**

downstairs ('daun'stɛəz) *adv.* 1. down the stairs; to or on a lower floor. ~*n.* 2. a. a lower or ground floor. b. (*as modifier*): *a downstairs room.* 3. *Brit. inf.* the servants of a household collectively.

downstream ('daun'striːm) *adv., adj.* in or towards the lower part of a stream; with the current.

down-to-earth *adj.* sensible; practical; realistic.

downtown ('daun'taun) *n.* 1. the central or lower part of a city, esp. the main commercial area. ~*adv.* 2. towards, to, or into this area. ~*adj.* 3. of, relating to, or situated in the downtown area: *a downtown cinema.*

downtrodden ('daun‚trɒdᵊn) *adj.* 1. subjugated; oppressed. 2. trodden down.

down under *n. Inf.* Australia or New Zealand.

downward ('daunwəd) *adj.* 1. descending from a higher to a lower level, condition, position, etc. 2. descending from a beginning. ~*adv.* 3. a variant of **downwards.** —'**downwardly** *adv.*

downwards ('daunwədz) *or* **downward** *adv.* 1. from a higher to a lower place, level, etc. 2. from an earlier time or source to a later.

downwind ('daun'wɪnd) *adv., adj.* in the same direction towards which the wind is blowing; with the wind from behind.

dowry ('dauərɪ) *n., pl.* **-ries.** 1. the property brought by a woman to her husband at marriage. 2. a natural talent or gift.

dowse (dauz) *vb.* (*intr.*) to search for underground water, minerals, etc., using a divining rod; divine. —'**dows-er** *n.*

doxology (dɒk'sɒlədʒɪ) *n., pl.* **-gies.** a hymn, verse, or form of words in Christian liturgy glorifying God. —**doxological** (‚dɒksə'lɒdʒɪkᵊl) *adj.*

doyen ('dɔɪən) *n.* the senior member of a group, profession, or society. —**doyenne** (dɔɪ'ɛn) *fem. n.*

doz. *abbrev. for* dozen.

doze (dəuz) *vb.* (*intr.*) 1. to sleep lightly or intermittently. 2. (often foll. by *off*) to fall into a light sleep. ~*n.* 3. a short sleep. —'**dozer** *n.*

dozen ('dʌzᵊn) *determiner.* 1. (preceded by *a* or a numeral) twelve or a group of twelve: *two dozen oranges.* ~*n., pl.* **dozens** *or* **dozen.** 2. **daily dozen.** *Brit.* regular physical exercises. 3. **by the dozen.** in large quantities. 4. **baker's dozen.** thirteen. 5. **talk nineteen to the dozen.** to talk without stopping. —'**dozenth** *adj.*

dozy ('dəuzɪ) *adj.* **dozier, doziest.** 1. drowsy. 2. *Brit. inf.* stupid. —'**dozily** *adv.* —'**doziness** *n.*

D.P. *abbrev. for:* 1. data processing. 2. displaced person.

D.Phil, D.Ph., *or* **DPh** *abbrev. for* Doctor of Philosophy. Also: **Ph.D., PhD**

DPP *or* **D.P.P.** (in Britain) *abbrev. for* Director of Public Prosecutions.

dr *or* **dr.** *abbrev. for* dram.

Dr. *abbrev. for:* 1. Doctor. 2. Drive.

drab¹ (dræb) *adj.* **drabber, drabbest.** 1. dull; dingy. 2. cheerless; dreary. 3. of the colour drab. ~*n.* 4. a light olive-brown colour. —'**drably** *adv.* —'**drabness** *n.*

drab² (dræb) *Arch.* ~*n.* 1. a slatternly woman. 2. a whore. ~*vb.* **drabbing, drabbed.** 3. (*intr.*) to consort with prostitutes.

drachm (dræm) *n.* 1. Also called: **fluid dram.** *Brit.* one eighth of a fluid ounce. 2. *U.S.* another name for **dram** (sense 2). 3. another name for **drachma.**

drachma ('drækmə) *n., pl.* **-mas** *or* **-mae** (-miː). 1. the standard monetary unit of Greece. 2. *U.S.* another name for **dram** (sense 2). 3. a silver coin of ancient Greece.

Draconian (dreɪ'kəunɪən) *or* **Draconic** (dreɪ'kɒnɪk) *adj.* (*sometimes not cap.*) 1. of or relating to Draco (Athenian statesman, 7th century B.C.), or his code of laws. 2. harsh.

draft (drɑːft) *n.* 1. a plan, sketch, or drawing of something. 2. a preliminary outline of a book, speech, etc. 3. another word for **bill of exchange.** 4. a demand or drain on something. 5. *U.S. & Austral.* selection for compulsory military service. 6. detachment of military personnel from one unit to another. 7. *Austral. & N.Z.* a group of livestock separated from the rest of the herd or flock. ~*vb.* (*tr.*) 8. to draw up an outline or sketch for something. 9. to prepare a plan or design of. 10. to detach (military personnel) from one unit to another. 11. *U.S.* to select for compulsory military service. 12. *Austral. & N.Z.* a. to select (cattle or sheep) from a herd or flock. b. to select (farm stock) for sale. ~*n., vb.* 13. the usual U.S. spelling of **draught.** —'**drafter** *n.*

drag (dræg) *vb.* **dragging, dragged.** 1. to pull or be pulled with force, esp. along the ground. 2. (*tr.*) often foll. by *away* or *from*) to persuade to come away. 3. to trail or cause to trail on the ground. 4. (*tr.*) to move with effort or difficulty. 5. to linger behind. 6. (when *intr.*, usually foll. by *for*) to search (the bed of a river, etc.) with a dragnet or hook. 7. (often foll. by *on* or *out*) to prolong tediously: *his talk dragged on for hours.* 8. (*tr.* foll. by *out* or *from*) to crush (clods) or level (a soil surface) by use of a drag. 9. (of hounds) to follow (a fox or its trail). 10. (*intr.*) *Sl.* to draw (on a cigarette, etc.). 11. (*tr.*) *U.S. sl.* to bore or annoy. 12. **drag anchor.** (of a vessel) to move away from its mooring because the anchor has failed to hold. 13. **drag one's feet** *or* **heels.** *Inf.* to act with deliberate slowness. ~*n.* 14. the act of dragging or the state of being dragged. 15. an implement, such as a dragnet, dredge, etc., used for dragging. 16. a type of harrow used to crush clods, level soil, etc. 17. a coach with seats inside and out, usually drawn by four horses. 18. a braking device. 19. a person or thing that slows up progress. 20. slow progress or movement. 21. *Aeronautics.* the resistance to the motion of a body passing through a fluid, esp. through air. 22. the trail of scent left by a fox, etc. 23. an artificial trail of scent drawn over the ground for hounds to follow. 24. *Sl.* a person or thing that is very tedious. 25. *Sl.* a car. 26. *Sl.* short for **drag race.** 27. *Sl.* a. women's clothes worn by a man (esp. in **in drag**). b. (*as modifier*): *a drag show.* c. clothes collectively. 28. *Inf.* a draw on a cigarette, etc. 29. *U.S. sl.* influence. 30. *Chiefly U.S. sl.* a street. ~See also **drag up.**

draggle ('drægᵊl) *vb.* 1. to make or become wet or dirty by trailing on the ground; bedraggle. 2. (*intr.*) to lag; dawdle.

dragnet ('dræg‚nɛt) *n.* 1. a net used to scour the bottom of a pond, river, etc., as when searching for something. 2. any system of coordinated efforts to track

---

THESAURUS

downpour cloudburst, deluge, flood, inundation, rainstorm, torrential rain

downright 1. absolute, blatant, categorical, clear, complete, explicit, out-and-out, outright, plain, positive, simple, thoroughgoing, total, undisguised, unequivocal, unqualified, utter 2. blunt, candid, forthright, frank, honest, open, outspoken, plain, sincere, straightforward, straight-from-the-shoulder

down-to-earth common-sense, hard-headed, matter-of-fact, mundane, no-nonsense, plain-spoken, practical, realistic, sane, sensible, unsentimental

downward *adj.* declining, descending,

earthward, heading down, sliding, slipping

doze 1. *v.* catnap, drop off (*Inf.*), drowse, kip (*Sl.*), nap, nod, nod off (*Inf.*), sleep, sleep lightly, slumber, snooze (*Inf.*), zizz (*Inf.*) 2. *n.* catnap, forty winks (*Inf.*), kip (*Sl.*), little sleep, nap, shuteye (*Sl.*), siesta, snooze (*Inf.*)

drab cheerless, colourless, dingy, dismal, dreary, dull, flat, gloomy, grey, lacklustre, shabby, sombre, uninspired, vapid

draft *v.* 1. compose, delineate, design, draw, draw up, formulate, outline, plan, sketch ~*n.* 2. abstract, delineation, outline, plan, preliminary form, rough, sketch, version 3. bill (*of exchange*), cheque, order, postal order

drag *v.* 1. draw, hale, haul, lug, pull, tow, trail, tug, yank 2. crawl, creep, go slowly, inch, limp along, shamble, shuffle 3. dawdle, draggle, lag behind, linger, loiter, straggle, trail behind 4. *With* **on** *or* **out** draw out, extend, keep going, lengthen, persist, prolong, protract, spin out, stretch out 5. **drag one's feet** *Inf.* block, hold back, obstruct, procrastinate, stall ~*n.* 6. *Sl.* annoyance, bore, bother, nuisance, pain (*Inf.*), pest

dragging boring, dull, going slowly, humdrum, monotonous, tedious, tiresome, wearisome

down wanted persons.

dragoman ('drægəʊmən) *n., pl.* **-mans** *or* **-men.** (in some Middle Eastern countries, esp. formerly) a professional interpreter or guide.

dragon ('drægən) *n.* **1.** a mythical monster usually represented as breathing fire and having a scaly reptilian body, wings, claws, and a long tail. **2.** *Inf.* a fierce person, esp. a woman. **3.** any of various very large lizards, esp. the Komodo dragon.

dragonfly ('drægən,flaɪ) *n., pl.* **-flies.** a predatory insect having a long slender body and two pairs of iridescent wings that are outspread at rest.

dragoon (drə'guːn) *n.* **1.** (originally) a mounted infantryman armed with a carbine. **2.** (*sometimes cap.*) a domestic fancy pigeon. **3. a.** a type of cavalryman. **b.** (*pl.; cap. when part of a name*): *the Royal Dragoons.* ~*vb.* (*tr.*) **4.** to coerce; force. **5.** to persecute by military force.

drag race *n.* a type of motor race in which specially built or modified cars are timed over a measured course. —**drag racing** *n.*

drag up *vb.* (*tr., adv.*) *Inf.* **1.** to rear (a child) poorly and in an undisciplined manner. **2.** to introduce or revive (an unpleasant fact or story).

drain (dreɪn) *n.* **1.** a pipe or channel that carries off water, sewage, etc. **2.** an instance or cause of continuous diminution in resources or energy; depletion. **3.** *Surgery.* a device, such as a tube, to drain off pus, etc. **4. down the drain.** wasted. ~*vb.* **5.** (*tr.*; often foll. by *off*) to draw off or remove (liquid) from. **6.** (*intr.*; often foll. by *away*) to flow (away) or filter (off). **7.** (*intr.*) to dry or be emptied as a result of liquid running off or flowing away. **8.** (*tr.*) to drink the entire contents of (a glass, cup, etc.). **9.** (*tr.*) to consume or make constant demands on (resources, energy, etc.); exhaust. **10.** (*intr.*) to disappear or leave, esp. gradually. **11.** (*tr.*) (of a river, etc.) to carry off the surface water from an area. **12.** (*intr.*) (of an area) to discharge its surface water into rivers, streams, etc. —**drainer** *n.*

drainage ('dreɪnɪdʒ) *n.* **1.** the process or a method of draining. **2.** a system of watercourses or drains. **3.** liquid, sewage, etc., that is drained away.

draining board *n.* a sloping grooved surface at one side of a sink, used for draining washed dishes, etc. Also called: **drainer.**

drainpipe ('dreɪn,paɪp) *n.* a pipe for carrying off rainwater, sewage, etc.; downpipe.

drake (dreɪk) *n.* the male of any duck.

dram (dræm) *n.* **1.** one sixteenth of an ounce (avoirdupois). 1 dram is equivalent to 0.0018 kilogram. **2.** *U.S.* one eighth of an apothecaries' ounce; 60 grains. 1 dram is equivalent to 0.0039 kilogram. **3.** a small amount of an alcoholic drink, esp. a spirit; tot.

drama ('drɑːmə) *n.* **1.** a work to be performed by actors; play. **2.** the genre of literature represented by works intended for the stage. **3.** the art of the writing and production of plays. **4.** a situation that is highly emotional, tragic, or turbulent.

dramatic (drə'mætɪk) *adj.* **1.** of drama. **2.** like a drama in suddenness, emotional impact, etc. **3.** striking; effective. **4.** acting or performed in a flamboyant way. —**dra'matically** *adv.*

dramatics (drə'mætɪks) *n.* **1.** (*functioning as sing. or pl.*) the art of acting or producing plays. **2.** dramatic productions. **3.** histrionic behaviour.

dramatis personae ('drɑːmətɪs pə'səʊnaɪ) *n.* the characters in a play.

dramatist ('dræmətɪst) *n.* a playwright.

dramatize *or* **-tise** ('dræmə,taɪz) *vb.* **1.** (*tr.*) to put into dramatic form. **2.** to express (something) in a dramatic or exaggerated way. —,**dramati'zation** *or* **-i'sation** *n.*

drank (dræŋk) *vb.* the past tense of **drink.**

drape (dreɪp) *vb.* **1.** (*tr.*) to hang or cover with material or fabric, usually in folds. **2.** to hang or arrange or be hung or arranged, esp. in folds. **3.** (*tr.*) to place casually and loosely. ~*n.* **4.** (*often pl.*) a cloth or hanging that covers something in folds. **5.** the way in which fabric hangs.

draper ('dreɪpə) *n.* **1.** *Brit.* a dealer in fabrics and sewing materials. **2.** *Arch.* a maker of cloth.

drapery ('dreɪpərɪ) *n., pl.* **-peries.** **1.** fabric or clothing arranged and draped. **2.** (*often pl.*) curtains or hangings that drape. **3.** *Brit.* the occupation or shop of a draper. **4.** fabrics and cloth collectively. —'**draperied** *adj.*

drastic ('dræstɪk) *adj.* extreme or forceful; severe. —'**drastically** *adv.*

drat (dræt) *interj.* *Sl.* an exclamation of annoyance.

draught *or U.S.* **draft** (drɑːft) *n.* **1.** a current of air, esp. in an enclosed space. **2. a.** the act of pulling a load, as by a vehicle or animal. **b.** (*as modifier*): *a draught horse.* **3.** the load or quantity drawn. **4.** a portion of liquid to be drunk, esp. a dose of medicine. **5.** the act or an instance of drinking; a gulp or swallow. **6.** the act or process of drawing air, etc., into the lungs. **7.** the amount of air, etc., inhaled. **8. a.** beer, wine, etc., stored in bulk, esp. in a cask. **b.** (*as modifier*): *draught beer.* **c. on draught.** drawn from a cask or keg. **9.** any one of the flat discs used in the game of draughts. *U.S.* equivalent: **checker.** **10.** the depth of a loaded vessel in the water. **11. feel the draught.** to be short of money.

draughtboard ('drɑːft,bɔːd) *n.* a square board divided into 64 squares of alternating colours, used for playing draughts or chess.

draughts (drɑːfts) *n.* a game for two players using a draughtboard and 12 draughtsmen each. *U.S.* name: **checkers.**

draughtsman *or U.S.* **draftsman** ('drɑːftsmən) *n., pl.* **-men.** **1.** a person employed to prepare detailed scale drawings of machinery, buildings, etc. **2.** a person skilled in drawing. **3.** *Brit.* any of the flat discs used in the game of draughts. *U.S.* equivalent: **checker.** —'**draughtsman,ship** *or U.S.* '**draftsman,ship** *n.*

draughty *or U.S.* **drafty** ('drɑːftɪ) *adj.* **draughtier, draughtiest** *or U.S.* **draftier, draftiest.** characterized by or exposed to draughts of air. —'**draughtily** *or U.S.* '**draftily** *adv.* —'**draughtiness** *or U.S.* '**draftiness** *n.*

Dravidian (drə'vɪdɪən) *n.* **1.** a family of languages spoken in S and central India and Ceylon, including Tamil, Malayalam, etc. **2.** a member of one of the aboriginal races of India, pushed south by the Indo-Europeans and now mixed with them. ~*adj.* **3.** of or denoting this family of languages or these peoples.

draw (drɔː) *vb.* **drawing, drew, drawn.** **1.** to cause (a person or thing) to move towards or away by pulling. **2.** to bring, take, or pull (something) out, as from a drawer, holster, etc. **3.** (*tr.*) to extract or pull or take out: *to draw teeth.* **4.** (*tr.*; often foll. by *off*) to take (liquid) out of a cask, etc., by means of a tap. **5.** (*intr.*) to move, esp. in a specified direction: *to draw alongside.* **6.** (*tr.*) to attract: *to draw attention.* **7.** (*tr.*) to cause to flow: *to draw blood.* **8.** to depict or sketch (a figure, picture, etc.) in lines, as with a pencil or pen. **9.** (*tr.*) to make, formulate, or derive: *to draw conclusions.* **10.** (*tr.*) to write (a legal document) in proper form. **11.** (*tr.*; sometimes foll. by

---

THESAURUS

dragoon *v.* browbeat, bully, coerce, compel, constrain, drive, force, impel, intimidate, strong-arm (*Inf.*)

drain *v.* **1.** bleed, draw off, dry, empty, evacuate, milk, pump off *or* out, remove, tap, withdraw **2.** consume, deplete, dissipate, empty, exhaust, sap, strain, tax, use up, weary **3.** discharge, effuse, exude, flow out, leak, ooze, seep, trickle, well out **4.** drink up, finish, gulp down, quaff, swallow ~*n.* **5.** channel, conduit, culvert, ditch, duct, outlet, pipe, sewer, sink, trench, watercourse **6.** depletion, drag, exhaustion, expenditure, reduction, sap, strain, withdrawal **7. down the drain** gone, gone for good, lost, ruined,

wasted

drainage bilge (water), seepage, sewage, sewerage, waste

dram drop, glass, measure, shot (*Inf.*), slug, snort (*Sl.*), tot

drama **1.** dramatization, play, show, stage play, stage show, theatrical piece **2.** acting, dramatic art, dramaturgy, stagecraft, theatre, Thespian art **3.** crisis, dramatics, excitement, histrionics, scene, spectacle, theatrics, turmoil

dramatic **1.** dramaturgic, dramaturgical, theatrical, Thespian **2.** breathtaking, climactic, electrifying, emotional, exciting, melodramatic, sensational, startling, sudden, sus-

penseful, tense, thrilling **3.** affecting, effective, expressive, impressive, moving, powerful, striking, vivid

dramatist dramaturge, playwright, scriptwriter

dramatize act, exaggerate, lay it on (thick) (*Sl.*), make a performance of, overdo, overstate, play-act, play to the gallery

drastic desperate, dire, extreme, forceful, harsh, radical, severe, strong

draught **1.** *Of air* current, flow, influx, movement, puff **2.** dragging, drawing, haulage, pulling, traction **3.** cup, dose, drench, drink, potion, quantity *in*) to suck or take in (air, etc.). **12.** (*intr.*) to induce or allow a draught to carry off air, smoke, etc. **13.** (*tr.*) to take or receive from a source: *to draw money from the bank.* **14.** (*tr.*) to earn: *draw interest.* **15.** (*tr.*) to write out (a bill of exchange, etc.): *to draw a cheque.* **16.** (*tr.*) to choose at random. **17.** (*tr.*) to reduce the diameter of (a wire) by pulling it through a die. **18.** (*tr.*) to shape (metal or glass) by rolling, by pulling through a die, or by stretching. **19.** *Archery.* to bend (a bow) by pulling the string. **20.** to steep (tea) or (of tea) to steep in boiling water. **21.** (*tr.*) to disembowel. **22.** (*tr.*) to cause (pus, etc.) to discharge from an abscess or wound. **23.** (*intr.*) (of two teams, etc.) to finish a game with an equal number of points, goals, etc.; tie. **24.** (*tr.*) *Bridge, whist.* to keep leading a suit. **25. draw trumps.** *Bridge, whist.* to play the trump suit until the opponents have none left. **26.** (*tr.*) *Billiards.* to cause (the cue ball) to spin back after a direct impact with another ball. **27.** (*tr.*) to search (a place) in order to find wild animals, etc., for hunting. **28.** *Golf.* to drive (the ball) too far to the left. **29.** (*tr.*) *Naut.* (of a vessel) to require (a certain depth) in which to float. **30. draw (a) blank.** to be unsuccessful; fail. **31. draw and quarter.** to disembowel and dismember (a person) after hanging. **32. draw stumps.** *Cricket.* to close play. **33. draw the line.** *Inf.* **a.** to fix a limit. **b.** to refuse to do. **34. draw the shot.** *Bowls.* to deliver the bowl in such a way that it approaches the jack. ~*n.* **35.** the act of drawing. **36.** *U.S.* a sum of money advanced to finance anticipated expenses. **37.** *Inf.* an event, act, etc., that attracts a large audience. **38.** a raffle or lottery. **39.** something taken at random, as a ticket in a lottery. **40.** a contest or game ending in a tie. **41.** *U.S.* a small natural drainage way or gully. ~See also **drawback, draw off,** etc.

drawback ('drɔːˌbæk) *n.* **1.** a disadvantage or hindrance. **2.** a refund of certain excise duties paid on imported goods that are re-exported. ~*vb.* **draw back.** (*intr., adv.; often foll. by from*) **3.** to retreat; move backwards. **4.** to turn aside from an undertaking.

drawbridge ('drɔːˌbrɪdʒ) *n.* a bridge that may be raised to prevent access or to enable vessels to pass.

drawee (drɔː'iː) *n.* the person or organization on which an order for payment is drawn.

drawer ('drɔːə) *n.* **1.** a person or thing that draws, esp. a draughtsman. **2.** a person who draws a cheque. **3.** a person who draws up a commercial paper. **4.** *Arch.* a person who draws beer, etc., in a bar. **5.** (drɔː). a boxlike container in a chest, table, etc., made for sliding in and out.

drawers (drɔːz) *pl. n.* a legged undergarment for either sex, worn below the waist.

drawing ('drɔːɪŋ) *n.* **1.** a picture or plan made by means of lines on a surface, esp. one made with a pencil or pen. **2.** a sketch or outline. **3.** the art of making drawings; draughtsmanship.

drawing pin *n. Brit.* a short tack with a broad smooth head for fastening papers to a drawing board, etc. U.S. names: **thumbtack, pushpin.**

drawing room *n.* **1.** a room where visitors are received and entertained; living room; sitting room. **2.** *Arch.* a formal reception.

drawl (drɔːl) *vb.* **1.** to speak or utter (words) slowly, esp. prolonging the vowel sounds. ~*n.* **2.** the way of speech of someone who drawls. —'**drawler** *n.*

drawn (drɔːn) *adj.* haggard, tired, or tense in appearance.

draw off *vb.* (*adv.*) **1.** (*tr.*) to cause (a liquid) to flow from something. **2.** to withdraw (troops).

draw on *vb.* **1.** (*intr., prep.*) to use or exploit (a source, fund, etc.). **2.** (*intr., adv.*) to come near. **3.** (*tr., prep.*) to withdraw (money) from (an account). **4.** (*tr., adv.*) to put on (clothes). **5.** (*tr., adv.*) to lead further; entice.

draw out *vb.* (*adv.*) **1.** to extend. **2.** (*tr.*) to cause (a person) to talk freely. **3.** (*tr.; foll. by of*) Also: **draw from.** to elicit (information) (from). **4.** (*tr.*) to withdraw (money) as from a bank account. **5.** (*intr.*) (of hours of daylight) to become longer. **6.** (*intr.*) (of a train) to leave a station. **7.** (*tr.*) to extend (troops) in line. **8.** (*intr.*) (of troops) to proceed from camp.

draw sheet *n.* a bed sheet that can be withdrawn while the bed is occupied.

drawstring ('drɔːˌstrɪŋ) *n.* a cord, etc., run through a hem around an opening, so that when it is pulled tighter, the opening closes.

draw up *vb.* (*adv.*) **1.** to come or cause to come to a halt. **2.** (*tr.*) **a.** to prepare a draft of (a document, etc.). **b.** to formulate and write out: *to draw up a contract.* **3.** (*used reflexively*) to straighten oneself. **4.** to form or arrange (a body of soldiers, etc.) in order or formation.

dray (dreɪ) *n.* **a.** a low cart used for carrying heavy loads. **b.** (*in combination*): *a drayman.*

dread (drɛd) *vb.* (*tr.*) **1.** to anticipate with apprehension or terror. **2.** to fear greatly. **3.** *Arch.* to be in awe of. ~*n.* **4.** great fear. **5.** an object of terror. **6.** *Arch.* deep reverence.

dreadful ('drɛdful) *adj.* **1.** extremely disagreeable, shocking, or bad. **2.** (*intensifier*): *a dreadful waste of time.* **3.** causing dread; terrifying. **4.** *Arch.* inspiring awe. —'**dreadfully** *adv.*

dreadnought ('drɛdˌnɔːt) *n.* **1.** a battleship armed with heavy guns of uniform calibre. **2.** an overcoat made of heavy cloth.

dream (driːm) *n.* **1. a.** mental activity, usually an imagined series of events, occurring during sleep. **b.** (*as modifier*): *a dream sequence.* **c.** (*in combination*): *dreamland.* **2. a.** a sequence of imaginative thoughts indulged in while awake; daydream; fantasy. **b.** (*as modifier*): *a dream world.* **3.** a person or thing seen or occurring in a dream. **4.** a cherished hope; aspiration. **5.** a vain hope. **6.** a person or thing that is as pleasant or seemingly unreal as a dream. **7. go like a dream.** to move, develop, or work very well. ~*vb.* **dreaming, dreamt** or **dreamed. 8.** (*may take a clause as object*) to undergo or experience (a dream or dreams). **9.** (*intr.*) to indulge in daydreams. **10.** to suffer delusions; be unrealistic. **11.** (when *intr.*, foll. by *of* or *about*) to have an image (of) or fantasy (about) in or as if in a dream. **12.** (*intr.; foll. by of*) to consider the possibility (of). —'**dreamer** *n.*

THESAURUS

draw *v.* **1.** drag, haul, pull, tow, tug **2.** delineate, depict, design, map out, mark out, outline, paint, portray, sketch, trace **3.** deduce, derive, get, infer, make, take **4.** allure, attract, bring forth, call forth, elicit, engage, entice, evoke, induce, influence, invite, persuade **5.** extort, extract, pull out, take out **6.** attenuate, elongate, extend, lengthen, stretch **7.** breathe in, drain, inhale, inspire, puff, pull, respire, suck **8.** compose, draft, formulate, frame, prepare, write **9.** choose, pick, select, single out, take ~*n.* **10.** *Inf.* attraction, enticement, lure, pull (*Inf.*) **11.** dead heat, deadlock, stalemate, tie

drawback defect, deficiency, detriment, difficulty, disadvantage, fault, flaw, fly in the ointment (*Inf.*), handicap, hindrance, hitch, impediment, imperfection, nuisance, obstacle, snag, stumbling block, trouble

draw back recoil, retract, retreat, shrink, start back, withdraw

drawing cartoon, delineation, depiction, illustration, outline, picture, portrayal, representation, sketch, study

drawl *v. Of speech sounds* drag out, draw out, extend, lengthen, prolong, protract

drawling dragging, drawly, droning, dull, twanging, twangy

drawn fatigued, fraught, haggard, harassed, harrowed, pinched, sapped, strained, stressed, taut, tense, tired, worn

draw on employ, exploit, extract, fall back on, have recourse to, make use of, rely on, take from, use

draw out drag out, extend, lengthen, make longer, prolong, prolongate, protract, spin out, stretch, string out

draw up **1.** bring to a stop, halt, pull up, run in, stop, stop short **2.** compose, draft, formulate, frame, prepare, write out

dread **1.** *v.* anticipate with horror, cringe at, fear, have cold feet (*Inf.*), quail, shrink from, shudder, tremble **2.** *n.* affright, alarm, apprehension, aversion, awe, dismay, fear, fright, funk (*Inf.*), heebie-jeebies (*Sl.*), horror, terror, trepidation **3.** *adj.* alarming, awe-inspiring, awful, dire, dreaded, dreadful, frightening, frightful, horrible, terrible, terrifying

dreadful alarming, appalling, awful, dire, distressing, fearful, formidable, frightful, ghastly, grievous, hideous, horrendous, horrible, monstrous, shocking, terrible, tragic, tremendous

dream *n.* **1.** daydream, delusion, fantasy, hallucination, illusion, imagination, pipe dream, reverie, speculation, trance, vagary, vision **2.** ambition, aspiration, design, desire, goal, hope, notion, wish **3.** beauty, delight, gem, joy, marvel, pleasure, treasure ~*v.* **4.** build castles in the air *or* in Spain, conjure up, daydream, envisage, fancy, fantasize, hallucinate, have dreams, imagine, stargaze, think, visualize

dreamer daydreamer, Don Quixote, fantasist, fantasizer, fantast, idealist, romancer,

dream up vb. (tr., adv.) Inf. to invent by ingenuity and imagination: to dream up an excuse.

dreamy ('dri:mɪ) adj. **dreamier, dreamiest.** **1.** vague or impractical. **2.** resembling a dream. **3.** relaxing; gentle: dreamy music. **4.** Inf. wonderful. **5.** having dreams, esp. daydreams. —**'dreamily** adv. —**'dreaminess** n.

dreary ('drɪərɪ) adj. **drearier, dreariest.** **1.** sad or dull; dismal. **2.** wearying; boring. ~Also (literary): **drear.** —**'drearily** adv. —**'dreariness** n.

dredge[1] (drɛdʒ) n. **1.** a machine used to scoop or suck up material from a riverbed, channel, etc. **2.** Also called: **dredger.** a vessel used for dredging. ~vb. **3.** to remove (material) from a riverbed, etc., by means of a dredge. **4.** (tr.) to search for (a submerged object) with or as if with a dredge; drag. —**'dredger** n.

dredge[2] (drɛdʒ) vb. to sprinkle or coat (food) with flour, etc. —**'dredger** n.

dredge up vb. (tr., adv.) **1.** Inf. to bring to notice, esp. with effort and from an obscure source. **2.** to raise, as with a dredge.

dregs (drɛgz) pl. n. **1.** solid particles that settle at the bottom of some liquids. **2.** residue or remains. **3.** Brit. sl. a despicable person.

drench (drɛntʃ) vb. (tr.) **1.** to make completely wet; soak. **2.** to give liquid medicine to (an animal). ~n. **3.** a soaking. **4.** a dose of liquid medicine given to an animal.

Dresden ('drɛzdən) n. **1.** a city in East Germany. **2.** Also called: **Dresden china.** delicate and decorative porcelain ware made near Dresden. ~adj. **3.** designating or of Dresden china.

dress (drɛs) vb. **1.** to put clothes on; attire. **2.** (intr.) to put on more formal attire. **3.** (tr.) to provide (someone) with clothing; clothe. **4.** (tr.) to arrange merchandise in (a shop window). **5.** (tr.) to arrange (the hair). **6.** (tr.) to apply protective or therapeutic covering to (a wound, sore, etc.). **7.** (tr.) to prepare (food, esp. fowl and fish) by cleaning, gutting, etc. **8.** (tr.) to put a finish on (stone, metal, etc.). **9.** (tr.) to cultivate (land), esp. by applying fertilizer. **10.** (tr.) to trim (trees, etc.). **11.** (tr.) to groom (a horse). **12.** (tr.) to convert (tanned hides) into leather. **13.** Mil. to bring (troops) into line or (of troops) to come into line (esp. in **dress ranks**). **14. dress ship.** Naut. to decorate a vessel by displaying signal flags on lines. ~n. **15.** a one-piece garment for a woman, consisting of a skirt and bodice. **16.** complete style of clothing; costume: military dress. **17.** (modifier) suitable for a formal occasion: a dress shirt. **18.** outer covering or appearance. ~See also **dress down, dress up.**

dressage ('drɛsɑ:ʒ) n. **a.** the training of a horse to perform manoeuvres in response to the rider's body signals. **b.** the manoeuvres performed.

dress circle n. a tier of seats in a theatre or other auditorium, usually the first gallery.

dress down vb. (tr., adv.) Inf. to reprimand severely or scold (a person).

dresser[1] ('drɛsə) n. **1.** a set of shelves, usually also with cupboards, for storing or displaying dishes, etc. **2.** a chest of drawers for storing clothing, often having a mirror on top.

dresser[2] ('drɛsə) n. **1.** a person who dresses in a speci-

fied way: a fashionable dresser. **2.** Theatre. a person employed to assist actors with their costumes. **3.** a tool used for dressing stone, etc. **4.** Brit. a person who assists a surgeon during operations. **5.** Brit. a window-dresser.

dressing ('drɛsɪŋ) n. **1.** a sauce for food, esp. for salad. **2.** the U.S. name for **stuffing** (sense 2). **3.** a covering for a wound, etc. **4.** fertilizer spread on land. **5.** size used for stiffening textiles. **6.** the processes in the conversion of hides into leather.

dressing-down n. Inf. a severe scolding.

dressing gown n. a full robe worn before dressing or for lounging.

dressing station n. Mil. a first-aid post close to a combat area.

dressing table n. a piece of bedroom furniture with a mirror and a set of drawers for clothes, cosmetics, etc.

dressmaker ('drɛs,meɪkə) n. a person whose occupation is making clothes, esp. for women. —**'dress-,making** n.

dress rehearsal n. **1.** the last rehearsal of a play, etc., using costumes, lighting, etc., as for the first night. **2.** any full-scale practice.

dress shirt n. a man's evening shirt, worn as part of formal evening dress.

dress suit n. a man's evening suit, esp. tails.

dress up vb. (adv.) **1.** to attire (oneself or another) in one's best clothes. **2.** to put fancy dress, etc., on. **3.** (tr.) to improve the appearance or impression of: to dress up the facts.

dressy ('drɛsɪ) adj. **dressier, dressiest.** Inf. **1.** (of clothes) elegant. **2.** (of persons) dressing stylishly. **3.** overelegant. —**'dressiness** n.

drew (dru:) vb. the past tense of **draw.**

drey or **dray** (dreɪ) n. a squirrel's nest.

dribble ('drɪbəl) vb. **1.** (usually intr.) to flow or allow to flow in a thin stream or drops; trickle. **2.** (intr.) to allow saliva to trickle from the mouth. **3.** (in soccer, basketball, hockey, etc.) to propel (the ball) by repeatedly tapping it with the hand, foot, or a stick. ~n. **4.** a small quantity of liquid falling in drops or flowing in a thin stream. **5.** a small quantity or supply. **6.** an act or instance of dribbling. —**'dribbler** n. —**'dribbly** adj.

driblet or **dribblet** ('drɪblɪt) n. a small amount.

dried (draɪd) vb. the past tense or past participle of **dry.**

drier[1] ('draɪə) adj. the comparative of **dry.**

drier[2] ('draɪə) n. a variant spelling of **dryer**[1].

driest ('draɪɪst) adj. the superlative of **dry.**

drift (drɪft) vb. (mainly intr.) **1.** (also tr.) to be carried along as by currents of air or water or (of a current) to carry (a vessel, etc.) along. **2.** to move aimlessly from one place or activity to another. **3.** to wander away from a fixed course or point; stray. **4.** (also tr.) (of snow, etc.) to accumulate in heaps or to drive (snow, etc.) into heaps. ~n. **5.** something piled up by the wind or current, as a snowdrift. **6.** tendency or meaning: the drift of the argument. **7.** a state of indecision or inaction. **8.** the extent to which a vessel, aircraft, etc. is driven off course by winds, etc. **9.** a general tendency of surface ocean water to flow in the direction of the prevailing winds. **10.** a driving movement, force, or influence; impulse. **11.** a controlled four-wheel skid used to take

---

THESAURUS

theorizer, utopian, visionary

dreamland cloud-cuckoo-land, cloud-land, dream world, fairyland, fantasy, illusion, land of dreams, land of make-believe, land of Nod, never-never land (Inf.), sleep

dream up concoct, contrive, cook up (Inf.), create, devise, hatch, imagine, invent, spin, think up

dreamy **1.** fanciful, imaginary, impractical, quixotic, speculative, vague, visionary **2.** chimerical, dreamlike, fantastic, intangible, misty, phantasmagoric, phantasmagorical, shadowy, unreal **3.** absent, abstracted, daydreaming, faraway, in a reverie, musing, pensive, preoccupied, with one's head in the clouds **4.** calming, gentle, lulling, relaxing, romantic, soothing

dreary **1.** bleak, cheerless, comfortless, depressing, dismal, doleful, downcast, drear, forlorn, gloomy, glum, joyless, lonely, lonesome, melancholy, mournful, sad, solitary,

sombre, sorrowful, wretched **2.** boring, colourless, drab, dull, humdrum, lifeless, monotonous, routine, tedious, uneventful, uninteresting, wearisome

dregs **1.** deposit, draff, dross, grounds, lees, residue, residuum, scourings, scum, sediment, trash, waste **2.** Sl. canaille, down-and-outs, good-for-nothings, outcasts, rabble, ragtag and bobtail, riffraff, scum

drench **1.** drown, duck, flood, imbrue, inundate, saturate, soak, souse, steep, wet **2.** Veterinary dose, physic, purge

dress n. **1.** costume, ensemble, frock, garment, get-up (Inf.), gown, outfit, rigout (Inf.), robe, suit **2.** apparel, attire, clothes, clothing, costume, garb, garments, gear (Sl.), guise, habiliment, raiment (Archaic), togs, vestment ~v. **3.** attire, change, clothe, don, garb, put on, robe, slip on or into **4.** adorn, apparel (Archaic), array, bedeck, deck, decorate, drape, embellish, furbish, ornament, rig,

trim **5.** adjust, align, arrange, comb (out), dispose, do (up), fit, groom, prepare, set, straighten **6.** bandage, bind up, plaster, treat

dress down berate, carpet (Inf.), castigate, haul over the coals, rebuke, reprimand, reprove, scold, tear (someone) off a strip, tell off (Inf.), upbraid

dressmaker couturier, modiste, seamstress, sewing woman, tailor

dress up **1.** doll up (Sl.), dress for dinner, dress formally, put on one's best bib and tucker (Inf.), put on one's glad rags (Sl.) **2.** disguise, play-act, put on fancy dress, wear a costume **3.** beautify, embellish, gild, improve, titivate, trick out or up

dribble **1.** drip, drop, fall in drops, leak, ooze, run, seep, trickle **2.** drip saliva, drivel, drool, slaver, slobber

bends at high speed. **12.** a deposit of sand, gravel, etc., esp. one transported and deposited by a glacier. **13.** a horizontal passage in a mine that follows the mineral vein. **14.** something, esp. a group of animals, driven along. **15.** a steel tool driven into holes to enlarge or align them. **16.** an uncontrolled slow change in some operating characteristic of a piece of equipment. **17.** *S. African.* a ford.

drifter ('drɪftə) *n.* **1.** a person or thing that drifts. **2.** *Inf.* a person who moves aimlessly from place to place. **3.** a boat used for drift-net fishing.

drift net *n.* a large fishing net that is allowed to drift with the tide or current.

driftwood ('drɪft‚wʊd) *n.* wood floating on or washed ashore by the sea or other body of water.

drill[1] (drɪl) *n.* **1.** a machine or tool for boring holes. **2.** *Mil.* training in procedures or movements, as for parades or the use of weapons. **3.** strict and often repetitious training or exercises used in teaching. **4.** *Inf.* correct procedure. **5.** a marine mollusc that preys on oysters. ~*vb.* **6.** to pierce, bore, or cut (a hole) in (material) with or as if with a drill. **7.** to instruct or be instructed in military procedures or movements. **8.** (*tr.*) to teach by rigorous exercises or training. **9.** (*tr.*) *Inf.* to riddle with bullets. —'**driller** *n.*

drill[2] (drɪl) *n.* **1.** a machine for planting seeds in rows. **2.** a furrow in which seeds are sown. **3.** a row of seeds planted by means of a drill. ~*vb.* **4.** to plant (seeds) by means of a drill. —'**driller** *n.*

drill[3] (drɪl) *n.* a hard-wearing twill-weave cotton cloth, used for uniforms, etc.

drill[4] (drɪl) *n.* an Old World monkey of W Africa, related to the mandrill.

drilling platform *n.* a structure, either fixed to the sea bed or mobile, which supports the machinery and equipment (**drilling rig**), together with the stores, etc., required for drilling an offshore oil well.

drilling rig *n.* **1.** the complete machinery, equipment, and structures needed to drill an oil well. **2.** a mobile drilling platform used for exploratory offshore drilling.

drily ('draɪlɪ) *adv.* a variant spelling of **dryly.**

drink (drɪŋk) *vb.* **drinking, drank, drunk. 1.** to swallow (a liquid). **2.** (*tr.*) to soak up (liquid); absorb. **3.** (*tr.; usually foll. by in*) to pay close attention (to). **4.** (*tr.*) to bring (oneself into a certain condition) by consuming alcohol. **5.** (*tr.; often foll. by away*) to dispose of or ruin by excessive expenditure on alcohol. **6.** (*intr.*) to consume alcohol, esp. to excess. **7.** (when *intr.*, foll. by *to*) to drink (a toast). **8. drink the health of.** to salute or celebrate with a toast. **9. drink with the flies.** *Austral. inf.* to drink alone. ~*n.* **10.** liquid suitable for drinking. **11.** alcohol or its habitual or excessive consumption. **12.** a portion of liquid for drinking; draught. **13. the drink.** *Inf.* the sea. —'**drinkable** *adj.* —'**drinker** *n.*

drip (drɪp) *vb.* **dripping, dripped. 1.** to fall or let fall in drops. ~*n.* **2.** the formation and falling of drops of liquid. **3.** the sound made by falling drops. **4.** a projection at the edge of a sill or cornice designed to throw water clear of the wall. **5.** *Inf.* an inane, insipid person. **6.**

Med. the usually intravenous drop-by-drop administration of a solution.

drip-dry *adj.* designating clothing or a fabric that will dry relatively free of creases if hung up when wet.

drip feed *vb.* (*tr.*) **1.** to feed someone a liquid drop by drop, esp. intravenously. ~*n.* **drip-feed. 2.** another term for **drip** (sense 6).

dripping ('drɪpɪŋ) *n.* **1.** the fat that exudes from meat while it is being roasted or fried. **2.** (*often pl.*) liquid that falls in drops. ~*adj.* **3.** (intensifier): *dripping wet.*

drippy ('drɪpɪ) *adj.* **-pier, -piest. 1.** tending to drip. **2.** *Inf.* mawkish, insipid, or inane.

drive (draɪv) *vb.* **driving, drove, driven. 1.** to push, propel, or be pushed or propelled. **2.** to guide the movement of (a vehicle, animal, etc.). **3.** (*tr.*) to compel or urge to work or act, esp. excessively. **4.** (*tr.*) to goad into a specified attitude or state: *work drove him to despair.* **5.** (*tr.*) to cause (an object) to make (a hole, crack, etc.). **6.** to move rapidly by striking or throwing with force. **7.** *Sport.* to hit (a ball) very hard and straight. **8.** *Golf.* to strike (the ball) with a driver. **9.** (*tr.*) to chase (game) from cover. **10.** to transport or be transported in a vehicle. **11.** (*intr.*) to rush or dash violently, esp. against an obstacle. **12.** (*tr.*) to transact with vigour (esp. in **drive a hard bargain**). **13.** (*tr.*) to force (a component) into or out of its location by means of blows or a press. **14.** (*tr.*) *Mining.* to excavate horizontally. **15. drive home. a.** to cause to penetrate to the fullest extent. **b.** to make clear by special emphasis. ~*n.* **16.** the act of driving. **17.** a journey in a driven vehicle. **18.** a road for vehicles, esp. a private road leading to a house. **19.** vigorous pressure, as in business. **20.** a united effort, esp. towards a common goal. **21.** *Brit.* a large gathering of persons to play whist, bridge, etc. **22.** energy, ambition, or initiative. **23.** a sustained and powerful military offensive. **24. a.** the means by which force, motion, etc. is transmitted in a mechanism: *fluid drive.* **b.** (*as modifier*): *a drive shaft.* **25.** *Sport.* a hard straight shot or stroke. **26.** a search for and chasing of game towards waiting guns. —'**drivable** *or* '**driveable** *adj.*

drive at *vb.* (*intr., prep.*) *Inf.* to aim at; intend or mean: *what are you driving at?*

drive-in *adj.* **1.** denoting a public facility or service designed to be used by patrons seated in their cars: *a drive-in bank.* ~*n.* **2.** *Chiefly U.S.* a cinema designed to be used in such a manner.

drivel ('drɪvəl) *vb.* **-elling, -elled** *or U.S.* **-eling, -eled. 1.** to allow (saliva) to flow from the mouth; dribble. **2.** (*intr.*) to speak foolishly. ~*n.* **3.** foolish or senseless talk. **4.** saliva flowing from the mouth; slaver. —'**driveller** *n.*

driven ('drɪvən) *vb.* the past participle of **drive.**

driver ('draɪvə) *n.* **1.** a person who drives a vehicle. **2.** a person who drives animals. **3.** a mechanical component that exerts a force on another to produce motion. **4.** *Golf.* a club, a No. 1 wood, used for tee shots. **5.** *Electronics.* a circuit whose output provides the input of another circuit. —'**driverless** *adj.*

driveway ('draɪv‚weɪ) *n.* a path for vehicles, often con-

THESAURUS

drift *v.* **1.** be carried along, coast, float, go (aimlessly), meander, stray, waft, wander **2.** accumulate, amass, bank up, drive, gather, pile up ~*n.* **3.** accumulation, bank, heap, mass, mound, pile **4.** course, current, direction, flow, impulse, movement, rush, sweep, trend **5.** *Fig.* aim, design, direction, gist, implication, import, intention, meaning, object, purport, scope, significance, tendency, tenor

drill *v.* **1.** discipline, exercise, instruct, practise, rehearse, teach, train ~*n.* **2.** discipline, exercise, instruction, practice, preparation, repetition, training ~*v.* **3.** bore, penetrate, perforate, pierce, puncture, sink in ~*n.* **4.** bit, borer, boring-tool, gimlet, rotary tool

drink *v.* **1.** absorb, drain, gulp, guzzle, imbibe, partake of, quaff, sip, suck, sup, swallow, swig, swill, toss off, wash down, wet one's whistle (*Inf.*) **2.** booze (*Inf.*), carouse, go on a binge *or* bender (*Inf.*), hit the bottle (*Inf.*), indulge, pub-crawl (*Chiefly Brit. sl.*), revel, tipple, tope, wassail ~*n.* **3.** beverage, liquid, potion, refreshment, thirst quencher

4. alcohol, booze (*Inf.*), hooch (*Sl.*), liquor, spirits, the bottle (*Inf.*) **5.** cup, draught, glass, gulp, sip, swallow, swig (*Inf.*), taste **6. the drink** *Inf.* the briny (*Inf.*), the deep, the main, the ocean, the sea

drinker alcoholic, bibber, boozer (*Inf.*), dipsomaniac, drunk, drunkard, guzzler, inebriate, lush (*Sl.*), soak (*Sl.*), sot, sponge (*Inf.*), tippler, toper, wino (*Sl.*)

drink in absorb, assimilate, be all ears (*Inf.*), be fascinated by, be rapt, hang on (someone's) words, hang on the lips of, pay attention

drink to pledge, pledge the health of, salute, toast

drip *v.* **1.** dribble, drizzle, drop, exude, filter, plop, splash, sprinkle, trickle ~*n.* **2.** dribble, dripping, drop, leak, trickle **3.** *Inf.* milksop, ninny, softy (*Inf.*), weakling, weed (*Inf.*), wet (*Inf.*)

drive *v.* **1.** herd, hurl, impel, propel, push, send, urge **2.** direct, go, guide, handle, manage, motor, operate, ride, steer, travel **3.** actuate, coerce, compel, constrain, force, goad,

harass, impel, motivate, oblige, overburden, overwork, press, prick, prod, rush, spur **4.** dash, dig, plunge, hammer, ram, sink, stab, thrust ~*n.* **5.** excursion, hurl (*Scot.*), jaunt, journey, outing, ride, run, spin (*Inf.*), trip, turn **6.** action, advance, appeal, campaign, crusade, effort, push (*Inf.*), surge **7.** ambition, effort, energy, enterprise, get-up-and-go (*Inf.*), initiative, motivation, pressure, push (*Inf.*), vigour, zip (*Inf.*)

drive at aim, allude to, get at (*Inf.*), have in mind, hint at, imply, indicate, intend, intimate, mean, refer to, signify, suggest

drivel *v.* **1.** dribble, drool, slaver, slobber **2.** babble, blether, gab (*Inf.*), gas (*Inf.*), maunder, prate, ramble, waffle (*Inf.*) ~*n.* **3.** balderdash, blah (*Sl.*), bosh (*Inf.*), bunk (*Inf.*), bunkum, fatuity, gibberish, nonsense, poppycock (*Inf.*), prating, rot, rubbish, stuff, twaddle, waffle (*Inf.*) **4.** saliva, slaver, slobber

driving compelling, dynamic, energetic, forceful, galvanic, sweeping, vigorous, violent

necting a house with a public road.
driving licence   *n.* an official document authorizing a person to drive a motor vehicle.
drizzle ('drɪzəl) *n.* **1.** very light rain. ~*vb.* **2.** (*intr.*) to rain lightly. —'**drizzly** *adj.*
droll (drəul) *adj.* amusing in a quaint or odd manner; comical. —'**drollery** *n.* —'**drollness** *n.* —'**drolly** *adv.*
-drome   *n. combining form.* **1.** a course, race course: *hippodrome.* **2.** a large place for a special purpose: *aerodrome.*
dromedary ('drʌmədərɪ) *n., pl.* **-daries.** a type of Arabian camel bred for racing and riding and having a single hump.
-dromous *adj. combining form.* moving or running: *anadromous; catadromous.*
drone[1] (drəun) *n.* **1.** a male honeybee whose sole function is to mate with the queen. **2.** *Brit.* a person who lives off the work of others. **3.** a pilotless radio-controlled aircraft.
drone[2] (drəun) *vb.* **1.** (*intr.*) to make a monotonous low dull sound. **2.** (when *intr.*, often foll. by *on*) to utter (words) in a monotonous tone, esp. to talk without stopping. ~*n.* **3.** a monotonous low dull sound. **4.** *Music.* a sustained bass note or chord. **5.** one of the single-reed pipes in a set of bagpipes. **6.** a person who speaks in a low monotonous tone.
drool (dru:l) *vb.* **1.** (*intr.; often foll. by over*) to show excessive enthusiasm (for) or pleasure (in); gloat (over). ~*vb., n.* **2.** another word for **drivel** (senses 1, 2, 4).
droop (dru:p) *vb.* **1.** to sag or allow to sag, as from weakness. **2.** (*intr.*) to be overcome by weariness. **3.** (*intr.*) to lose courage. ~*n.* **4.** the act or state of drooping. —'**droopy** *adj.*
drop (drɒp) *n.* **1.** a small quantity of liquid that forms or falls in a spherical mass. **2.** a very small quantity of liquid. **3.** a very small quantity of anything. **4.** something resembling a drop in shape or size. **5.** the act or an instance of falling; descent. **6.** a decrease in amount or value. **7.** the vertical distance that anything may fall. **8.** a steep incline or slope. **9.** the act of unloading troops, etc. by parachute. **10.** *Theatre.* See **drop curtain.** **11.** another word for **gallows.** **12.** *Chiefly U.S.* a slot through which an object can be dropped into a receptacle. **13.** *Austral. cricket sl.* a fall of the wicket. **14. at the drop of a hat.** without hesitation or delay. ~*vb.* **dropping, dropped.** **15.** (of liquids) to fall or allow to fall in globules. **16.** to fall or allow to fall vertically. **17.** (*tr.*) to allow to fall by letting go of. **18.** to sink or fall or cause to sink to the ground, as from a blow, weariness, etc. **19.** (*intr.;* foll. by *back, behind,* etc.) to move in a specified manner, direction, etc. **20.** (*intr.;* foll. by *in, by,* etc.) *Inf.* to pay a casual visit (to). **21.** to decrease in amount or value. **22.** to sink or cause to sink to a lower position. **23.** to make or become less in strength, volume, etc. **24.** (*intr.*) to decline in health or condition. **25.** (*intr.;* sometimes foll. by *into*) to pass easily into a condition: *to drop into a habit.* **26.** (*intr.*) to move gently as with a current of air. **27.** (*tr.*) to mention casually: *to drop a hint.* **28.** (*tr.*) to leave out (a word or letter). **29.** (*tr.*) to set down

(passengers or goods). **30.** (*tr.*) *Inf.* to send or post: *drop me a line.* **31.** (*tr.*) *Inf.* to discontinue: *let's drop the matter.* **32.** (*tr.*) *Inf.* to cease to associate with. **33.** (*tr.*) *Sl., chiefly U.S.* to cease to employ. **34.** (*tr.;* sometimes foll. by *in, off,* etc.) *Inf.* to leave or deposit. **35.** (of animals) to give birth to (offspring). **36.** *Sl., chiefly U.S.* to lose (money). **37.** (*tr.*) to lengthen (a hem, etc.). **38.** (*tr.*) to unload (troops, etc.) by parachute. **39.** (*tr.*) *Naut.* to sail out of sight of. **40.** (*tr.*) *Sport.* to omit (a player) from a team. **41.** (*tr.*) to lose (a game, etc.). **42.** (*tr.*) *Golf, basketball, etc.* to hit or throw (a ball) into a goal. ~See also **drop off, dropout.**
drop curtain   *n. Theatre.* a curtain that can be raised and lowered onto the stage.
drop off *vb.* (*adv.*) **1.** (*intr.*) to grow smaller or less. **2.** (*tr.*) to set down. **3.** (*intr.*) *Inf.* to fall asleep. ~*n.* **drop-off.** **4.** a steep descent. **5.** a sharp decrease.
dropout ('drɒpˌaut) *n.* **1.** a student who fails to complete a course. **2.** a person who rejects conventional society. **3. drop-out.** *Rugby.* a drop kick taken to restart play. ~*vb.* **drop out.** (*intr., adv.;* often foll. by *of*) **4.** to abandon or withdraw from (a school, job, etc.).
dropper ('drɒpə) *n.* **1.** a small tube having a rubber bulb at one end for dispensing drops of liquid. **2.** a person or thing that drops.
droppings ('drɒpɪŋz) *pl. n.* the dung of certain animals, such as rabbits, sheep, and birds.
drops (drɒps) *pl. n.* any liquid medication applied by means of a dropper.
drop scone   *n.* a scone made by dropping a spoonful of batter on a hot griddle.
dropsy ('drɒpsɪ) *n. Pathol.* a condition characterized by an accumulation of watery fluid in the tissues or in a body cavity. —**dropsical** ('drɒpsɪkəl) *adj.*
droshky ('drɒʃkɪ) *or* **drosky** ('drɒskɪ) *n., pl.* **-kies.** an open four-wheeled carriage, formerly used in Russia.
dross (drɒs) *n.* **1.** the scum formed on the surfaces of molten metals. **2.** worthless matter; waste. —'**drossy** *adj.* —'**drossiness** *n.*
drought (draut) *n.* **1.** a prolonged period of scanty rainfall. **2.** a prolonged shortage. —'**droughty** *adj.*
drove[1] (drəuv) *vb.* the past tense of **drive.**
drove[2] (drəuv) *n.* **1.** a herd of livestock being driven together. **2.** (*often pl.*) a moving crowd of people. ~*vb.* (*tr.*) **3.** to drive (livestock), usually for a considerable distance.
drover ('drəuvə) *n.* a person who drives sheep or cattle, esp. to and from market.
drown (draun) *vb.* **1.** to die or kill by immersion in liquid. **2.** (*tr.*) to get rid of: *he drowned his sorrows in drink.* **3.** (*tr.*) to drench thoroughly. **4.** (*tr.;* sometimes foll. by *out*) to render (a sound) inaudible by making a loud noise.
drowse (drauz) *vb.* **1.** to be or cause to be sleepy, dull, or sluggish. ~*n.* **2.** the state of being drowsy.
drowsy ('drauzɪ) *adj.* **drowsier, drowsiest.** **1.** heavy with sleepiness; sleepy. **2.** inducing sleep; soporific. **3.** sluggish or lethargic; dull. —'**drowsily** *adv.* —'**drowsi-**

THESAURUS

drizzle 1. *n.* fine rain, Scotch mist 2. *v.* mizzle (*Dialect*), rain, shower, spot *or* spit with rain, spray, sprinkle
droll amusing, clownish, comic, comical, diverting, eccentric, entertaining, farcical, funny, humorous, jocular, laughable, ludicrous, odd, quaint, ridiculous, risible, waggish, whimsical
drone[1] *n.* idler, leech, loafer, lounger, parasite, scrounger (*Inf.*), sluggard, sponger (*Inf.*)
drone[2] *v.* 1. buzz, hum, purr, thrum, vibrate, whirr 2. *Often with* **on** be boring, chant, drawl, intone, prose about, speak monotonously, talk interminably ~*n.* 3. buzz, hum, murmuring, purr, thrum, vibration, whirr, whirring
droop 1. bend, dangle, drop, fall down, hang (down), sag, sink 2. decline, diminish, fade, faint, flag, languish, slump, wilt, wither 3. despond, falter, give in, give up, lose heart *or* hope
drop *n.* 1. bead, bubble, driblet, drip, droplet, globule, pearl, tear 2. dab, dash, mouth-

ful, nip, pinch, shot (*Inf.*), sip, spot, taste, tot, trace, trickle 3. abyss, chasm, declivity, descent, fall, plunge, precipice, slope 4. cut, decline, decrease, deterioration, downturn, fall-off, lowering, reduction, slump ~*v.* 5. dribble, drip, fall in drops, trickle 6. decline, depress, descend, diminish, dive, droop, fall, lower, plummet, plunge, sink, tumble 7. abandon, cease, desert, discontinue, forsake, give up, kick (*Inf.*), leave, quit, relinquish, remit, terminate 8. *Inf.* disown, ignore, jilt, reject, renounce, repudiate, throw over 9. *Inf. Sometimes with* **off** deposit, leave, let off, set down, unload
drop in (on) blow in (*Inf.*), call, call in, go and see, look in (on), look up, pop in (*Inf.*), roll up (*Inf.*), stop, turn up, visit
drop off 1. decline, decrease, diminish, dwindle, fall off, lessen, slacken 2. allow to alight, deliver, leave, let off, set down 3. *Inf.* catnap, doze (off), drowse, fall asleep, have forty winks (*Inf.*), nod (off), snooze (*Inf.*)
drop out abandon, back out, forsake, give up, leave, quit, renege, stop, withdraw

drought 1. aridity, dehydration, drouth (*Archaic or Scot.*), dryness, dry spell, dry weather, parchedness 2. dearth, deficiency, insufficiency, lack, need, scarcity, shortage, want
drove collection, company, crowd, flock, gathering, herd, horde, mob, multitude, press, swarm, throng
drown 1. deluge, drench, engulf, flood, go down, go under, immerse, inundate, sink, submerge, swamp 2. *Fig.* deaden, engulf, muffle, obliterate, overcome, overpower, overwhelm, stifle, swallow up, wipe out
drowse 1. *v.* be drowsy, be lethargic, be sleepy, doze, drop off (*Inf.*), nap, nod, sleep, slumber, snooze (*Inf.*) 2. *n.* doze, forty winks (*Inf.*), nap, sleep, slumber
drowsy 1. comatose, dazed, dopey (*Sl.*), dozy, drugged, half asleep, heavy, lethargic, nodding, sleepy, somnolent, tired, torpid 2. dreamy, lulling, restful, sleepy, soothing, soporific

ness *n.*

drub (drʌb) *vb.* **drubbing, drubbed.** (*tr.*) **1.** to beat as
with a stick. **2.** to defeat utterly, as in a contest. **3.** to
drum or stamp (the feet). **4.** to instil with force or repetition. ~*n.* **5.** a blow, as from a stick.

drudge (drʌdʒ) *n.* **1.** a person who works hard at wearisome menial tasks. ~*vb.* **2.** (*intr.*) to toil at such tasks.
—'**drudger** *n.* —'**drudgingly** *adv.*

drudgery ('drʌdʒərɪ) *n., pl.* **-eries.** hard, menial, and
monotonous work.

drug (drʌg) *n.* **1.** any substance used in the treatment,
prevention, or diagnosis of disease. Related adj.: **pharmaceutical. 2.** a chemical substance, esp. a narcotic,
taken for the effects it produces. **3. drug on the market.**
a commodity available in excess of demand. ~*vb.* **drug-
ging, drugged.** (*tr.*) **4.** to mix a drug with (food, etc.).
5. to administer a drug to. **6.** to stupefy or poison with or
as if with a drug.

drug addict *n.* any person who is abnormally dependent on narcotic drugs.

drugget ('drʌgɪt) *n.* a coarse fabric used as a protective
floor covering, etc.

druggist ('drʌgɪst) *n.* a U.S. term for a pharmacist.

drugstore ('drʌgˌstɔː) *n. U.S.* a shop where medical prescriptions are made up and a wide variety of goods and
usually light meals are sold.

druid ('druːɪd) *n.* (*sometimes cap.*) **1.** a member of an
ancient order of priests in Gaul, Britain, and Ireland in
the pre-Christian era. **2.** a member of any of several
modern movements attempting to revive druidism.
—**druidess** ('druːɪdɪs) *fem. n.* —**dru'idic** *or* **dru'idical**
adj. —'**druid,ism** *n.*

drum (drʌm) *n.* **1.** a percussion instrument sounded by
striking a membrane stretched across the opening of a
hollow cylinder or hemisphere. **2.** the sound produced
by a drum or any similar sound. **3.** an object that resembles a drum in shape, such as a large spool or a cylindrical container. **4.** *Archit.* a cylindrical block of stone
used to construct the shaft of a column. **5.** short for **eardrum. 6.** any of various North American fishes that utter a drumming sound. **7.** a cylindrical object or structure, esp. the centre body of an axial-flow compressor
rotor. **8.** Also called: **magnetic drum.** *Computers.* a rotating cylindrical device on which data may be stored.
9. *Arch.* a drummer. **10.** *Austral. sl.* a brothel. **11. the
drum.** *Austral. inf.* the necessary information (esp. in
give (someone) the drum). ~*vb.* **drumming, drummed.**
12. to play (music) on or as if on a drum. **13.** to tap
rhythmically or regularly. **14.** (*tr.*; sometimes foll. by
up) to summon or call by drumming. **15.** (*tr.*) to instil by
constant repetition. **16. beat the drum for.** *Inf.* to attempt to arouse interest in.

drumbeat ('drʌm,biːt) *n.* the sound made by beating a
drum.

drumhead ('drʌm,hed) *n.* **1.** the part of a drum that is
actually struck. **2.** the head of a capstan. **3.** another
name for **eardrum.**

drumlin ('drʌmlɪn) *n.* a streamlined mound of glacial
drift.

drum major *n.* the noncommissioned officer, usually
of sergeant major's rank, who commands the corps of

drums of a military band and who is in command of both
the drums and the band when paraded together.

drummer ('drʌmə) *n.* **1.** a drum player. **2.** *Chiefly U.S.*
a travelling salesman.

drumstick ('drʌm,stɪk) *n.* **1.** a stick used for playing a
drum. **2.** the lower joint of the leg of a cooked fowl.

drum up *vb.* (*tr., adv.*) to obtain (support, business,
etc.) by solicitation or canvassing.

drunk (drʌŋk) *adj.* **1.** intoxicated with alcohol to the extent of losing control over normal functions. **2.** overwhelmed by strong influence or emotion. ~*n.* **3.** a person who is drunk. **4.** *Inf.* a drinking bout.

drunkard ('drʌŋkəd) *n.* a person who is frequently or
habitually drunk.

drunken ('drʌŋkən) *adj.* **1.** intoxicated. **2.** habitually
drunk. **3.** (*prenominal*) caused by or relating to alcoholic intoxication: *a drunken brawl.* —'**drunkenly** *adv.*
—'**drunkenness** *n.*

drupe (druːp) *n.* any fruit that has a fleshy or fibrous
part around a stone that encloses a seed, as the peach,
plum, and cherry. —**drupaceous** (druː'peɪʃəs) *adj.*

dry (draɪ) *adj.* **drier, driest** *or* **dryer, dryest. 1.** lacking
moisture; not damp or wet. **2.** having little or no rainfall. **3.** not in or under water. **4.** having the water
drained away or evaporated: *a dry river.* **5.** not providing milk: *a dry cow.* **6.** (of the eyes) free from tears. **7.
a.** thirsty. **b.** causing thirst. **8.** eaten without butter,
jam, etc.: *dry toast.* **9.** (of wine, etc.) not sweet. **10.** not
producing a mucous or watery discharge: *a dry cough.*
11. consisting of solid as opposed to liquid substances.
12. without adornment; plain: *dry facts.* **13.** lacking interest: *a dry book.* **14.** lacking warmth: *a dry greeting.*
15. (of humour) shrewd and keen in an impersonal, sarcastic, or laconic way. **16.** *Inf.* opposed to or prohibiting
the sale of alcoholic liquor: *a dry country.* ~*vb.* **drying,
dried. 17.** to make or become dry. **18.** (*tr.*) to preserve
(fruit, etc.) by removing the moisture. ~*n., pl.* **drys** *or*
dries. 19. the dry. *Austral. inf.* (*sometimes caps.*) the
dry season. ~See also **dry out, dry up.** —'**dryly** *or*
'**drily** *adv.* —'**dryness** *n.*

dryad ('draɪəd, -æd) *n., pl.* **-ads** *or* **-ades** (-ə,diːz). *Greek
myth.* a nymph or divinity of the woods.

dry battery *n.* an electric battery consisting of two or
more dry cells.

dry cell *n.* a primary cell in which the electrolyte is in
the form of a paste or is treated in some way to prevent
it from spilling.

dry-clean *vb.* (*tr.*) to clean (fabrics, etc.) with a solvent other than water. —,**dry-'cleaner** *n.*
—,**dry-'cleaning** *n.*

dry dock *n.* a dock that can be pumped dry for work
on a ship's bottom.

dryer[1] ('draɪə) *n.* **1.** a person or thing that dries. **2.** an
apparatus for removing moisture by forced draught,
heating, or centrifuging. **3.** any of certain chemicals
added to oils to accelerate their drying when used in
paints, etc.

dryer[2] ('draɪə) *adj.* a variant spelling of **drier**[1].

dry fly *n. Angling.* **a.** an artificial fly designed to be
floated on the surface of the water. **b.** (*as modifier*):

drubbing beating, clobbering (*Sl.*), defeat, flogging, hammering (*Inf.*), licking
(*Inf.*), pounding, pummelling, thrashing,
trouncing, walloping (*Inf.*), whipping

drudge 1. dogsbody (*Inf.*), factotum,
hack, maid *or* man of all work, menial, plodder, scullion (*Archaic*), servant, skivvy,
slave, toiler, worker **2.** *v.* grind (*Inf.*), keep
one's nose to the grindstone, labour, moil
(*Archaic or dialect*), plod, plug away (*Inf.*),
slave, toil, work

drudgery chore, donkey-work, fag (*Inf.*),
grind (*Inf.*), hack work, hard work, labour,
menial labour, skivvying, slavery, slog, sweat
(*Inf.*), sweated labour, toil

drug *n.* **1.** medicament, medication, medicine, physic, poison, remedy **2.** dope (*Sl.*),
narcotic, opiate ~*v.* **3.** administer a drug,
dope (*Sl.*), dose, medicate, treat **4.** anaesthetize, deaden, knock out, numb, poison, stupefy

drugged comatose, doped (*Sl.*), dopey

(*Sl.*), high (*Inf.*), on a trip (*Inf.*), spaced out
(*Sl.*), stoned (*Sl.*), stupefied, turned on (*Sl.*),
under the influence (*Inf.*), zonked (*Sl.*)

drum *v.* **1.** beat, pulsate, rap, reverberate,
tap, tattoo, throb **2.** *With* into din into, drive
home, hammer away, harp on, instil, reiterate

drum up attract, bid for, canvass, obtain,
petition, round up, solicit

drunk 1. *adj.* bacchic, canned (*Sl.*), drunk-
en, fu' (*Scot.*), fuddled, half seas over (*Inf.*),
inebriated, intoxicated, maudlin, merry
(*Inf.*), muddled, pie-eyed (*Sl.*), plastered (*Sl.*),
sloshed (*Sl.*), soaked (*Inf.*), stewed (*Sl.*),
stoned (*Sl.*), tiddly (*Sl.*), tight (*Inf.*), tipsy,
tired and emotional (*Euphemistic*), under
the influence (*Inf.*), well-oiled (*Sl.*) **2.** *n.* boozer (*Inf.*), drunkard, inebriate, lush (*Sl.*), soak
(*Sl.*), sot, toper, wino (*Sl.*)

drunkard alcoholic, carouser, dipsomaniac, drinker, drunk, lush (*Sl.*), soak (*Sl.*), sot,
tippler, toper, wino (*Sl.*)

drunken 1. bibulous, boozing (*Sl.*), drunk,
(gin-)sodden, inebriate, intoxicated, red-
nosed, sottish, tippling, toping, under the influence (*Inf.*) **2.** bacchanalian, bacchic, boozy
(*Sl.*), debauched, dionysian, dissipated, orgiastic, riotous, saturnalian

drunkenness alcoholism, bibulousness,
dipsomania, inebriety, insobriety, intemperance, intoxication, sottishness, tipsiness

dry *adj.* **1.** arid, barren, dehydrated, desiccated, dried up, juiceless, moistureless,
parched, sapless, thirsty, torrid, waterless **2.**
Fig. boring, dreary, dull, monotonous, plain,
tedious, tiresome, uninteresting **3.** *Fig.* cutting, deadpan, droll, keen, low-key, quietly
humorous, sarcastic, sharp, sly ~*v.* **4.** dehu-
midify, dehydrate, desiccate, drain, make
dry, parch, sear **5.** *With* out *or* up become
dry, become unproductive, harden, mummify, shrivel up, wilt, wither, wizen

dry-fly fishing.

dry goods *pl. n.* clothing, hardware, and related merchandise, as distinct from grocery items.

dry ice *n.* solid carbon dioxide used as a refrigerant. Also called: **carbon dioxide snow.**

dryly *or* **drily** ('draɪlɪ) *adv.* in a dry manner.

dry measure *n.* a unit or system of units for measuring dry goods, such as fruit, grains, etc.

dry out *vb.* (*adv.*) **1.** to make or become dry. **2.** *Inf.* to undergo or cause to undergo treatment for alcoholism or drug addiction.

dry rot *n.* **1.** crumbling and drying of timber, bulbs, potatoes, or fruit, caused by certain fungi. **2.** any fungus causing this decay. **3.** *Inf.* corrupt practices.

dry run *n.* **1.** *Mil.* practice in firing without live ammunition. **2.** *Inf.* a rehearsal.

dry-stone *adj.* (of a wall) made without mortar.

dry up *vb.* (*adv.*) **1.** (*intr.*) to become barren or unproductive; fail. **2.** to dry (dishes, cutlery, etc.) with a tea towel after they have been washed. **3.** (*intr.*) *Inf.* to stop talking or speaking.

D.S. *or* **d.s.** *Music. abbrev. for* dal segno.

D.Sc. *abbrev. for* Doctor of Science.

D.S.C. *Mil. abbrev. for* Distinguished Service Cross.

D.S.M. *Mil. abbrev. for* Distinguished Service Medal.

D.S.O. *Brit. mil. abbrev. for* Distinguished Service Order.

D.T.'s *Inf. abbrev. for* delirium tremens.

Du. *abbrev. for:* **1.** Duke. **2.** Dutch.

dual ('djuːəl) *adj.* **1.** relating to or denoting two. **2.** twofold; double. **3.** (in the grammar of some languages) denoting a form of a word indicating that exactly two referents are being referred to. ~*n.* **4.** *Grammar.* **a.** the dual number. **b.** a dual form of a word. —**dually** *adv.*

dual carriageway *n. Brit.* a road on which traffic travelling in opposite directions is separated by a central strip of turf, etc. *U.S. name:* **divided highway.**

dualism ('djuːə,lɪzəm) *n.* **1.** the state of being twofold or double. **2.** *Philosophy.* the doctrine that reality consists of two basic principles, usually taken to be mind and matter. **3.** *Theol.* **a.** the theory that the universe has been ruled from its origins by two conflicting powers, one good and one evil. **b.** the theory that there are two personalities, one human and one divine, in Christ. —**dualist** *n.* —**dual**ˈistic *adj.* —**duality** (djuːˈælɪtɪ) *n.*

dub[1] (dʌb) *vb.* **dubbing, dubbed.** **1.** (*tr.*) to invest (a person) with knighthood by tapping on the shoulder with a sword. **2.** (*tr.*) to invest with a title, name, or nickname. **3.** (*tr.*) to dress (leather) by rubbing. **4.** *Angling.* to dress (a fly).

dub[2] (dʌb) *Films.* ~*vb.* **dubbing, dubbed.** **1.** to alter the soundtrack of (a film, etc.). **2.** (*tr.*) to provide (a film) with a new soundtrack, esp. in a different language. **3.** (*tr.*) to provide (a film or tape) with a soundtrack. ~*n.* **4.** the new sounds added.

dubbin ('dʌbɪn) *n. Brit.* a greasy preparation applied to leather to soften it and make it waterproof.

dubiety (djuːˈbaɪɪtɪ) *n., pl.* **-ties.** **1.** the state of being doubtful. **2.** a doubtful matter.

dubious ('djuːbɪəs) *adj.* **1.** marked by or causing doubt. **2.** uncertain; doubtful. **3.** of doubtful quality; untrustworthy. **4.** not certain in outcome. —**dubiously** *adv.* —**dubiousness** *n.*

ducal ('djuːkəl) *adj.* of a duke or duchy.

ducat ('dʌkət) *n.* **1.** any of various former European gold or silver coins. **2.** (*pl.*) *Inf.* money.

duchess ('dʌtʃɪs) *n.* **1.** the wife or widow of a duke. **2.** a woman who holds the rank of duke in her own right.

duchy ('dʌtʃɪ) *n., pl.* **duchies.** the territory of a duke or duchess; dukedom.

duck[1] (dʌk) *n., pl.* **ducks** *or* **duck.** **1.** any of a family of aquatic birds, esp. those having short legs, webbed feet, and a broad blunt bill. **2.** the flesh of this bird, used as food. **3.** the female of such a bird, as opposed to the male (drake). **4.** Also: **ducks.** *Brit. inf.* dear or darling: used as a term of address. **5.** *Cricket.* a score of nothing by a batsman. **6. like water off a duck's back.** *Inf.* without effect.

duck[2] (dʌk) *vb.* **1.** to move (the head or body) quickly downwards or away, esp. to escape observation or evade a blow. **2.** to plunge suddenly under water. **3.** (when *intr.*, often foll. by *out*) *Inf.* to dodge or escape (a person, duty, etc.). **4.** (*intr.*) *Bridge.* to play a low card rather than trying to win a trick. ~*n.* **5.** the act or an instance of ducking. —ˈ**ducker** *n.*

duck[3] (dʌk) *n.* a heavy cotton fabric of plain weave, used for clothing, tents, etc.

duck-billed platypus *n.* an amphibious egg-laying mammal of E. Australia having dense fur, a broad bill and tail, and webbed feet.

duckboard ('dʌk,bɔːd) *n.* a board or boards laid so as to form a path over wet or muddy ground.

duckling ('dʌklɪŋ) *n.* a young duck.

ducks and drakes *n.* **1.** a game in which a flat stone is bounced across the surface of water. **2. make ducks and drakes of** *or* **play (at) ducks and drakes with.** *Inf.* to use recklessly; squander.

ducky *or* **duckie** ('dʌkɪ) *Inf.* ~*n., pl.* **duckies.** **1.** *Brit.* darling or dear: a term of endearment. ~*adj.* **2.** delightful; fine.

duct (dʌkt) *n.* **1.** a tube, pipe, or canal by means of which a substance, esp. a fluid or gas, is conveyed. **2.** any bodily passage, esp. one conveying secretions or excretions. **3.** a narrow tubular cavity in plants. **4.** a channel or pipe carrying electric wires. **5.** a passage through which air can flow, as in air conditioning. —ˈ**ductless** *adj.*

ductile ('dʌktaɪl) *adj.* **1.** (of a metal) able to sustain large deformations without fracture and able to be hammered into sheets or drawn out into wires. **2.** able to be moulded. **3.** easily led or influenced. —**ductility** (dʌkˈtɪlɪtɪ) *n.*

ductless gland *n. Anat.* See **endocrine gland.**

dud (dʌd) *Inf.* ~*n.* **1.** a person or thing that proves ineffectual. **2.** a shell, etc., that fails to explode. **3.** (*pl.*) clothes or other belongings. ~*adj.* **4.** failing in its purpose or function.

dude (djuːd) *n. Inf.* **1.** *Western U.S.* a city dweller, esp. one holidaying on a ranch. **2.** *U.S.* a dandy. **3.** *U.S.* any person. —ˈ**dudish** *adj.* —ˈ**dudishly** *adv.*

dudgeon ('dʌdʒən) *n.* anger or resentment (archaic, except **in high dudgeon**).

due (djuː) *adj.* **1.** (*postpositive*) immediately payable. **2.** (*postpositive*) owed as a debt. **3.** fitting; proper. **4.** (*prenominal*) adequate or sufficient. **5.** (*postpositive*) expected or appointed to be present or arrive. **6. due to.** attributable to or caused by. ~*n.* **7.** something that is owed, required, or due. **8. give (a person) his due.** to give or allow what is deserved or right. ~*adv.* **9.** directly or exactly. ~See also **dues.**

▷ **Usage.** There is considerable controversy over the use of *due to* and *owing to* as compound prepositions equivalent to *because of.* Careful users of English prefer *because of* or *on account of.* There is no dispute about the postpositive adjectival use of *due to* to mean *caused by*

THESAURUS

dryness aridity, aridness, dehumidification, dehydration, drought, thirst, thirstiness

dual binary, coupled, double, duplex, duplicate, matched, paired, twin, twofold

dub 1. bestow, confer, confer knighthood upon, entitle, knight 2. call, christen, denominate, designate, label, name, nickname, style, term

dubious 1. doubtful, hesitant, iffy (*Inf.*), sceptical, uncertain, unconvinced, undecided, unsure, wavering 2. ambiguous, debatable, doubtful, equivocal, indefinite, indeterminate, obscure, problematical, unclear, unsettled 3. fishy (*Inf.*), questionable, shady (*Inf.*), suspect, suspicious, undependable, unreliable, untrustworthy

duck 1. bend, bob, bow, crouch, dodge, drop, lower, stoop 2. dip, dive, douse, dunk, immerse, plunge, souse, submerge, wet 3. *Inf.* avoid, dodge, escape, evade, shirk, shun, sidestep

duct blood vessel, canal, channel, conduit, funnel, passage, pipe, tube

dud 1. *n.* failure, flop (*Inf.*), washout (*Inf.*) 2. *adj.* broken, bust (*Inf.*), duff (*Sl.*), failed, inoperative, kaput (*Inf.*), not functioning, valueless, worthless

dudgeon 1. *Archaic* indignation, ire, resentment, umbrage, wrath 2. **in high dudgeon** angry, fuming, indignant, offended, resentful, vexed

due *adj.* 1. in arrears, outstanding, owed, owing, payable, unpaid 2. appropriate, becoming, bounden, deserved, fit, fitting, just, justified, merited, obligatory, proper, requisite, right, rightful, suitable, well-earned 3. adequate, ample, enough, plenty of, sufficient 4. expected, expected to arrive, scheduled ~*n.* 5. comeuppance (*Sl.*), deserts, merits, prerogative, privilege, right(s) ~*adv.* 6. dead, direct, directly, exactly, straight, undeviatingly

(*the error was due to carelessness*), but *owing to* is not ordinarily used in this way.

duel ('dju:əl) *n.* **1.** a formal prearranged combat with deadly weapons between two people in the presence of seconds, usually to settle a quarrel. **2.** a contest or conflict between two persons or parties. ~*vb.* **duelling, duelled** *or U.S.* **dueling, dueled.** (*intr.*) **3.** to fight in a duel. **4.** to contest closely. —'**dueller** *or* '**duellist** *n.*

duenna (dju:'εnə) *n.* (in Spain and Portugal, etc.) an elderly woman retained by a family to act as governess and chaperon to girls.

dues (dju:z) *pl. n.* (*sometimes sing.*) charges, as for membership of a club or organization; fees.

duet (dju:'εt) *n.* **1.** a musical composition for two performers or voices. **2.** a pair of closely connected individuals; duo. —**du'ettist** *n.*

duff[1] (dʌf) *n.* **1.** a thick flour pudding boiled in a cloth bag. **2. up the duff.** *Sl., chiefly Austral.* pregnant.

duff[2] (dʌf) *Sl.* ~*vb.* (*tr.*) **1.** to give a false appearance to (old or stolen goods); fake. **2.** *Brit.* (foll. by *up*) to beat (a person) severely. **3.** *Austral.* to steal (cattle), altering the brand. **4.** *Golf.* to bungle a shot by hitting the ground behind the ball. ~*adj.* **5.** *Brit.* bad or useless: *a duff engine.*

duffel *or* **duffle** ('dʌfəl) *n.* **1.** a heavy woollen cloth. **2.** *Chiefly U.S.* equipment or supplies.

duffel coat *n.* a knee-length wool coat, usually with a hood and fastened with toggles.

duffer ('dʌfə) *n.* **1.** *Inf.* a dull or incompetent person. **2.** *Sl.* something worthless. **3.** *Austral. sl.* **a.** a mine that proves unproductive. **b.** a person who steals cattle.

dug[1] (dʌg) *vb.* the past tense or past participle of **dig.**

dug[2] (dʌg) *n.* a nipple, teat, udder, or breast.

dugong ('du:gɒŋ) *n.* a whalelike mammal occurring in shallow tropical waters from E Africa to Australia.

dugout ('dʌg,aʊt) *n.* **1.** a canoe, made by hollowing out a log. **2.** *Mil.* a covered excavation dug to provide shelter. **3.** in the Canadian prairies, a reservoir dug on a farm in which water from rain and snow is collected for use in irrigation, watering livestock, etc. **4.** *Sl.* a retired officer, etc., recalled to employment.

duiker *or* **duyker** ('daɪkə) *n., pl.* **-kers** *or* **-ker.** **1.** Also: **duikerbok.** any of various small African antelopes. **2.** *S. African.* any of several cormorants, esp. the long-tailed shag.

duke (dju:k) *n.* **1.** a nobleman of high rank: in the British Isles standing above the other grades of the nobility. **2.** the prince or ruler of a small principality or duchy. —'**dukedom** *n.*

dulcet ('dʌlsɪt) *adj.* (of a sound) soothing or pleasant; sweet.

dulcimer ('dʌlsɪmə) *n.* **1.** a tuned percussion instrument consisting of a set of strings stretched over a sounding board and struck with hammers. **2.** an instrument used in U.S. folk music, with an elliptical body and usually three strings plucked with a goose quill.

dull (dʌl) *adj.* **1.** slow to think or understand; stupid. **2.** lacking in interest. **3.** lacking in perception; insensitive. **4.** lacking sharpness. **5.** not acute, intense, or piercing. **6.** (of weather) not bright or clear. **7.** not active, busy, or

brisk. **8.** lacking in spirit; listless. **9.** (of colour) lacking brilliance; sombre. **10.** not loud or clear; muffled. ~*vb.* **11.** to make or become dull. —'**dullish** *adj.* —'**dullness** *or* '**dulness** *n.* —'**dully** *adv.*

dullard ('dʌləd) *n.* a dull or stupid person.

dulse (dʌls) *n.* any of several seaweeds that occur on rocks and have large red edible fronds.

duly ('dju:lɪ) *adv.* **1.** in a proper manner. **2.** at the proper time.

dumb (dʌm) *adj.* **1.** lacking the power to speak; mute. **2.** lacking the power of human speech: *dumb animals.* **3.** temporarily bereft of the power to speak: *struck dumb.* **4.** refraining from speech; uncommunicative. **5.** producing no sound: *a dumb piano.* **6.** made, done, or performed without speech. **7.** *Inf., chiefly U.S.* **a.** dim-witted. **b.** foolish. —'**dumbly** *adv.* —'**dumbness** *n.*

dumbbell ('dʌm,bεl) *n.* **1.** an exercising weight consisting of a single bar with a heavy ball or disc at either end. **2.** *Sl., chiefly U.S.* a fool.

dumbfound *or* **dumfound** (dʌm'faʊnd) *vb.* (*tr.*) to strike dumb with astonishment; amaze.

dumb show *n.* **1.** formerly, a part of a play acted in pantomime. **2.** meaningful gestures.

dumbwaiter ('dʌm,weɪtə) *n.* **1.** *Brit.* **a.** a stand placed near a dining table to hold food. **b.** a revolving circular tray placed on a table to hold food. U.S. name: **lazy Susan.** **2.** a lift for carrying food, rubbish, etc., between floors.

dumdum ('dʌm,dʌm) *n.* a soft-nosed bullet that expands on impact and inflicts extensive laceration.

dummy ('dʌmɪ) *n., pl.* **-mies.** **1.** a figure representing the human form, used for displaying clothes, as a target, etc. **2. a.** a copy of an object, often lacking some essential feature of the original. **b.** (*as modifier*): *a dummy drawer.* **3.** *Sl.* a stupid person. **4.** *Derog., sl.* a person without the power of speech. **5.** *Inf.* a person who says or does nothing. **6. a.** a person who appears to act for himself while acting on behalf of another. **b.** (*as modifier*): *a dummy buyer.* **7.** *Mil.* a blank round. **8.** *Bridge.* **a.** the hand exposed on the table by the declarer's partner and played by the declarer. **b.** the declarer's partner. **9. a.** a prototype of a book, indicating the appearance of the finished product. **b.** a designer's layout of a page. **10.** *Sport.* a feigned pass or move. **11.** *Brit.* a rubber teat for babies to suck or bite on. U.S. equivalent: **pacifier.** **12.** (*modifier*) counterfeit; sham. **13.** (*modifier*) (of a card game) played with one hand exposed or unplayed. **14. sell (someone) a dummy.** *Sport.* to use a dummy pass.

dummy run *n.* an experimental run; practice; rehearsal.

dump (dʌmp) *vb.* **1.** to drop, fall, or let fall heavily or in a mass. **2.** (*tr.*) to empty (objects or material) out of a container. **3.** to unload or empty (a container), as by overturning. **4.** (*tr.*) *Inf.* to dispose of. **5.** *Commerce.* to market (goods) in bulk and at low prices, esp. abroad, in order to maintain a high price in the home market and obtain a share of the foreign markets. **6.** (*tr.*) to store (supplies, etc.) temporarily. **7.** (*tr.*) *Austral.* (of a wave) to hurl a swimmer or surfer down. **8.** (*tr.*) *Austral.* to compact (bales of wool) by hydraulic pressure. **9.** (*tr.*)

THESAURUS

duel *n.* 1. affair of honour, single combat 2. clash, competition, contest, encounter, engagement, fight, rivalry ~*v.* 3. clash, compete, contend, contest, fight, rival, struggle, vie with

dues charge, charges, contribution, fee, levy, membership fee

duffer blunderer, booby, bungler, clod, clot (*Sl.*), galoot (*Sl., chiefly U.S.*), lubber, lummox (*Inf.*), oaf

dull *adj.* 1. dense, dim, dim-witted (*Inf.*), doltish, slow, stolid, stupid, thick, unintelligent 2. apathetic, blank, callous, dead, empty, heavy, indifferent, insensible, insensitive, lifeless, listless, passionless, slow, sluggish, unresponsive, unsympathetic, vacuous 3. boring, commonplace, dreary, dry, flat, humdrum, monotonous, plain, prosaic, run-of-the-mill, tedious, tiresome, unimaginative, uninteresting, vapid 4. blunt, blunted, dulled, edgeless, not keen, not sharp, unsharpened 5. cloudy, dim, dismal, gloomy, leaden, opaque,

overcast, turbid 6. depressed, inactive, slack, slow, sluggish, torpid, uneventful 7. drab, faded, feeble, indistinct, lacklustre, muffled, murky, muted, sombre, subdued, subfusc, toned-down ~*v.* 8. dampen, deject, depress, discourage, dishearten, dispirit, sadden 9. allay, alleviate, assuage, blunt, lessen, mitigate, moderate, palliate, paralyse, relieve, soften, stupefy, take the edge off 10. cloud, darken, dim, fade, obscure, stain, sully, tarnish

dullard blockhead, clod, dimwit (*Inf.*), dolt, dope (*Sl.*), dunce, nitwit, numskull, oaf

duly 1. accordingly, appropriately, befittingly, correctly, decorously, deservedly, fittingly, properly, rightfully, suitably 2. at the proper time, on time, punctually

dumb 1. at a loss for words, inarticulate, mum, mute, silent, soundless, speechless, tongue-tied, voiceless, wordless 2. *Inf.* dense, dim-witted (*Inf.*), dull, foolish, stupid, thick, unintelligent

dumbfound, dumfound amaze, astonish, astound, bewilder, bowl over (*Inf.*), confound, confuse, flabbergast (*Inf.*), nonplus, overwhelm, stagger, startle, stun, take aback

dumbfounded, dumfounded amazed, astonished, astounded, bewildered, bowled over (*Inf.*), breathless, confounded, confused, dumb, flabbergasted (*Inf.*), knocked for six (*Inf.*), knocked sideways (*Inf.*), nonplussed, overcome, overwhelmed, speechless, staggered, startled, stunned, taken aback, thrown, thunderstruck

dummy *n.* 1. figure, form, lay figure, manikin, mannequin, model 2. copy, counterfeit, duplicate, imitation, sham, substitute 3. *Sl.* blockhead, dimwit (*Inf.*), dolt, dullard, dunce, fool, numskull, simpleton ~*adj.* 4. artificial, bogus, fake, false, imitation, mock, phoney (*Sl.*), sham, simulated 5. mock, practice, simulated, trial

Computers. to record (the contents of the memory) on a storage device at a series of points during a computer run. ~*n.* **10.** a place or area where waste materials are dumped. **11.** a pile or accumulation of rubbish. **12.** the act of dumping. **13.** *Inf.* a dirty or unkempt place. **14.** *Mil.* a place where weapons, supplies, etc., are stored.

dumpling ('dʌmplɪŋ) *n.* **1.** a small ball of dough cooked and served with stew. **2.** a pudding consisting of a ball of dough filled with fruit: *apple dumpling.* **3.** *Inf.* a short plump person.

dumps (dʌmps) *pl. n. Inf.* a state of melancholy or depression (esp. in **down in the dumps**).

dumpy ('dʌmpɪ) *adj.* **dumpier, dumpiest.** short and plump; squat. —'**dumpily** *adv.* —'**dumpiness** *n.*

dun[1] (dʌn) *vb.* **dunning, dunned. 1.** (*tr.*) to press (a debtor) for payment. ~*n.* **2.** a person, esp. a hired agent, who importunes another for the payment of a debt. **3.** a demand for payment.

dun[2] (dʌn) *n.* **1.** a brownish-grey colour. **2.** a horse of this colour. **3.** *Angling.* an immature adult mayfly. ~*adj.* **dunner, dunnest. 4.** of a dun colour. **5.** dark and gloomy.

dunce (dʌns) *n.* a person who is stupid or slow to learn.

Dundee cake (dʌn'di:) *n. Chiefly Brit.* a fairly rich fruit cake decorated with almonds.

dunderhead ('dʌndə,hɛd) *n.* a slow-witted person. —'**dunder,headed** *adj.*

dune (dju:n) *n.* a mound or ridge of drifted sand.

dung (dʌŋ) *n.* **1.** excrement, esp. of animals; manure. **2.** something filthy. ~*vb.* **3.** (*tr.*) to cover with manure.

dungaree (,dʌŋgə'ri:) *n.* **1.** a coarse cotton fabric used chiefly for work clothes, etc. **2.** (*pl.*) **a.** a suit of workman's overalls made of this material. **b.** a child's playsuit. **3.** *U.S.* trousers.

dungeon ('dʌndʒən) *n.* **1.** a prison cell, often underground. **2.** a variant spelling of **donjon.**

dunghill ('dʌŋ,hɪl) *n.* **1.** a heap of dung. **2.** a foul place, condition, or person.

dunk (dʌŋk) *vb.* **1.** to dip (bread, etc.) in tea, soup, etc., before eating. **2.** to submerge. —'**dunker** *n.*

dunlin ('dʌnlɪn) *n.* a small sandpiper of northern and arctic regions, having a brown back and black breast in summer.

dunnock ('dʌnək) *n.* another name for a **hedge sparrow.**

duo ('dju:əʊ) *n., pl.* **duos** or **dui** ('dju:i:). **1.** *Music.* **a.** a pair of performers. **b.** a duet. **2.** a pair of actors, etc. **3.** *Inf.* a pair of closely connected individuals.

duo- *combining form.* indicating two.

duodecimal (,dju:əʊ'dɛsɪməl) *adj.* **1.** relating to twelve or twelfths. ~*n.* **2.** a twelfth. **3.** one of the numbers used in a duodecimal number system. —,**duo'decimally** *adv.*

duodenum (,dju:əʊ'di:nəm) *n., pl.* **-na** (-nə) *or* **-nums.** the first part of the small intestine, between the stomach and the jejunum. —,**duo'denal** *adj.*

duologue *or U.S. (sometimes)* **duolog** ('dju:ə,lɒg) *n.* **1.** a part or all of a play in which the speaking roles are limited to two actors. **2.** a less common word for **dialogue.**

dupe (dju:p) *n.* **1.** a person who is easily deceived. ~*vb.* **2.** (*tr.*) to deceive; cheat; fool. —'**dupable** *adj.*

—'**duper** *n.* —'**dupery** *n.*

duple ('dju:pəl) *adj.* **1.** a less common word for **double. 2.** *Music.* (of time or music) having two beats in a bar.

duplex ('dju:plɛks) *n.* **1.** *U.S.* a duplex apartment or house. ~*adj.* **2.** having two parts. **3.** having pairs of components of independent but identical function. **4.** permitting the transmission of simultaneous signals in both directions. —**du'plexity** *n.*

duplicate *adj.* ('dju:plɪkɪt). **1.** copied exactly from an original. **2.** identical. **3.** existing as a pair or in pairs. ~*n.* ('dju:plɪkɪt). **4.** an exact copy. **5.** something additional of the same kind. **6.** two exact copies (esp. in **in duplicate**). ~*vb.* ('dju:plɪ,keɪt). **7.** (*tr.*) to make a replica of. **8.** (*tr.*) to do or make again. **9.** (*tr.*) to make in a pair; make double. —**duplicable** ('dju:plɪkəbəl) *adj.* —,**dupli'cation** *n.*

duplicity (dju:'plɪsɪtɪ) *n., pl.* **-ties.** deception; double-dealing.

durable ('djʊərəbəl) *adj.* long-lasting; enduring. —,**dura'bility** *n.* —'**durably** *adv.*

durable goods *pl. n.* goods that require infrequent replacement. Also called: **durables.**

durance ('djʊərəns) *n. Arch. or literary.* **1.** imprisonment. **2.** duration.

duration (djʊ'reɪʃən) *n.* the length of time that something lasts or continues. —**du'rational** *adj.*

durbar ('dɜːbɑː, ,dɜː'bɑː) *n.* **a.** (formerly) the court of a native ruler or a governor in India. **b.** a levée at such a court.

duress (djʊ'rɛs, djʊə-) *n.* **1.** compulsion by use of force or threat; coercion (often in **under duress**). **2.** imprisonment.

during ('djʊərɪŋ) *prep.* **1.** concurrently with (some other activity). **2.** within the limit of (a period of time).

durst (dɜːst) *vb.* an archaic past tense of **dare.**

dusk (dʌsk) *n.* **1.** the darker part of twilight. **2.** *Poetic.* gloom; shade. ~*adj.* **3.** *Poetic.* shady; gloomy. ~*vb.* **4.** *Poetic.* to make or become dark.

dusky ('dʌskɪ) *adj.* **duskier, duskiest. 1.** dark in colour; swarthy. **2.** dim. —'**duskily** *adv.* —'**duskiness** *n.*

dust (dʌst) *n.* **1.** dry fine powdery material, such as particles of dirt, earth, or pollen. **2.** a cloud of such fine particles. **3.** *Christian theol.* **a.** the mortal body of man. **b.** the corpse of a dead person. **4.** the earth; ground. **5.** *Inf.* a disturbance; fuss (esp. in **kick up a dust, raise a dust**). **6.** something of little worth. **7.** short for **gold dust. 8.** ashes or household refuse. **9. bite the dust.** *Inf.* **a.** to suffer complete defeat. **b.** to die. **10. dust and ashes.** something that is very disappointing. **11. shake the dust off one's feet.** to depart angrily. **12. throw dust in the eyes of.** to confuse or mislead. ~*vb.* **13.** (*tr.*) to sprinkle or cover (something) with (dust or some other powdery substance). **14.** to remove dust by wiping, sweeping, or brushing. **15.** to make or become dirty with dust. —'**dustless** *adj.*

dustbin ('dʌst,bɪn) *n.* a large, usually cylindrical container for rubbish, esp. one used by a household. *U.S.* names: **garbage can, trash can.**

dust bowl *n.* a semiarid area in which the surface soil is exposed to wind erosion.

dustcart ('dʌst,kɑːt) *n.* a road vehicle for collecting ref-

---

THESAURUS

dump *v.* **1.** deposit, drop, fling down, let fall, throw down **2.** discharge, dispose of, ditch (*Sl.*), empty out, get rid of, jettison, scrap, throw away *or* out, tip, unload ~*n.* **3.** junkyard, refuse heap, rubbish heap, rubbish tip, tip **4.** *Inf.* hole (*Inf.*), hovel, joint (*Sl.*), mess, pigsty, shack, shanty, slum

dumps blues, dejection, depression, despondency, dolour, gloom, gloominess, low spirits, melancholy, mopes, sadness, unhappiness, woe

dun *v.* beset, importune, pester, plague, press, urge

dunce ass, blockhead, bonehead (*Sl.*), dimwit (*Inf.*), dolt, donkey, duffer (*Inf.*), dullard, dunderhead, goose (*Inf.*), halfwit, ignoramus, loon (*Inf.*), moron, nincompoop, numskull, simpleton, thickhead

dungeon cage, cell, donjon, lockup, oubliette, prison, vault

duplicate **1.** *adj.* corresponding, identical, matched, matching, twin, twofold **2.** *n.* carbon copy, clone, copy, double, facsimile, likeness, lookalike, match, mate, photocopy, Photostat (*Trademark*), replica, reproduction, ringer (*Sl.*), twin, Xerox (*Trademark*) **3.** *v.* clone, copy, double, echo, photocopy, Photostat (*Trademark*), repeat, replicate, reproduce, Xerox (*Trademark*)

durability constancy, durableness, endurance, imperishability, lastingness, permanence, persistence

durable abiding, constant, dependable, enduring, fast, firm, fixed, hard-wearing, lasting, long-lasting, permanent, persistent, reliable, resistant, sound, stable, strong, sturdy, substantial, tough

duress **1.** coercion, compulsion, constraint, pressure, threat **2.** captivity, confinement, constraint, hardship, imprisonment, incarceration, restraint

dusk **1.** dark, evening, eventide, gloaming,

nightfall, sundown, sunset, twilight **2.** *Poetic* darkness, gloom, murk, obscurity, shade, shadowiness

dusky **1.** dark, dark-complexioned, dark-hued, sable, swarthy **2.** caliginous (*Archaic*), cloudy, crepuscular, darkish, dim, gloomy, murky, obscure, overcast, shadowy, shady, tenebrous, twilight, twilit, veiled

dust *n.* **1.** fine fragments, grime, grit, particles, powder, powdery dirt **2.** dirt, earth, ground, soil **3.** *Inf.* commotion, disturbance, fuss, racket, row **4. bite the dust** *Inf.* die, drop dead, expire, fall in battle, pass away, perish **5. lick the dust** *Inf.* be servile, bootlick (*Inf.*), demean oneself, grovel, kowtow, toady **6. throw dust in the eyes of** con (*Sl.*), confuse, deceive, fool, have (someone) on, hoodwink, mislead, take in (*Inf.*) ~*v.* **7.** cover, dredge, powder, scatter, sift, spray, spread, sprinkle

use. U.S. name: **garbage truck.**

dust cover n. **1.** Also called: **dustsheet.** a large cloth used to protect furniture from dust. **2.** another name for **dust jacket. 3.** a perspex cover for a gramophone turntable.

duster ('dʌstə) n. **1.** a cloth used for dusting. U.S. name: **dust cloth. 2.** a machine for blowing out dust. **3.** a person or thing that dusts.

dust jacket or **cover** n. a removable paper cover used to protect a bound book.

dustman ('dʌstmən) n., pl. **-men.** Brit. a man whose job is to collect domestic refuse.

dustpan ('dʌst‚pæn) n. a short-handled hooded shovel into which dust is swept from floors, etc.

dust-up Inf. ~n. **1.** a fight or argument. ~vb. **dust up. 2.** (tr., adv.) to attack (someone).

dusty ('dʌstɪ) adj. **dustier, dustiest. 1.** covered with or involving dust. **2.** like dust. **3.** (of a colour) tinged with grey; pale. **4.** dull or unsatisfactory. —'**dustily** adv. —'**dustiness** n.

Dutch (dʌtʃ) n. **1.** the language of the Netherlands. **2. the Dutch.** (functioning as pl.) the natives, citizens, or inhabitants of the Netherlands. **3.** See **double Dutch. 4. in Dutch.** Sl. in trouble. ~adj. **5.** of the Netherlands, its inhabitants, or their language. ~adv. **6. go Dutch.** Inf. to share expenses equally.

Dutch auction n. an auction in which the price is lowered by stages until a buyer is found.

Dutch barn n. Brit. a farm building consisting of a steel frame and a curved roof.

Dutch courage n. **1.** false courage gained from drinking alcohol. **2.** alcoholic drink.

Dutch elm disease n. a fungal disease of elm trees characterized by withering of the foliage and stems and eventual death of the tree.

Dutchman ('dʌtʃmən) n., pl. **-men. 1.** a native, citizen, or inhabitant of the Netherlands. **2.** S. African derog. an Afrikaner.

Dutch medicine n. S. African. patent medicine, esp. made of herbs.

Dutch oven n. **1.** an iron or earthenware container with a cover, used for stews, etc. **2.** a metal box, open in front, for cooking in front of an open fire.

Dutch treat n. Inf. an entertainment, meal, etc., where each person pays for himself.

Dutch uncle n. Inf. a person who criticizes or reproves frankly and severely.

duteous ('dju:tɪəs) adj. Formal or arch. dutiful; obedient. —'**duteously** adv.

dutiable ('dju:tɪəb²l) adj. (of goods, etc.) liable to duty. —‚dutia'**bility** n.

dutiful ('dju:tɪful) adj. **1.** exhibiting or having a sense of duty. **2.** characterized by or resulting from a sense of duty: a dutiful answer.

duty ('dju:tɪ) n., pl. **-ties. 1.** a task or action that a person is bound to perform for moral or legal reasons. **2.** respect or obedience due to a superior, older persons, etc. **3.** the force that binds one morally or legally to one's obligations. **4.** a government tax, esp. on imports. **5.** Brit. **a.** the quantity of work for which a machine is designed. **b.** a measure of the efficiency of a machine. **6.** a job or service allocated. **7. do duty for.** to act as a substitute for. **8. on** (or **off**) **duty.** at (or not at) work.

duty-bound adj. morally obliged.

duty-free adj., adv. with exemption from customs or excise duties.

duty-free shop n. a shop, esp. one at a port or on board a ship, that sells perfume, tobacco, etc., at duty-free prices.

duvet ('du:veɪ) n. another name for **continental quilt.**

dwaal (dwɑːl) n. S. African. a state of befuddlement; daze.

dwarf (dwɔːf) n., pl. **dwarfs** or **dwarves** (dwɔːvz). **1.** an abnormally undersized person. **2. a.** an animal or plant much below the average height for the species. **b.** (as modifier): a dwarf tree. **3.** (in folklore) a small ugly manlike creature, often possessing magical powers. ~vb. **4.** to become or cause to become small in size, importance, etc. **5.** (tr.) to stunt the growth of. —'**dwarfish** adj.

dwell (dwɛl) vb. **dwelling, dwelt** or **dwelled.** (intr.) **1.** Formal, literary. to live as a permanent resident. **2.** to live (in a specified state): to dwell in poverty. ~n. **3.** a regular pause in the operation of a machine. —'**dweller** n.

dwelling ('dwɛlɪŋ) n. Formal, literary. a place of residence.

dwell on or **upon** vb. (intr., prep.) to think, speak, or write at length.

dwindle ('dwɪnd²l) vb. to grow or cause to grow less in size, intensity, or number.

Dy the chemical symbol for dysprosium.

dye (daɪ) n. **1.** a staining or colouring substance. **2.** a liquid that contains a colouring material and can be used to stain fabrics, skins, etc. **3.** the colour produced by dyeing. ~vb. **dyeing, dyed. 4.** (tr.) to impart a colour or stain to (fabric, hair, etc.) by or as if by the application of a dye. —'**dyable** or '**dyeable** adj. —'**dyer** n.

dyed-in-the-wool adj. **1.** extreme or unchanging in attitude, opinion, etc. **2.** (of a fabric) made of dyed yarn.

dyeing ('daɪɪŋ) n. the process or industry of colouring yarns, fabric, etc.

dying ('daɪɪŋ) vb. **1.** the present participle of **die**[1]. ~adj. **2.** relating to or occurring at the moment of death: a dying wish.

dyke[1] or esp. U.S. **dike** (daɪk) n. **1.** an embankment constructed to prevent flooding or keep out the sea. **2.** a ditch or watercourse. **3.** a bank made of earth alongside a ditch. **4.** a barrier or obstruction. **5.** a wall-like mass of igneous rock in older sedimentary rock. **6.** Austral. inf. a lavatory. ~vb. **7.** (tr.) to protect, enclose, or drain (land) with a dyke.

dyke[2] or **dike** (daɪk) n. Sl. a lesbian.

dynamic (daɪ'næmɪk) adj. **1.** of or concerned with energy or forces that produce motion, as opposed to static. **2.** of or concerned with dynamics. **3.** Also: **dynamical.** characterized by force of personality, ambition, energy, etc. **4.** Computers. (of a memory) needing its contents refreshed periodically. —dy'**namically** adv.

dynamics (daɪ'næmɪks) n. **1.** (functioning as sing.) the branch of mechanics concerned with the forces that change or produce the motions of bodies. **2.** (functioning as sing.) the branch of mechanics that includes statics and kinetics. **3.** (functioning as sing.) the branch of any science concerned with forces. **4.** those forces that produce change in any field or system. **5.** Music. **a.** the various degrees of loudness called for in performance. **b.** directions and symbols used to indicate degrees of

THESAURUS

dusty 1. dirty, grubby, sooty, unclean, undusted, unswept **2.** chalky, crumbly, friable, granular, powdery, sandy

dutiful compliant, conscientious, deferential, devoted, docile, duteous (Archaic), filial, obedient, punctilious, respectful, reverential, submissive

duty 1. assignment, business, calling, charge, engagement, function, mission, obligation, office, onus, province, responsibility, role, service, task, work **2.** allegiance, deference, loyalty, obedience, respect, reverence **3.** customs, due, excise, impost, levy, tariff, tax, toll **4. do duty for** stand in, substitute, take the place of **5. be the duty of** behove (Archaic), be incumbent upon, belong to, be (someone's) pigeon (Inf.), be up to (Inf.), devolve upon, pertain to, rest with **6. off duty** at

leisure, free, off, off work, on holiday **7. on duty** at work, busy, engaged

dwarf n. **1.** bantam, homunculus, hop-o'-my-thumb, Lilliputian, manikin, midget, pygmy, Tom Thumb **2.** gnome, goblin ~adj. **3.** baby, diminutive, dwarfed, Lilliputian, miniature, petite, pocket, small, tiny, undersized ~v. **4.** dim, diminish, dominate, minimize, overshadow, tower above or over **5.** check, cultivate by bonsai, lower, retard, stunt

dwell abide, establish oneself, hang out (Inf.), inhabit, live, lodge, quarter, remain, reside, rest, settle, sojourn, stay, stop

dwelling abode, domicile, dwelling house, establishment, habitation, home, house, lodging, quarters, residence

dwell on or **upon** be engrossed in, con-

tinue, elaborate, emphasize, expatiate, harp on, linger over, tarry over

dye 1. n. colorant, colour, colouring, pigment, stain, tinge, tint **2.** v. colour, pigment, stain, tincture, tinge, tint

dyed-in-the-wool complete, confirmed, deep-rooted, entrenched, established, inveterate, through-and-through

dying at death's door, ebbing, expiring, fading, failing, final, going, in extremis, moribund, mortal, passing, perishing, sinking

dynamic active, driving, electric, energetic, forceful, go-ahead, go-getting (Inf.), high-powered, lively, magnetic, powerful, vigorous, vital, zippy (Inf.)

loudness.

dynamism ('daɪnə‚mɪzəm) n. 1. Philosophy. any of several theories that attempt to explain phenomena in terms of an immanent force or energy. 2. the forcefulness of an energetic personality. —'dynamist n. —‚dyna'mistic adj.

dynamite ('daɪnə‚maɪt) n. 1. an explosive consisting of nitroglycerin mixed with an absorbent. 2. Inf. a spectacular or potentially dangerous person or thing. ~vb. 3. (tr.) to mine or blow up with dynamite. —'dyna‚miter n.

dynamo ('daɪnə‚məʊ) n., pl. -mos. 1. a device for converting mechanical energy into electrical energy. 2. Inf. an energetic hard-working person.

dynamoelectric (‚daɪnəməʊɪ'lɛktrɪk) or **dynamoelectrical** adj. of or concerned with the interconversion of mechanical and electrical energy.

dynamometer (‚daɪnə'mɒmɪtə) n. any of a number of instruments for measuring power.

dynast ('dɪnəst, -æst) n. a ruler, esp. a hereditary one.

dynasty ('dɪnəstɪ) n., pl. -ties. 1. a sequence of hereditary rulers. 2. any sequence of powerful leaders of the same family. —**dynastic** (dɪ'næstɪk) adj.

dyne (daɪn) n. the cgs unit of force; the force that imparts an acceleration of 1 centimetre per second per second to a mass of 1 gram. 1 dyne is equivalent to 10^{-5}

newton or 7.233×10^{-5} poundal.

dysentery ('dɪsəntrɪ) n. infection of the intestine marked by severe diarrhoea with the passage of mucus and blood. —**dysenteric** (‚dɪsən'tɛrɪk) adj.

dysfunction (dɪs'fʌŋkʃən) n. Med. any disturbance or abnormality in the function of an organ or part. —**dys'functional** adj.

dyslexia (dɪs'lɛksɪə) n. impaired ability to read, due to a disorder of the brain. —**dyslectic** (dɪs'lɛktɪk) adj., n. —**dys'lexic** adj.

dysmenorrhoea or esp. U.S. **dysmenorrhea** (‚dɪsmɛnə'rɪə) n. abnormally difficult or painful menstruation.

dyspepsia (dɪs'pɛpsɪə) n. indigestion or upset stomach. —**dys'peptic** adj., n.

dysphasia (dɪs'feɪzɪə) n. impaired coordination of speech. —**dys'phasic** adj., n.

dysprosium (dɪs'prəʊsɪəm) n. a metallic element of the lanthanide series: used in laser materials and as a neutron absorber in nuclear control rods. Symbol: Dy; atomic no.: 66; atomic wt.: 162.50.

dystrophy ('dɪstrəfɪ) n. any of various bodily disorders, characterized by wasting of tissues. See also **muscular dystrophy.** —**dystrophic** (dɪs'trɒfɪk) adj.

dz. abbrev. for dozen.

THESAURUS

dynasty ascendancy, dominion, empire, government, house, regime, rule, sovereignty, sway

E

e *or* **E** (iː) *n., pl.* **e's, E's,** *or* **Es. 1.** the fifth letter and second vowel of the English alphabet. **2.** any of several speech sounds represented by this letter, as in *he, bet,* or *below.*

e *symbol for:* **1.** *Maths.* a transcendental number used as the base of natural logarithms. Approximate value: 2.718 282... **2.** electron.

E *symbol for:* **1.** *Music.* **a.** the third note of the scale of C major. **b.** the major or minor key having this note as its tonic. **2.** *Physics.* **a.** energy. **b.** electromotive force. **3.** East. **4.** English. **5.** Egypt(ian).

e. *abbrev. for* engineer(ing).

E. *abbrev. for* Earl.

each (iːtʃ) *determiner.* **1. a.** every (one) of two or more considered individually: *each day; each person.* **b.** *(as pronoun): each gave according to his ability.* ~*adv.* **2.** for, to, or from each one; apiece: *four apples each.*

eager ('iːɡə) *adj.* **1.** *(postpositive; often foll. by to or for)* impatiently desirous (of); anxious or avid (for). **2.** characterized by or feeling expectancy or great desire: *an eager look.* **3.** *Arch.* biting; sharp. —**'eagerly** *adv.* —**'eagerness** *n.*

eager beaver *n. Inf.* a person who displays conspicuous diligence.

eagle ('iːɡəl) *n.* **1.** any of various birds of prey having large broad wings and strong soaring flight. Related adj.: **aquiline. 2.** a representation of an eagle used as an emblem, etc., esp. representing power: *the Roman eagle.* **3.** a standard, seal, etc., bearing the figure of an eagle. **4.** *Golf.* a score of two strokes under par for a hole. **5.** a former U.S. gold coin worth ten dollars.

eagle-eyed *adj.* having keen or piercing eyesight.

eaglet ('iːɡlɪt) *n.* a young eagle.

ear[1] (ɪə) *n.* **1.** the organ of hearing and balance in higher vertebrates (see **middle ear**). Related adj.: **aural. 2.** the outermost cartilaginous part of the ear in mammals, esp. man. **3.** the sense of hearing. **4.** sensitivity to musical sounds, poetic diction, etc.: *he has an ear for music.* **5.** attention, consideration (esp. in **give ear to, lend an ear**). **6.** an object resembling the external ear. **7. all ears.** *Inf.* very attentive; listening carefully. **8. by ear.** without reading from written music. **9. fall on deaf ears.** to be ignored or pass unnoticed. **10. in one ear and out the other.** *Inf.* heard but unheeded. **11. keep (or have) one's ear to the ground.** *Inf.* to be or try to be well informed about current trends and opinions. **12. out on one's ear.** *Inf.* dismissed unceremoniously. **13. play by ear. a.** *Inf.* to act according to the demands of a situation; improvise. **b.** to perform a musical piece on an instrument without written music. **14. a thick ear.** *Inf.* a blow on the ear. **15. turn a deaf ear.** *Inf.* to be unwilling to pay attention. **16. up to one's ears.** *Inf.* deeply involved, as in work or debt. —**eared** *adj.* —**'earless** *adj.*

ear[2] (ɪə) *n.* **1.** the part of a cereal plant, such as wheat or barley, that contains the seeds, grains, or kernels. ~*vb.* **2.** *(intr.)* (of cereal plants) to develop such parts.

earache ('ɪərˌeɪk) *n.* pain in the ear.

eardrum ('ɪəˌdrʌm) *n.* the nontechnical name for **tympanic membrane.**

earl (ɜːl) *n.* (in the British Isles) a nobleman ranking below a marquess and above a viscount. Female equivalent: **countess.** —**'earldom** *n.*

Earl Marshal *n.* an officer of the English peerage who presides over the College of Heralds and organizes royal processions and other important ceremonies.

early ('ɜːlɪ) *adj., adv.* **-lier, -liest. 1.** before the expected or usual time. **2.** occurring in or characteristic of the first part of a period or sequence. **3.** occurring in or characteristic of a period far back in time. **4.** occurring in the near future. **5. in the early days. a.** during the first years of any enterprise, such as marriage. **b.** *N.Z.* during the 19th-century pioneering period in New Zealand. —**'earliness** *n.*

Early English *n.* a style of architecture used in England in the 12th and 13th centuries, characterized by lancet arches and plate tracery.

earmark ('ɪəˌmɑːk) *vb. (tr.)* **1.** to set aside or mark out for a specific purpose. **2.** to make an identification mark on the ear of (a domestic animal). ~*n.* **3.** such a mark of identification. **4.** any distinguishing mark or characteristic.

earn (ɜːn) *vb.* **1.** to gain or be paid (money or other payment) in return for work or service. **2.** *(tr.)* to acquire or deserve through behaviour or action. **3.** *(tr.)* (of securities, investments, etc.) to gain (interest, profit, etc.). —**'earner** *n.*

earnest[1] ('ɜːnɪst) *adj.* **1.** serious in mind or intention. **2.** characterized by sincerity of intention. **3.** demanding or receiving serious attention. ~*n.* **4. in earnest.** with serious or sincere intentions. —**'earnestness** *n.*

earnest[2] ('ɜːnɪst) *n.* **1.** a part of something given in advance as a guarantee of the remainder. **2.** Also called: **earnest money.** *Contract law.* something given, usually a nominal sum of money, to confirm a contract. **3.** any token of something to follow.

earnings ('ɜːnɪŋz) *pl. n.* **1.** money or other payment earned. **2. a.** the profits of an enterprise. **b.** an individual's investment income.

earphone ('ɪəˌfəʊn) *n.* a device for converting electric currents into sound waves, held close to or inserted into the ear.

ear piercing *n.* the making of a hole in the lobe of an ear, using a sterilized needle, so that earrings may be worn fastened in the hole.

earplug ('ɪəˌplʌɡ) *n.* a piece of soft material placed in the ear to keep out noise or water.

earring ('ɪəˌrɪŋ) *n.* an ornament for the ear, usually clipped onto the lobe or fastened through a hole pierced in the lobe.

earshot ('ɪəˌʃɒt) *n.* the range or distance within which sound may be heard.

ear-splitting *or* **ear-piercing** *adj.* so loud or shrill as to hurt the ears.

earth (ɜːθ) *n.* **1.** *(sometimes cap.)* the third planet from the sun, the only planet on which life is known to exist. Related adjs.: **terrestrial, telluric. 2.** the inhabitants of this planet: *the whole earth rejoiced.* **3.** the dry surface of this planet; land; ground. **4.** the loose soft material on

---

the surface of the ground that consists of disintegrated rock particles, mould, clay, etc.; soil. **5.** worldly or temporal matters as opposed to the concerns of the spirit. **6.** the hole in which a burrowing animal, esp. a fox, lives. **7.** *Chem.* See **rare earth. 8. a.** a connection between an electrical circuit or device and the earth, which is at zero potential. **b.** a terminal to which this connection is made. **9.** (*modifier*) *Astrol.* of or relating to a group of three signs of the zodiac: Taurus, Virgo, and Capricorn. **10. come back** or **down to earth.** to return to reality from a fantasy or daydream. **11. on earth.** used as an intensifier in **what on earth, who on earth,** etc. **12. run to earth. a.** to hunt (an animal, esp. a fox) to its earth and trap it there. **b.** to hunt (a criminal, etc.) down. ~*vb.* **13.** (*tr.*) to connect (a circuit, device, etc.) to earth. ~See also **earth up.**

earthbound (ˈɜːθˌbaʊnd) *adj.* **1.** confined to the earth. **2.** heading towards the earth.

earth closet *n.* a type of lavatory in which earth is used to cover excreta.

earthen (ˈɜːθən) *adj.* (*prenominal*) **1.** made of baked clay: *an earthen pot.* **2.** made of earth.

earthenware (ˈɜːθənˌwɛə) *n.* **a.** vessels, etc., made of baked clay. **b.** (*as adj.*): *an earthenware pot.*

earthly (ˈɜːθlɪ) *adj.* **-lier, -liest. 1.** of or characteristic of the earth as opposed to heaven; materialistic; worldly. **2.** (*usually with a negative*) *Inf.* conceivable or possible (in **not an earthly** (**chance**), etc.). —**ˈearthliness** *n.*

earthnut (ˈɜːθˌnʌt) *n.* **1.** a perennial umbelliferous plant of Europe and Asia, having edible dark brown tubers. **2.** any of various plants having an edible root, tuber or underground pod, such as the peanut or truffle.

earthquake (ˈɜːθˌkweɪk) *n.* a series of vibrations at the earth's surface caused by movement along a fault plane, volcanic activity, etc. Related adj.: **seismic.**

earth science *n.* any of various sciences, such as geology and geography, that are concerned with the structure, age, etc. of the earth.

earth up *vb.* (*tr., adv.*) to cover (part of a plant) with soil to protect from frost, light, etc.

earthward (ˈɜːθwəd) *adj.* directed towards the earth. —**ˈearthwards** *adv.*

earthwork (ˈɜːθˌwɜːk) *n.* **1.** excavation of earth, as in engineering construction. **2.** a fortification made of earth.

earthworm (ˈɜːθˌwɜːm) *n.* any of numerous worms which burrow in the soil and help aerate and break up the ground.

earthy (ˈɜːθɪ) *adj.* **-ier, -iest. 1.** of, composed of, or characteristic of earth. **2.** unrefined, coarse, or crude. —**ˈearthily** *adv.* —**ˈearthiness** *n.*

ear trumpet *n.* a trumpet-shaped instrument held to the ear: an old form of hearing aid.

earwig (ˈɪəˌwɪg) *n.* **1.** any of various insects that typically have an elongated body with small leathery forewings, semicircular membranous hindwings, and curved forceps at the tip of the abdomen. ~*vb.* **-wigging, -wigged. 2.** (*tr.*) *Arch.* to attempt to influence (a person) by private insinuation.

ease (iːz) *n.* **1.** freedom from discomfort, worry, or anxiety. **2.** lack of difficulty, labour, or awkwardness. **3.** rest, leisure, or relaxation. **4.** freedom from poverty; affluence: *a life of ease.* **5.** lack of restraint, embarrassment, or stiffness: *ease of manner.* **6. at ease. a.** *Mil.* (of a standing soldier, etc.) in a relaxed position rather than at attention. **b.** a command to adopt such a position. **c.** in a relaxed attitude or frame of mind. ~*vb.* **7.** to make or become less burdensome. **8.** (*tr.*) to relieve (a person) of worry or care; comfort. **9.** (*tr.*) to make comfort-

able or give rest to. **10.** (*tr.*) to make less difficult; facilitate. **11.** to move or cause to move into, out of, etc., with careful manipulation. **12.** (when *intr.*, often foll. by *off* or *up*) to lessen or cause to lessen in severity, pressure, tension, or strain. **13. ease oneself** or **ease nature.** *Arch., euphemistic.* to urinate or defecate. —**ˈeaser** *n.* —**ˈeaseful** *adj.*

easel (ˈiːzəl) *n.* a frame, usually an upright tripod, for supporting or displaying an artist's canvas, a blackboard, etc.

easement (ˈiːzmənt) *n.* **1.** *Property law.* the right enjoyed by a landowner of making limited use of his neighbour's land, as by crossing it to reach his own property. **2.** the act of easing or something that brings ease.

easily (ˈiːzɪlɪ) *adv.* **1.** with ease; without difficulty or exertion. **2.** by far; undoubtedly: *easily the best.* **3.** probably; almost certainly.

▷ Usage. See at **easy.**

easiness (ˈiːzɪnɪs) *n.* **1.** the quality or condition of being easy to accomplish, do, obtain, etc. **2.** ease or relaxation of manner; nonchalance.

east (iːst) *n.* **1.** the direction along a parallel towards the sunrise, at 90° to north; the direction of the earth's rotation. **2. the east.** (*often cap.*) any area lying in or towards the east. Related adj.: **oriental.** ~*adj.* **3.** situated in, moving towards, or facing the east. **4.** (esp. of the wind) from the east. ~*adv.* **5.** in, to, or towards the east. **6. back East.** *Canad.* in or to E Canada, esp. east of Quebec.

East (iːst) *n.* **the. 1.** the continent of Asia regarded as culturally distinct from Europe and the West; the Orient. **2.** the countries under Communist rule, lying mainly in the E hemisphere. ~*adj.* **3.** of or denoting the eastern part of a specified country, area, etc.

eastbound (ˈiːstˌbaʊnd) *adj.* going or leading towards the east.

Easter (ˈiːstə) *n.* **1.** a festival of the Christian Church commemorating the Resurrection of Christ: falls on the Sunday following the first full moon after the vernal equinox. **2.** Also called: **Easter Sunday, Easter Day.** the day on which this festival is celebrated. **3.** the period between Good Friday and Easter Monday. Related adj.: **paschal.**

Easter egg *n.* an egg given to children at Easter, usually a chocolate egg or a hen's egg with its shell painted.

easterly (ˈiːstəlɪ) *adj.* **1.** of or in the east. ~*adv., adj.* **2.** towards the east. **3.** from the east: *an easterly wind.* ~*n., pl.* **-lies. 4.** a wind from the east.

eastern (ˈiːstən) *adj.* **1.** situated in or towards the east. **2.** facing or moving towards the east.

Eastern Church *n.* **1.** any of the Christian Churches of the former Byzantine Empire. **2.** any Church owing allegiance to the Orthodox Church. **3.** any Church having Eastern forms of liturgy and institutions.

eastern hemisphere *n.* (*often caps.*) **1.** that half of the globe containing Europe, Asia, Africa, and Australia, lying east of the Greenwich meridian. **2.** the lands in this, esp. Asia.

Eastertide (ˈiːstəˌtaɪd) *n.* the Easter season.

east-northeast *n.* **1.** the point on the compass or the direction midway between northeast and east. ~*adj., adv.* **2.** in, from, or towards this direction.

east-southeast *n.* **1.** the point on the compass or the direction midway between east and southeast. ~*adj., adv.* **2.** in, from, or towards this direction.

eastward (ˈiːstwəd) *adj.* **1.** situated or directed towards the east. ~*n.* **2.** the eastward part, direction, etc. —**ˈeastwardly** *adv., adj.* —**ˈeastwards** *adv.*

THESAURUS

earth 1. globe, orb, planet, sphere, terrestrial sphere, world **2.** clay, clod, dirt, ground, land, loam, mould, sod, soil, topsoil, turf

earthenware ceramics, crockery, crocks, pots, pottery, terra cotta

earthly 1. mundane, sublunary, tellurian, telluric, terrene, terrestrial, worldly **2.** human, material, mortal, non-spiritual, profane, secular, temporal, worldly **3.** base, carnal, fleshly, gross, low, materialistic, physical, sensual, sordid, vile **4.** *Inf.* conceivable, feasible, imaginable, likely, possible, practical

ease *n.* **1.** affluence, calmness, comfort,

content, contentment, enjoyment, happiness, leisure, peace, peace of mind, quiet, quietude, relaxation, repose, rest, restfulness, serenity, tranquillity **2.** easiness, effortlessness, facility, readiness, simplicity **3.** flexibility, freedom, informality, liberty, naturalness, unaffectedness, unconstraint, unreservedness **4.** aplomb, composure, insouciance, nonchalance, poise, relaxedness ~*v.* **5.** abate, allay, alleviate, appease, assuage, calm, comfort, disburden, lessen, lighten, mitigate, moderate, mollify, pacify, palliate, quiet, relax, relent, relieve, slacken, soothe, still, tranquillize **6.** aid, assist, expedite, facili-

tate, forward, further, lessen the labour of, make easier, simplify, smooth, speed up **7.** edge, guide, inch, manoeuvre, move carefully, slide, slip, squeeze, steer

easily 1. comfortably, effortlessly, facilely, readily, simply, smoothly, with ease, without difficulty, without trouble **2.** absolutely, beyond question, by far, certainly, clearly, definitely, doubtlessly, far and away, indisputably, indubitably, plainly, surely, undeniably, undoubtedly, unequivocally, unquestionably, without a doubt **3.** almost certainly, probably, well

easy ('iːzɪ) *adj.* **easier, easiest. 1.** not requiring much labour or effort; not difficult. **2.** free from pain, care, or anxiety. **3.** not restricting; lenient: *easy laws.* **4.** tolerant and undemanding; easy-going: *an easy disposition.* **5.** readily influenced; pliant: *an easy victim.* **6.** not constricting; loose: *an easy fit.* **7.** not strained or extreme; moderate: *an easy pace.* **8.** *Inf.* ready to fall in with any suggestion made; not predisposed: *he is easy about what to do.* **9. Easy Street.** *Inf.* a state of financial security. ~*adv.* **10.** *Inf.* in an easy or relaxed manner. **11. easy does it.** *Inf.* go slowly and carefully; be careful. **12. go easy.** (*usually imperative;* often foll. by *on*) *Inf.* to exercise moderation. **13. stand easy.** *Mil.* a command to soldiers standing at ease that they may relax further. **14. take it easy.** *Inf.* **a.** to avoid stress or undue hurry. **b.** to remain calm.
▷ **Usage.** *Easy* is not used as an adverb by careful speakers and writers except in certain set phrases: *to take it easy; easy does it.* Where a fixed expression is not involved, the usual adverbial form of *easy* is preferred: *this polish goes on more easily* (not *easier*) *than the other.*

easy chair *n.* a comfortable upholstered armchair.

easy-going ('iːzɪ'gəʊɪŋ) *adj.* **1.** relaxed in manner or attitude; excessively tolerant. **2.** moving at a comfortable pace: *an easy-going horse.*

eat (iːt) *vb.* **eating, ate, eaten. 1.** to take into the mouth and swallow (food, etc.), esp. after biting and chewing. **2.** (*tr.;* often foll. by *away* or *up*) to destroy as if by eating: *the damp had eaten away the woodwork.* **3.** (often foll. by *into*) to use up or waste: *taxes ate into his inheritance.* **4.** (often foll. by *into* or *through*) to make (a hole, passage, etc.) by eating or gnawing: *rats ate through the floor.* **5.** to take or have (a meal or meals): *we eat at six.* **6.** (*tr.*) to include as part of one's diet: *he doesn't eat fish.* **7.** (*tr.*) *Inf.* to cause to worry; make anxious: *what's eating you?* **8. eat one's hat if.** *Inf.* to be greatly surprised if (something happens). **9. eat one's heart out.** *Inf.* to pine with grief or longing. **10. eat one's words.** to take back something said; recant; retract. —'**eater** *n.*

eatable ('iːtəb³l) *adj.* fit or suitable for eating; edible.

eating ('iːtɪŋ) *n.* **1.** food, esp. in relation to quality or taste: *this fruit makes excellent eating.* ~*adj.* **2.** suitable for eating: *eating pears.* **3.** relating to or for eating: *an eating house.*

eat out *vb.* (*intr., adv.*) to eat away from home, esp. in a restaurant.

eats (iːts) *pl. n. Sl.* articles of food; provisions.

eat up *vb.* (*adv., mainly tr.*) **1.** (*also intr.*) to eat or consume entirely. **2.** *Inf.* to listen to with enthusiasm or appreciation: *the audience ate up his every word.* **3.** (often *passive*) *Inf.* to affect grossly: *she was eaten up by jealousy.* **4.** *Inf.* to travel a (distance) quickly: *we just ate up the miles.*

eau de Cologne (ˌəʊ də kə'ləʊn) *n.* See **cologne.**

eau de vie (ˌəʊ də 'viː) *n.* brandy or other spirits.

eaves (iːvz) *pl. n.* the edge of a roof that projects beyond the wall.

eavesdrop ('iːvzˌdrɒp) *vb.* **-dropping, -dropped.** (*intr.*) to listen secretly to the private conversation of others. —'**eavesˌdropper** *n.*

ebb (ɛb) *vb.* (*intr.*) **1.** (of tide water) to flow back or recede. Cf. **flow** (sense 8). **2.** to fall away or decline. ~*n.* **3. a.** the flowing back of the tide from high to low water or the period in which this takes place. **b.** (*as modifier*): *the ebb tide.* Cf. **flood** (sense 3). **4. at a low ebb.** in a state of weakness or decline.

ebony ('ɛbənɪ) *n., pl.* **-onies. 1.** any of various tropical and subtropical trees that have hard dark wood. **2.** the wood of such a tree. **3. a.** a black colour. **b.** (*as adj.*): *an ebony skin.*

ebullient (ɪ'bʌljənt, ɪ'bʊl-) *adj.* **1.** overflowing with enthusiasm or excitement. **2.** boiling. —e'**bullience** *or* e'**bulliency** *n.*

ebullition (ˌɛbə'lɪʃən) *n.* **1.** the process of boiling. **2.** a sudden outburst, as of intense emotion.

ec- *combining form.* out from; away from: *eccentric; ecdysis.*

EC *abbrev. for* East Central.

eccentric (ɪk'sɛntrɪk) *adj.* **1.** deviating or departing from convention; irregular or odd. **2.** situated away from the centre or the axis. **3.** not having a common centre: *eccentric circles.* **4.** not precisely circular. ~*n.* **5.** a person who deviates from normal forms of behaviour. **6.** a device for converting rotary motion to reciprocating motion. —ec'**centrically** *adv.*

eccentricity (ˌɛksɛn'trɪsɪtɪ) *n., pl.* **-ties. 1.** unconventional or irregular behaviour. **2.** the state of being eccentric. **3.** deviation from a circular path or orbit. **4.** *Geom.* a number that expresses the shape of a conic section. **5.** the degree of displacement of the geometric centre of a part from the true centre, esp. of the axis of rotation of a wheel.

Eccles. *or* **Eccl.** *Bible. abbrev. for* Ecclesiastes.

ecclesiastic (ɪˌkliːzɪ'æstɪk) *n.* **1.** a clergyman or other person in holy orders. ~*adj.* **2.** of or associated with the Christian Church or clergy.

ecclesiastical (ɪˌkliːzɪ'æstɪkəl) *adj.* of or relating to the Christian Church. —ecˌclesi'**astically** *adv.*

E.C.G. *abbrev. for:* **1.** electrocardiogram. **2.** electrocardiograph.

echelon ('ɛʃəˌlɒn) *n.* **1.** a level of command, responsibility, etc. (esp. in the **upper echelons**). **2.** *Mil.* **a.** a formation in which units follow one another but are offset sufficiently to allow each unit a line of fire ahead. **b.** a group formed in this way. ~*vb.* **3.** to assemble in echelon.

echidna (ɪ'kɪdnə) *n., pl.* **-nas** *or* **-nae** (-niː). a spine-covered monotreme mammal of Australia and New Guinea, having a long snout and claws. Also called: **spiny anteater.**

echinoderm (ɪ'kaɪnəʊˌdɜːm) *n.* any of various marine invertebrates characterized by tube feet, a calcite body-covering, and a five-part symmetrical body. The group

---

THESAURUS

easy 1. a piece of cake (*Inf.*), a pushover (*Sl.*), child's play (*Inf.*), clear, effortless, facile, light, no bother, not difficult, no trouble, painless, simple, smooth, straightforward, uncomplicated, undemanding **2.** calm, carefree, comfortable, contented, cushy (*Sl.*), easeful, leisurely, peaceful, pleasant, quiet, relaxed, satisfied, serene, tranquil, undisturbed, untroubled, unworried, well-to-do **3.** flexible, indulgent, lenient, liberal, light, mild, permissive, tolerant, unburdensome, unoppressive **4.** affable, casual, easy-going, friendly, gentle, graceful, gracious, informal, mild, natural, open, pleasant, relaxed, smooth, tolerant, unaffected, unceremonious, unconstrained, undemanding, unforced, unpretentious **5.** accommodating, amenable, biddable, compliant, docile, gullible, manageable, pliant, soft, submissive, suggestible, susceptible, tractable, trusting, yielding **6.** comfortable, gentle, leisurely, light, mild, moderate, temperate, undemanding, unexacting, unhurried

easy-going amenable, calm, carefree, casual, complacent, easy, even-tempered, flexible, happy-go-lucky, indulgent, insouci-

ant, laid-back (*Inf.*), lenient, liberal, mild, moderate, nonchalant, permissive, placid, relaxed, serene, tolerant, unconcerned, uncritical, undemanding, unhurried

eat 1. chew, consume, devour, ingest, munch, scoff (*Sl.*), swallow **2.** break bread, dine, feed, have a meal, take food, take nourishment **3.** corrode, crumble, decay, dissolve, erode, rot, waste away, wear away **4. eat one's words** abjure, recant, rescind, retract, take (statement) back

eavesdrop bug (*Inf.*), listen in, monitor, overhear, snoop (*Inf.*), spy, tap (*Inf.*)

ebb *v.* **1.** abate, fall away, fall back, flow back, go out, recede, retire, retreat, retrocede, sink, subside, wane, withdraw ~*n.* **2.** ebb tide, going out, low tide, low water, reflux, regression, retreat, retrocession, subsidence, wane, waning, withdrawal ~*v.* **3.** decay, decline, decrease, degenerate, deteriorate, diminish, drop, dwindle, fade away, fall away, flag, lessen, peter out, shrink, sink, slacken, weaken ~*n.* **4.** decay, decline, decrease, degeneration, deterioration, diminution, drop, dwindling, fading away, flagging, lessening, petering out,

shrinkage, sinking, slackening, weakening

eccentric 1. *adj.* aberrant, abnormal, anomalous, bizarre, capricious, erratic, freakish, idiosyncratic, irregular, odd, outlandish, peculiar, queer (*Inf.*), quirky, singular, strange, uncommon, unconventional, weird, whimsical **2.** *n.* case (*Inf.*), character (*Inf.*), crank (*Inf.*), freak (*Sl.*), nonconformist, odd fish (*Inf.*), oddity, weirdie *or* weirdo (*Inf.*)

eccentricity aberration, abnormality, anomaly, bizarreness, caprice, capriciousness, foible, freakishness, idiosyncrasy, irregularity, nonconformity, oddity, oddness, outlandishness, peculiarity, queerness (*Inf.*), quirk, singularity, strangeness, unconventionality, waywardness, weirdness, whimsicality, whimsicalness

ecclesiastic 1. *n.* churchman, clergyman, cleric, divine, holy man, man of the cloth, minister, parson, priest **2.** *adj.* Also **ecclesiastical** church, churchly, clerical, divine, holy, pastoral, priestly, religious, spiritual

includes the starfish, sea urchins, and sea cucumbers.

echo ('ɛkəʊ) n., pl. **-oes. 1. a.** the reflection of sound or other radiation by a reflecting medium, esp. a solid object. **b.** the sound so reflected. **2.** a repetition or imitation, esp. an unoriginal reproduction of another's opinions. **3.** something that evokes memories. **4.** (*sometimes pl.*) an effect that continues after the original cause has disappeared: *echoes of the French Revolution.* **5.** a person who copies another, esp. one who obsequiously agrees with another's opinions. **6. a.** the signal reflected by a radar target. **b.** the trace produced by such a signal on a radar screen. ~*vb.* **-oing, -oed. 7.** to resound or cause to resound with an echo. **8.** (*intr.*) (of sounds) to repeat or resound by echoes; reverberate. **9.** (*tr.*) (of persons) to repeat (words, opinions, etc.) in imitation, agreement, or flattery. **10.** (*tr.*) (of things) to resemble or imitate (another style, an earlier model, etc.). —'**echoless** adj. —'**echo,like** adj.

echo chamber n. Also called: **reverberation chamber.** a room with walls that reflect sound. It is used to make acoustic measurements and as a recording studio when echo effects are required.

echoic (ɛ'kəʊɪk) adj. **1.** characteristic of or resembling an echo. **2.** onomatopoeic; imitative.

echolocation (,ɛkəʊləʊ'keɪʃən) n. determination of the position of an object by measuring the time taken for an echo to return from it and its direction.

echo sounder n. a device for determining depth by measuring the time taken for a pulse of sound to reach the sea bed or a submerged object and for the echo to return. —**echo sounding** n.

éclair (eɪ'klɛə, ɪ'klɛə) n. a finger-shaped cake of choux pastry, usually filled with cream and covered with chocolate.

éclat (eɪ'klɑː) n. **1.** brilliant or conspicuous success, effect, etc. **2.** showy display; ostentation. **3.** social distinction. **4.** approval; acclaim; applause.

eclectic (ɪ'klɛktɪk, ɛ'klɛk-) adj. **1.** selecting from various styles, ideas, methods, etc. **2.** composed of elements drawn from a variety of sources, styles, etc. ~n. **3.** a person who favours an eclectic approach. —e'**clectically** adv. —e'**clecticism** n.

eclipse (ɪ'klɪps) n. **1.** the total or partial obscuring of one celestial body by another (**total eclipse** or **partial eclipse**). A **solar eclipse** occurs when the moon passes between the sun and the earth; a **lunar eclipse** when the earth passes between the sun and the moon. **2.** the period of time during which such a phenomenon occurs. **3.** any dimming or obstruction of light. **4.** a loss of importance, power, fame, etc., esp. through overshadowing by another. ~*vb.* (*tr.*) **5.** to cause an eclipse of. **6.** to cast a shadow upon; obscure. **7.** to overshadow or surpass. —e'**clipser** n.

ecliptic (ɪ'klɪptɪk) n. *Astron.* **a.** the great circle on the celestial sphere representing the apparent annual path of the sun relative to the stars. **b.** (*as modifier*): *the ecliptic plane.* **2.** an equivalent great circle on the terrestrial globe. ~*adj.* **3.** of or relating to an eclipse. —e'**cliptically** adv.

eclogue ('ɛklɒg) n. a pastoral or idyllic poem, usually in the form of a conversation.

eco- *combining form.* denoting ecology or ecological: *ecocide; ecosphere.*

ecology (ɪ'kɒlədʒɪ) n. **1.** the study of the relationships between living organisms and their environment. **2.** the set of relationships of a particular organism with its environment. —**ecological** (,iːkə'lɒdʒɪkəl) adj.

—e'**cologist** n.

econ. abbrev. for: **1.** economical. **2.** economics. **3.** economy.

economic (,iːkə'nɒmɪk, ,ɛkə-) adj. **1.** of or relating to an economy, economics, or finance. **2.** *Brit.* capable of being produced, operated, etc., for profit; profitable. **3.** concerning or affecting material resources or welfare: *economic pests.* **4.** concerned with or relating to the necessities of life; utilitarian. **5.** a variant of **economical.** **6.** *Inf.* inexpensive; cheap.

economical (,iːkə'nɒmɪkəl, ,ɛkə-) adj. **1.** using the minimum required; not wasteful. **2.** frugal; thrifty. **3.** a variant of **economic** (senses 1-4). —,eco'**nomically** adv.

economics (,iːkə'nɒmɪks, ,ɛkə-) n. **1.** (*functioning as sing.*) the social science concerned with the production and consumption of goods and services and the analysis of the commercial activities of a society. **2.** (*pl.*) financial aspects.

economist (ɪ'kɒnəmɪst) n. a specialist in economics.

economize or **-ise** (ɪ'kɒnə,maɪz) vb. (often foll. by on) to limit or reduce (expense, waste, etc.). —e,conomi'**zation** or **-i'sation** n.

economy (ɪ'kɒnəmɪ) n., pl. **-mies. 1.** careful management of resources to avoid unnecessary expenditure or waste; thrift. **2.** a means or instance of this; saving. **3.** sparing, restrained, or efficient use. **4. a.** the complex of activities undertaken for profit and concerned with the production, distribution, and consumption of goods and services. **b.** a particular type or branch of this: *a socialist economy.* **5.** the management of the resources, finances, income, and expenditure of a community, business enterprise, etc. **6. a.** a class of travel in aircraft, cheaper and less luxurious than first class. **b.** (*as modifier*): *economy class.* **7.** (*modifier*) purporting to offer a larger quantity for a lower price: *economy pack.* **8.** the orderly interplay between the parts of a system or structure.

ecosystem ('iːkəʊ,sɪstəm, 'ɛkəʊ-) n. *Ecology.* a system involving the interactions between a community and its non-living environment.

ecru ('ɛkruː, 'eɪkruː) n., adj. (of) a greyish-yellow to a light greyish colour.

ecstasy ('ɛkstəsɪ) n., pl. **-sies. 1.** (*often pl.*) a state of exalted delight, joy, etc.; rapture. **2.** intense emotion of any kind: *an ecstasy of rage.* **3.** *Psychol.* overpowering emotion sometimes involving temporary loss of consciousness: often associated with mysticism. —ec'**static** adj.

E.C.T. abbrev. for electroconvulsive therapy.

ecto- *combining form.* indicating outer, outside.

ectomorph ('ɛktəʊ,mɔːf) n. a type of person having a body build characterized by thinness, weakness, and a lack of weight. —,ecto'**morphic** adj. —'**ecto,morphy** n.

-ectomy n. *combining form.* indicating surgical excision of a part: *appendectomy.*

ectoplasm ('ɛktəʊ,plæzəm) n. **1.** *Cytology.* the outer layer of cytoplasm. **2.** *Spiritualism.* the substance supposedly emanating from the body of a medium during trances. —,ecto'**plasmic** adj.

ecumenical, oecumenical (,iːkjʊ'mɛnɪkəl, ,ɛk-) or **ecumenic, oecumenic** adj. **1.** of or relating to the Christian Church throughout the world, esp. with regard to its unity. **2.** tending to promote unity among Churches. —,ecu'**menically** or ,oecu'**menically** adv.

eczema ('ɛksɪmə) n. *Pathol.* a skin inflammation with

THESAURUS

echo v. **1.** repeat, resound, reverberate **2.** ape, copy, imitate, mirror, parallel, parrot, recall, reflect, reiterate, reproduce, resemble, ring, second ~n. **3.** answer, repetition, reverberation **4.** copy, imitation, mirror image, parallel, reflection, reiteration, reproduction, ringing **5.** allusion, evocation, hint, intimation, memory, reminder, suggestion, trace **6.** *Often plural* aftereffect, aftermath, consequence, repercussion

eclipse v. **1.** blot out, cloud, darken, dim, extinguish, obscure, overshadow, shroud, veil **2.** exceed, excel, outdo, outshine, surpass, transcend ~n. **3.** darkening, dimming, extinction, obscuration, occultation, shading **4.** decline, diminution, failure, fall, loss

economic 1. business, commercial, financial, industrial, mercantile, trade **2.** money-making, productive, profitable, profit-making, remunerative, solvent, viable **3.** bread-and-butter (*Inf.*), budgetary, financial, fiscal, material, monetary, pecuniary **4.** *Inf.* Also **economical** cheap, fair, inexpensive, low, low-priced, modest, reasonable

economical 1. cost-effective, efficient, money-saving, sparing, time-saving, unwasteful, work-saving **2.** careful, economizing, frugal, prudent, saving, scrimping, sparing, thrifty **3.** *Also* **economic** cheap, fair, inexpensive, low, low-priced, modest, reasonable

economize be economical, be frugal, be

sparing, cut back, husband, retrench, save, scrimp, tighten one's belt

economy frugality, husbandry, parsimony, providence, prudence, restraint, retrenchment, saving, sparingness, thrift, thriftiness

ecstasy bliss, delight, elation, enthusiasm, euphoria, exaltation, fervour, frenzy, joy, rapture, ravishment, rhapsody, seventh heaven, trance, transport

ecstatic blissful, delirious, elated, enraptured, enthusiastic, entranced, euphoric, fervent, frenzied, in exaltation, in transports of delight, joyful, joyous, on cloud nine (*Inf.*), overjoyed, rapturous, rhapsodic, transported

lesions that scale, crust, or ooze a serous fluid, often accompanied by intense itching. —**eczematous** (ɛkˈsɛmətəs) *adj.*

ed. *abbrev. for:* **1.** edited. **2.** (*pl.* **eds.**) edition. **3.** (*pl.* **eds.**) editor. **4.** education.

Edam (ˈiːdæm) *n.* a round yellow cheese with a red outside covering.

E.D.C. *abbrev. for* European Defence Community.

eddy (ˈɛdɪ) *n.*, *pl.* **-dies.** **1.** a movement in air, water, or other fluid in which the current doubles back on itself causing a miniature whirlwind or whirlpool. **2.** a deviation from or disturbance in the main trend of thought, life, etc. ~*vb.* **-dying, -died.** **3.** to move or cause to move against the main current.

edelweiss (ˈeɪdəlˌvaɪs) *n.* a small alpine flowering plant having white woolly oblong leaves and a tuft of floral leaves surrounding the flowers.

Eden (ˈiːdən) *n.* **1.** Also called: **Garden of Eden.** *Bible.* the garden in which Adam and Eve were placed at the Creation. **2.** a place or state of great delight or contentment.

edentate (iːˈdɛnteɪt) *n.* **1.** any mammal of the order *Edentata*, of tropical Central and South America, which have few or no teeth. The order includes anteaters, sloths, and armadillos. ~*adj.* **2.** of or relating to the order *Edentata*.

edge (ɛdʒ) *n.* **1.** a border, brim, or margin. **2.** a brink or verge. **3.** a line along which two faces or surfaces of a solid meet. **4.** the sharp cutting side of a blade. **5.** keenness, sharpness, or urgency. **6.** force, effectiveness, or incisiveness: *the performance lacked edge.* **7.** a ridge. **8. have the edge on** *or* **over.** to have a slight advantage or superiority (over). **9. on edge. a.** nervously irritable; tense. **b.** nervously excited or eager. **10. set (someone's) teeth on edge.** to make someone acutely irritated or uncomfortable. ~*vb.* **11.** (*tr.*) to provide an edge or border for. **12.** (*tr.*) to shape or trim (the edge or border of something). **13.** to push (one's way, someone, something, etc.) gradually, esp. edgeways. **14.** (*tr.*) *Cricket.* to hit (a bowled ball) with the edge of the bat. **15.** (*tr.*) to sharpen (a knife, etc.). —**'edger** *n.*

edgeways (ˈɛdʒˌweɪz) *or esp. U.S.* **edgewise** (ˈɛdʒˌwaɪz) *adv.* **1.** with the edge forwards or uppermost. **2.** on, by, with, or towards the edge. **3. get a word in edgeways.** (*usually with a negative*) *Inf.* to interrupt a conversation in which someone else is talking incessantly.

edging (ˈɛdʒɪŋ) *n.* **1.** anything placed along an edge to finish it, esp. as an ornament. **2.** the act of making an edge. ~*adj.* **3.** relating to or used for making an edge: *edging shears.*

edgy (ˈɛdʒɪ) *adj.* **-ier, -iest.** (*usually postpositive*) nervous, irritable, tense, or anxious. —**'edgily** *adv.* —**'edginess** *n.*

edible (ˈɛdɪbəl) *adj.* fit to be eaten; eatable. —ˌedi'bility *or* 'edibleness *n.*

edict (ˈiːdɪkt) *n.* **1.** a decree or order issued by any authority. **2.** any formal or authoritative command, proclamation, etc. —e'dictal *adj.*

edifice (ˈɛdɪfɪs) *n.* **1.** a building, esp. a large or imposing one. **2.** a complex or elaborate institution or organization.

edify (ˈɛdɪˌfaɪ) *vb.* **-fying, -fied.** (*tr.*) to improve the morality, intellect, etc., of, esp. by instruction. —ˌedifi'cation *n.* —'edi,fier *n.*

edit (ˈɛdɪt) *vb.* (*tr.*) **1.** to prepare (text) for publication by checking and improving its accuracy, clarity, etc. **2.** to be in charge of (a publication, esp. a periodical). **3.** to prepare (a film, tape, etc.) by rearrangement or selection of material. **4.** (often foll. by *out*) to remove, as from a manuscript or film.

edit. *abbrev. for:* **1.** edited. **2.** edition. **3.** editor.

edition (ɪˈdɪʃən) *n.* **1.** *Printing.* **a.** the entire number of copies of a book or other publication printed at one time. **b.** a copy from this number: *a first edition.* **2.** one of a number of printings of a book or other publication, issued at separate times with alterations, amendments, etc. **3. a.** an issue of a work identified by its format: *a leather-bound edition.* **b.** an issue of a work identified by its editor or publisher: *the Oxford edition.*

editor (ˈɛdɪtə) *n.* **1.** a person who edits written material for publication. **2.** a person in overall charge of a newspaper or periodical. **3.** a person in charge of one section of a newspaper or periodical: *the sports editor.* **4.** *Films.* a person who makes a selection and arrangement of shots. —'editor,ship *n.*

editorial (ˌɛdɪˈtɔːrɪəl) *adj.* **1.** of or relating to editing or editors. **2.** of, relating to, or expressed in an editorial. **3.** of or relating to the content of a publication. ~*n.* **4.** an article in a newspaper, etc., expressing the opinion of the editor or the publishers. —ˌedi'torialist *n.*

E.D.P. *abbrev. for* electronic data processing.

educable (ˈɛdjʊkəbəl) *or* **educatable** (ˈɛdjʊˌkeɪtəbəl) *adj.* capable of being trained or educated; able to learn. —ˌeduca'bility *or* ˌeducata'bility *n.*

educate (ˈɛdjʊˌkeɪt) *vb.* (*mainly tr.*) **1.** (*also intr.*) to impart knowledge by formal instruction to (a pupil); teach. **2.** to provide education for; pay for the schooling of. **3.** to improve or develop (a person, taste, skills, etc.). **4.** to train for some particular purpose or occupation. —'educative *adj.* —'edu,cator *n.*

educated (ˈɛdjʊˌkeɪtɪd) *adj.* **1.** having an education, esp. a good one. **2.** displaying culture, taste, and knowledge; cultivated. **3.** (*prenominal*) based on experience or information (esp. in **an educated guess**).

education (ˌɛdjʊˈkeɪʃən) *n.* **1.** the act or process of acquiring knowledge. **2.** the knowledge or training acquired by this process. **3.** the act or process of imparting knowledge to, esp. at a school, college, or university. **4.** the theory of teaching and learning. **5.** a particular kind of instruction or training: *a university education.* —ˌedu'cational *adj.* —ˌedu'cationalist *n.* —ˌedu'cationist *n.*

educe (ɪˈdjuːs) *vb.* (*tr.*) *Rare.* **1.** to evolve or develop. **2.** to draw out or elicit (information, solutions, etc.). **3.** *Logic.* to deduce. —e'ducible *adj.* —eductive (ɪˈdʌktɪv) *adj.*

Edwardian (ɛdˈwɔːdɪən) *adj.* of or characteristic of the reign of Edward VII, king of Great Britain and Ireland, 1901–10. —Ed'wardianism *n.*

-ee *suffix forming nouns.* **1.** indicating a recipient of an action (as opposed, esp. in legal terminology, to the agent): *assignee; lessee.* **2.** indicating a person in a

---

THESAURUS

eddy 1. *n.* counter-current, counterflow, swirl, vortex, whirlpool 2. *v.* swirl, whirl

edge *n.* 1. border, bound, boundary, brim, brink, contour, fringe, limit, line, lip, margin, outline, perimeter, periphery, rim, side, threshold, verge 2. acuteness, animation, bite, effectiveness, force, incisiveness, interest, keenness, point, pungency, sharpness, sting, urgency, zest 3. advantage, ascendancy, dominance, lead, superiority, upper hand 4. **on edge** apprehensive, eager, edgy, excited, ill at ease, impatient, irritable, keyed up, nervous, on tenterhooks, tense, uptight (*Inf.*) ~*v.* 5. bind, border, fringe, hem, rim, shape, trim 6. creep, ease, inch, sidle, steal, work, worm 7. hone, sharpen, strop, whet

edgy anxious, ill at ease, irascible, irritable, keyed up, nervous, on edge, restive, tense, touchy

edible comestible (*Rare*), digestible, eatable, esculent, fit to eat, good, harmless, pal-

atable, wholesome

edict act, command, decree, dictate, dictum, enactment, fiat, injunction, law, mandate, manifesto, order, ordinance, proclamation, pronouncement, pronunciamento, regulation, ruling, statute, ukase (*Rare*)

edifice building, construction, erection, fabric (*Rare*), habitation, house, pile, structure

edify educate, elevate, enlighten, guide, improve, inform, instruct, nurture, school, teach, uplift

edit 1. adapt, annotate, censor, check, condense, correct, emend, polish, redact, rephrase, revise, rewrite 2. assemble, compose, put together, rearrange, reorder, select

edition copy, impression, issue, number, printing, programme (*TV, Radio*), version, volume

educate civilize, coach, cultivate, develop, discipline, drill, edify, enlighten, exercise, foster, improve, indoctrinate, inform, in-

struct, mature, rear, school, teach, train, tutor

educated 1. coached, informed, instructed, nurtured, schooled, taught, tutored 2. civilized, cultivated, cultured, enlightened, experienced, informed, knowledgeable, learned, lettered, literary, polished, refined, tasteful

education breeding, civilization, coaching, cultivation, culture, development, discipline, drilling, edification, enlightenment, erudition, improvement, indoctrination, instruction, knowledge, nurture, scholarship, schooling, teaching, training, tuition, tutoring

educational cultural, didactic, edifying, educative, enlightening, heuristic, improving, informative, instructive

educative didactic, edifying, educational, enlightening, heuristic, improving, informative, instructive

specified state or condition: *absentee*. **3.** indicating a diminutive form of something: *bootee*.

EEC *abbrev. for* European Economic Community (the Common Market).

EEG *abbrev. for:* **1.** electroencephalogram. **2.** electroencephalograph.

eel (iːl) *n.* **1.** any teleost fish such as the European freshwater eel, having a long snakelike body, a smooth slimy skin, and reduced fins. **2.** any of various similar animals, such as the mud eel and the electric eel. **3.** an evasive or untrustworthy person. —'eel-,like *adj.* —'eely *adj.*

eelpout ('iːl,paʊt) *n.* **1.** a marine eel-like fish. **2.** another name for **burbot.**

e'en (iːn) *adv., n. Poetic or arch.* a contraction of **even²** or **evening.**

-eer *or* **-ier** *suffix.* **1.** (*forming nouns*) indicating a person who is concerned with or who does something specified: *auctioneer; engineer; profiteer; mutineer.* **2.** (*forming verbs*) to be concerned with something specified: *electioneer.*

e'er (ɛə) *adv. Poetic or arch.* a contraction of **ever.**

eerie ('ɪərɪ) *adj.* **eerier, eeriest.** uncannily frightening or disturbing; weird. —'**eerily** *adv.* —'**eeriness** *n.*

efface (ɪ'feɪs) *vb. (tr.)* **1.** to obliterate or make dim. **2.** to make (oneself) inconspicuous or humble. **3.** to rub out; erase. —ef'**faceable** *adj.* —ef'**facement** *n.* —ef'**facer** *n.*

effect (ɪ'fɛkt) *n.* **1.** something produced by a cause or agent; result. **2.** power to influence or produce a result. **3.** the condition of being operative (esp. in **in** or **into effect**). **4. take effect.** to become operative or begin to produce results. **5.** basic meaning or purpose (esp. in **to that effect**). **6.** an impression, usually contrived (esp. in **for effect**). **7.** a scientific phenomenon: *the Doppler effect.* **8. in effect. a.** in fact; actually. **b.** for all practical purposes. **9.** the overall impression or result. ~*vb.* **10.** (*tr.*) to cause to occur; accomplish. —ef'**fecter** *n.* —ef'**fectible** *adj.*

effective (ɪ'fɛktɪv) *adj.* **1.** productive of or capable of producing a result. **2.** in effect; operative. **3.** impressive: *an effective entrance.* **4.** (*prenominal*) actual rather than theoretical. **5.** (of a military force, etc.) equipped and prepared for action. ~*n.* **6.** a serviceman equipped and prepared for action. —ef'**fectively** *adv.* —ef'**fectiveness** *n.*

effects (ɪ'fɛkts) *pl. n.* **1.** Also called: **personal effects.** personal belongings. **2.** Also called: **special effects. a.** lighting, sounds, etc., to accompany a stage, film, or broadcast production. **b.** the devices used to produce these.

effectual (ɪ'fɛktjʊəl) *adj.* **1.** capable of or successful in producing an intended result; effective. **2.** (of documents, etc.) having legal force. —ef,**fectu'ality** *or* ef'**fectualness** *n.* —ef'**fectually** *adv.*

effectuate (ɪ'fɛktjuː,eɪt) *vb. (tr.)* to cause to happen; effect; accomplish. —ef,**fectu'ation** *n.*

effeminate (ɪ'fɛmɪnɪt) *adj.* (of a man or boy) displaying characteristics regarded as typical of a woman; not manly. —ef'**feminacy** *or* ef'**feminateness** *n.*

efferent ('ɛfərənt) *adj. Physiol.* carrying or conducting outwards, esp. from the brain or spinal cord. Cf. **afferent.** —'**efference** *n.*

effervesce (,ɛfə'vɛs) *vb. (intr.)* **1.** (of a liquid) to give off bubbles of gas. **2.** (of a gas) to issue in bubbles from a liquid. **3.** to exhibit great excitement, vivacity, etc. —,**effer'vescent** *adj.*

effete (ɪ'fiːt) *adj.* **1.** weak or decadent. **2.** exhausted; spent. **3.** (of animals or plants) no longer capable of reproduction. —ef'**feteness** *n.*

efficacious (,ɛfɪ'keɪʃəs) *adj.* capable of or successful in producing an intended result; effective. —**efficacy** ('ɛfɪkəsɪ) *or* ,**effi'caciousness** *n.*

efficient (ɪ'fɪʃənt) *adj.* **1.** functioning or producing effectively and with the least waste of effort; competent. **2.** *Philosophy.* producing a direct effect. —ef'**ficiency** *n.*

effigy ('ɛfɪdʒɪ) *n., pl.* **-gies. 1.** a portrait, esp. as a monument. **2.** a crude representation of someone, used as a focus for contempt or ridicule (often in **burn** or **hang in effigy**).

effloresce (,ɛflɔː'rɛs) *vb. (intr.)* **1.** to burst forth as into flower; bloom. **2.** to become powdery by loss of water crystallization. **3.** to become encrusted with powder or crystals as a result of chemical change or evaporation. —,**efflo'rescence** *n.*

effluence ('ɛfluəns) *or* **efflux** ('ɛflʌks) *n.* **1.** the act or process of flowing out. **2.** something that flows out.

effluent ('ɛfluənt) *n.* **1.** liquid discharged as waste, as from an industrial plant or sewage works. **2.** radioactive waste released from a nuclear power station. **3.** a stream that flows out of another body of water. **4.** something that flows out or forth. ~*adj.* **5.** flowing out or forth.

effluvium (ɛ'fluːvɪəm) *n., pl.* **-via** (-vɪə) *or* **-viums.** an unpleasant smell or exhalation, as of gaseous waste or decaying matter. —ef'**fluvial** *adj.*

effort ('ɛfət) *n.* **1.** physical or mental exertion. **2.** a determined attempt. **3.** achievement; creation. —'**effortful** *adj.* —'**effortless** *adj.*

THESAURUS

eerie awesome, creepy (*Inf.*), eldritch (*Poetic*), fearful, frightening, ghostly, mysterious, scary (*Inf.*), spectral, spooky (*Inf.*), strange, uncanny, unearthly, weird

efface **1.** annihilate, blot out, cancel, cross out, delete, destroy, dim, eradicate, erase, excise, expunge, extirpate, obliterate, raze, rub out, wipe out **2.** *Of oneself* be modest (bashful, diffident, retiring, timid, unassertive), humble, lower, make inconspicuous, withdraw

effect *n.* **1.** aftermath, conclusion, consequence, event, fruit, issue, outcome, result, upshot **2.** clout (*Inf.*), effectiveness, efficacy, efficiency, fact, force, influence, power, reality, strength, use, validity, vigour, weight **3.** drift, essence, impact, import, impression, meaning, purport, purpose, sense, significance, tenor **4.** action, enforcement, execution, force, implementation, operation **5. in effect** actually, effectively, essentially, for practical purposes, in actuality, in fact, in reality, in truth, really, to all intents and purposes, virtually **6. take effect** become operative, begin, come into force, produce results, work ~*v.* **7.** accomplish, achieve, actuate, bring about, carry out, cause, complete, consummate, create, effectuate, execute, fulfil, give rise to, initiate, make, perform, produce

effective **1.** able, active, adequate, capable, competent, effectual, efficacious, efficient, energetic, operative, productive, serviceable, useful **2.** cogent, compelling, convincing, emphatic, forceful, forcible, impressive, moving, persuasive, potent, powerful, striking, telling **3.** active, actual, current, in effect, in execution, in force, in operation, operative, real

effectiveness capability, clout (*Inf.*), cogency, effect, efficacy, efficiency, force, influence, potency, power, strength, success, use, validity, vigour, weight

effects belongings, chattels, furniture, gear, goods, movables, paraphernalia, possessions, property, things, trappings

effeminacy delicacy, femininity, softness, tenderness, unmanliness, weakness, womanishness, womanliness

effeminate delicate, feminine, sissy, soft, tender, unmanly, weak, womanish, womanlike, womanly

effervesce bubble, ferment, fizz, foam, froth, sparkle

effervescence **1.** bubbling, ferment, fermentation, fizz, foam, foaming, froth, frothing, sparkle **2.** animation, buoyancy, ebullience, enthusiasm, excitedness, excitement, exhilaration, exuberance, gaiety, high spirits, liveliness, vim (*Sl.*), vitality, vivacity, zing (*Inf.*)

effervescent **1.** bubbling, bubbly, carbonated, fermenting, fizzing, fizzy, foaming, foamy, frothing, frothy, sparkling **2.** animated, bubbly, buoyant, ebullient, enthusiastic, excited, exhilarated, exuberant, gay, in high spirits, irrepressible, lively, merry, vital, vivacious, zingy (*Inf.*)

effete **1.** corrupt, debased, decadent, decayed, decrepit, degenerate, dissipated, enervated, enfeebled, feeble, ineffectual, overrefined, spoiled, weak **2.** burnt out, drained, enervated, exhausted, played out, spent, used up, wasted, worn out **3.** barren, fruitless, infecund, infertile, sterile, unfruitful, unproductive, unprolific

efficacious active, adequate, capable, competent, effective, effectual, efficient, energetic, operative, potent, powerful, productive, serviceable, successful, useful

efficacy ability, capability, competence, effect, effectiveness, efficaciousness, efficiency, energy, force, influence, potency, power, strength, success, use, vigour, virtue, weight

efficiency ability, adeptness, capability, competence, economy, effectiveness, efficacy, power, productivity, proficiency, readiness, skilfulness, skill

efficient able, adept, businesslike, capable, competent, economic, effective, effectual, powerful, productive, proficient, ready, skilful, well-organized, workmanlike

effigy dummy, figure, guy, icon, idol, image, likeness, picture, portrait, representation, statue

effluent *n.* **1.** effluvium, pollutant, sewage, waste **2.** discharge, effluence, efflux, emanation, emission, exhalation, flow, outflow, outpouring ~*adj.* **3.** discharged, ema-

effrontery (ɪˈfrʌntərɪ) *n., pl.* **-ies.** shameless or insolent boldness.

effuse *vb.* (ɪˈfjuːz). **1.** to pour or flow out. **2.** to spread out; diffuse. ~*adj.* (ɪˈfjuːs). **3.** *Bot.* (esp. of an inflorescence) spreading out loosely.

effusion (ɪˈfjuːʒən) *n.* **1.** an unrestrained outpouring in speech or words. **2.** the act or process of being poured out. **3.** something that is poured out.

effusive (ɪˈfjuːsɪv) *adj.* **1.** extravagantly demonstrative of emotion; gushing. **2.** (of rock) formed by the solidification of magma. —**efˈfusively** *adv.* —**efˈfusiveness** *n.*

eft (ɛft) *n.* a dialect or archaic name for a **newt.**

EFTA (ˈɛftə) *n. acronym for* European Free Trade Association; established in 1960 to eliminate trade tariffs on industrial products; originally comprised Britain, Denmark, Norway, Sweden, Switzerland, Austria, and Portugal.

e.g. *abbrev. for* exempli gratia: for example.

egad (ɪˈgæd, iːˈgæd) *interj. Arch.* a mild oath.

egalitarian (ɪˌgælɪˈtɛərɪən) *adj.* **1.** of or upholding the doctrine of the equality of mankind. ~*n.* **2.** an adherent of egalitarian principles. —**eˌgaliˈtarianˌism** *n.*

egg[1] (ɛg) *n.* **1.** the oval or round reproductive body laid by the females of birds, reptiles, fishes, insects, and some other animals, consisting of a developing embryo, its food store, and sometimes jelly or albumen, all surrounded by an outer shell or membrane. **2.** Also called: **egg cell.** any female gamete; ovum. **3.** the egg of the domestic hen used as food. **4.** something resembling an egg, esp. in shape. **5. good** (or **bad**) **egg.** *Old-fashioned sl.* a good (or bad) person. **6. put** or **have all one's eggs in one basket.** to stake everything on a single venture. **7. teach one's grandmother to suck eggs.** *Inf.* to presume to teach someone something that he knows already.

egg[2] (ɛg) *vb.* (*tr.;* usually foll. by *on*) to urge or incite, esp. to daring or foolish acts.

egghead (ˈɛgˌhɛd) *n. Inf.* an intellectual.

eggnog (ˌɛgˈnɒg) *or* **egg-noggin** *n.* a drink made of eggs, milk, sugar, spice, and brandy, rum, or other spirit. Also called: **egg flip.**

eggplant (ˈɛgˌplɑːnt) *n.* another name (esp. U.S.) for **aubergine.**

eggshell (ˈɛgˌʃɛl) *n.* **1.** the hard porous outer layer of a bird's egg. **2.** (*modifier*) (of paint) having a matt finish similar to that of an egg.

eglantine (ˈɛglənˌtaɪn) *n.* another name for **sweetbrier.**

ego (ˈiːgəʊ, ˈɛgəʊ) *n., pl.* **egos.** **1.** the self of an individual person; the conscious subject. **2.** *Psychoanal.* the conscious mind, based on perception of the environment: responsible for modifying the antisocial instincts of the id and itself modified by the conscience (superego). **3.** *Inf.* one's image of oneself; morale. **4.** *Inf.* egotism; conceit.

egocentric (ˌiːgəʊˈsɛntrɪk, ˌɛg-) *adj.* **1.** regarding everything only in relation to oneself; self-centred. ~*n.* **2.** a self-centred person; egotist. —**ˌegocenˈtricity** *n.* —ˌegoˈcentrism *n.*

egoism (ˈiːgəʊˌɪzəm, ˈɛg-) *n.* **1.** concern for one's own interests and welfare. **2.** *Ethics.* the theory that the pursuit of one's own welfare is the highest good. **3.** self-centredness; egotism. —**ˈegoist** *n.*

egotism (ˈiːgəˌtɪzəm, ˈɛgə-) *n.* **1.** an inflated sense of self-importance or superiority; self-centredness. **2.** excessive reference to oneself. —**ˈegotist** *n.*

ego trip *n. Inf.* something undertaken to boost or draw attention to a person's own image or appraisal of himself.

egregious (ɪˈgriːdʒəs, -dʒɪəs) *adj.* **1.** outstandingly bad; flagrant. **2.** *Arch.* distinguished; eminent. —**eˈgregiousness** *n.*

egress (ˈiːgrɛs) *n.* **1.** Also: **egression.** the act of going or coming out; emergence. **2.** a way out; exit. **3.** the right to go out or depart.

egret (ˈiːgrɪt) *n.* any of various wading birds similar to herons but usually having white plumage and, in the breeding season, long feathery plumes.

Egyptian (ɪˈdʒɪpʃən) *adj.* **1.** of or relating to Egypt, a republic in NE Africa, its inhabitants, or their dialect of Arabic. **2.** of or characteristic of the ancient Egyptians, their language, or culture. ~*n.* **3.** a native or inhabitant of Egypt. **4.** a member of a people who established an advanced civilization in Egypt that flourished from the late fourth millennium B.C. **5.** the extinct language of the ancient Egyptians.

Egyptology (ˌiːdʒɪpˈtɒlədʒɪ) *n.* the study of the archaeology and language of ancient Egypt. —**ˌEgypˈtologist** *n.*

eh (eɪ) *interj.* an exclamation used to express questioning surprise or to seek the repetition or confirmation of a statement or question.

EHF *abbrev. for* extremely high frequency.

eider *or* **eider duck** (ˈaɪdə) *n.* any of several sea ducks of the N hemisphere. See **eiderdown.**

eiderdown (ˈaɪdəˌdaʊn) *n.* **1.** the breast down of the female eider duck, used for stuffing pillows, quilts, etc. **2.** a thick, warm cover for a bed, enclosing a soft filling.

eight (eɪt) *n.* **1.** the cardinal number that is the sum of one and seven and the product of two and four. **2.** a numeral 8, VIII, etc., representing this number. **3.** the amount or quantity that is one greater than seven. **4.** something representing, represented by, or consisting of eight units. **5.** *Rowing.* **a.** a racing shell propelled by eight oarsmen. **b.** the crew of such a shell. **6.** Also called: **eight o'clock.** eight hours after noon or midnight. **7. have one over the eight.** *Sl.* to be drunk. ~*determiner.* **8. a.** amounting to eight. **b.** (*as pronoun*): *I could only find eight.* —**eighth** *adj.*

eighteen (ˈeɪˈtiːn) *n.* **1.** the cardinal number that is the sum of ten and eight and the product of two and nine. **2.** a numeral 18, XVIII, etc., representing this number. **3.** the amount or quantity that is eight more than ten. **4.** something represented by, representing, or consisting of 18 units. ~*determiner.* **5. a.** amounting to eighteen: *eighteen weeks.* **b.** (*as pronoun*): *eighteen of them knew.* —**ˈeighˈteenth** *adj.*

eightfold (ˈeɪtˌfəʊld) *adj.* **1.** equal to or having eight times as many or as much. **2.** composed of eight parts. ~*adv.* **3.** by eight times as much.

eightsome reel (ˈeɪtsəm) *n.* a Scottish dance for eight people.

eighty (ˈeɪtɪ) *n., pl.* **-ies.** **1.** the cardinal number that is the product of ten and eight. **2.** a numeral 80, LXXX, etc., representing this number. **3.** (*pl.*) the numbers 80-89, esp. the 80th to the 89th year of a person's life or of a century. **4.** the amount or quantity that is eight times ten. **5.** something represented by, representing, or consisting of 80 units. ~*determiner.* **6. a.** amounting to eighty: *eighty pages of nonsense.* **b.** (*as pronoun*):

THESAURUS

nating, emitted, outflowing

effort **1.** application, endeavour, energy, exertion, force, labour, pains, power, strain, stress, stretch, striving, struggle, toil, travail (*Literary*), trouble, work **2.** attempt, endeavour, essay, go, shot (*Inf.*), stab (*Inf.*), try **3.** accomplishment, achievement, act, creation, deed, feat, job, product, production

effortless easy, facile, painless, simple, smooth, uncomplicated, undemanding, untroublesome

effulgent beaming, blazing, bright, brilliant, dazzling, flaming, fluorescent, fulgent (*Poetic*), glowing, incandescent, lucent, luminous, lustrous, radiant, refulgent (*Literary*), resplendent, shining, splendid, vivid

effusion **1.** discharge, effluence, efflux, emission, gush, outflow, outpouring, shedding, stream **2.** address, outpouring, speech,

talk, utterance, writing

effusive demonstrative, ebullient, enthusiastic, expansive, extravagant, exuberant, free-flowing, fulsome, gushing, lavish, overflowing, profuse, talkative, unreserved, unrestrained, wordy

egg on encourage, exhort, goad, incite, prod, prompt, push, spur, urge

egocentric egoistic, egoistical, egotistic, egotistical, self-centred, selfish

egoism egocentricity, egomania, egotism, narcissism, self-absorption, self-centredness, self-importance, self-interest, selfishness, self-love, self-regard, self-seeking

egoist egomaniac, egotist, narcissist, self-seeker

egoistic, egoistical egocentric, egomaniacal, egotistic, egotistical, narcissistic, self-absorbed, self-centred, self-important,

self-seeking

egotism conceitedness, egocentricity, egoism, egomania, narcissism, self-admiration, self-centredness, self-conceit, self-esteem, self-importance, self-love, self-praise, superiority, vainglory, vanity

egotist bighead (*Inf.*), blowhard (*Inf.*), boaster, braggadocio, braggart, egoist, egomaniac, self-admirer, swaggerer

egotistic, egotistical boasting, bragging, conceited, egocentric, egoistic, egoistical, egomaniacal, narcissistic, opinionated, self-admiring, self-centred, self-important, superior, vain, vainglorious

egress departure, emergence, escape, exit, exodus, issue, outlet, passage out, vent, way out, withdrawal

eighty are expected. —**'eightieth** *adj.*

einsteinium (aɪn'staɪnɪəm) *n.* a radioactive metallic transuranic element artificially produced from plutonium. Symbol: Es; atomic no.: 99; half-life of most stable isotope, ²⁵⁴Es: 276 days.

eisteddfod (aɪ'stɛdfəd) *n., pl.* **-fods** *or* **-fodau** (*Welsh* aɪ,stɛð'vɒdaɪ). any of a number of annual festivals in Wales in which competitions are held in music, poetry, drama, and the fine arts. —,**eistedd'fodic** *adj.*

either ('aɪðə, 'iːðə) *determiner.* **1. a.** one or the other (of two). **b.** (*as pronoun*): *either is acceptable.* **2.** both one and the other: *at either end of the table.* —*conj.* **3.** (*coordinating*) used preceding two or more possibilities joined by "*or*". ~*adv.* (*sentence modifier*) **4.** (*with a negative*) used to indicate that the clause immediately preceding is a partial reiteration of a previous clause: *John isn't a liar, but he isn't exactly honest either.*

▷ **Usage.** *Either* is followed by a singular verb in good usage: *either of these books is useful.* Careful writers and speakers are cautious in using *either* to mean *both* or *each* because of possible ambiguity, as in: *a ship could be moored on either side of the channel.* Agreement between verb and subject in *either...or...* constructions follows the pattern for *neither...nor...* See at **neither.**

ejaculate *vb.* (ɪ'dʒækjʊ,leɪt). **1.** to eject or discharge (semen) in orgasm. **2.** (*tr.*) to utter abruptly; blurt out. ~*n.* (ɪ'dʒækjʊlɪt). **3.** another word for **semen.** —e,**jacu-'lation** *n.* —**e'jacu,lator** *n.* —**e'jaculatory** *or* **e'jacula-tive** *adj.*

eject (ɪ'dʒɛkt) *vb.* **1.** (*tr.*) to force out; expel or emit. **2.** (*tr.*) to compel (a person) to leave; evict. **3.** (*tr.*) to dismiss, as from office. **4.** (*intr.*) to leave an aircraft rapidly, using an ejection seat or capsule. —**e'jection** *n.* —**e'jective** *adj.* —**e'jector** *n.*

ejection seat *or* **ejector seat** *n.* a seat, esp. in military aircraft, fired by a cartridge or rocket to eject the occupant in an emergency.

eke (iːk) *vb. Arch.* to increase, enlarge, or lengthen.

eke out *vb.* (*tr., adv.*) **1.** to make (a supply) last, esp. by frugal use. **2.** to support (existence) with difficulty and effort. **3.** to add to (something insufficient), esp. with effort.

elaborate *adj.* (ɪ'læbərɪt). **1.** planned with care and exactness. **2.** marked by complexity or detail. ~*vb.* (ɪ'læbə,reɪt). **3.** (*intr.; usually foll. by* on *or* upon) to add detail (to an account); expand (upon). **4.** (*tr.*) to work out in detail; develop. **5.** (*tr.*) to produce by careful labour. **6.** (*tr.*) *Physiol.* to change (food or simple substances) into more complex substances for use in the body. —**e'laborateness** *n.* —e,**labo'ration** *n.* —**elaborative** (ɪ'læbərətɪv) *adj.* —**e'labo,rator** *n.*

élan (eɪ'lɑːn) *n.* a combination of style and vigour.

eland ('iːlənd) *n.* **1.** a large spiral-horned antelope inhabiting bushland in eastern and southern Africa. **2. giant eland.** a similar but larger animal of central and W Africa.

elapse (ɪ'læps) *vb.* (*intr.*) (of time) to pass by.

elastic (ɪ'læstɪk) *adj.* **1.** (of a body or material) capable of returning to its original shape after compression, stretching, or other deformation. **2.** capable of adapting to change. **3.** quick to recover from fatigue, dejection, etc. **4.** springy or resilient. **5.** made of elastic. ~*n.* **6.** tape, cord, or fabric containing flexible rubber or similar substance allowing it to stretch and return to its original shape. —**e'lastically** *adv.* —,**elas'ticity** *n.*

elasticate (ɪ'læstɪ,keɪt) *vb.* (*tr.*) to insert elastic into (a fabric or garment). —e,**lasti'cation** *n.*

elastic band *n.* another name for **rubber band.**

elate (ɪ'leɪt) *vb.* (*tr.*) to fill with high spirits, exhilaration, pride, or optimism. —**e'latedly** *adv.* —**e'latedness** *n.* —**e'lation** *n.*

elbow ('ɛlbəʊ) *n.* **1.** the joint between the upper arm and the forearm. **2.** the corresponding joint of birds or mammals. **3.** the part of a garment that covers the elbow. **4.** something resembling an elbow, such as a sharp bend in a road. **5. at one's elbow.** within easy reach. **6. out at elbow(s).** ragged or impoverished. ~*vb.* **7.** to make (one's way) by shoving, jostling, etc. **8.** (*tr.*) to knock or shove as with the elbow.

elbow grease *n. Inf.* vigorous physical labour.

elbowroom ('ɛlbəʊ,ruːm, -,rʊm) *n.* sufficient scope to move or function.

elder[1] ('ɛldə) *adj.* **1.** born earlier; senior. **2.** (in certain card games) denoting or relating to the nondealer (the **elder hand),** who has certain advantages in the play. **3.** *Arch.* **a.** prior in rank or office. **b.** of a previous time. ~*n.* **4.** an older person; one's senior. **5.** *Anthropol.* a senior member of a tribe who has authority. **6.** (in certain Protestant Churches) a lay office. **7.** another word for **presbyter.** —'**elder,ship** *n.*

elder[2] ('ɛldə) *n.* Also called: **elderberry.** any of various shrubs or small trees having clusters of small white flowers and red, purple, or black berry-like fruits.

elderberry ('ɛldə,bɛrɪ) *n., pl.* **-ries. 1.** the fruit of the elder. **2.** another name for elder[2].

elderly ('ɛldəlɪ) *adj.* (of people) quite old; past middle age. —'**elderliness** *n.*

eldest ('ɛldɪst) *adj.* being the oldest, esp. the oldest surviving child of the same parents.

El Dorado (ɛl dɒ'rɑːdəʊ) *n.* **1.** a fabled city in South America, rich in treasure. **2.** Also: **eldorado.** any place of great riches or fabulous opportunity.

eldritch *or* **eldrich** ('ɛldrɪtʃ) *adj. Poetic.* unearthly; weird.

elect (ɪ'lɛkt) *vb.* **1.** (*tr.*) to choose (someone) to be (a representative or official) by voting. **2.** to select; choose. **3.** (*tr.*) (of God) to predestine for the grace of salvation. ~*adj.* **4.** (*immediately postpositive*) voted into office but not yet installed: *president elect.* **5. a.** chosen; elite. **b.** (*as collective n.* preceded by *the*): *the elect.* **6.** *Christian theol.* **a.** predestined by God to receive salvation. **b.** (*as collective n.* preceded by *the*): *the elect.*

elect. *or* **elec.** *abbrev. for:* **1.** electric(al). **2.** electricity.

election (ɪ'lɛkʃən) *n.* **1.** the selection by vote of a person or persons for a position, esp. a political office. **2.** a public vote. **3.** the act or an instance of choosing. **4.** *Christian theol.* **a.** the doctrine that God chooses individuals for salvation without reference to faith or works.

THESAURUS

eject 1. cast out, discharge, disgorge, emit, expel, spew, spout, throw out, vomit **2.** banish, boot out (*Inf.*), bounce (*Sl.*), deport, dispossess, drive out, evacuate, evict, exile, expel, oust, remove, throw out, turn out **3.** discharge, dislodge, dismiss, fire (*Inf.*), get rid of, kick out (*Inf.*), oust, sack (*Inf.*), throw out

ejection 1. casting out, disgorgement, expulsion, spouting, throwing out **2.** banishment, deportation, dispossession, evacuation, eviction, exile, expulsion, ouster (*Law*), removal **3.** discharge, dislodgement, dismissal, firing (*Inf.*), sacking (*Inf.*), the boot (*Sl.*), the sack (*Inf.*)

eke out 1. be economical with, be frugal with, be sparing with, economize on, husband, stretch out **2.** add to, enlarge, increase, make up (with), supplement

elaborate *adj.* **1.** careful, detailed, exact, intricate, laboured, minute, painstaking, perfected, precise, skilful, studied, thorough **2.** complex, complicated, decorated, detailed, extravagant, fancy, fussy, involved, ornamented, ornate, ostentatious, showy ~*v.* **3.** add detail, amplify, complicate, decorate, develop, devise, embellish, enhance, enlarge, expand (upon), flesh out, garnish, improve, ornament, polish, produce, refine, work out

elapse glide by, go, go by, lapse, pass, pass by, roll by, roll on, slip away, slip by

elastic 1. ductile, flexible, plastic, pliable, pliant, resilient, rubbery, springy, stretchable, stretchy, supple, yielding **2.** accommodating, adaptable, adjustable, complaisant, compliant, flexible, supple, tolerant, variable, yielding **3.** bouncy, buoyant, irrepressible, resilient

elated animated, blissful, cheered, delighted, ecstatic, elevated, euphoric, excited, exhilarated, exultant, gleeful, in high spirits, joyful, joyous, jubilant, overjoyed, proud, puffed up, roused

elation bliss, delight, ecstasy, euphoria, exaltation, exhilaration, exultation, glee, high spirits, joy, joyfulness, joyousness, jubilation, rapture

elbow *n.* **1.** angle, bend, corner, joint, turn **2. at one's elbow** at hand, close by, handy, near, to hand, within reach **3. out at elbow(s)** beggarly, down at heel, impoverished, in rags, ragged, seedy, shabby, tattered **4. rub elbows with** associate, fraternize, hang out (*Inf.*), hobnob, mingle, mix, socialize **5. up to the elbows** absorbed, busy, engaged, engrossed, immersed, occupied, tied up, up to the ears, wrapped up ~*v.* **6.** bump, crowd, hustle, jostle, knock, nudge, push, shoulder, shove

elbowroom freedom, latitude, leeway, play, room, scope, space

elder *adj.* **1.** ancient, earlier born, first-born, older, senior ~*n.* **2.** older person, senior **3.** *Presbyterianism* church official, office bearer, presbyter

elect 1. *v.* appoint, choose, decide upon, designate, determine, opt for, pick, pick out, prefer, select, settle on, vote **2.** *adj.* choice, chosen, elite, hand-picked, picked, preferred, select, selected

b. the doctrine that God chooses for salvation those who, by grace, persevere in faith and works.

electioneer (ɪˌlɛkʃəˈnɪə) vb. (intr.) **1.** to be active in a political election or campaign. ~n. **2.** a person who engages in this activity. —eˌlectionˈeering n., adj.

elective (ɪˈlɛktɪv) adj. **1.** of or based on selection by vote. **2.** selected by vote. **3.** having the power to elect. **4.** open to choice; optional. —**electivity** (ˌiːlɛkˈtɪvɪtɪ) or eˈlectiveness n.

elector (ɪˈlɛktə) n. **1.** someone who is eligible to vote in the election of a government. **2.** (often cap.) a member of the U.S. electoral college. **3.** (often cap.) (in the Holy Roman Empire) any of the German princes entitled to take part in the election of a new emperor. —eˈlectoral adj. —eˈlectorˌship n. —eˈlectress fem. n.

electorate (ɪˈlɛktərɪt) n. **1.** the body of all qualified voters. **2.** the rank, position, or territory of an elector of the Holy Roman Empire. **3.** Austral. & N.Z. the area represented by a Member of Parliament.

electric (ɪˈlɛktrɪk) adj. **1.** of, derived from, produced by, producing, transmitting, or powered by electricity. **2.** (of a musical instrument) amplified electronically. **3.** very tense or exciting; emotionally charged. ~n. **4.** Inf. an electric train, car, etc.
▷ **Usage.** See at **electronic**.

electrical (ɪˈlɛktrɪkəl) adj. of, relating to, or concerned with electricity. —eˈlectricalness n.
▷ **Usage.** See at **electronic**.

electrical engineering n. the branch of engineering concerned with practical applications of electricity. —**electrical engineer** n.

electric chair n. (in the U.S.) **a.** an electrified chair for executing criminals. **b.** (usually preceded by the) execution by this method.

electric eel n. an eel-like freshwater fish of N South America, having electric organs in the body.

electric field n. a field of force surrounding a charged particle within which another charged particle experiences a force.

electrician (ɪlɛkˈtrɪʃən, ˌiːlɛk-) n. a person whose occupation is the installation, maintenance, and repair of electrical devices.

electricity (ɪlɛkˈtrɪsɪtɪ, ˌiːlɛk-) n. **1.** a form of energy associated with stationary or moving electrons, protons, or other charged particles. **2.** the science of electricity. **3.** an electric current or charge. **4.** emotional tension or excitement.

electrify (ɪˈlɛktrɪˌfaɪ) vb. **-fying, -fied.** (tr.) **1.** to adapt or equip (a system, device, etc.) for operation by electrical power. **2.** to charge with or subject to electricity. **3.** to startle or excite intensely. —eˈlectriˌfiable adj. —eˌlectrifiˈcation n. —eˈlectriˌfier n.

electro (ɪˈlɛktrəʊ) n., pl. **-tros.** short for **electroplate** (sense 2) or **electrotype** (sense 1).

electro- or sometimes before a vowel **electr-** combining form. **1.** electric or electrically: electrodynamic. **2.** electrolytic: electrodialysis.

electrocardiograph (ɪˌlɛktrəʊˈkɑːdɪəʊˌɡrɑːf, -ˌɡræf) n. an instrument for making tracings (**electrocardiograms**) recording the electrical activity of the heart. —eˌlectroˌcardioˈgraphic or eˌlectroˌcardioˈgraphical adj. —**electrocardiography** (ɪˌlɛktrəʊˌkɑːdɪˈɒɡrəfɪ) n.

electrocute (ɪˈlɛktrəˌkjuːt) vb. (tr.) **1.** to kill as a result of an electric shock. **2.** U.S. to execute in the electric chair. —eˌlectroˈcution n.

electrode (ɪˈlɛktrəʊd) n. **1.** a conductor through which an electric current enters or leaves an electrolyte, an electric arc, or an electronic valve or tube. **2.** an element in a semiconducting device that emits, collects, or controls the movement of electrons or holes.

electrodynamics (ɪˌlɛktrəʊdaɪˈnæmɪks) n. (functioning as sing.) the branch of physics concerned with the interactions between electrical and mechanical forces.

electroencephalograph (ɪˌlɛktrəʊɛnˈsɛfələˌɡrɑːf, -ˌɡræf) n. an instrument for making tracings (**electroencephalograms**) recording the electrical activity of the brain, usually by means of electrodes placed on the scalp. See also **brain wave.** —eˌlectroenˌcephalo-

'graphic adj. —**electroencephalography** (ɪˌlɛktrəʊɛnˌsɛfəˈlɒɡrəfɪ) n.

electrolyse or U.S. **-yze** (ɪˈlɛktrəʊˌlaɪz) vb. (tr.) **1.** to decompose (a chemical compound) by electrolysis. **2.** to destroy (living tissue, such as hair roots) by electrolysis. —eˌlectrolyˈsation n. —eˈlectroˌlyser n.

electrolysis (ɪlɛkˈtrɒlɪsɪs) n. **1.** the conduction of electricity by an electrolyte, esp. the use of this process to induce chemical changes. **2.** the destruction of living tissue, such as hair roots, by an electric current, usually for cosmetic reasons.

electrolyte (ɪˈlɛktrəʊˌlaɪt) n. a solution or molten substance that conducts electricity.

electromagnet (ɪˌlɛktrəʊˈmæɡnɪt) n. a magnet consisting of an iron or steel core wound with a coil of wire, through which a current is passed.

electromagnetic (ɪˌlɛktrəʊmæɡˈnɛtɪk) adj. **1.** of, containing, or operated by an electromagnet. **2.** of, relating to, or consisting of electromagnetism. **3.** of or relating to electromagnetic radiation. —eˌlectromagˈnetically adv.

electromagnetism (ɪˌlɛktrəʊˈmæɡnɪˌtɪzəm) n. **1.** magnetism produced by electric current. **2.** the branch of physics concerned with this magnetism and with the interaction of electric and magnetic fields.

electromotive (ɪˌlɛktrəʊˈməʊtɪv) adj. of, concerned with, or producing an electric current.

electromotive force n. Physics. **a.** a source of energy that can cause current to flow in an electrical circuit. **b.** the rate at which energy is drawn from this source when unit current flows through the circuit, measured in volts.

electron (ɪˈlɛktrɒn) n. an elementary particle in all atoms, orbiting the nucleus in numbers equal to the atomic number of the element.

electronic (ɪlɛkˈtrɒnɪk, ˌiːlɛk-) adj. **1.** of, concerned with, using, or operated by devices, such as transistors, in which electrons are conducted through a semiconductor, vacuum, or gas. **2.** of or concerned with electronics. **3.** of or concerned with electrons. —elecˈtronically adv.
▷ **Usage.** Electronic is used to refer to equipment, such as television sets, computers, etc., in which current is controlled by transistors, valves, etc. and also to these components themselves. Electrical is used in a more general sense, often to refer to the use of electricity as opposed to other forms of energy: an electrical appliance. Electric, in many cases used interchangeably with electrical, is often restricted to the description of devices or to concepts relating to the flow of current: electric fire.

electronic music n. music consisting of sounds produced by electric currents either controlled from an instrument panel or keyboard or prerecorded on magnetic tape.

electronic organ n. Music. an instrument played by means of a keyboard, in which sounds are produced by electronic or electrical means.

electronics (ɪlɛkˈtrɒnɪks, ˌiːlɛk-) n. **1.** (functioning as sing.) the science and technology concerned with the development, behaviour, and applications of electronic devices and circuits. **2.** (functioning as pl.) the circuits and devices of a piece of electronic equipment.

electron microscope n. a powerful microscope that uses electrons, rather than light, and electron lenses to produce a magnified image.

electron tube n. an electrical device, such as a valve, in which a flow of electrons between electrodes takes place.

electronvolt (ɪˌlɛktrɒnˈvəʊlt) n. a unit of energy equal to the work done on an electron accelerated through a potential difference of 1 volt.

electroplate (ɪˈlɛktrəʊˌpleɪt) vb. **1.** (tr.) to plate (an object) by electrolysis. ~n. **2.** electroplated articles collectively, esp. when plated with silver. —eˈlectroˌplater n.

electrostatics (ɪˌlɛktrəʊˈstætɪks) n. the branch of physics concerned with static electricity. —eˌlectroˈstatic adj.

electrotype (ɪˈlɛktrəʊˌtaɪp) n. **1.** a duplicate printing

THESAURUS

election appointment, choice, choosing, decision, determination, judgment, preference, selection, vote, voting

elector chooser, constituent, selector,

voter

electric Fig. charged, dynamic, exciting, rousing, stimulating, stirring, tense, thrilling

electrify Fig. amaze, animate, astonish,

astound, excite, fire, galvanize, invigorate, jolt, rouse, shock, startle, stimulate, stir, take one's breath away, thrill

plate made by electrolytically depositing a layer of copper or nickel onto a mould of the original. ~*vb.* **2.** (*tr.*) to make an electrotype of (printed matter, etc.). —**e'lectro,typer** *n.*

electrum (ɪ'lɛktrəm) *n.* an alloy of gold and silver.

elegant ('ɛlɪgənt) *adj.* **1.** tasteful in dress, style, or design. **2.** dignified and graceful. **3.** cleverly simple; ingenious: *an elegant solution.* —**'elegance** *n.*

elegiac (,ɛlɪ'dʒaɪək) *adj.* **1.** resembling, characteristic of, relating to, or appropriate to an elegy. **2.** lamenting; mournful. **3.** denoting or written in elegiac couplets (which consist of a dactylic hexameter followed by a dactylic pentameter) or elegiac stanzas (which consist of a quatrain in iambic pentameters with alternate lines rhyming). ~*n.* **4.** (*often pl.*) an elegiac couplet or stanza.

elegy ('ɛlɪdʒɪ) *n., pl.* **-gies. 1.** a mournful poem or song, esp. a lament for the dead. **2.** poetry written in elegiac couplets or stanzas.

element ('ɛlɪmənt) *n.* **1.** any of the 105 known substances that consist of atoms with the same number of protons in their nuclei. **2.** one of the fundamental or irreducible components making up a whole. **3.** any group that is part of a larger unit, such as a military formation. **4.** a small amount; hint. **5.** a distinguishable section of a social group. **6.** the most favourable environment for an animal or plant. **7.** the situation in which a person is happiest or most effective (esp. in **in** or **out of one's element**). **8.** the resistance wire that constitutes the electrical heater in a cooker, heater, etc. **9.** one of the four substances thought in ancient and medieval cosmology to constitute the universe (earth, air, water, or fire). **10.** (*pl.*) atmospheric conditions, esp. wind, rain, and cold. **11.** (*pl.*) the basic principles. **12.** *Christianity.* the bread or wine consecrated in the Eucharist.

elemental (,ɛlɪ'mɛntəl) *adj.* **1.** fundamental; basic. **2.** motivated by or symbolic of primitive powerful natural forces or passions. **3.** of or relating to earth, air, water, and fire considered as elements. **4.** of or relating to atmospheric forces, esp. wind, rain, and cold. **5.** of or relating to a chemical element. ~*n.* **6.** *Rare.* a disembodied spirit. —,**ele'mental,ism** *n.*

elementary (,ɛlɪ'mɛntərɪ) *adj.* **1.** not difficult; rudimentary. **2.** of or concerned with the first principles of a subject; introductory or fundamental. **3.** *Chem.* another word for **elemental** (sense 5). —,**ele'mentariness** *n.*

elementary particle *n.* any of several entities, such as electrons, neutrons, or protons, that are less complex than atoms.

elementary school *n.* **1.** *Brit.* a former name for **primary school. 2.** *U.S.* a state school for the first six to eight years of a child's education.

elephant ('ɛlɪfənt) *n., pl.* **-phants** or **-phant.** either of two proboscidean mammals. The **African elephant** is the larger species, with large flapping ears and a less humped back than the **Indian elephant**, of S and SE Asia. —**'elephan,toid** *adj.*

elephantiasis (,ɛlɪfən'taɪəsɪs) *n. Pathol.* a complication of chronic filariasis, in which nematode worms block the lymphatic vessels, usually in the legs or scrotum, causing extreme enlargement of the affected area.

elephantine (,ɛlɪ'fæntaɪn) *adj.* **1.** denoting, relating to,

or characteristic of an elephant or elephants. **2.** huge, clumsy, or ponderous.

elevate ('ɛlɪ,veɪt) *vb.* (*tr.*) **1.** to move to a higher place. **2.** to raise in rank or status. **3.** to put in a cheerful mood; elate. **4.** to put on a higher cultural plane; uplift. **5.** to raise the axis of a gun. **6.** to raise the intensity or pitch of (the voice). —**'ele,vatory** *adj.*

elevation (,ɛlɪ'veɪʃən) *n.* **1.** the act of elevating or the state of being elevated. **2.** the height of something above a given place, esp. above sea level. **3.** a raised area; height. **4.** nobleness or grandeur. **5.** a drawing to scale of the external face of a building or structure. **6.** a ballet dancer's ability to leap high. **7.** *Astron.* another name for **altitude** (sense 3). **8.** the angle formed between the muzzle of a gun and the horizontal. —,**ele'vational** *adj.*

elevator ('ɛlɪ,veɪtə) *n.* **1.** a person or thing that elevates. **2.** a mechanical hoist, often consisting of a chain of scoops linked together on a conveyor belt. **3.** the U.S. name for **lift** (sense 12a). **4.** *Chiefly U.S.* a granary equipped with mechanical devices for hoisting grain. **5.** a control surface on the tailplane of an aircraft, for making it climb or descend.

eleven (ɪ'lɛvən) *n.* **1.** the cardinal number that is the sum of ten and one. **2.** a numeral 11, XI, etc., representing this number. **3.** something representing, represented by, or consisting of 11 units. **4.** (*functioning as sing. or pl.*) a team of 11 players in football, cricket, etc. **5.** Also called: **eleven o'clock.** eleven hours after noon or midnight. ~*determiner.* **6. a.** amounting to eleven. **b.** (*as pronoun*): *another eleven.* —**e'leventh** *adj.*

eleven-plus *n.* (esp. formerly) an examination, taken in England and Wales by children aged 11 or 12, that selects suitable candidates for grammar schools.

elevenses (ɪ'lɛvənzɪz) *pl. n. Brit. inf.* a light snack, usually with tea or coffee, taken in mid-morning.

elf (ɛlf) *n., pl.* **elves** (ɛlvz). **1.** (in folklore) one of a kind of legendary beings, usually characterized as small, manlike, and mischievous. **2.** a mischievous or whimsical child or girl. —**'elfish** *adj.*

elicit (ɪ'lɪsɪt) *vb.* (*tr.*) **1.** to give rise to; evoke. **2.** to bring to light. —**e'licitable** *adj.* —**e,lici'tation** *n.* —**e'licitor** *n.*

elide (ɪ'laɪd) *vb.* to undergo or cause to undergo elision. —**e'lidible** *adj.*

eligible ('ɛlɪdʒəbəl) *adj.* **1.** fit, worthy, or qualified, as for office. **2.** desirable, esp. as a spouse. —,**eligi'bility** *n.* —**'eligibly** *adv.*

eliminate (ɪ'lɪmɪ,neɪt) *vb.* (*tr.*) **1.** to remove or take out. **2.** to reject; omit from consideration. **3.** to remove (a competitor, team, etc.) from a contest, usually by defeat. **4.** *Sl.* to murder in cold blood. **5.** *Physiol.* to expel (waste) from the body. **6.** *Maths.* to remove (an unknown variable) from simultaneous equations. —**e'liminable** *adj.* —**e'liminant** *n.* —**e,limi'nation** *n.* —**e'liminative** or **e'liminatory** *adj.* —**e'limi,nator** *n.*

elision (ɪ'lɪʒən) *n.* **1.** omission of a syllable or vowel at the beginning or end of a word. **2.** omission of parts of a book.

elite or **élite** (ɪ'liːt, eɪ-) *n.* **1.** (*sometimes functioning as pl.*) the most powerful, rich or gifted members of a group, community, etc. **2.** a typewriter typesize having

---

THESAURUS

elegance, elegancy 1. beauty, courtliness, dignity, exquisiteness, gentility, grace, gracefulness, grandeur, luxury, polish, politeness, refinement, sumptuousness **2.** discernment, distinction, propriety, style, taste

elegant 1. à la mode, artistic, beautiful, chic, choice, comely, courtly, cultivated, delicate, exquisite, fashionable, fine, genteel, graceful, handsome, luxurious, modish, nice, polished, refined, stylish, sumptuous, tasteful **2.** appropriate, apt, clever, effective, ingenious, neat, simple

elegy coronach (*Scot., Irish*), dirge, keen, lament, plaint (*Archaic*), requiem, threnody

element 1. basis, component, constituent, essential factor, factor, feature, hint, ingredient, member, part, section, subdivision, trace, unit **2.** domain, environment, field, habitat, medium, milieu, sphere

elementary 1. clear, easy, facile, plain, rudimentary, simple, straightforward, un-

complicated **2.** basic, elemental, fundamental, initial, introductory, original, primary, rudimentary

elements 1. basics, essentials, foundations, fundamentals, principles, rudiments **2.** atmospheric conditions, atmospheric forces, powers of nature, weather

elevate 1. heighten, hoist, lift, lift up, raise, uplift, upraise **2.** advance, aggrandize, exalt, prefer, promote, upgrade **3.** animate, boost, brighten, buoy up, cheer, elate, excite, exhilarate, hearten, lift up, perk up, raise, rouse, uplift **4.** augment, boost, heighten, increase, intensify, magnify, swell

elevated 1. dignified, exalted, grand, high, high-flown, high-minded, inflated, lofty, noble, sublime **2.** animated, bright, cheerful, cheery, elated, excited, exhilarated, gleeful, in high spirits, overjoyed

elevation 1. altitude, height **2.** acclivity, eminence, height, hill, hillock, mountain,

rise, rising ground **3.** exaltedness, grandeur, loftiness, nobility, nobleness, sublimity **4.** advancement, aggrandizement, exaltation, preferment, promotion, upgrading

elicit bring forth, bring out, bring to light, call forth, cause, derive, draw out, educe, evoke, evolve, exact, extort, extract, give rise to, obtain, wrest

eligible acceptable, appropriate, desirable, fit, preferable, proper, qualified, suitable, suited, worthy

eliminate 1. cut out, dispose of, do away with, eradicate, exterminate, get rid of, remove, stamp out, take out **2.** dispense with, disregard, drop, eject, exclude, expel, ignore, knock out, leave out, omit, put out, reject, throw out **3.** *Sl.* annihilate, bump off (*Sl.*), kill, liquidate, murder, rub out (*U.S. sl.*), slay, terminate, waste (*U.S. sl.*)

12 characters to the inch. ~*adj.* **3.** of or suitable for an elite.

elitism (ɪ'liːtɪzəm, eɪ-) *n.* **1. a.** the belief that society should be governed by an elite. **b.** such government. **2.** pride in or awareness of being one of an elite group. —**e'litist** *n.*

elixir (ɪ'lɪksə) *n.* **1.** an alchemical preparation supposed to be capable of prolonging life (**elixir of life**) or of transmuting base metals into gold. **2.** anything that purports to be a sovereign remedy. **3.** a quintessence. **4.** a liquid containing a medicine with syrup, glycerin, or alcohol added to mask its unpleasant taste.

Elizabethan (ɪ,lɪzə'biːθən) *adj.* **1.** of, characteristic of, or relating to the reigns of Elizabeth I (queen of England, 1558–1603) or Elizabeth II (queen of Great Britain and N Ireland since 1952). **2.** of, relating to, or designating a style of architecture used in England during the reign of Elizabeth I. ~*n.* **3.** a person who lived in England during the reign of Elizabeth I.

elk (ɛlk) *n., pl.* **elks** or **elk. 1.** a large deer of N Europe and Asia: also occurs in N America, where it is called a moose. **2. American elk.** another name for **wapiti.**

ell (ɛl) *n.* an obsolete unit of length, approximately 45 inches.

ellipse (ɪ'lɪps) *n.* a closed conic section shaped like a flattened circle and formed by an inclined plane that does not cut the base of the cone.

ellipsis (ɪ'lɪpsɪs) *n., pl.* **-ses** (-siːz). **1.** omission of parts of a word or sentence. **2.** *Printing.* a sequence of three dots (...) indicating an omission in text.

ellipsoid (ɪ'lɪpsɔɪd) *n.* **a.** a geometric surface, symmetrical about the three coordinate axes, whose plane sections are ellipses or circles. **b.** a solid having this shape. —**ellipsoidal** (ɪlɪp'sɔɪdəl, ,ɛl-) *adj.*

elliptical (ɪ'lɪptɪkəl) *adj.* **1.** relating to or having the shape of an ellipse. **2.** relating to or resulting from ellipsis. **3.** (of speech, literary style, etc.) **a.** very concise, often so as to be obscure or ambiguous. **b.** circumlocutory. ~Also (for senses 1 and 2): **elliptic.** —**el'liptical-ness** *n.*

▷ **Usage.** The use of *elliptical* to mean *circumlocutory* is avoided by many careful speakers and writers.

elm (ɛlm) *n.* **1.** any tree of the genus *Ulmus*, occurring in the N hemisphere, having serrated leaves and winged fruits (samaras). **2.** the hard heavy wood of this tree.

elocution (,ɛlə'kjuːʃən) *n.* the art of public speaking. —,**elo'cutionary** *adj.* —,**elo'cutionist** *n.*

elongate ('iːlɒŋgeɪt) *vb.* **1.** to make or become longer; stretch. ~*adj.* **2.** long and narrow. **3.** lengthened or tapered. —'**elon,gative** *adj.* —,**elon'gation** *n.*

elope (ɪ'ləʊp) *vb.* (*intr.*) to run away secretly with a lover, esp. in order to marry. —**e'lopement** *n.* —**e'loper** *n.*

eloquence ('ɛləkwəns) *n.* **1.** ease in using language. **2.** powerful and effective language. **3.** the quality of being persuasive or moving.

eloquent ('ɛləkwənt) *adj.* **1.** (of speech, writing, etc.) fluent and persuasive. **2.** visibly or vividly expressive: *an eloquent yawn.* —'**eloquentness** *n.*

Elsan ('ɛlsæn) *n. Trademark.* a type of portable chemical lavatory.

else (ɛls) *determiner.* (*postpositive; used after an indefinite pronoun or an interrogative*) **1.** in addition; more: *there is nobody else here.* **2.** other; different: *where else could he be?* ~*adv.* **3. or else. a.** if not, then: *go away or else I won't finish my work today.* **b.** or something terrible will result: used as a threat: *sit down, or else!*

▷ **Usage.** The possessive of the expressions *anybody else, everybody else*, etc., is formed by adding 's to *else: somebody else's letter. Who else* is an exception in that *whose else* is an acceptable alternative to *who else's: whose else can it be?* or *who else's can it be?*

elsewhere (,ɛls'wɛə) *adv.* in or to another place; somewhere else.

elucidate (ɪ'luːsɪ,deɪt) *vb.* to make clear (something obscure or difficult); clarify. —**e,luci'dation** *n.* —**e'luci-,dative** or **e'luci,datory** *adj.* —**e'luci,dator** *n.*

elude (ɪ'luːd) *vb.* (*tr.*) **1.** to escape from or avoid, esp. by cunning. **2.** to avoid fulfilment of (a responsibility, obligation, etc.); evade. **3.** to escape discovery or understanding by; baffle. —**e'luder** *n.* —**elusion** (ɪ'luːʒən) *n.*

elusive (ɪ'luːsɪv) *adj.* **1.** difficult to catch. **2.** preferring or living in solitude and anonymity. **3.** difficult to remember. **4.** avoiding the issue: *an elusive answer.* —**e'lusiveness** *n.*

elver ('ɛlvə) *n.* a young eel, esp. one migrating up a river.

elves (ɛlvz) *n.* the plural of **elf.**

elvish ('ɛlvɪʃ) *adj.* a variant spelling of **elfish;** see **elf.**

Elysium (ɪ'lɪzɪəm) *n.* **1.** Also called: **Elysian fields.** *Greek myth.* the dwelling place of the blessed after death. **2.** a state or place of perfect bliss.

em (ɛm) *n. Printing.* **1.** the square of a body of any size of type, used as a unit of measurement. **2.** Also called: **pica em, pica.** a unit of measurement in printing, equal to one sixth of an inch.

emaciate (ɪ'meɪsɪ,eɪt) *vb.* (*usually tr.*) to become or cause to become abnormally thin. —**e,maci'ation** *n.*

emanate ('ɛmə,neɪt) *vb.* **1.** (*intr.; often foll. by from*) to issue or proceed from or as from a source. **2.** (*tr.*) to send forth; emit. —,**ema'nation** *n.* —**emanative** ('ɛmənətɪv) *adj.* —'**ema,nator** *n.* —**emanatory** ('ɛmə-,neɪtərɪ, -trɪ) *adj.*

emancipate (ɪ'mænsɪ,peɪt) *vb.* (*tr.*) **1.** to free from restriction or restraint, esp. social or legal restraint. **2.** (*often passive*) to free from the inhibitions of conventional morality. **3.** to liberate (a slave) from bondage. —**e,manci'pation** *n.* —**e'manci,pative** *adj.* —**e'manci,pator** or **e'manci,pator** *n.* —**emancipatory** (ɪ'mænsɪpətərɪ, -trɪ) *adj.*

emasculate (ɪ'mæskjʊ,leɪt) *vb.* (*tr.*) **1.** to remove the testicles of; castrate; geld. **2.** to deprive of vigour, effectiveness, etc. ~*adj.* (ɪ'mæskjʊlɪt, -,leɪt). **3.** castrated; gelded. **4.** deprived of strength, effectiveness, etc. —**e,mascu'lation** *n.* —**e'masculative** or **e'masculatory** *adj.* —**e'mascu,lator** *n.*

embalm (ɪm'bɑːm) *vb.* (*tr.*) **1.** to treat (a dead body) with preservatives to retard putrefaction. **2.** to preserve or cherish the memory of. **3.** *Poetic.* to give a sweet fragrance to. —**em'balmer** *n.* —**em'balmment** *n.*

THESAURUS

elite 1. *n.* aristocracy, best, cream, *crème de la crème*, elect, flower, gentry, high society, nobility, pick, upper class **2.** *adj.* aristocratic, best, choice, crack (*Sl.*), elect, exclusive, first-class, noble, pick, selected, upper-class

elocution articulation, declamation, delivery, diction, enunciation, oratory, pronunciation, public speaking, rhetoric, speech, speechmaking, utterance, voice production

elongate draw out, extend, lengthen, make longer, prolong, protract, stretch

elope abscond, bolt, decamp, disappear, escape, leave, run away, run off, slip away, steal away

eloquence expression, expressiveness, fluency, forcefulness, oratory, persuasiveness, rhetoric, way with words

eloquent 1. articulate, fluent, forceful, graceful, moving, persuasive, silver-tongued, stirring, well-expressed **2.** expressive, mean-

ingful, pregnant, revealing, suggestive, telling, vivid

elsewhere abroad, absent, away, hence (*Archaic*), in or to another place, not here, not present, somewhere else

elucidate annotate, clarify, clear up, explain, explicate, expound, gloss, illuminate, illustrate, interpret, make plain, shed or throw light upon, spell out, unfold

elucidation annotation, clarification, comment, commentary, explanation, explication, exposition, gloss, illumination, illustration, interpretation

elude 1. avoid, circumvent, dodge, duck (*Inf.*), escape, evade, flee, get away from, outrun, shirk, shun **2.** baffle, be beyond (someone), confound, escape, foil, frustrate, puzzle, stump, thwart

elusive 1. difficult to catch, shifty, slippery, tricky **2.** baffling, fleeting, indefinable, intangible, puzzling, subtle, transient, transi-

tory **3.** ambiguous, deceitful, deceptive, elusory, equivocal, evasive, fallacious, fraudulent, illusory, misleading, unspecific

emaciated atrophied, attenuate, attenuated, cadaverous, gaunt, haggard, lank, lean, meagre, pinched, scrawny, skeletal, thin, wasted

emaciation atrophy, attenuation, gauntness, haggardness, leanness, meagreness, scrawniness, thinness, wasting away

emanate 1. arise, come forth, derive, emerge, flow, issue, originate, proceed, spring, stem **2.** discharge, emit, exhale, give off, give out, issue, radiate, send forth

emanation 1. arising, derivation, emergence, flow, origination, proceeding **2.** discharge, effluent, efflux, effusion, emission, exhalation, radiation

emancipate deliver, discharge, disencumber, disenthral, enfranchise, free, liberate, manumit, release, set free, unchain, un-

embankment (ɪmˈbæŋkmənt) n. a man-made ridge of earth or stone that carries a road or railway or confines a waterway.

embargo (ɛmˈbɑːgəʊ) n., pl. **-goes.** 1. a government order prohibiting the departure or arrival of merchant ships in its ports. 2. any legal stoppage of commerce. 3. a restraint or prohibition. ~vb. **-going, -goed.** (tr.) 4. to lay an embargo upon. 5. to seize for use by the state.

embark (ɛmˈbɑːk) vb. 1. to board (a ship or aircraft). 2. (intr.; usually foll. by on or upon) to commence or engage (in) a new project, venture, etc. —ˌembarˈkation n. —emˈbarkment n.

embarrass (ɪmˈbærəs) vb. (mainly tr.) 1. to cause to feel confusion or self-consciousness; disconcert. 2. (usually passive) to involve in financial difficulties. 3. Arch. to complicate. 4. Arch. to impede or hamper. —emˈbarrassing adj. —emˈbarrassment n.

embassy (ˈɛmbəsɪ) n., pl. **-sies.** 1. the residence or place of business of an ambassador. 2. an ambassador and his entourage collectively. 3. the position, business, or mission of an ambassador. 4. any important or official mission.

embattle (ɪmˈbætəl) vb. (tr.) 1. to deploy (troops) for battle. 2. to fortify (a position, town, etc.). 3. to provide with battlements.

embed or **imbed** (ɪmˈbɛd) vb. **-bedding, -bedded.** 1. (usually foll. by in) to fix or become fixed firmly and deeply in a surrounding solid mass. 2. (tr.) to surround closely. 3. (tr.) to fix or retain (a thought, idea, etc.) in the mind. —emˈbedment or imˈbedment n.

embellish (ɪmˈbɛlɪʃ) vb. (tr.) 1. to beautify; adorn. 2. to make (a story, etc.) more interesting by adding detail. —emˈbellisher n. —emˈbellishment n.

ember (ˈɛmbə) n. 1. a glowing or smouldering piece of coal or wood, as in a dying fire. 2. the remains of a past emotion.

embezzle (ɪmˈbɛzəl) vb. to convert (money or property entrusted to one) fraudulently to one's own use. —emˈbezzlement n. —emˈbezzler n.

embitter (ɪmˈbɪtə) vb. (tr.) 1. to make (a person) bitter. 2. to aggravate (a hostile feeling, difficult situation, etc.). —emˈbitterment n.

emblazon (ɪmˈbleɪzən) vb. (tr.) 1. to portray heraldic arms on (a shield, one's notepaper, etc.). 2. to make bright or splendid, as with colours, flowers, etc. 3. to glorify, praise, or extol. —emˈblazonment n.

emblem (ˈɛmbləm) n. a visible object or representation that symbolizes a quality, type, group, etc. —ˌemblemˈatic or ˌemblemˈatical adj. —ˌemblemˈatically adv.

embody (ɪmˈbɒdɪ) vb. **-bodying, -bodied.** (tr.) 1. to give a tangible, bodily, or concrete form to (an abstract concept). 2. to be an example of or express (an idea, principle, etc.). 3. (often foll. by in) to collect or unite in a comprehensive whole. 4. Christian theol. to invest (a spiritual entity) with bodily form. —emˈbodiment n.

embolden (ɪmˈbəʊldən) vb. (tr.) to encourage; make bold.

embolism (ˈɛmbəˌlɪzəm) n. the occlusion of a blood vessel by an embolus. —emˈbolic adj.

embolus (ˈɛmbələs) n., pl. **-li** (-ˌlaɪ). material, such as part of a blood clot or an air bubble, that becomes lodged within a small blood vessel and impedes the circulation.

emboss (ɪmˈbɒs) vb. 1. to mould or carve (a decoration) on (a surface) so that it is raised above the surface in low relief. 2. to cause to bulge; make protrude. —emˈbosser n. —emˈbossment n.

embrace (ɪmˈbreɪs) vb. (mainly tr.) 1. (also intr.) (of a person) to take or clasp (another person) in the arms, or (of two people) to clasp each other, as in affection, greeting, etc.; hug. 2. to accept willingly or eagerly. 3. to take up (a new idea, faith, etc.); adopt. 4. to comprise or include as an integral part. 5. to encircle or enclose. 6. Rare. to perceive or understand. ~n. 7. the act of embracing. —emˈbraceable adj. —emˈbracement n. —emˈbracer n.

embrasure (ɪmˈbreɪʒə) n. 1. Fortifications. an opening or indentation, as in a battlement, for shooting through. 2. a door or window having splayed sides that increase the width of the opening in the interior. —emˈbrasured adj.

embrocate (ˈɛmbrəʊˌkeɪt) vb. (tr.) to apply a liniment or lotion to (a part of the body). —ˌembroˈcation n.

embroider (ɪmˈbrɔɪdə) vb. 1. to do decorative needlework upon (cloth, etc.). 2. to add fictitious or exaggerated detail to (a story, account, etc.). —emˈbroiderer n.

embroidery (ɪmˈbrɔɪdərɪ) n., pl. **-deries.** 1. decorative needlework done usually on loosely woven cloth or canvas, often being a picture or pattern. 2. elaboration or exaggeration, esp. in writing or reporting; embellishment.

embroil (ɪmˈbrɔɪl) vb. (tr.) 1. to involve (a person, oneself, etc.) in trouble, conflict, or argument. 2. to throw (affairs, etc.) into a state of confusion or disorder; complicate; entangle. —emˈbroiler n. —emˈbroilment n.

embryo (ˈɛmbrɪˌəʊ) n., pl. **-bryos.** 1. an animal in the early stages of development up to birth or hatching. 2. the human product of conception up to approximately the end of the second month of pregnancy. Cf. **foetus**. 3. a plant in the early stages of development. 4. an undeveloped or rudimentary state (esp. in **in embryo**). 5. something in an early stage of development. —ˈembry-

---

THESAURUS

fetter, unshackle

emancipation deliverance, discharge, enfranchisement, freedom, liberation, liberty, manumission, release

embalm 1. mummify, preserve 2. Of memories cherish, consecrate, conserve, enshrine, immortalize, store, treasure 3. Poetic make fragrant, perfume, scent

embargo 1. n. ban, bar, barrier, blockage, check, hindrance, impediment, interdict, interdiction, prohibition, proscription, restraint, restriction, stoppage 2. v. ban, bar, block, check, impede, interdict, prohibit, proscribe, restrict, stop

embark 1. board ship, go aboard, put on board, take on board, take ship 2. With on or upon begin, broach, commence, engage, enter, initiate, launch, plunge into, set about, set out, start, take up, undertake

embarrass abash, chagrin, confuse, discomfit, discompose, disconcert, discountenance, distress, fluster, mortify, put out of countenance, show up (Inf.)

embarrassing awkward, blush-making, compromising, discomfiting, disconcerting, distressing, humiliating, mortifying, sensitive, shameful, shaming, touchy, tricky, uncomfortable

embarrassment 1. awkwardness, bashfulness, chagrin, confusion, discomfiture, discomposure, distress, humiliation, mortification, self-consciousness, shame,

showing up (Inf.) 2. bind (Inf.), difficulty, mess, pickle (Inf.), predicament, scrape (Inf.) 3. excess, overabundance, superabundance, superfluity, surfeit, surplus

embellish adorn, beautify, bedeck, deck, decorate, dress up, elaborate, embroider, enhance, enrich, exaggerate, festoon, garnish, gild, grace, ornament, varnish

embellishment adornment, decoration, elaboration, embroidery, enhancement, enrichment, exaggeration, gilding, ornament, ornamentation

embezzle abstract, appropriate, defalcate (Law), filch, have one's hand in the till (Inf.), misapply, misappropriate, misuse, peculate, pilfer, purloin, steal

embezzlement abstraction, appropriation, defalcation (Law), filching, fraud, larceny, misapplication, misappropriation, misuse, peculation, pilferage, pilfering, purloining, stealing, theft, thieving

embitter 1. alienate, anger, disaffect, disillusion, envenom, make bitter or resentful, poison, sour 2. aggravate, exacerbate, exasperate, worsen

emblazon 1. adorn, blazon, colour, decorate, embellish, illuminate, ornament, paint 2. extol, glorify, laud (Literary), praise, proclaim, publicize, publish, trumpet

emblem badge, crest, device, figure, image, insignia, mark, representation, sigil (Rare), sign, symbol, token, type

embodiment 1. bodying forth, example, exemplar, exemplification, expression, incarnation, incorporation, manifestation, personification, realization, reification, representation, symbol, type 2. bringing together, codification, collection, combination, comprehension, concentration, consolidation, inclusion, incorporation, integration, organization, systematization

embolden animate, cheer, encourage, fire, hearten, inflame, inspirit, invigorate, nerve, reassure, rouse, stimulate, stir, strengthen, vitalize

embrace v. 1. clasp, cuddle, encircle, enfold, grasp, hold, hug, seize, squeeze, take or hold in one's arms 2. accept, adopt, avail oneself of, espouse, grab, make use of, receive, seize, take up, welcome 3. comprehend, comprise, contain, cover, deal with, embody, enclose, encompass, include, involve, provide for, subsume, take in, take into account ~n. 4. clasp, clinch (Sl.), cuddle, hug, squeeze

embroil complicate, compromise, confound, confuse, disorder, disturb, encumber, enmesh, ensnare, entangle, implicate, incriminate, involve, mire, mix up, muddle, perplex, trouble

embryo beginning, germ, nucleus, root, rudiment

,oid *adj.*

embryology (ˌɛmbrɪˈɒlədʒɪ) *n.* **1.** the scientific study of embryos. **2.** the structure and development of the embryo of a particular organism. —**embryological** (ˌɛmbrɪəˈlɒdʒɪkəl) *or* ˌembryoˈlogic *adj.* —ˌembryˈologist *n.*

embryonic (ˌɛmbrɪˈɒnɪk) *or* **embryonal** (ˈɛmbrɪənəl) *adj.* **1.** of or relating to an embryo. **2.** in an early stage; rudimentary; undeveloped. —ˌembryˈonically *adv.*

-eme *suffix forming nouns. Linguistics.* indicating a minimal distinctive unit of a specified type in a language: *morpheme; phoneme.*

emend (ɪˈmɛnd) *vb.* (*tr.*) to make corrections or improvements in (a text) by critical editing. —eˈmendable *adj.* —ˌemenˈdation *n.*

emerald (ˈɛmərəld, ˈɛmrəld) *n.* **1.** a green transparent variety of beryl: highly valued as a gem. **2.** its clear green colour.

Emerald Isle *n.* a poetic name for Ireland.

emerge (ɪˈmɜːdʒ) *vb.* (*intr.;* often foll. by *from*) **1.** to come up to the surface of or rise from water or other liquid. **2.** to come into view, as from concealment or obscurity. **3.** (foll. by *from*) to come out (of) or live (through (a difficult experience, etc.)). **4.** to become apparent. —eˈmergence *n.* —eˈmergent *adj.*

emergency (ɪˈmɜːdʒənsɪ) *n., pl.* **-cies. 1. a.** an unforeseen or sudden occurrence, esp. of danger demanding immediate action. **b.** (*as modifier*): *an emergency exit.* **2. a.** a patient requiring urgent treatment. **b.** (*as modifier*): *an emergency ward.* **3. state of emergency.** a condition, declared by a government, in which martial law applies, usually because of civil unrest or natural disaster. **4.** *N.Z.* a player selected to stand by to replace an injured member of a team; reserve.

emeritus (ɪˈmɛrɪtəs) *adj.* (*postpositive*) retired or honourably discharged from full-time work, but retaining one's title on an honorary basis: *a professor emeritus.*

emersion (ɪˈmɜːʃən) *n.* **1.** the act or an instance of emerging. **2.** *Astron.* the reappearance of a celestial body after an eclipse or occultation.

emery (ˈɛmərɪ) *n.* **a.** a hard greyish-black mineral consisting of corundum with either magnetite or haematite: used as an abrasive and polishing agent. **b.** (*as modifier*): *emery paper.*

emery board *n.* a strip of cardboard or wood with a rough surface of crushed emery, for filing one's nails.

emetic (ɪˈmɛtɪk) *adj.* **1.** causing vomiting. ~*n.* **2.** an emetic agent or drug.

emf *or* **EMF** *abbrev. for* electromotive force.

emigrate (ˈɛmɪˌɡreɪt) *vb.* (*intr.*) to leave one place, esp. one's native country, to settle in another. —ˈemigrant *n.* —ˌemiˈgration *n.* —ˈemiˌgratory *adj.*

émigré (ˈɛmɪˌɡreɪ) *n.* an emigrant, esp. one forced to leave his native country for political reasons.

eminence (ˈɛmɪnəns) *or* **eminency** *n., pl.* **-nences** *or* **-nencies. 1.** a position of superiority or fame. **2.** a high or raised piece of ground.

Eminence (ˈɛmɪnəns) *or* **Eminency** *n., pl.* **-nences** *or* **-nencies.** (preceded by *Your* or *His*) a title used to address or refer to a cardinal.

éminence grise *French.* (eminãs ˈɡriːz) *n., pl.* **éminences grises** (eminãs ˈɡriːz). a person who wields power and influence unofficially or behind the scenes.

eminent (ˈɛmɪnənt) *adj.* **1.** above others in rank, merit, or reputation; distinguished. **2.** (*prenominal*) noteworthy or outstanding. **3.** projecting or protruding; prominent.

emir (ɛˈmɪə) *n.* (in the Islamic world) **1.** an independent ruler or chieftain. **2.** a military commander or governor. **3.** a descendant of Mohammed. —eˈmirate *n.*

emissary (ˈɛmɪsərɪ, -ɪsrɪ) *n., pl.* **-saries. 1. a.** an agent sent on a mission; esp. one who represents a government or head of state. **b.** (*as modifier*): *an emissary delegation.* **2.** an agent sent on a secret mission, as a spy.

emission (ɪˈmɪʃən) *n.* **1.** the act of emitting or sending forth. **2.** energy, in the form of heat, light, radio waves, etc., emitted from a source. **3.** a substance, fluid, etc., that is emitted; discharge. **4.** *Physiol.* any bodily discharge, esp. of semen. —eˈmissive *adj.*

emit (ɪˈmɪt) *vb.* **emitting, emitted.** (*tr.*) **1.** to give or send forth; discharge. **2.** to give voice to; utter. **3.** *Physics.* to give off (radiation or particles).

Emmenthal (ˈɛmənˌtɑːl) *or* **Emmenthaler** *n.* a hard Swiss cheese with holes in it.

emollient (ɪˈmɒljənt) *adj.* **1.** softening or soothing, esp. to the skin. ~*n.* **2.** any preparation or substance that has this effect. —eˈmollience *n.*

emolument (ɪˈmɒljʊmənt) *n.* the profit arising from an office or employment; fees or wages.

emote (ɪˈməʊt) *vb.* (*intr.*) *Inf.* to display exaggerated emotion, as in acting. —eˈmoter *n.*

emotion (ɪˈməʊʃən) *n.* any strong feeling, as of joy, sorrow, or fear.

emotional (ɪˈməʊʃənəl) *adj.* **1.** of, characteristic of, or expressive of emotion. **2.** readily or excessively affected by emotion. **3.** appealing to or arousing emotion. **4.** caused or determined by emotion rather than reason: *an emotional argument.* —eˌmotionˈality *n.*

emotive (ɪˈməʊtɪv) *adj.* **1.** tending or designed to arouse emotion. **2.** of or characterized by emotion. —eˈmotiveness *or* ˌemoˈtivity *n.*

Emp. *abbrev. for:* **1.** Emperor. **2.** Empire. **3.** Empress.

empanel *or* **impanel** (ɪmˈpænəl) *vb.* **-elling, -elled** *or* *U.S.* **-eling, -eled.** (*tr.*) *Law.* **1.** to enter on a list (names of persons to be summoned for jury service). **2.** to select (a jury) from such a list. —emˈpanelment *or* imˈpanelment *n.*

empathy (ˈɛmpəθɪ) *n.* **1.** the power of understanding and imaginatively entering into another person's feelings. **2.** the attribution to an object, such as a work of art, of one's own feelings about it. —emˈpathic *or* ˌempaˈthetic *adj.* —ˈempathist *n.*

emperor (ˈɛmpərə) *n.* a monarch who rules or reigns

THESAURUS

emend amend, correct, edit, improve, rectify, redact, revise

emendation amendment, correction, editing, improvement, rectification, redaction, revision

emerge **1.** appear, arise, become visible, come forth, come into view, come out, come up, emanate, issue, proceed, rise, spring up, surface **2.** become apparent, become known, come out, come to light, crop up, develop, materialize, transpire, turn up

emergence advent, apparition, appearance, arrival, coming, dawn, development, disclosure, emanation, issue, materialization, rise

emergency crisis, danger, difficulty, exigency, extremity, necessity, pass, pinch, plight, predicament, quandary, scrape (*Inf.*), strait

emigrate migrate, move, move abroad, remove

emigration departure, exodus, migration, removal

eminence **1.** celebrity, dignity, distinction, esteem, fame, greatness, illustriousness, importance, notability, note, pre-eminence, prestige, prominence, rank, renown, reputation, repute, superiority **2.** elevation, height, high ground, hill, hillock, knoll, rise, summit

eminent celebrated, conspicuous, distinguished, elevated, esteemed, exalted, famous, grand, great, high, high-ranking, illustrious, important, notable, noted, noteworthy, outstanding, paramount, pre-eminent, prestigious, prominent, renowned, signal, superior, well-known

eminently conspicuously, exceedingly, exceptionally, extremely, greatly, highly, notably, outstandingly, prominently, remarkably, signally, strikingly, surpassingly, well

emission diffusion, discharge, ejaculation, ejection, emanation, exhalation, exudation, issuance, issue, radiation, shedding, transmission, utterance, venting

emit breathe forth, cast out, diffuse, discharge, eject, emanate, exhale, exude, give off, give out, give vent to, issue, radiate, send forth, send out, shed, throw out, transmit, utter, vent

emolument benefit, compensation, earnings, fee, gain, hire, pay, payment, profits, recompense, remuneration, return, reward, salary, stipend, wages

emotion agitation, ardour, excitement, feeling, fervour, passion, perturbation, sensation, sentiment, vehemence, warmth

emotional **1.** demonstrative, excitable, feeling, hot-blooded, passionate, responsive, sensitive, sentimental, susceptible, temperamental, tender, warm **2.** affecting, emotive, exciting, heart-warming, moving, pathetic, poignant, sentimental, stirring, tear-jerking (*Inf.*), thrilling, touching **3.** ardent, enthusiastic, fervent, fervid, fiery, heated, impassioned, passionate, roused, stirred, zealous

emotive **1.** argumentative, controversial, delicate, sensitive, touchy **2.** affecting, emotional, exciting, heart-warming, moving, pathetic, poignant, sentimental, stirring, tear-jerking (*Inf.*), thrilling, touching **3.** ardent, emotional, enthusiastic, fervent, fervid, fiery, heated, impassioned, passionate, roused, stirred, zealous

over an empire. —'**emperor,ship** n.

emperor penguin n. an Antarctic penguin with orange-yellow patches on the neck: the largest penguin, reaching a height of 1.3 m (4 ft.).

emphasis ('ɛmfəsɪs) n., pl. **-ses** (-siːz). **1.** special importance or significance. **2.** an object, idea, etc., that is given special importance or significance. **3.** stress on a particular syllable, word, or phrase in speaking. **4.** force or intensity of expression. **5.** sharpness or clarity of form or outline.

emphasize or **-ise** ('ɛmfə,saɪz) vb. (tr.) to give emphasis or prominence to; stress.

emphatic (ɪm'fætɪk) adj. **1.** expressed, spoken, or done with emphasis. **2.** forceful and positive; definite; direct. **3.** sharp or clear in form, contour, or outline. **4.** important or significant; stressed. —**em'phatically** adv.

emphysema (,ɛmfɪ'siːmə) n. Pathol. **1.** a condition in which the air sacs of the lungs are grossly enlarged, causing breathlessness and wheezing. **2.** the abnormal presence of air in a tissue or part.

empire ('ɛmpaɪə) n. **1.** an aggregate of peoples and territories under the rule of a single person, oligarchy, or sovereign state. **2.** any monarchy that has an emperor as head of state. **3.** the period during which a particular empire exists. **4.** supreme power; sovereignty. **5.** a large industrial organization with many ramifications.

Empire ('ɛmpaɪə) n. **the. 1.** the British Empire. **2.** French history. **a.** the period of imperial rule in France from 1804 to 1815 under Napoleon Bonaparte. **b.** Also called: **Second Empire.** the period from 1852 to 1870 when Napoleon III ruled as emperor. ~adj. **3.** denoting, characteristic of, or relating to the British Empire. **4.** denoting, characteristic of, or relating to either French Empire, esp. the first.

empire-builder n. Inf. a person who seeks extra power, esp. by increasing the number of his staff. —'**empire-,building** n., adj.

empirical (ɛm'pɪrɪkəl) adj. **1.** derived from or relating to experiment and observation rather than theory. **2.** (of medical treatment) based on practical experience rather than scientific proof. **3.** Philosophy. (of knowledge) derived from experience rather than by logic from first principles. **4.** of or relating to medical quackery. —**em'piricalness** n.

empiricism (ɛm'pɪrɪ,sɪzəm) n. **1.** Philosophy. the doctrine that all knowledge derives from experience. **2.** the use of empirical methods. **3.** medical quackery. —**em'piricist** n., adj.

emplacement (ɪm'pleɪsmənt) n. **1.** a prepared position for a gun or other weapon. **2.** the act of putting or state of being put in place.

emplane (ɪm'pleɪn) vb. to board or put on board an aeroplane.

employ (ɪm'plɔɪ) vb. (tr.) **1.** to engage or make use of the services of (a person) in return for money; hire. **2.** to provide work or occupation for; keep busy. **3.** to use as a means. ~n. **4.** the state of being employed (esp. in **in someone's employ**). —**em'ployable** adj. —**em,ploya'bility** n.

employee (ɛm'plɔɪiː, ,ɛmplɔɪ'iː) or **employé** n. a person who is hired to work for another or for a business, firm, etc., in return for payment.

employer (ɪm'plɔɪə) n. **1.** a person, firm, etc., that employs workers. **2.** a person who employs.

employment (ɪm'plɔɪmənt) n. **1.** the act of employing or state of being employed. **2.** a person's work or occupation.

emporium (ɛm'pɔːrɪəm) n., pl. **-riums** or **-ria** (-rɪə). a large retail shop offering for sale a wide variety of merchandise.

empower (ɪm'pauə) vb. (tr.) **1.** to give power or authority to; authorize. **2.** to give ability to; enable or permit. —**em'powerment** n.

empress ('ɛmprɪs) n. **1.** the wife or widow of an emperor. **2.** a woman who holds the rank of emperor in her own right.

empty ('ɛmptɪ) adj. **-tier, -tiest. 1.** containing nothing. **2.** without inhabitants; vacant or unoccupied. **3.** carrying no load, passengers, etc. **4.** without purpose, substance, or value: an empty life. **5.** insincere or trivial: empty words. **6.** not expressive or vital; vacant: an empty look. **7.** Inf. hungry. **8.** (postpositive, foll. by of) devoid; destitute. **9.** Inf. drained of energy or emotion. **10.** Maths, logic. (of a set or class) containing no members. ~vb. **-tying, -tied. 11.** to make or become empty. **12.** (when intr., foll. by into) to discharge (contents). **13.** (tr.; often foll. by of) to unburden or rid (oneself). ~n., pl. **-ties. 14.** Inf. an empty container, esp. a bottle or can. —'**emptiable** adj. —'**emptier** n. —'**emptily** adv. —'**emptiness** n.

empty-handed adj. **1.** carrying nothing in the hands. **2.** having gained nothing.

empty-headed adj. lacking sense; frivolous.

empyrean (,ɛmpaɪ'riːən) n. **1.** Arch. the highest part of the heavens, thought in ancient times to contain the pure element of fire and by early Christians to be the abode of God. **2.** Poetic. the heavens or sky. ~adj. also **empyreal. 3.** of or relating to the sky. **4.** heavenly or sublime.

emu ('iːmjuː) n. a large Australian flightless bird, similar to the ostrich.

emulate ('ɛmjʊ,leɪt) vb. (tr.) **1.** to attempt to equal or surpass, esp. by imitation. **2.** to rival or compete with. —'**emulative** adj. —,**emu'lation** n. —'**emu,lator** n.

emulous ('ɛmjʊləs) adj. **1.** desiring or aiming to equal or surpass another. **2.** characterized by or arising from emulation. —'**emulousness** n.

THESAURUS

emphasis accent, accentuation, attention, decidedness, force, importance, impressiveness, insistence, intensity, moment, positiveness, power, pre-eminence, priority, prominence, significance, strength, stress, underscoring, weight

emphasize accent, accentuate, dwell on, give priority to, highlight, insist on, lay stress on, play up, press home, put the accent on, stress, underline, underscore, weight

emphatic absolute, categorical, certain, decided, definite, direct, distinct, earnest, energetic, forceful, forcible, important, impressive, insistent, marked, momentous, positive, powerful, pronounced, resounding, significant, striking, strong, telling, unequivocal, unmistakable, vigorous

empire 1. commonwealth, domain, imperium (Rare), kingdom, realm **2.** authority, command, control, dominion, government, power, rule, sovereignty, supremacy, sway

empirical, empiric experiential, experimental, observed, practical, pragmatic

emplacement 1. location, lodgment, platform, position, site, situation, station **2.** placement, placing, positioning, putting in place, setting up, stationing

employ v. **1.** commission, engage, enlist, hire, retain, take on **2.** engage, fill, keep busy, make use of, occupy, spend, take up, use up **3.** apply, bring to bear, exercise, exert, make use of, ply, put to use, use, utilize ~n. **4.** employment, engagement, hire, service

employed active, busy, engaged, in a job, in employment, in work, occupied, working

employee hand, job-holder, staff member, wage-earner, worker, workman

employer boss (Inf.), business, company, establishment, firm, gaffer (Inf., chiefly Brit.), organization, outfit (Inf.), owner, patron, proprietor

employment 1. engagement, enlistment, hire, retaining, taking on **2.** application, exercise, exertion, use, utilization **3.** avocation (Archaic), business, calling, craft, employ, job, line, métier, occupation, profession, pursuit, service, trade, vocation, work

emporium bazaar, market, mart, shop, store

empower allow, authorize, commission, delegate, enable, entitle, license, permit, qualify, sanction, warrant

emptiness 1. bareness, blankness, desertedness, desolation, destitution, vacancy, vacuum, void, waste **2.** aimlessness, banality, barrenness, frivolity, futility, hollowness, inanity, ineffectiveness, meaninglessness, purposelessness, senselessness, silliness, unreality, unsatisfactoriness, unsubstantiality, vainness, valuelessness, vanity, worthlessness **3.** cheapness, hollowness, idleness, insincerity, triviality, trivialness **4.** absentness, blankness, expressionlessness, unintelligence, vacancy, vacantness, vacuity, vacuousness **5.** Inf. desire, hunger, ravening

empty adj. **1.** bare, blank, clear, deserted, desolate, destitute, hollow, unfurnished, uninhabited, unoccupied, untenanted, vacant, void, waste **2.** aimless, banal, bootless, frivolous, fruitless, futile, hollow, inane, ineffective, meaningless, purposeless, senseless, silly, unreal, unsatisfactory, unsubstantial, vain, valueless, worthless **3.** cheap, hollow, idle, insincere, trivial **4.** absent, blank, expressionless, unintelligent, vacant, vacuous **5.** Inf. famished, hungry, ravenous, starving (Inf.), unfed, unfilled ~v. **6.** clear, consume, deplete, discharge, drain, dump, evacuate, exhaust, gut, pour out, unburden, unload, up, vacate, void

empty-headed brainless, dizzy (Inf.), featherbrained, flighty, frivolous, giddy, harebrained, inane, scatterbrained, silly, skittish, vacuous

emulsify (ɪ'mʌlsɪ,faɪ) vb. -fying, -fied. to make or form into an emulsion. —e'mulsi,fiable or e'mulsible adj. —e,mulsifi'cation n. —e'mulsi,fier n.

emulsion (ɪ'mʌlʃən) n. 1. Photog. a light-sensitive coating on a base, such as paper or film, consisting of silver bromide suspended in gelatin. 2. Chem. a colloid in which both phases are liquids. 3. a type of paint in which the pigment is suspended in a vehicle that is dispersed in water as an emulsion. 4. Pharmacol. a mixture in which an oily medicine is dispersed in another liquid. 5. any liquid resembling milk. —e'mulsive adj.

en (ɛn) n. Printing. half the width of an em.

enable (ɪn'eɪbəl) vb. (tr.) 1. to provide (someone) with adequate power, means, opportunity, or authority (to do something). 2. to make possible or easy. —en'abler n.

enabling act n. a legislative act conferring certain specified powers on a person or organization.

enact (ɪn'ækt) vb. (tr.) 1. to make into an act or statute. 2. to establish by law; decree. 3. to represent or perform as in a play. —en'actable adj. —en'active or en-'actory adj. —en'actment or en'action n. —en'actor n.

enamel (ɪ'næməl) n. 1. a coloured glassy substance, translucent or opaque, fused to the surface of articles made of metal, glass, etc., for ornament or protection. 2. an article or articles ornamented with enamel. 3. an enamel-like paint or varnish. 4. any coating resembling enamel. 5. the hard white substance that covers the crown of each tooth. 6. (modifier) decorated or covered with enamel. —vb. -elling, -elled or U.S. -eling, -eled. (tr.) 7. to decorate with enamel. 8. to ornament with glossy variegated colours, as if with enamel. 9. to portray in enamel. —e'nameller, e'namellist or U.S. e'nameler, e'namelist n. —e'namel,work n.

enamour or U.S. **enamor** (ɪn'æmə) vb. (tr.; usually passive and foll. by of) to inspire with love; captivate. —en'amoured or U.S. en'amored adj.

en bloc French. (ã 'blɔk) adv. in a lump or block; as a body or whole; all together.

enc. abbrev. for: 1. enclosed. 2. enclosure.

encamp (ɪn'kæmp) vb. to lodge in a camp. —en'campment n.

encapsulate or **incapsulate** (ɪn'kæpsjʊ,leɪt) vb. 1. to enclose or be enclosed as in a capsule. 2. (tr.) to put in a short or concise form. —en,capsu'lation or in,capsu'lation n.

encase or **incase** (ɪn'keɪs) vb. (tr.) to place or enclose as in a case. —en'casement or in'casement n.

encash (ɪn'kæʃ) vb. (tr.) Brit., formal. to exchange (a cheque) for cash. —en'cashable adj. —en'cashment n.

encaustic (ɪn'kɔstɪk) Ceramics, etc. ~adj. 1. decorated by any process involving burning in colours, esp. by inlaying coloured clays and baking or by fusing wax colours to the surface. ~n. 2. the process of burning in colours. 3. a product of such a process. —en'caustically adv.

enceinte (ɒn'sænt) adj. another word for **pregnant**.

encephalitis (,ɛnsɛfə'laɪtɪs) n. inflammation of the brain. —**encephalitic** (,ɛnsɛfə'lɪtɪk) adj.

encephalo- or before a vowel **encephal-** combining form. indicating the brain: encephalogram; encephalitis.

encephalogram (ɛn'sɛfələ,græm) n. 1. an x-ray photograph of the brain, esp. one (a **pneumoencephalogram**) taken after replacing some of the cerebrospinal fluid with air or oxygen. 2. short for **electroencephalogram**; see **electroencephalograph**.

enchain (ɪn'tʃeɪn) vb. (tr.) 1. to bind with chains. 2. to hold fast or captivate (the attention, etc.). —en'chainment n.

enchant (ɪn'tʃɑnt) vb. (tr.) 1. to cast a spell on; bewitch. 2. to delight or captivate utterly. —en'chanter n. —en'chanting adj. —en'chantment n. —en'chantress fem. n.

encircle (ɪn'sɜkəl) vb. (tr.) to form a circle around; enclose within a circle; surround. —en'circlement n.

enclave ('ɛnkleɪv) n. a part of a country entirely surrounded by foreign territory: viewed from the position of the surrounding territories.

enclose or **inclose** (ɪn'kləʊz) vb. (tr.) 1. to close; hem in; surround. 2. to surround (land) with or as if with a fence. 3. to put in an envelope or wrapper, esp. together with a letter. 4. to contain or hold. —en'closable or in-'closable adj. —en'closer or in'closer n.

enclosure or **inclosure** (ɪn'kləʊʒə) n. 1. the act of enclosing or state of being enclosed. 2. an area enclosed as by a fence. 3. the act of appropriating land by setting up a fence around it. 4. a fence, wall, etc., that encloses. 5. something enclosed within an envelope or wrapper, esp. together with a letter. 6. Brit. a section of a sports ground, race course, etc., allotted to certain spectators.

encomium (ɛn'kəʊmɪəm) n., pl. **-miums** or **-mia** (-mɪə). a formal expression of praise; eulogy.

encompass (ɪn'kʌmpəs) vb. (tr.) 1. to enclose within a circle; surround. 2. to bring about: he encompassed the enemy's ruin. 3. to include entirely or comprehensively. —en'compassment n.

encore ('ɒŋkɔ) interj. 1. again: used by an audience to demand an extra or repeated performance. ~n. 2. an extra or repeated performance given in response to enthusiastic demand. ~vb. 3. (tr.) to demand an extra or repeated performance of (a work, piece of music, etc.) by (a performer).

encounter (ɪn'kaʊntə) vb. 1. to come upon or meet casually or unexpectedly. 2. to meet (an enemy, army, etc.) in battle or contest. 3. (tr.) to be faced with; contend with. ~n. 4. a casual or unexpected meeting. 5. a hostile meeting; contest. —en'counterer n.

encourage (ɪn'kʌrɪdʒ) vb. (tr.) 1. to inspire (someone) with the courage or confidence (to do something). 2. to stimulate (something or someone) by approval or help. —en'couragement n. —en'courager n. —en'couragingly adv.

THESAURUS

enable allow, authorize, capacitate, commission, empower, facilitate, fit, license, permit, prepare, qualify, sanction, warrant

enact 1. authorize, command, decree, establish, legislate, ordain, order, pass, proclaim, ratify, sanction 2. act, act out, appear as, depict, perform, personate, play, play the part of, portray, represent

enactment 1. authorization, command, commandment, decree, dictate, edict, law, legislation, order, ordinance, proclamation, ratification, regulation, statute 2. acting, depiction, performance, personation, playacting, playing, portrayal, representation

enamour bewitch, captivate, charm, enchant, endear, enrapture, entrance, fascinate, infatuate

enamoured bewitched, captivated, charmed, crazy about (Inf.), enchanted, enraptured, entranced, fascinated, fond, infatuated, in love, nuts on or about (Sl.), smitten, swept off one's feet, taken, wild about (Inf.)

encampment base, bivouac, camp, camping ground, campsite, cantonment, quarters, tents

encapsulate,   **incapsulate** abridge, compress, condense, digest, epitomize, précis, summarize, sum up

enchant beguile, bewitch, captivate, cast a spell on, charm, delight, enamour, enrapture, enthral, fascinate, hypnotize, mesmerize, spellbind

enchanter conjurer, magician, magus, necromancer, sorcerer, spellbinder, warlock, witch, wizard

enchanting alluring, appealing, attractive, bewitching, captivating, charming, delightful, endearing, entrancing, fascinating, lovely, pleasant, ravishing, winsome

enchantment 1. allure, allurement, beguilement, bliss, charm, delight, fascination, hypnotism, mesmerism, rapture, ravishment, transport 2. charm, conjuration, incantation, magic, necromancy, sorcery, spell, witchcraft, wizardry

enchantress 1. conjurer, lamia, magician, necromancer, sorceress, spellbinder, witch 2. charmer, femme fatale, seductress, siren, vamp (Inf.)

enclose, inclose 1. bound, circum-scribe, cover, encase, encircle, encompass, environ, fence, hedge, hem in, pen, shut in, wall in, wrap 2. include, insert, put in, send with 3. comprehend, contain, embrace, hold, include, incorporate

encompass 1. circle, circumscribe, encircle, enclose, envelop, environ, girdle, hem in, ring, surround 2. bring about, cause, contrive, devise, effect, manage 3. admit, comprehend, comprise, contain, cover, embody, embrace, hold, include, incorporate, involve, subsume, take in

encounter v. 1. bump into (Inf.), chance upon, come upon, confront, experience, face, happen on or upon, meet, run across, run into (Inf.) 2. attack, clash with, combat, come into conflict with, contend, cross swords with, do battle with, engage, fight, grapple with, strive, struggle ~n. 3. brush, confrontation, meeting 4. action, battle, clash, collision, combat, conflict, contest, dispute, engagement, fight, run-in (Inf.), set to (Inf.), skirmish

encourage 1. animate, buoy up, cheer, comfort, console, embolden, hearten, incite, inspire, inspirit, rally, reassure, rouse, stimu-

encroach (ɪnˈkrəʊtʃ) vb. (intr.) **1.** (often foll. by on or upon) to intrude gradually or stealthily upon the rights, property, etc., of another. **2.** to advance beyond certain limits. —en'croacher n. —en'croachment n.

encrust or **incrust** (ɪnˈkrʌst) vb. **1.** (tr.) to cover or overlay with or as with a crust or hard coating. **2.** to form or cause to form a crust or hard coating. **3.** (tr.) to decorate lavishly, as with jewels. —ˌencrus'tation or ˌincrus'tation n.

encumber or **incumber** (ɪnˈkʌmbə) vb. (tr.) **1.** to hinder or impede; hamper. **2.** to fill with superfluous or useless matter. **3.** to burden with debts, obligations, etc.

encumbrance or **incumbrance** (ɪnˈkʌmbrəns) n. **1.** a thing that impedes or is burdensome; hindrance. **2.** Law. a burden or charge upon property, such as a mortgage or lien.

ency., **encyc.**, or **encycl.** abbrev. for encyclopedia.

encyclical (enˈsɪklɪkəl) n. **1.** a letter sent by the pope to all Roman Catholic bishops. ~adj. also **encyclic. 2.** (of letters) intended for general circulation.

encyclopedia or **encyclopaedia** (enˌsaɪkləʊˈpiːdɪə) n. a book, often in many volumes, containing articles, often arranged in alphabetical order, dealing either with the whole range of human knowledge or with one particular subject. —enˌcyclo'pedic or enˌcyclo'paedic adj.

encyclopedist or **encyclopaedist** (enˌsaɪkləʊ-ˈpiːdɪst) n. a person who compiles or contributes to an encyclopedia. —enˌcyclo'pedism or enˌcyclo-'paedism n.

end (end) n. **1.** the extremity of the length of something, such as a road, line, etc. **2.** the surface at either extremity of an object **3.** the extreme extent, limit, or degree of something. **4.** the most distant place or time that can be imagined: the ends of the earth. **5.** the time at which something is concluded. **6.** the last section or part. **7.** a share or part. **8.** (often pl.) a remnant or fragment (esp. in odds and ends). **9.** a final state, esp. death; destruction. **10.** the purpose of an action or existence. **11.** Sport. either of the two defended areas of a playing field, rink, etc. **12.** Bowls. a section of play from one side of the green to the other. **13. at an end.** exhausted. **14. come to an end.** to become completed or exhausted. **15. in the end.** finally. **16. make (both) ends meet.** to spend no more than the money one has. **17. no end (of).** Inf. (intensifier): I had no end of work. **18. on end.** Inf. without pause or interruption. **19. the end.** Sl. the worst, esp. something that goes beyond the limits of endurance. ~vb. **20.** to bring or come to a finish; conclude. **21.** to die or cause to die. **22.** (tr.) to surpass or outdo: a novel to end all novels. **23. end it all.** Inf. to commit suicide. ~See also **end up.** —'ender n.

end- combining form. a variant of **endo-** before a vowel.

-end suffix forming nouns. See **-and.**

endanger (ɪnˈdeɪndʒə) vb. (tr.) to put in danger or peril;

imperil. —en'dangerment n.

endear (ɪnˈdɪə) vb. (tr.) to cause to be beloved or esteemed. —en'dearing adj.

endearment (ɪnˈdɪəmənt) n. something that endears, such as an affectionate utterance.

endeavour or U.S. **endeavor** (ɪnˈdevə) vb. **1.** to try (to do something). ~n. **2.** an effort to do or attain something. —en'deavourer or U.S. en'deavorer n.

endemic (enˈdemɪk) adj. also **endemial** (enˈdemɪəl) or **endemical. 1.** present within a localized area or peculiar to persons in such an area. ~n. **2.** an endemic disease or plant. —en'demically adv. —'endemism or ˌende'micity n.

ending ('endɪŋ) n. **1.** the act of bringing to or reaching an end. **2.** the last part of something. **3.** the final part of a word, esp. a suffix.

endive ('endaɪv) n. a plant cultivated for its crisp curly leaves, which are used in salads. Cf. **chicory.**

endless ('endlɪs) adj. **1.** having or seeming to have no end; eternal or infinite. **2.** continuing too long or continually recurring. **3.** formed with the ends joined. —'endlessness n.

endmost ('endˌməʊst) adj. nearest the end; most distant.

endo- or before a vowel **end-** combining form. inside; within: endocrine.

endocrine ('endəʊˌkraɪn, -krɪn) adj. also **endocrinal** (ˌendəʊˈkraɪnəl), **endocrinic** (ˌendəʊˈkrɪnɪk). **1.** of or denoting endocrine glands or their secretions. ~n. **2.** an endocrine gland.

endocrine gland n. any of the glands that secrete hormones directly into the blood stream, e.g. the pituitary, pineal, and thyroid.

endogenous (enˈdɒdʒɪnəs) adj. Biol. developing or originating within an organism or part of an organism. —en'dogeny n.

endomorph ('endəʊˌmɔːf) n. **1.** a type of person having a body build characterized by fatness and heaviness. **2.** a mineral that naturally occurs enclosed within another mineral. —ˌendo'morphic adj. —'endoˌmorphy n.

endorsation (ˌendɔːˈseɪʃən) n. Canad. approval or support.

endorse or **indorse** (ɪnˈdɔːs) vb. (tr.) **1.** to give approval or sanction to. **2.** to sign (one's name) on the back of (a cheque, etc.) to specify oneself as payee. **3.** Commerce. **a.** to sign the back of (a document) to transfer ownership of the rights to a specified payee. **b.** to specify (a sum) as transferable to another as payee. **4.** to write (a qualifying comment, etc.) on the back of a document. **5.** to sign a document, as when confirming receipt of payment. **6.** Chiefly Brit. to record (a conviction) on (a driving licence). —en'dorsable or in'dorsable adj. —en'dorser, en'dorsor or in'dorser, in'dorsor n. —ˌendor'see or ˌindor'see n. —en'dorsement n.

late **2.** abet, advance, advocate, aid, boost, egg on, favour, forward, foster, further, help, promote, spur, strengthen, succour, support, urge

encouragement advocacy, aid, boost, cheer, consolation, favour, help, incitement, inspiration, inspiritment, promotion, reassurance, stimulation, stimulus, succour, support, urging

encouraging bright, cheerful, cheering, comforting, good, heartening, hopeful, promising, reassuring, rosy, satisfactory, stimulating

encroach appropriate, arrogate, impinge, infringe, intrude, invade, make inroads, overstep, trench, trespass, usurp

encroachment appropriation, arrogation, impingement, incursion, infringement, inroad, intrusion, invasion, trespass, usurpation, violation

encumber burden, clog, cramp, embarrass, hamper, handicap, hinder, impede, incommode, inconvenience, make difficult, obstruct, oppress, overload, retard, saddle, slow down, trammel, weigh down

encumbrance burden, clog, difficulty, drag, embarrassment, handicap, hindrance,

impediment, inconvenience, liability, load, millstone, obstacle, obstruction

end n. **1.** bound, boundary, edge, extent, extreme, extremity, limit, point, terminus, tip **2.** attainment, cessation, close, closure, completion, conclusion, consequence, consummation, culmination, denouement, ending, expiration, expiry, finale, finish, issue, outcome, resolution, result, stop, termination, upshot, wind-up **3.** aim, aspiration, design, drift, goal, intent, intention, object, objective, point, purpose, reason **4.** part, piece, portion, responsibility, share, side **5.** bit, fragment, leftover, remainder, remnant, scrap, stub, tag end **6.** annihilation, death, demise, destruction, dissolution, doom, extermination, extinction, ruin, ruination **7. the end** Sl. beyond endurance, insufferable, intolerable, the final blow, the last straw, the limit (Inf.), the worst, too much (Inf.), unbearable, unendurable ~v. **8.** bring to an end, cease, close, complete, conclude, culminate, dissolve, expire, finish, resolve, stop, terminate, wind up **9.** abolish, annihilate, destroy, exterminate, extinguish, kill, put to death, ruin

endanger compromise, hazard, imperil, jeopardize, put at risk, put in danger, risk,

threaten

endear attach, attract, bind, captivate, charm, engage, win

endearing adorable, attractive, captivating, charming, engaging, lovable, sweet, winning, winsome

endearment 1. affectionate utterance, loving word, sweet nothing **2.** affection, attachment, fondness, love

endeavour 1. n. aim, attempt, crack (Inf.), effort, enterprise, essay, go, shot (Inf.), stab (Inf.), trial, try, undertaking, venture **2.** v. aim, aspire, attempt, do one's best, essay, have a go (crack, shot, stab), labour, make an effort, strive, struggle, take pains, try, undertake

ending catastrophe, cessation, close, completion, conclusion, consummation, culmination, denouement, end, finale, finish, resolution, termination, wind-up

endless 1. boundless, ceaseless, constant, continual, eternal, everlasting, immortal, incessant, infinite, interminable, limitless, measureless, perpetual, unbounded, unbroken, undying, unending, uninterrupted, unlimited **2.** interminable, monotonous, overlong **3.** continuous, unbroken, undivided,

endow (ɪn'daʊ) vb. (tr.) **1.** to provide with or bequeath a source of permanent income. **2.** (usually foll. by *with*) to provide (with qualities, characteristics, etc.). —**en'dower** n.

endowment (ɪn'daʊmənt) n. **1.** the income with which an institution, etc., is endowed. **2.** the act or process of endowing. **3.** (*usually pl.*) natural talents or qualities.

endowment assurance *or* **insurance** n. a form of life insurance that provides for the payment of a specified sum directly to the policyholder at a designated date or to his beneficiary should he die before this date.

endpaper ('ɛnd,peɪpə) n. either of two leaves at the front and back of a book pasted to the inside of the board covers and the first leaf of the book.

end product n. the final result of a process, series, etc., esp. in manufacturing.

endue *or* **indue** (ɪn'djuː) vb. **-duing, -dued.** (tr.) (usually foll. by *with*) to invest or provide, as with some quality or trait.

end up vb. (adv.) **1.** (*copula*) to become eventually; turn out to be. **2.** (*intr.*) to arrive, esp. by a circuitous or lengthy route or process.

endurance (ɪn'djʊərəns) n. **1.** the capacity, state, or an instance of enduring. **2.** something endured; a hardship, strain, or privation.

endure (ɪn'djʊə) vb. **1.** to undergo (hardship, strain, etc.) without yielding; bear. **2.** (tr.) to permit or tolerate. **3.** (*intr.*) to last or continue to exist. —**en'durable** adj. —**en,dura'bility** *or* **en'durableness** n.

enduring (ɪn'djʊərɪŋ) adj. **1.** permanent; lasting. **2.** having forbearance; long-suffering. —**en'duringly** adv. —**en'duringness** n.

endways ('ɛnd,weɪz) *or* esp. U.S. **endwise** ('ɛnd,waɪz) adv. **1.** having the end forwards or upwards. ~adj. **2.** vertical or upright. **3.** lengthways. **4.** standing or lying end to end.

-ene n. combining form. (in chemistry) indicating an unsaturated compound containing double bonds: *benzene; ethylene.*

enema ('ɛnɪmə) n., pl. **-mas** or **-mata** (-mətə). Med. **1.** the introduction of liquid into the rectum to evacuate the bowels, medicate, or nourish. **2.** the liquid so introduced.

enemy ('ɛnəmɪ) n., pl. **-mies. 1.** a person hostile or opposed to a policy, cause, person, or group. **2. a.** an armed adversary; opposing military force. **b.** (*as modifier*): *enemy aircraft.* **3. a.** a hostile nation or people. **b.** (*as modifier*): *an enemy alien.* **4.** something that harms or opposes. ~Related adj.: **inimical.**

energetic (,ɛnə'dʒɛtɪk) adj. having or showing energy; vigorous. —**,ener'getically** adv.

energize *or* **-ise** ('ɛnə,dʒaɪz) vb. **1.** to have or cause to have energy; invigorate. **2.** (tr.) to apply electric current or electromotive force to (a circuit, etc.). —**'ener,gizer** *or* **-iser** n.

energy ('ɛnədʒɪ) n., pl. **-gies. 1.** intensity or vitality of action or expression; forcefulness. **2.** capacity or tendency for intense activity; vigour. **3.** Physics. **a.** the capacity of a body or system to do work. **b.** a measure of this capacity, measured in joules (SI units).

enervate vb. ('ɛnə,veɪt). **1.** (tr.) to deprive of strength or vitality. ~adj. (ɪ'nɜːvɪt). **2.** deprived of strength or vitality. —**,ener'vation** n. —**'ener,vative** adj.

enfant terrible French. (ãfã tɛ'riːbl) n., pl. **enfants terribles** (ãfã tɛ'riːbl). a person given to unconventional conduct or indiscreet remarks.

enfeeble (ɪn'fiːbəl) vb. (tr.) to make weak. —**en'feeblement** n. —**en'feebler** n.

enfilade (,ɛnfɪ'leɪd) Mil. ~n. **1.** gunfire directed along the length of a position or formation. **2.** a position or formation subject to such fire. ~vb. (tr.) **3.** to attack (a position or formation) with enfilade.

enfold *or* **infold** (ɪn'fəʊld) vb. (tr.) **1.** to cover by enclosing. **2.** to embrace. —**en'folder** *or* **in'folder** n. —**en'foldment** *or* **in'foldment** n.

enforce (ɪn'fɔːs) vb. (tr.) **1.** to ensure obedience to (a law, decision, etc.). **2.** to impose (obedience, etc.) as by force. **3.** to emphasize or reinforce (an argument, etc.). —**en'forceable** adj. —**en,forcea'bility** n. —**enforcedly** (ɪn'fɔːsɪdlɪ) adv. —**en'forcement** n. —**en'forcer** n.

enfranchise (ɪn'fræntʃaɪz) vb. (tr.) **1.** to grant the power of voting to. **2.** to liberate, as from servitude. **3.** (in England) to invest (a town, city, etc.) with the right to be represented in Parliament. —**en'franchisement** n. —**en'franchiser** n.

Eng. abbrev. for: **1.** England. **2.** English.

engage (ɪn'geɪdʒ) vb. (mainly tr.) **1.** to secure the services of. **2.** to secure for use; reserve. **3.** to involve (a person or his attention) intensely. **4.** to attract (the affection) of (a person). **5.** to draw (somebody) into conversation. **6.** (intr.) to take part; participate. **7.** to promise (to do something). **8.** (*also intr.*) Mil. to begin an action with (an enemy). **9.** to bring (a mechanism) into operation. **10.** (*also intr.*) to undergo or cause to undergo interlocking, as of the components of a driving mechanism. **11.** Machinery. to locate (a locking device) in its operative position or to advance (a tool) into a workpiece to commence cutting. —**en'gager** n.

engagé *or* (fem.) **engagée** French. (ãga'ʒe) adj. (of an artist) committed to some ideology.

THESAURUS

whole

endorse, indorse 1. advocate, affirm, approve, authorize, back, champion, confirm, favour, ratify, recommend, sanction, subscribe to, support, sustain, vouch for, warrant **2.** countersign, sign, superscribe, undersign

endorsement, indorsement 1. comment, countersignature, qualification, signature, superscription **2.** advocacy, affirmation, approbation, approval, authorization, backing, championship, confirmation, favour, fiat, O.K. (*Inf.*), ratification, recommendation, sanction, seal of approval, subscription to, support, warrant

endow award, bequeath, bestow, confer, donate, endue, enrich, favour, finance, fund, furnish, give, grant, invest, leave, make over, provide, settle on, supply, will

endowment 1. award, benefaction, bequest, bestowal, boon, donation, fund, gift, grant, income, largess, legacy, presentation, property, provision, revenue **2.** *Often plural* ability, aptitude, attribute, capability, capacity, faculty, flair, genius, gift, power, qualification, quality, talent

end up 1. become eventually, finish as, finish up, turn out to be **2.** arrive finally, come to a halt, fetch up (*Inf.*), finish up, stop, wind up

endurable bearable, sufferable, supportable, sustainable, tolerable

endurance 1. bearing, fortitude, patience, perseverance, persistence, pertinacity, resignation, resolution, stamina, staying power, strength, submission, sufferance, tenacity, toleration **2.** continuation, continuity, durability, duration, immutability, lastingness, longevity, permanence, stability

endure 1. bear, brave, cope with, experience, go through, stand, stick it out (*Inf.*), suffer, support, sustain, take it (*Inf.*), thole (*Scot.*), undergo, weather, withstand **2.** abide, allow, bear, brook, countenance, permit, put up with, stand, stick (*Sl.*), stomach, submit to, suffer, swallow, take patiently, tolerate **3.** abide, be durable, continue, hold, last, live, live on, persist, prevail, remain, stand, stay, survive, wear well

enduring abiding, continuing, durable, eternal, firm, immortal, imperishable, lasting, living, long-lasting, perennial, permanent, persistent, persisting, prevailing, remaining, steadfast, steady, surviving, unfaltering, unwavering

enemy adversary, antagonist, competitor, foe, opponent, rival, the opposition, the other side

energetic active, animated, brisk, dynamic, forceful, forcible, high-powered, indefatigable, lively, potent, powerful, spirited, strenuous, strong, tireless, vigorous, zippy (*Inf.*)

energy activity, animation, ardour, brio, drive, efficiency, élan, exertion, fire, force, forcefulness, get-up-and-go (*Inf.*), go (*Inf.*), intensity, life, liveliness, pluck, power, spirit, stamina, strength, strenuousness, verve, vigour, vim (*Sl.*), vitality, vivacity, zeal, zest, zip (*Inf.*)

enfold, infold clasp, embrace, enclose, encompass, envelop, enwrap, fold, hold, hug, shroud, swathe, wrap, wrap up

enforce administer, apply, carry out, coerce, compel, constrain, exact, execute, implement, impose, insist on, oblige, prosecute, put in force, put into effect, reinforce, require, urge

enforced compelled, compulsory, constrained, dictated, imposed, involuntary, necessary, ordained, prescribed, required, unavoidable, unwilling

enforcement 1. administration, application, carrying out, exaction, execution, implementation, imposition, prosecution, reinforcement **2.** coercion, compulsion, constraint, insistence, obligation, pressure, requirement

enfranchise 1. give the vote to, grant suffrage to, grant the franchise to, grant voting rights to **2.** emancipate, free, liberate, manumit, release, set free

enfranchisement 1. giving the vote, granting suffrage *or* the franchise, granting voting rights **2.** emancipation, freedom, freeing, liberating, liberation, manumission, re-

engaged (ɪnˈgeɪdʒd) *adj.* **1.** pledged to be married; betrothed. **2.** occupied or busy. **3.** *Archit.* built against or attached to a wall or similar structure. **4.** (of a telephone line) in use.

engagement (ɪnˈgeɪdʒmənt) *n.* **1.** a pledge of marriage; betrothal. **2.** an appointment or arrangement, esp. for business or social purposes. **3.** the act of engaging or condition of being engaged. **4.** a promise, obligation, or other condition that binds. **5.** a period of employment, esp. a limited period. **6.** an action; battle.

engaging (ɪnˈgeɪdʒɪŋ) *adj.* pleasing, charming, or winning. —**enˈgagingness** *n.*

engender (ɪnˈdʒɛndə) *vb.* (*tr.*) to bring about or give rise to; cause to be born.

engine (ˈɛndʒɪn) *n.* **1.** any machine designed to convert energy into mechanical work. **2.** a railway locomotive. **3.** *Mil.* any piece of equipment formerly used in warfare, such as a battering ram. **4.** any instrument or device.

engineer (ˌɛndʒɪˈnɪə) *n.* **1.** a person trained in any branch of engineering. **2.** the originator or manager of a situation, system, etc. **3.** *U.S.* the driver of a railway locomotive. **4.** an officer responsible for a ship's engines. **5.** a member of the armed forces trained in engineering and construction work. ~*vb.* (*tr.*) **6.** to originate, cause, or plan in a clever or devious manner. **7.** to design, plan, or construct as a professional engineer.

engineering (ˌɛndʒɪˈnɪərɪŋ) *n.* the profession of applying scientific principles to the design, construction, and maintenance of engines, cars, machines, etc. (**mechanical engineering**), buildings, bridges, roads, etc. (**civil engineering**), electrical machines and communication systems (**electrical engineering**), chemical plant and machinery (**chemical engineering**), or aircraft (**aeronautical engineering**).

English (ˈɪŋglɪʃ) *n.* **1.** the official language of Britain, the U.S., most of the Commonwealth, and certain other countries. **2. the English.** (*functioning as pl.*) the natives or inhabitants of England collectively. **3.** (*often not cap.*) the usual U.S. term for **side** (in billiards). ~*adj.* **4.** of or relating to the English language. **5.** relating to or characteristic of England or the English. ~*vb.* (*tr.*) **6.** *Arch.* to translate or adapt into English. —ˈ**Englishness** *n.*

English horn *n. Music.* another name for **cor anglais.**

Englishman (ˈɪŋglɪʃmən) *or* (*fem.*) **Englishwoman** *n.*, *pl.* **-men** *or* **-women.** a native or inhabitant of England.

engorge (ɪnˈgɔːdʒ) *vb.* (*tr.*) **1.** *Pathol.* to congest with blood. **2.** to eat (food) greedily. **3.** to gorge (oneself); glut. —**enˈgorgement** *n.*

engraft *or* **ingraft** (ɪnˈgrɑːft) *vb.* (*tr.*) **1.** to graft (a shoot, bud, etc.) onto a stock. **2.** to incorporate in a firm or permanent way; implant. —ˌ**engrafˈtation**, ˌ**ingrafˈtation** *or* **enˈgraftment**, **inˈgraftment** *n.*

engrave (ɪnˈgreɪv) *vb.* (*tr.*) **1.** to inscribe (a design, writing, etc.) onto (a block, plate, or other printing surface) by carving, etching, or other process. **2.** to print (designs or characters) from a plate so made. **3.** to fix deeply or permanently in the mind. —**enˈgraver** *n.*

engraving (ɪnˈgreɪvɪŋ) *n.* **1.** the art of a person who engraves. **2.** a printing surface that has been engraved. **3.** a print made from this.

engross (ɪnˈgrəʊs) *vb.* (*tr.*) **1.** to occupy one's attention completely; absorb. **2.** to write or copy (manuscript) in large legible handwriting. **3.** *Law.* to write or type out formally (a document) preparatory to execution. —**grossedly** (ɪnˈgrəʊsɪdlɪ) *adv.* —**enˈgrossment** *n.* —**enˈgrosser** *n.*

engulf *or* **ingulf** (ɪnˈgʌlf) *vb.* (*tr.*) **1.** to immerse, plunge, bury, or swallow up. **2.** (*often passive*) to overwhelm. —**enˈgulfment** *n.*

enhance (ɪnˈhɑːns) *vb.* (*tr.*) to intensify or increase in quality, value, etc.; improve; augment. —**enˈhancement** *n.* —**enˈhancer** *n.*

enigma (ɪˈnɪgmə) *n.* a person, thing, or situation that is mysterious, puzzling, or ambiguous. —**enigmatic** (ˌɛnɪgˈmætɪk) *or* ˌ**enigˈmatical** *adj.* —ˌ**enigˈmatically** *adv.*

enjoin (ɪnˈdʒɔɪn) *vb.* (*tr.*) **1.** to order (someone) to do (something). **2.** to impose or prescribe (a mode of behaviour, etc.). **3.** *Law.* to require (a person) to do or refrain from (some act), esp. by an injunction. —**enˈjoiner** *n.* —**enˈjoinment** *n.*

enjoy (ɪnˈdʒɔɪ) *vb.* (*tr.*) **1.** to receive pleasure from; take joy in. **2.** to have the benefit of; use. **3.** to have as a condition; experience. **4. enjoy oneself.** to have a good time. —**enˈjoyable** *adj.* —**enˈjoyableness** *n.* —**enˈjoyably** *adv.* —**enˈjoyer** *n.* —**enˈjoyment** *n.*

enkindle (ɪnˈkɪndəl) *vb.* (*tr.*) **1.** to set on fire; kindle. **2.** to excite to activity or ardour; arouse.

enlace (ɪnˈleɪs) *vb.* (*tr.*) **1.** to bind or encircle with or as

---

THESAURUS

lease, setting free

engage 1. appoint, commission, employ, enlist, enrol, hire, retain, take on **2.** bespeak, book, charter, hire, lease, prearrange, rent, reserve, secure **3.** absorb, busy, engross, grip, involve, occupy, preoccupy, tie up **4.** allure, arrest, attach, attract, captivate, catch, charm, draw, enamour, enchant, fascinate, fix, gain, win **5.** embark on, enter into, join, partake, participate, practise, set about, take part, undertake **6.** affiance, agree, betroth (*Archaic*), bind, commit, contract, covenant, guarantee, obligate, oblige, pledge, promise, undertake, vouch, vow **7.** *Military* assail, attack, combat, come to close quarters with, encounter, fall on, fight with, give battle to, join battle with, meet, take on **8.** activate, apply, bring into operation, energize, set going, switch on **9.** dovetail, interact, interconnect, interlock, join, mesh

engaged 1. affianced, betrothed (*Archaic*), pledged, promised, spoken for **2.** absorbed, busy, committed, employed, engrossed, in use, involved, occupied, preoccupied, tied up, unavailable

engagement 1. assurance, betrothal, bond, compact, contract, oath, obligation, pact, pledge, promise, troth (*Archaic*), undertaking, vow, word **2.** appointment, arrangement, commitment, date, meeting **3.** commission, employment, gig (*Sl.*), job, post, situation, stint, work **4.** action, battle, combat, conflict, confrontation, contest, encounter, fight

engaging agreeable, appealing, attractive, captivating, charming, enchanting, fascinating, fetching (*Inf.*), likable, lovable, pleasant, pleasing, winning, winsome

engender 1. beget, breed, bring about, cause, create, excite, foment, generate, give rise to, hatch, incite, induce, instigate, lead to, make, occasion, precipitate, produce, provoke **2.** beget, breed, bring forth, father, generate, give birth to, procreate, propagate, sire, spawn

engine 1. machine, mechanism, motor **2.** agency, agent, apparatus, appliance, contrivance, device, implement, instrument, means, tool, weapon

engineer 1. *n.* architect, contriver, designer, deviser, director, inventor, manager, manipulator, originator, planner, schemer **2.** *v.* bring about, cause, concoct, contrive, control, create, devise, effect, encompass, finagle (*Inf.*), manage, manoeuvre, mastermind, originate, plan, plot, scheme, wangle (*Inf.*)

engrave 1. carve, chase, chisel, cut, enchase (*Rare*), etch, grave (*Archaic*), inscribe **2.** impress, imprint, print **3.** embed, fix, impress, imprint, infix, ingrain, lodge

engraving 1. carving, chasing, chiselling, cutting, dry point, enchasing (*Rare*), etching, inscribing, inscription **2.** block, carving, etching, inscription, plate, woodcut **3.** etching, impression, print

engross 1. absorb, arrest, engage, engulf, hold, immerse, involve, occupy, preoccupy **2.** corner, monopolize, sew up (*U.S.*)

engrossed absorbed, captivated, caught up, deep, enthralled, fascinated, gripped, immersed, intent, intrigued, lost, preoccupied, rapt, riveted

engrossing absorbing, captivating, compelling, enthralling, fascinating, gripping, interesting, intriguing, riveting

enhance add to, augment, boost, complement, elevate, embellish, exalt, heighten, improve, increase, intensify, lift, magnify, raise, reinforce, strengthen, swell

enigma conundrum, mystery, problem, puzzle, riddle

enigmatic, enigmatical ambiguous, cryptic, Delphic, doubtful, equivocal, incomprehensible, indecipherable, inexplicable, inscrutable, mysterious, obscure, perplexing, puzzling, recondite, sphinxlike, uncertain, unfathomable, unintelligible

enjoin 1. advise, bid, call upon, charge, command, counsel, demand, direct, instruct, order, prescribe, require, urge, warn **2.** *Law* ban, bar, disallow, forbid, interdict, place an injunction on, preclude, prohibit, proscribe, restrain

enjoy 1. appreciate, be entertained by, be pleased with, delight in, like, rejoice in, relish, revel in, take joy in, take pleasure in or from **2.** be blessed or favoured with, experience, have, have the benefit of, have the use of, own, possess, reap the benefits of, use **3. enjoy oneself** have a ball (*Inf.*), have a good time, have fun, make merry

enjoyable agreeable, amusing, delectable, delicious, delightful, entertaining, gratifying, pleasant, pleasing, pleasurable, satisfying, to one's liking

enjoyment 1. amusement, delectation, delight, diversion, entertainment, fun, gladness, gratification, gusto, happiness, indulgence, joy, pleasure, recreation, relish, satisfaction, zest **2.** advantage, benefit, exercise, ownership, possession, use

with laces. **2.** to entangle; intertwine. —**en'lacement** n.

enlarge (ɪn'lɑːdʒ) vb. **1.** to make or grow larger; increase or expand. **2.** (tr.) to make (a photographic print) of a larger size than the negative. **3.** (intr.; foll. by on or upon) to speak or write (about) in greater detail. —**en'largeable** adj. —**en'larger** n. —**en'largement** n.

enlighten (ɪn'laɪt⁹n) vb. (tr.) **1.** to give information or understanding to; instruct; edify. **2.** to give spiritual or religious revelation to. **3.** Poetic. to shed light on. —**en'lightener** n.

enlightenment (ɪn'laɪt⁹nmənt) n. the act or means of enlightening or the state of being enlightened.

Enlightenment (ɪn'laɪt⁹nmənt) n. **the.** an 18th-century philosophical movement stressing the importance of reason.

enlist (ɪn'lɪst) vb. **1.** to enter or persuade to enter the armed forces. **2.** (tr.) to engage or secure (a person or his support) for a venture, cause, etc. **3.** (intr.; foll. by in) to enter into or join an enterprise, cause, etc. —**en'lister** n. —**en'listment** n.

enliven (ɪn'laɪv⁹n) vb. (tr.) **1.** to make active, vivacious, or spirited. **2.** to make cheerful or bright; gladden. —**en'livener** n. —**en'liveningly** adv. —**en'livenment** n.

en masse (French ã 'mas) adv. in a group or mass; as a whole; all together.

enmesh, inmesh (ɪn'mɛʃ), or **immesh** (ɪ'mɛʃ) vb. (tr.) to catch or involve in or as if in a net or snare; entangle. —**en'meshment** n.

enmity ('ɛnmɪtɪ) n., pl. **-ties.** a feeling of hostility or ill will, as between enemies.

ennoble (ɪ'nəʊb⁹l) vb. (tr.) **1.** to make noble, honourable, or excellent; dignify; exalt. **2.** to raise to a noble rank. —**en'noblement** n. —**en'nobler** n.

ennui ('ɒnwiː) n. a feeling of listlessness and general dissatisfaction resulting from lack of activity or excitement.

enormity (ɪ'nɔːmɪtɪ) n., pl. **-ties. 1.** the quality or character of extreme wickedness. **2.** an act of great wickedness; atrocity. **3.** Inf. vastness of size or extent.
▷ **Usage.** In careful usage, the noun enormity is not employed to convey the idea of great size.

enormous (ɪ'nɔːməs) adj. **1.** unusually large in size, extent, or degree; immense; vast. **2.** Arch. extremely wicked; heinous. —**e'normously** adv. —**e'normousness** n.

enough (ɪ'nʌf) determiner. **1. a.** sufficient to answer a need, demand or supposition. **b.** (as pronoun): enough is now known. **2. that's enough!** that will do: used to put an end to an action, speech, performance, etc. ~adv. **3.** so as to be sufficient; as much as necessary. **4.** (not used with a negative) very or quite; rather. **5.** (intensifier): oddly enough. **6.** just adequately; tolerably.

enow (ɪ'naʊ) determiner, adv. an archaic word for **enough.**

en passant (ɒn pæ'sɑːnt) adv. in passing: in chess, said of capturing a pawn that has made an initial move of two squares. The capture is made as if the captured pawn had moved one square instead of two.

enplane (ɛn'pleɪn) vb. (intr.) to board an aircraft.

enquire (ɪn'kwaɪə) vb. (often foll. by of) **1.** to seek (information) by questioning; ask. **2.** See **inquire.** —**en'quirer** n. —**en'quiry** n.

enrage (ɪn'reɪdʒ) vb. (tr.) to provoke to fury; put into a rage. —**en'ragement** n.

enrapture (ɪn'ræptʃə) vb. (tr.) to fill with delight; enchant.

enrich (ɪn'rɪtʃ) vb. (tr.) **1.** to increase the wealth of. **2.** to endow with fine or desirable qualities. **3.** to make more beautiful; adorn; decorate. **4.** to improve in quality, colour, flavour, etc. **5.** to increase the food value of by adding nutrients. **6.** to fertilize (soil). **7.** Physics. to increase the concentration or abundance of one component or isotope in (a solution or mixture). —**en'richment** n.

enrol or U.S. **enroll** (ɪn'rəʊl) vb. **-rolling, -rolled.** (mainly tr.) **1.** to record or note in a roll or list. **2.** (also intr.) to become or cause to become a member; enlist; register. **3.** to put on record. —**,enrol'lee** n. —**en'roller** n. —**en'rolment** n.

en route (ɒn 'ruːt) adv. on or along the way.

ensconce (ɪn'skɒns) vb. (tr.; often passive) **1.** to establish or settle firmly or comfortably. **2.** to place in safety; hide.

ensemble (ɒn'sɒmb⁹l) n. **1.** all the parts of something considered together. **2.** a person's complete costume; outfit. **3.** the cast of a play other than the principals. **4.** Music. a group of soloists singing or playing together. **5.** Music. the degree of precision and unity exhibited by a group of instrumentalists or singers performing together. **6.** the general effect of something made up of individual parts. ~adv. **7.** all together or at once.

enshrine or **inshrine** (ɪn'ʃraɪn) vb. (tr.) **1.** to place or enclose as in a shrine. **2.** to hold as sacred; cherish; treasure. —**en'shrinement** n.

enshroud (ɪn'ʃraʊd) vb. (tr.) to cover or hide as with a shroud.

THESAURUS

enlarge 1. add to, amplify, augment, blow up (Inf.), broaden, diffuse, dilate, distend, elongate, expand, extend, grow, heighten, increase, inflate, lengthen, magnify, make or grow larger, multiply, stretch, swell, wax, widen **2.** amplify, descant, develop, dilate, elaborate, expand, expatiate, give details

enlighten advise, apprise, cause to understand, civilize, counsel, edify, educate, inform, instruct, make aware, teach

enlightened aware, broad-minded, civilized, cultivated, educated, informed, knowledgeable, liberal, literate, open-minded, reasonable, refined, sophisticated

enlightenment awareness, broadmindedness, civilization, comprehension, cultivation, edification, education, information, insight, instruction, knowledge, learning, literacy, open-mindedness, refinement, sophistication, teaching, understanding, wisdom

enlist engage, enrol, enter (into), gather, join, join up, muster, obtain, procure, recruit, register, secure, sign up, volunteer

enliven animate, brighten, buoy up, cheer, cheer up, excite, exhilarate, fire, gladden, hearten, inspire, inspirit, invigorate, pep up, perk up, quicken, rouse, spark, stimulate, vitalize, vivify, wake up

enmity acrimony, animosity, animus, antagonism, antipathy, aversion, bad blood, bitterness, hate, hatred, hostility, ill will, malevolence, malice, malignity, rancour, spite, venom

ennoble aggrandize, dignify, elevate, enhance, exalt, glorify, honour, magnify, raise

ennui boredom, dissatisfaction, lassitude, listlessness, tedium, the doldrums

enormity 1. atrociousness, atrocity, depravity, disgrace, evilness, heinousness, monstrousness, nefariousness, outrageousness, turpitude, viciousness, vileness, villainy, wickedness **2.** abomination, atrocity, crime, disgrace, evil, horror, monstrosity, outrage, villainy **3.** Inf. enormousness, greatness, hugeness, immensity, magnitude, massiveness, vastness

enormous 1. astronomic, Brobdingnagian, colossal, excessive, gargantuan, gigantic, gross, huge, immense, jumbo (Inf.), mammoth, massive, monstrous, mountainous, prodigious, titanic, tremendous, vast **2.** Archaic abominable, atrocious, depraved, disgraceful, evil, heinous, monstrous, nefarious, odious, outrageous, vicious, vile, villainous, wicked

enough 1. adj. abundant, adequate, ample, plenty, sufficient **2.** n. abundance, adequacy, ample supply, plenty, right amount, sufficiency **3.** adv. abundantly, adequately, amply, fairly, moderately, passably, reasonably, satisfactorily, sufficiently, tolerably

enquire 1. ask, query, question, request information, seek information **2.** Also inquire conduct an inquiry, examine, explore, inspect, investigate, look into, make inquiry, probe, scrutinize, search

enquiry 1. query, question **2.** Also inquiry

examination, exploration, inquest, inspection, investigation, probe, research, scrutiny, search, study, survey

enrage aggravate (Inf.), anger, exasperate, incense, incite, inflame, infuriate, irritate, madden, make one's blood boil, make one see red (Inf.), provoke

enraged aggravated (Inf.), angered, angry, boiling mad, exasperated, fuming, furious, incensed, inflamed, infuriated, irate, irritated, livid (Inf.), mad (Inf.), raging, raging mad, wild

enrich 1. make rich, make wealthy **2.** aggrandize, ameliorate, augment, cultivate, develop, endow, enhance, improve, refine, supplement **3.** adorn, decorate, embellish, grace, ornament

enrol 1. chronicle, inscribe, list, note, record **2.** accept, admit, engage, enlist, join up, matriculate, recruit, register, sign up or on, take on

enrolment acceptance, admission, engagement, enlistment, matriculation, recruitment, registration

en route in transit, on or along the way, on the road

ensemble n. **1.** aggregate, assemblage, collection, entirety, set, sum, total, totality, whole, whole thing **2.** costume, get-up (Inf.), outfit, suit **3.** band, cast, chorus, company, group, supporting cast, troupe ~adv. **4.** all at once, all together, as a group, as a whole, at once, at the same time, en masse, in concert

enshrine apotheosize, cherish, conse-

ensign ('ɛnsaɪn) n. 1. (also 'ɛnsən). a flag flown by a ship, branch of the armed forces, etc., to indicate nationality, allegiance, etc. See also Red Ensign. 2. any flag, standard, or banner. 3. a standard-bearer. 4. a symbol, token, or emblem; sign. 5. (in the U.S. Navy) a commissioned officer of the lowest rank. 6. (formerly in the British infantry) a commissioned officer of the lowest rank. —'ensign,ship or 'ensigncy n.

ensilage ('ɛnsɪlɪdʒ) n. 1. the process of ensiling green fodder. 2. a less common name for silage.

enslave (ɪn'sleɪv) vb. (tr.) to make a slave of; subjugate. —en'slavement n. —en'slaver n.

ensnare or **insnare** (ɪn'snɛə) vb. (tr.) to catch or trap as in a snare. —en'snarement n. —en'snarer n.

ensue (ɪn'sjuː) vb. -suing, -sued. 1. (intr.) to come next or afterwards. 2. (intr.) to occur as a consequence; result. 3. (tr.) Obs. to pursue. —en'suingly adv.

en suite French. (ɑ̃ 'sɥɪt) adv. forming a unit: a room with bathroom en suite.

ensure (ɛn'ʃʊə, -'ʃɔː) or (esp. U.S.) **insure** vb. (tr.) 1. (may take a clause as object) to make certain or sure; guarantee. 2. to make safe or secure; protect. —en'surer n.

E.N.T. Med. abbrev. for ear, nose, and throat.

entablature (ɛn'tæblətʃə) n. Archit. 1. the part of a classical temple above the columns, having an architrave, a frieze, and a cornice. 2. any similar construction.

entail (ɪn'teɪl) vb. (tr.) 1. to have as a necessary consequence: this task entails careful thought. 2. Property law. to restrict (the descent of an estate) to designated heirs. ~n. 3. Property law. a. such a limitation. b. an entailed estate. —en'tailer n. —en'tailment n.

entangle (ɪn'tæŋgəl) vb. (tr.) 1. to catch or involve in or as if in a tangle; ensnare or enmesh. 2. to make tangled or twisted; snarl. 3. to make complicated; confuse. 4. to involve in difficulties. —en'tanglement n. —en'tangler n.

entente (French ɑ̃'tɑ̃t) n. 1. short for **entente cordiale**. 2. the parties to an entente cordiale collectively.

entente cordiale (French ɑ̃'tɑ̃t kɔr'djal) n. 1. a friendly understanding between political powers. 2. (often caps.) the understanding reached by France and Britain in April 1904, over colonial disputes.

enter ('ɛntə) vb. 1. to come or go into (a place, house, etc.). 2. to penetrate or pierce. 3. (tr.) to introduce or insert. 4. to join (a party, organization, etc.). 5. (when intr., foll. by into) to become involved or take part (in). 6. (tr.) to record (an item) in a journal, account, etc. 7. (tr.) to record (a name, etc.) on a list. 8. (tr.) to present or submit: to enter a proposal. 9. (intr.) Theatre. to come on stage: used as a stage direction: enter Juliet. 10. (when intr., often foll. by into, on, or upon) to begin; start: to enter upon a new career. 11. (intr.; often foll. by upon) to come into possession (of). 12. (tr.) to place (evidence, etc.) before a court of law. —'enterable adj. —'enterer n.

enteric (ɛn'tɛrɪk) or **enteral** ('ɛntərəl) adj. intestinal.

enteritis (,ɛntə'raɪtɪs) n. inflammation of the intestine.

entero- or before a vowel **enter-** combining form. indicating an intestine: enterovirus; enteritis.

enterprise ('ɛntə,praɪz) n. 1. a project or undertaking, esp. one that requires boldness or effort. 2. participation in such projects. 3. readiness to embark on new ventures; boldness and energy. 4. a company or firm. —'enter,priser n.

enterprising ('ɛntə,praɪzɪŋ) adj. ready to embark on new ventures; full of boldness and initiative. —'enter,prisingly adv.

entertain (,ɛntə'teɪn) vb. 1. to provide amusement for (a person or audience). 2. to show hospitality to (guests). 3. (tr.) to hold in the mind.

entertainer (,ɛntə'teɪnə) n. 1. a professional performer in public entertainments. 2. any person who entertains.

entertaining (,ɛntə'teɪnɪŋ) adj. serving to entertain or give pleasure; diverting; amusing.

entertainment (,ɛntə'teɪnmənt) n. 1. the act or art of entertaining or state of being entertained. 2. an act, production, etc., that entertains; diversion; amusement.

enthral or U.S. **enthrall** (ɪn'θrɔːl) vb. -thralling, -thralled. (tr.) 1. to hold spellbound; enchant; captivate. 2. Obs. to hold as thrall; enslave. —en'thraller n. —en'thralment or U.S. en'thrallment n.

enthrone (ɛn'θrəʊn) vb. (tr.) 1. to place on a throne. 2. to honour or exalt. 3. to assign authority to. —en'thronement n.

enthuse (ɪn'θjuːz) vb. to feel or show or cause to feel or show enthusiasm.

enthusiasm (ɪn'θjuːzɪ,æzəm) n. 1. ardent and lively interest or eagerness. 2. an object of keen interest. 3. Arch. extravagant religious fervour.

enthusiast (ɪn'θjuːzɪ,æst) n. 1. a person motivated by enthusiasm; fanatic. 2. Arch. one whose zeal for religion

---

THESAURUS

crate, dedicate, embalm, exalt, hallow, preserve, revere, sanctify, treasure

enshroud cloak, cloud, conceal, cover, enclose, enfold, envelop, enwrap, hide, obscure, pall, shroud, veil, wrap

ensign badge, banner, colours, flag, jack, pennant, pennon, standard, streamer

enslave bind, dominate, enchain, enthral, reduce to slavery, subjugate, yoke

ensue arise, attend, be consequent on, befall, come after, come next, come to pass (Archaic), derive, flow, follow, issue, proceed, result, stem, succeed, supervene, turn out or up

ensure, insure 1. certify, confirm, effect, guarantee, make certain, make sure, secure, warrant 2. guard, make safe, protect, safeguard, secure

entail bring about, call for, cause, demand, encompass, give rise to, impose, involve, lead to, necessitate, occasion, require, result in

entangle 1. catch, compromise, embroil, enmesh, ensnare, entrap, foul, implicate, involve, knot, mat, mix up, ravel, snag, snare, tangle, trammel, trap 2. bewilder, complicate, confuse, jumble, mix up, muddle, perplex, puzzle, snarl, twist

entanglement 1. complication, confusion, ensnarement, entrapment, imbroglio (Obsolete), involvement, jumble, knot, mesh, mess, mix-up, muddle, snare, snarl-up (Inf.), tangle, toils, trap 2. difficulty, embarrassment, imbroglio, involvement, liaison, predicament, tie

enter 1. arrive, come or go in or into, insert, introduce, make an entrance, pass into, penetrate, pierce 2. become a member of, begin, commence, commit oneself to, embark upon, enlist, enrol, join, participate in, set about, set out on, sign up, start, take part in, take up 3. inscribe, list, log, note, record, register, set down, take down 4. offer, present, proffer, put forward, register, submit, tender

enterprise 1. adventure, effort, endeavour, essay, operation, plan, programme, project, undertaking, venture 2. activity, adventurousness, alertness, audacity, boldness, daring, dash, drive, eagerness, energy, enthusiasm, get-up-and-go (Inf.), gumption (Inf.), initiative, push (Inf.), readiness, resource, resourcefulness, spirit, vigour, zeal 3. business, company, concern, establishment, firm, operation

enterprising active, adventurous, alert, audacious, bold, daring, dashing, eager, energetic, enthusiastic, go-ahead, intrepid, keen, ready, resourceful, spirited, stirring, up-and-coming, venturesome, vigorous, zealous

entertain 1. amuse, charm, cheer, delight, divert, occupy, please, recreate (Rare), regale 2. accommodate, be host to, harbour, have company, have guests or visitors, lodge, put up, show hospitality to, treat 3. cherish, cogitate on, conceive, consider, contemplate, foster, harbour, hold, imagine, keep in mind, maintain, muse over, ponder, support, think about, think over

entertaining amusing, charming, cheering, delightful, diverting, funny, humorous, interesting, pleasant, pleasing, pleasurable, recreative (Rare), witty

entertainment amusement, cheer, distraction, diversion, enjoyment, fun, good time, leisure activity, pastime, play, pleasure, recreation, satisfaction, sport, treat

enthral beguile, captivate, charm, enchant, enrapture, entrance, fascinate, grip, hold spellbound, hypnotize, intrigue, mesmerize, rivet, spellbind

enthralling beguiling, captivating, charming, compelling, compulsive, enchanting, entrancing, fascinating, gripping, hypnotizing, intriguing, mesmerizing, riveting, spellbinding

enthusiasm 1. ardour, avidity, devotion, eagerness, earnestness, excitement, fervour, frenzy, interest, keenness, passion, relish, vehemence, warmth, zeal, zest 2. craze, fad (Inf.), hobby, hobbyhorse, interest, mania, passion, rage

enthusiast admirer, aficionado, buff (Inf.), devotee, fan, fanatic, fiend (Inf.), follower, freak (Sl.), lover, supporter, zealot

enthusiastic ardent, avid, devoted, eager, earnest, ebullient, excited, exuberant, fervent, fervid, forceful, hearty, keen, lively, passionate, spirited, unqualified, unstinting, vehement, vigorous, warm, wholehearted, zealous

is extravagant. —**en,thusi'astic** adj. —**en,thusi'asti-cally** adv.

entice (ın'taıs) vb. (tr.) to attract by exciting hope or desire; tempt; allure. —**en'ticement** n. —**en'ticer** n. —**en'ticingly** adv.

entire (ın'taıə) adj. **1.** (prenominal) whole; complete. **2.** (prenominal) without reservation or exception. **3.** not broken or damaged. **4.** undivided; continuous. **5.** (of leaves, petals, etc.) having a smooth margin not broken up into teeth or lobes. **6.** not castrated: an entire horse. **7.** Obs. unmixed; pure. ~n. **8.** an uncastrated horse. —**en'tirely** adv. —**en'tireness** n.

entirety (ın'taıərıtı) n., pl. **-ties. 1.** the state of being entire or whole; completeness. **2.** a thing, sum, amount, etc., that is entire; whole; total.

entitle (ın'taıt²l) vb. (tr.) **1.** to give (a person) the right to do or have something; qualify; allow. **2.** to give a name or title to. **3.** to confer a title of rank or honour upon. —**en'titlement** n.

entity ('ɛntıtı) n., pl. **-ties. 1.** something having real or distinct existence. **2.** existence or being. —**entitative** ('ɛntıtətıv) adj.

ento- combining form. inside; within: entoderm.

entomb (ın'tu:m) vb. (tr.) **1.** to place in or as if in a tomb; bury; inter. **2.** to serve as a tomb for. —**en'tombment** n.

entomo- combining form. indicating an insect: entomology.

entomology (,ɛntə'mɒlədʒı) n. the branch of science concerned with the study of insects. —**entomological** (,ɛntəmə'lɒdʒık²l) or ,**ento'logic** adj. —,**ento'mologist** n.

entourage (,ɒntu'rɑ:ʒ) n. **1.** a group of attendants or retainers; retinue. **2.** surroundings.

entr'acte (ɒn'trækt) n. **1.** an interval between two acts of a play or opera. **2.** (esp. formerly) an entertainment during such an interval.

entrails ('ɛntreılz) pl. n. **1.** the internal organs of a person or animal; intestines; guts. **2.** the innermost parts of anything.

entrain (ın'treın) vb. to board or put aboard a train. —**en'trainment** n.

entrance¹ ('ɛntrəns) n. **1.** the act or an instance of entering; entry. **2.** a place for entering, such as a door. **3. a.** the power, liberty, or right of entering. **b.** (as modifier): an entrance fee. **4.** the coming of an actor or other performer onto a stage.

entrance² (ın'trɑ:ns) vb. (tr.) **1.** to fill with wonder and delight; enchant. **2.** to put into a trance; hypnotize. —**en'trancement** n.

entrant ('ɛntrənt) n. a person who enters.

entrap (ın'træp) vb. **-trapping, -trapped.** (tr.) **1.** to catch or snare as in a trap. **2.** to trick into danger, difficulty, or embarrassment. —**en'trapment** n. —**en'trap-**

per n.

entreat or **intreat** (ın'tri:t) vb. **1.** to ask (a person) earnestly; beg or plead with; implore. **2.** to make an earnest request or petition for (something). **3.** an archaic word for **treat** (sense 4). —**en'treatment** or **in'treatment** n.

entreaty (ın'tri:tı) n., pl. **-treaties.** an earnest request or petition; supplication; plea.

entrecôte (French ãtrə'ko:t) n. a beefsteak cut from between the ribs.

entrée ('ɒntreı) n. **1.** a dish served before a main course. **2.** Chiefly U.S. the main course of a meal. **3.** the power or right of entry.

entrench or **intrench** (ın'trɛntʃ) vb. **1.** (tr.) to construct a defensive position by digging trenches around it. **2.** (tr.) to fix or establish firmly. **3.** (intr.; foll. by on or upon) to trespass or encroach. —**en'trenchment** or **in'trenchment** n. —**en'trencher** or **in'trencher** n.

entrepôt (French ãtrə'po) n. **1.** a warehouse for commercial goods. **2.** a trading centre or port at which goods are imported and re-exported without incurring duty.

entrepreneur (,ɒntrəprə'nɜ:) n. **1.** the owner or manager of a business enterprise who, by risk and initiative, attempts to make profits. **2.** a middleman or commercial intermediary. —,**entrepre'neurial** adj. —,**entrepre'neurship** n.

entropy ('ɛntrəpı) n., pl. **-pies. 1.** a thermodynamic quantity that changes in a reversible process by an amount equal to the heat absorbed or emitted divided by the thermodynamic temperature. It is measured in joules per kelvin. **2.** lack of pattern or organization; disorder.

entrust or **intrust** (ın'trʌst) vb. (tr.) **1.** (usually foll. by with) to invest or charge (with a duty, responsibility, etc.). **2.** (often foll. by to) to put into the care or protection of someone. —**en'trustment** or **in'trustment** n.

entry ('ɛntrı) n., pl. **-tries. 1.** the act or an instance of entering; entrance. **2.** a point or place for entering, such as a door, etc. **3. a.** the right or liberty of entering. **b.** (as modifier): an entry permit. **4.** the act of recording an item in a journal, account, etc. **5.** an item recorded, as in a diary, dictionary, or account. **6.** a person, horse, car, etc., entering a competition or contest. **7.** the competitors entering a contest considered collectively. **8.** the action of an actor in going on stage. **9.** Property law. the act of going upon land with the intention of asserting the right to possession. **10.** Cards. a card with which a player or hand can win a trick and so gain the lead. **11.** N Brit. dialect. a passage between the backs of two rows of houses.

entwine or **intwine** (ın'twaın) vb. (of two or more things) to twine together or (of one or more things) twine around (something else). —**en'twinement** or **in'twinement** n.

THESAURUS

entice allure, attract, beguile, cajole, coax, decoy, draw, inveigle, lead on, lure, persuade, prevail on, seduce, tempt, wheedle
entire 1. complete, full, total, whole **2.** absolute, full, outright, thorough, total, undiminished, unmitigated, unreserved, unrestricted **3.** intact, perfect, sound, unbroken, undamaged, unmarked, unmarred, whole, without a scratch **4.** continuous, integrated, unbroken, undivided, unified
entirely 1. absolutely, altogether, completely, fully, in every respect, perfectly, thoroughly, totally, unreservedly, utterly, wholly, without exception, without reservation **2.** exclusively, only, solely
entirety 1. absoluteness, completeness, fullness, totality, undividedness, unity, wholeness **2.** aggregate, sum, total, unity, whole
entitle 1. accredit, allow, authorize, empower, enable, enfranchise, fit for, license, make eligible, permit, qualify for, warrant **2.** call, characterize, christen, denominate, designate, dub, label, name, style, term, title
entity 1. being, body, creature, existence, individual, object, organism, presence, quantity, substance, thing **2.** essence, essential nature, quiddity (Philosophy), quintessence, real nature

entourage 1. associates, attendants, companions, company, cortege, court, escort, followers, following, retainers, retinue, staff, suite, train **2.** ambience, environment, environs, milieu, surroundings
entrails bowels, guts, innards (Inf.), insides (Inf.), intestines, offal, viscera
entrance¹ n. **1.** access, avenue, door, doorway, entry, gate, ingress, inlet, opening, passage, portal, way in **2.** appearance, arrival, coming in, entry, ingress, introduction **3.** access, admission, admittance, entrée, entry, ingress, permission to enter **4.** beginning, commencement, debut, initiation, introduction, outset, start
entrance² v. **1.** bewitch, captivate, charm, delight, enchant, enrapture, enthral, fascinate, gladden, ravish, spellbind, transport **2.** hypnotize, mesmerize, put in a trance
entrant 1. beginner, convert, initiate, neophyte, newcomer, new member, novice, probationer, tyro **2.** candidate, competitor, contestant, entry, participant, player
entreaty appeal, earnest request, exhortation, importunity, petition, plea, prayer, request, solicitation, suit, supplication
entrench, intrench 1. construct defences, dig in, dig trenches, fortify **2.** anchor,

dig in, embed, ensconce, establish, fix, implant, ingrain, install, lodge, plant, root, seat, set, settle **3.** encroach, impinge, infringe, interlope, intrude, make inroads, trespass
entrenched, intrenched deep-rooted, deep-seated, firm, fixed, indelible, ineradicable, ingrained, rooted, set, unshakable, well-established
entrust, intrust assign, authorize, charge, commend, commit, confide, consign, delegate, deliver, give custody of, hand over, invest, trust, turn over
entry 1. appearance, coming in, entering, entrance, initiation, introduction **2.** access, avenue, door, doorway, entrance, gate, ingress, inlet, opening, passage, passageway, portal, way in **3.** access, admission, entrance, entrée, free passage, permission to enter **4.** account, item, jotting, listing, memo, memorandum, minute, note, record, registration **5.** attempt, candidate, competitor, contestant, effort, entrant, participant, player, submission
entwine, intwine braid, embrace, encircle, entwist (Archaic), interlace, intertwine, interweave, knit, plait, surround, twine, twist, weave, wind

enumerate (ɪ'njuːmə,reɪt) vb. (tr.) 1. to name one by one; list. 2. to determine the number of; count. —e'**numerable** adj. —e,numer'**ation** n. —e'**numerative** adj.

enumerator (ɪ'njuːmə,reɪtə) n. 1. a person or thing that enumerates. 2. Brit. a person who issues and retrieves census forms.

enunciate (ɪ'nʌnsɪ,eɪt) vb. 1. to articulate or pronounce (words), esp. clearly and distinctly. 2. (tr.) to state precisely or formally. —e,nunci'**ation** n. —e'**nunciative** or e'**nunciatory** adj. —e'**nunci,ator** n.

enuresis (,ɛnjuˈriːsɪs) n. involuntary discharge of urine, esp. during sleep. —**enuretic** (,ɛnjuˈrɛtɪk) adj.

envelop (ɪn'vɛləp) vb. (tr.) 1. to wrap or enclose as in a covering. 2. to conceal or obscure. 3. to surround (an enemy force). —en'**velopment** n.

envelope ('ɛnvə,ləup, 'ɒn-) n. 1. a flat covering of paper, usually rectangular and with a flap that can be sealed, used to enclose a letter, etc. 2. any covering or wrapper. 3. Biol. any enclosing structure, such as a membrane, shell, or skin. 4. the bag enclosing gas in a balloon. 5. Maths. a curve or surface that is tangential to each one of a group of curves or surfaces.

enviable ('ɛnvɪəbəl) adj. exciting envy; fortunate or privileged. —'**enviableness** n.

envious ('ɛnvɪəs) adj. feeling, showing, or resulting from envy. —'**enviously** adv. —'**enviousness** n.

environment (ɪn'vaɪrənmənt) n. 1. external conditions or surroundings. 2. Ecology. the external surroundings in which a plant or animal lives, which influence its development and behaviour. 3. the state of being environed. —en,viron'**mental** adj.

environmentalist (ɪn,vaɪrən'mɛntəlɪst) n. a specialist in the maintenance of ecological balance and the conservation of the environment.

environs (ɪn'vaɪrənz) pl. n. a surrounding area or region, esp. the suburbs or outskirts of a city.

envisage (ɪn'vɪzɪdʒ) vb. (tr.) 1. to form a mental image of; visualize. 2. to conceive of as a possibility in the future. 3. Arch. to look in the face of. —en'**visagement** n.

▷ Usage. In careful English, envisage is usually used with a direct object rather than a clause to refer to conceptions of future possibilities: he envisaged great success for his project.

envoy[1] ('ɛnvɔɪ) n. 1. a diplomat ranking between an ambassador and a minister resident. 2. an accredited agent or representative. —'**envoyship** n.

envoy[2] or **envoi** ('ɛnvɔɪ) n. 1. a brief concluding stanza, notably in ballades. 2. a postscript in other forms of verse or prose.

envy ('ɛnvɪ) n., pl. -**vies.** 1. a feeling of grudging or somewhat admiring discontent aroused by the possessions, achievements, or qualities of another. 2. the desire to have something possessed by another; covetousness. 3. an object of envy. ~vb. -**vying, -vied.** 4. to be envious of (a person or thing). —'**envier** n. —'**envyingly** adv.

enzyme ('ɛnzaɪm) n. any of a group of complex proteins produced by living cells, that act as catalysts in specific biochemical reactions. —**enzymatic** (,ɛnzaɪ'mætɪk, -zɪ-) or **enzymic** (ɛn'zaɪmɪk, -'zɪm-) adj.

eo- combining form. early or primeval: Eocene; eohippus.

Eocene ('iːəʊ,siːn) adj. 1. of or denoting the second epoch of the Tertiary period, during which hooved mammals appeared. ~n. 2. **the Eocene.** the Eocene epoch or rock series.

Eolithic (,iːəʊ'lɪθɪk) adj. denoting or relating to the early part of the Stone Age, characterized by the use of crude stone tools (**eoliths**).

EP n. 1. Also called: **maxisingle.** an extended-play gramophone record: a longer recording than a single. ~adj. 2. denoting such a record.

epaulette or U.S. **epaulet** ('ɛpə,lɛt) n. a piece of ornamental material on the shoulder of a garment, esp. a military uniform.

épée ('ɛpeɪ) n. a sword similar to the foil but with a heavier blade. —'**épéeist** n.

epergne (ɪ'pɜːn) n. an ornamental centrepiece for a table, holding fruit, flowers, etc.

Eph. or **Ephes.** Bible. abbrev. for Ephesians.

ephedrine or **ephedrin** (ɪ'fɛdrɪn, 'ɛfɪ,driːn, -drɪn) n. a white crystalline alkaloid used for the treatment of asthma and hay fever.

ephemera (ɪ'fɛmərə) n., pl. -**eras** or -**erae** (-ə,riː). 1. a mayfly, esp. one of the genus Ephemera. 2. something transitory or short-lived.

ephemeral (ɪ'fɛmərəl) adj. 1. transitory; short-lived: ephemeral pleasure. ~n. 2. a short-lived organism, such as the mayfly. —e,phemer'**ality** or e'**phemeralness** n.

epi-, eph-, or before a vowel **ep-** prefix. 1. upon; above; over: epidermis; epicentre. 2. in addition to: epiphenomenon. 3. after: epilogue. 4. near; close to: epicalyx.

epic ('ɛpɪk) n. 1. a long narrative poem recounting in elevated style the deeds of a legendary hero. 2. the genre of epic poetry. 3. any work of literature, film, etc., having qualities associated with the epic. 4. an episode in the lives of men in which heroic deeds are performed. ~adj. 5. denoting, relating to, or characteristic of an epic or epics. 6. of heroic or impressive proportions.

epicene ('ɛpɪ,siːn) adj. 1. having the characteristics of both sexes. 2. of neither sex; sexless. 3. effeminate. 4. Grammar. a. denoting a noun that may refer to a male or a female. b. (in Latin, Greek, etc.) denoting a noun that retains the same gender regardless of the sex of the referent. —,epi'**cenism** n.

epicentre or U.S. **epicenter** ('ɛpɪ,sɛntə) n., pl. -**tres** or U.S. -**ters.** the area immediately above the origin of earthquake vibrations. —,epi'**central** adj.

epicure ('ɛpɪ,kjuə) n. 1. a person who cultivates a discriminating palate for good food and drink. 2. a person devoted to sensual pleasures. —'**epicur,ism** n.

epicurean (,ɛpɪkjuˈriːən) adj. 1. devoted to sensual pleasures, esp. food and drink. 2. suitable for an epicure. ~n. 3. an epicure; gourmet. —,epicu'**reanism** n.

Epicurean (,ɛpɪkjuˈriːən) adj. 1. of or relating to the philosophy of Epicurus (341–270 B.C.), Greek philosopher,

---

THESAURUS

enumerate 1. cite, detail, itemize, list, mention, name, quote, recapitulate, recite, recount, rehearse, relate, specify, spell out, tell 2. add up, calculate, compute, count, number, reckon, sum up, tally, total

enunciate 1. articulate, enounce, pronounce, say, sound, speak, utter, vocalize, voice 2. declare, proclaim, promulgate, pronounce, propound, publish, state

envelop blanket, cloak, conceal, cover, embrace, encase, encircle, enclose, encompass, enfold, engulf, enwrap, hide, obscure, sheathe, shroud, surround, swaddle, swathe, veil, wrap

envelope case, casing, coating, cover, covering, jacket, sheath, shell, skin, wrapper, wrapping

enviable advantageous, blessed, covetable, desirable, favoured, fortunate, lucky, much to be desired, privileged

envious begrudging, covetous, green-eyed, green with envy, grudging, jaundiced, jealous, malicious, resentful, spiteful

environ beset, besiege, encircle, enclose, encompass, engird, envelop, gird, hem, invest (Rare), ring, surround

environment atmosphere, background, conditions, context, domain, element, habitat, locale, medium, milieu, scene, setting, situation, surroundings, territory

environs district, locality, neighbourhood, outskirts, precincts, purlieus, suburbs, surrounding area, vicinity

envisage 1. conceive (of), conceptualize, contemplate, fancy, imagine, picture, think up, visualize 2. anticipate, envision, foresee, predict, see

envision anticipate, conceive of, contemplate, envisage, foresee, predict, see, visualize

envoy agent, ambassador, courier, delegate, deputy, diplomat, emissary, intermediary, legate, messenger, minister, plenipotentiary, representative

envy 1. n. covetousness, enviousness, grudge, hatred, ill will, jealousy, malice, malignity, resentfulness, resentment, spite, the green-eyed monster (Inf.) 2. v. be envious (of), begrudge, be jealous (of), covet, grudge, resent

ephemeral brief, evanescent, fleeting, flitting, fugacious, fugitive, impermanent, momentary, passing, short, short-lived, temporary, transient, transitory

epicure 1. bon vivant, epicurean, gastronome, gourmet 2. glutton, gourmand, hedonist, sensualist, sybarite, voluptuary

epicurean 1. adj. gluttonous, gourmandizing, hedonistic, libertine, luscious, lush, luxurious, pleasure-seeking, self-indulgent, sensual, sybaritic, voluptuous 2. n. bon vivant, epicure, gastronome, gourmet

who held that the highest good is pleasure or freedom from pain. ~*n.* **2.** a follower of the philosophy of Epicurus. —ˌEpicu'reanism *n.*

epidemic (ˌɛpɪ'dɛmɪk) *adj.* **1.** (esp. of a disease) attacking or affecting many persons simultaneously in a community or area. ~*n.* **2.** a widespread occurrence of a disease. **3.** a rapid development, spread, or growth of something. —epi'demically *adv.*

epidemiology (ˌɛpɪˌdiːmɪ'plədʒɪ) *n.* the branch of medical science concerned with epidemic diseases. —epidemiological (ˌɛpɪˌdiːmɪə'lɒdʒɪkəl) *adj.* —ˌepiˌdemi'ologist *n.*

epidermis (ˌɛpɪ'dɜːmɪs) *n.* **1.** the thin protective outer layer of the skin. **2.** the outer layer of cells of an invertebrate. **3.** the outer protective layer of cells of a plant. —ˌepi'dermal, ˌepi'dermic, *or* ˌepi'dermoid *adj.*

epidiascope (ˌɛpɪ'daɪəˌskəʊp) *n.* an optical device for projecting a magnified image onto a screen.

epidural (ˌɛpɪ'djʊərəl) *adj.* **1.** upon or outside the outermost membrane covering the brain and spinal chord (dura mater). ~*n.* **2.** Also: **epidural anaesthesia. a.** injection of anaesthetic into the space outside the dura mater enveloping the spinal cord. **b.** anaesthesia induced by this method.

epiglottis (ˌɛpɪ'glɒtɪs) *n., pl.* **-tises** *or* **-tides** (-tɪˌdiːz). a thin cartilaginous flap that covers the entrance to the larynx during swallowing, preventing food from entering the trachea. —ˌepi'glottal *or* ˌepi'glottic *adj.*

epigram ('ɛpɪˌɡræm) *n.* **1.** a witty, often paradoxical remark, concisely expressed. **2.** a short poem, esp. one having a witty and ingenious ending. —ˌepigram'matic *adj.* —ˌepigram'matically *adv.*

epigraph ('ɛpɪˌɡrɑːf, -ˌɡræf) *n.* **1.** a quotation at the beginning of a book, chapter, etc. **2.** an inscription on a monument or building. —**epigraphic** (ˌɛpɪ'ɡræfɪk) *or* ˌepi'graphical *adj.*

epilepsy ('ɛpɪˌlɛpsɪ) *n.* a disorder of the central nervous system characterized by periodic loss of consciousness with or without convulsions.

epileptic (ˌɛpɪ'lɛptɪk) *adj.* **1.** of, relating to, or having epilepsy. ~*n.* **2.** a person who has epilepsy. —ˌepi'leptically *adv.*

epilogue ('ɛpɪˌlɒɡ) *n.* **1. a.** a speech addressed to the audience by an actor at the end of a play. **b.** the actor speaking this. **2.** a short postscript to any literary work. **3.** *Brit.* the concluding programme of the day on a radio or television station. —**epilogist** (ɪ'pɪlədʒɪst) *n.*

Epiphany (ɪ'pɪfənɪ) *n., pl.* **-nies.** a Christian festival held on Jan. 6, commemorating, in the Western Church, the manifestation of Christ to the Magi.

epiphyte ('ɛpɪˌfaɪt) *n.* a plant that grows on another plant but is not parasitic on it. —**epiphytic** (ˌɛpɪ'fɪtɪk), ˌepi'phytal, *or* ˌepi'phytical *adj.*

Epis. *abbrev. for:* **1.** Also: **Episc.** Episcopal or Episcopalian. **2.** Epistle.

episcopacy (ɪ'pɪskəpəsɪ) *n., pl.* **-cies. 1.** government of a Church by bishops. **2.** another word for **episcopate.**

episcopal (ɪ'pɪskəpəl) *adj.* of, denoting, governed by, or relating to a bishop or bishops.

Episcopal (ɪ'pɪskəpəl) *adj.* of or denoting the Episcopal Church, an autonomous church of Scotland and the U.S. which is in full communion with the Church of England.

episcopalian (ɪˌpɪskə'peɪlɪən) *adj. also* **episcopal. 1.** practising or advocating the principle of Church government by bishops. ~*n.* **2.** an advocate of such Church government. —eˌpisco'palianism *n.*

Episcopalian (ɪˌpɪskə'peɪlɪən) *adj.* **1.** belonging to or denoting the Episcopal Church. ~*n.* **2.** a member or adherent of this Church.

episcopate (ɪ'pɪskəpɪt, -ˌpeɪt) *n.* **1.** the office, status, or term of office of a bishop. **2.** bishops collectively.

episode ('ɛpɪˌsəʊd) *n.* **1.** an event or series of events.

2. any of the sections into which a serialized novel or radio or television programme is divided. **3.** an incident or sequence that forms part of a narrative but may be a digression from the main story. **4.** (in ancient Greek tragedy) a section between two choric songs. **5.** *Music.* a contrasting section between statements of the subject, as in a fugue.

episodic (ˌɛpɪ'sɒdɪk) *or* **episodical** *adj.* **1.** resembling or relating to an episode. **2.** divided into episodes. **3.** irregular or sporadic. —ˌepi'sodically *adv.*

epistemology (ɪˌpɪstɪ'mɒlədʒɪ) *n.* the theory of knowledge, esp. the critical study of its validity, methods, and scope. —**epistemological** (ɪˌpɪstɪmə'lɒdʒɪkəl) *adj.* —eˌpiste'mologist *n.*

epistle (ɪ'pɪsəl) *n.* **1.** a letter, esp. one that is long, formal, or didactic. **2.** a literary work in letter form, esp. a verse letter.

Epistle (ɪ'pɪsəl) *n.* **1.** *Bible.* any of the letters of the apostles. **2.** a reading from one of the Epistles, part of the Eucharistic service in many Christian Churches.

epistolary (ɪ'pɪstələrɪ), **epistolic** (ˌɛpɪ'stɒlɪk), *or* **epistolatory** *adj.* **1.** relating to, denoting, conducted by, or contained in letters. **2.** (of a novel, etc.) in the form of a series of letters.

epitaph ('ɛpɪˌtɑːf, -ˌtæf) *n.* **1.** a commemorative inscription on a tombstone or monument. **2.** a commemorative speech or written passage. **3.** a final judgment on a person or thing. —**epitaphic** (ˌɛpɪ'tæfɪk) *adj.* —'epiˌtaphist *n.*

epithelium (ˌɛpɪ'θiːlɪəm) *n., pl.* **-liums** *or* **-lia** (-lɪə). an animal cellular tissue covering the external and internal surfaces of the body. —ˌepi'thelial *or* ˌepi'theliˌoid *adj.*

epithet ('ɛpɪˌθɛt) *n.* a descriptive word or phrase added to or substituted for a person's name. —ˌepi'thetic *or* ˌepi'thetical *adj.*

epitome (ɪ'pɪtəmɪ) *n.* **1.** a typical example of a characteristic or class; embodiment; personification. **2.** a summary of a written work; abstract. —**epitomical** (ˌɛpɪ'tɒmɪkəl) *or* ˌepi'tomic *adj.*

epitomize *or* **-ise** (ɪ'pɪtəˌmaɪz) *vb. (tr.)* **1.** to be a personification of; typify. **2.** to make an epitome of. —e'pitomist *n.* —eˌpitomi'zation *or* -i'sation *n.* —e'pitoˌmizer *or* -iser *n.*

E.P.N.S. *abbrev. for* electroplated nickel silver.

epoch ('iːpɒk) *n.* **1.** a point in time beginning a new or distinctive period. **2.** a long period of time marked by some predominant characteristic; era. **3.** *Astron.* a precise date to which information relating to a celestial body is referred. **4.** a unit of geological time within a period during which a series of rocks is formed. —**epochal** ('ɛpɒkəl) *adj.*

eponym ('ɛpənɪm) *n.* **1.** a name, esp. a place name, derived from the name of a real or mythical person. **2.** the name of the person from which such a name is derived. —**eponymous** (ɪ'pɒnɪməs) *adj.* —e'ponymously *adv.* —e'ponymy *n.*

epoxy (ɪ'pɒksɪ) *adj. Chem.* **1.** of, consisting of, or containing an oxygen atom joined to two different groups that are themselves joined to other groups: *epoxy group.* **2.** of, relating to, or consisting of an epoxy resin.

epoxy resin *n.* any of various tough resistant thermosetting synthetic resins containing epoxy groups: used in surface coatings, laminates, and adhesives.

epsilon ('ɛpsɪˌlɒn) *n.* the fifth letter of the Greek alphabet (Ε, ε).

Epsom salts ('ɛpsəm) *pl. n.* a medicinal preparation of hydrated magnesium sulphate, used as a purgative, etc.

equable ('ɛkwəbəl) *adj.* **1.** even-tempered; placid. **2.** unvarying; uniform: *an equable climate.* —ˌequa'bility *or* 'equableness *n.*

THESAURUS

epidemic 1. *adj.* general, pandemic, prevailing, prevalent, rampant, rife, sweeping, wide-ranging, widespread **2.** *n.* growth, outbreak, plague, rash, spread, upsurge, wave

epigram bon mot, quip, witticism

epilogue afterword, coda, concluding speech, conclusion, postscript

episode 1. adventure, affair, business, circumstance, event, experience, happening, incident, matter, occurrence **2.** chapter, instalment, part, passage, scene, section

epistle communication, letter, message, missive, note

epithet appellation, description, designation, name, nickname, sobriquet, tag, title

epitome 1. archetype, embodiment, essence, exemplar, personification, quintessence, representation, type, typical example **2.** abbreviation, abridgment, abstract, compendium, condensation, conspectus, contrac-

tion, digest, précis, résumé, summary, syllabus, synopsis

epitomize 1. embody, exemplify, illustrate, incarnate, personify, represent, symbolize, typify **2.** abbreviate, abridge, abstract, condense, contract, curtail, cut, encapsulate, précis, reduce, shorten, summarize, synopsize

epoch age, date, era, period, time

equable 1. agreeable, calm, composed,

equal ('iːkwəl) adj. 1. (often foll. by to or with) identical in size, quantity, degree, intensity, etc. 2. having identical privileges, rights, status, etc. 3. having uniform effect or application: equal opportunities. 4. evenly balanced or proportioned. 5. (usually foll. by to) having the necessary or adequate strength, ability, means, etc. (for). ~n. 6. a person or thing equal to another, esp. in merit, ability, etc. ~vb. **equalling, equalled** or U.S. **equaling, equaled.** 7. (tr.) to be equal to; match. 8. (intr.; usually foll. by out) to become equal. 9. (tr.) to make or do something equal to. —'**equally** adv.

equalitarian (ɪˌkwɒlɪ'tɛərɪən) adj., n. a less common word for egalitarian. —eˌquali'**tarianism** n.

equality (ɪ'kwɒlɪtɪ) n., pl. -**ties.** the state of being equal.

equalize or -**ise** ('iːkwəˌlaɪz) vb. 1. (tr.) to make equal or uniform. 2. (intr.) (in sports) to reach the same score as one's opponent or opponents. —ˌequali'**zation** or -i'**sation** n.

equanimity (ˌiːkwə'nɪmɪtɪ, ˌɛkwə-) n. calmness of mind or temper; composure. —**equanimous** (ɪ'kwænɪməs) adj.

equate (ɪ'kweɪt) vb. (mainly tr.) 1. to make or regard as equivalent or similar. 2. Maths. to indicate the equality of; form an equation from. 3. (intr.) to be equal. —e'**quatable** adj. —eˌquata'**bility** n.

equation (ɪ'kweɪʒən, -ʃən) n. 1. a mathematical statement that two expressions are equal. 2. the act of equating. 3. the state of being equal, equivalent, or equally balanced. 4. a representation of a chemical reaction using symbols of the elements. —e'**quational** adj. —e'**quationally** adv.

equator (ɪ'kweɪtə) n. 1. the great circle of the earth, equidistant from the poles, dividing the N and S hemispheres. 2. a circle dividing a sphere into two equal parts. 3. Astron. See **celestial equator.**

equatorial (ˌɛkwə'tɔːrɪəl) adj. 1. of, like, or existing at or near the equator. 2. (of a telescope) mounted on perpendicular axes, one of which is parallel to the earth's axis. ~n. 3. an equatorial telescope or its mounting.

equerry (ɪ'kwɛrɪ) n., pl. -**ries.** 1. an officer attendant upon the British sovereign. 2. an officer in a royal household responsible for the horses.

equestrian (ɪ'kwɛstrɪən) adj. 1. of or relating to horses and riding. 2. on horseback; mounted. 3. of, relating to, or composed of knights. ~n. 4. a person skilled in riding and horsemanship. —e'**questrianism** n.

equi- combining form. equal or equally: equidistant; equilateral.

equiangular (ˌiːkwɪ'æŋgjʊlə) adj. having all angles equal.

equidistant (ˌiːkwɪ'dɪstənt) adj. equally distant. —ˌequi'**distance** n. —ˌequi'**distantly** adv.

equilateral (ˌiːkwɪ'lætərəl) adj. 1. having all sides of equal length. ~n. 2. a geometric figure having all sides of equal length. 3. a side that is equal in length to other sides.

equilibrate (ˌiːkwɪ'laɪbreɪt, ɪ'kwɪlɪˌbreɪt) vb. to bring to or be in equilibrium; balance. —**equilibration** (ˌiːkwɪlaɪ-'breɪʃən, ɪˌkwɪlɪ-) n. —**equilibrator** (ɪ'kwɪlɪˌbreɪtə) n.

equilibrium (ˌiːkwɪ'lɪbrɪəm) n., pl. -**riums** or -**ria** (-rɪə). 1. a stable condition in which forces cancel one another. 2. any unchanging state of a body, system, etc., resulting from the balance of the influences to which it is subjected. 3. Physiol. a state of bodily balance, maintained primarily by receptors in the inner ear.

equine ('ɛkwaɪn) adj. of, relating to, or resembling a horse.

equinoctial (ˌiːkwɪ'nɒkʃəl) adj. 1. relating to or occurring at either or both equinoxes. 2. Astron. of or relating to the celestial equator. ~n. 3. a storm or gale at or near an equinox. 4. another name for **celestial equator.**

equinoctial circle or **line** n. another name for **celestial equator.**

equinox ('iːkwɪˌnɒks) n. either of the two occasions, six months apart, when day and night are of equal length. In the N hemisphere the **vernal equinox** occurs around March 21 (Sept. 23 in the S hemisphere). The **autumnal equinox** occurs around Sept. 23 in the N hemisphere (March 21 in the S hemisphere).

equip (ɪ'kwɪp) vb. **equipping, equipped.** (tr.) 1. to furnish with (necessary supplies, etc.). 2. (usually passive) to provide with abilities, understanding, etc. 3. to dress out; attire. —e'**quipment** n. —e'**quipper** n.

equipage ('ɛkwɪpɪdʒ) n. 1. a horse-drawn carriage, esp. one attended by liveried footmen. 2. the stores and equipment of a military unit. 3. Arch. a set of useful articles.

equipoise ('ɛkwɪˌpɔɪz) n. 1. even balance of weight; equilibrium. 2. a counterbalance; counterpoise. ~vb. 3. (tr.) to offset or balance.

equitable ('ɛkwɪtəbəl) adj. 1. fair; just. 2. Law. relating to or valid in equity, as distinct from common law or statute law. —'**equitableness** n.

equitation (ˌɛkwɪ'teɪʃən) n. the study and practice of riding and horsemanship.

equities ('ɛkwɪtɪz) pl. n. another name for **ordinary shares.**

equity ('ɛkwɪtɪ) n., pl. -**ties.** 1. the quality of being impartial; fairness. 2. an impartial or fair act, decision, etc. 3. Law. a system of jurisprudence founded on principles of natural justice and fair conduct. It supplements common law, as by providing a remedy where none exists at law. 4. Law. an equitable right or claim. 5. the interest of ordinary shareholders in a company. 6. the value of a debtor's property in excess of debts to which it is liable.

Equity ('ɛkwɪtɪ) n. Brit. the actors' trade union.

equiv. abbrev. for equivalent.

equivalent (ɪ'kwɪvələnt) adj. 1. equal in value, quantity, significance, etc. 2. having the same or a similar effect or meaning. 3. Logic, Maths. (of two propositions) having a biconditional between them. ~n. 4. something that is equivalent. 5. Also called: **equivalent weight.** the weight of a substance that will combine with or displace 8 grams of oxygen or 1.007 97 grams of hydrogen. —e'**quivalence** n. —e'**quivalently** adv.

THESAURUS

easy-going, even-tempered, imperturbable, level-headed, placid, serene, temperate, unexcitable, unflappable (Inf.), unruffled 2. consistent, constant, even, regular, smooth, stable, steady, temperate, tranquil, unchanging, uniform, unvarying

equal adj. 1. alike, commensurate, equivalent, identical, like, one and the same, proportionate, tantamount, the same, uniform 2. balanced, corresponding, egalitarian, even, evenly balanced, evenly matched, evenly proportioned, fifty-fifty (Inf.), level pegging (Brit. inf.), matched, regular, symmetrical, uniform, unvarying 3. able, adequate, capable, competent, fit, good enough, ready, strong enough, suitable, up to 4. egalitarian, equable, even-handed, fair, impartial, just, unbiased ~n. 5. brother, compeer, counterpart, equivalent, fellow, match, mate, parallel, peer, rival, twin ~v. 6. agree with, amount to, balance, be equal to, be even with, be level with, be tantamount to, come up to, correspond to, equalize, equate, even, level, match, parallel, rival, square with, tal-

ly with, tie with

equality balance, coequality, correspondence, egalitarianism, equal opportunity, equatability, equivalence, evenness, fairness, identity, likeness, parity, sameness, similarity, uniformity

equalize balance, equal, equate, even up, level, make equal, match, regularize, smooth, square, standardize

equate agree, balance, be commensurate, compare, correspond with or to, equalize, liken, make or be equal, match, offset, pair, parallel, square, tally, think of together

equation agreement, balancing, comparison, correspondence, equality, equalization, equating, equivalence, likeness, match, pairing, parallel

equestrian 1. adj. in the saddle, mounted, on horseback 2. n. cavalier (Archaic), horseman, knight, rider

equilibrium 1. balance, counterpoise, equipoise, evenness, rest, stability, steadiness, symmetry 2. calm, calmness, collected-

ness, composure, coolness, equanimity, poise, self-possession, serenity, stability, steadiness

equip accoutre, arm, array, attire, deck out, dress, endow, fit out, fit up, furnish, kit out, outfit, prepare, provide, rig, stock, supply

equipment accoutrements, apparatus, appurtenances, baggage, equipage, furnishings, furniture, gear, materiel, outfit, paraphernalia, rig, stuff, supplies, tackle, tools

equitable candid, disinterested, dispassionate, due, even-handed, fair, honest, impartial, just, nondiscriminatory, proper, proportionate, reasonable, right, rightful, unbiased, unprejudiced

equity disinterestedness, equitableness, even-handedness, fair-mindedness, fairness, fair play, honesty, impartiality, integrity, justice, reasonableness, rectitude, righteousness, uprightness

equivalence agreement, alikeness, conformity, correspondence, equality, evenness,

equivocal (ɪ'kwɪvəkəl) *adj.* **1.** capable of varying interpretations; ambiguous. **2.** deliberately misleading or vague. **3.** of doubtful character or sincerity. —e₁**quivo-**'**cality** or **equivocacy** (ɪ'kwɪvəkəsɪ) *n.* —e'**quivocalness** *n.*

equivocate (ɪ'kwɪvə₁keɪt) *vb.* (*intr.*) to use equivocal language, esp. to avoid speaking directly or honestly. —e'**quivo₁catingly** *adv.* —e₁**quivo**'**cation** *n.* —e'**quivo-** ₁**cator** *n.* —e'**quivocatory** *adj.*

er (ə, ɜː) *interj.* a sound made when hesitating in speech.

Er *the chemical symbol for* erbium.

E.R. *abbrev. for:* **1.** Elizabeth Regina. **2.** Eduardus Rex.

-er[1] *suffix forming nouns.* **1.** a person or thing that performs a specified action: *reader; lighter.* **2.** a person engaged in a profession, occupation, etc.: *writer; baker.* **3.** a native or inhabitant of: *Londoner; villager.* **4.** a person or thing having a certain characteristic: *newcomer; fiver.*

-er[2] *suffix.* forming the comparative degree of adjectives (*deeper, freer,* etc.) and adverbs (*faster, slower,* etc.).

era ('ɪərə) *n.* **1.** a period of time considered as being of a distinctive character; epoch. **2.** an extended period of time the years of which are numbered from a fixed point: *the Christian era.* **3.** a point in time beginning a new or distinctive period. **4.** a major division of geological time, divided into periods.

eradicate (ɪ'rædɪ₁keɪt) *vb.* (*tr.*) **1.** to obliterate. **2.** to pull up by the roots. —e'**radicable** *adj.* —e₁**radi**'**cation** *n.* —e'**radicative** *adj.* —e'**radi₁cator** *n.*

erase (ɪ'reɪz) *vb.* **1.** to obliterate or rub out (something written, typed, etc.). **2.** (*tr.*) to destroy all traces of. **3.** to remove (a recording) from (magnetic tape). —e'**rasable** *adj.*

eraser (ɪ'reɪzə) *n.* an object, such as a piece of rubber, for erasing something written, typed, etc.

erasure (ɪ'reɪʒə) *n.* **1.** the act or an instance of erasing. **2.** the place or mark, as on a piece of paper, where something has been erased.

erbium ('ɜːbɪəm) *n.* a soft malleable silvery-white element of the lanthanide series of metals. Symbol: Er; atomic no.: 68; atomic wt.: 167.26.

ere (ɛə) *conj., prep.* a poetic word for **before**.

erect (ɪ'rɛkt) *adj.* **1.** upright in posture or position. **2.** *Physiol.* (of the penis, clitoris, or nipples) firm or rigid after swelling with blood, esp. as a result of sexual excitement. **3.** (of plant parts) growing vertically or at right angles to the parts from which they arise. ~*vb.* (*mainly tr.*) **4.** to put up; build. **5.** to raise to an upright position. **6.** to found or form; set up. **7.** (*also intr.*) *Physiol.* to become or cause to become firm or rigid by filling with blood. **8.** to exalt. **9.** to draw or construct (a line, figure, etc.) on a given line or figure. —e'**rectable** *adj.* —e'**recter** *or* e'**rector** *n.* —e'**rection** *n.* —e'**rectness** *n.*

erectile (ɪ'rɛktaɪl) *adj.* **1.** *Physiol.* (of tissues or organs, such as the penis or clitoris) capable of becoming erect. **2.** capable of being erected. —**erectility** (ɪrɛk'tɪlɪtɪ,

₁iːrɛk-) *n.*

erelong (ɛə'lɒŋ) *adv. Arch. or poetic.* before long; soon.

eremite ('ɛrɪ₁maɪt) *n.* a Christian hermit or recluse. —**eremitic** (₁ɛrɪ'mɪtɪk) or ₁**ere**'**mitical** *adj.* —**eremitism** ('ɛrɪmaɪ₁tɪzəm) *n.*

erg (ɜːg) *n.* the cgs unit of work or energy; the work done when the point of application of a force of 1 dyne moves through 1 centimetre in the direction of the force.

ergo ('ɜːgəʊ) *sentence connector.* therefore; hence.

ergonomics (₁ɜːgə'nɒmɪks) *n.* (*functioning as sing.*) the study of the relationship between workers and their environment. —₁**ergo**'**nomic** *adj.* —**ergonomist** (ɜː'gɒnəmɪst) *n.*

ergot ('ɜːgət, -gɒt) *n.* **1.** a disease of cereals and other grasses caused by fungi of the genus *Claviceps.* **2.** any fungus causing this disease. **3.** the dried fungus, used as the source of certain alkaloids used in medicine.

Erin ('ɪərɪn, 'ɛərɪn) *n.* an archaic or poetic name for Ireland.

ermine ('ɜːmɪn) *n., pl.* **-mines** *or* **-mine.** **1.** the stoat in northern regions, where it has a white winter coat with a black-tipped tail. **2.** the fur of this animal. **3.** the dignity or office of a judge, noble, etc., whose state robes are trimmed with ermine.

erne *or* **ern** (ɜːn) *n.* a fish-eating sea eagle.

Ernie ('ɜːnɪ) *n.* (in Britain) a computer that randomly selects winning numbers of Premium Bonds.

erode (ɪ'rəʊd) *vb.* **1.** to grind or wear down or away or become ground or worn down or away. **2.** to deteriorate or cause to deteriorate. —e'**rodent** *adj.* —e'**rodible** *adj.*

erogenous (ɪ'rɒdʒɪnəs) *or* **erogenic** (₁ɛrə'dʒɛnɪk) *adj.* **1.** sensitive to sexual stimulation. **2.** arousing sexual desire or giving sexual pleasure. —**erogeneity** (₁ɛrədʒɪ-'niːɪtɪ) *n.*

erosion (ɪ'rəʊʒən) *n.* **1.** the wearing away of rocks, soil, etc. by the action of water, ice, wind, etc. **2.** the act or process of eroding or the state of being eroded. —e'**rosive** *or* e'**rosional** *adj.*

erotic (ɪ'rɒtɪk) *adj. also* **erotical. 1.** of, concerning, or arousing sexual desire or giving sexual pleasure. **2.** marked by strong sexual desire or being especially sensitive to sexual stimulation. —e'**rotically** *adv.*

erotica (ɪ'rɒtɪkə) *n.* explicitly sexual literature or art.

eroticism (ɪ'rɒtɪ₁sɪzəm) *or* **erotism** ('ɛrə₁tɪzəm) *n.* **1.** erotic quality or nature. **2.** the use of sexually arousing or pleasing symbolism in literature or art. **3.** sexual excitement or desire.

err (ɜː) *vb.* (*intr.*) **1.** to make a mistake; be incorrect. **2.** to deviate from a moral standard. **3.** to act with bias, esp. favourable bias: *to err on the right side.* —'**errancy** *n.*

errand ('ɛrənd) *n.* **1.** a short trip undertaken to perform a task or commission (esp. in **run errands**). **2.** the purpose or object of such a trip.

errant ('ɛrənt) *adj.* (*often postpositive*) **1.** *Arch. or literary.* wandering in search of adventure. **2.** erring or straying from the right course or accepted standards.

THESAURUS

identity, interchangeableness, likeness, match, parallel, parity, sameness, similarity, synonymy

equivalent 1. *adj.* alike, commensurate, comparable, correspondent, corresponding, equal, even, homologous, interchangeable, of a kind, same, similar, synonymous, tantamount **2.** *n.* correspondent, counterpart, equal, match, opposite number, parallel, peer, twin

equivocal ambiguous, ambivalent, doubtful, dubious, evasive, indefinite, indeterminate, misleading, oblique, obscure, questionable, suspicious, uncertain, vague

equivocate avoid the issue, beat about the bush (*Inf.*), dodge, evade, fence, fudge, hedge, parry, prevaricate, pussyfoot (*Inf.*), quibble, shuffle, sidestep, tergiversate, waffle (*Inf.*)

equivocation ambiguity, double talk, doubtfulness, evasion, hedging, prevarication, quibbling, shuffling, tergiversation, waffle (*Inf.*), weasel words (*Inf., chiefly U.S.*)

era age, cycle, date, day *or* days, epoch,

generation, period, stage, time

eradicate abolish, annihilate, deracinate, destroy, efface, eliminate, erase, expunge, exterminate, extinguish, extirpate, obliterate, remove, root out, stamp out, uproot, weed out, wipe out

eradication abolition, annihilation, deracination, destruction, effacement, elimination, erasure, expunction, extermination, extinction, extirpation, obliteration, removal

erase blot, cancel, delete, efface, expunge, obliterate, remove, rub out, scratch out, wipe out

erect *adj.* **1.** elevated, firm, perpendicular, pricked-up, raised, rigid, standing, stiff, straight, upright, vertical ~*v.* **2.** build, construct, elevate, lift, mount, pitch, put up, raise, rear, set up, stand up **3.** create, establish, form, found, initiate, institute, organize, set up

erection 1. assembly, building, construction, creation, elevation, establishment, fabrication, manufacture **2.** building, construction, edifice, pile, structure

erode abrade, consume, corrode, destroy, deteriorate, disintegrate, eat away, grind down, spoil, wear down *or* away

erosion abrasion, attrition, consumption, corrasion, corrosion, destruction, deterioration, disintegration, eating away, grinding down, spoiling, wear, wearing down *or* away

erotic amatory, aphrodisiac, carnal, erogenous, rousing, seductive, sensual, sexy (*Inf.*), stimulating, suggestive, titillating, voluptuous

err 1. be inaccurate, be incorrect, be in error, blunder, go astray, go wrong, make a mistake, misapprehend, miscalculate, misjudge, mistake, slip up (*Inf.*) **2.** deviate, do wrong, fall, go astray, lapse, misbehave, offend, sin, transgress, trespass

errand charge, commission, job, message, mission, task

errant 1. *Archaic* itinerant, journeying, peripatetic, rambling, roaming, roving, wandering **2.** aberrant, deviant, erring, offending, sinning, straying, wrong

—'**errantry** n.

erratic (ɪˈrætɪk) adj. **1.** irregular in performance, behaviour, or attitude; unpredictable. **2.** having no fixed or regular course. ~n. **3.** a piece of rock that has been transported from its place of origin, esp. by glacial action. —**er'ratically** adv.

erratum (ɪˈrɑːtəm) n., pl. **-ta** (-tə). **1.** an error in writing or printing. **2.** another name for **corrigendum.**

erroneous (ɪˈrəʊnɪəs) adj. based on or containing error; incorrect. —**er'roneousness** n.

error (ˈɛrə) n. **1.** a mistake or inaccuracy. **2.** an incorrect belief or wrong judgment. **3.** the condition of deviating from accuracy or correctness. **4.** deviation from a moral standard; wrongdoing. **5.** the amount of deviation by which something is incorrect or inaccurate. —'**error-ˌfree** adj.

ersatz (ˈɛəzæts, ˈɜː-) adj. **1.** made in imitation; artificial. ~n. **2.** an ersatz substance or article.

Erse (ɜːs) n. **1.** another name for **Gaelic** (sense 1). ~adj. **2.** of or relating to the Gaelic language.

erst (ɜːst) adv. Arch. **1.** long ago; formerly. **2.** at first.

erstwhile (ˈɜːstˌwaɪl) adj. **1.** former; one-time. ~adv. **2.** Arch. long ago; formerly.

eruct (ɪˈrʌkt) or **eructate** vb. **1.** to belch. **2.** (of a volcano) to pour out (fumes or volcanic matter). —**eructation** (ˌiːrʌkˈteɪʃən, ˌiːrʌk-) n.

erudite (ˈɛruˌdaɪt) adj. having or showing extensive scholarship; learned. —**erudition** (ˌɛruˈdɪʃən) or 'eru-ˌditeness n.

erupt (ɪˈrʌpt) vb. **1.** to eject (steam, water, and volcanic material) violently or (of volcanic material, etc.) to be so ejected. **2.** (intr.) (of a blemish) to appear on the skin. **3.** (intr.) (of a tooth) to emerge through the gum during normal tooth development. **4.** (intr.) to burst forth suddenly and violently. —**e'ruptible** adj. —**e'ruptive** adj. —**e'ruption** n.

erysipelas (ˌɛrɪˈsɪpɪləs) n. an acute streptococcal infectious disease of the skin, characterized by fever and purplish lesions.

erythro- or before a vowel **erythr-** combining form. red: erythrocyte.

erythrocyte (ɪˈrɪθrəʊˌsaɪt) n. a blood cell of vertebrates that transports oxygen and carbon dioxide, combined with haemoglobin. —**erythrocytic** (ɪˌrɪθrəʊˈsɪtɪk) adj.

Es the chemical symbol for einsteinium.

-es suffix. **1.** variant of **-s**[1] for nouns ending in ch, s, sh, z, postconsonantal y, for some nouns ending in a vowel, and nouns in f with v in the plural: ashes; heroes; calves. **2.** variant of **-s**[2] for verbs ending in ch, s, sh, z, postconsonantal y, or a vowel: preaches; steadies; echoes.

escalate (ˈɛskəˌleɪt) vb. to increase or be increased in extent, intensity, or magnitude. —ˌesca'lation n.

▷ **Usage.** Escalate is very commonly used in journalistic contexts in the sense of gradually increasing the intensity or scope of a war, etc. This word is, however, not yet completely accepted as appropriate in formal English.

escalator (ˈɛskəˌleɪtə) n. **1.** a moving staircase consisting of stair treads fixed to a conveyor belt. **2.** short for **escalator clause.**

escalator clause n. a clause in a contract stipulating an adjustment in wages, prices, etc., in the event of specified changes in conditions, such as a large rise in the cost of living.

escallop (ɛˈskɒləp, ɛˈskæl-) n., vb. another word for **scallop.**

escalope (ˈɛskəˌlɒp) n. a thin slice of meat, usually veal.

escapade (ˈɛskəˌpeɪd, ˌɛskəˈpeɪd) n. **1.** an adventure, esp. one that is mischievous or unlawful. **2.** a prank; romp.

escape (ɪˈskeɪp) vb. **1.** to get away or break free from (confinements, etc.). **2.** to manage to avoid (danger, etc.). **3.** (intr.; usually foll. by from) (of gases, liquids, etc.) to issue gradually, as from a crack; seep; leak. **4.** (tr.) to elude; be forgotten by: the figure escapes me. **5.** (tr.) to be articulated inadvertently or involuntarily: a roar escaped his lips. ~n. **6.** the act of escaping or state of having escaped. **7.** avoidance of injury, harm, etc. **8. a.** a means or way of escape. **b.** (as modifier): an escape route. **9.** a means of distraction or relief. **10.** a gradual outflow; leakage; seepage. **11.** Also called: **escape valve, escape cock.** a valve that releases air, steam, etc., above a certain pressure. **12.** a plant originally cultivated but now growing wild. —**es'capable** adj. —es,cap'ee n. —**es'caper** n.

escapement (ɪˈskeɪpmənt) n. **1.** a mechanism consisting of a toothed wheel (**escape wheel**) and anchor, used in timepieces to provide periodic impulses to the pendulum or balance. **2.** any similar mechanism that regulates movement. **3.** in pianos, the mechanism which allows the hammer to clear the string after striking, so the string can vibrate. **4.** Rare. an act or means of escaping.

escape road n. a road provided on a hill for a driver to drive into if his brakes fail or on a bend if he loses control of the turn.

escape velocity n. the minimum velocity necessary for a body to escape from the gravitational field of the earth or other celestial body.

escapism (ɪˈskeɪpɪzəm) n. an inclination to retreat from unpleasant reality, as through diversion or fantasy. —**es'capist** n., adj.

escapologist (ˌɛskəˈpɒlədʒɪst) n. an entertainer who specializes in freeing himself from confinement. —ˌesca'pology n.

escarpment (ɪˈskɑːpmənt) n. **1.** the long continuous steep face of a ridge or plateau formed by erosion or faulting; scarp. **2.** a steep artificial slope made around a fortified place.

-escent suffix forming adjectives. beginning to be, do, show, etc.: convalescent; luminescent. —**escence** suffix forming nouns.

eschatology (ˌɛskəˈtɒlədʒɪ) n. the branch of theology concerned with the end of the world. —**eschatological** (ˌɛskətəˈlɒdʒɪkəl) adj. —ˌescha'tologist n.

escheat (ɪsˈtʃiːt) Law. n. **1.** (before 1926) the reversion of property to the Crown in the absence of legal heirs. **2.** Feudalism. the reversion of property to the feudal lord in the absence of legal heirs. **3.** the property so reverting. ~vb. **4.** to take (land) by escheat or (of land) to revert by escheat. —**es'cheatable** adj. —**es'cheatage** n.

eschew (ɪsˈtʃuː) vb. (tr.) to keep clear of or abstain from (something disliked, injurious, etc.); shun; avoid. —**es'chewal** n. —**es'chewer** n.

escort n. (ˈɛskɔːt). **1.** one or more persons, soldiers,

THESAURUS

erratic 1. aberrant, abnormal, capricious, changeable, desultory, eccentric, fitful, inconsistent, irregular, shifting, unpredictable, unreliable, unstable, variable, wayward 2. directionless, meandering, planetary, wandering

erroneous amiss, fallacious, false, faulty, flawed, inaccurate, incorrect, inexact, invalid, mistaken, spurious, unfounded, unsound, untrue, wrong

error 1. bloomer (Inf.), blunder, boner (Sl.), boob (Sl.), delusion, erratum, fallacy, fault, flaw, howler (Inf.), inaccuracy, misapprehension, miscalculation, misconception, mistake, oversight, slip, solecism 2. delinquency, deviation, fault, lapse, misdeed, offence, sin, transgression, trespass, wrong, wrongdoing

erstwhile bygone, ex (Inf.), former, late, old, once, one-time, past, previous, quondam, sometime

erudite cultivated, cultured, educated, knowledgeable, learned, lettered, literate, scholarly, well-educated, well-read

erupt 1. be ejected, belch forth, blow up, break out, burst forth, burst into, burst out, discharge, explode, flare up, gush, pour forth, spew forth or out, spit out, spout, throw off, vent, vomit 2. Medical appear, break out

eruption 1. discharge, ejection, explosion, flare-up, outbreak, outburst, sally, venting 2. Medical inflammation, outbreak, rash

escalate amplify, ascend, be increased, enlarge, expand, extend, grow, heighten, increase, intensify, magnify, mount, raise, rise, step up

escapade adventure, antic, caper, fling, lark (Inf.), mischief, prank, romp, scrape (Inf.), spree, stunt, trick

escape v. 1. abscond, bolt, break free or out, decamp, do a bunk (Sl.), flee, fly, get away, make or effect one's escape, make one's getaway, run away or off, skip, slip away ~n. 2. bolt, break, break-out, decampment, flight, getaway ~v. 3. avoid, circumvent, dodge, duck, elude, evade, pass, shun, slip ~n. 4. avoidance, circumvention, elusion, evasion ~v. 5. discharge, drain, emanate, flow, gush, issue, leak, pour forth, seep, spurt ~n. 6. discharge, drain, effluence, efflux, emanation, emission, gush, leak, leakage, outflow, outpour, seepage, spurt ~v. 7. baffle, be beyond (someone), be forgotten by, elude, puzzle, stump ~n. 8. distraction, diversion, pastime, recreation, relief

eschew abandon, abjure, abstain from, avoid, elude, fight shy of, forgo, forswear, give up, have nothing to do with, keep or steer clear of, refrain from, renounce, shun, swear off

vehicles, etc., accompanying another or others for protection or as a mark of honour. **2.** a man or youth who accompanies a woman or girl on a social occasion. ~*vb.* (ɪsˈkɔːt). **3.** (*tr.*) to accompany or attend as an escort.

escritoire (ˌɛskrɪˈtwɑː) *n.* a writing desk with compartments and drawers.

escudo (ɛˈskuːdəʊ) *n., pl.* **-dos** (-dəʊz). **1.** the standard monetary unit of Portugal. **2.** the standard monetary unit of Chile. **3.** an old Spanish silver coin.

esculent (ˈɛskjʊlənt) *n.* **1.** any edible substance. ~*adj.* **2.** edible.

escutcheon (ɪˈskʌtʃən) *n.* **1.** a shield, esp. a heraldic one that displays a coat of arms. **2.** a plate or shield around a keyhole, door handle, etc. **3.** the place on the stern of a vessel where the name is shown. **4. blot on one's escutcheon.** a stain on one's honour. —**esˈcutcheoned** *adj.*

-ese *suffix forming adjectives and nouns.* indicating place of origin, language, or style: *Cantonese; Japanese; journalese.*

Eskimo (ˈɛskɪˌməʊ) *n.* **1.** (*pl.* **-mos** or **-mo**) a member of a group of peoples inhabiting N Canada, Greenland, Alaska, and E Siberia. The Eskimos are more properly referred to as the **Inuit. 2.** the language of these peoples. ~*adj.* **3.** of or relating to the Eskimos.

Eskimo dog *n.* a large powerful breed of sled dog with a long thick coat and curled tail.

E.S.N. *abbrev. for* educationally subnormal.

esoteric (ˌɛsəʊˈtɛrɪk) *adj.* **1.** restricted to or intended for an enlightened or initiated minority. **2.** difficult to understand; abstruse. **3.** not openly admitted; private. —ˌesoˈterically *adv.* —ˌesoˈteriˌcism *n.*

E.S.P. *abbrev. for* extrasensory perception.

esp. *abbrev. for* especially.

espadrille (ˌɛspəˈdrɪl) *n.* a light shoe with a canvas upper, esp. with a braided cord sole.

espalier (ɪˈspæljə) *n.* **1.** an ornamental shrub or fruit tree trained to grow flat, as against a wall. **2.** the trellis or framework on which such plants are trained. ~*vb.* **3.** (*tr.*) to train (a plant) on an espalier.

esparto or **esparto grass** (ɛˈspɑːtəʊ) *n., pl.* **-tos.** any of various grasses of S Europe and N Africa, used to make ropes, mats, etc.

especial (ɪˈspɛʃəl) *adj.* (*prenominal*) **1.** unusual; notable. **2.** applying to one person or thing in particular; specific; peculiar: *he had an especial dislike of relatives.* —**esˈpecially** *adv.*

▷ **Usage.** *Special* is always used in preference to *especial* when the sense is one of being out of the ordinary: *a special lesson. Special* is also used when something is referred to as being for a particular purpose: *the word was specially underlined for you.* Where an idea of preeminence or individuality is involved, either *especial* or *special* may be used: *he is my especial* (or *special*) *friend; he is especially* (or *specially*) *good at his job.* In informal English, however, *special* is usually preferred in all contexts.

Esperanto (ˌɛspəˈræntəʊ) *n.* an artificial language based on words common to the chief European languages. —ˌEspeˈrantist *n., adj.*

espionage (ˈɛspɪəˌnɑːʒ) *n.* **1.** the use of spies to obtain secret information, esp. by governments. **2.** the act of spying.

esplanade (ˌɛspləˈneɪd) *n.* **1.** a long open level stretch of ground for walking along, esp. beside the sea shore. Cf. **promenade** (sense 1). **2.** an open area in front of a fortified place.

espousal (ɪˈspauzəl) *n.* **1.** adoption or support: *an espousal of new beliefs.* **2.** (*sometimes pl.*) *Arch.* a marriage or betrothal ceremony.

espouse (ɪˈspauz) *vb.* (*tr.*) **1.** to adopt or give support to (a cause, ideal, etc.): *to espouse socialism.* **2.** *Arch.* (esp. of a man) to take as spouse; marry. —**esˈpouser** *n.*

espresso (ɛˈsprɛsəʊ) *n., pl.* **-sos. 1.** coffee made by forcing steam or boiling water through ground coffee beans. **2.** an apparatus for making coffee in this way.

esprit (ɛˈspriː) *n.* spirit and liveliness, esp. in wit.

esprit de corps (ɛˈspriː də ˈkɔː) *n.* consciousness of and pride in belonging to a particular group; the sense of shared purpose and fellowship.

espy (ɪˈspaɪ) *vb.* **-pying, -pied.** (*tr.*) to catch sight of or perceive; detect. —**esˈpier** *n.*

Esq. *abbrev. for* esquire.

-esque *suffix forming adjectives.* indicating a specified character, manner, style, or resemblance: *picturesque; Romanesque; statuesque.*

esquire (ɪˈskwaɪə) *n.* **1.** *Chiefly Brit.* a title of respect, usually abbreviated *Esq.*, placed after a man's name. **2.** (in medieval times) the attendant of a knight, subsequently often knighted himself.

ESRO (ˈɛzrəʊ) *n. acronym for* European Space Research Organization.

-ess *suffix forming nouns.* indicating a female: *actress; lioness.*

essay *n.* (ˈɛseɪ; *defs.* 2,3 *also* ɛˈseɪ). **1.** a short literary composition. **2.** an attempt; effort. **3.** a test or trial. ~*vb.* (ɛˈseɪ). (*tr.*) **4.** to attempt or try. **5.** to test or try out.

essayist (ˈɛseɪɪst) *n.* a person who writes essays.

essence (ˈɛsəns) *n.* **1.** the characteristic or intrinsic feature of a thing, which determines its identity; fundamental nature. **2.** a perfect or complete form of something. **3.** *Philosophy.* the unchanging inward nature of something. **4. a.** the constituent of a plant, usually an oil, alkaloid, or glycoside, that determines its chemical properties. **b.** an alcoholic solution of such a substance. **5.** a rare word for **perfume. 6. of the essence.** indispensable; vitally important.

essential (ɪˈsɛnʃəl) *adj.* **1.** vitally important; absolutely necessary. **2.** basic; fundamental. **3.** absolute; perfect. **4.** derived from or relating to an extract of a plant, drug, etc.: *an essential oil.* ~*n.* **5.** something fundamental or indispensable. —**essentiality** (ɪˌsɛnʃɪˈælɪtɪ) or es'sentialness *n.* —es'sentially *adv.*

essential oil *n.* any of various volatile oils in plants, having the odour or flavour of the plant from which they are extracted.

E.S.T. *abbrev. for:* **1.** (in the U.S. and Canada) Eastern Standard Time. **2.** electric-shock treatment.

est. *abbrev. for:* **1.** established. **2.** estimate(d).

-est *suffix.* forming the superlative degree of adjectives and adverbs: *fastest.*

establish (ɪˈstæblɪʃ) *vb.* (*tr.*) **1.** to make secure or per-

---

THESAURUS

escort *n.* **1.** bodyguard, company, convoy, cortege, entourage, guard, protection, retinue, safeguard, train **2.** attendant, beau, chaperon, companion, guide, partner, protector, squire (*Rare*) ~*v.* **3.** accompany, chaperon, conduct, convoy, guard, guide, lead, partner, protect, shepherd, squire, usher

especial 1. chief, distinguished, exceptional, extraordinary, marked, notable, noteworthy, outstanding, principal, signal, special, uncommon, unusual **2.** exclusive, express, individual, particular, peculiar, personal, private, singular, special, specific, unique

especially 1. chiefly, conspicuously, exceptionally, extraordinarily, mainly, markedly, notably, outstandingly, principally, remarkably, signally, specially, strikingly, supremely, uncommonly, unusually **2.** exclu-

sively, expressly, particularly, peculiarly, singularly, specifically, uniquely

espionage counter-intelligence, intelligence, spying, undercover work

espousal 1. adoption, advocacy, backing, championing, championship, defence, embracing, maintenance, support, taking up **2.** *Archaic* affiancing, betrothal, betrothing (*Archaic*), engagement, espousing (*Archaic*), marriage, nuptials, plighting, wedding

espouse 1. adopt, advocate, back, champion, defend, embrace, maintain, stand up for, support, take up **2.** *Archaic* betroth (*Archaic*), marry, take as spouse, take to wife, wed

essay article, composition, discourse, disquisition, dissertation, paper, piece, tract

essence 1. being, core, crux, entity, heart, kernel, life, lifeblood, meaning, nature, pith, principle, quiddity, quintessence, significance, soul, spirit, substance **2.** concentrate,

distillate, elixir, extract, spirits, tincture **3.** *Rare* cologne, fragrance, perfume, scent **4. in essence** basically, essentially, fundamentally, in effect, in substance, in the main, materially, substantially, to all intents and purposes; virtually **5. of the essence** crucial, essential, indispensable, of the utmost importance, vital, vitally important

essential *adj.* **1.** crucial, important, indispensable, necessary, needed, requisite, vital **2.** basic, cardinal, constitutional, elemental, elementary, fundamental, inherent, innate, intrinsic, key, main, principal **3.** absolute, complete, ideal, perfect, quintessential **4.** concentrated, distilled, extracted, rectified, refined, volatile ~*n.* **5.** basic, fundamental, must, necessity, prerequisite, principle, requisite, rudiment, *sine qua non*, vital part

manent in a certain place, condition, job, etc. **2.** to create or set up (an organization, etc.) as on a permanent basis. **3.** to prove correct; validate: *establish a fact.* **4.** to cause (a principle, theory, etc.) to be accepted: *establish a precedent.* **5.** to give (a Church) the status of a national institution. **—es'tablisher** n.

establishment (ɪ'stæblɪʃmənt) n. **1.** the act of establishing or state of being established. **2. a.** a business organization or other large institution. **b.** a place of business. **3.** the staff and equipment of an organization. **4.** any large organization or system. **5.** a household; residence. **6.** a body of employees or servants.

Establishment (ɪ'stæblɪʃmənt) n. **the.** a group or class having institutional authority within a society: usually seen as conservative.

estate (ɪ'steɪt) n. **1.** a large piece of landed property, esp. in the country. **2.** *Chiefly Brit.* a large area of property development, esp. of new houses or (**trading estate**) of factories. **3.** *Law.* **a.** property or possessions. **b.** the nature of interest that a person has in land or other property. **c.** the total extent of the property of a deceased person or bankrupt. **4.** Also called: **estate of the realm.** an order or class in a political community, regarded as a part of the body politic: the lords spiritual (**first estate**), lords temporal (peers) (**second estate**), and commons (**third estate**). See also **fourth estate. 5.** state, period, or position in life: *youth's estate; a poor man's estate.*

estate agent n. **1.** *Brit.* an agent concerned with the valuation, management, lease, and sale of property. **2.** the administrator of a large landed property; estate manager.

estate car n. *Brit.* a car containing a large carrying space, reached through a rear door: usually the back seats fold forward to increase the carrying space.

estate duty n. another name for **death duty.**

esteem (ɪ'stiːm) vb. *(tr.)* **1.** to have great respect or high regard for. **2.** *Formal.* to judge or consider; deem. ~n. **3.** high regard or respect; good opinion. **4.** *Arch.* judgment; opinion.

ester ('estə) n. *Chem.* any of a class of compounds produced by reaction between acids and alcohols with the elimination of water.

estimable ('estɪməbəl) adj. worthy of respect; deserving of admiration. **—'estimableness** n. **—'estimably** adv.

estimate vb. ('estɪˌmeɪt). **1.** to form an approximate idea of (size, cost, etc.); calculate roughly. **2.** *(tr.; may take a clause as object)* to form an opinion about; judge. **3.** to submit (an approximate price) for (a job) to a prospective client. ~n. ('estɪmɪt). **4.** an approximate calculation. **5.** a statement of the likely charge for certain work. **6.** a judgment; appraisal. **—'esti,mator** n. **—'estimative** adj.

estimation (ˌestɪ'meɪʃən) n. **1.** a considered opinion; judgment. **2.** esteem; respect. **3.** the act of estimating.

estoppel (ɪ'stɒpəl) n. *Law.* a rule of evidence whereby a person is precluded from denying the truth of a statement he has previously asserted.

estrange (ɪ'streɪndʒ) vb. *(tr.)* to antagonize or lose the affection of (someone previously friendly); alienate. **—es'trangement** n.

estuary ('estjʊərɪ) n., pl. **-aries.** the widening channel of a river where it nears the sea. **—estuarial** (ˌestjʊ'ɛərɪəl) adj. **—'estuarine** adj.

-et suffix of nouns. small or lesser: *islet; baronet.*

eta ('iːtə) n. the seventh letter in the Greek alphabet (H, η).

E.T.A. abbrev. for estimated time of arrival.

et al. abbrev. for: **1.** et alibi. **2.** et alii.

etc. abbrev. for et cetera.

et cetera (ɪt 'sɛtrə) n. and vb. substitute. **1.** and the rest; and others; and so forth. **2.** or the like; or something similar.

▷ **Usage.** Since *et cetera* (or *etc.*) means *and other things,* careful writers do not use the expression *and etc.* The repetition of *etc.,* as in *notebooks, etc., etc.,* is avoided in formal contexts.

etceteras (ɪt'sɛtrəz) pl. n. miscellaneous extra things or persons.

etch (etʃ) vb. **1.** *(tr.)* to wear away the surface of (a metal, glass, etc.) by the action of an acid. **2.** to cut or corrode (a design, etc.) on (a metal or other printing plate) by the action of acid on parts not covered by wax or other acid-resistant coating. **3.** *(tr.)* to cut as with a sharp implement. **4.** *(tr.; usually passive)* to imprint vividly. **—'etcher** n.

etching ('etʃɪŋ) n. **1.** the art, act, or process of preparing etched surfaces or of printing designs from them. **2.** an etched plate. **3.** an impression made from an etched plate.

eternal (ɪ'tɜːnəl)) adj. **1. a.** without beginning or end; lasting for ever. **b.** *(as n.): the eternal.* **2.** *(often cap.)* a name applied to God. **3.** unchanged by time; immutable: *eternal truths.* **4.** seemingly unceasing. **—ˌeter'nality** or e'ternalness n.

eternal triangle n. an emotional relationship in which there are conflicts involving a man and two women or a woman and two men.

eternity (ɪ'tɜːnɪtɪ) n., pl. **-ties. 1.** endless or infinite time. **2.** the quality, state, or condition of being eternal. **3.** *(usually pl.)* any aspect of life and thought considered timeless. **4.** *Theol.* the timeless existence, believed by some to characterize the afterlife. **5.** a seemingly endless period of time.

eternity ring n. a ring given as a token of lasting affection, esp. one set all around with stones to symbolize continuity.

ethane ('iːθeɪn, 'eθ-) n. a colourless odourless flammable gaseous alkane obtained from natural gas and petro-

---

THESAURUS

establish 1. base, constitute, create, decree, enact, ensconce, entrench, fix, form, found, ground, implant, inaugurate, install, institute, organize, plant, root, secure, settle, set up, start **2.** authenticate, certify, confirm, corroborate, demonstrate, prove, ratify, show, substantiate, validate, verify

establishment 1. creation, enactment, formation, foundation, founding, inauguration, installation, institution, organization, setting up **2.** business, company, concern, corporation, enterprise, firm, house, institute, institution, organization, outfit *(Inf.)*, setup *(Inf.)*, structure, system **3.** building, factory, house, office, plant, quarters **4.** abode, domicile, dwelling, home, house, household, residence **5. the Establishment** established order, institutionalized authority, ruling class, the powers that be, the system

estate 1. area, demesne, domain, holdings, lands, manor, property **2.** *Property law* assets, belongings, effects, fortune, goods, possessions, property, wealth **3.** caste, class, order, rank **4.** condition, lot, period, place, position, quality, rank, situation, standing, state, station, status

esteem v. **1.** admire, be fond of, cherish, honour, like, love, prize, regard highly, respect, revere, reverence, think highly of, treasure, value, venerate **2.** *Formal* account, believe, calculate, consider, deem, estimate, hold, judge, rate, reckon, regard, think, view ~n. **3.** admiration, consideration, credit, estimation, good opinion, honour, regard, respect, reverence, veneration

estimate v. **1.** appraise, assess, calculate roughly, evaluate, gauge, guess, judge, number, reckon, value **2.** assess, believe, conjecture, consider, form an opinion, guess, judge, rank, rate, reckon, surmise, think ~n. **3.** appraisal, appraisement, approximate calculation, assessment, evaluation, guess, guesstimate *(Inf.)*, judgment, reckoning, valuation **4.** appraisal, appraisement, assessment, belief, conjecture, educated guess, estimation, judgment, opinion, surmise, thought(s)

estimation 1. appraisal, appreciation, assessment, belief, consideration, considered opinion, estimate, evaluation, judgment, opinion, view **2.** admiration, credit, esteem, good opinion, honour, regard, respect, reverence, veneration

estrange alienate, antagonize, disaffect, disunite, divide, drive apart, lose *or* destroy the affection of, make hostile, part, separate, set at odds, withdraw, withhold

estrangement alienation, antagonization, breach, break-up, disaffection, dissociation, disunity, division, hostility, parting, separation, split, withdrawal, withholding

estuary creek, firth, fjord, inlet, mouth

et cetera and others, and so forth, and so on, and the like, and the rest, et al.

etch carve, corrode, cut, eat into, engrave, furrow, impress, imprint, incise, ingrain, inscribe, stamp

etching carving, engraving, impression, imprint, inscription, print

eternal 1. abiding, ceaseless, constant, deathless, endless, everlasting, immortal, infinite, interminable, never-ending, perennial, perpetual, sempiternal *(Literary)*, timeless, unceasing, undying, unending, unremitting, without end **2.** deathless, enduring, everlasting, immortal, immutable, imperishable, indestructible, lasting, permanent

eternity 1. age, ages, endlessness, for ever, immortality, infinitude, infinity, perpetuity, timelessness, time without end **2.** *Theology* heaven, paradise, the afterlife, the hereafter, the next world

leum: used as a fuel. Formula: C_2H_6.

ethanol ('ɛθə,nɒl, 'iːθə-) n. the technical name for **alcohol** (sense 1).

ethene ('ɛθiːn) n. the technical name for **ethylene**.

ether ('iːθə) n. 1. Also called: **diethyl ether, ethyl ether, ethoxyethane.** a colourless volatile highly flammable liquid: used as a solvent and anaesthetic. Formula: $C_2H_5OC_2H_5$. 2. any of a class of organic compounds with the general formula ROR', as in diethyl ether $C_2H_5OC_2H_5$. 3. **the ether.** the medium formerly believed to fill all space and to support the propagation of electromagnetic waves. 4. *Greek myth.* the upper regions of the atmosphere; clear sky or heaven. ~Also (for senses 3 and 4): **aether.** —**etheric** (iː'θɛrɪk) *adj.*

ethereal (ɪ'θɪərɪəl) *adj.* 1. extremely delicate or refined. 2. almost as light as air; airy. 3. celestial or spiritual. 4. of, containing, or dissolved in an ether, esp. diethyl ether. 5. of or relating to the ether. —**e,there'ality** or **e'therealness** n.

etherealize or **-ise** (ɪ'θɪərɪə,laɪz) vb. (tr.) 1. to make or regard as being ethereal. 2. to add ether to or make into ether. —**e,thereali'zation** or **-i'sation** n.

etherize or **-ise** ('iːθə,raɪz) vb. (tr.) Obs. to subject (a patient, etc.) to the anaesthetic influence of ether fumes; anaesthetize. —**etheri'zation** or **-i'sation** n. —**'ether,izer** or **-,iser** n.

ethic ('ɛθɪk) n. 1. a moral principle or set of moral values held by an individual or group. ~adj. 2. another word for **ethical.**

ethical ('ɛθɪkəl) *adj.* 1. in accordance with principles of conduct that are considered correct, esp. those of a given profession or group. 2. of or relating to ethics. 3. (of a medicinal agent) available legally only with a doctor's prescription. —**'ethicalness** or **,ethi'cality** n.

ethics ('ɛθɪks) n. 1. (functioning as sing.) the philosophical study of the moral value of human conduct and of the rules and principles that ought to govern it. 2. (functioning as pl.) a code of behaviour considered correct, esp. that of a particular group, profession, or individual. 3. (functioning as pl.) the moral fitness of a decision, course of action, etc. —**'ethicist** n.

Ethiopian (,iːθɪ'əʊpɪən) *adj.* 1. of or relating to Ethiopia (a state in NE Africa), its people, or any of their languages. ~n. 2. a native or inhabitant of Ethiopia. 3. any of the languages of Ethiopia, esp. Amharic. ~n., adj. 4. an archaic word for **Negro.**

ethnic ('ɛθnɪk) or **ethnical** *adj.* 1. of or relating to a human group having racial, religious, linguistic, and other traits in common. 2. relating to the classification of mankind into groups, esp. on the basis of racial characteristics. 3. denoting or deriving from the cultural traditions of a group of people. —**ethnicity** (ɛθ'nɪsɪtɪ) n.

ethno- combining form. indicating race, people, or culture.

ethnography (ɛθ'nɒgrəfɪ) n. the branch of anthropology that deals with the scientific description of individual human societies. —**eth'nographer** n. —**ethnographic** (,ɛθnəʊ'græfɪk) or **,ethno'graphical** *adj.*

ethnology (ɛθ'nɒlədʒɪ) n. the branch of anthropology that deals with races and peoples, their origins, characteristics, etc. —**ethnologic** (,ɛθnə'lɒdʒɪk) or **,ethno'logical** *adj.* —**eth'nologist** n.

ethos ('iːθɒs) n. the distinctive character, spirit, and attitudes of a people, culture, era, etc.: *the revolutionary ethos.*

ethyl ('iːθaɪl, 'ɛθɪl) n. (modifier) of, consisting of, or containing the monovalent group C_2H_5—. —**ethylic** (ɪ'θɪlɪk) *adj.*

ethyl alcohol n. another name for **alcohol** (sense 1).

ethylene ('ɛθɪ,liːn) or **ethene** ('ɛθiːn) n. a colourless flammable gaseous alkene used in the manufacture of polythene and other chemicals. Formula: $CH_2{:}CH_2$. —**ethylenic** (,ɛθɪ'liːnɪk) *adj.*

etiolate ('iːtɪəʊ,leɪt) vb. 1. Bot. to whiten (a green

plant) through lack of sunlight. 2. to become or cause to become pale and weak. —**,etio'lation** n.

etiquette ('ɛtɪ,kɛt, ,ɛtɪ'kɛt) n. 1. the customs or rules governing behaviour regarded as correct in social life. 2. a conventional code of practice followed in certain professions or groups.

Eton collar ('iːtən) n. a broad stiff white collar worn outside an Eton jacket.

Eton crop n. a very short mannish hair style worn by women in the 1920s.

Eton jacket n. a waist-length jacket, open in front, formerly worn by pupils of Eton College, a public school for boys in S England.

Etruscan (ɪ'trʌskən) or **Etrurian** (ɪ'trʊərɪən) n. 1. a member of an ancient people of Etruria in central Italy whose civilization greatly influenced the Romans. 2. the language of the ancient Etruscans. ~adj. 3. of or relating to Etruria, the Etruscans, their culture, or their language.

-ette suffix of nouns. 1. small: *cigarette.* 2. female: *majorette.* 3. (esp. in trade names) imitation: *Leatherette.*

étude ('eɪtjuːd) n. a short musical composition for a solo instrument, esp. one designed as an exercise or exploiting virtuosity.

ety., etym., or etymol. abbrev. for: 1. etymological. 2. etymology.

etymology (,ɛtɪ'mɒlədʒɪ) n., pl. **-gies.** 1. the study of the sources and development of words. 2. an account of the source and development of a word. —**etymological** (,ɛtɪmə'lɒdʒɪkəl) *adj.* —**,ety'mologist** n. —**,ety'mologize** or **-ise** vb.

Eu the chemical symbol for europium.

eu- prefix. well, pleasant, or good: *eupeptic; euphony.*

eucalyptus (,juːkə'lɪptəs) or **eucalypt** ('juːkə,lɪpt) n., pl. **-lyptuses, -lypti** (-'lɪptaɪ), or **-lypts.** any tree of the mostly Australian genus *Eucalyptus,* widely cultivated for timber, gum, as ornament, and for the medicinal oil in their leaves (**eucalyptus oil**).

Eucharist ('juːkərɪst) n. 1. the Christian sacrament in which Christ's Last Supper is commemorated by the consecration of bread and wine. 2. the consecrated elements of bread and wine offered in the sacrament. —**,Eucha'ristic** or **,Eucha'ristical** *adj.*

Euclidean or **Euclidian** (juː'klɪdɪən) *adj.* denoting a system of geometry based on the axioms of Euclid, 3rd century B.C. Greek mathematician, esp. upon the axiom that parallel lines meet at infinity.

eugenics (juː'dʒɛnɪks) n. (functioning as sing.) the study of methods of improving the quality of the human race, esp. by selective breeding. —**eu'genic** *adj.* —**eu'genically** *adv.* —**eu'genicist** n.

eulogize or **-ise** ('juːlə,dʒaɪz) vb. to praise (a person or thing) highly in speech or writing. —**'eulogist, 'eulo,gizer,** or **-iser** n. —**,eulo'gistic** or **,eulo'gistical** *adj.*

eulogy ('juːlədʒɪ) n., pl. **-gies.** 1. a speech or piece of writing praising a person or thing, esp. a person who has recently died. 2. high praise or commendation. ~Also called (archaic): **eulogium** (juː'ləʊdʒɪəm).

eunuch ('juːnək) n. 1. a man who has been castrated, esp. (formerly) for some office such as a guard in a harem. 2. Inf. an ineffective man.

euphemism ('juːfɪ,mɪzəm) n. 1. an inoffensive word or phrase substituted for one considered offensive or hurtful. 2. the use of such inoffensive words or phrases. —**'euphemist** n. —**,euphe'mistic** *adj.* —**,euphe'mistically** *adv.*

euphonic (juː'fɒnɪk) or **euphonious** (juː'fəʊnɪəs) *adj.* 1. denoting or relating to euphony; pleasing to the ear. 2. (of speech sounds) altered for ease of pronunciation. —**eu'phonically** or **eu'phoniously** *adv.* —**eu'phoniousness** n.

euphonium (juː'fəʊnɪəm) n. a brass musical instrument with four valves.

THESAURUS

ethical conscientious, correct, decent, fair, fitting, good, honest, honourable, just, moral, principled, proper, right, righteous, upright, virtuous

ethics conscience, moral code, morality, moral philosophy, moral values, principles, rules of conduct, standards

ethnic cultural, indigenous, national, native, racial, traditional

etiquette civility, code, convention, courtesy, customs, decorum, formalities, good or proper behaviour, manners, politeness, politesse, propriety, protocol, rules, usage

eulogize acclaim, applaud, commend, compliment, cry up, exalt, extol, glorify, laud, magnify (Archaic), panegyrize, pay

tribute to, praise, sing or sound the praises of

eulogy acclaim, acclamation, accolade, applause, commendation, compliment, encomium, exaltation, glorification, laudation, paean, panegyric, plaudit, praise, tribute

euphony ('ju:fənɪ) *n., pl.* **-nies.** **1.** the alteration of speech sounds, esp. by assimilation, so as to make them easier to pronounce. **2.** a pleasing sound, esp. in speech.

euphoria (ju:'fɔːrɪə) *n.* a feeling of great elation, esp. when exaggerated. —**euphoric** (ju:'forɪk) *adj.*

euphuism ('ju:fju:ˌɪzəm) *n.* **1.** an artificial prose style of the Elizabethan period, marked by extreme use of antithesis, alliteration, and extended similes and allusions. **2.** any stylish affectation in speech or writing. —'**euphuist** *n.* —ˌeuphu'istic *or* ˌeuphu'istical *adj.* —ˌeuphu'istically *adv.*

Eur. *abbrev. for* Europe(an).

Eur- *combining form.* variant of **Euro-** before a vowel.

Eurasian (juə'reɪʃən, -ʒən) *adj.* **1.** of or relating to Europe and Asia considered as a whole. **2.** of mixed European and Asian descent. ~*n.* **3.** a person of mixed European and Asian descent.

Euratom (juə'rætəm) *n.* short for **European Atomic Energy Commission;** an authority established by the Common Market to develop peaceful uses of nuclear energy.

eureka (ju'ri:kə) *interj.* an exclamation of triumph on discovering or solving something.

eurhythmics *or esp. U.S.* **eurythmics** (ju:'rɪðmɪks) *n. (functioning as sing.)* **1.** a system of training through physical movement to music. **2.** dancing of this style. —eu'rhythmy *or* eu'rythmy *n.*

Euro- ('juərəʊ-) *or before a vowel* **Eur-** *combining form.* Europe or European.

Eurodollar ('juərəʊˌdɒlə) *n.* a U.S. dollar as part of a European holding.

European (ˌjuərə'pɪən) *adj.* **1.** of or relating to Europe or its inhabitants. **2.** native to or derived from Europe. ~*n.* **3.** a native or inhabitant of Europe. **4.** a person of European descent. **5.** *S. African.* any white person. —ˌEuro'peanism *n.*

europium (ju'rəʊpɪəm) *n.* a silvery-white element of the lanthanide series of metals. Symbol: Eu; atomic no.: 63; atomic wt.: 151.96.

eurythmics (ju:'rɪðmɪks) *n.* a variant spelling (esp. U.S.) of **eurhythmics.**

Eustachian tube (ju:'steɪʃən) *n.* a tube that connects the middle ear with the pharynx and equalizes the pressure between the two sides of the eardrum.

euthanasia (ˌju:θə'neɪzɪə) *n.* the act of killing someone painlessly, esp. to relieve suffering from an incurable illness.

eV *abbrev. for* electronvolt.

evacuate (ɪ'vækjʊˌeɪt) *vb. (mainly tr.)* **1.** *(also intr.)* to withdraw or cause to withdraw (from a place of danger) to a place of safety. **2.** to make empty. **3.** *(also intr.) Physiol.* **a.** to eliminate or excrete (faeces). **b.** to discharge (any waste) from (the body). **4.** *(tr.)* to create a vacuum in (a bulb, flask, etc.). —eˌvacu'ation *n.* —e'vacuative *adj.* —e'vacuˌator *n.* —eˌvacu'ee *n.*

evade (ɪ'veɪd) *vb. (mainly tr.)* **1.** to get away from or avoid (imprisonment, captors, etc.). **2.** to get around, shirk, or dodge (the law, a duty, etc.). **3.** *(also intr.)* to avoid answering (a question). —e'vadable *adj.* —e'vader *n.* —e'vadingly *adv.*

evaluate (ɪ'væljʊˌeɪt) *vb. (tr.)* **1.** to ascertain or set the amount or value of. **2.** to judge or assess the worth of. —eˌvalu'ation *n.* —e'valuative *adj.* —e'valuˌator *n.*

evanesce (ˌevə'nes) *vb. (intr.)* (of smoke, mist, etc.) to fade gradually from sight; vanish.

evanescent (ˌevə'nesənt) *adj.* **1.** passing out of sight; fading away; vanishing. **2.** ephemeral or transitory. —ˌeva'nescence *n.*

evangel (ɪ'vændʒəl) *n.* **1.** *Arch.* the gospel of Christianity. **2.** *(often cap.)* any of the four Gospels of the New Testament. **3.** any body of teachings regarded as basic.

evangelical (ˌi:væn'dʒelɪkəl) *Christianity. adj.* **1.** of or following from the Gospels. **2.** denoting or relating to any of certain Protestant sects, which emphasize personal conversion and faith in atonement through the death of Christ as a means of salvation. **3.** denoting or relating to an evangelist. **4.** a member of an evangelical sect. —ˌevan'gelicalism *n.*

evangelism (ɪ'vændʒɪˌlɪzəm) *n.* **1.** the practice of spreading the Christian gospel. **2.** ardent or missionary zeal for a cause.

evangelist (ɪ'vændʒɪlɪst) *n.* **1.** an occasional preacher, sometimes itinerant. **2.** a preacher of the Christian gospel. —eˌvange'listic *adj.*

Evangelist (ɪ'vændʒɪlɪst) *n.* any of the writers of the New Testament Gospels: Matthew, Mark, Luke, or John.

evangelize *or* **-ise** (ɪ'vændʒɪˌlaɪz) *vb.* **1.** to preach the Christian gospel (to). **2.** *(intr.)* to advocate a cause with the object of making converts. —eˌvangeli'zation *or* **-i'sation** *n.* —e'vangeˌlizer *or* **-iser** *n.*

evaporate (ɪ'væpəˌreɪt) *vb.* **1.** to change or cause to change from a liquid or solid state to a vapour. **2.** to lose or cause to lose liquid by vaporization leaving a more concentrated residue. **3.** to disappear or cause to disappear. —e'vaporable *adj.* —eˌvapora'bility *n.* —eˌvapo'ration *n.* —e'vaporative *adj.* —e'vapoˌrator *n.*

evaporated milk *n.* thick unsweetened tinned milk from which some of the water has been evaporated.

evasion (ɪ'veɪʒən) *n.* **1.** the act of evading, esp. a distasteful duty, responsibility, etc., by cunning or by illegal means: *tax evasion.* **2.** cunning or deception used to dodge a question, duty, etc.; means of evading.

evasive (ɪ'veɪsɪv) *adj.* **1.** tending or seeking to evade; not straightforward. **2.** avoiding or seeking to avoid trouble or difficulties. **3.** hard to catch or obtain; elusive. —e'vasively *adv.* —e'vasiveness *n.*

eve (i:v) *n.* **1.** the evening or day before some special event. **2.** the period immediately before an event: *the eve of war.* **3.** an archaic word for **evening.**

even[1] ('i:vən) *adj.* **1.** level and regular; flat. **2.** *(postpositive;* foll. by *with)* on the same level or in the same plane (as). **3.** without variation or fluctuation; regular; constant. **4.** not readily moved or excited; calm: *an even temper.* **5.** equally balanced between two sides: *an even game.* **6.** equal or identical in number, quantity, etc. **7. a.** (of a number) divisible by two. **b.** characterized or indicated by such a number: *the even pages.* **8.** relating to or denoting two or either of two alternatives, events, etc., that have an equal probability: *an even chance of missing or catching a train.* **9.** having no balance of debt; neither owing nor being owed. **10.** just and impartial; fair. **11.** exact in number, amount, or extent: *an even pound.* **12.** equal, as in score; level. **13. even money. a.** a bet that wins an identical sum if it succeeds. **b.** *(as modifier):* the even-money favourite. **14. get even (with).** *Inf.* to exact revenge (on). ~*adv.* **15.** (intensifier; used to suggest that the content of a statement is unexpected or paradoxical): *even an idiot can do that.* **16.**

THESAURUS

euphoria bliss, ecstasy, elation, exaltation, exhilaration, exultation, glee, high spirits, intoxication, joy, joyousness, jubilation, rapture, transport

evacuate 1. abandon, clear, decamp, depart, desert, forsake, leave, move out, pull out, quit, relinquish, remove, vacate, withdraw 2. defecate, discharge, eject, eliminate, empty, excrete, expel, void

evade 1. avoid, circumvent, decline, dodge, duck, elude, escape, escape the clutches of, get away from, shirk, shun, sidestep, steer clear of 2. balk, circumvent, cop out (*Sl.*), equivocate, fence, fend off, fudge, hedge, parry, prevaricate, quibble, waffle (*Inf.*)

evaluate appraise, assay, assess, calculate, estimate, gauge, judge, rank, rate, reckon, size up (*Inf.*), value, weigh

evaluation appraisal, assessment, calculation, estimate, estimation, judgment, opinion, rating, valuation

evanescent brief, ephemeral, fading, fleeting, fugacious, fugitive, impermanent, momentary, passing, short-lived, transient, transitory, vanishing

evangelical, evangelistic crusading, missionary, propagandizing, proselytizing, zealous

evaporate 1. dehydrate, desiccate, dry, dry up, vaporize 2. dematerialize, disappear, dispel, disperse, dissipate, dissolve, evanesce, fade, fade away, melt, melt away, vanish

evaporation 1. dehydration, desiccation, drying, drying up, vaporization 2. dematerialization, disappearance, dispelling, dispersal, dissipation, dissolution, evanescence, fading, fading away, melting, melting away, vanishing

evasion artifice, avoidance, circumvention, cop-out (*Sl.*), cunning, dodge, elusion, equivocation, escape, evasiveness, excuse, fudging, obliqueness, pretext, prevarication, ruse, shift, shirking, shuffling, sophism, sophistry, subterfuge, trickery, waffle (*Inf.*)

evasive cagey (*Inf.*), casuistic, casuistical, cunning, deceitful, deceptive, devious, dissembling, elusive, elusory, equivocating, indirect, misleading, oblique, prevaricating, shifty, shuffling, slippery, sophistical, tricky

eve 1. day before, night before, vigil 2. brink, edge, point, threshold, verge

(intensifier; used with comparative forms): *even better.* **17.** notwithstanding; in spite of. **18.** used to introduce a more precise version of a word, phrase, or statement: *he is base, even depraved.* **19.** used preceding a clause of supposition or hypothesis to emphasize that whether or not the condition in it is fulfilled, the statement in the main clause remains valid: *even if she died he wouldn't care.* **20.** *Arch.* all the way; fully: *I love thee even unto death.* **21. even as.** (*conj.*) at the very same moment or in the very same way that. **22. even so.** in spite of any assertion to the contrary: nevertheless. ~See also **even out, even up.** —'**evener** *n.* —'**evenly** *adv.* —'**evenness** *n.*

even² ('i:vən) *n.* an archaic word for **eve** or **evening.**

even-handed *adj.* fair; impartial. —,**even-'handedly** *adv.* —,**even-'handedness** *n.*

evening ('i:vnɪŋ) *n.* **1.** the latter part of the day, esp. from late afternoon until nightfall. **2.** the latter or concluding period: *the evening of one's life.* **3.** the early part of the night spent in a specified way: *an evening at the theatre.* **4.** (*modifier*) of, used in, or occurring in the evening: *the evening papers.*

evening dress *n.* attire for a formal occasion during the evening.

evening primrose *n.* any plant of an American genus typically having yellow flowers that open in the evening.

evenings ('i:vnɪŋz) *adv. Inf.* in the evening, esp. regularly.

evening star *n.* a planet, usually Venus, seen shining brightly in the west just after sunset.

even out *vb.* (*adv.*) to make or become even, as by the removal of bumps, inequalities, etc.

evens ('i:vənz) *adj., adv.* **1.** (of a bet) winning an identical sum if successful. **2.** (of a runner) offered at such odds.

evensong ('i:vən,sɒŋ) *n.* **1.** Also called: **Evening Prayer.** *Church of England.* the daily evening service. **2.** *Chiefly R.C. Church.* another name for **vespers.**

event (ɪ'vɛnt) *n.* **1.** anything that takes place, esp. something important; an incident. **2.** the actual or final outcome (esp. in **in the event, after the event**). **3.** any one contest in a programme of sporting or other contests. **4. at all events** *or* **in any event.** regardless of circumstances; in any case. **5. in the event of.** in case of; if (such a thing) happens. **6. in the event that.** if it should happen that.

eventful (ɪ'vɛntfʊl) *adj.* full of events. —e'**ventfully** *adv.* —e'**ventfulness** *n.*

eventide ('i:vən,taɪd) *n. Arch. or poetic.* another word for **evening.**

eventing (ɪ'vɛntɪŋ) *n. Chiefly Brit.* the sport of taking part in equestrian competitions (esp. **three-day events**), usually involving cross-country riding, jumping, and dressage.

eventual (ɪ'vɛntʃʊəl) *adj.* **1.** (*prenominal*) happening in due course of time; ultimate. **2.** *Arch.* contingent or possible. —e'**ventually** *adv.*

eventuality (ɪ,vɛntʃʊ'ælɪtɪ) *n., pl.* **-ties.** a possible event, occurrence, or result; contingency.

eventuate (ɪ'vɛntʃʊ,eɪt) *vb.* (*intr.*) **1.** (often foll. by *in*) to result ultimately (in). **2.** to come about as a result. —e,ventu'**ation** *n.*

even up *vb.* (*adv.*) to make or become equal, esp. in respect of claims or debts.

ever ('ɛvə) *adv.* **1.** at any time. **2.** by any chance; in any case: *how did you ever find out?* **3.** at all times; always. **4.** in any possible way or manner: *come as fast as ever you can.* **5.** *Inf.*, *chiefly Brit.* (intensifier, in **ever so, ever such,** and **ever such a**). **6. is he** *or* **she ever!** *U.S. sl.* he *or* she displays the quality concerned in abundance. ~See also **for ever.**

evergreen ('ɛvə,gri:n) *adj.* **1.** (of certain trees and shrubs) bearing foliage throughout the year. Cf. **deciduous. 2.** remaining fresh and vital. ~*n.* **3.** an evergreen tree or shrub.

everlasting (,ɛvə'lɑ:stɪŋ) *adj.* **1.** never coming to an end; eternal. **2.** lasting for an indefinitely long period. **3.** lasting so long or occurring so often as to become tedious. ~*n.* **4.** eternity. **5.** Also called: **everlasting flower.** a plant whose blossoms keep their colour and shape when dried. —,**ever'lastingly** *adv.*

evermore (,ɛvə'mɔ:) *adv.* (often preceded by *for*) all time to come.

every ('ɛvrɪ) *determiner.* **1.** each one (of the class specified), without exception. **2.** (*not used with a negative*) the greatest or best possible: *every hope.* **3.** each: used before a noun phrase to indicate the recurrent, intermittent, or serial nature of a thing: *every third day.* **4. every bit.** (used in comparisons with *as*) quite; just; equally. **5. every other.** each alternate; every second. **6. every which way.** *U.S.* **a.** in all directions; everywhere. **b.** from all sides.

everybody ('ɛvrɪ,bɒdɪ) *pron.* every person; everyone. ▷ **Usage.** See at **everyone.**

everyday ('ɛvrɪ,deɪ) *adj.* **1.** happening each day. **2.** commonplace or usual. **3.** suitable for or used on ordinary days.

Everyman ('ɛvrɪ,mæn) *n.* **1.** a medieval English morality play in which the central figure represents man-

---

even *adj.* **1.** flat, flush, horizontal, level, parallel, plane, plumb, smooth, steady, straight, true, uniform **2.** constant, metrical, regular, smooth, steady, unbroken, uniform, uninterrupted, unvarying, unwavering **3.** calm, composed, cool, equable, equanimous, eventempered, imperturbable, peaceful, placid, serene, stable, steady, tranquil, undisturbed, unexcitable, unruffled, well-balanced **4.** coequal, commensurate, comparable, drawn, equal, equalized, equally balanced, fifty-fifty (*Inf.*), identical, level, level pegging (*Brit. inf.*), like, matching, neck and neck, on a par, parallel, similar, square, the same, tied, uniform **5.** balanced, disinterested, dispassionate, equitable, fair, fair and square, impartial, just, unbiased, unprejudiced **6. get even** (**with**) *Inf.* be revenged *or* revenge oneself, even the score, give tit for tat, pay back, reciprocate, repay, requite, return like for like, settle the score, take an eye for an eye, take vengeance ~*adv.* **7.** all the more, much, still, yet **8.** despite, disregarding, in spite of, notwithstanding **9. even as** at the same time as, at the time that, during the time that, exactly as, just as, while, whilst **10. even so all** the same, be that as it may, despite (that), however, in spite of (that), nevertheless, nonetheless, notwithstanding (that), still, yet ~*v.* **11.** *Often followed by* out *or* up align, balance, become level, equal, equalize, flatten, level, match, regularize, smooth, square, stabilize, steady **12. even the score** be re-venged *or* revenge oneself, equalize, get even (*Inf.*), give tit for tat, pay (someone) back, reciprocate, repay, requite, return like for like, settle the score, take an eye for an eye, take vengeance

even-handed balanced, disinterested, equitable, fair, fair and square, impartial, just, unbiased, unprejudiced

event **1.** adventure, affair, business, circumstance, episode, experience, fact, happening, incident, matter, milestone, occasion, occurrence **2.** conclusion, consequence, effect, end, issue, outcome, result, termination, upshot **3.** bout, competition, contest, game, tournament **4. at all events** at any rate, come what may, in any case, in any event, regardless, whatever happens

even-tempered calm, composed, cool, cool-headed, equable, imperturbable, levelheaded, peaceful, placid, serene, steady, tranquil, unexcitable, unruffled

eventful active, busy, consequential, critical, crucial, decisive, exciting, fateful, full, historic, important, lively, memorable, momentous, notable, noteworthy, remarkable, significant

eventual concluding, consequent, ensuing, final, future, later, overall, prospective, resulting, ultimate

eventuality case, chance, contingency, event, likelihood, possibility, probability

eventually after all, at the end of the day, finally, in the course of time, in the end,

in the long run, one day, some day, some time, sooner or later, ultimately, when all is said and done

ever **1.** at all, at any time (period, point), by any chance, in any case, on any occasion **2.** always, at all times, constantly, continually, endlessly, eternally, everlastingly, evermore, for ever, incessantly, perpetually, relentlessly, to the end of time, unceasingly, unendingly

everlasting **1.** abiding, deathless, endless, eternal, immortal, imperishable, indestructible, infinite, interminable, never-ending, perpetual, timeless, undying **2.** ceaseless, constant, continual, continuous, endless, incessant, interminable, never-ending, unceasing, uninterrupted, unremitting

evermore always, eternally, ever, for ever, *in perpetuum*, to the end of time

every all, each, each one, the whole number

everybody all and sundry, each one, each person, everyone, every person, one and all, the whole world

everyday **1.** daily, quotidian **2.** accustomed, common, common or garden (*Inf.*), commonplace, conventional, customary, dull, familiar, frequent, habitual, informal, mundane, ordinary, routine, run-of-the-mill, stock, unexceptional, unimaginative, usual, wonted, workaday

kind. **2.** (*often not cap.*) the ordinary person; common man.

every one *pron.* each person or thing in a group, without exception.

everyone ('ɛvrɪ‚wʌn, -wən) *pron.* every person; everybody.

▷ **Usage.** *Everybody, everyone, none, no one, nobody, somebody, someone,* and *each* function as singular in careful English: *everyone nodded his head* (not *their heads*). The use of *their* in such constructions is, however, common in informal English.

everything ('ɛvrɪ‚θɪŋ) *pron.* **1.** the entirety of a specified or implied class. **2.** a great deal, esp. of something very important.

everywhere ('ɛvrɪ‚wɛə) *adv.* to or in all parts or places.

evict (ɪ'vɪkt) *vb.* (*tr.*) **1.** to expel (a tenant) from property by process of law. **2.** to recover (property or the title to property) by judicial process or by virtue of a superior title. —e'**viction** *n.* —e'**victor** *n.*

evidence ('ɛvɪdəns) *n.* **1.** ground for belief or disbelief; data on which to base proof or to establish truth or falsehood. **2.** a mark or sign that makes evident. **3.** *Law.* matter produced before a court of law in an attempt to prove or disprove a point in issue. **4. turn queen's (king's, state's) evidence.** (of an accomplice) to act as witness for the prosecution and testify against those associated with him in crime. **5. in evidence.** on display; apparent. ~*vb.* (*tr.*) **6.** to make evident; show clearly. **7.** to give proof of or evidence for.

evident ('ɛvɪdənt) *adj.* easy to see or understand; apparent. —'**evidently** *adv.*

evidential (‚ɛvɪ'dɛnʃəl) *adj.* relating to, serving as, or based on evidence. —‚evi'**dentially** *adv.*

evil ('iːvəl) *adj.* **1.** morally wrong or bad; wicked. **2.** causing harm or injury. **3.** marked or accompanied by misfortune: *an evil fate.* **4.** (of temper, disposition, etc.) characterized by anger or spite. **5.** infamous: *an evil reputation.* **6.** offensive or unpleasant: *an evil smell.* ~*n.* **7.** the quality or an instance of being morally wrong; wickedness. **8.** (*sometimes cap.*) a force or power that brings about wickedness or harm. ~*adv.* **9.** (*now usually in combination*) in an evil manner; badly: *evil-smelling.* —'**evilly** *adv.* —'**evilness** *n.*

evildoer ('iːvəl‚duːə) *n.* a person who does evil. —'**evil‚doing** *n.*

evil eye *n.* **the. 1.** a look or glance superstitiously supposed to have the power of inflicting harm or injury. **2.** the power to inflict harm, etc., by such a look. —‚evil-'**eyed** *adj.*

evince (ɪ'vɪns) *vb.* (*tr.*) to make evident; show (something) clearly. —e'**vincible** *adj.* —e'**vincive** *adj.*

eviscerate (ɪ'vɪsə‚reɪt) *vb.* **1.** (*tr.*) to remove the internal organs of; disembowel. **2.** (*tr.*) to deprive of meaning or significance. —e‚viscer'**ation** *n.* —e'**viscer‚ator** *n.*

evocation (‚ɛvə'keɪʃən) *n.* the act or an instance of evoking. —**evocative** (ɪ'vɒkətɪv) *adj.*

evoke (ɪ'vəʊk) *vb.* (*tr.*) **1.** to call or summon up (a memory, feeling, etc.), esp. from the past. **2.** to provoke; elicit. **3.** to cause (spirits) to appear; conjure up. —**evocable** ('ɛvəkəbəl) *adj.* —e'**voker** *n.*

evolution (‚iːvə'luːʃən) *n.* **1.** *Biol.* a gradual change in the characteristics of a population of animals or plants over successive generations. **2.** a gradual development, esp. to a more complex form: *the evolution of modern art.* **3.** the act of throwing off, as heat, gas, vapour, etc. **4.** a pattern formed by a series of movements or something similar. **5.** an algebraic operation in which the root of a number, expression, etc., is extracted. **6.** *Mil.* an exercise carried out in accordance with a set procedure or plan. —‚evo'**lutionary** *or* ‚evo'**lutional** *adj.*

evolutionist (‚iːvə'luːʃənɪst) *n.* **1.** a person who believes in a theory of evolution. ~*adj.* **2.** of or relating to a theory of evolution. —‚evo'**lutionism** *n.* —‚evolu-tion'**istic** *adj.*

evolve (ɪ'vɒlv) *vb.* **1.** to develop or cause to develop gradually. **2.** (of animal or plant species) to undergo evolution of (organs or parts). **3.** (*tr.*) to yield, emit, or give off (heat, gas, vapour, etc.). —e'**volvable** *adj.* —e'**volvement** *n.*

ewe (juː) *n.* **a.** a female sheep. **b.** (*as modifier*): *a ewe lamb.*

ewer ('juːə) *n.* a large jug or pitcher with a wide mouth.

ex[1] (ɛks) *prep.* **1.** *Finance.* excluding; without: *ex dividend.* **2.** *Commerce.* without charge to the buyer until removed from: *ex warehouse.*

ex[2] (ɛks) *n. Inf.* (a person's) former wife, husband, etc.

ex-[1] *prefix.* **1.** out of; outside of; from: *exclosure; exurbia.* **2.** former: *ex-wife.*

ex-[2] *combining form.* variant of **exo-** before a vowel: *exergonic.*

Ex. *Bible. abbrev. for* Exodus.

exacerbate (ɪg'zæsə‚beɪt, ɪk'sæs-) *vb.* (*tr.*) **1.** to make (pain, disease, etc.) more intense; aggravate. **2.** to irritate (a person). —ex'**acer‚batingly** *adv.* —ex‚acer'**bation** *n.*

exact (ɪg'zækt) *adj.* **1.** correct in every detail; strictly accurate. **2.** precise, as opposed to approximate. **3.** (*prenominal*) specific; particular. **4.** operating with very great precision. **5.** allowing no deviation from a standard; rigorous; strict. **6.** based on measurement and the formulation of laws, as opposed to description and classification: *an exact science.* ~*vb.* (*tr.*) **7.** to force or compel (payment, etc.); extort: *to exact tribute.* **8.** to demand as a right; insist upon. **9.** to call for or require. —ex'**actable** *adj.* —ex'**actness** *n.* —ex'**actor** *or* ex'**acter** *n.*

exacting (ɪg'zæktɪŋ) *adj.* making rigorous or excessive demands. —ex'**actingness** *n.*

THESAURUS

everyone all and sundry, each one, each person, everybody, every person, one and all, the whole world

everything all, each thing, the aggregate, the entirety, the lot, the sum, the total, the whole caboodle (*Inf.*), the whole lot

everywhere all around, all over, far and wide *or* near, high and low, in each place, in every place, omnipresent, the world over, to *or* in all places, ubiquitous, ubiquitously

evict boot out (*Inf.*), chuck out (*Inf.*), dislodge, dispossess, eject, expel, kick out (*Inf.*), oust, put out, remove, show the door (to), throw on to the streets, throw out, turf out (*Inf.*), turn out

eviction clearance, dislodgement, dispossession, ejection, expulsion, ouster (*Law*), removal

evidence **1.** *n.* affirmation, attestation, averment, confirmation, corroboration, data, declaration, demonstration, deposition, grounds, indication, manifestation, mark, proof, sign, substantiation, testimony, token, witness **2.** *v.* demonstrate, denote, display, evince, exhibit, indicate, manifest, prove, reveal, show, signify, testify to, witness

evident apparent, clear, conspicuous, incontestable, incontrovertible, indisputable, manifest, noticeable, obvious, palpable, patent, perceptible, plain, tangible, unmistakable, visible

evidently **1.** clearly, doubtless, doubtlessly, incontestably, incontrovertibly, indisputably, manifestly, obviously, patently, plainly, undoubtedly, unmistakably, without question **2.** apparently, it seems, it would seem, ostensibly, outwardly, seemingly, to all appearances

evil *adj.* **1.** bad, base, corrupt, depraved, heinous, immoral, iniquitous, maleficent, malevolent, malicious, malignant, nefarious, reprobate, sinful, vicious, vile, villainous, wicked, wrong ~*n.* **2.** badness, baseness, corruption, curse, depravity, heinousness, immorality, iniquity, maleficence, malignity, sin, sinfulness, turpitude, vice, viciousness, villainy, wickedness, wrong, wrongdoing ~*adj.* **3.** baneful (*Archaic*), calamitous, catastrophic, deleterious, destructive, detrimental, dire, disastrous, harmful, hurtful, inauspicious, injurious, mischievous, painful, pernicious, ruinous, sorrowful, unfortunate, unlucky, woeful ~*n.* **4.** affliction, calamity, ca-

tastrophe, disaster, harm, hurt, ill, injury, mischief, misery, misfortune, pain, ruin, sorrow, suffering, woe ~*adj.* **5.** foul, mephitic, noxious, offensive, pestilential, putrid, unpleasant, vile

evoke **1.** arouse, awaken, call, excite, give rise to, induce, recall, rekindle, stimulate, stir up, summon up **2.** call forth, educe (*Rare*), elicit, produce, provoke **3.** arouse, call, call forth, conjure up, invoke, raise, summon

evolution development, enlargement, evolvement, expansion, growth, increase, maturation, progress, progression, unfolding, unrolling, working out

evolve develop, disclose, educe, elaborate, enlarge, expand, grow, increase, mature, open, progress, unfold, unroll, work out

exact *adj.* **1.** accurate, careful, correct, definite, explicit, express, faithful, faultless, identical, literal, methodical, orderly, particular, precise, right, specific, true, unequivocal, unerring, veracious, very **2.** careful, exacting, meticulous, painstaking, punctilious, rigorous, scrupulous, severe, strict ~*v.* **3.** call for, claim, command, compel, demand, extort, extract, force, impose, insist

exaction (ɪgˈzækʃən) *n.* **1.** the act or an instance of ex-acting. **2.** an excessive or harsh demand, esp. for mon-ey. **3.** a sum or payment exacted.

exactitude (ɪgˈzæktɪˌtjuːd) *n.* the quality of being exact; precision; accuracy.

exactly (ɪgˈzæktlɪ) *adv.* **1.** in an exact manner; accu-rately or precisely. **2.** in every respect; just. *~interj.* **3.** just so!, precisely! **4. not exactly.** *Ironical.* not at all; by no means.

exaggerate (ɪgˈzædʒəˌreɪt) *vb.* **1.** to regard or repre-sent as larger or greater, more important or more suc-cessful, etc., than is true. **2.** (*tr.*) to make greater, more noticeable, etc. —**exˈaggerˌatingly** *adv.* —**exˌaggerˈation** *n.* —**exˈaggerative** *or* **exˈaggeratory** *adj.* —**exˈaggerˌated** *adj.* —**exˈaggerˌator** *n.*

exalt (ɪgˈzɔːlt) *vb.* (*tr.*) **1.** to elevate in rank, dignity, etc. **2.** to praise highly; extol. **3.** to stimulate; excite. **4.** to fill with joy or delight; elate. —**exˈalted** *adj.* —**exˈalter** *n.* —ˌexalˈtation *n.*

exam (ɪgˈzæm) *n.* short for **examination** (sense 2).

examination (ɪgˌzæmɪˈneɪʃən) *n.* **1.** the act of examin-ing or state of being examined. **2.** *Education.* **a.** written exercises, oral questions, etc., set to test a candidate's knowledge and skill. **b.** (*as modifier*): *an examination paper.* **3.** *Med.* **a.** physical inspection of a patient. **b.** la-boratory study of secretory or excretory products, tissue samples, etc. **4.** *Law.* the formal interrogation of a per-son on oath. —**exˌamiˈnational** *adj.*

examine (ɪgˈzæmɪn) *vb.* (*tr.*) **1.** to inspect or scrutinize carefully or in detail; investigate. **2.** *Education.* to test the knowledge or skill of (a candidate) in (a subject or activity) by written or oral questions, etc. **3.** *Law.* to in-terrogate (a person) formally on oath. **4.** *Med.* to inves-tigate the state of health of (a patient). —**exˈaminable** *adj.* —**exˌamiˈnee** *n.* —**exˈaminer** *n.*

example (ɪgˈzɑːmpəl) *n.* **1.** a specimen or instance that is typical of its group or set; sample. **2.** a person, action, thing, etc., that is worthy of imitation; pattern. **3.** a prec-edent, illustration of a principle, or model. **4.** a punish-ment or the recipient of a punishment intended to serve as a warning. **5. for example.** as an illustration; for in-stance. *~vb.* **6.** (*tr.; now usually passive*) to present an example of; exemplify.

exasperate (ɪgˈzɑːspəˌreɪt) *vb.* (*tr.*) **1.** to cause great irritation or anger to. **2.** to cause (something unpleas-ant) to worsen; aggravate. —**exˈasperˌatedly** *adv.* —**exˈasperˌater** *n.* —**exˈasperˌatingly** *adv.* —**exˌas-perˈation** *n.*

ex cathedra (ɛks kəˈθiːdrə) *adj., adv.* **1.** with authority. **2.** *R.C. Church.* (of doctrines of faith or morals) defined by the pope as infallibly true, to be accepted by all Catholics.

excavate (ˈɛkskəˌveɪt) *vb.* **1.** to remove (soil, earth, etc.) by digging; dig out. **2.** to make (a hole or tunnel) in (solid matter) by hollowing. **3.** to unearth (buried ob-jects) methodically to discover information about the past. —ˌexcaˈvation *n.* —ˈexcaˌvator *n.*

exceed (ɪkˈsiːd) *vb.* **1.** to be superior to; excel. **2.** (*tr.*) to go beyond the limit or bounds of. **3.** to be greater in degree or quantity than. —**exˈceedable** *adj.* —**exˈceed-er** *n.*

exceeding (ɪkˈsiːdɪŋ) *adj.* **1.** very great; exceptional or excessive. *~adv.* **2.** *Arch.* to a great or unusual degree. —**exˈceedingly** *adv.*

excel (ɪkˈsɛl) *vb.* **-celling, -celled. 1.** to be superior to (another or others); surpass. **2.** (*intr.; foll.* by *in* or *at*) to be outstandingly good or proficient.

excellence (ˈɛksələns) *n.* **1.** the state or quality of ex-celling or being exceptionally good; extreme merit. **2.** an action, feature, etc., in which a person excels. —ˈex-cellent *adj.* —ˈexcellently *adv.*

Excellency (ˈɛksələnsɪ) *or* **Excellence** *n., pl.* **-lencies** *or* **-lences. 1.** (usually preceded by *Your, His,* or *Her*) a title used to address or refer to a high-ranking

upon, require, squeeze, wrest, wring

exacting demanding, difficult, hard, harsh, imperious, oppressive, painstaking, rigid, rigorous, severe, stern, strict, strin-gent, taxing, tough, unsparing

exactly *adv.* **1.** accurately, carefully, cor-rectly, definitely, explicitly, faithfully, fault-lessly, literally, methodically, precisely, rig-orously, scrupulously, severely, strictly, tru-ly, truthfully, unequivocally, unerringly, ve-raciously **2.** absolutely, bang, explicitly, ex-pressly, indeed, in every respect, just, par-ticularly, precisely, quite, specifically **3. not exactly** *Ironical* by no means, certainly not, hardly, in no manner, in no way, not at all, not by any means, not quite, not really *~interj.* **4.** absolutely, assuredly, as you say, certainly, indeed, just so, of course, precise-ly, quite, quite so, spot-on (*Inf.*), truly

exactness accuracy, carefulness, cor-rectness, exactitude, faithfulness, faultless-ness, nicety, orderliness, painstakingness, preciseness, precision, promptitude, regular-ity, rigorousness, rigour, scrupulousness, strictness, truth, unequivocalness, veracity

exaggerate amplify, embellish, embroi-der, emphasize, enlarge, exalt, hyperbolize, inflate, lay it on thick (*Inf.*), magnify, overdo, overemphasize, overestimate, overstate

exaggerated amplified, exalted, exces-sive, extravagant, highly coloured, hyperbol-ic, inflated, overblown, overdone, overesti-mated, overstated, pretentious, tall (*Inf.*)

exaggeration amplification, embellish-ment, emphasis, enlargement, exaltation, ex-cess, extravagance, hyperbole, inflation, magnification, overemphasis, overestima-tion, overstatement, pretension, pretentious-ness

exalt **1.** advance, aggrandize, dignify, el-evate, ennoble, honour, promote, raise, up-grade **2.** acclaim, apotheosize, applaud, bless, extol, glorify, idolize, laud, magnify (*Archa-ic*), pay homage to, pay tribute to, praise, reverence, set on a pedestal, worship **3.** ani-mate, arouse, electrify, elevate, excite, fire

the imagination (of), heighten, inspire, in-spirit, stimulate, uplift **4.** delight, elate, ex-hilarate, fill with joy, thrill

exaltation **1.** advancement, aggrandize-ment, dignity, elevation, eminence, ennoble-ment, grandeur, high rank, honour, loftiness, prestige, promotion, rise, upgrading **2.** ac-claim, acclamation, apotheosis, applause, blessing, extolment, glorification, glory, homage, idolization, laudation, lionization, magnification, panegyric, plaudits, praise, reverence, tribute, worship **3.** animation, elevation, excitement, inspiration, stimula-tion, uplift **4.** bliss, delight, ecstasy, elation, exhilaration, exultation, joy, joyousness, jubi-lation, rapture, transport

exalted **1.** august, dignified, elevated, emi-nent, grand, high, high-ranking, honoured, lofty, prestigious **2.** elevated, high-minded, ideal, intellectual, lofty, noble, sublime, su-perior, uplifting **3.** *Inf.* elevated, exaggerated, excessive, inflated, overblown, pretentious **4.** animated, blissful, ecstatic, elated, elevated, excited, exhilarated, exultant, in high spirits, in seventh heaven, inspired, inspirited, joy-ous, jubilant, on cloud nine (*Inf.*), rapturous, stimulated, transported, uplifted

examination analysis, assay, cat-echism, checkup, exploration, inquiry, inqui-sition, inspection, interrogation, investiga-tion, observation, perusal, probe, question-ing, quiz, research, review, scrutiny, search, study, survey, test, trial

examine **1.** analyse, appraise, assay, check, check out, consider, explore, go over or through, inspect, investigate, look over, peruse, ponder, pore over, probe, review, scan, scrutinize, sift, study, survey, take stock of, test, vet, weigh **2.** catechize, cross-examine, grill (*Inf.*), inquire, interrogate, question, quiz

example **1.** case, case in point, exemplifi-cation, illustration, instance, sample, speci-men **2.** archetype, exemplar, ideal, illustra-tion, model, paradigm, paragon, pattern, precedent, prototype, standard **3.** admoni-

tion, caution, lesson, warning **4. for example** as an illustration, by way of illustration, e.g., *exempli gratia*, for instance, to cite an in-stance, to illustrate

exasperate aggravate (*Inf.*), anger, an-noy, bug (*Inf.*), embitter, enrage, exacerbate, excite, gall, get (*Inf.*), incense, inflame, in-furiate, irk, irritate, madden, needle (*Inf.*), nettle, peeve (*Inf.*), pique, provoke, rankle, rile (*Inf.*), rouse, try the patience of, vex

exasperation aggravation (*Inf.*), anger, annoyance, exacerbation, fury, ire (*Liter-ary*), irritation, passion, pique, provocation, rage, vexation, wrath

excavate burrow, cut, delve, dig, dig out, dig up, gouge, hollow, mine, quarry, scoop, trench, tunnel, uncover, unearth

excavation burrow, cavity, cut, cutting, dig, diggings, ditch, dugout, hole, hollow, mine, pit, quarry, shaft, trench, trough

exceed **1.** beat, be superior to, better, cap (*Inf.*), eclipse, excel, go beyond, outdistance, outdo, outreach, outrun, outshine, outstrip, overtake, pass, surmount, surpass, top, trans-cend **2.** go beyond the bounds of, go over the limit of, go over the top, overstep

exceeding enormous, exceptional, ex-cessive, extraordinary, great, huge, pre-eminent, superior, superlative, surpassing, vast

exceedingly enormously, especially, exceptionally, excessively, extraordinarily, extremely, greatly, highly, hugely, inordi-nately, superlatively, surpassingly, unusually, vastly, very

excel **1.** beat, be superior, better, cap (*Inf.*), eclipse, exceed, go beyond, outdo, outrival, outshine, pass, surmount, surpass, top, trans-cend **2.** be good, be master of, be proficient, be skilful, be talented, predominate, shine, show talent, take precedence

excellence distinction, eminence, fine-ness, goodness, greatness, high quality, mer-it, perfection, pre-eminence, purity, superior-ity, supremacy, transcendence, virtue, worth

official, such as an ambassador. **2.** *R.C. Church.* a title of bishops and archbishops in many non-English-speaking countries.

except (ɪk'sɛpt) *prep.* **1.** Also: **except for.** other than; apart from. **2. except that.** (*conj.*) but for the fact that; were it not true that. ~*conj.* **3.** an archaic word for **unless. 4.** *Inf.; not standard in the U.S.* except that; but for the fact that. ~*vb.* **5.** (*tr.*) to leave out; omit; exclude. **6.** (*intr.; often foll. by* *to*) *Rare.* to take exception; object. —**ex'ceptable** *adj.*

excepting (ɪk'sɛptɪŋ) *prep.* **1.** except; except for (esp. in **not excepting**). ~*conj.* **2.** an archaic word for **unless.**

exception (ɪk'sɛpʃən) *n.* **1.** the act of excepting or fact of being excepted; omission. **2.** anything excluded from or not in conformance with a general rule, principle, class, etc. **3.** criticism, esp. adverse; objection. **4.** *Law.* (formerly) a formal objection in legal proceedings. **5. take exception. a.** (usually foll. by *to*) to make objections (to); demur (at). **b.** (often foll. by *at*) to be offended (by); be resentful (at).

exceptionable (ɪk'sɛpʃənəb'l) *adj.* open to or subject to objection; objectionable. —**ex'ceptionableness** *n.* —**ex'ceptionably** *adv.*

exceptional (ɪk'sɛpʃən'l) *adj.* **1.** forming an exception; not ordinary. **2.** having much more than average intelligence, ability, or skill.

excerpt *n.* ('ɛksɜːpt). **1.** a part or passage taken from a book, speech, etc.; extract. ~*vb.* (ɛk'sɜːpt). **2.** (*tr.*) to take (a part or passage) from a book, speech, etc. —**ex'cerpter** *or* **ex'cerptor** *n.* —**ex'cerptible** *adj.* —**ex'cerption** *n.*

excess *n.* (ɪk'sɛs, 'ɛksɛs). **1.** the state or act of going beyond normal, sufficient, or permitted limits. **2.** an immoderate or abnormal amount. **3.** the amount, number, etc. by which one thing exceeds another. **4.** overindulgence or intemperance. **5.** *Insurance, chiefly Brit.* a specified contribution towards the cost of a claim, payable by the policyholder. **6. in excess of.** of more than; over. **7. to excess.** to an inordinate extent; immoderately. ~*adj.* ('ɛksɛs, ɪk'sɛs). (*usually prenominal*) **8.** more than normal, necessary, or permitted; surplus: *excess weight.* **9.** payable as a result of previous underpayment: *excess postage.* —**ex'cessive** *adj.*

excess luggage *or* **baggage** *n.* luggage that is more in weight or number of pieces than an airline, etc. will carry free.

exchange (ɪks'tʃeɪndʒ) *vb.* **1.** (*tr.*) to give up or transfer (one thing) for an equivalent. **2.** (*tr.*) to give and receive (information, ideas, etc.); interchange. **3.** (*tr.*) to replace (one thing) with another, esp. to replace unsatisfactory goods. **4.** to hand over (goods) in return for the equivalent value in kind; barter; trade. ~*n.* **5.** the act or process of exchanging. **6. a.** anything given or received as an equivalent or substitute for something else. **b.** (*as modifier*): *an exchange student.* **7.** an argument or

quarrel. **8.** Also called: **telephone exchange.** a switching centre in which telephone lines are interconnected. **9.** a place where securities or commodities are sold, bought, or traded, esp. by brokers or merchants. **10. a.** the system by which commercial debts are settled by commercial documents, esp. bills of exchange, instead of by direct payment of money. **b.** the percentage or fee charged for accepting payment in this manner. **11.** a transfer or interchange of sums of money of equivalent value, as between different currencies. **12. win** (*or* **lose**) **the exchange.** *Chess.* to win (or lose) a rook in return for a bishop or knight. ~See also **bill of exchange, exchange rate, labour exchange.** —**ex'changeable** *adj.* —**ex,changea'bility** *n.* —**ex'changeably** *adv.* —**ex'changer** *n.*

exchange rate *n.* the rate at which the currency unit of one country may be exchanged for that of another.

exchequer (ɪks'tʃɛkə) *n.* **1.** (*often cap.*) *Government.* (in Britain and certain other countries) the accounting department of the Treasury. **2.** *Inf.* personal funds; finances.

excise[1] *n.* ('ɛksaɪz, ɛk'saɪz). **1.** Also called: **excise tax.** a tax on goods, such as spirits, produced for the home market. **2.** a tax paid for a licence to carry out various trades, sports, etc. **3.** *Brit.* that section of the government service responsible for the collection of excise, now the Board of Customs and Excise. ~*vb.* (ɪk'saɪz). **4.** (*tr.*) *Rare.* to compel (a person) to pay excise. —**excision** (ɛk'sɪʒən) *n.*

excise[2] (ɪk'saɪz) *vb.* (*tr.*) **1.** to delete (a passage, sentence, etc.). **2.** to remove (an organ or part) surgically.

exciseman ('ɛksaɪz,mæn) *n., pl.* **-men.** *Brit.* (formerly) a government agent whose function was to collect excise and prevent smuggling.

excitable (ɪk'saɪtəb'l) *adj.* **1.** easily excited; volatile. **2.** (esp. of a nerve) ready to respond to a stimulus. —**ex,cita'bility** *or* **ex'citableness** *n.*

excite (ɪk'saɪt) *vb.* (*tr.*) **1.** to arouse (a person), esp. to pleasurable anticipation or nervous agitation. **2.** to arouse or elicit (an emotion, response, etc.); evoke. **3.** to cause or bring about; stir up. **4.** to arouse sexually. **5.** *Physiol.* to cause a response in or increase the activity of (an organ, tissue, or part); stimulate. **6.** to raise (an atom, molecule, etc.) from the ground state to a higher energy level. **7.** to supply electricity to (the coils of a generator or motor) in order to create a magnetic field. —**ex'citant** *n.* —,**exci'tation** *n.* —**ex'citative** *or* **ex'citatory** *adj.* —**ex'citer** *or* **ex'citor** *n.*

excited (ɪk'saɪtɪd) *adj.* **1.** emotionally aroused, esp. to pleasure or agitation. **2.** characterized by excitement. **3.** sexually aroused. **4.** (of an atom, molecule, etc.) having an energy level above the ground state. —**ex'citedness** *n.*

excitement (ɪk'saɪtmənt) *n.* **1.** the state of being excited. **2.** a person or thing that excites.

exciting (ɪk'saɪtɪŋ) *adj.* causing excitement; stirring;

THESAURUS

excellent A1 (*Inf.*), admirable, capital, champion, choice, distinguished, estimable, exemplary, exquisite, fine, first-class, first-rate, good, great, meritorious, notable, noted, outstanding, prime, select, sterling, superb, superior, superlative, tiptop, top-notch (*Inf.*), worthy

except 1. prep. Also **except for** apart from, bar, barring, besides, but, excepting, excluding, exclusive of, omitting, other than, save (*Archaic*), saving, with the exception of **2. v.** ban, bar, disallow, exclude, leave out, omit, pass over, reject, rule out

exception 1. debarment, disallowment, excepting, exclusion, leaving out, omission, passing over, rejection **2.** anomaly, departure, deviation, freak, inconsistency, irregularity, oddity, peculiarity, quirk, special case **3. take exception** be offended, be resentful, demur, disagree, object, quibble, take offence, take umbrage

exceptional 1. aberrant, abnormal, anomalous, atypical, deviant, extraordinary, inconsistent, irregular, odd, peculiar, rare, singular, special, strange, uncommon, unusual **2.** excellent, extraordinary, marvellous, outstanding, phenomenal, prodigious,

remarkable, special, superior

excess *n.* **1.** glut, leftover, overabundance, overdose, overflow, overload, plethora, remainder, superabundance, superfluity, surfeit, surplus, too much **2.** debauchery, dissipation, dissoluteness, exorbitance, extravagance, immoderation, intemperance, overindulgence, prodigality, unrestraint ~*adj.* **3.** extra, leftover, redundant, remaining, residual, spare, superfluous, surplus

excessive disproportionate, enormous, exaggerated, exorbitant, extravagant, extreme, immoderate, inordinate, intemperate, needless, overdone, overmuch, prodigal, profligate, superfluous, too much, unconscionable, undue, unreasonable

exchange *v.* **1.** bandy, barter, change, commute, convert into, interchange, reciprocate, swap (*Inf.*), switch, trade, truck ~*n.* **2.** barter, dealing, interchange, quid pro quo, reciprocity, substitution, swap (*Inf.*), switch, tit for tat, trade, traffic, truck **3.** Bourse, market

excitable edgy, emotional, hasty, highly strung, hot-headed, hot-tempered, irascible, mercurial, nervous, passionate, quick-tempered, sensitive, susceptible, tempera-

mental, testy, touchy, violent, volatile

excite agitate, animate, arouse, awaken, discompose, disturb, electrify, elicit, evoke, fire, foment, galvanize, incite, inflame, inspire, instigate, kindle, move, provoke, quicken, rouse, stimulate, stir up, thrill, titillate, waken, whet

excited aflame, agitated, animated, aroused, awakened, discomposed, disturbed, enthusiastic, feverish, flurried, high (*Inf.*), hot and bothered (*Inf.*), moved, nervous, overwrought, roused, stimulated, stirred, thrilled, tumultuous, wild, worked up

excitement 1. action, activity, ado, adventure, agitation, animation, commotion, discomposure, elation, enthusiasm, ferment, fever, flurry, furore, heat, kicks (*Inf.*), passion, perturbation, thrill, tumult, warmth **2.** impulse, incitement, instigation, motivation, motive, provocation, stimulation, stimulus, urge

exciting electrifying, exhilarating, inspiring, intoxicating, moving, provocative, riproaring (*Inf.*), rousing, sensational, stimulating, stirring, thrilling, titillating

stimulating. —**ex'citingly** adv.

exclaim (ık'skleım) vb. to cry out or speak suddenly or excitedly, as from surprise, delight, horror, etc. —**ex-'claimer** n.

exclamation (,ɛksklə'meıʃən) n. 1. an abrupt or excited cry or utterance; ejaculation. 2. the act of exclaiming. —,**excla'mational** adj. —**ex'clamatory** adj.

exclamation mark or U.S. **point** n. 1. the punctuation mark ! used after exclamations and vehement commands. 2. this mark used for any other purpose, as to draw attention to an obvious mistake, in road warning signs, etc.

exclude (ık'sklu:d) vb. (tr.) 1. to keep out; prevent from entering. 2. to reject or not consider; leave out. 3. to expel forcibly; eject. —**ex'cludable** or **ex'cludible** adj. —**ex'cluder** n.

exclusion (ık'sklu:ʒən) n. the act or an instance of excluding or the state of being excluded. —**ex'clusionary** adj.

exclusive (ık'sklu:sıv) adj. 1. excluding all else; rejecting other considerations, events, etc. 2. belonging to a particular individual or group and to no other; not shared. 3. belonging to or catering for a privileged minority, esp. a fashionable clique. 4. (postpositive; foll. by to) limited (to); found only (in). 5. single; unique; only. 6. separate and incompatible. 7. (immediately postpositive) not including the numbers, dates, letters, etc., mentioned. 8. (postpositive; foll. by of) except (for); not taking account (of). 9. Logic. (of a disjunction) true if only one rather than both of its component propositions is true. ~n. 10. an exclusive story; a story reported in only one newspaper. —**ex'clusiveness** or **exclusivity** (,ɛksklu:'sıvıtı) n.

excommunicate R.C. Church. vb. (,ɛkskə'mju:nı,keıt). 1. (tr.) to sentence (a member of the Church) to exclusion from the communion of believers and from the privileges and public prayers of the Church. ~adj. (,ɛkskə'mju:nıkıt, -,keıt). 2. having incurred such a sentence. ~n. (,ɛkskə'mju:nıkıt, -,keıt). 3. an excommunicated person. —,**excom,muni'cation** n. —,**excom'municative** or ,**excom'municatory** adj. —,**excom'municator** n.

excoriate (ık'skɔ:rı,eıt) vb. (tr.) 1. to strip (the skin) from (a person or animal). 2. to denounce vehemently. —**ex,cori'ation** n.

excrement (ɛkskrımənt) n. waste matter discharged from the body, esp. faeces; excreta. —**excremental** (,ɛkskrı'mɛntəl) or **excrementitious** (,ɛkskrımɛn'tıʃəs) adj. —,**excre'mentally** adv.

excrescence (ık'skrɛsəns) n. a projection or protuberance, esp. an outgrowth from an organ or part of the body. —**ex'crescent** adj. —**excrescential** (,ɛkskrı'sɛnʃəl) adj.

excreta (ık'skri:tə) pl. n. waste matter, such as urine, faeces, or sweat, discharged from the body. —**ex'cretal** adj.

excrete (ık'skri:t) vb. 1. to discharge (waste matter, such as urine, sweat, or faeces) from the body. 2. (of plants) to eliminate (waste matter) through the leaves,

roots, etc. —**ex'creter** n. —**ex'cretion** n. —**ex'cretive** or **ex'cretory** adj.

excruciating (ık'skru:ʃı,eıtıŋ) adj. 1. unbearably painful; agonizing. 2. intense; extreme. 3. Inf. irritating; trying.

exculpate ('ɛkskʌl,peıt, ık'skʌlpeıt) vb. (tr.) to free from blame or guilt; vindicate or exonerate. —**exculpable** (ık'skʌlpəbəl) adj. —,**excul'pation** n. —**ex'culpatory** adj.

excursion (ık'skɜ:ʃən, -ʒən) n. 1. a short outward and return journey, esp. for sightseeing, etc.; outing. 2. a group going on such a journey. 3. (modifier) of or relating to reduced rates offered on certain journeys by rail: an excursion ticket. 4. a digression or deviation; diversion. 5. (formerly) a raid or attack. —**ex'cursionist** n.

excursive (ık'skɜ:sıv) adj. 1. tending to digress. 2. involving detours; rambling. —**ex'cursively** adv. —**ex'cursiveness** n.

excuse vb. (ık'skju:z). (tr.) 1. to pardon or forgive. 2. to seek pardon or exemption for (a person, esp. oneself). 3. to make allowances for: to excuse someone's ignorance. 4. to serve as an apology or explanation for; justify: her age excuses her. 5. to exempt from a task, obligation, etc. 6. to dismiss or allow to leave. 7. to seek permission for (someone, esp. oneself) to leave. 8. **be excused**. Euphemistic. to go to the lavatory. 9. **excuse me!** an expression used to catch someone's attention or to apologize for an interruption, disagreement, etc. ~n. (ık'skju:s). 10. an explanation offered in defence of some fault or as a reason for not fulfilling an obligation, etc. 11. Inf. an inferior example of something; makeshift substitute: she is a poor excuse for a hostess. 12. the act of excusing. —**ex'cusable** adj. —**ex'cusableness** n. —**ex'cusably** adv.

ex-directory adj. Chiefly Brit. not listed in a telephone directory, by request, and not disclosed to enquirers.

exeat ('ɛksıət) n. Brit. 1. leave of absence from school or some other institution. 2. a bishop's permission for a priest to leave his diocese in order to take up an appointment elsewhere.

exec. abbrev. for: 1. executive. 2. executor.

execrable ('ɛksıkrəbəl) adj. 1. deserving to be execrated; abhorrent. 2. of very poor quality. —'**execrableness** n. —'**execrably** adv.

execrate ('ɛksı,kreıt) vb. 1. (tr.) to loathe; detest; abhor. 2. (tr.) to denounce; deplore. 3. to curse (a person or thing); damn. —,**exe'cration** n. —'**exe,crative** or '**exe,cratory** adj. —'**exe,cratively** adv.

execute ('ɛksı,kju:t) vb. (tr.) 1. to put (a condemned person) to death; inflict capital punishment upon. 2. to carry out; complete. 3. to perform; accomplish; effect. 4. to make or produce: to execute a drawing. 5. to carry into effect (a judicial sentence, the law, etc.). 6. Law. to render (a deed, etc.) effective, as by signing, sealing, and delivering. 7. to carry out the terms of (a contract, will, etc.). —'**exe,cutable** adj. —**ex'ecutant** n. —'**exe,cuter** n.

THESAURUS

exclaim call, call out, cry, cry out, declare, ejaculate, proclaim, shout, utter, vociferate, yell

exclamation call, cry, ejaculation, expletive, interjection, outcry, shout, utterance, vociferation, yell

exclude 1. ban, bar, blackball, debar, disallow, embargo, forbid, interdict, keep out, ostracize, prohibit, proscribe, refuse, shut out, veto 2. count out, eliminate, except, ignore, leave out, omit, pass over, preclude, reject, repudiate, rule out, set aside 3. bounce (Sl.), drive out, eject, evict, expel, force out, get rid of, oust, remove, throw out

exclusion 1. ban, bar, debarment, embargo, forbiddance, interdict, nonadmission, preclusion, prohibition, proscription, refusal, veto 2. elimination, exception, omission, rejection, repudiation 3. eviction, expulsion, removal

exclusive 1. absolute, complete, entire, full, only, private, single, sole, total, undivided, unique, unshared, whole 2. aristocratic, chic, choice, clannish, classy (Sl.), cliquish,

closed, discriminative, elegant, fashionable, limited, narrow, posh (Inf.), private, restricted, restrictive, select, selfish, snobbish 3. confined, limited, peculiar, restricted, unique 4. debarring, except for, excepting, excluding, leaving aside, not counting, omitting, restricting, ruling out

excommunicate anathematize, ban, banish, cast out, denounce, eject, exclude, expel, proscribe, remove, repudiate, unchurch

excruciating acute, agonizing, burning, exquisite, extreme, harrowing, insufferable, intense, piercing, racking, searing, severe, tormenting, torturous, unbearable, unendurable, violent

exculpate absolve, acquit, clear, discharge, dismiss, excuse, exonerate, free, justify, pardon, release, vindicate

excursion 1. airing, day trip, expedition, jaunt, journey, outing, pleasure trip, ramble, tour, trip 2. detour, deviation, digression, episode, excursus, wandering

excusable allowable, defensible, forgiv-

able, justifiable, minor, pardonable, permissible, slight, understandable, venial, warrantable

excuse v. 1. absolve, acquit, bear with, exculpate, exonerate, extenuate, forgive, indulge, make allowances for, overlook, pardon, pass over, tolerate, turn a blind eye to, wink at 2. apologize for, condone, defend, explain, justify, mitigate, vindicate 3. absolve, discharge, exempt, free, let off, liberate, release, relieve, spare ~n. 4. apology, defence, explanation, grounds, justification, mitigation, plea, pretext, reason, vindication 5. copout (Sl.), disguise, evasion, expedient, makeshift, pretence, pretext, semblance, shift, subterfuge 6. Inf. apology, makeshift, mockery, substitute, travesty

execrate abhor, abominate, anathematize, condemn, curse, damn, denounce, deplore, despise, detest, excoriate, hate, imprecate, loathe, revile, vilify

execration abhorrence, abomination, anathema, condemnation, contempt, curse, damnation, detestation, excoriation, hate, ha-

execution (ˌɛksɪˈkjuːʃən) n. 1. the act or process of executing. 2. the carrying out or undergoing of a sentence of death. 3. the style or manner in which something is accomplished or performed; technique. 4. a. the enforcement of the judgment of a court of law. b. the writ ordering such enforcement.

executioner (ˌɛksɪˈkjuːʃənə) n. an official charged with carrying out the death sentence passed upon a condemned person.

executive (ɪgˈzɛkjʊtɪv) n. 1. a person or group responsible for the administration of a project, activity, or business. 2. a. the branch of government responsible for carrying out laws, decrees, etc. b. any administration. ~adj. 3. having the function of carrying plans, orders, laws, etc., into effect. —ex'ecutively adv.

executor (ɪgˈzɛkjʊtə) n. 1. Law. a person appointed by a testator to carry out his will. 2. a person who executes. —ex,ecu'torial adj. —ex'ecutory adj. —ex'ecutor,ship n. —ex'ecutrix fem n.

exegesis (ˌɛksɪˈdʒiːsɪs) n., pl. -ses (-siːz). explanation or critical interpretation of a text, esp. of the Bible. —ex-egetic (ˌɛksɪˈdʒɛtɪk) adj. —ˌexe'getics n.

exemplar (ɪgˈzɛmplə, -plɑː) n. 1. a person or thing to be copied or imitated; model. 2. a typical specimen or instance; example.

exemplary (ɪgˈzɛmplərɪ) adj. 1. fit for imitation; model. 2. serving as a warning; admonitory. 3. representative; typical. —ex'emplarily adv. —ex'emplariness n.

exemplify (ɪgˈzɛmplɪˌfaɪ) vb. -fying, -fied. (tr.) 1. to show by example. 2. to serve as an example of. 3. Law. to make an official copy of (a document) under seal. —ex'empli,fiable adj. —ex,emplifi'cation n. —ex'emplifi,cative adj. —ex'empli,fier n.

exempt (ɪgˈzɛmpt) vb. 1. (tr.) to release from an obligation, tax, etc.; excuse. ~adj. (postpositive) 2. freed from or not subject to an obligation, tax, etc.; excused. ~n. 3. a person who is exempt. —ex'emptible adj. —ex'emption n.

exequies (ˈɛksɪkwɪz) pl. n., sing. -quy. the rites and ceremonies used at funerals.

exercise (ˈɛksəˌsaɪz) vb. (mainly tr.) 1. to put into use; employ. 2. (intr.) to take exercise or perform exercises. 3. to practise using in order to develop or train. 4. to perform or make use of: to exercise one's rights. 5. to bring to bear: to exercise one's influence. 6. (often passive) to occupy the attentions of, esp. so as to worry or vex: to be exercised about a decision. 7. Mil. to carry out or cause to carry out practice, manoeuvres, drill, etc.

~n. 8. physical exertion, esp. for development, training, or keeping fit. 9. mental or other activity or practice, esp. to develop a skill. 10. a set of movements, tasks, etc., designed to train, improve, or test one's ability: piano exercises. 11. a performance or work of art done as practice or to demonstrate a technique. 12. the performance of a function: the exercise of one's rights. 13. (usually pl.) Mil. practice, manoeuvres, or drill. 14. Gymnastics. a particular event, such as the horizontal bar. —'exer,cisable adj. —'exer,ciser n.·

exert (ɪgˈzɜːt) vb. (tr.) to apply (oneself) diligently; make a strenuous effort. —ex'ertion n. —ex'ertive adj.

exeunt (ˈɛksɪˌʌnt) vb. Latin. they go out: used as a stage direction.

exeunt omnes (ˈɒmneɪz) Latin. they all go out: used as a stage direction.

ex gratia (ˈɡreɪʃə) adj. given as a favour or gratuitously where no legal obligation exists: an ex gratia payment.

exhale (ɛksˈheɪl, ɪgˈzeɪl) vb. 1. to expel (breath, smoke, etc.) from the lungs; breathe out. 2. to give off (air, fumes, etc.) or (of air, etc.) to be given off. —ex'halable adj. —ˌexha'lation n.

exhaust (ɪgˈzɔːst) vb. (mainly tr.) 1. to drain the energy of; tire out. 2. to deprive of resources, etc. 3. to deplete totally; consume. 4. to empty (a container) by drawing off or pumping out (the contents). 5. to develop or discuss thoroughly so that no further interest remains. 6. to remove gas from (a vessel, etc.) in order to reduce pressure or create a vacuum. 7. (intr.) (of steam or other gases) to be emitted or to escape from an engine after being expanded. ~n. 8. gases ejected from an engine as waste products. 9. the expulsion of expanded gas or steam from an engine. 10. a. the parts of an engine through which exhausted gases or steam pass. b. (as modifier): exhaust pipe. —ex'hauster n. —ex'haustible adj. —ex,hausti'bility n.

exhaustion (ɪgˈzɔːstʃən) n. 1. extreme tiredness. 2. the condition of being used up. 3. the act of exhausting or the state of being exhausted.

exhaustive (ɪgˈzɔːstɪv) adj. 1. comprehensive; thorough. 2. tending to exhaust. —ex'haustively adv. —ex'haustiveness n.

exhibit (ɪgˈzɪbɪt) vb. (mainly tr.) 1. (also intr.) to display (something) to the public. 2. to manifest; display; show. 3. Law. to produce (a document or object) in court as evidence. ~n. 4. an object or collection exhibited to the public. 5. Law. a document or object pro-

---

THESAURUS

tred, imprecation, loathing, malediction, odium, vilification

execute 1. behead, electrocute, guillotine, hang, kill, put to death, shoot 2. accomplish, achieve, administer, bring off, carry out, complete, consummate, discharge, do, effect, enact, enforce, finish, fulfil, implement, perform, prosecute, put into effect, realize, render 3. Law deliver, seal, serve, sign, validate

execution 1. accomplishment, achievement, administration, carrying out, completion, consummation, discharge, effect, enactment, enforcement, implementation, operation, performance, prosecution, realization, rendering 2. capital punishment, hanging, killing 3. delivery, manner, mode, performance, rendition, style, technique 4. Law warrant, writ

executioner 1. hangman, headsman 2. assassin, hit man (Sl.), killer, murderer, slayer

executive n. 1. administrator, director, manager, official 2. administration, directorate, directors, government, hierarchy, leadership, management ~adj. 3. administrative, controlling, decision-making, directing, governing, managerial

exemplary 1. admirable, commendable, correct, estimable, excellent, good, honourable, ideal, laudable, meritorious, model, praiseworthy, punctilious, sterling 2. admonitory, cautionary, monitory, warning 3. characteristic, illustrative, representative, typical

exemplify demonstrate, depict, display, embody, evidence, exhibit, illustrate, instance, manifest, represent, serve as an example of, show

exempt 1. v. absolve, discharge, except, excuse, exonerate, free, grant immunity, let off, liberate, release, relieve, spare 2. adj. absolved, clear, discharged, excepted, excused, favoured, free, immune, liberated, not liable, not subject, privileged, released, spared

exemption absolution, discharge, dispensation, exception, exoneration, freedom, immunity, privilege, release

exercise v. 1. apply, bring to bear, employ, enjoy, exert, practise, put to use, use, utilize, wield 2. discipline, drill, habituate, inure, practise, train, work out 3. afflict, agitate, annoy, burden, distress, disturb, occupy, pain, perturb, preoccupy, trouble, try, vex, worry ~n. 4. action, activity, discipline, drill, drilling, effort, labour, toil, training, work, work-out 5. accomplishment, application, discharge, employment, enjoyment, exertion, fulfilment, implementation, practice, use, utilization 6. drill, lesson, practice, problem, schooling, schoolwork, task, work

exert 1. bring into play, bring to bear, employ, exercise, expend, make use of, put forth, use, utilize, wield 2. exert oneself apply oneself, do one's best, endeavour, labour, make an effort, spare no effort, strain, strive, struggle, toil, try hard, work

exertion action, application, attempt, effort, employment, endeavour, exercise, industry, labour, pains, strain, stretch, struggle,

toil, travail (Literary), trial, use, utilization

exhaust 1. bankrupt, cripple, debilitate, disable, drain, enervate, enfeeble, fatigue, impoverish, prostrate, sap, tire, tire out, weaken, wear out 2. consume, deplete, dissipate, expend, finish, run through, spend, squander, use up, waste 3. drain, dry, empty, strain, void 4. be emitted, discharge, emanate, escape, issue

exhausted 1. all in (Sl.), beat (Sl.), crippled, dead (Inf.), dead beat (Inf.), dead tired, debilitated, disabled, dog-tired (Inf.), done in (Inf.), drained, enervated, enfeebled, fatigued, jaded, knackered (Sl.), out on one's feet, prostrated, ready to drop, sapped, spent, tired out, wasted, weak, worn out 2. at an end, consumed, depleted, dissipated, done, expended, finished, gone, spent, squandered, used up, wasted 3. bare, drained, dry, empty, void

exhausting arduous, backbreaking, crippling, debilitating, difficult, draining, enervating, fatiguing, gruelling, hard, laborious, punishing, sapping, strenuous, taxing, testing, tiring

exhaustion 1. debilitation, enervation, fatigue, feebleness, lassitude, prostration, tiredness, weariness 2. consumption, depletion, emptying

exhaustive all-embracing, all-inclusive, all-out (Inf.), complete, comprehensive, encyclopedic, extensive, far-reaching, full, fullscale, in-depth, intensive, sweeping, thorough, thoroughgoing, total

duced in court as evidence. —**ex'hibitor** *n.* —**ex'hibitory** *adj.*

exhibition (ˌɛksɪ'bɪʃən) *n.* **1.** a public display of art, skills, etc. **2.** the act of exhibiting or the state of being exhibited. **3. make an exhibition of oneself.** to behave so foolishly that one excites notice or ridicule. **4.** *Brit.* an allowance or scholarship awarded to a student at a university or school.

exhibitioner (ˌɛksɪ'bɪʃənə) *n. Brit.* a student who has been awarded an exhibition.

exhibitionism (ˌɛksɪ'bɪʃəˌnɪzəm) *n.* **1.** a compulsive desire to attract attention to oneself, esp. by exaggerated behaviour. **2.** a compulsive desire to expose one's genital organs publicly. —**exhi'bitionist** *n.* —**exhiˌbition-'istic** *adj.*

exhilarate (ɪg'zɪləˌreɪt) *vb.* (*tr.*) to make lively and cheerful; elate. —**ex'hilaˌratingly** *adv.* —**exˌhila'ration** *n.* —**ex'hilarative** or **ex'hilaratory** *adj.* —**ex'hilaˌrator** *n.*

exhort (ɪg'zɔːt) *vb.* to urge or persuade (someone) earnestly; advise strongly. —**exhortative** (ɪg'zɔːtətɪv) or **ex'hortatory** *adj.* —**exhor'tation** *n.* —**ex'horter** *n.*

exhume (ɛks'hjuːm) *vb.* (*tr.*) **1.** to dig up (something buried, esp. a corpse); disinter. **2.** to reveal; disclose. —**exhumation** (ˌɛkshjuː'meɪʃən) *n.* —**ex'humer** *n.*

ex hypothesi (ɛks haɪ'pɒθəsɪ) *adv.* in accordance with the hypothesis stated.

exigency ('ɛksɪdʒənsɪ, ɪg'zɪdʒənsɪ) or **exigence** ('ɛksɪdʒəns) *n., pl.* **-gencies** or **-gences. 1.** urgency. **2.** (*often pl.*) an urgent demand; pressing requirement. **3.** an emergency. —**'exigent** *adj.*

exiguous (ɪg'zɪgjʊəs, ɪk'sɪg-) *adj.* scanty or slender; meagre. —**exiguity** (ˌɛksɪ'gjuːɪtɪ) or **ex'iguousness** *n.*

exile ('ɛgzaɪl, 'ɛksaɪl) *n.* **1.** a prolonged, usually enforced absence from one's home or country. **2.** the official expulsion of a person from his native land. **3.** a person banished or living away from his home or country; expatriate. ~*vb.* **4.** to expel from home or country, esp. by official decree; banish. —**exilic** (ɛg'zɪlɪk, ɛk'sɪlɪk) or **ex'ilian** *adj.*

exist (ɪg'zɪst) *vb.* (*intr.*) **1.** to have being or reality; be. **2.** to eke out a living; stay alive. **3.** to be living; live. **4.** to be present under specified conditions or in a specified place.

existence (ɪg'zɪstəns) *n.* **1.** the fact or state of existing; being. **2.** the continuance or maintenance of life; living, esp. in adverse circumstances. **3.** something that exists; a being or entity. **4.** everything that exists. —**ex'istent** *adj.*

existential (ˌɛgzɪ'stɛnʃəl) *adj.* **1.** of or relating to existence, esp. human existence. **2.** *Philosophy.* based on personal experience. **3.** of a formula or proposition asserting the existence of at least one object fulfilling a given condition. **4.** of or relating to existentialism.

existentialism (ˌɛgzɪ'stɛnʃəˌlɪzəm) *n.* a modern philosophical movement stressing personal experience and responsibility and their demands on the individual, who is seen as a free agent in a deterministic and seemingly meaningless universe. —**exis'tentialist** *adj., n.*

exit ('ɛgzɪt, 'ɛksɪt) *n.* **1.** a way out. **2.** the act or an instance of going out. **3. a.** the act of leaving or right to leave a particular place. **b.** (*as modifier*): *an exit visa.* **4.** departure from life; death. **5.** *Theatre.* the act of going offstage. ~*vb.* (*intr.*) **6.** to go away or out; depart. **7.** *Theatre.* to go offstage: used as a stage direction: *exit Hamlet.*

ex libris (ɛks 'liːbrɪs) *adj.* **1.** from the collection or library of. ~*n.* **ex-libris. 2.** a bookplate bearing the owner's name, coat of arms, etc.

exo- *combining form.* external, outside, or beyond: *exothermal.*

exocrine ('ɛksəʊˌkraɪn) *adj.* **1.** of or relating to exocrine glands or their secretions. ~*n.* **2.** an exocrine gland.

Exod. *Bible. abbrev. for* Exodus.

exodus ('ɛksədəs) *n.* the act or an instance of going out.

Exodus ('ɛksədəs) *n.* **1. the.** the departure of the Israelites from Egypt. **2.** the second book of the Old Testament, recounting the events connected with this.

ex officio ('ɛks ə'fɪʃɪəʊ, ə'fɪsɪəʊ) *adv., adj.* by right of position or office.

exonerate (ɪg'zɒnəˌreɪt) *vb.* (*tr.*) **1.** to absolve from blame or a criminal charge. **2.** to relieve from an obligation. —**exˌoner'ation** *n.* —**ex'onerative** *adj.* —**ex'onerˌator** *n.*

exorbitant (ɪg'zɔːbɪtənt) *adj.* (of prices, demands, etc.) excessive; extravagant; immoderate. —**ex'orbitance** *n.* —**ex'orbitantly** *adv.*

exorcise or **-ize** ('ɛksɔːˌsaɪz) *vb.* (*tr.*) to expel (evil spirits) from (a person or place), by adjurations and religious rites. —**'exorˌciser** or **-izer** *n.* —**'exorcism** *n.* —**'exorcist** *n.*

exordium (ɛk'sɔːdɪəm) *n., pl.* **-diums** or **-dia** (-dɪə). an introductory part or beginning, esp. of an oration or discourse. —**ex'ordial** *adj.*

exotic (ɪg'zɒtɪk) *adj.* **1.** originating in a foreign country, esp. one in the tropics; not native: *an exotic plant.* **2.** *N.Z.* (of trees, esp. pine trees) native to the northern hemisphere but cultivated in New Zealand: *an exotic forest.* **3.** having a strange or bizarre allure, beauty, or quality. ~*n.* **4.** an exotic person or thing. —**ex'otically** *adv.* —**ex'otiˌcism** *n.* —**ex'oticness** *n.*

THESAURUS

exhibit 1. *v.* air, demonstrate, disclose, display, evidence, evince, expose, express, flaunt, indicate, make clear or plain, manifest, offer, parade, present, put on view, reveal, show **2.** *n.* display, exhibition, illustration, model, show

exhibition airing, demonstration, display, exhibit, expo (*Inf.*), exposition, fair, manifestation, performance, presentation, representation, show, showing, spectacle

exhilarating breathtaking, cheering, enlivening, exalting, exciting, exhilarant, exhilarative, exhilaratory, gladdening, invigorating, stimulating, thrilling, vitalizing

exhilaration animation, cheerfulness, delight, elation, exaltation, excitement, gaiety, gladness, gleefulness, high spirits, hilarity, joy, joyfulness, liveliness, mirth, sprightliness, vivacity

exhort admonish, advise, beseech, bid, call upon, caution, counsel, encourage, enjoin, entreat, goad, incite, persuade, press, spur, urge, warn

exhortation admonition, advice, beseeching, bidding, caution, counsel, encouragement, enjoinder (*Rare*), entreaty, goading, incitement, lecture, persuasion, sermon, urging, warning

exhume dig up, disentomb, disinter, unbury, unearth

exigency, exigence 1. acuteness, constraint, criticalness, demandingness, difficulty, distress, emergency, imperativeness, necessity, needfulness, pressingness, pressure, stress, urgency **2.** constraint, demand, necessity, need, requirement, wont **3.** crisis, difficulty, emergency, extremity, fix (*Inf.*), hardship, jam (*Inf.*), juncture, pass, pickle (*Inf.*), pinch, plight, predicament, quandary, scrape (*Inf.*), strait

exigent 1. acute, constraining, critical, crucial, imperative, importunate, insistent, necessary, needful, pressing, urgent **2.** arduous, demanding, difficult, exacting, hard, harsh, rigorous, severe, stiff, strict, stringent, taxing, tough

exile *n.* **1.** banishment, deportation, expatriation, expulsion, ostracism, proscription, separation **2.** deportee, émigré, expatriate, outcast, refugee ~*v.* **3.** banish, deport, drive out, eject, expatriate, expel, ostracize, oust, proscribe

exist 1. abide, be, be extant, be living, be present, breathe, continue, endure, happen, last, live, obtain, occur, prevail, remain, stand, survive **2.** eke out a living, get along *or* by, stay alive, subsist, survive

existence 1. actuality, animation, being, breath, continuance, continuation, duration, endurance, life, subsistence, survival **2.** being, creature, entity, thing **3.** creation, life, reality, the world

existent abiding, around, current, enduring, existing, extant, in existence, living, obtaining, present, prevailing, remaining, standing, surviving

exit *n.* **1.** door, egress, gate, outlet, passage out, vent, way out **2.** adieu, departure, evacuation, exodus, farewell, going, goodbye, leave-taking, retirement, retreat, withdrawal **3.** death, decease, demise, expiry, passing away ~*v.* **4.** bid farewell, depart, go away, go offstage (*Theatre*), go out, issue, leave, retire, retreat, say goodbye, take one's leave, withdraw

exodus departure, evacuation, exit, flight, going out, leaving, migration, retirement, retreat, withdrawal

exonerate 1. absolve, acquit, clear, discharge, dismiss, exculpate, excuse, justify, pardon, vindicate **2.** discharge, dismiss, except, excuse, exempt, free, let off, liberate, release, relieve

exorbitant enormous, excessive, extortionate, extravagant, extreme, immoderate, inordinate, outrageous, preposterous, unconscionable, undue, unreasonable, unwarranted

exorcise adjure, cast out, deliver (from), drive out, expel, purify

exorcism adjuration, casting out, deliverance, driving out, expulsion, purification

exotica (ɪgˈzɒtɪkə) pl. n. exotic objects, esp. when forming a collection.

expand (ɪkˈspænd) vb. **1.** to make or become greater in extent, volume, size, or scope. **2.** to spread out; unfold; stretch out. **3.** (intr.; often foll. by on) to enlarge or expatiate on (a story, topic, etc.). **4.** (intr.) to become increasingly relaxed, friendly, or talkative. **5.** Maths. to express (a function or expression) as the sum or product of terms. —exˈpandable or exˈpandible adj. —exˈpander n.

expanse (ɪkˈspæns) n. **1.** an uninterrupted surface of something that extends, esp. over a wide area; stretch. **2.** expansion or extension.

expansible (ɪkˈspænsəbəl) adj. able to expand or be expanded. —ex,pansiˈbility n.

expansion (ɪkˈspænʃən) n. **1.** the act of expanding or the state of being expanded. **2.** something expanded. **3.** the degree or amount by which something expands. **4.** an increase or development, esp. in the activities of a company. **5.** the increase in the dimensions of a body or substance when subjected to an increase in temperature, internal pressure, etc. —exˈpansionary adj.

expansionism (ɪkˈspænʃəˌnɪzəm) n. the doctrine or practice of expanding the economy or territory of a country. —exˈpansionist n., adj. —ex,pansionˈistic adj.

expansive (ɪkˈspænsɪv) adj. **1.** able or tending to expand or characterized by expansion. **2.** wide; extensive. **3.** friendly, open, or talkative. **4.** grand or extravagant. —exˈpansiveness or expansivity (,ɛkspænˈsɪvɪtɪ) n.

expatiate (ɪkˈspeɪʃɪˌeɪt) vb. (intr.) **1.** (foll. by on or upon) to enlarge (on a theme, topic, etc.); elaborate (on). **2.** Rare. to wander about. —ex,patiˈation n. —exˈpatiˌator n.

expatriate adj. (ɛksˈpætrɪɪt, -ˌeɪt). **1.** exiled or banished from one's native country. ~n. (ɛksˈpætrɪɪt, -ˌeɪt). **2.** an exile; expatriate person. ~vb. (ɛksˈpætrɪˌeɪt). (tr.) **3.** to exile (oneself) from one's native country or cause (another) to go into exile. —ex,patriˈation n.

expect (ɪkˈspɛkt) vb. (tr.; may take a clause as object or an infinitive) **1.** to regard as likely; anticipate. **2.** to look forward to or be waiting for. **3.** to decide that (something) is necessary; require: the teacher expects us to work late. —exˈpectable adj.

expectancy (ɪkˈspɛktənsɪ) or **expectance** n. **1.** something expected, esp. on the basis of a norm or average: his life expectancy was 30 years. **2.** anticipation;

expectation. **3.** the prospect of a future interest or possession.

expectant (ɪkˈspɛktənt) adj. **1.** expecting, anticipating, or hopeful. **2.** having expectations, esp. of possession of something. **3.** pregnant. ~n. **4.** a person who expects something.

expectation (,ɛkspɛkˈteɪʃən) n. **1.** the act or state of expecting or the state of being expected. **2.** (usually pl.) something looked forward to, whether feared or hoped for. **3.** an attitude of expectancy or hope. **4.** Statistics. the numerical probability that an event will occur. —expectative (ɪkˈspɛktətɪv) adj.

expectorant (ɪkˈspɛktərənt) Med. adj. **1.** promoting the secretion, liquefaction, or expulsion of sputum from the respiratory passages. ~n. **2.** an expectorant drug or agent.

expectorate (ɪkˈspɛktəˌreɪt) vb. to cough up and spit out (sputum from the respiratory passages). —ex,pectoˈration n. —exˈpectoˌrator n.

expediency (ɪkˈspiːdɪənsɪ) or **expedience** n., pl. **-encies** or **-ences**. **1.** appropriateness; suitability. **2.** the use of or inclination towards methods that are advantageous rather than fair or just. **3.** another word for **expedient** (sense 3).

expedient (ɪkˈspiːdɪənt) adj. **1.** suitable to the circumstances; appropriate. **2.** inclined towards methods that are advantageous rather than fair or just. ~n. also **expediency. 3.** something suitable or appropriate, esp. during an urgent situation.

expedite (ˈɛkspɪˌdaɪt) vb. (tr.) **1.** to facilitate the progress of; hasten or assist. **2.** to do or process with speed and efficiency. —ˈexpeˌditer or ˈexpeˌditor n.

expedition (,ɛkspɪˈdɪʃən) n. **1.** an organized journey or voyage, esp. for exploration or for a scientific or military purpose. **2.** the people and equipment comprising an expedition. **3.** promptness; dispatch. —,expeˈditionary adj.

expeditious (,ɛkspɪˈdɪʃəs) adj. characterized by or done with speed and efficiency; prompt; quick. —,expeˈditiously adv. —,expeˈditiousness n.

expel (ɪkˈspɛl) vb. **-pelling, -pelled.** (tr.) **1.** to eject or drive out with force. **2.** to deprive of participation in or membership of a school, club, etc. —exˈpellable adj. —expellee (,ɛkspɛˈliː) n. —exˈpeller n.

expend (ɪkˈspɛnd) vb. (tr.) **1.** to spend; disburse. **2.** to consume or use up. —exˈpender n.

═══════ THESAURUS ═══════

exotic 1. alien, external, extraneous, extrinsic, foreign, imported, introduced, naturalized, not native **2.** bizarre, colourful, curious, different, extraordinary, fascinating, glamorous, mysterious, outlandish, peculiar, strange, striking, unfamiliar, unusual

expand 1. amplify, augment, bloat, blow up, broaden, develop, dilate, distend, enlarge, extend, fatten, fill out, grow, heighten, increase, inflate, lengthen, magnify, multiply, prolong, protract, swell, thicken, wax, widen **2.** diffuse, open (out), outspread, spread (out), stretch (out), unfold, unfurl, unravel, unroll **3.** amplify, develop, dilate, elaborate, embellish, enlarge, expatiate, expound, flesh out, go into detail

expanse area, breadth, extent, field, plain, range, space, stretch, sweep, tract

expansion amplification, augmentation, development, diffusion, dilatation, distension, enlargement, expanse, growth, increase, inflation, magnification, multiplication, opening out, spread, swelling, unfolding, unfurling

expansive 1. dilating, distending, elastic, enlargeable, expanding, extendable, inflatable, stretching, stretchy, swelling **2.** all-embracing, broad, comprehensive, extensive, far-reaching, inclusive, thorough, voluminous, wide, wide-ranging, widespread **3.** affable, communicative, easy, effusive, free, friendly, garrulous, genial, loquacious, open, outgoing, sociable, talkative, unreserved, warm

expatiate amplify, descant, develop, dilate, dwell on, elaborate, embellish, enlarge, expound, go into detail

expatriate 1. adj. banished, emigrant, émigré, exiled, refugee **2.** n. emigrant, émigré, exile **3.** v. banish, exile, expel, ostracize, proscribe

expect 1. assume, believe, calculate, conjecture, forecast, foresee, imagine, presume, reckon, suppose, surmise, think, trust **2.** anticipate, await, bargain for, contemplate, envisage, hope for, look ahead to, look for, look forward to, predict, watch for **3.** call for, count on, demand, insist on, look for, rely upon, require, want, wish

expectancy 1. anticipation, assumption, belief, conjecture, expectation, hope, looking forward, prediction, presumption, probability, supposition, surmise, suspense, waiting **2.** likelihood, outlook, prospect

expectant 1. anticipating, anxious, apprehensive, awaiting, eager, expecting, hopeful, in suspense, ready, watchful **2.** enceinte, expecting (Inf.), gravid, pregnant

expectation 1. assumption, assurance, belief, calculation, confidence, conjecture, forecast, likelihood, presumption, probability, supposition, surmise, trust **2.** anticipation, apprehension, chance, expectancy, fear, hope, looking forward, outlook, possibility, prediction, promise, prospect, suspense **3.** demand, insistence, reliance, requirement, trust, want, wish

expecting enceinte, expectant, gravid, in the family way (Inf.), pregnant, with child

expediency, expedience 1. advantageousness, advisability, appropriateness, aptness, benefit, convenience, desirability, effectiveness, fitness, helpfulness, judiciousness, meetness, practicality, pragmatism, profitability, properness, propriety, prudence, suitability, usefulness, utilitarianism, utility **2.** contrivance, device, expedient, makeshift, manoeuvre, means, measure, method, resort, resource, scheme, shift, stopgap, stratagem, substitute

expedient 1. adj. advantageous, advisable, appropriate, beneficial, convenient, desirable, effective, fit, helpful, judicious, meet, opportune, politic, practical, pragmatic, profitable, proper, prudent, suitable, useful, utilitarian, worthwhile **2.** n. contrivance, device, expediency, makeshift, manoeuvre, means, measure, method, resort, resource, scheme, shift, stopgap, stratagem, substitute

expedite accelerate, advance, assist, dispatch, facilitate, forward, hasten, hurry, precipitate, press, promote, quicken, rush, speed (up), urge

expedition 1. enterprise, excursion, exploration, journey, mission, quest, safari, tour, trek, trip, undertaking, voyage **2.** company, crew, explorers, team, travellers, voyagers, wayfarers **3.** alacrity, celerity, dispatch, expeditiousness, haste, hurry, promptness, quickness, rapidity, readiness, speed, swiftness

expeditious active, alert, brisk, diligent, efficient, fast, hasty, immediate, instant, nimble, prompt, quick, rapid, ready, speedy, swift

expel 1. belch, cast out, discharge, dislodge, drive out, eject, remove, spew, throw out **2.** ban, banish, bar, blackball, discharge, dismiss, drum out, evict, exclude, exile, expatriate, oust, proscribe, send packing, throw out, turf out (Inf.)

expendable (ɪk'spɛndəbəl) *adj.* **1.** that may be expended or used up. **2.** able to be sacrificed to achieve an objective, esp. a military one. ~*n.* **3.** something expendable. —**ex,penda'bility** *n.*

expenditure (ɪk'spɛndɪtʃə) *n.* **1.** something expended, esp. money. **2.** the act of expending.

expense (ɪk'spɛns) *n.* **1.** a particular payment of money; expenditure. **2.** money needed for individual purchases; cost; charge. **3.** (*pl.*) money spent in the performance of a job, etc., usually reimbursed by an employer or allowable against tax. **4.** something requiring money for its purchase or upkeep. **5. at the expense of.** to the detriment of.

expense account *n.* **1.** an arrangement by which an employee's expenses are refunded by his employer or deducted from his income for tax purposes. **2.** a record of such expenses.

expensive (ɪk'spɛnsɪv) *adj.* high-priced; costly; dear. —**ex'pensiveness** *n.*

experience (ɪk'spɪərɪəns) *n.* **1.** direct personal participation or observation. **2.** a particular incident, feeling, etc., that a person has undergone. **3.** accumulated knowledge, esp. of practical matters. ~*vb.* (*tr.*) **4.** to participate in or undergo. **5.** to be moved by; feel. —**ex'perienceable** *adj.*

experienced (ɪk'spɪərɪənst) *adj.* having become skilful or knowledgeable from extensive participation or observation.

experiential (ɪk,spɪərɪ'ɛnʃəl) *adj.* relating to or derived from experience; empirical.

experiment *n.* (ɪk'spɛrɪmənt). **1.** a test or investigation, esp. one planned to provide evidence for or against a hypothesis. **2.** the act of conducting such an investigation or test; research. **3.** an attempt at something new or original. ~*vb.* (ɪk'spɛrɪ,mɛnt). **4.** (*intr.*) to make an experiment or experiments. —**ex,perimen'tation** *n.* —**ex'peri,menter** *n.*

experimental (ɪk,spɛrɪ'mɛntəl) *adj.* **1.** relating to, based on, or having the nature of experiment. **2.** based on or derived from experience; empirical. **3.** tending to experiment. **4.** tentative or provisional. —**ex,peri'mentalism** *n.*

expert ('ɛkspɜːt) *n.* **1.** a person who has extensive skill or knowledge in a particular field. ~*adj.* **2.** skilful or knowledgeable. **3.** of, involving, or done by an expert: *an expert job.* —**'expertly** *adv.* —**'expertness** *n.*

expertise (,ɛkspɜː'tiːz) *n.* special skill, knowledge, or judgment; expertness.

expiate ('ɛkspɪ,eɪt) *vb.* (*tr.*) to atone for (sin or wrongdoing); make amends for. —**'expi,ator** *n.* —**'expiable** *adj.* —,**expi'ation** *n.*

expiatory ('ɛkspɪətərɪ, -trɪ) *adj.* **1.** capable of making expiation. **2.** offered in expiation.

expiration (,ɛkspɪ'reɪʃən) *n.* **1.** the finish of something; expiry. **2.** the act, process, or sound of breathing out. —**ex'piratory** *adj.*

expire (ɪk'spaɪə) *vb.* **1.** (*intr.*) to finish or run out; come to an end. **2.** to breathe out (air). **3.** (*intr.*) to die. —**ex'pirer** *n.*

expiry (ɪk'spaɪərɪ) *n., pl.* **-ries.** **1. a.** a coming to an end, esp. of a contract period; termination. **b.** (*as modifier*): *the expiry date.* **2.** death.

explain (ɪk'spleɪn) *vb.* **1.** (when *tr.*, may take a clause as *object*) to make (something) comprehensible, esp. by giving a clear and detailed account of it. **2.** (*tr.*) to justify or attempt to justify (oneself) by reasons for one's actions. —**ex'plainable** *adj.* —**ex'plainer** *n.*

explanation (,ɛksplə'neɪʃən) *n.* **1.** the act or process of explaining. **2.** something that explains. **3.** a clarification of disputed points.

explanatory (ɪk'splænətərɪ, -trɪ) *or* **explanative** *adj.* serving or intended to serve as an explanation. —**ex'planatorily** *adv.*

expletive (ɪk'spliːtɪv) *n.* **1.** an exclamation or swearword; an oath or sound expressing emotion rather than meaning. **2.** any syllable, word, or phrase conveying no independent meaning, esp. one inserted in verse for the sake of metre. ~*adj. also* **expletory** (ɪk'spliːtərɪ). **3.** without particular meaning, esp. when filling out a line of verse.

explicable ('ɛksplɪkəbəl, ɪk'splɪk-) *adj.* capable of being explained.

explicate ('ɛksplɪ,keɪt) *vb.* (*tr.*) *Formal.* **1.** to make clear or explicit; explain. **2.** to formulate or develop (a theory, hypothesis, etc.). —**explicative** (ɪk'splɪkətɪv) *or* **explicatory** (ɪk'splɪkətərɪ, -trɪ) *adj.* —,**expli'cation** *n.* —'**expli,cator** *n.*

explicit (ɪk'splɪsɪt) *adj.* **1.** precisely and clearly expressed, leaving nothing to implication; fully stated. **2.** openly expressed without reservations; unreserved. —**ex'plicitly** *adv.* —**ex'plicitness** *n.*

explode (ɪk'spləʊd) *vb.* **1.** to burst or cause to burst with great violence, esp. through detonation of an explosive; blow up. **2.** to destroy or be destroyed in this manner. **3.** (of a gas) to undergo or cause (a gas) to undergo a sudden violent expansion, as a result of a fast exothermic chemical or nuclear reaction. **4.** (*intr.*) to react suddenly or violently with emotion, etc. **5.** (*intr.*) (esp. of a population) to increase rapidly. **6.** (*tr.*) to show (a theory, etc.) to be baseless. —**ex'ploder** *n.*

exploit *n.* ('ɛksplɔɪt). **1.** a notable deed or feat, esp. one that is heroic. ~*vb.* (ɪk'splɔɪt). (*tr.*) **2.** to take ad-

---

THESAURUS

expend consume, disburse, dissipate, employ, exhaust, fork out (*Sl.*), go through, lay out (*Inf.*), pay out, shell out (*Inf.*), spend, use (up)

expendable dispensable, inessential, nonessential, replaceable, unimportant

expenditure application, charge, consumption, cost, disbursement, expense, outgoings, outlay, output, payment, spending, use

expense charge, consumption, cost, disbursement, expenditure, loss, outlay, output, payment, sacrifice, spending, toll, use

expensive costly, dear, excessive, exorbitant, extravagant, high-priced, inordinate, lavish, overpriced, rich, steep (*Inf.*), stiff

experience *n.* **1.** contact, doing, evidence, exposure, familiarity, involvement, know-how (*Inf.*), knowledge, observation, participation, practice, proof, training, trial, understanding **2.** adventure, affair, encounter, episode, event, happening, incident, occurrence, ordeal, test, trial ~*v.* **3.** apprehend, become familiar with, behold, encounter, endure, face, feel, go through, have, know, live through, meet, observe, participate in, perceive, sample, sense, suffer, sustain, taste, try, undergo

experienced **1.** accomplished, adept, capable, competent, expert, familiar, knowledgeable, master, practised, professional, qualified, seasoned, skilful, tested, trained,

tried, veteran, well-versed **2.** knowing, mature, sophisticated, wise, worldly, worldly-wise

experiment **1.** *n.* assay, attempt, examination, experimentation, investigation, procedure, proof, research, test, trial, trial and error, trial run, venture **2.** *v.* assay, examine, investigate, put to the test, research, sample, test, try, verify

experimental empirical, exploratory, pilot, preliminary, probationary, provisional, speculative, tentative, test, trial, trial-and-error

expert **1.** *n.* ace (*Inf.*), adept, authority, connoisseur, dab hand (*Inf.*), master, past master, pro (*Inf.*), professional, specialist, virtuoso, wizard **2.** *adj.* able, adept, adroit, apt, clever, deft, dexterous, experienced, facile, handy, knowledgeable, master, masterly, practised, professional, proficient, qualified, skilful, skilled, trained, virtuoso

expertise ableness, adroitness, aptness, cleverness, command, deftness, dexterity, expertness, facility, judgment, knack, know-how (*Inf.*), knowledge, masterliness, mastery, proficiency, skilfulness, skill

expertness ableness, adroitness, aptness, command, deftness, dexterity, expertise, facility, judgment, know-how (*Inf.*), knowledge, masterliness, mastery, proficiency, skilfulness, skill

expire **1.** cease, close, come to an end,

conclude, end, finish, lapse, run out, stop, terminate **2.** breathe out, emit, exhale, expel **3.** decease, depart, die, kick the bucket (*Inf.*), pass away *or* on, perish

explain **1.** clarify, clear up, define, demonstrate, describe, disclose, elucidate, explicate (*Formal*), expound, illustrate, interpret, make clear *or* plain, resolve, solve, teach, unfold **2.** account for, excuse, give an explanation for, give a reason for, justify

explanation **1.** clarification, definition, demonstration, description, elucidation, explication, exposition, illustration, interpretation, resolution **2.** account, answer, cause, excuse, justification, meaning, mitigation, motive, reason, sense, significance, vindication

explanatory demonstrative, descriptive, elucidatory, explicative, expository, illuminative, illustrative, interpretive, justifying

explicit absolute, categorical, certain, clear, definite, direct, distinct, exact, express, frank, open, outspoken, patent, plain, positive, precise, specific, stated, straightforward, unambiguous, unequivocal, unqualified, unreserved

explode **1.** blow up, burst, detonate, discharge, erupt, go off, set off, shatter, shiver **2.** belie, debunk, discredit, disprove, give the lie to, invalidate, refute, repudiate

vantage of (a person, situation, etc.) for one's own ends. **3.** to make the best use of. —**ex'ploitable** *adj.* —**exploi'tation** *n.* —**ex'ploitive** *or* **ex'ploitative** *adj.*

explore (ɪk'splɔː) *vb.* **1.** (*tr.*) to examine or investigate, esp. systematically. **2.** to travel into (unfamiliar regions), esp. for scientific purposes. **3.** (*tr.*) *Med.* to examine (an organ or part) for diagnostic purposes. —,explo'ration *n.* —**ex'plorer** *n.*

explosion (ɪk'spləʊʒən) *n.* **1.** the act or an instance of exploding. **2.** a violent release of energy resulting from a rapid chemical or nuclear reaction. **3.** a sudden or violent outburst of activity, noise, emotion, etc. **4.** a rapid increase, esp. in a population.

explosive (ɪk'spləʊsɪv) *adj.* **1.** of, involving, or characterized by explosion. **2.** capable of exploding or tending to explode. **3.** potentially violent or hazardous: *an explosive situation.* ~*n.* **4.** a substance capable of exploding or tending to explode. —**ex'plosiveness** *n.*

expo ('ɛkspəʊ) *n., pl.* **-pos.** *Inf.* short for **exposition** (sense 3).

exponent (ɪk'spəʊnənt) *n.* **1.** (usually foll. by *of*) a person or thing that acts as an advocate (of an idea, cause, etc.). **2.** a person or thing that explains or interprets. **3.** a performer or artist. **4.** Also called: **power, index.** *Maths.* a number or variable placed as a superscript to another number or quantity indicating the number of times the number or quantity is to be multiplied by itself. ~*adj.* **5.** offering a declaration, explanation, or interpretation. —,expo'nential *adj.*

export *n.* ('ɛkspɔːt). **1.** (*often pl.*) **a.** goods (**visible exports**) or services (**invisible exports**) sold to a foreign country or countries. **b.** (*as modifier*): *an export licence.* ~*vb.* (ɪk'spɔːt, 'ɛkspɔːt). **2.** to sell (goods or services) or ship (goods) to a foreign country. **3.** (*tr.*) to transmit or spread (an idea, institution, etc.) abroad. —**ex'portable** *adj.* —**ex,porta'bility** *n.* —**ex'porter** *n.*

expose (ɪk'spəʊz) *vb.* (*tr.*) **1.** to display for viewing; exhibit. **2.** to bring to public notice; disclose. **3.** to divulge the identity of; unmask. **4.** (foll. by *to*) to make subject or susceptible (to attack, criticism, etc.). **5.** to abandon (a child, animal, etc.) in the open to die. **6.** (foll. by *to*) to introduce (to) or acquaint (with). **7.** *Photog.* to subject (a film or plate) to light, x-rays, etc. **8. expose oneself.** to display one's sexual organs in public. —**ex'posable** *adj.* —**ex'posal** *n.* —**ex'poser** *n.*

exposé (ɛks'pəʊzeɪ) *n.* the act or an instance of bringing a scandal, crime, etc., to public notice.

exposed (ɪk'spəʊzd) *adj.* **1.** not concealed; displayed for viewing. **2.** without shelter from the elements. **3.** susceptible to attack or criticism; vulnerable. —**exposedness** (ɪk'spəʊzɪdnɪs) *n.*

exposition (,ɛkspə'zɪʃən) *n.* **1.** a systematic, usually

written statement about or explanation of a subject. **2.** the act of expounding or setting forth information or a viewpoint. **3.** a large public exhibition, esp. of industrial products or arts and crafts. **4.** the act of exposing or the state of being exposed. **5.** *Music.* the first statement of the subjects or themes of a movement in sonata form or a fugue. **6.** *R.C. Church.* the exhibiting of the consecrated Eucharistic Host or a relic for public veneration. —,expo'sitional *adj.*

expository (ɪk'spɒzɪtərɪ, -trɪ) *or* **expositive** *adj.* of or involving exposition; explanatory. —**ex'positorily** *or* **ex'positively** *adv.*

ex post facto (ɛks 'pəʊst 'fæktəʊ) *adj.* having retrospective effect.

expostulate (ɪk'spɒstjʊ,leɪt) *vb.* (*intr.*; usually foll. by *with*) to argue or reason (with), esp. in order to dissuade. —ex,postu'lation *n.* —**ex'postu,lator** *n.* —**ex'postulatory** *or* **ex'postulative** *adj.*

exposure (ɪk'spəʊʒə) *n.* **1.** the act of exposing or the condition of being exposed. **2.** the position or outlook of a house, building, etc.: *a southern exposure.* **3.** lack of shelter from the weather, esp. the cold. **4.** a surface that is exposed. **5.** *Photog.* **a.** the act of exposing a film or plate to light, x-rays, etc. **b.** an area on a film or plate that has been exposed. **6.** *Photog.* **a.** the intensity of light falling on a film or plate multiplied by the time for which it is exposed. **b.** a combination of lens aperture and shutter speed used in taking a photograph. **7.** appearance before the public, as in a theatre, on television, etc.

exposure meter *n. Photog.* an instrument for measuring the intensity of light so that suitable camera settings can be determined. Also called: **light meter.**

expound (ɪk'spaʊnd) *vb.* (when *intr.*, foll. by *on* or *about*) to explain or set forth (an argument, theory, etc.) in detail. —**ex'pounder** *n.*

express (ɪk'sprɛs) *vb.* (*tr.*) **1.** to transform (ideas) into words; utter; verbalize. **2.** to show or reveal. **3.** to communicate (emotion, etc.) without words, as through music, painting, etc. **4.** to indicate through a symbol, formula, etc. **5.** to squeeze out: *to express the juice from an orange.* **6. express oneself.** to communicate one's thoughts or ideas. ~*adj.* (*prenominal*) **7.** clearly indicated; explicitly stated. **8.** done or planned for a definite reason; particular. **9.** of or designed for rapid transportation of people, mail, money, etc.: *express delivery.* ~*n.* **10. a.** a system for sending mail, money, etc., rapidly. **b.** mail, etc., conveyed by such a system. **c.** *Chiefly U.S.* an enterprise operating such a system. **11.** Also called: **express train.** a fast train stopping at no or only a few stations between its termini. ~*adv.* **12.** by means of express delivery. —**ex'presser** *n.* —**ex'pressible**

THESAURUS

exploit *n.* **1.** accomplishment, achievement, adventure, attainment, deed, feat, stunt ~*v.* **2.** abuse, impose upon, manipulate, milk, misuse, play on *or* upon, take advantage of **3.** capitalize on, cash in on (*Sl.*), make capital out of, make use of, profit by *or* from, put to use, turn to account, use, use to advantage, utilize

exploration 1. analysis, examination, inquiry, inspection, investigation, probe, research, scrutiny, search, study **2.** expedition, reconnaissance, survey, tour, travel, trip

exploratory analytic, experimental, fact-finding, investigative, probing, searching, trial

explore 1. analyse, examine, inquire into, inspect, investigate, look into, probe, prospect, research, scrutinize, search **2.** have *or* take a look around, range over, reconnoitre, scout, survey, tour, travel, traverse

explosion 1. bang, blast, burst, clap, crack, detonation, discharge, outburst, report **2.** eruption, fit, outbreak, outburst, paroxysm

explosive 1. unstable, volatile **2.** fiery, stormy, touchy, vehement, violent **3.** charged, dangerous, hazardous, overwrought, perilous, tense, ugly

exponent 1. advocate, backer, champion, defender, promoter, propagandist, proponent, spokesman, spokeswoman, supporter,

upholder **2.** commentator, demonstrator, elucidator, expositor, expounder, illustrator, interpreter **3.** example, exemplar, illustration, indication, model, sample, specimen, type **4.** executant, interpreter, performer, player, presenter

expose 1. display, exhibit, manifest, present, put on view, reveal, show, uncover, unveil **2.** air, betray, bring to light, denounce, detect, disclose, divulge, lay bare, let out, make known, reveal, show up, smoke out, uncover, unearth, unmask **3.** endanger, hazard, imperil, jeopardize, lay open, leave open, make vulnerable, risk, subject **4.** *With* **to** acquaint with, bring into contact with, familiarize with, introduce to, make conversant with

exposed 1. bare, exhibited, laid bare, made manifest, made public, on display, on show, on view, revealed, shown, unconcealed, uncovered, unveiled **2.** open, open to the elements, unprotected, unsheltered **3.** in danger, in peril, laid bare, laid open, left open, liable, open, susceptible, vulnerable

exposition 1. account, commentary, critique, description, elucidation, exegesis, explanation, explication, illustration, interpretation, presentation **2.** demonstration, display, exhibition, expo (*Inf.*), fair, presentation, show

expostulate argue (with), dissuade, pro-

test, reason (with), remonstrate (with)

exposure 1. baring, display, exhibition, manifestation, presentation, publicity, revelation, showing, uncovering, unveiling **2.** airing, betrayal, denunciation, detection, disclosure, divulgence, divulging, exposé, revelation, unmasking **3.** danger, hazard, jeopardy, risk, vulnerability **4.** acquaintance, contact, conversancy, experience, familiarity, introduction, knowledge **5.** aspect, frontage, location, outlook, position, setting, view

expound describe, elucidate, explain, explicate (*Formal*), illustrate, interpret, set forth, spell out, unfold

express *v.* **1.** articulate, assert, asseverate, communicate, couch, declare, enunciate, phrase, pronounce, put, put across, put into words, say, speak, state, tell, utter, verbalize, voice, word **2.** bespeak, convey, denote, depict, designate, disclose, divulge, embody, evince, exhibit, indicate, intimate, make known, manifest, represent, reveal, show, signify, stand for, symbolize, testify **3.** extract, force out, press out, squeeze out ~*adj.* **4.** accurate, categorical, certain, clear, definite, direct, distinct, exact, explicit, outright, plain, pointed, precise, unambiguous **5.** clearcut, especial, particular, singular, special **6.** direct, fast, high-speed, nonstop, quick, rapid, speedy, swift *adj.*

expression (ɪkˈsprɛʃən) *n.* **1.** the act or an instance of transforming ideas into words. **2.** a manifestation of an emotion, feeling, etc., without words. **3.** communication of emotion through music, painting, etc. **4.** a look on the face that indicates mood or emotion. **5.** the choice of words, intonation, etc., in communicating. **6.** a particular phrase used conventionally to express something. **7.** the act or process of squeezing out a liquid. **8.** *Maths.* a variable, function, or some combination of these. —**ex-ˈpressional** *adj.* —**exˈpressionless** *adj.*

expressionism (ɪkˈsprɛʃəˌnɪzəm) *n.* (*sometimes cap.*) an artistic and literary movement originating in the early 20th century, which sought to express emotions rather than to represent external reality: characterized by symbolism and distortion. —**exˈpressionist** *n., adj.* —**exˌpressionˈistic** *adj.*

expressive (ɪkˈsprɛsɪv) *adj.* **1.** of, involving, or full of expression. **2.** (*postpositive;* foll. by *of*) indicative or suggestive (of). **3.** having a particular meaning or force; significant. —**exˈpressiveness** *n.*

expressly (ɪkˈsprɛslɪ) *adv.* **1.** for an express purpose. **2.** plainly, exactly, or unmistakably.

expresso (ɪkˈsprɛsəʊ) *n.* variant of **espresso**.

expressway (ɪkˈsprɛsˌweɪ) *n. Chiefly U.S.* an urban motorway.

expropriate (ɛksˈprəʊprɪˌeɪt) *vb.* (*tr.*) to deprive (an owner) of (property), esp. by taking it for public use. —**exˌpropriˈation** *n.* —**exˈpropriˌator** *n.*

expulsion (ɪkˈspʌlʃən) *n.* the act of expelling or the fact or condition of being expelled. —**exˈpulsive** *adj.*

expunge (ɪkˈspʌndʒ) *vb.* (*tr.*) to delete or erase; blot out; obliterate. —**expunction** (ɪkˈspʌŋkʃən) *n.* —**exˈpunger** *n.*

expurgate (ˈɛkspəˌgeɪt) *vb.* (*tr.*) to amend (a book, text, etc.) by removing (offensive sections). —**expurˈgation** *n.* —**ˈexpurˌgator** *n.* —**expurgatory** (ɛksˈpɜːgətərɪ) *or* **expurgatorial** (ɛkˌspɜːgəˈtɔːrɪəl) *adj.*

exquisite (ɪkˈskwɪzɪt, ˈɛkskwɪzɪt) *adj.* **1.** possessing qualities of unusual delicacy and craftsmanship. **2.** extremely beautiful. **3.** outstanding or excellent. **4.** sensitive; discriminating. **5.** fastidious and refined. **6.** intense or sharp in feeling. ~*n.* **7.** *Obs.* a dandy. —**exˈquisiteness** *n.*

ex-serviceman *n., pl.* -**men.** a man who has served in the army, navy, or air force.

extant (ɛkˈstænt, ˈɛkstənt) *adj.* still in existence; surviving.
▷ **Usage.** Careful writers distinguish between *extant* and *existent.* Both are used of that which exists at the present time, but *extant* has a further connotation of survival.

extemporaneous (ɪkˌstɛmpəˈreɪnɪəs) *or* **extemporary** (ɪkˈstɛmpərərɪ) *adj.* **1.** spoken, performed, etc., without preparation; extempore. **2.** done in a temporary manner; improvised. —**exˌtempoˈraneously** *or* **exˈtemporarily** *adv.* —**exˌtempoˈraneousness** *or* **exˈtemporariness** *n.*

extempore (ɪkˈstɛmpərɪ) *adv., adj.* without planning or preparation.

extemporize *or* -**ise** (ɪkˈstɛmpəˌraɪz) *vb.* **1.** to perform, speak, or compose (an act, speech, music, etc.) without preparation. **2.** to use a temporary solution; improvise. —**exˌtemporiˈzation** *or* -**iˈsation** *n.* —**exˈtempoˌrizer** *or* -**iser** *n.*

extend (ɪkˈstɛnd) *vb.* **1.** to draw out or be drawn out; stretch. **2.** to last for a certain time. **3.** (*intr.*) to reach a certain point in time or distance. **4.** (*intr.*) to exist or occur. **5.** (*tr.*) to increase (a building, etc.) in size; add to or enlarge. **6.** (*tr.*) to broaden the meaning or scope of: *the law was extended.* **7.** (*tr.*) to present or offer. **8.** to stretch forth (an arm, etc.). **9.** (*tr.*) to lay out (a body) at full length. **10.** (*tr.*) to strain or exert (a person or animal) to the maximum. **11.** (*tr.*) to prolong (the time) for payment of (a debt or loan), completion of (a task), etc. —**exˈtendible** *or* **exˈtendable** *adj.* —**exˌtendiˈbility** *or* **exˌtendaˈbility** *n.*

extended family *n. Sociol., anthropol.* the nuclear family together with blood relatives, often spanning three or more generations.

extensible (ɪkˈstɛnsəbəl) *or* **extensile** (ɪkˈstɛnsaɪl) *adj.* capable of being extended. —**exˌtensiˈbility** *or* **exˈtensibleness** *n.*

extension (ɪkˈstɛnʃən) *n.* **1.** the act of extending or the condition of being extended. **2.** something that can be extended or that extends another object. **3.** the length, range, etc., over which something is extended. **4.** an additional telephone set connected to the same telephone line as another set. **5.** a room or rooms added to an existing building. **6.** a delay in the date originally set for payment of a debt or completion of a contract. **7.** the property of matter by which it occupies space. **8. a.** the act of straightening or extending an arm or leg. **b.** its position after being straightened or extended. **9. a.** a service by which the facilities of an educational establishment, library, etc., are offered to outsiders. **b.** (*as modifier*): *a university extension course.* **10.** *Logic.* another term for **denotation.** —**exˈtensional** *adj.* —**exˌtensionˈality** *or* **exˈtensionalˌism** *n.*

extensive (ɪkˈstɛnsɪv) *adj.* **1.** having a large extent, area, degree, etc. **2.** widespread. **3.** *Agriculture.* involving or farmed with minimum expenditure of capital or labour, esp. depending on a large extent of land. Cf. **intensive** (sense 3). **4.** of or relating to logical extension.

THESAURUS

expression 1. announcement, assertion, asseveration, communication, declaration, enunciation, mention, pronouncement, speaking, statement, utterance, verbalization, voicing **2.** demonstration, embodiment, exhibition, indication, manifestation, representation, show, sign, symbol, token **3.** air, appearance, aspect, countenance, face, look, mien (*Literary*) **4.** choice of words, delivery, diction, emphasis, execution, intonation, language, phraseology, phrasing, speech, style, wording **5.** idiom, locution, phrase, remark, set phrase, term, turn of phrase, word

expressive 1. eloquent, emphatic, energetic, forcible, lively, mobile, moving, poignant, striking, strong, sympathetic, telling, vivid **2.** allusive, demonstrative, indicative, meaningful, pointed, pregnant, revealing, significant, suggestive, thoughtful

expressly 1. especially, exactly, intentionally, on purpose, particularly, precisely, purposely, specially, specifically **2.** absolutely, categorically, clearly, decidedly, definitely, distinctly, explicitly, in no uncertain terms, manifestly, outright, plainly, pointedly, positively, unambiguously, unequivocally, unmistakably

expropriate appropriate, arrogate, assume, commandeer, confiscate, impound, requisition, seize, take, take over

expulsion banishment, debarment, discharge, dislodgment, dismissal, ejection, eviction, exclusion, exile, expatriation, extrusion, proscription, removal

expurgate blue-pencil, bowdlerize, censor, clean up (*Inf.*), cut, purge, purify

exquisite 1. beautiful, dainty, delicate, elegant, fine, lovely, precious **2.** attractive, beautiful, charming, comely, lovely, pleasing, striking **3.** admirable, choice, consummate, delicious, excellent, fine, flawless, incomparable, matchless, outstanding, peerless, perfect, rare, select, splendid, superb, superlative **4.** appreciative, consummate, cultivated, discerning, discriminating, fastidious, impeccable, meticulous, polished, refined, selective, sensitive **5.** acute, excruciating, intense, keen, piercing, poignant, sharp

extempore *adv./adj.* ad lib, extemporaneous, extemporary, freely, impromptu, improvised, offhand, off the cuff (*Inf.*), off the top of one's head, on the spot, spontaneously, unplanned, unpremeditated, unprepared

extemporize ad-lib, improvise, make up, play (it) by ear

extend 1. carry on, continue, drag out, draw out, elongate, lengthen, make longer, prolong, protract, spin out, spread out, stretch, unfurl, unroll **2.** carry on, continue, go on, last, take **3.** amount to, attain, go as far as, reach, spread **4.** add to, amplify, augment, broaden, develop, dilate, enhance, enlarge, expand, increase, spread, supplement, widen **5.** advance, bestow, confer, give, grant, hold out, impart, offer, present, proffer, put forth, reach out, stretch out, yield

extended 1. continued, drawn-out, elongated, enlarged, lengthened, long, prolonged, protracted, spread (out), stretched out, unfolded, unfurled, unrolled **2.** broad, comprehensive, enlarged, expanded, extensive, far-reaching, large-scale, sweeping, thorough, wide, widespread **3.** conferred, outstretched, proffered, stretched out

extension 1. amplification, augmentation, broadening, continuation, delay, development, dilatation, distension, elongation, enlargement, expansion, extent, increase, lengthening, postponement, prolongation, protraction, spread, stretching, widening **2.** addendum, addition, adjunct, annexe, appendage, appendix, branch, ell, supplement, wing

extensive all-inclusive, broad, capacious, commodious, comprehensive, expanded, extended, far-flung, far-reaching, general, great, huge, large, large-scale, lengthy, long, pervasive, prevalent, protracted, spacious, sweeping, thorough, universal, vast, voluminous, wholesale, wide, widespread

—ex'tensiveness *n.*

extensor (ɪkˈstɛnsə, -sɔː) *n.* any muscle that stretches or extends an arm, leg, or other bodily part.

extent (ɪkˈstɛnt) *n.* 1. the range over which something extends; scope. 2. an area or volume.

extenuate (ɪkˈstɛnjʊˌeɪt) *vb.* (*tr.*) 1. to represent (an offence, fault, etc.) as being less serious than it appears, as by showing mitigating circumstances. 2. to cause to be or appear less serious; mitigate. 3. *Arch.* **a.** to emaciate or weaken. **b.** to dilute or thin out. —ex'tenuˌatingly *adv.* —exˌtenuˈation *n.* —ex'tenuˌator *n.* —ex'tenuatory *adj.*

exterior (ɪkˈstɪərɪə) *n.* 1. a part, surface, or region that is on the outside. 2. the outward behaviour or appearance of a person. 3. a film or scene shot outside a studio. ~*adj.* 4. of, situated on, or suitable for the outside. 5. coming or acting from without. —ex'teriorly *adv.*

exterior angle *n.* 1. an angle of a polygon contained between one side extended and the adjacent side. 2. any of the four angles made by a transversal that are outside the region between the two intersected lines.

exterminate (ɪkˈstɜːmɪˌneɪt) *vb.* (*tr.*) to destroy (living things, esp. pests or vermin) completely; annihilate; eliminate. —ex'terminable *adj.* —exˌtermiˈnation *n.* —ex'terminative *or* ex'terminatory *adj.* —ex'termiˌnator *n.*

external (ɪkˈstɜːnəl) *adj.* 1. of, situated on, or suitable for the outside; outer. 2. coming or acting from without. 3. of or involving foreign nations. 4. of, relating to, or designating a medicine that is applied to the outside of the body. 5. *Anat.* situated on or near the outside of the body. 6. *Philosophy.* (of objects, etc.) taken to exist independently of a perceiving mind. ~*n.* 7. (*often pl.*) an external circumstance or aspect, esp. one that is superficial. —ˌexterˈnality *n.*

externalize (ɪkˈstɜːnəˌlaɪz), **exteriorize** (ɪkˈstɪərɪəˌraɪz) *or* **-ise** *vb.* (*tr.*) 1. to make external; give outward shape to. 2. *Psychol.* to attribute (one's feelings) to one's surroundings. —exˌternaliˈzation, exˌterioriˈzation *or* **-iˈsation** *n.*

extinct (ɪkˈstɪŋkt) *adj.* 1. (of an animal or plant species) having died out. 2. quenched or extinguished. 3. (of a volcano) no longer liable to erupt; inactive.

extinction (ɪkˈstɪŋkʃən) *n.* 1. the act of making extinct or the state of being extinct. 2. the act of extinguishing or the state of being extinguished. 3. complete destruction; annihilation. 4. *Physics.* reduction of the intensity of radiation as a result of absorption or scattering by matter.

extinguish (ɪkˈstɪŋgwɪʃ) *vb.* (*tr.*) 1. to put out or quench (a light, flames, etc.). 2. to remove or destroy entirely; annihilate. 3. *Arch.* to eclipse or obscure. —ex'tin-

guishable *adj.* —ex'tinguisher *n.* —ex'tinguishment *n.*

extirpate (ˈɛkstəˌpeɪt) *vb.* (*tr.*) 1. to remove or destroy completely. 2. to pull up or out; uproot. —ˌextir'pation *n.* —'extirˌpative *adj.* —'extirˌpator *n.*

extol *or U.S.* **extoll** (ɪkˈstəʊl) *vb.* **-tolling, -tolled.** (*tr.*) to praise lavishly; exalt. —ex'toller *n.* —ex'tolment *n.*

extort (ɪkˈstɔːt) *vb.* (*tr.*) 1. to secure (money, favours, etc.) by intimidation, violence, or the misuse of authority. 2. to obtain by importunate demands. —ex'tortion *n.* —ex'tortionate *adj.* —ex'tortioner, ex'tortionist, *or* ex'torter *n.* —ex'tortive *adj.*

extra (ˈɛkstrə) *adj.* 1. being more than what is usual or expected; additional. ~*n.* 2. a person or thing that is additional. 3. something for which an additional charge is made. 4. an additional edition of a newspaper, esp. to report a new development. 5. *Films.* a person temporarily engaged, usually for crowd scenes. 6. *Cricket.* a run not scored from the bat, such as a wide, no-ball, or bye. ~*adv.* 7. unusually; exceptionally: *an extra fast car.*

extra- *prefix.* outside or beyond an area or scope: *extrasensory; extraterritorial.*

extract *vb.* (ɪkˈstrækt). (*tr.*) 1. to pull out or uproot by force. 2. to remove or separate. 3. to derive (pleasure, information, etc.) from some source. 4. to deduce or develop (a doctrine, policy, etc.). 5. *Inf.* to extort (money, etc.). 6. to obtain (a substance) from a mixture or material by a process, such as digestion, distillation, mechanical separation, etc. 7. to cut out or copy out (an article, passage, etc.) from a publication. 8. to determine the value of (the root of a number). ~*n.* (ˈɛkstrækt). 9. something extracted, such as a passage from a book, etc. 10. a preparation containing the active principle or concentrated essence of a material. —exˌtractaˈbility *n.* —ex'tractable *adj.* —ex'traction *n.* —ex'tractive *adj.* —ex'tractor *n.*

extradite (ˈɛkstrəˌdaɪt) *vb.* (*tr.*) 1. to surrender (an alleged offender) for trial to a foreign state. 2. to procure the extradition of. —'extraˌditable *adj.* —ˌextra'dition *n.*

extramarital (ˌɛkstrəˈmærɪtəl) *adj.* (esp. of sexual relations) occurring outside marriage.

extramural (ˌɛkstrəˈmjʊərəl) *adj.* 1. connected with but outside the normal courses of a university, college, etc. 2. beyond the boundaries or walls of a city, castle, etc.

extraneous (ɪkˈstreɪnɪəs) *adj.* 1. not essential. 2. not pertinent; irrelevant. 3. coming from without. 4. not belonging. —ex'traneousness *n.*

extraordinary (ɪkˈstrɔːdənrɪ) *adj.* 1. very unusual or surprising. 2. not in an established manner or order. 3. employed for particular purposes. 4. (*usually postposi-*

THESAURUS

extent 1. bounds, compass, play, range, reach, scope, sphere, sweep 2. amount, amplitude, area, breadth, bulk, degree, duration, expanse, expansion, length, magnitude, measure, quantity, size, stretch, term, time, volume, width

extenuating justifying, mitigating, moderating, qualifying, serving as an excuse

exterior *n.* 1. appearance, aspect, coating, covering, façade, face, finish, outside, shell, skin, surface ~*adj.* 2. external, outer, outermost, outside, outward, superficial, surface 3. alien, exotic, external, extraneous, extrinsic, foreign, outside

exterminate abolish, annihilate, destroy, eliminate, eradicate, extirpate

external 1. apparent, exterior, outer, outermost, outside, outward, superficial, surface, visible 2. alien, exotic, exterior, extramural, extraneous, extrinsic, foreign, independent, outside

extinct 1. dead, defunct, gone, lost, vanished 2. doused, extinguished, inactive, out, quenched, snuffed out 3. abolished, defunct, ended, obsolete, terminated, void

extinction abolition, annihilation, death, destruction, dying out, eradication, excision, extermination, extirpation, obliteration, oblivion

extinguish 1. blow out, douse, put out, quench, smother, snuff out, stifle 2. abolish,

annihilate, destroy, eliminate, end, eradicate, erase, expunge, exterminate, extirpate, kill, obscure, remove, suppress, wipe out

extol acclaim, applaud, celebrate, commend, cry up, eulogize, exalt, glorify, laud, magnify (*Archaic*), panegyrize, pay tribute to, praise, sing the praises of

extort blackmail, bleed (*Inf.*), bully, coerce, exact, extract, force, squeeze, wrest, wring

extortion 1. blackmail, coercion, compulsion, demand, exaction, force, oppression, rapacity 2. enormity, exorbitance, expensiveness, overcharging

extortionate 1. excessive, exorbitant, extravagant, immoderate, inflated, inordinate, outrageous, preposterous, sky-high, unreasonable 2. blood-sucking (*Inf.*), exacting, grasping, hard, harsh, oppressive, rapacious, rigorous, severe, usurious

extra *adj.* 1. accessory, added, additional, ancillary, auxiliary, fresh, further, more, new, other, supplemental, supplementary 2. excess, extraneous, inessential, leftover, needless, redundant, reserve, spare, superogatory, superfluous, supernumerary, surplus, unnecessary, unneeded, unused ~*n.* 3. accessory, addendum, addition, adjunct, affix, appendage, appurtenance, attachment, bonus, complement, extension, supernumerary, supplement ~*adv.* 4. especially, excep-

tionally, extraordinarily, extremely, particularly, remarkably, uncommonly, unusually

extract *v.* 1. draw, extirpate, pluck out, pull, pull out, remove, take out, uproot, withdraw 2. bring out, derive, draw, elicit, evoke, exact, gather, get, glean, obtain, reap, wrest, wring 3. deduce, derive, develop, educe, elicit, evolve 4. distil, draw out, express, obtain, press out, separate out, squeeze, take out 5. abstract, choose, cite, copy out, cull, cut out, quote, select ~*n.* 6. concentrate, decoction, distillate, distillation, essence, juice 7. abstract, citation, clipping, cutting, excerpt, passage, quotation, selection

extraction 1. drawing, extirpation, pulling, removal, taking out, uprooting, withdrawal 2. derivation, distillation, separation 3. ancestry, birth, blood, derivation, descent, family, lineage, origin, parentage, pedigree, race, stock

extraneous 1. accidental, additional, adventitious, extra, incidental, inessential, needless, nonessential, peripheral, redundant, superfluous, supplementary, unessential, unnecessary, unneeded 2. beside the point, immaterial, impertinent, inadmissible, inapplicable, inapposite, inappropriate, inapt, irrelevant, off the subject, unconnected, unrelated 3. adventitious, alien, exotic, external, extrinsic, foreign, out of place, strange

tive) (of an official, etc.) additional or subordinate. —**ex'traordinarily** *adv.* —**ex'traordinariness** *n.*

extrapolate (ɪk'stræpə,leɪt) *vb.* **1.** *Maths.* to estimate (a value of a function etc.) beyond the known values, by the extension of a curve. Cf. **interpolate** (sense 4). **2.** to infer (something) by using but not strictly deducing from known facts. —**ex,trapo'lation** *n.* —**ex'trapolative** *or* **ex'trapolatory** *adj.* —**ex'trapo,lator** *n.*

extrasensory (,ɛkstrə'sɛnsəri) *adj.* of or relating to extrasensory perception.

extrasensory perception *n.* the supposed ability of certain individuals to obtain information about the environment without the use of normal sensory channels.

extravagant (ɪk'strævɪgənt) *adj.* **1.** spending money excessively or immoderately. **2.** going beyond usual bounds; unrestrained. **3.** ostentatious; showy. **4.** exorbitant in price; overpriced. —**ex'travagance** *n.*

extravaganza (ɪk,strævə'gænzə) *n.* **1.** an elaborately staged light entertainment. **2.** any lavish or fanciful display, literary composition, etc.

extreme (ɪk'striːm) *adj.* **1.** being of a high or of the highest degree or intensity. **2.** exceeding what is usual or reasonable; immoderate. **3.** very strict or severe; drastic. **4.** (*prenominal*) farthest or outermost. ~*n.* **5.** the highest or furthest degree (often in **in the extreme, go to extremes**). **6.** (*often pl.*) either of the two limits or ends of a scale or range. **7.** *Maths.* the first or last term of a series or a proportion. —**ex'tremeness** *n.* —**ex'tremely** *adv.* —**ex'tremist** *n.* —**extremity** (-'strɛm-) *n.*

extreme unction *n. R.C. Church.* a sacrament in which a person who is seriously ill or dying is anointed by a priest.

extricate ('ɛkstrɪ,keɪt) *vb.* (*tr.*) to remove or free from complication, hindrance, or difficulty; disentangle. —**'extricable** *adj.* —,**extri'cation** *n.*

extrinsic (ɛk'strɪnsɪk) *adj.* **1.** not contained or included within; extraneous. **2.** originating or acting from outside. —**ex'trinsically** *adv.*

extrovert *or* **extravert** ('ɛkstrə,vɜːt) *Psychol. n.* **1.** a person concerned more with external reality than inner feelings. ~*adj.* **2.** of or characterized by extroversion. —,**extro'version** *or* ,**extra'version** *n.* —'**extro,verted** *or* '**extra,verted** *adj.*

extrude (ɪk'struːd) *vb.* **1.** (*tr.*) to squeeze or force out. **2.** (*tr.*) to produce (moulded sections of plastic, metal, etc.) by ejection from a shaped nozzle or die. —**ex'trusion** *n.*

exuberant (ɪg'zjuːbərənt) *adj.* **1.** abounding in vigour and high spirits. **2.** lavish or effusive; excessively elaborate. **3.** growing luxuriantly or in profusion. —**ex'uberance** *n.*

exude (ɪg'zjuːd) *vb.* **1.** to release or be released through pores, incisions, etc., as sweat or sap. **2.** (*tr.*) to make apparent by mood or behaviour. —,**exu'dation** *n.*

exult (ɪg'zʌlt) *vb.* (*intr.*) **1.** to be joyful or jubilant, esp. because of triumph or success. **2.** (often foll. by *over*) to triumph (over). —**ex'ultant** *adj.* —**exultation** (,ɛgzʌl-'teɪʃən) *n.* —**ex'ultingly** *adv.*

-ey *suffix.* variant of **-y¹** and **-y²**.

eye (aɪ) *n.* **1.** the organ of sight of animals. Related adjs.: **ocular, ophthalmic. 2.** (*often pl.*) the ability to see; sense of vision. **3.** the external part of an eye, often including the area around it. **4.** a look, glance, expression, or gaze. **5.** a sexually inviting or provocative look (esp. in **give (someone) the (glad) eye; make eyes at**). **6.** attention or observation (often in **catch someone's eye; keep an eye on; cast an eye over**). **7.** ability to recognize, judge, or appreciate. **8.** (*often pl.*) opinion, judgment, point of view, or authority: *in the eyes of the law.* **9.** a structure or marking resembling an eye, such as the bud on a potato tuber or a spot on a butterfly wing. **10.** a small loop or hole, as at one end of a needle. **11.** a small area of low pressure and calm in the centre of a tornado. **12.** *Inf.* See **private eye. 13. all eyes.** *Inf.* acutely vigilant or observant. **14.** (**all**) **my eye.** *Inf.* rubbish; nonsense. **15. an eye for an eye.** retributive or vengeful justice; retaliation. **16. get one's eye in.** *Chiefly sports.* to become accustomed to the conditions, light, etc., with a consequent improvement in one's performance. **17. half an eye.** a modicum of perceptiveness. **18. have eyes for.** to be interested in. **19. in one's mind's eye.** pictured within the mind; imagined or remembered vividly. **20. in the public eye.** exposed to public curiosity or publicity. **21. keep an eye open** *or* **out (for).** to watch with special attention (for). **22. keep one's eyes skinned.** to watch vigilantly. **23. lay, clap,** *or* **set eyes on.** (*usually with a negative*) to see. **24. look (someone) in the eye.** to look openly and without shame or embarrassment at. **25. make sheep's eyes (at).** *Arch.* to ogle amorously. **26. more than meets the eye.** hidden motives, meaning, or facts. **27. see eye to eye (with).** to agree (with). **28. shut one's eyes to** *or* **turn a blind eye to.** to overlook or ignore deliberately. **29. up to one's eyes (in).** extremely busy (with). **30. with** *or* **having an eye to.** (*prep.*) **a.** regarding; with reference to. **b.** with the intention or purpose

THESAURUS

extraordinary amazing, bizarre, curious, exceptional, fantastic, marvellous, odd, outstanding, particular, peculiar, phenomenal, rare, remarkable, singular, special, strange, surprising, uncommon, unfamiliar, unheard-of, unique, unprecedented, unusual, unwonted, weird, wonderful

extravagance 1. improvidence, lavishness, overspending, prodigality, profligacy, profusion, squandering, waste, wastefulness **2.** absurdity, dissipation, exaggeration, excess, exorbitance, folly, immoderation, outrageousness, preposterousness, recklessness, unreasonableness, unrestraint, wildness

extravagant 1. excessive, improvident, imprudent, lavish, prodigal, profligate, spendthrift, wasteful **2.** absurd, exaggerated, excessive, exorbitant, fanciful, fantastic, foolish, immoderate, inordinate, outrageous, preposterous, reckless, unreasonable, unrestrained, wild **3.** fancy, flamboyant, flashy, garish, gaudy, grandiose, ornate, ostentatious, pretentious, showy **4.** costly, excessive, exorbitant, expensive, extortionate, inordinate, overpriced, steep (*Inf.*), unreasonable

extreme *adj.* **1.** acute, great, greatest, high, highest, intense, maximum, severe, supreme, ultimate, utmost, uttermost, worst **2.** downright, egregious, exaggerated, exceptional, excessive, extraordinary, extravagant, fanatical, immoderate, inordinate, intemperate, out-and-out, outrageous, radical, remarkable, sheer, uncommon, unconventional, unreasonable, unusual, utter, zealous **3.** dire, Draconian, drastic, harsh, radical,

rigid, severe, stern, strict, unbending, uncompromising **4.** faraway, far-off, farthest, final, last, most distant, outermost, remotest, terminal, ultimate, utmost, uttermost ~*n.* **5.** acme, apex, apogee, boundary, climax, consummation, depth, edge, end, excess, extremity, height, limit, maximum, minimum, nadir, pinnacle, pole, termination, top, ultimate, zenith

extremely acutely, awfully (*Inf.*), exceedingly, exceptionally, excessively, extraordinarily, greatly, highly, inordinately, intensely, markedly, quite, severely, terribly, to or in the extreme, ultra, uncommonly, unusually, utterly, very

extremist die-hard, fanatic, radical, ultra, zealot

extremity 1. acme, apex, apogee, border, bound, boundary, brim, brink, edge, end, extreme, frontier, limit, margin, maximum, minimum, nadir, pinnacle, pole, rim, terminal, termination, terminus, tip, top, ultimate, verge, zenith **2.** acuteness, climax, consummation, depth, excess, height **3.** adversity, crisis, dire straits, disaster, emergency, exigency, hardship, pinch, plight, setback, trouble **4. Plural** fingers and toes, hands and feet, limbs

extricate clear, deliver, disembarrass, disengage, disentangle, free, get out, get (someone) off the hook (*Sl.*), liberate, release, relieve, remove, rescue, withdraw, wriggle out of

exuberance 1. animation, buoyancy, cheerfulness, eagerness, ebullience, effer-

vescence, energy, enthusiasm, excitement, exhilaration, high spirits, life, liveliness, spirit, sprightliness, vigour, vitality, vivacity, zest **2.** effusiveness, exaggeration, excessiveness, fulsomeness, lavishness, prodigality, superfluity **3.** abundance, copiousness, lavishness, lushness, luxuriance, plenitude, profusion, rankness, richness, superabundance, teemingness

exuberant 1. animated, buoyant, cheerful, eager, ebullient, effervescent, elated, energetic, enthusiastic, excited, exhilarated, high-spirited, in high spirits, lively, sparkling, spirited, sprightly, vigorous, vivacious, zestful **2.** effusive, exaggerated, excessive, fulsome, lavish, overdone, prodigal, superfluous **3.** abundant, copious, lavish, lush, luxuriant, overflowing, plenteous, plentiful, profuse, rank, rich, superabundant, teeming

exult 1. be delighted, be elated, be in high spirits, be joyful, be jubilant, be overjoyed, celebrate, jubilate, jump for joy, make merry, rejoice **2.** boast, brag, crow, gloat, glory (in), revel, take delight in, taunt, triumph, vaunt

exultant cock-a-hoop, delighted, elated, exulting, flushed, gleeful, joyful, joyous, jubilant, overjoyed, rejoicing, revelling, transported, triumphant

exultation 1. celebration, delight, elation, glee, high spirits, joy, joyousness, jubilation, merriness, rejoicing, transport **2.** boasting, bragging, crowing, gloating, glory, glorying, revelling, triumph

of. **31. with one's eyes open.** in the full knowledge of all relevant facts. **32. with one's eyes shut. a.** with great ease, esp. as a result of thorough familiarity. **b.** without being aware of all the facts. ~*vb.* **eyeing** *or* **eying, eyed.** (*tr.*) **33.** to look at carefully or warily. **34.** to look at in a manner indicating sexual interest; ogle. —**'eyeless** *adj.* —**'eye,like** *adj.*

eyeball ('aɪ,bɔːl) *n.* **1.** the entire ball-shaped part of the eye. **2. eyeball to eyeball.** in close confrontation.

eyebrow ('aɪ,brau) *n.* **1.** the transverse bony ridge over each eye. **2.** the arch of hair that covers this ridge.

eye-catching *adj.* tending to attract attention; striking. —**'eye-,catcher** *n.*

eyed (aɪd) *adj.* **a.** having an eye or eyes (as specified). **b.** (*in combination*): *brown-eyed.*

eye dog *n.* *N.Z.* a dog trained to control sheep by staring fixedly at them. Also called: **strong-eye dog.**

eyeful ('aɪ,ful) *n.* *Inf.* **1.** a view, glance, or gaze. **2.** a beautiful or attractive sight, esp. a woman.

eyeglass ('aɪ,glɑːs) *n.* **1.** a lens for aiding or correcting defective vision, esp. a monocle. **2.** another word for **eyepiece.**

eyeglasses ('aɪ,glɑːsɪz) *pl. n.* Now chiefly *U.S.* another word for **spectacles.**

eyehole ('aɪ,houl) *n.* **1.** a hole through which a rope, hook, etc. is passed. **2.** *Inf.* the cavity that contains the eyeball.

eyelash ('aɪ,læʃ) *n.* **1.** any one of the short curved hairs that grow from the edge of the eyelids. **2.** a row or fringe of these hairs.

eyelet ('aɪlɪt) *n.* **1.** a small hole for a lace, cord, or hook to be passed through. **2.** a small metal ring or tube reinforcing an eyehole in fabric. **3.** a small opening, such as a peephole in a wall. **4.** *Embroidery.* a small hole with finely stitched edges. **5.** a small eye or eyelike marking. ~*vb.* **6.** (*tr.*) to supply with an eyelet or eyelets.

eyelevel ('aɪ,lɛvəl) *adj.* level with a person's eyes when looking straight ahead: *an eyelevel grill.*

eyelid ('aɪ,lɪd) *n.* either of the two muscular folds of skin that can be moved to cover the exposed portion of the eyeball.

eyeliner ('aɪ,laɪnə) *n.* a cosmetic used to outline the eyes.

eye-opener *n.* *Inf.* **1.** something startling or revealing. **2.** *U.S.* an alcoholic drink taken early in the morning.

eyepiece ('aɪ,piːs) *n.* the lens or lenses in an optical instrument nearest the eye of the observer.

eye rhyme *n.* a rhyme involving words that are similar in spelling but not in sound, such as *stone* and *none.*

eye shadow *n.* a coloured cosmetic put around the eyes.

eyeshot ('aɪ,ʃɒt) *n.* range of vision; view.

eyesight ('aɪ,saɪt) *n.* the ability to see; faculty of sight.

eyesore ('aɪ,sɔː) *n.* something very ugly.

eyespot ('aɪ,spɒt) *n.* **1.** a small area of light-sensitive pigment in some simple organisms. **2.** an eyelike marking, as on a butterfly wing.

eyestrain ('aɪ,streɪn) *n.* fatigue or irritation of the eyes, resulting from excessive use or uncorrected defects of vision.

Eyetie ('aɪtaɪ) *n., adj.* Brit. *sl.,* offensive. Italian.

eyetooth ('aɪ,tuːθ) *n., pl.* **-teeth. 1.** either of the two canine teeth in the upper jaw. **2. give one's eyeteeth for.** *Inf.* to go to any lengths to achieve or obtain (something).

eyewash ('aɪ,wɒʃ) *n.* **1.** a lotion for the eyes. **2.** *Inf.* nonsense; rubbish.

eyewitness ('aɪ,wɪtnɪs) *n.* a person present at an event who can describe what happened.

eyrie ('ɪərɪ, 'ɛərɪ, 'aɪərɪ) *or* **aerie** *n.* **1.** the nest of an eagle or other bird of prey, built in a high inaccessible place. **2.** any high isolated position or place.

eyrir ('eɪrɪə) *n., pl.* **aurar** ('ɔɪraː). an Icelandic monetary unit worth one hundredth of a krona.

THESAURUS

eye *n.* **1.** eyeball, optic (*Inf.*), orb (*Poetic*), peeper (*Sl.*) **2.** appreciation, discernment, discrimination, judgment, perception, recognition, taste **3.** *Often plural* belief, judgment, mind, opinion, point of view, viewpoint **4. keep an** *or* **one's eye on** guard, keep in view, keep tabs on (*Inf.*), keep under surveillance, look after, look out for, monitor, observe, pay attention to, regard, scrutinize, supervise, survey, watch, watch over **5. an eye for an eye** justice, reprisal, requital, retaliation, retribution, revenge, vengeance **6. lay, clap**

or **set eyes on** behold, come across, encounter, meet, notice, observe, run into, see **7. see eye to eye** accord, agree, back, be in unison, coincide, concur, fall in, get on, go along, harmonize, jibe (*Inf.*), subscribe to **8. up to one's eyes** busy, caught up, engaged, flooded out, fully occupied, inundated, overwhelmed, up to here, up to one's elbows, wrapped up in ~*v.* **9.** contemplate, gaze at, glance at, have *or* take a look at, inspect, look at, peruse, regard, scan, scrutinize, stare at, study, survey, view, watch **10. eye up, give** (someone) the

(glad) eye, leer at, make eyes at, ogle

eyesight observation, perception, range of vision, sight, vision

eyesore atrocity, blemish, blight, blot, disfigurement, disgrace, horror, mess, monstrosity, sight (*Inf.*), ugliness

eyewitness bystander, looker-on, observer, onlooker, passer-by, spectator, viewer, watcher, witness

F

f *or* **F** (εf) *n.*, *pl.* **f's**, **F's**, *or* **Fs**. **1.** the sixth letter of the English alphabet. **2.** a speech sound represented by this letter, as in *fat*.

f *symbol for:* **1.** *Music.* forte: an instruction to play loudly. **2.** *Physics.* frequency. **3.** *Maths.* function (of). **4.** *Physics.* femto-.

f, f/, *or* **f:** *symbol for* f number.

f. *or* **F.** *abbrev. for:* **1.** female. **2.** *Grammar.* feminine. **3.** (*pl.* **ff.** *or* **FF.**) folio. **4.** (*pl.* **ff.**) following (page). **5.** franc(s). **6.** furlong.

F *symbol for:* **1.** *Music.* **a.** the fourth note of the scale of C major. **b.** the major or minor key having this note as its tonic. **2.** Fahrenheit. **3.** *Chem.* fluorine. **4.** *Physics.* force. **5.** farad(s). **6.** *Genetics.* a generation of filial offspring, F_1 being the first generation of offspring.

fa *or* **fah** (fɑː) *Music.* **1.** (in the fixed system of solmization) the note F. **2.** (in tonic sol-fa) the fourth degree of any major scale.

FA (in Britain) *abbrev. for* Football Association.

f.a. *or* **F.A.** *abbrev. for* fanny adams.

Fabian ('feɪbɪən) *adj.* **1.** of or resembling the delaying tactics of Q. Fabius Maximus, Roman general who wore out the strength of Hannibal while avoiding a pitched battle; cautious. ~*n.* **2.** a member of or sympathizer with the Fabian Society. —**'Fabia,nism** *n.*

fable ('feɪbəl) *n.* **1.** a short moral story, esp. one with animals as characters. **2.** a false, fictitious, or improbable account. **3.** a story or legend about supernatural or mythical characters or events. **4.** legends or myths collectively. ~*vb.* **5.** to relate or tell (fables). **6.** (*intr.*) to tell lies. **7.** (*tr.*) to talk about or describe in the manner of a fable. —**'fabler** *n.*

fabled ('feɪbəld) *adj.* **1.** made famous in fable. **2.** fictitious.

fabric ('fæbrɪk) *n.* **1.** any cloth made from yarn or fibres by weaving, knitting, felting, etc. **2.** the texture of a cloth. **3.** a structure or framework: *the fabric of society.* **4.** a style or method of construction. **5.** *Rare.* a building.

fabricate ('fæbrɪ,keɪt) *vb.* (*tr.*) **1.** to make, build, or construct. **2.** to devise or concoct (a story, etc.). **3.** to fake or forge. —**,fabri'cation** *n.* —**'fabri,cator** *n.*

fabulous ('fæbjʊləs) *adj.* **1.** almost unbelievable; astounding; legendary: *fabulous wealth.* **2.** *Inf.* extremely good: *a fabulous time at the party.* **3.** of, relating to, or based upon fable: *a fabulous beast.* —**'fabulously** *adv.* —**'fabulousness** *n.*

façade *or* **facade** (fə'sɑːd, fæ-) *n.* **1.** the face of a building, esp. the main front. **2.** a front or outer appearance, esp. a deceptive one.

face (feɪs) *n.* **1. a.** the front of the head from the forehead to the lower jaw. **b.** (*as modifier*): *face flannel.* **2.**

a. the expression of the countenance: *a sad face.* **b.** a distorted expression, esp. to indicate disgust. **3.** *Inf.* make-up (esp. in **put one's face on**). **4.** outward appearance: *the face of the countryside is changing.* **5.** appearance or pretence (esp. in **put a bold, good, bad,** etc., **face on**). **6.** dignity (esp. in **lose** *or* **save face**). **7.** *Inf.* impudence or effrontery. **8.** the main side of an object, building, etc., or the front: *a cliff face.* **9.** the marked surface of an instrument, esp. the dial of a timepiece. **10.** the functional or working side of an object, as of a tool or playing card. **11. a.** the exposed area of a mine from which coal, ore, etc., may be mined. **b.** (*as modifier*): *face worker.* **12.** the uppermost part or surface: *the face of the earth.* **13.** Also called: **side.** any one of the plane surfaces of a crystal or other solid figure. **14.** Also called: **typeface.** *Printing.* **a.** the printing surface of any type character. **b.** the style or design of the character on the type. **15.** *N.Z.* the exposed slope of a hill. **16. face to face.** in confrontation. **17. in (the) face of.** despite. **18. on the face of it.** to all appearances. **19. set one's face against.** to oppose with determination. **20. show one's face.** to make an appearance. **21. to someone's face.** in someone's presence: *I told him the truth to his face.* ~*vb.* **22.** (when *intr.*, often foll. by *to, towards,* or *on*) to look or be situated or placed (in a specified direction): *the house faces onto the square.* **23.** to be opposite: *facing page 9.* **24.** (*tr.*) to be confronted by: *he faces many problems.* **25.** (*tr.*) to provide with a surface of a different material. **26.** to dress the surface of (stone or other material). **27.** (*tr.*) to expose (a card) with the face uppermost. **28.** *Mil.* to order (a formation) to turn in a certain direction or (of a formation) to turn as required: *right face!*

face card *n.* the usual U.S. term for **court card.**

faceless ('feɪslɪs) *adj.* **1.** without a face. **2.** without identity; anonymous. —**'facelessness** *n.*

face-lift *n.* **1.** cosmetic surgery for tightening sagging skin and smoothing wrinkles on the face. **2.** any improvement or renovation.

facer ('feɪsə) *n.* **1.** a person or thing that faces. **2.** *Brit. inf.* a difficulty or problem.

face-saving *adj.* maintaining dignity or prestige.

facet ('fæsɪt) *n.* **1.** any of the surfaces of a cut gemstone. **2.** an aspect or phase, as of a subject or personality. ~*vb.* **-eting, -eted** *or* **-etting, -etted.** **3.** (*tr.*) to cut facets in (a gemstone).

facetious (fə'siːʃəs) *adj.* **1.** characterized by love of joking. **2.** jocular or amusing, esp. at inappropriate times: *facetious remarks.* —**fa'cetiously** *adv.* —**fa'cetiousness** *n.*

THESAURUS

fable 1. allegory, apologue, legend, myth, parable, story, tale **2.** fabrication, fairy story (*Inf.*), falsehood, fantasy, fib, fiction, figment, invention, lie, romance, tall story (*Inf.*), untruth, white lie, yarn (*Inf.*)

fabric 1. cloth, material, stuff, textile, web **2.** constitution, construction, foundations, framework, infrastructure, make-up, organization, structure

fabricate 1. assemble, build, construct, erect, fashion, form, frame, make, manufacture, shape **2.** coin, concoct, devise, fake, falsify, feign, forge, invent, make up, trump up

fabrication 1. assemblage, assembly, building, construction, erection, manufacture, production **2.** cock-and-bull story (*Inf.*), concoction, fable, fairy story (*Inf.*), fake, falsehood, fiction, figment, forgery, invention, lie, myth, untruth

fabulous *n.* **1.** amazing, astounding, breathtaking, fictitious, immense, inconceivable, incredible, legendary, phenomenal, unbelievable **2.** *Inf.* fantastic (*Inf.*), marvellous, out-of-this-world (*Inf.*), spectacular, superb,

wonderful **3.** apocryphal, fantastic, fictitious, imaginary, invented, legendary, made-up, mythical, unreal

façade appearance, exterior, face, front, frontage, guise, mask, pretence, semblance, show, veneer

face *n.* **1.** clock (*Sl.*), countenance, dial (*Sl.*), features, kisser (*Sl.*), lineaments, mug (*Sl.*), phiz *or* phizog (*Sl.*), physiognomy, visage **2.** appearance, aspect, expression, frown, grimace, look, *moue,* pout, scowl, smirk **3.** air, appearance, disguise, display, exterior, façade, front, mask, pretence, semblance, show **4.** authority, dignity, honour, image, prestige, reputation, self-respect, standing, status **5.** *Inf.* assurance, audacity, boldness, brass neck (*Inf.*), cheek (*Inf.*), confidence, effrontery, gall (*Inf.*), impudence, nerve, presumption, sauce (*Inf.*) **6.** aspect, cover, exterior, facet, front, outside, right side, side, surface **7. face to face** *à deux,* confronting, eyeball to eyeball, in confrontation, opposite, tête-à-tête, vis-à-vis **8. fly in the face of** act in defiance of, defy, disobey, go against, oppose, rebel against, snap one's fingers at (*Inf.*) **9.**

on the face of it apparently, at first sight, seemingly, to all appearances, to the eye **10. pull** (*or* **make**) **a long face** frown, grimace, knit one's brows, look black (disapproving, displeased, put out, stern), lower, pout, scowl, sulk **11. show one's face** approach, be seen, come, put in *or* make an appearance, show up (*Inf.*), turn up **12. to one's face** directly, in one's presence, openly, straight ~*v.* **13.** be confronted by, brave, come up against, confront, cope with, deal with, defy, encounter, experience, meet, oppose **14.** be opposite, front onto, give towards *or* onto, look onto, overlook **15.** clad, coat, cover, dress, finish, level, line, overlay, sheathe, surface, veneer

facet angle, aspect, face, part, phase, plane, side, slant, surface

facetious amusing, comical, droll, flippant, frivolous, funny, humorous, jesting, jocose, jocular, merry, playful, pleasant, tongue in cheek, unserious, waggish, witty

face up to accept, acknowledge, come to terms with, confront, cope with, deal with,

face value n. 1. the value written or stamped on the face of a commercial paper or coin. 2. apparent worth or value.

facia ('feɪʃɪə) n. a variant spelling of **fascia**.

facial ('feɪʃəl) adj. 1. of or relating to the face. ~n. 2. a beauty treatment for the face, involving massage and cosmetic packs. —**'facially** adv.

-facient suffix forming adjectives and nouns. indicating a state or quality: absorbefacient.

facile ('fæsaɪl) adj. 1. easy to perform or achieve. 2. working or moving easily or smoothly. 3. superficial: a facile solution. —**'facilely** adv. —**'facileness** n.

facilitate (fə'sɪlɪˌteɪt) vb. (tr.) to assist the progress of. —**faˌciliˈtation** n.

facility (fə'sɪlɪtɪ) n., pl. -**ties**. 1. ease of action or performance. 2. ready skill or ease deriving from practice or familiarity. 3. (often pl.) the means or equipment facilitating the performance of an action. 4. Rare. easygoing disposition. 5. (usually pl.) a euphemistic word for lavatory.

facing ('feɪsɪŋ) n. 1. a piece of material used esp. to conceal the seam of a garment and prevent fraying. 2. (usually pl.) the collar, cuffs, etc., of the jacket of a military uniform. 3. an outer layer or coat of material applied to the surface of a wall.

facsimile (fæk'sɪmɪlɪ) n. 1. an exact copy or reproduction. 2. a telegraphic system in which a written or pictorial document is scanned photoelectrically, the resulting signals being transmitted and reproduced photographically. ~vb. -**leing**, -**led**. 3. (tr.) to make an exact copy of.

fact (fækt) n. 1. an event or thing known to have happened or existed. 2. a truth verifiable from experience or observation. 3. a piece of information: get me all the facts of this case. 4. Law. (often pl.) an actual event, happening, etc., as distinguished from its legal consequences. 5. after (or before) the fact. Criminal law. after (or before) the commission of the offence. 6. as a matter of fact, in fact, in point of fact. in reality or actuality. 7. fact of life. an inescapable truth, esp. an unpleasant one. See also facts of life.

faction ('fækʃən) n. 1. a group of people forming a minority within a larger body, esp. a dissentious group. 2. strife or dissension within a group. —**'factional** adj.

factious ('fækʃəs) adj. given to, producing, or characterized by faction. —**'factiously** adv.

factitious (fæk'tɪʃəs) adj. 1. artificial rather than natural. 2. not genuine; sham: factitious enthusiasm. —**fac'titiously** adv. —**fac'titiousness** n.

factor ('fæktə) n. 1. an element or cause that contributes to a result. 2. Maths. one of two or more integers or polynomials whose product is a given integer or polynomial: 2 and 3 are factors of 6. 3. a person who acts on another's behalf, esp. one who transacts business for another. 4. former name for a **gene**. 5. Commercial law. a person to whom goods are consigned for sale and who

is paid a factorage. 6. (in Scotland) the manager of an estate. ~vb. 7. (intr.) to engage in the business of a factor. —**'factorable** adj. —**'factorˌship** n.

factorial (fæk'tɔːrɪəl) Maths. ~n. 1. the product of all the positive integers from one up to and including a given integer: factorial four is $1 \times 2 \times 3 \times 4$. ~adj. 2. of or involving factorials or factors. —**fac'torially** adv.

factory ('fæktərɪ) n., pl. -**ries**. **a.** a building or group of buildings containing a plant assembly for the manufacture of goods. **b.** (as modifier): a factory worker. —**'factory-ˌlike** adj.

factory farm n. a farm in which animals are intensively reared using modern industrial methods. —**factory farming** n.

factory ship n. a vessel that processes fish supplied by a fleet.

factotum (fæk'təʊtəm) n. a person employed to do all kinds of work.

facts of life pl. n. the. the details of sexual behaviour and reproduction. See also fact (sense 7).

factual ('fæktʃʊəl) adj. 1. of, relating to, or characterized by facts. 2. real; actual. —**'factually** adv. —**'factualness** or ˌfactu'ality n.

faculty ('fækəltɪ) n., pl. -**ties**. 1. one of the inherent powers of the mind or body, such as memory, sight, or hearing. 2. any ability or power, whether acquired or inherent. 3. a conferred power or right. 4. **a.** a department within a university or college devoted to a particular branch of knowledge. **b.** the staff of such a department. **c.** Chiefly U.S. all administrative and teaching staff at a university, school, etc. 5. all members of a learned profession.

fad (fæd) n. Inf. 1. an intense but short-lived fashion. 2. a personal idiosyncrasy. —**'faddish** or **'faddy** adj.

fade (feɪd) vb. 1. to lose or cause to lose brightness, colour, or clarity. 2. (intr.) to lose vigour or youth. 3. (intr.; usually foll. by away or out) to vanish slowly. 4. to decrease the brightness or volume of (a television or radio programme) or (of a television programme, etc.) to decrease in this way. 5. (intr.) (of the brakes of a vehicle) to lose power. 6. to cause (a golf ball) to veer from a straight line or (of a golf ball) to veer from a straight flight. ~n. 7. the act or an instance of fading. —**'fadeless** adj. —**'fadedness** n.

fade-in n. 1. Films. an optical effect in which a shot appears gradually out of darkness. ~vb. **fade in** (adv.). 2. to increase or cause to increase gradually, as vision or sound in a film or broadcast.

fade-out n. 1. Films. an optical effect in which a shot slowly disappears into darkness. 2. a gradual and temporary loss of a radio or television signal. 3. a slow or gradual disappearance. ~vb. **fade out**. (adv.) 4. to decrease or cause to decrease gradually, as vision or sound in a film or broadcast.

THESAURUS

facile 1. adept, adroit, dexterous, easy, effortless, fluent, light, proficient, quick, ready, simple, skilful, smooth, uncomplicated 2. cursory, glib, hasty, shallow, slick, superficial

facilitate assist the progress of, ease, expedite, forward, further, help, make easy, promote, smooth the path of, speed up

facility 1. ability, adroitness, dexterity, ease, efficiency, effortlessness, expertness, fluency, knack, proficiency, quickness, readiness, skilfulness, skill, smoothness 2. Often plural advantage, aid, amenity, appliance, convenience, equipment, means, opportunity, resource

facing 1. adj. fronting, opposite, partnering 2. n. cladding, coating, façade, false front, front, overlay, plaster, reinforcement, revetment, stucco, surface, trimming, veneer

facsimile carbon, carbon copy, copy, duplicate, photocopy, Photostat (Trademark), print, replica, reproduction, transcript, Xerox (Trademark)

fact 1. act, deed, event, fait accompli, happening, incident, occurrence, performance 2. actuality, certainty, gospel (truth), naked truth, reality, truth 3. circumstance, detail,

feature, item, particular, point, specific 4. **in fact** actually, indeed, in point of fact, in reality, in truth, really, truly

faction 1. bloc, cabal, camp, caucus, clique, coalition, combination, confederacy, contingent, division, gang, ginger group, group, junta, lobby, minority, party, pressure group, section, sector, set, splinter group 2. conflict, disagreement, discord, disharmony, dissension, disunity, division, divisiveness, friction, infighting, rebellion, sedition, strife, tumult, turbulence

factious conflicting, contentious, disputatious, dissident, divisive, insurrectionary, litigious, malcontent, mutinous, partisan, rebellious, refractory, rival, sectarian, seditious, troublemaking, tumultuous, turbulent, warring

factor 1. aspect, cause, circumstance, component, consideration, determinant, element, influence, item, part, point, thing 2. Scot. agent, deputy, estate manager, middleman, reeve, steward

factory manufactory (Obsolete), mill, plant, works

factotum Girl Friday, handyman, jack of all trades, Man Friday, man of all work, odd

job man

facts data, details, gen (Inf.), info (Inf.), information, the lowdown (Inf.), the score (Inf.), the whole story

factual accurate, authentic, circumstantial, close, correct, credible, exact, faithful, genuine, literal, matter-of-fact, objective, precise, real, sure, true, true-to-life, unadorned, unbiased, veritable

faculties capabilities, intelligence, powers, reason, senses, wits

faculty 1. ability, adroitness, aptitude, bent, capability, capacity, cleverness, dexterity, facility, gift, knack, power, propensity, readiness, skill, talent, turn 2. branch of learning, department, discipline, profession, school, teaching staff (Chiefly U.S.) 3. authorization, licence, prerogative, privilege, right

fad affectation, craze, fancy, fashion, mania, mode, rage, trend, vogue, whim

fade 1. blanch, bleach, blench, dim, discolour, dull, grow dim, lose colour, lose lustre, pale, wash out 2. decline, die away, die out, dim, disappear, disperse, dissolve, droop, dwindle, ebb, etiolate, evanesce, fail, fall, flag, languish, melt away, perish, shrivel,

faeces *or esp. U.S.* **feces** ('fiːsiːz) *pl. n.* bodily waste matter discharged through the anus. —**faecal** *or esp. U.S.* **fecal** ('fiːkəl) *adj.*

faerie *or* **faery** ('feɪərɪ, 'feərɪ) *n., pl.* **-ries.** *Arch. or poetic.* **1.** the land of fairies. *~adj., n.* **2.** a variant spelling of **fairy.**

Faeroese *or* **Faroese** (,feərəʊ'iːz) *adj.* **1.** of or characteristic of the Faeroes, islands in the N Atlantic, their inhabitants, or their language. *~n.* **2.** the language of the Faeroes, closely related to Icelandic. **3.** (*pl.* **-ese**) a native or inhabitant of the Faeroes.

faff (fæf) *vb.* (*intr.; often foll. by about*) *Brit. inf.* to dither or fuss.

fag¹ (fæg) *n.* **1.** *Inf.* a boring or wearisome task. **2.** *Brit.* (*esp. formerly*) a young public school boy who performs menial chores for an older boy or prefect. *~vb.* **fagging, fagged. 3.** (when *tr.*, often foll. by *out*) *Inf.* to become or cause to become exhausted by hard work **4.** (*usually intr.*) *Brit.* to do or cause to do menial chores in a public school.

fag² (fæg) *n. Brit. sl.* a cigarette.

fag³ (fæg) *n. Sl., chiefly U.S.* short for **faggot².**

fag end *n.* **1.** the last and worst part. **2.** *Brit. inf.* the stub of a cigarette.

faggot¹ *or esp. U.S.* **fagot** ('fægət) *n.* **1.** a bundle of sticks or twigs, esp. when used as fuel. **2.** a bundle of iron bars, esp. to be forged into wrought iron. **3.** a ball of chopped meat bound with herbs and bread and eaten fried. *~vb.* (*tr.*) **4.** to collect into a bundle or bundles. **5.** *Needlework.* to do faggoting on (a garment, etc.).

faggot² ('fægət) *n. Sl., chiefly U.S.* a male homosexual.

Fah. *or* **Fahr.** *abbrev. for* Fahrenheit.

Fahrenheit ('færən,haɪt) *adj.* of or measured according to the Fahrenheit scale of temperature. Symbol: **F**

Fahrenheit scale *n.* a scale of temperatures in which 32° represents the melting point of ice and 212° represents the boiling point of pure water under standard atmospheric pressure. Cf. **Celsius scale.**

faïence (faɪ'ɑːns, feɪ-) *n.* tin-glazed earthenware, usually that of French, German, Italian, or Scandinavian origin.

fail (feɪl) *vb.* **1.** to be unsuccessful in an attempt (at something or to do something). **2.** (*intr.*) to stop operating or working properly: *the steering failed suddenly.* **3.** to judge or be judged as being below the officially accepted standard required in (a course, examination, etc.). **4.** (*tr.*) to prove disappointing or useless to (someone). **5.** (*tr.*) to neglect or be unable (to do something). **6.** (*intr.*) to prove insufficient in quantity or extent. **7.** (*intr.*) to weaken. **8.** (*intr.*) to go bankrupt. *~n.* **9.** a failure to attain the required standard. **10. without fail.** definitely.

failing ('feɪlɪŋ) *n.* **1.** a weak point. *~prep.* **2.** (*used to express a condition*) in default of: *failing a solution, the problem will have to wait until Monday.*

fail-safe *adj.* **1.** designed to return to a safe condition in the event of a failure or malfunction. **2.** safe from failure; foolproof.

failure ('feɪljə) *n.* **1.** the act or an instance of failing. **2.** a person or thing that is unsuccessful or disappointing. **3.** nonperformance of something required or expected: *failure to attend will be punished.* **4.** cessation of normal operation: *a power failure.* **5.** an insufficiency: *a crop failure.* **6.** a decline or loss, as in health. **7.** the fact of not reaching the required standard in an examination, test, etc. **8.** bankruptcy.

fain (feɪn) *adv.* **1.** (*usually with* would) *Arch.* gladly: *she would fain be dead. ~adj.* **2.** *Obs.* **a.** willing. **b.** compelled.

faint (feɪnt) *adj.* **1.** lacking clarity, brightness, volume, etc. **2.** lacking conviction or force: *faint praise.* **3.** feeling dizzy or weak as if about to lose consciousness. **4.** timid (esp. in **faint-hearted**). *~vb.* (*intr.*) **5.** to lose consciousness, as through weakness. **6.** *Arch. or poetic.* to become weak, esp. in courage. *~n.* **7.** a sudden spontaneous loss of consciousness caused by an insufficient supply of blood to the brain. —**'faintish** *adj.* —**'faintly** *adv.* —**'faintness** *n.*

fair¹ (feə) *adj.* **1.** free from discrimination, dishonesty, etc. **2.** in conformity with rules or standards: *a fair fight.* **3.** (of the hair or complexion) light in colour. **4.** beautiful to look at. **5.** quite good: *a fair piece of work.* **6.** unblemished; untainted. **7.** (of the tide or wind) favourable to the passage of a vessel. **8.** fine or cloudless. **9.** pleasant or courteous. **10.** apparently good or valuable: *fair words.* **11. fair and square.** in a correct or just way. **12. fair to middling.** about average. *~adv.* **13.** in a fair way: *act fair, now!* **14.** absolutely or squarely; quite. *~vb.* **15.** (*intr.*) *Dialect.* (of the weather) to become fine. *~n.* **16.** *Arch.* a person or thing that is beautiful or valuable. —**'fairish** *adj.* —**'fairness** *n.*

fair² (feə) *n.* **1.** a travelling entertainment with sideshows, rides, etc. **2.** a gathering of producers of and dealers in a given class of products to facilitate business: *a world fair.* **3.** a regular assembly at a specific place for the sale of goods, esp. livestock.

fairground ('feə,graʊnd) *n.* an open space used for a fair or exhibition.

fairing ('feərɪŋ) *n.* an external metal structure fitted around parts of an aircraft, car, etc., to reduce drag.

Fair Isle *n.* an intricate multicoloured pattern knitted with Shetland wool into various garments, such as sweaters.

fairly ('feəlɪ) *adv.* **1.** (*not used with a negative*) moderately. **2.** as deserved; justly. **3.** (*not used with a negative*) positively: *the hall fairly rang with applause.*

THESAURUS

vanish, vanish into thin air, wane, waste away, wilt, wither

faded bleached, dim, discoloured, dull, etiolated, indistinct, lustreless, pale, washed out

fading declining, decreasing, disappearing, dying, on the decline, vanishing

faeces bodily waste, droppings, dung, excrement, excreta, ordure, stools

fail 1. be defeated, be found lacking *or* wanting, be in vain, be unsuccessful, break down, come a cropper (*Inf.*), come to grief, come to naught, come to nothing, fall, fall short, fall short of, fall through, fizzle out (*Inf.*), flop (*Inf.*), founder, go astray, go down, go up in smoke (*Inf.*), meet with disaster, miscarry, misfire, miss, not make the grade (*Inf.*), run aground, turn out badly **2.** abandon, break one's word, desert, disappoint, forget, forsake, let down, neglect, omit **3.** be on one's last legs (*Inf.*), cease, conk out (*Inf.*), cut out, decline, die, disappear, droop, dwindle, fade, give out, give up, gutter, languish, peter out, sicken, sink, stop working, wane, weaken **4.** become insolvent, close down, crash, fold (*Inf.*), go bankrupt, go broke (*Inf.*), go bust (*Inf.*), go into receivership, go out of business, go to the wall, go under, smash **5. without fail** conscientiously, constantly, dependably, like clockwork, punctually, regularly, religiously, without exception

failing 1. *n.* blemish, blind spot, defect, deficiency, drawback, error, failure, fault, flaw, foible, frailty, imperfection, lapse, miscarriage, misfortune, shortcoming, weakness **2.** *prep.* in default of, in the absence of, lacking

failure 1. abortion, breakdown, collapse, defeat, downfall, fiasco, frustration, lack of success, miscarriage, overthrow, wreck **2.** black sheep, dead duck (*Inf.*), disappointment, dud (*Inf.*), flop (*Inf.*), incompetent, loser, ne'er-do-well, no-good, no-hoper (*Chiefly Aust.*), nonstarter, washout (*Inf.*) **3.** default, deficiency, dereliction, neglect, negligence, nonobservance, nonperformance, nonsuccess, omission, remissness, shortcoming, stoppage **4.** breakdown, decay, decline, deterioration, failing, loss **5.** bankruptcy, crash, downfall, folding (*Inf.*), insolvency, ruin

faint *adj.* **1.** bleached, delicate, dim, distant, dull, faded, faltering, feeble, hazy, hushed, ill-defined, indistinct, light, low, muffled, muted, soft, subdued, thin, vague, whispered **2.** feeble, remote, slight, unenthusiastic, weak **3.** dizzy, drooping, enervated, exhausted, faltering, fatigued, giddy, languid, lethargic, light-headed, muzzy, vertiginous, weak, woozy (*Inf.*) **4.** faint-hearted, lily-livered, spiritless, timid, timorous *~v.* **5.** black out, collapse, fade, fail, flake out (*Inf.*), keel over (*Inf.*), languish, lose consciousness, pass out, swoon

(*Literary*), weaken *~n.* **6.** blackout, collapse, swoon (*Literary*), syncope (*Medical*), unconsciousness

faint-hearted diffident, half-hearted, irresolute, timid, timorous, weak

faintly 1. feebly, in a whisper, indistinctly, softly, weakly **2.** a little, dimly, slightly, somewhat

fair¹ *adj.* **1.** above board, according to the rules, clean, disinterested, dispassionate, equal, equitable, even-handed, honest, honourable, impartial, just, lawful, legitimate, objective, on the level (*Inf.*), proper, square, trustworthy, unbiased, unprejudiced, upright **2.** blond, blonde, fair-haired, flaxen-haired, light, light-complexioned, tow-haired, tow-headed **3.** adequate, all right, average, decent, mediocre, middling, moderate, not bad, O.K. (*Inf.*), passable, reasonable, respectable, satisfactory, so-so (*Inf.*), tolerable **4.** beauteous, beautiful, bonny, comely, handsome, lovely, pretty, well-favoured **5.** bright, clear, clement, cloudless, dry, favourable, fine, sunny, sunshiny, unclouded

fair² *n.* bazaar, carnival, expo (*Inf.*), exposition, festival, fête, gala, market, show

fair-and-square above board, correct, honest, just, on the level (*Inf.*), straight

fairly 1. adequately, moderately, pretty

fair play n. 1. an established standard of decency, etc. 2. abidance by this standard.

fair sex n. **the.** women collectively.

fairway ('fɛə,weɪ) n. 1. (on a golf course) the avenue approaching a green bordered by rough. 2. Naut. the navigable part of a river, harbour, etc.

fair-weather adj. 1. suitable for use in fair weather only. 2. not reliable in situations of difficulty: *fair-weather friend.*

fairy ('fɛərɪ) n., pl. **fairies.** 1. an imaginary supernatural being, usually represented in diminutive human form and characterized as having magical powers. 2. Sl. a male homosexual. ~adj. (prenominal) 3. of a fairy or fairies. 4. resembling a fairy or fairies. —'**fairy-,like** adj.

fairy cycle n. a child's bicycle.

fairy godmother n. a benefactress, esp. an unknown one.

fairyland ('fɛərɪ,lænd) n. 1. the imaginary domain of the fairies. 2. a fantasy world, esp. one resulting from a person's wild imaginings.

fairy lights pl. n. small coloured electric bulbs strung together and used as decoration, esp. on a Christmas tree.

fairy ring n. a ring of dark luxuriant vegetation in grassy ground corresponding to the outer edge of an underground fungal mycelium.

fairy tale or **story** n. 1. a story about fairies or other mythical or magical beings. 2. a highly improbable account.

fait accompli French. (fε takɔ̃'pli) n., pl. **faits accomplis** (fε takɔ̃'pli). something already done and beyond alteration.

faith (feɪθ) n. 1. strong or unshakeable belief in something, esp. without proof. 2. a specific system of religious beliefs: *the Jewish faith.* 3. Christianity. trust in God and in his actions and promises. 4. a conviction of the truth of certain doctrines of religion. 5. complete confidence or trust in a person, remedy, etc. 6. loyalty, as to a person or cause (esp. in **keep faith, break faith**). 7. **bad faith.** dishonesty. 8. **good faith.** honesty. 9. (modifier) using or relating to the supposed ability to cure bodily ailments by means of religious faith: *a faith healer.* ~interj. 10. Arch. indeed.

faithful ('feɪθful) adj. 1. remaining true or loyal. 2. maintaining sexual loyalty to one's lover or spouse. 3. consistently reliable: *a faithful worker.* 4. reliable or truthful. 5. accurate in detail: *a faithful translation.* ~n. 6. **the faithful. a.** the believers in a religious faith, esp. Christianity. **b.** any group of loyal and steadfast followers. —'**faithfully** adv. —'**faithfulness** n.

faithless ('feɪθlɪs) adj. 1. unreliable or treacherous. 2. dishonest or disloyal. 3. lacking religious faith. —'**faithlessness** n.

fake (feɪk) vb. 1. (tr.) to cause (something inferior or not genuine) to appear more valuable or real by fraud or pretence. 2. to pretend to have (an illness, emotion, etc.). ~n. 3. an object, person, or act that is not genu-ine; sham. ~adj. 4. not genuine. —'**faker** n.

fakir (fə'kɪə, 'feɪkə) n. 1. a member of any religious order of Islam. 2. a Hindu ascetic mendicant.

Falange ('fælændʒ) n. the Fascist movement founded in Spain in 1933. —**Fa'langist** n., adj.

falcon ('fɔːlkən, 'fɔːkən) n. 1. a diurnal bird of prey such as the gyrfalcon, peregrine falcon, etc., having pointed wings and a long tail. 2. **a.** any of these or related birds, trained to hunt small game. **b.** the female of such a bird (cf. tercel).

falconry ('fɔːlkənrɪ, 'fɔːkən-) n. the art of keeping falcons and training them to return from flight to a lure or to hunt quarry. —'**falconer** n.

falderal ('fældɪ,ræl) or **folderol** ('fɒldɪ,rɒl) n. 1. a showy but worthless trifle. 2. foolish nonsense. 3. a nonsensical refrain in old songs.

fall (fɔːl) vb. **falling, fell, fallen.** (mainly intr.) 1. to descend by the force of gravity from a higher to a lower place. 2. to drop suddenly from an erect position. 3. to collapse to the ground, esp. in pieces. 4. to become less or lower in number, quality, etc.: *prices fell.* 5. to become lower in pitch. 6. to extend downwards: *her hair fell to her waist.* 7. to be badly wounded or killed. 8. to slope in a downward direction. 9. to yield to temptation or sin. 10. to diminish in status, estimation, etc. 11. to yield to attack: *the city fell under the assault.* 12. to lose power: *the government fell after the riots.* 13. to pass into or take on a specified condition: *to fall asleep.* 14. to adopt a despondent expression: *her face fell.* 15. to be averted: *her gaze fell.* 16. to come by chance or presumption: *suspicion fell on the butler.* 17. to occur; take place: *night fell.* 18. (foll. by back, behind, etc.) to move in a specified direction. 19. to occur at a specified place: *the accent falls on the last syllable.* 20. (foll. by to) to be inherited (by): *the estate falls to the eldest son.* 21. (often foll. by into, under, etc.) to be classified: *the subject falls into two main areas.* 22. to issue forth: *a curse fell from her lips.* 23. Cricket. (of a batsman's wicket) to be taken by the bowling side: *the sixth wicket fell for 96.* 24. **fall flat.** to fail to achieve a desired effect. 25. **fall foul of. a.** Naut. to come into collision with. **b.** to come into conflict with. 26. **fall short. a.** to prove inadequate. **b.** (often foll. by of) to fail to reach or measure up to (a standard). ~n. 27. an act or instance of falling. 28. something that falls: *a fall of snow.* 29. Chiefly U.S. autumn. 30. the distance that something falls: *a hundred-foot fall.* 31. a sudden drop from an upright position. 32. (often pl.) **a.** a waterfall or cataract. **b.** (cap. when part of a name): *Niagara Falls.* 33. a downward slope or decline. 34. a decrease in value, number, etc. 35. a decline in status or importance. 36. a capture or overthrow: *the fall of the city.* 37. Machinery, naut. the end of a tackle to which power is applied to hoist it. 38. Also called: **pinfall.** Wrestling. a scoring move, pinning both shoulders of one's opponent to the floor for a specified period. 39. **a.** the birth of an animal. **b.** the animals produced at a single birth. ~See also **fall about, fall away,** etc.

THESAURUS

well, quite, rather, reasonably, somewhat, tolerably 2. deservedly, equitably, honestly, impartially, justly, objectively, properly, without fear or favour 3. absolutely, in a manner of speaking, positively, really, veritably

fair-minded disinterested, even-handed, impartial, just, open-minded, unbiased, unprejudiced

fairness decency, disinterestedness, equitableness, equity, impartiality, justice, legitimacy, rightfulness, uprightness

fairy brownie, elf, hob, leprechaun, pixie, Robin Goodfellow, sprite

fairy tale or **fairy story** 1. folk tale, romance 2. cock-and-bull story (Inf.), fabrication, fantasy, fiction, invention, lie, tall story, untruth

faith 1. assurance, confidence, conviction, credence, credit, dependence, reliance, trust 2. belief, church, communion, creed, denomination, dogma, persuasion, religion 3. allegiance, constancy, faithfulness, fealty, fidelity, loyalty, truth, truthfulness 4. As in **keep**

faith, in good faith honour, pledge, promise, sincerity, vow, word, word of honour

faithful 1. attached, constant, dependable, devoted, loyal, reliable, staunch, steadfast, true, true-blue, trusty, truthful, unswerving, unwavering 2. accurate, close, exact, just, precise, strict, true 3. **the faithful** adherents, believers, brethren, communicants, congregation, followers, the elect

faithfulness 1. adherence, constancy, dependability, devotion, fealty, fidelity, loyalty, trustworthiness 2. accuracy, closeness, exactness, justice, strictness, truth

faithless disloyal, doubting, false, false-hearted, fickle, inconstant, perfidious, recreant (Archaic), traitorous, treacherous, unbelieving, unfaithful, unreliable, untrue, untrustworthy, untruthful

faithlessness betrayal, disloyalty, fickleness, inconstancy, infidelity, perfidy, treachery, unfaithfulness

fake 1. v. affect, assume, copy, counterfeit, fabricate, feign, forge, pretend, put on, sham, simulate 2. n. charlatan, copy, forgery, fraud, hoax, imitation, impostor, mountebank, phoney (Sl.), reproduction, sham 3. adj. affected, artificial, assumed, counterfeit, false, forged, imitation, mock, phoney (Sl.), pinchbeck, pseudo, reproduction, sham

fall v. 1. be precipitated, cascade, collapse, crash, descend, dive, drop, drop down, go head over heels, keel over, nose-dive, pitch, plummet, plunge, settle, sink, stumble, subside, topple, trip, trip over, tumble 2. abate, become lower, decline, decrease, depreciate, diminish, dwindle, ebb, fall off, flag, go down, lessen, slump, subside 3. be overthrown, be taken, capitulate, give in or up, give way, go out of office, pass into enemy hands, resign, succumb, surrender, yield 4. be a casualty, be killed, be lost, be slain, die, meet one's end, perish 5. become, befall, chance, come about, come to pass, fall out, happen, occur, take place 6. **fall foul of** brush with, come into conflict with, cross swords with, make trouble with, make an enemy of 7. **fall in love (with)** become attached to, become enamoured of, become fond of, become infatuated (with), be smitten by, conceive an affec-

Fall (fɔːl) *n.* **the.** *Theol.* Adam's sin of disobedience and the state of innate sinfulness ensuing from this for himself and all mankind.

fall about *vb.* (*intr.*, *adv.*) to behave in an uncontrolled manner: *we fell about laughing.*

fallacy ('fæləsɪ) *n.*, *pl.* **-cies.** **1.** an incorrect or misleading notion or opinion based on inaccurate facts or invalid reasoning. **2.** unsound reasoning. **3.** the tendency to mislead. **4.** *Logic.* an error in reasoning that renders an argument logically invalid.

fall away *vb.* (*intr.*, *adv.*) **1.** (of friendship, etc.) to be withdrawn. **2.** to slope down.

fall back *vb.* (*intr.*, *adv.*) **1.** to recede or retreat. **2.** (foll. by *on* or *upon*) to have recourse (to). ~*n.* **fallback. 3.** a retreat. **4.** a reserve, esp. money, that can be called upon in need.

fall behind *vb.* (*intr.*, *adv.*) **1.** to drop back; fail to keep up. **2.** to be in arrears, as with a payment.

fall down *vb.* (*intr.*, *adv.*) **1.** to drop suddenly or collapse. **2.** (often foll. by *on*) *Inf.* to fail.

fallen ('fɔːlən) *vb.* **1.** the past participle of **fall.** ~*adj.* **2.** having sunk in reputation or honour: *a fallen woman.* **3.** killed in battle with glory.

fall for *vb.* (*intr.*, *prep.*) **1.** to become infatuated with (a person). **2.** to allow oneself to be deceived by (a lie, trick, etc.).

fall guy *n. Inf.*, chiefly *U.S.* a person who is the victim of a confidence trick.

fallible ('fælɪbəl) *adj.* **1.** capable of being mistaken. **2.** liable to mislead. —,falli'bility *n.*

fall in *vb.* (*intr.*, *adv.*) **1.** to collapse. **2.** to adopt a military formation, esp. as a soldier taking his place in a line. **3.** (of a lease) to expire. **4.** (often foll. by *with*) **a.** to meet and join. **b.** to agree with or support a person, suggestion, etc.

falling sickness *or* **evil** *n.* a former name (nontechnical) for **epilepsy.**

falling star *n.* an informal name for **meteor.**

fall off *vb.* (*intr.*) **1.** to drop unintentionally to the ground from (a high object, bicycle, etc.), esp. after losing one's balance. **2.** (*adv.*) to diminish in size, intensity, etc.

fall on *vb.* (*intr.*, *prep.*) **1.** Also: **fall upon.** to attack or snatch (an army, booty, etc.). **2. fall flat on one's face.** to fail, esp. in a ridiculous manner. **3. fall on one's feet.** to emerge unexpectedly well from a difficult situation.

Fallopian tube (fə'ləupɪən) *n.* either of a pair of slender tubes through which ova pass from the ovaries to the uterus in female mammals.

fallout ('fɔːl,aut) *n.* **1.** the descent of radioactive material following a nuclear explosion. **2.** any particles that so descend. ~*vb.* **fall out.** (*intr.*, *adv.*) **3.** *Inf.* to disagree. **4.** (*intr.*) to occur. **5.** *Mil.* to leave a disciplinary formation.

fallow[1] ('fæləu) *adj.* **1.** (of land) left unseeded after being ploughed to regain fertility for a crop. **2.** (of an idea, etc.) undeveloped, but potentially useful. ~*n.* **3.** land treated in this way. ~*vb.* **4.** (*tr.*) to leave (land) unseeded after ploughing it. —'**fallowness** *n.*

fallow[2] ('fæləu) *adj.* of a light yellowish-brown colour.

fallow deer *n.* either of two species of deer, one of which is native to the Mediterranean region and the other to Persia. The summer coat is reddish with white spots.

fall through *vb.* (*intr.*, *adv.*) to fail.

fall to *vb.* (*intr.*) **1.** (*adv.*) to begin some activity, as eating, working, or fighting. **2.** (*prep.*) to devolve on (a person): *the task fell to me.*

false (fɔːls) *adj.* **1.** not in accordance with the truth or facts. **2.** irregular or invalid: *a false argument.* **3.** untruthful or lying: *a false account.* **4.** artificial; fake: *false eyelashes.* **5.** being or intended to be misleading or deceptive: *a false alarm.* **6.** treacherous: *a false friend.* **7.** based on mistaken or irrelevant ideas or facts: *a false hope.* **8.** (*prenominal*) (esp. of plants) superficially resembling the species specified: *false hellebore.* **9.** serving to supplement or replace, often temporarily: *a false keel.* **10.** *Music.* (of a note, interval, etc.) out of tune. ~*adv.* **11.** in a false or dishonest manner (esp. in **play** (someone) **false**). —'**falsely** *adv.* —'**falseness** *n.*

falsehood ('fɔːls,hud) *n.* **1.** the quality of being untrue. **2.** an untrue statement; lie. **3.** the act of deceiving or lying.

false pretences *pl. n.* a misrepresentation used to obtain anything, such as trust or affection (esp. in **under false pretences**).

falsetto (fɔːl'sɛtəu) *n.*, *pl.* **-tos.** a form of vocal production used by male singers to extend their range upwards by limiting the vibration of the vocal cords.

falsies ('fɔːlsɪz) *pl. n. Inf.* pads of soft material, such as foam rubber, worn to exaggerate the size of a woman's breasts.

falsify ('fɔːlsɪ,faɪ) *vb.* **-fying, -fied. 1.** (*tr.*) to make (a report, evidence, etc.) false or inaccurate by alteration. **2.** to render (the truth or facts) false or inaccurate in order to deceive. **3.** (*tr.*) to prove false. —'**falsi,fiable** *adj.* —**falsification** (,fɔːlsɪfɪ'keɪʃən) *n.*

falsity ('fɔːlsɪtɪ) *n.*, *pl.* **-ties. 1.** the state of being false or

---

THESAURUS

tion for, fall (for), lose one's heart (to), take a fancy to **8.** fall away, incline, incline downwards, slope **9.** backslide, err, go astray, lapse, offend, sin, transgress, trespass, yield to temptation ~*n.* **10.** descent, dive, drop, nose dive, plummet, plunge, slip, spill, tumble **11.** cut, decline, decrease, diminution, dip, drop, dwindling, falling off, lessening, lowering, reduction, slump **12.** capitulation, collapse, death, defeat, destruction, downfall, failure, overthrow, resignation, ruin, surrender **13.** declivity, descent, downgrade, incline, slant, slope **14.** degradation, failure, lapse, sin, slip, transgression

fallacious deceptive, delusive, delusory, erroneous, false, fictitious, illogical, illusory, incorrect, misleading, mistaken, sophistic, sophistical, spurious, untrue, wrong

fallacy casuistry, deceit, deception, delusion, error, falsehood, faultiness, flaw, illusion, inconsistency, misapprehension, misconception, mistake, sophism, sophistry, untruth

fall apart break up, crumble, disband, disintegrate, disperse, dissolve, fall to bits, go *or* come to pieces, lose cohesion, shatter

fall asleep doze off, drop off (*Inf.*), go to sleep, nod off (*Inf.*)

fall back on call upon, employ, have recourse to, make use of, press into service, resort to

fall behind be in arrears, drop back, get left behind, lag, lose one's place, trail

fall down disappoint, fail, fail to make the grade, fall short, go wrong, prove unsuccessful

fallen *adj.* **1.** collapsed, decayed, flat, on the ground, ruinous, sunken **2.** disgraced, dishonoured, immoral, loose, lost, ruined, shamed, sinful, unchaste **3.** dead, killed, lost, perished, slain, slaughtered

fall for 1. become infatuated with, desire, fall in love with, lose one's head over, succumb to the charms of **2.** accept, be deceived (duped, fooled, taken in) by, give credence to, swallow (*Inf.*)

fallible erring, frail, ignorant, imperfect, mortal, prone to error, uncertain, weak

fall in cave in, collapse, come down about one's ears, sink

falling off *n.* deceleration, decline, decrease, deterioration, downward trend, drop, slackening, slowing down, slump, waning, worsening

fall in with accept, agree with, assent, concur with, cooperate with, go along with, support

fall out 1. altercate, argue, clash, differ, disagree, fight, quarrel, squabble **2.** chance, come to pass, happen, occur, result, take place, turn out

fallow dormant, idle, inactive, inert, resting, uncultivated, undeveloped, unplanted, untilled, unused

fall short be deficient (lacking, wanting), fail, miss, prove inadequate

fall through come to nothing, fail, fizzle out (*Inf.*), miscarry

false 1. concocted, erroneous, faulty, fictitious, improper, inaccurate, incorrect, inexact, invalid, mistaken, unfounded, unreal, wrong **2.** lying, mendacious, truthless, unreliable, unsound, untrue, untrustworthy, untruthful **3.** artificial, bogus, counterfeit, ersatz, fake, feigned, forged, imitation, mock, pretended, sham, simulated, spurious, synthetic **4.** deceitful, deceiving, deceptive, delusive, fallacious, fraudulent, hypocritical, misleading, trumped up **5.** dishonest, dishonourable, disloyal, double-dealing, duplicitous, faithless, false-hearted, hypocritical, perfidious, treacherous, treasonable, two-faced, unfaithful, untrustworthy **6. play** (someone) **false** betray, cheat, deceive, double-cross, give the Judas kiss to, sell down the river (*Inf.*), stab in the back

falsehood 1. deceit, deception, dishonesty, dissimulation, inveracity (*Rare*), mendacity, perjury, prevarication, untruthfulness **2.** fabrication, fib, fiction, lie, misstatement, story, untruth

falsification adulteration, deceit, dissimulation, distortion, forgery, misrepresentation, perversion, tampering with

falsify alter, belie, cook (*Sl.*), counterfeit, distort, doctor, fake, forge, garble, misrepresent, misstate, pervert, tamper with

untrue. **2.** a lie or deception.

falter ('fɔːltə) vb. **1.** (intr.) to be hesitant, weak, or unsure. **2.** (intr.) to move unsteadily or hesitantly. **3.** to utter haltingly or hesitantly. ~n. **4.** hesitancy in speech or action. **5.** a quavering sound. —'**falterer** n. —'**falteringly** adv.

fame (feɪm) n. **1.** the state of being widely known or recognized. **2.** Arch. rumour or public report. ~vb. **3.** (tr.; now usually passive) to make famous: he was famed for his ruthlessness.

familial (fə'mɪlɪəl) adj. **1.** of or relating to the family. **2.** transmitted between individuals of a family: a familial disease.

familiar (fə'mɪlɪə) adj. **1.** well-known: a familiar figure. **2.** frequent or customary: a familiar excuse. **3.** (postpositive; foll. by with) acquainted. **4.** friendly; informal. **5.** close; intimate. **6.** more intimate than is acceptable; presumptuous. ~n. **7.** Also called: **familiar spirit.** a supernatural spirit supposed to attend and aid a witch, wizard, etc. **8.** a person attached to the household of the pope or a bishop, who renders service in return for support. **9.** a friend. —fa,mili'arity n. —fa'miliarly adv. —fa'miliarness n.

familiarize or **-rise** (fə'mɪljə,raɪz) vb. (tr.) **1.** to make (oneself or someone else) familiar, as with a particular subject. **2.** to make (something) generally known. —fa,miliari'zation or **-ri'sation** n.

family ('fæmɪlɪ, 'fæmlɪ) n., pl. **-lies. 1. a.** a primary social group consisting of parents and their offspring. **b.** (as modifier): a family unit. **2.** one's wife or husband and one's children. **3.** one's children, as distinguished from one's husband or wife. **4.** a group descended from a common ancestor. **5.** all the persons living together in one household. **6.** any group of related things or beings, esp. when scientifically categorized. **7.** Biol. any of the taxonomic groups into which an order is divided and which contains one or more genera. **8.** a group of historically related languages assumed to derive from one original language. **9.** Maths. a group of curves or surfaces whose equations differ from a given equation only in the values assigned to one or more constants. **10. in the family way.** Inf. pregnant.

Family Allowance n. **1.** (in Britain) a former name for **child benefit. 2.** (in Canada) an allowance paid by the Federal Government to the parents of dependent children.

family man n. a man who is married and has children, esp. one who is devoted to his family.

family name n. a surname, esp. when regarded as representing the family honour.

family planning n. the control of the number of children in a family and of the intervals between them, esp. by the use of contraceptives.

family tree n. a chart showing the genealogical relationships and lines of descent of a family. Also called:

genealogical tree.

famine ('fæmɪn) n. **1.** a severe shortage of food, as through crop failure or overpopulation. **2.** acute shortage of anything. **3.** violent hunger.

famish ('fæmɪʃ) vb. (now usually passive) to be or make very hungry or weak.

famous ('feɪməs) adj. **1.** known to or recognized by many people. **2.** Inf. excellent; splendid. —'**famously** adv. —'**famousness** n.

fan[1] (fæn) n. **1.** any device for creating a current of air by movement of a surface or number of surfaces, esp. a rotating device consisting of a number of blades attached to a central hub. **2.** any of various hand-agitated devices for cooling onself, esp. a collapsible semicircular series of flat segments of paper, ivory, etc. **3.** something shaped like such a fan, such as the tail of certain birds. **4.** Agriculture. a kind of basket formerly used for winnowing grain. ~vb. **fanning, fanned.** (mainly tr.) **5.** to cause a current of air to blow upon, as by means of a fan: to fan one's face. **6.** to agitate or move (air, etc.) with or as if with a fan. **7.** to make fiercer, more ardent, etc.: fan one's passion. **8.** (also intr.; often foll. by out) to spread out or cause to spread out in the shape of a fan. **9.** to winnow (grain) by blowing the chaff away from it. —'**fanlike** adj. —'**fanner** n.

fan[2] (fæn) n. **1.** an ardent admirer of a pop star, football team, etc. **2.** a devotee of a sport, hobby, etc.

Fanagalo ('fænəgələʊ) or **Fanakalo** n. a pidgin language widely used in southern Africa, having English, Afrikaans, and Zulu components.

fanatic (fə'nætɪk) n. **1.** a person whose enthusiasm or zeal for something is extreme or beyond normal limits. **2.** Inf. a person devoted to a particular hobby or pastime. ~adj. —fa'natical adj. —fa'nati,cism n.

fan belt n. the belt that drives a cooling fan in a car engine.

fancier ('fænsɪə) n. **1.** a person with a special interest in something. **2.** a person who breeds special varieties of plants or animals: a pigeon fancier.

fanciful ('fænsɪful) adj. **1.** not based on fact: fanciful notions. **2.** made or designed in a curious, intricate, or imaginative way. **3.** indulging in or influenced by fancy. —'**fancifully** adv. —'**fancifulness** n.

fancy ('fænsɪ) adj. **-cier, -ciest. 1.** ornamented or decorative: fancy clothes. **2.** requiring skill to perform: a fancy dance routine. **3.** capricious or illusory. **4.** (often used ironically) superior in quality. **5.** higher than expected: fancy prices. **6.** (of a domestic animal) bred for particular qualities. ~n., pl. **-cies. 7.** a sudden capricious idea. **8.** a sudden or irrational liking for a person or thing. **9.** the power to conceive and represent decorative and novel imagery, esp. in poetry. **10.** an idea or thing produced by this. **11.** a mental image. **12.** Music. a composition for solo lute, keyboard, etc, current during the 16th and 17th centuries. **13. the fancy.** Arch. those

---

THESAURUS

falter break, hesitate, shake, speak haltingly, stammer, stumble, stutter, totter, tremble, vacillate, waver

faltering broken, hesitant, irresolute, stammering, tentative, timid, uncertain, weak

fame celebrity, credit, eminence, glory, honour, illustriousness, name, prominence, public esteem, renown, reputation, repute, stardom

familiar 1. accustomed, common, common or garden (Inf.), conventional, customary, domestic, everyday, frequent, household, mundane, ordinary, recognizable, repeated, routine, stock, well-known **2. familiar with** abreast of, acquainted with, at home with, au courant, au fait, aware of, conscious of, conversant with, introduced, knowledgeable, no stranger to, on speaking terms with, versed in, well up in **3.** amicable, chummy (Inf.), close, confidential, cordial, easy, free, free-and-easy, friendly, hail-fellow-well-met, informal, intimate, near, open, relaxed, unceremonious, unconstrained, unreserved **4.** bold, disrespectful, forward, impudent, intrusive, overfree, presuming, presumptuous

familiarity 1. acquaintance, acquaintanceship, awareness, experience, grasp, understanding **2.** absence of reserve, closeness, ease, fellowship, freedom, friendliness, friendship, informality, intimacy, naturalness, openness, sociability, unceremoniousness **3.** boldness, disrespect, forwardness, liberties, liberty, presumption

familiarize accustom, bring into common use, coach, get to know (about), habituate, instruct, inure, make conversant, make used to, prime, school, season, train

family 1. brood, children, descendants, folk (Inf.), household, issue, kin, kindred, kinsmen, kith and kin, ménage, offspring, one's nearest and dearest, one's own flesh and blood, people, progeny, relations, relatives **2.** ancestors, ancestry, birth, blood, clan, descent, dynasty, extraction, forebears, forefathers, genealogy, house, line, lineage, parentage, pedigree, race, sept, stemma, stirps, strain, tribe **3.** class, classification, genre, group, kind, network, subdivision, system

family tree ancestry, extraction, genealogy, line, lineage, line of descent, pedigree, stemma, stirps

famine dearth, destitution, hunger, scarcity, starvation

famous acclaimed, celebrated, conspicuous, distinguished, eminent, excellent, far-famed, glorious, honoured, illustrious, legendary, lionized, much-publicized, notable, noted, prominent, remarkable, renowned, signal, well-known

fan[1] v. **1.** Often fig. add fuel to the flames, agitate, arouse, enkindle, excite, impassion, increase, provoke, rouse, stimulate, stir up, whip up, work up **2.** air-condition, air-cool, blow, cool, refresh, ventilate, winnow (Rare) ~n. **3.** air conditioner, blade, blower, propeller, punkah (In India), vane, ventilator

fan[2] adherent, admirer, aficionado, buff (Inf.), devotee, enthusiast, fiend (Inf.), follower, freak (Sl.), lover, rooter (U.S.), supporter, zealot

fanatic n. activist, addict, bigot, devotee, enthusiast, extremist, militant, visionary, zealot

fanatical bigoted, burning, enthusiastic, extreme, fervent, frenzied, immoderate, mad, obsessive, overenthusiastic, passionate, rabid, visionary, wild, zealous

fanciful capricious, chimerical, curious, extravagant, fabulous, fairy-tale, fantastic, ideal, imaginary, imaginative, mythical, poetic, romantic, unreal, visionary, whimsical, wild

who follow a particular sport, esp. prize fighting. ~*vb.* **-cying, -cied.** (*tr.*) **14.** to picture in the imagination. **15.** to imagine: *I fancy it will rain.* **16.** (*often used with a negative*) to like: *I don't fancy your chances!* **17.** (*reflexive*) to have a high or ill-founded opinion of oneself. **18.** *Inf.* to have a wish for: *she fancied some chocolate.* **19.** *Brit. inf.* to be physically attracted to (another person). **20.** to breed (animals) for particular characteristics. ~*interj.* **21.** Also: **fancy that!** an exclamation of surprise. —**'fancily** *adv.* —**'fanciness** *n.*

fancy dress *n.* **a.** costume worn at masquerades, etc., representing an historical figure, etc. **b.** (*as modifier*): *a fancy-dress ball.*

fancy-free *adj.* having no commitments.

fancy goods *pl. n.* small decorative gifts.

fancy man *n. Sl.* **1.** a woman's lover. **2.** a pimp.

fancy woman *n. Sl.* a mistress or prostitute.

fancywork ('fænsɪ,wɜːk) *n.* any ornamental needle-work, such as embroidery or crochet.

fandango (fæn'dæŋgəʊ) *n., pl.* **-gos.** **1.** an old Spanish courtship dance in triple time. **2.** a piece of music composed for or in the rhythm of this dance.

fanfare ('fænfɛə) *n.* **1.** a flourish or short tune played on brass instruments. **2.** an ostentatious flourish or display.

fang (fæŋ) *n.* **1.** the long pointed hollow or grooved tooth of a venomous snake through which venom is injected. **2.** any large pointed tooth, esp. the canine tooth of a carnivorous mammal. **3.** the root of a tooth. **4.** (*usually pl.*) *Brit. inf.* a tooth. —**fanged** *adj.* —**'fangless** *adj.*

fanjet ('fæn,dʒɛt) *n.* another name for **turbofan.**

fanlight ('fæn,laɪt) *n.* **1.** a semicircular window over a door or window, often having sash bars like the ribs of a fan. **2.** a small rectangular window over a door. U.S name: **transom.**

fanny ('fænɪ) *n., pl.* **-nies.** *Sl.* **1.** *Taboo, Brit.* the female pudendum. **2.** *Chiefly U.S.* the buttocks.

fanny adams *n. Brit. sl.* **1.** (*usually preceded by sweet*) absolutely nothing at all. **2.** *Chiefly naut.* (*formerly*) tinned meat.

fantail ('fæn,teɪl) *n.* **1.** a breed of domestic pigeon having a large tail that can be opened like a fan. **2.** an Old World flycatcher of Australia, New Zealand, and SE Asia, having a broad fan-shaped tail. **3.** a tail shaped like an outspread fan. **4.** an auxiliary sail on the upper portion of a windmill. **5.** *U.S.* a part of the deck projecting aft of the sternpost of a ship. —**'fan-,tailed** *adj.*

fantasia (fæn'teɪzɪə) *n.* **1.** any musical composition of a free or improvisatory nature. **2.** a potpourri of popular tunes woven loosely together.

fantasize *or* **-sise** ('fæntə,saɪz) *vb.* **1.** (when *tr.*, takes a clause as object) to conceive extravagant or whimsical ideas, images, etc. **2.** (*intr.*) to conceive pleasant mental images.

fantastic (fæn'tæstɪk) *adj. also* **fantastical. 1.** strange or fanciful in appearance, conception, etc. **2.** created in the mind; illusory. **3.** unrealistic: *fantastic plans.* **4.** incredible or preposterous: *a fantastic verdict.* **5.** *Inf.* very large or extreme: *a fantastic fortune.* **6.** *Inf.* very good; excellent. **7.** of or characterized by fantasy. **8.** capricious; fitful. —,**fantasti'cality** *or* **fan'tasticalness** *n.* —**fan'tastically** *adv.*

fantasy *or* **phantasy** ('fæntəsɪ) *n., pl.* **-sies. 1. a.** imagination unrestricted by reality. **b.** (*as modifier*): *a fantasy world.* **2.** a creation of the imagination, esp. a weird or bizarre one. **3.** *Psychol.* a series of pleasing mental images, usually serving to fulfil a need not gratified in reality. **4.** a whimsical or far-fetched notion. **5.** an illusion or phantom. **6.** a highly elaborate imaginative design or creation. **7.** *Music.* another word for **fantasia. 8.** literature having a large fantasy content. ~*vb.* **-sying, -sied. 9.** a less common word for **fantasize.**

fan vaulting *n. Archit.* vaulting having ribs that radiate like those of a fan and spring from the top of a capital. Also called: **palm vaulting.**

FAO *abbrev. for* Food and Agriculture Organization (of the United Nations).

far (fɑː) *adv., adj.* **farther** *or* **further, farthest** *or* **furthest.** *adv.* **1.** at, to, or from a great distance. **2.** at or to a remote time: *far in the future.* **3.** to a considerable degree: *a far better plan.* **4. as far as. a.** to the degree or extent that. **b.** to the distance or place of. **5. by far.** by a considerable margin. **6. far and away.** by a very great margin. **7. far and wide.** everywhere. **8. far be it from me.** on no account: *far be it from me to tell you what to do.* **9. few and far between.** infrequent. **10. go far. a.** to be successful: *your son will go far.* **b.** to be sufficient or last long: *the wine didn't go far.* **11. go too far.** to exceed reasonable limits. **12. so far. a.** up to the present moment. **b.** up to a certain point, extent, degree, etc. ~*adj.* (*prenominal*) **13.** remote in space or time: *in the far past.* **14.** extending a great distance. **15.** more distant: *the far end of the room.* **16. a far cry.** very different. **17. far from.** in a degree, state, etc. remote from: *he is far from happy.* —**'farness** *n.*

farad ('færəd) *n. Physics.* the derived SI unit of electric capacitance; the capacitance of a capacitor between the plates of which a potential of 1 volt is created by a charge of 1 coulomb. Symbol: F

faraway ('fɑːrə,weɪ) *adj.* (**far away** *when postpositive*). **1.** very distant. **2.** absent-minded.

farce (fɑːs) *n.* **1.** a broadly humorous play based on the exploitation of improbable situations. **2.** the genre of comedy represented by works of this kind. **3.** a ludicrous situation or action. **4.** another name for **forcemeat.** —**'farcical** *adj.*

fare (fɛə) *n.* **1.** the sum charged or paid for conveyance in a bus, train, etc. **2.** a paying passenger, esp. when carried by taxi. **3.** a range of food and drink. ~*vb.* (*intr.*) **4.** to get on (as specified): *he fared well.* **5.** (with *it* as a subject) to happen as specified: *it fared badly with him.* **6.** *Arch.* to eat: *we fared sumptuously.* **7.** (often foll. by *forth*) *Arch.* to travel. —**'farer** *n.*

THESAURUS

fancy *v.* **1.** be inclined to think, believe, conceive, conjecture, guess, imagine, infer, reckon, suppose, surmise, think, think likely **2.** be attracted to, crave, desire, dream of, hanker after, have a yen for, long for, relish, wish for, would like, yearn for **3.** *Inf.* be attracted to, be captivated by, desire, favour, go for (*Inf.*), have an eye for, like, lust after, prefer, take a liking to, take to ~*n.* **4.** caprice, desire, humour, idea, impulse, inclination, notion, thought, urge, whim **5.** fondness, hankering, inclination, liking, partiality, predilection, preference, relish **6.** conception, image, imagination, impression **7.** chimera, daydream, delusion, dream, fantasy, nightmare, phantasm, vision ~*adj.* **8.** baroque, decorated, decorative, elaborate, elegant, embellished, extravagant, fanciful, intricate, ornamental, ornamented, ornate **9.** capricious, chimerical, delusive, fanciful, fantastic, far-fetched, illusory, whimsical

fanfare ballyhoo, fanfaronade, flourish, trump (*Archaic*), trumpet call, tucket (*Archaic*)

fantastic 1. comical, eccentric, exotic, fanciful, freakish, grotesque, imaginative, odd, outlandish, peculiar, phantasmagorical, quaint, queer, rococo, strange, unreal, weird, whimsical **2.** ambitious, chimerical, extravagant, far-fetched, grandiose, illusory, ludicrous, ridiculous, unrealistic, visionary, wild **3.** absurd, capricious, implausible, incredible, irrational, mad, preposterous, unlikely **4.** *Inf.* enormous, extreme, great, overwhelming, severe, tremendous **5.** *Inf.* excellent, first-rate, marvellous, out of this world (*Inf.*), sensational, superb, wonderful

fantasy, phantasy 1. creativity, fancy, imagination, invention, originality **2.** apparition, daydream, delusion, dream, fancy, figment of the imagination, flight of fancy, hallucination, illusion, mirage, nightmare, pipe dream, reverie, vision

far *adv.* **1.** afar, a good way, a great distance, a long way, deep, miles **2.** considerably, decidedly, extremely, greatly, incomparably, much, very much **3. by far** by a long chalk (*Inf.*), by a long shot, by a long way, easily, far and away, immeasurably, incomparably, to a great degree, very much **4. far and wide** broadly, everywhere, extensively, far and near, here, there, and everywhere, widely, worldwide **5. so far** thus far, to date, until now, up to now, up to the present ~*adj.* **6.** distant, faraway, far-flung, far-off, far-removed, long, outlying, out-of-the-way, remote, removed

faraway 1. beyond the horizon, distant, far, far-flung, far-off, far-removed, outlying, remote **2.** absent, abstracted, distant, dreamy, lost

farce 1. broad comedy, buffoonery, burlesque, comedy, satire, slapstick **2.** absurdity, joke, mockery, nonsense, parody, ridiculousness, sham, travesty

farcical absurd, amusing, comic, custard-pie, derisory, diverting, droll, funny, laughable, ludicrous, nonsensical, preposterous, ridiculous, risible, slapstick

fare *n.* **1.** charge, passage money, price, ticket money, transport cost **2.** passenger, pick-up (*Inf.*), traveller **3.** commons, diet, eatables, food, meals, menu, provisions, rations, sustenance, table, victuals ~*v.* **4.** do, get along, get on, make out, manage, prosper **5.** *Used impersonally* go, happen, proceed, turn out

fare stage n. 1. a section of a bus journey for which a set charge is made. 2. the bus stop marking the end of such a section.

farewell (ˌfeəˈwɛl) sentence substitite. 1. goodbye; adieu. ~n. 2. a parting salutation. 3. an act of departure. 4. (modifier) expressing leave-taking: a farewell speech.

far-fetched adj. unlikely.

far-flung adj. 1. widely distributed. 2. far distant; remote.

farina (fəˈriːnə) n. 1. flour or meal made from any kind of cereal grain. 2. Chiefly Brit. starch.

farinaceous (ˌfærɪˈneɪʃəs) adj. 1. consisting or made of starch. 2. having a mealy texture or appearance. 3. containing starch: farinaceous seeds.

farm (fɑːm) n. 1. a. a tract of land, usually with house and buildings, cultivated as a unit or used to rear livestock. b. (as modifier): farm produce. c. (in combination): farmland. 2. a unit of land or water devoted to the growing or rearing of some particular type of vegetable, fruit, animal, or fish: a fish farm. 3. an installation for storage or disposal: a sewage farm. ~vb. 4. (tr.) a. to cultivate (land). b. to rear (stock, etc.) on a farm. 5. (intr.) to engage in agricultural work, esp. as a way of life. 6. (tr.) to look after a child for a fixed sum. 7. to collect the moneys due and retain the profits from (a tax district, business, etc.) for a specified period. ~See also **farm out**. —ˈfarmable adj.

farmer (ˈfɑːmə) n. 1. a person who operates or manages a farm. 2. a person who obtains the right to collect and retain a tax, rent, etc., on payment of a fee. 3. a person who looks after a child for a fixed sum.

farm hand n. a person who is hired to work on a farm.

farmhouse (ˈfɑːmˌhaʊs) n. a house attached to a farm, esp. the dwelling from which the farm is managed.

farming (ˈfɑːmɪŋ) n. a. the business or skill of agriculture. b. (as modifier): farming methods.

farm out vb. (tr., adv.) 1. to send (work) to be done by another person, firm, etc. 2. to put (a child, etc.) into the care of a private individual. 3. to lease to another for a fee the right to collect (taxes).

farmstead (ˈfɑːmˌstɛd) n. a farm or the part of a farm comprising its main buildings together with adjacent grounds.

farmyard (ˈfɑːmˌjɑːd) n. an area surrounded by or adjacent to farm buildings.

Far North n. the. the Arctic and sub-Arctic regions of the world.

faro (ˈfeərəʊ) n. a gambling game in which players bet against the dealer on what cards he will turn up.

far-off adj. (**far off** when postpositive). remote in space or time; distant.

far-out Sl. ~adj. (**far out** when postpositive) 1. bizarre or avant-garde. 2. wonderful. ~interj. **far out.** 3. an expression of amazement or delight.

far-reaching adj. extensive in influence, effect, or range.

farrier (ˈfærɪə) n. Chiefly Brit. 1. a person who shoes horses. 2. another name for **veterinary surgeon.** —ˈfarriery n.

farrow (ˈfærəʊ) n. 1. a litter of piglets. ~vb. 2. (of a sow) to give birth to (a litter).

far-seeing adj. having shrewd judgment.

far-sighted adj. 1. possessing prudence and fore-

sight. 2. Med. of or suffering from hyperopia. 3. another word for **long-sighted.** —ˌfar-ˈsightedly adv. —ˌfar-ˈsightedness n.

fart (fɑːt) Taboo. ~n. 1. an emission of intestinal gas from the anus. 2. Sl. a contemptible person. ~vb. (intr.) 3. to break wind. 4. **fart about** or **around.** Sl. a. to behave foolishly. b. to waste time.

farther (ˈfɑːðə) adv. 1. to or at a greater distance in space or time. 2. in addition. ~adj. 3. more distant in space or time. 4. additional.

▷ **Usage.** In careful usage, farther and farthest are preferred when referring to literal distance: the farthest planet. Further and furthest are regarded as more correct for figurative senses denoting greater amount, time, etc.: nothing could be further from the truth.

farthermost (ˈfɑːðəˌməʊst) adj. most distant or remote.

farthest (ˈfɑːðɪst) adv. 1. to or at the greatest distance in space or time. ~adj. 2. most distant in space or time. 3. most extended.

farthing (ˈfɑːðɪŋ) n. 1. a former British bronze coin worth a quarter of an old penny: withdrawn in 1961. 2. something of negligible value; jot.

farthingale (ˈfɑːðɪŋˌɡeɪl) n. a hoop or framework worn under skirts, esp. in the Elizabethan period, to shape and spread them.

fasces (ˈfæsiːz) pl. n., sing. **-cis** (-sɪs). 1. (in ancient Rome) one or more bundles of rods containing an axe with its blade protruding; a symbol of a magistrate's power. 2. (in modern Italy) such an object used as the symbol of Fascism.

fascia or **facia** (ˈfeɪʃɪə) n., pl. **-ciae** (-ʃɪˌiː). 1. the flat surface above a shop window. 2. Archit. a flat band or surface, esp. a part of an architrave. 3. (ˈfæʃɪə). fibrous connective tissue occurring in sheets between muscles. 4. Biol. a distinctive band of colour, as on an insect or plant. 5. Brit. the outer panel which covers the dashboard of a motor vehicle. —ˈfascial or ˈfacial adj.

fascicle (ˈfæsɪkəl) n. 1. a bundle of branches, leaves, etc. 2. Also called: **fasciculus.** Anat. a small bundle of fibres, esp. nerve fibres. —ˈfascicled adj. —**fascicular** (fəˈsɪkjʊlə) or **fasciculate** (fəˈsɪkjʊˌleɪt) adj. —ˌfasˌcicuˈlation n.

fascinate (ˈfæsɪˌneɪt) vb. (mainly tr.) 1. to attract and delight by arousing interest: his stories fascinated me for hours. 2. to render motionless, as by arousing terror or awe. 3. Arch. to put under a spell. —ˈfasciˌnating adj. —ˌfasciˈnation n.

Fascism (ˈfæʃɪzəm) n. 1. the authoritarian nationalistic political movement led by Benito Mussolini in Italy (1922–43). 2. (sometimes not cap.) any ideology or movement modelled on or inspired by this. 3. Inf. (often not cap.) any doctrine or system regarded as opposed to democracy and liberalism. —ˈFascist n.

fashion (ˈfæʃən) n. 1. a. style in clothes, behaviour, etc., esp. the latest style. b. (as modifier): a fashion magazine. 2. a. manner of performance: in a striking fashion. b. (in combination): crab-fashion. 3. a way of life that revolves around the activities, dress, interests, etc., that are most fashionable. 4. shape or form. 5. sort; kind. 6. **after** or **in a fashion.** in some manner, but not very well: I mended it, after a fashion. 7. **of fashion.** of high social standing. ~vb. (tr.) 8. to give a particular form to. 9. to make suitable or fitting. 10. Obs. to contrive. —ˈfashioner n.

THESAURUS

farewell adieu, adieux or adieus, departure, goodbye, leave-taking, parting, sendoff (Inf.), valediction

far-fetched doubtful, dubious, fantastic, hard to swallow (Inf.), implausible, improbable, incredible, preposterous, strained, unbelievable, unconvincing, unlikely, unnatural, unrealistic

farm 1. n. acreage, acres, croft (Scot.), farmstead, grange, holding, homestead, land, plantation, ranch (Chiefly North American), smallholding, station (Aust. & New Zealand) 2. v. bring under cultivation, cultivate, operate, plant, practise husbandry, till the soil, work

farmer agriculturist, agronomist, husbandman, smallholder, yeoman

farming agriculture, agronomy, hus-

bandry

far-reaching broad, extensive, important, momentous, pervasive, significant, sweeping, widespread

far-sighted acute, canny, cautious, discerning, far-seeing, judicious, politic, prescient, provident, prudent, sage, shrewd, wise

fascinate absorb, allure, beguile, bewitch, captivate, charm, delight, enamour, enchant, engross, enrapture, enravish, enthral, entrance, hold spellbound, hypnotize, infatuate, intrigue, mesmerize, rivet, spellbind, transfix

fascinated absorbed, beguiled, bewitched, captivated, charmed, engrossed, enthralled, entranced, hooked on, hypnotized, infatuated, smitten, spellbound, under a spell

fascinating alluring, bewitching, capti-

vating, compelling, enchanting, engaging, engrossing, enticing, gripping, intriguing, irresistible, ravishing, riveting, seductive

fascination allure, attraction, charm, enchantment, glamour, lure, magic, magnetism, pull, sorcery, spell

fashion n. 1. convention, craze, custom, fad, latest, latest style, look, mode, prevailing taste, rage, style, trend, usage, vogue 2. attitude, demeanour, manner, method, mode, style, way 3. appearance, configuration, cut, figure, form, guise (Archaic), line, make, model, mould, pattern, shape 4. description, kind, sort, type 5. beau monde, fashionable society, high society, jet set 6. **after a fashion** in a manner of speaking, in a way, moderately, somehow, somehow or other, to a degree, to some extent ~v. 7. construct, con-

fashionable ('fæ∫ənəbəl) adj. 1. conforming to fashion; in vogue. 2. of or patronized by people of fashion: a fashionable café. 3. (usually foll. by with) patronized (by). —'fashionableness n. —'fashionably adv.

fast[1] (fɑːst) adj. 1. acting or moving or capable of acting or moving quickly. 2. accomplished in or lasting a short time: a fast visit. 3. (prenominal) adapted to or facilitating rapid movement: the fast lane of a motorway. 4. (of a clock, etc.) indicating a time in advance of the correct time. 5. given to an active dissipated life. 6. of or characteristic of such activity: a fast life. 7. not easily moved; firmly fixed; secure. 8. firmly fastened or shut. 9. steadfast; constant (esp. in **fast friends**). 10. Sport. (of a playing surface, running track, etc.) conducive to rapid speed, as of a ball used on it or of competitors racing on it. 11. that will not fade or change colour readily. 12. proof against fading. 13. Photog. a. requiring a relatively short time of exposure to produce a given density: a fast film. b. permitting a short exposure time: a fast shutter. 14. **fast one**. Inf. a deceptive or unscrupulous trick (esp. in **pull a fast one**). 15. **fast worker**. a person who achieves results quickly, esp. in seductions. ~adv. 16. quickly; rapidly. 17. soundly; deeply: fast asleep. 18. firmly; tightly. 19. in quick succession. 20. in advance of the correct time: my watch is running fast. 21. in a reckless or dissipated way. 22. **fast by** or **beside**. Arch. close by. 23. **play fast and loose**. Inf. to behave in an insincere or unreliable manner.

fast[2] (fɑːst) vb. 1. (intr.) to abstain from eating all or certain foods or meals, esp. as a religious observance. ~n. 2. a. an act or period of fasting. b. (as modifier): a fast day. —'faster n.

fastback ('fɑːst,bæk) n. a car having a back that forms one continuous slope from roof to rear.

fast-breeder reactor n. a nuclear reactor that uses little or no moderator and produces more fissionable material than it consumes.

fasten ('fɑːsən) vb. 1. to make or become fast or secure. 2. to make or become attached or joined. 3. to close or become closed by fixing firmly in place, locking, etc. 4. (tr.; foll. by in or up) to enclose or imprison. 5. (tr.; usually foll. by on) to cause (blame, a nickname, etc.) to be attached (to). 6. (usually foll. by on or upon) to direct or be directed in a concentrated way. 7. (intr.; usually foll. by on) to take a firm hold (of). —'fastener n.

fastening ('fɑːsənɪŋ) n. something that fastens, such as a clasp or lock.

fast food n. a. food, esp. hamburgers, fried chicken, etc., that is prepared and served very quickly. b. (as modifier): a fast-food restaurant.

fastidious (fæ'stɪdɪəs) adj. 1. hard to please. 2. excessively particular about details. 3. exceedingly delicate. —fas'tidiously adv. —fas'tidiousness n.

fat (fæt) n. 1. any of a class of naturally occurring soft greasy solids that are present in some plants and animals, and are used in making soap and paint and in the food industry. 2. vegetable or animal tissue containing fat. 3. corpulence, obesity, or plumpness. 4. the best or richest part of something. 5. **chew the fat**. Sl. to chat. 6. **the fat is in the fire**. an irrevocable action has been taken from which dire consequences are expected. 7. **the fat of the land**. the best that is obtainable. ~adj. **fatter, fattest**. 8. having much or too much flesh or fat. 9. consisting of or containing fat; greasy. 10. profitable; lucrative. 11. affording great opportunities: a fat part in the play. 12. fertile or productive: a fat land. 13. thick, broad, or extended: a fat log of wood. 14. Sl. very little or none (in **a fat chance, a fat lot of good**, etc.). ~vb. **fatting, fatted**. 15. to make or become fat; fatten. —'fatless adj. —'fatly adv. —'fatness n. —'fattish adj.

fatal ('feɪtəl) adj. 1. resulting in death: a fatal accident. 2. bringing ruin. 3. decisively important. 4. inevitable. —'fatally adv.

fatalism ('feɪtə,lɪzəm) n. 1. the philosophical doctrine that all events are predetermined so that man is powerless to alter his destiny. 2. the acceptance of and submission to this doctrine. —'fatalist n. —,fatal'istic adj.

fatality (fə'tælɪtɪ) n., pl. **-ties**. 1. an accident or disaster resulting in death. 2. a person killed in an accident or disaster. 3. the power of causing death or disaster. 4. the quality or condition of being fated. 5. something caused by fate.

fate (feɪt) n. 1. the ultimate agency that predetermines the course of events. 2. the inevitable fortune that befalls a person or thing. 3. the end or final result. 4. death, destruction, or downfall. ~vb. 5. (tr.; usually passive) to predetermine: he was fated to lose.

fated ('feɪtɪd) adj. 1. destined. 2. doomed to death or destruction.

fateful ('feɪtful) adj. 1. having important consequences. 2. bringing death or disaster. 3. controlled by or as if by fate. 4. prophetic. —'fatefully adv. —'fatefulness n.

fathead ('fæt,hed) n. Inf. a stupid person; fool. —'fat,headed adj.

father ('fɑːðə) n. 1. a male parent. 2. a person who founds a line or family; forefather. 3. any male acting in a paternal capacity. 4. (often cap.) a respectful term of address for an old man. 5. a male who originates something: the father of modern psychology. 6. a leader of an association, council, etc.: a city father. 7. Brit. the eldest or most senior member in a union, profession, etc. 8. (often pl.) a senator in ancient Rome. ~vb. (tr.) 9. to procreate or generate (offspring). 10. to create, found, etc. 11. to act as a father to. 12. to acknowledge oneself as father or originator of. 13. (foll. by on or upon) to impose or foist upon. —'fatherhood n. —'fatherless adj.

THESAURUS

trive, create, design, forge, form, make, manufacture, mould, shape, work 8. accommodate, adapt, adjust, fit, suit, tailor

fashionable à la mode, all the go (Inf.), all the rage, chic, current, customary, genteel, in (Inf.), in vogue, latest, modern, modish, popular, prevailing, smart, stylish, trendsetting, trendy (Inf.), up-to-date, up-to-the-minute, usual, with it (Inf.)

fast[1] adj. 1. accelerated, brisk, fleet, flying, hasty, hurried, mercurial, nippy (Inf.), quick, rapid, speedy, swift, winged ~adv. 2. quick, hastily, hell for leather, hurriedly, in haste, like a bat out of hell (Inf.), like a flash, like a shot (Inf.), posthaste, presto, quickly, rapidly, speedily, swiftly, with all haste ~adj. 3. close, constant, fastened, firm, fixed, fortified, immovable, impregnable, lasting, loyal, permanent, secure, sound, staunch, steadfast, tight, unwavering ~adv. 4. deeply, firmly, fixedly, securely, soundly, tightly ~adj. 5. dissipated, dissolute, extravagant, gadabout, giddy, immoral, intemperate, licentious, loose, profligate, promiscuous, rakish, reckless, self-indulgent, wanton, wild ~adv. 6. extravagantly, intemperately, loosely, promiscuously, rakishly, recklessly, wildly 7. **pull a fast one** bamboozle (Inf.), cheat, con (Sl.),

deceive, defraud, hoodwink, put one over on (Inf.), swindle, take advantage of, take for a ride (Inf.), trick

fast[2] 1. v. abstain, deny oneself, go hungry, go without food, practise abstention, refrain from food or eating 2. n. abstinence, fasting

fasten 1. affix, anchor, attach, bind, bolt, chain, connect, fix, grip, join, lace, link, lock, make fast, make firm, seal, secure, tie, unite 2. Fig. aim, bend, concentrate, direct, fix, focus, rivet

fat adj. 1. beefy (Inf.), broad in the beam (Inf.), corpulent, elephantine, fleshy, gross, heavy, obese, overweight, plump, podgy, portly, roly-poly, rotund, solid, stout, tubby 2. adipose, fatty, greasy, oily, oleaginous, suety 3. affluent, cushy (Sl.), fertile, flourishing, fruitful, jammy (Sl.), lucrative, lush, productive, profitable, prosperous, remunerative, rich, thriving ~n. 4. adipose tissue, blubber, bulk, cellulite, corpulence, fatness, flab, flesh, obesity, overweight, paunch, weight problem

fatal 1. deadly, destructive, final, incurable, killing, lethal, malignant, mortal, pernicious, terminal 2. baleful, baneful, calamitous, catastrophic, disastrous, lethal, ruinous 3. critical, crucial, decisive, destined, determining,

doomed, fateful, final, foreordained, inevitable, predestined

fatalism acceptance, determinism, necessitarianism, passivity, predestinarianism, resignation, stoicism

fatality casualty, deadliness, death, disaster, fatal accident, lethalness, loss, mortality

fate 1. chance, destiny, divine will, fortune, kismet, nemesis, predestination, providence, weird (Archaic) 2. cup, fortune, horoscope, lot, portion, stars 3. end, future, issue, outcome, upshot 4. death, destruction, doom, downfall, end, ruin

fated destined, doomed, foreordained, ineluctable, inescapable, inevitable, marked down, predestined, pre-elected, preordained, sure, written

fateful 1. critical, crucial, decisive, important, portentous, significant 2. deadly, destructive, disastrous, fatal, lethal, ominous, ruinous

father n. 1. begetter, dad (Inf.), daddy (Inf.), governor (Inf.), old boy (Inf.), old man (Inf.), pa (Inf.), pater, paterfamilias, patriarch, pop (Inf.), sire 2. ancestor, forebear, forefather, predecessor, progenitor 3. architect, author, creator, founder, inventor, maker, originator, prime mover 4. city father, el-

Father ('fɑːðə) n. 1. God, esp. when considered as the first person of the Christian Trinity. 2. any of the early writers on Christian doctrine. 3. a title used for Christian priests.

father-in-law n., pl. **fathers-in-law.** the father of one's wife or husband.

fatherland ('fɑːðə,lænd) n. 1. a person's native country. 2. the country of a person's ancestors.

fatherly ('fɑːðəlı) adj. of, resembling, or suitable to a father. —'**fatherliness** n.

Father's Day n. the third Sunday in June, observed as a day in honour of fathers.

fathom ('fæðəm) n. 1. a unit of length equal to six feet, used to measure depths of water. ~vb. (tr.) 2. to measure the depth of, esp. with a sounding line. 3. to penetrate (a mystery, problem, etc.). —'**fathomable** adj. —'**fathomless** adj.

fatigue (fə'tiːg) n. 1. physical or mental exhaustion due to exertion. 2. a tiring activity or effort. 3. Physiol. the temporary inability of an organ or part to respond to a stimulus because of overactivity. 4. the weakening of a material subjected to alternating stresses, esp. vibrations. 5. any of the mainly domestic duties performed by military personnel, esp. as a punishment. 6. (pl.) special clothing worn by military personnel to carry out such duties. ~vb. -**tiguing, -tigued.** 7. to make or become weary or exhausted. —**fatigable** or **fatiguable** ('fætɪgəbəl) adj.

fat stock n. livestock fattened and ready for market.

fatten ('fætən) vb. 1. to grow or cause to grow fat or fatter. 2. (tr.) to cause (an animal or fowl) to become fat by feeding it. 3. (tr.) to make fuller or richer. 4. (tr.) to enrich (soil).

fatty ('fætı) adj. -**tier, -tiest.** 1. containing or derived from fat. 2. greasy; oily. 3. (esp. of tissues, organs, etc.) characterized by the excessive accumulation of fat. ~n., pl. -**ties.** 4. Inf. a fat person. —'**fattily** adv. —'**fattiness** n.

fatty acid n. any of a class of aliphatic carboxylic acids, such as palmitic acid, stearic acid, and oleic acid.

fatuity (fə'tjuːɪtɪ) n., pl. -**ties.** 1. inanity. 2. a fatuous remark, act, sentiment, etc. —**fa'tuitous** adj.

fatuous ('fætjuəs) adj. complacently or inanely foolish. —'**fatuously** adv. —'**fatuousness** n.

faucet ('fɔːsɪt) n. the U.S. name for a **tap²**.

fault (fɔːlt) n. 1. a failing or defect; flaw. 2. a mistake or error. 3. a misdeed. 4. responsibility for a mistake or misdeed. 5. Electronics. a defect in a circuit, component, or line, such as a short circuit. 6. Geol. a fracture in the earth's crust resulting in the relative displacement of the rocks on either side of it. 7. Tennis, squash, etc. an invalid serve. 8. (in showjumping) a penalty mark given for failing to clear, or refusing, a fence, etc. 9. **at fault.** guilty of error; culpable. 10. **find fault (with).** to seek out minor imperfections or errors (in). 11. **to a fault.** excessively. ~vb. 12. Geol. to undergo or cause to undergo a fault. 13. (tr.) to criticize or blame. 14. (intr.) to commit a fault. —'**faultless** adj.

fault-finding n. 1. continual criticism. ~adj. 2. given to finding fault. —'**fault-,finder** n.

faulty ('fɔːltı) adj. **faultier, faultiest.** defective or imperfect. —'**faultily** adv. —'**faultiness** n.

faun (fɔːn) n. (in Roman legend) a rural deity represented as a man with a goat's ears, horns, tail, and hind legs. —'**faun,like** adj.

fauna ('fɔːnə) n., pl. -**nas** or -**nae** (-niː). 1. all the animal life of a given place or time. 2. a descriptive list of such animals. —'**faunal** adj.

faux pas (fəʊ 'pɑː) n., pl. **faux pas** (fəʊ 'pɑːz). a social blunder.

favour or U.S. **favor** ('feɪvə) n. 1. an approving attitude; good will. 2. an act performed out of good will or mercy. 3. prejudice and partiality. 4. a condition of being regarded with approval (esp. in in favour, out of favour). 5. a token of love, good will, etc. 6. a small gift or toy given to a guest at a party. 7. History. a badge or ribbon worn or given to indicate loyalty. 8. **find favour with.** to be approved of by someone. 9. **in favour of. a.** approving. **b.** to the benefit of. **c.** (of a cheque, etc.) made out to. **d.** in order to show preference for. ~vb. (tr.) 10. to regard with especial kindness. 11. to treat with partiality. 12. to support; advocate. 13. to oblige. 14. to help; facilitate. 15. Inf. to resemble: he favours his father. 16. to wear habitually: she favours red. 17. to treat gingerly: a footballer favouring an injured leg. —'**favourer** or U.S. '**favorer** n.

favourable or U.S. **favorable** ('feɪvərəbəl) adj. 1. advantageous, encouraging or promising. 2. giving consent. —'**favourably** or U.S. '**favorably** adv.

-favoured adj. (in combination) having an appearance (as specified): ill-favoured.

THESAURUS

der, leader, patriarch, patron, senator 5. abbé, confessor, curé, padre (Inf.), pastor, priest ~v. 6. beget, get, procreate, sire 7. create, engender, establish, found, institute, invent, originate

fatherland homeland, land of one's birth, land of one's fathers, motherland, native land, old country

fatherly affectionate, benevolent, benign, forbearing, indulgent, kind, kindly, paternal, patriarchal, protective, supportive, tender

fathom 1. divine, estimate, gauge, measure, penetrate, plumb, probe, sound 2. comprehend, get to the bottom of, grasp, interpret, understand

fathomless abysmal, bottomless, deep, immeasurable, impenetrable, incomprehensible, profound, unfathomable, unplumbed

fatigue 1. v. drain, drain of energy, exhaust, fag (out) (Inf.), jade, overtire, take it out of (Inf.), tire, weaken, wear out, weary, whack (Inf.) 2. n. debility, ennui, heaviness, languor, lethargy, listlessness, overtiredness, tiredness

fatten 1. broaden, coarsen, expand, gain weight, grow fat, put on weight, spread, swell, thicken, thrive 2. Often with **up** bloat, build up, cram, distend, feed, feed up, nourish, overfeed, stuff

fatty adipose, fat, greasy, oily, oleaginous, rich

fatuous absurd, asinine, brainless, dense, dull, foolish, idiotic, inane, ludicrous, lunatic, mindless, moronic, puerile, silly, stupid, vacuous, weak-minded, witless

fault n. 1. blemish, defect, deficiency, draw-

back, failing, flaw, imperfection, infirmity, lack, shortcoming, snag, weakness, weak point 2. blunder, boob (Sl.), error, error of judgment, inaccuracy, indiscretion, lapse, mistake, negligence, offence, omission, oversight, slip, slip-up 3. accountability, culpability, liability, responsibility 4. delinquency, frailty, lapse, misconduct, misdeed, misdemeanour, offence, peccadillo, sin, transgression, trespass, wrong 5. **at fault** answerable, blamable, culpable, guilty, in the wrong, responsible, to blame 6. **find fault with** carp at, complain, criticize, pick holes in, pull to pieces, quibble, take to task 7. **to a fault** excessively, immoderately, in the extreme, needlessly, out of all proportion, overly (U.S.), overmuch, preposterously, ridiculously, unduly ~v. 8. blame, call to account, censure, criticize, find fault with, find lacking, hold (someone) accountable (responsible, to blame), impugn

fault-finding 1. n. carping, hairsplitting, nagging, niggling, nit-picking (Inf.) 2. adj. captious, carping, censorious, critical, hypercritical, pettifogging

faultless 1. accurate, classic, correct, exemplary, faithful, flawless, foolproof, impeccable, model, perfect, unblemished 2. above reproach, blameless, guiltless, immaculate, innocent, irreproachable, pure, sinless, spotless, stainless, unblemished, unspotted, unsullied

faulty bad, blemished, broken, damaged, defective, erroneous, fallacious, flawed, impaired, imperfect, imprecise, inaccurate, incorrect, invalid, malfunctioning, not working, out of order, unsound, weak, wrong

faux pas blunder, boob (Sl.), breach of etiquette, clanger (Inf.), gaffe, gaucherie, impropriety, indiscretion, solecism

favour n. 1. approbation, approval, backing, bias, championship, esteem, favouritism, friendliness, good opinion, good will, grace, kindness, kind regard, partiality, patronage, support 2. benefit, boon, courtesy, good turn, indulgence, kindness, obligement (Scot. or Archaic), service 3. **in favour of** all for (Inf.), backing, for, on the side of, pro, supporting, to the benefit of 4. gift, keepsake, love-token, memento, present, souvenir, token 5. badge, decoration, knot, ribbons, rosette ~v. 6. be partial to, esteem, have in one's good books, indulge, pamper, pull strings for (Inf.), reward, side with, smile upon, spoil, treat with partiality, value 7. advocate, approve, back, be in favour of, champion, choose, commend, countenance, encourage, fancy, incline towards, like, opt for, patronize, prefer, single out, support 8. abet, accommodate, advance, aid, assist, befriend, do a kindness to, facilitate, help, oblige, promote, succour 9. Inf. be the image or picture of, look like, resemble, take after 10. ease, extenuate, spare

favourable 1. advantageous, appropriate, auspicious, beneficial, convenient, encouraging, fair, fit, good, helpful, hopeful, opportune, promising, propitious, suitable, timely 2. affirmative, agreeable, amicable, approving, benign, encouraging, enthusiastic, friendly, kind, positive, reassuring, sympathetic, understanding, welcoming, well-disposed

favourably 1. advantageously, auspiciously, conveniently, fortunately, oppor-

favourite *or U.S.* **favorite** ('feɪvərɪt) *adj.* **1.** (*prenominal*) most liked. ~*n.* **2.** a person or thing regarded with especial preference or liking. **3.** *Sport.* a competitor thought likely to win.

favouritism *or U.S.* **favoritism** ('feɪvərɪˌtɪzəm) *n.* the practice of giving special treatment to a person or group.

fawn[1] (fɔːn) *n.* **1.** a young deer of either sex aged under one year. **2. a.** a light greyish-brown colour. **b.** (*as adj.*): *a fawn raincoat.* ~*vb.* **3.** (*tr.*) (of deer) to bear young. —'**fawn,like** *adj.*

fawn[2] (fɔːn) *vb.* (*intr.; often foll. by* on *or* upon) **1.** to seek attention and admiration (from) by cringing and flattering. **2.** (of animals, esp. dogs) to try to please by a show of extreme friendliness. —'**fawner** *n.* —'**fawning** *adj.*

fay (feɪ) *n.* a fairy or sprite.

F.B.I. (in the U.S.) *abbrev. for* Federal Bureau of Investigation; an agency responsible for investigating violations of Federal laws.

F.D. *abbrev. for* Fidei Defensor.

Fe *the chemical symbol for* iron.

fealty ('fiːəltɪ) *n., pl.* **-ties.** (in feudal society) the loyalty sworn to one's lord on becoming his vassal.

fear (fɪə) *n.* **1.** a feeling of distress, apprehension, or alarm caused by impending danger, pain, etc. **2.** a cause of this feeling. **3.** awe; reverence: *fear of God.* **4.** concern; anxiety. **5.** possibility; chance. **6. for fear of, that** *or* **lest.** to forestall or avoid. **7. no fear.** certainly not. ~*vb.* **8.** to be afraid (to do something) or of (a person or thing). **9.** (*tr.*) to revere; respect. **10.** (*tr.; takes a clause as object*) to be sorry: *I fear that you have not won.* **11.** (*intr.; foll. by* for) to feel anxiety about something. —'**fearless** *adj.* —'**fearlessly** *adv.* —'**fearlessness** *n.*

fearful ('fɪəful) *adj.* **1.** afraid. **2.** causing fear. **3.** *Inf.* very unpleasant: *a fearful cold.* —'**fearfully** *adv.* —'**fearfulness** *n.*

fearsome ('fɪəsəm) *adj.* **1.** frightening. **2.** timorous; afraid. —'**fearsomely** *adv.*

feasible ('fiːzəbəl) *adj.* **1.** able to be done or put into effect; possible. **2.** likely; probable. —,**feasi'bility** *n.* —'**feasibly** *adv.*

feast (fiːst) *n.* **1.** a large and sumptuous meal. **2.** a periodic religious celebration. **3.** something extremely pleasing: *a feast for the eyes.* **4. moveable feast.** a festival of variable date. ~*vb.* **5.** (*intr.*) **a.** to eat a feast. **b.** (usually foll. by *on*) to enjoy the eating (of): *to feast on cakes.* **6.** (*tr.*) to give a feast to. **7.** (*intr.; foll. by* on) to

take great delight (in): *to feast on beautiful paintings.* **8.** (*tr.*) to regale or delight: *to feast one's eyes.* —'**feaster** *n.*

feat (fiːt) *n.* a remarkable, skilful, or daring action.

feather ('fɛðə) *n.* **1.** any of the flat light waterproof structures forming the plumage of birds, each consisting of a hollow shaft having a vane of barbs on either side. **2.** something resembling a feather, such as a tuft of hair or grass. **3.** *Archery.* **a.** a bird's feather or artificial substitute fitted to an arrow to direct its flight. **b.** the feathered end of an arrow. **4.** *Rowing.* the position of an oar turned parallel to the water between strokes. **5.** condition of spirits; fettle: *in fine feather.* **6.** something of negligible value: *I don't care a feather.* **7. birds of a feather.** people of the same type or interests. **8. feather in one's cap.** a cause for pleasure at one's achievements. **9. white feather.** a sign of cowardice. ~*vb.* **10.** (*tr.*) to fit, cover, or supply with feathers. **11.** *Rowing.* to turn (an oar) parallel to the water during recovery between strokes, in order to lessen wind resistance. **12.** to change the pitch of (an aircraft propeller) so that the chord lines of the blades are in line with the airflow. **13.** (*intr.*) (of a bird) to grow feathers. **14. feather one's nest.** to provide oneself with comforts. —'**feathering** *n.* —'**feather-,like** *adj.* —'**feathery** *adj.*

feather bed *n.* **1.** a mattress filled with feathers or down. ~*vb.* **feather,bed, -bedding, -bedded.** **2.** (*tr.*) to pamper; spoil.

featherbrain ('fɛðə,breɪn) *or* **featherhead** *n.* a frivolous or forgetful person. —'**feather,brained** *or* '**feather,headed** *adj.*

featherweight ('fɛðə,weɪt) *n.* **1. a.** something very light or of little importance. **b.** (*as modifier*): *featherweight considerations.* **2. a.** a professional boxer weighing 118–126 pounds (53.5–57 kg). **b.** an amateur boxer weighing 54–57 kg (119–126 pounds). **3.** a wrestler weighing usually 126–139 pounds (57–63 kg).

feature ('fiːtʃə) *n.* **1.** any one of the parts of the face, such as the nose, chin, or mouth. **2.** a prominent or distinctive part, as of a landscape, book, etc. **3.** the principal film in a programme at a cinema. **4.** an item or article appearing at intervals in a newspaper, magazine, etc.: *a gardening feature.* **5.** Also called: **feature story.** a prominent story in a newspaper, etc.: *a feature on prison reform.* **6.** a programme given special prominence on radio or television. **7.** *Arch.* general form. ~*vb.* **8.** (*tr.*) to have as a feature or make a feature of. **9.** to give prominence to (an actor, famous event, etc.) in a film or (of an actor, etc.) to have prominence in a film. **10.** (*tr.*)

THESAURUS

tunely, profitably, to one's advantage, well **2.** agreeably, approvingly, enthusiastically, genially, graciously, helpfully, in a kindly manner, positively, with approval (approbation, cordiality), without prejudice

favourite 1. *adj.* best-loved, choice, dearest, esteemed, preferred **2.** *n.* beloved, blue-eyed boy (*Inf.*), choice, darling, dear, idol, pet, pick, preference, teacher's pet, the apple of one's eye

favouritism bias, jobs for the boys (*Inf.*), nepotism, one-sidedness, partiality, partisanship, preference, preferential treatment

fawn[1] *adj.* beige, buff, greyish-brown, neutral

fawn[2] *v.* Often with **on** *or* **upon** be obsequious, be servile, bow and scrape, court, crawl, creep, cringe, curry favour, dance attendance, flatter, grovel, ingratiate oneself, kneel, kowtow, lick (someone's) boots, pay court, toady, truckle

fawning abject, bootlicking (*Inf.*), bowing and scraping, crawling, cringing, deferential, flattering, grovelling, obsequious, prostrate, servile, slavish, sycophantic

fear *n.* **1.** alarm, apprehensiveness, awe, blue funk (*Inf.*), consternation, cravenness, dismay, dread, fright, horror, panic, qualms, terror, timidity, tremors, trepidation **2.** *bête noire*, bogey, bugbear, horror, nightmare, phobia, spectre **3.** agitation, anxiety, apprehension, concern, disquietude, distress, doubt, foreboding(s), misgiving(s), solicitude, suspicion, unease, uneasiness, worry **4.** awe,

reverence, veneration, wonder ~*v.* **5.** apprehend, be apprehensive (afraid, frightened, scared), be in a blue funk (*Inf.*), dare not, dread, have a horror of, have a phobia about, have butterflies in one's stomach (*Inf.*), have qualms, live in dread of, shake in one's shoes, shudder at, take fright, tremble at **6.** anticipate, apprehend, be afraid, expect, foresee, suspect **7.** *With* **for** be anxious (concerned, distressed) about, be disquieted over, feel concern for, tremble for, worry about **8.** respect, revere, reverence, stand in awe of, venerate

fearful 1. afraid, alarmed, anxious, apprehensive, diffident, faint-hearted, frightened, hesitant, intimidated, jittery (*Inf.*), jumpy, nervous, nervy, panicky, pusillanimous, scared, shrinking, tense, timid, timorous, uneasy **2.** appalling, atrocious, awful, dire, distressing, dreadful, frightful, ghastly, grievous, grim, gruesome, hair-raising, hideous, horrendous, horrible, horrific, monstrous, shocking, terrible, unspeakable

fearfully 1. apprehensively, diffidently, in fear and trembling, nervously, timidly, timorously, uneasily, with many misgivings *or* forebodings, with one's heart in one's mouth **2.** awfully, exceedingly, excessively, frightfully, terribly, tremendously, very

fearless bold, brave, confident, courageous, daring, dauntless, doughty, gallant, game (*Inf.*), gutsy (*Sl.*), heroic, indomitable, intrepid, lion-hearted, plucky, unabashed, unafraid, undaunted, unflinching, valiant, valorous

fearlessness boldness, bravery, confidence, courage, dauntlessness, guts (*Inf.*), indomitability, intrepidity, lion-heartedness, nerve, pluckiness

fearsome alarming, appalling, awe-inspiring, awesome, awful, daunting, dismaying, formidable, frightening, hair-raising, horrendous, horrifying, menacing, unnerving

feasibility expediency, practicability, usefulness, viability, workability

feasible achievable, attainable, likely, possible, practicable, realizable, reasonable, viable, workable

feast *n.* **1.** banquet, barbecue, beanfeast (*Brit. inf.*), beano (*Brit. sl.*), blowout (*Sl.*), carousal, carouse, dinner, entertainment, festive board, jollification, junket, repast, revels, slap-up meal (*Brit. inf.*), spread (*Inf.*), treat **2.** celebration, festival, fête, gala day, holiday, holy day, saint's day **3.** delight, enjoyment, gratification, pleasure, treat ~*v.* **4.** eat one's fill, eat to one's heart's content, fare sumptuously, gorge, gormandize, indulge, overindulge, stuff, stuff one's face (*Sl.*), wine and dine **5.** entertain, hold a reception for, kill the fatted calf for, regale, treat, wine and dine **6.** delight, gladden, gratify, rejoice, thrill

feat accomplishment, achievement, act, attainment, deed, exploit, performance

feathers down, plumage, plumes

feathery downy, feathered, fluffy, plumate *or* plumose (*Bot. & Zool.*), plumed, plumy, wispy

to draw the main features or parts of. —'**featureless** *adj.*

Feb. *abbrev. for* February.

febri- *combining form.* indicating fever: *febrifuge.*

febrile ('fiːbraɪl) *adj.* of or relating to fever; feverish. —**febrility** (fɪ'brɪlɪtɪ) *n.*

February ('fɛbrʊərɪ) *n., pl.* **-aries.** the second month of the year, consisting of 28 or (in a leap year) 29 days.

feckless ('fɛklɪs) *adj.* feeble; weak; ineffectual. —'**fecklessly** *adv.* —'**fecklessness** *n.*

fecund ('fiːkənd, 'fɛk-) *adj.* 1. fertile. 2. intellectually productive. —**fecundity** (fɪ'kʌndɪtɪ) *n.*

fecundate ('fiːkənˌdeɪt, 'fɛk-) *vb.* (*tr.*) 1. to make fruitful. 2. to fertilize. —ˌ**fecun'dation** *n.*

fed (fɛd) *vb.* 1. the past tense or past participle of **feed**. 2. **fed to death** *or* **fed (up) to the (back) teeth.** *Inf.* bored or annoyed.

Fed. *or* **fed.** *abbrev. for:* 1. Federal. 2. Federation. 3. Federated.

federal ('fɛdərəl) *adj.* 1. of or relating to a form of government or a country in which power is divided between one central and several regional governments. 2. of or relating to the central government of a federation. —'**federaˌlism** *n.* —'**federaˌlist** *n., adj.* —'**federally** *adv.*

Federal ('fɛdərəl) *adj.* 1. characteristic of or supporting the Union government during the American Civil War. ~*n.* 2. a supporter of the Union government during the American Civil War.

Federal Government *n.* the national government of a federated state, such as the Canadian national government located in Ottawa.

federalize *or* **-lise** ('fɛdərəˌlaɪz) *vb.* (*tr.*) 1. to unite in a federal union. 2. to subject to federal control. —ˌ**federali'zation** *or* **-li'sation** *n.*

federate *vb.* ('fɛdəˌreɪt) 1. to unite or cause to unite in a federal union. ~*adj.* ('fɛdərɪt). 2. federal; federated. —'**federative** *adj.*

federation (ˌfɛdə'reɪʃən) *n.* 1. the act of federating. 2. the union of several provinces, states, etc., to form a federal union. 3. a political unit formed in such a way. 4. any league, alliance, or confederacy.

fed up *adj.* (*usually postpositive*) annoyed or bored: *I'm fed up with your conduct.*

fee (fiː) *n.* 1. a payment asked by professional people or public servants for their services: *school fees.* 2. a charge made for a privilege: *an entrance fee.* 3. *Property law.* an interest in land capable of being inherited. The interest can be with unrestricted rights of disposal (**fee simple**) or with restricted rights to one class of heirs (**fee tail**). 4. (in feudal Europe) the land granted by a lord to his vassal. 5. **in fee.** *Law.* (of land) in absolute ownership. ~*vb.* **feeing, feed.** 6. *Rare.* to give a fee to. 7. *Chiefly Scot.* to hire for a fee.

feeble ('fiːbəl) *adj.* 1. lacking in physical or mental strength. 2. unconvincing: *feeble excuses.* 3. easily influenced. —'**feebleness** *n.* —'**feebly** *adv.*

feeble-minded *adj.* 1. lacking in intelligence. 2. mentally defective.

feed (fiːd) *vb.* **feeding, fed.** (*mainly tr.*) 1. to give food to: *to feed the cat.* 2. to give as food: *to feed meat to the cat.* 3. (*intr.*) to eat food: *the horses feed at noon.* 4. to provide food for. 5. to gratify; satisfy. 6. (*also intr.*) to supply (a machine, furnace, etc.) with (the necessary materials or fuel) for its operation, or (of such materials) to flow or move forwards into a machine, etc. 7. *Theatre, inf.* to cue (an actor, esp. a comedian) with lines. 8. *Sport.* to pass a ball to (a teammate). 9. (*also intr.; foll. by on or upon*) to eat or cause to eat. ~*n.* 10. the act or an instance of feeding. 11. food, esp. that of animals or babies. 12. the process of supplying a machine or furnace with a material or fuel. 13. the quantity of material or fuel so supplied. 14. *Theatre, inf.* a performer, esp. a straight man, who provides cues. 15. *Inf.* a meal. —'**feedable** *adj.*

feedback ('fiːdˌbæk) *n.* 1. a. the return of part of the output of an electronic circuit, device, or mechanical system to its input. In **negative feedback** a rise in output energy reduces the input energy; in **positive feedback** an increase in output energy reinforces the input energy. b. that part of the output signal fed back into the input. 2. the return of part of the sound output by a loudspeaker to the microphone, so that a high-pitched whistle is produced. 3. the whistling noise so produced. 4. the effect of a product or action in a cyclic biological reaction on another stage in the same reaction. 5. information in response to an enquiry, experiment, etc.

feeder ('fiːdə) *n.* 1. a person or thing that feeds or is fed. 2. a child's feeding bottle or bib. 3. a person or device that feeds the working material into a system or machine. 4. a tributary channel. 5. a road, service, etc., that links secondary areas to the main traffic network. 6. a power line for transmitting electrical power from a generating station to a distribution network.

feel (fiːl) *vb.* **feeling, felt.** 1. to perceive (something) by touching. 2. to have a physical or emotional sensation of (something): *to feel anger.* 3. (*tr.*) to examine (something) by touch. 4. (*tr.*) to find (one's way) by testing or cautious exploration. 5. (*copula*) to seem in respect of the sensation given: *it feels warm.* 6. to sense (esp. in **feel (it) in one's bones**). 7. to consider; believe; think. 8. (*intr.; foll. by for*) to show sympathy or compassion (towards): *I feel for you in your sorrow.* 9. (*tr.*) *Sl.* to pass one's hands over the sexual organs of. 10. **feel like.** to have an inclination (for something or doing something): *I don't feel like going to the pictures.* 11. **feel up to.** (*usually used with a negative or in a question*) to be fit enough for (something or doing something): *I don't feel up to going out.* ~*n.* 12. the act or an instance of feeling. 13. the quality of or an impression from something perceived through feeling: *a homely feel.* 14. the sense of touch.

▷ **Usage.** The verbs *feel, look,* and *smell* can be followed by an adverb or an adjective according to the sense in which they are used. Where a quality of the subject is involved, an adjective is used: *I feel sick; he looks strong.* For other senses an adverb would be used: *she feels strongly about that; I must look closely at his record.*

THESAURUS

feature *n.* 1. aspect, attribute, characteristic, facet, factor, hallmark, mark, peculiarity, point, property, quality, trait 2. attraction, crowd puller (*Inf.*), draw, highlight, innovation, main item, special, special attraction, speciality, specialty 3. article, column, comment, item, piece, report, story ~*v.* 4. accentuate, call attention to, emphasize, give prominence to, give the full works (*Sl.*), headline, play up, present, promote, set off, spotlight, star

features countenance, face, lineaments, physiognomy

feckless aimless, feeble, futile, hopeless, incompetent, ineffectual, irresponsible, shiftless, useless, weak, worthless

federate *v.* amalgamate, associate, combine, confederate, integrate, syndicate, unify, unite

federation alliance, amalgamation, association, *Bund,* coalition, combination, confederacy, copartnership, entente, federacy, league, syndicate, union

fed up (**with**) annoyed, blue, bored, brassed off (*Inf.*), browned-off (*Inf.*), depressed, discontented, dismal, dissatisfied, down, gloomy, glum, sick and tired of (*Inf.*), tired of, weary of

fee account, bill, charge, compensation, emolument, hire, honorarium, pay, payment, recompense, remuneration, reward, toll

feeble 1. debilitated, delicate, doddering, effete, enervated, enfeebled, etiolated, exhausted, failing, faint, frail, infirm, languid, powerless, puny, shilpit (*Scot.*), sickly, weak, weakened 2. flat, flimsy, inadequate, incompetent, indecisive, ineffective, ineffectual, inefficient, insignificant, insufficient, lame, paltry, poor, slight, tame, thin, unconvincing, weak

feeble-minded addle-pated, boneheaded (*Sl.*), deficient, dim-witted (*Inf.*), dull, dumb (*Inf.*), half-witted, idiotic, imbecilic, lacking, moronic, retarded, simple, slow on the uptake, slow-witted, soft in the head (*Inf.*), stupid, vacant, weak-minded

feebleness 1. debility, delicacy, effeteness, enervation, etiolation, exhaustion, frailness, frailty, incapacity, infirmity, lack of strength, languor, lassitude, sickliness, weakness 2. flimsiness, inadequacy, incompetence, indecisiveness, ineffectualness, insignificance, insufficiency, lameness, weakness

feed *v.* 1. cater for, nourish, provide for, provision, supply, sustain, victual, wine and dine 2. *Sometimes with* **on** devour, eat, exist on, fare, graze, live on, nurture, partake of, pasture, subsist, take nourishment 3. augment, bolster, encourage, foster, fuel, minister to, strengthen, supply ~*n.* 4. fodder, food, forage, pasturage, provender, silage 5. *Inf.* feast, meal, nosh (*Sl.*), nosh-up (*Brit. sl.*), repast, spread (*Inf.*), tuck-in (*Inf.*)

feel *v.* 1. caress, finger, fondle, handle, manipulate, maul, paw, run one's hands over, stroke, touch 2. be aware of, be sensible of, endure, enjoy, experience, go through, have, have a sensation of, know, notice, observe, perceive, suffer, take to heart, undergo 3. ex-

feeler ('fiːlə) n. **1.** a person or thing that feels. **2.** an organ in certain animals, such as an antenna, that is sensitive to touch. **3.** a remark designed to probe the reactions or intentions of others.

feeling ('fiːlɪŋ) n. **1.** the sense of touch. **2. a.** the ability to experience physical sensations, such as heat, etc. **b.** the sensation so experienced. **3.** a state of mind. **4.** a physical or mental impression: *a feeling of warmth.* **5.** fondness; sympathy: *to have a great deal of feeling for someone.* **6.** a sentiment: *a feeling that the project is feasible.* **7.** an emotional disturbance, esp. anger or dislike: *a lot of bad feeling.* **8.** intuitive appreciation and understanding: *a feeling for words.* **9.** sensibility in the performance of something. **10.** (*pl.*) emotional or moral sensitivity (esp. in **hurt** or **injure the feelings of**). ~*adj.* **11.** sentient; sensitive. **12.** expressing or containing emotion. —'**feelingly** *adv.*

feet (fiːt) n. **1.** the plural of **foot.** **2. at (someone's) feet.** as someone's disciple. **3. be run** or **rushed off one's feet.** to be very busy. **4. carry** or **sweep off one's feet.** to fill with enthusiasm. **5. feet of clay.** a weakness that is not widely known. **6. have** (or **keep**) **one's feet on the ground.** to be practical and reliable. **7. on one's** or **its feet. a.** standing up. **b.** in good health. **8. to stand on one's own feet.** to be independent.

feign (feɪn) vb. **1.** to pretend: *to feign innocence.* **2.** (*tr.*) to invent: *to feign an excuse.* **3.** (*tr.*) to copy; imitate. —'**feigningly** *adv.*

feint¹ (feɪnt) n. **1.** a mock attack or movement designed to distract an adversary, as in boxing, fencing, etc. **2.** a misleading action or appearance. ~*vb.* **3.** (*intr.*) to make a feint.

feint² (feɪnt) n. *Printing.* the narrowest rule used in the production of ruled paper.

feldspar ('fɛldˌspɑː, 'fɛlˌspɑː) or **felspar** n. any of a group of hard rock-forming minerals consisting of aluminium silicates of potassium, sodium, calcium, or barium: the principal constituents of igneous rocks. —**feldspathic** (fɛld'spæθɪk, fɛl'spæθ-) or **fel'spathic** *adj.*

felicitate (fɪ'lɪsɪˌteɪt) vb. to congratulate. —**fe‚lici'tation** n. —**fe'lici‚tator** n.

felicity (fɪ'lɪsɪtɪ) n., pl. **-ties. 1.** happiness. **2.** a cause of happiness. **3.** an appropriate expression or style. .**4.** the display of such expressions or style. —**fe'licitous** *adj.*

feline ('fiːlaɪn) adj. **1.** of, relating to, or belonging to a family of predatory mammals, including cats, lions, leopards, and cheetahs, having a round head and retractile claws. **2.** resembling or suggestive of a cat, esp. in stealth or grace. ~n. **3.** any member of the cat family; a cat. —'**felinely** *adv.* —**felinity** (fɪ'lɪnɪtɪ) n.

fell¹ (fɛl) vb. the past tense of **fall.**

fell² (fɛl) vb. (*tr.*) **1.** to cut or knock down: *to fell a tree.* **2.** *Needlework.* to fold the edges of a seam under and sew them flat. ~n. **3.** *U.S.* the timber felled in one season. **4.** a seam finished by felling. —'**feller** n.

fell³ (fɛl) adj. **1.** *Arch.* cruel or fierce. **2.** *Arch.* destructive or deadly. **3. one fell swoop.** a single hasty action or occurrence.

fell⁴ (fɛl) n. an animal skin or hide.

fell⁵ (fɛl) n. (*often pl.*) *Northern Brit.* **a.** a mountain, hill, or moor. **b.** (*in combination*): *fell-walking.*

fellatio (fɪ'leɪʃɪəʊ) n. a sexual activity in which the penis is stimulated by the mouth.

felloe ('fɛləʊ) or **felly** n., pl. **-loes** or **-lies.** a segment or the whole rim of a wooden wheel to which the spokes are attached.

fellow ('fɛləʊ) n. **1.** a man or boy. **2.** an informal word for **boyfriend.** **3.** *Inf.* one or oneself: *a fellow has to eat.* **4.** a person considered to be of little worth. **5. a.** (*often pl.*) a companion; associate. **b.** (*as modifier*): *fellow travellers.* **6.** a member of the governing body at any of various universities or colleges. **7.** a postgraduate student employed, esp. for a fixed period, to undertake research. **8. a.** a person in the same group, class, or condition: *the surgeon asked his fellows.* **b.** (*as modifier*): *a fellow sufferer.* **9.** one of a pair; counterpart; mate.

Fellow ('fɛləʊ) n. a member of any of various learned societies: *Fellow of the British Academy.*

fellow feeling n. **1.** mutual sympathy or friendship. **2.** an opinion held in common.

fellowship ('fɛləʊˌʃɪp) n. **1.** the state of sharing mutual interests, activities, etc. **2.** a society of people sharing mutual interests, activities, etc. **3.** companionship; friendship. **4.** the state or relationship of being a fellow. **5.** *Education.* **a.** a financed research post providing study facilities, privileges, etc., often in return for teaching services. **b.** an honorary title carrying certain privileges awarded to a postgraduate student.

fellow traveller n. **1.** a companion on a journey. **2.** a non-Communist who sympathizes with Communism.

felon ('fɛlən) n. **1.** *Criminal law.* (formerly) a person who has committed a felony. ~*adj.* **2.** *Arch.* evil.

felony ('fɛlənɪ) n., pl. **-nies.** *Criminal law.* (formerly) a serious crime, such as murder or arson. —**felonious** (-'ləʊn-) *adj.*

felspar ('fɛlˌspɑː) n. a variant spelling (esp. *Brit.*) of **feldspar.** —**felspathic** (fɛl'spæθɪk) *adj.*

felt¹ (fɛlt) vb. the past tense or past participle of **feel.**

felt² (fɛlt) n. **1.** a matted fabric of wool, hair, etc., made by working the fibres together under pressure or by heat or chemical action. **2.** any material, such as asbestos, made by a similar process of matting. ~*vb.* **3.** (*tr.*) to make into or cover with felt. **4.** (*intr.*) to become matted.

felt-tip pen n. a pen whose writing point is made from pressed fibres. Also called: **fibre-tip pen.**

fem. *abbrev. for:* **1.** female. **2.** feminine.

female ('fiːmeɪl) adj. **1.** of, relating to, or designating the sex producing gametes (ova) that can be fertilized by male gametes (spermatozoa). **2.** of or characteristic of a woman. **3.** for or composed of women or girls: *a female choir.* **4.** (of reproductive organs such as the ovary and carpel) capable of producing female gametes. **5.** (of flowers) lacking, or having nonfunctional, stamens. **6.** having an internal cavity into which a projecting male counterpart can be fitted: *a female thread.* ~n. **7.** a female animal or plant. —'**femaleness** n.

feminine ('fɛmɪnɪn) adj. **1.** suitable to or characteristic of a woman. **2.** possessing qualities or characteristics considered typical of or appropriate to a woman. **3.** effeminate; womanish. **4.** *Grammar.* **a.** denoting or belonging to a gender of nouns that includes all kinds of referents as well as some female animate referents. **b.** (*as n.*): *German Zeit "time" and Ehe "marriage" are feminines.* —'**femininely** *adv.* —‚femi'ninity or 'femi‚nineness n.

feminism ('fɛmɪˌnɪzəm) n. a doctrine or movement that advocates equal rights for women. —'**feminist** n., adj.

THESAURUS

plore, fumble, grope, sound, test, try **4.** be convinced, feel in one's bones, have a hunch, have the impression, intuit, sense **5.** believe, be of the opinion that, consider, deem, hold, judge, think **6.** appear, resemble, seem, strike one as **7.** *With* **for** be moved by, be sorry for, bleed for, commiserate, compassionate, condole with, empathize, feel compassion for, pity, sympathize with **8. feel like** could do with, desire, fancy, feel inclined, feel the need for, feel up to, have the inclination, want ~n. **9.** finish, surface, texture, touch **10.** air, ambience, atmosphere, feeling, impression, quality, sense, vibes (*Inf.*)

feeler 1. antenna, tentacle, whisker **2.** advance, approach, probe, trial balloon

feeling 1. feel, perception, sensation, sense, sense of touch, touch **2.** apprehension,

consciousness, hunch, idea, impression, inkling, notion, presentiment, sense, suspicion **3.** affection, ardour, emotion, fervour, fondness, heat, intensity, passion, sentiment, sentimentality, warmth **4.** appreciation, compassion, concern, empathy, pity, sensibility, sensitivity, sympathy, understanding **5.** inclination, instinct, opinion, point of view, view **6.** air, ambience, atmosphere, aura, feel, mood, quality **7. bad feeling** anger, dislike, distrust, enmity, hostility, upset

feelings ego, emotions, self-esteem, sensitivities, susceptibilities

feline 1. catlike, leonine **2.** graceful, sinuous, sleek, slinky, smooth, stealthy

fell v. cut, cut down, demolish, flatten, floor, hew, knock down, level, prostrate, raze, strike down

fellow n. **1.** bloke (*Inf.*), boy, chap (*Inf.*), character, customer (*Inf.*), guy (*Inf.*), individual, man, person **2.** associate, colleague, companion, compeer, comrade, co-worker, equal, friend, member, partner, peer **3.** brother, counterpart, double, duplicate, match, mate, twin ~*adj.* **4.** affiliated, akin, allied, associate, associated, co-, like, related, similar

fellowship 1. amity, brotherhood, camaraderie, communion, companionability, companionship, familiarity, fraternization, intercourse, intimacy, kindliness, sociability **2.** association, brotherhood, club, fraternity, guild, league, order, sisterhood, society, sodality

feminine 1. delicate, gentle, girlish, graceful, ladylike, modest, soft, tender, wom-

femur ('fiːmə) *n., pl.* **femurs** *or* **femora** ('fɛmərə). **1.** the longest thickest bone of the human skeleton, with the pelvis above and the knee below. Nontechnical name: **thighbone. 2.** the corresponding bone in other vertebrates or the corresponding segment of an insect's leg. —'**femoral** *adj.*

fen (fɛn) *n.* low-lying flat land that is marshy or artificially drained. —'**fenny** *adj.*

fence (fɛns) *n.* **1.** a structure that serves to enclose an area such as a garden or field, usually made of posts of timber, concrete, or metal connected by wire netting, rails, or boards. **2.** *Sl.* a dealer in stolen property. **3.** an obstacle for a horse to jump in steeplechasing or showjumping. **4.** *Machinery.* a guard or guide, esp. in a circular saw or plane. **5.** (**sit**) **on the fence.** (to be) unable or unwilling to commit oneself. ~*vb.* **6.** (*tr.*) to construct a fence on or around (a piece of land, etc.). **7.** (*tr.; foll. by in or off*) to close (in) or separate (off) with or as if with a fence: *he fenced in the livestock.* **8.** (*intr.*) to fight using swords or foils. **9.** (*intr.*) to evade a question or argument. **10.** (*intr.*) *Sl.* to receive stolen property. —'**fenceless** *adj.* —'**fencer** *n.*

fencing ('fɛnsɪŋ) *n.* **1.** the practice, art, or sport of fighting with foils, épées, sabres, etc. **2. a.** wire, stakes, etc., used as fences. **b.** fences collectively.

fend (fɛnd) *vb.* **1.** (*intr.; foll. by for*) to give support (to someone, esp. oneself). **2.** (*tr.; usually foll. by off*) to ward off or turn aside (blows, questions, etc.). ~*n.* **3.** *Scot. & N English dialect.* a shift or effort.

fender ('fɛndə) *n.* **1.** a low metal frame which confines falling coals to the hearth. **2.** a metal frame fitted to the front of locomotives to absorb shock, etc. **3.** a cushionlike device, such as a car tyre hung over the side of a vessel to reduce damage resulting from collision. **4.** the U.S. name for the wing of a car.

fenestration (ˌfɛnɪ'streɪʃən) *n.* **1.** the arrangement of windows in a building. **2.** an operation to restore hearing by making an artificial opening into the labyrinth of the ear.

Fenian ('fiːnɪən, 'fiːnjən) *n.* **1.** (formerly) a member of an Irish revolutionary organization founded in the U.S. in the 19th century to fight for an independent Ireland. ~*adj.* **2.** of or relating to the Fenians. —'**Fenianism** *n.*

fennel ('fɛnᵊl) *n.* a strong-smelling yellow-flowered umbelliferous plant whose seeds and feathery leaves are used to season and flavour food.

fenugreek ('fɛnjuˌgriːk) *n.* an annual heavily scented Mediterranean leguminous plant, with hairy stems and white flowers.

feoff (fiːf) *History.* ~*n.* **1.** a variant spelling of **fief.** ~*vb.* **2.** (*tr.*) to invest with a benefice or fief. —'**feoffee** *n.* —'**feoffment** *n.* —'**feoffor** *or* '**feoffer** *n.*

-fer *n. combining form.* indicating a person or thing that bears something specified: *crucifer; conifer.*

feral ('fɪərəl) *adj.* **1.** (of animals and plants) existing in a wild or uncultivated state. **2.** savage; brutal.

fermata (fə'mɑːtə) *n., pl.* **-tas** *or* **-te** (-tɪ). *Music.* another word for **pause.**

ferment *n.* ('fɜːmɛnt). **1.** any agent or substance, such as a bacterium, mould, yeast, or enzyme, that causes fermentation. **2.** another word for **fermentation. 3.** commotion; unrest. ~*vb.* (fə'mɛnt). **4.** to undergo or cause to undergo fermentation. **5.** to stir up or seethe with

excitement. —**fer'mentable** *adj.*

fermentation (ˌfɜːmɛn'teɪʃən) *n.* a chemical reaction in which an organic molecule splits into simpler substances, esp. the conversion of sugar to ethyl alcohol by yeast. —**fer'mentative** *adj.*

fermium ('fɜːmɪəm) *n.* a transuranic element artificially produced by neutron bombardment of plutonium. Symbol: Fm; atomic no.: 100; half-life of most stable isotope, ^{257}Fm: 80 days (approx.).

fern (fɜːn) *n.* **1.** a plant having roots, stems, and fronds and reproducing by spores formed in structures (sori) on the fronds. **2.** any of certain similar but unrelated plants, such as the sweet fern. —'**ferny** *adj.*

ferocious (fə'rəʊʃəs) *adj.* savagely fierce or cruel: *a ferocious tiger.* —**ferocity** (fə'rɒsɪtɪ) *n.*

-ferous *adj. combining form.* bearing or producing: *coniferous.*

ferret ('fɛrɪt) *n.* **1.** a domesticated albino variety of the polecat bred for hunting rats, rabbits, etc. ~*vb.* **2.** to hunt (rabbits, rats, etc.) with ferrets. **3.** (*tr.; usually foll. by out*) to drive from hiding: *to ferret out snipers.* **4.** (*tr.; usually foll. by out*) to find by persistent investigation. **5.** (*intr.*) to search around. —'**ferreter** *n.* —'**ferrety** *adj.*

ferri- *combining form.* indicating the presence of iron, esp. in the trivalent state: *ferricyanide; ferriferous.* Cf. **ferro-.**

Ferris wheel ('fɛrɪs) *n.* a fairground wheel having seats freely suspended from its rim.

ferro- *combining form.* **1.** indicating a property of iron or the presence of iron: *ferromagnetism.* **2.** indicating the presence of iron in the divalent state: *ferrocyanide.* Cf. **ferri-.**

ferroconcrete (ˌfɛrəʊ'kɒŋkriːt) *n.* another name for **reinforced concrete.**

ferrous sulphate *n.* an iron salt, usually obtained as greenish crystals: used in inks, tanning, etc. Also called: **copperas.**

ferruginous (fɛ'ruːdʒɪnəs) *adj.* **1.** (of minerals, rocks, etc.) containing iron: *a ferruginous clay.* **2.** rust-coloured.

ferrule ('fɛruːl) *n.* **1.** a metal ring, tube, or cap placed over the end of a stick or post for added strength or to increase wear. **2.** a small length of tube, etc., esp. one used for making a joint.

ferry ('fɛrɪ) *n., pl.* **-ries. 1.** Also called: **ferryboat.** a vessel for transporting passengers and usually vehicles across a body of water, esp. as a regular service. **2. a.** such a service. **b.** (*in combination*): *a ferryman.* **3.** the delivering of aircraft by flying them to their destination. ~*vb.* **-rying, -ried. 4.** to transport or go by ferry. **5.** to deliver (an aircraft) by flying it to its destination. **6.** (*tr.*) to convey (passengers, goods, etc.)

fertile ('fɜːtaɪl) *adj.* **1.** capable of producing offspring. **2. a.** (of land) capable of sustaining an abundant growth of plants. **b.** (of farm animals) capable of breeding stock. **3.** *Biol.* capable of undergoing growth and development: *fertile seeds; fertile eggs.* **4.** producing many offspring; prolific. **5.** highly productive: *a fertile brain.* **6.** *Physics.* (of a substance) able to be transformed into fissile or fissionable material. —'**fertilely** *adv.* —'**fertileness** *n.* —**fer'tility** *n.*

fertilize *or* **-lise** ('fɜːtɪˌlaɪz) *vb.* (*tr.*) **1.** to provide (an animal, plant, etc.) with sperm or pollen to bring about

---

THESAURUS

anly **2.** effeminate, effete, unmanly, unmasculine, weak, womanish

femme fatale charmer, Circe, enchantress, seductress, siren, vamp (*Inf.*)

fen bog, holm (*Dialect*), marsh, morass, moss (*Scot.*), quagmire, slough, swamp

fence *n.* **1.** barbed wire, barricade, barrier, defence, guard, hedge, paling, palisade, railings, rampart, shield, stockade, wall **2. on the fence** between two stools, irresolute, uncertain, uncommitted, undecided, vacillating ~*v.* **3.** *Often with* **in** *or* **off** bound, circumscribe, confine, coop, defend, encircle, enclose, fortify, guard, hedge, pen, protect, restrict, secure, separate, surround **4.** beat about the bush, cavil, dodge, equivocate, evade, hedge, parry, prevaricate, quibble, shift, stonewall, tergiversate

fencing *Fig.* beating about the bush, double talk, equivocation, evasiveness, hedging,

parrying, prevarication, quibbling, stonewalling, tergiversation, weasel words (*Inf., chiefly U.S.*)

ferment *v.* **1.** boil, brew, bubble, concoct, effervesce, foam, froth, heat, leaven, rise, seethe, work ~*n.* **2.** bacteria, barm, fermentation agent, leaven, leavening, mother, mother-of-vinegar, yeast ~*v.* **3.** *Fig.* agitate, boil, excite, fester, foment, heat, incite, inflame, provoke, rouse, seethe, smoulder, stir up ~*n.* **4.** *Fig.* agitation, brouhaha, commotion, disruption, excitement, fever, frenzy, furore, glow, heat, hubbub, imbroglio, state of unrest, stew, stir, tumult, turbulence, turmoil, unrest, uproar

ferocious 1. feral, fierce, predatory, rapacious, ravening, savage, violent, wild **2.** barbaric, barbarous, bloodthirsty, brutal, brutish, cruel, merciless, pitiless, relentless, ruthless, tigerish, vicious

ferocity barbarity, bloodthirstiness, brutality, cruelty, ferociousness, fierceness, inhumanity, rapacity, ruthlessness, savageness, savagery, viciousness, wildness

ferret out bring to light, dig up, disclose, discover, drive out, elicit, get at, nose out, root out, run to earth, search out, smell out, trace, track down, unearth

ferry 1. *n.* ferryboat, packet, packet boat **2.** *v.* carry, chauffeur, convey, run, ship, shuttle, transport

fertile abundant, fat, fecund, flowering, flowing with milk and honey, fruit-bearing, fruitful, generative, luxuriant, plenteous, plentiful, productive, prolific, rich, teeming, yielding

fertility abundance, fecundity, fruitfulness, luxuriance, productiveness, richness

fertilization. 2. to supply (soil or water) with nutrients to aid the growth of plants. **3.** to make fertile. —**ˌfertili-ˈzation** or **-liˈsation** n.

fertilizer or **-liser** (ˈfɜːtɪˌlaɪzə) n. **1.** any substance, such as manure, added to soil or water to increase its productivity. **2.** an object or organism that fertilizes an animal or plant.

ferule (ˈfɛruːl) n. **1.** a flat piece of wood, such as a ruler, used in some schools to cane children on the hand. ~vb. **2.** (tr.) to punish with a ferule.

fervent (ˈfɜːvənt) or **fervid** (ˈfɜːvɪd) adj. **1.** intensely passionate; ardent. **2.** Arch. or poetic. burning or glowing. —**ˈfervency** n. —**ˈfervently** or **ˈfervidly** adv.

fervour or U.S. **fervor** (ˈfɜːvə) n. **1.** great intensity of feeling or belief. **2.** Rare. intense heat.

festal (ˈfɛstəl) adj. another word for **festive.** —**ˈfestally** adv.

fester (ˈfɛstə) vb. **1.** to form or cause to form pus. **2.** (intr.) to become rotten; decay. **3.** to become or cause to become bitter, irritated, etc., esp. over a long period of time. ~n. **4.** a small ulcer or sore containing pus.

festival (ˈfɛstɪvəl) n. **1.** a day or period set aside for celebration or feasting, esp. one of religious significance. **2.** any occasion for celebration. **3.** an organized series of special events and performances: a festival of drama. **4.** Arch. a time of revelry. **5.** (modifier) relating to or characteristic of a festival.

festive (ˈfɛstɪv) adj. appropriate to or characteristic of a holiday, etc. —**ˈfestively** adv.

festivity (fɛsˈtɪvɪtɪ) n., pl. **-ties. 1.** merriment characteristic of a festival, etc. **2.** any festival or other celebration. **3.** (pl.) celebrations.

festoon (fɛˈstuːn) n. **1.** a decorative chain of flowers, ribbons, etc., suspended in loops. **2.** a carved or painted representation of this, as in architecture, furniture, or pottery. ~vb. (tr.) **3.** to decorate or join together with festoons. **4.** to form into festoons.

feta (ˈfɛtə) n. a white sheep or goat cheese popular in Greece.

fetch[1] (fɛtʃ) vb. (mainly tr.) **1.** to go after and bring back: to fetch help. **2.** to cause to come; bring or draw forth. **3.** (also intr.) to cost or sell for (a certain price): the table fetched six hundred pounds. **4.** to utter (a sigh, groan, etc.). **5.** Inf. to deal (a blow, slap, etc.). **6.** (used esp. as a command to dogs) to retrieve (an object thrown, etc.). **7.** fetch and carry. to perform menial tasks or run errands. ~n. **8.** the reach, stretch, etc., of a mechanism. **9.** a trick or stratagem. —**ˈfetcher** n.

fetch[2] (fɛtʃ) n. the ghost or apparition of a living person.

fetching (ˈfɛtʃɪŋ) adj. Inf. **1.** attractively befitting. **2.** charming.

fête or **fete** (feɪt) n. **1.** a gala, bazaar, or similar entertainment, esp. one held outdoors in aid of charity. **2.** a feast day or holiday, esp. one of religious significance. ~vb. **3.** (tr.) to honour or entertain with or as if with a fête: the author was fêted.

fetid or **foetid** (ˈfɛtɪd, ˈfiː-) adj. having a stale nauseating smell, as of decay. —**ˈfetidly** or **ˈfoetidly** adv.

—**ˈfetidness** or **ˈfoetidness** n.

fetish or **fetich** (ˈfɛtɪʃ, ˈfiːtɪʃ) n. **1.** something, esp. an inanimate object, that is believed to have magical powers. **2. a.** a form of behaviour involving fetishism. **b.** any object that is involved in fetishism. **3.** any object, activity, etc., to which one is excessively devoted. —**ˈfetishˌism** n.

fetlock (ˈfɛtˌlɒk) n. **1.** a projection behind and above a horse's hoof. **2.** Also called: **fetlock joint.** the joint at this part of the leg. **3.** the tuft of hair growing from this part.

fetter (ˈfɛtə) n. **1.** (often pl.) a chain or bond fastened round the ankle. **2.** (usually pl.) a check or restraint: in fetters. ~vb. (tr.) **3.** to restrict or confine. **4.** to bind in fetters.

fettle (ˈfɛtəl) vb. (tr.) **1.** to line or repair (the walls of a furnace). **2.** Brit. dialect. **a.** to prepare or arrange (a thing, oneself, etc.). **b.** to repair or mend (something). ~n. **3.** state of health, spirits, etc. (esp. in **in fine fettle**).

fetus (ˈfiːtəs) n. a variant spelling of **foetus.** —**ˈfetal** adj.

feu (fjuː) n. **1.** Scot. legal history. **a.** a feudal tenure of land for which rent was paid in money or grain instead of by the performance of military service. **b.** the land so held. **2.** Scot Law. a right to the use of land in return for a fixed annual payment (**feu duty**).

feud (fjuːd) n. **1.** long and bitter hostility between two families, clans, or individuals. **2.** a quarrel or dispute. ~vb. **3.** (intr.) to take part in or carry on a feud. —**ˈfeudist** n.

feudal[1] (ˈfjuːdəl) adj. **1.** of or characteristic of feudalism or its institutions. **2.** of or relating to a fief. **3.** Disparaging. old-fashioned.

feudal[2] (ˈfjuːdəl) adj. of or relating to a feud.

feudalism (ˈfjuːdəˌlɪzəm) n. the legal and social system that evolved in W Europe in the 8th and 9th centuries, in which vassals were protected and maintained by their lords, usually through the granting of fiefs, and were required to serve under them in war. Also called: **feudal system.** —**ˈfeudalist** n. —**ˌfeudalˈistic** adj.

fever (ˈfiːvə) n. **1.** an abnormally high body temperature, accompanied by a fast pulse rate, dry skin, etc. Related adj.: **febrile. 2.** any of various diseases, such as yellow fever or scarlet fever, characterized by a high temperature. **3.** intense nervous excitement. ~vb. **4.** (tr.) to affect with or as if with fever. —**ˈfevered** adj.

feverfew (ˈfiːvəˌfjuː) n. a bushy European strong-scented perennial plant with white flower heads, formerly used medicinally.

feverish (ˈfiːvərɪʃ) or **feverous** adj. **1.** suffering from fever. **2.** in a state of restless excitement. **3.** of, caused by, or causing fever. —**ˈfeverishly** or **ˈfeverously** adv.

fever pitch n. a state of intense excitement.

few (fjuː) determiner. **1.** hardly any: few men are so cruel. **b.** (as pronoun; functioning as pl.): many are called but few are chosen. **2.** (preceded by a) **a.** a small number of: a few drinks. **b.** (as pronoun; functioning as pl.): a few of you. **3. a good few.** Inf. several. **4. few and**

THESAURUS

fertilize 1. fecundate, fructify, impregnate, inseminate, make fruitful, make pregnant, pollinate **2.** compost, dress, enrich, feed, manure, mulch, top-dress

fertilizer compost, dressing, dung, guano, manure, marl

fervent, fervid animated, ardent, devout, eager, earnest, ecstatic, emotional, enthusiastic, excited, fiery, heartfelt, impassioned, intense, perfervid (Literary), vehement, warm, zealous

fervour animation, ardour, eagerness, earnestness, enthusiasm, excitement, fervency, intensity, passion, vehemence, warmth, zeal

festival 1. anniversary, commemoration, feast, fête, fiesta, holiday, holy day, saint's day **2.** carnival, celebration, entertainment, festivities, fête, field day, gala, jubilee, treat

festive back-slapping, carnival, celebratory, cheery, Christmassy, convivial, festal, gala, gay, gleeful, happy, hearty, holiday, jolly, jovial, joyful, joyous, jubilant, light-hearted, merry, mirthful, sportive

festivity 1. amusement, conviviality, fun, gaiety, jollification, joviality, joyfulness, merriment, merrymaking, mirth, pleasure, revelry, sport **2.** Often plural carousal, celebration, entertainment, festival, festive event, festive proceedings, fun and games, jollification, party

festoon 1. n. chaplet, garland, lei, swag, swathe, wreath **2.** v. array, bedeck, beribbon, deck, decorate, drape, garland, hang, swathe, wreathe

fetch 1. bring, carry, conduct, convey, deliver, escort, get, go for, lead, obtain, retrieve, transport **2.** draw forth, elicit, give rise to, produce **3.** bring in, earn, go for, make, realize, sell for, yield

fetching alluring, attractive, captivating, charming, cute, enchanting, enticing, fascinating, intriguing, sweet, taking, winsome

fête, fete 1. n. bazaar, fair, festival, gala, garden party, sale of work **2.** v. bring out the red carpet for (someone), entertain regally, hold a reception for (someone), honour, kill the fatted calf for (someone), lionize, make

much of, treat, wine and dine

fetish 1. amulet, cult object, talisman **2.** fixation, idée fixe, mania, obsession, thing (Inf.)

feud 1. n. argument, bad blood, bickering, broil, conflict, contention, disagreement, discord, dissension, enmity, estrangement, faction, falling out, grudge, hostility, quarrel, rivalry, strife, vendetta **2.** v. be at daggers drawn, be at odds, bicker, brawl, clash, contend, dispute, duel, fall out, quarrel, row, squabble, war

fever Fig. agitation, delirium, ecstasy, excitement, ferment, fervour, flush, frenzy, heat, intensity, passion, restlessness, turmoil, unrest

feverish 1. burning, febrile, fevered, flushed, hectic, hot, inflamed, pyretic (Medical) **2.** agitated, distracted, excited, frantic, frenetic, frenzied, impatient, obsessive, overwrought, restless

far between. a. widely spaced. **b.** scarce. **5. not** or **quite a few.** Inf. several. ~n. **6. the few.** a small number of people considered as a class: *the few who fell at Thermopylae.* —'**fewness** n.
▷ **Usage.** See at **less.**
fey (feɪ) adj. **1.** interested in or believing in the supernatural. **2.** clairvoyant; visionary. **3.** Chiefly Scot. fated to die; doomed. **4.** Chiefly Scot. in a state of high spirits. —'**feyness** n.
fez (fɛz) n., pl. **fezzes.** an originally Turkish brimless felt or wool cap, shaped like a truncated cone.
ff Music. symbol for fortissimo. See **f**
ff. 1. abbrev. for folios. **2.** symbol for and the following (pages, lines, etc.).
fiancé or (fem.) **fiancée** (fɪˈɒnseɪ) n. a person who is engaged to be married.
fiasco (fɪˈæskəʊ) n., pl. **-cos** or **-coes.** a complete failure, esp. one that is ignominious or humiliating.
fiat (ˈfaɪət) n. **1.** official sanction. **2.** an arbitrary order or decree.
fib (fɪb) n. **1.** a trivial and harmless lie. ~vb. **fibbing, fibbed. 2.** (intr.) to tell such a lie. —'**fibber** n.
fibre or U.S. **fiber** (ˈfaɪbə) n. **1.** a natural or synthetic filament that may be spun into yarn, such as cotton or nylon. **2.** cloth or other material made from such yarn. **3.** a long fine continuous thread or filament. **4.** the texture of any material or substance. **5.** essential substance or nature. **6.** strength of character (esp. in **moral fibre**). **7.** Bot. **a.** a narrow elongated thick-walled cell. **b.** a very small root or twig. **8.** a fibrous substance, such as bran, as part of someone's diet: *dietary fibre.* —'**fibred** or U.S. '**fibered** adj.
fibreboard or U.S. **fiberboard** (ˈfaɪbəˌbɔːd) n. a building material made of compressed wood or other plant fibres.
fibreglass (ˈfaɪbəˌglɑːs) n. **1.** material consisting of matted fine glass fibres, used as insulation in buildings, etc. **2.** a light strong material made by bonding fibreglass with a synthetic resin; used for car bodies, etc.
fibre optics n. (functioning as sing.) the use of bundles of long transparent glass fibres in transmitting light.
fibril (ˈfaɪbrɪl) or **fibrilla** (faɪˈbrɪlə) n., pl. **-brils** or **-brillae** (-ˈbrɪliː). **1.** a small fibre or part of a fibre. **2.** Biol. a root hair. —'**fibrillar** or **fi'brillose** adj.
fibrillation (ˌfaɪbrɪˈleɪʃən, ˌfɪb-) n. **1.** a local and uncontrollable twitching of muscle fibres. **2.** irregular twitchings of the muscular wall of the heart.
fibrin (ˈfɪbrɪn) n. a white insoluble elastic protein formed from fibrinogen when blood clots: forms a network that traps red cells and platelets.
fibro- combining form. **1.** indicating fibrous tissue: *fibrosis.* **2.** indicating fibre: *fibrocement.*
fibroid (ˈfaɪbrɔɪd) adj. **1.** Anat. of (structures or tissues) containing or resembling fibres. ~n. **2.** Also called: **fibroma.** a benign tumor derived from fibrous connective tissue.
fibrosis (faɪˈbrəʊsɪs) n. the formation of an abnormal amount of fibrous tissue in an organ or part.
fibrositis (ˌfaɪbrəˈsaɪtɪs) n. inflammation of white fibrous tissue, esp. that of muscle sheaths.

fibula (ˈfɪbjʊlə) n., pl. **-lae** (-ˌliː) or **-las. 1.** the outer and thinner of the two bones between the knee and ankle of the human leg. Cf. **tibia. 2.** the corresponding bone in other vertebrates. **3.** a metal brooch resembling a safety pin. —'**fibular** adj.
-fic suffix forming adjectives. making or producing: *honorific.*
fiche (fiːʃ) n. See **microfiche.**
fickle (ˈfɪkəl) adj. changeable in purpose, affections, etc. —'**fickleness** n.
fiction (ˈfɪkʃən) n. **1.** literary works invented by the imagination, such as novels or short stories. **2.** an invented story or explanation. **3.** the act of inventing a story. **4.** Law. something assumed to be true for the sake of convenience, though probably false. —'**fictional** adj. —'**fictionally** adv. —'**fictive** adj.
fictionalize or **-lise** (ˈfɪkʃənəˌlaɪz) vb. (tr.) to make into fiction. —ˌ**fictionali'zation** or **-li'sation** n.
fictitious (fɪkˈtɪʃəs) adj. **1.** not genuine or authentic: *to give a fictitious address.* **2.** of, related to, or characteristic of fiction. —**fic'titiously** adv. —**fic'titiousness** n.
fiddle (ˈfɪdəl) n. **1.** Inf. or disparaging. the violin. **2.** Naut. a small railing around the top of a table to prevent objects from falling off it. **3.** Brit. inf. an illegal transaction or arrangement. **4.** a manually delicate or tricky operation. **5. fit as a fiddle.** Inf. in very good health. **6. play second fiddle.** Inf. to play a minor part. ~vb. **7.** to play (a tune) on the fiddle. **8.** (intr.; often foll. by with) to make aimless movements with the hands. **9.** (when intr., often foll. by about or around) Inf. to waste (time). **10.** (often foll. by with) Inf. to interfere (with). **11.** Inf. to contrive to do (something) by illicit means or deception. **12.** (tr.) Inf. to falsify (accounts, etc.).
fiddle-faddle (ˈfɪdəlˌfædəl) n., interj. **1.** trivial matter. ~vb. **2.** (intr.) to fuss or waste time. —'**fiddle-ˌfaddler** n.
fiddler (ˈfɪdlə) n. **1.** a person who plays the fiddle. **2.** Inf. a petty rogue.
fiddlestick (ˈfɪdəlˌstɪk) n. **1.** Inf. a violin bow. **2.** any trifle. **3.** (pl.) interj. used to express annoyance or disagreement.
fiddling (ˈfɪdlɪŋ) adj. **1.** trifling or insignificant. **2.** another word for **fiddly.**
fiddly (ˈfɪdlɪ) adj. **-dlier, -dliest.** small and awkward to do or handle.
Fidei Defensor Latin. (ˈfaɪdɪˌaɪ dɪˈfɛnsɔː) n. defender of the faith; a title given to Henry VIII by Pope Leo X, and appearing on British coins as FID DEF (before decimalization) or FD (after decimalization).
fidelity (fɪˈdɛlɪtɪ) n., pl. **-ties. 1.** devotion to duties, obligations, etc. **2.** loyalty or devotion, as to a person or cause. **3.** faithfulness to one's spouse, lover, etc. **4.** accuracy in reporting detail. **5.** Electronics. the degree to which an amplifier or radio accurately reproduces the characteristics of the input signal.
fidget (ˈfɪdʒɪt) vb. **1.** (intr.) to move about restlessly. **2.** (intr.; often foll. by with) to make restless or uneasy movements (with something). **3.** (tr.) to cause to fidget. ~n. **4.** (often pl.) a state of restlessness or unease: *he's got the fidgets.* **5.** a person who fidgets. —'**fidgety** adj.

THESAURUS

few adj. **1.** hardly any, inconsiderable, infrequent, insufficient, meagre, negligible, not many, rare, scant, scanty, scarce, scarcely any, scattered, sparse, sporadic, thin **2. few and far between** at great intervals, hard to come by, infrequent, in short supply, irregular, rare, scarce, scattered, seldom met with, uncommon, unusual, widely spaced ~pron. **3.** handful, scarcely any, scattering, small number, some
fiancé, fiancée betrothed, intended, prospective spouse, wife- or husband-to-be
fiasco catastrophe, debacle, disaster, failure, flap (Inf.), mess, rout, ruin, washout (Inf.)
fib n. fiction, lie, prevarication, story, untruth, white lie, whopper (Inf.)
fibre 1. fibril, filament, pile, staple, strand, texture, thread **2.** Fig. essence, nature, quality, spirit, substance **3.** Fig., as in **moral fibre** resolution, stamina, strength, strength of character, toughness

fickle blowing hot and cold, capricious, changeable, faithless, fitful, flighty, inconstant, irresolute, mercurial, mutable, quicksilver, unfaithful, unpredictable, unstable, unsteady, vacillating, variable, volatile
fickleness capriciousness, fitfulness, flightiness, inconstancy, mutability, unfaithfulness, unpredictability, unsteadiness, volatility
fiction 1. fable, fantasy, legend, myth, novel, romance, story, storytelling, tale, work of imagination, yarn (Inf.) **2.** cock and bull story (Inf.), concoction, fabrication, falsehood, fancy, fantasy, figment of the imagination, imagination, improvisation, invention, lie, tall story, untruth
fictional imaginary, invented, legendary, made-up, nonexistent, unreal
fictitious apocryphal, artificial, assumed, bogus, counterfeit, fabricated, false, fanciful, feigned, imaginary, imagined, improvised, invented, made-up, make-believe, mythical,

spurious, unreal, untrue
fiddle v. **1.** Often with **with** fidget, finger, interfere with, mess about or around, play, tamper with, tinker, toy, trifle **2.** Inf. cheat, cook the books, diddle (Inf.), finagle (Inf.), fix, gerrymander, graft, manoeuvre, racketeer, swindle, wangle (Inf.) ~n. **3.** violin **4. fit as a fiddle** blooming, hale and hearty, healthy, in fine fettle, in good form, in good shape, in rude health, in the pink, sound, strong **5.** Inf. fix, fraud, graft, piece of sharp practice, racket, swindle, wangle (Inf.)
fiddling futile, insignificant, pettifogging, petty, trifling, trivial
fidelity 1. allegiance, constancy, dependability, devotedness, devotion, faith, faithfulness, fealty, integrity, lealty (Archaic or Scot.), loyalty, staunchness, trueheartedness, trustworthiness **2.** accuracy, adherence, closeness, correspondence, exactitude, exactness, faithfulness, preciseness, precision, scrupulousness

fiduciary (fɪ'dju:ʃɪərɪ) *Law.* ~*n.* **1.** a person bound to act for another's benefit, as a trustee. ~*adj.* **2. a.** having the nature of a trust. **b.** of or relating to a trust or trustee.

fie (faɪ) *interj. Obs. or facetious.* an exclamation of distaste or mock dismay.

fief *or* **feoff** (fi:f) *n.* (in feudal Europe) the property or fee granted to a vassal for his maintenance by his lord in return for service.

field (fi:ld) *n.* **1.** an open tract of uncultivated grassland; meadow. **2.** a piece of land cleared of trees and undergrowth used for pasture or growing crops: *a field of barley.* **3.** a limited or marked off area on which any of various sports, athletic competitions, etc., are held: *a soccer field.* **4.** an area that is rich in minerals or other natural resources: *a coalfield.* **5.** short for **battlefield** and **airfield.** **6.** the mounted followers that hunt with a pack of hounds. **7.** *Horse racing.* **a.** all the runners in a particular race. **b.** the runners in a race excluding the favourite. **8.** *Cricket.* the fielders collectively, esp. with regard to their positions. **9.** a wide or open expanse: *a field of snow.* **10. a.** an area of human activity: *the field of human knowledge.* **b.** a sphere or division of knowledge, etc.: *his field is physics.* **11.** a place away from the laboratory, office, library, etc., where practical work is done. **12.** the surface or background, as of a flag, coin, or heraldic shield, on which a design is displayed. **13.** Also called: **field of view.** the area within which an object may be observed with a telescope, etc. **14.** *Maths.* a set of entities, such as numbers, subject to two binary operations, addition and multiplication, such that the set is a commutative group under addition and the set, minus the zero, is a commutative group under multiplication. **15.** *Computers.* a set of one or more characters comprising a unit of information. **16. take the field.** to begin or carry on activity, esp. in sport or military operations. **17. play the field.** *Inf.* to disperse one's interests or attentions among a number of activities, people, or objects. **18.** (*modifier*) *Mil.* of or relating to equipment, personnel, etc., specifically trained for operations in the field: *a field gun.* ~*vb.* **19.** (*tr.*) *Sport.* to stop, catch, or return (the ball) as a fielder. **20.** (*tr.*) *Sport.* to send (a player or team) onto the field to play. **21.** (*intr.*) *Sport.* (of a player or team) to act or take turn as a fielder or fielders. **22.** (*tr.*) *Inf.* to deal with or handle: *to field a question.*

field day *n.* **1.** a day spent in some special outdoor activity, such as nature study. **2.** *Mil.* a day devoted to manoeuvres or exercises, esp. before an audience. **3.** *Inf.* a day or time of exciting activity: *the children had a field day with their new toys.*

fielder ('fi:ldə) *n. Cricket, etc.* **a.** a player in the field. **b.** a member of the fielding side.

field event *n.* a competition, such as the discus, etc., that takes place on a field or similar area as opposed to those on the running track.

fieldfare ('fi:ld,fɛə) *n.* a large Old World thrush having a pale grey head, brown wings and back, and a blackish tail.

field hockey *n. U.S. & Canad.* hockey played on a field, as distinguished from ice hockey.

field marshal *n.* an officer holding the highest rank in certain armies.

field officer *n.* an officer holding the rank of major, lieutenant colonel, or colonel.

fieldsman ('fi:ldzmən) *n., pl.* **-men.** *Cricket.* another name for **fielder.**

field sports *pl. n.* sports carried on in the countryside,

such as hunting or fishing.

fieldwork ('fi:ld,wɜ:k) *n. Mil.* a temporary structure used in fortifying a place or position.

field work *n.* an investigation or search for material, data, etc., made in the field as opposed to the classroom or laboratory. —**field worker** *n.*

fiend (fi:nd) *n.* **1.** an evil spirit. **2.** a cruel, brutal, or spiteful person. **3.** *Inf.* **a.** a person who is intensely interested in or fond of something: *a fresh-air fiend.* **b.** an addict: *a drug fiend.* —**'fiendish** *adj.*

Fiend (fi:nd) *n.* **the.** the devil; Satan.

fierce (fɪəs) *adj.* **1.** having a violent and unrestrained nature: *a fierce dog.* **2.** wild or turbulent in force, action, or intensity: *a fierce storm.* **3.** intense or strong: *fierce competition.* **4.** *Inf.* very unpleasant. —**'fiercely** *adv.* —**'fierceness** *n.*

fiery ('faɪərɪ) *adj.* **1.** of, containing, or composed of fire. **2.** resembling fire in heat, colour, ardour, etc.: *a fiery speaker.* **3.** easily angered or aroused: *a fiery temper.* **4.** (of food) producing a burning sensation: *a fiery curry.* **5.** (of the skin or a sore) inflamed. **6.** flammable.

fiesta (fɪ'estə) *n.* (esp. in Spain and Latin America) **1.** a religious festival or celebration. **2.** a holiday or carnival.

FIFA ('fi:fə) *n.* acronym for Fédération Internationale de Football Association.

fife (faɪf) *n.* **1.** a small high-pitched flute similar to the piccolo, used esp. in military bands. ~*vb.* **2.** to play (music) on a fife. —**'fifer** *n.*

fifteen ('fɪf'ti:n) *n.* **1.** the cardinal number that is the sum of ten and five. **2.** a numeral 15, XV, etc., representing this number. **3.** something represented by, representing, or consisting of 15 units. **4.** a rugby football team. ~*determiner.* **5. a.** amounting to fifteen: *fifteen jokes.* **b.** (*as pronoun*): *fifteen of us danced.* —**'fif-'teenth** *adj.*

fifth column *n.* **1.** (originally) a group of Falangist sympathizers in Madrid during the Spanish Civil War who were prepared to join the insurgents marching on the city. **2.** any group of hostile infiltrators. —**fifth columnist** *n.*

fifty ('fɪftɪ) *n., pl.* **-ties. 1.** the cardinal number that is the product of ten and five. **2.** a numeral 50, L, etc., representing this number. **3.** something represented by, representing, or consisting of 50 units. ~*determiner.* **4. a.** amounting to fifty: *fifty people.* **b.** (*as pronoun*): *fifty should be sufficient.* —**'fiftieth** *adj.*

fifty-fifty *adj., adv. Inf.* in equal parts.

fig (fɪg) *n.* **1.** a tree or shrub that produces a closed pear-shaped receptacle which becomes fleshy and edible when mature. **2.** the receptacle of any of these trees, having sweet flesh containing numerous seedlike fruits. **3.** (*used with a negative*) something of negligible value: *I don't care a fig for your opinion.*

fig. *abbrev. for:* **1.** figurative(ly). **2.** figure.

fight (faɪt) *vb.* **fighting, fought. 1.** to oppose or struggle against (an enemy) in battle. **2.** to oppose or struggle against (a person, cause, etc.) in any manner. **3.** (*tr.*) to engage in or carry on (a battle, contest, etc.). **4.** (when *intr.*, often foll. by *for*) to uphold or maintain (a cause, etc.) by fighting or struggling: *to fight for freedom.* **5.** (*tr.*) to make or achieve (a way) by fighting. **6.** to engage (another or others) in combat. **7. fight it out.** to contend until a decisive result is obtained. **8. fight shy.** to keep aloof from. ~*n.* **9.** a battle, struggle, or physical combat. **10.** a quarrel, dispute, or contest. **11.** resistance (esp. in **to put up a fight**). **12.** a boxing match.

THESAURUS

fidget 1. *v.* be like a cat on hot bricks (*Inf.*), bustle, chafe, fiddle, fret, jiggle, jitter (*Inf.*), move restlessly, squirm, twitch, worry **2.** *n.* Usually **the fidgets** fidgetiness, jitters (*Inf.*), nervousness, restlessness, unease, uneasiness

fidgety impatient, jerky, jittery (*Inf.*), jumpy, nervous, on edge, restive, restless, twitchy, uneasy

field *n.* **1.** grassland, green, greensward (*Archaic*), lea (*Literary*), mead (*Archaic*), meadow, pasture **2.** applicants, candidates, competition, competitors, contestants, entrants, possibilities, runners **3.** area, bailiwick, bounds, confines, department, discipline, domain, environment, limits, line, me-

tier, province, purview, range, scope, speciality, specialty, sphere of influence (activity, interest, study), territory ~*v.* **4.** catch, pick up, retrieve, return, stop **5.** *Fig.* deal with, deflect, handle, turn aside

fiend 1. demon, devil, evil spirit, hellhound **2.** barbarian, beast, brute, degenerate, monster, ogre, savage **3.** *Inf.* addict, enthusiast, fanatic, freak (*Sl.*), maniac

fiendish accursed, atrocious, blackhearted, cruel, demoniac, devilish, diabolical, hellish, implacable, infernal, inhuman, malevolent, malicious, malignant, monstrous, satanic, savage, ungodly, unspeakable, wicked

fierce 1. barbarous, brutal, cruel, danger-

ous, fell (*Archaic*), feral, ferocious, fiery, menacing, murderous, passionate, savage, threatening, tigerish, truculent, uncontrollable, untamed, vicious, wild **2.** blustery, boisterous, furious, howling, powerful, raging, stormy, strong, tempestuous, tumultuous, uncontrollable, violent **3.** cutthroat, intense, keen, relentless, strong

fiercely ferociously, frenziedly, furiously, in a frenzy, like cat and dog, menacingly, passionately, savagely, tempestuously, tigerishly, tooth and nail, uncontrolledly, viciously, with bared teeth, with no holds barred

fight *v.* **1.** assault, battle, bear arms against, box, brawl, carry on war, clash, close, combat, come to blows, conflict, con-

fighter ('faɪtə) n. **1.** a person who fights, esp. a professional boxer. **2.** a person who has determination. **3.** *Mil.* an armed aircraft designed for destroying other aircraft.

fighting chance n. a slight chance of success dependent on a struggle.

fight off vb. (tr., adv.) to struggle to avoid or repress: to fight off a cold.

fig leaf n. **1.** a leaf from a fig tree. **2.** a representation of a fig leaf used in sculpture, etc. to cover the genitals of nude figures. **3.** a device to conceal something regarded as shameful.

figment ('fɪgmənt) n. a fantastic notion or fabrication: a figment of the imagination.

figuration (ˌfɪgə'reɪʃən) n. **1.** *Music.* **a.** the employment of characteristic patterns of notes, esp. in variations on a theme. **b.** florid ornamentation. **2.** an instance of representing figuratively, as by means of allegory. **3.** a figurative representation. **4.** the act of decorating with a design.

figurative ('fɪgərətɪv) adj. **1.** involving a figure of speech; not literal; metaphorical. **2.** using or filled with figures of speech. **3.** representing by means of an emblem, likeness, etc. —**'figuratively** adv. —**'figurativeness** n.

figure ('fɪgə) n. **1.** any written symbol other than a letter, esp. a whole number. **2.** another name for **digit** (sense 2). **3.** an amount expressed numerically: a figure of £1800 was suggested. **4.** (pl.) calculations with numbers: he's good at figures. **5.** visible shape or form; outline. **6.** the human form: a girl with a slender figure. **7.** a slim bodily shape (esp. in **keep** or **lose one's figure**). **8.** a character or personage: a figure in politics. **9.** the impression created by a person through behaviour (esp. in **to cut a fine, bold,** etc., **figure**). **10. a.** a person as impressed on the mind. **b.** (in combination): father-figure. **11.** a representation in painting or sculpture, esp. of the human form. **12.** a representative object or symbol. **13.** a pattern or design, as in wood. **14.** a predetermined set of movements in dancing or skating. **15.** *Geom.* any combination of points, lines, curves, or planes. **16.** *Logic.* one of four possible arrangements of the terms in the major and minor premisses of a syllogism that give the same conclusion. **17.** *Music.* **a.** a numeral written above or below a note in a part. **b.** a characteristic short pattern of notes. ~vb. **18.** (when tr., often foll. by up) to calculate or compute (sums, amounts, etc.). **19.** (tr.; usually takes a clause as object) Inf., U.S. & N.Z. to consider. **20.** (tr.) to represent by a diagram or illustration. **21.** (tr.) to pattern or mark with a design. **22.** (tr.) to depict or portray in a painting, etc. **23.** (tr.) to imagine. **24.** (tr.) Music. to decorate (a melody line or part) with ornamentation. **25.** (intr.; usually foll. by in) to be included: his name figures in the article. **26.** (intr.) Inf. to accord

with expectation: it figures that he wouldn't come. —**'figurer** n.

figured ('fɪgəd) adj. **1.** depicted as a figure in painting or sculpture. **2.** decorated with a design. **3.** having a form. **4.** *Music.* **a.** ornamental. **b.** (of a bass part) provided with numerals indicating accompanying harmonies.

figurehead ('fɪgəˌhɛd) n. **1.** a person nominally having a prominent position, but no real authority. **2.** a carved bust on the bow of some sailing vessels.

figure of speech n. an expression of language, such as metaphor, by which the literal meaning of a word is not employed.

figure skating n. ice skating in which the skater traces outlines of selected patterns. —**figure skater** n.

figurine (ˌfɪgə'riːn) n. a small carved or moulded figure; statuette.

figwort ('fɪgˌwɜːt) n. a plant related to the foxglove having square stems and small greenish flowers.

filament ('fɪləmənt) n. **1.** the thin wire, usually tungsten, inside a light bulb that emits light when heated to incandescence by an electric current. **2.** *Electronics.* a high-resistance wire forming the cathode in some valves. **3.** a single strand of a natural or synthetic fibre. **4.** *Bot.* the stalk of a stamen. **5.** any slender structure or part. —**filamentary** (ˌfɪlə'mɛntərɪ) or ˌfila'mentous adj.

filbert ('fɪlbət) n. **1.** any of several N temperate shrubs that have edible rounded brown nuts. **2.** Also called: **hazelnut, cobnut.** the nut of any of these shrubs.

filch (fɪltʃ) vb. (tr.) to steal or take in small amounts. —**'filcher** n.

file¹ (faɪl) n. **1.** a folder, box, etc., used to keep documents or other items in order. **2.** the documents, etc., kept in this way. **3.** documents or information about a specific subject, person, etc. **4.** a line of people in marching formation, one behind another. **5.** any of the eight vertical rows of squares on a chessboard. **6.** Also called: **data set.** *Computers.* a block of data that can be accessed by means of its unique address from a storage device. **7. on file.** recorded or catalogued for reference, as in a file. ~vb. **8.** to place (a document, etc.) in a file. **9.** (tr.) to place (a legal document) on public or official record. **10.** (tr.) to bring (a suit, esp. a divorce suit) in a court of law. **11.** (tr.) to submit (copy) to a newspaper. **12.** (intr.) to march or walk in a file or files: the ants filed down the hill. —**'filer** n.

file² (faɪl) n. **1.** a hand tool consisting of a steel blade with small cutting teeth on some or all of its faces. It is used for shaping or smoothing. ~vb. **2.** (tr.) to shape or smooth (a surface) with a file. —**'filer** n.

filial ('fɪlɪəl) adj. **1.** of, resembling, or suitable to a son or daughter: filial affection. **2.** *Genetics.* designating any of the generations following the parental generation.

THESAURUS

fighter 1. fighting man, man-at-arms, soldier, warrior **2.** boxer, bruiser (Inf.), prize fighter, pugilist **3.** antagonist, battler, belligerent, combatant, contender, contestant, disputant, militant

fighting 1. adj. aggressive, argumentative, bellicose, belligerent, combative, contentious, disputatious, hawkish, martial, militant, pugnacious, sabre-rattling, truculent, warlike **2.** n. battle, bloodshed, blows struck, combat, conflict, hostilities, warfare

fight off beat off, keep or hold at bay, repel, repress, repulse, resist, stave off, ward off

figure n. **1.** character, cipher, digit, number, numeral, symbol **2.** amount, cost, price, sum, total, value **3.** form, outline, shadow, shape, silhouette **4.** body, build, chassis (Sl.), frame, physique, proportions, shape, torso **5.** depiction, design, device, diagram, drawing, emblem, illustration, motif, pattern, representation, sketch **6.** celebrity, character, dignitary, force, leader, notability, notable, personage, personality, presence, somebody, worthy ~v. **7.** Often with **up** add, calculate, compute, count, reckon, sum, tally, tot up, work out **8.** Usually with **in** act, appear, be conspicuous, be featured, be included, be mentioned, contribute to, feature, have a

place in, play a part **9. it figures** it follows, it goes without saying, it is to be expected

figurehead cipher, dummy, front man (Inf.), leader in name only, man of straw, mouthpiece, name, nonentity, puppet, straw man (Chiefly U.S.), titular or nominal head, token

figure of speech conceit, image, trope, turn of phrase

figure out 1. calculate, compute, reckon, work out **2.** comprehend, decipher, fathom, make head or tail of (Inf.), make out, resolve, see, understand

filament cilium (Biol. & Zool.), fibre, fibril, pile, staple, strand, string, thread, wire

filch abstract, crib (Inf.), embezzle, half-inch (Sl.), lift (Inf.), misappropriate, nick (Sl.), pilfer, pinch (Inf.), purloin, rip off (Sl.), snaffle (Inf.), steal, swipe (Sl.), take, thieve, walk off with

file¹ v. abrade, burnish, furbish, polish, rasp, refine, rub, rub down, scrape, shape, smooth

file² n. **1.** case, data, documents, dossier, folder, information, portfolio ~v. **2.** document, enter, pigeonhole, put in place, record, register, slot in ~n. **3.** column, line, list, queue, row, string ~v. **4.** march, parade, troop

tend, cross swords, do battle, engage, engage in hostilities, exchange blows, feud, go to war, grapple, joust, scrap (Inf.), spar, struggle, take the field, take up arms against, tilt, tussle, wage war, war, wrestle **2.** contest, defy, dispute, make a stand against, oppose, resist, stand up to, strive, struggle, withstand **3.** argue, bicker, dispute, fall out (Inf.), squabble, wrangle **4.** carry on, conduct, engage in, prosecute, wage **5. fight shy of** avoid, duck out of (Inf.), keep aloof from, keep at arm's length, shun, steer clear of ~n. **6.** action, affray (Law), altercation, battle, bout, brawl, brush, clash, combat, conflict, contest, dispute, dissension, dogfight, duel, encounter, engagement, exchange of blows, fracas, fray, free-for-all (Inf.), hostilities, joust, melee, passage of arms, riot, row, rumble (U.S. sl.), scrap (Inf.), scuffle, set-to (Inf.), skirmish, sparring match, struggle, tussle, war **7.** Fig. belligerence, gameness, mettle, militancy, pluck, resistance, spirit, will to resist

fight back 1. defend oneself, give tit for tat, put up a fight, reply, resist, retaliate **2.** bottle up, contain, control, curb, hold back, hold in check, restrain

fight down bottle up, control, curb, hold back, repress, restrain, suppress

—**'filially** adv.

filibuster ('fɪlɪˌbʌstə) n. 1. Chiefly U.S. the process of obstructing legislation by means of delaying tactics. 2. Also called: **filibusterer**. Chiefly U.S. a legislator who engages in such obstruction. 3. a freebooter or military adventurer, esp. in a foreign country. ~vb. 4. Chiefly U.S. to obstruct (legislation) with delaying tactics. 5. (intr.) to engage in unlawful military action. —**'fili,busterer** n.

filigree ('fɪlɪˌgriː) or **filagree** n. 1. delicate ornamental work of twisted gold, silver, or other wire. 2. any fanciful delicate ornamentation. ~adj. 3. made of or as if with filigree. —**'fili,greed** adj.

filings ('faɪlɪŋz) pl. n. shavings or particles removed by a file: iron filings.

Filipino (ˌfɪlɪ'piːnəʊ) n., pl. **-nos.** 1. a native or inhabitant of the Philippines. 2. another name for **Tagalog.** ~adj. 3. of or relating to the Philippines or their inhabitants.

fill (fɪl) vb. (mainly tr.; often foll. by up) 1. (also intr.) to make or become full: to fill up a bottle. 2. to occupy the whole of: the party filled the house. 3. to plug (a gap, crevice, etc.). 4. to meet (a requirement or need) satisfactorily. 5. to cover (a page or blank space) with writing, drawing, etc. 6. to hold and perform the duties of (an office or position). 7. to appoint or elect an occupant to (an office or position). 8. (also intr.) to swell or cause to swell with wind, as in manoeuvring the sails of a sailing vessel. 9. Chiefly U.S. to put together the necessary materials for (a prescription or order). 10. **fill the bill.** Inf. to serve or perform adequately. ~n. 11. material such as gravel, stones, etc., used to bring an area of ground up to a required level. 12. **one's fill.** the quantity needed to satisfy one. ~See also **fill in, fill out, fill up.**

filler ('fɪlə) n. 1. a person or thing that fills. 2. an object or substance used to add weight or size to something or to fill in a gap. 3. a paste, used for filling in cracks, holes, etc., in a surface before painting. 4. the inner portion of a cigar. 5. Journalism. articles, photographs, etc., to fill space between more important articles in a newspaper or magazine.

fillet ('fɪlɪt) n. 1. a. Also called: **fillet steak.** a strip of boneless meat. b. the boned side of a fish. 2. a narrow strip of any material. 3. a thin strip of ribbon, lace, etc., worn in the hair or around the neck. 4. a narrow flat moulding, esp. one between other mouldings. 5. a narrow band between flutings on the shaft of a column. 6. Heraldry. a horizontal division of a shield. 7. a narrow decorative line, impressed on the cover of a book. ~vb. (tr.) 8. to cut or prepare (meat or fish) as a fillet. 9. to cut fillets from (meat or fish). 10. to bind or decorate with or as if with a fillet. ~ Also (for senses 1-3): **filet.**

fill in vb. (adv.) 1. (tr.) to complete (a form, drawing, etc.). 2. (intr.) to act as a substitute. 3. (tr.) to put material into (a hole or cavity), esp. so as to make it level with a surface. 4. (tr.) Inf. to inform with facts or news. ~n. **fill-in.** 5. a substitute.

filling ('fɪlɪŋ) n. 1. the substance or thing used to fill a space or container: pie filling. 2. Dentistry. any of various substances (metal, plastic, etc.) for inserting into the prepared cavity of a tooth. 3. the woof in weaving.

filling station n. a place where petrol and other supplies for motorists are sold.

fillip ('fɪlɪp) n. 1. something that adds stimulation or enjoyment. 2. the action of holding a finger towards the palm with the thumb and suddenly releasing it outwards to produce a snapping sound. 3. a quick blow or tap

made by this. ~vb. 4. (tr.) to stimulate or excite. 5. (tr.) to strike or project sharply with a fillip. 6. (intr.) to make a fillip.

fill out vb. (adv.) 1. to make or become fuller, thicker, or rounder. 2. to make more substantial. 3. (tr.) U.S. to fill in (a form, etc.).

fill up vb. (adv.) 1. (tr.) to complete (a form, application, etc.). 2. to make or become full. ~n. **fill-up.** 3. the act of filling something completely, esp. the petrol tank of a car.

filly ('fɪlɪ) n., pl. **-lies.** a female horse or pony under the age of four.

film (fɪlm) n. 1. a. a sequence of images of moving objects photographed by a camera and providing the optical illusion of continuous movement when projected onto a screen. b. a form of entertainment, etc., composed of such a sequence of images. c. (as modifier): film techniques. 2. a thin flexible strip of cellulose coated with a photographic emulsion, used to make negatives and transparencies. 3. a thin coating or layer. 4. a thin sheet of any material, as of plastic for packaging. 5. a fine haze, mist, or blur. 6. a gauzy web of filaments or fine threads. ~vb. 7. a. to photograph with a cine camera. b. to make a film of (a screenplay, event, etc.). 8. to cover or become covered or coated with a film. —**'filmic** adj.

filmset ('fɪlmˌsɛt) vb. (tr.) **-setting, -set** Brit. to set (type matter) by filmsetting. —**'film,setter** n.

filmsetting ('fɪlmˌsɛtɪŋ) n. Brit., printing. typesetting by exposing type characters onto photographic film from which printing plates are made.

film strip n. a strip of film composed of different images projected separately as slides.

filmy ('fɪlmɪ) adj. **filmier, filmiest.** 1. transparent or gauzy. 2. hazy; blurred. —**'filmily** adv. —**'filminess** n.

filter ('fɪltə) n. 1. a porous substance, such as paper or sand, that allows fluid to pass but retains suspended solid particles. 2. any device containing such a porous substance for separating suspensions from fluids. 3. any of various porous substances built into the mouth end of a cigarette or cigar for absorbing impurities such as tar. 4. any electronic, optical, or acoustic device that blocks signals or radiations of certain frequencies while allowing others to pass. 5. any transparent disc of gelatin or glass used to eliminate or reduce the intensity of given frequencies from the light leaving a lamp, entering a camera, etc. 6. Brit. a traffic signal at a road junction which permits vehicles to turn either left or right when the main signals are red. ~vb. 7. (often foll. by out) to remove or separate (suspended particles, etc.) from (a liquid, gas, etc.) by the action of a filter. 8. (tr.) to obtain by filtering. 9. (intr.; foll. by through) to pass (through a filter or something like a filter). 10. (intr.) to flow slowly; trickle. ~See also **filter out.**

filter out or **through** vb. (intr., adv.) to become known gradually; leak.

filter paper n. a porous paper used for filtering liquids.

filter tip n. 1. an attachment to the mouth end of a cigarette for trapping impurities such as tar during smoking. 2. a cigarette having such an attachment. —**'filter-,tipped** adj.

filth (fɪlθ) n. 1. foul or disgusting dirt; refuse. 2. extreme physical or moral uncleanliness. 3. vulgarity or obscenity. —**'filthy** adj.

THESAURUS

filibuster n. 1. Chiefly U.S., with reference to legislation delay, hindrance, obstruction, postponement, procrastination ~v. 2. Chiefly U.S., with reference to legislation delay, hinder, obstruct, prevent, procrastinate, put off ~n. 3. adventurer, buccaneer, corsair, freebooter, pirate, sea robber, sea rover, soldier of fortune

fill 1. brim over, cram, crowd, furnish, glut, gorge, inflate, pack, pervade, replenish, sate, satiate, satisfy, stock, store, stuff, supply, swell 2. charge, imbue, impregnate, overspread, pervade, saturate, suffuse 3. block, bung, close, cork, plug, seal, stop 4. assign, carry out, discharge, engage, execute, fulfil, hold, occupy, officiate, perform, take up 5.

one's fill all one wants, ample, a sufficiency, enough, plenty, sufficient

fill in 1. answer, complete, fill out (U.S.), fill up 2. Inf. acquaint, apprise, bring up to date, give the facts or background, inform, put wise (Sl.) 3. deputize, replace, represent, stand in, sub, substitute, take the place of

filling 1. n. contents, filler, innards (Inf.), inside, insides, padding, stuffing, wadding 2. adj. ample, heavy, satisfying, square, substantial

film n. 1. coat, coating, covering, dusting, gauze, integument, layer, membrane, pellicle, scum, skin, tissue 2. blur, cloud, haze, haziness, mist, mistiness, opacity, veil 3. flick (Sl.), motion picture, movie (U.S. inf.) ~v. 4.

photograph, shoot, take 5. Often with over blear, blur, cloud, dull, haze, mist, veil

filmy 1. chiffon, cobwebby, delicate, diaphanous, fine, finespun, flimsy, floaty, fragile, gauzy, gossamer, insubstantial, seethrough, sheer, transparent 2. bleared, bleary, blurred, blurry, cloudy, dim, hazy, membranous, milky, misty, opalescent, opaque, pearly

filter v. 1. clarify, filtrate, purify, refine, screen, sieve, sift, strain, winnow 2. Often with through or out dribble, escape, exude, leach, leak, ooze, penetrate, percolate, seep, trickle, well ~n. 3. gauze, membrane, mesh, riddle, sieve, strainer

filth 1. carrion, contamination, defilement,

filtrate ('filtreit) *n.* **1.** a liquid or gas that has been filtered. ~*vb.* **2.** to filter. —**fil'tration** *n.*

fin (fin) *n.* **1.** any of the firm appendages that are the organs of locomotion and balance in fishes and some other aquatic animals. **2.** a part or appendage that resembles a fin. **3. a.** *Brit.* a vertical surface to which the rudder is attached at the rear of an aeroplane. **b.** an aerofoil fixed to a rocket or missile to give stability. **4.** *Naut.* a fixed or adjustable blade projecting under water from the hull of a vessel to give it stability or control. **5.** a projecting rib to dissipate heat from the surface of an engine cylinder or radiator. ~*vb.* **finning, finned. 6.** (*tr.*) to provide with fins. —**'finless** *adj.* —**finned** *adj.*

fin. *abbrev. for:* **1.** finance. **2.** financial.

Fin. *abbrev. for:* **1.** Finland. **2.** Finnish.

finagle (fi'neɪɡəl) *vb. Inf.* **1.** (*tr.*) to get or achieve by craftiness or persuasion. **2.** to use trickery on (a person). —**fi'nagler** *n.*

final ('faɪnəl) *adj.* **1.** of or occurring at the end; last. **2.** having no possibility of further discussion, action, or change: *a final decree of judgment.* **3.** relating to or constituting an end or purpose: *a final clause may be introduced by "in order to".* **4.** *Music.* another word for **perfect** (sense 9b.). ~*n.* **5.** a last thing; end. **6.** a deciding contest between the winners of previous rounds in a competition. —**fi'nality** *n.* —**'finally** *adv.*

finale (fi'nɑːli) *n.* **1.** the concluding part of any performance or presentation. **2.** the closing section or movement of a musical composition.

finalist ('faɪnəlɪst) *n.* a contestant who has reached the last stage of a competition.

finalize *or* **-lise** ('faɪnəˌlaɪz) *vb.* **1.** (*tr.*) to put into final form; settle: *to finalize plans for the merger.* **2.** to reach agreement on a transaction. —**ˌfinali'zation** *or* **-li'sation** *n.*

▷ **Usage.** Although *finalize* has been in widespread use for some time, it carries strong associations of bureaucratic or commercial jargon for many careful speakers and writers, who usually prefer *complete, conclude,* or *make final,* esp. in formal contexts.

finals ('faɪnəlz) *pl. n.* **1.** the deciding part of a competition. **2.** *Education.* the last examinations in an academic or professional course.

finance (fi'næns, 'faɪnæns) *n.* **1.** the system of money, credit, etc., esp. with respect to government revenues and expenditures. **2.** funds or the provision of funds. **3.** (*pl.*) financial condition. ~*vb.* **4.** (*tr.*) to provide or obtain funds or credit for.

financial (fi'nænʃəl, faɪ-) *adj.* **1.** of or relating to finance or finances. **2.** of or relating to persons who manage money, capital, or credit. **3.** *Austral. & N.Z. inf.* having money; in funds. **4.** *Austral. & N.Z.* (of a club member) fully paid-up. —**fi'nancially** *adv.*

financial year *n. Brit.* **1.** any annual period at the end of which a firm's accounts are made up. **2.** the annual period ending April 5, over which Budget estimates are made by the British Government. ~U.S. equivalent: **fiscal year.**

financier (fi'nænsɪə, faɪ-) *n.* a person who is engaged in large-scale financial operations.

finch (fintʃ) *n.* any of various songbirds having a short stout bill for feeding on seeds, such as the goldfinch, bullfinch, chaffinch, siskin, and canary.

find (faɪnd) *vb.* **finding, found.** (*mainly tr.*) **1.** to meet with or discover by chance. **2.** to discover or obtain, esp. by search or effort: *to find happiness.* **3.** (*may take a clause as object*) to realize: *he found that nobody knew.* **4.** (*may take a clause as object*) to consider: *I find this wine a little sour.* **5.** to look for and point out (something to be criticized). **6.** (*also intr.*) *Law.* to determine an issue and pronounce a verdict (upon): *the court found the accused guilty.* **7.** to regain (something lost or not functioning): *to find one's tongue.* **8.** to reach (a target): *the bullet found its mark.* **9.** to provide, esp. with difficulty: *we'll find room for you too.* **10.** to be able to pay: *I can't find that amount of money.* **11. find oneself.** to accept and make use of one's personality and interests. **12. find one's feet.** to become capable or confident. ~*n.* **13.** a person, thing, etc., that is found, esp. a valuable discovery.

finder ('faɪndə) *n.* **1.** a person or thing that finds. **2.** *Physics.* a small telescope fitted to a more powerful larger telescope. **3.** *Photog.* short for **viewfinder. 4. finders keepers.** *Inf.* whoever finds something has the right to keep it.

finding ('faɪndɪŋ) *n.* **1.** a thing that is found or discovered. **2.** *Law.* the conclusion reached after a judicial inquiry; verdict.

find out *vb.* (*adv.*) **1.** to gain knowledge of (something); learn. **2.** to detect the crime, deception, etc., of (someone).

fine¹ (faɪn) *adj.* **1.** very good of its kind: *a fine speech.* **2.** superior in skill or accomplishment: *a fine violinist.* **3.** (of weather) clear and dry. **4.** enjoyable or satisfying: *a fine time.* **5.** (*postpositive*) *Inf.* quite well: *I feel fine.* **6.** of delicate composition or careful workmanship: *fine crystal.* **7.** (of precious metals) pure or having a high degree of purity: *fine silver.* **8.** discriminating: *a fine eye for antique brasses.* **9.** abstruse or subtle: *a fine point.* **10.** very thin or slender: *fine hair.* **11.** very small: *fine print.* **12.** (of edges, blades, etc.) sharp; keen. **13.** ornate, showy, or smart. **14.** good-looking: *a fine young woman.* **15.** polished, elegant, or refined: *a fine gentleman.* **16.** *Cricket.* (of a fielding position) oblique to and behind the wicket: *fine leg.* **17.** (*prenominal*) *Inf.* disappointing or terrible: *a fine mess.* ~*adv.* **18.** *Inf.* all right: *that suits me fine.* **19.** finely. **20. cut it fine.** to allow little margin of time, space, etc. ~*vb.* **21.** to make or become finer; refine. **22.** (often foll. by *down* or *away*) to make or become smaller. —**'finely** *adv.* —**'fineness** *n.*

fine² (faɪn) *n.* **1.** a certain amount of money exacted as a penalty: *a parking fine.* **2.** a payment made by a tenant at the start of his tenancy to reduce his subsequent rent;

THESAURUS

dirt, dung, excrement, excreta, faeces, filthiness, foul matter, foulness, garbage, grime, muck, nastiness, ordure, pollution, putrefaction, putrescence, refuse, sewage, slime, sludge, squalor, uncleanness **2.** corruption, dirty-mindedness, impurity, indecency, obscenity, pornography, smut, vileness, vulgarity

filthy 1. dirty, faecal, feculent, foul, nasty, polluted, putrid, scummy, slimy, squalid, unclean, vile **2.** begrimed, black, blackened, grimy, grubby, miry, mucky, muddy, mudencrusted, smoky, sooty, unwashed **3.** bawdy, coarse, corrupt, depraved, dirty-minded, foul, foul-mouthed, impure, indecent, lewd, licentious, obscene, pornographic, smutty, suggestive **4.** base, contemptible, despicable, low, mean, offensive, scurvy, vicious, vile

final 1. closing, concluding, end, eventual, last, last-minute, latest, terminal, terminating, ultimate **2.** absolute, conclusive, decided, decisive, definite, definitive, determinate, finished, incontrovertible, irrevocable, settled

finale climax, close, conclusion, crowning glory, culmination, dénouement, epilogue,

finis, last act

finality certitude, conclusiveness, decidedness, decisiveness, definiteness, inevitableness, irrevocability, resolution, unavoidability

finalize agree, clinch (*Inf.*), complete, conclude, decide, settle, sew up (*Inf.*), tie up, work out, wrap up (*Inf.*)

finally 1. at last, at length, at long last, at the last, at the last moment, eventually, in the end, in the long run, lastly, ultimately, when all is said and done **2.** in conclusion, in summary, to conclude **3.** beyond the shadow of a doubt, completely, conclusively, convincingly, decisively, for all time, for ever, for good, inescapably, inexorably, irrevocably, once and for all, permanently

finance 1. *n.* accounts, banking, business, commerce, economics, financial affairs, investment, money, money management **2.** *v.* back, bankroll (*U.S.*), float, fund, guarantee, pay for, provide security for, set up in business, subsidize, support, underwrite

finances affairs, assets, capital, cash, financial condition, funds, money, resources, wherewithal

financial budgeting, economic, fiscal, monetary, money, pecuniary

find *v.* **1.** catch sight of, chance upon, come across, come up with, descry, discover, encounter, espy, expose, ferret out, hit upon, lay one's hand on, light upon, locate, meet, recognize, run to earth, spot, stumble upon, track down, turn up, uncover, unearth **2.** achieve, acquire, attain, earn, gain, get, obtain, procure, win **3.** get back, recover, regain, repossess, retrieve **4.** arrive at, ascertain, become aware, detect, discover, experience, learn, note, notice, observe, perceive, realise, remark **5.** be responsible for, bring, contribute, cough up (*Inf.*), furnish, provide, supply ~*n.* **6.** acquisition, asset, bargain, catch, discovery, good buy

finding award, conclusion, decision, decree, judgment, pronouncement, recommendation, verdict

find out 1. detect, discover, learn, note, observe, perceive, realize **2.** bring to light, catch, detect, disclose, expose, reveal, rumble (*Sl.*), suss out (*Sl.*), uncover, unmask

premium. **3. in fine. a.** in short. **b.** in conclusion. ~*vb.*
4. (*tr.*) to impose a fine on.

fine art *n.* **1.** art produced chiefly for its aesthetic value. **2.** (*often pl.*) any of the fields in which such art is produced, such as painting, sculpture, and engraving.

fine-drawn *adj.* **1.** (of arguments, distinctions, etc.) precise or subtle. **2.** (of wire, etc.) drawn out until very fine.

finery ('faɪnərɪ) *n.* elaborate or showy decoration, esp. clothing and jewellery.

fines herbes (*French* fin 'zɛrb) *pl. n.* a mixture of finely chopped herbs, used to flavour omelettes, salads, etc.

finespun ('faɪn'spʌn) *adj.* **1.** spun or drawn out to a fine thread. **2.** excessively subtle or refined.

finesse (fɪ'nɛs) *n.* **1.** elegant skill in style or performance. **2.** subtlety and tact in handling difficult situations. **3.** *Bridge, whist.* an attempt to win a trick when opponents hold a high card in the suit led by playing a lower card. **4.** a trick, artifice, or strategy. ~*vb.* **5.** to bring about with finesse. **6.** to play (a card) as a finesse.

fine-tooth comb *or* **fine-toothed comb** *n.* **1.** a comb with fine teeth set closely together. **2. go over** *or* **through with a fine-tooth(ed) comb.** to examine very thoroughly.

finger ('fɪŋɡə) *n.* **1. a.** any of the digits of the hand, often excluding the thumb. **b.** (*as modifier*): *a finger bowl.* **c.** (*in combination*): *a fingernail.* Related adj.: **digital.** **2.** the part of a glove made to cover a finger. **3.** something that resembles a finger in shape or function: *a finger of land.* **4.** the length or width of a finger used as a unit of measurement. **5.** a quantity of liquid in a glass, etc., as deep as a finger is wide. **6. get** *or* **pull one's finger out.** *Brit. inf.* to begin or speed up activity, esp. after initial delay. **7. have a** (*or* **one's**) **finger in the pie. a.** to have an interest in or take part in some activity. **b.** to meddle or interfere. **8. lay** *or* **put one's finger on.** to indicate or locate accurately. **9. not lift** (*or* **raise**) **a finger.** (*foll. by an infinitive*) not to make any effort (to do something). **10. twist** *or* **wrap around one's little finger.** to have easy and complete control or influence over. **11. put the finger on.** *Inf., U.S. & N.Z.* to inform on or identify, esp. for the police. ~*vb.* **12.** (*tr.*) to touch or manipulate with the fingers; handle. **13.** to use one's fingers in playing (an instrument, such as a piano or clarinet). **14.** to indicate on (a composition or part) the fingering required by a pianist, harpsichordist, etc. —**'fingerless** *adj.*

fingerboard ('fɪŋɡə,bɔːd) *n.* the long strip of hard wood on a violin, guitar, etc. upon which the strings are stopped by the fingers.

finger bowl *n.* a small bowl filled with water for rinsing the fingers at the table after a meal.

fingering ('fɪŋɡərɪŋ) *n.* **1.** the technique or art of using one's fingers in playing a musical instrument, esp. the piano. **2.** the numerals in a musical part indicating this.

fingernail ('fɪŋɡə,neɪl) *n.* a thin horny translucent plate covering part of the dorsal surface of the end joint of each finger.

fingerprint ('fɪŋɡə,prɪnt) *n.* **1.** an impression of the pattern of ridges on the surface of the end joint of each finger and thumb. **2.** any identifying characteristic. ~*vb.* **3.** (*tr.*) to take an inked impression of the fingerprints of (a person).

fingerstall ('fɪŋɡə,stɔːl) *n.* a protective covering for a finger. Also called: **cot.**

fingertip ('fɪŋɡə,tɪp) *n.* **1.** the end joint or tip of a finger. **2. at one's fingertips.** readily available.

finicky ('fɪnɪkɪ) *or* **finicking** *adj.* **1.** excessively particular; fussy. **2.** overelaborate.

finis ('fɪnɪs) *n.* the end; finish: used at the end of books, films, etc.

finish ('fɪnɪʃ) *vb.* (*mainly tr.*) **1.** to bring to an end; conclude or stop. **2.** (*intr.*; sometimes foll. by *up*) to be at or come to the end. **3.** to bring to a desired or complete condition. **4.** to put a particular surface texture on (wood, cloth, etc.). **5.** (*often foll. by off*) to destroy or defeat completely. **6.** to train (a person) in social graces and talents. **7.** (*intr.*; foll. by *with*) to end a relationship or association. ~*n.* **8.** the final or last stage or part; end. **9.** the death or absolute defeat of a person or one side in a conflict: *a fight to the finish.* **10.** the surface texture or appearance of wood, cloth, etc.: *a rough finish.* **11.** a thing, event, etc., that completes. **12.** completeness and high quality of workmanship. **13.** *Sport.* ability to sprint at the end of a race. —**'finished** *adj.* —**'finisher** *n.*

finishing school *n.* a private school for girls that teaches social graces.

finite ('faɪnaɪt) *adj.* **1.** bounded in magnitude or spatial or temporal extent. **2.** *Maths.* having a finite or countable number of digits, terms, etc. **3.** limited or restricted in nature: *human existence is finite.* **4.** denoting any form of a verb inflected for grammatical features such as person, number, and tense. —**'finitely** *adv.* —**'finiteness** *or* **finitude** ('faɪnɪ,tjuːd) *n.*

Finn (fɪn) *n.* a native, inhabitant, or citizen of Finland.

Finnish ('fɪnɪʃ) *adj.* **1.** of or characteristic of Finland, the Finns, or their language. ~*n.* **2.** the official language of Finland, belonging to the Finno-Ugric family.

fino ('fiːnəʊ) *n.* a very dry sherry.

fiord (fjɔːd) *n.* a variant spelling of **fjord.**

fipple flute *n.* an end-blown flute provided with a fipple, such as the recorder or flageolet.

fir (fɜː) *n.* **1.** any of a genus of pyramidal coniferous

THESAURUS

fine[1] *adj.* **1.** accomplished, admirable, beautiful, choice, excellent, exceptional, exquisite, first-class, first-rate, great, magnificent, masterly, ornate, outstanding, rare, select, showy, skilful, splendid, superior, supreme **2.** balmy, bright, clear, clement, cloudless, dry, fair, pleasant, sunny **3.** dainty, delicate, elegant, expensive, exquisite, fragile, quality **4.** abstruse, acute, critical, discriminating, fastidious, hairsplitting, intelligent, keen, minute, nice, precise, quick, refined, sensitive, sharp, subtle, tasteful, tenuous **5.** delicate, diaphanous, fine-grained, flimsy, gauzy, gossamer, light, lightweight, powdered, powdery, pulverized, sheer, slender, small, thin **6.** clear, pure, refined, solid, sterling, unadulterated, unalloyed, unpolluted **7.** attractive, bonny, good-looking, handsome, lovely, smart, striking, stylish, well-favoured **8.** acceptable, agreeable, all right, convenient, good, O.K. (*Inf.*), satisfactory, suitable **9.** brilliant, cutting, honed, keen, polished, razor-sharp, sharp

fine[2] **1.** *v.* amerce (*Archaic*), mulct, penalize, punish **2.** *n.* amercement (*Archaic*), damages, forfeit, penalty, punishment

finery best bib and tucker (*Inf.*), decorations, frippery, gear (*Inf.*), gewgaws, glad rags (*Sl.*), ornaments, showiness, splendour, Sunday best, trappings, trinkets

finesse *n.* **1.** adeptness, adroitness, artful-

ness, cleverness, craft, delicacy, diplomacy, discretion, know-how (*Inf.*), polish, quickness, savoir-faire, skill, sophistication, subtlety, tact **2.** artifice, bluff, feint, manoeuvre, ruse, stratagem, trick, wile ~*v.* **3.** bluff, manipulate, manoeuvre

finger *v.* **1.** feel, fiddle with (*Inf.*), handle, manipulate, maul, meddle with, paw (*Inf.*), play about with, touch, toy with **2. put one's finger on** bring to mind, discover, find out, hit the nail on the head, hit upon, identify, indicate, locate, pin down, place, recall, remember

finish *v.* **1.** accomplish, achieve, bring to a close *or* conclusion, carry through, cease, close, complete, conclude, culminate, deal with, discharge, do, end, execute, finalize, fulfil, get done, get out of the way, make short work of, put the finishing touch(es) to, round off, settle, stop, terminate, wind up (*Inf.*), wrap up (*Inf.*) **2.** *Sometimes with* **up** *or* **off** consume, deplete, devour, dispatch, dispose of, drain, drink, eat, empty, exhaust, expend, spend, use, use up **3.** *Often with* **off** administer *or* give the coup de grâce, annihilate, best, bring down, defeat, destroy, dispose of, drive to the wall, exterminate, get rid of, kill, overcome, overpower, put an end to, rout, ruin, worst ~*n.* **4.** cessation, close, closing, completion, conclusion, culmination, dénouement, end, ending, finale, last

stage(s), termination, winding up (*Inf.*), wind-up (*Inf., chiefly U.S.*) **5.** annihilation, bankruptcy, curtains (*Inf.*), death, defeat, end, end of the road, liquidation, ruin ~*v.* **6.** elaborate, perfect, polish, refine ~*n.* **7.** cultivation, culture, elaboration, perfection, polish, refinement ~*v.* **8.** coat, face, gild, lacquer, polish, smooth off, stain, texture, veneer, wax ~*n.* **9.** appearance, grain, lustre, patina, polish, shine, smoothness, surface, texture

finished 1. accomplished, classic, consummate, cultivated, elegant, expert, flawless, impeccable, masterly, perfected, polished, professional, proficient, refined, skilled, smooth, urbane **2.** accomplished, achieved, closed, complete, completed, concluded, done, ended, entire, final, finalized, full, in the past, over, over and done with, sewed up (*Inf.*), shut, terminated, through, tied up, wrapped up (*Inf.*) **3.** done, drained, empty, exhausted, gone, played out (*Inf.*), spent, used up **4.** bankrupt, defeated, devastated, done for (*Inf.*), doomed, gone, liquidated, lost, ruined, through, undone, washed up (*Inf., chiefly U.S.*), wiped out, wound up, wrecked

finite bounded, circumscribed, conditioned, delimited, demarcated, limited, restricted, subject to limitations, terminable

trees having single needle-like leaves and erect cones. **2.** any of various other related trees, such as the Douglas fir. **3.** the wood of any of these trees.

fire (faɪə) n. **1.** the state of combustion in which inflammable material burns, producing heat, flames, and often smoke. **2. a.** a mass of burning coal, wood, etc., used esp. in a hearth to heat a room. **b.** (*in combination*): *firelighter.* **3.** a destructive conflagration, as of a forest, building, etc. **4.** a device for heating a room, etc. **5.** something resembling a fire in light or brilliance: *a diamond's fire.* **6.** the act of discharging weapons, artillery, etc. **7.** a burst or rapid volley: *a fire of questions.* **8.** intense passion; ardour. **9.** liveliness, as of imagination, etc. **10.** fever and inflammation. **11.** a severe trial or torment (esp. in **go through fire and water**). **12. between two fires.** under attack from two sides. **13. catch fire.** to ignite. **14. hang fire.** to delay or be delayed. **15. on fire. a.** in a state of ignition. **b.** ardent or eager. **16. open fire.** to start firing a gun, artillery, etc. **17. play with fire.** to be involved in something risky. **18. set fire to** *or* **set on fire. a.** to ignite. **b.** to arouse or excite. **19. under fire.** being attacked, as by weapons or by harsh criticism. **20.** (*modifier*) *Astrol.* of or relating to a group of three signs of the zodiac, Aries, Leo, and Sagittarius. ~*vb.* **21.** to discharge (a firearm or projectile), or (of a firearm, etc.) to be discharged. **22.** to detonate (an explosive charge or device), or (of such a charge or device) to be detonated. **23.** (*tr.*) *Inf.* to dismiss from employment. **24.** (*tr.*) *Ceramics.* to bake in a kiln to harden the clay, etc. **25.** to kindle or be kindled. **26.** (*tr.*) to provide with fuel: *oil fires the heating system.* **27.** (*tr.*) to subject to heat. **28.** (*tr.*) to heat slowly so as to dry. **29.** (*tr.*) to arouse to strong emotion. **30.** to glow or cause to glow. ~*interj.* **31.** a cry to warn others of a fire. —'**firer** n.

fire alarm n. a device to give warning of fire, esp. a bell, siren, or hooter.

firearm ('faɪərˌɑːm) n. a weapon from which a projectile can be discharged by an explosion caused by igniting gunpowder, etc.

fireball ('faɪəˌbɔːl) n. **1.** a ball-shaped discharge of lightning. **2.** the region of hot ionized gas at the centre of a nuclear explosion. **3.** *Astron.* a large bright meteor. **4.** *Sl.* an energetic person.

firebomb ('faɪəˌbɒm) n. another name for **incendiary** (sense 6).

firebox ('faɪəˌbɒks) n. the furnace chamber of a boiler in a steam locomotive.

firebrand ('faɪəˌbrænd) n. **1.** a piece of burning wood. **2.** a person who causes unrest.

firebreak ('faɪəˌbreɪk) n. a strip of open land in forest or prairie, serving to arrest the advance of a fire.

firebrick ('faɪəˌbrɪk) n. a refractory brick made of fire clay, used for lining furnaces, flues, etc.

fire brigade n. *Chiefly Brit.* an organized body of firemen.

fire clay n. a heat-resistant clay used in the making of firebricks, furnace linings, etc.

firecracker ('faɪəˌkrækə) n. a small cardboard container filled with explosive powder.

firecrest ('faɪəˌkrɛst) n. a small European warbler having a crown striped with yellow, black, and white.

firedamp ('faɪəˌdæmp) n. a mixture of hydrocarbons, chiefly methane, formed in coal mines. See also **afterdamp.**

firedog ('faɪəˌdɒg) n. either of a pair of metal stands used to support logs in an open fire.

fire-eater n. **1.** a performer who simulates the swallowing of fire. **2.** a belligerent person.

fire engine n. a vehicle that carries firemen and firefighting equipment to a fire.

fire escape n. a means of evacuating persons from a building in the event of fire.

fire-extinguisher n. a portable device for extinguishing fires, usually consisting of a canister with a directional nozzle used to direct a spray of water, etc., onto the fire.

firefly ('faɪəˌflaɪ) n., pl. **-flies.** a nocturnal beetle common in warm and tropical regions, having luminescent abdominal organs.

fireguard ('faɪəˌgɑːd) n. a meshed frame put before an open fire to protect against falling logs, sparks, etc.

fire hall n. *Canad.* a fire station.

fire irons pl. n. metal fireside implements, such as poker, shovel, and tongs.

fireman ('faɪəmən) n., pl. **-men. 1.** a person who fights fires, usually a trained volunteer or public employee. **2. a.** (on steam locomotives) the man who stokes the fire. **b.** (on diesel and electric locomotives) the driver's assistant. **3.** a man who tends furnaces; stoker.

fireplace ('faɪəˌpleɪs) n. an open recess at the base of a chimney, etc., for a fire; hearth.

fire power n. *Mil.* the capability of delivering fire.

fire raiser n. a person who deliberately sets fire to property, etc. —**fire raising** n.

fire ship n. a vessel loaded with explosives and used, esp. formerly, as a bomb by igniting it and directing it to drift among an enemy's warships.

fireside ('faɪəˌsaɪd) n. **1.** the hearth. **2.** family life; the home.

fire station n. a building where fire-fighting vehicles and equipment are stationed. Also called (U.S.): **firehouse, station house.**

firetrap ('faɪəˌtræp) n. a building that would burn easily or one without fire escapes.

firewater ('faɪəˌwɔːtə) n. any strong spirit, esp. whisky.

fireworks ('faɪəˌwɜːks) pl. n. **1.** devices in which combustible materials are ignited and produce coloured flames, sparks, and smoke. **2.** a show in which large numbers of fireworks are let off. **3.** *Inf.* an exciting exhibition, as of musical virtuosity or wit. **4.** *Inf.* a burst of temper.

firing ('faɪərɪŋ) n. **1.** the process of baking ceramics, etc., in a kiln. **2.** the act of stoking a fire or furnace. **3.** a discharge of a firearm. **4.** something used as fuel, such as coal or wood.

firing line n. **1.** *Mil.* the positions from which fire is delivered. **2.** the leading or most advanced position in an activity.

firm¹ (fɜːm) adj. **1.** not soft or yielding to a touch or pressure. **2.** securely in position; stable or stationary. **3.** decided; settled. **4.** enduring or steady. **5.** having determination or strength. **6.** (of prices, markets, etc.) tending to rise. ~adv. **7.** in a secure or unyielding manner: *he stood firm.* ~vb. **8.** (sometimes foll. by *up*) to make or become firm. —'**firmly** adv. —'**firmness** n.

firm² (fɜːm) n. **1.** a commercial enterprise. **2.** a team of doctors and their assistants.

firmament ('fɜːməmənt) n. the expanse of the sky; heavens.

THESAURUS

fire n. **1.** blaze, combustion, conflagration, flames, inferno **2.** barrage, bombardment, cannonade, flak, fusillade, hail, salvo, shelling, sniping, volley **3.** *Fig.* animation, ardour, brio, burning passion, dash, eagerness, élan, enthusiasm, excitement, fervency, fervour, force, heat, impetuosity, intensity, life, light, lustre, passion, radiance, scintillation, sparkle, spirit, splendour, verve, vigour, virtuosity, vivacity **4. hanging fire** delayed, in abeyance, pending, postponed, put back, put off, shelved, suspended, undecided **5. on fire a.** ablaze, aflame, alight, blazing, burning, fiery, flaming, in flames **b.** ardent, eager, enthusiastic, excited, inspired, passionate ~v. **6.** enkindle, ignite, kindle, light, put a match to, set ablaze, set aflame, set alight, set fire to, set on fire **7.** detonate, discharge, eject, explode, hurl, launch, let off, loose, pull the trigger, set off, shell, shoot, touch off **8.** *Fig.* animate, arouse, electrify, enliven, excite, galvanize, impassion, incite, inflame, inspire, inspirit, irritate, quicken, rouse, stir **9.** *Inf.* cashier, discharge, dismiss, give marching orders, make redundant, sack (*Sl.*), show the door

firebrand *Fig.* agitator, demagogue, fomenter, incendiary, instigator, rabble-rouser, soapbox orator, tub-thumper

fireworks 1. illuminations, pyrotechnics **2.** *Fig.* fit of rage, hysterics, paroxysms, rage, rows, storm, temper, trouble, uproar

firm¹ adj. **1.** close-grained, compact, compressed, concentrated, congealed, dense, hard, inelastic, inflexible, jelled, jellified, rigid, set, solid, solidified, stiff, unyielding **2.** anchored, braced, cemented, embedded, fast, fastened, fixed, immovable, motionless, riveted, robust, rooted, secure, secured, stable, stationary, steady, strong, sturdy, taut, tight, unfluctuating, unmoving, unshakable **3.** adamant, constant, definite, fixed, inflexible, obdurate, resolute, resolved, set on, settled, staunch, steadfast, strict, true, unalterable, unbending, unfaltering, unflinching, unshakable, unshaken, unswerving, unwavering, unyielding

firm² n. association, business, company, concern, conglomerate, corporation, enterprise, house, organization, outfit (*Inf.*), partnership

first (fɜːst) adj. (usually prenominal) **1. a.** coming before all others. **b.** (as n.): I was the first to arrive. **2.** preceding all others in numbering or counting order; the ordinal number of one. Often written: 1st. **3.** rated, graded, or ranked above all other levels. **4.** denoting the lowest forward ratio of a gearbox in a motor vehicle. **5.** Music. **a.** denoting the highest part assigned to one of the voice parts in a chorus or one of the sections of an orchestra: the first violins. **b.** denoting the principal player in a specific orchestral section: he plays first horn. **6. first thing.** as the first action of the day: I'll see you first thing tomorrow. ~n. **7.** the beginning; outset: I couldn't see at first because of the mist. **8.** Education, chiefly Brit. an honours degree of the highest class. Full term: **first-class honours degree. 9.** the lowest forward ratio of a gearbox in a motor vehicle. ~adv. **10.** Also: **firstly.** before anything else in order, time, importance, etc.: do this first. **11. first and last.** on the whole. **12. from first to last.** throughout. **13.** for the first time: I've loved you since I first saw you. **14.** (sentence modifier) in the first place or beginning of a series of actions.

first aid n. **a.** immediate medical assistance given in an emergency. **b.** (as modifier): first-aid box.

first-born adj. **1.** eldest of the children in a family. ~n. **2.** the eldest child in a family.

first class n. **1.** the class or grade of the best or highest value, quality, etc. ~adj. (**first-class** when prenominal). **2.** of the best or highest class or grade: a first-class citizen. **3.** excellent. **4.** of or denoting the most comfortable class of accommodation in a hotel, aircraft, train, etc. **5.** (in Britain) of letters that are handled faster than second-class letters. ~adv. **first-class. 6.** by first-class mail, means of transportation, etc.

first-day cover n. Philately. an envelope postmarked on the first day of the issue of its stamps.

first-degree burn n. Pathol. the least severe type of burn, in which the skin surface is red and painful.

first-foot Chiefly Scot. ~n. Also **first-footer. 1.** the first person to enter a household in the New Year. ~vb. **2.** to enter (a house) as first-foot. —'**first**-'**footing** n.

first fruits pl. n. **1.** the first results or profits of an undertaking. **2.** fruit that ripens first.

first-hand adj., adv. **1.** from the original source: he got the news first-hand. **2. at first hand.** directly.

first lady n. (often caps.) U.S. the wife or official hostess of a state governor or a president.

firstly ('fɜːstlɪ) adv. another word for **first.**

first mate n. an officer second in command to the captain of a merchant ship.

first night n. **a.** the first public performance of a play, etc. **b.** (as modifier): first-night nerves. —,**first**-'**nighter** n.

first offender n. a person convicted of a criminal offence for the first time.

first officer n. **1.** another name for **first mate. 2.** the member of an aircraft crew who is second in command to the captain.

first person n. a grammatical category of pronouns and verbs used by the speaker to refer to or talk about himself.

first-rate adj. **1.** of the best or highest rated class or quality. **2.** Inf. very good; excellent.

first water n. **1.** the finest quality of diamond or other precious stone. **2.** the highest grade or best quality.

firth (fɜːθ) or **frith** n. a narrow inlet of the sea, esp. in Scotland.

fiscal ('fɪskəl) adj. **1.** of or relating to government finances, esp. tax revenues. **2.** of or involving financial matters. ~n. **3. a.** (in some countries) a public prosecutor. **b.** Scot. short for **procurator fiscal.** —'**fiscally** adv.

fiscal year n. the U.S. term for **financial year.**

fish (fɪʃ) n., pl. **fish** or **fishes. 1. a.** any of a large group of cold-blooded aquatic vertebrates having jaws, gills, and usually fins and a skin covered in scales: includes the sharks, rays, teleosts, lungfish, etc. **b.** (in combination): fishpond. Related adj.: **piscine. 2.** any of various similar but jawless vertebrates, such as the hagfish and lamprey. **3.** (not in technical use) any of various aquatic invertebrates, such as the cuttlefish and crayfish. **4.** the flesh of fish used as food. **5.** Inf. a person of little emotion or intelligence: a poor fish. **6. drink like a fish.** to drink to excess. **7. have other fish to fry.** to have other activities to do, esp. more important ones. **8. like a fish out of water.** out of one's usual place. **9. neither fish, flesh, nor fowl.** neither this nor that. ~vb. **10.** (intr.) to attempt to catch fish, as with a line and hook or with nets, traps, etc. **11.** (tr.) to fish in (a particular area of water). **12.** to search (a body of water) for something or to search for something, esp. in a body of water. **13.** (intr.; foll. by for) to seek something indirectly: to fish for compliments. ~See also **fish out.** —'**fish,like** adj.

fish cake n. a fried flattened ball of flaked fish mixed with mashed potatoes.

fisher ('fɪʃə) n. **1.** a fisherman. **2.** Also called: **pekan. a.** a large North American marten having dark brown fur. **b.** the fur of this animal.

fisherman ('fɪʃəmən) n., pl. -**men. 1.** a person who fishes as a profession or for sport. **2.** a vessel used for fishing.

fishery ('fɪʃərɪ) n., pl. -**eries. 1. a.** the industry of catching, processing, and selling fish. **b.** a place where this is carried on. **2.** a place where fish are reared. **3.** a fishing ground.

fish-eye lens n. Photog. a lens of small focal length, having a highly curved protruding front element, that covers almost 180°.

fishfinger ('fɪʃ,fɪŋgə) or U.S. **fish stick** n. an oblong piece of filleted or minced fish coated in breadcrumbs.

fishing ('fɪʃɪŋ) n. **a.** the occupation of catching fish. **b.** (as modifier): a fishing match.

fishing rod n. a long tapered flexible pole for use with a fishing line and, usually, a reel.

fish meal n. ground dried fish used as feed for farm animals, as a fertilizer, etc.

fishmonger ('fɪʃ,mʌŋgə) n. Chiefly Brit. a retailer of fish.

fishnet ('fɪʃ,nɛt) n. **a.** an open mesh fabric resembling netting. **b.** (as modifier): fishnet tights.

fish out vb. (tr., adv.) to find or extract (something): to fish keys out of a pocket.

fishplate ('fɪʃ,pleɪt) n. a flat piece of metal joining one rail or beam to the next, esp. on railway tracks.

fishtail ('fɪʃ,teɪl) n. **1.** an aeroplane manoeuvre in which the tail is moved from side to side to reduce speed. **2.** a nozzle having a long narrow slot at the top, placed over a Bunsen burner to produce a thin fanlike flame.

fishwife ('fɪʃ,waɪf) n., pl. -**wives. 1.** a woman who sells fish. **2.** a coarse scolding woman.

fishy ('fɪʃɪ) adj. **fishier, fishiest. 1.** of, involving, or suggestive of fish. **2.** abounding in fish. **3.** Inf. suspicious,

---

THESAURUS

firmament empyrean (Literary), heaven, heavens, sky, the blue, the skies, vault, vault of heaven, welkin (Archaic)

firmly 1. enduringly, immovably, like a rock, motionlessly, securely, steadily, tightly, unflinchingly, unshakably 2. determinedly, resolutely, staunchly, steadfastly, strictly, through thick and thin, unchangeably, unwaveringly, with a rod of iron, with decision

firmness 1. compactness, density, fixedness, hardness, inelasticity, inflexibility, resistance, rigidity, solidity, stiffness 2. immovability, soundness, stability, steadiness, strength, tautness, tensile strength, tension, tightness 3. constancy, fixedness, fixity of purpose, inflexibility, obduracy, resolution,

resolve, staunchness, steadfastness, strength of will, strictness

first adj. 1. chief, foremost, head, highest, leading, pre-eminent, prime, principal, ruling 2. earliest, initial, introductory, maiden, opening, original, premier, primeval, primitive, primordial, pristine 3. basic, cardinal, elementary, fundamental, key, primary, rudimentary ~adv. 4. at the beginning, at the outset, before all else, beforehand, firstly, initially, in the first place, to begin with, to start with ~n. 5. As in **from the first** beginning, commencement, inception, introduction, outset, start, starting point, word 'go' (Inf.)

firsthand direct, straight from the horse's mouth

first-rate admirable, A-one (Inf.), crack (Sl.), elite, excellent, exceptional, exclusive, first class, outstanding, prime, second to none, superb, superlative, tiptop, top, topnotch (Inf.), tops (Sl.)

fish out extract, extricate, find, haul out, produce, pull out

fishy 1. Inf. doubtful, dubious, funny (Inf.), implausible, improbable, odd, queer, questionable, suspect, suspicious, unlikely 2. blank, deadpan, dull, expressionless, glassy, glassy-eyed, inexpressive, lacklustre, lifeless, vacant, wooden 3. fishlike, piscatorial, piscatory, piscine

doubtful, or questionable. **4.** dull and lifeless: *a fishy look.* —**'fishily** *adv.*

fissile ('fɪsaɪl) *adj.* **1.** *Brit.* capable of undergoing nuclear fission. **2.** fissionable. **3.** tending to split or capable of being split.

fission ('fɪʃən) *n.* **1.** the act or process of splitting or breaking into parts. **2.** *Biol.* a form of asexual reproduction involving a division into two or more equal parts. **3.** short for **nuclear fission.** —**'fissionable** *adj.*

fissure ('fɪʃə) *n.* **1.** any long narrow cleft or crack, esp. in a rock. **2.** a weakness or flaw. **3.** *Anat.* a narrow split or groove that divides an organ such as the brain, lung, or liver into lobes. ~*vb.* **4.** to crack or split apart.

fist (fɪst) *n.* **1.** a hand with the fingers clenched into the palm, as for hitting. **2.** Also called: **fistful.** the quantity that can be held in a fist or hand. **3.** *Inf.* handwriting. **4.** an informal word for **index** (sense 9). ~*vb.* **5.** (*tr.*) to hit with the fist.

fisticuffs ('fɪstɪ,kʌfs) *pl. n.* combat with the fists.

fistula ('fɪstjʊlə) *n., pl.* **-las** *or* **-lae** (-,liː). *Pathol.* an abnormal opening between one hollow organ and another or between a hollow organ and the surface of the skin, caused by ulceration, malformation, etc. —**'fistulous** *or* **'fistular** *adj.*

fit[1] (fɪt) *vb.* **fitting, fitted. 1.** to be appropriate or suitable for (a situation, etc.). **2.** to be of the correct size or shape for (a container, etc.). **3.** (*tr.*) to adjust in order to render appropriate. **4.** (*tr.*) to supply with that which is needed. **5.** (*tr.*) to try clothes on (someone) in order to make adjustments if necessary. **6.** (*tr.*) to make competent or ready. **7.** (*tr.*) to locate with care. **8.** (*intr.*) to correspond with the facts or circumstances. ~*adj.* **fitter, fittest. 9.** appropriate. **10.** having the right qualifications; qualifying. **11.** in good health. **12.** worthy or deserving. **13.** (*foll. by an infinitive*) *Inf.* ready (to); strongly disposed (to): *she was fit to scream.* ~*n.* **14.** the manner in which something fits. **15.** the act or process of fitting. ~See also **fit in, fit out.** —**'fitly** *adv.* —**'fitness** *n.* —**'fittable** *adj.*

fit[2] (fɪt) *n.* **1.** *Pathol.* a sudden attack or convulsion, such as an epileptic seizure. **2.** a sudden spell of emotion: *a fit of anger.* **3.** an impulsive period of activity or lack of activity. **4. by fits (and starts).** in spasmodic spells. **5. have** *or* **throw a fit.** *Inf.* to become very angry.

fitful ('fɪtfʊl) *adj.* characterized by or occurring in irregular spells. —**'fitfully** *adv.*

fit in *vb.* **1.** (*tr.*) to give a place or time to. **2.** (*intr., adv.*) to belong or conform, esp. after adjustment: *he didn't fit in with their plans.*

fitment ('fɪtmənt) *n.* **1.** *Machinery.* an accessory attached to an assembly of parts. **2.** *Chiefly Brit.* a detachable part of the furnishings of a room.

fit out *vb.* (*tr., adv.*) to equip.

fitted ('fɪtɪd) *adj.* **1.** designed for excellent fit: *a fitted suit.* **2.** (of a carpet) cut or sewn to cover a floor completely. **3.** (of furniture) built to fit a particular space: *a fitted cupboard.*

fitter ('fɪtə) *n.* **1.** a person who fits a garment, esp.

when it is made for a particular person. **2.** a person who is skilled in the assembly and adjustment of machinery, esp. of a specified sort.

fitting ('fɪtɪŋ) *adj.* **1.** appropriate or proper. ~*n.* **2.** an accessory or part: *an electrical fitting.* **3.** (*pl.*) furnishings or accessories in a building. **4.** work carried out by a fitter. **5.** the act of trying on clothes so that they can be adjusted to fit. —**'fittingly** *adv.*

five (faɪv) *n.* **1.** the cardinal number that is the sum of four and one. **2.** a numeral, 5, V, etc., representing this number. **3.** the amount or quantity that is one greater than four. **4.** something representing, represented by, or consisting of five units, such as a playing card with five symbols on it. **5. five o'clock.** five hours after noon or midnight. ~*determiner.* **6. a.** amounting to five: *five nights.* **b.** (*as pronoun*): *choose any five you like.* —**fifth** *adj.*

fivefold ('faɪv,fəʊld) *adj.* **1.** equal to or having five times as many or as much. **2.** composed of five parts. ~*adv.* **3.** by or up to five times as many or as much.

fivepins ('faɪv,pɪnz) *n.* (*functioning as sing.*) a bowling game using five pins, played esp. in Canada. —**'five,pin** *adj.*

fiver ('faɪvə) *n.* *Inf. Brit.* a five-pound note.

fives (faɪvz) *n.* (*functioning as sing.*) a ball game similar to squash but played with bats or the hands.

Five-Year Plan *n.* (in socialist economies) a government plan for economic development over a period of five years.

fix (fɪks) *vb.* (*mainly tr.*) **1.** (*also intr.*) to make or become firm, stable, or secure. **2.** to attach or place permanently. **3.** (often foll. by *up*) to settle definitely; decide. **4.** to hold or direct (eyes, etc.) steadily: *he fixed his gaze on the woman.* **5.** to call to attention or rivet. **6.** to make rigid: *to fix one's jaw.* **7.** to place or ascribe: *to fix the blame.* **8.** to mend or repair. **9.** *Inf.* to provide or be provided with: *how are you fixed for supplies?* **10.** *Inf.* to influence (a person, etc.) unfairly, as by bribery. **11.** *Sl.* to take revenge on. **12.** *Inf.* to give (someone) his just deserts: *that'll fix him.* **13.** *Inf., chiefly U.S.* to prepare: *to fix a meal.* **14.** *Dialect or inf.* to spay or castrate (an animal). **15.** *Photog.* to treat (a film, plate, or paper) with fixer to make permanent the image rendered visible by developer. **16.** to convert (atmospheric nitrogen) into nitrogen compounds, as in the manufacture of fertilizers or the action of bacteria in the soil. **17.** to reduce (a substance) to a solid state or a less volatile state. **18.** (*intr.*) *Sl.* to inject a narcotic drug. ~*n.* **19.** *Inf.* a predicament; dilemma. **20.** the ascertaining of the navigational position, as of a ship, by radar, etc. **21.** *Sl.* an intravenous injection of a narcotic such as heroin. —**'fixable** *adj.*

fixation (fɪk'seɪʃən) *n.* **1.** the act of fixing or the state of being fixed. **2.** a preoccupation or obsession. **3.** *Psychol.* **a.** the situation of being set in a certain way of thinking or acting. **b.** a strong attachment of a person to another person or an object in early life. **4.** *Chem.* the conversion of nitrogen in the air into a compound, esp. a

---

═══ T H E S A U R U S ═══

fissure breach, break, chink, cleavage, cleft, crack, cranny, crevice, fault, fracture, gap, hole, interstice, opening, rent, rift, rupture, slit, split

fit[1] *adj.* 1. able, adapted, adequate, appropriate, apt, becoming, capable, competent, convenient, correct, deserving, equipped, expedient, fitted, fitting, good enough, meet (*Archaic*), prepared, proper, qualified, ready, right, seemly, suitable, trained, well-suited, worthy 2. able-bodied, hale, healthy, in good condition, in good shape, in good trim, robust, strapping, toned up, trim, well ~*v.* 3. accord, agree, be consonant, belong, concur, conform, correspond, dovetail, go, interlock, join, match, meet, suit, tally 4. *Often with* **out** *or* **up** accommodate, accoutre, arm, equip, fit out, kit out, outfit, prepare, provide, rig out 5. adapt, adjust, alter, arrange, dispose, fashion, modify, place, position, shape

fit[2] *n.* 1. attack, bout, convulsion, paroxysm, seizure, spasm 2. caprice, fancy, humour, mood, whim 3. bout, burst, outbreak, outburst, spell 4. **by fits and starts** erratically,

fitfully, intermittently, irregularly, on and off, spasmodically, sporadically, unsystematically

fitful broken, desultory, disturbed, erratic, flickering, fluctuating, haphazard, impulsive, intermittent, irregular, spasmodic, sporadic, unstable, variable

fitfully desultorily, erratically, in fits and starts, in snatches, intermittently, interruptedly, irregularly, off and on, spasmodically, sporadically

fitness 1. adaptation, applicability, appropriateness, aptness, competence, eligibility, pertinence, preparedness, propriety, qualifications, readiness, seemliness, suitability 2. good condition, good health, health, robustness, strength, vigour

fitted 1. adapted, cut out for, equipped, fit, qualified, right, suitable, tailor-made 2. *Often with* **with** accoutred, appointed, armed, equipped, furnished, outfitted, provided, rigged out, set up, supplied 3. built-in, permanent

fitting 1. *adj.* appropriate, becoming, *comme il faut*, correct, decent, decorous, de-

sirable, meet (*Archaic*), proper, right, seemly, suitable 2. *n.* accessory, attachment, component, connection, part, piece, unit

fix *v.* 1. anchor, embed, establish, implant, install, locate, place, plant, position, root, set, settle 2. attach, bind, cement, connect, couple, fasten, glue, link, make fast, pin, secure, stick, tie 3. agree on, appoint, arrange, arrive at, conclude, decide, define, determine, establish, limit, name, resolve, set, settle, specify 4. adjust, correct, mend, patch up, put to rights, regulate, repair, see to, sort 5. congeal, consolidate, harden, rigidify, set, solidify, stiffen, thicken 6. direct, focus, level at, rivet 7. *Inf.* bribe, fiddle, influence, manipulate, manoeuvre, pull strings (*Inf.*), rig 8. *Sl.* cook (someone's) goose (*Inf.*), get even with, get revenge on, pay back, settle (someone's) hash (*Inf.*), sort (someone) out (*Inf.*), take retribution on, wreak vengeance on ~*n.* 9. *Inf.* difficult situation, difficulty, dilemma, embarrassment, hole (*Sl.*), jam (*Inf.*), mess, pickle (*Inf.*), plight, predicament, quandary, spot (*Inf.*), ticklish situation

fertilizer. **5.** the reduction of a substance to a nonvolatile or solid form.

fixative ('fıksətıv) *adj.* **1.** serving or tending to fix. ~*n.* **2.** a fluid sprayed over drawings to prevent smudging or one that fixes tissues and cells for microscopic study. **3.** a substance added to a liquid, such as a perfume, to make it less volatile.

fixed (fıkst) *adj.* **1.** attached or placed so as to be immovable. **2.** stable: *fixed prices.* **3.** steadily directed: *a fixed expression.* **4.** established as to relative position: *a fixed point.* **5.** always at the same time: *a fixed holiday.* **6.** (of ideas, etc.) firmly maintained. **7.** (of an element) held in chemical combination: *fixed nitrogen.* **8.** (of a substance) nonvolatile. **9.** arranged. **10.** *Inf.* equipped or provided for, as with money, possessions, etc. **11.** *Inf.* illegally arranged: *a fixed trial.* —**fixedly** ('fıksıdlı) *adv.* —'**fixedness** *n.*

fixed star *n.* an extremely distant star whose position appears to be almost stationary over a long period of time.

fixer ('fıksə) *n.* **1.** *Photog.* a solution used to dissolve unexposed silver halides after developing. **2.** *Sl.* a person who makes arrangements, esp. by underhand or illegal means.

fixity ('fıksıtı) *n., pl.* **-ties.** **1.** the state or quality of being fixed. **2.** a fixture.

fixture ('fıkstʃə) *n.* **1.** an object firmly fixed in place, esp. a household appliance. **2.** a person or thing regarded as fixed in a particular place or position. **3.** *Property law.* an article attached to land and regarded as part of it. **4.** *Chiefly Brit.* **a.** a sports match or social occasion. **b.** the date of such an event.

fizz (fız) *vb.* (*intr.*) **1.** to make a hissing or bubbling sound. **2.** (of a drink) to produce bubbles of carbon dioxide. ~*n.* **3.** a hissing or bubbling sound. **4.** the bubbly quality of a drink; effervescence. **5.** any effervescent drink. —'**fizzy** *adj.* —'**fizziness** *n.*

fizzle ('fızl) *vb.* (*intr.*) **1.** to make a hissing or bubbling sound. **2.** (often foll. by *out*) *Inf.* to fail or die out, esp. after a promising start. ~*n.* **3.** a hissing or bubbling sound. **4.** *Inf.* a failure.

fjord *or* **fiord** (fjɔːd) *n.* a long narrow inlet of the sea between high steep cliffs, common in Norway.

fl. *abbrev. for:* **1.** floor. **2.** floruit. **3.** fluid.

flab (flæb) *n.* unsightly or unwanted fat on the body.

flabbergast ('flæbə,gɑːst) *vb.* (*tr.; usually passive*) *Inf.* to amaze utterly; astound.

flabby ('flæbı) *adj.* **-bier, -biest.** **1.** loose or yielding: *flabby muscles.* **2.** having flabby flesh, esp. through being overweight. **3.** lacking vitality; weak. —'**flabbiness** *n.*

flaccid ('flæksıd) *adj.* lacking firmness; soft and limp. —**flac'cidity** *n.*

flag[1] (flæg) *n.* **1.** a piece of cloth, esp. bunting, often attached to a pole or staff, decorated with a design and used as an emblem, symbol, or standard or as a means of signalling. **2.** a small piece of paper, etc., sold on flag days. **3.** the conspicuously marked or shaped tail of a deer or of certain dogs. **4.** *Brit., Austral.* the part of a taximeter that is raised when a taxi is for hire. **5. show the flag. a.** to assert a claim by military presence. **b.** *Inf.* to make an appearance. ~*vb.* **flagging, flagged.** (*tr.*) **6.** to decorate or mark with a flag or flags. **7.** (of-

ten foll. by *down*) to warn or signal (a vehicle) to stop. **8.** to send or communicate (messages, information, etc.) by flag. —'**flagger** *n.*

flag[2] (flæg) *n.* **1.** any of various plants that have long swordlike leaves, esp. an iris (**yellow flag**). **2.** the leaf of any such plant.

flag[3] (flæg) *vb.* **flagging, flagged.** (*intr.*) **1.** to hang down; droop. **2.** to become weak or tired.

flag[4] (flæg) *n.* **1.** short for **flagstone.** ~*vb.* **flagging, flagged.** **2.** (*tr.*) to furnish (a floor, etc.) with flagstones.

flag day *n.* a day on which money is collected by a charity and small flags or emblems are given to contributors.

flagellant ('flædʒılənt, flə'dʒɛlənt) *or* **flagellator** ('flædʒı,leıtə) *n.* a person who whips himself or others either as part of a religious penance or for sexual gratification.

flagellate *vb.* ('flædʒı,leıt). **1.** (*tr.*) to whip; flog. ~*adj.* ('flædʒılıt), *also* **flagellated.** **2.** possessing one or more flagella. **3.** whiplike. ~*n.* ('flædʒılıt). **4.** a flagellate organism. —,**flagel'lation** *n.*

flagellum (flə'dʒɛləm) *n., pl.* **-la** (-lə) *or* **-lums.** **1.** *Biol.* a long whiplike outgrowth from a cell that acts as an organ of locomotion: occurs in some protozoans, gametes, etc. **2.** *Bot.* a long thin shoot or runner. —**fla'gellar** *adj.*

flageolet (,flædʒə'lɛt) *n.* a high-pitched musical instrument of the recorder family.

flag of convenience *n.* a national flag flown by a ship registered in that country to gain financial or legal advantage.

flag of truce *n.* a white flag indicating an invitation to an enemy to negotiate.

flagon ('flægən) *n.* **1.** a large bottle of wine, cider, etc. **2.** a vessel having a handle, spout, and narrow neck.

flagpole ('flæg,pəʊl) *or* **flagstaff** ('flæg,stɑːf) *n., pl.* **-poles, -staffs,** *or* **-staves** (-,steıvz). a pole or staff on which a flag is hoisted and displayed.

flagrant ('fleıgrənt) *adj.* blatant; outrageous. —'**flagrancy** *n.* —'**flagrantly** *adv.*

flagship ('flæg,ʃıp) *n.* **1.** a ship, esp. in a fleet, aboard which the commander of the fleet is quartered. **2.** the most important ship belonging to a shipping company.

flagstone ('flæg,stəʊn) *n.* **1.** a hard fine-textured rock that can be split up into slabs for paving. **2.** a slab of such a rock.

flag-waving *n. Inf.* an emotional appeal intended to arouse patriotic feeling. —'**flag-,waver** *n.*

flail (fleıl) *n.* **1.** an implement used for threshing grain, consisting of a wooden handle with a free-swinging metal or wooden bar attached to it. ~*vb.* **2.** (*tr.*) to beat with or as if with a flail. **3.** to thresh about: *with arms flailing.*

flair (fleə) *n.* **1.** natural ability; talent. **2.** perceptiveness. **3.** *Inf.* stylishness or elegance: *to dress with flair.*

flak *or* **flack** (flæk) *n.* **1.** anti-aircraft fire or artillery. **2.** *Inf.* adverse criticism.

flake (fleık) *n.* **1.** a small thin piece or layer chipped off or detached from an object or substance. **2.** a small piece or particle: *a flake of snow.* **3.** *Archaeol.* a fragment removed by chipping from a larger stone used as a tool or weapon. ~*vb.* **4.** to peel or cause to peel off in flakes. **5.** to cover or become covered with or as with

fixation complex, hang-up (*Inf.*), *idée fixe*, infatuation, mania, obsession, preoccupation, thing (*Inf.*)

fixed **1.** anchored, attached, established, immovable, made fast, permanent, rigid, rooted, secure, set **2.** intent, level, resolute, steady, unbending, unblinking, undeviating, unflinching, unwavering **3.** agreed, arranged, decided, definite, established, planned, resolved, settled **4.** going, in working order, mended, put right, repaired, sorted **5.** *Inf.* framed, manipulated, packed, put-up, rigged

fix up **1.** agree on, arrange, fix, organize, plan, settle, sort out **2.** *Often with* **with** accommodate, arrange for, bring about, furnish, lay on, provide

fizz bubble, effervesce, fizzle, froth, hiss, sparkle, sputter

fizzle out abort, collapse, come to nothing, die away, end in disappointment, fail,

fall through, fold (*Inf.*), miss the mark, peter out

fizzy bubbling, bubbly, carbonated, effervescent, gassy, sparkling

flabbergasted abashed, amazed, astonished, astounded, bowled over (*Inf.*), confounded, dazed, disconcerted, dumbfounded, nonplussed, overcome, overwhelmed, rendered speechless, speechless, staggered, struck dumb, stunned

flag[1] *v.* abate, decline, die, droop, ebb, fade, fail, faint, fall, fall off, feel the pace, languish, peter out, pine, sag, sink, slump, succumb, taper off, wane, weaken, weary, wilt

flag[2] *n.* **1.** banderole, banner, colours, ensign, gonfalon, jack, pennant, pennon, standard, streamer ~*v.* **2.** *Sometimes with* **down** hail, salute, signal, warn, wave **3.** docket, indicate, label, mark, note, tab

flagging declining, decreasing, deterio-

rating, ebbing, fading, failing, faltering, giving up, sinking, slowing down, tiring, waning, weakening, wilting

flagrant arrant, atrocious, awful, barefaced, blatant, bold, brazen, crying, dreadful, egregious, enormous, flagitious, flaunting, glaring, heinous, immodest, infamous, notorious, open, ostentatious, out-and-out, outrageous, scandalous, shameless, undisguised

flagstone block, flag, paving stone, slab

flail *v.* beat, thrash, thresh, windmill

flair **1.** ability, accomplishment, aptitude, faculty, feel, genius, gift, knack, mastery, talent **2.** chic, dash, discernment, elegance, panache, style, stylishness, taste

flake **1.** *n.* disk, lamina, layer, peeling, scale, shaving, sliver, squama (*Biol.*), wafer **2.** *v.* blister, chip, desquamate, peel (off), scale (off)

flakes. **6.** (*tr.*) to form into flakes. —'**flaky** *adj.*

flake out *vb.* (*intr., adv.*) *Inf.* to become unconscious as through extreme exhaustion.

flambé (ˈflɑːmbeɪ) *adj.* (of food, such as steak or pancakes) served in flaming brandy, etc.

flamboyant (flæmˈbɔɪənt) *adj.* **1.** elaborate or extravagant; showy. **2.** rich or brilliant in colour. **3.** exuberant or ostentatious. **4.** of the French Gothic style of architecture characterized by flamelike tracery and elaborate carving. —**flam'boyance** *or* **flam'boyancy** *n.* —**flam'boyantly** *adv.*

flame (fleɪm) *n.* **1.** a hot usually luminous body of burning gas emanating in flickering streams from burning material or produced by a jet of ignited gas. **2.** (*often pl.*) the state or condition of burning with flames: *to burst into flames.* **3.** a brilliant light. **4.** a strong reddish-orange colour. **5.** intense passion or ardour. **6.** *Inf.* a lover or sweetheart (esp. in **an old flame**). ~*vb.* **7.** to burn or cause to burn brightly. **8.** (*intr.*) to become red or fiery: *his face flamed with anger.* **9.** (*intr.*) to become angry or excited. **10.** (*tr.*) to apply a flame to (something). —'**flame,like** *adj.* —'**flamy** *adj.*

flamenco (fləˈmɛŋkəʊ) *n., pl.* **-cos.** **1.** a type of dance music for vocal soloist and guitar, characterized by sad mood. **2.** the dance performed to such music.

flame-thrower *n.* a weapon that ejects a stream or spray of burning fluid.

flaming ('fleɪmɪŋ) *adj.* **1.** burning with or emitting flames. **2.** glowing brightly. **3.** intense or ardent: *a flaming temper.* **4.** *Inf.* (intensifier): *you flaming idiot.*

flamingo (fləˈmɪŋgəʊ) *n., pl.* **-gos** *or* **-goes.** a large wading bird having a pink-and-red plumage and downward-bent bill and inhabiting brackish lakes.

flammable ('flæməb'l) *adj.* readily combustible; inflammable. —,**flamma'bility** *n.*

▷ **Usage.** *Flammable* and *inflammable* are interchangeable when used of the properties of materials. *Flammable* is, however, often preferred for warning labels as there is less likelihood of misunderstanding (*inflammable* being sometimes taken to mean *not flammable*). The word that does mean *not flammable* is *nonflammable.*

flan (flæn) *n.* **1.** an open pastry or sponge tart filled with fruit or a savoury mixture. **2.** a piece of metal ready to receive the die or stamp in the production of coins.

flange (flændʒ) *n.* **1.** a radially projecting collar or rim on an object for strengthening it or for attaching it to another object. **2.** a flat outer face of a rolled-steel joist. ~*vb.* **3.** (*tr.*) to provide (a component) with a flange. —'**flangeless** *adj.*

flank (flæŋk) *n.* **1.** the side of a man or animal between the ribs and the hip. **2.** a cut of beef from the flank. **3.** the side of anything, such as a mountain or building. **4.** the side of a naval or military formation. ~*vb.* **5.** (when *intr.*, often foll. by *on* or *upon*) to be located at the side of (an object, etc.). **6.** *Mil.* to position or guard on or beside the flank of (a formation, etc.).

flannel ('flæn'l) *n.* **1.** a soft light woollen fabric with a slight nap, used for clothing, etc. **2.** (*pl.*) trousers or other garments made of flannel. **3.** *Brit.* a small piece of cloth used to wash the face and hands; face flannel. U.S. equivalent: **washcloth.** **4.** *Brit. inf.* indirect or evasive talk. ~*vb.* **-nelling, -nelled** *or U.S.* **-neling, -neled.** (*tr.*)

5. to cover or wrap with flannel. **6.** to rub or polish with flannel. **7.** *Brit. inf.* to flatter. —'**flannelly** *adj.*

flannelette (,flænəˈlɛt) *n.* a cotton imitation of flannel.

flap (flæp) *vb.* **flapping, flapped.** **1.** to move (wings or arms) up and down, esp. in or as if in flying, or (of wings or arms) to move in this way. **2.** to move or cause to move noisily back and forth or up and down: *the curtains flapped in the breeze.* **3.** (*intr.*) *Inf.* to become agitated or flustered. **4.** to deal (a person or thing) a blow with a broad flexible object. ~*n.* **5.** the action, motion, or noise made by flapping: *with one flap of its wings the bird was off.* **6.** a piece of material, etc., attached at one edge and usually used to cover an opening, as on a tent, envelope, or pocket. **7.** a blow dealt with a flat object. **8.** a movable surface fixed to an aircraft wing that increases lift during takeoff and drag during landing. **9.** *Inf.* a state of panic or agitation.

flapdoodle ('flæp,duːd'l) *n. Sl.* foolish talk; nonsense.

flapjack ('flæp,dʒæk) *n.* **1.** a chewy biscuit made with rolled oats. **2.** *Chiefly U.S.* another word for **pancake.**

flapper ('flæpə) *n.* (in the 1920s) a young woman, esp. one flaunting her unconventional behaviour.

flare (flɛə) *vb.* **1.** to burn or cause to burn with an unsteady or sudden bright flame. **2.** to burn off excess gas or oil. **3.** to spread or cause to spread outwards from a narrow to a wider shape. ~*n.* **4.** an unsteady flame. **5.** a sudden burst of flame. **6. a.** a blaze of light or fire used to illuminate, identify, alert, etc. **b.** the device producing such a blaze. **7.** a spreading shape or anything with a spreading shape: *a skirt with a flare.*

flare-up *n.* **1.** a sudden burst of fire or light. **2.** *Inf.* a sudden burst of emotion or violence. ~*vb.* **flare up.** (*intr., adv.*). **3.** to burst suddenly into fire or light. **4.** *Inf.* to burst into anger.

flash (flæʃ) *n.* **1.** a sudden short blaze of intense light or flame: *a flash of sunlight.* **2.** a sudden occurrence or display, esp. one suggestive of brilliance: *a flash of understanding.* **3.** a very brief space of time: *over in a flash.* **4.** Also called: **news flash.** a short news announcement concerning a new event. **5.** *Chiefly Brit.* an insignia or emblem worn on a uniform, vehicle, etc., to identify its military formation. **6.** a sudden rush of water down a river or watercourse. **7.** *Photog., inf.* short for **flashlight** (sense 2). **8.** (*modifier*) involving, using, or produced by a flash of heat, light, etc.: *flash distillation.* **9. flash in the pan.** a project, person, etc., that enjoys only short-lived success. ~*adj.* **10.** *Inf.* ostentatious or vulgar. **11.** sham or counterfeit. **12.** *Inf.* relating to or characteristic of the criminal underworld. ~*vb.* **13.** to burst or cause to burst suddenly or intermittently into flame. **14.** to emit or reflect or cause to emit or reflect light suddenly or intermittently. **15.** (*intr.*) to move very fast: *he flashed by on his bicycle.* **16.** (*intr.*) to come rapidly (into the mind or vision). **17.** (*intr.; foll. by out or up*) to appear like a sudden light. **18. a.** to signal or communicate very fast: *to flash a message.* **b.** to signal by use of a light, such as car headlights. **19.** (*tr.*) *Inf.* to display ostentatiously: *to flash money around.* **20.** (*tr.*) *Inf.* to show suddenly and briefly. **21.** (*intr.*) *Brit. sl.* to expose oneself indecently. **22.** to send a sudden rush of water down (a river, etc.), or to carry (a vessel) down by this method. —'**flasher** *n.*

THESAURUS

flake out collapse, faint, keel over, lose consciousness, pass out, swoon (*Literary*)

flamboyant 1. baroque, elaborate, extravagant, florid, ornate, ostentatious, rich, rococo, showy, theatrical 2. brilliant, colourful, dashing, dazzling, exciting, glamorous, swashbuckling

flame v. 1. blaze, burn, flare, flash, glare, glow, shine ~n. 2. blaze, brightness, fire, light 3. *Fig.* affection, ardour, enthusiasm, fervency, fervour, fire, intensity, keenness, passion, warmth 4. *Inf.* beau, beloved, boyfriend, girlfriend, heart-throb (*Brit.*), ladylove, lover, sweetheart

flameproof fire-resistant, incombustible, nonflammable, non-inflammable

flaming 1. ablaze, afire, blazing, brilliant, burning, fiery, glowing, ignited, in flames, raging, red, red-hot 2. angry, ardent, aroused, frenzied, hot, impassioned, intense, raging,

scintillating, vehement, vivid

flank n. 1. ham, haunch, hip, loin, quarter, side, thigh 2. side, wing ~v. 3. border, bound, edge, fringe, line, screen, skirt, wall

flannel *Fig.* 1. n. baloney (*Inf.*), blarney, equivocation, flattery, hedging, prevarication, soft soap (*Inf.*), sweet talk (*U.S. inf.*), waffle (*Inf.*), weasel words (*Inf., chiefly U.S.*) 2. v. blarney, butter up, equivocate, flatter, hedge, prevaricate, pull the wool over (someone's) eyes, soft-soap (*Inf.*), sweet-talk (*U.S. inf.*), waffle

flap v. 1. agitate, beat, flail, flutter, shake, swing, swish, thrash, thresh, vibrate, wag, wave ~n. 2. bang, banging, beating, flutter, shaking, swinging, swish, waving ~v. 3. *Inf.* dither, fuss, panic ~n. 4. *Inf.* agitation, commotion, fluster, panic, state (*Inf.*), stew (*Inf.*), sweat (*Inf.*), tizzy (*Inf.*), twitter 5. apron, cover, fly, fold, lapel, lappet, overlap,

skirt, tab, tail

flare v. 1. blaze, burn up, dazzle, flicker, flutter, glare, waver 2. *Often with* out broaden, spread out, widen ~n. 3. blaze, burst, dazzle, flame, flash, flicker, glare

flare up blaze, blow one's top (*Inf.*), boil over, break out, explode, fire up, fly off the handle (*Inf.*), lose control, lose one's cool (*Inf.*), lose one's temper, throw a tantrum

flash v. 1. blaze, coruscate, flare, flicker, glare, gleam, glint, glisten, glitter, light, scintillate, shimmer, sparkle, twinkle ~n. 2. blaze, burst, coruscation, dazzle, flare, flicker, gleam, ray, scintillation, shaft, shimmer, spark, sparkle, streak, twinkle ~v. 3. bolt, dart, dash, fly, race, shoot, speed, sprint, streak, sweep, whistle, zoom ~n. 4. instant, jiffy (*Inf.*), moment, second, shake, split second, trice, twinkling, twinkling of an eye, two shakes of a lamb's tail (*Inf.*) ~v. 5. display,

flashback ('flæʃ,bæk) n. a transition in a novel, film, etc., to an earlier scene or event.

flashbulb ('flæʃ,bʌlb) n. Photog. a small expendable glass light bulb that is triggered, usually electrically, to produce a bright flash of light.

flashcube ('flæʃ,kjuːb) n. a boxlike camera attachment, holding four flashbulbs, that turns so that each flashbulb can be used.

flash flood n. a sudden short-lived torrent, usually caused by a heavy storm, esp. in desert regions.

flash gun n. a device, sometimes incorporated in a camera, for holding and electrically firing a flashbulb as the shutter opens.

flashing ('flæʃɪŋ) n. a weatherproof material, esp. thin sheet metal, used to cover the valleys between the slopes of a roof, the junction between a chimney and a roof, etc.

flashlight ('flæʃ,laɪt) n. **1.** another word (esp. U.S.) for **torch**. **2.** Photog. the brief bright light emitted by a flashbulb or electronic flash. Often shortened to **flash**.

flash point n. **1.** the lowest temperature at which the vapour above a liquid can be ignited in air. **2.** a critical moment beyond which a situation will inevitably erupt into violence.

flashy ('flæʃɪ) adj. **flashier, flashiest. 1.** brilliant and dazzling, esp. for a short time or in a superficial way. **2.** cheap and ostentatious. —**'flashily** adv. —**'flashiness** n.

flask (flɑːsk) n. **1.** a bottle with a narrow neck, esp. used in a laboratory or for wine, oil, etc. **2.** Also called: **hip flask**. a small flattened container of glass or metal designed to be carried in a pocket, esp. for liquor. **3.** See **vacuum flask**.

flat[1] (flæt) adj. **flatter, flattest. 1.** horizontal; level: a flat roof. **2.** even or smooth, without projections or depressions: a flat surface. **3.** lying stretched out at full length: he lay flat on the ground. **4.** having little depth or thickness: a flat dish. **5.** (postpositive; often foll. by against) having a surface or side in complete contact with another surface: flat against the wall. **6.** (of a tyre) deflated. **7.** (of shoes) having an unraised heel. **8.** Chiefly Brit. **a.** (of races, racetracks, or racecourses) not having obstacles to be jumped. **b.** of, relating to, or connected with flat racing as opposed to steeplechasing and hurdling. **9.** without qualification; total: a flat denial. **10.** fixed: a flat rate. **11.** (prenominal or immediately postpositive) neither more nor less; exact: he did the journey in thirty minutes flat. **12.** unexciting: a flat joke. **13.** without variation or resonance; monotonous: a flat voice. **14.** (of beer, sparkling wines, etc.) having lost effervescence, as by exposure to air. **15.** (of trade, business, etc.) commercially inactive. **16.** (of a battery) fully discharged. **17.** (of a print, photograph, or painting) lacking contrast. **18.** (of paint) without gloss or lustre. **19.** Music. **a.** (immediately postpositive) denoting a note of a given letter name (or the sound it represents) that has been lowered in pitch by one chromatic semitone: B flat. **b.** (of an instrument, voice, etc.) out of tune by being too low in pitch. Cf. **sharp** (sense 12). **20.** Phonetics. flat **a.** the vowel sound of a as in the usual U.S. or S Brit. pronunciation of hand, cat. ~adv. **21.** in or into a prostrate, level, or flat state or position: he held his hand out flat. **22.** completely or utterly; absolutely. **23.** Music. **a.** lower than a standard pitch. **b.** too low in pitch: she sings flat. Cf. **sharp** (sense 15). **24. fall flat.** to prove a failure, not amusing, etc. **25. flat out.** Inf. **a.** with the maximum speed or effort. **b.** totally exhausted. ~n. **26.** a flat object, surface, or part. **27.** a low-lying tract of land, esp. a marsh or swamp. **28.** a mud bank exposed at low tide. **29.** Music. **a.** an accidental that lowers the pitch of the following note by one chromatic semitone. Usual symbol: ♭ **b.** a note affected by this accidental. Cf. **sharp** (sense 16). **30.** Theatre. a wooden frame covered with painted canvas, etc., used to form part of a stage setting. **31.** a punctured car tyre. **32.** (often cap.; preceded by the) Chiefly Brit. **a.** flat racing, esp. as opposed to steeplechasing and hurdling. **b.** the season of flat racing. ~vb. **flatting, flatted. 33.** to make or become flat. —**'flatly** adv. —**'flatness** n. —**'flattish** adj.

flat[2] (flæt) n. a set of rooms comprising a residence entirely on one floor of a building. Usual U.S. name: **apartment**.

flatboat ('flæt,bəʊt) n. any boat with a flat bottom, usually for transporting goods on a canal.

flatfish ('flæt,fɪʃ) n., pl. **-fish** or **-fishes**. any of an order of marine spiny-finned fish including the halibut, plaice, turbot, and sole, all of which have a flat body which has both eyes on the uppermost side.

flatfoot ('flæt,fʊt) n. **1.** a condition in which the instep arch of the foot is flattened. **2.** (pl. **-foots** or **-feet**.) a slang word (usually derogatory) for a **policeman**.

flat-footed (,flæt'fʊtɪd) adj. **1.** having flatfoot. **2.** Brit. inf. **a.** awkward. **b.** downright. **3.** Inf. off guard (often in **catch flat-footed**). —**,flat-'footedly** adv. —**,flat-'footedness** n.

flatiron ('flæt,aɪən) n. (formerly) an iron for pressing clothes that was heated by being placed on a stove, etc.

flatlet ('flætlɪt) n. a flat having only a few rooms.

flat racing n. **a.** the racing of horses on racecourses without jumps. **b.** (as modifier): the flat-racing season.

flats (flæts) pl. n. shoes with a flat heel or no heel.

flat spin n. **1.** an aircraft spin in which the longitudinal axis is more nearly horizontal than vertical. **2.** Inf. a state of confusion; dither.

flatten ('flæt²n) vb. **1.** (sometimes foll. by out) to make or become flat or flatter. **2.** (tr.) Inf. **a.** to knock down or injure. **b.** to crush or subdue. **3.** (tr.) Music. to lower the pitch of (a note) by one chromatic semitone. —**'flattener** n.

flatter ('flætə) vb. **1.** to praise insincerely, esp. in order to win favour or reward. **2.** to show to advantage: that dress flatters her. **3.** (tr.) to make to appear more attractive, etc., than in reality. **4.** to gratify the vanity of (a person). **5.** (tr.) to encourage, esp. falsely. **6.** (tr.) to deceive (oneself): I flatter myself that I am the best. —**'flatterable** adj. —**'flatterer** n.

flattery ('flætərɪ) n., pl. **-teries. 1.** the act of flattering. **2.** excessive or insincere praise.

flatulent ('flætjʊlənt) adj. **1.** suffering from or caused by an excessive amount of gas in the alimentary canal. **2.** generating excessive gas in the alimentary canal. **3.** pretentious. —**'flatulence** or **'flatulency** n. —**'flatulently** adv.

flatworm ('flæt,wɜːm) n. any parasitic or free-living invertebrate of the phylum Platyhelminthes, including flukes and tapeworms, having a flattened body.

flaunt (flɔːnt) vb. **1.** to display (possessions, oneself, etc.) ostentatiously. **2.** to wave or cause to wave freely. ~n. **3.** the act of flaunting.

THESAURUS

exhibit, expose, flaunt, flourish, show ~n. **6.** burst, demonstration, display, manifestation, outburst, show, sign, touch ~adj. **7.** Inf. cheap, glamorous, ostentatious, tacky (U.S. inf.), tasteless, vulgar

flashy cheap, cheap and nasty, flamboyant, flaunting, garish, gaudy, glittery, glitzy, in poor taste, jazzy (Inf.), loud, meretricious, ostentatious, showy, snazzy (Inf.), tasteless, tawdry, tinselly

flat[1] adj. **1.** even, horizontal, level, levelled, low, planar, plane, smooth, unbroken **2.** laid low, lying full length, outstretched, prostrate, reclining, recumbent, supine **3.** boring, dead, dull, flavourless, insipid, jejune, lacklustre, lifeless, monotonous, pointless, prosaic, spiritless, stale, tedious, uninteresting, vapid, watery, weak **4.** absolute, categorical, direct, downright, explicit, final, fixed, out-and-out,

peremptory, plain, positive, straight, unconditional, unequivocal, unmistakable, unqualified **5.** blown out, burst, collapsed, deflated, empty, punctured ~n. **6.** Often plural lowland, marsh, mud flat, plain, shallow, shoal, strand, swamp ~adv. **7.** absolutely, categorically, completely, exactly, point blank, precisely, utterly **8. flat out** all out, at full gallop, at full speed, at full tilt, for all one is worth, hell for leather, posthaste, under full steam

flat[2] apartment, rooms

flatly absolutely, categorically, completely, positively, unhesitatingly

flatness 1. evenness, horizontality, levelness, smoothness, uniformity **2.** dullness, emptiness, insipidity, monotony, staleness, tedium, vapidity

flatten 1. compress, even out, iron out, level, plaster, raze, roll, smooth off, squash,

trample **2.** bowl over, crush, fell, floor, knock down, knock off one's feet, prostrate, subdue

flatter 1. blandish, butter up, cajole, compliment, court, fawn, flannel (Inf.), humour, inveigle, lay it on (thick) (Sl.), praise, puff, soft-soap (Inf.), sweet-talk (U.S. inf.), wheedle **2.** become, do something for, enhance, set off, show to advantage, suit

flattering 1. becoming, effective, enhancing, kind, well-chosen **2.** adulatory, complimentary, fawning, fulsome, gratifying, honeyed, honey-tongued, ingratiating, laudatory, sugary

flattery adulation, blandishment, blarney, cajolery, false praise, fawning, flannel (Inf.), fulsomeness, honeyed words, obsequiousness, servility, soft-soap (Inf.), sweet-talk (U.S. inf.), sycophancy, toadyism

flautist ('flɔːtɪst) *or U.S.* **flutist** ('fluːtɪst) *n.* a player of the flute.

flavour *or U.S.* **flavor** ('fleɪvə) *n.* **1.** taste perceived in food or liquid in the mouth. **2.** a substance added to food, etc., to impart a specific taste. **3.** a distinctive quality or atmosphere. ~*vb.* **4.** (*tr.*) to impart a flavour or quality to. —'**flavourless** *or U.S.* '**flavorless** *adj.* —'**flavourful** *or U.S.* '**flavorful** *adj.*

flavouring *or U.S.* **flavoring** ('fleɪvərɪŋ) *n.* a substance used to impart a particular flavour to food: *rum flavouring.*

flaw[1] (flɔː) *n.* **1.** an imperfection or blemish. **2.** a crack or rift. **3.** *Law.* an invalidating defect in a document or proceeding. ~*vb.* **4.** to make or become blemished or imperfect. —'**flawless** *adj.*

flaw[2] (flɔː) *n.* a sudden short gust of wind; squall.

flax (flæks) *n.* **1.** a herbaceous plant or shrub that has blue flowers and is cultivated for its seeds (flaxseed) and for the fibres of its stems. **2.** the fibre of this plant, made into thread and woven into linen fabrics. **3.** any of various similar plants. **4.** *N.Z.* a swamp plant producing a fibre that is used by Maoris for decorative work, baskets, etc.

flaxen ('flæksən) *adj.* **1.** of or resembling flax. **2.** of a soft yellow colour: *flaxen hair.*

flay (fleɪ) *vb.* (*tr.*) **1.** to strip off the skin or outer covering of, esp. by whipping. **2.** to attack with savage criticism. —'**flayer** *n.*

flea (fliː) *n.* **1.** a small wingless parasitic blood-sucking jumping insect living on the skin of mammals and birds. **2. flea in one's ear.** *Inf.* a sharp rebuke.

fleabite ('fliː,baɪt) *n.* **1.** the bite of a flea. **2.** a slight or trifling annoyance or discomfort.

flea-bitten *adj.* **1.** bitten by or infested with fleas. **2.** *Inf.* shabby or decrepit.

flea market *n.* an open-air market selling cheap and often second-hand goods.

fleapit ('fliː,pɪt) *n. Inf.* a shabby cinema or theatre.

fleck (flɛk) *n.* **1.** a small marking or streak. **2.** a speck: *a fleck of dust.* ~*vb.* **3.** (*tr.*) Also: **flecker.** to speckle.

fled (flɛd) *vb.* the past tense or past participle of **flee.**

fledge (flɛdʒ) *vb.* **1.** (*tr.*) to feed and care for (a young bird) until it is able to fly. **2.** (*tr.*) Also called: **fletch.** to fit (something, esp. an arrow) with a feather or feathers. **3.** (*tr.*) to cover or adorn with or as if with feathers.

fledgling *or* **fledgeling** ('flɛdʒlɪŋ) *n.* **1.** a young bird that has grown feathers. **2.** a young and inexperienced person.

flee (fliː) *vb.* **fleeing, fled. 1.** to run away from (a place, danger, etc.). **2.** (*intr.*) to run or move quickly. —'**fleer** *n.*

fleece (fliːs) *n.* **1.** the coat of wool that covers the body of a sheep or similar animal. **2.** the wool removed from a single sheep. **3.** something resembling a fleece. **4.** sheepskin or a fabric with soft pile, used as a lining for coats, etc. ~*vb.* (*tr.*) **5.** to defraud or charge exorbitantly. **6.** another term for **shear** (sense 1). —'**fleecy** *adj.*

fleet[1] (fliːt) *n.* **1.** a number of warships organized as a tactical unit. **2.** all the warships of a nation. **3.** a number of aircraft, ships, buses, etc., operating together or under the same ownership.

fleet[2] (fliːt) *adj.* **1.** rapid in movement; swift. **2.** *Poetic.* fleeting. ~*vb.* **3.** (*intr.*) to move rapidly. **4.** (*tr.*) *Obs.* to cause (time) to pass rapidly. —'**fleetly** *adv.* —'**fleetness** *n.*

fleet chief petty officer *n.* a noncommissioned officer in the Royal Navy comparable in rank to a warrant officer in the army or the Royal Air Force.

fleeting ('fliːtɪŋ) *adj.* rapid and transient: *a fleeting glimpse of the sea.* —'**fleetingly** *adv.*

Fleming ('flɛmɪŋ) *n.* a native or inhabitant of Flanders, a medieval principality in the Low Countries, or of Flemish-speaking Belgium.

Flemish ('flɛmɪʃ) *n.* **1.** one of the two official languages of Belgium. **2. the.** (*functioning as pl.*) the Flemings collectively. ~*adj.* **3.** of or characteristic of Flanders, the Flemings, or their language.

flesh (flɛʃ) *n.* **1.** the soft part of the body of an animal or human, esp. muscular tissue, as distinct from bone and viscera. **2.** *Inf.* excess weight; fat. **3.** *Arch.* the edible tissue of animals as opposed to that of fish or, sometimes, fowl. **4.** the thick soft part of a fruit or vegetable. **5.** the human body and its physical or sensual nature as opposed to the soul or spirit. Related adj.: **carnal. 6.** mankind in general. **7.** animate creatures in general. **8.** one's own family; kin (esp. in **one's own flesh and blood**). **9.** a yellowish-pink colour. **10. in the flesh.** in person; actually present. ~*vb.* **11.** (*tr.*) *Hunting.* to stimulate the hunting instinct of (hounds or falcons) by giving them small quantities of raw flesh. **12.** *Arch. or poetic.* to accustom or incite to bloodshed or battle by initial experience. **13.** to fatten; fill out.

fleshly ('flɛʃlɪ) *adj.* **-lier, -liest. 1.** relating to the body; carnal: *fleshly desire.* **2.** worldly as opposed to spiritual. **3.** fat. —'**fleshliness** *n.*

fleshpots ('flɛʃ,pɒts) *pl. n. Often facetious.* **1.** luxurious living. **2.** places where bodily desires are gratified.

flesh wound (wuːnd) *n.* a wound affecting superficial tissues.

fleshy ('flɛʃɪ) *adj.* **fleshier, fleshiest. 1.** plump. **2.** related to or resembling flesh. **3.** *Bot.* (of some fruits, etc.) thick and pulpy. —'**fleshiness** *n.*

fleur-de-lis *or* **fleur-de-lys** (ˌflɜːdə'liː) *n., pl.* **fleurs-de-lis** *or* **fleurs-de-lys** (ˌflɜːdə'liːz). **1.** *Heraldry.* a charge representing a lily with three distinct petals. **2.** another name for **iris** (sense 2).

flew (fluː) *vb.* the past tense of **fly**[1].

flews (fluːz) *pl. n.* the fleshy hanging upper lip of a bloodhound or similar dog.

flex (flɛks) *n.* **1.** *Brit.* a flexible insulated electric cable, used esp. to connect appliances to mains. U.S. name: **cord.** ~*vb.* **2.** to bend or be bent: *he flexed his arm.* **3.** to contract (a muscle) or (of a muscle) to contract.

flexible ('flɛksɪbəl) *adj.* **1.** Also **flexile** ('flɛksaɪl). able to be bent easily without breaking. **2.** adaptable or variable: *flexible working hours.* **3.** able to be persuaded easily. —ˌflexi'bility *n.* —'**flexibly** *adv.*

THESAURUS

flavour *n.* **1.** aroma, essence, extract, flavouring, odour, piquancy, relish, savour, seasoning, smack, tang, taste, zest, zing (*Inf.*) **2.** aspect, character, essence, feel, feeling, property, quality, soupçon, stamp, style, suggestion, tinge, tone, touch ~*v.* **3.** ginger up, imbue, infuse, lace, leaven, season, spice

flavouring essence, extract, spirit, tincture, zest

flaw 1. blemish, defect, disfigurement, failing, fault, imperfection, speck, spot, weakness, weak spot **2.** breach, break, cleft, crack, crevice, fissure, fracture, rent, rift, scission, split, tear

flawed blemished, broken, chipped, cracked, damaged, defective, erroneous, faulty, imperfect, unsound

flawless 1. faultless, impeccable, perfect, spotless, unblemished, unsullied **2.** intact, sound, unbroken, undamaged, whole

fleabite drop in the ocean, nothing, piddling amount, pinprick, trifle

flea-bitten crawling, decrepit, fetid,

flea-ridden, frowsty, grotty (*Sl.*), grubby, infested, insalubrious, lousy, mean, mucky, pediculous (*Medical*), run-down, scabby, scruffy, scurfy, sleazy, slummy, sordid, squalid, tatty, unhygienic

flee abscond, avoid, beat a hasty retreat, bolt, cut and run (*Inf.*), decamp, depart, escape, fly, get away, leave, make a quick exit, make off, make oneself scarce (*Inf.*), make one's escape, make one's getaway, run away, scarper (*Sl.*), shun, skedaddle (*Inf.*), split (*Sl.*), take flight, take off (*Inf.*), take to one's heels, vanish

fleece 1. *Fig.* bleed (*Inf.*), cheat, con (*Sl.*), defraud, despoil, diddle (*Inf.*), mulct, overcharge, plunder, rifle, rip off (*Sl.*), rob, rook (*Sl.*), soak (*Sl., chiefly U.S.*), steal, swindle, take for a ride (*Inf.*), take to the cleaners (*Sl.*) **2.** clip, shear

fleet *n.* argosy, armada, flotilla, naval force, navy, sea power, squadron, task force, vessels, warships

fleeting brief, ephemeral, evanescent,

flitting, flying, fugacious, fugitive, here today, gone tomorrow, momentary, passing, short, short-lived, temporary, transient, transitory

fleetness celerity, lightning speed, nimble-footedness, nimbleness, quickness, rapidity, speed, speediness, swiftness, velocity

flesh 1. beef (*Inf.*), body, brawn, fat, fatness, food, meat, tissue, weight **2.** animality, body, carnality, flesh and blood, human nature, physicality, physical nature, sensuality **3.** homo sapiens, humankind, human race, living creatures, man, mankind, mortality, people, race, stock, world **4. one's own flesh and blood** blood, family, kin, kindred, kinsfolk, kith and kin, relations, relatives

flex *v.* angle, bend, contract, crook, curve, tighten

flexibility adaptability, adjustability, complaisance, elasticity, give (*Inf.*), pliability, pliancy, resilience, springiness, tensility

flexible 1. bendable, ductile, elastic, limber, lithe, mouldable, plastic, pliable, pliant,

flexitime ('flɛksɪˌtaɪm) *n.* a system permitting flexibility of working hours at the beginning or end of each day, provided an agreed number of hours (**core time**) are spent at work. Also called: **flextime**.

flibbertigibbet ('flɪbətɪˌdʒɪbɪt) *n.* an irresponsible, silly, or gossipy person.

flick[1] (flɪk) *vb.* 1. (*tr.*) to touch with or as if with the finger or hand in a quick jerky movement. 2. (*tr.*) to propel or remove by a quick jerky movement, usually of the fingers or hand. 3. to move or cause to move quickly or jerkily. 4. (*intr.;* foll. by *through*) to read or look at (a book, etc.) quickly or idly. ~*n.* 5. a tap or quick stroke with the fingers, a whip, etc. 6. the sound made by such a stroke. 7. a fleck or particle.

flick[2] (flɪk) *n. Sl.* 1. a cinema film. 2. (*pl.*) **the.** the cinema: *what's on at the flicks tonight?*

flicker ('flɪkə) *vb.* 1. (*intr.*) to shine with an unsteady or intermittent light. 2. (*intr.*) to move quickly to and fro. 3. (*tr.*) to cause to flicker. ~*n.* 4. an unsteady or brief light or flame. 5. a swift quivering or fluttering movement.

flick knife *n.* a knife with a retractable blade that springs out when a button is pressed.

flier *or* **flyer** ('flaɪə) *n.* 1. a person or thing that flies or moves very fast. 2. an aviator or pilot. 3. *Inf.* a long flying leap. 4. a rectangular step in a straight flight of stairs. 5. *Athletics. inf.* a flying start.

flight[1] (flaɪt) *n.* 1. the act, skill, or manner of flying. 2. a journey made by a flying animal or object. 3. a group of flying birds or aircraft: *a flight of swallows.* 4. the basic tactical unit of a military air force. 5. a journey through space, esp. of a spacecraft. 6. an aircraft flying on a scheduled journey. 7. a soaring mental journey above or beyond the normal everyday world: *a flight of fancy.* 8. a single line of hurdles across a track in a race. 9. a feather or plastic attachment fitted to an arrow or dart to give it stability in flight. 10. a set of steps or stairs between one landing or floor and the next. ~*vb.* 11. (*tr.*) *Sport.* to cause (a ball, dart, etc.) to float slowly towards its target. 12. (*tr.*) to shoot (a bird) in flight. 13. (*tr.*) to fledge (an arrow or dart).

flight[2] (flaɪt) *n.* 1. the act of fleeing or running away, as from danger. 2. **put to flight.** to cause to run away. 3. **take (to) flight.** to run away; flee.

flight deck *n.* 1. the crew compartment in an airliner. 2. the upper deck of an aircraft carrier from which aircraft take off.

flightless ('flaɪtlɪs) *adj.* (of certain birds and insects) unable to fly.

flight lieutenant *n.* an officer holding a commissioned rank senior to a flying officer and junior to a squadron leader in the Royal Air Force.

flight recorder *n.* an electronic device fitted to an aircraft for collecting and storing information concerning its performance in flight. It is often used to determine the cause of a crash. Also called: **black box.**

flight sergeant *n.* a noncommissioned officer in the Royal Air Force, junior in rank to that of master aircrew.

flighty ('flaɪtɪ) *adj.* **flightier, flightiest.** 1. frivolous and irresponsible. 2. mentally erratic or wandering. —'**flightiness** *n.*

flimsy ('flɪmzɪ) *adj.* **-sier, -siest.** 1. not strong or substantial: *a flimsy building.* 2. light and thin: *a flimsy dress.* 3. unconvincing; weak: *a flimsy excuse.* ~*n.* 4. thin paper used for making carbon copies of a letter, etc. 5. a copy made on such paper. —'**flimsiness** *n.*

flinch (flɪntʃ) *vb.* (*intr.*) 1. to draw back suddenly, as from pain, shock, etc.; wince. 2. (often foll. by *from*) to avoid contact (with): *he never flinched from his duty.* —'**flinchingly** *adv.*

fling (flɪŋ) *vb.* **flinging, flung.** (mainly *tr.*) 1. to throw, esp. with force or abandon. 2. to put or send without warning or preparation: *to fling someone into jail.* 3. (*also intr.*) to move (oneself or a part of the body) with abandon or speed. 4. (usually foll. by *into*) to apply (oneself) diligently and with vigour (to). 5. to cast aside: *she flung away her scruples.* ~*n.* 6. the act or an instance of flinging. 7. a period or occasion of unrestrained or extravagant behaviour. 8. any of various vigorous Scottish reels full of leaps and turns, such as the Highland fling. 9. a trial; try: *to have a fling at something different.* —'**flinger** *n.*

flint (flɪnt) *n.* 1. an impure greyish-black form of quartz that occurs in chalk. It produces sparks when struck with steel and is used in the manufacture of pottery and road-construction materials. Formula: SiO_2. 2. any piece of flint, esp. one used as a primitive tool or for striking fire. 3. a small cylindrical piece of an iron alloy, used in cigarette lighters. 4. Also called: **flint glass.** colourless glass other than plate glass. —'**flinty** *adj.*

flintlock ('flɪntˌlɒk) *n.* 1. an obsolete gunlock in which the charge is ignited by a spark produced by a flint in the hammer. 2. a firearm having such a lock.

flip (flɪp) *vb.* **flipping, flipped.** 1. to throw (something light or small) carelessly or briskly. 2. to throw or flick (an object such as a coin) so that it turns or spins in the air. 3. to flick: *to flip a crumb across the room.* 4. (foll. by *through*) to read or look at (a book, etc.) quickly, idly, or incompletely. 5. (*intr.*) to make a snapping movement or noise with the finger and thumb. 6. (*intr.*) *Sl.,* chiefly *U.S.* to fly into a rage or an emotional outburst (also in **flip one's lid, flip one's top**). ~*n.* 7. a snap or tap, usually with the fingers. 8. a rapid jerk. 9. any alcoholic drink containing beaten egg. ~*adj.* 10. *U.S. inf.* flippant or pert.

flip-flop *n.* 1. a backward handspring. 2. an electronic device or circuit that can assume either of two stable states by the application of a suitable pulse. 3. a complete change of opinion, policy, etc. 4. a repeated flapping noise. 5. Also called (esp. *U.S.*): **thong.** a rubber-soled sandal attached to the foot by a thong between the big toe and the next toe. ~*vb.* **-flopping, -flopped.** 6. (*intr.*) to move with repeated flaps.

flippant ('flɪpənt) *adj.* 1. marked by inappropriate levity; frivolous. 2. impertinent; saucy. —'**flippancy** *n.* —'**flippantly** *adv.*

flipper ('flɪpə) *n.* 1. the flat broad limb of seals, whales, etc., specialized for swimming. 2. (often *pl.*) either of a pair of rubber paddle-like devices worn on the feet as an aid in swimming.

flip side *n.* the less important side of a pop record.

flirt (flɜːt) *vb.* 1. (*intr.*) to behave or act amorously without emotional commitment. 2. (*intr.;* usually foll. by *with*) to deal playfully or carelessly (with something dangerous or serious): *the motorcyclist flirted with death.*

THESAURUS

springy, stretchy, supple, tensile, whippy, willowy, yielding 2. adaptable, adjustable, discretionary, open, variable 3. amenable, biddable, complaisant, compliant, docile, gentle, manageable, responsive, tractable

flick v. 1. dab, fillip, flip, hit, jab, peck, rap, strike, tap, touch 2. *With* **through** browse, flip, glance, skim, skip, thumb ~n. 3. fillip, flip, jab, peck, rap, tap, touch

flicker v. 1. flare, flash, glimmer, gutter, shimmer, sparkle, twinkle 2. flutter, quiver, vibrate, waver ~n. 3. flare, flash, gleam, glimmer, spark 4. atom, breath, drop, glimmer, iota, spark, trace, vestige

flickering fitful, guttering, twinkling, unsteady, wavering

flight[1] 1. flying, mounting, soaring, winging 2. *Of air travel* journey, trip, voyage 3. aerial navigation, aeronautics, air transport, aviation, flying 4. cloud, flock, formation, squad-ron, swarm, unit, wing

flight[2] 1. departure, escape, exit, exodus, fleeing, getaway, retreat, running away 2. **put to flight** chase off, disperse, drive off, rout, scare off, scatter, send packing, stampede 3. **take (to) flight** abscond, beat a retreat, bolt, decamp, do a bunk (*Sl.*), flee, light out (*Inf.*), make a hasty retreat, run away *or* off, withdraw hastily

flimsy 1. delicate, fragile, frail, gimcrack, insubstantial, makeshift, rickety, shaky, shallow, slight, superficial, unsubstantial 2. chiffon, gauzy, gossamer, light, sheer, thin, transparent 3. feeble, frivolous, implausible, inadequate, poor, thin, transparent, trivial, unconvincing, unsatisfactory, weak

flinch baulk, blench, cower, cringe, draw back, duck, flee, quail, recoil, retreat, shirk, shrink, shy away, start, swerve, wince, withdraw

fling v. 1. cast, catapult, chuck (*Inf.*), heave, hurl, jerk, let fly, lob (*Inf.*), pitch, precipitate, propel, send, shy, sling, throw, toss ~n. 2. cast, lob, pitch, shot, throw, toss 3. binge, bit of fun, good time, indulgence, spree 4. attempt, bash (*Inf.*), crack (*Inf.*), gamble, go, shot, stab, trial, try, venture, whirl (*Inf.*)

flip v./n. cast, flick, jerk, pitch, snap, spin, throw, toss, twist

flippancy cheek (*Inf.*), cheekiness, disrespectfulness, frivolity, impertinence, irreverence, levity, pertness, sauciness

flippant cheeky, disrespectful, flip (*Inf.,* chiefly *U.S.*), frivolous, glib, impertinent, impudent, irreverent, offhand, pert, rude, saucy, superficial

3. (*intr.;* usually foll. by *with*) to toy (with): *to flirt with the idea of leaving.* **4.** (*intr.*) to dart; flit. **5.** (*tr.*) to flick or toss. ~*n.* **6.** a person who acts flirtatiously. —'**flirter** *n.*

flirtation (flɜːˈteɪʃən) *n.* **1.** behaviour intended to arouse sexual feelings or advances without emotional commitment. **2.** any casual involvement.

flirtatious (flɜːˈteɪʃəs) *adj.* **1.** given to flirtation. **2.** expressive of playful sexual invitation: *a flirtatious glance.* —'**flir'tatiously** *adv.*

flit (flɪt) *vb.* **flitting, flitted.** (*intr.*) **1.** to move along rapidly and lightly. **2.** to fly rapidly and lightly. **3.** to pass quickly: *a memory flitted into his mind.* **4.** *Scot. & N English dialect.* to move house. **5.** *Brit. inf.* to depart hurriedly and stealthily in order to avoid obligations. ~*n.* **6.** the act or an instance of flitting. **7.** *Brit. inf.* a hurried and stealthy departure in order to avoid obligations. —'**flitter** *n.*

flitch (flɪtʃ) *n.* **1.** a side of pork salted and cured. **2.** a piece of timber cut lengthways from a tree trunk.

flitter ('flɪtə) *vb.* a less common word for **flutter.**

flittermouse ('flɪtəˌmaʊs) *n., pl.* **-mice.** a dialect name for **bat².**

float (fləʊt) *vb.* **1.** to rest or cause to rest on the surface of a fluid or in a fluid or space without sinking: *oil floats on water.* **2.** to move or cause to move buoyantly, lightly, or freely across a surface or through air, water, etc. **3.** to move about aimlessly, esp. in the mind: *thoughts floated before him.* **4.** (*tr.*) **a.** to launch or establish (a commercial enterprise, etc.). **b.** to offer for sale (stock or bond issues, etc.) on the stock market. **5.** (*tr.*) *Finance.* to allow (a currency) to fluctuate against other currencies in accordance with market forces. **6.** (*tr.*) to flood, inundate, or irrigate (land). ~*n.* **7.** something that floats. **8.** *Angling.* an indicator attached to a baited line that sits on the water and moves when a fish bites. **9.** a small hand tool with a rectangular blade used for smoothing plaster, etc. **10.** Also called: **paddle.** a blade of a paddle wheel. **11.** *Brit.* a buoyant garment or device to aid a person in staying afloat. **12.** a structure fitted to the underside of an aircraft to allow it to land on water. **13.** a motor vehicle used to carry a tableau or exhibit in a parade, esp. a civic parade. **14.** a small delivery vehicle, esp. one powered by batteries: *a milk float.* **15.** *Austral. & N.Z.* a vehicle for transporting horses. **16.** a sum of money used by shopkeepers to provide change at the start of the day's business. **17.** the hollow floating ball of a ballcock. —'**floatable** *adj.* —,**floata'bility** *n.* —'**floaty** *adj.*

floatation (fləʊˈteɪʃən) *n.* a variant spelling of **flotation.**

floating ('fləʊtɪŋ) *adj.* **1.** having little or no attachment. **2.** (of an organ or part) displaced from the normal position or abnormally movable: *a floating kidney.* **3.** uncommitted or unfixed: *floating voters.* **4.** *Finance.* **a.** (of capital) available for current use. **b.** (of debt) short-term and unfunded, usually raised to meet current expenses. **c.** (of a currency) free to fluctuate against other currencies in accordance with market forces. —'**floatingly** *adv.*

floats (fləʊts) *pl. n. Theatre.* another word for **footlights.**

flocculent ('flɒkjʊlənt) *adj.* **1.** like wool; fleecy. **2.** *Chem.* aggregated in woolly cloudlike masses: *a flocculent precipitate.* **3.** *Biol.* covered with tufts or flakes. —'**flocculence** *n.*

flock¹ (flɒk) *n.* (*sometimes functioning as pl.*) **1.** a group of animals of one kind, esp. sheep or birds. **2.** a large number of people. **3.** a body of Christians regarded as the pastoral charge of a priest, bishop, etc. ~*vb.* (*intr.*) **4.** to gather together or move in a flock. **5.** to go in large numbers: *people flocked to the church.*

flock² (flɒk) *n.* **1.** a tuft, as of wool, hair, cotton, etc. **2.** waste from fabrics such as cotton or wool used for stuffing mattresses, etc. **3.** Also called: **flocking.** very small tufts of wool applied to fabrics, wallpaper, etc., to give a raised pattern. —'**flocky** *adj.*

floe (fləʊ) *n.* See **ice floe.**

flog (flɒg) *vb.* **flogging, flogged.** **1.** (*tr.*) to beat harshly, esp. with a whip, strap, etc. **2.** *Brit. sl.* to sell. **3.** (*intr.*) to make progress by painful work. **4. flog a dead horse.** to pursue a line of attack or argument from which no results can come. —'**flogger** *n.*

flood (flʌd) *n.* **1. a.** the inundation of land that is normally dry through the overflowing of a body of water, esp. a river. **b.** the state of a river that is at an abnormally high level. Related adj.: **diluvial.** **2.** a great outpouring or flow: *a flood of words.* **3.** the rising of the tide from low to high water. **b.** (*as modifier*): *the flood tide.* Cf. **ebb** (sense 3). **4.** *Theatre.* short for **floodlight.** ~*vb.* **5.** (of water) to inundate or submerge (land) or (of land) to be inundated or submerged. **6.** to fill or be filled to overflowing, as with a flood. **7.** (*intr.*) to flow; surge: *relief flooded through him.* **8.** to supply an excessive quantity of petrol to (a carburettor or petrol engine) or (of a carburettor, etc.) to be supplied with such an excess. **9.** (*intr.*) to overflow. **10.** (*intr.*) to bleed profusely from the uterus, as following childbirth.

Flood (flʌd) *n. Old Testament.* **the.** the flood from which Noah and his family and livestock were saved in the ark (Genesis 7-8).

floodgate ('flʌdˌgeɪt) *n.* **1.** Also called: **head gate, water gate.** a gate in a sluice that is used to control the flow of water. **2.** (*often pl.*) a control or barrier against an outpouring or flow.

floodlight ('flʌdˌlaɪt) *n.* **1.** a broad intense beam of artificial light, esp. as used in the theatre or to illuminate the exterior of buildings. **2.** the lamp producing such light. ~*vb.* **-lighting, -lit.** **3.** (*tr.*) to illuminate as by floodlight.

floor (flɔː) *n.* **1.** Also called: **flooring.** the inner lower surface of a room. **2.** a storey of a building: *the second floor.* **3.** a flat bottom surface in or on any structure: *a dance floor.* **4.** the bottom surface of a tunnel, cave, sea, etc. **5.** that part of a legislative hall in which debate and other business is conducted. **6.** the right to speak in a legislative body (esp. in **get, have,** or **be given the floor**). **7.** the room in a stock exchange where trading takes place. **8.** the earth; ground. **9.** a minimum price charged or paid. **10. take the floor.** to begin dancing on a dance floor. ~*vb.* **11.** to cover with or construct a floor. **12.** (*tr.*) to knock to the floor or ground. **13.** (*tr.*) *Inf.* to disconcert, confound, or defeat.

floorboard ('flɔːˌbɔːd) *n.* one of the boards forming a floor.

flooring ('flɔːrɪŋ) *n.* **1.** the material used in making a floor. **2.** another word for **floor** (sense 1).

floor plan *n.* a drawing to scale of the arrangement of rooms on one floor of a building.

floor show *n.* a series of entertainments, such as singing and dancing, performed in a nightclub.

floozy, floozie, or **floosie** ('fluːzɪ) *n., pl.* **-zies** or **-sies.** *Sl.* a disreputable woman.

THESAURUS

flirt *v.* **1.** chat up (*Inf.*), coquet, dally, lead on, make advances, make eyes at, philander **2.** *Usually with* **with** consider, dabble in, entertain, expose oneself to, give a thought to, play with, toy with, trifle with ~*n.* **3.** coquette, heart-breaker, philanderer, tease, trifler, wanton

flirtation coquetry, dalliance, intrigue, philandering, teasing, toying, trifling

flirtatious amorous, arch, come-hither, come-on (*Inf.*), coquettish, coy, enticing, flirty, provocative, sportive, teasing

flirting amorous play, chatting up (*Inf.*), coquetry, dalliance, sport

float *v.* **1.** be *or* lie on the surface, be buoyant, displace water, hang, hover, poise, rest on water, stay afloat **2.** bob, drift, glide, move gently, sail, slide, slip along **3.** get going,

launch, promote, push off, set up

floating **1.** afloat, buoyant, buoyed up, nonsubmersible, ocean-going, sailing, swimming, unsinkable **2.** fluctuating, free, migratory, movable, unattached, uncommitted, unfixed, variable, wandering

flock *v.* **1.** collect, congregate, converge, crowd, gather, group, herd, huddle, mass, throng, troop ~*n.* **2.** colony, drove, flight, gaggle, herd, skein **3.** assembly, bevy, collection, company, congregation, convoy, crowd, gathering, group, herd, host, mass, multitude, throng

flog **1.** beat, castigate, chastise, flagellate, flay, lash, scourge, thrash, trounce, whack, whip **2.** drive, oppress, overexert, overtax, overwork, punish, push, strain, tax

flogging beating, caning, flagellation, hid-

ing (*Inf.*), horsewhipping, lashing, scourging, thrashing, trouncing, whipping

flood *v.* **1.** brim over, deluge, drown, immerse, inundate, overflow, pour over, submerge, swamp **2.** engulf, flow, gush, overwhelm, rush, surge, swarm, sweep **3.** choke, fill, glut, oversupply, saturate ~*n.* **4.** deluge, downpour, flash flood, freshet, inundation, overflow, spate, tide, torrent **5.** abundance, flow, glut, multitude, outpouring, profusion, rush, stream, torrent

floor **1.** *n.* level, stage, storey, tier **2.** *v. Fig.* baffle, beat, bewilder, bowl over (*Inf.*), bring up short, confound, conquer, defeat, discomfit, disconcert, dumbfound, knock down, nonplus, overthrow, perplex, prostrate, puzzle, stump, throw (*Inf.*)

flop ('flɒp) *vb.* **flopping, flopped.** **1.** (*intr.*) to bend, fall, or collapse loosely or carelessly: *his head flopped backwards.* **2.** (when *intr.*, often foll. by *into*, *onto*, etc.) to fall, cause to fall, or move with a sudden noise. **3.** (*intr.*) *Inf.* to fail: *the scheme flopped.* **4.** (*intr.*) to fall flat onto the surface of water. **5.** (*intr.*; often foll. by *out*) *Sl.* to go to sleep. ~*n.* **6.** the act of flopping. **7.** *Inf.* a complete failure. —'**floppy** *adj.*

floppy disk *n.* a flexible magnetic disk that stores information and can be used to store data in the memory of a digital computer.

flora ('flɔːrə) *n., pl.* **-ras** *or* **-rae** (-riː). **1.** all the plant life of a given place or time. **2.** a descriptive list of such plants, often including a key for identification.

floral ('flɔːrəl) *adj.* **1.** decorated with or consisting of flowers or patterns of flowers. **2.** of or associated with flowers. —'**florally** *adv.*

Florentine ('flɒrən‚taɪn) *adj.* **1.** of or relating to Florence, in Italy. ~*n.* **2.** a native or inhabitant of Florence.

floret ('flɔːrɪt) *n.* a small flower, esp. one of many making up the head of a composite flower.

floribunda (‚flɒrɪ'bʌndə) *n.* any of several varieties of cultivated hybrid roses whose flowers grow in large sprays.

florid ('flɒrɪd) *adj.* **1.** having a red or flushed complexion. **2.** excessively ornate; flowery: *florid architecture.* —flo'**ridity** *n.* —'**floridly** *adv.*

florin ('flɒrɪn) *n.* **1.** a former British coin, originally silver, equivalent to ten (new) pence. **2.** (formerly) another name for **guilder** (sense 1).

florist ('flɒrɪst) *n.* a person who grows or deals in flowers.

floss (flɒs) *n.* **1.** the mass of fine silky fibres obtained from cotton and similar plants. **2.** any similar fine silky material. **3.** untwisted silk thread used in embroidery, etc. **4.** Also called: **dental floss.** a waxed thread used to remove food particles from between teeth. —'**flossy** *adj.*

flotation *or* **floatation** (fləʊ'teɪʃən) *n.* **1. a.** the launching or financing of a commercial enterprise by bond or share issues. **b.** the raising of a loan or new capital by bond or share issues. **2.** power or ability to float. **3.** Also called: **froth flotation.** a process to concentrate the valuable ore in low-grade ores by using induced differences in surface tension to carry the valuable fraction to the surface.

flotilla (flə'tɪlə) *n.* a small fleet or a fleet of small vessels.

flotsam ('flɒtsəm) *n.* **1.** wreckage from a ship found floating. Cf. **jetsam.** **2.** odds and ends (esp. in **flotsam and jetsam**). **3.** vagrants.

flounce[1] (flaʊns) *vb.* **1.** (*intr.*; often foll. by *about, away, out,* etc.) to move or go with emphatic movements. ~*n.* **2.** the act of flouncing.

flounce[2] (flaʊns) *n.* an ornamental gathered ruffle sewn to a garment by its top edge.

flounder[1] ('flaʊndə) *vb.* (*intr.*) **1.** to move with difficulty, as in mud. **2.** to make mistakes. ~*n.* **3.** the act of floundering.

flounder[2] ('flaʊndə) *n., pl.* **-der** *or* **-ders.** a European flatfish having a greyish-brown body covered with prickly scales: an important food fish.

flour ('flaʊə) *n.* **1.** a powder, which may be either fine or coarse, prepared by grinding the meal of a grass, esp. wheat. **2.** any finely powdered substance. ~*vb.* **3.** (*tr.*) to make (grain, etc.) into flour. **4.** (*tr.*) to dredge or sprinkle (food or utensils) with flour. —'**floury** *adj.*

flourish ('flʌrɪʃ) *vb.* **1.** (*intr.*) to thrive; prosper. **2.** (*intr.*) to be at the peak of condition. **3.** (*intr.*) to be healthy: *plants flourish in the light.* **4.** to wave or cause to wave in the air with sweeping strokes. **5.** to display or make a display. **6.** to play (a fanfare, etc.) on a musical intrument. ~*n.* **7.** the act of waving or brandishing. **8.** a showy gesture: *he entered with a flourish.* **9.** an ornamental embellishment in writing. **10.** a display of ornamental language or speech. **11.** a grandiose passage of music. —'**flourisher** *n.*

flout (flaʊt) *vb.* (when *intr.*, usually foll. by *at*) to show contempt (for). —'**floutingly** *adv.*

flow (fləʊ) *vb.* (*mainly intr.*) **1.** (of liquids) to move or be conveyed as in a stream. **2.** (of blood) to circulate around the body. **3.** to move or progress freely as if in a stream: *the crowd flowed into the building.* **4.** to be produced continuously and effortlessly: *ideas flowed from her pen.* **5.** to be marked by smooth or easy movement. **6.** to hang freely or loosely: *her hair flowed down her back.* **7.** to be present in abundance: *wine flows at their parties.* **8.** (of tide water) to advance or rise. Cf. **ebb** (sense 1). **9.** (of rocks such as slate) to yield to pressure so that the structure and arrangement of the constituent minerals are altered. ~*n.* **10.** the act, rate, or manner of flowing: *a fast flow.* **11.** a continuous stream or discharge. **12.** continuous progression. **13.** the advancing of the tide. **14.** *Scot.* **a.** a marsh or swamp. **b.** an inlet or basin of the sea. **c.** (*cap.* when part of a name): *Scapa Flow.*

flow chart *or* **sheet** *n.* a diagrammatic representation of the sequence of operations in an industrial process, computer program, etc.

flower ('flaʊə) *n.* **1. a.** a bloom or blossom on a plant. **b.** a plant that bears blooms or blossoms. **2.** the reproductive structure of angiosperm plants, consisting of stamens and carpels surrounded by petals and sepals. In some plants it is brightly coloured and attracts insects for pollination. Related adj.: **floral. 3.** any similar reproductive structure in other plants. **4.** the prime; peak: *in the flower of his youth.* **5.** the choice or finest product, part, or representative. **6.** a decoration or embellishment. **7.** (*pl.*) fine powder, usually produced by sublimation: *flowers of sulphur.* ~*vb.* **8.** (*intr.*) to produce flowers; bloom. **9.** (*intr.*) to reach full growth or maturity. **10.** (*tr.*) to deck or decorate with flowers or floral designs. —'**flowerless** *adj.* —'**flower-‚like** *adj.*

flowered ('flaʊəd) *adj.* **1.** having flowers. **2.** decorated with flowers or a floral design.

flowerpot ('flaʊə‚pɒt) *n.* a pot in which plants are grown.

flowery ('flaʊərɪ) *adj.* **1.** abounding in flowers. **2.** decorated with flowers or floral patterns. **3.** like or suggestive of flowers. **4.** (of language or style) elaborate. —'**floweriness** *n.*

THESAURUS

flop *v.* **1.** collapse, dangle, droop, drop, fall, hang limply, sag, slump, topple, tumble **2.** *Inf.* bomb (*U.S. sl.*), close, come to nothing, fail, fall flat, fall short, fold (*Inf.*), founder, misfire ~*n.* **3.** *Inf.* cockup (*Brit. sl.*), debacle, disaster, failure, fiasco, loser, nonstarter, washout (*Inf.*)

floral flower-patterned, flowery

florid **1.** blowzy, flushed, high-coloured, high-complexioned, rubicund, ruddy **2.** baroque, busy, embellished, euphuistic, figurative, flamboyant, flowery, fussy, grandiloquent, high-flown, ornate, overelaborate

flotsam debris, detritus, jetsam, junk, odds and ends, sweepings, wreckage

flounder *v.* be in the dark, blunder, fumble, grope, muddle, plunge, struggle, stumble, thrash, toss, tumble, wallow

flourish *v.* **1.** bear fruit, be in one's prime, be successful, be vigorous, bloom, blossom, boom, burgeon, develop, do well, flower, get

ahead, get on, go great guns (*Sl.*), go up in the world, grow, grow fat, increase, prosper, succeed, thrive **2.** brandish, display, flaunt, flutter, shake, sweep, swing, swish, twirl, vaunt, wag, wave, wield ~*n.* **3.** brandishing, dash, display, fanfare, parade, shaking, show, showy gesture, twirling, wave **4.** curlicue, decoration, embellishment, ornamentation, plume, sweep

flourishing blooming, burgeoning, doing well, going strong, in the pink, in top form, lush, luxuriant, mushrooming, on the up and up (*Inf.*), prospering, rampant, successful, thriving

flout defy, deride, gibe at, insult, jeer at, laugh in the face of, mock, outrage, ridicule, scoff at, scorn, scout (*Archaic*), show contempt for, sneer at, spurn, taunt, treat with disdain

flow *v.* **1.** circulate, course, glide, gush, move, pour, purl, ripple, roll, run, rush, slide,

surge, sweep, swirl, whirl **2.** cascade, deluge, flood, inundate, overflow, pour, run, run out, spew, spill, spurt, squirt, stream, teem, well forth **3.** arise, emanate, emerge, issue, pour, proceed, result, spring ~*n.* **4.** course, current, drift, flood, flux, gush, outflow, outpouring, spate, stream, tide **5.** abundance, deluge, effusion, emanation, outflow, outpouring, plenty, plethora, succession, train

flower *n.* **1.** bloom, blossom, efflorescence **2.** *Fig.* best, choicest part, cream, elite, freshness, greatest *or* finest point, height, pick, vigour ~*v.* **3.** bloom, blossom, blow, burgeon, effloresce, flourish, mature, open, unfold

flowering *adj.* abloom, blooming, blossoming, florescent, in bloom, in blossom, in flower, open, out, ready

flowery baroque, embellished, euphuistic, fancy, figurative, florid, high-flown, ornate, overwrought, rhetorical

flowing **1.** falling, gushing, rolling, rush-

flown (fləun) *vb.* the past participle of **fly**[1].

fl. oz. *abbrev. for* fluid ounce.

flu (flu:) *n. Inf.* **1.** (often preceded by *the*) short for **influenza**. **2.** any of various viral infections, esp. a respiratory or intestinal infection.

fluctuate ('flʌktjʊˌeit) *vb.* **1.** to change or cause to change position constantly. **2.** (*intr.*) to rise and fall like a wave. —'**fluctuant** *adj.* —ˌfluctu'ation *n.*

flue (flu:) *n.* a shaft, tube, or pipe, esp. as used in a chimney, to carry off smoke, gas, etc.

fluent ('flu:ənt) *adj.* **1.** able to speak or write a specified foreign language with facility. **2.** spoken or written with facility. **3.** graceful in motion or shape. **4.** flowing or able to flow freely. —'**fluency** *n.* —'**fluently** *adv.*

fluff (flʌf) *n.* **1.** soft light particles, such as the down or nap of cotton or wool. **2.** any light downy substance. **3.** *Inf.* a mistake, esp. in speaking or reading lines or performing music. **4.** *Inf.* a young woman (esp. in **a bit of fluff**). ~*vb.* **5.** to make or become soft and puffy. **6.** *Inf.* to make a mistake in performing (an action, music, etc.). —'**fluffy** *adj.*

fluid ('flu:id) *n.* **1.** a substance, such as a liquid or gas, that can flow, has no fixed shape, and offers little resistance to an external stress. ~*adj.* **2.** capable of flowing and easily changing shape. **3.** of or using a fluid or fluids. **4.** constantly changing or apt to change. **5.** flowing. —'**fluidal** *adj.* —flu'idity *or* 'fluidness *n.*

fluid ounce *n.* **1.** *Brit.* a unit of capacity equal to one twentieth of an Imperial pint. **2.** *U.S.* a unit of capacity equal to one sixteenth of a U.S. pint.

fluke[1] (flu:k) *n.* **1.** a flat bladelike projection at the end of the arm of an anchor. **2.** either of the two lobes of the tail of a whale. **3.** the barb of a harpoon, arrow, etc.

fluke[2] (flu:k) *n.* **1.** an accidental stroke of luck. **2.** any chance happening. ~*vb.* **3.** (*tr.*) to gain, make, or hit by a fluke. —'**fluky** *adj.*

fluke[3] (flu:k) *n.* any parasitic flatworm, such as the blood fluke and liver fluke.

flummery ('flʌmərɪ) *n., pl.* **-meries.** **1.** *Inf.* meaningless flattery. **2.** *Chiefly Brit.* a cold pudding of oatmeal, etc.

flummox ('flʌməks) *vb.* (*tr.*) to perplex or bewilder.

flung (flʌŋ) *vb.* the past tense or past participle of **fling**.

flunk (flʌŋk) *Inf., U.S. & N.Z.* ~*vb.* **1.** to fail or cause to fail to reach the required standard in (an examination, course, etc.). **2.** (*intr.;* foll. by *out*) to be dismissed from a school.

flunky *or* **flunkey** ('flʌŋkɪ) *n., pl.* **flunkies** *or* **flunkeys.** **1.** a servile person. **2.** a person who performs menial tasks. **3.** *Usually derog.* a manservant in livery.

fluor ('flu:ɔ:) *n.* another name for **fluorspar**.

fluoresce (ˌfluə'rɛs) *vb.* (*intr.*) to exhibit fluorescence.

fluorescence (ˌfluə'rɛsəns) *n.* **1.** *Physics.* **a.** the emission of light or other radiation from atoms or molecules that are bombarded by particles, such as electrons, or by radiation from a separate source. **b.** such an emission of photons that ceases as soon as the bombarding radiation is discontinued. **2.** the radiation emitted as a result of fluorescence. Cf. **phosphorescence.** —ˌfluo'rescent *adj.*

fluorescent lamp *n.* a type of lamp in which ultraviolet radiation from an electrical gas discharge causes a thin layer of phosphor on a tube's inside surface to fluoresce.

fluoridate ('fluərɪˌdeit) *vb.* to subject (water) to fluoridation. —ˌfluori'dation *n.*

fluoride ('fluəˌraid) *n.* **1.** any salt of hydrofluoric acid, containing the fluoride ion, F⁻. **2.** any compound containing fluorine, such as methyl fluoride.

fluorinate ('fluərɪˌneit) *vb.* to treat or combine with fluorine. —ˌfluori'nation *n.*

fluorine ('fluəri:n) *n.* a toxic pungent pale yellow gas of the halogen group that is the most electronegative and reactive of all the elements: used in the production of uranium, fluorocarbons, and other chemicals. Symbol: F; atomic no.: 9; atomic wt.: 18.998.

fluorite ('fluərait) *n.* the U.S. name for **fluorspar**.

fluorspar ('fluəˌspɑ:), **fluor**, *or U.S.* **fluorite** *n.* a soft often fluorescent mineral consisting of calcium fluoride in crystalline form: the chief source of fluorine and its compounds.

flurry ('flʌrɪ) *n., pl.* **-ries.** **1.** a sudden commotion. **2.** a light gust of wind or rain or fall of snow. ~*vb.* **-rying, -ried.** **3.** to confuse or bewilder or be confused or bewildered.

flush[1] (flʌʃ) *vb.* **1.** to blush or cause to blush. **2.** to flow or flood or cause to flow or flood with or as if with water. **3.** to glow or shine or cause to glow or shine with a rosy colour. **4.** to send a volume of water quickly through (a pipe, etc.) or into (a toilet) for the purpose of cleansing, etc. **5.** (*tr.; usually passive*) to excite or elate. ~*n.* **6.** a rosy colour, esp. in the cheeks. **7.** a sudden flow or gush, as of water. **8.** a feeling of excitement or elation: *the flush of success.* **9.** freshness: *the flush of youth.* **10.** redness of the skin, as from the effects of a fever, alcohol, etc. —'**flusher** *n.*

flush[2] (flʌʃ) *adj.* (*usually postpositive*) **1.** level or even with another surface. **2.** directly adjacent; continuous. **3.** *Inf.* having plenty of money. **4.** *Inf.* abundant or plentiful, as money. **5.** full to the brim. ~*adv.* **6.** so as to be level or even. **7.** directly or squarely. ~*vb.* (*tr.*) **8.** to cause (surfaces) to be on the same level or in the same plane. ~*n.* **9.** a period of fresh growth of leaves, shoots, etc. —'**flushness** *n.*

flush[3] (flʌʃ) *vb.* (*tr.*) to rouse (game, etc.) and put to flight.

flush[4] (flʌʃ) *n.* (in poker and similar games) a hand containing only one suit.

fluster ('flʌstə) *vb.* **1.** to make or become nervous or upset. ~*n.* **2.** a state of confusion or agitation.

flute (flu:t) *n.* **1.** a wind instrument consisting of an open cylindrical tube of wood or metal having holes in the side stopped either by the fingers or by pads controlled by keys. The breath is directed across a mouth hole cut in the side. **2.** *Archit.* a rounded shallow concave groove on the shaft of a column, pilaster, etc. ~*vb.* **3.** to produce or utter (sounds) in the manner or tone of a flute. **4.** (*tr.*) to make grooves or furrows in. —'**fluteˌlike** *adj.* —'**fluty** *adj.*

THESAURUS

ing, smooth, streaming, sweeping **2.** continuous, cursive, easy, fluent, smooth, unbroken, uninterrupted **3.** abounding, brimming over, flooded, full, overrun, prolific, rich, teeming

fluctuate alter, alternate, change, ebb and flow, go up and down, hesitate, oscillate, rise and fall, seesaw, shift, swing, undulate, vacillate, vary, veer, waver

fluctuation alternation, change, fickleness, inconstancy, instability, oscillation, shift, swing, unsteadiness, vacillation, variation, wavering

fluency articulateness, assurance, command, control, ease, facility, glibness, readiness, slickness, smoothness, volubility

fluent articulate, easy, effortless, facile, flowing, glib, natural, ready, smooth, smooth-spoken, voluble, well-versed

fluff 1. *n.* down, dust, dustball, fuzz, lint, nap, oose (*Scot.*), pile **2.** *v. Inf.* bungle, cock up (*Sl.*), foul up (*Inf.*), make a mess off, mess up (*Inf.*), muddle, screw up (*Inf.*), spoil

fluid *adj.* **1.** aqueous, flowing, in solution,

liquefied, liquid, melted, molten, running, runny, watery **2.** adaptable, adjustable, changeable, flexible, floating, fluctuating, indefinite, mercurial, mobile, mutable, protean, shifting **3.** easy, elegant, feline, flowing, graceful, sinuous, smooth ~*n.* **4.** liquid, liquor, solution

flunky 1. assistant, drudge, hanger-on, menial, minion, slave, toady, tool, underling, yes man **2.** footman, lackey, manservant, valet

flurry *n.* **1.** *Fig.* ado, agitation, bustle, commotion, disturbance, excitement, ferment, flap, fluster, flutter, furore, fuss, hurry, stir, to-do, tumult, whirl **2.** flaw, gust, squall **3.** burst, outbreak, spell, spurt ~*v.* **4.** agitate, bewilder, bother, bustle, confuse, disconcert, disturb, fluster, flutter, fuss, hassle (*Inf.*), hurry, hustle, rattle (*Inf.*), ruffle, unsettle, upset

flush[1] *v.* **1.** blush, burn, colour, colour up, crimson, flame, glow, go red, redden, suffuse ~*n.* **2.** bloom, blush, colour, freshness, glow, redness, rosiness ~*v.* **3.** cleanse, douche, drench, eject, expel, flood, hose down, rinse

out, swab, syringe, wash out

flush[2] *adj.* **1.** even, flat, level, plane, square, true **2.** abundant, affluent, full, generous, lavish, liberal, overflowing, prodigal **3.** *Inf.* in funds, in the money (*Inf.*), moneyed, rich, rolling (*Sl.*), wealthy, well-heeled, well-off, well-supplied ~*adv.* **4.** even with, hard against, in contact with, level with, squarely, touching

flushed 1. blushing, burning, crimson, embarrassed, feverish, glowing, hot, red, rosy, rubicund, ruddy **2.** *Often with* **with** ablaze, animated, aroused, elated, enthused, excited, exhilarated, high (*Inf.*), inspired, intoxicated, thrilled

fluster 1. *v.* agitate, bother, bustle, confound, confuse, disturb, excite, flurry, hassle (*Inf.*), heat, hurry, make nervous, perturb, rattle (*Inf.*), ruffle, throw off balance, upset **2.** *n.* agitation, bustle, commotion, disturbance, dither, flap (*Inf.*), flurry, flutter, furore, perturbation, ruffle, state (*Inf.*), turmoil

fluting ('fluːtɪŋ) n. a design or decoration of flutes on a column, pilaster, etc.

flutter ('flʌtə) vb. **1.** to wave or cause to wave rapidly. **2.** (intr.) (of birds, butterflies, etc.) to flap the wings. **3.** (intr.) to move, esp. downwards, with an irregular motion. **4.** (intr.) Pathol. (of the heart) to beat abnormally rapidly, esp. in a regular rhythm. **5.** to be or make nervous or restless. **6.** (intr.) to move about restlessly. ~n. **7.** a quick flapping or vibrating motion. **8.** a state of nervous excitement or confusion. **9.** excited interest; stir. **10.** Brit. inf. a modest bet or wager. **11.** Pathol. an abnormally rapid beating of the heart, esp. in a regular rhythm. **12.** Electronics. a slow variation in pitch in a sound-reproducing system, similar to wow but occurring at higher frequencies. **13.** a potentially dangerous oscillation of an aircraft, or part of an aircraft. **14.** Also called: **flutter tonguing.** Music. a method of sounding a wind instrument, esp. the flute, with a rolling movement of the tongue. —'**flutterer** n. —'**fluttery** adj.

fluvial ('fluːvɪəl) adj. of or occurring in a river: fluvial deposits.

flux (flʌks) n. **1.** a flow or discharge. **2.** continuous change; instability. **3.** a substance, such as borax or salt, that gives a low melting-point mixture with a metal oxide to assist in fusion. **4.** Metallurgy. a chemical used to increase the fluidity of refining slags. **5.** Physics. **a.** the rate of flow of particles, energy, or a fluid, such as that of neutrons (**neutron flux**) or of light energy (**luminous flux**). **b.** the strength of a field in a given area: magnetic flux. **6.** Pathol. an excessive discharge of fluid from the body, such as watery faeces in diarrhoea. ~vb. **7.** to make or become fluid. **8.** (tr.) to apply flux to (a metal, soldered joint, etc.).

fly[1] (flaɪ) vb. **flying, flew, flown. 1.** (intr.) (of birds, aircraft, etc.) to move through the air in a controlled manner using aerodynamic forces. **2.** to travel over (an area of land or sea) in an aircraft. **3.** to operate (an aircraft or spacecraft). **4.** to float, flutter, or be displayed in the air or cause to float, etc., in this way: they flew the flag. **5.** to transport or be transported by or through the air by aircraft, wind, etc. **6.** (intr.) to move or be moved very quickly, or suddenly: the door flew open. **7.** (intr.) to pass swiftly: time flies. **8.** to escape from (an enemy, place, etc.); flee. **9.** (intr.; may be foll. by at or upon) to attack a person. **10. fly a kite. a.** to procure money by an accommodation bill. **b.** to experiment with something. **11. fly high.** Inf. **a.** to have a high aim. **b.** to prosper or flourish. **12. fly off the handle.** Inf. to lose one's temper. **13. let fly.** Inf. **a.** to lose one's temper (with a person): she really let fly at him. **b.** to shoot or throw (an object). ~n., pl. **flies. 14.** (often pl.) Also called: **fly front.** a closure that conceals a zip, buttons, or other fastening, by having one side overlapping, as on trousers. **15. a.** a flap forming the entrance to a tent. **b.** a piece of canvas drawn over the ridgepole of a tent to form an outer roof. **16.** short for **flywheel. 17. a.** the outer edge of a flag. **b.** the distance from the outer edge of a flag to the staff. **18.** Brit. a light one-horse covered carriage formerly let out on hire. **19.** (pl.) Theatre. the space above the stage out of view of the audience, used for storing scenery, etc. **20.** Rare. the act of flying. —'**flyable** adj.

fly[2] (flaɪ) n., pl. **flies. 1.** any dipterous insect, esp. the housefly, characterized by active flight. **2.** any of various similar but unrelated insects, such as the caddis fly, firefly, and dragonfly. **3.** Angling. a lure made from a

fish-hook dressed with feathers, tinsel, etc., to resemble any of various flies or nymphs: used in fly-fishing. **4. fly in the ointment.** Inf. a slight flaw that detracts from value or enjoyment. **5. there are no flies on him, her,** etc. Inf. he, she, etc., is no fool. —'**flyless** adj.

fly[3] (flaɪ) adj. Sl., chiefly Brit. knowing and sharp; smart.

flyaway ('flaɪəˌweɪ) adj. **1.** (of hair or clothing) loose and fluttering. **2.** frivolous or flighty; giddy.

flyblown ('flaɪˌbləʊn) adj. **1.** covered with flyblows. **2.** contaminated; tainted.

fly-by-night Inf. ~adj. **1.** unreliable or untrustworthy, esp. in finance. ~n. **2.** an untrustworthy person, esp. one who departs secretly or by night to avoid paying debts.

flycatcher ('flaɪˌkætʃə) n. **1.** a small insectivorous songbird of the Old World having a small slender bill fringed with bristles. **2.** an American passerine bird.

flyer ('flaɪə) n. a variant spelling of **flier.**

fly-fish vb. (intr.) Angling. to fish using artificial flies as lures. —'**fly-ˌfishing** n.

flying ('flaɪɪŋ) adj. **1.** (prenominal) hurried; fleeting: a flying visit. **2.** (prenominal) designed for fast action. **3.** hanging, waving, or floating freely: flying hair. ~n. **4.** the act of piloting, navigating, or travelling in an aircraft. **5.** (modifier) relating to, accustomed to, or adapted for flight: a flying machine. **6.** (modifier) moving or passing quickly on or as if on wings: flying hours.

flying boat n. a seaplane in which the fuselage consists of a hull that provides buoyancy.

flying buttress n. a buttress supporting a wall or other structure by an arch that transmits the thrust outwards and downwards.

flying colours pl. n. conspicuous success; triumph: he passed his test with flying colours.

flying doctor n. (in areas of sparse or scattered population) a doctor who visits patients by aircraft.

flying fish n. a fish common in warm and tropical seas, having enlarged winglike pectoral fins used for gliding above the surface of the water.

flying fox n. **1.** any large fruit bat of tropical Africa and Asia. **2.** Austral. a cable mechanism used for transportation across a river, gorge, etc.

flying officer n. an officer holding commissioned rank senior to a pilot officer but junior to a flight lieutenant in the British and certain other air forces.

flying saucer n. any unidentified disc-shaped flying object alleged to come from outer space.

flying squad n. a small group of police, soldiers, etc., ready to move into action quickly.

flying start n. **1.** (in sprinting) a start by a competitor anticipating the starting signal. **2.** a start to a race in which the competitor is already travelling at speed as he passes the starting line. **3.** any promising beginning. **4.** an initial advantage.

flying wing n. **1.** an aircraft consisting mainly of one large wing and no fuselage. **2.** in Canadian football, the twelfth player, who has a variable position behind the scrimmage line.

flyleaf ('flaɪˌliːf) n., pl. **-leaves.** the inner leaf of the endpaper of a book, pasted to the first leaf.

flyover ('flaɪˌəʊvə) n. **1.** Brit. an intersection of two roads at which one is carried over the other by a bridge. **2.** the U.S. name for a **fly-past.**

flypaper ('flaɪˌpeɪpə) n. paper with a sticky and poison-

THESAURUS

flutter v. **1.** agitate, bat, beat, flap, flicker, flit, flitter, fluctuate, hover, palpitate, quiver, ripple, ruffle, shiver, tremble, vibrate, waver ~n. **2.** palpitation, quiver, quivering, shiver, shudder, tremble, tremor, twitching, vibration **3.** agitation, commotion, confusion, dither, excitement, flurry, fluster, perturbation, state (Inf.), state of nervous excitement, tremble, tumult

fly v. **1.** flit, flutter, hover, mount, sail, soar, take to the air, take wing, wing **2.** aviate, be at the controls, control, manoeuvre, operate, pilot **3.** display, flap, float, flutter, show, wave **4.** elapse, flit, glide, pass, pass swiftly, roll on, run its course, slip away **5.** be off like a shot (Inf.), bolt, career, dart, dash, hare (Inf.), hasten, hurry, race, rush, scamper, scoot, shoot, speed, sprint, tear, whiz (Inf.), zoom **6.**

abscond, avoid, beat a retreat, clear out (Inf.), cut and run (Inf.), decamp, disappear, escape, flee, get away, hasten away, hightail (Inf., chiefly U.S.), light out (Inf.), make a getaway, make a quick exit, make one's escape, run, run for it, run from, show a clean pair of heels, shun, take flight, take off, take to one's heels **7. fly in the ointment** difficulty, drawback, flaw, hitch, problem, rub, small problem, snag **8. fly off the handle** blow one's top, explode, flip one's lid (Sl.), fly into a rage, have a tantrum, hit or go through the roof (Inf.), let fly (Inf.), lose one's cool (Inf.), lose one's temper **9. let fly a.** burst forth, give free reign, keep nothing back, lash out, let (someone) have it, lose one's temper, tear into (Inf.), vent **b.** cast, chuck, fire, fling, heave, hurl, hurtle, launch,

let off, lob (Inf.), shoot, sling, throw

fly at assail, assault, attack, fall upon, get stuck into (Inf.), go for, have a go at (Inf.), lay about, pitch into, rush at

fly-by-night adj. **1.** cowboy (Inf.), dubious, questionable, shady, undependable, unreliable, untrustworthy **2.** brief, here today, gone tomorrow, impermanent, short-lived

flying adj. **1.** brief, fleeting, fugacious, hasty, hurried, rushed, short-lived, transitory **2.** express, fast, fleet, mercurial, mobile, rapid, speedy, winged **3.** airborne, flapping, floating, fluttering, gliding, hovering, in the air, soaring, streaming, volitant, waving, windborne, winging

ous coating, usually hung from the ceiling to trap flies.

fly-past *n.* a ceremonial flight of aircraft over a given area.

fly sheet *n.* **1.** another term for **fly**[1] (sense 15). **2.** a short handbill.

fly spray *n.* a liquid used to destroy flies and other insects, sprayed from an aerosol.

flytrap ('flaɪ,træp) *n.* **1.** any of various insectivorous plants. **2.** a device for catching flies.

flyweight ('flaɪ,weɪt) *n.* **1. a.** a professional boxer weighing not more than 112 pounds (51 kg). **b.** an amateur boxer weighing 48–51 kg (106–112 pounds). **2.** (in Olympic wrestling) a wrestler not more than 115 pounds (52 kg).

flywheel ('flaɪ,wiːl) *n.* a heavy wheel that stores kinetic energy and smooths the operation of a reciprocating engine by maintaining a constant speed of rotation over the whole cycle.

Fm *the chemical symbol for* fermium.

FM *abbrev. for* frequency modulation.

fm. *abbrev. for:* **1.** Also: **fm** fathom. **2.** from.

F.M. *abbrev. for* Field Marshal.

f-number *or* **f number** *n. Photog.* the numerical value of the relative aperture. If the relative aperture is f8, 8 is the f-number.

fo. *abbrev. for* folio.

F.O. *abbrev. for:* **1.** *Army.* Field Officer. **2.** *Air Force.* Flying Officer. **3.** Foreign Office.

foal (fəʊl) *n.* **1.** the young of a horse or related animal. ~*vb.* **2.** to give birth to (a foal).

foam (fəʊm) *n.* **1.** a mass of small bubbles of gas formed on the surface of a liquid, such as the froth produced by a solution of soap or detergent in water. **2.** frothy saliva sometimes formed in and expelled from the mouth, as in rabies. **3.** the frothy sweat of a horse or similar animal. **4. a.** any of a number of light cellular solids made by creating bubbles of gas in the liquid material: used as insulation and packaging. **b.** (*as modifier*): *foam rubber; foam plastic.* ~*vb.* **5.** to produce or cause to produce foam; froth. **6.** (*intr.*) to be very angry (esp. in **foam at the mouth**). —'**foamless** *adj.* —'**foamy** *adj.*

fob[1] (fob) *n.* **1.** a chain or ribbon by which a pocket watch is attached to a waistcoat. **2.** any ornament hung on such a chain. **3.** a small pocket in a man's waistcoat, etc., for holding a watch.

fob[2] (fob) *vb.* **fobbing, fobbed.** (*tr.*) *Arch.* cheat.

f.o.b. *or* **F.O.B.** *Commerce. abbrev. for* free on board.

fob off *vb.* (*tr., adv.*) **1.** to trick (a person) with lies or excuses. **2.** to dispose of (goods) by trickery.

focal ('fəʊk²l) *adj.* **1.** of or relating to a focus. **2.** situated at or measured from the focus.

focal length *or* **distance** *n.* the distance from the focal point of a lens or mirror to the reflecting surface of the mirror or the centre point of the lens.

fo'c's'le *or* **fo'c'sle** ('fəʊks²l) *n.* a variant spelling of forecastle.

focus ('fəʊkəs) *n., pl.* **-cuses** *or* **-ci** (-saɪ). **1.** a point of convergence of light or sound waves, etc., or a point from which they appear to diverge. **2.** *Optics.* the state of an optical image when it is distinct and clearly defined or the state of an instrument producing this image: *the telescope is out of focus.* **3.** a point upon which attention, activity, etc., is concentrated. **4.** *Geom.* a fixed reference point on the concave side of a conic section, used when defining its eccentricity. **5.** the point beneath the earth's surface at which an earthquake originates. **6.** *Pathol.* the main site of an infection. ~*vb.* **-cusing, -cused.** **7.** to bring or come to a focus or into focus. **8.**

(*tr.; often foll. by on*) to concentrate. —'**focuser** *n.*

fodder ('fodə) *n.* **1.** bulk feed for livestock, esp. hay, straw, etc. ~*vb.* **2.** (*tr.*) to supply (livestock) with fodder.

foe (fəʊ) *n. Formal or literary.* another word for **enemy.**

foetid ('fɛtɪd, 'fiː-) *adj.* a variant spelling of **fetid.** —'**foetidly** *adv.* —'**foetidness** *n.*

foetus *or* **fetus** ('fiːtəs) *n., pl.* **-tuses.** the embryo of a mammal in the later stages of development, esp. a human embryo from the end of the second month of pregnancy until birth. —'**foetal** *adj.*

fog (fog) *n.* **1.** a mass of droplets of condensed water vapour suspended in the air, often greatly reducing visibility. **2.** a cloud of any substance in the atmosphere reducing visibility. **3.** a state of mental uncertainty. **4.** *Photog.* a blurred area on a developed negative, print, or transparency. ~*vb.* **fogging, fogged.** **5.** to envelop or become enveloped with or as if with fog. **6.** to confuse or become confused. **7.** *Photog.* to produce fog on (a negative, print, or transparency) or (of a negative, print, or transparency) to be affected by fog. —'**foggy** *adj.*

fog bank *n.* a distinct mass of fog, esp. at sea.

fogbound ('fog,baʊnd) *adj.* prevented from operation by fog: *the airport was fogbound.*

foghorn ('fog,hɔːn) *n.* **1.** a mechanical instrument sounded at intervals to serve as a warning to vessels in fog. **2.** *Inf.* a loud deep resounding voice.

fogy *or* **fogey** ('fəʊgɪ) *n., pl.* **-gies** *or* **-geys.** an extremely fussy or conservative person (esp. in **old fogy**). —'**fogyish** *or* '**fogeyish** *adj.*

foible ('fɔɪb²l) *n.* **1.** a slight peculiarity or minor weakness; idiosyncrasy. **2.** the most vulnerable part of a sword's blade, from the middle to the tip.

foil[1] (fɔɪl) *vb.* (*tr.*) **1.** to baffle or frustrate (a person, attempt, etc.). **2.** *Hunting.* (of hounds, hunters, etc.) to obliterate the scent left by a hunted animal or (of a hunted animal) to run back over its own trail. ~*n.* **3.** *Arch.* a setback or defeat. —'**foilable** *adj.*

foil[2] (fɔɪl) *n.* **1.** metal in the form of very thin sheets: *tin foil.* **2.** the thin metallic sheet forming the backing of a mirror. **3.** a thin leaf of shiny metal set under a gemstone to add brightness or colour. **4.** a person or thing that gives contrast to another. **5.** *Archit.* a small arc between cusps. **6.** short for **hydrofoil.** ~*vb.* (*tr.*) **7.** Also: **foliate.** *Archit.* to ornament (windows, etc.) with foils.

foil[3] (fɔɪl) *n.* a light slender flexible sword tipped by a button.

foist (fɔɪst) *vb.* (*tr.*) **1.** (often foll. by *off* or *on*) to sell or pass off (something, esp. an inferior article) as genuine, valuable, etc. **2.** (usually foll. by *in* or *into*) to insert surreptitiously or wrongfully.

fold[1] (fəʊld) *vb.* **1.** to bend or be bent double so that one part covers another. **2.** (*tr.*) to bring together and intertwine (the arms, legs, etc.). **3.** (*tr.*) (of birds, insects, etc.) to close (the wings) together from an extended position. **4.** (*tr.; often foll. by up or in*) to enclose in or as if in a surrounding material. **5.** (*tr.; foll. by in*) to clasp (a person) in the arms. **6.** (*tr.;* usually foll. by *round, about,* etc.) to wind (around); entwine. **7.** Also: **fold in.** (*tr.*) to mix (a whisked mixture) with other ingredients by gently turning one part over the other with a spoon. **8.** (*intr.; often foll. by up*) *Inf.* to collapse; fail: *the business folded.* ~*n.* **9.** a piece or section that has been folded: *a fold of cloth.* **10.** a mark, crease, or hollow made by folding. **11.** a hollow in undulating terrain. **12.** a bend in stratified rocks that results from movements within the earth's crust. **13.** a coil, as in a rope, etc. —'**foldable** *adj.*

fold[2] (fəʊld) *n.* **1. a.** a small enclosure or pen for sheep

---

THESAURUS

foam **1.** *n.* bubbles, froth, head, lather, spray, spume, suds **2.** *v.* boil, bubble, effervesce, fizz, froth, lather

focus *n.* **1.** bull's-eye, centre, centre of activity, centre of attraction, core, cynosure, focal point, headquarters, heart, hub, meeting place, target **2. in focus** clear, distinct, sharp-edged, sharply defined **3. out of focus** blurred, fuzzy, ill-defined, indistinct, muzzy, unclear ~*v.* **4.** aim, bring to bear, centre, concentrate, converge, direct, fix, join, meet, pinpoint, rivet, spotlight, zero in (*Inf.*), zoom in

foe adversary, antagonist, enemy, foeman

(*Archaic*), opponent, rival

fog *n.* **1.** gloom, miasma, mist, murk, murkiness, peasouper (*Inf.*), smog **2.** *Fig.* blindness, confusion, daze, haze, mist, obscurity, perplexity, stupor, trance ~*v.* **3.** becloud, bedim, befuddle, bewilder, blind, cloud, confuse, darken, daze, dim, muddle, obfuscate, obscure, perplex, stupefy **4.** cloud, mist over or up, steam up

foggy **1.** blurred, brumous (*Rare*), cloudy, dim, grey, hazy, indistinct, misty, murky, nebulous, obscure, smoggy, soupy, vaporous **2.** *Fig.* befuddled, bewildered, clouded, cloudy, confused, dark, dazed, dim, indistinct, muddled, obscure, stupefied, stupid, unclear, vague

foil[1] *v.* baffle, balk, check, checkmate, circumvent, counter, defeat, disappoint, elude, frustrate, nip in the bud, nullify, outwit, put a spoke in (someone's) wheel (*Brit.*), stop, thwart

foil[2] antithesis, background, complement, contrast, setting

foist fob off, get rid of, impose, insert, insinuate, interpolate, introduce, palm off, pass off, put over, sneak in, unload

or other livestock, where they can be gathered. **b.** a flock of sheep. **2.** a church or the members of it. ~*vb.* **3.** (*tr.*) to gather or confine (sheep, etc.) in a fold.

-fold *suffix forming adjectives and adverbs.* having so many parts or being so many times as much or as many: *three-hundredfold.*

foldaway ('fəʊldə,weɪ) *adj.* (*prenominal*) (of a bed, etc.) able to be folded away when not in use.

folder ('fəʊldə) *n.* **1.** a binder or file for holding loose papers, etc. **2.** a folded circular. **3.** a person or thing that folds.

folderol ('fəʊldə,rɒl) *n.* a variant spelling of **falderal.**

folding door *n.* a door in the form of two or more vertical hinged leaves that can be folded one against another.

foliaceous (,fəʊlɪ'eɪʃəs) *adj.* **1.** having the appearance of the leaf of a plant. **2.** bearing leaves or leaflike structures. **3.** *Geol.* consisting of thin layers.

foliage ('fəʊlɪɪdʒ) *n.* **1.** the green leaves of a plant. **2.** sprays of leaves used for decoration. **3.** an ornamental leaf-like design.

foliation (,fəʊlɪ'eɪʃən) *n.* **1.** *Bot.* **a.** the process of producing leaves. **b.** the state of being in leaf. **c.** the arrangement of leaves in a leaf bud. **2.** *Archit.* ornamentation consisting of cusps and foils. **3.** the consecutive numbering of the leaves of a book. **4.** *Geol.* the arrangement of the constituents of a rock in leaflike layers, as in schists.

folio ('fəʊlɪəʊ) *n., pl.* **-lios. 1.** a sheet of paper folded in half to make two leaves for a book. **2.** a book of the largest common size made up of such sheets. **3. a.** a leaf of paper numbered on the front side only. **b.** the page number of a book. **4.** *Law.* a unit of measurement of the length of legal documents, determined by the number of words, generally 72 or 90 in Britain and 100 in the U.S. ~*adj.* **5.** relating to or having the format of a folio: *a folio edition.*

folk (fəʊk) *n., pl.* **folk** or **folks. 1.** (*functioning as pl.; often pl. in form*) people in general, esp. those of a particular group or class: *country folk.* **2.** (*functioning as pl.; usually pl. in form*) *Inf.* members of a family. **3.** (*functioning as sing.*) *Inf.* short for **folk music. 4.** a people or tribe. **5.** (*modifier*) originating from or traditional to the common people of a country: *a folk song.* —'**folkish** *adj.*

folk dance *n.* **1.** any of various traditional rustic dances. **2.** a piece of music composed for such a dance. —**folk dancing** *n.*

folk etymology *n.* the gradual change in the form of a word through the influence of a more familiar word or phrase with which it becomes associated, as for example *sparrow-grass* for *asparagus.*

folklore ('fəʊk,lɔː) *n.* **1.** the unwritten literature of a people as expressed in folk tales, songs, etc. **2.** study of such materials. —'**folk,loric** *adj.* —'**folk,lorist** *n., adj.*

folk music *n.* **1.** music that is passed on from generation to generation. **2.** any music composed in this idiom.

folk song *n.* **1.** a song which has been handed down among the common people. **2.** a modern song which reflects the folk idiom.

folksy ('fəʊksɪ) *adj.* **-sier, -siest.** *Inf., chiefly U.S.* **1.** of or like ordinary people. **2.** friendly; affable.

follicle ('fɒlɪkəl) *n.* **1.** any small sac or cavity in the body having an excretory, secretory, or protective function: *a hair follicle.* **2.** *Bot.* a dry fruit that splits along one side only to release its seeds. —**follicular** (fɒ'lɪkjʊlə), **folliculate** (fɒ'lɪkjʊ,leɪt), or **fol'licu,lated** *adj.*

follow ('fɒləʊ) *vb.* **1.** to go or come after in the same direction. **2.** (*tr.*) to accompany: *she followed her sister everywhere.* **3.** to come after as a logical or natural consequence. **4.** (*tr.*) to keep to the course or track of: *she followed the towpath.* **5.** (*tr.*) to act in accordance with: *to follow instructions.* **6.** (*tr.*) to accept the ideas or beliefs of (a previous authority, etc.): *he followed Donne in most of his teachings.* **7.** to understand (an explanation, etc.): *the lesson was difficult to follow.* **8.** to watch closely or continuously: *she followed his progress.* **9.** (*tr.*) to have a keen interest in: *to follow athletics.* **10.** (*tr.*) to help in the cause of: *the men who followed Napoleon.* **11. follow suit. a.** *Cards.* to play a card of the suit led. **b.** to do the same as someone else.

follower ('fɒləʊə) *n.* **1.** a person who accepts the teachings of another: *a follower of Marx.* **2.** an attendant. **3.** a supporter, as of a sport or team. **4.** (*esp. formerly*) a male admirer.

following ('fɒləʊɪŋ) *adj.* **1. a.** (*prenominal*) about to be mentioned, specified, etc.: *the following items.* **b.** (*as n.*): *will the following please raise their hands?* **2.** (*of winds, currents, etc.*) moving in the same direction as a vessel. ~*n.* **3.** a group of supporters or enthusiasts: *he attracted a large following.*

follow-on *Cricket.* ~*n.* **1.** an immediate second innings forced on a team scoring a prescribed number of runs fewer than its opponents in the first innings. ~*vb.* **follow on. 2.** (*intr., adv.*) (of a team) to play a follow-on.

follow up *vb.* (*tr., adv.*) **1.** to pursue or investigate (a person, etc.) closely. **2.** to continue (action) after a beginning, esp. to increase its effect. ~*n.* **follow-up. 3. a.** something done to reinforce an initial action. **b.** (*as modifier*): *a follow-up letter.* **4.** *Med.* an examination of a patient at intervals after treatment.

folly ('fɒlɪ) *n., pl.* **-lies. 1.** the state or quality of being foolish. **2.** a foolish action, idea, etc. **3.** a building in the form of a castle, temple, etc., built to satisfy a fancy or conceit. **4.** (*pl.*) *Theatre.* an elaborately costumed review.

foment (fə'mɛnt) *vb.* (*tr.*) **1.** to encourage or instigate (trouble, discord, etc.). **2.** *Med.* to apply heat and moisture to (a part of the body) to relieve pain. —**fomentation** (,fəʊmɛn'teɪʃən) *n.* —fo'**menter** *n.*

fond (fɒnd) *adj.* **1.** (*postpositive;* foll. by *of*) having a liking (for). **2.** loving; tender. **3.** indulgent: *a fond mother.* **4.** *Arch.* or *dialect.* **a.** foolish. **b.** credulous. —'**fondly** *adv.* —'**fondness** *n.*

fondant ('fɒndənt) *n.* **1.** a thick flavoured paste of sugar and water, used in sweets and icings. **2.** a sweet made of this mixture.

fondle ('fɒndəl) *vb.* (*tr.*) to touch or stroke tenderly. —'**fondler** *n.*

THESAURUS

fold *v.* **1.** bend, crease, crumple, dog-ear, double, double over, gather, intertwine, overlap, pleat, tuck, turn under ~*n.* **2.** bend, crease, double thickness, folded portion, furrow, knife-edge, layer, overlap, pleat, turn, wrinkle ~*v.* **3.** do up, enclose, enfold, entwine, envelop, wrap, wrap up **4.** *Inf.* to be ruined, close, collapse, crash, fail, go bankrupt, go bust (*Inf.*), go to the wall, go under (*Inf.*), shut down

folder binder, envelope, file, portfolio

folk clan, ethnic group, family, kin, kindred, people, race, tribe

follow **1.** come after, come next, step into the shoes of, succeed, supersede, supplant, take the place of **2.** chase, dog, hound, hunt, pursue, run after, shadow, stalk, tail, track, trail **3.** accompany, attend, bring up the rear, come or go with, come after, escort, tag along, tread on the heels of **4.** act in accordance with, be guided by, comply, conform, give allegiance to, heed, mind, note, obey, observe, regard, watch **5.** appreciate, catch,

catch on (*Inf.*), comprehend, fathom, get, get the picture, grasp, keep up with, realize, see, take in, understand **6.** arise, be consequent, develop, emanate, ensue, flow, issue, proceed, result, spring, supervene **7.** adopt, copy, emulate, imitate, live up to, pattern oneself upon, take as example **8.** be a devotee *or* supporter of, be devoted to, be interested in, cultivate, keep abreast of, support

follower **1.** adherent, admirer, apostle, backer, believer, convert, devotee, disciple, fan, fancier, habitué, partisan, pupil, representative, supporter, votary, worshipper **2.** attendant, companion, hanger-on, helper, henchman, lackey, minion, retainer (*History*), sidekick (*Sl.*)

following **1.** *adj.* coming, consequent, consequential, ensuing, later, next, specified, subsequent, succeeding, successive **2.** *n.* audience, circle, clientele, coterie, entourage, fans, patronage, public, retinue, suite, support, supporters, train

follow up **1.** check out, find out about, in-

vestigate, look into, make inquiries, pursue **2.** consolidate, continue, make sure, reinforce

folly absurdity, daftness, fatuity, foolishness, idiocy, imbecility, imprudence, indiscretion, irrationality, lunacy, madness, nonsense, preposterousness, rashness, recklessness, silliness, stupidity

fond **1.** *With of* addicted to, attached to, enamoured of, have a liking (fancy, taste) for, have a soft spot for, hooked on, keen on, partial to, predisposed towards **2.** adoring, affectionate, amorous, caring, devoted, doting, indulgent, loving, tender, warm **3.** absurd, credulous, deluded, delusive, delusory, empty, foolish, indiscreet, naive, overoptimistic, vain

fondle caress, cuddle, dandle, pat, pet, stroke

fondly **1.** affectionately, dearly, indulgently, lovingly, possessively, tenderly, with affection **2.** credulously, foolishly, naively, stupidly, vainly

fondness **1.** attachment, fancy, liking,

fondue ('fɒndjuː; *French* fɔ̃'dy) *n.* a Swiss dish, consisting of melted cheese into which small pieces of bread are dipped.

font (fɒnt) *n.* **1.** a large bowl for baptismal water. **2.** the reservoir for oil in an oil lamp. **3.** *Arch. or poetic.* a fountain or well.

fontanelle *or* **fontanel** (ˌfɒntə'nɛl) *n. Anat.* any of the soft membranous gaps between the bones of the skull in a foetus or infant.

food (fuːd) *n.* **1.** any substance that can be ingested by a living organism and metabolized into energy and body tissue. Related adj.: **alimentary. 2.** nourishment in more or less solid form: *food and drink.* **3.** anything that provides mental nourishment or stimulus.

food poisoning *n.* an acute illness caused by food that is either naturally poisonous or contaminated by bacteria.

foodstuff ('fuːdˌstʌf) *n.* any material, substance, etc., that can be used as food.

fool[1] (fuːl) *n.* **1.** a person who lacks sense or judgement. **2.** a person who is made to appear ridiculous. **3.** (formerly) a professional jester living in a royal or noble household. **4.** *Obs.* an idiot or imbecile: *the village fool.* **5. act** *or* **play the fool.** to deliberately act foolishly. ~*vb.* **6.** (*tr.*) to deceive (someone), esp. in order to make him look ridiculous. **7.** (*intr.;* foll. by *with, around with,* or *about with*) *Inf.* to act or play (with) irresponsibly or aimlessly. **8.** (*intr.*) to speak or act in a playful or jesting manner. **9.** (*tr.;* foll. by *away*) to squander; fritter. ~*adj.* **10.** *U.S. inf.* short for **foolish.**

fool[2] (fuːl) *n. Chiefly Brit.* a dessert made from a purée of fruit with cream.

foolery ('fuːlərɪ) *n., pl.* **-eries. 1.** foolish behaviour. **2.** an instance of this.

foolhardy ('fuːlˌhɑːdɪ) *adj.* **-hardier, -hardiest.** heedlessly rash or adventurous. —**'fool,hardily** *adv.* —**'fool,hardiness** *n.*

foolish ('fuːlɪʃ) *adj.* **1.** unwise; silly. **2.** resulting from folly or stupidity. **3.** ridiculous or absurd. **4.** weakminded; simple. —**'foolishly** *adv.* —**'foolishness** *n.*

foolproof ('fuːlˌpruːf) *adj. Inf.* **1.** proof against failure. **2.** (esp. of machines, etc.) proof against human misuse, error, etc.

foolscap ('fuːlzˌkæp) *n. Chiefly Brit.* a size of writing or printing paper, 13½ by 17 inches.

fool's errand *n.* a fruitless undertaking.

fool's paradise *n.* illusory happiness.

fool's-parsley *n.* an evil-smelling Eurasian umbelliferous plant with small white flowers.

foot (fʊt) *n., pl.* **feet** (fiːt). **1.** the part of the vertebrate leg below the ankle joint that is in contact with the ground during standing and walking. Related adj.: **pedal. 2.** the part of a garment covering a foot. **3.** any of various organs of locomotion or attachment in invertebrates, including molluscs. **4.** *Bot.* the lower part of some plants or plant structures. **5.** a unit of length equal to one third of a yard or 12 inches. 1 foot is equivalent to 0.3048 metre. **6.** any part resembling a foot in form or function: *the foot of a chair.* **7.** the lower part of something; bottom: *the foot of a hill.* **8.** the end of a series or group: *the foot of the list.* **9.** manner of walking or moving: *a heavy foot.* **10. a.** infantry, esp. in the British army. **b.** (*as modifier*): *a foot soldier.* **11.** any of various attachments on a sewing machine that hold the fabric in position. **12.** *Prosody.* a group of two or more syllables in which one syllable has the major stress, forming the basic unit of poetic rhythm. **13. my foot!** an expression of disbelief, often of the speaker's own preceding statement. **14. of foot.** *Arch.* in manner of movement: *fleet of foot.* **15. on foot. a.** walking or running. **b.** astir; afoot. **16. one foot in the grave.** *Inf.* near to death. **17. put a foot wrong.** to make a mistake. **18. put one's best foot forward.** *Inf.* **a.** to try to do one's best, esp. in order to give a good impression. **b.** to hurry. **19. put one's foot down.** *Inf.* to act firmly. **20. put one's foot in it.** *Inf.* to blunder. **21. under foot.** on the ground; beneath one's feet. ~*vb.* **22.** to dance to music (esp. in **foot it**). **23.** (*tr.*) to walk over or set foot on (esp. in **foot it**). **24.** (*tr.*) to pay the entire cost of (esp. in **foot the bill**). —**'footless** *adj.*

footage ('fʊtɪdʒ) *n.* **1.** a length or distance measured in feet. **2.** the extent of film material shot and exposed.

foot-and-mouth disease *n.* an acute highly infectious viral disease of cattle, pigs, sheep, and goats, characterized by the formation of vesicular eruptions in the mouth and on the feet.

football ('fʊtˌbɔːl) *n.* **1. a.** any of various games played with a round or oval ball and usually based on two teams competing to kick, butt, carry, or otherwise propel the ball into each other's goal, territory, etc. **b.** (*as modifier*): *a football supporter.* **2.** the ball used in any of these games or their variants. **3.** a problem, issue, etc., that is passed from one group or person to another. —**'foot,baller** *n.*

footboard ('fʊtˌbɔːd) *n.* **1.** a treadle or foot-operated lever on a machine. **2.** a vertical board at the foot of a bed.

footbridge ('fʊtˌbrɪdʒ) *n.* a narrow bridge for the use of pedestrians.

footfall ('fʊtˌfɔːl) *n.* the sound of a footstep.

foothill ('fʊtˌhɪl) *n.* (*often pl.*) a relatively low hill at the foot of a mountain.

foothold ('fʊtˌhəʊld) *n.* **1.** a ledge or other place affording a secure grip, as during climbing. **2.** a secure position from which further progress may be made.

footing ('fʊtɪŋ) *n.* **1.** the basis or foundation on which something is established: *the business was on a secure footing.* **2.** the relationship or status existing between two persons, groups, etc. **3.** a secure grip by or for the feet. **4.** the lower part of a foundation of a column, wall, building, etc.

footle ('fuːtəl) *vb. Inf.* (*intr.;* often foll. by *around* or *about*) to loiter aimlessly. —**'footling** *adj.*

footlights ('fʊtˌlaɪts) *pl. n. Theatre.* lights set in a row

---

THESAURUS

love, partiality, penchant, predilection, preference, soft spot, susceptibility, taste, weakness **2**. affection, attachment, devotion, kindness, love, tenderness

food 1. aliment, board, bread, chow (*Inf.*), comestibles, commons, cooking, cuisine, diet, eatables (*Sl.*), eats (*Sl.*), edibles, fare, foodstuffs, grub (*Sl.*), larder, meat, menu, nosh (*Sl.*), nourishment, nutriment, nutrition, pabulum (*Rare*), provender, provisions, rations, refreshment, scoff (*Sl.*), stores, subsistence, sustenance, table, tuck (*Inf.*), viands, victuals **2**. *Cattle, etc.* feed, fodder, forage, provender

fool *n.* **1**. ass, bird-brain (*Inf.*), blockhead, bonehead (*Sl.*), chump (*Inf.*), clodpate (*Archaic*), clot (*Inf.*), dimwit (*Inf.*), dolt, dope (*Sl.*), dunce, dunderhead, fat-head (*Inf.*), goose (*Inf.*), halfwit, idiot, ignoramus, illiterate, imbecile (*Inf.*), jackass, loon, mooncalf, moron, nincompoop, ninny, nit (*Inf.*), nitwit, numskull, sap (*Sl.*), silly, simpleton, twerp (*Inf.*), twit (*Inf.*) **2**. butt, chump (*Inf.*), dupe, easy mark (*Sl.*), fall guy (*Inf., chiefly U.S.*), greenhorn (*Inf.*), gull (*Archaic*), laughing stock, mug (*Sl.*), stooge (*Sl.*), sucker (*Sl.*) **3**.

buffoon, clown, comic, harlequin, jester, merry-andrew, motley, pierrot, punchinello **4. act** *or* **play the fool** act up, be silly, cavort, clown, cut capers, frolic, lark about (*Inf.*), mess about, play the goat, show off ~*v.* **5**. bamboozle, beguile, bluff, cheat, con (*Sl.*), deceive, delude, dupe, gull (*Archaic*), have (someone) on, hoax, hoodwink, kid (*Inf.*), make a fool of, mislead, play a trick on, put one over on (*Inf.*), take in, trick **6**. act the fool, cut capers, feign, jest, joke, kid (*Inf.*), make believe, pretend, tease **7**. *With* **with, around with** *or* **about with** fiddle, meddle, mess, monkey, play, tamper, toy, trifle

foolery antics, capers, carry-on (*Inf.*), childishness, clowning, folly, fooling, horseplay, larks, mischief, monkey tricks (*Inf.*), nonsense, practical jokes, pranks, shenanigans (*Inf.*), silliness, tomfoolery

foolhardy adventurous, bold, hot-headed, impetuous, imprudent, incautious, irresponsible, madcap, precipitate, rash, reckless, temerarious, venturesome, venturous

foolish 1. absurd, ill-advised, ill-considered, ill-judged, imprudent, incautious, indiscreet, injudicious, nonsensical, sense-

less, short-sighted, silly, unintelligent, unreasonable, unwise **2**. brainless, crazy, daft (*Inf.*), doltish, fatuous, half-baked (*Inf.*), half-witted, harebrained, idiotic, imbecilic, ludicrous, mad, moronic, potty (*Brit. inf.*), ridiculous, senseless, silly, simple, stupid, weak, witless

foolishly absurdly, idiotically, illadvisedly, imprudently, incautiously, indiscreetly, injudiciously, like a fool, mistakenly, short-sightedly, stupidly, unwisely, without due consideration

foolishness 1. absurdity, folly, imprudence, inanity, indiscretion, irresponsibility, silliness, stupidity, weakness **2**. bunk (*Inf.*), bunkum, carrying-on (*Inf.*), claptrap (*Inf.*), foolery, nonsense, rigmarole, rubbish

foolproof certain, guaranteed, infallible, never-failing, safe, sure-fire (*Inf.*), unassailable, unbreakable

footing 1. basis, establishment, foot-hold, foundation, ground, groundwork, installation, settlement **2**. condition, grade, position, rank, relations, relationship, standing, state, status, terms

along the front of the stage floor.

footloose ('fut,luːs) *adj.* **1.** free to go or do as one wishes. **2.** restless: *to feel footloose.*

footman ('futmən) *n., pl.* **-men. 1.** a male servant, esp. one in livery. **2.** (formerly) a foot soldier.

footnote ('fut,nəut) *n.* **1.** a note printed at the bottom of a page, to which attention is drawn by means of a mark in the text. ~*vb.* **2.** (*tr.*) to supply (a page, etc.) with footnotes.

footpad ('fut,pæd) *n. Arch.* a robber or highwayman, on foot rather than horseback.

footpath ('fut,pɑːθ) *n.* a narrow path for walkers only.

footplate ('fut,pleit) *n. Chiefly Brit.* a platform in the cab of a locomotive on which the crew stand to operate the controls.

foot-pound *n.* an fps unit of work equal to the work done when a force of 1 pound moves through a distance of 1 foot. Abbrev.: **ft-lb.**

footprint ('fut,print) *n.* an indentation or outline of the foot of a person or animal on a surface.

footrest ('fut,rɛst) *n.* something that provides a support for the feet, such as a low stool, rail, etc.

footsie ('futsi) *n. Inf.* flirtation involving the touching together of feet, etc.

footsore ('fut,sɔː) *adj.* having sore or tired feet, esp. from much walking. —'**foot,soreness** *n.*

footstep ('fut,stɛp) *n.* **1.** the action of taking a step in walking. **2.** the sound made by walking. **3.** the distance covered with a step. **4.** a footmark. **5.** a single stair. **6. follow in someone's footsteps.** to continue the example of another.

footstool ('fut,stuːl) *n.* a low stool used for supporting or resting the feet of a seated person.

footwear ('fut,wɛə) *n.* anything worn to cover the feet.

footwork ('fut,wɜːk) *n.* skilful use of the feet, as in sports, dancing, etc.

fop (fop) *n.* a man who is excessively concerned with fashion and elegance. —'**foppery** *n.* —'**foppish** *adj.*

for (fɔː; *unstressed* fə) *prep.* **1.** directed or belonging to: *there's a phone call for you.* **2.** to the advantage of: *I only did it for you.* **3.** in the direction of: *heading for the border.* **4.** over a span of (time or distance): *working for six days.* **5.** in favour of: *vote for me.* **6.** in order to get or achieve: *I do it for money.* **7.** designed to meet the needs of: *these kennels are for puppies.* **8.** at a cost of: *I got it for hardly any money.* **9.** such as explains or results in: *his reason for changing his job was not given.* **10.** in place of: *a substitute for the injured player.* **11.** because of: *she wept for pure relief.* **12.** with regard or consideration to the usual characteristics of: *it's cool for this time of year.* **13.** concerning: *desire for money.* **14.** as being: *I know that for a fact.* **15.** at a specified time: *a date for the next evening.* **16.** to do or partake of: *an appointment for supper.* **17.** in the duty or task of: *that's for him to say.* **18.** to allow of: *too big a job for us to handle.* **19.** despite: *she's a good wife, for all her nagging.* **20.** in order to preserve, retain, etc.: *to fight for survival.* **21.** as a direct equivalent to: *word for word.* **22.** in order to become or enter: *to train for the priesthood.* **23.** in recompense for: *I paid for it last week.* **24. for it.** *Brit. inf.* liable for punishment or blame: *you'll be for it if she catches you.* ~*conj.* **25.** (*coordinating*) because; seeing that: *I couldn't stay, for the area was violent.*

for- *prefix.* **1.** indicating rejection or prohibition: *forbid.* **2.** indicating falsity: *forswear.* **3.** used to give intensive force: *forlorn.*

forage ('forɪdʒ) *n.* **1.** food for horses or cattle, esp. hay or straw. **2.** the act of searching for food or provisions. ~*vb.* **3.** to search (the countryside or a town) for food, etc. **4.** (*intr.*) *Mil.* to carry out a raid. **5.** (*tr.*) to obtain by searching about. **6.** (*tr.*) to give food or other provisions to. **7.** (*tr.*) to feed (cattle or horses) with such food. —'**forager** *n.*

forage cap *n.* a soldier's undress cap.

foramen (fo'reɪmɛn) *n., pl.* **-ramina** (-'ræmɪnə) *or* **-ramens.** a natural hole, esp. one in a bone.

foray ('forei) *n.* **1.** a short raid or incursion. ~*vb.* **2.** to raid or ravage (a town, district, etc.).

forbade (fə'bæd, -'beid) *or* **forbad** (fə'bæd) *vb.* the past tense of **forbid.**

forbear¹ (fɔː'bɛə) *vb.* **-bearing, -bore, -borne. 1.** (when *intr.*, often foll. by *from* or an infinitive) to cease or refrain (from doing something). **2.** *Arch.* to tolerate (misbehaviour, etc.). —**for'bearance** *n.*

forbear² ('fɔː,bɛə) *n.* a variant spelling of **forebear.**

forbid (fə'bid) *vb.* **-bidding, -bade** *or* **-bad, -bidden** *or* **-bid.** (*tr.*) **1.** to prohibit (a person) in a forceful or authoritative manner (from doing or having something). **2.** to make impossible. **3.** to shut out or exclude. —**for'bidden** *adj.* —**for'bidder** *n.*

forbidding (fə'bidiŋ) *adj.* **1.** hostile or unfriendly. **2.** dangerous or ominous.

forbore (fɔː'bɔː) *vb.* the past tense of **forbear¹.**

forborne (fɔː'bɔːn) *vb.* the past participle of **forbear¹.**

force¹ (fɔːs) *n.* **1.** strength or energy; power: *the force of the blow.* **2.** exertion or the use of exertion against a person or thing that resists. **3.** *Physics.* **a.** a dynamic influence that changes a body from a state of rest to one of motion or changes its rate of motion. **b.** a static influence that produces a strain in a body or system. Symbol: *F* **4. a.** intellectual, political, or moral influence or strength: *the force of his argument.* **b.** a person or thing with such influence: *he was a force in the land.* **5.** a group of persons organized for military or police functions: *armed forces.* **6.** (*sometimes cap.; preceded by the*) *Inf.* the police force. **7.** a group of persons organized for particular duties or tasks: *a work force.* **8.** *Criminal law.* violence unlawfully committed or threatened. **9. in force. a.** (of a law) having legal validity. **b.** in great strength or numbers. ~*vb.* (*tr.*) **10.** to compel or cause (a person, group, etc.) to do something through effort, superior strength, etc. **11.** to acquire or produce through effort, superior strength, etc.: *to force a confession.* **12.** to propel or drive despite resistance. **13.** to break down or open (a lock, door, etc.). **14.** to impose or inflict: *he forced his views on them.* **15.** to cause (plants or farm animals) to grow or fatten artificially at an increased rate. **16.** to strain to the utmost: *to force the voice.* **17.** to rape. **18.** *Cards.* **a.** to compel a player by the lead of a particular suit to play (a certain card). **b.** (in bridge) to induce (a bid) from one's partner. —'**forceable** *adj.* —'**forceless** *adj.* —'**forcer** *n.*

force² (fɔːs) *n. N Brit.* a waterfall.

forced (fɔːst) *adj.* **1.** done because of force: *forced labour.* **2.** false or unnatural: *a forced smile.* **3.** due to an

---

THESAURUS

footling fiddling, fussy, hairsplitting, immaterial, insignificant, irrelevant, minor, niggly, petty, pointless, silly, time-wasting, trifling, trivial, unimportant

footstep 1. footfall, step, tread 2. footmark, footprint, trace, track

forage 1. *n. Cattle, etc.* feed, fodder, food, foodstuffs, provender 2. *v.* cast about, explore, hunt, look round, plunder, raid, ransack, rummage, scour, scrounge (*Inf.*), search, seek

forbear abstain, avoid, cease, decline, desist, eschew, hold back, keep from, omit, pause, refrain, resist the temptation to, restrain oneself, stop, withhold

forbearance 1. indulgence, leniency, lenity, longanimity (*Rare*), long-suffering, mildness, moderation, patience, resignation, restraint, self-control, temperance, tolerance 2. abstinence, avoidance, refraining

forbearing clement, easy, forgiving, indulgent, lenient, long-suffering, merciful, mild, moderate, patient, tolerant

forbid ban, debar, disallow, exclude, hinder, inhibit, interdict, outlaw, preclude, prohibit, proscribe, rule out, veto

forbidden banned, outlawed, out of bounds, prohibited, proscribed, taboo, *verboten*, vetoed

forbidding 1. abhorrent, disagreeable, odious, offensive, off-putting (*Inf.*), repellent, repulsive 2. daunting, foreboding, frightening, grim, hostile, menacing, ominous, sinister, threatening, unfriendly

force *n.* 1. dynamism, energy, impact, impulse, life, might, momentum, muscle, potency, power, pressure, stimulus, strength, stress, vigour 2. arm-twisting (*Inf.*), coercion, compulsion, constraint, duress, enforcement, pressure, violence 3. bite, cogency, effect, ef-

fectiveness, efficacy, influence, persuasiveness, power, punch (*Inf.*), strength, validity, weight 4. drive, emphasis, fierceness, intensity, persistence, vehemence, vigour 5. army, battalion, body, corps, detachment, division, host, legion, patrol, regiment, squad, squadron, troop, unit 6. **in force a.** binding, current, effective, in operation, on the statute book, operative, valid, working **b.** all together, in full strength, in great numbers ~*v.* 7. bring pressure to bear upon, coerce, compel, constrain, drive, impel, impose, make, necessitate, obligate, oblige, overcome, press, press-gang, pressure, pressurize, put the squeeze on (*Inf.*), strong-arm (*Inf.*), urge 8. blast, break open, prise, propel, push, thrust, use violence on, wrench, wrest 9. drag, exact, extort, wring

emergency or necessity: *a forced landing.*

force-feed *vb.* **-feeding, -fed.** (*tr.*) to force (a person or animal) to eat or swallow (food).

forceful ('fɔːsfʊl) *adj.* **1.** powerful. **2.** persuasive or effective. —'**forcefully** *adv.* —'**forcefulness** *n.*

forcemeat ('fɔːsˌmiːt) *n.* a mixture of chopped ingredients used for stuffing. Also called: **farce.**

forceps ('fɔːsɪps) *n. pl.* **-ceps. 1. a.** a surgical instrument in the form of a pair of pincers, used esp. in the delivery of babies. **b.** (*as modifier*): *a forceps baby.* **2.** any part of an organism shaped like a forceps.

forcible ('fɔːsəbəl) *adj.* **1.** done by, involving, or having force. **2.** convincing or effective: *a forcible argument.* —'**forcibly** *adv.*

ford (fɔːd) *n.* **1.** a shallow area in a river that can be crossed by car, horseback, etc. ~*vb.* **2.** (*tr.*) to cross (a river, brook, etc.) over a shallow area. —'**fordable** *adj.*

fore[1] (fɔː) *adj.* **1.** (*usually in combination*) located at, in, or towards the front: *the forelegs of a horse.* ~*n.* **2.** the front part. **3.** something located at, or towards the front. **4. fore and aft.** located at both ends of a vessel: *a fore-and-aft rig.* **5. to the fore.** to the front or conspicuous position. ~*adv.* **6.** at or towards a ship's bow. **7.** *Obs.* before. ~*prep., conj.* **8.** a less common word for **before.**

fore[2] (fɔː) *interj.* (in golf) a warning shout made by a player about to make a shot.

fore- *prefix.* **1.** before in time or rank: *forefather.* **2.** at or near the front: *forecourt.*

forearm[1] ('fɔːrˌɑːm) *n.* the part of the arm from the elbow to the wrist.

forearm[2] (fɔːrˈɑːm) *vb.* (*tr.*) to prepare or arm (someone) in advance.

forebear *or* **forbear** ('fɔːˌbɛə) *n.* an ancestor.

forebode (fɔːˈbəʊd) *vb.* **1.** to warn of or indicate (an event, result, etc.) in advance. **2.** to have a premonition of (an event). —**fore**'**boding** *n., adj.*

forecast ('fɔːˌkɑːst) *vb.* **-casting, -cast** *or* **-casted. 1.** to predict or calculate (weather, events, etc.), in advance. **2.** (*tr.*) to serve as an early indication of. ~*n.* **3.** a statement of probable future weather calculated from meteorological data. **4.** a prediction. **5.** the practice or power of forecasting. —'**fore,caster** *n.*

forecastle, fo'c's'le, *or* **fo'c's'sle** ('fəʊksəl) *n.* the part of a vessel at the bow where the crew is quartered.

foreclose (fɔːˈkləʊz) *vb.* **1.** *Law.* to deprive (a mortgagor, etc.) of the right to redeem (a mortgage or pledge). **2.** (*tr.*) to shut out; bar. **3.** (*tr.*) to prevent or hinder. —**fore**'**closable** *adj.* —**foreclosure** (fɔːˈkləʊʒə) *n.*

forecourt ('fɔːˌkɔːt) *n.* **1.** a courtyard in front of a building, as one in a filling station. **2.** the section of the court in tennis, badminton, etc., between the service line and the net.

forefather ('fɔːˌfɑːðə) *n.* an ancestor, esp. a male. —'**fore,fatherly** *adj.*

forefinger ('fɔːˌfɪŋɡə) *n.* the finger next to the thumb. Also called: **index finger.**

forefoot ('fɔːˌfʊt) *n., pl.* **-feet.** either of the front feet of a quadruped.

forefront ('fɔːˌfrʌnt) *n.* **1.** the extreme front. **2.** the position of most prominence or action.

foregather (fɔːˈɡæðə) *vb.* a variant spelling of **forgather.**

forego[1] (fɔːˈɡəʊ) *vb.* **-going, -went, -gone.** to precede in

time, place, etc.

forego[2] (fɔːˈɡəʊ) *vb.* **-going, -went, -gone.** (*tr.*) a variant spelling of **forgo.**

foregoing (fɔːˈɡəʊɪŋ) *adj.* (*prenominal*) (esp. of writing or speech) going before; preceding.

foregone (fɔːˈɡɒn, 'fɔːˌɡɒn) *adj.* gone or completed; past. —**fore**'**goneness** *n.*

foregone conclusion *n.* an inevitable result or conclusion.

foreground ('fɔːˌɡraʊnd) *n.* **1.** the part of a scene situated towards the front or nearest to the viewer. **2.** a conspicuous position.

forehand ('fɔːˌhænd) *adj.* (*prenominal*) **1.** *Tennis, squash, etc.* (of a stroke) made with the palm of the hand facing the direction of the stroke. ~*n.* **2.** *Tennis, squash, etc.* **a.** a forehand stroke. **b.** the side on which such strokes are made. **3.** the part of a horse in front of the saddle.

forehead ('fɒrɪd) *n.* the part of the face between the natural hair line and the eyes. Related adj.: **frontal.**

foreign ('fɒrɪn) *adj.* **1.** of, located in, or coming from another country, area, people, etc.: *a foreign resident.* **2.** dealing or concerned with another country, area, people, etc.: *a foreign office.* **3.** not pertinent or related: *a matter foreign to the discussion.* **4.** not familiar: *strange.* **5.** in an abnormal place or position: *foreign matter.* —'**foreignness** *n.*

foreigner ('fɒrɪnə) *n.* **1.** a person from a foreign country. **2.** an outsider. **3.** something from a foreign country, such as a ship or product.

foreign minister *or* **secretary** *n.* (*often caps.*) a cabinet minister who is responsible for a country's dealings with other countries. U.S. equivalent: **secretary of state.**

foreign office *n.* the ministry of a country or state that is concerned with dealings with other states. U.S. equivalent: **state department.**

foreknow (fɔːˈnəʊ) *vb.* **-knowing, -knew, -known.** (*tr.*) to know in advance. —**fore**'**knowable** *adj.* —**fore**'**knowledge** *n.*

foreland ('fɔːlənd) *n.* **1.** a headland, cape, or promontory. **2.** land lying in front of something, such as water.

foreleg ('fɔːˌlɛɡ) *n.* either of the front legs of a horse, sheep, or other quadruped.

forelimb ('fɔːˌlɪm) *n.* either of the front or anterior limbs of a four-limbed vertebrate.

forelock ('fɔːˌlɒk) *n.* a lock of hair growing or falling over the forehead.

foreman ('fɔːmən) *n., pl.* **-men. 1.** a person, often experienced, who supervises other workmen. **2.** *Law.* the principal juror, who presides at the deliberations of a jury.

foremast ('fɔːˌmɑːst; *Naut.* 'fɔːməst) *n.* the mast nearest the bow on vessels with two or more masts.

foremost ('fɔːˌməʊst) *adj., adv.* first in time, place, rank, etc.

forenoon ('fɔːˌnuːn) *n.* the daylight hours before or just before noon.

forensic (fəˈrɛnsɪk) *adj.* used in, or connected with a court of law: *forensic science.* —**fo**'**rensically** *adv.*

forensic medicine *n.* the use of medical knowledge, esp. pathology, to the purposes of the law, as in determining the cause of death. Also called: **medical**

THESAURUS

forced 1. compulsory, conscripted, enforced, involuntary, mandatory, obligatory, slave, unwilling **2.** affected, artificial, contrived, false, insincere, laboured, stiff, strained, unnatural, wooden

forceful cogent, compelling, convincing, dynamic, effective, persuasive, pithy, potent, powerful, telling, vigorous, weighty

forcible 1. active, cogent, compelling, effective, efficient, energetic, forceful, impressive, mighty, potent, powerful, strong, telling, valid, weighty **2.** aggressive, armed, coercive, compulsory, drastic, violent

forcibly against one's will, by force, by main force, compulsorily, under compulsion, under protest, willy-nilly

forebear ancestor, father, forefather, forerunner, predecessor, progenitor

forebode augur, betoken, foreshadow,

foreshow, foretell, foretoken, forewarn, indicate, portend, predict, presage, prognosticate, promise, warn of

foreboding 1. anxiety, apprehension, apprehensiveness, chill, dread, fear, misgiving, premonition, presentiment **2.** augury, foreshadowing, foretoken, omen, portent, prediction, presage, prognostication, sign, token, warning

forecast 1. *v.* anticipate, augur, calculate, divine, estimate, foresee, foretell, plan, predict, prognosticate, prophesy **2.** *n.* anticipation, conjecture, foresight, forethought, guess, outlook, planning, prediction, prognosis, projection, prophecy

forefather ancestor, father, forebear, forerunner, predecessor, primogenitor, procreator, progenitor

forefront centre, fore, foreground, front,

lead, prominence, spearhead, van, vanguard

foregoing above, antecedent, anterior, former, preceding, previous, prior

foreground centre, forefront, front, limelight, prominence

foreign 1. alien, borrowed, distant, exotic, external, imported, outlandish, outside, overseas, remote, strange, unfamiliar, unknown **2.** extraneous, extrinsic, incongruous, irrelevant, unassimilable, uncharacteristic, unrelated

foreigner alien, immigrant, incomer, newcomer, outlander, stranger

foremost chief, first, front, headmost, highest, inaugural, initial, leading, paramount, pre-eminent, primary, prime, principal, supreme

jurisprudence.

forensics (fəˈrɛnsɪks) n. (functioning as sing. or pl.) the art or study of formal debating.

foreordain (ˌfɔːrɔːˈdeɪn) vb. (tr.; may take a clause as object) to determine (events, etc.) in the future. —**foreordination** (ˌfɔːrɔːdɪˈneɪʃən) n.

forepaw (ˈfɔːˌpɔː) n. either of the front feet of most land mammals that do not have hoofs.

forerunner (ˈfɔːˌrʌnə) n. 1. a person or thing that precedes another. 2. a person or thing coming in advance to herald the arrival of someone or something. 3. an omen; portent.

foresail (ˈfɔːˌseɪl; Naut. ˈfɔːsəl) n. Naut. 1. the aftermost headsail of a fore-and-aft rigged vessel. 2. the lowest sail set on the foremast of a square-rigged vessel.

foresee (fɔːˈsiː) vb. -seeing, -saw, -seen. (tr.; may take a clause as object) to see or know beforehand: he did not foresee that. —**foreseeable** adj. —**foreseer** n.

foreshadow (fɔːˈʃædəʊ) vb. (tr.) to show, indicate, or suggest in advance; presage.

foreshore (ˈfɔːˌʃɔː) n. the part of the shore that lies between the limits for high and low tides.

foreshorten (fɔːˈʃɔːtən) vb. (tr.) to represent (a line, form, object, etc.) as shorter than actual length in order to give an illusion of recession or projection.

foresight (ˈfɔːˌsaɪt) n. 1. provision for or insight into future problems, needs, etc. 2. the act or ability of foreseeing. 3. the act of looking forward. 4. Surveying. a reading taken looking forwards. 5. a sight on a firearm's muzzle. —**foresighted** adj. —**foresightedly** adv. —**foresightedness** n.

foreskin (ˈfɔːˌskɪn) n. Anat. the nontechnical name for prepuce.

forest (ˈfɒrɪst) n. 1. a large wooded area having a thick growth of trees and plants. 2. the trees of such an area. 3. N.Z. an area planted with pines or similar trees, not native trees. Cf. bush (sense 4). 4. something resembling a large wooded area, esp. in density: a forest of telegraph poles. 5. Law. (formerly) an area of woodland, esp. one owned by the sovereign and set apart as a hunting ground. 6. (modifier) of, involving, or living in a forest or forests: a forest glade. ~vb. 7. (tr.) to create a forest. —**forested** adj.

forestall (fɔːˈstɔːl) vb. (tr.) 1. to delay, stop, or guard against beforehand. 2. to anticipate. 3. to buy up merchandise for profitable resale. —**forestaller** n. —**forestalment** n.

forestation (ˌfɒrɪˈsteɪʃən) n. the planting of trees over a wide area.

forester (ˈfɒrɪstə) n. 1. a person skilled in forestry or in charge of a forest. 2. a person or animal that lives in a forest. 3. (cap.) a member of the Ancient Order of Foresters, a friendly society.

forestry (ˈfɒrɪstrɪ) n. 1. the science of planting and caring for trees. 2. the planting and management of forests. 3. Rare. forest land.

foretaste (ˈfɔːˌteɪst) n. an early but limited experience of something to come.

foretell (fɔːˈtɛl) vb. -telling, -told. (tr.; may take a clause as object) to tell or indicate (an event, result, etc.) beforehand.

forethought (ˈfɔːˌθɔːt) n. 1. advance consideration or deliberation. 2. thoughtful anticipation of future events.

foretoken n. (ˈfɔːˌtəʊkən). 1. a sign of a future event. ~vb. (fɔːˈtəʊkən). 2. (tr.) to foreshadow.

foretop (ˈfɔːˌtɒp; Naut. ˈfɔːtəp) n. Naut. a platform at the top of the foremast.

for ever or **forever** (fɔːˈrɛvə, fə-) adv. 1. without end; everlastingly. 2. at all times. 3. Inf. for a very long time: he went on speaking for ever. ~n. forever. 4. (as object) Inf. a very long time: it took him forever to reply.

forewarn (fɔːˈwɔːn) vb. (tr.) to warn beforehand. —**forewarner** n.

foreword (ˈfɔːˌwɜːd) n. an introductory statement to a book.

forfeit (ˈfɔːfɪt) n. 1. something lost or given up as a penalty for a fault, mistake, etc. 2. the act of losing or surrendering something in this manner. 3. Law. something confiscated as a penalty for an offence, etc. 4. (sometimes pl.) a. a game in which a player has to give up an object, perform a specified action, etc., if he commits a fault. b. an object so given up. ~vb. 5. (tr.) to lose or be liable to lose in consequence of a mistake, fault, etc. 6. (tr.) Law. to confiscate as punishment. ~adj. 7. surrendered or liable to be surrendered as a penalty. —**forfeiter** n.

forfeiture (ˈfɔːfɪtʃə) n. 1. something forfeited. 2. the act of forfeiting or paying a penalty.

forgather or **foregather** (fɔːˈɡæðə) vb. (intr.) 1. to gather together. 2. (foll. by with) to socialize.

forgave (fəˈɡeɪv) vb. the past tense of forgive.

forge[1] (fɔːdʒ) n. 1. a place in which metal is worked by heating and hammering; smithy. 2. a hearth or furnace used for heating metal. ~vb. 3. (tr.) to shape (metal) by heating and hammering. 4. (tr.) to form, make, or fashion (objects, etc.). 5. (tr.) to invent or devise (an agreement, etc.). 6. to make a fraudulent imitation of (a signature, etc.) or to commit forgery. —**forger** n.

forge[2] (fɔːdʒ) vb. (intr.) 1. to move at a steady pace. 2. **forge ahead.** to increase speed.

forgery (ˈfɔːdʒərɪ) n., pl. -geries. 1. the act of reproducing something for a fraudulent purpose. 2. something forged, such as an antique. 3. Criminal law. a. the false making or altering of a document, such as a cheque, etc., with intent to defraud. b. something forged.

forget (fəˈɡɛt) vb. -getting, -got, -gotten or -got. 1. (when tr., may take a clause as object or an infinitive) to fail to recall (someone or something once known). 2. (tr.; may take a clause as object or an infinitive) to neglect, either as the result of an unintentional error or intentionally. 3. (tr.) to leave behind by mistake. 4. **forget oneself.** a. to act in an improper manner. b. to be unselfish. c. to be deep in thought. —**forgettable** adj. —**forgetter** n.

forgetful (fəˈɡɛtful) adj. 1. tending to forget. 2. (often postpositive; foll. by of) inattentive (to) or neglectful (of). —**forgetfully** adv.

forget-me-not n. a temperate low-growing plant hav-

THESAURUS

foreordain doom, fate, foredoom, prearrange, predestine, predetermine, reserve

forerunner 1. ancestor, announcer, envoy, forebear, foregoer, harbinger, herald, precursor, predecessor, progenitor, prototype 2. augury, foretoken, indication, omen, portent, premonition, prognostic, sign, token

foresee anticipate, divine, envisage, forebode, forecast, foretell, predict, prophesy

foreshadow adumbrate, augur, betoken, bode, forebode, imply, indicate, portend, predict, prefigure, presage, promise, prophesy, signal

foresight anticipation, care, caution, circumspection, far-sightedness, forethought, precaution, premeditation, preparedness, prescience, prevision (Rare), provision, prudence

forestry arboriculture, dendrology (Bot.), silviculture, woodcraft, woodmanship

foretell adumbrate, augur, bode, forebode, forecast, foreshadow, foreshow, forewarn, portend, predict, presage, prognosti-

cate, prophesy, signify, soothsay

forethought anticipation, far-sightedness, foresight, precaution, providence, provision, prudence

forever 1. always, evermore, for all time, for good and all (Inf.), for keeps, in perpetuity, till Doomsday, till the cows come home (Inf.), till the end of time, world without end 2. all the time, constantly, continually, endlessly, eternally, everlastingly, incessantly, interminably, perpetually, unremittingly

forewarn admonish, advise, alert, apprise, caution, dissuade, give fair warning, put on guard, put on the qui vive, tip off

foreword introduction, preamble, preface, preliminary, prolegomenon, prologue

forfeit 1. n. amercement (Obsolete), damages, fine, forfeiture, loss, mulct, penalty 2. v. be deprived of, be stripped of, give up, lose, relinquish, renounce, surrender

forfeiture confiscation, giving up, loss, relinquishment, sequestration (Law), surrender

forge v. 1. construct, contrive, create, devise, fabricate, fashion, form, frame, hammer out, invent, make, mould, shape, work 2. coin, copy, counterfeit, fake, falsify, feign, imitate

forger coiner, counterfeiter, falsifier

forgery 1. coining, counterfeiting, falsification, fraudulence, fraudulent imitation 2. counterfeit, fake, falsification, imitation, phoney (Inf.), sham

forget 1. consign to oblivion, dismiss from one's mind, let bygones be bygones, let slip from the memory 2. leave behind, lose sight of, omit, overlook

forgetful absent-minded, apt to forget, careless, dreamy, heedless, inattentive, lax, neglectful, negligent, oblivious, unmindful

forgetfulness absent-mindedness, abstraction, carelessness, dreaminess, heedlessness, inattention, lapse of memory, laxness, oblivion, obliviousness, woolgathering

ing clusters of small blue flowers.

forgive (fəˈgɪv) vb. **-giving, -gave, -given. 1.** to cease to blame (someone or something). **2.** to grant pardon for (a mistake, etc.). **3.** (tr.) to free (someone) from penalty. **4.** (tr.) to free from the obligation of (a debt, etc.). —**forˈgivable** adj. —**forˈgiver** n.

forgiveness (fəˈgɪvnɪs) n. **1.** the act of forgiving or the state of being forgiven. **2.** willingness to forgive.

forgiving (fəˈgɪvɪŋ) adj. willing to forgive.

forgo or **forego** (fɔːˈgəʊ) vb. **-going, -went, -gone.** (tr.) to give up or do without.

forgot (fəˈgɒt) vb. **1.** the past tense of **forget. 2.** Arch. or dialect. a past participle of **forget.**

forgotten (fəˈgɒtⁿn) vb. the past participle of **forget.**

fork (fɔːk) n. **1.** a small usually metal implement consisting of two, three, or four long thin prongs on the end of a handle, used for lifting food to the mouth, etc. **2.** a similar-shaped agricultural tool, used for lifting, digging, etc. **3.** a pronged part of any machine, device, etc. **4.** (of a road, river, etc.) **a.** a division into two or more branches. **b.** the point where the division begins. **c.** such a branch. **5.** Chiefly U.S. the main tributary of a river. ~vb. **6.** (tr.) to pick up, dig, etc., with a fork. **7.** (tr.) Chess. to place (two enemy pieces) under attack with one of one's own pieces. **8.** (intr.) to be divided into two or more branches. **9.** to take one or other branch at a fork in a road, etc.

forked (fɔːkt) adj. **1. a.** having a fork or forklike parts. **b.** (in combination): two-forked. **2.** zigzag: forked lightning. —**forkedly** (ˈfɔːkɪdlɪ) adv.

fork-lift truck n. a vehicle having two power-operated horizontal prongs that can be raised and lowered for transporting, and unloading goods.

fork out, over, or **up** vb. (adv.) Sl. to pay (money, goods, etc.), esp. with reluctance.

forlorn (fəˈlɔːn) adj. **1.** miserable or cheerless. **2.** forsaken. **3.** (postpositive; foll. by of) bereft: forlorn of hope. **4.** desperate: the last forlorn attempt. —**forˈlornness** n.

forlorn hope n. **1.** a hopeless enterprise. **2.** a faint hope. **3.** Obs. a group of soldiers assigned to an extremely dangerous duty.

form (fɔːm) n. **1.** the shape or configuration of something as distinct from its colour, texture, etc. **2.** the particular mode, appearance, etc., in which a thing or person manifests itself: water in the form of ice. **3.** a type or kind: imprisonment is a form of punishment. **4.** a printed document, esp. one with spaces in which to insert facts or answers: an application form. **5.** physical or mental condition, esp. good condition, with reference to ability to perform: off form. **6.** the previous record of a horse, athlete, etc., esp. with regard to fitness. **7.** a fixed mode of artistic expression or representation in literary, musical, or other artistic works: sonata form. **8.** a mould, frame, etc., that gives shape to something. **9.** Education, chiefly Brit. a group of children who are

taught together. **10.** behaviour or procedure, esp. as governed by custom or etiquette: good form. **11.** formality or ceremony. **12.** a prescribed set or order of words, terms, etc., as in a religious ceremony or legal document. **13.** Philosophy. the essence of something, esp. as distinguished from matter. **14.** Logic. the pattern of an argument by which the reasoning can be shown to be logically valid or invalid. **15.** Brit. a bench, esp. one that is long, low, and backless. **16.** any of the various ways in which a word may be spelt or inflected. ~vb. **17.** to give shape or form to or to take shape or form, esp. a particular shape. **18.** to come or bring into existence: a scum formed. **19.** to make or construct or be made or constructed. **20.** to construct or develop in the mind: to form an opinion. **21.** (tr.) to train or mould by instruction or example. **22.** (tr.) to acquire or develop: to form a habit. **23.** (tr.) to be an element of or constitute: this plank will form a bridge. **24.** (tr.) to organize: to form a club.

-form adj. combining form. having the shape or form of or resembling: cruciform; vermiform.

formal (ˈfɔːməl) adj. **1.** of or following established forms, conventions, etc.: a formal document. **2.** characterized by observation of conventional forms of ceremony, behaviour, etc.: a formal dinner. **3.** methodical or stiff. **4.** suitable for occasions organized according to conventional ceremony: formal dress. **5.** denoting idiom, vocabulary, etc., used by educated speakers and writers of a language. **6.** acquired by study in academic institutions. **7.** symmetrical in form: a formal garden. **8.** of or relating to the appearance, form, etc., of something as distinguished from its substance. **9.** logically deductive: formal proof. **10.** denoting a second-person pronoun in some languages: in French the pronoun "vous" is formal, while "tu" is informal. —**ˈformally** adv. —**ˈformalness** n.

formaldehyde (fɔːˈmældɪˌhaɪd) n. a colourless poisonous irritating gas with a pungent characteristic odour, used as formalin and in the manufacture of synthetic resins.

formalism (ˈfɔːməˌlɪzəm) n. **1.** scrupulous or excessive adherence to outward form at the expense of content. **2.** the mathematical or logical structure of a scientific argument as distinguished from its subject matter. **3.** Theatre. a stylised mode of production. **4.** (in Marxist criticism, etc.) excessive concern with artistic technique at the expense of social values, etc. —**ˈformalist** n. —ˌformalˈistic adj.

formality (fɔːˈmælɪtɪ) n., pl. **-ties. 1.** a requirement of custom, etiquette, etc. **2.** the quality of being formal or conventional. **3.** strict or excessive observance of ceremony, etc.

formalize or **-lise** (ˈfɔːməˌlaɪz) vb. **1.** to be or make formal. **2.** (tr.) to make official or valid. **3.** (tr.) to give a definite shape or form to. —ˌformaliˈzation or -liˈsation n.

format (ˈfɔːmæt) n. **1.** the general appearance of a pub-

THESAURUS

forgive absolve, accept (someone's) apology, acquit, bear no malice, condone, excuse, exonerate, let bygones be bygones, let off (Inf.), pardon, remit

forgiveness absolution, acquittal, amnesty, condonation, exoneration, mercy, overlooking, pardon, remission

forgiving clement, compassionate, forbearing, humane, lenient, magnanimous, merciful, mild, soft-hearted, tolerant

forgo, forego abandon, abjure, cede, do without, give up, leave alone or out, relinquish, renounce, resign, sacrifice, surrender, waive, yield

forgotten blotted out, buried, bygone, consigned to oblivion, gone (clean) out of one's mind, left behind or out, lost, obliterated, omitted, past, past recall, unremembered

fork v. bifurcate, branch, branch off, diverge, divide, go separate ways, part, split

forked angled, bifurcate(d), branched, branching, divided, pronged, split, tined, zigzag

forlorn abandoned, bereft, cheerless, comfortless, deserted, desolate, destitute, disconsolate, forgotten, forsaken, friendless,

helpless, homeless, hopeless, lonely, lost, miserable, pathetic, pitiable, pitiful, unhappy, woebegone, wretched

form[1] v. **1.** assemble, bring about, build, concoct, construct, contrive, create, devise, establish, fabricate, fashion, forge, found, invent, make, manufacture, model, mould, produce, put together, set up, shape **2.** arrange, combine, design, dispose, draw up, frame, organize, pattern, plan, think up **3.** accumulate, appear, become visible, come into being, crystallize, grow, materialize, rise, settle, show up, take shape **4.** acquire, contract, cultivate, develop, get into (Inf.), pick up **5.** compose, comprise, constitute, make, make up, serve as **6.** bring up, discipline, educate, instruct, rear, school, teach, train

form[2] n. **1.** appearance, cast, configuration, construction, cut, fashion, formation, model, mould, pattern, shape, structure **2.** anatomy, being, body, build, figure, frame, outline, person, physique, shape, silhouette **3.** arrangement, character, description, design, guise, kind, manifestation, manner, method, mode, order, practice, semblance, sort, species, stamp, style, system, type, variety, way **4.**

format, framework, harmony, order, orderliness, organization, plan, proportion, structure, symmetry **5.** condition, fettle, fitness, good condition, good spirits, health, shape, trim **6. off form** below par, not in the pink (Inf.), not up to the mark, out of condition, stale, under the weather (Inf.), unfit **7.** behaviour, ceremony, conduct, convention, custom, done thing, etiquette, formality, manners, procedure, protocol, ritual, rule **8.** application, document, paper, sheet **9.** class, grade, rank

formal **1.** approved, ceremonial, explicit, express, fixed, lawful, legal, methodical, official, prescribed, pro forma , regular, rigid, ritualistic, set, solemn, strict **2.** affected, aloof, ceremonious, conventional, correct, exact, precise, prim, punctilious, reserved, starched, stiff, unbending

formality **1.** ceremony, convention, conventionality, custom, form, gesture, matter of form, procedure, red tape, rite, ritual **2.** ceremoniousness, correctness, decorum, etiquette, politesse, protocol, punctilio

lication, including type style, paper, binding, etc. **2.** style, plan, or arrangement, as of a television programme. **3.** *Computers.* the arrangement of data on magnetic tape, etc., to comply with a computer's input device. ~*vb.* **-matting, -matted.** (*tr.*) **4.** to arrange (a book, page, etc.) into a specified format.

formation (fɔːˈmeɪʃən) *n.* **1.** the act of giving or taking form or existence. **2.** something that is formed. **3.** the manner in which something is arranged. **4.** a formal arrangement of a number of persons or things acting as a unit, such as a troop of soldiers or a football team. **5.** a series of rocks with certain characteristics in common.

formative (ˈfɔːmətɪv) *adj.* **1.** of or relating to formation, development, or growth: *formative years.* **2.** shaping; moulding: *a formative experience.* **3.** functioning in the formation of derived, inflected, or compound words. ~*n.* **4.** an inflectional or derivational affix. —ˈformatively *adv.* —ˈformativeness *n.*

former (ˈfɔːmə) *adj.* (*prenominal*) **1.** belonging to or occurring in an earlier time: *former glory.* **2.** having been at a previous time: *a former colleague.* **3.** denoting the first or first mentioned of two. ~*n.* **4. the former.** the first or first mentioned of two: distinguished from *latter.*

formerly (ˈfɔːməlɪ) *adv.* at or in a former time; in the past.

formic (ˈfɔːmɪk) *adj.* **1.** of, relating to, or derived from ants. **2.** of, containing, or derived from formic acid.

Formica (fɔːˈmaɪkə) *n. Trademark.* any of various laminated plastic sheets used esp. for heat-resistant surfaces.

formidable (ˈfɔːmɪdəbəl) *adj.* **1.** arousing or likely to inspire fear or dread. **2.** extremely difficult to defeat, overcome, manage, etc. **3.** tending to inspire awe or admiration because of great size, excellence, etc. —ˈformidably *adv.*

formless (ˈfɔːmlɪs) *adj.* without a definite shape or form; amorphous. —ˈformlessly *adv.*

formula (ˈfɔːmjʊlə) *n., pl.* **-las** or **-lae** (-ˌliː). **1.** an established form or set of words, as used in religious ceremonies, legal proceedings, etc. **2.** *Maths., physics.* a general relationship, principle, or rule stated, often as an equation, in the form of symbols. **3.** *Chem.* a representation of molecules, radicals, ions, etc., expressed in the symbols of the atoms of their constituent elements. **4.** a method or rule for doing or producing something, often one proved to be successful. **5.** *U.S.* a prescription for making up a medicine, baby's food, etc. **6.** *Motor racing.* the category in which a type of car competes, judged according to engine size, weight, and fuel capacity. —**formulaic** (ˌfɔːmjʊˈleɪɪk) *adj.*

formulary (ˈfɔːmjʊlərɪ) *n., pl.* **-laries. 1.** a book of prescribed formulas, esp. relating to religious procedure or doctrine. **2.** a formula. **3.** *Pharmacol.* a book containing a list of pharmaceutical products with their formulas.

~*adj.* **4.** of or relating to a formula.

formulate (ˈfɔːmjʊˌleɪt) *vb.* (*tr.*) **1.** to put into or express in systematic terms; express in or as if in a formula. **2.** to devise. —ˌformuˈlation *n.*

fornicate (ˈfɔːnɪˌkeɪt) *vb.* (*intr.*) to commit fornication. —ˈforniˌcator *n.*

fornication (ˌfɔːnɪˈkeɪʃən) *n.* **1.** voluntary sexual intercourse outside marriage. **2.** *Bible.* sexual immorality in general, esp. adultery.

forsake (fəˈseɪk) *vb.* **-saking, -sook, -saken.** (*tr.*) **1.** to abandon. **2.** to give up (something valued or enjoyed). —forˈsaken *adj.* —forˈsaker *n.*

forsooth (fəˈsuːθ) *adv. Arch.* in truth; indeed.

forswear (fɔːˈsweə) *vb.* **-swearing, -swore, -sworn. 1.** (*tr.*) to reject or renounce with determination or as upon oath. **2.** (*tr.*) to deny or disavow absolutely or upon oath. **3.** to perjure (oneself). —forˈswearer *n.*

forsythia (fɔːˈsaɪθɪə) *n.* a shrub, native to China, Japan, and SE Europe but widely cultivated for its showy yellow bell-shaped flowers, which appear in spring before the foliage.

fort (fɔːt) *n.* **1.** a fortified enclosure, building, or position able to be defended against an enemy. **2. hold the fort.** *Inf.* to guard something temporarily.

forte[1] (fɔːt, ˈfɔːteɪ) *n.* **1.** something at which a person excels: *cooking is my forte.* **2.** *Fencing.* the stronger section of a sword, between the hilt and the middle.

forte[2] (ˈfɔːtɪ) *Music.* ~*adj., adv.* **1.** loud or loudly. ~*n.* **2.** a loud passage in music. Symbol: *f*

forth (fɔːθ) *adv.* **1.** forward in place, time, order, or degree. **2.** out, as from concealment or inaction. **3.** away, as from a place or country. **4. and so forth.** and so on. ~*prep.* **5.** *Arch.* out of.

forthcoming (ˌfɔːθˈkʌmɪŋ) *adj.* **1.** approaching in time: *the forthcoming debate.* **2.** about to appear: *his forthcoming book.* **3.** available or ready. **4.** open or sociable.

forthright *adj.* (ˈfɔːθˌraɪt). **1.** direct and outspoken. ~*adv.* (ˌfɔːθˈraɪt), *also* **forthrightly. 2.** in a direct manner; frankly. **3.** at once. —ˈforthˌrightness *n.*

forthwith (ˌfɔːθˈwɪθ) *adv.* at once.

fortification (ˌfɔːtɪfɪˈkeɪʃən) *n.* **1.** the act, art, or science of fortifying or strengthening. **2. a.** a wall, mound, etc., used to fortify a place. **b.** such works collectively.

fortify (ˈfɔːtɪˌfaɪ) *vb.* **-fying, -fied.** (*mainly tr.*) **1.** (*also intr.*) to make (a place) defensible, as by building walls, etc. **2.** to strengthen physically, mentally, or morally. **3.** to add alcohol to (wine), in order to produce sherry, port, etc. **4.** to increase the nutritious value of (a food), as by adding vitamins. **5.** to confirm: *to fortify an argument.* —ˈfortiˌfiable *adj.* —ˈfortiˌfier *n.*

fortissimo (fɔːˈtɪsɪˌməʊ) *Music.* ~*adj., adv.* **1.** very loud. ~*n.* **2.** a very loud passage in music. Symbol: *ff*

fortitude (ˈfɔːtɪˌtjuːd) *n.* strength and firmness of mind.

THESAURUS

formation 1. accumulation, compilation, composition, constitution, crystallization, development, establishment, evolution, forming, generation, genesis, manufacture, organization, production **2.** arrangement, configuration, design, disposition, figure, grouping, pattern, rank, structure

formative 1. impressionable, malleable, mouldable, pliant, sensitive, susceptible **2.** determinative, developmental, influential, moulding, shaping

former 1. antecedent, anterior, *ci-devant*, earlier, erstwhile, ex-, late, one-time, previous, prior, quondam, whilom (*Archaic*) **2.** ancient, bygone, departed, long ago, long gone, of yore, old, old-time, past **3.** above, aforementioned, aforesaid, first mentioned, foregoing, preceding

formerly aforetime (*Archaic*), already, at one time, before, heretofore, lately, once, previously

formidable 1. appalling, dangerous, daunting, dismaying, dreadful, fearful, frightful, horrible, intimidating, menacing, shocking, terrifying, threatening **2.** arduous, challenging, colossal, difficult, mammoth, onerous, overwhelming, staggering, toilsome **3.** awesome, great, impressive, indomitable, mighty, powerful, puissant, redoubtable, terrific, tremendous

formula 1. form of words, formulary, rite, ritual, rubric **2.** blueprint, method, modus operandi, precept, prescription, principle, procedure, recipe, rule, way

formulate 1. codify, define, detail, express, frame, give form to, particularize, set down, specify, systematize **2.** coin, develop, devise, evolve, forge, invent, map out, originate, plan, work out

forsake 1. abandon, cast off, desert, disown, jettison, jilt, leave, leave in the lurch, quit, repudiate, throw over **2.** abdicate, forgo, forswear, give up, have done with, relinquish, renounce, set aside, surrender, turn one's back on, yield

forsaken abandoned, cast off, deserted, destitute, disowned, forlorn, friendless, ignored, isolated, jilted, left behind, left in the lurch, lonely, marooned, outcast, solitary

fort 1. blockhouse, camp, castle, citadel, fastness, fortification, fortress, garrison, redoubt, station, stronghold **2. hold the fort** carry on, keep things moving, keep things on an even keel, maintain the status quo, stand in, take over the reins

forte gift, long suit (*Inf.*), métier, speciality, strength, strong point, talent

forth ahead, away, forward, into the open, onward, out, out of concealment, outward

forthcoming 1. approaching, coming, expected, future, imminent, impending, prospective **2.** accessible, at hand, available, in evidence, obtainable, on tap (*Inf.*), ready **3.** chatty, communicative, expansive, free, informative, open, sociable, talkative, unreserved

forthright above-board, blunt, candid, direct, frank, open, outspoken, plain-spoken, straightforward, straight from the shoulder (*Inf.*)

forthwith at once, directly, immediately, instantly, quickly, right away, straightaway, *tout de suite*, without delay

fortification 1. bastion, bulwark, castle, citadel, defence, fastness, fort, fortress, keep, protection, stronghold **2.** embattlement, reinforcement, strengthening

fortify 1. brace, buttress, embattle, garrison, protect, reinforce, secure, shore up, strengthen, support **2.** brace, cheer, confirm, embolden, encourage, hearten, invigorate, reassure, stiffen, strengthen, sustain

fortitude backbone, braveness, courage, dauntlessness, determination, endurance, fearlessness, firmness, grit, guts (*Inf.*), hardihood, intrepidity, patience, perseverance, pluck, resolution, staying power, stout-

fortnight ('fɔːtˌnaɪt) *n.* a period of 14 consecutive days; two weeks.

fortnightly ('fɔːtˌnaɪtlɪ) *Chiefly Brit.* ~*adj.* **1.** occurring or appearing once each fortnight. ~*adv.* **2.** once a fortnight. ~*n.*, *pl.* **-lies. 3.** a publication issued at intervals of two weeks.

FORTRAN ('fɔːtræn) *n.* a high-level computer programming language for mathematical and scientific purposes.

fortress ('fɔːtrɪs) *n.* **1.** a large fort or fortified town. **2.** a place or source of refuge or support. ~*vb.* **3.** (*tr.*) to protect.

fortuitous (fɔːˈtjuːɪtəs) *adj.* happening by chance, esp. by a lucky chance. —**forˈtuitously** *adv.*

fortuity (fɔːˈtjuːɪtɪ) *n.*, *pl.* **-ties. 1.** a chance or accidental occurrence. **2.** chance or accident.

fortunate ('fɔːtʃənɪt) *adj.* **1.** having good luck. **2.** occurring by or bringing good fortune or luck. —**ˈfortunately** *adv.*

fortune ('fɔːtʃən) *n.* **1.** an amount of wealth or material prosperity, esp. a great amount. **2. small fortune.** a large sum of money. **3.** a power or force, often personalized, regarded as being responsible for human affairs. **4.** luck, esp. when favourable. **5.** (*often pl.*) a person's destiny. ~*vb.* **6.** *Arch.* (*intr.*) to happen by chance.

fortune-teller *n.* a person who makes predictions about the future as by looking into a crystal ball, etc. —**ˈfortune-ˌtelling** *adj.*, *n.*

forty ('fɔːtɪ) *n.*, *pl.* **-ties. 1.** the cardinal number that is the product of ten and four. **2.** a numeral, 40, XL, etc., representing this number. **3.** something representing, represented by, or consisting of 40 units. ~*determiner.* **4. a.** amounting to forty: *forty thieves.* **b.** (*as pronoun*): *there were forty in the herd.* —**ˈfortieth** *adj.*

forty winks *n.* (*functioning as sing. or pl.*) *Inf.* a short light sleep; nap.

forum ('fɔːrəm) *n.*, *pl.* **-rums** *or* **-ra** (-rə). **1.** a meeting for the open discussion of subjects of public interest. **2.** a medium for open discussion, such as a magazine. **3.** a public meeting place for open discussion. **4.** a court; tribunal. **5.** (in ancient Italy) an open space serving as a city's marketplace and centre of public business.

Forum *or* **Forum Romanum** (rəʊˈmɑːnəm) *n.* **the.** the main forum of ancient Rome.

forward ('fɔːwəd) *adj.* **1.** directed or moving ahead. **2.** lying or situated in or near the front part of something. **3.** presumptuous, pert, or impudent. **4.** well developed or advanced, esp. in physical or intellectual development. **5.** (*often postpositive*) ready, eager, or willing. **6. a.** of or relating to the future or favouring change. **b.** (*in combination*): *forward-looking.* **7.** *Commerce.* relating to fulfilment at a future date. ~*n.* **8.** an attacking player in any of various sports, such as soccer. ~*adv.* **9.** a variant of **forwards. 10.** ('fɔːwəd; *Naut.* 'fɒrəd). towards the front or bow of an aircraft or ship. **11.** into a position of being subject to public scrutiny: *the witness came forward.* ~*vb.* (*tr.*) **12.** to send forward or pass on to an ultimate destination: *the letter was forwarded.* **13.** to advance or promote: *to forward one's career.* —**ˈforwarder** *n.* —**ˈforwardly** *adv.* —**ˈforwardness** *n.*

forwards ('fɔːwədz) *or* **forward** *adv.* **1.** towards or at a place ahead or in advance, esp. in space but also in time. **2.** towards the front.

fosse *or* **foss** (fɒs) *n.* a ditch or moat, esp. one dug as a fortification.

fossil ('fɒsəl) *n.* **1. a.** a relic or representation of a plant or animal that existed in a past geological age, occurring in the form of mineralized bones, shells, etc. **b.** (*as modifier*): *fossil insects.* **2.** *Inf.*, *derog.* a person, idea, thing, etc., that is outdated or incapable of change. **3.** *Linguistics.* a form once current but now appearing only in one or two special contexts.

fossilize *or* **-lise** ('fɒsɪˌlaɪz) *vb.* **1.** to convert or be converted into a fossil. **2.** to become or cause to become antiquated or inflexible. —**ˌfossiliˈzation** *or* **-liˈsation** *n.*

foster ('fɒstə) *vb.* (*tr.*) **1.** to promote the growth or development of. **2.** to bring up (a child, etc.). **3.** to cherish (a plan, hope, etc.) in one's mind. **4.** *Chiefly Brit.* **a.** to place (a child) in the care of foster parents. **b.** to bring up under fosterage. ~*adj.* **5.** (*in combination*) of or involved in the rearing of a child by persons other than his natural parents: *foster home.* —**ˈfosterer** *n.*

fought (fɔːt) *vb.* the past tense or past participle of **fight.**

foul (faʊl) *adj.* **1.** offensive to the senses; revolting. **2.** stinking. **3.** charged with or full of dirt or offensive matter. **4.** (of food) putrid; rotten. **5.** morally or spiritually offensive. **6.** obscene; vulgar: *foul language.* **7.** unfair: *to resort to foul means.* **8.** (esp. of weather) unpleasant or adverse. **9.** blocked or obstructed with dirt or foreign matter: *a foul drain.* **10.** (of the bottom of a vessel) covered with barnacles that slow forward motion. **11.** *Inf.* unsatisfactory; bad: *a foul book.* ~*n.* **12.** *Sport.* **a.** a violation of the rules. **b.** (*as modifier*): *a foul blow.* **13.** an entanglement or collision, esp. in sailing or fishing. ~*vb.* **14.** to make or become polluted. **15.** to become or cause to become entangled. **16.** (*tr.*) to disgrace. **17.** to become or cause to become clogged. **18.** (*tr.*) *Naut.* (of underwater growth) to cling to (the bottom of a vessel) so as to slow its motion. **19.** (*tr.*) *Sport.* to commit a foul against (an opponent). **20.** (*intr.*) *Sport.* to infringe the rules. **21.** to collide (with a boat, etc.). ~*adv.* **22.** in a foul manner. **23. fall foul of. a.** to get into trouble with. **b.** (of ships) to collide with. —**ˈfoully** *adv.* —**ˈfoulness** *n.*

foulard (fuːˈlɑːd) *n.* a soft light fabric of plain-weave or twill-weave silk or rayon, usually with a printed design.

foul play *n.* **1.** unfair conduct esp. with violence. **2.** a violation of the rules in a game or sport.

foul up ~*vb.* (*adv.*) **1.** (*tr.*) to bungle. **2.** (*tr.*) to contaminate. **3.** to be or cause to be blocked, choked, or en-

---

THESAURUS

heartedness, strength, strength of mind, valour

fortress castle, citadel, fastness, fort, redoubt, stronghold

fortunate 1. born with a silver spoon in one's mouth, bright, favoured, golden, happy, having a charmed life, in luck, lucky, prosperous, rosy, sitting pretty (*Inf.*), successful, well-off **2.** advantageous, auspicious, convenient, encouraging, favourable, felicitous, fortuitous, helpful, opportune, profitable, promising, propitious, providential, timely

fortunately by a happy chance, by good luck, happily, luckily, providentially

fortune 1. affluence, gold mine, opulence, possessions, property, prosperity, riches, treasure, wealth **2.** accident, chance, contingency, destiny, fate, fortuity, hap (*Archaic*), hazard, kismet, luck, providence **3.** *Often plural* adventures, circumstances, destiny, doom, expectation, experience(s), history, life, lot, portion, star, success **4.** bomb (*Sl.*), bundle (*Sl.*), king's ransom, mint, packet (*Sl.*), pile (*Sl.*), wealth

forward *adj.* **1.** advanced, advancing, early, forward-looking, onward, precocious, premature, progressive, well-developed **2.** advance, first, fore, foremost, front, head, leading **3.** assuming, bare-faced, bold, brash, brass-necked (*Inf.*), brazen, brazen-faced, cheeky, confident, familiar, fresh (*Inf.*), impertinent, impudent, overassertive, overweening, pert, presuming, presumptuous, pushy (*Inf.*) ~*adv.* **4.** *Also* **forwards** ahead, forth, on, onward **5.** into consideration, into prominence, into the open, into view, out, to light, to the fore, to the surface ~*v.* **6.** advance, aid, assist, back, encourage, expedite, favour, foster, further, hasten, help, hurry, promote, speed, support **7.** *Commerce* dispatch, freight, post, route, send, send on, ship, transmit

forward-looking dynamic, enlightened, enterprising, go-ahead, go-getting (*Inf.*), liberal, modern, progressive, reforming

forwardness boldness, brashness, brazenness, cheek (*Inf.*), cheekiness, impertinence, impudence, overconfidence, pertness, presumption

foster 1. cultivate, encourage, feed, foment, nurture, promote, stimulate, support, uphold **2.** bring up, mother, nurse, raise, rear, take care of **3.** accommodate, cherish, entertain, harbour, nourish, sustain

foul *adj.* **1.** contaminated, dirty, disgusting, fetid, filthy, impure, loathsome, malodorous, mephitic, nasty, nauseating, noisome, offensive, polluted, putrid, rank, repulsive, revolting, rotten, squalid, stinking, sullied, tainted, unclean **2.** abusive, blasphemous, blue, coarse, dirty, filthy, foul-mouthed, gross, indecent, lewd, low, obscene, profane, scatological, scurrilous, smutty, vulgar **3.** abhorrent, abominable, base, despicable, detestable, disgraceful, dishonourable, egregious, hateful, heinous, infamous, iniquitous, nefarious, notorious, offensive, scandalous, shameful, vicious, vile, wicked **4.** crooked, dirty, dishonest, fraudulent, inequitable, shady (*Inf.*), underhand, unfair, unjust, unscrupulous, unsportsmanlike **5.** bad, blustery, disagreeable, foggy, murky, rainy, rough, stormy, wet, wild ~*v.* **6.** begrime, besmear, besmirch, contaminate, defile, dirty, pollute, smear, soil, stain, sully, taint **7.** block, catch, choke, clog, ensnare, entangle, jam, snarl, twist

foul play chicanery, corruption, crime, deception, dirty work, double-dealing, duplicity, fraud, perfidy, roguery, sharp practice, skulduggery, treachery, villainy

tangled.

found[1] (faʊnd) *vb.* **1.** the past tense or past participle of **find.** *~adj.* **2.** furnished, or fitted out. **3.** *Brit.* with meals, heating, etc., provided without extra charge.

found[2] (faʊnd) *vb.* **1.** (*tr.*) to bring into being or establish (something, such as an institution, etc.). **2.** (*tr.*) to build or establish the foundation of. **3.** (*also intr.*; foll. by *on* or *upon*) to have a basis (in).

found[3] (faʊnd) *vb.* (*tr.*) **1.** to cast (a material, such as metal or glass) by melting and pouring into a mould. **2.** to make (articles) in this way.

foundation (faʊnˈdeɪʃən) *n.* **1.** that on which something is founded. **2.** (*often pl.*) a construction below the ground that distributes the load of a building, wall, etc. **3.** the base on which something stands. **4.** the act of founding or establishing or the state of being founded or established. **5.** an endowment for the support of an institution such as a school. **6.** an institution supported by an endowment, often one that provides funds for charities, research, etc. **7.** a cosmetic used as a base for make-up. —**founˈdational** *adj.*

founder[1] (ˈfaʊndə) *n.* a person who establishes an institution, society, etc.

founder[2] (ˈfaʊndə) *vb.* (*intr.*) **1.** (of a ship, etc.) to sink. **2.** to break down or fail: *the project foundered.* **3.** to sink into or become stuck in soft ground. **4.** to collapse. **5.** (of a horse) to stumble or go lame.

founder[3] (ˈfaʊndə) *n.* **a.** a person who makes metal castings. **b.** (*in combination*): *an iron founder.*

foundling (ˈfaʊndlɪŋ) *n.* an abandoned infant whose parents are not known.

foundry (ˈfaʊndrɪ) *n.*, *pl.* **-ries.** a place in which metal castings are produced.

fount[1] (faʊnt) *n.* **1.** *Poetic.* a spring or fountain. **2.** source.

fount[2] (faʊnt, fɒnt) *n.* *Printing.* a complete set of type of one style and size. Also called (esp. U.S.): **font.**

fountain (ˈfaʊntɪn) *n.* **1.** a jet or spray of water or some other liquid. **2.** a structure from which such a jet or a number of such jets spurt. **3.** a natural spring of water, esp. the source of a stream. **4.** a stream, jet, or cascade of sparks, lava, etc. **5.** a principal source. **6.** a reservoir, as for oil in a lamp. —**ˈfountained** *adj.*

fountainhead (ˈfaʊntɪnˌhɛd) *n.* **1.** a spring that is the source of a stream. **2.** a principal or original source.

fountain pen *n.* a pen the nib of which is supplied with ink from a cartridge or a reservoir in its barrel.

four (fɔː) *n.* **1.** the cardinal number that is the sum of three and one. **2.** a numeral, 4, IV, etc., representing this number. **3.** something representing, represented by, or consisting of four units, such as a playing card with four symbols on it. **4.** Also called: **four o'clock.** four hours after noon or midnight. **5.** *Cricket.* **a.** a shot that crosses the boundary after hitting the ground. **b.** the four runs scored for such a shot. **6.** *Rowing.* **a.** a racing shell propelled by four oarsmen. **b.** the crew of such a shell. *~determiner.* **7. a.** amounting to four: *four times.* **b.** (*as pronoun*): *four are ready.* —**fourth** *adj.*

fourfold (ˈfɔːˌfəʊld) *adj.* **1.** equal to or having four times as many or as much. **2.** composed of four parts. *~adv.* **3.** by up to four times as many or as much.

four-in-hand *n.* **1.** a road vehicle drawn by four horses and driven by one driver. **2.** a four-horse team. **3.** *U.S.* a long narrow tie tied in a flat slipknot with the ends dangling.

four-leaf clover or **four-leaved clover** *n.* a clover with four leaves rather than three, supposed to bring good luck.

four-letter word *n.* any of several short English words referring to sex or excrement: regarded generally as offensive or obscene.

four-poster *n.* a bed with posts at each corner supporting a canopy and curtains.

fourscore (ˌfɔːˈskɔː) *determiner.* an archaic word for **eighty.**

foursome (ˈfɔːsəm) *n.* **1.** a set or company of four. **2.** Also called: **fourball.** *Sport.* a game between two pairs of players, esp. in golf.

foursquare (ˌfɔːˈskwɛə) *adv.* **1.** squarely; firmly. *~adj.* **2.** solid and strong. **3.** forthright. **4.** a rare word for **square.**

four-stroke *adj.* designating an internal-combustion engine in which the piston makes four strokes for every explosion.

fourteen (ˈfɔːˈtiːn) *n.* **1.** the cardinal number that is the sum of ten and four. **2.** a numeral, 14, XIV, etc., representing this number. **3.** something represented by or consisting of 14 units. *~determiner.* **4. a.** amounting to fourteen: *fourteen cats.* **b.** (*as pronoun*): *the fourteen who remained.* —**ˈfourˈteenth** *adj.*

fourth dimension *n.* **1.** the dimension of time, which in addition to three spatial dimensions specifies the position of a point or particle. **2.** the concept in science fiction of a dimension in addition to three spatial dimensions. —**ˌfourth-diˈmensional** *adj.*

fourth estate *n.* (*sometimes caps.*) journalists or their profession; the press.

fowl (faʊl) *n.* **1.** Also called: **domestic fowl.** a domesticated gallinaceous bird occurring in many varieties. **2.** any other bird that is used as food or hunted as game. **3.** the flesh or meat of fowl, esp. of chicken. **4.** an archaic word for any **bird.** *~vb.* **5.** (*intr.*) to hunt or snare wildfowl. —**ˈfowler** *n.* —**ˈfowling** *n.*, *adj.*

fox (fɒks) *n.*, *pl.* **foxes** or **fox.** **1.** any canine mammal of the genus *Vulpes* and related genera. They are mostly predators and have a pointed muzzle and a bushy tail. **2.** the fur of any of these animals, usually reddish-brown or grey in colour. **3.** a person who is cunning and sly. *~vb.* **4.** (*tr.*) *Inf.* to perplex: *to fox a person with a problem.* **5.** to cause (paper, wood, etc.) to become discoloured with spots, or (of paper, etc.) to become discoloured. **6.** (*tr.*) to trick; deceive. **7.** (*intr.*) to act deceitfully or craftily. —**ˈfoxˌlike** *adj.*

foxglove (ˈfɒksˌglʌv) *n.* a plant having spikes of purple or white thimble-like flowers. The soft wrinkled leaves are a source of digitalis.

foxhole (ˈfɒksˌhəʊl) *n.* *Mil.* a small pit dug to provide shelter against hostile fire.

foxhound (ˈfɒksˌhaʊnd) *n.* a breed of short-haired hound, usually kept for hunting foxes.

fox hunt *n.* **1. a.** the hunting of foxes with hounds. **b.** an instance of this. **2.** an organization for fox hunting within a particular area. —**ˈfox-ˌhunter** *n.* —**ˈfox-ˌhunting** *n.*

fox terrier *n.* either of two breeds of small black-and-white terrier, the wire-haired and the smooth.

foxtrot (ˈfɒksˌtrɒt) *n.* **1.** a ballroom dance in quadruple time, combining short and long steps in various sequences. *~vb.* **-trotting, -trotted.** **2.** (*intr.*) to perform this dance.

foxy (ˈfɒksɪ) *adj.* **foxier, foxiest.** **1.** of or resembling a fox, esp. in craftiness. **2.** of a reddish-brown colour. **3.** (of paper, etc.) spotted, esp. by mildew. —**ˈfoxily** *adv.* —**ˈfoxiness** *n.*

foyer (ˈfɔɪeɪ, ˈfɔɪə) *n.* a hall, lobby, or anteroom, as in a hotel, theatre, cinema, etc.

f.p. or **fp** *abbrev. for* freezing point.

F.P. or **f.p.** *abbrev. for:* **1.** Also: **fp** freezing point. **2.** fully paid.

F.P.A. *abbrev. for* Family Planning Association.

f.p.s. *abbrev. for:* **1.** feet per second. **2.** foot-pound-second. **3.** *Photog.* frames per second.

THESAURUS

found 1. bring into being, constitute, construct, create, endow, erect, establish, fix, inaugurate, institute, organize, originate, plant, raise, settle, set up, start **2.** base, bottom, build, ground, rest, root, sustain

foundation 1. base, basis, bedrock, bottom, footing, groundwork, substructure, underpinning **2.** endowment, establishment, inauguration, institution, organization, setting up, settlement

founder[1] *n.* architect, author, beginner, benefactor, builder, constructor, designer, establisher, father, framer, generator, initiator, institutor, inventor, maker, organizer, originator, patriarch

founder[2] *v.* **1.** be lost, go down, go to the bottom, sink, submerge **2.** *Fig.* abort, break down, collapse, come to grief, come to nothing, fail, fall through, miscarry, misfire **3.** collapse, fall, go lame, lurch, sprawl, stagger, stumble, trip

foundling orphan, outcast, stray, waif

fountain 1. font, fount, jet, reservoir, spout, spray, spring, well **2.** *Fig.* beginning, cause, commencement, derivation, fountainhead, genesis, origin, rise, source, wellhead, wellspring

fountainhead *fons et origo*, fount, inspiration, mainspring, origin, source, spring, well, wellspring

Fr *the chemical symbol for* francium.

fr. *abbrev. for:* 1. fragment. 2. franc. 3. from.

Fr. *abbrev. for:* 1. *Christianity.* a. Father. b. Frater. 2. France. 3. French.

Fra (frɑː) *n.* brother: a title given to an Italian monk or friar.

fracas ('frækɑː) *n.* a noisy quarrel; brawl.

fraction ('frækʃən) *n.* 1. *Maths.* a ratio of two expressions or numbers other than zero. 2. any part or subdivision. 3. a small piece; fragment. 4. *Chem.* a component of a mixture separated by fractional distillation. 5. *Christianity.* the formal breaking of the bread in Communion. —'**fractional** *adj.* —'**fraction,ize** *or* -,**ise** *vb.*

fractious ('frækʃəs) *adj.* 1. irritable. 2. unruly. —'**fractiously** *adv.* —'**fractiousness** *n.*

fracture ('fræktʃə) *n.* 1. the act of breaking or the state of being broken. 2. a. the breaking or cracking of a bone or the tearing of a cartilage. b. the resulting condition. 3. a division, split, or breach. 4. *Mineralogy.* a. the characteristic appearance of the surface of a freshly broken mineral or rock. b. the way in which a mineral or rock naturally breaks. ~*vb.* 5. to break or cause to break. 6. to break or crack (a bone) or (of a bone) to become broken or cracked. —'**fractural** *adj.*

frae (freɪ) *prep.* a Scot. word for **from.**

fragile ('frædʒaɪl) *adj.* 1. able to be broken easily. 2. in a weakened physical state. 3. delicate; light: *a fragile touch.* 4. slight; tenuous. —'**fragilely** *adv.* —**fragility** (frə'dʒɪlɪtɪ) *n.*

fragment *n.* ('frægmənt). 1. a piece broken off or detached. 2. an incomplete piece: *fragments of a novel.* 3. a scrap; bit. ~*vb.* (fræg'mɛnt). 4. to break or cause to break into fragments. —,**fragmen'tation** *n.*

fragmentary ('frægməntərɪ) *adj.* made up of fragments; disconnected. Also: **fragmental.**

fragrance ('freɪgrəns) *or* **fragrancy** *n., pl.* -**grances** *or* -**grancies.** 1. a pleasant or sweet odour. 2. the state of being fragrant.

fragrant ('freɪgrənt) *adj.* having a pleasant or sweet smell. —'**fragrantly** *adv.*

frail (freɪl) *adj.* 1. physically weak and delicate. 2. fragile: *a frail craft.* 3. easily corrupted or tempted.

frailty ('freɪltɪ) *n., pl.* -**ties.** 1. physical or moral weakness. 2. (*often pl.*) a fault symptomatic of moral weakness.

frame (freɪm) *n.* 1. an open structure that gives shape and support to something, such as the ribs of a ship's hull or an aircraft's fuselage or the beams of a building. 2. an enclosing case or border into which something is fitted: *the frame of a picture.* 3. the system around which something is built up: *the frame of government.* 4. the structure of the human body. 5. a condition; state (esp. in **frame of mind**). 6. a. one of a series of exposures on film used in making motion pictures. b. an exposure on a film used in still photography. 7. a television picture scanned by one or more electron beams at a particular frequency. 8. *Snooker, etc.* a. the wooden triangle used to set up the balls. b. the balls when set up. c. a single game finished when all the balls have been potted. 9. short for **cold frame.** 10. one of the sections of which a beehive is composed, esp. one designed to hold a honeycomb. 11. *Sl.* another word for **frame-up.** 12. *Obs.* shape; form. ~*vb.* (*mainly tr.*) 13. to construct by fitting parts together. 14. to draw up the plans or basic details for: *to frame a policy.* 15. to compose or conceive: *to frame a reply.* 16. to provide, support, or enclose with a frame: *to frame a picture.* 17. to form (words) with the lips, esp. silently. 18. *Sl.* to conspire to incriminate (someone) on a false charge. —'**frameless** *adj.* —'**framer** *n.*

frame of reference *n.* 1. *Sociol.* a set of standards that determines and sanctions behaviour. 2. any set of planes or curves, such as the three coordinate axes, used to locate a point in space.

frame-up *n. Sl.* 1. a conspiracy to incriminate someone on a false charge. 2. a plot to bring about a dishonest result, as in a contest.

framework ('freɪm,wɜːk) *n.* 1. a structural plan or basis of a project. 2. a structure or frame supporting or containing something.

franc (fræŋk; *French* frɑ̃) *n.* 1. the standard monetary unit of France, French dependencies, and Monaco, divided into 100 centimes. 2. the standard monetary and currency unit, comprising 100 centimes, of various countries including Belgium, the Central African Republic, Gabon, Guinea, Liechtenstein, Luxembourg, Mauritania, Niger, the Republic of Congo, Senegal, Switzerland, Togo, etc. 3. a Moroccan monetary unit worth one hundredth of a dirham.

franchise ('fræntʃaɪz) *n.* 1. (usually preceded by *the*) the right to vote, esp. for representatives in a legislative body. 2. any exemption, privilege, or right granted to an individual or group by a public authority. 3. *Commerce.* authorization granted by a manufacturing enterprise to a distributor to market the manufacturer's products. 4. the full rights of citizenship. ~*vb.* 5. (*tr.*) *Commerce, chiefly U.S.* to grant (a person, firm, etc.) a franchise. —**franchisement** ('fræntʃɪzmənt) *n.*

Franciscan (fræn'sɪskən) *n.* a member of a Christian religious order of friars or nuns tracing their origins back to Saint Francis of Assisi.

francium ('frænsɪəm) *n.* an unstable radioactive element of the alkali-metal group, occurring in minute amounts in uranium ores. Symbol: Fr; atomic no.: 87; half-life of most stable isotope, ^{223}Fr: 22 minutes.

Franco- ('fræŋkəʊ-) *combining form.* indicating France or French: *Franco-Prussian.*

frank (fræŋk) *adj.* 1. honest and straightforward in speech or attitude: *a frank person.* 2. outspoken or blunt. 3. open and avowed: *frank interest.* ~*vb.* 4. *Chiefly Brit.* to put a mark on (a letter, etc.), either cancelling the postage stamp or in place of a stamp, ensuring free carriage. 5. to mark (a letter, etc.) with an official mark or signature, indicating the right of free delivery. 6. (*tr.*) to facilitate or assist (a person) to enter easily. 7. (*tr.*) to obtain immunity for (a person). ~*n.*

THESAURUS

foxy artful, astute, canny, crafty, cunning, devious, guileful, knowing, sharp, shrewd, sly, tricky, wily

foyer antechamber, anteroom, entrance hall, lobby, reception area, vestibule

fracas affray (*Law*), aggro (*Sl.*), brawl, disturbance, donnybrook, fight, free-for-all (*Inf.*), melee, quarrel, riot, row, rumpus, scrimmage, scuffle, trouble, uproar

fractious awkward, captious, crabby, cross, fretful, froward, grouchy (*Inf.*), irritable, peevish, pettish, petulant, querulous, recalcitrant, refractory, testy, touchy, unruly

fracture 1. *n.* breach, break, cleft, crack, fissure, gap, opening, rent, rift, rupture, schism, split 2. *v.* break, crack, rupture, splinter, split

fragile breakable, brittle, dainty, delicate, feeble, fine, flimsy, frail, frangible, infirm, slight, weak

fragility brittleness, delicacy, feebleness, frailty, frangibility, infirmity, weakness

fragment 1. *n.* bit, chip, fraction, morsel, part, particle, piece, portion, remnant, scrap,
shiver, sliver 2. *v.* break, break up, come apart, come to pieces, crumble, disintegrate, disunite, divide, shatter, shiver, splinter, split, split up

fragmentary bitty, broken, disconnected, discrete, disjointed, incoherent, incomplete, partial, piecemeal, scattered, scrappy, sketchy, unsystematic

fragrance aroma, balm, bouquet, fragrancy, perfume, redolence, scent, smell, sweet odour

fragrant ambrosial, aromatic, balmy, odoriferous, odorous, perfumed, redolent, sweet-scented, sweet-smelling

frail breakable, brittle, decrepit, delicate, feeble, flimsy, fragile, frangible, infirm, insubstantial, puny, slight, tender, unsound, vulnerable, weak, wispy

frailty 1. fallibility, feebleness, frailness, infirmity, peccability, puniness, susceptibility, weakness 2. blemish, defect, deficiency, failing, fault, flaw, foible, imperfection, peccadillo, shortcoming, vice, weak point

frame *v.* 1. assemble, build, constitute,
construct, fabricate, fashion, forge, form, institute, invent, make, manufacture, model, mould, put together, set up 2. block out, compose, conceive, concoct, contrive, cook up, devise, draft, draw up, form, formulate, hatch, map out, plan, shape, sketch 3. case, enclose, mount, surround ~*n.* 4. casing, construction, fabric, form, framework, scheme, shell, structure, system 5. anatomy, body, build, carcass, morphology, physique, skeleton 6. mount, mounting, setting 7. **frame of mind** attitude, disposition, fettle, humour, mood, outlook, spirit, state, temper

frame-up fabrication, fit-up (*Sl.*), put-up job, trumped-up charge

framework core, fabric, foundation, frame, frame of reference, groundwork, plan, schema, shell, skeleton, structure, the bare bones

franchise authorization, charter, exemption, freedom, immunity, prerogative, privilege, right, suffrage, vote

8. an official mark or signature affixed to a letter, etc., ensuring free delivery or delivery without stamps. —'**frankable** adj. —'**franker** n. —'**frankly** adv. —'**frankness** n.

Frank (fræŋk) n. a member of a group of West Germanic peoples who spread from the east in the late 4th century A.D. gradually conquering most of Gaul and Germany.

Frankenstein ('fræŋkɪn,staɪn) n. a thing that destroys its creator. Also called: **Frankenstein's monster.**

frankfurter ('fræŋk,fɜːtə) n. a smoked sausage, made of finely minced pork or beef.

frankincense ('fræŋkɪn,sɛns) n. an aromatic gum resin obtained from trees of the genus *Boswellia,* which occur in Asia and Africa.

Frankish ('fræŋkɪʃ) n. **1.** the ancient West Germanic language of the Franks. ~adj. **2.** of or relating to the Franks or their language.

frantic ('fræntɪk) adj. **1.** distracted with fear, pain, joy, etc. **2.** marked by or showing frenzy: *frantic efforts.* —'**frantically** or '**franticly** adv.

frappé ('fræpeɪ) n. **1.** a drink consisting of a liqueur, etc., poured over crushed ice. ~adj. **2.** (*postpositive*) (esp. of drinks) chilled.

fraternal (frə'tɜːnəl) adj. **1.** of or suitable to a brother; brotherly. **2.** of a fraternity. **3.** designating twins of the same or opposite sex that developed from two separate fertilized ova. Cf. **identical** (sense 3). —**fra'ternalism** n.

fraternity (frə'tɜːnɪtɪ) n., pl. **-ties. 1.** a body of people united in interests, aims, etc.: *the teaching fraternity.* **2.** brotherhood. **3.** *U.S.* a secret society joined by male students, functioning as a social club.

fraternize or **-nise** ('frætə,naɪz) vb. (*intr.;* often foll. by *with*) to associate on friendly terms. —**,fraterni'zation** or -**ni'sation** n. —'**frater,nizer** or -**,niser** n.

fratricide ('frætrɪ,saɪd, 'freɪ-) n. **1.** the act of killing one's brother. **2.** a person who kills his brother. —,**fratri'cidal** adj.

Frau (frau) n., pl. **Frauen** ('frauən) or **Fraus.** a married German woman: usually used as a title equivalent to *Mrs.*

fraud (frɔːd) n. **1.** deliberate deception, trickery, or cheating intended to gain an advantage. **2.** an act or instance of such deception. **3.** *Inf.* a person who acts in a false or deceitful way.

fraudulent ('frɔːdjʊlənt) adj. **1.** acting with or having the intent to deceive. **2.** relating to or proceeding from fraud. —'**fraudulence** n. —'**fraudulently** adv.

fraught (frɔːt) adj. (*usually postpositive* and foll. by *with*) filled or charged: *a venture fraught with peril.*

Fräulein (*German* 'frɔɪlaɪn) n., pl. **-lein** or *English* **-leins.** an unmarried German woman: often used as a title equivalent to *Miss.*

fray[1] (freɪ) n. **1.** a noisy quarrel. **2.** a fight or brawl.

fray[2] (freɪ) vb. **1.** to wear or cause to wear away into loose threads, esp. at an edge or end. **2.** to make or become strained or irritated. **3.** to rub or chafe (another object).

frazil ('freɪzɪl) n. spikes of ice that form in water moving turbulently enough to prevent the formation of a sheet of ice.

frazzle ('fræzəl) *Inf.* ~vb. **1.** to make or become exhausted or weary. ~n. **2.** the state of being frazzled or exhausted. **3. to a frazzle.** completely (esp. in **burnt to a frazzle**).

freak (friːk) n. **1.** a person, animal, or plant that is abnormal or deformed. **2. a.** an object, event, etc., that is abnormal. **b.** (*as modifier*): *a freak storm.* **3.** a personal whim or caprice. **4.** *Sl.* a person who acts or dresses in a markedly unconventional way. ~vb. **5.** See **freak out.** —'**freakish** adj. —'**freaky** adj.

freak out *Inf.* ~vb. (*adv.*) **1.** to experience or cause to experience radically altered perception esp. under the influence of drugs. **2.** to be or cause to be in a heightened emotional state. **3.** (*intr.*) to adopt an unconventional way of life. ~n. **freakout. 4.** a wild experience, esp. one induced by hallucinogenic drugs.

freckle ('frɛkəl) n. **1.** a small brownish spot on the skin developed by exposure to sunlight. Technical name: **lentigo. 2.** any small area of discoloration. ~vb. **3.** to mark or become marked with freckles or spots. —'**freckled** or '**freckly** adj.

free (friː) adj. **freer, freest. 1.** able to act at will; not under compulsion or restraint. **2. a.** not enslaved or confined. **b.** (*as n.*): *land of the free.* **3.** (*often postpositive* and foll. by *from*) not subject (to) or restricted (by some regulation, constraint, etc.): *free from pain.* **4.** (of a country, etc.) autonomous or independent. **5.** exempt from external direction: *free will.* **6.** not subject to conventional constraints: *free verse.* **7.** not exact or literal: *a free translation.* **8.** provided without charge: *free entertainment.* **9.** *Law.* (of property) **a.** not subject to payment of rent or performance of services; freehold. **b.** not subject to any burden or charge; unencumbered. **10.** (*postpositive;* often foll. by *of* or *with*) ready or generous in using or giving: *free with advice.* **11.** not occupied or in use; available: *a free cubicle.* **12.** (of a person) not busy. **13.** open or available to all. **14.** without charge to the subscriber or user: *freepost; freephone.* **15.** not fixed or joined; loose: *the free end of a chain.* **16.** without obstruction or impediment: *free passage.* **17.** *Chem.* chemically uncombined: *free nitrogen.* **18.** *Logic.* denoting an occurrence of a variable not bound by a quantifier. Cf. **bound**[1] (sense 7). **19. free and easy.** casual or tolerant; easy-going. **20. for free.** *Nonstandard.* without charge or cost. ~adv. **21.** in a free manner; freely. **22.** without charge or cost. **23.** *Naut.* with the wind blowing from the quarter. **24. make free with.** to behave too familiarly towards. ~vb. **freeing, freed.** (*tr.*) **25.** to set at liberty; release. **26.** to remove obstructions or impediments from. **27.** (often foll. by *of* or *from*) to relieve or rid (of obstacles, pain, etc.). —'**freely** adv. —'**freeness** n.

-free (-friː) adj. *combining form.* free from: *trouble-free; lead-free petrol.*

THESAURUS

frank artless, blunt, candid, direct, downright, forthright, free, honest, ingenuous, open, outright, outspoken, plain, plainspoken, sincere, straightforward, straight from the shoulder (*Inf.*), transparent, truthful, unconcealed, undisguised, unreserved, unrestricted

frankly 1. candidly, honestly, in truth, to be honest **2.** bluntly, directly, freely, openly, plainly, straight (*Inf.*), without reserve

frankness absence of reserve, bluntness, candour, forthrightness, ingenuousness, openness, outspokenness, plain speaking, truthfulness

frantic at one's wits' end, berserk, beside oneself, distracted, distraught, fraught (*Inf.*), frenetic, frenzied, furious, hectic, mad, overwrought, raging, raving, wild

fraternity association, brotherhood, camaraderie, circle, clan, club, companionship, company, comradeship, fellowship, guild, kinship, league, set, sodality, union

fraternize associate, concur, consort, cooperate, go around with, hang out (*Inf.*),

hobnob, keep company, mingle, mix, socialize, sympathize, unite

fraud 1. artifice, cheat, chicane, chicanery, craft, deceit, deception, double-dealing, duplicity, guile, hoax, humbug, imposture, sharp practice, spuriousness, stratagems, swindling, treachery, trickery **2.** bluffer, charlatan, cheat, counterfeit, double-dealer, fake, forgery, hoax, hoaxer, impostor, mountebank, phoney (*Inf.*), pretender, quack, sham, swindler

fraudulent counterfeit, crafty, criminal, crooked (*Inf.*), deceitful, deceptive, dishonest, double-dealing, duplicitous, false, knavish, phoney (*Inf.*), sham, spurious, swindling, treacherous

fray v. become threadbare, chafe, fret, rub, wear, wear away, wear thin

frayed frazzled, out at elbows, ragged, tattered, threadbare, worn

freak n. **1.** aberration, abnormality, aberration, anomaly, grotesque, malformation, monster, monstrosity, mutant, oddity, queer fish (*Inf.*), rara avis, sport, teratism, weirdo

or weirdie (*Inf.*) **2.** caprice, crotchet, fad, fancy, folly, humour, irregularity, quirk, turn, twist, vagary, whim, whimsy **3.** *Sl.* addict, aficionado, buff, devotee, enthusiast, fan, fanatic, fiend (*Inf.*), nut (*Sl.*) ~adj. **4.** aberrant, abnormal, atypical, bizarre, erratic, exceptional, fluky (*Inf.*), fortuitous, odd, queer, unaccountable, unexpected, unforeseen, unparalleled, unpredictable, unusual

free adj. **1.** complimentary, for free (*Inf.*), for nothing, free of charge, gratis, gratuitous, on the house, unpaid, without charge **2.** at large, at liberty, footloose, independent, liberated, loose, off the hook (*Inf.*), on the loose, uncommitted, unconstrained, unengaged, unfettered, unrestrained **3.** able, allowed, clear, disengaged, loose, open, permitted, unattached, unengaged, unhampered, unimpeded, unobstructed, unregulated, unrestricted, untrammelled **4.** *With* of above, beyond, deficient in, devoid of, exempt from, immune to, lacking (in), not liable to, safe from, sans (*Archaic*), unaffected by, unencumbered by, untouched by, without **5.** autarchic, autonomous, democratic, emancipated, independ-

freeboard ('fri:,bɔːd) *n.* the space or distance between the deck of a vessel and the waterline.

freebooter ('fri:,buːtə) *n.* a person, such as a pirate, living from plunder. —'**freeboot** *vb.* (*intr.*).

freeborn ('fri:,bɔːn) *adj.* 1. not born in slavery. 2. of or suitable for people not born in slavery.

Free Church *n. Chiefly Brit.* any Protestant Church, esp. the Presbyterian, other than the Established Church.

freedman ('fri:d,mæn) *n., pl.* -men. a man who has been freed from slavery.

freedom ('fri:dəm) *n.* 1. personal liberty, as from slavery, serfdom, etc. 2. liberation, as from confinement or bondage. 3. the quality or state of being free, esp. to enjoy political and civil liberties. 4. (usually foll. by *from*) exemption or immunity: *freedom from taxation.* 5. the right or privilege of unrestricted use or access: *the freedom of a city.* 6. autonomy, self-government, or independence. 7. the power or liberty to order one's own actions. 8. *Philosophy.* the quality, esp. of the will or the individual, of being unrestrained. 9. ease or frankness of manner: *she talked with complete freedom.* 10. excessive familiarity of manner. 11. ease and grace, as of movement.

free enterprise *n.* an economic system in which commercial organizations compete for profit with little state control.

free fall *n.* 1. free descent of a body in which the gravitational force is the only force acting on it. 2. the part of a parachute descent before the parachute opens.

free flight *n.* the flight of a rocket, missile, etc., when its engine has ceased to produce thrust.

free-for-all *n. Inf.* a disorganized brawl or argument, usually involving all those present.

free hand *n.* 1. unrestricted freedom to act (esp. in *give* (*someone*) *a free hand*). ~*adj., adv.* **freehand.** 2. (done) by hand without the use of guiding instruments: *a freehand drawing.*

free-handed *adj.* generous or liberal; unstinting. —,free-'handedly *adv.*

freehold ('fri:,həʊld) *Property law.* ~*n.* 1. a. tenure by which land is held in fee simple, fee tail, or for life. b. an estate held by such tenure. ~*adj.* 2. relating to or having the nature of freehold. —'**free,holder** *n.*

free house *n. Brit.* a public house not bound to sell only one brewer's products.

free kick *n. Soccer.* a place kick awarded for a foul or infringement.

freelance ('fri:,lɑːns) *n.* 1. a. Also called: **freelancer.** a self-employed person, esp. a writer or artist, who is hired to do specific assignments. b. (*as modifier*): *a freelance journalist.* 2. (in medieval Europe) a mercenary soldier or adventurer. ~*vb.* 3. to work as a freelance on (an assignment, etc.). ~*adv.* 4. as a freelance.

free-living *adj.* 1. given to ready indulgence of the appetites. 2. (of animals and plants) not parasitic. —,free-'liver *n.*

freeloader ('fri:,ləʊdə) *n. U.S. sl.* a person who habitually depends on others for food, shelter, etc.

free love *n.* the practice of sexual relationships without fidelity to a single partner.

freeman ('fri:mən) *n., pl.* -men. 1. a person who is not a slave. 2. a person who enjoys political and civil liberties. 3. a person who enjoys a privilege, such as the freedom of a city.

Freemason ('fri:,meɪsən) *n.* a member of the widespread secret order, founded in London in 1717, of **Free and Accepted Masons,** pledged to brotherliness and mutual aid. —'**Free,masonry** *n.*

free-range *adj. Chiefly Brit.* kept or produced in natural conditions: *free-range eggs.*

freesia ('fri:zɪə) *n.* a plant of Southern Africa, cultivated for its white, yellow, or pink tubular fragrant flowers.

free-spoken *adj.* speaking frankly or without restraint. —,free-'spokenly *adv.*

freestanding (,fri:'stændɪŋ) *adj.* not attached to or supported by another object.

freestyle ('fri:,staɪl) *n.* 1. a competition or race, as in swimming, in which each participant may use a style of his or her choice instead of a specified style. 2. a. **International freestyle.** an amateur style of wrestling with an agreed set of rules. b. Also called: **all-in wrestling.** a style of professional wrestling with no internationally agreed set of rules.

freethinker (,fri:'θɪŋkə) *n.* a person who forms his ideas and opinions independently of authority or accepted views, esp. in matters of religion. —**free thought** *n.*

free trade *n.* 1. international trade that is free of such government interference as protective tariffs. 2. *Arch.* smuggling.

free verse *n.* unrhymed verse without a metrical pattern.

freeway ('fri:,weɪ) *n. U.S.* 1. an expressway. 2. a major road that can be used without paying a toll.

freewheel (,fri:'wi:l) *n.* 1. a ratchet device in the rear hub of a bicycle wheel that permits the wheel to rotate freely while the pedals are stationary. ~*vb.* 2. (*intr.*) to coast on a bicycle using the freewheel.

free will *n.* 1. a. the apparent human ability to make choices that are not externally determined. b. the doctrine that human beings have such freedom of choice. Cf. **determinism.** 2. the ability to make a choice without outside coercion: *he left of his own free will.*

Free World *n.* **the.** the non-Communist countries collectively.

freeze (fri:z) *vb.* **freezing, froze, frozen.** 1. to change (a liquid) into a solid as a result of a reduction in temperature, or (of a liquid) to solidify in this way. 2. (when *intr.*, sometimes foll. by *over* or *up*) to cover, clog, or harden with ice, or become so covered, clogged, or hardened. 3. to fix fast or become fixed (to something) because of the action of frost. 4. (*tr.*) to preserve (food) by subjection to extreme cold, as in a freezer. 5. to feel or cause to feel the sensation or effects of extreme cold. 6. to die or cause to die of extreme cold. 7. to become or cause to become paralysed, fixed, or motionless, esp. through fear, shock, etc. 8. (*tr.*) to cause (moving film) to stop at a particular frame. 9. to make or become formal, haughty, etc., in manner. 10. (*tr.*) to fix (prices, incomes, etc.) at a particular level. 11. (*tr.*) to forbid by law the exchange, liquidation, or collection of (loans, assets, etc.). 12. (*tr.*) to stop (a process) at a particular stage of development. 13. (*intr.*; foll. by *onto*) *Inf., chiefly U.S.* to cling. ~*n.* 14. the act of freezing or state of being frozen. 15. *Meteorol.* a spell of temperatures below freezing point, usually over a wide area. 16. the fixing of incomes, prices, etc., by legislation. —'**freezable** *adj.*

THESAURUS

ent, self-governing, self-ruling, sovereign **6.** at leisure, available, empty, extra, idle, not tied down, spare, unemployed, uninhabited, unoccupied, unused, vacant **7.** casual, easy, familiar, forward, frank, free and easy, informal, laid-back (*Inf.*), lax, liberal, loose, natural, open, relaxed, spontaneous, unbidden, unceremonious, unconstrained, unforced, uninhibited **8.** big (*Inf.*), bounteous, bountiful, charitable, eager, generous, hospitable, lavish, liberal, munificent, open-handed, prodigal, unsparing, unstinting, willing **9. free and easy** casual, easy-going, informal, laid-back (*Inf.*), lax, lenient, liberal, relaxed, tolerant, unceremonious ~*adv.* **10.** at no cost, for love, gratis, without charge **11.** abundantly, copiously, freely, idly, loosely ~*v.* **12.** deliver, discharge, disenthrall, emancipate, let go, let out, liberate, loose, manumit, release, set

at liberty, set free, turn loose, uncage, unchain, unfetter, unleash, untie **13.** clear, cut loose, deliver, disengage, disentangle, exempt, extricate, ransom, redeem, relieve, rescue, rid, unburden, undo, unshackle

freedom **1.** autonomy, deliverance, emancipation, home rule, independence, liberty, manumission, release, self-government **2.** exemption, immunity, impunity, privilege **3.** ability, carte blanche, discretion, elbowroom, facility, flexibility, free rein, latitude, leeway, licence, opportunity, play, power, range, scope **4.** abandon, candour, directness, ease, familiarity, frankness, informality, ingenuousness, lack of restraint *or* reserve, openness, unconstraint **5.** boldness, brazenness, disrespect, forwardness, impertinence, laxity, licence, overfamiliarity,

presumption

free-for-all affray (*Law*), brawl, donnybrook, dust-up (*Inf.*), fight, fracas, melee, riot, row, shindy (*Sl.*)

free hand *n.* authority, carte blanche, discretion, freedom, latitude, liberty, scope

freely **1.** of one's own accord, of one's own free will, spontaneously, voluntarily, willingly, without prompting **2.** candidly, frankly, openly, plainly, unreservedly, without reserve **3.** as you please, unchallenged, without let or hindrance, without restraint **4.** abundantly, amply, bountifully, copiously, extravagantly, lavishly, liberally, like water, open-handedly, unstintingly, with a free hand **5.** cleanly, easily, loosely, readily, smoothly

freethinker agnostic, deist, doubter, infidel, sceptic, unbeliever

freeze-dry *vb.* **-drying, -dried.** (*tr.*) to preserve (a substance) by rapid freezing and subsequently drying in a vacuum.

freezer ('fri:zə) *n.* Also called: **deepfreeze.** an insulated cold-storage cabinet for long-term storage of perishable foodstuffs.

freezing point *n.* the temperature below which a liquid turns into a solid.

freight (freɪt) *n.* **1. a.** commercial transport that is slower and cheaper than express. **b.** the price charged for such transport. **c.** goods transported by this means. **d.** (*as modifier*): *freight transport.* **2.** *Chiefly Brit.* a ship's cargo or part of it. ~*vb.* (*tr.*) **3.** to load with goods for transport.

freighter ('freɪtə) *n.* **1.** a ship or aircraft designed for transporting cargo. **2.** a person concerned with the loading of a ship.

French (frɛntʃ) *n.* **1.** the official language of France: also an official language of Switzerland, Belgium, Canada, and certain other countries. Historically, French is an Indo-European language belonging to the Romance group. **2.** (preceded by *the*; *functioning as pl.*) the natives, citizens, or inhabitants of France collectively. ~*adj.* **3.** relating to, denoting, or characteristic of France, the French, or their language. **4.** (in Canada) of French Canadians. —'**Frenchness** *n.*

French bread *n.* white bread in a long slender loaf that has a crisp brown crust.

French Canadian *n.* **1.** a Canadian citizen whose native language is French. ~*adj.* **French-Canadian. 2.** of or relating to French Canadians or their language.

French chalk *n.* a variety of talc used to mark cloth or remove grease stains.

French dressing *n.* a salad dressing made from oil and vinegar with seasonings.

French fried potatoes *pl. n.* potato chips. Also called (U.S.): **French fries.**

French horn *n. Music.* a valved brass instrument with a funnel-shaped mouthpiece and a tube of conical bore coiled into a spiral.

Frenchify ('frɛntʃɪ,faɪ) *vb.* **-fying, -fied.** *Inf.* to make or become French in appearance, etc.

French leave *n.* an unauthorized absence or departure.

French letter *n. Brit.* a slang term for **condom.**

French-polish *vb.* to treat with French polish or give a French polish (to).

French polish *n.* **1.** a varnish for wood consisting of shellac dissolved in alcohol. **2.** the gloss finish produced by this polish.

French windows *pl. n.* (*sometimes sing.*) *Brit.* a pair of casement windows extending to floor level and opening onto a balcony, garden, etc.

frenetic (frɪ'nɛtɪk) *adj.* distracted or frantic. —**fre-'netically** *adv.*

frenzy ('frɛnzɪ) *n., pl.* **-zies. 1.** violent mental derangement. **2.** wild excitement or agitation. ~*vb.* **-zying, -zied. 3.** (*tr.*) to drive into a frenzy. —'**frenzied** *adj.*

frequency ('fri:kwənsɪ) *n., pl.* **-cies. 1.** the state of being frequent. **2.** the number of times that an event occurs within a given period. **3.** *Physics.* the number of times that a periodic function or vibration repeats itself in a specified time, often 1 second. It is usually measured in hertz. **4.** *Statistics.* **a.** the number of individuals in a class (**absolute frequency**). **b.** the ratio of this number to the total number of individuals under survey (**relative frequency**).

frequency modulation *n.* a method of transmitting information using a radio-frequency carrier wave. The frequency of the carrier wave is varied in accordance with the amplitude of the input signal, the amplitude of the carrier remaining unchanged. Cf. **amplitude modulation.**

frequent *adj.* ('fri:kwənt). **1.** recurring at short intervals. **2.** habitual. ~*vb.* (frɪ'kwɛnt). **3.** (*tr.*) to visit repeatedly or habitually. —,**frequen'tation** *n.* —**fre-'quenter** *n.* —'**frequently** *adv.*

frequentative (frɪ'kwɛntətɪv) *Grammar.* ~*adj.* **1.** denoting an aspect of verbs in some languages used to express repeated or habitual action. **2.** (in English) denoting a verb or an affix meaning repeated action, such as the verb *wrestle*, from *wrest.* ~*n.* **3.** a frequentative verb or affix.

fresco ('frɛskəʊ) *n., pl.* **-coes** or **-cos. 1.** a very durable method of wall-painting using watercolours on wet plaster. **2.** a painting done in this way.

fresh (frɛʃ) *adj.* **1.** newly made, harvested, etc.: *fresh bread; fresh strawberries.* **2.** newly acquired, found, etc.: *fresh publications.* **3.** novel; original: *a fresh outlook.* **4.** most recent: *fresh developments.* **5.** further; additional: *fresh supplies.* **6.** not canned, frozen, or otherwise preserved: *fresh fruit.* **7.** (of water) not salt. **8.** bright or clear: *a fresh morning.* **9.** chilly or invigorating: *a fresh breeze.* **10.** not tired; alert. **11.** not worn or faded: *fresh colours.* **12.** having a healthy or ruddy appearance. **13.** newly or just arrived: *fresh from the presses.* **14.** youthful or inexperienced. **15.** *Inf.* presumptuous or disrespectful; forward. ~*n.* **16.** the fresh part or time of something. **17.** another name for **freshet.** ~*adv.* **18.** in a fresh manner. —'**freshly** *adv.* —'**freshness** *n.*

freshen ('frɛʃən) *vb.* **1.** to make or become fresh or fresher. **2.** (often foll. by *up*) to refresh (oneself), esp. by washing. **3.** (*intr.*) (of the wind) to increase.

fresher ('frɛʃə) or **freshman** ('frɛʃmən) *n., pl.* **-ers** or **-men.** a first-year student at college or university.

freshet ('frɛʃɪt) *n.* **1.** the sudden overflowing of a river caused by heavy rain or melting snow. **2.** a stream of fresh water emptying into the sea.

freshwater ('frɛʃ,wɔːtə) *n.* (*modifier*) **1.** of or living in fresh water. **2.** (esp. of a sailor who has not sailed on the sea) inexperienced. **3.** *U.S.* little known: *a freshwater school.*

fret[1] (frɛt) *vb.* **fretting, fretted. 1.** to distress or be distressed. **2.** to rub or wear away. **3.** to feel or give annoyance or vexation. **4.** to eat away or be eaten away, as by chemical action. **5.** (*tr.*) to make by wearing away; erode. ~*n.* **6.** a state of irritation or anxiety.

fret[2] (frɛt) *n.* **1.** a repetitive geometrical figure, esp. one

---

THESAURUS

freeze **1.** benumb, chill, congeal, glaciate, harden, ice over *or* up, stiffen **2.** fix, hold up, inhibit, peg, stop, suspend

freezing arctic, biting, bitter, chill, chilled, cutting, frost-bound, frosty, glacial, icy, numbing, penetrating, polar, raw, Siberian, wintry

freight *n.* **1.** carriage, conveyance, shipment, transportation **2.** bales, bulk, burden, cargo, consignment, contents, goods, haul, lading, load, merchandise, payload, tonnage

French Gallic

frenzied agitated, all het up (*Inf.*), convulsive, distracted, distraught, excited, feverish, frantic, frenetic, furious, hysterical, mad, maniacal, rabid, uncontrolled, wild

frenzy **1.** aberration, agitation, delirium, derangement, distraction, fury, hysteria, insanity, lunacy, madness, mania, paroxysm, passion, rage, seizure, transport, turmoil **2.** bout, burst, convulsion, fit, outburst, paroxysm, spasm

frequency constancy, frequentness, periodicity, prevalence, recurrence, repetition

frequent[1] *adj.* common, constant, continual, customary, everyday, familiar, habitual, incessant, numerous, persistent, recurrent, recurring, reiterated, repeated, usual

frequent[2] *v.* attend, be a regular customer of, be found at, hang out at (*Inf.*), haunt, patronize, resort, visit

frequently commonly, customarily, habitually, many a time, many times, much, not infrequently, oft (*Literary*), often, oftentimes (*Archaic*), over and over again, repeatedly, thick and fast, very often

fresh **1.** different, latest, modern, modernistic, new, new-fangled, novel, original, recent, this season's, unconventional, unusual, up-to-date **2.** added, additional, auxiliary, extra, further, more, other, renewed, supplementary **3.** bracing, bright, brisk, clean, clear, cool, crisp, invigorating, pure, refreshing, spanking, sparkling, stiff, sweet, unpolluted **4.** alert, bouncing, bright, bright eyed and bushy tailed (*Inf.*), chipper (*Inf., chiefly U.S.*), energetic, full of vim and vigour (*Inf.*), invigorated, keen, like a new man, lively, refreshed, rested, restored, revived, sprightly, spry, vigorous, vital **5.** blooming, clear, fair, florid, glowing, good, hardy, healthy, rosy, ruddy, wholesome **6.** dewy, undimmed, unfaded, unwearied, unwithered, verdant, vivid, young **7.** artless, callow, green, inexperienced, natural, new, raw, uncultivated, untrained, untried, youthful **8.** crude, green, natural, raw, uncured, undried, unprocessed, unsalted **9.** *Inf.* bold, brazen, cheeky, disrespectful, familiar, flip (*Inf, chiefly U.S.*), forward, impudent, insolent, pert, presumptuous, saucy, smart-alecky (*Inf.*)

freshen **1.** enliven, freshen up, liven up, refresh, restore, revitalize, rouse, spruce up, titivate **2.** air, purify, ventilate

freshness **1.** innovativeness, inventiveness, newness, novelty, originality **2.** bloom, brightness, cleanness, clearness, dewiness, glow, shine, sparkle, vigour, wholesomeness

used as an ornamental border. **2.** such a pattern made in relief; fretwork. ~*vb.* **fretting, fretted.** **3.** (*tr.*) to ornament with fret or fretwork. —**'fretless** *adj.*

fret³ (fret) *n.* any of several small metal bars set across the fingerboard of a musical instrument of the lute, guitar, or viol family at various points along its length so as to produce the desired notes. —**'fretless** *adj.*

fretful ('fretful) *adj.* peevish, irritable, or upset. —**'fretfully** *adv.* —**'fretfulness** *n.*

fret saw *n.* a fine-toothed saw with a long thin narrow blade, used for cutting designs in thin wood or metal.

fretwork ('fret,wɜːk) *n.* decorative geometrical carving or openwork.

Freudian ('frɔɪdɪən) *adj.* **1.** of or relating to Sigmund Freud (1856–1939), Austrian psychiatrist, or his ideas. ~*n.* **2.** a person who follows or believes in the basic ideas of Sigmund Freud. —**'Freudianism** *n.*

Freudian slip *n.* any action, such as a slip of the tongue, that may reveal an unconscious thought.

Fri. *abbrev. for* Friday.

friable ('fraɪəbəl) *adj.* easily broken up; crumbly. —,**fria'bility** *or* **'friableness** *n.*

friar ('fraɪə) *n.* a member of any of various chiefly mendicant religious orders of the Roman Catholic Church.

friar's balsam *n.* a compound containing benzoin, mixed with hot water and used as an inhalant to relieve colds and sore throats.

friary ('fraɪərɪ) *n., pl.* **-aries.** *Christianity.* a convent or house of friars.

fricassee (,frɪkə'siː, 'frɪkəsɪ) *n.* **1.** stewed meat, esp. chicken or veal, served in a thick white sauce. ~*vb.* **-seeing, -seed.** **2.** (*tr.*) to prepare (meat, etc.) as a fricassee.

fricative ('frɪkətɪv) *n.* **1.** a consonant produced by partial occlusion of the airstream, such as (f) or (z). ~*adj.* **2.** relating to or denoting a fricative.

friction ('frɪkʃən) *n.* **1.** a resistance encountered when one body moves relative to another body with which it is in contact. **2.** the act, effect, or an instance of rubbing one object against another. **3.** disagreement or conflict. —**'frictional** *adj.* —**'frictionless** *adj.*

Friday ('fraɪdɪ) *n.* **1.** the sixth day of the week; fifth day of the working week. **2.** See **man Friday.**

fridge (frɪdʒ) *n. Inf.* short for **refrigerator.**

fried (fraɪd) *vb.* the past tense or past participle of **fry¹.**

friend (frend) *n.* **1.** a person known well to another and regarded with liking, affection, and loyalty. **2.** an acquaintance or associate. **3.** an ally in a fight or cause.

4. a fellow member of a party, society, etc. **5.** a patron or supporter. **6. be friends (with).** to be friendly (with). **7. make friends (with).** to become friendly (with). ~*vb.* **8.** (*tr.*) an archaic word for **befriend.** —**'friendless** *adj.* —**'friendship** *n.*

Friend (frend) *n.* a member of the Society of Friends; Quaker.

friendly ('frendlɪ) *adj.* **-lier, -liest.** **1.** showing or expressing liking, goodwill, or trust. **2.** tending or disposed to help or support: *a friendly breeze helped them escape.* ~*n., pl.* **-lies.** **3.** Also called: **friendly match.** *Sport.* a match played for its own sake. —**'friendlily** *adv.* —**'friendliness** *n.*

friendly society *n. Brit.* an association of people who pay regular dues or other sums in return for old-age pensions, sickness benefits, etc.

frier ('fraɪə) *n.* a variant spelling of **fryer.** See **fry¹.**

frieze (friːz) *n.* **1.** *Archit.* **a.** the horizontal band between the architrave and cornice of a classical entablature. **b.** the upper part of the wall of a room, below the cornice. **2.** any ornamental band on a wall.

frigate ('frɪgɪt) *n.* **1.** a medium-sized square-rigged warship of the 18th and 19th centuries. **2. a.** *Brit.* a warship smaller than a destroyer. **b.** *U.S.* a warship larger than a destroyer.

fright (fraɪt) *n.* **1.** sudden fear or alarm. **2.** a sudden alarming shock. **3.** *Inf.* a horrifying or ludicrous person or thing: *she looks a fright.* **4. take fright.** to become frightened. ~*vb.* **5.** (*tr.*) a poetic word for **frighten.**

frighten ('fraɪtən) *vb.* (*tr.*) **1.** to terrify; scare. **2.** to drive or force to go (away, off, out, in, etc.) by making afraid. —**'frightener** *n.* —**'frighteningly** *adv.*

frightful ('fraɪtful) *adj.* **1.** very alarming or horrifying. **2.** unpleasant, annoying, or extreme: *a frightful hurry.* —**'frightfully** *adv.* —**'frightfulness** *n.*

frigid ('frɪdʒɪd) *adj.* **1.** formal or stiff in behaviour or temperament. **2.** (esp. of women) lacking sexual responsiveness. **3.** characterized by physical coldness: *a frigid zone.* —**fri'gidity** *or* **'frigidness** *n.* —**'frigidly** *adv.*

Frigid Zone *n.* the cold region inside the Arctic or Antarctic Circle where the sun's rays are very oblique.

frill (frɪl) *n.* **1.** a gathered, ruched, or pleated strip of cloth sewn on at one edge only, as on garments, as ornament, or to give extra body. **2.** a ruff of hair or feathers around the neck of a dog or bird or a fold of skin around the neck of a reptile or amphibian. **3.** (*often pl.*) *Inf.* a superfluous or pretentious thing or manner; affectation: *he made a plain speech with no frills.* ~*vb.* **4.** (*tr.*) to

---

THESAURUS

fret 1. affront, agonize, anguish, annoy, brood, chagrin, goad, grieve, harass, irritate, lose sleep over, provoke, ruffle, torment, upset *or* distress oneself, worry 2. agitate, bother, distress, disturb, gall, irk, nag, nettle, peeve (*Inf.*), pique, rankle with, rile, trouble, vex

fretful captious, complaining, cross, crotchety (*Inf.*), edgy, fractious, irritable, out of sorts, peevish, petulant, querulous, short-tempered, splenetic, testy, touchy, uneasy

friction 1. abrasion, attrition, chafing, erosion, fretting, grating, irritation, rasping, resistance, rubbing, scraping, wearing away 2. animosity, antagonism, bad blood, bad feeling, bickering, conflict, disagreement, discontent, discord, disharmony, dispute, dissension, hostility, incompatibility, opposition, resentment, rivalry, wrangling

friend 1. Achates, alter ego, boon companion, bosom friend, buddy (*Inf.*), china (*Sl.*), chum (*Inf.*), companion, comrade, confidant, crony, familiar, intimate, mate (*Inf.*), pal, partner, playmate, soul mate 2. adherent, advocate, ally, associate, backer, benefactor, partisan, patron, supporter, well-wisher

friendless abandoned, alienated, all alone, alone, cut off, deserted, estranged, forlorn, forsaken, isolated, lonely, lonesome, ostracized, shunned, solitary, unattached, with no one to turn to, without a friend in the world, without ties

friendliness affability, amiability, companionability, congeniality, conviviality, ge-

niality, kindliness, mateyness (*Brit. inf.*), neighbourliness, open arms, sociability, warmth

friendly affable, affectionate, amiable, amicable, attached, attentive, auspicious, beneficial, benevolent, benign, chummy (*Inf.*), close, clubby, companionable, comradely, conciliatory, confiding, convivial, cordial, familiar, favourable, fond, fraternal, genial, good, helpful, intimate, kind, kindly, matey (*Brit. inf.*), neighbourly, on good terms, on visiting terms, outgoing, peaceable, propitious, receptive, sociable, sympathetic, thick (*Inf.*), welcoming, well-disposed

friendship affection, affinity, alliance, amity, attachment, benevolence, closeness, concord, familiarity, fondness, friendliness, good-fellowship, good will, harmony, intimacy, love, rapport, regard

fright 1. alarm, apprehension, (blue) funk (*Inf.*), cold sweat, consternation, dismay, dread, fear, fear and trembling, horror, panic, quaking, scare, shock, terror, the shivers, trepidation 2. *Inf.* eyesore, frump, mess (*Inf.*), scarecrow, sight (*Inf.*)

frighten affright (*Archaic*), alarm, appal, cow, daunt, dismay, freeze one's blood, intimidate, make one's blood run cold, make one's hair stand on end (*Inf.*), make (someone) jump out of his skin (*Inf.*), petrify, put the wind up (someone) (*Inf.*), scare, scare (someone) stiff, scare the living daylights out of (someone) (*Inf.*), shock, startle, terrify, terrorize, throw into a fright, throw into a

panic, unman, unnerve

frightened abashed, affrighted (*Archaic*), afraid, alarmed, cowed, dismayed, frozen, in a cold sweat, in a panic, in fear and trepidation, numb with fear, panicky, petrified, scared, scared stiff, startled, terrified, terrorized, terror-stricken, unnerved

frightening alarming, appalling, blood-curdling, daunting, dismaying, dreadful, fearful, fearsome, hair-raising, horrifying, intimidating, menacing, scary (*Inf.*), shocking, spooky (*Inf.*), terrifying, unnerving

frightful 1. alarming, appalling, awful, dire, dread, dreadful, fearful, ghastly, grim, grisly, gruesome, harrowing, hideous, horrendous, horrible, horrid, lurid, macabre, petrifying, shocking, terrible, terrifying, traumatic, unnerving, unspeakable 2. annoying, awful, disagreeable, dreadful, extreme, great, insufferable, terrible, terrific, unpleasant

frigid 1. arctic, chill, cold, cool, frost-bound, frosty, frozen, gelid, glacial, hyperboreal, icy, Siberian, wintry 2. aloof, austere, cold-hearted, forbidding, formal, icy, lifeless, passionless, passive, repellent, rigid, stiff, unapproachable, unbending, unfeeling, unloving, unresponsive

frigidity aloofness, austerity, chill, cold-heartedness, coldness, frostiness, iciness, impassivity, lack of response, lifelessness, passivity, touch-me-not attitude, unapproachability, unresponsiveness, wintriness

adorn or fit with a frill or frills. **5.** to form into a frill or frills. —**'frilliness** n. —**'frilly** adj.

fringe (frɪndʒ) n. **1.** an edging consisting of hanging threads, tassels, etc. **2. a.** an outer edge; periphery. **b.** (as modifier): a fringe area. **3.** (modifier) unofficial; not conventional in form: fringe theatre. **4.** Chiefly Brit. a section of the front hair cut short over the forehead. **5.** an ornamental border. **6.** Physics. any of the light and dark bands produced by diffraction or interference of light. ~vb. (tr.) **7.** to adorn with a fringe or fringes. **8.** to be a fringe for. —**'fringeless** adj.

fringe benefit n. an additional advantage, esp. a benefit provided by an employer to supplement an employee's regular pay.

frippery ('frɪpərɪ) n., pl. -peries. **1.** ornate or showy clothing or adornment. **2.** ostentation. **3.** trifles; trivia.

Frisbee ('frɪzbiː) n. Trademark. a light plastic disc thrown with a spinning motion for recreation or in competition.

Frisian ('frɪʒən) or **Friesian** n. **1.** a language spoken in the NW Netherlands and adjacent islands. **2.** a speaker of this language. ~adj. **3.** of or relating to this language or its speakers.

frisk (frɪsk) vb. **1.** (intr.) to leap, move about, or act in a playful manner. **2.** (tr.) (esp. of animals) to whisk or wave briskly: the dog frisked its tail. **3.** (tr.) Inf. to search (someone) by feeling for concealed weapons, etc. ~n. **4.** a playful antic or movement. **5.** Inf. an instance of frisking a person. —**'frisker** n.

frisky ('frɪskɪ) adj. **friskier, friskiest.** lively, high-spirited, or playful. —**'friskily** adv.

fritter[1] ('frɪtə) vb. (tr.) **1.** (usually foll. by away) to waste: to fritter away time. **2.** to break into small pieces.

fritter[2] ('frɪtə) n. a piece of food, such as apple, that is dipped in batter and fried in deep fat.

frivolous ('frɪvələs) adj. **1.** not serious or sensible in content, attitude, or behaviour. **2.** unworthy of serious or sensible treatment: frivolous details. —**'frivolously** adv. —**'frivolousness** or **frivolity** (frɪ'vɒlɪtɪ) n.

frizz (frɪz) vb. **1.** (of the hair, nap, etc.) to form or cause (the hair, etc.) to form tight curls or crisp tufts. ~n. **2.** hair that has been frizzed. **3.** the state of being frizzed. —**'frizzy** adj.

frizzle[1] ('frɪzəl) vb. **1.** to form (the hair) into tight crisp curls. ~n. **2.** a tight curl.

frizzle[2] ('frɪzəl) vb. **1.** to scorch or be scorched, esp. with a sizzling noise. **2.** (tr.) to fry (bacon, etc.) until crisp.

fro (frəʊ) adv. back or from.

frock (frɒk) n. **1.** a girl's or woman's dress. **2.** a loose garment of several types, such as a peasant's smock. **3.** a wide-sleeved outer garment worn by members of some religious orders. ~vb. **4.** (tr.) to invest (a person) with the office of a cleric.

frock coat n. a man's single- or double-breasted skirted coat, as worn in the 19th century.

frog[1] (frɒg) n. **1.** an insectivorous amphibian, having a short squat tailless body with a moist smooth skin and very long hind legs specialized for hopping. **2.** any of various similar amphibians, such as the tree frog. **3.** any spiked object used to support plant stems in a flower arrangement. **4.** a frog in one's throat. phlegm on the vocal cords that affects one's speech. —**'froggy** adj.

frog[2] (frɒg) n. **1.** (often pl.) a decorative fastening of looped braid or cord, as on a military uniform. **2.** an attachment on a belt to hold the scabbard of a sword, etc. —**'frogged** adj. —**'frogging** n.

frog[3] (frɒg) n. a tough elastic horny material in the centre of the sole of a horse's foot.

frog[4] (frɒg) n. a plate of iron or steel to guide train wheels over an intersection of railway lines.

Frog (frɒg) or **Froggy** ('frɒgɪ) n., pl. **Frogs** or **Froggies.** Brit. sl. a derogatory word for a French person.

frogman ('frɒgmən) n., pl. -men. a swimmer equipped with a rubber suit, flippers, and breathing equipment for working underwater.

frogmarch ('frɒg,mɑːtʃ) Chiefly Brit. ~n. **1.** a method of carrying a resisting person in which each limb is held and the victim is carried horizontally and face downwards. **2.** any method of making a person move against his will. ~vb. **3.** (tr.) to carry in a frogmarch or cause to move forward unwillingly.

frolic ('frɒlɪk) n. **1.** a light-hearted entertainment or occasion. **2.** light-hearted activity; gaiety. ~vb. -icking, -icked. **3.** (intr.) to caper about. ~adj. **4.** Arch. full of fun; gay. —**'frolicker** n.

frolicsome ('frɒlɪksəm) adj. merry and playful. —**'frolicsomely** adv.

from (frɒm; unstressed frəm) prep. **1.** used to indicate the original location, situation, etc.: from behind the bushes. **2.** in a period of time starting at: he lived from 1910 to 1970. **3.** used to indicate the distance between two things or places: a hundred miles from here. **4.** used to indicate a lower amount: from five to fifty pounds. **5.** showing the model of: painted from life. **6.** used with the gerund to mark prohibition, etc.: nothing prevents him from leaving. **7.** because of: exhausted from his walk. ▷ **Usage.** See at **off.**

frond (frɒnd) n. **1.** the compound leaf of a fern. **2.** the leaf of a palm.

front (frʌnt) n. **1.** that part or side that is forward, or most often seen or used. **2.** a position or place directly before or ahead: a fountain stood at the front of the building. **3.** the beginning, opening, or first part. **4.** the position of leadership: in the front of scientific knowledge. **5.** land bordering a lake, street, etc. **6.** land along a seashore or large lake, esp. a promenade. **7.** Mil. **a.** the total area in which opposing armies face each other. **b.** the space in which a military unit is operating: to advance on a broad front. **8.** Meteorol. the dividing line or plane between two air masses of different origins. **9.** outward aspect or bearing, as when dealing with a situation: a bold front. **10.** Inf. a business or other activity serving as a respectable cover for another, usually criminal, organization. **11.** Also called: **front man.** a nominal leader of an organization etc.; figurehead. **12.** Inf. outward appearance of rank or wealth. **13.** a particular field of activity: on the wages front. **14.** a group of people with a common goal: a national liberation front. **15.** a false fill-in for a jacket; a dickey. **16.** Arch. the forehead or the face. ~adj. (prenominal) **17.** of, at, or in the front: a front seat. **18.** Phonetics. of or denoting a vowel articulated with the tongue brought forward, as for the sound of ee in English see or a in English hat. ~vb. **19.** (when intr., foll. by on or onto) to face (onto): this house fronts the river. **20.** (tr.) to be a front of or for. **21.** (tr.) to appear as a presenter on a television show. **22.** (tr.) to confront. **23.** to supply a front for. **24.** (intr.; often foll. by up) Austral. inf. to appear (at): to front up at the police station. —**'frontless** adj.

---

frill n. flounce, furbelow, gathering, purfle, ruche, ruching, ruff, ruffle, tuck

frills additions, affectation(s), bits and pieces, decoration(s), dressing up, embellishment(s), extras, fanciness, fandangles, finery, frilliness, frippery, fuss, gewgaws, jazz (Sl.), mannerisms, nonsense, ornamentation, ostentation, superfluities, tomfoolery, trimmings

fringe n. **1.** binding, border, edging, hem, tassel, trimming **2.** borderline, edge, limits, march, marches, margin, outskirts, perimeter, periphery ~adj. **3.** unconventional, unofficial, unorthodox ~v. **4.** border, edge, enclose, skirt, surround, trim

frisk 1. bounce, caper, cavort, curvet, dance, frolic, gambol, hop, jump, play, prance, rollick, romp, skip, sport, trip **2.** Inf. check, inspect, run over, search, shake down (U.S. sl.)

frisky bouncy, coltish, frolicsome, full of beans (Inf.), full of joie de vivre, high-spirited, in high spirits, kittenish, lively, playful, rollicking, romping, spirited, sportive

fritter (away) dally away, dissipate, fool away, idle (away), misspend, run through, spend like water, squander, waste

frivolity childishness, flightiness, flippancy, flummery, folly, frivolousness, fun, gaiety, giddiness, jest, levity, light-heartedness, lightness, nonsense, puerility, shallowness, silliness, superficiality, trifling, triviality

frivolous 1. childish, dizzy, empty-headed, flighty, flip (Inf.), flippant, foolish, giddy, idle, ill-considered, juvenile, light-minded, nonserious, puerile, silly, superficial **2.** extravagant, impractical, light, minor, niggling, paltry, peripheral, petty, pointless, shallow, trifling, trivial, unimportant

frizzle crisp, fry, hiss, roast, scorch, sizzle, sputter

frolic v. **1.** caper, cavort, cut capers, frisk, gambol, lark, make merry, play, rollick, romp, sport ~n. **2.** antic, escapade, gambado, gambol, game, lark, prank, revel, romp, spree **3.** amusement, drollery, fun, fun and games, gaiety, high jinks, merriment, skylarking (Inf.), sport

frontage ('frʌntɪdʒ) n. 1. the façade of a building or the front of a plot of ground. 2. the extent of the front of a shop, plot of land, etc. 3. the direction in which a building faces.

frontal ('frʌntəl) adj. 1. of, at, or in the front. 2. of or relating to the forehead: frontal artery. ~n. 3. a decorative hanging for the front of an altar. —'frontally adv.

front bench n. 1. Brit. a. the foremost bench of either the Government or Opposition in the House of Commons. b. the leadership (frontbenchers) of either group, who occupy this bench. 2. the leadership of the government or opposition in various legislative assemblies.

frontier ('frʌntɪə, frʌn'tɪə) n. 1. a. the region of a country bordering on another or a line, barrier, etc., marking such a boundary. b. (as modifier): a frontier post. 2. U.S. the edge of the settled area of a country. 3. (often pl.) the limit of knowledge in a particular field: the frontiers of physics have been pushed back.

frontispiece ('frʌntɪsˌpiːs) n. 1. an illustration facing the title page of a book. 2. the principal façade of a building. 3. a pediment over a door, window, etc.

frontrunner ('frʌntˌrʌnə) n. Inf. the leader or a favoured contestant in a race, election, etc.

frost (frɒst) n. 1. a white deposit of ice particles, esp. one formed on objects out of doors at night. 2. an atmospheric temperature of below freezing point, characterized by the production of this deposit. 3. degrees of frost. degrees below freezing point. 4. Inf. something given a cold reception; failure. 5. Inf. coolness of manner. 6. the act of freezing. ~vb. 7. to cover or be covered with frost. 8. (tr.) to give a frostlike appearance to (glass, etc.), as by means of a fine-grained surface. 9. (tr.) Chiefly U.S. to decorate (cakes, etc.) with icing or frosting. 10. (tr.) to kill or damage (crops, etc.) with frost.

frostbite ('frɒstˌbaɪt) n. destruction of tissues, esp. those of the fingers, ears, toes, and nose, by freezing. —'frostˌbitten adj.

frosting ('frɒstɪŋ) n. 1. another word (esp. U.S.) for icing. 2. a rough or matt finish on glass, silver, etc.

frosty ('frɒstɪ) adj. frostier, frostiest. 1. characterized by frost: a frosty night. 2. covered by or decorated with frost. 3. lacking warmth or enthusiasm: the new plan had a frosty reception. —'frostily adv. —'frostiness n.

froth (frɒθ) n. 1. a mass of small bubbles of air or a gas in a liquid, produced by fermentation, etc. 2. a mixture of saliva and air bubbles formed at the lips in certain diseases, such as rabies. 3. trivial ideas or entertainment. ~vb. 4. to produce or cause to produce froth. 5. (tr.) to give out in the form of froth. —'frothy adj. —'frothily adv.

froward ('frəʊəd) adj. obstinate; contrary. —'frowardly adv. —'frowardness n.

frown (fraʊn) vb. 1. (intr.) to draw the brows together and wrinkle the forehead, esp. in worry, anger, or concentration. 2. (intr.; foll. by on or upon) to look disapprovingly (upon). 3. (tr.) to express (worry, etc.) by frowning. ~n. 4. the act of frowning. 5. a show of dislike or displeasure. —'frowner n. —'frowningly adv.

frowsty ('fraʊstɪ) adj. ill-smelling; stale; musty.

frowzy or **frowsy** ('fraʊzɪ) adj. frowzier, frowziest, or frowsier, frowsiest. 1. untidy or unkempt in appearance. 2. ill-smelling; frowsty. —'frowziness or 'frowsiness n.

froze (frəʊz) vb. the past tense of freeze.

frozen ('frəʊzən) vb. 1. the past participle of freeze. ~adj. 2. turned into or covered with ice. 3. killed or stiffened by extreme cold. 4. (of a region or climate) icy or snowy. 5. (of food) preserved by a freezing process. 6. a. (of prices, wages, etc.) arbitrarily pegged at a certain level. b. (of business assets) not convertible into cash. 7. frigid or disdainful in manner. 8. motionless or unyielding: he was frozen with horror. —'frozenly adv.

F.R.S. (in Britain) abbrev. for Fellow of the Royal Society.

fructify ('frʌktɪˌfaɪ) vb. -fying, -fied. 1. to bear or cause to bear fruit. 2. to make or become fruitful. —ˌfructifiˈcation n. —frucˈtiferous adj. —'fructiˌfier n.

fructose ('frʌktəʊs) n. a white crystalline sugar occurring in many fruits. Formula: $C_6H_{12}O_6$.

frugal ('fruːɡəl) adj. 1. practising economy; thrifty. 2. not costly; meagre. —fruˈgality n. —'frugally adv.

fruit (fruːt) n. 1. Bot. the ripened ovary of a flowering plant, containing one or more seeds. It may be dry, as in the poppy, or fleshy, as in the peach. 2. any fleshy part of a plant that supports the seeds and is edible, such as the strawberry. 3. any plant product useful to man, including grain, vegetables, etc. 4. (often pl.) the result or consequence of an action or effort. 5. Arch. offspring of man or animals. ~vb. 6. to bear or cause to bear fruit. —'fruitˌlike adj.

fruiterer ('fruːtərə) n. Chiefly Brit. a fruit dealer or seller.

fruitful ('fruːtfʊl) adj. 1. bearing fruit in abundance. 2. productive or prolific. 3. producing results or profits: a fruitful discussion. —'fruitfully adv. —'fruitfulness n.

fruition (fruːˈɪʃən) n. 1. the attainment of something worked for or desired. 2. enjoyment of this. 3. the act or condition of bearing fruit.

fruitless ('fruːtlɪs) adj. 1. yielding nothing or nothing of value; unproductive. 2. without fruit. —'fruitlessly adv. —'fruitlessness n.

fruit machine n. Brit. a gambling machine that pays out when certain combinations of diagrams, usually of fruit, appear on a dial.

fruit sugar n. another name for fructose.

fruity ('fruːtɪ) adj. fruitier, fruitiest. 1. of or resembling fruit. 2. (of a voice) mellow or rich. 3. Inf., chiefly

---

THESAURUS

frolicsome coltish, frisky, gay, kittenish, lively, merry, playful, rollicking, sportive, sprightly, wanton (Archaic)

front n. 1. anterior, exterior, façade, face, facing, foreground, forepart, frontage, obverse 2. beginning, fore, forefront, front line, head, lead, top, van, vanguard 3. air, appearance, aspect, bearing, countenance, demeanour, expression, exterior, face, manner, mien, show 4. blind, cover, cover-up, disguise, façade, mask, pretext, show 5. in front ahead, before, first, in advance, in the lead, in the van, leading, preceding, to the fore ~adj. 6. first, foremost, head, headmost, lead, leading, topmost ~v. 7. face (onto), look over or onto, overlook

frontier borderland, borderline, bound, boundary, confines, edge, limit, marches, perimeter, verge

frost freeze, freeze-up, hoarfrost, Jack Frost, rime

frosty 1. chilly, cold, frozen, hoar (Rare), ice-capped, icicled, icy, rimy, wintry 2. discouraging, frigid, off-putting, standoffish, unenthusiastic, unfriendly, unwelcoming

froth 1. n. bubbles, effervescence, foam, head, lather, scum, spume, suds 2. v. bubble

over, come to a head, effervesce, fizz, foam, lather

frothy 1. foaming, foamy, spumescent, spumous, spumy, sudsy 2. Fig. empty, frilly, frivolous, light, petty, slight, trifling, trivial, trumpery, unnecessary, unsubstantial, vain

frown 1. give a dirty look, glare, glower, knit one's brows, look daggers, lower, scowl 2. With on or upon disapprove of, discountenance, discourage, dislike, look askance at, not take kindly to, show disapproval or displeasure, take a dim view of, view with disfavour

frowsty close, fuggy, fusty, ill-smelling, musty, stale, stuffy

frowzy blowzy, dirty, draggletailed (Archaic), frumpish, messy, slatternly, sloppy, slovenly, sluttish, ungroomed, unkempt, untidy, unwashed

frozen 1. arctic, chilled, chilled to the marrow, frigid, frosted, icebound, ice-cold, ice-covered, icy, numb 2. fixed, pegged (of prices), petrified, rooted, stock-still, stopped, suspended, turned to stone

frugal abstemious, careful, cheeseparing, economical, meagre, niggardly, parsimonious, penny-wise, provident, prudent, saving, sparing, thrifty

fruit 1. crop, harvest, produce, product, yield 2. advantage, benefit, consequence, effect, outcome, profit, result, return, reward

fruitful 1. fecund, fertile, fructiferous 2. abundant, copious, flush, plenteous, plentiful, productive, profuse, prolific, rich, spawning 3. advantageous, beneficial, effective, gainful, productive, profitable, rewarding, successful, useful, well-spent, worthwhile

fruition actualization, attainment, completion, consummation, enjoyment, fulfilment, materialization, maturation, maturity, perfection, realization, ripeness

fruitless abortive, barren, bootless, futile, idle, ineffectual, in vain, pointless, profitless, to no avail, to no effect, unavailing, unfruitful, unproductive, unprofitable, unprolific, unsuccessful, useless, vain

fruity 1. full, mellow, resonant, rich 2. Inf. bawdy, blue, hot, indecent, indelicate, juicy, near the knuckle (Inf.), racy, ripe, risqué, salacious, sexy, smutty, spicy (Inf.), suggestive, titillating, vulgar

Brit. erotically stimulating; salacious. —**'fruitiness** *n.*

frump (frʌmp) *n.* a woman who is dowdy, drab, or unattractive. —**'frumpish** *or* **'frumpy** *adj.*

frustrate (frʌ'streit) *vb.* (*tr.*) **1.** to hinder or prevent (the efforts, plans, or desires) of. **2.** to upset, agitate, or tire. ~*adj.* **3.** *Arch.* frustrated or thwarted. —**frus'tration** *n.*

frustum ('frʌstəm) *n.*, *pl.* **-tums** *or* **-ta** (-tə). *Geom.* **a.** the part of a solid, such as a cone or pyramid, contained between the base and a plane parallel to the base that intersects the solid. **b.** the part of such a solid contained between two parallel planes intersecting the solid.

fry[1] (frai) *vb.* **frying, fried. 1.** (when *tr.*, sometimes foll. by *up*) to cook or be cooked in fat, oil, etc., usually over direct heat. **2.** *Sl., chiefly U.S.* to kill or be killed by electrocution. ~*n.*, *pl.* **fries. 3.** a dish of something fried, esp. the offal of a specified animal: *pig's fry.* **4. fry-up.** *Brit. inf.* the act of preparing a mixed fried dish or the dish itself. —**'fryer** *or* **'frier** *n.*

fry[2] (frai) *pl. n.* **1.** the young of various species of fish. **2.** the young of certain other animals, such as frogs.

frying pan *n.* **1.** a long-handled shallow pan used for frying. **2. out of the frying pan into the fire.** from a bad situation to a worse one.

f-stop ('εf,stɒp) *n.* any of the settings for the f-number of a camera.

ft. *abbrev. for:* **1.** foot *or* feet. **2.** fort.

fth. *or* **fthm.** *abbrev. for* fathom.

fuchsia ('fju:ʃə) *n.* **1.** a shrub widely cultivated for its showy drooping purple, red, or white flowers. **2** a reddish-purple to purplish-pink colour.

fuck (fʌk) *Taboo.* ~*vb.* **1.** to have sexual intercourse with (someone). ~*n.* **2.** an act of sexual intercourse. **3.** *Sl.* a partner in sexual intercourse. **4. not care** *or* **give a fuck.** not to care at all. ~*interj.* **5.** *Offens.* an expression of strong disgust or anger.

fuddle ('fʌdəl) *vb.* **1.** (*tr.; often passive*) to cause to be confused or intoxicated. ~*n.* **2.** a muddled or confused state.

fuddy-duddy ('fʌdɪ,dʌdɪ) *n.*, *pl.* **-dies.** *Inf.* a person, esp. an elderly one, who is extremely conservative or dull.

fudge[1] (fʌdʒ) *n.* a soft variously flavoured sweet made from sugar, butter, etc.

fudge[2] (fʌdʒ) *n.* **1.** foolishness; nonsense. ~*interj.* **2.** a mild exclamation of annoyance.

fuel (fjʊəl) *n.* **1.** any substance burned as a source of heat or power, such as coal or petrol. **2.** the material, containing a fissile substance such as uranium-235, that produces energy in a nuclear reactor. **3.** something that nourishes or builds up emotion, action, etc. ~*vb.* **fuelling, fuelled** *or U.S.* **fueling, fueled. 4.** to supply with or receive fuel.

fuel cell *n.* a cell in which chemical energy is converted directly into electrical energy.

fug (fʌg) *n. Chiefly Brit.* a hot, stale, or suffocating atmosphere. —**'fuggy** *adj.*

fugitive ('fju:dʒɪtɪv) *n.* **1.** a person who flees. **2.** a thing that is elusive or fleeting. ~*adj.* **3.** fleeing, esp. from arrest or pursuit. **4.** not permanent; fleeting. —**'fugitively** *adv.*

fugue (fju:g) *n.* **1.** a musical form consisting of a theme repeated a fifth above or a fourth below the continuing first statement. **2.** *Psychiatry.* a dreamlike altered state of consciousness, during which a person may wander away. —**'fugal** *adj.*

Führer *or* **Fuehrer** *German.* ('fy:rər) *n.* a leader: applied esp. to Adolf Hitler while he was Chancellor.

-ful *suffix.* **1.** (*forming adjectives*) full or characterized by: *painful; restful.* **2.** (*forming adjectives*) able or tending to: *useful.* **3.** (*forming nouns*) indicating as much as will fill the thing specified: *mouthful.*

▷ **Usage.** Where the amount held by a spoon, etc., is used as a rough unit of measurement, the correct form is *spoonful,* etc.: *take a spoonful of this medicine every day.* The plural of a word like spoonful is *spoonfuls* and not *spoonsful.*

fulcrum ('fulkrəm, 'fʌl-) *n.*, *pl.* **-crums** *or* **-cra** (-krə). **1.** the pivot about which a lever turns. **2.** something that supports or sustains; prop.

fulfil *or U.S.* **fulfill** (ful'fɪl) *vb.* **-filling, -filled.** (*tr.*) **1.** to bring about the completion or achievement of (a desire, promise, etc.). **2.** to carry out or execute (a request, etc.). **3.** to conform with or satisfy (regulations, etc.). **4.** to finish or reach the end of. **5. fulfil oneself.** to achieve one's potentials or desires. —**ful'filment** *or U.S.* **ful'fillment** *n.*

full[1] (ful) *adj.* **1.** holding or containing as much as possible. **2.** abundant in supply, quantity, number, etc.: *full of energy.* **3.** having consumed enough food or drink. **4.** (esp. of the face or figure) rounded or plump. **5.** (*prenominal*) complete: *a full dozen.* **6.** (*prenominal*) with all privileges, rights, etc.: *a full member.* **7.** (*prenominal*) having the same parents: *a full brother.* **8.** filled with emotion or sentiment: *a full heart.* **9.** (*postpositive;* foll. by *of*) occupied or engrossed (with): *full of his own projects.* **10.** *Music.* **a.** powerful or rich in volume and sound. **b.** completing a piece or section; concluding: *a full close.* **11.** (of a garment, esp. a skirt) containing a large amount of fabric. **12.** (of sails, etc.) distended by wind. **13.** (of wine, such as a burgundy) having a heavy body. **14.** (of a colour) rich; saturated. **15.** *Austral. inf.* drunk. **16. full of oneself.** full of pride or conceit. **17. full up.** filled to capacity. **18. in full cry.** (of a pack of hounds) in full pursuit of quarry. **19. in full swing.** at the height of activity: *the party was in full swing.* ~*adv.* **20. a.** completely; entirely. **b.** (*in combination*): *full-fledged.* **21.** directly; right: *he hit him full in the stomach.* **22.** very; extremely (esp. in **full well**). ~*n.* **23.** the greatest degree, extent, etc. **24. in full.** without omitting or shortening: *we paid in full for our mistake.* **25. to the full.** thoroughly; fully. ~*vb.* **26.** (*tr.*) *Needlework.* to gather or tuck. **27.** (*intr.*) (of the moon) to be fully illuminated. —**'fullness** *or esp. U.S.* **'fulness** *n.*

full[2] (ful) *vb.* (of cloth, yarn, etc.) to become or to make

---

THESAURUS

frustrate l. baffle, balk, block, check, circumvent, confront, counter, defeat, disappoint, foil, forestall, inhibit, neutralize, nullify, render null and void, stymie, thwart 2. depress, discourage, dishearten

frustrated carrying a chip on one's shoulder (*Inf.*), disappointed, discontented, discouraged, disheartened, embittered, foiled, irked, resentful

frustration l. blocking, circumvention, contravention, curbing, failure, foiling, nonfulfilment, nonsuccess, obstruction, thwarting 2. annoyance, disappointment, dissatisfaction, grievance, irritation, resentment, vexation

fuddled confused, drunk, inebriated, intoxicated, muddled, muzzy, sozzled (*Inf.*), stupefied, tipsy, woozy (*Inf.*)

fuddy-duddy n. back number (*Inf.*), conservative, dodo (*Inf.*), fossil, museum piece, (old) fogy, square (*Inf.*), stick-in-the-mud (*Inf.*), stuffed shirt (*Inf.*)

fudge v. avoid, cook (*Sl.*), dodge, equivocate, evade, fake, falsify, hedge, misrepresent, patch up, shuffle, slant, stall

fuel l. *n. Fig.* ammunition, encouragement, fodder, food, incitement, material, means, nourishment, provocation 2. *v.* charge, fan, feed, fire, incite, inflame, nourish, stoke up, sustain

fugitive l. *n.* deserter, escapee, refugee, runagate (*Archaic*), runaway 2. *adj.* brief, ephemeral, evanescent, fleeing, fleeting, flitting, flying, fugacious, momentary, passing, short, short-lived, temporary, transient, transitory, unstable

fulfil accomplish, achieve, answer, bring to completion, carry out, complete, comply with, conclude, conform to, discharge, effect, execute, fill, finish, keep, meet, obey, observe, perfect, perform, realise, satisfy

fulfilment accomplishment, achievement, attainment, carrying out or through, completion, consummation, crowning, discharge, discharging, effecting, end, implementation, observance, perfection, realization

full l. brimful, brimming, complete, entire, filled, gorged, intact, loaded, replete, sated, satiated, satisfied, saturated, stocked, suffi-

cient 2. abundant, adequate, all-inclusive, ample, broad, comprehensive, copious, detailed, exhaustive, extensive, generous, maximum, plenary, plenteous, plentiful, thorough, unabridged 3. chock-a-block, chock-full, crammed, crowded, in use, jammed, occupied, packed, taken 4. clear, deep, distinct, loud, resonant, rich, rounded 5. baggy, balloonlike, buxom, capacious, curvaceous, large, loose, plump, puffy, rounded, voluminous, voluptuous 6. in full completely, in its entirety, in total, *in toto,* without exception 7. to the full completely, entirely, fully, thoroughly, to the utmost, without reservation

full-blooded gutsy (*Sl.*), hearty, lusty, mettlesome, red-blooded, vigorous, virile

full-bodied fruity, full-flavoured, heady, heavy, mellow, redolent, rich, strong, well-matured

full-grown adult, developed, full-fledged, grown-up, in one's prime, marriageable, mature, nubile, of age, ripe

(cloth, yarn, etc.) more compact during manufacture through shrinking and pressing. —'**fuller**.

fullback ('fʊl,bæk) n. Soccer, hockey, rugby. **a.** a defensive player. **b.** the position held by this player.

full-blooded adj. **1.** (esp. of horses) of unmixed ancestry. **2.** having great vigour or health; hearty. —,**full-'bloodedness** n.

full-blown adj. **1.** characterized by the fullest, strongest, or best development. **2.** in full bloom.

full-bodied adj. having a full rich flavour or quality.

fuller's earth n. a natural absorbent clay used, after heating, for clarifying oils and fats, fulling cloth, etc.

full house n. **1.** Poker. a hand with three cards of the same value and another pair. **2.** a theatre, etc., filled to capacity. **3.** (in bingo, etc.) the set of numbers needed to win.

full-length n. (modifier) **1.** showing the complete length. **2.** not abridged

full moon n. one of the four phases of the moon when the moon is visible as a fully illuminated disc.

full pitch or **full toss** n. Cricket. a bowled ball that reaches the batsman without bouncing.

full-scale n. (modifier) **1.** (of a plan, etc.) of actual size. **2.** using all resources; all-out.

full stop or **full point** n. the punctuation mark (.) used at the end of a sentence that is not a question or exclamation, after abbreviations, etc. U.S. term: **period.**

full time n. the end of a football or other match.

full-time adj. **1.** for the entire time appropriate to an activity: a full-time job. ~adv. **full time. 2.** on a fulltime basis: he works full time. ~Cf. **part-time.**

fully ('fʊlɪ) adv. **1.** to the greatest degree or extent. **2.** amply; adequately: they were fully fed. **3.** at least: it was fully an hour before she came.

fully fashioned adj. (of stockings, seams, knitwear, etc.) shaped so as to fit closely.

fulmar ('fʊlmə) n. a heavily built short-tailed oceanic bird of polar regions.

fulminate ('fʌlmɪ,neɪt) vb. **1.** (intr.; often foll. by against) to make severe criticisms or denunciations; rail. **2.** to explode with noise and violence. ~n. **3.** any salt or ester of **fulminic acid,** an isomer of cyanic acid, which is used as a detonator. —'**fulminant** adj. —,**fulmi'nation** n. —'**fulmi,natory** adj.

fulsome ('fʊlsəm) adj. excessive or insincere, esp. in an offensive or distasteful way: fulsome compliments. —'**fulsomely** adv. —'**fulsomeness** n.

fumble ('fʌmbəl) vb. **1.** (intr.; often foll. by for or with) to grope about clumsily or blindly, esp. in searching. **2.** (intr.; foll. by at or with) to finger or play with, esp. in an

absent-minded way. **3.** to say or do awkwardly: he fumbled the introduction badly. **4.** to fail to catch or grasp (a ball, etc.) cleanly. ~n. **5.** the act of fumbling. —'**fumbler** n. —'**fumblingly** adv.

fume (fju:m) vb. **1.** (intr.) to be overcome with anger or fury. **2.** to give off (fumes) or (of fumes) to be given off, esp. during a chemical reaction. **3.** (tr.) to fumigate. ~n. **4.** (often pl.) a pungent or toxic vapour, gas, or smoke. **5.** a sharp or pungent odour. —'**fumeless** adj. —'**fumingly** adv. —'**fumy** adj.

fumigate ('fju:mɪ,geɪt) vb. to treat (something contaminated or infected) with fumes or smoke. —,**fumi'gation** n. —'**fumi,gator** n.

fun (fʌn) n. **1.** a source of enjoyment, amusement, diversion, etc. **2.** pleasure, gaiety, or merriment. **3.** jest or sport (esp. in **in** or **for fun). 4. fun and games.** Ironic or facetious. frivolous or hetic activity. **5. make fun of** or **poke fun at.** to ridicule or deride. **6.** (modifier) full of amusement, diversion, gaiety, etc.: a fun sport.

function ('fʌŋkʃən) n. **1.** the natural action or intended purpose of a person or thing in a specific role: the function of a hammer is to hit nails into wood. **2.** an official or formal social gathering or ceremony. **3.** a factor dependent upon another or other factors. **4.** Maths. **a.** a variable or expression whose value depends upon that of an independent variable or variables: y is a function of x, written $y = f(x)$. **b.** Also called: **map, mapping.** a relation between two sets such that a member of one set (the range) can be associated with a member of the other (the domain). **5.** to operate or perform as specified. **6.** (foll. by as) to perform the action or role (of something or someone else): a coin may function as a screwdriver.

functional ('fʌŋkʃənəl) adj. **1.** of, involving, or containing a function or functions. **2.** practical rather than decorative; utilitarian. **3.** capable of functioning; working. **4.** Med. affecting a function of an organ without structural change. —'**functionally** adv.

functionalism ('fʌŋkʃənə,lɪzəm) n. **1.** the theory of design that the form of a thing should be determined by its use. **2.** any doctrine that stresses purpose. —'**functionalist** n., adj.

functionary ('fʌŋkʃənərɪ) n., pl. **-aries.** a person acting in an official capacity, as for a government; an official.

fund (fʌnd) n. **1.** a reserve of money, etc., set aside for a certain purpose. **2.** a supply or store of something; stock: it exhausted his fund of wisdom. ~vb. (tr.) **3.** to furnish money to in the form of a fund. **4.** to place or store up in a fund. **5.** to convert (short-term floating debt) into long-term debt bearing fixed interest and represented by bonds. **6.** to accumulate a fund for the dis-

---

THESAURUS

fullness 1. abundance, adequateness, ampleness, copiousness, fill, glut, plenty, profusion, repletion, satiety, saturation, sufficiency **2.** broadness, completeness, comprehensiveness, entirety, extensiveness, plenitude, totality, vastness, wealth, wholeness **3.** clearness, loudness, resonance, richness, strength **4.** curvaceousness, dilation, distension, enlargement, roundness, swelling, tumescence, voluptuousness

full-scale all-encompassing, all-out, comprehensive, exhaustive, extensive, full-dress, in-depth, major, proper, sweeping, thorough, thoroughgoing, wide-ranging

fully 1. absolutely, altogether, completely, entirely, every inch, from first to last, heart and soul, in all respects, intimately, perfectly, positively, thoroughly, totally, utterly, wholly **2.** abundantly, adequately, amply, comprehensively, enough, plentifully, satisfactorily, sufficiently **3.** at least, quite, without (any) exaggeration, without a word of a lie (Inf.)

fully-fledged experienced, mature, professional, proficient, qualified, senior, time-served, trained

fulmination condemnation, denunciation, diatribe, invective, obloquy, philippic, reprobation, tirade

fulsome adulatory, cloying, excessive, extravagant, fawning, gross, immoderate, ingratiating, inordinate, insincere, nauseating,

overdone, saccharine, sickening, smarmy (Inf.), sycophantic, unctuous

fumble 1. bumble, feel around, flounder, grope, paw (Inf.), scrabble **2.** botch, bungle, make a hash of (Inf.), mess up, misfield, mishandle, mismanage, muff, spoil

fume Fig. **1.** v. boil, chafe, champ at the bit (Inf.), get hot under the collar (Inf.), get steamed up about (Sl.), rage, rant, rave, seethe, smoulder, storm **2.** n. agitation, dither, fit, fret, fury, passion, rage, stew (Inf.), storm

fumes effluvium, exhalation, exhaust, gas, haze, miasma, pollution, reek, smog, smoke, stench, vapour

fumigate clean out or up, cleanse, disinfect, purify, sanitize, sterilize

fuming all steamed up (Sl.), angry, at boiling point (Inf.), enraged, foaming at the mouth, in a rage, incensed, raging, roused, seething, up in arms

fun n. **1.** amusement, cheer, distraction, diversion, enjoyment, entertainment, frolic, gaiety, good time, high jinks, jollification, jollity, joy, junketing, living it up, merriment, merrymaking, mirth, pleasure, recreation, romp, sport, treat, whoopee (Inf.) **2.** buffoonery, clowning, foolery, game, horseplay, jesting, jocularity, joking, nonsense, play, playfulness, skylarking (Inf.), sport, teasing, tomfoolery **3. in** or **for fun** facetiously, for a joke, for a laugh, in jest, jokingly, light-heartedly,

mischievously, playfully, roguishly, teasingly, tongue in cheek, with a gleam or twinkle in one's eye, with a straight face **4. make fun of** deride, hold up to ridicule, lampoon, laugh at, make a fool of, make game of, make sport of, make the butt of, mock, parody, poke fun at, rag, rib (Inf.), ridicule, satirize, scoff at, send up (Brit. inf.), sneer at, take off, taunt ~adj. **5.** amusing, convivial, diverting, enjoyable, entertaining, lively, witty

function n. **1.** activity, business, capacity, charge, concern, duty, employment, exercise, job, mission, occupation, office, operation, part, post, province, purpose, raison d'être, responsibility, role, situation, task ~v. **2.** act, act the part of, behave, be in commission, be in operation or action, be in running order, do duty, go, officiate, operate, perform, run, serve, serve one's turn, work ~n. **3.** affair, do (Inf.), gathering, reception, social occasion

functional hard-wearing, operative, practical, serviceable, useful, utilitarian, utility, working

fund n. **1.** capital, endowment, foundation, kitty, pool, reserve, stock, store, supply **2.** hoard, mine, repository, reserve, reservoir, source, storehouse, treasury, vein ~v. **3.** capitalize, endow, finance, float, pay for, promote, stake, subsidize, support

charge of (a recurrent liability): *to fund a pension plan.*

fundamental (ˌfʌndəˈmɛntəl) *adj.* **1.** of, involving, or comprising a foundation; basic. **2.** of, involving, or comprising a source; primary. **3.** *Music.* denoting or relating to the principal or lowest note of a harmonic series. ~*n.* **4.** a principle, law, etc., that serves as the basis of an idea or system. **5. a.** the principal or lowest note of a harmonic series. **b.** the bass note of a chord in root position. —ˌfundamenˈtality *n.* —ˌfundaˈmentally *adv.*

fundamentalism (ˌfʌndəˈmɛntəˌlɪzəm) *n. Christianity.* the view that the Bible is divinely inspired and is therefore literally true. —ˌfundaˈmentalist *n., adj.*

fundamental particle *n.* another name for **elementary particle.**

funds (fʌndz) *pl. n.* **1.** money that is readily available. **2.** British government securities representing national debt.

funeral (ˈfjuːnərəl) *n.* **1. a.** a ceremony at which a dead person is buried or cremated. **b.** (*as modifier*): *a funeral service.* **2.** a procession of people escorting a corpse to burial. **3.** *Inf.* concern; affair: *that's your funeral.* —ˈfunerary *adj.*

funeral director *n.* an undertaker.

funereal (fjuːˈnɪərɪəl) *adj.* suggestive of a funeral; gloomy or mournful. Also: **funebrial.** —fuˈnereally *adv.*

funfair (ˈfʌnˌfɛə) *n. Brit.* an amusement park or fairground.

fungicide (ˈfʌndʒɪˌsaɪd) *n.* a substance or agent that destroys or is capable of destroying fungi. —ˌfungiˈcidal *adj.* —ˌfungiˈcidally *adv.*

fungoid (ˈfʌŋɡɔɪd) *adj.* resembling a fungus or fungi: *a fungoid growth.*

fungous (ˈfʌŋɡəs) *adj.* appearing suddenly and spreading quickly like a fungus.

fungus (ˈfʌŋɡəs) *n., pl.* **fungi** (ˈfʌndʒaɪ, ˈfʌŋɡaɪ) *or* **funguses.** **1.** any plant of the division *Fungi,* lacking chlorophyll, leaves, true stems, and roots, and reproducing by spores. The group includes moulds, yeasts, and mushrooms. **2.** something resembling a fungus, esp. in suddenly growing. **3.** *Pathol.* any soft tumorous growth. —ˈfungal *adj.*

funicular (fjuːˈnɪkjʊlə) *n.* **1.** Also called: **funicular railway.** a railway up the side of a mountain, consisting of two cars at either end of a cable passing round a driving wheel at the summit. ~*adj.* **2.** relating to or operated by a rope, etc.

funk (fʌŋk) *Inf., chiefly Brit.* ~*n.* **1.** Also called: **blue funk.** a state of nervousness, fear, or depression. **2.** a coward. ~*vb.* **3.** to flinch from (responsibility, etc.) through fear. **4.** (*tr.; usually passive*) to make afraid.

funnel (ˈfʌnəl) *n.* **1.** a hollow utensil with a wide mouth tapering to a small hole, used for pouring liquids, powders, etc., into a narrow-necked vessel. **2.** something resembling this in shape or function. **3.** a smokestack for smoke and exhaust gases, as on a steam locomotive. ~*vb.* **-nelling, -nelled** *or U.S.* **-neling, -neled. 4.** to move or cause to move or pour through or as if through a funnel. —ˈfunnel-,like *adj.*

funny (ˈfʌnɪ) *adj.* **-nier, -niest. 1.** causing amusement or laughter; humorous. **2.** peculiar; odd. **3.** suspicious or dubious (esp. in **funny business**). **4.** *Inf.* faint or ill. ~*n., pl.* **-nies. 5.** *Inf.* a joke or witticism. —ˈfunnily *adv.* —ˈfunniness *n.*

funny bone *n.* the area near the elbow where the ulnar nerve is close to the surface of the skin: when it is struck, a sharp tingling sensation is experienced.

fur (fɜː) *n.* **1.** the dense coat of fine silky hairs on such mammals as the cat, seal, and mink. **2. a.** the dressed skin of certain fur-bearing animals, with the hair left on. **b.** (*as modifier*): *a fur coat.* **3.** a garment made of fur, such as a stole. **4.** a pile fabric made in imitation of animal fur. **5.** *Heraldry.* any of various stylized representations of animal pelts used in coats of arms. **6. make the fur fly.** to cause a scene or disturbance. **7.** *Inf.* a whitish coating on the tongue, caused by excessive smoking, an upset stomach, etc. **8.** *Brit.* a whitish-grey deposit precipitated from hard water onto the insides of pipes, boilers, and kettles. ~*vb.* **furring, furred. 9.** (*tr.*) to line or trim a garment, etc., with fur. **10.** (often foll. by *up*) to cover or become covered with a furlike lining or deposit. —ˈfurless *adj.*

fur. *abbrev. for* furlong.

furbelow (ˈfɜːbɪˌləʊ) *n.* **1.** a flounce, ruffle, or other ornamental trim. **2.** (*often pl.*) showy ornamentation. ~*vb.* **3.** (*tr.*) to put a furbelow on (a garment, etc.).

furbish (ˈfɜːbɪʃ) *vb.* **1.** to make bright by polishing. **2.** (often foll. by *up*) to renovate; restore. —ˈfurbisher *n.*

furcate *vb.* (ˈfɜːkeɪt). **1.** to divide into two parts. ~*adj.* (ˈfɜːkeɪt). **2.** forked: *furcate branches.* —furˈcation *n.*

Furies (ˈfjʊərɪz) *pl. n., sing.* **Fury.** *Classical myth.* the snake-haired goddesses of vengeance, usually three in number, who pursued unpunished criminals. Also called: **Erinyes, Eumenides.**

furious (ˈfjʊərɪəs) *adj.* **1.** extremely angry or annoyed. **2.** violent or unrestrained, as in speed, energy, etc. —ˈfuriously *adv.* —ˈfuriousness *n.*

furl (fɜːl) *vb.* **1.** to roll up (an umbrella, flag, etc.) neatly and securely or (of an umbrella, flag, etc.) to be rolled up in this way. ~*n.* **2.** the act or an instance of furling. **3.** a single rolled-up section. —ˈfurlable *adj.*

furlong (ˈfɜːˌlɒŋ) *n.* a unit of length equal to 220 yards (201.168 metres).

furlough (ˈfɜːləʊ) *n.* **1.** leave of absence from military duty. ~*vb.* (*tr.*) **2.** to grant a furlough to.

furnace (ˈfɜːnɪs) *n.* **1.** an enclosed chamber in which heat is produced to destroy refuse, smelt or refine ores, etc. **2.** a very hot place.

furnish (ˈfɜːnɪʃ) *vb.* (*tr.*) **1.** to provide (a house, room, etc.) with furniture, etc. **2.** to equip with what is necessary. **3.** to supply: *the records furnished the information.* —ˈfurnisher *n.*

furnishings (ˈfɜːnɪʃɪŋz) *pl. n.* furniture, carpets, etc., with which a room or house is furnished.

furniture (ˈfɜːnɪtʃə) *n.* **1.** the movable articles that equip a room, house, etc. **2.** the equipment necessary for a ship, factory, etc. **3.** *Printing.* lengths of wood, plastic, or metal, used in assembling formes to surround the type. **4.** Also called: **door furniture.** locks, handles, etc., designed for use on doors.

furore (fjuːˈrɔːrɪ) *or esp. U.S.* **furor** (ˈfjʊərɔː) *n.* **1.** a public outburst; uproar. **2.** a sudden widespread enthusiasm; craze. **3.** frenzy; rage.

furrier (ˈfʌrɪə) *n.* a person whose occupation is selling, making, or repairing fur garments. —ˈfurriery *n.*

furrow (ˈfʌrəʊ) *n.* **1.** a long narrow trench made in the

THESAURUS

fundamental 1. *adj.* basic, cardinal, central, constitutional, crucial, elementary, essential, first, important, indispensable, integral, intrinsic, key, necessary, organic, primary, prime, principal, rudimentary, underlying, vital **2.** *n.* axiom, basic, cornerstone, essential, first principle, law, principle, rudiment, rule, *sine qua non*

fundamentally at bottom, at heart, basically, essentially, intrinsically, primarily, radically

funds 1. bread (*Sl.*), capital, cash, dough (*Sl.*), finance, hard cash, money, ready money, resources, savings, the ready (*Inf.*), the wherewithal **2. in funds** flush (*Inf.*), in the black, solvent, well-off, well-supplied

funeral burial, inhumation, interment, obsequies

funnel *v.* channel, conduct, convey, direct, filter, move, pass, pour

funny 1. absurd, amusing, a scream (card, caution) (*Inf.*), comic, comical, diverting, droll, entertaining, facetious, farcical, hilarious, humorous, jocose, jocular, jolly, killing (*Inf.*), laughable, ludicrous, rich, ridiculous, riotous, risible, side-splitting, silly, slapstick, waggish, witty **2.** curious, dubious, mysterious, odd, peculiar, perplexing, puzzling, queer, remarkable, strange, suspicious, unusual, weird ~*n.* **3.** *Inf.* crack (*Sl.*), jest, joke, play on words, pun, quip, wisecrack, witticism

furious 1. angry, beside oneself, boiling, enraged, frantic, frenzied, fuming, incensed, infuriated, in high dudgeon, livid (*Inf.*), mad, maddened, on the warpath (*Inf.*), raging, up in arms, wrathful, wroth (*Archaic*) **2.** agitated, boisterous, fierce, impetuous, intense, savage, stormy, tempestuous, tumultuous, turbulent, ungovernable, unrestrained, vehement, violent, wild

furnish 1. appoint, decorate, equip, fit (out, up), outfit, provide, provision, rig, stock, store, supply **2.** afford, bestow, endow, give, grant, offer, present, provide, reveal, supply

furniture appliances, appointments, chattels, effects, equipment, fittings, furnishings, goods, household goods, movable property, movables, possessions, things (*Inf.*)

furore 1. commotion, disturbance, excitement, flap (*Inf.*), frenzy, fury, hullabaloo, outburst, outcry, stir, to-do, uproar **2.** craze, enthusiasm, mania, rage

ground by a plough. **2.** any long deep groove, esp. a deep wrinkle on the forehead. ~*vb.* **3.** to develop or cause to develop furrows or wrinkles. **4.** to make a furrow or furrows in (land). —'**furrower** *n.* —'**furrowless** *adj.* —'**furrowy** *adj.*

furry ('fɜːrɪ) *adj.* **-rier, -riest. 1.** covered with fur or something furlike. **2.** of, relating to, or resembling fur. **3.** Also: **furred.** (of the tongue) coated with whitish cellular debris. —'**furrily** *adv.* —'**furriness** *n.*

further ('fɜːðə) *adv.* **1.** in addition; furthermore. **2.** to a greater degree or extent. **3.** to or at a more advanced point. **4.** to or at a greater distance in time or space. ~*adj.* **5.** additional; more. **6.** more distant or remote in time or space. ~*vb.* **7.** (*tr.*) to assist the progress of. ~See also **far, furthest.**

▷ **Usage.** See at **farther.**

further education *n.* (in Britain) formal education beyond school other than at a university or polytechnic.

furthermore ('fɜːðə,mɔː) *adv.* in addition; moreover.

furthest ('fɜːðɪst) *adv.* **1.** to the greatest degree or extent. **2.** to or at the greatest distance in time or space; farthest. ~*adj.* **3.** most distant or remote in time or space; farthest.

furtive ('fɜːtɪv) *adj.* characterized by stealth; sly and secretive. —'**furtively** *adv.* —'**furtiveness** *n.*

fury ('fjʊərɪ) *n., pl.* **-ries. 1.** violent or uncontrolled anger. **2.** an outburst of such anger. **3.** a person, esp. a woman, with a violent temper. **4.** See **Furies. 5.** like **fury.** *Inf.* violently; furiously.

furze (fɜːz) *n.* another name for **gorse.** —'**furzy** *adj.*

fuscous ('fʌskəs) *adj.* of a brownish-grey colour.

fuse[1] *or U.S.* **fuze** (fjuːz) *n.* **1.** a lead of combustible black powder (**safety fuse**), or a lead containing an explosive (**detonating fuse**), used to fire an explosive charge. **2.** any device by which an explosive charge is ignited. ~*vb.* **3.** (*tr.*) to equip with such a fuse. —'**fuseless** *adj.*

fuse[2] (fjuːz) *vb.* **1.** to unite or become united by melting, esp. by the action of heat. **2.** to become or cause to become liquid, esp. by the action of heat. **3.** to join or become combined. **4.** (*tr.*) to equip (a plug, etc.) with a fuse. **5.** *Brit.* to fail or cause to fail as a result of the blowing of a fuse: *the lights fused.* ~*n.* **6. a.** a protective device for safeguarding electric circuits, etc., containing a wire that melts and breaks the circuit when the current exceeds a certain value. **b.** any device performing a similar function.

fuselage ('fjuːzɪ,lɑːʒ) *n.* the main body of an aircraft.

fusible ('fjuːzəbəl) *adj.* capable of being fused or melted. —,**fusi'bility** *n.* —'**fusibly** *adv.*

fusilier (,fjuːzɪ'lɪə) *n.* **1.** (formerly) an infantryman armed with a light musket. **2.** Also: **fusileer. a.** a soldier, esp. a private, serving in any of certain British or other infantry regiments. **b.** (*pl.; cap. when part of a name*): *the Royal Welsh Fusiliers.*

fusillade (,fjuːzɪ'leɪd) *n.* **1.** a rapid continual discharge of firearms. **2.** a sudden outburst, as of criticism. ~*vb.*

3. (*tr.*) to attack with a fusillade.

fusion ('fjuːʒən) *n.* **1.** the act or process of fusing or melting together. **2.** the state of being fused. **3.** something produced by fusing. **4.** See **nuclear fusion. 5.** a coalition of political parties.

fuss (fʌs) *n.* **1.** nervous activity or agitation, esp. when unnecessary. **2.** complaint or objection: *he made a fuss over the bill.* **3.** an exhibition of affection or admiration: *they made a great fuss over the new baby.* **4.** a quarrel. ~*vb.* **5.** (*intr.*) to worry unnecessarily. **6.** (*intr.*) to be excessively concerned over trifles. **7.** (when *intr.*, usually foll. by *over*) to show great or excessive concern, affection, etc. (for). **8.** (*tr.*) to bother (a person). —'**fusser** *n.*

fusspot ('fʌs,pɒt) *n. Brit. inf.* a person who fusses unnecessarily.

fussy ('fʌsɪ) *adj.* **fussier, fussiest. 1.** inclined to fuss over minor points. **2.** very particular about detail. **3.** characterized by overelaborate detail. —'**fussily** *adv.* —'**fussiness** *n.*

fustian ('fʌstɪən) *n.* **1. a.** a hard-wearing fabric of cotton mixed with flax or wool. **b.** (*as modifier*): *a fustian jacket.* **2.** pompous talk or writing. ~*adj.* **3.** cheap; worthless. **4.** bombastic.

fusty ('fʌstɪ) *adj.* **-tier, -tiest. 1.** smelling of damp or mould. **2.** old-fashioned in attitude. —'**fustily** *adv.* —'**fustiness** *n.*

futile ('fjuːtaɪl) *adj.* **1.** having no effective result; unsuccessful. **2.** pointless; trifling. **3.** inane or foolish. —'**futilely** *adv.* —**futility** (fjuː'tɪlɪtɪ) *n.*

future ('fjuːtʃə) *n.* **1.** the time yet to come. **2.** undetermined events that will occur in that time. **3.** the condition of a person or thing at a later date: *the future of the school is undecided.* **4.** likelihood of later improvement: *he has a future as a singer.* **5.** Grammar. **a.** a tense of verbs used when the action or event described is to occur after the time of utterance. **b.** a verb in this tense. **6. in future.** from now on. ~*adj.* **7.** that is yet to come or be. **8.** of or expressing time yet to come. **9.** (*prenominal*) destined to become. **10.** Grammar. in or denoting the future as a tense of verbs. —'**futureless** *adj.*

future perfect Grammar. ~*adj.* **1.** denoting a tense of verbs describing an action that will have been performed by a certain time. ~*n.* **2. a.** the future perfect tense. **b.** a verb in this tense.

futures ('fjuːtʃəz) *pl.n.* commodities bought or sold at an agreed price for delivery at a specified future date.

futurism ('fjuːtʃə,rɪzəm) *n.* an artistic movement that arose in Italy in 1909 to replace traditional aesthetic values with the characteristics of the machine age. —'**futurist** *n., adj.*

futuristic (,fjuːtʃə'rɪstɪk) *adj.* **1.** denoting or relating to design, etc., that is thought likely to be fashionable at some future time. **2.** of or relating to futurism. —,**fu-tur'istically** *adv.*

futurity (fjuː'tjʊərɪtɪ) *n., pl.* **-ties. 1.** a less common word for **future. 2.** the quality of being in the future. **3.** a future event.

THESAURUS

furrow 1. *n.* channel, corrugation, crease, crow's-foot, fluting, groove, hollow, line, rut, seam, trench, wrinkle **2.** *v.* corrugate, crease, draw together, flute, knit, seam, wrinkle

further 1. *adj.* additional, extra, fresh, more, new, other, supplementary **2.** *adv.* additionally, also, as well as, besides, furthermore, in addition, moreover, on top of, over and above, to boot, what's more, yet **3.** *v.* advance, aid, assist, champion, contribute to, encourage, expedite, facilitate, forward, foster, hasten, help, lend support to, patronize, plug (*Inf.*), promote, push, speed, succour, work for

furtherance advancement, advocacy, backing, boosting, carrying-out, championship, promotion, prosecution, pursuit

furthermore additionally, as well, besides, further, in addition, into the bargain, moreover, not to mention, to boot, too, what's more

furthest extreme, farthest, furthermost, most distant, outermost, outmost, remotest, ultimate, uttermost

furtive clandestine, cloaked, conspirato-

rial, covert, hidden, secret, secretive, skulking, slinking, sly, sneaking, sneaky, stealthy, surreptitious, underhand, under-the-table

fury 1. anger, frenzy, impetuosity, ire, madness, passion, rage, wrath **2.** ferocity, fierceness, force, intensity, power, savagery, severity, tempestuousness, turbulence, vehemence, violence **3.** bacchante, hag, hellcat, shrew, spitfire, termagant, virago, vixen

fuse *v.* agglutinate, amalgamate, blend, coalesce, combine, commingle, dissolve, federate, integrate, intermingle, intermix, join, meld, melt, merge, run together, smelt, solder, unite, weld

fuss *n.* **1.** ado, agitation, bother, bustle, commotion, confusion, excitement, fidget, flap (*Inf.*), flurry, fluster, flutter, hurry, palaver, pother, stir, storm in a teacup (*Brit.*), to-do, upset, worry **2.** altercation, argument, bother, complaint, difficulty, display, furore, hassle (*Inf.*), objection, row, squabble, trouble, unrest, upset ~*v.* **3.** bustle, chafe, fidget, flap (*Inf.*), fret, fume, get in a stew (*Inf.*), get worked up, labour over, make a meal of (*Inf.*), make a thing of (*Inf.*), niggle, take

pains, worry

fussy 1. choosy (*Inf.*), dainty, difficult, discriminating, exacting, faddish, faddy, fastidious, finicky, hard to please, nit-picking (*Inf.*), old-maidish, old womanish, overparticular, particular, pernickety, squeamish **2.** busy, cluttered, overdecorated, overelaborate, overembellished, overworked, rococo

futile 1. abortive, barren, bootless, empty, forlorn, fruitless, hollow, ineffectual, in vain, nugatory, profitless, sterile, to no avail, unavailing, unproductive, unprofitable, unsuccessful, useless, vain, valueless, worthless **2.** idle, pointless, trifling, trivial, unimportant

futility 1. bootlessness, emptiness, fruitlessness, hollowness, ineffectiveness, uselessness **2.** pointlessness, triviality, unimportance, vanity

future 1. *n.* expectation, hereafter, outlook, prospect, time to come **2.** *adj.* approaching, coming, destined, eventual, expected, fated, forthcoming, impending, in the offing, later, prospective, subsequent, to be, to come, ultimate, unborn

futurology (ˌfjuːtʃəˈrɒlədʒɪ) *n.* the study or prediction of the future of mankind. —ˌfutur'ologist *n.*

fuzz[1] (fʌz) *n.* **1.** a mass or covering of fine or curly hairs, fibres, etc. **2.** a blur. ~*vb.* **3.** to make or become fuzzy. **4.** to make or become indistinct.

fuzz[2] (fʌz) *n.* a slang word for **police** or **policeman**.

fuzzy (ˈfʌzɪ) *adj.* **fuzzier, fuzziest.** **1.** of, resembling, or covered with fuzz. **2.** unclear or distorted. **3.** (of the hair) tightly curled or very wavy. —ˈfuzzily *adv.* —ˈfuzziness *n.*

fwd. *abbrev. for* forward.

-fy *suffix forming verbs.* to make or become: *beautify.*

THESAURUS

fuzzy **1.** down-covered, downy, flossy, fluffy, frizzy, linty, napped, woolly **2.** bleary, blurred, distorted, faint, ill-defined, indistinct, muffled, out of focus, shadowy, unclear

G

g *or* **G** (dʒiː) *n., pl.* **g's, G's,** *or* **Gs. 1.** the seventh letter of the English alphabet. **2.** a speech sound represented by this letter, usually either as in *grass*, or as in *page*.

g *symbol for:* **1.** gallon(s). **2.** gram(s). **3.** acceleration of free fall (due to gravity).

G *symbol for:* **1.** *Music.* **a.** the fifth note of the scale of C major. **b.** the major or minor key having this note as its tonic. **2.** gravitational constant. **3.** *Physics.* conductance. **4.** German. **5.** giga. **6.** good. **7.** *Sl., chiefly U.S.* grand (a thousand dollars or pounds).

G. *or* **g.** *abbrev. for:* **1.** gauges. **2.** gauss. **3.** gelding. **4.** Gulf. **5.** guilder(s). **6.** guinea(s).

Ga *the chemical symbol for* gallium.

gab (gæb) *Inf.* ~*vb.* **gabbing, gabbed. 1.** (*intr.*) to talk excessively or idly; gossip; chatter. ~*n.* **2.** idle or trivial talk. **3. gift of the gab.** ability to speak glibly or persuasively. —**'gabber** *n.*

gabble ('gæbəl) *vb.* **1.** to utter (words, etc.) rapidly and indistinctly; jabber. **2.** (*intr.*) (of geese, etc.) to utter rapid cackling noises. ~*n.* **3.** rapid and indistinct speech or noises. —**'gabbler** *n.*

gaberdine ('gæbə,diːn, ,gæbə'diːn) *n.* **1.** a twill-weave worsted, cotton, or spun-rayon fabric. **2.** Also called: **gabardine.** an ankle-length loose coat or frock worn by men, esp. by Jews, in the Middle Ages. **3.** any of various other garments made of gaberdine, esp. a child's raincoat.

gable ('geibəl) *n.* **1.** Also called: **gable end.** the triangular upper part of a wall between the sloping ends of a pitched roof (**gable roof**). **2.** a triangular ornamental feature, esp. as used over a door or window. —**'gabled** *adj.*

gad (gæd) *vb.* **gadding, gadded. 1.** (*intr.; often foll. by about* or *around*) to go out in search of pleasure; gallivant. ~*n.* **2.** carefree adventure (esp. in **on the gad**). —**'gadder** *n.*

gadabout ('gædə,baut) *n. Inf.* a person who restlessly seeks amusement, etc.

gadfly ('gæd,flai) *n., pl.* **-flies. 1.** any of various large dipterous flies, esp. the horsefly, that annoy livestock by sucking their blood. **2.** a constantly irritating person.

gadget ('gædʒit) *n.* **1.** a small mechanical device or appliance. **2.** any object that is interesting for its ingenuity.

gadoid ('geidoid) *adj.* **1.** of or belonging to an order of marine soft-finned fishes typically having the pectoral and pelvic fins close together and small cycloid scales. The group includes cod and hake. ~*n.* **2.** any gadoid fish.

gadolinium (,gædə'liniəm) *n.* a ductile malleable silvery-white ferromagnetic element of the lanthanide series of metals. Symbol: Gd; atomic no.: 64; atomic wt.: 157.25.

gadwall ('gæd,wɔːl) *n., pl.* **-walls** *or* **-wall.** a duck related to the mallard. The male has a grey body and black tail.

gadzooks (gæd'zuːks) *interj. Arch.* a mild oath.

Gael (geil) *n.* a person who speaks a Gaelic language, esp. a Highland Scot or a southern Irishman.

—**'Gaeldom** *n.*

Gaelic ('geilik) *n.* **1.** any of the closely related languages of the Celts in Ireland, Scotland, or the Isle of Man. ~*adj.* **2.** of, denoting, or relating to the Celtic people of Ireland, Scotland, or the Isle of Man or their language or customs.

gaff[1] (gæf) *n.* **1.** *Angling.* a stiff pole with a stout prong or hook attached for landing large fish. **2.** *Naut.* a boom hoisted aft of a mast to support a fore-and-aft sail. **3.** a metal spur fixed to the leg of a gamecock. ~*vb.* **4.** (*tr.*) *Angling.* to hook or land (a fish) with a gaff.

gaff[2] (gæf) *n.* **1.** *Sl.* nonsense. **2. blow the gaff.** *Brit. sl.* to divulge a secret.

gaffe (gæf) *n.* a social blunder, esp. a tactless remark.

gaffer ('gæfə) *n.* **1.** an old man: often used affectionately or patronizingly. **2.** *Inf., chiefly Brit.* a boss, foreman, or owner of a factory, etc. **3.** *Inf.* the senior electrician on a television or film set.

gag[1] (gæg) *vb.* **gagging, gagged. 1.** (*tr.*) to stop up (a person's mouth), esp. with a piece of cloth, etc., to prevent him from speaking or crying out. **2.** (*tr.*) *Inf.* to suppress or censor (free expression, information, etc.). **3.** *Sl.* to retch or cause to retch. **4.** (*intr.*) *Sl.* to struggle for breath; choke. ~*n.* **5.** a piece of cloth, rope, etc., stuffed into or tied across the mouth. **6.** *Inf.* any restraint on or suppression of information, free speech, etc. **7.** *Parliamentary procedure.* another word for **closure** (sense 4).

gag[2] (gæg) *Sl.* ~*n.* **1.** a joke or humorous story, esp. one told by a professional comedian. **2.** a hoax, practical joke, etc. ~*vb.* **gagging, gagged. 3.** (*intr.*) to tell jokes or funny stories, as comedians in nightclubs, etc.

gaga ('gɑːgɑː) *adj. Sl.* **1.** senile; doting. **2.** slightly crazy.

gage[1] (geidʒ) *n.* **1.** something deposited as security against the fulfilment of an obligation; pledge. **2.** (formerly) a glove or other object thrown down to indicate a challenge to combat. ~*vb.* **3.** (*tr.*) *Arch.* to stake, pledge, or wager.

gage[2] (geidʒ) *n.* short for **greengage.**

gage[3] (geidʒ) *n., vb. U.S.* a variant spelling (esp. in technical senses) of **gauge.**

gaggle ('gægəl) *vb.* **1.** (*intr.*) (of geese) to cackle. ~*n.* **2.** a flock of geese. **3.** *Inf.* a disorderly group of people.

gaiety ('geiəti) *n., pl.* **-ties. 1.** the state or condition of being gay. **2.** festivity; merrymaking. **3.** colourful bright appearance.

gaily ('geili) *adv.* **1.** in a gay manner; merrily. **2.** with bright colours; showily.

gain (gein) *vb.* **1.** (*tr.*) to acquire (something desirable); obtain. **2.** (*tr.*) to win in competition: *to gain the victory.* **3.** to increase, improve, or advance: *the car gained speed.* **4.** (*tr.*) to earn (a wage, living, etc.). **5.** (*intr.; usually foll. by on* or *upon*) **a.** to get nearer (to) or catch up (on). **b.** to get farther away (from). **6.** (*tr.*) (esp. of ships) to get to; reach: *the steamer gained port.* **7.** (of a timepiece) to operate too fast, so as to indicate a time ahead of the true time. ~*n.* **8.** something won, acquired, earned, etc.; profit; advantage. **9.** an increase in size, amount, etc. **10.** the act of gaining; attainment; acquisition. **11.** Also called: **amplification.** *Electronics.* the ratio of the output power of an amplifier to the power fed into it, usually measured in decibels.

gainful ('geɪnfʊl) *adj.* profitable; lucrative. —'**gainfully** *adv.* —'**gainfulness** *n.*

gainsay (geɪn'seɪ) *vb.* **-saying, -said.** (*tr.*) *Arch. or literary.* to deny (an allegation, statement, etc.); contradict. —**gain'sayer** *n.*

gait (geɪt) *n.* **1.** manner of walking or running, esp. a horse's walk, trot, canter, etc. ~*vb.* **2.** (*tr.*) to teach (a horse) a particular gait.

gaiter ('geɪtə) *n.* (*often pl.*) **1.** a cloth or leather covering for the leg or ankle. **2.** Also called: **spat.** a similar covering extending from the ankle to the instep.

gal (gæl) *n. Sl.* a girl.

gal or **gal.** *abbrev. for* gallon.

Gal. *abbrev. for* Galatians.

gala ('gɑːlə, 'geɪlə) *n.* **1. a.** a celebration; festive occasion. **b.** (*as modifier*): *a gala occasion.* **2.** *Chiefly Brit.* a sporting occasion involving competitions in several events: *a swimming gala.*

galactic (gə'læktɪk) *adj.* **1.** *Astron.* of or relating to a galaxy, esp. the Galaxy. **2. galactic plane.** the plane passing through the spiral arms of the Galaxy, contained by the great circle of the celestial sphere (**galactic equator**) and perpendicular to an imaginary line joining opposite points (**galactic poles**) on the celestial sphere. **3.** *Med.* of or relating to milk.

galantine ('gælən,tiːn) *n.* a cold dish of meat or poultry, which is boned, cooked, then pressed and glazed.

galaxy ('gæləksɪ) *n., pl.* **-axies. 1.** any of a vast number of star systems held together by gravitational attraction. **2.** a splendid gathering, esp. one of famous or distinguished people.

Galaxy ('gæləksɪ) *n.* **the.** the spiral galaxy that contains the solar system about three fifths of the distance from its centre. Also called: the **Milky Way System.**

gale (geɪl) *n.* **1.** a strong wind, specifically one of force 8 on the Beaufort scale or from 39-46 m.p.h. **2.** (*often pl.*) *Inf.* a loud outburst, esp. of laughter. **3.** *Arch. & poetic.* a gentle breeze.

galena (gə'liːnə) or **galenite** (gə'liːnaɪt) *n.* a soft heavy bluish-grey or black mineral consisting of lead sulphide: the chief source of lead. Formula: PbS.

gall[1] (gɔːl) *n.* **1.** *Inf.* impudence. **2.** bitterness; rancour. **3.** something bitter or disagreeable. **4.** *Physiol.* an obsolete term for **bile.** See also **gall bladder.**

gall[2] (gɔːl) *n.* **1.** a sore on the skin caused by chafing. **2.** something that causes vexation or annoyance. **3.** irritation; exasperation. ~*vb.* **4.** to abrade (the skin, etc.) as by rubbing. **5.** (*tr.*) to irritate or annoy; vex.

gall[3] (gɔːl) *n.* an abnormal outgrowth in plant tissue caused by certain parasitic insects, fungi, or bacteria.

gall. *abbrev. for* gallon.

gallant *adj.* ('gælənt). **1.** brave and high-spirited; cou-

rageous and honourable: *a gallant warrior.* **2.** (gə'lænt, 'gælənt). (of a man) attentive to women; chivalrous. **3.** imposing; dignified; stately: *a gallant ship.* **4.** *Arch.* showy in dress. ~*n.* ('gælənt, gə'lænt). **5.** a woman's lover or suitor. **6.** a dashing or fashionable young man, esp. one who pursues women. **7.** a brave, high-spirited, or adventurous man. ~*vb.* (gə'lænt, 'gælənt). *Rare.* **8.** (when *intr.*, usually foll. by *with*) to court or flirt (with). —'**gallantly** *adv.*

gallantry ('gæləntrɪ) *n., pl.* **-ries. 1.** conspicuous courage, esp. in war. **2.** polite attentiveness to women. **3.** a gallant action, speech, etc.

gall bladder *n.* a muscular sac, attached to the right lobe of the liver, that stores bile.

galleon ('gælɪən) *n.* a large sailing ship having three or more masts, used as a warship or trader from the 15th to the 18th centuries.

gallery ('gælərɪ) *n., pl.* **-leries. 1.** a covered passageway open on one side or on both sides. **2.** a balcony running along or around the inside wall of a church, hall, etc. **3.** *Theatre.* **a.** an upper floor that projects from the rear and contains the cheapest seats. **b.** the seats there. **c.** the audience seated there. **4.** a long narrow room, esp. one used for a specific purpose: *a shooting gallery.* **5.** a room or building for exhibiting works of art. **6.** an underground passage, as in a mine, etc. **7.** a small ornamental railing, esp. one surrounding the top of a desk, table, etc. **8.** any group of spectators, as at a golf match. **9. play to the gallery.** to try to gain popular favour, esp. by crude appeals. —'**galleried** *adj.*

galley ('gælɪ) *n.* **1.** any of various kinds of ship propelled by oars or sails used in ancient or medieval times. **2.** the kitchen of a ship, boat, or aircraft. **3.** any of various long rowing boats. **4.** *Printing.* **a.** a tray for holding composed type. **b.** short for **galley proof.**

galley proof *n.* a printer's proof, esp. one taken from type in a galley, used to make corrections before the matter has been split into pages. Often shortened to **galley.**

galley slave *n.* **1.** a criminal or slave condemned to row in a galley. **2.** *Inf.* a drudge.

galliard ('gæljəd) *n.* **1.** a spirited dance in triple time for two persons, popular in the 16th and 17th centuries. **2.** a piece of music for this dance.

Gallic ('gælɪk) *adj.* **1.** of or relating to France. **2.** of or relating to ancient Gaul or the Gauls.

Gallicism ('gælɪ,sɪzəm) *n.* a word or idiom borrowed from French.

gallinaceous (,gælɪ'neɪʃəs) *adj.* of, relating to, or belonging to an order of birds, including domestic fowl, pheasants, grouse, etc., having a heavy rounded body, short bill, and strong legs.

galling ('gɔːlɪŋ) *adj.* irritating, exasperating, or bitterly humiliating. —'**gallingly** *adv.*

THESAURUS

gain *v.* **1.** achieve, acquire, advance, attain, bag, build up, capture, collect, enlist, gather, get, glean, harvest, improve, increase, net, obtain, pick up, procure, profit, realize, reap, secure, win, win over **2.** acquire, bring in, clear, earn, get, make, net, obtain, produce, realize, win, yield **3.** *Usually with* **on a.** approach, catch up with, close with, get nearer, narrow the gap, overtake **b.** draw *or* pull away from, get farther away, leave behind, outdistance, recede, widen the gap **4.** arrive at, attain, come to, get to, reach **5. gain time** delay, procrastinate, stall, temporize, use delaying tactics ~*n.* **6.** accretion, achievement, acquisition, advance, advancement, advantage, attainment, benefit, dividend, earnings, emolument, growth, headway, improvement, income, increase, increment, lucre, proceeds, produce, profit, progress, return, rise, winnings, yield

gainful advantageous, beneficial, fruitful, lucrative, moneymaking, paying, productive, profitable, remunerative, rewarding, useful, worthwhile

gains booty, earnings, gainings, pickings, prize, proceeds, profits, revenue, takings, winnings

gainsay contradict, contravene, controvert, deny, disaffirm, disagree with, dispute

gait bearing, carriage, pace, step, stride, tread, walk

gala **1.** *n.* carnival, celebration, festival, festivity, fête, jamboree, pageant, party **2.** *adj.* celebratory, convivial, festal, festive, gay, jovial, joyful, merry

gale **1.** blast, cyclone, hurricane, squall, storm, tempest, tornado, typhoon **2.** *Inf.* burst, eruption, explosion, fit, howl, outbreak, outburst, peal, shout, shriek

gall[1] **1.** *Inf.* brass (*Inf.*), brass neck (*Inf.*), brazenness, cheek (*Inf.*), effrontery, impertinence, impudence, insolence, nerve (*Inf.*), sauciness **2.** acrimony, animosity, animus, antipathy, bad blood, bile, bitterness, enmity, hostility, malevolence, malice, malignity, rancour, sourness, spite, spleen, venom

gall[2] *n.* **1.** abrasion, chafe, excoriation, raw spot, scrape, sore, sore spot, wound **2.** aggravation (*Inf.*), annoyance, bother, botheration (*Inf.*), exasperation, harassment, irritant, irritation, nuisance, pest, provocation, vexation ~*v.* **3.** abrade, bark, chafe, excoriate, fret, graze, irritate, rub raw, scrape, skin **4.** aggravate (*Inf.*), annoy, bother, exasperate,

fret, harass, irk, irritate, nag, nettle, peeve (*Inf.*), pester, plague, provoke, rankle, rile (*Inf.*), rub up the wrong way, ruffle, vex

gallant *adj.* **1.** bold, brave, courageous, daring, dashing, dauntless, doughty, fearless, game (*Inf.*), heroic, high-spirited, honourable, intrepid, lion-hearted, manful, manly, mettlesome, noble, plucky, valiant, valorous **2.** attentive, chivalrous, courteous, courtly, gentlemanly, gracious, magnanimous, noble, polite **3.** august, dignified, elegant, glorious, grand, imposing, lofty, magnificent, noble, splendid, stately ~*n.* **4.** admirer, beau, boyfriend, escort, lover, paramour, suitor, wooer **5.** beau, blade (*Archaic*), buck (*Inf.*), dandy, fop, ladies' man, lady-killer (*Inf.*), man about town, man of fashion **6.** adventurer, cavalier, champion, daredevil, hero, knight, man of mettle, *preux chevalier*

gallantry **1.** audacity, boldness, bravery, courage, courageousness, daring, dauntlessness, derring-do (*Archaic*), fearlessness, heroism, intrepidity, manliness, mettle, nerve, pluck, prowess, spirit, valiance, valour **2.** attentiveness, chivalry, courteousness, courtesy, courtliness, elegance, gentlemanliness, graciousness, nobility, politeness

gallium ('gæliəm) *n.* a silvery metallic element that is liquid for a wide temperature range. It is used in high-temperature thermometers, semiconductors, and low-melting alloys. Symbol: Ga; atomic no.: 31; atomic wt.: 69.72.

gallivant ('gæli,vænt) *vb.* (*intr.*) to go about in search of pleasure, etc.; gad about.

gallnut ('gɔːl,nʌt) *or* **gall-apple** *n.* a type of plant gall that resembles a nut.

Gallo- ('gæləʊ-) *combining form.* denoting Gaul or France: *Gallo-Roman.*

gallon ('gælən) *n.* 1. Also called: **imperial gallon.** *Brit.* a unit of capacity equal to 277.42 cubic inches. 1 Brit. gallon is equivalent to 1.20 U.S. gallons or 4.55 litres. 2. *U.S.* a unit of capacity equal to 231 cubic inches. 1 U.S. gallon is equivalent to 0.83 imperial gallon or 3.79 litres. 3. (*pl.*) *Inf.* great quantities.

gallop ('gæləp) *vb.* 1. (of a horse or other quadruped) to run fast with a two-beat stride in which all four legs are off the ground at once. 2. to ride (a horse, etc.) at a gallop. 3. (*intr.*) *Inf.* to move, read, progress, etc., rapidly. ~*n.* 4. the fast two-beat gait of horses. 5. an instance of galloping. —'**galloper** *n.*

gallows ('gæləʊz) *n., pl.* **-lowses** *or* **-lows.** 1. a wooden structure usually consisting of two upright posts with a crossbeam, used for hanging criminals. 2. any timber structure resembling this. 3. **the gallows.** execution by hanging.

gallstone ('gɔːl,stəʊn) *n.* a small hard concretion formed in the gall bladder or its ducts.

Gallup Poll ('gæləp) *n.* a sampling of the views of a representative cross-section of the population, used esp. as a means of forecasting voting.

galop ('gæləp) *n.* 1. a 19th-century dance in quick duple time. 2. a piece of music for this dance.

galore (gə'lɔː) *determiner.* (*immediately postpositive*) *Inf.* in great numbers or quantity: *there were daffodils galore in the park.*

galoshes *or* **goloshes** (gə'lɒʃız) *pl. n.* (*sometimes sing.*) a pair of waterproof overshoes.

galumph (gə'lʌmpf, -'lʌmf) *vb.* (*intr.*) *Inf.* to leap or move about clumsily or joyfully.

galvanic (gæl'vænık) *adj.* 1. of, producing, or concerned with an electric current, esp. a direct current produced chemically. 2. *Inf.* resembling the effect of an electric shock; convulsive, startling, or energetic. —**gal'vanically** *adv.*

galvanism ('gælvə,nızəm) *n.* 1. *Obs.* electricity, esp. when produced by chemical means as in a cell or battery. 2. *Med.* treatment involving the application of electric currents to tissues.

galvanize *or* **-ise** ('gælvə,naız) *vb.* (*tr.*) 1. to stimulate to action; excite; startle. 2. to cover (iron, steel, etc.) with a protective zinc coating. 3. to stimulate by application of an electric current. —,**galvani'zation** *or* **-i'sation** *n.*

galvanometer (,gælvə'nɒmıtə) *n.* any sensitive instrument for detecting or measuring small electric currents. —**galvanometric** (,gælvənəʊ'metrık, gæl,vænə-) *adj.* —,**galva'nometry** *n.*

gambit ('gæmbıt) *n.* 1. *Chess.* an opening move in which a chessman, usually a pawn, is sacrificed to secure an advantageous position. 2. an opening comment, manoeuvre, etc., intended to secure an advantage.

gamble ('gæmb^al) *vb.* 1. (*intr.*) to play games of chance to win money, etc. 2. to risk or bet (money, etc.) on the

outcome of an event, sport, etc. 3. (*intr.*; often foll. by *on*) to act with the expectation of: *to gamble on its being a sunny day.* 4. (often foll. by *away*) to lose by or as if by betting; squander. ~*n.* 5. a risky act or venture. 6. a bet or wager. —'**gambler** *n.* —'**gambling** *n.*

gamboge (gæm'bəʊdʒ, -'buːʒ) *n.* 1. **a.** a gum resin used as the source of a yellow pigment and as a purgative. **b.** the pigment made from this resin. 2. **gamboge tree.** any of several tropical Asian trees that yield this resin.

gambol ('gæmb^al) *vb.* **-bolling, -bolled** *or U.S.* **-boling, -boled.** 1. (*intr.*) to skip or jump about in a playful manner; frolic. ~*n.* 2. a playful antic; frolic.

game[1] (geım) *n.* 1. an amusement or pastime; diversion. 2. a contest with rules, the result being determined by skill, strength, or chance. 3. a single period of play in such a contest, sport, etc. 4. the score needed to win a contest. 5. a single contest in a series; match. 6. equipment needed for playing certain games. 7. style or ability in playing a game. 8. a scheme, proceeding, etc., practised like a game: *the game of politics.* 9. an activity undertaken in a spirit of levity; joke: *marriage is just a game to him.* 10. **a.** wild animals, including birds and fish, hunted for sport, food, or profit. **b.** (*as modifier*): *game laws.* 11. the flesh of such animals, used as food. 12. an object of pursuit; quarry; prey (esp. in **fair game**). 13. *Inf.* work or occupation. 14. *Inf.* a trick, strategy, or device: *I can see through your little game.* 15. *Sl.,* chiefly *Brit.* prostitution (esp. in **on the game**). 16. **give the game away.** to reveal one's intentions or a secret. 17. **make (a) game of.** to make fun of; ridicule; mock. 18. **play the game.** *Inf.* to behave fairly or in accordance with the rules. 19. **the game is up.** there is no longer a chance of success. ~*adj.* 20. *Inf.* full of fighting spirit; plucky; brave. 21. (usually foll. by *for*) *Inf.* prepared or ready; willing: *I'm game for a try.* ~*vb.* 22. (*intr.*) to play games of chance for money, stakes, etc.; gamble. —'**gamely** *adv.* —'**gameness** *n.*

game[2] (geım) *adj.* a less common word for **lame** (esp. in **game leg**).

gamecock ('geım,kɒk) *n.* a cock bred and trained for fighting. Also called: **fighting cock.**

gamekeeper ('geım,kiːpə) *n.* a person employed to take care of game, as on an estate.

game laws *pl. n.* laws governing the hunting and preservation of game.

gamesmanship ('geımzmən,ʃıp) *n. Inf.* the art of winning games or defeating opponents by cunning practices without actually cheating.

gamesome ('geımsəm) *adj.* full of merriment; sportive. —'**gamesomeness** *n.*

gamester ('geımstə) *n.* a person who habitually plays games for money; gambler.

gamete ('gæmiːt, gə'miːt) *n.* a haploid reproductive cell that can undergo fertilization. —**gametic** (gə'metık) *adj.*

gamin ('gæmın) *n.* a street urchin.

gamine ('gæmiːn) *n.* a slim and boyish girl or young woman; an elfish tomboy.

gaming ('geımıŋ) *n.* **a.** gambling on games of chance. **b.** (*as modifier*): *gaming house.*

gamma ('gæmə) *n.* 1. the third letter in the Greek alphabet (Γ, γ). 2. the third in a group or series.

gamma rays *pl. n.* streams of **gamma radiation,** electromagnetic radiation of shorter wavelength and higher energy than x-rays.

gammer ('gæmə) *n. Rare, chiefly Brit.* a dialect word

THESAURUS

galling aggravating (*Inf.*), annoying, bitter, bothersome, exasperating, harassing, humiliating, irksome, irritating, nettlesome, plaguing, provoking, rankling, vexatious, vexing

gallop bolt, career, dart, dash, fly, hasten, hie (*Archaic*), hurry, race, run, rush, scud, shoot, speed, sprint, tear along, zoom

galore all over the place, aplenty, everywhere, in abundance, in great quantity, in numbers, in profusion, to spare

galvanize arouse, awaken, electrify, excite, fire, inspire, invigorate, jolt, move, provoke, quicken, shock, spur, startle, stimulate, stir, thrill, vitalize, wake

gamble *v.* 1. back, bet, game, have a flut-

ter (*Inf.*), lay *or* make a bet, play, punt, stake, try one's luck, wager 2. back, chance, hazard, put one's faith *or* trust in, risk, speculate, stake, stick one's neck out (*Inf.*), take a chance, venture ~*n.* 3. chance, leap in the dark, lottery, risk, speculation, uncertainty, venture 4. bet, flutter (*Inf.*), punt, wager

gambol 1. *v.* caper, cavort, curvet, cut a caper, frisk, frolic, hop, jump, prance, rollick, skip 2. *n.* antic, caper, frolic, gambado, hop, jump, prance, skip, spring

game[1] *n.* 1. amusement, distraction, diversion, entertainment, frolic, fun, jest, joke, lark, merriment, pastime, play, recreation, romp, sport 2. competition, contest, event, match, meeting, round, tournament 3. adven-

ture, business, enterprise, line, occupation, plan, proceeding, scheme, undertaking 4. chase, prey, quarry, wild animals 5. *Inf.* design, device, plan, plot, ploy, scheme, stratagem, strategy, tactic, trick 6. make (a) game of deride, make a fool of, make a laughing stock, make fun of, make sport of, mock, poke fun at, ridicule, send up (*Brit. inf.*)

game[2] *adj.* 1. bold, brave, courageous, dauntless, dogged, fearless, gallant, heroic, intrepid, persevering, persistent, plucky, resolute, spirited, unflinching, valiant, valorous 2. desirous, disposed, eager, inclined, interested, prepared, ready, willing

for an old woman: now chiefly humorous or contemptuous.

gammon[1] ('gæmən) n. 1. a cured or smoked ham. 2. the hindquarter of a side of bacon, cooked either whole or in rashers.

gammon[2] ('gæmən) Brit. inf. ~n. 1. deceitful nonsense; humbug. ~vb. 2. to deceive (a person).

gammy ('gæmɪ) adj. -mier, -miest. Brit. sl. (esp. of the leg) malfunctioning, injured, or lame; game.

gamp (gæmp) n. Brit. inf. an umbrella.

gamut ('gæmət) n. 1. entire range or scale, as of emotions. 2. Music. a. a scale, esp. (in medieval theory) one starting on the G on the bottom line of the bass staff. b. the whole range of notes.

gamy or **gamey** ('geɪmɪ) adj. **gamier, gamiest.** 1. having the smell or flavour of game, esp. high game. 2. Inf. spirited; plucky; brave. —'**gamily** adv. —'**gaminess** n.

-gamy n. combining form. denoting marriage or sexual union: bigamy. —**gamous** adj. combining form.

gander ('gændə) n. 1. a male goose. 2. Inf. a quick look (esp. in **take** (or **have**) **a gander**). 3. Inf. a simpleton.

gang[1] (gæŋ) n. 1. a group of people who associate together or act as an organized body, esp. for criminal or illegal purposes. 2. an organized group of workmen. 3. a series of similar tools arranged to work simultaneously in parallel. ~vb. 4. to form into, become part of, or act as a gang. ~See also **gang up.**

gang[2] (gæŋ) n. a variant spelling of **gangue.**

gang[3] (gæŋ) vb. (intr.) Scot. to go or walk.

gangland ('gæŋ,lænd, -lənd) n. Inf. the criminal underworld.

gangling ('gæŋglɪŋ) or **gangly** adj. tall, lanky, and awkward in movement.

ganglion ('gæŋglɪən) n., pl. **-glia** (-glɪə) or **-glions.** 1. an encapsulated collection of nerve-cell bodies, usually located outside the brain and spinal cord. 2. any concentration or centre of energy, activity, or strength. 3. a cystic tumour on a tendon sheath. —'**gangliar** adj. —,**gangli'onic** or '**gangli,ated** adj.

gangplank ('gæŋ,plæŋk) or **gangway** n. Naut. a portable bridge for boarding and leaving a vessel at dockside.

gangrene ('gæŋgriːn) n. death and decay of tissue as the result of interrupted blood supply, disease, or injury. —**gangrenous** ('gæŋgrɪnəs) adj.

gangster ('gæŋstə) n. a member of an organized gang of criminals.

gangue or **gang** (gæŋ) n. valueless and undesirable material in an ore.

gang up vb. (often foll. by on or against) Inf. to combine in a group (against).

gangway ('gæŋ,weɪ) n. 1. another word for **gangplank.** 2. Brit. an aisle between rows of seats. 3. temporary planks over mud or earth, as on a building site. ~interj. 4. clear a path!

gannet ('gænɪt) n. any of several heavily built marine birds having a long stout bill and typically white plumage with dark markings.

ganoid ('gænɔɪd) adj. 1. (of the scales of certain fishes) consisting of an inner bony layer and an outer layer of an enamel-like substance (ganoin). 2. denoting fishes, including the sturgeon and bowfin, having such scales. ~n. 3. a ganoid fish.

gantry ('gæntrɪ) or **gauntry** n., pl. **-tries.** 1. a bridgelike framework used to support a travelling crane,

signals over a railway track, etc. 2. Also called: **gantry scaffold.** the framework tower used to attend to a large rocket on its launching pad. 3. a supporting framework for a barrel.

gaol (dʒeɪl) n., vb. Brit. a variant spelling of **jail.** —'**gaoler** n.

gap (gæp) n. 1. a break or opening in a wall, fence, etc. 2. a break in continuity; interruption; hiatus. 3. a break in a line of hills or mountains affording a route through. 4. Chiefly U.S. a gorge or ravine. 5. a divergence or difference; disparity: the generation gap. 6. Electronics. a break in a magnetic circuit that increases the inductance and saturation point of the circuit. 7. **bridge, close, fill,** or **stop a gap.** to remedy a deficiency. ~vb. **gapping, gapped.** 8. (tr.) to make a breach or opening in.

gape (geɪp) vb. (intr.) 1. to stare in wonder, esp. with the mouth open. 2. to open the mouth wide, esp. involuntarily, as in yawning. 3. to be or become wide open: the crater gaped under his feet. ~n. 4. the act of gaping. 5. a wide opening. 6. the width of the widely opened mouth of a vertebrate. 7. a stare of astonishment. —'**gaper** n. —'**gapingly** adv.

garage ('gærɑːʒ, -rɪdʒ) n. 1. a building used to house a motor vehicle. 2. a commercial establishment in which motor vehicles are repaired, serviced, bought, and sold, and which usually also sells motor fuels. ~vb. 3. (tr.) to put into or keep in a garage.

garb (gɑːb) n. 1. clothes, esp. the distinctive attire of an occupation: clerical garb. 2. style of dress; fashion. 3. external appearance, covering, or attire. ~vb. 4. (tr.) to clothe; attire.

garbage ('gɑːbɪdʒ) n. 1. worthless, useless, or unwanted matter. 2. another word (esp. U.S.) for **rubbish.**

garble ('gɑːbəl) vb. (tr.) 1. to jumble (a story, quotation, etc.), esp. unintentionally. 2. to distort the meaning of (an account, text, etc.), as by making misleading omissions; corrupt. ~n. 3. a. the act of garbling. b. garbled matter. —'**garbler** n.

garçon (French garˈsɔ̃) n. a waiter or male servant, esp. if French.

garden ('gɑːdən) n. 1. Brit. a. an area of land, usually planted with grass, trees, flowerbeds, etc., adjoining a house. U.S. word: **yard.** b. (as modifier): a garden chair. 2. a. an area of land used for the cultivation of ornamental plants, herbs, fruit, vegetables, etc. b. (as modifier): garden tools. Related adj.: **horticultural.** 3. (often pl.) such an area of land that is open to the public, sometimes part of a park: botanical gardens. 4. a fertile and beautiful region. 5. **lead (a person) up the garden path.** Inf. to mislead or deceive. 6. **common or garden.** Inf. ordinary or commonplace. ~vb. 7. to work in, cultivate, or take care of (a garden, plot of land, etc.). —'**gardener** n.

garden centre n. a place where gardening tools and equipment, plants, seeds, etc., are sold.

garden city n. Brit. a planned town of limited size surrounded by a rural belt.

gardenia (gɑːˈdiːnɪə) n. 1. any evergreen shrub or tree of the Old World tropical genus Gardenia, cultivated for their large fragrant waxlike typically white flowers. 2. the flower of any of these shrubs.

gargantuan (gɑːˈgæntjʊən) adj. (sometimes cap.) huge; enormous.

gargle ('gɑːgəl) vb. 1. to rinse the mouth and throat with (a liquid, esp. a medicinal fluid) by slowly breathing through the liquid. ~n. 2. the liquid used for gargling. 3. the sound produced by gargling.

THESAURUS

gamut area, catalogue, compass, field, range, scale, scope, series, sweep

gang band, circle, clique, club, company, coterie, crew (Inf.), crowd, group, herd, horde, lot, mob, pack, party, ring, set, shift, squad, team, troupe

gangling, gangly angular, awkward, lanky, loose-jointed, rangy, rawboned, skinny, spindly, tall

gangster bandit, brigand, crook (Inf.), desperado, gang member, hood (U.S. sl.), hoodlum (Chiefly U.S. sl.), mobster (U.S. sl.), racketeer, robber, ruffian, thug, tough

gap 1. blank, breach, break, chink, cleft, crack, cranny, crevice, discontinuity, divide, hiatus, hole, interlude, intermission, inter-

ruption, interstice, interval, lacuna, lull, opening, pause, recess, rent, rift, space, vacuity, void 2. difference, disagreement, disparity, divergence, inconsistency

gape 1. gawk, gawp (Brit. sl.), goggle, stare, wonder 2. crack, open, split, yawn

gaping broad, cavernous, great, open, vast, wide, wide open, yawning

garb n. 1. apparel, array, attire, clothes, clothing, costume, dress, garment, gear (Sl.), habiliment, habit, outfit, raiment (Archaic), robes, uniform, vestments, wear 2. cut, fashion, look, mode, style 3. appearance, aspect, attire, covering, guise, outward form ~v. 4. apparel, attire, clothe, cover, dress, rig out, robe

garbage 1. bits and pieces, debris, detritus, junk, litter, odds and ends, rubbish, scraps 2. dross, filth, muck, offal, refuse, rubbish, scourings, slops, sweepings, swill, trash (Chiefly U.S.), waste

garble 1. confuse, jumble, mix up 2. corrupt, distort, doctor, falsify, misinterpret, misquote, misreport, misrepresent, misstate, mistranslate, mutilate, pervert, slant, tamper with, twist

gargantuan big, Brobdingnagian, colossal, elephantine, enormous, giant, gigantic, huge, immense, mammoth, massive, monstrous, monumental, mountainous, prodigious, titanic, towering, tremendous, vast

gargoyle ('gɑːgɔɪl) n. 1. a waterspout carved in the form of a grotesque face or creature and projecting from a roof gutter. 2. a person with a grotesque appearance.

garish ('gɛərɪʃ) adj. gay or colourful in a crude manner; gaudy. —'**garishly** adv. —'**garishness** n.

garland ('gɑːlənd) n. 1. a wreath of flowers, leaves, etc., worn round the head or neck or hung up. 2. a collection of short literary pieces, such as poems; anthology. ~vb. 3. (tr.) to adorn with a garland or garlands.

garlic ('gɑːlɪk) n. 1. a hardy widely cultivated Asian alliaceous plant having whitish flowers. 2. the bulb of this plant, made up of small segments (cloves) that have a strong odour and pungent taste and are used in cooking. —'**garlicky** adj.

garment ('gɑːmənt) n. 1. (often pl.) an article of clothing. 2. outer covering. ~vb. 3. (tr.; usually passive) to cover or clothe.

garner ('gɑːnə) vb. (tr.) 1. to gather or store as in a granary. ~n. 2. an archaic word for **granary.** 3. a place for storage.

garnet ('gɑːnɪt) n. any of a group of hard glassy red, yellow, or green minerals consisting of silicates in cubic crystalline form: used as a gemstone and abrasive.

garnish ('gɑːnɪʃ) vb. (tr.) 1. to decorate; trim. 2. to add something to (food) in order to improve its appearance or flavour. 3. Law. a. to serve with notice of proceedings; warn. b. to attach (a debt). ~n. 4. a decoration; trimming. 5. something, such as parsley, added to a dish for its flavour or decorative effect. —'**garnisher** n.

garret ('gærɪt) n. another word for **attic** (sense 1).

garrison ('gærɪsən) n. 1. the troops who maintain and guard a base or fortified place. 2. the place itself. ~vb. 3. (tr.) to station (troops) in (a fort, etc.).

garrotte or **garotte** (gə'rɒt) n. 1. a Spanish method of execution by strangulation. 2. the device, usually an iron collar, used in such executions. 3. Obs. strangulation of one's victim while committing robbery. ~vb. (tr.) 4. to execute by means of the garrotte. 5. to strangle, esp. in order to commit robbery. —**gar'rotter** or **ga-'rotter** n.

garrulous ('gærʊləs) adj. 1. given to constant chatter; talkative. 2. wordy or diffuse. —'**garrulously** adv. —'**garrulousness** or **garrulity** (gæ'ruːlɪtɪ) n.

garter ('gɑːtə) n. 1. a band, usually of elastic, worn round the leg to hold up a sock or stocking. 2. the U.S. word for **suspender.** ~vb. 3. (tr.) to fasten or secure as with a garter.

Garter ('gɑːtə) n. **the.** 1. **Order of the Garter.** the highest order of British knighthood. 2. (sometimes not cap.) a. the badge of this Order. b. membership of this Order.

garter stitch n. knitting in which all the rows are knitted in plain stitch.

garth (gɑːθ) n. 1. a courtyard surrounded by a cloister. 2. Arch. a yard or garden.

gas (gæs) n., pl. **gases** or **gasses.** 1. a substance in the physical state in which the attractive forces between its constituent atoms or molecules are not sufficiently strong to have a marked effect on their positions or mobility. 2. any substance that is gaseous at room temperature and atmospheric pressure. 3. any gaseous substance that is above its critical temperature and therefore not liquefiable by pressure alone. Cf. **vapour** (sense 2). 4. a. a fossil fuel in the form of a gas, used as a source of domestic and industrial heat. b. (as modifier): a gas cooker; gas fire. 5. a gaseous anaesthetic, such as

nitrous oxide. 6. Mining. firedamp or the explosive mixture of firedamp and air. 7. the usual U.S., Austral., & N.Z. word for **petrol.** 8. **step on the gas.** Inf. a. to accelerate a motor vehicle. b. to hurry. 9. a toxic, etc., substance in suspension in air used against an enemy, etc. 10. Sl. a. idle talk or boasting. b. Chiefly U.S. a delightful or successful person or thing: his latest record is a gas. ~vb. **gases** or **gasses, gassing, gassed.** 11. (tr.) to provide or fill with gas. 12. (tr.) to subject to gas fumes, esp. so as to asphyxiate or render unconscious. 13. (intr.; foll. by to) Inf. to talk in an idle or boastful way (to a person).

gasbag ('gæs,bæg) n. Sl. a person who talks in a vapid or empty way.

gas chamber or **oven** n. an airtight room into which poison gas is introduced to kill people or animals.

gaseous ('gæsɪəs, -ʃəs, -[jəs, 'geɪ-) adj. of, concerned with, or having the characteristics of a gas. —'**gaseousness** n.

gas gangrene n. gangrene resulting from infection of a wound by anaerobic bacteria that cause gas bubbles in the surrounding tissues.

gash (gæʃ) vb. 1. (tr.) to make a long deep cut in; slash. ~n. 2. a long deep cut.

gasholder ('gæs,həʊldə) n. 1. Also called: **gasometer.** a large tank for storing coal gas or natural gas prior to distribution to users. 2. any vessel for storing or measuring a gas.

gasify ('gæsɪ,faɪ) vb. **-fying, -fied.** to make into or become a gas. —,**gasifi'cation** n.

gasket ('gæskɪt) n. 1. a compressible packing piece of paper, rubber, asbestos, etc., sandwiched between the metal faces of a joint to provide a seal. 2. Naut. a piece of line used as a sail stop.

gaslight ('gæs,laɪt) n. 1. a type of lamp in which the illumination is produced by an incandescent mantle heated by a jet of gas. 2. the light produced by such a lamp.

gasman ('gæs,mæn) n., pl. **-men.** a man employed to read household gas meters, supervise gas fittings, etc.

gas mask n. a mask fitted with a chemical filter to enable the wearer to breathe air free of poisonous or corrosive gases.

gas meter n. an apparatus for measuring and recording the amount of gas passed through it.

gasoline or **gasolene** ('gæsə,liːn) n. the U.S. name for **petrol.**

gasometer (gæs'ɒmɪtə) n. a nontechnical name for **gasholder.**

gasp (gɑːsp) vb. 1. (intr.) to draw in the breath sharply or with effort, esp. in expressing awe, horror, etc. 2. (intr.; foll. by after or for) to crave. 3. (tr.; often foll. by out) to utter breathlessly. ~n. 4. a short convulsive intake of breath. 5. **at the last gasp. a.** at the point of death. **b.** at the last moment.

Gaspesian (gæ'speɪʒən) n. 1. a native or inhabitant of the Gaspé Peninsula in E Canada. ~adj. 2. of or relating to the Gaspé Peninsula or Gaspesians.

gas ring n. a circular assembly of gas jets, used esp. for cooking.

gassy ('gæsɪ) adj., **-sier, -siest.** 1. filled with, containing, or resembling gas. 2. Sl. full of idle or vapid talk. —'**gassiness** n.

gastric ('gæstrɪk) adj. of, relating to, near, or involving the stomach.

gastric juice n. a digestive fluid secreted by the stomach, containing hydrochloric acid, pepsin, rennin, etc.

THESAURUS

garish brassy, brummagem, cheap, flash (Inf.), flashy, flaunting, gaudy, glaring, glittering, loud, meretricious, raffish, showy, tasteless, tawdry, vulgar

garland 1. n. bays, chaplet, coronal, crown, festoon, honours, laurels, wreath 2. v. adorn, crown, deck, festoon, wreathe

garments apparel, array, articles of clothing, attire, clothes, clothing, costume, dress, duds (Inf.), garb, gear (Sl.), habiliment, habit, outfit, raiment (Archaic), robes, togs, uniform, vestments, wear

garner 1. v. accumulate, amass, assemble, collect, deposit, gather, hoard, husband, lay in or up, put by, reserve, save, stockpile, store, stow away, treasure 2. n. Literary depository, granary, store, storehouse, vault

garnish 1. v. adorn, beautify, bedeck, deck, decorate, embellish, enhance, grace, ornament, set off, trim 2. n. adornment, decoration, embellishment, enhancement, garniture, ornament, ornamentation, trim, trimming

garrison n. 1. armed force, command, detachment, troops, unit 2. base, camp, encampment, fort, fortification, fortress, post, station, stronghold ~v. 3. assign, mount, position, post, put on duty, station 4. defend, guard, man, occupy, protect, supply with troops

garrulity 1. babble, babbling, chatter, chattering, chattiness, effusiveness, gabbiness (Inf.), garrulousness, gift of the gab (Inf.), glibness, loquacity, mouthiness, prat-

ing, prattle, talkativeness, verbosity, volubility 2. diffuseness, long-windedness, prolixity, prosiness, verbosity, windiness, wordiness

garrulous 1. babbling, chattering, chatty, effusive, gabby (Inf.), glib, gossiping, gushing, loquacious, mouthy, prating, prattling, talkative, verbose, voluble 2. diffuse, gassy (Sl.), long-winded, prolix, prosy, verbose, windy, wordy

gash 1. v. cleave, cut, gouge, incise, lacerate, rend, slash, slit, tear, wound 2. n. cleft, cut, gouge, incision, laceration, rent, slash, slit, split, tear, wound

gasp 1. v. blow, catch one's breath, choke, fight for breath, gulp, pant, puff 2. n. blow, ejaculation, exclamation, gulp, pant, puff

gastric ulcer *n.* an ulcer of the mucous membrane lining the stomach.

gastritis (gæs'traɪtɪs) *n.* inflammation of the stomach.

gastro- *or often before a vowel* **gastr-** *combining form.* stomach: *gastroenteritis; gastritis.*

gastroenteritis (ˌgæstrəʊˌɛntə'raɪtɪs) *n.* inflammation of the stomach and intestines.

gastrointestinal (ˌgæstrəʊɪn'tɛstɪnəl) *adj.* of or relating to the stomach and intestinal tract.

gastronomy (gæs'trɒnəmɪ) *n.* the art of good eating. —**gastronomic** (ˌgæstrə'nɒmɪk) *or* ˌgastro'nomical *adj.* —ˌgastro'nomically *adv.*

gastropod ('gæstrəˌpɒd) *or* **gasteropod** ('gæstərəˌpɒd) *n.* any of a class of molluscs typically having a flattened muscular foot for locomotion and a head that bears stalked eyes. The class includes the snails, whelks, limpets, and slugs. —**gas'tropodous** *adj.*

gasworks ('gæsˌwɜːks) *n.* (*functioning as sing.*) a plant in which gas, esp. coal gas, is made.

gate (geɪt) *n.* **1.** a movable barrier, usually hinged, for closing an opening in a wall, fence, etc. **2.** an opening to allow passage into or out of an enclosed place. **3.** any means of entrance or access. **4.** a mountain pass or gap, esp. one providing entry into another country or region. **5.** a valve with a sliding or swinging component that regulates the flow of a liquid or gas in a pipe, etc. **6. a.** the number of people admitted to a sporting event or entertainment. **b.** the total entrance money received from them. **7.** *Electronics.* a logic circuit having one or more input terminals and one output terminal, the output being switched between two voltage levels determined by the combination of input signals. **8.** a component in a motion-picture camera or projector that holds each frame flat and momentarily stationary behind the lens. **9.** a slotted metal frame that controls the positions of the gear lever in a motor vehicle. ~*vb.* **10.** (*tr.*) *Brit.* to restrict (a student) to the school or college grounds as a punishment.

gâteau ('gætəʊ) *n., pl.* **-teaux** (-təʊz). any of various elaborate and rich cakes.

gatehouse ('geɪtˌhaʊs) *n.* a house built at or over a gateway, used as a fortification, etc.

gate-leg table *or* **gate-legged table** *n.* a table with one or two leaves supported by a hinged leg swung out from the frame.

gateway ('geɪtˌweɪ) *n.* **1.** an entrance that may be closed by or as by a gate. **2.** a means of entry or access: *Bombay, gateway to India.*

gather ('gæðə) *vb.* **1.** to assemble or cause to assemble. **2.** to collect or be collected gradually; muster. **3.** (*tr.*) to learn from information given; conclude or assume. **4.** (*tr.*) to pick or harvest (flowers, fruit, etc.). **5.** (*tr.*) to bring close (to). **6.** to increase or cause to increase gradually, as in force, speed, intensity, etc. **7.** to contract (the brow) or (of the brow) to become contracted into wrinkles; knit. **8.** (*tr.*) to assemble (sections of a book) in the correct sequence for binding. **9.** (*tr.*) to prepare or make ready: *to gather one's wits.* **10.** to draw (material) into a series of small tucks or folds. **11.** (*intr.*) *Inf.* (of a boil or other sore) to come to a head; form pus. ~*n.* **12. a.** the act of gathering. **b.** the amount gathered. **13.** a small fold in material, as made by a tightly pulled stitch; tuck. —**'gatherer** *n.*

gathering ('gæðərɪŋ) *n.* **1.** a group of people, things, etc., that are gathered together; assembly. **2.** *Sewing.* a series of gathers in material. **3.** *Inf.* **a.** the formation of pus in a boil. **b.** the pus so formed. **4.** *Printing.* an informal name for **section** (sense 15).

GATT (gæt) *n. acronym for* General Agreement on Tariffs and Trade: a multilateral international treaty signed in 1947 to promote trade.

gauche (gəʊʃ) *adj.* lacking ease of manner; tactless. —**'gauchely** *adv.* —**'gaucheness** *n.* —**gaucherie** (ˌgəʊʃə'riː, 'gəʊʃərɪ) *n.*

gaucho ('gaʊtʃəʊ) *n., pl.* **-chos.** a cowboy of the South American pampas, usually one of mixed Spanish and Indian descent.

gaud (gɔːd) *n.* an article of cheap finery.

gaudy[1] ('gɔːdɪ) *adj.* **gaudier, gaudiest.** bright or colourful in a crude or vulgar manner. —**'gaudily** *adv.* —**'gaudiness** *n.*

gaudy[2] ('gɔːdɪ) *n., pl.* **gaudies.** *Brit.* a celebratory feast held at some schools and colleges.

gauge *or* **gage** (geɪdʒ) *vb.* (*tr.*) **1.** to measure or determine the amount, quantity, size, condition, etc., of. **2.** to estimate or appraise; judge. **3.** to check for conformity or bring into conformity with a standard measurement, etc. ~*n.* **4.** a standard measurement, dimension, capacity, or quantity. **5.** any of various instruments for measuring a quantity: *a pressure gauge.* **6.** any of various devices used to check for conformity with a standard measurement. **7.** a standard or means for assessing; test; criterion. **8.** scope, capacity, or extent. **9.** the diameter of the barrel of a gun, esp. a shotgun. **10.** the thickness of sheet metal or the diameter of wire. **11.** the distance between the rails of a railway track. **12.** the distance between two wheels on the same axle of a vehicle, truck, etc. **13.** *Naut.* the position of a vessel in relation to the wind and another vessel. **14.** a measure of the fineness of woven or knitted fabric. ~*adj.* **15.** (of a pressure measurement) measured on a pressure gauge that registers zero at atmospheric pressure. —**'gaugeable** *or* **'gageable** *adj.*

Gaul (gɔːl) *n.* **1.** a native of ancient Gaul, a region in Roman times stretching from what is now N Italy to the S Netherlands. **2.** a Frenchman.

gaunt (gɔːnt) *adj.* **1.** bony and emaciated in appearance. **2.** (of places) bleak or desolate. —**'gauntly** *adv.* —**'gauntness** *n.*

gauntlet[1] ('gɔːntlɪt) *n.* **1.** a medieval armoured leather glove. **2.** a heavy glove with a long cuff. **3. take up** (*or* **throw down**) **the gauntlet.** to accept (or offer) a challenge.

gauntlet[2] ('gɔːntlɪt) *n.* **1.** a punishment in which the victim is forced to run between two rows of men who strike at him as he passes: formerly a military punishment. **2. run the gauntlet. a.** to suffer this punishment. **b.** to endure an onslaught, as of criticism. **3.** a testing ordeal.

gauntry ('gɔːntrɪ) *n., pl.* **-tries.** a variant spelling of **gantry.**

gauss (gaʊs) *n., pl.* **gauss.** the cgs unit of magnetic flux density. 1 gauss is equivalent to 10⁻⁴ tesla.

gauze (gɔːz) *n.* **1.** a transparent cloth of loose weave. **2.** a surgical dressing of muslin or similar material. **3.** any thin open-work material, such as wire. **4.** a fine mist or haze. —**'gauzy** *adj.*

gave (geɪv) *vb.* the past tense of **give.**

gavel ('gævəl) *n.* a small hammer used by a chairman, auctioneer, etc., to call for order or attention.

gavotte *or* **gavot** (gə'vɒt) *n.* **1.** an old formal dance in

---

THESAURUS

gate access, barrier, door, doorway, egress, entrance, exit, gateway, opening, passage, port (*Scot.*), portal

gather **1.** accumulate, amass, assemble, bring *or* get together, collect, congregate, convene, flock, forgather, garner, group, heap, hoard, marshal, mass, muster, pile up, round up, stack up, stockpile **2.** assume, be led to believe, conclude, deduce, draw, hear, infer, learn, make, surmise, understand **3.** clasp, draw, embrace, enfold, hold, hug **4.** crop, cull, garner, glean, harvest, pick, pluck, reap, select **5.** build, deepen, enlarge, expand, grow, heighten, increase, intensify, rise, swell, thicken, wax **6.** fold, pleat, pucker, ruffle, shirr, tuck

gathering **1.** assemblage, assembly, company, conclave, concourse, congrega-tion, congress, convention, convocation, crowd, flock, get-together (*Inf.*), group, knot, meeting, muster, party, rally, throng, turnout **2.** accumulation, acquisition, aggregate, collecting, collection, concentration, gain, heap, hoard, mass, pile, procuring, roundup, stock, stockpile **3.** *Inf.* abscess, boil, carbuncle, pimple, pustule, sore, spot, tumour, ulcer

gauche awkward, clumsy, graceless, ignorant, ill-bred, ill-mannered, inelegant, inept, insensitive, lacking in social graces, maladroit, tactless, uncultured, unpolished, unso-phisticated

gaudy bright, brilliant, brummagem, flash (*Inf.*), flashy, florid, garish, gay, glaring, loud, meretricious, ostentatious, raffish, showy, tasteless, tawdry, vulgar

gauge *v.* **1.** ascertain, calculate, check, compute, count, determine, measure, weigh **2.** adjudge, appraise, assess, estimate, evaluate, guess, judge, rate, reckon, value ~*n.* **3.** basis, criterion, example, exemplar, guide, guideline, indicator, measure, meter, model, pattern, rule, sample, standard, test, touchstone, yardstick **4.** bore, capacity, degree, depth, extent, height, magnitude, measure, scope, size, span, thickness, width

gaunt **1.** angular, attenuated, bony, cadaverous, emaciated, haggard, lank, lean, meagre, pinched, rawboned, scraggy, scrawny, skeletal, skinny, spare, thin, wasted **2.** bare, bleak, desolate, dismal, dreary, forbidding, forlorn, grim, harsh

quadruple time. **2.** a piece of music composed for or in the rhythm of this dance.

gawk (gɔːk) *n.* **1.** a clumsy stupid person; lout. ~*vb.* **2.** (*intr.*) to stare in a stupid way; gape.

gawky ('gɔːkı) *or* **gawkish** *adj.* **gawkier, gawkiest.** clumsy or ungainly; awkward. —'**gawkily** *or* '**gawkishly** *adv.* —'**gawkiness** *or* '**gawkishness** *n.*

gawp *or* **gaup** (gɔːp) *vb.* (*intr.*; often foll. by *at*) *Brit. sl.* to stare stupidly; gape.

gay (geı) *adj.* **1.** carefree and merry: *a gay temperament.* **2.** brightly coloured; brilliant: *a gay hat.* **3.** given to pleasure, esp. in social entertainment: *a gay life.* **4.** rakish or dissolute; licentious: *a gay old dog.* **5. a.** *Inf.* homosexual (used esp. by homosexuals of themselves). **b.** (*as n.*): *a group of gays.* —'**gayness** *n.*

gaze (geız) *vb.* **1.** (*intr.*) to look long and fixedly, esp. in wonder. ~*n.* **2.** a fixed look. —'**gazer** *n.*

gazebo (gə'ziːbəʊ) *n., pl.* **-bos** *or* **-boes.** a summerhouse, garden pavilion, or belvedere, sited to command a view.

gazelle (gə'zɛl) *n., pl.* **-zelles** *or* **-zelle.** any small graceful usually fawn-coloured antelope of Africa and Asia.

gazette (gə'zɛt) *n.* **1.** a newspaper or official journal. **2.** *Brit.* an official document containing public notices, appointments, etc. ~*vb.* **3.** (*tr.*) *Brit.* to announce or report (facts or an event) in a gazette.

gazetteer (ˌgæzı'tıə) *n.* **1.** a book or section of a book that lists and describes places. **2.** *Arch.* a writer for a gazette.

gazump (gə'zʌmp) *Brit.* ~*vb.* **1.** to raise the price of something, esp. a house, after agreeing a price verbally with (an intending buyer). **2.** (*tr.*) to swindle or overcharge. ~*n.* **3.** an act or instance of gazumping. —**ga-**'**zumper** *n.*

G.B. *abbrev. for* Great Britain.

G.B.E. *abbrev. for* (Knight or Dame) Grand Cross of the British Empire (a Brit. title).

g.b.h. *abbrev. for* grievous bodily harm.

G.C. *abbrev. for* George Cross (a Brit. award for bravery).

G.C.B. *abbrev. for* (Knight) Grand Cross of the Bath (a Brit. title).

G.C.E. *or* **GCE** **1.** (in Britain) *abbrev. for* General Certificate of Education: either of two public examinations in specified subjects taken as school-leaving qualifications or as qualifying examinations for entry into a university. See also **O level, A level.** ~*n.* **2.** *Inf.* any subject taken for one of these examinations.

G.C.M.G. *abbrev. for* (Knight or Dame) Grand Cross of the Order of St. Michael and St. George (a Brit. title).

G.C.V.O. *or* **GCVO** *abbrev. for* (Knight or Dame) Grand Cross of the Royal Victorian Order (a Brit. title).

Gd *the chemical symbol for* gadolinium.

Gdns. *abbrev. for* Gardens.

Ge *the chemical symbol for* germanium.

gear (gıə) *n.* **1.** a toothed wheel that engages with another toothed wheel or with a rack in order to change the speed or direction of transmitted motion. **2.** a mechanism for transmitting motion by gears. **3.** the engagement or specific ratio of a system of gears: *in gear; high gear.* **4.** equipment and supplies for a particular operation, sport, etc. **5.** *Naut.* all equipment or appurtenances belonging to a certain vessel, sailor, etc. **6.** short for **landing gear.** **7.** *Sl.* up-to-date clothes and accessories. **8.** a less common word for **harness** (sense 1). **9.** **out of gear.** out of order; not functioning properly. ~*vb.* **10.** (*tr.*) to adjust or adapt (one thing) so as to fit in or work with another: *to gear our output to current demand.* **11.** (*tr.*) to equip with or connect by gears. **12.**

(*intr.*) to be or come into gear. **13.** (*tr.*) to equip with harness.

gearbox ('gıəˌbɒks) *n.* **1.** the metal casing within which a train of gears is sealed. **2.** this metal casing and its contents, esp. in a motor vehicle.

gearing ('gıərıŋ) *n.* **1.** an assembly of gears designed to transmit motion. **2.** the act or technique of providing gears to transmit motion. **3.** *Accounting, Brit.* the ratio of a company's debt capital to its equity capital.

gear lever *or* *U.S.* **gearshift** ('gıəˌʃıft) *n.* a lever used to move gear wheels relative to each other, esp. in a motor vehicle.

gearwheel ('gıəˌwiːl) *n.* another name for **gear** (sense 1).

gecko ('gɛkəʊ) *n., pl.* **-os** *or* **-oes.** a small insectivorous terrestrial lizard of warm regions.

gee[1] (dʒiː) *interj.* **1.** Also: **gee up!** an exclamation, as to a horse or draught animal, to encourage it to turn to the right, go on, or go faster. ~*vb.* **geeing, geed.** **2.** (usually foll. by *up*) to move (an animal, esp. a horse) ahead; urge on.

gee[2] (dʒiː) *interj. U.S. inf.* a mild exclamation. Also: **gee whiz.**

geelbek ('xiːlˌbɛk) *n. S. African.* an edible marine fish with yellow jaws.

geese (giːs) *n.* the plural of **goose**[1].

geezer ('giːzə) *n. Inf.* a man, esp. an old one regarded as eccentric.

Geiger counter ('gaıgə) *or* **Geiger-Müller counter** ('mulə) *n.* an instrument for detecting and measuring the intensity of high-energy radiation.

geisha ('geıʃə) *n., pl.* **-sha** *or* **-shas.** a professional female companion for men in Japan, trained in music, dancing, and the art of conversation.

gel (dʒɛl) *n.* **1.** a semirigid jelly-like colloid in which a liquid is dispersed in a solid: *nondrip paint is a gel.* ~*vb.* **gelling, gelled.** **2.** to become or cause to become a gel. **3.** a variant spelling of **jell.**

gelatin ('dʒɛlətın) *or* **gelatine** ('dʒɛləˌtiːn) *n.* **1.** a colourless or yellowish water-soluble protein prepared by boiling animal hides and bones: used in foods, glue, photographic emulsions, etc. **2.** an edible jelly made of this substance.

gelatinize *or* **-ise** (dʒı'lætıˌnaız) *vb.* **1.** to make or become gelatinous. **2.** (*tr.*) *Photog.* to coat (glass, paper, etc.) with gelatin. —**ge**ˌlatini'**zation** *or* **-i'sation** *n.*

gelatinous (dʒı'lætınəs) *adj.* **1.** consisting of or resembling jelly; viscous. **2.** of, containing, or resembling gelatin. —**ge**'**latinously** *adv.* —**ge**'**latinousness** *n.*

geld (gɛld) *vb.* **gelding, gelded** *or* **gelt.** (*tr.*) **1.** to castrate (a horse or other animal). **2.** to deprive of virility or vitality; emasculate; weaken.

gelding ('gɛldıŋ) *n.* a castrated male horse.

gelignite ('dʒɛlıgˌnaıt) *n.* a type of dynamite in which the nitrogelatin is absorbed in a base of wood pulp and potassium or sodium nitrate. Also called (informal): **gelly.**

gem (dʒɛm) *n.* **1.** a precious or semiprecious stone used in jewellery as a decoration; jewel. **2.** a person or thing held to be a perfect example; treasure. ~*vb.* **gemming, gemmed.** **3.** (*tr.*) to set or ornament with gems. —'**gem,like** *adj.* —'**gemmy** *adj.*

geminate *adj.* ('dʒɛmınıt, -ˌneıt) *also* **geminated.** **1.** combined in pairs; doubled: *a geminate leaf.* ~*vb.* ('dʒɛmıˌneıt). **2.** to arrange or be arranged in pairs: *the "t"s in Italian "gatto" are geminated.* —'**geminately** *adv.* —ˌgemi'**nation** *n.*

Gemini ('dʒɛmıˌnaı, -'niː) *n.* **1.** *Astron.* a zodiacal con-

gawk 1. *n.* boor, churl, clod, clodhopper (*Inf.*), dolt, dunderhead, galoot (*Sl.*), ignoramus, lout, lubber, lummox (*Inf.*), oaf **2.** *v.* gape, gawp (*Sl.*), gaze open-mouthed, goggle, stare

gawky awkward, clownish, clumsy, gauche, loutish, lumbering, lumpish, maladroit, oafish, uncouth, ungainly

gay 1. animated, blithe, carefree, cheerful, debonair, glad, gleeful, happy, hilarious, insouciant, jolly, jovial, joyful, joyous, lighthearted, lively, merry, sparkling, sunny, vivacious **2.** bright, brilliant, colourful, flamboyant, flashy, fresh, garish, gaudy, rich,

showy, vivid **3.** convivial, festive, frivolous, frolicsome, fun-loving, gamesome, merry, playful, pleasure-seeking, rakish, rollicking, sportive, waggish

gaze 1. *v.* contemplate, gape, look, look fixedly, regard, stare, view, watch, wonder **2.** *n.* fixed look, look, stare

gazette journal, newspaper, news-sheet, organ, paper, periodical

gear *n.* **1.** cog, cogwheel, gearwheel, toothed wheel **2.** cogs, gearing, machinery, mechanism, works **3.** accessories, accoutrements, apparatus, equipment, harness, instruments, outfit, paraphernalia, rigging,

supplies, tackle, tools, trappings **4.** baggage, belongings, effects, kit, luggage, stuff, things **5.** *Sl.* apparel, array, attire, clothes, clothing, costume, dress, garb, garments, habit, outfit, rigout (*Inf.*), togs, wear ~*v.* **6.** adapt, adjust, equip, fit, rig, suit, tailor

gelatinous gluey, glutinous, gummy, jelly-like, mucilaginous, sticky, viscid, viscous

gelid arctic, chilly, cold, freezing, frigid, frosty, frozen, glacial, ice-cold, icy, polar

gem 1. jewel, precious stone, semiprecious stone, stone **2.** flower, jewel, masterpiece, pearl, pick, prize, treasure

stellation in the N hemisphere containing the stars Castor and Pollux. **2.** *Astrol.* Also called: the **Twins.** the third sign of the zodiac. The sun is in this sign between about May 21 and June 20.

gemsbok *or* **gemsbuck** ('gɛmz,bʌk) *n., pl.* **-bok, -boks** *or* **-buck, -bucks.** an oryx of southern Africa, marked with a broad black band along its flanks.

gen (dʒɛn) *n. Brit. inf.* information: *give me the gen on your latest project.* ~See also **gen up.**

gen. *abbrev. for:* **1.** gender. **2.** general(ly). **3.** generator. **4.** generic. **5.** genitive. **6.** genus.

Gen. *abbrev. for:* **1.** General. **2.** *Bible.* Genesis.

-gen *suffix forming nouns.* **1.** producing or that which produces: *hydrogen.* **2.** something produced: *antigen.*

gendarme ('ʒɒndɑːm) *n.* **1.** a member of the police force in France or in countries influenced or controlled by France. **2.** a slang word for a **policeman. 3.** a sharp pinnacle of rock on a mountain ridge.

gender ('dʒɛndə) *n.* **1.** a set of two or more grammatical categories into which the nouns of certain languages are divided. **2.** any of the categories, such as masculine, feminine, neuter, or common, within such a set. **3.** *Inf.* the state of being male, female, or neuter. **4.** *Inf.* all the members of one sex: *the female gender.*

gene (dʒiːn) *n.* a unit of heredity, capable of replication and mutation, occupying a fixed position on a chromosome and transmitted from parent to offspring during reproduction.

-gene *suffix forming nouns.* variant of **-gen.**

genealogy (,dʒiːnɪ'ælədʒɪ) *n., pl.* **-gies. 1.** the direct descent of an individual or group from an ancestor. **2.** the study of the evolutionary development of animals and plants from earlier forms. **3.** a chart showing the relationships and descent of an individual, group, etc. —**genealogical** (,dʒiːnɪə'lɒdʒɪkəl) *adj.* —,**genea'logically** *adv.* —,**gene'alogist** *n.*

general ('dʒɛnərəl, 'dʒɛnrəl) *adj.* **1.** common; widespread. **2.** of, applying to, or participated in by all or most of the members of a group, category, or community. **3.** relating to various branches of an activity, profession, etc.; not specialized: *general office work.* **4.** including various or miscellaneous items: *general knowledge; a general store.* **5.** not specific as to detail; overall: *a general description.* **6.** not definite; vague: *the general idea.* **7.** applicable or true in most cases; usual. **8.** (*prenominal or immediately postpositive*) having superior or extended authority or rank: *general manager; consul general.* ~*n.* **9.** an officer of a rank senior to lieutenant general, esp. one who commands a large military formation. **10.** any person who applies strategy or tactics. **11.** a general condition or principle: opposed to *particular.* **12.** a title for the head of a religious order, congregation, etc. **13.** *Arch.* the people; public. **14. in general.** generally; mostly or usually. —'**generalness** *n.*

general anaesthetic *n.* See **anaesthesia.**

general election *n.* **1.** an election in which representatives are chosen in all constituencies of a state. **2.** *U.S.* a final election from which successful candidates are sent to a legislative body. **3.** *U.S. & Canad.* a national, state, or provincial election.

generalissimo (,dʒɛnərə'lɪsɪ,məʊ, ,dʒɛnrə-) *n., pl.* **-mos.** a supreme commander of combined military, naval, and air forces.

generality (,dʒɛnə'rælɪtɪ) *n., pl.* **-ties. 1.** a principle or observation having general application. **2.** the state or quality of being general. **3.** *Arch.* the majority.

generalization *or* **-isation** (,dʒɛnrəlaɪ'zeɪʃən) *n.* **1.** a principle, theory, etc., with general application. **2.** the act or an instance of generalizing. **3.** *Logic.* a proposition asserting the truth of something either for all members of a class or for one or more particular members of a class.

generalize *or* **-ise** ('dʒɛnrə,laɪz) *vb.* **1.** to form (general principles or conclusions) from (detailed facts, experience, etc.); infer. **2.** (*intr.*) to think or speak in generalities, esp. in a prejudiced way. **3.** (*tr.; usually passive*) to cause to become widely used or known.

generally ('dʒɛnrəlɪ) *adv.* **1.** usually; as a rule. **2.** commonly or widely. **3.** without reference to specific details or facts; broadly.

general practitioner *n.* a physician who does not specialize but has a medical practice (**general practice**) in which he treats all illnesses. Informal name: **family doctor.** *Abbrev.:* **G.P.**

general staff *n.* officers assigned to advise senior officers in the planning and execution of military policy.

general strike *n.* a strike by all or most of the workers of a country, province, city, etc.

generate ('dʒɛnə,reɪt) *vb.* (*mainly tr.*) **1.** to produce or bring into being; create. **2.** (*also intr.*) to produce (electricity). **3.** to produce (a substance) by a chemical process. **4.** *Maths, linguistics.* to provide a precise criterion for membership in (a set): *these rules will generate all the noun phrases in English.* **5.** *Geom.* to trace or form by moving a point, line, or plane in a specific way: *circular motion of a line generates a cylinder.* —**generable** ('dʒɛnərəbəl) *adj.*

generation (,dʒɛnə'reɪʃən) *n.* **1.** the act or process of bringing into being; production or reproduction, esp. of offspring. **2.** a successive stage in natural descent of people or animals or the individuals produced at each stage. **3.** the average time between two such generations of a species: about 35 years for humans. **4.** all the people of approximately the same age, esp. when considered as sharing certain attitudes, etc. **5.** production of electricity, heat, etc. **6.** (*modifier, in combination*) **a.** belonging to a generation specified as having been born in or as having parents, grandparents, etc., born in a given country: *a third-generation American.* **b.** belonging to a specified stage of development in manufacture: *a second-generation computer.*

generation gap *n.* the years separating one generation from the next, esp. when regarded as representing the difference in outlook and the lack of understanding between them.

generative ('dʒɛnərətɪv) *adj.* **1.** of or relating to the production of offspring, parts, etc. **2.** capable of producing or originating.

generator ('dʒɛnə,reɪtə) *n.* **1.** *Physics.* **a.** any device for converting mechanical energy into electrical energy. **b.** a device for producing a voltage electrostatically. **2.** an apparatus for producing a gas. **3.** a person or thing that generates.

generic (dʒɪ'nɛrɪk) *adj.* **1.** applicable or referring to a whole class or group; general. **2.** *Biol.* of, relating to, or belonging to a genus: *the generic name.* **3.** (of a drug) not having a trademark. —**ge'nerically** *adv.*

generosity (,dʒɛnə'rɒsɪtɪ) *n., pl.* **-ties. 1.** willingness and liberality in giving away one's money, time, etc.; magnanimity. **2.** freedom from pettiness in character and mind. **3.** a generous act. **4.** abundance; plenty.

THESAURUS

genealogy ancestry, blood line, derivation, descent, extraction, family tree, line, lineage, pedigree, progeniture, stemma, stirps, stock, strain

general 1. accepted, broad, common, extensive, popular, prevailing, prevalent, public, universal, widespread **2.** accustomed, conventional, customary, everyday, habitual, normal, ordinary, regular, typical, usual **3.** approximate, ill-defined, imprecise, inaccurate, indefinite, inexact, loose, undetailed, unspecific, vague **4.** across-the-board, all-inclusive, blanket, broad, catholic, collective, comprehensive, encyclopedic, generic, indiscriminate, miscellaneous, panoramic, sweeping, total, universal

generality 1. abstract principle, gener-

alization, loose statement, sweeping statement, vague notion **2.** acceptedness, commonness, extensiveness, popularity, prevalence, universality **3.** approximateness, impreciseness, indefiniteness, inexactness, lack of detail, looseness, vagueness **4.** breadth, catholicity, comprehensiveness, miscellaneity, sweepingness, universality

generally 1. almost always, as a rule, by and large, conventionally, customarily, for the most part, habitually, in most cases, mainly, normally, on average, on the whole, ordinarily, regularly, typically, usually **2.** commonly, extensively, popularly, publicly, universally, widely **3.** approximately, broadly, chiefly, for the most part, in the main, largely, mainly, mostly, on the whole, pre-

dominantly, principally

generate beget, breed, bring about, cause, create, engender, form, give rise to, initiate, make, originate, procreate, produce, propagate, spawn, whip up

generation 1. begetting, breeding, creation, engenderment, formation, genesis, origination, procreation, production, propagation, reproduction **2.** age group, breed, crop **3.** age, day, days, epoch, era, period, time, times

generic all-encompassing, blanket, collective, common, comprehensive, general, inclusive, sweeping, universal, wide

generosity 1. beneficence, benevolence, bounteousness, bounty, charity, kindness, liberality, munificence, open-handedness **2.** dis-

generous ('dʒɛnərəs, 'dʒɛnrəs) *adj.* **1.** willing and liberal in giving away one's money, time, etc.; munificent. **2.** free from pettiness in character and mind. **3.** full or plentiful: *a generous portion.* **4.** (of wine) rich in alcohol. —'**generously** *adv.* —'**generousness** *n.*

genesis ('dʒɛnɪsɪs) *n., pl.* -**ses** (-ˌsiːz). a beginning or origin of anything.

Genesis ('dʒɛnɪsɪs) *n.* the first book of the Old Testament recounting the Creation of the world.

-**genesis** *n. combining form.* indicating genesis, development, or generation: *biogenesis; parthenogenesis.* —-**genetic** *or* -**genic** *adj. combining form.*

genetic (dʒɪ'nɛtɪk) *or* **genetical** *adj.* of or relating to genetics, genes, or the origin of something. —ge'**netically** *adv.*

genetic code *n. Biochem.* the order in which the four nitrogenous bases of DNA are arranged in the molecule, which determines the type and amount of protein synthesized in the cell.

genetics (dʒɪ'nɛtɪks) *n.* **1.** (*functioning as sing.*) the study of heredity and variation in organisms. **2.** the genetic features and constitution of a single organism, species, or group. —ge'**neticist** *n.*

Geneva Convention *n.* the international agreement, first formulated in 1864 at Geneva, establishing a code for wartime treatment of the sick or wounded: revised and extended to cover maritime warfare and prisoners of war.

genial ('dʒiːnjəl, -nɪəl) *adj.* **1.** cheerful, easygoing, and warm in manner. **2.** pleasantly warm, so as to give life, growth, or health. —**geniality** (ˌdʒiːnɪ'ælɪtɪ) *n.* —'**genially** *adv.*

genie ('dʒiːnɪ) *n.* **1.** (in fairy tales and stories) a servant who appears by magic and fulfils a person's wishes. **2.** another word for **jinni.**

genital ('dʒɛnɪtəl) *adj.* **1.** of or relating to the sexual organs or to reproduction. **2.** *Psychoanal.* relating to the mature stage of psychosexual development.

genitals ('dʒɛnɪtəlz) *or* **genitalia** (ˌdʒɛnɪ'teɪlɪə, -'teɪljə) *pl. n.* the external sexual organs.

genitive ('dʒɛnɪtɪv) *Grammar.* ~*adj.* **1.** denoting a case of nouns, pronouns, and adjectives in inflected languages used to indicate a relation of ownership or association. ~*n.* **2. a.** the genitive case. **b.** a word or speech element in this case. —**genitival** (ˌdʒɛnɪ'taɪvəl) *adj.* —ˌgeni'**tivally** *adv.*

genius ('dʒiːnɪəs, -njəs) *n., pl.* -**uses** *or for defs.* 5, 6 **genii** ('dʒiːnɪˌaɪ). **1.** a person with exceptional ability, esp. of a highly original kind. **2.** such ability. **3.** the distinctive spirit of a nation, era, language, etc. **4.** a person considered as exerting influence of a certain sort: *an evil genius.* **5.** *Roman myth.* **a.** the guiding spirit who attends a person from birth to death. **b.** the guardian spirit of a place. **6.** *Arabic myth.* (*usually pl.*) a demon; jinn.

genocide ('dʒɛnəʊˌsaɪd) *n.* the policy of deliberately killing a nationality or ethnic group. —ˌgeno'**cidal** *adj.*

-**genous** *adj. combining form.* **1.** yielding or generating: *erogenous.* **2.** generated by or issuing from: *endogenous.*

genre ('ʒɑːnrə) *n.* **1.** kind, category, or sort, esp. of literary or artistic work. **2. a.** a category of painting in which incidents from everyday life are depicted. **b.** (*as modifier*): *genre painting.*

gent (dʒɛnt) *n. Inf.* short for **gentleman.**

genteel (dʒɛn'tiːl) *adj.* **1.** respectable, polite, and well-bred. **2.** appropriate to polite or fashionable society. **3.** affectedly proper or refined; excessively polite. —gen'**teelly** *adv.* —gen'**teelness** *n.*

gentian ('dʒɛnʃən) *n.* **1.** any plant of the genus *Gentiana,* having blue, yellow, white, or red showy flowers. **2.** the bitter-tasting roots of the yellow gentian, which can be used as a tonic.

gentian violet *n.* a greenish crystalline substance that forms a violet solution in water, used as an indicator, antiseptic, and in the treatment of burns.

Gentile ('dʒɛntaɪl) *n.* **1.** a person, esp. a Christian, who is not a Jew. **2.** a Christian, as contrasted with a Jew. **3.** a person who is not a member of one's own church: used esp. by Mormons. **4.** a heathen or pagan. ~*adj.* **5.** of or relating to a race or religion that is not Jewish. **6.** Christian, as contrasted with Jewish. **7.** not being a member of one's own church: used esp. by Mormons. **8.** pagan or heathen.

gentility (dʒɛn'tɪlɪtɪ) *n., pl.* -**ties.** **1.** respectability and polite good breeding. **2.** affected politeness. **3.** noble birth or ancestry. **4.** people of noble birth.

gentle ('dʒɛntəl) *adj.* **1.** having a mild or kindly nature or character. **2.** soft or temperate; mild; moderate. **3.** gradual: *a gentle slope.* **4.** easily controlled; tame. **5.** *Arch.* of good breeding; noble: *gentle blood.* **6.** *Arch.* gallant; chivalrous. ~*vb.* (*tr.*) **7.** to tame or subdue (a horse, etc.). **8.** to appease or mollify. ~*n.* **9.** a maggot, esp. when used as bait in fishing. —'**gentleness** *n.* —'**gently** *adv.*

gentlefolk ('dʒɛntəlˌfəʊk) *or* **gentlefolks** *pl. n.* persons regarded as being of good breeding.

gentleman ('dʒɛntəlmən) *n., pl.* -**men.** **1.** a man regarded as having qualities of refinement associated with a good family. **2.** a man who is cultured, courteous, and well-educated. **3.** a polite name for a man. **4.** the personal servant of a gentleman (esp. in **gentleman's gentleman**). —'**gentlemanly** *adj.* —'**gentlemanliness** *n.*

gentry ('dʒɛntrɪ) *n.* **1.** *Brit.* persons just below the nobility in social rank. **2.** people of a particular class, esp. one considered to be inferior.

gents (dʒɛnts) *n.* (*functioning as sing.*) *Brit. inf.* a men's public lavatory.

genuflect ('dʒɛnjʊˌflɛkt) *vb.* (*intr.*) **1.** to act in a servile or deferential manner. **2.** *R.C. Church.* to bend one or both knees as a sign of reverence. —ˌgenu'**flection** *or* (*esp. Brit.*) ˌgenu'**flexion** *n.* —'genuˌ**flector** *n.*

genuine ('dʒɛnjʊɪn) *adj.* **1.** not fake or counterfeit; original; real; authentic. **2.** not pretending; frank; sincere. **3.** being of authentic or original stock. —'**genuinely** *adv.* —'**genuineness** *n.*

THESAURUS

interestedness, goodness, high-mindedness, magnanimity, nobleness, unselfishness

generous 1. beneficent, benevolent, bounteous, bountiful, charitable, free, hospitable, kind, lavish, liberal, munificent, open-handed, princely, ungrudging, unstinting **2.** big-hearted, disinterested, good, high-minded, lofty, magnanimous, noble, unselfish **3.** abundant, ample, copious, full, lavish, liberal, overflowing, plentiful, rich, unstinting

genesis beginning, birth, commencement, creation, dawn, engendering, formation, generation, inception, origin, outset, propagation, root, source, start

genial affable, agreeable, amiable, cheerful, cheery, congenial, convivial, cordial, easygoing, enlivening, friendly, glad, good-natured, happy, hearty, jolly, jovial, joyous, kind, kindly, merry, pleasant, sunny, warm, warm-hearted

geniality affability, agreeableness, amiability, cheerfulness, cheeriness, congeniality, conviviality, cordiality, friendliness, gladness, good cheer, good nature, happiness, heartiness, jollity, joviality, joy, joyous-

ness, kindliness, kindness, mirth, pleasantness, sunniness, warm-heartedness, warmth

genius 1. adept, brain (*Inf.*), expert, intellect (*Inf.*), maestro, master, master-hand, mastermind, virtuoso **2.** ability, aptitude, bent, brilliance, capacity, creative power, endowment, faculty, flair, gift, inclination, knack, propensity, talent, turn

genteel aristocratic, civil, courteous, courtly, cultivated, cultured, elegant, fashionable, formal, gentlemanly, ladylike, mannerly, polished, polite, refined, respectable, stylish, urbane, well-bred, well-mannered

gentility 1. civility, courtesy, courtliness, cultivation, culture, decorum, elegance, etiquette, formality, good breeding, good manners, mannerliness, polish, politeness, propriety, refinement, respectability, urbanity **2.** blue blood, gentle birth, good family, high birth, nobility, rank **3.** aristocracy, elite, gentlefolk, gentry, nobility, nobles, ruling class, upper class

gentle 1. amiable, benign, bland, compassionate, dove-like, humane, kind, kindly, lenient, meek, merciful, mild, pacific, peaceful,

placid, quiet, soft, sweet-tempered, tender **2.** balmy, calm, clement, easy, light, low, mild, moderate, muted, placid, quiet, serene, slight, smooth, soft, soothing, temperate, tranquil, untroubled **3.** easy, gradual, imperceptible, light, mild, moderate, slight, slow **4.** biddable, broken, docile, manageable, placid, tame, tractable **5.** *Archaic* aristocratic, courteous, cultured, elegant, genteel, gentleman-like, gentlemanly, high-born, ladylike, noble, polished, polite, refined, upper-class, well-born, well-bred

gentlemanly civil, civilized, courteous, cultivated, gallant, genteel, gentlemanlike, honourable, mannerly, noble, obliging, polished, polite, refined, reputable, suave, urbane, well-bred, well-mannered

genuine 1. actual, authentic, bona fide, honest, legitimate, natural, original, pure, real, sound, sterling, true, unadulterated, unalloyed, veritable **2.** artless, candid, earnest, frank, heartfelt, honest, sincere, unaffected, unfeigned

gen up vb. **genning up**, **genned up**. (tr.; adv.; often passive) Brit. inf. to brief (someone) in detail; give full information to.

genus ('dʒiːnəs) n., pl. **genera** ('dʒɛnərə) or **genuses**. **1.** Biol. any of the taxonomic groups into which a family is divided and which contains one or more species. **2.** Logic. a class of objects or individuals that can be divided into two or more groups or species. **3.** a class, group, etc., with common characteristics.

geo- combining form. indicating earth: geomorphology.

geocentric (,dʒiːəʊ'sɛntrɪk) adj. **1.** having the earth at its centre. **2.** measured as from the centre of the earth. —,**geo'centrically** adv.

geode ('dʒiːəʊd) n. a cavity, usually lined with crystals, within a rock mass or nodule. —**geodic** (dʒɪ'ɒdɪk) adj.

geodesic (,dʒiːəʊ'dɛsɪk, -'diː-) adj. **1.** Also: **geodetic**. relating to the geometry of curved surfaces. ~n. **2.** Also called: **geodesic line**. the shortest line between two points on a curved surface.

geodesy (dʒɪ'ɒdɪsɪ) n. the branch of science concerned with determining the exact position of geographical points and the shape and size of the earth. —**ge'odesist** n.

geog. abbrev. for: **1.** geographer. **2.** geographic(al). **3.** geography.

geographical mile n. another name for **nautical mile**.

geography (dʒɪ'ɒgrəfɪ) n., pl. **-phies**. **1.** the study of the natural features of the earth's surface, including topography, climate, soil, vegetation, etc., and man's response to them. **2.** the natural features of a region. —**ge'ographer** n. —**geographical** (,dʒɪə'græfɪkəl) or ,**geo'graphic** adj. —,**geo'graphically** adv.

geoid ('dʒiːɔɪd) n. **1.** a hypothetical surface that corresponds to mean sea level and extends under the continents. **2.** the shape of the earth.

geol. abbrev. for: **1.** geologic(al). **2.** geologist. **3.** geology.

geology (dʒɪ'ɒldʒɪ) n. **1.** the scientific study of the origin, structure, and composition of the earth. **2.** the geological features of a district or country. —**geological** (,dʒɪə'lɒdʒɪkəl) or ,**geo'logic** adj. —,**geo'logically** adv. —**ge'ologist** n.

geometric (,dʒɪə'mɛtrɪk) or **geometrical** adj. **1.** of, relating to, or following the methods and principles of geometry. **2.** consisting of, formed by, or characterized by points, lines, curves, or surfaces. **3.** (of design or ornamentation) composed predominantly of simple geometric forms, such as circles, rectangles, triangles, etc. —,**geo'metrically** adv.

geometric progression n. **1.** a sequence of numbers, each of which differs from the succeeding one by a constant ratio, as 1, 2, 4, 8, ... Cf. **arithmetic progression**. **2. geometric series**. such numbers written as a sum.

geometry (dʒɪ'ɒmɪtrɪ) n. **1.** the branch of mathematics concerned with the properties, relationships, and measurement of points, lines, curves, and surfaces. **2.** a shape, configuration, or arrangement. —**ge,ome'trician** n.

George Cross (dʒɔːdʒ) n. a British award for bravery. Abbrev.: **G.C.**

georgette or **georgette crepe** (dʒɔː'dʒɛt) n. a thin silk or cotton crepe fabric.

Georgian ('dʒɔːdʒən) adj. **1.** of or relating to any or all of the four kings who ruled Great Britain from 1714 to 1830, or to their reigns: Georgian architecture. **2.** of or relating to George V of Great Britain or his reign (1910–36): the Georgian poets. **3.** of or relating to the Georgian SSR, its people, or their language. **4.** of or relating to the American State of Georgia or its inhabitants. **5.** (of furniture, furnishings, etc.) in or imitative of the style prevalent in England during the 18th century. ~n. **6.** the official language of the Georgian SSR, belonging to the South Caucasian family. **7.** a native or inhabitant of the Georgian SSR. **8.** a native or inhabitant of the American State of Georgia.

geotropism (dʒɪ'ɒtrə,pɪzəm) n. the response of a plant part to the stimulus of gravity. Plant stems, which grow upwards irrespective of the position in which they are placed, show **negative geotropism**. —**geotropic** (,dʒiːəʊ'trɒpɪk) adj.

Ger. abbrev. for: **1.** German. **2.** Germany.

geranium (dʒɪ'reɪnɪəm) n. **1.** a cultivated plant having scarlet, pink, or white showy flowers. See also **pelargonium**. **2.** any plant such as cranesbill and herb Robert, having divided leaves and pink or purplish flowers.

gerbil or **gerbille** ('dʒɜːbɪl) n. a burrowing rodent inhabiting hot dry regions of Asia and Africa and having soft pale fur.

gerfalcon ('dʒɜː,fɔːlkən, -,fɔːkən) n. a variant spelling of **gyrfalcon**.

geriatrics (,dʒɛrɪ'ætrɪks) n. (functioning as sing.) the branch of medical science concerned with the diagnosis and treatment of diseases affecting elderly people. —,**geria'tric** adj. —,**geria'trician** n.

germ (dʒɜːm) n. **1.** a microorganism, esp. one that produces disease. **2.** (often pl.) the rudimentary or initial form of something: the germs of revolution. **3.** a simple structure that is capable of developing into a complete organism.

german ('dʒɜːmən) adj. **1.** (used in combination) **a.** having the same parents as oneself: a brother-german. **b.** having a parent that is a brother or sister of either of one's own parents: cousin-german. **2.** a less common word for **germane**.

German ('dʒɜːmən) n. **1.** the official language of East and West Germany and Austria and one of the official languages of Switzerland. **2.** a native, inhabitant, or citizen of East or West Germany. **3.** a person whose native language is German. ~adj. **4.** denoting, relating to, or using the German language. **5.** relating to, denoting, or characteristic of any German state or its people.

germander (dʒɜː'mændə) n. any of several plants of Europe, having two-lipped flowers with a very small upper lip.

germane (dʒɜː'meɪn) adj. (postpositive; usually foll. by to) related (to the topic being considered); akin; relevant. —**ger'manely** adv. —**ger'maneness** n.

Germanic (dʒɜː'mænɪk) n. **1.** a branch of the Indo-European family of languages that includes English, Dutch, German, the Scandinavian languages, and Gothic. Abbrev.: **Gmc**. **2.** Also called: **Proto-Germanic**. the unrecorded language from which all of these languages developed. ~adj. **3.** of, denoting, or relating to this group of languages. **4.** of, relating to, or characteristic of Germany, the German language, or any people that speaks a Germanic language.

germanium (dʒɜː'meɪnɪəm) n. a brittle crystalline grey element that is a semiconducting metalloid: used in transistors, and to strengthen alloys. Symbol: Ge; atomic no.: 32; atomic wt.: 72.59.

German measles n. a nontechnical name for **rubella**.

German silver n. another name for **nickel silver**.

germ cell n. a sexual reproductive cell.

germicide ('dʒɜːmɪ,saɪd) n. any substance that kills germs. —**germi'cidal** adj.

germinal ('dʒɜːmɪnəl) adj. **1.** of, relating to, or like germs or a germ cell. **2.** of, or in the earliest stage of development. —**'germinally** adv.

germinate ('dʒɜːmɪ,neɪt) vb. **1.** to cause (seeds or spores) to sprout or (of seeds or spores) to sprout. **2.** to grow or cause to grow; develop. **3.** to come or bring into existence; originate: the idea germinated with me. —**'germinative** adj. —,**germi'nation** n. —**'germi,nator** n.

germ warfare n. the use of bacteria against an enemy.

gerontology (,dʒɛrɒn'tɒlədʒɪ) n. the scientific study of ageing and the problems associated with elderly people. —**gerontological** (,dʒɛrɒntə'lɒdʒɪkəl) adj. —,**geron'tologist** n.

-gerous adj. combining form. bearing or producing: armigerous.

THESAURUS

germ 1. bacterium, bug (Inf.), microbe, microorganism, virus **2.** beginning, bud, cause, embryo, origin, root, rudiment, seed, source, spark **3.** bud, egg, embryo, nucleus, ovule, ovum, seed, spore, sprout

germane akin, allied, apposite, appropriate, apropos, apt, cognate, connected, fitting, kindred, material, pertinent, proper, related, relevant, suitable, to the point or purpose

germinate bud, develop, generate, grow, originate, pullulate, shoot, sprout, swell, vegetate

gerrymander ('dʒɛrɪˌmændə) vb. **1.** to divide the constituencies of (a voting area) so as to give one party an unfair advantage. **2.** to manipulate or adapt to one's advantage. ~n. **3.** an act or result of gerrymandering.

gerund ('dʒɛrənd) n. a noun formed from a verb, ending in -ing, denoting an action or state: the living is easy. —**gerundial** (dʒɪ'rʌndɪəl) adj.

gerundive (dʒɪ'rʌndɪv) n. **1.** (in Latin grammar) an adjective formed from a verb, expressing the desirability, etc., of the activity denoted by the verb. ~adj. **2.** of or relating to the gerund or gerundive. —**gerundival** (ˌdʒɛrən'daɪvəl) adj.

gesso ('dʒɛsəʊ) n. **1.** a white ground of plaster and size, used to prepare panels or canvas for painting or gilding. **2.** any white substance, esp. plaster of Paris, that forms a ground when mixed with water.

Gestapo (gɛ'stɑːpəʊ) n. the secret state police in Nazi Germany.

gestate ('dʒɛsteɪt) vb. to carry (developing young) in the uterus during pregnancy. —**ges'tation** n.

gesticulate (dʒɛ'stɪkjʊˌleɪt) vb. to express by or make gestures. —**ges,ticu'lation** n. —**ges'ticulative** adj. —**ges'ticu,lator** n.

gesture ('dʒɛstʃə) n. **1.** a motion of the hands, head, or body to express or emphasize an idea or emotion. **2.** something said or done as a formality or as an indication of intention. ~vb. **3.** to express by or make gestures; gesticulate. —**'gestural** adj. —**'gesturer** n.

get (gɛt) vb. **getting, got.** (mainly tr.) **1.** to come into possession of; receive or earn. **2.** to bring or fetch. **3.** to contract or be affected by: he got a chill. **4.** to capture or seize: the police got him. **5.** (also intr.) to become or cause to become or act as specified: to get one's hair cut; get wet. **6.** (intr.; foll. by a preposition or adverbial particle) to succeed in going, coming, leaving, etc.: get off the bus. **7.** (takes an infinitive) to manage or contrive: how did you get to be captain? **8.** to make ready or prepare: to get a meal. **9.** to hear, notice, or understand: I didn't get your meaning. **10.** to learn or master by study. **11.** (intr.; often foll. by to) to come (to) or arrive (at): we got home safely; to get to London. **12.** to catch or enter: to get a train. **13.** to induce or persuade: get him to leave. **14.** to reach by calculation: add 2 and 2 and you will get 4. **15.** to receive (a broadcast signal). **16.** to communicate with (a person or place), as by telephone. **17.** (also intr.; foll. by to) Inf. to have an emotional effect (on): that music really gets me. **18.** Inf. to annoy or irritate: her voice gets me. **19.** Inf. to bring a person into a difficult position from which he cannot escape. **20.** Inf. to hit: the blow got him in the back. **21.** Inf. to be revenged on, esp. by killing. **22.** Inf. to have the better of: your extravagant habits will get you in the end. **23.** (intr.; foll. by present participle) Inf. to begin: get moving. **24.** (used as a command) Inf. go! leave now! **25.** Arch. to beget or conceive. **26. get even with.** Inf. to settle an account with; pay back. **27. get with child.** Arch. to make pregnant. ~n. **28.** Rare. the act of begetting.

29. Rare. something begotten; offspring. **30.** Brit. sl. a variant of **git**. ~See also **get about, get across,** etc. —**'getable** or **'gettable** adj. —**'getter** n.

get about or **around** vb. (intr., adv.) **1.** to move around, as when recovering from an illness. **2.** to be socially active. **3.** (of news, rumour, etc.) to become known; spread.

get across vb. **1.** to cross or cause to cross. **2.** (adv.) to be or cause to be understood.

get at vb. (intr., prep.) **1.** to gain access to. **2.** to mean or intend: what are you getting at? **3.** to irritate or annoy persistently; criticize: she is always getting at him. **4.** to influence or seek to influence, esp. illegally by bribery, intimidation, etc.: someone had got at the witness before the trial.

get away vb. (adv., mainly intr.) **1.** to make an escape; leave. **2.** to make a start. **3. get away with. a.** to steal and escape (with money, goods, etc.). **b.** to do (something wrong, illegal, etc.) without being discovered or punished. ~interj. **4.** an exclamation indicating mild disbelief. ~n. **getaway. 5.** the act of escaping, esp. by criminals. **6.** a start or acceleration. **7.** (modifier) used for escaping: a getaway car.

get back vb. (adv.) **1.** (tr.) to recover or retrieve. **2.** (intr.; often foll. by to) to return, esp. to a former position or activity. **3.** (intr.; foll. by at) to retaliate (against); wreak vengeance (on). **4. get one's own back.** Inf. to obtain one's revenge.

get by vb. **1.** to pass; go past or overtake. **2.** (intr., adv.) Inf. to manage, esp. in spite of difficulties. **3.** (intr.) to be accepted or permitted: that book will never get by the authorities.

get in vb. (mainly adv.) **1.** (intr.) to enter a car, train, etc. **2.** (intr.) to arrive, esp. at one's home or place of work. **3.** (tr.) to bring in or inside: get the milk in. **4.** (tr.) to insert or slip in: he got his suggestion in before anyone else. **5.** (tr.) to gather or collect (crops, debts, etc.). **6.** to be elected or cause to be elected. **7.** (intr.) to obtain a place at university, college, etc. **8.** (foll. by on) to join or cause to join (an activity or organization).

get off vb. **1.** (intr., adv.) to escape the consequences of an action: he got off very lightly. **2.** (adv.) to be or cause to be acquitted: a good lawyer got him off. **3.** (adv.) to depart or cause to depart: to get the children off to school. **4.** (intr.) to descend (from a bus, train, etc.); dismount: she got off at the terminus. **5.** to move or cause to move to a distance (from): get off the field. **6.** (tr.) to remove; take off: get your coat off. **7.** (adv.) to go or send to sleep. **8.** (adv.) to send (letters) or (of letters) to be sent. **9. get off with.** Brit. inf. to establish a sexual relationship (with).

get on vb. (mainly adv.) **1.** Also (when prep.): onto. to board or cause or help to board (a bus, train, etc.). **2.** (tr.) to dress in (clothes as specified). **3.** (intr.) to grow late or (of time) to elapse: it's getting on and I must go. **4.** (intr.) (of a person) to grow old. **5.** (intr.; foll. by for) to approach (a time, age, amount, etc.): she

---

THESAURUS

gestation development, evolution, incubation, maturation, pregnancy, ripening

gesticulate gesture, indicate, make a sign, motion, sign, signal, wave

gesture 1. n. action, gesticulation, indication, motion, sign, signal **2.** v. gesticulate, indicate, motion, sign, signal, wave

get 1. achieve, acquire, attain, bag, bring, come by, come into possession of, earn, fall heir to, fetch, gain, glean, inherit, make, net, obtain, pick up, procure, realize, reap, receive, secure, succeed to, win **2.** be afflicted with, become infected with, be smitten by, catch, come down with, contract, fall victim to, take **3.** arrest, capture, collar (Inf.), grab, lay hold of, seize, take, trap **4.** become, come to be, grow, turn, wax **5.** catch, comprehend, fathom, follow, hear, notice, perceive, see, take in, understand, work out **6.** arrive, come, make it (Inf.), reach **7.** arrange, contrive, fix, manage, succeed, wangle (Inf.) **8.** coax, convince, induce, influence, persuade, prevail upon, sway, talk into, wheedle, win over **9.** communicate with, contact, get in touch with, reach **10.** Inf. affect, arouse, excite, have an effect on, impress, move, stimu-

late, stir, touch **11.** Inf. annoy, bother, bug (Inf.), get (someone's) goat (Sl.), irk, irritate, pique, rub (someone) up the wrong way, upset, vex **12.** baffle, confound, mystify, nonplus, perplex, puzzle, stump

get across 1. cross, ford, negotiate, pass over, traverse **2.** bring home to, communicate, convey, get (something) through to, impart, make clear or understood, put over, transmit

get ahead 1. advance, be successful, do well, flourish, get on, make good, progress, prosper, succeed, thrive **2.** excel, leave behind, outdo, outmanoeuvre, overtake, surpass

get along 1. agree, be compatible, be friendly, get on, harmonize, hit it off (Inf.) **2.** cope, develop, fare, get by (Inf.), make out (Inf.), manage, progress, shift **3.** be off, depart, go, go away, leave, move off

get at 1. acquire, attain, come to grips with, gain access to, get, get hold of, reach **2.** hint, imply, intend, lead up to, mean, suggest **3.** annoy, attack, blame, carp, criticize, find fault with, irritate, nag, pick on, taunt **4.** bribe, buy off, corrupt, influence, suborn,

tamper with

getaway break, break-out, decampment, escape, flight

get away break free, break out, decamp, depart, disappear, escape, flee, leave, make good one's escape

get back 1. recoup, recover, regain, repossess, retrieve **2.** arrive home, come back or home, return, revert, revisit **3.** With at be avenged, get even with, give tit for tat, retaliate, settle the score with, take vengeance on

get by 1. circumvent, get ahead of, go around, go past, overtake, pass, round **2.** Inf. contrive, cope, exist, fare, get along, make both ends meet, manage, subsist, survive

get down 1. alight, bring down, climb down, descend, disembark, dismount, get off, lower, step down **2.** bring down, depress, dishearten, dispirit

get in alight, appear, arrive, collect, come, embark, enter, include, infiltrate, insert, interpose, land, mount, penetrate

get off 1. alight, depart, descend, disembark, dismount, escape, exit, leave **2.** detach, remove, shed, take off

is getting on for seventy. **6.** (*intr.*) to make progress, manage, or fare: *how did you get on in your exam?* **7.** (*intr.; often foll. by with*) to establish a friendly relationship: *he gets on well with other people.* **8.** (*intr.; foll. by with*) to continue to do: *get on with your homework!*

get out *vb.* (*adv.*) **1.** to leave or escape or cause to leave or escape: used in the imperative when dismissing a person. **2.** to make or become known; publish or be published. **3.** (*tr.*) to express with difficulty. **4.** (*tr.; often foll. by of*) to extract (information or money) (from a person): *to get a confession out of a criminal.* **5.** (*tr.*) to gain or receive something, esp. something of significance or value. **6.** (foll. by *of*) to avoid or cause to avoid: *she always gets out of swimming.* **7.** *Cricket.* to dismiss or be dismissed.

get over *vb.* **1.** to cross or surmount (something). **2.** (*intr., prep.*) to recover from (an illness, shock, etc.). **3.** (*intr., prep.*) to overcome or master (a problem). **4.** (*intr., prep.*) to appreciate fully: *I just can't get over seeing you again.* **5.** (*tr., adv.*) to communicate effectively. **6.** (*tr., adv.*; sometimes foll. by *with*) to bring (something necessary but unpleasant) to an end: *let's get this job over with quickly.*

get round *or* **around** *vb.* (*intr.*) **1.** (*prep.*) to circumvent or overcome. **2.** (*prep.*) *Inf.* to have one's way with; cajole: *that girl can get round anyone.* **3.** (*prep.*) to evade (a law or rules). **4.** (*adv.; foll. by to*) to reach or come to at length: *I'll get round to that job in an hour.*

get through *vb.* **1.** to succeed or cause or help to succeed in an examination, test, etc. **2.** to bring or come to a destination, esp. after overcoming problems: *we got through the blizzards to the survivors.* **3.** (*adv.*) to contact or cause to contact, as by telephone. **4.** (*intr., prep.*) to use, spend, or consume (money, supplies, etc.). **5.** to complete or cause to complete (a task, process, etc.): *to get a bill through Parliament.* **6.** (*adv.; foll. by to*) to reach the awareness and understanding (of a person): *I just can't get the message through to him.*

get-together *Inf.* ~*n.* **1.** a small informal meeting or social gathering. ~*vb.* **get together.** (*adv.*) **2.** (*tr.*) to gather or collect. **3.** (*intr.*) (of people) to meet socially. **4.** (*intr.*) to discuss, esp. in order to reach an agreement.

get up *vb.* (*mainly adv.*) **1.** to wake and rise from one's bed or cause to wake and rise from bed. **2.** (*intr.*) to rise to one's feet; stand up. **3.** (*also prep.*) to ascend or cause to ascend. **4.** to increase or cause to increase in strength: *the wind got up at noon.* **5.** (*tr.*) *Inf.* to dress (oneself) in a particular way, esp. elaborately. **6.** (*tr.*) *Inf.* to devise or create: *to get up an entertainment for Christmas.* **7.** (*tr.*) *Inf.* to study or improve one's knowledge of: *I must get up my history.* **8.** (*intr.; foll. by to*) *Inf.* to be involved in: *he's always getting up to mischief.* ~*n.* **get-up. 9.** *Inf.* a costume or outfit. **10.** *Inf.* the arrangement or production of a book, etc.

get-up-and-go *n. Inf.* energy, drive, or ambition.

geum ('dʒi:əm) *n.* any herbaceous plant of the rose type, having compound leaves and red, orange, yellow, or white flowers.

geyser ('gi:zə; *U.S.* 'gaɪzər) *n.* **1.** a spring that discharges steam and hot water. **2.** *Brit.* a domestic gas water heater.

ghastly ('gɑːstlɪ) *adj.* **-lier, -liest. 1.** *Inf.* very bad or unpleasant. **2.** deathly pale; wan. **3.** *Inf.* extremely unwell; ill. **4.** terrifying; horrible. ~*adv.* **5.** unhealthily; sickly: *ghastly pale.* —'**ghastliness** *n.*

ghat (gɔːt) *n.* (in India) **1.** stairs or a passage leading down to a river. **2.** a place for bathing on the bank of a river. **3.** a mountain pass.

ghee (gi:) *n.* a clarified butter used in Indian cookery.

gherkin ('gɜːkɪn) *n.* **1.** the small immature fruit of any of various cucumbers, used for pickling. **2. a.** a tropical American climbing plant. **b.** its small spiny edible fruit.

ghetto ('gɛtəʊ) *n., pl.* **-tos** *or* **-toes. 1.** a densely populated slum area of a city inhabited by a socially and economically deprived minority. **2.** an area in a European city in which Jews were formerly required to live.

ghost (gəʊst) *n.* **1.** the disembodied spirit of a dead person, supposed to haunt the living as a pale or shadowy vision; phantom. Related adj.: **spectral. 2.** a haunting memory: *the ghost of his former life rose up before him.* **3.** a faint trace or possibility of something; glimmer: *a ghost of a smile.* **4.** the spirit; soul (archaic, except in **the Holy Ghost**). **5.** *Physics.* **a.** a faint secondary image produced by an optical system. **b.** a similar image on a television screen. **6. give up the ghost.** to die. ~*vb.* **7.** (*tr.*). to haunt. —'**ghost, like** *adj.* —'**ghostly** *adj.*

ghost town *n.* a deserted town, esp. one in the western U.S. that was formerly a boom town.

ghost word *n.* a word that has entered the language through the perpetuation, in dictionaries, etc., of an error.

ghoul (gu:l) *n.* **1.** a malevolent spirit or ghost. **2.** a person interested in morbid or disgusting things. **3.** a person who robs graves. **4.** (in Muslim legend) an evil demon thought to eat corpses. —'**ghoulish** *adj.* —'**ghoulishly** *adv.* —'**ghoulishness** *n.*

G.H.Q. *Mil. abbrev. for* General Headquarters.

ghyll (gɪl) *n.* a variant spelling of **gill²**.

gi *abbrev. for* gill (unit of measure).

GI *n. U.S. inf.* **1.** (*pl.* **GIs** *or* **GI's**). a soldier in the U.S. Army, esp. an enlisted man. ~*adj.* **2.** conforming to U.S. Army regulations.

G.I. *or* **g.i.** *abbrev. for* gastrointestinal.

giant ('dʒaɪənt) *n.* **1.** Also (fem.): **giantess** ('dʒaɪəntɪs). a mythical figure of superhuman size and strength, esp. in folklore or fairy tales. **2.** a person or thing of exceptional size, reputation, etc. ~*adj.* **3.** remarkably or supernaturally large.

giant panda *n.* See **panda.**

giaour ('dʒaʊə) *n.* a derogatory term for a non-Muslim, esp. a Christian.

Gib (dʒɪb) *n.* an informal name for Gibraltar.

gibber¹ ('dʒɪbə) *vb.* **1.** to utter rapidly and unintelligibly; prattle. **2.** (*intr.*) (of monkeys and related animals) to make characteristic chattering sounds.

gibber² ('dʒɪbə) *n. Austral.* **1.** a stone or boulder. **2.** (*modifier*) of or relating to a dry flat area of land covered with wind-polished stones: *gibber plains.*

gibberish ('dʒɪbərɪʃ) *n.* **1.** rapid chatter. **2.** incomprehensible talk; nonsense.

gibbet ('dʒɪbɪt) *n.* **1. a.** a wooden structure resembling a gallows, from which the bodies of executed criminals were formerly hung to public view. **b.** a gallows. ~*vb.* (*tr.*) **2.** to put to death by hanging on a gibbet. **3.** to hang (a corpse) on a gibbet. **4.** to expose to public ridicule.

gibbon ('gɪbən) *n.* a small agile arboreal anthropoid ape inhabiting forests in S Asia.

gibbous ('gɪbəs) *or* **gibbose** ('gɪbəʊs) *adj.* **1.** (of the

---

THESAURUS

get on 1. ascend, board, climb, embark, mount **2.** advance, cope, fare, get along, make out (*Inf.*), manage, progress, prosper, succeed **3.** agree, be compatible, be friendly, concur, get along, harmonize, hit it off (*Inf.*)

get out 1. alight, break out, clear out (*Inf.*), decamp, escape, evacuate, extricate oneself, free oneself, leave, vacate, withdraw

get out of avoid, dodge, escape, evade, shirk

get over 1. cross, ford, get across, pass, pass over, surmount, traverse **2.** come round, get better, mend, pull through, recover from, revive, survive **3.** defeat, get the better of, master, overcome, shake off **4.** communicate, convey, get *or* put across, impart, make clear *or* understood

get round 1. bypass, circumvent, edge,

evade, outmanoeuvre, skirt **2.** *Inf.* cajole, coax, convert, persuade, prevail upon, talk round, wheedle, win over

get together accumulate, assemble, collect, congregate, convene, converge, gather, join, meet, muster, rally, unite

get up arise, ascend, climb, increase, mount, rise, scale, stand

ghastly ashen, cadaverous, deathlike, deathly pale, dreadful, frightful, grim, grisly, gruesome, hideous, horrendous, horrible, horrid, livid, loathsome, pale, pallid, repellent, shocking, spectral, terrible, terrifying, wan

ghost 1. apparition, manes, phantasm, phantom, revenant, shade (*Literary*), soul, spectre, spirit, spook (*Inf.*), wraith **2.** glimmer, hint, possibility, semblance, shadow,

suggestion, trace

ghostly eerie, ghostlike, illusory, insubstantial, phantasmal, phantom, spectral, spooky (*Inf.*), supernatural, uncanny, unearthly, weird, wraithlike

giant 1. *n.* behemoth, colossus, Hercules, leviathan, monster, titan **2.** *adj.* Brobdingnagian, colossal, elephantine, enormous, gargantuan, gigantic, huge, immense, jumbo (*Inf.*), large, mammoth, monstrous, prodigious, titanic, vast

gibberish babble, balderdash, blather, double talk, drivel, gabble, gobbledegook (*Inf.*), jabber, jargon, mumbo jumbo, nonsense, prattle, twaddle, yammer (*Inf.*)

moon or a planet) more than half but less than fully illuminated. **2.** hunchbacked. **3.** bulging. —**'gibbously** *adv.* —**'gibbousness** *or* **gibbosity** (gɪ'bɒsɪtɪ) *n.*

gibe[1] *or* **jibe** (dʒaɪb) *vb.* **1.** to make jeering or scoffing remarks at; taunt. ~*n.* **2.** a derisive or provoking remark. —**'giber** *or* **'jiber** *n.*

gibe[2] (dʒaɪb) *vb., n. Naut.* a variant spelling of **gybe.**

giblets ('dʒɪblɪts) *pl. n.* (*sometimes sing.*) the gizzard, liver, heart, and neck of a fowl.

giddy ('gɪdɪ) *adj.* **-dier, -diest. 1.** affected with a reeling sensation and feeling as if about to fall; dizzy. **2.** causing or tending to cause vertigo. **3.** impulsive; scatter-brained. ~*vb.* **giddying, giddied. 4.** to make or become giddy. —**'giddily** *adv.* —**'giddiness** *n.*

gie (giː) *vb.* a Scot. word for **give.**

gift (gɪft) *n.* **1.** something given; a present. **2.** a special aptitude, ability, or power; talent. **3.** the power or right to give or bestow (esp. in **in the gift of,** in (someone's) **gift**). **4.** the act or process of giving. **5. look a gift-horse in the mouth.** (*usually negative*) to find fault with a free gift or chance benefit. ~*vb.* (*tr.*) **6.** to present (something) as a gift to (a person).

gifted ('gɪftɪd) *adj.* having or showing natural talent or aptitude: *a gifted musician.* —**'giftedly** *adv.* —**'giftedness** *n.*

giftwrap ('gɪft,ræp) *vb.* **-wrapping, -wrapped.** to wrap (a gift) attractively.

gig[1] (gɪg) *n.* **1.** a light two-wheeled one-horse carriage without a hood. **2.** *Naut.* a light tender for a vessel. **3.** a long light rowing boat, used esp. for racing. ~*vb.* **gigging, gigged. 4.** (*intr.*) to travel in a gig.

gig[2] (gɪg) *n. Inf.* **1.** a job, esp. a single booking for jazz or pop musicians. **2.** the performance itself. ~*vb.* **gigging, gigged. 3.** (*intr.*) to perform a gig.

giga- ('gɪgə, 'gaɪgə) *prefix.* denoting 10⁹: *gigavolt.* Symbol: G

gigantic (dʒaɪ'gæntɪk) *adj.* **1.** very large; enormous. **2.** Also: **gigantesque** (,dʒaɪgæn'tɛsk). of or suitable for giants. —**gi'gantically** *adv.*

giggle ('gɪgəl) *vb.* **1.** (*intr.*) to laugh nervously or foolishly. ~*n.* **2.** such a laugh. —**'giggler** *n.* —**'gigglingly** *adv.* —**'giggly** *adj.*

gigolo ('ʒɪgə,ləʊ) *n., pl.* **-los. 1.** a man who is kept by a woman, esp. an older woman. **2.** a man who is paid to dance with or escort women.

gigot ('dʒɪgət) *n.* **1.** a leg of lamb or mutton. **2.** a leg-of-mutton sleeve.

gild[1] (gɪld) *vb.* **gilding, gilded** *or* **gilt.** (*tr.*) **1.** to cover with or as if with gold. **2. gild the lily. a.** to adorn unnecessarily something already beautiful. **b.** to praise someone inordinately. **3.** to give a falsely attractive or valuable appearance to. —**'gilder** *n.*

gild[2] (gɪld) *n.* a variant spelling of **guild.**

gill[1] (gɪl) *n.* **1.** the respiratory organ in many aquatic animals. **2.** any of the radiating leaflike spore-producing structures on the undersurface of the cap of a mushroom. —**gilled** *adj.*

gill[2] (dʒɪl) *n.* a unit of liquid measure equal to one quarter of a pint.

gill[3] *or* **ghyll** (gɪl) *n. Brit. dialect.* **1.** a narrow stream; rivulet. **2.** a wooded ravine.

gillie, ghillie, *or* **gilly** ('gɪlɪ) *n., pl.* **-lies.** *Scot.* **1.** an attendant or guide for hunting or fishing. **2.** (formerly) a Highland chieftain's male attendant.

gills (gɪlz) *pl. n.* **1.** (*sometimes sing.*) the wattle of birds such as domestic fowl. **2.** the cheeks and jowls of a person. **3. green about the gills.** *Inf.* looking or feeling nauseated.

gilt[1] (gɪlt) *vb.* **1.** a past tense or past participle of **gild**[1]. ~*n.* **2.** gold or a substance simulating it, applied in gilding. **3.** superficial or false appearance of excellence. **4.** a gilt-edged security. ~*adj.* **5.** covered with or as if with gold or gilt; gilded.

gilt[2] (gɪlt) *n.* a young female pig, esp. one that has not had a litter.

gilt-edged *adj.* **1.** (of securities) dated over a short, medium, or long term, and characterized by minimum risk and usually issued by the Government. **2.** (of books, papers, etc.) having gilded edges.

gimbals ('dʒɪmbəlz, 'gɪm-) *pl. n.* a device, consisting of two or three pivoted rings at right angles to each other, that provides free suspension in all planes for a compass, chronometer, etc. Also called: **gimbal ring.**

gimcrack ('dʒɪm,kræk) *adj.* **1.** cheap; shoddy. ~*n.* **2.** a cheap showy trifle or gadget. —**'gim,crackery** *n.*

gimlet ('gɪmlɪt) *n.* **1.** a small hand tool consisting of a pointed spiral tip attached at right angles to a handle, used for boring small holes in wood. **2.** *U.S.* a cocktail consisting of half gin or vodka and half lime juice. ~*vb.* **3.** (*tr.*) to make holes in (wood) using a gimlet. ~*adj.* **4.** penetrating; piercing (esp. in **gimlet-eyed**).

gimmick ('gɪmɪk) *Inf.* ~*n.* **1.** something designed to attract extra attention, interest, or publicity. **2.** any clever device, gadget, or stratagem, esp. one used to deceive. —**'gimmickry** *n.* —**'gimmicky** *adj.*

gimp *or* **guimpe** (gɪmp) *n.* a tapelike trimming

gin[1] (dʒɪn) *n.* an alcoholic drink obtained by distillation of the grain of malted barley, rye, or maize, flavoured with juniper berries.

gin[2] (dʒɪn) *n.* **1.** a primitive engine in which a vertical shaft is turned by horses driving a horizontal beam in a circle. **2.** Also called: **cotton gin.** a machine of this type used for separating seeds from raw cotton. **3.** a trap for catching small mammals, consisting of a noose of thin strong wire. ~*vb.* **ginning, ginned.** (*tr.*) **4.** to free (cotton) of seeds with a gin. **5.** to trap or snare (game) with a gin. —**'ginner** *n.*

gin[3] (gɪn) *vb.* **ginning, gan, gun.** an archaic word for **begin.**

gin[4] (dʒɪn) *n. Austral. derog. sl.* an Aboriginal woman.

ginger ('dʒɪndʒə) *n.* **1.** any of several plants of the East Indies, cultivated throughout the tropics for their spicy hot-tasting underground stems. **2.** the underground stem of this plant, which is powdered and used as a seasoning or sugared and eaten as a sweetmeat. **3. a.** a reddish-brown or yellowish-brown colour. **b.** (*as adj.*): *ginger hair.* **4.** *Inf.* liveliness; vigour. —**'gingery** *adj.*

ginger ale *n.* a sweetened effervescent nonalcoholic drink flavoured with ginger extract.

ginger beer *n.* a slightly alcoholic drink made by fermenting a mixture of syrup and root ginger.

gingerbread ('dʒɪndʒə,brɛd) *n.* **1.** a moist brown cake, flavoured with ginger and treacle. **2. a.** a biscuit, similarly flavoured, cut into various shapes. **b.** (*as modifier*): *gingerbread man.* **3.** an elaborate but unsubstantial ornamentation.

ginger group *n. Chiefly Brit.* a group within a party, association, etc., that enlivens or radicalizes its parent body.

gingerly ('dʒɪndʒəlɪ) *adv.* **1.** in a cautious, reluctant, or timid manner. ~*adj.* **2.** cautious, reluctant, or timid.

ginger snap *or* **nut** *n.* a crisp biscuit flavoured with ginger.

gingham ('gɪŋəm) *n.* a cotton fabric, usually woven of

THESAURUS

gibe, jibe 1. *v.* deride, flout, jeer, make fun of, mock, poke fun at, ridicule, scoff, scorn, sneer, taunt, twit **2.** *n.* crack (*Sl.*), cutting remark, derision, dig, jeer, mockery, ridicule, sarcasm, scoffing, sneer, taunt

giddiness dizziness, faintness, light-headedness, vertigo

giddy 1. dizzy, dizzying, faint, light-headed, reeling, unsteady, vertiginous **2.** capricious, careless, changeable, changeful, erratic, fickle, flighty, frivolous, heedless, impulsive, inconstant, irresolute, irresponsible, reckless, scatterbrained, silly, thoughtless, unbalanced, unstable, unsteady, vacillating, volatile, wild

gift 1. benefaction, bequest, bonus, boon, bounty, contribution, donation, grant, gratuity, largess, legacy, offering, present **2.** ability, aptitude, attribute, bent, capability, capacity, endowment, faculty, flair, genius, knack, power, talent, turn

gifted able, accomplished, adroit, brilliant, capable, clever, expert, ingenious, intelligent, masterly, skilled, talented

gigantic Brobdingnagian, colossal, Cyclopean, elephantine, enormous, gargantuan, giant, herculean, huge, immense, mammoth, monstrous, prodigious, stupendous, titanic, tremendous, vast

giggle *v./n.* cackle, chortle, chuckle,

laugh, snigger, te-hee, titter, twitter

gild adorn, beautify, bedeck, brighten, coat, deck, dress up, embellish, embroider, enhance, enrich, garnish, grace, ornament

gimmick contrivance, device, dodge, gadget, gambit, gizmo (*Sl., chiefly U.S.*), ploy, scheme, stratagem, stunt, trick

gingerly 1. *adv.* carefully, cautiously, charily, circumspectly, daintily, delicately, fastidiously, hesitantly, reluctantly, squeamishly, suspiciously, timidly, warily **2.** *adj.* careful, cautious, chary, circumspect, dainty, delicate, fastidious, hesitant, reluctant, squeamish, suspicious, timid, wary

two coloured yarns in a checked or striped design.

gingivitis (ˌdʒɪndʒɪˈvaɪtɪs) n. inflammation of the gums.

ginkgo (ˈɡɪŋkɡəʊ) or **gingko** (ˈɡɪŋkəʊ) n., pl. **-goes** or **-koes.** a widely planted ornamental Chinese tree with fan-shaped deciduous leaves and fleshy yellow fruit. Also called: **maidenhair tree.**

gin palace (dʒɪn) n. (formerly) a gaudy drinking-house.

gin rummy (dʒɪn) n. a version of rummy in which a player may go out if the odd cards outside his sequences total less than ten points.

ginseng (ˈdʒɪnsɛŋ) n. 1. either of two plants of China or of North America, whose forked aromatic roots are used medicinally in China. 2. the root of either of these plants or a substance obtained from the roots.

gip (dʒɪp) vb. **gipping, gipped.** 1. a variant spelling of **gyp**¹. ~n. 2. a variant spelling of **gyp**².

Gipsy (ˈdʒɪpsɪ) n., pl. **-sies.** (sometimes not cap.) a variant spelling of **Gypsy.**

giraffe (dʒɪˈrɑːf, -ˈræf) n., pl. **-raffes** or **-raffe.** a large ruminant mammal inhabiting savannahs of tropical Africa: the tallest mammal, with very long legs and neck.

gird¹ (ɡɜːd) vb. **girding, girded** or **girt.** (tr.) 1. to put a belt, girdle, etc., around (the waist or hips). 2. to bind or secure with or as if with a belt: to gird on one's armour. 3. to surround; encircle. 4. to prepare (oneself) for action (esp. in **gird (up) one's loins**).

gird² (ɡɜːd) N Brit. dialect. ~vb. 1. (when intr., foll. by at) to jeer (at someone); mock. ~n. 2. a taunt; gibe.

girder (ˈɡɜːdə) n. a large beam, esp. one made of steel, used in the construction of bridges, buildings, etc.

girdle¹ (ˈɡɜːdəl) n. 1. a woman's elastic corset covering the waist to the thigh. 2. anything that surrounds or encircles. 3. a belt or sash. 4. Jewellery. the outer edge of a gem. 5. Anat. any encircling structure or part. 6. the mark left on a tree trunk after the removal of a ring of bark. ~vb. (tr.) 7. to put a girdle on or around. 8. to surround or encircle. 9. to remove a ring of bark from (a tree). —ˈgirdle-ˌlike adj.

girdle² (ˈɡɜːdəl) n. a less common word for **griddle.**

girl (ɡɜːl) n. 1. a female child from birth to young womanhood. 2. a young unmarried woman; lass; maid. 3. Inf. a sweetheart or girlfriend. 4. Inf. a woman of any age. 5. a female employee, esp. a female servant. 6. S. African derog. a Black female servant. —ˈgirlˌhood n. —ˈgirlish adj.

girlfriend (ˈɡɜːlˌfrɛnd) n. 1. a female friend with whom a man or boy is romantically or sexually involved. 2. any female friend.

Girl Guide n. See **Guide.**

girlie (ˈɡɜːlɪ) n. (modifier) Inf. featuring nude or scantily dressed women: a girlie magazine.

giro (ˈdʒaɪrəʊ) n., pl. **-ros.** the settlement of debts or other payments by transfers between accounts or by giro cheque, operated by post offices or banks.

girt¹ (ɡɜːt) vb. the past tense or past participle of **gird**¹.

girt² (ɡɜːt) vb. 1. (tr.) to bind or encircle; gird. 2. to measure the girth of (something).

girth (ɡɜːθ) n. 1. the distance around something; circumference. 2. a band around a horse's belly to keep the saddle in position. ~vb. 3. (usually foll. by up) to fasten a girth on (a horse). 4. (tr.) to encircle or surround.

gist (dʒɪst) n. the point or substance of an argument, speech, etc.

git (ɡɪt) n. Brit. sl. 1. a contemptible person, often a fool. 2. a bastard.

give (ɡɪv) vb. **giving, gave, given.** (mainly tr.) 1. (also intr.) to present or deliver voluntarily (something that is one's own) to another. 2. (often foll. by for) to transfer (something that is one's own, esp. money) to the possession of another as part of an exchange: to give fifty pounds for a painting. 3. to place in the temporary possession of another: I gave him my watch while I went swimming. 4. (when intr., foll. by of) to grant, provide, or bestow: give me some advice. 5. to administer: to give a reprimand. 6. to award or attribute: to give blame, praise, etc. 7. to be a source of: he gives no trouble. 8. to impart or communicate: to give news. 9. to utter or emit: to give a shout. 10. to perform, make, or do: the car gave a jolt. 11. to sacrifice or devote: he gave his life for his country. 12. to surrender: to give place to others. 13. to concede or yield: I will give you this game. 14. Inf. to happen: what gives? 15. (often foll. by to) to cause; lead: she gave me to believe that she would come. 16. to perform or present as an entertainment: to give a play. 17. to act as a host of (a party, etc.). 18. (intr.) to yield or break under force or pressure: this surface will give if you sit on it. 19. **give as good as one gets.** to respond to verbal or bodily blows to at least an equal extent as those received. 20. **give or take.** plus or minus: three thousand people came, give or take a few hundred. ~n. 21. Inf. tendency to yield under pressure; resilience. ~See also **give away, give in,** etc. —ˈgivable or ˈgiveable adj. —ˈgiver n.

give-and-take n. 1. mutual concessions, shared benefits, and cooperation. 2. a smoothly flowing exchange of ideas and talk. ~vb. **give and take.** 3. to make mutual concessions.

give away vb. (tr., adv.) 1. to donate or bestow as a gift, prize, etc. 2. to sell very cheaply. 3. to reveal or betray. 4. to fail to use (an opportunity) through folly or neglect. 5. to present (a bride) formally to her husband in a marriage ceremony. ~n. **giveaway.** 6. a betrayal or disclosure esp. when unintentional. 7. (modifier) very cheap (esp. in **giveaway prices**).

give in vb. (adv.) 1. (intr.) to yield; admit defeat. 2. (tr.) to submit or deliver (a document).

given (ˈɡɪvən) vb. 1. the past participle of **give.** ~adj. 2. (postpositive; foll. by to) tending (to); inclined or addicted (to). 3. specific or previously stated. 4. assumed as a premiss. 5. Maths. known or determined independently: a given volume. 6. (on official documents) issued or executed, as on a stated date.

give off vb. (tr., adv.) to emit or discharge: the mothballs gave off an acrid odour.

give out vb. (adv.) 1. (tr.) to emit or discharge. 2. (tr.) to publish or make known: the chairman gave out that he would resign. 3. (tr.) to hand out or distribute: they gave out free chewing gum. 4. (intr.) to become exhausted; fail: the supply of candles gave out.

give over vb. (adv.) 1. (tr.) to transfer, esp. to the care or custody of another. 2. (tr.) to assign or resign to a specific purpose or function: the day was given over to pleasure. 3. Inf. to cease (an activity): give over fighting, will you!

give up vb. (adv.) 1. to abandon hope (for). 2. (tr.) to renounce (an activity, belief, etc.): I have given up smoking. 3. to relinquish or resign from: he gave up the presidency. 4. (tr.; usually reflexive) to surrender: the escaped convict gave himself up. 5. (intr.) to admit one's defeat or inability to do something. 6. (tr.; often passive or reflexive) to devote completely (to): she gave herself up to caring for the sick.

THESAURUS

gird 1. belt, bind, girdle 2. blockade, encircle, enclose, encompass, enfold, engird, environ, hem in, pen, ring, surround 3. brace, fortify, make ready, prepare, ready, steel

girdle 1. n. band, belt, cincture, cummerbund, fillet, sash, waistband 2. v. bind, bound, encircle, enclose, encompass, engird, environ, gird, hem, ring, surround

girl bird (Sl.), chick (Sl.), colleen (Irish), damsel (Archaic), daughter, female child, lass, lassie (Inf.), maid (Archaic), maiden (Archaic), miss, wench

girth bulk, circumference, measure, size

gist core, drift, essence, force, idea, import, marrow, meaning, nub, pith, point, quintessence, sense, significance, substance

give 1. accord, administer, allow, award, bestow, commit, confer, consign, contribute, deliver, donate, entrust, furnish, grant, hand over or out, make over, permit, present, provide, supply, vouchsafe 2. announce, be a source of, communicate, emit, impart, issue, notify, pronounce, publish, render, transmit, utter 3. demonstrate, display, evidence, indicate, manifest, offer, proffer, provide, set forth, show 4. allow, cede, concede, devote, grant, hand over, lend, relinquish, surrender, yield 5. cause, do, engender, lead, make, occasion, perform, produce 6. bend, break, collapse, fall, recede, retire, sink

give away betray, disclose, divulge, expose, inform on, leak, let out, let slip,

reveal, uncover

give in admit defeat, capitulate, collapse, comply, concede, quit, submit, surrender, yield

given addicted, apt, disposed, inclined, liable, likely, prone

give off discharge, emit, exhale, exude, produce, release, send out, smell of, throw out, vent

give out 1. discharge, emit, exhale, exude, produce, release, send out, smell of, throw out, vent 2. announce, broadcast, communicate, disseminate, impart, make known, notify, publish, transmit, utter

give up abandon, capitulate, cease, cede, cut out, desist, despair, forswear, hand over,

gizzard ('gizəd) *n.* **1.** the thick-walled part of a bird's stomach, in which hard food is broken up. **2.** *Inf.* the stomach and entrails generally.

glacé ('glæsɪ) *adj.* **1.** crystallized or candied: *glacé cherries.* **2.** covered in icing. **3.** (of leather, silk, etc.) having a glossy finish. ∼*vb.* **-céing, -céed. 4.** (*tr.*) to ice or candy (cakes, fruits, etc.).

glacial ('gleɪsɪəl, -ʃəl) *adj.* **1.** characterized by the presence of masses of ice. **2.** relating to, caused by, or deposited by a glacier. **3.** extremely cold; icy. **4.** cold or hostile in manner. **5.** (of a chemical compound) of or tending to form crystals that resemble ice. **6.** very slow in progress: *a glacial pace.* —**'glacially** *adv.*

glaciate ('gleɪsɪˌeɪt) *vb.* **1.** to cover or become covered with glaciers or masses of ice. **2.** (*tr.*) to subject to the effects of glaciers, such as denudation and erosion. —**glaci'ation** *n.*

glacier ('glæsɪə, 'gleɪs-) *n.* a slowly moving mass of ice originating from an accumulation of snow.

glad¹ (glæd) *adj.* **gladder, gladdest. 1.** happy and pleased; contented. **2.** causing happiness or contentment. **3.** (*postpositive;* foll. by *to*) very willing: *he was glad to help.* ∼*vb.* **4.** (*tr.*) an archaic word for **gladden.** —**'gladly** *adv.* —**'gladness** *n.*

glad² (glæd) *n. Inf.* short for **gladiolus.**

gladden ('glædən) *vb.* to make or become glad and joyful. —**'gladdener** *n.*

glade (gleɪd) *n.* an open place in a forest; clearing.

glad eye *n. Inf.* an inviting or seductive glance (esp. in **give (someone) the glad eye**).

gladiator ('glædɪˌeɪtə) *n.* **1.** (in ancient Rome) a man trained to fight in arenas to provide entertainment. **2.** a person who supports and fights publicly for a cause. —**gladiatorial** (ˌglædɪə'tɔːrɪəl) *adj.*

gladiolus (ˌglædɪ'əʊləs) *n., pl.* **-lus, -li** (-laɪ), *or* **-luses.** any plant of a widely cultivated genus having swordshaped leaves and spikes of funnel-shaped brightly coloured flowers. Also called: **gladiola.**

gladrags ('glædˌrægz) *pl. n. Sl.* best clothes or clothes used on special occasions.

gladsome ('glædsəm) *adj.* an archaic word for **glad¹.** —**'gladsomely** *adv.* —**'gladsomeness** *n.*

glair (glɛə) *n.* **1.** white of egg, esp. when used as a size, glaze, or adhesive. **2.** any substance resembling this. ∼*vb.* **3.** (*tr.*) to apply glair to (something). —**'glairy** *or* **'glaireous** *adj.*

glamour *or U.S.* (*sometimes*) **glamor** ('glæmə) *n.* **1.** charm and allure; fascination. **2. a.** a fascinating or voluptuous beauty. **b.** (*as modifier*): *a glamour girl.* **3.** *Arch.* a magic spell; charm. —**'glamorous** *adj.*

glance¹ (glɑːns) *vb.* **1.** (*intr.*) to look hastily or briefly. **2.** (*intr.;* foll. by *over, through,* etc.) to look over briefly: *to glance through a report.* **3.** (*intr.*) to reflect, glint, or gleam: *the sun glanced on the water.* **4.** (*intr.;* usually foll. by *off*) to depart (from an object struck) at an oblique angle: *the arrow glanced off the tree.* ∼*n.* **5.** a hasty or brief look; peep. **6.** a flash or glint of light; gleam. **7.** the act or an instance of an object glancing off another. **8.** a brief allusion or reference. —**'glancingly** *adv.*

glance² (glɑːns) *n.* any mineral having a metallic lustre.

gland¹ (glænd) *n.* **1.** a cell or organ in man and other animals that synthesizes chemical substances and secretes them for the body to use or eliminate, either through a duct (exocrine gland) or directly into the bloodstream (endocrine gland). **2.** a structure, such as a lymph node, that resembles a gland in form. **3.** a cell or organ in plants that synthesizes and secretes a particular substance.

gland² (glænd) *n.* a device that prevents leakage of fluid from a point at which a rotating shaft emerges. It often consists of a flanged metal sleeve bedding into a stuffing box.

glanders ('glændəz) *n.* a highly infectious bacterial disease of horses, sometimes communicated to man, characterized by inflammation and ulceration of the mucous membranes of the air passages, skin and lymph glands.

glandular ('glændjʊlə) *or* **glandulous** ('glændjʊləs) *adj.* of, relating to, containing, functioning as, or affecting a gland. —**'glandularly** *or* **'glandulously** *adv.*

glandular fever *n.* another name for **infectious mononucleosis.**

glare (glɛə) *vb.* **1.** (*intr.*) to stare angrily; glower. **2.** (*tr.*) to express by glowering. **3.** (*intr.*) (of light, colour, etc.) to be very bright and intense. **4.** (*intr.*) to be dazzlingly ornamented or garish. ∼*n.* **5.** an angry stare. **6.** a dazzling light or brilliance. **7.** garish ornamentation or appearance. —**'glary** *adj.*

glaring ('glɛərɪŋ) *adj.* **1.** conspicuous: *a glaring omission.* **2.** dazzling or garish. —**'glaringly** *adv.* —**'glaringness** *n.*

glass (glɑːs) *n.* **1. a.** a hard brittle transparent or translucent noncrystalline solid, consisting of metal silicates or similar compounds. They are made from a fused mixture of oxides, such as lime, silicon dioxide, phosphorus pentoxide, etc. **b.** (*as modifier*): *a glass bottle.* Related adj.: **vitreous. 2.** something made of glass, esp. a drinking vessel, a barometer, or a mirror. **3.** Also called: **glassful.** the amount or volume contained in a drinking glass: *he drank a glass of wine.* **4.** glassware collectively. **5.** See **fibreglass.** ∼*vb.* **6.** (*tr.*) to cover with, enclose in, or fit with glass. —**'glassless** *adj.* —**'glass,like** *adj.*

glass-blowing *n.* the process of shaping a mass of molten glass by blowing air into it through a tube. —**'glass-,blower** *n.*

glasses ('glɑːsɪz) *pl. n.* a pair of lenses for correcting faulty vision, in a frame that rests on the bridge of the nose and hooks behind the ears. Also called: **spectacles, eyeglasses.**

glasshouse ('glɑːsˌhaʊs) *n.* **1.** *Brit.* a glass building, esp. a greenhouse, used for growing plants in protected or controlled conditions. **2.** *Inf., chiefly Brit.* a military detention centre.

glass wool *n.* fine spun glass massed into a wool-like bulk, used in insulation, filtering, etc.

glassy ('glɑːsɪ) *adj.* **-ier, -iest. 1.** resembling glass, esp. in smoothness or transparency. **2.** void of expression, life, or warmth: *a glassy stare.* —**'glassily** *adv.* —**'glassiness** *n.*

Glaswegian (glæz'wiːdʒən) *adj.* **1.** of or relating to Glasgow, a city in Scotland, or its inhabitants. ∼*n.* **2.** a native or inhabitant of Glasgow.

glaucoma (glɔː'kəʊmə) *n.* a disease of the eye in which increased pressure within the eyeball causes impaired

---

THESAURUS

leave off, quit, relinquish, renounce, resign, stop, surrender, throw in the towel, waive

glad 1. blithesome (*Literary*), cheerful, chuffed (*Sl.*), contented, delighted, gay, gleeful, gratified, happy, jocund, jovial, joyful, overjoyed, pleased, willing **2.** animated, cheerful, cheering, cheery, delightful, felicitous, gratifying, joyous, merry, pleasant, pleasing

gladden cheer, delight, elate, enliven, exhilarate, gratify, hearten, please, rejoice

gladly cheerfully, freely, gaily, gleefully, happily, jovially, joyfully, joyously, merrily, readily, willingly, with (a) good grace, with pleasure

gladness animation, blitheness, cheerfulness, delight, felicity, gaiety, glee, happiness, high spirits, hilarity, jollity, joy, joyousness, mirth, pleasure

glamorous alluring, attractive, beautiful, bewitching, captivating, charming, dazzling, elegant, enchanting, entrancing, exciting, fascinating, glittering, glossy, lovely, prestigious, smart

glamour allure, appeal, attraction, beauty, bewitchment, charm, enchantment, fascination, magnetism, prestige, ravishment, witchery

glance v. **1.** gaze, glimpse, look, peek, peep, scan, view **2.** flash, gleam, glimmer, glint, glisten, glitter, reflect, shimmer, shine, twinkle **3.** bounce, brush, graze, rebound, ricochet, skim **4.** With **over, through,** *etc.* browse, dip into, flip through, leaf through, riffle through, run over *or* through, scan, skim through, thumb through ∼*n.* **5.** brief look, dekko (*Sl.*), gander (*Inf.*), glimpse, look, peek, peep, quick look, squint, view **6.** flash, gleam, glimmer, glint, reflection, sparkle, twinkle **7.** allusion, passing mention,

reference

glare v. **1.** frown, give a dirty look, glower, look daggers, lower, scowl, stare angrily **2.** blaze, dazzle, flame, flare ∼*n.* **3.** angry stare, black look, dirty look, frown, glower, lower, scowl **4.** blaze, brilliance, dazzle, flame, flare, glow **5.** flashiness, floridness, gaudiness, loudness, meretriciousness, showiness, tawdriness

glaring 1. audacious, blatant, conspicuous, egregious, flagrant, gross, manifest, obvious, open, outrageous, outstanding, overt, patent, rank, unconcealed, visible **2.** blazing, bright, dazzling, flashy, florid, garish, glowing, loud

glassy 1. clear, glossy, icy, shiny, slick, slippery, smooth, transparent **2.** blank, cold, dazed, dull, empty, expressionless, fixed, glazed, lifeless, vacant

vision, sometimes progressing to blindness. **—glau'co-matous** *adj.*

glaucous ('glɔːkəs) *adj.* **1.** *Bot.* covered with a waxy or powdery bloom. **2.** bluish-green.

glaze (gleɪz) *vb.* **1.** (*tr.*) to fit or cover with glass. **2.** (*tr.*) *Ceramics.* to cover with a vitreous solution, rendering impervious to liquid. **3.** (*tr.*) to cover (foods) with a shiny coating by applying beaten egg, sugar, etc. **4.** (*tr.*) to make glossy or shiny. **5.** (when *intr.*, often foll. by *over*) to become or cause to become glassy: *his eyes were glazing over.* ~*n.* **6.** *Ceramics.* **a.** a vitreous coating. **b.** the substance used to produce such a coating. **7.** a smooth lustrous finish on a fabric produced by applying various chemicals. **8.** something used to give a glossy surface to foods: *a syrup glaze.* **—'glazer** *n.*

glazier ('gleɪzɪə) *n.* a person who fits windows, etc., with glass. **—'glaziery** *n.*

G.L.C. *abbrev. for* Greater London Council.

gleam (gliːm) *n.* **1.** a small beam or glow of light, esp. reflected light. **2.** a brief or dim indication: *a gleam of hope.* ~*vb.* (*intr.*) **3.** to send forth or reflect a beam of light. **4.** to appear, esp. briefly. **—'gleamingly** *adv.* **—'gleamy** *adj.*

glean (gliːn) *vb.* **1.** to gather (something) slowly and carefully in small pieces: *to glean information.* **2.** to gather (the useful remnants of a crop) from the field after harvesting. **—'gleaner** *n.*

gleanings ('gliːnɪŋz) *pl. n.* the useful remnants of a crop that can be gathered from the field after harvesting.

glebe (gliːb) *n.* **1.** *Brit.* land granted to a clergyman as part of his benefice. **2.** *Poetic.* land, esp. for growing things.

glee (gliː) *n.* **1.** great merriment; joy. **2.** a type of song originating in 18th-century England, sung by three or more unaccompanied voices.

gleeful ('gliːful) *adj.* full of glee; merry. **—'gleefully** *adv.* **—'gleefulness** *n.*

gleeman ('gliːmən) *n., pl.* **-men.** *Obs.* a minstrel.

glen (glɛn) *n.* a narrow and deep mountain valley, esp. in Scotland or Ireland.

glengarry (glɛn'gærɪ) *n., pl.* **-ries.** a brimless Scottish cap with a crease down the crown, often with ribbons at the back. Also called: **glengarry bonnet.**

glib (glɪb) *adj.* **glibber, glibbest.** fluent and easy, often in an insincere or deceptive way. **—'glibly** *adv.* **—'glibness** *n.*

glide (glaɪd) *vb.* **1.** to move or cause to move easily without jerks or hesitations. **2.** (*intr.*) to pass slowly or without perceptible change: *to glide into sleep.* **3.** to cause (an aircraft) to come into land without engine power, or (of an aircraft) to land in this way. **4.** (*intr.*) to fly a glider. **5.** *Music.* to execute a portamento from one note to another. **6.** (*intr.*) *Phonetics.* to produce a glide. ~*n.* **7.** a smooth easy movement. **8. a.** any of various dances featuring gliding steps. **b.** a step in such a dance. **9.** a manoeuvre in which an aircraft makes a gentle descent without engine power. **10.** the act or process of gliding. **11.** *Music.* a portamento or slur. **12.** *Phonetics.* a transitional sound as the speech organs pass from the articulatory position of one speech sound to that of the next. **—'glidingly** *adv.*

glider ('glaɪdə) *n.* **1.** an aircraft capable of gliding and soaring in air currents without the use of an engine. **2.** a person or thing that glides.

glimmer ('glɪmə) *vb.* (*intr.*) **1.** (of a light) to glow faintly or flickeringly. **2.** to be indicated faintly: *hope glimmered in his face.* ~*n.* **3.** a glow or twinkle of light. **4.** a faint indication. **—'glimmeringly** *adv.*

glimpse (glɪmps) *n.* **1.** a brief or incomplete view: *to catch a glimpse of the sea.* **2.** a vague indication. **3.** *Arch.* a glimmer of light. ~*vb.* **4.** (when *intr.*, usually foll. by *at*) to catch sight (of) momentarily. **—'glimpser** *n.*

glint (glɪnt) *vb.* **1.** to gleam or cause to gleam brightly. ~*n.* **2.** a bright gleam or flash. **3.** brightness or gloss. **4.** a brief indication.

glissade (glɪ'sɑːd, -'seɪd) *n.* **1.** a gliding step in ballet. **2.** a controlled descent over snow or ice. ~*vb.* **3.** (*intr.*) to perform a glissade.

glisten ('glɪsᵊn) *vb.* (*intr.*) **1.** (of a wet or glossy surface, etc.) to gleam by reflecting light. **2.** (of light) to reflect with brightness: *the sunlight glistens on wet leaves.* ~*n.* **3.** *Rare.* a gleam or gloss.

glister ('glɪstə) *vb., n.* an archaic word for **glitter.**

glitter ('glɪtə) *vb.* (*intr.*) **1.** (of a hard, wet, or polished surface) to reflect light in bright flashes. **2.** (of light) to be reflected in bright flashes. **3.** (usually foll. by *with*) to be decorated or enhanced by the glamour (of): *the show glitters with famous actors.* ~*n.* **4.** sparkle or brilliance. **5.** show and glamour. **6.** tiny pieces of shiny decorative material. **—'glitteringly** *adv.* **—'glittery** *adj.*

glitter ice *n. Canad.* ice formed from freezing rain. Also called: **silver thaw.**

gloaming ('gləʊmɪŋ) *n. Scot. or poetic.* twilight or dusk.

gloat (gləʊt) *vb.* **1.** (*intr.; often foll. by over*) to dwell (on) with malevolent smugness or exultation. ~*n.* **2.** the act of gloating. **—'gloater** *n.*

glob (glɒb) *n. Inf.* a rounded mass of some thick fluid substance.

global ('gləʊbᵊl) *adj.* **1.** covering or relating to the whole world. **2.** comprehensive. **—'globally** *adv.*

globe (gləʊb) *n.* **1.** a sphere on which a map of the world is drawn. **2. the globe.** the world; the earth. **3.** a planet or some other astronomical body. **4.** an object shaped like a sphere, such as a glass lampshade or fish bowl. **5.** an orb, usually of gold, symbolic of sovereignty. ~*vb.* **6.** to form or cause to form into a globe. **—'globe-like** *adj.*

globeflower ('gləʊb₁flaʊə) *n.* a plant having pale yellow, white, or orange globe-shaped flowers.

globetrotter ('gləʊb₁trɒtə) *n.* a habitual worldwide traveller, esp. a tourist. **—'globe₁trotting** *n., adj.*

globular ('glɒbjʊlə) *or* **globulous** *adj.* **1.** shaped like a globe or globule. **2.** having or consisting of globules. **—'globularly** *adv.*

globule ('glɒbjuːl) *n.* a small globe, esp. a drop of liquid.

globulin ('glɒbjʊlɪn) *n.* any of a group of simple proteins that are generally insoluble in water but soluble in salt solutions.

glockenspiel ('glɒkən₁spiːl, -₁ʃpiːl) *n.* a percussion in-

THESAURUS

glaze 1. *v.* burnish, coat, enamel, furbish, gloss, lacquer, polish, varnish 2. *n.* coat, enamel, finish, gloss, lacquer, lustre, patina, polish, shine, varnish

gleam *n.* 1. beam, flash, glimmer, glow, ray, sparkle 2. brightness, brilliance, coruscation, flash, gloss, lustre, sheen, splendour 3. flicker, glimmer, hint, inkling, ray, suggestion, trace ~*v.* 4. coruscate, flare, flash, glance, glimmer, glint, glisten, glitter, glow, scintillate, shimmer, shine, sparkle

glee cheerfulness, delight, elation, exhilaration, exuberance, exultation, fun, gaiety, gladness, hilarity, jocularity, jollity, joviality, joy, joyfulness, joyousness, liveliness, merriment, mirth, sprightliness, triumph, verve

gleeful cheerful, cock-a-hoop, delighted, elated, exuberant, exultant, gay, gratified, happy, jocund, jovial, joyful, joyous, jubilant, merry, mirthful, overjoyed, pleased, triumphant

glib artful, easy, fast-talking, fluent, garru-

lous, insincere, plausible, quick, ready, slick, slippery, smooth, smooth-tongued, suave, talkative, voluble

glide coast, drift, float, flow, fly, roll, run, sail, skate, skim, slide, slip, soar

glimmer *v.* 1. blink, flicker, gleam, glisten, glitter, glow, shimmer, shine, sparkle, twinkle ~*n.* 2. blink, flicker, gleam, glow, ray, shimmer, sparkle, twinkle 3. flicker, gleam, grain, hint, inkling, ray, suggestion, trace

glimpse 1. *n.* brief view, glance, look, peek, peep, quick look, sight, sighting, squint 2. *v.* catch sight of, descry, espy, sight, spot, spy, view

glint 1. *v.* flash, gleam, glimmer, glitter, shine, sparkle, twinkle 2. *n.* flash, gleam, glimmer, glitter, shine, sparkle, twinkle, twinkling

glisten coruscate, flash, glance, glare, gleam, glimmer, glint, glitter, scintillate, shimmer, shine, sparkle, twinkle

glitter *v.* 1. coruscate, flare, flash, glare, gleam, glimmer, glint, glisten, scintillate, shimmer, shine, sparkle, twinkle ~*n.* 2. beam, brightness, brilliance, flash, glare, gleam, lustre, radiance, scintillation, sheen, shimmer, shine, sparkle 3. display, gaudiness, glamour, pageantry, show, showiness, splendour, tinsel

gloat crow, exult, glory, relish, revel in, rub it in (*Inf.*), triumph, vaunt

global 1. international, pandemic, planetary, universal, world, worldwide 2. all-encompassing, all-inclusive, all-out, comprehensive, encyclopedic, exhaustive, general, thorough, total, unbounded, unlimited

globe ball, earth, orb, planet, round, sphere, world

globule bead, bubble, drop, droplet, particle, pearl, pellet

glomerate 426 glue

strument consisting of a set of tuned metal plates played with a pair of small hammers.

glomerate ('glɒmərɪt) *adj.* **1.** gathered into a compact rounded mass. **2.** *Anat.* (esp. of glands) conglomerate in structure. —ˌglome'ration *n.*

gloom (gluːm) *n.* **1.** partial or total darkness. **2.** a state of depression or melancholy. **3.** an appearance or expression of despondency or melancholy. **4.** *Poetic.* a dim or dark place. ~*vb.* **5.** (*intr.*) to look sullen or depressed. **6.** to make or become dark or gloomy.

gloomy ('gluːmɪ) *adj.* **gloomier, gloomiest. 1.** dark or dismal. **2.** causing depression, dejection, or gloom: *gloomy news.* **3.** despairing; sad. —'gloomily *adv.* —'gloominess *n.*

glorify ('glɔːrɪˌfaɪ) *vb.* **-fying, -fied.** (*tr.*) **1.** to make glorious. **2.** to make more splendid; adorn. **3.** to worship, exalt, or adore. **4.** to extol. **5.** to cause to seem more splendid or imposing than reality. —ˌglorifi'cation *n.* —'glori,fier *n.*

glorious ('glɔːrɪəs) *adj.* **1.** having or full of glory; illustrious. **2.** conferring glory or renown: *a glorious victory.* **3.** brilliantly beautiful. **4.** *Inf.* delightful or enjoyable. —'gloriously *adv.* —'gloriousness *n.*

glory ('glɔːrɪ) *n., pl.* **-ries. 1.** exaltation, praise, or honour. **2.** something that brings or is worthy of praise (esp. in **crowning glory**). **3.** thanksgiving, adoration, or worship: *glory be to God.* **4.** pomp; splendour: *the glory of the king's reign.* **5.** radiant beauty; resplendence: *the glory of the sunset.* **6.** the beauty and bliss of heaven. **7.** a state of extreme happiness or prosperity. **8.** another word for **halo** or **nimbus.** ~*vb.* **-rying, -ried. 9.** (*intr.; often foll. by in*) to triumph or exalt. ~*interj.* **10.** *Inf.* a mild interjection to express pleasure or surprise (often **glory be!**).

glory hole *n.* **1.** a cupboard or storeroom, esp. one which is very untidy. **2.** *Naut.* a storeroom or a small locker.

Glos. *abbrev. for* Gloucestershire.

gloss[1] (glɒs) *n.* **1. a.** lustre or sheen, as of a smooth surface. **b.** (*as modifier*): *gloss paint.* **2.** a superficially attractive appearance. **3.** a cosmetic used to give a sheen. ~*vb.* **4.** to give a gloss to or obtain a gloss. **5.** (*tr.; often foll. by over*) to hide under a deceptively attractive surface or appearance. —'glosser *n.*

gloss[2] (glɒs) *n.* **1.** a short or expanded explanation or interpretation of a word, expression, or foreign phrase in the margin or text of a manuscript, etc. **2.** an intentionally misleading explanation. **3.** short for **glossary.** ~*vb.* (*tr.*) **4.** to add glosses to. **5.** (often foll. by *over*) to give a false or misleading interpretation of. —'glosser *n.*

glossary ('glɒsərɪ) *n., pl.* **-ries.** an alphabetical list of terms peculiar to a field of knowledge with explanations.

—**glossarial** (glɒˈsɛərɪəl) *adj.* —'glossarist *n.*

glossy ('glɒsɪ) *adj.* **glossier, glossiest. 1.** smooth and shiny; lustrous. **2.** superficially attractive; plausible. **3.** (of a magazine) lavishly produced on shiny paper. ~*n., pl.* **glossies. 4.** Also called (U.S.): **slick.** an expensively produced magazine, printed on shiny paper and containing high quality colour photography. **5.** a photograph printed on paper that has a smooth shiny surface. —'glossily *adv.* —'glossiness *n.*

glottal stop *n.* a plosive speech sound produced by tightly closing the glottis and allowing the air pressure to build up before opening the glottis, causing the air to escape with force.

glottis ('glɒtɪs) *n., pl.* **-tises** or **-tides** (-tɪˌdiːz). the vocal apparatus of the larynx, consisting of the two true vocal cords and the opening between them. —'glottal *adj.*

glove (glʌv) *n.* **1.** (*often pl.*) a shaped covering for the hand with individual sheaths for the fingers and thumb, made of leather, fabric, etc. **2.** any of various large protective hand covers worn in sports, such as a boxing glove. ~*vb.* **3.** (*tr.*) to cover or provide with or as if with gloves.

glover ('glʌvə) *n.* a person who makes or sells gloves.

glow (gləʊ) *n.* **1.** light emitted by a substance or object at a high temperature. **2.** a steady even light without flames. **3.** brilliance of colour. **4.** brightness of complexion. **5.** a feeling of well-being or satisfaction. **6.** intensity of emotion. ~*vb.* (*intr.*) **7.** to emit a steady even light without flames. **8.** to shine intensely, as if from great heat. **9.** to be exuberant, as from excellent health or intense emotion. **10.** to experience a feeling of well-being or satisfaction: *to glow with pride.* **11.** (esp. of the complexion) to show a strong bright colour, esp. red. **12.** to be very hot.

glower ('glaʊə) *vb.* **1.** (*intr.*) to stare hard and angrily. ~*n.* **2.** a sullen or angry stare. —'gloweringly *adv.*

glow-worm *n.* a European beetle, the females and larvae of which bear luminescent organs producing a soft greenish light.

gloxinia (glɒkˈsɪnɪə) *n.* any of several tropical plants cultivated for their large white, red, or purple bell-shaped flowers.

glucose ('gluːkəʊz, -kəʊs) *n.* **1.** a white crystalline sugar, the most abundant form being dextrose. Formula: $C_6H_{12}O_6$. **2.** a yellowish syrup obtained by incomplete hydrolysis of starch: used in confectionery, fermentation, etc.

glue (gluː) *n.* **1.** any natural or synthetic adhesive, esp. a sticky gelatinous substance prepared by boiling animal products such as bones, skin, and horns. **2.** any other sticky or adhesive substance. ~*vb.* **gluing** or **glueing, glued. 3.** (*tr.*) to join or stick together as with glue. —'glue,like *adj.* —'gluer *n.* —'gluey *adj.*

THESAURUS

gloom 1. blackness, cloud, cloudiness, dark, darkness, dimness, dullness, dusk, duskiness, gloominess, murk, murkiness, obscurity, shade, shadow, twilight **2.** blues, dejection, depression, desolation, despair, despondency, downheartedness, low spirits, melancholy, misery, sadness, sorrow, unhappiness, woe

gloomy 1. black, crepuscular, dark, dim, dismal, dreary, dull, dusky, murky, obscure, overcast, shadowy, sombre, Stygian, tenebrous **2.** bad, black, cheerless, comfortless, depressing, disheartening, dispiriting, dreary, joyless, sad, saddening, sombre **3.** blue, chapfallen, cheerless, crestfallen, dejected, despondent, dismal, dispirited, down, downcast, downhearted, down in the dumps (*Inf.*), down in the mouth, glum, in low spirits, melancholy, miserable, moody, morose, pessimistic, sad, saturnine, sullen

glorify 1. add lustre to, adorn, aggrandize, augment, dignify, elevate, enhance, ennoble, illuminate, immortalize, lift up, magnify, raise **2.** adore, apotheosize, beatify, bless, canonize, deify, enshrine, exalt, honour, idolize, pay homage to, revere, sanctify, venerate, worship **3.** celebrate, cry up (*Inf.*), eulogize, extol, hymn, laud, lionize, magnify, panegyrize, praise, sing *or* sound the praises of

glorious 1. celebrated, distinguished, el-

evated, eminent, excellent, famed, famous, grand, honoured, illustrious, magnificent, majestic, noble, noted, renowned, sublime, triumphant **2.** beautiful, bright, brilliant, dazzling, divine, effulgent, gorgeous, radiant, resplendent, shining, splendid, superb **3.** *Inf.* delightful, enjoyable, excellent, fine, great, heavenly (*Inf.*), marvellous, pleasurable, splendid, wonderful

glory *n.* **1.** celebrity, dignity, distinction, eminence, exaltation, fame, honour, illustriousness, immortality, kudos, praise, prestige, renown **2.** adoration, benediction, blessing, gratitude, homage, laudation, praise, thanksgiving, veneration, worship **3.** grandeur, greatness, magnificence, majesty, nobility, pageantry, pomp, splendour, sublimity, triumph **4.** beauty, brilliance, effulgence, gorgeousness, lustre, radiance, resplendence ~*v.* **5.** boast, crow, exult, gloat, pride oneself, relish, revel, take delight, triumph

gloss[1] *n.* **1.** brightness, brilliance, burnish, gleam, lustre, polish, sheen, shine, varnish, veneer **2.** appearance, façade, front, mask, semblance, show, surface ~*v.* **3.** burnish, finish, furbish, glaze, lacquer, polish, shine, varnish, veneer **4.** camouflage, conceal, cover up, disguise, hide, mask, smooth over, veil, whitewash (*Inf.*)

gloss[2] **1.** *n.* annotation, comment, commen-

tary, elucidation, explanation, footnote, interpretation, note, scholium, translation **2.** *v.* annotate, comment, construe, elucidate, explain, interpret, translate

glossy bright, brilliant, burnished, glassy, glazed, lustrous, polished, sheeny, shining, shiny, silken, silky, sleek, smooth

glow *n.* **1.** burning, gleam, glimmer, incandescence, lambency, light, luminosity, phosphorescence **2.** brightness, brilliance, effulgence, radiance, splendour, vividness **3.** ardour, earnestness, enthusiasm, excitement, fervour, gusto, impetuosity, intensity, passion, vehemence, warmth **4.** bloom, blush, flush, reddening, rosiness ~*v.* **5.** brighten, burn, gleam, glimmer, redden, shine, smoulder **6.** be suffused, blush, colour, fill, flush, radiate, thrill, tingle

glower 1. *v.* frown, give a dirty look, glare, look daggers, lower, scowl **2.** *n.* angry stare, black look, dirty look, frown, glare, lower, scowl

glowing 1. aglow, beaming, bright, flaming, florid, flushed, lambent, luminous, red, rich, ruddy, suffused, vibrant, vivid, warm **2.** adulatory, complimentary, ecstatic, enthusiastic, eulogistic, laudatory, panegyrical, rave (*Inf.*), rhapsodic

glue 1. *n.* adhesive, cement, gum, mucilage, paste **2.** *v.* affix, agglutinate, cement, fix,

glum (glʌm) *adj.* **glummer, glummest.** silent or sullen, as from gloom. —'**glumly** *adv.* —'**glumness** *n.*

glut (glʌt) *n.* **1.** an excessive amount, as in the production of a crop. **2.** the act of glutting or state of being glutted. ~*vb.* **glutting, glutted.** (*tr.*) **3.** to feed or supply beyond capacity. **4.** to supply (a market, etc.) with a commodity in excess of the demand for it.

gluten ('gluːtən) *n.* a protein present in cereal grains, esp. wheat. —'**glutenous** *adj.*

glutinous ('gluːtɪnəs) *adj.* resembling glue in texture; sticky. —'**glutinously** *adv.*

glutton[1] ('glʌtən) *n.* **1.** a person devoted to eating and drinking to excess; greedy person. **2.** a person who has or appears to have a voracious appetite for something: *a glutton for punishment.* —'**gluttonous** *adj.* —'**gluttonously** *adv.*

glutton[2] ('glʌtən) *n.* another name for **wolverine.**

gluttony ('glʌtənɪ) *n., pl.* **-tonies.** the act or practice of eating to excess.

glyceride ('glɪsəˌraɪd) *n.* any fatty-acid ester of glycerol.

glycerin ('glɪsərɪn) *or* **glycerine** ('glɪsərɪn, ˌglɪsə'riːn) *n.* another name (not in technical usage) for **glycerol.**

glycerol ('glɪsəˌrɒl) *n.* a colourless odourless syrupy liquid: a by-product of soap manufacture, used as a solvent, antifreeze, plasticizer, and sweetener.

glyco- *or before a vowel* **glyc-** *combining form.* sugar: *glycogen.*

glycogen ('glaɪkəʊdʒən) *n.* a polysaccharide consisting of glucose units: the form in which carbohydrate is stored in animals. —**glycogenic** (ˌglaɪkəʊ'dʒɛnɪk) *adj.* —ˌglyco'genesis *n.*

G.M. *abbrev. for:* **1.** general manager. **2.** (in Britain) George Medal. **3.** Grand Master.

G-man *n., pl.* **G-men.** **1.** *U.S. sl.* an FBI agent. **2.** *Irish.* a political detective.

GMT *abbrev. for* Greenwich Mean Time.

gnarled (nɑːld) *or* **gnarly** *adj.* **1.** having gnarls: *the gnarled trunk of the old tree.* **2.** (esp. of hands) rough, twisted, and weather-beaten.

gnash (næʃ) *vb.* **1.** to grind (the teeth) together, as in pain or anger. **2.** (*tr.*) to bite or chew as by grinding the teeth. ~*n.* **3.** the act of gnashing the teeth.

gnat (næt) *n.* any of various small fragile biting two-winged insects.

gnaw (nɔː) *vb.* **gnawing, gnawed; gnawed** *or* **gnawn.** **1.** (when *intr.,* often foll. by *at* or *upon*) to bite (at) or chew (upon) constantly so as to wear away little by little. **2.** (*tr.*) to form by gnawing: *to gnaw a hole.* **3.** to cause erosion of (something). **4.** (when *intr.,* often foll. by *at*) to cause constant distress or anxiety (to). ~*n.* **5.** the act or an instance of gnawing.

gneiss (naɪs) *n.* any coarse-grained metamorphic rock that is banded or foliated. —'**gneissic, 'gneissoid,** *or* '**gneissose** *adj.*

gnome (nəʊm) *n.* **1.** one of a species of legendary creatures, usually resembling small misshapen old men, said to live in the depths of the earth and guard buried treasure. **2.** the statue of a gnome, esp. in a garden. **3.** a very small or ugly person. **4.** *Facetious or derog.* an international banker or financier (esp. in **gnomes of Zurich**). —'**gnomish** *adj.*

gnomic ('nəʊmɪk, 'nɒm-) *adj.* of or relating to aphorisms; pithy. —'**gnomically** *adv.*

gnomon ('nəʊmɒn) *n.* **1.** the stationary arm that projects the shadow on a sundial. **2.** a geometric figure remaining after a parallelogram has been removed from one corner of a larger parallelogram. —**gno'monic** *adj.*

gnostic ('nɒstɪk) *adj.* of, relating to, or possessing knowledge, esp. spiritual knowledge.

Gnostic ('nɒstɪk) *n.* **1.** an adherent of Gnosticism. ~*adj.* **2.** of or relating to Gnostics or to Gnosticism.

Gnosticism ('nɒstɪˌsɪzəm) *n.* a religious movement characterized by a belief in intuitive spiritual knowledge: regarded as a heresy by the Christian Church.

G.N.P. *abbrev. for* gross national product.

gnu (nuː) *n., pl.* **gnus** *or* **gnu.** either of two sturdy antelopes inhabiting the savannas of Africa, having an oxlike head and a long tufted tail. Also called: **wildebeest.**

go (gəʊ) *vb.* **going, went, gone.** (*mainly intr.*) **1.** to move or proceed, esp. to or from a point or in a certain direction: *to go home.* **2.** (*tr.; takes an infinitive,* often with *to* omitted or replaced by *and*) to proceed towards a particular person or place with some specified purpose: *I must go and get that book.* **3.** to depart: *we'll have to go at eleven.* **4.** to start, as in a race: often used in commands. **5.** to make regular journeys: *this train service goes to the East coast.* **6.** to operate or function effectively: *the radio won't go.* **7.** (*copula*) to become: *his face went red.* **8.** to make a noise as specified: *the gun went bang.* **9.** to enter into a specified state or condition: *to go into hysterics.* **10.** to be or continue to be in a specified state or condition: *to go in rags; to go in poverty.* **11.** to lead, extend, or afford access: *this route goes to the North.* **12.** to proceed towards an activity: *to go to sleep.* **13.** (*tr.; takes an infinitive*) to serve or contribute: *this letter goes to prove my point.* **14.** to follow a course as specified; fare: *the lecture went badly.* **15.** to be applied or allotted to a particular purpose or recipient: *his money went on drink.* **16.** to be sold: *the necklace went for three thousand pounds.* **17.** to be ranked; compare: *this meal is good as my meals go.* **18.** to blend or harmonize: *these chairs won't go with the rest of your furniture.* **19.** (foll. by *by* or *under*) to be known (by a name or disguise). **20.** to have a usual or proper place: *those books go on this shelf.* **21.** (of music, poetry, etc.) to be sounded; expressed, etc.: *how does that song go?* **22.** to fail or give way: *my eyesight is going.* **23.** to break down or collapse abruptly: *the ladder went at the critical moment.* **24.** to die: *the old man went at 2 a.m.* **25.** (often foll. by *by*) **a.** (of time, etc.) to elapse: *the hours go by so slowly.* **b.** to travel past: *the train goes by her house.* **c.** to be guided (by). **26.** to occur: *happiness does not always go with riches.* **27.** to be eliminated, abolished, or given up: *this entry must go to save space.* **28.** to be spent or finished: *all his money has gone.* **29.** to attend: *go to school.* **30.** to join a stated profession: *go on the stage.* **31.** (foll. by *to*) to have recourse (to); turn: *to go to arbitration.* **32.** (foll. by *to*) to subject or put oneself (to): *she goes to great pains to please him.* **33.** to proceed, esp. up to or beyond certain limits: *you will go too far one day and then you will be punished.* **34.** to be acceptable or tolerated: *anything goes.* **35.** to carry the weight of final authority: *what the boss says goes.* **36.** (foll. by *into*) to be contained in: *four goes into twelve three times.* **37.** (often foll. by *for*) to endure or last out: *we can't go for much longer without water.* **38.** (*tr.*) *Cards.* to bet or bid: *I go two hearts.* **39. go and.** *Inf.* to be so foolish or unlucky as to: *then she had to go and lose her hat.* **40. be going.** to intend or be about to start (to do or be doing something): often used as an alternative future construction: *what's going to happen to us?* **41. go bail.** to act as surety. **42. go it.** *Sl.* to do something or move energetically. **43. go it alone.** *Inf.* to act or proceed without allies or help. **44. go one better.** *Inf.* to surpass or outdo (someone). **45. let go. a.** to relax one's hold (on); release. **b.** to discuss or consider no further. **46. let oneself go. a.** to act in an uninhibited manner. **b.** to lose interest in one's appearance, manners, etc. **47. to go.** remaining. ~*n., pl.* **goes.** **48.** the act of going. **49. a.** an attempt or try: *he had a go at the stamp business.* **b.** an attempt at stopping a person suspected of a crime: *the police are not always in favour of the public having a go.* **50.** a turn: *it's my go next.* **51.** *Inf.* the quality of being active and energetic: *she has much more go than I.* **52.** *Inf.* hard or energetic work: *it's all go.* **53.** *Inf.* a successful venture or achievement: *he made a go of it.* **54.** *Inf.* a bargain or agreement. **55. from the word go.** *Inf.*

THESAURUS

gum, paste, seal, stick

glum chapfallen, churlish, crabbed, crestfallen, crusty, dejected, doleful, down, gloomy, gruff, grumpy, ill-humoured, low, moody, morose, pessimistic, saturnine, sour, sulky, sullen, surly

glut *n.* **1.** excess, overabundance, oversupply, saturation, superabundance, superfluity, surfeit, surplus ~*v.* **2.** cram, fill, gorge, over-

feed, satiate, stuff **3.** choke, clog, deluge, flood, inundate, overload, oversupply, saturate

glutton gannet (*Sl.*), gobbler, gorger, gormandizer, gourmand, pig (*Inf.*)

gluttony gormandizing, gourmandism, greed, greediness, piggishness, rapacity, voraciousness, voracity

gnarled contorted, knotted, knotty,

knurled, leathery, rough, rugged, twisted, weather-beaten, wrinkled

gnaw **1.** bite, chew, munch, nibble, worry **2.** consume, devour, eat away *or* into, erode, fret, wear away *or* down **3.** distress, fret, harry, haunt, nag, plague, prey on one's mind, trouble, worry

from the very beginning. **56. no go.** *Inf.* impossible; abortive or futile: *it's no go, I'm afraid.* **57. on the go.** *Inf.* active and energetic. ~*adj.* **58.** (*postpositive*) *Inf.* functioning properly and ready for action: esp. used in astronautics: *all systems are go.* ~See also **go about, go against,** etc.

go about *vb.* (*intr.*) **1.** (*prep.*) to busy oneself with: *to go about one's duties.* **2.** (*prep.*) to tackle (a problem or task). **3.** to circulate (in): *there's a lot of flu going about.* **4.** (*adv.*) (of a sailing ship) to change from one tack to another.

goad (gəʊd) *n.* **1.** a sharp pointed stick for urging on cattle, etc. **2.** anything that acts as a spur or incitement. ~*vb.* **3.** (*tr.*) to drive as if with a goad; spur; incite.

go against *vb.* (*intr.*, *prep.*) **1.** to be contrary to (principles or beliefs). **2.** to be unfavourable to (a person): *the case went against him.*

go-ahead *n.* **1.** (*usually preceded by the*) *Inf.* permission to proceed. ~*adj.* **2.** enterprising or ambitious.

goal (gəʊl) *n.* **1.** the aim or object towards which an endeavour is directed. **2.** the terminal point of a journey or race. **3.** (in various sports) the net, basket, etc. into or over which players try to propel the ball, puck, etc., to score. **4.** *Sport.* **a.** a successful attempt at scoring. **b.** the score so made. **5.** (in soccer, hockey, etc.) the position of goalkeeper. —'**goalless** *adj.*

goalkeeper ('gəʊl,ki:pə) *n. Sport.* a player in the goal whose duty is to prevent the ball, puck, etc., from entering or crossing it.

goal line *n. Sport.* the line marking each end of the pitch, on which the goals stand.

goat (gəʊt) *n.* **1.** any sure-footed agile ruminant mammal with hollow horns, naturally inhabiting rough stony ground in Europe, Asia, and N Africa. **2.** *Inf.* a lecherous man. **3.** a foolish person. **4. get (someone's) goat.** *Sl.* to cause annoyance to (someone). —'**goat,ish** *adj.*

Goat (gəʊt) *n.* **the.** the constellation Capricorn, the tenth sign of the zodiac.

go at *vb.* (*intr.*, *prep.*) **1.** to make an energetic attempt at (something). **2.** to attack vehemently.

goatee (gəʊ'ti:) *n.* a pointed tuftlike beard growing on the chin.

goatherd ('gəʊt,hɜːd) *n.* a person employed to tend or herd goats.

goatsbeard *or* **goat's-beard** ('gəʊts,bɪəd) *n.* **1.** Also called: **Jack-go-to-bed-at-noon.** a Eurasian plant of the composite family, with woolly stems and large heads of yellow rayed flowers. **2.** an American plant with long spikes of small white flowers.

goatskin ('gəʊt,skɪn) *n.* **1.** the hide of a goat. **2.** something made from the hide of a goat, such as leather or a container for wine.

goatsucker ('gəʊt,sʌkə) *n.* the U.S. name for **nightjar.**

gob¹ (gɒb) *n.* **1.** a lump or chunk, esp. of a soft substance. **2.** (*often pl.*) *Inf.* a great quantity or amount. **3.** *Inf.* a globule of spittle or saliva. ~*vb.* **gobbing, gobbed.** **4.** (*intr.*) *Brit. inf.* to spit.

gob² (gɒb) *n.* a slang word (esp. Brit.) for the **mouth.**

go back *vb.* (*intr.*, *adv.*) **1.** to return. **2.** (often foll. by *to*) to originate (in): *the links with France go back to the Norman Conquest.* **3.** (foll. by *on*) to change one's mind about; repudiate (esp. in **go back on one's word**).

gobbet ('gɒbɪt) *n.* a chunk, lump, or fragment, esp. of raw meat.

gobble¹ ('gɒbəl) *vb.* **1.** (when *tr.*, often foll. by *up*) to eat or swallow (food) hastily and in large mouthfuls. **2.** (*tr.*; often foll. by *up*) *Inf.* to snatch.

gobble² ('gɒbəl) *n.* **1.** the loud rapid gurgling sound made by male turkeys. ~*vb.* **2.** (*intr.*) (of a turkey) to make this sound.

gobbledegook *or* **gobbledygook** ('gɒbəldɪ,gu:k) *n. Inf.* pretentious language, esp. as characterized by obscure phraseology.

gobbler ('gɒblə) *n. Inf.* a male turkey.

Gobelin ('gəʊbəlɪn; *French* gɔ'blɛ̃) *adj.* **1.** of or resembling tapestry made at the Gobelins' factory in Paris, having vivid pictorial scenes. ~*n.* **2.** a tapestry of this kind.

go-between *n.* a person who acts as agent or intermediary for two people or groups in a transaction or dealing.

goblet ('gɒblɪt) *n.* **1.** a vessel for drinking, with a base and stem but without handles. **2.** *Arch.* a large drinking cup.

goblin ('gɒblɪn) *n.* (in folklore) a small grotesque supernatural creature, regarded as malevolent towards human beings.

goby ('gəʊbɪ) *n.*, *pl.* **-by** *or* **-bies.** a small spiny-finned fish of coastal or brackish waters, having a large head, an elongated tapering body, and the ventral fins modified as a sucker.

go-by *n. Sl.* a deliberate snub or slight (esp. in **give (a person) the go-by**).

go by *vb.* (*intr.*) **1.** to pass: *as the years go by.* **2.** (*prep.*) to be guided by: *in the darkness we could only go by the stars.* **3.** (*prep.*) to use as a basis for forming an opinion or judgement: *it's wise not to go only by appearances.*

go-cart *n. Motor racing.* See **kart.**

god (gɒd) *n.* **1.** a supernatural being, who is worshipped as the controller of some part of the universe or some aspect of life in the world or is the personification of some force. **2.** an image, idol, or symbolic representation of such a deity. **3.** any person or thing to which excessive attention is given: *money was his god.* **4.** a man who has qualities regarded as making him superior to other men. **5.** (*in pl.*) the gallery of a theatre. —'**goddess** *fem. n.* —'**god,like** *adj.*

God (gɒd) *n.* **1.** the sole Supreme Being, eternal, spiritual, and transcendent, who is the Creator and ruler of all and is infinite in all attributes; the object of worship in monotheistic religions. ~*interj.* **2.** an oath or exclamation used to indicate surprise, annoyance, etc. (and in such expressions as **My God!** or **God Almighty!**).

godchild ('gɒd,tʃaɪld) *n.*, *pl.* **-children.** a person who is sponsored by adults at baptism.

goddaughter ('gɒd,dɔːtə) *n.* a female godchild.

godetia (gə'di:ʃə) *n.* any plant of the American genus *Godetia*, esp. one grown as a showy-flowered annual garden plant.

godfather ('gɒd,fɑːðə) *n.* a male godparent.

god-fearing *adj.* pious; devout.

godforsaken ('gɒdfə,seɪkən) *adj.* **1.** (*usually prenominal*) desolate; dreary; forlorn. **2.** wicked.

THESAURUS

go *v.* **1.** advance, decamp, depart, fare (*Archaic*), journey, leave, make for, move, move out, pass, proceed, repair, set off, travel, withdraw **2.** function, move, operate, perform, run, work **3.** connect, extend, fit, give access, lead, reach, run, span, spread, incline, lead to, serve, tend, work towards **5.** develop, eventuate, fall out, fare, happen, proceed, result, turn out, work out **6.** accord, agree, blend, chime, complement, correspond, fit, harmonize, jibe (*Inf.*), match, suit **7.** die, expire, give up the ghost, pass away, perish **8.** elapse, expire, flow, lapse, pass, slip away ~*n.* **9.** attempt, bid, crack (*Inf.*), effort, essay, shot (*Inf.*), stab, try, turn, whack (*Inf.*), whirl (*Inf.*) **10.** *Inf.* activity, animation, drive, energy, force, get-up-and-go (*Inf.*), life, oomph (*Inf.*), pep, spirit, verve, vigour, vitality, vivacity

go about 1. circulate, move around, pass around, wander **2.** approach, begin, set about, tackle, undertake **3.** busy *or* occupy oneself with, devote oneself to

goad 1. *n.* impetus, incentive, incitement, irritation, motivation, pressure, spur, stimulation, stimulus, urge **2.** *v.* annoy, arouse, drive, egg on, exhort, harass, hound, impel, incite, instigate, irritate, lash, prick, prod, prompt, propel, spur, stimulate, sting, urge, worry

go-ahead 1. *n. Inf.* assent, authorization, consent, green light, leave, O.K. (*Inf.*), permission **2.** *adj.* ambitious, enterprising, go-getting (*Inf.*), pioneering, progressive, up-and-coming

go ahead advance, begin, continue, go forward, go on, proceed, progress

goal aim, ambition, design, destination, end, intention, limit, mark, object, objective, purpose, target

go along 1. acquiesce, agree, assent, concur, cooperate, follow **2.** accompany, carry on, escort, join, keep up, move, pass, travel

go away decamp, depart, exit, leave, move out, recede, withdraw

go back 1. return, revert **2.** change one's mind, desert, forsake, renege, repudiate, retract

gobble bolt, cram, devour, gorge, gulp, guzzle, stuff, swallow, wolf

go-between agent, broker, dealer, factor, intermediary, liaison, mediator, medium, middleman

go by 1. elapse, exceed, flow on, move onward, pass, proceed **2.** adopt, be guided by, follow, heed, judge from, observe, take as guide

Godhead ('gɒd,hɛd) n. (sometimes not cap.) **1.** the essential nature and condition of being God. **2. the Godhead.** God.

godless ('gɒdlɪs) adj. **1.** wicked or unprincipled. **2.** lacking a god. **3.** refusing to acknowledge God. —'**godlessly** adv. —'**godlessness** n.

godly ('gɒdlɪ) adj. **-lier, -liest.** having a religious character; pious; devout. —'**godliness** n.

godmother ('gɒd,mʌðə) n. a female godparent.

go down vb. (intr., mainly adv.) **1.** (also prep.) to move or lead to or as if to a lower place or level; sink, decline, decrease, etc. **2.** to be defeated; lose. **3.** to be remembered or recorded (esp. in **go down in history**). **4.** to be received: his speech went down well. **5.** (of food) to be swallowed. **6.** Brit. to leave (a college or university) at the end of a term. **7.** (usually foll. by with) Brit. to fall ill; be infected. **8.** (of a celestial body) to sink or set.

godparent ('gɒd,pɛərənt) n. a person who stands sponsor to another at baptism.

godsend ('gɒd,sɛnd) n. a person or thing that comes unexpectedly but is particularly welcome.

godson ('gɒd,sʌn) n. a male godchild.

Godspeed ('gɒd'spiːd) interj., n. an expression of good wishes for a person's success and safety.

godwit ('gɒdwɪt) n. a large shore bird of the sandpiper family having long legs and a long upturned bill.

goer ('gəʊə) n. **1. a.** a person who attends something regularly. **b.** (in combination): filmgoer. **2.** a person or thing that goes, esp. one that goes very fast. **3.** Austral. inf. an acceptable or feasible idea, proposal, etc. **4.** Austral. & N.Z. an energetic person.

goffer ('gəʊfə) vb. **1.** (tr.) to press pleats into (a frill). **2.** (tr.) to decorate (the edges of a book). ~n. **3.** an ornamental frill made by pressing pleats. **4.** the decoration formed by goffering books. **5.** the iron or tool used in making goffers.

go for vb. (intr., prep.) **1.** to go somewhere in order to have or fetch: he went for a drink. **2.** to seek to obtain: I'd go for that job if I were you. **3.** to prefer or choose; like: I really go for that new idea of yours. **4.** to make a physical or verbal attack on. **5.** to be considered to be of a stated importance or value: his twenty years went for nothing when he was made redundant.

go-getter n. Inf. an ambitious enterprising person.

goggle ('gɒgl) vb. **1.** (intr.) to stare fixedly, as in astonishment. **2.** to cause (the eyes) to roll or bulge or (of the eyes) to roll or bulge. ~n. **3.** a bulging stare. **4.** (pl.) spectacles, often of coloured glass or covered with gauze: used to protect the eyes. —'**goggle-eyed** adj.

gogglebox ('gɒgl,bɒks) n. Brit. sl. a television set.

go-go dancer n. a dancer, usually scantily dressed, who performs rhythmic and often erotic modern dance routines, esp. in a nightclub.

Goidelic (gɔɪ'dɛlɪk) n. **1.** the N group of Celtic languages, consisting of Irish Gaelic, Scottish Gaelic, and Manx. ~adj. **2.** of, relating to, or characteristic of this group of languages.

go in vb. (intr., adv.) **1.** to enter. **2.** (prep.) See **go into.** **3.** (of the sun, etc.) to become hidden behind a cloud. **4. go in for. a.** to enter as a competitor or contestant. **b.** to adopt as an activity, interest, or guiding principle: she went in for nursing.

going ('gəʊɪŋ) n. **1.** a departure or farewell. **2.** the condition of a surface such as a road or field with regard to walking, riding, etc.: muddy going. **3.** Inf. speed, progress, etc.: we made good going on the trip. ~adj. **4.** thriving (esp. in **a going concern**). **5.** current or accepted: the going rate. **6.** (postpositive) available: the best going.

going-over n., pl. **goings-over.** Inf. **1.** a check, examination, or investigation. **2.** a castigation or thrashing.

goings-on pl. n. Inf. **1.** actions or conduct, esp. when regarded with disapproval. **2.** happenings or events, esp. when mysterious or suspicious.

go into vb. (intr., prep.) **1.** to enter. **2.** to start a career in: to go into publishing. **3.** to investigate or examine. **4.** to be admitted to, esp. temporarily: she went into hospital. **5.** to enter a specified state: she went into fits of laughter.

goitre or U.S. **goiter** ('gɔɪtə) n. Pathol. a swelling of the thyroid gland, in some cases nearly doubling the size of the neck. —'**goitred** or U.S. '**goitered** adj. —'**goitrous** adj.

gold (gəʊld) n. **1. a.** a dense inert bright yellow element that is the most malleable and ductile metal, occurring in rocks and alluvial deposits: used as a monetary standard and in jewellery, dentistry, and plating. Symbol: Au; atomic no.: 79; atomic wt.: 196.97. Related adj.: **auric. b.** (as modifier): a gold mine. **2.** a coin or coins made of this metal. **3.** money; wealth. **4.** something precious, beautiful, etc., such as a noble nature (esp. in **heart of gold**). **5. a.** a deep yellow colour, sometimes with a brownish tinge. **b.** (as adj.): a gold carpet. **6.** short for **gold medal.**

goldcrest ('gəʊld,krɛst) n. a small Old World warbler having a greenish plumage and a bright yellow-and-black crown.

gold-digger n. **1.** a person who prospects or digs for gold. **2.** Inf. a woman who uses her sexual attractions to accumulate gifts and wealth.

gold dust n. gold in the form of small particles or powder.

golden ('gəʊldən) adj. **1.** of the yellowish colour of gold: golden hair. **2.** made from or largely consisting of gold: a golden statue. **3.** happy or prosperous: golden days. **4.** (sometimes cap.) (of anniversaries) the 50th in a series: Golden Jubilee; golden wedding. **5.** Inf. very successful or destined for success: the golden girl of tennis. **6.** extremely valuable or advantageous: a golden opportunity. —'**goldenly** adv. —'**goldenness** n.

golden age n. **1.** Classical myth. the first and best age of mankind, when existence was happy, prosperous, and innocent. **2.** the most flourishing and outstanding period, esp. in the history of an art or nation: the golden age of poetry.

golden eagle n. a large eagle of mountainous regions of the N hemisphere, having a plumage that is golden brown on the back.

Golden Fleece n. Greek myth. the fleece of a winged ram stolen by Jason and the Argonauts.

golden handshake n. Inf. a sum of money given to an employee, either on retirement or as compensation for loss of employment.

golden mean n. the middle course between extremes.

golden retriever n. a variety of retriever with a long silky wavy coat of a golden colour.

goldenrod (,gəʊldən'rɒd) n. a plant of the composite family of North America, Europe, and Asia, having spikes of small yellow flowers.

golden rule n. **1.** the rule of conduct formulated by Christ: Whatsoever ye would that men should do to you, do ye even so to them (Matthew 7:12). **2.** any important

---

THESAURUS

godforsaken abandoned, backward, bleak, deserted, desolate, dismal, dreary, forlorn, gloomy, lonely, neglected, remote, wretched

godless atheistic, depraved, evil, impious, irreligious, profane, ungodly, unprincipled, unrighteous, wicked

godlike celestial, deific, deiform, divine, heavenly, superhuman, transcendent

godly devout, god-fearing, good, holy, pious, religious, righteous, saintly

go down 1. be beaten, collapse, decline, decrease, drop, fall, founder, go under, lose, set, sink, submerge, submit, suffer defeat **2.** be commemorated (recalled, recorded, remembered)

godsend blessing, boon, manna, stroke of luck, windfall

go far advance, be successful, do well, get ahead (Inf.), get on (Inf.), make a name for oneself, progress, succeed

go for 1. clutch at, fetch, obtain, reach, seek, stretch for **2.** admire, be attracted to, be fond of, choose, favour, hold with, like, prefer **3.** assail, assault, attack, launch oneself at, rush upon, set about or upon, spring upon

go in (for) adopt, embrace, engage in, enter, espouse, practise, pursue, take up, undertake

go into 1. begin, develop, enter, participate in, undertake **2.** analyse, consider, delve into, discuss, examine, inquire into, investigate, look into, probe, pursue, review, scrutinize, study

golden 1. blond or blonde, bright, brilliant, flaxen, resplendent, shining, yellow **2.** best, blissful, delightful, flourishing, glorious, happy, joyful, joyous, precious, prosperous, rich, successful **3.** advantageous, auspicious, excellent, favourable, opportune, promising, propitious, rosy, valuable

principle: *a golden rule of sailing is to wear a life jacket.*

golden syrup *n. Brit.* a light golden coloured treacle produced by the evaporation of cane sugar juice, used to flavour cakes, puddings, etc.

goldfinch ('gəʊld‚fɪntʃ) *n.* a common European finch, the male of which has a red-and-white face and yellow-and-black wings.

goldfish ('gəʊld‚fɪʃ) *n., pl.* **-fish** *or* **-fishes.** a freshwater fish of E Europe and Asia, esp. China, widely introduced as a pond or aquarium fish. It resembles the carp and has a typically golden or orange-red coloration.

gold foil *n.* thin gold sheet that is thicker than gold leaf.

gold leaf *n.* very thin gold sheet produced by rolling or hammering gold and used for gilding woodwork, etc.

gold medal *n.* a medal of gold, awarded to the winner of a competition or race.

gold plate *n.* **1.** a thin coating of gold, usually produced by electroplating. **2.** vessels or utensils made of gold. —‚**gold-'plate** *vb.* (*tr.*)

gold rush *n.* a large-scale migration of people to a territory where gold has been found.

goldsmith ('gəʊld‚smɪθ) *n.* **a.** a dealer in articles made of gold. **b.** an artisan who makes such articles.

gold standard *n.* a monetary system in which the unit of currency is defined with reference to gold.

golf (gɒlf) *n.* **1.** a game played on a large open course, the object of which is to hit a ball using clubs, with as few strokes as possible, into each of usually 18 holes. ~*vb.* **2.** (*intr.*) to play golf. —'**golfer** *n.*

golf club *n.* **1.** any of various long-shafted clubs with wood or metal heads used to strike a golf ball. **2. a.** an association of golf players, usually having its own course and facilities. **b.** the premises of such an association.

golf course *or* **links** *n.* a large area of open land on which golf is played.

Goliath (gə'laɪəθ) *n. Bible.* a Philistine giant who was killed by David with a stone from his sling (I Samuel 17).

golliwog ('gɒlɪ‚wɒg) *n.* a soft doll with a black face, usually made of cloth or rags.

golly ('gɒlɪ) *interj.* an exclamation of mild surprise.

goloshes (gə'lɒʃɪz) *pl. n.* a less common spelling of **galoshes.**

-gon *n. combining form.* indicating a figure having a specified number of angles: *pentagon.*

gonad ('gɒnæd) *n.* an animal organ in which gametes are produced, such as a testis or an ovary. —'**gonadal,** **gonadial** (gɒ'neɪdɪəl). *adj.*

gondola ('gɒndələ) *n.* **1.** a long narrow flat-bottomed boat with a high ornamented stem: traditionally used on the canals of Venice. **2. a.** a car or cabin suspended from an airship or balloon. **b.** a moving cabin suspended from a cable across a valley, etc. **3.** a flat-bottomed barge used on canals and rivers of the U.S. **4.** *U.S.* a low, open, and flat-bottomed railway goods wagon. **5.** a set of island shelves in a self-service shop: used for displaying goods.

gondolier (‚gɒndə'lɪə) *n.* a man who propels a gondola.

gone (gɒn) *vb.* **1.** the past participle of **go.** ~*adj.* (*usually postpositive*) **2.** ended; past. **3.** lost; ruined. **4.** dead. **5.** spent; consumed; used up. **6.** *Inf.* faint or weak. **7.** *Inf.* having been pregnant (for a specified time): *six months gone.* **8.** (usually foll. by *on*) *Sl.* in love (with).

goner ('gɒnə) *n. Sl.* a person or thing beyond help or recovery, esp. a person who is about to die.

gonfalon ('gɒnfələn) *n.* **1.** a banner hanging from a crossbar, used esp. by certain medieval Italian republics. **2.** a battle flag suspended crosswise on a staff, usually having a serrated edge.

gong (gɒŋ) *n.* **1.** a percussion instrument consisting of a metal platelike disc struck with a soft-headed drumstick. **2.** a rimmed metal disc, hollow metal hemisphere, or metal strip, tube, or wire that produces a note when struck. **3.** a fixed saucer-shaped bell, as on an alarm clock, struck by a mechanically operated hammer. **4.** *Brit. sl.* a medal, esp. a military one. ~*vb.* **5.** (*intr.*) to sound a gong. **6.** (*tr.*) (of traffic police) to summon (a driver) to stop by sounding a gong.

gonorrhoea *or esp. U.S.* **gonorrhea** (‚gɒnə'rɪə) *n.* an infectious venereal disease characterized by a discharge of mucus and pus from the urethra or vagina. —‚**gonor-'rhoeal** *or esp. U.S.* ‚**gonor'rheal** *adj.*

-gony *n. combining form.* genesis, origin, or production: *cosmogony.*

goo (gu:) *n. Inf.* **1.** a sticky substance. **2.** coy or sentimental language or ideas.

good (gʊd) *adj.* **better, best.** **1.** having admirable, pleasing, superior, or positive qualities; not negative, bad, or mediocre: *a good teacher.* **2. a.** morally excellent or admirable; virtuous; righteous: *a good man.* **b.** (*as collective n.* preceded by *the*): *the good.* **3.** suitable or efficient for a purpose: *a good winter coat.* **4.** beneficial or advantageous: *vegetables are good for you.* **5.** not ruined or decayed: *the meat is still good.* **6.** kindly or approving: *you are good to him.* **7.** valid or genuine: *I would not do this without good reason.* **8.** honourable or held in high esteem: *a good family.* **9.** financially secure, sound, or safe: *a good investment.* **10.** (of a draft, etc.) drawn for a stated sum. **11.** (of debts) expected to be fully paid. **12.** clever, competent, or talented: *he's good at science.* **13.** obedient or well-behaved: *a good dog.* **14.** reliable, safe, or recommended: *a good make of clothes.* **15.** affording material pleasure: *the good life.* **16.** having a well-proportioned or generally fine appearance: *a good figure.* **17.** complete; full: *I took a good ten minutes to reach the house.* **18.** propitious; opportune: *a good time to ask for a rise.* **19.** satisfying or gratifying: *a good rest.* **20.** comfortable: *did you have a good night?* **21.** newest or of the best quality: *keep the good plates for guests.* **22.** fairly large, extensive, or long: *a good distance away.* **23.** sufficient; ample: *we have a good supply of food.* **24. a good one. a.** an unbelievable assertion. **b.** a very funny joke. **25. as good as.** virtually; practically: *it's as good as finished.* **26. good and.** *Inf.* (intensifier): *good and mad.* ~*interj.* **27.** an exclamation of approval, agreement, pleasure, etc. ~*n.* **28.** moral or material advantage or use; benefit or profit: *for the good of our workers; what is the good of worrying?* **29.** positive moral qualities; goodness; virtue; righteousness; piety. **30.** (*sometimes cap.*) the force that controls or effects positive moral qualities or virtue: *Good at work in the world.* **31.** a good thing. **32. for good (and all).** forever; permanently: *I have left them for good.* **33. make good. a.** to recompense or repair damage or injury. **b.** to be successful. **c.** to prove the truth of (a statement or accusation). **d.** to secure and retain (a position). **e.** to effect or fulfil (something intended or promised). **34. good on you.** *Austral. & N.Z.* well done, well said, etc.: a term of congratulation. ~See also **goods.** —'**goodish** *adj.*

▷ **Usage.** Careful speakers and writers of English do not use *good* and *bad* as adverbs: *she dances well* (not *good*);

THESAURUS

gone 1. elapsed, ended, finished, over, past **2.** absent, astray, away, lacking, lost, missing, vanished **3.** dead, deceased, defunct, departed, extinct, no more **4.** consumed, done, finished, spent, used up

good *adj.* **1.** acceptable, admirable, agreeable, capital, choice, commendable, excellent, fine, first-class, first-rate, great, pleasant, pleasing, positive, precious, satisfactory, splendid, super (*Inf.*), superior, tiptop, valuable, worthy **2.** admirable, estimable, ethical, exemplary, honest, honourable, moral, praiseworthy, right, righteous, upright, virtuous, worthy **3.** able, accomplished, adept, adroit, capable, clever, competent, dexterous, efficient, expert, first-rate, proficient, reliable, satisfactory, serviceable, skilled,

sound, suitable, talented, thorough, trustworthy, useful **4.** adequate, advantageous, auspicious, beneficial, convenient, favourable, fit, fitting, healthy, helpful, opportune, profitable, propitious, salubrious, salutary, suitable, useful, wholesome **5.** eatable, fit to eat, sound, uncorrupted, untainted, whole **6.** altruistic, approving, beneficent, benevolent, charitable, friendly, gracious, humane, kind, kind-hearted, kindly, merciful, obliging, well-disposed **7.** authentic, bona fide, dependable, genuine, honest, legitimate, proper, real, reliable, sound, true, trustworthy, valid **8.** decorous, dutiful, mannerly, obedient, orderly, polite, proper, seemly, well-behaved, well-mannered **9.** agreeable, cheerful, congenial, convivial, enjoyable, gratifying, happy, pleas-

ant, pleasing, pleasurable, satisfying **10.** adequate, ample, complete, considerable, entire, extensive, full, large, long, sizable, solid, substantial, sufficient, whole **11.** best, fancy, finest, newest, nicest, precious, smartest, special, valuable **12.** *Of weather* balmy, bright, calm, clear, clement, cloudless, fair, halcyon, mild, sunny, sunshiny, tranquil ~*n.* **13.** advantage, avail, behalf, benefit, gain, interest, profit, service, use, usefulness, welfare, wellbeing, worth **14.** excellence, goodness, merit, morality, probity, rectitude, right, righteousness, uprightness, virtue, worth **15. for good** finally, for ever, irrevocably, never to return, once and for all, permanently, *sine die*

he sings really badly (not *really bad*).

Good Book *n.* a name for the **Bible**.

goodbye (ˌgud'baɪ) *sentence substitute.* **1.** farewell: a conventional expression used at leave-taking or parting with people. *~n.* **2.** a leave-taking; parting: *they prolonged their goodbyes.* **3.** a farewell: *they said goodbyes to each other.*

good day *sentence substitute.* a conventional expression of greeting or farewell used during the day.

good-for-nothing *n.* **1.** an irresponsible or worthless person. *~adj.* **2.** irresponsible; worthless.

Good Friday *n.* the Friday before Easter, observed as a commemoration of the Crucifixion of Jesus.

goodies ('gudɪz) *pl. n.* **1.** any food or foods considered a special delight. **2.** a choice selection of an item or collection.

goodly ('gudlɪ) *adj.* **-lier, -liest.** **1.** considerable: *a goodly amount of money.* **2.** attractive, pleasing, or fine. **—'goodliness** *n.*

good morning *sentence substitute.* a conventional expression of greeting or farewell used in the morning.

goodness ('gudnɪs) *n.* **1.** the state or quality of being good. **2.** generosity; kindness. **3.** moral excellence; piety; virtue. **4.** what is good in something; essence. *~interj.* **5.** a euphemism for **God:** used as an exclamation of surprise.

good night *sentence substitute.* a conventional expression of farewell, used in the evening or at night, esp. when departing to bed.

goods (gudz) *pl. n.* **1.** possessions and personal property. **2.** (*sometimes sing.*) *Econ.* commodities that are tangible, usually movable, and generally not consumed at the same time as they are produced. **3.** articles of commerce; merchandise. **4.** *Chiefly Brit.* **a.** merchandise when transported, esp. by rail; freight. **b.** (*as modifier*): *a goods train.* **5.** *Sl.* that which is expected: *to deliver the goods.* **6. the goods.** *Sl.* the real thing. **7.** *U.S. sl.* incriminating evidence (esp. in **have the goods on someone**).

Good Samaritan *n.* **1.** *New Testament.* a figure in one of Christ's parables (Luke 10:30–37) who is an example of compassion towards those in distress. **2.** a kindly person who helps another in difficulty or distress.

Good Shepherd *n. New Testament.* a title given to Jesus Christ in John 10:11–12.

good-tempered *adj.* of a kindly and generous disposition.

good turn *n.* a helpful and friendly act; good deed; favour.

good will *n.* **1.** benevolence; kindliness. **2.** willingness or acquiescence. **3.** an intangible asset of an enterprise reflecting its commercial reputation, customer connections, etc.

goody[1] ('gudɪ) *interj.* **1.** a child's exclamation of pleasure. *~n., pl.* **goodies.** **2.** short for **goody-goody.** **3.** *Inf.* the hero in a film, book, etc.

goody[2] ('gudɪ) *n., pl.* **goodies.** *Arch., literary.* a married woman of low rank: used as a title: *Goody Two-Shoes.*

goody-goody *n., pl.* **-goodies.** **1.** *Inf.* a smugly virtuous or sanctimonious person. *~adj.* **2.** smug and sanctimonious.

gooey ('guːɪ) *adj.* **gooier, gooiest.** *Inf.* **1.** sticky, soft, and often sweet. **2.** oversweet and sentimental.

goof (guːf) *Inf.* *~n.* **1.** a foolish error. **2.** a stupid person. *~vb.* **3.** to bungle (something); botch. **4.** (*intr.; of-*

ten foll. by *about* or *around*) to fool (around); mess (about).

go off *vb.* (*intr.*) **1.** (*adv.*) (of power, a water supply, etc.) to cease to be available or functioning: *the lights suddenly went off.* **2.** (*adv.*) to explode. **3.** (*adv.*) to occur as specified: *the meeting went off well.* **4.** to leave (a place): *the actors went off stage.* **5.** (*adv.*) (of a sensation) to gradually cease to be felt. **6.** (*adv.*) to fall asleep. **7.** (*adv.*) (of concrete, mortar, etc.) to harden. **8.** (*adv.*) *Brit. inf.* (of food, etc.) to become stale or rotten. **9.** (*prep.*) *Brit. inf.* to cease to like.

goofy ('guːfɪ) *adj.* **goofier, goofiest.** *Inf.* foolish; silly. **—'goofily** *adv.* **—'goofiness** *n.*

googly ('guːglɪ) *n., pl.* **-lies.** *Cricket.* an off break bowled with a leg break action.

goon (guːn) *n.* **1.** a stupid or deliberately foolish person. **2.** *U.S. inf.* a thug hired to commit acts of violence or intimidation, esp. in an industrial dispute.

go on *vb.* (*intr., mostly adv.*) **1.** to continue or proceed. **2.** to happen or take place: *there's something peculiar going on here.* **3.** (*prep.*) to ride on, esp. as a treat: *children love to go on donkeys at the seaside.* **4.** *Theatre.* to make an entrance on stage. **5.** to talk excessively; chatter. **6.** to continue talking, esp. after a short pause. **7.** to criticize or nag: *stop going on at me all the time! ~interj.* **8.** I don't believe what you're saying.

goosander (guːˈsændə) *n.* a common merganser (a duck) of Europe and North America, having a dark head and white body in the male.

goose[1] (guːs) *n., pl.* **geese.** **1.** any of various web-footed long-necked birds typically larger and less aquatic than ducks. They are gregarious and migratory. **2.** the female of such a bird, as opposed to the male (gander). **3.** *Inf.* a silly person. **4.** (*pl.* **gooses**). a pressing iron with a long curving handle, used esp. by tailors. **5.** the flesh of the goose, used as food. **6. cook one's goose.** *Inf.* to spoil one's chances or plans completely.

goose[2] (guːs) *U.S. sl.* *~vb.* **1.** (*tr.*) to prod (a person) playfully in the behind. *~n., pl.* **gooses.** **2.** such a prod.

gooseberry ('guzbərɪ, -brɪ) *n., pl.* **-ries.** **1.** a Eurasian shrub having ovoid yellow-green or red-purple berries. **2. a.** the berry of this plant. **b.** (*as modifier*): *gooseberry jam.* **3.** *Brit. inf.* an unwanted single person, esp. a third person with a couple (often in **play gooseberry**).

goose flesh *n.* the bumpy condition of the skin induced by cold, fear, etc., caused by contraction of the muscles at the base of the hair follicles with consequent erection of papillae. Also called: **goose bumps, goose pimples, goose skin.**

goosegog ('guzgɒg) *n. Brit.* a dialect word for **gooseberry.**

goose step *n.* **1.** a military march step in which the leg is swung rigidly to an exaggerated height. *~vb.* **goose-step, -stepping, -stepped.** **2.** (*intr.*) to march in goose step.

go out *vb.* (*intr., adv.*) **1.** to depart from a room, house, country, etc. **2.** to cease to illuminate, burn, or function: *the fire has gone out.* **3.** to cease to be fashionable or popular: *that style went out ages ago!* **4.** (of a broadcast) to be transmitted. **5.** to go to entertainments, social functions, etc. **6.** (usually foll. by *with* or *together*) to associate (with a person of the opposite sex) regularly; date. **7.** (of workers) to begin to strike. **8.** *Card games, etc.* to get rid of the last card, token, etc., in one's hand.

go over *vb.* (*intr.*) **1.** to be received in a specified manner: *the concert went over very well.* **2.** (*prep.*)

THESAURUS

goodbye adieu, farewell, leave-taking, parting

good-for-nothing 1. *n.* black sheep, idler, layabout, ne'er-do-well, profligate, rapscallion, scapegrace, waster, wastrel 2. *adj.* feckless, idle, irresponsible, useless, worthless

good-humoured affable, amiable, cheerful, congenial, genial, good-tempered, happy, pleasant

good-looking attractive, comely, fair, handsome, personable, pretty, well-favoured

goodly 1. ample, considerable, large, significant, sizable, substantial, tidy (*Inf.*) 2. agreeable, attractive, comely, desirable, elegant, fine, good-looking, graceful, handsome, personable, pleasant, pleasing, well-

favoured

good-natured agreeable, benevolent, friendly, good-hearted, helpful, kind, kindly, tolerant, warm-hearted, well-disposed, willing to please

goodness 1. excellence, merit, quality, superiority, value, worth 2. beneficence, benevolence, friendliness, generosity, good will, graciousness, humaneness, kind-heartedness, kindliness, kindness, mercy, obligingness 3. honesty, honour, integrity, merit, morality, probity, rectitude, righteousness, uprightness, virtue 4. advantage, benefit, nourishment, nutrition, salubriousness, wholesomeness

goods 1. appurtenances, belongings, chattels, effects, furnishings, furniture, gear,

movables, paraphernalia, possessions, property, things, trappings 2. commodities, merchandise, stock, stuff, wares

good will amity, benevolence, favour, friendliness, friendship, heartiness, kindliness, zeal

go off 1. blow up, detonate, explode, fire 2. happen, occur, take place, 3. decamp, depart, go away, leave, move out, part, quit, 4. *Inf.* go bad, go stale, rot

go on 1. continue, endure, happen, last, occur, persist, proceed, stay 2. blether, carry on, chatter, prattle, ramble on, waffle, witter (on) (*Inf.*)

go out 1. depart, exit, leave 2. be extinguished, die out, expire, fade out

Also: **go through.** to examine and revise as necessary: *he went over the accounts.* **3.** (*prep.*) to check and repair: *can you go over my car please?* **4.** (*prep.*) Also: **go through.** to rehearse: *I'll go over my lines before the play.*

gopher ('gəʊfə) *n.* **1.** Also called: **pocket gopher.** a burrowing rodent of North and Central America, having a thickset body, short legs, and cheek pouches. **2.** a burrowing tortoise of SE North America.

Gordian knot ('gɔːdɪən) *n.* **1.** (in Greek legend) a complicated knot, tied by King Gordius of Phrygia, that Alexander the Great cut with a sword. **2.** a complicated and intricate problem (esp. in **cut the Gordian knot**).

gore¹ (gɔː) *n.* **1.** blood shed from a wound, esp. when coagulated. **2.** *Inf.* killing, fighting, etc.

gore² (gɔː) *vb.* (*tr.*) (of an animal, such as a bull) to pierce or stab (a person or another animal) with a horn or tusk.

gore³ (gɔː) *n.* **1.** a tapering or triangular piece of material used in making a shaped skirt, umbrella, etc. ~*vb.* **2.** (*tr.*) to make into or with a gore or gores.

gorge (gɔːdʒ) *n.* **1.** a deep ravine, esp. one through which a river runs. **2.** the contents of the stomach. **3.** feelings of disgust or resentment (esp. in **one's gorge rises**). **4.** an obstructing mass: *an ice gorge.* **5.** *Fortifications.* a narrow passage at the back of an outwork. **6.** *Arch.* the throat or gullet. ~*vb.* **7.** to swallow (food) ravenously. **8.** (*tr.*) to stuff (oneself) with food.

gorgeous ('gɔːdʒəs) *adj.* **1.** strikingly beautiful or magnificent: *gorgeous array; a gorgeous girl.* **2.** *Inf.* extremely pleasing, fine, or good: *gorgeous weather.* —'**gorgeously** *adv.* —'**gorgeousness** *n.*

Gorgon ('gɔːgən) *n.* **1.** *Greek myth.* any of three winged monstrous sisters who had live snakes for hair, huge teeth, and brazen claws. **2.** (*often not cap.*) *Inf.* a fierce or unpleasant woman.

Gorgonzola (ˌgɔːgən'zəʊlə) *n.* a semihard blue-veined cheese of sharp flavour, made from pressed milk.

gorilla (gə'rɪlə) *n.* **1.** the largest anthropoid ape, inhabiting the forests of central W Africa. It is stocky with a short muzzle and coarse dark hair. **2.** *Inf.* a large, strong, and brutal-looking man.

gormless ('gɔːmlɪs) *adj. Brit. inf.* stupid; dull.

go round *vb.* (*intr.*) **1.** (*adv.*) to be sufficient: *are there enough sweets to go round?* **2.** to circulate (in): *measles is going round the school.* **3.** to be long enough to encircle: *will that belt go round you?*

gorse (gɔːs) *n.* an evergreen shrub which has yellow flowers and thick green spines instead of leaves. Also called: **furze, whin.** —'**gorsy** *adj.*

gory ('gɔːrɪ) *adj.* **gorier, goriest. 1.** horrific or bloodthirsty: *a gory story.* **2.** involving bloodshed and killing: *a gory battle.* **3.** covered in gore. —'**gorily** *adv.* —'**goriness** *n.*

gosh (gɒʃ) *interj.* an exclamation of mild surprise or wonder.

goshawk ('gɒs,hɔːk) *n.* a large hawk of Europe, Asia, and North America, having a bluish-grey back and wings and paler underparts: used in falconry.

gosling ('gɒzlɪŋ) *n.* **1.** a young goose. **2.** an inexperienced or youthful person.

go-slow *n.* **1.** *Brit.* a deliberate slackening of the rate of production by organized labour as a tactic in industrial conflict. U.S. equivalent: **slowdown.** ~*vb.* **go slow. 2.** (*intr.*) to work deliberately slowly as a tactic in industrial conflict.

gospel ('gɒspəl) *n.* **1.** Also called: **gospel truth.** an unquestionable truth: *to take someone's word as gospel.* **2.** a doctrine maintained to be of great importance. **3.** Black religious music originating in the churches of the Southern states of the United States. **4.** the message or doctrine of a religious teacher. **5. a.** the story of Christ's life and teachings as narrated in the Gospels. **b.** the good news of salvation in Jesus Christ. **c.** (*as modifier*): *the gospel story.*

Gospel ('gɒspəl) *n.* **1.** any of the first four books of the New Testament, namely Matthew, Mark, Luke, and John. **2.** a reading from one of these in a religious service.

gossamer ('gɒsəmə) *n.* **1.** a gauze or silk fabric of the very finest texture. **2.** a filmy cobweb often seen on foliage or floating in the air. **3.** anything resembling gossamer in fineness or filminess.

gossip ('gɒsɪp) *n.* **1.** casual and idle chat. **2.** a conversation involving malicious chatter or rumours about other people. **3.** Also called: **gossipmonger.** a person who habitually talks about others, esp. maliciously. **4.** light easy communication: *to write a letter full of gossip.* **5.** *Arch.* a close woman friend. ~*vb.* **6.** (*intr.*; often foll. by *about*) to talk casually or maliciously (about other people). —'**gossiper** *n.* —'**gossipy** *adj.*

got (gɒt) *vb.* **1.** the past tense or past participle of **get.** **2. have got. a.** to possess. **b.** (*takes an infinitive*) used as an auxiliary to express compulsion: *I've got to get a new coat.*

Goth (gɒθ) *n.* **1.** a member of an East Germanic people from Scandinavia who invaded many parts of the Roman Empire from the 3rd to the 5th century. **2.** a rude or barbaric person.

Gothic ('gɒθɪk) *adj.* **1.** denoting, relating to, or resembling the style of architecture that was used in W Europe from the 12th to the 16th centuries, characterized by the lancet arch, the ribbed vault, and the flying buttress. **2.** (*sometimes not cap.*) of or relating to a literary style characterized by gloom, the grotesque, and the supernatural, popular esp. in the late 18th century. **3.** of, relating to, or characteristic of the Goths or their language. **4.** (*sometimes not cap.*) primitive and barbarous in style, behaviour, etc. **5.** of or relating to the Middle Ages. ~*n.* **6.** Gothic architecture or art. **7.** the extinct language of the ancient Goths; East Germanic. **8.** Also called (esp. Brit): **black letter.** the family of heavy script typefaces in use from about the 15th to 18th centuries. —'**Gothically** *adv.* —'**Gothi,cism** *n.*

go through *vb.* (*intr.*) **1.** (*adv.*) to be approved or accepted: *the amendment went through.* **2.** (*prep.*) to consume; exhaust: *we went through our supplies in a day.* **3.** (*prep.*) Also: **go over.** to examine: *he went through the figures.* **4.** (*prep.*) to suffer: *she went through tremendous pain.* **5.** (*prep.*) Also: **go over.** to rehearse: *let's just go through the details again.* **6.** (*prep.*) to search: *she went through the cupboards.* **7.** (*adv.*; foll by *with*) to bring to a successful conclusion, often by persistence.

go together *vb.* (*intr., adv.*) **1.** to be mutually suited; harmonize: *the colours go well together.* **2.** *Inf.* (of two people of opposite sex) to associate frequently with each other: *they had been going together for two years.*

gotten ('gɒtən) *vb. U.S.* the past participle of **get.**

gouache (gʊ'ɑːʃ) *n.* **1.** Also called: **body colour.** a painting technique using opaque watercolour in which the pigments are bound with glue. **2.** the paint used in this technique. **3.** a painting done by this method.

Gouda ('gaʊdə) *n.* a large flat round Dutch cheese, orig. made in the town of Gouda, mild and similar in taste to Edam.

gouge (gaʊdʒ) *vb.* (*mainly tr.*) **1.** (usually foll. by *out*) to scoop or force (something) out of its position. **2.** (some-

---

THESAURUS

go over 1. examine, inspect, rehearse, reiterate, review, revise, study **2.** peruse, read, scan, skim

gorge¹ *n.* canyon, cleft, clough (*Dialect*), defile, fissure, pass, ravine

gorge² *v.* bolt, cram, devour, feed, fill, glut, gobble, gormandize, gulp, guzzle, overeat, raven, sate, satiate, stuff, surfeit, swallow, wolf

gorgeous 1. beautiful, brilliant, dazzling, elegant, glittering, grand, luxuriant, magnificent, opulent, ravishing, resplendent, showy, splendid, stunning (*Inf.*), sumptuous, superb **2.** *Inf.* attractive, bright, delightful, enjoyable, exquisite, fine, glorious, good, good-looking,

lovely, pleasing

gory blood-soaked, bloodstained, bloodthirsty, bloody, ensanguined (*Literary*), murderous, sanguinary

gospel 1. certainty, fact, the last word, truth, verity **2.** credo, creed, doctrine, message, news, revelation, tidings

gossamer *adj.* airy, delicate, diaphanous, fine, flimsy, gauzy, light, sheer, silky, thin, transparent

gossip *n.* **1.** blether, chinwag (*Brit. inf.*), chitchat, clishmaclaver (*Scot.*), hearsay, idle talk, jaw (*Sl.*), newsmongering (*Old-fashioned*), prattle, scandal, small talk, tittle-

tattle **2.** babbler, blatherskite, blether, busybody, chatterbox (*Inf.*), chatterer, flibbertigibbet, gossipmonger, newsmonger (*Old-fashioned*), prattler, quidnunc, scandalmonger, tattler, telltale ~*v.* **3.** blather, blether, chat, gabble, jaw (*Sl.*), prate, prattle, tattle

go through 1. bear, brave, endure, experience, suffer, tolerate, undergo, withstand **2.** consume, exhaust, squander, use **3.** check, examine, explore, hunt, look, search

times foll. by *out*) to cut (a hole or groove) in (something) with a sharp instrument or tool. **3.** *U.S. inf.* to extort from. **4.** (*intr.*) *Austral.* to dig for (opal). ~*n.* **5.** a type of chisel with a blade that has a concavo-convex section. **6.** a mark or groove made as with a gouge. **7.** *U.S. inf.* extortion; swindling. —'**gouger** *n.*

goulash ('guːlæʃ) *n.* **1.** Also called: **Hungarian goulash.** a rich stew, originating in Hungary, made of beef, lamb, or veal highly seasoned with paprika. **2.** *Bridge.* a method of dealing in threes and fours without first shuffling the cards, to produce freak hands.

go up *vb.* (*intr., mainly adv.*) **1.** (*also prep.*) to move or lead as to a higher place or level; rise; increase: *prices are always going up.* **2.** to be destroyed: *the house went up in flames.* **3.** *Brit.* to go or return (to college or university).

gourd (guəd) *n.* **1.** the fruit of any of various plants of the cucumber family, esp. the bottle gourd and some squashes, whose dried shells are used for ornament, drinking cups, etc. **2.** any plant that bears this fruit. **3.** a bottle or flask made from the dried shell of the bottle gourd.

gourmand ('guəmənd) *or* **gormand** *n.* a person devoted to eating and drinking, esp. to excess. —'**gourmand,ism** *n.*

gourmandise *or* **-dize** (ˌgɔːmənˈdiːz) *n.* a love of and taste for good food.

gourmet ('guəmeɪ) *n.* a person who cultivates a discriminating palate for the enjoyment of good food and drink.

gout (gaut) *n.* **1.** a metabolic disease characterized by painful inflammation of certain joints, esp. of the big toe, caused by deposits of sodium urate. **2.** *Arch.* a drop or splash, esp. of blood. —'**gouty** *adj.* —'**goutily** *adv.* —'**goutiness** *n.*

Gov. *or* **gov.** *abbrev. for:* **1.** government. **2.** governor.

govern ('gʌvən) *vb.* (*mainly tr.*) **1.** (*also intr.*) to direct and control the actions, affairs, policies, functions, etc., of (an organization, nation, etc.); rule. **2.** to exercise restraint over; regulate or direct: *to govern one's temper.* **3.** to decide or determine (something): *his injury governed his decision to avoid sports.* **4.** to control the speed of an (engine, machine, etc.) using a governor. **5.** (of a word) to determine the inflection of (another word): *Latin nouns govern adjectives that modify them.* —'**governable** *adj.*

governance ('gʌvənəns) *n.* **1.** government, control, or authority. **2.** the action, manner, or system of governing.

governess ('gʌvənɪs) *n.* a woman teacher employed in a private household to teach and train the children.

government ('gʌvənmənt) *n.* **1.** the exercise of political authority over the actions, affairs, etc., of a political unit, people, etc.; the action of governing; political rule and administration. **2.** the system or form by which a community, etc., is ruled: *tyrannical government.* **3. a.** the executive policy-making body of a political unit, community, etc.; ministry or administration. **b.** (*cap. when of a specific country*): *the British Government.* **4. a.** the state and its administration: *blame it on the government.* **b.** (*as modifier*): *a government agency.* **5.** regulation; direction. **6.** *Grammar.* the determination of the form of one word by another word. —**governmental** (ˌgʌvənˈmɛntəl) *adj.* —ˌgovern'mentally *adv.*

governor ('gʌvənə) *n.* **1.** a person who governs. **2.** the ruler or chief magistrate of a colony, province, etc. **3.** the representative of the Crown in a British colony. **4.** *Brit.* the senior administrator of a society, prison, etc. **5.** the chief executive of any state in the U.S. **6.** a device that controls the speed of an engine, esp. by regulating the supply of fuel. **7.** *Brit. inf.* a name or title of respect to a father, employer, etc. —'**governor,ship** *n.*

governor general *n., pl.* **governors general** *or* **governor generals. 1.** the representative of the Crown in a dominion of the Commonwealth or a British colony; vicegerent. **2.** *Brit.* a governor with jurisdiction or precedence over other governors. —ˌgovernor-'general-ˌship *n.*

Govt. *or* **govt.** *abbrev. for* government.

go with *vb.* (*intr., prep.*) **1.** to accompany. **2.** to blend or harmonize: *that new wallpaper goes well with the furniture.* **3.** to be a normal part of: *three acres of land go with the house.* **4.** (of two people of the opposite sex) to associate frequently with each other.

go without *vb.* (*intr.*) *Chiefly Brit.* to be denied or deprived of (something, esp. food): *if you don't like your tea you can go without.*

gown (gaun) *n.* **1.** any of various outer garments, such as a woman's elegant or formal dress, a dressing robe, or a protective garment, esp. one worn by surgeons during operations. **2.** a loose wide garment indicating status, such as worn by academics. **3.** the members of a university as opposed to the other residents of the university town. ~*vb.* **4.** (*tr.*) to supply with or dress in a gown.

goy (gɔɪ) *n., pl.* **goyim** ('gɔɪɪm) *or* **goys.** *Sl.* a derogatory word used by Jews for a non-Jew. —'**goyish** *adj.*

G.P. *abbrev. for:* **1.** general practitioner. **2.** Gallup poll. **3.** (in Britain) graduated pension. **4.** Grand Prix. **5.** *Music.* general pause.

G.P.O. *abbrev. for* general post office.

Gr. *abbrev. for:* **1.** Grecian. **2.** Greece. **3.** Greek.

grab (græb) *vb.* **grabbing, grabbed. 1.** to seize hold of (something). **2.** (*tr.*) to seize illegally or unscrupulously. **3.** (*tr.*) to arrest; catch. **4.** (*tr.*) *Inf.* to catch the attention or interest of; impress. ~*n.* **5.** the act or an instance of grabbing. **6.** a mechanical device for gripping objects, esp. the hinged jaws of a mechanical excavator. **7.** something that is grabbed. —'**grabber** *n.*

grace (greɪs) *n.* **1.** elegance and beauty of movement, form, expression, or proportion. **2.** a pleasing or charming quality. **3.** goodwill or favour. **4.** a delay granted for the completion of a task or payment of a debt. **5.** a sense of propriety and consideration for others. **6.** (*pl.*) **a.** affectation of manner (esp. in **airs and graces**). **b. in (someone's) good graces.** regarded favourably and with kindness by (someone). **7.** mercy; clemency. **8.** *Christian theol.* **a.** the free and unmerited favour of God shown towards man. **b.** the divine assistance given to man in spiritual rebirth. **c.** the condition of being favoured or sanctified by God. **d.** an unmerited gift, favour, etc., granted by God. **9.** a short prayer recited before or after a meal to give thanks for it. **10.** *Music.* a melodic ornament or decoration. **11. with (a) bad grace.** unwillingly or grudgingly. **12. with (a) good grace.** willingly or cheerfully. ~*vb.* **13.** (*tr.*) to add elegance and beauty to: *flowers graced the room.* **14.** (*tr.*) to honour or favour: *to grace a party with one's presence.* **15.** to ornament or decorate (a melody, part, etc.) with nonessential notes. —'**graceless** *adj.*

go under default, die, drown, fail, fold (*Inf.*), founder, go down, sink, submerge, succumb

govern 1. administer, be in power, command, conduct, control, direct, guide, hold sway, lead, manage, order, oversee, pilot, reign, rule, steer, superintend, supervise **2.** bridle, check, contain, control, curb, direct, discipline, get the better of, hold in check, inhibit, master, regulate, restrain, subdue, tame **3.** decide, determine, guide, influence, rule, sway, underlie

government 1. administration, authority, dominion, execution, governance, law, polity, rule, sovereignty, state, statecraft **2.** administration, executive, ministry, powers-that-be, regime **3.** authority, command, control, direction, domination, guidance, man-agement, regulation, restraint, superintendence, supervision, sway

governor administrator, boss (*Inf.*), chief, commander, comptroller, controller, director, executive, head, leader, manager, overseer, ruler, superintendent, supervisor

go with accompany, agree, blend, complement, concur, correspond, fit, harmonize, match, suit

go without abstain, be denied, be deprived of, deny oneself, do without, go short, lack, want

gown costume, dress, frock, garb, garment, habit, robe

grab bag, capture, catch, catch *or* take hold of, clutch, grasp, grip, latch on to, nab (*Inf.*), pluck, seize, snap up, snatch

grace *n.* **1.** attractiveness, beauty, charm, comeliness, ease, elegance, finesse, gracefulness, loveliness, pleasantness, poise, polish, refinement, shapeliness, tastefulness **2.** benefaction, beneficence, benevolence, favour, generosity, goodness, good will, kindliness, kindness **3.** breeding, consideration, cultivation, decency, decorum, etiquette, mannerliness, manners, propriety, tact **4.** charity, clemency, compassion, forgiveness, indulgence, leniency, lenity, mercy, pardon, quarter, reprieve **5.** benediction, blessing, prayer, thanks, thanksgiving ~*v.* **6.** adorn, beautify, bedeck, deck, decorate, dignify, distinguish, elevate, embellish, enhance, enrich, favour, garnish, glorify, honour, ornament, set off

Grace (greis) *n.* (preceded by *your, his,* or *her*) a title used to address or refer to a duke, duchess, or archbishop.

grace-and-favour *n.* (*modifier*) *Brit.* (of a house, flat, etc.) owned by the sovereign and granted free of rent to a person to whom the sovereign wishes to express gratitude.

graceful ('greisful) *adj.* characterized by beauty of movement, style, form, etc. —**'gracefully** *adv.* —**'gracefulness** *n.*

grace note *n. Music.* a note printed in small type to indicate that it is melodically and harmonically nonessential.

Graces ('greisiz) *pl. n. Greek myth.* three sister goddesses, givers of charm and beauty.

gracious ('greiʃəs) *adj.* 1. characterized by or showing kindness and courtesy. 2. condescendingly courteous, benevolent, or indulgent. 3. characterized by or suitable for a life of elegance, ease, and indulgence: *gracious living.* 4. merciful or compassionate. ~*interj.* 5. an expression of mild surprise or wonder. —**'graciously** *adv.* —**'graciousness** *n.*

gradation (grə'deiʃən) *n.* 1. a series of systematic stages; gradual progression. 2. (*often pl.*) a stage or degree in such a series or progression. 3. the act or process of arranging or forming in stages, grades, etc., or of progressing evenly. 4. (in painting, drawing, or sculpture) transition from one colour, tone, or surface to another through a series of very slight changes. 5. *Linguistics.* any change in the quality or length of a vowel within a word indicating certain distinctions, such as inflectional or tense differentiations. See **ablaut.** —**gra'dational** *adj.* —**gra'dationally** *adv.*

grade (greid) *n.* 1. a position or degree in a scale, as of quality, rank, size, or progression: *high-grade timber.* 2. a group of people or things of the same category. 3. *Chiefly U.S.* a military or other rank. 4. a stage in a course of progression. 5. a mark or rating indicating achievement or the worth of work done, as at school. 6. *U.S.* a unit of pupils of similar age or ability taught together at school. 7. **make the grade.** *Inf.* **a.** to reach the required standard. **b.** to succeed. ~*vb.* 8. (*tr.*) to arrange according to quality, rank, etc. 9. (*tr.*) to determine the grade of or assign a grade to. 10. (*intr.*) to achieve or deserve a grade or rank. 11. to change or blend (something) gradually; merge. 12. (*tr.*) to level (ground, a road, etc.) to a suitable gradient.

-grade *adj. combining form.* indicating a kind or manner of movement or progression: *plantigrade; retrograde.*

gradient ('greidiənt) *n.* 1. Also called (esp. U.S.): **grade.** a part of a railway, road, etc., that slopes upwards or downwards; inclination. 2. Also called (esp. U.S.): **grade.** a measure of such a slope, esp. the ratio of the vertical distance between two points on the slope to the horizontal distance between them. 3. *Physics.* a measure of the change of some physical quantity, such as temperature or electric potential, over a specified distance. 4. *Maths.* (of a curve) the slope of the tangent at any point on a curve with respect to the horizontal axis. ~*adj.* 5. sloping uniformly.

gradual ('grædjuəl) *adj.* 1. occurring, developing, moving, etc., in small stages: *a gradual improvement in health.* 2. not steep or abrupt: *a gradual slope.* ~*n.* 3. (*often cap.*) *Christianity.* **a.** an antiphon usually from the Psalms, sung or recited immediately after the epistle at Mass. **b.** a book of plainsong containing the words and music of the parts of the Mass that are sung by the cantors and choir. —**'gradually** *adv.* —**'gradualness** *n.*

gradualism ('grædjuə,lizəm) *n.* 1. the policy of seeking to change something gradually, esp. in politics. 2. the theory that explains major changes in fossils, rock strata, etc., in terms of gradual evolutionary processes rather than sudden violent catastrophes. —**'gradualist** *n., adj.* —**gradual'istic** *adj.*

graduate *n.* ('grædjuit). 1. a person who has been awarded a first degree from a university or college. 2. *U.S.* a student who has completed a course of studies at a high school and received a diploma. ~*vb.* ('grædju,eit). 3. to receive or cause to receive a degree or diploma. 4. *Chiefly U.S.* to confer a degree, diploma, etc. upon. 5. (*tr.*) to mark (a thermometer, flask, etc.) with units of measurement; calibrate. 6. (*tr.*) to arrange or sort into groups according to type, quality, etc. 7. (*intr.;* often foll. by *to*) to change by degrees (from something to something else). —**'gradu,ator** *n.*

graduation (,grædju'eiʃən) *n.* 1. the act of graduating or the state of being graduated. 2. the ceremony at which school or college degrees and diplomas are conferred. 3. a mark or division or all the marks or divisions that indicate measure on an instrument or vessel.

Graeco- or esp. U.S. **Greco-** ('gri:kəʊ-, 'grekəʊ-) *combining form.* Greek: *Graeco-Roman.*

Graeco-Roman or esp. U.S. **Greco-Roman** *adj.* of, characteristic of, or relating to Greek and Roman influences.

graffito (græ'fi:təʊ) *n., pl.* **-ti** (-ti:). 1. *Archaeol.* any inscription or drawing scratched onto a surface, esp. rock or pottery. 2. (*pl.*) drawings, messages, etc., often obscene, scribbled on the walls of public lavatories, advertising posters, etc.

graft¹ (grɑ:ft) *n.* 1. *Horticulture.* **a.** a small piece of plant tissue (the scion) that is made to unite with an established plant (the stock), which supports and nourishes it. **b.** the plant resulting from the union of scion and stock. **c.** the point of union between the scion and the stock. 2. *Surgery.* a piece of tissue transplanted from a donor or from the patient's own body to an area of the body in need of the tissue. 3. the act of joining one thing to another as by grafting. ~*vb.* 4. *Horticulture.* **a.** to induce (a plant or part of a plant) to unite with another part or (of a plant or part of a plant) to unite in this way. **b.** to produce (fruit, flowers, etc.) by this means or (of fruit, etc.) to grow by this means. 5. to transplant (tissue) or (of tissue) to be transplanted. 6. to attach or incorporate or become attached or incorporated: *to graft a happy ending onto a sad tale.* —**'grafter** *n.* —**'grafting** *n.*

graft² (grɑ:ft) *n.* 1. *Inf.* work. (esp. in **hard graft**). 2. **a.** the acquisition of money, power, etc., by dishonest or unfair means, esp. by taking advantage of a position of trust. **b.** something gained in this way. **c.** a payment made to a person profiting by such a practice. ~*vb.* 3. (*intr.*) *Inf.* to work, esp. hard. 4. to acquire by or practise graft. —**'grafter** *n.*

Grail (greil) *n.* see **Holy Grail.**

grain (grein) *n.* 1. the small hard seedlike fruit of a grass, esp. a cereal plant. 2. a mass of such fruits, esp. when gathered for food. 3. the plants, collectively, from which such fruits are harvested. 4. a small hard particle: *a grain of sand.* 5. **a.** the general direction or arrangement of the fibres, layers, or particles in wood, leather, stone, etc. **b.** the pattern or texture resulting from such an arrangement. 6. the relative size of the particles of a substance: *sugar of fine grain.* 7. the granular texture of a rock, mineral, etc. 8. the outer layer of a hide or skin from which the hair or wool has been removed. 9. the smallest unit of weight in the avoirdu-

---

THESAURUS

graceful agile, beautiful, becoming, charming, comely, easy, elegant, fine, flowing, gracile (*Rare*), natural, pleasing, smooth, symmetrical, tasteful

gracious accommodating, affable, amiable, beneficent, benevolent, benign, benignant, charitable, chivalrous, civil, compassionate, considerate, cordial, courteous, courtly, friendly, hospitable, indulgent, kind, kindly, lenient, loving, merciful, mild, obliging, pleasing, polite, well-mannered

grade *n.* 1. brand, category, class, condition, degree, echelon, group, level, mark, notch, order, place, position, quality, rank,

rung, size, stage, station, step 2. **make the grade** *Inf.* come through with flying colours, come up to scratch (*Inf.*), measure up, measure up to expectations, pass muster, prove acceptable, succeed, win through 3. acclivity, bank, declivity, gradient, hill, incline, rise, slope ~*v.* 4. arrange, brand, class, classify, evaluate, group, order, range, rank, rate, sort, value

gradient acclivity, bank, declivity, grade, hill, incline, rise, slope

gradual continuous, even, gentle, graduated, moderate, piecemeal, progressive, regular, slow, steady, successive, unhurried

gradually bit by bit, by degrees, drop by drop, evenly, gently, little by little, moderately, piece by piece, piecemeal, progressively, slowly, steadily, step by step, unhurriedly

graduate *v.* 1. calibrate, grade, mark off, measure out, proportion, regulate 2. arrange, classify, grade, group, order, range, rank, sort

graft 1. *n.* bud, implant, scion, shoot, splice, sprout 2. *v.* affix, implant, ingraft, insert, join, splice, transplant

pois, Troy, and apothecaries' systems: equal to 0.0648 gram. **10.** the threads or direction of threads in a woven fabric. **11.** *Photog.* any of a large number of particles in a photographic emulsion. **12.** cleavage lines in crystalline material. **13.** *Chem.* any of a large number of small crystals forming a solid. **14.** a very small amount: *a grain of truth.* **15.** natural disposition, inclination, or character (esp. in **go against the grain**). **16.** *Astronautics.* a homogenous mass of solid propellant in a form designed to give the required combustion characteristics for a particular rocket. **17.** (*not in technical usage*) kermes or a red dye made from this insect. ~*vb.* (*mainly tr.*) **18.** (*also intr.*) to form grains or cause to form into grains; granulate; crystallize. **19.** to give a granular or roughened appearance or texture to. **20.** to paint, stain, etc., in imitation of the grain of wood or leather. **21. a.** to remove the hair or wool from (a hide or skin) before tanning. **b.** to raise the grain pattern on (leather).

grallatorial (ˌgrælə'tɔːrɪəl) *adj.* of or relating to long-legged wading birds.

gram[1] *or* **gramme** (græm) *n.* a metric unit of mass equal to one thousandth of a kilogram. Abbrev.: g

gram[2] (græm) *n.* **1.** any of several leguminous plants whose seeds are used as food in India. **2.** the seed of any of these plants.

gram. *abbrev. for:* **1.** grammar. **2.** grammatical.

-gram *n. combining form.* indicating a drawing or something written or recorded: *hexagram; telegram.*

gramineous (grə'mɪnɪəs) *adj.* **1.** of, relating to, or belonging to the grass family. **2.** resembling a grass; grasslike. ~Also: **graminaceous** (ˌgræmɪ'neɪʃəs).

graminivorous (ˌgræmɪ'nɪvərəs) *adj.* (of animals) feeding on grass.

grammar ('græmə) *n.* **1.** the branch of linguistics that deals with syntax and morphology, sometimes also phonology and semantics. **2.** the abstract system of rules in terms of which a person's mastery of his native language can be explained. **3.** a systematic description of the grammatical facts of a language. **4.** a book containing an account of the grammatical facts of a language or recommendations as to rules for the proper use of a language. **5.** the use of language with regard to its correctness or social propriety, esp. in syntax: *the teacher told him to watch his grammar.*

grammarian (grə'mɛərɪən) *n.* **1.** a person whose occupation is the study of grammar. **2.** the author of a grammar.

grammar school *n.* **1.** *Brit.* a state-maintained secondary school providing an education with an academic bias. **2.** *U.S.* another term for **elementary school**. **3.** *Austral.* a private school, esp. one controlled by a church. **4.** *N.Z.* a secondary school forming part of the public education system.

grammatical (grə'mætɪkəl) *adj.* **1.** of or relating to grammar. **2.** (of a sentence) well formed; regarded as correct. —**gram'matically** *adv.* —**gram'maticalness** *n.*

gramme (græm) *n.* a variant spelling of **gram**[1].

gramophone ('græmə,fəʊn) *n.* **a.** Also called: **record-player**. a device for reproducing the sounds stored on a record. A stylus vibrates in accordance with the undulations of the walls of the groove in the record as it rotates. U.S. word: **phonograph**. **b.** (*as modifier*): *a gramophone record.*

grampus ('græmpəs) *n., pl.* **-puses. 1.** a widely distributed slaty-grey dolphin with a blunt snout. **2.** another name for **killer whale**.

granary ('grænərɪ; *U.S.* 'greɪnərɪ) *n., pl.* **-ries. 1.** a building for storing threshed grain. **2.** a region that produces a large amount of grain.

grand (grænd) *adj.* **1.** large or impressive in size, extent, or consequence: *grand mountain scenery.* **2.** characterized by or attended with magnificence or display;

sumptuous: *a grand feast.* **3.** of great distinction or pretension; dignified or haughty. **4.** designed to impress: *grand gestures.* **5.** very good; wonderful. **6.** comprehensive; complete: *a grand total.* **7.** worthy of respect; fine: *a grand old man.* **8.** large or impressive in conception or execution: *grand ideas.* **9.** most important; chief: *the grand arena.* ~*n.* **10.** See **grand piano. 11.** (*pl.* **grand**) *Sl.,* chiefly *U.S.* a thousand pounds or dollars. —**'grandly** *adv.* —**'grandness** *n.*

grand- *prefix.* (in designations of kinship) one generation removed in ascent or descent: *grandson; grandfather.*

grandam ('grændəm, -dæm) *or* **grandame** ('grændeɪm, -dəm) *n.* an archaic word for **grandmother**.

grandaunt ('grænd,ɑːnt) *n.* another name for **great-aunt**.

grandchild ('græn,tʃaɪld) *n., pl.* **-children**. the son or daughter of one's child.

granddad ('græn,dæd) *or* **granddaddy** *n., pl.* **-dads** *or* **-daddies**. informal words for **grandfather**.

granddaughter ('græn,dɔːtə) *n.* a daughter of one's son or daughter.

grand duke *n.* **1.** a prince or nobleman who rules a territory, state, or principality. **2.** a son or a male descendant in the male line of a Russian tsar. **3.** a medieval Russian prince who ruled over other princes. —**grand duchess** *fem n.* —**grand duchy** *n.*

grande dame *French.* (grãd 'dam) *n.* a woman regarded as the most experienced, prominent, or venerable member of her profession, etc.

grandee (græn'diː) *n.* a Spanish prince or nobleman of the highest rank.

grandeur ('grændʒə) *n.* **1.** personal greatness, esp. when based on dignity, character, or accomplishments. **2.** magnificence; splendour. **3.** pretentious or bombastic behaviour.

grandfather ('græn,fɑːðə, 'grænd-) *n.* **1.** the father of one's father or mother. **2.** (*often pl.*) a male ancestor. **3.** (*often cap.*) a familiar term of address for an old man.

grandfather clock *n.* any of various types of long-pendulum clocks in tall standing wooden cases.

grandiloquent (græn'dɪləkwənt) *adj.* inflated, pompous, or bombastic in style or expression. —**gran'diloquence** *n.* —**gran'diloquently** *adv.*

grandiose ('grændɪ,əʊs) *adj.* **1.** pretentiously grand or stately. **2.** imposing in conception or execution. —**'grandiosely** *adv.* —**grandiosity** (ˌgrændɪ'ɒsɪtɪ) *n.*

grand jury *n. Law.* (esp. in the U.S.) a jury summoned to enquire into accusations of crime and ascertain whether the evidence is adequate to found an indictment. Abolished in England in 1948.

grandma, ('græn,mɑː) **grandmama,** *or* **grandmamma** ('grænmə,mɑː) *n.* informal words for **grandmother**.

grand mal ('grɒn 'mæl) *n.* a form of epilepsy characterized by loss of consciousness for up to five minutes and violent convulsions. Cf. **petit mal**.

grandmother ('græn,mʌðə, 'grænd-) *n.* **1.** the mother of one's father or mother. **2.** (*often pl.*) a female ancestor.

Grand National *n.* **the.** an annual steeplechase run at Aintree, Liverpool, since 1839.

grandnephew ('græn,nɛvjuː, -,nɛfjuː, 'grænd-) *n.* another name for **great-nephew**.

grandniece ('græn,niːs, 'grænd-) *n.* another name for **great-niece**.

grand opera *n.* an opera with a serious plot and fully composed text.

grandpa ('græn,pɑː) *or* **grandpapa** ('grænpə,pɑː) *n.* informal words for **grandfather**.

grandparent ('græn,pɛərənt, 'grænd-) *n.* the father or

---

grain 1. cereals, corn **2.** grist, kernel, seed **3.** atom, bit, crumb, fragment, granule, iota, jot, mite, modicum, molecule, morsel, mote, ounce, particle, piece, scintilla (*Rare*), scrap, scruple, spark, speck, suspicion, trace, whit **4.** fibre, nap, pattern, surface, texture, weave **5.** character, disposition, humour, inclination, make-up, temper

grand 1. ambitious, august, dignified, elevated, eminent, exalted, fine, glorious, grandiose, great, haughty, illustrious, imposing,

impressive, large, lofty, lordly, luxurious, magnificent, majestic, monumental, noble, opulent, ostentatious, palatial, pompous, pretentious, princely, regal, splendid, stately, striking, sublime, sumptuous **2.** admirable, excellent, fine, first-class, first-rate, great (*Inf.*), marvellous (*Inf.*), outstanding, smashing (*Inf.*), splendid, super (*Inf.*), superb, terrific (*Inf.*), very good, wonderful **3.** chief, head, highest, leading, main, pre-eminent, principal, supreme

grandeur augustness, dignity, greatness, importance, loftiness, magnificence, majesty, nobility, pomp, splendour, state, stateliness, sublimity

grandiose 1. affected, ambitious, bombastic, extravagant, flamboyant, high-flown, ostentatious, pompous, pretentious, showy **2.** ambitious, grand, imposing, impressive, lofty, magnificent, majestic, monumental, stately

mother of either of one's parents.

grand piano *n.* a form of piano in which the strings are arranged horizontally.

Grand Prix (*French* grã 'pri) *n.* any of a series of formula motor races to determine the annual Driver's World Championship.

grandsire ('græn,saɪə, 'grænd-) *n.* an archaic word for **grandfather.**

grandson ('grænsʌn, 'grænd-) *n.* a son of one's son or daughter.

grandstand ('græn,stænd, 'grænd-) *n.* 1. a terraced block of seats commanding the best view at racecourses, football pitches, etc. 2. the spectators in a grandstand.

grand tour *n.* 1. (formerly) an extended tour through the major cities of Europe, esp. one undertaken by a rich or aristocratic Englishman to complete his education. 2. *Inf.* an extended sightseeing trip, tour of inspection, etc.

granduncle ('grænd,ʌŋkəl) *n.* another name for **great-uncle.**

grange (greɪndʒ) *n.* 1. *Chiefly Brit.* a farm, esp. a farmhouse or country house with its various outbuildings. 2. *Arch.* a granary or barn.

granite ('grænɪt) *n.* 1. a light-coloured coarse-grained acid plutonic igneous rock consisting of quartz and feldspars: widely used for building. 2. great hardness, endurance, or resolution. —**granitic** (grə'nɪtɪk) *adj.*

granivorous (græ'nɪvərəs) *adj.* (of animals) feeding on seeds and grain. —**granivore** ('grænɪ,vɔː) *n.*

granny *or* **grannie** ('grænɪ) *n., pl.* -**nies.** 1. informal words for **grandmother.** Often shortened to **gran.** 2. *Inf.* an irritatingly fussy person. 3. See **granny knot.**

granny flat *n.* a flat built onto or constructed inside a house to accommodate an elderly parent.

granny knot *or* **granny's knot** *n.* a reef knot with the ends crossed the wrong way, making it liable to slip or jam.

grant (grɑːnt) *vb.* (*tr.*) 1. to consent to perform or fulfil: *to grant a wish.* 2. (*may take a clause as object*) to permit as a favour, indulgence, etc.: *to grant an interview.* 3. (*may take a clause as object*) to acknowledge the validity of; concede: *I grant what you say is true.* 4. to bestow, esp. in a formal manner. 5. to transfer (property) to another, esp. by deed; convey. 6. **take for granted. a.** to accept (something) as true and not requiring verification. **b.** to take advantage of the benefits of (something) without due appreciation. ~*n.* 7. a sum of money provided by a government or public fund to finance educational study, overseas aid, etc. 8. a privilege, right, etc., that has been granted. 9. the act of granting. 10. a transfer of property by deed; conveyance. —**'grantable** *adj.* —**gran'tee** *n.* —**'granter** *or* (*Law.*) **'grantor** *n.*

Granth (grʌnt) *n.* the sacred scripture of the Sikhs.

grant-in-aid *n., pl.* **grants-in-aid.** a sum of money granted by one government to a lower level of government for a programme, etc.

granular ('grænjʊlə) *adj.* 1. of, like, or containing granules. 2. having a grainy surface. —**granularity** (,grænjʊ'lærɪtɪ) *n.* —**'granularly** *adv.*

granulate ('grænjʊ,leɪt) *vb.* 1. to make into grains: *granulated sugar.* 2. to make or become roughened in surface texture. —**,granu'lation** *n.* —**'granulative** *adj.* —**'granu,lator** *or* **'granu,later** *n.*

granule ('grænjuːl) *n.* a small grain.

grape (greɪp) *n.* 1. the fruit of the grapevine, which has a purple or green skin and sweet flesh: eaten raw, dried to make raisins, currants, or sultanas, or used for making wine. 2. See **grapevine** (sense 1). 3. **the grape.** slang for **wine.** 4. See **grapeshot.** —**'grapey** *or* **'grapy** *adj.*

grapefruit ('greɪp,fruːt) *n., pl.* -**fruit** *or* -**fruits.** 1. a tropical or subtropical evergreen tree. 2. the large round edible fruit of this tree, which has yellow rind and juicy slightly bitter pulp.

grape hyacinth *n.* any of various Eurasian bulbous plants of the lily family with clusters of rounded blue flowers resembling tiny grapes.

grapeshot ('greɪp,ʃɒt) *n.* ammunition for cannons consisting of a number of or cluster of small projectiles.

grapevine ('greɪp,vaɪn) *n.* 1. any of several vines of E Asia, widely cultivated for its fruit (grapes). 2. *Inf.* an unofficial means of relaying information, esp. from person to person.

graph (grɑːf, græf) *n.* 1. Also called: **chart.** a drawing depicting the relation between certain sets of numbers or quantities by means of a series of dots, lines, etc., plotted with reference to a set of axes. 2. *Maths.* a drawing depicting a functional relation between two or three variables by means of a curve or surface containing only those points whose coordinates satisfy the relation. 3. *Linguistics.* a symbol in a writing system not further subdivisible into other such symbols. ~*vb.* 4. (*tr.*) to draw or represent in a graph.

-**graph** *n. combining form.* 1. an instrument that writes or records: *telegraph.* 2. a writing, record, or drawing: *autograph; lithograph.* —**-graphic** *or* —**-graphical** *adj. combining form.* —**-graphically** *adv. combining form.*

-**grapher** *n. combining form.* 1. indicating a person skilled in a subject: *geographer; photographer.* 2. indicating a person who writes or draws in a specified way: *stenographer; lithographer.*

graphic ('græfɪk) *or* **graphical** *adj.* 1. vividly or clearly described: *a graphic account of the disaster.* 2. of or relating to writing: *graphic symbols.* 3. *Maths.* using, relating to, or determined by a graph: *a graphic representation of the figures.* 4. of or relating to the graphic arts. 5. *Geol.* having or denoting a texture resembling writing: *graphic granite.* —**'graphically** *or* **'graphicly** *adv.* —**'graphicness** *n.*

graphic arts *pl. n.* any of the fine or applied visual arts based on drawing or the use of line, esp. illustration and print-making of all kinds.

graphics ('græfɪks) *n.* 1. (*functioning as sing.*) the process or art of drawing in accordance with mathematical principles. 2. (*functioning as sing.*) the study of writing systems. 3. (*functioning as pl.*) the drawings, photographs, etc., in the layout of a magazine or book.

graphite ('græfaɪt) *n.* a blackish soft form of carbon used in pencils, crucibles, and electrodes, as a lubricant, and as a moderator in nuclear reactors. —**graphitic** (grə'fɪtɪk) *adj.*

graphology (græ'fɒlədʒɪ) *n.* 1. the study of handwriting, esp. to analyse the writer's character. 2. *Linguistics.* the study of writing systems. —**,grapho'logical** *adj.* —**graph'ologist** *n.*

graph paper *n.* paper printed with intersecting lines for drawing graphs, diagrams, etc.

-**graphy** *n. combining form.* 1. indicating a form of writing, representing, etc.: *calligraphy; photography.* 2. indicating an art or descriptive science: *choreography; oceanography.*

grapnel ('græpnəl) *n.* 1. a device with a multiple hook at one end and attached to a rope, which is thrown or hooked over a firm mooring to secure an object attached to the other end of the rope. 2. a light anchor for small boats.

grapple ('græpəl) *vb.* 1. to come to grips with (one or more persons), esp. to struggle in hand-to-hand combat. 2. (*intr.; foll. by with*) to cope or contend: *to grapple with a financial problem.* 3. (*tr.*) to secure with a grapple. ~*n.* 4. any form of hook or metal instrument by which something is secured, such as a grapnel. 5. **a.** the act of gripping or seizing, as in wrestling. **b.** a grip or hold. —**'grappler** *n.*

grappling iron *or* **hook** ('græplɪŋ) *n.* a grapnel, esp. one used for securing ships.

grasp (grɑːsp) *vb.* 1. to grip (something) firmly as with

THESAURUS

grant *v.* 1. accede to, accord, acknowledge, admit, agree to, allocate, allot, allow, assign, award, bestow, cede, concede, confer, consent to, donate, give, impart, permit, present, vouchsafe, yield 2. *Law* assign, convey, transfer, transmit ~*n.* 3. admission, allocation, allotment, allowance, award, benefaction, bequest, boon, bounty, concession, donation, endowment, gift, present, subsidy

granule atom, crumb, fragment, grain, iota, jot, molecule, particle, scrap, speck

graphic 1. clear, descriptive, detailed, explicit, expressive, forcible, illustrative, lively, lucid, picturesque, striking, telling, vivid, well-drawn 2. delineated, diagrammatic, drawn, illustrative, pictorial, representational, seen, visible, visual

grapple 1. catch, clasp, clutch, come to

grips, fasten, grab, grasp, grip, hold, hug, lay *or* take hold, make fast, seize, wrestle 2. address oneself to, attack, battle, clash, combat, confront, contend, cope, deal with, do battle, encounter, engage, face, fight, struggle, tackle, take on, tussle, wrestle

the hands. **2.** (when *intr.*, often foll. by *at*) to struggle, snatch, or grope (for). **3.** (*tr.*) to understand, esp. with effort. ~*n.* **4.** the act of grasping. **5.** a grip or clasp, as of a hand. **6.** total rule or possession. **7.** understanding; comprehension. —**'graspable** *adj.* —**'grasper** *n.*

grasping ('grɑːspɪŋ) *adj.* greedy; avaricious. —**'graspingly** *adv.* —**'graspingness** *n.*

grass (grɑːs) *n.* **1.** any of a family of plants having jointed stems sheathed by long narrow leaves, flowers in spikes, and seedlike fruits. The family includes cereals, bamboo, etc. **2.** such plants collectively, in a lawn, meadow, etc. Related adj.: **verdant.** **3.** ground on which such grasses grow; a lawn, field, etc. **4.** ground on which animals are grazed; pasture. **5.** a slang word for **marijuana.** **6.** *Brit. sl.* a person who informs, esp. on criminals. **7. let the grass grow under one's feet.** to squander time or opportunity. ~*vb.* **8.** to cover or become covered with grass. **9.** to feed or be fed with grass. **10.** (*tr.*) to spread (cloth, etc.) out on grass for drying or bleaching in the sun. **11.** (when *intr.*, usually foll. by *on*) *Brit. sl.* to inform, esp. to the police. —**'grass,like** *adj.* —**'grassy** *adj.*

grass hockey *n.* in W Canada, field hockey, as contrasted with ice hockey.

grasshopper ('grɑːs,hɒpə) *n.* an insect having hind legs adapted for leaping: typically terrestrial, feeding on plants, and producing a ticking sound by rubbing the hind legs against the leathery forewings.

grassland ('grɑːs,lænd) *n.* **1.** land, such as a prairie, on which grass predominates. **2.** land reserved for natural grass pasture.

grass roots *pl. n.* **1.** the essentials. **2.** people considered to represent fundamental and practical views, esp. in politics.

grass snake *n.* **1.** a harmless nonvenomous European snake having a brownish-green body with variable markings. **2.** any of several similar related European snakes.

grass widow *or* (*masc.*) **grass widower** *n.* a person whose spouse is regularly away for a short period.

grate[1] (greɪt) *vb.* **1.** (*tr.*) to reduce to small shreds by rubbing against a rough or sharp perforated surface: *to grate carrots.* **2.** to scrape (an object) against or (objects) together, producing a harsh rasping sound, or (of objects) to scrape with such a sound. **3.** (when *intr.*, foll. by *on* or *upon*) to annoy. —**'grater** *n.*

grate[2] (greɪt) *n.* **1.** a framework of metal bars for holding fuel in a fireplace, stove, or furnace. **2.** a less common word for **fireplace** (sense 1). **3.** another name for **grating**[1]. ~*vb.* **4.** (*tr.*) to provide with a grate or grates.

grateful ('greɪtfʊl) *adj.* **1.** thankful for gifts, favours, etc.; appreciative. **2.** showing gratitude: *a grateful letter.* **3.** favourable or pleasant: *a grateful rest.* —**'gratefully** *adv.* —**'gratefulness** *n.*

gratify ('grætɪ,faɪ) *vb.* **-fying, -fied.** (*tr.*) **1.** to satisfy or please. **2.** to yield to or indulge (a desire, whim, etc.). —**,gratifi'cation** *n.* —**'grati,fier** *n.* —**'grati,fying** *adj.* —**'grati,fyingly** *adv.*

grating[1] ('greɪtɪŋ) *n.* Also called: **grate.** a framework of metal bars in the form of a grille set into a wall, pavement, etc., serving as a cover or guard but admitting air and sometimes light.

grating[2] ('greɪtɪŋ) *adj.* **1.** (of sounds) harsh and rasping. **2.** annoying; irritating. ~*n.* **3.** (*often pl.*) something produced by grating. —**'gratingly** *adv.*

gratis ('greɪtɪs, 'grætɪs, 'grɑːtɪs) *adv., adj.* (*postpositive*) without payment; free of charge.

gratitude ('grætɪ,tjuːd) *n.* a feeling of thankfulness, as for gifts or favours.

gratuitous (grə'tjuːɪtəs) *adj.* **1.** given or received without payment or obligation. **2.** without cause; unjustified. —**gra'tuitously** *adv.* —**gra'tuitousness** *n.*

gratuity (grə'tjuːɪtɪ) *n., pl.* **-ties.** **1.** a gift or reward, usually of money, for services rendered; tip. **2.** *Mil.* a financial award granted for long or meritorious service.

grav (græv) *n.* a unit of acceleration equal to the standard acceleration of free fall. 1 grav is equivalent to 9.806 65 metres per second per second. Symbol: G

gravamen (grə'veɪmɛn) *n., pl.* **-vamina** (-'væmɪnə). **1.** *Law.* that part of an accusation weighing most heavily against an accused. **2.** *Law.* the substance or material grounds of a complaint. **3.** a rare word for **grievance.**

grave[1] (greɪv) *n.* **1.** a place for the burial of a corpse, esp. beneath the ground and usually marked by a tombstone. Related adj.: **sepulchral.** **2.** something resembling a grave or resting place: *the ship went to its grave.* **3.** (often preceded by *the*) a poetic term for **death.** **4. to make (someone) turn in his grave.** to do something that would have shocked or distressed a person now dead.

grave[2] (greɪv) *adj.* **1.** serious and solemn: *a grave look.* **2.** full of or suggesting danger: *a grave situation.* **3.** important; crucial: *grave matters of state.* **4.** (of colours) sober or dull. **5.** (grɑːv). *Phonetics.* of or relating to an accent (`) over vowels, denoting a pronunciation with lower or falling musical pitch (as in ancient Greek), with certain special quality (as in French), or in a manner that gives the vowel status as a syllable (as in English agèd). ~*n.* **6.** (grɑːv). a grave accent. —**'gravely** *adv.* —**'graveness** *n.*

grave[3] (greɪv) *vb.* **graving, graved; graved** *or* **graven.** (*tr.*) *Arch.* **1.** to carve, sculpt, or engrave. **2.** to fix firmly in the mind.

gravel ('grævəl) *n.* **1.** a mixture of rock fragments and pebbles that is coarser than sand. **2.** *Pathol.* small rough calculi in the kidneys or bladder. ~*vb.* **-elling, -elled** *or* *U.S.* **-eling, -eled.** (*tr.*) **3.** to cover with gravel. **4.** to confound or confuse. **5.** *U.S. inf.* to annoy or disturb.

gravelly ('grævəlɪ) *adj.* **1.** consisting of or abounding in gravel. **2.** of or like gravel. **3.** (esp. of a voice) harsh and grating.

graven ('greɪvən) *vb.* **1.** a past participle of **grave**[3]. ~*adj.* **2.** strongly fixed.

graven image *n.* *Chiefly Bible.* a carved image used as an idol.

Graves (grɑːv) *n.* **1.** (*sometimes not cap.*) a white or red wine from the district around Bordeaux, France. **2.** a dry or medium sweet white wine from any country: *Spanish Graves.*

gravestone ('greɪv,stəʊn) *n.* a stone marking a grave.

THESAURUS

grasp *v.* **1.** catch, clasp, clinch, clutch, grab, grapple, grip, hold, lay *or* take hold of, seize, snatch **2.** catch *or* get the drift of, catch on, comprehend, follow, get, realize, see, take in, understand ~*n.* **3.** clasp, clutches, embrace, grip, hold, possession, tenure **4.** capacity, compass, control, extent, mastery, power, range, reach, scope, sway, sweep **5.** awareness, comprehension, ken, knowledge, mastery, perception, realization, understanding

grasping acquisitive, avaricious, close-fisted, covetous, greedy, mean, miserly, niggardly, penny-pinching (*Inf.*), rapacious, selfish, stingy, tightfisted, usurious, venal

grate *v.* **1.** mince, pulverize, shred, triturate **2.** creak, grind, rasp, rub, scrape, scratch **3.** annoy, chafe, exasperate, fret, gall, get one down, get on one's nerves (*Inf.*), irk, irritate, jar, nettle, peeve, rankle, rub one up the wrong way, set one's teeth on edge, vex

grateful **1.** appreciative, beholden, indebted, obliged, thankful **2.** acceptable, agreeable, favourable, gratifying, nice, pleasing, refreshing, restful, satisfactory, satisfying, welcome

gratify cater to, delight, favour, fulfil, give pleasure, gladden, humour, indulge, please, recompense, requite, satisfy, thrill

grating *adj.* annoying, disagreeable, discordant, displeasing, grinding, harsh, irksome, irritating, jarring, offensive, rasping, raucous, scraping, squeaky, strident, unpleasant, vexatious

gratis for nothing, free, freely, free of charge, gratuitously, on the house, unpaid

gratitude appreciation, gratefulness, indebtedness, obligation, recognition, sense of obligation, thankfulness, thanks

gratuitous **1.** complimentary, free, spontaneous, unasked-for, unpaid, unrewarded, voluntary **2.** assumed, baseless, causeless, groundless, irrelevant, needless, superfluous, uncalled-for, unfounded, unjustified, unmerited, unnecessary, unprovoked, unwarranted, wanton

gratuity baksheesh, benefaction, bonus, boon, bounty, donation, gift, largess, perquisite, *pourboire*, present, recompense, reward, tip

grave[1] *n.* burying place, crypt, last resting place, mausoleum, pit, sepulchre, tomb, vault

grave[2] **1.** dignified, dour, dull, earnest, gloomy, grim-faced, heavy, leaden, long-faced, muted, quiet, sage (*Obsolete*), sedate, serious, sober, solemn, sombre, staid, subdued, thoughtful, unsmiling **2.** acute, critical, crucial, dangerous, exigent, hazardous, important, life-and-death, momentous, of great consequence, perilous, pressing, serious, severe, significant, threatening, urgent, vital, weighty

graveyard boneyard (*Inf.*), burial ground, cemetery, charnel house, churchyard, God's acre (*Literary*), necropolis

graveyard ('greɪv,jɑːd) *n.* a place for graves; a burial ground, esp. a small one or one in a churchyard.

gravid ('grævɪd) *adj.* the technical word for **pregnant**.

gravimeter (grə'vɪmɪtə) *n.* **1.** an instrument for measuring the earth's gravitational field at points on its surface. **2.** an instrument for measuring relative density. —gra'vimetry *n.*

gravitate ('grævɪ,teɪt) *vb.* (*intr.*) **1.** *Physics.* to move under the influence of gravity. **2.** (usually foll. by *to* or *towards*) to be influenced or drawn, as by strong impulses. **3.** to sink or settle. —'gravi,tater *n.* —'gravi,tative *adj.*

gravitation (,grævɪ'teɪʃən) *n.* **1.** the force of attraction that bodies exert on one another as a result of their mass. **2.** any process or result caused by this interaction. ~Also called: **gravity.** —,gravi'tational *adj.* —,gravi'tationally *adv.*

gravity ('grævɪtɪ) *n., pl.* **-ties. 1.** the force of attraction that moves or tends to move bodies towards the centre of a celestial body, such as the earth or moon. **2.** the property of being heavy or having weight. **3.** another name for **gravitation. 4.** seriousness or importance, esp. as a consequence of an action or opinion. **5.** manner or conduct that is solemn or dignified. **6.** lowness in pitch. **7.** (*modifier*) of or relating to gravity or gravitation or their effects: *gravity feed.*

gravy ('greɪvɪ) *n., pl.* **-vies. 1. a.** the juices that exude from meat during cooking. **b.** the sauce made by thickening and flavouring such juices. **2.** *Sl., chiefly U.S.* money or gain acquired with little effort, esp. above that needed for ordinary living.

gravy boat *n.* a small often boat-shaped vessel for serving gravy or other sauces.

gray¹ (greɪ) *adj., n., vb.* a variant spelling (now esp. U.S.) of **grey.**

gray² (greɪ) *n.* the derived SI unit of the absorbed dose of ionizing radiation: equal to 1 joule per kilogram. Symbol: Gy

grayling ('greɪlɪŋ) *n., pl.* **-ling** or **-lings. 1.** a freshwater food fish of the salmon family of the N hemisphere, having a long spiny dorsal fin, a silvery back, and greyish-green sides. **2.** any of various European butterflies having grey or greyish-brown wings.

graze¹ (greɪz) *vb.* **1.** to allow (animals) to consume the vegetation on (an area of land), or (of animals) to feed thus. **2.** (*tr.*) to tend (livestock) while at pasture.

graze² (greɪz) *vb.* **1.** (when *intr.,* often foll. by *against* or *along*) to brush or scrape (against) gently, esp. in passing. **2.** (*tr.*) to break the skin of (a part of the body) by scraping. ~*n.* **3.** the act of grazing. **4.** a scrape or abrasion made by grazing.

grazier ('greɪzɪə) *n.* a rancher or farmer who rears or fattens cattle or sheep on grazing land.

grazing ('greɪzɪŋ) *n.* **1.** the vegetation on ranges or pastures that is available for livestock to feed upon. **2.** the land on which this is growing.

grease *n.* (griːs). **1.** animal fat in a soft or melted condition. **2.** any thick fatty oil, esp. one used as a lubricant for machinery, etc. ~*vb.* (griːs, griːz). (*tr.*) **3.** to soil, coat, or lubricate with grease. **4. grease the palm** (or **hand**) **of.** *Sl.* to bribe; influence by giving money to. —'greaser *n.* —'greaseless *adj.*

greasepaint ('griːs,peɪnt) *n.* **1.** a waxy or greasy substance used as make-up by actors. **2.** theatrical make-up.

greasy ('griːsɪ, -zɪ) *adj.* **greasier, greasiest. 1.** coated or soiled with or as if with grease. **2.** composed of or full of grease. **3.** resembling grease. **4.** unctuous or oily in manner. —'greasily *adv.* —'greasiness *n.*

great (greɪt) *adj.* **1.** relatively large in size or extent; big. **2.** relatively large in number; having many parts or members: *a great assembly.* **3.** of relatively long duration: *a great wait.* **4.** of larger size or more importance than others of its kind: *the great auk.* **5.** extreme or more than usual: *great worry.* **6.** of significant importance or consequence: *a great decision.* **7. a.** of exceptional talents or achievements; remarkable: *a great writer.* **b.** (*as n.*): *the great; one of the greats.* **8.** arising from or possessing idealism in thought, action, etc.; heroic: *great deeds.* **9.** illustrious or eminent: *a great history.* **10.** impressive or striking: *a great show of wealth.* **11.** active or enthusiastic: *a great walker.* **12.** (often foll. by *at*) skilful or adroit: *a great carpenter; you are great at singing.* **13.** *Inf.* excellent; fantastic. ~*n.* **14.** Also called: **great organ.** the principal manual on an organ. —'greatly *adv.* —'greatness *n.*

great- *prefix.* **1.** being the parent of a person's grandparent (in the combinations **great-grandfather, great-grandmother, great-grandparent**). **2.** being the child of a person's grandchild (in the combinations **great-grandson, great-granddaughter, great-grandchild**).

great auk *n.* a large flightless auk, extinct since the middle of the 19th century.

great-aunt or **grandaunt** *n.* an aunt of one's father or mother; sister of one's grandfather or grandmother.

Great Bear *n.* **the.** the English name for **Ursa Major.**

great circle *n.* a circular section of a sphere that has a radius equal to that of the sphere.

greatcoat ('greɪt,kəʊt) *n.* a heavy overcoat.

Great Dane *n.* one of a very large rangy breed of dog with a short coat.

great-nephew or **grandnephew** *n.* a son of one's nephew or niece; grandson of one's brother or sister. —**great-niece** or **'grandniece** *n.* (*fem.*).

Great Russian *n.* **1.** *Linguistics.* the technical name for **Russian. 2.** a member of the chief East Slavonic people of Russia. ~*adj.* **3.** of or relating to this people or their language.

Greats (greɪts) *pl. n.* (at Oxford University) **1.** the Honour School of Literae Humaniores, involving the study of Greek and Roman history and literature and philosophy. **2.** the final examinations at the end of this course.

great seal *n.* (*often caps.*) the principal seal of a nation, sovereign, etc., used to authenticate documents of the highest importance.

great tit *n.* a Eurasian tit with yellow-and-black underparts and a black-and-white head.

great-uncle or **granduncle** *n.* an uncle of one's fa-

THESAURUS

gravitate 1. *With to* or *towards* be influenced (attracted, drawn, pulled), incline, lean, move, tend **2.** be precipitated, descend, drop, fall, precipitate, settle, sink

gravity 1. acuteness, consequence, exigency, hazardousness, importance, moment, momentousness, perilousness, pressingness, seriousness, severity, significance, urgency, weightiness **2.** demureness, dignity, earnestness, gloom, grimness, reserve, sedateness, seriousness, sobriety, solemnity, thoughtfulness

graze *v.* **1.** brush, glance off, kiss, rub, scrape, shave, skim, touch **2.** abrade, bark, chafe, scrape, scratch, skin ~*n.* **3.** abrasion, scrape, scratch

greasy 1. fatty, oily, slick, slimy, slippery **2.** fawning, glib, grovelling, ingratiating, oily, slick, smarmy (*Brit. inf.*), smooth, sycophantish, toadying, unctuous

great 1. big, bulky, colossal, enormous, extensive, gigantic, huge, immense, large, mammoth, prodigious, stupendous, tremen-dous, vast, voluminous **2.** extended, lengthy, long, prolonged, protracted **3.** capital, chief, grand, leading, main, major, paramount, primary, principal, prominent, superior **4.** considerable, decided, excessive, extravagant, extreme, grievous, high, inordinate, prodigious, pronounced, strong **5.** consequential, critical, crucial, grave, heavy, important, momentous, serious, significant, weighty **6.** celebrated, distinguished, eminent, exalted, excellent, famed, famous, glorious, illustrious, notable, noteworthy, outstanding, prominent, remarkable, renowned, superlative, talented **7.** august, chivalrous, dignified, distinguished, exalted, fine, glorious, grand, heroic, high-minded, idealistic, impressive, lofty, magnanimous, noble, princely, sublime **8.** active, devoted, enthusiastic, keen, zealous **9.** able, adept, adroit, crack (*Sl.*), expert, good, masterly, proficient, skilful, skilled **10.** *Inf.* admirable, excellent, fantastic (*Inf.*), fine, first-rate, good, marvellous (*Inf.*), terrific (*Inf.*), tremendous (*Inf.*), wonderful **11.** absolute, arrant, complete, consummate, down-right, egregious, flagrant, out-and-out, perfect, positive, thoroughgoing, thundering (*Inf.*), total, unmitigated, unqualified, utter

greatly abundantly, by leaps and bounds, by much, considerably, enormously, exceedingly, extremely, highly, hugely, immensely, markedly, mightily, much, notably, powerfully, remarkably, tremendously, vastly, very much

greatness 1. bulk, enormity, hugeness, immensity, largeness, length, magnitude, mass, prodigiousness, size, vastness **2.** amplitude, force, high degree, intensity, potency, power, strength **3.** gravity, heaviness, import, importance, moment, momentousness, seriousness, significance, urgency, weight **4.** celebrity, distinction, eminence, fame, glory, grandeur, illustriousness, lustre, note, renown **5.** chivalry, dignity, disinterestedness, generosity, grandeur, heroism, high-mindedness, idealism, loftiness, majesty, nobility, nobleness, stateliness, sublimity

ther or mother; brother of one's grandfather or grand-mother.

Great War *n.* another name for **World War I.**

grebe (griːb) *n.* an aquatic bird, such as the great crested grebe and little grebe, similar to the divers but with lobate rather than webbed toes and a vestigial tail.

Grecian ('griːʃən) *adj.* 1. (esp. of beauty or architecture) conforming to Greek ideals. ~*n.* 2. a scholar of Greek. ~*adj.*, *n.* 3. another word for **Greek.**

Greco- ('griːkəʊ-, 'grɛkəʊ-) *combining form.* a variant (esp. U.S.) of **Graeco-.**

greed (griːd) *n.* 1. excessive consumption of or desire for food. 2. excessive desire, as for wealth or power.

greedy ('griːdɪ) *adj.* **greedier, greediest.** 1. excessively desirous of food or wealth, esp. in large amounts; voracious. 2. (*postpositive*; foll. by *for*) eager (for): *a man greedy for success.* —'**greedily** *adv.* —'**greediness** *n.*

Greek (griːk) *n.* 1. the official language of Greece, constituting the Hellenic branch of the Indo-European family of languages. 2. a native or inhabitant of Greece or a descendant of such a native. 3. a member of the Greek Orthodox Church. 4. *Inf.* anything incomprehensible (esp. in **it's (all) Greek to me**). ~*adj.* 5. denoting, relating to, or characteristic of Greece, the Greeks, or the Greek language; Hellenic. 6. of, relating to, or designating the Greek Orthodox Church. —'**Greekness** *n.*

Greek cross *n.* a cross with each of the four arms of the same length.

Greek fire *n.* a Byzantine weapon consisting of a mixture that caught fire when wetted.

green (griːn) *n.* 1. any of a group of colours, such as that of fresh grass, that lie between yellow and blue in the visible spectrum. Related *adj.*: **verdant.** 2. a dye or pigment of or producing these colours. 3. something of the colour green. 4. a small area of grassland, esp. in the centre of a village. 5. an area of smooth turf kept for a special purpose: *a putting green.* 6. (*pl.*) **a.** the edible leaves and stems of certain plants, eaten as a vegetable. **b.** freshly cut branches of ornamental trees, shrubs, etc., used as a decoration. ~*adj.* 7. of the colour green. 8. greenish in colour or having parts or marks that are greenish. 9. vigorous; not faded: *a green old age.* 10. envious or jealous. 11. immature, unsophisticated, or gullible. 12. characterized by foliage or green plants: *a green wood; a green salad.* 13. fresh, raw, or unripe: *green bananas.* 14. unhealthily pale in appearance: *he was green after his boat trip.* 15. (of meat) not smoked or cured: *green bacon.* 16. (of timber) freshly felled; not dried or seasoned. ~*vb.* 17. to make or become green. —'**greenish** *adj.* —'**greenly** *adv.* —'**greenness** *n.* —'**greeny** *adj.*

green bean *n.* any bean plant, such as the French bean, having narrow green edible pods.

green belt *n.* a zone of farmland, parks, and open country surrounding a town or city.

Green Cross Code *n. Brit.* a code for children giving rules for road safety.

greenery ('griːnərɪ) *n., pl.* **-eries.** green foliage, esp. when used for decoration.

green-eyed *adj.* 1. jealous or envious. 2. **the green-eyed monster.** jealousy or envy.

greenfinch ('griːn,fɪntʃ) *n.* a common European finch, the male of which has a dull green plumage with yellow patches on the wings and tail.

green fingers *pl. n.* considerable talent or ability to grow plants.

greenfly ('griːn,flaɪ) *n., pl.* **-flies.** a greenish aphid commonly occurring as a pest on garden and crop plants.

greengage ('griːn,geɪdʒ) *n.* 1. a cultivated variety of plum tree with edible green plumlike fruits. 2. the fruit of this tree.

greengrocer ('griːn,grəʊsə) *n. Chiefly Brit.* a retail trader in fruit and vegetables. —'**green,grocery** *n.*

greenhorn ('griːn,hɔːn) *n. Inf.* 1. an inexperienced person, esp. one who is extremely gullible. 2. a newcomer or novice.

greenhouse ('griːn,haʊs) *n.* a building with glass walls and roof for the cultivation of plants under controlled conditions.

greenkeeper ('griːn,kiːpə) *n.* a person responsible for maintaining a golf course or bowling green.

green light *n.* 1. a signal to go, esp. a green traffic light. 2. permission to proceed with a project, etc.

green paper *n.* (*often caps.*) (in Britain) a government document containing policy proposals to be discussed, esp. by Parliament.

green pepper *n.* the green unripe fruit of the sweet pepper, eaten raw or cooked.

green pound *n.* a unit of account used in calculating Britain's contributions to and payments from the Community Agricultural Fund of the EEC.

greenroom ('griːn,ruːm, -,rʊm) *n.* (esp. formerly) a backstage room in a theatre where performers may rest or receive visitors.

greenshank ('griːn,ʃæŋk) *n.* a large European sandpiper with greenish legs and a slightly upturned bill.

greenstick fracture ('griːn,stɪk) *n.* a fracture in children in which the bone is partly bent and splinters only on the convex side of the bend.

greensward ('griːn,swɔːd) *n. Arch.* or *literary.* fresh green turf or an area of such turf.

green tea *n.* a sharp tea made from tea leaves that have been dried quickly without fermenting.

greet[1] (griːt) *vb.* (*tr.*) 1. to meet or receive with expressions of gladness or welcome. 2. to send a message of friendship to. 3. to receive in a specified manner: *her remarks were greeted by silence.* 4. to become apparent to: *the smell of bread greeted him.* —'**greeter** *n.*

greet[2] (griːt) *Arch.* or *dialect.* ~*vb.* 1. (*intr.*) to weep; lament. ~*n.* 2. weeping; lamentation.

greeting ('griːtɪŋ) *n.* 1. the act or an instance of welcoming or saluting on meeting. 2. (*often pl.*) **a.** an expression of friendly salutation. **b.** (*as modifier*): *a greetings card.*

gregarious (grɪ'gɛərɪəs) *adj.* 1. enjoying the company of others. 2. (of animals) living together in herds or flocks. 3. (of plants) growing close together. 4. of, relating to, or characteristic of crowds or communities. —gre'**gariously** *adv.* —gre'**gariousness** *n.*

Gregorian calendar (grɪ'gɔːrɪən) *n.* the revision of the Julian calendar introduced in 1582 by Pope Gregory XIII and still in force, whereby the ordinary year is made to consist of 365 days.

Gregorian chant *n.* another name for **plainsong.**

gremlin ('grɛmlɪn) *n.* 1. an imaginary imp jokingly said to be responsible for mechanical troubles in aircraft, esp. in World War II. 2. any mischievous troublemaker.

grenade (grɪ'neɪd) *n.* 1. a small container filled with explosive thrown by hand or fired from a rifle. 2. a sealed glass vessel that is thrown and shatters to release chemicals, such as tear gas.

grenadier (,grɛnə'dɪə) *n.* 1. *Mil.* **a.** (in the British Army) a member of the senior regiment of infantry in the Household Brigade. **b.** (formerly) a member of a

---

THESAURUS

greed, greediness 1. edacity, esurience, gluttony, gormandizing, hunger, insatiableness, ravenousness, voracity 2. acquisitiveness, avidity, covetousness, craving, cupidity, desire, eagerness, graspingness, longing, rapacity, selfishness

greedy 1. edacious, esurient, gluttonous, gormandizing, hoggish, hungry, insatiable, piggish, ravenous, voracious 2. acquisitive, avaricious, avid, covetous, craving, desirous, eager, grasping, hungry, impatient, rapacious, selfish

Greek 1. *n.* Hellene 2. *adj.* Hellenic

green *adj.* 1. blooming, budding, flourish-

ing, fresh, grassy, leafy, new, undecayed, verdant, verdurous 2. fresh, immature, new, raw, recent, unripe 3. callow, credulous, gullible, ignorant, immature, inexperienced, inexpert, ingenuous, innocent, naive, new, raw, unpolished, unpractised, unskilful, unsophisticated, untrained, unversed, wet behind the ears (*Inf.*) 4. covetous, envious, grudging, jealous, resentful 5. ill, nauseous, pale, sick, unhealthy, wan 6. immature, pliable, supple, tender, undried, unseasoned, young ~*n.* 7. common, grassplot, lawn, sward, turf

green light approval, authorization, blessing, clearance, confirmation, go-ahead

(*Inf.*), imprimatur, O.K. (*Inf.*), okay (*Inf.*), permission, sanction

greet accost, address, compliment, hail, meet, nod to, receive, salute, tip one's hat to, welcome

greeting 1. address, hail, reception, salutation, salute, welcome 2. *Plural* best wishes, compliments, devoirs, good wishes, regards, respects, salutations

gregarious affable, companionable, convivial, cordial, friendly, outgoing, sociable, social

special formation, usually selected for strength and height. **c.** (formerly) a soldier trained to throw grenades. **2.** any of various deep-sea fish, typically having a large head and a long tapering tail.

grew (gruː) *vb.* the past tense of **grow.**

grey *or U.S.* **gray** (greɪ) *adj.* **1.** of a neutral tone, intermediate between black and white, that has no hue and reflects and transmits only a little light. **2.** greyish in colour or having greyish marks. **3.** dismal or dark, esp. from lack of light; gloomy. **4.** neutral or dull, esp. in character or opinion. **5.** having grey hair. **6.** of or characteristic of old age; wise. **7.** ancient; venerable. ~*n.* **8.** any of a group of grey tones. **9.** grey cloth or clothing. **10.** an animal, esp. a horse, that is grey or whitish. ~*vb.* **11.** to become or make grey. —'**greyish** *or U.S.* '**grayish** *adj.* —'**greyly** *or U.S.* '**grayly** *adv.* —'**greyness** *or U.S.* '**grayness** *n.*

Grey Cup *n.* the annual championship game of the Canadian Football league or the trophy awarded to the winner.

Grey Friar *n.* a Franciscan friar.

greyhound ('greɪ,haʊnd) *n.* a tall slender fast-moving breed of hound.

greylag *or* **greylag goose** ('greɪ,læg) *n.* a large grey Eurasian goose: the ancestor of many domestic breeds of goose. U.S. spelling: **graylag.**

grey matter *n.* **1.** the greyish tissue of the brain and spinal cord, containing nerve cell bodies and fibres. **2.** *Inf.* brains or intellect.

grey squirrel *n.* a grey-furred squirrel, native to E North America but now widely established.

grid (grɪd) *n.* **1.** See **gridiron. 2.** a network of horizontal and vertical lines superimposed over a map, building plan, etc., for locating points. **3. the grid.** the national network of transmission lines, pipes, etc., by which electricity, gas, or water is distributed. **4.** Also called: **control grid.** *Electronics.* an electrode usually consisting of a cylindrical mesh of wires, that controls the flow of electrons between the cathode and anode of a valve. **5.** any interconnecting system of links: *the bus service formed a grid across the country.*

griddle ('grɪdªl) *n.* **1.** Also called: **girdle.** *Brit.* a thick round iron plate with a half hoop handle over the top, for making scones, etc. **2.** any flat heated surface, esp. on the top of a stove, for cooking food. ~*vb.* **3.** (*tr.*) to cook (food) on a griddle.

gridiron ('grɪd,aɪən) *n.* **1.** a utensil of parallel metal bars, used to grill meat, fish, etc. **2.** any framework resembling this utensil. **3.** a framework above the stage in a theatre from which suspended scenery, lights, etc., are manipulated. **4.** the field of play in American football. ~Often shortened to **grid.**

grief (griːf) *n.* **1.** deep or intense sorrow, esp. at the death of someone. **2.** something that causes keen distress. **3. come to grief.** *Inf.* to end unsuccessfully or disastrously.

grievance ('griːvəns) *n.* **1.** a real or imaginary wrong causing resentment and regarded as grounds for complaint. **2.** a feeling of resentment or injustice at having been unfairly treated.

grieve (griːv) *vb.* to feel or cause to feel great sorrow or distress, esp. at the death of someone. —'**griever** *n.*

grievous ('griːvəs) *adj.* **1.** very severe or painful: *a grievous injury.* **2.** very serious; heinous: *a grievous sin.* **3.** showing or marked by grief. **4.** causing great pain or suffering. —'**grievously** *adv.* —'**grievousness** *n.*

grievous bodily harm *n. Criminal law.* serious injury caused by one person to another.

griffin ('grɪfɪn), **griffon,** *or* **gryphon** *n.* a winged monster with an eagle-like head and the body of a lion.

griffon ('grɪfən) *n.* **1.** any of various small wire-haired breeds of dog, originally from Belgium. **2.** a large vulture of Africa, S Europe, and SW Asia, having a pale plumage with black wings.

grill (grɪl) *vb.* **1.** to cook (meat, etc.) by direct heat, as under a grill or over a hot fire, or (of meat, etc.) to be cooked in this way. Usual U.S. word: **broil. 2.** (*tr., usually passive*) to torment with or as if with extreme heat: *the travellers were grilled by the scorching sun.* **3.** (*tr.*) *Inf.* to subject to insistent or prolonged questioning. ~*n.* **4.** a device with parallel bars of thin metal on which meat, etc., may be cooked by a fire; gridiron. **5.** a device on a cooker that radiates heat downwards for grilling meat, etc. **6.** food cooked by grilling. **7.** See **grillroom.** —**grilled** *adj.* —'**griller** *n.*

grille *or* **grill** (grɪl) *n.* **1.** a framework, esp. of metal bars arranged to form an ornamental pattern, used as a screen or partition. **2.** Also called: **radiator grille.** a grating that admits cooling air to the radiator of a motor vehicle. **3.** a metal or wooden openwork grating used as a screen or divider. **4.** a protective screen, usually plastic or metal, in front of the loudspeaker in a radio, record player, etc.

grillroom ('grɪl,ruːm, -,rʊm) *n.* a restaurant where grilled steaks and other meat are served.

grilse (grɪls) *n., pl.* **grilses** *or* **grilse.** a salmon at the stage when it returns for the first time from the sea to fresh water.

grim (grɪm) *adj.* **grimmer, grimmest. 1.** stern; resolute: *grim determination.* **2.** harsh or formidable in manner or appearance. **3.** harshly ironic or sinister: *grim laughter.* **4.** cruel, severe, or ghastly: *a grim accident.* **5.** *Arch. or poetic.* fierce: *a grim warrior.* **6.** *Inf.* unpleasant; disagreeable. —'**grimly** *adv.* —'**grimness** *n.*

grimace (grɪ'meɪs) *n.* **1.** an ugly or distorted facial expression, as of wry humour, disgust, etc. ~*vb.* **2.** (*intr.*) to contort the face. —**gri'macer** *n.*

grimalkin (grɪ'mælkɪn, -'mɔːl-) *n.* **1.** an old cat, esp. an old female cat. **2.** a crotchety or shrewish old woman.

grime (graɪm) *n.* **1.** dirt, soot, or filth, esp. when ingrained. ~*vb.* **2.** (*tr.*) to make dirty or coat with filth. —'**grimy** *adj.*

grin (grɪn) *vb.* **grinning, grinned. 1.** to smile with the lips drawn back revealing the teeth or express (something) by such a smile: *to grin a welcome.* **2.** (*intr.*) to draw back the lips revealing the teeth, as in a snarl or grimace. **3. grin and bear it.** *Inf.* to suffer trouble or hardship without complaint. ~*n.* **4.** a broad smile. **5.** a snarl or grimace. —'**grinner** *n.* —'**grinningly** *adv.*

grind (graɪnd) *vb.* **grinding, ground. 1.** to reduce or be reduced to small particles by pounding or abrading: *to grind corn.* **2.** (*tr.*) to smooth, sharpen, or polish by friction or abrasion: *to grind a knife.* **3.** to scrape or grate together (two things, esp. the teeth) with a harsh rasping sound or (of such objects) to be scraped together. **4.** (*tr.; foll. by out*) to speak or say something in a rough voice. **5.** (*tr.; often foll. by down*) to hold down; oppress; tyrannize. **6.** (*tr.*) to operate (a machine) by turning a handle. **7.** (*tr.; foll. by out*) to produce in a routine or uninspired manner: *he ground out his weekly article for the paper.* **8.** (*intr.*) *Inf.* to study or work laboriously. ~*n.* **9.** *Inf.* la-

---

THESAURUS

grey 1. ashen, bloodless, colourless, livid, pale, pallid, wan **2.** cheerless, cloudy, dark, depressing, dim, dismal, drab, dreary, dull, foggy, gloomy, misty, murky, overcast, sunless **3.** anonymous, characterless, colourless, dull, indistinct, neutral, unclear, unidentifiable **4.** aged, ancient, elderly, experienced, hoary, mature, old, venerable

grief 1. affliction, agony, anguish, bereavement, dejection, distress, grievance, heartache, heartbreak, misery, mournfulness, mourning, pain, regret, remorse, sadness, sorrow, suffering, trial, tribulation, trouble, woe **2. come to grief** *Inf.* come unstuck, fail, meet with disaster, miscarry

grievance affliction, beef (*Sl.*), complaint, damage, distress, grief, gripe (*Inf.*),

hardship, injury, injustice, resentment, sorrow, trial, tribulation, trouble, unhappiness, wrong

grieve 1. ache, bemoan, bewail, complain, deplore, lament, mourn, regret, rue, sorrow, suffer, wail, weep **2.** afflict, agonize, break the heart of, crush, distress, hurt, injure, make one's heart bleed, pain, sadden, wound

grievous 1. afflicting, calamitous, damaging, distressing, dreadful, grave, harmful, heavy, hurtful, injurious, lamentable, oppressive, painful, severe, wounding **2.** appalling, atrocious, deplorable, dreadful, egregious, flagrant, glaring, heinous, intolerable, lamentable, monstrous, offensive, outrageous, shameful, shocking, unbearable **3.** agonized, grief-stricken, heart-rending, mournful, piti-

ful, sorrowful, tragic

grim cruel, ferocious, fierce, forbidding, formidable, frightful, ghastly, grisly, gruesome, harsh, hideous, horrible, horrid, implacable, merciless, morose, relentless, resolute, ruthless, severe, shocking, sinister, stern, sullen, surly, terrible, unrelenting, unyielding

grimace 1. *n.* face, frown, mouth, scowl, sneer, wry face **2.** *v.* frown, make a face *or* faces, mouth, scowl, sneer

grime dirt, filth, smut, soot

grimy begrimed, besmeared, besmirched, dirty, filthy, foul, grubby, smutty, soiled, sooty, unclean

borious or routine work or study. **10.** a specific grade of pulverization, as of coffee beans: *coarse grind.* **11.** the act or sound of grinding. —**'grindingly** *adv.*

grinder ('graɪndə) *n.* **1.** a person who grinds, esp. one who grinds cutting tools. **2.** a machine for grinding. **3.** a molar tooth.

grindstone ('graɪnd,stəʊn) *n.* **1. a.** a machine having a circular block of stone rotated for sharpening tools or grinding metal. **b.** the stone used in this machine. **c.** any stone used for sharpening; whetstone. **2. keep** *or* **have one's nose to the grindstone.** to work hard and perseveringly.

grip (grɪp) *n.* **1.** the act or an instance of grasping and holding firmly: *he lost his grip on the slope.* **2.** Also called: **handgrip.** the strength or pressure of such a grasp, as in a handshake. **3.** the style or manner of grasping an object, such as a tennis racket. **4.** understanding, control, or mastery of a subject, problem, etc. **5. come** *or* **get to grips.** (often foll. by *with*) **a.** to deal with (a problem or subject). **b.** to tackle (an assailant). **6.** Also called: **handgrip.** a part by which an object is grasped; handle. **7.** Also called: **handgrip.** a travelling bag or holdall. **8.** See **hairgrip. 9.** any device that holds by friction, such as certain types of brake. ~*vb.* **gripping, gripped** *or* **gript. 10.** to take hold of firmly or tightly, as by a clutch. **11.** to hold the interest or attention of: *to grip an audience.* —**'gripper** *n.* —**'gripping-ly** *adv.*

gripe (graɪp) *vb.* **1.** (*intr.*) *Inf.* to complain, esp. in a persistent nagging manner. **2.** to cause sudden intense pain in the intestines of (a person) or (of a person) to experience this pain. **3.** *Arch.* to clutch; grasp. **4.** (*tr.*) *Arch.* to afflict. ~*n.* **5.** (usually *pl.*) a sudden intense pain in the intestines; colic. **6.** *Inf.* a complaint or grievance. **7.** *Now rare.* **a.** the act of gripping. **b.** a firm grip. **c.** a device that grips. —**'griper** *n.* —**'gripingly** *adv.*

grippe *or* **grip** (grɪp) *n.* a former name for **influenza.**

grisly ('grɪzlɪ) *adj.* **-lier, -liest.** causing horror or dread; gruesome. —**'grisliness** *n.*

grist (grɪst) *n.* **1. a.** grain intended to be or that has been ground. **b.** the quantity of such grain processed in one grinding. **2.** *Brewing.* malt grains that have been cleaned and cracked. **3. grist to** (*or* **for**) **the** (*or* **one's**) **mill.** anything that can be turned to profit or advantage.

gristle ('grɪsəl) *n.* cartilage, esp. when in meat. —**'gristly** *adj.* —**'gristliness** *n.*

grit (grɪt) *n.* **1.** small hard particles of sand, earth, stone, etc. **2.** Also called: **gritstone.** any coarse sandstone that can be used as a grindstone or millstone. **3.** indomitable courage, toughness, or resolution. ~*vb.* **gritting, gritted. 4.** to clench or grind together (two objects, esp. the teeth). **5.** to cover (a surface, such as icy roads) with grit. —**'gritter** *n.* —**'gritty** *adj.*

Grit (grɪt) *n., adj. Canad.* an informal word for **Liberal.**

grits (grɪts) *pl. n.* hulled or coarsely ground grain.

grizzle[1] ('grɪzəl) *vb.* **1.** to make or become grey. ~*n.* **2.** a grey colour. **3.** grey hair.

grizzle[2] ('grɪzəl) *vb.* (*intr.*) *Inf., chiefly Brit.* (esp. of a child) to fret; whine. —**'grizzler** *n.*

grizzled ('grɪzəld) *adj.* **1.** streaked or mixed with grey; grizzly. **2.** having grey hair.

grizzly ('grɪzlɪ) *adj.* **-zlier, -zliest. 1.** somewhat grey;

grizzled. ~*n., pl.* **-zlies. 2.** See **grizzly bear.**

grizzly bear *n.* a greyish-brown variety of the brown bear, formerly widespread in W North America. Often shortened to **grizzly.**

groan (grəʊn) *n.* **1.** a prolonged stressed dull cry expressive of agony, pain, or disapproval. **2.** a loud harsh creaking sound, as of a tree bending in the wind. **3.** *Inf.* a grumble or complaint, esp. a persistent one. ~*vb.* **4.** to utter (low inarticulate sounds) expressive of pain, grief, disapproval, etc. **5.** (*intr.*) to make a sound like a groan. **6.** (*intr.,* usually foll. by *beneath* or *under*) to be weighed down (by) or suffer greatly (under). **7.** (*intr.*) *Inf.* to complain or grumble. —**'groaner** *n.* —**'groan-ingly** *adv.*

groat (grəʊt) *n.* an obsolete English silver coin worth four pennies.

groats (grəʊts) *pl. n.* the hulled and crushed grain of oats, wheat, or certain other cereals.

grocer ('grəʊsə) *n.* a dealer in foodstuffs and other household supplies.

groceries ('grəʊsərɪz) *pl. n.* merchandise, esp. foodstuffs, sold by a grocer.

grocery ('grəʊsərɪ) *n., pl.* **-ceries.** the business or premises of a grocer.

grog (grɒg) *n.* **1.** diluted spirit, usually rum, as an alcoholic drink. **2.** *Austral. & N.Z. inf.* alcoholic drink in general, esp. spirits.

groggy ('grɒgɪ) *adj.* **-gier, -giest.** *Inf.* **1.** dazed or staggering, as from exhaustion, blows, or drunkenness. **2.** faint or weak. —**'groggily** *adv.* —**'grogginess** *n.*

grogram ('grɒgrəm) *n.* a coarse fabric of silk, wool, or silk mixed with wool or mohair, often stiffened with gum, formerly used for clothing.

groin (grɔɪn) *n.* **1.** the depression or fold where the legs join the abdomen. **2.** *Euphemistic.* the genitals, esp. the testicles. **3.** a variant spelling (esp. U.S.) of **groyne. 4.** *Archit.* a curved arris formed where two intersecting vaults meet. ~*vb.* **5.** (*tr.*) *Archit.* to provide or construct with groins.

grommet ('grɒmɪt) *or* **grummet** *n.* a ring of rubber or plastic or a metal eyelet designed to line a hole to prevent a cable or pipe passed through it from chafing.

groom (gru:m, grʊm) *n.* **1.** a person employed to clean and look after horses. **2.** See **bridegroom. 3.** any of various officers of a royal or noble household. **4.** *Arch.* a male servant. ~*vb.* (*tr.*) **5.** to make or keep (clothes, appearance, etc.) clean and tidy. **6.** to rub down, clean, and smarten (a horse, dog, etc.). **7.** to train or prepare for a particular task, occupation, etc.: *to groom someone for the Presidency.*

groomsman ('gru:mzmən, 'grʊmz-) *n., pl.* **-men.** a man who attends the bridegroom at a wedding, usually the best man.

groove (gru:v) *n.* **1.** a long narrow channel or furrow, esp. one cut into wood by a tool. **2.** the spiral channel in a gramophone record. **3.** a settled existence, routine, etc., to which one is suited or accustomed. **4.** *Sl.* an experience, event, etc., that is groovy. **5. in the groove. a.** *Jazz.* playing well and apparently effortlessly, with a good beat, etc. **b.** *U.S.* fashionable. ~*vb.* **6.** (*tr.*) to form or cut a groove in. **7.** (*intr.*) *Sl.* to enjoy oneself or feel in rapport with one's surroundings. **8.** (*tr.*) *Sl.* to ex-

---

THESAURUS

grind *v.* **1.** abrade, comminute, crush, granulate, grate, kibble, mill, pound, powder, pulverize, triturate **2.** file, polish, sand, sharpen, smooth, whet **3.** gnash, grate, grit, scrape **4.** *With* **down** afflict, harass, hold down, hound, oppress, persecute, plague, trouble, tyrannize (over) ~*n.* **5.** *Inf.* chore, drudgery, hard work, labour, sweat (*Inf.*), task, toil

grip *n.* **1.** clasp, handclasp (*U.S.*), purchase **2.** clutches, comprehension, control, domination, grasp, hold, influence, keeping, mastery, perception, possession, power, tenure, understanding **3. come** *or* **get to grips (with)** close with, confront, contend with, cope with, deal with, encounter, face up to, grapple with, grasp, handle, meet, tackle, take on, undertake ~*v.* **4.** clasp, clutch, grasp, hold, latch on to, seize, take hold of **5.** catch up, compel, engross, enthral, entrance, fascinate, hold, involve, mesmerize, rivet, spellbind

gripping compelling, compulsive, engrossing, enthralling, entrancing, exciting, fascinating, riveting, spellbinding, thrilling, unputdownable (*Inf.*)

grisly abominable, appalling, awful, dreadful, frightful, ghastly, grim, gruesome, hideous, horrible, horrid, macabre, shocking, sickening, terrible, terrifying

grit *n.* **1.** dust, gravel, pebbles, sand **2.** backbone, courage, determination, doggedness, fortitude, gameness, guts (*Inf.*), hardihood, mettle, nerve, perseverance, pluck, resolution, spirit, tenacity, toughness ~*v.* **3.** clench, gnash, grate, grind

gritty 1. abrasive, dusty, grainy, granular, gravelly, rasping, rough, sandy **2.** brave, courageous, determined, dogged, game, hardy, mettlesome, plucky, resolute, spirited, steadfast, tenacious, tough

groan *n.* **1.** cry, moan, sigh, whine **2.** *Inf.* beef (*Sl.*), complaint, gripe (*Inf.*), grouse,

grumble, objection ~*v.* **3.** cry, moan, sigh, whine **4.** *Inf.* beef (*Sl.*), bemoan, bitch (*Sl.*), complain, gripe (*Inf.*), grouse, grumble, lament, object

groggy befuddled, confused, dazed, dizzy, faint, muzzy, punch-drunk, reeling, shaky, staggering, stunned, stupefied, unsteady, weak, wobbly, woozy (*Inf.*)

groom *n.* **1.** currier (*Rare*), hostler *or* ostler (*Archaic*), stableboy, stableman ~*v.* **2.** clean, dress, get up (*Inf.*), preen, primp, smarten up, spruce up, tidy, turn out **3.** brush, clean, curry, rub down, tend **4.** coach, drill, educate, make ready, nurture, prepare, prime, ready, train

groove channel, cut, cutting, flute, furrow, gutter, hollow, indentation, rebate, rut, score, trench

cite. **9.** (*intr.*) *Sl.* to progress or develop. **10.** (*intr.*) *Jazz.* to play well, with a good beat, etc.

groovy ('gruːvɪ) *adj.* **groovier, grooviest.** *Sl.* attractive, fashionable, or exciting.

grope (grəʊp) *vb.* **1.** (*intr.* usually foll. by *for*) to feel or search about uncertainly (for something) with the hands. **2.** (usually foll. by *for* or *after*) to search uncertainly or with difficulty (for a solution, answer, etc.). ~*n.* **3.** the act of groping. —'**gropingly** *adv.*

grosbeak ('grəʊs.biːk, 'grɒs-) *n.* any of various finches that have a massive powerful bill.

grosgrain ('grəʊ.greɪn) *n.* a heavy ribbed silk or rayon fabric or tape for trimming clothes, etc.

gros point (grəʊ) *n.* **1.** a needlepoint stitch covering two horizontal and two vertical threads. **2.** work done in this stitch.

gross (grəʊs) *adj.* **1.** repellently or excessively fat or bulky. **2.** with no deductions for expenses, tax, etc.; total: *gross sales.* Cf. **net²**. **3.** (of personal qualities, tastes, etc.) conspicuously coarse or vulgar. **4.** obviously or exceptionally culpable or wrong; flagrant: *gross inefficiency.* **5.** lacking in perception, sensitivity, or discrimination: *gross judgments.* **6.** (esp. of vegetation) dense; thick; luxuriant. ~*n.* **7.** *pl.* **gross.** a unit of quantity equal to 12 dozen. **8.** *pl.* **grosses. a.** the entire amount. **b.** the great majority. ~*vb.* (*tr.*) **9.** to earn as total revenue, before deductions for expenses, tax, etc. —'**grossly** *adv.* —'**grossness** *n.*

gross domestic product *n.* the total value of all goods and services produced domestically by a nation during a year. It is equivalent to gross national product minus net investment incomes from foreign nations. Abbrev.: **GDP**

gross national product *n.* the total value of all final goods and services produced annually by a nation. Abbrev.: **GNP**

gross profit *n.* *Accounting.* the difference between total revenue from sales and the total cost of purchases or materials, with an adjustment for stock.

grotesque (grəʊˈtɛsk) *adj.* **1.** strangely or fantastically distorted; bizarre. **2.** of or characteristic of the grotesque in art. **3.** absurdly incongruous; in a ludicrous context. ~*n.* **4.** a 16th-century decorative style in which parts of human, animal, and plant forms are distorted and mixed. **5.** a decorative device, as in painting or sculpture, in this style. **6.** *Printing.* the family of 19th-century sans serif display types. **7.** any grotesque person or thing. —gro'**tesquely** *adv.* —gro'**tesqueness** *n.* —gro'**tesquery** *or* gro'**tesquerie** *n.*

grotto ('grɒtəʊ) *n.*, *pl.* **-toes** *or* **-tos.** **1.** a small cave, esp. one with attractive features. **2.** a construction in the form of a cave, esp. as in landscaped gardens during the 18th century.

grotty ('grɒtɪ) *adj.* **-tier, -tiest.** *Brit. sl.* unpleasant, nasty, or unattractive.

grouch (graʊtʃ) *Inf.* ~*vb.* **1.** to complain; grumble. ~*n.* **2.** a complaint, esp. a persistent one. **3.** a person who is always grumbling. —'**grouchy** *adj.* —'**grouchily** *adv.* —'**grouchiness** *n.*

ground¹ (graʊnd) *n.* **1.** the land surface. **2.** earth or soil. **3.** (*pl.*) the land around a dwelling house or other building. **4.** (*sometimes pl.*) an area of land given over to a purpose: *football ground.* **5.** land having a particular characteristic: *high ground.* **6.** matter for consideration or debate; field of research or enquiry: *the report covered a lot of ground.* **7.** a position or viewpoint, as in an argument or controversy (esp. in **give ground, hold, stand,** *or* **shift one's ground**). **8.** position or advantage,

as in a subject or competition (esp. in **gain ground, lose ground,** etc.). **9.** (*often pl.*) reason; justification: *grounds for complaint.* **10.** *Arts.* **a.** the prepared surface applied to a wall, canvas, etc., to prevent it reacting with or absorbing the paint. **b.** the background of a painting against which the other parts of a work of art appear superimposed. **11. a.** the first coat of paint applied to a surface. **b.** (*as modifier*): *ground colour.* **12.** the bottom of a river or the sea. **13.** (*pl.*) sediment or dregs, esp. from coffee. **14.** *Chiefly Brit.* the floor of a room. **15.** *Cricket.* the area from the popping crease back past the stumps, in which a batsman may legally stand. **16.** *Electrical.* the usual U.S. word for **earth** (sense 8). **17. break new ground.** to do something that has not been done before. **18. common ground.** a subject about which there is agreement or similar thinking. **19. cut the ground from under someone's feet.** to anticipate someone's action and thus make it irrelevant or meaningless. **20. (down) to the ground.** *Brit. inf.* completely; absolutely: *it suited him down to the ground.* **21. home ground.** a familiar area or topic. **22. into the ground.** beyond what is requisite or can be endured; to exhaustion. **23.** (*modifier*) on or concerned with the ground: *ground frost; ground forces.* ~*vb.* **24.** (*tr.*) to put or place on the ground. **25.** (*tr.*) to instruct in fundamentals. **26.** (*tr.*) to provide a basis or foundation for; establish. **27.** (*tr.*) to confine (an aircraft, pilot, etc.) to the ground. **28.** the usual U.S. word for **earth** (sense 13). **29.** (*tr.*) *Naut.* to run (a vessel) aground. **30.** (*intr.*) to hit or reach the ground.

ground² (graʊnd) *vb.* **1.** the past tense or past participle of **grind.** ~*adj.* **2.** having the surface finished, thickness reduced, or an edge sharpened by grinding. **3.** reduced to fine particles by grinding.

ground bass (beɪs) *n.* *Music.* a short melodic bass line that is repeated over and over again.

ground control *n.* **1.** the personnel, radar, computers, etc., on the ground that monitor the progress of aircraft or spacecraft. **2.** a system for feeding continuous radio messages to an aircraft pilot to enable him to make a blind landing.

ground cover *n.* the mass of dense low herbaceous plants and shrubs that grow over the surface of the ground.

ground floor *n.* **1.** the floor of a building level or almost level with the ground. **2. get in on the ground floor.** *Inf.* to be in a project, undertaking, etc., from its inception.

grounding ('graʊndɪŋ) *n.* a foundation, esp. the basic general knowledge of a subject.

ground ivy *n.* a creeping or trailing Eurasian aromatic herbaceous plant with scalloped leaves and purplish-blue flowers.

groundless ('graʊndlɪs) *adj.* without reason or justification: *his suspicions were groundless.* —'**groundlessly** *adv.* —'**groundlessness** *n.*

groundnut ('graʊnd.nʌt) *n.* **1.** a North American climbing leguminous plant with small edible underground tubers. **2.** the tuber of this plant. **3.** *Brit.* another name for **peanut.**

groundsel ('graʊnsəl) *n.* any of certain plants of the composite family, esp. a Eurasian weed with heads of small yellow flowers.

groundsheet ('graʊnd.ʃiːt) *n.* a waterproof rubber, plastic, or polythene sheet placed on the ground in a tent, etc., to keep out damp.

groundsman ('graʊndzmən) *n.*, *pl.* **-men.** a person employed to maintain a sports ground, park, etc.

THESAURUS

grope cast about, feel, finger, fish, flounder, fumble, grabble, scrabble, search

gross *adj.* **1.** big, bulky, corpulent, dense, fat, great, heavy, hulking, large, lumpish, massive, obese, overweight, thick **2.** aggregate, before deductions, before tax, entire, total, whole **3.** coarse, crude, improper, impure, indecent, indelicate, lewd, low, obscene, offensive, ribald, rude, sensual, smutty, unseemly, vulgar **4.** apparent, arrant, blatant, downright, egregious, flagrant, glaring, grievous, heinous, manifest, obvious, outrageous, plain, rank, serious, shameful, sheer, shocking, unmitigated, unqualified, utter **5.** boorish, callous, coarse, crass, dull, ignorant,

imperceptive, insensitive, tasteless, uncultured, undiscriminating, unfeeling, unrefined, unsophisticated ~*v.* **6.** bring in, earn, make, rake in (*Inf.*), take

grotesque absurd, bizarre, deformed, distorted, extravagant, fanciful, fantastic, freakish, incongruous, ludicrous, malformed, misshapen, odd, outlandish, preposterous, ridiculous, strange, unnatural, weird, whimsical

ground *n.* **1.** clod, dirt, dry land, dust, earth, field, land, loam, mould, sod, soil, terra firma, terrain, turf **2.** *Often plural* area, country, district, domain, estate, fields, gardens, habitat, holding, land, property, realm, terrain, territory, tract **3.** *Usually plural* account, argument, base, basis, call, cause, excuse, factor, foundation, inducement, justification, motive, occasion, premise, pretext, rationale, reason **4.** *Usually plural* deposit, dregs, grouts, lees, sediment, settlings **5.** arena, field, park (*Inf.*), pitch, stadium ~*v.* **6.** base, establish, fix, found, set, settle **7.** acquaint with, coach, familiarize with, inform, initiate, instruct, prepare, teach, train, tutor

groundless baseless, chimerical, empty, false, idle, illusory, imaginary, unauthorized, uncalled-for, unfounded, unjustified, unprovoked, unsupported, unwarranted

ground swell n. 1. a considerable swell of the sea, often caused by a distant storm or earthquake. 2. a rapidly developing general feeling or opinion.

groundwork ('graund,wɜːk) n. 1. preliminary work as a foundation or basis. 2. the ground or background of a painting, etc.

group (gruːp) n. 1. a number of persons or things considered as a collective unit. 2. a. a number of persons bound together by common social standards, interests, etc. b. (as modifier): group behaviour. 3. a small band of players or singers, esp. of pop music. 4. a number of animals or plants considered as a unit because of common characteristics, habits, etc. 5. an association of companies under a single ownership and control. 6. two or more figures or objects forming a design in a painting or sculpture. 7. a military formation comprising complementary arms and services: a brigade group. 8. an air force organization of higher level than a squadron. 9. Also called: **radical**. Chem. two or more atoms that are bound together in a molecule and behave as a single unit: a methyl group -CH₃. 10. a vertical column of elements in the periodic table that all have similar electronic structures, properties, and valencies: the halogen group. 11. Maths. a set under an operation involving any two members of the set such that the set is closed, associative, and contains both an identity and the inverse of each member. 12. See **blood group**. ~vb. 13. to arrange or place (things, people, etc.) in or into a group, or (of things, etc.) to form into a group.

group captain n. an officer holding commissioned rank senior to a wing commander but junior to an air commodore in the British R.A.F. and certain other air forces.

group therapy n. Psychiatry. the simultaneous treatment of a number of individuals who are brought together to share their problems in group discussion.

grouse[1] (graus) n., pl. **grouse** or **grouses**. a game bird occurring mainly in the N hemisphere, having a stocky body and feathered legs and feet.

grouse[2] (graus) vb. 1. (intr.) to grumble; complain. ~n. 2. a persistent complaint. —'**grouser** n.

grout (graut) n. 1. a thin mortar for filling joints between tiles, masonry, etc. 2. a fine plaster used as a finishing coat. 3. (pl.) sediment or dregs. ~vb. 4. (tr.) to fill (joints) or finish (walls, etc.) with grout. —'**grouter** n.

grove (grəuv) n. 1. a small wooded area or plantation. 2. a road lined with houses and often trees, esp. in a suburban area.

grovel ('grɒvəl) vb. **-elling, -elled** or U.S. **-eling, -eled**. (intr.) 1. to humble or abase oneself, as in making apologies or showing respect. 2. to lie or crawl face downwards, as in fear or humility. 3. (often foll. by in) to indulge or take pleasure (in sensuality or vice). —'**groveller** n.

grow (grəu) vb. **growing, grew, grown**. 1. (of an organism or part of an organism) to increase in size or develop (hair, leaves, or other structures). 2. (intr.; usually foll. by out of or from) to originate, as from an initial cause or source: the federation grew out of the Empire. 3. (intr.) to increase in size, number, degree, etc.: the population is growing rapidly. 4. (intr.) to change in

length or amount in a specified direction: some plants grow downwards. 5. (copula; may take an infinitive) (esp. of emotions, physical states, etc.) to develop or come into existence or being gradually: to grow cold; he grew to like her. 6. (intr.; foll. by together) to be joined gradually by or as by growth: the branches on the tree grew together. 7. (when intr., foll. by with) to become covered with a growth: the path grew with weeds. 8. to produce (plants) by controlling or encouraging their growth, esp. for home consumption or on a commercial basis. ~ See also **grow into, grow on**, etc. —'**growable** adj. —'**grower** n.

growing pains pl. n. 1. pains in muscles or joints sometimes experienced by growing children. 2. difficulties besetting a new enterprise in its early stages.

grow into vb. (intr., prep.) to become big or mature enough for: his clothes were always big enough for him to grow into.

growl (graul) vb. 1. (of animals, esp. when hostile) to utter (sounds) in a low inarticulate manner: the dog growled. 2. to utter (words) in a gruff or angry manner. 3. (intr.) to make sounds suggestive of an animal growling: the thunder growled. ~n. 4. the act or sound of growling. —'**growler** n. —'**growlingly** adv.

grown (grəun) adj. a. developed or advanced: fully grown. b. (in combination): half-grown.

grown-up adj. 1. having reached maturity; adult. 2. suitable for or characteristic of an adult. ~n. 3. an adult.

grow on vb. (intr., prep.) to become progressively more acceptable or pleasant to.

grow out of vb. (intr., adv. + prep.) to become too big or mature for: she soon grew out of her girlish ways.

growth (grəuθ) n. 1. the process or act of growing. 2. an increase in size, number, significance, etc. 3. something grown or growing: a new growth of hair. 4. a stage of development: a full growth. 5. any abnormal tissue, such as a tumour. 6. (modifier) of, relating to, or characterized by growth: a growth industry.

grow up vb. (intr., adv.) 1. to reach maturity; become adult. 2. to come into existence; develop.

groyne or esp. U.S. **groin** (grɔɪn) n. a wall or jetty built out from a riverbank or seashore to control erosion. Also called: **spur, breakwater**.

grub (grʌb) vb. **grubbing, grubbed**. 1. (when tr., often foll. by up or out) to search for and pull up (roots, stumps, etc.) by digging in the ground. 2. to dig up the surface of (ground, soil, etc.), esp. to clear away roots, stumps, etc. 3. (intr.; often foll. by in or among) to search carefully. 4. (intr.) to work unceasingly, esp. at a dull task. ~n. 5. the short legless larva of certain insects, esp. beetles. 6. Sl. food; victuals. 7. a person who works hard, esp. in a plodding way. —'**grubber** n.

grubby ('grʌbɪ) adj. **-bier, -biest**. 1. dirty; slovenly. 2. mean; beggarly. 3. infested with grubs. —'**grubbily** adv. —'**grubbiness** n.

grudge (grʌdʒ) n. 1. a persistent feeling of resentment, esp. one due to an insult or injury. ~vb. 2. (tr.) to give unwillingly. 3. to feel resentful or envious about (someone else's success, possessions, etc.). —'**grudger** n. —'**grudgingly** adv.

THESAURUS

groundwork base, basis, cornerstone, footing, foundation, fundamentals, preliminaries, preparation, spadework, underpinnings

group n. 1. aggregation, assemblage, association, band, batch, bunch, category, circle, class, clique, clump, cluster, collection, company, congregation, coterie, crowd, faction, formation, gang, gathering, organization, pack, party, set, troop ~v. 2. arrange, assemble, associate, assort, bracket, class, classify, dispose, gather, marshal, order, organize, put together, range, sort 3. associate, band together, cluster, congregate, consort, fraternize, gather, get together

grouse 1. v. beef (Sl.), bellyache (Sl.), bitch (Sl.), carp, complain, find fault, gripe (Inf.), grouch (Inf.), grumble, moan, whine 2. n. beef (Sl.), complaint, grievance, gripe (Inf.), grouch (Inf.), grumble, moan, objection

grovel abase oneself, bootlick (Inf.), bow and scrape, cower, crawl, creep, cringe, crouch, demean oneself, fawn, flatter, humble oneself, kowtow, sneak, toady

grow 1. develop, enlarge, expand, extend, fill out, get bigger, get taller, heighten, increase, multiply, spread, stretch, swell, thicken, widen 2. develop, flourish, germinate, shoot, spring up, sprout, vegetate 3. arise, issue, originate, spring, stem 4. advance, expand, flourish, improve, progress, prosper, succeed, thrive 5. become, come to be, develop (into), get, turn, wax 6. breed, cultivate, farm, nurture, produce, propagate, raise

grown-up 1. adj. adult, fully-grown, mature, of age 2. n. adult, man, woman

growth 1. aggrandizement, augmentation, development, enlargement, evolution, expansion, extension, growing, heightening, increase, multiplication, proliferation, stretching, thickening, widening 2. crop, cultivation,

development, germination, produce, production, shooting, sprouting, vegetation 3. advance, advancement, expansion, improvement, progress, prosperity, rise, success 4. Medicine excrescence, lump, tumour

grub v. 1. burrow, dig up, probe, pull up, root (Inf.), rootle (Brit.), search for, uproot 2. ferret, forage, hunt, rummage, scour, search, uncover, unearth 3. drudge, grind (Inf.), labour, plod, slave, slog, sweat, toil ~n. 4. caterpillar, larva, maggot 5. Sl. eats (Sl.), food, nosh (Sl.), rations, sustenance, victuals

grubby besmeared, dirty, filthy, frowzy, grimy, manky (Scot. dialect), mean, messy, mucky, scruffy, seedy, shabby, slovenly, smutty, soiled, sordid, squalid, unkempt, untidy, unwashed

grudge 1. n. animosity, animus, antipathy, aversion, bitterness, dislike, enmity, grievance, hard feelings, hate, ill will, malevolence, malice, pique, rancour, resentment,

gruel ('gru:əl) *n.* a drink or thin porridge made by boiling meal, esp. oatmeal, in water or milk.

gruelling *or U.S.* **grueling** ('gru:əlɪŋ) *adj.* **1.** extremely severe or tiring. ~*n.* **2.** *Inf.* a severe or tiring experience, esp. punishment.

gruesome ('gru:səm) *adj.* inspiring repugnance and horror; ghastly. —'**gruesomely** *adv.* —'**gruesomeness** *n.*

gruff (grʌf) *adj.* **1.** rough or surly in manner, speech, etc. **2.** (of a voice, bark, etc.) low and throaty. —'**gruffly** *adv.* —'**gruffness** *n.*

grumble ('grʌmbəl) *vb.* **1.** to utter (complaints) in a nagging way. **2.** (*intr.*) to make low dull rumbling sounds. ~*n.* **3.** a complaint; grouse. **4.** a low rumbling sound. —'**grumbler** *n.* —'**grumblingly** *adv.* —'**grumbly** *adj.*

grumpy ('grʌmpɪ) *or* **grumpish** *adj.* **grumpier, grumpiest.** peevish; sulky. —'**grumpily** *or* '**grumpishly** *adv.* —'**grumpiness** *or* '**grumpishness** *n.*

Grundy ('grʌndɪ) *n.* a narrow-minded person who keeps critical watch on the propriety of others.

grunt (grʌnt) *vb.* **1.** (*intr.*) (esp. of pigs and some other animals) to emit a low short gruff noise. **2.** (when *tr.*, may take a clause as object) to express something gruffly: *he grunted his answer.* ~*n.* **3.** the characteristic low short gruff noise of pigs, etc., or a similar sound, as of disgust. **4.** any of various mainly tropical marine fishes that utter a grunting sound when caught. —'**grunter** *n.*

Gruyère *or* **Gruyère cheese** ('gru:jɛə) *n.* a hard flat whole-milk cheese, pale yellow in colour and with holes.

gryphon ('grɪfən) *n.* a variant spelling of **griffin.**

G.S. *abbrev. for:* **1.** General Secretary. **2.** General Staff.

G-string *n.* **1.** a piece of cloth worn by striptease artistes covering the pubic area only and attached to a very narrow waistband. **2.** a strip of cloth attached to the front and back of a waistband and covering the loins. **3.** *Music.* a string tuned to G.

G-suit *n.* a close-fitting garment that is worn by the crew of high-speed aircraft and can be pressurized to prevent blackout during certain manoeuvres.

GT *abbrev. for* gran turismo: a touring car; usually a fast sports car with a hard fixed roof.

guanaco (gwɑ:'nɑːkəʊ) *n., pl.* -**cos.** a cud-chewing South American mammal closely related to the domesticated llama.

guano ('gwɑːnəʊ) *n., pl.* -**nos.** **1.** the dried excrement of fish-eating sea birds, deposited in rocky coastal regions of South America: used as a fertilizer. **2.** any similar but artificially produced fertilizer.

guarantee (ˌgærən'tiː) *n.* **1.** a formal assurance, esp. in writing, that a product, service, etc., will meet certain standards or specifications. **2.** *Law.* a promise, esp. a collateral agreement, to answer for the debt, default, or miscarriage of another. **3. a.** a person, company, etc., to whom a guarantee is made. **b.** a person, company, etc., who gives a guarantee. **4.** a person who acts as a guarantor. **5.** something that makes a specified condition or outcome certain. **6.** a variant spelling of **guaranty.** ~*vb.* -**teeing, -teed.** (*mainly tr.*) **7.** (*also intr.*) to take responsibility for (someone else's debts, obligations, etc.). **8.** to serve as a guarantee for. **9.** to secure or furnish security for: *a small deposit will guarantee any dress.* **10.** (usually foll. by *from* or *against*) to undertake to protect or keep secure, as against injury, loss, etc. **11.** to ensure: *good planning will guarantee success.* **12.** (*may take a clause as object or an infinitive*) to promise or make certain.

guarantor (ˌgærən'tɔː) *n.* a person who gives or is bound by a guarantee or guaranty; surety.

guaranty ('gærəntɪ) *n., pl.* -**ties.** **1.** a pledge of responsibility for fulfilling another person's obligations in case of that person's default. **2.** a thing given or taken as security for a guaranty. **3.** the act of providing security. **4.** a person who acts as a guarantor. ~*vb.* -**tying, -tied.** **5.** a variant spelling of **guarantee.**

guard (gɑːd) *vb.* **1.** to watch over or shield (a person or thing) from danger or harm; protect. **2.** to keep watch over (a prisoner or other potentially dangerous person or thing), as to prevent escape. **3.** (*tr.*) to control: *to guard one's tongue.* **4.** (*intr.;* usually foll. by *against*) to take precautions. **5.** to control entrance and exit through (a gate, door, etc.). **6.** (*tr.*) to provide (machinery, etc.) with a device to protect the operator. **7.** (*tr.*) **a.** *Chess, cards.* to protect or cover (a chess man or card) with another. **b.** *Curling, bowling.* to protect or cover (a stone or bowl) by placing one's own stone or bowl between it and another player. ~*n.* **8.** a person or group who keeps a protecting, supervising, or restraining watch or control over people, such as prisoners, things, etc. Related adj.: **custodial. 9.** a person or group of people, such as soldiers, who form a ceremonial escort. **10.** *Brit.* the official in charge of a train. **11. a.** the act or duty of protecting, restraining, or supervising. **b.** (*as modifier*): *guard duty.* **12.** a device, part, or attachment on an object, such as a weapon or machine tool, designed to protect the user against injury. **13.** anything that provides or is intended to provide protection: *a guard against infection.* **14.** *Sport.* an article of light tough material worn to protect any of various parts of the body. **15.** the posture of defence or readiness in fencing, boxing, cricket, etc. **16. off (one's) guard.** having one's defences down; unprepared. **17. on (one's) guard.** prepared to face danger, difficulties, etc. **18. stand guard.** (of a military sentry, etc.) to keep watch. **19. mount guard.** *Chiefly mil.* (of a sentry, etc.) to begin to keep watch. —'**guarder** *n.*

guarded ('gɑːdɪd) *adj.* **1.** protected or kept under surveillance. **2.** prudent, restrained, or noncommittal: *a guarded reply.* —'**guardedly** *adv.* —'**guardedness** *n.*

guardhouse ('gɑːdˌhaʊs) *n. Mil.* a building serving as headquarters for military police and in which military prisoners are detained.

guardian ('gɑːdɪən) *n.* **1.** one who looks after, protects, or defends: *the guardian of public morals.* **2.** *Law.* someone legally appointed to manage the affairs of a person incapable of acting for himself, as an infant or person of unsound mind. ~*adj.* **3.** protecting or safeguarding. —'**guardianˌship** *n.*

guardsman ('gɑːdzmən) *n., pl.* -**men.** **1.** (in Britain) a member of a Guards battalion or regiment. **2.** (in the

---

THESAURUS

spite, venom **2.** *v.* begrudge, be reluctant, complain, covet, envy, hold back, mind, resent, stint

gruelling arduous, backbreaking, brutal, crushing, demanding, difficult, exhausting, fatiguing, fierce, grinding, hard, harsh, laborious, punishing, severe, stiff, strenuous, taxing, tiring, trying

gruesome abominable, awful, fearful, ghastly, grim, grisly, hideous, horrendous, horrible, horrid, horrific, horrifying,. loathsome, macabre, repugnant, repulsive, shocking, spine-chilling, terrible

gruff **1.** bad-tempered, bearish, blunt, brusque, churlish, crabbed, crusty, curt, discourteous, grouchy (*Inf.*), grumpy, illhumoured, ill-natured, impolite, rough, rude, sour, sullen, surly, uncivil, ungracious, unmannerly **2.** croaking, guttural, harsh, hoarse, husky, low, rasping, rough, throaty

grumble *v.* **1.** beef (*Sl.*), bellyache (*Sl.*), bitch (*Sl.*), carp, complain, find fault, gripe (*Inf.*), grouch (*Inf.*), grouse, moan, repine, whine **2.** growl, gurgle, murmur, mutter, roar, rumble ~*n.* **3.** beef (*Sl.*), complaint, grievance, gripe (*Inf.*), grouch (*Inf.*), grouse, moan, objection **4.** growl, gurgle, murmur, muttering, roar, rumble

guarantee **1.** *n.* assurance, bond, certainty, collateral, covenant, earnest, guaranty, pledge, promise, security, surety, undertaking, warranty, word, word of honour **2.** *v.* answer for, assure, certify, ensure, insure, maintain, make certain, pledge, promise, protect, secure, stand behind, swear, vouch for, warrant

guarantor backer, bailsman (*Rare*), bondsman (*Law*), guarantee, sponsor, supporter, surety, underwriter, voucher, warrantor

guard *v.* **1.** cover, defend, escort, keep, mind, oversee, patrol, police, preserve, protect, safeguard, save, screen, secure, shelter, shield, supervise, tend, watch, watch over

~*n.* **2.** custodian, defender, lookout, picket, protector, sentinel, sentry, warder, watch, watchman **3.** convoy, escort, patrol **4.** buffer, bulwark, bumper, defence, pad, protection, rampart, safeguard, screen, security, shield **5.** attention, care, caution, heed, vigilance, wariness, watchfulness **6. off (one's) guard** napping, unprepared, unready, unwary, with one's defences down **7. on (one's) guard** alert, cautious, circumspect, on the alert, on the lookout, on the qui vive, prepared, ready, vigilant, wary, watchful

guarded cagey (*Inf.*), careful, cautious, circumspect, discreet, noncommittal, prudent, reserved, restrained, reticent, suspicious, wary

guardian attendant, champion, curator, custodian, defender, escort, guard, keeper, preserver, protector, trustee, warden, warder

U.S.) a member of the National Guard. **3.** a guard.

guard's van *n. Railways, Brit. & N.Z.* the van in which the guard travels, usually attached to the rear of a train. U.S. equivalent: **caboose.**

guava ('gwɑːvə) *n.* **1.** any of various tropical American trees, grown esp. for their edible fruit. **2.** the fruit of such a tree, having yellow skin and pink pulp.

gubbins ('gʌbɪnz) *n.* **1.** an object of little value. **2.** a small gadget. **3.** *Inf.* a silly person.

gubernatorial (ˌgjuːbənə'tɔːrɪəl, ˌguː-) *adj. Chiefly U.S.* of or relating to a governor.

gudgeon[1] ('gʌdʒən) *n.* **1.** a small slender European freshwater fish with a barbel on each side of the mouth: used as bait by anglers. **2.** any of various other fishes, such as the goby. **3.** *Sl.* a person who is easy to trick or cheat. ~*vb.* **4.** (*tr.*) *Sl.* to trick or cheat.

gudgeon[2] ('gʌdʒən) *n.* **1.** the female or socket portion of a pinned hinge. **2.** *Naut.* one of two or more looplike sockets, fixed to the transom of a boat, into which the pintles of a rudder are fitted.

guelder-rose ('gɛldəˌrəʊz) *n.* a Eurasian shrub with clusters of white flowers and small red fruits.

Guernsey ('gɜːnzɪ) *n.* **1.** an island in the English Channel: the second largest of the Channel Islands. **2.** a breed of dairy cattle producing rich creamy milk, originating from the island of Guernsey. **3.** (*sometimes not cap.*) a seaman's knitted woollen sweater. **4.** (*not cap.*) *Austral.* a sleeveless woollen shirt or jumper worn by a football player. **5. get a guernsey.** *Austral.* to be selected for a team or gain recognition for something.

guerrilla *or* **guerilla** (gə'rɪlə) *n.* **a.** a member of an irregular usually politically motivated armed force that combats stronger regular forces. **b.** (*as modifier*): *guerrilla warfare.*

guess (gɛs) *vb.* (*when tr., may take a clause as object*) **1.** (*when intr., often foll. by at or about*) to form or express an uncertain estimate or conclusion (about something), based on insufficient information: *guess what we're having for dinner.* **2.** to arrive at a correct estimate of (something) by guessing: *he guessed my age.* **3.** *Inf., chiefly U.S.* to believe, think, or suppose (something): *I guess I'll go now.* ~*n.* **4.** an estimate or conclusion arrived at by guessing: *a bad guess.* **5.** the act of guessing. —**'guesser** *n.*

guesswork ('gɛsˌwɜːk) *n.* **1.** a set of conclusions, estimates, etc., arrived at by guessing. **2.** the process of making guesses.

guest (gɛst) *n.* **1.** a person who is entertained, taken out to eat, etc., and paid for by another. **2. a.** a person who receives hospitality at the home of another. **b.** (*as modifier*): *the guest room.* **3. a.** a person who receives the hospitality of a government, establishment, or organization. **b.** (*as modifier*): *a guest speaker.* **4. a.** an actor, contestant, entertainer, etc., taking part as a visitor in a programme in which there are also regular participants. **b.** (*as modifier*): *a guest appearance.* **5.** a patron of a hotel, boarding house, restaurant, etc. ~*vb.* **6.** (*intr.*) *Inf.* (in theatre and broadcasting) to be a guest: *to guest on a show.*

guesthouse ('gɛstˌhaʊs) *n.* a private home or boarding house offering accommodation.

guff (gʌf) *n. Sl.* ridiculous or insolent talk.

guffaw (gʌ'fɔː) *n.* **1.** a crude and boisterous laugh. ~*vb.* **2.** to laugh or express (something) in this way.

guidance ('gaɪdəns) *n.* **1.** leadership, instruction, or direction. **2. a.** counselling or advice on educational, vocational, or psychological matters. **b.** (*as modifier*): *the marriage-guidance counsellor.* **3.** something that guides. **4.** any process by which the flight path of a missile is controlled in flight.

guide (gaɪd) *vb.* **1.** to lead the way for (a person). **2.** to control the movement or course of (an animal, vehicle, etc.) by physical action; steer. **3.** to supervise or instruct (a person). **4.** (*tr.*) to direct the affairs of (a person, company, nation, etc.). **5.** (*tr.*) to advise or influence (a person) in his standards or opinions: *let truth guide you.* ~*n.* **6. a.** a person, animal, or thing that guides. **b.** (*as modifier*): *a guide dog.* **7.** a person, usually past, who conducts tour expeditions, etc. **8.** a model or criterion, as in moral standards or accuracy. **9.** Also called: **guidebook.** a handbook with information for visitors to a place. **10.** a book that instructs or explains the fundamentals of a subject or skill. **11.** any device that directs the motion of a tool or machine part. **12.** a mark, sign, etc., that points the way. **13. a.** *Naval.* a ship in a formation used as a reference for manoeuvres. **b.** *Mil.* a soldier stationed to one side of a column or line to regulate alignment, show the way, etc. —**'guidable** *adj.* —**'guider** *n.*

Guide (gaɪd) *n.* (*sometimes not cap.*) a member of the organization for girls equivalent to the Scouts. U.S. equivalent: **Girl Scout.**

guided missile *n.* a missile, esp. one that is rocket-propelled, having a flight path controlled either by radio signals or by internal preset or self-actuating homing devices.

guideline ('gaɪdˌlaɪn) *n.* a principle put forward to set standards or determine a course of action.

guidepost ('gaɪdˌpəʊst) *n.* **1.** a sign on a post by a road indicating directions. **2.** a principle or guideline.

guidon ('gaɪdən) *n.* **1.** a small pennant, used as a marker or standard, esp. by cavalry regiments. **2.** the man or vehicle that carries this.

guild *or* **gild** (gɪld) *n.* **1.** an organization, club, or fellowship. **2.** (esp. in medieval Europe) an association of men sharing the same interests, such as merchants or artisans: formed for mutual aid and protection and to maintain craft standards. —**'guildsman, 'gildsman** *or* (*fem.*) **'guildswoman, 'gildswoman** *n.*

guilder ('gɪldə) *or* **gulden** *n., pl.* **-ders, -der** *or* **-dens, -den.** **1.** Also: **gilder.** the standard monetary unit of the Netherlands, divided into 100 cents. **2.** any of various former gold or silver coins of Germany, Austria, or the Netherlands.

guildhall ('gɪldˌhɔːl) *n. Brit.* **a.** the hall of a guild or corporation. **b.** a town hall.

guile (gaɪl) *n.* clever or crafty character or behaviour. —**'guileful** *adj.* —**'guilefully** *adv.* —**'guilefulness** *n.* —**'guileless** *adj.* —**'guilelessly** *adv.* —**'guilelessness** *n.*

guillemot ('gɪlɪˌmɒt) *n.* a northern oceanic diving bird having a black-and-white plumage and long narrow bill.

guillotine *n.* ('gɪləˌtiːn). **1. a.** a device for beheading persons, consisting of a weighted blade set between two upright posts. **b. the guillotine.** execution by this instrument. **2.** a device for cutting or trimming sheet material, such as paper or sheet metal, consisting of a long rigid blade that descends onto the sheet. **3.** a surgical instrument for removing tonsils, growths in the throat, etc.

THESAURUS

guerrilla freedom fighter, irregular, member of the underground *or* resistance, partisan, underground fighter

guess *v.* **1.** conjecture, estimate, fathom, hypothesize, penetrate, predict, solve, speculate, work out **2.** believe, conjecture, dare say, deem, divine, fancy, hazard, imagine, judge, reckon, suppose, surmise, suspect, think ~*n.* **3.** conjecture, feeling, hypothesis, judgment, notion, prediction, reckoning, speculation, supposition, surmise, suspicion, theory

guesswork conjecture, estimation, presumption, speculation, supposition, surmise, suspicion, theory

guest boarder, caller, company, lodger, visitant, visitor

guidance advice, auspices, conduct, con-

trol, counsel, counselling, direction, government, help, instruction, intelligence, leadership, management, teaching

guide *v.* **1.** accompany, attend, conduct, convoy, direct, escort, lead, pilot, shepherd, show the way, steer, usher **2.** command, control, direct, handle, manage, manoeuvre, steer **3.** advise, counsel, educate, govern, influence, instruct, oversee, regulate, rule, superintend, supervise, sway, teach, train ~*n.* **4.** adviser, attendant, chaperon, cicerone, conductor, controller, counsellor, director, escort, leader, mentor, monitor, pilot, steersman, teacher, usher **5.** criterion, example, exemplar, ideal, inspiration, lodestar, master, model, paradigm, standard **6.** beacon, clue, guiding light, key, landmark, lodestar, mark, marker, pointer, sign, signal,

signpost **7.** catalogue, directory, guidebook, handbook, instructions, key, manual, vade mecum

guild association, brotherhood, club, company, corporation, fellowship, fraternity, league, lodge, order, organization, society, union

guile art, artfulness, artifice, cleverness, craft, craftiness, cunning, deceit, deception, duplicity, gamesmanship (*Inf.*), knavery, ruse, sharp practice, slyness, treachery, trickery, trickiness, wiliness

guileful artful, clever, crafty, cunning, deceitful, duplicitous, foxy, sly, sneaky, treacherous, tricky, underhand, wily

4. (in Parliament, etc.) a form of closure under which a bill is divided into compartments, groups of which must be completely dealt with each day. ~*vb.* (ˌgɪləˈtiːn). (*tr.*) **5.** to behead (a person) by guillotine. **6.** (in Parliament, etc.) to limit debate on (a bill, motion, etc.) by the guillotine. —ˌguilloˈtiner *n.*

guilt (gɪlt) *n.* **1.** the fact or state of having done wrong or committed an offence. **2.** responsibility for a criminal or moral offence deserving punishment or a penalty. **3.** remorse or self-reproach caused by feeling that one is responsible for a wrong or offence. **4.** *Arch.* sin or crime.

guiltless (ˈgɪltlɪs) *adj.* free of all responsibility for wrongdoing or crime; innocent. —ˈguiltlessly *adv.* —ˈguiltlessness *n.*

guilty (ˈgɪltɪ) *adj.* **guiltier, guiltiest. 1.** responsible for an offence or misdeed. **2.** *Law.* having committed an offence or adjudged to have done so: *the accused was found guilty.* **3.** of, showing, or characterized by guilt. —ˈguiltily *adv.* —ˈguiltiness *n.*

guinea (ˈgɪnɪ) *n.* **1. a.** a British gold coin taken out of circulation in 1813, worth 21 shillings. **b.** the sum of 21 shillings (£1.05), still used in quoting professional fees. **2.** See **guinea fowl.**

guinea fowl *or* **guinea** *n.* a domestic fowl of Africa and SW Asia, having a dark plumage mottled with white, a naked head and neck, and a heavy rounded body.

guinea pig *n.* **1.** a domesticated cavy, commonly kept as a pet and used in scientific experiments. **2.** *Inf.* a person or thing used for experimentation.

guipure (gɪˈpjuə) *n.* **1.** Also called: **guipure lace.** any of many types of heavy lace that have their pattern connected by threads, rather than supported on a net mesh. **2.** a heavy corded trimming; gimp.

guise (gaɪz) *n.* **1.** semblance or pretence: *under the guise of friendship.* **2.** external appearance in general. **3.** *Arch.* manner or style of dress.

guitar (gɪˈtɑː) *n.* a plucked stringed instrument originating in Spain, usually having six strings, a flat sounding board with a circular sound hole in the centre, a flat back, and a fretted fingerboard. —guiˈtarist *n.*

Gulag (ˈguːlæg) *n.* the central administrative department of the Soviet security service, responsible for maintaining prisons and labour camps.

gulch (gʌltʃ) *n. U.S.* a narrow ravine cut by a fast stream.

gulf (gʌlf) *n.* **1.** a large deep bay. **2.** a deep chasm. **3.** something that divides or separates, such as a lack of understanding. **4.** something that engulfs, such as a whirlpool. ~*vb.* **5.** (*tr.*) to swallow up; engulf.

Gulf Stream *n.* a relatively warm ocean current flowing northeastwards from the Gulf of Mexico towards NW Europe. Also called: **North Atlantic Drift.**

gulfweed (ˈgʌlf,wiːd) *n.* a brown seaweed having air bladders and forming dense floating masses in tropical Atlantic waters, esp. the Gulf Stream. Also called: **sargasso, sargasso weed.**

gull¹ (gʌl) *n.* an aquatic bird such as the common gull or mew having long pointed wings, short legs, and a mostly white plumage.

gull² (gʌl) *Arch.* ~*n.* **1.** a person who is easily fooled or cheated. ~*vb.* **2.** (*tr.*) to fool, cheat, or hoax.

gullet (ˈgʌlɪt) *n.* **1.** a less formal name for the **oesophagus. 2.** the throat or pharynx.

gullible (ˈgʌləbəl) *adj.* easily taken in or tricked. —ˌgulliˈbility *n.* —ˈgullibly *adv.*

gully (ˈgʌlɪ) *n., pl.* **-lies. 1.** a channel or small valley,

esp. one cut by heavy rainwater. **2.** *N.Z.* a bush-clad small valley. **3.** *Cricket.* **a.** a fielding position between the slips and point. **b.** a fielder in this position. ~*vb.* **-lying, -lied. 4.** (*tr.*) to make (channels) in (the ground, sand, etc.).

gulp (gʌlp) *vb.* **1.** (*tr.*; often foll. by *down*) to swallow rapidly, esp. in large mouthfuls. **2.** (*tr.*; often foll. by *back*) to stifle or choke: *to gulp back sobs.* **3.** (*intr.*) to swallow air convulsively because of nervousness, surprise, etc. **4.** (*intr.*) to make a noise, as when swallowing too quickly. ~*n.* **5.** the act of gulping. **6.** the quantity taken in a gulp. —ˈgulper *n.* —ˈgulpingly *adv.* —ˈgulpy *adj.*

gum¹ (gʌm) *n.* **1.** any of various sticky substances that exude from certain plants, hardening on exposure to air and dissolving or forming viscous masses in water. **2.** any of various products, such as adhesives, that are made from such substances. **3.** any sticky substance used as an adhesive; mucilage; glue. **4.** See **chewing gum, bubble gum,** and **gumtree. 5.** *Chiefly Brit.* a gumdrop. ~*vb.* **gumming, gummed. 6.** to cover or become covered, clogged, or stiffened as with gum. **7.** (*tr.*) to stick together or in place with gum. **8.** (*intr.*) to emit or form gum. ~See also **gum up.**

gum² (gʌm) *n.* the fleshy tissue that covers the jaw bones around the bases of the teeth.

gum arabic *n.* a gum exuded by certain acacia trees, used in the manufacture of ink, food thickeners, pills, emulsifiers, etc.

gumboil (ˈgʌm,bɔɪl) *n.* an abscess on the gums.

gumboots (ˈgʌm,buːts) *pl. n.* knee-length or calf-length rubber boots, worn esp. in wet conditions. Also called (esp. Brit.): **Wellington boots.**

gummy¹ (ˈgʌmɪ) *adj.* **-mier, -miest. 1.** sticky or tacky. **2.** consisting of, coated with, or clogged by gum or a similar substance. **3.** producing gum. —ˈgumminess *n.*

gummy² (ˈgʌmɪ) *adj.* **-mier, -miest. 1.** toothless. ~*n., pl.* **-mies. 2.** *Austral.* Also called: **gummy shark.** a small crustacean-eating shark with flat crushing teeth.

gumption (ˈgʌmpʃən) *n. Inf.* **1.** *Brit.* common sense or resourcefulness. **2.** initiative or courage.

gum resin *n.* a mixture of resin and gum obtained from various plants and trees.

gumtree (ˈgʌm,triː) *n.* **1.** any of various trees that yield gum, such as the eucalyptus, sweet gum, and sour gum. Sometimes shortened to **gum. 2. up a gumtree.** *Sl.* in a very awkward position; in difficulties.

gum up *vb.* (*tr., adv.*) **1.** to cover, dab, or stiffen with gum. **2.** *Inf.* to make a mess of; bungle (often in **gum up the works**).

gun (gʌn) *n.* **1. a.** a weapon with a metallic tube or barrel from which a missile is discharged, usually by force of an explosion. It may be portable or mounted. **b.** (*as modifier*): *a gun barrel.* **2.** the firing of a gun as a salute or signal, as in military ceremonial. **3.** a member of or a place in a shooting party or syndicate. **4.** any device used to project something under pressure: *a spray gun.* **5.** *U.S. sl.* an armed criminal; gunman. **6.** *Austral. sl.* **a.** an expert. **b.** (*as modifier*): *a gun shearer.* **7. give it the gun.** *Sl.* to increase speed, effort, etc., to a considerable or maximum degree. **8. go great guns.** *Sl.* to act or function with great speed, intensity, etc. **9. jump** *or* **beat the gun. a.** (of a runner, etc.) to set off before the starting signal is given. **b.** *Inf.* to act prematurely. **10. stick to one's guns.** *Inf.* to maintain one's opinions or intentions in spite of opposition. ~*vb.* **gunning, gunned. 11.** (when *tr.,* often foll. by *down*) to shoot (someone) with a gun. **12.** (*tr.*) to press hard on the accelerator of (an en-

---

THESAURUS

guilt 1. blame, blameworthiness, criminality, culpability, delinquency, guiltiness, iniquity, misconduct, responsibility, sinfulness, wickedness, wrong, wrongdoing **2.** bad conscience, contrition, disgrace, dishonour, guiltiness, guilty conscience, infamy, regret, remorse, self-condemnation, self-reproach, shame, stigma

guiltless blameless, clean (*Sl.*), clear, immaculate, impeccable, innocent, irreproachable, pure, sinless, spotless, unimpeachable, unsullied, untainted, untarnished

guilty 1. at fault, blameworthy, convicted, criminal, culpable, delinquent, erring, evil, felonious, iniquitous, offending, reprehen-

sible, responsible, sinful, to blame, wicked, wrong **2.** ashamed, conscience-stricken, contrite, hangdog, regretful, remorseful, rueful, shamefaced, sheepish, sorry

gulf 1. bay, bight, sea inlet **2.** abyss, breach, chasm, cleft, gap, opening, rent, rift, separation, split, void, whirlpool

gullibility credulity, innocence, naiveté, simplicity, trustingness

gullible born yesterday, credulous, easily taken in, foolish, green, innocent, naive, silly, simple, trusting, unsceptical, unsophisticated, unsuspecting

gully channel, ditch, gutter, watercourse

gulp *v.* **1.** bolt, devour, gobble, guzzle, knock

back (*Inf.*), quaff, swallow, swig (*Inf.*), swill, toss off, wolf **2.** choke, gasp, stifle, swallow ~*n.* **3.** draught, mouthful, swallow, swig (*Inf.*)

gum 1. *n.* adhesive, cement, exudate, glue, mucilage, paste, resin **2.** *v.* affix, cement, clog, glue, paste, stick, stiffen

gumption ability, acumen, astuteness, cleverness, common sense, discernment, enterprise, get-up-and-go (*Inf.*), horse sense, initiative, mother wit, nous (*Brit. sl.*), resourcefulness, sagacity, savvy (*Sl.*), shrewdness, spirit, wit(s)

gine): *to gun the engine of a car.* **13.** (*intr.*) to hunt with a gun. ~See also **gun for.**

gunboat ('gʌn,bəʊt) *n.* a small shallow-draft vessel carrying mounted guns and used by coastal patrols, etc.

gunboat diplomacy *n.* diplomacy conducted by threats of military intervention.

guncotton ('gʌn,kɒtən) *n.* cellulose nitrate containing a relatively large amount of nitrogen: used as an explosive.

gun dog *n.* **1.** a dog trained to work with a hunter or gamekeeper, esp. in retrieving, pointing at, or flushing game. **2.** a dog belonging to any breed adapted to these activities.

gunfire ('gʌn,faɪə) *n.* **1.** the firing of one or more guns, esp. when done repeatedly. **2.** the use of firearms, as contrasted with other military tactics.

gun for *vb.* (*intr., prep.*) **1.** to search for in order to reprimand, punish, or kill. **2.** to try earnestly for: *he was gunning for promotion.*

gunge (gʌndʒ) *Inf.* ~*n.* **1.** sticky, rubbery, or congealed matter. ~*vb.* **2.** (*tr.; usually passive;* foll by *up*) to block or encrust with gunge; clog. —'**gungy** *adj.*

gunk (gʌŋk) *n. Inf.* slimy, oily, or filthy matter.

gunman ('gʌnmən) *n., pl.* -**men. 1.** a man who is armed with a gun, esp. unlawfully. **2.** a man who is skilled with a gun.

gunmetal ('gʌn,metəl) *n.* **1.** a type of bronze containing copper, tin, and zinc. **2.** a dark grey colour.

gunnel¹ ('gʌnəl) *n.* any eel-like fish occurring in coastal regions of northern seas.

gunnel² ('gʌnəl) *n.* a variant spelling of **gunwale.**

gunner ('gʌnə) *n.* **1.** a serviceman who works with, uses, or specializes in guns. **2.** *Naval.* (formerly) a warrant officer responsible for the training of gun crews, their performance in action, and accounting for ammunition. **3.** (in the British Army) an artilleryman, esp. a private. **4.** a person who hunts with a rifle or shotgun.

gunnery ('gʌnərɪ) *n.* **1.** the art and science of the efficient design and use of ordnance, esp. artillery. **2.** guns collectively. **3.** the use and firing of guns.

gunny ('gʌnɪ) *n., pl.* -**nies.** *Chiefly U.S.* **1.** a coarse hard-wearing fabric usually made from jute and used for sacks, etc. **2.** Also called: **gunny sack.** a sack made from this fabric.

gunpoint ('gʌn,pɔɪnt) *n.* **1.** the muzzle of a gun. **2. at gunpoint.** being under or using the threat of being shot.

gunpowder ('gʌn,paʊdə) *n.* an explosive mixture of potassium nitrate, charcoal, and sulphur: used in time fuses and in fireworks.

gunrunning ('gʌn,rʌnɪŋ) *n.* the smuggling of guns and ammunition or other weapons of war into a country. —'**gun,runner** *n.*

gunshot ('gʌn,ʃɒt) *n.* **1. a.** shot fired from a gun. **b.** (*as modifier*): *gunshot wounds.* **2.** the range of a gun. **3.** the shooting of a gun.

gunslinger ('gʌn,slɪŋə) *n. U.S. sl.* a gunfighter or gunman, esp. in the Old West.

gunstock ('gʌn,stɒk) *n.* the wooden handle or support to which is attached the barrel of a rifle.

gunwale *or* **gunnel** ('gʌnəl) *n. Naut.* the top of the side of a boat or ship.

guppy ('gʌpɪ) *n., pl.* -**pies.** a small brightly coloured freshwater fish of N South America and the West Indies: a popular aquarium fish.

gurgle ('gɜːgəl) *vb.* **1.** (*intr.*) (of liquids, esp. of streams, etc.) to make low bubbling noises when flowing. **2.** to ut-

ter low throaty bubbling noises, esp. as a sign of contentment: *the baby gurgled with delight.* ~*n.* **3.** the act or sound of gurgling.

gurnard ('gɜːnəd) *or* **gurnet** ('gɜːnɪt) *n., pl.* -**nard, -nards** *or* -**net, -nets.** a European marine fish having a heavily armoured head and finger-like pectoral fins.

guru ('gʊruː, 'guːruː) *n.* **1.** a Hindu or Sikh religious teacher or leader, giving personal spiritual guidance to his disciples. **2.** *Often derog.* a leader or chief theoretician of a movement, esp. a spiritual or religious cult.

gush (gʌʃ) *vb.* **1.** to pour out or cause to pour out suddenly and profusely, usually with a rushing sound. **2.** to act or utter in an overeffusive, affected, or sentimental manner. ~*n.* **3.** a sudden copious flow or emission, esp. of liquid. **4.** something that flows out or is emitted. **5.** an extravagant and insincere expression of admiration, sentiment, etc. —'**gushingly** *adv.*

gusher ('gʌʃə) *n.* **1.** a person who gushes, as in being effusive or sentimental. **2.** something, such as a spurting oil well, that gushes.

gusset ('gʌsɪt) *n.* **1.** an inset piece of material used esp. to strengthen or enlarge a garment. **2.** a triangular metal plate for strengthening a corner joint. ~*vb.* **3.** (*tr.*) to put a gusset in (a garment).

gust (gʌst) *n.* **1.** a sudden blast of wind. **2.** a sudden rush of smoke, sound, etc. **3.** an outburst of emotion. ~*vb.* **4.** (*intr.*) to blow in gusts. —'**gusty** *adj.*

gusto ('gʌstəʊ) *n.* vigorous enjoyment, zest, or relish: *the aria was sung with great gusto.*

gut (gʌt) *n.* **1. a.** the lower part of the alimentary canal; intestine. **b.** the entire alimentary canal. Related adj.: **visceral. 2.** (*often pl.*) the bowels or entrails, esp. of an animal. **3.** See **catgut. 4.** a silky fibrous substance extracted from silkworms, used in the manufacture of fishing tackle. **5.** a narrow channel or passage. **6.** (*pl.*) *Inf.* courage, willpower, or daring; forcefulness. **7.** (*pl.*) *Inf.* the essential part: *the guts of a problem.* ~*vb.* **gutting, gutted.** (*tr.*) **8.** to remove the entrails from (fish, etc.). **9.** (esp. of fire) to destroy the inside of (a building). **10.** to take out the central points of (an article, etc.), esp. in summary form. ~*adj.* **11.** *Inf.* arising from or characterized by what is basic, essential, or natural: *a gut problem; a gut reaction.*

gutless ('gʌtlɪs) *adj. Inf.* lacking courage or determination.

gutsy ('gʌtsɪ) *adj.* **gutsier, gutsiest.** *Sl.* **1.** gluttonous; greedy. **2.** full of courage or boldness. **3.** passionate; lusty.

gutta-percha ('gʌtə'pɜːtʃə) *n.* **1.** any of several tropical trees with leathery leaves. **2.** a whitish rubber substance derived from the coagulated milky latex of any of these trees: used in electrical insulation, waterproofing and dentistry.

gutter ('gʌtə) *n.* **1.** a channel along the eaves or on the roof of a building, used to collect and carry away rainwater. **2.** a channel running along the kerb or the centre of a road to collect and carry away rainwater. **3.** either of the two channels running parallel to a tenpin bowling lane. **4.** *Printing.* the white space between the facing pages of an open book. **5.** *Surfing.* a dangerous deep channel formed by currents and waves. **6. the gutter.** *Inf.* a poverty-stricken, degraded, or criminal environment. ~*vb.* **7.** (*tr.*) to make gutters in. **8.** (*intr.*) to flow in a stream or rivulet. —'**guttering** *n.*

gutter press *n.* the section of the popular press that seeks sensationalism in its coverage.

guttersnipe ('gʌtə,snaɪp) *n.* a child who spends most of

THESAURUS

gunman assassin, bandit, bravo, desperado, gangster, gunslinger (*U.S. sl.*), hit man (*Sl.*), killer, mobster (*U.S. sl.*), murderer, terrorist, thug

gurgle 1. *v.* babble, bubble, burble, crow, lap, murmur, plash, purl, ripple, splash 2. *n.* babble, murmur, purl, ripple

guru authority, guiding light, leader, maharishi, master, mentor, sage, swami, teacher, tutor

gush *v.* 1. burst, cascade, flood, flow, jet, pour, run, rush, spout, spurt, stream 2. babble, blather, chatter, effervesce, effuse, enthuse, jabber, overstate, spout ~*n.* 3. burst, cascade, flood, flow, jet, outburst, outflow, rush, spout, spurt, stream, torrent 4. babble,

blather, chatter, effusion, exuberance

gust *n.* 1. blast, blow, breeze, flurry, gale, puff, rush, squall 2. burst, eruption, explosion, fit, gale, outburst, paroxysm, passion, storm, surge ~*v.* 3. blast, blow, puff, squall

gusto appetite, appreciation, brio, delight, enjoyment, enthusiasm, exhilaration, fervour, liking, pleasure, relish, savour, verve, zeal, zest

gusty blowy, blustering, blustery, breezy, squally, stormy, tempestuous, windy

gut *n.* 1. *Often plural* belly, bowels, entrails, innards (*Inf.*), insides (*Inf.*), intestines, inwards, paunch, stomach, viscera 2. *Plural. Inf.* audacity, backbone, boldness, bottle (*Sl.*), courage, daring, forcefulness, grit, hardi-

hood, mettle, nerve, pluck, spirit, spunk (*Inf.*), willpower ~*v.* 3. clean, disembowel, draw, dress, eviscerate 4. clean out, despoil, empty, pillage, plunder, ransack, ravage, rifle, sack, strip ~*adj.* 5. *Inf.* basic, deepseated, emotional, heartfelt, innate, instinctive, intuitive, involuntary, natural, spontaneous, unthinking, visceral

gutless abject, chicken (*Sl.*), cowardly, craven, faint-hearted, feeble, irresolute, lily-livered, spineless, submissive, timid, weak

gutter channel, conduit, ditch, drain, duct, pipe, sluice, trench, trough, tube

guttersnipe gamin, mudlark (*Sl.*), ragamuffin, street Arab, street urchin, waif

his time in the streets, esp. in a slum area.

guttural ('gʌtərəl) *adj.* **1.** *Anat.* of or relating to the throat. **2.** *Phonetics.* pronounced in the throat or the back of the mouth. **3.** raucous. ~*n.* **4.** *Phonetics.* a guttural consonant. —'**gutturally** *adv.*

guy[1] (gaɪ) *n.* **1.** *Inf.* a man or youth. **2.** *Brit.* a crude effigy of Guy Fawkes, usually made of old clothes stuffed with straw or rags, that is burnt on top of a bonfire on Guy Fawkes Day (November 5). **3.** *Brit.* a person in shabby or ludicrously odd clothes. ~*vb.* **4.** (*tr.*) to make fun of; ridicule.

guy[2] (gaɪ) *n.* **1.** a rope, chain, wire, etc., for anchoring an object in position or for steadying or guiding it. ~*vb.* **2.** (*tr.*) to anchor, steady, or guide with a guy or guys.

guzzle ('gʌzəl) *vb.* to consume (food or drink) excessively or greedily. —'**guzzler** *n.*

gybe *or* **jibe** (dʒaɪb) *Naut.* ~*vb.* **1.** (*intr.*) (of a fore-and-aft sail) to shift suddenly from one side of the vessel to the other when running before the wind. **2.** to cause (a sailing vessel) to gybe or (of a sailing vessel) to undergo gybing. ~*n.* **3.** an instance of gybing.

gym (dʒɪm) *n.* short for **gymnasium, gymnastics.**

gymkhana (dʒɪm'kɑːnə) *n. Chiefly Brit.* **1.** an event in which horses and riders display skill and aptitude in various races and contests. **2.** the place where this event is held.

gymnasium (dʒɪm'neɪzɪəm) *n., pl.* -**siums** *or* -**sia** (-zɪə). **1.** a large room or hall equipped with bars, weights, ropes, etc., for physical training. **2.** (in various European countries) a secondary school that prepares pupils for university.

gymnast ('dʒɪmnæst) *n.* a person who is skilled or trained in gymnastics. —**gym'nastic** *adj.*

gymnastics (dʒɪm'næstɪks) *n.* **1.** (*functioning as sing.*) practice or training in exercises that develop physical strength and agility or mental capacity. **2.** (*functioning as pl.*) gymnastic exercises.

gymnosperm ('dʒɪmnəʊˌspɜːm, 'gɪm-) *n.* any seed-bearing plant in which the ovules are borne naked on open scales, which are often arranged in cones; any conifer or related plant. Cf. **angiosperm.** —ˌ**gymno'spermous** *adj.*

gym shoe *n.* another name for **plimsoll.**

gymslip ('dʒɪmˌslɪp) *n.* a tunic or pinafore dress worn by schoolgirls, often part of a school uniform.

gyn- *combining form.* variant of **gyno-** before a vowel.

gynaeco- *or U.S.* **gyneco-** *combining form.* relating to women; female: *gynaecology.*

gynaecology *or U.S.* **gynecology** (ˌgaɪnɪ'kɒlədʒɪ) *n.*

the branch of medicine concerned with diseases in women. —**gynaecological** (ˌgaɪnɪkə'lɒdʒɪkəl), **gynaeco'logic** *or U.S.* **ˌgyneco'logical,** **ˌgyneco'logic** *adj.* —ˌ**gynae-'cologist** *or U.S.* **ˌgyne'cologist** *n.*

gyno- *or before a vowel* **gyn-** *combining form.* **1.** relating to women; female: *gynarchy.* **2.** denoting a female reproductive organ: *gynophore.*

gyp[1] (dʒɪp) *Sl.* ~*vb.* **gypping, gypped.** **1.** (*tr.*) to swindle, cheat, or defraud. ~*n.* **2.** an act of cheating. **3.** a person who gyps.

gyp[2] (dʒɪp) *n. Brit. & N.Z. sl.* severe pain; torture: *his arthritis gave him gyp.*

gypsum ('dʒɪpsəm) *n.* a mineral consisting of hydrated calcium sulphate that occurs in sedimentary rocks and clay and is used principally in making plasters and cements, esp. plaster of Paris. Formula: $CaSO_4.2H_2O$. —**gypseous** ('dʒɪpsɪəs) *adj.*

Gypsy *or* **Gipsy** ('dʒɪpsɪ) *n., pl.* -**sies.** (*sometimes not cap.*) **1. a.** a member of a people scattered throughout Europe and North America, who maintain a nomadic way of life in industrialized societies. They migrated from NW India about the 9th century onwards. **b.** (*as modifier*): *a Gypsy fortune-teller.* **2.** the language of the Gypsies; Romany. **3.** a person who looks or behaves like a Gypsy. —'**Gypsyish** *or* '**Gipsyish** *adj.*

gyrate *vb.* (dʒaɪ'reɪt). **1.** (*intr.*) to rotate or spiral, esp. about a fixed point or axis. ~*adj.* ('dʒaɪrɪt) **2.** *Biol.* curved or coiled into a circle. —**gy'ration** *n.* —**gy'rator** *n.* —**gyratory** ('dʒaɪrətərɪ) *adj.*

gyrfalcon *or* **gerfalcon** ('dʒɜːˌfɔːlkən, -ˌfɔːkən) *n.* a very large rare falcon of northern and arctic regions.

gyro ('dʒaɪrəʊ) *n., pl.* -**ros.** **1.** See **gyrocompass.** **2.** See **gyroscope.**

gyro- *or before a vowel* **gyr-** *combining form.* **1.** indicating rotating or gyrating motion: *gyroscope.* **2.** indicating a gyroscope: *gyrocompass.*

gyrocompass ('dʒaɪrəʊˌkʌmpəs) *n.* a nonmagnetic compass that uses a motor-driven gyroscope to indicate true north.

gyroscope ('dʒaɪrəˌskəʊp) *n.* a device containing a disc rotating on an axis that can turn freely in any direction so that the disc maintains the same orientation irrespective of the movement of the surrounding structure. —**gyroscopic** (ˌdʒaɪrə'skɒpɪk) *adj.* —ˌ**gyro'scopically** *adv.*

gyrostabilizer *or* -**liser** (ˌdʒaɪrəʊ'steɪbɪˌlaɪzə) *n.* a gyroscopic device used to stabilize the rolling motion of a ship.

gyve (dʒaɪv) *Arch.* ~*vb.* **1.** (*tr.*) to shackle or fetter. ~*n.* **2.** (*usually pl.*) fetters.

THESAURUS

guttural deep, gravelly, gruff, hoarse, husky, low, rasping, rough, thick, throaty

guy 1. *n. Inf.* bloke (*Brit. inf.*), cat (*Sl.*), chap, fellow, lad, man, person, youth 2. *v.* caricature, make (a) game of, make fun of, mock, poke fun at, rib (*Inf.*), ridicule, send up (*Brit inf.*), take off (*Inf.*)

Gypsy, Gipsy Bohemian, nomad, rambler, roamer, Romany, rover, traveller, vagabond, vagrant, wanderer

H

h or **H** (eɪtʃ) n., pl. **h's**, **H's**, or **Hs**. **1.** the eighth letter of the English alphabet. **2.** a speech sound represented by this letter. **3. a.** something shaped like an H. **b.** (in combination): an H-beam.

h symbol for: **1.** Physics. Planck constant. **2.** hecto-. **3.** hour.

H symbol for: **1.** Chem. hydrogen. **2.** Physics. magnetic field strength. **3.** Electronics. henry. **4.** (on Brit. pencils, signifying degree of hardness of lead) hard.

h. or **H.** abbrev. for: **1.** harbour. **2.** height. **3.** high. **4.** hour. **5.** hundred. **6.** husband.

ha or **hah** (haː) interj. **1.** an exclamation expressing derision, triumph, surprise, etc. **2.** (reiterated) a representation of the sound of laughter.

ha abbrev. for hectare.

habeas corpus ('heɪbɪəs 'kɔːpəs) n. Law. a writ ordering a person to be brought before a court or judge, esp. so that the court may ascertain whether his detention is lawful.

haberdasher ('hæbə,dæʃə) n. **1.** Brit. a dealer in small articles for sewing, such as buttons, zips, and ribbons. **2.** U.S. a men's outfitter.

habiliment (hə'bɪlɪmənt) n. (often pl.) dress or attire.

habit ('hæbɪt) n. **1.** a tendency or disposition to act in a particular way. **2.** established custom, usual practice, etc. **3.** Psychol. a learned behavioural response to a particular situation. **4.** mental disposition or attitude: a good working habit of mind. **5. a.** a practice or substance to which a person is addicted: drink has become a habit with him. **b.** the state of being dependent on something, esp. a drug. **6.** Bot., zool. method of growth, type of existence, or general appearance: a burrowing habit. **7.** the customary apparel of a particular occupation, rank, etc., now esp. the costume of a nun or monk. **8.** Also called: **riding habit**. a woman's riding dress. ~vb. (tr.) **9.** to clothe. **10.** an archaic word for **inhabit**.

habitable ('hæbɪtəbəl) adj. able to be lived in. —,habita'bility or 'habitableness n. —'habitably adv.

habitant ('hæbɪtənt) n. **1.** a less common word for **inhabitant**. **2. a.** one of the original French settlers in Canada or Louisiana. **b.** a descendant of these settlers, esp. a farmer.

habitat ('hæbɪˌtæt) n. **1.** the natural home of an animal or plant. **2.** the place in which a person, group, class, etc., is normally found.

habitation (,hæbɪ'teɪʃən) n. **1.** a dwelling place. **2.** occupation of a dwelling place.

habit-forming adj. tending to become a habit or addiction.

habitual (hə'bɪtjʊəl) adj. **1.** (usually prenominal) done or experienced regularly and repeatedly: the habitual Sunday walk. **2.** (usually prenominal) by habit: a habitual drinker. **3.** customary; usual. —ha'bitually adv. —ha'bitualness n.

habituate (hə'bɪtjʊ,eɪt) vb. **1.** to accustom; make used to. **2.** U.S. inf. to frequent. —ha,bitu'ation n.

habitué (hə'bɪtjʊ,eɪ) n. a frequent visitor to a place.

hachure (hæ'ʃjʊə) n. shading of short lines drawn on a relief map to indicate gradients.

hacienda (,hæsɪ'ɛndə) n. **1.** (in Spain or Spanish-speaking countries) **a.** a ranch or large estate. **b.** any substantial manufacturing establishment in the country. **2.** the main house on such a ranch or establishment.

hack¹ (hæk) vb. **1.** (when intr., usually foll. by at or away) to chop (at) roughly or violently. **2.** to cut and clear (a way), as through undergrowth. **3.** (in sport, esp. rugby) to foul (an opposing player) by kicking his shins. **4.** Basketball. to commit the foul of striking (an opposing player) on the arm. **5.** (intr.) Inf. to cough in short dry bursts. **6.** (tr.) to cut (a story, article, etc.) in a damaging way. ~n. **7.** a cut or gash. **8.** any tool used for shallow digging, such as a mattock or pick. **9.** a chopping blow. **10.** Inf. a dry spasmodic cough. **11.** a kick on the shins, as in rugby.

hack² (hæk) n. **1.** a horse kept for riding. **2.** an old or overworked horse. **3.** a horse kept for hire. **4.** Brit. a country ride on horseback. **5.** a drudge. **6.** a person who produces mediocre literary work. **7.** U.S. inf. **a.** a cabdriver. **b.** a taxi. ~vb. **8.** Brit. to ride (a horse) cross-country for pleasure. **9.** (tr.) Inf. to write (an article, etc.) in the manner of a hack. ~adj. (prenominal) **10.** banal, mediocre, or unoriginal: hack writing.

hackle ('hækəl) n. **1.** any of the long slender feathers on the neck of the turkey, pheasant, etc. **2.** Angling. parts of an artificial fly made from hackle feathers, representing the legs of a real fly. **3.** a steel flax comb. ~vb. (tr.) **4.** to comb (flax) using a hackle.

hackles ('hækəlz) pl. n. **1.** the hairs on the back of the neck and the back of a dog, cat, etc., which rise when the animal is angry or afraid. **2.** anger or resentment: to make one's hackles rise.

hackney ('hæknɪ) n. **1.** a compact breed of harness horse with a high-stepping trot. **2.** a coach or carriage that is for hire. **3.** a popular term for **hack²** (sense 1). ~vb. **4.** (tr.; usually passive) to make commonplace and banal by too frequent use.

hackneyed ('hæknɪd) adj. used so often as to be trite, dull, and stereotyped.

hacksaw ('hæk,sɔː) n. a handsaw for cutting metal, with a blade in a frame under tension.

had (hæd) vb. the past tense or past participle of **have**.

haddock ('hædək) n., pl. **-docks** or **-dock**. a North Atlantic gadoid food fish similar to but smaller than the cod.

hadedah ('hɑːdɪ,dɑː) n. a large grey-green S. African ibis.

Hades ('heɪdiːz) n. **1.** Greek myth. **a.** the underworld abode of the souls of the dead. **b.** Pluto, the god of the underworld, brother of Zeus and husband of Persephone. **2.** (often not cap.) hell.

hadj (hædʒ) n., pl. **hadjes**. a variant spelling of **hajj**.

hadji ('hædʒɪ) n., pl. **hadjis**. a variant spelling of **hajji**.

haem- combining form. a variant of **haemo-** before a vowel. Also (esp. U.S.): **hem-**.

haemal or U.S. **hemal** ('hiːməl) adj. **1.** of the blood.

THESAURUS

habit n. **1.** bent, custom, disposition, manner, mannerism, practice, proclivity, propensity, quirk, tendency, way **2.** convention, custom, mode, practice, routine, rule, second nature, usage, wont **3.** constitution, disposition, frame of mind, make-up, nature **4.** addiction, dependence, fixation, obsession, weakness **5.** apparel, dress, garb, garment, habiliment, riding dress ~v. **6.** array, attire, clothe, dress, equip

habitation **1.** abode, domicile, dwelling, dwelling house, home, house, living quarters, lodging, quarters, residence **2.** inhabitance, inhabitancy, occupancy, occupation, tenancy

habitual **1.** accustomed, common, customary, familiar, fixed, natural, normal, ordinary, regular, routine, standard, traditional, usual, wonted **2.** chronic, confirmed, constant, established, frequent, hardened, ingrained, inveterate, persistent, recurrent

habituate acclimatize, accustom, break in, condition, discipline, familiarize, harden, inure, make used to, school, season, train

habituated acclimatized, accustomed, adapted, broken in, conditioned, disciplined, familiarized, hardened, inured, schooled, seasoned, trained, used (to)

habitué constant customer, frequenter, frequent visitor, regular (Inf.), regular patron

hack¹ v. **1.** chop, cut, gash, hew, kick, lacerate, mangle, mutilate, notch, slash ~n. **2.** chop, cut, gash, notch, slash ~v./n. **3.** Inf. bark, cough, rasp

hack² adj. **1.** banal, mediocre, pedestrian, poor, stereotyped, tired, undistinguished, uninspired, unoriginal ~n. **2.** Grub Street writer, literary hack, penny-a-liner, scribbler **3.** drudge, plodder, slave **4.** crock, hired horse, horse, jade, nag, poor old tired horse

hackles make one's hackles rise anger, annoy, bridle at, cause resentment, get one's dander up (Sl.), make one see red (Inf.)

hackneyed banal, clichéd, common, commonplace, overworked, pedestrian, played out (Inf.), run-of-the-mill, stale, stereotyped, stock, threadbare, timeworn, tired, trite, unoriginal, worn-out

2. denoting or relating to the region of the body containing the heart.

haematic or U.S. **hematic** (hiː'mætɪk) adj. Also: **haemic.** relating to, acting on, having the colour of, or containing blood.

haematite or U.S. **hematite** ('hiːmə‚taɪt, 'hɛm-) n. a red or reddish-black mineral consisting of ferric oxide in hexagonal crystalline form: the principal ore of iron.

haemato- or before a vowel **haemat-** combining form. indicating blood: haematology. Also: **haemo-** or (U.S.): **hemato-, hemat-.**

haematology or U.S. **hematology** (‚hiːmə'tɒlədʒɪ) n. the branch of medical science concerned with diseases of the blood. —**haematologic** (‚hiːmətə'lɒdʒɪk), **‚haemato'logical** or U.S. **‚hemato'logic, ‚hemato'logical** adj.

haemo-, haema-, or before a vowel **haem-** combining form. denoting blood. Also: (U.S.) **hemo-, hema-** or **hem-.**

haemoglobin or U.S. **hemoglobin** (‚hiːməʊ'gləʊbɪn) n. a protein that gives red blood cells their characteristic colour. It combines reversibly with oxygen and is thus very important in the transportation of oxygen to tissues.

haemophilia or U.S. **hemophilia** (‚hiːməʊ'fɪlɪə) n. an inheritable disease, usually affecting only males, characterized by loss or impairment of the normal clotting ability of blood. —**‚haemo'philiac** or U.S. **‚hemo'philiac** n. —**‚haemo'philic** or U.S. **‚hemo'philic** adj.

haemoptysis or U.S. **hemoptysis** (hɪ'mɒptɪsɪs) n., pl. **-ses** (-‚siːz). spitting or coughing up of blood, as in tuberculosis.

haemorrhage or U.S. **hemorrhage** ('hɛmərɪdʒ) n. **1.** profuse bleeding from ruptured blood vessels. ~vb. **2.** (intr.) to bleed profusely.

haemorrhoids or U.S. **hemorrhoids** ('hɛmə‚rɔɪdz) pl. n. Pathol. swollen and twisted veins in the region of the anus. Nontechnical name: **piles.** —**‚haemor'rhoidal** or U.S. **‚hemor'rhoidal** adj.

hafnium ('hæfnɪəm) n. a bright metallic element found in zirconium ores. Symbol: Hf; atomic no.: 72; atomic wt.: 178.49.

haft (hɑːft) n. **1.** the handle of an axe, knife, etc. ~vb. **2.** (tr.) to provide with a haft.

hag (hæg) n. **1.** an unpleasant or ugly old woman. **2.** a witch. —**'haggish** adj.

Hag. Bible. abbrev. for Haggai.

haggard ('hægəd) adj. **1.** careworn or gaunt, as from anxiety or starvation. **2.** wild or unruly. **3.** (of a hawk) having reached maturity in the wild before being caught. ~n. **4.** Falconry. a haggard hawk. —**'haggardly** adv. —**'haggardness** n.

haggis ('hægɪs) n. a Scottish dish made from sheep's or calf's offal, oatmeal, suet, and seasonings boiled in a skin made from the animal's stomach.

haggle ('hægəl) vb. (intr.; often foll. by over) to bargain or wrangle (over a price, terms of an agreement, etc.); barter. —**'haggler** n.

hagio- or before a vowel **hagi-** combining form. indicating a saint, saints, or holiness: hagiography.

hagiography (‚hægɪ'ɒgrəfɪ) n., pl. **-phies.** the writing of the lives of the saints. —**‚hagi'ographer** n. —**hagiographic** (‚hægɪə'græfɪk) or **‚hagio'graphical** adj.

hagiology (‚hægɪ'ɒlədʒɪ) n., pl. **-gies.** literature concerned with the lives and legends of saints. —**hagiological** (‚hægɪə'lɒdʒɪkəl) adj. —**‚hagi'ologist** n.

hag-ridden adj. tormented or worried, as if by a witch.

hah (hɑː) interj. a variant spelling of **ha.**

ha-ha¹ ('hɑː 'hɑː) or **haw-haw** interj. **1.** a representation of the sound of laughter. **2.** an exclamation expressing derision, mockery, etc.

ha-ha² ('hɑː‚hɑː) or **haw-haw** n. a sunken fence bordering a garden or park, that allows uninterrupted views from within.

haiku ('haɪkuː) or **hokku** n., pl. **-ku.** an epigrammatic Japanese verse form in 17 syllables.

hail¹ (heɪl) n. **1.** small pellets of ice falling from cumulonimbus clouds when there are strong rising air currents. **2.** a storm of such pellets. **3.** words, ideas, missiles, etc., directed with force and in great quantity: a hail of abuse. ~vb. **4.** (intr.; with it as subject) to be the case that hail is falling. **5.** (often with it as subject) to fall or cause to fall as or like hail.

hail² (heɪl) vb. (mainly tr.) **1.** to greet, esp. enthusiastically: the crowd hailed the actress with joy. **2.** to acclaim or acknowledge: they hailed him as their hero. **3.** to attract the attention of by shouting or gesturing: to hail a taxi. **4.** (intr.; foll. by from) to be a native of: she hails from India. ~n. **5.** the act or an instance of hailing. **6.** a distance across which one can attract attention (esp. in **within hail**). ~interj. **7.** Poetic. an exclamation of greeting. —**'hailer** n.

Hail Mary n. another term for the **Ave Maria.**

hailstone ('heɪl‚stəʊn) n. a pellet of hail.

hailstorm ('heɪl‚stɔːm) n. a storm during which hail falls.

hair (hɛə) n. **1.** any of the threadlike structures that grow from follicles beneath the skin of mammals. **2.** a growth of such structures, as on an animal's body, which helps prevent heat loss. **3.** Bot. any threadlike outgrowth, such as a root hair. **4. a.** a fabric made from the hair of some animals. **b.** (as modifier): a hair shirt. **5.** another word for **hair's-breadth:** to lose by a hair. **6. get in someone's hair.** Inf. to annoy someone persistently. **7. hair of the dog (that bit one).** an alcoholic drink taken as an antidote to a hangover. **8. keep your hair on!** Brit. inf. keep calm. **9. let one's hair down.** to behave without reserve. **10. not turn a hair.** to show no surprise, anger, fear, etc. **11. split hairs.** to make petty and unnecessary distinctions. —**'hairless** adj. —**'hair‚like** adj.

haircloth ('hɛə‚klɒθ) n. a cloth woven from horsehair, used (esp. formerly) in upholstery, etc.

hairdo ('hɛə‚duː) n., pl. **-dos.** the arrangement of a woman's hair, esp. after styling and setting.

hairdresser ('hɛə‚drɛsə) n. **1.** a person whose business is cutting, colouring and arranging hair. **2.** a hairdresser's establishment. ~Related adj.: **tonsorial.** —**'hair‚dressing** n.

-haired adj. having hair as specified: long-haired.

hairgrip ('hɛə‚grɪp) n. Chiefly Brit. a small tightly bent metal hair clip. Also called (esp. U.S.): **bobby pin.**

hairline ('hɛə‚laɪn) n. **1.** the natural margin formed by hair on the head. **2. a.** a very narrow line. **b.** (as modifier): a hairline crack.

hairpiece ('hɛə‚piːs) n. **1.** a wig or toupee. **2.** a section of extra hair attached to a woman's real hair to give it greater bulk or length.

hairpin ('hɛə‚pɪn) n. **1.** a thin double-pronged pin used to fasten the hair. **2.** (modifier) (esp. of a bend in a road) curving very sharply.

hair-raising adj. inspiring horror; terrifying: a hair-raising drop of 600 feet.

hair's-breadth n. **a.** a very short or imperceptible margin or distance. **b.** (as modifier): a hair's-breadth escape.

THESAURUS

hag beldam (Archaic), crone, fury, harridan, Jezebel, shrew, termagant, virago, vixen, witch

haggard careworn, drawn, emaciated, gaunt, ghastly, hollow-eyed, pinched, shrunken, thin, wan, wasted, wrinkled

haggle 1. bargain, barter, beat down, chaffer, dicker (Chiefly U.S.), higgle, palter 2. bicker, dispute, quarrel, squabble, wrangle

hail¹ Fig. 1. n. barrage, bombardment, pelting, rain, shower, storm, volley 2. v. barrage, batter, beat down upon, bombard, pelt, rain, rain down on, shower, storm, volley

hail² 1. acclaim, acknowledge, applaud, cheer, exalt, glorify, greet, honour, salute, welcome 2. accost, address, call, flag down, halloo, shout to, signal to, sing out, speak to, wave down 3. With from be a native of, be born in, come from, originate in

hair 1. head of hair, locks, mane, mop, shock, tresses 2. by a hair by a fraction of an inch, by a hair's-breadth, by a narrow margin, by a split second, by a whisker, by the skin of one's teeth 3. get in one's hair annoy, exasperate, harass, irritate, pester, plague 4. let one's hair down let it all hang out (Inf.), let off steam (Inf.), let oneself go, relax 5. not turn a hair keep one's cool (Sl.), keep one's hair on (Brit. inf.), not bat an eyelid, remain calm 6. split hairs cavil, find fault, overrefine, pettifog, quibble

hairless bald, baldheaded, beardless, clean-shaven, depilated, glabrous or glabrate (Biol.), shorn, tonsured

hair-raising alarming, bloodcurdling, breathtaking, creepy, exciting, frightening, horrifying, petrifying, scary, shocking, spine-chilling, startling, terrifying, thrilling

hair's-breadth 1. n. fraction, hair, jot, narrow margin, whisker 2. adj. close, hazardous, narrow

hair slide *n.* a hinged clip with a tortoiseshell, bone, or similar back, used to fasten a girl's hair.

hairsplitting ('hɛə,splɪtɪŋ) *n.* 1. the making of petty distinctions. ~*adj.* 2. occupied with or based on petty distinctions. —'hair,splitter *n.*

hairspring ('hɛə,sprɪŋ) *n.* a fine spiral spring in a timepiece, used to regulate the balance wheel.

hair trigger *n.* 1. a trigger of a firearm that responds to very slight pressure. 2. *Inf.* any mechanism, reaction, etc., set in operation by slight provocation.

hairy ('hɛərɪ) *adj.* **hairier, hairiest.** 1. covered with hair. 2. *Sl.* **a.** difficult or problematic. **b.** dangerous or exciting. —'**hairiness** *n.*

hajj *or* **hadj** (hædʒ) *n., pl.* **hajjes** *or* **hadjes.** the pilgrimage to Mecca that every Muslim is required to make at least once in his life.

hajji, hadji, *or* **haji** ('hædʒɪ) *n., pl.* **hajjis, hadjis,** *or* **hajis.** 1. a Muslim who has made a pilgrimage to Mecca: also used as a title. 2. a Christian who has visited Jerusalem.

hake (heɪk) *n., pl.* **hake** *or* **hakes.** 1. a gadoid food fish of the N hemisphere, having an elongated body with a large head and two dorsal fins. 2. a similar North American fish.

halberd ('hælbəd) *or* **halbert** *n.* a spear fitted with an axe head, used in 15th- and 16th-century warfare. —,**halber'dier** *n.*

halcyon ('hælsɪən) *adj.* 1. peaceful, gentle, and calm. ~*n.* 2. *Greek myth.* a fabulous bird associated with the winter solstice. 3. a poetic name for the **kingfisher.** 4. **halcyon days. a.** a fortnight of calm weather during the winter solstice. **b.** a period of peace and happiness.

hale¹ (heɪl) *adj.* healthy and robust (esp. in **hale and hearty**). —'**haleness** *n.*

hale² (heɪl) *vb.* (*tr.*) to pull or drag. —'**haler** *n.*

half (hɑːf) *n., pl.* **halves** (hɑːvz). 1. **a.** either of two equal or corresponding parts that together comprise a whole. **b.** a quantity equalling such a part: *half a dozen.* 2. half a pint, esp. of beer. 3. *Scot.* a small drink of spirits, esp. whisky. 4. *Football, hockey, etc.* the half of the pitch regarded as belonging to one team. 5. *Golf.* an equal score with an opponent. 6. (in various games) either of two periods of play separated by an interval. 7. a half-price ticket on a bus, etc. 8. short for **half-hour.** 9. *Sport.* short for **halfback.** 10. *Obs.* a half-year period. 11. **by halves.** (*used with a negative*) without being thorough: *we don't do things by halves.* 12. **go halves.** (often foll. by *on, in,* etc.) **a.** to share expenses. **b.** to share the whole amount (of something): *to go halves on an orange.* ~*determiner.* 13. **a.** being a half or approximately a half: *half the kingdom.* **b.** (*as pronoun; functioning as sing. or pl.*): *half of them came.* ~*adj.* 14. not perfect or complete: *he only did a half job on it.* ~*adv.* 15. to the amount or extent of a half. 16. to a great amount or extent. 17. partially; to an extent. 18. **by half.** to an excessive degree: *he's too arrogant by half.* 19. **half two,** *etc. Inf.* 30 minutes after two o'clock, etc. 20. **have half a mind to.** to have a vague intention to. 21. **not half.** *Inf.* **a.** not in any way: *he's not half clever enough.* **b.** *Brit.* very; indeed: *he isn't half stupid.* **c.** *sentence substitute.* yes, indeed.

half-and-half *n.* 1. a mixture of half one thing and

half another thing. 2. a drink consisting of equal parts of beer (or ale) and porter.

halfback ('hɑːf,bæk) *n.* 1. *Soccer.* any of three players positioned behind the line of forwards and in front of the fullbacks. 2. *Rugby.* either the scrum half or the stand-off half. 3. any of certain similar players in other team sports.

half-baked *adj.* 1. insufficiently baked. 2. *Inf.* foolish; stupid. 3. *Inf.* poorly planned.

half-binding *n.* a type of bookbinding in which the backs are bound in one material and the sides in another.

half-blood *n.* 1. **a.** the relationship between individuals having only one parent in common. **b.** an individual having such a relationship. 2. a less common name for a **half-breed.** —,**half-'blooded** *adj.*

half board *n.* the daily provision by a hotel of bed, breakfast, and one main meal. Also called: **demipension.**

half-breed *n.* 1. a person whose parents are of different races, esp. the offspring of a White person and an American Indian. ~*adj. also* **half-bred.** 2. of, relating to, or designating offspring of people or animals of different races or breeds.

half-brother *n.* the son of either of one's parents by another partner.

half-caste *n.* 1. a person having parents of different races, esp. the offspring of a European and an Indian. ~*adj.* 2. of, relating to, or designating such a person.

half-cock *n.* 1. the halfway position of a firearm's hammer when the trigger is cocked by the hammer and the hammer cannot reach the primer to fire the weapon. 2. **go off at half-cock** *or* **half-cocked.** to fail as a result of inadequate preparation or premature starting.

half-crown *n.* a former British coin worth 12½ (new) pence. Also called: **half-a-crown.**

half-hearted *adj.* without enthusiasm or determination. —,**half-'heartedly** *adv.*

half-hitch *n.* a knot made by passing the end of a piece of rope around itself and through the loop thus made.

half-hour *n.* 1. a period of 30 minutes. 2. the point of time 30 minutes after the beginning of an hour. —,**half-'hourly** *adv., adj.*

half-life *n.* the time taken for half of the atoms in a radioactive material to undergo decay.

half-mast *n.* the halfway position to which a flag is lowered on a mast to mourn the dead

half-moon *n.* 1. the moon at first or last quarter when half its face is illuminated. 2. the time at which a half-moon occurs. 3. something shaped like a half-moon.

halfpenny ('heɪpnɪ) *n.* 1. (*pl.* -**pennies.**) a small British coin worth half a new penny. 2. (*pl.* -**pennies.**) an old British coin worth half an old penny. 3. (*pl.* -**pence.**) something of negligible value. —**halfpennyworth** *or* **ha'p'orth** ('heɪpəð) *n.*

half-sister *n.* the daughter of either of one's parents by another partner.

half-size *n.* any size, esp. in clothing, that is halfway between two sizes.

half term *n. Brit. education.* a short holiday midway through an academic term.

half-asleep *adj.*	**half-crazy** *adj.*	**half-finished** *adj.*	**half-raw** *adj.*
half-blind *adj.*	**half-day** *n.*	**half-frozen** *adj.*	**half-remembered** *adj.*
half-century *n.*	**half-done** *adj.*	**half-full** *adj.*	**half-shut** *adj.*
half-clothed *adj.*	**half-drowned** *adj.*	**half-grown** *adj.*	**half-starved** *adj.*
half-completed *adj.*	**half-drunk** *adj.*	**half-inclined** *adj.*	**half-submerged** *adj.*
half-conscious *adj.*	**half-eaten** *adj.*	**half-naked** *adj.*	**half-understood** *adj.*
half-cooked *adj.*	**half-filled** *adj.*	**half-open** *adj.*	**half-used** *adj.*

THESAURUS

hairsplitting *adj.* captious, carping, cavilling, fault-finding, fine, finicky, nice, niggling, nit-picking (*Inf.*), overrefined, pettifogging, quibbling, subtle

hairy 1. bearded, bewhiskered, bushy, fleecy, furry, hirsute, pileous (*Biol.*), pilose (*Biol.*), shaggy, stubbly, unshaven, woolly 2. *Sl.* dangerous, difficult, hazardous, perilous, risky, scaring

halcyon 1. calm, gentle, mild, pacific, peaceful, placid, quiet, serene, still, tranquil, undisturbed, unruffled 2. *Fig.* carefree, flour-

ishing, golden, happy, palmy, prosperous

hale able-bodied, blooming, fit, flourishing, healthy, hearty, in fine fettle, in the pink, robust, sound, strong, vigorous, well

half 1. *n.* bisection, division, equal part, fifty per cent, fraction, hemisphere, portion, section 2. *adj.* divided, fractional, halved, incomplete, limited, moderate, partial 3. *adv.* after a fashion, all but, barely, inadequately, incompletely, in part, partially, partly, pretty nearly, slightly 4. **by half** considerably, excessively, very much

half-baked 1. brainless, crazy, foolish, harebrained, senseless, silly, stupid 2. ill-conceived, ill-judged, impractical, poorly planned, short-sighted, unformed, unthought out *or* through

half-hearted apathetic, cool, indifferent, lacklustre, listless, lukewarm, neutral, passive, perfunctory, spiritless, tame, unenthusiastic, uninterested

half-timbered or **half-timber** adj. (of a building) having an exposed timber framework filled with brick, stone, or plastered laths, as in Tudor architecture. —ˌhalf-ˈtimbering n.

halftime n. Sport. **a.** a rest period between the two halves of a game. **b.** (as modifier): the half-time score.

half-title n. **1.** the short title of a book as printed on the right-hand page preceding the title page. **2.** a title on a separate page preceding a section of a book.

halftone (ˈhɑːfˌtəʊn) n. **1.** a process used to reproduce an illustration by photographing it through a fine screen to break it up into dots. **2.** the print obtained.

half-track n. a vehicle with caterpillar tracks on the wheels that supply motive power only.

half-truth n. a partially true statement intended to mislead. —ˈhalf-ˈtrue adj.

halfway (ˌhɑːfˈweɪ) adv., adj. **1.** at or to half the distance. **2.** in or of an incomplete manner. **3. meet halfway.** to compromise with.

halfway house n. **1.** a place to rest midway on a journey. **2.** the halfway point in any progression. **3.** a centre or hostel designed to facilitate the readjustment to private life of released prisoners, mental patients, etc.

halfwit (ˈhɑːfˌwɪt) n. **1.** a feeble-minded person. **2.** a foolish or inane person. —ˌhalfˈwitted adj.

halibut (ˈhælɪbət) n., pl. **-buts** or **-but**. **1.** the largest flatfish: a dark green North Atlantic species that is a very important food fish. **2.** any of several similar and related flatfishes such as the **Greenland halibut**.

halitosis (ˌhælɪˈtəʊsɪs) n. the state or condition of having bad breath.

hall (hɔːl) n. **1.** a room serving as an entry area. **2.** (sometimes cap.) a building for public meetings. **3.** (often cap.) the great house of an estate; manor. **4.** a large building or room used for assemblies, dances, etc. **5.** a residential building in a university. **6. a.** a large room, esp. for dining, in a college or university. **b.** a meal eaten in this room. **7.** the large room of a house, castle, etc. **8.** U.S. a corridor into which rooms open. **9.** (often pl.) Inf. short for **music hall.**

hallelujah, halleluiah (ˌhælɪˈluːjə), or **alleluia** (ˌælɪˈluːjə) interj. **1.** an exclamation of praise to God. ~n. **2.** an exclamation of "Hallelujah". **3.** a musical composition that uses the word Hallelujah as its text.

halliard (ˈhæljəd) n. a variant spelling of **halyard.**

hallmark (ˈhɔːlˌmɑːk) n. **1.** Brit. an official series of marks stamped by the London Guild of Goldsmiths on gold, silver, or platinum articles to guarantee purity, date of manufacture, etc. **2.** a mark of authenticity or excellence. **3.** an outstanding feature. ~vb. **4.** (tr.) to stamp with or as if with a hallmark.

hallo (həˈləʊ) interj., n. **1.** a variant spelling of **hello.** ~interj., n., vb. **2.** a variant spelling of **halloo.**

halloo (həˈluː), **hallo,** or **halloa** (həˈləʊ) sentence substitute. **1.** a shout to attract attention, esp. to call hounds at a hunt. ~n., pl. **-loos, -los,** or **-loas. 2.** a shout of "halloo". ~vb. **-looing, -looed; -loing, -loed,** or **-loaing, -loaed. 3.** to shout. **4.** (tr.) to urge on (dogs) with shouts.

hallow (ˈhæləʊ) vb. (tr.) **1.** to consecrate or set apart as being holy. **2.** to venerate as being holy. —ˈhallower n.

Hallowe'en or **Halloween** (ˌhæləʊˈiːn) n. the eve of All Saints' Day celebrated on Oct. 31; Allhallows Eve.

hallucinate (həˈluːsɪˌneɪt) vb. (intr.) to experience hallucinations. —halˈluciˌnator n.

hallucination (həˌluːsɪˈneɪʃən) n. the alleged perception of an object when no object is present, occurring under hypnosis, in some mental disorders, etc. —halˈlucinatory adj.

hallucinogen (həˈluːsɪnəˌdʒɛn) n. any drug that induces hallucinations. —**hallucinogenic** (həˌluːsɪnəˈdʒɛnɪk) adj.

hallway (ˈhɔːlˌweɪ) n. a hall or corridor.

halm (hɔːm) n. a variant spelling of **haulm.**

halo (ˈheɪləʊ) n., pl. **-loes** or **-los. 1.** a disc or ring of light around the head of an angel, saint, etc., as in painting. **2.** the aura surrounding a famous or admired person, thing, or event. **3.** a circle of light around the sun or moon, caused by the refraction of light by particles of ice. ~vb. **-loes** or **-los, -loing, -loed. 4.** to surround with or form a halo.

halogen (ˈhæləˌdʒɛn) n. any of the chemical elements fluorine, chlorine, bromine, iodine, and astatine. They are all monovalent and readily form negative ions. —**halogenous** (həˈlɒdʒɪnəs) adj.

halt[1] (hɔːlt) n. **1.** an interruption or end to movement or progress. **2.** Chiefly Brit. a minor railway station, without permanent buildings. **3. call a halt (to).** to put an end (to); stop. ~n., interj. **4.** a command to halt, esp. as an order when marching. ~vb. **5.** to come or bring to a halt.

halt[2] (hɔːlt) vb. (intr.) **1.** (esp. of verse) to falter or be defective. **2.** to be unsure. **3.** Arch. to be lame. ~adj. **4.** Arch. lame. ~n. **5. the halt.** Arch. lame persons collectively.

halter (ˈhɔːltə) n. **1.** headgear for a horse, usually with a rope for leading. **2.** a style of woman's top fastened behind the neck and waist, leaving the back and arms bare. **3.** a rope having a noose for hanging a person. **4.** death by hanging. ~vb. (tr.) **5.** to put on a halter. **6.** to hang (someone).

halting (ˈhɔːltɪŋ) adj. **1.** hesitant: halting speech. **2.** lame. —ˈhaltingly adv.

halve (hɑːv) vb. (tr.) **1.** to divide into two approximately equal parts. **2.** to share equally. **3.** to reduce by half, as by cutting. **4.** Golf. to take the same number of strokes on (a hole or round) as one's opponent.

halyard or **halliard** (ˈhæljəd) n. Naut. a line for hoisting or lowering a sail, flag, or spar.

ham[1] (hæm) n. **1.** the part of the hindquarters of a pig between the hock and the hip. **2.** the meat of this part. **3.** Inf. the back of the leg above the knee.

ham[2] (hæm) n. **1.** Theatre, inf. **a.** an actor who overacts or relies on stock gestures. **b.** overacting or clumsy acting. **c.** (as modifier): a ham actor. **2.** Inf. a licensed amateur radio operator. ~vb. **hamming, hammed. 3.** Inf. to overact.

hamadryad (ˌhæməˈdraɪəd) n. **1.** Classical myth. a nymph which inhabits a tree and dies with it. **2.** a venomous snake of tropical Asia.

hamburger (ˈhæmˌbɜːgə) n. a cake of minced beef, often served in a bread roll. Also called: **beefburger.**

Hamitic (hæˈmɪtɪk, hə-) n. **1.** a group of N African languages related to Semitic. ~adj. **2.** denoting or belonging to this group of languages. **3.** denoting or characteristic of the Hamites, a group of peoples of N Africa, including the ancient Egyptians, supposedly descended from Noah's son Ham.

hamlet (ˈhæmlɪt) n. a small village, esp. (in Britain) one without its own church.

hammer (ˈhæmə) n. **1.** a hand tool consisting of a

THESAURUS

halfway adv. **1.** midway, to or in the middle, to the midpoint **2.** incompletely, moderately, nearly, partially, partly, rather **3. meet halfway** accommodate, come to terms, compromise, concede, give and take, strike a balance, trade off ~adj. **4.** central, equidistant, intermediate, mid, middle, midway **5.** imperfect, incomplete, moderate, partial, part-way

halfwit dimwit (Inf.), dolt, dullard, dunce, dunderhead, fool, idiot, imbecile (Inf.), mental defective, moron, nitwit, simpleton

half-witted addle-brained, barmy (Sl.), batty (Sl.), crazy, doltish, dull, dull-witted, feeble-minded, foolish, idiotic, moronic, silly, simple, simple-minded, stupid

hall 1. corridor, entrance hall, entry, foyer, hallway, lobby, passage, passageway, vestibule **2.** assembly room, auditorium, chamber, concert hall, meeting place

hallmark 1. authentication, device, endorsement, mark, seal, sign, stamp, symbol **2.** badge, emblem, indication, sure sign, telltale sign

hallucination aberration, apparition, delusion, dream, fantasy, figment of the imagination, illusion, mirage, phantasmagoria, vision

halo aura, aureole or aureola, corona, halation (Photog.), nimbus, radiance, ring of light

halt[1] v. **1.** break off, call it a day, cease, close down, come to an end, desist, draw up, pull up, rest, stand still, stop, wait **2.** arrest, block, bring to an end, check, curb, cut short, end, hold back, impede, obstruct, stem, terminate ~n. **3.** arrest, break, close, end, impasse, interruption, pause, stand, standstill, stop, stoppage, termination

halt[2] v. **1.** be defective, falter, hobble, limp, stumble **2.** be unsure, boggle, dither, haver, hesitate, pause, stammer, swither (Scot. dialect), think twice, waver ~adj. **3.** Archaic crippled, lame, limping

halting awkward, faltering, hesitant, imperfect, laboured, stammering, stumbling, stuttering

halve 1. bisect, cut in half, divide equally, reduce by fifty per cent, share equally, split in two **2. by halves** imperfectly, incompletely, scrappily, skimpily

heavy usually steel head held transversely on the end of a handle, used for driving in nails, etc. **2.** any tool or device with a similar function, such as the striking head on a bell. **3.** a power-driven striking tool, esp. one used in forging. **4.** a part of a gunlock that strikes the primer or percussion cap when the trigger is pulled. **5.** *Field sports.* **a.** a heavy metal ball attached to a flexible wire: thrown in competitions. **b.** the sport of throwing the hammer. **6.** an auctioneer's gavel. **7.** a device on a piano that is made to strike a string or group of strings causing them to vibrate. **8.** *Anat.* the nontechnical name for **malleus.** **9. go under the hammer.** to be offered for sale by an auctioneer. **10. hammer and tongs.** with great effort or energy. **11. on someone's hammer.** *Austral. & N.Z. sl.* in hot pursuit of someone. ~*vb.* **12.** to strike or beat with or as if with a hammer. **13.** (*tr.*) to shape with or as if with a hammer. **14.** (when *intr.*, foll. by *away*) to force (facts, ideas, etc.) into (someone) through constant repetition. **15.** (*intr.*) to feel or sound like hammering. **16.** (*intr.*; often foll. by *away*) to work at constantly. **17.** (*tr.*) *Brit.* to criticize severely. **18.** *Inf.* to defeat. **19.** (*tr.*) *Stock Exchange.* **a.** to announce the default of (a member). **b.** to cause prices of (securities, the market, etc.) to fall by bearish selling. —'**hammer-,like** *adj.*

hammer and sickle *n.* the emblem on the flag of the Soviet Union, representing the industrial workers and the peasants respectively.

hammerhead ('hæmə,hɛd) *n.* **1.** a ferocious shark having a flattened hammer-shaped head. **2.** a tropical African wading bird having a dark plumage and a long backward-pointing crest. **3.** a large African fruit bat with a hammer-shaped muzzle. —'**hammer,headed** *adj.*

hammer out *vb.* (*tr.*, *adv.*) **1.** to shape or remove with or as if with a hammer. **2.** to settle or reconcile (differences, problems, etc.)

hammertoe ('hæmə,təʊ) *n.* a deformity causing the toe to be bent in a clawlike arch.

hammock ('hæmək) *n.* a length of canvas, net, etc., suspended at the ends and used as a bed.

hammy ('hæmɪ) *adj.* **-mier, -miest.** *Inf.* **1.** (of an actor) tending to overact. **2.** (of a play, performance, etc.) overacted or exaggerated.

hamper[1] ('hæmpə) *vb.* **1.** (*tr.*) to prevent the progress or free movement of. ~*n.* **2.** *Naut.* gear aboard a vessel that, though essential, is often in the way.

hamper[2] ('hæmpə) *n.* **1.** a large basket, usually with a cover. **2.** *Brit.* a selection of food and drink packed in a hamper or other container.

hamster ('hæmstə) *n.* a Eurasian burrowing rodent having a stocky body, short tail, and cheek pouches: a popular pet.

hamstring ('hæm,strɪŋ) *n.* **1.** one of the tendons at the back of the knee. **2.** the large tendon at the back of the hind leg of a horse, etc. ~*vb.* **-stringing, -strung. 3.** to cripple by cutting the hamstring of. **4.** to thwart.

hand (hænd) *n.* **1.** the prehensile part of the body at the end of the arm, consisting of a thumb, four fingers, and a palm. Related adj.: **manual. 2.** the corresponding part in animals. **3.** something resembling this in shape or function. **4. a.** the cards dealt in one round of a card game. **b.** a player holding such cards. **c.** one round of a card game. **5.** agency or influence: *the hand of God.* **6.** a part in something done: *he had a hand in the victory.* **7.** assistance: *to give someone a hand.* **8.** a pointer on a dial, indicator, or gauge, esp. on a clock. **9.** acceptance or pledge of partnership, as in marriage. **10.** a position indicated by its location to the side of an object or the observer: *on the right hand.* **11.** a contrastive aspect, condition, etc.: *on the other hand.* **12.** source or origin: *a story heard at third hand.* **13.** a person, esp. one who creates something: *a good hand at painting.* **14.** a manual worker. **15.** a member of a ship's crew: *all hands on deck.* **16.** a person's handwriting: *the letter was in his own hand.* **17.** a round of applause: *give him a hand.* **18.** a characteristic way of doing something: *the hand of a master.* **19.** a unit of length equalling four inches, used for measuring the height of horses. **20.** a cluster of bananas. **21. a free hand.** freedom to do as desired. **22. a heavy hand.** tyranny or oppression: *he ruled with a heavy hand.* **23. a high hand.** a dictatorial manner. **24. (near) at hand.** very close, esp. in time. **25. by hand. a.** by manual rather than mechanical means. **b.** by messenger or personally: *the letter was delivered by hand.* **26. force someone's hand.** to force someone to act. **27. from hand to mouth. a.** in poverty: *living from hand to mouth.* **b.** without preparation or planning. **28. hand and foot.** in all ways possible; completely: *they waited on him hand and foot.* **29. hand in glove.** in close association. **30. hand over fist. a.** in an easy manner. **b.** in large amounts: *he squanders money hand over fist.* **31. hold one's hand.** to stop or postpone a planned action or punishment. **32. hold someone's hand.** to support, help, or guide someone, esp. by giving sympathy. **33. in hand. a.** under control. **b.** receiving attention. **c.** available in reserve. **d.** with deferred payment: *he works a week in hand.* **34. keep one's hand in.** to continue or practise. **35. on hand.** close by; present. **36. out of hand. a.** beyond control. **b.** without reservation or deeper examination: *he condemned him out of hand.* **37. show one's hand.** to reveal one's stand, opinion, or plans. **38. take in hand.** to discipline; control. **39. throw one's hand in.** to give up a venture, game, etc. **40. to hand.** accessible. **41. try one's hand.** to attempt to do something. **42.** (*modifier*) **a.** of or involving the hand: *a hand grenade.* **b.** carried in or worn on the hand: *hand luggage.* **c.** operated by hand: *a hand drill.* **43.** (*in combination*) made by hand rather than machine: *hand-sewn.* ~*vb.* (*tr.*) **44.** to transmit or offer by the hand or hands. **45.** to help or lead with the hand. **46.** *Naut.* to furl (a sail). **47. hand it to someone.** to give credit to someone. ~See also **hand down, hand in,** etc. —'**handless** *adj.*

handbag ('hænd,bæg) *n.* **1.** Also called: **bag, purse** (U.S.), **pocketbook** (U.S.). a woman's small bag carried to contain personal articles. **2.** a small suitcase that can be carried by hand.

handball ('hænd,bɔːl) *n.* **1.** a game in which two or four people strike a ball against a wall with the hand. **2.** the small hard rubber ball used. ~*vb.* (*tr.*) **3.** *Australian Rules football.* to pass (the ball) with a blow of the fist.

handbill ('hænd,bɪl) *n.* a small printed notice for distribution by hand.

handbook ('hænd,bʊk) *n.* a reference book listing brief facts on a subject or place or directions for maintenance or repair, as of a car.

handbrake ('hænd,breɪk) *n.* **1.** a brake operated by a hand lever. **2.** the lever that operates the handbrake.

handbreadth ('hænd,brɛtθ, -,brɛdθ) *or* **hand's-breadth** *n.* the width of a hand used as an indication of length.

THESAURUS

hammer *v.* **1.** bang, beat, drive, hit, knock, strike, tap **2.** beat out, fashion, forge, form, make, shape **3.** *Often with* **into** din into, drive home, drub into, drum into, grind into, impress upon, instruct, repeat **4.** *Often with* **away** (**at**) beaver away (*Brit. inf.*), drudge, grind, keep on, peg away (*Chiefly Brit.*), persevere, persist, plug away (*Inf.*), pound away, stick at, work **5.** *Inf.* beat, clobber (*Sl.*), defeat, drub, slate (*Inf.*), thrash, trounce, worst

hammer out accomplish, bring about, come to a conclusion, complete, excogitate, finish, form a resolution, make a decision, negotiate, produce, settle, sort out, thrash out, work out

hamper *v.* bind, cramp, curb, embarrass, encumber, entangle, fetter, frustrate, ham-string, handicap, hinder, hold up, impede, interfere with, obstruct, prevent, restrain, restrict, slow down, thwart, trammel

hamstring **1.** cripple, disable, hock, injure, lame **2.** balk, foil, frustrate, prevent, ruin, stop, thwart

hamstrung at a loss, crippled, disabled, helpless, *hors de combat*, incapacitated, paralysed

hand *n.* **1.** fist, mitt (*Sl.*), palm, paw (*Inf.*) **2.** agency, direction, influence, part, participation, share **3.** aid, assistance, help, support **4.** artificer, artisan, craftsman, employee, hired man, labourer, operative, worker, workman **5.** calligraphy, chirography, handwriting, longhand, penmanship, script **6.** clap, ovation, round of applause **7.** ability, art, artistry, skill **8. at** *or* **on hand** approaching, available, close, handy, imminent, near, nearby, on tap (*Inf.*), ready, within reach **9. from hand to mouth** by necessity, improvidently, in poverty, insecurely, on the breadline (*Inf.*), precariously, uncertainly **10. hand in glove** allied, in cahoots (*Inf.*), in league, in partnership **11. hand over fist** by leaps and bounds, easily, steadily, swiftly **12. in hand a.** in order, receiving attention, under control **b.** available for use, in reserve, put by, ready ~*v.* **13.** deliver, hand over, pass **14.** aid, assist, conduct, convey, give, guide, help, lead, present, transmit

handbook Baedeker, guide, guidebook, instruction book, manual, vade mecum

handcart ('hænd,kɑ:t) n. a simple cart, usually with one or two wheels, pushed or drawn by hand.

handcraft ('hænd,krɑ:ft) n. 1. another word for **handicraft**. ~vb. 2. (tr.) to make by handicraft.

handcuff ('hænd,kʌf) vb. 1. (tr.) to put handcuffs on (a person); manacle. ~n. 2. (pl.) a pair of locking metal rings joined by a short bar or chain for securing prisoners, etc.

hand down vb. (tr., adv.) 1. to bequeath. 2. to pass (an outgrown garment) on from one member of a family to a younger one. 3. U.S. law. to announce (a verdict).

-handed adj. having a hand or hands as specified: a four-handed game of cards.

handful ('hænd,fʊl) n., pl. **-fuls.** 1. the amount or number that can be held in the hand. 2. a small number or quantity. 3. Inf. a person or thing difficult to manage or control.

handicap ('hændɪ,kæp) n. 1. something that hampers or hinders. 2. a contest, esp. a race, in which competitors are given advantages or disadvantages of weight, distance, etc., in an attempt to equalize their chances. 3. the advantage or disadvantage prescribed. 4. Golf. the average number of strokes by which a player exceeds par. 5. any disability, esp. one affecting the normal ability to move. ~vb. **-capping, -capped.** (tr.) 6. to be a hindrance or disadvantage to. 7. to assign a handicap to. 8. to organize (a contest) by handicapping. —'handi,capper n.

handicapped ('hændɪ,kæpt) adj. 1. physically or mentally disabled. 2. (of a competitor) assigned a handicap. ~n. 3. (often preceded by **the**) people with an appreciable and lasting physical or mental disability.

handicraft ('hændɪ,krɑ:ft) n. 1. skill in working with the hands. 2. a particular skill performed with the hands, such as weaving. 3. the work so produced. ~Also called: **handcraft.**

hand in vb. (tr., adv.) to return or submit (something, such as an examination paper).

handiwork ('hændɪ,wɜ:k) n. 1. work produced by hand. 2. the result of the action or endeavours of a person or thing.

handkerchief ('hæŋkətʃɪf, -,tʃi:f) n. a small square of soft absorbent material carried and used to wipe the nose, etc.

handle ('hændəl) n. 1. the part of a utensil, drawer, etc., designed to be held in order to move, use, or pick up the object. 2. N.Z. a glass beer mug with a handle. 3. Sl. a title put before a person's name. 4. an excuse for doing something: his background served as a handle for their mockery. 5. the quality, as of textiles, perceived by feeling. 6. **fly off the handle.** Inf. to become suddenly extremely angry. ~vb. (mainly tr.) 7. to hold, move, or touch with the hands. 8. to operate using the hands: the boy handled the reins well. 9. to control: my wife handles my investments. 10. to manage successfully: a secretary must be able to handle clients. 11. to discuss (a theme, subject, etc.). 12. to deal with in a specified way: I was handled with great tact. 13. to trade or deal in (specified merchandise). 14. (intr.) to react in a specified way to operation: the car handles well on bends. —'handled adj. —'handling n.

handlebars ('hændəl,bɑ:z) pl. n. (sometimes sing.) a metal bar having its ends curved to form handles, used for steering a bicycle, etc.

handler ('hændlə) n. 1. a person who trains and controls an animal, esp. a police dog. 2. a person who holds or incites a dog, gamecock, etc., in a contest. 3. the trainer or second of a boxer.

handmade (,hænd'meɪd) adj. made by hand, not by machine, esp. with care or craftsmanship.

handmaiden ('hænd,meɪdən) or **handmaid** n. 1. a person or thing that serves a useful but subordinate purpose. 2. Arch. a female servant.

hand-me-down n. Inf. 1. something, esp. an outgrown garment, passed down from one person to another. 2. anything that has already been used by another.

hand on vb. (tr., adv.) to pass to the next in a succession.

hand-out n. 1. clothing, food, or money given to a needy person. 2. a leaflet, free sample, etc., given out to publicize something. 3. a statement distributed to the press to confirm or replace an oral presentation. ~vb. **hand out.** 4. (tr., adv.) to distribute.

hand over vb. (tr., adv.) to surrender possession of; transfer.

hand-pick vb. (tr.) to select with great care, as for a special job. —,hand-'picked adj.

handrail ('hænd,reɪl) n. a rail alongside a stairway, etc., to provide support.

hands (hændz) n. 1. power or keeping: your welfare is in his hands. 2. Also called: **handling.** Soccer. the infringement of touching the ball with the hand or arm. 3. **change hands.** to pass from the possession of one person to another. 4. **hands down.** without effort; easily. 5. **have one's hands full. a.** to be completely occupied. **b.** to be beset with problems. 6. **have one's hands tied.** to be unable to act. 7. **lay hands on** or **upon. a.** to get possession of. **b.** to beat up; assault. **c.** to find. **d.** Christianity. to confirm or ordain by the imposition of hands. 8. **off one's hands.** for which one is no longer responsible. 9. **on one's hands. a.** for which one is responsible: I've got too much on my hands to help. **b.** to spare: time on my hands. 10. **wash one's hands of.** to have nothing more to do with.

handset ('hænd,sɛt) n. a telephone mouthpiece and earpiece mounted as a single unit.

handshake ('hænd,ʃeɪk) n. the act of grasping and shaking a person's hand, as when being introduced or agreeing on a deal.

handsome ('hændsəm) adj. 1. (of a man) good-looking. 2. (of a woman) fine-looking in a dignified way. 3. well-proportioned; stately: a handsome room. 4. liberal: a handsome allowance. 5. gracious or generous: a handsome action. —'handsomely adv. —'handsomeness n.

handspring ('hænd,sprɪŋ) n. a gymnastic feat in which a person starts from a standing position and leaps forwards or backwards into a handstand and then onto his feet.

handstand ('hænd,stænd) n. the act of supporting the body on the hands in an upside-down position.

hand-to-hand adj., adv. at close quarters.

hand-to-mouth adj., adv. with barely enough money or food to satisfy immediate needs.

THESAURUS

handcuff 1. v. fetter, manacle, shackle 2. n. Plural bracelets (Sl.), cuffs (Inf.), fetters, manacles, shackles

hand down or **on** bequeath, give, grant, pass on or down, transfer, will

handful few, small number, small quantity, smattering, sprinkling

handicap n. 1. barrier, block, disadvantage, drawback, encumbrance, hindrance, impediment, limitation, millstone, obstacle, restriction, shortcoming, stumbling block 2. advantage, edge, head start, odds, penalty, upper hand 3. defect, disability, impairment ~v. 4. burden, encumber, hamper, hamstring, hinder, hold back, impede, limit, place at a disadvantage, restrict, retard

handicraft art, artisanship, craft, craftsmanship, handiwork, skill, workmanship

handiwork 1. craft, handicraft, handiwork 2. achievement, artefact, creation, design, invention, product, production, result

handle n. 1. grip, haft, handgrip, helve, hilt, knob, stock ~v. 2. feel, finger, fondle, grasp, hold, maul, paw (Inf.), pick up, poke, touch 3. control, direct, guide, manage, manipulate, manoeuvre, operate, steer, use, wield 4. administer, conduct, cope with, deal with, manage, supervise, take care of, treat 5. discourse, discuss, treat 6. carry, deal in, market, sell, stock, trade, traffic in

handling administration, approach, conduct, direction, management, manipulation, running, treatment

hand-me-down adj. handed down, inherited, passed on, second-hand, used, worn

hand-out 1. alms, charity, dole 2. bulletin, circular, free sample, leaflet, literature (Inf.), press release

hand out deal out, disburse, dish out (Inf.), dispense, disseminate, distribute, give out, mete

hand over deliver, donate, fork out or up

(Sl.), present, release, surrender, turn over, yield

hand-picked choice, chosen, elect, elite, recherché, select, selected

hands 1. authority, care, charge, command, control, custody, disposal, guardianship, keeping, possession, power, supervision 2. **hands down** easily, effortlessly, with no contest

handsome 1. admirable, attractive, becoming, comely, elegant, fine, good-looking, graceful, majestic, personable, stately, well-proportioned 2. abundant, ample, bountiful, considerable, generous, gracious, large, liberal, magnanimous, plentiful, sizable

handsomely abundantly, amply, bountifully, generously, liberally, magnanimously, munificently, plentifully, richly

handwork ('hænd,wɜːk) n. work done by hand rather than by machine. —'hand,worked adj.

handwriting ('hænd,raɪtɪŋ) n. 1. writing by hand rather than by typing or printing. 2. a person's characteristic writing style: that is in my handwriting. —'hand,written adj.

handy ('hændɪ) adj. handier, handiest. 1. conveniently within reach. 2. easy to handle or use. 3. skilful with one's hands. —'handily adv. —'handiness n.

handyman ('hændɪ,mæn) n., pl. -men. a man employed to do or skilled in odd jobs, etc.

hang (hæŋ) vb. hanging, hung. 1. to fasten or be fastened from above, esp. by a cord, chain, etc. 2. to place or be placed in position as by a hinge so as to allow free movement: to hang a door. 3. (intr.; sometimes foll. by over) to be suspended; hover: a pall of smoke hung over the city. 4. (intr.; sometimes foll. by over) to threaten. 5. (intr.) to be or remain doubtful (esp. in **hang in the balance**). 6. (p.t. & p.p. hanged) to suspend or be suspended by the neck until dead. 7. (tr.) to decorate, furnish, or cover with something suspended. 8. (tr.) to fasten to a wall: to hang wallpaper. 9. to exhibit or be exhibited in an art gallery, etc. 10. to droop or allow to droop: to hang one's head. 11. (of cloth, clothing, etc.) to drape, fall, or flow: her skirt hangs well. 12. (tr.) to suspend (game such as pheasant) so that it becomes slightly decomposed and therefore more tasty. 13. (of a jury) to prevent or be prevented from reaching a verdict. 14. (p.t. & p.p. hanged) Sl. to damn or be damned: used in mild curses or interjections. 15. (intr.) to pass slowly (esp. in **time hangs heavily**). 16. **hang fire.** to procrastinate or delay. ~n. 17. the way in which something hangs. 18. (usually used with a negative) Sl. a damn: I don't care a hang. 19. **get the hang of.** Inf. a. to understand the technique of doing something. b. to perceive the meaning of. ~See also **hang about, hang back,** etc.

hang about or **around** vb. (intr.) 1. to waste time; loiter. 2. (adv., foll. by with) to frequent the company (of someone).

hangar ('hæŋə) n. a large building for storing and maintaining aircraft.

hang back vb. (intr., adv.; often foll. by from) to be reluctant to go forward or carry on.

hangdog ('hæŋ,dɒg) adj. downcast, furtive, or guilty in appearance or manner.

hanger ('hæŋə) n. 1. a. any support, such as a peg or loop, on or by which something may be hung. b. Also called: **coat hanger.** a curved piece of wood, wire, etc., with a hook, used to hang up clothes. 2. a. a person who hangs something. b. (in combination): paperhanger. 3. a type of dagger worn on a sword belt. 4. Brit. a wood on a steep hillside.

hanger-on n., pl. hangers-on. a sycophantic follower or dependant.

hang-glider n. an unpowered aircraft consisting of a large cloth wing stretched over a light framework from which the pilot hangs in a harness. —'hang-gliding n.

hanging ('hæŋɪŋ) n. 1. a. the putting of a person to death by suspending the body by the neck. b. (as modifier): a hanging offence. 2. (often pl.) a decorative drapery hung on a wall or over a window. ~adj. 3. not sup-

ported from below; suspended. 4. undecided; still under discussion. 5. projecting downwards; overhanging. 6. situated on a steep slope. 7. (prenominal) given to issuing death sentences: a hanging judge.

hangman ('hæŋmən) n., pl. -men. an official who carries out a sentence of hanging.

hangnail ('hæŋ,neɪl) n. a piece of skin torn away from, but still attached to, the base or side of a fingernail.

hang on vb. (intr.) 1. (adv.) to continue or persist, esp. with effort or difficulty. 2. (adv.) to grasp or hold. 3. (prep.) to depend on: everything hangs on this deal. 4. (prep.) Also: **hang onto, hang upon.** to listen attentively to. 5. (adv.) Inf. to wait: hang on for a few minutes.

hang out vb. (adv.) 1. to suspend, be suspended, or lean. 2. (intr.) Inf. to frequent a place. 3. **let it all hang out.** Inf., chiefly U.S. a. to relax completely in an unassuming way. b. to act or speak freely. ~n. **hang-out.** 4. Inf. a place that one frequents.

hangover ('hæŋ,əʊvə) n. 1. the delayed aftereffects of drinking too much alcohol. 2. a person or thing left over from or influenced by a past age.

hang together vb. (intr., adv.) 1. to be cohesive or united. 2. to be consistent: your statements don't quite hang together.

hang up vb. (adv.) 1. (tr.) to put on a hook, hanger, etc. 2. to replace (a telephone receiver) on its cradle at the end of a conversation. 3. (tr.; usually passive; usually foll. by on) Inf. to cause to have an emotional or psychological preoccupation or problem: he's really hung up on his mother. ~n. **hang-up.** Inf. 4. an emotional or psychological preoccupation or problem. 5. a persistent cause of annoyance.

hank (hæŋk) n. 1. a loop, coil, or skein, as of rope. 2. Naut. a ringlike fitting that can be opened to admit a stay for attaching the luff of a sail. 3. a unit of measurement of cloth, yarn, etc., such as a length of 840 yards (767 m) of cotton or 560 yards (512 m) of worsted yarn.

hanker ('hæŋkə) vb. (foll. by for, after, or an infinitive) to have a yearning. —'hankerer n.

hanky or **hankie** ('hæŋkɪ) n., pl. hankies. Inf. short for handkerchief.

hanky-panky ('hæŋkɪ'pæŋkɪ) n. Inf. 1. dubious or foolish behaviour. 2. illicit sexual relations.

Hansard ('hænsɑːd) n. 1. the official verbatim report of the proceedings of the British Parliament. 2. a similar report kept by the Canadian House of Commons and other legislative bodies.

Hanseatic League n. a commercial organization of towns in N Germany formed in the mid-14th century to protect and control trade.

hansom ('hænsəm) n. (sometimes cap.) a two-wheeled one-horse carriage with a fixed hood. The driver sits on a high outside seat at the rear. Also called: **hansom cab.**

Hants. (hænts) abbrev. for Hampshire.

hap (hæp) Arch. n. 1. luck; chance. 2. an occurrence. ~vb. **happing, happed.** 3. (intr.) to happen.

ha'penny ('heɪpnɪ) n., pl. -nies. Brit. a variant spelling of **halfpenny.**

haphazard (hæp'hæzəd) adv., adj. 1. at random. ~adj. 2. careless; slipshod. —hap'hazardly adv

---

THESAURUS

handwriting calligraphy, chirography, fist, hand, longhand, penmanship, scrawl, script

handy 1. accessible, at or on hand, available, close, convenient, near, nearby, within reach 2. convenient, easy to use, helpful, manageable, neat, practical, serviceable, useful 3. adept, adroit, clever, deft, dexterous, expert, nimble, proficient, ready, skilful, skilled

hang 1. be pendent, dangle, depend, droop, incline, suspend 2. execute, gibbet, send to the gallows, string up (Inf.) 3. adhere, cling, hold, rest, stick 4. attach, cover, deck, decorate, drape, fasten, fix, furnish 5. be poised, drift, float, hover, remain, swing 6. bend downward, bend forward, bow, dangle, drop, incline, lean over, let droop, loll, lower, sag, trail 7. **hang fire** be slow, be suspended, delay, hang back, procrastinate, stall, stick, vacillate 8. **get the hang of** comprehend, get the knack or technique, grasp, understand

hang about or **around** 1. dally, linger, loiter, roam, tarry, waste time 2. associate with, frequent, haunt, resort

hang back be backward, be reluctant, demur, hesitate, hold back, recoil

hangdog adj. abject, browbeaten, cowed, cringing, defeated, downcast, furtive, guilty, shamefaced, sneaking, wretched

hanger-on dependant, follower, freeloader (Sl., chiefly U.S.), lackey, leech, minion, parasite, sponger (Inf.), sycophant

hanging adj. 1. dangling, drooping, flapping, flopping, floppy, loose, pendent, suspended, swinging, unattached, unsupported 2. undecided, unresolved, unsettled, up in the air (Inf.) 3. beetle, beetling, jutting, overhanging, projecting

hang on 1. carry on, continue, endure, go on, hold on, hold out, persevere, persist, remain 2. cling, clutch, grasp, grip, hold fast 3. be conditional upon, be contingent on, be dependent on, be determined by, depend on,

hinge, rest, turn on 4. Also **hang onto, hang upon** be rapt, give ear, listen attentively 5. Inf. hold on, hold the line, remain, stop, wait

hangover aftereffects, crapulence, head (Inf.), morning after (Inf.)

hang over be imminent, impend, loom, menace, threaten

hang-up block, difficulty, inhibition, obsession, preoccupation, problem, thing (Inf.)

hank coil, length, loop, piece, roll, skein

hanker With for or after covet, crave, desire, hunger, itch, long, lust, pine, thirst, want, wish, yearn, yen (Inf.)

hankering craving, desire, hunger, itch, longing, pining, thirst, urge, wish, yearning, yen (Inf.)

haphazard 1. accidental, arbitrary, chance, fluky (Inf.), random 2. aimless, careless, casual, disorderly, disorganized, hit or miss (Inf.), indiscriminate, slapdash, slipshod, unmethodical, unsystematic

—**hap'hazardness** n.

hapless ('hæplɪs) adj. unfortunate; wretched. —**haplessly** adv. —**'haplessness** n.

happen ('hæpən) vb. 1. (intr.) to take place; occur. 2. (intr.; foll. by to) (of some unforeseen event, esp. death), to fall to the lot (of): if anything happens to me it'll be your fault. 3. (tr.) to chance (to be or do something): I happen to know him. 4. (tr.; takes a clause as object) to be the case, esp. by chance: it happens that I know him. ~adv., sentence substitute. N English dialect. 5. another word for **perhaps**.
▷ Usage. See at **occur**.

happening ('hæpənɪŋ, 'hæpnɪŋ) n. 1. an event. 2. an improvised or spontaneous performance consisting of bizarre events.

happy ('hæpɪ) adj. **-pier, -piest.** 1. feeling or expressing joy; pleased. 2. causing joy or gladness. 3. fortunate: the happy position of not having to work. 4. aptly expressed; appropriate: a happy turn of phrase. 5. (postpositive) Inf. slightly intoxicated. 6. **happy event.** Inf. the birth of a child. 7. **happy medium.** a course or state that avoids extremes. —**'happily** adv. —**'happiness** n.

happy-go-lucky adj. carefree or easygoing.

harakiri (ˌhærə'kɪrɪ) or **harikari** (ˌhærɪ'kɑːrɪ) n. (formerly, in Japan) ritual suicide by disembowelment when disgraced or under sentence of death.

harangue (hə'ræŋ) vb. 1. to address (a person or crowd) in an angry, vehement, or forcefully persuasive way. ~n. 2. a loud, forceful, or angry speech. —**ha'ranguer** n.

harass ('hærəs) vb. (tr.) to trouble, torment, or confuse by continual persistent attacks, questions, etc. —**'harasser** n. —**'harassment** n.

harbinger ('hɑːbɪndʒə) n. 1. a person or thing that announces or indicates the approach of something; forerunner. ~vb. 2. (tr.) to announce the approach or arrival of.

harbour or U.S. **harbor** ('hɑːbə) n. 1. a sheltered port. 2. a place of refuge or safety. ~vb. 3. (tr.) to give shelter to: to harbour a criminal. 4. (tr.) to maintain secretly: to harbour a grudge. 5. to shelter (a vessel) in a harbour or (of a vessel) to seek shelter.

harbour master n. an official in charge of a harbour.

hard (hɑːd) adj. 1. firm or rigid. 2. toughened; not soft or smooth: hard skin. 3. difficult to do or accomplish: a hard task. 4. difficult to understand: a hard question. 5. showing or requiring considerable effort or application: hard work. 6. demanding: a hard master. 7. harsh; cruel: a hard fate. 8. inflicting pain, sorrow, or hardship: hard times. 9. tough or adamant: a hard man. 10. violent: a hard knock. 11. cool or uncompromising: we took a long hard look at our profit factor. 12. indisputable; real: hard facts. 13. Chem. (of water) impairing the formation of a lather by soap. 14. practical, shrewd, or calculating: he is a hard man in business. 15. harsh: hard light. 16. a. (of currency) high and stable in exchange value. b. (of credit) difficult to obtain; tight. 17. (of alcoholic drink) being a spirit rather than a wine, beer, etc. 18. (of a drug) highly addictive. 19. Physics. (of radiation) having high energy and the ability to penetrate solids. 20. Chiefly U.S. (of goods) durable. 21. short for **hard-core**. 22. Phonetics. (not in technical usage) denoting the consonants c and g when they are pronounced as in cat and got. 23. a. heavily fortified. b. (of nuclear armament) located underground. 24. Brit. inf. incorrigible or disreputable (esp. in a **hard case**). 25. a **hard nut to crack.** a. a person not easily won over. b. a thing not easily understood. 26. **hard by.** close by. 27. **hard of hearing.** slightly deaf. 28. **hard up.** Inf. a. in need of money. b. (foll. by for) in great need (of): hard up for suggestions. ~adv. 29. with great energy, force, or vigour: the team always played hard. 30. as far as possible: hard left. 31. earnestly or intently: she thought hard about the formula. 32. with great intensity: his son's death hit him hard. 33. (foll. by on, upon, by, or after) close; near: hard on his heels. 34. (foll. by at) assiduously; devotedly. 35. a. with effort or difficulty: their victory was hard won. b. (in combination): hard-earned. 36. slowly: prejudice dies hard. 37. **go hard with.** to cause pain or difficulty to (someone). 38. **hard put (to it).** scarcely having the capacity (to do something). ~n. 39. Brit. a roadway across a foreshore. 40. Sl. hard labour. 41. Taboo sl. an erection of the penis (esp. in **get** or **have a hard on**). —**'hardness** n.

hardback ('hɑːdˌbæk) n. 1. a book with covers of cloth, cardboard, or leather. ~adj. 2. Also: **casebound, hardbound, hardcover.** of or denoting a hardback or the publication of hardbacks.

hard-bitten adj. Inf. tough and realistic.

hardboard ('hɑːdˌbɔːd) n. a thin stiff sheet made of

▬▬▬ THESAURUS ▬▬▬

happen 1. appear, arise, come about, come off (Inf.), come to pass, crop up (Inf.), develop, ensue, eventuate, follow, materialize, occur, present itself, result, take place, transpire (Inf.) 2. become of, befall, betide 3. chance, fall out, have the fortune to be, supervene, turn out

happening accident, adventure, affair, case, chance, episode, event, experience, incident, occasion, occurrence, phenomenon, proceeding, scene

happily 1. agreeably, contentedly, delightedly, enthusiastically, freely, gladly, heartily, willingly, with pleasure 2. blithely, cheerfully, gaily, gleefully, joyfully, joyously, merrily 3. auspiciously, favourably, fortunately, luckily, opportunely, propitiously, providentially, seasonably 4. appropriately, aptly, felicitously, gracefully, successfully

happiness beatitude, blessedness, bliss, cheer, cheerfulness, cheeriness, contentment, delight, ecstasy, elation, enjoyment, exuberance, felicity, gaiety, gladness, high spirits, joy, jubilation, light-heartedness, merriment, pleasure, prosperity, satisfaction, wellbeing

happy 1. blessed, blest, blissful, blithe, cheerful, content, contented, delighted, ecstatic, elated, glad, gratified, jolly, joyful, joyous, jubilant, merry, overjoyed, over the moon (Inf.), pleased, sunny, thrilled, walking on air (Inf.) 2. advantageous, appropriate, apt, auspicious, befitting, convenient, enviable, favourable, felicitous, fortunate, lucky, opportune, promising, propitious, satisfactory, seasonable, successful, timely, welltimed

happy-go-lucky blithe, carefree, casual, devil-may-care, easy-going, heedless, improvident, insouciant, irresponsible, lighthearted, nonchalant, unconcerned, untroubled

harangue 1. n. address, declamation, diatribe, exhortation, lecture, oration, philippic, screed, speech, spiel (Inf.), tirade 2. v. address, declaim, exhort, hold forth, lecture, rant, spout (Inf.)

harass annoy, badger, bait, beleaguer, bother, chivvy (Brit.), devil (Inf.), disturb, exasperate, exhaust, fatigue, harry, hassle (Inf.), hound, perplex, persecute, pester, plague, tease, tire, torment, trouble, vex, weary, worry

harassed careworn, distraught, harried, hassled (Inf.), plagued, strained, tormented, troubled, under pressure, under stress, vexed, worried

harassment aggravation (Inf.), annoyance, badgering, bedevilment, bother, hassle (Inf.), irritation, molestation, nuisance, persecution, pestering, torment, trouble, vexation

harbour n. 1. anchorage, destination, haven, port 2. asylum, covert, haven, refuge, retreat, sanctuary, sanctum, security, shelter ~v. 3. conceal, hide, lodge, protect, provide refuge, relieve, secrete, shelter, shield 4. believe, brood over, cherish, cling to, entertain, foster, hold, imagine, maintain, nurse, nurture, retain

hard adj. 1. compact, dense, firm, impenetrable, inflexible, rigid, rocklike, solid, stiff, stony, strong, tough, unyielding 2. arduous, backbreaking, burdensome, exacting, exhausting, fatiguing, formidable, Herculean, laborious, rigorous, strenuous, toilsome, tough, uphill, wearying 3. baffling, complex, complicated, difficult, intricate, involved, knotty, perplexing, puzzling, tangled, thorny, unfathomable 4. callous, cold, cruel, exacting, grim, hardhearted, harsh, implacable, obdurate, pitiless, ruthless, severe, stern, strict, stubborn, unfeeling, unjust, unkind, unrelenting, unsparing, unsympathetic 5. calamitous, dark, disagreeable, disastrous, distressing, grievous, grim, intolerable, painful, unpleasant 6. driving, fierce, forceful, heavy, powerful, strong, violent 7. Of feelings or words acrimonious, angry, antagonistic, bitter, hostile, rancorous, resentful 8. Of truth or facts actual, bare, cold, definite, indisputable, plain, undeniable, unvarnished, verified ~adv. 9. energetically, fiercely, forcefully, forcibly, heavily, intensely, powerfully, severely, sharply, strongly, vigorously, violently, with all one's might, with might and main 10. assiduously, determinedly, diligently, doggedly, earnestly, industriously, intently, persistently, steadily, strenuously, untiringly 11. agonizingly, badly, distressingly, harshly, laboriously, painfully, roughly, severely, with difficulty 12. bitterly, hardly, keenly, rancorously, reluctantly, resentfully, slowly, sorely

hard and fast binding, immutable, incontrovertible, inflexible, invariable, rigid, set, strict, stringent, unalterable

hard-bitten or **hard-boiled** casehardened, cynical, down-to-earth, hardheaded, hard-nosed (Sl.), matter-of-fact, practical, realistic, shrewd, tough, unsentimental

hard-core 1. dedicated, die-hard, dyed-in-the-wool, extreme, intransigent, obstinate, rigid, staunch, steadfast 2. explicit, obscene

compressed sawdust and woodchips bound together under heat and pressure.

hard-boiled *adj.* **1.** (of an egg) boiled until solid. **2.** *Inf.* **a.** tough, realistic. **b.** cynical.

hard cash *n.* money or payment in money, as opposed to payment by cheque, credit, etc.

hard copy *n.* computer output that can be read by the eye, as contrasted with machine-readable output such as magnetic tape.

hard core *n.* **1.** the members of a group who form an intransigent nucleus resisting change. **2.** material, such as broken stones, used to form a foundation for a road, etc. ~*adj.* **hard-core. 3.** (of pornography) describing or depicting sexual acts in explicit detail. **4.** completely established in a belief, etc.: *hard-core Communists.*

hard disk *n.* another name for **Winchester disk.**

harden ('hɑːdən) *vb.* **1.** to make or become hard or harder; freeze, stiffen, or set. **2.** to make or become tough or unfeeling. **3.** to make or become stronger or firmer. **4.** (*intr.*) *Commerce.* **a.** (of prices, a market, etc.) to cease to fluctuate. **b.** (of price) to rise higher. —'**hardener** *n.*

hardened ('hɑːdənd) *adj.* **1.** rigidly set, as in a mode of behaviour. **2.** toughened; seasoned.

hard hat *n.* **1.** a hat made of a hard material for protection, worn esp. by construction workers. **2.** *Inf., chiefly U.S.* a construction worker.

hard-headed *adj.* tough, realistic, or shrewd; not moved by sentiment.

hardhearted (ˌhɑːd'hɑːtɪd) *adj.* unkind or intolerant. —ˌhard'**heartedness** *n.*

hard labour *n. Criminal law.* (formerly) the penalty of compulsory physical labour imposed in addition to a sentence of imprisonment.

hard line *n.* an uncompromising course or policy. —ˌhard'**liner** *n.*

hardly ('hɑːdlɪ) *adv.* **1.** scarcely; barely: *we hardly knew the family.* **2.** only just: *he could hardly hold the cup.* **3.** *Often used ironically.* not at all: *he will hardly incriminate himself.* **4.** with difficulty. **5.** *Rare.* harshly or cruelly.

▷ **Usage.** Since *hardly, scarcely,* and *barely* already have negative force, it is redundant to use another negative in the same clause: *he had hardly had* (not *he hadn't hardly had) time to think.*

hard pad *n.* an old-fashioned name for **canine distemper.** See **distemper**[1].

hard palate *n.* the anterior bony portion of the roof of the mouth.

hard-pressed *adj.* **1.** in difficulties. **2.** subject to severe competition or attack. **3.** closely pursued.

hard sell *n.* an aggressive insistent technique of selling or advertising.

hardship ('hɑːdʃɪp) *n.* **1.** conditions of life difficult to endure. **2.** something that causes suffering or privation.

hard shoulder *n. Brit.* a surfaced verge running along the edge of a motorway for emergency stops.

hardtack ('hɑːdˌtæk) *n.* a kind of hard saltless biscuit, formerly eaten esp. by sailors as a staple aboard ship. Also called: **ship's biscuit, sea biscuit.**

hardware ('hɑːdˌwɛə) *n.* **1.** metal tools, implements, etc., esp. cutlery or cooking utensils. **2.** *Computers.* the physical equipment used in a computer system, such as the central processing unit, peripheral devices, and memory. Cf. **software. 3.** mechanical equipment, components, etc. **4.** heavy military equipment, such as tanks and missiles. **5.** *Inf.* a gun.

hardwood ('hɑːdˌwʊd) *n.* **1.** the wood of any of numerous broad-leaved trees, such as oak, beech, ash, etc., as distinguished from the wood of a conifer. **2.** any tree from which this wood is obtained.

hardy ('hɑːdɪ) *adj.* **-dier, -diest. 1.** having or demanding a tough constitution; robust. **2.** bold; courageous. **3.** foolhardy; rash. **4.** (of plants) able to live out of doors throughout the winter. —'**hardily** *adv.* —'**hardiness** *n.*

hare (hɛə) *n., pl.* **hares** *or* **hare. 1.** a solitary mammal which is larger than a rabbit, has longer ears and legs, and lives in a shallow nest (form). **2. start a hare.** to raise a topic for conversation. **3. run with the hare and hunt with the hounds.** to be on good terms with both sides. ~*vb.* **4.** (*intr.;* often foll. by *off, after,* etc.) *Brit. inf.* to run fast or wildly. —'**hare**ˌ**like** *adj.*

hare and hounds *n.* (*functioning as sing.*) a game in which certain players (**hares**) run across country scattering pieces of paper that the other players (**hounds**) follow in an attempt to catch the hares.

harebell ('hɛəˌbɛl) *n.* a N temperate plant having slender stems and leaves, and bell-shaped blue flowers.

harebrained *or* **hairbrained** ('hɛəˌbreɪnd) *adj.* rash, foolish, or badly thought out.

harelip ('hɛəˌlɪp) *n.* a congenital cleft or fissure in the midline of the upper lip, often occurring with cleft palate. —'**hare**ˌ**lipped** *adj.*

harem ('hɛərəm, hɑː'riːm) *or* **hareem** (hɑː'riːm) *n.* **1.** the part of an Oriental house reserved strictly for wives, concubines, etc. **2.** a Muslim's wives and concubines collectively. **3.** a group of female animals that are the mates of a single male.

haricot ('hærɪˌkəʊ) *n.* a variety of French bean with light-coloured edible seeds, which can be dried and stored.

harikari (ˌhærɪ'kɑːrɪ) *n.* a variant spelling of **harakiri.**

hark (hɑːk) *vb.* (*intr.; usually imperative*) to listen; pay attention.

hark back *vb.* (*intr., adv.*) to return to an earlier subject in speech or thought.

harlequin ('hɑːlɪkwɪn) *n.* **1.** (*sometimes cap.*) *Theatre.* a stock comic character originating in the commedia dell'arte; the foppish lover of Columbine in the English harlequinade. He is usually represented in diamond-patterned multicoloured tights, wearing a black mask. **2.** a clown or buffoon. ~*adj.* **3.** varied in colour or decoration.

harlequinade (ˌhɑːlɪkwɪ'neɪd) *n.* **1.** (*sometimes cap.*) *Theatre.* a play in which harlequin has a leading role. **2.** buffoonery.

Harley Street ('hɑːlɪ) *n.* a street in central London famous for its large number of medical specialists' consulting rooms.

harlot ('hɑːlət) *n.* a prostitute. —'**harlotry** *n.*

harm (hɑːm) *n.* **1.** physical or mental injury. **2.** moral wrongdoing. ~*vb.* **3.** (*tr.*) to injure physically, morally, or mentally.

THESAURUS

harden 1. anneal, bake, cake, freeze, set, solidify, stiffen **2.** brace, buttress, fortify, gird, indurate, nerve, reinforce, steel, strengthen, toughen **3.** accustom, brutalize, case-harden, habituate, inure, season, train

hardened 1. chronic, fixed, habitual, incorrigible, inveterate, irredeemable, reprobate, set, shameless **2.** accustomed, habituated, inured, seasoned, toughened

hard-headed astute, cool, hard-boiled (*Inf.*), level-headed, practical, pragmatic, realistic, sensible, shrewd, tough, unsentimental

hardhearted callous, cold, cruel, hard, heartless, indifferent, inhuman, insensitive, intolerant, merciless, pitiless, stony, uncaring, unfeeling, unkind, unsympathetic

hard-hitting critical, no holds barred, pulling no punches, strongly worded, tough, unsparing, vigorous

hardiness boldness, courage, fortitude, intrepidity, resilience, resolution, robustness, ruggedness, sturdiness, toughness, valour

hardline definite, inflexible, intransigent, tough, uncompromising, undeviating, unyielding

hardly almost not, barely, by no means, faintly, infrequently, just, not at all, not quite, no way, only, only just, scarcely, with difficulty

hard-pressed harried, hotly pursued, in difficulties, pushed (*Inf.*), under attack, under pressure, up against it (*Inf.*), with one's back to the wall

hardship adversity, affliction, austerity, burden, calamity, destitution, difficulty, fatigue, grievance, labour, misery, misfortune, need, oppression, persecution, privation, suffering, toil, torment, trial, tribulation, trouble, want

hard up bankrupt, broke (*Inf.*), bust (*Inf.*), cleaned out (*Sl.*), impecunious, impoverished, in the red (*Inf.*), on one's uppers (*Inf.*), out of pocket, penniless, poor, short, short of cash *or* funds, skint (*Brit. sl.*)

hard-wearing durable, resilient, rugged, stout, strong, tough, well-made

hard-working assiduous, busy, conscientious, diligent, energetic, indefatigable, industrious, sedulous, zealous

hardy 1. firm, fit, hale, healthy, hearty, in fine fettle, lusty, robust, rugged, sound, stalwart, stout, strong, sturdy, tough, vigorous **2.** bold, brave, courageous, daring, heroic, intrepid, manly, plucky, resolute, stouthearted, valiant, valorous **3.** audacious, brazen, foolhardy, headstrong, impudent, rash, reckless

hark back look back, recall, recollect, regress, remember, revert, think back

harlot call girl, fallen woman, hussy, loose

harmful ('hɑːmfʊl) *adj.* causing or tending to cause harm; injurious. —'**harmfully** *adv.*

harmless ('hɑːmlɪs) *adj.* not causing or tending to cause harm. —'**harmlessly** *adv.*

harmonic (hɑː'mɒnɪk) *adj.* 1. of, producing, or characterized by harmony; harmonious. 2. *Music.* of or belonging to harmony. 3. *Maths.* a. capable of expression in the form of sine and cosine functions. b. of or relating to numbers whose reciprocals form an arithmetic progression. 4. *Physics.* of or concerned with a harmonic or harmonics. ~*n.* 5. *Physics, music.* a component of a periodic quantity, such as a musical tone, with a frequency that is an integral multiple of the fundamental frequency. 6. *Music.* (*not in technical use*) overtone. —**har'monically** *adv.*

harmonica (hɑː'mɒnɪkə) *n.* a small wind instrument in which reeds of graduated lengths set into a metal plate enclosed in a narrow oblong box are made to vibrate by blowing and suction.

harmonics (hɑː'mɒnɪks) *n.* 1. (*functioning as sing.*) the science of musical sounds and their acoustic properties. 2. (*functioning as pl.*) the overtones of a fundamental note, as produced by lightly touching the string of a stringed instrument at one of its node points while playing.

harmonious (hɑː'məʊnɪəs) *adj.* 1. (esp. of colours or sounds) fitting together well. 2. having agreement. 3. tuneful or melodious.

harmonium (hɑː'məʊnɪəm) *n.* a musical keyboard instrument in which air from pedal-operated bellows causes the reeds to vibrate.

harmonize *or* **-nise** ('hɑːmə,naɪz) *vb.* 1. to make or become harmonious. 2. (*tr.*) *Music.* to provide a harmony for (a tune, etc.). 3. (*intr.*) to sing in harmony, as with other singers. 4. to collate parallel narratives. —,**harmoni'zation** *or* **-ni'sation** *n.*

harmony ('hɑːmənɪ) *n., pl.* **-nies.** 1. agreement in action, opinion, feeling, etc. 2. order or congruity of parts to their whole or to one another. 3. agreeable sounds. 4. *Music.* a. any combination of notes sounded simultaneously. b. the vertically represented structure of a piece of music. Cf. **melody** (sense 1b.). c. the art or science concerned with combinations of chords. 5. a collation of parallel narratives, esp. of the four Gospels.

harness ('hɑːnɪs) *n.* 1. an arrangement of straps fitted to a draught animal in order that the animal can be attached to and pull a cart. 2. something resembling this, esp. for attaching something to the body: *a parachute harness.* 3. *Weaving.* the part of a loom that raises and lowers the warp threads. 4. *Arch.* armour. 5. **in harness.** at one's routine work. ~*vb.* (*tr.*) 6. to put harness on (a horse). 7. (usually foll. by *to*) to attach (a draught animal) to (a cart, etc.). 8. to control so as to employ the energy or potential power of: *to harness the atom.* 9. to equip with armour. —'**harnesser** *n.*

harp (hɑːp) *n.* 1. a large triangular plucked stringed instrument consisting of a soundboard connected to an upright pillar by means of a curved crossbar from which

the strings extend downwards. ~*vb.* 2. (*intr.*) to play the harp. 3. (*intr.;* foll. by *on* or *upon*) to speak or write in a persistent and tedious manner. —'**harper** *or* '**harpist** *n.*

harpoon (hɑː'puːn) *n.* 1. a. a barbed missile attached to a long cord and hurled or fired from a gun when hunting whales, etc. b. (*as modifier*): *a harpoon gun.* ~*vb.* 2. (*tr.*) to spear with or as if with a harpoon. —**har'pooner** *or* ,**harpoon'eer** *n.*

harp seal *n.* a brownish-grey North Atlantic and Arctic seal, having a dark mark on its back.

harpsichord ('hɑːpsɪ,kɔːd) *n.* a horizontally strung stringed keyboard instrument, triangular in shape, with strings plucked by plectra mounted on pivoted jacks. —'**harpsi,chordist** *n.*

harpy ('hɑːpɪ) *n., pl.* **-pies.** a cruel grasping person.

Harpy ('hɑːpɪ) *n., pl.* **-pies.** *Greek myth.* a ravenous creature with a woman's head and trunk and a bird's wings and claws.

harquebus ('hɑːkwɪbəs) *n., pl.* **-buses.** a variant spelling of **arquebus.** —,**harquebu'sier** *n.*

harridan ('hærɪdən) *n.* a scolding old woman; nag.

harrier[1] ('hærɪə) *n.* 1. a person or thing that harries. 2. a diurnal bird of prey having broad wings and long legs and tail.

harrier[2] ('hærɪə) *n.* 1. a smallish breed of hound used originally for hare-hunting. 2. a cross-country runner.

harrow ('hærəʊ) *n.* 1. any of various implements used to level the ground, stir the soil, break up clods, destroy weeds, etc., in soil. ~*vb.* (*tr.*) 2. to draw a harrow over (land). 3. to distress; vex. —'**harrower** *n.* —'**harrowing** *adj.* —'**harrowingly** *adv.*

harry ('hærɪ) *vb.* **-rying, -ried.** 1. (*tr.*) to harass; worry. 2. to ravage (a town, etc.), esp. in war.

harsh (hɑːʃ) *adj.* 1. rough or grating to the senses. 2. stern, severe, or cruel. —'**harshly** *adv.* —'**harshness** *n.*

hart (hɑːt) *n., pl.* **harts** *or* **hart.** the male of the deer, esp. the red deer aged five years or more.

hartal (hɑː'tɑːl) *n.* (in India) the act of closing shops or suspending work, esp. in political protest.

hartebeest ('hɑːtɪ,biːst) *or* **hartbeest** ('hɑːt,biːst) *n.* 1. either of two large African antelopes having an elongated muzzle, lyre-shaped horns, and a fawn-coloured coat. 2. any similar and related animal, such as **Hunter's hartebeest.**

hartshorn ('hɑːts,hɔːn) *n.* an obsolete name for **sal volatile** (sense 2).

harum-scarum ('hɛərəm'skɛərəm) *adj., adv.* 1. in a reckless way or of a reckless nature. ~*n.* 2. a person who is impetuous or rash.

harvest ('hɑːvɪst) *n.* 1. the gathering of a ripened crop. 2. the crop itself. 3. the season for gathering crops. 4. the product of an effort, action, etc.: *a harvest of love.* ~*vb.* 5. to gather (a ripened crop) from (the place where it has been growing). 6. (*tr.*) to receive (consequences). —'**harvesting** *n.*

THESAURUS

woman, pro (*Inf.*), prostitute, scrubber (*Sl.*), streetwalker, strumpet, tart (*Inf.*), tramp (*Sl.*), whore

harm *n.* 1. abuse, damage, detriment, disservice, hurt, ill, impairment, injury, loss, mischief, misfortune 2. evil, immorality, iniquity, sin, sinfulness, vice, wickedness, wrong ~*v.* 3. abuse, blemish, damage, hurt, ill-treat, ill-use, impair, injure, maltreat, mar, molest, ruin, spoil, wound

harmful baleful, baneful, damaging, deleterious, destructive, detrimental, disadvantageous, evil, hurtful, injurious, noxious, pernicious

harmless gentle, innocent, innocuous, innoxious, inoffensive, nontoxic, not dangerous, safe, unobjectionable

harmonious 1. agreeable, compatible, concordant, congruous, consonant, coordinated, correspondent, dulcet, euphonious, harmonic, harmonizing, matching, mellifluous, melodious, musical, sweet-sounding, symphonious (*Literary*), tuneful 2. agreeable, amicable, compatible, concordant, congenial, cordial, *en rapport*, fraternal, friend-

ly, in accord, in harmony, in unison, of one mind, sympathetic

harmonize accord, adapt, agree, arrange, attune, be in unison, be of one mind, blend, chime with, cohere, compose, coordinate, correspond, match, reconcile, suit, tally, tone in with

harmony 1. accord, agreement, amicability, amity, compatibility, concord, conformity, consensus, cooperation, friendship, good will, like-mindedness, peace, rapport, sympathy, unanimity, understanding, unity 2. balance, compatibility, concord, congruity, consistency, consonance, coordination, correspondence, fitness, parallelism, suitability, symmetry 3. euphony, melodiousness, melody, tune, tunefulness

harness *n.* 1. equipment, gear, tack, tackle, trappings 2. **in harness** active, at work, busy, in action, working ~*v.* 3. couple, hitch up, put in harness, saddle, yoke 4. apply, channel, control, employ, exploit, make productive, mobilize, render useful, turn to account, utilize

harp **With on** *or* **upon** dwell on, go on, la-

bour, press, reiterate, renew, repeat

harrowing agonizing, alarming, chilling, distressing, disturbing, excruciating, frightening, heartbreaking, heart-rending, nerveracking, painful, racking, soaring, terrifying, tormenting, traumatic

harry 1. annoy, badger, bedevil, chivvy, disturb, fret, harass, hassle (*Inf.*), molest, persecute, pester, plague, tease, torment, trouble, vex, worry 2. depredate (*Rare*), despoil, devastate, pillage, plunder, raid, ravage, rob, sack

harsh 1. coarse, croaking, crude, discordant, dissonant, glaring, grating, guttural, jarring, rasping, raucous, rough, strident, unmelodious 2. abusive, austere, bitter, bleak, brutal, comfortless, cruel, dour, Draconian, grim, hard, pitiless, punitive, relentless, ruthless, severe, sharp, Spartan, stern, stringent, unfeeling, unkind, unpleasant, unrelenting

harshly brutally, cruelly, grimly, roughly, severely, sharply, sternly, strictly

harshness acerbity, acrimony, asperity, austerity, bitterness, brutality, churlishness, coarseness, crudity, hardness, ill-temper, rig-

harvester ('hɑːvɪstə) n. 1. a person who harvests. 2. a harvesting machine, esp. a combine harvester.

harvest home n. 1. the bringing in of the harvest. 2. Chiefly Brit. a harvest supper.

harvest moon n. the full moon occurring nearest to the autumnal equinox.

harvest mouse n. a very small reddish-brown Eurasian mouse inhabiting cornfields, hedgerows, etc.

has (hæz) vb. (used with he, she, it, or a singular noun) a form of the present tense (indicative mood) of **have**.

has-been n. Inf. a person or thing that is no longer popular, successful, effective, etc.

hash[1] (hæʃ) n. 1. a dish of diced cooked meat, vegetables, etc., reheated in a sauce. 2. a reuse or rework of old material. 3. **make a hash of.** Inf. to mess up or destroy. 4. **settle someone's hash.** Inf. to subdue or get even with someone. ~vb. (tr.) 5. to chop into small pieces. 6. to mess up.

hash[2] (hæʃ) n. Sl. short for **hashish**.

hashish ('hæʃiːʃ, -ɪʃ) or **hasheesh** n. a resinous extract of the dried flower tops of the female hemp plant, used as a hallucinogenic. See also **cannabis**.

haslet ('hæzlɪt) or **harslet** n. a loaf of cooked minced pig's offal, eaten cold.

hasp (hɑːsp) n. 1. a metal fastening consisting of a hinged strap with a slot that fits over a staple and is secured by a pin, bolt, or padlock. ~vb. 2. (tr.) to secure (a door, window, etc.) with a hasp.

hassle ('hæsəl) Inf. ~n. 1. a quarrel or fight. 2. a great deal of trouble. ~vb. 3. to quarrel or struggle with (someone). 4. to cause annoyance or trouble to (someone); harass.

hassock ('hæsək) n. 1. a firm upholstered cushion used for kneeling on, esp. in church. 2. a thick clump of grass.

haste (heɪst) n. 1. speed, esp. in an action. 2. the act of hurrying in a careless manner. 3. a necessity for hurrying; urgency. 4. **make haste.** to hurry; rush. ~vb. 5. a poetic word for **hasten**.

hasten ('heɪsən) vb. 1. (may take an infinitive) to hurry or cause to hurry; rush. 2. (tr.) to be anxious (to say something). —'**hastener** n.

hasty ('heɪstɪ) adj. **-tier, -tiest.** 1. rapid; swift; quick. 2. excessively or rashly quick. 3. short-tempered. 4. showing irritation or anger: hasty words. —'**hastily** adv. —'**hastiness** n.

hat (hæt) n. 1. a head covering, esp. one with a brim and a shaped crown. 2. Inf. a role or capacity. 3. **at the drop of a hat.** immediately. 4. **eat one's hat.** Sl. to be shocked or proved wrong if a certain event or result happens. 5. **keep (something) under one's hat.** to keep (something) secret. 6. **old hat.** something stale or old-fashioned. 7. **pass (or send) the hat round.** to collect money, as for a cause. 8. **take off one's hat to.** to admire

or congratulate. 9. **talk through one's hat. a.** to talk foolishly. **b.** to deceive or bluff. ~vb. **hatting, hatted.** 10. (tr.) to supply (a person, etc.) with a hat or put a hat on (someone). —'**hatless** adj.

hatband ('hæt,bænd) n. a band or ribbon around the base of the crown of a hat.

hatch[1] (hætʃ) vb. 1. to cause (the young of various animals, esp. birds) to emerge from the egg or (of young birds, etc.) to emerge from the egg. 2. to cause (eggs) to break and release the fully developed young or (of eggs) to break and release the young animal within. 3. (tr.) to contrive or devise (a scheme, plot, etc.). ~n. 4. the act or process of hatching. 5. a group of newly hatched animals.

hatch[2] (hætʃ) n. 1. a covering for a hatchway. 2. **a.** short for **hatchway. b.** a door in an aircraft or spacecraft. 3. Also called: **serving hatch.** an opening in a wall separating a kitchen from a dining area. 4. the lower half of a divided door. 5. a sluice in a dam, dyke, or weir. 6. **down the hatch.** Sl. (used as a toast) drink up! 7. **under hatches. a.** below decks. **b.** out of sight. **c.** dead.

hatch[3] (hætʃ) vb. Drawing, engraving, etc. to mark (a figure, etc.) with fine parallel or crossed lines to indicate shading. —'**hatching** n.

hatchback ('hætʃ,bæk) n. 1. a sloping rear end of a car having a single door that is lifted to open. 2. a car having such a rear end.

hatchet ('hætʃɪt) n. 1. a short axe used for chopping wood, etc. 2. a tomahawk. 3. (modifier) of narrow dimensions and sharp features: a hatchet face. 4. **bury the hatchet.** to make peace.

hatchet man n. Inf. 1. a person carrying out unpleasant assignments for an employer or superior. 2. a severe or malicious critic.

hatchway ('hætʃ,weɪ) n. 1. an opening in the deck of a vessel to provide access below. 2. a similar opening in a wall, floor, ceiling, or roof.

hate (heɪt) vb. 1. to dislike (something) intensely; detest. 2. (intr.) to be unwilling (to be or do something). ~n. 3. intense dislike. 4. Inf. a person or thing that is hated (esp. in pet hate). —'**hateable** or '**hatable** adj.

hateful ('heɪtful) adj. 1. causing or deserving hate; loathsome; detestable. 2. Arch. full of hate. —'**hatefully** adv. —'**hatefulness** n.

hatred ('heɪtrɪd) n. intense dislike; enmity.

hatter ('hætə) n. 1. a person who makes and sells hats. 2. **mad as a hatter.** eccentric.

hat trick n. 1. Cricket. the achievement of a bowler in taking three wickets with three successive balls. 2. any achievement of three successive points, victories, etc.

hauberk ('hɔːbɜːk) n. a long coat of mail, often sleeveless.

haughty ('hɔːtɪ) adj. **-tier, -tiest.** having or showing

THESAURUS

our, roughness, severity, sourness, sternness

harvest n. 1. harvesting, harvest-time, ingathering, reaping 2. crop, produce, yield 3. Fig. consequence, effect, fruition, product, result, return ~v. 4. gather, mow, pick, pluck, reap 5. accumulate, acquire, amass, collect, garner

hash 1. confusion, hotchpotch, jumble, mess, mishmash, mix-up, muddle, shambles 2. **make a hash of** Inf. botch, bungle, jumble, mess up, mishandle, mismanage, mix, muddle

hassle n. 1. altercation, argument, bickering, disagreement, dispute, fight, quarrel, squabble, tussle, wrangle 2. bother, difficulty, inconvenience, problem, struggle, trial, trouble, upset ~v. 3. annoy, badger, bother, bug (Inf.), harass, harry, hound, pester

haste 1. alacrity, briskness, celerity, dispatch, expedition, fleetness, nimbleness, promptitude, quickness, rapidity, rapidness, speed, swiftness, urgency, velocity 2. bustle, hastiness, helter-skelter, hurry, hustle, impetuosity, precipitateness, rashness, recklessness, rush

hasten 1. bolt, dash, fly, haste, hurry (up), make haste, race, run, rush, scurry, scuttle, speed, sprint, step on it (Inf.), tear (along) 2.

accelerate, advance, dispatch, expedite, goad, hurry (up), precipitate, press, push forward, quicken, speed (up), step up (Inf.), urge

hastily 1. apace, double-quick, fast, posthaste, promptly, quickly, rapidly, speedily, straightaway 2. heedlessly, hurriedly, impetuously, impulsively, on the spur of the moment, precipitately, rashly, recklessly, too quickly

hasty 1. brisk, eager, expeditious, fast, fleet, hurried, prompt, rapid, speedy, swift, urgent 2. brief, cursory, fleeting, passing, perfunctory, rushed, short, superficial 3. foolhardy, headlong, heedless, impetuous, impulsive, indiscreet, precipitate, rash, reckless, thoughtless, unduly quick 4. brusque, excited, fiery, hot-headed, hot-tempered, impatient, irascible, irritable, passionate, quick-tempered, snappy

hatch 1. breed, bring forth, brood, incubate 2. Fig. conceive, concoct, contrive, cook up (Inf.), design, devise, dream up (Inf.), plan, plot, project, scheme, think up

hatchet man assassin, bravo, calumniator, cutthroat, debunker, defamer, destroyer, detractor, gunman, hired assassin, hit man (Sl.), killer, murderer, smear campaign-

er, thug, traducer

hate v. 1. abhor, abominate, be hostile to, be repelled by, be sick of, despise, detest, dislike, execrate, have an aversion to, loathe, recoil from 2. be loath, be reluctant, be sorry, be unwilling, dislike, feel disinclined, have no stomach for, shrink from ~n. 3. abhorrence, abomination, animosity, animus, antagonism, antipathy, aversion, detestation, dislike, enmity, execration, hatred, hostility, loathing, odium

hateful abhorrent, abominable, despicable, detestable, disgusting, execrable, forbidding, foul, heinous, horrible, loathsome, obnoxious, odious, offensive, repellent, repugnant, repulsive, revolting, vile

hatred abomination, animosity, animus, antagonism, antipathy, aversion, detestation, dislike, enmity, execration, hate, ill will, odium, repugnance, revulsion

haughty arrogant, assuming, conceited, contemptuous, disdainful, high, high and mighty (Inf.), hoity-toity (Inf.), imperious, lofty, overweening, proud, scornful, snobbish, snooty (Inf.), stuck-up (Inf.), supercilious, uppish (Brit. inf.)

arrogance. —'**haughtily** adv. —'**haughtiness** n.

haul (hɔːl) vb. **1.** to drag (something) with effort. **2.** (tr.) to transport, as in a lorry. **3.** Naut. to alter the course of (a vessel), esp. so as to sail closer to the wind. **4.** (intr.) Naut. (of the wind) to blow from a direction nearer the bow. ~n. **5.** the act of dragging with effort. **6.** (esp. of fish) the amount caught at a single time. **7.** something that is hauled. **8.** a distance of hauling or travelling. —'**hauler** n.

haulage ('hɔːlɪdʒ) n. **1.** the act or labour of hauling. **2.** a rate or charge levied for the transportation of goods, esp. by rail.

haulier ('hɔːljə) n. **1.** Brit. a person or firm that transports goods by road. **2.** a mine worker who conveys coal from the workings to the foot of the shaft.

haulm or **halm** (hɔːm) n. **1.** the stalks of beans, peas, potatoes, grasses, etc., collectively. **2.** a single stem of such a plant.

haunch (hɔːntʃ) n. **1.** the human hip or fleshy hindquarter of an animal. **2.** the leg and loin of an animal, used for food. **3.** Also called: **hance**. Archit. the part of an arch between the impost and the apex.

haunt (hɔːnt) vb. **1.** to visit (a person or place) in the form of a ghost. **2.** (tr.) to recur to (the memory, thoughts, etc.): he was haunted by the fear of insanity. **3.** to visit (a place) frequently. **4.** to associate with (someone) frequently. ~n. **5.** (often pl.) a place visited frequently. **6.** a place to which animals habitually resort for food, drink, shelter, etc.

haunted ('hɔːntɪd) adj. **1.** frequented or visited by ghosts. **2.** (postpositive) obsessed or worried.

haunting ('hɔːntɪŋ) adj. **1.** (of memories) poignant or persistent. **2.** poignantly sentimental; eerily evocative. —'**hauntingly** adv.

hautboy ('əʊbɔɪ) n. **1.** a strawberry with large fruit. **2.** an archaic word for **oboe**.

haute couture French. (ot ku'tyːr) n. high fashion.

hauteur (əʊ'tɜː) n. pride; haughtiness.

have (hæv) vb. **has, having, had.** (mainly tr.) **1.** to be in possession of; own: he has two cars. **2.** to possess as a quality or attribute: he has dark hair. **3.** to receive, take, or obtain: she had a present; have a look. **4.** to hold in the mind: to have an idea. **5.** to possess a knowledge of: I have no German. **6.** to experience: to have a shock. **7.** to suffer from: to have a cold. **8.** to gain control of or advantage over: you have me on that point. **9.** (usually passive) Sl. to cheat or outwit: he was had by that dishonest salesman. **10.** (foll. by on) to exhibit (mercy, etc., towards). **11.** to take part in: to have a conversation. **12.** to arrange or hold: to have a party. **13.** to cause, compel, or require to (be, do, or be done): have my shoes mended. **14.** (takes an infinitive with to) used as an auxiliary to express compulsion or necessity: I had to run quickly to escape him. **15.** to eat, drink, or partake of. **16.** Taboo sl. to have sexual intercourse with. **17.** (used with a negative) to tolerate or allow: I won't have all this noise. **18.** to state or assert: rumour has it that they will marry. **19.** to place: I'll have the sofa in this room. **20.** to receive as a guest: to have people to stay. **21.** to beget or bear (offspring). **22.** (takes a past participle) used as an auxiliary to form compound tenses expressing completed action: I have gone; I had gone. **23. had better** or **best.** ought to: you had better go. **24. had rather** or **sooner.** to consider preferable that: I had rather you left

at once. **25. have had it.** Inf. **a.** to be exhausted, defeated, or killed. **b.** to have lost one's last chance. **c.** to become unfashionable. **26. have it away** (or off). Taboo, Brit. sl. to have sexual intercourse. **27. have it coming.** Inf. to be about to receive or to merit retribution. **28. have it in for.** Inf. to wish or intend harm towards. **29. have it so good.** to have so many material benefits. **30. have to do with. a.** to have dealings with. **b.** to be of relevance to. **31. let (someone) have it.** Sl. to launch an attack on (someone). ~n. **32.** (usually pl.) Inf. a person or group in possession of wealth, security, etc.: the haves and the have-nots.

haven ('heɪvən) n. **1.** a harbour or other sheltered place for shipping. **2.** a place of safety; shelter. ~vb. **3.** (tr.) to shelter as in a haven.

have on vb. (tr.) **1.** (usually adv.) to wear. **2.** (usually adv.) to have a commitment: what does your boss have on this afternoon? **3.** (adv.) to trick or tease (a person). **4.** (prep.) to have available (information, esp. when incriminating) about (a person).

have out vb. (tr., adv.) **1.** to settle (a matter) or come to (a final decision), esp. by fighting or by frank discussion (often in **have it out**). **2.** to have extracted or removed.

haver ('heɪvə) vb. (intr.) Brit. **1.** Scot. & N English dialect. to babble; talk nonsense. **2.** to dither. ~n. **3.** (usually pl.) Scot. nonsense.

haversack ('hævə,sæk) n. a canvas bag for provisions or equipment, carried on the back or shoulder.

have up vb. (tr., adv.; usually passive) to cause to appear for trial: he was had up for breaking and entering.

havoc ('hævək) n. **1.** destruction; devastation; ruin. **2.** Inf. confusion; chaos. **3. cry havoc.** Arch. to give the signal for pillage and destruction. **4. play havoc.** (often foll. by with) to cause a great deal of damage, distress, or confusion (to).

haw[1] (hɔː) n. **1.** the fruit of the hawthorn. **2.** another name for **hawthorn**.

haw[2] (hɔː) n., interj. **1.** an inarticulate utterance, as of hesitation, embarrassment, etc.; hem. ~vb. **2.** (intr.) to make this sound. **3. hem (or hum) and haw.** See **hem**[2] (sense 3).

hawfinch ('hɔː,fɪntʃ) n. an uncommon European finch having a very stout bill.

hawk[1] (hɔːk) n. **1.** any of various diurnal birds of prey of the family Accipitridae, typically having short rounded wings and a long tail. **2.** a person who advocates or supports war or warlike policies. **3.** a ruthless or rapacious person. ~vb. **4.** (intr.) to hunt with falcons, hawks, etc. **5.** (intr.) (of falcons or hawks) to fly in quest of prey. **6.** to pursue or attack on the wing, as a hawk. —'**hawking** n. —'**hawkish** adj. —'**hawk,like** adj.

hawk[2] (hɔːk) vb. **1.** to offer (goods) for sale, as in the street. **2.** (tr.; often foll. by about) to spread (news, gossip, etc.).

hawk[3] (hɔːk) vb. **1.** (intr.) to clear (the throat) noisily. **2.** (tr.) to force (phlegm, etc.) up from the throat.

hawker[1] ('hɔːkə) n. a person who travels from place to place selling goods.

hawker[2] ('hɔːkə) n. a person who hunts with hawks, falcons, etc.

hawk-eyed adj. **1.** having extremely keen sight. **2.** vigilant, watchful, or observant.

THESAURUS

haul v. **1.** drag, draw, hale, heave, lug, pull, tow, trail, tug **2.** carry, cart, convey, hump (Brit. sl.), move, transport ~n. **3.** drag, heave, pull, tug **4.** booty, catch, find, gain, harvest, loot, spoils, takings, yield

haunt v. **1.** visit, walk **2.** beset, come back, obsess, plague, possess, prey on, recur, stay with, torment, trouble, weigh on **3.** frequent, hang around or about, repair, resort, visit ~n. **4.** den, gathering place, hangout (Inf.), meeting place, rendezvous, resort, stamping ground

haunted **1.** cursed, eerie, ghostly, jinxed, possessed, spooky (Inf.) **2.** obsessed, plagued, preoccupied, tormented, troubled, worried

haunting disturbing, eerie, evocative, indelible, nostalgic, persistent, poignant, recurrent, recurring, unforgettable

have **1.** hold, keep, obtain, occupy, own,

possess, retain **2.** accept, acquire, gain, get, obtain, procure, receive, secure, take **3.** comprehend, comprise, contain, embody, include, take in **4.** endure, enjoy, experience, feel, meet with, suffer, sustain, undergo **5.** Sl. cheat, deceive, dupe, fool, outwit, swindle, take in (Inf.), trick **6.** Usually **have to** be bound, be compelled, be forced, be obliged, have got to, must, ought, should **7.** allow, consider, entertain, permit, put up with (Inf.), think about, tolerate **8.** bear, beget, bring forth, bring into the world, deliver, give birth to **9. have had it** Inf. be defeated, be exhausted, be finished, be out, be past it (Inf.)

haven **1.** anchorage, harbour, port, roads (Nautical) **2.** Fig. asylum, refuge, retreat, sanctuary, sanctum, shelter

have on **1.** be clothed in, be dressed in, wear **2.** be committed to, be engaged to,

have on the agenda, have planned **3.** Of a person deceive, kid (Inf.), play a joke on, tease, trick

havoc **1.** carnage, damage, desolation, despoliation, destruction, devastation, rack and ruin, ravages, ruin, slaughter, waste, wreck **2.** Inf. chaos, confusion, disorder, disruption, mayhem, shambles **3. play havoc (with)** bring into chaos, confuse, demolish, destroy, devastate, disorganize, disrupt, wreck

hawk v. **1.** bark (Inf.), cry, market, peddle, sell, tout (Inf.), vend **2.** Often **with about** bandy about (Inf.), bruit about (Archaic), buzz, noise abroad, put about, retail, rumour

hawker barrow boy (Brit.), cheap-jack (Inf.), colporteur, crier, huckster, pedlar, vendor

hawk moth *n.* any of various moths having long narrow wings and powerful flight, with the ability to hover over flowers when feeding from the nectar.

hawse (hɔːz) *Naut. n.* **1.** the part of the bows of a vessel where the hawseholes are. **2.** in full: **hawsehole.** one of the holes in the upper part of the bows of a vessel through which the anchor rope passes. **3.** the distance from the bow of an anchored vessel to the anchor. **4.** the arrangement of port and starboard anchor ropes when a vessel is riding on both anchors.

hawser ('hɔːzə) *n. Naut.* a large heavy rope.

hawthorn ('hɔː,θɔːn) *n.* any of various thorny trees or shrubs of a N temperate genus, having white or pink flowers and reddish fruits (haws). Also called (in Britain): **may, may tree, mayflower.**

hay (heɪ) *n.* **1. a.** grass, clover, etc., cut and dried as fodder. **b.** (*in combination*): *a hayfield.* **2. hit the hay.** *Sl.* to go to bed. **3. make hay of.** to throw into confusion. **4. make hay while the sun shines.** *Inf.* to take full advantage of an opportunity. **5. roll in the hay.** *Inf.* sexual intercourse or heavy petting. ~*vb.* **6.** to cut, dry, and store (grass, etc.) as fodder.

haybox ('heɪ,bɒks) *n.* an airtight box full of hay used for cooking by retained heat.

hay fever *n.* an allergic reaction to pollen, dust, etc., characterized by sneezing, runny nose, and watery eyes due to inflammation of the mucous membranes of the eyes and nose.

haymaker ('heɪ,meɪkə) *n.* **1.** a person who helps to cut, turn, or carry hay. **2.** either of two machines, one designed to crush stems of hay, the other to break and bend them, in order to cause more rapid and even drying. **3.** *Boxing sl.* a wild swinging punch. —'hay-,making *adj., n.*

haystack ('heɪ,stæk) *or* **hayrick** *n.* a large pile of hay, esp. one built in the open air and covered with thatch.

haywire ('heɪ,waɪə) *adj.* (*postpositive*) *Inf.* **1.** (of things) not functioning properly. **2.** (of people) erratic or crazy.

hazard ('hæzəd) *n.* **1.** exposure or vulnerability to injury, loss, etc. **2. at hazard.** at risk; in danger. **3.** a thing likely to cause injury, etc. **4.** *Golf.* an obstacle such as a bunker, a sand pit, etc. **5.** chance; accident. **6.** a gambling game played with two dice. **7.** *Real tennis.* **a.** the receiver's side of the court. **b.** one of the winning openings. **8.** *Billiards.* a scoring stroke made either when a ball other than the striker's is pocketed (**winning hazard**) or the striker's cue ball itself (**losing hazard**). ~*vb.* (*tr.*) **9.** to risk. **10.** to venture (an opinion, guess, etc.). **11.** to expose to danger.

hazardous ('hæzədəs) *adj.* **1.** involving great risk. **2.** depending on chance. —'**hazardously** *adv.* —'**hazardousness** *n.*

haze (heɪz) *n.* **1.** *Meteorol.* reduced visibility in the air as a result of condensed water vapour, dust, etc., in the atmosphere. **2.** obscurity of perception, feeling, etc. ~*vb.* **3.** (when *intr.*, often foll. by *over*) to make or become hazy.

hazel ('heɪzəl) *n.* **1.** Also called: **cob.** any of several shrubs of a N temperate genus, having edible rounded nuts. **2.** the wood of any of these trees. **3.** short for **hazelnut.** **4. a.** a light yellowish-brown colour. **b.** (*as adj.*): *hazel eyes.*

hazelnut ('heɪzəl,nʌt) *n.* the nut of a hazel shrub, having a smooth shiny hard shell. Also called: **filbert** or (in Britain) **cobnut, cob.**

hazy ('heɪzɪ) *adj.* **-zier, -ziest.** misty; indistinct; vague. —'**hazily** *adv.* —'**haziness** *n.*

Hb *symbol for* haemoglobin.

HB (on Brit. pencils) *symbol for* hard-black: denoting a medium-hard lead.

H.B.C. *abbrev. for* Hudson's Bay Company.

H-bomb *n.* short for **hydrogen bomb.**

H.C. *abbrev. for:* **1.** Holy Communion. **2.** (in Britain) House of Commons.

H.C.F. *or* **h.c.f.** *abbrev. for* highest common factor.

he (hiː; *unstressed* iː) *pron.* (*subjective*) **1.** refers to a male person or animal. **2.** refers to an indefinite antecedent such as *whoever* or *anybody*: *everybody can do as he likes.* **3.** refers to a person or animal of unknown or unspecified sex: *a member may vote as he sees fit.* ~*n.* **4. a.** a male person or animal. **b.** (*in combination*): *he-goat.*

He *the chemical symbol for* helium.

HE *or* **H.E.** *abbrev. for:* **1.** high explosive. **2.** His Eminence. **3.** His (*or* Her) Excellency.

head (hɛd) *n.* **1.** the upper or front part of the body in vertebrates, including man, that contains and protects the brain, eyes, mouth, and nose and ears. Related adj.: **cephalic. 2.** the corresponding part of an invertebrate animal. **3.** something resembling a head in form or function, such as the top of a tool. **4. a.** the person commanding most authority within a group, organization, etc. **b.** (*as modifier*): *head buyer.* **c.** (*in combination*): *headwaiter.* **5.** the position of leadership or command. **6.** the most forward part of a thing; front: *the head of a queue.* **7.** the highest part of a thing; upper end: *the head of the pass.* **8.** the froth on the top of a glass of beer. **9.** aptitude, intelligence, and emotions (esp. in **over one's head, lose one's head,** etc.): *she has a good head for figures.* **10.** (*pl.* **head**) a person or animal considered as a unit: *the show was two pounds per head; six hundred head of cattle.* **11.** the head considered as a measure: *he's a head taller than his mother.* **12.** *Bot.* **a.** a dense inflorescence such as that of the daisy. **b.** any other compact terminal part of a plant, such as the leaves of a cabbage. **13.** a culmination or crisis (esp. in **bring** *or* **come to a head**). **14.** the pus-filled tip or central part of a pimple, boil, etc. **15.** the source of a river or stream. **16.** (*cap. when part of name*) a headland or promontory. **17.** the obverse of a coin, usually bearing a portrait of the head of a monarch, etc. **18.** a main point of an argument, discourse, etc. **19.** (*often pl.*) a headline or heading. **20.** *Naut.* (*often pl.*) a lavatory. **21.** the taut membrane of a drum, tambourine, etc. **22. a.** the height of the surface of liquid above a specific point, esp. as a measure of the pressure at that point: *a head of four feet.* **b.** any pressure: *a head of steam in the boiler.* **23.** *Sl.* **a.** a person who regularly takes drugs, esp. LSD or cannabis. **b.** (*in combination*): *an acid-head.* **24.** *Mining.* a road driven into the coal face. **25. a.** the terminal point of a route. **b.** (*in combination*): *railhead.* **26.** a device on a turning or boring machine equipped with one or more cutting tools held to the work by this device. **27.** **cylinder head.** See **cylinder** (sense 4). **28.** an electromagnet that can read, write, or erase information on a magnetic medium, used in computers, tape recorders, etc. **29.** *Inf.* short for **headmaster. 30.** a narrow margin of victory (esp. in (**win**) **by a head**). **31.** *Inf.* short for **headache. 32. bite** *or* **snap someone's head off.** *Inf.* to speak sharply to someone. **33. give someone** (*or* **something**) **his head. a.** to allow a person greater freedom or responsibility. **b.** to allow a horse to gallop by lengthening the reins. **34. go to one's head. a.** to make one dizzy or confused, as might an alcoholic drink. **b.** to make one conceited: *his success has gone to his head.* **35. head and shoulders above.** greatly superior to. **36. head over heels. a.** turning a complete somersault. **b.** completely; utterly (esp. in **head over heels in love**). **37. hold up one's head.** to be unashamed. **38. keep one's head.** to remain calm. **39. keep one's head above water.** to manage to survive a difficult experience. **40. not make head nor tail of.** *Inf.* to fail to understand (a problem, etc.). **41. off** (*or* **out of**) **one's head.** *Sl.* insane or delirious. **42. off the top of one's head.** without previous thought; impromptu. **43. on one's** (*own*) **head.** at a person's (own) risk or responsibility. **44. over someone's head. a.** without a person in the obvious position being considered: *the graduate was promoted over the heads of several of his seniors.* **b.** without consulting a person in the obvious position but referring to a higher authority: *he went straight to the director, over the head of his immediate boss.* **c.** beyond a person's comprehension. **45. put** (**our, their,** *etc.*) **heads together.** *Inf.* to consult together. **46. take it into one's head.** to conceive a notion (to do something). **47.**

THESAURUS

hazardous 1. dangerous, dicey (*Sl., chiefly Brit.*), difficult, fraught with danger, hairy (*Sl.*), insecure, perilous, precarious, risky, unsafe **2.** chancy (*Inf.*), haphazard, precarious, uncertain, unpredictable

haze cloud, dimness, film, fog, mist, obscurity, smog, smokiness, steam, vapour

hazy 1. blurry, cloudy, dim, dull, faint, foggy, misty, nebulous, obscure, overcast, smoky, veiled **2.** *Fig.* fuzzy, ill-defined, indefinite, indistinct, loose, muddled, muzzy, nebulous, uncertain, unclear, vague

turn someone's head. to make someone vain, conceited, etc. ~vb. **48.** (tr.) to be at the front or top of: *to head the field.* **49.** (tr.; often foll. by *up*) to be in the commanding or most important position. **50.** (often foll. by *for*) to go or cause to go (towards): *where are you heading?* **51.** to turn or steer (a vessel) as specified: *to head into the wind.* **52.** *Soccer.* to propel (the ball) by striking it with the head. **53.** (tr.) to provide with a head or heading. **54.** (tr.) to cut the head off (something): *to head celery.* **55.** (intr.) to form a head, as a plant. **56.** (intr.; often foll. by *in*) (of streams, rivers, etc.) to originate or rise in. ~See also **head off, heads.** —'**headless** *adj.* —'**head,like** *adj.*

headache ('hɛd,eɪk) *n.* **1.** a continuous pain in the head. **2.** *Inf.* any cause of worry, difficulty, or annoyance. —'**head,achy** *adj.*

headboard ('hɛd,bɔːd) *n.* a vertical board or terminal at the head of a bed.

headdress ('hɛd,drɛs) *n.* any head covering, esp. an ornate one or one denoting a rank.

headed ('hɛdɪd) *adj.* **1. a.** having a head or heads. **b.** (in combination): *two-headed; bullet-headed.* **2.** having a heading: *headed notepaper.*

header ('hɛdə) *n.* **1.** a machine that trims the heads from castings, forgings, etc., or one that forms heads, as in wire, to make nails. **2.** a person who operates such a machine. **3.** Also called: **header tank.** a reservoir that maintains a gravity feed or a static fluid pressure in an apparatus. **4.** a brick or stone laid across a wall so that its end is flush with the outer surface. **5.** the action of striking a ball with the head. **6.** *Inf.* a headlong fall or dive.

headfirst ('hɛd'fɜːst) *adj., adv.* **1.** with the head foremost; headlong. ~*adv.* **2.** rashly.

headgear ('hɛd,gɪə) *n.* **1.** a hat. **2.** any part of a horse's harness that is worn on the head. **3.** the hoisting mechanism at the pithead of a mine.

head-hunting *n.* **1.** the practice among certain peoples of removing the heads of slain enemies and preserving them as trophies. **2.** *U.S. sl.* the destruction or neutralization of political opponents. **3.** (of a company or corporation) the recruitment of, or a drive to recruit, new high-level personnel, esp. in management or in specialist fields. —'**head-,hunter** *n.*

heading ('hɛdɪŋ) *n.* **1.** a title for a page, chapter, etc. **2.** a main division, as of a speech. **3.** *Mining.* **a.** a horizontal tunnel. **b.** the end of such a tunnel. **4.** the angle between the direction of an aircraft and a specified meridian, often due north. **5.** the compass direction parallel to the keel of a vessel. **6.** the act of heading.

headland *n.* **1.** ('hɛdlənd). a narrow area of land jutting out into a sea, lake, etc. **2.** ('hɛd,lænd). a strip of land along the edge of an arable field left unploughed to allow space for machines.

headlight ('hɛd,laɪt) or **headlamp** *n.* a powerful light, equipped with a reflector and attached to the front of a motor vehicle, etc.

headline ('hɛd,laɪn) *n.* **1. a.** a phrase at the top of a newspaper or magazine article indicating the subject of the article, usually in larger and heavier type. **b.** a line

at the top of a page indicating the title, page number, etc. **2. hit the headlines.** to become prominent in the news. **3.** (usually pl.) the main points of a television or radio news broadcast, read out before the full broadcast.

headlong ('hɛd,lɒŋ) *adv., adj.* **1.** with the head foremost; headfirst. **2.** with great haste. ~*adj.* **3.** *Arch.* (of slopes, etc.) very steep; precipitous.

headmaster (,hɛd'mɑːstə) or (fem.) **headmistress** *n.* the principal of a school.

headmost ('hɛd,məʊst) *adj.* foremost.

head off *vb.* (tr., adv.) **1.** to intercept and force to change direction: *to head off the stampede.* **2.** to prevent or forestall.

head-on *adv., adj.* **1.** front foremost: *a head-on collision.* **2.** with directness or without compromise: *in his usual head-on fashion.*

headphones ('hɛd,fəʊnz) *pl. n.* an electrical device consisting of two earphones held in position by a flexible metallic strap passing over the head. Informal name: **cans.**

headquarters (,hɛd'kwɔːtəz) *pl. n.* (sometimes functioning as sing.) **1.** any centre from which operations are directed, as in the police. **2.** a military formation comprising the commander and his staff. ~Abbrev.: **HQ, H.Q., h.q.**

headroom ('hɛd,rʊm, -,ruːm) or **headway** *n.* the height of a bridge, room, etc.; clearance.

heads (hɛdz) *interj., adv.* *Inf.* with the obverse side of a coin uppermost, esp. if it has a head on it: used as a call before tossing a coin.

headship ('hɛd,ʃɪp) *n.* **1.** the position or state of being a leader; command. **2.** *Brit.* the position of headmaster or headmistress of a school.

headshrinker ('hɛd,ʃrɪŋkə) *n.* **1.** *Sl.* a psychiatrist. Often shortened to **shrink.** **2.** a headhunter who shrinks the heads of his victims.

headstall ('hɛd,stɔːl) *n.* the part of a bridle that fits round a horse's head.

head start *n.* an initial advantage in a competitive situation.

headstone ('hɛd,stəʊn) *n.* **1.** a memorial stone at the head of a grave. **2.** *Archit.* another name for **keystone.**

headstrong ('hɛd,strɒŋ) *adj.* **1.** self-willed; obstinate. **2.** (of an action) heedless; rash.

headwaters ('hɛd,wɔːtəz) *pl. n.* the tributary streams of a river in the area in which it rises.

headway ('hɛd,weɪ) *n.* **1.** motion forward: *the vessel made no headway.* **2.** progress: *he made no headway with the problem.* **3.** another name for **headroom.** **4.** the interval between consecutive trains, buses, etc., on the same route.

headwind ('hɛd,wɪnd) *n.* a wind blowing directly against the course of an aircraft or ship.

headword ('hɛd,wɜːd) *n.* a key word placed at the beginning of a line, paragraph, etc., as in a dictionary entry.

heady ('hɛdɪ) *adj.* **headier, headiest.** **1.** (of alcoholic drink) intoxicating. **2.** strongly affecting the senses; extremely exciting. **3.** rash; impetuous. —'**headily** *adv.*

THESAURUS

head *n.* **1.** conk (*Sl.*), cranium, crown, loaf (*Sl.*), noddle (*Inf.*, chiefly *Brit.*), nut (*Sl.*), pate, skull **2.** boss (*Inf.*), captain, chief, chieftain, commander, director, headmaster, headmistress, head teacher, leader, manager, master, principal, superintendent, supervisor **3.** apex, crest, crown, height, peak, pitch, summit, tip, top, vertex **4.** first place, fore, forefront, front, van, vanguard **5.** beginning, commencement, origin, rise, source, start **6.** ability, aptitude, brain, brains (*Inf.*), capacity, faculty, flair, intellect, intelligence, mentality, mind, talent, thought, understanding **7.** branch, category, class, department, division, heading, section, subject, topic **8.** climax, conclusion, crisis, culmination, end, turning point **9.** *Geog.* cape, foreland, headland, point, promontory **10. go to one's head** dizzy, excite, intoxicate, make conceited, puff up **11. head over heels** completely, intensely, thoroughly, uncontrollably, utterly, wholeheartedly **12. put (our, their, etc.) heads together** *Inf.* confab (*Inf.*), confabulate, confer, consult, deliberate, discuss, palaver, powwow, talk over ~*adj.* **13.** arch, chief, first, foremost, front, highest, leading, main, pre-eminent, premier, prime, principal, supreme, topmost ~*v.* **14.** be *or* go first, cap, crown, lead, lead the way, precede, top **15.** be in charge of, command, control, direct, govern, guide, lead, manage, rule, run, supervise **16.** *Often with* for aim, go to, make a beeline for, make for, point, set off for, set out, start towards, steer, turn

headache 1. cephalalgia (*Medical*), migraine, neuralgia **2.** *Inf.* bane, bother, inconvenience, nuisance, problem, trouble, vexation, worry

headfirst 1. *adj./adv.* diving, headlong, head-on **2.** *adv.* carelessly, hastily, head over heels, precipitately, rashly, recklessly

heading 1. caption, headline, name, rubric, title **2.** category, class, division, section

headlong 1. *adj./adv.* headfirst, headforemost, head-on **2.** *adj.* breakneck, dangerous, hasty, impetuous, impulsive, inconsiderate,

precipitate, reckless, thoughtless **3.** *adv.* hastily, heedlessly, helter-skelter, hurriedly, pell-mell, precipitately, rashly, thoughtlessly, wildly

head off 1. block off, cut off, deflect, divert, intercept, interpose, intervene **2.** avert, fend off, forestall, parry, prevent, stop, ward off

headstrong contrary, foolhardy, froward, heedless, imprudent, impulsive, intractable, mulish, obstinate, perverse, pigheaded, rash, reckless, self-willed, stubborn, ungovernable, unruly, wilful

headway 1. advance, improvement, progress, progression, way **2. make headway** advance, come *or* get on, cover ground, develop, gain, gain ground, make strides, progress

heady 1. inebriating, intoxicating, potent, spirituous, strong **2.** exciting, exhilarating, intoxicating, overwhelming, stimulating, thrilling **3.** hasty, impetuous, impulsive, inconsiderate, precipitate, rash, reckless, thoughtless

—'**headiness** n.

heal (hi:l) vb. **1.** to restore or be restored to health. **2.** (intr.; often foll. by over or up) (of a wound) to repair by natural processes, as by scar formation. **3.** (tr.) to cure (a disease or disorder). **4.** to restore or be restored to friendly relations, harmony, etc. —'**healer** n.

health (hɛlθ) n. **1.** the state of being bodily and mentally vigorous and free from disease. **2.** the general condition of body and mind: in poor health. **3.** the condition of any unit, society, etc.: the economic health of a nation. **4.** a toast to a person. **5.** (modifier) of or relating to food or other goods reputed to be beneficial to the health: health food. **6.** (modifier) of or relating to health: health resort; health service.

health centre n. the surgery and offices of a group medical practice.

healthful ('hɛlθful) adj. a less common word for **healthy** (senses 1–3).

health visitor n. Brit. a nurse who visits and helps the old and the sick in their homes.

healthy ('hɛlθɪ) adj. **healthier, healthiest. 1.** enjoying good health. **2.** sound: the company's finances are not very healthy. **3.** conducive to health. **4.** indicating soundness of body or mind: a healthy appetite. **5.** Inf. considerable: a healthy sum. —'**healthily** adv. —'**healthiness** n.

heap (hi:p) n. **1.** a collection of articles or mass of material gathered in a pile. **2.** (often pl.; usually foll. by of) Inf. a large number or quantity. **3.** Inf. a thing that is very old, unreliable, etc.: the car was a heap. ~adv. **4. heaps.** (intensifier): he was heaps better. ~vb. **5.** (often foll. by up or together) to collect or be collected into or as if into a pile. **6.** (tr.; often foll. by with, on, or upon) to load (with) abundantly: to heap with riches.

hear (hɪə) vb. **hearing, heard. 1.** (tr.) to perceive (a sound) with the sense of hearing. **2.** (tr.; may take a clause as object) to listen to: did you hear what I said? **3.** (when intr., sometimes foll. by of or about; when tr., may take a clause as object) to be informed (of); receive information (about). **4.** Law. to give a hearing to (a case). **5.** (when intr., usually foll. by of and used with a negative) to listen (to) with favour, assent, etc.: she wouldn't hear of it. **6.** (intr.; foll. by from) to receive a letter (from). **7. hear! hear!** (interj.) an exclamation of approval. **8. hear tell (of).** Dialect. to be told (about). —'**hearer** n.

hearing ('hɪərɪŋ) n. **1.** the sense by which sound is perceived. **2.** an opportunity to be listened to. **3.** the range within which sound can be heard; earshot. **4.** the investigation of a matter by a court of law, esp. the preliminary inquiry into an indictable crime by magistrates.

hearing aid n. a device for assisting the hearing of partially deaf persons, typically a small battery-powered amplifier worn in or behind the ear.

hearken or U.S. (sometimes) **harken** ('hɑ:kən) vb.

Arch. to listen to (something).

hear out vb. (tr., adv.) to listen in regard to every detail and give a proper or full hearing to.

hearsay ('hɪə,seɪ) n. gossip; rumour.

hearsay evidence n. Law. evidence based on what has been reported to a witness by others rather than what he has himself observed.

hearse (hɜːs) n. a vehicle, such as a car or carriage, used to carry a coffin to the grave.

heart (hɑːt) n. **1.** the hollow muscular organ in vertebrates whose contractions propel the blood through the circulatory system. Related adj.: **cardiac. 2.** the corresponding organ in invertebrates. **3.** this organ considered as the seat of emotions, esp. love. **4.** emotional mood: a change of heart. **5.** tenderness or pity: you have no heart. **6.** courage or spirit. **7.** the most central part: the heart of the city. **8.** the most important part: the heart of the matter. **9.** (of vegetables, such as cabbage) the inner compact part. **10.** the breast: she held him to her heart. **11.** a dearly loved person: dearest heart. **12.** a conventionalized representation of the heart, having two rounded lobes at the top meeting in a point at the bottom. **13. a.** a red heart-shaped symbol on a playing card. **b.** a card with one or more of these symbols or (when pl.) the suit of cards so marked. **14.** a fertile condition in land (esp. in **in good heart**). **15. after one's own heart.** appealing to one's own disposition or taste. **16. break one's (or someone's) heart.** to grieve (or cause to grieve) very deeply, esp. through love. **17. by heart.** by committing to memory. **18. eat one's heart out.** to grieve inconsolably. **19. from (the bottom of) one's heart.** very sincerely or deeply. **20. have one's heart in one's mouth (or throat).** to be full of apprehension, excitement, or fear. **21. have one's heart in the right place.** to be kind, thoughtful, or generous. **22. have the heart.** (usually used with a negative) to have the necessary will, callousness, etc., (to do something): I didn't have the heart to tell him. **23. heart of hearts.** the depths of one's conscience or emotions. **24. heart of oak.** a brave person. **25. lose heart.** to become despondent or disillusioned (over something). **26. lose one's heart to.** to fall in love with. **27. set one's heart on.** to have as one's ambition to obtain; covet. **28. take heart.** to become encouraged. **29. take to heart.** to take seriously or be upset about. **30. wear one's heart on one's sleeve.** to show one's feelings openly. **31. with all one's heart.** very willingly. ~vb. (intr.) **32.** (of vegetables) to form a heart.

heartache ('hɑːt,eɪk) n. intense anguish or mental suffering.

heart attack n. any sudden severe instance of abnormal heart functioning, esp. coronary thrombosis.

heartbeat ('hɑːt,biːt) n. one complete pulsation of the heart.

heartbreak ('hɑːt,breɪk) n. intense and overwhelming

THESAURUS

heal 1. cure, make well, mend, regenerate, remedy, restore, treat **2.** alleviate, ameliorate, compose, conciliate, harmonize, patch up, reconcile, settle, soothe

healing 1. analeptic, curative, medicinal, remedial, restorative, restoring, sanative, therapeutic **2.** assuaging, comforting, emollient, gentle, lenitive, mild, mitigative, palliative, soothing

health 1. fitness, good condition, haleness, healthiness, robustness, salubrity, soundness, strength, vigour, wellbeing **2.** condition, constitution, fettle, form, shape, state, tone

healthy 1. active, blooming, fit, flourishing, hale, hale and hearty, hardy, hearty, in fine fettle, in fine fettle, in fine form, in good condition, in good shape (Inf.), in the pink, physically fit, robust, sound, strong, sturdy, vigorous, well **2.** beneficial, bracing, good for one, healthful, health-giving, hygienic, invigorating, nourishing, nutritious, salubrious, salutary, wholesome

heap n. **1.** accumulation, aggregation, collection, hoard, lot, mass, mound, mountain, pile, stack, stockpile, store **2.** Often plural Inf. abundance, a lot, great deal, lashings (Brit. inf.), load(s) (Inf.), lots (Inf.), mass, mint, ocean(s), oodles (Inf.), plenty, pot(s) (Inf.),

quantities, stack(s), tons ~v. **3.** accumulate, amass, augment, bank, collect, gather, hoard, increase, mound, pile, stack, stockpile, store **4.** assign, bestow, burden, confer, load, shower upon

hear 1. attend, be all ears (Inf.), catch, eavesdrop, give attention, hark, hearken (Archaic), heed, listen in, listen to, overhear **2.** ascertain, be informed, be told of, discover, find out, gather, get wind of (Inf.), hear tell (Dialect), learn, pick up, understand **3.** Law examine, investigate, judge, try

hearing 1. audition, auditory, ear, perception **2.** audience, audition, chance to speak, interview **3.** auditory range, earshot, hearing distance, range, reach, sound **4.** inquiry, investigation, review, trial

hearsay buzz, gossip, grapevine (Inf.), idle talk, mere talk, on dit, report, rumour, talk, talk of the town, tittle-tattle, word of mouth

heart 1. character, disposition, emotion, feeling, inclination, nature, sentiment, soul, sympathy, temperament **2.** affection, benevolence, compassion, concern, humanity, love, pity, tenderness, understanding **3.** boldness, bravery, courage, fortitude, guts (Inf.), mettle, mind, nerve, pluck, purpose, resolu-

tion, spirit, spunk (Inf.), will **4.** central part, centre, core, crux, essence, hub, kernel, marrow, middle, nucleus, pith, quintessence, root **5. at heart** au fond, basically, essentially, fundamentally, in essence, in reality, really, truly **6. by heart** by memory, by rote, off pat, parrot-fashion (Inf.), pat, word for word **7. eat one's heart out** agonize, brood, grieve, mope, mourn, pine, regret, repine, sorrow **8. from (the bottom of) one's heart** deeply, devoutly, fervently, heart and soul, heartily, sincerely, with all one's heart **9. heart and soul** absolutely, completely, devotedly, entirely, gladly, wholeheartedly **10. take heart** be comforted, be encouraged, be heartened, brighten up, buck up (Inf.), cheer up, perk up, revive

heartbreaking agonizing, bitter, desolating, disappointing, distressing, grievous, heart-rending, pitiful, poignant, sad, tragic

heartbroken brokenhearted, crestfallen, crushed, dejected, desolate, despondent, disappointed, disconsolate, disheartened, dispirited, downcast, grieved, heartsick, miserable

grief, esp. through disappointment in love. —'heart-,breaker n. —'heart,breaking adj.

heartburn ('hɑːt,bɜːn) n. a burning sensation beneath the breastbone caused by irritation of the oesophagus. Technical names: **cardialgia, pyrosis.**

-hearted adj. having a heart or disposition as specified: cold-hearted; heavy-hearted.

hearten ('hɑːtən) vb. to make or become cheerful. —'hearteningly adv.

heart failure n. 1. a condition in which the heart is unable to pump an adequate amount of blood to the tissues. 2. sudden cessation of the heartbeat, resulting in death.

heartfelt ('hɑːt,fɛlt) adj. sincerely and strongly felt.

hearth (hɑːθ) n. 1. **a.** the floor of a fireplace, esp. one that extends outwards into the room. **b.** (as modifier): hearth rug. 2. this as a symbol of the home, etc. 3. the bottom part of a metallurgical furnace in which the molten metal is produced or contained.

heartless ('hɑːtlɪs) adj. unkind or cruel. —'heartlessly adv. —'heartlessness n.

heart-rending adj. causing great mental pain and sorrow. —'heart-,rendingly adv.

hearts (hɑːts) n. (functioning as sing.) a card game in which players must avoid winning tricks containing hearts or the queen of spades. Also called: **Black Maria.**

heart-searching n. examination of one's feelings or conscience.

heartstrings ('hɑːt,strɪŋz) pl. n. Often facetious. deep emotions.

heart-throb n. 1. Brit. an object of infatuation. 2. a heart beat.

heart-to-heart adj. 1. (esp. of a conversation) concerned with personal problems or intimate feelings. ~n. 2. an intimate conversation.

heart-warming adj. 1. pleasing; gratifying. 2. emotionally moving.

heartwood ('hɑːt,wʊd) n. the central core of dark hard wood in tree trunks, consisting of nonfunctioning xylem tissue that has become blocked with resins, tannins, and oils.

hearty ('hɑːtɪ) adj. **heartier, heartiest.** 1. warm and unreserved in manner. 2. vigorous and heartfelt: hearty dislike. 3. healthy and strong (esp. in **hale and hearty**). 4. substantial and nourishing. ~n. Inf. 5. a comrade, esp. a sailor. 6. a vigorous sporting man: a rugby hearty. —'heartily adv. —'heartiness n.

heat (hiːt) n. 1. a form of energy that is transferred by a difference in temperature: it is equal to the total kinetic energy of the atoms or molecules of a system. Related adjs.: **thermal, calorific.** 2. the sensation caused by heat energy; warmth. 3. the state of being hot. 4. hot weather: the heat of summer. 5. intensity of feeling: the heat of rage. 6. the most intense part: the heat of the battle. 7. a period of sexual excitement in female mammals that occurs at oestrus. 8. Sport. **a.** a preliminary eliminating contest in a competition. **b.** a single section of a contest. 9. Sl. police activity after a crime: the heat is off. 10. in

the heat of the moment. without pausing to think. ~vb. 11. to make or become hot or warm. 12. to make or become excited or intense.

heated ('hiːtɪd) adj. 1. made hot. 2. impassioned or highly emotional. —'heatedly adv.

heater ('hiːtə) n. 1. any device for supplying heat, such as a convector. 2. U.S. sl. a pistol. 3. Electronics. a conductor carrying a current that indirectly heats the cathode in some types of valve.

heath (hiːθ) n. 1. Brit. a large open area, usually with sandy soil and scrubby vegetation, esp. heather. 2. Also called: **heather.** a low-growing evergreen shrub having small bell-shaped typically pink or purple flowers. 3. any of several heathlike plants, such as sea heath. —'heath,like adj. —'heathy adj.

heathen ('hiːðən) n., pl.-thens or -then. 1. a person who does not acknowledge the God of Christianity, Judaism, or Islam; pagan. 2. an uncivilized or barbaric person. ~adj. 3. irreligious; pagan. 4. uncivilized; barbaric. 5. of or relating to heathen peoples or their customs and beliefs. —'heathendom n. —'heathenism or 'heathenry n.

heather ('hɛðə) n. 1. Also called: **ling, heath.** a low-growing evergreen Eurasian shrub that grows in dense masses on open ground and has clusters of small bell-shaped typically pinkish-purple flowers. 2. a purplish-red to pinkish-purple colour. ~adj. 3. of a heather colour. 4. of or relating to interwoven yarns of mixed colours: heather mixture. —'heathery adj.

Heath Robinson (hiːθ 'rɒbɪnsən) adj. (of a mechanical device) absurdly complicated in design and having a simple function.

heatstroke ('hiːt,strəʊk) n. a condition resulting from prolonged exposure to intense heat, characterized by high fever.

heat wave n. 1. a continuous spell of abnormally hot weather. 2. an extensive slow-moving air mass at a relatively high temperature.

heave (hiːv) vb. **heaving, heaved** or **hove.** 1. (tr.) to lift or move with a great effort. 2. (tr.) to throw (something heavy) with effort. 3. to utter (sounds) noisily or unhappily: to heave a sigh. 4. to rise and fall or cause to rise and fall heavily. 5. (p.t. & p.p. **hove**) Naut. **a.** to move or cause to move in a specified direction: to heave in sight. **b.** (intr.) (of a vessel) to pitch or roll. 6. (tr.) to displace (rock strata, etc.) in a horizontal direction. 7. (intr.) to retch. ~n. 8. the act of heaving. 9. a horizontal displacement of rock strata at a fault. —'heaver n.

heaven ('hɛvən) n. 1. (sometimes cap.) Christianity. **a.** the abode of God and the angels. **b.** a state of communion with God after death. 2. (usually pl.) the firmament surrounding the earth. 3. (in various mythologies) a place, such as Elysium or Valhalla, to which those who have died in the gods' favour are brought to dwell in happiness. 4. a place or state of happiness. 5. (sing. or pl.; sometimes cap.) God or the gods, used in exclamatory phrases: for heaven's sake. 6. **in seventh heaven.** ecstatically happy. 7. **move heaven and earth.** to do everything possible (to achieve something).

THESAURUS

heartfelt ardent, cordial, deep, devout, earnest, fervent, genuine, hearty, honest, profound, sincere, unfeigned, warm, wholehearted

heartily 1. cordially, deeply, feelingly, genuinely, profoundly, sincerely, unfeignedly, warmly 2. eagerly, earnestly, enthusiastically, resolutely, vigorously, zealously 3. absolutely, completely, thoroughly, totally, very

heartless brutal, callous, cold, cold-blooded, cold-hearted, cruel, hard, hardhearted, harsh, inhuman, merciless, pitiless, uncaring, unfeeling, unkind

heart-rending affecting, distressing, harrowing, heartbreaking, moving, pathetic, piteous, pitiful, poignant, sad, tragic

heartsick dejected, despondent, dispirited, downcast, heartsore, heavy-hearted, sick at heart

heart-to-heart 1. adj. candid, intimate, open, personal, sincere, unreserved 2. n. cosy chat, tête-à-tête

heart-warming 1. gratifying, pleasing, rewarding, satisfying 2. affecting, cheering, encouraging, heartening, moving, touching, warming

hearty 1. affable, ardent, back-slapping, cordial, eager, ebullient, effusive, enthusiastic, friendly, generous, genial, jovial, unreserved, warm 2. earnest, genuine, heartfelt, honest, real, sincere, true, unfeigned, wholehearted 3. active, energetic, hale, hardy, healthy, robust, sound, strong, vigorous, well 4. ample, filling, nourishing, sizable, solid, square, substantial

heat n. 1. calefaction, fever, fieriness, high temperature, hotness, hot spell, sultriness, swelter, torridity, warmness, warmth 2. Fig. agitation, ardour, earnestness, excitement, fervour, fever, fury, impetuosity, intensity, passion, vehemence, violence, warmth, zeal ~v. 3. become warm, chafe, flush, glow, grow hot, make hot, reheat, warm up 4. animate, excite, impassion, inflame, inspirit, rouse, stimulate, stir, warm

heated angry, bitter, excited, fierce, fiery, frenzied, furious, impassioned, intense, passionate, raging, stormy, tempestuous, vehement, violent

heathen n. 1. idolater, idolatress, infidel, pagan, unbeliever 2. barbarian, philistine, savage ~adj. 3. godless, heathenish, idolatrous, infidel, irreligious, pagan 4. barbaric, philistine, savage, uncivilized, unenlightened

heave 1. drag (up), elevate, haul (up), heft (Inf.), hoist, lever, lift, pull (up), raise, tug 2. cast, fling, hurl, pitch, send, sling, throw, toss 3. breathe heavily, groan, puff, sigh, sob, suspire (Archaic), utter wearily 4. billow, breathe, dilate, exhale, expand, palpitate, pant, rise, surge, swell, throb 5. gag (Sl.), retch, spew, throw up (Inf.), vomit

heaven 1. abode of God, bliss, Elysium or Elysian fields (Greek myth), happy hunting ground (Amerind legend), hereafter, life everlasting, life to come, next world, nirvana (Buddhism, Hinduism), paradise, Valhalla (Norse myth), Zion (Christianity) 2. Usually

heavenly ('hɛvənlɪ) *adj.* **1.** *Inf.* wonderful. **2.** of or occurring in space: *a heavenly body.* **3.** holy. —'**heavenliness** *n.*

heave to *vb.* (*adv.*) to stop (a vessel) or (of a vessel) to stop, as by trimming the sails, etc.

heavy ('hɛvɪ) *adj.* **heavier, heaviest.** **1.** of comparatively great weight. **2.** having a relatively high density: *lead is a heavy metal.* **3.** great in yield, quality, or quantity: *heavy traffic.* **4.** considerable: *heavy emphasis.* **5.** hard to bear or fulfil: *heavy demands.* **6.** sad or dejected: *heavy at heart.* **7.** coarse or broad: *heavy features.* **8.** (of soil) having a high clay content; cloggy. **9.** solid or fat: *heavy legs.* **10.** (of an industry) engaged in the large-scale complex manufacture of capital goods or extraction of raw materials. **11.** serious; grave. **12.** *Mil.* **a.** equipped with large weapons, armour, etc. **b.** (of guns, etc.) of a large and powerful type. **13.** (of a syllable) having stress or accentuation. **14.** dull and uninteresting: *a heavy style.* **15.** prodigious: *a heavy drinker.* **16.** (of cakes, etc.) insufficiently leavened. **17.** deep and loud: *a heavy thud.* **18.** (of music, literature, etc.). **a.** dramatic and powerful. **b.** not immediately comprehensible or appealing. **19.** *Sl.* (of rock music) having a powerful beat; hard. **20.** burdened: *heavy with child.* **21.** **heavy on.** *Inf.* using large quantities of: *this car is very heavy on petrol.* **22.** clumsy and slow: *heavy going.* **23.** cloudy or overcast: *heavy skies.* **24.** not easily digestible: *a heavy meal.* **25.** (of an element or compound) being or containing an isotope with greater atomic weight than that of the naturally occurring element: *heavy water.* **26.** (of the going on a racecourse) soft and muddy. **27.** *Sl.* using, or prepared to use, violence or brutality. ~*n., pl.* **heavies. 28. a.** a villainous role. **b.** an actor who plays such a part. **29.** *Mil.* **a.** a large fleet unit, esp. an aircraft carrier or battleship. **b.** a large piece of artillery. **30.** *Inf.* a heavyweight boxer, wrestler, etc. —'**heavily** *adv.* —'**heaviness** *n.*

heavy-duty *n.* (*modifier*) made to withstand hard wear, bad weather, etc.

heavy-handed *adj.* **1.** clumsy. **2.** harsh and oppressive. —ˌ**heavy-'handedly** *adv.*

heavy-hearted *adj.* sad; melancholy.

heavy hydrogen *n.* another name for **deuterium.**

heavy water *n.* water whose molecules contain deuterium atoms rather than hydrogen atoms. Also called: **deuterium oxide.**

heavyweight ('hɛvɪˌweɪt) *n.* **1.** a person or thing that is heavier than average. **2. a.** a professional boxer weighing more than 175 pounds (79 kg). **b.** an amateur boxer weighing more than 81 kg (179 pounds). **3.** a wrestler weighing usually over 214 pounds (97 kg). **4.** *Inf.* an important or highly influential person.

Heb. *or* **Hebr.** *abbrev. for:* **1.** Hebrew (language). **2.** *Bible.* Hebrews.

hebdomadal (hɛb'dɒmədəl) *adj.* weekly.

Hebraic (hɪ'breɪɪk) *or* **Hebraical** *adj.* of, relating to, or characteristic of the Hebrews or their language or culture. —**He'braically** *adv.*

Hebrew ('hiːbruː) *n.* **1.** a member of an ancient Semitic people claiming descent from Abraham; an Israelite. **2.** the ancient language of the Hebrews, revived as the official language of Israel. ~*adj.* **3.** of or relating to the Hebrews or their language.

heck (hɛk) *interj.* a mild exclamation of surprise, irritation, etc.

heckle ('hɛkəl) *vb.* **1.** to interrupt (a public speaker, etc.) by comments, questions, or taunts. **2.** (*tr.*) Also: **hackle, hatchel.** to comb (hemp or flax). ~*n.* **3.** an instrument for combing flax or hemp. —'**heckler** *n.*

hectare ('hɛktɑː) *n.* one hundred ares (10 000 square metres or 2.471 acres). Symbol: ha

hectic ('hɛktɪk) *adj.* **1.** characterized by extreme activity or excitement. **2.** associated with or symptomatic of tuberculosis (esp. in **hectic fever, hectic flush**). ~*n.* **3.** a hectic fever or flush. **4.** *Rare.* a person who is consumptive. —'**hectically** *adv.*

hecto- *or before a vowel* **hect-** *prefix.* denoting 100: *hectogram.* Symbol: h

hectog *abbrev. for* hectogram.

hector ('hɛktə) *vb.* **1.** to bully or torment by teasing. ~*n.* **2.** a blustering bully.

he'd (hiːd; *unstressed* iːd, hɪd, ɪd) *contraction of* he had *or* he would.

heddle ('hɛdəl) *n.* one of a set of frames of vertical wires on a loom, each wire having an eye through which a warp thread can be passed.

hedge (hɛdʒ) *n.* **1.** a row of shrubs or bushes forming a boundary. **2.** a barrier or protection against something. **3.** the act or a method of reducing the risk of loss on an investment, etc. **4.** a cautious or evasive statement. **5.** (*as modifier*) low, inferior, or illiterate: *hedge priest.* ~*vb.* **6.** (*tr.*) to enclose or separate with or as if with a hedge. **7.** (*intr.*) to trim or prune a hedge. **8.** (*tr.*) to hinder or restrict. **9.** (*intr.*) to evade decision, esp. by making noncommittal statements. **10.** (*tr.*) to guard against the risk of loss in (a bet, etc.), esp. by laying bets with other bookmakers. **11.** (*intr.*) to protect against loss through future price fluctuations, as by investing in futures. —'**hedger** *n.*

hedgehog ('hɛdʒˌhɒg) *n.* **1.** a small nocturnal Old World mammal having a protective covering of spines on the back. **2.** *U.S.* any of various other spiny animals, esp. the porcupine.

hedgehop ('hɛdʒˌhɒp) *vb.* - hopping, - hopped. (*intr.*) (of an aircraft) to fly close to the ground, as in crop spraying. —'**hedgeˌhopping** *n., adj.*

hedgerow ('hɛdʒˌrəʊ) *n.* a hedge of shrubs or low trees, esp. one bordering a field.

hedge sparrow *n.* a small brownish European songbird. Also called: **dunnock.**

hedonism ('hiːdəˌnɪzəm, 'hɛd-) *n.* **1.** *Ethics.* the doctrine that the pursuit of pleasure is the highest good. **2.** indulgence in sensual pleasures. —ˌ**hedon'istic** *adj.* —'**hedonist** *n.*

THESAURUS

plural empyrean (*Poetic*), ether, firmament, sky, welkin (*Archaic*) **3.** *Fig.* bliss, dreamland, ecstasy, enchantment, felicity, happiness, paradise, rapture, seventh heaven, sheer bliss, transport, utopia

heavenly 1. *Inf.* alluring, beautiful, blissful, delightful, divine (*Inf.*), entrancing, exquisite, glorious, lovely, rapturous, ravishing, sublime, wonderful **2.** angelic, beatific, blessed, blest, celestial, cherubic, divine, empyrean, extraterrestrial, godlike, holy, immortal, paradisaical, seraphic, superhuman, supernal (*Literary*), supernatural

heavily 1. awkwardly, clumsily, ponderously, weightily **2.** laboriously, painfully, with difficulty **3.** completely, decisively, roundly, thoroughly, utterly **4.** dejectedly, dully, gloomily, sluggishly, woodenly **5.** closely, compactly, densely, fast, hard, thick, thickly **6.** deep, deeply, profoundly, sound, soundly **7.** a great deal, considerably, copiously, excessively, frequently, to excess, very much

heaviness 1. gravity, heftiness, ponderousness, weight **2.** arduousness, burdensomeness, grievousness, onerousness, oppressiveness, severity, weightiness **3.** deadness, dullness, languor, lassitude, numbness, sluggishness, torpor **4.** dejection, depression, despondency, gloom, gloominess, glumness, melancholy, sadness, seriousness

heavy 1. bulky, hefty, massive, ponderous, portly, weighty **2.** burdensome, difficult, grievous, hard, harsh, intolerable, laborious, onerous, oppressive, severe, tedious, vexatious, wearisome **3.** apathetic, drowsy, dull, inactive, indolent, inert, listless, slow, sluggish, stupid, torpid, wooden **4.** crestfallen, dejected, depressed, despondent, disconsolate, downcast, gloomy, grieving, melancholy, sad, sorrowful **5.** complex, deep, difficult, grave, profound, serious, solemn, weighty **6.** abundant, considerable, copious, excessive, large, profuse **7.** burdened, encumbered, laden, loaded, oppressed, weighted **8.** boisterous, rough, stormy, tempestuous, turbulent, violent, wild **9.** dull, gloomy, leaden, louring, lowering, overcast

heavy-handed 1. awkward, bungling, clumsy, graceless, ham-fisted (*Inf.*), ham-handed (*Inf.*), inept, inexpert, like a bull in a china shop (*Inf.*), maladroit, unhandy **2.** bungling, inconsiderate, insensitive, tactless, thoughtless **3.** autocratic, domineering, harsh, oppressive, overbearing

heckle bait, barrack (*Inf.*), disrupt, interrupt, jeer, pester, shout down, taunt

hectic animated, boisterous, chaotic, excited, fevered, feverish, flurrying, flustering, frantic, frenetic, frenzied, furious, heated, riotous, rumbustious, tumultuous, turbulent, wild

hector bluster, boast, browbeat, bully, bullyrag, harass, huff and puff, intimidate, menace, provoke, ride roughshod over, roister, threaten, worry

hedge *n.* **1.** hedgerow, quickset **2.** barrier, boundary, screen, windbreak **3.** compensation, counterbalance, guard, insurance cover, protection ~*v.* **4.** border, edge, enclose, fence, surround **5.** block, confine, hem in (about, around), hinder, obstruct, restrict **6.** beg the question, be noncommittal, dodge, duck, equivocate, evade, prevaricate, pussyfoot (*Inf.*), quibble, sidestep, temporize, waffle (*Inf.*) **7.** cover, fortify, guard, insure, protect, safeguard, shield

-hedron *n. combining form.* indicating a solid having a specified number of surfaces: *tetrahedron.* —**-hedral** *adj. combining form.*

heebie-jeebies ('hi:bɪ'dʒi:bɪz) *pl. n.* **the.** *Sl.* apprehension and nervousness.

heed (hi:d) *n.* **1.** careful attention; notice: *to take heed.* ~*vb.* **2.** to pay close attention to. —**'heedful** *adj.* —**'heedfully** *adv.* —**'heedfulness** *n.*

heedless ('hi:dlɪs) *adj.* taking no notice; careless or thoughtless. —**'heedlessly** *adv.* —**'heedlessness** *n.*

heehaw ('hi:,hɔ:) *interj.* an imitation or representation of the braying sound of a donkey.

heel[1] (hi:l) *n.* **1.** the back part of the human foot. **2.** the corresponding part in other vertebrates. **3.** the part of a stocking, etc., designed to fit the heel. **4.** the outer part of a shoe underneath the heel. **5.** the end or back section of something: *the heel of a loaf.* **6.** *Horticulture.* the small part of the parent plant that remains attached to a young shoot cut for propagation. **7.** the back part of a golf club head where it bends to join the shaft. **8.** *Sl.* a contemptible person. **9. at** (*or* **on**) **one's heels.** following closely. **10. cool** (*or* **kick**) **one's heels.** to be kept waiting, esp. deliberately. **11. down at heel. a.** shabby or worn. **b.** slovenly. **12. take to one's heels.** to run off. **13. to heel.** under control, as a dog walking by a person's heel. ~*vb.* **14.** (*tr.*) to repair or replace the heel of (shoes, etc.). **15.** (*tr.*) *Golf.* to strike (the ball) with the heel of the club. **16.** to follow at the heels of (a person). —**'heelless** *adj.*

heel[2] (hi:l) *vb.* **1.** (of a vessel) to lean over; list. ~*n.* **2.** inclined position from the vertical.

heelball ('hi:l,bɔ:l) *n.* **a.** a mixture of beeswax and lampblack used by shoemakers to blacken the edges of heels and soles. **b.** a similar substance used to take rubbings, esp. brass rubbings.

heeled (hi:ld) *adj.* **1. a.** having a heel or heels. **b.** (*in combination*): *high-heeled.* **2. well-heeled.** wealthy.

hefty ('hɛftɪ) *adj.* **heftier, heftiest.** *Inf.* **1.** big and strong. **2.** characterized by vigour or force: *a hefty blow.* **3.** bulky or heavy. —**'heftily** *adv.*

hegemony (hɪ'gɛmənɪ) *n., pl.* **-nies.** ascendancy or domination of one power or state within a league, confederation, etc. —**hegemonic** (,hɛgə'mɒnɪk) *adj.*

Hegira *or* **Hejira** ('hɛdʒɪrə) *n.* **1.** the flight of Mohammed from Mecca to Medina in 622 A.D.; the starting point of the Muslim era. **2.** the Muslim era itself. **3.** (*often not cap.*) an escape or flight.

heifer ('hɛfə) *n.* a young cow.

height (haɪt) *n.* **1.** the vertical distance from the bottom of something to the top. **2.** the vertical distance of a place above sea level. **3.** relatively great altitude. **4.** the topmost point; summit. **5.** *Astron.* the angular distance of a celestial body above the horizon. **6.** the period of greatest intensity: *the height of the battle.* **7.** an extreme example: *the height of rudeness.* **8.** (*often pl.*) an area of high ground.

heighten ('haɪtən) *vb.* to make or become higher or more intense.

height of land *n. U.S. & Canad.* a watershed.

heinous ('heɪnəs, 'hi:-) *adj.* evil; atrocious. —**'heinously** *adv.*

heir (ɛə) *n.* **1.** the person legally succeeding to all property of a deceased person. **2.** any person or thing that carries on some tradition, circumstance, etc., from a forerunner. —**'heirdom** *or* **'heirship** *n.* —**'heiress** *fem. n.*

heir apparent *n., pl.* **heirs apparent.** a person whose right to succeed to certain property cannot be defeated, provided such person survives his ancestor.

heirloom ('ɛə,lu:m) *n.* **1.** an object that has been in a family for generations. **2.** an item of personal property inherited in accordance with the terms of a will.

heir presumptive *n. Property law.* a person who expects to succeed to an estate but whose right may be defeated by the birth of one nearer in blood to the ancestor.

Hejira ('hɛdʒɪrə) *n.* a variant spelling of **Hegira.**

held (hɛld) *vb.* the past tense or past participle of **hold**[1].

helical ('hɛlɪkəl) *adj.* of or like a helix; spiral.

helicopter ('hɛlɪ,kɒptə) *n.* an aircraft without wings that is capable of moving vertically and hovering, obtaining its lift from the rotation of overhead blades.

helio- *or before a vowel* **heli-** *combining form.* indicating the sun: *heliocentric.*

heliocentric (,hi:lɪəʊ'sɛntrɪk) *adj.* **1.** having the sun at its centre. **2.** measured from or in relation to the sun. —**,helio'centrically** *adv.*

heliograph ('hi:lɪəʊ,grɑ:f) *n.* **1.** an instrument for sending messages (**heliograms**) by means of flashes of light. **2.** a device used to photograph the sun. —**,heli'ography** *n.*

heliotrope ('hi:lɪə,trəʊp, 'hɛljə-) *n.* **1.** any plant of the genus *Heliotropium,* esp. the South American variety, cultivated for its small fragrant purple flowers. **2.** a bluish-violet to purple colour. **3.** another name for **bloodstone.**

heliotropism (,hi:lɪ'ɒtrə,pɪzəm) *n.* the growth of a plant in response to the stimulus of sunlight. —**heliotropic** (,hi:lɪəʊ'trɒpɪk) *adj.*

heliport ('hɛlɪ,pɔ:t) *n.* an airport for helicopters.

helium ('hi:lɪəm) *n.* a very light nonflammable colourless odourless element that is an inert gas, occurring in certain natural gases. Symbol: He; atomic no.: 2; atomic wt.: 4.0026.

helix ('hi:lɪks) *n., pl.* **helices** ('hɛlɪ,si:z) *or* **helixes.** **1.** a spiral. **2.** the incurving fold that forms the margin of the external ear. **3.** another name for **volute** (sense 2). **4.** any terrestrial mollusc of the genus *Helix,* which includes the garden snail.

hell (hɛl) *n.* **1.** *Christianity.* (*sometimes cap.*) **a.** the place or state of eternal punishment of the wicked after death. **b.** forces of evil regarded as residing there. **2.** (*sometimes cap.*) (in various religions and cultures) the abode of the spirits of the dead. **3.** pain, extreme difficulty, etc. **4.** *Inf.* a cause of such suffering: *war is hell.* **5.** *U.S.* high spirits or mischievousness. **6.** *Now rare.* a gambling house. **7. for the hell of it.** *Inf.* for the fun of it. **8. give someone hell.** *Inf.* **a.** to give someone a severe reprimand or punishment. **b.** to be a source of torment to someone. **9. hell for leather.** at great speed. **10. (come) hell or high water.** *Inf.* whatever difficulties may arise. **11. hell to pay.** *Inf.* serious consequences, as of a foolish action. **12. raise hell.** *Inf.* **a.** to create a noisy disturbance. **b.** to react strongly and unfavourably. **13. the hell.** *Inf.* **a.** (intensifier): used in such phrases as **what the hell,** etc. **b.** an expression of strong disagreement: *the hell I will.* ~*interj.* **14.** *Inf.* an exclamation of anger, surprise, etc.

he'll (hi:l; *unstressed* i:l, hɪl, ɪl) *contraction of* he will *or* he shall.

THESAURUS

heed 1. *n.* attention, care, caution, consideration, ear, heedfulness, mind, note, notice, regard, respect, thought, watchfulness **2.** *v.* attend, bear in mind, be guided by, consider, follow, give ear to, listen to, mark, mind, note, obey, observe, pay attention to, regard, take notice of, take to heart

heedful attentive, careful, cautious, chary, circumspect, mindful, observant, prudent, vigilant, wary, watchful

heedless careless, foolhardy, imprudent, inattentive, incautious, neglectful, negligent, oblivious, precipitate, rash, reckless, thoughtless, unmindful, unobservant, unthinking

heel[1] *n.* **1.** crust, end, remainder, rump,

stub, stump **2.** *Sl.* blackguard, bounder (*Brit. inf.*), cad (*Brit inf.*), rotter (*Sl., chiefly Brit.*), scoundrel, swine **3. down at heel** dowdy, impoverished, out at elbows, run-down, seedy, shabby, slipshod, slovenly, worn **4. take to one's heels** escape, flee, run away *or* off, show a clean pair of heels, skedaddle (*Inf.*), take flight, vamoose (*Sl., chiefly U.S.*) **5. well-heeled** affluent, flush (*Inf.*), moneyed, prosperous, rich, wealthy, well-off, well-to-do

heel[2] cant, careen, incline, keel over, lean over, list, tilt

hefty 1. beefy (*Inf.*), big, brawny, burly, hulking, husky (*Inf.*), massive, muscular, robust, strapping, strong **2.** forceful, heavy, powerful, thumping (*Sl.*), vigorous **3.** ample, awkward, bulky, colossal, cumbersome,

heavy, large, massive, ponderous, substantial, tremendous, unwieldy, weighty

height 1. altitude, elevation, highness, loftiness, stature, tallness **2.** apex, apogee, crest, crown, elevation, hill, mountain, peak, pinnacle, summit, top, vertex, zenith **3.** acme, dignity, eminence, exaltation, grandeur, loftiness, prominence **4.** climax, culmination, extremity, limit, maximum, ne plus *ultra,* ultimate, utmost degree, uttermost

heighten 1. add to, aggravate, amplify, augment, enhance, improve, increase, intensify, magnify, sharpen, strengthen **2.** elevate, enhance, ennoble, exalt, magnify, raise, uplift

heir beneficiary, heiress (*Fem.*), inheritor,

hellbent (ˌhɛlˈbɛnt) adj. (postpositive and foll. by on) Inf. strongly or rashly intent.

hellebore (ˈhɛlɪˌbɔː) n. 1. any plant of the Eurasian genus Helleborus, typically having showy flowers and poisonous parts. See also **Christmas rose**. 2. any of various plants which yield alkaloids used in the treatment of heart disease.

Hellene (ˈhɛliːn) or **Hellenian** (hɛˈliːnɪən) n. another name for a **Greek**.

Hellenism (ˈhɛlɪˌnɪzəm) n. 1. the principles, ideals, and pursuits associated with classical Greek civilization. 2. the spirit or national character of the Greeks. 3. imitation of or devotion to the culture of ancient Greece. —**ˈHellenist** n.

Hellenistic (ˌhɛlɪˈnɪstɪk) or **Hellenistical** adj. characteristic of or relating to Greek civilization in the Mediterranean world, esp. from the death of Alexander the Great (323 B.C.) to the defeat of Antony and Cleopatra (30 B.C.). —ˌHellenˈistically adv.

hellfire (ˈhɛlˌfaɪə) n. 1. the torment of hell, envisaged as eternal fire. 2. (modifier) characterizing sermons that emphasize this.

hellish (ˈhɛlɪʃ) adj. 1. of or resembling hell. 2. wicked; cruel. 3. Inf. very unpleasant. ~adv. 4. Brit. inf. (intensifier): a hellish good idea.

hello, hallo, or **hullo** (hɛˈləʊ, həˈ; ˈhɛləʊ) sentence substitute. 1. an expression of greeting. 2. a call used to attract attention. 3. an expression of surprise. ~n., pl. -los. 4. the act of saying or calling "hello."

Hell's Angel n. a member of a motorcycle gang who typically dress in Nazi-style paraphernalia and are noted for their lawless behaviour.

helm¹ (hɛlm) n. 1. Naut. a. the wheel or entire apparatus by which a vessel is steered. b. the position of the helm: that is, on the side of the keel opposite from that of the rudder. 2. a position of leadership or control (esp. in **at the helm**). ~vb. 3. (tr.) to steer. —**ˈhelmsman** n.

helm² (hɛlm) n. an archaic or poetic word for **helmet**.

helmet (ˈhɛlmɪt) n. 1. a piece of protective or defensive armour for the head worn by soldiers, policemen, firemen, divers, etc. 2. Biol. a part or structure resembling a helmet, esp. the upper part of the calyx of certain flowers. —**ˈhelmeted** adj.

helminth (ˈhɛlmɪnθ) n. any parasitic worm, esp. a nematode or fluke. —**helˈminthic** or **helminthoid** (ˈhɛlmɪnˌθɔɪd, hɛlˈmɪnθɔɪd) adj.

help (hɛlp) vb. 1. to assist (someone to do something), esp. by sharing the work, cost, or burden of something. 2. to alleviate the burden of (someone else) by giving assistance. 3. (tr.) to assist (a person) to go in a specified direction: help the old lady up. 4. to contribute to: to help the relief operations. 5. to improve (a situation, etc.): crying won't help. 6. (tr.; preceded by can, could, etc.; usually used with a negative) a. to refrain from: we can't help wondering who he is. b. (usually foll. by it) to be responsible for: I can't help it if it rains. 7. to alleviate (an illness, etc.). 8. (tr.) to serve (a customer). 9. (tr.; foll. by to) a. to serve (someone with food, etc.) (usually in **help oneself**). b. to provide (oneself with) without permission. 10. **cannot help but**. to be unable to do anything else except: I cannot help but laugh. 11. **so help me. a.** on my honour. **b.** no matter what: so help me, I'll get revenge. ~n. 12. the act of helping, or being helped, or a person or thing that helps. 13. a. a person hired for a job, esp. a farm worker or domestic servant. b. (functioning as sing.) several employees collectively. 14. a remedy: there's no help for it. ~interj. 15. used to ask for assistance. —**ˈhelper** n.

helpful (ˈhɛlpfʊl) adj. giving help. —**ˈhelpfully** adv. —**ˈhelpfulness** n.

helping (ˈhɛlpɪŋ) n. a single portion of food.

helpless (ˈhɛlplɪs) adj. 1. unable to manage independently. 2. made weak: they were helpless from giggling. —**ˈhelplessly** adv. —**ˈhelplessness** n.

helpmate (ˈhɛlpˌmeɪt) n. a companion and helper, esp. a wife.

helpmeet (ˈhɛlpˌmiːt) n. a less common word for **helpmate**.

help out vb. (adv.) to assist, esp. by sharing the burden or cost of something with (another person).

helter-skelter (ˈhɛltəˈskɛltə) adj. 1. haphazard or careless. ~adv. 2. in a helter-skelter manner. ~n. 3. Brit. a high spiral slide, as at a fairground. 4. disorder.

helve (hɛlv) n. the handle of a hand tool such as an axe or pick.

hem¹ (hɛm) n. 1. an edge to a piece of cloth, made by folding the raw edge under and stitching it down. 2. short for **hemline**. ~vb. **hemming, hemmed.** (tr.) 3. to provide with a hem. 4. (usually foll. by in, around, or about) to enclose or confine. —**ˈhemmer** n.

hem² (hɛm) n., interj. 1. a representation of the sound of clearing the throat, used to gain attention, etc. ~vb. **hemming, hemmed.** 2. (intr.) to utter this sound. 3. **hem (or hum) and haw**. to hesitate in speaking.

he-man n., pl. **-men.** Inf. a strongly built muscular man.

hemato- or before a vowel **hemat-** combining form. U.S. variants of **haemato-**.

hemi- prefix. half: hemicycle; hemisphere.

-hemia n. combining form. U.S. variant of **-aemia**.

hemiplegia (ˌhɛmɪˈpliːdʒɪə) n. paralysis of one side of the body. —**ˈhemiˈplegic** adj.

hemipteran (hɪˈmɪptərən) n. any hemipterous insect.

hemisphere (ˈhɛmɪˌsfɪə) n. 1. one half of a sphere. 2. a. half of the terrestrial globe, divided into **northern** and **southern hemispheres** by the equator or into **eastern** and **western hemispheres** by some meridians, usually 0° and 180°. b. a map or projection of one of the hemispheres. 3. Anat. short for **cerebral hemisphere,** a half of the cerebrum. —**hemispheric** (ˌhɛmɪˈsfɛrɪk) or ˌhemiˈspherical adj.

hemline (ˈhɛmˌlaɪn) n. the level to which the hem of a skirt or dress hangs.

hemlock (ˈhɛmˌlɒk) n. 1. an umbelliferous poisonous Eurasian plant having finely divided leaves, spotted stems, and small white flowers. 2. a poisonous drug derived from this plant. 3. Also called: **hemlock spruce.** a coniferous tree of North America and Asia.

hemp (hɛmp) n. 1. Also called: **cannabis, marijuana.**

THESAURUS

inheritress or inheritrix (Fem.), next in line, scion, successor

hell 1. Abaddon, abode of the damned, abyss, Acheron (Greek myth), bottomless pit, fire and brimstone, Gehenna (New Testament, Judaism), Hades (Greek myth), hellfire, infernal regions, inferno, lower world, nether world, Tartarus (Greek myth), underworld 2. affliction, agony, anguish, martyrdom, misery, nightmare, ordeal, suffering, torment, trial, wretchedness 3. **hell for leather** at the double, full-tilt, headlong, hotfoot, hurriedly, like a bat out of hell (Inf.), pell-mell, posthaste, quickly, speedily, swiftly

hellish 1. damnable, damned, demoniacal, devilish, diabolical, fiendish, infernal 2. abominable, accursed, atrocious, barbarous, cruel, detestable, execrable, inhuman, monstrous, nefarious, vicious, wicked

helm 1. Nautical rudder, steering gear, tiller, wheel 2. Fig. command, control, direction, leadership, rule 3. **at the helm** at the wheel, directing, in charge, in command, in

control, in the driving seat, in the saddle

help v. 1. abet, aid, assist, back, befriend, cooperate, lend a hand, promote, relieve, save, second, serve, stand by, succour, support 2. alleviate, ameliorate, cure, ease, facilitate, heal, improve, mitigate, relieve, remedy, restore 3. abstain, avoid, control, eschew, forbear, hinder, keep from, prevent, refrain from, resist, shun, withstand ~n. 4. advice, aid, assistance, avail, benefit, cooperation, guidance, helping hand, service, support, use, utility 5. assistant, employee, hand, helper, worker 6. balm, corrective, cure, relief, remedy, restorative, salve, succour

helper abettor, adjutant, aide, aider, ally, assistant, attendant, auxiliary, coadjutor, collaborator, colleague, deputy, helpmate, mate, partner, right-hand man, second, subsidiary, supporter

helpful 1. advantageous, beneficial, constructive, favourable, fortunate, practical, productive, profitable, serviceable, timely,

useful 2. accommodating, beneficent, benevolent, caring, considerate, cooperative, friendly, kind, neighbourly, supportive, sympathetic

helping n. dollop (Inf.), piece, plateful, portion, ration, serving

helpless 1. abandoned, defenceless, dependent, destitute, exposed, forlorn, unprotected, vulnerable 2. debilitated, disabled, feeble, impotent, incapable, incompetent, infirm, paralysed, powerless, unfit, weak

helter-skelter 1. adv. carelessly, hastily, headlong, hurriedly, pell-mell, rashly, recklessly, wildly 2. adj. anyhow, confused, disordered, haphazard, higgledy-piggledy (Inf.), hit-or-miss, jumbled, muddled, random, topsy-turvy

hem 1. n. border, edge, fringe, margin, trimming 2. v. Usually with **in** beset, border, circumscribe, confine, edge, enclose, environ, hedge in, restrict, shut in, skirt, surround

an Asian plant having tough fibres, deeply lobed leaves, and small greenish flowers. See also **Indian hemp. 2.** the fibre of this plant, used to make canvas, rope, etc. **3.** any of several narcotic drugs obtained from some varieties of this plant, esp. from Indian hemp. —'**hempen** or '**hemp,like** adj.

hemstitch ('hɛm,stɪtʃ) n. **1.** a decorative edging stitch, usually for a hem, in which the cross threads are stitched in groups. ~vb. **2.** to decorate (a hem, etc.) with hemstitches.

hen (hɛn) n. **1.** the female of any bird, esp. of the domestic fowl. **2.** the female of certain other animals, such as the lobster. **3.** Scot. dialect. a term of affectionate address, used to women.

henbane ('hɛn,beɪn) n. a poisonous Mediterranean plant with sticky hairy leaves: yields the drug hyoscyamine.

hence (hɛns) n. **1.** sentence connector. for this reason; therefore. ~adv. **2.** from this time: a year hence. **3.** Arch. from here; away. ~interj. **4.** Arch. begone!, away!

henceforth ('hɛns'fɔːθ), **henceforwards,** or **henceforward** adv. from now on.

henchman ('hɛntʃmən) n., pl. -**men. 1.** a faithful attendant or supporter. **2.** Arch. a squire; page.

henge (hɛndʒ) n. a circular monument, often containing a circle of stones, dating from the Neolithic and Bronze Ages.

hen harrier n. a common harrier that nests in marshes and open land. U.S. names: **marsh hawk, marsh harrier.**

henna ('hɛnə) n. **1.** a shrub or tree of Asia and N Africa. **2.** a reddish dye obtained from the powdered leaves of this plant, used as a cosmetic and industrial dye. **3.** a reddish-brown colour. ~vb. **4.** (tr.) to dye with henna.

henpeck ('hɛn,pɛk) vb. (tr.) (of a woman) to harass or torment (a man, esp. her husband) by persistent nagging. —'**hen,pecked** adj.

henry ('hɛnrɪ) n., pl. -**ry, -ries,** or -**rys.** the derived SI unit of electric inductance; the inductance of a closed circuit in which an emf of 1 volt is produced when the current varies uniformly at the rate of 1 ampere per second. Symbol: H

hep (hɛp) adj. **hepper, heppest.** Sl. an earlier word for **hip⁴.**

hepatic (hɪ'pætɪk) adj. **1.** of the liver. **2.** having the colour of liver. ~n. **3.** any of various drugs for use in treating diseases of the liver.

hepatitis (,hɛpə'taɪtɪs) n. inflammation of the liver.

hepta- or before a vowel **hept-** combining form. seven: heptameter.

heptagon ('hɛptəgən) n. a polygon having seven sides. —**heptagonal** (hɛp'tægənəl) adj.

her (hɜː; unstressed hə, ə) pron. (objective) **1.** refers to a female person or animal: he loves her. **2.** refers to things personified as feminine or traditionally to ships and nations. ~determiner. **3.** of, belonging to, or associated with her: her hair.

▷ **Usage.** See at **me.**

herald ('hɛrəld) n. **1.** a person who announces important news. **2.** Often literary. a forerunner; harbinger. **3.** the intermediate rank of heraldic officer, between king-of-arms and pursuivant. **4.** (in the Middle Ages) an official at a tournament. ~vb. (tr.) **5.** to announce publicly. **6.** to precede or usher in. —**he'raldic** adj.

heraldry ('hɛrəldrɪ) n., pl. -**ries. 1.** the study concerned with the classification of armorial bearings, the tracing of genealogies, etc. **2.** armorial bearings, insignia, etc. **3.** the show and ceremony of heraldry. —'**heraldist** n.

herb (hɜːb; U.S. ɜːrb) n. **1.** a plant whose aerial parts do

not persist above ground at the end of the growing season; herbaceous plant. **2.** any of various usually aromatic plants, such as parsley and rosemary, that are used in cookery and medicine. —'**herb,like** adj. —'**herby** adj.

herbaceous (hɜː'beɪʃəs) adj. **1.** designating or relating to plants that are fleshy as opposed to woody: a herbaceous plant. **2.** (of petals and sepals) green and leaflike.

herbaceous border n. a flower bed that contains perennials rather than annuals.

herbage ('hɜːbɪdʒ) n. **1.** herbaceous plants collectively, esp. the edible parts on which cattle, sheep, etc., graze. **2.** the vegetation of pasture land; pasturage.

herbal ('hɜːbəl) adj. **1.** of herbs. ~n. **2.** a book describing the properties of plants.

herbalist ('hɜːbəlɪst) n. **1.** a person who grows or specializes in the use of herbs, esp. medicinal herbs. **2.** (formerly) a descriptive botanist.

herbicide ('hɜːbɪ,saɪd) n. a chemical that destroys plants, esp. one used to control weeds.

herbivore ('hɜːbɪ,vɔː) n. an animal that feeds on grass and other plants. —**herbivorous** (hɜː'bɪvərəs) adj.

herculean (,hɜːkjʊ'liːən) adj. **1.** requiring tremendous effort, strength, etc. **2.** (sometimes cap.) resembling Hercules, hero of classical myth, in strength, courage, etc.

herd (hɜːd) n. **1.** a large group of mammals living and feeding together, esp. cattle. **2.** Often disparaging. a large group of people. **3. a.** Arch. or dialect. a man who tends livestock. **b.** (in combination): swineherd. ~vb. **4.** to collect or be collected into or as if into a herd. **5.** (tr.) to drive forward in a large group. **6.** (tr.) to look after (livestock). —'**herder** n.

herd instinct n. Psychol. the inborn tendency to associate with others and follow the group's behaviour.

herdsman ('hɜːdzmən) n., pl. -**men.** Chiefly Brit. a person who breeds or cares for cattle or (rarely) other livestock. U.S. equivalent: **herder.**

here (hɪə) adv. **1.** in, at, or to this place, point, case, or respect: we come here every summer; here comes Roy. **2. here and there.** at several places in or throughout an area. **3. here's to.** a formula used in proposing a toast to someone or something. **4. neither here nor there.** of no relevance or importance.

hereabouts ('hɪərə,baʊts) or **hereabout** adv. in this region or neighbourhood.

hereafter (,hɪər'ɑːftə) adv. **1.** Formal or law. in a subsequent part of this document, matter, case, etc. **2.** a less common word for **henceforth. 3.** at some time in the future. **4.** in a future life after death. ~n. (usually preceded by the) **5.** life after death. **6.** the future.

hereby (,hɪə'baɪ) adv. (used in official statements, etc.) by means of or as a result of this.

hereditable (hɪ'rɛdɪtəbəl) adj. a less common word for **heritable.** —**he,redita'bility** n.

hereditary (hɪ'rɛdɪtərɪ, -trɪ) adj. **1.** of or denoting factors that can be transmitted genetically from one generation to another. **2.** Law. **a.** descending to succeeding generations by inheritance. **b.** transmitted according to established rules of descent. **3.** derived from one's ancestors; traditional: hereditary feuds. —**he'reditarily** adv. —**he'reditariness** n.

heredity (hɪ'rɛdɪtɪ) n., pl. -**ties. 1.** the transmission from one generation to another of genetic factors that determine individual characteristics. **2.** the sum total of the inherited factors in an organism.

herein (,hɪər'ɪn) adv. **1.** Formal or law. in or into this place, thing, document, etc. **2.** Rare. in this respect, circumstance, etc.

hereinafter (,hɪərɪn'ɑːftə) adv. Formal or law. from this point on in this document, etc.

THESAURUS

hence ergo, for this reason, on that account, therefore, thus

henceforth from now on, from this day forward, hence, hereafter, hereinafter, in the future

henpecked browbeaten, bullied, cringing, dominated, led by the nose, meek, subject, subjugated, timid, treated like dirt

herald n. **1.** bearer of tidings, crier, messenger **2.** forerunner, harbinger, indication, omen, precursor, sign, signal, token ~v. **3.** advertise, announce, broadcast, proclaim,

publicize, publish, trumpet **4.** foretoken, harbinger, indicate, pave the way, portend, precede, presage, promise, show, usher in

herd n. **1.** assemblage, collection, crowd, crush, drove, flock, horde, mass, mob, multitude, press, swarm, throng **2.** mob, populace, rabble, riffraff, the hoi polloi, the masses, the plebs ~v. **3.** assemble, associate, collect, congregate, flock, gather, huddle, muster, rally **4.** drive, force, goad, guide, lead, shepherd, spur

hereafter 1. adv. after this, from now on,

hence, henceforth, henceforward, in future **2.** n. afterlife, future life, life after death, next world, the beyond

hereditary 1. family, genetic, inborn, inbred, inheritable, transmissible **2.** ancestral, bequeathed, handed down, inherited, patrimonial, traditional, transmitted, willed

heredity congenital traits, constitution, genetic make-up, genetics, inheritance

hereof (ˌhɪərˈɒv) adv. Formal or law. of or concerning this.

heresy (ˈhɛrəsɪ) n., pl. **-sies. 1. a.** an opinion contrary to the orthodox tenets of a religious body. **b.** the act of maintaining such an opinion. **2.** any belief that is or is thought to be contrary to official or established theory. **3.** adherence to unorthodox opinion.

heretic (ˈhɛrətɪk) n. **1.** Now chiefly R.C. Church. a person who maintains beliefs contrary to the established teachings of his Church. **2.** a person who holds unorthodox opinions in any field. —**heretical** (hɪˈrɛtɪkəl) adj. —**heˈretically** adv.

hereto (ˌhɪəˈtuː) adv. Formal or law. to this place, thing, matter, document, etc.

heretofore (ˌhɪətuˈfɔː) adv. Formal or law. until now; before this time.

hereupon (ˌhɪərəˈpɒn) adv. **1.** following immediately after this; at this stage. **2.** Formal or law. upon this thing, point, subject, etc.

herewith (ˌhɪəˈwɪð, -ˈwɪθ) adv. Rare or formal. together with this: we send you herewith your statement of account.

heritable (ˈhɛrɪtəbəl) adj. **1.** capable of being inherited; inheritable. **2.** Chiefly law. capable of inheriting. —ˌheritaˈbility n. —ˈheritably adv.

heritage (ˈhɛrɪtɪdʒ) n. **1.** something inherited at birth. **2.** anything that has been transmitted from the past or handed down by tradition. **3.** Law. any property, esp. land, that by law has descended or may descend to an heir.

hermaphrodite (hɜːˈmæfrəˌdaɪt) n. **1.** Biol. an animal or flower that has both male and female reproductive organs. **2.** a person having both male and female sexual characteristics. **3.** a person or thing in which two opposite qualities are combined. ~adj. **4.** having the characteristics of an hermaphrodite. —herˌmaphroˈditic or herˌmaphroˈditical adj. —herˈmaphroditˌism n.

hermetic (hɜːˈmɛtɪk) or **hermetical** adj. sealed so as to be airtight. —herˈmetically adv.

hermit (ˈhɜːmɪt) n. **1.** one of the early Christian recluses. **2.** any person living in solitude. —herˈmitic or herˈmitical adj.

hermitage (ˈhɜːmɪtɪdʒ) n. **1.** the abode of a hermit. **2.** any retreat.

hermit crab n. a small soft-bodied crustacean living in and carrying about the empty shells of whelks or similar molluscs.

hernia (ˈhɜːnɪə) n., pl. **-nias** or **-niae** (-nɪˌiː). the projection of an organ or part through the lining of the cavity in which it is normally situated, esp. the intestine through the front wall of the abdominal cavity. Also called: **rupture.** —ˈhernial adj. —ˈherniˌated adj.

hero (ˈhɪərəʊ) n., pl. **-roes. 1.** a man distinguished by exceptional courage, nobility, etc. **2.** a man who is idealized for possessing superior qualities in any field. **3.** Classical myth. a being of extraordinary strength and courage, often the offspring of a mortal and a god. **4.** the principal male character in a novel, play, etc.

heroic (hɪˈrəʊɪk) or **heroical** adj. **1.** of, like, or befitting a hero. **2.** courageous but desperate. **3.** treating of heroes and their deeds. **4.** of or resembling the heroes of classical mythology. **5.** (of language, manner, etc.) extravagant. **6.** Prosody. of or resembling heroic verse.

7. (of the arts, esp. sculpture) larger than life-size; smaller than colossal. —heˈroically adv.

heroics (hɪˈrəʊɪks) pl. n. **1.** Prosody. short for **heroic verse. 2.** extravagant or melodramatic language, behaviour, etc.

heroic verse n. Prosody. a type of verse suitable for epic or heroic subjects, such as the classical hexameter or the French Alexandrine.

heroin (ˈhɛrəʊɪn) n. a white bitter-tasting crystalline powder derived from morphine: a highly addictive narcotic.

heroine (ˈhɛrəʊɪn) n. **1.** a woman possessing heroic qualities. **2.** a woman idealized for possessing superior qualities. **3.** the main female character in a novel, play, film, etc.

heroism (ˈhɛrəʊˌɪzəm) n. the state or quality of being a hero.

heron (ˈhɛrən) n. any of various wading birds having a long neck, slim body, and a plumage that is commonly grey or white.

heronry (ˈhɛrənrɪ) n., pl. **-ries.** a colony of breeding herons.

hero worship n. **1.** admiration for heroes or idealized persons. **2.** worship by the ancient Greeks and Romans of heroes. ~vb. **hero-worship, -shipping, -shipped** or U.S. **-shiping, -shiped. 3.** (tr.) to feel admiration or adulation for. —ˈhero-ˌworshipper n.

herpes (ˈhɜːpiːz) n. any of several inflammatory diseases of the skin, esp. herpes simplex. —**herpetic** (hɜːˈpɛtɪk) adj.

herpes simplex (ˈsɪmplɛks) n. an acute viral disease characterized by formation of clusters of watery blisters.

herpes zoster (ˈzɒstə) n. a technical name for **shingles.**

herring (ˈhɛrɪŋ) n., pl. **-rings** or **-ring.** an important food fish of northern seas, having an elongated body covered with large silvery scales.

herringbone (ˈhɛrɪŋˌbəʊn) n. **1. a.** a pattern consisting of two or more rows of short parallel strokes slanting in alternate directions to form a series of zigzags. **b.** (as modifier): a herringbone pattern. **2.** Skiing. a method of ascending a slope by walking with the skis pointing outwards and one's weight on the inside edges. ~vb. **3.** to decorate (textiles, brickwork, etc.) with herringbone. **4.** (intr.) Skiing. to ascend a slope in herringbone fashion.

herring gull n. a common gull that has a white plumage with black-tipped wings.

hers (hɜːz) pron. **1.** something or someone belonging to her: hers is the nicest dress; that cat is hers. **2. of hers.** belonging to her.

herself (həˈsɛlf) pron. **1. a.** the reflexive form of she or her. **b.** (intensifier): the queen herself signed. **2.** (preceded by a copula) her normal self: she looks herself again after the operation.
▷ **Usage.** See at **myself.**

hertz (hɜːts) n., pl. **hertz.** the derived SI unit of frequency; the frequency of a periodic phenomenon that has a periodic time of 1 second; 1 cycle per second. Symbol: Hz

he's (hiːz) contraction of he is or he has.

hesitant (ˈhɛzɪtənt) adj. wavering, hesitating, or irresolute. —ˈhesitantly adv.

hesitate (ˈhɛzɪˌteɪt) vb. (intr.) **1.** to be slow in acting;

THESAURUS

heresy apostasy, dissidence, error, heterodoxy, iconoclasm, impiety, revisionism, schism, unorthodoxy

heretic apostate, dissenter, dissident, nonconformist, renegade, revisionist, schismatic, sectarian, separatist

heretical freethinking, heterodox, iconoclastic, idolatrous, impious, revisionist, schismatic, unorthodox

heritage bequest, birthright, endowment, estate, inheritance, legacy, lot, patrimony, portion, share, tradition

hermit anchoret, anchorite, eremite, monk, recluse, solitary, stylite

hero 1. celebrity, champion, conqueror, exemplar, great man, heart-throb (Brit.), idol, man of the hour, popular figure, star, superstar, victor **2.** lead actor, leading man, male lead, principal male character, protagonist

heroic 1. bold, brave, courageous, daring, dauntless, doughty, fearless, gallant, intrepid, lion-hearted, stouthearted, undaunted, valiant, valorous **2.** classical, Homeric, legendary, mythological **3.** classic, elevated, epic, exaggerated, extravagant, grand, grandiose, high-flown, inflated

heroine 1. celebrity, goddess, ideal, woman of the hour **2.** diva, female lead, lead actress, leading lady, prima donna, principal female character, protagonist

heroism boldness, bravery, courage, courageousness, daring, fearlessness, fortitude, gallantry, intrepidity, prowess, spirit, valour

hero worship admiration, adoration, adulation, idealization, idolization, putting on a pedestal, veneration

hesitant diffident, doubtful, half-hearted, halting, hanging back, hesitating, irresolute,

lacking confidence, reluctant, sceptical, shy, timid, uncertain, unsure, vacillating, wavering

hesitate 1. be uncertain, delay, dither, doubt, haver (Brit.), pause, shillyshally (Inf.), swither (Scot. dialect), vacillate, wait, waver **2.** balk, be reluctant, be unwilling, boggle, demur, hang back, scruple, shrink from, think twice **3.** falter, fumble, hem and haw, stammer, stumble, stutter

hesitation 1. delay, doubt, dubiety, hesitancy, indecision, irresolution, uncertainty, vacillation **2.** demurral, misgiving(s), qualm(s), reluctance, scruple(s), unwillingness **3.** faltering, fumbling, hemming and hawing, stammering, stuttering

be uncertain. **2.** to be reluctant (to do something). **3.** to stammer or pause in speaking. —**hesitancy** ('hɛzɪtənsɪ) or ˌhesi'tation n. —'hesiˌtatingly adv.

Hesperus ('hɛspərəs) n. an evening star, esp. Venus.

hessian ('hɛsɪən) n. a coarse jute fabric similar to sacking.

hest (hɛst) n. an archaic word for **behest.**

hetero- combining form. other, another, or different: heterosexual.

heterodox ('hɛtərəʊˌdɒks) adj. **1.** at variance with established or accepted doctrines or beliefs. **2.** holding unorthodox opinions. —'heteroˌdoxy n.

heterodyne ('hɛtərəʊˌdaɪn) vb. **1.** Electronics. to mix (two alternating signals) to produce two signals having frequencies corresponding to the sum and the difference of the original frequencies. ~adj. **2.** produced by, operating by, or involved in heterodyning two signals.

heterogeneous (ˌhɛtərəʊ'dʒiːnɪəs) adj. **1.** composed of unrelated parts. **2.** not of the same type. —**heterogeneity** (ˌhɛtərəʊdʒɪ'niːɪtɪ) or ˌhetero'geneousness n.

heteromorphic (ˌhɛtərəʊ'mɔːfɪk) or **heteromorphous** adj. Biol. **1.** differing from the normal form. **2.** (esp. of insects) having different forms at different stages of the life cycle. —ˌhetero'morphism n.

heterosexual (ˌhɛtərəʊ'sɛksjʊəl) n. **1.** a person who is sexually attracted to the opposite sex. ~adj. **2.** of or relating to heterosexuality. —ˌheteroˌsexu'ality n.

het up adj. Inf. angry; excited: don't get het up.

heuristic (hjʊə'rɪstɪk) adj. **1.** helping to learn; guiding in investigation. **2.** (of a method of teaching) allowing pupils to learn things for themselves. **3.** Maths., science. using or obtained by reasoning from past experience since no algorithm exists. ~n. **4.** (pl.) the science of heuristic procedure. —heu'ristically adv.

hew (hjuː) vb. **hewing, hewed, hewed** or **hewn. 1.** to strike (something, esp. wood) with cutting blows, as with an axe. **2.** (tr.; often foll. by out) to carve from a substance. **3.** (tr.; often foll. by away, off, etc.) to sever from a larger portion. **4.** (intr.; often foll. by to) U.S. to conform. —'hewer n.

hexa- or before a vowel **hex-** combining form. six: hexachord; hexameter.

hexagon ('hɛksəgən) n. a polygon having six sides. —hex'agonal adj.

hexagram ('hɛksəˌgræm) n. a star-shaped figure formed by extending the sides of a regular hexagon to meet at six points.

hexameter (hɛk'sæmɪtə) n. Prosody. **1.** a verse line consisting of six metrical feet. **2.** (in Greek and Latin epic poetry) a verse line of six metrical feet, of which the first four are usually dactyls or spondees, the fifth a dactyl, and the sixth a spondee or trochee. —**hexametric** (ˌhɛksə'mɛtrɪk) or ˌhexa'metrical adj.

hexapod ('hɛksəˌpɒd) n. an insect.

hey (heɪ) interj. **1.** an expression indicating surprise, dismay, discovery, etc. **2. hey presto.** an exclamation used by conjurors to herald the climax of a trick.

heyday ('heɪˌdeɪ) n. the time of most power, popularity, vigour, etc.

Hf the chemical symbol for hafnium.

HF, H.F., hf, or **h.f.** abbrev. for high frequency.

Hg the chemical symbol for mercury.

HGV (in Britain) abbrev. for heavy goods vehicle.

H.H. abbrev. for: **1.** His (or Her) Highness. **2.** His Holiness (title of the Pope).

HH (on pencils) abbrev. for double hard.

hi (haɪ) sentence substitute. Chiefly U.S. an informal word for **hello.**

hiatus (haɪ'eɪtəs) n., pl. **-tuses** or **-tus. 1.** (esp. in manuscripts) a break or interruption in continuity. **2.** a break between adjacent vowels in the pronunciation of a word.

hiatus hernia n. protrusion of part of the stomach through the diaphragm at the oesophageal opening.

hibernate ('haɪbəˌneɪt) vb. (intr.) **1.** (of some animals) to pass the winter in a dormant condition with metabolism greatly slowed down. **2.** to cease from activity. —ˌhiber'nation n. —'hiberˌnator n.

Hibernia (haɪ'bɜːnɪə) n. the Roman name for **Ireland:** used poetically in later times. —Hi'bernian adj., n.

hibiscus (hɪ'bɪskəs) n., pl. **-cuses.** any plant of the chiefly tropical and subtropical genus Hibiscus, cultivated for its large brightly coloured flowers.

hiccup ('hɪkʌp) n. **1.** a spasm of the diaphragm producing a sudden breathing in of air resulting in a characteristic sharp sound. **2.** the state of having such spasms. **3.** Inf. a minor difficulty. ~vb. **-cuping, -cuped** or **-cupping, -cupped. 4.** (intr.) to make a hiccup or hiccups. **5.** (tr.) to utter with a hiccup. ~Also: **hiccough.**

hick (hɪk) n. Inf., chiefly U.S. a country bumpkin.

hickory ('hɪkərɪ) n., pl. **-ries. 1.** a tree of a chiefly North American genus, having nuts with edible kernels and hard smooth shells. **2.** the hard tough wood of any of these trees.

hidalgo (hɪ'dælgəʊ) n., pl. **-gos.** a member of the lower nobility in Spain.

hidden ('hɪdən) vb. **1.** the past participle of **hide¹.** ~adj. **2.** concealed or obscured: a hidden cave; a hidden meaning.

hide¹ (haɪd) vb. **hiding, hid, hidden** or **hid. 1.** to conceal (oneself or an object) from view or discovery: to hide a pencil; to hide from the police. **2.** (tr.) to obscure: clouds hid the sun. **3.** (tr.) to keep secret. **4.** (tr.) to turn (one's eyes, etc.) away. ~n. **5.** Brit. a place of concealment, usually disguised to appear as part of the natural environment, used by hunters, birdwatchers, etc. U.S. equivalent: **blind.** —'hider n.

hide² (haɪd) n. **1.** the skin of an animal, either tanned or raw. **2.** Inf. the human skin. ~vb. **hiding, hided. 3.** (tr.) Inf. to flog. —'hideless adj.

hide-and-seek or U.S. **hide-and-go-seek** n. a game in which one player covers his eyes while the others hide, and then tries to find them.

hideaway ('haɪdəˌweɪ) n. a hiding place or secluded spot.

hidebound ('haɪdˌbaʊnd) adj. **1.** restricted by petty rules, a conservative attitude, etc. **2.** (of cattle, etc.) having the skin closely attached to the flesh as a result of poor feeding.

hideous ('hɪdɪəs) adj. **1.** extremely ugly; repulsive. **2.** terrifying and horrific. —'hideously adv. —'hideousness n.

hide-out n. a hiding place, esp. a remote place used by outlaws, etc.; hideaway.

hiding¹ ('haɪdɪŋ) n. **1.** the state of concealment: in hiding. **2. hiding place.** a place of concealment.

hiding² ('haɪdɪŋ) n. Inf. a flogging; beating.

hie (haɪ) vb. **hieing** or **hying, hied.** Arch. or poetic. to hurry; speed.

hierarchy ('haɪəˌrɑːkɪ) n., pl. **-chies. 1.** a system of persons or things arranged in a graded order. **2.** a body of persons in holy orders organized into graded ranks. **3.** the collective body of those so organized. **4.** a series of ordered groupings within a system, such as the arrangement of plants into classes, orders, etc. **5.** government by a priesthood. —ˌhier'archical or ˌhier'archic adj. —'hierˌarchism n.

THESAURUS

hew **1.** axe, chop, cut, hack, lop, split **2.** carve, fashion, form, make, model, sculpt, sculpture, shape, smooth

heyday bloom, flowering, pink, prime, prime of life, salad days

hiatus aperture, blank, breach, break, chasm, discontinuity, gap, interruption, interval, lacuna, lapse, opening, rift, space

hibernate hole up, lie dormant, overwinter, remain torpid, sleep snug, vegetate, winter

hidden abstruse, clandestine, close, concealed, covered, covert, cryptic, dark, hermetic, hermetical, masked, mysterious, mystic, mystical, obscure, occult, recondite, secret, shrouded, ulterior, unrevealed, unseen, veiled

hide¹ **1.** cache, conceal, go into hiding, go to ground, go underground, hole up, lie low, secrete, take cover **2.** blot out, bury, camouflage, cloak, conceal, cover, disguise, eclipse, mask, obscure, screen, shelter, shroud, veil **3.** hush up, keep secret, suppress, withhold

hide² fell, pelt, skin

hidebound brassbound, conventional, narrow, narrow-minded, rigid, set, set in one's ways, strait-laced, ultraconservative

hideous **1.** ghastly, grim, grisly, grotesque, gruesome, monstrous, repulsive, revolting, ugly, unsightly **2.** abominable, appalling, awful, detestable, disgusting, dreadful, horrendous, horrible, horrid, loathsome, macabre, odious, shocking, sickening, terrible, terrifying

hide-out den, hideaway, hiding place, lair, secret place, shelter

hiding n. beating, caning, drubbing, flogging, larruping (Brit. dialect), lathering (Inf.), licking (Inf.), spanking, tanning (Sl.), thrashing, walloping (Inf.), whaling, whipping

hierarchy grading, pecking order,

hieratic (ˌhaɪəˈrætɪk) *adj.* **1.** of priests. **2.** of a cursive form of hieroglyphics used by priests in ancient Egypt. **3.** of styles in art that adhere to certain fixed types, as in ancient Egypt. ~*n.* **4.** the hieratic script of ancient Egypt. —ˌhier'atically *adv.*

hiero- *or before a vowel* **hier-** *combining form.* holy or divine: *hierarchy.*

hieroglyphic (ˌhaɪərəˈglɪfɪk) *adj. also* **hieroglyphical.** **1.** of or relating to a form of writing using picture symbols, esp. as used in ancient Egypt. **2.** difficult to decipher. ~*n. also* **hieroglyph. 3.** a picture or symbol representing an object, concept, or sound. **4.** a symbol that is difficult to decipher. —ˌhiero'glyphically *adv.*

hieroglyphics (ˌhaɪərəˈglɪfɪks) *n. (functioning as sing.)* **1.** a form of writing, esp. as used in ancient Egypt, in which pictures or symbols are used to represent objects, concepts, or sounds. **2.** difficult or undecipherable writing.

hi-fi (ˈhaɪˈfaɪ) *n. Inf.* **1. a.** short for **high fidelity. b.** *(as modifier):* **hi-fi equipment. 2.** a set of high-quality sound-reproducing equipment.

higgledy-piggledy (ˈhɪgəldɪˈpɪgəldɪ) *Inf.* ~*adj., adv.* **1.** in a jumble. ~*n.* **2.** a muddle.

high (haɪ) *adj.* **1.** being a relatively great distance from top to bottom; tall: *a high building.* **2.** situated at a relatively great distance above sea level: *a high plateau.* **3.** *(postpositive)* being a specified distance from top to bottom: *three feet high.* **4.** extending from or performed at an elevation: *a high dive.* **5.** *(in combination)* coming up to a specified level: *knee-high.* **6.** being at its peak: *high noon.* **7.** of greater than average height: *a high collar.* **8.** greater than normal in intensity or amount: *a high wind; high mileage.* **9.** (of sound) acute in pitch. **10.** (of latitudes) relatively far north or south from the equator. **11.** (of meat) slightly decomposed, regarded as enhancing the flavour of game. **12.** very important: *the high priestess.* **13.** exalted in style or character: *high drama.* **14.** expressing contempt or arrogance: *high words.* **15.** elated; cheerful: *high spirits.* **16.** *Inf.* being in a state of altered consciousness induced by alcohol, narcotics, etc. **17.** luxurious or extravagant: *high life.* **18.** advanced in complexity: *high finance.* **19.** (of a gear) providing a relatively great forward speed for a given engine speed. **20.** *Phonetics.* denoting a vowel whose articulation is produced by raising the tongue, such as for the *ee* in *see* or *oo* in *moon.* **21.** *(cap. when part of name)* formal and elaborate: *High Mass.* **22.** *(usually cap.)* relating to the High Church. **23.** *Cards.* having a relatively great value in a suit. **24. high and dry.** stranded; destitute. **25. high and mighty.** *Inf.* arrogant. **26. high opinion.** a favourable opinion. ~*adv.* **27.** at or to a height: *he jumped high.* **28.** in a high manner. **29.** *Naut.* close to the wind with sails full. ~*n.* **30.** a high place or level. **31.** *Inf.* a state of altered consciousness induced by alcohol, narcotics, etc. **32.** another word for **anticyclone. 33. on high. a.** at a height. **b.** in heaven.

highball (ˈhaɪˌbɔːl) *n. U.S.* a long iced drink consisting of a spirit base with soda water, etc.

highbrow (ˈhaɪˌbraʊ) *Often disparaging.* ~*n.* **1.** a person of scholarly and erudite tastes. ~*adj. also* **high-**browed. **2.** appealing to highbrows.

highchair (ˈhaɪˌtʃɛə) *n.* a long-legged chair for a child, esp. one with a table-like tray.

High Church *n.* **1.** the party or movement within the Church of England stressing continuity with Catholic Christendom, the authority of bishops, and the importance of sacraments. ~*adj.* **High-Church. 2.** of or relating to this party or movement. —ˈHigh-ˈChurchman *n.*

high commissioner *n.* the senior diplomatic representative sent by one Commonwealth country to another instead of an ambassador.

High Court *n.* **1.** (in England) Also called: **High Court of Justice.** the supreme court dealing with civil law cases. **2.** (in Scotland) Also called: **High Court of Justiciary.** the supreme court dealing with criminal law cases. **3.** (in Australia) the highest court of appeal, deciding esp. constitutional issues. **4.** (in New Zealand) Formerly called: **Supreme Court.** a court of law that is superior to a District Court.

higher education *n.* education and training at colleges, universities, polytechnics, etc.

higher-up *n. Inf.* a person of higher rank or in a superior position.

highest common factor *n.* the largest number or quantity that is a factor of each member of a group of numbers or quantities.

high explosive *n.* an extremely powerful chemical explosive, such as TNT or gelignite.

highfalutin (ˌhaɪfəˈluːtɪn) *or* **highfaluting** *adj. Inf.* pompous or pretentious.

high fidelity *n.* **a.** the reproduction of sound using electronic equipment that gives faithful reproduction with little or no distortion. **b.** *(as modifier):* a high-fidelity amplifier. Often shortened to **hi-fi.**

high-flier *or* **high-flyer** *n.* **1.** a person who is extreme in aims, ambition, etc. **2.** a person of great ability, esp. in a career. —ˈhigh-ˌflying *n.*

high-flown *adj.* extravagant or pretentious in conception or intention: *high-flown ideas.*

high frequency *n.* a radio-frequency lying between 30 and 3 megahertz. Abbrev.: **HF**

high-handed *adj.* tactlessly overbearing and inconsiderate. —ˌhigh-ˈhandedness *n.*

highjack (ˈhaɪˌdʒæk) *vb.* a less common spelling of **hijack.** —ˈhighˌjacker *n.*

high jump *n.* **1.** (usually preceded by *the*) an athletic event in which a competitor has to jump over a high bar. **2. the high jump.** *Brit. inf.* a severe reprimand or punishment. —**high jumper** *n.* —**high jumping** *n.*

highland (ˈhaɪlənd) *n.* **1.** relatively high ground. **2.** *(modifier)* of or relating to a highland. —ˈhighlander *n.*

Highland (ˈhaɪlənd) *n. (modifier)* of or denoting the Highlands of Scotland. —ˈHighlander *n.*

Highland cattle *n.* a breed of cattle with shaggy reddish-brown hair and long horns.

Highland fling *n.* a vigorous Scottish solo dance.

high-level language *n.* a computer programming language that is closer to human language or mathematical notation than to machine language.

THESAURUS

ranking

hieroglyphic *adj.* enigmatical, figurative, indecipherable, obscure, runic, symbolical

high *adj.* **1.** elevated, lofty, soaring, steep, tall, towering **2.** excessive, extraordinary, extreme, great, intensified, sharp, strong **3.** arch, chief, consequential, distinguished, eminent, exalted, important, influential, leading, powerful, prominent, ruling, significant, superior **4.** arrogant, boastful, bragging, despotic, domineering, haughty, lofty, lordly, ostentatious, overbearing, proud, tyrannical, vainglorious **5.** capital, extreme, grave, important, serious **6.** boisterous, bouncy (*Inf.*), cheerful, elated, excited, exhilarated, exuberant, joyful, light-hearted, merry, strong, tumultuous, turbulent **7.** *Inf.* delirious, euphoric, freaked out (*Inf.*), hyped up (*Sl.*), inebriated, intoxicated, on a trip (*Inf.*), spaced out (*Sl.*), stoned (*Sl.*), tripping (*Inf.*), turned on (*Sl.*) **8.** costly, dear, exorbitant, expensive, high-priced, steep (*Inf.*), stiff **9.**

acute, high-pitched, penetrating, piercing, piping, sharp, shrill, soprano, strident, treble **10.** extravagant, grand, lavish, luxurious, rich **11.** gamy, niffy (*Sl.*), pongy (*Brit. sl.*), strong-flavoured, tainted, whiffy (*Inf.*) **12. high and dry** abandoned, bereft, destitute, helpless, stranded **13. high and low** all over, everywhere, exhaustively, far and wide, in every nook and cranny **14. high and mighty** *Inf.* arrogant, cavalier, conceited, disdainful, haughty, imperious, overbearing, self-important, snobbish, stuck-up (*Inf.*), superior ~*adv.* **15.** aloft, at great height, far up, way up ~*n.* **16.** apex, height, peak, record level, summit, top **17.** *Inf.* delirium, ecstasy, euphoria, intoxication, trip (*Inf.*)

highbrow 1. *n.* aesthete, Brahmin (*U.S.*), brain (*Inf.*), brainbox (*Sl.*), egghead (*Inf.*), intellectual, mastermind, savant, scholar **2.** *adj.* bookish, brainy (*Inf.*), cultivated, cultured, deep, highbrowed, intellectual, sophisticated

high-class A-one (*Inf.*), choice, classy

(*Sl.*), elite, exclusive, first-rate, high-quality, posh (*Inf., chiefly Brit.*), select, superior, tip-top, top-flight, tops (*Sl.*), U (*Brit. inf.*), upper-class

highfalutin, highfaluting big, bombastic, florid, grandiose, high-flown, high-sounding, lofty, magniloquent, pompous, pretentious, supercilious, swanky (*Inf.*)

high-flown elaborate, exaggerated, extravagant, florid, grandiose, highfalutin (*Inf.*), inflated, lofty, magniloquent, over-blown, pretentious

high-handed arbitrary, autocratic, bossy (*Inf.*), despotic, dictatorial, domineering, imperious, inconsiderate, oppressive, overbearing, peremptory, self-willed, tyrannical, wilful

highland *n.* heights, hill country, hills, mountainous region, plateau, tableland, uplands

highlight ('haɪ,laɪt) n. 1. an area of the lightest tone in a painting, photograph, etc. 2. Also called: **high spot.** the most exciting or memorable part or time. 3. (pl.) a lightened or brightened effect produced in the hair by bleaching selected strands. ~vb. (tr.) 4. Painting, photog., etc. to mark with light tone. 5. to bring emphasis to. 6. to produce highlights in (the hair).

highliner ('haɪ,laɪnər) n. Canad. in the Maritime Provinces, the fishing boat or fisherman bringing in the most fish.

highly ('haɪlɪ) adv. 1. (intensifier): highly disappointed. 2. with great approbation: we spoke highly of it. 3. in a high position: placed highly in class. 4. at or for a high cost.

highly strung or U.S. **high-strung** adj. tense and easily upset; excitable; nervous.

High Mass n. a solemn and elaborate sung Mass.

high-minded adj. 1. having or characterized by high moral principles. 2. Arch. arrogant; haughty. —,high-'mindedness n.

highness ('haɪnɪs) n. the condition of being high.

Highness ('haɪnɪs) n. (preceded by Your, His, or Her) a title used to address or refer to a royal person.

high-octane adj. (of petrol) having a high octane number.

high-pitched adj. 1. pitched high in tone. 2. (of a roof) having steeply sloping sides. 3. (of an argument, style, etc.) lofty or intense.

high-powered adj. 1. (of an optical instrument or lens) having a high magnification. 2. dynamic and energetic; highly capable.

high-pressure adj. 1. having, using, or designed to withstand pressure above normal. 2. Inf. (of selling) persuasive in an aggressive and persistent manner.

high priest n. 1. Judaism. the priest of highest rank who alone was permitted to enter the holy of holies of the Temple. 2. the head of a cult. —**high priesthood** n.

high-rise adj. (prenominal) of or relating to a building that has many storeys, esp. one used for flats or offices: a high-rise block.

highroad ('haɪ,rəʊd) n. 1. a main road; highway. 2. (usually preceded by the) the sure way: the highroad to fame.

high school n. 1. Brit. another term for **grammar school.** 2. U.S. & N.Z. a secondary school.

high seas pl. n. (sometimes sing.) the open seas, outside the jurisdiction of any one nation.

high season n. the most popular time of year at a holiday resort, etc.

high-sounding adj. another term for **high-flown.**

high-spirited adj. vivacious, bold, or lively. —,high-'spiritedness n.

high table n. (sometimes cap.) the table in the dining hall of a school, college, etc., at which the principal teachers, fellows, etc., sit.

high tea n. Brit. a substantial early evening meal consisting of a cooked dish, cakes, etc., and usually accompanied by tea.

high-tension n. (modifier) carrying or operating at a relatively high voltage.

high tide n. 1. the tide at its highest level. 2. a culminating point.

high time Inf. ~adv. 1. the latest possible time: it's high time you mended this shelf. ~n. 2. Also: **high old time.** an enjoyable and exciting time.

high treason n. an act of treason directly affecting a sovereign or state.

highveld ('haɪ,fɛlt) n. **the.** the high grassland region of the Transvaal, South Africa.

high-water mark n. 1. the level reached by sea water at high tide or by other stretches of water in flood. 2. the highest point.

highway ('haɪ,weɪ) n. 1. Now chiefly U.S. except in legal contexts. a main road, esp. one that connects towns. 2. a direct path or course.

highwayman ('haɪweɪmən) n., pl. **-men.** (formerly) a robber, usually on horseback, who held up travellers on public roads.

hijack or **highjack** ('haɪ,dʒæk) vb. 1. (tr.) to seize, divert, or appropriate (a vehicle or the goods it carries) while in transit: to hijack an aircraft. ~n. 2. the act or an instance of hijacking. —'hi,jacker or 'high,jacker n.

hike (haɪk) vb. 1. (intr.) to walk a long way, usually for pleasure, esp. in the country. 2. (usually foll. by up) **a.** to pull or be pulled; hitch. **b.** to raise (prices). ~n. 3. a long walk. 4. a rise in price. —'hiker n.

hilarious (hɪ'lɛərɪəs) adj. very funny. —hi'lariously adv. —hi'lariousness or hilarity (hɪ'lærɪtɪ) n.

Hilary term ('hɪlərɪ) n. the spring term at Oxford University and some other educational establishments.

hill (hɪl) n. 1. **a.** a natural elevation of the earth's surface, less high or craggy than a mountain. **b.** (in combination): a hillside. 2. **a.** a heap or mound. **b.** (in combination): a dunghill. 3. an incline; slope. 4. **hill and dale.** (of gramophone records) having vertical groove undulations. 5. **over the hill.** Sl. **a.** beyond one's prime. **b.** Mil. absent without leave or deserting. ~vb. (tr.) 6. to form into a hill. 7. to cover or surround with a heap of earth. —'hilly adj.

hillbilly ('hɪl,bɪlɪ) n., pl. **-lies.** 1. Usually disparaging. an unsophisticated person, esp. from the mountainous areas in the southeastern U.S. 2. another name for **country-and-western.**

hillock ('hɪlək) n. a small hill or mound. —'hillocked or 'hillocky adj.

hills (hɪlz) pl. n. 1. **the.** a hilly and often remote region. 2. **as old as the hills.** very old.

hilt (hɪlt) n. 1. the handle or shaft of a sword, dagger, etc. 2. **to the hilt.** to the full. ~vb. 3. (tr.) to supply with a hilt.

hilum ('haɪləm) n., pl. **-la** (-lə). Bot. a scar on a seed marking its point of attachment to the seed stalk.

THESAURUS

highlight 1. n. best part, climax, feature, focal point, focus, high point, high spot, main feature, memorable part, peak 2. v. accent, accentuate, bring to the fore, emphasize, feature, focus attention on, give prominence to, play up, set off, show up, spotlight, stress, underline

highly 1. decidedly, eminently, exceptionally, extraordinarily, extremely, greatly, immensely, supremely, tremendously, vastly, very, very much 2. appreciatively, approvingly, enthusiastically, favourably, warmly, well

highly strung easily upset, edgy, excitable, irascible, irritable, nervous, nervy (Brit. inf.), neurotic, restless, sensitive, stressed, taut, temperamental, tense

high-minded elevated, ethical, fair, good, honourable, idealistic, magnanimous, moral, noble, principled, pure, righteous, upright, virtuous, worthy

high-powered aggressive, driving, dynamic, effective, energetic, enterprising, forceful, go-ahead, go-getting (Inf.), highly capable, vigorous

high-pressure Of salesmanship aggressive, bludgeoning, coercive, compelling, forceful, high-powered, importunate, insistent, intensive, persistent, persuasive, pushy (Inf.)

high-sounding affected, artificial, bombastic, extravagant, flamboyant, florid, grandiloquent, grandiose, high-flown, imposing, magniloquent, ostentatious, overblown, pompous, pretentious, stilted, strained

high-speed brisk, express, fast, hotted-up (Inf.), quick, rapid, souped-up (Inf.), streamlined, swift

high-spirited animated, boisterous, bold, bouncy, daring, dashing, ebullient, effervescent, energetic, exuberant, frolicsome, full of life, fun-loving, gallant, lively, mettlesome, spirited, spunky (Inf.), vibrant, vital, vivacious

high spirits abandon, boisterousness, exhilaration, exuberance, good cheer, hilarity, joie de vivre, rare good humour

hijack commandeer, expropriate, seize, skyjack, take over

hike v. 1. back-pack, hoof it (Sl.), leg it (Inf.), ramble, tramp, walk 2. Usually with up hitch up, jack up, lift, pull up, raise ~n. 3. journey on foot, march, ramble, tramp, trek, walk

hilarious amusing, comical, convivial, entertaining, exhilarated, funny, gay, happy, humorous, jolly, jovial, joyful, joyous, merry, mirthful, noisy, rollicking, side-splitting, uproarious

hilarity amusement, boisterousness, cheerfulness, conviviality, exhilaration, exuberance, gaiety, glee, high spirits, jollification, jollity, joviality, joyousness, laughter, levity, merriment, mirth

hill 1. brae (Scot.), down (Archaic), elevation, eminence, fell, height, hillock, hilltop, knoll, mound, mount, prominence, tor 2. drift, heap, hummock, mound, pile, stack 3. acclivity, brae (Scot.), climb, gradient, incline, rise, slope

hillock barrow, hummock, knap (Dialect), knoll, monticule, mound, tump (Western Brit. dialect)

hilt 1. grip, haft, handgrip, handle, helve 2. **to the hilt** completely, entirely, fully, totally, wholly

him (hım; *unstressed* ım) *pron.* (*objective*) refers to a male person or animal: *they needed him; she baked him a cake; not him again!*
▷ **Usage.** See at **me.**

himself (hɪm'sɛlf; *medially often* ɪm'sɛlf) *pron.* **1. a.** the reflexive form of *he* or *him.* **b.** (intensifier): *the king himself waved to me.* **2.** (*preceded by a copula*) his normal self: *he seems himself once more.*
▷ **Usage.** See at **myself.**

hind[1] (haɪnd) *adj.* **hinder, hindmost** *or* **hindermost.** (*prenominal*) (esp. of parts of the body) situated at the back: *a hind leg.*

hind[2] (haɪnd) *n., pl.* **hinds** *or* **hind.** **1.** the female of the deer, esp. the red deer when aged three years or more. **2.** any of several marine fishes related to the grouper.

hinder[1] ('hɪndə) *vb.* **1.** to be or get in the way of (someone or something); hamper. **2.** (*tr.*) to prevent.

hinder[2] ('haɪndə) *adj.* (*prenominal*) situated at or further towards the back; posterior.

Hindi ('hɪndɪ) *n.* **1.** a language or group of dialects of N central India. See also **Hindustani.** **2.** a formal literary dialect of this language, the official language of India. **3.** a person whose native language is Hindi.

hindmost ('haɪnd,məʊst) *or* **hindermost** ('hɪndə-,məʊst) *adj.* furthest back; last.

hindrance ('hɪndrəns) *n.* **1.** an obstruction or snag; impediment. **2.** the act of hindering.

hindsight ('haɪnd,saɪt) *n.* **1.** the ability to understand, after something has happened, what should have been done. **2.** a firearm's rear sight.

Hindu *or* **Hindoo** ('hɪnduː; hɪn'duː) *n., pl.* **-dus** *or* **-doos.** **1.** a person who adheres to Hinduism. **2.** an inhabitant or native of Hindustan or India. ~*adj.* **3.** relating to Hinduism, Hindus, or India.

Hinduism *or* **Hindooism** ('hɪndʊ,ɪzəm) *n.* the complex of beliefs and customs comprising the dominant religion of India, characterized by the worship of many gods, a caste system, belief in reincarnation, etc.

Hindustani, Hindoostani (,hɪndʊ'stɑːnɪ), *or* **Hindostani** *n.* **1.** the dialect of Hindi spoken in Delhi: used as a lingua franca throughout India. **2.** all the spoken forms of Hindi and Urdu considered together. ~*adj.* **3.** of or relating to these languages or Hindustan.

hinge (hɪndʒ) *n.* **1.** a device for holding together two parts such that one can swing relative to the other. **2.** a natural joint, such as the knee joint, that functions in only one plane. **3.** something on which events, opinions, etc., turn. **4.** Also called: **mount.** *Philately.* a small transparent strip of gummed paper for affixing a stamp to a page. ~*vb.* **5.** (*tr.*) to fit a hinge to (something). **6.** (*intr.*; usually foll. by *on* or *upon*) to depend (on). **7.** (*intr.*) to hang or turn on or as if on a hinge. —**hinged** *adj.*

hinny[1] ('hɪnɪ) *n., pl.* **-nies.** the sterile hybrid offspring of a male horse and a female donkey.

hinny[2] ('hɪnɪ) *n. N English dialect.* a term of endearment, esp. for a woman.

hint (hɪnt) *n.* **1.** a suggestion given in an indirect or subtle manner. **2.** a helpful piece of advice. **3.** a small amount; trace. ~*vb.* **4.** (when *intr.*, often foll. by *at*; when *tr.*, takes a clause as object) to suggest indirectly.

hinterland ('hɪntə,lænd) *n.* **1.** land lying behind something, esp. a coast or the shore of a river. **2.** remote or undeveloped areas. **3.** an area near and dependent on a large city, esp. a port.

hip[1] (hɪp) *n.* **1.** (*often pl.*) either side of the body below the waist and above the thigh. **2.** another name for **pelvis** (sense 1). **3.** short for **hip joint. 4.** the angle formed where two sloping sides of a roof meet. —**'hipless** *adj.*

hip[2] (hɪp) *n.* the berry-like brightly coloured fruit of a rose plant. Also called: **rosehip.**

hip[3] (hɪp) *interj.* an exclamation used to introduce cheers (in **hip, hip, hurrah**).

hip[4] (hɪp) *adj.* **hipper, hippest** *Sl.* **1.** aware of or following the latest trends. **2.** (*often postpositive;* foll. by *to*) informed (about).

hip bath *n.* a portable bath in which the bather sits.

hipbone ('hɪp,bəʊn) *n.* the nontechnical name for **innominate bone.**

hip joint *n.* the ball-and-socket joint that connects each leg to the trunk of the body.

hipped (hɪpt) *adj.* **1. a.** having a hip or hips. **b.** (*in combination*): *broad-hipped.* **2.** (esp. of cows, sheep, etc.) having an injury to the hip, such as a dislocation. **3.** *Archit.* having a hip or hips: *hipped roof.*

hippie *or* **hippy** ('hɪpɪ) *n., pl.* **-pies.** (esp. during the 1960s) a person whose behaviour, dress, use of drugs, etc., implied a rejection of conventional values.

hippo ('hɪpəʊ) *n., pl.* **-pos.** *Inf.* short for **hippopotamus.**

Hippocratic oath (,hɪpəʊ'krætɪk) *n.* an oath taken by a doctor to observe a code of medical ethics derived from that of Hippocrates, (?460–?377 B.C.), Greek physician.

hippodrome ('hɪpə,drəʊm) *n.* **1.** a music hall, variety theatre, or circus. **2.** (in ancient Greece or Rome) an open-air course for horse and chariot races.

hippopotamus (,hɪpə'pɒtəməs) *n., pl.* **-muses** *or* **-mi** (-,maɪ). a very large gregarious mammal living in or around the rivers of tropical Africa.

hippy[1] ('hɪpɪ) *adj.* **-pier, -piest.** *Inf.* (esp. of a woman) having large hips.

hippy[2] ('hɪpɪ) *n., pl.* **-pies.** a variant spelling of **hippie.**

hip roof *n.* a roof having sloping ends and sides.

hipster ('hɪpstə) *n.* **1.** *Sl.* an outmoded word for **hippie. 2.** (*modifier*) (of trousers) cut so that the top encircles the hips.

hipsters ('hɪpstəz) *pl. n. Brit.* trousers cut so that the top encircles the hips. Usual U.S. word: **hip-huggers.**

hire (haɪə) *vb.* (*tr.*) **1.** to acquire the temporary use of (a thing) or the services of (a person) in exchange for payment. **2.** (often foll. by *out*) to provide (something) or the services of (oneself or others) for payment, usually for an agreed period. **3.** (*tr.*; foll. by *out*) Chiefly Brit. to pay independent contractors for (work to be done). ~*n.* **4. a.** the act of hiring or the state of being hired. **b.** (*as modifier*): *a hire car.* **5.** the price for a person's services or the temporary use of something. **6. for** *or* **on hire.** available for hire. —**'hirable** *or* **'hireable** *adj.* —**'hirer** *n.*

hireling ('haɪəlɪŋ) *n. Derog.* a person who works only for money.

hire-purchase *n. Brit.* a system in which a buyer takes possession of merchandise on payment of a deposit and completes the purchase by paying a series of instalments while the seller retains ownership until the final instalment is paid. Abbrev.: **H.P., h.p.** U.S. equivalent: **instalment buying.**

hirsute ('hɜːsjuːt) *adj.* **1.** covered with hair. **2.** (of plants) covered with long but not stiff hairs. —**'hirsuteness** *n.*

his (hɪz; *unstressed* ɪz) *determiner.* **1. a.** of, belonging to, or associated with him: *his knee; I don't like his being out so late.* **b.** (*as pronoun*): *his is on the left; that book is his.* **2. his and hers.** for a man and woman respectively. ~*pron.* **3. of his.** belonging to him.

Hispanic (hɪ'spænɪk) *adj.* of or derived from Spain or the Spanish. —**Hi'spanicism** *n.*

hiss (hɪs) *n.* **1.** a sound like that of a prolonged *s.* **2.** such a sound as an exclamation of derision, contempt, etc. ~*vb.* **3.** (*intr.*) to produce or utter a hiss. **4.** (*tr.*) to

---

THESAURUS

hind after, back, caudal (*Anat.*), hinder, posterior, rear

hinder arrest, check, debar, delay, deter, encumber, frustrate, hamper, hamstring, handicap, hold up *or* back, impede, interrupt, obstruct, oppose, prevent, retard, slow down, stop, stymie, thwart, trammel

hindmost concluding, final, furthest, furthest behind, last, most remote, rearmost, terminal, trailing, ultimate

hindrance bar, barrier, check, deterrent, difficulty, drag, drawback, encumbrance, handicap, hitch, impediment, interruption, limitation, obstacle, obstruction, restraint, restriction, snag, stoppage, stumbling block, trammel

hinge *v.* be contingent, be subject to, depend, hang, pivot, rest, revolve around, turn

hint *n.* **1.** allusion, clue, implication, indication, inkling, innuendo, insinuation, intimation, mention, reminder, suggestion, tip-off, word to the wise **2.** advice, help, pointer, suggestion, tip, wrinkle (*Inf.*) **3.** breath, dash, soupçon, speck, suggestion, suspicion, taste, tinge, touch, trace, undertone, whiff, whisper ~*v.* **4.** allude, cue, imply, indicate, insinuate, intimate, let it be known, mention, prompt, suggest, tip off

hippie beatnik, bohemian, dropout, flower child

hire *v.* **1.** appoint, commission, employ, engage, sign up, take on **2.** charter, engage, lease, let, rent ~*n.* **3.** charge, cost, fee, price, rent, rental

express with a hiss. **5.** (*tr.*) to show derision or anger towards (a speaker, performer, etc.) by hissing. —'**hisser** *n.*

hist (hıst) *interj.* an exclamation used to attract attention or as a warning to be silent.

histamine ('hıstə,miːn) *n.* an amine released by the body tissues in allergic reactions, causing irritation. Formula: $C_5H_9N_3$. —**histaminic** (,hıstə'mınık) *adj.*

histo- *or before a vowel* **hist-** *combining form.* indicating animal or plant tissue: *histology; histamine.*

histogram ('hıstə,græm) *n.* a figure that represents a frequency distribution, consisting of contiguous rectangles whose width is in proportion to the class interval under consideration and whose height is the associated frequency.

histology (hı'stɒlədʒı) *n.* the study of the tissues of an animal or plant. —**histological** (,hıstə'lɒdʒıkəl) *or* ,**histo'logic** *adj.*

historian (hı'stɔːrıən) *n.* a person who writes or studies history, esp. one who is an authority on it.

historic (hı'stɒrık) *adj.* **1.** famous in history; significant. **2.** *Linguistics.* (of Latin, Greek, or Sanskrit verb tenses) referring to past time.

▷ **Usage.** A distinction is made between *historic* (important, significant) and *historical* (pertaining to history): *a historic decision; a historical perspective.*

historical (hı'stɒrıkəl) *adj.* **1.** belonging to or typical of the study of history: *historical methods.* **2.** concerned with events of the past: *historical accounts.* **3.** based on or constituting factual material as distinct from legend or supposition. **4.** based on history: *a historical novel.* **5.** occurring in history. —**his'torically** *adv.*

▷ **Usage.** See at **historic.**

historicism (hı'stɒrı,sızəm) *n.* **1.** the belief that natural laws govern historical events. **2.** the theory that each period in history has its own values, inapplicable to other periods. **3.** excessive emphasis on history, past styles, etc. —**his'toricist** *n., adj.*

historicity (,hıstɒ'rısıtı) *n.* historical authenticity.

historiographer (hı,stɔːrı'ɒgrəfə) *n.* **1.** a historian, esp. one concerned with historical method. **2.** a historian employed to write the history of a group or public institution. —**hi,stori'ography** *n.*

history ('hıstərı) *n., pl.* -**ries. 1.** a record or account of past events, developments, etc. **2.** all that is preserved of the past, esp. in written form. **3.** the discipline of recording and interpreting past events. **4.** past events, esp. when considered as an aggregate. **5.** an event in the past, esp. one that has been reduced in importance: *their quarrel was just history.* **6.** the past, previous experiences, etc., of a thing or person: *the house had a strange history.* **7.** a play that depicts historical events. **8.** a narrative relating the events of a character's life: *the history of Joseph Andrews.*

histrionic (,hıstrı'ɒnık) *adj.* **1.** excessively dramatic or artificial: *histrionic gestures.* **2.** *Now rare.* dramatic. ~*n.* **3.** (*pl.*) melodramatic displays of temperament. **4.** *Rare.* (*pl., functioning as sing.*) dramatics. —,**histri'onically** *adv.*

hit (hıt) *vb.* **hitting, hit.** (*mainly tr.*) **1.** (*also intr.*) to deal (a blow) to (a person or thing); strike. **2.** to come

into violent contact with: *the car hit the tree.* **3.** to strike with a missile: *to hit a target.* **4.** to knock or bump: *I hit my arm on the table.* **5.** to propel by striking: *to hit a ball.* **6.** *Cricket.* to score (runs). **7.** to affect (a person, place, or thing), esp. suddenly or adversely: *his illness hit his wife very hard.* **8.** to reach: *unemployment hit a new high.* **9.** to experience: *I've hit a slight snag here.* **10.** *U.S. sl.* to murder (a rival criminal) in fulfilment of an underworld vendetta. **11.** *Inf.* to set out on: *let's hit the road.* **12.** *Inf.* to arrive: *he will hit town tomorrow.* **13.** *Inf., chiefly U.S.* to demand or request from: *he hit me for a pound.* **14. hit the bottle.** *Sl.* to drink an excessive amount of alcohol. **15. hit the sack** (*or* **hay**). *Sl.* to go to bed. ~*n.* **16.** an impact or collision. **17. a.** a shot, blow, etc., that reaches its object. **b.** (*as modifier*): *a hit list; a hit squad.* **18.** an apt, witty, or telling remark. **19.** *Inf.* **a.** a person or thing that gains wide appeal: *she's a hit with everyone.* **b.** (*as modifier*): *a hit record.* **20.** *Inf.* a stroke of luck. **21.** *U.S. sl.* a murder carried out as the result of an underworld vendetta. **22. make a hit with.** *Inf.* to make a favourable impression on. ~See also **hit off, hit on, hit out.** —'**hitter** *n.*

hit-and-run *adj.* (*prenominal*) **1.** denoting a motor-vehicle accident in which the driver leaves the scene without stopping to give assistance, inform the police, etc. **2.** (of an attack, raid, etc.) relying on surprise allied to a rapid departure from the scene of operations: *hit-and-run tactics.*

hitch (hıtʃ) *vb.* **1.** to fasten or become fastened with a knot or tie. **2.** (*tr.*; often foll. by *up*) to pull up (the trousers, etc.) with a quick jerk. **3.** (*intr.*) *Chiefly U.S.* to move in a halting manner. **4.** (*tr.*; *passive*) *Inf.* to marry (esp. in **get hitched**). **5.** *Inf.* to obtain (a ride) by hitchhiking. ~*n.* **6.** an impediment or obstacle, esp. one that is temporary or minor. **7.** a knot that can be undone by pulling against the direction of the strain that holds it. **8.** a sudden jerk: *he gave it a hitch and it came loose.* **9.** *Inf.* a ride obtained by hitchhiking. —'**hitcher** *n.*

hitchhike ('hıtʃ,haık) *vb.* (*intr.*) to travel by obtaining free lifts in motor vehicles. —'**hitch,hiker** *n.*

hither ('hıðə) *adv.* **1.** to or towards this place (esp. in **come hither**). **2. hither and thither.** this way and that, as in confusion. ~*adj.* **3.** *Arch. or dialect.* (of a side or part) nearer; closer.

hitherto ('hıðə'tuː) *adv.* until this time: *hitherto, there have been no problems.*

hit man *n.* a hired assassin.

hit off *vb.* **1.** (*tr., adv.*) to represent or mimic accurately. **2. hit it off.** *Inf.* to have a good relationship with.

hit on *vb.* (*intr., prep.*) to discover unexpectedly or guess correctly. Also: **hit upon.**

hit or miss *adj.* (**hit-or-miss** *when prenominal*) *Inf.* random; casual; haphazard. Also: **hit and miss.**

hit out *vb.* (*intr., adv.*; often foll. by *at*) **1.** to direct blows forcefully and vigorously. **2.** to make a verbal attack (upon someone).

Hittite ('hıtaıt) *n.* **1.** a member of an ancient people of Anatolia, who built a great empire in N Syria and Asia Minor in the second millennium B.C. **2.** the extinct language of this people. ~*adj.* **3.** of or relating to this peo-

---

THESAURUS

hiss *n.* 1. buzz, hissing, sibilance, sibilation 2. boo, catcall, contempt, derision, jeer, raspberry ~*v.* 3. rasp, shrill, sibilate, wheeze, whirr, whistle, whiz 4. blow a raspberry, boo, catcall, condemn, damn, decry, deride, hoot, jeer, mock, revile, ridicule

historian annalist, biographer, chronicler, historiographer, recorder

historic celebrated, consequential, epoch-making, extraordinary, famous, momentous, notable, outstanding, red-letter, remarkable, significant

historical actual, archival, attested, authentic, chronicled, documented, factual, real, veritable

history 1. account, annals, autobiography, biography, chronicle, memoirs, narration, narrative, recapitulation, recital, record, relation, saga, story 2. ancient history, antiquity, bygone times, days of old, days of yore, olden days, the good old days, the old days, the past, yesterday, yesteryear

hit *v.* 1. bang, bash (*Inf.*), batter, beat, belt (*Sl.*), clip (*Sl.*), clobber (*Sl.*), clout (*Inf.*), cuff, flog, knock, lob, punch, slap, smack, smite (*Archaic*), sock (*Sl.*), strike, swat, thump, wallop (*Inf.*), whack 2. bang into, bump, clash with, collide with, crash against, meet head-on, run into, smash into 3. accomplish, achieve, arrive at, attain, gain, reach, secure, strike, touch 4. affect, damage, devastate, impinge on, influence, leave a mark on, make an impact *or* impression on, move, overwhelm, touch ~*n.* 5. blow, bump, clash, clout (*Inf.*), collision, cuff, impact, knock, rap, shot, slap, smack, stroke, swipe (*Inf.*), wallop (*Inf.*) 6. *Inf.* sellout, sensation, smash (*Inf.*), success, triumph, winner

hitch *v.* 1. attach, connect, couple, fasten, harness, join, make fast, tether, tie, unite, yoke 2. *Often with* up hoick, jerk, pull, tug, yank 3. *Inf.* hitchhike, thumb a lift ~*n.* 4. catch, check, delay, difficulty, drawback, hindrance, hold-up, impediment, mishap, prob-

lem, snag, stoppage, trouble

hither close, closer, here, near, nearer, nigh (*Archaic*), over here, to this place

hitherto heretofore, previously, so far, thus far, till now, until now, up to now

hit off 1. capture, catch, impersonate, mimic, represent, take off (*Inf.*) 2. **hit it off** *Inf.* be on good terms, click (*Sl.*), get on (well) with, take to, warm to

hit on *or* **upon** arrive at, chance upon, come upon, discover, guess, invent, light upon, realize, strike upon, stumble on, think up

hit or miss aimless, casual, cursory, disorganized, haphazard, indiscriminate, perfunctory, random, undirected, uneven

hit out (at) assail, attack, castigate, condemn, denounce, inveigh against, lash out, rail against, strike out at

ple, their civilization, or their language.

hive (haɪv) *n.* **1.** a structure in which social bees live. **2.** a colony of social bees. **3.** a place showing signs of great industry (esp. in **a hive of activity**). **4.** a teeming multitude. ~*vb.* **5.** to cause (bees) to collect or (of bees) to collect inside a hive. **6.** to live or cause to live in or as if in a hive. **7.** (*tr.;* often foll. by *up* or *away*) to store, esp. for future use. —'**hive,like** *adj.*

hive off *vb.* (*adv.*) **1.** to transfer or be transferred from a larger group or unit. **2.** (*usually tr.*) to transfer (profitable activities of a nationalized industry) back to private ownership.

H.L. (in Britain) *abbrev. for* House of Lords.

H.M. *abbrev. for:* **1.** His (*or* Her) Majesty. **2.** headmaster; headmistress.

H.M.A.S. *abbrev. for* His (*or* Her) Majesty's Australian Ship.

H.M.C.S. *abbrev. for* His (*or* Her) Majesty's Canadian Ship.

H.M.I. (in Britain) *abbrev. for* Her Majesty's Inspector; a government official who examines and supervises schools.

H.M.S. *abbrev. for:* **1.** His (*or* Her) Majesty's Service. **2.** His (*or* Her) Majesty's Ship.

H.M.S.O. (in Britain) *abbrev. for* His (*or* Her) Majesty's Stationery Office.

H.N.C. (in Britain) *abbrev. for* Higher National Certificate; a qualification recognized by many national technical and professional institutions.

H.N.D. (in Britain) *abbrev. for* Higher National Diploma; a qualification in technical subjects equivalent to an ordinary degree.

ho (həʊ) *interj.* **1.** Also: **ho-ho.** an imitation or representation of the sound of a deep laugh. **2.** an exclamation used to attract attention, etc.

Ho *the chemical symbol for* holmium.

hoar (hɔː) *n.* **1.** short for **hoarfrost.** ~*adj.* **2.** *Rare.* covered with hoarfrost. **3.** *Arch.* a poetic variant of **hoary.**

hoard (hɔːd) *n.* **1.** an accumulated store hidden away for future use. **2.** a cache of ancient coins, treasure, etc. ~*vb.* **3.** to gather or accumulate (a hoard). —'**hoarder** *n.*

hoarding ('hɔːdɪŋ) *n.* **1.** Also called (esp. U.S.): **billboard.** a large board used for displaying advertising posters, as by a road. **2.** a temporary wooden fence erected around an area while construction or repairs are in progress.

hoarfrost ('hɔː,frɒst) *n.* a deposit of needle-like ice crystals formed on the ground by direct condensation at temperatures below freezing point. Also called: **white frost.**

hoarse (hɔːs) *adj.* **1.** gratingly harsh in tone. **2.** having a husky voice, as through illness, shouting, etc. —'**hoarsely** *adv.* —'**hoarseness** *n.*

hoary ('hɔːrɪ) *adj.* **hoarier, hoariest. 1.** having grey or white hair. **2.** white or whitish-grey in colour. **3.** ancient or venerable. —'**hoariness** *n.*

hoax (həʊks) *n.* **1.** a deception, esp. a practical joke. ~*vb.* **2.** (*tr.*) to deceive or play a joke on (someone). —'**hoaxer** *n.*

hob[1] (hɒb) *n.* **1.** the flat top part of a cooking stove, or a separate flat surface, containing hotplates or burners. **2.** a shelf beside an open fire, for keeping kettles, etc., hot. **3.** a steel pattern used in forming a mould or die in cold metal.

hob[2] (hɒb) *n.* **1.** a hobgoblin or elf. **2. raise** *or* **play hob.** *U.S. inf.* to cause mischief.

hobble ('hɒbəl) *vb.* **1.** (*intr.*) to walk with a lame awkward movement. **2.** (*tr.*) to fetter the legs of (a horse) in order to restrict movement. **3.** to progress with difficul-

ty. ~*n.* **4.** a strap, rope, etc., used to hobble a horse. **5.** a limping gait. ~Also (for senses 2, 4): **hopple.** —'**hobbler** *n.*

hobby ('hɒbɪ) *n., pl.* **-bies. 1.** an activity pursued in spare time for pleasure or relaxation. **2.** *Arch.* a small horse. **3.** short for **hobbyhorse** (sense 1). **4.** an early form of bicycle, without pedals. —'**hobbyist** *n.*

hobbyhorse ('hɒbɪ,hɔːs) *n.* **1.** a toy consisting of a stick with a figure of a horse's head at one end. **2.** a rocking horse. **3.** a figure of a horse attached to a performer's waist in a morris dance, etc. **4.** a favourite topic (esp. in **on one's hobbyhorse**).

hobgoblin (hɒb'gɒblɪn) *n.* **1.** a mischievous goblin. **2.** bogy.

hobnail ('hɒb,neɪl) *n.* **a.** a short nail with a large head for protecting the soles of heavy footwear. **b.** (*as modifier*): **hobnail boots.** —'**hob,nailed** *adj.*

hobnob ('hɒb,nɒb) *vb.* **-nobbing, -nobbed.** (*intr.;* often foll. by *with*) **1.** to socialize or talk informally. **2.** *Obs.* to drink (with).

hobo ('həʊbəʊ) *n., pl.* **-bos** *or* **-boes.** *Chiefly U.S.* **1.** a tramp; vagrant. **2.** a migratory worker. —'**hoboism** *n.*

Hobson's choice ('hɒbsənz) *n.* the choice of taking what is offered or nothing at all.

hock[1] (hɒk) *n.* **1.** the joint at the tarsus of a horse or similar animal, corresponding to the human ankle. ~*vb.* **2.** another word for **hamstring.**

hock[2] (hɒk) *n.* any of several white wines from the German Rhine.

hock[3] (hɒk) *Inf., chiefly U.S.* ~*vb.* **1.** (*tr.*) to pawn or pledge. ~*n.* **2.** the state of being in pawn. **3. in hock. a.** in prison. **b.** in debt. **c.** in pawn. —'**hocker** *n.*

hockey ('hɒkɪ) *n.* **1.** Also called (esp. U.S. & Canad.): **field hockey.** a game played on a field by two opposing teams of 11 players each, who try to hit a ball into their opponents' goal using long sticks curved at the end. **2.** See **ice hockey.**

hocus-pocus ('həʊkəs'pəʊkəs) *n.* **1.** trickery or chicanery. **2.** an incantation used by conjurers or magicians. **3.** conjuring skill. ~*vb.* **-cusing, -cused** *or* **-cussing, -cussed. 4.** to deceive or trick (someone).

hod (hɒd) *n.* **1.** an open wooden box attached to a pole, for carrying bricks, mortar, etc. **2.** a tall narrow coal scuttle.

hodgepodge ('hɒdʒ,pɒdʒ) *n.* a variant spelling (esp. U.S.) of **hotchpotch.**

Hodgkin's disease ('hɒdʒkɪnz) *n.* a malignant disease characterized by enlargement of the lymph nodes, spleen, and liver.

hodometer (hɒ'dɒmɪtə) *n.* another name for **odometer.** —ho'**dometry** *n.*

hoe (həʊ) *n.* **1.** any of several kinds of long-handled hand implement used to till the soil, weed, etc. ~*vb.* **hoeing, hoed. 2.** to dig, scrape, weed, or till (surface soil) with or as if with a hoe. —'**hoer** *n.*

hog (hɒg) *n.* **1.** a domesticated pig, esp. a castrated male. **2.** *U.S.* any mammal of the family *Suidae;* pig. **3.** Also: **hogget** ('hɒgɪt), **hogg.** *Brit. dialect.* a young sheep that has yet to be sheared. **4.** *Inf.* a greedy person. **5. go the whole hog.** *Sl.* to do something thoroughly or unreservedly. ~*vb.* **hogging, hogged. 6.** *Sl.* to take more than one's share of. **7.** (*tr.*) to arch (the back) like a hog. **8.** (*tr.*) to cut (the mane) of (a horse) very short. —'**hogger** *n.* —'**hog,like** *adj.*

hogback ('hɒg,bæk) *n.* **1.** Also called: **hog's back.** a narrow ridge with steep sides. **2.** *Archaeol.* a tomb with sloping sides.

Hogmanay (,hɒgmə'neɪ) *n.* (*sometimes not cap.*) New Year's Eve in Scotland.

hogshead ('hɒgz,hed) *n.* **1.** a unit of capacity, used esp.

THESAURUS

hoard 1. *n.* accumulation, cache, fund, heap, mass, pile, reserve, stockpile, store, supply, treasure-trove **2.** *v.* accumulate, amass, buy up, cache, collect, deposit, garner, gather, hive, lay up, put away, put by, save, stash away (*Inf.*), stockpile, store, treasure

hoarder collector, magpie (*Brit.*), miser, niggard, saver, squirrel (*Inf.*)

hoarse croaky, discordant, grating, gravelly, growling, gruff, guttural, harsh, husky, rasping, raucous, rough, throaty

hoary 1. frosty, grey, grey-haired, grizzled, hoar, silvery, white, white-haired **2.** aged, ancient, antiquated, antique, old, venerable

hoax 1. *n.* cheat, con (*Sl.*), deception, fast one (*Inf.*), fraud, imposture, joke, practical joke, prank, ruse, spoof (*Inf.*), swindle, trick **2.** *v.* bamboozle (*Inf.*), befool, bluff, con (*Sl.*), deceive, delude, dupe, fool, gammon (*Inf.*), gull, (*Archaic*), hoodwink, hornswoggle (*Sl.*), swindle, take in (*Inf.*), take (someone) for a ride (*Inf.*), trick

hobby diversion, favourite occupation, (lei-

sure) activity, leisure pursuit, pastime, relaxation, sideline

hobnob associate, consort, fraternize, hang about, keep company, mingle, mix, socialize

hogwash balderdash, bilge (*Inf.*), bunk (*Inf.*), drivel, hooey (*Sl.*), nonsense, piffle (*Inf.*), rot, rubbish, tosh (*Brit. inf.*), trash, tripe (*Inf.*), twaddle

for alcoholic beverages. It has several values. **2.** a large cask.

hogwash ('hɒg‚wɒʃ) *n.* **1.** nonsense. **2.** pigswill.

hoick (hɔɪk) *vb.* to rise or raise abruptly and sharply.

hoi polloi ('hɔɪ pə'lɔɪ) *n.* **the.** *Often derog.* the masses; common people.

hoist (hɔɪst) *vb.* **1.** (*tr.*) to raise or lift up, esp. by mechanical means. **2. hoist with one's own petard.** See **petard.** ~*n.* **3.** any apparatus or device for hoisting. **4.** the act of hoisting. **5.** *Austral.* a rotary apparatus on which clothes can be hung to dry. **6.** *Naut.* a group of signal flags. **7.** the inner edge of a flag next to the staff. —'**hoister** *n.*

hoity-toity (‚hɔɪtɪ'tɔɪtɪ) *adj. Inf.* arrogant or haughty.

hokum ('həʊkəm) *n. U.S. sl.* **1.** claptrap; bunk. **2.** obvious or hackneyed material of a sentimental nature in a play, film, etc.

hold[1] (həʊld) *vb.* **holding, held.** **1.** to have or keep (an object) with or within the hands, arms, etc.; clasp. **2.** (*tr.*) to support: *to hold a drowning man's head above water.* **3.** to maintain or be maintained in a specified state: *to hold firm.* **4.** (*tr.*) to set aside or reserve: *they will hold our tickets until tomorrow.* **5.** (when *intr.,* usually used in commands) to restrain or be restrained from motion, action, departure, etc.: *hold that man until the police come.* **6.** (*intr.*) to remain fast or unbroken: *that cable won't hold much longer.* **7.** (*intr.*) (of the weather) to remain dry and bright. **8.** (*tr.*) to keep the attention of. **9.** (*tr.*) to engage in or carry on: *to hold a meeting.* **10.** (*tr.*) to have the ownership, possession, etc., of: *he holds a law degree; who's holding the ace?* **11.** (*tr.*) to have the use of or responsibility for: *to hold office.* **12.** (*tr.*) to have the capacity for: *the carton will hold eight books.* **13.** (*tr.*) to be able to control the outward effects of drinking beer, spirits, etc. **14.** (often foll. by *to* or *by*) to remain or cause to remain committed to: *hold him to his promise.* **15.** (*tr.; takes a clause as object*) to claim: *he holds that the theory is incorrect.* **16.** (*intr.*) to remain relevant, valid, or true: *the old philosophies don't hold nowadays.* **17.** (*tr.*) to consider in a specified manner: *I hold him very dear.* **18.** (*tr.*) to defend successfully: *hold the fort against the attack.* **19.** (sometimes foll. by *on*) *Music.* to sustain the sound of (a note) throughout its specified duration. **20.** (*tr.*) *Computers.* to retain (data) in a storage device after copying onto another storage device or location. **21. hold (good) for.** to apply or be relevant to: *the same rules hold for everyone.* **22. hold one's own. a.** to maintain one's position. **b.** to be sufficiently competent: *she can't hold her own in the top class.* **23. hold one's peace** or **tongue.** *Inf.* to be silent. **24. hold water.** to stand up to examination. **25. there is no holding him.** he is so spirited that he cannot be restrained. ~*n.* **26.** the act or method of holding fast or grasping. **27.** something to hold onto, as for support or control. **28.** an object or device that holds fast or grips something else. **29.** controlling influence: *she has a hold on him.* **30.** a short pause. **31.** a prison or a cell in a prison. **32.** *Wrestling.* a way of seizing one's opponent. **33.** *Music.* a pause or fermata. **34. a.** a tenure, esp. of

land. **b.** (*in combination*): *freehold.* **35.** *Arch.* a fortified place. **36. no holds barred.** all limitations removed. ~See also **hold back, hold down,** etc. —'**holdable** *adj.* —'**holder** *n.*

hold[2] (həʊld) *n.* the space in a ship or aircraft for storing cargo.

holdall ('həʊld‚ɔːl) *n. Brit.* a large strong bag or basket. Usual U.S. name: **carryall.**

hold back *vb.* (*adv.*) **1.** to restrain or be restrained. **2.** (*tr.*) to withhold: *he held back part of the payment.*

hold down *vb.* (*tr., adv.*) **1.** to restrain or control. **2.** *Inf.* to manage to retain or keep possession of: *to hold down two jobs at once.*

holdfast ('həʊld‚fɑːst) *n.* **1.** the act of gripping strongly. **2.** any device used to secure an object, such as a hook, clamp, etc. **3.** the organ of attachment of a seaweed or related plant.

hold forth *vb.* (*adv.*) **1.** (*intr.*) to speak for a long time or in public. **2.** (*tr.*) to offer (an attraction or enticement).

hold in *vb.* (*tr., adv.*) **1.** to curb, control, or keep in check. **2.** to conceal (feelings).

holding ('həʊldɪŋ) *n.* **1.** land held under a lease. **2.** (*often pl.*) property to which the holder has legal title, such as land, stocks, shares, and other investments. **3.** *Sport.* the obstruction of an opponent with the hands or arms, esp. in boxing.

holding company *n.* a company with controlling shareholdings in one or more other companies.

hold off *vb.* (*adv.*) **1.** (*tr.*) to keep apart or at a distance. **2.** (*intr.;* often foll. by *from*) to refrain (from doing something).

hold on *vb.* (*intr., adv.*) **1.** to maintain a firm grasp. **2.** to continue or persist. **3.** (foll. by *to*) to keep or retain: *hold on to those stamps as they'll soon be valuable.* **4.** *Inf.* to keep a telephone line open. ~*interj.* **5.** *Inf.* stop! wait!

hold out *vb.* (*adv.*) **1.** (*tr.*) to offer. **2.** (*intr.*) to last or endure. **3.** (*intr.*) to continue to stand firm, as a person refusing to succumb to persuasion. **4.** *Chiefly U.S.* to withhold (something due). **5. hold out for.** *Inf.* to wait patiently for (the fulfilment of one's demands). **6. hold out on.** *Inf.* to keep from telling (a person) some important information.

hold over *vb.* (*tr., mainly adv.*) **1.** to defer or postpone. **2.** (*prep.*) to intimidate (a person) with (a threat).

hold-up *n.* **1.** a robbery, esp. an armed one. **2.** a delay; stoppage. ~*vb.* **hold up.** (*adv.*) **3.** (*tr.*) to delay; hinder. **4.** (*tr.*) to support. **5.** (*tr.*) to waylay in order to rob, esp. using a weapon. **6.** (*tr.*) to exhibit or present.

hold with *vb.* (*intr., prep.*) to support; approve of.

hole (həʊl) *n.* **1.** an area hollowed out in a solid. **2.** an opening in or through something. **3.** an animal's burrow. **4.** *Inf.* an unattractive place, such as a town. **5.** a fault: *he picked holes in my argument.* **6.** *Sl.* a difficult and embarrassing situation. **7.** the cavity in various games into which the ball must be thrust. **8.** (on a golf course) **a.** each of the divisions of a course (usually 18) represented by the distance between the tee and a green. **b.**

THESAURUS

hoi polloi admass, *canaille,* commonalty, riffraff, the (common) herd, the common people, the great unwashed (*Inf. and derogatory*), the lower orders, the masses, the plebs, the populace, the proles (*Derogatory sl., chiefly Brit.*), the proletariat, the rabble, the third estate

hoist 1. *v.* elevate, erect, heave, lift, raise, rear, upraise 2. *n.* crane, elevator, lift, tackle, winch

hold *v.* 1. have, keep, maintain, occupy, own, possess, retain 2. adhere, clasp, cleave, clinch, cling, clutch, cradle, embrace, enfold, grasp, grip, stick 3. arrest, bind, check, confine, curb, detain, imprison, restrain, stay, stop, suspend 4. assume, believe, consider, deem, entertain, esteem, judge, maintain, presume, reckon, regard, think, view 5. continue, endure, last, persevere, persist, remain, resist, stay, wear 6. assemble, call, carry on, celebrate, conduct, convene, have, officiate at, preside over, run, solemnize 7. bear, brace, carry, prop, shoulder, support, sustain, take 8. accommodate, comprise,

contain, have a capacity for, seat, take 9. apply, be in force, be the case, exist, hold good, operate, remain true, remain valid, stand up 10. **hold one's own** do well, hold fast, hold out, keep one's head above water, keep pace, keep up, maintain one's position, stand firm, stand one's ground, stay put, stick to one's guns (*Inf.*) ~*n.* 11. clasp, clutch, grasp, grip 12. anchorage, foothold, footing, leverage, prop, purchase, stay, support, vantage 13. ascendancy, authority, clout (*Inf.*), control, dominance, dominion, influence, mastery, pull (*Inf.*), sway

hold back 1. check, control, curb, inhibit, repress, restrain, suppress 2. desist, forbear, keep back, refuse, withhold

holder 1. bearer, custodian, incumbent, keeper, occupant, owner, possessor, proprietor, purchaser 2. case, container, cover, housing, receptacle, sheath

hold forth declaim, descant, discourse, go on (*Inf.*), harangue, lecture, orate, preach, speak, speechify, spiel (*Inf.*), spout (*Inf.*)

hold off 1. avoid, defer, delay, keep from,

postpone, put off, refrain 2. fend off, keep off, rebuff, repel, repulse, stave off

hold out 1. extend, give, offer, present, proffer 2. carry on, continue, endure, hang on, last, persevere, persist, stand fast, withstand

hold over adjourn, defer, delay, postpone, put off, suspend, waive

hold-up 1. bottleneck, delay, difficulty, hitch, obstruction, setback, snag, stoppage, traffic jam, trouble, wait 2. burglary, mugging (*Inf.*), robbery, stick-up (*Sl.*), theft

hold up 1. delay, detain, hinder, impede, retard, set back, slow down, stop 2. brace, buttress, jack up, prop, shore up, support, sustain 3. mug (*Inf.*), rob, stick up (*Sl.*), waylay 4. display, exhibit, flaunt, present, show 5. bear up, endure, last, survive, wear

hold with agree to *or* with, approve of, be in favour of, countenance, subscribe to, support, take kindly to

the score made in striking the ball from the tee into the hole. **9.** *Physics.* a vacancy in a normally filled band of electron energies that behaves as a carrier of charge and is mathematically equivalent to a positron. **10. hole in the wall.** *Inf.* a small dingy place, esp. one difficult to find. **11. make a hole in.** to consume or use a great amount of (food, drink, money, etc.). ~*vb.* **12.** to make a hole or holes in (something). **13.** (when *intr.*, often foll. by *out*) *Golf.* to hit (the ball) into the hole. —**'holey** *adj.*

hole-and-corner *adj.* (*usually prenominal*) *Inf.* furtive or secretive.

hole up *vb.* (*intr., adv.*) *Chiefly U.S.* **1.** (of an animal) to hibernate. **2.** to hide or remain secluded.

holiday ('hɒlɪˌdeɪ) *n.* **1.** (*often pl.*) *Chiefly Brit.* a period in which a break is taken from work or studies for rest, travel, or recreation. U.S. word: **vacation. 2.** a day on which work is suspended by law or custom, such as a religious festival, bank holiday, etc. Related adj.: **ferial.** ~*vb.* **3.** (*intr.*) *Chiefly Brit.* to spend a holiday.

holiness ('həʊlɪnɪs) *n.* the state or quality of being holy.

Holiness ('həʊlɪnɪs) *n.* (preceded by *his* or *your*) a title reserved for the pope.

holism ('həʊlɪzəm) *n. Philosophy.* the idea that the whole is greater than the sum of its parts. —**ho'listic** *adj.*

holland ('hɒlənd) *n.* a coarse linen cloth.

hollandaise sauce (ˌhɒlənˈdeɪz, ˈhɒlənˌdeɪz) *n.* a rich sauce of egg yolks, butter, vinegar, etc.

Hollands ('hɒləndz) *n.* Dutch gin, often sold in stone bottles.

holler ('hɒlə) *Inf.* ~*vb.* **1.** to shout or yell (something). ~*n.* **2.** a shout; call.

hollo ('hɒləʊ) *or* **holla** ('hɒlə) *n., pl.* **-los** *or* **-las.** *interj.* **1.** a cry for attention, or of encouragement. ~*vb.* **2.** (*intr.*) to shout.

hollow ('hɒləʊ) *adj.* **1.** having a hole or space within; not solid. **2.** having a sunken area; concave. **3.** deeply set: *hollow cheeks.* **4.** (of sounds) as if resounding in a hollow place. **5.** without substance or validity. **6.** hungry or empty. **7.** insincere; cynical. **8. beat (someone) hollow.** *Brit. inf.* to defeat thoroughly. ~*n.* **9.** a cavity, opening, or space in or within something. **10.** a depression in the land. ~*vb.* (*often foll. by out,* usually when *tr.*) **11.** to make or become hollow. **12.** to form (a hole, cavity, etc.) or (of a hole, etc.) to be formed. —**'hollowly** *adv.* —**'hollowness** *n.*

holly ('hɒlɪ) *n., pl.* **-lies. 1.** a tree or shrub having bright red berries and shiny evergreen leaves with prickly edges. **2.** its branches, used for Christmas decorations. **3. holly oak.** another name for **holm oak.**

hollyhock ('hɒlɪˌhɒk) *n.* a tall plant with stout hairy stems and spikes of white, yellow, red, or purple flowers. Also called (U.S.): **rose mallow.**

holmium ('hɒlmɪəm) *n.* a malleable silver-white metallic element of the lanthanide series. Symbol: Ho; atomic no.: 67; atomic wt.: 164.93.

holm oak (həʊm) *n.* an evergreen Mediterranean oak tree with prickly leaves resembling holly. Also called: **holm, holly oak, ilex.**

holo- *or before a vowel* **hol-** *combining form.* whole or wholly: *holograph.*

holocaust ('hɒləˌkɔːst) *n.* **1.** great destruction or loss of life or the source of such destruction, esp. fire. **2.** (*usually cap.*) **the.** the mass murder of Jews in Nazi Germany.

holograph ('hɒləˌgræf, -ˌgrɑːf) *n.* a book or document handwritten by its author; original manuscript; autograph.

holography (hɒˈlɒgrəfɪ) *n.* the science of producing a photographic record (**hologram**) by illuminating the object with coherent light and exposing a film to light reflected from this object and to a direct beam of the coherent light. When interference patterns on the film are illuminated by the coherent light a three-dimensional image is produced. —**holographic** (ˌhɒlə-ˈgræfɪk) *adj.* —ˌholo'graphically *adv.*

hols (hɒlz) *pl. n. Brit. school sl.* holidays.

holster ('həʊlstə) *n.* a sheathlike leather case for a pistol, attached to a belt or saddle.

holy ('həʊlɪ) *adj.* **-lier, -liest. 1.** of or associated with God or a deity; sacred. **2.** endowed or invested with extreme purity. **3.** devout or virtuous. **4. holier-than-thou.** offensively sanctimonious or self-righteous. ~*n., pl.* **-lies. 5.** a sacred place.

Holy Communion *n.* **1.** the celebration of the Eucharist. **2.** the consecrated elements.

Holy Ghost *or* **Spirit** *n. Christianity.* the third person of the Trinity.

Holy Grail *n.* (in medieval legend) the bowl used by Jesus at the Last Supper. It was brought to Britain by Joseph of Arimathea, where it became the quest of many knights. Also called: **Grail, Sangraal.**

Holy Land *n.* **the.** another name for Palestine.

holy of holies *n.* **1.** any place of special sanctity. **2.** the innermost compartment of the Jewish tabernacle, where the Ark was enshrined.

holy orders *n.* **1.** the sacrament whereby a person is admitted to the Christian ministry. **2.** the grades of the Christian ministry. **3.** the status of an ordained Christian minister.

Holy See *n. R.C. Church.* **1.** the see of the pope as bishop of Rome. **2.** the Roman curia.

Holy Spirit *n.* another name for the **Holy Ghost.**

Holy Week *n.* the week preceding Easter Sunday.

homage ('hɒmɪdʒ) *n.* **1.** a public show of respect or honour towards someone or something (esp. in **pay** *or* **do homage to**). **2.** (in feudal society) the act of respect and allegiance made by a vassal to his lord.

homburg ('hɒmbɜːg) *n.* a man's hat of soft felt with a dented crown and a stiff upturned brim.

home (həʊm) *n.* **1.** the place where one lives. **2.** a house or other dwelling. **3.** a family or other group living in a house. **4.** a person's country, city, etc., esp. viewed as a birthplace or a place dear to one. **5.** the habitat of an animal. **6.** the place where something is invented, founded, or developed. **7.** a building or organization set up to care for people in a certain category, such as orphans, the aged, etc. **8.** *Sport.* one's own ground: *the match is at home.* **9. a.** the objective towards which a player strives in certain sports. **b.** an area where a player is safe from attack. **10. a home from home.** a place other than one's own home where one can be at ease. **11. at home. a.** in one's own home or country. **b.**

THESAURUS

hole 1. aperture, breach, break, crack, fissure, gap, opening, orifice, outlet, perforation, puncture, rent, split, tear, vent **2.** cave, cavern, cavity, chamber, depression, excavation, hollow, pit, pocket, scoop, shaft **3.** burrow, covert, den, earth, lair, nest, retreat, shelter **4.** *Inf.* dive (*Sl.*), dump (*Sl.*), hovel, joint (*Sl.*), slum **5.** *Inf.* cell, dungeon, oubliette, prison **6.** defect, discrepancy, error, fallacy, fault, flaw, inconsistency, loophole **7.** *Sl.* dilemma, fix (*Inf.*), imbroglio, jam (*Inf.*), mess, predicament, quandary, scrape (*Inf.*), tangle, (tight) spot (*Inf.*) **8. pick holes in** cavil, crab (*Inf.*), criticize, denigrate, disparage, disprove, find fault, niggle, pull to pieces, run down, slate (*Inf.*)

hole-and-corner backstairs, clandestine, furtive, secret, secretive, sneaky (*Inf.*), stealthy, surreptitious, underhand, under the counter (*Inf.*)

holiday 1. break, leave, recess, time off,

vacation **2.** anniversary, bank holiday, celebration, feast, festival, festivity, fête, gala, public holiday, saint's day

holier-than-thou goody-goody (*Inf.*), pietistic, pietistical, priggish, religiose, sanctimonious, self-righteous, self-satisfied, smug, unctuous

holiness blessedness, devoutness, divinity, godliness, piety, purity, religiousness, righteousness, sacredness, saintliness, sanctity, spirituality, virtuousness

hollow *adj.* **1.** empty, not solid, unfilled, vacant, void **2.** cavernous, concave, deep-set, depressed, indented, sunken **3.** deep, dull, expressionless, flat, low, muffled, muted, reverberant, rumbling, sepulchral, toneless **4.** empty, fruitless, futile, meaningless, pointless, Pyrrhic, specious, unavailing, useless, vain, worthless **5.** empty, famished, hungry, ravenous, starved **6.** artificial, cynical, deceitful, faithless, false, flimsy, hollow-

hearted, hypocritical, insincere, treacherous, unsound, weak **7. beat (someone) hollow** *Inf.* defeat, hammer (*Inf.*), outdo, overcome, rout, thrash, trounce, worst ~*n.* **8.** basin, bowl, cave, cavern, cavity, concavity, crater, cup, den, dent, depression, dimple, excavation, hole, indentation, pit, trough **9.** bottom, dale, dell, dingle, glen, valley ~*v.* **10.** channel, dig, dish, excavate, furrow, gouge, groove, pit, scoop

holocaust annihilation, carnage, conflagration, destruction, devastation, genocide, inferno, massacre, mass murder

holy 1. devout, divine, faithful, god-fearing, godly, hallowed, pious, pure, religious, righteous, saintly, sublime, virtuous **2.** blessed, consecrated, dedicated, hallowed, sacred, sacrosanct, sanctified, venerable, venerated

at ease. **c.** giving an informal party at one's own home. **d.** *Brit.* such a party. **12. at home in, on,** *or* **with.** familiar with. **13. home and dry.** *Brit. sl.* definitely safe or successful. Austral. & N.Z. equivalent: **home and hosed. 14. near home.** concerning one deeply. ~*adj.* (*usually prenominal*) **15.** of one's home, country, etc.; domestic. **16.** *Sport.* relating to one's own ground: *a home game.* **17.** *U.S.* central; principal: *the company's home office.* ~*adv.* **18.** to or at home: *I'll be home tomorrow.* **19.** to or on the point. **20.** to the fullest extent: *hammer the nail home.* **21. bring home to. a.** to make clear to. **b.** to place the blame on. **22. to write home about.** to be of particular interest: *the film was nothing to write home about.* ~*vb.* **23.** (*intr.*) (of birds and other animals) to return home accurately from a distance. **24.** (often foll. by *in on* or *onto*) to direct or be directed onto a point or target, esp. by automatic navigational aids. **25.** to send or go home. **26.** to furnish with a home. **27.** (*intr.;* often foll. by *in* or *in on*) to be directed towards a goal, target, etc. —**'homeless** *adj., n.* —**'homelessness** *n.*

home-brew *n.* **1.** a beer or other alcoholic drink brewed at home rather than commercially. **2.** *Canad. inf.* a professional football player who was born in Canada and is not an import. —**'home-'brewed** *adj.*

Home Counties *pl. n.* the counties surrounding London.

home economics *n.* the study of diet, budgeting, child care, and other subjects concerned with running a home.

home farm *n. Brit.* (esp. formerly) a farm attached to and providing food for a large country house.

Home Guard *n.* a volunteer part-time military force recruited for the defence of the United Kingdom in World War II.

home help *n. Brit.* a woman employed, esp. by a local authority, to do housework in a person's home.

homeland ('həʊm,lænd) *n.* **1.** the country in which one lives or was born. **2.** the official name for a **Bantustan**.

homely ('həʊmlɪ) *adj.* **-lier, -liest. 1.** characteristic of or suited to the ordinary home; unpretentious. **2.** (of a person) **a.** *Brit.* warm and domesticated. **b.** *Chiefly U.S.* plain. —**'homeliness** *n.*

home-made *adj.* **1.** (esp. of foods) made at home or on the premises, esp. of high-quality ingredients. **2.** crudely fashioned.

homeo-, homoeo-, *or* **homoio-** *combining form.* like or similar: *homeomorphism.*

Home Office *n. Brit. government.* the department responsible for the maintenance of law and order, and all other domestic affairs not specifically assigned to another department.

homeopathy *or* **homoeopathy** (,həʊmɪ'ɒpəθɪ) *n.* a method of treating disease by the use of small amounts of a drug that, in healthy persons, produces symptoms similar to those of the disease being treated. —**homeopathic** *or* **homoeopathic** (,həʊmɪə'pæθɪk) *adj.* —**homeopathist** *or* **homoeopathist** (,həʊmɪ'ɒpəθɪst) *n.*

homeostasis *or* **homoeostasis** (,həʊmɪəʊ'steɪsɪs) *n.* **1.** the maintenance of metabolic equilibrium within an animal by a tendency to compensate for disrupting changes. **2.** the maintenance of equilibrium within a social group, person, etc.

Homeric (hɒʊ'mɛrɪk) *adj.* **1.** of, relating to, or resembling Homer, Greek poet (circa 800 B.C.), to whom are attributed the Iliad and the Odyssey, or his poems. **2.** imposing or heroic. —**Ho'merically** *adv.*

home rule *n.* **1.** self-government, esp. in domestic affairs. **2.** the partial autonomy sometimes granted to a national minority or a colony.

Home Secretary *n. Brit. government.* the head of the Home Office.

homesick ('həʊm,sɪk) *adj.* depressed or melancholy at being away from home and family. —**'home,sickness** *n.*

homespun ('həʊm,spʌn) *adj.* **1.** having plain or unsophisticated character. **2.** woven or spun at home. ~*n.* **3.** cloth made at home or made of yarn spun at home.

homestead ('həʊm,stɛd, -stɪd) *n.* **1.** a house or estate and the adjoining land, buildings, etc., esp. a farm. **2.** (in the U.S. & Canada) a house and adjoining land designated by the owner as his fixed residence and exempt under the homestead laws from seizure and forced sale for debts. **3.** *Austral. & N.Z.* (on a sheep or cattle station) the owner's or manager's residence; in New Zealand, the term includes all outbuildings.

homesteader ('həʊm,stɪdə) *n. U.S. and Canada.* a person holding land under a homestead law.

homestead law *n.* (in the U.S. & Canada) any of various laws conferring privileges on homesteaders.

homeward ('həʊmwəd) *adj.* **1.** going home. **2.** (of a voyage, etc.) returning to the home port. ~*adv. also* **homewards. 3.** towards home.

homework ('həʊm,wɜːk) *n.* **1.** school work done at home. **2.** any preparatory study.

homicide ('hɒmɪ,saɪd) *n.* **1.** the killing of a human being by another person. **2.** a person who kills another. —**,homi'cidal** *adj.*

homily ('hɒmɪlɪ) *n., pl.* **-lies. 1.** a sermon. **2.** moralizing talk or writing. —**,homi'letic** *adj.* —**'homilist** *n.*

homing ('həʊmɪŋ) *n.* (*modifier*) **1.** *Zool.* relating to the ability to return home after travelling great distances. **2.** (of an aircraft, missile, etc.) capable of guiding itself onto a target.

homing pigeon *n.* any breed of pigeon developed for its homing instinct, used for racing. Also called: **homer.**

hominid ('hɒmɪnɪd) *n.* **1.** any primate of the family *Hominidae,* which includes modern man (*Homo sapiens*) and the extinct precursors of man. ~*adj.* **2.** of or belonging to the *Hominidae.*

hominoid ('hɒmɪ,nɔɪd) *adj.* **1.** of or like man; manlike. **2.** of or belonging to the primate family, which includes the anthropoid apes and man. ~*n.* **3.** a hominoid animal.

homo ('həʊməʊ) *n., pl.* **-mos.** *Inf.* short for **homosexual.**

Homo ('həʊməʊ) *n.* any primate of the hominid genus *Homo,* including modern man (see **Homo sapiens**).

homo- *combining form.* same or like: *homologous; homosexual.*

homoeo- *combining form.* variant of **homeo-.**

homogeneous (,həʊmə'dʒiːnɪəs, ,hɒm-) *adj.* **1.** composed of similar or identical parts or elements. **2.** of uniform nature. **3.** similar in kind or nature. **4.** *Maths.* containing terms of the same degree with respect to all the variables, as in $x^2 + 2xy + y^2$. —**homogeneity** (,həʊməʊdʒɪ'niːɪtɪ, ,hɒm-) *n.* —**,homo'geneousness** *n.*

homogenize *or* **-nise** (hɒ'mɒdʒɪ,naɪz) *vb.* **1.** (*tr.*) to break up the fat globules in (milk or cream) so that they are evenly distributed. **2.** to make or become homogeneous. —**ho,mogeni'zation** *or* **-ni'sation** *n.*

homograph ('hɒmə,grɑːf) *n.* one of a group of words spelt in the same way but having different meanings.

THESAURUS

home *n.* **1.** abode, domicile, dwelling, dwelling place, habitation, house, residence **2.** birthplace, family, fireside, hearth, homestead, home town, household **3.** abode, element, environment, habitat, habitation, haunt, home ground, range, stamping ground, territory **4. at home a.** available, in, present **b.** at ease, comfortable, familiar, relaxed **c.** entertaining, giving a party, having guests, receiving **d.** *As a noun* party, reception, soirée **5. at home in, on,** *or* **with** conversant with, familiar with, knowledgeable, proficient, skilled, well-versed **6. bring home to** drive home, emphasize, impress upon, make clear, press home ~*adj.* **7.** central, domestic, familiar, family, household, inland, internal, local, national, native

homeland country of origin, fatherland, mother country, motherland, native land

homeless 1. *adj.* abandoned, destitute, displaced, dispossessed, down-and-out, exiled, forlorn, forsaken, outcast, unsettled **2.** *n.* **the homeless** dossers (*Sl.*), squatters, vagrants

homelike cheerful, comfortable, cosy, easy, familiar, homy, informal, intimate, relaxing, snug

homely comfortable, comfy (*Inf.*), cosy, domestic, everyday, familiar, friendly, homelike, homespun, homy, informal, modest, natural, ordinary, plain, simple, unaffected, unassuming, unpretentious, welcoming

homespun artless, coarse, homely, home-made, inelegant, plain, rough, rude,

rustic, unpolished, unsophisticated

homicidal deadly, death-dealing, lethal, maniacal, mortal, murderous

homicide 1. bloodshed, killing, manslaughter, murder, slaying **2.** killer, murderer, slayer

homily address, discourse, lecture, preaching, preachment, sermon

homogeneity analogousness, comparability, consistency, correspondence, identicalness, oneness, sameness, similarity, uniformity

homogeneous akin, alike, analogous, cognate, comparable, consistent, identical, kindred, similar, uniform, unvarying

homologous (hɒʊˈmɒləɡəs, hɒ-), **homological** (ˌhɒʊməˈlɒdʒɪkəl, ˌhɒm-), *or* **homologic** *adj.* 1. having a related or similar position, structure, etc. 2. *Biol.* (of organs and parts) having the same evolutionary origin but different functions: *the wing of a bat and the paddle of a whale are homologous.* —ˌhomoˈlogically *adv.* —ˈhomoˌlogue *n.*

homology (hɒʊˈmɒlədʒɪ) *n., pl.* -gies. the condition of being homologous.

homonym (ˈhɒmənɪm) *n.* 1. one of a group of words pronounced or spelt in the same way but having different meanings. Cf. **homograph.** 2. *Biol.* a specific or generic name that has been used for two or more different organisms. —ˌhomoˈnymic *or* hoˈmonymous *adj.*

Homo sapiens (ˈsæpɪˌɛnz) *n.* the specific name of modern man; the only extant species of the genus *Homo.* This species also includes extinct types of primitive man such as Cro-Magnon man.

homosexual (ˌhɒʊməʊˈsɛksjʊəl, ˌhɒm-) *n.* 1. a person who is sexually attracted to members of the same sex. ~adj. 2. of or relating to homosexuals or homosexuality. 3. of or relating to the same sex. —ˌhomoˌsexuˈality *n.*

homy *or esp. U.S.* **homey** (ˈhɒʊmɪ) *adj.* **homier, homiest.** like a home; cosy. —ˈhominess *or esp. U.S.* ˈhomeyness *n.*

hon *or* **hon.** *abbrev. for:* 1. honorary. 2. honourable.

Hon *or* **Hon.** *abbrev. for* Honourable (title).

hone (hɒʊn) *n.* 1. a fine whetstone for sharpening. ~vb. 2. (tr.) to sharpen or polish with or as if with a hone.

honest (ˈɒnɪst) *adj.* 1. not given to lying, cheating, stealing, etc.; trustworthy. 2. not false or misleading; genuine. 3. just or fair: *honest wages.* 4. characterized by sincerity: *an honest appraisal.* 5. without pretensions: *honest farmers.* 6. *Arch.* (of a woman) respectable. 7. **honest broker.** a mediator in disputes, esp. international ones. 8. **make an honest woman of.** to marry (a woman, esp. one who is pregnant) to prevent scandal.

honestly (ˈɒnɪstlɪ) *adv.* 1. in an honest manner. 2. (intensifier): *I honestly don't believe it.*

honesty (ˈɒnɪstɪ) *n., pl.* -ties. 1. the condition of being honest. 2. *Arch.* virtue or respect. 3. a purple-flowered European plant cultivated for its flattened silvery pods, which are used for indoor decoration. Also called: **moonwort, satinpod.**

honey (ˈhʌnɪ) *n.* 1. a sweet viscid substance made by bees from nectar and stored in their nests or hives as food. 2. anything that is sweet or delightful. 3. (often *cap.*) *Chiefly U.S.* a term of endearment. 4. *Inf., chiefly U.S.* something very good of its kind. ~vb. **honeying, honeyed** *or* **honied.** 5. (tr.) to sweeten with or as if with honey. 6. (often foll. by *up*) to talk to (someone) in a flattering way. —ˈhoneyˌlike *adj.*

honeybee (ˈhʌnɪˌbiː) *n.* any of various social bees widely domesticated as a source of honey and beeswax. Also called: **hive bee.**

honeycomb (ˈhʌnɪˌkɒʊm) *n.* 1. a waxy structure, constructed by bees in a hive, that consists of adjacent hexagonal cells in which honey is stored, eggs are laid, and larvae develop. 2. something resembling this in structure. ~vb. (tr.) 3. to pierce with holes, cavities, etc. 4. to permeate: *honeycombed with spies.*

honeydew (ˈhʌnɪˌdjuː) *n.* 1. a sugary substance excreted by aphids and similar insects. 2. a similar substance exuded by certain plants.

honeyed *or* **honied** (ˈhʌnɪd) *adj. Poetic.* 1. flattering or soothing. 2. made sweet or agreeable: *honeyed words.* 3. full of honey.

honeymoon (ˈhʌnɪˌmuːn) *n.* 1. a holiday taken by a newly married couple. 2. a holiday considered to resemble a honeymoon: *a second honeymoon.* 3. the early, usually calm period of a relationship or enterprise. ~vb. 4. (intr.) to take a honeymoon. —ˈhoneyˌmooner *n.*

honeysuckle (ˈhʌnɪˌsʌkəl) *n.* 1. a temperate shrub or vine with fragrant white, yellow, or pink tubular flowers. 2. any of various Australian trees or shrubs of the genus *Banksia,* having flowers in dense spikes.

honied (ˈhʌnɪd) *adj.* a variant spelling of **honeyed.** —ˈhoniedly *adv.*

honk (hɒŋk) *n.* 1. a representation of the sound made by a goose. 2. any sound resembling this. ~vb. 3. to make or cause (something) to make such a sound. 4. (intr.) *Brit. sl.* to vomit.

honky-tonk (ˈhɒŋkɪˌtɒŋk) *n.* 1. *U.S. sl.* a cheap disreputable nightclub, bar, etc. 2. **a.** a style of ragtime piano-playing, esp. on a tinny-sounding piano. **b.** (as modifier): *honky-tonk music.*

honorarium (ˌɒnəˈrɛərɪəm) *n., pl.* -iums *or* -ia (-ɪə). a fee paid for a nominally free service.

honorary (ˈɒnərərɪ) *adj.* (usually prenominal) 1. **a.** held or given only as an honour, without the normal privileges or duties: *an honorary degree.* **b.** (of a secretary, treasurer, etc.) unpaid. 2. having such a position or title. 3. depending on honour rather than legal agreement.

honorific (ˌɒnəˈrɪfɪk) *adj.* 1. showing respect. 2. **a.** (of a pronoun, verb inflection, etc.) indicating the speaker's respect for the addressee. **b.** (as n.): *a Japanese honorific.* —ˌhonorˈifically *adv.*

honour *or U.S.* **honor** (ˈɒnə) *n.* 1. personal integrity; allegiance to moral principles. 2. **a.** fame or glory. **b.** a person who wins this for his country, school, etc. 3. (often *pl.*) great respect, esteem, etc., or an outward sign of this. 4. (often *pl.*) high or noble rank. 5. a privilege or pleasure: *it is an honour to serve you.* 6. a woman's chastity. 7. **a.** *Bridge, etc.* any of the top five cards in a suit or any of the four aces at no trumps. **b.** *Whist.* any of the top four cards. 8. *Golf.* the right to tee off first. 9. **do the honours. a.** to serve as host or hostess. **b.** to perform a social act, such as carving meat, etc. 10. **in honour bound.** under a moral obligation. 11. **in honour of.** out of respect for. 12. **on one's honour.** on the pledge of one's word or good name. ~vb. (tr.) 13. to hold in respect. 14. to show courteous behaviour towards. 15. to worship. 16. to confer a distinction upon. 17. to accept and then pay when due (a cheque, draft, etc.). 18. to bow or curtsy to (one's dancing partner).

Honour (ˈɒnə) *n.* (preceded by *Your, His,* or *Her*) a title used to or of certain judges.

honourable *or U.S.* **honorable** (ˈɒnərəbəl) *adj.* 1. possessing or characterized by high principles. 2. worthy of honour or esteem. 3. consistent with or bestowing honour. —ˈhonourably *or U.S.* ˈhonorably *adv.*

Honourable *or U.S.* **Honorable** (ˈɒnərəbəl) *adj.* (pre-

THESAURUS

homosexual *adj.* bent (Sl.), camp (Inf.), gay (Inf.), homoerotic, lesbian, queer (Inf.), sapphic

honest 1. conscientious, decent, ethical, high-minded, honourable, law-abiding, reliable, reputable, scrupulous, trustworthy, trusty, truthful, upright, veracious, virtuous 2. above board, authentic, bona fide, genuine, honest to goodness, on the level (Inf.), on the up and up, proper, real, straight, true 3. equitable, fair, fair and square, impartial, just 4. candid, direct, forthright, frank, ingenuous, open, outright, plain, sincere, straightforward, undisguised, unfeigned

honestly 1. by fair means, cleanly, ethically, honourably, in good faith, lawfully, legally, legitimately, on the level (Inf.), with clean hands 2. candidly, frankly, in all sincerity, in plain English, plainly, straight (out), to one's face, truthfully

honesty 1. faithfulness, fidelity, honour,

incorruptibility, integrity, morality, probity, rectitude, reputability, scrupulousness, straightness, trustworthiness, truthfulness, uprightness, veracity, virtue 2. bluntness, candour, equity, even-handedness, fairness, frankness, genuineness, openness, outspokenness, plainness, sincerity, straightforwardness

honorary complimentary, ex officio, formal, *honoris causa,* in name *or* title only, nominal, titular, unofficial, unpaid

honour *n.* 1. credit, dignity, distinction, elevation, esteem, fame, glory, high standing, prestige, rank, renown, reputation, repute 2. acclaim, accolade, adoration, commendation, deference, homage, kudos, praise, recognition, regard, respect, reverence, tribute, veneration 3. decency, fairness, goodness, honesty, integrity, morality, principles, probity, rectitude, righteousness, trustworthiness, uprightness 4. compliment,

credit, favour, pleasure, privilege, source of pride *or* satisfaction 5. chastity, innocence, modesty, purity, virginity, virtue ~v. 6. admire, adore, appreciate, esteem, exalt, glorify, hallow, prize, respect, revere, reverence, value, venerate, worship 7. be as good as (Inf.), be faithful to, be true to, carry out, discharge, fulfil, keep, live up to, observe 8. acclaim, celebrate, commemorate, commend, compliment, decorate, dignify, exalt, glorify, laud, lionize, praise 9. accept, acknowledge, cash, clear, credit, pass, pay, take

honourable 1. ethical, fair, high-minded, honest, just, moral, principled, true, trustworthy, trusty, upright, upstanding, virtuous 2. distinguished, eminent, great, illustrious, noble, notable, noted, prestigious, renowned, venerable 3. creditable, estimable, proper, reputable, respectable, respected, right, righteous, virtuous

nominal) **the.** a title of respect placed before a name: used of various officials in the English-speaking world, as a courtesy title in Britain for the children of certain peers, and in Parliament by one member speaking of another. Abbrev.: **Hon.**

honours *or U.S.* **honors** ('ɒnəz) *pl. n.* **1.** observances of respect. **2.** (*often cap.*) *Brit.* **a.** (in a university degree course) a rank of the highest academic standard. **b.** (*as modifier*): *an honours degree.* Abbrev.: **Hons. 3.** a high mark awarded for an examination; distinction. **4. last** (*or funeral*) **honours.** observances of respect at a funeral. **5. military honours.** marks of respect paid by or to soldiers, etc.

hooch *or* **hootch** (hu:tʃ) *n. U.S. sl.* alcoholic drink, esp. illicitly distilled spirits.

hood[1] (hʊd) *n.* **1.** a loose head covering either attached to a cloak or coat or made as a separate garment. **2.** something resembling this in shape or use. **3.** the U.S. name for **bonnet** (of a car). **4.** the folding roof of a convertible car. **5.** a hoodlike garment worn over an academic gown, indicating its wearer's degree and university. **6.** *Biol.* a hoodlike structure, such as the fold of skin on the head of a cobra ~*vb.* **7.** (*tr.*) to cover with or as if with a hood. —'**hooded** *adj.* —'**hood,like** *adj.*

hood[2] (hʊd) *n. U.S. sl.* short for **hoodlum.**

-hood *suffix forming nouns.* **1.** indicating state or condition: *manhood.* **2.** indicating a body of persons: *knighthood; priesthood.*

hooded crow *n.* a crow that has a grey body and black head, wings, and tail. Also called (*Scot.*): **hoodie** ('hʊdɪ), **hoodie crow.**

hoodlum ('hu:dləm) *n.* **1.** a petty gangster. **2.** a lawless youth.

hoodoo ('hu:du:) *n., pl.* **-doos. 1.** a variant of **voodoo. 2.** *Inf.* a person or thing that brings bad luck. **3.** *Inf.* bad luck. ~*vb.* **-dooing, -dooed. 4.** (*tr.*) *Inf.* to bring bad luck to.

hoodwink ('hʊd,wɪŋk) *vb.* (*tr.*) **1.** to dupe; trick. **2.** *Obs.* to cover or hide.

hooey ('hu:ɪ) *n., interj. Sl.* nonsense.

hoof (hu:f) *n., pl.* **hooves** *or* **hoofs. 1. a.** the horny covering of the end of the foot in the horse, deer, and all other ungulate mammals. **b.** (*in combination*): *a hoofbeat.* Related adj.: **ungular. 2.** the foot of an ungulate mammal. **3.** a hoofed animal. **4.** *Facetious.* a person's foot. **5. on the hoof** (of livestock) alive. ~*vb.* **6. hoof it.** *Sl.* **a.** to walk. **b.** (*intr.*) to dance. —**hoofed** *adj.*

hoo-ha ('hu:,hɑ:) *n.* a noisy commotion or fuss.

hook (hʊk) *n.* **1.** a curved piece of material, usually metal, used to suspend, hold, or pull something. **2.** Also called **fish-hook.** a sharp hook used in angling, esp. one with a barb. **3.** a trap or snare. **4.** something resembling a hook in design or use. **5. a.** a sharp bend, esp. in a river. **b.** a sharply curved spit of land. **6.** *Boxing.* a short swinging blow delivered with the elbow bent. **7.** *Cricket.* a shot in which the ball is hit square on the leg side with the bat held horizontally. **8.** *Golf.* a shot that causes the ball to go to the player's left. **9.** a hookshaped stroke used in writing, such as a part of a letter extending above or below the line. **10.** *Music.* a stroke added to the stem of a note to indicate time values shorter than a crotchet. **11.** a sickle. **12.** *Naut.* an anchor. **13. by hook or (by) crook.** by any means. **14. hook, line, and sinker.** *Inf.* completely: *he fell for it hook, line, and sinker.* **15. off the hook.** *Sl.* free from obligation or guilt. **16. sling one's hook.** *Brit. sl.* to leave. ~*vb.* **17.** (*often foll. by up*) to fasten or be fastened with or as if with a hook or hooks. **18.** (*tr.*) to catch (something, such as a fish) on a hook. **19.** to curve like or into the shape of a hook. **20.** (*tr.*) to make (a rug) by hooking yarn through a stiff fabric backing with a special instrument. **21.** *Boxing.* to hit (an opponent) with a hook. **22.** *Cricket, etc.* to play (a ball) with a hook. **23.** *Rugby.* to obtain and pass

(the ball) backwards from a scrum, using the feet. **24.** (*tr.*) *Sl.* to steal. ~See also **hook-up.** —'**hook,like** *adj.*

hookah *or* **hooka** ('hʊkə) *n.* an oriental pipe for smoking marijuana, tobacco, etc., consisting of one or more long flexible stems connected to a container of water or other liquid through which smoke is drawn and cooled. Also called: **hubble-bubble, water pipe.**

hooked (hʊkt) *adj.* **1.** bent like a hook. **2.** having a hook or hooks. **3.** caught or trapped. **4.** a slang word for **married. 5.** *Sl.* addicted to a drug. **6.** (*often foll. by on*) obsessed (with).

hooker ('hʊkə) *n.* **1.** a person or thing that hooks. **2.** *U.S. sl.* a prostitute. **3.** *Rugby.* the central forward in the front row of a scrum whose main job is to hook the ball.

hook-up *n.* **1.** the contact of an aircraft in flight with the refuelling hose of a tanker aircraft. **2.** an alliance or relationship. **3.** the linking of broadcasting equipment or stations to transmit a special programme. ~*vb.* **hook up** (*adv.*) **4.** to connect (two or more people or things).

hookworm ('hʊk,wɜ:m) *n.* any of various parasitic blood-sucking worms which cause disease. They have hooked mouthparts and enter their hosts by boring through the skin.

hooligan ('hu:lɪgən) *n. Sl.* a rough lawless young person. —'**hooliganism** *n.*

hoop (hu:p) *n.* **1.** a rigid circular band of metal or wood. **2.** something resembling this. **3.** a band of iron that holds the staves of a barrel together. **4.** a child's toy shaped like a hoop and rolled on the ground or whirled around the body. **5.** *Croquet.* any of the iron arches through which the ball is driven. **6. a.** a light curved frame to spread out a skirt. **b.** (*as modifier*): *a hoop skirt.* **7.** *Basketball.* the round metal frame to which the net is attached to form the basket. **8.** a large ring with paper stretched over it through which performers or animals jump. **9. go through the hoop.** to be subjected to an ordeal. ~*vb.* **10.** (*tr.*) to surround with or as if with a hoop. —**hooped** *adj.*

hoopla ('hu:plɑ:) *n.* **1.** *Brit.* a fairground game in which a player tries to throw a hoop over an object and so win it. **2.** *U.S. sl.* **a.** noise; bustle. **b.** nonsense; ballyhoo.

hoopoe ('hu:pu:) *n.* an Old World bird having a pinkish-brown plumage with black-and-white wings and an erectile crest.

hooray (hu:'reɪ) *or* **hoorah** (hu:'rɑ:) *interj., n., vb.* **1.** variant spellings of **hurrah.** ~*interj.* **2.** Also: **hooroo** (hu:'ru:). *Austral. & N.Z.* cheerio.

hoot (hu:t) *n.* **1.** the mournful wavering cry of some owls. **2.** a similar sound, such as that of a train whistle. **3.** a jeer of derision. **4.** *Inf.* an amusing person or thing. ~*vb.* **5.** (*often foll. by at*) to jeer or yell (something) contemptuously (at someone). **6.** (*tr.*) to drive (speakers, actors on stage, etc.) off by hooting. **7.** (*intr.*) to make a hoot. **8.** (*intr.*) *Brit.* to blow a horn.

hooter ('hu:tə) *n. Chiefly Brit.* **1.** a person or thing that hoots, esp. a car horn. **2.** *Sl.* a nose.

Hoover ('hu:və) *n.* **1.** *Trademark.* a type of vacuum cleaner. ~*vb.* (*usually not cap.*) **2.** to vacuum-clean (a carpet, etc.).

hooves (hu:vz) *n.* a plural of **hoof.**

hop[1] (hɒp) *vb.* **hopping, hopped. 1.** (*intr.*) to jump forwards or upwards on one foot. **2.** (*intr.*) (esp. of frogs, birds, etc.) to move forwards in short jumps. **3.** (*tr.*) to jump over. **4.** (*intr.*) *Inf.* to move quickly (in, on, out of, etc.): *hop on a bus.* **5.** (*tr.*) *Inf.* to cross (an ocean) in an aircraft. **6.** (*tr.*) *U.S. inf.* to travel by means of: *he hopped a train to Chicago.* **7.** (*intr.*) another word for **limp**[1]. **8. hop it** (*or off*). *Brit. sl.* to go away. ~*n.* **9.** the act or an instance of hopping. **10.** *Inf.* an informal dance. **11.** *Inf.* a trip, esp. in an aircraft. **12. on the hop.** *Inf.* **a.** active or busy. **b.** *Brit.* unawares or unprepared.

hop[2] (hɒp) *n.* **1.** a climbing plant which has green conelike female flowers and clusters of small male flow-

honours adornments, awards, decorations, dignities, distinctions, laurels, titles

hoodwink bamboozle (*Inf.*), befool, cheat, con (*Sl.*), cozen, delude, dupe, fool, gull (*Archaic*), hoax, impose, lead up the garden path (*Inf.*), mislead, pull a fast one on (*Inf.*), rook (*Sl.*), swindle, trick

hook *n.* 1. catch, clasp, fastener, hasp, holder, link, lock, peg 2. noose, snare, springe, trap 3. **by hook or by crook** by any means,

by fair means or foul, somehow, somehow or other, someway 4. **hook, line, and sinker** *Inf.* completely, entirely, thoroughly, through and through, totally, utterly, wholly 5. **off the hook** *Sl.* acquitted, cleared, exonerated, in the clear, let off, under no obligation, vindicated ~*v.* 6. catch, clasp, fasten, fix, hasp, secure 7. catch, enmesh, ensnare, entrap, snare, trap

hooligan delinquent, hoodlum (*Chiefly*

U.S.), rowdy, ruffian, tough, vandal, yob *or* yobbo (*Brit. sl.*)

hoop band, circlet, girdle, loop, ring, wheel

hoot *n.* 1. call, cry, toot 2. boo, catcall, hiss, jeer, yell 3. *Inf.* card (*Inf.*), caution (*Inf.*), laugh (*Inf.*), scream (*Inf.*) ~*v.* 4. boo, catcall, condemn, decry, denounce, execrate, hiss, howl down, jeer, yell at 5. cry, scream, shout, shriek, toot, whoop, yell

ers. See also **hops**. **2. hop garden**. a field of hops. **3**. *Sl*. opium or any other narcotic drug. —**'hop-,picker** *n*.

hope (həʊp) *n*. **1**. (*sometimes pl*.) a feeling of desire for something and confidence in the possibility of its fulfilment: *his hope for peace was justified*. **2**. a reasonable ground for this feeling: *there is still hope*. **3**. a person or thing that gives cause for hope. **4**. a thing, situation, or event that is desired: *my hope is that prices will fall*. **5. not a hope** or **some hope**. used ironically to express little confidence that expectations will be fulfilled. ~*vb*. **6**. (*tr.; takes a clause as object or an infinitive*) to desire (something) with some possibility of fulfilment: *I hope to tell you*. **7**. (*intr.; often foll. by for*) to have a wish. **8**. (*tr.; takes a clause as object*) to trust or believe: *we hope that this is satisfactory*. —**'hoper** *n*.

hopeful ('həʊpfʊl) *adj*. **1**. having or expressing hope. **2**. inspiring hope; promising. ~*n*. **3**. a person considered to be on the brink of success (esp. in **a young hopeful**). —**'hopefulness** *n*.

hopefully ('həʊpfʊlɪ) *adv*. **1**. in a hopeful manner. **2**. *Inf*. it is hoped: *hopefully they will be married soon*.

▷ **Usage**. The use of *hopefully* to mean 'it is hoped that' is not universally accepted as standard. It does, however, represent a construction well-established in colloquial English, as in the use of *happily* in *the two vehicles crashed, but happily no one was injured*.

hopeless ('həʊplɪs) *adj*. **1**. having or offering no hope. **2**. impossible to solve. **3**. unable to learn, function, etc. **4**. *Inf*. without skill or ability. —**'hopelessly** *adv*. —**'hopelessness** *n*.

hopper ('hɒpə) *n*. **1**. a person or thing that hops. **2**. a funnel-shaped reservoir from which solid materials can be discharged into a receptacle below, esp. for feeding fuel to a furnace, loading a truck, etc. **3**. a machine used for picking hops; a hop-picker. **4**. any of various long-legged hopping insects. **5**. an open-topped railway truck for loose minerals, etc., unloaded through doors on the underside. **6**. *S. African*. another name for **cocopan**. **7**. *Computers*. a device for holding punched cards and feeding them to a card reader.

hops (hɒps) *pl. n*. the dried flowers of the hop plant, used to give a bitter taste to beer.

hopscotch ('hɒp,skɒtʃ) *n*. a children's game in which a player throws a small stone or other object to land in one of a pattern of squares marked on the ground and then hops over to it to pick it up.

horde (hɔːd) *n*. **1**. a vast crowd; throng; mob. **2**. a nomadic group of people, esp. an Asiatic group. **3**. a large moving mass of animals, esp. insects.

horehound or **hoarhound** ('hɔː,haʊnd) *n*. a downy herbaceous Old World plant with small white flowers that contain a bitter juice formerly used as a cough medicine and flavouring.

horizon (hə'raɪzᵊn) *n*. **1**. Also called: **visible horizon, apparent horizon**. the apparent line that divides the earth and the sky. **2**. *Astron*. **a**. Also called: **sensible horizon**. the circular intersection with the celestial sphere of the plane tangential to the earth at the position of the observer. **b**. Also called: **celestial horizon**. the great circle on the celestial sphere, the plane of which passes through the centre of the earth and is parallel to the sensible horizon. **3**. the range or limit of scope, interest, knowledge, etc. **4**. a layer of rock within a stratum that has a particular composition by which the stratum may be dated.

horizontal (,hɒrɪ'zɒntᵊl) *adj*. **1**. parallel to the plane of the horizon; level; flat. **2**. of or relating to the horizon. **3**. in a plane parallel to that of the horizon. **4**. applied uniformly to all members of a group. **5**. *Econ*. relating to identical stages of commercial activity: *horizontal integration*. ~*n*. **6**. a horizontal plane, position, line, etc.

—,**horizon'tality** *n*. —,**hori'zontally** *adv*.

hormone ('hɔːməʊn) *n*. **1**. a chemical substance produced in an endocrine gland and transported in the blood to a certain tissue, on which it exerts a specific effect. **2**. an organic compound produced by a plant that is essential for growth. **3**. any synthetic substance having the same effects. —**hor'monal** *adj*.

horn (hɔːn) *n*. **1**. either of a pair of permanent bony outgrowths on the heads of cattle, antelopes, etc. Related adj.: **corneous**. **2**. the outgrowth from the nasal bone of a rhinoceros, consisting of a mass of fused hairs. **3**. any hornlike projection, such as the eyestalk of a snail. **4**. the antler of a deer. **5**. **a**. the constituent substance, mainly keratin, of horns, hoofs, etc. **b**. (*in combination*): *horn-rimmed spectacles*. **6**. a container or device made from this substance or an artificial substitute: *a drinking horn*. **7**. an object resembling a horn in shape, such as a cornucopia. **8**. a primitive musical wind instrument made from horn. **9**. any musical instrument consisting of a pipe or tube of brass fitted with a mouthpiece. See **French horn, cor anglais**. **10**. *Jazz sl*. any wind instrument. **11**. **a**. a device for producing a warning or signalling noise. **b**. (*in combination*): *a foghorn*. **12**. (*usually pl*.) the imaginary hornlike parts formerly supposed to appear on the forehead of a cuckold. **13**. **a**. a hollow conical device coupled to a gramophone to control the direction and quality of the sound. **b**. a similar device attached to an electrical loudspeaker, esp. in a public address system. **14**. a stretch of land or water shaped like a horn. **15**. *Brit. taboo sl*. an erection of the penis. **16. on the horns of a dilemma**. involving a choice between equally unpalatable alternatives. ~*vb*. (*tr*.) **17**. to provide with a horn or horns. **18**. to gore or butt with a horn. **19**. (*tr*.) to remove or shorten the horns of (cattle, etc.). —**horned** *adj*. —**'hornless** *adj*. —**'horn,like** *adj*.

hornbeam ('hɔːn,biːm) *n*. **1**. a tree of Europe and Asia having smooth grey bark and hard white wood. **2**. its wood. ~Also called: **ironwood**.

hornbill ('hɔːn,bɪl) *n*. a bird of tropical Africa and Asia, having a very large bill with a basal bony protuberance.

hornblende ('hɔːn,blɛnd) *n*. a mineral of the amphibole group consisting of the aluminium silicates of calcium, sodium, magnesium, and iron: varies in colour from green to black.

hornbook ('hɔːn,bʊk) *n*. a page bearing a religious text or the alphabet, held in a frame with a thin window of horn over it.

hornet ('hɔːnɪt) *n*. **1**. any of various large social wasps that can inflict a severe sting. **2. hornet's nest**. a strongly unfavourable reaction (often in **stir up a hornet's nest**).

horn of plenty *n*. another term for **cornucopia**.

hornpipe ('hɔːn,paɪp) *n*. **1**. an obsolete reed instrument with a mouthpiece made of horn. **2**. an old British solo dance to a hornpipe accompaniment, traditionally performed by sailors. **3**. a piece of music for such a dance.

horny ('hɔːnɪ) *adj*. **hornier, horniest. 1**. of, like, or hard as horn. **2**. having a horn or horns. **3**. *Sl*. aroused sexually. —**'horniness** *n*.

horology (hɒ'rɒlədʒɪ) *n*. the art or science of making timepieces or of measuring time. —**horologic** (,hɒrə'lɒdʒɪk) or ,**horo'logical** *adj*.

horoscope ('hɒrə,skəʊp) *n*. **1**. the prediction of a person's future based on zodiacal data for the time of birth. **2**. the configuration of the planets, sun, and moon in the sky at a particular moment. **3**. a diagram showing the positions of the planets, sun, moon, etc., at a particular time and place. —**horoscopic** (,hɒrə'skɒpɪk) *adj*. —**horoscopy** (hɒ'rɒskəpɪ) *n*.

horrendous (hɒ'rɛndəs) *adj*. another word for **horrific**.

THESAURUS

hop 1. *v*. bound, caper, dance, jump, leap, skip, spring, vault **2**. *n*. bounce, bound, jump, leap, skip, spring, step, vault

hope 1. *n*. ambition, anticipation, assumption, belief, confidence, desire, dream, expectancy, expectation, faith, longing **2**. *v*. anticipate, aspire, await, believe, contemplate, count on, desire, expect, foresee, long, look forward to, rely, trust

hopeful 1. anticipating, assured, buoyant, confident, expectant, looking forward to, optimistic, sanguine **2**. auspicious, bright,

cheerful, encouraging, heartening, promising, propitious, reassuring, rosy

hopefully 1. confidently, expectantly, optimistically, sanguinely **2**. *Inf*. all being well, conceivably, expectedly, feasibly, probably

hopeless 1. defeatist, dejected, demoralized, despairing, desperate, despondent, disconsolate, downhearted, forlorn, in despair, pessimistic, woebegone **2**. helpless, incurable, irremediable, irreparable, irreversible, lost, past remedy, remediless **3**. forlorn, futile, impossible, impracticable, pointless, un-

achievable, unattainable, useless, vain **4**. *Inf*. inadequate, incompetent, ineffectual, inferior, no good, poor, useless (*Inf*.)

horde band, crew, crowd, drove, gang, host, mob, multitude, pack, press, swarm, throng, troop

horizon 1. field of vision, skyline, vista **2**. compass, ken, perspective, prospect, purview, range, realm, scope, sphere, stretch

—hor'rendously *adv.*

horrible ('hɒrəbəl) *adj.* **1.** causing horror; dreadful. **2.** disagreeable. **3.** *Inf.* cruel or unkind. —'**horribleness** *n.* —'**horribly** *adv.*

horrid ('hɒrɪd) *adj.* **1.** disagreeable; unpleasant: *a horrid meal.* **2.** repulsive or frightening. **3.** *Inf.* unkind. —'**horridly** *adv.* —'**horridness** *n.*

horrific (hɒ'rɪfɪk, hə-) *adj.* provoking horror; horrible. —hor'**rifically** *adv.*

horrify ('hɒrɪ,faɪ) *vb.* -**fying, -fied.** (*tr.*) **1.** to cause feelings of horror; terrify. **2.** to shock greatly. —,horrifi'**cation** *n.* —'**horri,fyingly** *adv.*

horror ('hɒrə) *n.* **1.** extreme fear; terror; dread. **2.** intense hatred. **3.** (*often pl.*) a thing or person causing fear, loathing, etc. **4.** (*modifier*) having a frightening subject: *a horror film.*

horrors ('hɒrəz) *pl. n.* **1.** *Sl.* a fit of depression or anxiety. **2.** *Inf.* See **delirium tremens.** ~*interj.* **3.** an expression of dismay, sometimes facetious.

hors d'oeuvre (ɔː 'dɜːvr) *n., pl.* **hors d'oeuvre** *or* **hors d'oeuvres** ('dɜːvr). an appetizer, usually served before the main meal.

horse (hɔːs) *n.* **1.** a solid-hoofed, herbivorous, domesticated mammal used for draught work and riding. Related adj.: **equine. 2.** the adult male of this species; stallion. **3. Przewalski's horse.** a rare species of wild horse. **4.** (*functioning as pl.*) horsemen, esp. cavalry: *a regiment of horse.* **5.** Also called: **buck.** *Gymnastics.* a padded apparatus on legs, used for vaulting, etc. **6.** a narrow board supported by a pair of legs at each end, used as a frame for sawing or as a trestle, barrier, etc. **7.** a contrivance on which a person may ride and exercise. **8.** a slang word for **heroin. 9.** *Mining.* a mass of rock within a vein of ore. **10.** *Naut.* a rod, rope, or cable, fixed at the ends, along which something may slide; traveller. **11.** *Inf.* short for **horsepower. 12.** (*modifier*) drawn by a horse or horses: *a horse cart.* **13. be** (*or* **get**) **on one's high horse.** *Inf.* to act disdainfully aloof. **14. flog a dead horse.** *Chiefly Brit.* **a.** to harp on some long discarded subject. **b.** to pursue the solution of a problem long realized to be insoluble. **15. hold one's horses.** to restrain oneself. **16. a horse of another** *or* **a different colour.** a completely different topic, argument, etc. **17. the horse's mouth.** the most reliable source. ~*vb.* **18.** (*tr.*) to provide with a horse or horses. **19.** to put or be put on horseback. —'**horse,like** *adj.*

horseback ('hɔːs,bæk) *n.* **a.** a horse's back (esp. in **on horseback**). **b.** *Chiefly U.S.* (*as modifier*): *horseback riding.*

horsebox ('hɔːs,bɒks) *n. Brit.* a van or trailer used for carrying horses.

horse brass *n.* a decorative brass ornament, originally attached to a horse's harness.

horse chestnut *n.* **1.** a tree having palmate leaves, erect clusters of white, pink, or red flowers, and brown shiny inedible nuts enclosed in a spiky bur. **2.** Also called: **conker.** the nut of this tree.

horseflesh ('hɔːs,fleʃ) *n.* **1.** horses collectively. **2.** the flesh of a horse, esp. edible horse meat.

horsefly ('hɔːs,flaɪ) *n., pl.* -**flies.** a large stout-bodied dipterous fly, the female of which sucks the blood of mammals, esp. horses, cattle, and man. Also called: **gadfly, cleg.**

horsehair ('hɔːs,heə) *n.* hair taken chiefly from the tail or mane of a horse, used in upholstery and for fabric, etc.

horse laugh *n.* a coarse or raucous laugh.

horseman ('hɔːsmən) *n., pl.* -**men. 1.** a person skilled in riding. **2.** a person who rides a horse. —'**horseman,ship** *n.* —'**horse,woman** *fem. n.*

horseplay ('hɔːs,pleɪ) *n.* rough or rowdy play.

horsepower ('hɔːs,pauə) *n.* an fps unit of power, equal to 550 foot-pounds per second (equivalent to 745.7 watts). ~Abbrevs.: **HP, H.P., h.p., hp.**

horseradish ('hɔːs,rædɪʃ) *n.* a coarse Eurasian plant cultivated for its thick white pungent root, which is ground and combined with vinegar, etc., to make a sauce.

horse sense *n.* another term for **common sense.**

horseshoe ('hɔːs,ʃuː) *n.* **1.** a piece of iron shaped like a U nailed to the underside of the hoof of a horse to protect the soft part of the foot: commonly thought to be a token of good luck. **2.** an object of similar shape.

horsetail ('hɔːs,teɪl) *n.* **1.** a plant having jointed stems with whorls of small dark toothlike leaves. **2.** a stylized horse's tail formerly used as the emblem of a pasha.

horsewhip ('hɔːs,wɪp) *n.* **1.** a whip, usually with a long thong, used for managing horses. ~*vb.* -**whipping,** -**whipped. 2.** (*tr.*) to flog with such a whip. —'**horse,whipper** *n.*

horsy *or* **horsey** ('hɔːsɪ) *adj.* **horsier, horsiest. 1.** of or relating to horses: *a horsy smell.* **2.** dealing with or devoted to horses. **3.** like a horse: *a horsy face.* —'**horsily** *adv.* —'**horsiness** *n.*

hortatory ('hɔːtətərɪ) *or* **hortative** ('hɔːtətɪv) *adj.* tending to exhort; encouraging. —**hor'tation** *n.* —'**hortatorily** *or* '**hortatively** *adv.*

horticulture ('hɔːtɪ,kʌltʃə) *n.* the art or science of cultivating gardens. —,horti'**cultural** *adj.* —,horti'**culturist** *n.*

Hos. *Bible. abbrev. for* Hosea.

hosanna (həʊ'zænə) *interj.* an exclamation of praise, esp. one to God.

hose[1] (həʊz) *n.* **1.** a flexible pipe, for conveying a liquid or gas. ~*vb.* **2.** (sometimes foll. by *down*) to wash, water, or sprinkle (a person or thing) with or as if with a hose.

hose[2] (həʊz) *n., pl.* **hose** *or* **hosen. 1.** stockings, socks, and tights collectively. **2.** *History.* a man's garment covering the legs and reaching up to the waist. **3. half-hose.** socks.

hosier ('həʊzɪə) *n.* a person who sells stockings, etc.

hosiery ('həʊzɪərɪ) *n.* stockings, socks, and knitted underclothing collectively.

hospice ('hɒspɪs) *n., pl.* **hospices. 1.** *Arch.* a place of shelter for travellers, esp. one kept by a monastic order. **2.** *Brit.* a home for the care of people in need, esp. the terminally ill.

hospitable ('hɒspɪtəbəl, hɒ'spɪt-) *adj.* **1.** welcoming to guests or strangers. **2.** fond of entertaining. —'**hospitableness** *n.* —'**hospitably** *adv.*

hospital ('hɒspɪtəl) *n.* **1.** an institution for the medical or psychiatric care and treatment of patients. **2.** (*modifier*) having the function of a hospital: *a hospital ship.* **3.** a repair shop for something specified: *a dolls' hospital.* **4.** *Arch.* a charitable home, hospice, or school.

hospitality (,hɒspɪ'tælɪtɪ) *n., pl.* -**ties.** kindness in welcoming strangers or guests.

hospitalize *or* -**lise** ('hɒspɪtə,laɪz) *vb.* (*tr.*) to admit or send (a person) into a hospital. —,hospitali'**zation** *or* -**li'sation** *n.*

hospitaller *or U.S.* **hospitaler** ('hɒspɪtələ) *n.* a per-

---

THESAURUS

horrible 1. abhorrent, abominable, appalling, awful, dreadful, fearful, frightful, ghastly, grim, grisly, gruesome, heinous, hideous, horrid, loathsome, repulsive, revolting, shameful, shocking, terrible, terrifying **2.** *Inf.* awful, beastly (*Inf.*), cruel, disagreeable, dreadful, ghastly (*Inf.*), mean, nasty, terrible, unkind, unpleasant

horrid 1. awful, disagreeable, disgusting, dreadful, horrible, nasty, offensive, terrible, unpleasant **2.** abominable, alarming, appalling, formidable, frightening, hair-raising, harrowing, hideous, horrific, odious, repulsive, revolting, shocking, terrifying, terrorizing **3.** *Inf.* beastly (*Inf.*), cruel, mean, nasty, unkind

horrify 1. affright, alarm, frighten, intimidate, petrify, scare, terrify, terrorize **2.** appal, disgust, dismay, outrage, shock, sicken

horror 1. alarm, apprehension, awe, consternation, dismay, dread, fear, fright, panic, terror **2.** abhorrence, abomination, antipathy, aversion, detestation, disgust, hatred, loathing, repugnance, revulsion

horror-struck *or* **horror-stricken** aghast, appalled, awe-struck, frightened to death, horrified, petrified, scared out of one's wits, shocked

horseman cavalier, cavalryman, dragoon, equestrian, horse-soldier, rider

horseplay buffoonery, clowning, fooling around, high jinks, pranks, romping, rough-and-tumble, roughhousing (*Sl.*), skylarking (*Inf.*)

horse sense common sense, gumption (*Inf.*), judgment, mother wit, nous (*Inf.*), practicality

hospitable 1. amicable, bountiful, cordial, friendly, generous, genial, gracious, kind, liberal, sociable, welcoming **2.** accessible, amenable, open-minded, receptive, responsive, tolerant

hospitality cheer, conviviality, cordiality, friendliness, heartiness, hospitableness, neighbourliness, sociability, warmth, welcome

son, esp. a member of certain religious orders, dedicated to hospital work, ambulance services, etc.

host¹ ('həust) *n.* **1.** a person who receives or entertains guests, esp. in his own home. **2.** the compere of a show or television programme. **3.** *Biol.* **a.** an animal or plant that supports a parasite. **b.** an animal into which tissue is experimentally grafted. **4.** the owner or manager of an inn. ~*vb.* **5.** to be the host of (a party, programme, etc.): *to host one's own show.*

host² ('həust) *n.* **1.** a great number; multitude. **2.** an archaic word for **army.**

Host (həust) *n. Christianity.* the wafer of unleavened bread consecrated in the Eucharist.

hostage ('hɒstɪdʒ) *n.* **1.** a person given to or held by another as a security or pledge. **2.** the state of being held as a hostage. **3.** any security or pledge.

hostel ('hɒstəl) *n.* **1.** a building providing overnight accommodation, as for homeless people. **2.** See **youth hostel. 3.** *Brit.* a supervised lodging house for nurses, workers, etc. —'**hosteller** or *U.S.* '**hosteler** *n.* —'**hostelling** or *U.S.* '**hosteling** *n.*

hostess ('həustɪs) *n.* **1.** a woman acting as host. **2.** a woman who receives and entertains patrons of a club, restaurant, etc. **3.** See **air hostess.**

hostile ('hɒstaɪl) *adj.* **1.** antagonistic; opposed. **2.** of or relating to an enemy. **3.** unfriendly. —'**hostilely** *adv.*

hostility (hɒ'stɪlɪtɪ) *n., pl.* -**ties. 1.** enmity. **2.** an act expressing enmity. **3.** (*pl.*) fighting; warfare.

hot (hɒt) *adj.* **hotter, hottest. 1.** having a relatively high temperature. **2.** having a temperature higher than desirable. **3.** causing a sensation of bodily heat. **4.** causing a burning sensation on the tongue: *a hot curry.* **5.** expressing or feeling intense emotion, such as anger or lust. **6.** intense or vehement. **7.** recent; new: *hot from the press.* **8.** *Ball games.* (of a ball) thrown or struck hard, and so difficult to respond to. **9.** much favoured: *a hot favourite.* **10.** *Inf.* having a dangerously high level of radioactivity. **11.** *Sl.* stolen or otherwise illegally obtained. **12.** *Sl.* (of people) being sought by the police. **13.** (of a colour) intense; striking: *hot pink.* **14.** following closely: *hot on the scent.* **15.** *Inf.* at a dangerously high electric potential. **16.** *Sl.* good (esp. in **not so hot**). **17.** *Jazz sl.* arousing great excitement by inspired improvisation, strong rhythms, etc. **18.** *Inf.* dangerous or unpleasant (esp. in **make it hot for someone**). **19.** (in various games) very near the answer. **20.** *Metallurgy.* (of a process) at a sufficiently high temperature for metal to be in a soft workable state. **21.** *Austral. & N.Z. inf.* (of a price, etc.) excessive. **22. hot under the collar.** *Inf.* aroused with anger, annoyance, etc. **23. in hot water.** *Inf.* in trouble. ~*adv.* **24.** in a hot manner; hotly. —'**hottish** *adj.* —'**hotly** *adv.* —'**hotness** *n.*

hot air *n. Inf.* empty and usually boastful talk.

hotbed ('hɒt,bɛd) *n.* **1.** a glass-covered bed of soil, usually heated, for propagating plants, forcing early vegetables, etc. **2.** a place offering ideal conditions for the growth of an idea, activity, etc., esp. one considered bad.

hot-blooded *adj.* **1.** passionate or excitable. **2.** (of a horse) being of thoroughbred stock.

hotchpotch ('hɒtʃ,pɒtʃ) or *esp. U.S.* **hodgepodge** *n.* **1.** a jumbled mixture. **2.** a thick soup or stew.

hot cross bun *n.* a yeast bun marked with a cross and traditionally eaten on Good Friday.

hot dog *n.* a sausage, esp. a frankfurter, usually served hot in a long roll split lengthways.

hotel (həu'tɛl) *n.* **1.** a commercially run establishment providing lodging and usually meals for guests. **2.** *Austral. & N.Z.* a public house.

hotelier (hə'tɛljeɪ) *n.* an owner or manager of one or more hotels.

hotfoot ('hɒt,fut) *adv.* with all possible speed.

hot-headed *adj.* impetuous, rash, or hot-tempered. —,**hot-'headedness** *n.*

hothouse ('hɒt,haus) *n.* **1. a.** a greenhouse in which the temperature is maintained at a fixed level. **b.** (*as modifier): a hothouse plant.* **2.** (*modifier*) *Inf.*, often disparaging. sensitive or delicate.

hot line *n.* a direct telephone, teletype, or other communications link between heads of government, etc., for emergency use.

hot money *n.* capital that is transferred from one commercial centre to another seeking the best opportunity for short-term gain.

hotplate ('hɒt,pleɪt) *n.* **1.** an electrically heated plate on a cooker or one set into a working surface. **2.** a portable device on which food can be kept warm.

hotpot ('hɒt,pɒt) *n. Brit.* a casserole covered with a layer of potatoes.

hot rod *n.* a car with an engine that has been radically modified to produce increased power.

hot seat *n.* **1.** *Inf.* a difficult or dangerous position. **2.** *U.S.* a slang term for **electric chair.**

hot stuff *n. Inf.* **1.** a person, object, etc., considered important, attractive, etc. **2.** a pornographic or erotic book, play, film, etc.

Hottentot ('hɒtⁿn,tɒt) *n.* **1.** (*pl.* -**tot** or -**tots**) a member of a race of people of southern Africa, who formerly occupied the region near the Cape of Good Hope and are now almost extinct. **2.** any of the languages of this people. **3.** *S. African derog.* a non-White person.

hot up *vb.* (*adv.*) *Inf.* **1.** to make or become more exciting, active, or intense. **2.** (*tr.*) another term for **soup up.**

hot-water bottle *n.* a receptacle, esp. one made of rubber, designed to be filled with hot water, used for warming a bed.

hound (haund) *n.* **1. a.** any of several breeds of dog used for hunting. **b.** (*in combination): a deerhound.* **2. the hounds.** a pack of foxhounds, etc. **3.** a dog, esp. one regarded as annoying. **4.** a despicable person. **5.** (in hare and hounds) a runner who pursues a hare. **6.** *Sl., chiefly U.S.* an enthusiast: *an autograph hound.* **7. ride to hounds** or **follow the hounds.** to take part in a fox hunt. ~*vb.* (*tr.*) **8.** to pursue relentlessly. **9.** to urge on. —'**hounder** *n.*

hour (auə) *n.* **1.** a period of time equal to 3600 seconds; 1/24th of a calendar day. Related adj.: **horary. 2.** any of the points on the face of a timepiece that indicate intervals of 60 minutes. **3. the hour.** an exact number of complete hours: *the bus leaves on the hour.* **4.** the time. **5.** the time allowed for or used for something: *the lunch hour.* **6.** a special moment: *our finest hour.* **7.** the dis-

---

THESAURUS

host¹ *n.* **1.** entertainer, innkeeper, landlord, master of ceremonies, proprietor **2.** anchor man, compere (*Brit.*), presenter ~*v.* **3.** compere (*Brit.*), introduce, present

host² array, drove, horde, legion, multitude, myriad, swarm, throng

hostage captive, gage, pawn, pledge, prisoner, security, surety

hostile 1. antagonistic, anti (*Inf.*), bellicose, belligerent, contrary, ill-disposed, inimical, malevolent, opposed, opposite, rancorous, unkind, warlike **2.** adverse, alien, inhospitable, unfriendly, unpropitious, unsympathetic, unwelcoming

hostilities conflict, fighting, state of war, war, warfare

hostility abhorrence, animosity, animus, antagonism, antipathy, aversion, detestation, enmity, hatred, ill will, malevolence, malice, opposition, resentment, unfriendliness

hot 1. blistering, boiling, burning, fiery,

flaming, heated, piping hot, roasting, scalding, scorching, searing, steaming, sultry, sweltering, torrid, warm **2.** acrid, biting, peppery, piquant, pungent, sharp, spicy **3.** *Fig.* animated, ardent, excited, fervent, fervid, fierce, fiery, impetuous, inflamed, intense, irascible, lustful, passionate, raging, stormy, touchy, vehement, violent **4.** fresh, just out, latest, new, recent, up to the minute **5.** approved, favoured, in demand, in vogue, popular, sought-after **6.** close, following closely, in hot pursuit, near

hot air blather, blether, bombast, bosh (*Inf.*), bunkum, claptrap (*Inf.*), empty talk, gas (*Sl.*), guff (*Sl.*), rant, tall talk (*Inf.*), verbiage, wind

hotbed breeding ground, den, forcing house, nest, nursery, seedbed

hot-blooded ardent, excitable, fervent, fiery, heated, impulsive, passionate, rash, spirited, temperamental, wild

hotchpotch conglomeration, farrago, gallimaufry, hash, jumble, medley, *mélange*, mess, miscellany, mishmash, mixture, olio, olla podrida, potpourri

hotfoot hastily, helter-skelter, hurriedly, pell-mell, posthaste, quickly, speedily

hothead daredevil, desperado, hotspur, madcap, tearaway

hot-headed fiery, foolhardy, hasty, hot-tempered, impetuous, precipitate, quick-tempered, rash, reckless, unruly, volatile

hothouse 1. *n.* conservatory, glasshouse, greenhouse **2.** *adj.* coddled, dainty, delicate, exotic, fragile, frail, overprotected, pampered, sensitive

hound *v.* **1.** chase, drive, give chase, hunt, hunt down, pursue **2.** badger, goad, harass, harry, impel, persecute, pester, prod, provoke

tance covered in an hour: *we live an hour from the city.* **8.** *Astron.* an angular measurement of right ascension equal to 15° or a 24th part of the celestial equator. **9. one's last hour.** the time of one's death.

hourglass ('auə‚glɑːs) *n.* **1.** a device consisting of two transparent chambers linked by a narrow channel, containing a quantity of sand that takes a specified time to trickle from one chamber to the other. **2.** (*modifier*) well-proportioned with a small waist: *an hourglass figure.*

houri ('huərɪ) *n., pl.* **-ris.** **1.** (in Muslim belief) any of the nymphs of Paradise. **2.** any alluring woman.

hourly ('auəlɪ) *adj.* **1.** of, occurring, or done every hour. **2.** done in or measured by the hour: *an hourly rate.* **3.** continual or frequent. ~*adv.* **4.** every hour. **5.** at any moment.

hours (auəz) *pl. n.* **1.** a period regularly appointed for work, etc. **2.** one's times of rising and going to bed: *he keeps late hours.* **3. the small hours.** the hours just after midnight. **4. till all hours.** until very late. **5.** an indefinite time. **6.** Also called (in the Roman Catholic Church): **canonical hours. a.** the seven times of the day laid down for the recitation of the prayers of the divine office. **b.** the prayers recited at these times.

house *n.* (haus), *pl.* **houses** ('hauzɪz). **1. a.** a building used as a home; dwelling. **b.** (*as modifier*): *house dog.* **2.** the people present in a house. **3. a.** a building for some specific purpose. **b.** (*in combination*): *a schoolhouse.* **4.** (*often cap.*) a family or dynasty: *the House of York.* **5. a.** a commercial company: *a publishing house.* **b.** (*as modifier*): *a house journal.* **6.** a legislative body. **7.** a quorum in such a body (esp. in **make a house**). **8.** a dwelling for a religious community. **9.** *Astrol.* any of the 12 divisions of the zodiac. **10.** any of several divisions of a large school. **11.** a hotel, restaurant, club, etc., or the management of such an establishment: *drinks on the house.* **12.** the audience in a theatre or cinema. **13.** an informal word for **brothel.** **14.** a hall in which a legislative body meets. **15.** See **full house.** **16.** *Naut.* any structure or shelter on the weather deck of a vessel. **17. bring the house down.** *Theatre.* to win great applause. **18. like a house on fire.** *Inf.* very well. **19. open house.** free or general hospitality. **20. put one's house in order.** to settle or organize one's affairs. **21. safe as houses.** *Brit.* very secure. ~*vb.* (hauz). **22.** (*tr.*) to provide with or serve as accommodation. **23.** to give or receive lodging. **24.** (*tr.*) to contain or cover; protect. **25.** (*tr.*) to fit (a piece of wood) into a mortise, joint, etc. —'**houseless** *adj.*

house arrest *n.* confinement to one's own home rather than in prison.

houseboat ('haus‚bəut) *n.* a stationary boat or barge used as a home.

housebound ('haus‚baund) *adj.* unable to leave one's house because of illness, injury, etc.

housebreaking ('haus‚breɪkɪŋ) *n. Criminal law.* the act of entering a building as a trespasser for an unlawful purpose. Assimilated with burglary, 1968. —'**house‚breaker** *n.*

housecoat ('haus‚kəut) *n.* a woman's loose robelike informal garment.

housefly ('haus‚flaɪ) *n., pl.* **-flies.** a common dipterous fly that frequents human habitations, spreads disease, and lays its eggs in carrion, decaying vegetables, etc.

household ('haus‚həuld) *n.* **1.** the people living together in one house. **2.** (*modifier*) relating to the running of a household: *household management.*

householder ('haus‚həuldə) *n.* a person who owns or rents a house. —'**house‚holder‚ship** *n.*

household name *or* **word** *n.* a person or thing that is very well known.

housekeeper ('haus‚kiːpə) *n.* a person, esp. a woman,

employed to run a household.

housekeeping ('haus‚kiːpɪŋ) *n.* **1.** the running of a household. **2.** money allotted for this.

housemaid ('haus‚meɪd) *n.* a girl or woman employed to do housework, esp. one who is resident in the household.

housemaid's knee *n.* inflammation and swelling of the bursa in front of the kneecap, caused esp. by constant kneeling on a hard surface. Technical name: **prepatellar bursitis.**

houseman ('hausmən) *n., pl.* **-men.** *Med.* a junior doctor who is a member of the medical staff of a hospital. U.S. equivalent: **intern.**

house martin *n.* a Eurasian swallow with a slightly forked tail.

House of Commons *n.* (in Britain, Canada, etc.) the lower chamber of Parliament.

House of Keys *n.* the lower chamber of the legislature of the Isle of Man.

House of Lords *n.* (in Britain) the upper chamber of Parliament, composed of the peers of the realm.

house party *n.* **1.** a party, usually in a country house, at which guests are invited to stay for several days. **2.** the guests who are invited.

house-proud *adj.* proud of the appearance, cleanliness, etc., of one's house, sometimes excessively so.

housetop ('haus‚tɒp) *n.* **1.** the roof of a house. **2. proclaim from the housetops.** to announce (something) publicly.

house-warming *n.* a party given after moving into a new home.

housewife *n., pl.* **-wives.** **1.** ('haus‚waɪf) a woman who keeps house. **2.** ('hʌzɪf) Also called: **hussy, huswife.** *Chiefly Brit.* a small sewing kit. —**housewifery** ('haus‚wɪfərɪ) *n.* —'**housewifely** *adj.*

housework ('haus‚wɜːk) *n.* the work of running a home, such as cleaning, cooking, etc.

housing[1] ('hauzɪŋ) *n.* **1. a.** houses collectively. **b.** (*as modifier*): *a housing problem.* **2.** the act of providing with accommodation. **3.** a hole or slot made in one wooden member to receive another. **4.** a part designed to contain or support a component or mechanism: *a wheel housing.*

housing[2] ('hauzɪŋ) *n.* (*often pl.*) *Arch.* another word for **trappings** (sense 2).

hove (həuv) *vb. Chiefly naut.* a past tense or past participle of **heave.**

hovel ('hɒvəl) *n.* **1.** a ramshackle dwelling place. **2.** an open shed for livestock, carts, etc. **3.** the conical building enclosing a kiln.

hover ('hɒvə) *vb.* (*intr.*) **1.** to remain suspended in one place. **2.** (of certain birds, esp. hawks) to remain in one place in the air by rapidly beating the wings. **3.** to linger uncertainly. **4.** to be in a state of indecision. ~*n.* **5.** the act of hovering. —'**hoverer** *n.*

hovercraft ('hɒvə‚krɑːft) *n.* a vehicle that is able to travel across both land and water on a cushion of air.

how (hau) *adv.* **1.** in what way? by what means?: *how did it happen?* Also used in indirect questions: *tell me how he did it.* **2.** to what extent?: *how tall is he?* **3.** how good? how well? what...like?: *how did she sing? how was the holiday?* **4.** how about? used to suggest something: *how about a cup of tea?* **5. how are you?** what is your state of health? **6. how come?** *Inf.* what is the reason (that)?: *how come you told him?* **7. how's that? a.** what is your opinion? **b.** *Cricket.* (an appeal to the umpire) is the batsman out? **8. how now?** *or* **how so?** *Arch.* what is the meaning of this? **9.** in whatever way: *do it how you wish.* **10. and how!** (intensifier) very much so! ~*n.* **11.** the way a thing is done: *the how of it.*

howbeit (hau'biːɪt) *Arch.* ~ **1.** sentence connector.

THESAURUS

house *n.* **1.** abode, building, domicile, dwelling, edifice, habitation, home, homestead, residence **2.** family, household, ménage **3.** ancestry, clan, dynasty, family tree, kindred, line, lineage, race, tribe **4.** business, company, concern, establishment, firm, organization, outfit (*Inf.*), partnership **5.** Commons, legislative body, parliament **6.** hotel, inn, public house, tavern **7. on the house** for nothing, free, gratis, without expense ~*v.* **8.** accommodate, billet, board, domicile,

harbour, lodge, put up, quarter, take in **9.** contain, cover, keep, protect, sheathe, shelter, store

household **1.** *n.* family, home, house, ménage **2.** *adj.* domestic, domiciliary, family, ordinary, plain

householder homeowner, occupant, resident, tenant

housekeeping home economy, homemaking (*U.S.*), housecraft, household management, housewifery

housing **1.** accommodation, dwellings, homes, houses **2.** case, casing, container, cover, covering, enclosure, sheath

hovel cabin, den, hole, hut, shack, shanty, shed

hover **1.** be suspended, drift, float, flutter, fly, hang, poise **2.** hang about, linger, wait nearby **3.** alternate, dither, falter, fluctuate, haver (*Brit.*), oscillate, pause, seesaw, swither (*Scot. dialect*), vacillate, waver

however. ~*conj.* **2.** (*subordinating*) though; although.

howdah ('haʊdə) *n.* a seat for riding on an elephant's back, esp. one with a canopy.

however (haʊ'ɛvə) **1.** *sentence connector.* still; nevertheless. **2.** *sentence connector.* on the other hand; yet. ~*adv.* **3.** by whatever means. **4.** (*used with adjectives of quantity or degree*) no matter how: *however long it takes, finish it.* **5.** an emphatic form of **how** (sense 1).

howitzer ('haʊɪtsə) *n.* a cannon having a short barrel with a low muzzle velocity and a steep angle of fire.

howl (haʊl) *n.* **1.** a long plaintive cry characteristic of a wolf or hound. **2.** a similar cry of pain or sorrow. **3.** a prolonged outburst of laughter. **4.** *Electronics.* an unwanted high-pitched sound produced by a sound-producing system as a result of feedback. ~*vb.* **5.** to express in a howl or utter such cries. **6.** (*intr.*) (of the wind, etc.) to make a wailing noise. **7.** (*intr.*) *Inf.* to shout or laugh.

howl down *vb.* (*tr., adv.*) to prevent (a speaker) from being heard by shouting disapprovingly.

howler ('haʊlə) *n.* **1.** Also called: **howler monkey.** a large New World monkey inhabiting tropical forests in South America and having a loud howling cry. **2.** *Inf.* a glaring mistake. **3.** a person or thing that howls.

howling ('haʊlɪŋ) *adj.* (*prenominal*) *Inf.* (intensifier): *a howling success; a howling error.*

howsoever (,haʊsəʊ'ɛvə) *sentence connector, adv.* a less common word for **however.**

hoy (hɔɪ) *interj.* a cry used to attract attention or drive animals.

hoyden *or* **hoiden** ('hɔɪdən) *n.* a wild boisterous girl; tomboy. —'**hoydenish** *or* '**hoidenish** *adj.*

H.P. *abbrev. for:* **1.** *Brit.* hire purchase. **2.** Also: **hp** horsepower. **3.** high pressure. **4.** (in Britain) Houses of Parliament. ~Also (for senses 1-3): **h.p.**

H.Q. *or* **h.q.** *abbrev. for* headquarters.

hr. *or* **hr** *abbrev. for* hour.

H.R.H. *abbrev. for* His (*or* Her) Royal Highness.

HT *Physics. abbrev. for* high tension.

hub (hʌb) *n.* **1.** the central portion of a wheel, propeller, fan, etc., through which the axle passes. **2.** the focal point.

hubble-bubble ('hʌbəl'bʌbəl) *n.* **1.** another name for **hookah.** **2.** turmoil. **3.** a gargling sound.

hubbub ('hʌbʌb) *n.* **1.** a confused noise of many voices. **2.** tumult; uproar.

hubby ('hʌbɪ) *n., pl.* **-bies.** an informal word for **husband.**

hubris ('hjuːbrɪs) *or* **hybris** ('haɪbrɪs) *n.* **1.** pride or arrogance. **2.** (in Greek tragedy) an excess of ambition, pride, etc., ultimately causing the transgressor's ruin. —**hu'bristic** *or* **hy'bristic** *adj.*

huckaback ('hʌkə,bæk) *n.* a coarse absorbent linen or cotton fabric used for towels, etc. Also: **huck** (hʌk).

huckster ('hʌkstə) *n.* **1.** a person who uses aggressive or questionable methods of selling. **2.** *Now rare.* a person who sells small articles or fruit in the street. **3.** *U.S.* a person who writes for radio or television advertisements. ~*vb.* **4.** (*tr.*) to peddle. **5.** (*tr.*) to sell or advertise aggressively or questionably. **6.** to haggle over.

huddle ('hʌdəl) *n.* **1.** a heaped or crowded mass of people or things. **2.** *Inf.* a private or impromptu conference (esp. in **go into a huddle**). ~*vb.* **3.** to crowd or nestle closely together. **4.** (often foll. by *up*) to hunch (oneself), as through cold. **5.** (*intr.*) *Inf.* to confer privately. **6.**

(*tr.*) *Chiefly Brit.* to do (something) in a careless way. **7.** (*tr.*) *Rare.* to put on (clothes) hurriedly. —**'huddler** *n.*

hue (hjuː) *n.* **1.** the attribute of colour that enables an observer to classify it as red, blue, etc., and excludes white, black, and grey. **2.** a shade of a colour. **3.** aspect: *a different hue on matters.* —**hued** *adj.*

hue and cry *n.* **1.** (formerly) the pursuit of a suspected criminal with loud cries in order to raise the alarm. **2.** any loud public outcry.

huff (hʌf) *n.* **1.** a passing mood of anger or pique (esp. in **in a huff**). ~*vb.* **2.** to make or become angry or resentful. **3.** (*intr.*) to blow or puff heavily. **4.** Also: **blow.** *Draughts.* to remove (an opponent's draught) from the board for failure to make a capture. **5.** (*tr.*) *Obs.* to bully. —**'huffish** *or* **'huffy** *adj.*

hug (hʌg) *vb.* **hugging, hugged.** (*mainly tr.*) **1.** (*also intr.*) to clasp tightly, usually with affection; embrace. **2.** to keep close to a shore, kerb, etc. **3.** to cling to (beliefs, etc.); cherish. **4.** to congratulate (oneself). ~*n.* **5.** a tight or fond embrace. —**'huggable** *adj.*

huge (hjuːdʒ) *adj.* extremely large. —**'hugely** *adv.* —**'hugeness** *n.*

huggermugger ('hʌgə,mʌgə) *n.* **1.** confusion. **2.** *Rare.* secrecy. ~*adj., adv. Arch.* **3.** with secrecy. **4.** in confusion. ~*vb. Obs.* **5.** (*tr.*) to keep secret. **6.** (*intr.*) to act secretly.

Huguenot ('hjuːgə,nəʊ, -,nɒt) *n.* **1.** a French Calvinist, esp. of the 16th or 17th centuries. ~*adj.* **2.** designating the French Protestant Church.

huh (*spelling pron.* hʌ) *interj.* an exclamation of derision, bewilderment, enquiry, etc.

hula ('huːlə) *or* **hula-hula** *n.* a Hawaiian dance performed by a woman.

hulk (hʌlk) *n.* **1.** the body of an abandoned vessel. **2.** *Disparaging.* a large or unwieldy vessel. **3.** *Disparaging.* a large ungainly person or thing. **4.** (*often pl.*) the hull of a ship, used as a storehouse, etc., or (esp. in 19th-century Britain) as a prison.

hulking ('hʌlkɪŋ) *adj.* big and ungainly.

hull (hʌl) *n.* **1.** the main body of a vessel, tank, etc. **2.** the calyx at the base of a strawberry, raspberry, or similar fruit. **3.** the outer casing of a missile, rocket, etc. ~*vb.* **4.** to remove the hulls from (fruit). **5.** (*tr.*) to pierce the hull of (a vessel, tank, etc.). —**'huller** *n.*

hullabaloo *or* **hullaballoo** (,hʌləbə'luː) *n., pl.* **-loos.** loud confused noise; commotion.

hullo (hʌ'ləʊ) *sentence substitute, n.* a variant spelling of **hello.**

hum (hʌm) *vb.* **humming, hummed.** **1.** (*intr.*) to make a low continuous vibrating sound. **2.** (*intr.*) (of a person) to sing with the lips closed. **3.** (*intr.*) to utter an indistinct sound, as in hesitation; hem. **4.** (*intr.*) *Sl.* to be in a state of feverish activity. **5.** (*intr.*) *Sl.* to smell unpleasant. **6. hum and haw.** See **hem²** (sense 3). ~*n.* **7.** a low continuous murmuring sound. **8.** *Electronics.* an undesired low-frequency noise in the output of an amplifier or receiver. ~*interj., n.* **9.** an indistinct sound of hesitation, embarrassment, etc.; hem. —**'hummer** *n.*

human ('hjuːmən) *adj.* **1.** of or relating to mankind: *human nature.* **2.** consisting of people: *a human chain.* **3.** having the attributes of man as opposed to animals, divine beings, or machines: *human failings.* **4. a.** kind or considerate. **b.** natural. ~*n.* **5.** a human being; person. —**'humanness** *n.*

THESAURUS

however after all, anyhow, be that as it may, but, nevertheless, nonetheless, notwithstanding, on the other hand, still, though, yet

howl 1. *n.* bay, bellow, clamour, cry, groan, hoot, outcry, roar, scream, shriek, ululation, wail, yelp, yowl **2.** *v.* bellow, cry, cry out, lament, quest (*used of hounds*), roar, scream, shout, shriek, ululate, wail, weep, yell, yelp

howler bloomer (*Brit. inf.*), blunder, boner (*Sl.*), bull (*Sl.*), clanger (*Inf.*), error, malapropism, mistake, schoolboy howler

hub centre, core, focal point, focus, heart, middle, nerve centre, pivot

huddle *n.* **1.** confusion, crowd, disorder, heap, jumble, mass, mess, muddle **2.** *Inf.* confab (*Inf.*), conference, discussion, meeting ~*v.* **3.** cluster, converge, crowd, flock, gath-

er, press, throng **4.** crouch, cuddle, curl up, hunch up, make oneself small, nestle, snuggle

hue 1. colour, dye, shade, tincture, tinge, tint, tone **2.** aspect, cast, complexion, light

hue and cry brouhaha, clamour, furore, hullabaloo, much ado, outcry, ruction (*Inf.*), rumpus, uproar

hug *v.* **1.** clasp, cuddle, embrace, enfold, hold close, squeeze, take in one's arms **2.** cling to, follow closely, keep close, stay near **3.** cherish, cling, hold onto, nurse, retain ~*n.* **4.** bear hug, clasp, clinch (*Sl.*), embrace, squeeze

huge Brobdingnagian, bulky, colossal, enormous, extensive, gargantuan, giant, gigantic, great, immense, jumbo (*Inf.*), large,

mammoth, massive, monumental, mountainous, prodigious, stupendous, titanic, tremendous, vast

hulk 1. derelict, frame, hull, shell, shipwreck, wreck **2.** lout, lubber, lump (*Inf.*), oaf

hull *n.* **1.** body, casing, covering, frame, framework, skeleton **2.** husk, peel, pod, rind, shell, shuck, skin ~*v.* **3.** husk, peel, shell, shuck, skin, trim

hullabaloo babel, bedlam, brouhaha, clamour, commotion, confusion, din, disturbance, furore, hubbub, hue and cry, hurlyburly, noise, outcry, pandemonium, racket, ruckus (*Inf.*), ruction (*Inf.*), rumpus, to-do, tumult, turmoil, uproar

hum 1. bombinate *or* bombilate (*Literary*), buzz, croon, drone, mumble, murmur, purr,

human being *n.* a member of any of the races of *Homo sapiens;* person; man, woman, or child.

humane (hjuːˈmeɪn) *adj.* 1. characterized by kindness, sympathy, etc. 2. inflicting as little pain as possible: *a humane killing.* 3. civilizing or liberal: *humane studies.* —hu'manely *adv.* —hu'maneness *n.*

humanism (ˈhjuːməˌnɪzəm) *n.* 1. a school of philosophy that believes in human effort and ingenuity rather than religion. 2. (*often cap.*) a cultural movement of the Renaissance, based on classical studies. 3. interest in the welfare of people. —'humanist *n.* —human'istic *adj.*

humanitarian (hjuːˌmænɪˈtɛərɪən) *adj.* 1. having the interests of mankind at heart. ~*n.* 2. a philanthropist. —hu,mani'tarianism *n.*

humanity (hjuːˈmænɪtɪ) *n., pl.* -ties. 1. the human race. 2. the quality of being human. 3. kindness or mercy. 4. (*pl.*) (usually preceded by *the*) the study of literature, philosophy, and the arts, esp. study of Ancient Greece and Rome.

humanize *or* -nise (ˈhjuːməˌnaɪz) *vb.* 1. to make or become human. 2. to make or become humane. —,humani'zation *or* -ni'sation *n.*

humankind (ˌhjuːmənˈkaɪnd) *n.* the human race; humanity.

humanly (ˈhjuːmənlɪ) *adv.* 1. by human powers or means. 2. in a human or humane manner.

humanoid (ˈhjuːməˌnɔɪd) *adj.* 1. like a human being in appearance. ~*n.* 2. a being with human rather than anthropoid characteristics. 3. (in science fiction) a robot or creature resembling a human being.

human rights *pl. n.* the rights of individuals to liberty, justice, etc.

humble (ˈhʌmbəl) *adj.* 1. conscious of one's failings. 2. unpretentious; lowly: *a humble cottage; my humble opinion.* 3. deferential or servile. ~*vb.* (*tr.*) 4. to cause to become humble; humiliate. 5. to lower in status. —'humbleness *n.* —'humbly *adv.*

humble pie *n.* 1. (formerly) a pie made from the heart, entrails, etc., of a deer. 2. **eat humble pie.** to be forced to behave humbly; be humiliated.

humbug (ˈhʌmˌbʌg) *n.* 1. a person or thing that deceives. 2. nonsense. 3. *Brit.* a hard boiled sweet, usually having a striped pattern. ~*vb.* -bugging, -bugged. 4. to cheat or deceive (someone). —'hum,bugger *n.* —'hum,buggery *n.*

humdinger (ˈhʌmˌdɪŋə) *n. Sl.* an excellent person or thing.

humdrum (ˈhʌmˌdrʌm) *adj.* 1. ordinary; dull. ~*n.* 2. a monotonous routine, task, or person.

humerus (ˈhjuːmərəs) *n., pl.* -meri (-məˌraɪ). 1. the bone that extends from the shoulder to the elbow in man. 2. the corresponding bone in other vertebrates. —'humeral *adj.*

humid (ˈhjuːmɪd) *adj.* moist; damp. —'humidly *adv.* —'humidness *n.*

humidex (ˈhjuːmɪdɛks) *n. Canad.* an index of discomfort showing the combined effect of humidity and temperature.

humidify (hjuːˈmɪdɪˌfaɪ) *vb.* -fying, -fied. (*tr.*) to make (air, etc.) humid or damp. —hu,midifi'cation *n.* —hu'midifier *n.*

humidity (hjuːˈmɪdɪtɪ) *n.* 1. dampness. 2. a measure of the amount of moisture in the air.

humiliate (hjuːˈmɪlɪˌeɪt) *vb.* (*tr.*) to lower or hurt the dignity or pride of. —hu'mili,atingly *adv.* —hu,mili'ation *n.* —hu'mili,ator *n.*

humility (hjuːˈmɪlɪtɪ) *n., pl.* -ties. the state or quality of being humble.

hummingbird (ˈhʌmɪŋˌbɜːd) *n.* a very small American bird having a brilliant iridescent plumage, long slender bill, and wings specialized for very powerful vibrating flight.

hummock (ˈhʌmək) *n.* 1. a hillock; knoll. 2. a ridge or mound of ice in an ice field. 3. *Chiefly southern U.S.* a wooded area lying above the level of an adjacent marsh. —'hummocky *adj.*

humoresque (ˌhjuːməˈrɛsk) *n.* a short lively piece of music.

humorist (ˈhjuːmərɪst) *n.* a person who acts, speaks, or writes in a humorous way.

humorous (ˈhjuːmərəs) *adj.* 1. funny; comical; amusing. 2. displaying or creating humour. —'humorously *adv.* —'humorousness *n.*

humour *or U.S.* **humor** (ˈhjuːmə) *n.* 1. the quality of being funny. 2. Also called: **sense of humour.** the ability to appreciate or express that which is humorous. 3. situations, speech, or writings that are humorous. 4. a. a state of mind; mood. b. (*in combination*): *good humour.* 5. temperament or disposition. 6. a caprice or whim. 7. any of various fluids in the body: *aqueous humour.* 8. *Arch.* Also called: **cardinal humour.** any of the four bodily fluids (blood, phlegm, choler or yellow bile, melancholy or black bile) formerly thought to determine emotional and physical disposition. 9. **out of humour.** in a bad mood. ~*vb.* (*tr.*) 10. to gratify; indulge: *he humoured the boy's whims.* 11. to adapt oneself to: *to humour someone's fantasies.* —'humourless *or U.S.* 'humorless *adj.*

THESAURUS

sing, throb, thrum, vibrate, whir 2. be active, be busy, bustle, buzz, move, pulsate, pulse, stir, vibrate

human *adj.* 1. anthropoid, fleshly, manlike, mortal 2. approachable, compassionate, considerate, fallible, forgivable, humane, kind, kindly, natural, understandable, understanding, vulnerable ~*n.* 3. body, child, creature, human being, individual, man, mortal, person, soul, wight (*Archaic*), woman

humane benevolent, benign, charitable, clement, compassionate, forbearing, forgiving, gentle, good, good-natured, kind, kindhearted, kindly, lenient, merciful, mild, sympathetic, tender, understanding

humanitarian 1. *adj.* altruistic, beneficent, benevolent, charitable, compassionate, humane, philanthropic, public-spirited 2. *n.* altruist, benefactor, Good Samaritan, philanthropist

humanitarianism beneficence, benevolence, charity, generosity, good will, humanism, philanthropy

humanities classical studies, classics, liberal arts, literae humaniores

humanity 1. flesh, Homo sapiens, humankind, human race, man, mankind, men, mortality, people 2. human nature, humanness, mortality 3. benevolence, benignity, brotherly love, charity, compassion, fellow feeling, kind-heartedness, kindness, mercy, philanthropy, sympathy, tenderness, tolerance, understanding

humanize civilize, cultivate, educate, enlighten, improve, mellow, polish, reclaim, refine, soften, tame

humble *adj.* 1. meek, modest, self-effacing, submissive, unassuming, unostentatious, unpretentious 2. common, commonplace, insignificant, low, low-born, lowly, mean, modest, obscure, ordinary, plebeian, poor, simple, undistinguished, unimportant, unpretentious 3. courteous, deferential, obliging, obsequious, polite, respectful, servile, subservient ~*v.* 4. abase, abash, break, bring down, chagrin, chasten, crush, debase, degrade, demean, disgrace, humiliate, lower, mortify, put down (*Sl.*), reduce, shame, sink, subdue, take down a peg (*Inf.*) 5. **humble oneself** abase oneself, eat crow (*U.S. inf.*), eat humble pie, go on bended knee, grovel, swallow one's pride

humbug *n.* 1. bluff, cheat, deceit, deception, dodge, feint, fraud, hoax, imposition, imposture, ruse, sham, swindle, trick, trickery, wile 2. charlatan, cheat, con man (*Sl.*), faker, fraud, impostor, phoney (*Sl.*), quack, swindler, trickster 3. baloney (*Inf.*), cant, charlatanry, claptrap (*Inf.*), eyewash (*Inf.*), gammon (*Brit. inf.*), hypocrisy, nonsense, quackery, rubbish ~*v.* 4. bamboozle (*Inf.*), befool, beguile, cheat, cozen, deceive, delude, dupe, fool, gull (*Archaic*), hoax, hoodwink, impose, mislead, swindle, take in (*Inf.*), trick

humdrum boring, commonplace, dreary, dull, monotonous, mundane, ordinary, repetitious, routine, tedious, tiresome, uneventful, uninteresting, unvaried, wearisome

humid clammy, damp, dank, moist, muggy, steamy, sticky, sultry, watery, wet

humidity clamminess, damp, dampness, dankness, dew, humidness, moistness, moisture, mugginess, sogginess, wetness

humiliate abase, abash, bring low, chagrin, chasten, crush, debase, degrade, discomfit, disgrace, embarrass, humble, make (someone) eat humble pie, mortify, put down (*Sl.*), shame, subdue, take down a peg (*Inf.*)

humiliating crushing, degrading, disgracing, embarrassing, humbling, ignominious, mortifying, shaming

humiliation abasement, affront, chagrin, condescension, degradation, disgrace, dishonour, embarrassment, humbling, ignominy, indignity, loss of face, mortification, put-down, resignation, self-abasement, shame, submission, submissiveness

humility diffidence, humbleness, lack of pride, lowliness, meekness, modesty, self-abasement, servility, submissiveness, unpretentiousness

humorist comedian, comic, droll, eccentric, funny man, jester, joker, wag, wit

humorous amusing, comic, comical, entertaining, facetious, farcical, funny, hilarious, jocose, jocular, laughable, ludicrous,

hump ('hʌmp) n. **1.** a rounded protuberance or projection. **2.** a rounded deformity of the back, consisting of a spinal curvature. **3.** a rounded protuberance on the back of a camel or related animal. **4. the hump.** Brit. inf. a fit of sulking. ~vb. **5.** to form or become a hump; hunch; arch. **6.** (tr.) Sl. to carry or heave. **7.** Taboo sl. to have sexual intercourse with (someone). —'hump,like adj. —'humpy adj.

humpback ('hʌmp,bæk) n. **1.** another word for **hunchback. 2.** Also called: **humpback whale.** a large whalebone whale with a humped back and long flippers. **3.** a Pacific salmon, the male of which has a humped back. **4.** Also: **humpback bridge.** Brit. a road bridge having a sharp incline and decline and usually a narrow roadway. —'hump,backed adj.

humph (spelling pron. hʌmf) interj. an exclamation of annoyance, indecision, etc.

humus ('hju:məs) n. a dark brown or black colloidal mass of partially decomposed organic matter in the soil. It improves the fertility and water retention of the soil.

Hun (hʌn) n. **1.** a member of any of several Asiatic nomadic peoples who dominated much of Asia and E Europe from before 3000 B.C. invading the Roman Empire in the 4th and 5th centuries A.D. **2.** Inf. a derogatory name for a German. **3.** Inf. a vandal. —'Hunnish adj. —'Hun,like adj.

hunch (hʌntʃ) n. **1.** an intuitive guess or feeling. **2.** another word for **hump. 3.** a lump or large piece. ~vb. **4.** to draw (oneself or a part of the body) up or together. **5.** (intr.; usually foll. by up) to sit in a hunched position.

hunchback ('hʌntʃ,bæk) n. **1.** a person having an abnormal curvature of the spine. **2.** such a curvature. ~Also called: **humpback.** —'hunch,backed adj.

hundred ('hʌndrəd) n., pl. **-dreds** or **-dred. 1.** the cardinal number that is the product of ten and ten; five score. **2.** a numeral, 100, C, etc., representing this number. **3.** (often pl.) a large but unspecified number, amount, or quantity. **4.** (pl.) the 100 years of a specified century: in the sixteen hundreds. **5.** something representing, represented by, or consisting of 100 units. **6.** Maths. the position containing a digit representing that number followed by two zeros: in 4376, 3 is in the hundred's place. **7.** an ancient division of a county. ~determiner. **8.** amounting to or approximately a hundred: a hundred reasons for that. —'hundredth adj.

hundreds and thousands pl. n. tiny beads of coloured sugar, used in decorating cakes, etc.

hundredweight ('hʌndrəd,weit) n., pl. **-weights** or **-weight. 1.** Also called: **long hundredweight.** Brit. a unit of weight equal to 112 pounds (50.802 kg). **2.** Also called: **short hundredweight.** U.S. a unit of weight equal to 100 pounds (45.359 kg). **3.** Also called: **metric hundredweight.** a metric unit of weight equal to 50 kilograms. ~Abbrev. (for senses 1, 2): **cwt**

hung (hʌŋ) vb. **1.** the past tense or past participle of **hang** (except in the sense of to execute). ~adj. **2.** (of a political party, jury, etc.) not having a majority: a hung parliament. **3. hung over.** Inf. suffering from the effects of a hangover. **4. hung up.** Sl. impeded by some difficulty or delay. **b.** emotionally disturbed. **5. hung up on.** Sl., chiefly U.S. obsessively or exclusively interested in.

Hungarian (hʌŋ'gɛərɪən) n. **1.** the official language of Hungary, also spoken in Rumania and elsewhere, belonging to the Finno-Ugric family. **2.** a native, inhabitant, or citizen of Hungary. ~adj. **3.** of or relating to Hungary, its people, or their language. ~Cf. **Magyar.**

hunger ('hʌŋɡə) n. **1.** a feeling of emptiness or weakness induced by lack of food. **2.** desire or craving: hunger for a woman. ~vb. **3.** (intr.; usually foll. by for or after) to have a great appetite or desire (for).

hunger strike n. a voluntary fast undertaken, usually by a prisoner, as a means of protest. —**hunger striker** n.

hungry ('hʌŋɡrɪ) adj. **-grier, -griest. 1.** desiring food. **2.** (postpositive; foll. by for) having a craving, desire, or need (for). **3.** expressing or appearing to express greed, craving, or desire. **4.** lacking fertility; poor. **5.** Austral. & N.Z. greedy; mean. **6.** N.Z. (of timber) dry and bare. —'hungrily adv. —'hungriness n.

hunk (hʌŋk) n. **1.** a large piece. **2.** Sl., chiefly U.S. a sexually attractive man.

hunkers ('hʌŋkəz) pl. n. Scot. & N. English dialect. haunches.

hunt (hʌnt) vb. **1.** to seek out and kill (animals) for food or sport. **2.** (intr.; often foll. by for) to search (for): to hunt for a book. **3.** (tr.) to use (hounds, horses, etc.) in the pursuit of wild animals, game, etc.: to hunt a pack of hounds. **4.** (tr.) to search (country) to hunt game, etc.: to hunt the parkland. **5.** (tr.; often foll. by down) to track diligently so as to capture: to hunt down a criminal. **6.** (tr.; usually passive) to persecute; hound. **7.** (intr.) (of a gauge indicator, etc.) to oscillate about a mean value or position. **8.** (intr.) (of an aircraft, rocket, etc.) to oscillate about a flight path. ~n. **9.** the act or an instance of hunting. **10.** chase or search, esp. of animals. **11.** the area of a hunt. **12.** a party or institution organized for the pursuit of wild animals, esp. for sport. **13.** the members of such a party or institution.

hunter ('hʌntə) n. **1.** a person or animal that seeks out and kills or captures game. Fem.: **huntress** ('hʌntrɪs). **2. a.** a person who looks diligently for something. **b.** (in combination): a fortune-hunter. **3.** a specially bred horse used in hunting, characterized by strength and stamina. **4.** a watch with a hinged metal lid or case (**hunting case**) to protect the crystal.

hunter's moon n. the full moon following the harvest moon.

huntsman ('hʌntsmən) n., pl. **-men. 1.** a person who hunts. **2.** a person who trains hounds, beagles, etc., and manages them during a hunt.

hurdle ('hɜ:dəl) n. **1. a.** Athletics. one of a number of light barriers over which runners leap in certain events. **b.** a low barrier used in certain horse races. **2.** an obstacle: the next hurdle in his career. **3.** a light framework of interlaced osiers, etc., used as a temporary fence. **4.** a sledge on which criminals were dragged to their executions. ~vb. **5.** to jump (a hurdle). **6.** (tr.) to surround with hurdles. **7.** (tr.) to overcome. —'hurdler n.

hurdy-gurdy ('hɜ:dɪ'gɜ:dɪ) n., pl. **-dies.** any mechanical musical instrument, such as a barrel organ.

hurl (hɜ:l) vb. **1.** (tr.) to throw with great force. **2.** (tr.) to utter with force; yell: to hurl insults. ~n. **3.** the act of hurling.

hurling ('hɜ:lɪŋ) or **hurley** n. a traditional Irish game resembling hockey, played with sticks and a ball between two teams of 15 players.

hurly-burly ('hɜ:lɪ'bɜ:lɪ) n., pl. **hurly-burlies.** confusion or commotion.

THESAURUS

merry, playful, pleasant, side-splitting, waggish, whimsical, witty

humour n. **1.** amusement, comedy, drollery, facetiousness, fun, funniness, jocularity, ludicrousness, wit **2.** comedy, farce, gags (Sl.), jesting, jests, jokes, joking, pleasantry, wisecracks (Inf.), wit, witticisms, wittiness **3.** disposition, frame of mind, mood, spirits, temper **4.** bent, bias, fancy, freak, mood, propensity, quirk, vagary, whim ~v. **5.** accommodate, cosset, favour, flatter, go along with, gratify, indulge, mollify, pamper, spoil

hump n. **1.** bulge, bump, knob, mound, projection, protrusion, protuberance, swelling **2. the hump** Brit. inf. megrims (Rare), the blues, the doldrums, the dumps (Inf.), the grumps (Inf.), the mopes, the sulks ~v. **3.** arch, curve, form a hump, hunch, lift, tense

4. Sl. carry, heave, hoist, lug, shoulder

hunch 1. n. feeling, idea, impression, inkling, intuition, premonition, presentiment, suspicion **2.** v. arch, bend, crouch, curve, draw in, huddle, hump, squat, stoop, tense

hunchback crookback (Rare), crouchback (Archaic), humpback, kyphosis (Pathol.), Quasimodo

hunger n. **1.** appetite, emptiness, esurience, famine, hungriness, ravenousness, starvation, voracity **2.** appetence, appetite, craving, desire, greediness, itch, lust, yearning, yen (Inf.) ~v. **3.** crave, desire, hanker, itch, long, pine, starve, thirst, want, wish, yearn

hungry 1. empty, famished, famishing, hollow, peckish (Inf., chiefly Brit.), ravenous, sharp-set, starved, starving, voracious **2.**

athirst, avid, covetous, craving, desirous, eager, greedy, keen, yearning

hunk block, chunk, gobbet, lump, mass, piece, slab, wedge, wodge (Brit. inf.)

hunt v. **1.** chase, gun for, hound, pursue, stalk, track, trail **2.** ferret about, forage, go in quest of, look, look high and low, rummage through, scour, search, seek, try to find ~n. **3.** chase, hunting, investigation, pursuit, quest, search

hunted careworn, desperate, distraught, gaunt, haggard, harassed, harried, persecuted, stricken, terror-stricken, tormented, worn

hurdle n. **1.** barricade, barrier, fence, hedge, wall **2.** barrier, complication, difficulty, handicap, hindrance, impediment, obstacle, obstruction, snag, stumbling block

hurrah (huˈrɑː), **hooray** (huːˈreɪ), *or* **hoorah** (huːˈrɑː) *interj., n.* **1.** a cheer of joy, victory, etc. ~*vb.* **2.** to shout "hurrah".

hurricane (ˈhʌrɪkən) *n.* **1.** a severe, often destructive storm, esp. a tropical cyclone. **2.** a wind of force 12 on the Beaufort scale, with speeds over 72 m.p.h.

hurricane deck *n.* a ship's deck that is covered by a light deck as a sunshade.

hurricane lamp *n.* a paraffin lamp with a glass covering. Also called: **storm lantern.**

hurried (ˈhʌrɪd) *adj.* performed with great or excessive haste. —ˈ**hurriedly** *adv.* —ˈ**hurriedness** *n.*

hurry (ˈhʌrɪ) *vb.* **-rying, -ried.** **1.** (*intr.;* often foll. by *up*) to hasten; rush. **2.** (*tr.;* often foll. by *along*) to speed up the completion, progress, etc., of. ~*n., pl.* **-ries.** **3.** haste. **4.** urgency or eagerness. **5. in a hurry.** *Inf.* **a.** easily: *you won't beat him in a hurry.* **b.** willingly: *we won't go there again in a hurry.*

hurst (hɜːst) *n. Arch.* **1.** a wood. **2.** a sandbank.

hurt (hɜːt) *vb.* **hurting, hurt.** **1.** to cause physical or mental injury to. **2.** to produce a painful sensation: *the bruise hurts.* **3.** (*intr.*) *Inf.* to feel pain. ~*n.* **4.** physical or mental pain or suffering. **5.** a wound, cut, or sore. **6.** damage or injury; harm. —ˈ**hurter** *n.* —ˈ**hurtful** *adj.*

hurtle (ˈhɜːtəl) *vb.* to project or be projected very quickly, noisily, or violently.

husband (ˈhʌzbənd) *n.* **1.** a woman's partner in marriage. **2.** *Arch.* a manager of an estate. ~*vb.* **3.** to manage or use (resources, finances, etc.) thriftily. **4.** *Arch.* (*tr.*) to find a husband for. **5.** (*tr.*) *Obs.* to till (the soil). —ˈ**husbander** *n.*

husbandry (ˈhʌzbəndrɪ) *n.* **1.** farming, esp. when regarded as a science, skill, or art. **2.** management of affairs and resources.

hush (hʌʃ) *vb.* **1.** to make or become silent; quieten; soothe. ~*n.* **2.** stillness; silence. ~*interj.* **3.** a plea or demand for silence.

hush-hush *adj. Inf.* (esp. of official work, documents, etc.) secret; confidential.

hush money *n. Sl.* money given to a person to ensure that something is kept secret.

hush up *vb.* (*tr., adv.*) to suppress information or rumours about.

husk (hʌsk) *n.* **1.** the external green or membranous covering of certain fruits and seeds. **2.** any worthless outer covering. ~*vb.* **3.** (*tr.*) to remove the husk from.

husky[1] (ˈhʌskɪ) *adj.* **huskier, huskiest.** **1.** (of a voice, utterance, etc.) slightly hoarse or rasping. **2.** of or containing husks. **3.** *Inf.* big and strong. —ˈ**huskily** *adv.* —ˈ**huskiness** *n.*

husky[2] (ˈhʌskɪ) *n., pl.* **huskies.** **1.** a breed of Arctic sled dog with a thick dense coat, pricked ears, and a curled tail. **2.** *Canad. sl.* **a.** a member of the Inuit people. **b.** their language.

hussar (huˈzɑː) *n.* **1.** a member of any of various light cavalry regiments, renowned for their elegant dress. **2.**

a Hungarian horseman of the 15th century.

hussy (ˈhʌsɪ, -zɪ) *n., pl.* **-sies.** *Contemptuous.* a shameless or promiscuous woman.

hustings (ˈhʌstɪŋz) *n.* (*functioning as pl. or sing.*) **1.** *Brit.* (before 1872) the platform on which candidates were nominated for Parliament and from which they addressed the electors. **2.** the proceedings at a parliamentary election.

hustle (ˈhʌsəl) *vb.* **1.** to shove or crowd (someone) roughly. **2.** to move hurriedly or furtively: *he hustled her out of sight.* **3.** (*tr.*) to deal with hurriedly: *to hustle legislation through.* **4.** (*intr.*) *Sl.* to obtain (something) forcefully. **5.** *U.S. sl.* (of procurers and prostitutes) to solicit. ~*n.* **6.** an instance of hustling. —ˈ**hustler** *n.*

hut (hʌt) *n.* **1.** a small house or shelter. ~*vb.* **2.** to furnish with or live in a hut. —ˈ**hut-like** *adj.*

hutch (hʌtʃ) *n.* **1.** a cage, usually of wood and wire mesh, for small animals. **2.** *Inf., derog.* a small house. **3.** a cart for carrying ore.

huzzah (həˈzɑː) *interj., n., vb.* an archaic word for **hurrah.**

hyacinth (ˈhaɪəsɪnθ) *n.* **1.** any plant of the Mediterranean genus *Hyacinthus,* esp. a cultivated variety having a thick flower stalk bearing bell-shaped fragrant flowers. **2.** the flower or bulb of such a plant. **3.** any similar plant, such as the grape hyacinth. **4.** Also called: **jacinth.** a reddish transparent variety of the mineral zircon, used as a gemstone. **5.** a purplish-blue colour. —**hyacinthine** (ˌhaɪəˈsɪnθaɪn) *adj.*

hybrid (ˈhaɪbrɪd) *n.* **1.** an animal or plant resulting from a cross between genetically unlike individuals; usually sterile. **2.** anything of mixed ancestry. **3.** a word, part of which is derived from one language and part from another, such as *monolingual.* ~*adj.* **4.** denoting or being a hybrid; of mixed origin. —ˈ**hybridism** *n.* —hyˈbridity *n.*

hybridize *or* **-ise** (ˈhaɪbrɪˌdaɪz) *vb.* to produce or cause to produce hybrids; crossbreed. —ˌhybridiˈzation *or* -iˈsation *n.*

hydra (ˈhaɪdrə) *n., pl.* **-dras** *or* **-drae** (-driː). **1.** a freshwater coelenterate in which the body is a slender polyp with tentacles around the mouth. **2.** a persistent trouble or evil.

hydrangea (haɪˈdreɪndʒə) *n.* a shrub or tree of an Asian and American genus cultivated for their large clusters of white, pink, or blue flowers.

hydrant (ˈhaɪdrənt) *n.* an outlet from a water main, usually an upright pipe with a valve attached, from which water can be tapped for fighting fires, etc.

hydrate (ˈhaɪdreɪt) *n.* **1.** a chemical compound containing water that is chemically combined with a substance and can usually be expelled without changing the constitution of the substance. **2.** a chemical compound that can dissociate reversibly into water and another compound. ~*vb.* **3.** to undergo or cause to undergo treatment or impregnation with water. —hyˈdration *n.* —ˈ**hydrator** *n.*

THESAURUS

hurl cast, chuck (*Inf.*), fire, fling, heave, launch, let fly, pitch, project, propel, send, shy, sling, throw, toss

hurly-burly bedlam, brouhaha, chaos, commotion, confusion, disorder, furore, hubbub, pandemonium, tumult, turbulence, turmoil, uproar

hurricane cyclone, gale, storm, tempest, tornado, twister (*U.S. inf.*), typhoon, willy-willy (*Aust.*), windstorm

hurried breakneck, brief, cursory, hasty, hectic, perfunctory, precipitate, quick, rushed, short, slapdash, speedy, superficial, swift

hurry v. **1.** dash, fly, get a move on (*Inf.*), lose no time, make haste, rush, scoot, scurry, step on it (*Inf.*) **2.** accelerate, expedite, goad, hasten, hustle, push on, quicken, speed (up), urge ~n. **3.** bustle, celerity, commotion, dispatch, expedition, flurry, haste, precipitation, promptitude, quickness, rush, speed, urgency

hurt v. **1.** bruise, damage, disable, harm, impair, injure, mar, spoil, wound **2.** ache, be sore, be tender, burn, pain, smart, sting, throb **3.** afflict, aggrieve, annoy, cut to the

quick, distress, grieve, pain, sadden, sting, upset, wound ~n. **4.** discomfort, distress, pain, pang, soreness, suffering **5.** bruise, sore, wound **6.** damage, detriment, disadvantage, harm, injury, loss, mischief, wrong ~adj. **7.** bruised, cut, damaged, grazed, harmed, injured, scarred, scraped, scratched, wounded **8.** aggrieved, crushed, injured, miffed (*Inf.*), offended, pained, piqued, rueful, sad, wounded

hurtful cruel, cutting, damaging, destructive, detrimental, disadvantageous, distressing, harmful, injurious, malicious, mean, mischievous, nasty, pernicious, prejudicial, spiteful, unkind, upsetting, wounding

husband v. budget, conserve, economize, hoard, manage thriftily, save, store, use sparingly

husbandry **1.** agriculture, agronomy, cultivation, farming, land management, tillage **2.** careful management, economy, frugality, good housekeeping, thrift

hush v. **1.** mute, muzzle, quieten, shush, silence, still, suppress **2.** allay, appease, calm, compose, mollify, soothe ~n. **3.** calm, peace, peacefulness, quiet, silence, still (*Poetic*),

stillness, tranquillity

hush-hush classified, confidential, restricted, secret, top-secret

husk bark, chaff, covering, glume, hull, rind, shuck

huskiness dryness, harshness, hoarseness, raspingness, roughness

husky **1.** croaking, croaky, gruff, guttural, harsh, hoarse, rasping, raucous, rough, throaty **2.** *Inf.* beefy (*Inf.*), brawny, burly, hefty, muscular, powerful, rugged, stocky, strapping, thickset

hussy baggage (*Inf., old-fashioned*), floozy (*Sl.*), jade, minx, quean (*Archaic*), scrubber (*Brit. sl.*), slut, strumpet, tart (*Inf.*), tramp (*Sl.*), trollop, wanton, wench (*Archaic*)

hustle bustle, crowd, elbow, force, haste, hasten, hurry, impel, jog, jostle, push, rush, shove, thrust

hut cabin, den, hovel, lean-to, refuge, shanty, shed, shelter

hybrid *n.* amalgam, composite, compound, cross, crossbreed, half-blood, half-breed, mixture, mongrel, mule

hydraulic (haɪˈdrɒlɪk) *adj.* **1.** operated by pressure transmitted through a pipe by a liquid, such as water or oil. **2.** of or employing liquids in motion. **3.** of hydraulics. **4.** hardening under water: *hydraulic cement.* —**hyˈdraulically** *adv.*

hydraulics (haɪˈdrɒlɪks) *n.* (*functioning as sing.*) the study of the mechanical and flow properties of fluids, esp. as they apply to practical engineering. Also called: **fluid mechanics.**

hydride (ˈhaɪdraɪd) *n.* any compound of hydrogen with another element.

hydro (ˈhaɪdrəʊ) *n., pl.* **-dros.** *Brit.* a hotel or resort, often near a spa, offering facilities for hydropathic treatment.

Hydro (ˈhaɪdrəʊ) *n.* (esp. in Canada) a hydroelectric power company or board.

hydro- *or before a vowel* **hydr-** *combining form.* **1.** indicating water or fluid: *hydrodynamics.* **2.** indicating hydrogen in a chemical compound: *hydrochloric acid.* **3.** indicating a hydroid: *hydrozoan.*

hydrocarbon (ˌhaɪdrəʊˈkɑːbən) *n.* any organic compound containing only carbon and hydrogen.

hydrocephalus (ˌhaɪdrəʊˈsɛfələs) *or* **hydrocephaly** (ˌhaɪdrəʊˈsɛfəlɪ) *n.* accumulation of cerebrospinal fluid within the ventricles of the brain because its normal outlet has been blocked by congenital malformation or disease. Nontechnical name: **water on the brain.** —**hydrocephalic** (ˌhaɪdrəʊsɛˈfælɪk) *or* **hydroˈcephalous** *adj.*

hydrochloric acid (ˌhaɪdrəˈklɒrɪk) *n.* the aqueous solution of hydrogen chloride: a strong acid used in many industrial and laboratory processes.

hydrodynamics (ˌhaɪdrəʊdaɪˈnæmɪks, -dɪ-) *n.* (*functioning as sing.*) the branch of science concerned with the mechanical properties of fluids, esp. liquids. Also called: **hydromechanics.**

hydroelectric (ˌhaɪdrəʊɪˈlɛktrɪk) *adj.* **1.** generated by the pressure of falling water: *hydroelectric power.* **2.** of the generation of electricity by water pressure: *a hydroelectric scheme.* —**hydroelectricity** (ˌhaɪdrəʊɪlɛkˈtrɪsɪtɪ) *n.*

hydrofoil (ˈhaɪdrəˌfɔɪl) *n.* **1.** a fast light vessel the hull of which is raised out of the water on one or more pairs of fixed vanes. **2.** any of these vanes.

hydrogen (ˈhaɪdrɪdʒən) *n.* **a.** a flammable colourless gas that is the lightest and most abundant element in the universe. It occurs in water and in most organic compounds. Symbol: H; atomic no.: 1; atomic wt.: 1.007 97. **b.** (*as modifier*): *hydrogen bomb.* —**hydrogenous** (hɪˈdrɒdʒɪnəs) *adj.*

hydrogenate (ˈhaɪdrədʒɪˌneɪt, haɪˈdrɒdʒɪˌneɪt) *vb.* to undergo or cause to undergo a reaction with hydrogen: *to hydrogenate ethylene.* —**hydrogenˈation** *n.*

hydrogen bomb *n.* a type of bomb in which energy is released by fusion of hydrogen nuclei to give helium nuclei. The energy required to initiate the fusion is provided by an atom bomb, which is surrounded by a hydrogen-containing substance. Also called: **H-bomb.**

hydrogen peroxide *n.* a colourless oily unstable liquid used as a bleach and as an oxidizer in rocket fuels. Formula: H_2O_2.

hydrography (haɪˈdrɒgrəfɪ) *n.* the study, surveying, and mapping of the oceans, seas, and rivers. —**hyˈdrographer** *n.* —**hydrographic** (ˌhaɪdrəˈgræfɪk) *adj.*

hydrology (haɪˈdrɒlədʒɪ) *n.* the study of the distribution, conservation, use, etc., of the water of the earth and its atmosphere. —**hydrologic** (ˌhaɪdrəˈlɒdʒɪk) *adj.* —**hyˈdrologist** *n.*

hydrolysis (haɪˈdrɒlɪsɪs) *n.* a chemical reaction in which a compound reacts with water to produce other compounds. —**hydrolytic** (ˌhaɪdrəˈlɪtɪk) *adj.*

hydrometer (haɪˈdrɒmɪtə) *n.* an instrument for measuring the relative density of a liquid. —**hydrometric** (ˌhaɪdrəʊˈmɛtrɪk) *or* **hydroˈmetrical** *adj.*

hydropathy (haɪˈdrɒpəθɪ) *n.* a pseudoscientific method of treating disease by the use of large quantities of water both internally and externally. —**hydropathic** (ˌhaɪdrəʊˈpæθɪk) *adj.*

hydrophilic (ˌhaɪdrəʊˈfɪlɪk) *adj. Chem.* tending to dissolve in, mix with, or be wetted by water: *a hydrophilic colloid.* —**ˈhydroˌphile** *n.*

hydrophobia (ˌhaɪdrəˈfəʊbɪə) *n.* **1.** another name for **rabies. 2.** a fear of drinking fluids, esp. that of a person with rabies, because of painful spasms when trying to swallow. —**ˌhydroˈphobic** *adj.*

hydroplane (ˈhaɪdrəʊˌpleɪn) *n.* **1.** a motorboat equipped with hydrofoils or with a shaped bottom that raises its hull out of the water at high speeds. **2.** an attachment to an aircraft to enable it to glide along the surface of the water. **3.** another name for a **seaplane. 4.** a horizontal vane on the hull of a submarine for controlling its vertical motion. ~*vb.* **5.** (*intr.*) (of a boat) to rise out of the water in the manner of a hydroplane.

hydroponics (ˌhaɪdrəʊˈpɒnɪks) *n.* (*functioning as sing.*) a method of cultivating plants by growing them in gravel, etc., through which water containing dissolved inorganic nutrient salts is pumped. —**ˌhydroˈponic** *adj.* —**ˌhydroˈponically** *adv.*

hydrosphere (ˈhaɪdrəˌsfɪə) *n.* the watery part of the earth's surface, including oceans, lakes, water vapour in the atmosphere, etc.

hydrostatics (ˌhaɪdrəʊˈstætɪks) *n.* (*functioning as sing.*) the branch of science concerned with the mechanical properties and behaviour of fluids that are not in motion. —**ˌhydroˈstatic** *adj.*

hydrotherapy (ˌhaɪdrəʊˈθɛrəpɪ) *n. Med.* the treatment of certain diseases by the external application of water, as for mobilizing stiff joints or strengthening weakened muscles. —**hydrotherapic** (ˌhaɪdrəʊθɪˈræpɪk) *adj.* —**ˌhydroˈtherapist** *n.*

hydrotropism (haɪˈdrɒtrəˌpɪzəm) *n.* the directional growth of plants in response to the stimulus of water.

hydrous (ˈhaɪdrəs) *adj.* containing water.

hydroxide (haɪˈdrɒksaɪd) *n.* **1.** a base or alkali containing the ion OH^-. **2.** any compound containing an -OH group.

hydroxyl (haɪˈdrɒksɪl) *n.* (*modifier*) of, consisting of, or containing the monovalent group -OH or the ion OH^-: *a hydroxyl group or radical.*

hydrozoan (ˌhaɪdrəʊˈzəʊən) *n.* **1.** any coelenterate of the class *Hydrozoa,* which includes the hydra and the Portuguese man-of-war. ~*adj.* **2.** of the *Hydrozoa.*

hyena *or* **hyaena** (haɪˈiːnə) *n.* any of several long-legged carnivorous doglike mammals such as the spotted or laughing hyena, of Africa and S Asia. —**hyˈenic** *or* **hyˈaenic** *adj.*

hygiene (ˈhaɪdʒiːn) *n.* **1.** Also called: **hygienics.** the science concerned with the maintenance of health. **2.** clean or healthy practices or thinking: *personal hygiene.* —**hyˈgienic** *adj.* —**ˈhygienist** *n.*

hygro- *or before a vowel* **hygr-** *combining form.* indicating moisture: *hygrometer.*

hygrometer (haɪˈgrɒmɪtə) *n.* any of various instruments for measuring humidity. —**hygrometric** (ˌhaɪgrəˈmetrɪk) *adj.*

hygroscope (ˈhaɪgrəˌskəʊp) *n.* any device that indicates the humidity of the air without necessarily measuring it.

hygroscopic (ˌhaɪgrəˈskɒpɪk) *adj.* (of a substance) tending to absorb water from the air. —**ˌhygroˈscopically** *adv.*

hying (ˈhaɪɪŋ) *vb.* the present participle of **hie.**

hymen (ˈhaɪmɛn) *n. Anat.* a fold of mucous membrane that partly covers the entrance to the vagina and is usually ruptured when sexual intercourse takes place for the first time. —**ˈhymenal** *adj.*

hymenopteran (ˌhaɪmɪˈnɒptərən) *or* **hymenopteron** *n., pl.* **-terans, -tera** (-tərə), *or* **-terons.** any of a large order of insects including wasps, bees, ants, etc., which have four membranous wings.

hymn (hɪm) *n.* **1.** a Christian song of praise sung to God or a saint. **2.** a similar song praising other gods, a nation, etc. ~*vb.* **3.** to express (praises, thanks, etc.) by singing hymns. —**hymnic** (ˈhɪmnɪk) *adj.*

hymnal (ˈhɪmnəl) *n.* **1.** Also: **hymn book.** a book of hymns. ~*adj.* **2.** of, relating to, or characteristic of hymns.

hymnody (ˈhɪmnədɪ) *n.* **1.** the composition or singing of hymns. **2.** hymns collectively. ~Also called: **hymnology.**

hymnology (hɪmˈnɒlədʒɪ) *n.* **1.** the study of hymn com-

THESAURUS

hygiene cleanliness, hygienics, sanitary measures, sanitation

hygienic aseptic, clean, disinfected, germ-free, healthy, pure, salutary, sanitary

position. **2.** another word for **hymnody.** —**hym'nologist** n.

hyoscyamine (ˌhaɪəˈsaɪəˌmiːn) n. a poisonous alkaloid occurring in henbane and related plants: used in medicine.

hype (haɪp) Sl. ~n. **1.** a deception or racket. **2.** an intensive or exaggerated publicity or sales promotion. ~vb. **3.** (tr.) to market or promote (a product) using exaggerated or intensive publicity.

hyped up adj. Sl. stimulated or excited by or as if by the effect of a stimulating drug.

hyper- prefix. **1.** above, over, or in excess: hypercritical. **2.** denoting an abnormal excess: hyperacidity. **3.** indicating that a chemical compound contains a greater than usual amount of an element: hyperoxide.

hyperactive (ˌhaɪpərˈæktɪv) adj. abnormally active. —ˌhyperac'tivity n.

hyperbola (haɪˈpɜːbələ) n., pl. **-las** or **-le** (-ˌliː). a conic section formed by a plane that cuts a cone at a steeper angle to its base than its side.

hyperbole (haɪˈpɜːbəlɪ) n. a deliberate exaggeration used for effect: he embraced her a thousand times. —**hy'perbolism** n.

hyperbolic (ˌhaɪpəˈbɒlɪk) or **hyperbolical** adj. **1.** of a hyperbola. **2.** Rhetoric. of a hyperbole. —ˌhyper-'bolically adv.

Hyperborean (ˌhaɪpəˈbɔːrɪən) n. **1.** Greek myth. one of a people believed to have lived beyond the North Wind in a sunny land. **2.** an inhabitant of the extreme north. ~adj. **3.** (sometimes not cap.) of or relating to the extreme north.

hypercritical (ˌhaɪpəˈkrɪtɪkəl) adj. excessively or severely critical. —ˌhyper'critically adv.

hyperglycaemia or U.S. **hyperglycemia** (ˌhaɪpəglaɪˈsiːmɪə) n. Pathol. an abnormally large amount of sugar in the blood. —ˌhypergly'caemic or U.S. ˌhypergly'cemic adj.

hypermarket (ˈhaɪpəˌmɑːkɪt) n. Brit. a huge self-service store, usually built on the outskirts of a town.

hyperon (ˈhaɪpəˌrɒn) n. Physics. any baryon that is not a nucleon.

hypersensitive (ˌhaɪpəˈsɛnsɪtɪv) adj. **1.** having unduly vulnerable feelings. **2.** abnormally sensitive to an allergen, a drug, or other agent. —ˌhyper'sensitiveness or ˌhyperˌsensi'tivity n.

hypersonic (ˌhaɪpəˈsɒnɪk) adj. concerned with or having a velocity of at least five times that of sound in the same medium under the same conditions. —ˌhyper-'sonics n.

hypertension (ˌhaɪpəˈtɛnʃən) n. Pathol. abnormally high blood pressure. —**hypertensive** (ˌhaɪpəˈtɛnsɪv) adj., n.

hypertrophy (haɪˈpɜːtrəfɪ) n., pl. **-phies. 1.** enlargement of an organ or part resulting from an increase in the size of the cells. ~vb. **-phying, -phied. 2.** to undergo or cause to undergo this condition.

hyperventilation (ˌhaɪpəˌvɛntɪˈleɪʃən) n. an increase in the rate of breathing, sometimes resulting in cramp and dizziness.

hyphen (ˈhaɪfən) n. **1.** the punctuation mark (-), used to separate parts of compound words, to link the words of a phrase, and between syllables of a word split between two consecutive lines. ~vb. **2.** (tr.) another word for **hyphenate.**

hyphenate (ˈhaɪfəˌneɪt) vb. (tr.) to separate (words, etc.) with a hyphen. —ˌhyphen'ation n.

hypno- or before a vowel **hypn-** combining form. **1.** indicating sleep: hypnopaedia. **2.** relating to hypnosis: hypnotherapy.

hypnosis (hɪpˈnəʊsɪs) n., pl. **-ses** (-siːz). an artificially induced state of semiconsciousness characterized by an increased suggestibility to the words of the hypnotist.

hypnotherapy (ˌhɪpnəʊˈθɛrəpɪ) n. the use of hypnosis in the treatment of physical or mental disorders.

hypnotic (hɪpˈnɒtɪk) adj. **1.** of or producing hypnosis or sleep. **2.** (of a person) susceptible to hypnotism. ~n. **3.** a drug that induces sleep. **4.** a person susceptible to hypnosis. —**hyp'notically** adv.

hypnotism (ˈhɪpnəˌtɪzəm) n. **1.** the scientific study and practice of hypnosis. **2.** the process of inducing hypnosis. —'hypnotist n.

hypnotize or **-tise** (ˈhɪpnəˌtaɪz) vb. (tr.) **1.** to induce hypnosis in (a person). **2.** to charm or beguile; fascinate. —ˌhypnoti'zation or -ti'sation n. —'hypnoˌtizer or -ˌtiser n.

hypo (ˈhaɪpəʊ) n., pl. **-pos.** Inf. short for **hypodermic syringe.**

hypo- or before a vowel **hyp-** prefix. **1.** beneath or below: hypodermic. **2.** lower: hypogastrium. **3.** less than; denoting a deficiency: hypothyroid. **4.** indicating that a chemical compound contains an element in a lower oxidation state than usual: hypochlorous acid.

hypocaust (ˈhaɪpəˌkɔːst) n. an ancient Roman heating system in which hot air circulated under the floor and between double walls.

hypochondria (ˌhaɪpəˈkɒndrɪə) n. chronic abnormal anxiety concerning the state of one's health. Also called: **hypochondriasis** (ˌhaɪpəʊkɒnˈdraɪəsɪs).

hypochondriac (ˌhaɪpəˈkɒndrɪˌæk) n. **1.** a person suffering from hypochondria. ~adj. also **hypochondriacal** (ˌhaɪpəʊkɒnˈdraɪəkəl). **2.** relating to or suffering from hypochondria.

hypocrisy (hɪˈpɒkrəsɪ) n., pl. **-sies. 1.** the practice of professing standards, beliefs, etc., contrary to one's real character or actual behaviour. **2.** an act or instance of this.

hypocycloid (ˌhaɪpəˈsaɪklɔɪd) n. a curve described by a point on the circumference of a circle as the circle rolls around the inside of a fixed coplanar circle. —ˌhypocy-'cloidal adj.

hypodermic (ˌhaɪpəˈdɜːmɪk) adj. **1.** of or relating to the region of the skin beneath the epidermis. **2.** injected beneath the skin. ~n. **3.** a hypodermic syringe or needle. **4.** a hypodermic injection. —ˌhypo'dermically adv.

hypodermic syringe n. Med. a type of syringe consisting of a hollow cylinder, usually of glass or plastic, a tightly fitting piston, and a hollow needle (**hypodermic needle**), used for withdrawing blood samples, etc.

hypostasis (haɪˈpɒstəsɪs) n., pl. **-ses** (-ˌsiːz). **1.** Metaphysics. the essential nature of anything. **2.** Christianity. **a.** any of the three persons of the Godhead. **b.** the one person of Christ in which the divine and human natures are united. **3.** the accumulation of blood in an organ or part as the result of poor circulation. —**hypostatic** (ˌhaɪpəˈstætɪk) or ˌhypo'statical adj.

hypotension (ˌhaɪpəʊˈtɛnʃən) n. Pathol. abnormally low blood pressure. —**hypotensive** (ˌhaɪpəʊˈtɛnsɪv) adj.

hypotenuse (haɪˈpɒtɪˌnjuːs) n. the side in a right-angled triangle that is opposite the right angle. Abbrev.: **hyp.**

hypothecate (haɪˈpɒθɪˌkeɪt) vb. (tr.) Law. to pledge (personal property or a ship) as security for a debt without transferring possession or title. —hyˌpothe'cation n. —hy'potheˌcator n.

hypothermia (ˌhaɪpəʊˈθɜːmɪə) n. **1.** Pathol. an abnormally low body temperature, as induced in the elderly by exposure to cold weather. **2.** Med. the intentional reduction of normal body temperature to reduce the patient's metabolic rate.

hypothesis (haɪˈpɒθɪsɪs) n., pl. **-ses** (-ˌsiːz). **1.** a suggested explanation for a group of facts or phenomena, either accepted as a basis for further verification (**working hypothesis**) or accepted as likely to be true. **2.** an assumption used in an argument; supposition. —**hy'pothesist** n.

THESAURUS

hype ballyhoo (Inf.), brouhaha, build-up, plugging (Inf.), publicity, puffing, racket, razzmatazz (Sl.)

hypnotic mesmeric, mesmerizing, narcotic, opiate, sleep-inducing, somniferous, soothing, soporific, spellbinding

hypnotize 1. mesmerize, put in a trance, put to sleep **2.** entrance, fascinate, magnetize, spellbind

hypochondriac adj./n. valetudinarian

hypocrisy cant, deceit, deceitfulness, deception, dissembling, duplicity, falsity, imposture, insincerity, pharisaism, phariseeism, phoneyness (Sl.), pretence, sanctimoniousness, speciousness, two-facedness

hypocrite charlatan, deceiver, dissembler, fraud, Holy Willie, impostor, Pecksniff, pharisee, phoney (Sl.), pretender, Tartuffe, whited sepulchre

hypocritical canting, deceitful, decep-

tive, dissembling, duplicitous, false, fraudulent, hollow, insincere, Janus-faced, pharisaical, phoney (Sl.), sanctimonious, specious, spurious, two-faced

hypothesis assumption, postulate, premise, premiss, proposition, supposition, theory, thesis

hypothesize *or* **-ise** (haɪˈpɒθɪˌsaɪz) *vb.* to form or assume as a hypothesis. **—hyˈpotheˌsizer** *or* **-iser** *n.*

hypothetical (ˌhaɪpəˈθɛtɪkəl) *or* **hypothetic** *adj.* **1.** having the nature of a hypothesis. **2.** assumed or thought to exist. **3.** *Logic.* another word for **conditional** (sense 4). **—ˌhypoˈthetically** *adv.*

hypso- *or before a vowel* **hyps-** *combining form.* indicating height: *hypsometry.*

hyrax (ˈhaɪræks) *n.* any of various rodent-like herbivorous mammals of Africa and SW Asia.

hyssop (ˈhɪsəp) *n.* **1.** a widely cultivated Asian plant with spikes of small blue flowers and aromatic leaves, used as a condiment and in perfumery and folk medicine. **2.** a Biblical plant, used for sprinkling in the ritual practices of the Hebrews.

hysterectomy (ˌhɪstəˈrɛktəmɪ) *n., pl.* **-mies.** surgical removal of the uterus.

hysteresis (ˌhɪstəˈriːsɪs) *n. Physics.* the lag in a variable property of a system with respect to the effect producing it as this effect varies, esp. the phenomenon in which the magnetic induction of a ferromagnetic material lags behind the changing external field. **—hysteretic** (ˌhɪstəˈrɛtɪk) *adj.*

hysteria (hɪˈstɪərɪə) *n.* **1.** a mental disorder characterized by emotional outbursts and, often, physical symptoms such as paralysis. **2.** any frenzied emotional state, esp. of laughter or crying.

hysteric (hɪˈstɛrɪk) *n.* **1.** a hysterical person. **~adj.** **2.** hysterical.

hysterical (hɪˈstɛrɪkəl) *adj.* **1.** suggesting hysteria: *hysterical cries.* **2.** suffering from hysteria. **3.** *Inf.* wildly funny. **—hysˈterically** *adv.*

hysterics (hɪˈstɛrɪks) *n.* **1.** an attack of hysteria. **2.** *Inf.* wild uncontrollable bursts of laughter.

hystero- *or before a vowel* **hyster-** *combining form.* the uterus: *hysterectomy.*

Hz *abbrev. for* hertz.

THESAURUS

hypothetical academic, assumed, conjectural, imaginary, putative, speculative, supposed, theoretical

hysteria agitation, delirium, frenzy, hysterics, madness, panic, unreason

hysterical **1.** berserk, beside oneself, convulsive, crazed, distracted, distraught, frantic, frenzied, mad, overwrought, raving, uncontrollable **2.** *Inf.* comical, farcical, hilarious, screaming, side-splitting, uproarious, wildly funny

I

i *or* **I** (aı) *n., pl.* **i's, I's,** *or* **Is.** **1.** the ninth letter and third vowel of the English alphabet. **2.** any of several speech sounds represented by this letter. **3. a.** something shaped like an I. **b.** (*in combination*): *an I-beam.* **4. dot one's i's and cross one's t's.** to pay attention to detail.

I (aı) *pron.* (*subjective*) refers to the speaker or writer.

I *symbol for:* **1.** *Chem.* iodine. **2.** *Physics.* current. **3.** *Physics.* isospin. **~** **4.** *the Roman numeral for* one. See **Roman numerals.**

I. *abbrev. for:* **1.** Independence. **2.** Independent. **3.** Institute. **4.** International. **5.** Island; Isle.

-ia *suffix forming nouns.* **1.** in place names: *Columbia.* **2.** in names of diseases: *pneumonia.* **3.** in words denoting condition or quality: *utopia.* **4.** in names of botanical genera and zoological classes: *Reptilia.* **5.** in collective nouns borrowed from Latin: *regalia.*

IAEA *abbrev. for* International Atomic Energy Agency.

-ial *suffix forming adjectives.* of or relating to: *managerial.*

iamb ('aıæm, 'aıæmb) *or* **iambus** (aı'æmbəs) *n., pl.* **iambs, iambi** (aı'æmbaı), *or* **iambuses.** *Prosody.* **1.** a metrical foot of two syllables, a short one followed by a long one. **2.** a line of verse of such feet.

iambic (aı'æmbık) *Prosody.* *~adj.* **1.** of, relating to, or using an iamb. **2.** (in Greek literature) denoting a satirical verse written in iambs. *~n.* **3.** a metrical foot, line, or stanza consisting of iambs. **4.** an ancient Greek satirical verse written in iambs.

-ian *suffix.* variant of **-an:** *Etonian.*

-iasis *or* **-asis** *n. combining form.* (in medicine) indicating a diseased condition: *psoriasis.* Cf. **-osis** (sense 2).

-iatrics *n. combining form.* indicating medical care or treatment: *paediatrics.*

iatrogenic (aı,ætrəʊ'dʒɛnık) *adj. Med.* (of an illness) induced in a patient as the result of a physician's action. **—iatrogenicity** (aı,ætrəʊdʒı'nısıtı) *n.*

-iatry *n. combining form.* indicating healing or medical treatment: *psychiatry.* Cf. **-iatrics.** **—-iatric** *adj. combining form.*

I.B.A. (in Britain) *abbrev. for* Independent Broadcasting Authority.

Iberian (aı'bıərıən) *n.* **1.** a member of a group of ancient Caucasoid peoples who inhabited the Iberian Peninsula, in SW Europe in classical times. **2.** a native or inhabitant of the Iberian Peninsula; a Spaniard or Portuguese. **3.** a native or inhabitant of ancient Iberia. *~adj.* **4.** relating to the pre-Roman peoples of the Iberian Peninsula or of Caucasian Iberia. **5.** of or relating to the Iberian Peninsula, its inhabitants, or any of their languages.

ibex ('aıbɛks) *n., pl.* **ibexes, ibices** ('ıbı,siːz, 'aı-), *or* **ibex.** any of three species of wild goat of mountainous regions of Europe, Asia, and North Africa, having large backward-curving horns.

ibid. *or* **ib.** (referring to a book, etc., previously cited) *abbrev. for* ibidem: in the same place.

ibis ('aıbıs) *n., pl.* **ibises** *or* **ibis.** any of various wading birds such as the sacred ibis, that occur in warm regions and have a long thin down-curved bill.

-ible *suffix forming adjectives.* variant of **-able.** **—-ibly** *suffix forming adverbs.* **—-ibility** *suffix forming nouns.*

Ibo *or* **Igbo** ('iːbəʊ) *n.* **1.** (*pl.* **-bos** *or* **-bo**) a member of a Negroid people of W Africa, living in S Nigeria. **2.** their language, belonging to the Niger-Congo family.

i/c *abbrev. for:* **1.** in charge (of). **2.** internal combustion.

-ic *suffix forming adjectives.* **1.** of, relating to, or resembling: *periodic.* See also **-ical.** **2.** (in chemistry) indicating that an element is chemically combined in the higher of two possible valence states: *ferric.* Cf. **-ous** (sense 2).

I.C.A. *abbrev. for:* **1.** (in Britain) Institute of Contemporary Arts. **2.** Institute of Chartered Accountants.

-ical *suffix forming adjectives.* variant of **-ic,** but having a less literal application than corresponding adjectives ending in *-ic: economical.* **—-ically** *suffix forming adverbs.*

ICBM *abbrev. for* intercontinental ballistic missile.

ice (aıs) *n.* **1.** water in the solid state, formed by freezing liquid water. Related adj.: **glacial.** **2.** a portion of ice cream. **3. break the ice. a.** to relieve shyness, etc., esp. between strangers. **b.** to be the first of a group to do something. **4. cut no ice.** *Inf.* to fail to make an impression. **5. on ice.** in abeyance; pending. **6. on thin ice.** unsafe; vulnerable. *~vb.* **7.** (often foll. by *up, over,* etc.) to form ice; freeze. **8.** (*tr.*) to mix with ice or chill (a drink, etc.). **9.** (*tr.*) to cover (a cake, etc.) with icing. **—iced** *adj.*

I.C.E. (in Britain) *abbrev. for* Institution of Civil Engineers.

Ice. *abbrev. for* Iceland(ic).

ice age *n.* any period of time during which a large part of the earth's surface was covered with ice, because of the advance of glaciers. Also called: **glacial period.**

iceberg ('aısbɜːg) *n.* **1.** a large mass of ice floating in the sea. **2. tip of the iceberg.** the small visible part of something, esp. a problem, that is much larger. **3.** *Sl., chiefly U.S.* a person considered to have a cold or reserved manner. **4.** *Austral. inf.* a person who swims or surfs in winter or takes cold showers.

icebound ('aıs,baʊnd) *adj.* covered or made immobile by ice; frozen in: *an icebound ship.*

icebox ('aıs,bɒks) *n.* **1.** a compartment in a refrigerator for storing or making ice. **2.** an insulated cabinet packed with ice for storing food.

icebreaker ('aıs,breıkə) *n.* **1.** Also called: **iceboat.** a vessel with a reinforced bow for breaking up the ice in bodies of water. **2.** a device for breaking ice into smaller pieces.

icecap ('aıs,kæp) *n.* a thick mass of glacial ice that permanently covers an area, such as the polar regions or the peak of a mountain.

ice cream *n.* a sweetened frozen liquid, made from cream, milk, or a custard base, flavoured in various ways.

ice field *n.* **1.** a large ice floe. **2.** a large mass of ice permanently covering an extensive area of land.

ice floe *n.* a sheet of ice, of variable size, floating in the sea. See also **ice field** (sense 1).

ice hockey *n.* a game played on ice by two teams wearing skates, who try to propel a flat puck into their opponents' goal with long sticks.

Icelandic (aıs'lændık) *adj.* **1.** of or relating to Iceland, its people, or their language. *~n.* **2.** the official language of Iceland.

ice lolly *n. Brit. inf.* a water ice or an ice cream on a stick. Also called: **lolly.**

ice pack *n.* **1.** a bag or folded cloth containing ice, applied to a part of the body to reduce swelling, etc. **2.** another name for **pack ice.** **3.** a sachet containing a gel that retains its temperature for an extended period of time, used esp. in cool bags.

ice skate *n.* **1.** a boot having a steel blade fitted to the sole to enable the wearer to glide over ice. **2.** the steel blade on such a boot. *~vb.* **ice-skate. 3.** (*intr.*) to glide over ice on ice skates. **—'ice-,skater** *n.*

I.Chem.E. *abbrev. for* Institution of Chemical Engineers.

THESAURUS

ichor ('aıkɔː) n. **1.** *Greek myth.* the fluid said to flow in the veins of the gods. **2.** *Pathol.* a foul-smelling watery discharge from a wound or ulcer. —'**ichorous** *adj.*

ichthyo- *or before a vowel* **ichthy-** *combining form.* indicating or relating to fishes: *ichthyology.*

ichthyology (ˌıkθı'ɒlədʒı) n. the study of fishes. —**ichthyologic** (ˌıkθıə'lɒdʒık) *or* ˌ**ichthyo'logical** *adj.* —ˌ**ichthy'ologist** n.

I.C.I. *abbrev. for* Imperial Chemical Industries.

-ician *suffix forming nouns.* indicating a person skilled or involved in a subject or activity: *physician; beautician.*

icicle ('aısıkəl) n. a hanging spike of ice formed by the freezing of dripping water.

icing ('aısıŋ) n. **1.** Also called (esp. U.S.): **frosting.** a sugar preparation, variously flavoured and coloured, for coating and decorating cakes, etc. **2.** the formation of ice, as on a ship, due to the freezing of moisture in the atmosphere.

icing sugar n. *Brit.* a very finely ground sugar used for icings, confections, etc. U.S. term: **confectioners' sugar.**

icon *or* **ikon** ('aıkɒn) n. **1.** a representation of Christ or a saint, esp. one painted in oil on a wooden panel in a traditional Byzantine style and venerated in the Eastern Church. **2.** an image, picture, etc. **3.** a symbol resembling or analogous to the thing it represents.

icono- *or before a vowel* **icon-** *combining form.* indicating an image or likeness: *iconology.*

iconoclast (aı'kɒnəˌklæst) n. **1.** a person who attacks established or traditional concepts, principles, etc. **2. a.** a destroyer of religious images or objects. **b.** an adherent of a heretical iconoclastic movement within the Greek Orthodox Church from 725 to 842 A.D. —iˌ**cono-'clastic** *adj.* —iˌ**cono'clastically** *adv.* —i'**conoˌclasm** n.

icosahedron (ˌaıkɒsə'hiːdrən) n., pl. **-drons** *or* **-dra** (-drə). a solid figure having 20 faces. —ˌ**icosa'hedral** *adj.*

-ics *suffix forming nouns; functioning as sing.* **1.** indicating a science, art, or matters relating to a particular subject: *politics.* **2.** indicating certain activities: *acrobatics.*

icy ('aısı) *adj.* **icier, iciest. 1.** made of, covered with, or containing ice. **2.** resembling ice. **3.** freezing or very cold. **4.** cold or reserved in manner; aloof. —'**icily** *adv.* —'**iciness** n.

id (ıd) n. *Psychoanal.* the primitive instincts and energies in the unconscious mind that, modified by the ego and the superego, underlie all psychic activity.

ID *abbrev. for* identification.

id. *abbrev. for* idem.

I'd (aıd) *contraction of* I had *or* I would.

-id¹ *suffix forming nouns and adjectives.* indicating members of a zoological family: *cyprinid.*

-id² *suffix forming nouns.* variant of **-ide.**

-idae *suffix forming nouns.* indicating names of zoological families: *Felidae.*

-ide *or* **-id** *suffix forming nouns.* **1.** (added to the combining form of the nonmetallic or electronegative elements) indicating a binary compound: *sodium chloride.* **2.** indicating an organic compound derived from another: *acetanilide.* **3.** indicating one of a class of compounds or elements: *peptide.*

idea (aı'dıə) n. **1.** the product of mental activity whereby the mind consciously conceives a thought; conception. **2.** an impression established in the mind by something perceived; notion. **3.** a belief; opinion. **4.** a scheme, intention, plan, etc. **5.** a vague notion; inkling: *he had no idea of the truth.* **6.** significance or purpose: *the idea of the game is to discover the murderer.* **7.** *Philosophy.* **a.** an immediate object of thought or perception. **b.** (*sometimes cap.*) (in Plato) the universal essence or archetype of any class of things or concepts. **8. get ideas.** to become ambitious, restless, etc. **9. not one's idea of.** not what one regards as (hard work, a holiday, etc.). **10. that's an idea.** that is worth considering. **11. the very idea!** that is preposterous, unreasonable, etc.

ideal (aı'dıəl) n. **1.** a conception of something that is perfect. **2.** a person or thing considered to represent perfection. **3.** something existing only as an idea. **4.** a pattern or model, esp. of ethical behaviour. ~*adj.* **5.** conforming to an ideal. **6.** of, involving, or existing in the form of an idea. **7.** *Philosophy.* **a.** of or relating to a highly desirable and possible state of affairs. **b.** of or relating to idealism. —i'**deally** *adv.* —i'**dealness** n.

idealism (aı'dıəˌlızəm) n. **1.** belief in or pursuance of ideals. **2.** the tendency to represent things in their ideal forms, rather than as they are. **3.** *Philosophy.* the doctrine that thought or the mind is the only reality and that external objects consist merely of ideas. —i'**dealist** n. —iˌ**deal'istic** *adj.* —iˌ**deal'istically** *adv.*

idealize *or* **-ise** (aı'dıəˌlaız) vb. **1.** to consider or represent (something) as ideal. **2.** (*tr.*) to portray as ideal; glorify. **3.** (*intr.*) to form an ideal or ideals. —iˌ**deali'zation** *or* -i'**sation** n. —i'**dealˌizer** *or* -ˌ**iser** n.

idée fixe *French.* (ide 'fiks) n., pl. **idées fixes** (ide 'fiks). a fixed idea; obsession.

idem *Latin.* ('aıdɛm, 'ıdɛm) *pron., adj.* the same: used to refer to an article, chapter, etc., previously cited.

identical (aı'dɛntıkəl) *adj.* **1.** being the same. **2.** exactly alike or equal. **3.** designating either or both of a pair of twins of the same sex who developed from a single fertilized ovum that split into two. Cf. **fraternal** (sense 3). —i'**dentically** *adv.* —i'**denticalness** n.

identification (aıˌdɛntıfı'keıʃən) n. **1.** the act of identifying or the state of being identified. **2. a.** something that identifies a person or thing. **b.** (*as modifier*): *an identification card.* **3.** *Psychol.* **a.** the process of recognizing specific objects as the result of remembering. **b.** the process by which one incorporates aspects of another person's personality. **c.** the transferring of a response from one situation to another because the two bear similar features.

identification parade n. a group of persons assembled for the purpose of discovering whether a witness can identify the suspect.

identify (aı'dɛntıˌfaı) vb. **-fying, -fied.** (*mainly tr.*) **1.** to prove or recognize as being a certain person or thing; determine the identity of. **2.** to consider as the same or equivalent. **3.** (*also intr.; often foll. by with*) to consider (oneself) as similar to another. **4.** to determine the taxonomic classification of (a plant or animal). **5.** (*intr.;* usually foll. by *with*) *Psychol.* to engage in identification. —i'**dentiˌfiable** *adj.* —i'**dentiˌfier** n.

THESAURUS

icy 1. arctic, biting, bitter, chill, chilling, chilly, cold, freezing, frost-bound, frosty, frozen over, ice-cold, raw **2.** glacial, glassy, like a sheet of glass, rimy, slippery, slippy (*Inf.*) **3.** *Fig.* aloof, cold, distant, forbidding, frigid, frosty, glacial, hostile, indifferent, steely, stony, unfriendly, unwelcoming

idea 1. abstraction, concept, conception, conclusion, fancy, impression, judgment, perception, thought, understanding **2.** belief, conviction, doctrine, interpretation, notion, opinion, teaching, view, viewpoint **3.** approximation, clue, estimate, guess, hint, impression, inkling, intimation, notion, suspicion **4.** aim, end, import, intention, meaning, object, objective, plan, purpose, *raison d'être*, reason, sense, significance **5.** design, hypothesis, plan, recommendation, scheme, solution, suggestion, theory **6.** archetype, essence, form, pattern

ideal n. **1.** archetype, criterion, epitome, example, exemplar, last word, model, nonpareil, paradigm, paragon, pattern, perfection, prototype, standard, standard of perfection **2.** *Often plural* moral value, principle, standard ~*adj.* **3.** archetypal, classic, complete, consummate, model, optimal, perfect, quintessential, supreme **4.** abstract, conceptual, hypothetical, intellectual, mental, theoretical, transcendental **5.** fanciful, imaginary, impractical, ivory-tower, unattainable, unreal, Utopian, visionary

idealist n. romantic, Utopian, visionary

idealistic impracticable, optimistic, perfectionist, quixotic, romantic, starry-eyed, Utopian, visionary

ideally all things being equal, if one had one's way, in a perfect world, under the best of circumstances

identical alike, corresponding, duplicate, equal, equivalent, indistinguishable, interchangeable, like, matching, selfsame, the same, twin

identification 1. cataloguing, classifying, establishment of identity, labelling, naming, pinpointing, recognition **2.** association, connection, empathy, fellow feeling, involvement, rapport, relationship, sympathy **3.** credentials, ID, letters of introduction, papers

identify 1. catalogue, classify, diagnose, label, make out, name, pick out, pinpoint, place, put one's finger on (*Inf.*), recognize, single out, spot, tag **2.** *Often with* **with** ally, associate, empathize, feel for, put in the same category, put oneself in the place *or* shoes of, relate to, respond to, see through another's eyes, think of in connection (with)

Identikit (aɪˈdɛntɪˌkɪt) n. *Trademark*. **a.** a set of transparencies of typical facial characteristics that can be superimposed on one another to build up a picture of a person sought by the police. **b.** (*as modifier*): *an Identikit picture*.

identity (aɪˈdɛntɪtɪ) n., pl. **ties**. **1. a.** the state of having unique identifying characteristics. **b.** (*as modifier*): *an identity card*. **2.** the individual characteristics by which a person or thing is recognized. **3.** the state of being the same in nature, quality, etc.: *linked by the identity of their tastes*. **4.** *Maths*. **a.** an equation that is valid for all values of its variables, as in $(x -y)(x + y) = x^2 - y^2$. Often denoted by the symbol ≡ **b.** Also called: **identity element**. a member of a set that when operating on another member, *x*, produces that member *x*: the identity for multiplication of numbers is 1 since $x.1 = 1.x = x$. **5.** *Logic*. the relationship between an object and itself. **6.** *Austral. inf.* a well-known local person; figure: *a Barwidgee identity*. **7.** *Austral. & N.Z. inf.* an eccentric; character: *an old identity in the town*.

ideo- *combining form*. of or indicating idea or ideas: *ideology*.

ideogram (ˈɪdɪəʊˌɡræm) *or* **ideograph** (ˈɪdɪəʊˌɡrɑːf) n. **1.** a sign or symbol, used in a writing system such as that of China, that directly represents a concept or thing, rather than a word for it. **2.** any graphic sign or symbol, such as %, &, etc.

ideology (ˌaɪdɪˈɒlədʒɪ) n., pl. **-gies**. **1.** a body of ideas that reflects the beliefs of a nation, political system, etc. **2.** *Philosophy*. an idea that is false or held for the wrong reasons but is believed with such conviction as to be irrefutable. **3.** speculation that is imaginary or visionary. **4.** the study of the nature and origin of ideas. —**ideological** (ˌaɪdɪəˈlɒdʒɪkəl) *or* ˌideoˈlogic adj. —ˌideoˈlogically adv. —ˌideˈologist n.

ides (aɪdz) n. (*functioning as sing.*) (in the Roman calendar) the 15th day in March, May, July, and October and the 13th day of each other month.

id est *Latin*. (ɪd ˈɛst) the full form of **i.e.**

idiocy (ˈɪdɪəsɪ) n., pl. **-cies**. **1.** (*not in technical usage*) severe mental retardation. **2.** foolishness; stupidity. **3.** a foolish act or remark.

idiom (ˈɪdɪəm) n. **1.** a group of words whose meaning cannot be predicted from the constituent words: (*It was raining*) *cats and dogs*. **2.** linguistic usage that is grammatical and natural to native speakers. **3.** the characteristic vocabulary or usage of a specific human group or subject. **4.** the characteristic artistic style of an individual, school, etc. —**idiomatic** (ˌɪdɪəˈmætɪk) adj. —ˌidioˈmatically adv.

idiosyncrasy (ˌɪdɪəʊˈsɪŋkrəsɪ) n., pl. **-sies**. **1.** a tendency, type of behaviour, etc., of a person; quirk. **2.** the composite physical or psychological make-up of a person. **3.** an abnormal reaction of an individual to specific foods, drugs, or other agents. —**idiosyncratic** (ˌɪdɪəʊsɪŋˈkrætɪk) adj. —ˌidiosynˈcratically adv.

idiot (ˈɪdɪət) n. **1.** a person with severe mental retardation. **2.** a foolish or senseless person.

idiotic (ˌɪdɪˈɒtɪk) adj. of or resembling an idiot; foolish; senseless. —ˌidiˈotically adv.

idle (ˈaɪdəl) adj. **1.** unemployed or unoccupied; inactive. **2.** not operating or being used. **3.** not wanting to work; lazy. **4.** (*usually prenominal*) frivolous or trivial: *idle pleasures*. **5.** ineffective or powerless; vain. **6.** without basis; unfounded. ~vb. **7.** (when *tr.*, often foll. by *away*) to waste or pass (time) fruitlessly or inactively. **8.** (*intr.*) (of a shaft, etc.) to turn without doing useful work. **9.** (*intr.*) (of an engine) to run at low speed with the transmission disengaged. —**idleness** n. —**idly** adv.

idler (ˈaɪdlə) n. **1.** a person who idles. **2.** a gearwheel placed between two others to transfer motion.

idol (ˈaɪdəl) n. **1.** a material object that is worshipped as a god. **2.** *Christianity, Judaism*. any being (other than the one God) to which divine honour is paid. **3.** a person who is revered, admired, or highly loved.

idolatry (aɪˈdɒlətrɪ) n. **1.** the worship of idols. **2.** great devotion or reverence. —**i'dolater** n. *or* **i'dolatress** fem. n. —**i'dolatrous** adj.

idolize *or* **-ise** (ˈaɪdəˌlaɪz) vb. **1.** (*tr.*) to admire or revere greatly. **2.** (*tr.*) to worship as an idol. **3.** (*intr.*) to worship idols. —**idolism**, ˌidoliˈzation *or* -iˈsation n. —ˈidolist, ˈidolˌizer *or* -ˌiser n.

idyll *or U.S.* (*sometimes*) **idyl** (ˈɪdɪl) n. **1.** a poem or prose work describing an idealized rural life, pastoral scenes, etc. **2.** a charming or picturesque scene or event. **3.** a piece of music with a pastoral character. —**i'dyllic** adj. —**i'dyllically** adv.

i.e. *abbrev. for* id est: that is.

-ie *suffix forming nouns*. variant of -y²: used to form informal words (esp. in Australia): *surfie*.

I.E.E. *abbrev. for* Institution of Electrical Engineers.

-ier *suffix forming nouns*. variant of **-eer**: *brigadier*.

if (ɪf) conj. (*subordinating*) **1.** in case that, or on condition that: *if you try hard it might work*. **2.** used to introduce an indirect question. In this sense, *if* approaches the meaning of *whether*. **3.** even though: *an attractive if awkward girl*. **4. a.** used to introduce expressions of desire, with *only*: *if I had only known*. **b.** used to introduce exclamations of surprise, dismay, etc.: *if this doesn't top everything!* **5. as if**. as it would be if; as though: *he treats me as if I were stupid*. ~n. **6.** an uncertainty or doubt: *the big if is whether our plan will work*. **7.** a condition or stipulation: *I won't have any ifs or buts*.

-ify *suffix forming verbs*. variant of **-fy**: *intensify*. —**-ification** suffix forming nouns.

igloo *or* **iglu** (ˈɪɡluː) n., pl. **-loos** *or* **-lus**. **1.** a dome-shaped Eskimo house, built of blocks of solid snow. **2.** a hollow made by a seal in the snow over its breathing hole in the ice.

igneous (ˈɪɡnɪəs) adj. **1.** (of rocks) derived from magma or lava that has solidified on or below the earth's surface. **2.** of or relating to fire.

ignis fatuus (ˈɪɡnɪs ˈfætjʊəs) n., pl. **ignes fatui** (ˈɪɡniːz ˈfætjʊˌaɪ). another name for **will-o'-the-wisp**.

ignite (ɪɡˈnaɪt) vb. **1.** to catch fire or set fire to; burn or

---

◼◼◼ T H E S A U R U S ◼◼◼

identity 1. distinctiveness, existence, individuality, oneness, particularity, personality, self, selfhood, singularity, uniqueness 2. accord, correspondence, empathy, rapport, sameness, unanimity, unity

idiocy abject stupidity, asininity, fatuity, fatuousness, foolishness, imbecility, inanity, insanity, lunacy, senselessness, tomfoolery

idiom 1. expression, locution, phrase, set phrase, turn of phrase 2. jargon, language, mode of expression, parlance, style, talk, usage, vernacular

idiomatic dialectal, native, vernacular

idiosyncrasy affectation, characteristic, eccentricity, habit, mannerism, oddity, peculiarity, personal trait, quirk, singularity, trick

idiot ass, blockhead, booby, cretin, dimwit (*Inf.*), dunderhead, fool, halfwit, imbecile, mooncalf, moron, nincompoop, nitwit, simpleton

idiotic asinine, crazy, daft (*Inf.*), dumb (*Inf.*), fatuous, foolhardy, foolish, halfwitted, harebrained, imbecile, imbecilic, inane, in-sane, lunatic, moronic, senseless, stupid, unintelligent

idle adj. 1. dead, empty, gathering dust, inactive, jobless, mothballed, out of action *or* operation, out of work, redundant, stationary, ticking over, unemployed, unoccupied, unused, vacant 2. indolent, lackadaisical, lazy, shiftless, slothful, sluggish 3. frivolous, insignificant, irrelevant, nugatory, superficial, trivial, unhelpful, unnecessary 4. abortive, bootless, fruitless, futile, groundless, ineffective, of no avail, otiose, pointless, unavailing, unproductive, unsuccessful, useless, vain, worthless ~v. 5. *Often followed by away* dally, dawdle, fool, fritter, kill time, laze, loiter, lounge, potter, waste, while 6. coast, drift, mark time, shirk, sit back and do nothing, skive (*Brit. sl.*), slack, slow down, take it easy (*Inf.*), vegetate

idleness 1. inaction, inactivity, leisure, time on one's hands, unemployment 2. hibernation, inertia, laziness, shiftlessness, sloth, sluggishness, torpor, vegetating 3. dilly-dallying (*Inf.*), lazing, loafing, pottering, skiving (*Brit sl.*), time-wasting, trifling

idling adj. dawdling, drifting, loafing, pottering, resting, resting on one's oars, taking it easy (*Inf.*), ticking over

idol 1. deity, god, graven image, image, pagan symbol 2. *Fig.* beloved, darling, favourite, hero, pet, pin-up (*Sl.*), superstar

idolater 1. heathen, idol-worshipper, pagan 2. admirer, adorer, devotee, idolizer, votary, worshipper

idolatrous adoring, adulatory, reverential, uncritical, worshipful

idolatry adoration, adulation, apotheosis, deification, exaltation, glorification, hero worship, idolizing

idolize admire, adore, apotheosize, bow down before, deify, dote upon, exalt, glorify, hero-worship, look up to, love, revere, reverence, venerate, worship, worship to excess

if 1. conj. admitting, allowing, assuming, granting, in case, on condition that, on the assumption that, provided, providing, supposing, though, whenever, wherever, whether 2. n. condition, doubt, hesitation, stipulation, uncertainty

cause to burn. **2.** (*tr.*) *Chem.* to heat strongly. —**ig'nitable** *or* **ig'nitible** *adj.* —**ig,nita'bility** *or* **ig,niti'bility** *n.* —**ig'niter** *n.*

ignition (ɪg'nɪʃən) *n.* **1.** the act or process of initiating combustion. **2.** the process of igniting the fuel in an internal-combustion engine. **3.** (preceded by *the*) the devices used to ignite the fuel in an internal-combustion engine.

ignoble (ɪg'nəʊbəl) *adj.* **1.** dishonourable; base; despicable. **2.** of low birth or origins; humble; common. **3.** of low quality; inferior. —**,igno'bility** *or* **ig'nobleness** *n.* —**ig'nobly** *adv.*

ignominy ('ɪgnə,mɪnɪ) *n.*, *pl.* **-minies.** **1.** disgrace or public shame; dishonour. **2.** a cause of disgrace; a shameful act. —**,igno'minious** *adj.* —**,igno'miniously** *adv.* —**,igno'miniousness** *n.*

ignoramus (,ɪgnə'reɪməs) *n.*, *pl.* **-muses.** an ignorant person; fool.

ignorance ('ɪgnərəns) *n.* lack of knowledge, information, or education; the state of being ignorant.

ignorant ('ɪgnərənt) *adj.* **1.** lacking in knowledge or education; unenlightened. **2.** (*postpositive*; often foll. by *of*) lacking in awareness or knowledge (of): *ignorant of the law.* **3.** resulting from or showing lack of knowledge or awareness: *an ignorant remark.* —**'ignorantly** *adv.*

ignore (ɪg'nɔː) *vb.* (*tr.*) to fail or refuse to notice; disregard. —**ig'norer** *n.*

iguana (ɪ'gwɑːnə) *n.* either of two large tropical American arboreal herbivorous lizards, esp. the common iguana, having a greyish-green body with a row of spines along the back. —**i'guanian** *n.*, *adj.*

IHS the first three letters of the name Jesus in Greek (ΙΗΣΟΥΣ), often used as a Christian emblem.

ikebana (,iːkə'bɑːnə) *n.* the Japanese decorative art of flower arrangement.

ikon ('aɪkɒn) *n.* a variant spelling of **icon.**

il- *prefix.* variant of **in-¹** and **in-²** before *l.*

-il *suffix forming nouns.* variant of **-ile.**

-ile *or* **-il** *suffix forming adjectives and nouns.* indicating capability, liability, or a relationship with something: *agile; juvenile.* —**-ility** *suffix forming nouns.*

ileum ('ɪlɪəm) *n.* the part of the small intestine between the jejunum and the caecum. —**'ileac** *adj.*

ilex ('aɪlɛks) *n.* **1.** any of a genus of trees or shrubs such as the holly and inkberry. **2.** another name for the **holm oak.**

ilium ('ɪlɪəm) *n.*, *pl.* **-ia** (-ɪə). the uppermost and widest of the three sections of the hipbone.

ilk (ɪlk) *n.* **1.** a type; class; sort (esp. in **of that, his,** etc., **ilk**): *people of that ilk should not be allowed here.* **2. of that ilk.** *Scot.* of the place of the same name: to indicate that the person is laird of the place named: *Moncrieff of that ilk.*

▷ **Usage.** Although the use of *ilk* in sense 1 is often condemned as being the result of a misunderstanding of the original Scottish expression, it is nevertheless well established and generally acceptable.

ill (ɪl) *adj.* **worse, worst.** **1.** (*usually postpositive*) not in good health; sick. **2.** characterized by or intending harm, etc.; hostile: *ill deeds.* **3.** causing pain, harm, adversity, etc. **4.** ascribing or imputing evil to something referred to: *ill repute.* **5.** promising an unfavourable outcome; unpropitious: *an ill omen.* **6.** harsh; lacking kindness: *ill will.* **7.** not up to an acceptable standard; faulty: *ill manners.* **8. ill at ease.** unable to relax; uncomfortable. ~*n.* **9.** evil or harm; misfortune; trouble. **10.** a mild disease. ~*adv.* **11.** badly: *the title ill befits him.* **12.** with difficulty; hardly: *he can ill afford the money.*

ill. *abbrev. for:* **1.** illustrated. **2.** illustration.

I'll (aɪl) contraction of *I will* or *I shall.*

ill-advised *adj.* **1.** acting without reasonable care or thought: *you would be ill-advised to sell your house now.* **2.** badly thought out; not or insufficiently considered: *an ill-advised plan of action.* —**,ill-ad'visedly** *adv.*

ill-bred *adj.* badly brought up; lacking good manners. —**,ill-'breeding** *n.*

ill-considered *adj.* done without due consideration; not thought out: *an ill-considered decision.*

ill-disposed *adj.* (often foll. by *towards*) not kindly disposed.

illegal (ɪ'liːgəl) *adj.* **1.** forbidden by law; unlawful; illicit. **2.** unauthorized or prohibited by a code of official or accepted rules. —**il'legally** *adv.* —**,ille'gality** *n.*

illegible (ɪ'lɛdʒɪbəl) *adj.* unable to be read or deciphered. —**il,legi'bility** *or* **il'legibleness** *n.* —**il'legibly** *adv.*

illegitimate (,ɪlɪ'dʒɪtɪmɪt) *adj.* **1.** born of parents who were not married to each other at the time of birth; bastard. **2.** illegal; unlawful. **3.** contrary to logic; incorrectly reasoned. —**,ille'gitimacy** *or* **,ille'gitimateness** *n.* —**,ille'gitimately** *adv.*

ill-fated *adj.* doomed or unlucky.

ill-favoured *adj.* **1.** unattractive or repulsive in ap-

THESAURUS

ignite burn, burst into flames, catch fire, fire, flare up, inflame, kindle, light, put a match to (*Inf.*), set alight, set fire to, take fire, touch off

ignominious abject, despicable, discreditable, disgraceful, dishonourable, disreputable, humiliating, indecorous, inglorious, mortifying, scandalous, shameful, sorry, undignified

ignominy bad odour, contempt, discredit, disgrace, dishonour, disrepute, humiliation, infamy, mortification, obloquy, odium, opprobrium, reproach, shame, stigma

ignorance **1.** greenness, inexperience, innocence, nescience (*Literary*), oblivion, unawareness, unconsciousness, unfamiliarity **2.** benightedness, blindness, illiteracy, lack of education, mental darkness, unenlightenment, unintelligence

ignorant **1.** benighted, blind to, inexperienced, innocent, in the dark about, oblivious, unaware, unconscious, unenlightened, uninformed, uninitiated, unknowing, unschooled, unwitting **2.** green, illiterate, naive, unaware, uncultivated, uneducated, unknowledgeable, unlearned, unlettered, unread, untaught, untrained, untutored **3.** crass, crude, gross, half-baked (*Inf.*), insensitive, rude, shallow, superficial, uncomprehending, unscholarly

ignore be oblivious to, bury one's head in the sand, cold-shoulder, cut (*Inf.*), disregard, give the cold shoulder to, neglect, overlook, pass over, pay no attention to, reject, send (someone) to Coventry, shut one's eyes to, take no notice of, turn a blind eye to, turn a deaf ear to, turn one's back on

ill *adj.* **1.** ailing, dicky (*Sl.*), diseased, funny (*Inf.*), indisposed, infirm, laid up (*Inf.*), not up to snuff (*Inf.*), off-colour, on the sick list (*Inf.*), out of sorts (*Inf.*), poorly (*Inf.*), queasy, queer, seedy (*Inf.*), sick, under the weather (*Inf.*), unhealthy, unwell, valetudinarian **2.** bad, damaging, deleterious, detrimental, evil, foul, harmful, iniquitous, injurious, ruinous, unfortunate, unlucky, vile, wicked, wrong **3.** acrimonious, adverse, antagonistic, cantankerous, cross, harsh, hateful, hostile, hurtful, inimical, malevolent, malicious, sullen, surly, unfriendly, unkind **4.** disturbing, foreboding, inauspicious, ominous, sinister, threatening, unfavourable, unhealthy, unlucky, unpromising, unpropitious, unwholesome ~*n.* **5.** affliction, harm, hurt, injury, misery, misfortune, pain, trial, tribulation, trouble, unpleasantness, woe **6.** ailment, complaint, disease, disorder, illness, indisposition, infirmity, malady, malaise, sickness **7.** abuse, badness, cruelty, damage, depravity, destruction, evil, ill usage, malice, mischief, suffering, wickedness ~*adv.* **8.** badly, hard, inauspiciously, poorly, unfavourably, unfortunately, unluckily **9.** barely, by no means, hardly, insufficiently, scantily **10.** *As in* ill-gotten criminally, dishonestly, foully, fraudulently, illegally, illegitimately, illicitly, unlawfully, unscrupulously

ill-advised foolhardy, foolish, ill-considered, ill-judged, impolitic, imprudent, inappropriate, incautious, indiscreet, injudicious, misguided, overhasty, rash, reckless, short-sighted, thoughtless, unseemly, unwise, wrong-headed

ill-assorted incompatible, incongruous, inharmonious, mismatched, uncongenial, unsuited

ill at ease anxious, awkward, disquieted, disturbed, edgy, faltering, fidgety, hesitant, nervous, on edge, on pins and needles (*Inf.*), on tenterhooks, out of place, restless, self-conscious, strange, tense, uncomfortable, uneasy, unquiet, unrelaxed, unsettled, unsure

ill-bred bad-mannered, boorish, churlish, coarse, crass, discourteous, ill-mannered, impolite, indelicate, rude, uncivil, uncivilized, uncouth, ungallant, ungentlemanly, unladylike, unmannerly, unrefined, vulgar

ill-defined blurred, dim, fuzzy, indistinct, nebulous, shadowy, unclear, vague, woolly

ill-disposed against, antagonistic, anti (*Inf.*), antipathetic, averse, disobliging, down on (*Inf.*), hostile, inimical, opposed, uncooperative, unfriendly, unwelcoming

illegal actionable (*Law*), banned, black-market, bootleg, criminal, felonious, forbidden, illicit, lawless, outlawed, prohibited, proscribed, unauthorized, unconstitutional, under the counter, unlawful, unlicensed, unofficial, wrongful

illegality crime, criminality, felony, illegitimacy, illicitness, lawlessness, unlawfulness, wrong, wrongness

illegible crabbed, faint, hard to make out, hieroglyphic, indecipherable, obscure, scrawled, undecipherable, unreadable

pearance; ugly. **2.** offensive, disagreeable, or objectionable. —,ill-'favouredly *adv.* —,ill-'favouredness *n.*
ill-founded *adj.* not founded on true or reliable premisses; unsubstantiated.
ill-gotten *adj.* obtained dishonestly or illegally (esp. in **ill-gotten gains**).
ill humour *n.* a disagreeable or sullen mood; bad temper. —,ill-'humoured *adj.* —,ill'humouredly *adv.*
illiberal (ɪ'lɪbərəl) *adj.* **1.** narrow-minded; prejudiced; intolerant. **2.** not generous; mean. **3.** lacking in culture or refinement. —il,liber'ality *n.* —il'liberally *adv.*
illicit (ɪ'lɪsɪt) *adj.* **1.** another word for **illegal**. **2.** not allowed or approved by common custom, rule, or standard: *illicit sexual relations.* —il'licitly *adv.* —il'licitness *n.*
illiterate (ɪ'lɪtərɪt) *adj.* **1.** unable to read and write. **2.** violating accepted standards in reading and writing: *an illiterate scrawl.* **3.** uneducated, ignorant, or uncultured: *scientifically illiterate.* ~*n.* **4.** an illiterate person. —il'literacy *or* il'literateness *n.* —il'literately *adv.*
ill-mannered *adj.* having bad manners; rude; impolite. —,ill-'manneredly *adv.*
illness ('ɪlnɪs) *n.* **1.** a disease or indisposition; sickness. **2.** a state of ill health.
illogical (ɪ'lɒdʒɪkəl) *adj.* **1.** characterized by lack of logic; senseless or unreasonable. **2.** disregarding logical principles. —illogicality (ɪ,lɒdʒɪ'kælɪtɪ) *or* il'logicalness *n.* —il'logically *adv.*
ill-starred *adj.* unlucky; unfortunate; ill-fated.
ill-timed *adj.* occurring at or planned for an unsuitable time.
ill-treat *vb.* (*tr.*) to behave cruelly or harshly towards; misuse; maltreat. —,ill-'treatment *n.*
illuminant (ɪ'lu:mɪnənt) *n.* **1.** something that provides or gives off light. ~*adj.* **2.** giving off light; illuminating.
illuminate *vb.* (ɪ'lu:mɪ,neɪt). **1.** (*tr.*) to throw light in or into; light up. **2.** (*tr.*) to make easily understood; clarify. **3.** to adorn, decorate, or be decorated with lights. **4.** (*tr.*) to decorate (a letter, etc.) by the application of colours, gold, or silver. **5.** (*intr.*) to become lighted up. ~*adj.* (ɪ'lu:mɪnɪt, -,neɪt). **6.** *Arch.* made clear or bright

with light. ~*n.* (ɪ'lu:mɪnɪt, -,neɪt). **7.** a person who claims to have special enlightenment. —il'lumi,nating-ly *adv.* —il'luminative *adj.* —il'lumi,nator *n.*
illumination (ɪ,lu:mɪ'neɪʃən) *n.* **1.** the act of illuminating or the state of being illuminated. **2.** a source of light. **3.** (*often pl.*) *Chiefly Brit.* a light or lights used as decoration in streets, parks, etc. **4.** spiritual or intellectual enlightenment; insight or understanding. **5.** the act of making understood; clarification. **6.** decoration in colours, gold, or silver used on some manuscripts. **7.** *Physics.* another name (not in technical usage) for **illuminance.**
illumine (ɪ'lu:mɪn) *vb.* a literary word for **illuminate.** —il'luminable *adj.*
ill-use *vb.* ('ɪl'ju:z). **1.** to use badly or cruelly; abuse; maltreat. ~*n.* ('ɪl'ju:s), *also* **ill-usage. 2.** harsh or cruel treatment; abuse.
illusion (ɪ'lu:ʒən) *n.* **1.** a false appearance or deceptive impression of reality: *the mirror gives an illusion of depth.* **2.** a false or misleading perception or belief; delusion. **3.** *Psychol.* a perception that is not true to reality, having been altered subjectively in the mind of the perceiver. See also **hallucination.** —il'lusionary *or* il-'lusional *adj.* —il'lusioned *adj.* —illusory (-'lu:s-) *or* il-'lusive *adj.* —il'lusoriness *n.*
illusionist (ɪ'lu:ʒənɪst) *n.* **1.** a person given to illusions; visionary; dreamer. **2.** *Philosophy.* a person who believes in illusionism. **3.** an artist who practises illusionism. **4.** a conjuror; magician. —il,lusion'istic *adj.*
illustrate ('ɪlə,streɪt) *vb.* **1.** to clarify or explain by use of examples, analogy, etc. **2.** (*tr.*) to be an example of. **3.** (*tr.*) to explain or decorate (a book, text, etc.) with pictures. —'illus,trative *adj.* —'illus,trator *n.*
illustration (,ɪlə'streɪʃən) *n.* **1.** pictorial matter used to explain or decorate a text. **2.** an example: *an illustration of his ability.* **3.** the act of illustrating or the state of being illustrated. —,illus'trational *adj.*
illustrious (ɪ'lʌstrɪəs) *adj.* **1.** of great renown; famous and distinguished. **2.** glorious or great: *illustrious deeds.* —il'lustriously *adv.* —il'lustriousness *n.*

THESAURUS

illegitimate 1. illegal, illicit, improper, unauthorized, unconstitutional, unlawful, unsanctioned **2.** baseborn (*Archaic*), bastard, born on the wrong side of the blanket, born out of wedlock, fatherless, misbegotten (*Literary*), natural, spurious (*Rare*) **3.** illogical, incorrect, invalid, spurious, unsound
ill-fated blighted, doomed, hapless, ill-omened, ill-starred, luckless, star-crossed, unfortunate, unhappy, unlucky
ill feeling animosity, animus, antagonism, bad blood, bitterness, disgruntlement, dissatisfaction, dudgeon (*Archaic*), enmity, frustration, hard feelings, hostility, ill will, indignation, offence, rancour, resentment
ill-founded baseless, empty, groundless, idle, unjustified, unproven, unreliable, unsubstantiated, unsupported
ill-humoured acrimonious, bad-tempered, crabbed, crabby, cross, disagreeable, grumpy, huffy, impatient, irascible, irritable, like a bear with a sore head (*Inf.*), mardy (*Dialect*), moody, morose, out of sorts, out of temper, petulant, sharp, snappish, snappy, sulky, sullen, tart, testy, thin-skinned, touchy, waspish
illiberal 1. bigoted, hidebound, intolerant, narrow-minded, prejudiced, reactionary, small-minded, uncharitable, ungenerous **2.** close-fisted, mean, miserly, niggardly, parsimonious, selfish, sordid, stingy, tight, tight-fisted, ungenerous
illicit 1. black-market, bootleg, contraband, criminal, felonious, illegal, illegitimate, prohibited, unauthorized, unlawful, unlicensed **2.** clandestine, forbidden, furtive, guilty, immoral, improper, wrong
illiteracy benightedness, ignorance, illiterateness, lack of education
illiterate benighted, ignorant, uncultured, uneducated, unlettered, untaught,

untutored
ill-judged foolish, ill-advised, ill-considered, injudicious, misguided, over-hasty, rash, short-sighted, unwise, wrong-headed
ill-mannered badly behaved, boorish, churlish, coarse, discourteous, ill-behaved, ill-bred, impolite, insolent, loutish, rude, uncivil, uncouth, unmannerly
ill-natured bad-tempered, catty (*Inf.*), churlish, crabbed, cross, cross-grained, disagreeable, disobliging, malevolent, malicious, mean, nasty, perverse, petulant, spiteful, sulky, sullen, surly, unfriendly, unkind, unpleasant
illness affliction, ailment, attack, complaint, disability, disease, disorder, ill health, indisposition, infirmity, malady, malaise, poor health, sickness
illogical absurd, fallacious, faulty, inconclusive, inconsistent, incorrect, invalid, irrational, meaningless, senseless, sophistical, specious, spurious, unreasonable, unscientific, unsound
ill-starred doomed, ill-fated, ill-omened, inauspicious, star-crossed, unfortunate, unhappy, unlucky
ill temper annoyance, bad temper, crossness, curtness, impatience, irascibility, irritability, petulance, sharpness, spitefulness, tetchiness
ill-tempered annoyed, bad-tempered, choleric, cross, curt, grumpy, ill-humoured, impatient, irascible, irritable, sharp, spiteful, testy, tetchy, touchy
ill-timed awkward, inappropriate, inconvenient, inept, inopportune, unseasonable, untimely, unwelcome
ill-treat abuse, damage, handle roughly, harass, harm, harry, ill-use, injure, knock about, maltreat, mishandle, misuse, op-

press, wrong
ill-treatment abuse, damage, harm, ill-use, injury, mistreatment, misuse, rough handling
illuminate 1. brighten, illumine (*Literary*), irradiate, light, light up **2.** clarify, clear up, elucidate, enlighten, explain, give insight into, instruct, make clear, shed light on **3.** adorn, decorate, illustrate, ornament
illuminating enlightening, explanatory, helpful, informative, instructive, revealing
illumination 1. beam, brightening, brightness, light, lighting, lighting up, lights, radiance, ray **2.** awareness, clarification, edification, enlightenment, insight, inspiration, instruction, perception, revelation, understanding
illusion 1. chimera, daydream, fantasy, figment of the imagination, hallucination, ignis fatuus, mirage, mockery, phantasm, semblance, will-o'-the-wisp **2.** deception, delusion, error, fallacy, false impression, fancy, misapprehension, misconception
illusory *or* **illusive** apparent, Barmecide, beguiling, chimerical, deceitful, deceptive, delusive, fallacious, false, hallucinatory, misleading, mistaken, seeming, sham, unreal, untrue
illustrate 1. bring home, clarify, demonstrate, elucidate, emphasize, exemplify, exhibit, explain, instance, interpret, make clear, make plain, point up, show **2.** adorn, decorate, depict, draw, ornament, picture, sketch
illustrated decorated, embellished, graphic, illuminated, pictorial, picture, pictured, with illustrations
illustration 1. analogy, case, case in point, clarification, demonstration, elucidation, example, exemplification, explanation,

ill will n. hostile feeling; enmity; antagonism.

I.L.O. abbrev. for International Labour Organization.

I'm (aɪm) n. contraction of I am.

im- prefix. variant of **in-¹** and **in-²** before b, m, and p.

image ('ɪmɪdʒ) n. 1. a representation or likeness of a person or thing, esp. in sculpture. 2. an optically formed reproduction of an object, such as one formed by a lens or mirror. 3. a person or thing that resembles another closely; double or copy. 4. a mental picture; idea produced by the imagination. 5. the personality presented to the public by a person: a politician's image. 6. the pattern of light that is focused onto the retina. 7. Psychol. the mental experience of something that is not immediately present to the senses, often involving memory. See also **imagery**. 8. a personification of a specified quality; epitome: the image of good breeding. 9. a mental picture or association of ideas evoked in a literary work. ~vb. (tr.) Rare. 10. to picture in the mind; imagine. 11. to make or reflect an image of. 12. to portray or describe. 13. to be an example or epitome of; typify. —'**imageable** adj. —'**imageless** adj.

imagery ('ɪmɪdʒrɪ, -dʒərɪ) n., pl. **-ries.** 1. descriptive language in a literary work, esp. that appealing to the senses. 2. images collectively. 3. Psychol. **a.** the materials or general processes of the imagination. **b.** the characteristic kind of mental images formed by a particular individual. See also **image** (sense 7), **imagination** (sense 1).

imaginary (ɪ'mædʒɪnərɪ, -dʒɪnrɪ) adj. 1. existing in the imagination; unreal; illusory. 2. Maths. involving or containing imaginary numbers. —im'**aginarily** adv. —im'**aginariness** n.

imagination (ɪ,mædʒɪ'neɪʃən) n. 1. the faculty or action of producing mental images of what is not present or has not been experienced. 2. mental creative ability. 3. the ability to deal resourcefully with unexpected or unusual problems, circumstances, etc.

imaginative (ɪ'mædʒɪnətɪv) adj. 1. produced by or indicative of a creative imagination. 2. having a vivid imagination. —im'**aginatively** adv. —im'**aginativeness** n.

imagine (ɪ'mædʒɪn) vb. 1. (when tr., may take a clause as object) to form a mental image of. 2. (when tr., may take a clause as object) to think, believe, or guess. 3. (tr.; takes a clause as object) to suppose; assume: I imagine he'll come. —im'**aginable** adj. —im'**aginably** adv. —im'**aginer** n.

imago (ɪ'meɪgəʊ) n., pl. **imagoes** or **imagines** (ɪ'mædʒə-,niːz). 1. an adult sexually mature insect. 2. Psychoanal. an idealized image of another person, usually a parent, carried in the unconscious.

imam (ɪ'mɑːm) or **imaum** (ɪ'mɑːm, ɪ'mɔːm) n. Islam. 1. a leader of congregational prayer in a mosque. 2. a caliph, as leader of a Muslim community.

imbalance (ɪm'bæləns) n. a lack of balance, as in emphasis, proportion, etc.: the political imbalance of the programme.

imbecile ('ɪmbɪ,siːl, -,saɪl) n. 1. Psychol. a person of very low intelligence (I.Q. of 25 to 50). 2. Inf. an extremely stupid person; dolt. ~adj. also **imbecilic** (,ɪmbɪ-'sɪlɪk). 3. of or like an imbecile; mentally deficient; feeble-minded. 4. stupid or senseless: an imbecile thing to do. —'**imbe,cilely** or ,**imbe'cilically** adv. —,**imbe'cility** n.

imbed (ɪm'bɛd) vb. **-bedding, -bedded.** a less common spelling of **embed.**

imbibe (ɪm'baɪb) vb. 1. to drink (esp. alcoholic drinks). 2. Literary. to take in or assimilate (ideas, etc.): to imbibe the spirit of the Renaissance. 3. (tr.) to take in as if by drinking: to imbibe fresh air. 4. to absorb or cause to absorb liquid or moisture; assimilate or saturate. —im'**biber** n.

imbroglio (ɪm'brəʊlɪ,əʊ) n., pl. **-glios.** 1. a confused or perplexing political or interpersonal situation. 2. Obs. a confused heap; jumble.

imbue (ɪm'bjuː) vb. **-buing, -bued.** (tr.; usually foll. by with) 1. to instil or inspire (with ideals, principles, etc.). 2. Rare. to soak, esp. with dye, etc. —im'**buement** n.

I. Mech. E. abbrev. for Institution of Mechanical Engineers.

IMF abbrev. for International Monetary Fund.

imitate ('ɪmɪ,teɪt) vb. (tr.) 1. to try to follow the manner, style, etc., of or take as a model: many writers imitated the language of Shakespeare. 2. to pretend to be or to impersonate, esp. for humour; mimic. 3. to make a copy or reproduction of; duplicate. —**imitable** ('ɪmɪtəb²l) adj. —,**imita'bility** n. —'**imi,tator** n.

imitation (,ɪmɪ'teɪʃən) n. 1. the act or practice of imitating; mimicry. 2. an instance or product of imitating, such as a copy of the manner of a person; impression. 3. **a.** a copy of a genuine article; counterfeit. **b.** (as modifier): imitation jewellery. 4. Music. the repetition of a phrase or figure in one part after its appearance in another, as in a fugue. —,**imi'tational** adj.

imitative ('ɪmɪtətɪv) adj. 1. imitating or tending to copy. 2. characterized by imitation. 3. copying or reproducing an original, esp. in an inferior manner: imitative painting. 4. another word for **onomatopoeic.** —'**imitatively** adv. —'**imitativeness** n.

immaculate (ɪ'mækjʊlɪt) adj. 1. completely clean; extremely tidy: his clothes were immaculate. 2. completely flawless, etc.: an immaculate rendering of the sym-

THESAURUS

instance, interpretation, specimen 2. adornment, decoration, figure, picture, plate, sketch

illustrious brilliant, celebrated, distinguished, eminent, exalted, famed, famous, glorious, great, noble, notable, noted, prominent, remarkable, renowned, resplendent, signal, splendid

ill will acrimony, animosity, animus, antagonism, antipathy, aversion, bad blood, dislike, enmity, envy, grudge, hard feelings, hatred, hostility, malevolence, malice, no love lost, rancour, resentment, spite, unfriendliness, venom

image 1. appearance, effigy, figure, icon, idol, likeness, picture, portrait, reflection, representation, statue 2. chip off the old block (Inf.), counterpart, (dead) ringer (Sl.), Doppelgänger, double, facsimile, replica, similitude, spit (Inf.), spitting image or spit and image (Inf.) 3. conceit, concept, conception, figure, idea, impression, mental picture, perception, trope

imaginable believable, comprehensible, conceivable, credible, likely, plausible, possible, supposable, thinkable, under the sun, within the bounds of possibility

imaginary assumed, chimerical, dreamlike, fancied, fanciful, fictional, fictitious, hallucinatory, hypothetical, ideal, illusive, illusory, imagined, invented, legendary, made-up, mythological, nonexistent, phantasmal,

shadowy, supposed, suppositious, supposititious, unreal, unsubstantial, visionary

imagination 1. creativity, enterprise, fancy, ingenuity, insight, inspiration, invention, inventiveness, originality, resourcefulness, vision, wit, wittiness 2. chimera, conception, idea, ideality, illusion, image, invention, notion, supposition, unreality

imaginative clever, creative, dreamy, enterprising, fanciful, fantastic, ingenious, inspired, inventive, original, poetical, visionary, vivid, whimsical

imagine 1. conceive, conceptualize, conjure up, create, devise, dream up (Inf.), envisage, fantasize, form a mental picture of, frame, invent, picture, plan, project, scheme, see in the mind's eye, think of, think up, visualize 2. apprehend, assume, believe, conjecture, deduce, deem, fancy, gather, guess, infer, realize, suppose, surmise, suspect, take for granted, take it, think

imbecile 1. n. bungler, cretin, dolt, dotard, fool, halfwit, idiot, moron, thickhead 2. adj. asinine, fatuous, feeble-minded, foolish, idiotic, imbecilic, inane, ludicrous, moronic, simple, stupid, thick, witless

imbecility asininity, childishness, cretinism, fatuity, foolishness, idiocy, inanity, incompetency, stupidity

imbibe 1. consume, drink, knock back (Inf.), quaff, sink (Inf.), suck, swallow, swig (Inf.) 2. Literary absorb, acquire, assimilate,

gain, gather, ingest, receive, take in

imbroglio complexity, complication, embarrassment, entanglement, involvement, misunderstanding, quandary

imitate affect, ape, burlesque, caricature, copy, counterfeit, do (Inf.), do an impression of, duplicate, echo, emulate, follow, follow in the footsteps of, follow suit, impersonate, mimic, mirror, mock, parody, personate, repeat, send up (Brit. inf.), simulate, spoof (Inf.), take a leaf out of (someone's) book, take off (Inf.), travesty

imitation n. 1. aping, copy, counterfeit, counterfeiting, duplication, echoing, likeness, mimicry, resemblance, simulation 2. fake, forgery, impersonation, impression, mockery, parody, reflection, replica, reproduction, sham, substitution, takeoff (Inf.), travesty ~adj. 3. artificial, dummy, ersatz, man-made, mock, phoney (Inf.), pseudo (Inf.), repro, reproduction, sham, simulated, synthetic

imitative copied, copycat (Inf.), copying, derivative, echoic, mimetic, mimicking, mock, onomatopoeic, parrotlike, plagiarized, pseudo (Inf.), put-on, second-hand, simulated, unoriginal

imitator aper, copier, copycat (Inf.), echo, epigone (Rare), follower, impersonator, impressionist, mimic, parrot, shadow

phony. **3.** morally pure; free from sin or corruption. **4.** *Biol.* with no spots or markings. **—im'maculacy** *or* **im'maculateness** *n.* **—im'maculately** *adv.*

immanent ('ɪmənənt) *adj.* **1.** existing, operating, or remaining within; inherent. **2.** *Philosophy.* (of a mental act) occurring entirely within the mind. **3.** (of God) present throughout the universe. **—'immanence** *or* **'immanency** *n.* **—'immanently** *adv.* **—'immanen₁tism** *n.*

immaterial (₁ɪmə'tɪərɪəl) *adj.* **1.** of no real importance; inconsequential. **2.** not formed of matter; incorporeal; spiritual. **—₁imma₁teri'ality** *n.* **—₁imma'terially** *adv.*

immature (₁ɪmə'tjʊə, -'tʃʊə) *adj.* **1.** not fully grown or developed. **2.** deficient in maturity; lacking wisdom, insight, emotional stability, etc. **—₁imma'turity** *or* **₁imma'tureness** *n.* **—₁imma'turely** *adv.*

immeasurable (ɪ'mɛʒərəbəl) *adj.* incapable of being measured, esp. by virtue of great size; limitless. **—im₁measura'bility** *or* **im'measurableness** *n.* **—im'measurably** *adv.*

immediate (ɪ'miːdɪət) *adj.* (*usually prenominal*) **1.** taking place or accomplished without delay: *an immediate reaction.* **2.** closest or most direct in effect or relationship: *the immediate cause of his downfall.* **3.** having no intervening medium; direct in effect: *an immediate influence.* **4.** contiguous in space, time, or relationship: *our immediate neighbour.* **5.** *Philosophy.* of or relating to a concept that is directly known or intuited. **—im'mediacy** *or* **im'mediateness** *n.*

immemorial (₁ɪmɪ'mɔːrɪəl) *adj.* originating in the distant past; ancient (*postpositive in* **time immemorial**). **—₁imme'morially** *adv.*

immense (ɪ'mɛns) *adj.* **1.** unusually large; huge; vast. **2.** without limits; immeasurable. **3.** *Inf.* very good; excellent. **—im'mensely** *adv.* **—im'menseness** *n.*

immerse (ɪ'mɜːs) *vb.* (*tr.*) **1.** (often foll. by *in*) to plunge or dip into liquid. **2.** (*often passive; often foll. by in*) to involve deeply; engross: *to immerse oneself in a problem.* **3.** to baptize by dipping the whole body into water. **—im'mersible** *adj.* **—im'mersion** *n.*

immersion heater (ɪ'mɜːʃən) *n.* an electrical device, usually thermostatically controlled, for heating the liquid in which it is immersed.

immigrant ('ɪmɪgrənt) *n.* **1. a.** a person who immigrates. **b.** (*as modifier*): *an immigrant community.* **2.**

Brit. a person who has been settled in a country of which he is not a native for less than ten years.

immigrate ('ɪmɪ₁greɪt) *vb.* **1.** (*intr.*) to come to a place or country of which one is not a native in order to settle there. **2.** (*tr.*) to introduce or bring in as an immigrant. **—₁immi'gration** *n.* **—'immi₁gratory** *adj.* **—'immi₁grator** *n.*

imminent ('ɪmɪnənt) *adj.* **1.** liable to happen soon; impending. **2.** *Obs.* overhanging. **—'imminence** *n.* **—'imminently** *adv.*

immiscible (ɪ'mɪsɪbəl) *adj.* (of liquids) incapable of being mixed: *oil and water are immiscible.* **—im₁misci'bility** *n.* **—im'miscibly** *adv.*

immobile (ɪ'məʊbaɪl) *adj.* **1.** not moving; motionless. **2.** not able to move or be moved; fixed. **—immobility** (₁ɪməʊ'bɪlɪtɪ) *n.*

immobilize *or* **-ise** (ɪ'məʊbɪ₁laɪz) *vb.* (*tr.*) **1.** to make immobile: *to immobilize a car.* **2.** *Finance.* to convert (circulating capital) into fixed capital. **—im₁mobili'zation** *or* **-i'sation** *n.* **—im'mobi₁lizer** *or* **-i₁liser** *n.*

immoderate (ɪ'mɒdərɪt, ɪ'mɒdrɪt) *adj.* lacking in moderation; excessive: *immoderate demands.* **—im'moderately** *adv.* **—im₁moder'ation** *or* **im'moderateness** *n.*

immodest (ɪ'mɒdɪst) *adj.* **1.** indecent, esp. with regard to sexual propriety; improper. **2.** bold, impudent, or shameless. **—im'modestly** *adv.* **—im'modesty** *n.*

immolate ('ɪməʊ₁leɪt) *vb.* (*tr.*) **1.** to kill or offer as a sacrifice. **2.** *Literary.* to sacrifice (something highly valued). **—₁immo'lation** *n.* **—'immo₁lator** *n.*

immoral (ɪ'mɒrəl) *adj.* **1.** transgressing accepted moral rules; corrupt. **2.** sexually dissolute; profligate or promiscuous. **3.** unscrupulous or unethical: *immoral trading.* **4.** tending to corrupt or resulting from corruption: *immoral earnings.* **—₁immo'rality** *n.* **—im'morally** *adv.*

▷ **Usage.** See at **amoral.**

immortal (ɪ'mɔːtəl) *adj.* **1.** not subject to death or decay; having perpetual life. **2.** having everlasting fame; remembered throughout time. **3.** everlasting; perpetual; constant. **4.** of or relating to immortal beings or concepts. ~*n.* **5.** an immortal being. **6.** (*often pl.*) a person who is remembered enduringly, esp. an author. **—₁immor'tality** *n.* **—im'mortally** *adv.*

immortalize *or* **-ise** (ɪ'mɔːtə₁laɪz) *vb.* (*tr.*) **1.** to give

---

THESAURUS

immaculate 1. clean, impeccable, neat, neat as a new pin, spick-and-span, spruce, trim, unexceptionable **2.** above reproach, faultless, flawless, guiltless, incorrupt, innocent, perfect, pure, sinless, spotless, stainless, unblemished, uncontaminated, undefiled, unpolluted, unsullied, untarnished, virtuous

immaterial 1. a matter of indifference, extraneous, impertinent, inapposite, inconsequential, inconsiderable, inessential, insignificant, irrelevant, of little account, of no consequence, of no importance, trifling, trivial, unimportant, unnecessary **2.** airy, disembodied, ethereal, ghostly, incorporeal, metaphysical, spiritual, unembodied, unsubstantial

immature 1. adolescent, crude, green, imperfect, premature, raw, undeveloped, unfinished, unfledged, unformed, unripe, unseasonable, untimely, young **2.** babyish, callow, childish, inexperienced, infantile, jejune, juvenile, puerile, wet behind the ears (*Inf.*)

immaturity 1. crudeness, crudity, greenness, imperfection, rawness, unpreparedness, unripeness **2.** babyishness, callowness, childishness, inexperience, juvenility, puerility

immeasurable bottomless, boundless, endless, illimitable, immense, incalculable, inestimable, inexhaustible, infinite, limitless, measureless, unbounded, unfathomable, unlimited, vast

immediate 1. instant, instantaneous **2.** adjacent, close, contiguous, direct, near, nearest, next, primary, proximate, recent **3.** actual, current, existing, extant, on hand, present, pressing, up to date, urgent

immediately 1. at once, before you

could say Jack Robinson (*Inf.*), directly, forthwith, instantly, now, promptly, pronto (*Inf.*), right away, right now, straight away, this instant, this very minute, *tout de suite,* unhesitatingly, without delay, without hesitation **2.** at first hand, closely, directly, nearly

immemorial age-old, ancient, archaic, fixed, long-standing, of yore, olden (*Archaic*), rooted, time-honoured, traditional

immense Brobdingnagian, colossal, elephantine, enormous, extensive, giant, gigantic, great, huge, illimitable, immeasurable, infinite, interminable, jumbo (*Inf.*), large, mammoth, massive, monstrous, monumental, prodigious, stupendous, titanic, tremendous, vast

immensity bulk, enormity, expanse, extent, greatness, hugeness, infinity, magnitude, massiveness, scope, size, sweep, vastness

immersion 1. baptism, bathe, dip, dipping, dousing, ducking, dunking, plunging, submerging **2.** *Fig.* absorption, concentration, involvement, preoccupation

immigrant incomer, newcomer, settler

imminent at hand, brewing, close, coming, fast-approaching, forthcoming, gathering, impending, in the air, in the offing, looming, menacing, near, nigh (*Archaic*), on the horizon, on the way, threatening

immobile at a standstill, at rest, fixed, frozen, immobilized, immotile, immovable, like a statue, motionless, rigid, riveted, rooted, stable, static, stationary, stiff, still, stock-still, stolid, unmoving

immobility absence of movement, firmness, fixity, immovability, inertness, motionlessness, stability, steadiness, stillness

immobilize bring to a standstill, cripple,

disable, freeze, halt, lay up (*Inf.*), paralyse, put out of action, render inoperative, stop, transfix

immoderate egregious, enormous, exaggerated, excessive, exorbitant, extravagant, extreme, inordinate, intemperate, over the odds (*Inf.*), profligate, steep (*Inf.*), uncalled-for, unconscionable, uncontrolled, undue, unjustified, unreasonable, unrestrained, unwarranted, wanton

immodesty 1. bawdiness, coarseness, impurity, indecorousness, indelicacy, lewdness, obscenity **2.** audacity, boldness, brass neck (*Sl.*), forwardness, gall (*Inf.*), impudence, shamelessness, temerity

immoral abandoned, bad, corrupt, debauched, degenerate, depraved, dishonest, dissolute, evil, impure, indecent, iniquitous, lewd, licentious, nefarious, obscene, of easy virtue, pornographic, profligate, reprobate, sinful, unchaste, unethical, unprincipled, vicious, vile, wicked, wrong

immorality badness, corruption, debauchery, depravity, dissoluteness, evil, iniquity, licentiousness, profligacy, sin, turpitude, vice, wickedness, wrong

immortal *adj.* **1.** abiding, constant, death-defying, deathless, endless, enduring, eternal, everlasting, imperishable, incorruptible, indestructible, lasting, perennial, perpetual, sempiternal (*Literary*), timeless, undying, unfading ~*n.* **2.** god, goddess, Olympian **3.** genius, great (*Usually plural*), hero, paragon

immortality 1. deathlessness, endlessness, eternity, everlasting life, incorruptibility, indestructibility, perpetuity, timelessness **2.** celebrity, fame, glorification, gloriousness, glory, greatness, renown

everlasting fame to, as by treating in a literary work: *Macbeth was immortalized by Shakespeare.* **2.** to give immortality to. —**im͵mortali'zation** or **-i'sation** n. —**im'mortal͵izer** or **-͵iser** n.

immovable or **immoveable** (ɪ'muːvəbᵊl) adj. **1.** unable to move or be moved; immobile. **2.** unable to be diverted from one's intentions; steadfast. **3.** unaffected by feeling; impassive. **4.** unchanging; unalterable. **5.** (of feasts, etc.) on the same date every year. **6.** *Law.* **a.** (of property) not liable to be removed; fixed. **b.** of or relating to immovable property. —**im͵mova'bility, im͵movea'bility** or **im'movableness, im'moveableness** n. —**im'movably** or **im'moveably** adv.

immune (ɪ'mjuːn) adj. **1.** protected against a specific disease by inoculation or as the result of innate or acquired resistance. **2.** relating to or conferring immunity: *an immune body* (see **antibody**). **3.** (usually postpositive; foll. by *to*) unsusceptible (to) or secure (against): *immune to inflation.* **4.** exempt from obligation, penalty, etc. ~n. **5.** an immune person or animal.

immunity (ɪ'mjuːnɪtɪ) n., pl. **-ties. 1.** the ability of an organism to resist disease, as by producing its own antibodies or as a result of inoculation. **2.** freedom from obligation or duty, esp. exemption from tax, legal liability, etc.

immunize or **-nise** ('ɪmjuˌnaɪz) vb. (tr.) to make immune, esp. by inoculation. —͵**immuni'zation** or **-ni'sation** n. —'**immu͵nizer** or **-͵niser** n.

immuno- or before a vowel **immun-** combining form. indicating immunity or immune: *immunology.*

immunology (͵ɪmjuˈnɒlədʒɪ) n. the branch of biological science concerned with the study of immunity. —**immunologic** (͵ɪmjunəˈlɒdʒɪk) or ͵**immuno'logical** adj. —͵**immuno'logically** adv. —͵**immu'nologist** n.

immure (ɪ'mjuə) vb. (tr.) **1.** *Arch.* or *literary.* to enclose within or as if within walls; imprison. **2.** to shut (oneself) away from society. —**im'murement** n.

immutable (ɪ'mjuːtəbᵊl) adj. unchanging through time; unalterable; ageless: *immutable laws.* —**im͵muta'bility** or **im'mutableness** n.

imp (ɪmp) n. **1.** a small demon or devil; mischievous sprite. **2.** a mischievous child. ~vb. **3.** (tr.) *Falconry.* to insert (new feathers) in order to repair the wing of a falcon.

imp. abbrev. for: **1.** imperative. **2.** imperfect. **3.** imperial. **4.** impersonal. **5.** import. **6.** importer.

impact n. ('ɪmpækt). **1.** the act of one body, etc., striking another; collision. **2.** the force with which one thing hits another. **3.** the impression made by an idea, social group, etc. ~vb. (ɪm'pækt). **4.** to drive or press (an object) firmly into (another object, thing, etc.) or (of two objects) to be driven or pressed firmly together. —**im'paction** n.

impacted (ɪm'pæktɪd) adj. **1.** (of a tooth) unable to erupt, esp. because of being wedged against another tooth below the gum. **2.** (of a fracture) having the jagged broken ends wedged into each other.

impair (ɪm'pɛə) vb. (tr.) to reduce or weaken in strength, quality, etc.: *his hearing was impaired by an accident.* —**im'pairable** adj. —**im'pairer** n. —**im'pairment** n.

impala (ɪm'pɑːlə) n., pl. **-las** or **-la.** an antelope of southern and eastern Africa, having lyre-shaped horns and able to move with enormous leaps.

impale or **empale** (ɪm'peɪl) vb. (tr.) **1.** (often foll. by *on, upon,* or *with*) to pierce with a sharp instrument: *they impaled his severed head on a spear.* **2.** *Heraldry.* to charge (a shield) with two coats of arms placed side by side. —**im'palement** or **em'palement** n.

impalpable (ɪm'pælpəbᵊl) adj. **1.** imperceptible, esp. to the touch: *impalpable shadows.* **2.** difficult to understand; abstruse. —**im͵palpa'bility** n. —**im'palpably** adv.

impanel (ɪm'pænᵊl) vb. **-elling, -elled** or U.S. **-eling, -eled.** a variant spelling (esp. U.S.) of **empanel.** —**im'panelment** n.

impart (ɪm'pɑːt) vb. (tr.) **1.** to communicate (information, etc.); relate. **2.** to give or bestow (an abstract quality): *to impart wisdom.* —**im'partable** adj. —͵**impar'tation** or **im'partment** n.

impartial (ɪm'pɑːʃəl) adj. not prejudiced towards or against any particular side; fair; unbiased. —**im͵parti'ality** or **im'partialness** n. —**im'partially** adv.

impassable (ɪm'pɑːsəbᵊl) adj. (of terrain, roads, etc.) not able to be travelled through or over. —**im͵passa'bility** or **im'passableness** n. —**im'passably** adv.

impasse (ɪm'pɑːs, æm'pɑːs) n. a situation in which progress is blocked; an insurmountable difficulty; stalemate; deadlock.

impassible (ɪm'pæsəbᵊl) adj. *Rare.* **1.** not susceptible to pain or injury. **2.** impassive or unmoved. —**im͵passi'bility** or **im'passibleness** n. —**im'passibly** adv.

impassioned (ɪm'pæʃənd) adj. filled with passion; fiery; inflamed: *an impassioned appeal.* —**im'passionedly** adv. —**im'passionedness** n.

impassive (ɪm'pæsɪv) adj. **1.** not revealing or affected by emotion; reserved. **2.** calm; serene; imperturbable. —**im'passively** adv. —**im'passiveness** or **impassivity** (͵ɪmpæ'sɪvɪtɪ) n.

impasto (ɪm'pæstəʊ) n. **1.** paint applied thickly, so that brush marks are evident. **2.** the technique of painting in this way.

impatience (ɪm'peɪʃəns) n. **1.** lack of patience; intolerance of or irritability with anything that impedes or delays. **2.** restless desire for change and excitement.

impatient (ɪm'peɪʃənt) adj. **1.** lacking patience; easily irritated at delay, etc. **2.** exhibiting lack of patience. **3.** (postpositive; foll. by *of*) intolerant (of) or indignant (at): *impatient of indecision.* **4.** (postpositive; often foll. by *for*) restlessly eager (for *or* to do something). —**im'patiently** adv.

impeach (ɪm'piːtʃ) vb. (tr.) **1.** *Criminal law.* to bring a charge or accusation against. **2.** *Brit. criminal law.* to

---

THESAURUS

immortalize apotheosize, celebrate, commemorate, enshrine, eternalize, eternize, exalt, glorify, memorialize, perpetuate, solemnize

immovable 1. fast, firm, fixed, immutable, jammed, rooted, secure, set, stable, stationary, stuck, unbudgeable 2. adamant, constant, impassive, inflexible, obdurate, resolute, steadfast, stony-hearted, unchangeable, unimpressionable, unshakable, unshaken, unwavering, unyielding

immune clear, exempt, free, insusceptible, invulnerable, let off (*Inf.*), not affected, not liable, not subject, proof (against), protected, resistant, safe, unaffected

immunity 1. amnesty, charter, exemption, exoneration, franchise, freedom, indemnity, invulnerability, liberty, licence, prerogative, privilege, release, right 2. immunization, protection, resistance

immunize inoculate, protect, safeguard, vaccinate

imp brat, demon, devil, gamin, minx, rascal, rogue, scamp, sprite, urchin

impact n. 1. bang, blow, bump, collision, concussion, contact, crash, force, jolt, knock, shock, smash, stroke, thump 2. brunt, burden, consequences, effect, full force, impression, influence, meaning, power, repercussions, significance, thrust, weight ~v. 3. clash, collide, crash, crush, hit, strike

impair blunt, damage, debilitate, decrease, deteriorate, diminish, enervate, enfeeble, harm, hinder, injure, lessen, mar, reduce, spoil, undermine, vitiate, weaken, worsen

impaired damaged, defective, faulty, flawed, imperfect, unsound

impart 1. communicate, convey, disclose, discover, divulge, make known, pass on, relate, reveal, tell 2. accord, afford, bestow, confer, contribute, give, grant, lend, offer, yield

impartial detached, disinterested, equal, equitable, even-handed, fair, just, neutral, nondiscriminating, nonpartisan, objective, open-minded, unbiased, unprejudiced, without fear or favour

impartiality detachment, disinterest, disinterestedness, dispassion, equality, equity, even-handedness, fairness, lack of bias, neutrality, nonpartisanship, objectivity, open-mindedness

impassable blocked, closed, impenetrable, obstructed, pathless, trackless, unnavigable

impasse blind alley (*Inf.*), dead end, deadlock, stalemate, standoff, standstill

impassioned animated, ardent, blazing, excited, fervent, fervid, fiery, furious, glowing, heated, inflamed, inspired, intense, passionate, rousing, stirring, vehement, violent, vivid, warm, worked up

impatience 1. haste, hastiness, heat, impetuosity, intolerance, irritability, irritableness, quick temper, rashness, shortness, snappiness, vehemence, violence 2. agitation, anxiety, avidity, disquietude, eagerness, edginess, fretfulness, nervousness, restiveness, restlessness, uneasiness

impatient 1. abrupt, brusque, curt, demanding, edgy, hasty, hot-tempered, indignant, intolerant, irritable, quick-tempered, snappy, sudden, testy, vehement, violent 2. agog, athirst, chafing, eager, fretful, headlong, impetuous, like a cat on hot bricks (*Inf.*), restless, straining at the leash

accuse of a crime against the state. **3.** *Chiefly U.S.* to charge (a public official) with an offence committed in office. **4.** to challenge or question (a person's honesty, integrity, etc.). —**im'peachable** *adj.* —**im'peachment** *n.*

impeccable (ɪm'pɛkəbəl) *adj.* **1.** without flaw or error; faultless: *an impeccable record.* **2.** *Rare.* incapable of sinning. —**im,pecca'bility** *n.* —**im'peccably** *adv.*

impecunious (,ɪmpɪ'kjuːnɪəs) *adj.* without money; penniless. —**,impe'cuniously** *adv.* —**,impe'cuniousness** or **impecuniosity** (,ɪmpɪkjuːnɪ'ɒsɪtɪ) *n.*

impedance (ɪm'piːdəns) *n.* **1.** a measure of the opposition to the flow of an alternating current equal to the square root of the sum of the squares of the resistance and the reactance, expressed in ohms. **2.** the ratio of the sound pressure in a medium to the rate of alternating flow through a specified surface due to the sound wave. **3.** the ratio of the mechanical force to the velocity of the resulting vibration.

impede (ɪm'piːd) *vb.* (*tr.*) to restrict or retard in action, progress, etc.; obstruct. —**im'peder** *n.* —**im'pedingly** *adv.*

impediment (ɪm'pɛdɪmənt) *n.* **1.** a hindrance or obstruction. **2.** a physical defect, esp. one of speech, such as a stammer. **3.** (*pl.* **-ments** or **-menta** (-'mɛntə)) *Law.* an obstruction to the making of a contract, esp. one of marriage. —**im,pedi'mental** or **im,pedi'mentary** *adj.*

impedimenta (ɪm,pɛdɪ'mɛntə) *pl. n.* **1.** any objects that impede progress, esp. the baggage and equipment carried by an army. **2.** a plural of **impediment** (sense 3).

impel (ɪm'pɛl) *vb.* **-pelling, -pelled.** (*tr.*) **1.** to urge or force (a person) to an action; constrain or motivate. **2.** to push, drive, or force into motion. —**im'pellent** *n., adj.*

impend (ɪm'pɛnd) *vb.* (*intr.*) **1.** (esp. of something threatening) to be imminent. **2.** (foll. by *over*) *Rare.* to be suspended; hang. —**im'pendence** or **im'pendency** *n.* —**im'pending** *adj.*

impenetrable (ɪm'pɛnɪtrəbəl) *adj.* **1.** incapable of being pierced through or penetrated: *an impenetrable forest.* **2.** incapable of being understood; incomprehensible. **3.** incapable of being seen through: *impenetrable gloom.* **4.** not susceptible to ideas, influence, etc.: *impenetrable ignorance.* **5.** *Physics.* (of a body) incapable of occupying the same space as another body. —**im,penetra'bility** *n.* —**im'penetrableness** *n.* —**im'penetrably** *adv.*

impenitent (ɪm'pɛnɪtənt) *adj.* not sorry or penitent; unrepentant. —**im'penitence, im'penitency,** or **im'penitentness** *n.* —**im'penitently** *adv.*

imper. *abbrev. for* imperative.

imperative (ɪm'pɛrətɪv) *adj.* **1.** extremely urgent or important; essential. **2.** peremptory or authoritative: *an imperative tone of voice.* **3.** Also: **imperatival** (ɪm,pɛrə'taɪvəl). *Grammar.* denoting a mood of verbs used in giving orders, making requests, etc. ~*n.* **4.** something that

is urgent or essential. **5.** an order or command. **6.** *Grammar.* **a.** the imperative mood. **b.** a verb in this mood. —**im'peratively** *adv.* —**im'perativeness** *n.*

imperator (,ɪmpə'rɑːtɔː) *n.* (in ancient Rome) a title bestowed upon generals and, later, emperors. —**imperatorial** (ɪm,pɛrə'tɔːrɪəl) *adj.* —**,impe'rator,ship** *n.*

imperceptible (,ɪmpə'sɛptɪbəl) *adj.* too slight, subtle, gradual, etc., to be perceived. —**,imper,cepti'bility** or **,imper'ceptibleness** *n.* —**,imper'ceptibly** *adv.*

imperf. *abbrev. for:* **1.** imperfect. **2.** (of stamps) imperforate.

imperfect (ɪm'pɜːfɪkt) *adj.* **1.** exhibiting or characterized by faults, mistakes, etc.; defective. **2.** not complete or finished; deficient. **3.** *Grammar.* denoting a tense of verbs used most commonly in describing continuous or repeated past actions or events. **4.** *Law.* legally unenforceable. **5.** *Music.* **a.** proceeding to the dominant from the tonic, subdominant, or any chord other than the dominant. **b.** of or relating to all intervals other than the fourth, fifth, and octave. Cf. **perfect** (sense 9). ~*n.* **6.** *Grammar.* **a.** the imperfect tense. **b.** a verb in this tense. —**im'perfectly** *adv.* —**im'perfectness** *n.*

imperfection (,ɪmpə'fɛkʃən) *n.* **1.** the condition or quality of being imperfect. **2.** a fault or defect.

imperial (ɪm'pɪərɪəl) *adj.* **1.** of or relating to an empire, emperor, or empress. **2.** characteristic of an emperor; majestic; commanding. **3.** exercising supreme authority; imperious. **4.** (esp. of products) of a superior size or quality. **5.** (*usually prenominal*) (of weights, measures, etc.) conforming to standards legally established in Great Britain. ~*n.* **6.** a book size, esp. 7½ by 11 inches or 11 by 15 inches. **7.** a size of writing paper, 23 by 31 inches (U.S.) or 22 by 30 inches (Brit.). **8.** *U.S.* **a.** the top of a carriage. **b.** a luggage case carried there. **9.** a small tufted beard popularized by the French emperor Napoleon III. —**im'perially** *adv.* —**im'perialness** *n.*

imperialism (ɪm'pɪərɪə,lɪzəm) *n.* **1.** the policy or practice of extending a state's rule over other territories. **2.** the extension or attempted extension of authority, influence, power, etc., by any person, country, institution, etc.: *cultural imperialism.* **3.** a system of imperial government or rule by an emperor. **4.** the spirit, character, authority, etc., of an empire. —**im'perialist** *adj., n.* —**im,perial'istic** *adj.* —**im,perial'istically** *adv.*

imperil (ɪm'pɛrɪl) *vb.* (*tr.*) to place in danger or jeopardy; endanger. —**im'perilment** *n.*

imperious (ɪm'pɪərɪəs) *adj.* **1.** domineering; arrogant; overbearing. **2.** *Rare.* urgent; imperative. —**im'periously** *adv.* —**im'periousness** *n.*

impermanent (ɪm'pɜːmənənt) *adj.* not permanent; fleeting; transitory. —**im'permanence** or **im'permanency** *n.* —**im'permanently** *adv.*

impermeable (ɪm'pɜːmɪəbəl) *adj.* (of a substance) not allowing the passage of a fluid through interstices; not

---

THESAURUS

impeach 1. accuse, arraign, blame, censure, charge, criminate (*Rare*), denounce, indict, tax 2. call into question, cast aspersions on, cast doubt on, challenge, disparage, impugn, question

impeachment accusation, arraignment, indictment

impeccable above suspicion, exact, exquisite, faultless, flawless, immaculate, incorrupt, innocent, irreproachable, perfect, precise, pure, sinless, stainless, unblemished, unerring, unimpeachable

impecunious broke (*Inf.*), cleaned out (*Sl.*), destitute, indigent, insolvent, penniless, poverty-stricken, skint (*Sl.*), stony (*Sl.*), strapped (*Sl.*)

impede bar, block, brake, check, clog, curb, delay, disrupt, hamper, hinder, hold up, obstruct, restrain, retard, slow (down), stop, throw a spanner in the works (*Inf.*), thwart

impediment bar, barrier, block, check, clog, curb, defect, difficulty, encumbrance, hindrance, obstacle, obstruction, snag, stumbling block

impedimenta accoutrements, baggage, belongings, effects, equipment, gear, junk (*Inf.*), luggage, movables, odds and ends, paraphernalia, possessions, stuff, things, trappings, traps

impel actuate, compel, constrain, drive, force, goad, incite, induce, influence, inspire, instigate, motivate, move, oblige, power, prod, prompt, propel, push, require, spur, stimulate, urge

impending approaching, brewing, coming, forthcoming, gathering, hovering, imminent, in the offing, looming, menacing, near, nearing, on the horizon, threatening

impenetrable 1. dense, hermetic, impassable, impermeable, impervious, inviolable, solid, thick, unpierceable 2. arcane, baffling, cabbalistic, dark, enigmatic, enigmatical, hidden, incomprehensible, indiscernible, inexplicable, inscrutable, mysterious, obscure, unfathomable, unintelligible

imperative 1. compulsory, crucial, essential, exigent, indispensable, insistent, obligatory, pressing, urgent, vital 2. authoritative, autocratic, commanding, dictatorial, domineering, high-handed, imperious, lordly, magisterial, peremptory

imperceptible faint, fine, gradual, impalpable, inappreciable, inaudible, indiscernible, indistinguishable, infinitesimal, insensible, invisible, microscopic, minute, shadowy, slight, small, subtle, tiny, undetectable, unnoticeable

imperceptibly by a hair's-breadth, in-

appreciably, indiscernibly, invisibly, little by little, slowly, subtly, unnoticeably, unobtrusively, unseen

imperfect broken, damaged, defective, deficient, faulty, flawed, immature, impaired, incomplete, inexact, limited, partial, patchy, rudimentary, sketchy, undeveloped, unfinished

imperfection blemish, defect, deficiency, failing, fallibility, fault, flaw, foible, frailty, inadequacy, incompleteness, infirmity, insufficiency, peccadillo, shortcoming, stain, taint, weakness, weak point

imperial 1. kingly, majestic, princely, queenly, regal, royal, sovereign 2. august, exalted, grand, great, high, imperious, lofty, magnificent, noble, superior, supreme

imperil endanger, expose, hazard, jeopardize, risk

imperishable abiding, enduring, eternal, everlasting, immortal, indestructible, perennial, permanent, perpetual, undying, unfading, unforgettable

impermeable hermetic, impassable, impenetrable, impervious, nonporous, proof, resistant

permeable. —**im,permea'bility** or **im'permeableness** n. —**im'permeably** adv.

impermissible (,impə'misibəl) adj. not permissible; not allowed. —**,imper,missi'bility** n.

impersonal (im'pɜːsənəl) adj. **1.** without reference to any individual person; objective: an impersonal assessment. **2.** devoid of human warmth or sympathy; cold: an impersonal manner. **3.** not having human characteristics: an impersonal God. **4.** Grammar. (of a verb) having no logical subject: it is raining. **5.** Grammar. (of a pronoun) not denoting a person. —**im,person'ality** n. —**im'personally** adv.

impersonate (im'pɜːsə,neit) vb. (tr.) **1.** to pretend to be (another person). **2.** to imitate the character, mannerisms, etc., of (another person). **3.** Rare. to play the part or character of. **4.** an archaic word for **personify**. —**im,person'ation** n. —**im'person,ator** n.

impertinent (im'pɜːtinənt) adj. **1.** rude; insolent; impudent. **2.** irrelevant or inappropriate. —**im'pertinence** n. —**im'pertinently** adv.

imperturbable (,impɜː'tɜːbəbəl) adj. not easily perturbed; calm; unruffled. —**,imper,turba'bility** or **,imper'turbableness** n. —**,imper'turbably** adv.

impervious (im'pɜːviəs) or **imperviable** adj. **1.** not able to be penetrated, as by water, light, etc.; impermeable. **2.** (often postpositive; foll. by to) not able to be influenced (by) or not receptive (to): impervious to argument. —**im'perviously** adv. —**im'perviousness** n.

impetigo (,impi'taigəʊ) n. a contagious pustular skin disease. —**impetiginous** (,impi'tidʒinəs) adj.

impetuous (im'petjʊəs) adj. **1.** liable to act without consideration; rash; impulsive. **2.** resulting from or characterized by rashness or haste. **3.** Poetic. moving with great force or violence; rushing: the impetuous stream hurtled down the valley. —**im'petuously** adv. —**im'petuousness** or **impetuosity** (im,petjʊ'ɒsiti) n.

impetus ('impitəs) n., pl. **-tuses.** **1.** an impelling movement or force; incentive or impulse; stimulus. **2.** Physics. the force that sets a body in motion or that tends to resist changes in a body's motion.

impi ('impi) n., pl. **-pi** or **-pies.** a group of Bantu warriors.

impiety (im'paiiti) n., pl. **-ties.** **1.** lack of reverence or proper respect for a god. **2.** any lack of proper respect. **3.** an impious act.

impinge (im'pindʒ) vb. **1.** (intr.; usually foll. by on or upon) to encroach or infringe; trespass: to impinge on someone's time. **2.** (intr.; usually foll. by on, against, or upon) to collide (with); strike. —**im'pingement** n. —**im'pinger** n.

impious ('impiəs) adj. **1.** lacking piety or reverence for a god. **2.** lacking respect; undutiful. —**'impiously** adv. —**'impiousness** n.

impish ('impiʃ) adj. of or like an imp; mischievous. —**'impishly** adv. —**'impishness** n.

implacable (im'plækəbəl) adj. **1.** incapable of being placated or pacified; unappeasable. **2.** inflexible; intractable. —**im,placa'bility** n. —**im'placably** adv.

implant vb. (im'plɑːnt). (tr.) **1.** to inculcate; instil: to implant sound moral principles. **2.** to plant or embed; infix; entrench. **3.** Surgery. to graft or insert (a tissue, hormone, etc.) into the body. ~n. ('im,plɑːnt). **4.** anything implanted, esp. surgically, such as a tissue graft. —**,implan'tation** n.

implausible (im'plɔːzəbəl) adj. not plausible; provoking disbelief; unlikely. —**im,plausi'bility** or **im'plausibleness** n. —**im'plausibly** adv.

implement n. ('implimənt). **1.** a piece of equipment; tool or utensil: gardening implements. **2.** a means to achieve a purpose; agent. ~vb. ('impli,ment). (tr.) **3.** to carry out; put into action: to implement a plan. **4.** Rare. to supply with tools. —**,imple'mental** adj. —**,implemen'tation** n.

implicate ('impli,keit) vb. (tr.) **1.** to show to be involved, esp. in a crime. **2.** to imply: his protest implicated censure by the authorities. **3.** Rare. to entangle. —**,impli'cation** n. —**implicative** (im'plikətiv) adj. —**im'plicatively** adv.

implicit (im'plisit) adj. **1.** not explicit; implied; indirect. **2.** absolute and unreserved; unquestioning: implicit trust. **3.** (when postpositive, foll. by in) contained or inherent: to bring out the anger implicit in the argument. —**im'plicitly** adv. —**im'plicitness** n.

implied (im'plaid) adj. hinted at or suggested; not directly expressed: an implied criticism.

implode (im'pləʊd) vb. to collapse inwards. Cf. **explode**.

implore (im'plɔː) vb. (tr.) to beg or ask (someone) earnestly (to do something); plead with; beseech; supplicate. —**,implo'ration** n. —**im'ploratory** adj. —**im'ploringly** adv.

THESAURUS

impersonal bureaucratic, businesslike, cold, detached, dispassionate, formal, inhuman, neutral, remote

impersonate act, ape, do (Inf.), do an impression of, enact, imitate, masquerade as, mimic, pass oneself off as, personate, pose as (Inf.), take off (Inf.)

impersonation caricature, imitation, impression, mimicry, parody, takeoff (Inf.)

impertinence assurance, audacity, backchat (Inf.), boldness, brass neck (Sl.), brazenness, cheek (Inf.), disrespect, effrontery, forwardness, impudence, incivility, insolence, nerve (Inf.), pertness, presumption, rudeness, sauce (Inf.)

impertinent **1.** bold, brazen, cheeky (Inf.), discourteous, disrespectful, flip (Inf.), forward, fresh (Inf.), impolite, impudent, insolent, interfering, pert, presumptuous, rude, saucy (Inf.), uncivil, unmannerly **2.** inapplicable, inappropriate, incongruous, irrelevant

imperturbable calm, collected, complacent, composed, cool, equanimous, nerveless, sedate, self-possessed, stoical, tranquil, undisturbed, unexcitable, unflappable (Inf.), unmoved, unruffled

impervious **1.** hermetic, impassable, impenetrable, impermeable, imperviable, invulnerable, resistant, sealed **2.** closed to, immune, invulnerable, proof against, unaffected by, unmoved by, unreceptive, unswayable, untouched by

impetuosity haste, hastiness, impulsiveness, precipitancy, precipitateness, rashness, vehemence, violence

impetuous ardent, eager, fierce, furious, hasty, headlong, impassioned, impulsive, pas-

sionate, precipitate, rash, spontaneous, spur-of-the-moment, unbridled, unplanned, unpremeditated, unreflecting, unrestrained, unthinking, vehement, violent

impetuously helter-skelter, impulsively, in the heat of the moment, on the spur of the moment, passionately, rashly, recklessly, spontaneously, unthinkingly, vehemently, without thinking

impetus **1.** catalyst, goad, impulse, impulsion, incentive, motivation, push, spur, stimulus **2.** energy, force, momentum, power

impiety godlessness, iniquity, irreligion, irreverence, profaneness, profanity, sacrilege, sinfulness, ungodliness, unholiness, unrighteousness, wickedness

impinge **1.** encroach, invade, make inroads, obtrude, trespass, violate **2.** affect, bear upon, have a bearing on, influence, infringe, relate to, touch, touch upon **3.** clash, collide, dash, strike

impious blasphemous, godless, iniquitous, irreligious, irreverent, profane, sacrilegious, sinful, ungodly, unholy, unrighteous, wicked

impish devilish, elfin, mischievous, prankish, puckish, rascally, roguish, sportive, waggish

implacability implacableness, inexorability, inflexibility, intractability, mercilessness, pitilessness, relentlessness, ruthlessness, unforgivingness, vengefulness

implacable cruel, inexorable, inflexible, intractable, merciless, pitiless, rancorous, relentless, remorseless, ruthless, unappeasable, unbending, uncompromising, unforgiving, unrelenting, unyielding

implant **1.** inculcate, infix, infuse, insemi-

nate, instil, sow **2.** embed, fix, graft, ingraft, insert, place, plant, root, sow

implement **1.** n. agent, apparatus, appliance, device, gadget, instrument, tool, utensil **2.** v. bring about, carry out, complete, effect, enforce, execute, fulfil, perform, put into action or effect, realize

implementation accomplishment, carrying out, discharge, effecting, enforcement, execution, fulfilment, performance, performing, realization

implicate associate, compromise, concern, embroil, entangle, imply, include, incriminate, inculpate, involve, mire, tie up with

implicated incriminated, involved, suspected, under suspicion

implication **1.** association, connection, entanglement, incrimination, involvement **2.** conclusion, inference, innuendo, meaning, overtone, presumption, ramification, significance, signification, suggestion

implicit **1.** contained, implied, inferred, inherent, latent, tacit, taken for granted, undeclared, understood, unspoken **2.** absolute, constant, entire, firm, fixed, full, steadfast, total, unhesitating, unqualified, unreserved, unshakable, unshaken, wholehearted

implicitly absolutely, completely, firmly, unconditionally, unhesitatingly, unreservedly, utterly, without reservation

implied hinted at, implicit, indirect, inherent, insinuated, suggested, tacit, undeclared, unexpressed, unspoken, unstated

implore beg, beseech, conjure, crave, entreat, go on bended knee to, importune, plead with, pray, solicit, supplicate

imply (ɪm'plaɪ) *vb.* **-plying, -plied.** (*tr.; may take a clause as object*) **1.** to express or indicate by a hint; suggest. **2.** to suggest or involve as a necessary consequence or connotation.
▷ Usage. See at **infer.**
impolite (ˌɪmpə'laɪt) *adj.* discourteous; rude; uncivil. —ˌimpo'litely *adv.* —ˌimpo'liteness *n.*
impolitic (ɪm'pɒlɪtɪk) *adj.* not politic or expedient; unwise. —im'politicly *adv.*
imponderable (ɪm'pɒndərəbəl, -drəbəl) *adj.* **1.** unable to be weighed or assessed. —*n.* **2.** something difficult or impossible to assess. —im,pondera'bility *or* im'ponderableness *n.* —im'ponderably *adv.*
import *vb.* (ɪm'pɔːt, 'ɪmpɔːt). **1.** to buy or bring in (goods or services) from a foreign country. **2.** (*tr.*) to bring in from an outside source: *to import foreign words into the language.* **3.** *Rare.* to signify; mean: *to import doom.* —*n.* ('ɪmpɔːt). **4.** (*often pl.*) **a.** goods or services that are bought from foreign countries. **b.** (*as modifier*): *an import licence.* **5.** importance: *a man of great import.* **6.** meaning. **7.** *Canad. sl.* a sportsman who is not native to the area where he plays. —im'portable *adj.* —im'porter *n.*
importance (ɪm'pɔːtəns) *n.* **1.** the state of being important; significance. **2.** social status; standing; esteem: *a man of importance.* **3.** *Obs.* **a.** meaning or signification. **b.** an important matter. **c.** importunity.
important (ɪm'pɔːtənt) *adj.* **1.** of great significance or value; outstanding. **2.** of social significance; notable; eminent; esteemed: *an important man in the town.* **3.** (when postpositive, usually foll. by *to*) of great concern (to); valued highly (by): *your wishes are important to me.* —im'portantly *adv.*
▷ Usage. In a sentence such as *he changed the financial structure of the parent company and, more important, he altered its social policy,* careful writers often prefer *more important* to *more importantly,* since the *-ly* ending of the adverb is unnecessary in parenthetical constructions. This is also true of *first, second, last,* etc., which are often preferred to *firstly, secondly, lastly,* etc.; *first, he introduced the sonnet to his homeland; second, he intiated influential poetic experiments; last and most important, he was able to create an atmosphere of sincerity in his poetry.*
importation (ˌɪmpɔː'teɪʃən) *n.* **1.** the act, business, or process of importing goods or services. **2.** an imported product or service.
importunate (ɪm'pɔːtjʊnɪt) *adj.* **1.** persistent or demanding; insistent. **2.** *Rare.* troublesome; annoying. —im'portunately *adv.* —im'portunateness *n.*
importune (ɪm'pɔːtjuːn) *vb.* (*tr.*) **1.** to harass with per-

sistent requests; demand of (someone) insistently. **2.** to beg for persistently; request with insistence. —im'portunely *adv.* —im'portuner *n.* —ˌimpor'tunity *or* im'portunacy *n.*
impose (ɪm'pəʊz) *vb.* (usually foll. by *on* or *upon*) **1.** (*tr.*) to establish as something to be obeyed or complied with; enforce. **2.** to force (oneself, one's presence, etc.) on others; obtrude. **3.** (*intr.*) to take advantage, as of a person or quality: *to impose on someone's kindness.* **4.** (*tr.*) *Printing.* to arrange (pages, type, etc.) in a chase so that the pages will be in the correct order. **5.** (*tr.*) to pass off deceptively; foist. —im'posable *adj.* —im'poser *n.*
imposing (ɪm'pəʊzɪŋ) *adj.* grand or impressive: *an imposing building.* —im'posingly *adv.* —im'posingness *n.*
imposition (ˌɪmpə'zɪʃən) *n.* **1.** the act of imposing. **2.** something imposed unfairly on someone. **3.** a task set as a school punishment. **4.** the arrangement of pages for printing.
impossibility (ɪmˌpɒsə'bɪlɪtɪ, ˌɪmpɒs-) *n., pl.* **-ties.** **1.** the state or quality of being impossible. **2.** something that is impossible.
impossible (ɪm'pɒsəbəl) *adj.* **1.** incapable of being done, undertaken, or experienced. **2.** incapable of occurring or happening. **3.** absurd or inconceivable; unreasonable. **4.** *Inf.* intolerable; outrageous: *those children are impossible.* —im'possibleness *n.* —im'possibly *adv.*
impost[1] ('ɪmpəʊst) *n.* **1.** a tax, esp. a customs duty. **2.** the weight that a horse must carry in a handicap race. —*vb.* **3.** (*tr.*) *U.S.* to classify (imported goods) according to the duty payable on them. —'imposter *n.*
impost[2] ('ɪmpəʊst) *n. Archit.* a member at the top of a column that supports an arch.
impostor *or* **imposter** (ɪm'pɒstə) *n.* a person who deceives others, esp. by assuming a false identity; charlatan.
imposture (ɪm'pɒstʃə) *n.* the act or an instance of deceiving others, esp. by assuming a false identity. —im'postrous (ɪm'pɒstrəs), **impostorous** (ɪm'pɒstərəs) *adj.*
impotent ('ɪmpətənt) *adj.* **1.** (when *postpositive,* often takes an infinitive) lacking sufficient strength; powerless. **2.** (esp. of males) unable to perform sexual intercourse. —'impotence, 'impotency *n.* —'impotently *adv.*
impound (ɪm'paʊnd) *vb.* (*tr.*) **1.** to confine (animals, etc.) in a pound. **2.** to take legal possession of (a document, evidence, etc.). **3.** to collect (water) in a reservoir or dam. —im'poundable *adj.* —im'poundage *or* im'poundment *n.* —im'pounder *n.*
impoverish *or* **empoverish** (ɪm'pɒvərɪʃ) *vb.* (*tr.*) **1.**

THESAURUS

imply 1. connote, give (someone) to understand, hint, insinuate, intimate, signify, suggest **2.** betoken, denote, entail, evidence, import, include, indicate, involve, mean, point to, presuppose
impolite bad-mannered, boorish, churlish, discourteous, disrespectful, ill-bred, ill-mannered, indecorous, indelicate, insolent, loutish, rough, rude, uncivil, ungallant, ungentlemanly, ungracious, unladylike, unmannerly, unrefined
impoliteness bad manners, boorishness, churlishness, discourtesy, disrespect, incivility, indelicacy, insolence, rudeness, unmannerliness
impolitic ill-advised, ill-judged, imprudent, indiscreet, inexpedient, injudicious, maladroit, misguided, undiplomatic, untimely, unwise
import *n.* **1.** bearing, drift, gist, implication, intention, meaning, message, purport, sense, significance, thrust **2.** consequence, importance, magnitude, moment, significance, substance, weight ~*v.* **3.** bring in, introduce, land
importance 1. concern, consequence, import, interest, moment, momentousness, significance, substance, value, weight **2.** distinction, eminence, esteem, influence, mark, pre-eminence, prestige, prominence, standing, status, usefulness, worth
important 1. far-reaching, grave, large,

material, meaningful, momentous, of substance, primary, salient, serious, signal, significant, substantial, urgent, weighty **2.** eminent, foremost, high-level, high-ranking, influential, leading, notable, noteworthy, of note, outstanding, powerful, pre-eminent, prominent, seminal **3.** *Usually with* to basic, essential, of concern *or* interest, relevant, valuable, valued
importunate burning, clamant, clamorous, demanding, dogged, earnest, exigent, insistent, persistent, pertinacious, pressing, solicitous, troublesome, urgent
impose 1. decree, establish, exact, fix, institute, introduce, lay, levy, ordain, place, promulgate, put, set **2.** appoint, charge with, dictate, enforce, enjoin, inflict, prescribe, saddle (someone) with **3.** *With on* or *upon* butt in, encroach, foist, force oneself, gatecrash (*Inf.*), horn in (*Inf.*), intrude, obtrude, presume, take liberties, trespass **4.** *With on or upon* **a.** abuse, exploit, play on, take advantage of, use **b.** con (*Inf.*), deceive, dupe, hoodwink, pull the wool over (somebody's) eyes, trick
imposing august, commanding, dignified, effective, grand, impressive, majestic, stately, striking
imposition 1. application, decree, introduction, laying on, levying, promulgation **2.** cheek (*Inf.*), encroachment, intrusion, liberty, presumption **3.** artifice, cheating, con

(*Inf.*), deception, dissimulation, fraud, hoax, imposture, stratagem, trickery **4.** burden, charge, constraint, duty, levy, tax

impossibility hopelessness, impracticability, inability, inconceivability

impossible 1. beyond one, beyond the bounds of possibility, hopeless, impracticable, inconceivable, not to be thought of, out of the question, unachievable, unattainable, unobtainable, unthinkable **2.** absurd, inadmissible, insoluble, intolerable, ludicrous, outrageous, preposterous, unacceptable, unanswerable, ungovernable, unreasonable, unsuitable, unworkable

impostor charlatan, cheat, deceiver, fake, fraud, hypocrite, impersonator, knave (*Archaic*), phoney (*Sl.*), pretender, quack, rogue, sham, trickster

impotence disability, enervation, feebleness, frailty, helplessness, inability, inadequacy, incapacity, incompetence, ineffectiveness, inefficacy, inefficiency, infirmity, paralysis, powerlessness, uselessness, weakness

impotent disabled, emasculate, enervated, feeble, frail, helpless, incapable, incapacitated, incompetent, ineffective, infirm, nerveless, paralysed, powerless, unable, unmanned, weak

to make poor or diminish the quality of: *to impoverish society by cutting the grant to the arts.* **2.** to deprive (soil, etc.) of fertility. —**im'poverishment** *or* **em'poverishment** *n.*

impracticable (ɪm'præktɪkəbəl) *adj.* **1.** incapable of being put into practice or accomplished; not feasible. **2.** unsuitable for a desired use; unfit. —**im,practica'bility** *or* **im'practicableness** *n.* —**im'practicably** *adv.*

impractical (ɪm'præktɪkəl) *adj.* **1.** not practical or workable: *an impractical solution.* **2.** not given to practical matters or gifted with practical skills. —**im,practi'cality** *or* **im'practicalness** *n.* —**im'practically** *adv.*

imprecate ('ɪmprɪ,keɪt) *vb.* **1.** (*intr.*) to swear or curse. **2.** (*tr.*) to invoke or bring down (evil, a curse, etc.). —**'impre,catory** *adj.* —**,impre'cation** *n.*

imprecise (,ɪmprɪ'saɪs) *adj.* not precise; inexact or inaccurate. —**,impre'cisely** *adv.* —**imprecision** (,ɪmprɪ'sɪʒən) *or* **,impre'ciseness** *n.*

impregnable (ɪm'prɛgnəbəl) *adj.* **1.** unable to be broken into or taken by force: *an impregnable castle.* **2.** unshakable: *impregnable self-confidence.* **3.** incapable of being refuted: *an impregnable argument.* —**im,preg-na'bility** *n.* —**im'pregnably** *adv.*

impregnate *vb.* ('ɪmprɛg,neɪt). (*tr.*) **1.** to saturate, soak, or infuse. **2.** to imbue or permeate; pervade. **3.** to cause to conceive; make pregnant; fertilize. **4.** to make (land, soil, etc.) fruitful. ~*adj.* (ɪm'prɛgnɪt, -neɪt). **5.** pregnant or fertilized. —**,impreg'nation** *n.* —**im'pregnator** *n.*

impresario (,ɪmprɪ'sɑːrɪ,əʊ) *n., pl.* **-sarios.** the director or manager of an opera, ballet, etc.

impress¹ *vb.* (ɪm'prɛs). (*tr.*) **1.** to make an impression on; have a strong, lasting, or favourable effect on: *I am impressed by your work.* **2.** to produce (an imprint, etc.) by pressure in or on (something): *to impress a seal in wax.* **3.** (often foll. by *on*) to stress (something to a person); urge; emphasize. **4.** to exert pressure on; press. ~*n.* ('ɪmprɛs). **5.** the act or an instance of impressing. **6.** a mark, imprint, or effect produced by impressing. —**im'presser** *n.* —**im'pressible** *adj.*

impress² *vb.* (ɪm'prɛs). **1.** to commandeer or coerce (men or things) into government service; press-gang. ~*n.* ('ɪmprɛs). **2.** the act of commandeering or coercing into government service.

impression (ɪm'prɛʃən) *n.* **1.** an effect produced in the mind by a stimulus; sensation: *he gave the impression of wanting to help.* **2.** an imprint or mark produced by pressing. **3.** a vague idea, consciousness, or belief: *I had the impression we had met before.* **4.** a strong, favourable, or remarkable effect. **5.** the act of impressing or the state of being impressed. **6.** *Printing.* **a.** the act, process, or result of printing from type, plates, etc. **b.** the total number of copies of a publication printed at one time. **7.** an imprint of the teeth and gums for preparing crowns, dentures, etc. **8.** an imitation or impersonation. —**im'pressional** *adj.* —**im'pressionally** *adv.*

impressionable (ɪm'prɛʃənəbəl, -'prɛʃnə-) *adj.* easily influenced or characterized by susceptibility to influence: *an impressionable age.* —**im,pressiona'bility** *or* **im'pressionableness** *n.*

impressionism (ɪm'prɛʃə,nɪzəm) *n.* (*often cap.*) a 19th-century movement in French painting, having the aim of objectively recording experience by a system of fleeting impressions, esp. of natural light effects. —**im'pressionist** *n.*

impressive (ɪm'prɛsɪv) *adj.* capable of impressing, esp. by size, magnificence, etc.; awe-inspiring; commanding. —**im'pressively** *adv.* —**im'pressiveness** *n.*

imprimatur (,ɪmprɪ'meɪtə, -'mɑː-) *n.* **1.** sanction or approval for something to be printed. **2.** *R.C. Church.* a licence certifying the Church's approval.

imprint *n.* ('ɪmprɪnt). **1.** a mark or impression produced by pressure, printing, or stamping. **2.** a characteristic mark or indication; stamp: *the imprint of great sadness on his face.* **3.** the publisher's or printer's name and address in a book, etc. ~*vb.* (ɪm'prɪnt). **4.** to produce (a mark, impression, etc.) on (a surface) by pressure, printing, or stamping: *to imprint a seal on wax.* **5.** to establish firmly; impress: *to imprint the details on one's mind.*

imprison (ɪm'prɪzən) *vb.* (*tr.*) to confine in or as if in prison. —**im'prisonment** *n.*

improbable (ɪm'prɒbəbəl) *adj.* not likely or probable; doubtful; unlikely. —**im,proba'bility** *or* **im'probableness** *n.* —**im'probably** *adv.*

improbity (ɪm'prəʊbɪtɪ) *n., pl.* **-ties.** dishonesty, wickedness, or unscrupulousness.

impromptu (ɪm'prɒmptjuː) *adj.* **1.** unrehearsed; spontaneous; extempore. **2.** produced or done without care or planning; improvised. ~*adv.* **3.** in a spontaneous or improvised way: *he spoke impromptu.* ~*n.* **4.** something that is impromptu. **5.** a short piece of instrumental music, sometimes improvisatory in character.

improper (ɪm'prɒpə) *adj.* **1.** lacking propriety; not seemly or fitting. **2.** unsuitable for a certain use or occasion; inappropriate. **3.** irregular or abnormal. —**im-**

THESAURUS

impoverish 1. bankrupt, beggar, break, ruin 2. deplete, diminish, drain, exhaust, pauperize, reduce, sap, use up, wear out

impoverished 1. bankrupt, destitute, distressed, impecunious, indigent, in reduced *or* straitened circumstances, necessitous, needy, on one's uppers, penurious, poverty-stricken, ruined, straitened 2. barren, denuded, depleted, drained, empty, exhausted, played out, reduced, spent, sterile, worn out

impracticability futility, hopelessness, impossibility, impracticality, unsuitableness, unworkability, uselessness

impracticable 1. impossible, out of the question, unachievable, unattainable, unfeasible, unworkable 2. awkward, impractical, inapplicable, inconvenient, unserviceable, unsuitable, useless

impractical 1. impossible, impracticable, inoperable, nonviable, unrealistic, unserviceable, unworkable, visionary, wild 2. idealistic, romantic, starry-eyed, unbusinesslike, unrealistic, visionary

impracticality hopelessness, impossibility, inapplicability, romanticism, unworkability

imprecise ambiguous, blurred round the edges, careless, equivocal, estimated, fluctuating, hazy, ill-defined, inaccurate, indefinite, indeterminate, inexact, inexplicit, loose, rough, sloppy (*Inf.*), vague, wide of the mark, woolly

impregnable immovable, impenetrable, indestructible, invincible, invulnerable, secure, strong, unassailable, unbeatable, unconquerable, unshakable

impregnate 1. fill, imbrue (*Rare*), imbue, infuse, percolate, permeate, pervade, saturate, soak, steep, suffuse 2. fecundate, fertilize, fructify, get with child, inseminate, make pregnant

impress 1. affect, excite, grab (*Sl.*), influence, inspire, make an impression, move, stir, strike, sway, touch 2. *Often with* on *or* upon bring home to, emphasize, fix, inculcate, instil into, stress 3. emboss, engrave, imprint, indent, mark, print, stamp

impression 1. effect, feeling, impact, influence, reaction, sway 2. **make an impression** arouse comment, be conspicuous, cause a stir, excite notice, find favour, make a hit (*Inf.*), make an impact, stand out 3. belief, concept, conviction, fancy, feeling, funny feeling (*Inf.*), hunch, idea, memory, notion, opinion, recollection, sense, suspicion 4. brand, dent, hollow, impress, imprint, indentation, mark, outline, stamp, stamping 5. edition, imprinting, issue, printing 6. imitation, impersonation, parody, send-up (*Brit. inf.*), takeoff (*Inf.*)

impressionable feeling, gullible, ingenuous, open, receptive, responsive, sensitive, suggestible, susceptible, vulnerable

impressive affecting, exciting, forcible, moving, powerful, stirring, touching

imprint 1. *n.* impression, indentation, mark, print, sign, stamp 2. *v.* engrave, establish, etch, fix, impress, print, stamp

imprison confine, constrain, detain, immure, incarcerate, intern, jail, lock up, put away, put under lock and key, send down (*Inf.*), send to prison

imprisoned behind bars, captive, confined, immured, incarcerated, in irons, in jail, inside (*Sl.*), interned, jailed, locked up, put away, under lock and key

imprisonment confinement, custody, detention, durance (*Archaic*), duress, incarceration, internment, porridge (*Sl.*)

improbability doubt, doubtfulness, dubiety, uncertainty, unlikelihood

improbable doubtful, dubious, fanciful, far-fetched, implausible, questionable, unbelievable, uncertain, unconvincing, unlikely, weak

impromptu 1. *adj.* ad-lib, extemporaneous, extempore, extemporized, improvised, offhand, off the cuff (*Inf.*), spontaneous, unpremeditated, unprepared, unrehearsed, unscripted, unstudied 2. *adv.* ad lib, off the cuff (*Inf.*), off the top of one's head (*Inf.*), on the spur of the moment, spontaneously, without preparation

improper 1. impolite, indecent, indecorous, indelicate, off-colour, risqué, smutty, suggestive, unbecoming, unfitting, unseemly, untoward, vulgar 2. ill-timed, inapplicable, inapposite, inappropriate, inapt, incongruous, infelicitous, inopportune, malapropos, out of place, uncalled-for, unfit, unseasonable, unsuitable, unsuited, unwarranted 3. abnormal, erroneous, false, inaccurate, incorrect, irregular, wrong

'**properly** *adv.* —**im'properness** *n.*

improper fraction *n.* a fraction in which the numerator is greater than the denominator, as 7/6.

impropriate *vb.* (ɪm'prəʊprɪˌeɪt). **1.** (*tr.*) to transfer (property, rights, etc.) from the Church into lay hands. ~*adj.* (ɪm'prəʊprɪɪt, -ˌeɪt). **2.** transferred in this way. —**im,propri'ation** *n.* —**im'propri,ator** *n.*

impropriety (ˌɪmprə'praɪɪtɪ) *n., pl.* **-ties. 1.** lack of propriety; indecency; indecorum. **2.** an improper act or use. **3.** the state of being improper.

improve (ɪm'pruːv) *vb.* **1.** to make or become better in quality; ameliorate. **2.** (*tr.*) to make (buildings, land, etc.) more valuable by additions or betterment. **3.** (*intr.*; usually foll. by *on* or *upon*) to achieve a better standard or quality in comparison (with): *to improve on last year's crop.* —**im'provable** *adj.* —**im,prova'bility** *or* **im'provableness** *n.* —**im'prover** *n.*

improvement (ɪm'pruːvmənt) *n.* **1.** the act of improving or the state of being improved. **2.** something that improves, esp. an addition or alteration. **3.** *Austral. & N.Z.* a building on a piece of land, adding to its value.

improvident (ɪm'prɒvɪdənt) *adj.* **1.** not provident; thriftless, imprudent, or prodigal. **2.** heedless or incautious; rash. —**im'providence** *n.* —**im'providently** *adv.*

improvise ('ɪmprəˌvaɪz) *vb.* **1.** to perform or make quickly from materials and sources available, without previous planning. **2.** to perform (a poem, play, piece of music, etc.), composing as one goes along. —'**impro,viser** *n.* —**improvi'sation** *n.* —**improvisatory** (ˌɪmprə'vaɪzətərɪ, -'vɪz-, ˌɪmprəvaɪz'eɪtərɪ) *adj.*

imprudent (ɪm'pruːdənt) *adj.* not prudent; rash, heedless, or indiscreet. —**im'prudence** *n.* —**im'prudently** *adv.*

impudent ('ɪmpjʊdənt) *adj.* **1.** mischievous, impertinent, or disrespectful. **2.** an obsolete word for **immodest.** —'**impudence** *n.* —'**impudently** *adv.* —'**impudentness** *n.*

impugn (ɪm'pjuːn) *vb.* (*tr.*) to challenge or attack as false; criticize. —**im'pugnable** *adj.* —**im'pugnment** *n.* —**im'pugner** *n.*

impulse ('ɪmpʌls) *n.* **1.** an impelling force or motion; thrust; impetus. **2.** a sudden desire, whim, or inclination. **3.** an instinctive drive; urge. **4.** tendency; current; trend. **5.** *Physics.* **a.** the product of the average magnitude of a force acting on a body and the time for which it acts. **b.** the change in the momentum of a body as a result of a force acting upon it. **6. on impulse.** spontaneously or impulsively.

impulsive (ɪm'pʌlsɪv) *adj.* **1.** characterized by actions based on sudden desires, whims, or inclinations: *an impulsive man.* **2.** based on emotional impulses or whims; spontaneous. **3.** forceful, inciting, or impelling. **4.** (of

physical forces) acting for a short time; not continuous. —**im'pulsively** *adv.* —**im'pulsiveness** *n.*

impunity (ɪm'pjuːnɪtɪ) *n., pl.* **-ties. 1.** exemption or immunity from punishment, recrimination, or other unpleasant consequences. **2. with impunity.** with no care or heed for such consequences.

impure (ɪm'pjʊə) *adj.* **1.** not pure; combined with something else; tainted or sullied. **2.** (in certain religions) ritually unclean. **3.** (of a colour) mixed with another colour. **4.** of more than one origin or style, as of architecture. —**im'purely** *adv.* —**im'pureness** *n.*

impurity (ɪm'pjʊərɪtɪ) *n., pl.* **-ties. 1.** the quality of being impure. **2.** an impure thing, constituent, or element: *impurities in the water.* **3.** *Electronics.* a small quantity of an element added to a pure semiconductor crystal to control its electrical conductivity.

impute (ɪm'pjuːt) *vb.* (*tr.*) **1.** to attribute or ascribe (something dishonest or dishonourable) to a person. **2.** to attribute to a source or cause: *I impute your success to nepotism.* —,**impu'tation** *n.* —**im'putative** *adj.* —**im'puter** *n.* —**im'putable** *adj.*

I.Mun.E. *abbrev.. for* Institution of Municipal Engineers.

in (ɪn) *prep.* **1.** inside; within: *no smoking in the auditorium.* **2.** at a place where there is: *in the shade; in the rain.* **3.** indicating a state, situation, or condition: *in silence.* **4.** when (a period of time) has elapsed: *come back in one year.* **5.** using: *written in code.* **6.** concerned with, esp. as an occupation: *in journalism.* **7.** while or by performing the action of: *in crossing the street he was run over.* **8.** used to indicate purpose: *in honour of the president.* **9.** (of certain animals) pregnant with: *in calf.* **10.** a variant of **into**: *she fell in the water.* **11. have it in one.** (often foll. by an infinitive) to have the ability (to do something). **12. in that** *or* **in so far as.** (*conj.*) because or to the extent that: *I regret my remark in that it upset you.* **13. nothing in it.** no difference or interval between two things. ~*adv.* (*particle*) **14.** in or into a particular place; inward or indoors: *come in.* **15.** so as to achieve office or power: *the Conservatives got in at the last election.* **16.** so as to enclose: *block in.* **17.** (in certain games) so as to take one's turn of the play: *you have to get the other side out before you go in.* **18.** *Brit.* (of a fire) alight. **19.** (*in combination*) indicating an activity or gathering: *teach-in; work-in.* **20. in at.** present at (the beginning, end, etc.). **21. in for.** about to be affected by (something, esp. something unpleasant): *you're in for a shock.* **22. in on.** acquainted with or sharing in: *I was in on all his plans.* **23. in with.** associated with; friendly with; regarded highly by. **24. have (got) it in for.** to be seeking to give vent to a grievance against (someone). ~*adj.* **25.** (*stressed*) fashion-

---

THESAURUS

impropriety 1. bad taste, immodesty, incongruity, indecency, indecorum, unsuitability, vulgarity **2.** blunder, faux pas, gaffe, gaucherie, mistake, slip, solecism

improve 1. advance, ameliorate, amend, augment, better, correct, help, mend, polish, rectify, touch up, upgrade **2.** develop, enhance, gain strength, increase, look up (*Inf.*), make strides, perk up, pick up, progress, rally, reform, rise, take a turn for the better (*Inf.*), take on a new lease of life (*Inf.*) **3.** convalesce, gain ground, gain strength, grow better, make progress, mend, recover, recuperate, turn the corner

improvement 1. advancement, amelioration, amendment, augmentation, betterment, correction, gain, rectification **2.** advance, development, enhancement, furtherance, increase, progress, rally, recovery, reformation, rise, upswing

improvident careless, heedless, imprudent, inconsiderate, negligent, prodigal, profligate, reckless, shiftless, short-sighted, spendthrift, thoughtless, thriftless, uneconomical, unthrifty, wasteful

improvisation ad-lib, ad-libbing, expedient, extemporizing, impromptu, invention, makeshift, spontaneity

improvise 1. ad-lib, coin, extemporize, invent, play it by ear (*Inf.*), speak off the cuff (*Inf.*) **2.** concoct, contrive, devise, make do,

throw together

improvised ad-lib, extemporaneous, extempore, extemporized, makeshift, off the cuff (*Inf.*), spontaneous, spur-of-the-moment, unprepared, unrehearsed

imprudent careless, foolhardy, foolish, heedless, ill-advised, ill-considered, ill-judged, impolitic, improvident, incautious, inconsiderate, indiscreet, injudicious, irresponsible, overhasty, rash, reckless, temerarious, unthinking, unwise

impudence assurance, audacity, backchat (*Inf.*), boldness, brass neck (*Sl.*), bumptiousness, cheek (*Inf.*), effrontery, face (*Inf.*), impertinence, insolence, lip (*Sl.*), nerve (*Inf.*), pertness, presumption, rudeness, sauciness, shamelessness

impudent audacious, bold, bold-faced, brazen, bumptious, cheeky (*Inf.*), cocky (*Inf.*), forward, fresh (*Inf.*), immodest, impertinent, insolent, pert, presumptuous, rude, saucy (*Inf.*), shameless

impulse 1. catalyst, force, impetus, momentum, movement, pressure, push, stimulus, surge, thrust **2.** *Fig.* caprice, drive, feeling, incitement, inclination, influence, instinct, motive, notion, passion, resolve, urge, whim, wish

impulsive devil-may-care, emotional, hasty, headlong, impetuous, instinctive, intuitive, passionate, precipitate, quick, rash,

spontaneous, unconsidered, unpredictable, unpremeditated

impunity dispensation, exemption, freedom, immunity, liberty, licence, nonliability, permission, security

impure 1. admixed, adulterated, alloyed, debased, mixed, unrefined **2.** contaminated, defiled, dirty, filthy, foul, infected, polluted, sullied, tainted, unclean, unwholesome, vitiated **3.** carnal, coarse, corrupt, gross, immodest, immoral, indecent, indelicate, lascivious, lewd, licentious, lustful, obscene, prurient, ribald, salacious, smutty, unchaste, unclean

impurity 1. admixture, adulteration, mixture **2.** befoulment, contamination, defilement, dirtiness, filth, foulness, infection, pollution, taint, uncleanness **3.** *Often plural* bits, contaminant, dirt, dross, foreign body, foreign matter, grime, marks, pollutant, scum, spots, stains **4.** carnality, coarseness, corruption, grossness, immodesty, immorality, indecency, lasciviousness, lewdness, licentiousness, obscenity, prurience, salaciousness, smuttiness, unchastity, vulgarity

imputation accusation, ascription, aspersion, attribution, blame, censure, charge, insinuation, reproach, slander, slur

impute accredit, ascribe, assign, attribute, credit, lay at the door of, refer, set down to

able; modish: *the in thing to do.* *~n.* **26. ins and outs.** intricacies or complications; details.

In *the chemical symbol for* indium.

in. *abbrev. for* inch(es).

in-¹, il-, im-, *or* **ir-** *prefix.* **a.** not; non-: *incredible; illegal; imperfect; irregular.* **b.** lack of: *inexperience.* The list at the bottom of the page contains words which may be easily understood if "not" or "lack of" is used with the meaning of the basic word. Cf. **un-.**

in-², il-, im-, *or* **ir-** *prefix.* **1.** in; into; towards; within; on: *infiltrate; immigrate.* **2.** having an intensive or causative function: *inflame; imperil.*

-in *suffix forming nouns.* **1.** indicating a neutral organic compound, including proteins, glucosides, and glycerides: *insulin; tripalmitin.* **2.** indicating an enzyme in certain nonsystematic names: *pepsin.* **3.** indicating a pharmaceutical substance: *penicillin; aspirin.* **4.** indicating a chemical substance in certain nonsystematic names: *coumarin.*

in absentia *Latin.* (ɪn æbˈsɛntɪə) *adv.* in the absence of (someone indicated).

inaccessible (ˌɪnækˈsɛsəbəl) *adj.* not accessible; unapproachable. **—ˌinacˌcessiˈbility** *or* **ˌinacˈcessibleness** *n.* **—ˌinacˈcessibly** *adv.*

inaccuracy (ɪnˈækjurəsɪ) *n., pl.* **-cies. 1.** lack of accuracy; imprecision. **2.** an error, mistake, or slip. **—inˈaccurate** *adj.*

inaction (ɪnˈækʃən) *n.* lack of action; idleness; inertia.

inactive (ɪnˈæktɪv) *adj.* **1.** idle or inert; not active. **2.** sluggish, passive, or indolent. **3.** *Mil.* of or relating to persons or equipment not in active service. **4.** *Chem.* (of a substance) having little or no reactivity. **—inˈactively** *adv.* **—ˌinacˈtivity** *n.*

inadequate (ɪnˈædɪkwɪt) *adj.* **1.** not adequate; insufficient. **2.** not capable or competent; lacking. **—inˈad-**

equacy *n.* **—inˈadequately** *adv.*

inadvertent (ˌɪnədˈvɜːtənt) *adj.* **1.** failing to act carefully or considerately; inattentive. **2.** resulting from heedless action; unintentional. **—ˌinadˈvertence** *n.* **—ˌinadˈvertently** *adv.*

-inae *suffix forming plural proper nouns.* occurring in names of zoological subfamilies: *Felinae.*

inalienable (ɪnˈeɪljənəbəl) *adj.* not able to be transferred to another; not alienable: *the inalienable rights of the citizen.* **—inˌalienaˈbility** *or* **inˈalienableness** *n.* **—inˈalienably** *adv.*

inamorata (ɪnˌæməˈrɑːtə, ˌɪnæmə-) *or* (*masc.*) **inamorato** (ɪnˌæməˈrɑːtəʊ, ˌɪnæmə-) *n., pl.* **-tas** *or* (*masc.*) **-tos.** a person with whom one is in love; lover.

inane (ɪˈneɪn) *adj.* **1.** senseless, unimaginative, or empty; unintelligent: *inane remarks.* *~n.* **2.** *Arch.* something empty or vacant, esp. the void of space. **—inˈanely** *adv.* **—inanity** (-ˈnæn-) *n.*

inanimate (ɪnˈænɪmɪt) *adj.* **1.** lacking the qualities of living beings; not animate: *inanimate objects.* **2.** lacking any sign of life or consciousness; appearing dead. **3.** lacking vitality; spiritless; dull. **—inˈanimately** *adv.* **—inˈanimateness** *or* **inanimation** (ɪnˌænɪˈmeɪʃən) *n.*

inanition (ˌɪnəˈnɪʃən) *n.* **1.** exhaustion resulting from lack of food. **2.** mental, social, or spiritual weakness or lassitude.

inapposite (ɪnˈæpəzɪt) *adj.* not appropriate or pertinent; unsuitable. **—inˈappositely** *adv.* **—inˈappositeness** *n.*

inapt (ɪnˈæpt) *adj.* **1.** not apt or fitting; inappropriate. **2.** lacking skill; inept. **—inˈaptiˌtude** *or* **inˈaptness** *n.* **—inˈaptly** *adv.*

inasmuch as (ˌɪnəzˈmʌtʃ) *conj.* (*subordinating*) **1.** in view of the fact that; seeing that; since. **2.** to the extent or degree that; insofar as.

---

inability *n.*	**inconstant** *adj.*	**inessential** *adj. n.*	**ingratitude** *n.*
inadmissible *adj.*	**incontestable** *adj.*	**inexact** *adj.*	**inharmonious** *adj.*
inadvisable *adj.*	**inconvenience** *n. vb.*	**inexcusable** *adj.*	**inhospitable** *adj.*
inapplicable *adj.*	**inconvenient** *adj.*	**inexpedient** *adj.*	**inhospitality** *n.*
inappropriate *adj.*	**incorrect** *adj.*	**inexpensive** *adj.*	**injudicious** *adj.*
inarticulate *adj.*	**indefinable** *adj.*	**inexperience** *n.*	**inoffensive** *adj.*
inartistic *adj.*	**indestructible** *adj.*	**inexpert** *adj.*	**inoperative** *adj.*
inattentive *adj.*	**indiscernible** *adj.*	**inexplicable** *adj.*	**inopportune** *adj.*
inaudible *adj.*	**indisputable** *adj.*	**infelicitous** *adj.*	**insensitive** *adj.*
inauspicious *adj.*	**indissoluble** *adj.*	**infelicity** *n.*	**inseparable** *adj.*
incapable *adj.*	**inefficient** *adj.*	**infertile** *adj.*	**instability** *n.*
incombustible *adj.*	**inelastic** *adj.*	**infertility** *n.*	**insufficient** *adj.*
incomplete *adj.*	**inelegant** *adj.*	**inflexible** *adj.*	**insurmountable** *adj.*
incomprehensible *adj.*	**ineligible** *adj. n.*	**infrequent** *adj.*	**intolerable** *adj.*
inconclusive *adj.*	**inequitable** *adj.*	**inglorious** *adj.*	**intolerant** *adj.*

THESAURUS

inability disability, disqualification, impotence, inadequacy, incapability, incapacity, incompetence, ineptitude, powerlessness

inaccessible impassable, out of reach, out of the way, remote, unapproachable, unattainable, un-get-at-able (*Inf.*), unreachable

inaccuracy 1. erroneousness, imprecision, incorrectness, inexactness, unfaithfulness, unreliability 2. blunder, corrigendum, defect, erratum, error, fault, howler (*Inf.*), literal (*Printing*), miscalculation, mistake, slip, typo (*Inf., printing*)

inaccurate careless, defective, discrepant, erroneous, faulty, imprecise, incorrect, in error, inexact, mistaken, out, unfaithful, unreliable, unsound, wide of the mark, wild, wrong

inaccurately carelessly, clumsily, imprecisely, inexactly, unfaithfully, unreliably

inaction dormancy, idleness, immobility, inactivity, inertia, rest, torpidity, torpor

inactive 1. abeyant, dormant, idle, immobile, inert, inoperative, jobless, kicking one's heels, latent, mothballed, out of service, out of work, unemployed, unoccupied, unused 2. dull, indolent, lazy, lethargic, low-key (*Inf.*), passive, quiet, sedentary, slothful, slow, sluggish, somnolent, torpid

inactivity 1. dormancy, hibernation, immobility, inaction, passivity, unemployment 2. dilatoriness, *dolce far niente*, dullness, heaviness, indolence, inertia, inertness, lassi-

tude, laziness, lethargy, quiescence, sloth, sluggishness, stagnation, torpor, vegetation

inadequacy 1. dearth, deficiency, inadequateness, incompleteness, insufficiency, meagreness, paucity, poverty, scantiness, shortage, skimpiness 2. defectiveness, faultiness, inability, inaptness, incapacity, incompetence, incompetency, ineffectiveness, inefficacy, unfitness, unsuitableness 3. defect, failing, imperfection, lack, shortage, shortcoming, weakness

inadequate 1. defective, deficient, faulty, imperfect, incommensurate, incomplete, insubstantial, insufficient, meagre, niggardly, scanty, short, sketchy, skimpy, sparse 2. found wanting, inapt, incapable, incompetent, not up to scratch (*Inf.*), unequal, unfitted, unqualified

inadequately imperfectly, insufficiently, meagerly, poorly, scantily, sketchily, skimpily, sparsely, thinly

inadmissible immaterial, improper, inappropriate, incompetent, irrelevant, unacceptable, unallowable, unqualified, unreasonable

inadvertently 1. carelessly, heedlessly, in an unguarded moment, negligently, thoughtlessly, unguardedly, unthinkingly 2. accidentally, by accident, by mistake, involuntarily, mistakenly, unintentionally, unwittingly

inadvisable ill-advised, impolitic, im-

prudent, inexpedient, injudicious, unwise

inane asinine, daft (*Inf.*), devoid of intelligence, empty, fatuous, frivolous, futile, idiotic, imbecilic, mindless, puerile, senseless, silly, stupid, trifling, unintelligent, vacuous, vain, vapid, worthless

inanimate cold, dead, defunct, extinct, inactive, inert, insensate, insentient, lifeless, quiescent, soulless, spiritless

inanity asininity, bêtise (*Rare*), daftness (*Inf.*), emptiness, fatuity, folly, frivolity, imbecility, puerility, senselessness, silliness, vacuity, vapidity, worthlessness

inapplicable inapposite, inappropriate, inapt, irrelevant, unsuitable, unsuited

inappropriate disproportionate, ill-fitted, ill-suited, ill-timed, improper, incongruous, malapropos, out of place, tasteless, unbecoming, unbefitting, unfit, unfitting, unseemly, unsuitable, untimely

inapt 1. ill-fitted, ill-suited, inapposite, inappropriate, infelicitous, unsuitable, unsuited 2. awkward, clumsy, dull, gauche, incompetent, inept, inexpert, maladroit, slow, stupid

inarticulate 1. blurred, incoherent, incomprehensible, indistinct, muffled, mumbled, unclear, unintelligible 2. dumb, mute, silent, speechless, tongue-tied, unspoken, unuttered, unvoiced, voiceless, wordless 3. faltering, halting, hesitant, poorly spoken

inattention absent-mindedness, care-

inaugural (ɪnˈɔːgjʊrəl) *adj.* 1. characterizing or relating to an inauguration. ~*n.* 2. a speech made at an inauguration, esp. by a president of the U.S.

inaugurate (ɪnˈɔːgjʊˌreɪt) *vb.* (*tr.*) 1. to commence officially or formally; initiate. 2. to place in office formally and ceremonially; induct. 3. to open ceremonially; dedicate formally: *to inaugurate a factory.* —**inˌauguˈration** *n.* —**inˈauguˌrator** *n.* —**inauguratory** (ɪnˈɔːgjʊrətərɪ, -trɪ) *adj.*

inboard (ˈɪnˌbɔːd) *adj.* 1. (esp. of a boat's motor or engine) situated within the hull. 2. situated between the wing tip of an aircraft and its fuselage: *an inboard engine.* ~*adv.* 3. towards the centre line of or within a vessel, aircraft, etc.

inborn (ˈɪnˈbɔːn) *adj.* existing from birth; congenital; innate.

inbred (ˈɪnˈbrɛd) *adj.* 1. produced as a result of inbreeding. 2. deeply ingrained; innate: *inbred good manners.*

inbreed (ˈɪnˈbriːd) *vb.* **-breeding, -bred.** 1. to breed from unions between closely related individuals, esp. over several generations. 2. (*tr.*) to develop within; engender. —**ˈinˈbreeding** *n., adj.*

inc. *abbrev. for:* 1. including. 2. inclusive. 3. income. 4. increase.

Inc. (esp. U.S.) *abbrev. for* incorporated. Brit. equivalent: **Ltd.**

incalculable (ɪnˈkælkjʊləbəl) *adj.* beyond calculation; unable to be predicted or determined. —**inˌcalculaˈbility** *n.* —**inˈcalculably** *adv.*

incandescent (ˌɪnkænˈdɛsənt) *adj.* emitting light as a result of being heated; red-hot or white-hot. —**incanˈdescently** *adv.* —**incanˈdescence** *n.*

incandescent lamp *n.* a source of light that contains a heated solid, such as an electrically heated filament.

incantation (ˌɪnkænˈteɪʃən) *n.* 1. ritual recitation of magic words or sounds. 2. the formulaic words or sounds used; a magic spell. —**ˌincanˈtational** *or* **inˈcantatory** *adj.*

incapacitate (ˌɪnkəˈpæsɪˌteɪt) *vb.* (*tr.*) 1. to deprive of power, strength, or capacity; disable. 2. to deprive of legal capacity or eligibility. —**ˌincaˌpaciˈtation** *n.*

incapacity (ˌɪnkəˈpæsɪtɪ) *n., pl.* **-ties.** 1. lack of power, strength, or capacity; inability. 2. *Law.* legal disqualification or ineligibility.

incarcerate (ɪnˈkɑːsəˌreɪt) *vb.* (*tr.*) to confine or imprison. —**inˌcarcerˈation** *n.* —**inˈcarcerˌator** *n.*

incarnadine (ɪnˈkɑːnəˌdaɪn) *Arch. or literary.* ~*vb.* 1. (*tr.*) to tinge or stain with red. ~*adj.* 2. of a pinkish or reddish colour similar to that of flesh or blood.

incarnate *adj.* (ɪnˈkɑːnɪt, -neɪt). (*usually immediately postpositive*) 1. possessing bodily form, esp. the human form: *a devil incarnate.* 2. personified or typified: *stupidity incarnate.* ~*vb.* (ɪnˈkɑːneɪt). (*tr.*) 3. to give a bodily or concrete form to. 4. to be representative or typical of.

incarnation (ˌɪnkɑːˈneɪʃən) *n.* 1. the act of manifesting or state of being manifested in bodily form, esp. human form. 2. a bodily form assumed by a god, etc. 3. a person or thing that typifies or represents some quality, idea, etc.

Incarnation (ˌɪnkɑːˈneɪʃən) *n. Christian theol.* the assuming of a human body by the Son of God.

incendiary (ɪnˈsɛndɪərɪ) *adj.* 1. of or relating to the illegal burning of property, goods, etc. 2. tending to create strife, violence, etc. 3. (of a substance) capable of catching fire or burning readily. ~*n., pl.* **-aries.** 4. a person who illegally sets fire to property, goods, etc.; arsonist. 5. (esp. formerly) a person who stirs up civil strife, violence, etc.; agitator. 6. Also called: **incendiary bomb.** a bomb that is designed to start fires. 7. an incendiary substance, such as phosphorus. —**inˈcendiaˌrism** *n.*

incense[1] (ˈɪnsɛns) *n.* 1. any of various aromatic substances burnt for their fragrant odour, esp. in religious ceremonies. 2. the odour or smoke so produced. 3. any pleasant fragrant odour; aroma. ~*vb.* 4. to burn incense in honour of (a deity). 5. (*tr.*) to perfume or fumigate with incense.

incense[2] (ɪnˈsɛns) *vb.* (*tr.*) to enrage greatly. —**inˈcensement** *n.*

incentive (ɪnˈsɛntɪv) *n.* 1. a motivating influence; stimulus. 2. **a.** an additional payment made to employees to increase production. **b.** (*as modifier*): *an incentive scheme.* ~*adj.* 3. serving to incite to action.

inception (ɪnˈsɛpʃən) *n.* the beginning, as of a project or undertaking.

incessant (ɪnˈsɛsənt) *adj.* not ceasing; continual. —**in-**

lessness, daydreaming, disregard, forgetfulness, heedlessness, inadvertence, inattentiveness, indifference, neglect, preoccupation, thoughtlessness, woolgathering

inattentive absent-minded, careless, distracted, distrait, dreamy, heedless, inadvertent, neglectful, negligent, preoccupied, regardless, remiss, thoughtless, unheeding, unmindful, unobservant, vague

inaudible indistinct, low, mumbling, out of earshot, stifled, unheard

inaugural dedicatory, first, initial, introductory, maiden, opening

inaugurate 1. begin, commence, get under way, initiate, institute, introduce, kick off (*Inf.*), launch, originate, set in motion, set up, usher in 2. induct, install, instate, invest 3. commission, dedicate, open, ordain

inauguration 1. initiation, institution, launch, launching, opening, setting up 2. induction, installation, investiture

inauspicious bad, black, discouraging, ill-omened, ominous, unfavourable, unfortunate, unlucky, unpromising, unpropitious, untoward

inborn congenital, connate, hereditary, inbred, ingrained, inherent, inherited, innate, instinctive, intuitive, native, natural

inbred constitutional, deep-seated, ingrained, inherent, innate, native, natural

incalculable boundless, countless, enormous, immense, incomputable, inestimable, infinite, innumerable, limitless, measureless, numberless, uncountable, untold, vast, without number

incantation abracadabra, chant, charm, conjuration, formula, hex (*U.S. dialect*), invocation, spell

incapable 1. feeble, inadequate, incompetent, ineffective, inept, inexpert, insufficient, not equal to, not up to, unfit, unfitted, unqualified, weak 2. helpless, impotent, powerless, unable, unfit 3. *With of* impervious, not admitting of, not susceptible to, resistant

incapacitate cripple, disable, disqualify, immobilize, lay up (*Inf.*), paralyse, prostrate, put out of action (*Inf.*), scupper (*Brit. sl.*), unfit (*Rare*)

incapacitated disqualified, *hors de combat,* immobilized, indisposed, laid up (*Inf.*), out of action (*Inf.*), unfit

incapacity disqualification, feebleness, impotence, inability, inadequacy, incapability, incompetency, ineffectiveness, powerlessness, unfitness, weakness

incarcerate commit, confine, coop up, detain, gaol, immure, impound, imprison, intern, jail, lock up, put under lock and key, restrain, restrict, send down (*Brit.*), throw in jail

incarceration bondage, captivity, confinement, detention, imprisonment, internment, restraint

incarnate 1. in bodily form, in human form, in the flesh, made flesh 2. embodied, personified, typified

incarnation avatar, bodily form, embodiment, exemplification, impersonation, manifestation, personification, type

incautious careless, hasty, heedless, ill-advised, ill-judged, improvident, imprudent, impulsive, inconsiderate, indiscreet, injudicious, negligent, precipitate, rash, reckless, thoughtless, unguarded, unthinking, unwary

incautiously imprudently, impulsively, indiscreetly, precipitately, rashly, recklessly,

thoughtlessly, unthinkingly

incendiary *adj.* 1. dissentious, inflammatory, provocative, rabble-rousing, seditious, subversive ~*n.* 2. arsonist, firebug (*Inf.*), fire raiser, pyromaniac 3. agitator, demagogue, firebrand, insurgent, rabble-rouser, revolutionary

incense[1] *v.* anger, enrage, exasperate, excite, get one's hackles up, inflame, infuriate, irritate, madden, make one's blood boil (*Inf.*), make one see red (*Inf.*), make one's hackles rise, provoke, raise one's hackles, rile (*Inf.*)

incense[2] *n.* aroma, balm, bouquet, fragrance, perfume, redolence, scent

incensed angry, enraged, exasperated, fuming, furious, indignant, infuriated, irate, ireful (*Literary*), mad (*Inf.*), maddened, on the warpath (*Inf.*), steamed up (*Sl.*), up in arms, wrathful

incentive bait, carrot (*Inf.*), encouragement, enticement, goad, impetus, impulse, inducement, lure, motivation, motive, spur, stimulant, stimulus

inception beginning, birth, commencement, dawn, inauguration, initiation, kickoff (*Inf.*), origin, outset, rise, start

incessant ceaseless, constant, continual, continuous, endless, eternal, everlasting, interminable, never-ending, nonstop, perpetual, persistent, relentless, unbroken, unceasing, unending, unrelenting, unremitting

incessantly all the time, ceaselessly, constantly, continually, endlessly, eternally, everlastingly, interminably, nonstop, perpetually, persistently, without a break

'cessancy n. —in'cessantly adv.

incest ('ınsɛst) n. sexual intercourse between two persons who are too closely related to marry. —in'cestuous adj.

inch¹ (ıntʃ) n. 1. a unit of length equal to one twelfth of a foot or 0.0254 metre. 2. Meteorol. a. an amount of precipitation that would cover a surface with water one inch deep. b. a unit of pressure equal to a mercury column one inch high in a barometer. 3. a very small distance, degree, or amount. 4. every inch. in every way; completely: every inch an aristocrat. 5. inch by inch. gradually; little by little. 6. within an inch of one's life almost to death ~vb. 7. to move or be moved very slowly or in very small steps: the car inched forward.

inch² (ıntʃ) n. Scot. & Irish. a small island.

inchmeal ('ıntʃ,miːl) adv. gradually; inch by inch or little by little.

inchoate adj. (ın'kəʊeıt, -'kəʊıt). 1. just beginning; incipient. 2. undeveloped; immature; rudimentary. ~vb. (ın'kəʊeıt). (tr.) 3. to begin. —in'choately adv. —in'choateness n. —,incho'ation n. —inchoative (ın'kəʊətıv) adj.

incidence ('ınsıdəns) n. 1. degree, extent, or frequency of occurrence; amount: a high incidence of death from pneumonia. 2. the act or manner of impinging on or affecting by proximity or influence. 3. Physics. the arrival of a beam of light or particles at a surface. See also angle of incidence. 4. Geom. the partial coincidence of two configurations, such as a point on a circle.

incident ('ınsıdənt) n. 1. a definite occurrence; event. 2. a minor, subsidiary, or related event. 3. a relatively insignificant event that might have serious consequences. 4. a public disturbance. ~adj. 5. (postpositive; foll. by to) related (to) or dependent (on). 6. (when postpositive, often foll. by to) having a subsidiary or minor relationship (with). 7. (esp. of a beam of light or particles) arriving at or striking a surface.

incidental (,ınsı'dɛntəl) adj. 1. happening in connection with or resulting from something more important; casual or fortuitous. 2. (postpositive; foll. by to) found in connection (with); related (to). 3. (postpositive; foll. by upon) caused (by). 4. occasional or minor: incidental expenses. ~n. 5. (often pl.) a minor expense, event, or action. —,inci'dentally adv. —,inci'dentalness n.

incidental music n. background music for a film, etc.

incinerate (ın'sınə,reıt) vb. to burn up completely; reduce to ashes. —in,ciner'ation n.

incinerator (ın'sınə,reıtə) n. a furnace or apparatus for incinerating something, esp. refuse.

incipient (ın'sıpıənt) adj. just starting to be or happen; beginning. —in'cipience or in'cipiency n. —in'cipiently adv.

incise (ın'saız) vb. (tr.) to produce (lines, a design, etc.) by cutting into the surface of (something) with a sharp tool.

incision (ın'sıʒən) n. 1. the act of incising. 2. a cut, gash, or notch. 3. a cut made with a knife during a surgical operation.

incisive (ın'saısıv) adj. 1. keen, penetrating, or acute. 2. biting or sarcastic; mordant: an incisive remark. 3. having a sharp cutting edge: incisive teeth. —in'cisively adv. —in'cisiveness n.

incisor (ın'saızə) n. a chisel-edged tooth at the front of the mouth.

incite (ın'saıt) vb. (tr.) to stir up or provoke to action. —,inci'tation n. —in'citement n. —in'citer n. —in'citingly adv.

incl. abbrev. for: 1. including. 2. inclusive.

inclement (ın'klɛmənt) adj. 1. (of weather) stormy, severe, or tempestuous. 2. harsh, severe, or merciless. —in'clemency n. —in'clemently adv.

inclination (,ınklı'neıʃən) n. 1. (often foll. by for, to, towards, or an infinitive) a particular disposition, esp. a liking; tendency: I've no inclination for such dull work. 2. the degree of deviation from a particular plane, esp. a horizontal or vertical plane. 3. a sloping or slanting surface; incline. 4. the act of inclining or the state of being inclined. 5. another name for dip (sense 27). —,incli'national adj.

incline vb. (ın'klaın). 1. to deviate from a particular plane, esp. a vertical or horizontal plane; slope or slant. 2. (when tr., may take an infinitive) to be disposed or cause to be disposed (towards some attitude or to do something): that does not incline me to think that you are right. 3. to bend or lower (part of the body, esp. the head), as in a bow or in order to listen. 4. incline one's ear. to listen favourably (to). ~n. ('ınklaın, ın'klaın). 5. an inclined surface or slope; gradient. —in'clined adj. —in'cliner n.

inclined plane n. a plane whose angle to the horizontal is less than a right angle.

inclose (ın'kləʊz) vb. a less common spelling of enclose. —in'closure n.

include (ın'kluːd) vb. (tr.) 1. to have as contents or part of the contents; be made up of or contain. 2. to add as part of something else; put in as part of a set, group, or category. 3. to contain as a secondary or minor ingredient or element. —in'cludable or in'cludible adj.

inclusion (ın'kluːʒən) n. 1. the act of including or the state of being included. 2. something included.

inclusive (ın'kluːsıv) adj. 1. (postpositive; foll. by of) considered together (with): capital inclusive of profit. 2. (postpositive) including the limits specified: Monday to Friday inclusive. 3. comprehensive. 4. Logic. (of a disjunction) true if at least one of its component propositions is true. —in'clusively adv. —in'clusiveness n.

THESAURUS

incidence amount, degree, extent, frequency, occurrence, prevalence, rate

incident 1. adventure, circumstance, episode, event, fact, happening, matter, occasion, occurrence 2. brush, clash, commotion, confrontation, contretemps, disturbance, mishap, scene, skirmish

incidental 1. accidental, casual, chance, fortuitous, odd, random 2. With to accompanying, attendant, by-the-way, concomitant, contingent, contributory, related 3. ancillary, minor, nonessential, occasional, secondary, subordinate, subsidiary

incidentally 1. accidentally, by chance, casually, fortuitously 2. by the bye, by the way, in passing, parenthetically

incidentals contingencies, extras, minutiae, odds and ends

incinerate burn up, carbonize, char, consume by fire, cremate, reduce to ashes

incipient beginning, commencing, developing, embryonic, inceptive, inchoate, nascent, originating, starting

incise carve, chisel, cut (into), engrave, etch

incision cut, gash, notch, opening, slash, slit

incisive 1. acute, keen, penetrating, perspicacious, piercing, trenchant 2. acid, biting, caustic, cutting, mordant, sarcastic, sardonic, satirical, severe, sharp

incisiveness 1. keenness, penetration, perspicacity, sharpness, trenchancy 2. acidity, pungency, sarcasm

incite agitate for or against, animate, drive, egg on, encourage, excite, foment, goad, impel, inflame, instigate, prompt, provoke, put up to, rouse, set on, spur, stimulate, stir up, urge, whip up

incitement agitation, encouragement, goad, impetus, impulse, inducement, instigation, motivation, motive, prompting, provocation, spur, stimulus

incivility bad manners, boorishness, discourteousness, discourtesy, disrespect, ill-breeding, impoliteness, rudeness, unmannerliness

inclemency 1. bitterness, boisterousness, rawness, rigour, roughness, severity, storminess 2. callousness, cruelty, harshness, mercilessness, severity, tyranny, unfeelingness

inclement 1. bitter, boisterous, foul, harsh, intemperate, rigorous, rough, severe, stormy, tempestuous 2. callous, cruel, draconian, harsh, intemperate, merciless, pitiless, rigorous, severe, tyrannical, unfeeling, unmerciful

inclination 1. affection, aptitude, bent, bias, desire, disposition, fancy, fondness, leaning, liking, partiality, penchant, predilection, predisposition, prejudice, proclivity, proneness, propensity, stomach, taste, tendency, turn, turn of mind, wish 2. bending, bow, bowing, nod 3. angle, bend, bending, deviation, gradient, incline, leaning, pitch, slant, slope, tilt

incline v. 1. be disposed or predisposed, bias, influence, persuade, predispose, prejudice, sway, tend, turn 2. bend, bow, lower, nod, stoop 3. bend, bevel, cant, deviate, diverge, lean, slant, slope, tend, tilt, tip, veer ~n. 4. acclivity, ascent, declivity, descent, dip, grade, gradient, ramp, rise, slope

inclined apt, disposed, given, liable, likely, minded, of a mind (Inf.), predisposed, prone, willing

inclose see ENCLOSE

include 1. comprehend, comprise, contain, cover, embody, embrace, encompass, incorporate, involve, subsume, take in, take into account 2. add, allow for, build in, count, enter, insert, introduce, number among

including as well as, containing, counting, inclusive of, plus, together with, with

inclusion addition, incorporation,

incognito (ˌɪnkɒgˈniːtəʊ) or (fem.) **incognita** adv., adj. (postpositive) **1.** under an assumed name or appearance; in disguise. ~n., pl. -tos or (fem.) -tas. **2.** a person who is incognito. **3.** the assumed name or disguise of such a person.

incognizant (ɪnˈkɒgnɪzənt) adj. (when postpositive, often foll. by of) unaware (of). —in**ˈcognizance** n.

incoherent (ˌɪnkəʊˈhɪərənt) adj. **1.** lacking in clarity or organization; disordered. **2.** unable to express oneself clearly; inarticulate. —**inco'herence** or **inco'herency** n. —**inco'herently** adv.

income (ˈɪnkʌm, ˈɪnkəm) n. **1.** the amount of monetary or other returns, either earned or unearned, accruing over a given period of time. **2.** receipts; revenue.

income tax n. a personal tax levied on annual income subject to certain deductions.

incoming (ˈɪnˌkʌmɪŋ) adj. **1.** coming in; entering. **2.** about to come into office; succeeding. **3.** (of interest, dividends, etc.) being received; accruing. ~n. **4.** the act of coming in; entrance. **5.** (usually pl.) income or revenue.

incommensurable (ˌɪnkəˈmɛnʃərəbəl) adj. **1.** incapable of being judged, measured, or considered comparatively. **2.** (postpositive; foll. by with) not in accordance; incommensurate. **3.** Maths. not having a common factor other than 1, such as 2 and √-5. ~n. **4.** something incommensurable. —ˌincom,mensura'bility n. —ˌincom'mensurably adv.

incommensurate (ˌɪnkəˈmɛnʃərɪt) adj. **1.** (when postpositive, often foll. by with) not commensurate; disproportionate. **2.** incommensurable. —ˌincom'mensurately adv. —ˌincom'mensurateness n.

incommode (ˌɪnkəˈməʊd) vb. (tr.) to bother, disturb, or inconvenience.

incommodious (ˌɪnkəˈməʊdɪəs) adj. **1.** insufficiently spacious; cramped. **2.** troublesome or inconvenient. —ˌincom'modiously adv.

incommunicado (ˌɪnkəˌmjuːnɪˈkɑːdəʊ) adv., adj. (postpositive) deprived of communication with other people, as while in solitary confinement.

incomparable (ɪnˈkɒmpərəbəl, -prəbəl) adj. **1.** beyond or above comparison; matchless; unequalled. **2.** lacking a basis for comparison; not having qualities or features that can be compared. —in,compara'bility or in'comparableness n. —in'comparably adv.

incompatible (ˌɪnkəmˈpætəbəl) adj. **1.** incapable of living or existing together in harmony; conflicting or antagonistic. **2.** opposed in nature or quality; inconsistent. **3.** Med. (esp. of two drugs or two types of blood) incapable of being combined or used together; antagonistic. **4.** Logic. (of two propositions) unable to be both true at the same time. **5.** (of plants) incapable of self-fertilization. ~n. **6.** (often pl.) a person or thing that is incompatible with another. —ˌincom,pati'bility or ˌincom'patibleness n. —ˌincom'patibly adv.

incompetent (ɪnˈkɒmpɪtənt) adj. **1.** not possessing the necessary ability, skill, etc. to do or carry out a task; incapable. **2.** marked by lack of ability, skill, etc. **3.** Law. not legally qualified: an incompetent witness. ~n. **4.** an incompetent person. —in'competence or in'competency n. —in'competently adv.

inconceivable (ˌɪnkənˈsiːvəbəl) adj. incapable of being conceived, imagined, or considered. —ˌincon,ceiva'bility or ˌincon'ceivableness n. —ˌincon'ceivably adv.

incongruous (ɪnˈkɒŋgrʊəs) or **incongruent** adj. **1.** (when postpositive, foll. by with or to) incompatible with (what is suitable); inappropriate. **2.** containing disparate or discordant elements or parts. —in'congruously adv. —in'congruousness or incongruity (ˌɪnkɒŋˈgruːɪtɪ) n.

inconnu (ˈɪnkənjuː, ˈɪnkənuː) n. Canad. a whitefish of Far Northern waters.

inconsequential (ˌɪnkɒnsɪˈkwɛnʃəl, ɪnˌkɒn-) or **inconsequent** (ɪnˈkɒnsɪkwənt) adj. **1.** not following logically as a consequence. **2.** trivial or insignificant. **3.** not in a logical sequence; haphazard. —ˌinconse,quenti'ality, ˌinconse'quentialness, or in'consequence n. —ˌinconse'quentially or in'consequently adv.

inconsiderable (ˌɪnkənˈsɪdərəbəl) adj. **1.** relatively small. **2.** not worthy of consideration; insignificant. —ˌincon'siderableness n. —ˌincon'siderably adv.

inconsiderate (ˌɪnkənˈsɪdərɪt) adj. lacking in care or thought for others; thoughtless. —ˌincon'siderately adv. —ˌincon'siderateness or ˌincon,sider'ation n.

inconsistent (ˌɪnkənˈsɪstənt) adj. **1.** lacking in consistency, agreement, or compatibility; at variance. **2.** containing contradictory elements. **3.** irregular or fickle in behaviour or mood. **4.** Logic. (of a set of axioms) leading to at least one proposition that can be shown to be true by one axiom and false by another. —ˌincon'sistency n. —ˌincon'sistently adv.

inconsolable (ˌɪnkənˈsəʊləbəl) adj. incapable of being consoled or comforted; disconsolate. —ˌincon,sola'bility

---

THESAURUS

inclusive across-the-board, all-embracing, all in, all together, blanket, catch-all (Chiefly U.S.), comprehensive, full, general, in toto, overall, sweeping, umbrella, without exception

incognito disguised, in disguise, under an assumed name, unknown, unrecognized

incoherence disconnectedness, disjointedness, inarticulateness, unintelligibility

incoherent confused, disconnected, disjointed, disordered, inarticulate, inconsistent, jumbled, loose, muddled, rambling, stammering, stuttering, unconnected, uncoordinated, unintelligible, wandering, wild

incombustible fireproof, flameproof, noncombustible, nonflammable, noninflammable

income earnings, gains, interest, means, pay, proceeds, profits, receipts, revenue, salary, takings, wages

incoming approaching, arriving, entering, homeward, landing, new, returning, succeeding

incomparable beyond compare, inimitable, matchless, paramount, peerless, superlative, supreme, transcendent, unequalled, unmatched, unparalleled, unrivalled

incomparably beyond compare, by far, easily, eminently, far and away, immeasurably

incompatibility antagonism, conflict, discrepancy, disparateness, incongruity, inconsistency, irreconcilability, uncongeniality

incompatible antagonistic, antipathetic, conflicting, contradictory, discordant, discrepant, disparate, ill-assorted, incongruous, inconsistent, inconsonant, irreconcilable, mismatched, uncongenial, unsuitable, unsuited

incompetence inability, inadequacy, incapability, incapacity, incompetency, ineffectiveness, ineptitude, ineptness, insufficiency, skill-lessness, unfitness, uselessness

incompetent bungling, floundering, incapable, incapacitated, ineffectual, inept, inexpert, insufficient, skill-less, unable, unfit, unfitted, unskilful, useless

incomplete broken, defective, deficient, fragmentary, imperfect, insufficient, lacking, partial, short, unaccomplished, undeveloped, undone, unexecuted, unfinished, wanting

incomprehensible above one's head, all Greek to (Inf.), baffling, beyond comprehension, beyond one's grasp, enigmatic, impenetrable, inconceivable, inscrutable, mysterious, obscure, opaque, perplexing, puzzling, unfathomable, unimaginable, unintelligible, unthinkable

inconceivable beyond belief, impossible, incomprehensible, incredible, mind-boggling (Sl.), not to be thought of, out of the question, staggering (Inf.), unbelievable, unheard-of, unimaginable, unknowable, unthinkable

inconclusive ambiguous, indecisive, indeterminate, open, uncertain, unconvincing, undecided, unsettled, up in the air (Inf.), vague

incongruity conflict, discrepancy, disparity, inappropriateness, inaptness, incompatibility, inconsistency, inharmoniousness, unsuitability

incongruous absurd, conflicting, contradictory, contrary, disconsonant, discordant, extraneous, improper, inappropriate, inapt, incoherent, incompatible, inconsistent, out of keeping, out of place, unbecoming, unsuitable, unsuited

inconsiderable exiguous, inconsequential, insignificant, light, minor, negligible, petty, slight, small, small-time (Inf.), trifling, trivial, unimportant

inconsiderate careless, indelicate, insensitive, intolerant, rude, self-centred, selfish, tactless, thoughtless, uncharitable, ungracious, unkind, unthinking

inconsistency 1. contrariety, disagreement, discrepancy, disparity, divergence, incompatibility, incongruity, inconsonance, paradox, variance 2. fickleness, instability, unpredictability, unreliability, unsteadiness

inconsistent 1. at odds, at variance, conflicting, contradictory, contrary, discordant, discrepant, incoherent, incompatible, in conflict, incongruous, irreconcilable, out of step 2. capricious, changeable, erratic, fickle, inconstant, irregular, unpredictable, unstable, unsteady, vagarious (Rare), variable

inconsistently contradictorily, differently, eccentrically, erratically, inequably, randomly, unequally, unfairly, unpredictably, variably

inconsolable brokenhearted, desolate, despairing, heartbroken, heartsick, prostrate with grief, sick at heart

or ˌincon'solableness *n.* —ˌincon'solably *adv.*

inconspicuous (ˌɪnkən'spɪkjʊəs) *adj.* not easily noticed or seen; not prominent or striking. —ˌincon'spicuously *adv.* —ˌincon'spicuousness *n.*

incontinent (ɪn'kɒntɪnənt) *adj.* **1.** relating to or exhibiting involuntary urination or defecation. **2.** lacking in restraint or control, esp. sexually. **3.** (foll. by *of*) having little or no control (over). **4.** unrestrained; uncontrolled. —in'continence *n.* —in'continently *adv.*

incontrovertible (ˌɪnkɒntrə'vɜːtəbəl, ɪnˌkɒn-) *adj.* incapable of being contradicted or disputed; undeniable. —ˌincontro'vertibility *n.* —ˌincontro'vertibly *adv.*

incorporate *vb.* (ɪn'kɔːpəˌreɪt) **1.** to include or be included as a part or member of a united whole. **2.** to form a united whole or mass; merge or blend. **3.** to form into a corporation or other organization with a separate legal identity. ~*adj.* (ɪn'kɔːpərɪt, -prɪt) **4.** combined into a whole; incorporated. **5.** formed into or constituted as a corporation. —in'corporative *adj.* —inˌcorpo'ration *n.* —in'corpoˌrated *adj.*

incorporeal (ˌɪnkɔː'pɔːrɪəl) *adj.* **1.** without material form, body, or substance. **2.** spiritual or metaphysical. **3.** *Law.* having no material existence but existing by reason of its annexation of something material: *an incorporeal hereditament.* —ˌincor'poreally *adv.* —ˌincorpo'reity (ɪnˌkɔːpə'riːɪtɪ) *or* ˌincorpore'ality *n.*

incorrigible (ɪn'kɒrɪdʒəbəl) *adj.* **1.** beyond correction, reform, or alteration. **2.** firmly rooted; ineradicable. ~*n.* **3.** a person or animal that is incorrigible. —inˌcorrigi'bility *or* in'corrigibleness *n.* —in'corrigibly *adv.*

incorruptible (ˌɪnkə'rʌptəbəl) *adj.* **1.** incapable of being corrupted; honest; just. **2.** not subject to decay or decomposition. —inˌcorrupti'bility *n.* —in'corruptibly *adv.*

increase *vb.* (ɪn'kriːs). **1.** to make or become greater in size, degree, frequency, etc.; grow or expand. ~*n.* ('ɪnkriːs). **2.** the act of increasing; augmentation. **3.** the amount by which something increases. **4. on the increase.** increasing, esp. becoming more frequent. —in'creasable *adj.* —in'creasedly (ɪn'kriːsɪdlɪ) *or* in'creasingly *adv.* —in'creaser *n.*

incredible (ɪn'krɛdəbəl) *adj.* **1.** beyond belief or understanding; unbelievable. **2.** *Inf.* marvellous; amazing. —inˌcredi'bility *or* in'credibleness *n.* —in'credibly *adv.*

incredulity (ˌɪnkrɪ'djuːlɪtɪ) *n.* lack of belief; scepticism.

incredulous (ɪn'krɛdʒʊləs) *adj.* (often foll. by *of*) not prepared or willing to believe (something); unbelieving. —in'credulously *adv.* —in'credulousness *n.*

increment ('ɪnkrɪmənt) *n.* **1.** an increase or addition, esp. one of a series. **2.** the act of increasing; augmentation. **3.** *Maths.* a small positive or negative change in a variable or function. —ˌincre'mental (ˌɪnkrɪ'mɛntəl) *adj.*

incriminate (ɪn'krɪmɪˌneɪt) *vb.* (*tr.*) **1.** to imply or suggest the guilt or error of (someone). **2.** to charge with a crime or fault. —in'crimiˌnation *n.* —in'crimiˌnator *n.* —in'criminatory *adj.*

incrust (ɪn'krʌst) *vb.* a variant spelling of **encrust.** —in'crustant *n.*, *adj.* —ˌincrus'tation *n.*

incubate ('ɪnkjʊˌbeɪt) *vb.* **1.** (of birds) to supply (eggs) with heat for their development, esp. by sitting on them. **2.** to cause (bacteria, etc.) to develop, esp. in an incubator or culture medium. **3.** (*intr.*) (of embryos, etc.) to develop in favourable conditions, esp. in an incubator. **4.** (*intr.*) (of disease germs) to remain inactive in an animal or human before causing disease. **5.** to develop gradually; foment or be fomented. —ˌincu'bation *n.* —ˌincu'bational *adj.* —'incuˌbative *or* 'incuˌbatory *adj.*

incubator ('ɪnkjʊˌbeɪtə) *n.* **1.** *Med.* an apparatus for housing prematurely born babies until they are strong enough to survive. **2.** a container in which birds' eggs can be artificially hatched or bacterial cultures grown. **3.** a person, animal, or thing that incubates.

incubus ('ɪnkjʊbəs) *n.*, *pl.* **-bi** (-ˌbaɪ) *or* **-buses.** **1.** a demon believed in folklore to have sexual intercourse with sleeping women. Cf. **succubus.** **2.** something that oppresses or disturbs greatly, esp. a nightmare or obsession.

inculcate ('ɪnkʌlˌkeɪt, ɪn'kʌlkeɪt) *vb.* (*tr.*) to instil by insistent repetition. —ˌincul'cation *n.* —'inculˌcator *n.*

inculpate ('ɪnkʌlˌpeɪt, ɪn'kʌlpeɪt) *vb.* (*tr.*) to incriminate; cause blame to be imputed to. —ˌincul'pation *n.* —inculpative (ɪn'kʌlpətɪv) *or* inculpatory (ɪn'kʌlpətərɪ, -trɪ) *adj.*

incumbency (ɪn'kʌmbənsɪ) *n.*, *pl.* **-cies.** **1.** the state or quality of being incumbent. **2.** the office, duty, or tenure of an incumbent.

incumbent (ɪn'kʌmbənt) *adj.* **1.** *Formal.* (often *postpositive* and foll. by *on* or *upon* and an infinitive) morally binding; obligatory: *it is incumbent on me to attend.* **2.** (usually *postpositive* and foll. by *on*) resting or lying (on). **3.** (usually *prenominal*) occupying or holding an office. ~*n.* **4.** a person who holds an office, esp. a clergyman holding a benefice.

incunabula (ˌɪnkjʊ'næbjʊlə) *pl. n.*, *sing.* **-lum** (-ləm). **1.** any book printed before 1500. **2.** the earliest stages of something; beginnings. —ˌincu'nabular *adj.*

incur (ɪn'kɜː) *vb.* **-curring, -curred.** (*tr.*) **1.** to make oneself subject to (something undesirable); bring upon oneself. **2.** to run into or encounter. —in'currable *adj.*

inconspicuous camouflaged, hidden, insignificant, modest, muted, ordinary, plain, quiet, retiring, unassuming, unnoticeable, unobtrusive, unostentatious

incontestable beyond doubt, beyond question, certain, incontrovertible, indisputable, indubitable, irrefutable, self-evident, sure, undeniable, unquestionable

incontinent 1. unbridled, unchecked, uncontrollable, uncontrolled, ungovernable, ungoverned, unrestrained 2. debauched, lascivious, lecherous, lewd, loose, lustful, profligate, promiscuous, unchaste, wanton

incontrovertible beyond dispute, certain, established, incontestable, indisputable, indubitable, irrefutable, positive, sure, undeniable, unquestionable, unshakable

inconvenience n. 1. annoyance, awkwardness, bother, difficulty, disadvantage, disruption, disturbance, drawback, fuss, hindrance, nuisance, trouble, uneasiness, upset, vexation 2. awkwardness, cumbersomeness, unfitness, unhandiness, unsuitableness, untimeliness, unwieldiness ~v. 3. bother, discommode, disrupt, disturb, give (someone) bother *or* trouble, irk, make (someone) go out of his way, put out, put to trouble, trouble, upset

inconvenient 1. annoying, awkward, bothersome, disadvantageous, disturbing, embarrassing, inopportune, tiresome, troublesome, unseasonable, unsuitable, untimely, vexatious 2. awkward, cumbersome, difficult, unhandy, unmanageable, unwieldy

incorporate absorb, amalgamate, assimilate, blend, coalesce, combine, consolidate, embody, fuse, include, integrate, merge, mix, subsume, unite

incorrect erroneous, false, faulty, flawed, improper, inaccurate, inappropriate, inexact, mistaken, out, specious, unfitting, unsuitable, untrue, wide of the mark (*Inf.*), wrong

incorrectness erroneousness, error, fallacy, faultiness, impreciseness, imprecision, impropriety, inaccuracy, inexactness, speciousness, unsoundness, unsuitability, wrongness

incorrigible hardened, hopeless, incurable, intractable, inveterate, irredeemable, unreformed

incorruptibility honesty, honour, integrity, justness, uprightness

incorruptible 1. above suspicion, honest, honourable, just, straight, trustworthy, unbribable, upright 2. everlasting, imperishable, undecaying

increase v. 1. add to, advance, aggrandize, amplify, augment, boost, build up, develop, dilate, enhance, enlarge, escalate, expand, extend, grow, heighten, inflate, intensify, magnify, mount, multiply, prolong, raise, snowball, spread, step up (*Inf.*), strengthen, swell, wax ~n. 2. addition, augmentation, boost, development, enlargement, escalation, expansion, extension, gain,

growth, increment, intensification, rise, upsurge, upturn 3. **on the increase** developing, escalating, expanding, growing, increasing, multiplying, on the rise, proliferating, spreading

increasingly more and more, progressively, to an increasing extent

incredible 1. absurd, beyond belief, farfetched, implausible, impossible, improbable, inconceivable, preposterous, unbelievable, unimaginable, unthinkable 2. *Inf.* ace (*Inf.*), amazing, astonishing, astounding, awe-inspiring, extraordinary, far-out (*Sl.*), great, marvellous, prodigious, superhuman, wonderful

incredulity disbelief, distrust, doubt, scepticism, unbelief

incredulous disbelieving, distrustful, doubtful, doubting, dubious, mistrustful, sceptical, suspicious, unbelieving, unconvinced

increment accretion, accrual, accruement, addition, advancement, augmentation, enlargement, gain, increase, step (up)

incriminate accuse, arraign, blacken the name of, blame, charge, impeach, implicate, inculpate, indict, involve, point the finger at (*Inf.*), stigmatize

incumbent binding, compulsory, mandatory, necessary, obligatory

incur arouse, bring (upon oneself), contract, draw, earn, expose oneself to, gain, induce, lay oneself open to, meet with, provoke

incurable (ɪn'kjuərəbəl) *adj.* **1.** (esp. of a disease) not curable; unresponsive to treatment. ~*n.* **2.** a person having an incurable disease. —**in,cura'bility** *or* **in'curableness** *n.* —**in'curably** *adv.*

incursion (ɪn'kɜːʃən) *n.* **1.** a sudden invasion, attack, or raid. **2.** the act of running or leaking into; penetration. —**incursive** (ɪn'kɜːsɪv) *adj.*

ind. *abbrev. for:* **1.** independence. **2.** independent. **3.** index. **4.** indicative. **5.** indirect. **6.** industrial. **7.** industry.

Ind. *abbrev. for:* **1.** Independent. **2.** India. **3.** Indian. **4.** Indies.

indaba (ɪn'dɑːbə) *n.* **1.** (among Bantu peoples of southern Africa) a meeting to discuss a serious topic. **2.** *S. African inf.* a matter of concern or for discussion.

indebted (ɪn'dɛtɪd) *adj.* (*postpositive*) **1.** owing gratitude for help, favours, etc.; obligated. **2.** owing money.

indebtedness (ɪn'dɛtɪdnɪs) *n.* **1.** the state of being indebted. **2.** the total of a person's debts.

indecency (ɪn'diːsənsɪ) *n., pl.* **-cies. 1.** the state or quality of being indecent. **2.** an indecent act, etc.

indecent (ɪn'diːsənt) *adj.* **1.** offensive to standards of decency, esp. in sexual matters. **2.** unseemly or improper (esp. in **indecent haste**). —**in'decently** *adv.*

indecisive (,ɪndɪ'saɪsɪv) *adj.* **1.** (of a person) vacillating; irresolute. **2.** not decisive or conclusive. —**,inde'cision** *or* **,inde'cisiveness** *n.* —**,inde'cisively** *adv.*

indeed (ɪn'diːd) **1.** (*sentence connector*) certainly; actually: *indeed, it may never happen.* ~*adv.* **2.** (intensifier): *that is indeed amazing.* **3.** or rather; what is more: *a comfortable, indeed wealthy family.* ~*interj.* **4.** an expression of doubt, surprise, etc.

indef. *abbrev. for* indefinite.

indefatigable (,ɪndɪ'fætɪgəbəl) *adj.* unable to be tired out; unflagging. —**,inde,fatiga'bility** *n.* —**,inde'fatigably** *adv.*

indefensible (,ɪndɪ'fɛnsəbəl) *adj.* **1.** not justifiable or excusable. **2.** capable of being disagreed with; untenable. **3.** incapable of defence against attack. —**,inde,fensi'bility** *n.* —**,inde'fensibly** *adv.*

indefinite (ɪn'dɛfɪnɪt) *adj.* **1.** not certain or determined; unsettled. **2.** without exact limits; indeterminate: *an indefinite number.* **3.** vague, evasive, or unclear. **4.** in traditional logic, a proposition in which it is not stated whether the subject is universal or particular, as in *men are mortal.* —**in'definitely** *adv.* —**in'definiteness** *n.*

indefinite article *n. Grammar.* a determiner that expresses nonspecificity of reference, such as *a, an,* or *some.*

indelible (ɪn'dɛlɪbəl) *adj.* **1.** incapable of being erased or obliterated. **2.** making indelible marks: *indelible ink.* —**in,deli'bility** *or* **in'delibleness** *n.* —**in'delibly** *adv.*

indelicate (ɪn'dɛlɪkɪt) *adj.* **1.** coarse, crude, or rough. **2.** offensive, embarrassing, or tasteless. —**in'delicacy** *or*

in'delicateness *n.* —**in'delicately** *adv.*

indemnify (ɪn'dɛmnɪ,faɪ) *vb.* **-fying, -fied.** (*tr.*) **1.** to secure against future loss, damage, or liability; give security for; insure. **2.** to compensate for loss, etc.; reimburse. —**in,demnifi'cation** *n.* —**in'demni,fier** *n.*

indemnity (ɪn'dɛmnɪtɪ) *n., pl.* **-ties. 1.** compensation for loss or damage; reimbursement. **2.** protection or insurance against future loss or damage. **3.** legal exemption from penalties incurred through one's acts or defaults. **4.** *Canad.* the annual salary paid by the government to a member of Parliament or of a provincial legislature.

indent[1] *vb.* (ɪn'dɛnt). (*mainly tr.*) **1.** to place (written matter, etc.) in from the margin. **2.** to cut (a document in duplicate) so that the irregular lines may be matched. **3.** *Chiefly Brit.* (in foreign trade) to place an order for (foreign goods). **4.** (when *intr.*, foll. by *for,* on, or *upon*) *Chiefly Brit.* to make an order on (a source of supply) or for (something). **5.** to notch (an edge, border, etc.); make jagged. **6.** to bind (an apprentice, etc.) by indenture. ~*n.* ('ɪn,dɛnt). **7.** *Chiefly Brit.* (in foreign trade) an order for foreign merchandise. **8.** *Chiefly Brit.* an official order for goods. —**in'denter** *or* **in'dentor** *n.*

indent[2] *vb.* (ɪn'dɛnt). **1.** (*tr.*) to make a dent or depression in. ~*n.* ('ɪn,dɛnt). **2.** a dent or depression.

indentation (,ɪndɛn'teɪʃən) *n.* **1.** a hollowed, notched, or cut place, as on an edge or on a coastline. **2.** a series of hollows, notches, or cuts. **3.** the act of indenting or the condition of being indented. **4.** Also called: **indention, indent.** the leaving of space or the amount of space left between a margin and the start of an indented line.

indention (ɪn'dɛnʃən) *n.* another word for **indentation** (sense 4).

indenture (ɪn'dɛntʃə) *n.* **1.** any deed, contract, or sealed agreement between two or more parties. **2.** (formerly) a deed drawn up in duplicate, each part having correspondingly indented edges for identification and security. **3.** (*often pl.*) a contract between an apprentice and his master. **4.** a less common word for **indentation.** ~*vb.* **5.** (*intr.*) to enter into an agreement by indenture. **6.** (*tr.*) to bind (an apprentice, servant, etc.) by indenture. —**in'denture,ship** *n.*

independence (,ɪndɪ'pɛndəns) *n.* the state or quality of being independent. Also: **independency.**

independent (,ɪndɪ'pɛndənt) *adj.* **1.** free from control in action, judgment, etc.; autonomous. **2.** not dependent on anything else for function, validity, etc.; separate. **3.** not reliant on the support, esp. financial support, of others. **4.** capable of acting for oneself or on one's own: *a very independent little girl.* **5.** providing a large unearned sum towards one's support (esp. in **independent income, independent means**). **6.** living on an unearned income. **7.** *Maths.* (of a system of equations) not all satisfied by the same set of values for the variables. **8.** *Logic.* (of two or more propositions) unrelated. ~*n.* **9.** an independent person or thing. **10.** a person who is not af-

═══════ **THESAURUS** ═══════

incurable *adj.* **1.** dyed-in-the-wool, hopeless, incorrigible, inveterate **2.** fatal, inoperable, irrecoverable, irremediable, remediless, terminal

indebted beholden, grateful, in debt, obligated, obliged, under an obligation

indecency bawdiness, coarseness, crudity, foulness, grossness, immodesty, impropriety, impurity, indecorum, indelicacy, lewdness, licentiousness, obscenity, outrageousness, pornography, smut, smuttiness, unseemliness, vileness, vulgarity

indecent **1.** blue, coarse, crude, dirty, filthy, foul, gross, immodest, improper, impure, indelicate, lewd, licentious, pornographic, salacious, scatological, smutty, vile **2.** ill-bred, improper, in bad taste, indecorous, offensive, outrageous, tasteless, unbecoming, unseemly, vulgar

indecipherable crabbed, illegible, indistinguishable, unintelligible, unreadable

indecision ambivalence, doubt, hesitancy, hesitation, indecisiveness, irresolution, shilly-shallying (*Inf.*), uncertainty, vacillation, wavering

indecisive 1. doubtful, faltering, hesitating, in two minds (*Inf.*), irresolute, pussyfoot-

ing (*Inf.*), tentative, uncertain, undecided, undetermined, vacillating, wavering **2.** inconclusive, indefinite, indeterminate, unclear, undecided

indeed actually, certainly, doubtlessly, in point of fact, in truth, positively, really, strictly, to be sure, truly, undeniably, undoubtedly, verily (*Archaic*), veritably

indefensible faulty, inexcusable, insupportable, unforgivable, unjustifiable, unpardonable, untenable, unwarrantable, wrong

indefinable dim, hazy, impalpable, indescribable, indistinct, inexpressible, nameless, obscure, unrealized, vague

indefinite ambiguous, confused, doubtful, equivocal, evasive, general, ill-defined, imprecise, indeterminate, indistinct, inexact, loose, obscure, uncertain, unclear, undefined, undetermined, unfixed, unknown, unlimited, unsettled, vague

indefinitely continually, endlessly, for ever, *sine die*

indelible enduring, indestructible, ineffaceable, ineradicable, inexpungible, inextirpable, ingrained, lasting, permanent

indelicacy bad taste, coarseness, crudity, grossness, immodesty, impropriety, inde-

cency, obscenity, offensiveness, rudeness, smuttiness, suggestiveness, tastelessness, vulgarity

indelicate blue, coarse, crude, embarrassing, gross, immodest, improper, indecent, indecorous, low, near the knuckle (*Inf.*), obscene, off-colour, offensive, risqué, rude, suggestive, tasteless, unbecoming, unseemly, untoward, vulgar

indemnify 1. endorse, guarantee, insure, protect, secure, underwrite **2.** compensate, pay, reimburse, remunerate, repair, repay, requite, satisfy

indemnity 1. guarantee, insurance, protection, security **2.** compensation, redress, reimbursement, remuneration, reparation, requital, restitution, satisfaction **3.** *Law* exemption, immunity, impunity, privilege

indent *v.* **1.** ask for, order, request, requisition **2.** cut, dint, mark, nick, notch, pink, scallop, score, serrate

independence autarchy, autonomy, freedom, home rule, liberty, self-determination, self-government, self-reliance, self-rule, self-sufficiency, separation, sovereignty

filiated to or who acts independently of a political party. —,inde'pendently adv.

independent clause n. Grammar. a main or coordinate clause.

independent school n. (in Britain) a school that is neither financed nor controlled by the government or local authorities.

indescribable (,ındı'skraıbəbəl) adj. beyond description; too intense, extreme, etc., for words. —,inde,scriba'bility n. —,inde'scribably adv.

indeterminate (,ındı'tɜ:mınıt) adj. 1. uncertain in extent, amount, or nature. 2. not definite; inconclusive: an indeterminate reply. 3. unable to be predicted, calculated, or deduced. 4. Maths. a. having no numerical meaning, as 0/0. b. (of an equation) having more than one variable and an unlimited number of solutions. —,inde'terminacy or ,inde'terminateness n. —,inde'terminately adv.

index ('ındɛks) n., pl. -dexes or -dices (-dı,si:z). 1. an alphabetical list of persons, subjects, etc., mentioned in a printed work, usually at the back, and indicating where they are referred to. 2. See **thumb index.** 3. Library science. a systematic list of book titles or authors' names, giving cross-references and the location of each book; catalogue. 4. an indication, sign, or token. 5. a pointer, needle, or other indicator, as on an instrument. 6. Maths. a. another name for **exponent** (sense 4). b. a number or variable placed as a superscript to the left of a radical sign indicating the root to be extracted, as in $^3\sqrt{8} = 2$. 7. a numerical scale by means of which levels of the cost of living can be compared with some base number. 8. a number or ratio indicating a specific characteristic, property, etc.: refractive index. 9. Also called: **fist.** a printer's mark ☞ used to indicate notes, paragraphs, etc. ~vb. (tr.) 10. to put an index in (a book). 11. to enter (a word, item, etc.) in an index. 12. to point out; indicate. —'indexer n. —in'dexical adj. —'indexless adj.

indexation (,ındɛk'seıʃən) or **index-linking** n. the act of making wages, interest rates, etc., index-linked.

index finger n. the finger next to the thumb. Also called: **forefinger.**

index-linked adj. (of wages, interest, etc.) directly related to the cost-of-living index and rising accordingly.

Indiaman ('ındıəmən) n., pl. -men. (formerly) a large merchant ship engaged in trade with India.

Indian ('ındıən) n. 1. a native or inhabitant of the Republic of India, in a subcontinent of Asia. 2. an American Indian. 3. (not in scholarly usage) any of the languages of the American Indians. ~adj. 4. of or relating to India, its inhabitants, or any of their languages. 5. of or relating to the American Indians or any of their languages.

Indian club n. a bottle-shaped club, usually used in pairs by gymnasts, jugglers, etc.

Indian corn n. another name for **maize** (sense 1).

Indian file n. another term for **single file.**

Indian hemp n. another name for **hemp,** esp. the variety **cannabis indica,** from which several narcotic drugs are obtained.

Indian ink or esp. U.S. **India ink** ('ındıə) n. 1. a black pigment made from a mixture of lampblack and a binding agent such as gelatin or glue: usually formed into solid cakes and sticks. 2. a black liquid ink made from this pigment.

Indian list n. Inf. (in Canada) a list of persons to whom spirits may not be sold.

Indian summer n. a period of unusually warm weather, esp. in the autumn.

India paper n. a thin soft opaque printing paper made in the Orient.

Indic ('ındık) adj. 1. denoting, belonging to, or relating to a branch of Indo-European consisting of certain languages of India, including Sanskrit, Hindi and Urdu. ~n. 2. this group of languages. ~Also: **Indo-Aryan.**

indicate ('ındı,keıt) vb. (tr.) 1. (may take a clause as object) to be or give a sign or symptom of; imply: cold hands indicate a warm heart. 2. to point out or show. 3. (may take a clause as object) to state briefly; suggest. 4. (of instruments) to show a reading of. 5. (usually passive) to recommend or require: surgery seems to be indicated for this patient. —'indi,catable adj. —indicatory (ın'dıkətərı, -trı) adj.

indication (,ındı'keıʃən) n. 1. something that serves to indicate or suggest; sign: an indication of foul play. 2. the degree or quantity represented on a measuring instrument or device. 3. the action of indicating. 4. something that is indicated as advisable, necessary, or expedient.

indicative (ın'dıkətıv) adj. 1. (usually postpositive; foll. by of) serving as a sign; suggestive: indicative of trouble ahead. 2. Grammar. denoting a mood of verbs used chiefly to make statements. ~n. 3. Grammar. a. the indicative mood. b. a verb in the indicative mood. ~Abbrev.: **indic.** —in'dicatively adv.

indicator ('ındı,keıtə) n. 1. a device to attract attention, such as the pointer of a gauge or a warning lamp. 2. an instrument that displays certain operating conditions in a machine, such as a gauge showing temperature, etc. 3. Also called: **blinkers.** a device for indicating that a motor vehicle is about to turn left or right, esp. two pairs of lights that flash. 4. a delicate measuring instrument used to determine small differences in the height of mechanical components. 5. Chem. a substance used to indicate the completion of a chemical reaction, usually by a change of colour.

indices ('ındı,si:z) n. a plural of **index.**

indict (ın'daıt) vb. (tr.) to charge (a person) with crime, esp. formally in writing; accuse. —indict'ee n. —in'dicter or in'dictor n. —in'dictable adj.

indictment (ın'daıtmənt) n. Criminal law. 1. a formal written charge of crime formerly referred to and presented on oath by a grand jury. 2. any formal accusation of crime. 3. the act of indicting or the state of being indicted.

indifference (ın'dıfrəns, -fərəns) n. 1. the fact or state of being indifferent; lack of care or concern. 2. lack of quality; mediocrity. 3. lack of importance; insignificance.

indifferent (ın'dıfrənt, -fərənt) adj. 1. (often foll. by to) showing no care or concern; uninterested: he was indifferent to my pleas. 2. unimportant; immaterial. 3. a. of only average or moderate size, extent, quality, etc. b. not at all good; poor. 4. showing or having no preferences; impartial. —in'differently adv.

THESAURUS

independent 1. absolute, free, liberated, separate, unconnected, unconstrained, uncontrolled, unrelated 2. autarchic, autarchical, autonomous, decontrolled, nonaligned, self-determining, self-governing, separated, sovereign 3. bold, individualistic, liberated, self-contained, self-reliant, self-sufficient, self-supporting, unaided, unconventional

independently alone, autonomously, by oneself, individually, on one's own, separately, solo, unaided

indescribable beggaring description, beyond description, beyond words, incommunicable, indefinable, ineffable, inexpressible, unutterable

indestructible abiding, durable, enduring, everlasting, immortal, imperishable, incorruptible, indelible, indissoluble, lasting, nonperishable, permanent, unbreakable,

unfading

indeterminate imprecise, inconclusive, indefinite, inexact, uncertain, undefined, undetermined, unfixed, unspecified, unstipulated, vague

index 1. clue, guide, indication, mark, sign, symptom, token 2. director, forefinger, hand, indicator, needle, pointer

indicate 1. add up to (Inf.), bespeak, be symptomatic of, betoken, denote, evince, imply, manifest, point to, reveal, show, signify, suggest 2. designate, point out, point to, specify 3. display, express, mark, read, record, register, show

indication clue, evidence, explanation, forewarning, hint, index, inkling, intimation, manifestation, mark, note, omen, portent, sign, signal, suggestion, symptom, warning

indicative exhibitive, indicatory, indi-

cial, pointing to, significant, suggestive, symptomatic

indicator display, gauge, guide, index, mark, marker, meter, pointer, sign, signal, signpost, symbol

indict accuse, arraign, charge, impeach, prosecute, serve with a summons, summon, summons, tax

indictment accusation, allegation, charge, impeachment, prosecution, summons

indifference 1. absence of feeling, aloofness, apathy, callousness, carelessness, coldness, coolness, detachment, disregard, heedlessness, inattention, lack of interest, negligence, stoicalness, unconcern 2. disinterestedness, dispassion, equity, impartiality, neutrality, objectivity 3. insignificance, irrelevance, triviality, unimportance

indigenous (ɪnˈdɪdʒɪnəs) adj. (when postpositive, foll. by to) **1.** originating or occurring naturally (in a country, etc.); native. **2.** innate (to); inherent (in). —in'digenously adv. —in'digenousness n.

indigent ('ɪndɪdʒənt) adj. **1.** so poor as to lack even necessities; very needy. **2.** (usually foll. by of) Arch. lacking (in) or destitute (of). ~n. **3.** an impoverished person. —'indigence n. —'indigently adv.

indigestible (ˌɪndɪˈdʒɛstəbəl) adj. **1.** incapable of being digested or difficult to digest. **2.** difficult to understand or absorb mentally: an indigestible book. —ˌindiˌgesti'bility n. —ˌindi'gestibly adv.

indigestion (ˌɪndɪˈdʒɛstʃən) n. difficulty in digesting food, accompanied by abdominal pain, heartburn, and belching.

indignant (ɪnˈdɪgnənt) adj. feeling or showing indignation. —in'dignantly adv.

indignation (ˌɪndɪgˈneɪʃən) n. anger or scorn aroused by something felt to be unfair, unworthy, or wrong.

indignity (ɪnˈdɪgnɪtɪ) n., pl. -ties. injury to one's self-esteem or dignity; humiliation.

indigo ('ɪndɪˌgəʊ) n., pl. -gos or -goes. **1.** a blue vat dye originally obtained from plants but now made synthetically. **2.** any of various leguminous tropical plants, such as the anil, that yield this dye. **3.** a. any of a group of colours that have the same blue-violet hue; a spectral colour. b. (as adj.): an indigo carpet. —indigotic (ˌɪndɪˈgɒtɪk) adj.

indirect (ˌɪndɪˈrɛkt) adj. **1.** deviating from a direct course or line; roundabout; circuitous. **2.** not coming as a direct effect or consequence; secondary: indirect benefits. **3.** not straightforward, open, or fair; devious or evasive. —ˌindi'rectly adv. —ˌindi'rectness n.

indirect lighting n. reflected or diffused light from a concealed source.

indirect object n. Grammar. a noun, pronoun, or noun phrase indicating the recipient or beneficiary of the action of a verb and its direct object, as John in the sentence I bought John a newspaper.

indirect speech or esp. U.S. **indirect discourse** n. the reporting of something said or written by conveying what was meant rather than repeating the exact words, as in the sentence He asked me whether I would go as opposed to He asked me, "Will you go?" Also called: **reported speech.**

indirect tax n. a tax levied on goods or services ra-

ther than on individuals or companies.

indiscreet (ˌɪndɪˈskriːt) adj. not discreet; imprudent or tactless. —ˌindis'creetly adv. —ˌindis'creetness n.

indiscrete (ˌɪndɪˈskriːt) adj. not divisible or divided into parts.

indiscretion (ˌɪndɪˈskrɛʃən) n. **1.** the characteristic or state of being indiscreet. **2.** an indiscreet act, remark, etc.

indiscriminate (ˌɪndɪˈskrɪmɪnɪt) adj. **1.** lacking discrimination or careful choice; random or promiscuous. **2.** jumbled; confused. —ˌindis'criminately adv. —ˌindis'criminateness n. —ˌindis,crimi'nation n.

indispensable (ˌɪndɪˈspɛnsəbəl) adj. **1.** absolutely necessary; essential. **2.** not to be disregarded or escaped: an indispensable role. ~n. **3.** an indispensable person or thing. —ˌindis,pensa'bility or ˌindis'pensableness n. —ˌindis'pensably adv.

indisposed (ˌɪndɪˈspəʊzd) adj. **1.** sick or ill. **2.** unwilling. —**indisposition** (ˌɪndɪspəˈzɪʃən) n.

indistinct (ˌɪndɪˈstɪŋkt) adj. incapable of being clearly distinguished, as by the eyes, ears, or mind; not distinct. —ˌindis'tinctly adv. —ˌindis'tinctness n.

indite (ɪnˈdaɪt) vb. (tr.) Arch. to write. —in'ditement n. —in'diter n.

indium ('ɪndɪəm) n. a rare soft silvery metallic element associated with zinc ores: used in alloys, electronics, and electroplating. Symbol: In; atomic no.: 49; atomic wt.: 114.82.

individual (ˌɪndɪˈvɪdjʊəl) adj. **1.** of, relating to, characteristic of, or meant for a single person or thing. **2.** separate or distinct, esp. from others of its kind; particular: please mark the individual pages. **3.** characterized by unusual and striking qualities; distinctive. **4.** Obs. indivisible; inseparable. ~n. **5.** a single person, esp. when regarded as distinct from others. **6.** Biol. a single animal or plant, esp. as distinct from a species. —ˌindi'vidually adv.

▷ **Usage.** In careful speech and writing, the noun individual is not loosely used as a synonym of person, although it is appropriate in that sense when a single person is being considered in contrast to a group, as in in mass democracy the rights of the individual must be protected.

individualism (ˌɪndɪˈvɪdjʊəˌlɪzəm) n. **1.** the principle of asserting one's independence and individuality; egoism. **2.** an individual quirk. **3.** another word for laissez faire (sense 1). **4.** Philosophy. the doctrine that only individual things exist. —ˌindi'vidualist n.

THESAURUS

indifferent 1. aloof, apathetic, callous, careless, cold, cool, detached, distant, heedless, impervious, inattentive, regardless, uncaring, unconcerned, unimpressed, uninterested, unmoved, unresponsive, unsympathetic **2.** immaterial, insignificant, of no consequence, unimportant **3.** average, fair, mediocre, middling, moderate, ordinary, passable, perfunctory, so-so (Inf.), undistinguished, uninspired **4.** disinterested, dispassionate, equitable, impartial, neutral, nonaligned, nonpartisan, objective, unbiased, uninvolved, unprejudiced

indigent destitute, impecunious, impoverished, in want, necessitous, needy, on one's uppers (Inf.), penniless, penurious, poor, poverty-stricken, straitened

indigestion dyspepsia, dyspepsy, upset stomach

indignant angry, annoyed, disgruntled, exasperated, fuming (Inf.), furious, heated, huffy (Inf.), in a huff, incensed, in high dudgeon, irate, livid (Inf.), mad (Inf.), miffed (Inf.), narked (Sl.), peeved (Inf.), provoked, resentful, riled, scornful, seeing red (Inf.), sore (Inf.), up in arms (Inf.), wrathful

indignation anger, exasperation, fury, ire (Literary), pique, rage, resentment, righteous anger, scorn, umbrage, wrath

indignity abuse, affront, contumely, dishonour, disrespect, humiliation, injury, insult, obloquy, opprobrium, outrage, reproach, slap in the face (Inf.), slight, snub

indirect 1. backhanded, circuitous, circumlocutory, crooked, devious, long-drawn-out, meandering, oblique, periphrastic, ram-

bling, roundabout, tortuous, wandering, winding, zigzag **2.** ancillary, collateral, contingent, incidental, secondary, subsidiary, unintended

indirectly by implication, circumlocutorily, in a roundabout way, obliquely, periphrastically, second-hand

indiscernible hidden, impalpable, imperceptible, indistinct, indistinguishable, invisible, unapparent, undiscernible

indiscreet foolish, hasty, heedless, ill-advised, ill-considered, ill-judged, impolitic, imprudent, incautious, injudicious, naive, rash, reckless, tactless, undiplomatic, unthinking, unwise

indiscretion error, faux pas, folly, foolishness, gaffe, gaucherie, imprudence, mistake, rashness, recklessness, slip, slip of the tongue, tactlessness

indiscriminate 1. aimless, careless, desultory, general, hit or miss (Inf.), random, sweeping, uncritical, undiscriminating, unmethodical, unselective, unsystematic, wholesale **2.** chaotic, confused, haphazard, higgledy-piggledy (Inf.), jumbled, mingled, miscellaneous, mixed, mongrel, motley, promiscuous, undistinguishable

indispensable crucial, essential, imperative, key, necessary, needed, needful, requisite, vital

indisposed 1. ailing, confined to bed, ill, laid up (Inf.), on the sick list (Inf.), poorly (Inf.), sick, unwell **2.** averse, disinclined, loath, reluctant, unwilling

indisposition 1. ailment, ill health, illness, sickness **2.** aversion, disinclination, dis-

like, distaste, hesitancy, reluctance, unwillingness

indisputable absolute, beyond doubt, certain, evident, incontestable, incontrovertible, indubitable, irrefutable, positive, sure, unassailable, undeniable, unquestionable

indissoluble abiding, binding, enduring, eternal, fixed, imperishable, incorruptible, indestructible, inseparable, lasting, permanent, solid, unbreakable

indistinct ambiguous, bleary, blurred, confused, dim, doubtful, faint, fuzzy, hazy, ill-defined, indefinite, indeterminate, indiscernible, indistinguishable, misty, muffled, obscure, out of focus, shadowy, unclear, undefined, unintelligible, vague, weak

indistinguishable 1. alike, identical, like as two peas in a pod (Inf.), (the) same, twin **2.** imperceptible, indiscernible, invisible, obscure

individual 1. adj. characteristic, discrete, distinct, distinctive, exclusive, identical, idiosyncratic, own, particular, peculiar, personal, personalized, proper, respective, separate, several, single, singular, special, specific, unique **2.** n. being, body (Inf.), character, creature, mortal, party, person, personage, soul, type, unit

individualism egocentricity, egoism, freethinking, independence, originality, self-direction, self-interest, self-reliance

individualist freethinker, independent, loner, lone wolf, maverick, nonconformist, original

individuality (ˌɪndɪˌvɪdjʊˈælɪtɪ) n., pl. **-ties.** **1.** distinctive or unique character or personality: *a work of great individuality.* **2.** the qualities that distinguish one person or thing from another; identity. **3.** the state or quality of being a separate entity; discreteness.

individualize or **-ise** (ˌɪndɪˈvɪdjʊəˌlaɪz) vb. (tr.) **1.** to make or mark as individual or distinctive in character. **2.** to consider or treat individually; particularize. **3.** to make or modify so as to meet the special requirements of a person. —ˌindiˌvidualiˈzation or -iˈsation n. —ˌindi-ˈvidualˌizer or -ˌiser n.

indivisible (ˌɪndɪˈvɪzəbəl) adj. **1.** unable to be divided. **2.** Maths. leaving a remainder when divided by a given number. —ˌindiˌvisiˈbility n. —ˌindiˈvisibly adv.

Indo- (ˈɪndəʊ-) combining form. denoting India or Indian: *Indo-European.*

indoctrinate (ɪnˈdɒktrɪˌneɪt) vb. (tr.) **1.** to teach (a person or group of people) systematically to accept doctrines, esp. uncritically. **2.** Rare. to instruct. —inˌdoctriˈnation n. —inˈdoctriˌnator n.

Indo-European adj. **1.** denoting, belonging to, or relating to a family of languages that includes English: characteristically marked by inflection showing gender, number, and case. **2.** denoting or relating to the hypothetical parent language of this family, primitive Indo-European. **3.** denoting, belonging to, or relating to any of the peoples speaking these languages. ~n. **4.** the Indo-European family of languages. **5.** the reconstructed hypothetical parent language of this family.

indolent (ˈɪndələnt) adj. **1.** disliking work or effort; lazy; idle. **2.** Pathol. causing little pain: *an indolent tumour.* **3.** (esp. of a painless ulcer) slow to heal. —ˈindolence n. —ˈindolently adv.

indomitable (ɪnˈdɒmɪtəbəl) adj. (of courage, pride, etc.) difficult or impossible to defeat or subdue. —inˌdomitaˈbility or inˈdomitableness n. —inˈdomitably adv.

Indonesian (ˌɪndəʊˈniːzɪən) adj. **1.** of or relating to Indonesia, a republic in SE Asia, its people, or their language. ~n. **2.** a native or inhabitant of Indonesia. **3.** a branch of the Malayo-Polynesian family of languages.

indoor (ˈɪnˌdɔː) adj. (prenominal) of, situated in, or appropriate to the inside of a house or other building: *an indoor tennis court; indoor amusements.*

indoors (ˌɪnˈdɔːz) adv., adj. (postpositive) inside or into a house or other building.

indorse (ɪnˈdɔːs) vb. a variant spelling of **endorse**.

indrawn (ˌɪnˈdrɔːn) adj. **1.** drawn or pulled in. **2.** inward-looking or introspective.

indubitable (ɪnˈdjuːbɪtəbəl) adj. incapable of being doubted; unquestionable. —inˈdubitably adv.

induce (ɪnˈdjuːs) vb. (tr.) **1.** (often foll. by an infinitive) to persuade or use influence on. **2.** to cause or bring about. **3.** Med. to initiate or hasten (labour), as by administering a drug to stimulate uterine contractions. **4.** Logic. to assert or establish (a general proposition, etc.) by induction. **5.** to produce (an electromotive force or electrical current) by induction. **6.** to transmit (magnetism) by induction. —inˈducer n. —inˈducible adj.

inducement (ɪnˈdjuːsmənt) n. **1.** the act of inducing. **2.** a means of inducing; persuasion; incentive. **3.** Law. the introductory part that leads up to and explains the matter in dispute.

induct (ɪnˈdʌkt) vb. (tr.) **1.** to bring in formally or install in an office, place, etc.; invest. **2.** (foll. by to or into) to initiate in knowledge (of). **3.** U.S. to enlist for military service. **4.** Physics. another word for **induce** (senses 5, 6).

inductance (ɪnˈdʌktəns) n. **1.** the property of an electric circuit as a result of which an electromotive force is created by a change of current in the same or in a neighbouring circuit. **2.** a component, such as a coil, in an electrical circuit, the main function of which is to produce inductance.

induction (ɪnˈdʌkʃən) n. **1.** the act of inducting or state of being inducted. **2.** the act of inducing. **3.** Logic. **a.** a process of reasoning by which a general conclusion is drawn from a set of premises, based mainly on experience or experimental evidence. **b.** a conclusion reached by this process of reasoning. **4.** the process by which electrical or magnetic properties are transferred, without physical contact, from one circuit or body to another. See also **inductance**. **5.** Maths. a method of proving a proposition P(n) by showing that it is true for all preceding values of n and for n + 1. **6.** a formal introduction or entry into an office or position. **7.** U.S. the enlistment of a civilian into military service. —inˈductional adj.

induction coil n. a transformer for producing a high voltage from a low voltage. It consists of a cylindrical primary winding of few turns, a concentric secondary winding of many turns, and often a common soft-iron core.

inductive (ɪnˈdʌktɪv) adj. **1.** relating to or operated by electrical or magnetic induction: *an inductive reactance.* **2.** Logic, maths. of, relating to, or using induction: *inductive reasoning.* **3.** serving to induce or cause. —inˈductively adv. —inˈductiveness n.

inductor (ɪnˈdʌktə) n. **1.** a person or thing that inducts. **2.** another name for an **inductance** (sense 2).

indue (ɪnˈdjuː) vb. a variant spelling of **endue**.

indulge (ɪnˈdʌldʒ) vb. **1.** (when intr., often foll. by in) to yield to or gratify (a whim or desire for): *to indulge in new clothes.* **2.** (tr.) to yield to the wishes of; pamper: *to indulge a child.* **3.** (tr.) to allow oneself the pleasure of: *he indulged himself.* **4.** (intr.) Inf. to take alcoholic drink, esp. to excess. —inˈdulger n. —inˈdulgingly adv.

indulgence (ɪnˈdʌldʒəns) n. **1.** the act of indulging or state of being indulgent. **2.** a pleasure, habit, etc., indulged in; extravagance. **3.** liberal or tolerant treatment. **4.** something granted as a favour or privilege. **5.** R.C. Church. a remission of the temporal punishment for sin after its guilt has been forgiven. **6.** Also called: **Declaration of Indulgence.** a royal grant during the reigns of Charles II and James II of England giving Nonconformists and Roman Catholics a measure of religious freedom.

indulgent (ɪnˈdʌldʒənt) adj. showing or characterized by indulgence. —inˈdulgently adv.

indurate vb. (ˈɪndjʊˌreɪt). **1.** to make or become hard or callous. **2.** to make or become hardy. ~adj. (ˈɪndjʊrɪt). **3.** hardened, callous, or unfeeling. —ˌinduˈration n. —ˈinduˌrative adj.

industrial (ɪnˈdʌstrɪəl) adj. **1.** of, relating to, or derived from industry. **2.** employed in industry: *the industrial work force.* **3.** relating to or concerned with workers in industry: *industrial conditions.* **4.** used in industry: *industrial chemicals.* —inˈdustrially adv.

industrial estate n. Brit. an area of land set aside for

THESAURUS

individuality character, discreteness, distinction, distinctiveness, originality, peculiarity, personality, separateness, singularity, uniqueness

individually apart, independently, one at a time, one by one, personally, separately, severally, singly

indoctrinate brainwash, drill, ground, imbue, initiate, instruct, school, teach, train

indoctrination brainwashing, drilling, grounding, inculcation, instruction, schooling, training

indolent fainéant, idle, inactive, inert, lackadaisical, languid, lazy, lethargic, listless, lumpish, slack, slothful, slow, sluggish, torpid, workshy

indomitable invincible, resolute, staunch, steadfast, unbeatable, unconquerable, unflinching, untameable, unyielding

indubitable certain, evident, incontestable, incontrovertible, indisputable, irrefutable, obvious, sure, unarguable, undeniable, undoubted, unquestionable, veritable

induce 1. actuate, convince, draw, encourage, get, impel, incite, influence, instigate, move, persuade, press, prevail upon, prompt, talk into 2. bring about, cause, effect, engender, generate, give rise to, lead to, occasion, produce, set in motion

inducement attraction, bait, carrot (Inf.), cause, come-on (Inf.), consideration, encouragement, impulse, incentive, incitement, influence, lure, motive, reward, spur, stimulus, urge

indulge 1. cater to, give way to, gratify, pander to, regale, satiate, satisfy, treat oneself to, yield to 2. With in bask in, give free rein to, give oneself up to, luxuriate in, revel

in, wallow in 3. baby, coddle, cosset, favour, foster, give in to, go along with, humour, mollycoddle, pamper, pet, spoil

indulgence 1. excess, fondness, immoderation, intemperance, intemperateness, kindness, leniency, pampering, partiality, permissiveness, profligacy, profligateness, spoiling 2. appeasement, fulfilment, gratification, satiation, satisfaction 3. extravagance, favour, luxury, privilege, treat 4. courtesy, forbearance, good will, patience, tolerance, understanding

indulgent compliant, easy-going, favourable, fond, forbearing, gentle, gratifying, kind, kindly, lenient, liberal, mild, permissive, tender, tolerant, understanding

industry and business. U.S. equivalent: **industrial park.**

industrialism (ɪnˈdʌstrɪəˌlɪzəm) n. an organization of society characterized by large-scale mechanized manufacturing industry rather than trade, farming, etc.

industrialist (ɪnˈdʌstrɪəlɪst) n. a person who has a substantial interest in the ownership or control of industrial enterprise.

industrialize or **-ise** (ɪnˈdʌstrɪəˌlaɪz) vb. **1.** (tr.) to develop industry on an extensive scale in (a country, region, etc.). **2.** (intr.) (of a country, region, etc.) to undergo the development of industry on an extensive scale. —**in‚dustriali'zation** or **-i'sation** n.

industrious (ɪnˈdʌstrɪəs) adj. hard-working, diligent, or assiduous. —**in'dustriously** adv. —**in'dustriousness** n.

industry (ˈɪndəstrɪ) n., pl. **-tries. 1.** organized economic activity concerned with manufacture, processing of raw materials, or construction. **2.** a branch of commercial enterprise concerned with the output of a specified product: *the steel industry.* **3. a.** industrial ownership and management interests collectively. **b.** manufacturing enterprise collectively, as opposed to agriculture. **4.** diligence; assiduity.

-ine¹ *suffix forming adjectives.* **1.** of, relating to, or belonging to: *saturnine.* **2.** consisting of or resembling: *crystalline.*

-ine² *suffix forming nouns.* **1.** indicating a halogen: *chlorine.* **2.** indicating a nitrogenous organic compound, including amino acids, alkaloids, and certain other bases: *nicotine.* **3.** Also: **-in.** indicating a chemical substance in certain nonsystematic names: *glycerine.* **4.** indicating a mixture of hydrocarbons: *benzine.* **5.** indicating feminine form: *heroine.*

inebriate vb. (ɪnˈiːbrɪˌeɪt). (tr.) **1.** to make drunk; intoxicate. **2.** to arouse emotionally; make excited. ~n. (ɪnˈiːbrɪt). **3.** a person who is drunk, esp. habitually. ~adj. (ɪnˈiːbrɪt), *also* **inebriated. 4.** drunk, esp. habitually. —**in‚ebri'ation** n. —**inebriety** (ˌɪnɪˈbraɪɪtɪ) n.

inedible (ɪnˈɛdɪbəl) adj. not fit to be eaten. —**in‚edi'bility** n.

▷ **Usage.** In careful speech and writing, *inedible* is not synonymous with *uneatable. Inedible* implies that something is of a sort not suitable for eating, while *uneatable* implies that it is so disgusting as to be beyond eating.

ineducable (ɪnˈɛdjʊkəbəl) adj. incapable of being educated, esp. on account of mental retardation. —**in‚edu-**

ca'bility n.

ineffable (ɪnˈɛfəbəl) adj. **1.** too great or intense to be expressed in words; unutterable. **2.** too sacred to be uttered. **3.** indescribable; indefinable. —**in‚effa'bility** or **in'effableness** n. —**in'effably** adv.

ineluctable (ˌɪnɪˈlʌktəbəl) adj. (esp. of fate) incapable of being avoided; inescapable. —**ine‚lucta'bility** n. —**ine'luctably** adv.

inept (ɪnˈɛpt) adj. **1.** not suitable, appropriate, or fitting; out of place. **2.** awkward, clumsy, or incompetent. —**in'epti‚tude** n. —**in'eptly** adv. —**in'eptness** n.

inequable (ɪnˈɛkwəbəl) adj. uneven; not uniform.

inequality (ˌɪnɪˈkwɒlɪtɪ) n., pl. **-ties. 1.** the state or quality of being unequal; disparity. **2.** an instance of disparity. **3.** lack of smoothness or regularity. **4.** social or economic disparity. **5.** *Maths.* **a.** a statement indicating that the value of one quantity or expression is not equal to another. **b.** the relation of being unequal.

inert (ɪnˈɜːt) adj. **1.** having no inherent ability to move or to resist motion. **2.** inactive, lazy, or sluggish. **3.** having only a limited ability to react chemically; unreactive. —**in'ertly** adv. —**in'ertness** n.

inertia (ɪnˈɜːʃə, -ʃɪə) n. **1.** the state of being inert; inactivity. **2.** *Physics.* **a.** the tendency of a body to preserve its state of rest or uniform motion unless acted upon by an external force. **b.** an analogous property of other physical quantities that resist change: *thermal inertia.* —**in'ertial** adj.

inertia selling n. the practice of sending unrequested goods to householders, followed by a bill for the goods if they do not return them.

inescapable (ˌɪnɪˈskeɪpəbəl) adj. incapable of being escaped or avoided. —**‚ines'capably** adv.

inestimable (ɪnˈɛstɪməbəl) adj. **1.** not able to be estimated; immeasurable. **2.** of immeasurable value. —**in‚estima'bility** or **in'estimableness** n. —**in'estimably** adv.

inevitable (ɪnˈɛvɪtəbəl) adj. **1.** unavoidable. **2.** sure to happen; certain. ~n. **3.** (often preceded by *the*) something that is unavoidable. —**in‚evita'bility** or **in'evitableness** n. —**in'evitably** adv.

inexorable (ɪnˈɛksərəbəl) adj. **1.** not able to be moved by entreaty or persuasion. **2.** relentless. —**in‚exora'bility** n. —**in'exorably** adv.

THESAURUS

industrialist baron, big businessman, boss, capitalist, captain of industry, financier, magnate, manufacturer, producer, tycoon

industrious active, assiduous, busy, conscientious, diligent, energetic, hard-working, laborious, persevering, persistent, productive, purposeful, sedulous, steady, tireless, zealous

industriously assiduously, conscientiously, diligently, doggedly, hard, like a Trojan, nose to the grindstone (*Inf.*), perseveringly, sedulously, steadily, without slacking

industry 1. business, commerce, commercial enterprise, manufacturing, production, trade **2.** activity, application, assiduity, determination, diligence, effort, labour, perseverance, persistence, tirelessness, toil, vigour, zeal

inebriated befuddled, blind drunk, blotto (*Sl.*), drunk, fou or fu' (*Scot.*), half-cut (*Inf.*), half seas over (*Inf.*), high (*Inf.*), high as a kite (*Inf.*), inebriate, in one's cups, intoxicated, legless (*Inf.*), merry, paralytic (*Inf.*), pie-eyed (*Sl.*), plastered (*Sl.*), smashed (*Sl.*), sozzled (*Inf.*), stoned (*Sl.*), the worse for drink, three sheets in the wind (*Inf.*), tight (*Inf.*), tipsy, under the influence (*Inf.*), under the weather (*Inf.*)

ineffective barren, bootless, feeble, fruitless, futile, idle, impotent, inadequate, ineffectual, inefficacious, inefficient, unavailing, unproductive, useless, vain, weak, worthless

ineffectual abortive, bootless, emasculate, feeble, fruitless, futile, idle, impotent, inadequate, incompetent, ineffective, inefficacious, inefficient, inept, lame, powerless, unavailing, useless, vain, weak

inefficiency carelessness, disorganization, incompetence, muddle, slackness

inefficient disorganized, feeble, incapable, incompetent, ineffectual, inefficacious, inept, inexpert, slipshod, sloppy, wasteful, weak

ineligible disqualified, incompetent (*Law*), objectionable, ruled out, unacceptable, undesirable, unequipped, unfit, unfitted, unqualified, unsuitable

inept 1. awkward, bumbling, bungling, cack-handed (*Inf.*), clumsy, gauche, incompetent, inexpert, maladroit, unhandy, unskilful, unworkmanlike **2.** absurd, improper, inappropriate, inapt, infelicitous, malapropos, meaningless, out of place, pointless, ridiculous, unfit, unsuitable

ineptitude 1. clumsiness, gaucheness, incapacity, incompetence, inexpertness, unfitness, unhandiness **2.** absurdity, inappropriateness, pointlessness, uselessness

inequality bias, difference, disparity, disproportion, diversity, imparity, irregularity, lack of balance, preferentiality, prejudice, unevenness

inequitable biased, discriminatory, one-sided, partial, partisan, preferential, prejudiced, unfair, unjust

inert dead, dormant, dull, idle, immobile, inactive, inanimate, indolent, lazy, leaden, lifeless, motionless, passive, quiescent, slack, slothful, sluggish, slumberous (*Chiefly poetic*), static, still, torpid, unmoving, unreactive, unresponsive

inertia apathy, deadness, disinclination to move, drowsiness, dullness, idleness, immobility, inactivity, indolence, languor, lassitude, laziness, lethargy, listlessness, passivity, sloth, sluggishness, stillness, stupor, torpor, unresponsiveness

inescapable certain, destined, fated, ineluctable, ineludible (*Rare*), inevitable, inexorable, sure, unavoidable

inestimable beyond price, immeasurable, incalculable, invaluable, precious, priceless, prodigious

inevitable assured, certain, decreed, destined, fixed, ineluctable, inescapable, inexorable, necessary, ordained, settled, sure, unavoidable, unpreventable

inevitably as a necessary consequence, as a result, automatically, certainly, necessarily, of necessity, perforce, surely, unavoidably, willy-nilly

inexcusable indefensible, inexpiable, outrageous, unforgivable, unjustifiable, unpardonable, unwarrantable

inexhaustible 1. bottomless, boundless, endless, illimitable, infinite, limitless, measureless, never-ending, unbounded **2.** indefatigable, tireless, undaunted, unfailing, unflagging, untiring, unwearied, unwearying

inexorable adamant, cruel, hard, harsh, immovable, implacable, ineluctable, inescapable, inflexible, merciless, obdurate, pitiless, relentless, remorseless, severe, unappeasable, unbending, unrelenting, unyielding

inexorably implacably, inevitably, irresistibly, relentlessly, remorselessly, unrelentingly

inexpensive bargain, budget, cheap, economical, low-cost, low-priced, modest,

inexpiable (ɪn'ɛkspɪəbəl) *adj.* **1.** incapable of being expiated; unpardonable. **2.** *Arch.* implacable. —**in'expiableness** *n.*

in extenso *Latin.* (ɪn ɪk'stɛnsəʊ) *adv.* at full length.

in extremis *Latin.* (ɪn ɪk'striːmɪs) *adv.* **1.** in extremity; in dire straits. **2.** at the point of death.

inextricable (ˌɪnɛks'trɪkəbəl) *adj.* **1.** not able to be escaped from: *an inextricable dilemma.* **2.** not able to be disentangled, etc.: *an inextricable knot.* **3.** extremely involved or intricate. —ˌinextrica'bility *or* ˌinex'tricableness *n.* —ˌinex'tricably *adv.*

inf. *abbrev. for:* **1.** inferior. **2.** infinitive. **3.** information.

Inf. *or* **inf.** *abbrev. for* infantry.

infallible (ɪn'fæləbəl) *adj.* **1.** not fallible; not liable to error. **2.** not liable to failure; certain; sure: *an infallible cure.* ~*n.* **3.** a person or thing that is incapable of error or failure. —**in,falli'bility** *or* **in'fallibleness** *n.* —**in'fallibly** *adv.*

infamous ('ɪnfəməs) *adj.* **1.** having a bad reputation; notorious. **2.** causing or deserving a bad reputation; shocking: *infamous conduct.* —**'infamously** *adv.* —**'infamousness** *n.*

infamy ('ɪnfəmɪ) *n., pl.* **-mies.** **1.** the state or condition of being infamous. **2.** an infamous act or event.

infancy ('ɪnfənsɪ) *n., pl.* **-cies.** **1.** the state or period of being an infant; childhood. **2.** an early stage of growth or development. **3.** infants collectively. **4.** the period of life prior to attaining legal majority; minority nonage.

infant ('ɪnfənt) *n.* **1.** a child at the earliest stage of its life; baby. **2.** *Law.* another word for **minor** (sense 9). **3.** *Brit.* a young schoolchild. **4.** a person who is beginning or inexperienced in an activity. **5.** (*modifier*) **a.** of or relating to young children or infancy. **b.** designed or intended for young children. **6.** in an early stage of development; nascent: *an infant science.* **7.** *Law.* of or relating to the legal status of infancy. —**'infant,hood** *n.*

infanta (ɪn'fæntə) *n.* **1.** (formerly) a daughter of a king of Spain or Portugal. **2.** the wife of an infante.

infante (ɪn'fæntɪ) *n.* (formerly) a son of a king of Spain or Portugal, esp. one not heir to the throne.

infanticide (ɪn'fæntɪˌsaɪd) *n.* **1.** the killing of an infant. **2.** the practice of killing newborn infants, still prevalent in some primitive tribes. **3.** a person who kills an infant. —**in,fanti'cidal** *adj.*

infantile ('ɪnfənˌtaɪl) *adj.* **1.** like a child in action or behaviour; childishly immature; puerile. **2.** of, relating to, or characteristic of infants or infancy. **3.** in an early stage of development. —**infantility** (ˌɪnfən'tɪlɪtɪ) *n.*

infantile paralysis *n.* another name for **poliomyelitis.**

infantry ('ɪnfəntrɪ) *n., pl.* **-tries.** **a.** soldiers or units of soldiers who fight on foot with small arms. **b.** (*as modifi-*

er): *an infantry unit.*

infant school *n. Brit.* a school for children aged between 5 and 7.

infatuate *vb.* (ɪn'fætjʊˌeɪt). (*tr.*) **1.** to inspire or fill with foolish, shallow, or extravagant passion. **2.** to cause to act foolishly. ~*n.* (ɪn'fætjʊɪt, -ˌeɪt). **3.** *Literary.* a person who is infatuated. —**in,fatu'ation** *n.*

infatuated (ɪn'fætjʊˌeɪtɪd) *adj.* (often foll. by *with*) possessed by a foolish or extravagant passion, esp. for another person.

infect (ɪn'fɛkt) *vb.* (*mainly tr.*) **1.** to cause infection in; contaminate (an organism, wound, etc.) with pathogenic microorganisms. **2.** (*also intr.*) to affect or become affected with a communicable disease. **3.** to taint, pollute, or contaminate. **4.** to affect, esp. adversely, as if by contagion. ~*adj.* **5.** *Arch.* contaminated or polluted with or as if with a disease; infected. —**in'fector** *or* **in'fecter** *n.*

infection (ɪn'fɛkʃən) *n.* **1.** invasion of the body by pathogenic microorganisms. **2.** the resulting condition in the tissues. **3.** an infectious disease. **4.** the act of infecting or state of being infected. **5.** an agent or influence that infects. **6.** persuasion or corruption, as by ideas, perverse influences, etc.

infectious (ɪn'fɛkʃəs) *adj.* **1.** (of a disease) capable of being transmitted. **2.** (of a disease) caused by microorganisms, such as bacteria, viruses, or protozoa. **3.** causing or transmitting infection. **4.** tending or apt to spread, as from one person to another: *infectious mirth.* —**in'fectiously** *adv.* —**in'fectiousness** *n.*

infectious hepatitis *n.* an acute infectious viral disease characterized by inflammation of the liver, fever, and jaundice.

infectious mononucleosis *n.* an acute infectious disease, probably caused by a virus, characterized by fever, sore throat, swollen and painful lymph nodes, and abnormal lymphocytes in the blood. Also called: **glandular fever.**

infective (ɪn'fɛktɪv) *adj.* **1.** capable of causing infection. **2.** a less common word for **infectious.** —**in'fectively** *adv.* —**in'fectiveness** *n.*

infer (ɪn'fɜː) *vb.* **-ferring, -ferred.** (when *tr., may take a clause as object*) **1.** to conclude (a state of affairs, supposition, etc.) by reasoning from evidence; deduce. **2.** (*tr.*) to have or lead to as a necessary or logical consequence; indicate. **3.** (*tr.*) to hint or imply. —**in'ferable,** *or* **in'ferrable** *adj.* —**in'ferrer** *n.*

▷ **Usage.** The use of *infer* in the sense of *imply* often occurs in both speech and writing but is avoided by all careful speakers and writers of English.

inference ('ɪnfərəns, -frəns) *n.* **1.** *Logic.* a process of reasoning in which a conclusion is obtained in some way from certain facts or premisses. **2.** the act or process of inferring. **3.** an inferred conclusion, deduction, etc.

THESAURUS

reasonable

inexperience callowness, greenness, ignorance, newness, rawness, unexpertness, unfamiliarity

inexperienced amateur, callow, fresh, green, immature, new, raw, unaccustomed, unacquainted, unfamiliar, unfledged, unpractised, unschooled, unseasoned, unskilled, untrained, untried, unused, unversed, wet behind the ears (*Inf.*)

inexpert amateurish, awkward, bungling, cack-handed (*Inf.*), clumsy, inept, maladroit, skill-less, unhandy, unpractised, unprofessional, unskilful, unskilled, unworkmanlike

inexplicable baffling, beyond comprehension, enigmatic, incomprehensible, inscrutable, insoluble, mysterious, mystifying, strange, unaccountable, unfathomable, unintelligible

inexpressible incommunicable, indefinable, indescribable, ineffable, unspeakable, unutterable

inexpressive bland, blank, cold, dead, deadpan, emotionless, empty, expressionless, impassive, inanimate, inscrutable, lifeless, stony, vacant

inextinguishable enduring, eternal, immortal, imperishable, indestructible, irrepressible, undying, unquenchable, unsup-

pressible

inextricably indissolubly, indistinguishably, inseparably, intricately, irretrievably, totally

infallibility 1. faultlessness, impeccability, irrefutability, omniscience, perfection, supremacy, unerringness **2.** dependability, reliability, safety, sureness, trustworthiness

infallible 1. faultless, impeccable, omniscient, perfect, unerring, unimpeachable **2.** certain, dependable, foolproof, reliable, sure, sure-fire (*Inf.*), trustworthy, unbeatable, unfailing

infamous abominable, atrocious, base, detestable, disgraceful, dishonourable, disreputable, egregious, flagitious, hateful, heinous, ignominious, ill-famed, iniquitous, loathsome, monstrous, nefarious, notorious, odious, opprobrious, outrageous, scandalous, scurvy, shameful, shocking, vile, villainous, wicked

infancy 1. babyhood, early childhood **2.** beginnings, cradle, dawn, early stages, emergence, inception, origins, outset, start

infant 1. *n.* babe, baby, bairn (*Scot.*), child, little one, neonate, newborn child, suckling, toddler, tot, wean (*Scot.*) **2.** *adj.* baby, dawning, developing, early, emergent, growing, immature, initial, nascent, newborn, un-

fledged, young

infantile babyish, childish, immature, puerile, tender, weak, young

infatuate befool, beguile, besot, bewitch, captivate, delude, enchant, enrapture, enravish, fascinate, make a fool of, mislead, obsess, stupefy, sweep one off one's feet, turn (someone's) head

infatuated beguiled, besotted, bewitched, captivated, carried away, crazy about (*Inf.*), enamoured, enraptured, fascinated, head over heels in love with, inflamed, intoxicated, obsessed, possessed, smitten (*Inf.*), spellbound, swept off one's feet, under the spell of

infatuation crush (*Inf.*), fixation, folly, foolishness, madness, obsession, passion, thing (*Inf.*)

infect affect, blight, contaminate, corrupt, defile, influence, poison, pollute, spread to *or* among, taint, touch, vitiate

infection contagion, contamination, corruption, defilement, poison, pollution, septicity, virus

infectious catching, communicable, contagious, contaminating, corrupting, defiling, infective, pestilential, poisoning, polluting, spreading, transmittable, virulent, vitiating

infer conclude, conjecture, deduce, derive,

inferential (ˌɪnfəˈrɛnʃəl) adj. of, relating to, or derived from inference. —ˌinferˈentially adv.

inferior (ɪnˈfɪərɪə) adj. **1.** lower in value or quality. **2.** lower in rank, position, or status; subordinate. **3.** not of the best; mediocre; commonplace. **4.** lower in position; situated beneath. **5.** (of a plant ovary) situated below the other floral parts. **6.** Astron. **a.** orbiting between the sun and the earth: an inferior planet. **b.** lying below the horizon. **7.** Printing. (of a character) printed at the foot of an ordinary character. ~n. **8.** an inferior person. **9.** Printing. an inferior character. —**inferiority** (ɪnˌfɪərɪˈɒrɪtɪ) n. —inˈferiorly adv.

inferiority complex n. Psychiatry. a disorder arising from the conflict between the desire to be noticed and the fear of being humiliated, characterized by aggressiveness or withdrawal into oneself.

infernal (ɪnˈfɜːnəl) adj. **1.** of or relating to an underworld of the dead. **2.** deserving or befitting hell; diabolic; fiendish. **3.** Inf. irritating; confounded. —ˌinferˈnality n. —inˈfernally adv.

infernal machine n. Arch. an explosive device (usually disguised) or booby trap.

inferno (ɪnˈfɜːnəʊ) n., pl. -nos. **1.** (sometimes cap.; usually preceded by the) hell; the infernal region. **2.** any place or state resembling hell, esp. a conflagration.

infest (ɪnˈfɛst) vb. (tr.) **1.** to inhabit or overrun in unpleasantly large numbers. **2.** (of parasites such as lice) to invade and live on or in (a host). —ˌinfesˈtation n. —inˈfester n.

infidel (ˈɪnfɪdəl) n. **1.** a person who has no religious belief; unbeliever. ~adj. **2.** rejecting a specific religion, esp. Christianity or Islam. **3.** of or relating to unbelievers or unbelief.

infidelity (ˌɪnfɪˈdɛlɪtɪ) n., pl. -ties. **1.** lack of faith or constancy, esp. sexual faithfulness. **2.** lack of religious faith; disbelief. **3.** an act or instance of disloyalty.

infield (ˈɪnˌfiːld) n. **1.** Cricket. the area of the field near the pitch. **2.** Baseball. the area of the playing field enclosed by the base lines. **3.** Agriculture. the part of a farm nearest to the farm buildings. —ˈinˌfielder n.

infighting (ˈɪnˌfaɪtɪŋ) n. **1.** Boxing. combat at close quarters in which proper blows are inhibited. **2.** intense competition, as between members of the same organization. —ˈinˌfighter n.

infiltrate (ˈɪnfɪlˌtreɪt) vb. **1.** to undergo the process in which a fluid passes into the pores or interstices of a solid; permeate. **2.** Mil. to pass undetected through (an enemy-held line or position). **3.** to gain or cause to gain entrance or access surreptitiously: they infiltrated the party structure. ~n. **2.** something that infiltrates. —ˌinfilˈtration n. —ˈinfilˌtrative adj. —ˈinfilˌtrator n.

infin. abbrev. for infinitive.

infinite (ˈɪnfɪnɪt) adj. **1. a.** having no limits or boundaries in time, space, extent, or magnitude. **b.** (as collective n. preceded by the): the infinite. **2.** extremely or immeasurably great or numerous: infinite wealth. **3.** all-embracing, absolute, or total: God's infinite wisdom. **4.** Maths. having an unlimited or uncountable number of digits, factors, terms, members, etc. —ˈinfinitely adv. —ˈinfiniteness n.

infinitesimal (ˌɪnfɪnɪˈtɛsɪməl) adj. **1.** infinitely or immeasurably small. **2.** Maths. of, relating to, or involving a small change in the value of a variable that approaches zero as a limit. ~n. **3.** Maths. an infinitesimal quantity. —ˌinfiniˈtesimally adv.

infinitive (ɪnˈfɪnɪtɪv) n. Grammar. a form of the verb not inflected for grammatical categories such as tense and person and used without an overt subject. In English, the infinitive usually consists of the word to followed by the verb. —**infinitival** (ˌɪnfɪnɪˈtaɪvəl) adj. —inˈfinitively or ˌinfiniˈtivally adv.

infinitude (ɪnˈfɪnɪˌtjuːd) n. **1.** the state or quality of being infinite. **2.** an infinite extent, quantity, degree, etc.

infinity (ɪnˈfɪnɪtɪ) n., pl. -ties. **1.** the state or quality of being infinite. **2.** endless time, space, or quantity. **3.** an infinitely or indefinitely great number or amount. **4.** Maths. **a.** the concept of a value greater than any finite numerical value. **b.** the reciprocal of zero. **c.** the limit of an infinite sequence of numbers.

infirm (ɪnˈfɜːm) adj. **1.** weak in health or body, esp. from old age. **2.** lacking moral certainty; indecisive or irresolute. **3.** not stable, sound, or secure: an infirm structure. **4.** Law. (of a law, etc.) lacking legal force; invalid. —inˈfirmly adv. —inˈfirmness n.

infirmary (ɪnˈfɜːmərɪ) n., pl. -ries. a place for the treatment of the sick or injured; dispensary; hospital.

infirmity (ɪnˈfɜːmɪtɪ) n., pl. -ties. **1.** the state or quality of being infirm. **2.** physical weakness or debility; frailty. **3.** a moral flaw or failing.

infix vb. (ɪnˈfɪks, ˈɪnˌfɪks). **1.** (tr.) to fix firmly in. **2.** (tr.) to instil or inculcate. **3.** Grammar. to insert (an affix) into the middle of a word. ~n. (ˈɪnˌfɪks). **4.** Grammar. an affix inserted into the middle of a word. —ˌinfixˈation or infixion (ɪnˈfɪkʃən) n.

inflame (ɪnˈfleɪm) vb. **1.** to arouse or become aroused to violent emotion. **2.** (tr.) to increase or intensify; aggravate. **3.** to produce inflammation in (a tissue, organ, or part) or (of a tissue, etc.) to become inflamed. **4.** to set or be set on fire. **5.** (tr.) to cause to redden. —inˈflamer n.

inflammable (ɪnˈflæməbəl) adj. **1.** liable to catch fire; flammable. **2.** readily aroused to anger or passion. ~n. **3.** something that is liable to catch fire. —ˌinˌflammaˈbility or inˈflammableness n. —inˈflammably adv.
▷ **Usage.** See at flammable.

inflammation (ˌɪnfləˈmeɪʃən) n. **1.** the reaction of living tissue to injury or infection, characterized by heat, redness, swelling, and pain. **2.** the act of inflaming or the state of being inflamed.

inflammatory (ɪnˈflæmətərɪ, -trɪ) adj. **1.** characterized by or caused by inflammation. **2.** tending to arouse vio-

---

THESAURUS

gather, presume, read between the lines, surmise, understand

inference assumption, conclusion, conjecture, consequence, corollary, deduction, illation (Rare), presumption, reading, surmise

inferior adj. **1.** junior, lesser, lower, menial, minor, secondary, subordinate, subsidiary, under, underneath **2.** bad, imperfect, indifferent, low-grade, mean, mediocre, poor, poorer, second-class, second-rate, shoddy, substandard, worse ~n. **3.** junior, menial, subordinate, underling

inferiority 1. badness, deficiency, imperfection, inadequacy, insignificance, meanness, mediocrity, shoddiness, unimportance, worthlessness **2.** abasement, inferior status or standing, lowliness, subordination, subservience

infernal 1. chthonian, Hadean, hellish, lower, nether, Plutonian, Stygian, Tartarean (Literary), underworld **2.** accursed, damnable, damned, demonic, devilish, diabolical, fiendish, hellish, malevolent, malicious, satanic

infertile barren, infecund, nonproductive, sterile, unfruitful, unproductive

infertility barrenness, infecundity, sterility, unfruitfulness, unproductiveness

infest beset, flood, invade, overrun, penetrate, ravage, swarm, throng

infested alive, beset, crawling, lousy, overrun, pervaded, plagued, ravaged, ridden, swarming, teeming

infiltrate creep in, filter through, insinuate oneself, penetrate, percolate, permeate, pervade, sneak in (Inf.), work or worm one's way into

infinite absolute, all-embracing, bottomless, boundless, enormous, eternal, everlasting, illimitable, immeasurable, immense, inestimable, inexhaustible, interminable, limitless, measureless, never-ending, numberless, perpetual, stupendous, total, unbounded, uncounted, untold, vast, wide, without end, without number

infinitesimal atomic, inappreciable, insignificant, microscopic, minuscule, minute, negligible, teeny, tiny, unnoticeable, wee

infinity boundlessness, endlessness, eternity, immensity, infinitude, perpetuity, vastness

infirm 1. ailing, debilitated, decrepit, doddering, doddery, enfeebled, failing, feeble, frail, lame, weak **2.** faltering, indecisive, insecure, irresolute, shaky, unsound, unstable, vacillating, wavering, weak, wobbly

infirmity 1. debility, decrepitude, deficiency, feebleness, frailty, ill health, imperfection, sickliness, vulnerability **2.** ailment, defect, disorder, failing, fault, malady, sickness, weakness

inflame 1. agitate, anger, arouse, embitter, enrage, exasperate, excite, fire, foment, heat, ignite, impassion, incense, infuriate, intoxicate, kindle, madden, provoke, rile, rouse, stimulate **2.** aggravate, exacerbate, exasperate, fan, increase, intensify, worsen

inflamed angry, chafing, festering, fevered, heated, hot, infected, red, septic, sore, swollen

inflammable combustible, flammable, incendiary

inflammation burning, heat, painfulness, rash, redness, sore, soreness, tenderness

inflammatory anarchic, demagogic, explosive, fiery, incendiary, inflaming, instigative, insurgent, intemperate, provocative, rabble-rousing, rabid, riotous, seditious

lence, strong emotion, etc. —in'flammatorily *adv.*

inflatable (ɪn'fleɪtəbəl) *n.* 1. any of various large air-filled objects made of strong plastic or rubber. ~*adj.* 2. capable of being inflated.

inflate (ɪn'fleɪt) *vb.* 1. to expand or cause to expand by filling with gas or air. 2. (*tr.*) to cause to increase excessively; puff up; swell: *to inflate one's opinion of oneself.* 3. (*tr.*) to cause inflation of (prices, money, etc.). 4. (*tr.*) to raise in spirits; elate. 5. (*intr.*) to undergo economic inflation. —in'flatedly *adv.* —in'flatedness *n.* —in'flater *or* in'flator *n.*

inflation (ɪn'fleɪʃən) *n.* 1. the act of inflating or state of being inflated. 2. *Econ.* a progressive increase in the general level of prices brought about by an expansion in demand or the money supply or by autonomous increases in costs. 3. *Inf.* the rate of increase of prices. —in'flationary *adj.*

inflect (ɪn'flɛkt) *vb.* 1. *Grammar.* to change (the form of a word) by inflection. 2. (*tr.*) to change (the voice) in tone or pitch; modulate. 3. (*tr.*) to cause to deviate from a straight or normal line or course; bend. —in'flectedness *n.* —in'flective *adj.* —in'flector *n.*

inflection *or* **inflexion** (ɪn'flɛkʃən) *n.* 1. modulation of the voice. 2. *Grammar.* a change in the form of a word, signalling change in such grammatical functions as tense, person, gender, number, or case. 3. an angle or bend. 4. the act of inflecting or the state of being inflected. 5. *Maths.* a change in curvature from concave to convex or vice versa. —in'flectional *or* in'flexional *adj.* —in'flectionally *or* in'flexionally *adv.* —in'flectionless *or* in'flexionless *adj.*

inflict (ɪn'flɪkt) *vb.* (*tr.*) 1. (often foll. by *on* or *upon*) to impose (something unwelcome, such as pain, oneself, etc.). 2. to deal out (blows, lashes, etc.). —in'flictable *adj.* —in'flicter *or* in'flictor *n.* —in'fliction *n.*

in-flight *adj.* provided during flight in an aircraft: *in-flight meals.*

inflorescence (ˌɪnflɔː'rɛsəns) *n.* 1. the part of a plant that consists of the flower-bearing stalks. 2. the arrangement of the flowers on the stalks. 3. the process of flowering; blossoming. —ˌinflo'rescent *adj.*

inflow ('ɪn,fləʊ) *n.* 1. something, such as a liquid or gas, that flows in. 2. Also called: **inflowing.** the act of flowing in; influx.

influence ('ɪnfluəns) *n.* 1. an effect of one person or thing on another. 2. the power of a person or thing to have such an effect. 3. power or sway resulting from ability, wealth, position, etc. 4. a person or thing having influence. 5. *Astrol.* an ethereal fluid regarded as emanating from the stars and affecting a person's future. 6. **under the influence.** *Inf.* drunk. ~*vb.* (*tr.*) 7. to per-

suade or induce. 8. to have an effect upon (actions, events, etc.); affect. —'influenceable *adj.* —'influencer *n.*

influential (ˌɪnflu'ɛnʃəl) *adj.* having or exerting influence. —ˌinflu'entially *adv.*

influenza (ˌɪnflu'ɛnzə) *n.* a highly contagious viral disease characterized by fever, muscular aches and pains, and inflammation of the respiratory passages. —ˌinflu'enzal *adj.*

influx ('ɪn,flʌks) *n.* 1. the arrival or entry of many people or things. 2. the act of flowing in; inflow. 3. the mouth of a stream or river.

info ('ɪnfəʊ) *n. Inf.* short for **information.**

infold (ɪn'fəʊld) *vb.* (*tr.*) a variant spelling of **enfold.**

inform (ɪn'fɔːm) *vb.* 1. (*tr.; often foll. by of or about*) to give information to; tell. 2. (*tr.; often foll. by of or about*) to make conversant (with). 3. (*intr.; often foll. by against or on*) to give information regarding criminals, to the police, etc. 4. (*tr.*) to give form to. 5. (*tr.*) to impart some essential or formative characteristic to. 6. (*tr.*) to animate or inspire. —in'formable *adj.*

informal (ɪn'fɔːməl) *adj.* 1. not of a formal, official, or stiffly conventional nature. 2. appropriate to everyday life or use: *informal clothes.* 3. denoting or characterized by idiom, vocabulary, etc., appropriate to conversational language rather than to formal written language. 4. denoting a second-person pronoun in some languages used when the addressee is regarded as a friend or social inferior. —ˌin'formality *n.* —in'formally *adv.*

informal vote *n. Austral.* an invalid vote or ballot.

informant (ɪn'fɔːmənt) *n.* a person who gives information.

information (ˌɪnfə'meɪʃən) *n.* 1. knowledge acquired through experience or study. 2. knowledge of specific and timely events or situations; news. 3. the act of informing or the condition of being informed. 4. **a.** an office, agency, etc., providing information. **b.** (*as modifier*): *information service.* 5. a charge or complaint made before justices of the peace, usually on oath, to institute summary criminal proceedings. 6. *Computers.* **a.** the results derived from the processing of data according to programmed instructions. **b.** another word for **data** (sense 2). —ˌinfor'mational *adj.*

information theory *n.* a collection of mathematical theories concerned with coding, transmitting, storing, retrieving, and decoding information.

informative (ɪn'fɔːmətɪv) *or* **informatory** *adj.* providing information; instructive. —in'formatively *adv.* —in'formativeness *n.*

informer (ɪn'fɔːmə) *n.* 1. a person who informs against

THESAURUS

inflate aerate, aggrandize, amplify, balloon, bloat, blow up, boost, dilate, distend, enlarge, escalate, exaggerate, expand, increase, puff up *or* out, pump up, swell

inflated bombastic, exaggerated, grandiloquent, ostentatious, overblown, swollen

inflation aggrandizement, blowing up, distension, enhancement, enlargement, escalation, expansion, extension, increase, intensification, puffiness, rise, spread, swelling, tumefaction

inflection 1. accentuation, bend, bow, crook, curvature, intonation, modulation 2. *Gram.* conjugation, declension 3. angle, arc, arch

inflexibility 1. hardness, immovability, inelasticity, rigidity, stiffness, stringency 2. fixity, intransigence, obduracy, obstinacy, steeliness

inflexible 1. adamant, brassbound, dyed-in-the-wool, firm, fixed, hard and fast, immovable, immutable, implacable, inexorable, intractable, iron, obdurate, obstinate, relentless, resolute, rigorous, set, set in one's ways, steadfast, steely, strict, stringent, stubborn, unadaptable, unbending, unchangeable, uncompromising, unyielding 2. hard, hardened, inelastic, nonflexible, rigid, stiff, taut

inflict administer, apply, deliver, exact, impose, levy, mete *or* deal out, visit, wreak

infliction 1. administration, exaction, imposition, perpetration, wreaking 2. affliction, penalty, punishment, trouble, visitation, worry

influence *n.* 1. agency, ascendancy, authority, control, credit, direction, domination, effect, guidance, magnetism, mastery, power, pressure, rule, spell, sway, weight 2. clout (*Inf.*), connections, good offices, hold, importance, leverage, power, prestige, pull (*Inf.*), weight ~*v.* 1. act *or* work upon, affect, arouse, bias, control, count, direct, dispose, guide, impel, impress, incite, incline, induce, instigate, lead to believe, manipulate, modify, move, persuade, predispose, prompt, rouse, sway 2. bring pressure to bear upon, carry weight with, make oneself felt, pull strings (*Inf.*)

influential authoritative, controlling, effective, efficacious, forcible, guiding, important, instrumental, leading, meaningful, momentous, moving, persuasive, potent, powerful, significant, telling, weighty

influx arrival, convergence, flow, incursion, inflow, inrush, inundation, invasion, rush

inform 1. acquaint, advise, apprise, communicate, enlighten, give (someone) to understand, instruct, leak to, let know, make conversant (with), notify, put (someone) in the picture (*Inf.*), send word to, teach, tell, tip off 2. Often with *against* or *on* betray, blab, blow the whistle on (*U.S. inf.*), clype

(*Scot.*), denounce, grass (*Brit. sl.*), incriminate, inculpate, nark (*Brit. sl.*), peach (*Sl.*), rat, snitch (*Sl.*), squeal (*Sl.*), tell on (*Inf.*) 3. animate, characterize, illuminate, imbue, inspire, permeate, suffuse, typify

informal casual, colloquial, easy, familiar, natural, relaxed, simple, unceremonious, unconstrained, unofficial

informality casualness, ease, familiarity, lack of ceremony, naturalness, relaxation, simplicity

information advice, counsel, data, dope (*Sl.*), facts, gen (*Brit. inf.*), info (*Inf.*), inside story, instruction, intelligence, knowledge, lowdown (*Inf.*), material, message, news, notice, report, tidings, word

informative chatty, communicative, edifying, educational, enlightening, forthcoming, gossipy, illuminating, instructive, newsy, revealing

informed abreast, acquainted, *au courant, au fait,* briefed, conversant, enlightened, erudite, expert, familiar, genned up (*Brit. inf.*), in the know (*Inf.*), knowledgeable, learned, posted, primed, reliable, up, up to date, versed, well-read

informer accuser, betrayer, grass (*Brit. sl.*), Judas, nark (*Brit. sl.*), sneak, squealer (*Sl.*), stool pigeon

someone, esp. a criminal. **2.** a person who provides information.

infra- *prefix.* below; beneath; after: *infrasonic.*

infra dig ('ɪnfrə 'dɪg) *adj. (postpositive) Inf.* beneath one's dignity.

infrangible (ɪn'frændʒɪbəl) *adj.* **1.** incapable of being broken. **2.** not capable of being violated or infringed. —in,frangi'bility *or* in'frangibleness *n.* —in'frangibly *adv.*

infrared (ˌɪnfrə'rɛd) *n.* **1.** the part of the electromagnetic spectrum with a longer wavelength than light but a shorter wavelength than radio waves. ~*adj.* **2.** of, relating to, or consisting of radiation lying within the infrared.

infrasonic (ˌɪnfrə'sɒnɪk) *adj.* having a frequency below that of sound.

infrastructure ('ɪnfrəˌstrʌktʃə) *n.* **1.** the basic structure of an organization, system, etc. **2.** the stock of fixed capital equipment in a country, including factories, roads, schools, etc., considered as a determinant of economic growth.

infringe (ɪn'frɪndʒ) *vb.* **1.** (*tr.*) to violate or break (a law, agreement, etc.). **2.** (*intr.; foll. by* on *or* upon) to encroach or trespass. —in'fringement *n.* —in'fringer *n.*

infuriate *vb.* (ɪn'fjʊərɪˌeɪt). **1.** (*tr.*) to anger; annoy. ~*adj.* (ɪn'fjʊərɪɪt). **2.** *Arch.* furious; infuriated. —in-'furiatingly *adv.* —in,furi'ation *n.*

infuse (ɪn'fjuːz) *vb.* **1.** (*tr.; often foll. by* into) to instil or inculcate. **2.** (*tr.; foll. by* with) to inspire; emotionally charge. **3.** to soak or be soaked in order to extract flavour or other properties. **4.** *Rare.* (foll. by *into*) to pour. —in'fuser *n.*

infusible (ɪn'fjuːzəbəl) *adj.* not fusible; not easily melted; having a high melting point. —in,fusi'bility *or* in'fusibleness *n.*

infusion (ɪn'fjuːʒən) *n.* **1.** the act of infusing. **2.** something infused. **3.** an extract obtained by soaking. —in'fusive (ɪn'fjuːsɪv) *adj.*

-ing[1] *suffix forming nouns.* **1.** (*from verbs*) the action of, process of, result of, or something connected with the verb: *meeting; a wedding; winnings.* **2.** (*from other nouns*) something used in, consisting of, involving, etc.: *tubing; soldiering.* **3.** (*from other parts of speech*): *an outing.*

-ing[2] *suffix.* **1.** forming the present participle of verbs: *walking; believing.* **2.** forming participial adjectives: *a growing boy; a sinking ship.* **3.** forming adjectives not derived from verbs: *swashbuckling.*

-ing[3] *suffix forming nouns.* a person or thing having a certain quality or being of a certain kind: *sweeting; whiting.*

ingenious (ɪn'dʒiːnjəs, -nɪəs) *adj.* possessing or done with ingenuity; skilful or clever. —in'geniously *adv.* —in'geniousness *n.*

ingénue (ˌænʒeɪ'njuː) *n.* an artless, innocent, or inexperienced girl or young woman.

ingenuity (ˌɪndʒɪ'njuːɪtɪ) *n., pl.* -ties. **1.** inventive talent; cleverness. **2.** an ingenious device, act, etc. **3.** *Arch.* frankness; candour.

ingenuous (ɪn'dʒɛnjʊəs) *adj.* **1.** naive, artless, or innocent. **2.** candid; frank; straightforward. —in'genuously

adv. —in'genuousness *n.*

ingest (ɪn'dʒɛst) *vb.* (*tr.*) to take (food or liquid) into the body. —in'gestible *adj.* —in'gestion *n.* —in'gestive *adj.*

ingle ('ɪŋgəl) *n. Arch. or dialect.* a fire in a room or a fireplace.

inglenook ('ɪŋgəlˌnʊk) *n. Brit.* a corner by a fireplace; chimney corner.

ingoing ('ɪnˌgəʊɪŋ) *adj.* coming or going in; entering.

ingot ('ɪŋgət) *n.* a piece of cast metal obtained from a mould in a form suitable for storage, etc.

ingraft (ɪn'grɑːft) *vb.* a variant spelling of **engraft.** —in'graftment *or* ˌingraf'tation *n.*

ingrain *or* **engrain** *vb.* (ɪn'greɪn). (*tr.*) **1.** to impress deeply on the mind or nature; instil. **2.** *Arch.* to dye into the fibre of (a fabric). ~*adj.* ('ɪnˌgreɪn). **3.** (of woven or knitted articles) made of dyed yarn or of fibre that is dyed before being spun into yarn. ~*n.* ('ɪnˌgreɪn). **4.** a carpet made from ingrained yarn.

ingrained *or* **engrained** (ɪn'greɪnd) *adj.* **1.** deeply impressed or instilled. **2.** (*prenominal*) complete or inveterate; utter. **3.** (esp. of dirt) worked into or through the fibre, grain, pores, etc. —ingrainedly *or* engrainedly (ɪn'greɪnɪdlɪ) *adv.* —in'grainedness *or* en'grainedness *n.*

ingratiate (ɪn'greɪʃɪˌeɪt) *vb.* (*tr.; often foll. by* with) to place (oneself) purposely in the favour (of another). —in'grati,ating *or* in'gratiatory *adj.* —in'grati,atingly *adv.* —in,grati'ation *n.*

ingredient (ɪn'griːdɪənt) *n.* a component of a mixture, compound, etc., esp. in cooking.

ingress ('ɪngrɛs) *n.* **1.** the act of going or coming in; entering. **2.** a way in; entrance. **3.** the right or permission to enter. —ingression (ɪn'grɛʃən) *n.*

ingrowing ('ɪnˌgrəʊɪŋ) *adj.* **1.** (esp. of a toenail) growing abnormally into the flesh. **2.** growing within or into. —'in,growth *n.*

ingrown ('ɪnˌgrəʊn, ɪn'grəʊn) *adj.* **1.** (esp. of a toenail) grown abnormally into the flesh; covered by adjacent tissues. **2.** grown within; native; innate.

inguinal ('ɪŋgwɪnəl) *adj. Anat.* of or relating to the groin.

inhabit (ɪn'hæbɪt) *vb.* (*tr.*) to live or dwell in; occupy. —in'habitable *adj.* —in,habita'bility *n.* —in,habi'tation *n.*

inhabitant (ɪn'hæbɪtənt) *n.* a person or animal that is a permanent resident of a particular place or region. —in'habitancy *or* in'habitance *n.*

inhalant (ɪn'heɪlənt) *adj.* **1.** (esp. of a medicinal preparation) inhaled for its therapeutic effect. **2.** inhaling. ~*n.* **3.** an inhalant medicinal preparation.

inhale (ɪn'heɪl) *vb.* to draw (breath, etc.) into the lungs; breathe in. —ˌinha'lation *n.*

inhaler (ɪn'heɪlə) *n.* **1.** a device for breathing in therapeutic vapours, esp. one for relieving nasal congestion. **2.** a person who inhales.

inhere (ɪn'hɪə) *vb.* (*intr.; foll. by* in) to be an inseparable part (of).

inherent (ɪn'hɪərənt, -'hɛr-) *adj.* existing as an inseparable part; intrinsic. —in'herently *adv.*

THESAURUS

infrequent few and far between, occasional, rare, sporadic, uncommon, unusual

infringe 1. break, contravene, disobey, transgress, violate 2. *With* on *or* upon encroach, intrude, trespass

infringement breach, contravention, infraction, noncompliance, nonobservance, transgression, trespass, violation

infuriate anger, be like a red rag to a bull, enrage, exasperate, get one's back up (*Inf.*), get one's goat (*Sl.*), incense, irritate, madden, make one's blood boil, make one see red (*Inf.*), make one's hackles rise, provoke, raise one's hackles, rile

infuriating aggravating (*Inf.*), annoying, exasperating, galling, irritating, maddening, mortifying, pestilential, provoking, vexatious

ingenious adroit, bright, brilliant, clever, crafty, creative, dexterous, fertile, inventive, masterly, original, ready, resourceful,

shrewd, skilful, subtle

ingenuity adroitness, cleverness, faculty, flair, genius, gift, ingeniousness, inventiveness, knack, originality, resourcefulness, sharpness, shrewdness, skill, turn

ingenuous artless, candid, childlike, frank, guileless, honest, innocent, naive, open, plain, simple, sincere, trustful, trusting, unreserved, unsophisticated, unstudied

ingenuousness artlessness, candour, frankness, guilelessness, innocence, naivety, openness, trustingness, unsuspiciousness

inglorious discreditable, disgraceful, dishonourable, disreputable, failed, humiliating, ignoble, ignominious, infamous, obscure, shameful, unheroic, unknown, unsuccessful, unsung

ingratiate be a yes man, blandish, crawl, curry favour, fawn, flatter, get in with (*Inf.*), get on the right side of, grovel, insinuate oneself, lick (someone's) boots, play up

to, rub (someone) up the right way (*Inf.*), seek the favour (of someone), suck up to (*Inf.*), toady, worm oneself into (someone's) favour

ingratiating bootlicking (*Inf.*), crawling, fawning, flattering, humble, obsequious, servile, sycophantic, timeserving, toadying, unctuous

ingratitude thanklessness, unappreciativeness, ungratefulness

ingredient component, constituent, element, part

inhabit abide, dwell, live, lodge, make one's home, occupy, people, populate, possess, reside, take up residence in, tenant

inhabitant aborigine, citizen, denizen, dweller, indigene, indweller, inmate, native, occupant, occupier, resident, tenant

inhabited colonized, developed, held, occupied, peopled, populated, settled, tenanted

inhale breathe in, draw in, gasp, respire,

inherit (ɪnˈhɛrɪt) vb. **1.** to receive (property, etc.) by succession or under a will. **2.** (intr.) to succeed as heir. **3.** (tr.) to possess (a characteristic) through genetic transmission. **4.** (tr.) to receive (a position, etc.) from a predecessor. —in'herited adj. —in'heritor n. —in-'heritress or in'heritrix fem. n.

inheritable (ɪnˈhɛrɪtəbəl) adj. **1.** capable of being transmitted by heredity from one generation to a later one. **2.** capable of being inherited. **3.** Rare. having the right to inherit. —in,herita'bility or in'heritableness n. —in'heritably adv.

inheritance (ɪnˈhɛrɪtəns) n. **1.** Law. **a.** hereditary succession to an estate, title, etc. **b.** the right of an heir to succeed on the death of an ancestor. **c.** something that may legally be transmitted to an heir. **2.** the act of inheriting. **3.** something inherited; heritage. **4.** the derivation of characteristics of one generation from an earlier one by heredity.

inhibit (ɪnˈhɪbɪt) vb. (tr.) **1.** to restrain or hinder (an impulse, desire, etc.). **2.** to prohibit, forbid, or prevent. **3.** to stop, prevent, or decrease the rate of (a chemical reaction). —in'hibitable adj. —in'hibiter or in'hibitor n. —in'hibitive or in'hibitory adj.

inhibition (,ɪnɪˈbɪʃən, ,ɪnhɪ-) n. **1.** the act of inhibiting or the condition of being inhibited. **2.** Psychol. a mental state or condition in which the varieties of expression and behaviour of an individual become restricted. **3.** the process of stopping or retarding a chemical reaction. **4.** Physiol. the suppression of the function or action of an organ or part, as by stimulation of its nerve supply.

inhuman (ɪnˈhjuːmən) adj. **1.** Also: **inhumane** (,ɪnhjuː-ˈmeɪn). lacking humane feelings, such as sympathy, understanding, etc.; cruel; brutal. **2.** not human. —,inhu'manely adv. —in'humanly adv. —in'humanness n.

inhumanity (,ɪnhjuːˈmænɪti) n., pl. -ties. **1.** lack of humane qualities. **2.** an inhumane act, decision, etc.

inhume (ɪnˈhjuːm) vb. (tr.) to inter; bury. —,inhu'mation n. —in'humer n.

inimical (ɪˈnɪmɪkəl) adj. **1.** adverse or unfavourable. **2.** not friendly; hostile. —in'imically adv. —in'imicalness or in,imi'cality n.

inimitable (ɪˈnɪmɪtəbəl) adj. incapable of being duplicated or imitated; unique. —in,imita'bility or in'imi-

tableness n. —in'imitably adv.

iniquity (ɪˈnɪkwɪti) n., pl. -ties. **1.** lack of justice or righteousness; wickedness; injustice. **2.** a wicked act; sin. —in'iquitous adj. —in'iquitously adv. —in'iquitousness n.

initial (ɪˈnɪʃəl) adj. **1.** of, at, or concerning the beginning. ~n. **2.** the first letter of a word, esp. a person's name. **3.** Printing. a large letter set at the beginning of a chapter or work. **4.** Bot. a cell from which tissues and organs develop by division and differentiation. ~vb. -tialling, -tialled or U.S. -tialing, -tialed. **5.** (tr.) to sign with one's initials, esp. to indicate approval; endorse. —in'itialer or in'itialler n. —in'itially adv.

initiate vb. (ɪˈnɪʃɪˌeɪt). (tr.) **1.** to begin or originate. **2.** to accept (new members) into an organization such as a club, through often secret ceremonies. **3.** to teach fundamentals to. ~adj. (ɪˈnɪʃɪt, -ˌeɪt). **4.** initiated; begun. ~n. (ɪˈnɪʃɪt, -ˌeɪt). **5.** a person who has been initiated, esp. recently. **6.** a beginner; novice. —in,iti'ation n. —in'iti,ator n. —in'itiatory adj.

initiative (ɪˈnɪʃɪətɪv, -ˈnɪʃətɪv) n. **1.** the first step or action of a matter; commencing move: a peace initiative. **2.** the right or power to begin or initiate something: he has the initiative. **3.** the ability or attitude required to begin or initiate something. **4.** Government. the right of citizens to introduce legislation, etc., in a legislative body, as in Switzerland. **5. on one's own initiative.** without being prompted. ~adj. **6.** of or concerning initiation or serving to initiate; initiatory. —in'itiatively adv.

inject (ɪnˈdʒɛkt) vb. (tr.) **1.** Med. to introduce (a fluid) into (the body) by means of a syringe. **2.** (foll. by into) to introduce (a new aspect or element): to inject humour into a scene. **3.** to interject (a comment, idea, etc.). —in'jectable adj. —in'jection n. —in'jector n.

injunction (ɪnˈdʒʌŋkʃən) n. **1.** Law. an instruction or order issued by a court to a party to an action, esp. to refrain from some act. **2.** a command, admonition, etc. **3.** the act of enjoining. —in'junctive adj. —in'junctively adv.

injure (ˈɪndʒə) vb. (tr.) **1.** to cause physical or mental harm or suffering to; hurt or wound. **2.** to offend, esp. by an injustice. —'injurable adj. —'injured adj. —'injurer n.

suck in

inherent basic, congenital, connate, essential, hereditary, inborn, inbred, inbuilt, ingrained, inherited, innate, instinctive, intrinsic, native, natural

inherit accede to, be bequeathed, be left, come into, fall heir to, succeed to

inheritance bequest, birthright, heritage, legacy, patrimony

inhibit arrest, bar, bridle, check, constrain, cramp (someone's) style (Inf.), curb, debar, discourage, forbid, frustrate, hinder, hold back or in, impede, obstruct, prevent, prohibit, restrain, stop

inhibited constrained, frustrated, guarded, repressed, reserved, reticent, self-conscious, shy, subdued, uptight (Inf.), withdrawn

inhibition bar, check, embargo, hang-up (Sl.), hindrance, interdict, mental blockage, obstacle, prohibition, reserve, restraint, restriction, reticence, self-consciousness, shyness

inhospitable 1. cool, uncongenial, unfriendly, ungenerous, unkind, unreceptive, unsociable, unwelcoming, xenophobic **2.** bare, barren, bleak, desolate, empty, forbidding, hostile, lonely, sterile, unfavourable, uninhabitable

inhuman animal, barbaric, barbarous, bestial, brutal, cold-blooded, cruel, diabolical, fiendish, heartless, merciless, pitiless, remorseless, ruthless, savage, unfeeling, vicious

inhumane brutal, cruel, heartless, pitiless, uncompassionate, unfeeling, unkind, unsympathetic

inhumanity atrocity, barbarism, brutality, brutishness, cold-bloodedness, cold-

heartedness, cruelty, hardheartedness, heartlessness, pitilessness, ruthlessness, unkindness, viciousness

inhume bury, entomb, inter, lay to rest, sepulchre

inimical adverse, antagonistic, antipathetic, contrary, destructive, disaffected, harmful, hostile, hurtful, ill-disposed, injurious, noxious, opposed, oppugnant (Rare), pernicious, repugnant, unfavourable, unfriendly, unwelcoming

inimitable consummate, incomparable, matchless, nonpareil, peerless, supreme, unequalled, unexampled, unique, unmatched, unparalleled, unrivalled, unsurpassable

iniquitous abominable, accursed, atrocious, base, criminal, evil, heinous, immoral, infamous, nefarious, reprehensible, reprobate, sinful, unjust, unrighteous, vicious, wicked

iniquity abomination, baseness, crime, evil, evildoing, heinousness, infamy, injustice, misdeed, offence, sin, sinfulness, unrighteousness, wickedness, wrong, wrongdoing

initial adj. beginning, commencing, early, first, inaugural, inceptive, inchoate, incipient, introductory, opening, primary

initially at or in the beginning, at first, at the outset, at the start, first, firstly, in the early stages, originally, primarily, to begin with

initiate v. **1.** begin, break the ice, commence, get under way, inaugurate, institute, kick off (Inf.), launch, lay the foundations of, open, originate, pioneer, set going, set in motion, set the ball rolling, start **2.** coach, familiarize with, indoctrinate, induct, instate, instruct, introduce, invest, teach, train ~n. **3.**

beginner, convert, entrant, learner, member, novice, probationer, proselyte, tyro

initiation admission, commencement, debut, enrolment, entrance, inauguration, inception, induction, installation, instatement, introduction, investiture

initiative 1. advantage, beginning, commencement, first move, first step, lead **2.** ambition, drive, dynamism, enterprise, get-up-and-go (Inf.), inventiveness, leadership, originality, push (Inf.), resource, resourcefulness

inject 1. inoculate, jab (Inf.), shoot (Inf.), vaccinate **2.** bring in, infuse, insert, instil, interject, introduce

injection 1. inoculation, jab (Inf.), shot (Inf.), vaccination, vaccine **2.** dose, infusion, insertion, interjection, introduction

injudicious foolish, hasty, ill-advised, ill-judged, ill-timed, impolitic, imprudent, incautious, inconsiderate, indiscreet, inexpedient, rash, unthinking, unwise

injunction admonition, command, dictate, exhortation, instruction, mandate, order, precept, ruling

injure abuse, blemish, blight, break, damage, deface, disable, harm, hurt, impair, maltreat, mar, ruin, spoil, tarnish, undermine, vitiate, weaken, wound, wrong

injured 1. broken, disabled, hurt, lamed, undermined, weakened, wounded **2.** cut to the quick, disgruntled, displeased, hurt, long-suffering, put out, reproachful, stung, unhappy, upset, wounded **3.** abused, blackened, blemished, defamed, ill-treated, maligned, maltreated, offended, tarnished, vilified, wronged

injurious (ɪn'dʒʊərɪəs) *adj.* **1.** causing damage or harm; deleterious; hurtful. **2.** abusive, slanderous, or libellous. —**in'juriously** *adv.* —**in'juriousness** *n.*

injury ('ɪndʒərɪ) *n., pl.* **-ries. 1.** physical damage or hurt. **2.** a specific instance of this: *a leg injury.* **3.** harm done to a reputation. **4.** *Law.* a violation or infringement of another person's rights that causes him harm and is actionable at law.

injury time *n. Soccer.* extra playing time added on to compensate for time spent attending to injured players during the match.

injustice (ɪn'dʒʌstɪs) *n.* **1.** the condition or practice of being unjust or unfair. **2.** an unjust act.

ink (ɪŋk) *n.* **1.** a fluid or paste used for printing, writing, and drawing. **2.** a dark brown fluid ejected into the water for self-concealment by an octopus or related mollusc. ~*vb.* (*tr.*) **3.** to mark with ink. **4.** to coat (a printing surface) with ink. —**'inker** *n.*

inkling ('ɪŋklɪŋ) *n.* a slight intimation or suggestion; suspicion.

inkosi (ɪŋ'kɔːsɪ) *n. S. African.* a chief; leader.

inkstand ('ɪŋk,stænd) *n.* a stand or tray on which are kept writing implements and containers for ink.

inkwell ('ɪŋk,wɛl) *n.* a small container for pen ink, often let into the surface of a desk.

inky ('ɪŋkɪ) *adj.* **inkier, inkiest. 1.** resembling ink, esp. in colour; dark or black. **2.** of, containing, or stained with ink. —**'inkiness** *n.*

inlaid ('ɪn,leɪd, ɪn'leɪd) *adj.* **1.** set in the surface, as a design in wood. **2.** having such a design or inlay: *an inlaid table.*

inland *adj.* ('ɪnlənd). **1.** of or located in the interior of a country or region away from a sea or border. **2.** *Chiefly Brit.* operating within a country or region; domestic; not foreign. ~*n.* ('ɪn,lænd, -lənd). **3.** the interior of a country or region. ~*adv.* ('ɪn,lænd, -lənd). **4.** towards or into the interior of a country or region. —**'inlander** *n.*

Inland Revenue *n.* (in Britain) a government board that administers and collects major direct taxes, such as income tax.

in-law *n.* **1.** a relative by marriage. ~*adj.* **2.** (*postpositive; in combination*) related by marriage: *a father-in-law.*

inlay *vb.* (ɪn'leɪ) **-laying, -laid.** (*tr.*) **1.** to decorate (an article, esp. of furniture) by inserting pieces of wood, ivory, etc., into slots in the surface. ~*n.* ('ɪn,leɪ). **2.** *Dentistry.* a filling inserted into a cavity and held in position by cement. **3.** decoration made by inlaying. **4.** an inlaid article, surface, etc. —**'in,layer** *n.*

inlet *n.* ('ɪn,lɛt). **1.** a narrow inland opening of the coastline. **2.** an entrance or opening. **3.** the act of letting someone or something in. **4.** something let in or inserted. **5. a.** a passage or valve through which a substance, esp. a fluid, enters a machine. **b.** (*as modifier*): *an inlet valve.* ~*vb.* (ɪn'lɛt), **-letting, -let.** **6.** (*tr.*) to insert or inlay.

in loco parentis *Latin.* (ɪn 'ləʊkəʊ pə'rɛntɪs) in place of a parent: said of a person acting in a parental capacity.

inly ('ɪnlɪ) *adv. Poetic.* inwardly; intimately.

inmate ('ɪn,meɪt) *n.* a person who is confined to an institution such as a prison or hospital.

inmost ('ɪn,məʊst) *adj.* another word for **innermost.**

inn (ɪn) *n.* a pub or small hotel providing food and accommodation. —**'innless** *adj.*

innards ('ɪnədz) *pl. n. Inf.* **1.** the internal organs of the body, esp. the viscera. **2.** the interior parts or components of anything, esp. the working parts.

innate (ɪ'neɪt, 'ɪneɪt) *adj.* **1.** existing from birth; congenital; inborn. **2.** being an essential part of the character of a person or thing. **3.** instinctive; not learned: *innate ideas.* —**in'nately** *adv.* —**in'nateness** *n.*

inner ('ɪnə) *adj.* (*prenominal*) **1.** being or located further inside: *an inner room.* **2.** happening or occurring inside. **3.** relating to the soul, mind, spirit, etc. **4.** more profound or obscure; less apparent: *the inner meaning.* **5.** exclusive or private: *inner regions of the party.* ~*n.* **6.** *Archery.* **a.** the red innermost ring on a target. **b.** a shot which hits this ring. —**'innerly** *adv.* —**'innerness** *n.*

inner man *n. or* **inner woman** *fem. n.* **1.** the mind or soul. **2.** *Jocular.* the stomach or appetite.

innermost ('ɪnə,məʊst) *adj.* **1.** being or located furthest within; central. **2.** intimate; private.

inner tube *n.* an inflatable rubber tube that fits inside a pneumatic tyre casing.

innings ('ɪnɪŋz) *n.* **1.** (*functioning as sing.*) *Cricket, etc.* **a.** the batting turn of a player or team. **b.** the runs scored during such a turn. **2.** (*sometimes sing.*) a period of opportunity or action.

innkeeper ('ɪn,kiːpə) *n.* an owner or manager of an inn.

innocence ('ɪnəsəns) *n.* the quality or state of being innocent. Archaic word: **innocency** ('ɪnəsənsɪ).

innocent ('ɪnəsənt) *adj.* **1.** not corrupted or tainted with evil; sinless; pure. **2.** not guilty of a particular crime; blameless. **3.** (*postpositive;* foll. by *of*) free (of); lacking: *innocent of all knowledge of history.* **4.** harmless or innocuous: *an innocent game.* **5.** credulous, naive, or artless. **6.** simple-minded; slow-witted. ~*n.* **7.** an innocent person, esp. a young child or an ingenuous adult. **8.** a simple-minded person; simpleton. —**'innocently** *adv.*

innocuous (ɪ'nɒkjʊəs) *adj.* having little or no adverse or harmful effect; harmless. —**in'nocuously** *adv.* —**in'nocuousness** *or* **innocuity** (,ɪnə'kjuːɪtɪ) *n.*

innominate bone (ɪ'nɒmɪnɪt) *n.* either of the two bones that form the sides of the pelvis, consisting of the ilium, ischium, and pubis. Nontechnical name: **hipbone.**

innovate ('ɪnə,veɪt) *vb.* to invent or begin to apply (methods, ideas, etc.). —**'inno,vative** *or* **'inno,vatory** *adj.* —**'inno,vator** *n.*

innovation (,ɪnə'veɪʃən) *n.* **1.** something newly introduced, such as a new method or device. **2.** the act of innovating. —**,inno'vational** *adj.* —**,inno'vationist** *n.*

innuendo (,ɪnjʊ'ɛndəʊ) *n., pl.* **-dos** *or* **-does. 1.** an indirect or subtle reference, esp. one made maliciously or indicating criticism or disapproval; insinuation. **2.** *Law.* (in an action for defamation) an explanation of the construction put upon words alleged to be defamatory where this meaning is not apparent.

THESAURUS

injury abuse, damage, detriment, disservice, evil, grievance, harm, hurt, ill, injustice, mischief, ruin, wound, wrong

injustice bias, discrimination, favouritism, inequality, inequity, iniquity, one-sidedness, oppression, partiality, partisanship, prejudice, unfairness, unjustness, unlawfulness, wrong

inkling clue, conception, faintest *or* foggiest idea, glimmering, hint, idea, indication, intimation, notion, suggestion, suspicion, whisper

inland *adj.* domestic, interior, internal, up-country

inlet arm (of the sea), bay, bight, cove, creek, entrance, firth *or* frith (*Scot.*), ingress, passage, sea loch (*Scot.*)

inmost *or* **innermost** basic, buried, central, deep, deepest, essential, intimate, personal, private, secret

innate congenital, connate, constitutional, essential, inborn, inbred, indigenous, in-grained, inherent, inherited, instinctive, intrinsic, intuitive, native, natural

inner **1.** central, essential, inside, interior, internal, intestinal, inward, middle **2.** esoteric, hidden, intimate, personal, private, repressed, secret, unrevealed **3.** emotional, mental, psychological, spiritual

innkeeper host, hostess, hotelier, landlady, landlord, mine host, publican

innocence 1. blamelessness, chastity, clean hands, guiltlessness, incorruptibility, probity, purity, righteousness, sinlessness, stainlessness, uprightness, virginity, virtue **2.** harmlessness, innocuousness, innoxiousness, inoffensiveness **3.** artlessness, credulousness, freshness, guilelessness, gullibility, inexperience, ingenuousness, naïveté, simplicity, unsophistication, unworldliness **4.** ignorance, lack of knowledge, nescience (*Literary*), unawareness, unfamiliarity

innocent *adj.* **1.** blameless, clear, faultless, guiltless, honest, in the clear, not guilty, uninvolved, unoffending **2.** chaste, immaculate, impeccable, incorrupt, pristine, pure, righteous, sinless, spotless, stainless, unblemished, unsullied, upright, virgin, virginal **3.** *With of* clear of, empty of, free from, ignorant, lacking, nescient, unacquainted with, unaware, unfamiliar with, untouched by **4.** harmless, innocuous, inoffensive, unmalicious, unobjectionable, well-intentioned, well-meant **5.** artless, childlike, credulous, frank, guileless, gullible, ingenuous, naive, open, simple, unsuspicious, unworldly, wet behind the ears (*Inf.*) ~*n.* **6.** babe (in arms) (*Inf.*), child, greenhorn (*Inf.*), ingénue (*fem.*)

innovation alteration, change, departure, introduction, modernism, modernization, newness, novelty, variation

innuendo aspersion, hint, implication, imputation, insinuation, intimation, overtone, suggestion, whisper

Innuit ('ınjuːɪt) n. a variant spelling of **Inuit**.

innumerable (ɪ'njuːmərəbəl, ɪ'njuːmrəbəl) or **innumerous** adj. so many as to be uncountable; extremely numerous. —**in,numera'bility** or **in'numerableness** n. —**in'numerably** adv.

innumerate (ɪ'njuːmərɪt) adj. **1.** having neither knowledge nor understanding of mathematics or science. ~n. **2.** an innumerate person. —**in'numeracy** n.

inoculate (ɪ'nɒkjuˌleɪt) vb. **1.** to introduce (the causative agent of a disease) into the body in order to induce immunity. **2.** (tr.) to introduce (microorganisms, esp. bacteria) into (a culture medium). **3.** (tr.) to cause to be influenced or imbued, as with ideas. —**in,ocu'lation** n. —**in'oculative** adj. —**in'ocu,lator** n.

inoperable (ɪn'ɒpərəbəl, -'ɒprə-) adj. **1.** incapable of being implemented or operated. **2.** Surgery. not suitable for operation without risk, esp. because of metastasis. —**in,opera'bility** or **in'operableness** n. —**in'operably** adv.

inordinate (ɪn'ɔːdɪnɪt) adj. **1.** exceeding normal limits; immoderate. **2.** unrestrained, as in behaviour or emotion; intemperate. **3.** irregular or disordered. —**in'ordinacy** or **in'ordinateness** n. —**in'ordinately** adv.

inorganic (ˌɪnɔː'gænɪk) adj. **1.** not having the structure or characteristics of living organisms; not organic. **2.** relating to or denoting chemical compounds that do not contain carbon. **3.** not having a system, structure, or ordered relation of parts; amorphous. **4.** not resulting from or produced by growth; artificial. —**,inor'ganically** adv.

inorganic chemistry n. the branch of chemistry concerned with the elements and all their compounds except those containing carbon.

inpatient ('ɪnˌpeɪʃənt) n. a patient living in the hospital where he is being treated.

in perpetuum Latin. (ɪn pɜː'petjuəm) for ever.

input ('ɪnˌpʊt) n. **1.** the act of putting in. **2.** that which is put in. **3.** (often pl.) a resource required for industrial production, such as capital goods, etc. **4.** Electronics. the signal or current fed into a component or circuit. **5.** Computers. **a.** the data fed into a computer from a peripheral device. **b.** the devices and operations involved in transferring the data. **6.** (modifier) of or relating to electronic, computer, or other input: input program. ~vb. **7.** (tr.) to insert (data) into a computer.

inquest ('ɪnˌkwɛst) n. **1.** an inquiry into the cause of an unexplained, sudden, or violent death, held by a jury before a coroner. **2.** Inf. any inquiry or investigation.

inquietude (ɪn'kwaɪɪˌtjuːd) n. restlessness, uneasiness, or anxiety. —**inquiet** (ɪn'kwaɪət) adj. —**in'quietly** adv.

inquire (ɪn'kwaɪə) vb. **1.** (intr.; often foll. by into) to make a search or investigation. **2.** See **enquire.** —**in'quirer** n. —**in'quiry** n.

inquisition (ˌɪnkwɪ'zɪʃən) n. **1.** the act of inquiring deeply or searchingly; investigation. **2.** a deep or searching inquiry, esp. a ruthless official investigation in order to suppress revolt or root out the unorthodox. **3.** an official inquiry, esp. one held by a jury before an officer of the Crown. —**,inqui'sitional** adj. —**,inqui'sitionist** n.

Inquisition (ˌɪnkwɪ'zɪʃən) n. History. a judicial institution of the Roman Catholic Church (1232–1820) founded to suppress heresy.

inquisitive (ɪn'kwɪzɪtɪv) adj. **1.** excessively curious, esp. about the affairs of others; prying. **2.** eager to learn; inquiring. —**in'quisitively** adv. —**in'quisitiveness** n.

inquisitor (ɪn'kwɪzɪtə) n. **1.** a person who inquires, esp. deeply, searchingly, or ruthlessly. **2.** (often cap.) an official of the ecclesiastical court of the Inquisition.

inquisitorial (ɪnˌkwɪzɪ'tɔːrɪəl) adj. **1.** of, relating to, or resembling inquisition or an inquisitor. **2.** offensively curious; prying. **3.** Law. denoting criminal procedure in which one party is both prosecutor and judge, or in which the trial is held in secret. Cf. **accusatorial** (sense 2). —**in,quisi'torially** adv. —**in,quisi'torialness** n.

in re (ɪn 'reɪ) in the matter of: used esp. in bankruptcy proceedings.

INRI abbrev. for Iesus Nazarenus Rex Iudaeorum (the inscription placed over Christ's head during the Crucifixion).

inroad ('ɪnˌrəʊd) n. **1.** an invasion or hostile attack; raid or incursion. **2.** an encroachment or intrusion.

inrush ('ɪnˌrʌʃ) n. a sudden usually overwhelming inward flow or rush; influx. —**'inˌrushing** n., adj.

ins. abbrev. for: **1.** inches. **2.** insulated. **3.** insurance.

insane (ɪn'seɪn) adj. **1. a.** mentally deranged; crazy; of unsound mind. **b.** (as collective n. preceded by the): the insane. **2.** characteristic of a person of unsound mind: an insane stare. **3.** irresponsible; very foolish; stupid. —**in'sanely** adv. —**in'saneness** n.

insanity (ɪn'sænɪtɪ) n., pl. **-ties. 1.** relatively permanent disorder of the mind; state or condition of being insane. **2.** utter folly; stupidity.

insatiable (ɪn'seɪʃəbəl, -ʃɪə-) or **insatiate** (ɪn'seɪʃɪɪt) adj. not able to be satisfied or satiated; greedy or unappeasable. —**in,satia'bility** or **in'satiateness** n. —**in'satiably** or **in'satiately** adv.

inscribe (ɪn'skraɪb) vb. (tr.) **1.** to make, carve, or engrave (writing, letters, etc.) on (a surface such as wood, stone, or paper). **2.** to enter (a name) on a list or in a register. **3.** to sign one's name on (a book, etc.) before presentation to another person. **4.** to draw (a geometric construction) inside another construction so that the two are in contact but do not intersect. —**in'scribable** adj. —**in'scribableness** n. —**in'scriber** n.

inscription (ɪn'skrɪpʃən) n. **1.** something inscribed, esp. words carved or engraved on a coin, tomb, etc. **2.** a signature or brief dedication in a book or on a work of art. **3.** the act of inscribing. —**in'scriptional** or **in'scriptive** adj. —**in'scriptively** adv.

THESAURUS

innumerable beyond number, countless, incalculable, infinite, many, multitudinous, myriad, numberless, numerous, unnumbered, untold

inoffensive harmless, humble, innocent, innocuous, innoxious, mild, neutral, nonprovocative, peaceable, quiet, retiring, unobjectionable, unobtrusive, unoffending

inoperative broken, broken-down, defective, hors de combat, ineffective, ineffectual, inefficacious, invalid, nonactive, null and void, out of action, out of commission, out of order, out of service, unserviceable, unworkable, useless

inopportune ill-chosen, ill-timed, inappropriate, inauspicious, inconvenient, malapropos, mistimed, unfavourable, unfortunate, unpropitious, unseasonable, unsuitable, untimely

inordinate disproportionate, excessive, exorbitant, extravagant, immoderate, intemperate, preposterous, unconscionable, undue, unreasonable, unrestrained, unwarranted

inorganic artificial, chemical, man-made, mineral

inquest inquiry, inquisition, investigation,

probe

inquire 1. examine, explore, inspect, investigate, look into, make inquiries, probe, scrutinize, search **2.** Also **enquire** ask, query, question, request information, seek information

inquiring analytical, curious, doubtful, inquisitive, interested, investigative, outward-looking, probing, questioning, searching, wondering

inquiry 1. examination, exploration, inquest, interrogation, investigation, probe, research, scrutiny, search, study, survey **2.** Also **enquiry** query, question

inquisition cross-examination, examination, grilling (Inf.), inquest, inquiry, investigation, question, quizzing, third degree (Inf.)

inquisitive curious, inquiring, intrusive, nosy (Inf.), nosy-parkering (Inf.), peering, probing, prying, questioning, scrutinizing, snooping (Inf.), snoopy (Inf.)

inroad 1. advance, encroachment, foray, incursion, intrusion, invasion, irruption, onslaught, raid **2. make inroads upon** consume, eat away, eat up or into, encroach

upon, use up

insane 1. crazed, crazy, demented, deranged, mad, mentally disordered, mentally ill, non compos mentis, of unsound mind, out of one's mind, unhinged **2.** barmy (Sl.), batty (Sl.), bonkers (Sl.), cracked (Sl.), crackers (Sl.), cuckoo (Inf.), loony (Sl.), loopy (Inf.), mental (Sl.), nuts (Sl.), nutty (Sl.), off one's chump (Inf.), off one's head (Inf.), off one's nut (Inf.), off one's rocker (Inf.), round the bend (Inf.), round the twist (Inf.), screwy (Inf.) **3.** bizarre, daft (Inf.), fatuous, foolish, idiotic, impractical, irrational, irresponsible, lunatic (Inf.), preposterous, senseless, stupid

insanitary contaminated, dirtied, dirty, disease-ridden, feculent, filthy, impure, infected, infested, insalubrious, noxious, polluted, unclean, unhealthy, unhygienic

insanity 1. aberration, craziness, delirium, dementia, frenzy, madness, mental derangement, mental disorder, mental illness **2.** folly, irresponsibility, lunacy, preposterousness, senselessness, stupidity

insatiable gluttonous, greedy, insatiate, intemperate, quenchless, rapacious, ravenous, unappeasable, unquenchable, voracious

inscribe 1. carve, cut, engrave, etch, im-

inscrutable (ɪnˈskruːtəbəl) *adj.* mysterious or enigmatic; incomprehensible. —**inˌscrutaˈbility** *or* **inˈscrutableness** *n.* —**inˈscrutably** *adv.*

insect (ˈɪnsɛkt) *n.* **1.** any of a class of small airbreathing arthropods, having a body divided into head, thorax, and abdomen, three pairs of legs, and (in most species) two pairs of wings. **2.** (loosely) any similar invertebrate, such as a spider, tick, or centipede. **3.** a contemptible, loathsome, or insignificant person. —**inˈsectile** *adj.* —**ˈinsect-ˌlike** *adj.*

insecticide (ɪnˈsɛktɪˌsaɪd) *n.* a substance used to destroy insect pests. —**inˌsectiˈcidal** *adj.*

insectivore (ɪnˈsɛktɪˌvɔː) *n.* **1.** any of an order of placental mammals, being typically small, with simple teeth, and feeding on invertebrates. The group includes shrews, moles, and hedgehogs. **2.** any animal or plant that derives nourishment from insects. —ˌ**insecˈtivorous** *adj.*

insecure (ˌɪnsɪˈkjʊə) *adj.* **1.** anxious or afraid; not confident or certain. **2.** not adequately protected: *an insecure fortress.* **3.** unstable or shaky. —**inseˈcurely** *adv.* —**inseˈcureness** *n.* —**inseˈcurity** *n.*

inseminate (ɪnˈsɛmɪˌneɪt) *vb.* (*tr.*) **1.** to impregnate (a female) with semen. **2.** to introduce (ideas or attitudes) into the mind of (a person or group). —**inˌsemiˈnation** *n.* —**inˈsemiˌnator** *n.*

insensate (ɪnˈsɛnseɪt, -sɪt) *adj.* **1.** lacking sensation or consciousness. **2.** insensitive; unfeeling. **3.** foolish; senseless. —**inˈsensately** *adv.* —**inˈsensateness** *n.*

insensible (ɪnˈsɛnsəbəl) *adj.* **1.** lacking sensation or consciousness. **2.** (foll. by *of* or *to*) unaware (of) or indifferent (to): *insensible to suffering.* **3.** thoughtless or callous. **4.** a less common word for **imperceptible.** —**inˌsensiˈbility** *or* **inˈsensibleness** *n.* —**inˈsensibly** *adv.*

insert *vb.* (ɪnˈsɜːt). (*tr.*) **1.** to put in or between; introduce. **2.** to introduce into text, as in a newspaper; interpolate. ~*n.* (ˈɪnsɜːt). **3.** something inserted. **4. a. a.** a folded section placed in another for binding in with a book. **b.** a printed sheet, esp. one bearing advertising, placed loose between the leaves of a book, periodical, etc. —**inˈsertable** *adj.* —**inˈserter** *n.*

insertion (ɪnˈsɜːʃən) *n.* **1.** the act of inserting or something that is inserted. **2.** a word, sentence, correction, etc., inserted into text, such as a newspaper. **3.** a strip of lace, embroidery, etc., between two pieces of material. **4.** *Anat.* the point or manner of attachment of a muscle to the bone that it moves. —**inˈsertional** *adj.*

in-service *adj.* denoting training that is given in the working environment to employees: *in-service training*

for teachers.

inset *vb.* (ɪnˈsɛt), **-setting, -set. 1.** (*tr.*) to set or place in or within; insert. ~*n.* (ˈɪnˌsɛt). **2.** something inserted. **3.** *Printing.* **a.** a small map or diagram set within the borders of a larger one. **b.** another name for **insert** (sense 4). **4.** a piece of fabric inserted into a garment, as to shape it or for decoration. —**ˈinˌsetter** *n.*

inshore (ˈɪnˈʃɔː) *adj.* **1.** in or on the water, but close to the shore: *inshore weather.* ~*adv., adj.* **2.** towards the shore from the water: *an inshore wind; we swam inshore.*

inside *n.* (ˈɪnˈsaɪd). **1.** the interior; inner or enclosed part or surface. **2.** the side of a path away from the road or adjacent to a wall. **3.** (*also pl.*) *Inf.* the internal organs of the body, esp. the stomach and bowels. **4. inside of.** in a period of time less than; within. **5. inside out.** with the inside facing outwards. **6. know (something) inside out.** to know thoroughly or perfectly. ~*prep.* (ˌɪnˈsaɪd). **7.** in or to the interior of; within or to within; on the inside of. ~*adj.* (ˈɪnˌsaɪd). **8.** on or of an interior; on the inside: *an inside door.* **9.** (*prenominal*) arranged or provided by someone within an organization or building, esp. illicitly: *the raid was an inside job; inside information.* ~*adv.* (ˌɪnˈsaɪd). **10.** within or to within in a thing or place; indoors. **11.** *Sl.* in or into prison.

▷ **Usage.** See at **outside.**

inside job *n. Inf.* a crime committed with the assistance of someone associated with the victim.

insider (ɪnˈsaɪdə) *n.* **1.** a member of a specified group. **2.** a person with access to exclusive information.

insidious (ɪnˈsɪdɪəs) *adj.* **1.** stealthy, subtle, cunning, or treacherous. **2.** working in a subtle or apparently innocuous way, but nevertheless deadly: *an insidious illness.* —**inˈsidiously** *adv.* —**inˈsidiousness** *n.*

insight (ˈɪnˌsaɪt) *n.* **1.** the ability to perceive clearly or deeply; penetration. **2.** a penetrating and often sudden understanding, as of a complex situation or problem. **3.** *Psychol.* the capacity for understanding one's own or another's mental processes. **4.** *Psychiatry.* the ability to understand one's own problems. —**ˈinˌsightful** *adj.*

insignia (ɪnˈsɪgnɪə) *n., pl.* **-nias** *or* **-nia. 1.** a badge or emblem of membership, office, or dignity. **2.** a distinguishing sign or mark.

insignificant (ˌɪnsɪgˈnɪfɪkənt) *adj.* **1.** having little or no importance; trifling. **2.** almost or relatively meaningless. **3.** small or inadequate: *an insignificant wage.* **4.** not distinctive in character, etc. —ˌ**insigˈnificance** *or* ˌ**insigˈnificancy** *n.* —ˌ**insigˈnificantly** *adv.*

insincere (ˌɪnsɪnˈsɪə) *adj.* lacking sincerity; hypocritical. —ˌ**insinˈcerely** *adv.* —**insincerity** (ˌɪnsɪnˈsɛrɪtɪ) *n.*

THESAURUS

press, imprint **2.** engross, enlist, enrol, enter, record, register, write **3.** address, dedicate

inscription dedication, engraving, label, legend, lettering, saying, words

inscrutable 1. blank, deadpan, enigmatic, impenetrable, poker-faced (*Inf.*), sphinxlike, unreadable **2.** hidden, incomprehensible, inexplicable, mysterious, undiscoverable, unexplainable, unfathomable, unintelligible

insecure 1. afraid, anxious, uncertain, unconfident, unsure **2.** dangerous, defenceless, exposed, hazardous, ill-protected, open to attack, perilous, unguarded, unprotected, unsafe, unshielded, vulnerable **3.** built upon sand, flimsy, frail, insubstantial, loose, on thin ice, precarious, rickety, rocky, shaky, unreliable, unsound, unstable, unsteady, weak, wobbly

insecurity 1. anxiety, fear, uncertainty, unsureness, worry **2.** danger, defencelessness, hazard, peril, risk, uncertainty, vulnerability, weakness **3.** dubiety, frailness, instability, precariousness, shakiness, uncertainty, unreliability, unsteadiness, weakness

insensibility 1. apathy, callousness, dullness, indifference, insensitivity, lethargy, thoughtlessness, torpor **2.** inertness, numbness, unconsciousness

insensible 1. anaesthetized, benumbed, dull, inert, insensate, numbed, senseless, stupid, torpid **2.** apathetic, callous, cold, deaf, hard-hearted, impassive, impervious, indif-

ferent, oblivious, unaffected, unaware, unconscious, unfeeling, unmindful, unmoved, unresponsive, unsusceptible, untouched **3.** imperceivable, imperceptible, minuscule, negligible, unnoticeable

insensitive 1. callous, crass, hardened, imperceptive, indifferent, obtuse, tactless, thick-skinned, tough, uncaring, unconcerned, unfeeling, unresponsive, unsusceptible **2.** *With* **to** dead to, immune to, impervious to, nonreactive, proof against, unaffected by, unmoved by

inseparable 1. conjoined, inalienable, indissoluble, indivisible, inseverable **2.** bosom, close, devoted, intimate

insert embed, enter, implant, infix, interject, interpolate, interpose, introduce, place, pop in (*Inf.*), put, set, stick in, tuck in, work in

insertion addition, implant, inclusion, insert, inset, interpolation, introduction, supplement

inside *n.* **1.** contents, inner part, interior **2.** *Often plural. Inf.* belly, bowels, entrails, gut, guts, innards (*Inf.*), internal organs, stomach, viscera, vitals ~*adv.* **3.** indoors, under cover, within ~*adj.* **4.** inner, innermost, interior, internal, intramural, inward **5.** classified, confidential, esoteric, exclusive, internal, limited, private, restricted, secret

insidious artful, crafty, crooked, cunning, deceitful, deceptive, designing, disingenuous, duplicitous, guileful, intriguing,

Machiavellian, slick, sly, smooth, sneaking, stealthy, subtle, surreptitious, treacherous, tricky, wily

insight acumen, awareness, comprehension, discernment, intuition, intuitiveness, judgment, observation, penetration, perception, perspicacity, understanding, vision

insignia badge, crest, decoration, distinguishing mark, earmark, emblem, ensign, symbol

insignificance immateriality, inconsequence, irrelevance, meaninglessness, negligibility, paltriness, pettiness, triviality, unimportance, worthlessness

insignificant flimsy, immaterial, inconsequential, inconsiderable, irrelevant, meagre, meaningless, minor, negligible, nondescript, nonessential, not worth mentioning, nugatory, of no account (consequence, moment), paltry, petty, scanty, trifling, trivial, unimportant, unsubstantial

insincere deceitful, deceptive, devious, dishonest, disingenuous, dissembling, dissimulating, double-dealing, duplicitous, evasive, faithless, false, hollow, hypocritical, Janus-faced, lying, mendacious, perfidious, pretended, two-faced, unfaithful, untrue, untruthful

insincerity deceitfulness, deviousness, dishonesty, disingenuousness, dissimulation, duplicity, faithlessness, hypocrisy, lip service, mendacity, perfidy, pretence, untruthfulness

insinuate (ɪnˈsɪnjʊˌeɪt) vb. **1.** (may take a clause as object) to suggest by indirect allusion, hints, innuendo, etc. **2.** (tr.) to introduce subtly or deviously. **3.** (tr.) to cause (someone, esp. oneself) to be accepted by gradual approaches or manoeuvres. —**inˈsinuative** or **inˈsinuatory** adj. —**inˈsinuˌator** n.

insinuation (ɪnˌsɪnjʊˈeɪʃən) n. **1.** an indirect or devious hint or suggestion. **2.** the act or practice of insinuating.

insipid (ɪnˈsɪpɪd) adj. **1.** lacking spirit or interest; boring. **2.** lacking taste; unpalatable. —ˌinsiˈpidity or inˈsipidness n. —inˈsipidly adv.

insist (ɪnˈsɪst) vb. (when tr., takes a clause as object; when intr., usually foll. by on or upon) **1.** to make a determined demand (for): he insisted on his rights. **2.** to express a convinced belief (in) or assertion (of). —inˈsister n. —inˈsistingly adv.

insistent (ɪnˈsɪstənt) adj. **1.** making continual and persistent demands. **2.** demanding notice or attention; compelling: the insistent cry of a bird. —inˈsistence or inˈsistency n. —inˈsistently adv.

in situ Latin. (ɪn ˈsɪtjuː) adv., adj. (postpositive) in the natural, original, or appropriate position.

in so far or U.S. **insofar** adv. (usually foll. by as or that) to the degree or extent (that).

insole (ˈɪnˌsəʊl) n. **1.** the inner sole of a shoe or boot. **2.** a loose additional inner sole used to give extra warmth or to make a shoe fit.

insolent (ˈɪnsələnt) adj. offensive, impudent, or disrespectful. —ˈinsolence n. —ˈinsolently adv.

insoluble (ɪnˈsɒljʊbəl) adj. **1.** incapable of being dissolved; incapable of forming a solution, esp. in water. **2.** incapable of being solved. —inˌsoluˈbility or inˈsolubleness n. —inˈsolubly adv.

insolvent (ɪnˈsɒlvənt) adj. **1.** having insufficient assets to meet debts and liabilities; bankrupt. **2.** of or relating to bankrupts or bankruptcy. ~n. **3.** a person who is insolvent; bankrupt. —inˈsolvency n.

insomnia (ɪnˈsɒmnɪə) n. chronic inability to fall asleep or to enjoy uninterrupted sleep. —inˈsomnious adj. —inˈsomniˌac n., adj.

insomuch (ˌɪnsəʊˈmʌtʃ) adv. **1.** (foll. by as or that) to such an extent or degree. **2.** (foll. by as) because of the fact (that); inasmuch (as).

insouciant (ɪnˈsuːsɪənt) adj. carefree or unconcerned; light-hearted. —inˈsouciance n. —inˈsouciantly adv.

inspan (ɪnˈspæn) vb. **-spanning, -spanned.** (tr.) Chiefly S. African. **1.** to harness (animals) to (a vehicle); yoke. **2.** to press (people) into service.

inspect (ɪnˈspɛkt) vb. (tr.) **1.** to examine closely, esp. for faults or errors. **2.** to scrutinize officially (a document, military personnel on ceremonial parade, etc.). —inˈspectable adj. —inˈspection n. —inˈspective adj.

inspector (ɪnˈspɛktə) n. **1.** a person who inspects, esp. an official who examines for compliance with regulations, standards, etc. **2.** a police officer ranking below a superintendent and above a sergeant. —inˈspectoral or **inspectorial** (ˌɪnspɛkˈtɔːrɪəl) adj. —inˈspectorˌship n.

inspectorate (ɪnˈspɛktərɪt) n. **1.** the office, rank, or duties of an inspector. **2.** a body of inspectors. **3.** a district under an inspector.

inspiration (ˌɪnspɪˈreɪʃən) n. **1.** stimulation or arousal of the mind, feelings, etc., to special activity or creativity. **2.** the state or quality of being so stimulated or aroused. **3.** someone or something that causes this state. **4.** an idea or action resulting from such a state. **5.** the act or process of inhaling; breathing in.

inspiratory (ɪnˈspaɪərətərɪ, -trɪ) adj. of or relating to inhalation or the drawing in of air.

inspire (ɪnˈspaɪə) vb. **1.** to exert a stimulating or beneficial effect upon (a person, etc.); animate or invigorate. **2.** (tr.; foll. by with or to; may take an infinitive) to arouse (with a particular emotion or to a particular action); stir. **3.** (tr.) to prompt or instigate; give rise to. **4.** (tr.; often passive) to guide or arouse by divine influence or inspiration. **5.** to take or draw (air, gas, etc.) into the lungs; inhale. **6.** (tr.) Arch. to breathe into or upon. —inˈspirable adj. —inˈspirative adj. —inˈspirer n. —inˈspiringly adv.

inst. abbrev. for: **1.** instant (this month). **2.** instantaneous. **3.** instrumental.

install or **instal** (ɪnˈstɔːl) vb. **-stalling, -stalled.** (tr.) **1.** to place (equipment) in position and connect and adjust for use. **2.** to put in a position, rank, etc. **3.** to settle (a person, esp. oneself) in a position or state: she installed herself in an armchair. —ˌinstalˈlation n. —inˈstaller n.

installment plan n. the U.S. name for **hire-purchase.**

instalment or U.S. **installment** (ɪnˈstɔːlmənt) n. **1.** one of the portions into which a debt is divided for pay-

═══ THESAURUS ═══

insinuate 1. allude, hint, imply, indicate, intimate, suggest **2.** infiltrate, infuse, inject, instil, introduce **3.** curry favour, get in with (Inf.), ingratiate, worm or work one's way in

insinuation 1. allusion, aspersion, hint, implication, innuendo, slur, suggestion **2.** infiltration, infusion, ingratiating, injection, instillation, introduction

insipid 1. anaemic, banal, bland, characterless, colourless, drab, dry, dull, flat, jejune, lifeless, limp, pointless, prosaic, prosy, spiritless, stale, stupid, tame, tedious, trite, unimaginative, uninteresting, vapid, weak, wearisome, wishy-washy (Inf.) **2.** bland, flavourless, savourless, tasteless, unappetizing, watered down, watery, wishy-washy (Inf.)

insipidity, insipidness 1. banality, colourlessness, dullness, flatness, lack of imagination, pointlessness, staleness, tameness, tediousness, triteness, uninterestingness, vapidity **2.** blandness, flavourlessness, lack of flavour, tastelessness

insist 1. be firm, brook no refusal, demand, lay down the law, not take no for an answer, persist, press (someone), require, stand firm, stand one's ground, take or make a stand, urge **2.** assert, asseverate, aver, claim, contend, hold, maintain, reiterate, repeat, swear, urge, vow

insistence assertion, contention, demands, emphasis, importunity, insistency, persistence, pressing, reiteration, stress, urging

insistent demanding, dogged, emphatic, exigent, forceful, importunate, incessant, peremptory, persevering, persistent, pressing, unrelenting, urgent

insolence abuse, audacity, backchat (Inf.), boldness, cheek (Inf.), chutzpah (U.S. inf.), contemptuousness, contumely, disrespect, effrontery, gall (Inf.), impertinence, impudence, incivility, insubordination, offensiveness, pertness, rudeness, sauce (Inf.), uncivility

insolent abusive, bold, brazen-faced, contemptuous, fresh (Inf.), impertinent, impudent, insubordinate, insulting, pert, rude, saucy, uncivil

insoluble baffling, impenetrable, indecipherable, inexplicable, mysterious, mystifying, obscure, unaccountable, unfathomable, unsolvable

insolvency bankruptcy, failure, liquidation, ruin

insolvent bankrupt, broke (Inf.), failed, gone bust (Inf.), gone to the wall (Inf.), in queer street (Inf.), in receivership, in the hands of the receivers, on the rocks (Inf.), ruined

insomnia sleeplessness, wakefulness

inspect check, examine, give (something or someone) the once-over (Inf.), go over or through, investigate, look over, oversee, scan, scrutinize, search, superintend, supervise, survey, vet

inspection check, checkup, examination, investigation, look-over, once-over (Inf.), review, scan, scrutiny, search, superintendence, supervision, surveillance, survey

inspector censor, checker, critic, examiner, investigator, overseer, scrutineer, scrutinizer, superintendent, supervisor

inspiration 1. arousal, awakening, encouragement, influence, muse, spur, stimulus **2.** afflatus, creativity, elevation, enthusiasm, exaltation, genius, illumination, insight, revelation, stimulation

inspire 1. animate, be responsible for, encourage, enliven, fire or touch the imagination of, galvanize, hearten, imbue, influence, infuse, inspirit, instil, spark off, spur, stimulate **2.** arouse, enkindle, excite, give rise to, produce, quicken, stir

inspired 1. brilliant, dazzling, enthralling, exciting, impressive, memorable, of genius, outstanding, superlative, thrilling, wonderful **2.** Of a guess instinctive, instinctual, intuitive **3.** aroused, elated, enthused, exalted, exhilarated, galvanized, possessed, stimulated, stirred up, uplifted

inspiring affecting, encouraging, exciting, exhilarating, heartening, moving, rousing, stimulating, stirring, uplifting

instability capriciousness, changeableness, disequilibrium, fickleness, fitfulness, fluctuation, fluidity, frailty, imbalance, impermanence, inconstancy, insecurity, irresolution, mutability, oscillation, precariousness, restlessness, shakiness, transience, unpredictability, unsteadiness, vacillation, variability, volatility, wavering, weakness

install, instal 1. fix, lay, lodge, place, position, put in, set up, station **2.** establish, inaugurate, induct, instate, institute, introduce, invest, set up **3.** ensconce, position, settle

installation 1. establishment, fitting, instalment, placing, positioning, setting up **2.** inauguration, induction, instatement, investiture **3.** equipment, machinery, plant, system **4.** Military base, establishment, post, station

ment at specified intervals over a fixed period. **2.** a portion of something that is issued, broadcast, or published in parts.

instance ('ınstəns) *n.* **1.** a case or particular example. **2. for instance.** for or as an example. **3.** a specified stage in proceedings; step (in **in the first, second,** etc., **instance**). **4.** urgent request or demand (esp. in **at the instance of**). ~*vb.* (*tr.*) **5.** to cite as an example.

instant ('ınstənt) *n.* **1.** a very brief time; moment. **2.** a particular moment or point in time: *at the same instant.* **3. on the instant.** immediately; without delay. ~*adj.* **4.** immediate; instantaneous. **5.** urgent or imperative. **6.** (esp. of foods) prepared or designed for preparation with very little time and effort: *instant coffee.* **7.** (*postpositive*) of the present month: *a letter of the 7th instant.* Abbrev.: **inst.**

instantaneous (,ınstən'teınıəs) *adj.* **1.** occurring with almost no delay; immediate. **2.** happening or completed within a moment: *instantaneous death.* —,**instan'taneously** *adv.* —,**instan'taneousness** or **instantaneity** (ın,stæntə'ni:ıtı) *n.*

instantly ('ınstəntlı) *adv.* **1.** immediately; at once. **2.** *Arch.* urgently or insistently.

instead (ın'stɛd) *adv.* **1.** as a replacement, substitute, or alternative. **2. instead of.** (*prep.*) in place of or as an alternative to.

instep ('ın,stɛp) *n.* **1.** the middle section of the human foot, forming the arch between the ankle and toes. **2.** the part of a shoe, stocking, etc., covering this.

instigate ('ınstı,geıt) *vb.* (*tr.*) **1.** to bring about, as by incitement or urging: *to instigate rebellion.* **2.** to urge on to some drastic or unadvisable action. —,**insti'gation** *n.* —'**insti,gative** *adj.* —'**insti,gator** *n.*

instil or (*esp. U.S.*) **instill** (ın'stıl) *vb.* (*tr.*) **1.** to introduce gradually; implant or infuse. **2.** *Rare.* to pour in or inject in drops. —**in'stiller** *n.* —**in'stilment, in'stillment,** or ,**instil'lation** *n.*

instinct ('ınstıŋkt) *n.* **1.** the innate capacity of an animal to respond to a given stimulus in a relatively fixed way. **2.** inborn intuitive power. ~*adj.* **3.** *Rare.* (*postpositive;* often foll. by *with*) **a.** animated or impelled (by). **b.** imbued or infused (with). —**in'stinctive** *adj.* —**in'stinctively** *adv.*

institute ('ınstı,tju:t) *vb.* (*tr.*) **1.** to organize; establish. **2.** to initiate: *to institute a practice.* **3.** to establish in a position or office; induct. ~*n.* **4.** an organization founded for particular work, such as education, promotion of the arts, or scientific research. **5.** the building where such an organization is situated. **6.** something instituted, esp. a rule, custom, or precedent. —'**insti,tutor** or '**insti,tuter** *n.*

institution (,ınstı'tju:ʃən) *n.* **1.** the act of instituting. **2.** an organization or establishment founded for a specific purpose, such as a hospital, church, or college. **3.** the building where such an organization is situated. **4.** an established custom, law, or relationship in a society or community. **5.** *Inf.* a constant feature or practice: *Jones's drink at the bar was an institution.* **6.** the appointment of an incumbent to an ecclesiastical office or pastoral charge. —,**insti'tutionary** *adj.*

institutional (,ınstı'tju:ʃənəl) *adj.* **1.** of, relating to, or characteristic of institutions. **2.** dull, routine, and uniform: *institutional meals.* **3.** relating to principles or institutes, esp. of law. —,**insti'tutionally** *adv.* —,**insti'tutiona,lism** *n.* —,**insti'tutional,ize** or *-ise vb.*

instruct (ın'strʌkt) *vb.* (*tr.*) **1.** to direct to do something; order. **2.** to teach (someone) how to do (something). **3.** to furnish with information; apprise. **4.** *Law, chiefly Brit.* (esp. of a client to his solicitor or a solicitor to a barrister) to give relevant facts or information to. —**in'structible** *adj.*

instruction (ın'strʌkʃən) *n.* **1.** a direction; order. **2.** the process or act of imparting knowledge; teaching; education. **3.** *Computers.* a part of a program consisting of coded commands to the computer to perform a specified function. —**in'structional** *adj.*

instructions (ın'strʌkʃənz) *pl. n.* **1.** directions, orders, or recommended rules for guidance, use, etc. **2.** *Law.* the facts and details relating to a case given by a client to his solicitor or by a solicitor to a barrister.

instructive (ın'strʌktıv) *adj.* serving to instruct or enlighten; conveying information. —**in'structively** *adv.* —**in'structiveness** *n.*

instructor (ın'strʌktə) *n.* **1.** someone who instructs; teacher. **2.** *U.S.* a university teacher ranking below assistant professor. —**in'structor,ship** *n.* —**instructress**

THESAURUS

instalment chapter, division, episode, part, portion, repayment, section

instance *n.* **1.** case, case in point, example, illustration, occasion, occurrence, precedent, situation, time **2.** application, behest, demand, entreaty, importunity, impulse, incitement, insistence, instigation, pressure, prompting, request, solicitation, urging ~*v.* **3.** adduce, cite, mention, name, quote, specify

instant *n.* **1.** flash, jiffy (*Inf.*), moment, second, shake (*Inf.*), split second, tick (*Brit. inf.*), trice, twinkling, twinkling of an eye (*Inf.*), two shakes of a lamb's tail (*Inf.*) **2.** on the instant forthwith, immediately, instantly, now, right away, without delay **3.** juncture, moment, occasion, point, time ~*adj.* **4.** direct, immediate, instantaneous, on-the-spot, prompt, quick, split-second, urgent **5.** convenience, fast, precooked, ready-mixed **6.** burning, exigent, imperative, importunate, pressing, urgent

instantaneous direct, immediate, instant, on-the-spot

instantaneously at once, forthwith, immediately, in a fraction of a second, instantly, in the same breath, in the twinkling of an eye (*Inf.*), like greased lightning (*Inf.*), on the instant, on the spot, promptly, quick as lightning, straight away, then and there

instantly at once, directly, forthwith, immediately, instantaneously, instanter (*Law*), now, on the spot, pronto (*Inf.*), right away, right now, straight away, there and then, this minute, *tout de suite,* without delay

instead **1.** alternatively, in lieu, in preference, on second thoughts, preferably, rather **2.** *With* **of** as an alternative *or* equivalent to, in lieu of, in place of, rather than

instigate actuate, bring about, encour-

age, foment, impel, incite, influence, initiate, kindle, move, persuade, prompt, provoke, rouse, set on, spur, start, stimulate, stir up, urge, whip up

instigation behest, bidding, encouragement, incentive, incitement, prompting, urging

instigator agitator, firebrand, fomenter, goad, incendiary, inciter, leader, mischief-maker, motivator, prime mover, ringleader, spur, troublemaker

instil, instill engender, engraft, imbue, implant, impress, inculcate, infix, infuse, insinuate, introduce

instinct aptitude, faculty, feeling, gift, gut feeling (*Inf.*), gut reaction (*Inf.*), impulse, intuition, knack, natural inclination, predisposition, proclivity, sixth sense, talent, tendency, urge

instinctive automatic, inborn, inherent, innate, instinctual, intuitional, intuitive, involuntary, mechanical, native, natural, reflex, spontaneous, unlearned, unpremeditated, unthinking, visceral

instinctively automatically, by instinct, intuitively, involuntarily, naturally, without thinking

institute[1] *v.* appoint, begin, bring into being, commence, constitute, enact, establish, fix, found, induct, initiate, install, introduce, invest, launch, ordain, organize, originate, pioneer, put into operation, set in motion, settle, set up, start

institute[2] *n.* **1.** academy, association, college, conservatory, foundation, guild, institution, school, seat of learning, seminary, society **2.** custom, decree, doctrine, dogma, edict, law, maxim, precedent, precept, principle, regulation, rule, tenet

institution **1.** constitution, creation, en-

actment, establishment, formation, foundation, initiation, introduction, investiture, investment, organization **2.** academy, college, establishment, foundation, hospital, institute, school, seminary, society, university **3.** convention, custom, fixture, law, practice, ritual, rule, tradition

institutional **1.** accepted, bureaucratic, conventional, established, establishment (*Inf.*), formal, organized, orthodox, societal **2.** cheerless, clinical, cold, drab, dreary, dull, forbidding, formal, impersonal, monotonous, regimented, routine, uniform, unwelcoming

instruct **1.** bid, charge, command, direct, enjoin, order, tell **2.** coach, discipline, drill, educate, enlighten, ground, guide, inform, school, teach, train, tutor **3.** acquaint, advise, apprise, brief, counsel, inform, notify, tell

instruction **1.** apprenticeship, coaching, discipline, drilling, education, enlightenment, grounding, guidance, information, lesson(s), preparation, schooling, teaching, training, tuition, tutelage **2.** briefing, command, direction, directive, injunction, mandate, order, ruling

instructions advice, directions, guidance, information, key, orders, recommendations, rules

instructive cautionary, didactic, edifying, educational, enlightening, helpful, illuminating, informative, instructional, revealing, useful

instructor adviser, coach, demonstrator, exponent, guide, master, mentor, mistress, pedagogue, preceptor (*Rare*), schoolmaster, schoolmistress, teacher, trainer, tutor

(ɪn'strʌktrɪs) *fem. n.*
instrument *n.* ('ɪnstrəmənt). **1.** a mechanical implement or tool, esp. one used for precision work. **2.** *Music.* any of various contrivances or mechanisms that can be played to produce musical tones or sounds. **3.** an important factor or agency in something: *her evidence was an instrument in his arrest.* **4.** *Inf.* a person used by another to gain an end; dupe. **5.** a measuring device, such as a pressure gauge. **6. a.** a device or system for use in navigation or control, esp. of aircraft. **b.** *(as modifier): instrument landing.* **7.** a formal legal document. ~*vb.* ('ɪnstrəˌmɛnt). *(tr.)* **8.** another word for **orchestrate** (sense 1). **9.** to equip with instruments.
instrumental (ˌɪnstrə'mɛntəl) *adj.* **1.** serving as a means or influence; helpful. **2.** of, relating to, or characterized by an instrument. **3.** played by or composed for musical instruments. **4.** *Grammar.* denoting a case of nouns, etc. indicating the instrument used in performing an action, usually using the prepositions *with* or *by means of.* ~*n.* **5.** a piece of music composed for instruments rather than for voices. **6.** *Grammar.* the instrumental case. —ˌinstrumen'tality *n.* —ˌinstru'mentally *adv.*
instrumentalist (ˌɪnstrə'mɛntəlɪst) *n.* a person who plays a musical instrument.
instrumentation (ˌɪnstrəmɛn'teɪʃən) *n.* **1.** the instruments specified in a musical score or arrangement. **2.** the study of the characteristics of musical instruments. **3.** the use of instruments or tools.
instrument panel or **board** *n.* **1.** a panel on which instruments are mounted, as on a car. See also **dashboard.** **2.** an array of instruments, gauges, etc., mounted to display the condition or performance of a machine.
insubordinate (ˌɪnsə'bɔːdɪnɪt) *adj.* **1.** not submissive to authority; disobedient or rebellious. **2.** not in a subordinate position or rank. ~*n.* **3.** an insubordinate person. —ˌinsub'ordinately *adv.* —ˌinsubˌordi'nation *n.*
insubstantial (ˌɪnsəb'stænʃəl) *adj.* **1.** not substantial; flimsy, tenuous, or slight. **2.** imaginary; unreal. —ˌinsubˌstanti'ality *n.* —ˌinsub'stantially *adv.*
insufferable (ɪn'sʌfərəbəl) *adj.* intolerable; unendurable. —in'sufferableness *n.* —in'sufferably *adv.*
insufficiency (ˌɪnsə'fɪʃənsɪ) *n.* **1.** Also: ˌinsuf'ficience. the state of being insufficient. **2.** *Pathol.* failure in the functioning of an organ, tissue, etc.: *cardiac insufficiency.*
insular ('ɪnsjʊlə) *adj.* **1.** of, relating to, or resembling an island. **2.** remote, detached, or aloof. **3.** illiberal or narrow-minded. **4.** isolated or separated. —'insularism *or* insularity (ˌɪnsjʊ'lærɪtɪ) *n.* —'insularly *adv.*
insulate ('ɪnsjʊˌleɪt) *vb. (tr.)* **1.** to prevent the transmission of electricity, heat, or sound to or from (a body or device) by surrounding with a nonconducting material. **2.** to isolate or detach. —'insuˌlator *n.*
insulation (ˌɪnsjʊ'leɪʃən) *n.* **1.** Also called: **insulant** ('ɪnsjʊlənt). material used to insulate a body or device. **2.** the act or process of insulating.

insulin ('ɪnsjʊlɪn) *n.* a protein hormone, secreted in the pancreas by the islets of Langerhans, that controls the concentration of glucose in the blood.
insult *vb.* (ɪn'sʌlt). *(tr.)* **1.** to treat, mention, or speak to rudely; offend; affront. ~*n.* ('ɪnsʌlt). **2.** an offensive or contemptuous remark or action; affront; slight. **3.** a person or thing producing the effect of an affront: *some television is an insult to intelligence.* **4.** *Med.* an injury or trauma. —in'sulter *n.*
insuperable (ɪn'suːpərəbəl, -prəbəl, -'sjuː-) *adj.* incapable of being overcome; insurmountable. —inˌsupera'bility *n.* —in'superably *adv.*
insupportable (ˌɪnsə'pɔːtəbəl) *adj.* **1.** incapable of being endured; intolerable; insufferable. **2.** incapable of being supported or justified; indefensible. —ˌinsup'portableness *n.* —ˌinsup'portably *adv.*
insurance (ɪn'ʃʊərəns, -'ʃɔː-) *n.* **1. a.** the act, system, or business of providing financial protection against specified contingencies, such as death, loss, or damage. **b.** the state of having such protection. **c.** Also called: **insurance policy.** the policy providing such protection. **d.** the pecuniary amount of such protection. **e.** the premium payable in return for such protection. **f.** *(as modifier): insurance agent; insurance company; insurance stamp.* **2.** a means of protecting or safeguarding against risk or injury.
insure (ɪn'ʃʊə, -'ʃɔː) *vb.* **1.** (often foll. by *against*) to guarantee or protect (against risk, loss, etc.). **2.** (often foll. by *against*) to issue (a person) with an insurance policy or take out an insurance policy (on): *his house was heavily insured against fire.* **3.** another word for (esp. U.S.) for **ensure.** ~Also (rare) (for senses 1, 2): **ensure.** —in'surable *adj.* —inˌsura'bility *n.*
insured (ɪn'ʃʊəd, -'ʃɔːd) *adj.* **1.** covered by insurance: *an insured risk.* ~*n.* **2.** the person, persons, or organization covered by an insurance policy.
insurer (ɪn'ʃʊərə, -'ʃɔː-) *n.* **1.** a person or company offering insurance policies in return for premiums. **2.** a person or thing that insures.
insurgence (ɪn'sɜːdʒəns) *n.* rebellion, uprising, or riot.
insurgent (ɪn'sɜːdʒənt) *adj.* **1.** rebellious or in revolt, as against a government in power or the civil authorities. ~*n.* **2.** a person who takes part in an uprising or rebellion; insurrectionist. —in'surgency *n.*
insurrection (ˌɪnsə'rɛkʃən) *n.* the act or an instance of rebelling against a government in power or the civil authorities; insurgency. —ˌinsur'rectional *adj.* —ˌinsur'rectionary *n., adj.* —ˌinsur'rectionist *n., adj.*
int. *abbrev. for:* **1.** interest. **2.** interior. **3.** internal. **4.** Also: **Int.** international.
intact (ɪn'tækt) *adj.* untouched or unimpaired; left complete or perfect. —in'tactness *n.*
intaglio (ɪn'tɑːlɪ,əʊ) *n., pl.* **-lios** *or* **-li** (-ljiː). **1.** a seal, gem, etc., ornamented with a sunken or incised design. **2.** the art or process of incised carving. **3.** a design, figure, or ornamentation carved, engraved, or etched into the surface of the material used. **4.** any of various printing

instrument 1. apparatus, appliance, contraption *(Inf.)*, contrivance, device, gadget, implement, mechanism, tool, utensil **2.** agency, agent, channel, factor, force, means, mechanism, medium, organ, vehicle **3.** *Inf.* cat's-paw, dupe, pawn, puppet, tool
instrumental active, assisting, auxiliary, conducive, contributory, helpful, helping, influential, involved, of help *or* service, subsidiary, useful
insubordinate contumacious, defiant, disobedient, disorderly, fractious, insurgent, mutinous, rebellious, recalcitrant, refractory, riotous, seditious, turbulent, undisciplined, ungovernable, unruly
insubordination defiance, disobedience, indiscipline, insurrection, mutinousness, mutiny, rebellion, recalcitrance, revolt, riotousness, sedition, ungovernability
insubstantial 1. feeble, flimsy, frail, poor, slight, tenuous, thin, weak **2.** chimerical, ephemeral, false, fanciful, idle, illusory, imaginary, immaterial, incorporeal, unreal
insufferable detestable, dreadful, enough to test the patience of a saint, enough to try the patience of Job, impos

sible, insupportable, intolerable, more than flesh and blood can stand, outrageous, past bearing, too much, unbearable, unendurable, unspeakable
insufficient deficient, inadequate, incapable, incommensurate, incompetent, lacking, short, unfitted, unqualified
insular *Fig.* blinkered, circumscribed, closed, contracted, cut off, illiberal, inward-looking, isolated, limited, narrow, narrow-minded, parish-pump, parochial, petty, prejudiced, provincial
insulate *Fig.* close off, cocoon, cushion, cut off, isolate, protect, sequester, shield, wrap up in cotton wool
insult 1. *n.* abuse, affront, aspersion, contumely, indignity, insolence, offence, outrage, rudeness, slap in the face *(Inf.)*, slight, snub **2.** *v.* abuse, affront, call names, give offence to, injure, miscall *(Dialect)*, offend, outrage, revile, slag *(Sl.)*, slander, slight, snub
insulting abusive, affronting, contemptuous, degrading, disparaging, insolent, offensive, rude, scurrilous, slighting
insuperable impassable, insurmountable, invincible, unconquerable

insupportable 1. insufferable, intolerable, past bearing, unbearable, unendurable **2.** indefensible, unjustifiable, untenable
insurance assurance, cover, coverage, guarantee, indemnification, indemnity, protection, provision, safeguard, security, something to fall back on *(Inf.)*, warranty
insure assure, cover, guarantee, indemnify, underwrite, warrant
insurgent 1. insurrectionist, mutineer, rebel, resister, revolter, revolutionary, revolutionist, rioter **2.** *adj.* disobedient, insubordinate, insurrectionary, mutinous, rebellious, revolting, revolutionary, riotous, seditious
insurmountable hopeless, impassable, impossible, insuperable, invincible, overwhelming, unconquerable
insurrection coup, insurgency, mutiny, putsch, rebellion, revolt, revolution, riot, rising, sedition, uprising
intact all in one piece, complete, entire, perfect, scatheless, sound, together, unbroken, undamaged, undefiled, unharmed, unhurt, unimpaired, uninjured, unscathed, untouched, unviolated, virgin, whole

techniques using an etched or engraved plate. **5.** an incised die used to make a design in relief. —**intagliated** (ınˈtɑːlɪˌeɪtɪd) adj.

intake (ˈınˌteɪk) n. **1.** a thing or a quantity taken in: an intake of students. **2.** the act of taking in. **3.** the opening through which fluid enters a duct or channel, esp. the air inlet of a jet engine. **4.** a ventilation shaft in a mine. **5.** a contraction or narrowing: an intake in a garment.

intangible (ınˈtændʒıbəl) adj. **1.** incapable of being perceived by touch; impalpable. **2.** imprecise or unclear to the mind: intangible ideas. **3.** (of property or a business asset) saleable though not possessing intrinsic productive value. ~n. **4.** something that is intangible. —inˌtangiˈbility n. —inˈtangibly adv.

integer (ˈıntıdʒə) n. **1.** any rational number that can be expressed as the sum or difference of a finite number of units, as 1, 2, 3, etc. **2.** an individual entity or whole unit.

integral (ˈıntıgrəl) adj. **1.** (often foll. by to) being an essential part (of); intrinsic (to). **2.** intact; entire. **3.** formed of constituent parts; united. **4.** Maths. **a.** of or involving an integral. **b.** involving or being an integer. ~n. **5.** Maths. the sum of a large number of infinitesimally small quantities, summed either between stated limits (**definite integral**) or in the absence of limits (**indefinite integral**). **6.** a complete thing; whole. —integrality (ˌıntıˈgrælıtı) n. —ˈintegrally adv.

integral calculus n. the branch of calculus concerned with the determination of integrals (**integration**) and their application to the solution of differential equations.

integrate vb. (ˈıntıˌgreıt). **1.** to make or be made into a whole; incorporate or be incorporated. **2.** (tr.) to designate (a school, park, etc.) for use by all races or groups; desegregate. **3.** to amalgamate or mix (a racial or religious group) with an existing community. **4.** Maths. to determine the integral of a function or variable. ~adj. (ˈıntıgrıt). **5.** made up of parts; integrated. —**integrable** (ˈıntəgrəbəl) adj. —ˌintegraˈbility n. —ˌinteˈgration n. —ˈinteˌgrative adj.

integrated circuit n. a very small electronic circuit consisting of an assembly of elements made from a chip of semiconducting material.

integrity (ınˈtegrıtı) n. **1.** adherence to moral principles; honesty. **2.** the quality of being unimpaired; soundness. **3.** unity; wholeness.

integument (ınˈtegjumənt) n. any outer protective layer or covering, such as a cuticle, seed coat, rind, or shell. —inˌteguˈmental or inˌteguˈmentary adj.

intellect (ˈıntıˌlekt) n. **1.** the capacity for understanding, thinking, and reasoning. **2.** a mind or intelligence, esp. a brilliant one: his intellect is wasted on that job. **3.** Inf. a person possessing a brilliant mind; brain. —ˌintelˈlective adj. —ˌintelˈlectively adv.

intellectual (ˌıntıˈlektʃuəl) adj. **1.** of or relating to the intellect. **2.** appealing to or characteristic of people with a developed intellect: intellectual literature. **3.** expressing or enjoying mental activity. ~n. **4.** a person

who enjoys mental activity and has highly developed tastes in art, etc. **5.** a person who uses his intellect. **6.** a highly intelligent person. —ˌintelˌlectuˈality or ˌintelˈlectualness n. —ˌintelˈlectually adv. —ˌintelˈlectualˌize or -ˌise vb.

intelligence (ınˈtelıdʒəns) n. **1.** the capacity for understanding; ability to perceive and comprehend meaning. **2.** Old-fashioned. news; information. **3.** military information about enemies, spies, etc. **4.** a group or department that gathers or deals with such information. **5.** (often cap.) an intelligent being, esp. one that is not embodied. **6.** (modifier) of or relating to intelligence: an intelligence network. —inˌtelliˈgential adj.

intelligence quotient n. a measure of the intelligence of an individual. The quotient is derived by dividing an individual's mental age by his actual age and multiplying the result by 100. Abbrev.: **I.Q.**

intelligent (ınˈtelıdʒənt) adj. **1.** having or indicating intelligence; clever. **2.** indicating high intelligence; perceptive: an intelligent guess. **3.** (postpositive; foll. by of) Arch. having knowledge or information. —inˈtelligently adv.

intelligentsia (ınˌtelıˈdʒentsıə) n. (usually preceded by the) the educated or intellectual people in a society or community.

intelligible (ınˈtelıdʒəbəl) adj. **1.** able to be understood; comprehensible. **2.** Philosophy. capable of being apprehended by the mind or intellect alone. —inˌtelliˈbility n. —inˈtelligibly adv.

intemperate (ınˈtempərıt, -prıt) adj. **1.** consuming alcoholic drink habitually or to excess; immoderate. **2.** unrestrained: intemperate rage. **3.** extreme or severe: an intemperate climate. —inˈtemperance or inˈtemperateness n. —inˈtemperately adv.

intend (ınˈtend) vb. **1.** (may take a clause as object) to propose or plan (something or to do something); have in mind; mean. **2.** (tr.; often foll. by for) to design or destine (for a certain purpose, person, etc.). **3.** (tr.) to mean to express or indicate: what do his words intend? **4.** (intr.) to have a purpose as specified; mean: he intends well. —inˈtender n.

intended (ınˈtendıd) adj. **1.** planned or future. ~n. **2.** Inf. a person whom one is to marry; fiancé or fiancée.

intense (ınˈtens) adj. **1.** of extreme force, strength, degree, or amount: intense heat. **2.** characterized by deep or forceful feelings: an intense person. —inˈtensely adv. —inˈtenseness n.

intensifier (ınˈtensıˌfaıə) n. **1.** a person or thing that intensifies. **2.** a word, esp. an adjective or adverb, that serves to intensify the meaning of the word or phrase that it modifies. **3.** a substance, esp. one containing silver or uranium, used to increase the density of a photographic film or plate.

intensify (ınˈtensıˌfaı) vb. **-fying, -fied. 1.** to make or become intense or more intense. **2.** (tr.) to increase the density of (a photographic film or plate). —inˌtensifiˈcation n.

THESAURUS

integral 1. basic, component, constituent, elemental, essential, fundamental, indispensable, intrinsic, necessary, requisite 2. complete, entire, full, intact, undivided, whole

integrate accommodate, amalgamate, assimilate, blend, coalesce, combine, fuse, harmonize, incorporate, intermix, join, knit, merge, mesh, unite

integration amalgamation, assimilation, blending, combining, commingling, fusing, harmony, incorporation, mixing, unification

integrity 1. candour, goodness, honesty, honour, incorruptibility, principle, probity, purity, rectitude, righteousness, uprightness, virtue 2. coherence, cohesion, completeness, soundness, unity, wholeness

intellect 1. brains (Inf.), intelligence, judgment, mind, reason, sense, understanding 2. Inf. brain (Inf.), egghead (Inf.), genius, intellectual, intelligence, mind, thinker

intellectual 1. adj. bookish, cerebral, highbrow, intelligent, mental, rational, scholarly, studious, thoughtful 2. n. academic, egghead (Inf.), highbrow, thinker

intelligence 1. acumen, alertness, apti-

tude, brain power, brains (Inf.), brightness, capacity, cleverness, comprehension, discernment, grey matter (Inf.), intellect, mind, nous (Brit. sl.), penetration, perception, quickness, reason, understanding 2. advice, data, disclosure, facts, findings, gen (Inf.), information, knowledge, low-down (Inf.), news, notice, notification, report, rumour, tidings, tip-off, word

intelligent acute, alert, apt, brainy (Inf.), bright, clever, discerning, enlightened, instructed, knowing, penetrating, perspicacious, quick, quick-witted, rational, sharp, smart, thinking, well-informed

intelligentsia eggheads (Inf.), highbrows, illuminati, intellectuals, literati, masterminds, the learned

intelligibility clarity, clearness, comprehensibility, distinctness, explicitness, lucidity, plainness, precision, simplicity

intelligible clear, comprehensible, distinct, lucid, open, plain, understandable

intemperate excessive, extravagant, extreme, immoderate, incontinent, inordinate, intoxicated, passionate, prodigal, profligate, self-indulgent, severe, tempestuous, un-

bridled, uncontrollable, ungovernable, unrestrained, violent, wild

intend 1. aim, be resolved or determined, contemplate, determine, have in mind or view, mean, meditate, plan, propose, purpose, scheme 2. Often with for aim, consign, design, destine, earmark, mark out, mean, set apart

intense 1. acute, agonizing, close, concentrated, deep, excessive, exquisite, extreme, fierce, forceful, great, harsh, intensive, powerful, profound, protracted, severe, strained 2. ardent, burning, consuming, eager, earnest, energetic, fanatical, fervent, fervid, fierce, forcible, heightened, impassioned, keen, passionate, speaking, vehement

intensely deeply, extremely, fiercely, passionately, profoundly, strongly

intensify add fuel to the flames (Inf.), add to, aggravate, boost, concentrate, deepen, emphasize, enhance, escalate, exacerbate, heighten, increase, magnify, quicken, redouble, reinforce, set off, sharpen, step up (Inf.), strengthen, whet

intensity (ɪnˈtɛnsɪtɪ) n., pl. **-ties. 1.** the state or quality of being intense. **2.** extreme force, degree, or amount. **3.** Physics. **a.** a measure of field strength or of the energy transmitted by radiation. **b.** (of sound in a specified direction) the average rate of flow of sound energy for one period through unit area at right angles to the specified direction.

intensive (ɪnˈtɛnsɪv) adj. **1.** of, relating to, or characterized by intensity: intensive training. **2.** (usually in combination) using one factor of production proportionately more than others, as specified: capital-intensive; labour-intensive. **3.** Agriculture. involving or farmed using large amounts of capital or labour to increase production from a particular area. Cf. **extensive** (sense 3). **4.** denoting or relating to a grammatical intensifier. **5.** denoting or belonging to a class of pronouns used to emphasize a noun or personal pronoun. **6.** of or relating to intension. ~n. **7.** an intensifier or intensive pronoun or grammatical construction. —in'**tensively** adv. —in-'**tensiveness** n.

intensive care n. extensive and continual care provided for an acutely ill patient in a hospital.

intent (ɪnˈtɛnt) n. **1.** something that is intended; aim; purpose; design. **2.** the act of intending. **3.** Law. the will or purpose with which one does an act. **4.** implicit meaning; connotation. **5. to all intents and purposes.** for all practical purposes; virtually. ~adj. **6.** firmly fixed; determined; concentrated: an intent look. **7.** (postpositive; usually foll. by on or upon) having the fixed intention (of); directing one's mind or energy (to): intent on committing a crime. —in'**tently** adv. —in-'**tentness** n.

intention (ɪnˈtɛnʃən) n. **1.** a purpose or goal; aim: it is his intention to reform. **2.** the act of intending. **3.** Med. a natural healing process in which the edges of a wound cling together with no tissue between (**first intention**), or in which the edges adhere with tissue between (**second intention**). **4.** (usually pl.) design or purpose with respect to a proposal of marriage (esp. in **honourable intentions**).

intentional (ɪnˈtɛnʃənᵊl) adj. **1.** performed by or expressing intention; deliberate. **2.** of or relating to intention or purpose. —in,**tention'ality** n. —in'**tentionally** adv.

inter (ɪnˈtɜː) vb. **-terring, -terred.** (tr.) to place (a body, etc.) in the earth; bury, esp. with funeral rites.

inter- prefix. **1.** between or among: international. **2.** together, mutually, or reciprocally: interdependent; interchange.

interact (ˌɪntərˈækt) vb. (intr.) to act on or in close relation with each other. —,**inter'active** adj.

inter alia Latin. (ˈɪntər ˈeɪlɪə) adv. among other things.

interbreed (ˌɪntəˈbriːd) vb. **-breeding, -bred. 1.** to breed within a single family or strain so as to produce particular characteristics in the offspring. **2.** another term for **crossbreed** (sense 1).

intercede (ˌɪntəˈsiːd) vb. (intr.; often foll. by in) to come between parties or act as mediator or advocate: to intercede in the strike. —,**inter'ceder** n.

intercept vb. (ˌɪntəˈsɛpt). (tr.) **1.** to stop, deflect, or seize on the way from one place to another; prevent from arriving or proceeding. **2.** Sport. to seize or cut off (a pass) on its way from one opponent to another. **3.** Maths. to cut off, mark off, or bound (some part of a line, curve, plane, or surface). ~n. (ˈɪntəˌsɛpt). **4.** Maths. **a.** a point at which two figures intersect. **b.** the distance from the origin to the point at which a line, curve, or surface cuts a coordinate axis. **5.** Sport, U.S. the act of intercepting an opponent's pass. —,**inter'ception** n. —,**inter'ceptive** adj. —,**inter'ceptor** or ,**inter'cepter** n.

intercession (ˌɪntəˈsɛʃən) n. **1.** the act or an instance of interceding. **2.** the act of interceding or offering petitionary prayer to God on behalf of others. **3.** such petitionary prayer. —,**inter'cessional** or ,**inter'cessory** adj. —,**inter'cessor** n. —,**interces'sorial** adj.

interchange vb. (ˌɪntəˈtʃeɪndʒ). **1.** to change places or cause to change places; alternate; exchange; switch. ~n. (ˈɪntəˌtʃeɪndʒ). **2.** the act of interchanging; exchange or alternation. **3.** a motorway junction of interconnecting roads and bridges designed to prevent streams of traffic crossing one another. —,**inter'changeable** adj. —,**inter,changea'bility** or ,**inter'changeableness** n. —,**inter'changeably** adv.

intercom (ˈɪntəˌkɒm) n. Inf. an internal telephone system for communicating within a building, aircraft, etc.

intercommunicate (ˌɪntəkəˈmjuːnɪˌkeɪt) vb. (intr.) **1.** to communicate mutually. **2.** to interconnect or have access, as two rooms, etc. —,**intercom'municable** adj. —,**intercom,muni'cation** n. —,**intercom'municative** adj.

intercommunion (ˌɪntəkəˈmjuːnjən) n. association between Churches, involving esp. mutual reception of Holy Communion.

intercourse (ˈɪntəˌkɔːs) n. **1.** communication or exchange between individuals; mutual dealings. **2.** See **sexual intercourse**.

interdict n. (ˈɪntəˌdɪkt). **1.** R.C. Church. the exclusion of a person in a particular place from certain sacraments, although not from communion. **2.** Civil law. any order made by a court or official prohibiting an act. **3.** Scot. law. an order having the effect of an injunction. ~vb. (ˌɪntəˈdɪkt) (tr.) **4.** to place under legal or ecclesiastical sanction; prohibit; forbid. **5.** Mil. to destroy (an enemy's lines of communication) by firepower. —,**inter'dictive** or ,**inter'dictory** adj. —,**inter'dictively** adv. —,**inter'dictor** n. —,**inter'diction** n.

interdisciplinary (ˌɪntəˈdɪsɪplɪnərɪ) adj. involving two or more academic disciplines.

interest (ˈɪntrɪst, -tərɪst) n. **1.** the sense of curiosity about or concern with something or someone. **2.** the power of stimulating such a sense: to have great interest. **3.** the quality of such stimulation. **4.** something in which

intercity adj. n.	**interdepartmental** adj.	**interknit** vb.	**interstellar** adj.
intercollegiate adj.	**interdepartmentally** adv.	**interlace** vb.	**intertribal** adj.
interconnect vb.	**interdepend** vb.	**intermesh** vb.	**intertwine** vb.
interconnection n.	**interdependence** n.	**intermingle** vb.	**intervarsity** adj.
intercontinental adj.	**interdependent** adj.	**intermix** vb.	**interwar** adj.
interdenominational adj.	**intergalactic** adj.	**interplanetary** adj.	**interweave** vb.

THESAURUS

intensity ardour, concentration, depth, earnestness, emotion, energy, excess, extremity, fanaticism, fervency, fervour, fierceness, fire, force, intenseness, keenness, passion, potency, power, severity, strain, strength, tension, vehemence, vigour

intensive all-out, comprehensive, concentrated, demanding, exhaustive, in-depth, thorough, thoroughgoing

intent adj. **1.** absorbed, alert, attentive, committed, concentrated, determined, eager, earnest, engrossed, fixed, industrious, intense, occupied, piercing, preoccupied, rapt, resolute, resolved, steadfast, steady, watchful, wrapped up **2.** bent, hellbent (Inf.), set ~n. **3.** aim, design, end, goal, intention, meaning, object, objective, plan, purpose **4. to all intents and purposes** as good as, practically, virtually

intention aim, design, end, end in view, goal, idea, intent, meaning, object, objective, point, purpose, scope, target, view

intentional calculated, deliberate, designed, done on purpose, intended, meant, planned, prearranged, preconcerted, premeditated, purposed, studied, wilful

intentionally by design, deliberately, designedly, on purpose, wilfully

intently attentively, closely, fixedly, hard, keenly, searchingly, steadily, watchfully

inter bury, entomb, inhume, inurn, lay to rest, sepulchre

intercede advocate, arbitrate, interpose, intervene, mediate, plead, speak

intercept arrest, block, catch, check, cut off, deflect, head off, interrupt, obstruct, seize, stop, take

intercession advocacy, entreaty, good offices, intervention, mediation, plea, pleading, prayer, solicitation, supplication

interchange 1. v. alternate, bandy, barter, exchange, reciprocate, swap (Inf.), switch, trade **2.** n. alternation, crossfire, exchange, give and take, intersection, junction, reciprocation

interchangeable commutable, equivalent, exchangeable, identical, reciprocal, synonymous, the same, transposable

intercourse 1. association, commerce, communication, communion, connection, contact, converse, correspondence, dealings, intercommunication, trade, traffic, truck **2.** carnal knowledge, coition, coitus, congress, copulation, intimacy, sex (Inf.), sexual act, sexual intercourse, sexual relations

one is interested; a hobby or pursuit. **5.** (*often pl.*) benefit; advantage: *in one's own interest.* **6.** (*often pl.*) a right, share, or claim, esp. in a business or property. **7. a.** a charge for the use of credit or borrowed money. **b.** such a charge expressed as a percentage per time unit of the sum borrowed or used. **8.** (*often pl.*) a section of a community, etc., whose members have common aims: *the landed interest.* **9. declare an interest.** to make known one's connection, esp. a prejudicial connection, with an affair. ~*vb.* (*tr.*) **10.** to arouse or excite the curiosity or concern of. **11.** to cause to become involved in something; concern.

interested ('intristid, -təris-) *adj.* **1.** showing or having interest. **2.** (*usually prenominal*) personally involved or implicated: *the interested parties met to discuss the business.* —'**interestedly** *adv.* —'**interestedness** *n.*

interesting ('intristiŋ, -təris-) *adj.* inspiring interest; absorbing. —'**interestingly** *adv.* —'**interestingness** *n.*

interface ('intə,feis) *n.* **1.** *Physical chem.* a surface that forms the boundary between two liquids or chemical phases. **2.** a common point or boundary between two things. **3.** an electrical circuit linking one device, esp. a computer, with another. —**interfacial** (,intə-'feiʃəl) *adj.* —,**inter'facially** *adv.*

interfacing ('intə,feisiŋ) *n.* **1.** a piece of fabric sewn beneath the facing of a garment, usually at the inside of the neck, armholes, etc., to give shape and firmness. **2.** another name for **interlining.**

interfere (,intə'fiə) *vb.* (*intr.*) **1.** (often foll. by *in*) to interpose; meddlesomely or unwarrantedly; intervene. **2.** (often foll. by *with*) to come between or into opposition; hinder. **3.** (foll. by *with*) *Euphemistic.* to assault sexually. **4.** to strike one against the other, as a horse's legs. **5.** *Physics.* to cause or produce interference. —,**inter'ferer** *n.* —,**inter'feringly** *adv.*

interference (,intə'fiərəns) *n.* **1.** the act or an instance of interfering. **2.** *Physics.* the process in which two or more waves of the same frequency and phase combine to form a resultant wave in which a series of stationary nodes or antinodes, known as **interference patterns,** are formed. **3.** any undesired signal that tends to interfere with the reception of radio waves. —**interferential** (,intəfə'renʃəl) *adj.*

interferon (,intə'fiərɒn) *n. Biochem.* any of a family of proteins made by cells in response to virus infection that prevent the growth of the virus.

interfuse (,intə'fju:z) *vb.* **1.** to diffuse or mix throughout or become so diffused or mixed; intermingle. **2.** to blend or fuse or become blended or fused. —,**inter'fusion** *n.*

interim ('intərim) *adj.* **1.** (*prenominal*) temporary, provisional, or intervening: *interim measures to deal with the emergency.* ~*n.* **2.** (usually preceded by *the*) the intervening time; the meantime (esp. in **in the interim**). ~*adv.* **3.** *Rare.* meantime.

interior (in'tiəriə) *n.* **1.** a part, surface, or region that is inside or on the inside: *the interior of Africa.* **2.** inner character or nature. **3.** a film or scene shot inside a building, studio, etc. **4.** a picture of the inside of a room or building, as in a painting or stage design. **5.** the inside of a building or room, with respect to design and decoration. ~*adj.* **6.** of, situated on, or suitable for the inside;

inner. **7.** coming or acting from within; internal. **8.** of or involving a nation's domestic affairs; internal. **9.** (esp. of one's spiritual or mental life) secret or private; not observable. —**in'teriorly** *adv.*

interior angle *n.* an angle of a polygon contained between two adjacent sides.

interior decoration *n.* **1.** the colours, furniture, etc., of the interior of a house, etc. **2.** Also called: **interior design.** the art or business of an interior decorator.

interj. *abbrev. for* interjection.

interject (,intə'dʒɛkt) *vb.* (*tr.*) to interpose abruptly or sharply; interrupt with; throw in: *she interjected clever remarks.* —,**inter'jector** *n.*

interjection (,intə'dʒɛkʃən) *n.* **1.** the act of interjecting. **2.** a word or phrase that is used in syntactic isolation and that expresses sudden emotion; expletive. Abbrev.: **interj.** —,**inter'jectional** *or* ,**inter'jectory** *adj.* —,**inter'jectionally** *adv.*

interlard (,intə'lɑ:d) *vb.* (*tr.*) **1.** to scatter thickly in or between; intersperse: *to interlard one's writing with foreign phrases.* **2.** to occur frequently in; be scattered in or through: *foreign phrases interlard his writings.*

interlay (,intə'lei) *vb.* **-laying, -laid.** (*tr.*) to insert (layers) between; interpose: *to interlay gold among the silver; to interlay the silver with gold.*

interleaf ('intə,li:f) *n., pl.* **-leaves.** a blank leaf inserted between the leaves of a book. —,**inter'leave** *vb.*

interline[1] (,intə'lain) *or* **interlineate** (,intə'lini,eit) *vb.* (*tr.*) to write or print (matter) between the lines of (a text, book, etc.). —'**inter,lining** *or* ,**inter,line'ation** *n.*

interline[2] (,intə'lain) *vb.* (*tr.*) to provide (a part of a garment) with a second lining, esp. of stiffened material. —'**inter,liner** *n.*

interlining ('intə,lainiŋ) *n.* the material used to interline parts of garments, now often made of reinforced paper.

interlock *vb.* (,intə'lɒk) **1.** to join or be joined firmly, as by a mutual interconnection of parts. ~*n.* ('intə,lɒk). **2.** the act of interlocking or the state of being interlocked. **3.** a device, esp. one operated electromechanically, used in a logic circuit to prevent an activity being initiated unless preceded by certain events. ~*adj.* **4.** closely knitted. —'**inter,locker** *n.*

interlocutor (,intə'lɒkjutə) *n.* **1.** a person who takes part in a conversation. **2.** the man in the centre of a troupe of minstrels who engages the others in talk or acts as announcer. **3.** *Scot. law.* a decree by a judge. —,**inter'locutress,** ,**inter'locutrice,** *or* ,**inter'locutrix** *fem. n.*

interlocutory (,intə'lɒkjutəri, -tri) *adj.* **1.** *Law.* pronounced during the course of proceedings; provisional: *an interlocutory injunction.* **2.** interposed, as into a conversation, narrative, etc. **3.** of, relating to, or characteristic of dialogue. —,**inter'locutorily** *adv.*

interlude ('intə,lu:d) *n.* **1.** a period of time or different activity between longer periods, processes, or events; episode or interval. **2.** *Theatre.* a short dramatic piece played separately or as part of a longer entertainment, common in 16th-century England. **3.** a brief piece of music, dance, etc., given between the sections of another performance.

intermarry (,intə'mæri) *vb.* **-rying, -ried.** (*intr.*) **1.** to

---

THESAURUS

interest *n.* **1.** affection, attention, attentiveness, attraction, concern, curiosity, notice, regard, suspicion, sympathy **2.** concern, consequence, importance, moment, note, relevance, significance, weight **3.** activity, diversion, hobby, leisure activity, pastime, preoccupation, pursuit, relaxation **4.** advantage, benefit, gain, good, profit **5. in the interest of** for the sake of, on behalf of, on the part of, profitable to, to the advantage of **6.** authority, claim, commitment, influence, investment, involvement, participation, portion, right, share, stake **7.** *Often plural* affair, business, care, concern, matter ~*v.* **8.** amuse, arouse one's curiosity, attract, divert, engross, fascinate, hold the attention of, intrigue, move, touch **9.** affect, concern, engage, involve

interested 1. affected, attentive, attracted, curious, drawn, excited, fascinated, intent, keen, moved, responsive, stimulated **2.**

biased, concerned, implicated, involved, partial, partisan, predisposed, prejudiced

interesting absorbing, amusing, appealing, attractive, compelling, curious, engaging, engrossing, entertaining, gripping, intriguing, pleasing, provocative, stimulating, suspicious, thought-provoking, unusual

interfere 1. butt in, get involved, intermeddle, intervene, intrude, meddle, poke one's nose in (*Inf.*), stick one's oar in (*Inf.*), tamper **2.** *Often with* **with** be a drag upon (*Sl.*), block, clash, collide, conflict, cramp, frustrate, get in the way of, hamper, handicap, hinder, impede, inhibit, obstruct, trammel

interference 1. intermeddling, intervention, intrusion, meddlesomeness, meddling, prying **2.** clashing, collision, conflict, impedance, obstruction, opposition

interim 1. *adj.* acting, caretaker, improvised, intervening, makeshift, pro tem, pro-

visional, stopgap, temporary **2.** *n.* interregnum, interval, meantime, meanwhile

interior *adj.* **1.** inner, inside, internal, inward **2.** *Geog.* central, inland, remote, upcountry **3.** *Politics* domestic, home **4.** hidden, inner, intimate, mental, personal, private, secret, spiritual ~*n.* **5.** bosom, centre, contents, core, heart, innards (*Inf.*), inside **6.** *Geog.* centre, heartland, upcountry

interjection cry, ejaculation, exclamation, interpolation, interposition

interloper gate-crasher (*Inf.*), intermeddler, intruder, meddler, trespasser, uninvited guest, unwanted visitor

interlude break, breathing space, delay, episode, halt, hiatus, intermission, interval, pause, respite, rest, spell, stop, stoppage, wait

become joined to someone from another group, race, religion, creed, etc. by marriage. **2.** to marry within one's own family, clan, group, etc. —,**inter'marriage** n.

intermediary (,ɪntə'miːdɪərɪ) n., pl. **-aries. 1.** a person who acts as a mediator or agent between parties. **2.** something that acts as a medium or means. *~adj.* **3.** acting as an intermediary. **4.** situated, acting, or coming between; intermediate.

intermediate adj. (,ɪntə'miːdɪɪt). **1.** occurring or situated between two points, extremes, places, etc.; in between. *~n.* (,ɪntə'miːdɪɪt). **2.** something intermediate. **3.** a substance formed during one of the stages of a chemical process before the desired product is obtained. *~vb.* (,ɪntə'miːdɪˌeɪt). **4.** (*intr.*) to act as an intermediary or mediator. —,**inter'mediacy** or ,**inter'mediateness** n. —,**inter'mediately** adv. —,**intermedi'ation** n. —,**inter'medi,ator** n.

interment (ɪn'tɜːmənt) n. burial, esp. with ceremonial rites.

intermezzo (,ɪntə'mɛtsəʊ) n., pl. **-zos** or **-zi** (-siː). **1.** a short piece of instrumental music composed for performance between the acts or scenes of an opera, drama, etc. **2.** an instrumental piece either inserted between two longer movements in an extended composition or intended for independent performance.

interminable (ɪn'tɜːmɪnəbəl) adj. endless or seemingly endless because of monotony or tiresome length. —**in'terminableness** n. —**in'terminably** adv.

intermission (,ɪntə'mɪʃən) n. **1.** an interval, as between parts of a film, etc. **2.** a period between events or activities; pause. **3.** the act of intermitting or the state of being intermitted. —,**inter'missive** adj.

intermittent (,ɪntə'mɪtənt) adj. occurring occasionally or at regular or irregular intervals; periodic. —,**inter'mittence** or ,**inter'mittency** n. —,**inter'mittently** adv.

intern vb. **1.** (ɪn'tɜːn). (*tr.*) to detain or confine within a country or a limited area, esp. during wartime. **2.** ('ɪntɜːn). (*intr.*) *Chiefly U.S.* to serve or train as an intern. *~n.* ('ɪntɜːn). **3.** another word for **internee. 4.** Also: **interne.** the approximate U.S. equivalent of a British **houseman.** —**in'ternment** n. —'**intern,ship** or '**interne,ship** n.

internal (ɪn'tɜːnəl) adj. **1.** of, situated on, or suitable for the inside; inner. **2.** coming or acting from within; interior. **3.** involving the spiritual or mental life; subjective. **4.** of or involving a nation's domestic as opposed to foreign affairs. **5.** situated within, affecting, or relating to the inside of the body. *~n.* **6.** *Euphemistic.* a medical examination of the vagina or uterus. —,**inter'nality** or **in'ternalness** n. —**in'ternally** adv.

internal-combustion engine n. a heat engine in which combustion occurs within the engine rather than in an external furnace.

international (,ɪntə'næʃənəl) adj. **1.** of, concerning, or involving two or more nations or nationalities. **2.** established by, controlling, or legislating for several nations: *an international court.* **3.** available for use by all nations: *international waters. ~n.* **4.** *Sport.* **a.** a contest between two national teams. **b.** a member of a national team. —,**inter,nation'ality** n. —,**inter'nationally** adv.

International (,ɪntə'næʃənəl) n. **1.** any of several international socialist organizations. **2.** a member of any of these organizations.

internationalism (,ɪntə'næʃənəˌlɪzəm) n. **1.** the ideal or practice of cooperation and understanding between

nations. **2.** the state or quality of being international. —,**inter'nationalist** n.

International Phonetic Alphabet n. a series of signs and letters for the representation of human speech sounds. It is based on the Roman alphabet but supplemented by modified signs or symbols from other writing systems.

internecine (,ɪntə'niːsaɪn) adj. **1.** mutually destructive or ruinous; maiming both or all sides: *internecine war.* **2.** of or relating to slaughter or carnage; bloody. **3.** of or involving conflict within a group or organization.

internee (,ɪntɜː'niː) n. a person who is interned, esp. an enemy citizen in wartime or a terrorism suspect.

internist ('ɪntɜːnɪst, ɪn'tɜːnɪst) n. a physician who specializes in internal medicine.

interpenetrate (,ɪntə'pɛnɪˌtreɪt) vb. **1.** to penetrate (something) thoroughly; pervade. **2.** to penetrate each other or one another mutually. —,**inter'penetrable** adj. —,**inter'penetrant** adj. —,**inter,pene'tration** n. —,**inter'penetrative** adj. —,**inter'penetratively** adv.

interplay ('ɪntəˌpleɪ) n. reciprocal and mutual action and reaction, as in circumstances, events, or personal relations.

Interpol ('ɪntəˌpɒl) n. acronym for International Criminal Police Organization, an association of over 100 national police forces, devoted chiefly to fighting international crime.

interpolate (ɪn'tɜːpəˌleɪt) vb. **1.** to insert or introduce (a comment, passage, etc.) into (a conversation, text, etc.). **2.** to falsify or alter (a text, manuscript, etc.) by the later addition of (material, esp. spurious passages). **3.** (*intr.*) to make additions, interruptions, or insertions. **4.** *Maths.* to estimate (a value of a function) between the values already known or determined. Cf. **extrapolate** (sense 1). —**in'terpo,later** or **in'terpo,lator** n. —**in'terpolative** adj.

interpose (,ɪntə'pəʊz) vb. **1.** to put or place between or among other things. **2.** to introduce (comments, questions, etc.) into a speech or conversation; interject. **3.** to exert or use influence or action in order to alter or intervene in (a situation). —,**inter'posal** n. —,**inter'poser** n. —,**interpo'sition** n.

interpret (ɪn'tɜːprɪt) vb. **1.** to clarify or explain the meaning of; elucidate. **2.** to construe the significance or intention of. **3.** to convey or represent the spirit or meaning of (a poem, song, etc.) in performance. **4.** (*intr.*) to act as an interpreter; translate orally. —**in'terpretable** adj. —**in,terpreta'bility** or **in'terpretableness** n. —**in'terpretably** adv.

interpretation (ɪn,tɜːprɪ'teɪʃən) n. **1.** the act or process of interpreting or explaining; elucidation. **2.** the result of interpreting; an explanation. **3.** a particular view of an artistic work, esp. as expressed by stylistic individuality in its performance. —**in,terpre'tational** adj.

interpreter (ɪn'tɜːprɪtə) n. **1.** a person who translates orally from one language into another. **2.** a person who interprets the work of others. —**in'terpreter,ship** n. —**in'terpretress** fem. n.

interregnum (,ɪntə'rɛgnəm) n., pl. **-nums** or **-na** (-nə). **1.** an interval between two reigns, governments, etc. **2.** any period in which a state lacks a ruler, government, etc. **3.** a period of absence of some control, authority, etc. **4.** a gap in a continuity. —,**inter'regnal** adj.

interrelate (,ɪntərɪ'leɪt) vb. to place in or come into a mutual or reciprocal relationship. —,**interre'lation** n.

THESAURUS

intermediary n. agent, broker, entrepreneur, go-between, mediator, middleman

intermediate halfway, in-between (*Inf.*), intermediary, interposed, intervening, mean, mid, middle, midway, transitional

interment burial, burying, funeral, inhumation, sepulture

interminable boundless, ceaseless, dragging, endless, everlasting, immeasurable, infinite, limitless, long, long-drawn-out, long-winded, never-ending, perpetual, protracted, unbounded, unlimited, wearisome

intermingle amalgamate, blend, combine, commingle, commix, fuse, interlace, intermix, interweave, merge, mix

intermission break, cessation, entr'acte, interlude, interruption, interval, let-up (*Inf.*), lull, pause, recess, respite, rest,

stop, stoppage, suspense, suspension

intermittent broken, discontinuous, fitful, irregular, occasional, periodic, punctuated, recurrent, recurring, spasmodic, sporadic, stop-go (*Inf.*)

intern confine, detain, hold, hold in custody

internal **1.** inner, inside, interior, intimate, private, subjective **2.** civic, domestic, home, in-house, intramural

international cosmopolitan, ecumenical (*Rare*), global, intercontinental, universal, worldwide

interpolate add, insert, intercalate, introduce

interpolation addition, aside, insert, insertion, intercalation, interjection, introduction

interpose **1.** come or place between, intercede, interfere, intermediate, intervene, intrude, step in **2.** insert, interject, interrupt (with), introduce, put forth

interpret adapt, clarify, construe, decipher, decode, define, elucidate, explain, explicate, expound, make sense of, paraphrase, read, render, solve, spell out, take, throw light on, translate, understand

interpretation analysis, clarification, construction, diagnosis, elucidation, exegesis, explanation, explication, exposition, meaning, performance, portrayal, reading, rendering, rendition, sense, signification, translation, understanding, version

interpreter annotator, commentator, exponent, scholiast, translator

—ˌinterreˈlationˌship n.

interrogate (ɪnˈtɛrəˌgeɪt) vb. to ask questions (of), esp. to question (a witness in court, spy, etc.) closely. —inˈterroˌgator n. —inˌterroˈgation n.

interrogation mark n. a less common term for **question mark.**

interrogative (ˌɪntəˈrɒgətɪv) adj. 1. asking or having the nature of a question. 2. denoting a form or construction used in asking a question. 3. denoting or belonging to a class of words, such as which and whom, that serve to question which individual referent is intended. ~n. 4. an interrogative word, phrase, sentence, or construction. 5. a question mark. —ˌinterˈrogatively adv.

interrogatory (ˌɪntəˈrɒgətərɪ, -trɪ) adj. 1. expressing or involving a question. ~n. 2. a question or interrogation.

interrupt (ˌɪntəˈrʌpt) vb. 1. to break the continuity of (an action, event, etc.) or hinder (a person) by intrusion. 2. (tr.) to cease to perform (some action). 3. (tr.) to obstruct (a view, etc.). 4. to prevent or disturb (a conversation, discussion, etc.) by questions, interjections, or comment. —ˌinterˈruptible adj. —ˌinterˈruptive adj. —ˌinterˈruptively adv. —ˌinterˈrupted adj.

interrupter or **interruptor** (ˌɪntəˈrʌptə) n. 1. a person or thing that interrupts. 2. an electromechanical device for opening and closing an electric circuit.

interruption (ˌɪntəˈrʌpʃən) n. 1. something that interrupts, such as a comment, question, or action. 2. an interval or intermission. 3. the act of interrupting or the state of being interrupted.

interscholastic (ˌɪntəskəˈlæstɪk) adj. 1. (of sports events, competitions, etc.) occurring between two or more schools. 2. representative of various schools.

intersect (ˌɪntəˈsɛkt) vb. 1. to divide, cut, or mark off by passing through or across. 2. (esp. of roads) to cross (each other). 3. Maths. (often foll. by with) to have one or more points in common (with another configuration).

intersection (ˌɪntəˈsɛkʃən, ˈɪntəˌsɛk-) n. 1. a point at which things intersect, esp. a road junction. 2. the act of intersecting or the state of being intersected. 3. Maths. a. a point or set of points common to two or more geometric configurations. b. Also called: **product.** the elements that are common to two or more sets. —ˌinterˈsectional adj.

interspace vb. (ˌɪntəˈspeɪs). 1. (tr.) to make or occupy a space between. ~n. (ˈɪntəˌspeɪs). 2. space between or among things. —**interspatial** (ˌɪntəˈspeɪʃəl) adj. —ˌinterˈspatially adv.

intersperse (ˌɪntəˈspɜːs) vb. (tr.) to scatter or distribute among, between, or on. —**interspersedly** (ˌɪntəˈspɜːsɪdlɪ) adv. —**interspersion** (ˌɪntəˈspɜːʃən) or ˌinterˈspersal n.

interstice (ɪnˈtɜːstɪs) n. (usually pl.) 1. a minute opening or crevice between things. 2. Physics. the space between adjacent atoms in a crystal lattice. —**interstitial**

(ˌɪntəˈstɪʃəl) adj.

interval (ˈɪntəvəl) n. 1. the period of time between two events, instants, etc. 2. the distance between two points, objects, etc. 3. a pause or interlude, as between periods of intense activity. 4. Brit. a short period between parts of a play, etc.; intermission. 5. Music. the difference of pitch between two notes, either sounded simultaneously or in succession as in a musical part. 6. the ratio of the frequencies of two sounds. 7. at intervals. a. occasionally or intermittently. b. with spaces between. —**intervallic** (ˌɪntəˈvælɪk) adj.

intervene (ˌɪntəˈviːn) vb. (intr.) 1. (often foll. by in) to take a decisive or intrusive role (in) in order to determine events. 2. (foll. by in or between) to come or be (among or between). 3. (of a period of time) to occur between events or points in time. 4. (of an event) to disturb or hinder a course of action. 5. Law. to interpose and become a party to a legal action between others, esp. in order to protect one's interests. —**interˈvener** or ˌinterˈvenor n.

intervention (ˌɪntəˈvɛnʃən) n. 1. an act of intervening. 2. any interference in the affairs of others, esp. by one state in the affairs of another. 3. Econ. the action of a central bank in supporting the international value of a currency by buying large quantities of the currency to keep the price up.

interview (ˈɪntəˌvjuː) n. 1. a conversation with or questioning of a person, usually conducted for television or a newspaper. 2. a formal discussion, esp. one in which an employer assesses a job applicant. ~vb. 3. to conduct an interview with (someone). —ˌinterviewˈee n. —ˈinterˌviewer n.

intestate (ɪnˈtɛsteɪt, -tɪt) adj. 1. a. (of a person) not having made a will. b. (of property) not disposed of by will. ~n. 2. a person who dies without having made a will. —inˈtestacy n.

intestine (ɪnˈtɛstɪn) n. (usually pl.) the part of the alimentary canal between the stomach and the anus. See **large intestine, small intestine.** —**intestinal** (ɪnˈtɛstɪnəl, ˌɪntɛsˈtaɪnəl) adj.

intimacy (ˈɪntɪməsɪ) n., pl. **-cies.** 1. close or warm friendship or understanding; personal relationship. 2. (often pl.) Euphemistic. sexual relations.

intimate¹ (ˈɪntɪmɪt) adj. 1. characterized by a close or warm personal relationship: an intimate friend. 2. deeply personal, private, or secret. 3. (often postpositive; foll. by with) Euphemistic. having sexual relations (with). 4. (postpositive; foll. by with) having a deep or unusual knowledge (of). 5. having a friendly, warm, or informal atmosphere: an intimate nightclub. 6. of or relating to the essential part or nature of something; intrinsic. —ˈintimately adv. —ˈintimateness n.

intimate² (ˈɪntɪˌmeɪt) vb. (tr.; may take a clause as object) 1. to hint; suggest. 2. Rare. to proclaim. —ˈintiˌmater n. —ˌintiˈmation n.

THESAURUS

interrogate ask, catechize, cross-examine, cross-question, enquire, examine, give (someone) the third degree (Inf.), grill (Inf.), inquire, investigate, pump, put the screws on (Inf.), question, quiz

interrogation cross-examination, cross-questioning, enquiry, examination, grilling (Inf.), inquiry, inquisition, probing, questioning, third degree (Inf.)

interrogative curious, inquiring, inquisitive, inquisitorial, questioning, quizzical

interrupt barge in (Inf.), break, break in, break off, break (someone's) train of thought, butt in, check, cut, cut off, cut short, delay, disconnect, discontinue, disjoin, disturb, disunite, divide, heckle, hinder, hold up, interfere (with), intrude, lay aside, obstruct, punctuate, separate, sever, stay, stop, suspend

interrupted broken, cut off, disconnected, discontinuous, disturbed, incomplete, intermittent, uneven

interruption break, cessation, disconnection, discontinuance, disruption, dissolution, disturbance, disuniting, division, halt, hiatus, hindrance, hitch, impediment, intrusion, obstacle, obstruction, pause, separation, severance, stop, stoppage, suspension

intersect bisect, crisscross, cross, cut, cut across, divide, meet

intersection crossing, crossroads, interchange, junction

interval break, delay, distance, gap, hiatus, interim, interlude, intermission, meantime, meanwhile, opening, pause, period, playtime, rest, season, space, spell, term, time, wait

intervene 1. arbitrate, intercede, interfere, interpose oneself, intrude, involve oneself, mediate, step in (Inf.), take a hand (Inf.) 2. befall, come to pass, ensue, happen, occur, succeed, supervene, take place

intervention agency, intercession, interference, interposition, intrusion, mediation

interview 1. n. audience, conference, consultation, dialogue, evaluation, meeting, oral (examination), press conference, talk 2. v. examine, interrogate, question, sound out, talk to

interviewer examiner, interlocutor, interrogator, investigator, questioner, reporter

interwoven blended, connected, entwined, inmixed, interconnected, interlaced, interlocked, intermingled, knit

intestinal abdominal, coeliac, duodenal, gut (Inf.), inner, stomachic, visceral

intestines bowels, entrails, guts, innards (Inf.), insides (Inf.), internal organs, viscera, vitals

intimacy closeness, confidence, confidentiality, familiarity, fraternization, understanding

intimate¹ adj. 1. bosom, cherished, close, confidential, dear, friendly, near, nearest and dearest, thick (Inf.), warm 2. confidential, personal, private, privy, secret 3. deep, detailed, exhaustive, experienced, first-hand, immediate, in-depth, penetrating, personal, profound, thorough 4. comfy (Inf.), cosy, friendly, informal, snug, tête-à-tête, warm ~n. 5. bosom friend, buddy (Inf.), china (Brit. sl.), chum (Inf.), close friend, comrade, confidant, confidante, (constant) companion, crony, familiar, friend, mate (Inf.), mucker (Brit. sl.), pal

intimate² v. allude, announce, communicate, declare, drop a hint, give (someone) to understand, hint, impart, imply, indicate, insinuate, let it be known, make known, remind, state, suggest, tip (someone) the wink (Brit. inf.), warn

intimately 1. affectionately, closely,

intimidate (ɪn'tɪmɪˌdeɪt) vb. (tr.) **1.** to make timid or frightened, as by threats; scare. **2.** to discourage, restrain, or silence unscrupulously, as by threats or blackmail. —in,timi'dation n. —in'timi,dator n.

into ('ɪntʊ; unstressed 'ɪntə) prep. **1.** to the interior or inner parts of: to look into a case. **2.** to the middle or midst of so as to be surrounded by: into the bushes. **3.** against; up against: he drove into a wall. **4.** used to indicate the result of a change: he changed into a monster. **5.** Maths. used to indicate a dividend: three into six is two. **6.** Inf. interested in: I'm really into Freud.

intonation (ˌɪntəʊ'neɪʃən) n. **1.** the sound pattern of phrases and sentences produced by pitch variation in the voice. **2.** the act or manner of intoning. **3.** an intoned, chanted, or monotonous utterance; incantation. **4.** Music. the opening of a piece of plainsong, sung by a soloist. **5.** Music. the capacity to play or sing in tune. —ˌinto'national adj.

intone (ɪn'təʊn) or **intonate** vb. **1.** to utter, recite, or sing (a chant, prayer, etc.) in a monotonous or incantatory tone. **2.** to speak with a particular or characteristic intonation or tone. **3.** to sing (the opening phrase of a psalm, etc.) in plainsong. —in'toner n.

in toto Latin. (ɪn 'təʊtəʊ) adv. totally; entirely; completely.

intoxicant (ɪn'tɒksɪkənt) n. **1.** anything that causes intoxication. ~adj. **2.** causing intoxication.

intoxicate (ɪn'tɒksɪˌkeɪt) vb. (tr.) **1.** (of an alcoholic drink) to produce in (a person) a state ranging from euphoria to stupor; make drunk; inebriate. **2.** to stimulate, excite, or elate so as to overwhelm. **3.** (of a drug, etc.) to poison. —in'toxicable adj. —in'toxi,catingly adv.

intoxication (ɪnˌtɒksɪ'keɪʃən) n. **1.** drunkenness; inebriation. **2.** great elation. **3.** the act of intoxicating. **4.** poisoning.

intr. abbrev. for intransitive.

intra- prefix. within; inside: intramuscular; intrastate; intravenous.

intractable (ɪn'træktəbəl) adj. **1.** difficult to influence or direct: an intractable disposition. **2.** (of a problem, illness, etc.) difficult to solve, alleviate, or cure. —inˌtracta'bility or in'tractableness n. —in'tractably adv.

intrados (ɪn'treɪdɒs) n., pl. **-dos** or **-doses**. Archit. the inner curve or surface of an arch.

intramural (ˌɪntrə'mjʊərəl) adj. Education, chiefly U.S. operating within or involving those in a single establishment. —ˌintra'murally adv.

intrans. abbrev. for intransitive.

intransigent (ɪn'trænsɪdʒənt) adj. **1.** not willing to compromise; obstinately maintaining an attitude. ~n. **2.** an intransigent person, esp. in politics. —in'transigence or in'transigency n. —in'transigently adv.

intransitive (ɪn'trænsɪtɪv) adj. **1. a.** denoting a verb that does not require a direct object. **b.** (as n.) such a verb. **2.** denoting an adjective or noun that does not require any particular noun phrase as a referent. **3.** having the property that although one object is related to a second that bears the same relationship to a third, the first does not bear this relationship to the third: "being the mother of" is an intransitive relationship. ~Cf. **transitive**. —in'transitively adv. —inˌtransi'tivity or in'transitiveness n.

intrauterine (ˌɪntrə'juːtərain) adj. within the womb.

intrauterine device n. a metal or plastic device, in the shape of a loop, coil, or ring, inserted into the uterus to prevent conception. Abbrev.: I.U.D.

intravenous (ˌɪntrə'viːnəs) adj. Anat. within a vein: an intravenous injection. Abbrev. (esp. of an injection): I.V., i.v. —ˌintra'venously adv.

in-tray n. a tray for incoming papers, etc., requiring attention.

intrepid (ɪn'trepɪd) adj. fearless; daring; bold. —ˌintre'pidity n. —in'trepidly adv.

intricate ('ɪntrɪkɪt) adj. **1.** difficult to understand; obscure; complex; puzzling. **2.** entangled or involved: intricate patterns. —'intricacy or 'intricateness n. —'intricately adv.

intrigue vb. (ɪn'triːg), **-triguing, -trigued. 1.** (tr.) to make interested or curious. **2.** (intr.) to make secret plots or employ underhand methods; conspire. **3.** (intr.; often foll. by with) to carry on a clandestine love affair. ~n. (ɪn'triːg, 'ɪntriːg). **4.** the act or an instance of secret plotting, etc. **5.** a clandestine love affair. **6.** the quality of arousing interest or curiosity; beguilement. —in'triguer n. —in'triguingly adv.

intrinsic (ɪn'trɪnsɪk) or **intrinsical** adj. **1.** of or relating to the essential nature of a thing; inherent. **2.** Anat. situated within or peculiar to a part: intrinsic muscles. —in'trinsically adv.

intro ('ɪntrəʊ) n., pl. **-tros.** Inf. short for **introduction.**

intro- prefix. in, into, or inward: introvert.

introduce (ˌɪntrə'djuːs) vb. (tr.) **1.** (often foll. by to) to present (someone) by name (to another person). **2.** (foll. by to) to cause to experience for the first time: to introduce a visitor to beer. **3.** to present for consideration or approval, esp. before a legislative body: to introduce a bill in parliament. **4.** to bring in; establish: to introduce decimal currency. **5.** to present (a radio or television programme, etc.) verbally. **6.** (foll. by with) to

---

THESAURUS

confidentially, confidingly, familiarly, personally, tenderly, very well, warmly **2.** fully, in detail, inside out, thoroughly, through and through, to the core, very well

intimation 1. allusion, hint, indication, inkling, insinuation, reminder, suggestion, warning **2.** announcement, communication, declaration, notice

intimidate affright (Archaic), alarm, appal, browbeat, bully, coerce, cow, daunt, dishearten, dismay, dispirit, frighten, lean on (Inf.), overawe, scare, scare off (Inf.), subdue, terrify, terrorize, threaten, twist someone's arm (Inf.)

intimidation arm-twisting (Inf.), browbeating, bullying, coercion, fear, menaces, pressure, terror, terrorization, threat(s)

intolerable beyond bearing, excruciating, impossible, insufferable, insupportable, more than flesh and blood can stand, not to be borne, painful, unbearable, unendurable

intolerance bigotry, chauvinism, discrimination, dogmatism, fanaticism, illiberality, impatience, jingoism, narrow-mindedness, narrowness, prejudice, racialism, racism, xenophobia

intolerant bigoted, chauvinistic, dictatorial, dogmatic, fanatical, illiberal, impatient, narrow, narrow-minded, one-sided, prejudiced, racialist, racist, small-minded, uncharitable, xenophobic

intonation 1. accentuation, cadence, in-

flection, modulation, tone **2.** chant, incantation

intone chant, croon, intonate, recite, sing

intoxicate 1. addle, befuddle, fuddle, go to one's head, inebriate, put (someone) under the table (Inf.), stupefy **2.** Fig. elate, excite, exhilarate, inflame, make one's head spin, stimulate

intoxicated 1. blotto (Sl.), canned (Sl.), cut (Brit. sl.), drunk, drunken, fuddled, half seas over (Brit. inf.), high (Inf.), inebriated, in one's cups (Inf.), lit up (Sl.), plastered (Sl.), smashed (Sl.), sozzled (Inf.), stewed (Sl.), stiff (Sl.), stoned (Sl.), the worse for drink, three sheets in the wind (Inf.), tight (Inf.), tipsy, under the influence **2.** Fig. dizzy, elated, enraptured, euphoric, excited, exhilarated, high (Inf.), infatuated, sent (Sl.), stimulated

intoxicating 1. alcoholic, inebriant, intoxicant, spirituous, strong **2.** Fig. exciting, exhilarating, heady, stimulating, thrilling

intoxication 1. drunkenness, inebriation, inebriety, insobriety, tipsiness **2.** Fig. delirium, elation, euphoria, exaltation, excitement, exhilaration, infatuation

intransigent hardline, immovable, intractable, obdurate, obstinate, stubborn, tenacious, tough, unbending, unbudgeable, uncompromising, unyielding

intrepid audacious, bold, brave, courageous, daring, dauntless, doughty, fearless, gallant, game (Inf.), heroic, lion-hearted,

nerveless, plucky, resolute, stalwart, stouthearted, unafraid, undaunted, unflinching, valiant, valorous

intricacy complexity, complication, convolutions, elaborateness, entanglement, intricateness, involution, involvement, knottiness, obscurity

intricate baroque, Byzantine, complex, complicated, convoluted, daedal (Literary), difficult, elaborate, fancy, involved, knotty, labyrinthine, obscure, perplexing, rococo, sophisticated, tangled, tortuous

intrigue v. **1.** arouse the curiosity of, attract, charm, fascinate, interest, pique, rivet, tickle one's fancy, titillate **2.** connive, conspire, machinate, manoeuvre, plot, scheme ~n. **3.** cabal, chicanery, collusion, conspiracy, double-dealing, knavery, machination, manipulation, manoeuvre, plot, ruse, scheme, sharp practice, stratagem, trickery, wile **4.** affair, amour, intimacy, liaison, romance

intriguing beguiling, compelling, diverting, exciting, fascinating, interesting, tantalizing, titillating

intrinsic basic, built-in, central, congenital, constitutional, elemental, essential, fundamental, genuine, inborn, inbred, inherent, native, natural, real, true, underlying

start: *he introduced his talk with some music.* **7.** (often foll. by *into*) to insert or inject: *he introduced the needle into his arm.* —ˌintroˈducer *n.* —ˌintroˈducible *adj.*

introduction (ˌintrəˈdʌkʃən) *n.* **1.** the act of introducing or fact of being introduced. **2.** a presentation of one person to another or others. **3.** a means of presenting a person to another person, such as a letter of introduction or reference. **4.** a preliminary part, as of a book, speech, etc. **5.** *Music.* an opening passage in a movement or composition that precedes the main material. **6.** a basic or elementary work of instruction, reference, etc.

introductory (ˌintrəˈdʌktəri, -tri) *adj.* serving as an introduction; preliminary; prefatory.

introit (ˈintrɔit) *n. R.C. Church, Church of England.* a short prayer said or sung as the celebrant is entering the sanctuary to celebrate Mass or Holy Communion. —inˈtroital *adj.*

introspection (ˌintrəˈspɛkʃən) *n.* the examination of one's own thoughts, impressions, and feelings. —ˌintroˈspective *adj.* —ˌintroˈspectively *adv.*

introversion (ˌintrəˈvɜːʃən) *n. Psychol.* the directing of interest inwards towards one's own thoughts and feelings.

introvert *n.* (ˈintrəˌvɜːt). **1.** *Psychol.* a person prone to introversion. ~*adj.* (ˈintrəˌvɜːt). **2.** Also: **introverted**. characterized by introversion. ~*vb.* (ˌintrəˈvɜːt). **3.** (*tr.*) *Pathol.* to turn (a hollow organ or part) inside out.

intrude (inˈtruːd) *vb.* **1.** (often foll. by *into*, *on*, or *upon*) to put forward or interpose (oneself, one's views, something) abruptly or without invitation. **2.** *Geol.* to force or thrust (molten magma) between solid rocks. —inˈtruder *n.* —inˈtrudingly *adv.*

intrusion (inˈtruːʒən) *n.* **1.** the act or an instance of intruding; an unwelcome visit, etc.: *an intrusion on one's privacy.* **2. a.** the movement of magma into spaces in the overlying strata to form igneous rock. **b.** any igneous rock formed in this way. **3.** *Property law.* an unlawful entry onto land by a stranger after determination of a particular estate of freehold. —inˈtrusional *or* inˈtrusive *adj.*

intrust (inˈtrʌst) *vb.* a less common spelling of **entrust**.

intuition (ˌintjuˈiʃən) *n.* **1.** knowledge or perception not gained by reasoning and intelligence; instinctive knowledge or insight. **2.** anything learned or perceived in this way. —ˌintuˈitional *adj.* —ˌintuˈitionally *adv.*

intuitive (inˈtjuːitiv) *adj.* **1.** resulting from intuition: *an intuitive awareness.* **2.** of, characterized by, or involving intuition. **3.** *Philosophy.* (of knowledge) obtained by intuition, not empirically or discursively. —inˈtuitively

adv. —inˈtuitiveness *n.*

Inuit (ˈinjuːit) *n., pl.* **-it** *or* **-its.** an Eskimo of N America or Greenland, as distinguished from one from Asia or the Aleuts.

inundate (ˈinʌnˌdeit) *vb.* (*tr.*) **1.** to cover completely with water; overflow; flood; swamp. **2.** to overwhelm, as if with a flood: *to be inundated with requests.* —ˈinundant *or* inˈundatory *adj.* —ˌinunˈdation *n.* —ˈinunˌdator *n.*

inure *or* **enure** (iˈnjuə) *vb.* **1.** (*tr.; often passive;* often foll. by *to*) to cause to accept or become hardened to; habituate. **2.** (*intr.*) (esp. of a law, etc.) to come into operation; take effect. —inˈurement *or* enˈurement *n.*

in vacuo Latin. (in ˈvækjuˌəu) *adv.* in a vacuum.

invade (inˈveid) *vb.* **1.** to enter (a country, territory, etc.) by military force. **2.** (*tr.*) to occupy in large numbers; overrun; infest. **3.** (*tr.*) to trespass or encroach upon (privacy, etc.). **4.** (*tr.*) to enter and spread throughout, esp. harmfully; pervade. —inˈvadable *adj.* —inˈvader *n.*

invalid¹ (ˈinvəˌliːd, -lid) *n.* **1. a.** a person suffering from disablement or chronic ill health. **b.** (*as modifier*): *an invalid chair.* ~*adj.* **2.** suffering from or disabled by injury, sickness, etc. ~*vb.* (*tr.*) **3.** to cause to become an invalid; disable. **4.** (usually foll. by *out; often passive*) *Chiefly Brit.* to require (a member of the armed forces) to retire from active service through wounds or illness.

invalid² (inˈvælid) *adj.* **1.** not valid; having no cogency or legal force. **2.** *Logic.* having a conclusion that does not necessarily follow from its premisses; not valid. —inˈvalidity (ˌinvəˈliditi) *or* inˈvalidness *n.* —inˈvalidly *adv.*

invalidate (inˈvæliˌdeit) *vb.* (*tr.*) **1.** to render weak or ineffective, as an argument. **2.** to take away the legal force or effectiveness of; annul, as a contract. —inˌvaliˈdation *n.* —inˈvaliˌdator *n.*

invaluable (inˈvæljuəbəl) *adj.* having great value that is impossible to calculate; priceless. —inˈvaluableness *n.* —inˈvaluably *adv.*

invariable (inˈvɛəriəbəl) *adj.* **1.** not subject to alteration; unchanging. ~*n.* **2.** a mathematical quantity having an unchanging value; a constant. —inˌvariaˈbility *or* inˈvariableness *n.* —inˈvariably *adv.*

invasion (inˈveiʒən) *n.* **1.** the act of invading with armed forces. **2.** any encroachment or intrusion: *an invasion of rats.* **3.** the onset or advent of something harmful, esp. of a disease. —inˈvasive (inˈveisiv) *adj.*

invective (inˈvɛktiv) *n.* **1.** vehement accusation or denunciation, esp. of a bitterly abusive or sarcastic kind. ~*adj.* **2.** characterized by or using abusive language, bit-

---

THESAURUS

introduce 1. acquaint, do the honours, familiarize, make known, make the introduction, present **2.** begin, bring in, commence, establish, found, inaugurate, initiate, institute, launch, organize, pioneer, set up, start, usher in **3.** advance, air, bring up, broach, moot, offer, propose, put forward, recommend, set forth, submit, suggest, ventilate **4.** announce, lead into, lead off, open, preface **5.** add, inject, insert, interpolate, interpose, put in, throw in (*Inf.*)

introduction 1. baptism, debut, establishment, first acquaintance, inauguration, induction, initiation, institution, launch, pioneering, presentation **2.** commencement, exordium, foreword, intro (*Inf.*), lead-in, opening, opening passage, opening remarks, overture, preamble, preface, preliminaries, prelude, proem, prolegomena, prolegomenon, prologue **3.** addition, insertion, interpolation

introductory early, elementary, first, inaugural, initial, initiatory, opening, precursory, prefatory, preliminary, preparatory, starting

introspective brooding, contemplative, inner-directed, introverted, inward-looking, meditative, pensive, subjective

introverted indrawn, inner-directed, introspective, inward-looking, self-centred, self-contained, withdrawn

intrude butt in, encroach, infringe, inter-

fere, interrupt, meddle, obtrude, push in, thrust oneself in *or* forward, trespass, violate

intruder burglar, gate-crasher (*Inf.*), infiltrator, interloper, invader, prowler, raider, snooper (*Inf.*), squatter, thief, trespasser

intrusion encroachment, infringement, interference, interruption, invasion, trespass, violation

intrusive disturbing, forward, impertinent, importunate, interfering, invasive, meddlesome, nosy (*Inf.*), officious, presumptuous, pushy (*Inf.*), uncalled-for, unwanted

intuition discernment, hunch, insight, instinct, perception, presentiment, sixth sense

intuitive innate, instinctive, instinctual, involuntary, spontaneous, unreflecting, untaught

inundate deluge, drown, engulf, flood, glut, immerse, overflow, overrun, overwhelm, submerge, swamp

inundation deluge, flood, overflow, tidal wave, torrent

invade 1. assail, assault, attack, burst in, descend upon, encroach, infringe, make inroads, occupy, raid, violate **2.** infect, infest, overrun, overspread, penetrate, permeate, pervade, swarm over

invader aggressor, alien, attacker, looter, plunderer, raider, trespasser

invalid¹ 1. *adj.* ailing, bedridden, disabled, feeble, frail, ill, infirm, poorly (*Inf.*), sick, sickly, valetudinarian, weak **2.** *n.* convales-

cent, patient, valetudinarian

invalid² *adj.* baseless, fallacious, false, ill-founded, illogical, inoperative, irrational, not binding, nugatory, null, null and void, unfounded, unscientific, unsound, untrue, void, worthless

invalidate abrogate, annul, cancel, nullify, overrule, overthrow, quash, render null and void, rescind, undermine, undo, weaken

invaluable beyond price, costly, inestimable, precious, priceless, valuable

invariable changeless, consistent, constant, fixed, immutable, inflexible, regular, rigid, set, unalterable, unchangeable, unchanging, unfailing, uniform, unvarying, unwavering

invariably always, consistently, customarily, day in, day out, ever, every time, habitually, inevitably, on every occasion, perpetually, regularly, unfailingly, without exception

invasion 1. aggression, assault, attack, foray, incursion, inroad, irruption, offensive, onslaught, raid **2.** breach, encroachment, infiltration, infraction, infringement, intrusion, overstepping, usurpation, violation

invective abuse, berating, billingsgate, castigation, censure, contumely, denunciation, diatribe, obloquy, philippic(s), reproach, revilement, sarcasm, tirade, tongue-lashing, vilification, vituperation

ter sarcasm, etc. —**in'vectively** adv. —**in'vective-
ness** n.

inveigh (ın'veı) vb. (intr.; foll. by against) to speak with
violent or invective language; rail. —**in'veigher** n.

inveigle (ın'viːgəl, -'veı-) vb. (tr.; often foll. by into or an
infinitive) to lead (someone into a situation) or persuade
(to do something) by cleverness or trickery; cajole.
—**in'veiglement** n. —**in'veigler** n.

invent (ın'vɛnt) vb. 1. to create or devise (new ideas,
machines, etc.). 2. to make up (falsehoods, etc.);
fabricate. —**in'ventable** adj. —**in'ventor** n.

invention (ın'vɛnʃən) n. 1. the act or process of inventing. 2. something that is invented. 3. Patent law.
the discovery or production of some new or improved
process or machine. 4. creative power or ability; inventive skill. 5. Euphemistic. a fabrication; lie. 6. Music. a
short piece consisting of two or three parts usually in
imitative counterpoint. —**in'ventional** adj. —**in'ven-
tionless** adj.

inventive (ın'vɛntɪv) adj. 1. skilled or quick at contriving; ingenious; resourceful. 2. characterized by inventive skill: an inventive programme of work. 3. of or relating to invention. —**in'ventively** adv. —**in'ventive-
ness** n.

inventory ('ınvəntərı, -trı) n. 1. a detailed list of articles, goods, property, etc. 2. (often pl.) Accounting,
chiefly U.S. **a.** the amount or value of a firm's current assets that consist of raw materials, work in progress, and
finished goods; stock. **b.** such assets individually. ~vb.
3. (tr.) to enter (items) in an inventory; make a list of.
—'**inventoriable** adj. —,**inven'torial** adj. —,**inven'torially** adv.

inverse (ın'vɜːs, 'ınvɜːs) adj. 1. opposite or contrary in
effect, sequence, direction, etc. 2. Maths. **a.** (of a relationship) containing two variables such that an increase
in one results in a decrease in the other. **b.** (of an element) operating on a specified member of a set to produce the identity of the set: the additive inverse element
of x is -x. 3. (usually prenominal) upside down; inverted: in an inverse position. ~n. 4. Maths. an inverse
element. —**in'versely** adv.

inversion (ın'vɜːʃən) n. 1. the act of inverting or state
of being inverted. 2. something inverted, esp. a reversal
of order, mutual functions, etc.: an inversion of their previous relationship. 3. Also called: **anastrophe**. Rhetoric.
the reversal of a normal order of words. 4. Chem. **a.** the
conversion of a dextrorotatory solution of sucrose into a
laevorotatory solution of glucose and fructose by hydrolysis. **b.** any similar reaction in which the optical
properties of the reactants are opposite to those of the
products. 5. Music. **a.** the process or result of transpos-
ing the notes of a chord such that the root, originally in
the bass, is placed in an upper part. **b.** the modification
of an interval in which the higher note becomes the lower or the lower one the higher. 6. Pathol. abnormal positioning of an organ or part, as in being upside down or
turned inside out. 7. Psychiatry. **a.** the adoption of the
role or characteristics of the opposite sex. **b.** another
word for **homosexuality**. 8. Meteorol. an abnormal condition in which the layer of air next to the earth's surface
is cooler than an overlying layer. 9. Also called: **negation**. Computers. an operation by which each digit of a
binary number is changed to the alternative digit, as

10110 to 01001. —**in'versive** adj.

invert vb. (ın'vɜːt). 1. to turn or cause to turn upside
down or inside out. 2. (tr.) to reverse in effect, sequence, direction, etc. 3. (tr.) Phonetics. to turn (the tip
of the tongue) up and back to pronounce (a speech
sound). ~n. ('ınvɜːt). 4. Psychiatry. **a.** a person who
adopts the role of the opposite sex. **b.** another word for
homosexual. 5. Archit. **a.** the lower inner surface of a
drain, sewer, etc. **b.** an arch that is concave upwards,
esp. one used in foundations. —**in'vertible** adj.
—**in,verti'bility** n.

invertebrate (ın'vɜːtɪbrɪt, -,breɪt) n. 1. any animal
lacking a backbone, including all species not classified as
vertebrates. ~adj. also **invertebral**. 2. of, relating to,
or designating invertebrates.

inverted comma or **turned comma** n. another
term for **quotation mark**.

invest (ın'vɛst) vb. 1. (often foll. by in) to lay out (money or capital in an enterprise) with the expectation of
profit. 2. (tr.; often foll. by in) to devote (effort, resources, etc., to a project). 3. (tr.; often foll. by in or
with) Arch. or ceremonial. to clothe or adorn (in some
garment, esp. the robes of an office). 4. (tr.; often foll.
by in) to install formally or ceremoniously (in an official
position, rank, etc.). 5. (tr.; foll. by in or with) to place
(power, authority, etc., in) or provide (with power or
authority): to invest new rights in the monarchy. 6. (tr.;
usually passive; foll. by in or with) to provide or endow
(a person with qualities, characteristics, etc.). 7. (tr.;
foll. by with) Usually poetic. to cover or adorn, as if with
a coat or garment: when spring invests the trees with
leaves. 8. (tr.) Rare. to surround with military forces;
besiege. 9. (intr.; foll. by in) Inf. to purchase; buy. —**in-
'vestable** or **in'vestible** adj. —**in'vestor** n.

investigate (ın'vɛstɪ,geɪt) vb. to inquire into (a situation or problem, esp. a crime or death) thoroughly; examine systematically, esp. in order to discover the truth.
—**in'vesti,gative** or **in'vestigatory** adj. —**in'vesti,ga-
tor** n.

investigation (ın,vɛstɪ'geɪʃən) n. the act or process of
investigating; a careful search or examination in order
to discover facts, etc.

investiture (ın'vɛstɪtʃə) n. 1. the act of presenting with
a title or with the robes and insignia of an office or rank.
2. (in feudal society) the formal bestowal of the possesso-
ry right to a fief. —**in'vestitive** adj.

investment (ın'vɛstmənt) n. 1. **a.** the act of investing
money. **b.** the amount invested. **c.** an enterprise, asset,
etc., in which money is or can be invested. 2. Biol. the
outer layer or covering of an organ, part, or organism.
3. a less common word for **investiture** (sense 1). 4. the
act of investing or state of being invested, as with an official robe, specific quality, etc. 5. Rare. the act of besieging with military forces, works, etc.

investment trust n. a financial enterprise that invests its subscribed capital in securities for its investors'
benefit.

inveterate (ın'vɛtərıt) adj. 1. long established, esp. so
as to be deep-rooted or ingrained: an inveterate feeling
of hostility. 2. (prenominal) settled or confirmed in a
habit or practice, esp. a bad one; hardened. —**in'vet-
eracy** n. —**in'veterately** adv.

THESAURUS

invent 1. coin, come up with (Inf.), conceive, contrive, create, design, devise, discover, dream up (Inf.), formulate, imagine,
improvise, originate, think up 2. concoct,
cook up (Inf.), fabricate, feign, forge, make
up, trump up

invention 1. brainchild (Inf.), contraption, contrivance, creation, design, development, device, discovery, gadget 2. coinage,
creativeness, creativity, genius, imagination,
ingenuity, inspiration, inventiveness, originality, resourcefulness 3. deceit, fabrication,
fake, falsehood, fantasy, fib (Inf.), fiction, figment or product of (someone's) imagination,
forgery, lie, prevarication, sham, story, tall
story (Inf.), untruth, yarn

inventive creative, fertile, gifted, imaginative, ingenious, innovative, inspired, original, resourceful

inventor architect, author, coiner, crea-

tor, designer, father, framer, maker, originator

inventory n. account, catalogue, file, list,
record, register, roll, roster, schedule, stock
book

inverse adj. contrary, converse, inverted,
opposite, reverse, reversed, transposed

inversion antipode, antithesis, contraposition, contrariety, contrary, opposite, reversal, transposal, transposition

invert capsize, introvert, intussuscept
(Pathol.), invaginate (Pathol.), overset, overturn, reverse, transpose, turn inside out, turn
turtle, turn upside down, upset, upturn

invest 1. advance, devote, lay out, put in,
sink, spend 2. endow, endue, provide, supply
3. authorize, charge, empower, license, sanction, vest 4. adopt, consecrate, enthrone, establish, inaugurate, induct, install, ordain 5.
Mil. beleaguer, beset, besiege, enclose, lay

siege to, surround 6. Archaic array, bedeck,
bedizen (Archaic), clothe, deck, drape, dress,
robe

investigate consider, enquire into, examine, explore, go into, inquire into, inspect,
look into, make enquiries, probe, put to the
test, scrutinize, search, sift, study

investigation analysis, enquiry, examination, exploration, fact finding, hearing, inquest, inquiry, inspection, probe, research,
review, scrutiny, search, study, survey

investigator dick (Sl.), examiner, gumshoe (U.S. sl.), inquirer, (private) detective,
private eye (Inf.), researcher, reviewer,
sleuth or sleuthhound (Inf.)

investiture admission, enthronement,
inauguration, induction, installation, instatement, investing, investment, ordination

investment 1. asset, investing, speculation, transaction, venture 2. ante (Inf.), con-

invidious (ɪn'vɪdɪəs) *adj.* **1.** incurring or tending to arouse resentment, unpopularity, etc.: *an invidious task.* **2.** (of comparisons or distinctions) unfairly or offensively discriminating. —**in'vidiously** *adv.* —**in'vidiousness** *n.*

invigilate (ɪn'vɪdʒɪ,leɪt) *vb.* (*intr.*) **1.** *Brit.* to watch examination candidates, esp. to prevent cheating. U.S. word: **proctor.** **2.** *Arch.* to keep watch. —**in,vigi'lation** *n.* —**in'vigi,lator** *n.*

invigorate (ɪn'vɪgə,reɪt) *vb.* (*tr.*) to give vitality and vigour to; animate; brace; refresh: *to be invigorated by fresh air.* —**in'vigor,atingly** *adv.* —**in,vigor'ation** *n.* —**in'vigorative** *adj.* —**in'vigor,ator** *n.*

invincible (ɪn'vɪnsəb°l) *adj.* incapable of being defeated; unconquerable; insuperable. —**in,vinci'bility** *or* **in'vincibleness** *n.* —**in'vincibly** *adv.*

inviolable (ɪn'vaɪələb°l) *adj.* that must not or cannot be transgressed, dishonoured, or broken; to be kept sacred: *an inviolable oath.* —**in,viola'bility** *n.* —**in'violably** *adv.*

inviolate (ɪn'vaɪəlɪt, -,leɪt) *adj.* **1.** free from violation, injury, disturbance, etc. **2.** a less common word for **inviolable.** —**in'violacy** *or* **in'violateness** *n.* —**in'violately** *adv.*

invisible (ɪn'vɪzəb°l) *adj.* **1.** not visible; not able to be perceived by the eye: *invisible rays.* **2.** concealed from sight; hidden. **3.** not easily seen or noticed: *invisible mending.* **4.** kept hidden from public view; secret; clandestine. **5.** *Econ.* of or relating to services, such as insurance and freight, rather than goods: *invisible earnings.* ~*n.* **6.** *Econ.* an invisible item of trade; service. —**in,visi'bility** *or* **in'visibleness** *n.* —**in'visibly** *adv.*

invitation (,ɪnvɪ'teɪʃən) *n.* **1. a.** the act of inviting, such as an offer of entertainment or hospitality. **b.** (*as modifier*): *an invitation race.* **2.** the act of enticing or attracting; allurement.

invite *vb.* (ɪn'vaɪt). (*tr.*) **1.** to ask (a person) in a friendly or polite way (to do something, attend an event, etc.). **2.** to make a request for, esp. publicly or formally: *to invite applications.* **3.** to bring on or provoke; give occasion for: *you invite disaster by your actions.* **4.** to welcome or tempt. ~*n.* ('ɪnvaɪt). **5.** an informal word for **invitation.** —**in'viter** *n.*

inviting (ɪn'vaɪtɪŋ) *adj.* tempting; alluring; attractive. —**in'vitingness** *n.*

invocation (,ɪnvə'keɪʃən) *n.* **1.** the act of invoking or calling upon some agent for assistance. **2.** a prayer asking God for help, forgiveness, etc. **3.** an appeal for inspiration from a Muse or deity at the beginning of a poem. **4. a.** the act of summoning a spirit from another world by ritual incantation or magic. **b.** the incantation used in this act. —**,invo'cational** *adj.* —**invocatory** (ɪn'vɒkətərɪ, -trɪ) *adj.*

invoice ('ɪnvɔɪs) *n.* **1.** a document issued by a seller to a buyer listing the goods or services supplied and stating the sum of money due. **2.** *Rare.* a consignment of invoiced merchandise. ~*vb.* **3.** (*tr.*) **a.** to present (a customer, etc.) with an invoice. **b.** to list (merchandise sold) on an invoice.

invoke (ɪn'vəʊk) *vb.* (*tr.*) **1.** to call upon (an agent, esp. God or another deity) for help, inspiration, etc. **2.** to appeal to (an outside authority) for confirmation, corroboration, etc. **3.** to implore or beg (help, etc.). **4.** to summon (a spirit, etc.); conjure up. —**in'vocable** *adj.* —**in'voker** *n.*

involuntary (ɪn'vɒləntərɪ, -trɪ) *adj.* **1.** carried out without one's conscious wishes; not voluntary; unintentional. **2.** *Physiol.* (esp. of a movement or muscle) performed or acting without conscious control. —**in'voluntarily** *adv.* —**in'voluntariness** *n.*

involute *adj.* ('ɪnvə,luːt), *also* **involuted.** **1.** complex, intricate, or involved. **2.** *Bot.* (esp. of petals, leaves, etc., in bud) having margins that are rolled inwards. **3.** (of certain shells) closely coiled so that the axis is obscured. ~*n.* ('ɪnvə,luːt). **4.** *Geom.* the curve described by the free end of a thread as it is wound around another curve, the **evolute,** such that its normals are tangential to the evolute. ~*vb.* (,ɪnvə'luːt). **5.** (*intr.*) to become involute. —**'invo,lutely** *adv.* —**'invo,lutedly** *adv.* —**,invo'lution** *n.*

involve (ɪn'vɒlv) *vb.* (*tr.*) **1.** to include or contain as a necessary part. **2.** to have an effect on; spread to: *the investigation involved many innocent people.* **3.** (*often passive;* usually foll. by *in* or *with*) to concern or associate significantly: *many people were involved in the crime.* **4.** (*often passive*) to make complicated; tangle. **5.** *Rare, often poetic.* to wrap or surround. **6.** *Maths., obs.* to raise to a specified power. —**in'volvement** *n.* —**in'volver** *n.*

invulnerable (ɪn'vʌlnərəb°l, -vʌlnrəb°l) *adj.* **1.** incapable of being wounded, hurt, damaged, etc. **2.** incapable of being damaged or captured: *an invulnerable fortress.* —**in,vulnera'bility** *or* **in'vulnerableness** *n.* —**in'vulnerably** *adv.*

inward ('ɪnwəd) *adj.* **1.** going or directed towards the middle of or into something. **2.** situated within; inside. **3.** of, relating to, or existing in the mind or spirit: *inward meditation.* ~*adv.* **4.** a variant of **inwards.** ~*n.* **5.** the inward part; inside. —**'inwardness** *n.*

inwardly ('ɪnwədlɪ) *adv.* **1.** within the private thoughts or feelings; secretly. **2.** not aloud: *to laugh inwardly.* **3.** with reference to the inside or inner part; internally.

inwards *adv.* ('ɪnwədz), *also* **inward.** **1.** towards the

---

THESAURUS

tribution, stake **3.** *Mil.* beleaguering, besieging, blockading, siege, surrounding

inveterate chronic, confirmed, deep-dyed, deep-rooted, deep-seated, dyed-in-the-wool, entrenched, established, habitual, hard-core, hardened, incorrigible, incurable, ineradicable, ingrained, long-standing, obstinate

invidious discriminatory, envious (*Obsolete*), hateful, obnoxious, odious, offensive, repugnant, slighting, undesirable

invigorate animate, brace, buck up (*Inf.*), energize, enliven, exhilarate, fortify, freshen (up), galvanize, harden, liven up, nerve, pep up, perk up, put new heart into, quicken, refresh, rejuvenate, revitalize, stimulate, strengthen

invincible impregnable, indestructible, indomitable, inseparable, insuperable, invulnerable, unassailable, unbeatable, unconquerable, unsurmountable, unyielding

inviolable hallowed, holy, inalienable, sacred, sacrosanct, unalterable

inviolate entire, intact, pure, sacred, stainless, unbroken, undefiled, undisturbed, unhurt, unpolluted, unstained, unsullied, untouched, virgin, whole

invisible **1.** imperceptible, indiscernible, out of sight, unperceivable, unseen **2.** concealed, disguised, hidden, inappreciable, inconspicuous, infinitesimal, microscopic

invitation **1.** asking, begging, bidding, call, invite (*Inf.*), request, solicitation, summons, supplication **2.** allurement, challenge, come-on (*Inf.*), coquetry, enticement, glad eye (*Inf.*), incitement, inducement, open door, overture, provocation, temptation

invite **1.** ask, beg, bid, call, request, request the pleasure of (someone's) company, solicit, summon **2.** allure, ask for (*Inf.*), attract, bring on, court, draw, encourage, entice, lead, leave the door open to, provoke, solicit, tempt, welcome

inviting alluring, appealing, attractive, beguiling, captivating, delightful, engaging, enticing, fascinating, intriguing, magnetic, mouthwatering, pleasing, seductive, tempting, warm, welcoming, winning

invocation appeal, beseeching, entreaty, petition, prayer, supplication

invoke **1.** adjure, appeal to, beg, beseech, call upon, conjure, entreat, implore, petition, pray, solicit, supplicate **2.** apply, call in, have recourse to, implement, initiate, put into effect, resort to, use

involuntary **1.** compulsory, forced, obligatory, reluctant, unwilling **2.** automatic, blind, conditioned, instinctive, instinctual, reflex, spontaneous, unconscious, uncontrolled, unintentional, unthinking

involve **1.** entail, imply, mean, necessitate, presuppose, require **2.** affect, associate, compromise, concern, connect, draw in, implicate, incriminate, inculpate, mix up (*Inf.*),

touch **3.** comprehend, comprise, contain, cover, embrace, include, incorporate, number among, take in **4.** absorb, bind, commit, engage, engross, grip, hold, preoccupy, rivet, wrap up **5.** complicate, embroil, enmesh, entangle, link, mire, mix up, snarl up, tangle

involved **1.** Byzantine, complex, complicated, confusing, convoluted, difficult, elaborate, intricate, knotty, labyrinthine, sophisticated, tangled, tortuous **2.** caught (up), concerned, implicated, in on (*Inf.*), mixed up in *or* with, occupied, participating, taking part

involvement **1.** association, commitment, concern, connection, dedication, interest, participation, responsibility **2.** complexity, complication, difficulty, embarrassment, entanglement, imbroglio, intricacy, problem, ramification

invulnerable impenetrable, indestructible, insusceptible, invincible, proof against, safe, secure, unassailable

inward *adj.* **1.** entering, inbound, incoming, inflowing, ingoing, inpouring, penetrating **2.** confidential, hidden, inmost, inner, innermost, inside, interior, internal, personal, private, privy, secret

inwardly at heart, deep down, in one's head, in one's inmost heart, inside, privately, secretly, to oneself, within

interior or middle of something. **2.** in, into, or towards the mind or spirit. ~*pl. n.* (ˈɪnədz). **3.** a variant of **innards.**

inwrought (ˌɪnˈrɔːt) *adj.* **1.** worked or woven into material, esp. decoratively. **2.** *Rare.* blended with other things.

Io *Chem. the symbol for* ionium.

iodide (ˈaɪəˌdaɪd) *n.* **1.** a salt of hydriodic acid, containing the iodide ion, I⁻. **2.** a compound containing an iodine atom, such as methyl iodide.

iodine (ˈaɪəˌdiːn) *n.* a bluish-black element of the halogen group that sublimates into a violet irritating gas. Its compounds are used in medicine and photography and in dyes. The radioisotope **iodine-131** is used in the treatment of thyroid disease. Symbol: I; atomic no.: 53; atomic wt.: 126.90.

iodize *or* **-ise** (ˈaɪəˌdaɪz) *vb.* (*tr.*) to treat or react with iodine or an iodine compound. Also: **iodate.** —ˌiodiˈzation *or* -iˈsation *n.* —ˈioˌdizer *or* -ˌdiser *n.*

I.O.M. *abbrev. for* Isle of Man.

ion (ˈaɪən, -ɒn) *n.* an electrically charged atom or group of atoms formed by the loss or gain of one or more electrons. See also **cation, anion.**

-ion *suffix forming nouns.* indicating an action, process, or state: *creation; objection.* Cf. **-ation, -tion.**

ion exchange *n.* the process in which ions are exchanged between a solution and an insoluble solid, usually a resin. It is used to soften water.

Ionic (aɪˈɒnɪk) *adj.* **1.** of, denoting, or relating to one of the five classical orders of architecture, characterized by fluted columns and capitals with scroll-like ornaments. **2.** of or relating to Ionia, on the coast of Asia Minor, its inhabitants or their dialect of Ancient Greek. ~*n.* **3.** one of four chief dialects of Ancient Greek; the dialect spoken in Ionia.

ionize *or* **-ise** (ˈaɪəˌnaɪz) *vb.* to change or become changed into ions. —ˈionˌizable *or* -ˌisable *adj.* —ˌioniˈzation *or* -iˈsation *n.*

ionosphere (aɪˈɒnəˌsfɪə) *n.* a region of the earth's atmosphere, extending from about 60 to 1000 km above the earth's surface, in which there is a high concentration of free electrons formed as a result of ionizing radiation entering the atmosphere from space. —**ionospheric** (aɪˌɒnəˈsfɛrɪk) *adj.*

iota (aɪˈəʊtə) *n.* **1.** the ninth letter in the Greek alphabet (I, ι), a vowel or semivowel. **2.** (*usually used with a negative*) a very small amount; jot (esp. in **not one** *or* **an iota**).

IOU *n.* a written promise or reminder to pay a debt.

-ious *suffix forming adjectives from nouns.* characterized by or full of: *ambitious; suspicious.*

I.O.W. *abbrev. for* Isle of Wight.

IPA *abbrev. for* International Phonetic Alphabet.

ipecac (ˈɪpɪˌkæk) *or* **ipecacuanha** (ˌɪpɪˌkækjuˈænə) *n.* **1.** a low-growing South American shrub. **2.** a drug prepared from the dried roots of this plant, used as a purgative and emetic.

ipso facto (ˈɪpsəʊ ˈfæktəʊ) *adv.* by that very fact or act.

I.Q. *abbrev. for* intelligence quotient.

Ir *the chemical symbol for* iridium.

Ir. *abbrev. for:* **1.** Ireland. **2.** Irish.

ir- *prefix.* variant of **in-¹** and **in-²** before *r.*

I.R.A. *abbrev. for* Irish Republican Army.

Iranian (ɪˈreɪnɪən) *n.* **1.** a native or inhabitant of Iran, in SW Asia. **2.** a branch of the Indo-European family of languages, including Persian. **3.** the modern Persian language. ~*adj.* **4.** relating to or characteristic of Iran, its inhabitants, or their language; Persian. **5.** belonging to or relating to the Iranian branch of Indo-European.

irascible (ɪˈræsɪbəl) *adj.* **1.** easily angered; irritable. **2.** showing irritability: *an irascible action.* —ˌirasciˈbility *or* iˈrascibleness *n.* —iˈrascibly *adv.*

irate (aɪˈreɪt) *adj.* **1.** incensed with anger; furious. **2.** marked by extreme anger: *an irate letter.* —iˈrately *adv.*

ire (aɪə) *n. Literary.* anger; wrath. —ˈireful *adj.* —ˈirefulness *n.*

iridaceous (ˌɪrɪˈdeɪʃəs, ˌaɪ-) *adj.* of, relating to, or belonging to the family of monocotyledonous plants, including the iris, having swordlike leaves and showy flowers.

iridescent (ˌɪrɪˈdɛsənt) *adj.* displaying a spectrum of colours that shimmer and change due to interference and scattering as the observer's position changes. —ˌiriˈdescence *n.* —ˌiriˈdescently *adv.*

iridium (aɪˈrɪdɪəm, ɪˈrɪd-) *n.* a very hard yellowish-white transition element that is the most corrosion-resistant metal known. It occurs in platinum ores and is used as an alloy with platinum. Symbol: Ir; atomic no.: 77; atomic wt.: 192.2.

iris (ˈaɪrɪs) *n., pl.* **irises** *or* **irides** (ˈaɪrɪˌdiːz, ˈɪrɪ-). **1.** the coloured muscular diaphragm that surrounds and controls the size of the pupil. **2.** Also called: **fleur-de-lis.** any iridaceous plant having brightly coloured flowers composed of three petals and three drooping sepals. **3.** a poetic word for **rainbow.**

Irish (ˈaɪrɪʃ) *adj.* **1.** of, relating to, or characteristic of Ireland, its people, their Celtic language, or their dialect of English. ~*n.* **2. the.** (*functioning as pl.*) the natives or inhabitants of Ireland. **3.** another name for **Irish Gaelic. 4.** the dialect of English spoken in Ireland.

Irish bull *n.* a ludicrously illogical statement.

Irish coffee *n.* hot coffee mixed with whiskey and topped with double cream.

Irish Gaelic *n.* the Goidelic language of the Celts of Ireland, still spoken in the southwest; an official language of the Republic of Ireland since 1921.

Irish stew *n.* a stew made of mutton, lamb, or beef, with potatoes, onions, etc.

irk (ɜːk) *vb.* (*tr.*) to irritate, vex, or annoy.

irksome (ˈɜːksəm) *adj.* causing vexation, annoyance, or boredom; troublesome or tedious. —ˈirksomely *adv.* —ˈirksomeness *n.*

I.R.O. *abbrev. for:* **1.** (in Brit.) Inland Revenue Office. **2.** International Refugee Organization.

iron (ˈaɪən) *n.* **1. a.** a malleable ductile silvery-white ferromagnetic metallic element. It is widely used for structural and engineering purposes. Symbol: Fe; atomic no.: 26; atomic wt.: 55.847. Related adjs.: **ferric, ferrous.** Related prefix: **ferro-. b.** (*as modifier*): *iron railings.* **2.** any of certain tools or implements made of iron or steel, esp. for use when hot: *a grappling iron; a soldering iron.* **3.** an appliance for pressing fabrics using dry heat or steam, esp. a small electrically heated device with a handle and a weighted flat bottom. **4.** any of various golf clubs with metal heads, numbered from 2 to 10 according to the slant of the face. **5.** a splint-like support for a malformed leg. **6.** great hardness, strength, or resolve: *a will of iron.* **7. strike while the iron is hot.** to act at an opportune moment. ~*adj.* **8.** very hard, immovable, or implacable: *iron determination.* **9.** very strong; extremely robust: *an iron constitution.* **10.** cruel or unyielding: *he ruled with an iron hand.* ~*vb.* **11.** to smooth (clothes or fabric) by removing (creases or wrinkles) using a heated iron; press. **12.** (*tr.*) to furnish or clothe with iron. **13.** (*tr.*) *Rare.* to place (a prisoner) in irons. ~See also **iron out, irons.** —ˈironer *n.* —ˈironless *adj.* —ˈironˌlike *adj.*

Iron Age *n.* **a.** the period following the Bronze Age characterized by the extremely rapid spread of iron tools and weapons. **b.** (*modifier*) of or relating to this period.

ironclad *adj.* (ˌaɪənˈklæd). **1.** covered or protected with iron: *an ironclad warship.* **2.** inflexible; rigid: *an ironclad rule.* ~*n.* (ˈaɪənˌklæd). **3.** a large wooden 19th-century warship with armoured plating.

Iron Curtain *n.* **1. a.** the guarded border between the countries of the Soviet bloc and the rest of Europe. **b.** (*as modifier*): *Iron Curtain countries.* **2.** (*sometimes not caps.*) any barrier that separates communities or ideologies.

iron hand *n.* harsh or rigorous control; overbearing or autocratic force.

iron horse *n. Inf., rare.* a steamdriven railway locomotive.

ironic (aɪˈrɒnɪk) *or* **ironical** *adj.* of, characterized by, or using irony. —iˈronically *adv.* —iˈronicalness *n.*

THESAURUS

Irish Hibernian

irksome annoying, boring, bothersome, burdensome, disagreeable, exasperating, irritating, tedious, tiresome, troublesome, un-

interesting, unwelcome, vexatious, vexing, wearisome

iron *adj.* **1.** chalybeate, ferric, ferrous, irony **2.** *Fig.* adamant, cruel, hard, heavy, immov-

able, implacable, indomitable, inflexible, obdurate, rigid, robust, steel, steely, strong, tough, unbending, unyielding

ironic, ironical 1. double-edged,

ironing board *n.* a board, usually on legs, with a suitable covering on which to iron clothes.

iron lung *n.* an airtight metal cylinder enclosing the entire body up to the neck and providing artificial respiration.

iron maiden *n.* a medieval instrument of torture, consisting of an enclosed space lined with iron spikes, into which the victim was locked.

ironmaster ('aɪən‚mɑːstə) *n. Brit.* a manufacturer of iron.

ironmonger ('aɪən‚mʌŋgə) *n. Brit.* a dealer in metal utensils, hardware, locks, etc. *U.S.* equivalent: **hardware dealer.** —'**iron‚mongery** *n.*

iron out *vb.* (*tr., adv.*) **1.** to smooth, using a heated iron. **2.** to put right or settle (a problem or difficulty) as a result of negotiations or discussions. **3.** *Austral. inf.* to knock (a person) out.

iron pyrites *n.* another name for **pyrite.**

iron rations *pl. n.* emergency food supplies, esp. for military personnel in action.

irons ('aɪənz) *pl. n.* **1.** fetters or chains (often in **in** or **into irons**). **2. have several irons in the fire.** to be involved in many projects, activities, etc.

ironsides ('aɪən‚saɪdz) *n.* **1.** a person with great stamina or resistance. **2.** an ironclad ship. **3.** (*often cap.*) (in the English Civil War) **a.** the cavalry regiment trained and commanded by Oliver Cromwell. **b.** Cromwell's entire army.

ironstone ('aɪən‚stəʊn) *n.* **1.** any rock consisting mainly of an iron-bearing ore. **2.** a tough durable earthenware.

ironware ('aɪən‚wɛə) *n.* domestic articles made of iron.

ironwood ('aɪən‚wʊd) *n.* **1.** any of various trees, such as hornbeam, that have very hard wood. **2.** a Californian rosaceous tree with very hard wood. **3.** the wood of any of these trees.

ironwork ('aɪən‚wɜːk) *n.* **1.** work done in iron, esp. decorative work. **2.** the craft or practice of working in iron.

ironworks ('aɪən‚wɜːks) *n.* (*sometimes functioning as sing.*) a building in which iron is smelted, cast, or wrought.

irony[1] ('aɪrənɪ) *n., pl.* **-nies. 1.** the humorous or mildly sarcastic use of words to imply the opposite of what they normally mean. **2.** an instance of this, used to draw attention to some incongruity or irrationality. **3.** incongruity between what is expected to be and what actually is, or a situation or result showing such incongruity.

irony[2] ('aɪənɪ) *adj.* of, resembling, or containing iron.

irradiate (ɪ'reɪdɪ‚eɪt) *vb.* **1.** (*tr.*) *Physics.* to subject to or treat with light or other electromagnetic radiation or with beams of particles. **2.** (*tr.*) to make clear or bright intellectually or spiritually; illumine. **3.** a less common word for **radiate** (sense 1). **4.** (*intr.*) *Obs.* to become radiant. —**ir'radiance** *n.* —**ir'radiative** *adj.* —**ir'radi‚ator** *n.*

irrational (ɪ'ræʃənəl) *adj.* **1.** inconsistent with reason or logic; illogical; absurd. **2.** incapable of reasoning. **3.** *Maths.* (of an equation, etc.) containing one or more variables in irreducible radical form or raised to a fractional power: $\sqrt{(x^2 + 1)} = x^{3/3}$. **b.** (*as n.*): *an irrational.* —**ir'rationally** *adv.* —**ir‚ration'ality** *n.*

irrational number *n.* any real number that cannot be expressed as the ratio of two integers, such as π.

irreconcilable (ɪ'rɛkən‚saɪləbəl, ɪ‚rɛkən'saɪ-) *adj.* **1.** not able to be reconciled; uncompromisingly conflicting; incompatible. ~*n.* **2.** a person or thing that is implacably hostile or uncompromisingly opposed. **3.** (*usually pl.*) one of various principles, ideas, etc., that are incapable of being brought into agreement. —**ir‚recon'cila'bility** *or* **ir'recon‚cilableness** *n.* —**ir'recon‚cilably** *adv.*

irrecoverable (‚ɪrɪ'kʌvərəbəl, -'kʌvrə-) *adj.* **1.** not able to be recovered or regained. **2.** not able to be remedied or rectified. —**‚irre'coverableness** *n.* —**‚irre'coverably** *adv.*

irredeemable (‚ɪrɪ'diːməbəl) *adj.* **1.** (of bonds, shares, etc.) without a date of redemption of capital; incapable of being bought back directly or paid off. **2.** (of paper money) not convertible into specie. **3.** (of a loss) not able to be recovered; irretrievable. **4.** not able to be improved or rectified; irreparable. —**‚irre‚deema'bility** *or* **‚irre'deemableness** *n.* —**‚irre'deemably** *adv.*

irredentist (‚ɪrɪ'dɛntɪst) *n.* **1.** (*sometimes cap.*) a person, esp. a member of a 19th-century Italian association, who favoured the acquisition of territory that had once been part of his country or was considered to have been. ~*adj.* **2.** of, relating to, or advocating irredentism. —**‚irre'dentism** *n.*

irreducible (‚ɪrɪ'djuːsɪbəl) *adj.* **1.** not able to be reduced or lessened. **2.** not able to be brought to a simpler or reduced form. **3.** *Maths.* (of a polynomial) unable to be factorized into polynomials of lower degree, as $(x^2 + 1)$. —**‚irre‚duci'bility** *n.* —**‚irre'ducibly** *adv.*

irrefutable (ɪ'rɛfjʊtəbəl, ‚ɪrɪ'fjuːtəbəl) *adj.* impossible to deny or disprove; incontrovertible. —**ir‚refuta'bility** *n.* —**ir'refutably** *adv.*

irreg. *abbrev. for* irregular(ly).

irregular (ɪ'rɛgjʊlə) *adj.* **1.** lacking uniformity or symmetry; uneven in shape, position, arrangement, etc. **2.** not occurring at expected or equal intervals: *an irregular pulse.* **3.** differing from the normal or accepted practice or routine; unconventional. **4.** (of the formation, inflections, or derivations of a word) not following the usual pattern of formation in a language. **5.** of or relating to guerrillas or volunteers not belonging to regular forces: *irregular troops.* **6.** (of flowers) having any of their petals differing in size, shape, etc. **7.** *U.S.* (of merchandise) not up to the manufacturer's standards or specifications; imperfect. ~*n.* **8.** a soldier not in a regular army. **9.** (*often pl.*) *U.S.* imperfect or flawed merchandise. —**ir‚regu'larity** *n.* —**ir'regularly** *adv.*

irrelevant (ɪ'rɛləvənt) *adj.* not relating or pertinent to the matter at hand; not important. —**ir'relevance** *or* **ir'relevancy** *n.* —**ir'relevantly** *adv.*

THESAURUS

mocking, sarcastic, sardonic, satirical, scoffing, sneering, wry **2.** incongruous, paradoxical

iron out clear up, eliminate, eradicate, erase, expedite, get rid of, harmonize, put right, reconcile, resolve, settle, simplify, smooth over, sort out, straighten out, unravel

irons bonds, chains, fetters, gyves (*Archaic*), manacles, shackles

irony 1. mockery, sarcasm, satire **2.** contrariness, incongruity, paradox

irrational 1. absurd, crazy, foolish, illogical, injudicious, nonsensical, preposterous, silly, unreasonable, unreasoning, unsound, unthinking, unwise **2.** aberrant, brainless, crazy, demented, insane, mindless, muddleheaded, raving, senseless, unstable, wild

irrationality absurdity, brainlessness, illogicality, insanity, lack of judgment, lunacy, madness, preposterousness, senselessness, unreasonableness, unsoundness

irreconcilable 1. hardline, implacable, inexorable, inflexible, intransigent, unappeasable, uncompromising **2.** clashing, conflicting, diametrically opposed, incompatible, incongruous, inconsistent, opposed

irrecoverable gone for ever, irreclaimable, irredeemable, irremediable, irreparable, irretrievable, lost, unregainable, unsalvageable, unsavable

irrefutable apodeictic, apodictic, beyond question, certain, incontestable, incontrovertible, indisputable, indubitable, invincible, irrefragable, irresistible, sure, unanswerable, unassailable, undeniable, unquestionable

irregular *adj.* **1.** desultory, disconnected, eccentric, erratic, fitful, fluctuating, fragmentary, haphazard, intermittent, nonuniform, occasional, out of order, patchy, random, shifting, spasmodic, sporadic, uncertain, unmethodical, unpunctual, unsteady, unsystematic, variable, wavering **2.** abnormal, anomalous, capricious, disorderly, eccentric, exceptional, extraordinary, immoderate, improper, inappropriate, inordinate, odd, peculiar, queer, quirky, unconventional, unofficial, unorthodox, unsuitable, unusual **3.**

asymmetrical, broken, bumpy, craggy, crooked, elliptic, elliptical, holey, jagged, lopsided, lumpy, pitted, ragged, rough, serrated, unequal, uneven, unsymmetrical ~*n.* **4.** guerrilla, partisan, volunteer

irregularity 1. asymmetry, bumpiness, crookedness, jaggedness, lack of symmetry, lopsidedness, lumpiness, patchiness, raggedness, roughness, unevenness **2.** aberration, abnormality, anomaly, breach, deviation, eccentricity, freak, malfunction, malpractice, oddity, peculiarity, singularity, unconventionality, unorthodoxy **3.** confusion, desultoriness, disorderliness, disorganization, haphazardness, lack of method, randomness, uncertainty, unpunctuality, unsteadiness

irregularly anyhow, by fits and starts, disconnectedly, eccentrically, erratically, fitfully, haphazardly, in snatches, intermittently, jerkily, now and again, occasionally, off and on, out of sequence, spasmodically, unevenly, unmethodically, unpunctually

irrelevance, irrelevancy inappositeness, inappropriateness, inaptness, in-

irreligion (ˌɪrɪˈlɪdʒən) n. 1. lack of religious faith. 2. indifference or opposition to religion. —**irreˈligionist** n. —**irreˈligious** adj. —**irreˈligiously** adv. —**irreˈligiousness** n.

irremediable (ˌɪrɪˈmiːdɪəbəl) adj. not able to be remedied; incurable or irreparable. —**irreˈmediableness** n. —**irreˈmediably** adv.

irremissible (ˌɪrɪˈmɪsəbəl) adj. 1. unpardonable; inexcusable. 2. that must be done, as through duty or obligation. —**irreˌmissiˈbility** or ˌirreˈmissibleness n. —ˌirreˈmissibly adv.

irremovable (ˌɪrɪˈmuːvəbəl) adj. not able to be removed. —ˌirreˌmovaˈbility n. —ˌirreˈmovably adv.

irreparable (ɪˈrɛpərəbəl, ɪˈrɛprəbəl) adj. not able to be repaired or remedied; beyond repair. — irˌrepara'bility or ir'reparableness n. —ir'reparably adv.

irreplaceable (ˌɪrɪˈpleɪsəbəl) adj. not able to be replaced: an irreplaceable antique. —ˌirreˈplaceably adv.

irrepressible (ˌɪrɪˈprɛsəbəl) adj. not capable of being repressed, controlled, or restrained. —ˌirreˌpressiˈbility or ˌirreˈpressibleness n. —ˌirreˈpressibly adv.

irreproachable (ˌɪrɪˈprəʊtʃəbəl) adj. not deserving reproach; blameless. —ˌirreˌproachaˈbility or ˌirreˈproachableness n. —ˌirreˈproachably adv.

irresistible (ˌɪrɪˈzɪstəbəl) adj. 1. not able to be resisted or refused; overpowering: an irresistible impulse. 2. very fascinating or alluring: an irresistible woman. —ˌirreˌsistiˈbility or ˌirreˈsistibleness n. —ˌirreˈsistibly adv.

irresolute (ɪˈrɛzəˌluːt) adj. lacking resolution; wavering; hesitating. —irˈresoˌlutely adv. —irˈresoˌluteness or irˌresoˈlution n.

irrespective (ˌɪrɪˈspɛktɪv) adj. 1. **irrespective of** (prep.) without taking account of; regardless of. ~adv. 2. Inf. regardless; without due consideration: he carried on with his plan irrespective. —ˌirreˈspectively adv.

irresponsible (ˌɪrɪˈspɒnsəbəl) adj. 1. not showing or done with due care for the consequences of one's actions or attitudes; reckless. 2. not capable of bearing responsibility. —ˌirreˌsponsiˈbility or ˌirreˈsponsibleness n. —ˌirreˈsponsibly adv.

irretrievable (ˌɪrɪˈtriːvəbəl) adj. not able to be retrieved, recovered, or repaired. —ˌirreˌtrievaˈbility n. —ˌirreˈtrievably adv.

irreverence (ɪˈrɛvərəns, ɪˈrɛvrəns) n. 1. lack of due respect or veneration; disrespect. 2. a disrespectful remark or act. —irˈreverent or irˌreveˈrential adj. —irˈreverently adv.

irreversible (ˌɪrɪˈvɜːsəbəl) adj. 1. not able to be reversed: the irreversible flow of time. 2. not able to be revoked or repealed; irrevocable. 3. Chem., physics. capable of changing or producing a change in one direction only: an irreversible reaction. —ˌirreˌversiˈbility or ˌirreˈversibleness n. —ˌirreˈversibly adv.

irrevocable (ɪˈrɛvəkəbəl) adj. not able to be revoked, changed, or undone; unalterable. —irˌrevocaˈbility or irˈrevocableness n. —irˈrevocably adv.

irrigate (ˈɪrɪˌgeɪt) vb. 1. to supply (land) with water by means of artificial canals, ditches, etc., esp. to promote the growth of food crops. 2. Med. to bathe or wash out (a bodily part, cavity, or wound). 3. (tr.) to make fertile, fresh, or vital by or as if by watering. —ˈirrigable adj. —ˌirriˈgation n. —ˈirriˌgative adj. —ˈirriˌgator n.

irritable (ˈɪrɪtəbəl) adj. 1. quickly irritated; easily annoyed; peevish. 2. (of all living organisms) capable of responding to such stimuli as heat, light, and touch. 3. Pathol. abnormally sensitive. —ˌirritaˈbility n. —ˈirritableness n. —ˈirritably adv.

irritant (ˈɪrɪtənt) adj. 1. causing irritation; irritating. ~n. 2. something irritant. —ˈirritancy n.

irritate (ˈɪrɪˌteɪt) vb. 1. to annoy or anger (someone). 2. (tr.) Biol. to stimulate (an organism or part) to respond in a characteristic manner. 3. (tr.) Pathol. to cause (a bodily organ or part) to become excessively stimulated, resulting in inflammation, tenderness, etc. —ˌirriˈtation n. —ˈirriˌtator n.

irrupt (ɪˈrʌpt) vb. (intr.) 1. to enter forcibly or suddenly. 2. (of population) to increase suddenly in numbers. —irˈruption n. —irˈruptive adj.

is (ɪz) vb. (used with he, she, it, and with singular nouns) a form of the present tense (indicative mood) of **be**.

Is. abbrev. for: 1. Also: **Isa.** Bible. Isaiah. 2. **Island(s)** or **Isle(s)**.

is- combining form. variant of iso- before a vowel: isentropic.

I.S.B.N., ISBN abbrev. for International Standard Book Number.

-ise suffix forming verbs. a variant of **-ize**.
▷ Usage. See at **-ize**.

-ish suffix forming adjectives. 1. of or belonging to a nationality: Scottish. 2. Often derog. having the manner or qualities of; resembling: slavish; boyish. 3. somewhat; approximately: yellowish; sevenish. 4. concerned or preoccupied with: bookish.

isinglass (ˈaɪzɪŋˌɡlɑːs) n. 1. a gelatin made from the air bladders of freshwater fish, used as a clarifying agent and adhesive. 2. another name for **mica**.

Isl. abbrev. for: 1. Island. 2. Isle.

THESAURUS

irrelevant beside the point, extraneous, immaterial, impertinent, inapplicable, inapposite, inappropriate, inapt, inconsequent, neither here nor there, unconnected, unrelated

irreparable beyond repair, incurable, irrecoverable, irremediable, irreplaceable, irretrievable, irreversible

irreplaceable indispensable, invaluable, priceless, unique, vital

irrepressible boisterous, bubbling over, buoyant, ebullient, effervescent, insuppressible, uncontainable, uncontrollable, unmanageable, unquenchable, unrestrainable, unstoppable

irreproachable beyond reproach, blameless, faultless, guiltless, impeccable, inculpable, innocent, irreprehensible, irreprovable, perfect, pure, unblemished, unimpeachable

irresistible 1. compelling, imperative, overmastering, overpowering, overwhelming, potent, urgent 2. ineluctable, inescapable, inevitable, inexorable, unavoidable 3. alluring, beckoning, enchanting, fascinating, ravishing, seductive, tempting

irresolute doubtful, fickle, half-hearted, hesitant, hesitating, indecisive, infirm, in two minds, tentative, undecided, undetermined, unsettled, unstable, unsteady, vacillating, wavering, weak

irrespective of apart from, despite, discounting, in spite of, notwithstanding, regardless of, without reference to, without regard to

irresponsible careless, featherbrained, flighty, giddy, harebrained, harumscarum, ill-considered, immature, reckless, scatter-brained, shiftless, thoughtless, undependable, unreliable, untrustworthy, wild

irreverence cheek (Inf.), cheekiness (Inf.), derision, disrespect, flippancy, impertinence, impudence, lack of respect, mockery, sauce (Inf.)

irreverent cheeky (Inf.), contemptuous, derisive, disrespectful, flip (Inf.), flippant, iconoclastic, impertinent, impious, impudent, mocking, saucy, tongue-in-cheek

irreversible final, incurable, irreparable, irrevocable, unalterable

irrevocable changeless, fated, fixed, immutable, invariable, irremediable, irretrievable, irreversible, predestined, predetermined, settled, unalterable, unchangeable, unreversible

irrigate flood, inundate, moisten, water, wet

irritability bad temper, ill humour, impatience, irascibility, peevishness, petulance, prickliness, testiness, tetchiness, touchiness

irritable bad-tempered, cantankerous, choleric, crabbed, crabby, cross, crotchety (Inf.), dyspeptic, exasperated, fiery, fretful, hasty, hot, ill-humoured, ill-tempered, irascible, narky (Inf.), out of humour, oversensi-

tive, peevish, petulant, prickly, snappish, snappy, snarling, tense, testy, touchy

irritate 1. aggravate (Inf.), anger, annoy, bother, drive one up the wall (Inf.), enrage, exasperate, fret, get in one's hair (Inf.), get one's back up (Inf.), get one's hackles up, get on one's nerves (Inf.), harass, incense, inflame, infuriate, needle (Inf.), nettle, offend, pester, provoke, raise one's hackles, rankle with, rub up the wrong way (Inf.), ruffle, try one's patience, vex 2. aggravate, chafe, fret, inflame, intensify, pain, rub

irritated angry, annoyed, bothered, cross, displeased, exasperated, flustered, harassed, impatient, irritable, nettled, out of humour, peeved (Inf.), piqued, put out, ruffled, vexed

irritating aggravating (Inf.), annoying, displeasing, disquieting, disturbing, galling, infuriating, irksome, maddening, nagging, pestilential, provoking, thorny, troublesome, trying, upsetting, vexatious, worrisome

irritation 1. anger, annoyance, crossness, displeasure, exasperation, ill humour, ill temper, impatience, indignation, irritability, resentment, shortness, snappiness, testiness, vexation, wrath 2. aggravation (Inf.), annoyance, goad, irritant, nuisance, pain (Inf.), pain in the neck (Inf.), pest, provocation, tease, thorn in one's flesh

Islam ('ɪzlɑːm) n. 1. Also called: **Islamism**. the religion of Muslims, teaching that there is only one God and that Mohammed is his prophet; Mohammedanism. 2. a. Muslims collectively and their civilization. b. the countries where the Muslim religion is predominant. —**Is'lamic** adj.

island ('aɪlənd) n. 1. a mass of land that is surrounded by water and is smaller than a continent. 2. something resembling this: a traffic island. 3. Anat. a part, structure, or group of cells distinct in constitution from its immediate surroundings. ~Related adj.: **insular.** ~vb. (tr.) Rare. 4. to cause to become an island. 5. to intersperse with islands, 6. to place on an island; insulate; isolate. —**'island-,like** adj.

islander ('aɪləndə) n. a native or inhabitant of an island.

isle (aɪl) n. Poetic except when cap. and part of place name. an island, esp. a small one.

islet ('aɪlɪt) n. a small island.

ism ('ɪzəm) n. Inf., often derog. an unspecified doctrine, system, or practice.

-ism suffix forming nouns. 1. indicating an action, process, or result: criticism. 2. indicating a state or condition: paganism. 3. indicating a doctrine, system, or body of principles and practices: Leninism; spiritualism. 4. indicating behaviour or a characteristic quality: heroism. 5. indicating a characteristic usage, esp. of a language: Scotticism.

iso- or before a vowel **is-** combining form. 1. equal or identical: isomagnetic. 2. indicating that a chemical compound is an isomer of a specified compound: isobutane.

isobar ('aɪsəʊ,bɑː) n. 1. a line on a map connecting places of equal atmospheric pressure, usually reduced to sea level for purposes of comparison, at a given time or period. 2. Physics. any of two or more atoms that have the same mass number but different atomic numbers. Cf. **isotope.** —**'isobarism** n. —,**iso'baric** adj.

isochronal (aɪ'sɒkrənəl) or **isochronous** adj. 1. having the same duration; equal in time. 2. occurring at equal time intervals; having a uniform period of vibration. —**i'sochronally** or **i'sochronously** adv. —**i'sochronism** n.

isolate vb. ('aɪsə,leɪt) (tr.) 1. to place apart; cause to be alone. 2. Med. to quarantine (a person or animal) having a contagious disease. 3. to obtain (a compound) in an uncombined form. 4. to obtain pure cultures of (bacteria, esp. those causing a particular disease). 5. Electronics. to prevent interaction between (circuits, components, etc.); insulate. ~n. ('aɪsəlɪt). 6. an isolated person or group. —**'isolable** adj. —,**isola'bility** n. —**'iso,lator** n. —,**iso'lation** n.

isomer ('aɪsəmə) n. 1. Chem. a compound that exhibits isomerism with one or more other compounds. 2. Physics. a nuclide that exhibits isomerism with one or more other nuclides. —**isomeric** (,aɪsə'mɛrɪk) adj.

isometric (,aɪsəʊ'mɛtrɪk) adj. also **isometrical**. 1. having equal dimensions or measurements. 2. Physiol. of or relating to muscular contraction that does not produce shortening of the muscle. 3. (of a crystal or system of crystallization) having three mutually perpendicular equal axes. 4. (of a method of projecting a drawing in three dimensions) having the three axes equally inclined and all lines drawn to scale. ~n. 5. Also called: isometric **drawing**. a drawing made in this way. —,**iso'metrically** adv.

isomorphism (,aɪsəʊ'mɔːfɪzəm) n. 1. Biol. similarity of form, as in different generations of the same life cycle. 2. Chem. the existence of two or more substances of different composition in a similar crystalline form. 3. Maths. a one-to-one correspondence between the el-

ements of two or more sets, such as those of Arabic and Roman numerals. —,**iso'morphic** or ,**iso'morphous** adj. —**'iso,morph** n.

isosceles (aɪ'sɒsɪ,liːz) adj. (of a triangle) having two sides of equal length.

isotherm ('aɪsəʊ,θɜːm) n. 1. a line on a map linking places of equal temperature. 2. Physics. a curve on a graph that connects points of equal temperature. ~Also called: **isothermal, isothermal line.**

isotope ('aɪsə,təʊp) n. one of two or more atoms with the same atomic number that contain different numbers of neutrons. —**isotopic** (,aɪsə'tɒpɪk) adj. —,**iso'topically** adv. —**isotopy** (aɪ'sɒtəpɪ) n.

isotropic (,aɪsəʊ'trɒpɪk) or **isotropous** (aɪ'sɒtrəpəs) adj. 1. having uniform physical properties in all directions. 2. Biol. not having predetermined axes: isotropic eggs. —,**iso'tropically** adv. —**i'sotropy** n.

Israel ('ɪzreɪəl, -rɪəl) n. 1. a. a republic in SW Asia, established as the modern state of Israel. b. the ancient kingdom of the Jews in this region. 2. **Children of Israel.** the Jewish people or nation.

Israelite ('ɪzrɪə,laɪt, -rə-) n. 1. Bible. a member of the ethnic group claiming descent from Jacob; a Hebrew. 2. a member of any of various Christian sects who regard themselves as God's chosen people. 3. an archaic word for a Jew.

issue ('ɪʃuː) n. 1. the act of sending or giving out something; supply; delivery. 2. something issued; an edition of stamps, a magazine, etc. 3. the act of emerging; outflow; discharge. 4. something flowing out, such as a river. 5. a place of outflow; outlet. 6. the descendants of a person; offspring; progeny. 7. a topic of interest or discussion. 8. an important subject requiring a decision. 9. an outcome or consequence; result. 10. Pathol. discharge from a wound. 11. Law. the matter remaining in dispute between the parties to an action after the pleadings. 12. the yield from or profits arising out of land or other property. 13. **at issue. a.** under discussion. **b.** in disagreement. 14. **force the issue.** to compel decision on some matter. 15. **join issue.** to join in controversy. 16. **take issue.** to disagree. ~vb. **-suing, -sued.** 17. to come forth or emerge or cause to come forth or emerge. 18. to publish or deliver (a newspaper, magazine, etc.). 19. (tr.) to make known or announce. 20. (intr.) to originate or proceed. 21. (intr.) to be a consequence; result. 22. (intr.; foll. by in) to end or terminate. 23. (tr.) (foll. by with) to supply officially (with). —**'issuer** n. —**'issuable** adj.

-ist suffix. 1. (forming nouns) a person who performs a certain action or is concerned with something specified: motorist; soloist. 2. (forming nouns) a person who practises in a specific field: physicist. 3. (forming nouns and adjectives) a person who advocates a particular doctrine, system, etc., or relating to such a person or the doctrine advocated: socialist. 4. (forming nouns and adjectives) a person characterized by a specified trait, tendency, etc., or relating to such a person or trait: purist.

isthmian ('ɪsθmɪən) adj. relating to or situated in an isthmus.

isthmus ('ɪsməs) n., pl. **-muses** or **-mi** (-maɪ). 1. a narrow strip of land connecting two relatively large land areas. 2. Anat. **a.** a narrow band of tissue connecting two larger parts of a structure. **b.** a narrow passage connecting two cavities. —**'isthmian** or **'isthmoid** adj.

-istic suffix forming adjectives. equivalent to a combination of -ist and -ic but in some words having a less specific or literal application and sometimes a mildly pejorative force, as compared with corresponding adjectives ending in -ist: communistic; impressionistic.

it (ɪt) pron. (subjective or objective) 1. refers to a nonhu-

---

THESAURUS

isolate cut off, detach, disconnect, divorce, insulate, quarantine, segregate, separate, sequester, set apart

isolated 1. backwoods, hidden, incommunicado, lonely, off the beaten track, outlying, out-of-the-way, remote, retired, secluded, unfrequented 2. abnormal, anomalous, exceptional, freak, random, single, solitary, special, unique, unrelated, untypical, unusual

isolation aloofness, detachment, disconnection, exile, insularity, insulation, loneliness, quarantine, remoteness, retirement, seclusion, segregation, self-sufficiency, separa-

tion, solitude, withdrawal

issue n. 1. affair, argument, concern, controversy, matter, matter of contention, point, point in question, problem, question, subject, topic 2. **at issue** at variance, controversial, in disagreement, in dispute, to be decided, under discussion, unsettled 3. **take issue** challenge, disagree, dispute, object, oppose, raise an objection, take exception 4. conclusion, consequence, culmination, effect, end, finale, outcome, pay-off (Inf.), result, termination, upshot 5. copy, edition, impression, instalment, number, printing 6. cir-

culation, delivery, dispersion, dissemination, distribution, granting, issuance, issuing, publication, sending out, supply, supplying 7. children, descendants, heirs, offspring, progeny, scions, seed (Biblical) ~v. 8. announce, broadcast, circulate, deliver, distribute, emit, give out, promulgate, publish, put in circulation, put out, release 9. arise, be a consequence of, come forth, emanate, emerge, flow, originate, proceed, rise, spring, stem

man, animal, plant, or inanimate thing, or sometimes to a small baby: *it looks dangerous; give it a bone.* **2.** refers to an unspecified or implied antecedent or to a previous or understood clause, phrase, etc.: *it is impossible; I knew it.* **3.** used to represent human life or experience in respect of the present situation: *how's it going? I've had it; to brazen it out.* **4.** used as a formal subject (or object), referring to a following clause, phrase, or word: *it helps to know the truth; I consider it dangerous to go on.* **5.** used in the nominative as the formal grammatical subject of impersonal verbs: *it is raining; it hurts.* **6.** (used as complement with *be*) *Inf.* the crucial or ultimate point: *the steering failed and I thought that was it.* ~*n.* **7.** (in children's games) the player whose turn it is to try to touch another. **8.** *Inf.* **a.** sexual intercourse. **b.** sex appeal.

It. *abbrev. for:* **1.** Italian. **2.** Italy.

i.t.a. *or* **I.T.A.** *abbrev. for* initial teaching alphabet, a partly phonetic alphabet used to teach reading.

I.T.A. (in Britain) *abbrev. for* Independent Television Authority: now superseded by the I.B.A.

ital. *abbrev. for* italic.

Ital. *abbrev. for:* **1.** Italian. **2.** Italy.

Italian (ɪˈtæljən) *n.* **1.** the official language of Italy and one of the official languages of Switzerland. **2.** a native or inhabitant of Italy or a descendant of one. ~*adj.* **3.** relating to, denoting, or characteristic of Italy, its inhabitants, or their language.

Italianate (ɪˈtæljənɪt, -ˌneɪt) *or* **Italianesque** *adj.* Italian in style or character.

italic (ɪˈtælɪk) *adj.* **1.** Also: **Italian.** of, relating to, or denoting a style of handwriting with the letters slanting to the right. **2.** a style of printing type modelled on this, chiefly used to indicate emphasis, a foreign word, etc. Cf. **roman.** ~*n.* **3.** (*often pl.*) italic type or print.

italicize *or* **-ise** (ɪˈtælɪˌsaɪz) *vb.* **1.** to print (textual matter) in italic type. **2.** (*tr.*) to underline (words, etc.) with a single line to indicate italics. —iˌtaliciˈzation *or* -iˈsation *n.*

itch (ɪtʃ) *n.* **1.** an irritation or tickling sensation of the skin causing a desire to scratch. **2.** a restless desire. **3.** any skin disorder, such as scabies, characterized by intense itching. ~*vb.* **4.** to feel or produce an irritating or tickling sensation. **5.** to have a restless desire (to do something). **6. itching palm.** a grasping nature; avarice. —ˈitchy *adj.* —ˈitchiness *n.*

-ite¹ *suffix forming nouns.* **1.** a native or inhabitant of: *Israelite.* **2.** a follower or advocate of; a supporter of a group: *Luddite; labourite.* **3.** (in biology) indicating a division of a body or organ: *neurite; somite.* **4.** indicating a mineral or rock: *nephrite; peridotite.* **5.** indicating a commercial product: *vulcanite.*

-ite² *suffix of nouns.* indicating a salt or ester of an acid having a name ending in *-ous: a nitrite is a salt of nitrous acid.*

item *n.* (ˈaɪtəm). **1.** a thing or unit, esp. included in a list or collection. **2.** *Bookkeeping.* an entry in an account. **3.** a piece of information, detail, or note: *a news item.* ~*vb.* **4.** (*tr.*) an archaic word for **itemize.** ~*adv.* (ˈaɪtem). **5.** likewise; also.

itemize *or* **-ise** (ˈaɪtəˌmaɪz) *vb.* (*tr.*) to put on a list or make a list of. —ˌitemiˈzation *or* -iˈsation *n.* —ˈitemˌizer *or* -ˌiser *n.*

iterate (ˈɪtəˌreɪt) *vb.* (*tr.*) to say or do again; repeat. —ˈiterant *adj.* —ˌiterˈation *n.* —ˈiterative *adj.*

itinerant (ɪˈtɪnərənt, aɪ-) *adj.* **1.** itinerating. **2.** working for a short time in various places, esp. as a casual labourer. ~*n.* **3.** an itinerant worker or other person.

—iˈtinerantly *adv.*

itinerary (aɪˈtɪnərərɪ, ɪ-) *n., pl.* **-aries. 1.** a plan or line of travel; route. **2.** a record of a journey. **3.** a guidebook for travellers. ~*adj.* **4.** of or relating to travel or routes of travel.

-ition *suffix forming nouns.* a variant of **-ation:** *fruition.*

-itis *suffix forming nouns.* indicating inflammation of a specified part: *tonsillitis.*

it'll (ˈɪtəl) *contraction of* it will *or* it shall.

-itol *suffix forming nouns.* indicating that certain chemical compounds are alcohols containing two or more hydroxyl groups: *inisitol; sorbitol.*

its (ɪts) *determiner.* **a.** of, belonging to, or associated in some way with it: *its left rear wheel; I can see its logical consequence.* **b.** (*as pronoun*): *its is over there.*
▷ **Usage.** The possessive adjective and pronoun *its* is never written with an apostrophe: *the cat has hurt its ear.* The contraction of *it is, it's,* always has an apostrophe: *it's a pity that the cat has hurt its ear.*

it's (ɪts) *contraction of* it is.

itself (ɪtˈsɛlf) *pron.* **1. a.** the reflexive form of **it. b.** (intensifier): *even the money itself won't convince me.* **2.** (*preceded by a copula*) its normal or usual self: *my cat doesn't seem itself these days.*
▷ **Usage.** See at **myself.**

ITV (in Britain) *abbrev. for* Independent Television.

-ity *suffix forming nouns.* indicating state or condition: *technicality.*

-ium *or sometimes* **-um** *suffix forming nouns.* **1.** indicating a metallic element: *platinum; barium.* **2.** (in chemistry) indicating groups forming positive ions: *ammonium chloride; hydroxonium ion.* **3.** indicating a biological structure: *syncytium.*

-ive *suffix.* **1.** (*forming adjectives*) indicating a tendency, inclination, character, or quality: *divisive; festive; massive.* **2.** (*forming nouns of adjectival origin*): *detective; expletive.*

I've (aɪv) *contraction of* I have.

ivories (ˈaɪvərɪz, -vrɪz) *pl. n. Sl.* **1.** the keys of a piano. **2.** billiard balls. **3.** another word for **teeth. 4.** another word for **dice.**

ivory (ˈaɪvərɪ, -vrɪ) *n., pl.* **-ries. 1. a.** a hard smooth creamy white variety of dentine that makes up a major part of the tusks of elephants and walruses. **b.** (*as modifier*): *ivory ornaments.* **2.** a tusk made of ivory. **3. a.** a yellowish-white colour; cream. **b.** (*as adj.*): *ivory shoes.* **4.** a substance resembling elephant tusk. **5.** an ornament, etc., made of ivory. **6. black ivory.** *Obs.* Negro slaves collectively. —ˈivory-ˌlike *adj.*

ivory tower (ˈaɪvə) *n.* seclusion or remoteness of attitude regarding problems, everyday life, etc.

ivy (ˈaɪvɪ) *n., pl.* **ivies. 1.** a woody climbing or trailing plant having lobed evergreen leaves and black berry-like fruits. **2.** any of various other climbing or creeping plants, such as poison ivy and ground ivy. —ˈivy-ˌlike *adj.*

ixia (ˈɪksɪə) *n.* an iridaceous plant of southern Africa, having showy ornamental funnel-shaped flowers.

-ize *or* **-ise** *suffix forming verbs.* **1.** to cause to become, resemble, or agree with: *legalize.* **2.** to become; change into: *crystallize.* **3.** to affect in a specified way; subject to: *hypnotize.* **4.** to act according to some practice, principle, policy, etc.: *economize.*
▷ **Usage.** In the U.S. and in Britain, *-ize* is the standard ending for many verbs, but *-ise* is equally acceptable in British English. Certain words are, however, always spelt with *-ise* in both the U.S. and in Britain: *revise.*

THESAURUS

itch *v.* **1.** crawl, irritate, prickle, tickle, tingle **2.** ache, burn, crave, hanker, hunger, long, lust, pant, pine, yearn ~*n.* **3.** irritation, itchiness, prickling, tingling **4.** craving, desire, hankering, hunger, longing, lust, passion, restlessness, yearning, yen (*Inf.*)

itching agog, aquiver, atremble, avid, burning, consumed with curiosity, eager, impatient, inquisitive, longing, mad keen (*Inf.*), raring, spoiling for

itchy eager, edgy, fidgety, impatient, restive, restless, unsettled

item 1. article, aspect, component, consideration, detail, entry, matter, particular, point, thing **2.** account, article, bulletin, dispatch, feature, note, notice, paragraph, piece, report

itemize count, detail, document, enumerate, instance, inventory, list, number, particularize, record, set out, specify

itinerant *adj.* ambulatory, Gypsy, journeying, migratory, nomadic, peripatetic,

roaming, roving, travelling, unsettled, vagabond, vagrant, wandering, wayfaring

itinerary 1. circuit, journey, line, programme, route, schedule, tour **2.** Baedeker, guide, guidebook

ivory tower cloister, refuge, remoteness, retreat, sanctum, seclusion, splendid isolation, unreality, world of one's own

J

j or **J** (dʒeɪ) *n.*, *pl.* **j's**, **J's**, or **Js.** **1.** the tenth letter of the English alphabet. **2.** a speech sound represented by this letter.

J *symbol for:* **1.** *Cards.* jack. **2.** joule(s).

jab (dʒæb) *vb.* **jabbing**, **jabbed.** **1.** to poke or thrust sharply. **2.** to strike with a quick short blow or blows. ~*n.* **3.** a sharp poke or stab. **4.** a quick short blow. **5.** *Inf.* an injection: *polio jabs.* —'**jabbingly** *adv.*

jabber ('dʒæbə) *vb.* **1.** to speak or say rapidly, incoherently, and without making sense; chatter. ~*n.* **2.** such talk.

jabot ('ʒæbəʊ) *n.* a frill or ruffle on the breast or throat of a garment.

jacinth ('dʒæsɪnθ) *n.* another name for **hyacinth** (sense 4).

jack (dʒæk) *n.* **1.** a man or fellow. **2.** a sailor. **3.** the male of certain animals, esp. of the ass or donkey. **4.** a mechanical or hydraulic device for exerting a large force, esp. to raise a heavy weight such as a motor vehicle. **5.** any of several mechanical devices that replace manpower, such as a contrivance for rotating meat on a spit. **6.** one of four playing cards in a pack, one for each suit; knave. **7.** *Bowls.* a small usually white bowl at which the players aim with their own bowls. **8.** *Electrical engineering.* a socket and plug connection in electrical equipment. **9.** a flag, esp. a small flag flown at the bow of a ship indicating the ship's nationality. **10.** *Austral. sl.* venereal disease. **11.** a part of the action of a harpsichord, consisting of a fork-shaped device on the end of a pivoted lever on which a plectrum is mounted. **12. a.** any of various tropical and subtropical fishes. **b.** an immature pike. **13.** Also called: **jackstone.** one of the pieces used in the game of jacks. **14.** *U.S.* a slang word for **money. 15. every man jack.** everyone without exception. ~*adj.* **16.** *Austral. sl.* tired or fed up (esp. in **to be jack of** something). ~*vb.* **17.** (*tr.*) to lift or push (an object) with a jack. ~See also **jack in, jack up.**

jackal ('dʒɔːl) *n.* **1.** any of several African or S Asian mammals closely related to the dog, having long legs and pointed ears and muzzle: they are predators and carrion-eaters. **2.** a person who does menial tasks for another.

jackanapes ('dʒækə,neɪps) *n.* **1.** a conceited impertinent person. **2.** a mischievous child. **3.** *Arch.* a monkey.

jackass ('dʒæk,æs) *n.* **1.** a male donkey. **2.** a fool.

jackboot ('dʒæk,buːt) *n.* **1.** an all-leather military boot, extending up to or above the knee. **2.** authoritarian rule. —'**jack,booted** *adj.*

jackdaw ('dʒæk,dɔː) *n.* a large common Eurasian bird, related to the crow, in which the plumage is black and dark grey: noted for its thieving habits.

jacket ('dʒækɪt) *n.* **1.** a short coat, esp. one that is hip-length and has a front opening and sleeves. **2.** something that resembles this: *a life jacket.* **3.** any exterior covering or casing, such as the insulating cover of a boiler. **4.** See **dust jacket. 5. a.** the skin of a baked potato. **b.** (*as modifier*): *jacket potatoes.* **6.** *Oil Industry.* the support structure, esp. the legs, of an oil platform. ~*vb.* **7.** (*tr.*) to put a jacket on (someone or something). —'**jacketed** *adj.*

Jack Frost *n.* a personification of frost.

jack in *vb.* (*tr., adv.*) to abandon or leave (an attempt or enterprise).

jack-in-office *n.* a self-important petty official.

jack-in-the-box *n., pl.* **jack-in-the-boxes** or **jacks-in-the-box.** a toy consisting of a figure on a tight spring in a box, which springs out when the lid is opened.

jackknife ('dʒæk,naɪf) *n., pl.* -**knives. 1.** a knife with the blade pivoted to fold into a recess in the handle. **2.** a former name for a type of dive in which the diver bends at the waist in midair; forward pike dive. ~*vb.* (*intr.*) **3.** (of an articulated lorry) to go out of control in such a way that the trailer swings round at an angle to the tractor.

jack of all trades *n., pl.* **jacks of all trades.** a person who undertakes many different kinds of work.

jack-o'-lantern *n.* **1.** a lantern made from a hollowed pumpkin, which has holes cut in it to represent a human face. **2.** a will-o'-the-wisp.

jackpot ('dʒæk,pɒt) *n.* **1.** any large prize, kitty, or accumulated stake that may be won in gambling. **2. hit the jackpot.** *Sl.* **a.** to win a jackpot. **b.** to achieve great success, esp. through luck.

jack rabbit *n.* any of various W North American hares having long hind legs and large ears.

jacks (dʒæks) *pl. n.* a game in which bone or metal pieces (**jackstones**) are thrown and then picked up between bounces or throws of a small ball.

Jack Tar *n. Now chiefly literary.* a sailor.

jack up *vb.* (*adv.*) **1.** (*tr.*) to increase (prices, salaries, etc.). **2.** (*tr.*) to raise an object, such as a car, with or as with a jack. **3.** (*intr.*) *Austral. inf.* to refuse to comply.

Jacobean (,dʒækə'bɪən) *adj.* **1.** *History.* relating to James I of England or to the period of his rule (1603–25). **2.** of or relating to the style of furniture current at this time, characterized by the use of dark brown carved oak. **3.** relating to or having the style of architecture used in England during this period.

Jacobin ('dʒækəbɪn) *n.* **1.** a member of the most radical club founded during the French Revolution, which instituted the Reign of Terror. **2.** an extreme political radical. **3.** a French Dominican friar. ~*adj.* **4.** of or relating to the Jacobins or their policies. —,**Jaco'binic** or ,**Jaco'binical** *adj.* —'**Jacobinism** *n.*

Jacobite ('dʒækə,baɪt) *n. British history.* an adherent of James II after his overthrow in 1688, or of his descendants in their attempts to regain the throne. —**Jacobitic** (,dʒækə'bɪtɪk) *adj.*

Jacquard ('dʒækɑːd, dʒə'kɑːd) *n.* **1.** Also called: **Jacquard weave.** a fabric in which the design is incorporated into the weave. **2.** Also called: **Jacquard loom.** the loom that produces this fabric.

Jacuzzi (dʒə'kuːzɪ) *n.* **1.** *Trademark.* a device which swirls water in a bath. **2.** a bath containing such a device.

jade[1] (dʒeɪd) *n.* **1.** a semiprecious stone which varies in colour from white to green and is used for making ornaments and jewellery. **2.** the green colour of jade.

jade[2] (dʒeɪd) *n.* **1.** an old overworked horse. **2.** *Derog.* a woman considered to be disreputable. ~*vb.* **3.** to exhaust or make exhausted from work or use. —'**jadish** *adj.*

jaded ('dʒeɪdɪd) *adj.* **1.** exhausted or dissipated. **2.** satiated. —'**jadedly** *adv.* —'**jadedness** *n.*

Jaffa ('dʒæfə, 'dʒɑː-) *n.* **1.** a port in W Israel, on the Mediterranean. **2.** a large variety of orange, having a thick skin.

jag[1] (dʒæg) *vb.* **jagging**, **jagged. 1.** (*tr.*) to cut unevenly. ~*n.*, *vb.* **2.** an informal word for **jab.** ~*n.* **3.** a jagged notch or projection.

jag[2] (dʒæg) *n. Sl.* **a.** intoxication from drugs or alcohol. **b.** a bout of drinking or drug taking.

jagged ('dʒægɪd) *adj.* having sharp projecting notches. —'**jaggedly** *adv.*

THESAURUS

jab *v./n.* dig, lunge, nudge, poke, prod, punch, stab, tap, thrust

jacket case, casing, coat, covering, envelope, folder, sheath, skin, wrapper, wrapping

jackpot award, bonanza, kitty, pool, pot, prize, reward, winnings

jack up 1. elevate, heave, hoist, lift, lift up, raise, rear **2.** accelerate, augment, boost, escalate, increase, inflate, put up, raise

jade harridan, hussy, nag, shrew, slattern, slut, trollop, vixen, wench

jaded 1. exhausted, fagged (out) (*Inf.*), fatigued, spent, tired, tired-out, weary **2.** bored, cloyed, dulled, glutted, gorged, sated, satiated, surfeited, tired

jagged barbed, broken, cleft, craggy, denticulate, indented, notched, pointed, ragged, ridged, rough, serrated, snaggy, spiked, toothed, uneven

jaguar ('dʒægjʊə) n. a large feline mammal of S North America, Central America, and N South America, similar to the leopard but with larger spots on its coat.

jail or **gaol** (dʒeɪl) n. 1. a place for the confinement of persons convicted and sentenced to imprisonment or of persons awaiting trial. ~vb. 2. (tr.) to confine in prison.

jailbird or **gaolbird** ('dʒeɪl‚bɜːd) n. a person who is or has been confined to jail, esp. repeatedly; convict.

jailer, jailor, or **gaoler** ('dʒeɪlə) n. a person in charge of prisoners in a jail.

jalap or **jalop** ('dʒæləp) n. 1. a Mexican climbing plant. 2. the dried and powdered root of any of these plants, used as a purgative. —**jalapic** (dʒə'læpɪk) adj.

jalopy or **jaloppy** (dʒə'lɒpɪ) n., pl. **-lopies** or **-loppies.** Inf. a dilapidated old car.

jalousie ('ʒæluˌziː) n. 1. a window blind or shutter constructed from angled slats of wood, etc. 2. a window made of angled slats of glass.

jam¹ (dʒæm) vb. **jamming, jammed.** 1. (tr.) to cram or wedge into or against something: to jam paper into an incinerator. 2. (tr.) to crowd or pack: cars jammed the roads. 3. to make or become stuck or locked. 4. (tr.; often foll. by on) to activate suddenly (esp. in **jam on the brakes**). 5. (tr.) to block; congest. 6. (tr.) to crush or squeeze. 7. Radio. to prevent the clear reception of (radio communications) by transmitting other signals on the same frequency. 8. (intr.) Sl. to play in a jam session. ~n. 9. a crowd or congestion in a confined space: a traffic jam. 10. the act of jamming or the state of being jammed. 11. Inf. a predicament: to help a friend out of a jam. 12. See **jam session.** —'**jammer** n.

jam² (dʒæm) n. a preserve containing fruit, which has been boiled with sugar until the mixture sets.

jamb or **jambe** (dʒæm) n. a vertical side member of a door frame, window frame, or lining.

jamboree (‚dʒæmbə'riː) n. 1. a large and often international gathering of Scouts. 2. a party or spree.

jammy ('dʒæmɪ) adj. **-mier, -miest.** Brit. sl. 1. pleasant; desirable. 2. lucky.

jam-packed adj. packed or filled to capacity.

jam session n. Sl. a gathering of jazz or pop musicians in which music is improvised.

Jan. abbrev. for January.

jangle ('dʒæŋgəl) vb. 1. to sound or cause to sound discordantly, harshly, or unpleasantly. 2. (tr.) to produce a jarring effect on: the accident jangled his nerves. 3. Arch. to wrangle. —'**jangler** n.

janitor ('dʒænɪtə) n. 1. Scot. the caretaker of a building, esp. a school. 2. Chiefly U.S. a person employed to clean and maintain a building. —**janitorial** (‚dʒænɪ'tɔːrɪəl) adj.

January ('dʒænjʊərɪ) n., pl. **-aries.** the first month of the year, consisting of 31 days.

japan (dʒə'pæn) n. 1. a glossy durable black lacquer originally from the Orient, used on wood, metal, etc. 2. work decorated and varnished in the Japanese manner. ~vb. **-panning, -panned.** 3. (tr.) to lacquer with japan or any similar varnish.

Japanese (‚dʒæpə'niːz) adj. 1. of or characteristic of Japan, its people, or their language. ~n. 2. pl. **-nese.** a native or inhabitant of Japan. 3. the official language of Japan.

jape (dʒeɪp) n. 1. a jest or joke. ~vb. 2. to joke or jest (about). —'**japer** n. —'**japery** n.

japonica (dʒə'pɒnɪkə) n. 1. Also called: **Japanese quince.** a Japanese shrub cultivated for its red flowers and yellowish fruit. 2. another name for the **camellia.**

jar¹ (dʒɑː) n. 1. a wide-mouthed container that is usually cylindrical, made of glass or earthenware, and without handles. 2. Also: **jarful.** the contents or quantity contained in a jar. 3. Brit. inf. a glass of beer.

jar² (dʒɑː) vb. **jarring, jarred.** 1. to vibrate or cause to vibrate. 2. to make or cause to make a harsh discordant sound. 3. (often foll. by on) to have a disturbing or painful effect (on the nerves, mind, etc.). 4. (intr.) to disagree; clash. ~n. 5. a jolt or shock. 6. a harsh discordant sound.

jar³ (dʒɑː) n. **on a** (or **the**) **jar.** (of a door) slightly open; ajar.

jardinière (‚ʒɑːdɪ'njɛə) n. 1. an ornamental pot or trough for plants. 2. a garnish of fresh vegetables for a dish of meat.

jargon ('dʒɑːgən) n. 1. specialized language concerned with a particular subject, culture, or profession. 2. language characterized by pretentious vocabulary or meaning. 3. gibberish.

jasmine ('dʒæsmɪn, 'dʒæz-) n. 1. Also called: **jessamine.** any tropical or subtropical oleaceous shrub or climbing plant widely cultivated for their white, yellow, or red fragrant flowers. 2. any of several other shrubs with fragrant flowers, such as the Cape jasmine, yellow jasmine, and frangipani (**red jasmine**).

jasper ('dʒæspə) n. 1. an opaque impure form of quartz, red, yellow, brown, or dark green in colour, used as a gemstone and for ornamental decoration. 2. Also called: **jasper ware.** a dense hard stoneware.

jaundice ('dʒɔːndɪs) n. 1. Also called: **icterus.** yellowing of the skin due to the abnormal presence of bile pigments in the blood, as in hepatitis. 2. jealousy, envy, and ill humour. ~vb. 3. to distort (the judgment, etc.) adversely: jealousy had jaundiced his mind. 4. to affect with or as if with jaundice.

jaunt (dʒɔːnt) n. 1. a short pleasurable excursion; outing. ~vb. 2. (intr.) to go on such an excursion.

jaunting car n. a light two-wheeled one-horse car, formerly widely used in Ireland.

jaunty ('dʒɔːntɪ) adj. **-tier, -tiest.** 1. sprightly and cheerful: a jaunty step. 2. smart; trim: a jaunty hat. —'**jauntily** adv. —'**jauntiness** n.

Javanese (‚dʒɑːvə'niːz) adj. 1. of or relating to the island of Java, in Indonesia. ~n. 2. a native or inhabitant of Java. 3. the Malayan language of Java.

javelin ('dʒævlɪn) n. 1. a long pointed spear thrown as a weapon or in competitive field events. 2. **the javelin.** the event or sport of throwing the javelin.

jaw (dʒɔː) n. 1. the part of the skull of a vertebrate that frames the mouth and holds the teeth. 2. the corresponding part of an invertebrate, esp. an insect. 3. a pair or either of a pair of hinged or sliding components of a machine or tool designed to grip an object. 4. Sl. **a.** impudent talk. **b.** idle conversation. **c.** a lecture. ~vb. 5. (intr.) Sl. **a.** to chat; gossip. **b.** to lecture.

jawbone ('dʒɔː‚bəʊn) n. a nontechnical name for **mandible** or (less commonly) **maxilla.**

jaws (dʒɔːz) pl. n. 1. the narrow opening of some confined place such as a gorge. 2. **the jaws.** a dangerously close position: the jaws of death.

THESAURUS

jail, gaol 1. n. borstal, brig (Chiefly U.S.), clink (Sl.), cooler (Sl.), inside (Sl.), jailhouse (Southern U.S.), jug (Sl.), lockup, nick (Sl.), penitentiary (U.S.), prison, quod (Sl.), reformatory, stir (Sl.) 2. v. confine, detain, immure, impound, imprison, incarcerate, lock up, send down

jailer, gaoler captor, guard, keeper, screw (Sl.), turnkey (Archaic), warden, warder

jam v. 1. cram, crowd, crush, force, pack, press, ram, squeeze, stuff, throng, wedge 2. block, cease, clog, congest, halt, obstruct, stall, stick ~n. 3. crowd, crush, horde, mass, mob, multitude, pack, press, swarm, throng 4. bind, dilemma, fix (Inf.), hole (Sl.), pickle (Inf.), plight, predicament, quandary, scrape (Inf.), spot (Inf.), strait, trouble

jamboree carnival, carouse, celebration, festival, festivity, fête, frolic, jubilee, merriment, party, revelry, spree

jangle 1. v. chime, clank, clash, clatter, jingle, rattle, vibrate 2. n. cacophony, clang, clangour, clash, din, dissonance, jar, racket, rattle, reverberation

janitor caretaker, concierge, custodian, doorkeeper, porter

jar¹ amphora, carafe, container, crock, flagon, jug, pitcher, pot, receptacle, urn, vase, vessel

jar² v. 1. bicker, clash, contend, disagree, interfere, oppose, quarrel, wrangle 2. agitate, convulse, disturb, grate, irritate, jolt, offend, rasp, rattle (Inf.), rock, shake, vibrate 3. annoy, clash, discompose, grate, grind, irk, irritate, nettle ~n. 4. agitation, altercation,

bickering, disagreement, discord, grating, irritation, jolt, quarrel, rasping, wrangling

jargon 1. argot, cant, dialect, idiom, lingo (Inf.), parlance, patois, slang, tongue, usage 2. balderdash, bunkum (Inf.), drivel, gabble, gibberish, gobbledegook, mumbo jumbo, nonsense, palaver, rigmarole, twaddle

jaundiced 1. cynical, preconceived, sceptical 2. biased, bigoted, bitter, distorted, envious, hostile, jealous, partial, prejudiced, resentful, spiteful, suspicious

jaunt airing, excursion, expedition, outing, promenade, ramble, stroll, tour, trip

jaunty airy, breezy, buoyant, carefree, dapper, gay, high-spirited, lively, perky, self-confident, showy, smart, sprightly, spruce, trim

jaw v. 1. babble, chat, chatter, gossip, lec-

jay (dʒeɪ) *n.* **1.** a passerine bird related to the crow having a pinkish-brown body, blue-and-black wings, and a black-and-white crest. **2.** a foolish or gullible person.

jaywalk ('dʒeɪ,wɔːk) *vb.* (*intr.*) to cross or walk in a street recklessly or illegally. —'**jay,walker** *n.* —'**jay,walking** *n.*

jazz (dʒæz) *n.* **1. a.** a kind of music of American Negro origin, characterized by syncopated rhythms, solo and group improvisation, and a variety of harmonic idioms and instrumental techniques. **b.** (*as modifier*): *a jazz band.* **c.** (*in combination*): *a jazzman.* **2.** *Sl.* rigmarole: *legal papers and all that jazz.* ~*vb.* **3.** (*intr.*) to play or dance to jazz music. —'**jazzer** *n.* —'**jazzy** *adj.* —'**jazzily** *adv.* —'**jazziness** *n.*

jazz up *vb.* (*tr., adv.*) *Inf.* **1.** to imbue (a piece of music) with jazz qualities, esp. by a quicker tempo. **2.** to make more lively or appealing.

jealous ('dʒeləs) *adj.* **1.** suspicious or fearful of being displaced by a rival. **2.** (often *postpositive* and foll. by *of*) resentful (of) or vindictive (towards). **3.** (often *postpositive* and foll. by *of*) possessive and watchful in the protection (of): *jealous of one's reputation.* **4.** characterized by or resulting from jealousy. **5.** *Obsolete except in biblical use.* demanding exclusive loyalty: *a jealous God.* —'**jealously** *adv.*

jealousy ('dʒeləsɪ) *n., pl.* -**ousies.** the state or quality of being jealous.

jean (dʒiːn) *n.* a tough twill-weave cotton fabric used for hard-wearing trousers, overalls, etc.

jeans (dʒiːnz) *pl. n.* informal trousers for casual wear, made esp. of denim or corduroy.

Jeep (dʒiːp) *n. Trademark.* a small road vehicle with four-wheel drive.

jeer (dʒɪə) *vb.* **1.** (often foll. by *at*) to laugh or scoff (at a person or thing). ~*n.* **2.** a remark or cry of derision.

Jehovah (dʒɪ'həʊvə) *n. Old Testament.* the personal name of God, revealed to Moses on Mount Horeb (Exodus 3).

jejune (dʒɪ'dʒuːn) *adj.* **1.** naive; unsophisticated. **2.** insipid; dull. **3.** lacking, nourishment. —je'**junely** *adv.* —je'**juneness** *n.*

Jekyll and Hyde ('dʒekəl; haɪd) *n.* **a.** a person with two distinct personalities, one good, the other evil. **b.** (*as modifier*): *a Jekyll-and-Hyde personality.*

jell *or* **gel** (dʒel) *vb.* **jelling, jelled** *or* **gelling, gelled.** **1.** to make or become gelatinous; congeal. **2.** to assume definite form: *his ideas have jelled.*

jellaba *or* **jellabah** ('dʒeləbə) *n.* a kind of loose cloak with a hood, worn esp. in North Africa.

jellify ('dʒelɪ,faɪ) *vb.* -**fies, -fying, -fied.** to make into or become jelly. —,jellifi'**cation** *n.*

jelly[1] ('dʒelɪ) *n., pl.* -**lies.** **1.** a fruit-flavoured clear dessert set with gelatine. **2.** a preserve made from the juice of fruit boiled with sugar and used as jam. **3.** a savoury food preparation set with gelatine or with a strong gelatinous stock: *calf's-foot jelly.* ~*vb.* -**lying, -lied.** **4.** to jellify. —'**jellied** *adj.* —'**jelly-,like** *adj.*

jelly[2] ('dʒelɪ) *n. Brit.* a slang name for **gelignite.**

jellyfish ('dʒelɪ,fɪʃ) *n., pl.* -**fish** *or* -**fishes.** **1.** any marine coelenterate having a gelatinous umbrella-shaped body with trailing tentacles. **2.** *Inf.* a weak indecisive person.

jemmy ('dʒemɪ) *or U.S.* **jimmy** *n., pl.* -**mies.** **1.** a short steel crowbar used, esp. by burglars, for forcing

doors and windows. ~*vb.* -**mying, -mied.** **2.** (*tr.*) to prise (something) open with a jemmy.

jenny ('dʒenɪ) *n., pl.* -**nies.** **1.** a machine for turning up the edge of a piece of sheet metal in preparation for making a joint. **2.** the female of certain animals or birds, esp. a donkey, ass, or wren. **3.** short for **spinning jenny.** **4.** *Billiards, etc.* an in-off.

jeopardize *or* -**ise** ('dʒepə,daɪz) *vb.* **1.** to risk; hazard: *he jeopardized his job by being persistently unpunctual.* **2.** (*tr.*) to put in danger.

jeopardy ('dʒepədɪ) *n.* (usually preceded by *in*) **1.** danger of injury, loss, death, etc.: *his health was in jeopardy.* **2.** *Law.* danger of being convicted and punished for a criminal offence.

Jer. *Bible. abbrev. for* Jeremiah.

jerbil ('dʒɜːbɪl) *n.* a variant spelling of **gerbil.**

jerboa (dʒɜː'bəʊə) *n.* any small nocturnal burrowing rodent inhabiting dry regions of Asia and N Africa, having long hind legs specialized for jumping.

jeremiad (,dʒerɪ'maɪəd) *n.* a long mournful lamentation or complaint.

jerk[1] (dʒɜːk) *vb.* **1.** to move or cause to move with an irregular or spasmodic motion. **2.** to throw, twist, pull, or push (something) abruptly or spasmodically. **3.** (*tr.; often foll. by out*) to utter (words, etc.) in a spasmodic or breathless manner. ~*n.* **4.** an abrupt or spasmodic movement. **5.** an irregular jolting motion: *the car moved with a jerk.* **6.** (*pl.*) Also called: **physical jerks.** *Brit. inf.* physical exercises. **7.** *Sl., chiefly U.S.* a stupid or ignorant person. —'**jerker** *n.*

jerk[2] (dʒɜːk) *vb.* **1.** to preserve beef, etc., by cutting into thin strips and drying in the sun. ~*n.* **2.** Also called: **jerky.** jerked meat.

jerkin ('dʒɜːkɪn) *n.* **1.** a sleeveless short jacket worn by men or women. **2.** a man's sleeveless fitted jacket, often made of leather, worn in the 16th and 17th centuries.

jerky ('dʒɜːkɪ) *adj.* **jerkier, jerkiest.** characterized by jerks. —'**jerkily** *adv.* —'**jerkiness** *n.*

Jerry ('dʒerɪ) *n., pl.* -**ries.** *Brit. sl.* **1.** a German, esp. a German soldier. **2.** the Germans collectively.

jerry-build *vb.* -**building, -built.** (*tr.*) to build (houses, flats, etc.) badly using cheap materials. —'**jerry-,builder** *n.*

jerry can *n.* a flat-sided can used for storing or transporting liquids, esp. motor fuel.

jersey ('dʒɜːzɪ) *n.* **1.** a knitted garment covering the upper part of the body. **2. a.** a machine-knitted slightly elastic cloth of wool, silk, nylon, etc., used for clothing. **b.** (*as modifier*): *a jersey suit.* **3.** *N.Z.* a football strip.

Jersey ('dʒɜːzɪ) *n.* **1.** an island in the English Channel, the largest of the Channel Islands. **2.** a breed of dairy cattle producing milk with a high butterfat content, originating from the island of Jersey.

Jerusalem artichoke (dʒə'ruːsələm) *n.* **1.** a North American sunflower widely cultivated for its underground edible tubers. **2.** the tuber of this plant, which is eaten as a vegetable.

jest (dʒest) *n.* **1.** something done or said for amusement; joke. **2.** playfulness; fun: *to act in jest.* **3.** a jeer or taunt. **4.** an object of derision. ~*vb.* **5.** to act or speak in an amusing or frivolous way. **6.** to make fun of (a person or thing). —'**jestful** *adj.*

jester ('dʒestə) *n.* a professional clown employed by a king or nobleman during the Middle Ages.

THESAURUS

ture, talk **2.** abuse, censure, criticize, revile, scold ~*n.* **3.** chat, chinwag (*Brit. inf.*), conversation, gossip, natter, talk

jaws abyss, aperture, entrance, gates, ingress, maw, mouth, opening, orifice

jazz up animate, enhance, enliven, heighten, improve

jazzy animated, fancy, flashy, gaudy, lively, smart, snazzy (*Inf.*), spirited, vivacious, wild, zestful

jealous 1. covetous, desirous, emulous, envious, green, green-eyed, grudging, intolerant, invidious, resentful, rival **2.** anxious, apprehensive, attentive, guarded, mistrustful, protective, solicitous, suspicious, vigilant, wary, watchful, zealous

jealousy covetousness, distrust, envy, heart-burning, ill-will, mistrust, possessive-

ness, resentment, spite, suspicion

jeer 1. *v.* banter, barrack, cock a snook at (*Brit.*), contemn, deride, flout, gibe, heckle, hector, knock (*Sl.*), mock, ridicule, scoff, sneer, taunt **2.** *n.* abuse, aspersion, catcall, derision, gibe, hiss, hoot, obloquy, ridicule, scoff, sneer, taunt

jell 1. congeal, harden, set, solidify, thicken **2.** come together, crystallize, finalize, form, materialize, take shape

jeopardize chance, endanger, expose, gamble, hazard, imperil, risk, stake, venture

jeopardy danger, endangerment, exposure, hazard, insecurity, liability, peril, precariousness, risk, venture, vulnerability

jeremiad complaint, groan, keen, lament, lamentation, moan, plaint, wail

jerk *v./n.* jolt, lurch, pull, throw, thrust, tug,

tweak, twitch, wrench, yank

jerky bouncy, bumpy, convulsive, fitful, jolting, jumpy, rough, shaky, spasmodic, tremulous, twitchy, uncontrolled

jerry-built cheap, defective, faulty, flimsy, ramshackle, rickety, shabby, slipshod, thrown together, unsubstantial

jest 1. *n.* banter, bon mot, crack (*Sl.*), fun, gag (*Sl.*), hoax, jape, joke, play, pleasantry, prank, quip, sally, sport, wisecrack (*Inf.*), witticism **2.** *v.* banter, chaff, deride, gibe, jeer, joke, kid (*Inf.*), mock, quip, scoff, sneer, tease

jester 1. comedian, comic, humorist, joker, quipster, wag, wit **2.** buffoon, clown, fool, harlequin, madcap, mummer, pantaloon, prankster, zany

Jesuit ('dʒɛzjuɪt) n. 1. a member of a Roman Catholic religious order (the **Society of Jesus**) founded by Ignatius Loyola in 1534 with the aim of defending Catholicism against the Reformation. 2. (*sometimes not cap.*) *Inf., offens.* a person given to subtle and equivocating arguments. —**Jesu'itical** *adj.*

Jesus ('dʒiːzəs) n. 1. Also called: **Jesus Christ, Jesus of Nazareth.** ?4 B.C.–?29 A.D., founder of Christianity, born in Galilee and brought up as a Jew. He is believed by Christians to be the Son of God. ~*interj. also* **Jesus wept.** 2. used to express intense surprise, dismay, etc.

jet[1] (dʒɛt) n. 1. a thin stream of liquid or gas forced out of a small aperture. 2. an outlet or nozzle for emitting such a stream. 3. a jet-propelled aircraft. ~*vb.* **jetting, jetted.** 4. to issue or cause to issue in a jet: *water jetted from the hose.* 5. to transport or be transported by jet aircraft.

jet[2] (dʒɛt) n. **a.** a hard black variety of lignite that takes a brilliant polish and is used for jewellery, etc. **b.** (*as modifier*): *jet earrings.*

jet black n. **a.** a deep black colour. **b.** (*as adj.*): *jet-black hair.*

jet engine n. a gas turbine, esp. one fitted to an aircraft.

jet lag n. a general feeling of fatigue often experienced by travellers by jet aircraft who cross several time zones in relatively few hours.

jet propulsion n. 1. propulsion by means of a jet of fluid. 2. propulsion by means of a gas turbine, esp. when the exhaust gases provide the propulsive thrust. —,**jet-pro'pelled** *adj.*

jetsam ('dʒɛtsəm) n. 1. that portion of the cargo of a vessel thrown overboard to lighten her, as during a storm. Cf. **flotsam.** 2. another word for **flotsam** (sense 2).

jet set n. a rich and fashionable social set, the members of which travel widely for pleasure. —'**jet,setter** n.

jettison ('dʒɛtɪsən, -zən) vb. (tr.) 1. to abandon: *to jettison old clothes.* 2. to throw overboard. ~n. 3. another word for **jetsam** (sense 1).

jetty ('dʒɛtɪ) n., pl. **-ties.** a pier, dock, groyne, mole, or other structure extending into the water from the shore.

Jew (dʒuː) n. 1. a member of the Semitic people who are descended from the ancient Israelites. 2. a person whose religion is Judaism. 3. a member of the ancient tribe or nation of Judah. 4. (*modifier*) *Offens.* Jewish: *a Jew boy.* 5. (*sometimes not cap.*) *Offens.* **a.** a person who drives a hard bargain. **b.** a miserly person. ~*vb.* 6. (*tr.; often not cap.*) *Offens.* to drive a hard bargain.

jewel ('dʒuːəl) n. 1. a precious or semiprecious stone; gem. 2. a person or thing resembling a jewel in preciousness, brilliance, etc. 3. a gemstone used as a bearing in a watch. 4. a piece of jewellery. ~*vb.* **-elling, -elled** or U.S. **-eling, -eled.** 5. (tr.) to fit or decorate with a jewel or jewels.

jeweller or U.S. **jeweler** ('dʒuːələ) n. a person whose business is the cutting or setting of gemstones or the making or selling of jewellery.

jewellery or U.S. **jewelry** ('dʒuːəlrɪ) n. objects that are worn for personal adornment, such as bracelets, rings, necklaces, etc., considered collectively.

Jewish ('dʒuːɪʃ) adj. 1. of or characteristic of Jews. 2. *Offens.* miserly. —'**Jewishly** *adv.* —'**Jewishness** *n.*

Jewry ('dʒʊərɪ) n., pl. **-ries.** 1. **a.** Jews collectively. **b.** the Jewish religion or culture. 2. a quarter of a town inhabited by Jews.

jew's-harp n. a musical instrument consisting of a small lyre-shaped metal frame held between the teeth, with a steel tongue plucked with the finger.

Jezebel ('dʒɛzə,bɛl) n. 1. *Old Testament.* the wife of Ahab, king of Israel. 2. (*sometimes not cap.*) a shameless or scheming woman.

jib[1] (dʒɪb) n. 1. *Naut.* any triangular sail set forward of the foremast of a vessel. 2. **cut of someone's jib.** someone's manner, style, etc.

jib[2] (dʒɪb) vb. **jibbing, jibbed.** (intr.) *Chiefly Brit.* 1. (often foll. by *at*) to be reluctant (to). 2. (of an animal) to stop short and refuse to go forwards. 3. *Naut.* variant of **gybe.** —'**jibber** n.

jib[3] (dʒɪb) n. the projecting arm of a crane or the boom of a derrick.

jib boom n. *Naut.* a spar forming an extension of the bowsprit.

jibe[1] (dʒaɪb) or **jib** (dʒɪb) vb., n. *Naut.* variant spellings of **gybe.**

jibe[2] (dʒaɪb) vb. a variant spelling of **gibe**[1].

jibe[3] (dʒaɪb) vb. (intr.) *Inf.* to agree; accord; harmonize.

jiffy ('dʒɪfɪ) or **jiff** n., pl. **jiffies** or **jiffs.** *Inf.* a very short time: *wait a jiffy.*

jig (dʒɪg) n. 1. any of several old rustic kicking and leaping dances. 2. a piece of music composed for or in the rhythm of this dance. 3. a mechanical device designed to hold and locate a component during machining. 4. *Angling.* any of various spinning lures that wobble when drawn through the water. 5. Also called: **jigger.** *Mining.* a device for separating ore or coal from waste material by agitation in water. ~*vb.* **jigging, jigged.** 6. to dance (a jig). 7. to jerk or cause to jerk up and down rapidly. 8. (often foll. by *up*) to fit or be fitted in a jig. 9. (tr.) to drill or cut (a workpiece) in a jig. 10. *Mining.* to separate ore or coal from waste material using a jig.

jigger ('dʒɪgə) n. 1. a person or thing that jigs. 2. *Golf.* a club, an iron, usually No. 4. 3. any of a number of mechanical devices having a vibratory motion. 4. a light lifting tackle used on ships. 5. a small glass, esp. for whisky. 6. *Billiards.* another word for **bridge**[1]. 7. *N.Z.* a hand or power-propelled runabout used on railway lines.

jiggered ('dʒɪgəd) adj. (*postpositive*) *Inf.* damned; blowed: *I'm jiggered if he'll get away with it.*

jiggery-pokery ('dʒɪgərɪ'pəukərɪ) n. *Inf., chiefly Brit.* dishonest or deceitful behaviour.

jiggle ('dʒɪgəl) vb. to move or cause to move up and down or to and fro with a short jerky motion. —'**jiggly** *adj.*

jigsaw ('dʒɪg,sɔ:) n. 1. a mechanical saw with a fine steel blade for cutting intricate curves in sheets of material. 2. See **jigsaw puzzle.**

jigsaw puzzle n. a puzzle in which the player has to reassemble a picture that has been cut into a large number of irregularly shaped interlocking pieces.

jilt (dʒɪlt) vb. 1. (tr.) to leave or reject (a lover), esp. without previous warning. ~n. 2. a woman who jilts a lover.

jim crow ('dʒɪm 'krəu) (*often caps.*) U.S. ~n. 1. **a.** the policy or practice of segregating Negroes. **b.** (*as modifier*): *jim-crow laws.* 2. a derogatory term for Negro. 3. an implement for bending iron bars or rails. —'**jim-'crowism** n.

jimjams ('dʒɪm,dʒæmz) pl. n. 1. *Sl.* delirium tremens. 2. a state of nervous tension or anxiety.

jingle ('dʒɪŋgəl) vb. 1. to ring or cause to ring lightly and repeatedly. 2. (intr.) to sound in a manner suggestive of jingling: *a jingling verse.* ~n. 3. a sound of metal jingling. 4. a rhythmical verse, etc., esp. one used in advertising. —'**jingly** *adj.*

jingo ('dʒɪŋgəu) n., pl. **-goes.** 1. a loud and bellicose patriot. 2. jingoism. 3. **by jingo.** (*interj.*) an exclamation of surprise.

jingoism ('dʒɪŋgəu,ɪzəm) n. the belligerent spirit or foreign policy of jingoes. —'**jingoist** n., adj. —,**jingo'istic** *adj.*

jink (dʒɪŋk) vb. 1. to move swiftly or turn in order to

THESAURUS

jet[1] black, coal-black, ebony, inky, pitch-black, raven, sable

jet[2] n. 1. flow, fountain, gush, spout, spray, spring, stream 2. atomizer, nose, nozzle, rose, spout, sprayer, sprinkler ~v. 3. flow, gush, issue, rush, shoot, spew, spout, squirt, stream, surge 4. fly, soar, zoom

jettison abandon, discard, dump, eject, expel, heave, scrap, throw overboard, unload

jetty breakwater, dock, groyne, mole, pier, quay, wharf

jewel 1. brilliant, gemstone, ornament, precious stone, rock (*Sl.*), sparkler (*Inf.*), trinket 2. charm, find, gem, humdinger (*Sl.*), masterpiece, paragon, pearl, prize, rarity, treasure (*Fig.*), wonder

jewellery finery, gems, jewels, ornaments, precious stones, regalia, treasure, trinkets

Jezebel harlot, harridan, hussy, jade, virago, wanton, witch

jib balk, recoil, refuse, retreat, shrink, stop short

jig v. bob, bounce, caper, jiggle, jounce, prance, shake, skip, twitch, wiggle, wobble

jingle v. 1. chime, clatter, clink, jangle, rattle, ring, tinkle, tintinnabulate ~n. 2. clang, clangour, clink, rattle, reverberation, ringing, tinkle 3. chorus, ditty, doggerel, limerick, melody, song, tune

dodge. ~n. **2.** a jinking movement.

jinks (dʒɪŋks) pl. n. boisterous or mischievous play (esp. in **high jinks**).

jinn (dʒɪn) n. (often functioning as sing.) the plural of **jinni**.

jinni, jinnee or **djinni** (dʒɪˈniː) n., pl. **jinn** or **djinn** (dʒɪn). a spirit in Muslim mythology who could assume human or animal form and influence man by supernatural powers.

jinx (dʒɪŋks) n. **1.** an unlucky force, person, or thing. ~vb. **2.** (tr.) to be or put a jinx on.

jitter (ˈdʒɪtə) Inf. ~vb. **1.** (intr.) to be anxious or nervous. ~n. **2. the jitters.** nervousness and anxiety. —ˈ**jittery** adj.

jitterbug (ˈdʒɪtəˌbʌɡ) n. **1.** a fast jerky American dance, usually to a jazz accompaniment, that was popular in the 1940s. **2.** a person who dances the jitterbug. ~vb. **-bugging, -bugged. 3.** (intr.) to perform such a dance.

jiujitsu or **jiujutsu** (dʒuːˈdʒɪtsuː) n. variant spellings of **jujitsu.**

jive (dʒaɪv) n. **1.** a style of lively and jerky dance, popular esp. in the 1940s and 1950s. ~vb. **2.** (intr.) to dance the jive. —ˈ**jiver** n.

job (dʒɒb) n. **1.** an individual piece of work or task. **2.** an occupation. **3.** an object worked on or a result produced from working. **4.** a duty or responsibility: her job was to cook the dinner. **5.** Inf. a difficult task or problem: I had a job to contact him. **6.** Inf. a particular type of something: a four-wheel drive job. **7.** Inf. a crime, esp. a robbery. **8.** Computers. a unit of work for a computer. **9.** Inf. a state of affairs: make the best of a bad job. **10. on the job.** actively engaged in one's employment. **11. just the job.** exactly what was required. ~vb. **jobbing, jobbed. 12.** (intr.) to work by the piece or at casual jobs. **13.** to make a private profit out of (a public office, etc.). **14.** (tr.; usually foll. by in) **a.** to buy and sell (goods or services) as a middleman: he jobs in government surplus. **b.** Brit. to buy and sell stocks and shares as a stockjobber. **15.** Austral. sl. to punch. —ˈ**jobless** adj.

jobber (ˈdʒɒbə) n. **1.** Brit. short for **stockjobber** (sense 1). **2.** a person who jobs.

jobbery (ˈdʒɒbərɪ) n. the practice of making private profit out of a public office.

jobbing (ˈdʒɒbɪŋ) adj. working by the piece, not regularly employed: a jobbing gardener.

Jobcentre (ˈdʒɒbˌsɛntə) or **job centre** n. Brit. any of a number of government offices forming a section of the Employment Service Agency, having premises situated in the main shopping area of a town in which people seeking jobs can consult displayed advertisements in informal surroundings.

job lot n. **1.** a miscellaneous collection of articles sold as a lot. **2.** a collection of cheap or trivial items.

Job's comforter (dʒəʊbz) n. a person who, while purporting to give sympathy, succeeds only in adding to distress.

jock (dʒɒk) n. Inf. short for **jockey** or **jockstrap.**

Jock (dʒɒk) n. a slang word or name for a Scot.

jockey (ˈdʒɒkɪ) n. **1.** a person who rides horses in races, esp. as a profession. ~vb. **2. a.** (tr.) to ride (a horse) in a race. **b.** (intr.) to ride as a jockey. **3.** (often foll. by for) to try to obtain an advantage by manoeuvring (esp. in **jockey for position**). **4.** to trick or cheat (a person).

jockstrap (ˈdʒɒkˌstræp) n. a piece of elasticated material worn by men, esp. athletes, to support the genitals. Also called: **athletic support.**

jocose (dʒəˈkəʊs) adj. characterized by humour. —jo-ˈcosely adv. —**jocosity** (dʒəˈkɒsɪtɪ) n.

jocular (ˈdʒɒkjʊlə) adj. **1.** characterized by joking and good humour. **2.** meant lightly or humorously. —**jocularity** (ˌdʒɒkjʊˈlærɪtɪ) n. —ˈ**jocularly** adv.

jocund (ˈdʒɒkənd) adj. of a humorous temperament; merry. —**jocundity** (dʒəʊˈkʌndɪtɪ) n. —ˈ**jocundly** adv.

jodhpurs (ˈdʒɒdpəz) pl. n. riding breeches, loose-fitting around the hips and tight-fitting from the thighs to the ankles.

jog (dʒɒɡ) vb. **jogging, jogged. 1.** (intr.) to run or move slowly or at a jog trot, esp. for physical exercise. **2.** (intr.; foll. by on or along) to continue in a plodding way. **3.** (tr.) to jar or nudge slightly. **4.** (tr.) to remind: jog my memory. ~n. **5.** the act of jogging. **6.** a slight jar or nudge. **7.** a jogging motion; trot. —ˈ**jogger** n.

jogging (ˈdʒɒɡɪŋ) n. a slow run or trot, esp. as a keep-fit exercise.

joggle (ˈdʒɒɡəl) vb. **1.** to shake or move (someone or something) with a slightly jolting motion. **2.** (tr.) to join or fasten (two pieces of building material) by means of a joggle. ~n. **3.** the act of joggling. **4.** a slight irregular shake. **5.** a joint between two pieces of building material by means of a projection on one piece that fits into a notch in the other. —ˈ**joggler** n.

jog trot n. **1.** an easy bouncy gait, esp. of a horse, midway between a walk and a trot. **2.** a regular way of living or doing something.

john (dʒɒn) n. U.S. a slang word for **lavatory.**

John Bull n. **1.** a personification of England or the English people. **2.** a typical Englishman.

johnny (ˈdʒɒnɪ) n., pl. **-nies.** Brit. inf. (often cap.) a man or boy; chap.

Johnsonian (dʒɒnˈsəʊnɪən) adj. of, relating to, or characteristic of Samuel Johnson, 18th century English lexicographer, his works, or his style of writing.

joie de vivre French. (ʒwad ˈvivr) n. joy of living; enjoyment of life; ebullience.

join (dʒɔɪn) vb. **1.** to come or bring together. **2.** to become a member of (a club, etc.). **3.** (intr.; often foll. by with) to become associated or allied. **4.** (intr.; usually foll. by in) to take part. **5.** (tr.) to meet (someone) as a companion. **6.** (tr.) to become part of. **7.** (tr.) to unite (two people) in marriage. **8.** (tr.) Geom. to connect with a straight line or a curve. **9. join battle.** to engage in conflict or competition. **10. join hands. a.** to hold one's own hands together. **b.** (of two people) to hold each other's hands. **c.** (usually foll. by with) to work together in an enterprise. ~n. **11.** a joint; seam. **12.** the act of joining. ~See **join up.**

joinder (ˈdʒɔɪndə) n. **1.** the act of joining, esp. in legal contexts. **2.** Law. **a.** (in pleading) the stage at which the parties join issue (**joinder of issue**). **b.** the joining of two or more persons as coplaintiffs or codefendants (**joinder of parties**).

joiner (ˈdʒɔɪnə) n. **1.** Chiefly Brit. a person skilled in making finished woodwork, such as windows and stairs. **2.** a person or thing that joins. **3.** Inf. a person who joins many clubs, etc.

joinery (ˈdʒɔɪnərɪ) n. **1.** the skill or craft of a joiner. **2.** work made by a joiner.

joint (dʒɔɪnt) n. **1.** a junction of two or more parts or objects. **2.** Anat. the junction between two or more bones. **3.** the point of connection between movable parts in in-

---

THESAURUS

jinx 1. n. black magic, curse, evil eye, hex (U.S.), nemesis, plague, voodoo **2.** v. bewitch, curse, hex (U.S.)

jitters anxiety, fidgets, nerves, nervousness, tenseness, the shakes (Inf.), the willies (Inf.)

jittery agitated, anxious, fidgety, jumpy, nervous, quivering, shaky, trembling

job 1. affair, assignment, charge, chore, concern, contribution, duty, enterprise, errand, function, pursuit, responsibility, role, stint, task, undertaking, venture, work **2.** activity, business, calling, capacity, career, craft, employment, function, livelihood, métier, occupation, office, position, post, profession, situation, trade, vocation **3.** allotment, assign-

ment, batch, commission, consignment, contract, lot, output, piece, portion, product, share

jobless idle, inactive, out of work, unemployed, unoccupied

jockey 1. bamboozle, cheat, con (Sl.), deceive, dupe, fool, hoax, hoodwink, trick **2.** cajole, engineer, finagle (Inf.), ingratiate, insinuate, manage, manipulate, manoeuvre, negotiate, trim, wheedle

jocular amusing, comical, droll, facetious, frolicsome, funny, humorous, jesting, jocose, jocund, joking, jolly, jovial, playful, roguish, sportive, teasing, waggish, whimsical, witty

jog 1. activate, arouse, nudge, prod, prompt, push, remind, shake, stimulate, stir, suggest

2. bounce, jar, jerk, jiggle, joggle, jolt, jostle, jounce, rock, shake **3.** canter, dogtrot, lope, run, trot **4.** lumber, plod, traipse (Inf.), tramp, trudge

joie de vivre ebullience, enjoyment, enthusiasm, gaiety, gusto, joy, joyfulness, pleasure, relish, zest

join 1. accompany, add, adhere, annex, append, attack, cement, combine, connect, couple, fasten, knit, link, marry, splice, tie, unite, yoke **2.** affiliate with, associate with, enlist, enrol, enter, sign up **3.** adjoin, border, border on, butt, conjoin, extend, meet, reach, touch, verge on

vertebrates. **4.** the part of a plant stem from which a branch or leaf grows. **5.** one of the parts into which a carcass of meat is cut by the butcher, esp. for roasting. **6.** *Geol.* a crack in a rock along which no displacement has occurred. **7.** *Sl.* **a.** a bar or nightclub. **b.** *Often facetious.* a dwelling or meeting place. **8.** *Sl.* a marijuana cigarette. **9. out of joint. a.** dislocated. **b.** out of order. ~*adj.* **10.** shared by or belonging to two or more: *joint property.* **11.** created by combined effort. **12.** sharing with others or with one another: *joint rulers.* ~*vb.* (*tr.*) **13.** to provide with or fasten by a joint or joints. **14.** to plane the edge of (a board, etc.) into the correct shape for a joint. **15.** to cut or divide (meat, etc.) into joints. —'**jointed** *adj.* —'**jointly** *adv.*

joint stock *n.* capital funds held in common and usually divided into shares.

joint-stock company *n.* **1.** *Brit.* a business enterprise characterized by the sharing of ownership between shareholders, whose liability is limited. **2.** *U.S.* a business enterprise whose owners are issued shares of transferable stock but do not enjoy limited liability.

jointure ('dʒɔɪntʃə) *n. Law.* **a.** provision made by a husband for his wife by settling property upon her at marriage for her use after his death. **b.** the property so settled.

join up *vb.* (*adv.*) **1.** (*intr.*) to become a member of a military or other organization; enlist. **2.** (often foll. by *with*) to unite or connect.

joist (dʒɔɪst) *n.* a beam made of timber, steel, or reinforced concrete, used in the construction of floors, roofs, etc.

joke (dʒəʊk) *n.* **1.** a humorous anecdote. **2.** something that is said or done for fun. **3.** a ridiculous or humorous circumstance. **4.** a person or thing inspiring ridicule or amusement. **5. no joke.** something very serious. ~*vb.* **6.** (*intr.*) to tell jokes. **7.** (*intr.*) to speak or act facetiously. **8.** to make fun of (someone). —'**jokey** *or* '**joky** *adj.* —'**jokingly** *adv.*

joker ('dʒəʊkə) *n.* **1.** a person who jokes, esp. in an obnoxious manner. **2.** *Sl.* a man; fellow. **3.** an extra playing card in a pack, which in many card games can rank above any other card.

jollify ('dʒɒlɪ,faɪ) *vb.* **-fying, -fied.** to be or cause to be jolly. —,**jollifi'cation** *n.*

jollity ('dʒɒlɪtɪ) *n., pl.* **-ties.** the condition of being jolly.

jolly ('dʒɒlɪ) *adj.* **-lier, -liest. 1.** full of good humour. **2.** having or provoking gaiety and merrymaking. **3.** pleasing. ~*adv.* **4.** *Brit.* (intensifier): *you're jolly nice.* ~*vb.* **-lying, -lied.** (*tr.*) *Inf.* **5.** (often foll. by *up* or *along*) to try to make or keep (someone) cheerful. **6.** to make good-natured fun of. —'**jolliness** *n.*

Jolly Roger *n.* the traditional pirate flag, consisting of a white skull and crossbones on a black field.

jolt (dʒəʊlt) *vb.* (*tr.*) **1.** to bump against with a jarring blow. **2.** to move in a jolting manner. **3.** to surprise or shock. ~*n.* **4.** a sudden jar or blow. **5.** an emotional shock.

Jonah ('dʒəʊnə) *or* **Jonas** ('dʒəʊnəs) *n.* **1.** *Old Testament.* a Hebrew prophet who, having been thrown overboard from a ship was swallowed by a whale and vomited onto dry land. **2.** a person believed to bring bad luck to those around him.

jonquil ('dʒɒŋkwɪl) *n.* a Eurasian variety of narcissus

with long fragrant yellow or white short-tubed flowers.

josh (dʒɒʃ) *U.S. sl.* ~*vb.* **1.** to tease (someone) in a bantering way. ~*n.* **2.** a teasing joke. —'**josher** *n.*

Josh. *Bible. abbrev. for* Joshua.

joss (dʒɒs) *n.* a Chinese deity worshipped in the form of an idol.

joss stick *n.* a stick of dried perfumed paste, giving off a fragrant odour when burnt as incense.

jostle ('dʒɒsəl) *or* **justle** ('dʒʌsəl) *vb.* **1.** to bump or push (someone) roughly. **2.** to come or bring into contact. **3.** to force (one's way) by pushing. ~*n.* **4.** the act of jostling. **5.** a rough bump or push.

jot (dʒɒt) *vb.* **jotting, jotted. 1.** (*tr.;* usually foll. by *down*) to write a brief note of. ~*n.* **2.** (*used with a negative*) a little bit (in **not to care** (*or* **give**) **a jot**).

jotter ('dʒɒtə) *n.* a small notebook.

jotting ('dʒɒtɪŋ) *n.* something jotted down.

joule (dʒuːl) *n.* the derived SI unit of work or energy; the work done when the point of application of a force of 1 newton is displaced through a distance of 1 metre in the direction of the force. Symbol: **J**

journal ('dʒɜːnəl) *n.* **1.** a newspaper or periodical. **2.** a book in which a daily record of happenings, etc., is kept. **3.** an official record of the proceedings of a legislative body. **4.** *Book-keeping.* one of several books in which transactions are initially recorded to facilitate subsequent entry in the ledger. **5.** the part of a shaft or axle in contact with or enclosed by a bearing.

journalese (,dʒɜːnə'liːz) *n. Derog.* a superficial style of writing regarded as typical of newspapers, etc.

journalism ('dʒɜːnə,lɪzəm) *n.* **1.** the profession or practice of reporting about, photographing, or editing news stories for one of the mass media. **2.** newspapers and magazines collectively. —'**journalist** *n.*

journey ('dʒɜːnɪ) *n.* **1.** a travelling from one place to another. **2. a.** the distance travelled in a journey. **b.** the time taken to make a journey. ~*vb.* **3.** (*intr.*) to make a journey. —'**journeyer** *n.*

journeyman ('dʒɜːnɪmən) *n., pl.* **-men. 1.** a craftsman, artisan, etc., who is qualified to work at his trade in the employment of another. **2.** a competent workman.

joust (dʒaʊst) *History.* ~*n.* **1.** a combat between two mounted knights tilting against each other with lances. ~*vb.* **2.** (*intr.;* often foll. by *against* or *with*) to encounter or engage in such a tournament: *he jousted with five opponents.* —'**jouster** *n.*

Jove (dʒəʊv) *n.* **1.** another name for **Jupiter**[1]. **2. by Jove.** an exclamation of surprise or excitement. —'**Jovian** *adj.*

jovial ('dʒəʊvɪəl) *adj.* having or expressing convivial humour. —,**jovi'ality** *n.* —'**jovially** *adv.*

jowl[1] (dʒaʊl) *n.* **1.** the jaw, esp. the lower one. **2.** (*often pl.*) a cheek. **3. cheek by jowl.** See **cheek.** —**jowled** *adj.*

jowl[2] (dʒaʊl) *n.* **1.** fatty flesh hanging from the lower jaw. **2.** a similar fleshy part in animals, such as the dewlap of a bull.

joy (dʒɔɪ) *n.* **1.** a deep feeling or condition of happiness or contentment. **2.** something causing such a feeling. **3.** an outward show of pleasure or delight. **4.** *Brit. inf.* success; luck: *I went for a loan, but got no joy.* ~*vb.* **5.** (*intr.*) to feel joy. **6.** (*tr.*) *Obs.* to gladden.

THESAURUS

joint *n.* **1.** articulation, connection, hinge, intersection, junction, juncture, knot, nexus, node, seam, union ~*adj.* **2.** collective, combined, communal, concerted, consolidated, cooperative, joined, mutual, shared, united ~*v.* **3.** connect, couple, fasten, fit, join, unite **4.** carve, cut up, dismember, dissect, divide, segment, sever, sunder

jointly as one, collectively, in common, in conjunction, in league, in partnership, mutually, together, unitedly

joke *n.* **1.** frolic, fun, gag (*Sl.*), jape, jest, lark, play, pun, quip, quirk, sally, sport, whimsy, wisecrack (*Inf.*), witticism, yarn **2.** buffoon, butt, clown, laughing stock, simpleton, target ~*v.* **3.** banter, chaff, deride, frolic, gambol, jest, kid (*Inf.*), mock, quip, ridicule, taunt, tease

joker buffoon, clown, comedian, comic, humorist, jester, kidder (*Inf.*), prankster, trick-

ster, wag, wit

jolly blithesome, carefree, cheerful, convivial, festive, frolicsome, funny, gay, gladsome, hilarious, jocund, jovial, joyful, joyous, jubilant, merry, mirthful, playful, sportive, sprightly

jolt *v.* **1.** jar, jerk, jog, jostle, knock, push, shake, shove **2.** astonish, discompose, disturb, perturb, stagger, startle, stun, surprise, upset ~*n.* **3.** bump, jar, jerk, jog, jump, lurch, quiver, shake, start **4.** blow, bolt from the blue, bombshell, reversal, setback, shock, surprise, thunderbolt

jostle bump, butt, crowd, elbow, hustle, jog, joggle, jolt, press, push, scramble, shake, shove, squeeze, throng, thrust

jot **1.** *n.* ace, atom, bit, detail, fraction, grain, iota, mite, morsel, particle, scintilla, scrap, smidgen (*U.S.*), speck, tittle, trifle, whit **2.** *v.* list, note, note down, record, register, scrib-

ble, tally

journal **1.** chronicle, daily, gazette, magazine, monthly, newspaper, paper, periodical, record, register, review, tabloid, weekly **2.** chronicle, commonplace book, daybook, diary, log, record

journalist broadcaster, columnist, commentator, contributor, correspondent, hack, newsman, newspaperman, pressman, reporter, scribe (*Inf.*), stringer

journey **1.** *n.* excursion, expedition, jaunt, odyssey, outing, passage, peregrination, pilgrimage, progress, ramble, tour, travel, trek, trip, voyage **2.** *v.* fare, fly, go, peregrinate, proceed, ramble, range, roam, rove, tour, travel, traverse, trek, voyage, wander, wend

jovial airy, animated, blithe, buoyant, cheery, convivial, cordial, gay, glad, happy, hilarious, jocose, jocund, jolly, jubilant, merry, mirthful

joyful ('dʒɔɪful) *adj.* **1.** full of joy; elated. **2.** expressing or producing joy: *a joyful look; a joyful occasion.* —'**joyfully** *adv.* —'**joyfulness** *n.*

joyless ('dʒɔɪlɪs) *adj.* having or producing no joy or pleasure. —'**joylessly** *adv.*

joyous ('dʒɔɪəs) *adj.* **1.** having a happy nature or mood. **2.** joyful. —'**joyously** *adv.*

joy ride *Inf.* ~*n.* **1.** an enjoyable ride taken in a car, esp. in a stolen car driven recklessly. ~*vb.* **joy-ride, -riding, -rode, -ridden. 2.** (*intr.*) to take such a ride. —'**joy,rider** *n.*

joy stick *n. Inf.* the control stick of an aircraft.

J.P. *abbrev. for* Justice of the Peace.

Jr. *or* **jr.** *abbrev. for* junior.

jubilant ('dʒuːbɪlənt) *adj.* feeling or expressing great joy. —'**jubilance** *n.* —'**jubilantly** *adv.*

jubilate ('dʒuːbɪˌleɪt) *vb.* (*intr.*) **1.** to have or express great joy; rejoice. **2.** to celebrate a jubilee. —ˌjubi'la-tion *n.*

jubilee ('dʒuːbɪˌliː) *n.* **1.** a time or season for rejoicing. **2.** a special anniversary, esp. a 25th or 50th one. **3.** *R.C. Church.* a specially appointed period in which special indulgences are granted. **4.** *Old Testament.* a year that was to be observed every 50th year, during which Hebrew slaves were to be liberated, etc.

Jud. *Bible. abbrev. for:* **1.** Also: **Judg.** Judges. **2.** Judith.

Judaic (dʒuː'deɪɪk) *adj.* of or relating to the Jews or Judaism. —**Ju'daically** *adv.*

Judaism ('dʒuːdeɪˌɪzəm) *n.* **1.** the religion of the Jews, based on the Old Testament and the Talmud and having as its central point a belief in one God **2.** the religious and cultural traditions of the Jews. **3.** the Jews collectively. —'**Judaist** *n.* —ˌJuda'istic *adj.*

Judas ('dʒuːdəs) *n.* **1.** *New Testament.* the apostle who betrayed Jesus to his enemies for 30 pieces of silver (Luke 22:3–6, 47–48). **2.** a person who betrays a friend; traitor.

judder ('dʒʌdə) *Inf., chiefly Brit.* ~*vb.* **1.** (*intr.*) to shake or vibrate. ~*n.* **2.** abnormal vibration in a mechanical system. **3.** a juddering motion.

judge (dʒʌdʒ) *n.* **1.** a public official with authority to hear cases in a court of law and pronounce judgment upon them. **2.** a person who is appointed to determine the result of contests or competitions. **3.** a person qualified to comment critically: *a good judge of antiques.* **4.** a leader of the peoples of Israel from Joshua's death to the accession of Saul. ~*vb.* **5.** to hear and decide upon (a case at law). **6.** (*tr.*) to pass judgment on. **7.** (when *tr., may take a clause as object or an infinitive*) to decide (something) after inquiry. **8.** to determine the result of (a contest or competition). **9.** to appraise (something) critically. **10.** (*tr.; takes a clause as object*) to believe something to be the case. —'**judge,like** *adj.* —'**judger** *n.* —'**judgeship** *n.*

judgment *or* **judgement** ('dʒʌdʒmənt) *n.* **1.** the faculty of being able to make critical distinctions and achieve a balanced viewpoint. **2. a.** the verdict pronounced by a court of law. **b.** an obligation arising as a result of such a verdict, such as a debt. **c.** (*as modifier*):

a judgment debtor. **3.** the formal decision of one or more judges at a contest or competition. **4.** a particular decision formed in a case in dispute or doubt. **5.** an estimation: *a good judgment of distance.* **6.** criticism or censure. **7. against one's better judgment.** contrary to a preferred course of action. **8. sit in judgment. a.** to preside as judge. **b.** to assume the position of critic. —**judgmental** *or* **judgemental** (dʒʌdʒ'mɛntəl) *adj.*

Judgment ('dʒʌdʒmənt) *n.* **1.** the estimate by God of the ultimate worthiness or unworthiness of the individual or of all mankind. **2.** God's subsequent decision determining the final destinies of all individuals.

Judgment Day *n.* the occasion of the Last Judgment by God at the end of the world. Also called: **Day of Judgment.** See **Last Judgment.**

judicature ('dʒuːdɪkətʃə) *n.* **1.** the administration of justice. **2.** the office, function, or power of a judge. **3.** the extent of authority of a court or judge. **4.** a body of judges; judiciary. **5.** a court of justice or such courts collectively.

judicial (dʒuː'dɪʃəl) *adj.* **1.** of or relating to the administration of justice. **2.** of or relating to judgment in a court of law or to a judge exercising this function. **3.** allowed or enforced by a court of law: *judicial separation.* **4.** having qualities appropriate to a judge. **5.** giving or seeking judgment. —**ju'dicially** *adv.*

judiciary (dʒuː'dɪʃərɪ) *adj.* **1.** of or relating to courts of law, judgment, or judges. ~*n., pl.* **-aries. 2.** the branch of the central authority in a state concerned with the administration of justice. **3.** the system of courts in a country. **4.** the judges collectively.

judicious (dʒuː'dɪʃəs) *adj.* having or proceeding from good judgment. —**ju'diciously** *adv.* —**ju'diciousness** *n.*

judo ('dʒuːdəʊ) *n.* **a.** the modern sport derived from jujitsu, in which the object is to force an opponent to submit using the minimum of physical effort. **b.** (*as modifier*): *a judo throw.* —'**judoist** *n.*

jug (dʒʌg) *n.* **1.** a vessel for holding or pouring liquids, usually having a handle and a lip. U.S. equivalent: **pitcher. 2.** *Austral. & N.Z.* a container in which water is boiled, esp. an electric kettle. **3.** *U.S.* a large vessel with a narrow mouth. **4.** Also called: **jugful.** the amount of liquid held by a jug. **5.** *Brit. inf.* a glass of beer. **6.** *Sl.* jail. ~*vb.* **jugging, jugged. 7.** to stew or boil (meat, esp. hare) in an earthenware container. **8.** (*tr.*) *Sl.* to put in jail.

juggernaut ('dʒʌgəˌnɔːt) *n.* **1.** any terrible force, esp. one that demands complete self-sacrifice. **2.** *Brit.* a very large heavy lorry.

juggins ('dʒʌgɪnz) *n. Brit. inf.* a silly fellow.

juggle ('dʒʌgəl) *vb.* **1.** to throw and catch (several objects) continuously so that most are in the air all the time. **2.** to manipulate (facts, etc.) so as to give a false picture. **3.** (*tr.*) to keep (several activities) in progress, esp. with difficulty. ~*n.* **4.** an act of juggling. —'**juggler** *n.*

jugular ('dʒʌgjʊlə) *adj.* **1.** of, relating to, or situated near the throat or neck. ~*n.* **2.** Also called: **jugular vein.** any of the large veins in the neck carrying blood to the heart from the head.

juice (dʒuːs) *n.* **1.** any liquid that occurs naturally in or

---

THESAURUS

joy 1. bliss, delight, ecstasy, elation, exaltation, exultation, felicity, festivity, gaiety, gladness, glee, hilarity, pleasure, rapture, ravishment, satisfaction, transport 2. charm, delight, gem, jewel, pride, prize, treasure, treat, wonder

joyful blithesome, delighted, elated, enraptured, glad, gladsome, gratified, happy, jocund, jolly, jovial, jubilant, light-hearted, merry, pleased, satisfied

joyless cheerless, dejected, depressed, dismal, dispirited, downcast, dreary, gloomy, miserable, sad, unhappy

joyous cheerful, festive, heartening, joyful, merry, rapturous

jubilant elated, enraptured, euphoric, excited, exuberant, exultant, glad, joyous, overjoyed, rejoicing, rhapsodic, thrilled, triumphal, triumphant

jubilation celebration, ecstasy, elation, excitement, exultation, festivity, jamboree, joy, jubilee, triumph

jubilee carnival, celebration, festival, festivity, fête, gala, holiday

judge *n.* 1. adjudicator, arbiter, arbitrator, moderator, referee, umpire 2. appraiser, arbiter, assessor, authority, connoisseur, critic, evaluator, expert 3. beak (*Brit. sl.*), justice, magistrate ~*v.* 4. adjudge, adjudicate, arbitrate, ascertain, conclude, decide, determine, discern, distinguish, mediate, referee, umpire 5. appraise, appreciate, assess, consider, criticize, esteem, estimate, evaluate, examine, rate, review, value 6. adjudge, condemn, decree, doom, find, pass sentence, pronounce sentence, rule, sentence, sit, try

judgment 1. acumen, common sense, discernment, discrimination, intelligence, penetration, percipience, perspicacity, prudence, sagacity, sense, shrewdness, taste, understanding, wisdom 2. arbitration, award, conclusion, decision, decree, determination, finding, order, result, ruling, sentence, verdict 3. assessment, belief, conviction, deduc-

tion, diagnosis, estimate, finding, opinion, valuation, view 4. damnation, doom, fate, misfortune, retribution

judicial 1. judiciary, juridical, legal, official 2. discriminating, distinguished, impartial, judgelike, magisterial, magistral

judicious acute, astute, careful, cautious, circumspect, considered, diplomatic, discerning, discreet, discriminating, enlightened, expedient, informed, politic, prudent, rational, reasonable, sagacious, sage, sane, sapient, sensible, shrewd, skilful, sober, sound, thoughtful, well-advised, well-judged, wise

jug carafe, container, crock, ewer, jar, pitcher, urn, vessel

juggle alter, change, disguise, doctor (*Inf.*), falsify, fix (*Inf.*), manipulate, manoeuvre, misrepresent, modify, tamper with

is secreted by plant or animal tissue: *the juice of an orange*. **2.** *Inf.* **a.** petrol. **b.** electricity. **c.** alcoholic drink. **3.** vigour or vitality. —'**juiceless** *adj.*

juicy ('dʒuːsɪ) *adj.* **juicier, juiciest.** **1.** full of juice. **2.** provocatively interesting; spicy: *juicy gossip.* **3.** *Chiefly U.S.* profitable: *a juicy contract.* —'**juicily** *adv.* —'**juiciness** *n.*

jujitsu, jujutsu, *or* **jiujutsu** (dʒuːˈdʒɪtsuː) *n.* the traditional Japanese system of unarmed self-defence perfected by the samurai. See also **judo.**

juju ('dʒuːdʒuː) *n.* **1.** an object superstitiously revered by certain West African peoples and used as a charm or fetish. **2.** the power associated with a juju.

jujube ('dʒuːdʒuːb) *n.* **1.** any of several Old World spiny trees that have small yellowish flowers and dark red edible fruits. **2.** the fruit of any of these trees. **3.** a chewy sweet made of flavoured gelatine and sometimes medicated to soothe sore throats.

jukebox ('dʒuːkˌbɒks) *n.* an automatic gramophone, usually in a large case, in which records may be selected by inserting coins and pressing appropriate buttons.

jukskei ('dʒʊkˌskeɪ) *n.* a S. African game in which a peg is thrown over a fixed distance at a stake driven into the ground.

Julian calendar ('dʒuːljən) *n.* the calendar introduced by Julius Caesar in 46 B.C., in which leap years occurred every fourth year and in every centenary year. Cf. **Gregorian calendar.**

julienne (ˌdʒuːlɪˈɛn) *adj.* **1.** (of vegetables) cut into thin shreds. ~*n.* **2.** a clear consommé to which such vegetables have been added.

July (dʒuːˈlaɪ) *n., pl.* **-lies.** the seventh month of the year, consisting of 31 days.

jumble ('dʒʌmbəl) *vb.* **1.** to mingle (objects, etc.) in a state of disorder. **2.** (*tr.; usually passive*) to remember in a confused form. ~*n.* **3.** a disordered mass, state, etc. **4.** articles donated for a jumble sale. —'**jumbly** *adj.*

jumble sale *n.* a sale of miscellaneous articles, usually secondhand, in aid of charity. U.S. equivalent: **rummage sale.**

jumbo ('dʒʌmbəʊ) *n., pl.* **-bos.** **1.** *Inf.* **a.** a very large person or thing. **b.** (*as modifier*): *a jumbo box of detergent.* **2.** See **jumbo jet.**

jumbo jet *n.* *Inf.* a type of large jet-propelled airliner.

jump (dʒʌmp) *vb.* **1.** (*intr.*) to leap or spring clear of the ground or other surface by using the muscles in the legs and feet. **2.** (*tr.*) to leap over or clear (an obstacle): *to jump a gap.* **3.** (*tr.*) to cause to leap over an obstacle: *to jump a horse over a hedge.* **4.** to move or proceed hastily (into, onto, out of, etc.): *she jumped into a taxi.* **5.** (*tr.*) *Inf.* to board so as to travel illegally on: *he jumped the train as it was leaving.* **6.** (*intr.*) to parachute from an aircraft. **7.** (*intr.*) to jerk or start, as with astonishment, surprise, etc. **8.** to rise or cause to rise suddenly or abruptly. **9.** to pass or skip over (intervening objects or matter): *she jumped a few lines and then continued reading.* **10.** (*intr.*) to change from one thing to another, esp. from one subject to another. **11.** *Draughts.* to capture (an opponent's piece) by moving one of one's own pieces over it to an unoccupied square. **12.** (*intr.*) *Bridge.* to bid in response to one's partner at a higher level than is necessary, to indicate a strong hand. **13.** (*tr.*) to come off (a track, etc.): *the locomotive jumped the rails.* **14.** (*intr.*) (of the stylus of a record player) to be jerked out of the groove. **15.** (*intr.*) *Sl.* to be lively: *the party was jumping.* **16.** (*tr.*) *Inf.* to attack without warning: *thieves jumped the old man.* **17.** (*tr.*) *Inf.* (of a driver or a motor vehicle) to pass through (a red traffic light) or move away from (traffic lights) before they change to green. **18. jump bail.** to forfeit one's bail by failing to appear in court. **19. jump down someone's throat.** *Inf.* to address someone sharply. **20. jump ship.** to desert, esp. to leave a ship in which one is legally bound to serve. **21. jump the queue.** *Inf.* to obtain some advantage out of turn or unfairly. **22. jump to it.** *Inf.* to begin something quickly and efficiently. ~*n.* **23.** an act or instance of jumping. **24.** a space, distance, or obstacle to be jumped or that has been jumped. **25.** a descent by parachute from an aircraft. **26.** *Sport.* any of several contests involving a jump: *the high jump.* **27.** a sudden rise: *the jump in prices last month.* **28.** a sudden or abrupt transition. **29.** a sudden jerk or involuntary muscular spasm, esp. as a reaction of surprise. **30.** a step or degree: *one jump ahead.* **31.** *Draughts.* a move that captures an opponent's piece by jumping over it. **32.** *Films.* **a.** a break in continuity in the normal sequence of shots. **b.** (*as modifier*): *a jump cut.* **33. on the jump.** *Inf., chiefly U.S.* **a.** in a hurry. **b.** busy. ~See also **jump at, jump on.**

jump at *vb.* (*intr., prep.*) to be glad to accept: *I would jump at the chance of going.*

jumped-up *adj.* *Inf.* suddenly risen in significance, esp. when appearing arrogant.

jumper[1] ('dʒʌmpə) *n.* *Chiefly Brit.* a sweater or pullover.

jumper[2] ('dʒʌmpə) *n.* **1.** a boring tool that works by repeated impact, such as a steel bit in a drill used in boring rock. **2.** Also called: **jumper cable, jumper lead.** a short length of wire used to make a connection, usually temporarily. **3.** a person or animal that jumps.

jump jet *n.* *Inf.* a fixed-wing jet aircraft that is capable of landing and taking off vertically.

jump leads (liːdz) *pl. n.* two heavy cables fitted with crocodile clips used to start a motor vehicle with a discharged battery by connecting the battery to an external battery.

jump on *vb.* (*intr., prep.*) *Inf.* to berate or reprimand.

jump-start *vb.* **1.** to start the engine of (a car) by pushing or rolling it and then engaging the gears or (of a car) to start in this way. ~*n.* **2.** the act of starting a car in this way. ~Also called (in Brit.): **bump-start.**

jump suit *n.* a one-piece garment of combined trousers and jacket or shirt.

jumpy ('dʒʌmpɪ) *adj.* **jumpier, jumpiest.** **1.** nervous or apprehensive. **2.** moving jerkily or fitfully. —'**jumpily** *adv.* —'**jumpiness** *n.*

Jun. *abbrev. for:* **1.** June. **2.** Also: **jun.** junior.

junction ('dʒʌŋkʃən) *n.* **1. a.** a place where several routes or lines meet, link, or cross each other: *a railway junction.* **b.** a place where roads meet and cross: *a motorway junction.* **2.** *Electronics.* **a.** a contact between two different metals or other materials: *a thermocouple junction.* **b.** a transition region in a semiconductor. **3.** the act of joining or the state of being joined.

juncture ('dʒʌŋktʃə) *n.* **1.** a point in time, esp. a critical one (often in **at this juncture**). **2.** *Linguistics.* the set of phonological features signalling a division between words, such as those that distinguish *a name* from *an aim.* **3.** a less common word for **junction.**

June (dʒuːn) *n.* the sixth month of the year, consisting of 30 days.

jungle ('dʒʌŋɡəl) *n.* **1.** an equatorial forest area with luxuriant vegetation. **2.** any dense or tangled thicket or growth. **3.** a place of intense or ruthless struggle for survival: *the concrete jungle.* —'**jungly** *adj.*

junior ('dʒuːnjə) *adj.* **1.** lower in rank or length of service; subordinate. **2.** younger in years. **3.** of or relating to youth or childhood. **4.** *Brit.* of schoolchildren between the ages of 7 and 11 approximately. **5.** *U.S.* of or designating the third year of a four-year course at college or high school. ~*n.* **6.** *Law.* (in England) any barrister below the rank of Queen's Counsel. **7.** a junior person. **8.** *Brit.* a junior schoolchild. **9.** *U.S.* a junior student.

Junior ('dʒuːnjə) *adj. Chiefly U.S.* being the younger: usually used after a name to distinguish the son from the father: *Charles Parker, Junior.* Abbrev.: **Jnr., Jr.**

juniper ('dʒuːnɪpə) *n.* a coniferous shrub or small tree of the N hemisphere, having purple berry-like cones. The cones of the **common** or **dwarf juniper** are used as a flavouring in making gin.

junk[1] (dʒʌŋk) *n.* **1.** discarded objects, etc., collectively. **2.** *Inf.* rubbish: *the play was absolute junk.* **3.** *Sl.* any narcotic drug, esp. heroin. ~*vb.* **4.** (*tr.*) *Inf.,* chiefly *U.S.* to discard as junk.

junk[2] (dʒʌŋk) *n.* a sailing vessel used in Chinese waters and characterized by a very high poop, flat bottom, and square sails supported by battens.

Junker ('juŋkə) *n.* **1.** *History.* any of the aristocratic landowners of Prussia who were devoted to maintaining their privileges. **2.** an arrogant and tyrannical German army officer or official. **3.** (formerly) a young German nobleman. —'**Junkerdom** *n.*

junket ('dʒʌŋkɪt) *n.* **1.** a sweet dessert made of flavoured milk set to a curd with rennet. **2.** a feast. **3.** *U.S.* an excursion, esp. one made for pleasure at public expense. ~*vb.* **4.** to have or entertain with a feast. **5.** (*intr.*) *U.S.* (of a public official, etc.) to go on a junket. —'**junketing** *n.*

junk food *n.* food which is eaten in addition to or instead of regular meals, and which often has a low nutritional value.

junkie *or* **junky** ('dʒʌŋkɪ) *n., pl.* **junkies.** an informal word for **drug addict.**

junta ('dʒʊntə) *n.* **1.** a group of military officers holding the power in a country, esp. after a coup d'état. **2.** Also called: **junto.** a small group of men. **3.** a legislative or executive council in some parts of Latin America.

Jupiter[1] ('dʒuːpɪtə) *n.* (in Roman tradition) the king and ruler of the Olympian gods.

Jupiter[2] ('dʒuːpɪtə) *n.* the largest of the planets and the fifth from the sun.

Jurassic (dʒʊ'ræsɪk) *adj.* **1.** of or formed in the second period of the Mesozoic era, during which dinosaurs and ammonites flourished. ~*n.* **2. the.** the Jurassic period or rock system.

juridical (dʒʊ'rɪdɪkəl) *adj.* of or relating to law or to the administration of justice; legal. —**ju'ridically** *adv.*

jurisdiction (ˌdʒʊərɪs'dɪkʃən) *n.* **1.** the right or power to administer justice and to apply laws. **2.** the exercise or extent of such right or power. **3.** authority in general. —ˌjuris'dictional *adj.*

jurisprudence (ˌdʒʊərɪs'pruːdəns) *n.* **1.** the science or philosophy of law. **2.** a system or body of law. **3.** a branch of law: *medical jurisprudence.* —**jurispruden-tial** (ˌdʒʊərɪspruː'denʃəl) *adj.*

jurist ('dʒʊərɪst) *n.* a person versed in the science of law, esp. Roman or civil law.

juror ('dʒʊərə) *n.* **1.** a member of a jury. **2.** a person who takes an oath.

jury[1] ('dʒʊərɪ) *n., pl.* **-ries.** **1.** a group of, usually, twelve people sworn to deliver a true verdict according to the evidence upon a case presented in a court of law. **2.** a body of persons appointed to judge a competition and award prizes.

jury[2] ('dʒʊərɪ) *adj. Chiefly naut.* (in combination) makeshift: *jury-rigged.*

jury box *n.* an enclosure where the jury sit in court.

jury-rigged *adj. Chiefly naut.* set up in a makeshift manner.

just *adj.* (dʒʌst). **1. a.** fair or impartial in action or judgment. **b.** (*as n.*): *the just.* **2.** conforming to high moral standards; honest. **3.** consistent with justice: *a just action.* **4.** rightly applied or given: *a just reward.* **5.** legally valid; lawful: *a just inheritance.* **6.** well-founded: *just criticism.* **7.** correct or true: *a just account.* ~*adv.* (dʒʌst; *unstressed* dʒəst). **8.** used with forms of *have* to indicate an action performed in the very recent past: *I have just closed the door.* **9.** at this very instant: *he's just coming in to land.* **10.** no more than; only: *just an ordinary car.* **11.** exactly: *that's just what I mean.* **12.** barely: *he just got there in time.* **13. just about. a.** at the point of starting (to do something). **b.** almost: *I've just about had enough.* **14. just a moment, second,** *or* **minute.** an expression requesting the hearer to wait or pause for a brief period of time. —'**justly** *adv.* —'**just-ness** *n.*

justice ('dʒʌstɪs) *n.* **1.** the quality or fact of being just. **2.** *Ethics.* the moral principle that determines the fairness of actions, etc. **3.** the administration of law according to prescribed and accepted principles. **4.** conformity to the law. **5.** a judge of the Supreme Court of Judicature. **6.** short for **justice of the peace. 7.** good reason (esp. in **with justice**). **8. do justice to. a.** to show to full advantage. **b.** to show full appreciation of by action. **c.** to treat or judge fairly. **9. do oneself justice.** to make full use of one's abilities. **10. bring to justice.** to capture, try, and usually punish (a criminal, etc.). —'**justice-ˌship** *n.*

justice of the peace *n.* a lay magistrate whose function is to preserve the peace in his area and try summarily such cases as are within his jurisdiction.

justiciary (dʒʌ'stɪʃɪərɪ) *adj.* **1.** of or relating to the administration of justice. ~*n., pl.* **-aries. 2.** an officer or administrator of justice; judge.

justifiable ('dʒʌstɪˌfaɪəbəl) *adj.* capable of being justified. —ˌjustiˌfia'bility *n.* —'justiˌfiably *adv.*

justify ('dʒʌstɪˌfaɪ) *vb.* **-fying, -fied.** **1.** (*often passive*) to prove or see to be just or valid; vindicate. **2.** to show to be reasonable: *his behaviour justifies our suspicion.* **3.** to declare or show to be free from blame or guilt. **4.** *Law.* to show good reason in court for (some action taken). **5.** (*also intr.*) *Printing.* to adjust the spaces between words in (a line of type) so that it is of the required length or (of a line of type) to fit exactly. **6. a.** *Protestant theol.* to declare righteous by the imputation of Christ's merits to the sinner. **b.** *R.C. theol.* to change from sinfulness to righteousness by the transforming effects of grace. **7.** (*also intr.*) *Law.* to prove (a person) to have sufficient means to act as surety, etc., or (of a person) to qualify to provide bail or surety. —ˌjustifi'cation *n.* —'justiˌfier *n.*

justle ('dʒʌsəl) *vb., n.* a less common word for **jostle.**

jut (dʒʌt) *vb.* **jutting, jutted.** **1.** (*intr.; often foll. by out*) to stick out or overhang beyond the surface or main part. ~*n.* **2.** something that juts out. —'**jutting** *adj.*

jute (dʒuːt) *n.* **1.** either of two Old World tropical yellow-flowered herbaceous plants, cultivated for their strong fibre. **2.** this fibre, used in making sacks, rope, etc.

juvenile ('dʒuːvɪˌnaɪl) *adj.* **1.** young, youthful, or imma-

---

THESAURUS

junior inferior, lesser, lower, minor, secondary, subordinate, younger

junk clutter, debris, leavings, litter, oddments, odds and ends, refuse, rubbish, rummage, scrap, trash, waste

jurisdiction 1. authority, command, control, dominion, influence, power, prerogative, rule, say, sway 2. area, bounds, circuit, compass, district, dominion, field, orbit, province, range, scope, sphere, zone

just *adj.* 1. blameless, conscientious, decent, equitable, fair, fairminded, good, honest, honourable, impartial, lawful, pure, right, righteous, unbiased, upright, virtuous 2. accurate, correct, exact, faithful, normal, precise, proper, regular, sound, true 3. appropriate, apt, condign, deserved, due, fitting, justified,

legitimate, merited, proper, reasonable, rightful, suitable, well-deserved ~*adv.* 4. absolutely, completely, entirely, exactly, perfectly, precisely 5. hardly, lately, only now, recently, scarcely 6. at most, but, merely, no more than, nothing but, only, simply, solely

just about all but, almost, around, close to, nearly, not quite, practically, well-nigh

justice 1. equity, fairness, honesty, impartiality, integrity, justness, law, legality, legitimacy, reasonableness, rectitude, right 2. amends, compensation, correction, penalty, recompense, redress, reparation 3. judge, magistrate

justifiable acceptable, defensible, excusable, fit, lawful, legitimate, proper, reasonable, right, sound, tenable, understandable,

valid, vindicable, warrantable, well-founded

justification 1. absolution, apology, approval, defence, exculpation, excuse, exoneration, explanation, extenuation, plea, rationalization, vindication 2. basis, defence, grounds, plea, reason, warrant

justify absolve, acquit, approve, confirm, defend, establish, exculpate, excuse, exonerate, explain, legalize, legitimize, maintain, substantiate, sustain, uphold, validate, vindicate, warrant

justly accurately, correctly, equally, equitably, fairly, honestly, impartially, lawfully, properly

jut bulge, extend, impend, overhang, poke, project, protrude, stick out

ture. **2.** suitable or designed for young people: *juvenile pastimes.* ~*n.* **3.** a juvenile person, animal, or plant. **4.** an actor who performs youthful roles. **5.** a book intended for young readers. —'**juve**,**nilely** *adv.*

juvenile delinquency *n.* antisocial or criminal conduct by juvenile delinquents.

juvenilia (ˌdʒuːvɪˈnɪlɪə) *pl. n.* works of art, literature, or music produced in youth, before the artist, author, or composer has formed a mature style.

juxtapose (ˌdʒʌkstəˈpəʊz) *vb.* (*tr.*) to place close together or side by side. —ˌjuxtapoˈsition *n.* —ˌjuxtapoˈsitional *adj.*

THESAURUS

juvenile 1. *n.* adolescent, boy, child, girl, infant, minor, youth **2.** *adj.* babyish, boyish, callow, childish, girlish, immature, inexperienced, infantile, jejune, puerile, undeveloped, unsophisticated, young, youthful

juxtaposition adjacency, closeness, contact, contiguity, nearness, propinquity, proximity, vicinity

K

k *or* **K** (keɪ) *n., pl.* **k's, K's,** *or* **Ks. 1.** the 11th letter and 8th consonant of the English alphabet. **2.** a speech sound represented by this letter, usually a voiceless velar stop, as in *kitten.*

k *symbol for:* **1.** kilo(s). **2.** *Maths.* the unit vector along the z-axis.

K *symbol for:* **1.** kelvin(s). **2.** *Chess.* king. **3.** *Chem.* potassium. **4.** *Physics.* kaon. **5.** one thousand. **6.** *Computers.* a unit of 1024 words, bytes, or bits.

K. *or* **k.** *abbrev. for:* **1.** (*not cap.*) karat. **2.** king. **3.** *Currency.* **a.** kopeck. **b.** krona. **c.** krone. **4.** knight. **5.** (*cap.*) Köchel: indicating the serial number in the catalogue of the works of Mozart made by Ludwig von Köchel, 1800–77.

Kaffir *or* **Kafir** ('kæfə) *n., pl.* **-firs, -fir** *or* **-irs, -ir. 1.** *Offens.* **a.** (in southern Africa) any Black African. **b.** (*as modifier*): *Kaffir farming.* **2.** a former name for the **Xhosa** language.

kaffir beer *n. S. African.* beer made from sorghum (kaffir corn) or millet.

kaffirboom ('kæfə,buəm) *n.* a S. African deciduous flowering tree.

kaffir corn *n.* a southern African variety of sorghum, cultivated in dry regions for its grain and as fodder. Sometimes shortened to **kaffir.**

Kafir ('kæfə) *n., pl.* **-irs** *or* **-ir. 1.** a member of a people inhabiting E Afghanistan. **2.** a variant spelling of **Kaffir.**

kaftan *or* **caftan** ('kæftæn) *n.* **1.** a long coatlike garment, usually with a belt, worn in the East. **2.** an imitation of this, worn esp. by women, consisting of a loose dress with long wide sleeves.

Kaiser ('kaɪzə) *n.* (*sometimes not cap.*) *History.* **1.** any of the three German emperors. **2.** *Obs.* any Austro-Hungarian emperor.

kale *or* **kail** (keɪl) *n.* **1.** a cultivated variety of cabbage with crinkled leaves. **2.** *Scot.* a cabbage. ~Cf. **sea kale.**

kaleidoscope (kə'laɪdə,skəup) *n.* **1.** an optical toy for producing symmetrical patterns by multiple reflections in inclined mirrors enclosed in a tube. Loose pieces of coloured glass, paper, etc., are placed in the tube between the mirrors. **2.** any complex pattern of frequently changing shapes and colours. —**kaleidoscopic** (kə,laɪdə'skɒpɪk) *adj.*

kaleyard *or* **kailyard** ('keɪl,jɑːd) *n. Scot.* a vegetable garden.

Kamasutra (,kɑːmə'suːtrə) *n.* **the.** an ancient Hindu text on erotic pleasure.

kamikaze (,kæmɪ'kɑːzɪ) *n.* (*often cap.*) (in World War II) **a.** one of a group of Japanese pilots who performed suicidal missions. **b.** (*as modifier*): *a kamikaze attack.*

kangaroo (,kæŋgə'ruː) *n., pl.* **-roos.** a large herbivorous marsupial of Australia and New Guinea, having large powerful hind legs used for leaping, and a long thick tail. —,**kanga'roo-,like** *adj.*

kangaroo closure *n. Parliamentary procedure.* a form of closure in which the chairman or speaker selects certain amendments for discussion and excludes others.

kangaroo court *n.* an irregular court, esp. one set up by strikers.

KANU ('kɑːnuː) *n.* acronym for Kenya African National Union.

kaolin ('keɪəlɪn) *n.* a fine white clay used for the manufacture of hard-paste porcelain and bone china and in medicine as a poultice. Also called: **china clay.** —,**kao'linic** *adj.*

kapok ('keɪpɒk) *n.* a silky fibre obtained from the hairs covering the seeds of a tropical tree (**kapok tree**): used for stuffing pillows, etc.

kappa ('kæpə) *n.* the tenth letter in the Greek alphabet (K, κ).

kaput (kæ'put) *adj.* (*postpositive*) *Inf.* ruined, broken, or not functioning.

karabiner (,kærə'biːnə) *n. Mountaineering.* a metal clip with a spring for attaching to a piton. Also called: **snap ring.**

karakul *or* **caracul** ('kærəkəl) *n.* **1.** a breed of sheep of central Asia having coarse black, grey, or brown hair: the lambs have soft curled hair. **2.** the fur prepared from these lambs. ~See also **Persian lamb.**

karate (kə'rɑːtɪ) *n.* a traditional Japanese system of unarmed combat, employing smashes, chops, kicks, etc., with the hands, feet, elbows, or legs.

karma ('kɑːmə) *n.* **1.** *Hinduism, Buddhism.* the principle of retributive justice determining a person's state of life and the state of his reincarnations as the effect of his past deeds. **2.** destiny or fate. **3.** *Inf.* an aura or quality that a person, place, or thing is felt to have. —'**karmic** *adj.*

kart (kɑːt) *n.* a light low-framed vehicle with small wheels and engine used for recreational racing (**karting**). Also called: **go-cart, go-kart.**

kasbah *or* **casbah** ('kæzbɑː) (*sometimes cap.*) *n.* **1.** the citadel of various North African cities. **2.** the quarter in which a kasbah is located.

katydid ('keɪtɪ,dɪd) *n.* a green long-horned grasshopper living among the foliage of trees in North America.

kauri ('kaurɪ) *n., pl.* **-ris.** a New Zealand coniferous tree with oval leaves and round cones, cultivated for wood and resin.

kayak *or* **kaiak** ('kaɪæk) *n.* a canoe-like boat used by Eskimos, consisting of a frame covered with animal skins.

kayo *or* **KO** ('keɪ'əu) *n., vb. Boxing, sl.* another term for **knockout** or **knock out.**

kazoo (kə'zuː) *n., pl.* **-zoos.** a cigar-shaped musical instrument of metal or plastic with a membranous diaphragm of thin paper that vibrates with a nasal sound when the player hums into it.

K.B.E. *abbrev. for* Knight (Commander of the Order) of the British Empire.

kc *abbrev. for* kilocycle.

K.C. (in Britain) *abbrev. for* King's Counsel.

kcal *abbrev. for* kilocalorie.

K.C.B. *abbrev. for* Knight Commander of the Bath (a Brit. title).

K.C.M.G. *abbrev. for* Knight Commander (of the Order) of St. Michael and St. George (a Brit. title).

kea ('keɪə) *n.* a large New Zealand parrot with brownish-green plumage.

kebab (kə'bæb) *n.* a dish consisting of small pieces of meat, tomatoes, onions, etc., threaded onto skewers and grilled. Also called: **shish kebab.**

kedge (kɛdʒ) *Naut.* ~*vb.* **1.** to draw (a vessel) along by hauling in on the cable of a light anchor, or (of a vessel) to be drawn in this fashion. ~*n.* **2.** a light anchor, used esp. for kedging.

kedgeree (,kɛdʒə'riː) *n. Chiefly Brit.* a dish consisting of rice, cooked flaked fish, and hard-boiled eggs.

keek (kiːk) *n., vb.* a Scot. word for **peep**[1].

keel (kiːl) *n.* **1.** one of the main longitudinal structural members of a vessel to which the frames are fastened. **2. on an even keel.** well-balanced; steady. **3.** any structure corresponding to or resembling the keel of a ship. **4.** *Biol.* a ridgelike part; carina. ~*vb.* **5.** See **keel over.**

keelhaul ('kiːl,hɔːl) *vb.* (*tr.*) **1.** to drag (a person) by a rope from one side of a vessel to the other through the water under the keel. **2.** to rebuke harshly.

keel over *vb.* (*adv.*) **1.** to turn upside down; capsize. **2.** *Inf.* to collapse suddenly.

keelson ('kɛlsən, 'kiːl-) *or* **kelson** ('kɛlsən) *n.* a longitu-

---

dinal beam fastened to the keel of a vessel for strength and stiffness.

keen[1] (kiːn) *adj.* **1.** eager or enthusiastic. **2.** (*postpositive;* foll. by *on*) fond (of); devoted (to): *keen on golf.* **3.** intellectually acute: *a keen wit.* **4.** (of sight, smell, hearing, etc.) capable of recognizing fine distinctions. **5.** having a sharp cutting edge or point. **6.** extremely cold and penetrating: *a keen wind.* **7.** intense or strong: *a keen desire.* **8.** *Chiefly Brit.* extremely competitive: *keen prices.* —'**keenly** *adv.* —'**keenness** *n.*

keen[2] (kiːn) *vb.* **1.** to lament the dead. ~*n.* **2.** a dirge or lament for the dead. —'**keener** *n.*

keep (kiːp) *vb.* **keeping, kept. 1.** (*tr.*) to have or retain possession of. **2.** (*tr.*) to have temporary possession or charge of: *keep my watch for me.* **3.** (*tr.*) to store in a customary place: *I keep my books in the desk.* **4.** to remain or cause to remain in a specified state or condition: *keep ready.* **5.** to continue or cause to continue: *keep in step.* **6.** (*tr.*) to have or take charge or care of: *keep the shop for me till I return.* **7.** (*tr.*) to look after or maintain for use, pleasure, etc.: *to keep chickens.* **8.** (*tr.*) to provide for the upkeep or livelihood of. **9.** (*tr.*) to support financially, esp. in return for sexual favours. **10.** to confine or detain or be confined or detained. **11.** to withhold or reserve or admit of withholding or reserving: *your news will keep.* **12.** (*tr.*) to refrain from divulging or violating: *to keep a secret.* **13.** to preserve or admit of preservation. **14.** (*tr.;* sometimes foll. by *up*) to observe with due rites or ceremonies. **15.** (*tr.*) to maintain by writing regular records in: *to keep a diary.* **16.** (when *intr.*, foll. by *in, on, to,* etc.) to stay in, on, or at (a place or position): *keep to the path.* **17.** (*tr.*) to associate with (esp. in **keep bad company**). **18.** (*tr.*) to maintain in existence: *to keep court in the palace.* **19.** (*tr.*) *Chiefly Brit.* to have habitually in stock: *this shop keeps all kinds of wool.* **20. how are you keeping?** how are you? **21. keep tabs on** (or **track of**). *Inf.* to continue to be informed about. ~*n.* **22.** living or support. **23.** charge or care: *the dog is in your keep.* **24.** Also called: **dungeon, donjon.** the main tower within the walls of a medieval castle or fortress. **25. for keeps.** *Inf.* **a.** permanently. **b.** for the winner or possessor to keep permanently.

keep at *vb.* (*prep.*) **1.** (*intr.*) to persist in. **2.** (*tr.*) to constrain (a person) to continue doing (a task).

keep away *vb.* (*adv.;* often foll. by *from*) to refrain or prevent from coming (near).

keep back *vb.* (*adv.;* often foll. by *from*) **1.** (*tr.*) to refuse to reveal or disclose. **2.** to prevent or be prevented from advancing, entering, etc.

keep down *vb.* (*adv.,* mainly *tr.*) **1.** to repress. **2.** to restrain or control: *he had difficulty keeping his anger down.* **3.** to cause not to increase or rise. **4.** (*intr.*) to lie low. **5.** not to vomit.

keeper ('kiːpə) *n.* **1.** a person in charge of animals, esp. in a zoo. **2.** a person in charge of a museum, collection, or section of a museum. **3.** a person in charge of other people, such as a warder in a jail. **4.** See **goalkeeper, wicketkeeper, gamekeeper. 5.** a person who keeps

something. **6.** a bar placed across the poles of a permanent magnet to close the magnetic circuit when it is not in use.

keep from *vb.* (*prep.*) **1.** (foll. by a gerund) to prevent or restrain (oneself or another); refrain or cause to refrain. **2.** (*tr.*) to preserve or protect.

keeping ('kiːpɪŋ) *n.* **1.** conformity or harmony (esp. in **in** *or* **out of keeping**). **2.** charge or care: *valuables in the keeping of a bank.*

keep off *vb.* **1.** to stay or cause to stay at a distance (from). **2.** (*prep.*) not to eat or drink or to prevent from eating or drinking. **3.** (*prep.*) to avoid or cause to avoid (a topic).

keep on *vb.* (*adv.*) **1.** to continue or persist in (doing something): *keep on running.* **2.** (*tr.*) to continue to wear. **3.** (*tr.*) to continue to employ: *the firm kept on only ten men.* **4.** (*intr.;* foll. by *about*) to persist in talking (about). **5.** (*intr.;* foll. by *at*) to nag (a person).

keep out *vb.* (*adv.*) **1.** to remain or cause to remain outside. **2. keep out of. a.** to remain or cause to remain unexposed to. **b.** to avoid or cause to avoid: *keep out of his way.*

keepsake ('kiːpˌseɪk) *n.* a gift that evokes memories of a person or event.

keep to *vb.* (*prep.*) **1.** to adhere to or stand by or cause to adhere to or stand by. **2.** to confine or be confined to. **3. keep to oneself. a.** (*intr.*) to avoid the society of others. **b.** (*tr.*) to refrain from sharing or disclosing. **4. keep oneself to oneself.** to avoid the society of others.

keep up *vb.* (*adv.*) **1.** (*tr.*) to maintain (prices, one's morale) at the present level. **2.** (*intr.*) to maintain a pace or rate set by another. **3.** (*intr.;* often foll. by *with*) to remain informed: *to keep up with developments.* **4.** (*tr.*) to maintain in good condition. **5.** (*tr.*) to hinder (a person) from going to bed at night. **6. keep it up.** to continue a good performance. **7. keep up with.** to remain in contact, esp. by letter. **8. keep up with (the Joneses).** *Inf.* to compete with (one's neighbours) in material possessions, etc.

keg (kɛg) *n.* **1.** a small barrel with a capacity of between five and ten gallons. **2.** *Brit.* an aluminium container in which beer is transported and stored.

kelp (kɛlp) *n.* **1.** any large brown seaweed. **2.** the ash of such seaweed, used as a source of iodine and potash.

kelpie[1] *or* **kelpy** ('kɛlpɪ) *n., pl.* -**pies.** a breed of sheepdog with pointed ears, originally from Australia.

kelpie[2] ('kɛlpɪ) *n.* (in Scottish folklore) a water spirit in the form of a horse.

kelson ('kɛlsən) *n.* a variant spelling of **keelson.**

kelt (kɛlt) *n.* a salmon that has recently spawned.

Kelt (kɛlt) *n.* a variant spelling of **Celt.**

kelvin ('kɛlvɪn) *n.* the basic SI unit of thermodynamic temperature; the fraction 1/273.16 of the thermodynamic temperature of the triple point of water. Symbol: K

Kelvin scale *n.* a scale of temperature in which the degree is equal to that on the Celsius scale and the zero value is −273.15°C. Also called: **absolute scale.**

THESAURUS

keen 1. ardent, avid, devoted to, eager, earnest, ebullient, enthusiastic, fervid, fierce, fond of, impassioned, intense, zealous **2.** acid, acute, biting, caustic, cutting, edged, finely honed, incisive, penetrating, piercing, pointed, razorlike, sardonic, satirical, sharp, tart, trenchant **3.** astute, brilliant, canny, clever, discerning, discriminating, perceptive, perspicacious, quick, sagacious, sapient, sensitive, shrewd, wise

keenness 1. ardour, avidity, avidness, diligence, eagerness, earnestness, ebullience, enthusiasm, fervour, impatience, intensity, passion, zeal, zest **2.** acerbity, harshness, incisiveness, mordancy, penetration, pungency, rigour, severity, sharpness, sternness, trenchancy, unkindness, virulence **3.** astuteness, canniness, cleverness, discernment, insight, sagacity, sapience, sensitivity, shrewdness, wisdom

keep *v.* **1.** conserve, control, hold, maintain, possess, preserve, retain **2.** accumulate, amass, carry, deal in, deposit, furnish, garner, heap, hold, pile, place, stack, stock, store, trade in **3.** care for, defend, guard, look

after, maintain, manage, mind, operate, protect, safeguard, shelter, shield, tend, watch over **4.** board, feed, foster, maintain, nourish, nurture, provide for, provision, subsidize, support, sustain, victual **5.** accompany, associate with, consort with, fraternize with **6.** arrest, block, check, constrain, control, curb, delay, detain, deter, hamper, hamstring, hinder, hold, hold back, impede, inhibit, keep back, limit, obstruct, prevent, restrain, retard, shackle, stall, withhold **7.** adhere to, celebrate, commemorate, comply with, fulfil, hold, honour, obey, observe, perform, respect, ritualize, solemnize ~*n.* **8.** board, food, livelihood, living, maintenance, means, nourishment, subsistence, support **9.** castle, citadel, donjon, dungeon, fastness, stronghold, tower

keep at be steadfast, carry on, complete, continue, drudge, endure, finish, grind, labour, last, maintain, persevere, persist, remain, slave, stay, stick, toil

keep back 1. check, constrain, control, curb, delay, hold back, limit, prohibit, restrain, restrict, retard, withhold **2.** censor,

conceal, hide, reserve, suppress, withhold

keeper attendant, caretaker, curator, custodian, defender, gaoler, governor, guard, guardian, jailer, overseer, preserver, steward, superintendent, warden, warder

keeping 1. aegis, auspices, care, charge, custody, guardianship, keep, maintenance, patronage, possession, protection, safekeeping, trust **2.** accord, agreement, balance, compliance, conformity, congruity, consistency, correspondence, harmony, observance, proportion

keep on carry on, continue, endure, last, persevere, persist, prolong, remain

keepsake emblem, favour, memento, relic, remembrance, reminder, souvenir, symbol, token

keep up balance, compete, contend, continue, emulate, keep pace, maintain, match, persevere, preserve, rival, sustain, vie

keg barrel, cask, drum, firkin, hogshead, tun, vat

ken (kɛn) n. **1.** range of knowledge or perception (esp. in **beyond** or **in one's ken**). ~vb. **kenning, kenned** or **kent. 2.** (tr.) Northern Brit. dialect. to know. **3.** Northern Brit. dialect. to understand.

kennel ('kɛnᵊl) n. **1.** a hutlike shelter for a dog. U.S. name: **doghouse. 2.** (usually pl.) an establishment where dogs are bred, trained, boarded, etc. **3.** a hovel. **4.** a pack of hounds. ~vb. **-nelling, -nelled** or U.S. **-neling, -neled. 5.** to keep or stay in a kennel.

kepi ('keɪpiː) n., pl. **kepis.** a military cap with a circular top and a horizontal peak.

kept (kɛpt) vb. **1.** the past tense or past participle of **keep. 2. kept woman.** Censorious. a woman maintained by a man as his mistress.

kerb or U.S. **curb** (kɜːb) n. a line of stone or concrete forming an edge between a pavement and a roadway. —'**kerbing** n.

kerbstone or U.S. **curbstone** ('kɜːb,stəʊn) n. one of a series of stones that form a kerb.

kerchief ('kɜːtʃɪf) n. a piece of cloth worn over the head. —'**kerchiefed** adj.

kerfuffle (kə'fʌfᵊl) n. Inf., chiefly Brit. commotion; disorder.

kermes ('kɜːmɪz) n. **1.** the dried bodies of female scale insects used as a red dyestuff. **2.** a small evergreen Eurasian oak tree: the host plant of kermes scale insects.

kernel ('kɜːnᵊl) n. **1.** the edible seed of a nut or fruit within the shell or stone. **2.** the grain of a cereal, esp. wheat, consisting of the seed in a hard husk. **3.** the central or essential part of something. —'**kernel-less** adj.

kerosene or **kerosine** ('kɛrə,siːn) n. another name for **paraffin,** except when used as a fuel for jet aircraft.

kestrel ('kɛstrəl) n. any of several small falcons that feed on small mammals and tend to hover against the wind.

ketch (kɛtʃ) n. a two-masted sailing vessel, fore-and-aft rigged, with a tall mainmast.

ketchup ('kɛtʃəp), **catchup,** or **catsup** n. any of various sauces containing vinegar: tomato ketchup.

ketone ('kiːtəʊn) n. any of a class of compounds with the general formula R'COR, where R and R' are usually alkyl or aryl groups. —**ketonic** (kɪ'tɒnɪk) adj.

kettle ('kɛtᵊl) n. **1.** a metal container with a handle and spout for boiling water. **2.** any of various metal containers for heating liquids, cooking fish, etc.

kettledrum ('kɛtᵊl,drʌm) n. a percussion instrument consisting of a hollow bowl-like hemisphere covered with a skin or membrane, supported on a tripod. The pitch may be adjusted by means of screws, which alter the tension of the skin. —'**kettle,drummer** n.

kettle of fish n. **a pretty kettle of fish.** an awkward situation; mess.

key¹ (kiː) n. **1.** a metal instrument, usually of a specifically contoured shape, that is made to fit a lock and, when rotated, operates the lock's mechanism. **2.** any instrument that is rotated to operate a valve, clock winding mechanism, etc. **3.** a small metal peg or wedge inserted to prevent relative motion. **4.** any of a set of levers operating a typewriter, computer, etc. **5.** any of the visible parts of the lever mechanism of a musical keyboard instrument that when depressed cause the instrument to sound. **6. a.** Also called: **tonality.** any of the 24 major and minor diatonic scales considered as a corpus of notes upon which a piece of music draws for its tonal framework. **b.** the main tonal centre in an extended composition: a symphony in the key of F major. **7.** something that is crucial in providing an explanation or interpretation. **8.** a means of achieving a desired end: the key to happiness. **9.** a means of access or control: Gibraltar is the key to the Mediterranean. **10.** a list of explanations of symbols, codes, etc. **11.** a text that explains or gives information about a work of literature, art, or music. **12.** Electrical engineering. a hand-operated device for opening or closing a circuit, esp. for transmitting Morse code. **13.** the grooving or scratching of a surface or the application of a rough coat of plaster, etc., to provide a bond for a subsequent finish. **14.** pitch:

he spoke in a low key. **15.** a mood or style: a poem in a melancholic key. **16.** short for **keystone** (sense 1). **17.** Bot. any dry winged fruit, esp. that of the ash. **18.** (modifier) of great importance: a key issue. ~vb. (tr.) **19.** (foll. by to) to harmonize (with): to key one's actions to the prevailing mood. **20.** to adjust or fasten with a key or some similar device. **21.** to provide with a key or keys. **22.** to include a distinguishing device in (an advertisement, etc.), so that responses to it can be identified. ~See also **key up.** —'**keyless** adj.

key² (kiː) n. a variant spelling of **cay.**

keyboard ('kiː,bɔːd) n. **1. a.** a set of keys, usually hand-operated, as on a piano, typewriter, or typesetting machine. **b.** (as modifier): a keyboard instrument. ~vb. **2.** (tr.) to set (a text) in type by using a keyboard machine.

keyhole ('kiː,həʊl) n. an aperture in a door or a lock case through which a key may be passed to engage the lock mechanism.

key money n. a fee payment required from a new tenant of a house or flat before he moves in.

keynote ('kiː,nəʊt) n. **1. a.** a central or determining principle in a speech, literary work, etc. **b.** (as modifier): a keynote speech. **2.** the note upon which a scale or key is based; tonic. ~vb. (tr.) **3.** to deliver a keynote address to (a political convention, etc.).

keypad ('kiː,pæd) n. a small panel with a set of buttons for operating a teletext system, electronic calculator, etc.

key punch n. **1.** Also called: **card punch.** a device having a keyboard that is operated manually to transfer data onto punched cards, paper tape, etc. ~vb. **key-punch. 2.** to transfer (data) by using a key punch.

key signature n. Music. a group of sharps or flats appearing at the beginning of each stave line to indicate the key in which a piece, section, etc., is to be performed.

keystone ('kiː,stəʊn) n. **1.** the central stone at the top of an arch or the top stone of a dome or vault. **2.** something that is necessary to connect other related things.

key up vb. (tr., adv.) to raise the intensity, excitement, tension, etc., of.

kg or **kg.** abbrev. for kilogram.

K.G. abbrev. for Knight of the Order of the Garter (a Brit. title).

K.G.B. abbrev. for Komitet Gosudarstvennoi Bezopasnosti: the Soviet secret police since 1954.

khaki ('kɑːkɪ) n., pl. **-kis. 1.** a dull yellowish-brown colour. **2. a.** a hard-wearing fabric of this colour, used esp. for military uniforms. **b.** (as modifier): a khaki jacket.

khan (kɑːn) n. **1. a.** (formerly) a title borne by medieval Chinese emperors and Mongol and Turkic rulers. **b.** such a ruler. **2.** a title of respect borne by important personages in Afghanistan and central Asia. —'**khanate** n.

khedive (kɪ'diːv) n. the viceroy of Egypt under Ottoman suzerainty (1867-1914). —**khe'dival** or **khe'divial** adj.

kHz abbrev. for kilohertz.

kibbutz (kɪ'bʊts) n., pl. **kibbutzim** (,kɪbʊt'siːm). a collective agricultural settlement in modern Israel, owned and administered communally by its members.

kibosh ('kaɪ,bɒʃ) n. Sl. **put the kibosh on.** to put a stop to; prevent from continuing; halt.

kick (kɪk) vb. **1.** (tr.) to drive or impel with the foot. **2.** (tr.) to hit with the foot or feet. **3.** (intr.) to strike out or thrash about with the feet, as in fighting or swimming. **4.** (intr.) to raise a leg high, as in dancing. **5.** (of a gun, etc.) to recoil or strike in recoiling when fired. **6.** (tr.) Rugby. to make (a conversion or a drop goal) by means of a kick. **7.** (tr.) Soccer. to score (a goal) by a kick. **8.** (intr.; sometimes foll. by against) Inf. to object or resist. **9.** (intr.) Inf. to be active and in good health (esp. in **alive and kicking**). **10.** Inf. to change gear in a car: he kicked into third. **11.** (tr.) Inf. to free oneself of (an addiction, etc.): to kick the habit. **12. kick one's heels.** to be idle or be kept waiting. **13. kick up one's heels.** Inf. to enjoy oneself without inhibition. ~n. **14.** a thrust or blow with the foot. **15.** any of certain rhythmic leg movements

---

THESAURUS

kernel core, essence, germ, gist, grain, marrow, nub, pith, seed, substance

key n. **1.** latchkey, opener **2.** Fig. answer, clue, cue, explanation, guide, indicator, inter-

pretation, lead, means, pointer, sign, solution, translation ~adj. **3.** basic, chief, crucial, decisive, essential, fundamental, important, leading, main, major, pivotal, principal

keynote centre, core, essence, gist, heart, kernel, marrow, pith, substance, theme

used in swimming. **16.** the recoil of a gun or other firearm. **17.** *Inf.* exciting quality or effect (esp. in **get a kick out of, for kicks**). **18.** *Inf.* the sudden stimulating effect of strong alcoholic drink or certain drugs. **19.** *Inf.* power or force. **20. kick in the teeth.** *Sl.* a humiliating rebuff. —'**kickable** *adj.*

kick about *or* **around** *vb.* (*mainly adv.*) *Inf.* **1.** (*tr.*) to treat harshly. **2.** (*tr.*) to discuss (ideas, etc.) informally. **3.** (*intr.*) to wander aimlessly. **4.** (*intr.*) to lie neglected or forgotten.

kickback ('kɪk,bæk) *n.* **1.** a strong reaction. **2.** *U.S.* part of an income paid to a person having influence over the size or payment of the income, esp. by some illegal arrangement. ~*vb.* **kick back.** (*adv.*) **3.** (*intr.*) to have a strong reaction. **4.** (*intr.*) (esp. of a gun) to recoil. **5.** *U.S.* to pay a kickback to (someone).

kick off *vb.* (*intr., adv.*) **1.** to start play in a game of football by kicking the ball from the centre of the field. **2.** *Inf.* to commence (a discussion, job, etc.). ~*n.* **kick-off. 3. a.** a place kick from the centre of the field in a game of football. **b.** the time at which the first such kick is due to take place.

kick out *vb.* (*tr., adv.*) *Inf.* to eject or dismiss.

kickstand ('kɪk,stænd) *n.* a short metal bar attached to the frame of a motorcycle or bicycle, which when kicked into a vertical position holds the stationary vehicle upright.

kick up *vb.* (*adv.*) *Inf.* to cause (trouble, etc.).

kid[1] (kɪd) *n.* **1.** the young of a goat or of a related animal, such as an antelope. **2.** soft smooth leather made from the hide of a kid. **3.** *Inf.* **a.** a young person; child. **b.** (*modifier*) younger or being still a child: *kid brother.* ~*vb.* **kidding, kidded. 4.** (of a goat) to give birth to (young). —'**kiddishness** *n.* —'**kid,like** *adj.*

kid[2] (kɪd) *Inf.* ~*vb.* **kidding, kidded. 1.** (*tr.*) to tease or deceive. **2.** (*intr.*) to behave or speak deceptively for fun. —'**kidder** *n.* —'**kiddingly** *adv.*

kiddy *or* **kiddie** ('kɪdɪ) *n., pl.* -**dies.** *Inf.* an affectionate word for **child.**

kid glove *n.* **1.** a glove made of kidskin. **2. handle with kid gloves.** to treat with great tact or caution. ~*adj.* **kidglove. 3.** overdelicate. **4.** diplomatic; tactful: *a kidglove approach.*

kidnap ('kɪdnæp) *vb.* **-napping, -napped** *or U.S.* **-naping, -naped.** (*tr.*) to carry off and hold (a person), usually for ransom. —'**kidnapper** *n.*

kidney ('kɪdnɪ) *n.* **1.** either of two bean-shaped organs at the back of the abdominal cavity in man. They filter waste products from the blood, which are excreted as urine. Related adj.: **renal. 2.** the corresponding organ in other animals. **3.** the kidneys of certain animals used as food. **4.** class, type, or disposition (esp. in **of the same** *or* **a different kidney**).

kidney bean *n.* **1.** any of certain bean plants having kidney-shaped seeds, esp. the scarlet runner. **2.** the seed of any of these beans.

kidney machine *n.* a machine carrying out the functions of a kidney, esp. used in haemodialysis.

kidney stone *n.* *Pathol.* a hard mass formed in the kidney, usually composed of oxalates, phosphates, and carbonates.

kill (kɪl) *vb.* (*mainly tr.*) **1.** (*also intr.; when tr.,* sometimes foll. by *off*) to cause the death of (a person or animal). **2.** to put an end to: *to kill someone's interest.* **3.** to make (time) pass quickly, esp. while waiting for something. **4.** to deaden (sound). **5.** *Inf.* to tire out: *the effort killed him.* **6.** *Inf.* to cause to suffer pain or discomfort: *my shoes are killing me.* **7.** *Inf.* to quash or veto: *the bill was killed in the House of Lords.* **8.** *Inf.* to switch off; stop. **9.** (*also intr.*) *Inf.* to overcome with attraction, laughter, surprise, etc.: *she was dressed to kill.* **10.** *Tennis, squash, etc.* to hit (a ball) so hard or so accurately that the opponent cannot return it. **11.** *Soccer.* to bring (a moving ball) under control. **12. kill oneself.** *Inf.* to overexert oneself: *don't kill yourself.* **13. kill two birds with one stone.** to achieve two results with one action. ~*n.* **14.** the act of causing death, esp. at the end of a hunt, bullfight, etc. **15.** the animal or animals killed during a hunt. **16.** *N.Z.* a seasonal tally of the number of stock killed at a meatworks. **17.** the destruction of a battleship, tank, etc. **18. in at the kill.** present at the end of some undertaking. —'**killer** *n.*

killer whale *n.* a ferocious black-and-white toothed whale most common in cold seas.

killing ('kɪlɪŋ) *Inf.* ~*adj.* **1.** very tiring: *a killing pace.* **2.** extremely funny. ~*n.* **3.** a sudden stroke of success, as in speculations on the stock market (esp. in **make a killing**).

kill-joy *n.* a person who spoils other people's pleasure.

kiln (kɪln) *n.* a large oven for burning, drying, or processing something, such as porcelain or bricks.

kilo ('ki:ləʊ) *n., pl.* -**los.** short for **kilogram** *or* **kilometre.**

kilo- *prefix.* **1.** denoting 10^3 (1000): *kilogram.* Symbol: k **2.** (in computers) denoting 2^{10} (1024) with reference to storage size: *kilobyte.*

kilocycle ('kɪləʊ,saɪkəl) *n.* short for kilocycle per second: a former unit of frequency equal to 1 kilohertz.

kilogram *or* **kilogramme** ('kɪləʊ,græm) *n.* **1.** one thousand grams. **2.** the basic SI unit of mass, equal to the mass of the international prototype held by the *Bureau International des Poids et Mesures.* Symbol: kg

kilohertz ('kɪləʊ,hɜːts) *n.* one thousand hertz; one thousand cycles per second. Symbol: kHz

kilolitre ('kɪlə,liːtə) *n.* one thousand litres. Symbol: kl

kilometre *or U.S.* **kilometer** ('kɪlə,miːtə, kɪ'lɒmɪtə) *n.* one thousand metres. Symbol: km —**kilometric** (,kɪləʊ'mɛtrɪk) *adj.*

kiloton ('kɪləʊ,tʌn) *n.* **1.** one thousand tons. **2.** an explosive power, esp. of a nuclear weapon, equal to the power of 1000 tons of TNT.

kilowatt ('kɪləʊ,wɒt) *n.* one thousand watts. Symbol: kW

kilowatt-hour *n.* a unit of energy equal to the work done by a power of 1000 watts in one hour. Symbol: kWh

kilt (kɪlt) *n.* **1.** a knee-length pleated skirt, esp. one in plaid, as worn by men in the Scottish Highlands. ~*vb.* (*tr.*) **2.** to tuck (the skirt) up around one's body. **3.** to put pleats in (cloth, etc.). —'**kilted** *adj.*

kimono (kɪ'məʊnəʊ) *n., pl.* -**nos.** a loose sashed ankle-length garment with wide sleeves, worn in Japan. —**ki'monoed** *adj.*

kin (kɪn) *n.* **1.** a person's relatives collectively. **2.** a class or group with similar characteristics. **3.** See **next of kin.** ~*adj.* **4.** (*postpositive*) related by blood.

-kin *suffix forming nouns.* small: *lambkin.*

THESAURUS

kick *v.* 1. boot, punt 2. *Fig.* complain, gripe (*Inf.*), grumble, object, oppose, protest, rebel, resist, spurn 3. *Inf.* abandon, desist from, give up, leave off, quit, stop ~*n.* 4. force, intensity, pep, power, punch, pungency, snap (*Inf.*), sparkle, strength, tang, verve, vitality, zest 5. buzz (*Sl.*), enjoyment, excitement, fun, gratification, pleasure, stimulation, thrill

kickoff *n.* beginning, commencement, opening, outset, start

kick off *v.* begin, commence, get under way, initiate, open, start

kick out *v.* discharge, dismiss, eject, evict, expel, get rid of, oust, reject, remove, sack, toss out

kid 1. *n.* baby, bairn, boy, child, girl, infant, lad, little one, stripling, teenager, tot, youngster, youth 2. *v.* bamboozle, beguile, cozen, delude, fool, gull (*Archaic*), hoax, hoodwink, jest, joke, mock, plague, pretend, rag (*Sl.*), ridicule, tease, trick

kidnap abduct, capture, hijack, hold to ransom, remove, seize, skyjack, steal

kill 1. annihilate, assassinate, bump off (*Sl.*), butcher, destroy, dispatch, do away with, do in (*Sl.*), eradicate, execute, exterminate, extirpate, knock off (*Sl.*), liquidate, massacre, murder, neutralize, obliterate, slaughter, slay, take (someone's) life, waste (*Sl.*) 2. *Fig.* cancel, cease, deaden, defeat, extinguish, halt, quash, quell, ruin, scotch, smother, stifle, still, stop, suppress, veto

killer assassin, butcher, cutthroat, destroyer, executioner, exterminator, gunman, hit man (*Sl.*), liquidator, murderer, slaughterer, slayer

killing *n.* 1. bloodshed, carnage, execution, extermination, fatality, homicide, man-slaughter, massacre, murder, slaughter, slaying 2. *Inf.* bomb (*Sl.*), bonanza, cleanup (*Inf.*), coup, gain, profit, success, windfall ~*adj.* 3. deadly, death-dealing, deathly, fatal, lethal, mortal, murderous 4. *Inf.* debilitating, enervating, exhausting, fatiguing, punishing, tiring 5. *Inf.* absurd, amusing, comical, hilarious, ludicrous, uproarious

kill-joy dampener, damper, spoilsport, wet blanket (*Inf.*)

kin *n.* 1. affinity, blood, connection, consanguinity, extraction, kinship, lineage, relationship, stock 2. connections, family, kindred, kinsfolk, kinsmen, kith, people, relations, relatives ~*adj.* 3. akin, allied, close, cognate, consanguine, consanguineous, kindred, near, related

kind[1] (kaɪnd) *adj.* **1.** having a friendly nature or attitude. **2.** helpful to others or to another: *a kind deed.* **3.** considerate or humane. **4.** cordial; courteous (esp. in **kind regards**). **5.** pleasant; mild: *a kind climate.* **6.** *Inf.* beneficial or not harmful.

kind[2] (kaɪnd) *n.* **1.** a class or group having characteristics in common; sort; type: *two of a kind.* **2.** an instance or example of a class or group, esp. a rudimentary one: *heating of a kind.* **3.** essential nature or character: *the difference is one of kind rather than degree.* **4.** *Arch.* nature; the natural order. **5. in kind. a.** (of payment) in goods or produce rather than in money. **b.** with something of the same sort: *to return an insult in kind.*

▷ **Usage.** Careful users of English avoid the mixture of plural and singular constructions frequently used with *kind,* as in *those kind* (instead of *kinds*) *of buildings seem badly designed.*

kindergarten ('kɪndəˌɡɑːtən) *n.* a class or small school for young children, usually between the ages of four and six.

kind-hearted *adj.* sympathetic. **—ˌkind-'heartedly** *adv.* **—ˌkind-'heartedness** *n.*

kindle ('kɪndəl) *vb.* **1.** to set alight or start to burn. **2.** to arouse or be aroused: *the project kindled his interest.* **3.** to make or become bright. **—'kindler** *n.*

kindling ('kɪndlɪŋ) *n.* material for starting a fire, such as dry wood, straw, etc.

kindly ('kaɪndlɪ) *adj.* **-lier, -liest. 1.** having a sympathetic or warm-hearted nature. **2.** motivated by warm and sympathetic feelings. **3.** pleasant: *a kindly climate.* **4.** *Arch.* natural; normal. **~***adv.* **5.** in a considerate or humane way. **6.** with tolerance: *he kindly forgave my rudeness.* **7.** cordially: *he greeted us kindly.* **8.** please (often used to express impatience or formality): *will you kindly behave yourself!* **9.** *Arch.* appropriately. **10. take kindly.** to react favourably. **—'kindliness** *n.*

kindness ('kaɪndnɪs) *n.* **1.** the practice or quality of being kind. **2.** a kind or helpful act.

kindred ('kɪndrɪd) *adj.* **1.** having similar or common qualities, origin, etc. **2.** related by blood or marriage. **3. kindred spirit.** a person with whom one has something in common. **~***n.* **4.** relationship by blood. **5.** similarity in character. **6.** a person's relatives collectively.

kine (kaɪn) *n.* (*functioning as pl.*) an archaic word for cows or cattle.

kinematics (ˌkɪnɪ'mætɪks) *n.* (*functioning as sing.*) the study of the motion of bodies without reference to mass or force. **—ˌkine'matic** *adj.* **—ˌkine'matically** *adv.*

kinetic (kɪ'nɛtɪk) *adj.* relating to or caused by motion. **—ki'netically** *adv.*

kinetic art *n.* art, esp. sculpture, that moves or has moving parts.

kinetics (kɪ'nɛtɪks, kaɪ-) *n.* (*functioning as sing.*) **1.** another name for **dynamics** (sense 2). **2.** the branch of mechanics, including both dynamics and kinematics, concerned with the study of bodies in motion. **3.** the branch of dynamics that excludes the study of bodies at rest.

kinfolk ('kɪnˌfəʊk) *pl. n. Chiefly U.S.* another word for **kinsfolk.**

king (kɪŋ) *n.* **1.** a male sovereign prince who is the official ruler of an independent state; monarch. Related adjs.: **royal, regal. 2. a.** a ruler or chief: *king of the fairies.* **b.** (*in combination*): *the pirate king.* **3.** a person, animal, or thing considered as the best or most important of its kind. **4.** any of four playing cards in a pack, one for each suit, bearing the picture of a king. **5.** the most important chess piece. **6.** *Draughts.* a piece that has moved entirely across the board and has been crowned, after which it may move backwards as well as forwards. **7. king of kings. a.** God. **b.** a title of any of various oriental monarchs. **~***vb.* (*tr.*) **8.** to make (someone) a king. **9. king it.** to act in a superior fashion. **—'king,hood** *n.* **—'king,like** *adj.* **—'kingly** *adj.* **—'kingship** *n.*

King Charles spaniel (tʃɑːlz) *n.* a toy breed of spaniel with very long ears.

kingcup ('kɪŋˌkʌp) *n. Brit.* any of several yellow-flowered plants, esp. the marsh marigold.

kingdom ('kɪŋdəm) *n.* **1.** a territory, state, people, or community ruled or reigned over by a king or queen. **2.** any of the three groups into which natural objects may be divided: the animal, plant, and mineral kingdoms. **3.** *Theol.* the eternal sovereignty of God. **4.** an area of activity: *the kingdom of the mind.*

kingfisher ('kɪŋˌfɪʃə) *n.* a bird which has a greenish-blue and orange plumage, a large head, short tail, and long sharp bill, and feeds on fish.

kingklip ('kɪŋˌklɪp) *n.* an edible eel-like marine fish.

king-of-arms *n., pl.* **kings-of-arms. 1.** the highest rank of heraldic officer. **2.** a person holding this rank.

kingpin ('kɪŋˌpɪn) *n.* **1.** Also called (Brit.): **swivel pin.** a pivot pin that provides a steering joint in a motor vehicle by securing the stub axle to the axle beam. **2.** *Tenpin bowling.* the front pin in the triangular arrangement of the ten pins. **3.** *Inf.* the most important person in an organization. **4.** (in ninepins) the central pin in the diamond pattern of the nine pins.

king-size or **king-sized** *adj.* larger or longer than a standard size.

king's post *n. Canad. history.* any of the fur-trading and fishing posts in Quebec.

kink (kɪŋk) *n.* **1.** a sharp twist or bend in a wire, rope, hair, etc. **2.** a crick in the neck or similar muscular spasm. **3.** a flaw or minor difficulty in some undertaking. **4.** a flaw or idiosyncrasy of personality.

kinky ('kɪŋkɪ) *adj.* **kinkier, kinkiest. 1.** *Sl.* given to unusual, abnormal, or deviant sexual practices. **2.** *Sl.* exhibiting unusual idiosyncrasies of personality. **3.** *Sl.* attractive or provocative in a bizarre way: *kinky clothes.* **4.** tightly looped, as a wire or rope. **5.** tightly curled, as hair. **—'kinkily** *adv.* **—'kinkiness** *n.*

kinsfolk ('kɪnzˌfəʊk) *pl. n.* one's family or relatives.

kinship ('kɪnʃɪp) *n.* **1.** blood relationship. **2.** the state of having common characteristics.

THESAURUS

kind[1] *n.* **1.** brand, breed, class, family, genus, ilk, race, set, sort, species, variety **2.** character, description, essence, habit, manner, mould, nature, persuasion, sort, style, temperament, type

kind[2] *adj.* affectionate, amiable, amicable, beneficent, benevolent, benign, bounteous, charitable, clement, compassionate, congenial, considerate, cordial, courteous, friendly, generous, gentle, good, gracious, humane, indulgent, kind-hearted, kindly, lenient, loving, mild, neighbourly, obliging, philanthropic, propitious, sympathetic, tender-hearted, thoughtful, understanding

kind-hearted altruistic, amicable, compassionate, considerate, generous, good-natured, gracious, helpful, humane, kind, sympathetic, tender-hearted

kindle **1.** fire, ignite, inflame, light, set fire to **2.** *Fig.* agitate, animate, arouse, awaken, bestir, enkindle, exasperate, excite, foment, incite, induce, inflame, inspire, provoke, rouse, sharpen, stimulate, stir, thrill

kindliness amiability, beneficence, benevolence, benignity, charity, compassion,

friendliness, gentleness, humanity, kind-heartedness, kindness, sympathy

kindly **1.** *adj.* beneficial, benevolent, benign, compassionate, cordial, favourable, genial, gentle, good-natured, hearty, helpful, kind, mild, pleasant, polite, sympathetic, warm **2.** *adv.* agreeably, cordially, graciously, politely, tenderly, thoughtfully

kindness **1.** affection, amiability, beneficence, benevolence, charity, clemency, compassion, decency, fellow-feeling, generosity, gentleness, goodness, good will, grace, hospitality, humanity, indulgence, kindliness, magnanimity, patience, philanthropy, tenderness, tolerance, understanding **2.** aid, assistance, benefaction, bounty, favour, generosity, good deed, help, service

kindred *n.* **1.** affinity, consanguinity, relationship **2.** connections, family, flesh, kin, kinsfolk, kinsmen, lineage, relations, relatives **~***adj.* **3.** affiliated, akin, allied, cognate, congenial, corresponding, kin, like, matching, related, similar

king crowned head, emperor, majesty, monarch, overlord, prince, ruler, sovereign

kingdom **1.** dominion, dynasty, empire, monarchy, realm, reign, sovereignty **2.** commonwealth, county, division, nation, province, state, territory, tract **3.** area, domain, field, province, sphere, territory

kink **1.** bend, coil, corkscrew, crimp, entanglement, frizz, knot, tangle, twist, wrinkle **2.** cramp, crick, pang, pinch, spasm, stab, tweak, twinge **3.** complication, defect, difficulty, flaw, hitch, imperfection, knot, tangle **4.** crotchet, eccentricity, fetish, foible, idiosyncrasy, quirk, singularity, vagary, whim

kinky **1.** bizarre, eccentric, odd, outlandish, peculiar, queer, quirky, strange, unconventional, weird **2.** degenerated, depraved, deviant, licentious, perverted, unnatural, warped **3.** coiled, crimped, curled, curly, frizzled, frizzy, tangled, twisted

kinsfolk connections, family, kin, kindred, kinsmen, relations, relatives

kinship **1.** blood relationship, consanguinity, kin, relation, ties of blood **2.** affinity, alliance, association, bearing, connection, correspondence, relationship, similarity

kinsman ('kınzmən) n., pl. **-men**. a blood relation or a relation by marriage. —'**kins,woman** fem. n.

kiosk ('ki:ɒsk) n. **1.** a small sometimes movable booth from which cigarettes, newspapers, sweets, etc., are sold. **2.** Chiefly Brit. a telephone box. **3.** (in Turkey, Iran, etc.) a light open-sided pavilion.

kip (kıp) Brit. sl. ~n. **1.** sleep or slumber: to get some kip. **2.** a bed or lodging. ~vb. (intr.) **3.** to sleep or take a nap. **4.** (foll. by down) to prepare for sleep.

kipper ('kıpə) n. **1.** a fish, esp. a herring, that has been cleaned, salted, and smoked. **2.** a male salmon during the spawning season. ~vb. **3.** (tr.) to cure (herrings, etc.) by salting and smoking.

kirk (kɜ:k) n. **1.** a Scottish word for **church**. **2.** a Scottish church.

Kirsch (kıəʃ) or **Kirschwasser** ('kıəʃ,va:sə) n. a brandy distilled from cherries, made chiefly in the Black Forest in Germany.

kismet ('kızmɛt, 'kıs-) n. **1.** Islam. the will of Allah. **2.** fate or destiny.

kiss (kıs) vb. **1.** (tr.) to touch with the lips or press the lips against as an expression of love, greeting, respect, etc. **2.** (intr.) to join lips with another person in an act of love or desire. **3.** to touch (each other) lightly. ~n. **4.** a caress with the lips. **5.** a light touch. —'**kissable** adj.

kiss curl n. Brit. a circular curl of hair pressed flat against the cheek or forehead.

kisser ('kısə) n. **1.** a person who kisses, esp. in a way specified. **2.** a slang word for **mouth** or **face**.

kiss of life n. the. Inf. mouth-to-mouth resuscitation in which a person blows gently into the victim's mouth, allowing the lungs to deflate after each blow.

kist (kıst) n. S. African. a large wooden chest in which linen is stored, esp. one used to store a bride's trousseau.

kit (kıt) n. **1.** a set of tools, supplies, etc., for use together or for a purpose: a first-aid kit. **2.** a set of pieces of equipment sold ready to be assembled. **3.** the case or container for such a set. **4.** clothing and other personal effects, esp. those of a traveller or soldier: safari kit. ~See also **kit out**.

kitbag ('kıt,bæg) n. a canvas or other bag for a serviceman's kit.

kitchen ('kıtʃın) n. **a.** a room or part of a building equipped for preparing and cooking food. **b.** (as modifier): a kitchen table.

kitchen Dutch n. S. African derog. an impoverished form of Afrikaans often mixed with words from other languages, as English.

kitchenette (,kıtʃı'nɛt) n. a small kitchen or part of a room equipped for use as a kitchen.

kitchen garden n. a garden where vegetables and sometimes also fruit are grown.

kite (kaıt) n. **1.** a light frame covered with a thin material flown in the wind at the end of a length of string. **2.** Brit. sl. an aeroplane. **3.** (pl.) Naut. any of various light sails used in addition to the working sails of a vessel. **4.** a bird of prey having a long forked tail and long broad wings and usually preying on small mammals and insects. **5.** Arch. a person who preys on others. **6.** Commerce. a negotiable paper drawn without any actual transaction or assets and designed to obtain money on credit. ~vb. **7.** to issue (fictitious papers) to obtain credit or money. **8.** (intr.) to soar and glide.

Kite mark n. Brit. the official mark of quality and reliability, in the form of a kite, on articles approved by the British Standards Institution.

kith (kıθ) n. **kith and kin**. one's friends and relations.

kit out or **up** vb. kitting, kitted. (tr., adv.) Chiefly Brit. to provide with or acquire (a kit of personal effects and necessities).

kitsch (kıtʃ) n. tawdry, vulgarized, or pretentious art, literature, etc., usually with popular appeal.

kitten ('kıtən) n. **1.** a young cat. **2. have kittens**. Brit. inf. to react with disapproval, anxiety, etc.: she had kittens when she got the bill. ~vb. **3.** (of cats) to give birth to (young).

kittenish ('kıtənıʃ) adj. **1.** like a kitten; lively. **2.** (of a woman) flirtatious, esp. coyly flirtatious.

kittiwake ('kıtı,weık) n. either of two oceanic gulls having pale grey black-tipped wings and a square-cut tail.

kitty[1] ('kıtı) n., pl. **-ties**. a diminutive or affectionate name for a **kitten** or **cat**.

kitty[2] ('kıtı) n., pl. **-ties**. **1.** the pool of bets in certain gambling games. **2.** any shared fund of money. **3.** (in bowls) the jack.

kiwi ('ki:wı) n., pl. **-wis**. **1.** a nocturnal flightless New Zealand bird having a long beak, stout legs, and weakly barbed feathers. **2.** Inf. a New Zealander. **3.** N.Z. inf. a lottery.

kiwi fruit n. the fuzzy edible fruit of an Asian climbing plant. Also called: **Chinese gooseberry**.

kl. abbrev. for kilolitre.

klaxon ('klæksən) n. a type of loud horn formerly used on motor vehicles.

kleptomania (,klɛptəʊ'meınıə) n. Psychol. a strong impulse to steal, esp. when there is no obvious motivation. —,klepto'mani,ac n.

klipspringer ('klıp,sprıŋə) n. a small agile antelope inhabiting rocky regions of Africa south of the Sahara.

kloof (klu:f) n. a mountain pass or gorge in southern Africa.

km or **km.** abbrev. for kilometre.

knack (næk) n. **1.** a skilful, ingenious, or resourceful way of doing something. **2.** a particular talent or aptitude, esp. an intuitive one.

knacker ('nækə) Brit. ~n. **1.** a person who buys up old horses for slaughter. **2.** a person who buys up old buildings and breaks them up for scrap. ~vb. **3.** (tr.; usually passive) Sl. to tire. —'**knackery** n.

knapsack ('næp,sæk) n. a canvas or leather bag carried strapped on the back or shoulder.

knapweed ('næp,wi:d) n. any of several plants having purplish thistle-like flowers.

knave (neıv) n. **1.** Arch. a dishonest man. **2.** another word for **jack** (the playing card). **3.** Obs. a male servant. —'**knavish** adj.

knavery ('neıvərı) n., pl. **-eries**. **1.** a deceitful or dishonest act. **2.** dishonest conduct; trickery.

knead (ni:d) vb. (tr.) **1.** to work and press (a soft substance, such as bread dough) into a uniform mixture with the hands. **2.** to squeeze or press with the hands. **3.** to make by kneading. —'**kneader** n.

knee (ni:) n. **1.** the joint of the human leg connecting the tibia and fibula with the femur and protected in front by the patella. **2. a.** the area surrounding and above this joint. **b.** (modifier) reaching or covering the knee: knee socks. **3.** the upper surface of a sitting person's thigh: the child sat on her mother's knee. **4.** a corresponding or similar part in other vertebrates. **5.** the part of a garment that covers the knee. **6.** anything resembling a knee in action or shape. **7.** any of the hollow rounded protuberances that project upwards from the roots of the swamp cypress. **8. bend** or **bow the knee**. to kneel or submit. **9. bring someone to his knees**. to force someone into submission. ~vb. **kneeing, kneed**. **10.** (tr.) to strike, nudge, or push with the knee.

kneecap ('ni:,kæp) n. **1.** Anat. a nontechnical name for

kinsman blood relative, fellow clansman, fellow tribesman, relation, relative

kiosk bookstall, booth, counter, newsstand, stall, stand

kiss v. 1. buss (Archaic), canoodle (Inf.), greet, neck (Inf.), osculate, peck (Inf.), salute, smooch (Inf.) 2. brush, caress, glance, graze, scrape, touch ~n. 3. buss (Archaic), osculation, peck (Inf.), smacker (Sl.)

kit accoutrements, apparatus, effects, equipment, gear, impedimenta, implements, instruments, outfit, paraphernalia, provisions, rig, supplies, tackle, tools, trappings, utensils

kitchen cookhouse, galley, kitchenette

kit out or **up** accoutre, arm, deck out, equip, fit out, fix up, furnish, outfit, provide with, supply

knack ability, adroitness, aptitude, bent, capacity, dexterity, expertise, expertness, facility, flair, forte, genius, gift, handiness, ingenuity, propensity, quickness, skilfulness, skill, talent, trick

knave blackguard, bounder (Inf.), cheat, rapscallion, rascal, reprobate, rogue, rotter (Sl.), scallywag (Inf.), scamp, scapegrace, scoundrel, swindler, varlet (Archaic), villain

knavery chicanery, corruption, deceit, deception, dishonesty, double-dealing, duplicity, fraud, imposture, rascality, roguery, trickery, villainy

knavish deceitful, deceptive, dishonest, dishonourable, fraudulent, lying, rascally, roguish, scoundrelly, tricky, unprincipled, unscrupulous, villainous

knead blend, form, manipulate, massage, mould, press, rub, shape, squeeze, stroke, work

patella. ~*vb.* **-capping, -capped.** (*tr.*) **2.** (esp. of certain terrorist groups) to shoot (a person) in the kneecap.

knee-deep *adj.* **1.** so deep as to reach or cover the knees. **2.** (*postpositive; often foll. by in*) **a.** sunk or covered to the knees: *knee-deep in sand.* **b.** deeply involved: *knee-deep in work.*

knee-high *adj.* another word for **knee-deep** (sense 1).

kneel (niːl) *vb.* **kneeling, knelt** *or* **kneeled. 1.** (*intr.*) to rest, fall, or support oneself on one's knees. ~*n.* **2.** the act or position of kneeling. —'**kneeler** *n.*

knell (nɛl) *n.* **1.** the sound of a bell rung to announce a death or a funeral. **2.** something that precipitates or indicates death or destruction. ~*vb.* **3.** (*intr.*) to ring a knell. **4.** (*tr.*) to proclaim by or as if by a tolling bell.

knelt (nɛlt) *vb.* a past tense or past participle of **kneel.**

knew (njuː) *vb.* the past tense of **know.**

knickerbockers ('nɪkəˌbɒkəz) *pl. n.* baggy breeches fastened with a band at the knee or above the ankle. Also called: **knickers.**

knickers ('nɪkəz) *pl. n.* any pants for women, esp. baggy wool or silk ones held up by elastic.

knickknack ('nɪkˌnæk) *n.* **1.** a cheap ornament. **2.** an ornamental article of furniture, dress, etc.

knife (naɪf) *n., pl.* **knives** (naɪvz). **1.** a cutting instrument consisting of a sharp-edged blade of metal fitted into a handle or onto a machine. **2.** a similar instrument used as a weapon. **3. have one's knife into someone.** to have a grudge against someone. **4. under the knife.** undergoing a surgical operation. ~*vb.* (*tr.*) **5.** to stab or kill with a knife. **6.** to betray or depose in an underhand way. —'**knifeˌlike** *adj.*

knife edge *n.* **1.** the sharp cutting edge of a knife. **2.** any sharp edge, esp. an arête. **3.** a sharp-edged wedge of hard material on which the beam of a balance pivots. **4.** a critical point.

knight (naɪt) *n.* **1.** (in medieval Europe) **a.** (originally) a person who served his lord as a mounted and heavily armed soldier. **b.** (later) a gentleman with the military and social standing of this rank. **2.** (in modern times) a person invested by a sovereign with a nonhereditary rank and dignity usually in recognition of personal services, achievements, etc. **3.** a chess piece, usually shaped like a horse's head. **4.** a champion of a lady or of a cause or principle. **5.** a member of the Roman class below the senators. ~*vb.* **6.** (*tr.*) to make (a person) a knight.

knight errant *n., pl.* **knights errant.** (esp. in medieval romance) a knight who wanders in search of deeds of courage, chivalry, etc. —**knight errantry** *n.*

knighthood ('naɪthʊd) *n.* **1.** the order, dignity, or rank of a knight. **2.** the qualities of a knight.

knightly ('naɪtlɪ) *adj.* of, relating to, resembling, or befitting a knight. —'**knightliness** *n.*

knit (nɪt) *vb.* **knitting, knitted** *or* **knit. 1.** to make (a garment, etc.) by looping and entwining (wool) by hand by means of long eyeless needles (**knitting needles**) or by machine (**knitting machine**). **2.** to join or be joined together closely. **3.** to draw (the brows) together or (of the brows) to come together, as in frowning or concentrating. ~*n.* **4.** a fabric made by knitting. **b.** (*in combination*): *a heavy knit.* —'**knitter** *n.*

knitting ('nɪtɪŋ) *n.* knitted work or the process of producing it.

knitwear ('nɪtˌwɛə) *n.* knitted clothes, esp. sweaters.

knives (naɪvz) *n.* the plural of **knife.**

knob (nɒb) *n.* **1.** a rounded projection from a surface, such as a lump on a tree trunk. **2.** a handle of a door,

drawer, etc., esp. one that is rounded. **3.** a round hill or knoll. ~*vb.* **knobbing, knobbed. 4.** (*tr.*) to supply or ornament with knobs. **5.** (*intr.*) to bulge. —'**knobbly** *adj.* —'**knobby** *adj.* —'**knobˌlike** *adj.*

knock (nɒk) *vb.* **1.** (*tr.*) to give a blow or push to. **2.** (*intr.*) to rap sharply with the knuckles, a hard object, etc.: *to knock at the door.* **3.** (*tr.*) to make or force by striking: *to knock a hole in the wall.* **4.** (*intr.; usually foll. by against*) to collide (with). **5.** (*tr.*) to bring into a certain condition by hitting: *to knock someone unconscious.* **6.** (*tr.*) *Inf.* to criticize adversely. **7.** (*intr.*) Also **pink.** (of an internal-combustion engine) to emit a metallic noise as a result of faulty combustion. **8.** (*intr.*) (of a bearing, esp. one in an engine) to emit a regular characteristic sound as a result of wear. **9.** *Brit. sl.* to have sexual intercourse with (a person). **10. knock (a person) into the middle of next week.** *Inf.* to hit (a person) with a very heavy blow. **11. knock on the head. a.** to daze or kill (a person) by striking on the head. **b.** to prevent the further development of (a plan). ~*n.* **12. a.** a blow, push, or rap: *he gave the table a knock.* **b.** the sound so caused. **13.** the sound of knocking in an engine or bearing.

knock about *or* **around** *vb.* **1.** (*intr., adv.*) to wander about aimlessly. **2.** (*intr., prep.*) to travel about, esp. as resulting in varied experience: *he's knocked about the world.* **3.** (*intr., adv.; foll. by with*) to associate. **4.** (*tr., adv.*) to treat brutally: *he knocks his wife about.* **5.** (*tr., adv.*) to consider or discuss informally.

knock back *vb.* (*tr., adv.*) *Inf.* **1.** to drink, esp. quickly. **2.** to cost. **3.** to shock; disconcert. **4.** to reject or refuse. ~*n.* **knockback. 5.** *Prison sl.* failure to obtain parole. **6.** *Sl.* a refusal or rejection.

knock down *vb.* (*tr., adv.*) **1.** to strike to the ground with a blow, as in boxing. **2.** (in auctions) to declare (an article) sold. **3.** to demolish. **4.** to dismantle for ease of transport. **5.** *Inf.* to reduce (a price, etc.). ~*adj.* **knockdown.** (*prenominal*) **6.** powerful: *a knockdown blow.* **7.** *Chiefly Brit.* cheap: *a knockdown price.* **8.** easily dismantled: *knockdown furniture.*

knocker ('nɒkə) *n.* **1.** an object, usually made of metal, attached to a door by a hinge and used for knocking. **2.** (*usually pl.*) *Sl.* a female breast. **3.** a person or thing that knocks. **4. on the knocker.** *Austral. & N.Z. inf.* promptly: *you pay on the knocker here.*

knock-knee *n.* a condition in which the legs are bent inwards causing the knees to touch when standing. —ˌ**knock-'kneed** *adj.*

knock off *vb.* (*mainly adv.*) **1.** (*intr., also prep.*) *Inf.* to finish work: *we knocked off an hour early.* **2.** (*tr.*) *Inf.* to make or do hastily or easily: *to knock off a novel in a week.* **3.** (*tr.; also prep.*) *Inf.* to reduce the price of (an article). **4.** (*tr.*) *Sl.* to kill. **5.** (*tr.*) *Sl.* to rob or steal: *knock off a bank.* **6.** (*tr.*) *Sl.* to stop doing something, used as a command: *knock it off!*

knock-on *Rugby.* ~*n.* **1.** the infringement of playing the ball forward with the hand or arm. ~*vb.* **knock on.** (*adv.*) **2.** to play (the ball) forward with the hand or arm.

knock-on effect *n.* the indirect result of an action: *the number of redundancies was not great but there were as many again from the knock-on effect.*

knockout ('nɒkˌaʊt) *n.* **1.** the act of rendering unconscious. **2.** a blow that renders an opponent unconscious. **3. a.** a competition in which competitors are eliminated progressively. **b.** (*as modifier*): *a knockout contest.* **4.** *Inf.* a person or thing that is overwhelmingly impressive

---

THESAURUS

kneel bow, bow down, curtsey, genuflect, get down on one's knees, kowtow, make obeisance, stoop

knell 1. *v.* announce, chime, herald, peal, resound, ring, sound, toll 2. *n.* chime, peal, ringing, sound, toll

knickers bloomers, briefs, drawers, panties, smalls, underwear

knickknack bagatelle, bauble, bibelot, bric-a-brac, gewgaw, gimcrack, kickshaw, plaything, trifle, trinket

knife 1. *n.* blade, cutter, cutting tool 2. *v.* cut, impale, lacerate, pierce, slash, stab, wound

knit 1. affix, ally, bind, connect, contract, fasten, heal, interlace, intertwine, join, link,

loop, mend, secure, tie, unite, weave 2. crease, furrow, knot, wrinkle

knob boss, bulk, bump, bunch, door-handle, knot, knurl, lump, nub, projection, protrusion, protuberance, snag, stud, swell, swelling, tumour

knock *v.* 1. buffet, clap, cuff, hit, punch, rap, slap, smack, smite (*Archaic*), strike, thump, thwack ~*n.* 2. blow, box, clip, clout, cuff, hammering, rap, slap, smack, thump ~*v.* 3. *Inf.* abuse, belittle, carp, cavil, censure, condemn, criticize, deprecate, disparage, find fault, lambaste, run down, slam (*Sl.*) ~*n.* 4. blame, censure, condemnation, criticism, defeat, failure, rebuff, rejection, reversal, setback, stricture

knock about *or* **around** 1. ramble, range, roam, rove, traipse, travel, wander 2. abuse, batter, beat up (*Inf.*), bruise, buffet, damage, hit, hurt, maltreat, manhandle, maul, mistreat, strike, wound

knock down batter, clout (*Inf.*), demolish, destroy, fell, floor, level, pound, raze, smash, wallop (*Inf.*), wreck

knock off 1. clock off, clock out, complete, conclude, finish, stop work, terminate 2. filch, nick (*Sl.*), pilfer, pinch, purloin, rob, steal, thieve 3. assassinate, bump off (*Sl.*), do away with, do in (*Sl.*), kill, liquidate, murder, slay, waste (*Sl.*)

or attractive: *she's a knockout.* ~*vb.* **knock out.** (*tr.,*
adv.) **5.** to render unconscious, esp. by a blow. **6.** *Box-*
ing. to defeat (an opponent) by a knockout. **7.** to destroy
or injure badly. **8.** to eliminate, esp. in a knockout competition. **9.** *Inf.* to overwhelm or amaze: *I was knocked*
out by that new song. **10. knock the bottom out of.** *Inf.*
to invalidate (an argument).

knock up *vb.* (*adv., mainly tr.*) **1.** Also: **knock togeth-**
er. *Inf.* to assemble quickly: *to knock up a set of shelves.*
2. *Brit. inf.* to waken; rouse: *to knock someone up early.*
3. *Sl.* to make pregnant. **4.** *Brit. inf.* to exhaust. **5.** *Crick-*
et. to score (runs). **6.** (*intr.*) *Tennis, squash, etc.* to practise, esp. before a match. ~*n.* **knock-up.** **7.** a practice
session at tennis, squash, etc.

knoll (nəʊl) *n.* a small rounded hill.

knot¹ (nɒt) *n.* **1.** any of various fastenings formed by
looping and tying a piece of rope, cord, etc., in upon itself or to another piece of rope. **2.** a prescribed method
of tying a particular knot. **3.** a decorative bow, as of ribbon. **4.** a small closely knit group. **5.** a tie or bond: *the*
marriage knot. **6.** a difficult problem. **7. a.** a hard mass
of wood where a branch joins the trunk of a tree. **b.** a
cross section of this visible on a piece of timber. **8.**
Pathol. a lump of vessels or fibres formed in a part, as in
a muscle. **9.** a unit of speed used by nautical vessels and
aircraft, being one nautical mile (about 1.15 statute miles
or 1.85km) per hour. **10.** another term (not in technical
use) for **nautical mile.** **11. at a rate of knots.** very fast.
12. tie (someone) **in knots.** to completely perplex (someone). ~*vb.* **knotting, knotted.** **13.** (*tr.*) to tie or fasten in
a knot. **14.** to form or cause to form into a knot. **15.** (*tr.*)
to entangle or become entangled. —**'knotted** *adj.*
—**'knotter** *n.* —**'knotless** *adj.*

knot² (nɒt) *n.* a small northern sandpiper with a short
bill and grey plumage.

knotgrass ('nɒt,grɑːs) *n.* **1.** Also called: **allseed.** a
weed whose small green flowers produce numerous
seeds. **2.** any of several related plants.

knothole ('nɒt,həʊl) *n.* a hole in a piece of wood where
a knot has been.

knotty ('nɒtɪ) *adj.* **knottier, knottiest.** **1.** (of wood, rope,
etc.) full of or characterized by knots. **2.** extremely difficult or intricate.

know (nəʊ) *vb.* **knowing, knew, known.** (*mainly tr.*) **1.**
(*also intr.; may take a clause as object*) to be or feel certain of the truth or accuracy of (a fact, etc.). **2.** to be acquainted or familiar with: *she's known him five years.*
3. to have a familiarity or grasp of: *he knows French.* **4.**
(*also intr.; may take a clause as object*) to understand or
perceive (facts, etc.): *he knows the answer now.* **5.** (foll.
by *how*) to be sure or aware of (how to be or do something). **6.** to experience, esp. deeply: *to know poverty.*
7. to be intelligent, informed, or sensible enough (to do
something). **8.** (*may take a clause as object*) to be able
to distinguish or discriminate. **9.** *Arch.* to have sexual
intercourse with. **10. know what's what.** to know how
one thing or things in general work. **11. you never**
know. things are uncertain. ~*n.* **12. in the know.** *Inf.*
aware or informed. —**'knowable** *adj.* —**'knower** *n.*

know-how *n.* *Inf.* **1.** ingenuity, aptitude, or skill. **2.**
commercial and saleable knowledge of how to do a particular thing.

knowing ('nəʊɪŋ) *adj.* **1.** suggesting secret knowledge.
2. wise, shrewd, or clever. **3.** deliberate. ~*n.* **4.** there

is **no knowing.** one cannot tell. —**'knowingly** *adv.*
—**'knowingness** *n.*

knowledge ('nɒlɪdʒ) *n.* **1.** the facts or experiences
known by a person or group of people. **2.** the state of
knowing. **3.** consciousness or familiarity gained by experience or learning. **4.** erudition or informed learning.
5. specific information about a subject. **6. to my (his,**
etc.) **knowledge. a.** as I understand it. **b.** as I know.

knowledgeable *or* **knowledgable** ('nɒlɪdʒəbəl) *adj.*
possessing or indicating much knowledge. —**'knowl-**
edgeably *adv.*

known (nəʊn) *vb.* **1.** the past participle of **know.** ~*adj.*
2. identified: *a known criminal.*

knuckle ('nʌkəl) *n.* **1.** a joint of a finger, esp. that connecting a finger to the hand. **2.** a joint of veal, pork, etc.,
consisting of the part of the leg below the knee joint. **3.**
near the knuckle. *Inf.* approaching indecency. ~*vb.* **4.**
(*tr.*) to rub or press with the knuckles. **5.** (*intr.*) to keep
the knuckles on the ground while shooting a marble.
—**'knuckly** *adj.*

knuckle down *vb.* (*intr., adv.*) *Inf.* to apply oneself
diligently: *to knuckle down to some work.*

knuckle-duster *n.* (*often pl.*) a metal bar fitted over
the knuckles, often with holes for the fingers, for inflicting injury by a blow with the fist.

knuckle under *vb.* (*intr., adv.*) to give way under
pressure or authority; yield.

knurl *or* **nurl** (nɜːl) *vb.* (*tr.*) **1.** to impress with a series
of fine ridges or serrations. ~*n.* **2.** a small ridge, esp.
one of a series.

KO, K.O., *or* **k.o.** ('keɪ'əʊ) *vb.* **KO'ing, KO'd; K.O.'ing,**
K.O.'d; k.o.'ing, k.o.'d, *n., pl.* **KO's, K.O.'s,** *or* **k.o.'s.** a
slang term for **knock out** or **knockout.**

koala *or* **koala bear** (kəʊ'ɑːlə) *n.* a slow-moving Australian arboreal marsupial, having dense greyish fur and
feeding on eucalyptus leaves. Also called (in Australia):
native bear.

kohl (kəʊl) *n.* a cosmetic powder used esp. in Muslim
and Asian countries to darken the area around the eyes.

kohlrabi (kəʊl'rɑːbɪ) *n., pl.* **-bies.** a cultivated variety
of cabbage whose thickened stem is eaten as a vegetable. Also called: **turnip cabbage.**

kokanee (kəʊ'kænɪ) *n.* a landlocked salmon of lakes in
W North America: a variety of sockeye.

kola ('kəʊlə) *n.* a variant spelling of **cola.**

kolinsky (kə'lɪnskɪ) *n., pl.* **-skies.** **1.** any of various
Asian minks. **2.** the rich tawny fur of this animal.

kolkhoz (kɒl'hɔːz) *n.* a Russian collective farm.

kook (kuːk) *n.* *U.S. inf.* an eccentric or foolish person.
—**'kooky** *or* **'kookie** *adj.*

kookaburra ('kʊkə,bʌrə) *n.* a large Australian kingfisher with a cackling cry. Also called: **laughing**
jackass.

kopeck *or* **copeck** ('kəʊpɛk) *n.* a Soviet monetary unit
worth one hundredth of a rouble.

Koran (kɔː'rɑːn) *n.* the sacred book of Islam, believed
by Muslims to be the infallible word of God dictated to
Mohammed. Also: **Qur'an.** —**Ko'ranic** *adj.*

Korean (kə'rɪən) *adj.* **1.** of or relating to Korea in SE
Asia, its people, or their language. ~*n.* **2.** a native or in-
habitant of Korea. **3.** the official language of North and
South Korea.

kosher ('kəʊʃə) *adj.* **1.** *Judaism.* prepared according to

---

THESAURUS

knockout 1. *coup de grâce*, kayo (*Sl.*),
K.O. (*Sl.*) 2. hit, sensation, smash, smash-hit,
stunner (*Inf.*), success, triumph, winner

knot *v.* 1. bind, complicate, entangle, knit,
loop, secure, tether, tie, weave ~*n.* 2. bond,
bow, braid, connection, joint, ligature, loop,
rosette, tie 3. aggregation, bunch, clump,
cluster, collection, heap, mass, pile, tuft 4. assemblage, band, circle, clique, company,
crew (*Inf.*), crowd, gang, group, mob, pack,
set, squad

know 1. apprehend, comprehend, experience, fathom, feel certain, ken (*Scot.*), learn,
notice, perceive, realize, recognize, see,
undergo, understand 2. associate with, be acquainted with, be familiar with, fraternize
with, have dealings with, have knowledge of,
recognize 3. differentiate, discern, distinguish, identify, make out, perceive, recog-

nize, see, tell

know-how ability, adroitness, aptitude,
capability, dexterity, experience, expertise,
faculty, flair, ingenuity, knack, knowledge,
proficiency, savoir-faire, skill, talent

knowing 1. astute, clever, competent, discerning, experienced, expert, intelligent,
qualified, skilful, well-informed 2. acute, cunning, eloquent, expressive, meaningful, perceptive, sagacious, shrewd, significant 3.
aware, conscious, deliberate, intended, intentional

knowingly consciously, deliberately, intentionally, on purpose, purposely, wilfully,
wittingly

knowledge 1. education, enlightenment,
erudition, instruction, intelligence, learning,
scholarship, schooling, science, tuition, wisdom 2. ability, apprehension, cognition, com-

prehension, consciousness, discernment,
grasp, judgment, recognition, understanding
3. acquaintance, cognizance, familiarity, information, intimacy, notice

knowledgeable 1. acquainted, *au cou-*
rant, au fait, aware, cognizant, conscious,
conversant, experienced, familiar, in the
know (*Inf.*), understanding, well-informed 2.
educated, erudite, intelligent, learned, lettered, scholarly

known acknowledged, admitted, avowed,
celebrated, common, confessed, familiar, famous, manifest, noted, obvious, patent, plain,
popular, published, recognized, well-known

knuckle under *v.* accede, acquiesce,
capitulate, give in, give way, submit, succumb, surrender, yield

or conforming to Jewish dietary laws. **2.** *Inf.* **a.** genuine or authentic. **b.** legitimate. ~*n.* **3.** kosher food.

kowtow ('kautau) *vb.* (*intr.*) **1.** to touch the forehead to the ground as a sign of respect or deference: a former Chinese custom. **2.** (often foll. by *to*) to be servile (towards). ~*n.* **3.** the act of kowtowing.

Kr *the chemical symbol for* krypton.

kraal (krɑːl) *n. S. African.* **1.** a hut village in southern Africa, esp. one surrounded by a stockade. **2.** an enclosure for livestock.

kremlin ('krɛmlɪn) *n.* the citadel of any Russian city.

Kremlin ('krɛmlɪn) *n.* **1.** the 12th-century citadel in Moscow, containing the offices of the Soviet government. **2.** the central government of the Soviet Union.

krill (krɪl) *n., pl.* **krill.** any small shrimplike marine crustacean: the principal food of whalebone whales.

kris (krɪs) *n.* a Malayan and Indonesian stabbing or slashing knife with a scalloped edge. Also called: **crease, creese.**

krona ('krəunə) *n., pl.* **-nor** (-nə). the standard monetary unit of Sweden.

króna ('krəunə) *n., pl.* **-nur** (nə). the standard monetary unit of Iceland.

krone ('krəunə) *n., pl.* **-ner** (-nə). **1.** the standard monetary unit of Denmark. **2.** the standard monetary unit of Norway.

krypton ('krɪptɒn) *n.* an inert gaseous element occurring in trace amounts in air and used in fluorescent lights and lasers. Symbol: Kr; atomic no.: 36; atomic wt.: 83.80.

Kt *Chess. abbrev. for* knight. Also: **N**

kt. *abbrev. for:* **1.** karat. **2.** *Naut.* knot.

Kt. *or* **Knt.** *abbrev. for* knight.

kudos ('kjuːdɒs) *n.* (*functioning as sing.*) acclaim, glory,

or prestige.

kudu *or* **koodoo** ('kuːduː) *n.* either of two spiral-horned antelopes (**greater kudu** or **lesser kudu**), which inhabit the bush of Africa.

Ku Klux Klan ('kuː 'klʌks 'klæn) *n.* **1.** a secret organization of white Southerners formed after the U.S. Civil War to fight Black emancipation. **2.** a secret organization of White Protestant Americans, mainly in the South, who use violence against Blacks, Jews, etc. —**Ku Klux Klanner** *n.*

kukri ('kukrı) *n.* a knife with a curved blade that broadens towards the point, esp. as used by Gurkhas.

kulak ('kuːlæk) *n.* (in Russia after 1906) a member of the class of peasants who became proprietors of their own farms. In 1929 Stalin initiated their liquidation.

kümmel ('kuməl) *n.* a German liqueur flavoured with aniseed and cumin.

kumquat *or* **cumquat** ('kʌmkwɒt) *n.* **1.** a small Chinese citrus tree. **2.** the small round orange fruit of such a tree, with a sweet rind, used in preserves and confections.

kung fu ('kʌŋ 'fuː) *n.* a Chinese martial art combining principles of karate and judo.

kW *or* **kw** *abbrev. for* kilowatt.

kwashiorkor (ˌkwæʃɪˈɔːkə) *n.* severe malnutrition of infants and young children, resulting from dietary deficiency of protein.

kWh, kwh, *or* **kw-h** *abbrev. for* kilowatt-hour.

kyle (kaɪl) *n. Scot.* (esp. in place names) a narrow strait or channel: *Kyle of Lochalsh.*

Kyrie eleison ('kɪrɪ əˈleɪsən) *n.* **1.** a formal invocation used in the liturgies of the Roman Catholic, Greek Orthodox, and Anglican Churches. **2.** a musical setting of this. Often shortened to **Kyrie.**

L

l or **L** (ɛl) n., pl. **l's**, **L's**, or **Ls**. **1.** the 12th letter of the English alphabet. **2.** a speech sound represented by this letter. **3. a.** something shaped like an L. **b.** (in combination): an L-shaped room.

L symbol for: **1.** lambert(s). **2.** large. **3.** Latin. **4.** (on British motor vehicles) learner driver. **5.** Physics. length. **6.** Usually written: £. libra: pound. . **7.** longitude. **8.** Electronics. inductor (in circuit diagrams). **9.** Physics. **a.** latent heat. **b.** self-inductance. ~**10.** the Roman numeral for 50. See **Roman numerals**.

L. or **l.** abbrev. for: **1.** lake. **2.** latitude. **3.** law. **4.** leaf. **5.** league. **6.** left. **7.** length. **8.** (pl. LL or ll.) line. **9.** link. **10.** lire. **11.** litre(s). **12.** low.

la (lɑː) n. Music. an alternative spelling of **lah**.

La the chemical symbol for lanthanum.

laager (ˈlɑːgə) n. **1.** (in Africa) a camp, esp. one defended by a circular formation of wagons. **2.** Mil. a place where armoured vehicles are parked. ~vb. **3.** to form (wagons) into a laager. **4.** (tr.) to park (armoured vehicles) in a laager.

lab (læb) n. Inf. short for **laboratory**.

Lab. abbrev. for: **1.** Politics. Labour. **2.** Labrador.

label (ˈleɪbəl) n. **1.** a piece of paper, card, or other material attached to an object to identify it or give instructions or details concerning its ownership, use, nature, destination, etc.; tag. **2.** a brief descriptive phrase or term given to a person, group, school of thought, etc.: the label "Romantic" is applied to many different kinds of poetry. **3.** a word or phrase heading a piece of text to indicate or summarize its contents. **4.** a trademark or company or brand name on certain goods, esp. on gramophone records. **5.** Computers. a set of characters by which a file is identified by the central processing unit. **6.** Chem. a radioactive element used in a compound to trace the mechanism of a chemical reaction. ~vb. **-belling**, **-belled** or U.S. **-beling**, **-beled**. (tr.) **7.** to fasten a label to. **8.** to mark with a label. **9.** to describe or classify in a word or phrase: to label someone a liar. **10.** to make (one or more atoms in a compound) radioactive, for use in determining the mechanism of a reaction. —**ˈlabeller** n.

labia (ˈleɪbɪə) n. the plural of **labium**.

labial (ˈleɪbɪəl) adj. **1.** of, relating to, or near lips or labia. **2.** Music. producing sounds by the action of an air stream over a narrow liplike fissure, as in a flue pipe of an organ. **3.** Phonetics. relating to a speech sound whose articulation involves movement or use of the lips. ~n. **4.** Also called: **labial pipe**. Music. an organ pipe with a liplike fissure. **5.** Phonetics. a speech sound such as English p or m, whose articulation involves movement or use of the lips. —**ˈlabially** adv.

labiate (ˈleɪbɪˌeɪt, -ɪt) n. **1.** any plant of the family Labiatae, having square stems, aromatic leaves, and a two-lipped corolla: includes mint, thyme, sage, rosemary, etc. ~adj. **2.** of, relating to, or belonging to the family Labiatae.

labium (ˈleɪbɪəm) n., pl. **-bia** (-bɪə). **1.** a lip or liplike structure. **2.** any one of the four lip-shaped folds of the female vulva, comprising an outer pair (**labia majora**), and an inner pair (**labia minora**).

laboratory (ləˈbɒrətərɪ, -trɪ; U.S. ˈlæbrəˌtɔːrɪ) n., pl. **-ries**. **1. a.** a building or room equipped for conducting scientific research or for teaching practical science. **b.** (as modifier): laboratory equipment. **2.** a place where chemicals or medicines are manufactured. ~Often shortened to **lab**.

laborious (ləˈbɔːrɪəs) adj. **1.** involving great exertion or long effort. **2.** given to working hard. **3.** (of literary style, etc.) not fluent. —**laˈboriously** adv. —**laˈboriousness** n.

labour or U.S. **labor** (ˈleɪbə) n. **1.** productive work, esp. physical toil done for wages. **2. a.** the people, class, or workers involved in this, esp. as opposed to management, capital, etc. **b.** (as modifier): labour relations. **3. a.** difficult or arduous work or effort. **b.** (in combination): labour-saving. **4.** a particular job or task, esp. of a difficult nature. **5.** the pain or effort of childbirth or the time during which this takes place. ~vb. **6.** (intr.) to perform labour; work. **7.** (intr.; foll. by for, etc.) to strive or work hard (for something). **8.** (intr.; usually foll. by under) to be burdened (by) or be at a disadvantage (because of): to labour under a misapprehension. **9.** (intr.) to make one's way with difficulty. **10.** (tr.) to deal with too persistently: to labour a point. **11.** (intr.) (of a woman) to be in labour. **12.** (intr.) (of a ship) to pitch and toss.

Labour Day n. a public holiday in many countries in honour of labour, usually held on May 1.

laboured or U.S. **labored** (ˈleɪbəd) adj. **1.** (of breathing) performed with difficulty. **2.** showing effort.

labourer or U.S. **laborer** (ˈleɪbərə) n. a person engaged in physical work, esp. unskilled work.

labour exchange n. Brit. a former name for the **Employment Service Agency**.

Labour Party n. **1.** a British political party, formed in 1900 as an amalgam of various trade unions and socialist groups, generally supporting the interests of organized labour. **2.** any similar party in any of various other countries.

Labrador retriever (ˈlæbrəˌdɔː) n. a variety of retriever with a short black or golden-brown coat. Often shortened to **Labrador**.

laburnum (ləˈbɜːnəm) n. any tree or shrub of a Eurasian genus having clusters of yellow drooping flowers: all parts of the plant are poisonous.

labyrinth (ˈlæbərɪnθ) n. **1.** a mazelike network of tunnels, chambers, or paths, either natural or man-made. **2.** any complex or confusing system of streets, passages, etc. **3.** a complex or intricate situation. **4.** any system of interconnecting cavities, esp. those comprising the internal ear. **5.** Electronics. an enclosure behind a high-performance loudspeaker, consisting of a series of air chambers designed to absorb unwanted sound waves.

lac¹ (læk) n. a resinous substance secreted by certain insects (**lac insects**), used in the manufacture of shellac.

lac² (lɑːk) n. a variant spelling of **lakh**.

lace (leɪs) n. **1.** a delicate decorative fabric made from cotton, silk, etc., woven in an open web of different symmetrical patterns and figures. **2.** a cord or string drawn through eyelets or around hooks to fasten a shoe or garment. **3.** ornamental braid often used on military uniforms, etc. ~vb. **4.** to fasten (shoes, etc.) with a lace. **5.** (tr.) to draw (a cord or thread) through holes, eyes, etc., as when tying shoes. **6.** (tr.) to compress the waist

---

═ THESAURUS ═

label n. **1.** docket (Chiefly Brit.), marker, sticker, tag, tally, ticket **2.** characterization, classification, description, epithet **3.** brand, company, mark, trademark ~v. **4.** docket (Chiefly Brit.), mark, stamp, sticker, tag, tally **5.** brand, call, characterize, class, classify, define, describe, designate, identify, name

labour n. **1.** industry, toil, work **2.** employees, hands, labourers, workers, work force, workmen **3.** donkey-work, drudgery, effort, exertion, grind (Inf.), industry, pains, painstaking, sweat (Inf.), toil, travail **4.**

chore, job, task, undertaking **5.** childbirth, contractions, delivery, labour pains, pains, parturition, throes, travail ~v. **6.** drudge, endeavour, grind (Inf.), peg along or away (Chiefly Brit.), plod, plug along or away (Inf.), slave, strive, struggle, sweat (Inf.), toil, travail, work **7.** Usually with **under** be a victim of, be burdened by, be disadvantaged, suffer **8.** dwell on, elaborate, overdo, overemphasize, strain **9.** Of a ship heave, pitch, roll, toss

laboured **1.** awkward, difficult, forced,

heavy, stiff, strained **2.** affected, contrived, overdone, overwrought, ponderous, studied, unnatural

labourer blue-collar worker, drudge, hand, labouring man, manual worker, navvy (Brit. inf.), unskilled worker, worker, working man, workman

labyrinth coil, complexity, complication, convolution, entanglement, intricacy, jungle, knotty problem, maze, perplexity, puzzle, riddle, snarl, tangle, windings

of (someone), as with a corset. **7.** (*tr.*) to add a dash of spirits to (a beverage). **8.** (*tr.; usually passive* and foll. by *with*) to streak or mark with lines or colours: *the sky was laced with red.* **9.** (*tr.*) to intertwine; interlace. **10.** (*tr.*) *Inf.* to give a sound beating to.

lacerate *vb.* ('læsə‚reɪt). (*tr.*) **1.** to tear (the flesh, etc.) jaggedly. **2.** to hurt or harrow (the feelings, etc.). ~*adj.* ('læsə‚reɪt, -rɪt). **3.** having edges that are jagged: *lacerate leaves.*

lace up *vb.* **1.** (*tr., adv.*) to tighten or fasten (clothes or footwear) with laces. ~*adj.* **lace-up.** **2.** (of footwear) to be fastened with laces. ~*n.* **3.** a lace-up shoe or boot.

lachrymal ('lækrɪməl) *adj.* a variant spelling of **lacrimal.**

lachrymose ('lækrɪ‚məus) *adj.* **1.** given to weeping; tearful. **2.** mournful; sad. —**'lachry‚mosely** *adv.*

lacing ('leɪsɪŋ) *n.* **1.** *Chiefly Brit.* a course of bricks, stone, etc., for strengthening a rubble or flint wall. **2.** another word for **lace** (senses 2, 3). **3.** *Inf.* a severe beating.

lack (læk) *n.* **1.** an insufficiency, shortage, or absence of something required or desired. **2.** something that is required but is absent or in short supply. ~*vb.* **3.** (when *intr.*, often foll. by *in* or *for*) to be deficient (in) or have need (of).

lackadaisical (‚lækə'deɪzɪkəl) *adj.* **1.** lacking vitality and purpose. **2.** lazy esp, in a dreamy way. —‚**lacka-'daisically** *adv.*

lackey ('lækɪ) *n.* **1.** a servile follower; hanger-on. **2.** a liveried male servant or valet. **3.** a person who is treated like a servant. ~*vb.* **4.** (when *intr.*, often foll. by *for*) to act as a lackey (to).

lacklustre *or U.S.* **lackluster** ('læk‚lʌstə) *adj.* lacking force, brilliance, or vitality.

laconic (lə'kɒnɪk) *adj.* (of a person's speech) using few words; terse. —**la'conically** *adv.*

lacquer ('lækə) *n.* **1.** a hard glossy coating made by dissolving cellulose derivatives or natural resins in a volatile solvent. **2.** a black resinous substance, obtained from certain trees (**lacquer trees**), used to give a hard glossy finish to wooden furniture. **3.** Also called: **hair lacquer.** a mixture of shellac and alcohol for spraying onto the hair to hold a style in place. **4.** *Art.* decorative objects coated with such lacquer, often inlaid. —**'lac-querer** *n.*

lacrimal, lachrymal, *or* **lacrymal** ('lækrɪməl) *adj.* of or relating to tears or to the glands that secrete tears.

lacrimation (‚lækrɪ'meɪʃən) *n.* the secretion of tears.

lactate[1] ('lækteɪt) *n.* an ester or salt of lactic acid.

lactate[2] ('lækteɪt) *vb.* (*intr.*) (of mammals) to produce or secrete milk.

lactation (læk'teɪʃən) *n.* **1.** the secretion of milk from the mammary glands after parturition. **2.** the period during which milk is secreted.

lacteal ('læktɪəl) *adj.* **1.** of, relating to, or resembling milk. **2.** (of lymphatic vessels) conveying or containing chyle. ~*n.* **3.** any of the lymphatic vessels conveying chyle from the small intestine to the thoracic duct.

lactic ('læktɪk) *adj.* relating to or derived from milk.

lactic acid *n.* a colourless syrupy carboxylic acid found in sour milk and many fruits.

lacto- *or before a vowel* **lact-** *combining form.* indicating milk: *lactobacillus.*

lactose ('læktəus, -təuz) *n.* a white crystalline sugar occurring in milk and used in pharmaceuticals and baby foods. Formula: $C_{12}H_{22}O_{11}$.

lacuna (lə'kju:nə) *n., pl.* **-nae** (-ni:) *or* **-nas.** **1.** a gap or space, esp. in a book or manuscript. **2.** *Biol.* a cavity or depression, such as any of the spaces in the matrix of bone. —**la'cunose, la'cunal, la'cunar,** *or* **la'cunary** *adj.*

lacy ('leɪsɪ) *adj.* **lacier, laciest.** made of or resembling lace. —**'lacily** *adv.* —**'laciness** *n.*

lad (læd) *n.* **1.** a boy or young man. **2.** *Inf.* a familiar form of address for any male. **3.** *Brit.* a boy or man who looks after horses.

ladder ('lædə) *n.* **1.** a portable framework of wood, metal, rope, etc., in the form of two long parallel members connected by rungs or steps fixed to them at right angles, for climbing up or down. **2.** any hierarchy conceived of as having a series of ascending stages, levels, etc.: *the social ladder.* **3.** Also called: **run.** *Chiefly Brit.* a line of connected stitches that have come undone in knitted material, esp. stockings. ~*vb.* **4.** *Chiefly Brit.* to cause a line of interconnected stitches in (stockings, etc.) to undo, as by snagging, or (of a stocking) to come undone in this way.

ladder back *n.* a type of chair in which the back is constructed of horizontal slats between two uprights.

laddie ('lædɪ) *n. Chiefly Scot.* a familiar term for a male, esp. a boy; lad.

lade (leɪd) *vb.* **lading, laded, laden** *or* **laded.** **1.** to put cargo or freight on board (a ship, etc.) or (of a ship, etc.) to take on cargo or freight. **2.** (*tr.; usually passive* and foll. by *with*) to burden or oppress. **3.** (*tr.; usually passive* and foll. by *with*) to fill or load. **4.** to remove (liquid) with or as if with a ladle.

laden ('leɪdən) **1.** a past participle of **lade.** ~*adj.* **2.** weighed down with a load; loaded. **3.** encumbered; burdened.

la-di-da, lah-di-dah, *or* **la-de-da** (‚lɑ:di:'dɑ:) *adj. Inf.* affecting exaggeratedly genteel manners or speech.

ladies *or* **ladies' room** *n.* (*functioning as sing.*) *Inf.* a women's public lavatory.

lading ('leɪdɪŋ) *n.* a load; cargo; freight.

ladle ('leɪdəl) *n.* **1.** a long-handled spoon having a deep bowl for serving or transferring liquids. **2.** a large bucket-shaped container for transferring molten metal. ~*vb.* **3.** (*tr.*; often foll. by *out*) to serve out as with a ladle. —**'ladle‚ful** *n.* —**'ladler** *n.*

ladle out *vb.* (*tr., adv.*) *Inf.* to distribute (money, gifts, etc.) generously.

lady ('leɪdɪ) *n., pl.* **-dies. 1.** a woman regarded as having the characteristics of a good family and high social position. **2.** *a.* a polite name for a woman. *b.* (*as modifier*): *a lady doctor.* **3.** an informal name for **wife. 4. lady of the house.** the female head of the household. **5.** *History.* a woman with proprietary rights and authority, as over a manor.

Lady ('leɪdɪ) *n., pl.* **-dies. 1.** (in Britain) a title of honour borne by various classes of women of the peerage. **2. my lady.** a term of address to holders of the title Lady. **3. Our Lady.** a title of the Virgin Mary.

ladybird ('leɪdɪ‚bɜ:d) *n.* any of various small brightly coloured beetles, esp. one having red elytra with black spots.

Lady Day *n.* Also called: **Annunciation Day.** March 25, the feast of the Annunciation of the Virgin Mary.

lady-in-waiting *n., pl.* **ladies-in-waiting.** a lady who attends a queen or princess.

lady-killer *n. Inf.* a man who believes he is irresistibly fascinating to women.

THESAURUS

lace *n.* **1.** filigree, netting, openwork, tatting **2.** bootlace, cord, shoelace, string, thong, tie ~*v.* **3.** attach, bind, close, do up, fasten, intertwine, interweave, thread, tie, twine **4.** add to, fortify, mix in, spike

lacerate 1. claw, cut, gash, jag, maim, mangle, rend, rip, slash, tear, wound **2.** *Fig.* afflict, distress, harrow, rend, torment, torture, wound

laceration cut, gash, injury, mutilation, rent, rip, slash, tear, wound

lachrymose crying, dolorous, lugubrious, mournful, sad, tearful, weeping, weepy (*Inf.*), woeful

lack 1. *n.* absence, dearth, deficiency, deprivation, destitution, insufficiency, need, priva-

tion, scantiness, scarcity, shortage, shortcoming, shortness, want **2.** *v.* be deficient in, be short of, be without, miss, need, require, want

lackadaisical 1. apathetic, dull, enervated, half-hearted, indifferent, languid, languorous, lethargic, limp, listless, spiritless **2.** abstracted, dreamy, idle, indolent, inert, lazy

lackey 1. creature, fawner, flatterer, flunky, hanger-on, instrument, menial, minion, parasite, pawn, sycophant, toady, tool, yes man **2.** attendant, flunky, footman, manservant, valet

lacking defective, deficient, flawed, impaired, inadequate, minus (*Inf.*), missing, needing, sans (*Archaic*), wanting, without

lacklustre boring, dim, drab, dry, dull, flat, leaden, lifeless, lustreless, muted, prosaic, sombre, unimaginative, uninspired, vapid

laconic brief, compact, concise, crisp, curt, pithy, sententious, short, succinct, terse, to the point

lad boy, chap (*Inf.*), fellow, guy (*Inf.*), juvenile, kid, laddie (*Scot.*), schoolboy, shaver (*Inf.*), stripling, youngster, youth

laden burdened, charged, encumbered, fraught, full, hampered, loaded, oppressed, taxed, weighed down, weighted

lady-killer Casanova, Don Juan, heartbreaker, ladies' man, libertine, Lothario, philanderer, rake, roué, wolf (*Inf.*), womanizer

ladylike ('leɪdɪˌlaɪk) *adj.* like or befitting a lady.

lady's finger *n.* another name for **bhindi**.

Ladyship ('leɪdɪˌʃɪp) *n.* (preceded by *your* or *her*) a title used to address or refer to any peeress except a duchess.

lady's-slipper *n.* any of various orchids having reddish or purple flowers.

laevo- *or U.S.* **levo-** *combining form.* **1.** on or towards the left: *laevorotatory.* **2.** (in chemistry) denoting a laevorotatory compound.

lag¹ (læg) *vb.* **lagging, lagged.** (*intr.*) **1.** (often foll. by *behind*) to hang (back) or fall (behind) in movement, progress, development, etc. **2.** to fall away in strength or intensity. ~*n.* **3.** the act or state of slowing down or falling behind. **4.** the interval of time between two events, esp. between an action and its effect.

lag² (læg) *Sl.* ~*n.* **1.** a convict or ex-convict (esp. in **old lag**). **2.** a term of imprisonment. ~*vb.* **lagging, lagged.** **3.** (*tr.*) to arrest or put in prison.

lag³ (læg) *vb.* **lagging, lagged.** **1.** (*tr.*) to cover (a pipe, cylinder, etc.) with lagging to prevent loss of heat. ~*n.* **2.** the insulating casing of a steam cylinder, boiler, etc. **3.** a stave.

lager ('lɑːgə) *n.* a light-bodied effervescent beer, stored for varying periods before use.

laggard ('lægəd) *n.* **1.** a person who lags behind. ~*adj.* **2.** *Rare.* sluggish, slow, or dawdling. —'**laggardly** *adv.* —'**laggardness** *n.*

lagging ('lægɪŋ) *n.* **1.** insulating material wrapped around pipes, boilers, etc., or laid in a roof loft, to prevent loss of heat. **2.** the act or process of applying lagging.

lagoon (lə'guːn) *n.* **1.** a body of water cut off from the open sea by coral reefs or sand bars. **2.** any small body of water, esp. one adjoining a larger one.

lah (lɑː) *n. Music.* (in tonic sol-fa) the sixth note of any major scale; submediant.

laid (leɪd) *vb.* the past tense or past participle of **lay¹**.

laid-back *adj.* relaxed in style or character; easygoing and unhurried.

laid paper *n.* paper with a regular mesh impressed upon it.

lain (leɪn) *vb.* the past participle of **lie²**.

lair (lɛə) *n.* **1.** the resting place of a wild animal. **2.** *Inf.* a place of seclusion or hiding. ~*vb.* **3.** (*intr.*) (esp. of a wild animal) to retreat to or rest in a lair. **4.** (*tr.*) to drive or place (an animal) in a lair.

laird (lɛəd) *n. Scot.* a landowner, esp. of a large estate.

laissez faire *or* **laisser faire** *French.* (ˌlɛseɪ 'fɛə) *n.* **1. a.** Also called: **individualism.** the doctrine of unrestricted freedom in commerce, esp. for private interests. **b.** (*as modifier*): *a laissez-faire economy.* **2.** indifference or noninterference, esp. in the affairs of others.

laity ('leɪɪtɪ) *n.* **1.** laymen, as distinguished from clergymen. **2.** all people not of a specific occupation.

lake¹ (leɪk) *n.* **1.** an expanse of water entirely surrounded by land and unconnected to the sea except by rivers or streams. Related adj.: **lacustrine.** **2.** anything resembling this. **3.** a surplus of a liquid commodity in the European Economic Community: *a wine lake.*

lake² (leɪk) *n.* **1.** a bright pigment produced by the combination of an organic colouring matter with an inorganic compound, usually a metallic salt, oxide, or hydroxide. **2.** a red dye obtained by combining a metallic compound with cochineal.

Lake District *n.* a region of lakes and mountains in NW England, in Cumbria. Also called: **Lakeland, the Lakes.**

lake trout *n.* a yellow-spotted char of the Great Lakes region of Canada.

lakh *or* **lac** (lɑːk) *n.* (in India) the number 100000, esp. referring to this sum of rupees.

lam¹ (læm) *vb.* **lamming, lammed.** *Sl.* **1.** (*tr.*) to thrash or beat. **2.** (*intr.;* usually foll. by *into* or *out*) to make a sweeping stroke or blow.

lam² (læm) ~*n. U.S. sl.* **1.** a sudden flight or escape, esp. to avoid arrest. **2. on the lam.** making an escape.

Lam. *Bible. abbrev. for* Lamentations.

lama ('lɑːmə) *n.* a priest or monk of Lamaism.

Lamaism ('lɑːməˌɪzəm) *n.* the Mahayana form of Buddhism of Tibet and Mongolia. —'**Lamaist** *n., adj.* —ˌLama'**istic** *adj.*

lamb (læm) *n.* **1.** the young of a sheep. **2.** the meat of a young sheep. **3.** a person, esp. a child, who is innocent, meek, good, etc. **4.** a person easily deceived. ~*vb.* **5.** (*intr.*) (of a ewe) to give birth. —'**lamb**ˌ**like** *adj.*

Lamb (læm) *n.* **the.** A title given to Christ in the New Testament.

lambaste *or* **lambast** (læm'beɪst) *vb.* (*tr.*) *Sl.* **1.** to beat or whip severely. **2.** to reprimand or scold.

lambda ('læmdə) *n.* the 11th letter of the Greek alphabet (Λ, λ).

lambent ('læmbənt) *adj.* **1.** (esp. of a flame) flickering softly over a surface. **2.** glowing with soft radiance. **3.** (of wit or humour) light or brilliant. —'**lambency** *n.* —'**lambently** *adv.*

lambkin ('læmkɪn) *n.* **1.** a small lamb. **2.** a term of affection for a small endearing child.

lambskin ('læmˌskɪn) *n.* **1.** the skin of a lamb, esp. with the wool still on. **2.** a material or garment prepared from this skin.

lame (leɪm) *adj.* **1.** disabled or crippled in the legs or feet. **2.** painful or weak: *a lame back.* **3.** not effective or enthusiastic: *a lame try.* **4.** *U.S. sl.* conventional or uninspiring. ~*vb.* **5.** (*tr.*) to make lame. —'**lamely** *adv.* —'**lameness** *n.*

lamé ('lɑːmeɪ) *n.* a fabric of silk, cotton, or wool interwoven with threads of metal.

lame duck *n. Inf.* **1.** a person or thing that is disabled or ineffectual. **2.** *Stock Exchange.* a speculator who cannot discharge his liabilities. **3.** *U.S.* an elected official or body of officials remaining in office in the interval between the election and inauguration of a successor.

lament (lə'mɛnt) *vb.* **1.** to feel or express sorrow, remorse, or regret (for or over). ~*n.* **2.** an expression of sorrow. **3.** a poem or song in which a death is lamented. —ˌlamen'**tation** *n.* —la'**menter** *n.* —la'**mentingly** *adv.*

lamentable ('læməntəbəl) *adj.* **1.** wretched, deplorable, or distressing. **2.** an archaic word for **mournful.** —'**lamentably** *adv.*

lamented (lə'mɛntɪd) *adj.* grieved for or regretted (often in **late lamented**): *our late lamented employer.* —la'**mentedly** *adv.*

lamina ('læmɪnə) *n., pl.* **-nae** (-ˌniː) *or* **-nas.** **1.** a thin plate, esp. of bone or mineral. **2.** *Bot.* the flat blade of a leaf. —'**laminar** *or* **laminose** ('læmɪˌnəʊs, -ˌnəʊz) *adj.*

laminate *vb.* ('læmɪˌneɪt). **1.** (*tr.*) to make (material in sheet form) by bonding together two or more thin sheets. **2.** to split or be split into thin sheets. **3.** (*tr.*) to beat, form, or press (material, esp. metal) into thin sheets. **4.** (*tr.*) to cover or overlay with a thin sheet of material. ~*n.* ('læmɪˌneɪt, -nɪt). **5.** a material made by bonding together two or more sheets. ~*adj.* ('læmɪˌneɪt, -nɪt). **6.** having or composed of lamina; laminated. —'**laminable** ('læmɪnəbəl) *adj.* —ˌlami'**nation** *n.*

THESAURUS

ladylike courtly, cultured, decorous, elegant, genteel, modest, polite, proper, refined, respectable, well-bred

lag 1. be behind, dawdle, delay, drag (behind), drag one's feet, hang back, idle, linger, loiter, saunter, straggle, tarry, trail **2.** decrease, diminish, ebb, fail, fall off, flag, lose strength, slacken, wane

laggard dawdler, idler, lingerer, loafer, loiterer, lounger, saunterer, slowcoach (*Brit. inf.*), sluggard, snail, straggler

laid-back at ease, casual, easy-going, free and easy, relaxed, unflappable (*Inf.*), unhurried

laid up bedridden, disabled, housebound,

ill, immobilized, incapacitated, injured, on the sick list, out of action (*Inf.*), sick

lair 1. burrow, den, earth, form, hole, nest, resting place **2.** *Inf.* den, hide-out, refuge, retreat, sanctuary

laissez faire *n.* free enterprise, free trade, individualism, live and let live, non-intervention

lame 1. crippled, defective, disabled, game, halt (*Archaic*), handicapped, hobbling, limping **2.** *Fig.* feeble, flimsy, inadequate, insufficient, poor, thin, unconvincing, unsatisfactory, weak

lament *v.* **1.** bemoan, bewail, complain, deplore, grieve, mourn, regret, sorrow, wail,

weep ~*n.* **2.** complaint, keening, lamentation, moan, moaning, plaint, ululation, wail, wailing **3.** coronach (*Scot., Irish*), dirge, elegy, monody, requiem, threnody

lamentable 1. deplorable, distressing, grievous, mournful, regrettable, sorrowful, tragic, unfortunate, woeful **2.** low, meagre, mean, miserable, pitiful, poor, unsatisfactory, wretched

lamentation dirge, grief, grieving, keening, lament, moan, mourning, plaint, sobbing, sorrow, ululation, wailing, weeping

—'lami,nator n.

laminated ('læmɪ,neɪtɪd) adj. 1. composed of many layers of plastic, wood, etc., bonded together. 2. covered with a thin protective layer of plastic, etc.

Lammas ('læməs) n. 1. R.C. Church. Aug. 1, held as a feast, commemorating St. Peter's miraculous deliverance from prison. 2. Also called: **Lammas Day.** the same day formerly observed in England as a harvest festival.

lamp (læmp) n. 1. a. any of a number of devices that produce illumination: an electric lamp; a gas lamp; an oil lamp. b. (in combination): lampshade. 2. a device for holding one or more electric light bulbs: a table lamp. 3. a vessel in which a liquid fuel is burned to supply illumination. 4. any of a variety of devices that produce radiation, esp. for therapeutic purposes: an ultraviolet lamp.

lampblack ('læmp,blæk) n. a finely divided form of almost pure carbon produced by the incomplete combustion of organic compounds, such as natural gas, used in making carbon electrodes and dynamo brushes and as a pigment.

lamplighter ('læmp,laɪtə) n. 1. (formerly) a person who lit and extinguished street lamps, esp. gas ones. 2. Chiefly U.S. any of various devices used to light lamps.

lampoon (læm'puːn) n. 1. a satire in prose or verse ridiculing a person, literary work, etc. ~vb. 2. (tr.) to attack or satirize in a lampoon. —**lam'pooner** or **lam'poonist** n. —**lam'poonery** n.

lamppost ('læmp,pəʊst) n. a post supporting a lamp, esp. in a street.

lamprey ('læmprɪ) n. any eel-like vertebrate having a round sucking mouth for clinging to and feeding on the blood of other animals. Also called: **lamper eel.**

Lancastrian (læŋ'kæstrɪən) n. 1. a native or resident of Lancashire or Lancaster. 2. an adherent of the house of Lancaster in the Wars of the Roses. ~adj. 3. of or relating to Lancashire or Lancaster. 4. of or relating to the house of Lancaster.

lance (lɑːns) n. 1. a long weapon with a pointed head used by horsemen. 2. a similar weapon used for hunting, whaling, etc. 3. Surgery. another name for **lancet** (sense 1). ~vb. (tr.) 4. to pierce (an abscess or boil) with a lancet. 5. to pierce as with a lance.

lance corporal n. a noncommissioned officer of the lowest rank in the British Army.

lanceolate ('lɑːnsɪə,leɪt, -lɪt) adj. narrow and tapering to a point at each end: lanceolate leaves.

lancer ('lɑːnsə) n. 1. (formerly) a cavalryman armed with a lance. 2. a member of a regiment retaining such a title.

lancers ('lɑːnsəz) n. (functioning as sing.) 1. a quadrille for eight or sixteen couples. 2. a piece of music composed for this dance.

lancet ('lɑːnsɪt) n. 1. Also called: **lance.** a pointed surgical knife with two sharp edges. 2. short for **lancet arch** or **lancet window.**

lancet arch n. a narrow acutely pointed arch.

lancet window n. a narrow window having a lancet arch. Sometimes shortened to **lancet.**

Lancs. (læŋks) abbrev. for Lancashire.

land (lænd) n. 1. the solid part of the surface of the earth as distinct from seas, lakes, etc. Related adj.: **terrestrial.** 2. ground, esp. with reference to its use, quality, etc. 3. rural or agricultural areas as contrasted with urban ones. 4. farming as an occupation or way of life. 5. Law. any tract of ground capable of being owned as property. 6. a. a country, region, or area. b. the people of a country, etc. 7. Econ. the factor of production consisting of all natural resources. ~vb. 8. to transfer (something) or go from a ship or boat to the shore: land the cargo. 9. (intr.) to come to or touch shore. 10.

(intr.) (in Canada), to be legally admitted to the country, as an immigrant, or **landed immigrant.** 11. to come down or bring (something) down to earth after a flight or jump. 12. to come or bring to some point, condition, or state. 13. (tr.) Angling. to retrieve (a hooked fish) from the water. 14. (tr.) Inf. to win or obtain: to land a job. 15. (tr.) Inf. to deliver (a blow). ~See also **land up.** —'**landless** adj.

land agent n. 1. a person who administers a landed estate and its tenancies. 2. a person who acts as an agent for the sale of land. —**land agency** n.

landau ('lændɔː) n. a four-wheeled horse-drawn carriage with two folding hoods over the passenger compartment.

landed ('lændɪd) adj. 1. owning land: landed gentry. 2. consisting of or including land: a landed estate.

landfall ('lænd,fɔːl) n. 1. the act of sighting or nearing land, esp. from the sea. 2. the land sighted or neared.

landfill ('lænd,fɪl) adj. of or denoting low-lying sites or tips being filled up with alternate layers of rubbish and earth.

land girl n. a girl or woman who does farm work, esp. in wartime.

landgrave ('lænd,greɪv) n. German history. 1. (from the 13th century to 1806) a count who ruled over a specified territory. 2. (after 1806) the title of any of various sovereign princes.

land-holder n. a person who owns or occupies land. —'**land-,holding** adj., n.

landing ('lændɪŋ) n. 1. a. the act of coming to land, esp. after a sea voyage. b. (as modifier): landing place. 2. a place of disembarkation. 3. the floor area at the top of a flight of stairs.

landing field n. an area of land on which aircraft land and from which they take off.

landing gear n. the usual U.S. name for **undercarriage.**

landlady ('lænd,leɪdɪ) n., pl. **-dies.** 1. a woman who owns and leases property. 2. a woman who owns or runs a lodging house, inn, etc.

landlocked ('lænd,lɒkt) adj. 1. (esp. of lakes) completely surrounded by land. 2. (esp. of certain salmon) living in fresh water that is permanently isolated from the sea.

landlord ('lænd,lɔːd) n. 1. a man who owns and leases property. 2. a man who owns or runs a lodging house, inn, etc.

landlubber ('lænd,lʌbə) n. Naut. any person having no experience at sea.

landmark ('lænd,mɑːk) n. 1. a prominent or well-known object in or feature of a particular landscape. 2. an important or unique decision, event, fact, discovery, etc. 3. a boundary marker.

landmass ('lænd,mæs) n. a large continuous area of land, as opposed to seas or islands.

land mine n. Mil. an explosive charge placed in the ground, usually detonated by stepping or driving on it.

landowner ('lænd,əʊnə) n. a person who owns land. —'**land,owner,ship** n. —'**land,owning** n., adj.

landscape ('lænd,skeɪp) n. 1. an extensive area of scenery as viewed from a single aspect. 2. a painting, drawing, photograph, etc., depicting natural scenery. 3. the genre including such pictures. ~vb. 4. (tr.) to improve the natural features of (a garden, park, etc.), as by creating contoured features and planting trees. 5. (intr.) to work as a landscape gardener.

landscape gardening n. the art of laying out grounds in imitation of natural scenery. Also called: **landscape architecture.** —**landscape gardener** n.

landslide ('lænd,slaɪd) n. 1. Also called: **landslip. a.** the sliding of a large mass of rock material, soil, etc., down the side of a mountain or cliff. **b.** the material dis-

---

THESAURUS

lampoon 1. n. burlesque, caricature, parody, pasquinade, satire, send-up (Brit. inf.), skit, squib, takeoff (Inf.) 2. v. burlesque, caricature, make fun of, mock, parody, pasquinade, ridicule, satirize, send up (Brit. inf.), squib, take off (Inf.)

land n. 1. dry land, earth, ground, terra firma 2. dirt, ground, loam, soil 3. countryside, farming, farmland, rural districts 4. acres, estate, grounds, property, real property, re-

alty 5. country, district, fatherland, motherland, nation, province, region, territory, tract ~v. 6. alight, arrive, berth, come to rest, debark, disembark, dock, touch down 7. Sometimes with up arrive, bring, carry, cause, end up, lead, turn up, wind up 8. Inf. acquire, gain, get, obtain, secure, win

landlord 1. host, hotelier, hotel-keeper, innkeeper 2. freeholder, lessor, owner, proprietor

landmark 1. feature, monument 2. crisis, milestone, turning point, watershed 3. benchmark, boundary, cairn, milepost, signpost

landscape countryside, outlook, panorama, prospect, scene, scenery, view, vista

landslide 1. n. avalanche, landslip, rockfall 2. adj. decisive, overwhelming, runaway

lodged in this way. **2.** an overwhelming electoral victory.

land up vb. (adv., usually intr.) to arrive or cause to arrive at a final point or condition.

landward ('lændwəd) adj. **1.** lying, facing, or moving towards land. **2.** in the direction of the land. ~adv. **3.** a variant of **landwards**.

landwards ('lændwədz) or **landward** adv. towards land.

lane (leɪn) n. **1.** a narrow road or way between buildings, hedges, fences, etc. **2.** any narrow well-defined track or course, as for lines of traffic in a road, or for ships or aircraft. **3.** one of the parallel strips into which a running track or swimming bath is divided for races. **4.** the long strip of wooden flooring down which balls are bowled in a bowling alley.

lang. abbrev. for language.

langlauf ('lɑːŋ,laʊf) n. cross-country skiing. —**langläufer** ('lɑːŋ,lɔɪfə) n.

language ('læŋgwɪdʒ) n. **1.** a system for the expression of thoughts, feelings, etc., by the use of spoken sounds or conventional symbols. **2.** the faculty for the use of such systems, which is a distinguishing characteristic of man as compared with other animals. **3.** the language of a particular nation or people. **4.** any other means of communicating, such as gesture or animal sounds: the language of love. **5.** the specialized vocabulary used by a particular group: medical language. **6.** a particular manner or style of verbal expression: your language is disgusting. **7.** Computers. See **programming language**.

language laboratory n. a room equipped with tape recorders, etc., for learning foreign languages.

languid ('læŋgwɪd) adj. **1.** without energy or spirit. **2.** without interest or enthusiasm. **3.** sluggish; inactive. —**languidly** adv. —**languidness** n.

languish ('læŋgwɪʃ) vb. (intr.) **1.** to lose or diminish in strength or energy. **2.** (often foll. by for) to be listless with desire; pine. **3.** to suffer deprivation, hardship, or neglect: to languish in prison. **4.** to put on a tender, nostalgic, or melancholic expression. —**languisher** n. —**languishment** n.

languor ('læŋgə) n. **1.** physical or mental laziness or weariness. **2.** a feeling of dreaminess and relaxation. **3.** oppressive silence or stillness. —**languorous** adj.

lank (læŋk) adj. **1.** long and limp. **2.** thin or gaunt. —**lankly** adv. —**lankness** n.

lanky ('læŋkɪ) adj. **-ier, -iest.** tall, thin, and loose-jointed. —**lankily** adv. —**lankiness** n.

lanolin ('lænəlɪn) or **lanoline** ('lænəlɪn, -,liːn) n. a yellowish viscous substance extracted from wool: used in some ointments.

lantern ('læntən) n. **1.** a light with a transparent protective case. **2.** a structure on top of a dome or roof having openings or windows to admit light or air. **3.** the upper part of a lighthouse that houses the light.

lantern jaw n. (when pl., refers to upper and lower jaw; when sing. usually to lower jaw) a long hollow jaw that gives the face a drawn appearance. —**lantern-,jawed** adj.

lanthanide series ('lænθə,naɪd) n. a class of 15 chemically related elements (**lanthanides**) with atomic numbers from 57 (lanthanum) to 71 (lutecium).

lanthanum ('lænθənəm) n. a silvery-white ductile metallic element of the lanthanide series: used in pyrophoric alloys, electronic devices, and in glass manufacture. Symbol: La; atomic no.: 57; atomic wt.: 138.91.

lanyard or **laniard** ('lænjəd) n. **1.** a cord, esp. one worn around the neck, to hold a whistle, knife, etc. **2.** a

cord used in firing certain types of cannon. **3.** Naut. a line for extending or tightening standing rigging.

laodicean (,leɪəʊdɪ'sɪən) adj. **1.** lukewarm and indifferent, esp. in religious matters. ~n. **2.** a person having a lukewarm attitude towards religious matters.

lap[1] (læp) n. **1.** the area formed by the upper surface of the thighs of a seated person. **2.** Also called: **lapful**. the amount held in one's lap. **3.** a protected place or environment: in the lap of luxury. **4.** the part of one's clothing that covers the lap. **5. drop in someone's lap.** give someone the responsibility of.

lap[2] (læp) n. **1.** one circuit of a racecourse or track. **2.** a stage or part of a journey, race, etc. **3. a.** an overlapping part or projection. **b.** the extent of overlap. **4.** the length of material needed to go around an object. **5.** a rotating disc coated with fine abrasive for polishing gemstones. ~vb. **lapping, lapped. 6.** (tr.) to wrap or fold (around or over): he lapped a bandage around his wrist. **7.** (tr.) to enclose or envelop in: he lapped his wrist in a bandage. **8.** to place or lie partly or completely over or project beyond. **9.** (tr.; usually passive) to envelop or surround with comfort, love, etc.: lapped in luxury. **10.** (intr.) to be folded. **11.** (tr.) to overtake (an opponent) in a race so as to be one or more circuits ahead. **12.** (tr.) to polish or cut (a workpiece, gemstone, etc.) with a fine abrasive. —**lapper** n.

lap[3] (læp) vb. **lapping, lapped. 1.** (of small waves) to wash against (a shore, boat, etc.), usually with light splashing sounds. **2.** (often foll. by up) (esp. of animals) to scoop (a liquid) into the mouth with the tongue. ~n. **3.** the act or sound of lapping. **4.** a thin food for dogs or other animals. ~See also **lap up**. —**lapper** n.

lap dog n. a pet dog small and docile enough to be cuddled in the lap.

lapel (lə'pɛl) n. the continuation of the turned or folded back collar on a suit, coat, jacket, etc. —**la'pelled** adj.

lapidary ('læpɪdərɪ) n., pl. **-daries. 1.** a person whose business is to cut, polish, set, or deal in gemstones. ~adj. **2.** of or relating to gemstones or the work of a lapidary. **3.** Also **lapidarian** (,læpɪ'deərɪən). engraved, cut, or inscribed in a stone or gemstone. **4.** of sufficiently high quality to be engraved on a stone: a lapidary inscription.

lapis lazuli ('læpɪs 'læzjʊ,laɪ) n. **1.** a brilliant blue mineral used as a gemstone. **2.** the deep blue colour of lapis lazuli.

lap joint n. a joint made by placing one member over another and fastening them together. Also called: **lapped joint.** —**lap-,jointed** adj.

lap of honour n. a ceremonial circuit of a racing track, etc., by the winner of a race.

Lapp (læp) n. **1.** Also: **Laplander.** a member of a nomadic people living chiefly in N Scandinavia and the Kola Peninsula of the Soviet Union. **2.** the language of this people. ~adj. **3.** of or relating to this people or their language. —**Lappish** adj., n.

lappet ('læpɪt) n. **1.** a small hanging flap or piece of lace, etc. **2.** Zool. a lobelike hanging structure, such as the wattle on a bird's head.

lapse (læps) n. **1.** a drop in standard of an isolated or temporary nature: a lapse of justice. **2.** a break in occurrence, usage, etc.: a lapse of five weeks between letters. **3.** a gradual decline or a drop to a lower degree, condition, or state: a lapse from high office. **4.** a moral fall. **5.** Law. the termination of some right, interest, or privilege, as by neglecting to exercise it or through failure of some contingency. **6.** Insurance. the termination of coverage following a failure to pay the premiums. ~vb. (intr.) **7.** to drop in standard or fail to maintain a

---

THESAURUS

language 1. communication, conversation, discourse, expression, interchange, parlance, speech, talk, utterance, verbalization, vocalization **2.** argot, cant, dialect, idiom, jargon, lingo (Inf.), lingua franca, patois, speech, terminology, tongue, vernacular, vocabulary **3.** diction, expression, phraseology, phrasing, style, wording

languid 1. drooping, faint, feeble, languorous, limp, pining, sickly, weak, weary **2.** indifferent, lackadaisical, languorous, lazy, listless, spiritless, unenthusiastic, uninterested **3.** dull, heavy, inactive, inert, lethargic, sluggish, torpid

languish 1. decline, droop, fade, fail, faint, flag, sicken, waste, weaken, wilt, wither **2.** Often with **for** desire, hanker, hunger, long, pine, sigh, want, yearn **3.** be abandoned, be disregarded, be neglected, rot, suffer, waste away **4.** brood, despond, grieve, repine, sorrow

languishing 1. declining, deteriorating, drooping, droopy, fading, failing, flagging, sickening, sinking, wasting away, weak, weakening, wilting, withering **2.** dreamy, longing, lovelorn, lovesick, melancholic, nostalgic, pensive, pining, soulful, tender, wistful, woebegone, yearning

lank 1. dull, lifeless, limp, long, lustreless, straggling **2.** attenuated, emaciated, gaunt, lanky, lean, rawboned, scraggy, scrawny, skinny, slender, slim, spare, thin

lanky angular, bony, gangling, gaunt, loose-jointed, rangy, rawboned, scraggy, scrawny, spare, tall, thin, weedy (Inf.)

lap[1] **1.** n. circle, circuit, course, distance, loop, orbit, round, tour **2.** v. cover, enfold, envelop, fold, swaddle, swathe, turn, twist, wrap

lap[2] **1.** gurgle, plash, purl, ripple, slap, splash, swish, wash **2.** drink, lick, sip, sup

norm. **8.** to decline gradually or fall in status, condition, etc. **9.** to be discontinued, esp. through negligence or other failure. **10.** (usually foll. by *into*) to drift or slide (into a condition): *to lapse into sleep.* **11.** (often foll. by *from*) to turn away (from beliefs or norms). **12.** (of time) to slip away. —**'lapsable** *or* **'lapsible** *adj.* —**'lapser** *n.*

lap up *vb.* (*tr., adv.*) *Inf.* **1.** to eat or drink. **2.** to relish or delight in: *he laps up horror films.* **3.** to believe or accept uncritically: *he laps up stories.*

lapwing ('læp,wɪŋ) *n.* any of several plovers, typically having a crested head, wattles, and spurs. Also called: **green plover, peewit.**

larboard ('lɑːbəd) *n., adj. Naut.* a former word for **port**².

larceny ('lɑːsɪnɪ) *n., pl.* **-nies.** *Law.* (formerly) a technical word for **theft.** —**'larcenist** *or* **'larcener** *n.* —**'larcenous** *adj.*

larch (lɑːtʃ) *n.* **1.** any coniferous tree having deciduous needle-like leaves and egg-shaped cones. **2.** the wood of any of these trees.

lard (lɑːd) *n.* **1.** the rendered fat from a pig, used in cooking. ~*vb.* (*tr.*) **2.** to prepare (lean meat, poultry, etc.) by inserting small strips of bacon or fat before cooking. **3.** to cover or smear (foods) with lard. **4.** to add extra material to (speech or writing); embellish. —**'lardy** *adj.*

larder ('lɑːdə) *n.* a room or cupboard, used as a store for food.

lardy cake ('lɑːdɪ) *n. Brit.* a rich sweet cake made of bread dough, lard, sugar, and dried fruit.

lares and penates ('lɛərɪːz, 'lɑː-; pə'nɑːtiːz) *pl. n.* **1.** *Roman myth.* **a.** household gods. **b.** statues of these gods kept in the home. **2.** the valued possessions of a household.

large (lɑːdʒ) *adj.* **1.** having a relatively great size, quantity, extent, etc.; big. **2.** of wide or broad scope, capacity, or range; comprehensive. **3.** having or showing great breadth of understanding. ~*n.* **4. at large. a.** (esp. of a dangerous criminal or wild animal) free; not confined. **b.** roaming freely, as in a foreign country. **c.** as a whole; in general. **d.** in full detail; exhaustively. **e.** *U.S.* representing or assigned to a state, district, or nation: *an ambassador at large.* —**'largeness** *n.*

large intestine *n.* the part of the alimentary canal consisting of the caecum, colon, and rectum.

largely ('lɑːdʒlɪ) *adv.* **1.** principally; to a great extent. **2.** on a large scale or in a large manner.

large-scale *adj.* **1.** wide-ranging or extensive. **2.** (of maps and models) constructed or drawn to a big scale.

largess *or* **largesse** (lɑː'dʒes) *n.* **1.** the generous bestowal of gifts, favours, or money. **2.** the things so bestowed. **3.** generosity of spirit or attitude.

largish ('lɑːdʒɪʃ) *adj.* fairly large.

largo ('lɑːgəʊ) *Music.* ~*adj., adv.* **1.** to be performed slowly and broadly. ~*n., pl.* **-gos.** **2.** a piece or passage to be performed in this way.

lariat ('lærɪət) *n. U.S.* **1.** another word for **lasso** (sense 1). **2.** a rope for tethering animals.

lark¹ (lɑːk) *n.* any brown bird of a predominantly Old World family of songbirds, esp. the skylark: noted for their singing.

lark² (lɑːk) *Inf.* ~*n.* **1.** a carefree adventure or frolic. **2.** a harmless piece of mischief. ~*vb.* **3.** (*intr.; often* foll. by *about*) to have a good time by frolicking. **4.** (*intr.*) to play a prank. —**'larkish** *or* **'larky** *adj.*

larkspur ('lɑːk,spɜː) *n.* any of various plants related to the delphinium, with spikes of blue, pink, or white irregular spurred flowers.

larrigan ('lærɪgən) *n.* a knee-high oiled leather moccasin boot worn by trappers, etc.

larrikin ('lærɪkɪn) *n. Austral. & N.Z. sl.* **a.** a hooligan. **b.** (*as modifier*): *a larrikin bloke.*

larva ('lɑːvə) *n., pl.* **-vae** (-viː). an immature free-living form of many animals that develops into a different adult form by metamorphosis. —**'larval** *adj.*

laryngeal (,lærɪn'dʒiːəl, lə'rɪndʒɪəl) *or* **laryngal** (lə'rɪŋgəl) *adj.* **1.** of or relating to the larynx. **2.** *Phonetics.* articulated at the larynx; glottal.

laryngitis (,lærɪn'dʒaɪtɪs) *n.* inflammation of the larynx. —**laryngitic** (,lærɪn'dʒɪtɪk) *adj.*

laryngo- *or before a vowel* **laryng-** *combining form.* indicating the larynx: *laryngoscope.*

larynx ('lærɪŋks) *n., pl.* **larynges** (lə'rɪndʒiːz) *or* **larynxes.** a cartilaginous and muscular hollow organ forming part of the air passage to the lungs: in higher vertebrates it contains the vocal cords.

lasagne *or* **lasagna** (lə'zænjə, -'sæn-) *n.* **1.** a form of pasta consisting of wide flat sheets. **2.** any of several dishes made from layers of lasagne and meat, cheese, etc.

lascar ('læskə) *n.* a sailor from the East Indies.

lascivious (lə'sɪvɪəs) *adj.* **1.** lustful; lecherous. **2.** exciting sexual desire. —**las'civiously** *adv.* —**las'civiousness** *n.*

laser ('leɪzə) *n.* **1.** Also called: **optical maser.** a device for converting light of mixed frequencies into an intense narrow monochromatic beam of coherent light. **2.** any similar device for producing a beam of any electromagnetic radiation, such as infrared or microwave radiation.

lash¹ (læʃ) *n.* **1.** a sharp cutting blow from a whip or other flexible object. **2.** the flexible end or ends of a whip. **3.** a cutting or hurtful blow to the feelings, as one caused by ridicule or scolding. **4.** a forceful beating or impact, as of wind, rain, or waves against something. **5. have a lash (at).** *Austral. & N.Z. inf.* to make an attempt at or take part in (something). **6.** See **eyelash.** ~*vb.* (*tr.*) **7.** to hit (a person or thing) sharply with a whip, rope, etc., esp, formerly, as punishment. **8.** (of wind, waves, etc.) to beat forcefully against. **9.** to attack with words, ridicule, etc. **10.** to flick or wave sharply to and fro: *the panther lashed his tail.* **11.** to urge or drive as with a whip: *to lash the audience into a violent mood.* —**'lasher** *n.*

lash² (læʃ) *vb.* (*tr.*) to bind or secure with rope, string, etc.

lashing¹ ('læʃɪŋ) *n.* **1.** a whipping; flogging. **2.** a scolding. **3.** (*pl.; usually* foll. by *of*) *Brit. inf.* large amounts; lots.

lashing² ('læʃɪŋ) *n.* rope, cord, etc., used for binding or securing.

lash out *vb.* (*intr., adv.*) **1.** to burst into or resort to verbal or physical attack. **2.** *Inf.* to be extravagant, as in spending.

lash-up ('læʃ,ʌp) *n.* a temporary connection of equip-

THESAURUS

lapse *n.* **1.** error, failing, fault, indiscretion, mistake, negligence, omission, oversight, slip **2.** break, gap, intermission, interruption, interval, lull, passage, pause **3.** backsliding, decline, descent, deterioration, drop, fall, relapse ~*v.* **4.** decline, degenerate, deteriorate, drop, fail, fall, sink, slide, slip **5.** become obsolete, become void, end, expire, run out, stop, terminate

lapsed 1. discontinued, ended, expired, finished, invalid, out of date, run out, unrenewed **2.** backsliding, lacking faith, nonpractising

larceny burglary, misappropriation, pilfering, purloining, robbery, stealing, theft

large 1. big, bulky, colossal, considerable, enormous, giant, gigantic, goodly, great, huge, immense, jumbo (*Inf.*), king-size, mansize, massive, monumental, sizable, substantial, tidy (*Inf.*), vast **2.** abundant, ample, broad, capacious, comprehensive, copious, extensive, full, generous, grand, grandiose, liberal, plentiful, roomy, spacious, sweeping, wide **3. at large a.** at liberty, free, on the loose, on the run, roaming, unconfined **b.** as a whole, chiefly, generally, in general, in the main, mainly **c.** at length, considerably, exhaustively, greatly, in full detail

largely as a rule, by and large, chiefly, considerably, extensively, generally, mainly, mostly, predominantly, primarily, principally, to a great extent, widely

large-scale broad, extensive, far-reaching, global, sweeping, vast, wholesale, wide, wide-ranging

largess 1. alms-giving, benefaction, bounty, charity, generosity, liberality, munificence, open-handedness, philanthropy **2.** bequest, bounty, donation, endowment, gift, grant, present

lark 1. *n.* antic, caper, escapade, fling, frolic, fun, gambol, game, jape, mischief, prank, revel, rollick, romp, skylark, spree **2.** *v.* caper, cavort, cut capers, frolic, gambol, have fun, make mischief, play, rollick, romp, sport

lash¹ **1.** *n.* blow, hit, stripe, stroke, swipe (*Inf.*) ~*v.* **2.** beat, birch, chastise, flagellate, flog, horsewhip, lam (*Sl.*), scourge, thrash, whip **3.** beat, buffet, dash, drum, hammer, hit, knock, larrup (*Dialect*), pound, smack, strike **4.** attack, belabour, berate, castigate, censure, criticize, flay, lambaste, lampoon, ridicule, satirize, scold, tear into (*Inf.*), upbraid

lash² bind, fasten, join, make fast, rope, secure, strap, tie

lass bird (*Sl.*), chick (*Sl.*), colleen (*Irish*), damsel, girl, lassie (*Scot.*), maid, maiden, miss, schoolgirl, young woman

ment for experimental or emergency use.

lass (læs) *n.* a girl or young woman.

Lassa fever ('læsə) *n.* a serious viral disease of Central West Africa, characterized by high fever and muscular pains.

lassie ('læsɪ) *n. Inf.* a little lass; girl.

lassitude ('læsɪˌtjuːd) *n.* physical or mental weariness.

lasso (læ'suː, 'læsəʊ) *n., pl.* **-sos** *or* **-soes.** 1. a long rope or thong with a running noose at one end, used (esp. in America) for roping horses, cattle, etc.; lariat. ~*vb.* **-soing, -soed.** 2. (*tr.*) to catch as with a lasso. —**las'soer** *n.*

last[1] (lɑːst) *adj.* (*often prenominal*) 1. being, happening, or coming at the end or after all others: *the last horse in the race.* 2. being or occurring just before the present; most recent: *last Thursday.* 3. only remaining: *one's last cigarette.* 4. most extreme; utmost. 5. least suitable, appropriate, or likely: *he was the last person I would have chosen.* 6. (esp. relating to the end of a person's life or of the world) final or ultimate: *last rites.* ~*adv.* 7. after all others; at or in the end: *he came last.* 8. most recently: *he was last seen in the mountains.* 9. (*sentence modifier*) as the last or latest item. ~*n.* 10. the **last. a.** a person or thing that is last. **b.** the final moment; end. 11. one's last moments before death. 12. the final appearance, mention, or occurrence: *we've seen the last of him.* 13. **at last.** in the end; finally. 14. **at long last.** finally, after difficulty, delay, or irritation.

last[2] (lɑːst) *vb.* 1. (when *intr.*, often foll. by *for*) to remain in being (for a length of time); continue: *his hatred lasted for several years.* 2. to be sufficient for the needs of (a person) for (a length of time): *it will last us until Friday.* 3. (when *intr.*, often foll. by *for*) to remain fresh, uninjured, or unaltered (for a certain time). —**'laster** *n.*

last[3] (lɑːst) *n.* 1. the wooden or metal form on which a shoe or boot is fashioned or repaired. ~*vb.* 2. (*tr.*) to fit (a shoe or boot) on a last. —**'laster** *n.*

last-ditch *n.* (*modifier*) made or done as a last desperate effort in the face of opposition.

lasting ('lɑːstɪŋ) *adj.* permanent or enduring. —**'lastingly** *adv.* —**'lastingness** *n.*

Last Judgment *n.* **the.** the occasion, after the resurrection of the dead at the end of the world, when, according to biblical tradition, God will decree the final destinies of all men according to the good and evil in their earthly lives. Also called: **the Last Day, Doomsday, Judgment Day.**

lastly ('lɑːstlɪ) *adv.* 1. at the end or at the last point. ~*sentence connector.* 2. finally.

last name *n.* another term for **surname.**

last out *vb.* (*intr., adv.*) 1. to be sufficient for one's needs: *how long will our supplies last out?* 2. to endure or survive: *some old people don't last out the winter.*

last post *n.* (in the British military services) 1. a bugle call that orders men to retire for sleep. 2. a similar call sounded at military funerals.

last rites *pl. n. Christianity.* religious rites prescribed for those close to death.

last straw *n.* **the.** the final irritation or problem that stretches one's endurance or patience beyond the limit.

lat. *abbrev. for* latitude.

Lat. *abbrev. for* Latin.

latch (lætʃ) *n.* 1. a fastening for a gate or door that consists of a bar that may be slid or lowered into a groove, hole, etc. 2. a spring-loaded door lock that can be opened by a key from outside. 3. Also called: **latch circuit.** *Electronics.* a logic circuit that transfers the input states to the output states when signalled. ~*vb.* 4. to fasten, fit, or be fitted as with a latch.

latchkey child ('lætʃˌkiː) *n.* a child who has to let himself in at home on returning from school, as his parents are out at work.

latch on *vb.* (*intr., adv.; often foll. by to*) 1. to attach oneself (to). 2. to understand.

late (leɪt) *adj.* 1. occurring or arriving after the correct or expected time: *the train was late.* 2. (*prenominal*) occurring at, scheduled for, or being at a relatively advanced time: *a late marriage.* 3. (*prenominal*) towards or near the end: *the late evening.* 4. at an advanced time in the evening or at night: *it was late.* 5. (*prenominal*) occurring or being just previous to the present time: *his late remarks on industry.* 6. (*prenominal*) having died, esp. recently: *my late grandfather.* 7. (*prenominal*) just preceding the present or existing person or thing; former: *the late manager of this firm.* 8. **of late.** recently; lately. ~*adv.* 9. after the correct or expected time: *he arrived late.* 10. at a relatively advanced age: *she married late.* 11. recently; lately: *as late as yesterday he was selling books.* 12. **late in the day. a.** at a late or advanced stage. **b.** too late. —**'lateness** *n.*

lateen (lə'tiːn) *adj. Naut.* denoting a rig with a triangular sail (**lateen sail**) bent to a yard hoisted to the head of a low mast, used esp. in the Mediterranean.

Late Greek *n.* the Greek language from about the 3rd to the 8th centuries A.D.

Late Latin *n.* the form of written Latin used from the 3rd to the 7th centuries A.D.

lately ('leɪtlɪ) *adv.* in recent times; of late.

latent ('leɪt³nt) *adj.* 1. potential but not obvious or explicit. 2. (of buds, spores, etc.) dormant. 3. *Pathol.* (esp. of an infectious disease) not yet revealed or manifest. —**'latency** *n.* —**'latently** *adv.*

later ('leɪtə) *adj., adv.* 1. the comparative of **late.** ~*adv.* 2. afterwards; subsequently.

lateral ('læt³rəl) *adj.* 1. of or relating to the side or sides: *a lateral blow.* ~*n.* 2. a lateral object, part, passage, or movement. —**'laterally** *adv.*

lateral thinking *n.* a way of solving problems by employing unorthodox and apparently illogical means.

latest ('leɪtɪst) *adj., adv.* 1. the superlative of **late.** ~*adj.* 2. most recent, modern, or new: *the latest fashions.* ~*n.* 3. **at the latest.** no later than the time specified. 4. **the latest.** *Inf.* the most recent fashion or development.

latex ('leɪtɛks) *n., pl.* **latexes** *or* **latices** ('læti,siːz). 1. a whitish milky fluid containing protein, starch, alkaloids, etc., that is produced by many plants. Latex from the rubber tree is used in the manufacture of rubber. 2. a suspension of synthetic rubber or plastic in water, used in the manufacture of synthetic rubber products, etc.

lath (lɑːθ) *n., pl.* **laths** (lɑːðz, lɑːθs). 1. one of several thin narrow strips of wood used to provide a supporting framework for plaster, tiles, etc. 2. expanded sheet metal, wire mesh, etc., used to provide backing for plaster or rendering. 3. any thin strip of wood. ~*vb.* 4. (*tr.*) to attach laths to (a ceiling, roof, floor, etc.).

lathe (leɪð) *n.* 1. a machine for shaping or boring metal, wood, etc., in which the workpiece is turned about a horizontal axis against a fixed tool. ~*vb.* 2. (*tr.*) to shape or

---

THESAURUS

last[1] *adj.* 1. aftermost, at the end, hindmost, rearmost 2. latest, most recent 3. closing, concluding, extreme, final, furthest, remotest, terminal, ultimate, utmost ~*adv.* 4. after, behind, bringing up the rear, in or at the end, in the rear ~*n.* 5. close, completion, conclusion, end, ending, finale, finish, termination 6. **at last** at length, eventually, finally, in conclusion, in the end, ultimately

last[2] *v.* abide, carry on, continue, endure, hold on, hold out, keep, keep on, persist, remain, stand up, survive, wear

last-ditch all-out (*Inf.*), desperate, final, frantic, heroic, straining, struggling

lasting abiding, continuing, deep-rooted, durable, enduring, indelible, lifelong, longstanding, long-term, perennial, permanent, perpetual, unceasing, undying, unending

lastly after all, all in all, at last, finally, in conclusion, in the end, to conclude, to sum up, ultimately

last word, the 1. final say, finis, summation, ultimatum 2. best, cream, *crème de la crème*, crown, epitome, *ne plus ultra*, perfection, quintessence, ultimate 3. *dernier cri*, fashion, latest, newest, rage, vogue

latch 1. *n.* bar, bolt, catch, clamp, fastening, hasp, hook, lock, sneck (*Dialect*) 2. *v.* bar, bolt, fasten, lock, make fast, secure, sneck (*Dialect*)

late *adj.* 1. behind, behindhand, belated, delayed, last-minute, overdue, slow, tardy, unpunctual 2. advanced, fresh, modern, new, recent 3. dead, deceased, defunct, departed, ex-, former, old, past, preceding, previous ~*adv.* 4. at the last minute, behindhand, behind time, belatedly, dilatorily, slowly, tardily, unpunctually

lately in recent times, just now, latterly, not long ago, of late, recently

lateness advanced hour, belatedness, delay, late date, retardation, tardiness, unpunctuality

later *adv.* after, afterwards, by and by, in a while, in time, later on, next, subsequently, thereafter

lateral edgeways, flanking, side, sideward, sideways

latest *adj.* current, fashionable, in, modern, most recent, newest, now, up-to-date, up-to-the-minute, with it (*Inf.*)

bore (a workpiece) on a lathe.

lather ('lɑːðə) *n.* **1.** foam formed by the action of soap or a detergent in water. **2.** foam formed by other liquid, such as the saliva of a horse. **3.** *Inf.* a state of agitation. ~*vb.* **4.** to coat or become coated with lather. **5.** (*intr.*) to form a lather. **6.** (*tr.*) *Inf.* to beat; flog. —**'lathery** *adj.*

Latin ('lætɪn) *n.* **1.** the language of ancient Rome and the Roman Empire and of the educated in medieval Europe. Having originally been the language of Latium in W central Italy, belonging to the Italic branch of the Indo-European family, it later formed the basis of the Romance group. **2.** a member of any of those peoples whose languages are derived from Latin. **3.** an inhabitant of ancient Latium. ~*adj.* **4.** of or relating to the Latin language, the ancient Latins, or Latium. **5.** characteristic of or relating to those peoples whose languages are derived from Latin. **6.** of or relating to the Roman Catholic Church.

Latinate ('lætɪˌneɪt) *adj.* (of writing vocabulary, etc.) imitative of or derived from Latin.

latish ('leɪtɪʃ) *adj.* rather late.

latitude ('lætɪˌtjuːd) *n.* **1. a.** an angular distance measured in degrees north or south of the equator (latitude 0°). **b.** (*often pl.*) a region considered with regard to its distance from the equator. **2.** scope for freedom of action, thought, etc.; freedom from restriction: *his parents gave him a great deal of latitude.* —ˌlati'tudinal *adj.* —ˌlati'tudinally *adv.*

latitudinarian (ˌlætɪˌtjuːdɪ'nɛərɪən) *adj.* **1.** permitting or marked by freedom of attitude or behaviour, esp. in religious matters. ~*n.* **2.** a person with latitudinarian views. —ˌlati,tudi'narianism *n.*

latrine (lə'triːn) *n.* a lavatory, as in a barracks, camp, etc.

-latry *n. combining form.* indicating worship of or excessive veneration of: *idolatry; Mariolatry.* —**-latrous** *adj. combining form.*

latter ('lætə) *adj.* (*prenominal*) **1. a.** denoting the second or second mentioned of two: distinguished from *former.* **b.** (*as n.; functioning as sing. or pl.*): *the latter is not important.* **2.** near or nearer the end: *the latter part of a film.* **3.** more advanced in time or sequence; later.
▷ *Usage.* In careful usage, *latter* is used when only two items are in question: *he gave the money to Christopher and not to John, the latter being less in need of it. Last-named* is used to refer to the last-named of three or more items.

latter-day *adj.* present-day; modern.

latterly ('lætəlɪ) *adv.* recently; lately.

lattice ('lætɪs) *n.* **1.** Also called: **latticework.** an open framework of strips of wood, metal, etc., arranged to form an ornamental pattern. **2. a.** a gate, screen, etc., formed of such a framework. **b.** (*as modifier*): *a lattice window.* **3.** something, such as a decorative or heraldic device, resembling such a framework. **4.** an array of objects or points in a periodic pattern in two or three dimensions, esp. an array of atoms, ions, etc., in a crystal or an array of points indicating their positions in space. ~*vb.* **5.** to make, adorn, or supply with a lattice or lattices. —**'latticed** *adj.*

laud (lɔːd) *Literary.* ~*vb.* **1.** (*tr.*) to praise or glorify. ~*n.* **2.** praise or glorification.

laudable ('lɔːdəbəl) *adj.* deserving or worthy of praise; admirable; commendable. —**'laudableness** *or* ˌlauda'bility *n.* —**'laudably** *adv.*

laudanum ('lɔːdənəm) *n.* **1.** a tincture of opium. **2.** (formerly) any medicine of which opium was the main ingredient.

laudatory ('lɔːdətərɪ, -trɪ) *or* **laudative** *adj.* expressing or containing praise; eulogistic.

laugh (lɑːf) *vb.* **1.** (*intr.*) to express or manifest emotion, esp. mirth or amusement, typically by expelling air from the lungs in short bursts to produce an inarticulate voiced noise, with the mouth open. **2.** (*intr.*) (esp. of certain mammals or birds) to make a noise resembling a laugh. **3.** (*tr.*) to utter or express with laughter: *he laughed his derision at the play.* **4.** (*tr.*) to bring or force (someone, esp. oneself) into a certain condition by laughter: *he laughed himself sick.* **5.** (*intr.;* foll. by *at*) to make fun (of); jeer (at). **6. laugh up one's sleeve.** to laugh or have grounds for amusement, self-satisfaction, etc., secretly. **7. laugh on the other side of one's face.** to show sudden disappointment or shame after appearing cheerful or confident. ~*n.* **8.** the act or an instance of laughing. **9.** a manner of laughter. **10.** *Inf.* a person or thing that causes laughter: *that holiday was a laugh.* **11. the last laugh.** the final success in an argument, situation, etc., after previous defeat. —**'laugher** *n.* —**'laughingly** *adv.*

laughable ('lɑːfəbəl) *adj.* **1.** producing scorn; ludicrous: *he offered me a laughable sum for the picture.* **2.** arousing laughter. —**'laughableness** *n.* —**'laughably** *adv.*

laughing gas *n.* another name for **nitrous oxide.**

laughing stock *n.* an object of humiliating ridicule.

laugh off *vb.* (*tr., adv.*) to treat or dismiss lightly, esp. with stoicism.

laughter ('lɑːftə) *n.* **1.** the action of or noise produced by laughing. **2.** the experience or manifestation of mirth, amusement, scorn, or joy.

launch[1] (lɔːntʃ) *vb.* **1.** to move (a vessel) into the water. **2.** to move (a newly built vessel) into the water for the first time. **3.** (*tr.*) to start off or set in motion: *to launch a scheme.* **4.** (*tr.*) to propel with force. **5.** to involve (oneself) totally and enthusiastically: *to launch oneself into work.* **6.** (*tr.*) to set (a missile, spacecraft, etc.) into motion. **7.** (*intr.;* foll. by *into*) to start talking or writing (about): *he launched into a story.* **8.** (*intr.;* usually foll. by *out*) to start (out) on a fresh course. ~*n.* **9.** an act or instance of launching. —**'launcher** *n.*

launch[2] (lɔːntʃ) *n.* **1.** a motor driven boat used chiefly as a transport boat. **2.** the largest of the boats of a man-of-war.

launching pad *or* **launch pad** *n.* a platform from which a spacecraft, rocket, etc., is launched.

launder ('lɔːndə) *vb.* **1.** to wash and often also to iron (clothes, linen, etc.). **2.** (*tr.*) *Chiefly U.S. sl.* to make (money illegally obtained) appear to be legally gained by passing it through foreign banks or legitimate enterprises. —**'launderer** *n.*

Launderette (ˌlɔːndə'rɛt, lɔːn'drɛt) *or* *U.S., Austral., & N.Z.* **Laundromat** ('lɔːndrəˌmæt) *n. Trademark.* a commercial establishment where clothes can be washed and dried, using coin-operated machines.

laundress ('lɔːndrɪs) *n.* a woman who launders clothes,

═══ THESAURUS ═══

lather *n.* **1.** bubbles, foam, froth, soap, soapsuds, suds **2.** *Inf.* dither, fever, flap (*Inf.*), fluster, fuss, pother, state (*Inf.*), stew (*Inf.*), sweat, tizzy (*Inf.*), twitter ~*v.* **3.** foam, froth, soap **4.** *Inf.* beat, cane, drub, flog, lambaste, strike, thrash, whip

lathery bubbly, foamy, frothy, soapy, sudsy

latitude **1.** breadth, compass, extent, range, reach, room, scope, space, span, spread, sweep, width **2.** elbowroom, freedom, indulgence, laxity, leeway, liberty, licence, play, unrestrictedness

latter closing, concluding, last, last-mentioned, later, latest, modern, recent, second

latterly hitherto, lately, of late, recently

lattice fretwork, grating, grid, grille, latticework, mesh, network, openwork, reticulation, tracery, trellis, web

laudable admirable, commendable, creditable, estimable, excellent, meritorious, of note, praiseworthy, worthy

laudatory acclamatory, adulatory, approbatory, approving, commendatory, complimentary, eulogistic, panegyrical

laugh *v.* **1.** be convulsed (*Inf.*), be in stitches, chortle, chuckle, crease up (*Inf.*), giggle, guffaw, roar with laughter, snigger, split one's sides, titter **2. laugh at** belittle, deride, jeer, lampoon, make a mock of, make fun of, mock, ridicule, scoff at, take the mickey (out of) (*Inf.*), taunt ~*n.* **3.** belly laugh (*Inf.*), chortle, chuckle, giggle, guffaw, roar or shriek of laughter, snigger, titter **4.** *Inf.* card (*Inf.*), caution (*Inf.*), clown, comedian, comic, entertainer, hoot (*Inf.*), humorist, joke, lark, scream (*Inf.*), wag, wit

laughable **1.** absurd, derisive, derisory, ludicrous, nonsensical, preposterous, ridiculous, worthy of scorn **2.** amusing, comical, diverting, droll, farcical, funny, hilarious, humorous, mirthful, risible

laughing stock Aunt Sally (*Brit.*), butt, everybody's fool, fair game, figure of fun, target, victim

laugh off brush aside, dismiss, disregard, ignore, minimize, pooh-pooh, shrug off

laughter **1.** cachinnation, chortling, chuckling, giggling, guffawing, laughing, tittering **2.** amusement, glee, hilarity, merriment, mirth

launch **1.** cast, discharge, dispatch, fire, project, propel, send off, set afloat, set in motion, throw **2.** begin, commence, embark upon, inaugurate, initiate, instigate, introduce, open, start

sheets, etc., for a living.

laundry ('lɔːndrɪ) *n., pl.* **-dries. 1.** a place where clothes and linen are washed and ironed. **2.** the clothes or linen washed and ironed. **3.** the act of laundering.

laureate ('lɔːrɪɪt) *adj.* (*usually immediately postpositive*) **1.** *Literary.* crowned with laurel leaves as a sign of honour. ~*n.* **2.** short for **poet laureate. 3.** *Rare.* a person honoured with the laurel crown or wreath. —'**laureate,ship** *n.*

laurel ('lɒrəl) *n.* **1.** Also called: **bay, bay laurel, sweet bay, true laurel.** a small Mediterranean evergreen tree with glossy aromatic leaves, used for flavouring in cooking, and small blackish berries. **2.** a similar and related tree of the Canary Islands and Azores. **3. spurge laurel.** a European evergreen shrub, *Daphne laureola*, with glossy leaves and small green flowers. **4.** (*pl.*) a wreath of true laurel, worn on the head as an emblem of victory or honour in classical times. **5.** (*pl.*) honour, distinction, or fame. **6. look to one's laurels.** to be on guard against one's rivals. **7. rest on one's laurels.** to be satisfied with distinction won by past achievements. ~*vb.* **-relling, -relled** *or U.S.* **-reling, -reled. 8.** (*tr.*) to crown with laurels.

Laurentian (lɔː'rɛnʃən) *adj.* **1.** Also: **Lawrentian.** of or resembling the style of D. H. or T. E. Lawrence. **2.** of, relating to, or situated near the St. Lawrence River.

Laurentian Shield *n.* another name for the **Canadian Shield.** Also: **Laurentian Plateau.**

lav (læv) *n. Brit. inf.* short for **lavatory.**

lava ('lɑːvə) *n.* **1.** magma emanating from volcanoes. **2.** any extrusive igneous rock formed by the solidification of lava.

lavatory ('lævətərɪ, -trɪ) *n., pl.* **-ries. a.** a sanitary installation for receiving and disposing of urine and faeces, consisting of a bowl fitted with a water-flushing device and connected to a drain. **b.** a room containing such an installation. Also called: **toilet, water closet, W.C.**

lave (leɪv) *vb.* an archaic word for **wash.**

lavender ('lævəndə) *n.* **1.** any of various perennial shrubs or herbaceous plants of the labiate family, esp. *Lavandula vera*, cultivated for its mauve or blue flowers and as the source of a fragrant oil (**oil of lavender**). **2.** the dried parts of *L. vera*, used to perfume clothes. **3.** a pale or light bluish-purple colour. **4.** perfume scented with lavender.

lavish ('lævɪʃ) *adj.* **1.** prolific, abundant, or profuse. **2.** generous; unstinting; liberal. **3.** extravagant; prodigal; wasteful: *lavish expenditure.* ~*vb.* **4.** (*tr.*) to give, expend, or apply abundantly, generously, or in profusion. —'**lavisher** *n.* —'**lavishly** *adv.* —'**lavishness** *n.*

law (lɔː) *n.* **1.** a rule or set of rules instituted by act of Parliament, custom, or practice in order to punish those who offend the conventions of society. **2. a.** a rule or body of rules made by the legislature. See **statute law. b.** a rule or body of rules made by a municipal or other authority. See **bylaw. 3. a.** the condition and control enforced by such rules. **b.** (*in combination*): *lawcourt.* **4. law and order. a.** the policy of strict enforcement of the law, esp. against crime and violence. **b.** (*as modifier*): *law-and-order candidate. 5.* a code of conduct: *a law of etiquette.* **6.** one of a set of rules governing a particular field of activity: *the laws of tennis.* **7. the law. a.** the legal or judicial system. **b.** the profession or practice of law. **c.** *Inf.* the police or a policeman. **8.** Also called: **law of nature.** a generalization based on a recurring fact or event. **9.** the science or knowledge of law; jurisprudence. **10.** the principles originating and formerly applied only in courts of common law. Cf. **equity** (sense 3). **11.** a general principle, formula, or rule describing a phenomenon in mathematics, science, philosophy, etc.: *the laws of thermodynamics.* **12.** (*often cap.;* preceded by *the*) the body of laws contained in the first five books of the Old Testament. Also called: **Law of Moses. 13. go to law.** to resort to legal proceedings on some matter. **14. lay down the law.** to speak in an authoritative or dogmatic manner. ~Related adjs.: **judicial, juridical, legal.**

law-abiding *adj.* adhering more or less strictly to the laws: *a law-abiding citizen.*

law agent *n.* (in Scotland) a solicitor entitled to appear for a client in any Sheriff Court.

lawbreaker ('lɔː,breɪkə) *n.* a person who breaks the law. —'**law,breaking** *n., adj.*

lawful ('lɔːful) *adj.* allowed, recognized, or sanctioned by law; legal. —'**lawfully** *adv.* —'**lawfulness** *n.*

lawgiver ('lɔː,gɪvə) *n.* **1.** the giver of a code of laws. **2.** Also called: **lawmaker.** a maker of laws. —'**law,giving** *n., adj.*

lawless ('lɔːlɪs) *adj.* **1.** without law. **2.** disobedient to the law. **3.** contrary to or heedless of the law. **4.** uncontrolled; unbridled: *lawless rage.* —'**lawlessly** *adv.* —'**lawlessness** *n.*

lawn[1] (lɔːn) *n.* a flat and usually level area of mown and cultivated grass. —'**lawny** *adj.*

lawn[2] (lɔːn) *n.* a fine linen or cotton fabric, used for clothing. —'**lawny** *adj.*

lawn mower *n.* a hand-operated or power-operated machine for cutting grass on lawns.

lawn tennis *n.* **1.** tennis played on a grass court. **2.** the formal name for **tennis.**

lawrencium (lɒ'rɛnsɪəm) *n.* an element artificially produced from californium. Symbol: Lr; atomic no.: 103; half-life of most stable isotope, ^{256}Lr: 35 seconds.

lawsuit ('lɔː,suːt, -,sjuːt) *n.* a proceeding in a court of law brought by one party against another, esp. a civil action.

law term *n.* **1.** an expression or word used in law. **2.** any of various periods of time appointed for the sitting of law courts.

lawyer ('lɔːjə, 'lɔɪə) *n.* a member of the legal profession, esp. a solicitor.

lax (læks) *adj.* **1.** lacking firmness; not strict. **2.** lacking precision or definition. **3.** not taut. **4.** *Phonetics.* (of a speech sound) pronounced with little muscular effort. —'**laxly** *adv.* —'**laxity** *or* '**laxness** *n.*

laxative ('læksətɪv) *n.* **1.** an agent stimulating evacuation of faeces. ~*adj.* **2.** stimulating evacuation of faeces.

lay[1] (leɪ) *vb.* **laying, laid.** (*mainly tr.*) **1.** to put in a low or horizontal position; cause to lie: *to lay a cover on a bed.* **2.** to place, put, or be in a particular state or position: *he laid his finger on his lips.* **3.** (*intr.*) *Dialect or not standard.* to be in a horizontal position; lie: *he often lays in bed all the morning.* **4.** (sometimes foll. by *down*) to establish as a basis: *to lay a foundation for discussion.* **5.** to place or dispose in the proper position: *to lay a carpet.* **6.** to arrange (a table) for eating a meal. **7.** to prepare for lighting by placing fuel in the grate, etc.: *lay the fire.* **8.** (*also intr.*) (of birds, esp. the domestic hen) to produce (eggs). **9.** to present or put forward: *he laid his*

---

laurels acclaim, awards, bays, commendation, credit, distinction, fame, glory, honour, kudos, praise, prestige, recognition, renown, reward

lavatory bathroom, bog (*Brit. sl.*), can (*U.S. sl.*), cloakroom (*Brit.*), Gents, head(s) (*Nautical sl.*), john (*U.S. sl.*), Ladies, latrine, loo (*Brit. inf.*), powder room, (public) convenience, toilet, washroom, water closet, W.C.

lavish *adj.* **1.** abundant, copious, exuberant, lush, luxuriant, opulent, plentiful, profuse, prolific, sumptuous **2.** bountiful, effusive, free, generous, liberal, munificent, open-handed, unstinting **3.** exaggerated, excessive, extravagant, immoderate, improvident, intemperate, prodigal, thriftless, unreasonable, unrestrained, wasteful, wild ~*v.* **4.** deluge, dissipate, expend, heap, pour, shower, spend, squander, waste

law 1. charter, code, constitution, jurisprudence **2.** act, code, command, commandment, covenant, decree, edict, enactment, order, ordinance, rule, statute **3.** axiom, canon, criterion, formula, precept, principle, regulation, standard **4. lay down the law** dictate, dogmatize, emphasize, pontificate

law-abiding compliant, dutiful, good, honest, honourable, lawful, obedient, orderly, peaceable, peaceful

lawbreaker convict, criminal, crook (*Inf.*), culprit, delinquent, felon (*Formerly criminal law*), miscreant, offender, sinner, transgressor, trespasser, violater, wrongdoer

lawful allowable, authorized, constitutional, just, legal, legalized, legitimate, licit, permissible, proper, rightful, valid, warranted

lawless anarchic, chaotic, disorderly, insubordinate, insurgent, mutinous, rebellious, reckless, riotous, seditious, ungoverned, unrestrained, unruly, wild

lawsuit action, argument, case, cause, contest, dispute, litigation, proceedings, prosecution, suit, trial

lawyer advocate, attorney, barrister, counsel, counsellor, legal adviser, solicitor

lax 1. careless, casual, easy-going, lenient, neglectful, negligent, overindulgent, remiss, slack, slipshod **2.** broad, general, imprecise, inaccurate, indefinite, inexact, nonspecific, shapeless, vague **3.** flabby, flaccid, loose, slack, soft, yielding

case before the magistrate. **10.** to impute or attribute: *all the blame was laid on him.* **11.** to arrange, devise, or prepare: *to lay a trap.* **12.** to place, set, or locate: *the scene is laid in London.* **13.** to make (a bet) with (someone): *I lay you five to one on Prince.* **14.** to cause to settle: *to lay the dust.* **15.** to allay; suppress: *to lay a rumour.* **16.** to bring down forcefully: *to lay a whip on someone's back.* **17.** *Taboo sl.* to have sexual intercourse with. **18.** to press down or make smooth: *to lay the nap of cloth.* **19.** (*intr.*) *Naut.* to move or go, esp. into a specified position or direction: *to lay close to the wind.* **20. lay bare.** to reveal or explain: *he laid bare his plans.* **21. lay hands on.** See **hands.** **22. lay hold of.** to seize or grasp. **23. lay oneself open.** to make oneself vulnerable (to criticism, attack, etc.). **24. lay open.** to reveal or disclose. **25. lay siege to.** to besiege (a city, etc.). ~*n.* **26.** the manner or position in which something lies or is placed. **27.** *Taboo sl.* **a.** an act of sexual intercourse. **b.** a sexual partner. ~See also **layabout, lay aside,** etc.

▷ **Usage.** In careful English, the verb *lay* is used with an object and *lie* without one: *the soldier laid down his arms; the book was lying on the table.* In informal English, *lay* is frequently used for *lie: the book was laying on the table.*

lay² (leɪ) *vb.* the past tense of **lie².**

lay³ (leɪ) *adj.* **1.** of, involving, or belonging to people who are not clergymen. **2.** nonprofessional; amateur.

lay⁴ (leɪ) *n.* **1.** a ballad or short narrative poem, esp. one intended to be sung. **2.** a song or melody.

layabout (ˈleɪəˌbaʊt) *n.* a lazy person; loafer.

lay aside *vb.* (*tr., adv.*) **1.** to abandon or reject. **2.** to store or reserve for future use.

lay-by *n.* **1.** *Brit.* a place for drivers to stop at the side of a main road. **2.** *Naut.* an anchorage in a narrow waterway, away from the channel. **3.** a small railway siding where rolling stock may be stored or parked. **4.** *Chiefly Austral. & N.Z.* a system of payment whereby a buyer pays a deposit on an article, which is reserved for him until he has paid the full price. ~*vb.* **lay by** (*tr., adv.*) **5.** to set aside or save for future needs.

lay down *vb.* (*tr., adv.*) **1.** to place on the ground, etc. **2.** to relinquish or discard: *to lay down one's life.* **3.** to formulate (a rule, principle, etc.). **4.** to build or begin to build: *the railway was laid down as far as Chester.* **5.** to record (plans) on paper. **6.** to convert (land) into pasture. **7.** to store or stock: *to lay down wine.* **8.** *Inf.* to wager or bet.

layer (ˈleɪə) *n.* **1.** a thickness of some homogeneous substance, such as a stratum or a coating on a surface. **2.** a laying hen. **3.** *Horticulture.* a shoot or branch rooted during layering. ~*vb.* **4.** to form or make a layer of (something). **5.** to take root or cause to take root by layering.

layette (leɪˈɛt) *n.* a complete set of articles, including clothing, bedclothes, and other accessories, for a newborn baby.

lay figure *n.* **1.** an artist's jointed dummy, used in place of a live model, esp. for studying effects of dra-

pery. **2.** a person considered to be subservient or unimportant.

lay in *vb.* (*tr., adv.*) to accumulate and store: *we must lay in food for the party.*

lay into *vb.* (*intr., prep.*) **1.** to attack forcefully. **2.** to berate severely.

layman (ˈleɪmən) *or* (*fem.*) **laywoman** *n., pl.* -**men** *or* -**women.** **1.** a person who is not a clergyman. **2.** a person who does not have specialized or professional knowledge of a subject: *science for the layman.*

lay off *vb.* **1.** (*tr., adv.*) to dismiss from employment, esp. temporarily: *the firm had to lay off 100 men.* **2.** (*intr.*) *Inf.* to leave (a person, thing, or activity) alone: *lay off me, will you!* **3.** (*tr., adv.*) to mark off the boundaries of. ~*n.* **lay-off.** **4.** the act of dismissing employees. **5.** a period of imposed unemployment.

lay on *vb.* (*tr., adv.*) **1.** to provide or supply: *to lay on entertainment.* **2.** *Brit.* to install: *to lay on electricity.* **3. lay it on.** *Sl.* **a.** to exaggerate, esp. when flattering. **b.** to charge an exorbitant price. **c.** to punish or strike harshly.

lay out *vb.* (*tr., adv.*) **1.** to arrange or spread out. **2.** to prepare (a corpse) for burial. **3.** to plan or contrive. **4.** *Inf.* to spend (money), esp. lavishly. **5.** *Inf.* to knock unconscious. ~*n.* **layout.** **6.** the act of laying out. **7.** something laid out. **8.** the arrangement of written material, photographs, or other artwork on an advertisement or page in a book, newspaper, etc. **9.** a preliminary plan indicating this. **10.** a drawing showing the relative disposition of parts in a machine, etc.

lay reader *n.* **1.** *Church of England.* a person licensed by a bishop to conduct religious services other than the Eucharist. **2.** *R.C. Church.* a layman chosen from among the congregation to read the epistle at Mass.

lay up *vb.* (*tr., adv.*) **1.** to store or reserve for future use. **2.** (*usually passive*) *Inf.* to incapacitate or confine through illness.

laze (leɪz) *vb.* **1.** (*intr.*) to be indolent or lazy. **2.** (*tr.; often foll. by* away) to spend (time) in indolence. ~*n.* **3.** the act or an instance of lazing.

lazy (ˈleɪzɪ) *adj.* -**zier,** -**ziest.** **1.** not inclined to work or exertion. **2.** conducive to or causing indolence. **3.** moving in a languid or sluggish manner: *a lazy river.* —**lazily** *adv.* —**laziness** *n.*

lazybones (ˈleɪzɪˌbəʊnz) *n.* *Inf.* a lazy person.

lb *or* **lb.** *abbrev. for* libra: pound (weight).

l.b.w. *Cricket. abbrev. for* leg before wicket.

l.c. *abbrev. for:* **1.** left centre (of a stage, etc.). **2.** loco citato: in the place cited. **3.** *Printing.* lower case.

l.c.d., lcd, L.C.D., *or* **LCD** *abbrev. for* lowest common denominator.

LCD *abbrev. for* liquid crystal display.

L.C.J. (in Britain) *abbrev. for* Lord Chief Justice.

l.c.m. *or* **L.C.M.** *abbrev. for* lowest common multiple.

L/Cpl. *abbrev. for* lance corporal.

L.D.S. *abbrev. for:* **1.** Latter-day Saints. **2.** Also **LDS** (in Britain) Licentiate in Dental Surgery.

THESAURUS

lay¹ 1. deposit, establish, leave, place, plant, posit, put, set, set down, settle, spread **2.** arrange, dispose, locate, organize, position, set out **3.** bear, deposit, produce **4.** advance, bring forward, lodge, offer, present, put forward, submit **5.** allocate, allot, ascribe, assign, attribute, charge, impute **6.** concoct, contrive, design, devise, hatch, plan, plot, prepare, work out **7.** apply, assess, burden, charge, encumber, impose, saddle, tax **8.** bet, gamble, give odds, hazard, risk, stake, wager **9.** allay, alleviate, appease, assuage, calm, quiet, relieve, soothe, still, suppress **10. lay bare** disclose, divulge, explain, expose, reveal, show, unveil **11. lay hands on a.** acquire, get, get hold of, grab, grasp, seize **b.** assault, attack, beat up, lay into, set on **c.** discover, find, unearth **d.** *Christianity* bless, confirm, consecrate, ordain **12. lay hold of** get, get hold of, grab, grasp, grip, seize, snatch

lay² **1.** laic, laical, nonclerical, secular **2.** amateur, inexpert, nonprofessional, nonspecialist

layabout beachcomber, good-for-nothing,

idler, laggard, loafer, lounger, ne'er-do-well, shirker, skiver (*Brit. sl.*), slubberdegullion (*Archaic*), vagrant, wastrel

lay aside abandon, cast aside, dismiss, postpone, put aside, put off, reject, shelve

lay down **1.** discard, drop, give, give up, relinquish, surrender, yield **2.** affirm, assume, establish, formulate, ordain, postulate, prescribe, stipulate

layer 1. bed, ply, row, seam, stratum, thickness, tier **2.** blanket, coat, coating, cover, covering, film, mantle, sheet

lay in accumulate, amass, build up, collect, hoard, stockpile, stock up, store (up)

lay into assail, attack, belabour, hit out at, lambaste, let fly at, pitch into, set about

layman amateur, lay person, nonprofessional, outsider

lay-off discharge, dismissal, unemployment

lay off 1. discharge, dismiss, drop, let go, make redundant, oust, pay off **2.** *Inf.* cease, desist, give it a rest (*Inf.*), give over (*Inf.*),

give up, leave alone, leave off, let up, quit, stop

lay on 1. cater (for), furnish, give, provide, supply **2. lay it on** *Sl.* butter up, exaggerate, flatter, overdo it, overpraise, soft-soap

layout arrangement, design, draft, formation, geography, outline, plan

lay out 1. arrange, design, display, exhibit, plan, spread out **2.** *Inf.* disburse, expend, fork out (*Sl.*), invest, pay, shell out (*Inf.*), spend **3.** *Inf.* kayo (*Sl.*), knock for six (*Inf.*), knock out, knock unconscious, KO (*Sl.*)

laziness dilatoriness, do-nothingness, faineance, faineancy, idleness, inactivity, indolence, lackadaisicalness, slackness, sloth, slothfulness, slowness, sluggishness, tardiness

lazy 1. idle, inactive, indolent, inert, remiss, shiftless, slack, slothful, slow, workshy **2.** drowsy, languid, languorous, lethargic, sleepy, slow-moving, sluggish, somnolent, torpid

lea (li:) *n.* **1.** *Poetic.* a meadow or field. **2.** land that has been sown with grass seed.

LEA (in Britain) *abbrev. for* Local Education Authority.

leach (li:tʃ) *vb.* **1.** to remove or be removed from a substance by a percolating liquid. **2.** to lose or cause to lose soluble substances by the action of a percolating liquid. ~*n.* **3.** the act or process of leaching. **4.** a substance that is leached or the constituents removed by leaching. **5.** a porous vessel for leaching. —**'leacher** *n.*

lead¹ (li:d) *vb.* **leading, led. 1.** to show the way to (an individual or a group) by going with or ahead: *lead the party into the garden.* **2.** to guide or be guided by holding, pulling, etc.: *he led the horse by its reins.* **3.** (*tr.*) to cause to act, feel, think, or behave in a certain way; induce; influence: *he led me to believe that he would go.* **4.** (when *intr.*, foll. by *to*) (of a road, route, etc.) to serve as the means of reaching a place. **5.** (*tr.*) to go ahead so as to indicate (esp. in **lead the way**). **6.** to guide, control, or direct: *to lead an army.* **7.** (*tr.*) to direct the course of or conduct (water, a rope, or wire, etc.) along or as if along a channel. **8.** to initiate the action of (something); have the principal part in (something): *to lead a discussion.* **9.** to go at the head of or have the top position in (something): *he leads his class in geography.* **10.** (*intr.*; foll. by *with*) to have as the first or principal item: *the newspaper led with the royal birth.* **11.** *Music. Brit.* to play first violin in (an orchestra). **12.** to direct and guide (one's partner) in a dance. **13.** (*tr.*) **a.** to pass or spend: *I lead a miserable life.* **b.** to cause to pass a life of a particular kind: *to lead a person a dog's life.* **14.** (*intr.*; foll. by *to*) to tend (to) or result (in): *this will only lead to misery.* **15.** to initiate a round of cards by putting down (the first card) or to have the right to do this: *she led a diamond.* **16.** (*intr.*) *Boxing.* to make an offensive blow, esp. as one's habitual attacking punch. ~*n.* **17. a.** the first, foremost, or most prominent place. **b.** (*as modifier*): *lead singer.* **18.** example, precedence, or leadership: *the class followed the teacher's lead.* **19.** an advance or advantage held over others: *the runner had a lead of twenty yards.* **20.** anything that guides or directs; indication; clue. **21.** another name for **leash. 22.** the act or prerogative of playing the first card in a round of cards or the card so played. **23.** the principal role in a play, film, etc., or the person playing such a role. **24. a.** the principal news story in a newspaper: *the scandal was the lead in the papers.* **b.** (*as modifier*): *lead story.* **25.** *Music.* an important entry assigned to one part. **26.** a wire, cable, or other conductor for making an electrical connection. **27.** *Boxing.* **a.** one's habitual attacking punch. **b.** a blow made with this. **28.** a deposit of metal or ore; lode. ~See also **lead off, lead on, lead up to.**

lead² (lɛd) *n.* **1.** a heavy toxic bluish-white metallic element that is highly malleable: used in alloys, accumulators, cable sheaths, paints, and as a radiation shield. Symbol: Pb; atomic no.: 82; atomic wt.: 207.2. **2.** a lead weight suspended on a line used to take soundings of the depth of water. **3.** lead weights or shot, as used in cartridges, fishing lines, etc. **4.** a thin grooved strip of lead for holding small panes of glass or pieces of stained glass. **5.** (*pl.*) **a.** thin sheets or strips of lead used as a roof covering. **b.** a flat or low-pitched roof covered with such sheets. **6.** Also called: **leading.** *Printing.* a thin strip of type metal used for spacing between lines. **7. a.** graphite used for drawing. **b.** a thin stick of this material, esp. the core of a pencil. **8.** (*modifier*) of, consisting of, relating to, or containing lead. ~*vb.* (*tr.*) **9.** to fill or treat with lead. **10.** to surround, cover, or secure with lead or leads. **11.** *Printing.* to space (type) by use of leads.

leaden ('lɛdən) *adj.* **1.** heavy and inert. **2.** laboured or sluggish: *leaden steps.* **3.** gloomy, spiritless, or lifeless. **4.** made partly or wholly of lead. **5.** of a dull greyish colour: *a leaden sky.* —**'leadenly** *adv.* —**'leadenness** *n.*

leader ('li:də) *n.* **1.** a person who rules, guides, or inspires others; head. **2.** *Music.* **a.** Also called (esp. U.S.): **concertmaster.** the principal first violinist of an orchestra, who plays solo parts, and acts as the conductor's deputy and spokesman for the orchestra. **b.** *U.S.* a conductor or director of an orchestra or chorus. **3.** the leading horse or dog in a team. **4.** *Chiefly Brit.* the leading editorial in a newspaper. Usual U.S. term: **leading article. 5.** *Angling.* another word for **trace²** (sense 2). **6.** a strip of blank film or tape used to facilitate threading a projector, developing machine, etc. **7.** (*pl.*) *Printing.* rows of dots or hyphens used to guide the reader's eye across a page, as in a table of contents. **8.** *Bot.* any of the long slender shoots that grow from the stem or branch of a tree. **9.** *Brit.* a member of the Government having primary authority in initiating legislative business (esp. in **Leader of the House of Commons** and **Leader of the House of Lords**). —**'leaderless** *adj.* —**'leader,ship** *n.*

lead-in ('li:d,ɪn) *n.* **1.** an introduction to a subject. **2.** the connection between a radio transmitter, receiver, etc., and the aerial or transmission line.

leading ('li:dɪŋ) *adj.* **1.** capable of guiding, directing, or influencing. **2.** (*prenominal*) principal or primary. **3.** in the first position. —**'leadingly** *adv.*

leading aircraftman ('li:dɪŋ) *n. Brit. airforce.* the rank above aircraftman. —**leading aircraftwoman** *fem. n.*

leading light ('li:dɪŋ) *n. Inf.* an important or outstanding person, esp. in an organization.

leading note ('li:dɪŋ) *n. Music.* **1.** another word for **subtonic. 2.** (esp. in cadences) a note that tends most naturally to resolve to the note lying one semitone above it.

leading question ('li:dɪŋ) *n.* a question phrased in a manner that tends to suggest the desired answer, such as *What do you think of the horrible effects of pollution?*

leading rating ('li:dɪŋ) *n.* a rank in the Royal Navy comparable but junior to that of a corporal in the army.

lead off (li:d) *vb.* (*adv.*) **1.** to initiate the action of (something); begin. ~*n.* **lead-off. 2.** an initial move or action.

lead on (li:d) *vb.* (*tr., adv.*) to lure or entice, esp. into trouble or wrongdoing.

lead pencil (lɛd) *n.* a pencil containing a thin stick of a graphite compound.

lead poisoning (lɛd) *n.* **1.** acute or chronic poisoning by lead, characterized by abdominal pain, vomiting, convulsions, and coma. **2.** *U.S. sl.* death or injury resulting from being shot with bullets.

lead time (li:d) *n.* **1.** *Manufacturing, chiefly U.S.* the time between the design of a product and its production. **2.** *Commerce.* the time from the placing of an order to the delivery of the goods.

lead up to (li:d) *vb.* (*intr., adv. + prep.*) **1.** to act as a preliminary or introduction to. **2.** to approach (a topic) gradually or cautiously.

leaf (li:f) *n., pl.* **leaves** (li:vz). **1.** the main organ of photosynthesis and transpiration in higher plants, usually consisting of a flat green blade attached to the stem directly or by a stalk. **2.** foliage collectively. **3. in leaf.** (of shrubs, trees, etc.) having a full complement of foliage leaves. **4.** one of the sheets of paper in a book. **5.** a hinged, sliding, or detachable part, such as an extension to a table. **6.** metal in the form of a very thin flexible

---

leach drain, extract, filter, filtrate, lixiviate (*Chem.*), percolate, seep, strain

lead *v.* **1.** conduct, escort, guide, pilot, precede, show the way, steer, usher **2.** cause, dispose, draw, incline, induce, influence, persuade, prevail, prompt **3.** command, direct, govern, head, manage, preside over, supervise **4.** be ahead (of), blaze a trail, come first, exceed, excel, outdo, outstrip, surpass, transcend **5.** experience, have, live, pass, spend, undergo **6.** bring on, cause, conduce, contribute, produce, result in, serve, tend ~*n.* **7.** advance, advantage, edge, first place, margin, precedence, primacy, priority, start, supremacy, van, vanguard **8.** direction, example, guidance, leadership, model **9.** clue, guide, hint, indication, suggestion, tip, trace **10.** leading role, principal, protagonist, star part, title role ~*adj.* **11.** chief, first, foremost, head, leading, main, most important, premier, primary, prime, principal

leader bellwether, boss (*Inf.*), captain, chief, chieftain, commander, conductor, counsellor, director, guide, head, number one, principal, ringleader, ruler, superior

leadership **1.** administration, direction, directorship, domination, guidance, management, running, superintendency **2.** authority, command, control, influence, initiative, pre-eminence, supremacy, sway

leading chief, dominant, first, foremost, governing, greatest, highest, main, number one, outstanding, pre-eminent, primary, principal, ruling, superior

lead on beguile, deceive, draw on, entice, inveigle, lure, seduce, string along (*Inf.*), tempt

lead up to approach, intimate, introduce, make advances, make overtures, pave the way, prepare for, prepare the way, work round to

sheet: *gold leaf*. **7. take a leaf out of** (*or* **from**) **someone's book.** to imitate someone, esp. in one particular course of action. **8. turn over a new leaf.** to change or resolve to improve one's behaviour. ~*vb*. **9.** (when *intr*., usually foll. by *through*) to turn (through pages, sheets, etc.) cursorily. **10.** (*intr*.) (of plants) to produce leaves. —'**leafless** *adj*. —'**leaf,like** *adj*.

leafage ('li:fɪdʒ) *n*. a less common word for **foliage**.

leaflet ('li:flɪt) *n*. **1.** a printed and usually folded sheet of paper for distribution, esp. for advertising. **2.** any of the subdivisions of a compound leaf such as a fern leaf. **3.** any small leaf or leaflike part. ~*vb*. **4.** (*intr*.) to distribute leaflets.

leaf mould *n*. **1.** a nitrogen-rich material consisting of decayed leaves, etc., used as a fertilizer. **2.** any of various fungus diseases affecting the leaves of certain plants.

leafy ('li:fɪ) *adj*. **leafier, leafiest. 1.** covered with or having leaves. **2.** resembling a leaf or leaves. —'**leafiness** *n*.

league[1] (li:g) *n*. **1.** an association or union of persons, nations, etc., formed to promote the interests of its members. **2.** an association of sporting clubs that organizes matches between member teams. **3.** a class, category, or level: *he is not in the same league*. **4. in league** (**with**). working or planning together with. **5.** (*modifier*) of, involving, or belonging to a league: *a league game; a league table*. ~*vb*. **leaguing, leagued. 6.** to form or be formed into a league.

league[2] (li:g) *n*. an obsolete unit of distance of varying length. It is commonly equal to 3 miles.

leak (li:k) *n*. **1. a.** a crack, hole, etc., that allows the accidental escape or entrance of fluid, light, etc. **b.** such escaping or entering fluid, light, etc. **2. spring a leak.** to develop a leak. **3.** something resembling this in effect: *a leak in the defence system*. **4.** the loss of current from an electrical conductor because of faulty insulation, etc. **5.** a disclosure of secret information. **6.** the act or an instance of leaking. **7.** *Sl.* an act of urinating. ~*vb*. **8.** to enter or escape or allow to enter or escape through a crack, hole, etc. **9.** (when *intr*., often foll. by *out*) to disclose (secret information) or (of secret information) to be disclosed. **10.** (*intr*.) *Sl.* to urinate. —'**leaker** *n*. —'**leaky** *adj*.

leakage ('li:kɪdʒ) *n*. **1.** the act or an instance of leaking. **2.** something that escapes or enters by a leak. **3.** *Physics*. an undesired flow of electric current, neutrons, etc.

lean[1] (li:n) *vb*. **leaning; leant** *or* **leaned. 1.** (foll. by *against, on*, or *upon*) to rest or cause to rest against a support. **2.** to incline or cause to incline from a vertical position. **3.** (*intr*.; foll. by *to* or *towards*) to have or express a tendency or leaning. **4.** (*intr*.; foll. by *on* or *upon*) to depend for advice, support, etc. ~*n*. **5.** the condition of inclining from a vertical position.

lean[2] (li:n) *adj*. **1.** not fat or full. **2.** (of meat) having little or no fat. **3.** not rich, abundant, or satisfying. ~*n*. **4.** the part of meat that contains little or no fat. —'**leanly** *adv*. —'**leanness** *n*.

leaning ('li:nɪŋ) *n*. a tendency or inclination.

leant (lɛnt) *vb*. a past tense or past participle of **lean**[1].

lean-to *n., pl.* **-tos. 1.** a roof that has a single slope adjoining a wall or building. **2.** a shed or outbuilding with such a roof.

leap (li:p) *vb*. **leaping; leapt** *or* **leaped. 1.** (*intr*.) to jump suddenly from one place to another. **2.** (*intr*.; often foll. by *at*) to move or react quickly. **3.** (*tr*.) to jump over. **4.** to come into prominence rapidly: *the thought leapt into his mind*. **5.** (*tr*.) to cause (an animal, esp. a horse) to jump a barrier. ~*n*. **6.** the act of jumping. **7.** a spot from which a leap was or may be made. **8.** an abrupt change or increase. **9. a leap in the dark.** an action performed without knowledge of the consequences. **10. by leaps and bounds.** extremely fast. —'**leaper** *n*.

leapfrog ('li:p,frɒg) *n*. **1.** a children's game in which each player in turn leaps over the others' bent backs. ~*vb*. **-frogging, -frogged. 2. a.** (*intr*.) to play leapfrog. **b.** (*tr*.) to leap in this way over (something). **3.** to advance or cause to advance by jumps or stages.

leap year *n*. a calendar year of 366 days, February 29 (**leap day**) being the additional day, that occurs every four years (those whose number is divisible by four).

learn (lɜ:n) *vb*. **learning; learnt** *or* **learned** (lɜ:nd). **1.** (when *tr*., may take a clause as object) to gain knowledge of (something) or acquire skill in (some art or practice). **2.** (*tr*.) to commit to memory. **3.** (*tr*.) to gain by experience, example, etc. **4.** (*intr*.; often foll. by *of* or *about*) to become informed; know. **5.** *Not standard*. to teach. —'**learnable** *adj*. —'**learner** *n*.

▷ **Usage.** Educated writers and speakers of English do not use *learn* for *teach*: *that will teach* (not *learn*) *him a lesson*.

learned ('lɜ:nɪd) *adj*. **1.** having great knowledge or erudition. **2.** involving or characterized by scholarship. **3.** (*prenominal*) a title applied in referring to a member of the legal profession, esp. to a barrister: *my learned friend*. —'**learnedly** *adv*. —'**learnedness** *n*.

learning ('lɜ:nɪŋ) *n*. **1.** knowledge gained by study; instruction or scholarship. **2.** the act of gaining knowledge.

lease (li:s) *n*. **1.** a contract by which property is conveyed to a person for a specified period, usually for rent. **2.** the instrument by which such property is conveyed. **3.** the period of time for which it is conveyed. **4.** a prospect of renewed health, happiness, etc.: *a new lease of life*. ~*vb*. (*tr*.) **5.** to grant possession of (land, buildings, etc.) by lease. **6.** to take a lease of (property); hold under a lease. —'**leasable** *adj*. —'**leaser** *n*.

leasehold ('li:s,həʊld) *n*. **1.** land or property held under a lease. **2.** the tenure by which such property is held. **3.** (*modifier*) held under a lease. —'**lease,holder** *n*.

leash (li:ʃ) *n*. **1.** a line or rope used to walk or control a dog or other animal; lead. **2.** something resembling this in function: *he kept a tight leash on his emotions*. **3. straining at the leash.** eagerly impatient to begin something. ~*vb*. **4.** (*tr*.) to control or secure as by a leash.

THESAURUS

leaf *n*. **1.** blade, bract, flag, foliole, frond, needle, pad **2.** folio, page, sheet **3. turn over a new leaf** amend, begin anew, change, change one's ways, improve, reform ~*v*. **4.** bud, green, put out leaves, turn green **5.** browse, flip, glance, riffle, skim, thumb (through)

leaflet advert (*Brit. inf.*), bill, booklet, brochure, circular, handbill, pamphlet

league *n*. **1.** alliance, association, band, coalition, combination, combine, compact, confederacy, confederation, consortium, federation, fellowship, fraternity, group, guild, partnership, union **2.** ability group, category, class, level **3. in league** (**with**) allied, collaborating, hand in glove, in cahoots (*Inf.*), leagued ~*v*. **4.** ally, amalgamate, associate, band, collaborate, combine, confederate, join forces, unite

leak *n*. **1.** aperture, chink, crack, crevice, fissure, hole, opening, puncture **2.** drip, leakage, leaking, oozing, percolation, seepage **3.** disclosure, divulgence ~*v*. **4.** discharge, drip, escape, exude, ooze, pass, percolate,

seep, spill, trickle **5.** disclose, divulge, give away, let slip, let the cat out of the bag, make known, make public, pass on, reveal, spill the beans (*Inf.*), tell

leaky cracked, holey, leaking, not watertight, perforated, porous, punctured, split, waterlogged

lean[1] *v*. **1.** be supported, prop, recline, repose, rest **2.** bend, incline, slant, slope, tilt, tip **3.** be disposed to, be prone to, favour, gravitate towards, have a propensity, prefer, tend **4.** confide, count on, depend, have faith in, rely, trust

lean[2] *adj*. **1.** angular, bony, emaciated, gaunt, lank, rangy, scraggy, scrawny, skinny, slender, slim, spare, thin, unfatty, wiry **2.** bare, barren, inadequate, infertile, meagre, pitiful, poor, scanty, sparse, unfruitful, unproductive

leaning aptitude, bent, bias, disposition, inclination, liking, partiality, penchant, predilection, proclivity, proneness, propensity, taste, tendency

leap *v*. **1.** bounce, bound, caper, cavort,

frisk, gambol, hop, jump, skip, spring **2.** *Fig.* arrive at, come to, form hastily, hasten, hurry, jump, reach, rush **3.** clear, jump (over), vault **4.** advance, become prominent, escalate, gain attention, increase, rocket, soar, surge ~*n*. **5.** bound, caper, frisk, hop, jump, skip, spring, vault **6.** escalation, increase, rise, surge, upsurge, upswing

learn 1. acquire, attain, become able, grasp, imbibe, master, pick up **2.** commit to memory, con (*Archaic*), get off pat, get (something) word-perfect, learn by heart, memorize **3.** ascertain, detect, determine, discern, discover, find out, gain, gather, hear, understand

learned academic, cultured, erudite, experienced, expert, highbrow, intellectual, lettered, literate, scholarly, skilled, versed, well-informed, well-read

learner apprentice, beginner, disciple, neophyte, novice, pupil, scholar, student, trainee, tyro

learning acquirements, attainments, culture, education, erudition, information,

least ('li:st) *determiner.* **1. a. the.** the superlative of **lit-tle:** *you have the least talent of anyone.* **b.** (*as pronoun; functioning as sing.*): *least isn't necessarily worst.* **2. at least. a.** if nothing else: *you should at least try.* **b.** at the least. **3. at the least.** Also: **at least.** at the minimum: *at the least you should earn a hundred pounds.* **4. in the least.** (*usually used with a negative*) in the slightest degree; at all: *I don't mind in the least.* ~*adv.* **5. the least.** superlative of **little:** *they travel the least.* ~*adj.* **6.** of very little importance.

leastways ('li:st₁weɪz) *or U.S.* **leastwise** *adv. Inf.* at least; anyway; at any rate.

leather ('lɛðə) *n.* **1. a.** a material consisting of the skin of an animal made smooth and flexible by tanning, removing the hair, etc. **b.** (*as modifier*): *leather goods.* **2.** something, such as a garment, made of leather. ~*vb.* (*tr.*) **3.** to cover with leather. **4.** to whip as with a leather strap.

leatherjacket ('lɛðə₁dʒækɪt) *n.* **1.** any of various tropical fishes having a leathery skin. **2.** the greyish-brown tough-skinned larva of certain craneflies, which destroy the roots of grasses, etc.

leathery ('lɛðərɪ) *adj.* having the appearance or texture of leather, esp. in toughness. —**leatheriness** *n.*

leave[1] ('li:v) *vb.* **leaving, left.** (*mainly tr.*) **1.** (*also intr.*) to go or depart (from a person or place). **2.** to cause to remain behind, often by mistake, in a place: *he often leaves his keys in his coat.* **3.** to cause to be or remain in a specified state: *paying the bill left him penniless.* **4.** to renounce or abandon: *to leave a political movement.* **5.** to refrain from consuming or doing something: *the things we have left undone.* **6.** to result in; cause: *childhood problems often leave emotional scars.* **7.** to entrust or commit: *leave the shopping to her.* **8.** to pass in a specified direction: *flying out of the country, we left the cliffs on our left.* **9.** to be survived by (members of one's family): *he leaves a wife and two children.* **10.** to bequeath: *he left his investments to his children.* **11.** (*tr.*) to have as a remainder: *37 –14 leaves 23.* **12.** *Not standard.* to permit; let. **13. leave (someone) alone. a.** to refrain from persecuting, bothering, etc. **b.** to permit to stay or be alone. —**leaver** *n.*
▷ **Usage.** In educated usage, *leave* is not used in the sense of *let* (allow): *let him go,* not *leave him go.*

leave[2] ('li:v) *n.* **1.** permission to do something: *he was granted leave to speak.* **2. by** or **with your leave.** with your permission. **3.** permission to be absent, as from a place of work: *leave of absence.* **4.** the duration of such absence: *ten days' leave.* **5.** a farewell or departure (esp. in **take (one's) leave**). **6. on leave.** officially excused from work or duty. **7. take leave (of).** to say farewell (to).

leave[3] ('li:v) *vb.* **leaving, leaved.** (*intr.*) to produce or grow leaves.

leaven ('lɛvən) *n. also* **leavening. 1.** any substance that produces fermentation in dough or batter, such as yeast, and causes it to rise. **2.** a piece of such a substance kept

to ferment a new batch of dough. **3.** an agency or influence that produces a gradual change. ~*vb.* (*tr.*) **4.** to cause fermentation in (dough or batter). **5.** to pervade, causing a gradual change.

leave off *vb.* **1.** (*intr.*) to stop; cease. **2.** (*tr., adv.*) to stop wearing or using.

leave out *vb.* (*tr., adv.*) **1.** to cause to remain in the open. **2.** to omit or exclude.

leaves (li:vz) *n.* the plural of **leaf.**

leave-taking *n.* the act of departing; a farewell.

leavings ('li:vɪŋz) *pl. n.* something remaining, such as food on a plate, residue, refuse, etc.

lecher ('lɛtʃə) *n.* a promiscuous or lewd man. —**lecherous** *adj.* —**lechery** *n.*

lecithin ('lɛsɪθɪn) *n. Biochem.* any of a group of yellow-brown compounds that are found in many plant and animal tissues, esp. egg yolk: used in making candles, cosmetics, and inks.

lectern ('lɛktən) *n.* **1.** a reading desk in a church. **2.** any similar desk or support.

lecture ('lɛktʃə) *n.* **1.** a discourse on a particular subject given or read to an audience. **2.** the text of such a discourse. **3.** a method of teaching by formal discourse. **4.** a lengthy reprimand or scolding. ~*vb.* **5.** to give or read a lecture (to an audience or class). **6.** (*tr.*) to reprimand at length. —**lecturer** *n.* —**lectureship** *n.*

led (lɛd) *vb.* the past tense or past participle of **lead**[1].

LED *Electronics. abbrev. for* light-emitting diode.

ledge (lɛdʒ) *n.* **1.** a narrow horizontal surface resembling a shelf and projecting from a wall, window, etc. **2.** a layer of rock that contains an ore; vein. **3.** a ridge of rock that lies beneath the surface of the sea. **4.** a narrow shelflike projection on a cliff or mountain. —**ledgy** *or* **ledged** *adj.*

ledger ('lɛdʒə) *n.* **1.** *Book-keeping.* the principal book in which the commercial transactions of a company are recorded. **2.** *Angling.* a wire trace that allows the weight to rest on the bottom and the bait to float freely. ~*vb.* **3.** (*intr.*) *Angling.* to fish using a ledger.

ledger line *n. Music.* a short line placed above or below the staff to accommodate notes representing pitches above or below the staff.

lee (li:) *n.* **1.** a sheltered part or side; the side away from the direction from which the wind is blowing. ~*adj.* **2.** (*prenominal*) *Naut.* on, at, or towards the side or part away from the wind: *on a lee shore.* Cf. **weather** (sense 4).

leech (li:tʃ) *n.* **1.** an annelid worm which has a sucker at each end of the body and feeds on the blood or tissues of other animals. **2.** a person who clings to or preys on another person. **3. a.** an archaic word for **physician. b.** (*in combination*): *leechcraft.* ~*vb.* (*tr.*) **4.** to use leeches to suck the blood of (a person), as a method of medical treatment.

leek (li:k) *n.* **1.** a vegetable with a slender white bulb, cylindrical stem, and broad flat overlapping leaves. **2.**

---

knowledge, letters, literature, lore, research, scholarship, schooling, study, tuition, wisdom

lease *v.* charter, hire, let, loan, rent

leash *n.* **1.** lead, rein, tether **2.** check, control, curb, hold, restraint ~*v.* **3.** fasten, secure, tether, tie up **4.** check, control, curb, hold back, restrain, suppress

least feeblest, fewest, last, lowest, meanest, minimum, minutest, poorest, slightest, smallest, tiniest

leathery coriaceous, durable, hard, hardened, leatherlike, leathern (*Archaic*), rough, rugged, tough, wrinkled

leave[1] *v.* **1.** abandon, decamp, depart, desert, disappear, do a bunk (*Brit. sl.*), exit, flit (*Inf.*), forsake, go, go away, move, pull out, quit, relinquish, retire, set out, take off (*Inf.*), withdraw **2.** forget, lay down, leave behind, mislay **3.** cause, deposit, generate, produce, result in **4.** abandon, cease, desert, desist, drop, evacuate, forbear, give up, refrain, relinquish, renounce, stop, surrender **5.** allot, assign, cede, commit, consign, entrust, give over, refer **6.** bequeath, demise, devise (*Law*), hand down, transmit, will

leave[2] *n.* **1.** allowance, authorization, con-

cession, consent, dispensation, freedom, liberty, permission, sanction **2.** furlough, holiday, leave of absence, sabbatical, time off, vacation **3.** adieu, departure, farewell, goodbye, leave-taking, parting, retirement, withdrawal

leaven *n.* **1.** barm, ferment, leavening, yeast **2.** *Fig.* catalyst, influence, inspiration ~*v.* **3.** ferment, lighten, raise, work **4.** *Fig.* elevate, imbue, inspire, permeate, pervade, quicken, stimulate, suffuse

leave off abstain, break off, cease, desist, discontinue, end, give over (*Inf.*), give up, halt, knock off (*Inf.*), refrain, stop

leave out bar, cast aside, count out, disregard, except, exclude, ignore, neglect, omit, overlook, reject

leavings bits, dregs, fragments, leftovers, orts (*Archaic or dialect*), pieces, refuse, remains, remnants, residue, scraps, spoil, sweepings, waste

lecherous carnal, concupiscent, goatish (*Archaic*), lascivious, lewd, libidinous, licentious, lubricious, lustful, prurient, randy (*Sl., chiefly Brit.*), raunchy (*U.S. Sl.*), ruttish, salacious, unchaste, wanton

lechery carnality, concupiscence, debauchery, lasciviousness, lecherousness, leching (*Inf.*), lewdness, libertinism, libidinousness, licentiousness, lubricity, lust, lustfulness, profligacy, prurience, rakishness, randiness (*Sl., chiefly Brit.*), salaciousness, sensuality, wantonness, womanizing

lecture *n.* **1.** address, discourse, disquisition, harangue, instruction, lesson, speech, talk ~*v.* **2.** address, discourse, expound, give a talk, harangue, hold forth, speak, talk, teach ~*n.* **3.** castigation, censure, chiding, dressing-down (*Inf.*), going-over (*Inf.*), rebuke, reprimand, reproof, scolding, talking-to (*Inf.*), telling off (*Inf.*), wigging (*Brit. sl.*) ~*v.* **4.** admonish, berate, carpet (*Inf.*), castigate, censure, chide, rate, reprimand, reprove, scold, tell off (*Inf.*)

ledge mantle, projection, ridge, shelf, sill, step

leech *Fig.* bloodsucker (*Inf.*), freeloader (*U.S. sl.*), hanger-on, parasite, sponger (*Inf.*), sycophant

the national emblem of Wales.

leer (lɪə) *vb.* **1.** (*intr.*) to give an oblique, sneering, or suggestive look or grin. ~*n.* **2.** such a look. —**'leeringly** *adv.*

leery ('lɪərɪ) *adj.* **leerier, leeriest** **1.** *Now chiefly dialect.* knowing or sly. **2.** *Sl.* (foll. by *of*) suspicious or wary. —**'leeriness** *n.*

lees (liːz) *pl. n.* the sediment from an alcoholic drink.

leet (liːt) *n. Scot.* a list of candidates for an office.

leeward ('liːwəd; *Naut.* 'luːəd) *Chiefly naut.* ~*adj.* **1.** of, in, or moving to the quarter towards which the wind blows. ~*n.* **2.** the point or quarter towards which the wind blows. **3.** the side towards the lee. ~*adv.* **4.** towards the lee. ~Cf. **windward.**

leeway ('liːˌweɪ) *n.* **1.** room for free movement within limits, as in action or expenditure. **2.** sideways drift of a boat or aircraft.

left[1] (lɛft) *adj.* **1.** (*usually prenominal*) of or designating the side of something or someone that faces west when the front is turned towards the north. **2.** (*usually prenominal*) worn on a left hand, foot, etc. **3.** (*sometimes cap.*) of or relating to the political left. **4.** (*sometimes cap.*) radical or progressive. ~*adv.* **5.** on or in the direction of the left. ~*n.* **6.** a left side, direction, position, area, or part. **7.** (*often cap.*) the supporters or advocates of varying degrees of social, political, or economic change, reform, or revolution. **8.** *Boxing.* **a.** a blow with the left hand. **b.** the left hand.

left[2] (lɛft) *vb.* the past tense or past participle of **leave**[1].

left-hand *adj.* (*prenominal*) **1.** of, relating to, located on, or moving towards the left. **2.** for use by the left hand; left-handed.

left-handed *adj.* **1.** using the left hand with greater ease than the right. **2.** performed with the left hand. **3.** designed or adapted for use by the left hand. **4.** awkward or clumsy. **5.** ironically ambiguous: *a left-handed compliment.* **6.** turning from right to left; anticlockwise. ~*adv.* **7.** with the left hand. —**left-'handedly** *adv.* —ˌleft-'handedness *n.* —ˌleft-'hander *n.*

leftist ('lɛftɪst) *adj.* **1.** of, tending towards, or relating to the political left or its principles. ~*n.* **2.** a person who supports or belongs to the political left. —**'leftism** *n.*

left-luggage office *n. Brit.* a place at a railway station, etc., where luggage may be left for a small charge. U.S. name: **checkroom.**

leftover ('lɛftˌəʊvə) *n.* **1.** (*often pl.*) an unused portion or remnant, as of material or of cooked food. ~*adj.* **2.** left as an unused portion.

leftward ('lɛftwəd) *adj.* **1.** on or towards the left. ~*adv.* **2.** a variant of **leftwards.**

leftwards ('lɛftwədz) *or* **leftward** *adv.* towards or on the left.

left wing *n.* **1.** (*often cap.*) the leftist faction of an assembly, party, group, etc.; the radical or progressive wing. **2.** *Sports.* **a.** the left-hand side of the field of play from the point of view of either team facing its opponents' goal. **b.** a player positioned in this area in certain games. ~*adj.* **left-wing. 3.** of, belonging to, or relating to the political left wing. —ˌleft-'winger *n.*

lefty ('lɛftɪ) *n., pl.* **lefties.** *Inf.* **1.** a left-winger. **2.** *Chiefly U.S.* a left-handed person.

leg (lɛg) *n.* **1.** either of the two lower limbs in humans,

or any similar or analogous structure in animals that is used for locomotion or support. **2.** this part of an animal, esp. the thigh, used for food: *leg of lamb.* **3.** something similar to a leg in appearance or function, such as one of the four supporting members of a chair. **4.** a branch, limb, or part of a forked or jointed object. **5.** the part of a garment that covers the leg. **6.** a section or part of a journey or course. **7.** a single stage, lap, length, etc., in a relay race. **8.** either the opposite or adjacent side of a right-angled triangle. **9.** one of a series of games, matches, or parts of games. **10.** *N.Z. & Austral.* either one of two races on which a cumulative bet has been placed. **11.** *Cricket.* **a.** the side of the field to the left of and behind a right-handed batsman as he faces the bowler. **b.** (*as modifier*): *a leg slip; leg stump.* **12. not have a leg to stand on.** *Inf.* to have no reasonable or logical basis for an opinion or argument. **13. on his, its,** etc., **last legs.** (of a person or thing) worn out; exhausted. **14. pull someone's leg.** *Inf.* to tease, fool, or make fun of someone. **15. shake a leg.** *Sl.* to hurry up: usually used in the imperative. **16. stretch one's legs.** to stand up or walk around, esp. after sitting for some time. ~*vb.* **legging, legged. 17. leg it.** *Inf.* to walk, run, or hurry. —**'leggy** *adj.* —**'legless** *adj.*

legacy ('lɛgəsɪ) *n., pl.* **-cies.** **1.** a gift by will, esp. of money or personal property. **2.** something handed down or received from an ancestor or predecessor.

legal ('liːg²l) *adj.* **1.** established by or founded upon law; lawful. **2.** of or relating to law. **3.** recognized, enforceable, or having a remedy at law rather than in equity. **4.** relating to or characteristic of the profession of law. —**'legally** *adv.*

legal aid *n.* financial assistance available to persons unable to meet the full cost of legal proceedings.

legalese (ˌliːgə'liːz) *n.* the conventional language in which legal documents are written.

legalism ('liːgəˌlɪzəm) *n.* strict adherence to the law, esp. the letter of the law rather than its spirit. —**'legalist** *n., adj.* —ˌlegal'istic *adj.*

legality (lɪ'gælɪtɪ) *n., pl.* **-ties.** **1.** the state or quality of being legal or lawful. **2.** adherence to legal principles.

legalize *or* **-ise** ('liːgəˌlaɪz) *vb.* (*tr.*) to make lawful or legal. —ˌlegali'zation *or* **-i'sation** *n.*

legal tender *n.* currency that a creditor must by law accept in redemption of a debt.

legate ('lɛgɪt) *n.* **1.** a messenger, envoy, or delegate. **2.** *R.C. Church.* an emissary representing the Pope. —**'legateˌship** *n.*

legatee (ˌlɛgə'tiː) *n.* a person to whom a legacy is bequeathed.

legation (lɪ'geɪʃən) *n.* **1.** a diplomatic mission headed by a minister. **2.** the official residence and office of a diplomatic minister. **3.** the act of sending forth a diplomatic envoy. **4.** the mission of a diplomatic envoy. **5.** the rank or office of a legate.

legato (lɪ'gɑːtəʊ) *Music.* ~*adj., adv.* **1.** to be performed smoothly and connectedly. ~*n., pl.* **-tos. 2. a.** a style of playing with no perceptible gaps between notes. **b.** (*as modifier*): *a legato passage.*

leg before wicket *n. Cricket.* a manner of dismissal on the grounds that a batsman has been struck on the leg by a bowled ball that otherwise would have hit the wick-

---

THESAURUS

leer *n./v.* eye, gloat, goggle, grin, ogle, smirk, squint, stare, wink

lees deposit, dregs, grounds, precipitate, refuse, sediment, settlings

leeway elbowroom, latitude, margin, play, room, scope, space

left *adj.* **1.** larboard (*Nautical*), left-hand, port, sinistral **2.** *Of politics* leftist, left-wing, liberal, progressive, radical, socialist

left-handed 1. awkward, cack-handed (*Inf.*), careless, clumsy, fumbling, gauche, maladroit **2.** ambiguous, backhanded, double-edged, enigmatic, equivocal, indirect, ironic, sardonic

leftover *n.* **1.** legacy, remainder, residue, surplus, survivor **2.** *Plural* leavings, oddments, odds and ends, remains, remnants, scraps ~*adj.* **3.** excess, extra, remaining, surplus, uneaten, unused, unwanted

leg 1. limb, lower limb, member, pin (*Inf.*),

stump (*Inf.*) **2.** brace, prop, support, upright **3.** lap, part, portion, section, segment, stage, stretch **4. a leg up** assistance, boost, help, helping hand, push, support **5. not have a leg to stand on** *Inf.* be defenceless, be full of holes, be illogical, be invalid, be undermined, be vulnerable, lack support **6. on one's (its) last legs** about to break down, about to collapse, at death's door, dying, exhausted, failing, giving up the ghost, worn out **7. pull someone's leg** *Inf.* chaff, deceive, fool, make fun of, tease, trick **8. shake a leg** *Sl.* **a.** get a move on (*Inf.*), get cracking (*Inf.*), hasten, hurry, look lively (*Inf.*), rush, stir one's stumps **b.** dance, hoof it (*Sl.*), trip the light fantastic **9. stretch one's legs** exercise, go for a walk, move about, promenade, stroll, take a walk, take the air **10. leg it** *Inf.* go on foot, hotfoot, hurry, run, skedaddle (*Inf.*), walk

legacy 1. bequest, devise (*Law*), estate,

gift, heirloom, inheritance **2.** birthright, endowment, heritage, inheritance, patrimony, throwback, tradition

legal 1. allowable, allowed, authorized, constitutional, lawful, legalized, legitimate, licit, permissible, proper, rightful, sanctioned, valid **2.** forensic, judicial, juridical

legality accordance with the law, admissibleness, lawfulness, legitimacy, permissibility, rightfulness, validity

legalize allow, approve, authorize, decriminalize, legitimate, legitimatize, license, permit, sanction, validate

legatee beneficiary, heir, inheritor, recipient

legation consulate, delegation, diplomatic mission, embassy, envoys, ministry, representation

et. Abbrev.: **l.b.w.**

legend ('lɛdʒənd) n. **1.** a popular story handed down from earlier times whose truth has not been ascertained. **2.** a group of such stories: *the Arthurian legend.* **3.** a modern story that has the characteristics of a traditional tale. **4.** a person whose fame or notoriety makes him a source of exaggerated or romanticized tales. **5.** an inscription or title, as on a coin or beneath a coat of arms. **6.** explanatory matter accompanying a table, map, chart, etc.

legendary ('lɛdʒəndərɪ, -drɪ) adj. **1.** of or relating to legend. **2.** celebrated or described in a legend or legends. **3.** very famous or notorious.

legerdemain (ˌlɛdʒədə'meɪn) n. **1.** another name for **sleight of hand. 2.** cunning deception or trickery.

leger line ('lɛdʒə) n. a variant spelling of **ledger line.**

legged ('lɛgɪd, lɛgd) adj. **a.** having a leg or legs. **b.** (in combination): *three-legged; long-legged.*

leggings ('lɛgɪŋz) pl. n. an extra outer covering for the lower legs.

Leghorn n. **1.** ('lɛgˌhɔːn). the English name for Livorno, a port in W central Italy. **2.** (lɛ'gɔːn). a breed of domestic fowl.

leghorn ('lɛgˌhɔːn) n. **1.** a type of Italian wheat straw that is woven into hats. **2.** any hat made from this straw.

legible ('lɛdʒəbəl) adj. (of handwriting, print, etc.) able to be read or deciphered. —ˌlegi'bility n. —'legibly adv.

legion ('liːdʒən) n. **1.** a unit in the ancient Roman army of infantry with supporting cavalry of three to six thousand men. **2.** any large military force: *the French Foreign Legion.* **3.** (usually cap.) an association of ex-servicemen: *the British Legion.* **4.** (often pl.) any very large number. —adj. **5.** (usually postpositive) very numerous. —'legionary adj., n.

legionnaire (ˌliːdʒə'nɛə) n. (often cap.) a member of certain military forces or associations.

Legionnaire's disease (ˌliːdʒə'nɛəz) n. a serious, sometimes fatal bacterial infection which has symptoms similar to those of pneumonia.

legislate ('lɛdʒɪsˌleɪt) vb. **1.** (intr.) to make or pass laws. **2.** (tr.) to bring into effect by legislation. —'legisˌlator n.

legislation (ˌlɛdʒɪs'leɪʃən) n. **1.** the act or process of making laws. **2.** the laws so made.

legislative ('lɛdʒɪslətɪv) adj. **1.** of or relating to legislation. **2.** having the power or function of legislating: *a legislative assembly.* **3.** of or relating to a legislature. —'legislatively adv.

legislative assembly n. (often cap.) **1.** the bicameral legislature in 28 states of the U.S. **2.** the unicameral legislature in most Canadian provinces. **3.** the lower chamber of the bicameral state legislatures in several other Commonwealth countries, such as Australia. **4.** any assembly with legislative powers.

legislature ('lɛdʒɪsˌleɪtʃə) n. a body of persons vested with power to make and repeal laws.

legitimate adj. (lɪ'dʒɪtɪmɪt). **1.** born in lawful wedlock. **2.** conforming to established standards of usage, behaviour, etc. **3.** based on correct or acceptable principles of reasoning. **4.** authorized by or in accordance with law. **5.** of, relating to, or ruling by hereditary right: *a legitimate monarch.* **6.** of or relating to serious drama as distinct from films, television, vaudeville, etc. ~vb. (lɪ'dʒɪtɪˌmeɪt). **7.** (tr.) to make, pronounce, or show to be legitimate. —le'gitimacy n. —le'gitimately adv. —leˌgiti'mation n.

legitimatize, -tise (lɪ'dʒɪtɪməˌtaɪz) or **legitimize, -mise** (lɪ'dʒɪtɪˌmaɪz) vb. (tr.) to make legitimate; legalize. —leˌgitimati'zation, -ti'sation or leˌgitimi'zation, -mi'sation n.

leg-pull n. Brit. inf. a practical joke or mild deception.

legroom ('lɛgˌruːm) n. room to move one's legs comfortably, as in a car.

leguan ('lɛguˌɑːn) n. a large amphibious S African lizard.

legume ('lɛgjuːm, lɪ'gjuːm) n. **1.** the long dry fruit produced by leguminous plants; a pod. **2.** any of various table vegetables, esp. beans or peas. **3.** any leguminous plant.

leguminous (lɪ'gjuːmɪnəs) adj. of, relating to, or belonging to any family of flowering plants having pods (or legumes) as fruits and root nodules enabling storage of nitrogen-rich material.

lei (leɪ) n. (in Hawaii) a garland of flowers, worn around the neck.

Leics. abbrev. for Leicestershire.

leisure ('lɛʒə) n. **1. a.** time or opportunity for ease, relaxation, etc. **b.** (as modifier): *leisure activities.* **2.** ease or leisureliness. **3. at leisure. a.** having free time. **b.** not occupied or engaged. **c.** without hurrying. **4. at one's leisure.** when one has free time. —'leisured adj.

leisurely ('lɛʒəlɪ) adj. **1.** unhurried; relaxed. ~adv. **2.** without haste; in a relaxed way. —'leisureliness n.

leitmotiv or **leitmotif** ('laɪtməʊˌtiːf) n. **1.** Music. a recurring short melodic phrase used, esp. in Wagnerian music dramas, to suggest a character, thing, etc. **2.** an often repeated image or theme in a literary work.

L.E.M. (lɛm) n. acronym for lunar excursion module.

lemming ('lɛmɪŋ) n. any of various volelike rodents of northern and arctic regions of Europe, Asia, and North America.

lemon ('lɛmən) n. **1.** a small Asian evergreen tree widely cultivated in warm and tropical regions for its edible fruits. Related adjs.: **citric, citrine, citrous. 2. a.** the yellow oval fruit of this tree, having juicy acidic flesh. **b.** (as modifier): *a lemon jelly.* **3.** Also called: **lemon yellow. a.** a greenish-yellow or pale yellow colour. **b.** (as adj.): *lemon wallpaper.* **4.** a distinctive tart flavour made from or in imitation of the lemon. **5.** Sl. a person or thing considered to be useless or defective. —'lemony adj.

lemonade (ˌlɛmə'neɪd) n. a drink made from lemon juice, sugar, and water or from carbonated water, citric acid, etc.

lemon sole n. a European flatfish with a variegated brown body: highly valued as a food fish.

lemon squash n. Brit. a drink made from a sweetened lemon concentrate and water.

lemur ('liːmə) n. **1.** any of a family of Madagascan pro-

THESAURUS

legend 1. fable, fiction, folk tale, myth, narrative, saga, story, tale **2.** celebrity, luminary, marvel, phenomenon, prodigy, spectacle, wonder **3.** caption, device, inscription, motto **4.** cipher, code, key, table of symbols

legendary 1. apocryphal, fabled, fabulous, fanciful, fictitious, mythical, romantic, storied, traditional **2.** celebrated, famed, famous, illustrious, immortal, renowned, well-known

legibility clarity, decipherability, ease of reading, legibleness, neatness, plainness, readability, readableness

legible clear, decipherable, distinct, easily read, easy to read, neat, plain, readable

legion n. **1.** army, brigade, company, division, force, troop **2.** drove, horde, host, mass, multitude, myriad, number, throng ~adj. **3.** countless, multitudinous, myriad, numberless, numerous, very many

legislate codify, constitute, enact, establish, make laws, ordain, pass laws, prescribe, put in force

legislation 1. codification, enactment, lawmaking, prescription, regulation **2.** act, bill, charter, law, measure, regulation, ruling, statute

legislative adj. congressional, judicial, juridical, jurisdictive, lawgiving, lawmaking, ordaining, parliamentary

legislator lawgiver, lawmaker, parliamentarian

legislature assembly, chamber, congress, diet, house, lawmaking body, parliament, senate

legitimate adj. **1.** acknowledged, authentic, authorized, genuine, lawful, legal, legit (Sl.), licit, proper, real, rightful, sanctioned, statutory, true **2.** admissible, correct, just, justifiable, logical, reasonable, sensible, valid, warranted, well-founded ~v. **3.** authorize, legalize, legitimatize, legitimize, permit, pronounce lawful, sanction

legitimatize, legitimize authorize, legalize, legitimate, permit, pronounce lawful, sanction

leisure 1. breathing space, ease, freedom, free time, holiday, liberty, opportunity, pause, quiet, recreation, relaxation, respite, rest, retirement, spare moments, spare time, time off, vacation **2. at leisure a.** available, free, not booked up, on holiday, unengaged, unoccupied **b.** Also **at one's leisure** at an unhurried pace, at one's convenience, deliberately, in one's own (good) time, unhurriedly, when it suits one, when one gets round to it (Inf.), without hurry

leisurely 1. adj. comfortable, easy, gentle, laid-back (Inf.), lazy, relaxed, restful, slow, unhurried **2.** adv. at one's convenience, at one's leisure, comfortably, deliberately, easily, indolently, lazily, lingeringly, slowly, unhurriedly, without haste

simian primates such as the ring-tailed lemur. They are typically arboreal, having foxy faces and long tails. **2.** any similar or closely related animal, such as a loris or indris. —**'lemu,roid** ('lɛmjʊ,rɔɪd) *n., adj.*

lend (lɛnd) *vb.* **lending, lent. 1.** (*tr.*) to permit the use of (something) with the expectation of its return. **2.** to provide (money) temporarily, often at interest. **3.** (*intr.*) to provide loans, esp. as a profession. **4.** (*tr.*) to impart or contribute (something, esp. some abstract quality): *her presence lent beauty.* **5. lend an ear.** to listen. **6. lend oneself** or **itself.** to possess the right characteristics or qualities for: *the novel lends itself to serialization.* —**'lender** *n.*

▷ **Usage.** Although the use of *loan* as a verb equivalent to *lend* is widespread, it is avoided by careful speakers and writers except when referring to the formal lending of money: *the bank loaned him the money.*

length (lɛŋkθ, lɛŋθ) *n.* **1.** the linear extent or measurement of something from end to end, usually being the longest dimension. **2.** the extent of something from beginning to end, measured in some more or less regular units or intervals: *the book was 600 pages in length.* **3.** a specified distance, esp. between two positions: *the length of a race.* **4.** a period of time, as between specified limits or moments. **5.** a piece or section of something narrow and long: *a length of tubing.* **6.** the quality, state, or fact of being long rather than short. **7.** (*usually pl.*) the amount of trouble taken in pursuing or achieving something (esp. in **to great lengths**). **8.** (*often pl.*) the extreme or limit of action (esp. in **to any length(s)**). **9.** *Prosody, phonetics.* the metrical quantity or temporal duration of a vowel or syllable. **10.** the distance from one end of a rectangular swimming bath to the other. **11. at length. a.** in depth; fully. **b.** eventually.

lengthen ('lɛŋkθən, 'lɛŋθən) *vb.* to make or become longer. —**'lengthener** *n.*

lengthways ('lɛŋkθ,weɪz, 'lɛŋθ-) or *U.S.* **lengthwise** *adv., adj.* in, according to, or along the direction of length.

lengthy ('lɛŋkθɪ, 'lɛŋθɪ) *adj.* **lengthier, lengthiest.** of relatively great or tiresome extent or duration. —**'lengthily** *adv.* —**'lengthiness** *n.*

lenient ('liːnɪənt) *adj.* showing or characterized by mercy or tolerance. —**'leniency** or **'lenience** *n.* —**'leniently** *adv.*

lenitive ('lɛnɪtɪv) *adj.* **1.** soothing or alleviating pain or distress. ~*n.* **2.** a lenitive drug.

lenity ('lɛnɪtɪ) *n., pl.* **-ties.** the state or quality of being lenient.

lens (lɛnz) *n.* **1.** a piece of glass or other transparent material, used to converge or diverge transmitted light and form optical images. **2.** Also called: **compound lens.** a combination of such lenses for forming images or concentrating a beam of light. **3.** a device that diverges or converges a beam of electromagnetic radiation, sound, or particles.

lent (lɛnt) *vb.* the past tense or past participle of **lend.**

Lent (lɛnt) *n. Christianity.* the period of forty weekdays lasting from Ash Wednesday to Holy Saturday, observed as a time of penance and fasting commemorating Jesus' fasting in the wilderness. —**'lenten** *adj.*

lentil ('lɛntɪl) *n.* **1.** a small annual leguminous plant of the Mediterranean region and W Asia, having edible convex seeds. **2.** any of the seeds of this plant, which are cooked and eaten in soups, etc.

lento ('lɛntəʊ) *Music.* ~*adj., adv.* **1.** to be performed slowly. ~*n., pl.* **-tos. 2.** a movement or passage performed in this way.

Leo ('liːəʊ) *n., Latin genitive* **Leonis** (liː'əʊnɪs). **1.**

Astron. a zodiacal constellation in the N hemisphere, lying between Cancer and Virgo. **2.** *Astrol.* Also called: the **Lion.** the fifth sign of the zodiac. The sun is in this sign between about July 23 and Aug. 22.

leonine ('liːə,naɪn) *adj.* of, characteristic of, or resembling a lion.

leontopodium (liː,ɒntə'pəʊdɪəm) *n.* another name for **edelweiss.**

leopard ('lɛpəd) *n.* **1.** Also called: **panther.** a large feline mammal of forests of Africa and Asia, usually having a tawny yellow coat with black rosette-like spots. **2.** any of several similar felines, such as the snow leopard and cheetah. **3.** *Heraldry.* a stylized leopard, painted as a lion with the face turned towards the front. —**'leopardess** *fem. n.*

leotard ('lɪə,tɑːd) *n.* a tight-fitting garment covering the body from the shoulders down to the thighs and worn by acrobats, ballet dancers, etc.

leper ('lɛpə) *n.* **1.** a person who has leprosy. **2.** a person who is ignored or despised.

lepidopteran (,lɛpɪ'dɒptərən) *n., pl.* **-terans** or **-tera** (-tərə). **1.** any of a large order of insects typically having two pairs of wings covered with fragile scales: comprises the butterflies and moths. ~*adj.* also **lepidopterous. 2.** of, relating to, or belonging to this order.

lepidopterist (,lɛpɪ'dɒptərɪst) *n.* a person who studies or collects moths and butterflies.

leprechaun ('lɛprə,kɔːn) *n.* (in Irish folklore) a mischievous elf, often believed to have a treasure hoard.

leprosy ('lɛprəsɪ) *n. Pathol.* a chronic infectious disease occurring mainly in tropical and subtropical regions, characterized by the formation of painful inflamed nodules beneath the skin and disfigurement and wasting of affected parts.

leprous ('lɛprəs) *adj.* **1.** having leprosy. **2.** relating to or resembling leprosy.

lepton ('lɛptɒn) *n. Physics.* any of a group of elementary particles and their antiparticles, such as an electron, muon, or neutrino, that participate in weak interactions.

lesbian ('lɛzbɪən) *n.* **1.** a female homosexual. ~*adj.* **2.** of or characteristic of lesbians. —**'lesbianism** *n.*

lese-majesty ('liːz'mædʒɪstɪ) *n.* **1.** any of various offences committed against the sovereign power in a state; treason. **2.** an attack on authority or position.

lesion ('liːʒən) *n.* **1.** any structural change in a bodily part resulting from injury or disease. **2.** an injury or wound.

less (lɛs) *determiner.* **1. a.** the comparative of **little** (sense 1): *less sugar; less spirit than before.* **b.** (as pronoun; functioning as sing. or pl.): *she has less than she needs; the less you eat, the less you want.* **2.** (usually preceded by *no*) lower in rank or importance: *no less a man than the president.* **3. less of.** to a smaller extent or degree: *we see less of John these days; less of a success than I'd hoped.* ~*adv.* **4.** the comparative of *a little: she walks less than she should; less quickly; less beautiful.* ~*prep.* **5.** subtracting; minus: *three weeks less a day.*

▷ **Usage.** *Less* should not be confused with *fewer. Less* means less in quantity: *there is less water than before. Fewer* means smaller in number: *there are fewer people than before.*

-less *suffix forming adjectives.* **1.** without; lacking: *speechless.* **2.** not able to (do something) or not able to be (done, performed, etc.): *countless.*

lessee (lɛ'siː) *n.* a person to whom a lease is granted; a tenant under a lease.

lessen ('lɛsən) *vb.* **1.** to make or become less. **2.** (*tr.*) to make little of.

THESAURUS

lend 1. accommodate one with, advance, loan **2.** add, afford, bestow, confer, contribute, furnish, give, grant, impart, present, provide, supply **3. lend an ear** give ear, hearken (*Archaic*), heed, listen, take notice **4. lend a hand** aid, assist, give a (helping) hand, help, help out **5. lend itself to** be adaptable, be appropriate, be serviceable, fit, present opportunities of, suit **6. lend oneself to** agree, consent, cooperate, countenance, espouse, support

length 1. *Of linear extent* distance, extent, longitude, measure, reach, span **2.** *Of time* duration, period, space, span, stretch, term **3.**

measure, piece, portion, section, segment **4.** elongation, extensiveness, lengthiness, protractedness **5. at length a.** completely, fully, in depth, in detail, thoroughly, to the full **b.** for ages, for a long time, for hours, interminably **c.** at last, at long last, eventually, finally, in the end

lengthen continue, draw out, elongate, expand, extend, increase, make longer, prolong, protract, spin out, stretch

lengthy diffuse, drawn-out, extended, interminable, lengthened, long, long-drawn-out, long-winded, overlong, prolix, prolonged, protracted, tedious, verbose, very long

leniency, lenience clemency, compassion, forbearance, gentleness, indulgence, lenity, mercy, mildness, moderation, tenderness, tolerance

lenient clement, compassionate, forbearing, forgiving, gentle, indulgent, kind, merciful, mild, sparing, tender, tolerant

lesbian 1. *n.* butch (*Sl.*), dyke (*Sl.*), sapphist, tribade **2.** *adj.* butch (*Sl.*), gay (*Inf.*), homosexual, sapphic, tribadic

less *adj.* **1.** shorter, slighter, smaller **2.** inferior, minor, secondary, subordinate ~*adv.* **3.** barely, little, meagrely, to a smaller extent

lesser ('lɛsə) *adj.* not as great in quantity, size, or worth.

lesson ('lɛsən) *n.* **1. a.** a unit, or single period of instruction in a subject; class: *an hour-long music lesson.* **b.** the content of such a unit. **2.** material assigned for individual study. **3.** something from which useful knowledge or principles can be learned; example. **4.** the principles, knowledge, etc., gained. **5.** a reprimand or punishment intended to correct. **6.** a portion of Scripture appointed to be read at divine service.

lessor ('lɛsɔː, lɛ'sɔː) *n.* a person who grants a lease of property.

lest (lɛst) *conj. (subordinating; takes a subjunctive vb.) Arch.* **1.** so as to prevent any possibility that: *keep down lest anyone see us.* **2.** *(after vbs. or phrases expressing fear, worry, anxiety, etc.)* for fear that; in case: *he was alarmed lest she should find out.*

let[1] (lɛt) *vb.* **letting, let.** *(tr.; usually takes an infinitive without to or an implied infinitive)* **1.** to permit; allow: *she lets him roam around.* **2.** *(imperative or dependent imperative)* **a.** used as an auxiliary to express a request, proposal, or command, or to convey a warning or threat: *let's get on; just let me catch you here again!* **b.** (in mathematical or philosophical discourse) used as an auxiliary to express an assumption or hypothesis: *let "a" equal "b".* **c.** used as an auxiliary to express resigned acceptance of the inevitable: *let the worst happen.* **3. a.** to allow the occupation of (accommodation) in return for rent. **b.** to assign (a contract for work). **4.** to allow or cause the movement of (something) in a specified direction: *to let air out of a tyre.* **5. let alone.** *(conj.)* much less; not to mention: *I can't afford wine, let alone champagne.* **6. let alone** *or* **be.** to leave (something) undisturbed or unchanged: *let the poor cat alone.* **7. let go.** See **go.** **8. let loose.** to set free. ~See also **let down, let off,** etc.

let[2] (lɛt) *n.* **1.** an impediment or obstruction (esp. in **without let or hindrance**). **2.** *Tennis, squash, etc.* **a.** a minor infringement or obstruction of the ball, requiring a point to be replayed. **b.** the point so replayed. ~*vb.* **letting, letted** *or* **let.** **3.** *(tr.) Arch.* to hinder; impede.

-let *suffix forming nouns.* **1.** small or lesser: *booklet.* **2.** an ornament worn on a specified part of the body: *anklet.*

let down *vb. (tr., mainly adv.)* **1.** *(also prep.)* to lower. **2.** to fail to fulfil the expectations of (a person); disappoint. **3.** to undo, shorten, and resew (the hem) so as to lengthen (a dress, skirt, etc.). **4.** to untie (long hair that is bound up) and allow to fall loose. **5.** to deflate: *to let down a tyre.* ~*n.* **letdown.** **6.** a disappointment.

lethal ('liːθəl) *adj.* **1.** able to cause or causing death. **2.** of or suggestive of death. —**lethality** (liː'θælɪtɪ) *n.* —**'lethally** *adv.*

lethargy ('lɛθədʒɪ) *n., pl.* **-gies.** **1.** sluggishness, slowness, or dullness. **2.** an abnormal lack of energy. —**lethargic** (lɪ'θɑːdʒɪk) *adj.* —**le'thargically** *adv.*

Lethe ('liːθɪ) *n.* **1.** *Greek myth.* a river in Hades that caused forgetfulness in those who drank its waters. **2.** forgetfulness. —**Lethean** (lɪ'θiːən) *adj.*

let off *vb. (tr., mainly adv.)* **1.** *(also prep.)* to allow to disembark or leave. **2.** to explode or fire (a bomb, gun, etc.). **3.** *(also prep.)* to excuse from (work or other responsibilities): *I'll let you off for a week.* **4.** *Inf.* to allow to get away without the expected punishment, work, etc. **5.** to let (accommodation) in portions. **6.** to release (liquid, air, etc.).

let on *vb. (adv.; when tr., takes a clause as object)* **1.** to allow (something, such as a secret) to be known; reveal: *he never let on that he was married.* **2.** *(tr.)* to pretend.

let out *vb. (adv., mainly tr.)* **1.** to give vent to; emit: *to let out a howl.* **2.** to allow to go or run free; release. **3.** *(may take a clause as object)* to reveal (a secret). **4.** to make available to tenants, hirers, or contractors. **5.** to permit to flow out: *to let air out of the tyres.* **6.** to make (a garment) larger, as by unpicking (the seams) and sewing nearer the outer edge. ~*n.* **let-out.** **7.** a chance to escape.

letter ('lɛtə) *n.* **1.** any of a set of conventional symbols used in writing or printing a language, each symbol being associated with a group of phonetic values; character of the alphabet. **2.** a written or printed communication addressed to a person, company, etc., usually sent by post. **3.** (often preceded by *the*) the strict legalistic or pedantic interpretation of the meaning of an agreement, document, etc.; exact wording as distinct from actual intention (esp. in **the letter of the law**). **4. to the letter. a.** following the literal interpretation or wording exactly. **b.** attending to every detail. ~*vb.* **5.** to write or mark letters on (a sign, etc.), esp. by hand. **6.** *(tr.)* to set down or print using letters. —**'letterer** *n.*

letter bomb *n.* an explosive device in an envelope, detonated when the envelope is opened.

letter box *n. Chiefly Brit.* **a.** a private box into which letters, etc., are delivered. **b.** a public box into which letters, etc., are put for collection.

lettered ('lɛtəd) *adj.* **1.** well educated in literature, the arts, etc. **2.** literate. **3.** of or characterized by learning or culture. **4.** printed or marked with letters.

letterhead ('lɛtə,hɛd) *n.* a sheet of writing paper printed with one's address, name, etc.

letter of credit *n.* a letter issued by a bank entitling the bearer to draw funds up to a specified maximum from that bank or its agencies.

letterpress ('lɛtə,prɛs) *n.* **1. a.** a method of printing in which ink is transferred from raised surfaces to paper by pressure. **b.** matter so printed. **2.** text matter as distinct from illustrations.

letters ('lɛtəz) *n.* **1.** literary knowledge, ability, or learning: *a man of letters.* **2.** literary culture in general. **3.** an official title, degree, etc., indicated by an abbreviation: *letters after one's name.*

letters patent *n.* See **patent** (senses 1,4).

lettuce ('lɛtɪs) *n.* **1.** any of various plants of the composite family cultivated in many varieties for their large

THESAURUS

~*prep.* **4.** excepting, lacking, minus, subtracting, without

lessen abate, abridge, contract, curtail, decrease, de-escalate, degrade, die down, diminish, dwindle, ease, erode, grow less, impair, lighten, lower, minimize, moderate, narrow, reduce, shrink, slacken, slow down, weaken, wind down

lessening abatement, contraction, curtailment, decline, decrease, de-escalation, diminution, dwindling, ebbing, erosion, let-up (*Inf.*), minimization, moderation, petering out, reduction, shrinkage, slackening, slowing down, waning, weakening

lesser inferior, less important, lower, minor, secondary, slighter, subordinate, under-

lesson 1. class, coaching, instruction, period, schooling, teaching, tutoring **2.** assignment, drill, exercise, homework, lecture, practice, reading, recitation, task **3.** deterrent, example, exemplar, message, model, moral, precept **4.** admonition, censure, chiding, punishment, rebuke, reprimand, reproof, scolding, warning

let[1] *v.* **1.** allow, authorize, give leave, give permission, give the go-ahead (green light,

O.K.) (*Inf.*), grant, permit, sanction, suffer (*Archaic*), tolerate, warrant **2.** hire, lease, rent **3.** allow, cause, enable, grant, make, permit

let[2] *n.* constraint, hindrance, impediment, interference, obstacle, obstruction, prohibition, restriction

letdown anticlimax, bitter pill, blow, comedown (*Inf.*), disappointment, disgruntlement, disillusionment, frustration, setback, washout (*Inf.*)

let down disappoint, disenchant, disillusion, dissatisfy, fail, fall short, leave in the lurch, leave stranded

lethal baleful, dangerous, deadly, deathly, destructive, devastating, fatal, mortal, murderous, noxious, pernicious, poisonous, virulent

lethargic apathetic, comatose, debilitated, drowsy, dull, enervated, heavy, inactive, indifferent, inert, languid, lazy, listless, sleepy, slothful, slow, sluggish, somnolent, stupefied, torpid

lethargy apathy, drowsiness, dullness, hebetude (*Rare*), inaction, indifference, inertia, languor, lassitude, listlessness, sleepi-

ness, sloth, slowness, sluggishness, stupor, torpidity, torpor

let in admit, allow to enter, give access to, greet, include, incorporate, receive, take in, welcome

let off 1. detonate, discharge, emit, explode, exude, fire, give off, leak, release **2.** absolve, discharge, dispense, excuse, exempt, exonerate, forgive, pardon, release, spare

let out 1. emit, give vent to, produce **2.** discharge, free, let go, liberate, release **3.** betray, disclose, leak, let fall, let slip, make known, reveal

letter 1. character, sign, symbol **2.** acknowledgment, answer, billet (*Archaic*), communication, dispatch, epistle, line, message, missive, note, reply **3. to the letter** accurately, exactly, literally, precisely, strictly, word for word

letters belles-lettres, culture, erudition, humanities, learning, literature, scholarship

let-up abatement, break, cessation, interval, lessening, lull, pause, recess, remission, respite, slackening

edible leaves. **2.** the leaves of any of these varieties, which are eaten in salads. **3.** any of various plants that resemble true lettuce, such as lamb's lettuce.

let up vb. (intr., adv.) **1.** to diminish, slacken, or stop. **2.** (foll. by on) Inf. to be less harsh (towards someone). ~n. **let-up. 3.** Inf. a lessening or abatement.

leuco-, leuko- or before a vowel **leuc-, leuk-** combining form. white or lacking colour: leucocyte; leukaemia.

leucocyte or esp. U.S. **leukocyte** ('lu:kə,saɪt) n. any of the large unpigmented cells in the blood of vertebrates. Also called: **white blood cell, white (blood) corpuscle.** —**leucocytic** or esp. U.S. **leukocytic** (,lu:kə-'sɪtɪk) adj.

leucotomy (lu:'kɒtəmɪ) n. the surgical operation of cutting some of the nerve fibres within the brain for treating intractable mental disorders.

leukaemia or esp. U.S. **leukemia** (lu:'ki:mɪə) n. an acute or chronic disease characterized by a gross proliferation of leucocytes, which crowd into the bone marrow, spleen, lymph nodes, etc., and suppress the blood-forming apparatus.

Lev. Bible. abbrev. for Leviticus.

Levant (lɪ'vænt) n. **the.** a former name for the area of the E Mediterranean now occupied by Lebanon, Syria, and Israel. —**Levantine** ('lɛvən,taɪn) adj., n.

levanter (lɪ'væntə) n. (sometimes cap.) **1.** an easterly wind in the W Mediterranean area. **2.** an inhabitant of the Levant.

levee[1] ('lɛvɪ) n. **1.** an embankment alongside a river constructed to prevent flooding. **2.** an embankment that surrounds a field that is to be irrigated. **3.** a landing place on a river; quay.

levee[2] ('lɛvɪ, 'lɛveɪ) n. **1.** a formal reception held by a sovereign just after rising from bed. **2.** (in Britain) a public court reception for men.

level ('lɛvəl) adj. **1.** on a horizontal plane. **2.** having a surface of completely equal height. **3.** being of the same height as something else. **4.** (of quantities to be measured, as in recipes) even with the top of the cup, spoon, etc. **5.** equal to or even with (something or someone else). **6.** not having or showing inconsistency or irregularities. **7.** Also: **level-headed.** even-tempered; steady. **8. one's level best.** the best one can do. ~vb. **-elling, -elled** or U.S. **-eling, -eled. 9.** (tr.; sometimes foll. by off) to make (a surface) horizontal, level, or even. **10.** to make (two or more people or things) equal, as in position or status. **11.** (tr.) to raze to the ground. **12.** (tr.) to knock (a person) down as by a blow. **13.** (tr.) to direct (a gaze, criticism, etc.) emphatically at someone. **14.** (intr.; often foll. by with) Inf. to be straightforward and frank. **15.** (intr.; foll. by off or out) to manoeuvre an aircraft into a horizontal flight path after a dive, climb, or glide. **16.** (often foll. by at) to aim (a weapon) horizontally. ~n. **17.** a horizontal datum line or plane. **18.** a device, such as a spirit level, for determining whether a surface is horizontal. **19.** a surveying instrument used for measuring relative heights of land. **20.** position or status in a scale of values. **21.** amount or degree of progress; stage. **22.** a specified vertical position; altitude. **23.** a horizontal line or plane with respect to which measurement of elevation is based: sea level. **24.** a flat even surface or area of land. **25.** Physics. the ratio of the magnitude of a physical quantity to an arbitrary magnitude: sound-pressure level. **26. on the level.** Inf. sincere or genuine. —**leveller** or U.S. **leveler** n. —**levelly** adv. —**levelness** n.

level crossing n. Brit. a point at which a railway and a road cross, esp. one with barriers that close the road when a train is due to pass.

level-headed adj. even-tempered, balanced, and reliable; steady. —,level-'headedly adv. —,level-'headedness n.

lever ('li:və) n. **1.** a rigid bar pivoted about a fulcrum, used to transfer a force to a load and usually to provide a mechanical advantage. **2.** any of a number of mechanical devices employing this principle. **3.** a means of exerting pressure in order to accomplish something. ~vb. **4.** to prise or move (an object) with a lever.

leverage ('li:vərɪdʒ, -vrɪdʒ) n. **1.** the action of a lever. **2.** the mechanical advantage gained by employing a lever. **3.** strategic advantage.

leveret ('lɛvərɪt, -vrɪt) n. a young hare, esp. one less than one year old.

leviathan (lɪ'vaɪəθən) n. **1.** Bible. a monstrous beast, esp. a sea monster. **2.** any huge or powerful thing.

Levis ('li:vaɪz) pl. n. Trademark. jeans, usually blue and made of denim.

levitate ('lɛvɪ,teɪt) vb. to rise or cause to rise and float in the air, usually attributed to supernatural intervention. —,levi'tation n. —'levi,tator n.

levity ('lɛvɪtɪ) n., pl. **-ties. 1.** inappropriate lack of seriousness. **2.** fickleness or instability. **3.** Arch. lightness in weight.

levy ('lɛvɪ) vb. **levying, levied.** (tr.) **1.** to impose and collect (a tax, tariff, fine, etc.). **2.** to conscript troops for service. **3.** to seize or attach (property) in accordance with the judgment of a court. ~n., pl. **levies. 4. a.** the act of imposing and collecting a tax, tariff, etc. **b.** the money so raised. **5. a.** the conscription of troops for service. **b.** a person conscripted in this way.

lewd (lu:d) adj. characterized by or intended to excite crude sexual desire; obscene. —'lewdly adv. —'lewdness n.

lexical ('lɛksɪkəl) adj. **1.** of or relating to items of vocabulary in a language. **2.** of or relating to a lexicon. —'lexically adv.

lexicography (,lɛksɪ'kɒgrəfɪ) n. the process or profession of writing or compiling dictionaries. —,lexi'cographer n. —**lexicographic** (,lɛksɪkə'græfɪk) or ,lexico-'graphical adj.

lexicon ('lɛksɪkən) n. **1.** a dictionary, esp. one of an ancient language such as Greek or Hebrew. **2.** a list of terms relating to a particular subject. **3.** Linguistics. the set of all the morphemes of a language.

ley (leɪ, li:) n. **1.** arable land temporarily under grass. **2.** Also: **ley line.** a line joining two prominent points in the landscape, thought to be the line of a prehistoric track.

Leyden jar ('laɪdən) n. Physics. an early type of capacitor consisting of a glass jar with the lower part of the inside and outside coated with tinfoil.

L.F. Radio. abbrev. for low frequency.

l.h. or **L.H.** abbrev. for left hand.

Li the chemical symbol for lithium.

liabilities (,laɪə'bɪlɪtɪz) pl. n. Accounting. business obligations not discharged and shown as balanced against assets on the balance sheet.

THESAURUS

let up abate, decrease, diminish, ease (up), moderate, slacken, stop, subside

level adj. **1.** consistent, even, flat, horizontal, plain, plane, smooth, uniform **2.** aligned, balanced, commensurate, comparable, equivalent, even, flush, in line, neck and neck, on a line, on a par, proportionate **3.** calm, equable, even, even-tempered, stable, steady ~v. **4.** even off or out, flatten, make flat, plane, smooth **5.** bulldoze, demolish, destroy, devastate, equalize, flatten, knock down, lay low, pull down, raze, smooth, tear down, wreck **6.** aim, beam, direct, focus, point, train **7.** Inf. be above board, be frank, be honest, be open, be straightforward, be up front (Sl.), come clean (Inf.), keep nothing back ~n. **8.** altitude, elevation, height, vertical position **9.** achievement, degree, grade, position, rank, stage, standard, standing, status **10.** bed, floor, layer, storey, stratum, zone **11.** flat surface, horizontal, plain, plane **12. on the level** Inf. above board, fair, genuine, honest, open, sincere, square, straight, straightforward, up front (Sl.)

level-headed balanced, calm, collected, composed, cool, dependable, even-tempered, reasonable, sane, self-possessed, sensible, steady, together (Sl., chiefly U.S.), unflappable (Inf.)

lever 1. n. bar, crowbar, handle, handspike, jemmy **2.** v. force, jemmy, move, prise, pry (U.S.), purchase, raise

leverage ascendancy, authority, clout (Inf.), influence, pull (Inf.), purchasing power, rank, weight

levity buoyancy, facetiousness, fickleness, flightiness, flippancy, frivolity, giddiness, light-heartedness, light-mindedness, silliness, skittishness, triviality

levy v. **1.** charge, collect, demand, exact, gather, impose, tax **2.** call, call up, conscript, mobilize, muster, press, raise, summon ~n. **3.** assessment, collection, exaction, gathering, imposition **4.** assessment, duty, excise, fee, imposition, impost, tariff, tax, toll

lewd bawdy, blue, dirty, impure, indecent, lascivious, libidinous, licentious, loose, lustful, obscene, pornographic, profligate, salacious, smutty, unchaste, vile, vulgar, wanton, wicked

lewdness bawdiness, carnality, crudity, debauchery, depravity, impurity, indecency, lasciviousness, lechery, licentiousness, lubricity, obscenity, pornography, profligacy, salaciousness, smut, smuttiness, unchastity, vulgarity, wantonness

liability (ˌlaɪəˈbɪlɪtɪ) n., pl. **-ties. 1.** the state of being liable. **2.** a financial obligation. **3.** a hindrance or disadvantage.

liable (ˈlaɪəbəl) adj. (postpositive) **1.** legally obliged or responsible; answerable. **2.** susceptible or exposed; subject. **3.** probable or likely: it's liable to happen soon.

▷ **Usage.** Careful users of English take liable to mean responsible for and subject to in sentences such as he was liable for his employees' accidents and he was liable to accidents. The use of liable in the sense of likely is avoided: he was likely (not liable) to have accidents.

liaise (lɪˈeɪz) vb. (intr.; usually foll. by with) to communicate and maintain contact (with).

liaison (lɪˈeɪzɒn) n. **1.** communication and contact between groups or units. **2.** a secretive or adulterous sexual relationship. **3.** the relationship between military units necessary to ensure unity of purpose. **4.** (esp. in French) the pronunciation of a normally silent consonant at the end of a word immediately before another word commencing with a vowel, in such a way that the consonant is taken over as the initial sound of the following word, as in ils ont (iːlˈzɔ̃). **5.** any thickening for soups, sauces, etc., such as egg yolks or cream.

liana (lɪˈɑːnə) or **liane** (lɪˈɑːn) n. any of various woody climbing plants of tropical forests.

liar (ˈlaɪə) n. a person who tells lies.

lib (lɪb) n. Inf. short for **liberation** (see liberate).

lib. abbrev. for: **1.** liber: book. **2.** librarian. **3.** library.

Lib. abbrev. for Liberal.

libation (laɪˈbeɪʃən) n. **1. a.** the pouring-out of wine, etc., in honour of a deity. **b.** the liquid so poured out. **2.** Usually facetious. an alcoholic drink.

libel (ˈlaɪbəl) n. **1.** Law. **a.** the publication of defamatory matter in permanent form, as by a written or printed statement, picture, etc. **b.** the act of publishing such matter. **2.** any defamatory or unflattering representation or statement. ~vb. **-belling, -belled** or U.S. **-beling, -beled.** (tr.) **3.** Law. to make or publish a defamatory statement or representation about (a person). **4.** to misrepresent injuriously. —**ˈlibeller** or **ˈlibelist** n. —**ˈlibellous** or **ˈlibelous** adj.

liberal (ˈlɪbərəl, ˈlɪbrəl) adj. **1.** relating to or having social and political views that favour progress and reform. **2.** relating to or having policies or views advocating individual freedom. **3.** giving and generous in temperament or behaviour. **4.** tolerant of other people. **5.** abundant; lavish: a liberal helping of cream. **6.** not strict; free: a liberal translation. **7.** of or relating to an education that aims to develop general cultural interests and intellectual ability. ~n. **8.** a person who has liberal ideas or opinions. —**ˈliberally** adv. —**ˈliberalness** n.

Liberal (ˈlɪbərəl, ˈlɪbrəl) n. **1.** a member or supporter of

a Liberal Party. ~adj. **2.** of or relating to a Liberal Party.

liberality (ˌlɪbəˈrælɪtɪ) n., pl. **-ties. 1.** generosity; bounty. **2.** the quality or condition of being liberal.

liberalize or **-ise** (ˈlɪbərəˌlaɪz, ˈlɪbrə-) vb. to make or become liberal. —**ˌliberaliˈzation** or **-iˈsation** n. —**ˈliberalˌizer** or **-ˌiser** n.

liberate (ˈlɪbəˌreɪt) vb. (tr.) **1.** to give liberty to; make free. **2.** to release (something, esp. a gas) from chemical combination. **3.** to release from occupation or subjugation by a foreign power. —**ˌliberˈation** n. —**ˈliberˌator** n.

libertine (ˈlɪbəˌtiːn, -ˌtaɪn) n. **1.** a morally dissolute person. ~adj. **2.** morally dissolute. —**ˈliberˌtinage** or **ˈlibertinˌism** n.

liberty (ˈlɪbətɪ) n., pl. **-ties. 1.** the power of choosing, thinking, and acting for oneself; freedom from control or restriction. **2.** the right or privilege of access to a particular place; freedom. **3.** (often pl.) a social action regarded as being familiar, forward, or improper. **4.** (often pl.) an action that is unauthorized: he took liberties with the translation. **5. a.** authorized leave granted to a sailor. **b.** (as modifier): liberty man; liberty boat. **6. at liberty.** free, unoccupied, or unrestricted. **7. take liberties (with).** to be overfamiliar or overpresumptuous.

libidinous (lɪˈbɪdɪnəs) adj. characterized by excessive sexual desire. —**liˈbidinously** adv. —**liˈbidinousness** n.

libido (lɪˈbiːdəʊ) n., pl. **-dos. 1.** Psychoanal. psychic energy emanating from the id. **2.** sexual urge or desire. —**libidinal** (lɪˈbɪdɪnəl) adj. —**liˈbidinally** adv.

Libra (ˈliːbrə) n., Latin genitive **Librae** (ˈliːbriː). **1.** Astron. a small faint zodiacal constellation in the S hemisphere, lying between Virgo and Scorpius. **2.** Astrol. Also called: the **Scales,** the **Balance.** the seventh sign of the zodiac. The sun is in this sign between about Sept. 23 and Oct. 22.

librarian (laɪˈbrɛərɪən) n. a person in charge of a library. —**liˈbrarianˌship** n.

library (ˈlaɪbrərɪ) n., pl. **-braries. 1.** a room or set of rooms where books and other literary materials are kept. **2.** a collection of literary materials, films, tapes, gramophone records, etc., kept for reference or borrowing. **3.** the building or institution that houses such a collection: a public library. **4.** a set of books published as a series, often in a similar format. **5.** Computers. a collection of standard programs and subroutines, usually stored on disk.

libretto (lɪˈbretəʊ) n., pl. **-tos** or **-ti** (-tiː). a text written for and set to music in an opera, etc. —**liˈbrettist** n.

lice (laɪs) n. the plural of **louse.**

licence or U.S. **license** (ˈlaɪsəns) n. **1.** a certificate, tag, document, etc., giving official permission to do

---

THESAURUS

liability 1. accountability, answerability, culpability, duty, obligation, onus, responsibility **2.** arrear, debit, debt, indebtedness, obligation **3.** burden, disadvantage, drag, drawback, encumbrance, handicap, hindrance, impediment, inconvenience, millstone, minus (Inf.), nuisance **4.** likelihood, probability, proneness, susceptibility, tendency

liable 1. accountable, amenable, answerable, bound, chargeable, obligated, responsible **2.** exposed, open, subject, susceptible, vulnerable **3.** apt, disposed, inclined, likely, prone, tending **4. render oneself liable to** expose oneself to, incur, lay oneself open to, run the risk of

liaison 1. communication, connection, contact, go-between, hook-up, interchange, intermediary **2.** affair, amour, entanglement, illicit romance, intrigue, love affair, romance

liar fabricator, falsifier, fibber, perjurer, prevaricator, storyteller (Inf.)

libel 1. n. aspersion, calumny, defamation, denigration, obloquy, slander, smear, vituperation **2.** v. blacken, calumniate, defame, derogate, drag (someone's) name through the mud, malign, revile, slander, slur, smear, traduce, vilify

libellous aspersive, calumniatory, calumnious, defamatory, derogatory, false, injurious, malicious, maligning, scurrilous, slanderous, traducing, untrue, vilifying, vituperative

liberal 1. advanced, humanistic, latitudinarian, libertarian, progressive, radical, reformist **2.** altruistic, beneficent, bounteous, bountiful, charitable, free-handed, generous, kind, open-handed, open-hearted, unstinting **3.** advanced, broad-minded, catholic, enlightened, high-minded, humanitarian, indulgent, magnanimous, permissive, tolerant, unbiased, unbigoted, unprejudiced **4.** abundant, ample, bountiful, copious, handsome, lavish, munificent, plentiful, profuse, rich **5.** broad, flexible, free, general, inexact, lenient, loose, not close, not literal, not strict

liberality 1. altruism, beneficence, benevolence, bounty, charity, free-handedness, generosity, kindness, largess, munificence, open-handedness, philanthropy **2.** breadth, broad-mindedness, candour, catholicity, impartiality, latitude, liberalism, libertarianism, magnanimity, permissiveness, progressivism, toleration

liberalize ameliorate, broaden, ease, expand, extend, loosen, mitigate, moderate, modify, relax, slacken, soften, stretch

liberate deliver, discharge, disenthral, emancipate, free, let loose, let out, manumit, redeem, release, rescue, set free

liberation deliverance, emancipation,

enfranchisement, freedom, freeing, liberating, liberty, manumission, redemption, release, unfettering, unshackling

liberator deliverer, emancipator, freer, manumitter, redeemer, rescuer, saviour

libertine 1. n. debauchee, lecher, loose liver, profligate, rake, reprobate, roué, seducer, sensualist, voluptuary, womanizer **2.** adj. abandoned, corrupt, debauched, decadent, degenerate, depraved, dissolute, immoral, licentious, profligate, rakish, reprobate, voluptuous, wanton

liberty 1. autonomy, emancipation, freedom, immunity, independence, liberation, release, self-determination, sovereignty **2.** authorization, carte blanche, dispensation, exemption, franchise, freedom, leave, licence, permission, prerogative, privilege, right, sanction **3.** Often plural disrespect, familiarity, forwardness, impertinence, impropriety, impudence, insolence, overfamiliarity, presumption, presumptuousness **4. at liberty** free, not confined, on the loose, unlimited, unoccupied, unrestricted

libidinous carnal, concupiscent, debauched, impure, incontinent, lascivious, lecherous, lickerish (Archaic), loose, lustful, prurient, randy (Sl., chiefly Brit.), ruttish, salacious, sensual, unchaste, wanton, wicked

something. **2.** formal permission or exemption. **3.** liberty of action or thought; freedom. **4.** intentional disregard of conventional rules to achieve a certain effect: *poetic licence.* **5.** excessive freedom.

license ('laɪsəns) *vb.* (*tr.*) **1.** to grant or give a licence for (something, such as the sale of alcohol). **2.** to give permission to or for. —'**licensable** *adj.* —'**licenser** *or* '**licensor** *n.*

licensee (,laɪsən'siː) *n.* a person who holds a licence, esp. one to sell alcoholic drink.

licentiate (laɪ'sɛnʃɪɪt) *n.* **1.** a person who holds a licence to practise a certain profession. **2.** a higher degree awarded by certain universities. **3.** a person who holds this degree. **4.** *Chiefly Presbyterian Church.* a person holding a licence to preach. —li'**centiate**,**ship** *n.*

licentious (laɪ'sɛnʃəs) *adj.* **1.** sexually unrestrained or promiscuous. **2.** *Now rare.* showing disregard for convention. —li'**centiously** *adv.* —li'**centiousness** *n.*

lichee (,laɪ'tʃiː) *n.* a variant spelling of **litchi.**

lichen ('laɪkən, 'lɪtʃən) *n.* any of various small plants which are formed by the symbiotic association of a fungus and an alga and occur as crusty patches or bushy growths on tree trunks, bare ground, etc. —'**lichened** *adj.* —'**lichenous** *adj.*

lich gate *or* **lych gate** (lɪtʃ) *n.* a roofed gate to a churchyard, formerly used as a temporary shelter for the bier.

licit ('lɪsɪt) *adj.* a less common word for **lawful.** —'**licitly** *adv.* —'**licitness** *n.*

lick (lɪk) *vb.* **1.** (*tr.*) to pass the tongue over, esp. in order to taste or consume. **2.** to flicker or move lightly over or round (something): *the flames licked around the door.* **3.** (*tr.*) *Inf.* **a.** to defeat or vanquish. **b.** to flog or thrash. **c.** to be or do much better than. **4. lick into shape.** to put into a satisfactory condition. **5. lick one's lips.** to anticipate or recall something with pleasure. **6. lick one's wounds.** to retire after a defeat. ~*n.* **7.** an instance of passing the tongue over something. **8.** a small amount: *a lick of paint.* **9.** short for **salt lick. 10.** *Inf.* a hit; blow. **11.** an informal word for **speed. 12. a lick and a promise.** something hastily done, esp. a hurried wash. —'**licker** *n.*

lickspittle ('lɪk,spɪtəl) *n.* a flattering or servile person.

licorice ('lɪkərɪs) *n.* the usual U.S. spelling of **liquorice.**

lid (lɪd) *n.* **1.** a cover, usually removable or hinged, for a receptacle: *a saucepan lid; a desk lid.* **2.** short for **eyelid. 3. put the lid on.** *Inf.* **a.** *Brit.* to be the final blow to. **b.** to curb, prevent, or discourage. —'**lidded** *adj.* —'**lidless** *adj.*

lido ('liːdəʊ) *n., pl.* **-dos.** *Brit.* a public place of recreation, including a swimming pool.

lie¹ (laɪ) *vb.* **lying, lied. 1.** (*intr.*) to speak untruthfully with intent to mislead or deceive. **2.** (*intr.*) to convey a false impression or practise deception: *the camera does not lie.* ~*n.* **3.** an untrue or deceptive statement deliberately used to mislead. **4.** something that is deliberately intended to deceive. **5. give the lie to. a.** to disprove. **b.** to accuse of lying.

lie² (laɪ) *vb.* **lying, lay, lain.** (*intr.*) **1.** (often foll. by *down*) to place oneself or be in a prostrate position, horizontal to the ground. **2.** to be situated, esp. on a horizontal surface: *the pencil is lying on the desk; India lies to the south of Russia.* **3.** to be buried: *here lies Jane Brown.* **4.** (*copula*) to be and remain (in a particular state or condition): *to lie dormant.* **5.** to stretch or extend: *the city lies before us.* **6.** (usually foll. by *on* or *upon*) to rest or weigh: *my sins lie heavily on my mind.* **7.** (usually foll. by *in*) to exist or consist inherently: *strength lies in unity.* **8.** (foll. by *with*) **a.** to be or rest (with): *the ultimate decision lies with you.* **b.** *Arch.* to have sexual intercourse (with). **9.** (of an action, claim, appeal, etc.) to subsist; be maintainable or admissible. **10.** *Arch.* to stay temporarily. ~*n.* **11.** the manner, place, or style in which something is situated. **12.** the hiding place or lair of an animal. **13. lie of the land. a.** the topography of the land. **b.** the way in which a situation is developing. ~See also **lie down, lie in.**

▷ **Usage.** See at **lay¹.**

lied (liːd; *German* liːt) *n., pl.* **lieder** ('liːdə; *German* 'liːdər). *Music.* any of various musical settings for solo voice and piano of a romantic or lyrical poem.

lie detector *n. Inf.* a polygraph used esp. by a police interrogator to detect false or devious answers to questions, a sudden change in one or more involuntary physiological responses being considered a manifestation of guilt, fear, etc.

lie down *vb.* (*intr., adv.*) **1.** to place oneself or be in a prostrate position in order to rest. **2.** to accept without protest or opposition (esp. in **take something lying down**). ~*n.* **lie-down. 3.** a rest.

lief (liːf) *adv.* **1.** *Now rare.* gladly; willingly: *I'd as lief go today as tomorrow.* ~*adj.* **2.** *Arch.* **a.** ready; glad. **b.** dear; beloved.

liege (liːdʒ) *adj.* **1.** (of a lord) owed feudal allegiance (esp. in **liege lord**). **2.** (of a vassal or servant) owing feudal allegiance: *a liege subject.* **3.** faithful; loyal. ~*n.* **4.** a liege lord. **5.** a liegeman or true subject.

lie in *vb.* (*intr., adv.*) **1.** to remain in bed late in the morning. **2.** to be confined in childbirth. ~*n.* **lie-in. 3.** a long stay in bed in the morning.

lien (lɪən, 'liːən) *n. Law.* a right to retain possession of another's property pending discharge of a debt.

lieu (ljuː, luː) *n.* stead; place (esp. in **in lieu, in lieu of**).

lieutenant (lɛf'tɛnənt; in the Navy, lə'tɛnənt; *U.S.* luː'tɛnənt) *n.* **1.** a military officer holding commissioned rank immediately junior to a captain. **2.** a naval officer holding commissioned rank immediately junior to a lieutenant commander. **3.** *U.S.* an officer in a police or fire department ranking immediately junior to a captain. **4.** a person who holds an office in subordination to or in place of a superior. —lieu'**tenancy** *n.*

lieutenant colonel *n.* an officer holding commissioned rank immediately junior to a colonel in certain armies, air forces, and marine corps.

lieutenant commander *n.* an officer holding commissioned rank in certain navies immediately junior to a commander.

lieutenant general *n.* an officer holding commissioned rank in certain armies, air forces, and marine corps immediately junior to a general.

lieutenant governor *n.* **1.** a deputy governor. **2.** (in the U.S.) an elected official who acts as deputy to a state governor. **3.** (in Canada) the representative of the Crown in a province: appointed by the federal government.

life (laɪf) *n., pl.* **lives** (laɪvz). **1.** the state or quality that

---

THESAURUS

licence *n.* **1.** authority, authorization, carte blanche, certificate, charter, dispensation, entitlement, exemption, immunity, leave, liberty, permission, permit, privilege, right, warrant **2.** freedom, independence, latitude, liberty, self-determination **3.** abandon, anarchy, disorder, excess, immoderation, impropriety, indulgence, irresponsibility, lawlessness, laxity, profligacy, unruliness

license *v.* accredit, allow, authorize, certify, commission, empower, permit, sanction, warrant

licentious abandoned, debauched, disorderly, dissolute, immoral, impure, lascivious, lax, lewd, libertine, libidinous, lubricous, lustful, profligate, promiscuous, sensual, uncontrollable, uncontrolled, uncurbed, unruly, wanton

licentiousness abandon, debauchery, dissipation, dissoluteness, lechery, lewdness,
libertinism, libidinousness, lubricity, lust, lustfulness, profligacy, promiscuity, prurience, salaciousness, salacity, wantonness

lick *v.* **1.** brush, lap, taste, tongue, touch, wash **2.** *Of flames* dart, flick, flicker, ignite, kindle, play over, ripple, touch **3.** *Inf.* **a.** defeat, overcome, rout, trounce, vanquish, wipe the floor with (*Inf.*) **b.** beat, flog, slap, spank, strike, thrash, wallop (*Inf.*) **c.** beat, best, excel, outdo, outstrip, surpass, top ~*n.* **4.** bit, brush, dab, little, sample, speck, stroke, taste, touch **5.** *Inf.* clip (*Inf.*), pace, rate, speed

licking 1. beating, drubbing, flogging, hiding (*Inf.*), spanking, tanning (*Sl.*), thrashing, whipping **2.** beating, defeat, drubbing, trouncing

lie¹ 1. *v.* dissimulate, equivocate, fabricate, falsify, fib, forswear oneself, invent, misrepresent, perjure, prevaricate, tell a lie, tell untruths **2.** *n.* deceit, fabrication, falsehood, falsification, falsity, fib, fiction, invention, mendacity, prevarication, untruth, white lie

lie² *v.* **1.** be prone, be prostrate, be recumbent, be supine, couch, loll, lounge, recline, repose, rest, sprawl, stretch out **2.** be, be buried, be found, be interred, be located, belong, be placed, be situated, exist, extend, remain **3.** *Usually with on or upon* burden, oppress, press, rest, weigh **4.** *Usually with in* be present, consist, dwell, exist, inhere, pertain **5.** lie low conceal oneself, go to earth, go underground, hide, hide away, hide out, hole up, keep a low profile, keep out of sight, lurk, skulk, take cover

liege chieftain, feudal lord, master, overlord, seigneur, sovereign, superior, suzerain

distinguishes living beings or organisms from dead ones and from inorganic matter, characterized chiefly by metabolism, growth, and the ability to reproduce and respond to stimuli. Related adj.: **animate.** **2.** the period between birth and death. **3.** a living person or being: *to save a life.* **4.** the time between birth and the present time. **5. a.** the remainder or extent of one's life. **b.** (*as modifier*): *a life sentence; life membership; life work.* **6.** the amount of time that something is active or functioning: *the life of a battery.* **7.** a present condition, state, or mode of existence: *my life is very dull here.* **8. a.** a biography. **b.** (*as modifier*): *a life story.* **9.** a characteristic state or mode of existence: *town life.* **10.** the sum or course of human events and activities. **11.** liveliness or high spirits: *full of life.* **12.** a source of strength, animation, or vitality: *he was the life of the show.* **13.** all living things, taken as a whole: *there is no life on Mars; plant life.* **14.** (*modifier*) *Arts.* drawn or taken from a living model: *life drawing.* **15.** (in certain games) one of a number of opportunities for participation. **16. as large as life.** *Inf.* real and living. **17. for dear life.** *Inf.* urgently or with extreme vigour or desperation. **18. for the life of me (him, her,** etc.) though trying desperately. **19. a matter of life and death.** a matter of extreme urgency. **20. not on your life.** *Inf.* certainly not. **21. to the life.** (of a copy or image) resembling the original exactly. **22. the time of one's life.** a memorably enjoyable time. **23. true to life.** faithful to reality.

life belt *n.* a buoyant ring used to keep a person afloat when in danger of drowning.

lifeblood ('laɪf,blʌd) *n.* **1.** the blood, considered as vital to life. **2.** the essential or animating force.

lifeboat ('laɪf,bəʊt) *n.* a boat used for rescuing people at sea, escaping from a sinking ship, etc.

life buoy *n.* any of various kinds of buoyant device for keeping people afloat in an emergency.

lifeguard ('laɪf,gɑːd) *n.* a person at a beach or pool to guard people against the risk of drowning.

life jacket *n.* an inflatable sleeveless jacket worn to keep a person afloat when in danger of drowning.

lifeless ('laɪflɪs) *adj.* **1.** without life; inanimate; dead. **2.** not sustaining living organisms. **3.** having no vitality or animation. **4.** unconscious. —'**lifelessly** *adv.* —'**lifelessness** *n.*

lifelike ('laɪf,laɪk) *adj.* closely resembling or representing life. —'**life,likeness** *n.*

lifeline ('laɪf,laɪn) *n.* **1.** a line thrown or fired aboard a vessel for hauling in a hawser for a breeches buoy. **2.** a line by which a deep-sea diver is raised or lowered. **3.** a vital line of access or communication.

lifelong ('laɪf,lɒŋ) *adj.* lasting for or as if for a lifetime.

life peer *n. Brit.* a peer whose title lapses at his death.

life preserver *n.* **1.** *Brit.* a club or bludgeon, esp. one kept for self-defence. **2.** *U.S.* a life belt or life jacket.

lifer ('laɪfə) *n. Inf.* a prisoner sentenced to life imprisonment.

life raft *n.* a raft for emergency use at sea.

life-saver *n.* **1.** the saver of a person's life. **2.** *Austral.* an expert swimmer, esp. a member of a surf lifesaving club at a surfing beach, who rescues surfers or swimmers from drowning. **3.** *Inf.* a person or thing that

gives help in time of need. —'**life-,saving** *adj., n.*

life-size *or* **life-sized** *adj.* representing actual size.

life style *n.* the particular attitudes, habits, or behaviour associated with an individual or group.

lifetime ('laɪf,taɪm) *n.* **1. a.** the length of time a person or animal is alive. **b.** (*as modifier*): *a lifetime supply.* **2.** the length of time that something functions, is useful, etc. **3.** *Physics.* Also called: **life.** the average time of existence of an unstable or reactive entity.

lift (lɪft) *vb.* **1.** to rise or cause to rise upwards from the ground or another support to a higher place: *to lift a sack.* **2.** to move or cause to move upwards: *to lift one's eyes.* **3.** (*tr.*) to take hold of in order to carry or remove: *to lift something down from a shelf.* **4.** (*tr.*) to raise in status, spirituality, estimation, etc.: *his position lifted him from the common crowd.* **5.** (*tr.*) to revoke or rescind: *to lift tax restrictions.* **6.** (*tr.*) to take (plants or underground crops) out of the ground for transplanting or harvesting. **7.** (*intr.*) to disappear by lifting or as if by lifting: *the fog lifted.* **8.** (*tr.*) *Inf.* to take unlawfully or dishonourably; steal. **9.** (*tr.*) to perform a face-lift on. ~*n.* **10.** the act or an instance of lifting. **11.** the power or force available or used for lifting. **12. a.** *Brit.* a platform, compartment, or cage raised or lowered in a vertical shaft to transport persons or goods in a building. *U.S.* word: **elevator. b.** See **chair lift, ski lift. 13.** the distance or degree to which something is lifted. **14.** a ride in a car or other vehicle for part or all of a passenger's journey. **15.** a rise in the height of the ground. **16.** an elevation of the spirits or temperament. **17.** the force required to lift an object. **18.** a layer inserted in the heel of a shoe, etc., to give the wearer added height. **19.** aid; help. **20.** the component of the aerodynamic forces acting on an aerofoil, etc., at right angles to the airflow and opposing gravity. —'**lifter** *n.*

liftoff ('lɪft,ɒf) *n.* **1.** the initial movement of a rocket from its launching pad. **2.** the instant at which this occurs. ~*vb.* **lift off. 3.** (*intr., adv.*) (of a rocket) to leave its launching pad.

ligament ('lɪgəmənt) *n.* **1.** *Anat.* any one of the bands of tough fibrous connective tissue that restrict movement in joints, connect various bones or cartilages, support muscles, etc. **2.** any physical or abstract bond.

ligature ('lɪgətʃə, -,tʃʊə) *n.* **1.** the act of binding or tying up. **2.** something used to bind. **3.** a link, bond, or tie. **4.** *Surgery.* a thread or wire for tying around a vessel, duct, etc., as for constricting the flow of blood. **5.** *Printing.* a character of two or more joined letters, such as fl, fi, ffl. **6.** *Music.* a slur or the group of notes connected by it. ~*vb.* **7.** (*tr.*) to bind with a ligature; ligate.

light[1] (laɪt) *n.* **1.** the medium of illumination that makes sight possible. **2.** Also called: **visible radiation.** electromagnetic radiation that is capable of causing a visual sensation. **3.** (*not in technical usage*) electromagnetic radiation that has a wavelength outside this range, esp. ultraviolet radiation: *ultraviolet light.* **4.** the sensation experienced when electromagnetic radiation within the visible spectrum falls on the retina of the eye. **5.** anything that illuminates, such as a lamp or candle. **6.** See **traffic light. 7.** a particular quality or type of light: *a good light for reading.* **8. a.** illumination from the sun

---

THESAURUS

life 1. animation, being, breath, entity, growth, sentience, viability, vitality **2.** being, career, continuance, course, duration, existence, lifetime, span, time **3.** human, human being, individual, mortal, person, soul **4.** autobiography, biography, career, confessions, history, life story, memoirs, story **5.** behaviour, conduct, life style, way of life **6.** the human condition, the times, the world, this mortal coil, trials and tribulations, vicissitudes **7.** activity, animation, brio, energy, get-up-and-go (*Inf.*), go (*Inf.*), high spirits, liveliness, oomph (*Inf.*), sparkle, spirit, verve, vigour, vitality, vivacity, zest **8.** animating spirit, *élan vital*, essence, heart, lifeblood, soul, spirit, vital spark **9.** creatures, living beings, living things, organisms, wildlife **10. come to life** awaken, become animated, revive, rouse, show signs of life **11. for dear life** *Inf.* desperately, for all one is worth, intensely, quickly, urgently, vigorously

lifeblood animating force, driving force,

essence, guts (*Inf.*), heart, inspiration, life, stimulus, vital spark

lifeless 1. cold, dead, deceased, defunct, extinct, inanimate, inert **2.** bare, barren, desert, empty, sterile, uninhabited, unproductive, waste **3.** cold, colourless, dull, flat, heavy, hollow, lacklustre, lethargic, listless, passive, pointless, slow, sluggish, spent, spiritless, static, stiff, torpid, wooden **4.** comatose, dead to the world, in a faint, inert, insensate, insensible, out cold, out for six, unconscious

lifelike authentic, exact, faithful, graphic, natural, photographic, real, realistic, true-to-life, undistorted, vivid

lifelong constant, deep-rooted, enduring, for all one's life, for life, lasting, lifetime, long-lasting, long-standing, perennial, permanent, persistent

lifetime all one's born days, career, course, day(s), existence, life span, one's natural life, period, span, time

life work business, calling, career, interest, mission, occupation, profession, purpose, pursuit, vocation, work

lift v. **1.** bear aloft, buoy up, draw up, elevate, heft (*Inf.*), hoist, pick up, raise, raise high, rear, upheave, uplift, upraise **2.** advance, ameliorate, boost, dignify, elevate, enhance, exalt, improve, promote, raise, upgrade **3.** annul, cancel, countermand, end, relax, remove, rescind, revoke, stop, terminate **4.** ascend, be dispelled, climb, disappear, disperse, dissipate, mount, rise, vanish **5.** *Inf.* appropriate, copy, crib (*Inf.*), half-inch (*Brit. sl.*), nick (*Sl., chiefly Brit.*), pilfer, pinch (*Inf.*), pirate, plagiarize, pocket, purloin, steal, take, thieve ~n. **6.** car ride, drive, ride, run, transport **7.** boost, encouragement, fillip, pick-me-up, reassurance, shot in the arm (*Inf.*), uplift **8.** elevator (*Chiefly U.S.*)

during the day; daylight. **b.** the time this appears; daybreak; dawn. **9.** anything that allows the entrance of light, such as a window or compartment of a window. **10.** the condition of being visible or known (esp. in **bring** or **come to light**). **11.** an aspect or view: *he saw it in a different light.* **12.** mental understanding or spiritual insight. **13.** a person considered to be an authority or leader. **14.** brightness of countenance, esp. a sparkle in the eyes. **15. a.** the act of igniting or kindling something, such as a cigarette. **b.** something that ignites or kindles, esp. in a specified manner, such as a spark or flame. **c.** something used for igniting or kindling, such as a match. **16.** See **lighthouse**. **17. in (the) light of.** in view of; taking into account; considering. **18. see the light (of day). a.** to come into being. **b.** to come to public notice. **c.** to acquire insight. **19. strike a light. a.** (*vb.*) to ignite something, esp. a match, by friction. **b.** (*interj.*) *Brit.* an exclamation of surprise. *~adj.* **20.** full of light; well-lighted. **21.** (of a colour) reflecting or transmitting a large amount of light: *light yellow. ~vb.* **lighting, lighted** *or* **lit. 22.** to ignite or cause to ignite. **23.** (often foll. by *up*) to illuminate or cause to illuminate. **24.** to make or become cheerful or animated. **25.** (*tr.*) to guide or lead by light. *~See also* **light up.** — '**lightish** *adj.* — '**lightless** *adj.*

light² (laɪt) *adj.* **1.** not heavy; weighing relatively little. **2.** having relatively low density: *magnesium is a light metal.* **3.** lacking sufficient weight; not agreeing with standard or official weights. **4.** not great in degree, intensity, or number: *light rain.* **5.** without burdens, difficulties, or problems; easily borne or done: *a light heart; light work.* **6.** graceful, agile, or deft: *light fingers.* **7.** not bulky or clumsy. **8.** not serious or profound; entertaining: *light music; light verse.* **9.** without importance or consequence; insignificant: *no light matter.* **10.** frivolous or capricious. **11.** loose in morals. **12.** dizzy or unclear: *a light head.* **13.** (of bread, cake, etc.) spongy or well leavened. **14.** easily digested: *a light meal.* **15.** relatively low in alcoholic content: *a light wine.* **16.** (of a soil) having a crumbly texture. **17.** (of a vessel, lorry, etc.) **a.** designed to carry light loads. **b.** not loaded. **18.** carrying light arms or equipment: *light infantry.* **19.** (of an industry) engaged in the production of small consumer goods using light machinery. **20.** *Phonetics, prosody.* (of a syllable, vowel, etc.) unaccented or weakly stressed; short. **21. light on.** *Austral. & N.Z. inf.* lacking a sufficient quantity of (something). **22. make light of.** to treat as insignificant or trifling. *~adv.* **23.** with little equipment, baggage, etc.: *to travel light. ~vb.* **lighting, lighted** *or* **lit.** (*intr.*) **24.** (esp. of birds) to settle or land after flight. **25.** to get down from a horse, vehicle, etc. **26.** (foll. by *on* or *upon*) to come upon unexpectedly. **27.**

to strike or fall on: *the choice lighted on me.* — '**lightish** *adj.* — '**lightly** *adv.* — '**lightness** *n.*

lighten¹ ('laɪt°n) *vb.* **1.** to become or make light. **2.** (*intr.*) to shine; glow. **3.** (*intr.*) (of lightning) to flash. **4.** (*tr.*) *Arch.* to cause to flash.

lighten² ('laɪt°n) *vb.* **1.** to make or become less heavy. **2.** to make or become less burdensome or oppressive; mitigate. **3.** to make or become more cheerful or lively.

lighter¹ ('laɪtə) *n.* **1.** a small portable device for providing a naked flame to light cigarettes, etc. **2.** a person or thing that ignites something.

lighter² ('laɪtə) *n.* a flat-bottomed barge used for transporting cargo, esp. in loading or unloading a ship.

light-fingered *adj.* having nimble or agile fingers, esp. for thieving or picking pockets.

light flyweight *n.* an amateur boxer weighing not more than 48 kg (106 pounds).

light-footed *adj.* having a light or nimble tread. — '**light-'footedly** *adv.*

light-headed *adj.* **1.** frivolous. **2.** giddy; feeling faint or slightly delirious. — '**light-'headedly** *adv.* — '**light-'headedness** *n.*

light-hearted *adj.* cheerful or carefree in mood or disposition. — '**light-'heartedly** *adv.* — '**light-'heartedness** *n.*

light heavyweight *n.* **1.** Also (in Britain): **cruiserweight. a.** a professional boxer weighing 160–175 pounds (72.5–79.5 kg). **b.** an amateur boxer weighing 75–81 kg (165–179 pounds). **2.** a wrestler weighing usually 192–214 pounds (87–97 kg).

lighthouse ('laɪt,haʊs) *n.* a fixed structure in the form of a tower equipped with a light visible to mariners for warning them of obstructions, etc.

lighting ('laɪtɪŋ) *n.* **1.** the act or quality of illumination or ignition. **2.** the apparatus for supplying artificial light effects to a stage, film, or television set. **3.** the distribution of light on an object or figure, as in painting, photography, etc.

lighting-up time *n.* the time when vehicles are required by law to have their lights on.

light middleweight *n.* an amateur boxer weighing 67–71 kg (148–157 pounds).

lightness ('laɪtnɪs) *n.* the attribute of an object or colour that enables an observer to judge the extent to which the object or colour reflects or transmits incident light.

lightning ('laɪtnɪŋ) *n.* **1.** a flash of light in the sky, occurring during a thunderstorm and caused by a discharge of electricity, either between clouds or between a cloud and the earth. **2.** (*modifier*) fast and sudden: *a lightning raid.*

lightning conductor *or* **rod** *n.* a metal strip termi-

THESAURUS

light¹ *n.* **1.** blaze, brightness, brilliance, effulgence, flash, glare, gleam, glint, glow, illumination, incandescence, lambency, luminescence, luminosity, lustre, phosphorescence, radiance, ray, refulgence, scintillation, shine, sparkle **2.** beacon, bulb, candle, flare, lamp, lantern, lighthouse, star, taper, torch, windowpane **3.** broad day, cockcrow, dawn, daybreak, daylight, daytime, morn (*Poetic*), morning, sun, sunbeam, sunrise, sunshine **4.** *Fig.* angle, approach, aspect, attitude, context, interpretation, point of view, slant, vantage point, viewpoint **5.** awareness, comprehension, elucidation, explanation, illustration, information, insight, knowledge, understanding **6.** example, exemplar, guiding light, model, paragon, shining example **7.** flame, lighter, match **8. bring to light** disclose, discover, expose, reveal, show, uncover, unearth, unveil **9. come to light** appear, be disclosed, be discovered, be revealed, come out, transpire, turn up **10. in (the) light of** bearing in mind, because of, considering, in view of, taking into account, with knowledge of **11. shed** *or* **throw light on** clarify, clear up, elucidate, explain, simplify *~adj.* **12.** aglow, bright, brilliant, glowing, illuminated, luminous, lustrous, shining, sunny, well-lighted, well-lit **13.** bleached, blond, faded, fair, light-hued, light-toned, pale, pastel *~v.* **14.** fire, ignite, inflame, kindle, set a match to **15.** brighten, clarify, floodlight,

flood with light, illuminate, illumine, irradiate, lighten, light up, put on, switch on, turn on **16.** animate, brighten, cheer, irradiate, lighten

light² *adj.* **1.** airy, buoyant, delicate, easy, flimsy, imponderous, insubstantial, lightsome, lightweight, portable, slight, underweight **2.** faint, gentle, indistinct, mild, moderate, slight, soft, weak **3.** inconsequential, inconsiderable, insignificant, minute, scanty, slight, small, thin, tiny, trifling, trivial, unsubstantial, wee **4.** cushy (*Sl.*), easy, effortless, manageable, moderate, simple, undemanding, unexacting, untaxing **5.** agile, airy, graceful, light-footed, lithe, nimble, sprightly, sylphlike **6.** amusing, diverting, entertaining, frivolous, funny, gay, humorous, light-hearted, pleasing, superficial, trifling, trivial, witty **7.** airy, animated, blithe, carefree, cheerful, cheery, fickle, frivolous, gay, lively, merry, sunny **8.** dizzy, giddy, light-headed, reeling, unsteady, volatile **9.** digestible, frugal, modest, not heavy, not rich, restricted, small **10.** crumbly, friable, loose, porous, sandy, spongy *~v.* **11.** alight, land, perch, settle **12. With** *on* **or** *upon* chance, come across, discover, encounter, find, happen upon, hit upon, stumble on

lighten¹ become light, brighten, flash, gleam, illuminate, irradiate, light up, make bright, shine

lighten² **1.** disburden, ease, make lighter,

reduce in weight, unload **2.** alleviate, ameliorate, assuage, ease, facilitate, lessen, mitigate, reduce, relieve **3.** brighten, buoy up, cheer, elate, encourage, gladden, hearten, inspire, lift, perk up, revive

light-fingered crafty, crooked (*Inf.*), dishonest, furtive, pilfering, pinching (*Inf.*), shifty, sly, stealing, thieving, underhand

light-headed **1.** bird-brained (*Inf.*), featherbrained, fickle, flighty, flippant, foolish, frivolous, giddy, inane, rattlebrained (*Inf.*), shallow, silly, superficial, trifling **2.** delirious, dizzy, faint, giddy, hazy, vertiginous, woozy (*Inf.*)

light-hearted blithe, blithesome (*Literary*), bright, carefree, cheerful, effervescent, frolicsome, gay, glad, gleeful, happy-go-lucky, insouciant, jocund, jolly, jovial, joyful, joyous, merry, playful, sunny, untroubled, upbeat (*Inf.*)

lightless caliginous (*Archaic*), dark, dim, dusky, gloomy, inky, jet black, murky, pitch-black, pitch-dark, pitchy, Stygian, sunless, tenebrous, unilluminated, unlighted, unlit

lightly **1.** airily, delicately, faintly, gently, gingerly, slightly, softly, timidly **2.** moderately, sparingly, sparsely, thinly **3.** easily, effortlessly, readily, simply **4.** breezily, carelessly, flippantly, frivolously, heedlessly, indifferently, slightingly, thoughtlessly

nating in sharp points, attached to the highest part of a building, etc., to provide a safe path to earth for lightning discharges.

light opera *n.* another term for **operetta**.

lights[1] (laits) *pl. n.* a person's ideas, knowledge, or understanding: *he did it according to his lights*.

lights[2] (laits) *pl. n.* the lungs, esp. of sheep, bullocks, and pigs, used esp. for feeding pets.

lights out *n.* 1. the time when those resident at an institution, such as soldiers in barracks or children at a boarding school, are expected to retire to bed. 2. a signal indicating this.

light up *vb.* (*adv.*) 1. to light a cigarette, pipe, etc. 2. to illuminate or cause to illuminate. 3. to make or become cheerful or animated.

lightweight ('lait,weit) *adj.* 1. of a relatively light weight. 2. not serious; trivial. ~*n.* 3. a person or animal of a relatively light weight. 4. **a.** a professional boxer weighing 130–135 pounds (59–61 kg). **b.** an amateur boxer weighing 57–60 kg (126–132 pounds). 5. a wrestler weighing usually 115–126 pounds (52–57 kg). 6. *Inf.* an incompetent and unimportant person.

light welterweight *n.* an amateur boxer weighing 60–63.5 kg (132–140 pounds).

light year *n.* a unit of distance used in astronomy, equal to the distance travelled by light in one mean solar year, i.e. 9.4607×10^{15} metres or 5.8784×10^{12} miles.

ligneous ('lignias) *adj.* of or resembling wood.

lignite ('lignait) *n.* a brown carbonaceous sedimentary rock with woody texture that consists of accumulated layers of partially decomposed vegetation: used as a fuel. Also called: **brown coal.** —**lignitic** (lig'nitik) *adj.*

lignum vitae ('lignam 'vaiti) *n.* 1. either of two tropical American trees having blue or purple flowers. 2. the heavy resinous wood of either of these trees.

like[1] (laik) *adj.* 1. (*prenominal*) similar; resembling. ~*prep.* 2. similar to; similarly to; in the manner of: *acting like a maniac; he's so like his father.* 3. used correlatively to express similarity: *like mother, like daughter.* 4. such as: *there are lots of games—like draughts, for instance.* ~*adv.* 5. a dialect word for **likely.** ~*conj.* 6. *Not standard.* as though; as if: *you look like you've just seen a ghost.* 7. in the same way as; in the same way that: *she doesn't dance like you do.* 8. **the like.** similar things: *dogs, foxes, and the like.* 9. **the likes** (or **like**) **of.** people or things similar to (someone or something specified): *we don't want the likes of you around here.*

▷ *Usage.* The use of *like* as a conjunction (*he behaves like his father did*) is avoided in good usage, *as, as if,* or *as though* being preferred. Many careful writers and speakers do accept, however, the use of *like* as a preposition in constructions where no verb is expressed: *he looks like his father.*

like[2] (laik) *vb.* 1. (*tr.*) to find (something) enjoyable or agreeable or find it enjoyable or agreeable (to do something): *he likes boxing; he likes to hear music.* 2. (*tr.*) to be fond of. 3. (*tr.*) to prefer or wish (to do something): *we would like you to go.* 4. (*tr.*) to feel towards; consider; regard: *how did she like it?* 5. (*intr.*) to feel disposed or inclined; choose; wish. ~*n.* 6. (*usually pl.*) a favourable feeling, desire, preference, etc. (esp. in **likes and dislikes**). —'**likable** *or* '**likeable** *adj.*

-like *suffix forming adjectives.* 1. resembling or simi-

lar to: *lifelike.* 2. having the characteristics of: *childlike.*

likelihood ('laikli,hud) *or* **likeliness** *n.* 1. the condition of being likely or probable; probability. 2. something that is probable.

likely ('laikli) *adj.* 1. (usually foll. by an infinitive) tending or inclined; apt: *likely to rain.* 2. probable: *a likely result.* 3. believable or feasible; plausible. 4. appropriate for a purpose or activity. 5. having good possibilities of success: *a likely candidate.* ~*adv.* 6. probably or presumably.

like-minded *adj.* agreeing in opinions, goals, etc. —,like-'mindedly *adv.* —,like-'mindedness *n.*

liken ('laikan) *vb.* (*tr.*) to see or represent as the same or similar; compare.

likeness ('laiknis) *n.* 1. the condition of being alike; similarity. 2. a painted, carved, moulded, or graphic image of a person or thing. 3. an imitative appearance; semblance.

likewise ('laik,waiz) *adv.* 1. in addition; moreover; also. 2. in like manner; similarly.

liking ('laikiŋ) *n.* 1. the feeling of a person who likes; fondness. 2. a preference, inclination, or pleasure.

lilac ('lailak) *n.* 1. any of various Eurasian shrubs or small trees of the olive family which have large sprays of purple or white fragrant flowers. 2. a light or moderate purple colour.

Lilliputian (,lili'pju:fian) *n.* 1. a tiny person or being. ~*adj.* 2. tiny; very small. 3. petty or trivial.

Lilo ('lai,lau) *n., pl.* -**los.** *Trademark.* a type of inflatable plastic or rubber mattress.

lilt (lilt) *n.* 1. (in music) a jaunty rhythm. 2. a buoyant motion. ~*vb.* (*intr.*) 3. (of a melody) to have a lilt. 4. to move in a buoyant manner.

lily ('lili) *n., pl.* **lilies.** 1. any perennial plant of a N temperate genus, such as the tiger lily, having scaly bulbs and showy typically pendulous flowers. 2. the bulb or flower of any of these plants. 3. any of various similar or related plants, such as the water lily. —'**lily-**,**like** *adj.*

lily-livered *adj.* cowardly; timid.

lily of the valley *n., pl.* **lilies of the valley.** a small liliaceous plant of Eurasia and North America cultivated for its spikes of fragrant white bell-shaped flowers.

lima bean ('laima) *n.* 1. any of several varieties of the bean plant native to tropical America, cultivated for its flat pods containing pale green edible seeds. 2. the seed of such a plant.

limb[1] (lim) *n.* 1. an arm or leg, or the analogous part on an animal, such as a wing. 2. any of the main branches of a tree. 3. a branching or projecting section or member; extension. 4. a person or thing considered to be a member, part, or agent of a larger group or thing. 5. **out on a limb. a.** in a precarious or questionable position. **b.** *Brit.* isolated, esp. because of unpopular opinions. —'**limbless** *adj.*

limb[2] (lim) *n.* 1. the edge of the apparent disc of the sun, a moon, or a planet. 2. a graduated arc attached to instruments, such as the sextant, used for measuring angles. 3. *Bot.* the expanded part of a leaf, petal, or sepal.

limbed (limd) *adj.* **a.** having limbs. **b.** (*in combination*): *short-limbed; strong-limbed.*

limber[1] ('limba) *adj.* 1. capable of being easily bent or flexed; pliant. 2. able to move or bend freely; agile.

lightweight *adj.* inconsequential, insignificant, of no account, paltry, petty, slight, trifling, trivial, unimportant, worthless

likable, likeable agreeable, amiable, appealing, attractive, charming, engaging, friendly, genial, nice, pleasant, pleasing, sympathetic, winning, winsome

like[1] 1. *adj.* akin, alike, allied, analogous, approximating, cognate, corresponding, equivalent, identical, parallel, relating, resembling, same, similar 2. *n.* counterpart, equal, fellow, match, parallel, twin

like[2] *v.* 1. adore (*Inf.*), be fond of, be keen on, be partial to, delight in, dig (*Sl.*), enjoy, go for (*Sl.*), love, relish, revel in 2. admire, appreciate, approve, cherish, esteem, hold dear, prize, take a shine to (*Inf.*), take to 3. care to, choose, choose to, desire, fancy, feel inclined, prefer, select, want, wish ~*n.* 4.

Usually *plural* cup of tea (*Inf.*), favourite, liking, partiality, predilection, preference

likelihood chance, good chance, liability, likeliness, possibility, probability, prospect, reasonableness, strong possibility

likely *adj.* 1. anticipated, apt, disposed, expected, in a fair way, inclined, liable, on the cards, possible, probable, prone, tending, to be expected 2. be *or* seem likely be in the running for, bid fair, incline towards, promise, stand a good chance, suggest, tend 3. believable, credible, feasible, plausible, reasonable, verisimilar 4. acceptable, agreeable, appropriate, befitting, fit, pleasing, proper, qualified, suitable 5. fair, favourite, hopeful, odds-on, promising, up-and-coming ~*adv.* 6. doubtlessly, in all probability, like as not (*Inf.*), like enough (*Inf.*), no doubt, presumably, probably

liken compare, equate, juxtapose, match, parallel, relate, set beside

likeness 1. affinity, correspondence, resemblance, similarity, similitude 2. copy, counterpart, delineation, depiction, effigy, facsimile, image, model, photograph, picture, portrait, replica, representation, reproduction, study 3. appearance, form, guise, semblance

liking affection, affinity, appreciation, attraction, bent, bias, desire, fondness, inclination, love, partiality, penchant, predilection, preference, proneness, propensity, soft spot, stomach, taste, tendency, weakness

limb 1. appendage, arm, extension, extremity, leg, member, part, wing 2. bough, branch, offshoot, projection, spur

—'**limberness** n.

limber[2] ('lɪmbə) n. **1.** part of a gun carriage, consisting of an axle, pole, and two wheels. ~vb. **2.** (usually foll. by up) to attach the limber (to a gun, etc.).

limber up vb. (intr., adv.) (esp. in sports) to exercise in order to be limber and agile.

limbo[1] ('lɪmbəʊ) n., pl. -**bos. 1.** (often cap.) Christianity. the supposed abode of infants dying without baptism and the just who died before Christ. **2.** an imaginary place for lost, forgotten, or unwanted persons or things. **3.** an unknown intermediate place or condition between two extremes: in limbo.

limbo[2] ('lɪmbəʊ) n., pl. -**bos.** a West Indian dance in which dancers pass, while leaning backwards, under a bar.

lime[1] (laɪm) n. **1.** short for **quicklime, birdlime, slaked lime. 2.** Agriculture. any of certain calcium compounds, esp. calcium hydroxide, spread as a dressing on lime-deficient land. ~vb. (tr.) **3.** to spread (twigs, etc.) with birdlime. **4.** to spread a calcium compound upon (land) to improve plant growth. **5.** to catch (animals, esp. birds) as with birdlime. **6.** to whitewash (a wall, ceiling, etc.) with a mixture of lime and water (**limewash**).

lime[2] (laɪm) n. **1.** a small Asian citrus tree with stiff sharp spines and small round or oval greenish fruits. **2. a.** the fruit of this tree, having acid fleshy pulp rich in vitamin C. **b.** (as modifier): lime juice. ~adj. **3.** having the flavour of lime fruit.

lime[3] (laɪm) n. a European linden tree planted in many varieties for ornament.

lime green n. **a.** a moderate greenish-yellow colour. **b.** (as adj.): a lime-green dress.

limekiln ('laɪmˌkɪln) n. a kiln in which calcium carbonate is calcined to produce quicklime.

limelight ('laɪmˌlaɪt) n. **1. the.** a position of public attention or notice (esp. in **in the limelight**). **2. a.** a type of lamp, formerly used in stage lighting, in which light is produced by heating lime to white heat. **b.** Also called: **calcium light.** brilliant white light produced in this way.

limerick ('lɪmərɪk) n. a form of comic verse consisting of five anapaestic lines.

limestone ('laɪmˌstəʊn) n. a sedimentary rock consisting mainly of calcium carbonate: used as a building stone and in the manufacture of cement, lime, etc.

limey ('laɪmɪ) U.S. sl. ~n. **1.** a British person. **2.** a British sailor or ship. ~adj. **3.** British.

limit ('lɪmɪt) n. **1.** (sometimes pl.) the ultimate extent, degree, or amount of something: the limit of endurance. **2.** (often pl.) the boundary or edge of a specific area: the city limits. **3.** (often pl.) the area of premises within specific boundaries. **4.** the largest quantity or amount allowed. **5.** Maths. **a.** a value to which a function approaches as the independent variable approaches a specified value or infinity. **b.** a value to which a sequence a_n approaches as n approaches infinity. **c.** the limit of a sequence of partial sums of a convergent infinite series. **6.** Maths. one of the two specified values between which a definite integral is evaluated. **7. the limit.** Inf. a person or thing that is intolerably exasperating. ~vb. (tr.) **8.** to restrict or confine, as to area, extent, time, etc. —'**limitable** adj. —'**limiter** n. —'**limitless** adj. —'**limitlessly** adv. —'**limitlessness** n.

limitation (ˌlɪmɪ'teɪʃən) n. **1.** something that limits a quality or achievement. **2.** the act of limiting or the condition of being limited. **3.** Law. a certain period of time, legally defined, within which an action, claim, etc., must be commenced.

limited ('lɪmɪtɪd) adj. **1.** having a limit; restricted; confined. **2.** without fullness or scope; narrow. **3.** (of gov-erning powers, sovereignty, etc.) restricted or checked, by or as if by a constitution, laws, or an assembly: limited government. **4.** Chiefly Brit. (of a business enterprise) owned by shareholders whose liability for the enterprise's debts is restricted. —'**limitedly** adv. —'**limitedness** n.

limited liability n. Brit. liability restricted to the un-paid portion (if any) of the par value of the shares of a limited company.

limn (lɪm) vb. (tr.) **1.** to represent in drawing or painting. **2.** Arch. to describe in words. —**limner** ('lɪmnə) n.

limousine ('lɪməˌziːn, ˌlɪmə'ziːn) n. any large and luxurious car, esp. one that has a glass division between the driver and passengers.

limp[1] (lɪmp) vb. (intr.) **1.** to walk with an uneven step, esp. with a weak or injured leg. **2.** to advance in a labouring or faltering manner. ~n. **3.** an uneven walk or progress. —'**limper** n. —'**limpingly** adv.

limp[2] (lɪmp) adj. **1.** not firm or stiff. **2.** not energetic or vital. **3.** (of the binding of a book) not stiffened with boards. —'**limply** adv. —'**limpness** n.

limpet ('lɪmpɪt) n. **1.** any of numerous marine gastropods, such as the common limpet and keyhole limpet, that have a conical shell and are found clinging to rocks. **2.** (modifier) relating to or denoting certain weapons that are attached to their targets by magnetic or adhesive properties and resist removal: limpet mines.

limpid ('lɪmpɪd) adj. **1.** clear or transparent. **2.** (esp. of writings, style, etc.) free from obscurity. **3.** calm; peaceful. —**lim'pidity** or '**limpidness** n. —'**limpidly** adv.

limy[1] ('laɪmɪ) adj. **limier, limiest.** of, like, or smeared with birdlime. —'**liminess** n.

limy[2] ('laɪmɪ) adj. **limier, limiest.** of or tasting of lime (the fruit).

linage ('laɪnɪdʒ) n. **1.** the number of lines in a piece of written or printed matter. **2.** payment for written material calculated according to the number of lines.

linchpin ('lɪntʃˌpɪn) n. **1.** a pin placed transversely through an axle to keep a wheel in position. **2.** a person or thing regarded as an essential or coordinating element: the linchpin of the company.

Lincs. (lɪŋks) abbrev. for Lincolnshire.

linctus ('lɪŋktəs) n., pl. -**tuses.** a syrupy medicinal preparation, taken to relieve coughs and sore throats.

linden ('lɪndən) n. any of various deciduous trees of a N temperate genus having heart-shaped leaves and small fragrant yellowish flowers: cultivated for timber and as shade trees. See also **lime**[3].

line[1] (laɪn) n. **1.** a narrow continuous mark, as one made by a pencil, pen, or brush across a surface. **2.** such a mark cut into or raised from a surface. **3.** a thin indented mark or wrinkle. **4.** a straight or curved continuous trace having no breadth that is produced by a moving point. **5.** Maths. **a.** any straight one-dimensional geometrical element whose identity is determined by two points. A **line segment** lies between any two points on a line. **b.** a set of points (x, y) that satisfies the equation $y = mx + c$, where m is the gradient and c is the intercept with the y-axis. **6.** a border or boundary: the county line. **7.** Sport. **a.** a white or coloured band indicating a boundary or division on a field, track, etc. **b.** a mark or imaginary mark at which a race begins or ends. **8.** American football. **a.** Also called: **line of scrimmage.** an imaginary line, parallel to the goal lines, on which the ball is placed at the start of each play and on either side of which the teams line up. **b.** the players arranged in a row on either side of the line of scrimmage at the start of each play. **9.** a specified point of change or limit: the dividing

THESAURUS

limelight attention, celebrity, fame, glare of publicity, prominence, public eye, publicity, public notice, recognition, stardom, the spotlight

limit n. **1.** bound, breaking point, cutoff point, deadline, end, end point, furthest bound, greatest extent, termination, the bitter end, ultimate, utmost **2.** Often plural border, boundary, confines, edge, end, extent, frontier, perimeter, periphery, precinct **3.** ceiling, check, curb, limitation, maximum, obstruction, restraint, restriction **4. the limit** Inf. enough, it (Inf.), the end, the last straw ~v. **5.** bound, check, circumscribe, confine,

curb, delimit, demarcate, fix, hem in, hinder, ration, restrain, restrict, specify

limitation block, check, condition, constraint, control, curb, disadvantage, drawback, impediment, obstruction, qualification, reservation, restraint, restriction, sna

limited 1. bounded, checked, circumscribed, confined, constrained, controlled, curbed, defined, finite, fixed, hampered, hemmed in, restricted **2.** cramped, diminished, inadequate, insufficient, minimal, narrow, reduced, restricted, short, unsatisfactory

limitless boundless, countless, endless, il-

limitable, immeasurable, immense, inexhaustible, infinite, measureless, never-ending, numberless, unbounded, uncalculable, undefined, unending, unlimited, untold, vast

limp[1] **1.** v. falter, halt (Archaic), hobble, hop, shamble, shuffle **2.** n. hobble, lameness

limp[2] adj. **1.** drooping, flabby, flaccid, flexible, floppy, lax, limber, loose, pliable, relaxed, slack, soft **2.** debilitated, enervated, exhausted, lethargic, spent, tired, weak, worn out

line between sanity and madness. **10. a.** the edge or contour of a shape. **b.** the sum or type of such contours, characteristic of a style or design: *the line of a building.* **11.** anything long, flexible, and thin, such as a wire or string: *a washing line; a fishing line.* **12.** a telephone connection: *a direct line to New York.* **13.** a conducting wire, cable, or circuit for making connections between pieces of electrical apparatus, such as a cable for electric-power transmission, telecommunications, etc. **14.** a system of travel or transportation, esp. over agreed routes: *a shipping line.* **15.** a company operating such a system. **16.** a route between two points on a railway. **17.** *Chiefly Brit.* a railway track, including the roadbed, sleepers, etc. **18.** a course or direction of movement or advance: *the line of flight of a bullet.* **19.** a course or method of action, behaviour, etc.: *take a new line with him.* **20.** a policy or prescribed course of action or way of thinking (often in **bring** *or* **come into line**). **21.** a field of study, interest, occupation, trade, or profession: *this book is in your line.* **22.** alignment; true (esp. in **in line, out of line**). **23.** one kind of product or article: *a nice line in hats.* **24.** a row of persons or things: *a line of cakes on the conveyor belt.* **25.** a chronological or ancestral series, esp. of people: *a line of prime ministers.* **26.** a row of words printed or written across a page or column. **27.** a unit of verse consisting of the number of feet appropriate to the metre being used and written or printed with the words in a single row. **28.** a short letter; note: *just a line to say thank you.* **29.** a piece of useful information or hint about something: *give me a line on his work.* **30.** one of a number of narrow horizontal bands forming a television picture. **31.** a narrow band in an electromagnetic spectrum, resulting from a transition in an atom of a gas. **32.** *Music.* **a.** any of the five horizontal marks that make up the stave. **b.** the musical part or melody notated on one such set. **c.** a discernible shape formed by sequences of notes or musical sounds: *a meandering melodic line.* **d.** (in polyphonic music) a set of staves that are held together with a bracket or brace. **33.** a defensive or fortified position, esp. one that marks the most forward position in war or a national boundary: *the front line.* **34.** a formation adopted by a body or a number of military units when drawn up abreast. **35.** the combatant forces of certain armies and navies, excluding supporting arms. **36. a.** the equator (esp. in **crossing the line**). **b.** any circle or arc on the terrestrial or celestial sphere. **37.** the U.S. word for **queue**. **38. all along the line. a.** at every stage in a series. **b.** in every detail. **39. draw the line (at).** to object (to) or set a limit (on): *her father draws the line at her coming in after midnight.* **40. get a line on.** *Inf.* to obtain information about. **41. hold the line. a.** to keep a telephone line open. **b.** *Football.* to prevent the opponents from taking the ball forward. **c.** (of soldiers) to keep formation, as when under fire. **42. in line for.** in the running for; a candidate for: *he's in line for a directorship.* **43. in line with.** conforming to. **44. lay** *or* **put on the line. a.** to pay money. **b.** to speak frankly and directly. **c.** to risk (one's career, reputation, etc.) on something. ~*vb.* **45.** (*tr.*) to mark with a line or lines. **46.** (*tr.*) to draw or represent with a line or lines. **47.** (*tr.*) to be or put as a border to: *tulips lined the lawns.* **48.** to place in or form a row, series, or alignment. ~See also **lines, line-up.** —'**linable** *or* '**lineable** *adj.* —'**lined** *adj.*

line² (laın) *vb.* (*tr.*) **1.** to attach an inside covering to (a garment, curtain, etc.), as for protection, to hide the seaming, or so that it should hang well. **2.** to cover or fit the inside of: *to line the walls with books.* **3.** to fill plentifully: *a purse lined with money.*

lineage ('lınııdʒ) *n.* direct descent from an ancestor, esp. a line of descendants from one ancestor.

lineal ('lınıəl) *adj.* **1.** being in a direct line of descent from an ancestor. **2.** of, involving, or derived from direct descent. **3.** a less common word for **linear.** —'**lineally** *adv.*

lineament ('lınıəmənt) *n.* (*often pl.*) **1.** a facial outline or feature. **2.** a distinctive feature.

linear ('lınıə) *adj.* **1.** of, in, along, or relating to a line. **2.** of or relating to length. **3.** resembling, represented by, or consisting of a line or lines. **4.** having one dimension. **5.** designating a style in the arts, esp. painting, that obtains its effects through line rather than colour or light. **6.** *Maths.* of or relating to the first degree: *a linear equation.* **7.** narrow and having parallel edges: *a linear leaf.* **8.** *Electronics.* **a.** Also: **analogue.** (of a circuit, etc.) having an output that is directly proportional to input: *linear amplifier.* **b.** having components arranged in a line. —**linearity** (,lını'ærıtı) *n.* —'**linearly** *adv.*

linear measure *n.* a unit or system of units for the measurement of length.

lineation (,lını'eıʃən) *n.* **1.** the act of marking with lines. **2.** an arrangement of or division into lines.

line drawing *n.* a drawing made with lines only.

linen ('lının) *n.* **1. a.** a hard-wearing fabric woven from the spun fibres of flax. **b.** (*as modifier*): *a linen table-cloth.* **2.** yarn or thread spun from flax fibre. **3.** clothes, sheets, tablecloths, etc., made from linen cloth or from cotton.

line of fire *n.* the flight path of a missile discharged or to be discharged from a firearm.

line printer *n.* an electromechanical device that prints a line of characters at a time: used in printing and in computer systems.

liner ('laınə) *n.* **1.** a passenger ship or aircraft, esp. one that is part of a commercial fleet. **2.** Also called: **eyeliner.** a cosmetic used to outline the eyes. **3.** a person or thing that uses lines, esp. in drawing or copying.

lines (laınz) *pl. n.* **1.** general appearance or outline: *a car with fine lines.* **2.** a plan of procedure or construction: *built on traditional lines.* **3. a.** the spoken words of a theatrical presentation. **b.** the words of a particular role: *he forgot his lines.* **4.** *Inf., chiefly Brit.* a marriage certificate: *marriage lines.* **5.** a defensive position, row of trenches, or other fortification: *we broke through the enemy lines.* **6.** a school punishment of writing the same sentence or phrase out a specified number of times. **7. read between the lines.** to understand or find an implicit meaning in addition to the obvious one.

linesman ('laınzmən) *n., pl.* -**men.** **1.** an official who helps the referee or umpire in various sports, esp. by indicating when the ball has gone out of play. **2.** *Chiefly Brit.* a person who installs, maintains, or repairs telephone or electric-power lines. U.S. name: **lineman.**

line-up *n.* **1.** a row or arrangement of people or things assembled for a particular purpose: *the line-up for the football match.* **2.** the members of such a row or arrangement. ~*vb.* **line up.** (*adv.*) **3.** to form, put into, or organize a line-up. **4.** (*tr.*) to produce, organize, and assemble: *they lined up some questions.* **5.** (*tr.*) to align.

ling¹ (lıŋ) *n., pl.* **ling** *or* **lings.** **1.** any of several northern coastal food fishes having an elongated body with long

---

THESAURUS

line¹ *n.* **1.** band, bar, channel, dash, groove, mark, rule, score, scratch, streak, stripe, stroke, underline **2.** crease, crow's foot, furrow, mark, wrinkle **3.** border, borderline, boundary, demarcation, edge, frontier, limit, mark **4.** configuration, contour, features, figure, outline, profile, silhouette **5.** cable, cord, filament, rope, strand, string, thread, wire **6.** axis, course, direction, path, route, track, trajectory **7.** approach, avenue, belief, course, course of action, ideology, method, policy, position, practice, procedure, scheme, system **8.** activity, area, business, calling, department, employment, field, forte, interest, job, occupation, profession, province, pursuit, specialization, trade, vocation **9.** column, crocodile (*Brit.*), file, procession, queue, rank, row, sequence, series **10.** ances-

try, breed, family, lineage, race, stock, strain, succession **11.** card, letter, message, note, postcard, report, word **12.** clue, hint, indication, information, lead **13.** *Military* disposition, firing line, formation, front, front line, position, trenches **14. draw the line** lay down the law, object, prohibit, put one's foot down, restrict, set a limit **15. in line a.** in alignment, in a row, plumb, straight, true **b.** in accord, in agreement, in conformity, in harmony, in step **16. in line for** a candidate for, being considered for, due for, in the running for, next in succession to, on the short list for ~*v.* **17.** crease, cut, draw, furrow, inscribe, mark, rule, score, trace, underline **18.** border, bound, edge, fringe, rank, rim, skirt, verge

line² *v.* ceil, cover, face, fill, interline

lineaments configuration, countenance, face, features, line, outline, phiz *or* phizog (*Sl., chiefly Brit.*), physiognomy, trait, visage

lined 1. feint, ruled **2.** furrowed, wizened, worn, wrinkled

lines 1. appearance, configuration, contour, cut, outline, shape, style **2.** convention, example, model, pattern, plan, principle, procedure **3.** part, script, words

line-up arrangement, array, row, selection, team

line up 1. fall in, form ranks, queue up **2.** assemble, come up with, lay on, obtain, organize, prepare, procure, produce, secure **3.** align, arrange, array, marshal, order, range, regiment, straighten

fins. **2.** another name for **burbot** (a fish).

ling² (lɪŋ) *n.* another name for **heather.**

ling. *abbrev. for* linguistics.

-ling¹ *suffix forming nouns.* **1.** *Often disparaging.* a person or thing belonging to or associated with the group, activity, or quality specified: *nestling; underling.* **2.** used as a diminutive: *duckling.*

-ling² *suffix forming adverbs.* in a specified condition, manner, or direction: *darkling.*

linger ('lɪŋgə) *vb.* (*mainly intr.*) **1.** to delay or prolong departure. **2.** to go in a slow or leisurely manner; saunter. **3.** to remain just alive for some time prior to death. **4.** to persist or continue, esp. in the mind. **5.** to be slow to act; dither. —**'lingerer** *n.* —**'lingeringly** *adv.*

lingerie ('lænʒərɪ) *n.* women's underwear and nightwear.

lingo ('lɪŋgəʊ) *n., pl.* **-goes.** *Inf.* any foreign or unfamiliar language, jargon, etc.

lingua franca ('lɪŋgwə 'fræŋkə) *n., pl.* **lingua francas** *or* **linguae francae** ('lɪŋgwiː 'frænsiː). **1.** a language used for communication among people of different mother tongues. **2.** a hybrid language containing elements from several different languages used in this way. **3.** any system of communication providing mutual understanding.

lingual ('lɪŋgwəl) *adj.* **1.** *Anat.* of or relating to the tongue. **2. a.** *Rare.* of or relating to language or languages. **b.** (*in combination*): *polylingual.* **3.** articulated with the tongue. ~*n.* **4.** a lingual consonant, such as Scots (r). —**'lingually** *adv.*

linguist ('lɪŋgwɪst) *n.* **1.** a person who is skilled in foreign languages. **2.** a person who studies linguistics.

linguistic (lɪŋ'gwɪstɪk) *adj.* **1.** of or relating to language. **2.** of or relating to linguistics. —**lin'guistically** *adv.*

linguistics (lɪŋ'gwɪstɪks) *n.* (*functioning as sing.*) the scientific study of language.

liniment ('lɪnɪmənt) *n.* a medicated liquid, usually containing alcohol, camphor, and an oil, applied to the skin to relieve pain, stiffness, etc.

lining ('laɪnɪŋ) *n.* **1.** material used to line a garment, curtain, etc. **2.** any material used as an interior covering.

link (lɪŋk) *n.* **1.** any of the separate rings, loops, or pieces that connect or make up a chain. **2.** something that resembles such a ring, loop, or piece. **3.** a connecting part or episode. **4.** a connecting piece in a mechanism. **5.** Also called: **radio link.** a system of transmitters and receivers that connect two locations by means of radio and television signals. **6.** a unit of length equal to one hundredth of a chain. 1 link of a Gunter's chain is equal to 7.92 inches, and of an engineer's chain to 1 foot. ~*vb.* **7.** (often foll. by *up*) to connect or be connected with or as if with links. **8.** (*tr.*) to connect by association, etc.

linkage ('lɪŋkɪdʒ) *n.* **1.** the act of linking or the state of being linked. **2.** a system of interconnected levers or rods for transmitting or regulating the motion of a mechanism. **3.** *Electronics.* the product of the total number of lines of magnetic flux and the number of turns in a coil or circuit through which they pass. **4.** *Genetics.* the occurrence of two genes close together on the same chromosome so that they tend to be inherited as a single unit.

linkman ('lɪŋkmən) *n., pl.* **-men.** a presenter of a television or radio programme, esp. a sports transmission, consisting of a number of outside broadcasts from different locations.

links (lɪŋks) *pl. n.* **1.** short for **golf links.** See golf

course. **2.** *Chiefly Scot.* undulating sandy ground near the shore.

link-up ('lɪŋk,ʌp) *n.* a joining or linking together of two factions, objects, etc.

linnet ('lɪnɪt) *n.* a brownish Old World finch: the male has a red breast and forehead.

lino ('laɪnəʊ) *n.* short for **linoleum.**

linocut ('laɪnəʊ,kʌt) *n.* **1.** a design cut in relief on a block of linoleum. **2.** a print made from such a block.

linoleum (lɪ'nəʊlɪəm) *n.* a sheet material made of hessian, jute, etc., coated with a mixture of powdered cork, linseed oil, rosin, and pigment, used as a floor covering. Often shortened to **lino.**

Linotype ('laɪnəʊ,taɪp) *n.* **1.** *Trademark.* a typesetting machine, operated by a keyboard, that casts an entire line on one solid slug of metal. **2.** type produced by such a machine.

linseed ('lɪn,siːd) *n.* the seed of flax

linseed oil *n.* a yellow oil extracted from seeds of the flax plant. It is used in making oil paints, printer's ink, linoleum, etc.

linsey-woolsey ('lɪnzɪ'wʊlzɪ) *n.* a thin rough fabric of linen warp and coarse wool or cotton filling.

lint (lɪnt) *n.* **1.** an absorbent cotton or linen fabric with the nap raised on one side, used to dress wounds, etc. **2.** shreds of fibre, yarn, etc. —**'linty** *adj.*

lintel ('lɪntəl) *n.* a horizontal beam, as over a door or window.

lion ('laɪən) *n.* **1.** a large gregarious predatory feline mammal of open country in parts of Africa and India, having a tawny yellow coat and, in the male, a shaggy mane. Related adj.: **leonine. 2.** a conventionalized lion, the principal beast used as an emblem in heraldry. **3.** a courageous, strong, or bellicose person. **4.** a celebrity or idol who attracts much publicity and a large following. **5. the lion's share.** the largest portion. —**'lioness** *fem. n.*

lion-hearted *adj.* very brave; courageous.

lionize *or* **-ise** ('laɪə,naɪz) *vb.* (*tr.*) to treat as or make into a celebrity. —,**lioni'zation** *or* **-i'sation** *n.* —**'lion-,izer** *or* **-,iser** *n.*

lip (lɪp) *n.* **1.** *Anat.* **a.** either of the two fleshy folds surrounding the mouth. Related adj.: **labial. b.** (*as modifier*): *lip salve.* **2.** the corresponding part in animals, esp. mammals. **3.** any structure resembling a lip, such as the rim of a crater, the margin of a gastropod shell, etc. **4.** a nontechnical word for **labium. 5.** *Sl.* impudent talk or backchat. **6. bite one's lip. a.** to stifle one's feelings. **b.** to be annoyed or irritated. **7. keep a stiff upper lip.** to show courage or composure. **8. smack one's lips.** to anticipate or recall something with glee or relish. ~*vb.* **lipping, lipped. 9.** (*tr.*) to touch with the lip or lips. **10.** (*tr.*) to form or be a lip or lips for. **11.** (*tr.*) *Rare.* to murmur or whisper. **12.** (*intr.*) to use the lips in playing a wind instrument. —**'lipless** *adj.* —**'lip,like** *adj.*

lipo- *or before a vowel* **lip-** *combining form.* fat or fatty: *lipoprotein.*

-lipped *adj.* having a lip or lips as specified: *tight-lipped.*

lip-read ('lɪp,riːd) *vb.* **-reading, -read** (-'red). to interpret (words) by lip-reading.

lip-reading *n.* a method used by the deaf to comprehend spoken words by interpreting movements of the speaker's lips. Also called: **speech-reading.** —**'lip-,reader** *n.*

lip service *n.* insincere tribute or respect.

lipstick ('lɪp,stɪk)·*n.* a cosmetic for colouring the lips, usually in the form of a stick.

liquefy *or* **liquify** ('lɪkwɪ,faɪ) *vb.* **-fying, -fied.** (esp. of a gas) to become or cause to become liquid. —**liquefac-**

THESAURUS

linger 1. hang around, loiter, remain, stay, stop, tarry, wait **2.** dally, dawdle, delay, idle, lag, procrastinate, take one's time **3.** cling to life, die slowly, hang on, last, survive **4.** abide, continue, endure, persist, remain, stay

lingering dragging, long-drawn-out, persistent, protracted, remaining, slow

link *n.* **1.** component, constituent, division, element, member, part, piece **2.** association, attachment, bond, connection, joint, knot, relationship, tie, tie-up, vinculum ~*v.* **3.** attach, bind, connect, couple, fasten, join, tie, unite,

yoke **4.** associate, bracket, connect, identify, relate

lion *Fig.* **1.** brave man, champion, conqueror, fighter, hero, warrior **2.** big name, celebrity, idol, luminary, notable, prodigy, star, superstar, V.I.P., wonder **3. beard the lion in his den** brave, confront, court destruction, defy danger, face, stand up to, tempt providence

lion-hearted bold, brave, courageous, daring, dauntless, heroic, intrepid, resolute, stalwart, valiant, valorous

lionize acclaim, adulate, aggrandize, celebrate, eulogize, exalt, fête, glorify, heroworship, honour, idolize, make much of, mob, sing *or* sound the praises of

lip 1. brim, brink, edge, margin, rim **2.** *Sl.* backchat (*Inf.*), cheek (*Inf.*), effrontery, impertinence, insolence, rudeness, sauce (*Inf.*) **3.** *Music* control, embouchure **4. smack** *or* **lick one's lips** anticipate, delight in, drool over, enjoy, gloat over, relish, savour, slaver over

tion *or* **liquifaction** (ˌlɪkwɪˈfækʃən) *n.* —ˈliqueˌfiable *or* ˈliquiˌfiable *adj.* —ˈliqueˌfier *or* ˈliquiˌfier *n.*

liqueur (lɪˈkjuə; *French* liˈkœːr) *n.* **1. a.** any of several highly flavoured sweetened spirits such as kirsch or cointreau, intended to be drunk after a meal. **b.** (*as modifier*): *liqueur glass.* **2.** a small hollow chocolate sweet containing liqueur.

liquid (ˈlɪkwɪd) *n.* **1.** a substance in a physical state in which it can easily change its shape but cannot be expanded or compressed. Cf. **gas** (sense 1), **solid** (sense 1). **2.** a substance that is a liquid at room temperature and atmospheric pressure. **3.** *Phonetics.* a frictionless continuant, esp. (l) or (r). ~*adj.* **4.** of, concerned with, or being a liquid or having the characteristic state of liquids: *liquid wax.* **5.** shining, transparent, or brilliant. **6.** flowing, fluent, or smooth. **7.** (of assets) in the form of money or easily convertible into money. —**ˈliˈquidity** *or* **ˈliquidness** *n.* —**ˈliquidly** *adv.*

liquidate (ˈlɪkwɪˌdeɪt) *vb.* **1.** to settle or pay off (a debt, claim, etc.). **2. a.** to terminate the operations of (a commercial firm, bankrupt estate, etc.) by assessment of liabilities and appropriation of assets for their settlement. **b.** (of a commercial firm, etc.) to terminate operations in this manner. **3.** (*tr.*) to convert (assets) into cash. **4.** (*tr.*) to eliminate or kill. —**ˈliquiˌdator** *n.*

liquidation (ˌlɪkwɪˈdeɪʃən) *n.* **1. a.** the process of terminating the affairs of a business firm, etc., by realizing its assets to discharge its liabilities. **b.** the state of a business firm, etc., having its affairs so terminated (esp. in **to go into liquidation**). **2.** destruction; elimination.

liquidize *or* **-dise** (ˈlɪkwɪˌdaɪz) *vb.* **1.** to make or become liquid; liquefy. **2.** (*tr.*) to pulverize (food) in a liquidizer so as to produce a fluid.

liquidizer *or* **-diser** (ˈlɪkwɪˌdaɪzə) *n.* a kitchen appliance with blades for puréeing vegetables, blending liquids, etc. Also called: **blender.**

liquid measure *n.* a unit or system of units for measuring volumes of liquids or their containers.

liquid paraffin *n.* an oily liquid obtained by petroleum distillation and used as a laxative.

liquor (ˈlɪkə) *n.* **1.** any alcoholic drink, esp. spirits, or such drinks collectively. **2.** any liquid substance, esp. that in which food has been cooked. **3.** *Pharmacol.* a solution of a pure substance in water. **4. in liquor.** drunk.

liquorice *or* *U.S.* **licorice** (ˈlɪkərɪs, -ərɪʃ) *n.* **1.** a perennial Mediterranean leguminous shrub. **2.** the dried root of this plant, used as a laxative and in confectionery. **3.** a sweet having a liquorice flavour.

lira (ˈlɪərə; *Italian* ˈliːra) *n., pl.* **lire** (ˈlɪərɪ; *Italian* ˈliːre) *or* **liras. 1.** the standard monetary unit of Italy. **2.** Also called: **pound.** the standard monetary unit of Turkey.

lisle (laɪl) *n.* **a.** a strong fine cotton thread or fabric. **b.** (*as modifier*): *lisle stockings.*

lisp (lɪsp) *n.* **1.** the articulation of *s* and *z* like or nearly like the *th* sounds in English *thin* and *then* respectively. **2.** the habit or speech defect of pronouncing *s* and *z* in this manner. **3.** the sound of a lisp in pronunciation. ~*vb.* **4.** to use a lisp in the pronunciation of (speech). **5.** to speak or pronounce imperfectly or haltingly. —**ˈlisper** *n.* —**ˈlispingly** *adv.*

lissom *or* **lissome** (ˈlɪsəm) *adj.* **1.** supple in the limbs or body; lithe; flexible. **2.** agile; nimble. —**ˈlissomly** *or* **ˈlissomely** *adv.* —**ˈlissomness** *or* **ˈlissomeness** *n.*

list¹ (lɪst) *n.* **1.** an item-by-item record of names or things, usually written or printed one under the other. ~*vb.* **2.** (*tr.*) to make a list of. **3.** (*tr.*) to include in a list.

4. (*tr.*) *Stock Exchange.* to obtain an official quotation for (a security) so that it may be traded on the recognized market. **5.** an archaic word for **enlist.** —**ˈlistable** *adj.* —**ˈlisting** *n.*

list² (lɪst) *n.* **1.** a border or edging strip, esp. of cloth. **2.** a less common word for **selvage.** ~*vb.* (*tr.*) **3.** to border with or as if with a list or lists.

list³ (lɪst) *vb.* **1.** (esp. of ships) to lean over or cause to lean over to one side. ~*n.* **2.** the act or an instance of leaning to one side.

list⁴ (lɪst) *Arch.* ~*vb.* **1.** to be pleasing to (a person). **2.** (*tr.*) to desire or choose. ~*n.* **3.** a liking or desire.

list⁵ (lɪst) *vb.* an archaic or poetic word for **listen.**

listed building *n.* (in Britain) a building officially recognized as having special historical or architectural interest and therefore protected from demolition or alteration.

listen (ˈlɪsən) *vb.* (*intr.*) **1.** to concentrate on hearing something. **2.** to take heed; pay attention: *I warned you but you wouldn't listen.* —**ˈlistener** *n.*

listen in *vb.* (*intr., adv.; often foll. by to*) **1.** to listen to the radio. **2.** to intercept radio communications. **3.** to listen but not contribute (to a discussion), esp. surreptitiously.

listless (ˈlɪstlɪs) *adj.* having or showing no interest; lacking vigour or energy. —**ˈlistlessly** *adv.* —**ˈlistlessness** *n.*

list price *n.* the selling price of merchandise as quoted in a catalogue or advertisement.

lists (lɪsts) *pl. n.* **1.** *History.* **a.** the enclosed field of combat at a tournament. **b.** the barriers enclosing the field at a tournament. **2.** any arena or scene of conflict, controversy, etc. **3. enter the lists.** to engage in a conflict, controversy, etc.

lit (lɪt) *vb.* **1.** a past tense or past participle of **light¹. 2.** a past tense or past participle of **light².**

lit. *abbrev. for:* **1.** literal(ly). **2.** literary. **3.** literature. **4.** litre.

litany (ˈlɪtənɪ) *n., pl.* **-nies. 1.** *Christianity.* **a.** a form of prayer consisting of a series of invocations, each followed by an unvarying response. **b. the Litany.** the general supplication in this form in the Book of Common Prayer. **2.** any tedious recital.

litchi, lichee, *or* **lychee** (ˌlaɪˈtʃiː) *n.* **1.** a Chinese tree cultivated for its round edible fruits. **2.** the fruit of this tree, which has whitish juicy pulp and is usually eaten dried or as a preserve. **3. litchi nut.** the dried fruit of this tree.

-lite *n. combining form.* (in names of minerals) stone: *chrysolite.*

liter (ˈliːtə) *n.* the U.S. spelling of **litre.**

literacy (ˈlɪtərəsɪ) *n.* **1.** the ability to read and write. **2.** the ability to use language proficiently.

literal (ˈlɪtərəl) *adj.* **1.** in exact accordance with or limited to the primary or explicit meaning of a word or text. **2.** word for word. **3.** dull, factual, or prosaic. **4.** consisting of, concerning, or indicated by letters. **5.** true; actual. ~*n.* **6.** Also called: **literal error.** a misprint or misspelling in a text. —**ˈliterally** *adv.* —**ˈliteralness** *or* **literality** (ˌlɪtəˈrælɪtɪ) *n.*

literalism (ˈlɪtərəˌlɪzəm) *n.* **1.** the disposition to take words and statements in their literal sense. **2.** literal or realistic portrayal in art or literature. —**ˈliteralist** *n.* —**ˌliteralˈistic** *adj.*

THESAURUS

liquid *n.* **1.** fluid, juice, liquor, solution ~*adj.* **2.** aqueous, flowing, fluid, liquefied, melted, molten, running, runny, thawed, wet **3.** bright, brilliant, clear, limpid, shining, translucent, transparent **4.** dulcet, fluent, mellifluent, mellifluous, melting, smooth, soft, sweet **5.** *Of assets* convertible, negotiable

liquidate 1. clear, discharge, honour, pay, pay off, settle, square **2.** abolish, annul, cancel, dissolve, terminate **3.** cash, convert to cash, realize, sell off, sell up **4.** annihilate, bump off (*Sl.*), destroy, dispatch, do away with, do in (*Sl.*), eliminate, exterminate, finish off, get rid of, kill, murder, remove, rub out (*U.S. sl.*), silence, wipe out (*Inf.*)

liquor 1. alcohol, booze (*Inf.*), drink, grog,

hard stuff (*Inf.*), hooch (*Sl., chiefly U.S.*), intoxicant, juice (*Inf.*), spirits, strong drink **2.** broth, extract, gravy, infusion, juice, liquid, stock

list¹ 1. *n.* catalogue, directory, file, index, inventory, invoice, leet (*Scot.*), listing, record, register, roll, schedule, series, syllabus, tabulation, tally **2.** *v.* bill, book, catalogue, enrol, enter, enumerate, file, index, itemize, note, record, register, schedule, set down, tabulate, write down

list² 1. *v.* cant, careen, heel, heel over, incline, lean, tilt, tip **2.** *n.* cant, leaning, slant, tilt

listen 1. attend, be all ears, be attentive, give ear, hang on (someone's) words, hark, hear, hearken (*Archaic*), keep one's ears

open, lend an ear, pin back one's ears (*Inf.*), prick up one's ears **2.** concentrate, do as one is told, give heed to, heed, mind, obey, observe, pay attention, take notice

listless apathetic, enervated, heavy, impassive, inattentive, indifferent, indolent, inert, languid, languishing, lethargic, lifeless, limp, lymphatic, mopish, sluggish, spiritless, supine, torpid, vacant

literacy ability, articulacy, articulateness, cultivation, education, knowledge, learning, proficiency, scholarship

literal 1. accurate, close, exact, faithful, strict, verbatim, word for word **2.** boring, colourless, down-to-earth, dull, factual, matter-of-fact, prosaic, prosy, unimaginative, uninspired **3.** actual, bona fide, genuine, gospel,

literary ('lɪtərərɪ, 'lɪtrərɪ) *adj.* **1.** of, relating to, concerned with, or characteristic of literature or scholarly writing: *a literary style.* **2.** versed in or knowledgeable about literature. **3.** (of a word) formal; not colloquial. —'**literarily** *adv.* —'**literariness** *n.*

literate ('lɪtərɪt) *adj.* **1.** able to read and write. **2.** educated; learned. ~*n.* **3.** a literate person. —'**literately** *adv.*

literati (,lɪtə'rɑːtiː) *pl. n.* literary or scholarly people.

literature ('lɪtərɪtʃə, 'lɪtrɪ-) *n.* **1.** written material such as poetry, novels, essays, etc. **2.** the body of written work of a particular culture or people: *Scandinavian literature.* **3.** written or printed matter of a particular type or genre: *scientific literature.* **4.** the art or profession of a writer. **5.** *Inf.* printed matter on any subject.

-lith *n. combining form.* indicating stone or rock: *megalith.*

lithe (laɪð) *adj.* flexible or supple. —'**lithely** *adv.* —'**litheness** *n.*

lithium ('lɪθɪəm) *n.* a soft silvery element of the alkali metal series: the lightest known metal, used as an alloy hardener, as a reducing agent, and in batteries. Symbol: Li; atomic no.: 3; atomic wt.: 6.941.

litho ('laɪθəʊ) *n., pl.* **-thos.** *adj., adv.* short for **lithography, lithograph, lithographic,** or **lithographically.**

litho- *or before a vowel* **lith-** *combining form.* stone: *lithograph.*

lithograph ('lɪθə,grɑːf) *n.* **1.** a print made by lithography. ~*vb.* **2.** (*tr.*) to reproduce (pictures, text, etc.) by lithography. —**lithographic** (,lɪθə'græfɪk) *adj.* —,**litho-**'**graphically** *adv.*

lithography (lɪ'θɒgrəfɪ) *n.* a method of printing from a metal or stone surface on which the printing areas are not raised but made ink-receptive as opposed to ink-repellent. —li'**thographer** *n.*

litigant ('lɪtɪgənt) *n.* **1.** a party to a lawsuit. ~*adj.* **2.** engaged in litigation.

litigate ('lɪtɪ,geɪt) *vb.* **1.** to bring or contest (a claim, action, etc.) in a lawsuit. **2.** (*intr.*) to engage in legal proceedings. —'**liti,gator** *n.*

litigation (,lɪtɪ'geɪʃən) *n.* **1.** the act or process of bringing or contesting a lawsuit. **2.** a judicial proceeding or contest.

litmus ('lɪtməs) *n.* a soluble powder obtained from certain lichens. It turns red under acid conditions and blue under basic conditions. Absorbent paper treated with it (**litmus paper**) is used as an indicator.

litotes ('laɪtəʊ,tiːz) *n., pl.* **-tes.** understatement for rhetorical effect, esp. using negation with a term in place of using an antonym of that term, as in "She was not a little upset" for "She was extremely upset".

litre *or U.S.* **liter** ('liːtə) *n.* **1.** one cubic decimetre. **2.** (formerly), the volume occupied by 1 kilogram of pure water. This is equivalent to 1.000 028 cubic decimetres or about 1.76 pints.

Litt.D. *or* **Lit.D.** *abbrev. for* Doctor of Letters *or* Doctor of Literature.

litter ('lɪtə) *n.* **1. a.** small refuse or waste materials carelessly dropped, esp. in public places. **b.** (*as modifier*): *litter bin.* **2.** a disordered or untidy condition or a collection of objects in this condition. **3.** a group of offspring produced at one birth by a mammal such as a sow. **4.** a layer of partly decomposed leaves, twigs, etc., on the ground in a wood or forest. **5.** straw, hay, or simi-

lar material used as bedding, protection, etc., by animals or plants. **6.** a means of conveying people, esp. sick or wounded people, consisting of a light bed or seat held between parallel sticks. ~*vb.* **7.** to make (a place) untidy by strewing (refuse). **8.** to scatter (objects, etc.) about or (of objects) to lie around or upon (anything) in an untidy fashion. **9.** (of pigs, cats, etc.) to give birth to (offspring). **10.** (*tr.*) to provide (an animal or plant) with straw or hay for bedding, protection, etc.

litter lout *or U.S.* **litterbug** ('lɪtə,bʌg) *n. Sl.* a person who tends to drop refuse in public places.

little ('lɪt³l) *determiner.* **1.** (often preceded by *a*) **a.** a small quantity, extent, or duration of: *the little hope there is left; very little milk.* **b.** (*as pronoun*): *save a little for me.* **2.** not much: *little damage was done.* **3. make little of.** to regard or treat as insignificant; dismiss. **4. not a little. a.** very. **b.** a lot. **5. think little of.** to have a low opinion of. ~*adj.* **6.** of small or less than average size. **7.** young: *a little boy.* **8.** endearingly familiar; dear: *my husband's little ways.* **9.** contemptible, mean, or disagreeable: *your filthy little mind.* ~*adv.* **10.** (usually preceded by *a*) in a small amount; to a small extent or degree; not a lot: *to laugh a little.* **11.** (*used preceding a verb*) not at all, or hardly: *he little realized his fate.* **12.** not much or often: *we go there very little now.* **13. little by little.** by small degrees. ~See also **less, lesser, least.**

Little Bear *n. the.* the English name for **Ursa Minor.**

little people *pl. n. Folklore.* small supernatural beings, such as elves or leprechauns.

little woman *n. the. Brit., old-fashioned.* a facetious term for **wife.**

littoral ('lɪtərəl) *adj.* **1.** of or relating to the shore of a sea, lake, or ocean. ~*n.* **2.** a coastal or shore region.

liturgy ('lɪtədʒɪ) *n., pl.* **-gies. 1.** the forms of public services officially prescribed by a Church. **2.** (*often cap.*) Also called: **Divine Liturgy.** *Chiefly Eastern Churches.* the Eucharistic celebration. **3.** a particular order or form of public service laid down by a Church. —li'**turgical** *adj.*

livable *or* **liveable** ('lɪvəb³l) *adj.* **1.** (of a room, house, etc.) suitable for living in. **2.** worth living; tolerable. **3.** (foll. by *with*) pleasant to live (with). —'**livableness,** '**liveableness** *or* ,**liva**'**bility,** ,**livea**'**bility** *n.*

live[1] (lɪv) *vb.* (*mainly intr.*) **1.** to show the characteristics of life; be alive. **2.** to remain alive or in existence. **3.** to exist in a specified way: *to live poorly.* **4.** (usually foll. by *in* or *at*) to reside or dwell: *to live in London.* **5.** (often foll. by *on*) to continue or last: *the pain still lives in her memory.* **6.** (usually foll. by *by*) to order one's life (according to a certain philosophy, religion, etc.). **7.** (foll. by *on, upon,* or *by*) to support one's style of life; subsist: *to live by writing.* **8.** (foll. by *with*) to endure the effects (of a crime, mistake, etc.). **9.** (foll. by *through*) to experience and survive: *he lived through the war.* **10.** (*tr.*) to pass or spend (one's life, etc.). **11.** to enjoy life to the full: *he knows how to live.* **12.** (*tr.*) to put into practice in one's daily life; express: *he lives religion every day.* **13. live and let live.** to refrain from interfering in others' lives; be tolerant. ~See also **live down, live in,** etc.

live[2] (laɪv) *adj.* **1.** (*prenominal*) showing the characteristics of life. **2.** (*usually prenominal*) of, relating to, or abounding in life: *the live weight of an animal.* **3.** (*usually prenominal*) of current interest; controversial: *a live*

THESAURUS

plain, real, simple, true, unexaggerated, unvarnished

literally actually, exactly, faithfully, plainly, precisely, really, simply, strictly, to the letter, truly, verbatim, word for word

literary bookish, erudite, formal, learned, lettered, literate, scholarly, well-read

literate cultivated, cultured, educated, erudite, informed, knowledgeable, learned, lettered, scholarly, well-informed, well-read

literature 1. belles-lettres, letters, lore, writings, written works **2.** brochure, information, leaflet, pamphlet

lithe flexible, limber, lissom, loose-jointed, loose-limbed, pliable, pliant, supple

litigant claimant, contestant, disputant, litigator, party, plaintiff

litigate contest at law, file a suit, go to court, go to law, institute legal proceedings, press charges, prosecute, sue

litigation action, case, contending, disputing, lawsuit, process, prosecution

litigious argumentative, belligerent, contentious, disputatious, quarrelsome

litter *n.* **1.** debris, detritus, fragments, muck, refuse, rubbish, shreds **2.** clutter, confusion, disarray, disorder, jumble, mess, scatter, untidiness **3.** brood, family, offspring, progeny, young **4.** bedding, couch, floor cover, mulch, straw-bed **5.** palanquin, stretcher ~*v.* **6.** clutter, derange, disarrange, disorder, mess up, scatter, strew

little *adj.* **1.** diminutive, dwarf, elfin, infinitesimal, Lilliputian, mini, miniature, minute, petite, pygmy, short, slender, small, tiny,

wee **2.** babyish, immature, infant, junior, undeveloped, young **3.** hardly any, insufficient, meagre, scant, skimpy, small, sparse **4.** brief, fleeting, hasty, passing, short, short-lived **5.** inconsiderable, insignificant, minor, negligible, paltry, trifling, trivial, unimportant **6.** base, cheap, illiberal, mean, narrow-minded, petty, small-minded ~*adv.* **7.** barely, hardly, not much, not quite, only just **8.** hardly ever, not often, rarely, scarcely, seldom **9. little by little** bit by bit, by degrees, gradually, imperceptibly, piecemeal, progressively, slowly, step by step ~*n.* **10.** bit, dab, dash, fragment, hint, modicum, particle, pinch, small amount, snippet, speck, spot, taste, touch, trace, trifle

issue. **4.** actual: *a real live cowboy.* **5.** *Inf.* full of life and energy. **6.** (of a coal, ember, etc.) glowing or burning. **7.** (esp. of a volcano) not extinct. **8.** loaded or capable of exploding: *a live bomb.* **9.** *Radio, television, etc.* transmitted or present at the time of performance, rather than being a recording: *a live show.* **10.** connected to a source of electric power: *a live circuit.* **11.** being in a state of motion or transmitting power.

-lived (-lɪvd) *adj.* having or having had a life as specified: *short-lived.*

live down (lɪv) *vb.* (*tr., adv.*) to withstand the effects of (a crime, mistake, etc.) by waiting until others forget or forgive it.

live in *or* **out** (lɪv) *vb.* (*intr., adv.*) (of an employee) to dwell at (or away from) one's place of employment.

livelihood ('laɪvlɪ,hud) *n.* occupation or employment.

livelong ('lɪv,lɒŋ) *adj.* Chiefly poetic. **1.** (of time) long or seemingly long (esp. in **all the livelong day**). **2.** whole; entire.

lively ('laɪvlɪ) *adj.* **-lier, -liest. 1.** full of life or vigour. **2.** vivacious or animated, esp. when in company. **3.** busy; eventful. **4.** characterized by mental or emotional intensity; vivid. **5.** having a striking effect on the mind or senses. **6.** refreshing or invigorating: *a lively breeze.* **7.** springy or bouncy or encouraging springiness: *a lively ball.* ~*adv.* Also: **'livelily. 8.** in a brisk or lively manner: *step lively.* —**'liveliness** *n.*

liven ('laɪvən) *vb.* (usually foll. by *up*) to make or become lively; enliven. —**'livener** *n.*

liver¹ ('lɪvə) *n.* **1.** a multilobed highly vascular reddish-brown glandular organ in the human abdominal cavity. Its main function is the metabolic transformation of nutrients. It also secretes bile, stores glycogen, and detoxifies certain poisons. Related adj.: **hepatic. 2.** the corresponding organ in animals. **3.** the liver of certain animals used as food. **4.** a reddish-brown colour.

liver² ('lɪvə) *n.* a person who lives in a specified way: *a fast liver.*

liveried ('lɪvərɪd) *adj.* (esp. of servants or footmen) wearing livery.

liverish ('lɪvərɪʃ) *adj.* **1.** *Inf.* having a disorder of the liver. **2.** disagreeable; peevish. —**'liverishness** *n.*

liver sausage *or esp. U.S.* **liverwurst** ('lɪvə,wɜːst) *n.* a sausage containing liver.

liverwort ('lɪvə,wɜːt) *n.* any of a class of plants growing in wet places and resembling green seaweeds or leafy mosses.

livery ('lɪvərɪ) *n., pl.* **-eries. 1.** the identifying uniform, badge, etc., of a member of a guild or one of the servants of a feudal lord. **2.** a uniform worn by some menservants. **3.** an individual or group that wears such a uniform. **4.** distinctive dress or outward appearance. **5. a.** the stabling, keeping, or hiring out of horses for money. **b.** (*as modifier*): *a livery horse.* **6. at livery.** being kept in a livery stable.

lives (laɪvz) *n.* the plural of **life.**

livestock ('laɪv,stɒk) *n.* (*functioning as sing. or pl.*) cattle, horses, and similar animals kept for domestic use but

not as pets, esp. on a farm.

live together (lɪv) *vb.* (*intr., adv.*) (esp. of an unmarried couple) to dwell in the same house or flat; cohabit. Also: **live with.**

live up (lɪv) *vb.* **1.** (*intr., adv.;* foll. by *to*) to fulfil (an expectation, obligation, principle, etc.). **2. live it up.** *Inf.* to enjoy oneself, esp. flamboyantly.

live wire (laɪv) *n.* **1.** *Sl.* an energetic or enterprising person. **2.** a wire carrying an electric current.

livid ('lɪvɪd) *adj.* **1.** (of the skin) discoloured, as from a bruise or contusion. **2.** of a greyish tinge or colour. **3.** *Inf.* angry or furious. —**'lividly** *adv.* —**'lividness** *or* **li'vidity** *n.*

living ('lɪvɪŋ) *adj.* **1. a.** possessing life; not dead. **b.** (*as collective n.* preceded by *the*): *the living.* **2.** having the characteristics of life (used esp. to distinguish organisms from nonliving matter). **3.** currently in use or valid: *living language.* **4.** seeming to be real: *a living image.* **5.** (of animals or plants) existing in the present age. **6.** presented by actors before a live audience: *living theatre.* **7.** (*prenominal*) (intensifier): *the living daylights.* ~*n.* **8.** the condition of being alive. **9.** the manner in which one conducts one's life: *fast living.* **10.** the means, esp. the financial means, whereby one lives. **11.** *Church of England.* another term for **benefice. 12.** (*modifier*) of, involving, or characteristic of everyday life: *living area.* **13.** (*modifier*) of or involving those now alive (esp. in **living memory**).

living room *n.* a room in a private house or flat used for relaxation and entertainment.

living wage *n.* a wage adequate to maintain a person and his family in reasonable comfort.

lizard ('lɪzəd) *n.* any of a group of reptiles typically having an elongated body, four limbs, and a long tail: includes the geckos, iguanas, chameleons, monitors, and slowworms.

L.J. (in Britain) *abbrev. for* Lord Justice.

L.L. *abbrev. for:* **1.** Late Latin. **2.** Low Latin. **3.** Lord Lieutenant.

ll. *abbrev. for* lines (of written matter).

llama ('lɑːmə) *n.* **1.** a domesticated South American cud-chewing mammal of the camel family, that is used as a beast of burden and is valued for its hair, flesh, and hide. **2.** the cloth made from the wool of this animal.

LL.B. *abbrev. for* Bachelor of Laws.

LL.D. *abbrev. for* Doctor of Laws.

LL.M. *abbrev. for* Master of Laws.

Lloyd's (lɔɪdz) *n.* an association of London underwriters, set up in the late 17th century. Originally concerned with marine insurance and shipping information, it now subscribes a variety of insurance policies and publishes a daily list (**Lloyd's List**) of shipping data and news.

lo (ləʊ) *interj.* Look! See! (now often in **lo and behold**).

loach (ləʊtʃ) *n.* a carplike freshwater fish of Eurasia and Africa, having a long narrow body with barbels around the mouth.

THESAURUS

live¹ *v.* **1.** be, be alive, breathe, draw breath, exist, have life **2.** be permanent, be remembered, last, persist, prevail, remain alive **3.** *Sometimes with* **in** abide, dwell, hang out (*Inf.*), inhabit, lodge, occupy, reside, settle, stay (*Chiefly Scot.*) **4.** abide, continue, earn a living, endure, fare, feed, get along, lead, make ends meet, pass, remain, subsist, support oneself, survive **5.** be happy, enjoy life, flourish, luxuriate, make the most of life, prosper, thrive **6. live it up** *Inf.* celebrate, enjoy oneself, have a ball (*Inf.*), have fun, make whoopee (*Inf.*), paint the town red, push the boat out (*Brit. inf.*), revel

live² *adj.* **1.** alive, animate, breathing, existent, living, quick (*Archaic*), vital **2.** active, burning, controversial, current, hot, pertinent, pressing, prevalent, topical, unsettled, vital **3.** *Inf.* active, alert, brisk, dynamic, earnest, energetic, lively, vigorous, vivid, wide-awake **4.** active, alight, blazing, burning, connected, glowing, hot, ignited, smouldering, switched on

livelihood employment, job, living, maintenance, means, (means of) support, oc-

cupation, (source of) income, subsistence, sustenance, work

liveliness activity, animation, boisterousness, briskness, dynamism, energy, gaiety, quickness, smartness, spirit, sprightliness, vitality, vivacity

lively 1. active, agile, alert, brisk, chipper (*Inf.*), chirpy, energetic, full of pep (*Inf.*), keen, nimble, perky, quick, sprightly, spry, vigorous **2.** animated, blithe, blithesome, cheerful, frisky, frolicsome, gay, merry, sparkling, spirited, vivacious **3.** astir, bustling, busy, buzzing, crowded, eventful, moving, stirring **4.** bright, colourful, exciting, forceful, invigorating, racy, refreshing, stimulating, vivid

liven animate, brighten, buck up (*Inf.*), enliven, hot up (*Inf.*), pep up, perk up, put life into, rouse, stir, vitalize, vivify

liverish 1. bilious, queasy, sick **2.** crotchety (*Inf.*), crusty, disagreeable, fratchy (*Inf.*), grumpy, ill-humoured, irascible, irritable, peevish, snappy, splenetic

livery attire, clothing, costume, dress,

garb, raiment (*Poetic*), regalia, suit, uniform, vestments

live wire ball of fire (*Inf.*), dynamo, go-getter (*Inf.*), hustler (*U.S.*), life and soul of the party, self-starter

livid 1. angry, black-and-blue, bruised, contused, discoloured, purple **2.** ashen, blanched, bloodless, doughy, greyish, leaden, pale, pallid, pasty, wan, waxen **3.** *Inf.* angry, beside oneself, boiling, enraged, exasperated, fuming, furious, incensed, indignant, infuriated, mad (*Inf.*), outraged

living *adj.* **1.** active, alive, animated, breathing, existing, in the land of the living (*Inf.*), lively, quick (*Archaic*), strong, vigorous, vital **2.** active, contemporary, continuing, current, developing, extant, in use, ongoing, operative, persisting ~*n.* **3.** animation, being, existence, existing, life, subsistence **4.** life style, mode of living, way of life **5.** job, livelihood, maintenance, (means of) support, occupation, (source of) income, subsistence, sustenance, work **6.** *Church of England* benefice **7. the living** flesh and blood, the quick (*Archaic*)

load (ləʊd) *n.* **1.** something to be borne or conveyed; weight. **2. a.** the usual amount borne or conveyed. **b.** (*in combination*): *a carload.* **3.** something that weighs down, oppresses, or burdens: *that's a load off my mind.* **4.** a single charge of a firearm. **5.** the weight that is carried by a structure. **6.** *Electrical engineering, electronics.* **a.** a device that receives or dissipates the power from an amplifier, oscillator, generator, or some other source of signals. **b.** the power delivered by a machine, generator, circuit, etc. **7.** the resistance overcome by an engine or motor when it is driving a machine, etc. **8.** an external force applied to a component or mechanism. **9. a load of.** *Inf.* a quantity of: *a load of nonsense.* **10. get a load of.** *Inf.* pay attention to. **11. have a load on.** *U.S. sl.* to be intoxicated. ~*vb.* (*mainly tr.*) **12.** (*also intr.*) to place or receive (cargo, goods, etc.) upon (a ship, lorry, etc.). **13.** to burden or oppress. **14.** to supply in abundance: *load with gifts.* **15.** to cause to be prejudicial: *to load a question.* **16.** (*also intr.*) to put an ammunition charge into (a firearm). **17.** *Photog.* to position (a film, cartridge, or plate) in (a camera). **18.** to weight or bias (a roulette wheel, dice, etc.). **19.** *Insurance.* to increase (a premium) to cover expenses, etc. **20.** *Computers.* to transfer (a program) to a memory. **21. load the dice. a.** to add weights to dice in order to bias them. **b.** to arrange to have a favourable or unfavourable position. —'**loader** *n.*

loaded ('ləʊdɪd) *adj.* **1.** carrying a load. **2.** (of dice, a roulette wheel, etc.) weighted or otherwise biased. **3.** (of a question or statement) containing a hidden trap or implication. **4.** charged with ammunition. **5.** *Sl.* wealthy. **6.** (*postpositive*) *Sl., chiefly U.S.* **a.** drunk. **b.** drugged.

loads (ləʊdz) *Inf.* ~*pl. n.* **1.** (often foll. by *of*) a lot. ~*adv.* **2.** (*intensifier*): *loads better.*

loadstar ('ləʊd,stɑː) *n.* a variant spelling of **lodestar.**

loadstone ('ləʊd,stəʊn) *n.* a variant spelling of **lodestone.**

loaf[1] (ləʊf) *n., pl.* **loaves** (ləʊvz). **1.** a shaped mass of baked bread. **2.** any shaped or moulded mass of food, such as sugar, cooked meat, etc. **3.** *Sl.* the head; sense: *use your loaf!*

loaf[2] (ləʊf) *vb.* **1.** (*intr.*) to loiter or lounge around in an idle way. **2.** (*tr.*; foll. by *away*) to spend (time) idly: *he loafed away his life.*

loafer ('ləʊfə) *n.* **1.** a person who avoids work; idler. **2.** *Chiefly U.S.* a moccasin-like shoe.

loam (ləʊm) *n.* **1.** rich soil consisting of a mixture of sand, clay, and decaying organic material. **2.** a paste of clay and sand used for making moulds in a foundry, plastering walls, etc. ~*vb.* **3.** (*tr.*) to cover, treat, or fill with loam. —'**loamy** *adj.* —'**loaminess** *n.*

loan (ləʊn) *n.* **1.** the act of lending: *the loan of a car.* **2.** property lent, esp. money lent at interest for a period of time. **3.** the adoption by speakers of one language of a form current in another language. **4. on loan.** lent out; borrowed. ~*vb.* **5.** to lend (something, esp. money). —'**loaner** *n.*

▷ **Usage.** See at **lend.**

loath *or* **loth** (ləʊθ) *adj.* **1.** (usually foll. by *to*) reluctant or unwilling. **2. nothing loath.** willing.

loathe (ləʊð) *vb.* (*tr.*) to feel strong hatred or disgust for. —'**loather** *n.*

loathing ('ləʊðɪŋ) *n.* abhorrence; disgust.

loathsome ('ləʊðsəm) *adj.* causing loathing; abhorrent.

—'**loathsomely** *adv.* —'**loathsomeness** *n.*

loaves (ləʊvz) *n.* the plural of **loaf**[1].

lob (lɒb) *Sport.* ~*n.* **1.** a ball struck in a high arc. **2.** *Cricket.* a ball bowled in a slow high arc. ~*vb.* **lobbing, lobbed.** **3.** to hit or kick a ball in a high arc. **4.** *Inf.* to throw.

lobar ('ləʊbə) *adj.* of, relating to, or affecting a lobe.

lobate ('ləʊbeɪt) *adj.* **1.** having or resembling lobes. **2.** (of birds) having separate toes that are each fringed with a weblike lobe. —'**lobately** *adv.* —**lo'bation** *n.*

lobby ('lɒbɪ) *n., pl.* **-bies.** **1.** a room or corridor used as an entrance hall, vestibule, etc. **2.** *Chiefly Brit.* a hall in a legislative building used for meetings between the legislators and members of the public. **3.** Also called: **division lobby.** *Chiefly Brit.* one of two corridors in a legislative building in which members vote. **4.** a group of persons who attempt to influence legislators on behalf of a particular interest. ~*vb.* **-bying, -bied.** **5.** to attempt to influence (legislators, etc.) in the formulation of policy. **6.** (*intr.*) to act in the manner of a lobbyist. **7.** (*tr.*) to apply pressure for the passage of (a bill, etc.). —'**lobbyer** *n.*

lobbyist ('lɒbɪɪst) *n. Chiefly U.S.* a person employed by a particular interest to lobby. —'**lobby,ism** *n.*

lobe (ləʊb) *n.* **1.** any rounded projection forming part of a larger structure. **2.** any of the subdivisions of a bodily organ or part, delineated by shape or connective tissue. **3.** Also called: **ear lobe.** the fleshy lower part of the external ear. **4.** any of the parts, not entirely separate from each other, into which a flattened plant part, such as a leaf, is divided.

lobelia (ləʊ'biːlɪə) *n.* any of a genus of plants having red, blue, white, or yellow five-lobed flowers with the three lower lobes forming a lip.

lobotomy (ləʊ'bɒtəmɪ) *n., pl.* **-mies.** **1.** surgical incision into a lobe of any organ. **2.** Also called: **prefrontal leucotomy.** surgical interruption of one or more nerve tracts in the frontal lobe of the brain: used in the treatment of intractable mental disorders.

lobscouse ('lɒb,skaʊs) *n.* a sailor's stew of meat, vegetables, and hardtack.

lobster ('lɒbstə) *n., pl.* **-sters** *or* **-ster.** **1.** any of several large marine decapod crustaceans occurring on rocky shores and having the first pair of limbs modified as large pincers. **2.** any of several similar crustaceans, esp. the spiny lobster. **3.** the flesh of any of these crustaceans, eaten as a delicacy.

local ('ləʊkəl) *adj.* **1.** characteristic of or associated with a particular locality or area. **2.** of, concerned with, or relating to a particular place or point in space. **3.** *Med.* of, affecting, or confined to a limited area or part. **4.** (of a train, bus, etc.) stopping at all stations or stops. ~*n.* **5.** a train, bus, etc., that stops at all stations or stops. **6.** an inhabitant of a specified locality. **7.** *Brit. inf.* a pub close to one's home or place of work. **8.** *Med.* short for **local anaesthetic** (see **anaesthesia**). **9.** *U.S.* an item of local interest in a newspaper. —'**locally** *adv.* —'**localness** *n.*

local anaesthetic *n. Med.* See **anaesthesia.**

local authority *n. Brit.* the governing body of a county, district, etc. U.S. equivalent: **local government.**

locale (ləʊ'kɑːl) *n.* a place or area, esp. with reference to events connected with it.

locality (ləʊ'kælɪtɪ) *n., pl.* **-ties.** **1.** a neighbourhood or area. **2.** the site or scene of an event. **3.** the fact or condition of having a location or position in space.

THESAURUS

load *n.* 1. bale, cargo, consignment, freight, lading, shipment 2. affliction, burden, encumbrance, incubus, millstone, onus, oppression, pressure, trouble, weight, worry ~*v.* 3. cram, fill, freight, heap, lade, pack, pile, stack, stuff 4. burden, encumber, hamper, oppress, saddle with, trouble, weigh down, worry 5. *Of firearms* charge, make ready, prepare to fire, prime 6. **load the dice** fix, rig, set up

loaded 1. burdened, charged, freighted, full, laden, weighted 2. biased, distorted, weighted 3. artful, insidious, manipulative, prejudicial, tricky 4. at the ready, charged, primed, ready to shoot *or* fire 5. *Sl.* affluent, flush (*Inf.*), moneyed, rich, rolling (*Sl.*), wealthy, well-heeled (*Sl.*), well off, well-to-do

loaf *n.* 1. block, cake, cube, lump, slab 2. *Sl.*

block (*Inf.*), chump (*Brit. sl.*), gumption (*Inf.*), head, noddle (*Inf., chiefly Brit.*), nous (*Brit. sl.*), sense

loan 1. *n.* accommodation, advance, allowance, credit, mortgage, touch (*Sl.*) 2. *v.* accommodate, advance, allow, credit, lend, let out

loath, loth against, averse, backward, counter, disinclined, indisposed, opposed, reluctant, resisting, unwilling

loathing abhorrence, abomination, antipathy, aversion, detestation, disgust, execration, hatred, horror, odium, repugnance, repulsion, revulsion

loathsome abhorrent, abominable, detestable, disgusting, execrable, hateful, horrible, nasty, nauseating, obnoxious, odious, offensive, repugnant, repulsive, revolting, vile

lobby *n.* 1. corridor, entrance hall, foyer, hall, hallway, passage, passageway, porch, vestibule 2. pressure group ~*v.* 3. bring pressure to bear, campaign for, exert influence, influence, persuade, press for, pressure, promote, pull strings (*Brit. inf.*), push for, solicit votes, urge

local *adj.* 1. community, district, neighbourhood, parish, provincial, regional 2. confined, limited, narrow, parish, parochial, provincial, pump, restricted, small-town ~*n.* 3. character (*Inf.*), inhabitant, local yokel (*Disparaging*), native, resident

locality 1. area, district, neck of the woods (*Inf.*), neighbourhood, region, vicinity 2. locale, location, place, position, scene, setting, site, spot

localize *or* **-ise** ('ləʊkə,laɪz) *vb.* **1.** to make or become local in attitude, behaviour, etc. **2.** (*tr.*) to restrict or confine (something) to a particular area or part. **3.** (*tr.*) to assign or ascribe to a particular region. —'**local,iz-able** *or* **-,isable** *adj.* —,**locali'zation** *or* **-i'sation** *n.* —'**local,izer** *or* **-,iser** *n.*

locate (ləʊ'keɪt) *vb.* **1.** (*tr.*) to discover the position, situation, or whereabouts of; find. **2.** (*tr.; often passive*) to situate or place: *located on the edge of the city.* **3.** (*intr.*) *U.S.* to become established or settled. —**lo'cater** *n.*

location (ləʊ'keɪʃən) *n.* **1.** a site or position; situation. **2.** the act or process of locating or the state of being located. **3.** a place outside a studio where filming is done: *shot on location.* **4.** (in South Africa) **a.** a Black African or Coloured township, usually located near a small town. **b.** a Black African tribal reserve in the E Cape Province. **5.** *Computers.* a position in a memory capable of holding a unit of information, such as a word, and identified by its address.

locative ('lɒkətɪv) *Grammar.* ~*adj.* **1.** (of a word or phrase) indicating place or direction. **2.** denoting a case of nouns, etc., that refers to the place at which the action described by the verb occurs. ~*n.* **3. a.** the locative case. **b.** a word or speech element in this case.

loc. cit. (in textual annotation) *abbrev. for* loco citato.

loch (lɒk, lɒx) *n.* **1.** a Scot. word for **lake**[1]. **2.** a long narrow bay or arm of the sea in Scotland.

loci ('ləʊsaɪ) *n.* a plural of **locus**.

lock[1] (lɒk) *n.* **1.** a device fitted to a gate, door, drawer, lid, etc., to keep it firmly closed. **2.** a similar device attached to a machine, vehicle, etc. **3. a.** a section of a canal or river that may be closed off by gates to control the water level and the raising and lowering of vessels that pass through it. **b.** (*as modifier*): *a lock gate; a lock keeper.* **4.** the jamming, fastening, or locking together of parts. **5.** *Brit.* the extent to which a vehicle's front wheels will turn: *this car has a good lock.* **6.** a mechanism that detonates the charge of a gun. **7. lock, stock, and barrel.** completely; entirely. **8.** any wrestling hold in which a wrestler seizes a part of his opponent's body. **9.** Also called: **lock forward.** *Rugby.* **a.** a player in the second row of the scrum. **b.** this position. **10.** a gas bubble in a hydraulic system or a liquid bubble in a pneumatic system that stops the fluid flow in a pipe, capillary, etc.: *an air lock.* ~*vb.* **11.** to fasten (a door, gate, etc.) or (of a door, etc.) to become fastened with a lock, bolt, etc., so as to prevent entry or exit. **12.** (*tr.*) to secure (a building) by locking all doors, windows, etc. **13.** to fix or become fixed together securely or inextricably. **14.** to become or cause to become rigid or immovable: *the front wheels of the car locked.* **15.** (when *tr., often passive*) to clasp or entangle (someone or each other) in a struggle or embrace. **16.** (*tr.*) to furnish (a canal) with locks. **17.** (*tr.*) to move (a vessel) through a system of locks. —'**lockable** *adj.*

lock[2] (lɒk) *n.* **1.** a strand, curl, or cluster of hair. **2.** a tuft or wisp of wool, cotton, etc. **3.** (*pl.*) *Chiefly literary.* hair, esp. when curly or fine.

locker ('lɒkə) *n.* **1. a.** a small compartment or drawer that may be locked, as one of several in a gymnasium, etc., for clothes and valuables. **b.** (*as modifier*): *a locker room.* **2.** a person or thing that locks.

locket ('lɒkɪt) *n.* a small ornamental case, usually on a necklace or chain, that holds a picture, keepsake, etc.

lockjaw ('lɒk,dʒɔː) *n. Pathol.* a nontechnical name for **trismus** and (often) **tetanus**.

lock out *vb.* (*tr., adv.*) **1.** to prevent from entering by locking a door. **2.** to prevent (employees) from working during an industrial dispute, as by closing a factory. ~*n.* **lockout.** **3.** the closing of a place of employment by an employer, in order to bring pressure on employees to agree to terms.

locksmith ('lɒk,smɪθ) *n.* a person who makes or repairs locks.

lock up *vb.* (*adv.*) **1.** (*tr.*) Also: **lock in, lock away.** to imprison or confine. **2.** to lock or secure the doors, windows, etc., of (a building). **3.** (*tr.*) to keep or store securely: *secrets locked up in history.* **4.** (*tr.*) to invest (funds) so that conversion into cash is difficult. ~*n.* **lockup** **5.** the action or time of locking up. **6.** a jail or block of cells. **7.** *Brit.* a small shop with no attached quarters for the owner. **8.** *Brit.* a garage or storage place separate from the main premises. **9.** *Printing.* the pages of type held in a chase by the positioning of quoins.

loco[1] ('ləʊkəʊ) *n. Inf.* short for **locomotive**.

loco[2] ('ləʊkəʊ) *adj.* **1.** *Sl., chiefly U.S.* insane. ~*vb.* (*tr.*) **2.** *U.S. sl.* to make insane.

locomotion (,ləʊkə'məʊʃən) *n.* the act, fact, ability, or power of moving.

locomotive (,ləʊkə'məʊtɪv) *n.* **1. a.** Also called: **locomotive engine.** a self-propelled engine driven by steam, electricity, or diesel power and used for drawing trains along railway tracks. **b.** (*as modifier*): *a locomotive shed; a locomotive works.* ~*adj.* **2.** of or relating to locomotion. **3.** moving or able to move, as by self-propulsion.

locum tenens ('ləʊkəm 'tiːnɛnz) *n., pl.* **locum tenentes** (tə'nɛntiːz). *Chiefly Brit.* a person who stands in temporarily for another member of the same profession, esp. for a physician, chemist, or clergyman. Often shortened to **locum.**

locus ('ləʊkəs) *n., pl.* **loci** ('ləʊsaɪ). **1.** (in many legal phrases) a place or area, esp. the place where something occurred. **2.** *Maths.* a set of points or lines whose location satisfies or is determined by one or more specified conditions: *the locus of points equidistant from a given point is a circle.* **3.** *Genetics.* the position of a particular gene on a chromosome.

locust ('ləʊkəst) *n.* **1.** any of numerous insects, related to the grasshopper, of warm and tropical regions of the Old World, which travel in vast swarms, stripping large areas of vegetation. **2.** Also called: **locust tree.** a North American leguminous tree having prickly branches, hanging clusters of white fragrant flowers, and reddish-brown seed pods. **3.** the yellowish durable wood of this tree. **4.** any of several similar trees, such as the honey locust and carob.

locution (ləʊ'kjuːʃən) *n.* **1.** a word, phrase, or expression. **2.** manner or style of speech.

lode (ləʊd) *n.* **1.** a deposit of valuable ore occurring between definite limits in the surrounding rock; vein. **2.** a deposit of metallic ore filling a fissure in the surrounding rock.

lodestar *or* **loadstar** ('ləʊd,stɑː) *n.* **1.** a star, esp. the North Star, used in navigation or astronomy as a point of reference. **2.** something that serves as a guide or model.

lodestone *or* **loadstone** ('ləʊd,stəʊn) *n.* **1. a.** magnetite that is naturally magnetic. **b.** a piece of this, which can be used as a magnet. **2.** a person or thing regarded as a focus of attraction.

lodge (lɒdʒ) *n.* **1.** *Chiefly Brit.* a small house at the entrance to the grounds of a country mansion, usually occupied by a gatekeeper or gardener. **2.** a house or cabin used occasionally, as for some seasonal activity. **3.** (*cap. when part of a name*) a large house or hotel. **4.** a room for the use of porters in a university, college, etc. **5.** a local branch or chapter of certain societies. **6.** the building used as the meeting place of such a society. **7.** the dwelling place of certain animals, esp. beavers. **8.** a hut or tent of certain North American Indian peoples. ~*vb.* **9.** to provide or be provided with accommodation or shelter, esp. rented accommodation. **10.** (*intr.*) to live temporarily, esp. in rented accommodation. **11.** to implant, embed, or fix or be implanted, embedded, or fixed. **12.**

▬▬▬ THESAURUS ▬▬▬

localize **1.** circumscribe, concentrate, confine, contain, delimit, delimitate, limit, restrain, restrict **2.** ascribe, assign, narrow down, pinpoint, specify

locate **1.** come across, detect, discover, find, lay one's hands on, pin down, pinpoint, run to earth, track down, unearth **2.** establish, fix, place, put, seat, set, settle, situate

location bearings, locale, locus, place,

point, position, site, situation, spot, venue, whereabouts

lock[1] *n.* **1.** bolt, clasp, fastening, padlock ~*v.* **2.** bolt, close, fasten, latch, seal, secure, shut, sneck (*Dialect*) **3.** clench, engage, entangle, entwine, join, link, mesh, unite **4.** clasp, clutch, embrace, encircle, enclose, grapple, grasp, hug, press

lock[2] curl, ringlet, strand, tress, tuft

lock out ban, bar, debar, exclude, keep

out, refuse admittance to, shut out

lockup cell, cooler (*Sl.*), gaol, jail, jug (*Sl.*), police cell

lock up cage, confine, detain, imprison, incarcerate, jail, put behind bars, shut up

locution **1.** collocation, expression, idiom, phrase, term, turn of speech, wording **2.** accent, articulation, diction, inflection, intonation, manner of speech, phrasing, style

(*tr.*) to deposit or leave for safety, storage, etc. **13.** (*tr.*) to bring (a charge or accusation) against someone. **14.** (*tr.; often foll. by in or with*) to place (authority, power, etc.) in the control (of someone).

lodger ('lɒdʒə) *n.* a person who pays rent in return for accommodation in someone else's house.

lodging ('lɒdʒɪŋ) *n.* **1.** a temporary residence. **2.** (*sometimes pl.*) sleeping accommodation.

lodgment *or* **lodgement** ('lɒdʒmənt) *n.* **1.** the act of lodging or the state of being lodged. **2.** a blockage or accumulation. **3.** a small area gained and held in enemy territory.

loft (lɒft) *n.* **1.** the space inside a roof. **2.** a gallery, esp. one for the choir in a church. **3.** a room over a stable used to store hay. **4.** *U.S.* an upper storey of a warehouse or factory. **5.** a raised house or coop in which pigeons are kept. **6.** *Sport.* **a.** (in golf) the angle from the vertical made by the club face to give elevation to a ball. **b.** elevation imparted to a ball. **c.** a lofting stroke or shot. ~*vb.* (*tr.*) **7.** *Sport.* to strike or kick (a ball) high in the air. **8.** to store or place in a loft. **9.** *Golf.* to slant (the face of a golf club).

lofty ('lɒftɪ) *adj.* **loftier, loftiest. 1.** of majestic or imposing height. **2.** exalted or noble in character or nature. **3.** haughty or supercilious. **4.** elevated, eminent, or superior. —'**loftily** *adv.* —'**loftiness** *n.*

log[1] (lɒg) *n.* **1. a.** a section of the trunk or a main branch of a tree, when stripped of branches. **b.** (*modifier*) constructed out of logs: *a log cabin.* **2. a.** a detailed record of a voyage of a ship or aircraft. **b.** a record of the hours flown by pilots and aircrews. **c.** a book in which these records are made; logbook. **3.** a written record of information about transmissions kept by radio stations, amateur radio operators, etc. **4.** Also called: **chip log.** a device consisting of a float with an attached line, formerly used to measure the speed of a ship. **5. like a log.** without stirring or being disturbed (in **sleep like a log**). ~*vb.* **logging, logged. 6.** (*tr.*) to fell the trees of (a forest, area, etc.) for timber. **7.** (*tr.*) to saw logs from (trees). **8.** (*intr.*) to work at the felling of timber. **9.** (*tr.*) to enter (a distance, event, etc.) in a logbook or log. **10.** (*tr.*) to travel (a specified distance or time) or move at (a specified speed).

log[2] (lɒg) *n.* short for **logarithm.**

▷ **Usage.** In mathematical usage *log* is followed by a subscript number indicating the base. The absence of this number implies that the logarithm is a common logarithm.

-log *combining form.* U.S. variant of **-logue.**

loganberry ('ləʊgənbərɪ, -brɪ) *n., pl.* **-ries. 1.** a trailing prickly hybrid plant of the rose family, cultivated for its edible fruit. **2.** the purplish-red acid fruit of this plant.

logarithm ('lɒgə,rɪðəm) *n.* the exponent indicating the power to which a fixed number, the base, must be raised to obtain a given number or variable. It is used esp. to simplify multiplication and division. Often shortened to **log.** —**logarithmic** (,lɒgə'rɪðmɪk) *adj.*

logbook ('lɒg,bʊk) *n.* **1.** a book containing the official record of trips made by a ship or aircraft. **2.** *Brit.* (formerly) a document listing the registration, manufacture, etc., of a motor vehicle.

logger ('lɒgə) *n.* another word for **lumberjack.**

loggerhead ('lɒgə,hɛd) *n.* **1.** Also called: **loggerhead turtle.** a large-headed turtle occurring in most seas. **2.** a

tool consisting of a large metal sphere attached to a long handle, used for warming liquids, melting tar, etc. **3.** *Arch. or dialect.* a blockhead; dunce. **4. at loggerheads.** engaged in dispute or confrontation.

loggia ('lɒdʒə, 'lɒdʒɪə) *n., pl.* **-gias** *or* **-gie** (-dʒɛ). a covered area on the side of a building.

logging ('lɒgɪŋ) *n.* the work of felling, trimming, and transporting timber.

logic ('lɒdʒɪk) *n.* **1.** the branch of philosophy concerned with analysing the patterns of reasoning by which a conclusion is drawn from a set of premisses, without reference to meaning or context. **2.** the system and principles of reasoning used in a specific field of study. **3.** a particular method of argument or reasoning. **4.** force or effectiveness in argument or dispute. **5.** reasoned thought or argument, as distinguished from irrationality. **6.** the relationship and interdependence of a series of events, facts, etc. **7.** *Electronics, computers.* the principles underlying the units in a computer system that perform arithmetical and logical operations.

logical ('lɒdʒɪkəl) *adj.* **1.** relating to, used in, or characteristic of logic: *logical connective.* **2.** using, according to, or deduced from the principles of logic: *a logical conclusion.* **3.** capable of or characterized by clear or valid reasoning. **4.** reasonable or necessary because of facts, events, etc.: *the logical candidate.* **5.** *Computers.* of, performed by, used in, or relating to the logic circuits in a computer. —,**logi'cality** *or* '**logicalness** *n.* —'**logically** *adv.*

logician (lɒ'dʒɪʃən) *n.* a person who specializes in or is skilled at logic.

logistics (lɒ'dʒɪstɪks) *n.* **1.** (*functioning as sing. or pl.*) the science of the movement and maintenance of military forces. **2.** the handling of an operation involving the movement of labour and materials, etc. —**lo'gistical** *adj.*

log jam *n. Chiefly U.S.* **1.** blockage caused by the crowding together of a number of logs floating in a river. **2.** a deadlock; standstill.

-logue *or* **U.S. -log** *n. combining form.* indicating speech or discourse of a particular kind: *travelogue; monologue.*

-logy *n. combining form.* **1.** indicating the science or study of: *musicology.* **2.** indicating writing, discourse, or body of writings: *trilogy; phraseology; martyrology.* —**-logical** *or* **-logic** *adj. combining form.* —**-logist** *n. combining form.*

loin (lɔɪn) *n.* **1.** *Anat.* the lower back and sides between the pelvis and the ribs. Related adj.: **lumbar. 2.** a cut of meat from this part of an animal.

loincloth ('lɔɪn,klɒθ) *n.* a piece of cloth worn round the loins. Also called: **breechcloth.**

loins (lɔɪnz) *pl. n.* **1.** the hips and the inner surface of the legs where they join the trunk of the body; crotch. **2.** *Euphemistic.* the reproductive organs.

loiter ('lɔɪtə) *vb.* (*intr.*) to stand or act aimlessly or idly. —'**loiterer** *n.*

loll (lɒl) *vb.* **1.** (*intr.*) to lie, lean, or lounge in a lazy or relaxed manner. **2.** to hang or allow to hang loosely. ~*n.* **3.** an act or instance of lolling. —'**loller** *n.* —'**lollingly** *adv.*

Lollard ('lɒləd) *n. English history.* a follower of John Wycliffe (?1330–84), English religious reformer, during the 14th, 15th, and 16th centuries. —'**Lollardism** *n.*

THESAURUS

lodge *n.* **1.** cabin, chalet, cottage, gatehouse, house, hunting lodge, hut, shelter **2.** assemblage, association, branch, chapter, club, group, society **3.** den, haunt, lair, retreat ~*v.* **4.** accommodate, billet, board, entertain, harbour, put up, quarter, room, shelter, sojourn, stay, stop **5.** become fixed, catch, come to rest, imbed, implant, stick **6.** deposit, file, lay, place, put, put on record, register, set, submit

lodger boarder, guest, paying guest, P.G., resident, roomer, tenant

lodging *Often plural* abode, accommodation, apartments, boarding, digs (*Brit. inf.*), dwelling, habitation, quarters, residence, rooms, shelter

lofty **1.** elevated, high, raised, sky-high, soaring, tall, towering **2.** dignified, distinguished, elevated, exalted, grand, illustrious,

imposing, majestic, noble, renowned, stately, sublime, superior **3.** arrogant, condescending, disdainful, haughty, high and mighty (*Inf.*), lordly, patronizing, proud, snooty (*Inf.*), supercilious, toffee-nosed (*Brit. sl.*)

log *n.* **1.** block, bole, chunk, piece of timber, stump, trunk ~*v.* **2.** chop, cut, fell, hew ~*n.* **3.** account, chart, daybook, journal, listing, logbook, record, tally ~*v.* **4.** book, chart, make a note of, note, record, register, report, set down, tally

loggerhead **at loggerheads** at daggers drawn, at each other's throats, at enmity, at odds, estranged, feuding, in dispute, opposed, quarrelling

logic **1.** argumentation, deduction, dialectics, ratiocination, science of reasoning, syllogistic reasoning **2.** good reason, good sense, reason, sense, sound judgment **3.**

chain of thought, coherence, connection, link, rationale, relationship

logical **1.** clear, cogent, coherent, consistent, deducible, pertinent, rational, reasonable, relevant, sound, valid, well-organized **2.** judicious, most likely, necessary, obvious, plausible, reasonable, sensible, wise

logistics coordination, engineering, management, masterminding, orchestration, organization, plans, strategy

loiter dally, dawdle, delay, dilly-dally (*Inf.*), hang about *or* around, idle, lag, linger, loaf, loll, saunter, skulk, stroll

loll **1.** flop, lean, loaf, lounge, recline, relax, slouch, slump, sprawl **2.** dangle, droop, drop, flap, flop, hang, hang loosely, sag

lollipop ('lɒlɪˌpɒp) n. **1.** a boiled sweet or toffee stuck on a small wooden stick. **2.** *Brit.* another word for **ice lolly.**

lollipop man n. *Brit. inf.* a person holding a circular sign on a pole who stops traffic so that children may cross the road. Also (*fem.*): **lollipop lady.**

lollop ('lɒləp) vb. (intr.) *Chiefly Brit.* **1.** to walk or run with a clumsy or relaxed bouncing movement. **2.** a less common word for **lounge.**

lolly ('lɒlɪ) n., pl. **-lies. 1.** an informal word for **lollipop.** **2.** *Brit.* short for **ice lolly. 3.** *Brit.* a slang word for **money. 4.** *Austral. & N.Z. inf.* a sweet, esp. a boiled one. **5. do the** (or **one's**) **lolly.** *Austral. inf.* to lose one's temper.

Lombard Street n. the British financial and banking world.

London pride ('lʌndən) n. a type of saxifrage plant having a basal rosette of leaves and pinkish-white flowers.

lone (ləʊn) adj. (prenominal) **1.** unaccompanied; solitary. **2.** single or isolated: *a lone house.* **3.** a literary word for **lonely. 4.** *Rare.* unmarried or widowed. —'**loneness** n.

lonely ('ləʊnlɪ) adj. **-lier, -liest. 1.** unhappy as a result of being without companions. **2.** causing or resulting from the state of being alone. **3.** isolated, unfrequented, or desolate. **4.** without companions; solitary. —'**loneliness** n.

loner ('ləʊnə) n. *Inf.* a person who avoids the company of others or prefers to be alone.

lonesome ('ləʊnsəm) adj. **1.** *Chiefly U.S.* another word for **lonely.** ~n. **2. by one's lonesome.** *U.S. inf.* on one's own. —'**lonesomely** adv. —'**lonesomeness** n.

long[1] (lɒŋ) adj. **1.** having relatively great extent in space or duration in time. **2. a.** (postpositive) of a specified number of units in extent or duration: *three hours long.* **b.** (in combination): *a two-foot-long line.* **3.** having or consisting of a relatively large number of items or parts: *a long list.* **4.** having greater than the average or expected range, extent, or duration: *a long match.* **5. a.** (of drinks) containing a large quantity of nonalcoholic beverage. **b.** beer as opposed to spirits. **6.** *Inf.* (foll. by *on*) plentifully supplied or endowed (with): *long on good ideas.* **7.** *Phonetics.* (of a speech sound, esp. a vowel) **a.** of relatively considerable duration. **b.** (in popular usage) denoting the qualities of the five English vowels in such words as *mate, mete, mite, moat, moot,* and *mute.* **8.** from end to end; lengthwise. **9.** unlikely to win, happen, succeed, etc.: *a long chance.* **10.** *Prosody.* **a.** denoting a vowel of relatively great duration. **b.** denoting a syllable containing such a vowel. **c.** carrying the emphasis. **11.** *Finance.* having or characterized by large holdings of securities or commodities in anticipation of rising prices. **12.** *Cricket.* (of a fielding position) near the boundary: *long leg.* **13. in the long run.** ultimately; after or over a period of time. ~adv. **14.** for a certain time or period: *how long will it last?* **15.** for or during an extensive period of time: *long into the next year.* **16.** at a distant time; quite a bit of time: *long before I met you; long ago.* **17.** *Finance.* into a position with more security or commodity holdings than are required by sale contracts and therefore dependent on rising prices for profit: *to go long.* **18. as** (or **so**) **long as. a.** for or during just the length of time that. **b.** inasmuch as; since. **c.** provided that; if. **19. no longer.** not any more; formerly but not now. ~n. **20.** a long time (esp. in **for long**). **21.** a relatively long thing, such as a signal in Morse code. **22.** *Phonetics.* a long vowel or syllable. **23.** *Finance.* a person with large holdings of a security or commodity in ex-

pectation of a rise in its price; bull. **24. before long.** soon. **25. the long and the short of it.** the essential points or facts. —'**longish** adj.

long[2] (lɒŋ) vb. (intr.; foll. by *for* or an infinitive) to have a strong desire.

long. abbrev. for longitude.

long- adv. (in combination) for or lasting a long time: *long-awaited; long-established; long-lasting.*

longbow ('lɒŋˌbəʊ) n. a large powerful hand-drawn bow, esp. as used in medieval England.

long-distance n. **1.** (modifier) covering relatively long distances: *a long-distance driver.* **2.** (modifier) (of telephone calls, lines, etc.) connecting points a relatively long way apart. **3.** *Chiefly U.S.* a long-distance telephone call. **4.** a long-distance telephone system or its operator. ~adv. **5.** by a long-distance telephone line: *he phoned long-distance.*

longevity (lɒn'dʒɛvɪtɪ) n. **1.** long life. **2.** relatively long duration of employment, service, etc.

longhand ('lɒŋˌhænd) n. a form of handwriting in which letters, words, etc., are set down in full.

long-headed adj. astute; shrewd; sagacious. —ˌlong-'headedly adv. —ˌlong-'headedness n.

longing ('lɒŋɪŋ) n. **1.** a prolonged unfulfilled desire or need. ~adj. **2.** having or showing desire or need: *a longing look.* —'**longingly** adv.

longitude ('lɒndʒɪˌtjuːd) n. distance in degrees east or west of the prime meridian at 0° measured by the angle between the plane of the prime meridian and that of the meridian through the point in question, or by the time difference.

longitudinal (ˌlɒndʒɪ'tjuːdɪnəl) adj. **1.** of or relating to longitude or length. **2.** placed or extended lengthways. —ˌlongi'tudinally adv.

long johns pl. n. *Inf.* underpants with long legs.

long jump n. an athletic contest in which competitors try to cover the farthest distance possible with a running jump from a fixed board or mark. U.S. equivalent: **broad jump.**

long-lived adj. having long life, existence, or currency. —ˌlong-'livedness n.

long-playing adj. of or relating to an LP (long player).

long-range adj. **1.** of or extending into the future: *a long-range weather forecast.* **2.** (of vehicles, aircraft, etc.) capable of covering great distances without refuelling. **3.** (of weapons) made to be fired at a distant target.

longs (lɒŋz) pl. n. **1.** full-length trousers. **2.** long-dated gilt-edged securities.

long shot n. **1.** a competitor, as in a race, considered to be unlikely to win. **2.** a bet against heavy odds. **3.** an undertaking, guess, or possibility with little chance of success. **4.** *Films.* a shot where the camera is or appears to be distant from the object to be photographed. **5. by a long shot.** by any means: *he still hasn't finished by a long shot.*

long-sighted adj. **1.** related to or suffering from hyperopia. **2.** able to see distant objects in focus. **3.** having foresight. —ˌlong-'sightedly adv. —ˌlong-'sightedness n.

long-standing adj. existing for a long time.

long-suffering adj. **1.** enduring pain, unhappiness, etc., without complaint. ~n. **2.** long and patient endurance. —ˌlong-'sufferingly adv.

long-term adj. **1.** lasting or extending over a long time: *long-term prospects.* **2.** *Finance.* maturing after a long period: *a long-term bond.*

longtime ('lɒŋ‚taɪm) *adj.* of long standing.

long ton *n.* the full name for **ton**[1].

long wave *n.* **a.** a radio wave with a wavelength greater than 1000 metres. **b.** (*as modifier*): *a long-wave broadcast.*

longways ('lɒŋ‚weɪz) *or U.S.* **longwise** *adv.* another word for **lengthways.**

long-winded *adj.* **1.** tiresomely long. **2.** capable of energetic activity without becoming short of breath. —‚**long-'windedly** *adv.* —‚**long-'windedness** *n.*

loo (lu:) *n., pl.* **-loos.** *Brit.* an informal word for **lavatory.**

loofah ('lu:fə) *n.* the fibrous interior of the fruit of a type of gourd, which is dried and used as a bath sponge or for scrubbing. Also (esp. U.S.): **loofa, luffa.**

look (luk) *vb.* (*mainly intr.*) **1.** (often foll. by *at*) to direct the eyes (towards): *to look at the sea.* **2.** (often foll. by *at*) to direct one's attention (towards): *let's look at the circumstances.* **3.** (often foll. by *to*) to turn one's interests or expectations (towards): *to look to the future.* **4.** (*copula*) to give the impression of being by appearance to the eye or mind; seem: *that looks interesting.* **5.** to face in a particular direction: *the house looks north.* **6.** to expect or hope (to do something): *I look to hear from you soon.* **7.** (foll. by *for*) **a.** to search or seek: *I looked for you everywhere.* **b.** to cherish the expectation (of); hope (for): *I look for success.* **8.** (foll. by *to*) **a.** to be mindful (of): *to look to the promise one has made.* **b.** to have recourse (to): *look to your swords, men!* **9.** (foll. by *into*) to carry out an investigation. **10.** (*tr.*) to direct a look at (someone) in a specified way: *she looked her rival up and down.* **11.** (*tr.*) to accord in appearance with (something): *to look one's age.* **12. look alive** *or* **lively.** to hurry up; get busy. **13. look here.** an expression used to attract someone's attention, add emphasis to a statement, etc. **14. look sharp** *or* **smart.** to hurry up; make haste. ~*n.* **15.** the act or an instance of looking: *a look of despair.* **16.** a view or sight (of something): *let's have a look.* **17.** (*often pl.*) appearance to the eye or mind; aspect: *the look of innocence; I don't like the looks of this place.* ~See also **look after, look back,** etc. —'**looker** *n.*

▷ Usage. See at **feel.**

look after *vb.* (*intr., prep.*) **1.** to take care of; be responsible for. **2.** to follow with the eyes.

look back *vb.* (*intr., adv.*) **1.** to cast one's mind to the past. **2.** (*usually used with a negative*) to cease to make progress: *after his first book was published, he never looked back.*

look down *vb.* (*intr., adv.;* foll. by *on* or *upon*) to express or show contempt or disdain (for).

look forward to *vb.* (*intr., adv.* + *prep.*) to wait or hope for, esp. with pleasure.

look-in *Inf.* ~*n.* **1.** a chance to be chosen, participate, etc. **2.** a short visit. ~*vb.* **look in. 3.** (*intr., adv.;* often foll. by *on*) to pay a short visit.

looking glass *n.* a mirror.

look on *vb.* (*intr.*) **1.** (*adv.*) to be a spectator at an event or incident. **2.** (*prep.*) Also: **look upon.** to consider or regard: *she looked on the whole affair as a joke.*

—‚**looker-'on** *n.*

lookout ('luk‚aut) *n.* **1.** the act of keeping watch against danger, etc. **2.** a person or persons instructed or employed to keep such a watch, esp. on a ship. **3.** a strategic point from which a watch is kept. **4.** *Inf.* worry or concern: *that's his lookout.* **5.** *Chiefly Brit.* outlook, chances, or view. ~*vb.* **look out.** (*adv., mainly intr.*) **6.** to heed one's behaviour; be careful. **7.** to be on the watch: *look out for my mother at the station.* **8.** (*tr.*) to search for and find. **9.** (foll. by *on* or *over*) to face in a particular direction: *the house looks out over the moor.*

look over *vb.* **1.** (*intr., prep.*) to inspect by making a tour of (a factory, house, etc.). **2.** (*tr., adv.*) to examine (a document, letter, etc.).

look-see *n. Sl.* a brief inspection or look.

look up *vb.* (*adv.*) **1.** (*tr.*) to discover (something required to be known) by resorting to a work of reference, such as a dictionary. **2.** (*intr.*) to increase, as in quality or value: *things are looking up.* **3.** (*intr.;* foll. by *to*) to have respect (for): *I've always wanted a girlfriend I could look up to.* **4.** (*tr.*) to visit or make contact with (a person): *I'll look you up when I'm in town.*

loom[1] (lu:m) *n.* an apparatus, worked by hand or mechanically (**power loom**), for weaving yarn into a textile.

loom[2] (lu:m) *vb.* (*intr.*) **1.** to come into view indistinctly with an enlarged and often threatening aspect. **2.** (of an event) to seem ominously close. **3.** (often foll. by *over*) (of large objects) to dominate or overhang. ~*n.* **4.** a rising appearance, as of something far away.

loon (lu:n) *n.* the U.S. name for **diver** (the bird).

loony *or* **looney** ('lu:nɪ) *Sl.* ~*adj.* **loonier, looniest. 1.** lunatic; insane. **2.** foolish or ridiculous. ~*n., pl.* **loonies** *or* **looneys. 3.** a foolish or insane person. —'**looniness** *n.*

loop (lu:p) *n.* **1.** the round or oval shape formed by a line, string, etc., that curves around to cross itself. **2.** any round or oval-shaped thing that is closed or nearly closed. **3.** an intrauterine contraceptive device in the shape of a loop. **4.** *Electronics.* a closed electric or magnetic circuit through which a signal can circulate, as in a feedback control system. **5.** a flight manoeuvre in which an aircraft flies one complete circle in the vertical plane. **6.** Also called: **loop line.** *Chiefly Brit.* a railway branch line which leaves the main line and rejoins it after a short distance. **7.** *Maths., physics.* a closed curve on a graph: *hysteresis loop.* **8.** a continuous strip of cinematographic film. **9.** *Computers.* a series of instructions in a program, performed repeatedly until some specified condition is satisfied. ~*vb.* **10.** (*tr.*) to make a loop in or of (a line, string, etc.). **11.** (*tr.*) to fasten or encircle with a loop or something like a loop. **12.** Also: **loop the loop.** to cause (an aircraft) to perform a loop or (of an aircraft) to perform a loop. **13.** (*intr.*) to move in loops or in a path like a loop. —'**looper** *n.*

loophole ('lu:p‚həul) *n.* **1.** an ambiguity, omission, etc., as in a law, by which one can avoid a penalty or responsibility. **2.** a small gap or hole in a wall, esp. one in a fortified wall. ~*vb.* **3.** (*tr.*) to provide with loopholes.

THESAURUS

look *v.* **1.** behold (*Archaic*), consider, contemplate, examine, eye, feast one's eyes upon, gaze, glance, inspect, observe, peep, regard, scan, scrutinize, see, study, survey, take a gander at (*Inf.*), view, watch **2.** appear, display, evidence, exhibit, look like, make clear, manifest, present, seem, seem to be, show, strike one as **3.** face, front, front on, give onto, overlook **4.** anticipate, await, expect, hope, reckon on **5.** forage, hunt, search, seek **6.** gape, gawk, gawp (*Brit. sl.*), glower, goggle, rubberneck (*Sl.*), ogle, stare **7.** look like be the image of, favour, make one think of, put one in mind of, remind one of, resemble, take after ~*n.* **8.** examination, eyeful (*Inf.*), gaze, glance, glimpse, inspection, look-see (*Sl.*), observation, once-over (*Inf.*), peek, review, sight, squint (*Inf.*), survey, view **9.** air, appearance, aspect, bearing, cast, complexion, countenance, demeanour, effect, expression, face, fashion, guise, manner, mien (*Literary*), semblance

look after attend to, care for, guard, keep an eye on, mind, nurse, protect, sit with, supervise, take care of, take charge of, tend, watch

look down on *or* **upon** contemn, despise, disdain, hold in contempt, look down one's nose at (*Inf.*), misprize, scorn, sneer, spurn, treat with contempt, turn one's nose up (at) (*Inf.*)

look forward to anticipate, await, count on, count the days until, expect, hope for, long for, look for, wait for

look into check out, delve into, examine, explore, follow up, go into, inquire about, inspect, investigate, look over, make enquiries, probe, research, scrutinize, study

lookout 1. guard, qui vive, readiness, vigil, watch **2.** guard, sentinel, sentry, vedette (*Military*), watchman **3.** beacon, citadel, observation post, post, tower, watchtower **4.** *Inf.* business, concern, funeral (*Inf.*), pigeon (*Brit. inf.*), worry **5.** chances, future, likelihood, outlook, prospect, view

look out be alert, be careful, be on guard, be on the qui vive, be vigilant, beware, keep an eye out, keep one's eyes open (peeled,

skinned), pay attention, watch out

look over cast an eye over, check, examine, flick through, inspect, look through, monitor, peruse, scan, view

look up 1. find, hunt for, research, search for, seek out, track down **2.** ameliorate, come along, get better, improve, perk up, pick up, progress, shape up, show improvement **3.** *With* **to** admire, defer to, esteem, have a high opinion of, honour, regard highly, respect, revere **4.** call (on), drop in on (*Inf.*), go to see, look in on, pay a visit to, visit

loom 1. appear, become visible, be imminent, bulk, emerge, hover, impend, menace, take shape, threaten **2.** dominate, hang over, mount, overhang, overshadow, overtop, rise, soar, tower

loop 1. *n.* bend, circle, coil, convolution, curl, curve, eyelet, hoop, kink, loophole, noose, ring, spiral, twirl, twist, whorl **2.** *v.* bend, braid, circle, coil, connect, curl, curve round, encircle, fold, join, knot, roll, spiral, turn, twist, wind round

loophole 1. aperture, knothole, opening,

loopy ('lu:pɪ) *adj.* **loopier, loopiest. 1.** full of loops; curly or twisted. **2.** *Inf.* slightly mad, crazy.

loose (lu:s) *adj.* **1.** free or released from confinement or restraint. **2.** not close, compact, or tight in structure or arrangement. **3.** not fitted or fitting closely: *loose clothing is cooler.* **4.** not bundled, packaged, fastened, or put in a container: *loose nails.* **5.** inexact; imprecise: *a loose translation.* **6.** (of funds, cash, etc.) not allocated or locked away; readily available: *loose change.* **7. a.** (esp. of women) promiscuous or easy. **b.** (of attitudes, ways of life, etc.) immoral or dissolute. **8. a.** lacking a sense of responsibility or propriety: *loose talk.* **b.** (*in combination*): *loosetongued.* **9. a.** (of the bowels) emptying easily, esp. excessively. **b.** (of a cough) accompanied by phlegm, mucus, etc. **10.** *Inf., chiefly U.S.* very relaxed; easy. ~*n.* **11. the loose.** *Rugby.* the part of play when the forwards close round the ball in a ruck or loose scrum. **12. on the loose. a.** free from confinement or restraint. **b.** *Inf.* on a spree. ~*adv.* **13. a.** in a loose manner; loosely. **b.** (*in combination*): *loose-fitting.* ~*vb.* **14.** (*tr.*) to set free or release, as from confinement, restraint, or obligation. **15.** (*tr.*) to unfasten or untie. **16.** to make or become less strict, tight, firmly attached, compact, etc. **17.** (when *intr.*, often foll. by *off*) to let fly (a bullet, arrow, or other missile). —**'loosely** *adv.* —**'looseness** *n.*

loose-jointed *adj.* **1.** supple and easy in movement. **2.** loosely built; with ill-fitting joints. —ˌloose-'jointed-ness *n.*

loose-leaf *adj.* (of a binder, album, etc.) capable of being opened to allow removal and addition of pages.

loosen ('lu:sən) *vb.* **1.** to make or become less tight, fixed, etc. **2.** (often foll. by *up*) to make or become less firm, compact, or rigid. **3.** (*tr.*) to untie. **4.** (*tr.*) to let loose; set free. **5.** (often foll. by *up*) to make or become less strict, severe, etc. **6.** (*tr.*) to rid or relieve (the bowels) of constipation. —**'loosener** *n.*

loot (lu:t) *n.* **1.** goods stolen during pillaging, as in wartime, during riots, etc. **2.** goods, money, etc., obtained illegally. **3.** *Inf.* money or wealth. ~*vb.* **4.** to pillage (a city, etc.) during war or riots. **5.** to steal (money or goods), esp. during pillaging. —**'looter** *n.*

lop[1] (lɒp) *vb.* **lopping, lopped.** (*tr.; usually foll. by off*) **1.** to sever (parts) from a tree, body, etc., esp. with swift strokes. **2.** to cut out or eliminate from as excessive. ~*n.* **3.** a part or parts lopped off, as from a tree. —**'lopper** *n.*

lop[2] (lɒp) *vb.* **lopping, lopped. 1.** to hang or allow to hang loosely. **2.** (*intr.*) to slouch about or move awkwardly.

lope (ləup) *vb.* **1.** (*intr.*) (of a person) to move or run with a long swinging stride. **2.** (*intr.*) (of four-legged animals) to run with a regular bounding movement. **3.** to cause (a horse) to canter with a long easy stride or (of a horse) to canter in this manner. ~*n.* **4.** a long steady gait or stride.

lop-eared *adj.* (of animals) having ears that droop.

lopsided (ˌlɒp'saɪdɪd) *adj.* **1.** leaning to one side. **2.** greater in weight, height, or size on one side. —ˌlop-'sidedly *adv.* —ˌlop'sidedness *n.*

loquacious (lɒ'kweɪʃəs) *adj.* characterized by or showing a tendency to talk a great deal. —lo'quaciously *adv.* —loquacity (lɒ'kwæsɪtɪ) *or* lo'quaciousness *n.*

lor (lɔ:) *interj. Not standard.* an exclamation of surprise or dismay.

loran ('lɔ:rən) *n.* a radio navigation system operating over long distances. Synchronized pulses are transmitted from widely spaced radio stations to aircraft or shipping, the time of arrival of the pulses being used to determine position.

lord (lɔ:d) *n.* **1.** a person who has power or authority over others, such as a monarch or master. **2.** a male member of the nobility, esp. in Britain. **3.** (in medieval Europe) a feudal superior, esp. the master of a manor. **4.** a husband considered as head of the household (archaic except in the facetious phrase **lord and master**). **5. my lord.** a respectful form of address used to a judge, bishop, or nobleman. ~*vb.* **6.** (*tr.*) *Now rare.* to make a lord of (a person). **7.** to act in a superior manner towards (esp. in **lord it over**). —**'lordless** *adj.* —**'lord,like** *adj.*

Lord (lɔ:d) *n.* **1.** a title given to God or Jesus Christ. **2.** *Brit.* **a.** a title given to men of high birth, specifically to an earl, marquess, baron, or viscount. **b.** a courtesy title given to the younger sons of a duke or marquess. **c.** the ceremonial title of certain high officials or of a bishop or archbishop: *Lord Mayor; Lord Bishop of Durham.* ~*interj.* **3.** (*sometimes not cap.*) an exclamation of dismay, surprise, etc.: *Good Lord!*

Lord Chief Justice *n.* the judge who is second only to the Lord Chancellor in the English legal hierarchy; president of one division of the High Court of Justice.

Lord High Chancellor *n.* another name for the **Lord Chancellor.**

Lord Lieutenant *n.* **1.** (in Britain) the representative of the Crown in a county. **2.** (formerly) the British viceroy in Ireland.

lordly ('lɔ:dlɪ) *adj.* **-lier, -liest. 1.** haughty; arrogant; proud. **2.** of or befitting a lord. ~*adv.* **3.** *Arch.* in the manner of a lord. —**'lordliness** *n.*

Lord Mayor *n.* the mayor in the City of London and in certain other boroughs.

Lord of Misrule *n.* (formerly, in England) a person appointed master of revels at a Christmas celebration.

Lord Privy Seal *n.* (in Britain) the senior cabinet minister without official duties.

Lords (lɔ:dz) *n.* the short for **House of Lords.**

Lord's (lɔ:dz) *n.* a cricket ground in N London; headquarters of the M.C.C.

Lord's Day *n.* **the.** the Christian Sabbath; Sunday.

lordship ('lɔ:dʃɪp) *n.* the position or authority of a lord.

Lordship ('lɔ:dʃɪp) *n.* (preceded by *Your* or *His*) *Brit.* a title used to address or refer to a bishop, a judge of the high court, or any peer except a duke.

Lord's Prayer *n.* **the.** the prayer taught by Jesus Christ to his disciples, as in Matthew 6:9–13, Luke 11:2–4. Also called: **Our Father, Paternoster** (esp. Latin version).

Lords Spiritual *pl. n.* the Anglican bishops of England and Wales who are members of the House of Lords.

Lord's Supper *n.* **the.** another term for **Holy Communion** (I Corinthians 11:20).

Lords Temporal *pl. n.* **the.** (in Britain) peers other than bishops in their capacity as members of the House of Lords.

lore (lɔ:) *n.* **1.** collective knowledge or wisdom on a particular subject, esp. of a traditional nature. **2.** knowledge or learning.

THESAURUS

slot **2.** *Fig.* avoidance, escape, evasion, excuse, let-out, means of escape, plea, pretence, pretext, subterfuge

loose *adj.* **1.** floating, free, insecure, movable, released, unattached, unbound, unconfined, unfastened, unfettered, unrestricted, unsecured, untied, wobbly **2.** baggy, easy, hanging, loosened, not fitting, not tight, relaxed, slack, slackened, sloppy **3.** diffuse, disconnected, disordered, ill-defined, imprecise, inaccurate, indefinite, indistinct, inexact, rambling, random, vague **4.** abandoned, debauched, disreputable, dissipated, dissolute, fast, immoral, lewd, libertine, licentious, profligate, promiscuous, unchaste, wanton **5.** careless, heedless, imprudent, lax, negligent, rash, thoughtless, unmindful ~*v.* **6.** detach, disconnect, disengage, ease, free, let go, lib-

erate, loosen, release, set free, slacken, unbind, undo, unfasten, unleash, unloose, untie

loosen 1. detach, let out, separate, slacken, unbind, undo, unloose, unstick, untie, work free, work loose **2.** deliver, free, let go, liberate, release, set free **3.** *Often with* up ease up *or* off, go easy (*Inf.*), lessen, let up, mitigate, moderate, relax, soften, weaken

loot 1. *n.* booty, goods, haul, plunder, prize, spoils, swag (*Sl.*) **2.** *v.* despoil, pillage, plunder, raid, ransack, ravage, rifle, rob, sack

lopsided askew, asymmetrical, awry, cockeyed, crooked, disproportionate, off balance, one-sided, out of shape, out of true, squint, tilting, unbalanced, unequal, uneven, warped

lord 1. commander, governor, king, leader, liege, master, monarch, overlord, potentate,

prince, ruler, seigneur, sovereign, superior **2.** earl, noble, nobleman, peer, viscount **3. lord it over** act big (*Sl.*), be overbearing, boss around (*Inf.*), domineer, order around, play the lord, pull rank, put on airs, swagger

Lord, Our *or* **The** Christ, God, Jehovah, Jesus Christ, the Almighty

lordly 1. arrogant, condescending, despotic, dictatorial, disdainful, domineering, haughty, high and mighty (*Inf.*), high-handed, hoity-toity (*Inf.*), imperious, lofty, overbearing, patronizing, proud, stuck-up (*Inf.*), supercilious, toffee-nosed (*Sl., chiefly Brit.*), tyrannical **2.** aristocratic, dignified, exalted, gracious, grand, imperial, lofty, majestic, noble, princely, regal, stately

lore 1. beliefs, doctrine, experience, folk-wisdom, mythos, saws, sayings, teaching, tra-

lorgnette (lɔːˈnjɛt) *n.* a pair of spectacles or opera glasses mounted on a handle.

lorry (ˈlɒrɪ) *n., pl.* **-ries. 1.** a large motor vehicle designed to carry heavy loads, esp. one with a flat platform. U.S. name: **truck. 2.** any of various vehicles with a flat load-carrying surface, esp. one designed to run on rails.

lose (luːz) *vb.* **losing, lost.** (*mainly tr.*) **1.** to part with or come to be without, as through theft, accident, negligence, etc. **2.** to fail to keep or maintain: *to lose one's balance.* **3.** to suffer the loss or deprivation of: *to lose a parent.* **4.** to cease to have or possess. **5.** to fail to get or make use of: *to lose a chance.* **6.** (*also intr.*) to fail to gain or win (a contest, game, etc.): *to lose the match.* **7.** to fail to see, hear, perceive, or understand: *I lost the gist of his speech.* **8.** to waste: *to lose money gambling.* **9.** to wander from so as to be unable to find: *to lose one's way.* **10.** to cause the loss of: *his delay lost him the battle.* **11.** to allow to go astray or out of sight: *we lost him in the crowd.* **12.** (*usually passive*) to absorb or engross: *he was lost in contemplation.* **13.** (*usually passive*) to cause the death or destruction of: *two men were lost in the crash.* **14.** to outdistance or elude: *he soon lost his pursuers.* **15.** (*intr.*) to decrease or depreciate in value or effectiveness: *poetry always loses in translation.* **16.** (*also intr.*) (of a timepiece) to run slow (by a specified amount). **17.** (of a woman) to fail to give birth to (a viable baby), esp. as the result of a miscarriage. —**ˈlosable** *adj.*

lose out *vb. Inf.* **1.** (*intr., adv.*) to be defeated or unsuccessful. **2. lose out on.** to fail to secure or make use of: *we lost out on the sale.*

loser (ˈluːzə) *n.* **1.** a person or thing that loses. **2.** *Inf.* a person or thing that seems destined to be taken advantage of, fail, etc.: *a born loser.*

losing (ˈluːzɪŋ) *adj.* unprofitable; failing: *the business was a losing concern.*

loss (lɒs) *n.* **1.** the act or an instance of losing. **2.** the disadvantage or deprivation resulting from losing: *a loss of reputation.* **3.** the person, thing, or amount lost: *a large loss.* **4.** (*pl.*) military personnel lost by death or capture. **5.** (*sometimes pl.*) the amount by which the costs of a business transaction or operation exceed its revenue. **6.** *Insurance.* **a.** an occurrence of something that has been insured against, thus giving rise to a claim by a policyholder. **b.** the amount of the resulting claim. **7. at a loss. a.** unable or too perplexed to do something). **b.** bewildered. **c.** rendered helpless (for lack of something): *at a loss for words.* **8. dead loss.** *Sl.* a useless or contemptible person, thing, etc.

loss leader *n.* an article offered below cost to attract customers.

lost (lɒst) *adj.* **1.** unable to be found or recovered. **2.** unable to find one's way or ascertain one's whereabouts. **3.** confused, bewildered, or helpless: *he is lost in discussions of theory.* **4.** (*sometimes foll. by on*) not utilized, noticed, or taken advantage of (by): *rational arguments are lost on her.* **5.** no longer possessed or existing because of defeat, misfortune, or the passage of time: *a lost art.* **6.** destroyed physically: *the lost platoon.* **7.** (foll. by *to*) no longer available or open (to). **8.** (foll. by *to*) insensible or impervious (to a sense of shame, justice, etc.). **9.** (foll. by *in*) engrossed (in): *he was lost in his book.* **10.** morally fallen: *a lost woman.* **11.** damned: *a lost soul.*

lot (lɒt) *pron.* **1.** (*functioning as sing. or pl.; preceded by a*) a great number or quantity: *a lot to do; a lot of people.* ~*n.* **2.** a collection of objects, items, or people: *a nice lot of youngsters.* **3.** portion in life; destiny; fortune: *it falls to my lot to be poor.* **4.** any object, such as a straw or slip of paper, drawn from others at random to make a selection or choice (esp. in **draw** or **cast lots**). **5.** the use of lots in making a selection or choice (esp. in **by lot**). **6.** an assigned or apportioned share. **7.** an item or set of items for sale in an auction. **8.** an area of land: *a parking lot.* **9.** U.S. a film studio. **10. a bad lot.** an unpleasant or disreputable person. **11. cast** *or* **throw in one's lot with.** to join with voluntarily and share the fortunes of. **12. the lot.** the entire amount or number. ~*adv.* (preceded by *a*) *Inf.* **13.** to a considerable extent, degree, or amount; very much: *to delay a lot.* **14.** a great deal of the time or often: *to sing madrigals a lot.* ~*vb.* **lotting, lotted. 15.** to draw lots for (something). **16.** (*tr.*) to divide (land, etc.) into lots. **17.** (*tr.*) another word for **allot.**

loth (ləʊθ) *adj.* a variant spelling of **loath.**

Lothario (ləʊˈθɑːrɪˌəʊ) *n., pl.* **-os.** (*sometimes not cap.*) a rake, libertine, or seducer.

lotion (ˈləʊʃən) *n.* a liquid preparation having a soothing, cleansing, or antiseptic action, applied to the skin, eyes, etc.

lots (lɒts) *pl. n. Inf.* **1.** (often foll. by *of*) great numbers or quantities: *lots of people; to eat lots.* ~*adv.* **2.** a great deal. **3.** (*intensifier*): *the journey is lots quicker by train.*

lottery (ˈlɒtərɪ) *n., pl.* **-teries. 1.** a game of chance in which tickets are sold, which may later qualify the holder for a prize. **2.** an endeavour the success of which is regarded as a matter of luck.

lotto (ˈlɒtəʊ) *n.* a children's game in which numbered discs are drawn at random and called out, while the players cover the corresponding numbers on cards, the winner being the first to cover all the numbers, a particular row, etc.

lotus *or* **lotos** (ˈləʊtəs) *n.* **1.** (in Greek mythology) a fruit that induces forgetfulness and a dreamy languor in those who eat it. **2.** any of several water lilies of tropical Africa and Asia, esp. the **white lotus**, which was regarded as sacred in ancient Egypt. **3.** a related plant which is the sacred lotus of India, China, and Tibet. **4.** a representation of such a plant, common in Hindu, Buddhist, and ancient Egyptian art. **5.** any of a genus of leguminous plants of the legume family of the Old World and North America, having yellow, pink, or white pealike flowers.

lotus-eater *n. Greek myth.* one of a people encountered by Odysseus in North Africa who lived in indolent forgetfulness, drugged by the fruit of the legendary lotus.

THESAURUS

ditional wisdom, traditions, wisdom **2.** erudition, knowhow (*Inf.*), knowledge, learning, letters, scholarship

lose 1. be deprived of, displace, drop, fail to keep, forget, mislay, misplace, miss, suffer loss **2.** capitulate, default, fail, fall short, forfeit, lose out on (*Inf.*), miss, pass up (*Inf.*), yield **3.** be defeated, be the loser, be worsted, come a cropper (*Inf.*), come to grief, get the worst of, lose out, suffer defeat, take a licking (*Inf.*) **4.** consume, deplete, dissipate, drain, exhaust, expend, lavish, misspend, squander, use up, waste **5.** confuse, miss, stray from, wander from **6.** lap, leave behind, outdistance, outrun, outstrip, overtake, pass **7.** dodge, duck, elude, escape, evade, give someone the slip, shake off, slip away, throw off

loser also-ran, dud (*Inf.*), failure, flop (*Inf.*), lemon (*Sl.*), no-hoper (*Austral. sl.*), underdog, washout (*Inf.*)

loss 1. bereavement, deprivation, disappearance, failure, forfeiture, losing, misfortune, mislaying, privation, squandering, waste **2.** cost, damage, defeat, destruction,

detriment, disadvantage, harm, hurt, impairment, injury, ruin **3.** *Plural* casualties, dead, death toll, fatalities, number killed (captured, injured, missing, wounded) **4.** *Sometimes plural* debit, debt, deficiency, deficit, depletion, losings, shrinkage **5. at a loss** at one's wits' end, baffled, bewildered, confused, helpless, nonplussed, perplexed, puzzled, stuck (*Inf.*), stumped

lost 1. disappeared, forfeited, mislaid, misplaced, missed, missing, strayed, vanished, wayward **2.** adrift, astray, at sea, disoriented, off-course, off-track **3.** baffled, bewildered, clueless (*Sl.*), confused, helpless, ignorant, mystified, perplexed, puzzled **4.** abolished, annihilated, demolished, destroyed, devastated, eradicated, exterminated, obliterated, perished, ruined, wasted, wiped out, wrecked **5.** absent, absorbed, abstracted, distracted, dreamy, engrossed, entranced, preoccupied, rapt, spellbound, taken up **6.** consumed, dissipated, frittered away, misapplied, misdirected, misspent, misused, squandered, wasted **7.** bygone, dead, extinct, forgotten, gone, lapsed, obsolete, out-of-date, past, unremem-

bered **8.** abandoned, corrupt, damned, depraved, dissolute, fallen, irreclaimable, licentious, profligate, unchaste, wanton

lot 1. assortment, batch, bunch (*Inf.*), collection, consignment, crowd, group, quantity, set **2.** accident, chance, destiny, doom, fate, fortune, hazard, plight, portion **3.** allowance, cut (*Inf.*), parcel, part, percentage, piece, portion, quota, ration, share **4. a lot** *or* **lots** abundance, a great deal, heap(s), large amount, load(s) (*Inf.*), masses (*Inf.*), numbers, ocean(s), oodles (*Inf.*), piles, plenty, quantities, reams (*Inf.*), scores, stack(s) **5. draw lots** choose, cut for aces, cut straws (*Inf.*), decide, pick, select, spin a coin, toss up **6. throw in one's lot with** ally *or* align oneself with, join, join forces with, join fortunes with, make common cause with, support

lotion balm, cream, embrocation, liniment, salve, solution

lottery 1. draw, raffle, sweepstake **2.** chance, gamble, hazard, risk, toss-up (*Inf.*), venture

lotus position n. a seated cross-legged position used in yoga, meditation, etc.

loud (laʊd) adj. **1.** (of sound) relatively great in volume: a loud shout. **2.** making or able to make sounds of relatively great volume: a loud engine. **3.** clamorous, insistent, and emphatic: loud protests. **4.** (of colours, designs, etc.) offensive or obtrusive to look at. **5.** characterized by noisy, vulgar, and offensive behaviour. ~adv. **6.** in a loud manner. **7.** out loud. Inf. audibly, as distinct from silently. —'loudish adj. —'loudly adv. —'loudness n.

loudspeaker (ˌlaʊd'spiːkə) n. a device for converting audio-frequency signals into sound waves. Often shortened to **speaker.**

lough (lɒk, lɒx) n. **1.** an Irish word for **lake**[1]. **2.** a long narrow bay or arm of the sea in Ireland.

lounge (laʊndʒ) vb. **1.** (intr.; often foll. by about or around) to sit, lie, walk, or stand in a relaxed manner. **2.** to pass (time) lazily or idly. ~n. **3.** a communal room in a hotel, ship, etc., used for waiting or relaxing in. **4.** Chiefly Brit. a living room in a private house. **5.** Also called: **lounge bar, saloon bar.** Brit. a more expensive bar in a pub or hotel. **6.** a sofa or couch. **7.** the act or an instance of lounging. —'lounger n.

lounge suit n. a man's suit of matching jacket and trousers worn for the normal business day.

lour (laʊə) vb. a variant spelling of **lower**[2].

lourie ('laʊrɪ) n. a type of African bird with bright plumage.

louse (laʊs) n., pl. **-lice** (laɪs). **1.** a wingless bloodsucking insect, such as the head louse, body louse, and crab louse, all of which infest man. **2. biting** or **bird louse.** a wingless insect, such as the chicken louse: external parasites of birds and mammals, with biting mouthparts. **3.** any of various similar but unrelated insects. **4.** pl. **louses.** Sl. an unpleasant or mean person. ~vb. (tr.) **5.** to remove lice from. **6.** (foll. by up) Sl. to ruin or spoil.

lousy ('laʊzɪ) adj. **lousier, lousiest. 1.** Sl. very mean or unpleasant. **2.** Sl. inferior or bad. **3.** infested with lice. **4.** (foll. by with) Sl. provided with an excessive amount (of): he's lousy with money. —'lousily adv. —'lousiness n.

lout (laʊt) n. a crude or oafish person; boor. —'loutish adj.

louvre or U.S. **louver** ('luːvə) n. **1. a.** any of a set of horizontal parallel slats in a door or window, sloping outwards to throw off rain and admit air. **b.** Also called: **louvre boards.** the slats and frame supporting them. **2.** Archit. a turret that allows smoke to escape. —'louvred or U.S. 'louvered adj.

lovage ('lʌvɪdʒ) n. a European umbelliferous plant with greenish-white flowers and aromatic fruits, which are used for flavouring food.

love (lʌv) vb. **1.** (tr.) to have a great attachment to and affection for. **2.** (tr.) to have passionate desire, longing, and feelings for. **3.** (tr.) to like or desire (to do something) very much. **4.** (tr.) to make love to. **5.** (intr.) to be in love. ~n. **6. a.** an intense emotion of affection, warmth, fondness, and regard towards a person or thing.

b. (as modifier): love story. **7.** a deep feeling of sexual attraction and desire. **8.** wholehearted liking for or pleasure in something. **9.** Christianity. God's benevolent attitude towards man. **10.** Also: **my love.** a beloved person: used esp. as an endearment. **11.** Brit. inf. a term of address, not necessarily for a person regarded as likable. **12.** (in tennis, squash, etc.) a score of zero. **13. fall in love.** to become in love. **14. for love.** without payment. **15. for love or money.** by any means. **16. for the love of.** for the sake of. **17. in love.** in a state of strong emotional attachment and usually sexual attraction. **18. make love (to). a.** to have sexual intercourse (with). **b.** Now arch. to make advances (to). —'lovable or 'loveable adj. —'loveless adj.

lovebird ('lʌvˌbɜːd) n. any of several small African parrots often kept as cagebirds.

love child n. Euphemistic. an illegitimate child; bastard.

love-lies-bleeding n. any of several plants having drooping spikes of small red flowers.

lovelorn ('lʌvˌlɔːn) adj. miserable because of unrequited love or unhappiness in love.

lovely ('lʌvlɪ) adj. **-lier, -liest. 1.** very attractive or beautiful. **2.** highly pleasing or enjoyable: a lovely time. **3.** inspiring love; lovable. ~n. **4.** Sl. a lovely woman. —'loveliness n.

lovemaking ('lʌvˌmeɪkɪŋ) n. **1.** sexual play and activity between lovers, esp. including sexual intercourse. **2.** an archaic word for **courtship.**

lover ('lʌvə) n. **1.** a person, now esp. a man, who has an extramarital or premarital sexual relationship with another person. **2.** (often pl.) either of the two people involved in a love affair. **3. a.** someone who loves a specified person or thing: a lover of music. **b.** (in combination): a music-lover; cat-lover.

lovesick ('lʌvˌsɪk) adj. pining or languishing because of love. —'loveˌsickness n.

lovey-dovey adj. making an excessive or ostentatious display of affection.

loving ('lʌvɪŋ) adj. feeling or showing love and affection. —'lovingly adv. —'lovingness n.

loving cup n. **1.** a large vessel, usually two-handled, out of which people drink in turn at a banquet. **2.** a similar cup awarded to the winner of a competition.

low[1] (ləʊ) adj. **1.** having a relatively small distance from base to top; not tall or high: a low hill; a low building. **2. a.** situated at a relatively short distance above the ground, sea level, the horizon, or other reference position: low cloud. **b.** (in combination): low-lying. **3.** of less than usual height, depth, or degree: low temperature. **4. a.** (of numbers) small. **b.** (of measurements) expressed in small numbers. **5. a.** involving or containing a relatively small amount of something: a low supply. **b.** (in combination): low-powered. **6. a.** having little value or quality. **b.** (in combination): low-grade. **7.** coarse or vulgar: a low conversation. **8. a.** inferior in culture or status. **b.** (in combination): low-class. **9.** in a physically or mentally depressed or weakened state. **10.** low-

---

necked: *a low dress.* **11.** with a hushed tone; quiet or soft: *a low whisper.* **12.** of relatively small price or monetary value: *low cost.* **13.** *Music.* relating to or characterized by a relatively low pitch. **14.** (of latitudes) situated not far north or south of the equator. **15.** having little or no money. **16.** abject or servile. **17.** unfavourable: *a low opinion.* **18.** not advanced in evolution: *a low form of plant life.* **19.** deep: *a low bow.* **20.** *Phonetics.* of, relating to, or denoting a vowel whose articulation is produced by moving the back of the tongue away from the soft palate, such as for the *a* in English *father.* **21.** (of a gear) providing a relatively low forward speed for a given engine speed. **22.** (*usually cap.*) of or relating to the Low Church. ~*adv.* **23.** in a low position, level, degree, intensity, etc.: *to bring someone low.* **24.** at a low pitch; deep: *to sing low.* **25.** at a low price; cheaply: *to buy low.* **26.** lay low. **a.** to cause to fall by a blow. **b.** to overcome, defeat, or destroy. **27.** lie low. **a.** to keep or be concealed or quiet. **b.** to wait for a favourable opportunity. ~*n.* **28.** a low position, level, or degree: *an all-time low.* **29.** an area of relatively low atmospheric pressure, esp. a depression. —'**lowness** *n.*

low² (ləʊ) *n. also* **lowing. 1.** the sound uttered by cattle; moo. ~*vb.* **2.** to make or express by a low or moo.

lowborn (ˌləʊˈbɔːn) *or* **lowbred** (ˌləʊˈbrɛd) *adj. Now rare.* of ignoble or common parentage.

lowbrow ('ləʊˌbraʊ) *Disparaging.* ~*n.* **1.** a person who has uncultivated or nonintellectual tastes. ~*adj. also* **lowbrowed. 2.** of or characteristic of such a person.

Low Church *n.* **1.** the school of thought in the Church of England stressing evangelical beliefs and practices. ~*adj.* **Low-Church. 2.** of or relating to this school.

low comedy *n.* comedy characterized by slapstick and physical action.

low-down *Inf.* ~*adj.* **1.** mean, underhand, or despicable. ~*n.* **lowdown. 2. the.** information.

lower¹ ('ləʊə) *adj.* **1.** being below one or more other things: *the lower shelf.* **2.** reduced in amount or value: *a lower price.* **3.** *Maths.* (of a limit or bound) less than or equal to one or more numbers or variables. **4.** (*sometimes cap.*) *Geol.* denoting the early part of a period, formation, etc.: *Lower Silurian.* ~*vb.* **5.** (*tr.*) to cause to become low or on a lower level; bring, put, or cause to move down. **6.** (*tr.*) to reduce or bring down in estimation, dignity, value, etc.: *to lower oneself.* **7.** to reduce or be reduced: *to lower one's confidence.* **8.** (*tr.*) to make quieter: *to lower the radio.* **9.** (*tr.*) to reduce the pitch of. **10.** (*intr.*) to diminish or become less.

lower² *or* **lour** ('laʊə) *vb.* (*intr.*) **1.** (esp. of the sky, weather, etc.) to be overcast, dark, and menacing. **2.** to scowl or frown. ~*n.* **3.** a menacing scowl or appearance. —'**loweringly** *or* '**louringly** *adv.*

Lower Canada *n.* (from 1791 to 1841) the official name of the S region of the present-day province of Quebec.

lower case *n.* **1.** the bottom half of a compositor's type case, in which the small letters are kept. ~*adj.* **lower-case. 2.** of or relating to small letters. ~*vb.* **lower-case. 3.** (*tr.*) to print with lower-case letters.

lower class *n.* **1.** the social stratum having the lowest position in the social hierarchy. ~*adj.* **lower-class.**

2. of or relating to the lower class. **3.** inferior or vulgar.

lower house *n.* one of the houses of a bicameral legislature: usually the larger and more representative. Also called: **lower chamber.**

lowest common denominator *n.* the smallest integer or polynomial that is exactly divisible by each denominator of a set of fractions. Abbrev.: **l.c.d., L.C.D.** Also called: **least common denominator.**

lowest common multiple *n.* the smallest number or quantity that is exactly divisible by each member of a set of numbers or quantities. Abbrev.: **l.c.m., L.C.M.** Also called: **least common multiple.**

low frequency *n.* a radio-frequency band or a frequency lying between 300 and 30 kilohertz.

low-key *or* **low-keyed** *adj.* **1.** having a low intensity or tone. **2.** restrained or subdued.

lowland ('ləʊlənd) *n.* **1.** relatively low ground. **2.** (*often pl.*) a low generally flat region. ~*adj.* **3.** of or relating to a lowland or lowlands. —'**lowlander** *n.*

Lowland ('ləʊlənd) *adj.* of or relating to the Lowlands of Scotland or the dialect of English spoken there.

Low Latin *n.* any form of Latin other than the classical, such as Medieval Latin.

lowly ('ləʊlɪ) ~*adj.* **-lier, -liest. 1.** humble or low in position, rank, status, etc. **2.** full of humility; meek. **3.** simple, unpretentious, or plain. ~*adv.* **4.** in a low or lowly manner. —'**lowliness** *n.*

Low Mass *n.* a Mass that has a simplified ceremonial form and is spoken rather than sung.

low-minded *adj.* having a vulgar or crude mind and character. —ˌlow-'**mindedly** *adv.* —ˌlow-'**mindedness** *n.*

low-pitched *adj.* **1.** pitched low in tone. **2.** (of a roof) having sides with a shallow slope.

low-pressure *adj.* **1.** having, using, or involving a pressure below normal: *a low-pressure gas.* **2.** relaxed or calm.

low profile *n.* a position or attitude characterized by a deliberate avoidance of prominence or publicity.

low-spirited *adj.* depressed or dejected. —ˌlow-'**spiritedly** *adv.* —ˌlow-'**spiritedness** *n.*

low tide *n.* **1.** the tide when it is at its lowest level or the time at which it reaches this. **2.** a lowest point.

lowveld ('ləʊˌfɛlt) *n.* (in South Africa) the low grasslands of the Transvaal province.

low water *n.* **1.** another name for **low tide. 2.** the state of any stretch of water at its lowest level.

lox¹ (lɒks) *n.* a kind of smoked salmon.

lox² (lɒks) *n.* short for **liquid oxygen,** esp. when used as an oxidizer for rocket fuels.

loyal ('lɔɪəl) *adj.* **1.** showing allegiance. **2.** faithful to one's country, government, etc. **3.** of or expressing loyalty. —'**loyally** *adv.*

loyalist ('lɔɪəlɪst) *n.* a patriotic supporter of his sovereign or government. —'**loyalism** *n.*

Loyalist ('lɔɪəlɪst) *n.* **1.** (in Northern Ireland) any of the Protestants wishing to retain Ulster's link with Britain. **2.** (in North America) an American colonist who supported Britain during the War of American Independence. **3.** (during the Spanish Civil War) a supporter of

---

THESAURUS

low 1. little, short, small, squat, stunted **2.** deep, depressed, ground-level, low-lying, shallow, subsided, sunken **3.** depleted, insignificant, little, meagre, paltry, reduced, scant, small, sparse, trifling **4.** deficient, inadequate, inferior, low-grade, mediocre, poor, puny, second-rate, shoddy, substandard, worthless **5.** coarse, common, crude, disgraceful, dishonourable, disreputable, gross, ill-bred, obscene, rough, rude, unbecoming, undignified, unrefined, vulgar **6.** humble, lowborn, lowly, meek, obscure, plain, plebeian, poor, simple, unpretentious **7.** blue, brassed off (*Inf.*), dejected, depressed, despondent, disheartened, down, downcast, down in the dumps (*Inf.*), fed up, forlorn, gloomy, glum, miserable, morose, sad, unhappy **8.** debilitated, dying, exhausted, feeble, frail, ill, prostrate, reduced, sinking, stricken, weak **9.** gentle, hushed, muffled, muted, quiet, soft, subdued, whispered **10.** cheap, economical, inexpensive, moderate, modest, reasonable

11. abject, base, contemptible, dastardly, degraded, depraved, despicable, ignoble, mean, menial, nasty, scurvy, servile, sordid, unworthy, vile, vulgar

lowdown dope (*Sl.*), gen (*Brit. inf.*), info (*Inf.*), information, inside story, intelligence

lower¹ *adj.* **1.** inferior, junior, lesser, low-level, minor, secondary, second-class, smaller, subordinate, under **2.** curtailed, decreased, diminished, lessened, pared down, reduced ~*v.* **3.** depress, drop, fall, let down, make lower, sink, submerge, take down **4.** abase, belittle, condescend, debase, degrade, deign, demean, devalue, disgrace, downgrade, humble, humiliate, stoop **5.** abate, curtail, cut, decrease, diminish, lessen, minimize, moderate, prune, reduce, slash **6.** soften, tone down

lower², lour 1. be brewing, blacken, cloud up *or* over, darken, loom, menace, threaten **2.** frown, give a dirty look, glare, glower, look daggers, look sullen, scowl

low-key low-pitched, muffled, muted, played down, quiet, restrained, subdued, toned down, understated

lowly 1. ignoble, inferior, lowborn, mean, obscure, plebeian, proletarian, subordinate **2.** docile, dutiful, gentle, humble, meek, mild, modest, submissive, unassuming **3.** average, common, homespun, modest, ordinary, plain, poor, simple, unpretentious

low-spirited apathetic, blue, brassed off (*Inf.*), dejected, depressed, despondent, down, down-hearted, down in the dumps (*Inf.*), fed up, gloomy, heavy-hearted, low, miserable, moody, sad, unhappy

loyal attached, constant, dependable, devoted, dutiful, faithful, patriotic, staunch, steadfast, tried and true, true, true-blue, true-hearted, trustworthy, trusty, unswerving, unwavering

the republican government.

loyalty ('lɔɪəltɪ) n., pl. **-ties.** 1. the state or quality of being loyal. 2. (often pl.) allegiance.

lozenge ('lɒzɪndʒ) n. 1. Med. a medicated tablet held in the mouth until it has dissolved. 2. Geom. another name for **rhombus.** 3. Heraldry. a diamond-shaped charge. —'**lozenged** or '**lozengy** adj.

LP n. a. Also called: **long player.** a long-playing gramophone record: one designed to rotate at 33 revolutions per minute. **b.** (as modifier): an LP sleeve.

L.P. abbrev. for: 1. Also: **LP** (in Britain) Lord Provost. 2. Also: **l.p.** low pressure.

Lr the chemical symbol for lawrencium.

LSD n. lysergic acid diethylamide; a crystalline compound prepared from lysergic acid, used in experimental medicine and taken illegally as a hallucinogenic drug. Informal name: **acid.**

L.S.D., £.s.d., or **l.s.d.** (in Britain, esp. formerly) abbrev. for Latin librae, solidi, denarii: pounds, shillings, pence.

L.S.E. abbrev. for London School of Economics.

Lt. abbrev. for Lieutenant.

Ltd. or **ltd.** abbrev. for limited (liability). U.S. equivalent: **Inc.**

Lu the chemical symbol for lutetium.

lubber ('lʌbə) n. 1. a big, awkward, or stupid person. 2. short for **landlubber.** —'**lubberly** adj., adv. —'**lubberliness** n.

lubricant ('lu:brɪkənt) n. 1. a lubricating substance, such as oil. ~adj. 2. serving to lubricate.

lubricate ('lu:brɪ‚keɪt) vb. 1. (tr.) to cover or treat with an oily substance so as to lessen friction. 2. (tr.) to make greasy, slippery, or smooth. 3. (intr.) to act as a lubricant. —‚**lubri'cation** n. —'**lubri‚cative** adj. —'**lubri‚cator** n.

lubricity (lu:'brɪsɪtɪ) n. 1. Formal or literary. lewdness or salaciousness. 2. Rare. smoothness or slipperiness. —**lubricous** ('lu:brɪkəs) or **lubricious** (lu:'brɪʃəs) adj.

lucerne (lu:'sɜ:n) n. Brit. another name for **alfalfa.**

lucid ('lu:sɪd) adj. 1. readily understood; clear. 2. shining or glowing. 3. of or relating to a period of normality between periods of insane behaviour. —**lu'cidity** or '**lucidness** n. —'**lucidly** adv.

lucifer ('lu:sɪfə) n. a friction match: originally a trade name.

Lucifer ('lu:sɪfə) n. 1. the leader of the rebellion of the angels; Satan. 2. the planet Venus when it rises as the morning star.

luck (lʌk) n. 1. events that are beyond control and seem subject to chance; fortune. 2. success or good fortune. 3. something considered to bring good luck. 4. **down on one's luck.** having little or no good luck to the point of suffering hardships. 5. **no such luck.** unfortunately not. 6. **try one's luck.** to attempt something that is uncertain.

lucky ('lʌkɪ) adj. **-ier, -iest.** 1. having or bringing good fortune. 2. happening by chance, esp. as desired. —'**luckily** adv. —'**luckiness** n.

lucky dip n. Brit. 1. a box filled with sawdust containing small prizes for which children search. 2. Inf. an undertaking of uncertain outcome.

lucrative ('lu:krətɪv) adj. producing a profit; profitable. —'**lucratively** adv. —'**lucrativeness** n.

lucre ('lu:kə) n. Usually facetious. money or wealth (esp. in **filthy lucre**).

Luddite ('lʌdaɪt) n. English history. 1. any of the textile workers opposed to mechanization who organized machine-breaking between 1811 and 1816. 2. any opponent of industrial change or innovation. ~adj. 3. of or relating to the Luddites.

ludicrous ('lu:dɪkrəs) adj. absurd or incongruous to the point of provoking laughter. —'**ludicrously** adv. —'**ludicrousness** n.

ludo ('lu:dəʊ) n. Brit. a simple board game in which players advance counters by throwing dice.

luff (lʌf) n. 1. Naut. the leading edge of a fore-and-aft sail. ~vb. 2. Naut. to head a (sailing vessel) into the wind so that her sails flap. 3. (intr.) Naut. (of a sail) to flap when the wind is blowing equally on both sides. 4. to move the jib of (a crane) in order to shift a load.

lug[1] (lʌg) vb. **lugging, lugged.** 1. to carry or drag (something heavy) with great effort. 2. (tr.) to introduce (an irrelevant topic) into a conversation or discussion. ~n. 3. the act or an instance of lugging.

lug[2] (lʌg) n. 1. a projecting piece by which something is connected, supported, or lifted. 2. a box or basket for vegetables or fruit. 3. Brit. inf. or Scot. another word for **ear**[1]. 4. Sl. a man, esp. a stupid or awkward one.

luggage ('lʌgɪdʒ) n. suitcases, trunks, etc.

lugger ('lʌgə) n. Naut. a small working boat rigged with a lugsail.

lugsail ('lʌgsəl) n. Naut. a four-sided sail bent and hoisted on a yard.

lugubrious (lʊ'gu:brɪəs) adj. excessively mournful; doleful. —**lu'gubriously** adv. —**lu'gubriousness** n.

lugworm ('lʌg‚wɜ:m) n. a worm living in burrows on sandy shores and having tufted gills: much used as bait. Sometimes shortened to **lug.**

lukewarm (‚lu:k'wɔ:m) adj. 1. (esp. of water) moderately warm; tepid. 2. having or expressing little enthusiasm or conviction. —‚**luke'warmly** adv. —‚**luke'warmness** n.

lull (lʌl) vb. (tr.) 1. to soothe (a person or animal) by soft sounds or motions (esp. in **lull to sleep**). 2. to calm (someone or someone's fears, suspicions, etc.), esp. by deception. ~n. 3. a short period of calm or diminished activity.

lullaby ('lʌlə‚baɪ) n., pl. **-bies.** 1. a quiet song to lull a child to sleep. ~vb. **-bying, -bied.** 2. (tr.) to quiet or soothe as with a lullaby.

lumbago (lʌm'beɪgəʊ) n. pain in the lower back; backache.

lumbar ('lʌmbə) adj. of, near, or relating to the part of the body between the lowest ribs and the hipbones.

lumbar puncture n. Med. insertion of a hollow needle into the lower spinal cord to withdraw cerebrospinal fluid, introduce drugs, etc.

lumber[1] ('lʌmbə) n. 1. Chiefly U.S. & Canad. **a.** logs; sawn timber. **b.** (as modifier): the lumber trade. 2. Brit. **a.** useless household articles that are stored away. **b.** (as modifier): lumber room. ~vb. 3. (tr.) to pile to-

---

THESAURUS

loyalty allegiance, constancy, dependability, devotion, faithfulness, fealty, fidelity, patriotism, reliability, staunchness, steadfastness, true-heartedness, trueness, trustiness, trustworthiness

lubricate grease, make slippery, make smooth, oil, oil the wheels, smear, smooth the way

lucid 1. clear, clear-cut, comprehensible, crystal clear, distinct, evident, explicit, intelligible, limpid, obvious, pellucid, plain, transparent 2. beaming, bright, brilliant, effulgent, gleaming, luminous, radiant, resplendent, shining 3. clear, crystalline, diaphanous, glassy, limpid, pellucid, pure, translucent, transparent 4. all there, clear-headed, compos mentis, in one's right mind, rational, reasonable, sane, sensible, sober, sound

luck 1. accident, chance, destiny, fate, fortuity, fortune, hap (Archaic), hazard 2. advantage, blessing, break (Inf.), fluke, godsend, good fortune, good luck, prosperity,

serendipity, stroke, success, windfall

luckily 1. favourably, fortunately, happily, opportunely, propitiously, providentially 2. as it chanced, as luck would have it, by chance, fortuitously

luckless calamitous, cursed, disastrous, doomed, hapless, hopeless, ill-fated, ill-starred, jinxed, star-crossed, unfortunate, unhappy, unlucky, unpropitious, unsuccessful

lucky 1. advantageous, blessed, charmed, favoured, fortunate, prosperous, serendipitous, successful 2. adventitious, auspicious, fortuitous, opportune, propitious, providential, timely

lucrative advantageous, fat, fruitful, gainful, high-income, money-making, paying, productive, profitable, remunerative, well-paid

ludicrous absurd, burlesque, comic, comical, crazy, droll, farcical, funny, incongruous, laughable, nonsensical, odd, outlandish, preposterous, ridiculous, silly, zany

luggage baggage, bags, cases, gear, impedimenta, paraphernalia, suitcases, things, trunks

lugubrious dirgelike, dismal, doleful, dreary, funereal, gloomy, melancholy, morose, mournful, sad, serious, sombre, sorrowful, woebegone, woeful

lukewarm 1. blood-warm, tepid, warm 2. Fig. apathetic, cold, cool, half-hearted, indifferent, laodicean, phlegmatic, unconcerned, unenthusiastic, uninterested, unresponsive

lull v. 1. allay, calm, compose, hush, lullaby, pacify, quell, quiet, rock to sleep, soothe, still, subdue, tranquillize 2. abate, cease, decrease, diminish, dwindle, ease off, let up, moderate, quieten down, slacken, subside, wane ~n. 3. calm, calmness, hush, let-up (Inf.), pause, quiet, respite, silence, stillness, tranquillity

lullaby berceuse, cradlesong

gether in a disorderly manner. **4.** (*tr.*) to fill up or encumber with useless household articles. **5.** *Chiefly U.S. & Canad.* to convert (the trees) of (a forest) into marketable timber. **6.** (*tr.*) *Brit. inf.* to burden with something unpleasant, tedious, etc. —**'lumberer** *n.* —**'lumbering** *n.*

lumber² ('lʌmbə) *vb.* (*intr.*) **1.** to move or proceed in an awkward heavy manner. **2.** an obsolete word for **rumble.** —**'lumbering** *adj.*

lumberjack ('lʌmbə,dʒæk) *n.* (esp. in North America) a person whose work involves felling trees, transporting the timber, etc.

lumen ('lu:mɪn) *n., pl.* **-mens** *or* **-mina** (-mɪnə). **1.** the derived SI unit of luminous flux; the flux emitted in a solid angle of 1 steradian by a point source having a uniform intensity of 1 candela. Symbol: lm **2.** *Anat.* a passage, duct, or cavity in a tubular organ. **3.** a cavity within a plant cell. —**'luminal** *adj.*

luminary ('lu:mɪnərɪ) *n., pl.* **-naries. 1.** a person who enlightens or influences others. **2.** a famous person. **3.** *Literary.* something, such as the sun or moon, that gives off light.

luminescence (,lu:mɪ'nɛsəns) *n. Physics.* the emission of light at low temperatures by any process other than incandescence. —,**lumi'nescent** *adj.*

luminous ('lu:mɪnəs) *adj.* **1.** radiating or reflecting light; shining; glowing: *luminous colours.* **2.** (*not in technical use*) exhibiting luminescence: *luminous paint.* **3.** full of light; well-lit. **4.** (of a physical quantity in photometry) evaluated according to the visual sensation produced in an observer rather than by absolute energy measurements: *luminous intensity.* **5.** easily understood; lucid; clear. **6.** enlightening or wise. —**luminosity** (,lu:mɪ'nɒsɪtɪ) *n.* —**'luminously** *adv.* —**'luminousness** *n.*

lump¹ (lʌmp) *n.* **1.** a small solid mass without definite shape. **2.** *Pathol.* any small swelling or tumour. **3.** a collection of things; aggregate. **4.** *Inf.* an awkward, heavy, or stupid person. **5. the lump.** *Brit.* self-employed workers in the building trade considered collectively. **6.** (*modifier*) in the form of a lump or lumps: *lump sugar.* **7. a lump in one's throat.** a tight dry feeling in one's throat, usually caused by great emotion. **8. in the lump.** collectively; en masse. ~*vb.* **9.** (*tr.*; often foll. by *together*) to collect into a mass or group. **10.** (*intr.*) to grow into lumps or become lumpy. **11.** (*tr.*) to consider as a single group, often without justification. **12.** (*tr.*) to make or cause lumps in or on. **13.** (*intr.*; often foll. by *along*) to move in a heavy manner.

lump² (lʌmp) *vb.* (*tr.*) *Inf.* to tolerate or put up with; endure (in **lump it**).

lumpish ('lʌmpɪʃ) *adj.* **1.** resembling a lump. **2.** stupid, clumsy, or heavy. —**'lumpishly** *adv.* —**'lumpishness** *n.*

lump sum *n.* a relatively large sum of money, paid at one time, esp. in cash.

lumpy ('lʌmpɪ) *adj.* **lumpier, lumpiest. 1.** full of or having lumps. **2.** (esp. of the sea) rough. **3.** (of a person) heavy or bulky. —**'lumpily** *adv.* —**'lumpiness** *n.*

lunacy ('lu:nəsɪ) *n., pl.* **-cies. 1.** (formerly) any severe mental illness. **2.** foolishness.

lunar ('lu:nə) *adj.* **1.** of or relating to the moon. **2.** occuring on or used on the moon: *lunar module.* **3.** relat-

ing to, caused by, or measured by the position or orbital motion of the moon.

lunatic ('lu:nətɪk) *adj.* **1.** an informal or archaic word for **insane.** ~*n.* **2.** a person who is insane.

lunatic asylum *n.* another name, usually regarded as offensive, for an institution for the mentally ill.

lunatic fringe *n.* the members of a society who adopt views regarded as fanatical.

lunch (lʌntʃ) *n.* **1.** a meal eaten during the middle of the day. ~*vb.* **2.** (*intr.*) to eat lunch. **3.** (*tr.*) to provide or buy lunch for. —**'luncher** *n.*

luncheon ('lʌntʃən) *n.* a lunch, esp. a formal one.

luncheon meat *n.* a ground mixture of meat (often pork) and cereal, usually tinned.

luncheon voucher *n.* a voucher worth a specified amount issued to employees and redeemable at a restaurant for food. Abbrev.: **LV**

lung (lʌŋ) *n.* **1.** either one of a pair of spongy saclike respiratory organs within the thorax of higher vertebrates, which oxygenate the blood and remove its carbon dioxide. **2. at the top of one's lungs.** in one's loudest voice; yelling.

lunge (lʌndʒ) *n.* **1.** *Fencing.* a thrust made by advancing the front foot and straightening the back leg, extending the sword arm forwards. **2.** a sudden forward motion. ~*vb.* **3.** (*intr.*) *Fencing.* to make a lunge. **4.** to move or cause to move with a lunge. —**'lunger** *n.*

lupin *or U.S.* **lupine** ('lu:pɪn) *n.* a leguminous plant of North America, Europe, and Africa, with large spikes of brightly coloured flowers and flattened pods.

lupine ('lu:paɪn) *adj.* of, relating to, or resembling a wolf.

lupus ('lu:pəs) *n.* any of various ulcerative skin diseases.

lurch¹ (lɜ:tʃ) *vb.* (*intr.*) **1.** to lean or pitch suddenly to one side. **2.** to stagger. ~*n.* **3.** the act or an instance of lurching.

lurch² (lɜ:tʃ) *n.* **1. leave (someone) in the lurch.** to desert (someone) in trouble. **2.** *Cribbage.* the state of a losing player with less than 30 points at the end of a game.

lurcher ('lɜ:tʃə) *n.* **1.** a person who prowls or lurks. **2.** a crossbred hunting dog, esp. one trained to hunt silently.

lure (luə) *vb.* (*tr.*) **1.** (sometimes foll. by *away* or *into*) to tempt or attract by the promise of some type of reward. **2.** *Falconry.* to entice (a hawk or falcon) from the air to the falconer by a lure. ~*n.* **3.** a person or thing that lures. **4.** *Angling.* any of various types of brightly coloured artificial spinning baits. **5.** *Falconry.* a feathered decoy to which small pieces of meat can be attached. —**'lurer** *n.*

lurid ('luərɪd) *adj.* **1.** vivid in shocking detail; sensational. **2.** horrible in savagery or violence. **3.** pallid in colour; wan. **4.** glowing with an unnatural glare. —**'luridly** *adv.* —**'luridness** *n.*

lurk (lɜ:k) *vb.* (*intr.*) **1.** to move stealthily or be concealed, esp. for evil purposes. **2.** to be present in an unobtrusive way; be latent. ~*n.* **3.** *Austral. & N.Z. sl.* a scheme for success. —**'lurker** *n.*

luscious ('lʌʃəs) *adj.* **1.** extremely pleasurable, esp. to the taste or smell. **2.** very attractive. **3.** *Arch.* cloying. —**'lusciously** *adv.* —**'lusciousness** *n.*

THESAURUS

lumber¹ 1. *n.* castoffs, clutter, discards, jumble, junk, refuse, rubbish, trash, trumpery, white elephants **2.** *v. Brit. sl.* burden, encumber, impose upon, land, load, saddle

lumber² *v.* clump, lump along, plod, shamble, shuffle, stump, trudge, trundle, waddle

lumbering awkward, blundering, bovine, bumbling, clumsy, elephantine, heavy, heavy-footed, hulking, lubberly, overgrown, ponderous, ungainly, unwieldy

luminous bright, brilliant, glowing, illuminated, lighted, lit, luminescent, lustrous, radiant, resplendent, shining, vivid **2.** clear, evident, intelligible, lucid, obvious, perspicuous, plain, transparent

lump¹ *n.* **1.** ball, bunch, cake, chunk, clod, cluster, dab, gob, gobbet, group, hunk, mass, nugget, piece, spot, wedge **2.** bulge, bump, growth, protrusion, protuberance, swelling, tumescence, tumour ~*v.* **3.** agglutinate, aggregate, batch, bunch, coalesce, collect,

combine, conglomerate, consolidate, group, mass, pool, unite

lump² *v.* bear, brook, endure, put up with, stand, suffer, take, thole (*Northern dialect*), tolerate

lunacy 1. dementia, derangement, idiocy, insanity, madness, mania, psychosis **2.** aberration, absurdity, craziness, folly, foolhardiness, foolishness, idiocy, imbecility, madness, senselessness, stupidity, tomfoolery

lunatic 1. *adj.* barmy (*Sl.*), bonkers (*Sl.*), crackbrained, crazy, daft, demented, deranged, insane, irrational, mad, maniacal, nuts (*Sl.*), psychotic, unhinged **2.** *n.* loony (*Sl.*), madman, maniac, nut (*Sl.*), nutcase (*Sl.*), nutter (*Sl.*), psychopath

lunge 1. *n.* charge, cut, jab, pass, pounce, spring, stab, swing, swipe, thrust **2.** *v.* bound, charge, cut, dash, dive, fall upon, hit at, jab, leap, pitch into, plunge, poke, pounce, set upon, stab, strike at, thrust

lure 1. *v.* allure, attract, beckon, decoy,

draw, ensnare, entice, inveigle, invite, lead on, seduce, tempt **2.** *n.* allurement, attraction, bait, carrot (*Inf.*), come-on (*Inf.*), decoy, enticement, inducement, magnet, siren song, temptation

lurid 1. exaggerated, graphic, melodramatic, sensational, shocking, startling, unrestrained, vivid, yellow (*Of journalism*) **2.** disgusting, ghastly, gory, grim, grisly, gruesome, macabre, revolting, savage, violent **3.** ashen, ghastly, pale, pallid, sallow, wan **4.** bloody, fiery, flaming, glaring, glowering, intense, livid, overbright, sanguine

lurk conceal oneself, crouch, go furtively, hide, lie in wait, move with stealth, prowl, skulk, slink, sneak, snoop

luscious appetizing, delectable, delicious, honeyed, juicy, mouth-watering, palatable, rich, savoury, scrumptious (*Inf.*), succulent, sweet, toothsome, yummy (*Sl.*)

lush¹ (lʌʃ) *adj.* **1.** (of vegetation) abounding in lavish growth. **2.** (esp. of fruits) succulent and fleshy. **3.** luxurious, elaborate, or opulent. —**'lushly** *adv.* —**'lushness** *n.*

lush² (lʌʃ) *U.S. sl.* ~*n.* **1.** a heavy drinker, esp. an alcoholic. **2.** alcoholic drink. ~*vb.* **3.** to drink (alcohol) to excess.

lust (lʌst) *n.* **1.** a strong desire for sexual gratification. **2.** a strong desire or drive. ~*vb.* **3.** (*intr.; often foll. by after or for*) to have a lust (for). —**'lustful** *adj.* —**'lustfully** *adv.* —**'lustfulness** *n.*

lustre *or U.S.* **luster** ('lʌstə) *n.* **1.** reflected light; sheen; gloss. **2.** radiance or brilliance of light. **3.** great splendour of accomplishment, beauty, etc. **4.** a dress fabric of cotton and wool with a glossy surface. **5.** a vase or chandelier from which hang cut-glass drops. **6.** a drop-shaded piece of cut glass or crystal used as such a decoration. **7.** a shiny metallic surface on some pottery and porcelain. **8.** *Mineralogy.* the way in which light is reflected from the surface of a mineral. ~*vb.* **9.** to make, be, or become lustrous. —**'lustreless** *or U.S.* **'lusterless** *adj.* —**'lustrous** *adj.*

lusty ('lʌstɪ) *adj.* **lustier, lustiest. 1.** having or characterized by robust health. **2.** strong or invigorating. —**'lustily** *adv.* —**'lustiness** *n.*

lute¹ (luːt) *n.* an ancient plucked stringed instrument, with a long fretted fingerboard and a body shaped like a sliced pear. —**'lutenist** *or* **'lutanist** *n.*

lute² (luːt) *n.* **1.** a mixture of cement and clay used to seal the joints between pipes, etc. ~*vb.* **2.** (*tr.*) to seal (a joint or surface) with lute.

lutetium *or* **lutecium** (luːˈtiːʃɪəm) *n.* a silvery-white metallic element of the lanthanide series. Symbol: Lu; atomic no.: 71; atomic wt.: 174.97.

Lutheran ('luːθərən) *n.* **1.** a follower of Luther (1483-1546), German leader of the Protestant Reformation, or a member of a Lutheran Church. ~*adj.* **2.** of or relating to Luther or his doctrines. **3.** of or relating to a Lutheran Church. —**'Lutheranism** *n.*

lux (lʌks) *n., pl.* **lux.** the derived SI unit of illumination equal to a luminous flux of 1 lumen per square metre.

luxuriant (lʌgˈzjʊərɪənt) *adj.* **1.** rich and abundant; lush. **2.** very elaborate or ornate. **3.** extremely productive or fertile. —**lux'uriance** *n.* —**lux'uriantly** *adv.*

luxuriate (lʌgˈzjʊərɪˌeɪt) *vb.* (*intr.*) **1.** (foll. by *in*) to take voluptuous pleasure; revel. **2.** to flourish profusely. **3.** to live in a sumptuous way. —**lux‚uri'ation** *n.*

luxurious (lʌgˈzjʊərɪəs) *adj.* **1.** characterized by luxury. **2.** enjoying or devoted to luxury. —**lux'uriously** *adv.* —**lux'uriousness** *n.*

luxury ('lʌkʃərɪ) *n., pl.* **-ries. 1.** indulgence in and enjoyment of rich, comfortable, and sumptuous living. **2.** (*sometimes pl.*) something considered an indulgence rather than a necessity. **3.** (*modifier*) relating to, indicating, or supplying luxury: *a luxury liner.*

LV *abbrev. for* luncheon voucher.

-ly¹ *suffix forming adjectives.* **1.** having the nature or qualities of: *godly.* **2.** occurring at certain intervals; every: *daily.*

-ly² *suffix forming adverbs.* in a certain manner; to a certain degree: *quickly; recently; chiefly.*

lyceum (laɪˈsɪəm) *n.* (now chiefly in the names of buildings) **1.** a public building for concerts, lectures, etc. **2.** *U.S.* a cultural organization responsible for presenting concerts, lectures, etc.

lychee (ˌlaɪˈtʃiː) *n.* a variant spelling of **litchi.**

lych gate (lɪtʃ) *n.* a variant spelling of **lich gate.**

lye (laɪ) *n.* **1.** any solution obtained by leaching, such as the caustic solution obtained by leaching wood ash. **2.** a concentrated solution of sodium hydroxide or potassium hydroxide.

lying¹ ('laɪɪŋ) *vb.* the present participle and gerund of **lie¹.**

lying² ('laɪɪŋ) *vb.* the present participle and gerund of **lie².**

lying-in *n., pl.* **lyings-in.** confinement in childbirth

lymph (lɪmf) *n.* the almost colourless fluid, containing chiefly white blood cells, that is collected from the tissues of the body and transported in the lymphatic system.

lymphatic (lɪmˈfætɪk) *adj.* **1.** of, relating to, or containing lymph. **2.** of or relating to the lymphatic system. **3.** sluggish or lacking vigour. ~*n.* **4.** a lymphatic vessel.

lymph node *n.* any of numerous bean-shaped masses of tissue, situated along the course of lymphatic vessels, that help to protect against infection and are a source of lymphocytes.

lympho- *or before a vowel* **lymph-** *combining form.* indicating lymph or the lymphatic system: *lymphocyte.*

lynch (lɪntʃ) *vb.* (*tr.*) (of a mob) to kill (a person) for some supposed offence. —**'lyncher** *n.* —**'lynching** *n.*

lynx (lɪŋks) *n., pl.* **lynxes** *or* **lynx. 1.** a feline mammal of Europe and North America, with grey-brown mottled fur, tufted ears, and a short tail. **2.** the fur of this animal. **3. bay lynx.** another name for **bobcat. 4. desert lynx.** another name for **caracal.** —**'lynx‚like** *adj.*

lynx-eyed *adj.* having keen sight.

lyre (laɪə) *n.* an ancient Greek stringed instrument consisting of a resonating tortoise shell to which a crossbar was attached by two projecting arms. It was plucked with a plectrum and used for accompanying songs.

lyrebird ('laɪəˌbɜːd) *n.* either of two pheasant-like Australian birds: during courtship displays, the male spreads its tail into the shape of a lyre.

lyric ('lɪrɪk) *adj.* **1.** (of poetry) **a.** expressing the writer's personal feelings and thoughts. **b.** having the form and manner of a song. **2.** of or relating to such poetry. **3.** (of a singing voice) having a light quality and tone. **4.** intended for singing, esp. (in classical Greece) to the accompaniment of the lyre. ~*n.* **5.** a short poem of song-like quality. **6.** (*pl.*) the words of a popular song. ~*Also* (*for senses 1-3*): **lyrical.** —**'lyrically** *adv.* —**'lyricalness** *n.*

lyrical ('lɪrɪk(ə)l) *adj.* **1.** another word for **lyric** (senses 1-3). **2.** enthusiastic; effusive.

lyricism ('lɪrɪˌsɪzəm) *n.* **1.** the quality or style of lyric poetry. **2.** emotional outpouring.

lyricist ('lɪrɪsɪst) *n.* **1.** a person who writes the words for a song, opera, or musical play. **2.** Also called: **lyrist.** a lyric poet.

THESAURUS

lush 1. abundant, dense, flourishing, green, lavish, overgrown, prolific, rank, teeming, verdant **2.** fresh, juicy, ripe, succulent, tender **3.** elaborate, extravagant, grand, lavish, luxurious, opulent, ornate, palatial, plush (*Inf.*), ritzy (*Sl.*), sumptuous

lust *n.* **1.** carnality, concupiscence, lasciviousness, lechery, lewdness, libido, licentiousness, pruriency, randiness (*Sl., chiefly Brit.*), salaciousness, sensuality, wantonness **2.** appetence, appetite, avidity, covetousness, craving, cupidity, desire, greed, longing, passion, thirst ~*v.* **3.** be consumed with desire for, covet, crave, desire, hunger for *or* after, lech after (*Inf.*), need, slaver over, want, yearn

lustre 1. burnish, gleam, glint, glitter, gloss, glow, sheen, shimmer, shine, sparkle **2.** brightness, brilliance, dazzle, lambency, lu-

minousness, radiance, resplendence **3.** distinction, fame, glory, honour, illustriousness, prestige, renown

lusty brawny, energetic, hale, healthy, hearty, in fine fettle, powerful, red-blooded (*Inf.*), robust, rugged, stalwart, stout, strapping, strong, sturdy, vigorous, virile

luxuriant 1. abundant, ample, copious, excessive, lavish, plenteous, plentiful, prodigal, profuse, superabundant **2.** baroque, corinthian, decorated, elaborate, extravagant, fancy, festooned, flamboyant, florid, flowery, ornate, rococo, sumptuous **3.** dense, exuberant, fecund, fertile, flourishing, fruitful, lush, overflowing, productive, prolific, rank, rich, riotous, teeming, thriving

luxurious 1. comfortable, costly, de luxe, expensive, lavish, magnificent, opulent, plush (*Inf.*), rich, ritzy (*Sl.*), splendid, sumptu-

ous, well-appointed **2.** epicurean, pampered, pleasure-loving, self-indulgent, sensual, sybaritic, voluptuous

luxury 1. affluence, hedonism, opulence, richness, splendour, sumptuousness, voluptuousness **2.** bliss, comfort, delight, enjoyment, gratification, indulgence, pleasure, satisfaction, wellbeing **3.** extra, extravagance, frill, indulgence, nonessential, treat

lying 1. *n.* deceit, dishonesty, dissimulation, double-dealing, duplicity, fabrication, falsity, fibbing, guile, mendacity, perjury, prevarication, untruthfulness **2.** *adj.* deceitful, dishonest, dissembling, double-dealing, false, guileful, mendacious, perfidious, treacherous, two-faced, untruthful

lyrical carried away, ecstatic, effusive, emotional, enthusiastic, expressive, impassioned, inspired, poetic, rapturous, rhapsodic

M

m *or* **M** (εm) *n.*, *pl.* **m's, M's,** *or* **Ms. 1.** the 13th letter of
the English alphabet. **2.** a speech sound represented by
this letter, as in *mat.*

m *symbol for:* **1.** metre(s). **2.** mile(s). **3.** milli-. **4.**
minute(s).

M *symbol for:* **1.** mach. **2.** mega-. **3.** *Currency.*
mark(s). **4.** million. **5.** (in Britain) motorway. **6.** *the
Roman numeral for* 1000.

m. *abbrev. for:* **1.** *Cricket.* maiden (over). **2.** male. **3.**
mare. **4.** married. **5.** masculine. **6.** meridian. **7.**
month.

M. *abbrev. for:* **1.** Majesty. **2.** Master. **3.** Medieval. **4.**
(in titles) Member. **5.** million. **6.** (*pl.* **MM.** *or* **MM**)
Also: **M** *French.* Monsieur.

M'- *prefix.* a variant of **Mac-.**

ma (mɑ:) *n.* an informal word for **mother.**

M.A. *abbrev. for:* **1.** Master of Arts. **2.** Military Academy.

ma'am (mæm, mɑːm; *unstressed* məm) *n.* short for
madam: used as a title of respect, esp. for female royalty.

mac *or* **mack** (mæk) *n. Inf.* short for **mackintosh.**

Mac (mæk) *n. Chiefly U.S.* an informal term of address
to a man.

Mac-, Mc- *or* **M'-** *prefix.* (in surnames of Gaelic origin) son of: *MacDonald.*

macabre (məˈkɑːbə, -brə) *adj.* gruesome; ghastly; grim.

macadam (məˈkædəm) *n.* a road surface made of compressed layers of small broken stones, esp. one that is
bound together with tar or asphalt. —**macˈadam,ize** *or*
-,**ise** *vb.*

macaroni *or* **maccaroni** (,mækəˈrəʊnɪ) *n.*, *pl.* **-nis** *or*
-nies. 1. pasta tubes made from wheat flour. **2.** (in 18th-
century Britain) a dandy who affected foreign manners
and style.

macaroon (,mækəˈruːn) *n.* a kind of sweet biscuit made
of ground almonds, sugar, and egg whites.

macaw (məˈkɔː) *n.* a large tropical American parrot
having a long tail and brilliant plumage.

Macc. *abbrev. for* Maccabees (books of the Apocrypha).

mace¹ (meɪs) *n.* **1.** a club, usually having a spiked metal
head, used esp. in the Middle Ages. **2.** a ceremonial staff
of office carried by certain officials. **3.** an early form of
billiard cue.

mace² (meɪs) *n.* a spice made from the dried aril round
the nutmeg seed.

macebearer (ˈmeɪs,bɛərə) *n.* a person who carries a
mace in processions or ceremonies.

macerate (ˈmæsə,reɪt) *vb.* **1.** to soften or separate or
be softened or separated as a result of soaking. **2.** to become or cause to become thin. —**ˈmacer,ator** *n.*
—,**macerˈation** *n.*

Mach (mæk) *n.* short for **Mach number.**

machete (məˈʃɛtɪ, -ˈtʃeɪ-) *n.* a broad heavy knife used for
cutting or as a weapon, esp. in parts of Central and South
America.

Machiavellian (,mækɪəˈvɛlɪən) *adj.* **1.** of or relating to
the alleged political principles of the Florentine statesman Machiavelli (1469–1527); cunning, amoral, and opportunist. ~*n.* **2.** a cunning, amoral, and opportunist
person, esp. a politician. —,**Machiaˈvellianism** *n.*

machicolation (mə,tʃɪkəˈleɪʃən) *n.* **1.** (esp. in medieval castles) a projecting gallery or parapet having
openings through which missiles could be dropped. **2.**
any such opening.

machinate (ˈmækɪ,neɪt) *vb.* (*usually tr.*) to contrive,
plan, or devise (schemes, plots, etc.). —,**machiˈnation**
n. —ˈ**machi,nator** *n.*

machine (məˈʃiːn) *n.* **1.** an assembly of interconnected
components arranged to transmit or modify force in order to perform useful work. **2.** a device for altering the
magnitude or direction of a force, esp. a lever, screw,
wedge, or pulley. **3.** a mechanically operated device or
means of transport, such as a car, aircraft, etc. **4.** any
mechanical or electrical device that automatically performs tasks or assists in performing tasks. **5.** any intricate structure or agency. **6.** a mechanically efficient,
rigid, or obedient person. **7.** an organized body of people
that controls activities, policies, etc. ~*vb.* **8.** (*tr.*) to
shape, cut, or remove (excess material) from (a workpiece) using a machine tool. **9.** to use a machine to carry out a process on (something). —**maˈchinable** *or*
maˈchineable *adj.* —**ma,chinaˈbility** *or* **ma,chine-
aˈbility** *n.*

machine gun *n.* **1. a.** a rapid-firing automatic gun,
using small-arms ammunition. **b.** (*as modifier*):
machine-gun fire. ~*vb.* **machine-gun, -gunning,
-gunned. 2.** (*tr.*) to shoot or fire at with a machine gun.
—**machine gunner** *n.*

machine language *or* **code** *n.* instructions for a
computer in binary code.

machinery (məˈʃiːnərɪ) *n.*, *pl.* **-eries. 1.** machines, machine parts, or machine systems collectively. **2.** a particular machine system or set of machines. **3.** a system
similar to a machine.

machine shop *n.* a workshop in which machine tools
are operated.

machine tool *n.* a power-driven machine, such as a
lathe, for cutting, shaping, and finishing metals, etc.
—**maˈchine-,tooled** *adj.*

machinist (məˈʃiːnɪst) *n.* **1.** a person who operates machines to cut or process materials. **2.** a maker or repair-
er of machines.

machismo (mæˈkɪzməʊ, -ˈtʃɪz-) *n.* strong or exaggerated
masculinity.

Mach number *n.* (*often not cap.*) the ratio of the
speed of a body in a particular medium to the speed of
sound in that medium. Mach number 1 corresponds to
the speed of sound.

macho (ˈmætʃəʊ) *n.*, *pl.* **machos. 1.** a strong virile man.
~*adj.* **2.** strongly or exaggeratedly masculine.

mack (mæk) *n. Brit. inf.* short for **mackintosh.**

mackerel (ˈmækrəl) *n.*, *pl.* **-rel** *or* **-rels. 1.** a spiny-
finned food fish occurring in northern coastal regions of
the Atlantic and in the Mediterranean. It has a deeply
forked tail and a greenish-blue body marked with wavy
dark bands on the back. **2.** any of various related fishes.

mackintosh *or* **macintosh** (ˈmækɪn,tɒʃ) *n.* **1.** a
waterproof raincoat made of rubberized cloth. **2.** such
cloth. **3.** any raincoat.

macramé (məˈkrɑːmɪ) *n.* a type of ornamental work
made by knotting and weaving coarse thread.

macro- *or before a vowel* **macr-** *combining form.* **1.**
large, long, or great in size or duration: *macroscopic.* **2.**
Pathol. indicating abnormal enlargement or over-
development: *macrocephaly.*

macrobiotics (,mækrəʊbaɪˈɒtɪks) *n.* (*functioning as
sing.*) a dietary system which advocates whole grains
and vegetables grown without chemical additives.
—,**macrobiˈotic** *adj.*

macrocosm (ˈmækrə,kɒzəm) *n.* a complex structure,
such as the universe or society, regarded as an entirety.

THESAURUS

macabre cadaverous, deathlike, deathly,
dreadful, eerie, frightening, frightful, ghastly,
ghostly, ghoulish, grim, grisly, gruesome, hideous, horrid, morbid, unearthly, weird

machination artifice, cabal, conspiracy, design, device, dodge, intrigue, manoeu-

vre, plot, ploy, ruse, scheme, stratagem,
trick

machine 1. apparatus, appliance, contraption, contrivance, device, engine, instrument, mechanism, tool **2.** agency, machinery, organization, party, setup (*Inf.*), structure, system **3.** *Fig.* agent, automaton, me-

chanical man, puppet, robot, zombie

machinery 1. apparatus, equipment,
gear, instruments, mechanism, tackle, tools,
works **2.** agency, channels, machine, organization, procedure, structure, system

~Cf. **microcosm.** —ˌmacro'**cosmic** *adj.* —ˌmacro'**cosmically** *adv.*

macron ('mækrɒn) *n.* a diacritical mark (¯) placed over a letter to represent a long vowel.

macroscopic (ˌmækrəʊ'skɒpɪk) *adj.* **1.** large enough to be visible to the naked eye. **2.** comprehensive; concerned with large units. —ˌmacro'**scopically** *adv.*

macula ('mækjʊlə) *or* **macule** ('mækjuːl) *n., pl.* **-ulae** (-juˌliː) *or* **-ules.** *Anat.* **1.** a small spot or area of distinct colour, esp. the macula lutea. **2.** any small discoloured spot or blemish on the skin, such as a freckle. —'**macular** *adj.* —ˌmacu'**lation** *n.*

mad (mæd) *adj.* **madder, maddest. 1.** mentally deranged; insane. **2.** senseless; foolish. **3.** (often foll. by *at*) *Inf.* angry; resentful. **4.** (foll. by *about, on,* or *over;* often postpositive) wildly enthusiastic (about) or fond (of). **5.** extremely excited or confused; frantic: *a mad rush.* **6.** wildly gay: *a mad party.* **7.** temporarily overpowered by violent reactions, emotions, etc.: *mad with grief.* **8.** (of animals) **a.** unusually ferocious: *a mad buffalo.* **b.** afflicted with rabies. **9. like mad.** *Inf.* with great energy, enthusiasm, or haste. **10. mad as a hatter.** crazy. ~*vb.* **madding, madded. 11.** *U.S. or arch.* to make or become mad; act or cause to act as if mad. —'**madness** *n.*

madam ('mædəm) *n.* **1.** a polite term of address for a woman, esp. one of relatively high social status. **2.** a woman who runs a brothel. **3.** *Brit. inf.* a precocious or pompous little girl.

madame ('mædəm) *n., pl.* **mesdames** ('meɪˌdæm). a married Frenchwoman: used as a title equivalent to *Mrs.,* and sometimes extended to older unmarried women to show respect.

madcap ('mædˌkæp) *adj.* **1.** impulsive, reckless, or lively. ~*n.* **2.** an impulsive, reckless, or lively person.

madden ('mædⁿn) *vb.* to make or become mad or angry. —'**maddening** *adj.* —'**maddeningly** *adv.*

madder ('mædə) *n.* **1.** a plant having small yellow flowers and a red fleshy root. **2.** the root. **3.** a dark reddish-purple dye formerly obtained from this root. **4.** a red lake obtained from alizarin and an inorganic base; used as a pigment in inks and paints.

made (meɪd) *vb.* **1.** the past tense and past participle of **make. 2.** artificially produced. **3.** (*in combination*) produced or shaped as specified: *handmade.* **4. get** *or* **have it made.** *Sl.* to be assured of success.

Madeira (mə'dɪərə) *n.* a rich strong fortified white wine made on Madeira, a Portuguese island in the N Atlantic.

mademoiselle (ˌmædmwə'zɛl) *n., pl.* **mesdemoiselles** (ˌmeɪdmwə'zɛl). **1.** a young unmarried French girl or woman: used as a title equivalent to *Miss.* **2.** a French teacher or governess.

made-up *adj.* **1.** invented; fictional. **2.** wearing make-up. **3.** put together. **4.** (of a road) surfaced with tarmac, concrete, etc.

madhouse ('mædˌhaʊs) *n. Inf.* **1.** a mental hospital or asylum. **2.** a state of uproar or confusion.

madly ('mædlɪ) *adv.* **1.** in an insane or foolish manner. **2.** with great speed and energy. **3.** *Inf.* extremely or excessively: *I love you madly.*

madman ('mædmən) *or* (*fem.*) **madwoman** *n., pl.* **-men** *or* **-women.** a person who is insane.

Madonna (mə'dɒnə) *n.* **1.** *Chiefly R.C. Church.* a designation of the Virgin Mary. **2.** (*sometimes not cap.*) a picture or statue of the Virgin Mary.

madrigal ('mædrɪgəl) *n.* **1.** *Music.* a type of 16th- or 17th-century part song for unaccompanied voices, with an amatory or pastoral text. **2.** a short love poem. —ˌmadrigal'**esque** *adj.* —**madrigalian** (ˌmædrɪ'gælɪən, -'geɪ-) *adj.* —'**madrigalist** *n.*

maelstrom ('meɪlstrəʊm) *n.* **1.** a large powerful whirlpool. **2.** any turbulent confusion.

maenad ('miːnæd) *n.* **1.** *Classical history.* a woman participant in the orgiastic rites of Dionysus, Greek god of wine. **2.** a frenzied woman. —**mae'nadic** *adj.*

maestro ('maɪstrəʊ) *n., pl.* **-tri** (-trɪ) *or* **-tros. 1.** a distinguished music teacher, conductor, or musician. **2.** any master of an art: often used as a term of address.

mae west (meɪ) *n. Sl.* an inflatable life jacket, esp. as issued to the U.S. armed forces.

Mafia ('mæfɪə) *n.* **1. the.** an international secret criminal organization founded in Sicily, and carried to the U.S. by Italian immigrants. **2.** any group considered to resemble the Mafia.

magazine (ˌmægə'ziːn) *n.* **1.** a periodic paperback publication containing articles, fiction, photographs, etc. **2. a.** a metal case holding several cartridges used in some automatic firearms. **b.** this compartment itself. **3.** a building or compartment for storing weapons, explosives, military provisions, etc. **4.** a stock of ammunition. **5.** *Photog.* another name for **cartridge** (sense 3). **6.** a rack for automatically feeding slides through a projector.

magenta (mə'dʒɛntə) *n.* **a.** a deep purplish red. **b.** (*as adj.*): *a magenta filter.*

maggot ('mægət) *n.* **1.** the limbless larva of dipterous insects, esp. the housefly and blowfly. **2.** *Rare.* a fancy or whim. —'**maggoty** *adj.*

magi ('meɪdʒaɪ) *pl. n., sing.* **-gus** (-gəs). **1.** the Zoroastrian priests of the ancient Medes and Persians. **2. the three Magi.** the wise men from the East who came to do homage to the infant Jesus (Matthew 2:1–12). —**magian** ('meɪdʒɪən) *adj.*

magic ('mædʒɪk) *n.* **1.** the art that, by use of spells, supposedly invokes supernatural powers to influence events; sorcery. **2.** the practice of this art. **3.** the practice of illusory tricks to entertain; conjuring. **4.** any mysterious or extraordinary quality or power. **5. like magic.** very quickly. ~*adj. also* **magical. 6.** of or relating to magic. **7.** possessing or considered to possess mysterious powers. **8.** unaccountably enchanting. ~*vb.* **-icking, -icked. 9.** (*tr.*) to transform or produce by or as if by magic. **10.** (*tr.; foll. by away*) to cause to disappear as if by magic. —'**magically** *adv.*

THESAURUS

mad 1. aberrant, bananas (*Sl.*), barmy (*Sl.*), batty (*Sl.*), bonkers (*Sl.*), crackers (*Sl.*), crazed, crazy (*Inf.*), cuckoo (*Inf.*), delirious, demented, deranged, distracted, frantic, frenzied, insane, loony (*Sl.*), loopy (*Inf.*), lunatic, mental (*Sl.*), non compos mentis, nuts (*Sl.*), nutty (*Sl.*), off one's chump (*Sl.*), off one's head, off one's nut (*Sl.*), off one's rocker (*Sl.*), off one's trolley (*Sl.*), of unsound mind, out of one's mind, psychotic, rabid, raving, round the bend (*Brit. sl.*), round the twist (*Brit. sl.*), screwy (*Inf.*), unbalanced, unhinged, unstable **2.** absurd, daft (*Inf.*), foolhardy, foolish, imprudent, irrational, ludicrous, nonsensical, preposterous, senseless, unreasonable, unsafe, unsound, wild **3.** *Inf.* angry, berserk, enraged, exasperated, fuming, furious, in a wax (*Inf.*), incensed, infuriated, irate, irritated, livid (*Inf.*), raging, resentful, seeing red (*Inf.*), wild, wrathful **4.** ardent, avid, crazy, daft (*Inf.*), devoted, dotty (*Brit. sl.*), enamoured, enthusiastic, fanatical, fond, hooked (*Sl.*), impassioned, infatuated, in love with, keen, nuts (*Sl.*), wild, zealous **5.** abandoned, agitated, boisterous, ebullient, energetic, excited, frenetic, frenzied, gay, riotous, uncontrolled, unrestrained, wild **6. like mad** *Inf.* energetically, enthusiastically, excitedly, furiously, madly, quickly, rapidly, speedily, unrestrainedly, violently, wildly

madden annoy, craze, derange, drive one crazy (*off one's head, out of one's mind, round the bend* (*Brit. sl.*), *round the twist* (*Brit. sl.*)*, to distraction*), enrage, exasperate, get one's hackles up, incense, inflame, infuriate, irritate, make one's blood boil, make one see red (*Inf.*), make one's hackles rise, provoke, raise one's hackles, unhinge, upset, vex

made-up fabricated, false, fictional, imaginary, invented, make-believe, mythical, specious, trumped-up, unreal, untrue

madly 1. crazily, deliriously, dementedly, distractedly, frantically, frenziedly, hysterically, insanely, rabidly **2.** absurdly, foolishly, irrationally, ludicrously, nonsensically, senselessly, unreasonably, wildly **3.** energetically, excitedly, furiously, hastily, hurriedly, like mad, quickly, rapidly, recklessly, speedily, violently, wildly **4.** *Inf.* desperately, devotedly, exceedingly, excessively, extremely, intensely, passionately, to distraction

madman *or* **madwoman** loony (*Sl.*), lunatic, maniac, mental case (*Sl.*), nut (*Sl.*), nutcase (*Sl.*), nutter (*Sl.*), psycho (*Sl.*), psychopath, psychotic

madness 1. aberration, craziness, delusion, dementia, derangement, distraction, insanity, lunacy, mania, mental illness, psychopathy, psychosis **2.** absurdity, daftness (*Inf.*), folly, foolhardiness, foolishness, nonsense, preposterousness, wildness **3.** anger, exasperation, frenzy, fury, ire, rage, raving, wildness, wrath **4.** ardour, craze, enthusiasm, fanaticism, fondness, infatuation, keenness, passion, rage, zeal **5.** abandon, agitation, excitement, frenzy, furore, intoxication, riot, unrestraint, uproar

magazine 1. journal, pamphlet, paper, periodical **2.** ammunition dump, arsenal, depot, powder-room (*Obsolete*), store, storehouse, warehouse

magic *n.* **1.** black art, enchantment, necromancy, occultism, sorcery, sortilege, spell, theurgy, witchcraft, wizardry **2.** conjuring, hocus-pocus, illusion, jiggery-pokery (*Inf., chiefly Brit.*), jugglery, legerdemain, prestidigitation, sleight of hand, trickery **3.** allurement, charm, enchantment, fascination,

magician (mə'dʒɪʃən) n. **1.** another term for **conjurer.** **2.** a person who practises magic. **3.** a person with extraordinary skill, influence, etc.

magic lantern n. an early type of slide projector.

magisterial (ˌmædʒɪ'stɪərɪəl) adj. **1.** commanding; authoritative. **2.** domineering; dictatorial. **3.** of or relating to a teacher or person of similar status. **4.** of or relating to a magistrate. —ˌmagis'terially adv.

magistracy ('mædʒɪstrəsɪ) or **magistrature** ('mædʒɪstrəˌtjʊə) n., pl. **-cies** or **-tures.** **1.** the office or function of a magistrate. **2.** magistrates collectively. **3.** the district under the jurisdiction of a magistrate.

magistrate ('mædʒɪˌstreɪt, -strɪt) n. **1.** a public officer concerned with the administration of law. **2.** another name for **justice of the peace.** —'magisˌtrateship n.

magistrates' court n. (in England) a court held before two or more justices of the peace or a stipendiary magistrate to deal with minor crimes, certain civil actions, and preliminary hearings.

magma ('mægmə) n., pl. **-mas** or **-mata** (-mətə). **1.** a paste or suspension consisting of a finely divided solid dispersed in a liquid. **2.** a hot viscous liquid within the earth's crust which solidifies to form igneous rock. —**magmatic** (mæg'mætɪk) adj.

Magna Carta ('mægnə 'kɑːtə) or **Magna Charta** n. English history. the charter granted by King John at Runnymede in 1215, recognizing the rights and privileges of the barons, church, and freemen.

magnanimous (mæg'nænɪməs) adj. generous and noble. —ˌmagna'nimity n. —**mag'nanimously** adv.

magnate ('mægneɪt, -nɪt) n. **1.** a person of power and rank, esp. in industry. **2.** History. a great nobleman. —'magnateˌship n.

magnesia (mæg'niːʃə) n. a white tasteless substance used as an antacid and laxative and in refractory materials. Formula: MgO. Also called: **magnesium oxide.** —mag'nesian or **magnesic** (mæg'niːsɪk) adj.

magnesium (mæg'niːzɪəm) n. a light silvery-white metallic element of the alkaline earth series that burns with an intense white flame: used in light structural alloys, flash bulbs, flares, and fireworks. Symbol: Mg; atomic no.: 12; atomic wt.: 24.312.

magnet ('mægnɪt) n. **1.** a body that can attract certain substances, such as iron or steel, as a result of a magnetic field; a piece of ferromagnetic substance. See also **electromagnet. 2.** a person or thing that exerts a great attraction.

magnetic (mæg'nɛtɪk) adj. **1.** of, producing, or operated by means of magnetism. **2.** of or concerned with a magnet. **3.** of or concerned with the magnetism of the earth: the magnetic equator. **4.** capable of being magnetized. **5.** exerting a powerful attraction: a magnetic personality. —**mag'netically** adv.

magnetic disk n. another name for **disk** (sense 2).

magnetic field n. a field of force surrounding a permanent magnet or a moving charged particle, in which another permanent magnet or moving charge experiences a force.

magnetic mine n. a mine designed to activate when a magnetic field such as that generated by the metal of a ship's hull is detected.

magnetic needle n. a slender magnetized rod used in certain instruments, such as the magnetic compass, for indicating the direction of a magnetic field.

magnetic north n. the direction in which a compass needle points, at an angle (the declination) from the direction of true (geographic) north.

magnetic pole n. **1.** either of two regions in a magnet where the magnetic induction is concentrated. **2.** either of two variable points on the earth's surface towards which a magnetic needle points, where the lines of force of the earth's magnetic field are vertical.

magnetic storm n. a sudden severe disturbance of the earth's magnetic field, caused by emission of charged particles from the sun.

magnetic tape n. a long narrow plastic strip coated with iron oxide, chrome dioxide, etc., used to record sound or video signals or to store information in computers.

magnetism ('mægnɪˌtɪzəm) n. **1.** the property of attraction displayed by magnets. **2.** any of a class of phenomena in which a field of force is caused by a moving electric charge. **3.** the branch of physics concerned with magnetic phenomena. **4.** powerful attraction.

magnetite ('mægnɪˌtaɪt) n. a black magnetizable mineral that is an important source of iron.

magnetize or **-ise** ('mægnɪˌtaɪz) vb. (tr.) **1.** to make (a substance or object) magnetic. **2.** to attract strongly. —'magnetˌizable or -ˌisable adj. —ˌmagneti'zation or -i'sation n. —'magnetˌizer or -ˌiser n.

magneto (mæg'niːtəʊ) n., pl. **-tos.** a small electric generator in which the magnetic field is produced by a permanent magnet, esp. one for providing the spark in an internal-combustion engine.

magnetron ('mægnɪˌtrɒn) n. a two-electrode electronic valve used with an applied magnetic field to generate high-power microwave oscillations, esp. for use in radar.

Magnificat (mæg'nɪfɪˌkæt) n. Christianity. the hymn of the Virgin Mary (Luke 1:46-55), used as a canticle.

magnification (ˌmægnɪfɪ'keɪʃən) n. **1.** the act of magnifying or the state of being magnified. **2.** the degree to which something is magnified. **3.** a magnified copy, photograph, drawing, etc., of something. **4.** a measure of the ability of a lens or other optical instrument to magnify.

magnificent (mæg'nɪfɪsənt) adj. **1.** splendid or impressive in appearance. **2.** superb or very fine. **3.** (esp. of ideas) noble or elevated. —**mag'nificence** n. —**mag'nificently** adv.

magnify ('mægnɪˌfaɪ) vb. **-fying, -fied. 1.** to increase, cause to increase, or be increased in apparent size, as through the action of a lens, microscope, etc. **2.** to exaggerate or become exaggerated in importance: don't magnify your troubles. **3.** (tr.) Arch. to glorify. —'magniˌfiable adj. —'magniˌfier n.

magnifying glass or **magnifier** n. a convex lens

THESAURUS

glamour, magnetism, power ~adj. **4.** Also **magical** bewitching, charismatic, charming, enchanting, entrancing, fascinating, magnetic, marvellous, miraculous, sorcerous, spellbinding

magician 1. archimage (Rare), conjurer, conjuror, enchanter, enchantress, illusionist, necromancer, sorcerer, thaumaturge (Rare), theurgist, warlock, witch, wizard **2.** genius, marvel, miracle-worker, spellbinder, virtuoso, wizard, wonder-worker

magisterial arrogant, assertive, authoritative, bossy (Inf.), commanding, dictatorial, domineering, high-handed, imperious, lordly, masterful, overbearing, peremptory

magistrate bailie (Scot.), J.P., judge, justice, justice of the peace, provost (Scot.)

magnanimity beneficence, big-heartedness, bountifulness, charitableness, generosity, high-mindedness, largess, munificence, nobility, open-handedness, selflessness, unselfishness

magnanimous beneficent, big, big-hearted, bountiful, charitable, free, generous, great-hearted, handsome, high-minded, kind, kindly, munificent, noble, open-handed, selfless, ungrudging, unselfish, unstinting

magnate 1. baron, big cheese (Sl.), big noise (Sl.), big shot (Sl.), big wheel (Sl.), bigwig (Sl.), captain of industry, chief, fat cat (Sl.), leader, mogul, Mr. Big (Sl.), nabob (Inf.), notable, plutocrat, tycoon, V.I.P. **2.** aristocrat, baron, bashaw, grandee, magnifico, merchant, noble, notable, personage, prince

magnetic alluring, attractive, captivating, charismatic, charming, enchanting, entrancing, fascinating, hypnotic, irresistible, mesmerizing, seductive

magnetism allure, appeal, attraction, attractiveness, captivatingness, charisma, charm, draw, drawing power, enchantment, fascination, hypnotism, magic, mesmerism, power, pull, seductiveness, spell

magnification aggrandizement, amplification, augmentation, blow-up (Inf.), boost, build-up, deepening, dilation, enhance-ment, enlargement, exaggeration, expansion, heightening, increase, inflation, intensification

magnificence brilliance, glory, gorgeousness, grandeur, luxuriousness, luxury, majesty, nobility, opulence, pomp, resplendence, splendour, stateliness, sublimity, sumptuousness

magnificent august, brilliant, elegant, elevated, exalted, excellent, fine, glorious, gorgeous, grand, grandiose, imposing, impressive, lavish, luxurious, majestic, noble, opulent, outstanding, princely, regal, resplendent, rich, splendid, stately, sublime, sumptuous, superb, superior, transcendent

magnify 1. aggrandize, amplify, augment, blow up (Inf.), boost, build up, deepen, dilate, enlarge, expand, heighten, increase, intensify **2.** aggravate, blow up, blow up out of all proportion, dramatize, enhance, exaggerate, inflate, make a mountain out of a molehill, overdo, overemphasize, overestimate, overplay, overrate, overstate

used to produce an enlarged image of an object.

magniloquent (mægˈnɪləkwənt) *adj.* (of speech) lofty in style; grandiloquent. —**magˈniloquence** *n.* —**magˈniloquently** *adv.*

magnitude (ˈmægnɪˌtjuːd) *n.* **1.** relative importance or significance: *a problem of the first magnitude.* **2.** relative size or extent. **3.** *Maths.* a number assigned to a quantity as a basis of comparison for the measurement of similar quantities. **4.** Also called: **apparent magnitude.** *Astron.* the apparent brightness of a celestial body expressed on a numerical scale on which bright stars have a low value.

magnolia (mægˈnəʊlɪə) *n.* **1.** any tree or shrub of the genus *Magnolia* of Asia and North America: cultivated for their white, pink, purple, or yellow showy flowers. **2.** the flower of any of these plants.

magnum (ˈmægnəm) *n., pl.* -**nums.** a wine bottle holding the equivalent of two normal bottles (approximately 52 fluid ounces).

magnum opus *n.* a great work of art or literature, esp. the greatest single work of an artist.

magpie (ˈmægˌpaɪ) *n.* **1.** any of various birds having a black-and-white plumage, long tail, and a chattering call. **2.** any of various similar birds of Australia. **3.** *Brit.* a person who hoards small objects. **4.** a person who chatters. **5. a.** the outmost ring but one on a target. **b.** a shot that hits this ring.

magus (ˈmeɪgəs) *n., pl.* -**gi** (-dʒaɪ). **1.** a Zoroastrian priest. **2.** an astrologer, sorcerer, or magician of ancient times.

Magyar (ˈmægjɑː) *n.* **1.** (*pl.* -**yars**) a member of the predominant ethnic group of Hungary. **2.** the Hungarian language. ~*adj.* **3.** of or relating to the Magyars or their language. **4.** *Sewing.* of or relating to a style of sleeve cut in one piece with the bodice.

maharajah *or* **maharaja** (ˌmɑːhəˈrɑːdʒə) *n.* any of various Indian princes, esp. any of the rulers of the former native states.

maharani *or* **maharanee** (ˌmɑːhəˈrɑːniː) *n.* **1.** the wife of a maharajah. **2.** a woman holding the rank of maharajah.

maharishi (ˌmɑːhɑːˈriːʃɪ, məˈhɑːriːʃɪ) *n. Hinduism.* a Hindu teacher of religious and mystical knowledge.

mahatma (məˈhɑːtmə) *n.* (*sometimes cap.*) **1.** *Hinduism.* a Brahman sage. **2.** *Theosophy.* an adept or sage.

mahjong *or* **mah-jongg** (ˌmɑːˈdʒɒŋ) *n.* a game of Chinese origin, usually played by four people, using tiles bearing various designs.

mahogany (məˈhɒgənɪ) *n., pl.* -**nies.** **1.** any of various tropical American trees valued for their hard reddish-brown wood. **2.** any of several trees with similar wood, such as African mahogany and Philippine mahogany. **3. a.** the wood of any of these trees. **b.** (*as modifier*): *a mahogany table.* **4.** a reddish-brown colour.

mahout (məˈhaʊt) *n.* (in India and the East Indies) an elephant driver or keeper.

maid (meɪd) *n.* **1.** *Arch. or literary.* a young unmarried girl; maiden. **2. a.** a female servant. **b.** (*in combination*): *a housemaid.* **3.** a spinster.

maiden (ˈmeɪdən) *n.* **1.** *Arch. or literary.* **a.** a young unmarried girl, esp. a virgin. **b.** (*as modifier*): *a maiden blush.* **2.** *Horse racing.* **a.** a horse that has never won a race. **b.** (*as modifier*): *a maiden race.* **3.** *Cricket.* See **maiden over. 4.** (*modifier*) of or relating to an older unmarried woman: *a maiden aunt.* **5.** (*modifier*) of or involving an initial experience or attempt: *a maiden voyage.* **6.** (*modifier*) (of a person or thing) untried; unused.

7. (*modifier*) (of a place) never trodden, penetrated, or captured. —**ˈmaidenˌhood** *n.* —**ˈmaidenish** *adj.* —**ˈmaidenˌlike** *adj.* —**ˈmaidenly** *adj.*

maidenhair fern *or* **maidenhair** (ˈmeɪdənˌhɛə) *n.* any of various ferns of tropical and warm regions, having delicate fan-shaped fronds with small pale green leaflets.

maidenhead (ˈmeɪdənˌhɛd) *n.* **1.** a nontechnical word for the **hymen. 2.** virginity; maidenhood.

maiden name *n.* a woman's surname before marriage.

maiden over *n. Cricket.* an over in which no runs are scored.

maid of honour *n.* **1.** *U.S.* the principal unmarried attendant of a bride. **2.** *Brit.* a small tart with an almond-flavoured filling. **3.** an unmarried lady attending a queen or princess.

maidservant (ˈmeɪdˌsɜːvənt) *n.* a female servant.

mail[1] (meɪl) *n.* **1.** Also called (esp. *Brit.*): **post.** letters, packages, etc., that are transported and delivered by the post office. **2.** the postal system. **3.** a single collection or delivery of mail. **4.** a train, ship, or aircraft that carries mail. **5.** (*modifier*) of, involving, or used to convey mail: *a mail train.* ~*vb.* **6.** (*tr.*) *Chiefly U.S.* to send by mail. —**ˈmailable** *adj.*

mail[2] (meɪl) *n.* **1.** a type of flexible armour consisting of riveted metal rings or links. **2.** the hard protective shell of such animals as the turtle and lobster. ~*vb.* **3.** (*tr.*) to clothe or arm with mail.

mailbag (ˈmeɪlˌbæg) *or* **mailsack** *n.* a large bag for transporting or delivering mail.

mailing list *n.* a register of names and addresses to which advertising matter, etc., is sent by post.

mail order *n.* **1.** an order for merchandise sent by post. **2. a.** a system of buying and selling merchandise through the post. **b.** (*as modifier*): *a mail-order firm.*

maim (meɪm) *vb.* (*tr.*) **1.** to mutilate, cripple, or disable a part of the body of (a person or animal). **2.** to make defective.

main[1] (meɪn) *adj.* (*prenominal*) **1.** chief or principal. **2.** sheer or utmost (esp. in **by main force**). **3.** *Naut.* of, relating to, or denoting any gear, such as a stay or sail, belonging to the mainmast. ~*n.* **4.** a principal pipe, conduit, duct, or line in a system used to distribute water, electricity, etc. **5.** (*pl.*) **a.** the main distribution network for water, gas, or electricity. **b.** (*as modifier*): *mains voltage.* **6.** the chief or most important part or consideration. **7.** great strength or force (now chiefly in **might and main**). **8.** *Literary.* the open ocean. **9.** *Arch.* short for **Spanish Main. 10.** *Arch.* short for **mainland. 11. in** (*or* **for**) **the main.** on the whole; for the most part.

main[2] (meɪn) *n.* **1.** a throw of the dice in dice games. **2.** a cockfighting contest. **3.** a match in archery, boxing, etc.

main chance *n.* self-interest (esp. in the phrase **have an eye to the main chance**).

main clause *n. Grammar.* a clause that can stand alone as a sentence.

mainframe *Computers.* ~*adj.* **1.** denoting a high-speed general-purpose computer, usually with a large store capacity. ~*n.* **2.** such a computer. **3.** the central processing unit of a computer.

mainland (ˈmeɪnlənd) *n.* the main part of a land mass as opposed to an island or peninsula. —**ˈmainlander** *n.*

main line *n.* **1.** *Railways.* **a.** the trunk route between two points, usually fed by branch lines. **b.** (*as modifier*): *a*

THESAURUS

magniloquent bombastic, declamatory, elevated, exalted, grandiloquent, high-flown, high-sounding, lofty, orotund, overblown, pompous, pretentious, rhetorical, sonorous, stilted, turgid

magnitude 1. consequence, eminence, grandeur, greatness, importance, mark, moment, note, significance, weight 2. amount, amplitude, bigness, bulk, capacity, dimensions, enormity, expanse, extent, hugeness, immensity, intensity, largeness, mass, measure, proportions, quantity, size, space, strength, vastness, volume

maid 1. damsel, girl, lass, lassie (*Inf.*), maiden, miss, nymph (*Poetic*), wench 2. abigail (*Archaic*), handmaiden (*Archaic*),

housemaid, maid-servant, servant, serving-maid

maiden *n.* 1. damsel, girl, lass, lassie (*Inf.*), maid, miss, nymph, virgin, wench ~*adj.* 2. chaste, intact, pure, undefiled, unmarried, unwed, virgin, virginal 3. first, inaugural, initial, initiatory, introductory 4. fresh, new, unbroached, untapped, untried, unused

maidenly chaste, decent, decorous, demure, gentle, girlish, modest, pure, reserved, undefiled, unsullied, vestal, virginal, virtuous

mail *n.* 1. correspondence, letters, packages, parcels, post 2. post, postal service, postal system ~*v.* 3. dispatch, forward, post, send, send by mail *or* post

maim cripple, disable, hamstring, hurt, impair, incapacitate, injure, lame, mangle, mar, mutilate, put out of action, wound

main *adj.* 1. capital, cardinal, central, chief, critical, crucial, essential, foremost, head, leading, necessary, outstanding, paramount, particular, predominant, pre-eminent, premier, primary, prime, principal, special, supreme, vital 2. absolute, brute, direct, downright, entire, mere, pure, sheer, undisguised, utmost, utter ~*n.* 3. cable, channel, conduit, duct, line, pipe 4. effort, force, might, potency, power, puissance, strength 5. in (*or* for) the main for the most part, generally, in general, mainly, mostly, on the whole *main-line station.* **2.** *U.S.* a main road. **3.** *Sl.* a main vein, into which a narcotic drug, esp. heroin, can be injected. ~*vb.* **mainline. 4.** (*intr.*) *Sl.* to inject a drug thus. ~*adj.* **mainline. 5.** having an important or moderate position; principal. —'**main,liner** *n.*

mainly ('meɪnlɪ) *adv.* for the most part; to the greatest extent; principally.

mainmast ('meɪn,mɑːst) *n. Naut.* the chief mast of a sailing vessel with two or more masts.

mainsail ('meɪn,seɪl; *Naut.* 'meɪnsəl) *n. Naut.* the largest and lowermost sail on the mainmast.

mainspring ('meɪn,sprɪŋ) *n.* **1.** the principal spring of a mechanism, esp. in a watch or clock. **2.** the chief cause or motive of something.

mainstay ('meɪn,steɪ) *n.* **1.** *Naut.* the forestay that braces the mainmast. **2.** a chief support of something.

mainstream ('meɪn,striːm) *n.* **1.** the main current (of a river, cultural trend, etc.). ~*adj.* **2.** of or relating to the style of jazz that lies between the traditional and the modern.

maintain (meɪn'teɪn) *vb.* (*tr.*) **1.** to continue or retain; keep in existence. **2.** to keep in proper or good condition. **3.** to enable (a person) to support a style of living: *the money maintained us for a month.* **4.** (*takes a clause as object*) to state or assert. **5.** to defend against contradiction; uphold: *she maintained her innocence.* **6.** to defend against physical attack. —**main'tainable** *adj.* —**main'tainer** *n.*

maintenance ('meɪntɪnəns) *n.* **1.** the act of maintaining or the state of being maintained. **2.** a means of support; livelihood. **3.** (*modifier*) of or relating to the maintaining of buildings, machinery, etc.: *maintenance man.* **4.** *Law.* the interference in a legal action by a person having no interest in it, as by providing funds to continue the action. **5.** *Law.* a provision ordered to be made by way of periodical payments or a lump sum, as for a spouse after a divorce.

maisonette *or* **maisonnette** (,meɪzə'nɛt) *n.* self-contained living accommodation often occupying two floors of a larger house and having its own outside entrance.

maître d'hôtel (,mɛtrə dəʊ'tɛl) *n., pl.* **maîtres d'hôtel.** **1.** a head waiter or steward. **2.** the manager or owner of a hotel.

maize (meɪz) *n.* **1.** Also called: **sweet corn, Indian corn.** **a.** a tall annual grass cultivated for its yellow edible grains, which develop on a spike. **b.** the grain of this plant, used for food, for fodder, and as a source of oil. **2.** a yellow colour.

Maj. *abbrev. for* Major.

majesty ('mædʒɪstɪ) *n.* **1.** great dignity of bearing; loftiness; grandeur. **2.** supreme power or authority. —**ma'jestic** *adj.*

Majesty ('mædʒɪstɪ) *n., pl.* **-ties.** (preceded by *Your, His, Her,* or *Their*) a title used to address or refer to a sovereign or the wife or widow of a sovereign.

majolica (mə'dʒɒlɪkə, mə'jɒl-) *or* **maiolica** *n.* a type of porous pottery glazed with bright metallic oxides that originated in Majorca and was extensively made in Renaissance Italy.

major ('meɪdʒə) *n.* **1.** *Mil.* an officer immediately junior to a lieutenant colonel. **2.** a person who is superior in a group or class. **3.** (often preceded by *the*) *Music.* a major key, chord, mode, or scale. **4.** *U.S., Austral. & N.Z.* **a.** the principal field of study of a student. **b.** a student who is studying a particular subject as his principal field: *a*

sociology major. **5.** a person who has reached the age of legal majority. **6.** *Logic.* a major term or premiss. ~*adj.* **7.** larger in extent, number, etc. **8.** of greater importance or priority. **9.** very serious or significant. **10.** of, involving, or making up a majority. **11.** *Music.* **a.** (of a scale or mode) having notes separated by a whole tone, except for the third and fourth degrees, and seventh and eighth degrees, which are separated by a semitone. **b.** relating to or employing notes from the major scale: *a major key.* **c.** (*postpositive*) denoting a specified key or scale as being major: *C major.* **d.** denoting a chord or triad having a major third above the root. **e.** (in jazz) denoting a major chord with a major seventh added above the root. **12.** *Logic.* (of a term or premiss) having greater generality or scope than another term or proposition. **13.** *Chiefly U.S. & Austral.* of or relating to a student's principal field of study at a university, etc. **14.** *Brit.* the elder: used after a schoolboy's surname if he has one or more younger brothers in the same school: *Price major.* **15.** of full legal age. ~*vb.* **16.** (*intr.;* usually foll. by *in*) *U.S., Austral., & N.Z.* to do one's principal study (in a particular subject): *to major in English literature.* —'**majorship** *n.*

major-domo (,meɪdʒə'dəʊməʊ) *n., pl.* **-mos.** **1.** the chief steward or butler of a great household. **2.** *Facetious.* a steward or butler.

major general *n. Mil.* an officer immediately junior to a lieutenant general. —'**major-'general,ship** *or* '**major-'generalcy** *n.*

majority (mə'dʒɒrɪtɪ) *n., pl.* **-ties. 1.** the greater number or part of something. **2.** (in an election) the number of votes or seats by which the strongest party or candidate beats the combined opposition or the runner-up. **3.** the largest party or group that votes together in a legislative or deliberative assembly. **4.** the time of reaching or state of having reached full legal age. **5.** the rank, office, or commission of major. **6.** *Euphemistic.* the dead (esp. in **join the majority, go** *or* **pass over to the majority**). **7.** (*modifier*) of, involving, or being a majority: *a majority decision.* **8. in the majority.** forming or part of the greater number of something.

make (meɪk) *vb.* **making, made.** (*mainly tr.*) **1.** to bring into being by shaping, changing, or combining materials, ideas, etc.; form or fashion. **2.** to draw up, establish, or form: *to make one's will.* **3.** to cause to exist, bring about, or produce: *don't make a noise.* **4.** to cause, compel, or induce: *please make him go away.* **5.** to appoint or assign: *they made him chairman.* **6.** to constitute: *one swallow doesn't make a summer.* **7.** (*also intr.*) to come or cause to come into a specified state or condition: *to make merry.* **8.** (*copula*) to be or become through development: *he will make a good teacher.* **9.** to cause or ensure the success of: *your news has made my day.* **10.** to amount to: *twelve inches make a foot.* **11.** to serve as or be suitable for: *that piece of cloth will make a coat.* **12.** to prepare or put into a fit condition for use: *to make a bed.* **13.** to be the essential element in or part of: *charm makes a good salesman.* **14.** to carry out, effect, or do. **15.** (*intr.;* foll. by *to, as if to,* or *as though to*) to act with the intention or with a show of doing something: *he made as if to hit her.* **16.** to use for a specified purpose: *I will make this town my base.* **17.** to deliver or pronounce: *to make a speech.* **18.** to give information or an opinion: *what time do you make it?* **19.** to cause to seem or represent as being. **20.** to earn, acquire, or win for oneself: *to make friends.* **21.** to engage in: *to make war.* **22.** to traverse or cover (distance) by

mainly above all, chiefly, first and foremost, for the most part, generally, in general, in the main, largely, mostly, most of all, on the whole, overall, predominantly, primarily, principally, substantially, to the greatest extent, usually

mainstay anchor, backbone, bulwark, buttress, chief support, linchpin, pillar, prop

maintain 1. care for, carry on, conserve, continue, finance, keep, keep up, prolong, look after, nurture, perpetuate, preserve, provide, retain, supply, support, sustain, take care of, uphold 2. affirm, allege, assert, asseverate, aver, avow, claim, contend, declare, hold, insist, profess, state 3. advocate, argue for, back, champion, defend, fight for, justify, plead for, stand by, take up the cudg-

els for, uphold, vindicate

maintenance 1. care, carrying-on, conservation, continuance, continuation, keeping, nurture, perpetuation, preservation, prolongation, provision, repairs, retainment, supply, support, sustainment, sustention, upkeep 2. aliment, alimony, allowance, food, keep, livelihood, living, subsistence, support, sustenance, upkeep

majestic august, awesome, dignified, elevated, exalted, grand, grandiose, imperial, imposing, impressive, kingly, lofty, magnificent, monumental, noble, pompous, princely, regal, royal, splendid, stately, sublime, superb

majesty augustness, awesomeness, dignity, exaltedness, glory, grandeur, imposing-

ness, impressiveness, kingliness, loftiness, magnificence, nobility, pomp, queenliness, royalty, splendour, state, stateliness, sublimity

major 1. better, bigger, chief, elder, greater, higher, larger, leading, main, most, senior, superior, supreme, uppermost 2. critical, crucial, grave, great, important, notable, outstanding, pre-eminent, radical, serious, significant, vital, weighty

majority 1. best part, bulk, greater number, mass, more, most, plurality, preponderance, superiority 2. adulthood, manhood, maturity, seniority, womanhood

travelling: *we can make a hundred miles by nightfall.* **23.** to arrive in time for: *he didn't make the first act of the play.* **24.** *Cards.* **a.** to win a trick with (a specified card). **b.** to shuffle (the cards). **c.** *Bridge.* to fulfil (a contract) by winning the necessary number of tricks. **25.** *Cricket.* to score (runs). **26.** *Electronics.* to close (a circuit) permitting a flow of current. **27.** (*intr.*) to increase in depth: *the water in the hold was making a foot a minute.* **28.** *Inf.* to gain a place or position on or in: *to make the headlines.* **29.** *Inf., chiefly U.S.* to achieve the rank of. **30.** *Taboo sl.* to succeed in having sexual intercourse with (a girl). **31. make a book.** to take bets on a race or another contest. **32. make a day,** etc., **of it.** to cause an activity to last a day, etc. **33. make do.** See do¹ (sense 29). **34. make eyes at.** to flirt with or ogle. **35. make good. a.** to repair or provide restitution for. **b.** to be successful in (a plan, activity, etc.): *he made good his intention.* **36. make heavy weather (of). a.** *Naut.* to roll and pitch in heavy seas. **b.** *Inf.* to carry out with great difficulty or unnecessarily great effort. **37. make it. a.** *Inf.* to be successful in doing something. **b.** (foll. by *with*) *Taboo sl.* to have sexual intercourse. **38. make like.** *Sl., chiefly U.S.* to imitate. **39. make love (to). a.** to have sexual intercourse (with). **b.** to engage in courtship (with). **40. make time.** See time (sense 38). **41. make water. a.** another term for urinate. **b.** (of a boat, hull, etc.) to let in water. ~*n.* **42.** brand, type, or style. **43.** the manner or way in which something is made. **44.** disposition or character; make-up. **45.** the act or process of making. **46.** the amount or number made. **47.** *Cards.* a player's turn to shuffle. **48. on the make.** *Sl.* **a.** out for profit or conquest. **b.** in search of a sexual partner. ~See also **make away, make for,** etc. —'**makable** *adj.*

make away *vb.* (*intr., adv.*) **1.** to depart in haste. **2. make away with. a.** to steal or abduct. **b.** to kill, destroy, or get rid of.

make believe *vb.* **1.** to pretend or enact a fantasy. ~*n.* **make-believe. 2. a.** a fantasy or pretence. **b.** (*as modifier*): *a make-believe world.*

make for *vb.* (*intr., prep.*) **1.** to head towards. **2.** to prepare to attack. **3.** to help bring about.

make of *vb.* (*tr., prep.*) **1.** to interpret as the meaning of. **2.** to produce or construct from: *houses made of brick.* **3. make little, much,** etc. **of. a.** to gain little,

much, etc., benefit from. **b.** to attribute little, much, etc., significance to.

make off *vb.* **1.** (*intr., adv.*) to go or run away in haste. **2. make off with.** to steal or abduct.

make out *vb.* (*adv.*) **1.** (*tr.*) to discern or perceive. **2.** (*tr.*) to understand or comprehend. **3.** (*tr.*) to write out: *he made out a cheque.* **4.** (*tr.*) to attempt to establish or prove: *he made me out to be a liar.* **5.** (*intr.*) to pretend: *he made out that he could cook.* **6.** (*intr.*) to manage or fare.

maker ('meɪkə) *n.* a person who executes a legal document, esp. one who signs a promissory note.

Maker ('meɪkə) *n.* **1.** a title given to God (as Creator). **2. (go to) meet one's Maker.** to die.

makeshift ('meɪk,ʃɪft) *adj.* **1.** serving as a temporary or expedient means. ~*n.* **2.** something serving in this capacity.

make-up *n.* **1.** cosmetics, such as powder, lipstick, etc., applied to the face. **2. a.** the cosmetics, false hair, etc., used by an actor to adapt his appearance. **b.** the art or result of applying such cosmetics. **3.** the manner of arrangement of the parts or qualities of someone or something. **4.** the arrangement of type matter and illustrations on a page or in a book. **5.** mental or physical constitution. ~*vb.* **make up.** (*adv.*) **6.** (*tr.*) to form or constitute: *these arguments make up the case for the defence.* **7.** (*tr.*) to devise, construct, or compose, sometimes with the intent to deceive: *to make up an excuse.* **8.** (*tr.*) to supply what is lacking or deficient in; complete: *these extra people will make up our total.* **9.** (*tr.*) to put in order, arrange, or prepare: *to make up a bed.* **10.** (*intr.; foll.* by *for*) to compensate or atone (for). **11.** to settle (differences) amicably (often in **make it up**). **12.** to apply cosmetics to (the face, etc.) to enhance one's appearance or for a theatrical role. **13.** to assemble (type and illustrations) into (columns or pages). **14.** (*tr.*) to surface (a road) with tarmac, concrete, etc. **15. make up one's mind.** to make a decision about something or to do something. **16. make up to.** *Inf.* **a.** to make friendly overtures to. **b.** to flirt with.

makeweight ('meɪk,weɪt) *n.* **1.** something put on a scale to make up a required weight. **2.** an unimportant person or thing added to make up a lack.

making ('meɪkɪŋ) *n.* **1. a.** the act of a person or thing that makes or the process of being made. **b.** (*in combi-*

THESAURUS

make *v.* **1.** assemble, build, compose, constitute, construct, create, fabricate, fashion, forge, form, frame, manufacture, mould, originate, produce, put together, shape, synthesize **2.** accomplish, beget, bring about, cause, create, effect, engender, generate, give rise to, lead to, occasion, produce **3.** cause, coerce, compel, constrain, dragoon, drive, force, impel, induce, oblige, press, pressurize, prevail upon, require **4.** appoint, assign, create, designate, elect, install, invest, nominate, ordain **5.** draw up, enact, establish, fix, form, frame, pass **6.** add up to, amount to, compose, constitute, embody, form, represent **7.** act, carry out, do, effect, engage in, execute, perform, practise, prosecute **8.** calculate, estimate, gauge, judge, reckon, suppose, think **9.** acquire, clear, earn, gain, get, net, obtain, realize, secure, take in, win **10.** arrive at, arrive in time for, attain, catch, get to, meet, reach **11. make it** *Inf.* arrive (*Inf.*), be successful, come through, get on, get somewhere, prosper, pull through, succeed, survive ~*n.* **12.** brand, build, character, composition, constitution, construction, cut, designation, form, kind, make-up, mark, model, shape, sort, structure, style, type, variety **13.** cast of mind, character, disposition, frame of mind, humour, kidney, make-up, nature, stamp, temper, temperament

make as if *or* **though** act as if or though, affect, feign, feint, give the impression that, make a show of, pretend

make away 1. abscond, beat a hasty retreat, clear out (*Inf.*), cut and run (*Inf.*), decamp, depart, flee, fly, make off, run away *or* off, run for it (*Inf.*), scoot, skedaddle (*Inf.*),

take to one's heels **2.** *With* with abduct, carry off, filch, kidnap, knock off (*Sl.*), make off with, nab (*Inf.*), nick (*Sl.*), pilfer, pinch (*Inf.*), purloin, steal, swipe (*Sl.*) **3.** *With* with bump off (*Sl.*), destroy, dispose of, do away with, do in (*Sl.*), eliminate, get rid of, kill, murder

make-believe 1. *n.* charade, dream, fantasy, imagination, play-acting, pretence, unreality **2.** *adj.* dream, fantasized, fantasy, imaginary, imagined, made-up, mock, pretend, pretended, sham, unreal

make believe act as if *or* though, dream, enact, fantasize, imagine, play, play-act, pretend

make do cope, get along *or* by, improvise, manage, muddle through, scrape along *or* by

make for 1. aim for, be bound for, head for *or* towards, proceed towards, steer (a course) for **2.** assail, assault, attack, fall on, fly at, go for, have a go at (*Inf.*), lunge at, set upon **3.** be conducive to, conduce to, contribute to, facilitate, favour, promote

make off 1. abscond, beat a hasty retreat, bolt, clear out (*Inf.*), cut and run (*Inf.*), decamp, flee, fly, make away, run away *or* off, run for it (*Inf.*), take to one's heels **2.** *With* with abduct, carry off, filch, kidnap, knock off (*Sl.*), make away with, nab (*Inf.*), nick (*Sl.*), pilfer, pinch (*Inf.*), purloin, run away *or* off with, steal, swipe (*Sl.*)

make out 1. descry, detect, discern, discover, distinguish, espy, perceive, recognize, see **2.** comprehend, decipher, fathom, follow, grasp, perceive, realize, see, understand, work out **3.** complete, draw up, fill in *or* out, inscribe, write (out) **4.** demonstrate, describe, prove, represent, show **5.** assert,

claim, let on, make as if *or* though, pretend **6.** fare, get on, manage, prosper, succeed, thrive

maker author, builder, constructor, director, fabricator, framer, manufacturer, producer

Maker Creator, God

makeshift 1. *adj.* expedient, jury (*Chiefly nautical*), make-do, provisional, rough and ready, stopgap, substitute, temporary **2.** *n.* expedient, shift, stopgap, substitute

make-up 1. cosmetics, face (*Inf.*), greasepaint (*Theatre*), maquillage, paint (*Inf.*), powder, war paint (*Inf., humorous*) **2.** arrangement, assembly, composition, configuration, constitution, construction, form, format, formation, organization, structure **3.** build, cast of mind, character, constitution, disposition, figure, frame of mind, make, nature, stamp, temper, temperament

make up 1. compose, comprise, constitute, form **2.** coin, compose, concoct, construct, cook up (*Inf.*), create, devise, dream up, fabricate, formulate, frame, hatch, invent, originate, trump up, write **3.** complete, fill, meet, supply **4.** *With* for atone, balance, compensate, make amends, offset, recompense, redeem, redress, requite **5.** bury the hatchet, call it quits, come to terms, compose, forgive and forget, make peace, mend, reconcile, settle, shake hands **6. make up one's mind** choose, come to a decision, decide, determine, make a decision, reach a decision, resolve, settle **7. make up to** *Inf.* chat up (*Inf.*), court, curry favour with, flirt with, make overtures to, woo

nation): *watchmaking*. **2. be the making of.** to cause the success of. **3. in the making.** in the process of becoming or being made. **4.** something made or the quantity of something made at one time.

makings ('meɪkɪŋz) *pl. n.* **1.** potentials, qualities, or materials: *he had the makings of a leader.* **2.** Also called: **rollings**. *U.S., Austral., & N.Z. sl.* the tobacco and cigarette paper used for rolling a cigarette. **3.** profits; earnings.

Mal. *abbrev. for:* **1.** *Bible*. Malachi. **2.** Malay(an).

mal- *combining form*. bad or badly; wrong or wrongly; imperfect or defective: *maladjusted; malfunction*.

malachite ('mæləˌkaɪt) *n.* a green mineral consisting of hydrated basic copper carbonate: a source of copper, also used for making ornaments.

maladjustment (ˌmæləˈdʒʌstmənt) *n.* **1.** *Psychol*. a failure to meet the demands of society, such as coping with problems and social relationships. **2.** faulty or bad adjustment. —ˌmaladˈjusted *adj.*

maladminister (ˌmælədˈmɪnɪstə) *vb.* (*tr.*) to administer badly, inefficiently, or dishonestly. —ˌmaladˌminisˈtration *n.*

maladroit (ˌmæləˈdrɔɪt) *adj.* **1.** clumsy; not dexterous. **2.** tactless and insensitive. —ˌmalaˈdroitly *adv.* —ˌmalaˈdroitness *n.*

malady ('mælədɪ) *n., pl.* **-dies.** **1.** any disease or illness. **2.** any unhealthy, morbid, or desperate condition.

Málaga ('mæləgə) *n.* a sweet fortified dessert wine from Málaga, a port in S Spain.

malaise (mæˈleɪz) *n.* a feeling of unease, mild sickness, or depression.

malapropism ('mæləprɒpˌɪzəm) *or* **malaprop** *n.* **1.** the unintentional misuse of a word by confusion with one of similar sound, esp. when creating a ridiculous effect, as in *under the affluence of alcohol*. **2.** the habit of misusing words in this manner.

malaria (məˈlɛərɪə) *n.* an infectious disease characterized by recurring attacks of chills and fever, caused by the bite of an anopheles mosquito infected with any of certain protozoans. —**maˈlarial, maˈlarian**, *or* **maˈlarious** *adj.*

malarkey *or* **malarky** (məˈlɑːkɪ) *n. Inf.* nonsense; rubbish.

Malathion (ˌmæləˈθaɪɒn) *n. Trademark*. an insecticide consisting of an organic phosphate.

Malay (məˈleɪ) *n.* **1.** a member of a people living chiefly in Malaysia and Indonesia. **2.** the language of this people. *~adj.* **3.** of or relating to the Malays or their language.

malcontent ('mælkənˌtɛnt) *adj.* **1.** disgusted or discontented. *~n.* **2.** a person who is malcontent.

male (meɪl) *adj.* **1.** of, relating to, or designating the sex producing gametes (spermatozoa) that can fertilize female gametes (ova). **2.** of, relating to, or characteristic of a man. **3.** for or composed of men or boys: *a male choir*. **4.** (of gametes) capable of fertilizing an egg cell.

5. (of reproductive organs) capable of producing male gametes. **6.** (of flowers) bearing stamens but lacking a functional pistil. **7.** *Electronics, engineering*. having a projecting part or parts that fit into a female counterpart: *a male plug*. *~n.* **8.** a male person, animal, or plant. —'**maleness** *n.*

male chauvinism *n.* the belief, held or alleged to be held by certain men, that men are superior to women. —**male chauvinist** *n.*

malediction (ˌmælɪˈdɪkʃən) *n.* **1.** the utterance of a curse against someone or something. **2.** a slanderous accusation or comment. —ˌmaleˈdictive *or* ˌmaleˈdictory *adj.*

malefactor ('mælɪˌfæktə) *n.* a criminal; wrongdoer. —ˌmaleˈfaction *n.*

malevolent (məˈlɛvələnt) *adj.* wishing or appearing to wish evil to others; malicious. —maˈlevolence *n.* —maˈlevolently *adv.*

malfeasance (mælˈfiːzəns) *n. Law*. the doing of a wrongful or illegal act, esp. by a public official. Cf. **misfeasance**. —malˈfeasant *n., adj.*

malformation (ˌmælfɔːˈmeɪʃən) *n.* **1.** the condition of being faulty or abnormal in form or shape. **2.** *Pathol*. a deformity, esp. when congenital. —malˈformed *adj.*

malfunction (mælˈfʌŋkʃən) *vb.* **1.** (*intr.*) to function imperfectly or fail to function. *~n.* **2.** failure to function or defective functioning.

malice ('mælɪs) *n.* **1.** the desire to do harm or mischief. **2.** evil intent. **3.** *Law*. the state of mind with which an act is committed and from which the intent to do wrong may be inferred. —**malicious** (məˈlɪʃəs) *adj.*

malign (məˈlaɪn) *adj.* **1.** evil in influence, intention, or effect. *~vb.* **2.** (*tr.*) to slander or defame. —maˈligner *n.* —maˈlignly *adv.*

malignant (məˈlɪgnənt) *adj.* **1.** having or showing desire to harm others. **2.** tending to cause great harm; injurious. **3.** *Pathol*. (of a tumour, etc.) uncontrollable or resistant to therapy. —maˈlignancy *n.* —maˈlignantly *adv.*

malignity (məˈlɪgnɪtɪ) *n., pl.* **-ties.** **1.** the condition or quality of being malign or deadly. **2.** (*often pl.*) a malign or malicious act or feeling.

malinger (məˈlɪŋgə) *vb.* (*intr.*) to pretend or exaggerate illness, esp. to avoid work. —maˈlingerer *n.*

mall (mɔːl, mæl) *n.* **1.** a shaded avenue, esp. one open to the public. **2.** a street or area lined with shops and closed to vehicles. **3.** See **pall-mall**.

mallard ('mælɑːd) *n., pl.* **-lard** *or* **-lards.** a duck common over most of the N hemisphere, the male of which has a dark green head and reddish-brown breast: the ancestor of all domestic breeds of duck.

malleable ('mælɪəbªl) *adj.* **1.** (esp. of metal) able to be worked, hammered, or shaped under pressure or blows without breaking. **2.** able to be influenced; pliable or tractable. —ˌmalleaˈbility *or* 'malleableness *n.* —'malleably *adv.*

THESAURUS

making 1. assembly, building, composition, construction, creation, fabrication, forging, manufacture, production 2. **in the making** budding, coming, emergent, growing, nascent, potential

makings 1. beginnings, capability, capacity, ingredients, materials, potentiality, potential(s), qualities 2. earnings, income, proceeds, profits, returns, revenue, takings

maladjusted alienated, disturbed, estranged, hung-up (*Sl.*), neurotic, unstable

maladministration blundering, bungling, corruption, dishonesty, incompetence, inefficiency, malfeasance (*Law*), malpractice, misgovernment, mismanagement, misrule

malady affliction, ailment, complaint, disease, disorder, ill, illness, indisposition, infirmity, sickness

malaise angst, anxiety, depression, discomfort, disquiet, doldrums, enervation, illness, lassitude, melancholy, sickness, unease, weakness

malcontent 1. *adj.* disaffected, discontented, disgruntled, disgusted, dissatisfied, dissentious, factious, ill-disposed, rebellious,

resentful, restive, unhappy, unsatisfied 2. *n.* agitator, complainer, fault-finder, grouch (*Inf.*), grouser, grumbler, mischief-maker, rebel, troublemaker

male manful, manlike, manly, masculine, virile

malefactor convict, criminal, crook (*Inf.*), culprit, delinquent, evildoer, felon, lawbreaker, miscreant, offender, outlaw, transgressor, villain, wrongdoer

malevolence hate, hatred, ill will, malice, maliciousness, malignity, rancour, spite, spitefulness, vengefulness, vindictiveness

malevolent baleful, evil-minded, hateful (*Archaic*), hostile, ill-natured, malicious, malign, malignant, pernicious, rancorous, spiteful, vengeful, vicious, vindictive

malformation crookedness, deformity, distortion, misshape, misshapenness

malformed abnormal, contorted, crooked, deformed, distorted, irregular, misshapen, twisted

malfunction 1. *v.* break down, develop a fault, fail, go wrong 2. *n.* breakdown, defect, failure, fault, flaw, impairment

malice animosity, animus, bad blood, bit-

terness, enmity, evil intent, hate, hatred, ill will, malevolence, maliciousness, malignity, rancour, spite, spitefulness, spleen, vengefulness, venom, vindictiveness

malicious baleful, bitchy (*Sl.*), bitter, catty (*Inf.*), evil-minded, hateful, ill-disposed, ill-natured, injurious, malevolent, malignant, mischievous, pernicious, rancorous, resentful, spiteful, vengeful, vicious

malign 1. *adj.* bad, baleful, baneful, deleterious, destructive, evil, harmful, hostile, hurtful, injurious, malevolent, malignant, pernicious, vicious, wicked 2. *v.* abuse, blacken (someone's name), calumniate, defame, denigrate, derogate, disparage, do a hatchet job on (*Inf.*), harm, injure, libel, revile, run down, slander, smear, speak ill of, traduce, vilify

malignant 1. baleful, bitter, destructive, harmful, hostile, hurtful, inimical, injurious, malevolent, malicious, malign, of evil intent, pernicious, spiteful, vicious 2. *Medical* cancerous, dangerous, deadly, evil, fatal, irremediable, metastatic, uncontrollable, virulent

mallet ('mælɪt) n. 1. a tool resembling a hammer but having a large head of wood, copper, lead, leather, etc., used for driving chisels, beating sheet metal, etc. 2. a long stick with a head like a hammer used to strike the ball in croquet or polo.

mallow ('mæləʊ) n. 1. any of several malvaceous plants of Europe, having purple, pink, or white flowers. 2. any of various related plants, such as the marsh mallow.

malmsey ('mɑːmzɪ) n. a sweet Madeira wine.

malnutrition (ˌmælnjuːˈtrɪʃən) n. lack of adequate nutrition resulting from insufficient food, unbalanced diet, or defective assimilation.

malodorous (mælˈəʊdərəs) adj. having a bad smell.

malpractice (mælˈpræktɪs) n. 1. immoral, illegal, or unethical professional conduct or neglect of professional duty. 2. any instance of improper professional conduct.

malt (mɔːlt) n. 1. cereal grain, such as barley, that is kiln-dried after it has germinated by soaking in water. 2. Also called: **malt liquor.** any alcoholic drink brewed from malt. ~vb. 3. to make into or become malt. 4. to make (something, esp. liquor) with malt. —'malty adj.

Maltese (mɔːlˈtiːz) adj. 1. of or relating to Malta, its inhabitants, or their language. ~n. 2. (pl. -tese) a native or inhabitant of Malta. 3. the official language of Malta, a form of Arabic with borrowings from Italian, etc.

Maltese cross n. a cross with triangular arms that taper towards the centre, sometimes having indented outer sides.

Malthusian (mælˈθjuːzɪən) adj. 1. of or relating to the theory of T. R. Malthus (1766–1834), English economist, stating that increases in population tend to exceed increases in the means of subsistence and that therefore sexual restraint should be exercised. ~n. 2. a supporter of this theory. —Mal'thusianism n.

maltose ('mɔːltəʊz) n. a sugar formed by the enzymic hydrolysis of starch.

maltreat (mælˈtriːt) vb. (tr.) to treat badly, cruelly, or inconsiderately. —mal'treater n. —mal'treatment n.

malversation (ˌmælvɜːˈseɪʃən) n. Rare. professional or public misconduct.

mam (mæm) n. Brit. dialect. another word for **mother.**

mama or esp. U.S. **mamma** (məˈmɑː) n. Old-fashioned. an informal word for **mother.**

mamba ('mæmbə) n. any of various partly arboreal tropical African venomous snakes, esp. the **green** and **black mambas.**

mambo ('mæmbəʊ) n., pl. -**bos.** 1. a modern Latin American dance, resembling the rumba. ~vb. 2. (intr.) to perform this dance.

Mameluke or **Mamaluke** ('mæmɪˌluːk) n. 1. a member of a military class, originally of Turkish slaves, ruling in Egypt from about 1250 to 1517 and remaining powerful until 1811. 2. (in Muslim countries) a slave.

mamilla or U.S. **mammilla** (mæˈmɪlə) n., pl. -**lae** (-liː). 1. a nipple or teat. 2. any nipple-shaped prominence. —'mamillary or U.S. 'mammillary adj.

mamma ('mæmə) n., pl. -**mae** (-miː). the milk-secreting organ of female mammals: the breast in women, the udder in cows, etc. —'mammary adj.

mammal ('mæməl) n. any animal of the Mammalia, a large class of warm-blooded vertebrates having mammary glands in the female. —mammalian (mæˈmeɪlɪən) adj., n.

mammon ('mæmən) n. riches or wealth regarded as a source of evil and corruption. —'mammonish adj. —'mammonism n. —'mammonist or 'mammonite n.

Mammon ('mæmən) n. Bible. the personification of riches and greed in the form of a false god.

mammoth ('mæməθ) n. 1. any large extinct elephant of the Pleistocene epoch, such as the **woolly mammoth,** having a hairy coat and long curved tusks. ~adj. 2. of gigantic size or importance.

man (mæn) n., pl. **men** (mɛn). 1. an adult male human being, as distinguished from a woman. 2. (modifier) male; masculine: a man child. 3. a human being, considered as representative of mankind. 4. human beings collectively; mankind. 5. Also called: **modern man. a.** a member of any of the living races of Homo sapiens, characterized by erect bipedal posture, a highly developed brain, and powers of articulate speech, abstract reasoning, and imagination. **b.** any extinct member of the species Homo sapiens, such as Cro-Magnon man. 6. a member of any of the extinct species of the genus Homo, such as Java man. 7. an adult male human being with qualities associated with the male, such as courage or virility: be a man. 8. manly qualities or virtues: the man in him was outraged. 9. a. a subordinate, servant, or employee. b. (in combination): the man-days required to complete a job. 10. (usually pl.) a member of the armed forces who does not hold commissioned, warrant, or noncommissioned rank (as in **officers and men**). 11. a member of a group, team, etc. 12. a husband, boyfriend, etc. 13. an expression used parenthetically by hippies, etc., to indicate an informal relationship between speaker and hearer. 14. a movable piece in various games, such as draughts. 15. a vassal of a feudal lord. 16. S. African sl. any person. 17. **as one man.** with unanimous action or response. 18. **be one's own man.** to be independent or free. 19. **he's your man.** he's the person needed. 20. **man and boy.** from childhood. 21. **sort out** or **separate the men from the boys.** to separate the experienced from the inexperienced. 22. **to a man.** without exception. ~interj. 23. Inf. an exclamation or expletive, often indicating surprise or pleasure. ~vb. **manning, manned.** (tr.) 24. to provide with sufficient men for operation, defence, etc. 25. to take one's place at or near in readiness for action. —'manhood n.

Man. abbrev. for: 1. Manila (paper). 2. Manitoba.

manacle ('mænək^əl) n. 1. (usually pl.) a shackle, handcuff, or fetter, used to secure the hands of a prisoner, convict, etc. ~vb. (tr.) 2. to put manacles on. 3. to confine or constrain.

manage ('mænɪdʒ) vb. (mainly tr.) 1. (also intr.) to be in charge (of); administer: to manage a shop. 2. to succeed in being able (to do something); contrive. 3. to have room, time, etc., for: can you manage dinner tomorrow? 4. to exercise control or domination over. 5. (intr.) to contrive to carry on despite difficulties, esp. financial ones. 6. to wield or handle (a weapon). —'manageable adj.

management ('mænɪdʒmənt) n. 1. the members of the executive or administration of an organization or business. 2. managers or employers collectively. 3. the technique, practice, or science of managing or controlling. 4. the skilful or resourceful use of materials, time, etc. 5. the specific treatment of a disease, etc.

manager ('mænɪdʒə) n. 1. a person who directs or manages an organization, industry, shop, etc. 2. a per-

---

THESAURUS

malpractice 1. abuse, dereliction, misbehaviour, misconduct, mismanagement, negligence 2. abuse, misdeed, offence, transgression

maltreat abuse, bully, damage, handle roughly, harm, hurt, ill-treat, injure, mistreat

mammoth Brobdingnagian, colossal, enormous, gargantuan, giant, gigantic, huge, immense, jumbo (Inf.), massive, mighty, monumental, mountainous, prodigious, stupendous, titanic, vast

man n. 1. bloke (Brit. inf.), chap (Inf.), gentleman, guy (Inf.), male 2. adult, being, body, human, human being, individual, one, person, personage, somebody, soul 3. Homo sapiens, humanity, humankind, human race, mankind, mortals, people 4. attendant, employee, follower, hand, hireling, manservant,

retainer, servant, soldier, subject, subordinate, valet, vassal, worker, workman 5. beau, boyfriend, husband, lover, partner, spouse 6. **to a man** bar none, every one, one and all, unanimously, without exception ~v. 7. crew, fill, furnish with men, garrison, occupy, people, staff

manacle 1. n. bond, chain, fetter, gyve (Archaic), handcuff, iron, shackle, tie 2. v. bind, chain, check, clap or put in irons, confine, constrain, curb, fetter, hamper, handcuff, inhibit, put in chains, restrain, shackle, tie one's hands

manage 1. administer, be in charge (of), command, concert, conduct, direct, govern, manipulate, oversee, preside over, rule, run, superintend, supervise 2. accomplish, arrange, bring about or off, contrive, cope

with, deal with, effect, engineer, succeed 3. control, dominate, govern, guide, handle, influence, manipulate, operate, pilot, ply, steer, train, use, wield 4. carry on, cope, fare, get along, get by, get on, make do, make out, muddle through, shift, survive

manageable amenable, compliant, controllable, convenient, docile, easy, governable, handy, submissive, tamable, tractable, wieldy

management 1. administration, board, bosses (Inf.), directorate, directors, employers, executive(s) 2. administration, care, charge, command, conduct, control, governance, government, guidance, handling, manipulation, operation, rule, running, superintendence, supervision

son who controls the business affairs of an actor, entertainer, etc. **3.** a person who controls the training of a sportsman or team. **4.** a person who has a talent for managing efficiently. **5.** (in Britain) a member of either House of Parliament appointed to arrange a matter in which both Houses are concerned. —**managerial** (ˌmænəˈdʒɪərɪəl) adj. —ˈmanagerˌship n.

managing (ˈmænɪdʒɪŋ) adj. having administrative control or authority: a managing director.

mañana Spanish. (məˈnjɑːnə) n., adv. **a.** tomorrow. **b.** some other and later time.

man-at-arms n., pl. **men-at-arms.** a soldier, esp. a heavily armed mounted soldier in medieval times.

manatee (ˌmænəˈtiː) n. a sirenian mammal occurring in tropical coastal waters of America, the West Indies, and Africa, having a prehensile upper lip and a broad flattened tail.

Manchu (mænˈtʃuː) n. **1.** (pl. -chus or -chu) a member of a Mongoloid people of Manchuria, a region of NE China, who conquered China in the 17th century, establishing an imperial dynasty that lasted until 1912. **2.** the language of this people. ~adj. **3.** Also: **Ching.** of or relating to the dynasty of the Manchus.

Mancunian (mæŋˈkjuːnɪən) n. **1.** a native or inhabitant of Manchester, a city in NW England. ~adj. **2.** of or relating to Manchester.

-mancy n. combining form. indicating divination of a particular kind: chiromancy. —**-mantic** adj. combining form.

mandala (ˈmændələ, mænˈdɑːlə) n. Hindu and Buddhist art. any of various designs symbolizing the universe, usually circular.

mandamus (mænˈdeɪməs) n., pl. -muses. Law. (formerly) a writ, now a prerogative order, from a superior court commanding an inferior tribunal, public official, etc., to take some specified action.

mandarin (ˈmændərɪn) n. **1.** (in the Chinese Empire) a member of a senior grade of the bureaucracy. **2.** a high-ranking official whose powers are extensive and thought to be outside political control. **3. a.** a small citrus tree cultivated for its edible fruit. **b.** the fruit, resembling the tangerine. —ˈmandarinate n.

Mandarin Chinese or **Mandarin** n. the official language of China since 1917.

mandate n. (ˈmændeɪt, -dɪt). **1.** an official or authoritative instruction or command. **2.** Politics. the support or commission given to a government and its policies or an elected representative and his policies through an electoral victory. **3.** (often cap.) Also called: **mandated territory.** (formerly) any of the territories under the trusteeship of the League of Nations administered by one of its member states. **4. a.** Roman law. a contract by which one person commissions another to act for him gratuitously. **b.** Contract law. a contract under which a party entrusted with goods undertakes to perform gratuitously some service in respect of such goods. **c.** Scot. law. a contract by which a person is engaged to act in the management of the affairs of another. ~vb. (ˈmændeɪt). (tr.) **5.** to assign (territory) to a nation under a mandate. **6.** to delegate authority to. —ˈmanˌdator n.

mandatory (ˈmændətərɪ, -trɪ) adj. also **mandatary. 1.** having the nature or powers of a mandate. **2.** obligatory; compulsory. **3.** (of a state) having received a mandate over some territory. ~n., pl. -ries. **4.** a person or state holding a mandate. —ˈmandatorily adv.

mandible (ˈmændɪbəl) n. **1.** the lower jawbone in vertebrates. **2.** either of a pair of mouthparts in insects and other arthropods that are usually used for biting and crushing food. **3.** Ornithol. either part of the bill, esp. the

lower part. —**mandibular** (mænˈdɪbjʊlə) adj. —**mandibulate** (mænˈdɪbjʊlɪt, -ˌleɪt) n., adj.

mandolin or **mandoline** (ˌmændəˈlɪn) n. a plucked stringed instrument having four pairs of strings stretched over a small light body with a fretted finger board. It is usually played with a plectrum. —ˌmandoˈlinist n.

mandrake (ˈmændreɪk) or **mandragora** (mænˈdrægərə) n. a Eurasian plant with purplish flowers and a forked root. It was formerly thought to have magic powers and a narcotic was prepared from its root.

mandrel or **mandril** (ˈmændrəl) n. **1.** a spindle on which a workpiece is supported during machining operations. **2.** a shaft or arbor on which a machining tool is mounted.

mandrill (ˈmændrɪl) n. an Old World monkey of W Africa. It has a short tail and brown hair, and the ridged muzzle, nose, and hindquarters are red and blue.

mane (meɪn) n. **1.** the long coarse hair that grows from the crest of the neck in such mammals as the lion and horse. **2.** long thick human hair. —**maned** adj.

manège or **manege** (mæˈneɪʒ) n. **1.** the art of training horses and riders. **2.** a riding school.

man Friday n. **1.** a loyal male servant or assistant. **2.** Also: **Girl Friday, Person Friday.** any factotum, esp. in an office.

manful (ˈmænfʊl) adj. resolute, strong; manly. —ˈmanfully adv. —ˈmanfulness n.

manganese (ˌmæŋgəˈniːz) n. a brittle greyish-white metallic element: used in making steel and ferromagnetic alloys. Symbol: Mn; atomic no.: 25; atomic wt.: 54.938.

mange (meɪndʒ) n. an infectious disorder mainly affecting domestic animals, characterized by itching and loss of hair: caused by parasitic mites.

mangelwurzel (ˈmæŋgəlˌwɜːzəl) or **mangoldwurzel** (ˈmæŋgəʊldˌwɜːzəl) n. a Eurasian variety of beet, cultivated as a cattle food, having a large yellowish root.

manger (ˈmeɪndʒə) n. a trough or box in a stable, barn, etc., from which horses or cattle feed.

mangle¹ (ˈmæŋgəl) vb. (tr.) **1.** to mutilate, disfigure, or destroy by cutting, crushing, or tearing. **2.** to ruin, spoil, or mar. —ˈmangler n.

mangle² (ˈmæŋgəl) n. **1.** a machine for pressing or drying textiles, clothes, etc., consisting of two heavy rollers between which the cloth is passed. **2.** Chiefly Brit. another word for **wringer.** ~vb. (tr.) **3.** to press or dry in a mangle.

mango (ˈmæŋgəʊ) n., pl. -goes or -gos. **1.** a tropical Asian evergreen tree, cultivated in the tropics for its fruit. **2.** the ovoid edible fruit of this tree, having a smooth rind and sweet juicy flesh.

mangrove (ˈmæŋgrəʊv, ˈmæn-) n. any of various tropical evergreen trees or shrubs, having stiltlike intertwining aerial roots and forming dense thickets along coasts.

mangy or **mangey** (ˈmeɪndʒɪ) adj. -gier, -giest. **1.** having or caused by mange. **2.** scruffy or shabby. —ˈmangily adv. —ˈmanginess n.

manhandle (ˈmænˌhændəl, ˌmænˈhændəl) vb. (tr.) **1.** to handle or push (someone) about roughly. **2.** to move or do by manpower rather than by machinery.

manhole (ˈmænˌhəʊl) n. **1.** Also called: **inspection chamber.** a shaft with a removable cover that leads down to a sewer or drain. **2.** a hole, usually with a detachable cover, through which a man can enter a boiler, tank, etc.

man-hour n. a unit of work in industry, equal to the work done by one man in one hour.

manhunt (ˈmænˌhʌnt) n. an organized search, usually

manager administrator, boss (Inf.), comptroller, conductor, controller, director, executive, gaffer (Inf.), governor, head, organizer, overseer, proprietor, superintendent, supervisor

mandate authority, authorization, bidding, charge, command, commission, decree, directive, edict, fiat, injunction, instruction, order, precept, sanction, warrant

mandatory binding, compulsory, obligatory, required, requisite

manful bold, brave, courageous, daring, determined, gallant, hardy, heroic, indomi-

table, intrepid, manly, noble, powerful, resolute, stalwart, stout, stout-hearted, strong, valiant, vigorous

manfully boldly, bravely, courageously, desperately, determinedly, gallantly, hard, heroically, intrepidly, like a Trojan, like one possessed, like the devil, nobly, powerfully, resolutely, stalwartly, stoutly, strongly, to the best of one's ability, valiantly, vigorously, with might and main

mangle butcher, cripple, crush, cut, deform, destroy, disfigure, distort, hack, lacer-

ate, maim, mar, maul, mutilate, rend, ruin, spoil, tear, wreck

mangy dirty, mean, moth-eaten, scabby (Inf.), scruffy, seedy, shabby, shoddy, squalid

manhandle 1. handle roughly, knock about, maul, paw (Inf.), pull, push, rough up 2. carry, haul, heave, hump (Brit. sl.), lift, manoeuvre, pull, push, shove, tug

manhood bravery, courage, determination, firmness, fortitude, hardihood, manfulness, manliness, masculinity, maturity, mettle, resolution, spirit, strength, valour, virility

by police, for a wanted man or fugitive.

mania ('meɪnɪə) *n.* **1.** a mental disorder characterized by great excitement and occasionally violent behaviour. **2.** obsessional enthusiasm or partiality. —'**manic** *adj.*

-mania *n. combining form.* indicating extreme desire or pleasure of a specified kind or an abnormal excitement aroused by something: *kleptomania; nymphomania; pyromania.* —-**maniac** *n. and adj. combining form.*

maniac ('meɪnɪˌæk) *n.* **1.** *Inf.* a wild disorderly person. **2.** *Inf.* a person who has a great craving or enthusiasm for something. **3.** *Psychiatry, obs.* a person afflicted with mania. —**maniacal** (mə'naɪəkᵊl) *or* '**maniac** *adj.* —**ma'niacally** *adv.*

manic-depressive *Psychiatry.* ~*adj.* **1.** denoting a mental disorder characterized by an alternation between extreme excitement and confidence and deep depression. ~*n.* **2.** a person afflicted with this disorder.

manicure ('mænɪˌkjʊə) *n.* **1.** care of the hands and fingernails, involving shaping the nails, removing cuticles, etc. **2.** Also called: **manicurist.** a person who gives manicures, esp. as a profession. ~*vb.* **3.** to care for (the hands and fingernails) in this way.

manifest ('mænɪˌfɛst) *adj.* **1.** easily noticed or perceived; obvious. ~*vb.* **2.** (*tr.*) to show plainly; reveal or display. **3.** (*tr.*) to prove beyond doubt. **4.** (*intr.*) (of a disembodied spirit) to appear in visible form. ~*n.* **5.** a customs document containing particulars of a ship, its cargo, and its destination. **6.** *Chiefly U.S.* **a.** a list of cargo, passengers, etc., on an aeroplane. **b.** a list of railway trucks or their cargo. —'**mani,festable** *adj.* —,**manifes'tation** *n.* —'**mani,festly** *adv.*

manifesto (ˌmænɪ'fɛstəʊ) *n., pl.* **-toes** *or* **-tos.** a public declaration of intent, policy, aims, etc., as issued by a political party, government, or movement.

manifold ('mænɪˌfəʊld) *adj. Formal.* **1.** of several different kinds; multiple. **2.** having many different forms, features, or elements. ~*n.* **3.** something having many varied parts, forms, or features. **4.** a chamber or pipe with a number of inlets or outlets used to collect or distribute a fluid. In an internal-combustion engine the **inlet manifold** carries the vaporized fuel from the carburettor to the inlet ports and the **exhaust manifold** carries the exhaust gases away. ~*vb.* **5.** (*tr.*) to duplicate (a page, book, etc.). **6.** to make manifold; multiply. —'**mani,foldly** *adv.* —'**mani,foldness** *n.*

manikin, manakin, *or* **mannikin** ('mænɪkɪn) *n.* **1.** a little man; dwarf or child. **2.** an anatomical model of the body or a part of the body, esp. for use in medical or art instruction. **3.** variants of **mannequin.**

Manila hemp *or* **Manilla hemp** *n.* a fibre obtained from the plant abaca, used for rope, paper, etc.

Manila paper *or* **Manilla paper** *n.* a strong usually brown paper made from Manila hemp or similar fibres.

man in the street *n.* the typical or ordinary person.

manipulate (mə'nɪpjʊˌleɪt) *vb.* **1.** (*tr.*) to handle or use, esp. with some skill. **2.** to control or influence (something) cleverly or skilfully. **3.** to falsify (accounts, etc.) for one's own advantage. **4.** (in physiotherapy) to examine or treat manually, as in loosening a joint. —**manipu-**

lability (məˌnɪpjʊlə'bɪlɪtɪ) *n.* —**ma'nipu,latable** *or* **ma'nipulable** *adj.* —**ma,nipu'lation** *n.* —**ma'nipulative** *adj.* —**ma'nipu,lator** *n.* —**ma'nipulatory** *adj.*

Manitoban (ˌmænɪ'təʊbən) *adj.* **1.** of or denoting Manitoba, a province of W Canada. ~*n.* **2.** a native or inhabitant of Manitoba.

mankind (ˌmæn'kaɪnd) *n.* **1.** human beings collectively; humanity. **2.** men collectively, as opposed to womankind.

manly ('mænlɪ) *adj.* **-lier, -liest. 1.** possessing qualities, such as vigour or courage, generally regarded as appropriate to or typical of a man; masculine. **2.** characteristic of or befitting a man. —'**manliness** *n.*

man-made *adj.* made by man; artificial.

manna ('mænə) *n.* **1.** *Old Testament.* the miraculous food which sustained the Israelites in the wilderness (Exodus 16:14–36). **2.** any spiritual or divine nourishment. **3.** a sweet substance obtained from various plants, esp. from the **manna** or **flowering ash** of S Europe, used as a mild laxative.

manned (mænd) *adj.* **1.** supplied or equipped with men, esp. soldiers. **2.** (of spacecraft, etc.) having a human crew.

mannequin ('mænɪkɪn) *n.* **1.** a woman who wears the clothes displayed at a fashion show; model. **2.** a life-size dummy of the human body used to fit or display clothes.

manner ('mænə) *n.* **1.** a way of doing or being. **2.** a person's bearing and behaviour. **3.** the style or customary way of doing or accomplishing something. **4.** type or kind. **5.** mannered style, as in art; mannerism. **6. by all manner of means.** certainly; of course. **7. by no manner of means.** under no circumstances. **8. in a manner of speaking.** in a way; so to speak. **9. to the manner born.** naturally fitted to a specified role or activity.

mannered ('mænəd) *adj.* **1.** having idiosyncrasies or mannerisms; affected. **2.** (*in combination*) having manners as specified: *ill-mannered.*

mannerism ('mænəˌrɪzəm) *n.* **1.** a distinctive and individual gesture or trait. **2.** (*often cap.*) a principally Italian movement in art and architecture between the High Renaissance and Baroque periods (1520–1600), using distortion and exaggeration of human proportions, perspective, etc. **3.** adherence to a distinctive or affected manner, esp. in art or literature. —'**mannerist** *n., adj.* —,**manner'istic** *adj.* —,**manner'istically** *adv.*

mannerless ('mænəlɪs) *adj.* having bad manners; boorish. —'**mannerlessness** *n.*

mannerly ('mænəlɪ) *adj.* **1.** well-mannered; polite. ~*adv.* **2.** *Now rare.* with good manners; politely. —'**mannerliness** *n.*

manners ('mænəz) *pl. n.* **1.** social conduct. **2.** a socially acceptable way of behaving.

mannish ('mænɪʃ) *adj.* **1.** (of a woman) displaying qualities regarded as typical of a man. **2.** of or resembling a man. —'**mannishly** *adv.* —'**mannishness** *n.*

manoeuvre *or U.S.* **maneuver** (mə'nu:və) *n.* **1.** a contrived, complicated, and possibly deceptive plan or action. **2.** a movement or action requiring dexterity and

---

THESAURUS

mania **1.** aberration, craziness, delirium, dementia, derangement, disorder, frenzy, insanity, lunacy, madness **2.** cacoethes, craving, craze, desire, enthusiasm, fad (*Inf.*), fetish, fixation, obsession, partiality, passion, preoccupation, rage, thing (*Inf.*)

maniac **1.** loony (*Sl.*), lunatic, madman, madwoman, nutcase (*Sl.*), nutter (*Brit. sl.*), psycho (*Sl.*), psychopath **2.** enthusiast, fan, fanatic, fiend (*Inf.*), freak (*Sl.*)

manifest 1. *adj.* apparent, clear, conspicuous, distinct, evident, glaring, noticeable, obvious, open, palpable, patent, plain, unmistakable, visible **2.** *v.* declare, demonstrate, display, establish, evince, exhibit, expose, express, make plain, prove, reveal, set forth, show

manifestation appearance, demonstration, disclosure, display, exhibition, exposure, expression, indication, instance, mark, materialization, revelation, show, sign, symptom, token

manifold abundant, assorted, copious, di-

verse, diversified, many, multifarious, multifold, multiple, multiplied, multitudinous, numerous, varied, various

manipulate 1. employ, handle, operate, ply, use, wield, work **2.** conduct, control, direct, engineer, guide, influence, manoeuvre, negotiate, steer

mankind Homo sapiens, humanity, humankind, human race, man, people

manliness boldness, bravery, courage, fearlessness, firmness, hardihood, heroism, independence, intrepidity, manfulness, manhood, masculinity, mettle, resolution, stoutheartedness, valour, vigour, virility

manly bold, brave, courageous, daring, dauntless, fearless, gallant, hardy, heroic, male, manful, masculine, muscular, noble, powerful, red-blooded (*Inf.*), resolute, robust, stout-hearted, strapping, strong, valiant, valorous, vigorous, virile, well-built

man-made artificial, ersatz, manufactured, plastic (*Sl.*), synthetic

manner 1. air, appearance, aspect, bear-

ing, behaviour, comportment, conduct, demeanour, deportment, look, mien (*Literary*), presence, tone **2.** approach, custom, fashion, form, genre, habit, line, means, method, mode, practice, procedure, process, routine, style, tack, tenor, usage, way, wont **3.** brand, breed, category, form, kind, nature, sort, type, variety

mannered affected, artificial, posed, pretentious, pseudo (*Inf.*), put-on, stilted

mannerism characteristic, foible, habit, idiosyncrasy, peculiarity, quirk, trait, trick

mannerly civil, civilized, courteous, decorous, genteel, gentlemanly, gracious, ladylike, polished, polite, refined, respectful, well-behaved, well-bred, well-mannered

manners 1. bearing, behaviour, breeding, carriage, comportment, conduct, demeanour, deportment **2.** ceremony, courtesy, decorum, etiquette, formalities, good form, polish, politeness, politesse, proprieties, protocol, refinement, social graces, the done thing

skill. **3. a.** a tactic or movement of a military or naval unit. **b.** (*pl.*) tactical exercises, usually on a large scale. **4.** a planned movement of an aircraft in flight. ~*vb.* **5.** (*tr.*) to contrive or accomplish with skill or cunning. **6.** (*intr.*) to manipulate situations, etc., in order to gain some end. **7.** (*intr.*) to perform a manoeuvre or manoeuvres. **8.** to move or deploy or be moved or deployed, as military units, etc. —**ma'noeuvrable** *or U.S.* **ma'neuverable** *adj.* —**ma,noeuvra'bility** *or U.S.* **ma,neuvera'bility** *n.* —**ma'noeuvrer** *or U.S.* **ma'neuverer** *n.*

man-of-war *or* **man o' war** *n., pl.* **men-of-war, men o' war.** **1.** a warship. **2.** See **Portuguese man-of-war.**

manor ('mænə) *n.* **1.** (in medieval Europe) the manor house of a lord and the lands attached to it. **2.** a manor house. **3.** a landed estate. **4.** *Brit. inf.* a police district. —**manorial** (mə'nɔːrɪəl) *adj.*

manor house *or* **seat** *n.* (esp. formerly) the house of the lord of a manor.

manpower ('mæn,pauə) *n.* **1.** power supplied by men. **2.** a unit of power based on the rate at which a man can work; approximately 75 watts. **3.** the number of people needed or available for a job.

manqué *French.* ('mɒŋkeɪ) *adj.* (*postpositive*) unfulfilled; potential; would-be: *the manager is an actor manqué.*

mansard ('mænsɑːd, -səd) *n.* Also called: **mansard roof.** a roof having two slopes on both sides and both ends, the lower slopes being steeper than the upper.

manse (mæns) *n.* (in certain religious denominations) the house provided for a minister.

manservant ('mæn,sɜːvənt) *n., pl.* **menservants.** a male servant, esp. a valet.

mansion ('mænʃən) *n.* **1.** Also called: **mansion house.** a large and imposing house. **2.** a less common word for **manor house.** **3.** (*pl.*) a block of flats.

Mansion House *n.* **the.** the residence of the Lord Mayor of London.

manslaughter ('mæn,slɔːtə) *n.* **1.** *Law.* the unlawful killing of one human being by another without malice aforethought. Cf. **murder.** **2.** (loosely) the killing of a human being.

mantel *or* **mantle** ('mæntəl) *n.* **1.** a wooden or stone frame around the opening of a fireplace, together with its decorative facing. **2.** Also called: **mantel shelf.** a shelf above this frame.

mantelpiece ('mæntəl,piːs) *n.* **1.** Also called: **mantel shelf, chimneypiece.** a shelf above a fireplace often forming part of the mantel. **2.** another word for **mantel** (sense 1).

mantic ('mæntɪk) *adj.* **1.** of or relating to divination and prophecy. **2.** having divining or prophetic powers. —**'mantically** *adv.*

-mantic *adj. combining form.* forming adjectives from nouns ending in **-mancy.**

mantilla (mæn'tɪlə) *n.* a woman's lace or silk scarf covering the shoulders and head, worn esp. in Spain.

mantis ('mæntɪs) *n., pl.* **-tises** *or* **-tes** (-tiːz). any carnivorous typically green insect of warm and tropical regions, having a long body and large eyes and resting with the first pair of legs raised as if in prayer. Also called: **praying mantis.**

mantissa (mæn'tɪsə) *n.* the fractional part of a common logarithm representing the digits of the associated number but not its magnitude: *the mantissa of 2.4771 is .4771.*

mantle ('mæntəl) *n.* **1.** *Arch.* a loose wrap or cloak. **2.** anything that covers completely or envelops. **3.** a small

dome-shaped or cylindrical mesh, used to increase illumination in a gas or oil lamp by becoming incandescent. **4.** *Zool.* a protective layer of epidermis in molluscs and brachiopods that secretes a substance forming the shell. **5.** *Ornithol.* the feathers of the folded wings and back, esp. when of a different colour from the remaining feathers. **6.** *Geol.* the part of the earth between the crust and the core. **7.** a less common spelling of **mantel.** ~*vb.* **8.** (*tr.*) to envelop or supply with a mantle. **9.** to spread over or become spread over. **10.** (*intr.*) to blush; flush.

mantra ('mæntrə, 'mʌn-) *n.* **1.** *Hinduism.* any of those parts of the Vedic literature which consist of the metrical psalms of praise. **2.** *Hinduism, Buddhism.* any sacred word or syllable used as an object of concentration.

manual ('mænjʊəl) *adj.* **1.** of or relating to a hand or hands. **2.** operated or done by hand. **3.** physical, as opposed to mental or mechanical: *manual labour.* **4.** by human labour rather than automatic or computer-aided means. ~*n.* **5.** a book, esp. of instructions or information. **6.** *Music.* one of the keyboards played by hand on an organ. **7.** *Mil.* the prescribed drill with small arms. —**'manually** *adv.*

manufactory (,mænjʊ'fæktərɪ, -trɪ) *n., pl.* **-ries.** an obsolete word for **factory.**

manufacture (,mænjʊ'fæktʃə) *vb.* **1.** to process or make (a product) from a raw material, esp. as a large-scale operation using machinery. **2.** (*tr.*) to invent or concoct. ~*n.* **3.** the production of goods, esp. by industrial processes. **4.** a manufactured product. **5.** the creation or production of anything. —**,manu'facturer** *n.*

manumit (,mænjʊ'mɪt) *vb.* **-mitting, -mitted.** (*tr.*) to free from slavery, servitude, etc.; emancipate. —**manumission** (,mænjʊ'mɪʃən) *n.*

manure (mə'njʊə) *n.* **1.** animal excreta, usually with straw, etc., used to fertilize land. **2.** *Chiefly Brit.* any material, esp. chemical fertilizer, used to fertilize land. ~*vb.* **3.** (*tr.*) to spread manure upon (fields or soil). —**ma'nurer** *n.*

manuscript ('mænjʊ,skrɪpt) *n.* **1.** a book or other document written by hand. **2.** the original handwritten or typed version of a book, article, etc., as submitted by an author for publication. **3.** handwriting, as opposed to printing.

Manx (mæŋks) *adj.* **1.** of or relating to the Isle of Man (an island in the British Isles), its inhabitants, their former language, or their dialect of English. ~*n.* **2.** a former language of the Isle of Man, closely related to Scottish Gaelic.

Manx cat *n.* a short-haired tailless variety of cat, believed to originate on the Isle of Man.

many ('mɛnɪ) *determiner.* **1.** (sometimes preceded by *a great* or *a good*) **a.** a large number of: *many times.* **b.** (*as pronoun; functioning as pl.*): *many are seated already.* **2.** (foll. by *a, an,* or *another,* and a sing. noun) each of a considerable number of: *many a man.* **3.** (preceded by *as, too, that,* etc.) **a.** a great number of: *as many apples as you like.* **b.** (*as pronoun; functioning as pl.*): *I have as many as you.* ~*n.* **4. the many.** the majority of mankind, esp. the common people.

Maoism ('mauɪzəm) *n.* Marxism-Leninism as interpreted by Mao Tse-tung (1893–1976), Chinese statesman: distinguished by its theory of guerrilla warfare and its emphasis on the revolutionary potential of the peasantry. —**'Maoist** *n., adj.*

Maori ('maurɪ, 'mɑːrɪ) *n.* **1.** (*pl.* **-ris** *or* **-ri**) a member of the people of Polynesian origin living in New Zealand since before the arrival of European settlers. **2.** the lan-

---

THESAURUS

manoeuvre *n.* **1.** action, artifice, dodge, intrigue, machination, move, movement, plan, plot, ploy, ruse, scheme, stratagem, subterfuge, tactic, trick **2.** deployment, evolution, exercise, movement, operation ~*v.* **3.** contrive, devise, engineer, intrigue, machinate, manage, manipulate, plan, plot, pull strings, scheme, wangle (*Inf.*) **4.** deploy, exercise, move **5.** direct, drive, guide, handle, navigate, negotiate, pilot, steer

mansion abode, dwelling, habitation, hall, manor, residence, seat, villa

mantle *n.* **1.** *Archaic* cape, cloak, hood, shawl, wrap **2.** blanket, canopy, cloud, cover, covering, curtain, envelope, pall, screen, shroud, veil ~*v.* **3.** blanket, cloak, cloud, cov-

er, disguise, envelop, hide, mask, overspread, screen, shroud, veil, wrap

manual **1.** *adj.* done by hand, hand-operated, human, physical **2.** *n.* bible, enchiridion (*Rare*), guide, guidebook, handbook, instructions, workbook

manufacture *v.* **1.** assemble, build, compose, construct, create, fabricate, forge, form, make, mass-produce, mould, process, produce, put together, shape, turn out **2.** concoct, cook up (*Inf.*), devise, fabricate, hatch, invent, make up, think up, trump up ~*n.* **3.** assembly, construction, creation, fabrication, making, mass-production, produce, production

manufacturer builder, constructor,

creator, fabricator, factory-owner, industrialist, maker, producer

manure compost, droppings, dung, muck, ordure

many *adj.* **1.** abundant, copious, countless, divers (*Archaic*), frequent, innumerable, manifold, multifarious, multifold, multitudinous, myriad, numerous, profuse, sundry, umpteen (*Inf.*), varied, various ~*n.* **2.** a horde, a lot, a mass, a multitude, a thousand and one, heaps (*Inf.*), large numbers, lots (*Inf.*), piles (*Inf.*), plenty, scores, tons (*Inf.*), umpteen (*Inf.*) **3. the many** crowd, hoi polloi, majority, masses, multitude, people, rank and file

map 611 **marguerite**

guage of this people, belonging to the Malayo-Polynesian family. ~*adj.* **3.** of or relating to this people or their language. —'**Maori,land** *n.*

map (mæp) *n.* **1.** a diagrammatic representation of the earth's surface or part of it, showing the geographical distributions, positions, etc., of features such as roads, towns, relief, rainfall, etc. **2.** a diagrammatic representation of the stars or of the surface of a celestial body. **3.** a maplike drawing of anything. **4.** *Maths.* another name for **function** (sense 4b.). **5.** a slang word for **face** (sense 1). **6. put on the map.** to make (a town, company, etc.) well-known. ~*vb.* **mapping, mapped.** (*tr.*) **7.** to make a map of. **8.** *Maths.* to represent or transform (a function, figure, set, etc.).

maple ('meipəl) *n.* **1.** any tree or shrub of a N temperate genus, having winged seeds borne in pairs and lobed leaves. **2.** the hard wood of any of these trees, used for furniture and flooring. **3.** the flavour of the sap of the sugar maple. ~See also **sugar maple.**

maple leaf *n.* the leaf of the maple tree, the national emblem of Canada.

maple syrup *n. Chiefly U.S.* a very sweet syrup made from the sap of the sugar maple.

map out *vb.* (*tr., adv.*) to plan or design.

mapping ('mæpɪŋ) *n. Maths.* another name for **function** (sense 4b.)

maquis (mɑː'kiː) *n., pl.* **-quis** (-'kiː). **1.** shrubby, mostly evergreen, vegetation found in coastal regions of the Mediterranean. **2.** (*often cap.*) **a.** the French underground movement that fought against the German occupying forces in World War II. **b.** a member of this movement.

mar (mɑː) *vb.* **marring, marred.** (*tr.*) to cause harm to; spoil or impair. —'**marrer** *n.*

Mar. *abbrev. for* March.

marabou ('mærə,buː) *n.* **1.** a large black-and-white African carrion-eating stork. **2.** a down feather of this bird, used to trim garments.

maraca (mə'rækə) *n.* a percussion instrument, usually one of a pair, consisting of a gourd or plastic shell filled with dried seeds, etc.

maraschino (,mærə'skiːnəʊ) *n.* a liqueur made from marasca cherries, having a taste like bitter almonds.

marathon ('mærəθən) *n.* **1.** a race on foot of 26 miles 385 yards (42.195 kilometres). **2. a.** any long or arduous task, etc. **b.** (*as modifier*): *a marathon effort.*

maraud (mə'rɔːd) *vb.* to wander or raid in search of plunder. —**ma'rauder** *n.*

marble ('mɑːbəl) *n.* **1. a.** a hard crystalline metamorphic rock resulting from the recrystallization of a limestone. **b.** (*as modifier*): *a marble bust.* **2.** a block or work of art of marble. **3.** a small round glass or stone ball used in playing marbles. ~*vb.* **4.** (*tr.*) to mottle with variegated streaks in imitation of marble. —'**marbled** *adj.*

marbles ('mɑːbəlz) *n.* **1.** (*functioning as sing.*) a game in which marbles are rolled at one another, similar to bowls. **2.** *Inf.* wits: *to lose one's marbles.*

marbling ('mɑːblɪŋ) *n.* **1.** a mottled effect or pattern resembling marble. **2.** such an effect obtained by transferring floating colours from a gum solution. **3.** the streaks of fat in lean meat.

marc (mɑːk) *n.* **1.** the remains of grapes or other fruit that have been pressed for wine-making. **2.** a brandy distilled from these.

marcasite ('mɑːkə,saɪt) *n.* **1.** a metallic pale yellow mineral consisting of iron pyrites in crystalline form used in jewellery. **2.** a cut and polished form of steel or any white metal used for making jewellery.

march[1] (mɑːtʃ) *vb.* **1.** (*intr.*) to walk or proceed with stately or regular steps, usually in a procession or mili-

tary formation. **2.** (*tr.*) to make (a person or group) proceed. **3.** (*tr.*) to traverse or cover by marching. ~*n.* **4.** the act or an instance of marching. **5.** a regular stride. **6.** a long or exhausting walk. **7.** advance; progression (of troops, etc.). **8.** a distance or route covered by marching. **9.** a piece of music, as for a march. **10. steal a march on.** to gain an advantage over, esp. by a secret enterprise. —'**marcher** *n.*

march[2] (mɑːtʃ) *n.* **1.** a frontier, border, or boundary or the land lying along it, often of disputed ownership. ~*vb.* **2.** (*intr.;* often foll. by *upon* or *with*) to share a common border (with).

March (mɑːtʃ) *n.* the third month of the year, consisting of 31 days.

March hare *n.* a hare during its breeding season in March, noted for its wild and excitable behaviour (esp. in **mad as a March hare**).

marching orders *pl. n.* **1.** military orders, esp. to infantry, giving instructions about a march, its destination, etc. **2.** *Inf.* any dismissal, esp. notice of dismissal from employment.

marchioness ('mɑːʃənɪs, ,mɑːʃə'nɛs) *n.* **1.** the wife or widow of a marquis. **2.** a woman who holds the rank of marquis.

marchpane ('mɑːtʃ,peɪn) *n.* an archaic word for **marzipan.**

Mardi Gras ('mɑːdɪ 'grɑː) *n.* the festival of Shrove Tuesday, celebrated in some cities with great revelry.

mare[1] (mɛə) *n.* the adult female of a horse or zebra.

mare[2] ('mɑːreɪ, -rɪ) *n., pl.* **maria** ('mɑːrɪə). **1.** (*cap. when part of a name*) any of a large number of huge dry plains on the surface of the moon, visible as dark markings and once thought to be seas. **2.** a similar area on the surface of Mars.

mare's-nest *n.* **1.** a discovery imagined to be important but proving worthless. **2.** a disordered situation.

margarine (,mɑːdʒə'riːn, ,mɑː-g-) *or* **margarin** ('mɑːdʒərɪn, 'mɑː-g-, ,mɑːdʒə'riːn, ,mɑː-g-) *n.* a substitute for butter, prepared from vegetable and animal fats with added small amounts of milk, salt, vitamins, colouring matter, etc.

marge (mɑːdʒ) *n. Brit. inf.* short for **margarine.**

margin ('mɑːdʒɪn) *n.* **1.** an edge or rim, and the area immediately adjacent to it; border. **2.** the blank space surrounding the text on a page. **3.** a vertical line on a page delineating this space. **4.** an additional amount or one beyond the minimum necessary: *a margin of error.* **5.** *Austral.* a payment made in addition to a basic wage, esp. for special skill or responsibility. **6.** a bound or limit. **7.** the amount by which one thing differs from another. **8.** *Commerce.* the profit on a transaction. **9.** *Econ.* the minimum return below which an enterprise becomes unprofitable. **10.** *Finance.* collateral deposited by a client with a broker as security. ~Also (*archaic*): **margent** ('mɑːdʒənt). ~*vb.* (*tr.*) **11.** to provide with a margin; border. **12.** *Finance.* to deposit a margin upon.

marginal ('mɑːdʒɪnəl) *adj.* **1.** of, in, on, or constituting a margin. **2.** close to a limit, esp. a lower limit: *marginal legal ability.* **3.** *Econ.* relating to goods or services produced and sold at the margin of profitability: *marginal cost.* **4.** *Politics, chiefly Brit.* of or designating a constituency in which elections tend to be won by small margins: *a marginal seat.* **5.** designating agricultural land on the margin of cultivated zones. —**marginality** (,mɑːdʒɪ'nælɪtɪ) *n.* —'**marginally** *adv.*

margrave ('mɑː,greɪv) *n.* a German nobleman ranking above a count. Margraves were originally counts appointed to govern frontier provinces, but all eventually became princes of the Holy Roman Empire. —**margravate** ('mɑːgrəvɪt) *n.*

marguerite (,mɑːgə'riːt) *n.* **1.** a cultivated garden plant whose flower heads have white or pale yellow rays

---

THESAURUS

mar blemish, blight, blot, damage, deface, detract from, disfigure, harm, hurt, impair, injure, maim, mangle, mutilate, ruin, scar, spoil, stain, sully, taint, tarnish, vitiate

maraud despoil, forage, foray, harry, loot, pillage, plunder, raid, ransack, ravage, reive (*Dialect*), sack

marauder bandit, brigand, buccaneer, cateran (*Scot.*), corsair, freebooter, mosstrooper, outlaw, pillager, pirate, plunderer, raider, ravager, reiver (*Dialect*), robber

march *v.* **1.** file, footslog, pace, parade, stalk, stride, strut, tramp, tread, walk ~*n.* **2.** hike, routemarch, tramp, trek, walk **3.** demo (*Inf.*), demonstration, parade, procession **4.** gait, pace, step, stride **5.** advance, development, evolution, progress, progression **6. on the march** advancing, afoot, astir, en route, marching, on one's way, on the way, proceeding, progressing, under way

marches borderland, borders, boundaries, confines, frontiers, limits, marchlands

margin **1.** border, bound, boundary, brim, brink, confine, edge, limit, perimeter, periphery, rim, side, verge **2.** allowance, compass, elbowroom, extra, latitude, leeway, play, room, scope, space, surplus

marginal **1.** bordering, borderline, on the edge, peripheral **2.** insignificant, low, minimal, minor, negligible, slight, small

around a yellow disc. **2.** any of various related plants with daisy-like flowers.

marigold ('mærɪˌgəʊld) n. **1.** any of various tropical American plants cultivated for their yellow or orange flower heads and strongly scented foliage. **2.** any of various similar or related plants, such as the marsh marigold.

marijuana (ˌmærɪjʊˈɑːnə) or **marihuana** (ˌmærɪˈhwɑːnə) n. **1.** the dried leaves and flowers of the hemp plant, used as a narcotic, esp. in cigarettes. See also **cannabis. 2.** U.S. another name for **hemp** (the plant).

marimba (məˈrɪmbə) n. a Latin American percussion instrument consisting of a set of hardwood plates placed over tuned metal resonators, played with soft-head hammers.

marina (məˈriːnə) n. an elaborate docking facility for yachts and other pleasure boats.

marinade n. (ˌmærɪˈneɪd). **1.** a spiced liquid mixture of oil, wine, vinegar, etc., in which meat or fish is soaked before cooking. **2.** meat or fish soaked in this. ~vb. ('mærɪˌneɪd). **3.** a variant of **marinate.**

marinate ('mærɪˌneɪt) vb. to soak in marinade. —ˌmariˈnation n.

marine (məˈriːn) adj. (usually prenominal) **1.** of, found in, or relating to the sea. **2.** of or relating to shipping, navigation, etc. **3.** of or relating to a body of seagoing troops or a government department concerned with maritime affairs. **4.** used or adapted for use at sea. ~n. **5.** shipping and navigation in general. **6.** (cap. when part of a name) **a.** a member of a marine corps or similar body. **b.** the branch of the army connected with the sea. **7.** a picture of a ship, seascape, etc. **8. tell it to the marines.** Inf. an expression of disbelief.

mariner ('mærɪnə) n. a formal or literary word for **seaman.**

marionette (ˌmærɪəˈnɛt) n. a puppet or doll whose jointed limbs are moved by strings.

marital ('mærɪtəl) adj. **1.** of or relating to marriage. **2.** of or relating to a husband. —ˈmaritally adv.

maritime ('mærɪˌtaɪm) adj. **1.** of or relating to navigation, shipping, etc. **2.** of, relating to, near, or living near the sea. **3.** (of a climate) having small temperature differences between summer and winter.

Maritime Provinces or **Maritimes** pl. n. the. certain of the Canadian provinces with coasts facing the Gulf of St. Lawrence or the Atlantic: New Brunswick, Nova Scotia, Prince Edward Island, and sometimes Newfoundland.

Maritimer ('mærɪˌtaɪmə) n. a native or inhabitant of the Maritime Provinces of Canada.

marjoram ('mɑːdʒərəm) n. **1.** Also called: **sweet marjoram.** an aromatic Mediterranean plant with sweet-scented leaves, used for seasoning food and in salads. **2.** Also called: **wild marjoram, pot marjoram, origan.** a similar and related European plant. See also **oregano.**

mark¹ (mɑːk) n. **1.** a visible impression, stain, etc., on a surface, such as a spot or scratch. **2** a sign, symbol, or other indication that distinguishes something. **3.** a cross or other symbol made instead of a signature. **4.** a written or printed sign or symbol, as for punctuation. **5.** a letter, number, or percentage used to grade academic work. **6.** a thing that indicates position or directs; mark-

er. **7.** a desired or recognized standard: up to the mark. **8.** an indication of some quality, feature, or prowess. **9.** quality or importance: a person of little mark. **10.** a target or goal. **11.** impression or influence. **12.** Sl. a suitable victim, esp. for swindling. **13.** (often cap.) (in trade names) a model, brand, or type. **14.** Naut. one of the intervals distinctively marked on a sounding lead. **15.** Rugby. an impression on the ground made with the heel by a player on catching a forward kick, throw, or knock by an opponent, which entitles him to a free kick. **16.** Australian Rules football. **a.** a catch of the ball from a kick of at least 10 yards, after which a free kick is taken. **b.** the spot where this occurs. **17. the mark.** Boxing. the middle of the stomach. **18.** (in medieval England and Germany) a piece of land held in common by the free men of a community. **19. make one's mark.** to succeed or achieve recognition. **20. on your mark** or **marks.** a command given to runners in a race to prepare themselves at the starting line. ~vb. **21.** to make or receive (a visible impression, trace, or stain) on (a surface). **22.** (tr.) to characterize or distinguish. **23.** (often foll. by off or out) to set boundaries or limits (on). **24.** (tr.) to select, designate, or doom by or as if by a mark: to mark someone as a criminal. **25.** (tr.) to put identifying or designating labels, stamps, etc., on, esp. to indicate price. **26.** (tr.) to pay heed or attention to: mark my words. **27.** to observe; notice. **28.** to grade or evaluate (scholastic work). **29.** Brit. football, etc. to stay close to (an opponent) to hamper his play. **30.** to keep (score) in some games. **31. mark time. a.** to move the feet alternately as in marching but without advancing. **b.** to act in a mechanical and routine way. **c.** to halt progress temporarily. ~See also **markdown, mark-up.** —ˈmarker n.

mark² (mɑːk) n. **1.** See **Deutsche Mark. 2.** a former monetary unit and coin in England and Scotland worth two thirds of a pound sterling. **3.** a silver coin of Germany until 1924.

markdown ('mɑːkˌdaʊn) n. **1.** a price reduction. ~vb. **mark down. 2.** (tr., adv.) to reduce in price.

marked (mɑːkt) adj. **1.** obvious, evident, or noticeable. **2.** singled out, esp. as the target of attack: a marked man. **3.** Linguistics. distinguished by a specific feature, as in phonology. For example, of the two phonemes /t/ and /d/, the /d/ is marked because it exhibits the feature of voice. —**markedly** ('mɑːkɪdlɪ) adv. —ˈmarkedness n.

market ('mɑːkɪt) n. **1. a.** an event or occasion, usually held at regular intervals, at which people meet to buy and sell merchandise. **b.** (as modifier): market day. **2.** a place at which a market is held. **3.** a shop that sells a particular merchandise: an antique market. **4. the market.** business or trade in a commodity as specified: the sugar market. **5.** the trading or selling opportunities provided by a particular group of people: the foreign market. **6.** demand for a particular product or commodity. **7.** See **stock market. 8.** See **market price, market value. 9. be in the market for.** to wish to buy or acquire. **10. on the market.** available for purchase. **11. seller's (or buyer's) market.** a market characterized by excess demand (or supply) and thus favourable to sellers (or buyers). ~vb. **12.** to offer or produce for sale. **13.** (intr.) to buy or deal in a market. —ˈmarketable adj. —ˈmarketer n.

market garden n. Chiefly Brit. an establishment

THESAURUS

marijuana bhang, cannabis, charas, dope (Sl.), ganja, grass (Sl.), hash (Sl.), hashish, hemp, kif, leaf (Sl.), mary jane (U.S. sl.), pot (Sl.), smoke (Inf.), stuff (Sl.), tea (U.S. sl.), weed (Sl.)

marine maritime, nautical, naval, oceangoing, oceanic, pelagic, saltwater, sea, seafaring, seagoing, thalassic

mariner bluejacket, gob (Inf.), hand, Jack Tar, matelot (Brit. sl.), navigator, sailor, salt, sea dog, seafarer, seafaring man, seaman, tar

marital conjugal, connubial, married, matrimonial, nuptial, spousal, wedded

maritime 1. marine, nautical, naval, oceanic, sea, seafaring 2. coastal, littoral, seaside

mark n. 1. blemish, blot, blotch, bruise, dent, impression, line, nick, pock, scar, scratch, smudge, splotch, spot, stain, streak

2. badge, blaze, brand, characteristic, device, earmark, emblem, evidence, feature, hallmark, impression, incision, index, indication, label, note, print, proof, seal, sign, stamp, symbol, symptom, token 3. criterion, level, measure, norm, standard, yardstick 4. aim, end, goal, object, objective, purpose, target 5. consequence, dignity, distinction, eminence, fame, importance, influence, notability, note, notice, prestige, quality, regard, standing 6. footmark, footprint, sign, trace, track, trail, vestige 7. **make one's mark** achieve recognition, be a success, find a place in the sun, get on in the world, make a success of oneself, make good, make it (Inf.), make something of oneself, prosper, succeed ~v. 8. blemish, blot, blotch, brand, bruise, dent, impress, imprint, nick, scar, scratch, smudge, splotch, stain, streak 9. brand, characterize, identify, label, stamp 10. betoken, denote, distinguish, evince, exemplify, illustrate, show 11. attend,

hearken (Archaic), mind, note, notice, observe, pay attention, pay heed, regard, remark, watch 12. appraise, assess, correct, evaluate, grade

marked apparent, clear, considerable, conspicuous, decided, distinct, evident, manifest, notable, noted, noticeable, obvious, outstanding, patent, prominent, pronounced, remarkable, salient, signal, striking

markedly clearly, considerably, conspicuously, decidedly, distinctly, evidently, greatly, manifestly, notably, noticeably, obviously, outstandingly, patently, remarkably, signally, strikingly, to a great extent

market 1. n. bazaar, fair, mart 2. v. offer for sale, retail, sell, vend

marketable in demand, merchantable, salable, sought after, vendible, wanted

where fruit and vegetables are grown for sale. —**market gardener** n. —**market gardening** n.

marketing ('mɑ:kɪtɪŋ) n. the business of selling goods, including advertising, packaging, etc.

marketplace ('mɑ:kɪt,pleɪs) n. **1.** a place where a public market is held. **2.** any centre where ideas, opinions, etc., are exchanged. **3.** the commercial world of buying and selling.

market price n. the prevailing price, as determined by supply and demand, at which goods, services, etc., may be bought or sold.

market research n. the collection and analysis of data relating to the demand for a product, often undertaken before marketing it.

market town n. Chiefly Brit. a town that holds a market, esp. an agricultural centre.

market value n. the amount obtainable on the open market for the sale of property, financial assets, or goods and services.

marking ('mɑ:kɪŋ) n. **1.** a mark or series of marks. **2.** the arrangement of colours on an animal, plant, etc.

marksman ('mɑ:ksmən) n., pl. **-men. 1.** a person skilled in shooting. **2.** a serviceman selected for his skill in shooting. —**marksman,ship** n.

mark-up n. **1.** an amount added to the cost of a commodity to provide the seller with a profit. **2. a.** an increase in the price of a commodity. **b.** the amount of this. ~vb. **mark up.** (tr., adv.) **3.** to add a percentage for profit to the cost of (a commodity). **4.** to increase the price of.

marl (mɑ:l) n. **1.** a fine-grained sedimentary rock consisting of clay minerals, calcium carbonate, and silt: used as a fertilizer. ~vb. **2.** (tr.) to fertilize (land) with marl. —**'marly** adj.

marlinespike, marlinspike ('mɑ:lɪn,spaɪk), or **marlingspike** ('mɑ:lɪŋ,spaɪk) n. Naut. a pointed metal tool used in separating strands of rope, etc.

marmalade ('mɑ:mə,leɪd) n. a preserve made by boiling the pulp and rind of citrus fruits, esp. oranges, with sugar.

marmoreal (mɑ:'mɔ:rɪəl) or **marmorean** adj. of, relating to, or resembling marble.

marmoset ('mɑ:mə,zɛt) n. **1.** any of various small South American monkeys, having long hairy tails. **2. pygmy marmoset.** a related form: the smallest monkey, inhabiting tropical forests of the Amazon.

marmot ('mɑ:mət) n. **1.** any of various burrowing rodents of Europe, Asia, and North America. They are heavily built and have coarse fur. **2. prairie marmot.** another name for **prairie dog.**

maroon[1] (mə'ru:n) vb. (tr.) **1.** to abandon ashore, esp. on an island. **2.** to isolate without resources. ~n. **3.** a descendant of a group of runaway slaves living in the remoter areas of the West Indies or Guyana.

maroon[2] (mə'ru:n) n. **1. a.** a dark red to purplish-red colour. **b.** (as adj.): a maroon carpet. **2.** an exploding firework, esp. one used as a warning signal.

marque (mɑ:k) n. a brand of product, esp. of a car.

marquee (mɑ:'ki:) n. **1.** a large tent used for entertainment, etc. **2.** Also called: **marquise.** Chiefly U.S. a canopy over the entrance to a theatre, hotel, etc.

marquess ('mɑ:kwɪs) n. **1.** (in the British Isles) a nobleman ranking between a duke and an earl. **2.** See **marquis.**

marquetry or **marqueterie** ('mɑ:kɪtrɪ) n., pl. **-quetries** or **-queteries.** a pattern of inlaid veneers of wood, brass, ivory, etc., used chiefly as ornamentation in furniture.

marquis ('mɑ:kwɪs, mɑ:'ki:) n., pl. **-quises** or **-quis.** (in various countries) a nobleman ranking above a count, corresponding to a British marquess. The title of mar-

quis is often used in place of that of marquess.

marquise (mɑ:'ki:z) n. **1.** (in various countries) another word for **marchioness. 2. a.** a gemstone, esp. a diamond, cut in a pointed oval shape and usually faceted. **b.** a piece of jewellery, esp. a ring, set with such a stone or with an oval cluster of stones. **3.** another name for **marquee** (sense 2).

marriage ('mærɪdʒ) n. **1.** the state or relationship of being husband and wife. **2. a.** the legal union or contract made by a man and woman to live as husband and wife. **b.** (as modifier): marriage certificate. **3.** the ceremony formalizing this union; wedding. **4.** a close or intimate union, relationship, etc.

marriageable ('mærɪdʒəbəl) adj. (esp. of women) suitable for marriage, usually with reference to age. —,**marriagea'bility** n.

marriage guidance n. advice given to couples who have problems in their married life.

married ('mærɪd) adj. **1.** having a husband or wife. **2.** joined in marriage. **3.** of or involving marriage or married persons. **4.** closely or intimately united. ~n. **5.** (usually pl.) a married person (esp. in **young marrieds**).

marrow ('mærəʊ) n. **1.** the fatty network of connective tissue that fills the cavities of bones. **2.** the vital part; essence. **3.** Brit. short for **vegetable marrow.** —**'marrowy** adj.

marrowfat ('mærəʊ,fæt) or **marrow pea** n. **1.** any of several varieties of pea plant that have large seeds. **2.** the seed of such a plant.

marry[1] ('mærɪ) vb. **-rying, -ried. 1.** to take (someone as one's husband or wife) in marriage. **2.** (tr.) to join or give in marriage. **3.** to unite closely or intimately. **4.** (tr.) Naut. to match up (the strands) of ropes before splicing.

marry[2] ('mærɪ) interj. Arch. an exclamation of surprise, anger, etc.

marry off vb. (tr., adv.) to find a husband or wife for (a person, esp. one's son or daughter).

Mars (mɑ:z) n. **1.** the fourth planet from the sun. **2.** the Roman god of war.

Marsala (mɑ:'sɑ:lə) n. a dark sweet dessert wine from Marsala, a port in Sicily.

Marseillaise (,mɑ:sə'leɪz) n. **the.** the French national anthem, written in 1792 by C. J. Rouget de Lisle for the Rhine army of revolutionary France.

marsh (mɑ:ʃ) n. low poorly drained land that is sometimes flooded and often lies at the edge of lakes, etc. Cf. **swamp** (sense 1).

marshal ('mɑ:ʃəl) n. **1.** (in some armies and air forces) an officer of the highest rank. **2.** (in England) an officer who accompanies a judge on circuit and performs secretarial duties. **3.** (in the U.S.) **a.** a Federal court officer assigned to a judicial district whose functions are similar to those of a sheriff. **b.** (in some states) the chief police or fire officer. **4.** an officer who organizes or conducts ceremonies, parades, etc. **5.** Also called: **knight marshal.** (formerly in England) an officer of the royal family or court, esp. one in charge of protocol. ~vb. **-shalling, -shalled** or U.S. **-shaling, -shaled.** (tr.) **6.** to arrange in order: to marshal the facts. **7.** to assemble and organize (troops, vehicles, etc.) prior to onward movement. **8.** to guide or lead, esp. in a ceremonious way. **9.** to combine (coats of arms) on one shield. —**'marshalcy** or **'marshal,ship** n.

marshalling yard n. Railways. a place or depot where railway wagons are shunted and made up into trains.

Marshal of the Royal Air Force n. a rank in the Royal Air Force comparable to that of a field marshal in the army.

marsh gas n. a gas largely composed of methane pro-

THESAURUS

marksman, -woman crack shot (Inf.), deadeye (Inf., chiefly U.S.), dead shot (Inf.), good shot, sharpshooter

maroon abandon, cast ashore, cast away, desert, leave, leave high and dry (Inf.), strand

marriage 1. espousal, match, matrimony, nuptial rites, nuptials, wedding, wedding ceremony, wedlock 2. alliance, amalgamation, association, confederation, coupling, link, merger, union

married 1. hitched (Inf.), joined, one, spliced (Inf.), united, wed, wedded 2. conjugal, connubial, husbandly, marital, matrimonial, nuptial, spousal, wifely

marrow core, cream, essence, gist, heart, kernel, pith, quick, quintessence, soul, spirit, substance

marry 1. become man and wife, espouse, get hitched (Inf.), get spliced (Inf.), take the plunge (Inf.), take to wife, tie the knot (Inf.), walk down the aisle (Inf.), wed, wive (Archa-

ic) 2. ally, bond, join, knit, link, match, merge, splice, tie, unify, unite, yoke

marsh bog, fen, morass, moss (Scot. & northern English dialect), quagmire, slough, swamp

marshal 1. align, arrange, array, assemble, collect, deploy, dispose, draw up, gather, group, line up, muster, order, organize, rank 2. conduct, escort, guide, lead, shepherd, usher

duced when vegetation decomposes under water.

marsh mallow *n.* a malvaceous plant, that grows in salt marshes and has pale pink flowers. The roots yield a mucilage formerly used to make marshmallows.

marshmallow (ˌmɑːʃˈmæləʊ) *n.* **1.** a spongy sweet containing gum arabic or gelatine, sugar, etc. **2.** a sweetened paste or confection made from the root of the marsh mallow.

marsh marigold *n.* a yellow-flowered plant that grows in swampy places.

marsupial (mɑːˈsjuːpɪəl, -ˈsuː-) *n.* **1.** any mammal of an order in which the young are born in an immature state and continue development in the marsupium. The order occurs mainly in Australia and South and Central America and includes the opossums and kangaroos. ~*adj.* **2.** of, relating to, or belonging to marsupials. **3.** of or relating to a marsupium.

marsupium (mɑːˈsjuːpɪəm, -ˈsuː-) *n., pl.* **-pia** (-pɪə). an external pouch in most female marsupials within which the newly born offspring complete their development.

mart (mɑːt) *n.* a market or trading centre.

Martello tower (mɑːˈtɛləʊ) *n.* a small circular tower for coastal defence.

marten (ˈmɑːtɪn) *n., pl.* **-tens** *or* **-ten. 1.** any of several agile arboreal mammals of Europe, Asia, and North America, having bushy tails and golden brown to blackish fur. **2.** the highly valued fur of these animals. ~See also **sable** (sense 1).

martial (ˈmɑːʃəl) *adj.* of, relating to, or characteristic of war, soldiers, or the military life. —**ˈmartialism** *n.* —**ˈmartialist** *n.* —**ˈmartially** *adv.*

martial law *n.* rule of law maintained by the military in the absence of civil law.

Martian (ˈmɑːʃən) *adj.* **1.** of, occurring on, or relating to the planet Mars. ~*n.* **2.** an inhabitant of Mars, esp. in science fiction.

martin (ˈmɑːtɪn) *n.* any of various birds of the swallow family, having a square or slightly forked tail. See also **house martin.**

martinet (ˌmɑːtɪˈnɛt) *n.* a person who maintains strict discipline, esp. in a military force.

martingale (ˈmɑːtɪnˌɡeɪl) *n.* **1.** a strap from the reins to the girth of a horse, preventing it from carrying its head too high. **2.** any gambling system in which the stakes are raised, usually doubled, after each loss. **3.** *Naut.* a chain or cable running from a bowsprit to the stern, and serving to counteract the strain of the headstays.

martini (mɑːˈtiːnɪ) *n., pl.* **-nis. 1.** (*often cap.*) *Trademark.* an Italian vermouth. **2.** a cocktail of gin and vermouth.

Martinmas (ˈmɑːtɪnməs) *n.* the feast of St. Martin on Nov. 11; a quarter day in Scotland.

martyr (ˈmɑːtə) *n.* **1.** a person who suffers death rather than renounce his religious beliefs. **2.** a person who suffers greatly or dies for a cause, belief, etc. **3.** a person who suffers from poor health, misfortune, etc.: *a martyr to rheumatism.* ~*vb. also* **ˈmartyrize** *or* **-ise.** (*tr.*) **4.** to kill as a martyr. **5.** to make a martyr of. —**ˈmartyrdom** *n.* —ˌmartyriˈzation *or* -iˈsation *n.*

marvel (ˈmɑːvəl) *vb.* **-velling, -velled** *or U.S.* **-veling, -veled. 1.** (when *intr.,* often foll. by *at* or *about;* when *tr.,* takes a clause as object) to be filled with surprise or wonder. ~*n.* **2.** something that causes wonder. **3.** *Arch.* astonishment.

marvellous *or U.S.* **marvelous** (ˈmɑːvələs) *adj.* **1.** causing great wonder, surprise, etc.; extraordinary. **2.** improbable or incredible. **3.** *Inf.* excellent; splendid. —**ˈmarvellously** *or U.S.* **ˈmarvelously** *adv.* —**ˈmarvellousness** *or U.S.* **ˈmarvelousness** *n.*

Marxism (ˈmɑːksɪzəm) *n.* the economic and political theory and practice originated by Karl Marx (1818–83) and Friedrich Engels (1820–95), German political philosophers. It holds that actions and human institutions are economically determined, that the class struggle is the basic agency of historical change, and that capitalism will ultimately be superseded by communism. —**ˈMarxist** *n., adj.*

marzipan (ˈmɑːzɪˌpæn) *n.* a paste made from ground almonds, sugar, and egg whites, used to coat fruit cakes or moulded into sweets.

-mas *n. combining form.* indicating a Christian festival: *Christmas; Michaelmas.*

Masai (ˈmɑːsaɪ, mɑːˈsaɪ) *n.* **1.** (*pl.* **-sais** *or* **-sai**) a member of a Nilotic people, formerly noted as warriors, living chiefly in Kenya and Tanzania. **2.** the language of this people.

masc. *abbrev. for* masculine.

mascara (mæˈskɑːrə) *n.* a cosmetic for darkening the eyelashes.

mascot (ˈmæskət) *n.* a person, animal, or thing considered to bring good luck.

masculine (ˈmæskjʊlɪn) *adj.* **1.** possessing qualities or characteristics considered typical of or appropriate to a man; manly. **2.** unwomanly. **3.** *Grammar.* denoting a gender of nouns that includes all kinds of referents as well as some male animate referents. **4.** *Prosody.* denoting an ending consisting of a single stressed syllable. **5.** *Prosody.* denoting a rhyme between pairs of single final stressed syllables. —**ˈmasculinely** *adv.* —ˌmascuˈlinity *n.*

maser (ˈmeɪzə) *n.* a device for amplifying microwaves, working on the same principle as a laser.

mash (mæʃ) *n.* **1.** a soft pulpy mass or consistency. **2.** *Agriculture.* a feed of bran, meal, or malt mixed with water and fed to horses, cattle, or poultry. **3.** (esp. in brewing) a mixture of mashed malt grains and hot water, from which malt is extracted. **4.** *Brit.* mashed potatoes. ~*vb.* (*tr.*) **5.** to beat or crush into a mash. **6.** to steep (malt grains) in hot water in order to extract malt. **7.** *Northern Brit. dialect.* to brew (tea). —**ˈmasher** *n.*

mashie *or* **mashy** (ˈmæʃɪ) *n., pl.* **mashies.** *Golf.* an iron for lofting shots, usually No. 5.

mask (mɑːsk) *n.* **1.** any covering for the whole or a part of the face worn for amusement, protection, disguise, etc. **2.** a fact, action, etc., that conceals something. **3.** another name for **masquerade. 4.** a likeness of a face or head, either sculpted or moulded, such as a death mask. **5.** an image of a face worn by an actor, esp. in classical drama, in order to symbolize a character. **6.** a variant spelling of **masque. 7.** *Surgery.* a sterile gauze covering for the nose and mouth worn to minimize the spread of germs. **8.** *Sport.* a protective covering for the face worn for fencing, ice hockey, etc. **9.** a carving in the form of a face or head, used as an ornament. **10.** a device placed over the nose and mouth to facilitate or prevent inhalation of a gas. **11.** *Photog.* a shield of paper, paint, etc., placed over an area of unexposed photographic surface to stop light falling on it. **12.** the face or head of an animal, such as a fox. **13.** *Rare.* a person wearing a mask. ~*vb.* **14.** to cover with or put on a mask. **15.** (*tr.*) to conceal; disguise: *to mask an odour.* **16.** (*tr.*) *Photog.* to shield a particular area of (an unexposed photographic surface) to prevent or reduce the action of light there. —**masked** *adj.* —**ˈmasker** *n.*

masking tape *n.* an adhesive tape used to protect surfaces surrounding an area to be painted.

maskinonge (ˈmæskəˌnɒndʒ) *n.* another name for **muskellunge.**

masochism (ˈmæsəˌkɪzəm) *n.* **1.** *Psychiatry.* an abnormal condition in which pleasure, esp. sexual pleasure, is

---

THESAURUS

marshy boggy, fenny, miry, quaggy, spongy, swampy, waterlogged, wet

martial bellicose, belligerent, brave, heroic, military, soldierly, warlike

martinet disciplinarian, drillmaster, stickler

martyrdom agony, anguish, ordeal, persecution, suffering, torment, torture

marvel 1. *v.* be amazed, be awed, be filled with surprise, gape, gaze, goggle, wonder **2.** *n.* genius, miracle, phenomenon, portent, prodigy, whiz (*Inf.*), wonder

marvellous 1. amazing, astonishing, astounding, breathtaking, extraordinary, miraculous, phenomenal, prodigious, remarkable, singular, spectacular, stupendous, wondrous **2.** difficult *or* hard to believe, fabulous, fantastic, implausible, improbable, incredible, surprising, unbelievable, unlikely **3.** *Inf.* colossal, excellent, fabulous (*Inf.*), fantastic (*Inf.*), glorious, great (*Inf.*), magnificent, sensational, smashing (*Inf.*), splendid, stupendous, super (*Inf.*), superb, terrific (*Inf.*), wonderful

masculine 1. male, manful, manlike, manly, mannish, virile **2.** bold, brave, gallant, hardy, muscular, powerful, red-blooded (*Inf.*), resolute, robust, stout-hearted, strapping, strong, vigorous, well-built

mask *n.* **1.** domino, false face, visor, vizard (*Archaic*) **2.** blind, camouflage, cloak, concealment, cover, cover-up, disguise, façade, front, guise, screen, semblance, show, veil, veneer ~*v.* **3.** camouflage, cloak, conceal, cover, disguise, hide, obscure, screen, veil

derived from pain or from humiliation, domination, etc., by another person. **2.** a tendency to take pleasure from one's own suffering. Cf. **sadism.** —ˈmasochist n. —ˌmasoˈchistic adj. —ˌmasoˈchistically adv.

mason (ˈmeɪsən) n. **1.** a person skilled in building with stone. **2.** a person who dresses stone. ~vb. **3.** (tr.) to construct or strengthen with masonry.

Mason (ˈmeɪsən) n. short for **Freemason.**

masonic (məˈsɒnɪk) adj. **1.** (often cap.) of or relating to Freemasons or Freemasonry. **2.** of or relating to masons or masonry. —maˈsonically adv.

masonry (ˈmeɪsənrɪ) n., pl. -ries. **1.** the craft of a mason. **2.** work that is built by a mason; stonework or brickwork. **3.** (often cap.) Also called: **Freemasonry. a.** the institutions, rites, practices, etc., of Freemasons. **b.** Freemasons collectively.

masque or **mask** (mɑːsk) n. **1.** a dramatic entertainment of the 16th to 17th centuries, consisting of pantomime, dancing, dialogue, and song. **2.** the words and music for this. **3.** short for **masquerade.**

masquerade (ˌmæskəˈreɪd) n. **1.** a party or other gathering at which the guests wear masks and costumes. **2.** the disguise worn at such a function. **3.** a pretence or disguise. ~vb. (intr.) **4.** to participate in a masquerade; disguise oneself. **5.** to dissemble. —ˌmasquerˈader n.

mass (mæs) n. **1.** a large coherent body of matter without a definite shape. **2.** a collection of the component parts of something. **3.** a large amount or number, as of people. **4.** the main part or majority. **5. in the mass.** in the main; collectively. **6.** the size of a body; bulk. **7.** Physics. a physical quantity expressing the amount of matter in a body. It is a measure of a body's resistance to changes in velocity (**inertial mass**) and also of the force experienced in a gravitational field (**gravitational mass**). **8.** (in painting, drawing, etc.) an area of unified colour, shade, or intensity, usually denoting a solid form or plane. ~(modifier) **9.** done or occurring on a large scale: mass hysteria. **10.** consisting of a mass or large number, esp. of people: a mass meeting. ~vb. **11.** to form (people or things) or (of people or things) to join together into a mass.

Mass (mæs, mɑːs) n. **1.** (in the Roman Catholic Church and certain Protestant Churches) the celebration of the Eucharist. See also **High Mass, Low Mass. 2.** a musical setting of those parts of the Eucharistic service sung by choir or congregation.

massacre (ˈmæsəkə) n. **1.** the wanton or savage killing of large numbers of people, as in battle. **2.** Inf. an overwhelming defeat, as in a game. ~vb. (tr.) **3.** to kill indiscriminately or in large numbers. **4.** Inf. to defeat overwhelmingly.

massage (ˈmæsɑːʒ, -sɑːdʒ) n. **1.** the act of kneading, rubbing, etc., parts of the body to promote circulation, suppleness, or relaxation. ~vb. (tr.) **2.** to give a massage to. **3.** to treat (stiffness, etc.) by a massage.

massasauga (ˌmæsəˈsɔːgə) n. a North American venomous snake that has a horny rattle at the end of the tail.

masses (ˈmæsɪz) pl. n. **1.** (preceded by the) the body of common people. **2.** (often foll. by of) Inf., chiefly Brit. great numbers or quantities: masses of food.

masseur (mæˈsɜː) or (fem.) **masseuse** (mæˈsɜːz) n. a person who gives massages, esp. as a profession.

massif (ˈmæsiːf) n. a mass of rock or a series of connected masses forming a mountain range.

massive (ˈmæsɪv) adj. **1.** (of objects) large in mass; bulky, heavy, and usually solid. **2.** impressive or imposing. **3.** relatively intensive or large; considerable: a massive dose. **4.** Geol. **a.** (of igneous rocks) having no stratification, cleavage, etc.; homogeneous. **b.** (of sedimentary rocks) arranged in thick poorly defined strata. **5.** Mineralogy. without obvious crystalline structure. —ˈmassively adv. —ˈmassiveness n.

mass media pl. n. the means of communication that reach large numbers of people, such as television, newspapers, magazines, and radio.

mass noun n. a noun that refers to an extended substance rather than to each of a set of objects, e.g., water as opposed to lake. In English when used indefinitely they are characteristically preceded by some rather than a or an; they do not have plural forms. Cf. **count noun.**

mass-produce vb. (tr.) to manufacture (goods) to a standardized pattern on a large scale by means of extensive mechanization and division of labour. —ˌmass-proˈduced adj. —ˌmass-proˈducer n. —mass production n.

mass spectrometer or **spectroscope** n. an instrument in which ions, produced from a sample, are separated by electric or magnetic fields according to their ratios of charge to mass. A record is produced (**mass spectrum**) of the types of ion present and their amounts.

mast¹ (mɑːst) n. **1.** Naut. any vertical spar for supporting sails, rigging, flags, etc., above the deck of a vessel. **2.** any sturdy upright pole used as a support. **3. before the mast.** Naut. as an apprentice seaman. ~vb. **4.** (tr.) Naut. to equip with a mast or masts.

mast² (mɑːst) n. the fruit of forest trees, such as beech, oak, etc., used as food for pigs.

mastaba or **mastabah** (ˈmæstəbə) n. a mudbrick superstructure above tombs in ancient Egypt.

mastectomy (mæˈstɛktəmɪ) n., pl. -mies. the surgical removal of a breast.

master (ˈmɑːstə) n. **1.** the man in authority, such as the head of a household, the employer of servants, or the owner of slaves or animals. **2. a.** a person with exceptional skill at a certain thing. **b.** (as modifier): a master thief. **3. a.** a person who has complete control of a situation, etc. **b.** an abstract thing regarded as having power or influence: they regarded fate as the master of their lives. **4. a.** a workman or craftsman fully qualified to practise his trade and to train others. **b.** (as modifier): master carpenter. **5. a.** an original copy, stencil, etc., from which duplicates are made. **b.** (as modifier): master copy. **6.** a player of a game, esp. chess or bridge, who has won a specified number of tournament games. **7.** the principal of some colleges. **8.** a highly regarded teacher or leader. **9.** a graduate holding a master's degree. **10.** the chief executive officer aboard a merchant ship. **11.** a person presiding over a function, organization, or institution. **12.** Chiefly Brit. a male teacher. **13.** an officer of the Supreme Court of Judicature subordinate to a judge. **14.** the superior person or side in a contest. **15.** (often cap.) the heir apparent of a Scottish viscount or baron. ~(modifier) **16.** overall or controlling: master plan. **17.** designating a device or mechanism that controls others: master switch. **18.** main; principal: master bedroom. ~vb. (tr.) **19.** to become thoroughly

---

THESAURUS

mass n. **1.** block, chunk, concretion, hunk, lump, piece **2.** aggregate, body, collection, entirety, sum, sum total, totality, whole **3.** accumulation, aggregation, assemblage, batch, bunch, collection, combination, conglomeration, heap, load, lot, pile, quantity, stack **4.** assemblage, band, body, bunch (Inf.), crowd, group, horde, host, lot, mob, number, throng, troop **5.** body, bulk, greater part, lion's share, majority, preponderance **6.** bulk, dimension, greatness, magnitude, size **7. the masses** commonalty, common people, crowd, hoi polloi, multitude ~adj. **8.** extensive, general, indiscriminate, large-scale, pandemic, popular, wholesale, widespread ~v. **9.** accumulate, amass, assemble, collect, congregate, forgather, gather, mob, muster, rally, swarm, throng

massacre 1. n. annihilation, blood bath,

butchery, carnage, extermination, killing, mass slaughter, murder, slaughter **2.** v. annihilate, butcher, cut to pieces, exterminate, kill, mow down, murder, slaughter, slay, wipe out

massage 1. n. kneading, manipulation, rubbing, rub-down **2.** v. knead, manipulate, rub, rub down

massive big, bulky, colossal, enormous, extensive, gargantuan, gigantic, great, heavy, hefty, huge, hulking, immense, imposing, impressive, mammoth, monster, monumental, ponderous, solid, substantial, titanic, vast, weighty, whacking (Inf.), whopping (Inf.)

master n. **1.** boss (Inf.), captain, chief, commander, controller, director, employer, governor, head, lord, manager, overlord, overseer, owner, principal, ruler, skipper

(Inf.), superintendent **2.** ace (Inf.), adept, dab hand (Brit. inf.), doyen, expert, genius, maestro, past master, pro (Inf.), virtuoso, wizard **3.** guide, guru, instructor, pedagogue, preceptor, schoolmaster, spiritual leader, swami, teacher, tutor ~adj. **4.** adept, crack (Inf.), expert, masterly, proficient, skilful, skilled **5.** chief, controlling, foremost, grand, great, leading, main, predominant, prime, principal ~v. **6.** acquire, become proficient in, get the hang of (Inf.), grasp, learn **7.** bridle, check, conquer, curb, defeat, overcome, overpower, quash, quell, subdue, subjugate, suppress, tame, triumph over, vanquish **8.** command, control, direct, dominate, govern, manage, regulate, rule

proficient in. **20.** to overcome; defeat. **21.** to rule or control as master.

Master ('mɑːstə) *n.* **1.** a title of address for a boy. **2.** a term of address, esp. as used by disciples addressing or referring to a religious teacher. **3.** an archaic equivalent of **Mr.**

masterful ('mɑːstəful) *adj.* **1.** having or showing mastery. **2.** fond of playing the master; imperious. —'**masterfully** *adv.* —'**masterfulness** *n.*

master key *n.* a key that opens all the locks of a set. Also called: **passkey.**

masterly ('mɑːstəli) *adj.* of the skill befitting a master. —'**masterliness** *n.*

mastermind ('mɑːstə,maɪnd) *vb.* **1.** (*tr.*) to plan and direct (a complex undertaking). —*n.* **2.** a person of great intelligence or executive talent, esp. one who directs an undertaking.

Master of Arts *n.* a degree, usually postgraduate and in a nonscientific subject, or the holder of this degree. Abbrev.: **M.A.**

master of ceremonies *n.* a person who presides over a public ceremony, formal dinner, or entertainment, introducing the events, performers, etc.

Master of the Rolls *n.* (in England) a judge of the court of appeal: the senior civil judge in the country and the Keeper of the Records at the Public Record Office.

masterpiece ('mɑːstə,piːs) *or* **masterwork** *n.* **1.** an outstanding work or performance. **2.** the most outstanding piece of work of a creative artist, craftsman, etc.

masterstroke ('mɑːstə,strəʊk) *n.* an outstanding piece of strategy, skill, talent, etc.

mastery ('mɑːstəri) *n., pl.* **-teries.** **1.** full command or understanding of a subject. **2.** outstanding skill; expertise. **3.** the power of command; control. **4.** victory or superiority.

masthead ('mɑːst,hed) *n.* **1.** *Naut.* the head of a mast. **2.** the name of a newspaper or periodical, its proprietors, staff, etc., printed at the top of the front page. —*vb.* (*tr.*) **3.** to send (a sailor) to the masthead as a punishment. **4.** to raise (a sail) to the masthead.

mastic ('mæstɪk) *n.* **1.** an aromatic resin obtained from the mastic tree and used as an astringent and to make varnishes and lacquers. **2. mastic tree.** a small Mediterranean evergreen tree that yields the resin mastic. **3.** any of several putty-like substances used as a filler, adhesive, or seal in wood, plaster, or masonry. **4.** a liquor flavoured with mastic gum.

masticate ('mæstɪ,keɪt) *vb.* **1.** to chew (food). **2.** to reduce (materials such as rubber) to a pulp by crushing, grinding, or kneading. —,**masti'cation** *n.* —'**masti,cator** *n.*

mastiff ('mæstɪf) *n.* a breed of large powerful short-haired dog, usually fawn brown.

mastitis (mæ'staɪtɪs) *n.* inflammation of a breast or an udder.

masto- *or before a vowel* **mast-** *combining form.* indicating the breast, mammary glands, or something resembling a breast or nipple: *mastodon; mastoid.*

mastodon ('mæstə,dɒn) *n.* an extinct elephant-like mammal common in Pliocene times.

mastoid ('mæstɔɪd) *adj.* **1.** shaped like a nipple or breast. **2.** designating or relating to a nipple-like process of the temporal bone behind the ear. —*n.* **3.** the mastoid process. **4.** *Inf.* mastoiditis.

mastoiditis (,mæstɔɪ'daɪtɪs) *n.* inflammation of the mastoid process.

masturbate ('mæstə,beɪt) *vb.* to stimulate the genital organs of (oneself or another) to achieve sexual pleasure. —,**mastur'bation** *n.* —'**mastur,bator** *n.* —**masturbatory** ('mæstə,beɪtəri) *adj.*

mat¹ (mæt) *n.* **1.** a thick flat piece of fabric used as a floor covering, a place to wipe one's shoes, etc. **2.** a smaller pad of material used to protect a surface from the heat, etc., of an object placed upon it. **3.** a large piece of thick padded material put on the floor as a surface for wrestling, judo, etc. **4.** any surface or mass that is densely interwoven or tangled: *a mat of weeds.* —*vb.* **matting, matted.** **5.** to tangle or weave or become tangled or woven into a dense mass. **6.** (*tr.*) to cover with a mat or mats.

mat² (mæt) *n.* **1.** a border of cardboard, cloth, etc., placed around a picture as a frame or between picture and frame. —*adj.* **2.** having a dull, lustreless, or roughened surface. —*vb.* **matting, matted.** (*tr.*) **3.** to furnish (a picture) with a mat. **4.** to give (a surface) a mat finish. —Also (for senses 2 & 4): **matt.**

matador ('mætə,dɔː) *n.* **1.** the principal bullfighter who kills the bull. **2.** (in some card games) one of the highest cards. **3.** a game played with dominoes in which the dots on adjacent halves must total seven.

match¹ (mætʃ) *n.* **1.** a formal game or sports event in which people, teams, etc., compete. **2.** a person or thing able to provide competition for another: *she's met her match.* **3.** a person or thing that resembles, harmonizes with, or is equivalent to another in a specified respect. **4.** a person or thing that is an exact copy or equal of another. **5. a.** a partnership between a man and a woman, as in marriage. **b.** an arrangement for such a partnership. **6.** a person regarded as a possible partner, as in marriage. —*vb.* (*mainly tr.*) **7.** to fit (parts) together. **8.** (*also intr.; sometimes foll. by up*) to resemble, harmonize with, correspond to, or equal (one another or something else). **9.** (sometimes foll. by *with* or *against*) to compare in order to determine which is the superior. **10.** (often foll. by *to* or *with*) to adapt so as to correspond with: *to match hope with reality.* **11.** (often foll. by *with* or *against*) to arrange a competition between. **12.** to find a match for. **13.** *Electronics.* to connect (two circuits) so that their impedances are equal, to produce a maximum transfer of energy. —'**matchable** *adj.*

match² (mætʃ) *n.* **1.** a thin strip of wood or cardboard tipped with a chemical that ignites by friction on a rough surface or a surface coated with a suitable chemical (see **safety match**). **2.** a length of cord or wick impregnated with a chemical so that it burns slowly. It is used to fire cannons, etc.

matchbox ('mætʃ,bɒks) *n.* a small box for holding matches.

matchless ('mætʃlɪs) *adj.* unequalled; incomparable; peerless. —'**matchlessly** *adv.*

matchlock ('mætʃ,lɒk) *n.* **1.** an obsolete type of gunlock igniting the powder by means of a slow match. **2.** a gun having such a lock.

matchmaker ('mætʃ,meɪkə) *n.* **1.** a person who brings

THESAURUS

masterful **1.** adept, adroit, clever, consummate, crack (*Inf.*), deft, dexterous, excellent, expert, exquisite, fine, finished, first-rate, masterly, skilful, skilled, superior, superlative, supreme **2.** arrogant, authoritative, bossy (*Inf.*), despotic, dictatorial, domineering, high-handed, imperious, magisterial, overbearing, overweening, peremptory, self-willed, tyrannical

masterly adept, adroit, clever, consummate, crack (*Inf.*), dexterous, excellent, expert, exquisite, fine, finished, first-rate, masterful, skilful, skilled, superior, superlative, supreme

mastermind **1.** *v.* be the brains behind (*Inf.*), conceive, devise, direct, manage, organize, plan **2.** *n.* architect, authority, brain(s) (*Inf.*), director, engineer, genius, intellect, manager, organizer, planner, virtuoso

masterpiece *chef d'oeuvre,* classic, jewel, magnum opus, master work, *pièce de résistance, tour de force*

mastery **1.** command, comprehension, familiarity, grasp, knowledge, understanding **2.** ability, acquirement, attainment, cleverness, deftness, dexterity, expertise, finesse, know-how (*Inf.*), proficiency, prowess, skill, virtuosity **3.** ascendancy, authority, command, conquest, control, domination, dominion, pre-eminence, rule, superiority, supremacy, sway, triumph, upper hand, victory, whip hand

match *n.* **1.** bout, competition, contest, game, test, trial **2.** competitor, counterpart, equal, equivalent, peer, rival **3.** companion, complement, counterpart, equal, equivalent, fellow, mate, tally **4.** copy, dead ringer (*Sl.*), double, duplicate, equal, lookalike, replica, ringer (*Sl.*), spit (*Inf.*), spit and image (*Inf.*),

spitting image (*Inf.*), twin **5.** affiliation, alliance, combination, couple, duet, marriage, pair, pairing, partnership, union —*v.* **6.** ally, combine, couple, join, link, marry, mate, pair, unite, yoke **7.** accompany, accord, adapt, agree, blend, coordinate, correspond, fit, go with, harmonize, suit, tally, tone with **8.** compare, compete, contend, emulate, equal, measure up to, oppose, pit against, rival, vie

matching analogous, comparable, coordinating, corresponding, double, duplicate, equal, equivalent, identical, like, paired, parallel, same, toning, twin

matchless consummate, exquisite, incomparable, inimitable, peerless, perfect, superlative, supreme, unequalled, unique, unmatched, unparalleled, unrivalled

together suitable partners for marriage. **2.** a person who arranges competitive matches. —**'match,making** *n., adj.*

match play *n. Golf.* scoring according to the number of holes won and lost —**match player** *n.*

matchstick ('mætʃ,stik) *n.* the wooden part of a match.

matchwood ('mætʃ,wʊd) *n.* **1.** wood suitable for making matches. **2.** splinters or fragments.

mate¹ (meɪt) *n.* **1.** the sexual partner of an animal. **2.** a marriage partner. **3. a.** *Inf., chiefly Brit. & Austral.* a friend, usually of the same sex: often used to any male in direct address. **b.** (*in combination*) an associate, colleague, fellow sharer, etc.: *a classmate.* **4.** one of a pair of matching items. **5.** *Naut.* **a.** short for **first mate. b.** any officer below the master on a commercial ship. **6.** (in some professions) an assistant: *a plumber's mate.* ~*vb.* **7.** to pair (a male and female animal) or (of animals) to pair for reproduction. **8.** to marry or join in marriage. **9.** (*tr.*) to join as a pair.

mate² (meɪt) *n., vb. Chess.* See **checkmate.**

matelot, matlo, *or* **matlow** ('mætləʊ) *n. Sl., chiefly Brit.* a sailor.

mater ('meɪtə) *n. Brit. sl.* a word for **mother:** often used facetiously.

material (mə'tɪərɪəl) *n.* **1.** the substance of which a thing is made or composed; component or constituent matter. **2.** facts, etc., that a finished work may be based on or derived from. **3.** cloth or fabric. **4.** a person who has qualities suitable for a given occupation, training, etc.: *that boy is university material.* ~*adj.* **5.** of, relating to, or composed of physical substance. **6.** of, relating to, or affecting economic or physical well-being: *material ease.* **7.** of or concerned with physical rather than spiritual interests. **8.** of great import or consequence: *material benefit.* **9.** (often foll. by *to*) relevant. **10.** *Philosophy.* of or relating to matter as opposed to form. —**ma,teri'ality** *n.*

materialism (mə'tɪərɪə,lɪzəm) *n.* **1.** interest in and desire for money, possessions, etc., rather than spiritual or ethical values. **2.** *Philosophy.* the doctrine that matter is the only reality and that the mind, the emotions, etc., are merely functions of it. Cf. **idealism. 3.** *Ethics.* the rejection of any religious or supernatural account of things. —**ma'terialist** *n.* —**ma,terial'istic** *adj.* —**ma,terial'istically** *adv.*

materialize *or* **-ise** (mə'tɪərɪə,laɪz) *vb.* **1.** (*intr.*) to become fact; actually happen. **2.** to invest or become invested with a physical shape or form. **3.** to cause (a spirit, as of a dead person) to appear in material form or (of a spirit) to appear in such form. **4.** (*intr.*) to take shape; become tangible. —**ma,teriali'zation** *or* **-i'sation** *n.* —**ma'terial,izer** *or* **-,iser** *n.*

▷ **Usage.** Careful writers and speakers avoid using *materialize* to mean *happen* or *occur,* esp. in formal contexts: *they talked for several hours but nothing happened* (not *materialized*). The word is often used, however, in the sense of taking shape: *after many hours of discussion, the project finally began to materialize.*

materially (mə'tɪərɪəlɪ) *adv.* **1.** to a significant extent; considerably. **2.** with respect to material objects. **3.** *Philosophy.* with respect to substance as distinct from form.

materials (mə'tɪərɪəlz) *pl. n.* the equipment necessary for a particular activity.

materiel *or* **matériel** (mə,tɪərɪ'ɛl) *n.* the materials and equipment of an organization, esp. of a military force.

maternal (mə'tɜːnəl) *adj.* **1.** of, relating to, or characteristic of a mother. **2.** related through the mother's side of the family: *his maternal uncle.* —**ma'ternalism** *n.* —**ma,ternal'istic** *adj.* —**ma'ternally** *adv.*

maternity (mə'tɜːnɪtɪ) *n.* **1.** motherhood. **2.** the characteristics associated with motherhood; motherliness. **3.** (*modifier*) relating to pregnant women or women at the time of childbirth: *a maternity ward.*

matey ('meɪtɪ) *Brit. inf.* ~*adj.* **1.** friendly or intimate. ~*n.* **2.** friend or fellow: usually used in direct address. —**'mateyness** *or* **'matiness** *n.*

math (mæθ) *n. U.S. inf.* short for **mathematics.** Brit. equivalent: **maths**

mathematical (,mæθə'mætɪkəl) *or* **mathematic** *adj.* **1.** of, used in, or relating to mathematics. **2.** characterized by or using the precision of mathematics. **3.** using, determined by, or in accordance with the principles of mathematics. —**,mathe'matically** *adv.*

mathematician (,mæθəmə'tɪʃən) *n.* an expert or specialist in mathematics.

mathematics (,mæθə'mætɪks) *n.* **1.** (*functioning as sing.*) a group of related sciences, including algebra, geometry, and calculus, concerned with the study of number, quantity, shape, and space and their interrelationships by using a specialized notation. **2.** (*functioning as sing. or pl.*) mathematical operations and processes involved in the solution of a problem or study of some scientific field.

maths (mæθs) *n. Brit. inf.* short for **mathematics.** U.S. equivalent: **math**

matinée ('mætɪ,neɪ) *n.* a daytime, esp. afternoon, performance of a play, concert, etc.

matinée coat *n.* a short coat for a baby.

matins *or* **mattins** ('mætɪnz) *n.* (*functioning as sing. or pl.*) **1. a.** *Chiefly R.C. Church.* the first of the seven canonical hours of prayer. **b.** the service of morning prayer in the Church of England. **2.** *Literary.* a morning song, esp. of birds.

matri- *combining form.* mother or motherhood: *matriarchy.*

matriarch ('meɪtrɪ,ɑːk) *n.* **1.** a woman who dominates an organization, community, etc. **2.** the female head of a tribe or family. **3.** a very old or venerable woman. —**'matri,archal** *or* **'matri,archic** *adj.*

matriarchy ('meɪtrɪ,ɑːkɪ) *n., pl.* **-chies. 1.** a form of social organization in which a female is head of the family or society, and descent and kinship are traced through the female line. **2.** any society dominated by women.

matricide ('mætrɪ,saɪd, 'meɪ-) *n.* **1.** the act of killing one's own mother. **2.** a person who kills his mother. —**,matri'cidal** *adj.*

matriculate (mə'trɪkjʊ,leɪt) *vb.* **1.** to enrol or be enrolled in an institution, esp. a college or university. **2.** (*intr.*) to attain the academic standard required for a course at such an institution. —**ma,tricu'lation** *n.*

matrilineal (,mætrɪ'lɪnɪəl, ,meɪ-) *adj.* relating to descent or kinship through the female line.

matrimony ('mætrɪmənɪ) *n., pl.* **-nies. 1.** the state or condition of being married. **2.** the ceremony of marriage. **3. a.** a card game in which the king and queen together are a winning combination. **b.** such a combination. —**,matri'monial** *adj.*

matrix ('meɪtrɪks, 'mæ-) *n., pl.* **matrices** ('meɪtrɪ,siːz, 'mæ-) *or* **matrixes. 1.** a substance, situation, or environment in which something has its origin, takes form, or is enclosed. **2.** the intercellular substance of bone, cartilage, connective tissue, etc. **3.** the rock in which fossils, pebbles, etc., are embedded. **4.** *Printing.* **a.** a metal mould for casting type. **b.** a papier-mâché or plastic mould impressed from the forme and used for stereotyping. **5.** a mould used in the production of gramophone records. **6.** a bed of perforated material placed beneath a workpiece in a press or stamping machine against which the punch operates. **7.** *Maths.* a rectangular array of elements set out in rows and columns,

---

THESAURUS

mate *n.* **1.** better half (*Humorous*), husband, partner, spouse, wife **2.** *Inf.* buddy (*Inf.*), china (*Brit. sl.*), chum (*Inf.*), comrade, crony, friend, pal (*Inf.*) **3.** associate, colleague, companion, compeer, co-worker, fellow-worker **4.** assistant, helper, subordinate **5.** companion, double, fellow, match, twin ~*v.* **6.** breed, copulate, couple, pair **7.** marry, match, wed **8.** couple, join, match, pair, yoke

material *n.* **1.** body, constituents, element, matter, stuff, substance **2.** data, evidence, facts, information, notes, work **3.** cloth, fabric, stuff ~*adj.* **4.** bodily, concrete, corporeal, fleshly, nonspiritual, palpable, physical, substantial, tangible, worldly **5.** consequential, essential, grave, important, indispensable, key, meaningful, momentous, serious, significant, vital, weighty **6.** applicable, apposite, apropos, germane, pertinent, relevant

materialize appear, come about, come into being, come to pass, happen, occur, take place, take shape, turn up

materially considerably, essentially, gravely, greatly, much, seriously, significantly, substantially

maternal motherly

maternity motherhood, motherliness

matrimonial conjugal, connubial, hymeneal, marital, married, nuptial, spousal, wedded, wedding

matrimony marital rites, marriage, nuptials, wedding ceremony, wedlock

used to facilitate the solution of problems, such as transformation of coordinates. **8.** *Obs.* the womb.

matron ('meɪtrən) *n.* **1.** a married woman regarded as staid or dignified. **2.** a woman in charge of the domestic or medical arrangements in an institution. **3.** *U.S.* a wardress in a prison. **4.** *Brit.* the administrative head of the nursing staff in a hospital. Official name: **nursing officer.** —'**matronal** *or* '**matronly** *adj.* —'**matron,hood** *or* '**matron,ship** *n.*

matron of honour   *n., pl.* **matrons of honour.** a married woman serving as chief attendant to a bride.

matt *or* **matte** (mæt) *adj., vb.* variant spellings of **mat²** (senses 2 & 4).

Matt. *Bible. abbrev. for* Matthew.

matted ('mætɪd) *adj.* **1.** tangled into a thick mass. **2.** covered with or formed of matting.

matter ('mætə) *n.* **1.** that which makes up something, esp. a physical object; material. **2.** substance that occupies space and has mass, as distinguished from substance that is mental, spiritual, etc. **3.** substance of a specified type: *vegetable matter.* **4.** (sometimes foll. by *of* or *for*) thing; affair; concern; question: *a matter of taste.* **5.** a quantity or amount: *a matter of a few pence.* **6.** the content of written or verbal material as distinct from its style or form. **7.** (*used with a negative*) importance; consequence. **8.** *Philosophy.* **a.** (in the writings of Aristotle and the Scholastics) that which is itself formless but can receive form and become substance. **b.** that which is organized into chemical substances and living things. **c.** (in the Cartesian tradition) one of two basic modes of existence, the other being **mind. 9.** *Printing.* **a.** type set up. **b.** copy to be set in type. **10.** a secretion or discharge, such as pus. **11.** *Law.* **a.** something to be proved. **b.** statements or allegations to be considered by a court. **12. for that matter.** as regards that. **13. no matter. a.** regardless of; irrespective of: *no matter what the excuse, you must not be late.* **b.** (*sentence substitute*) it is unimportant. **14. the matter.** wrong; the trouble: *there's nothing the matter.* ~*vb.* (*intr.*) **15.** to be of consequence or importance. **16.** to form and discharge pus.

matter of fact   *n.* **1.** a fact that is undeniably true. **2.** *Law.* a statement of facts the truth of which the court must determine on the basis of the evidence before it. **3. as a matter of fact.** actually; in fact. ~*adj.* **matter-of-fact. 4.** unimaginative or emotionless: *he gave a matter-of-fact account of the murder.*

matting ('mætɪŋ) *n.* **1.** a coarsely woven fabric, usually made of a natural fibre such as straw or hemp and used as a floor covering, packing material, etc. **2.** the act or process of making mats. **3.** material for mats.

mattins ('mætɪnz) *n.* a variant spelling of **matins.**

mattock ('mætək) *n.* a type of large pick that has one end of its blade shaped like an adze, used for loosening soil, cutting roots, etc.

mattress ('mætrɪs) *n.* **1.** a large flat pad with a strong cover, filled with straw, foam rubber, etc., and often incorporating coiled springs, used as a bed or as part of a bed. **2.** a woven mat of brushwood, poles, etc., used to protect an embankment, dyke, etc., from scour. **3.** a concrete or steel raft or slab used as a foundation or footing.

maturate ('mætjʊˌreɪt, 'mætʃʊ-) *vb.* **1.** to mature or

bring to maturity. **2.** a less common word for **suppurate.** —ˌ**matu'ration** *n.* —**maturative** (məˈtjʊərətɪv, məˈtʃʊə-) *adj.*

mature (məˈtjʊə, -ˈtʃʊə) *adj.* **1.** relatively advanced physically, mentally, etc.; grown-up. **2.** (of plans, theories, etc.) fully considered; perfected. **3.** due or payable: *a mature debenture.* **4.** *Biol.* **a.** fully developed or differentiated: *a mature cell.* **b.** fully grown; adult: *a mature animal.* **5.** (of fruit, wine, cheese, etc.) ripe or fully aged. ~*vb.* **6.** to make or become mature. **7.** (*intr.*) (of notes, bonds, etc.) to become due for payment or repayment. —**ma'turely** *adv.* —**ma'tureness** *or* **ma'turity** *n.*

matutinal (ˌmætjʊˈtaɪnəl) *adj.* of, occurring in, or during the morning.

matzo, matzoh ('mætsəʊ) *or* **matza, matzah** ('mætsə) *n., pl.* **matzos, matzohs, matzas, matzahs,** *or* **matzoth** (*Hebrew* maˈtsɔt). a large brittle very thin biscuit of unleavened bread, traditionally eaten during the Jewish Passover.

maudlin ('mɔːdlɪn) *adj.* foolishly tearful or sentimental, as when drunk, etc.

maul (mɔːl) *vb.* (*tr.*) **1.** to handle clumsily; paw. **2.** to batter or lacerate. ~*n.* **3.** a heavy two-handed hammer. **4.** *Rugby.* a loose scrum. —'**mauler** *n.*

maunder ('mɔːndə) *vb.* (*intr.*) to move, talk, or act aimlessly or idly.

Maundy money ('mɔːndɪ) *n.* specially minted coins given by the British sovereign to poor people on the Thursday before Easter (**Maundy Thursday**).

mausoleum (ˌmɔːsəˈlɪəm) *n., pl.* **-leums** *or* **-lea** (-ˈlɪə). a large stately tomb.

mauve (məʊv) *n.* **1. a.** any of various pale to moderate pinkish-purple or bluish-purple colours. **b.** (*as adj.*): *a mauve flower.* **2.** a reddish-purple aniline dye.

maverick ('mævərɪk) *n.* **1.** (in the U.S.) an unbranded animal, esp. a stray calf. **2. a.** a person of independent or unorthodox views. **b.** (*as modifier*): *a maverick politician.*

mavis ('meɪvɪs) *n.* a popular name for the **song thrush.**

maw (mɔː) *n.* **1.** the mouth, throat, crop, or stomach of an animal, esp. of a voracious animal. **2.** *Inf.* the mouth or stomach of a greedy person.

mawkish ('mɔːkɪʃ) *adj.* **1.** falsely sentimental, esp. in a weak or maudlin way. **2.** nauseating or insipid. —'**mawkishly** *adv.* —'**mawkishness** *n.*

max. *abbrev. for* maximum.

maxi ('mæksɪ) *adj.* **1. a.** (of a garment) reaching the ankle. **b.** (*as n.*): *she wore a maxi.* **c.** (*in combination*): *a maxidress.* **2.** large or considerable.

maxilla (mækˈsɪlə) *n., pl.* **-lae** (-liː). **1.** the upper jawbone in vertebrates. **2.** any member of one or two pairs of mouthparts in insects and other arthropods. —**max'illary** *adj.*

maxim ('mæksɪm) *n.* a brief expression of a general truth, principle, or rule of conduct.

maximize *or* **-ise** ('mæksɪˌmaɪz) *vb.* (*tr.*) to make as high or great as possible; increase to a maximum. —ˌ**maximi'zation** *or* **-i'sation** *n.* —'**maxi,mizer** *or* **-iser** *n.*

maximum ('mæksɪməm) *n., pl.* **-mums** *or* **-ma** (-mə). **1.** the greatest possible amount, degree, etc. **2.** the highest value of a variable quantity. ~*adj.* **3.** of, being, or show-

---

THESAURUS

matrix forge, mould, origin, source, womb

matted knotted, tangled, tousled, uncombed

matter *n.* **1.** body, material, stuff, substance **2.** affair, business, concern, episode, event, incident, issue, occurrence, proceeding, question, situation, subject, thing, topic, transaction **3.** amount, quantity, sum **4.** argument, context, purport, sense, subject, substance, text, thesis **5.** consequence, import, importance, moment, note, significance, weight **6.** complication, difficulty, distress, problem, trouble, upset, worry **7.** *Medical* discharge, purulence, pus, secretion ~*v.* **8.** be important, be of consequence, carry weight, count, have influence, make a difference, mean something, signify

matter-of-fact deadpan, down-to-earth, dry, dull, emotionless, flat, lifeless, mundane, plain, prosaic, sober, unembel-

lished, unimaginative, unsentimental, unvarnished

mature 1. *adj.* adult, complete, fit, full-blown, fully fledged, full-grown, grown, grown-up, matured, mellow, of age, perfect, prepared, ready, ripe, ripened, seasoned **2.** *v.* age, become adult, bloom, come of age, develop, grow up, maturate, mellow, perfect, reach adulthood, ripen, season

maturity adulthood, completion, experience, full bloom, full growth, fullness, majority, manhood, maturation, matureness, perfection, ripeness, wisdom, womanhood

maudlin lachrymose, mawkish, mushy (*Inf.*), overemotional, sentimental, slushy (*Inf.*), soppy (*Brit. inf.*), tearful, weepy (*Inf.*)

maul 1. abuse, handle roughly, ill-treat, manhandle, molest, paw **2.** batter, beat, beat up (*Inf.*), claw, knock about, lacerate, mangle, pummel, rough up, thrash

maunder 1. dawdle, dilly-dally (*Inf.*), drift, idle, loaf, meander, mooch (*Sl.*), potter, ramble, straggle, stray, traipse (*Inf.*) **2.** babble, blather, blether, chatter, gabble, prattle, rabbit (*Brit. sl.*), ramble, rattle on, witter (*Inf.*)

mawkish 1. emotional, feeble, gushy (*Inf.*), maudlin, mushy (*Inf.*), schmaltzy (*Sl.*), sentimental, slushy (*Inf.*), soppy (*Brit. inf.*) **2.** disgusting, flat, foul, insipid, jejune, loathsome, nauseous, offensive, stale, vapid

maxim adage, aphorism, apophthegm, axiom, byword, gnome, motto, proverb, rule, saw, saying

maximum 1. *n.* apogee, ceiling, crest, extremity, height, most, peak, pinnacle, summit, top, upper limit, utmost, uttermost, zenith **2.** *adj.* greatest, highest, maximal, most, paramount, supreme, topmost, utmost

ing a maximum or maximums. ~Abbrev.: **max.**

maxwell ('mækswəl) n. the cgs unit of magnetic flux equal to the flux through one square centimetre normal to a field of one gauss. It is equivalent to 10^{-8} weber. Abbrev.: **Mx**

may[1] (meı) vb. past **might.** (takes an infinitive without to or an implied infinitive) used as an auxiliary **1.** to indicate that permission is requested by or granted to someone: he may go. **2.** (often foll. by well) to indicate possibility: the rope may break. **3.** to indicate ability or capacity, esp. in questions: may I help you? **4.** to express a strong wish: long may she reign. **5.** to indicate result or purpose: used only in clauses introduced by that or so that: he writes so that the average reader may understand. **6.** to express courtesy in a question: whose child may this little girl be? **7. be that as it may.** in spite of that: a sentence connector conceding the possible truth of a previous statement and introducing an adversative clause: be that as it may, I still think he should come. **8. come what may.** whatever happens. **9. that's as may be.** (foll. by a clause introduced by but) that may be so.

▷ **Usage.** In careful written usage, may is used rather than can when reference is made to permission rather than to capability. He may do it is, for this reason, more appropriate than he can do it when the desired sense is he is allowed to do it. In spoken English, however, can is often used where the correct use of may results in forms that are considered to be awkward. Can't I? is preferred on this ground to mayn't I? in speech. The difference between may and might is one of emphasis: he might be coming usually indicates less certainty than he may be coming. Similarly, might I have it? is felt to be more hesitant than may I have it?

may[2] or **may tree** (meı) n. a Brit. name for **hawthorn.**

May (meı) n. the fifth month of the year, consisting of 31 days.

Maya ('maıə) n. **1.** (pl. **-ya** or **-yas**) Also called: **Mayan.** a member of an American Indian people of Yucatán, Belize, and N Guatemala, once having an advanced civilization. **2.** the language of this people.

maybe ('meı,biː) adv. **1.** perhaps. ~sentence substitute. **2.** possibly; neither yes nor no.

Mayday ('meı,deı) n. the international radiotelephone distress signal.

May Day n. the first day of May, traditionally a celebration of the coming of spring: in some countries now observed as a holiday in honour of workers.

mayfly ('meı,flaı) n., pl. **-flies.** any of an order of short-lived insects having large transparent wings.

mayhap ('meı,hæp) adv. an archaic word for **perhaps.**

mayhem or **maihem** ('meıhɛm) n. **1.** Law. the wilful and unlawful infliction of injury upon a person, esp. (formerly) the injuring or removing of a limb rendering him less capable of defending himself against attack. **2.** any violent destruction or confusion.

mayn't ('meıənt, meınt) contraction of may not.

mayonnaise (,meıə'neız) n. a thick creamy sauce made from egg yolks, oil, and vinegar or lemon juice.

mayor (mɛə) n. the chief officer of a municipal corporation in many countries. Scot. equivalent: **provost.** —'mayoral adj. —'mayor,ship n.

mayoralty ('mɛərəltı) n., pl. **-ties.** the office or term of office of a mayor.

mayoress ('mɛərıs) n. **1.** Chiefly Brit. the wife of a mayor. **2.** a female mayor.

maypole ('meı,pəʊl) n. a tall pole around which people dance during May-Day celebrations.

May queen n. a girl chosen, esp. for her beauty, to preside over May-Day celebrations.

maze (meız) n. **1.** a complex network of paths or passages, esp. one with high hedges in a garden, designed to puzzle those walking through it. **2.** a similar system represented diagrammatically as a pattern of lines. **3.** any confusing network of streets, etc. **4.** a state of confusion.

~vb. **5.** an archaic or dialect word for **amaze.** —'mazement n. —'mazy adj.

mazurka or **mazourka** (mə'zɜːkə) n. **1.** a Polish national dance in triple time. **2.** a piece of music composed for this dance.

M.B. abbrev. for Bachelor of Medicine.

M.B.E. abbrev. for Member of the Order of the British Empire (a Brit. title).

M.C. abbrev. for: **1.** Master of Ceremonies. **2.** (in the U.S.) Member of Congress. **3.** (in Britain) Military Cross.

Mc- prefix. a variant of **Mac-.**

M.C.C. (in Britain) abbrev. for Marylebone Cricket Club.

McCoy (mə'kɔı) n. Sl. the genuine person or thing (esp. in **the real McCoy**).

M.Ch. abbrev. for Master of Surgery.

Md the chemical symbol for mendelevium.

M.D. abbrev. for: **1.** Doctor of Medicine. **2.** mentally deficient. **3.** Managing Director.

M.D.T. (in the U.S. and Canada) abbrev. for Mountain Daylight Time.

me (miː; unstressed mı) pron. (objective) **1.** refers to the speaker or writer: that shocks me. ~n. **2.** Inf. the personality of the speaker or writer or something that expresses it: the real me.

▷ **Usage.** Although the nominative case is traditionally required after the verb to be, even careful speakers say it is me (or him, her, etc.) rather than it is I in informal contexts. The use of me, etc., before an -ing form of the verb (he disapproved of me coming) is common, but careful speakers and writers use the possessive form: he disapproved of my coming.

ME or **M.E.** abbrev. for Middle English.

mea culpa Latin. ('meıɑː 'kʊlpɑː) my fault: an acknowledgment of guilt.

mead[1] (miːd) n. a wine made by fermenting a solution of honey, often with spices added.

mead[2] (miːd) n. an archaic or poetic word for **meadow.**

meadow ('mɛdəʊ) n. **1.** an area of grassland, often used for hay or for grazing of animals. **2.** a low-lying piece of grassland, often boggy and near a river. —'meadowy adj.

meadowsweet ('mɛdəʊ,swiːt) n. **1.** a Eurasian plant with dense heads of small fragrant cream-coloured flowers. **2.** any of several related North American plants.

meagre or U.S. **meager** ('miːgə) adj. **1.** deficient in amount, quality, or extent. **2.** thin or emaciated. **3.** lacking in richness or strength. —'meagrely or U.S. 'meagerly adv.

meal[1] (miːl) n. **1. a.** any of the regular occasions, such as breakfast, lunch, dinner, etc., when food is served and eaten. **b.** (in combination): mealtime. **2.** the food served and eaten. **3. make a meal of.** Inf. to perform (a task) with unnecessarily great effort.

meal[2] (miːl) n. **1.** the edible part of a grain or pulse (excluding wheat) ground to a coarse powder. **2.** Scot. oatmeal. **3.** U.S. maize flour. —'mealy adj.

mealie ('miːlı) n. a South African word for **maize.**

mealie-meal n. S. African. meal made from finely ground maize.

meals-on-wheels n. (in Britain) a service taking hot meals to the elderly, infirm, etc. in their own homes.

meal ticket n. **1.** the U.S. equivalent of **luncheon voucher. 2.** Sl. a person, situation, etc., providing a source of livelihood or income.

mealy-mouthed adj. hesitant or afraid to speak plainly; not outspoken.

mean[1] (miːn) vb. meaning, meant. (mainly tr.) **1.** (may take a clause as object or an infinitive) to intend to convey or express. **2.** (may take a clause as object or an infinitive) to intend: she didn't mean to hurt it. **3.** (may take a clause as object) to say or do in all seriousness: the boss means what he says. **4.** (often passive; often foll. by for) to destine or design (for a certain person or purpose): she was meant for greater things. **5.** (may take a clause as object) to denote or connote; signify; represent. **6.** (may take a clause as object) to produce; cause: the weather will mean long traffic delays. **7.** to have the importance of: money means nothing to him. **8.** (intr.) to have the intention of behaving or acting (esp. in **mean well** or **mean ill**). **9. mean business.** to be serious about something.

mean² (miːn) adj. **1.** Chiefly Brit. miserly, ungenerous, or petty. **2.** despicable, ignoble, or callous: a mean action. **3.** poor or shabby: a mean abode. **4.** Inf., chiefly U.S. bad-tempered; vicious. **5.** Inf. ashamed: he felt mean. **6.** Sl. excellent; skilful: he plays a mean trombone. **7. no mean. a.** of high quality: no mean performer. **b.** difficult: no mean feat. —'**meanly** adv. —'**meanness** n.

mean³ (miːn) n. **1.** the middle point, state, or course between limits or extremes. **2.** moderation. **3.** Maths. **a.** the second and third terms of a proportion, as b and c in $a/b = c/d$. **b.** another name for **average** (sense 2). **4.** Statistics. a statistic obtained by multiplying each possible value of a variable by its probability and then taking the sum or integral over the range of the variable. ~adj. **5.** intermediate or medium in size, quantity, etc. **6.** occurring halfway between extremes or limits; average.

meander (mɪˈændə) vb. (intr.) **1.** to follow a winding course. **2.** to wander without definite aim or direction. ~n. **3.** (often pl.) a curve or bend, as in a river. **4.** (often pl.) a winding course or movement. **5.** an ornamental pattern, esp. as used in ancient Greek architecture.

mean deviation n. Statistics. **1.** the difference between an observed value of a variable and its mean. **2.** Also called: **mean deviation from the mean** (or **median**), **average deviation.** a measure of dispersion derived by computing the mean of the absolute values of the differences between observed values of a variable and the variable's mean.

meaning (ˈmiːnɪŋ) n. **1.** the sense or significance of a word, sentence, symbol, etc.; import. **2.** the purpose behind speech, action, etc. **3.** the inner, symbolic, or true interpretation, value, or message. **4.** valid content; efficacy. ~adj. **5.** expressive of some sense, intention, criticism, etc.: a meaning look. ~See also **well-meaning.**

meaningful (ˈmiːnɪŋful) adj. having great meaning or validity. —'**meaningfully** adv. —'**meaningfulness** n.

meaningless (ˈmiːnɪŋlɪs) adj. futile or empty of meaning. —'**meaninglessly** adv. —'**meaninglessness** n.

means (miːnz) n. **1.** (functioning as sing. or pl.) the medium, method, or instrument used to obtain a result or achieve an end: a means of communication. **2.** (functioning as pl.) resources or income. **3.** (functioning as pl.) considerable wealth or income: a man of means. **4. by all means.** without hesitation or doubt; certainly. **5. by means of.** with the use or help of. **6. by no manner of means.** definitely not. **7. by no** (or **not by any**) **means.** on no account; in no way.

means test n. the checking of a person's income to determine whether he qualifies for financial or social aid from a government.

meant (mɛnt) vb. the past tense or past participle of **mean¹**.

mean time or **mean solar time** n. the times, at a particular place, measured in terms of the passage of the mean sun, giving 24-hour days (mean solar days) throughout a year.

meantime (ˈmiːnˌtaɪm) or **meanwhile** (ˈmiːnˌwaɪl) n. **1.** the intervening time or period (esp. in **in the meantime**). ~adv. **2.** during the intervening time or period. **3.** at the same time, esp. in another place.
▷ **Usage.** In formal usage, in the meantime is preferred to meantime, although meantime is very common in informal spoken English. The most usual one-word form of the adverb in written English is meanwhile: in the meantime (or meanwhile not meantime), the king had not been idle.

meany or **meanie** (ˈmiːnɪ) n., pl. **meanies.** Inf. **1.** Chiefly Brit. a miserly or stingy person. **2.** Chiefly U.S. a nasty ill-tempered person.

measles (ˈmiːzəlz) n. **1.** a highly contagious viral disease common in children, characterized by fever, profuse nasal discharge of mucus, conjunctivitis, and a rash of small red spots. See also **German measles. 2.** a disease of cattle, sheep, and pigs, caused by infestation with tapeworm larvae.

measly (ˈmiːzlɪ) adj. **-slier, -sliest. 1.** Inf. meagre in quality or quantity. **2.** (of meat) infested with tapeworm larvae. **3.** having or relating to measles.

measure (ˈmɛʒə) n. **1.** the extent, quantity, amount, or degree of something, as determined by measurement or calculation. **2.** a device for measuring distance, volume, etc., such as a graduated scale or container. **3.** a system

---

THESAURUS

mean¹ v. **1.** betoken, connote, convey, denote, drive at, express, hint at, imply, indicate, purport, represent, say, signify, spell, stand for, suggest, symbolize **2.** aim, aspire, contemplate, design, desire, have in mind, intend, plan, propose, purpose, set out, want, wish **3.** design, destine, fate, fit, make, match, predestine, preordain, suit **4.** bring about, cause, engender, entail, give rise to, involve, lead to, necessitate, produce, result in **5.** adumbrate, augur, betoken, foreshadow, foretell, herald, portend, presage, promise

mean² adj. **1.** beggarly, close, mercenary, mingy (Brit. inf.), miserly, near (Inf.), niggardly, parsimonious, penny-pinching, penurious, selfish, stingy, tight, tight-fisted, ungenerous **2.** bad-tempered, cantankerous, churlish, disagreeable, hostile, ill-tempered, malicious, nasty, rude, sour, unfriendly, unpleasant **3.** abject, base, callous, contemptible, degenerate, degraded, despicable, disgraceful, dishonourable, hard-hearted, ignoble, low-minded, narrow-minded, petty, scurvy, shabby, shameful, sordid, vile, wretched **4.** beggarly, contemptible, down-at-heel, insignificant, miserable, paltry, petty, poor, rundown, scruffy, seedy, shabby, sordid, squalid, tawdry, wretched **5.** base, baseborn (Archaic), common, humble, ignoble, inferior, low, lowborn, lowly, menial, modest, obscure, ordinary, plebeian, proletarian, servile, undistinguished, vulgar

mean³ 1. n. average, balance, compromise, happy medium, median, middle, middle course or way, mid-point, norm **2.** adj. average, intermediate, medial, median, medium, middle, middling, normal, standard

meander 1. v. ramble, snake, stravaig (Scot.), stray, stroll, turn, wander, wind, zigzag **2.** n. bend, coil, curve, loop, turn, twist, zigzag

meandering anfractuous, circuitous, convoluted, indirect, roundabout, serpentine, snaking, tortuous, wandering, winding

meaning n. **1.** connotation, denotation, drift, explanation, gist, implication, import, interpretation, message, purport, sense, significance, signification, substance, upshot, value **2.** aim, design, end, goal, idea, intention, object, plan, point, purpose, trend **3.** effect, efficacy, force, point, thrust, use, usefulness, validity, value, worth ~adj. **4.** eloquent, expressive, meaningful, pointed, pregnant, speaking, suggestive

meaningful 1. important, material, purposeful, relevant, serious, significant, useful, valid, worthwhile **2.** eloquent, expressive, meaning, pointed, pregnant, speaking, suggestive

meaningless aimless, empty, futile, hollow, inane, inconsequential, insignificant, insubstantial, nonsensical, nugatory, pointless, purposeless, senseless, trifling, trivial, useless, vain, valueless, worthless

meanness 1. minginess (Brit. inf.), miserliness, niggardliness, parsimony, penuriousness, selfishness, stinginess, tightfistedness **2.** bad temper, cantankerousness, churlishness, disagreeableness, hostility, ill temper, malice, maliciousness, nastiness, rudeness, sourness, unfriendliness, unpleasantness **3.** abjectness, baseness, degeneracy, degradation, despicableness, disgracefulness, dishonourableness, low-mindedness,

narrow-mindedness, pettiness, scurviness, shabbiness, shamefulness, sordidness, vileness, wretchedness **4.** beggarliness, contemptibleness, insignificance, paltriness, pettiness, poorness, scruffiness, seediness, shabbiness, sordidness, squalor, tawdriness, wretchedness **5.** baseness, humbleness, lowliness, obscurity, servility

means 1. agency, avenue, channel, course, expedient, instrument, measure, medium, method, mode, process, way **2.** affluence, capital, estate, fortune, funds, income, money, property, resources, riches, substance, wealth, wherewithal **3. by all means** absolutely, certainly, definitely, doubtlessly, of course, positively, surely **4. by means of** by dint of, by way of, through, using, utilizing, via, with the aid of **5. by no means** absolutely not, definitely not, in no way, not at all, not in the least, not in the slightest, not the least bit, on no account

meantime at the same time, concurrently, for now, for the duration, for the moment, for then, in the interim, in the interval, in the intervening time, in the meantime, in the meanwhile, simultaneously

meanwhile at the same time, concurrently, for now, for the duration, for the moment, for then, in the interim, in the interval, in the intervening time, in the meantime, in the meanwhile, simultaneously

measurable assessable, computable, determinable, gaugeable, material, mensurable, perceptible, quantifiable, quantitative, significant

of measurement: *metric measure.* **4.** a standard used in a system of measurements. **5.** a specific or standard amount of something: *a measure of grain; full measure.* **6.** a basis or standard for comparison. **7.** reasonable or permissible limit or bounds: *within measure.* **8.** degree or extent (often in **in some measure, in a measure,** etc.): *a measure of freedom.* **9.** (*often pl.*) a particular action intended to achieve an effect. **10.** a legislative bill, act, or resolution. **11.** *Music.* another word for **bar**[1] (sense 15). **12.** *Prosody.* poetic rhythm or cadence; metre. **13.** a metrical foot. **14.** *Poetic.* a melody or tune. **15.** the act of measuring; measurement. **16.** *Arch.* a dance. **17.** *Printing.* the width of a page or column of type. **18. for good measure.** as an extra precaution or beyond requirements. **19. made to measure.** (of clothes) made to fit an individual purchaser. ~*vb.* **20.** (*tr.; often foll. by up*) to determine the size, amount, etc., of by measurement. **21.** (*intr.*) to make a measurement. **22.** (*tr.*) to estimate or determine. **23.** (*tr.*) to function as a measurement of: *the ohm measures electrical resistance.* **24.** (*tr.*) to bring into competition or conflict with: *he measured his strength against that of his opponent.* **25.** (*intr.*) to be as specified in extent, amount, etc.: *the room measures six feet.* **26.** (*tr.*) to travel or move over as if measuring. —**'measurable** *adj.* —**'measureless** *adj.*

measured (*'mɛʒəd*) *adj.* **1.** determined by measurement. **2.** slow or stately. **3.** carefully considered; deliberate. —**'measuredly** *adv.*

measurement (*'mɛʒəmənt*) *n.* **1.** the act or process of measuring. **2.** an amount, extent, or size determined by measuring. **3.** a system of measures based on a particular standard.

measures (*'mɛʒəz*) *pl. n.* rock strata that are characterized by a particular type of sediment or deposit: *coal measures.*

measure up *vb.* **1.** (*adv.*) to determine the size, etc., (of) by measurement. **2. measure up to.** to fulfil (expectations, standards, etc.).

meat (*miːt*) *n.* **1.** the flesh of mammals used as food. **2.** anything edible, esp. flesh with the texture of meat: *crab meat.* **3.** food, as opposed to drink. **4.** the essence or gist. **5.** an archaic word for **meal**[1]. **6. meat and drink.** a source of pleasure. —**'meatless** *adj.*

meatball (*'miːtˌbɔːl*) *n.* **1.** minced beef, shaped into a ball before cooking. **2.** *U.S. sl.* a stupid or boring person.

meaty (*'miːtɪ*) *adj.* **meatier, meatiest. 1.** of, relating to, or full of meat. **2.** heavily built; fleshy or brawny. **3.** full of import or interest: *a meaty discussion.* —**'meatily** *adv.* —**'meatiness** *n.*

Mecca (*'mɛkə*) *n.* **1.** a city in W Saudi Arabia: birthplace of Mohammed; the holiest city of Islam. **2.** (*sometimes not cap.*) a place that attracts many visitors.

Meccano (*mɪ'kɑːnəʊ*) *n. Trademark.* a construction set of miniature metal or plastic parts from which mechanical models can be made.

mech. *abbrev. for:* **1.** mechanical. **2.** mechanics. **3.** mechanism.

mechanic (*mɪ'kænɪk*) *n.* a person skilled in maintaining or operating machinery, motors, etc.

mechanical (*mɪ'kænɪkəl*) *adj.* **1.** made, performed, or operated by or as if by a machine or machinery. **2.** concerned with machines or machinery. **3.** relating to or controlled or operated by physical forces. **4.** of or concerned with mechanics. **5.** (of a gesture, etc.) automatic; lacking thought, feeling, etc. **6.** *Philosophy.* accounting for phenomena by physically determining forces. —**me'chanicalism** *n.* —**me'chanically** *adv.* —**me-'chanicalness** *n.*

mechanical drawing *n.* a drawing to scale of a machine, machine component, architectural plan, etc., from which dimensions can be taken.

mechanical engineering *n.* the branch of engineering concerned with the design, construction, and operation of machines.

mechanics (*mɪ'kænɪks*) *n.* **1.** (*functioning as sing.*) the branch of science, divided into statics, dynamics, and kinematics, concerned with the equilibrium or motion of bodies in a particular frame of reference. **2.** (*functioning as sing.*) the science of designing, constructing, and operating machines. **3.** the working parts of a machine. **4.** the technical aspects of something.

mechanism (*'mɛkəˌnɪzəm*) *n.* **1.** a system or structure of moving parts that performs some function, esp. in a machine. **2.** something resembling a machine in the arrangement and working of its parts. **3.** any mechanical device or part of such a device. **4.** a process or technique: *the mechanism of novel writing.* **5.** *Philosophy.* the attempt to explain phenomena in mechanical terms. **6.** *Psychoanal.* **a.** the ways in which psychological forces interact and operate. **b.** a structure having an influence on the behaviour of a person, such as a defence mechanism.

mechanistic (*ˌmɛkə'nɪstɪk*) *adj.* **1.** *Philosophy.* of or relating to the theory of mechanism. **2.** *Maths.* of or relating to mechanics. —**'mechanist** *n.* —**ˌmecha'nistically** *adv.*

mechanize *or* **-ise** (*'mɛkəˌnaɪz*) *vb.* (*tr.*) **1.** to equip (a factory, etc.) with machinery. **2.** to make mechanical, automatic, or monotonous. **3.** to equip (an army, etc.) with motorized or armoured vehicles. —**ˌmechani'zation** *or* **-i'sation** *n.* —**'mecha,nizer** *or* **-iser** *n.*

med. *abbrev. for:* **1.** medical. **2.** medicine. **3.** medieval. **4.** medium.

Med (*mɛd*) *n. Inf.* the Mediterranean region.

M.Ed. *abbrev. for* Master of Education.

medal (*'mɛdəl*) *n.* a small flat piece of metal bearing an inscription or image, given as an award or commemoration of some outstanding event, etc. —**'medallist** *n.*

medallion (*mɪ'dæljən*) *n.* **1.** a large medal. **2.** an oval or circular decorative device resembling a medal, usually bearing a portrait or relief moulding, used in architecture and textile design.

meddle (*'mɛdəl*) *vb.* **1.** (*intr.; usually foll. by with*) to interfere officiously or annoyingly. **2.** (*intr.; usually foll. by in*) to involve oneself unwarrantedly. —**'meddler** *n.*

THESAURUS

measure *n.* **1.** allotment, allowance, amount, amplitude, capacity, degree, extent, magnitude, portion, proportion, quantity, quota, range, ration, reach, scope, share, size **2.** gauge, metre, rule, scale, yardstick **3.** method, standard, system **4.** criterion, example, model, norm, standard, test, touchstone, yardstick **5.** bounds, control, limit, limitation, moderation, restraint **6.** act, action, course, deed, expedient, manoeuvre, means, procedure, proceeding, step **7.** act, bill, enactment, law, resolution, statute **8.** beat, cadence, foot, metre, rhythm, verse **9. for good measure** as a bonus, besides, in addition, into the bargain, to boot ~*v.* **10.** appraise, assess, calculate, calibrate, compute, determine, estimate, evaluate, gauge, judge, mark out, quantify, rate, size, sound, survey, value, weigh **11.** adapt, adjust, calculate, choose, fit, judge, tailor

measureless beyond measure, boundless, endless, immeasurable, immense, incalculable, inestimable, infinite, limitless, unbounded, vast

measurement **1.** appraisal, assessment, calculation, calibration, computation, estimation, evaluation, judgment, mensuration, metage, survey, valuation **2.** amount, amplitude, area, capacity, depth, dimension, extent, height, length, magnitude, size, volume, weight, width

measure out allot, apportion, assign, deal out, dispense, distribute, divide, dole out, issue, mete out, parcel out, pour out, share out

measure up (to) be adequate, be capable, be equal to, be fit, be suitable, be suited, come up to scratch (*Inf.*), come up to standard, compare, cut the mustard (*U.S. sl.*), equal, fit *or* fill the bill, fulfil the expectations, make the grade (*Inf.*), match, meet, rival

meat **1.** aliment, cheer, chow (*Inf.*), comestibles, eats (*Sl.*), fare, flesh, food, grub (*Inf.*), nourishment, nutriment, provender, provisions, rations, subsistence, sustenance, viands, victuals **2.** core, essence, gist, heart, kernel, marrow, nub, nucleus, pith, point, substance

meaty **1.** hearty, nourishing, rich, substan-tial **2.** beefy (*Inf.*), brawny, burly, fleshy, heavily built, heavy, husky (*Inf.*), muscular, solid, strapping, sturdy **3.** interesting, meaningful, pithy, profound, rich, significant, substantial

mechanical **1.** automated, automatic, machine-driven **2.** automatic, cold, cursory, dead, emotionless, habitual, impersonal, instinctive, involuntary, lacklustre, lifeless, machine-like, matter-of-fact, perfunctory, routine, spiritless, unconscious, unfeeling, unthinking

mechanism **1.** apparatus, appliance, contrivance, device, instrument, machine, structure, system, tool **2.** action, components, gears, innards (*Inf.*), machinery, motor, workings, works **3.** agency, execution, functioning, means, medium, method, operation, performance, procedure, process, system, technique, workings

meddle butt in, interfere, intermeddle, interpose, intervene, intrude, pry, put one's oar in, stick one's nose in (*Inf.*), tamper

—'**meddlesome** adj.

media ('miːdɪə) n. 1. a plural of **medium**. 2. Inf. the mass media collectively.

mediaeval (ˌmɛdɪ'iːvəl) adj. a variant spelling of **medieval**.

medial ('miːdɪəl) adj. 1. of or situated in the middle. 2. ordinary or average in size. 3. Maths. relating to an average. 4. another word for **median** (senses 1, 2). —'**medially** adv.

median ('miːdɪən) adj. 1. of, relating to, situated in, or directed towards the middle. 2. Statistics. of or relating to the median. ~n. 3. a middle point, plane, or part. 4. Geom. a. a straight line joining one vertex of a triangle to the midpoint of the opposite side. b. a straight line joining the midpoints of the nonparallel sides of a trapezium. 5. Statistics. the middle value in a frequency distribution, below and above which lie values with equal total frequencies. 6. Statistics. the middle number or average of the two middle numbers in an ordered sequence of numbers. —'**medianly** adv.

mediant ('miːdɪənt) n. Music. a. the third degree of a minor scale. b. (as modifier): a mediant chord.

mediate vb. ('miːdɪˌeɪt). 1. (intr.; usually foll. by between or in) to intervene (between parties or in a dispute) in order to bring about agreement. 2. to bring about (an agreement) between parties in a dispute. 3. to resolve (differences) by mediation. 4. (intr.) to be in an intermediate position. 5. (tr.) to serve as a medium for causing (a result) or transferring (objects, information, etc.). ~adj. ('miːdɪɪt). 6. occurring as a result of or dependent upon mediation. —'**mediately** adv. —ˌmedi'ation n. —'medi,ator n.

medic ('mɛdɪk) n. Inf. a doctor, medical orderly, or medical student.

medical ('mɛdɪkəl) adj. 1. of or relating to the science of medicine or to the treatment of patients by drugs, etc., as opposed to surgery. ~n. 2. Inf. a medical examination. —'**medically** adv.

medical certificate n. 1. a document stating the result of a satisfactory medical examination. 2. a doctor's certificate giving evidence of a person's unfitness for work, etc.

medicate ('mɛdɪˌkeɪt) vb. (tr.) 1. to cover or impregnate (a wound, etc.) with an ointment, etc. 2. to treat (a patient) with a medicine. 3. to add a medication to (a bandage, shampoo, etc.). —'**medicative** adj.

medication (ˌmɛdɪ'keɪʃən) n. 1. treatment with drugs or remedies. 2. a drug or remedy.

medicinal (mɛ'dɪsɪnəl) adj. 1. relating to or having therapeutic properties. ~n. 2. a medicinal substance. —me'**dicinally** adv.

medicine ('mɛdsɪn, 'mɛdsɪn) n. 1. any drug or remedy for use in treating, preventing, or alleviating the symptoms of disease. 2. the science of preventing, diagnosing, alleviating, or curing disease. 3. any nonsurgical branch of medical science. 4. the practice or profession of medicine. 5. something regarded by primitive people as having magical or remedial properties. 6. **take one's medicine**. to accept a deserved punishment. 7. **a taste** (or dose) **of one's own medicine**. an unpleasant experience in retaliation for a similar unkind or aggressive act.

medicine man n. (among certain peoples, esp. North American Indians) a person believed to have supernatural powers of healing; a magician or sorcerer.

medico ('mɛdɪˌkəʊ) n., pl. -cos. Inf. a doctor or medical student.

medieval or **mediaeval** (ˌmɛdɪ'iːvəl) adj. 1. of, relating to, or in the style of the Middle Ages. 2. Inf. old-fashioned; primitive. —ˌmedi'**evalist** or ˌmedi'**aevalist** n.

Medieval Greek n. the Greek language from the 7th century A.D. to shortly after the sacking of Constantinople in 1204. Also called: **Middle Greek, Byzantine Greek.**

Medieval Latin n. the Latin language as used throughout Europe in the Middle Ages.

mediocre (ˌmiːdɪ'əʊkə) adj. Often derog. average or ordinary in quality. —**mediocrity** (-'ɒkrɪtɪ) n.

meditate ('mɛdɪˌteɪt) vb. (intr.) 1. (foll. by on or upon) to think about something deeply. 2. to reflect deeply on spiritual matters, esp. as a religious act. —'**meditative** adj. —'**meditatively** adv. —'medi,tator n.

meditation (ˌmɛdɪ'teɪʃən) n. 1. the act of meditating; reflection. 2. contemplation of spiritual matters, esp. as a religious practice.

Mediterranean (ˌmɛdɪtə'reɪnɪən) n. 1. short for the **Mediterranean Sea**, the sea between S Europe, N Africa, and SW Asia. 2. a native or inhabitant of a Mediterranean country. ~adj. 3. of, relating to, situated or dwelling near the Mediterranean Sea. 4. denoting a postulated subdivision of the Caucasoid race, characterized by slender build and dark complexion. 5. Meteorol. (of a climate) characterized by hot summers and relatively warm winters when most of the annual rainfall occurs. 6. (often not cap.) Obs. situated in the middle of a land mass; inland.

medium ('miːdɪəm) adj. 1. midway between extremes; average. ~n., pl. -dia (-dɪə) or -diums. 2. an intermediate or middle state, degree, or condition; mean: the happy medium. 3. an intervening substance or agency for transmitting or producing an effect; vehicle. 4. a means or agency for communicating or diffusing information, etc., to the public. 5. a person supposedly used as a spiritual intermediary between the dead and the living. 6. the substance in which specimens of animals and plants are preserved or displayed. 7. Biol. Also called: **culture medium**. a nutritive substance in which cultures of bacteria or fungi are grown. 8. the substance or surroundings in which an organism naturally lives or grows. 9. Art. a. the category of a work of art, as determined by its materials and methods of production. b. the materials used in a work of art. 10. any solvent in which pigments are mixed and thinned.

▷ **Usage.** Careful writers and speakers do not use media as a singular noun when referring to a medium of mass communication: television is a valuable medium (not media) for advertising.

medium wave n. a. a radio wave with a wavelength between 100 and 1000 metres. b. (as modifier): a medium-wave broadcast.

medlar ('mɛdlə) n. 1. a small Eurasian tree. 2. its fruit, which resembles the crab apple and is not edible until it has begun to decay.

medley ('mɛdlɪ) n. 1. a mixture of various types or elements. 2. a musical composition consisting of various tunes arranged as a continuous whole. 3. Also called: **medley relay. a.** Swimming. a race in which a different stroke is used for each length. b. Athletics. a relay race in which each leg has a different distance.

THESAURUS

mediate act as middleman, arbitrate, bring to an agreement, bring to terms, conciliate, intercede, interpose, intervene, make peace between, moderate, reconcile, referee, resolve, restore harmony, settle, step in (Inf.), umpire

mediator advocate, arbiter, arbitrator, go-between, honest broker, interceder, intermediary, judge, middleman, moderator, negotiator, peacemaker, referee, umpire

medicinal analeptic, curative, healing, medical, remedial, restorative, roborant, sanatory, therapeutic

medicine cure, drug, medicament, medication, physic, remedy

medieval 1. Gothic 2. Inf. antediluvian, antiquated, antique, archaic, old-fashioned, primitive, unenlightened

mediocre average, commonplace, fair to middling (Inf.), indifferent, inferior, insignificant, mean, medium, middling, ordinary, passable, pedestrian, run-of-the-mill, second-rate, so-so (Inf.), tolerable, undistinguished, uninspired

mediocrity 1. commonplaceness, indifference, inferiority, insignificance, ordinariness, poorness, unimportance 2. cipher, lightweight (Inf.), nobody, nonentity, second-rater

meditate 1. be in a brown study, cogitate, consider, contemplate, deliberate, muse, ponder, reflect, ruminate, study, think 2. consider, contemplate, design, devise, have in mind, intend, mull over, plan, purpose, scheme, think over

meditation brown study, cerebration, cogitation, concentration, contemplation, musing, pondering, reflection, reverie, ruminating, rumination, study, thought

medium adj. 1. average, fair, intermediate, mean, medial, median, mediocre, middle, middling, midway ~n. 2. average, centre, compromise, mean, middle, middle course (ground, path, way), midpoint 3. agency, avenue, channel, form, instrument, instrumentality, means, mode, organ, vehicle, way 4. atmosphere, conditions, element, environment, habitat, influences, milieu, setting, surroundings 5. spiritist, spiritualist

medley assortment, confusion, farrago, gallimaufry, hodgepodge, hotchpotch, jumble, mélange, miscellany, mishmash, mixed bag (Inf.), mixture, olio, omnium-gatherum, pastiche, patchwork, potpourri, salmagundi

medulla (mɪˈdʌlə) n., pl. -las or -lae (-liː). **1.** Anat. the innermost part of an organ or structure. **2.** Bot. another name for **pith** (sense 4). —me'**dullary** or me'**dullar** adj.
medusa (mɪˈdjuːzə) n., pl. -sas or -sae (-ziː). another name for **jellyfish**. —me'**dusoid** adj., n.
meek (miːk) adj. **1.** patient, long-suffering, or submissive; humble. **2.** spineless or spiritless; compliant. —'**meekly** adv. —'**meekness** n.
meerkat ('mɪəˌkæt) n. any of several South African mongooses, esp. the slender-tailed meerkat or suricate, which has a lemur-like face and four-toed feet.
meerschaum ('mɪəʃəm) n. **1.** a white, yellowish, or pink compact earthy mineral consisting of hydrated magnesium silicate: used to make tobacco pipes and as a building stone. **2.** a tobacco pipe having a bowl made of this mineral.
meet[1] (miːt) vb. **meeting, met. 1.** (sometimes foll. by up or with) to come together (with), either by design or by accident; encounter. **2.** to come into or be in conjunction or contact with (something or each other). **3.** (tr.) to come to or be at the place of arrival of: to meet a train. **4.** to make the acquaintance of or be introduced to (someone or each other). **5.** to gather in the company of (someone or each other). **6.** to come into the presence of (someone or each other) as opponents. **7.** (tr.) to cope with effectively; satisfy: to meet someone's demands. **8.** (tr.) to be apparent to (esp. in **meet the eye**). **9.** (tr.) to return or counter: to meet a blow with another. **10.** to agree with (someone or each other): we met him on the price he suggested. **11.** (tr.) to experience; suffer: he met his death in a road accident. **12.** to occur together: courage and kindliness met in him. ~n. **13.** the assembly of hounds, huntsmen, etc., prior to a hunt. **14.** a meeting, esp. a sports meeting. —'**meeter** n.
meet[2] (miːt) adj. Arch. proper, fitting, or correct. —'**meetly** adv.
meeting ('miːtɪŋ) n. **1.** an act of coming together; encounter. **2.** an assembly or gathering. **3.** a conjunction or union.
mega- combining form. **1.** denoting 10[6]: megawatt. Symbol: M **2.** (in computer technology) denoting 2^{20} (1 048 576): megabyte. **3.** large or great: megalith.
megadeath ('mɛɡəˌdɛθ) n. the death of a million people, esp. in a nuclear war or attack.
megahertz ('mɛɡəˌhɜːts) n., pl. **megahertz.** one million hertz. Former name: **megacycle.**
megalith ('mɛɡəlɪθ) n. a stone of great size, esp. one forming part of a prehistoric monument. —ˌmega'**lithic** adj.
megalo- or before a vowel **megal-** combining form. indicating greatness, or abnormal size: megalopolis.
megalomania (ˌmɛɡələʊˈmeɪnɪə) n. a mental illness characterized by delusions of grandeur, power, wealth, etc. —ˌmegalo'**maniac** adj., n. —**megalomaniacal** (ˌmɛɡələʊməˈnaɪəkəl) adj.
megalopolis (ˌmɛɡəˈlɒpəlɪs) n. an urban complex, usually comprising several large towns. —**megalopolitan** (ˌmɛɡəˈlɒpɪtən) adj., n.
megaphone ('mɛɡəˌfəʊn) n. a funnel-shaped instrument used to amplify the voice. Also called: **loud-hailer.** —**megaphonic** (ˌmɛɡəˈfɒnɪk) adj.
megaton ('mɛɡəˌtʌn) n. **1.** one million tons. **2.** an explosive power, esp. of a nuclear weapon, equal to the power of one million tons of TNT.
megawatt ('mɛɡəˌwɒt) n. one million watts.
meiosis (maɪˈəʊsɪs) n., pl. -ses (-ˌsiːz). **1.** a type of cell division in which a nucleus divides into four daughter nuclei, each containing half the chromosome number of the parent nucleus. **2.** Rhetoric. another word for **litotes.** —**meiotic** (maɪˈɒtɪk) adj. —**mei'otically** adv.
melamine ('mɛləˌmiːn) n. **1.** a colourless crystalline compound used in making synthetic resins. **2.** a resin produced from melamine (**melamine resin**) or a material made from this resin.
melancholia (ˌmɛlənˈkəʊlɪə) n. Psychiatry. a mental state characterized by depression and irrational fears. —ˌmelan'**choliˌac** adj., n.
melancholy ('mɛlənkəlɪ) n., pl. -cholies. **1.** a tendency to gloominess or depression. **2.** a sad thoughtful state of mind. **3.** Arch. **a.** a gloomy character. **b.** one of the four bodily humours; black bile. ~adj. **4.** characterized by, causing, or expressing sadness, dejection, etc. —ˌmel-an'**cholic** adj., n.
Melanesian (ˌmɛləˈniːzɪən) adj. **1.** of or relating to Melanesia (a division of islands in the Pacific), its people, or their languages. ~n. **2.** a native or inhabitant of Melanesia: generally Negroid with frizzy hair and small stature. **3.** a group or branch of languages spoken in Melanesia.
mélange French. (meˈlɑ̃ːʒ) n. a mixture; confusion.
melanin ('mɛlənɪn) n. any of a group of black or dark brown pigments present in the hair, skin, and eyes of man and animals: produced in excess in certain skin diseases and in melanomas.
melano- or before a vowel **melan-** combining form. black or dark: melanin; melanism; melanoma.
melanoma (ˌmɛləˈnəʊmə) n., pl. -mas or -mata (-mətə). Pathol. a tumour composed of darkly pigmented cells.
Melba toast ('mɛlbə) n. very thin crisp toast.
melee or **mêlée** ('mɛleɪ) n. a noisy riotous fight or brawl; a lively debate.
meliorate ('miːlɪəˌreɪt) vb. a variant of **ameliorate.** —ˌmelio'**ration** n. —**meliorative** ('miːlɪərətɪv) adj., n.
melliferous (mɪˈlɪfərəs) or **mellific** (mɪˈlɪfɪk) adj. forming or producing honey.
mellifluous (mɪˈlɪflʊəs) or **mellifluent** adj. (of sounds or utterances) smooth or honeyed; sweet. —**mel'lifluously** adv. —**mel'lifluousness** or **mel'lifluence** n.
mellow ('mɛləʊ) adj. **1.** (esp. of fruits) full-flavoured; sweet; ripe. **2.** (esp. of wines) well-matured. **3.** (esp. of colours or sounds) soft or rich. **4.** kind-hearted, esp. through maturity or old age. **5.** genial, as through the effects of alcohol. **6.** (of soil) soft and loamy. ~vb. **7.** to make or become mellow. —'**mellowness** n.
melodeon or **melodion** (mɪˈləʊdɪən) n. Music. **1.** a type of small accordion. **2.** a type of keyboard instrument similar to the harmonium.
melodic (mɪˈlɒdɪk) adj. **1.** of or relating to melody. **2.** of or relating to a part in a piece of music. **3.** melodious. —me'**lodically** adv.
melodious (mɪˈləʊdɪəs) adj. **1.** having a tune that is pleasant to the ear. **2.** of or relating to melody; melodic. —me'**lodiously** adv. —me'**lodiousness** n.
melodrama ('mɛləˌdrɑːmə) n. **1.** a play, film, etc.,

THESAURUS

meek 1. deferential, docile, forbearing, gentle, humble, long-suffering, mild, modest, patient, peaceful, soft, submissive, unassuming, unpretentious, yielding **2.** acquiescent, compliant, resigned, spineless, spiritless, tame, timid, unresisting, weak, weak-kneed (Inf.)
meekness 1. deference, docility, forbearance, gentleness, humbleness, humility, long-suffering, lowliness, mildness, modesty, patience, peacefulness, resignation, softness, submission, submissiveness **2.** acquiescence, compliance, resignation, spinelessness, spiritlessness, tameness, timidity, weakness
meet 1. bump into, chance on, come across, confront, contact, encounter, find, happen on, run across, run into **2.** abut, adjoin, come together, connect, converge, cross, intersect, join, link up, touch, unite **3.** answer, carry out, come up to, comply, cope

with, discharge, equal, fulfil, gratify, handle, match, measure up, perform, satisfy **4.** assemble, collect, come together, congregate, convene, forgather, gather, muster, rally **5.** bear, encounter, endure, experience, face, go through, suffer, undergo
meeting 1. assignation, confrontation, encounter, engagement, introduction, rendezvous, tryst (Archaic) **2.** assembly, audience, company, conclave, conference, congregation, convention, convocation, gathering, get-together (Inf.), meet, rally, reunion, session **3.** concourse, confluence, conjunction, convergence, crossing, intersection, junction, union
melancholy 1. n. blues, dejection, depression, despondency, gloom, gloominess, low spirits, pensiveness, sadness, sorrow, unhappiness, woe **2.** adj. blue, dejected, depressed, despondent, disconsolate, dismal,

dispirited, doleful, down, downcast, downhearted, down in the dumps (Inf.), down in the mouth, gloomy, glum, heavy-hearted, joyless, low, low-spirited, lugubrious, melancholic, miserable, moody, mournful, pensive, sad, sombre, sorrowful, unhappy, woebegone, woeful
mellow adj. **1.** delicate, full-flavoured, juicy, mature, perfect, rich, ripe, soft, sweet, well-matured **2.** dulcet, full, mellifluous, melodious, rich, rounded, smooth, sweet, tuneful, well-tuned **3.** cheerful, cordial, elevated, expansive, genial, half-tipsy, happy, jolly, jovial, merry (Brit. inf.), relaxed ~v. **4.** develop, improve, mature, perfect, ripen, season, soften, sweeten
melodious concordant, dulcet, euphonious, harmonious, melodic, musical, silvery, sweet-sounding, sweet-toned, tuneful

characterized by extravagant action and emotion. **2.** (formerly) a romantic drama characterized by sensational incident, music, and song. **3.** overdramatic emotion or behaviour. —**melodramatic** (ˌmɛlədrəˈmætɪk) *adj.* —ˌ**melodra'matically** *adv.* —ˌ**melodra'matics** *pl. n.* —**melodramatist** (ˌmɛləˈdræmətɪst) *n.*

melody (ˈmɛlədɪ) *n., pl.* **-dies. 1.** *Music.* **a.** a succession of notes forming a distinctive sequence; tune. **b.** the horizontally represented aspect of the structure of a piece of music. Cf. **harmony** (sense 4b). **2.** sounds that are pleasant because of tone or arrangement, esp. words of poetry.

melon (ˈmɛlən) *n.* **1.** any of several varieties of trailing plants (see **muskmelon, watermelon**), cultivated for their edible fruit. **2.** the fruit of any of these plants, which has a hard rind and juicy flesh.

Melpomene (mɛlˈpɒmɪnɪ) *n. Greek myth.* the Muse of tragedy.

melt (mɛlt) *vb.* **melting, melted; melted** *or* **molten. 1.** to liquefy (a solid) or (of a solid) to become liquefied, as a result of the action of heat. **2.** to become or make liquid; dissolve. **3.** (often foll. by *away*) to disappear; fade. **4.** (foll. by *down*) to melt (metal scrap) for reuse. **5.** (often foll. by *into*) to blend or cause to blend gradually. **6.** to make or become emotional or sentimental; soften. ~*n.* **7.** the act or process of melting. **8.** something melted or an amount melted. —**meltable** *adj.* —**'melter** *n.* —**'meltingly** *adv.*

melting point *n.* the temperature at which a solid turns into a liquid.

melting pot *n.* **1.** a pot in which metals or other substances are melted, esp. in order to mix them. **2.** an area in which many races, ideas, etc., are mixed.

meltwater (ˈmɛltˌwɔːtə) *n.* melted snow or ice.

mem. *abbrev. for:* **1.** member. **2.** memoir. **3.** memorandum. **4.** memorial.

member (ˈmɛmbə) *n.* **1.** a person who belongs to a club, political party, etc. **2.** any individual plant or animal in a taxonomic group. **3.** any part of an animal body, such as a limb. **4.** any part of a plant, such as a petal, root, etc. **5.** *Maths., Logic.* any individual object belonging to a set or logical class. **6.** a component part of a building or construction. —**'memberless** *adj.*

Member of Parliament *n.* a member of the House of Commons or similar legislative body, as in many Commonwealth countries.

membership (ˈmɛmbəˌʃɪp) *n.* **1.** the members of an organization collectively. **2.** the state of being a member.

membrane (ˈmɛmbreɪn) *n.* **1.** any thin pliable sheet of material. **2.** a pliable sheetlike usually fibrous tissue that covers, lines, or connects plant and animal organs or cells. —**membranous** (ˈmɛmbrənəs) *or* **membraneous** (mɛmˈbreɪnɪəs) *adj.*

memento (mɪˈmɛntəʊ) *n., pl.* **-tos** *or* **-toes.** something that reminds one of past events; a souvenir.

memento mori (ˈmɔːriː) *n.* an object, such as a skull, intended to remind people of death.

memo (ˈmɛməʊ, ˈmiːməʊ) *n., pl.* **memos.** short for **memorandum.**

memoir (ˈmɛmwɑː) *n.* **1.** a biography or historical account, esp. one based on personal knowledge. **2.** an essay, as on a specialized topic. —**'memoirist** *n.*

memoirs (ˈmɛmwɑːz) *pl. n.* **1.** a collection of reminiscences about a period, series of events, etc., written from personal experience or special sources. **2.** an autobiographical record. **3.** a record, as of transactions of a society, etc.

memorabilia (ˌmɛmərəˈbɪlɪə) *pl. n., sing.* **-rabile** (-ˈræbɪlɪ). memorable events or things.

memorable (ˈmɛmərəbəl) *adj.* worth remembering or easily remembered. —ˌ**memora'bility** *n.* —**'memorably** *adv.*

memorandum (ˌmɛməˈrændəm) *n., pl.* **-dums** *or* **-da** (-də). **1.** a written statement, record, or communication. **2.** a note of things to be remembered. **3.** an informal diplomatic communication. **4.** *Law.,* a short written summary of the terms of a transaction. ~Often (esp. for senses 1 and 2) shortened to **memo.**

memorial (mɪˈmɔːrɪəl) *adj.* **1.** serving to preserve the memory of the dead or a past event. **2.** of or involving memory. ~*n.* **3.** something serving as a remembrance. **4.** a written statement of facts submitted to a government, authority, etc., in conjunction with a petition. **5.** an informal diplomatic paper. —**me'morially** *adv.*

memorize *or* **-ise** (ˈmɛməˌraɪz) *vb.* (*tr.*) to commit to memory; learn so as to remember.

memory (ˈmɛmərɪ) *n., pl.* **-ries. 1.** the ability of the brain to store and recall past sensations, thoughts, knowledge, etc.: *he can do it from memory.* **2.** the sum of everything retained by the mind. **3.** a particular recollection of an event, person, etc. **4.** the time over which recollection extends: *within his memory.* **5.** commemoration or remembrance: *in memory of our leader.* **6.** the state of being remembered, as after death. **7.** Also called: **memory bank.** a part of a computer in which information is stored for immediate use by the central processing unit.

memsahib (ˈmɛmˌsɑːɪb, -hɪb) *n.* (formerly in India) a term of respect used of a European married woman.

men (mɛn) *n.* the plural of **man.**

menace (ˈmɛnɪs) *vb.* **1.** to threaten with violence, danger, etc. ~*n.* **2.** *Literary.* a threat. **3.** something menacing; a source of danger. **4.** *Inf.* a nuisance. —**'menacingly** *adv.*

ménage (meɪˈnɑːʒ) *n.* the persons of a household.

ménage à trois *French.* (menaːʒ a ˈtrwa) *n., pl.* **ménages à trois** (menaːʒ a ˈtrwa). a sexual arrangement involving a married couple and the lover of one of them.

menagerie (mɪˈnædʒərɪ) *n.* **1.** a collection of wild animals kept for exhibition. **2.** the place where such animals are housed.

mend (mɛnd) *vb.* **1.** (*tr.*) to repair (something broken or unserviceable). **2.** to improve or undergo improvement; reform (often in **mend one's ways**). **3.** (*intr.*) to heal or recover. **4.** (of conditions) to improve; become better. ~*n.* **5.** the act of repairing. **6.** a mended area, esp. on a garment. **7. on the mend.** becoming better, esp. in health. —**'mendable** *adj.* —**'mender** *n.*

THESAURUS

melodramatic blood-and-thunder, extravagant, hammy (*Inf.*), histrionic, overdramatic, overemotional, sensational, stagy, theatrical

melody 1. air, descant, music, refrain, song, strain, theme, tune **2.** euphony, harmony, melodiousness, music, musicality, tunefulness

melt 1. deliquesce, diffuse, dissolve, flux, fuse, liquefy, soften, thaw **2.** *Often with* away disappear, disperse, dissolve, evanesce, evaporate, fade, vanish **3.** disarm, mollify, relax, soften, touch

member 1. associate, fellow, representative **2.** appendage, arm, component, constituent, element, extremity, leg, limb, organ, part, portion

membership 1. associates, body, fellows, members **2.** belonging, enrolment, fellowship, participation

memento keepsake, memorial, relic, remembrance, reminder, souvenir, token, trophy

memoir account, biography, essay, journal, life, monograph, narrative, record, register

memoirs 1. autobiography, diary, experiences, journals, life, life story, memories, recollections, reminiscences **2.** annals, chronicles, records, transactions

memorable catchy, celebrated, distinguished, extraordinary, famous, historic, illustrious, important, impressive, momentous, notable, noteworthy, remarkable, signal, significant, striking, unforgettable

memorial *adj.* **1.** commemorative, monumental ~*n.* **2.** cairn, memento, monument, plaque, record, remembrance, souvenir **3.** address, memorandum, petition, statement

memorize commit to memory, con (*Archaic*), get by heart, learn, learn by heart, learn by rote, remember

memory 1. recall, recollection, remembrance, reminiscence, retention **2.** commemoration, honour, remembrance **3.** celebrity, fame, glory, name, renown, reputation, repute

menace *v.* **1.** alarm, bode ill, browbeat, bully, frighten, impend, intimidate, loom, lour, lower, terrorize, threaten, utter threats to ~*n.* **2.** commination, intimidation, scare, threat, warning **3.** danger, hazard, jeopardy, peril **4.** *Inf.* annoyance, nuisance, pest, plague, troublemaker

menacing alarming, dangerous, frightening, intimidating, intimidatory, looming, louring, lowering, minacious, minatory, ominous, threatening

mend *v.* **1.** cure, darn, fix, heal, patch, rectify, refit, reform, remedy, renew, renovate, repair, restore, retouch **2.** ameliorate, amend, better, correct, emend, improve, rectify, reform, revise **3.** convalesce, get better, heal, recover, recuperate ~*n.* **4.** darn, patch, repair, stitch **5. on the mend** convalescent,

mendacity (mɛn'dæsɪtɪ) n., pl. **-ties.** **1.** the tendency to be untruthful. **2.** a falsehood. —**mendacious** (mɛn-'deɪʃəs) adj. —**men'daciously** adv.

mendelevium (ˌmɛndɪ'liːvɪəm) n. a transuranic element artificially produced by bombardment of einsteinium. Symbol: Md; atomic no.: 101; half-life of most stable isotope, [258]Md: 60 days (approx.).

Mendel's laws ('mɛndəlz) pl. n. the principles of heredity proposed by Gregor Mendel (1822–84), Austrian monk and botanist. The **Law of Segregation** states that every somatic cell of an individual carries a pair of hereditary units for each character: the pairs separate during meiosis so that each gamete carries only one unit of each pair. The **Law of Independent Assortment** states that the separation of the units of each pair is not influenced by that of any other pair.

mendicant ('mɛndɪkənt) adj. **1.** begging. **2.** (of a member of a religious order) dependent on alms for sustenance. ~n. **3.** a mendicant friar. **4.** a less common word for **beggar.** —'**mendicancy** or **mendicity** (mɛn-'dɪsɪtɪ) n.

menfolk ('mɛnˌfəʊk) pl. n. men collectively, esp. the men of a particular family.

menhir ('mɛnhɪə) n. a single standing stone, dating from prehistoric times.

menial ('miːnɪəl) adj. **1.** consisting of or occupied with work requiring little skill, esp. domestic duties. **2.** of, involving, or befitting servants. **3.** servile. ~n. **4.** a domestic servant. **5.** a servile person.

meninges (mɪ'nɪndʒiːz) pl. n., sing. **meninx** ('miːnɪŋks). the three membranes (**dura mater, arachnoid, pia mater**) that envelop the brain and spinal cord. —**meningeal** (mɪ'nɪndʒɪəl) adj.

meningitis (ˌmɛnɪn'dʒaɪtɪs) n. inflammation of the membranes that surround the brain or spinal cord, caused by infection. —**meningitic** (ˌmɛnɪn'dʒɪtɪk) adj.

meniscus (mɪ'nɪskəs) n., pl. **-nisci** (-'nɪsaɪ) or **-niscuses.** **1.** the curved upper surface of a liquid standing in a tube, produced by the surface tension. **2.** a crescent-shaped lens; a concavo-convex or convexo-concave lens. —**me'niscoid** adj.

meno- combining form. menstruation.

menopause ('mɛnəʊˌpɔːz) n. the period during which a woman's menstrual cycle ceases, normally at an age of 45 to 50. —ˌmeno'pausal adj.

menorah (mɪ'nɔːrə) n. Judaism. **1.** a seven-branched candelabrum used in ceremonies. **2.** a stand with nine lamps used during the Hanukkah festival.

menses ('mɛnsiːz) n., pl. **menses.** **1.** another name for **menstruation.** See **menstruate.** **2.** the period of time during which one menstruation occurs. **3.** the matter discharged during menstruation.

menstruate ('mɛnstrʊˌeɪt) vb. (intr.) to undergo menstruation. —ˌmenstru'ation n.

mensuration (ˌmɛnsjə'reɪʃən) n. **1.** the study of the measurement of geometric magnitudes such as length. **2.** the act or process of measuring. —**mensurative** ('mɛnʃərətɪv) adj.

-ment suffix forming nouns, esp. from verbs. **1.** indicating state, condition, or quality: enjoyment. **2.** indicating the result or product of an action: embankment. **3.** indicating process or action: management.

mental ('mɛntəl) adj. **1.** of or involving the mind. **2.** occurring only in the mind: mental arithmetic. **3.** affected by mental illness: a mental patient. **4.** concerned with mental illness: a mental hospital. **5.** Sl. insane. —'**mentally** adv.

mental deficiency n. Psychiatry. a condition of low intellectual development requiring special education and employment. Also called: **mental handicap, mental retardation, mental subnormality.**

mentality (mɛn'tælɪtɪ) n., pl. **-ties.** **1.** the state or quality of mental or intellectual ability. **2.** a way of thinking; mental inclination or character.

menthol ('mɛnθɒl) n. an organic compound found in peppermint oil and used as an antiseptic, in inhalants, and as an analgesic.

mention ('mɛnʃən) vb. (tr.) **1.** to refer to or speak about briefly or incidentally. **2.** to acknowledge or honour. **3. not to mention (something).** to say nothing of (something too obvious to mention). ~n. **4.** a recognition or acknowledgment. **5.** a slight reference or allusion. **6.** the act of mentioning. —'**mentionable** adj.

mentor ('mɛntɔː) n. a wise or trusted adviser or guide.

menu ('mɛnjuː) n. a list of dishes served at a meal or that can be ordered in a restaurant.

meow, miaou, miaow (mɪ'aʊ, mjaʊ), or **miaul** (mɪ-'aʊl, mjaʊl) vb. **1.** (intr.) (of a cat) to make a characteristic crying sound. ~interj. **2.** an imitation of this sound.

MEP abbrev. for Member of the European Parliament.

Mephistopheles (ˌmɛfɪ'stɒfɪˌliːz) or **Mephisto** (mə-'fɪstəʊ) n. a devil in medieval mythology and the one to whom Faust sold his soul in German legend. —**Mephistophelean** or **Mephistophelian** (ˌmɛfɪstə'fiːlɪən) adj.

-mer suffix forming nouns. Chem. denoting a substance of a particular class: monomer; polymer.

mercantile ('mɜːkənˌtaɪl) adj. **1.** of, relating to, or characteristic of trade or traders; commercial. **2.** of or relating to mercantilism.

mercantilism ('mɜːkəntɪˌlɪzəm) n. Econ. a theory prevalent in Europe during the 17th and 18th centuries asserting that the wealth of a nation depends on possession of precious metals and therefore that a government must maximize foreign trade surplus and foster national commercial interests, a merchant marine, the establishment of colonies, etc. —'**mercantilist** n., adj.

Mercator projection (mɜː'keɪtə) n. a map projection on which parallels and meridians form a rectangular grid, scale being exaggerated with increasing distance from the equator. Also called: **Mercator's projection.**

mercenary ('mɜːsɪnərɪ, -sɪnrɪ) adj. **1.** influenced by greed or gain. **2.** of or relating to a mercenary or mercenaries. ~n., pl. **-naries.** **3.** a man hired to fight for a foreign army, etc. **4.** Rare. any person who works solely for pay.

mercer ('mɜːsə) n. Brit. a dealer in textile fabrics and fine cloth. —'**mercery** n.

mercerize or **-ise** ('mɜːsəˌraɪz) vb. (tr.) to treat (cotton yarn) with an alkali to increase its strength and reception to dye and impart a lustrous silky appearance.

merchandise n. ('mɜːtʃənˌdaɪs, -ˌdaɪz). **1.** commercial goods; commodities. ~vb. ('mɜːtʃənˌdaɪz). **2.** to engage in the commercial purchase and sale of (goods or services); trade.

THESAURUS

convalescing, getting better, improving, recovering, recuperating

mendacious deceitful, deceptive, dishonest, duplicitous, fallacious, false, fraudulent, insincere, lying, perfidious, perjured, untrue, untruthful

menial adj. **1.** boring, dull, humdrum, low-status, routine, unskilled **2.** abject, base, degrading, demeaning, fawning, grovelling, humble, ignoble, ignominious, low, lowly, mean, obsequious, servile, slavish, sorry, subservient, sycophantic, vile ~n. **3.** attendant, dogsbody (Inf.), domestic, drudge, flunky, labourer, lackey, serf, servant, skivvy (Brit.), slave, underling

menstruation catamenia (Physiology), courses (Physiology), flow (Inf.), menses, menstrual cycle, monthly (Inf.), period, the curse (Inf.)

mental 1. cerebral, intellectual **2.** deranged, disturbed, insane, lunatic, mad, mentally ill, psychiatric, psychotic, unbalanced, unstable

mentality 1. brainpower, brains, comprehension, grey matter (Inf.), intellect, intelligence quotient, I.Q., mental age, mind, rationality, understanding, wit **2.** attitude, cast of mind, character, disposition, frame of mind, make-up, outlook, personality, psychology, turn of mind, way of thinking

mentally in one's head, intellectually, in the mind, inwardly, psychologically, rationally, subjectively

mention v. **1.** acknowledge, adduce, allude to, bring up, broach, call attention to, cite, communicate, declare, disclose, divulge, hint at, impart, intimate, make known, name, point out, recount, refer to, report, reveal, speak about or of, state, tell, touch upon **2. not to mention** as well as, besides, not counting, to say nothing of ~n. **3.** acknowledgment, citation, recognition, tribute **4.** allusion, announcement, indication, notification, observation, reference, remark

mentor adviser, coach, counsellor, guide, guru, instructor, teacher, tutor

menu bill of fare, carte du jour, tariff (Chiefly Brit.)

mercantile commercial, marketable, trade, trading

mercenary adj. **1.** acquisitive, avaricious, bribable, covetous, grasping, greedy, money-grubbing (Inf.), sordid, venal **2.** bought, hired, paid, venal ~n. **3.** condottiere (Hist.), free companion (Hist.), freelance (Hist.), hireling, soldier of fortune

merchandise 1. n. commodities, goods,

merchant (ˈmɜːtʃənt) n. **1.** a person engaged in the purchase and sale of commodities for profit; trader. **2.** U.S. & Scot. a person engaged in retail trade. **3.** (esp. in historical contexts) any trader. **4.** Derog. a person dealing or involved in something undesirable: a gossip merchant. **5.** (modifier) **a.** of the merchant navy: a merchant sailor. **b.** of or concerned with trade: a merchant ship. ~vb. **6.** (tr.) to conduct trade in; deal in.

merchant bank n. Brit. a financial institution engaged primarily in accepting foreign bills and underwriting new security issues. —**merchant banker** n.

merchantman (ˈmɜːtʃəntmən) n., pl. -**men.** a merchant ship.

merchant navy or **marine** n. the ships or crew engaged in a nation's commercial shipping.

merciful (ˈmɜːsɪfʊl) adj. showing or giving mercy; compassionate. —**mercifully** adv. —**mercifulness** n.

merciless (ˈmɜːsɪlɪs) adj. without mercy; pitiless, cruel, or heartless. —**mercilessly** adv. —**mercilessness** n.

mercurial (mɜːˈkjʊərɪəl) adj. **1.** of, like, containing, or relating to mercury. **2.** volatile; lively: a mercurial temperament. **3.** (sometimes cap.) of, like, or relating to the god or the planet Mercury. ~n. **4.** Med. any salt of mercury for use as a medicine. —**mer‚curiˈality** n. —**merˈcurially** adv.

mercuric (mɜːˈkjʊərɪk) adj. of or containing mercury in the divalent state.

mercurous (ˈmɜːkjʊrəs) adj. of or containing mercury in the monovalent state.

mercury (ˈmɜːkjʊrɪ) n., pl. -**ries. 1.** Also called: **quicksilver.** a heavy silvery-white toxic liquid metallic element: used in thermometers, barometers, mercury-vapour lamps, and dental amalgams. Symbol: Hg; atomic no.: 80; atomic wt.: 200.59. **2.** any plant of the genus Mercurialis. **3.** Arch. a messenger or courier.

Mercury[1] (ˈmɜːkjʊrɪ) n. Roman myth. the messenger of the gods.

Mercury[2] (ˈmɜːkjʊrɪ) n. the smallest planet and the nearest to the sun.

mercy (ˈmɜːsɪ) n., pl. -**cies. 1.** compassionate treatment of or attitude towards an offender, adversary, etc., who is in one's power or care; clemency; pity. **2.** the power to show mercy. **3.** a relieving or welcome occurrence or state of affairs. **4. at the mercy of.** in the power of.

mercy flight n. an aircraft flight to bring a seriously ill or injured person to hospital from an isolated community.

mercy killing n. another term for **euthanasia.**

mere[1] (mɪə) adj. superlative **merest.** being nothing more than something specified: she is a mere child. —ˈ**merely** adv.

mere[2] (mɪə) n. **1.** Brit. dialect or arch. a lake or marsh. **2.** Obs. the sea or an inlet of it.

meretricious (‚mɛrɪˈtrɪʃəs) adj. **1.** superficially or garishly attractive. **2.** insincere. **3.** Arch. of, like, or relating to a prostitute. —‚**mereˈtriciously** adv. —‚**mereˈtriciousness** n.

merganser (mɜːˈgænsə) n., pl. -**sers** or -**ser.** any of several typically crested large marine diving ducks, having a long slender hooked bill with serrated edges.

merge (mɜːdʒ) vb. **1.** to meet and join or cause to meet and join. **2.** to blend or cause to blend; fuse. —ˈ**mergence** n.

merger (ˈmɜːdʒə) n. **1.** Commerce. the combination of two or more companies. **2.** Law. the absorption of an estate, interest, offence, etc., into a greater one. **3.** the act of merging or the state of being merged.

meridian (məˈrɪdɪən) n. **1. a.** one of the imaginary lines joining the north and south poles at right angles to the equator, designated by degrees of longitude from 0° at Greenwich to 180°. **b.** the. great circle running through both poles. **2.** Astron. the great circle on the celestial sphere passing through the north and south celestial poles and the zenith and nadir of the observer. **3.** the peak; zenith: the meridian of his achievements. **4.** Obs. noon. ~adj. **5.** along or relating to a meridian. **6.** of or happening at noon. **7.** relating to the peak of something.

meridional (məˈrɪdɪənəl) adj. **1.** along, relating to, or resembling a meridian. **2.** characteristic of or located in the south, esp. of Europe. ~n. **3.** an inhabitant of the south, esp. of France.

meringue (məˈræŋ) n. **1.** stiffly beaten egg whites mixed with sugar and baked. **2.** a small cake or shell of this mixture, often filled with cream.

merino (məˈriːnəʊ) n., pl. -**nos. 1.** a breed of sheep originating in Spain. **2.** the long fine wool of this sheep. **3.** the yarn made from this wool, often mixed with cotton. ~adj. **4.** made from merino wool.

merit (ˈmɛrɪt) n. **1.** worth or superior quality; excellence. **2.** (often pl.) a deserving or commendable quality or act. **3.** Theol. spiritual credit granted or received for good works. **4.** the fact or state of deserving; desert. ~vb. **5.** (tr.) to be worthy of; deserve.

meritocracy (‚mɛrɪˈtɒkrəsɪ) n., pl. -**cies. 1.** rule by persons chosen for their superior talents or intellect. **2.** the persons constituting such a group. **3.** a social system formed on such a basis.

meritorious (‚mɛrɪˈtɔːrɪəs) adj. praiseworthy;. showing merit. —‚**meriˈtoriously** adv. —‚**meriˈtoriousness** n.

merits (ˈmɛrɪts) pl. n. **1.** the actual and intrinsic rights and wrongs of an issue, esp. in a law case. **2. on its (his, her,** etc.) **merits.** on the intrinsic qualities or virtues.

merlin (ˈmɜːlɪn) n. a small falcon that has a dark plumage with a black-barred tail.

mermaid (ˈmɜː‚meɪd) n. an imaginary sea creature fabled to have a woman's head and upper body and a fish's tail.

-merous adj. combining form. (in biology) having a certain number or kind of parts.

merry (ˈmɛrɪ) adj. -**rier,** -**riest. 1.** cheerful; jolly. **2.** very funny; hilarious. **3.** Brit. inf. slightly drunk. **4. play merry hell with.** Inf. to disturb greatly; disrupt. —ˈ**merrily** adv. —ˈ**merriment** n. —ˈ**merriness** n.

THESAURUS

produce, products, staples, stock, stock in trade, truck, vendibles, wares **2.** v. buy and sell, deal in, distribute, do business in, market, retail, sell, trade, traffic in, vend

merchant broker, dealer, retailer, salesman, seller, shopkeeper, trader, tradesman, trafficker, vendor, wholesaler

merciful beneficent, benignant, clement, compassionate, forbearing, forgiving, generous, gracious, humane, kind, lenient, liberal, mild, pitying, soft, sparing, sympathetic, tender-hearted

merciless barbarous, callous, cruel, fell (Archaic), hard, hard-hearted, harsh, heartless, implacable, inexorable, inhumane, pitiless, relentless, ruthless, severe, unappeasable, unfeeling, unforgiving, unmerciful, unpitying, unsparing, unsympathetic

mercurial active, capricious, changeable, erratic, fickle, flighty, gay, impulsive, inconstant, irrepressible, light-hearted, lively, mobile, quicksilver, spirited, sprightly, temperamental, unpredictable, unstable, variable, volatile

mercy 1. benevolence, charity, clemency, compassion, favour, forbearance, forgiveness, grace, kindness, leniency, pity, quarter **2.** benison (Archaic), blessing, boon, godsend, piece of luck, relief **3. at the mercy of** defenceless against, exposed to, in the clutches of, in the power of, naked before, open to, prey to, subject to, threatened by, unprotected against, vulnerable to

mere adj. absolute, bare, common, complete, entire, nothing more than, plain, pure, pure and simple, sheer, simple, stark, unadulterated, unmitigated, unmixed, utter

merge amalgamate, be swallowed up by, become lost in, blend, coalesce, combine, consolidate, converge, fuse, incorporate, intermix, join, meet, meld, melt into, mingle, mix, tone with, unite

merger amalgamation, coalition, combination, consolidation, fusion, incorporation, union

merit n. **1.** advantage, asset, excellence, good, goodness, integrity, quality, strong point, talent, value, virtue, worth, worthiness **2.** claim, credit, desert, due, right ~v. **3.** be entitled to, be worthy of, deserve, earn, have

a claim to, have a right to, have coming to one, incur, rate, warrant

meritorious admirable, commendable, creditable, deserving, excellent, exemplary, good, honourable, laudable, praiseworthy, right, righteous, virtuous, worthy

merriment amusement, conviviality, festivity, frolic, fun, gaiety, glee, hilarity, jocularity, jollity, joviality, laughter, levity, liveliness, merry-making, mirth, revelry, sport

merry 1. blithe, blithesome, carefree, cheerful, convivial, festive, frolicsome, fun-loving, gay, glad, gleeful, happy, jocund, jolly, joyful, joyous, light-hearted, mirthful, rollicking, sportive, vivacious **2.** amusing, comic, comical, facetious, funny, hilarious, humorous, jocular, mirthful **3.** Brit. inf. elevated (Inf.), happy, mellow, squiffy (Brit. inf.), tiddly (Brit. sl.), tipsy **4.** make merry carouse, celebrate, enjoy oneself, feast, frolic, have a good time, have fun, make whoopee (Inf.), revel

merry-andrew (-'ændruː) *n.* a joker, clown, or buffoon.

merry-go-round *n.* **1.** another name for **roundabout** (sense 1). **2.** a whirl of activity.

merrymaking ('mɛrɪˌmeɪkɪŋ) *n.* fun, revelry, or festivity. —'**merry**ˌ**maker** *n.*

mésalliance (mɛˈzælɪəns) *n.* a marriage with a person of lower social status.

mescal (mɛˈskæl) *n.* **1.** Also called: **peyote.** a spineless globe-shaped cactus of Mexico and the southwestern U.S. Its button-like tubercles (**mescal buttons**) are chewed by certain Indian tribes for their hallucinogenic effects. **2.** a colourless alcholic spirit distilled from the fermented juice of certain agave plants.

mescaline *or* **mescalin** ('mɛskəˌliːn, -lɪn) *n.* a hallucinogenic drug derived from mescal buttons.

mesdames ('meɪˌdæm) *n.* the plural of **madame.**

mesdemoiselles (ˌmeɪdmwɔˈzɛl) *n.* the plural of **mademoiselle.**

mesentery ('mɛsəntərɪ, 'mɛz-) *n., pl.* **-teries.** the double layer of peritoneum that is attached to the back wall of the abdominal cavity and supports most of the small intestine. —ˌmesen'teric *adj.* —mesˌente'ritis *n.*

mesh (mɛʃ) *n.* **1.** a network; net. **2.** an open space between the strands of a network. **3.** (*often pl.*) the strands surrounding these spaces. **4.** anything that ensnares, or holds like a net. **5.** the engagement of teeth on interacting gearwheels: *the gears are in mesh.* —*vb.* **6.** to entangle or become entangled. **7.** (of gear teeth) to engage or cause to engage. **8.** (*intr.; often foll. by with*) to coordinate (with). **9.** to work or cause to work in harmony.

mesmerize *or* **-ise** ('mɛzməˌraɪz) *vb.* (*tr.*) **1.** a former word for **hypnotize.** **2.** to hold (someone) as if spellbound. —ˌmesmeri'zation *or* -i'sation *n.* —'mesmerˌizer *or* -ˌiser *n.*

meso- *or before a vowel* **mes-** *combining form.* middle or intermediate: *mesomorph.*

Mesolithic (ˌmɛsəʊˈlɪθɪk) *n.* **1.** the period between the Palaeolithic and the Neolithic, in Europe from about 12 000 to 3000 B.C. ~*adj.* **2.** of or relating to the Mesolithic.

mesomorph ('mɛsəʊˌmɔːf) *n.* a type of person having a muscular body build with a relatively prominent underlying bone structure.

mesomorphic (ˌmɛsəʊˈmɔːfɪk) *adj. also* **mesomorphous.** **1.** *Chem.* existing in or concerned with an intermediate state of matter between a true liquid and a true solid. **2.** relating to or being a mesomorph. —ˌmeso'morphism *n.*

meson ('miːzɒn) *n.* any of a group of elementary particles that has a rest mass between those of an electron and a proton, and an integral spin. —me'sonic *or* 'mesic *adj.*

mesosphere ('mɛsəʊˌsfɪə) *n.* the atmospheric layer lying between the stratosphere and the thermosphere.

Mesozoic (ˌmɛsəʊˈzəʊɪk) *adj.* **1.** of, denoting, or relating to an era of geological time that began 225 000 000 years ago and lasted about 155 000 000 years. ~*n.* **2.** the. the Mesozoic era.

mess (mɛs) *n.* **1.** a state of confusion or untidiness, esp. if dirty or unpleasant. **2.** a chaotic or troublesome state of affairs; muddle. **3.** *Inf.* a dirty or untidy person or thing. **4.** *Arch.* a portion of food, esp. soft or semiliquid food. **5.** a place where service personnel eat or take recreation. **6.** a group of people, usually servicemen, who eat together. **7.** the meal so taken. ~*vb.* **8.** (*tr.; often*

foll. by *up*) to muddle or dirty. **9.** (*intr.*) to make a mess. **10.** (*intr.*) (often foll. by *with*) to interfere; meddle. **11.** (*intr.*) (often foll. by *with* or *together*) *Mil.* to group together, esp. for eating.

mess about *or* **around** *vb.* (*adv.*) **1.** (*intr.*) to occupy oneself trivially; potter. **2.** (when *intr.*, often foll. by *with*) to interfere or meddle (with).

message ('mɛsɪdʒ) *n.* **1.** a communication, usually brief, from one person or group to another. **2.** an implicit meaning, as in a work of art. **3.** a formal communiqué. **4.** an inspired communication of a prophet or religious leader. **5.** a mission; errand. **6. get the message.** *Inf.* to understand. ~*vb.* **7.** (*tr.*) to send as a message.

messages ('mɛsɪdʒɪz) *pl. n. Scot. & NE English dialect.* errands to buy food, etc.; household shopping.

messenger ('mɛsɪndʒə) *n.* **1.** a person who takes messages from one person or group to another. **2.** a person who runs errands. **3.** a carrier of official dispatches; courier.

Messiah (mɪˈsaɪə) *n.* **1.** *Judaism.* the awaited king of the Jews, to be sent by God to free them. **2.** Jesus Christ, when regarded in this role. **3.** an exceptional liberator of a country or people. —Mes'siahˌship *n.* —Messianic *or* messianic (ˌmɛsɪˈænɪk) *adj.*

messieurs ('mɛsəz) *n.* the plural of **monsieur.**

mess jacket *n.* a waist-length jacket, worn by officers in the mess for formal dinners.

mess kit *n. Mil.* **1.** *Brit.* formal evening wear for officers. **2.** Also called: **mess gear.** eating utensils used esp. in the field.

Messrs. ('mɛsəz) *n.* the plural of **Mr.**

messy ('mɛsɪ) *adj.* **messier, messiest.** dirty, confused, or untidy. —'messily *adv.* —'messiness *n.*

met (mɛt) *vb.* the past tense or past participle of **meet**[1].

met. *abbrev. for:* **1.** meteorological. **2.** meteorology. **3.** metropolitan.

meta- *or sometimes before a vowel* **met-** *prefix.* **1.** indicating change or alternation: *metabolism; metamorphosis.* **2.** transcending or going beyond: *metapsychology.* **3.** occurring or situated behind or after: *metaphysics.* **4.** (*often in italics*) denoting that an organic compound contains a benzene ring with substituents in the 1,3-positions: *meta-cresol.* **5.** denoting an isomer, polymer, or compound related to a specified compound: *metaldehyde.* **6.** denoting an oxyacid that is the least hydrated form of the anhydride or a salt of such an acid: *metaphosphoric acid.*

metabolism (mɪˈtæbəˌlɪzəm) *n.* **1.** the sum total of the chemical processes that occur in living organisms, resulting in growth, production of energy, elimination of waste material, etc. **2.** the sum total of the chemical processes affecting a particular substance in the body: *carbohydrate metabolism.* —**metabolic** (ˌmɛtəˈbɒlɪk) *adj.* —ˌmeta'bolically *adv.*

metacarpus (ˌmɛtəˈkɑːpəs) *n., pl.* **-pi** (-paɪ). **1.** the skeleton of the hand between the wrist and the fingers, consisting of five long bones. **2.** the corresponding bones in other vertebrates. —ˌmeta'carpal *adj., n.*

metal ('mɛtᵊl) *n.* **1. a.** any of a number of chemical elements, such as iron or copper, that are often lustrous ductile solids, have basic oxides, form positive ions, and are good conductors of heat and electricity. **b.** an alloy, such as brass or steel, containing one or more of these elements. **2.** the substance of glass in a molten state or as the finished product. **3.** *N.Z.* an unsealed road surface: *the car skidded off the metal.* **4.** *Heraldry.* gold or silver. **5.** the basic quality of a person or thing; stuff. **6.**

THESAURUS

mesh *n.* **1.** net, netting, network, plexus, reticulation, tracery, web **2.** entanglement, snare, tangle, toils, trap, web ~*v.* **3.** catch, enmesh, ensnare, entangle, net, snare, tangle, trap **4.** combine, come together, connect, coordinate, dovetail, engage, fit together, harmonize, interlock, knit

mesmerize captivate, enthral, entrance, fascinate, grip, hold spellbound, hypnotize, magnetize, spellbind

mess *n.* **1.** botch, chaos, clutter, confusion, dirtiness, disarray, disorder, disorganization, hash (*Inf.*), jumble, litter, mishmash, shambles, turmoil, untidiness **2.** difficulty, dilemma, fine kettle of fish (*Inf.*), fix (*Inf.*), imbro-

glio, jam (*Inf.*), mix-up, muddle, perplexity, pickle (*Inf.*), plight, predicament, stew (*Inf.*) ~*v.* **3.** *Often with up* befoul, besmirch, botch, bungle, clutter, dirty, disarrange, dishevel, foul, litter, make a hash of (*Inf.*), muck up (*Brit. sl.*), muddle, pollute, scramble **4.** *Often with* with fiddle (*Inf.*), interfere, meddle, play, tamper, tinker

mess about *or* **around 1.** amuse oneself, dabble, footle (*Inf.*), muck about (*Inf.*), play about *or* around, potter, trifle **2.** fiddle (*Inf.*), interfere, meddle, play, tamper, tinker, toy

message 1. bulletin, communication, communiqué, dispatch, intimation, letter,

memorandum, missive, note, notice, tidings, word **2.** idea, import, meaning, moral, point, purport, theme **3.** commission, errand, job, mission, task **4. get the message** catch on (*Inf.*), comprehend, get it (*Inf.*), get the point, see, take the hint, understand

messenger agent, bearer, carrier, courier, delivery boy, emissary, envoy, errandboy, go-between, harbinger, herald, runner

messy chaotic, cluttered, confused, dirty, dishevelled, disordered, disorganized, grubby, littered, muddled, shambolic (*Inf.*), sloppy (*Inf.*), slovenly, unkempt, untidy

(pl.) the rails of a railway. ~adj. 7. made of metal. ~vb. -**alling**, -**alled** or U.S. -**aling**, -**aled**. (tr.) 8. to fit or cover with metal.

metal. or **metall.** abbrev. for: 1. metallurgical. 2. metallurgy.

metallic (mɪ'tælɪk) adj. 1. of, concerned with, or consisting of metal or a metal. 2. suggestive of a metal: a metallic click; metallic lustre. 3. Chem. (of a metal element) existing in the free state rather than in combination: metallic copper.

metalliferous (ˌmɛtə'lɪfərəs) adj. containing a metallic element.

metallography (ˌmɛtə'lɒgrəfɪ) n. the branch of metallurgy concerned with the composition and structure of metals and alloys. —**metallographic** (mɪˌtælə'græfɪk) adj.

metalloid ('mɛtəˌlɔɪd) n. 1. a nonmetallic element, such as arsenic or silicon, that has some of the properties of a metal. ~adj. also **metalloidal** (ˌmɛtə'lɔɪdəl). 2. of or being a metalloid. 3. resembling a metal.

metallurgy (mɛ'tælədʒɪ) n. the scientific study of the extraction, refining, alloying, and fabrication of metals and of their structure and properties. —**metal'lurgic** or ˌ**metal'lurgical** adj. —**metallurgist** (mɛ'tælədʒɪst, 'mɛtəˌlɜːdʒɪst) n.

metalwork ('mɛtəlˌwɜːk) n. 1. the craft of working in metal. 2. work in metal or articles made from metal. —'**metal,worker** n.

metamorphic (ˌmɛtə'mɔːfɪk) or **metamorphous** adj. 1. relating to or resulting from metamorphosis or metamorphism. 2. (of rocks) altered considerably from the original structure and composition by pressure and heat.

metamorphism (ˌmɛtə'mɔːfɪzəm) n. 1. the process by which metamorphic rocks are formed. 2. a variant of **metamorphosis.**

metamorphose (ˌmɛtə'mɔːfəuz) vb. to undergo or cause to undergo metamorphosis or metamorphism.

metamorphosis (ˌmɛtə'mɔːfəsɪs) n., pl. -**ses** (-ˌsiːz). 1. a complete change of physical form or substance. 2. a complete change of character, appearance, etc. 3. a person or thing that has undergone metamorphosis. 4. Zool. the rapid transformation of a larva into an adult that occurs in certain animals, for example the stage between chrysalis and butterfly.

metaphor ('mɛtəfə, -ˌfɔː) n. a figure of speech in which a word or phrase is applied to an object or action that it does not literally denote in order to imply a resemblance, for example he is a lion in battle. Cf. **simile.** —**metaphoric** (ˌmɛtə'fɒrɪk) or ˌ**meta'phorical** adj. —ˌ**meta'phorically** adv.

metaphysical (ˌmɛtə'fɪzɪkəl) adj. 1. of or relating to metaphysics. 2. based on abstract reasoning. 3. overtheoretical. 4. incorporeal; supernatural. —ˌ**meta'physically** adv.

Metaphysical (ˌmɛtə'fɪzɪkəl) adj. 1. denoting or relating to certain 17th-century poets who combined intense feeling with elaborate imagery. ~n. 2. a poet of this group.

metaphysics (ˌmɛtə'fɪzɪks) n. (functioning as sing.) 1. the branch of philosophy that deals with first principles, esp. of being and knowing. 2. (popularly) abstract or subtle discussion or reasoning. —**metaphysician** (ˌmɛtəfɪ'zɪʃən) or **metaphysicist** (ˌmɛtə'fɪzɪsɪst) n.

metastasis (mɪ'tæstəsɪs) n., pl. -**ses** (-ˌsiːz). Pathol. the spreading of a disease, esp. cancer cells, from one part of the body to another. —**me'tasta,size** or -**ise** vb. —**metastatic** (ˌmɛtə'stætɪk) adj. —ˌ**meta'statically** adv.

metatarsus (ˌmɛtə'tɑːsəs) n., pl. -**si** (-saɪ). 1. the skeleton of the foot between the toes and the tarsus, consisting of five long bones. 2. the corresponding skeletal part in other vertebrates. —ˌ**meta'tarsal** adj., n.

metathesis (mɪ'tæθəsɪs) n., pl. -**ses** (-ˌsiːz). the transposition of two sounds or letters in a word or of two words in a sentence. —**metathetic** (ˌmɛtə'θɛtɪk) or ˌ**meta'thetical** adj.

metazoan (ˌmɛtə'zəuən) n. 1. any animal having a body composed of many cells: includes all animals except sponges and protozoans. ~adj. also **metazoic.** 2. of or relating to the metazoans.

mete (miːt) vb. (tr.) 1. (usually foll. by out) Formal. to distribute or allot (something, often unpleasant). 2. Poetic, dialect. to measure.

metempsychosis (ˌmɛtəmsaɪ'kəusɪs) n., pl. -**ses** (-siːz). the migration of a soul from one body to another. —ˌ**metempsy'chosist** n.

meteor ('miːtɪə) n. 1. a very small meteoroid that has entered the earth's atmosphere. 2. Also called: **shooting star, falling star.** the bright streak of light appearing in the sky due to the incandescence of such a body heated by friction at its surface.

meteoric (ˌmiːtɪ'ɒrɪk) adj. 1. of, formed by, or relating to meteors. 2. like a meteor in brilliance, speed, or transience. 3. Rare. of weather; meteorological. —ˌ**me-te'orically** adv.

meteorite ('miːtɪəˌraɪt) n. a rocklike object consisting of the remains of a meteoroid that has fallen on earth. —**meteoritic** (ˌmiːtɪə'rɪtɪk) adj.

meteoroid ('miːtɪəˌrɔɪd) n. any of the small celestial bodies that are thought to orbit the sun. When they enter the earth's atmosphere, they become visible as meteors. —ˌ**meteor'oidal** adj.

meteorol. or **meteor.** abbrev for: 1. meteorological. 2. meteorology.

meteorology (ˌmiːtɪə'rɒlədʒɪ) n. the study of the earth's atmosphere, esp. of weather-forming processes and weather forecasting. —**meteorological** (ˌmiːtɪərə'lɒdʒɪkəl) or ˌ**meteoro'logic** adj. —ˌ**meteoro'logically** adv. —ˌ**meteor'ologist** n.

meteor shower n. a transient rain of meteors occurring at regular intervals and coming from a particular region in the sky.

meter[1] ('miːtə) n. the U.S. spelling of **metre**[1].

meter[2] ('miːtə) n. the U.S. spelling of **metre**[2].

meter[3] ('miːtə) n. 1. any device that measures and records a quantity, such as of gas, current, voltage, etc. that has passed through it during a specified period. 2. See **parking meter.** ~vb. (tr.) 3. to measure (a rate of flow) with a meter.

-**meter** n. combining form. 1. indicating an instrument for measuring: barometer. 2. Prosody. indicating a verse having a specified number of feet: pentameter.

Meth. abbrev. for Methodist.

methadone ('mɛθəˌdəun) or **methadon** ('mɛθəˌdɒn) n. a narcotic analgesic drug similar to morphine but less habit-forming.

methane ('miːθeɪn) n. a colourless odourless flammable gas, the main constituent of natural gas: used as a fuel.

methane series n. any of a series of saturated aliphatic hydrocarbons with the general formula $C_nH_{2n+1}A_2$. Also called: **alkane series.**

methanol ('mɛθəˌnɒl) n. a colourless volatile poisonous liquid compound used as a solvent and fuel. Formula: CH_3OH. Also called: **methyl alcohol, wood alcohol.**

methinks (mɪ'θɪŋks) vb. past **methought.** (tr.) (takes a clause as object) Arch. it seems to me.

method ('mɛθəd) n. 1. a way of proceeding or doing something, esp. a systematic or regular one. 2. orderliness of thought, action, etc. 3. (often pl.) the techniques or arrangement of work for a particular field or subject. —'**methodist** n.

Method n. (sometimes not cap.) a. a technique of acting in which the actor bases his role on the inner motiva-

---

THESAURUS

tion of the character played. **b.** (*as modifier*): *a Method actor.*

methodical (mɪˈθɒdɪkəl) *or* **methodic** *adj.* characterized by method or orderliness; systematic. —**meˈthodically** *adv.*

Methodist (ˈmɛθədɪst) *n.* **1.** a member of any of the Nonconformist denominations that derive from the system of faith and practice initiated by John Wesley and his followers. ~*adj.* *also* **ˌMethodˈistic** *or* **ˌMethodˈistical.** **2.** of or relating to Methodism or the Methodist Church. —ˈ**Method,ism** *n.*

methodology (ˌmɛθəˈdɒlədʒɪ) *n.*, *pl.* **-gies.** **1.** the system of methods and principles used in a particular discipline. **2.** the branch of philosophy concerned with the science of method. —**methodological** (ˌmɛθədəˈlɒdʒɪkəl) *adj.* —**ˌmethodoˈlogically** *adv.* —ˌ**methodˈologist** *n.*

methought (mɪˈθɔːt) *vb. Arch.* the past tense of **methinks.**

meths (mɛθs) *n. Chiefly Brit.* an informal name for **methylated spirits.**

methyl (ˈmiːθaɪl, ˈmɛθɪl) *n.* **1.** (*modifier*) of, consisting of, or containing the monovalent group of atoms CH_3. **2.** a compound in which methyl groups are bound directly to a metal atom. —**methylic** (məˈθɪlɪk) *adj.*

methyl acetate *n.* a colourless volatile flammable liquid ester ,used as a solvent, esp. in paint removers. Formula: CH_3COOCH_3.

methyl alcohol *n.* another name for **methanol.**

methylate (ˈmɛθɪˌleɪt) *vb.* (*tr.*) to mix with methanol.

methylated spirits *n.* alcohol that has been denatured by the addition of methanol and pyridine and a violet dye.

methyl chloride *n.* a colourless gas with an etherlike odour, used as a refrigerant and anaesthetic. Formula: CH_3Cl.

methylene (ˈmɛθɪˌliːn) *n.* (*modifier*) of, consisting of, or containing the divalent group of atoms $=CH_2$: *a methylene group or radical.*

meticulous (mɪˈtɪkjʊləs) *adj.* very precise about details; painstaking. —**meˈticulously** *adv.* —**meˈticulousness** *n.*

métier (ˈmɛtɪeɪ) *n.* **1.** a profession or trade. **2.** a person's strong point or speciality.

Métis (meɪˈtiːs) *n.*, *pl.* **-tis** (-ˈtiːs, -ˈtiːz). a person of mixed parentage, esp. the offspring of a French Canadian and a North American Indian. —**Métisse** (meɪˈtiːs) *fem. n.*

metonymy (mɪˈtɒnɪmɪ) *n.*, *pl.* **-mies.** the substitution of a word referring to an attribute for the thing that is meant, e.g. *the crown,* used to refer to a monarch. Cf. **synecdoche.** —**metonymical** (ˌmɛtəˈnɪmɪkəl) *or* ˌ**metoˈnymic** *adj.*

metre[1] *or U.S.* **meter** (ˈmiːtə) *n.* **1.** a metric unit of length equal to approximately 1.094 yards. **2.** the basic SI unit of length; the length of the path travelled by light in free space during a time interval of 1/299 792 458 of a second. Symbol: m

metre[2] *or U.S.* **meter** (ˈmiːtə) *n.* **1.** *Prosody.* the rhythmic arrangement of syllables in verse, usually according to the number and kind of feet in a line. **2.** *Music.* another word (esp. U.S.) for **time** (sense 22).

metre-kilogram-second *n.* See **mks units.**

metric (ˈmɛtrɪk) *adj.* of or relating to the metre or metric system.

metrical (ˈmɛtrɪkəl) *or* **metric** (ˈmɛtrɪk) *adj.* **1.** of or relating to measurement. **2.** of or in poetic metre. —ˈ**metrically** *adv.*

metricate (ˈmɛtrɪˌkeɪt) *vb.* to convert (a measuring system, instrument, etc.) from nonmetric to metric units. —ˌ**metriˈcation** *n.*

metric system *n.* any decimal system of units based on the metre. For scientific purposes SI units are used.

metric ton *n.* a unit of mass equal to 1000 kilograms or 2204.6 pounds. Also called: **tonne.**

metro (ˈmɛtrəʊ) *or* **métro** *n.*, *pl.* **-ros.** an underground railway system in certain cities, such as that in Paris.

Metro (ˈmɛtrəʊ) *n. Canad.* a metropolitan city administration, esp. Metropolitan Toronto.

metronome (ˈmɛtrəˌnəʊm) *n.* a device which indicates the tempo of music by producing a clicking sound from a pendulum with an adjustable period of swing. —**metronomic** (ˌmɛtrəˈnɒmɪk) *adj.*

metronymic (ˌmɛtrəˈnɪmɪk) *or* **matronymic** *adj.* **1.** (of a name) derived from the name of the mother or other female ancestor. ~*n.* **2.** a metronymic name.

metropolis (mɪˈtrɒpəlɪs) *n.*, *pl.* **-lises.** **1.** the main city, esp. of a country or region. **2.** a centre of activity. **3.** the chief see in an ecclesiastical province.

metropolitan (ˌmɛtrəˈpɒlɪtən) *adj.* **1.** of or characteristic of a metropolis. **2.** constituting a city and its suburbs. **3.** of, relating to, or designating an ecclesiastical metropolis. **4.** of or belonging to the home territories of a country, as opposed to overseas territories: *metropolitan France.* ~*n.* **5.** *a. Eastern Churches.* the head of an ecclesiastical province, ranking between archbishop and patriarch. **b.** *Church of England.* an archbishop. **c.** *R.C. Church.* an archbishop or bishop having authority over the dioceses in his province. —ˌ**metroˈpolitanism** *n.*

-metry *n. combining form.* indicating the process or science of measuring: *geometry.* —**-metric** *adj. combining form.*

mettle (ˈmɛtəl) *n.* **1.** courage; spirit. **2.** character. **3.** **on one's mettle.** roused to making one's best efforts. —ˈ**mettled** *or* ˈ**mettlesome** *adj.*

MeV *abbrev. for* million electronvolts (10^6 electronvolts).

mew[1] (mjuː) *vb.* **1.** (*intr.*) (esp. of a cat) to make a characteristic high-pitched cry. ~*n.* **2.** such a sound.

mew[2] (mjuː) *n.* any sea gull, esp. the common gull.

mewl (mjuːl) *vb.* **1.** (*intr.*) (esp. of a baby) to cry weakly; whimper. ~*n.* **2.** such a cry.

mews (mjuːz) *n. Chiefly Brit.* **1.** a yard or street lined by buildings originally used as stables but now often converted into dwellings. **2.** the buildings around a mews.

Mex. *abbrev. for:* **1.** Mexican. **2.** Mexico.

Mexican (ˈmɛksɪkən) *adj.* **1.** of or relating to Mexico, in Central America. ~*n.* **2.** a native or inhabitant of Mexico.

mezcal (mɛˈskæl) *n.* a variant spelling of **mescal.**

mezcaline (ˈmɛzkəˌliːn) *n.* a variant spelling of **mescaline.**

mezzanine (ˈmɛzəˌniːn, ˈmɛtsəˌniːn) *n.* **1.** Also called: **mezzanine floor.** an intermediate storey, esp. a low one between the ground and first floor of a building. **2.** *Theatre, U.S.* the first balcony. **3.** *Theatre, Brit.* a room or floor beneath the stage.

mezzo (ˈmɛtsəʊ) *adv. Music.* moderately; quite: *mezzo piano.*

mezzo-soprano *n.*, *pl.* **-nos.** **1.** a female voice intermediate between a soprano and contralto. **2.** a singer with such a voice.

mezzotint (ˈmɛtsəʊˌtɪnt) *n.* **1.** a method of engraving a copper plate by scraping and burnishing the roughened surface. **2.** a print made from a plate so treated. ~*vb.* **3.** (*tr.*) to engrave (a copper plate) in this fashion.

mf *Music. abbrev. for* mezzo forte.

MF *abbrev. for:* **1.** *Radio.* medium frequency. **2.** Middle French.

mg *or* **mg.** *abbrev. for* milligram.

Mg *the chemical symbol for* magnesium.

M. Glam. *abbrev. for* Mid Glamorgan.

Mgr. *abbrev. for:* **1.** manager. **2.** Monseigneur. **3.** Monsignor.

MHG *abbrev. for* Middle High German.

MHz *abbrev. for* megahertz.

mi *or* **me** (miː) *n. Music.* (in tonic sol-fa) the third degree of any major scale; a mediant.

MI *abbrev. for* Military Intelligence.

MI5 *abbrev. for* Military Intelligence, section five; a former name for the counterintelligence agency of the

---

THESAURUS

methodical businesslike, deliberate, disciplined, efficient, meticulous, neat, ordered, orderly, organized, painstaking, planned, precise, regular, structured, systematic, tidy, well-regulated

meticulous detailed, exact, fastidious, fussy, microscopic, painstaking, particular, perfectionist, precise, punctilious, scrupulous, strict, thorough

métier 1. calling, craft, line, occupation, profession, pursuit, trade, vocation 2. forte, long suit (*Inf.*), speciality, specialty, strong point, strong suit

metropolis capital, city

mettle 1. ardour, boldness, bottle (*Brit. sl.*), bravery, courage, daring, fire, fortitude, gallantry, gameness, grit, guts (*Inf.*), hardihood, heart, indomitability, life, nerve, pluck, resolution, resolve, spirit, spunk (*Inf.*), valour, vigour 2. calibre, character, disposition, kidney, make-up, nature, quality, stamp, temperament, temper

British Government.

MI6 *abbrev. for* Military Intelligence, section six; a former name for the intelligence and espionage agency of the British Government.

miaou *or* **miaow** (mɪˈaʊ, mjaʊ) *vb., interj.* variant spellings of **meow**.

miasma (mɪˈæzmə) *n., pl.* **-mata** (-mətə) *or* **-mas.** **1.** an unwholesome or foreboding atmosphere. **2.** pollution in the atmosphere, esp. noxious vapours from decomposing organic matter. —**mi'asmal** *or* **miasmatic** (ˌmiːəzˈmætɪk) *adj.*

Mic. *Bible. abbrev. for* Micah.

mica (ˈmaɪkə) *n.* any of a group of minerals consisting of hydrous silicates of aluminium, potassium, etc., in monoclinic crystalline form, occurring in igneous and metamorphic rock. Because of their resistance to electricity and heat they are used as dielectrics, in heating elements, etc. Also called: **isinglass.** —**micaceous** (maɪˈkeɪʃəs) *adj.*

mice (maɪs) *n.* the plural of **mouse**.

Mich. *abbrev. for:* **1.** Michaelmas. **2.** Michigan.

Michaelmas (ˈmɪkəlməs) *n.* Sept. 29, the feast of St. Michael the archangel; in England, Ireland, and Wales, one of the four quarter days.

Michaelmas daisy *n. Brit.* any of various composite plants that have small autumn-blooming purple, pink, or white flowers.

Mick (mɪk) *n. (sometimes not cap.)* **1.** Also: **Mickey.** *Derog.* a slang name for an Irishman or a Roman Catholic. **2.** *Austral.* the tails side of a coin.

mickey *or* **micky** (ˈmɪkɪ) *n. Inf.* **take the mickey** *or* **micky out of.** to tease.

Mickey Finn *n. Sl.* **a.** a drink containing a drug to make the drinker unconscious. **b.** the drug itself. Often shortened to **Mickey.**

mickle (ˈmɪkəl) *or* **muckle** (ˈmʌkəl) *Arch. or N Brit. dialect.* ~*adj.* **1.** great or abundant. ~*adv.* **2.** much; greatly. ~*n.* **3.** a great amount, esp. in the proverb, *many a little makes a mickle.*

micro- *or before a vowel* **micr-** *combining form.* **1.** small or minute: *microdot.* **2.** indicating magnification or amplification: *microscope; microphone.* **3.** involving the use of a microscope: *microscopy.* **4.** indicating a method or instrument for dealing with small quantities: *micrometer.* **5.** (in pathology) indicating abnormal smallness or underdevelopment: *microcephaly.* **6.** denoting 10^{-6}: *microsecond.* Symbol: μ

microbe (ˈmaɪkrəʊb) *n.* any microscopic organism, esp. a disease-causing bacterium. —**mi'crobial, mi'crobic,** *or* **mi'crobian** *adj.*

microbiology (ˌmaɪkrəʊbaɪˈɒlədʒɪ) *n.* the branch of biology involving the study of microorganisms. —**microbiological** (ˌmaɪkrəˌbaɪəˈlɒdʒɪkəl) *or* ˌmicro.bio'logic *adj.* —ˌmicro.bio'logically *adv.* —ˌmicrobi'ologist *n.*

microcephaly (ˌmaɪkrəʊˈsɛfəlɪ) *n.* the condition of having an abnormally small head or cranial capacity. —**microcephalic** (ˌmaɪkrəʊsɪˈfælɪk) *adj., n.* —ˌmicro'cephalous *adj.*

microchemistry (ˌmaɪkrəʊˈkɛmɪstrɪ) *n.* chemical experimentation with minute quantities of material. —ˌmicro'chemical *adj.*

microchip (ˈmaɪkrəʊˌtʃɪp) *n.* another word for **chip** (sense 7).

microcircuit (ˈmaɪkrəʊˌsɜːkɪt) *n.* a miniature electronic circuit, esp. one in which a number of circuit components are contained in one small chip of semiconducting material. See **integrated circuit.** —ˌmicro'circuitry *n.*

microcomputer (ˌmaɪkrəʊkəmˈpjuːtə) *n.* a computer in which the central processing unit is contained in one or more silicon chips.

microcosm (ˈmaɪkrəʊˌkɒzəm) *or* **microcosmos** (ˌmaɪkrəʊˈkɒzmɒs) *n.* **1.** a miniature representation of something. **2.** man regarded as epitomizing the universe. ~*Cf.* **macrocosm.** —ˌmicro'cosmic *or* ˌmicro'cosmical *adj.*

microdot (ˈmaɪkrəʊˌdɒt) *n.* a greatly reduced photographic copy (about the size of a pinhead) of a document, etc. used esp. in espionage.

microelectronics (ˌmaɪkrəʊɪlɛkˈtrɒnɪks) *n. (function-*

ing as sing.) the branch of electronics concerned with microcircuits.

microfiche (ˈmaɪkrəʊˌfiːʃ) *n.* a sheet of film, usually the size of a filing card, on which books, newspapers, documents, etc., can be recorded in miniaturized form.

microfilm (ˈmaɪkrəʊˌfɪlm) *n.* **1.** a strip of film on which books, documents, etc., can be recorded in miniaturized form. ~*vb.* **2.** to photograph (a page, document, etc.) on microfilm.

micrometer (maɪˈkrɒmɪtə) *n.* **1.** any of various instruments or devices for the accurate measurement of distances or angles. **2.** Also called: **micrometer gauge, micrometer calliper.** a type of gauge for the accurate measurement of small distances, thicknesses, etc. The gap between its measuring faces is adjusted by a fine screw (**micrometer screw**). —**micrometric** (ˌmaɪkrəʊˈmɛtrɪk) *or* ˌmicro'metrical *adj.* —**mi'crometry** *n.*

microminiaturization *or* **-isation** (ˌmaɪkrəʊˌmɪnɪtʃəraɪˈzeɪʃən) *n.* the production and application of very small components and the circuits and equipment in which they are used. —ˌmicro'miniatuˌrize *or* **-ise** *vb.*

micron (ˈmaɪkrɒn) *n.* a unit of length equal to 10^{-6} metre. It is being replaced by the micrometre, the equivalent SI unit.

Micronesian (ˌmaɪkrəʊˈniːzɪən) *adj.* **1.** of or relating to Micronesia (a division of islands in the Pacific), its inhabitants, or their languages. ~*n.* **2.** a member of the people that inhabit Micronesia. **3.** a group of languages spoken in Micronesia.

microorganism (ˌmaɪkrəʊˈɔːɡəˌnɪzəm) *n.* any organism, such as a virus, of microscopic size.

microphone (ˈmaɪkrəˌfəʊn) *n.* a device used in sound-reproduction systems for converting sound into electrical energy. —**microphonic** (ˌmaɪkrəˈfɒnɪk) *adj.*

microprint (ˈmaɪkrəʊˌprɪnt) *n.* a greatly reduced photographic copy of print, read by a magnifying device. It is used in order to reduce the size of large books, etc.

microprocessor (ˌmaɪkrəʊˈprəʊsɛsə) *n. Computers.* a single integrated circuit performing the basic functions of the central processing unit in a small computer.

microscope (ˈmaɪkrəˌskəʊp) *n.* **1.** an optical instrument that uses a lens or combination of lenses to produce a magnified image of a small, close object. **2.** any instrument, such as the electron microscope, for producing a magnified visual image of a small object. —**mi'croscopy** *n.*

microscopic (ˌmaɪkrəˈskɒpɪk) *or* **microscopical** *adj.* **1.** not large enough to be seen with the naked eye but visible under a microscope. **2.** very small; minute. **3.** of, concerned with, or using a microscope. —ˌmicro'scopically *adv.*

microsecond (ˈmaɪkrəʊˌsɛkənd) *n.* one millionth of a second.

microstructure (ˈmaɪkrəʊˌstrʌktʃə) *n.* structure on a microscopic scale, esp. the structure of an alloy as observed by etching, polishing, and observation under a microscope.

microwave (ˈmaɪkrəʊˌweɪv) *n.* **a.** electromagnetic radiation in the wavelength range 0.3 to 0.001 metres; used in radar, cooking, etc. **b.** (*as modifier*): *microwave oven.*

micturate (ˈmɪktjʊˌreɪt) *vb.* (*intr.*) a less common word for **urinate.** —**micturition** (ˌmɪktjʊˈrɪʃən) *n.*

mid¹ (mɪd) *adj.* **1.** *Phonetics.* of, relating to, or denoting a vowel whose articulation lies approximately halfway between high and low, such as *e* in English *bet.* ~*n.* **2.** an archaic word for **middle.**

mid² *or* **'mid** (mɪd) *prep.* a poetic word for **amid.**

mid- *combining form.* indicating a middle part, point, time, or position: *midday; mid-April.*

midair (ˌmɪdˈɛə) *n.* **a.** some point above ground level, in the air. **b.** (*as modifier*): *a midair collision of aircraft.*

midday (ˈmɪdˈdeɪ) *n.* **a.** the middle of the day; noon. **b.** (*as modifier*): *a midday meal.*

middelskot (ˈmɪdəlˌskɒt) *n.* (in South Africa) an intermediate payment to a farmers' cooperative for a crop or wool clip.

midden (ˈmɪdən) *n.* **a.** *Arch. or dialect.* a dunghill or

━━━━━━━━━━━━ **THESAURUS** ━━━━━━━━━━━━

microbe bacillus, bacterium, bug (*Inf.*), germ, microorganism, virus

microscopic imperceptible, infinitesi-

mal, invisible, minuscule, minute, negligible, tiny

midday noon, noonday, noontide, noon-

time, twelve noon, twelve o'clock

pile of refuse. **b.** *Brit. dialect.* a dustbin.

middle ('mɪdᵊl) *adj.* **1.** equally distant from the ends or periphery of something; central. **2.** intermediate in status, situation, etc. **3.** located between the early and late parts of a series, time sequence, etc. **4.** not extreme, esp. in size; medium. **5.** (esp. in Greek and Sanskrit grammar) denoting a voice of verbs expressing reciprocal or reflexive action. **6.** (*usually cap.*) (of a language) intermediate between the earliest and the modern forms. ~*n.* **7.** an area or point equal in distance from the ends or periphery or in time between the early and late parts. **8.** an intermediate part or section, such as the waist. **9.** *Grammar.* the middle voice. ~*vb.* (*tr.*) **10.** to place in the middle. **11.** *Naut.* to fold in two. **12.** *Football.* to return (the ball) from the wing to midfield. **13.** *Cricket.* to hit (the ball) with the middle of the bat.

middle age *n.* the period of life between youth and old age, usually (in man) considered to occur approximately between the ages of 40 and 60. —,middle-'aged *adj.*

Middle Ages *n.* **the.** *European history.* **1.** (broadly) the period from the deposition of the last W Roman emperor in 476 A.D. to the Italian Renaissance (or the fall of Constantinople in 1453). **2.** (narrowly) the period from about 1000 A.D. to the 15th century.

Middle America *n.* **1.** the territories between the U.S. and South America: Mexico, Central America, and the Antilles. **2.** the U.S. middle class, esp. those groups that are politically conservative. —**Middle American** *adj., n.*

middlebrow ('mɪdᵊl,braʊ) *Disparaging.* ~*n.* **1.** a person with conventional tastes and limited cultural appreciation. ~*adj. also* **middlebrowed.** **2.** of or appealing to middlebrows.

middle C *n.* *Music.* the note written on the first ledger line below the treble staff or the first ledger line above the bass staff.

middle class *n.* **1.** Also called: **bourgeoisie.** a social stratum between the lower and upper classes. It consists of businessmen, professional people, etc., along with their families, and is marked by bourgeois values. ~*adj.* **middle-class.** **2.** of, relating to, or characteristic of the middle class.

middle ear *n.* the sound-conducting part of the ear, containing the malleus, incus, and stapes.

Middle East *n.* **1.** (loosely) the area around the E Mediterranean, esp. Israel and the Arab countries from Turkey to North Africa and eastwards to Iran. **2.** (formerly) the area extending from the Tigris and Euphrates to Burma. —**Middle Eastern** *adj.*

Middle English *n.* the English language from about 1100 to about 1450.

Middle High German *n.* High German from about 1200 to about 1500.

Middle Low German *n.* Low German from about 1200 to about 1500.

middleman ('mɪdᵊl,mæn) *n., pl.* **-men.** **1.** a trader engaged in the distribution of goods from producer to consumer. **2.** an intermediary.

middlemost ('mɪdᵊl,məʊst) *adj., adv.* another word for **midmost.**

middle-of-the-road *adj.* not extreme, esp. in political views; moderate.

middle school *n.* *Brit.* a school for children aged between 8 or 9 and 12 or 13.

middleweight ('mɪdᵊl,weɪt) *n.* **1. a.** a professional boxer weighing 154-160 pounds (70-72.5 kg). **b.** an amateur boxer weighing 71-75 kg (157-165 pounds). **2.** a wrestler weighing usually 172-192 pounds (78-87 kg).

Middle West *n.* another name for the **Midwest.** —**Middle Western** *adj.* —**Middle Westerner** *n.*

middling ('mɪdlɪŋ) *adj.* **1.** mediocre in quality, size, etc.; neither good nor bad, esp. in health (often in **fair to middling**). ~*adv.* **2.** *Inf.* moderately: *middling well.*

—'middlingly *adv.*

Middx. *abbrev. for* Middlesex.

midfield (,mɪd'fiːld) *n.* *Soccer.* **a.** the general area between the two opposing defences. **b.** (*as modifier*): *a midfield player.*

midge (mɪdʒ) *n.* **1.** a mosquito-like dipterous insect occurring in dancing swarms, esp. near water. **2.** a small or diminutive person or animal.

midget ('mɪdʒɪt) *n.* **1.** a dwarf whose skeleton and features are of normal proportions. **2. a.** something small of its kind. **b.** (*as modifier*): *a midget car.*

midi ('mɪdɪ) *adj.* **a.** (of a skirt, etc.) reaching to below the knee or midcalf. **b.** (*as n.*): *she wore her new midi.*

midiron ('mɪd,aɪən) *n.* *Golf.* a club, a No. 2 iron, used for approach shots.

midland ('mɪdlənd) *n.* **a.** the central or inland part of a country. **b.** (*as modifier*): *a midland region.*

Midlands ('mɪdləndz) *n.* **the.** the central counties of England: characterized by manufacturing industries. —'**Midlander** *n.*

midmost ('mɪd,məʊst) *adj., adv.* in the middle or midst.

midnight ('mɪd,naɪt) *n.* **1. a.** the middle of the night; 12 o'clock at night. **b.** (*as modifier*): *the midnight hour.* **2. burn the midnight oil.** to work or study late into the night.

midnight sun *n.* the sun visible at midnight during the summer inside the Arctic and Antarctic circles.

mid-off *n.* *Cricket.* the fielding position on the off side closest to the bowler.

mid-on *n.* *Cricket.* the fielding position on the on side closest to the bowler.

midpoint ('mɪd,pɔɪnt) *n.* **1.** the point on a line that is at an equal distance from either end. **2.** a point in time halfway between the beginning and end of an event.

midrib ('mɪd,rɪb) *n.* the main vein of a leaf, running down the centre of the blade.

midriff ('mɪdrɪf) *n.* **1. a.** the middle part of the human body, esp. between waist and bust. **b.** (*as modifier*): *midriff bulge.* **2.** *Anat.* another name for the **diaphragm.** **3.** the part of a woman's garment covering the midriff.

midshipman ('mɪd,ʃɪpmən) *n., pl.* **-men.** a probationary rank held by young naval officers under training, or an officer holding such a rank.

midships ('mɪd,ʃɪps) *adv., adj.* *Naut.* See **amidships.**

midst (mɪdst) *n.* **1. in the midst of.** surrounded or enveloped by; at a point during. **2. in our midst.** among us.

midsummer ('mɪd'sʌmə) *n.* **1. a.** the middle or height of the summer. **b.** (*as modifier*): *a midsummer carnival.* **2.** another name for **summer solstice.**

Midsummer Day *or* **Midsummer's Day** *n.* June 24, the feast of St. John the Baptist; in England, Ireland, and Wales, one of the four quarter days. See also **summer solstice.**

midterm ('mɪd'tɜːm) *n.* **1. a.** the middle of a term in a school, university, etc. **b.** (*as modifier*): midterm exam. **2.** *U.S. Politics.* **a.** the middle of a term of office, esp. of a presidential term, when congressional and local elections are held. **b.** (*as modifier*): midterm elections. **3. a.** the middle of the gestation period. **b.** (*as modifier*): midterm pregnancy. See **term** (sense 6).

midway ('mɪd,weɪ *or, for adv., n.* ,mɪd'weɪ) *adj.* **1.** in or at the middle of the distance; halfway. ~*adv.* **2.** to the middle of the distance. ~*n.* **3.** *Obs.* a middle place, way, etc.

midweek ('mɪd'wiːk) *n.* **a.** the middle of the week. **b.** (*as modifier*): a midweek holiday.

Midwest ('mɪd'wɛst) *or* **Middle West** *n.* the N central part of the U.S.; the states from Ohio westwards that border on the Great Lakes, and often the upper Mississippi and Missouri valleys. —'**Mid**western *adj.* —'**Mid**westerner *n.*

mid-wicket *n.* *Cricket.* the fielding position on the on

THESAURUS

middle *adj.* **1.** central, halfway, inner, inside, intermediate, intervening, mean, medial, median, medium, mid ~*n.* **2.** centre, focus, halfway point, heart, inside, mean, midpoint, midsection, midst, thick **3.** midriff, midsection, waist

middleman broker, distributor, entrepreneur, go-between, intermediary

middling adequate, all right, average, fair, indifferent, mediocre, medium, moderate, modest, O.K. (*Inf.*), okay (*Inf.*), ordinary, passable, run-of-the-mill, so-so (*Inf.*), tolerable, unexceptional, unremarkable

midget **1.** dwarf, gnome, homuncule, homunculus, manikin, pygmy, shrimp (*Inf.*), Tom Thumb **2.** *adj.* baby, dwarf, Lilliputian, little, miniature, pocket, pygmy, small, tiny

midnight dead of night, middle of the

night, the witching hour, twelve o'clock (at night)

midst 1. bosom, centre, core, depths, heart, hub, interior, middle, thick **2. in the midst of** among, during, enveloped by, in the middle of, in the thick of, surrounded by

midway betwixt and between, halfway, in the middle

side, midway between square leg and mid-on.

midwife ('mɪd,waɪf) n., pl. **-wives. 1.** a nurse qualified to deliver babies and to care for women before, during, and after childbirth. **2.** a woman skilled in aiding in the delivery of babies. —**midwifery** ('mɪd,wɪfərɪ) n.

midwinter ('mɪd'wɪntə) n. **1. a.** the middle or depth of the winter. **b.** (as modifier): a midwinter festival. **2.** another name for **winter solstice.**

mien (miːn) n. Literary. a person's manner, bearing, or appearance.

miff (mɪf) Inf. ~vb. **1.** to take offence or to offend. ~n. **2.** a petulant mood. **3.** a petty quarrel.

might[1] (maɪt) vb. (takes an implied infinitive or an infinitive without to) used as an auxiliary: **1.** making the past tense or subjunctive mood of **may**[1]: he might have come. **2.** (often foll. by well) expressing possibility: he might well come. In this sense might looks to the future and functions as a weak form of may. See **may**[1] (sense 2).

▷ Usage. See at **may**[1].

might[2] (maɪt) n. **1.** power, force, or vigour, esp. of a great or supreme kind. **2.** physical strength. **3.** (**with**) **might and main.** See **main**[1] (sense-7).

mighty ('maɪtɪ) adj. **mightier, mightiest. 1. a.** having or indicating might; powerful or strong. **b.** (as collective n.): the mighty. **2.** very large; vast. **3.** Inf. very great in extent, importance, etc. ~adv. **4.** Inf., chiefly U.S. (intensifier): mighty tired. —'**mightily** adv. —'**mightiness** n.

▷ Usage. Mighty is used by many speakers, esp. in the south of the U.S. and in various dialects, as an intensifier equivalent to very. This use of mighty is nevertheless avoided outside informal speech by careful users of English.

mignonette (,mɪnjə'nɛt) n. **1.** any of various mainly Mediterranean plants, such as **garden mignonette**, that have spikes of small greenish-white flowers. **2.** a type of fine pillow lace. ~adj. **3.** of a greyish-green colour.

migraine ('miːgreɪn, 'maɪ-) n. a throbbing headache usually affecting only one side of the head and commonly accompanied by nausea and visual disturbances. —'**migrainous** adj.

migrate (maɪ'greɪt) vb. (intr.) **1.** to go from one place to settle in another, esp. in a foreign country. **2.** (of birds, fishes, etc.) to journey between different habitats at specific times of the year. —'**migrant** n., adj. —mi-'**gration** n. —'**migrator** n. —**migratory** ('maɪgrətərɪ, -trɪ) adj.

mikado (mɪ'kɑːdəʊ) n., pl. **-dos.** (often cap.) Arch. the Japanese emperor.

mike (maɪk) n. Inf. short for **microphone.**

mil (mɪl) n. **1.** a unit of length equal to one thousandth of an inch. **2.** a unit of angular measure, used in gunnery, equal to one six-thousand-four-hundredth of a circumference.

milady or **miladi** (mɪ'leɪdɪ) n., pl. **-dies.** (formerly) a continental title used for an English gentlewoman.

milage ('maɪlɪdʒ) n. a variant spelling of **mileage.**

milch (mɪltʃ) n. **1.** (modifier) (esp. of cattle) yielding milk. **2. milch cow.** Inf. a source of easy income, esp. a person.

mild (maɪld) adj. **1.** (of a taste, sensation, etc.) not pow-

erful or strong; bland. **2.** gentle or temperate in character, climate, behaviour, etc. **3.** not extreme; moderate. **4.** feeble; unassertive. ~n. **5.** Brit. draught beer, of darker colour than bitter and flavoured with fewer hops. —'**mildly** adv. —'**mildness** n.

mildew ('mɪl,djuː) n. **1.** any of various diseases of plants that affect mainly the leaves and are caused by parasitic fungi. **2.** any fungus causing this. **3.** another name for **mould**[2]. ~vb. **4.** to affect or become affected with mildew. —'**mil,dewy** adj.

mild steel n. any of a class of strong tough steels that contain a low quantity of carbon.

mile (maɪl) n. **1.** Also called: **statute mile.** a unit of length used in English-speaking countries, equal to 1760 yards. 1 mile is equivalent to 1.609 34 kilometres. **2.** See **nautical mile. 3.** the Roman mile, equivalent to 1620 yards. **4.** (often pl.) Inf. a great distance; great deal: he missed by a mile. **5.** a race extending over a mile. ~adv. **6.** miles. (intensifier): that's miles better.

mileage or **milage** ('maɪlɪdʒ) n. **1.** a distance expressed in miles. **2.** the total number of miles that a motor vehicle has travelled. **3.** allowance for travelling expenses, esp. as a fixed rate per mile. **4.** the number of miles a motor vehicle will travel on one gallon of fuel. **5.** Inf. use, benefit, or service provided by something.

mileometer or **milometer** (maɪ'lɒmɪtə) n. a device that records the number of miles that a bicycle or motor vehicle has travelled.

milepost ('maɪl,pəʊst) n. **1.** Horse racing. a marking post on a racecourse a mile before the finishing line. **2.** Chiefly U.S. a signpost that shows the distance in miles to or from a place.

miler ('maɪlə) n. an athlete, horse, etc., that runs or specializes in races of one mile.

milestone ('maɪl,stəʊn) n. **1.** a stone pillar that shows the distance in miles to or from a place. **2.** a significant event in life, history, etc.

milfoil ('mɪl,fɔɪl) n. another name for **yarrow.**

miliaria (,mɪlɪ'ɛərɪə) n. an acute itching eruption of the skin, caused by blockage of the sweat glands.

milieu ('miːljɜː) n., pl. **milieus** or French **milieux** (mi-'ljə). surroundings, location, or setting.

militant ('mɪlɪtənt) adj. **1.** aggressive or vigorous, esp. in the support of a cause. **2.** warring; engaged in warfare. ~n. **3.** a militant person. —'**militancy** n. —'**militantly** adv.

militarism ('mɪlɪtə,rɪzəm) n. **1.** military spirit; pursuit of military ideals. **2.** domination by the military, esp. on a political level. —'**militarist** n. —,**militar'istic** adj.

military ('mɪlɪtərɪ, -trɪ) adj. **1.** of or relating to the armed forces, warlike matters, etc. **2.** of or characteristic of soldiers. ~n., pl. **-taries** or **-tary. 3.** (preceded by the) the armed services. —'**militarily** adv. —,**militari-'zation** or **-i'sation** n. —'**milita,rize** or **-ise** vb.

military police n. a corps within an army that performs police and disciplinary duties. —**military police-man** n.

militate ('mɪlɪ,teɪt) vb. (intr.; usually foll. by against or for) (of facts, etc.) to have influence or effect: the evidence militated against his release.

THESAURUS

might 1. ability, capability, capacity, clout (Sl.), efficacy, efficiency, energy, force, potency, power, prowess, puissance, strength, sway, valour, vigour **2.** (**with**) **might and main** as hard as one can, as hard as possible, forcefully, full blast, full force, lustily, manfully, mightily, vigorously, with all one's might or strength

mightily 1. decidedly, exceedingly, extremely, greatly, highly, hugely, intensely, much, very, very much **2.** energetically, forcefully, lustily, manfully, powerfully, strongly, vigorously, with all one's might and main, with all one's strength

mighty 1. doughty, forceful, hardy, indomitable, lusty, manful, potent, powerful, puissant, robust, stalwart, stout, strapping, strong, sturdy, vigorous **2.** bulky, colossal, enormous, gigantic, grand, great, huge, immense, large, massive, monumental, prodi-

gious, stupendous, titanic, towering, tremendous, vast

migrant 1. n. drifter, emigrant, gypsy, immigrant, itinerant, nomad, rover, tinker, transient, vagrant, wanderer **2.** adj. drifting, gypsy, immigrant, itinerant, migratory, nomadic, roving, shifting, transient, travelling, vagrant, wandering

migrate drift, emigrate, journey, move, roam, rove, shift, travel, trek, voyage, wander

migration emigration, journey, movement, roving, shift, travel, trek, voyage, wandering

migratory gypsy, itinerant, migrant, nomadic, peripatetic, roving, shifting, transient, travelling, unsettled, vagrant, wandering

mild 1. amiable, balmy, bland, calm, clement, compassionate, docile, easy, easy-going,

equable, forbearing, forgiving, gentle, indulgent, kind, meek, mellow, merciful, moderate, pacific, peaceable, placid, pleasant, serene, smooth, soft, temperate, tender, tranquil, warm **2.** demulcent, emollient, lenitive, mollifying, soothing

mildness blandness, calmness, clemency, docility, forbearance, gentleness, indulgence, kindness, leniency, lenity, meekness, mellowness, moderation, placidity, smoothness, softness, temperateness, tenderness, tranquillity, warmth

milieu background, element, environment, locale, location, mise en scène, scene, setting, sphere, surroundings

militant adj. **1.** active, aggressive, assertive, combative, vigorous **2.** belligerent, combating, contending, embattled, fighting, in arms, warring ~n. **3.** activist, partisan **4.** belligerent, combatant, fighter, warrior

militia (mɪ'lɪʃə) *n.* **1.** a body of citizen (as opposed to professional) soldiers. **2.** an organization containing men enlisted for service in emergency only. —**mi'litia-man** *n.*

milk (mɪlk) *n.* **1. a.** a whitish fluid secreted by the mammary glands of mature female mammals and used for feeding their young until weaned. **b.** the milk of cows, goats, etc., used by man as a food or in the production of butter, cheese, etc. **2.** any similar fluid in plants, such as the juice of a coconut. **3.** a milklike pharmaceutical preparation, such as milk of magnesia. **4. cry over spilt milk.** to lament something that cannot be altered. ~*vb.* **5.** to draw milk from the udder of (an animal). **6.** (*intr.*) (of animals) to yield milk. **7.** (*tr.*) to draw off or tap in small quantities: *to milk the petty cash.* **8.** (*tr.*) to extract as much money, help, etc., as possible from: *to milk a situation of its news value.* **9.** (*tr.*) to extract venom, sap, etc., from. —**'milker** *n.* —**'milkiness** *n.* —**'milking** *n.* —**'milky** *adj.*

milk-and-water *adj.* (**milk and water** when postpositive). weak, feeble, or insipid.

milk bar *n.* **a.** a snack bar at which milk drinks and light refreshments are served. **b.** (in Australia) a shop selling, in addition to milk, basic provisions and other items.

milk chocolate *n.* chocolate that has been made with milk, having a creamy taste.

milk float *n. Brit.* a small motor vehicle used to deliver milk to houses.

milkmaid ('mɪlk,meɪd) *n.* a girl or woman who milks cows.

milkman ('mɪlkmən) *n., pl.* **-men.** a man who delivers or sells milk.

milk of magnesia *n.* a suspension of magnesium hydroxide in water, used as an antacid and laxative.

milk pudding *n. Chiefly Brit.* a pudding made by boiling or baking milk with a grain, esp. rice.

milk run *n. Aeronautics, inf.* a routine and uneventful flight.

milk shake *n.* a cold frothy drink made of milk, flavouring, and sometimes ice cream, whisked or beaten together.

milksop ('mɪlk,sɒp) *n.* a feeble or ineffectual man or youth.

milk tooth *n.* any of the first teeth to erupt; a deciduous tooth. Also called: **baby tooth.**

Milky Way *n.* **the.** the diffuse band of light stretching across the night sky that consists of millions of faint stars, nebulae, etc., and forms part of the Galaxy.

mill (mɪl) *n.* **1.** a building fitted with machinery for processing materials, manufacturing goods, etc.; factory. **2. a.** a machine that processes materials, manufactures goods, etc., by performing a continuous or repetitive operation, such as a machine to grind flour, pulverize solids, or press fruit. **3.** a machine that tools or polishes metal. **4.** a small machine for grinding solids: *a pepper mill.* **5.** a system, institution, etc., that influences people or things in the manner of a factory: *the educational mill.* **6.** an unpleasant experience; ordeal (esp. in **go** *or* **be put through the mill**). **7.** a fist fight. **8. run of the mill.** ordinary or routine. ~*vb.* **9.** (*usually tr.*) to grind, press, or pulverize in or as if in a mill. **10.** (*usually tr.*) to process or produce in or with a mill. **11.** to cut or roll (metal) with or as if with a milling machine. **12.** (*tr.*) to groove or flute the edge of (a coin). **13.** (often foll. by *about* or *around*) to move about or cause to move about in a confused manner. **14.** *Arch. sl.* to fight, esp. with the fists. —**'millable** *adj.* —**milled** *adj.*

milldam ('mɪl,dæm) *n.* a dam built in a stream to raise the water level sufficiently for it to turn a millwheel.

millefeuille *French.* (mil'fœːj) *n. Brit.* a small iced cake made of puff pastry filled with jam and cream.

millennium (mɪ'lɛnɪəm) *n., pl.* **-niums** *or* **-nia** (-nɪə). **the.** *Christianity.* the period of a thousand years of Christ's awaited reign upon earth. **2.** a period or cycle of one thousand years. **3.** a time of peace and happiness, esp. in the distant future. —**mil'lennial** *adj.* —**mil'lennialist** *n.*

millepede ('mɪlɪ,piːd) *or* **milleped** ('mɪlɪ,pɛd) *n.* variant spellings of **millipede.**

miller ('mɪlə) *n.* **1.** a person who keeps, operates, or works in a mill, esp. a corn mill. **2.** a person who operates a milling machine.

miller's thumb *n.* any of several small freshwater European fishes having a flattened body.

millesimal (mɪ'lɛsɪməl) *adj.* **1. a.** denoting a thousandth. **b.** (*as n.*): *a millesimal.* **2.** of, consisting of, or relating to a thousandth.

millet ('mɪlɪt) *n.* **1.** a cereal grass cultivated for grain and animal fodder. **2. a.** an Indian annual grass cultivated for grain and forage, having pale round shiny seeds. **b.** the seed of this plant. **3.** any of various similar or related grasses.

milli- *prefix.* denoting 10^{-3}: *millimetre.* Symbol: m

milliard ('mɪlɪ,ɑːd, 'mɪljɑːd) *n. Brit.* a thousand million. U.S. equivalent: **billion.**

millibar ('mɪlɪ,bɑː) *n.* a cgs unit of atmospheric pressure equal to 10^{-3} bar, 100 newtons per square metre or 0.750617 millimetres of mercury.

milligram *or* **milligramme** ('mɪlɪ,græm) *n.* one thousandth of a gram.

millilitre *or U.S.* **milliliter** ('mɪlɪ,liːtə) *n.* one thousandth of a litre.

millimetre *or U.S.* **millimeter** ('mɪlɪ,miːtə) *n.* one thousandth of a metre.

milliner ('mɪlɪnə) *n.* a person who makes or sells women's hats. —**'millinery** *n.*

milling ('mɪlɪŋ) *n.* **1.** the act or process of grinding, pressing, or crushing in a mill. **2.** the grooves or fluting on the edge of a coin, etc.

million ('mɪljən) *n., pl.* **-lions** *or* **-lion.** **1.** the cardinal number that is the product of 1000 multiplied by 1000. **2.** a numeral, 1 000 000, 10^6, M̅, etc., representing this number. **3.** (*often pl.*) an extremely large but unspecified number or amount: *I have millions of things to do.* ~*determiner.* **4.** (preceded by *a* or by a numeral) **a.** amounting to a million: *a million light years.* **b.** (*as pronoun*): *I can see a million.* —**'millionth** *adj.*

millionaire (,mɪljə'nɛə) *n.* a person whose assets are worth at least a million of the standard monetary units of his country. —**,million'airess** *fem. n.*

millipede, millepede ('mɪlɪ,piːd), *or* **milleped** ('mɪlɪ,pɛd) *n.* any of various terrestrial herbivorous arthropods, having a cylindrical body, each segment of which bears two pairs of legs.

millisecond ('mɪlɪ,sɛkənd) *n.* one thousandth of a second.

millpond ('mɪl,pɒnd) *n.* **1.** a pool formed by damming a stream to provide water to turn a millwheel. **2.** any expanse of calm water.

millrace ('mɪl,reɪs) *or* **millrun** *n.* **1.** the current of water that turns a millwheel. **2.** the channel for this water.

millstone ('mɪl,stəʊn) *n.* **1.** one of a pair of heavy flat disc-shaped stones that are rotated one against the other to grind grain. **2.** a heavy burden, such as a responsibility or obligation.

millstream ('mɪl,striːm) *n.* a stream of water used to turn a millwheel.

millwheel ('mɪl,wiːl) *n.* a wheel, esp. a waterwheel, that drives a mill.

milometer (maɪ'lɒmɪtə) *n.* a variant spelling of **mileometer.**

milord (mɪ'lɔːd) *n.* (formerly) a continental title used

THESAURUS

military 1. *adj.* armed, martial, soldier-like, soldierly, warlike **2.** *n.* armed forces, army, forces, services

militate 1. *With* **against** be detrimental to, conflict with, contend, count, counter, counteract, oppose, resist, tell, weigh **2.** *With* **for** advance, aid, further, help, promote

militia fencibles (*History*), National Guard (*U.S.*), reserve(s), Territorial Army (*Brit.*), trainband (*History*), yeomanry (*History*)

milk *v.* **1.** drain, draw off, express, extract, let out, press, siphon, tap **2.** bleed, drain, exploit, extract, impose on, pump, take advantage of, use, wring

milk-and-water feeble, innocuous, insipid, jejune, vapid, weak, wishy-washy (*Inf.*)

milksop chinless wonder (*Brit. inf.*), coward, dastard (*Archaic*), mollycoddle, namby-pamby, sissy, weakling

mill *n.* **1.** factory, foundry, plant, shop,

works **2.** crusher, grinder **3. run of the mill** average, commonplace, everyday, fair, middling, ordinary, routine, unexceptional, unremarkable ~*v.* **4.** comminute, crush, granulate, grate, grind, pound, powder, press, pulverize **5.** crowd, seethe, swarm, throng

millstone 1. grindstone, quernstone **2.** affliction, burden, dead weight, drag, encumbrance, load, weight

for an English gentleman.

milt (mɪlt) *n.* **1.** the testis of a fish. **2.** the spermatozoa and seminal fluid produced by a fish. **3.** *Rare.* the spleen, esp. of fowls and pigs. ~*vb.* **4.** to fertilize (fish roe) with milt, esp. artificially. —'**milter** *n.*

mime (maɪm) *n.* **1.** the theatrical technique of expressing an idea or mood or portraying a character entirely by gesture and bodily movement without the use of words. **2.** Also called: **mime artist.** a performer specializing in this. **3.** a dramatic presentation using such a technique. **4.** (in the classical theatre) **a.** a comic performance with exaggerated gesture and physical action. **b.** an actor in such a performance. ~*vb.* **5.** to express (an idea, etc.) in actions or gestures without speech. **6.** (of singers or musicians) to perform as if singing a song or playing a piece of music that is actually prerecorded. —'**mimer** *n.*

Mimeograph ('mɪmɪə,græf) *n.* **1.** *Trademark.* an office machine for printing multiple copies of text or line drawings from a stencil. **2.** a copy produced by this. ~*vb.* **3.** to print copies from (a prepared stencil) using this machine.

mimesis (mɪ'miːsɪs) *n.* **1.** *Art, literature.* the imitative representation of nature or human behaviour. **2.** *Biol.* another name for **mimicry** (sense 2). **3.** *Rhetoric.* representation of another person's alleged words in a speech. —**mimetic** (mɪ'mɛtɪk) *adj.*

mimic ('mɪmɪk) *vb.* -**icking,** -**icked.** (*tr.*) **1.** to imitate (a person, a manner, etc.), esp. for satirical effect; ape. **2.** to take on the appearance of: *certain flies mimic wasps.* **3.** to copy closely or in a servile manner. ~*n.* **4.** a person or an animal, such as a parrot, that is clever at mimicking. **5.** an animal that displays mimicry. ~*adj.* **6.** of, relating to, or using mimicry. **7.** simulated, make-believe, or mock. —'**mimicker** *n.*

mimicry ('mɪmɪkrɪ) *n., pl.* -**ries.** **1.** the act or art of copying or imitating closely; mimicking. **2.** the resemblance shown by one animal species to another, which protects it from predators.

M.I.Min.E. *abbrev. for* Member of the Institute of Mining Engineers.

mimosa (mɪ'məʊsə, -zə) *n.* any of various tropical shrubs or trees having ball-like clusters of typically yellow flowers and leaves that are often sensitive to touch or light.

min. *abbrev. for:* **1.** mineralogy. **2.** minimum. **3.** mining. **4.** minute or minutes.

Min. *abbrev. for:* **1.** Minister. **2.** Ministry.

mina ('maɪnə) *n.* a variant spelling of **myna** (bird).

minaret (,mɪnə'rɛt, 'mɪnə,rɛt) *n.* a slender tower of a mosque having one or more balconies. —,**mina'reted** *adj.*

minatory ('mɪnətərɪ, -trɪ) *or* **minatorial** *adj.* threatening or menacing.

mince (mɪns) *vb.* **1.** (*tr.*) to chop, grind, or cut into very small pieces. **2.** (*tr.*) to soften or moderate: *I didn't mince my words.* **3.** (*intr.*) to walk or speak in an affected dainty manner. ~*n.* **4.** *Chiefly Brit.* minced meat. —'**mincer** *n.*

mincemeat ('mɪns,miːt) *n.* **1.** a mixture of dried fruit, spices, etc., used esp. for filling pies. **2.** **make mincemeat of.** to defeat completely.

mince pie *n.* a small round pastry tart filled with mincemeat.

mincing ('mɪnsɪŋ) *adj.* (of a person) affectedly elegant in gait, manner, or speech. —'**mincingly** *adv.*

mind (maɪnd) *n.* **1.** the entity in an individual responsible for thought, feelings, and speech. **2.** intelligence or the intellect, esp. as opposed to feelings or wishes. **3.** recollection or remembrance: *it comes to mind.* **4.** the faculty of original or creative thought; imagination: *it's all in the mind.* **5.** a person considered as an intellectual being: *great minds.* **6.** condition, state, or manner of feeling or thought: *his state of mind.* **7.** an inclination, desire, or purpose: *I have a mind to go.* **8.** attention or thoughts: *keep your mind on your work.* **9.** a sound mental state; sanity: *to lose your mind.* **10.** (in Cartesian philosophy) one of two basic modes of existence, the other being matter. **11. blow someone's mind.** *Sl.* **a.** to cause someone to have a psychedelic experience. **b.** to astound or surprise someone. **12. in** *or* **of two minds.** undecided; wavering. **13. make up one's mind.** to decide (something or to do something). **14. on one's mind.** in one's thoughts. **15. piece of one's mind.** an expression of one's candid opinion, esp. a rebuke. ~*vb.* **16.** (when *tr.*, *may take a clause as object*) to take offence at: *do you mind if I smoke?* **17.** to pay attention to (something); heed; notice: *to mind one's own business.* **18.** (*tr.; takes a clause as object*) to make certain; ensure: *mind you tell her.* **19.** (*tr.*) to take care of; have charge of: *to mind the shop.* **20.** (when *tr.*, *may take a clause as object*) to be cautious or careful about (something): *mind how you go.* **21.** (*tr.*) to obey (someone or something); heed: *mind your father!* **22.** to be concerned (about); be troubled (about): *never mind about your hat.* **23. mind you.** an expression qualifying a previous statement: *Dogs are nice. Mind you, I don't like all dogs.* ~Related adj.: **mental.** ~See also **mind out.** —'**minder** *n.*

minded ('maɪndɪd) *adj.* **1.** having a mind, inclination, intention, etc., as specified: *politically minded.* **2.** (in combination): *money-minded.*

mindful ('maɪndfʊl) *adj.* (usually *postpositive* and foll. by *of*) keeping aware; heedful: *mindful of your duty.* —'**mindfully** *adv.* —'**mindfulness** *n.*

mindless ('maɪndlɪs) *adj.* **1.** stupid or careless. **2.** requiring little or no intellectual effort. —'**mindlessly** *adv.* —'**mindlessness** *n.*

mind out *vb.* (*intr., adv.*) *Brit.* to be careful or pay attention.

mind-reader *n.* a person seemingly able to discern the thoughts of another. —'**mind-,reading** *n.*

mind's eye *n.* the visual memory or the imagination.

mine¹ (maɪn) *pron.* **1.** something or someone belonging to or associated with me: *mine is best.* **2. of mine.** belonging to or associated with me. ~*determiner.* **3.** (*preceding a vowel*) an archaic word for **my:** *mine eyes.*

mine² (maɪn) *n.* **1.** a system of excavations made for the extraction of minerals, esp. coal, ores, or precious

---

THESAURUS

mime 1. *n.* dumb show, gesture, mummery, pantomime 2. *v.* act out, gesture, pantomime, represent, simulate

mimic *v.* 1. ape, caricature, imitate, impersonate, parody, take off (*Inf.*) 2. echo, look like, mirror, resemble, simulate, take on the appearance of ~*n.* 3. caricaturist, copycat (*Inf.*), imitator, impersonator, impressionist, parodist, parrot ~*adj.* 4. echoic, imitation, imitative, make-believe, mimetic, mock, sham, simulated

mince 1. chop, crumble, cut, grind, hash 2. diminish, euphemize, extenuate, hold back, moderate, palliate, soften, spare, tone down, weaken 3. attitudinize, give oneself airs, ponce (*Sl.*), pose, posture

mincing affected, dainty, effeminate, foppish, lah-di-dah (*Inf.*), nice, niminy-piminy, poncy (*Sl.*), precious, pretentious, sissy

mind *n.* 1. brain(s) (*Inf.*), grey matter (*Inf.*), intellect, intelligence, mentality, ratiocination, reason, sense, spirit, understanding, wits 2. memory, recollection, remem-

brance 3. brain, head, imagination, psyche 4. brain (*Inf.*), genius, intellect, intellectual, thinker 5. attitude, belief, feeling, judgment, opinion, outlook, point of view, sentiment, thoughts, view, way of thinking 6. bent, desire, disposition, fancy, inclination, intention, leaning, notion, purpose, tendency, urge, will, wish 7. attention, concentration, thinking, thoughts 8. judgment, marbles (*Inf.*), mental balance, rationality, reason, sanity, senses, wits 9. **in** *or* **of two minds** dithering, hesitant, shillyshallying (*Inf.*), swithering (*Scot.*), uncertain, undecided, unsure, vacillating, wavering 10. **make up one's mind** choose, come to a decision, decide, determine, reach a decision, resolve 11. **bear** *or* **keep in mind** be cognizant of, be mindful of, remember, take note of ~*v.* 12. be affronted, be bothered, care, disapprove, dislike, look askance at, object, resent, take offence 13. adhere to, attend, comply with, follow, heed, listen to, mark, note, notice, obey, observe, pay attention, pay heed to, regard, respect, take heed, watch 14. be sure, ensure, make

certain 15. attend to, guard, have charge of, keep an eye on, look after, take care of, tend, watch 16. be careful, be cautious, be on (one's) guard, be wary, take care, watch 17. **never mind** disregard, do not concern yourself, don't bother, don't give (it) a second thought, forget (it), it does not matter, it's none of your business, it's nothing to do with you, pay no attention

mindful alert, alive to, attentive, aware, careful, chary, cognizant, conscious, heedful, regardful, respectful, sensible, thoughtful, wary, watchful

mindless 1. asinine, brutish, careless, foolish, forgetful, gratuitous, heedless, idiotic, imbecilic, inattentive, moronic, neglectful, negligent, oblivious, obtuse, stupid, thoughtless, unintelligent, unmindful, unthinking, witless 2. automatic, brainless, mechanical

mind out be careful, be on one's guard, beware, keep one's eyes open, look out, pay attention, take care, watch

stones. **2.** any deposit of ore or minerals. **3.** a lucrative source or abundant supply: *a mine of information.* **4.** a device containing explosive designed to destroy ships, vehicles, or personnel, usually laid beneath the ground or in water. **5.** a tunnel dug to undermine a fortification, etc. ~*vb.* **6.** to dig into (the earth) for (minerals). **7.** to make (a hole, tunnel, etc.) by digging or boring. **8.** to place explosive mines in position below the surface of (the sea or land). **9.** to undermine (a fortification, etc.) by digging mines. **10.** another word for **undermine.**

mine detector *n.* an instrument designed to detect explosive mines. —**mine detection** *n.*

mine-dump *n. S. African.* a large mound of residue, esp. from gold-mining operations.

minefield ('maın,fi:ld) *n.* an area of ground or water containing explosive mines.

minelayer ('maın,leıə) *n.* a warship or aircraft designed for the carrying and laying of mines.

miner ('maınə) *n.* **1.** a person who works in a mine. **2.** any of various insects or insect larvae that bore into and feed on plant tissues. **3.** *Austral.* any of several honey-eaters.

mineral ('mınərəl, 'mınrəl) *n.* **1.** any of a class of naturally occurring solid inorganic substances with a characteristic crystalline form and a homogeneous chemical composition. **2.** any inorganic matter. **3.** any substance obtained by mining, esp. a metal ore. **4.** (*often pl.*) *Brit.* short for **mineral water. 5.** *Brit.* a soft drink containing carbonated water and flavourings. ~*adj.* **6.** of, relating to, containing, or resembling minerals.

mineralogy (,mınə'rælədʒı) *n.* the branch of geology concerned with the study of minerals. —**mineralogical** (,mınərə'lodʒıkəl) *or* ,**mineral'ogic** *adj.* —,**miner'alogist** *n.*

mineral water *n.* water containing dissolved mineral salts or gases, usually having medicinal properties.

minestrone (,mını'strəunı) *n.* a soup made from a variety of vegetables and pasta.

minesweeper ('maın,swi:pə) *n.* a naval vessel equipped to clear mines. —'**mine,sweeping** *n.*

Ming (mıŋ) *n.* **1.** the imperial dynasty of China from 1368 to 1644. ~*adj.* **2.** of or relating to Chinese porcelain produced during the Ming dynasty.

mingle ('mıŋgəl) *vb.* **1.** to mix or cause to mix. **2.** (*intr.; often foll. by* with) to come into close association. —'**mingler** *n.*

mingy ('mındʒı) *adj.* **-gier, -giest.** *Brit. inf.* miserly, stingy, or niggardly.

mini ('mını) *adj.* **1.** (of a woman's dress, skirt, etc.) very short; thigh-length. **2.** (*prenominal*) small; miniature. ~*n.* **3.** something very small of its kind, esp. a small car or a miniskirt.

mini- *combining form.* smaller or shorter than the standard size: *minibus; miniskirt.*

miniature ('mınıtʃə) *n.* **1.** a model, copy, or representation on a very small scale. **2.** anything that is very small of its kind. **3.** a very small painting, esp. a portrait. **4.** an illuminated decoration in a manuscript. **5. in miniature.** on a small scale. ~*adj.* **6.** greatly reduced in size, etc. **7.** on a small scale; minute. —'**miniaturist** *n.* —,**miniaturi'zation** *or* **-i'sation** *n.* —'**miniatu,rize** *or* **-ise** *vb.*

minibus ('mını,bʌs) *n.* a small bus able to carry ap-

proximately ten passengers.

minicab ('mını,kæb) *n.* a small saloon car used as a taxi.

minicomputer (,mınıkəm'pju:tə) *n.* a small comparatively cheap digital computer.

minim ('mınım) *n.* **1.** a unit of fluid measure equal to one sixtieth of a drachm. It is approximately equal to one drop. Symbol: M, ♍ **2.** *Music.* a note having the time value of half a semibreve. **3.** a small or insignificant thing. **4.** a downward stroke in calligraphy.

minimize *or* **-ise** ('mını,maız) *vb.* (*tr.*) **1.** to reduce to or estimate at the least possible degree or amount. **2.** to rank or treat at less than the true worth; belittle. —,**minimi'zation** *or* **-i'sation** *n.* —'**mini,mizer** *or* **-iser** *n.*

minimum ('mınıməm) *n., pl.* **-mums** *or* **-ma** (-mə). **1.** the least possible amount, degree, or quantity. **2.** the least amount recorded, allowed, or reached. **3.** (*modifier*) being the least possible, recorded, allowed, etc.: *minimum age.* ~*adj.* **4.** of or relating to a minimum or minimums. —'**minimal** *adj.* —'**minimally** *adv.*

minimum lending rate *n.* (formerly) the minimum rate at which the Bank of England discounted approved bills.

minimum wage *n.* the lowest wage that an employer is permitted to pay by law or union contract.

mining ('maınıŋ) *n.* **1.** the act, process, or industry of extracting ore, ores, etc., from the earth. **2.** *Mil.* the process of laying mines.

minion ('mınjən) *n.* **1.** a favourite or dependant, esp. a servile or fawning one. **2.** a servile agent.

miniskirt ('mını,skɜːt) *n.* a very short skirt, originally in the 1960s, one at least four inches above the knee. Often shortened to **mini.**

minister ('mınıstə) *n.* **1.** (esp. in Presbyterian and some Nonconformist Churches) a clergyman. **2.** a head of a government department. **3.** any diplomatic agent accredited to a foreign government or head of state. **4.** short for **minister plenipotentiary.** See **envoy¹** (sense 1). **5.** Also called: **minister resident.** a diplomat ranking after an envoy. **6.** a person who attends to the needs of others, esp. in religious matters. **7.** a person who acts as the agent or servant of a person or thing. ~*vb.* **8.** (*intr.; often foll. by to*) to attend to the needs (of); take care (of). **9.** (*tr.*) *Arch.* to provide; supply. —,**minis'terial** *adj.* —'**ministrant** *adj.*

minister of state *n.* **1.** (in the British Parliament) a minister, usually below cabinet rank, appointed to assist a senior minister. **2.** any government minister.

Minister of the Crown *n. Brit.* any Government minister of cabinet rank.

minister plenipotentiary *n., pl.* **ministers plenipotentiary.** another term for **envoy¹** (sense 1).

ministration (,mını'streıʃən) *n.* **1.** the act or an instance of serving or giving aid. **2.** the act or an instance of ministering religiously. —**ministrative** ('mınıstrətıv) *adj.*

ministry ('mınıstrı) *n., pl.* **-tries. 1. a.** the profession or duties of a minister of religion. **b.** his performance of these duties. **2.** ministers of religion or government ministers considered collectively. **3.** the tenure of a minister. **4. a.** a government department headed by a minister. **b.** the buildings of such a department.

THESAURUS

mine *n.* **1.** coalfield, colliery, deposit, excavation, lode, pit, shaft, vein **2.** abundance, fund, hoard, reserve, source, stock, store, supply, treasury, wealth **3.** sap, trench, tunnel ~*v.* **4.** delve, dig for, dig up, excavate, extract, hew, quarry, unearth **5.** lay mines in *or* under, sow with mines **6.** sap, subvert, tunnel, undermine, weaken

miner coalminer, collier (*Brit.*), pitman (*Brit.*)

mingle 1. alloy, blend, coalesce, combine, commingle, compound, intermingle, intermix, interweave, join, marry, merge, mix, unite **2.** associate, circulate, consort, fraternize, hang about *or* around, hang out (*Inf.*), hobnob, rub shoulders (*Inf.*), socialize

miniature *adj.* baby, diminutive, dwarf, Lilliputian, little, midget, mini, minuscule, minute, pocket, pygmy, reduced, scaled-

down, small, tiny, toy, wee

minimal least, least possible, littlest, minimum, nominal, slightest, smallest, token

minimize 1. abbreviate, attenuate, curtail, decrease, diminish, miniaturize, prune, reduce, shrink **2.** belittle, decry, deprecate, depreciate, discount, disparage, make light or little of, play down, underestimate, underrate

minimum 1. *n.* bottom, depth, least, lowest, nadir, slightest **2.** *adj.* least, least possible, littlest, lowest, minimal, slightest, smallest

minion bootlicker (*Inf.*), creature, darling, dependant, favourite, flatterer, flunky, follower, hanger-on, henchman, hireling, lackey, lickspittle, myrmidon, parasite, pet, sycophant, toady, underling, yes man

minister *n.* **1.** churchman, clergyman,

cleric, divine, ecclesiastic, parson, pastor, preacher, priest, vicar **2.** administrator, ambassador, cabinet member, delegate, diplomat, envoy, executive, office-holder, official, plenipotentiary **3.** agent, aide, assistant, lieutenant, servant, subordinate, underling ~*v.* **4.** accommodate, administer, answer, attend, be solicitous of, cater to, pander to, serve, take care of, tend

ministration aid, assistance, favour, help, patronage, relief, service, succour, support

ministry 1. administration, cabinet, council, government, holy orders, the church, the priesthood, the pulpit **2.** bureau, department, office

miniver ('mınıvə) *n.* white fur, used in ceremonial costumes.

mink (mıŋk) *n.* **1.** any of several mammals of Europe, Asia, and North America, having slightly webbed feet. **2.** their highly valued fur, esp. that of the American mink. **3.** a garment made of this, esp. a woman's coat or stole.

minnesinger ('mını,sıŋə) *n.* one of the German lyric poets and musicians of the 12th to 14th centuries.

minnow ('mınəʊ) *n., pl.* **-nows** *or* **-now. 1.** a small slender European freshwater cyprinid fish. **2.** a small or insignificant person.

Minoan (mı'nəʊən) *adj.* **1.** of or denoting the Bronze Age culture of Crete from about 3000 B.C. to about 1100 B.C. ~*n.* **2.** a Cretan belonging to the Minoan culture.

minor ('maınə) *adj.* **1.** lesser or secondary in amount, extent, importance, or degree. **2.** of or relating to the minority. **3.** below the age of legal majority. **4.** *Music.* **a.** (of a scale) having a semitone between the second and third and fifth and sixth degrees (**natural minor**). **b.** (of a key) based on the minor scale. **c.** (*postpositive*) denoting a specified key based on the minor scale: *C minor.* **d.** (of an interval) reduced by a semitone from the major. **e.** (of a chord, esp. a triad) having a minor third above the root. **f.** (esp. in jazz) of or relating to a chord built upon a minor triad and containing a minor seventh: *a minor ninth.* **5.** *Logic.* (of a term or premiss) having less generality or scope than another term or proposition. **6.** *U.S. education.* of or relating to an additional secondary subject taken by a student. **7.** *Brit.* the younger or junior: sometimes used after the surname of a schoolboy if he has an older brother in the same school. ~*n.* **8.** a person or thing that is lesser or secondary. **9.** a person below the age of legal majority. **10.** *U.S. education.* a subsidiary subject. **11.** *Music.* a minor key, chord, mode, or scale. **12.** *Logic.* a minor term or premiss. ~*vb.* **13.** (*intr.*; usually foll. by *in*) *U.S. education.* to take a minor.

minority (maı'nɒrıtı, mı-) *n., pl.* **-ties. 1.** the smaller of two parts, factions, or groups. **2.** a group that is different racially, politically, etc., from a larger group of which it is a part. **3. a.** the state of being a minor. **b.** the period during which a person is below legal age. **4.** (*modifier*) relating to or being a minority: *a minority opinion.*

minster ('mınstə) *n. Brit.* any of certain cathedrals and large churches, usually originally connected to a monastery.

minstrel ('mınstrəl) *n.* **1.** a medieval musician who performed songs or recited poetry with instrumental accompaniment. **2.** a performer in a minstrel show. **3.** *Arch. or poetic.* any poet, musician, or singer. —'**minstrelsy** *n.*

minstrel show *n.* a theatrical entertainment consisting of songs, dances, etc., performed by actors wearing black face make-up.

mint[1] (mınt) *n.* **1.** any N temperate plant of a genus having aromatic leaves. The leaves of some species are used for seasoning and flavouring. See also **peppermint, spearmint. 2.** a sweet flavoured with mint. —'**minty** *adj.*

mint[2] (mınt) *n.* **1.** a place where money is coined by governmental authority. **2.** a very large amount of money. **3.** (*modifier*) **in mint condition.** in perfect condition; as if new. ~*adj.* **4.** (of coins, postage stamps, etc.) in perfect condition as issued. ~*vb.* **5.** to make (coins) by stamping metal. **6.** (*tr.*) to invent (esp. phrases or words). —'**minter** *n.*

mint julep ('dʒu:lɪp) *n. Chiefly U.S.* a long drink consisting of bourbon whiskey, crushed ice, sugar, and sprigs of mint.

minuend ('mınjʊ,ɛnd) *n.* the number from which another number, the **subtrahend,** is to be subtracted.

minuet (,mınju'ɛt) *n.* **1.** a stately court dance of the 17th and 18th centuries in triple time. **2.** a piece of music composed for or in the rhythm of this dance.

minus ('maınəs) *prep.* **1.** reduced by the subtraction of: *four minus two* (written 4 - 2). **2.** *Inf.* deprived of; lacking: *minus the trimmings.* ~*adj.* **3. a.** indicating or involving subtraction: *a minus sign.* **b.** Also: **negative.** having a value or designating a quantity less than zero: *a minus number.* **4.** involving a disadvantage, harm, etc.: *a minus factor.* **5.** (*postpositive*) *Education.* slightly below the standard of a particular grade: *a B minus.* **6.** denoting a negative electric charge. ~*n.* **7.** short for **minus sign. 8.** a negative quantity. **9.** a disadvantage, loss, or deficit. **10.** *Inf.* something detrimental or negative. ~Mathematical symbol: -

minuscule ('mınə,skju:l) *n.* **1.** a lower-case letter. **2.** writing using such letters. **3.** a small cursive 7th-century style of lettering. ~*adj.* **4.** relating to, printed in, or written in small letters. **5.** very small. **6.** (of letters) lower-case. —**minuscular** (mı'nʌskjʊlə) *adj.*

minus sign *n.* the symbol -, indicating subtraction or a negative quantity.

minute[1] ('mınıt) *n.* **1.** a period of time equal to 60 seconds; one sixtieth of an hour. **2.** Also called: **minute of arc.** a unit of angular measure equal to one sixtieth of a degree. Symbol: ′. **3.** any very short period of time; moment. **4.** a short note or memorandum. **5.** the distance that can be travelled in a minute: *it's only two minutes away.* **6. up to the minute** (**up-to-the-minute** when prenominal). the very latest or newest. ~*vb.* (*tr.*) **7.** to record in minutes: *to minute a meeting.* **8.** to time in terms of minutes. ~See also **minutes.** —'**minutely** *adv.*

minute[2] (maı'nju:t) *adj.* **1.** very small; diminutive; tiny. **2.** unimportant; petty. **3.** precise or detailed. —**mi'nuteness** *n.* —**mi'nutely** *adv.*

minute hand ('mınıt) *n.* the pointer on a timepiece that indicates minutes.

minutes ('mınıts) *pl. n.* an official record of the proceedings of a meeting, conference, etc.

minute steak ('mınıt) *n.* a small piece of steak that can be cooked quickly.

minutiae (mı'nju:ʃı,i:) *pl. n., sing.* **-tia** (-ʃıə). small, precise, or trifling details.

minx (mıŋks) *n.* a bold, flirtatious, or scheming woman.

Miocene ('maıə,si:n) *adj.* **1.** of or denoting the fourth epoch of the Tertiary period. ~*n.* **2. the Miocene.** this epoch or rock series.

miracle ('mırəkəl) *n.* **1.** a marvellous event attributed to a supernatural cause. **2.** any amazing or wonderful event. **3.** a marvellous example of something: *a miracle of engineering.* **4.** short for **miracle play. 5.** (*modifier*) being or seeming a miracle: *a miracle cure.*

miracle play *n.* a medieval play based on a biblical story or the life of a saint. Cf. **mystery play.**

miraculous (mı'rækjʊləs) *adj.* **1.** of, like, or caused by a miracle; marvellous. **2.** surprising. **3.** having the power to work miracles. —**mi'raculously** *adv.* —**mi'raculousness** *n.*

mirage ('mıra:ʒ) *n.* **1.** an image of a distant object or sheet of water, often inverted or distorted, caused by atmospheric refraction by hot air. **2.** something illusory.

THESAURUS

minor inconsequential, inconsiderable, inferior, insignificant, junior, lesser, light, negligible, paltry, petty, secondary, slight, small, smaller, subordinate, trifling, trivial, unimportant, younger

minstrel bard, harper, jongleur, musician, singer, troubadour

mint *n.* 1. bomb (*Brit. sl.*), bundle (*Sl.*), fortune, heap (*Inf.*), King's ransom, million, packet (*Sl.*), pile (*Inf.*) ~*adj.* 2. brand-new, excellent, first-class, fresh, perfect, unblemished, undamaged, untarnished ~*v.* 3. cast, coin, make, produce, punch, stamp, strike 4. coin, construct, devise, fabricate, fashion, forge, invent, make up, produce, think up

minute[1] *n.* 1. sixtieth of an hour, sixty sec-

onds 2. flash, instant, jiffy (*Inf.*), moment, second, shake (*Inf.*), tick (*Inf.*), trice 3. any minute any moment, any second, any time, at any time, before long, very soon 4. up to the minute all the rage, in, latest, modish, (most) fashionable, newest, now (*Inf.*), smart, stylish, trendiest, trendy, up to date, vogue, with it (*Inf.*)

minute[2] *adj.* 1. diminutive, fine, infinitesimal, Lilliputian, little, microscopic, miniature, minuscule, slender, small, tiny 2. inconsiderable, negligible, paltry, petty, picayune (*U.S.*), piddling (*Inf.*), puny, slight, trifling, trivial, unimportant 3. close, critical, detailed, exact, exhaustive, meticulous, painstaking, precise, punctilious

minutely closely, critically, exactly, exhaustively, in detail, meticulously, painstakingly, precisely, with a fine-tooth comb

minutes memorandum, notes, proceedings, record(s), transactions, transcript

minutiae details, finer points, niceties, particulars, subtleties, trifles, trivia

minx baggage (*Inf.*), coquette, flirt, hoyden, hussy, jade, tomboy, wanton

miracle marvel, phenomenon, prodigy, thaumaturgy, wonder

miraculous amazing, astonishing, astounding, extraordinary, incredible, inexplicable, magical, marvellous, phenomenal, preternatural, prodigious, superhuman, supernatural, thaumaturgic, unaccountable,

mire (maɪə) n. **1.** a boggy or marshy area. ~vb. **2.** to sink or cause to sink in a mire. **3.** (tr.) to make dirty or muddy. **4.** (tr.) to involve, esp. in difficulties, etc. —'**miry** adj.

mirk (mɜːk) n. a variant spelling of **murk.** —'**mirkily** adv. —'**mirkiness** n. —'**mirky** adj.

mirror ('mɪrə) n. **1.** a surface, such as polished metal or glass coated with a metal film, that reflects an image of an object placed in front of it. **2.** such a reflecting surface mounted in a frame. **3.** any reflecting surface. **4.** a thing that reflects or depicts something else. ~vb. **5.** (tr.) to reflect, represent, or depict faithfully: he mirrors his teacher's ideals.

mirror image n. **1.** an image as observed in a mirror. **2.** an object that corresponds to another as it would to its image in a mirror.

mirror writing n. backward writing that forms a mirror image of normal writing.

mirth (mɜːθ) n. laughter, gaiety, or merriment. —'**mirthful** adj. —'**mirthfulness** n. —'**mirthless** adj. —'**mirthlessness** n.

mis- prefix. **1.** wrong or bad; wrongly or badly: misunderstanding; misfortune; mistreat; mislead. **2.** lack of; not: mistrust.

misadventure (ˌmɪsəd'ventʃə) n. **1.** an unlucky event; misfortune. **2.** Law. accidental death not due to crime or negligence.

misalliance (ˌmɪsə'laɪəns) n. an unsuitable alliance or marriage. —ˌmisal'ly vb.

misanthrope ('mɪzənˌθrəʊp) or **misanthropist** (mɪ-'zænθrəpɪst) n. a person who dislikes or distrusts other people or mankind in general. —**misanthropic** (ˌmɪzən-'θrɒpɪk) or ˌmisan'thropical adj. —**misanthropy** (mɪ-'zænθrəpɪ) n.

misapply (ˌmɪsə'plaɪ) vb. **-plying, -plied.** (tr.) **1.** to apply wrongly or badly. **2.** another word for **misappropriate.** —**misapplication** (ˌmɪsæplɪ'keɪʃən) n.

misapprehend (ˌmɪsæprɪ'hend) vb. (tr.) to misunderstand. —**misapprehension** (ˌmɪsæprɪ'henʃən) n. —ˌmisappre'hensive adj. —ˌmisappre'hensiveness n.

misappropriate (ˌmɪsə'prəʊprɪˌeɪt) vb. (tr.) to appropriate for a wrong or dishonest use; embezzle or steal. —ˌmisap,propri'ation n.

misbegotten (ˌmɪsbɪ'gɒtən) adj. **1.** unlawfully obtained. **2.** badly conceived, planned, or designed. **3.** Literary and dialect. illegitimate; bastard.

misbehave (ˌmɪsbɪ'heɪv) vb. to behave (oneself) badly. —ˌmisbe'haver n. —**misbehaviour** (ˌmɪsbɪ'heɪvjə) n.

miscalculate (ˌmɪs'kælkjʊˌleɪt) vb. (tr.) to calculate wrongly. —ˌmiscalcu'lation n.

miscall (ˌmɪs'kɔːl) vb. (tr.) **1.** to call by the wrong name. **2.** Brit. dialect. to abuse or malign. —ˌmis'caller n.

miscarriage (mɪs'kærɪdʒ) n. **1.** (mɪs'kærɪdʒ, 'mɪskær-). spontaneous expulsion of a foetus from the womb, esp. prior to the 20th week of pregnancy. **2.** an act of mismanagement or failure: a miscarriage of justice. **3.** Brit. the failure of freight to reach its destination. —**mis'carry** vb.

miscast (ˌmɪs'kɑːst) vb. **-casting, -cast.** (tr.) **1.** to cast badly. **2.** (often passive) a. to cast (a role) in (a play, film, etc.) inappropriately: Falstaff was miscast. b. to assign an inappropriate role to: he was miscast as Othello.

miscegenation (ˌmɪsɪdʒɪ'neɪʃən) n. interbreeding of races, esp. where differences of pigmentation are involved.

miscellanea (ˌmɪsə'leɪnɪə) pl. n. a collection of miscellaneous items, esp. literary works.

miscellaneous (ˌmɪsə'leɪnɪəs) adj. **1.** composed of or containing a variety of things; mixed. **2.** having varied capabilities, sides, etc. —ˌmiscel'laneously adv. —ˌmiscel'laneousness n. —**miscellanist** (mɪ'sɛlən-ɪst) n.

miscellany (mɪ'sɛlənɪ; U.S. 'mɪsəˌleɪnɪ) n., pl. **-nies.** (sometimes pl.) a miscellaneous collection of items, esp. essays, poems, etc.

mischance (mɪs'tʃɑːns) n. **1.** bad luck. **2.** a stroke of bad luck.

mischief ('mɪstʃɪf) n. **1.** wayward but not malicious behaviour, usually of children, that causes trouble, etc. **2.** a playful inclination to behave in this way or to tease or disturb. **3.** a person who causes mischief. **4.** injury or harm caused by a person or thing. **5.** a source of trouble, difficulty, etc.

mischievous ('mɪstʃɪvəs) adj. **1.** inclined to acts of mis-

misaddress vb.	**miscount** n.	**misidentification** n.	**misperception** n.
misadministration n.	**misemploy** vb.	**misidentify** vb.	**misremember** vb.
misalign vb.	**misgovern** vb.	**mismanage** vb.	**misreport** vb.
misalignment n.	**misgovernment** n.	**mismanagement** n.	**misstatement** n.
miscount vb.	**mishear** vb.	**misname** vb.	**mistype** vb.

THESAURUS

unbelievable, wonderful, wondrous

mirage hallucination, illusion, optical illusion, phantasm

mire n. **1.** bog, marsh, morass, quagmire, swamp **2.** dirt, muck, mud, ooze, slime **3.** in the mire encumbered, entangled, in difficulties, in trouble ~v. **4.** bog down, flounder, sink, stick in the mud **5.** begrime, besmirch, bespatter, cake, dirty, muddy, soil **6.** catch up, enmesh, entangle, involve

mirror n. **1.** glass, looking-glass, reflector, speculum **2.** copy, double, image, likeness, reflection, replica, representation, twin ~v. **3.** copy, depict, echo, emulate, follow, reflect, represent, show

mirth amusement, cheerfulness, festivity, frolic, fun, gaiety, gladness, glee, hilarity, jocularity, jollity, joviality, joyousness, laughter, levity, merriment, merrymaking, pleasure, rejoicing, revelry, sport

mirthful amused, amusing, blithe, cheerful, cheery, festive, frolicsome, funny, gay, glad, gladsome (Archaic), happy, hilarious, jocund, jolly, jovial, laughable, light-hearted, merry, playful, sportive, uproarious, vivacious

misadventure accident, bad break (Inf.), bad luck, calamity, catastrophe, debacle, disaster, failure, ill fortune, ill luck, mischance, misfortune, mishap, reverse, setback

misanthrope cynic, egoist, egotist, mankind-hater, misanthropist

misapprehend get the wrong idea or impression, misconceive, misconstrue, misinterpret, misread, mistake, misunderstand

misapprehension delusion, error, fallacy, false belief, false impression, misconception, misconstruction, misinterpretation, misreading, mistake, misunderstanding, wrong idea or impression

misappropriate defalcate (Law), embezzle, misapply, misspend, misuse, peculate, pocket, steal, swindle

misbegotten 1. dishonest, disreputable, ill-gotten, illicit, purloined, shady (Inf.), stolen, unlawful, unrespectable **2.** abortive, harebrained, ill-advised, ill-conceived, poorly thought-out **3.** Literary bastard, born out of wedlock, illegitimate, natural, spurious (Rare)

misbehave act up (Inf.), be bad, be insubordinate, be naughty, carry on (Inf.), get up to mischief, muck about (Brit. sl.)

misbehaviour acting up (Inf.), bad behaviour, impropriety, incivility, indiscipline, insubordination, misconduct, misdeeds, misdemeanour, monkey business (Inf.), naughtiness, rudeness, shenanigans (Inf.)

misbelief delusion, error, fallacy, false belief, heresy, unorthodoxy

miscalculate blunder, calculate wrongly, err, get (it) wrong (Inf.), go wrong, make a mistake, misjudge, overestimate, overrate, slip up, underestimate, underrate

miscarriage 1. miss (Inf.), spontaneous

abortion **2.** botch (Inf.), breakdown, error, failure, misadventure, mischance, misfire, mishap, mismanagement, nonsuccess, perversion, thwarting, undoing

miscarry 1. abort **2.** come to grief, come to nothing, fail, fall through, gang agley (Scot.), go amiss, go astray, go awry, go wrong, misfire

miscellaneous assorted, confused, diverse, diversified, farraginous, heterogeneous, indiscriminate, jumbled, many, mingled, mixed, motley, multifarious, multiform, promiscuous, sundry, varied, various

miscellany anthology, assortment, collection, diversity, farrago, gallimaufry, hotchpotch, jumble, medley, mélange, mixed bag, mixture, omnium-gatherum, potpourri, salmagundi, variety

mischance accident, bad break (Inf.), bad luck, calamity, contretemps, disaster, ill chance, ill fortune, ill luck, infelicity, misadventure, misfortune, mishap

mischief 1. devilment, impishness, misbehaviour, monkey business (Inf.), naughtiness, pranks, roguery, roguishness, shenanigans (Inf.), trouble, waywardness **2.** devil, imp, monkey, nuisance, pest, rascal, rogue, scallywag (Inf.), scamp, tyke (Inf.), villain **3.** damage, detriment, disadvantage, disruption, evil, harm, hurt, injury, misfortune, trouble

chief. **2.** teasing; slightly malicious. **3.** causing or intended to cause harm. —'**mischievously** adv. —'**mischievousness** n.

miscible ('mɪsɪbəl) adj. capable of mixing: miscible with water. —ˌmisci'**bility** n.

misconception (ˌmɪskən'sɛpʃən) n. a false or mistaken view, opinion, or attitude. —**misconceive** (ˌmɪskən'siːv) vb.

misconduct n. (mɪs'kɒndʌkt). **1.** behaviour, such as adultery or professional negligence, that is regarded as immoral or unethical. ~vb. (ˌmɪskən'dʌkt). (tr.) **2.** to conduct (oneself) in such a way. **3.** to manage (something) badly.

misconstrue (ˌmɪskən'struː) vb. -**struing**, -**strued**. (tr.) to interpret mistakenly. —ˌmiscon'**struction** n.

miscreant ('mɪskrɪənt) n. **1.** a wrongdoer or villain. **2.** Arch. an unbeliever or heretic. ~adj. **3.** evil or villainous. **4.** Arch. unbelieving or heretical.

misdeal (ˌmɪs'diːl) vb. -**dealing**, -**dealt**. **1.** (intr.) to deal out cards incorrectly. ~n. **2.** a faulty deal. —ˌmis'**dealer** n.

misdeed (ˌmɪs'diːd) n. an evil or illegal action.

misdemeanour or U.S. **misdemeanor** (ˌmɪsdɪ'miːnə) n. **1.** Criminal law. (formerly) an offence generally less heinous than a felony. **2.** any minor offence or transgression.

misdirect (ˌmɪsdɪ'rɛkt) vb. (tr.) **1.** to give (a person) wrong directions or instructions. **2.** to address (a letter, parcel, etc.) wrongly. —ˌmisdi'**rection** n.

misdoubt (mɪs'daʊt) vb. an archaic word for **doubt** or **suspect**.

mise en scène French. (miz ã 'sɛn) n. **1. a.** the arrangement of properties, scenery, etc., in a play. **b.** the objects so arranged; stage setting. **2.** the environment of an event.

miser ('maɪzə) n. **1.** a person who hoards money or possessions, often living miserably. **2.** a selfish person. —'**miserliness** n. —'**miserly** adj.

miserable ('mɪzərəbəl) adj. **1.** unhappy or depressed; wretched. **2.** causing misery, discomfort, etc.: a miserable life. **3.** contemptible: a miserable villain. **4.** sordid or squalid: miserable living conditions. **5.** mean; stingy. —'**miserableness** n. —'**miserably** adv.

misericord or **misericorde** (mɪ'zɛrɪˌkɔːd) n. **1.** a ledge projecting from the underside of the hinged seat of a choir stall in a church, on which the occupant can support himself while standing. **2.** Christianity. **a.** a relaxation of certain monastic rules for infirm or aged monks or nuns. **b.** a monastery or room where this can be enjoyed. **3.** a medieval dagger used to give the death stroke to a wounded foe.

misery ('mɪzərɪ) n., pl. -**eries**. **1.** intense unhappiness, discomfort, or suffering. **2.** a cause of such unhappiness, etc. **3.** squalid or poverty-stricken conditions. **4.** Brit. inf. a person who is habitually depressed: he is such a misery.

misfeasance (mɪs'fiːzəns) n. Law. the improper performance of an act that is lawful in itself. Cf. **malfeasance**.

misfire (ˌmɪs'faɪə) vb. (intr.) **1.** (of a firearm or its projectile) to fail to fire or explode as expected. **2.** (of a motor engine or vehicle, etc.) to fail to fire at the appropriate time. **3.** to fail to operate or occur as intended. ~n. **4.** the act or an instance of misfiring.

misfit n. ('mɪsˌfɪt). **1.** a person not suited to a particular social environment. **2.** something that does not fit or fits badly. ~vb. (ˌmɪs'fɪt), -**fitting**, -**fitted**. **3.** to fail to fit or be fitted.

misfortune (mɪs'fɔːtʃən) n. **1.** evil fortune; bad luck. **2.** an unfortunate or disastrous event.

misgiving (mɪs'gɪvɪŋ) n. (often pl.) a feeling of uncertainty, apprehension, or doubt.

misguide (ˌmɪs'gaɪd) vb. (tr.) to guide or direct wrongly or badly.

misguided (ˌmɪs'gaɪdɪd) adj. foolish or unreasonable, esp. in action or behaviour. —ˌmis'**guidedly** adv.

mishandle (ˌmɪs'hændəl) vb. (tr.) to handle or treat badly or inefficiently.

mishap ('mɪshæp) n. **1.** an unfortunate accident. **2.** bad luck.

mishit Sport. ~n. ('mɪsˌhɪt). **1.** a faulty shot or stroke. ~vb. (ˌmɪs'hɪt), -**hitting**, -**hit**. **2.** to hit (a ball) with a faulty stroke.

mishmash ('mɪʃˌmæʃ) n. a confused collection or mixture.

misinform (ˌmɪsɪn'fɔːm) vb. (tr.) to give incorrect information to. —**misinformation** (ˌmɪsɪnfə'meɪʃən) n.

misinterpret (ˌmɪsɪn'tɜːprɪt) vb. (tr.) to interpret badly, misleadingly, or incorrectly. —ˌmisin,terpre'**tation** n.

THESAURUS

mischievous 1. arch, bad, badly behaved, exasperating, frolicsome, impish, naughty, playful, puckish, rascally, roguish, sportive, teasing, troublesome, vexatious, wayward **2.** bad, damaging, deleterious, destructive, detrimental, evil, harmful, hurtful, injurious, malicious, malignant, pernicious, sinful, spiteful, troublesome, vicious, wicked

misconception delusion, error, fallacy, misapprehension, misconstruction, mistaken belief, misunderstanding, wrong end of the stick (Inf.), wrong idea

misconduct 1. n. delinquency, dereliction, immorality, impropriety, malfeasance (Law), malpractice, malversation (Rare), misbehaviour, misdemeanour, mismanagement, naughtiness, rudeness, transgression, unethical behaviour, wrongdoing **2.** v. behave badly, botch (up), bungle, err, make a mess of, misdirect, mismanage, sin

misconstrue get a false impression, make a wrong interpretation, misapprehend, misconceive, misinterpret, misjudge, misread, mistake, mistranslate, misunderstand, take the wrong way (Inf.)

miscreant 1. n. blackguard, caitiff (Archaic), criminal, evildoer, knave (Archaic), malefactor, rascal, reprobate, rogue, scoundrel, sinner, vagabond, villain, wrongdoer **2.** adj. corrupt, criminal, depraved, evil, iniquitous, nefarious, rascally, reprehensible, reprobate, scoundrelly, unprincipled, vicious, villainous, wicked

misdeed crime, fault, misconduct, misdemeanour, offence, sin, transgression, trespass, villainy, wrong

misdemeanour fault, infringement, misbehaviour, misconduct, misdeed, offence,

peccadillo, transgression, trespass

miser cheapskate (Inf.), churl, curmudgeon, hunks (Rare), niggard, penny-pincher (Inf.), screw (Sl.), Scrooge, skinflint, tightwad (U.S. sl.)

miserable 1. afflicted, broken-hearted, crestfallen, dejected, depressed, desolate, despondent, disconsolate, distressed, doleful, down, downcast, down in the mouth (Inf.), forlorn, gloomy, heartbroken, melancholy, mournful, sorrowful, unhappy, woebegone, wretched **2.** destitute, impoverished, indigent, meagre, needy, penniless, poor, poverty-stricken, scanty **3.** abject, bad, contemptible, deplorable, despicable, detestable, disgraceful, lamentable, low, mean, pathetic, piteous, pitiable, scurvy, shabby, shameful, sordid, sorry, squalid, vile, worthless, wretched

miserly avaricious, beggarly, close, close-fisted, covetous, grasping, illiberal, mean, mingy (Brit. inf.), near, niggardly, parsimonious, penny-pinching (Inf.), penurious, sordid, stingy, tightfisted, ungenerous

misery 1. agony, anguish, depression, desolation, despair, discomfort, distress, gloom, grief, hardship, melancholy, sadness, sorrow, suffering, torment, torture, unhappiness, woe, wretchedness **2.** affliction, bitter pill (Inf.), burden, calamity, catastrophe, curse, disaster, load, misfortune, ordeal, sorrow, trial, tribulation, trouble, woe **3.** destitution, indigence, need, penury, poverty, privation, sordidness, squalor, want, wretchedness **4.** Brit. inf. grouch (Inf.), killjoy, moaner, pessimist, prophet of doom, sourpuss (Inf.), spoilsport, wet blanket (Inf.)

misfire fail, fail to go off, fall through, go

phut (Inf.), go wrong, miscarry

misfit eccentric, fish out of water (Inf.), nonconformist, square peg (in a round hole) (Inf.)

misfortune 1. bad luck, evil fortune, hard luck, ill luck, infelicity **2.** accident, adversity, affliction, blow, calamity, disaster, evil chance, failure, hardship, harm, loss, misadventure, mischance, misery, mishap, reverse, setback, stroke of bad luck, tragedy, trial, tribulation, trouble

misgiving anxiety, apprehension, distrust, doubt, hesitation, qualm, reservation, scruple, suspicion, uncertainty, unease, worry

misguided deluded, erroneous, foolish, ill-advised, imprudent, injudicious, labouring under a delusion or misapprehension, misled, misplaced, mistaken, uncalled-for, unreasonable, unwarranted, unwise

mishandle botch, bungle, make a hash of (Inf.), make a mess of, mess up (Inf.), mismanage, muff, screw (up) (Inf.)

mishap accident, adversity, bad luck, calamity, contretemps, disaster, evil chance, evil fortune, hard luck, ill fortune, ill luck, infelicity, misadventure, mischance, misfortune

misinform deceive, give (someone) a bum steer (Sl.), give (someone) duff gen (Brit. inf.), misdirect, misguide, mislead

misinterpret distort, falsify, get wrong, misapprehend, misconceive, misconstrue, misjudge, misread, misrepresent, mistake, misunderstand, pervert

n. —ˌmisin'terpreter n.

misjudge (ˌmɪs'dʒʌdʒ) vb. to judge (a person or persons) wrongly or unfairly. —ˌmis'judger n. —ˌmis'judgment or ˌmis'judgement n.

mislay (mɪs'leɪ) vb. -laying, -laid. (tr.) 1. to lose (something) temporarily, esp. by forgetting where it is. 2. to lay (something) badly.

mislead (mɪs'liːd) vb. -leading, -led. (tr.) 1. to give false or confusing information to. 2. to lead or guide in the wrong direction. —mis'leader n. —mis'leading adj. —mis'leadingly adv.

mismatch (ˌmɪs'mætʃ) vb. 1. to match badly, esp. in marriage. ~n. 2. a bad match.

misnomer (ˌmɪs'nəʊmə) n. 1. an incorrect or unsuitable name for a person or thing. 2. the act of referring to a person by the wrong name.

miso- or before a vowel **mis-** combining form. indicating hatred: misogyny.

misogamy (mɪ'sɒɡəmɪ, maɪ-) n. hatred of marriage. —mi'sogamist n.

misogyny (mɪ'sɒdʒɪnɪ, maɪ-) n. hatred of women. —mi'sogynist n. —mi'sogynous adj.

misplace (ˌmɪs'pleɪs) vb. (tr.) 1. to put (something) in the wrong place, esp. to lose (something) temporarily by forgetting where it was placed. 2. (often passive) to bestow (trust, affection, etc.) inadvisedly. —ˌmis'placement n.

misprint n. ('mɪsˌprɪnt). 1. an error in printing, made through damaged type, careless reading, etc. ~vb. (ˌmɪs'prɪnt). 2. (tr.) to print (a letter) incorrectly.

misprision (mɪs'prɪʒən) n. **a.** a failure to inform the authorities of the commission of an act of treason. **b.** the deliberate concealment of the commission of a felony.

mispronounce (ˌmɪsprə'naʊns) vb. to pronounce (a word) wrongly. —**mispronunciation** (ˌmɪsprəˌnʌnsɪ'eɪʃən) n.

misquote (ˌmɪs'kwəʊt) vb. to quote (a text, speech, etc.) inaccurately. —ˌmisquo'tation n.

misread (ˌmɪs'riːd) vb. -reading, -read (-'rɛd). (tr.) 1. to read incorrectly. 2. to misinterpret.

misrepresent (ˌmɪsrɛprɪ'zɛnt) vb. (tr.) to represent wrongly or inaccurately. —ˌmisrepresen'tation n. —ˌmisrepre'sentative adj.

misrule (ˌmɪs'ruːl) vb. 1. (tr.) to govern inefficiently or without justice. ~n. 2. inefficient or unjust government. 3. disorder.

miss¹ (mɪs) vb. 1. to fail to reach, hit, meet, find, or attain (some aim, goal, target, etc.). 2. (tr.) to fail to attend or be present for: to miss an appointment. 3. (tr.) to fail to see, hear, understand, or perceive. 4. (tr.) to lose, overlook, or fail to take advantage of: to miss an opportunity. 5. (tr.) to leave out; omit: to miss an entry in a list. 6. (tr.) to discover or regret the loss or absence of:`she missed him. 7. (tr.) to escape or avoid (something, esp. a danger), usually narrowly: he missed death by inches. 8. miss the boat. to lose an opportunity. ~n. 9. a failure to reach, hit, meet, find, etc. 10. give (something) a miss. Inf. to avoid (something): give the pudding a miss. ~See also miss out.

miss² (mɪs) n. Inf. or fashion trade use. 1. an unmarried woman or girl. 2. a size in young women's clothes.

Miss (mɪs) n. a title of an unmarried woman or girl, usually used before the surname or sometimes alone in direct address.

▷ **Usage.** When reference is made to two or more unmarried women with the same surname, the Misses Smith is more formal than the Miss Smiths.

missal ('mɪsəl) n. R.C. Church. a book containing the prayers, etc., of the Masses for a complete year.

misshape vb. (ˌmɪs'ʃeɪp). 1. -shaping, -shaped or -shapen. (tr.) to shape badly; deform. ~n. ('mɪsˌʃeɪp). 2. something that is badly shaped.

misshapen (ˌmɪs'ʃeɪpən) adj. badly shaped; deformed. —ˌmis'shapenness n.

missile ('mɪsaɪl) n. 1. any object or weapon that is thrown at a target or shot from an engine, gun, etc. 2. a rocket-propelled weapon that flies either in a fixed trajectory (ballistic missile) or in a trajectory controlled during flight (guided missile).

missing ('mɪsɪŋ) adj. 1. not present; absent or lost. 2. not able to be traced and not known to be dead: nine men were missing after the attack.

missing link n. 1. (sometimes cap.; usually preceded by the) a hypothetical extinct animal, formerly thought to be intermediate between the anthropoid apes and man. 2. any missing section or part in a series.

mission ('mɪʃən) n. 1. a specific task or duty assigned to a person or group of people. 2. a person's vocation (often in **mission in life**). 3. a group of persons representing or working for a particular country, business, etc., in a foreign country. 4. a special embassy sent to a foreign country for a specific purpose. 5. **a.** a group of people sent by·a religious body, esp. a Christian church, to a foreign country to do religious and social work. **b.** the campaign undertaken by such a group. 6. **a.** a building in which missionary work is performed. **b.** the area assigned to a particular missionary. 7. the dispatch of aircraft or spacecraft to achieve a particular task. 8. a charitable centre that offers shelter or aid to the destitute or underprivileged. 9. (modifier) of or relating to an ecclesiastical mission: a mission station. ~vb. 10. (tr.) to direct a mission to or establish a mission in (a given region).

missionary ('mɪʃənərɪ) n., pl. -aries. **a.** Also called: **missioner.** a member of a religious mission. **b.** (as modifier): missionary work.

missis or **missus** ('mɪsɪz, -ɪs) n. (usually preceded by the) Inf. one's wife or the wife of the person addressed or referred to.

missive ('mɪsɪv) n. 1. a formal or official letter. 2. a formal word for **letter**.

miss out vb. 1. (tr., adv.) to leave out; overlook. 2. (intr., adv.; often foll. by on) to fail to experience: you missed out on the celebrations.

misspell (ˌmɪs'spɛl) vb. -spelling, -spelt or -spelled. to spell (a word or words) wrongly. —ˌmis'spelling n.

misspend (ˌmɪs'spɛnd) vb. -spending, -spent. to spend thoughtlessly or wastefully.

THESAURUS

misjudge be wrong about, get the wrong idea about, miscalculate, overestimate, overrate, underestimate, underrate

mislay be unable to find, be unable to put or lay one's hand on, forget the whereabouts of, lose, lose track of, misplace, miss

mislead beguile, bluff, deceive, delude, fool, give (someone) a bum steer (Sl.), hoodwink, lead astray, misdirect, misguide, misinform, pull the wool over (someone's) eyes (Inf.), take in (Inf.)

misleading ambiguous, casuistical, confusing, deceitful, deceptive, delusive, delusory, disingenuous, evasive, false, sophistical, specious, spurious, tricky (Inf.), unstraightforward

mismanage be incompetent, be inefficient, botch, bungle, make a hash of (Inf.), make a mess of, maladminister, mess up, misconduct, misdirect, misgovern, mishandle

misplace 1. be unable to find, be unable

to put or lay one's hand on, forget the whereabouts of, lose, lose track of, misfile, mislay, miss, put in the wrong place 2. place unwisely, place wrongly

misprint corrigendum, erratum, literal, mistake, printing error, typo (Inf.), typographical error

misquote distort, falsify, garble, mangle, misreport, misrepresent, misstate, muddle, pervert, quote or take out of context, twist

misrepresent belie, disguise, distort, falsify, garble, misinterpret, misstate, pervert, twist

misrule 1. bad government, maladministration, misgovernment, mismanagement 2. anarchy, chaos, confusion, disorder, lawlessness, tumult, turmoil

miss¹ v. 1. avoid, be late for, blunder, err, escape, evade, fail, fail to grasp, fail to notice, forego, lack, leave out, let go, let slip, lose, miscarry, mistake, omit, overlook, pass over, pass up, skip, slip, trip 2. feel the loss

of, long for, need, pine for, want, wish, yearn for ~n. 3. blunder, error, failure, fault, loss, mistake, omission, oversight, want

miss² damsel, girl, lass, lassie (Inf.), maid, maiden, schoolgirl, spinster, young lady

misshapen contorted, crippled, crooked, deformed, distorted, grotesque, ill-made, ill-proportioned, malformed, twisted, ugly, ungainly, unshapely, unsightly, warped, wry

missile projectile, rocket, weapon

missing absent, astray, gone, lacking, left behind, left out, lost, mislaid, misplaced, not present, nowhere to be found, unaccounted-for, wanting

mission 1. aim, assignment, business, calling, charge, commission, duty, errand, goal, job, office, operation, purpose, pursuit, quest, task, trust, undertaking, vocation, work 2. commission, delegation, deputation, embassy, legation, ministry, task force

missionary apostle, converter, evangelist, preacher, propagandist, proselytizer

missy ('mɪsɪ) *n., pl.* **missies.** *Inf.* an affectionate or disparaging form of address to a young girl.

mist (mɪst) *n.* **1.** a thin fog resulting from condensation in the air near the earth's surface. **2.** *Meteorol.* such an atmospheric condition with a horizontal visibility of 1–2 kilometres. **3.** a fine spray of liquid, such as that produced by an aerosol container. **4.** condensed water vapour on a surface. **5.** something that causes haziness or lack of clarity, such as a film of tears. ~*vb.* **6.** to cover or be covered with or as if with mist. —'**mistily** *adv.* —'**mistiness** *n.* —'**misty** *adj.*

mistake (mɪ'steɪk) *n.* **1.** an error or blunder in action, opinion, or judgment. **2.** a misconception or misunderstanding. ~*vb.*-**taking,**-**took,**-**taken. 3.** (*tr.*) to misunderstand; misinterpret: *she mistook his meaning.* **4.** (*tr.; foll. by for*) to take (for), interpret (as), or confuse (with): *she mistook his direct manner for honesty.* **5.** (*tr.*) to choose badly or incorrectly: *he mistook his path.* **6.** (*intr.*) to make a mistake. —**mis'takable** *adj.*

mistaken (mɪ'steɪkən) *adj.* **1.** (*usually predicative*) wrong in opinion, judgment, etc. **2.** arising from error in judgment, etc.: *a mistaken viewpoint.* —**mis'takenly** *adv.* —**mis'takenness** *n.*

mister ('mɪstə) (*sometimes cap.*) ~*n.* **1.** an informal form of address for a man. **2.** *Naval.* **a.** the official form of address for subordinate or senior warrant officers. **b.** the official form of address for all officers in a merchant ship, other than the captain. **3.** *Brit.* the form of address for a surgeon. **4.** the form of address for officials holding certain positions: *mister chairman.* ~*vb.* **5.** (*tr.*) *Inf.* to call (someone) mister.

Mister ('mɪstə) *n.* the full form of **Mr.**

mistime (ˌmɪs'taɪm) *vb.* (*tr.*) to time (an action, utterance, etc.) wrongly.

mistle thrush *or* **missel thrush** ('mɪsəl) *n.* a large European thrush with a brown back and spotted breast, noted for feeding on mistletoe berries.

mistletoe ('mɪsəl,təʊ) *n.* **1.** a Eurasian evergreen shrub with waxy white berries: grows as a partial parasite on various trees: used as a Christmas decoration. **2.** any of several similar and related American plants.

mistook (mɪ'stʊk) *vb.* the past tense of **mistake.**

mistral ('mɪstrəl, mɪ'strɑːl) *n.* a strong cold dry wind that blows through the Rhône valley and S France to the Mediterranean coast, mainly in the winter.

mistreat (ˌmɪs'triːt) *vb.* (*tr.*) to treat badly. —**mis'treatment** *n.*

mistress ('mɪstrɪs) *n.* **1.** a woman who has a continuing extramarital sexual relationship with a man. **2.** a woman in a position of authority, ownership, or control. **3.** a woman having control over something specified: *mistress of her own destiny.* **4.** *Chiefly Brit.* short for **schoolmistress** (see **schoolmaster**). **5.** an archaic or dialect word for **sweetheart.**

Mistress ('mɪstrɪs) *n.* an archaic or dialect title equivalent to **Mrs.**

Mistress of the Robes *n. Brit.* a lady of high rank in charge of the Queen's wardrobe.

mistrial (mɪs'traɪəl) *n.* **1.** a trial made void because of some error. **2.** (*U.S.*) an inconclusive trial, as when a jury cannot agree on a verdict.

mistrust (ˌmɪs'trʌst) *vb.* **1.** to have doubts or suspicions about (someone or something). ~*n.* **2.** distrust. —**mis'trustful** *adj.* —**mis'trustfully** *adv.* —**mis'trustfulness** *n.*

misunderstanding (ˌmɪsʌndə'stændɪŋ) *n.* **1.** a failure to understand properly. **2.** a disagreement. —**misunder'stand** *vb.*

misunderstood (ˌmɪsʌndə'stʊd) *adj.* not properly or sympathetically understood: *a misunderstood adolescent.*

misuse *n.* (ˌmɪs'juːs), *also* **misusage. 1.** erroneous, improper, or unorthodox use: *misuse of words.* **2.** cruel or inhumane treatment. ~*vb.* (ˌmɪs'juːz). (*tr.*) **3.** to use wrongly. **4.** to treat badly or harshly. —**mis'user** *n.*

mite[1] (maɪt) *n.* any of numerous small terrestrial or aquatic free-living or parasitic arachnids.

mite[2] (maɪt) *n.* **1.** a very small particle, creature, or object. **2.** a very small contribution or sum of money. **3.** a former Flemish coin of small value. **4.** a mite. (*adv.*) *Inf.* somewhat: *he's a mite foolish.*

mitigate ('mɪtɪ,geɪt) *vb.* to make or become less severe or harsh; moderate. —**mitigable** ('mɪtɪgəbəl) *adj.* —**miti'gation** *n.* —'**miti,gative** *or* '**miti,gatory** *adj.* —'**miti,gator** *n.*

mitigating circumstances *pl.n.* circumstances that may be held to lessen the culpability of an offender.

mitosis (maɪ'təʊsɪs, mɪ-) *n.* a method of cell division, in which the nucleus divides into daughter nuclei, each containing the same number of chromosomes as the parent nucleus. —**mitotic** (maɪ'tɒtɪk, mɪ-) *adj.*

mitre *or U.S.* **miter** ('maɪtə) *n.* **1.** *Christianity.* the liturgical headdress of a bishop or abbot, consisting of a tall pointed cleft cap with two bands hanging down at the back. **2.** Also called: **mitre joint.** a corner joint formed by cutting bevels of equal angles at the ends of each

---

THESAURUS

missive communication, dispatch, epistle, letter, memorandum, message, note, report

misspent dissipated, idle, imprudent, misapplied, prodigal, profitless, squandered, thrown away, wasted

mist 1. *n.* cloud, condensation, dew, drizzle, film, fog, haar (*Eastern Brit.*), haze, smog, smur *or* smir (*Scot.*), spray, steam, vapour **2.** *v.* becloud, befog, blur, cloud, film, fog, obscure, steam (up)

mistake *n.* **1.** bloomer (*Brit. inf.*), blunder, boob (*Brit. sl.*), boo-boo (*Inf.*), clanger (*Inf.*), erratum, error, error of judgment, false move, fault, faux pas, gaffe, goof (*Inf.*), howler (*Inf.*), inaccuracy, miscalculation, misconception, misstep, misunderstanding, oversight, slip, slip-up (*Inf.*), solecism ~*v.* **2.** get wrong, misapprehend, misconceive, misconstrue, misinterpret, misjudge, misread, misunderstand **3.** accept as, confound, confuse with, misinterpret as, mix up with, take for **4.** be wide of *or* be off the mark, be wrong, blunder, drop a clanger (*Inf.*), err, goof (*Inf.*), miscalculate, misjudge, put one's foot in it (*Inf.*), slip up (*Inf.*)

mistaken barking up the wrong tree (*Inf.*), erroneous, fallacious, false, faulty, inaccurate, inappropriate, incorrect, in the wrong, labouring under a misapprehension, misguided, misinformed, mislead, off target, off the mark, unfounded, unsound, wide of the mark, wrong

mistakenly by mistake, erroneously, fallaciously, falsely, inaccurately, inappropriately, incorrectly, in error, misguidedly, wrongly

mistimed badly timed, ill-timed, inconvenient, inopportune, unseasonable, unsynchronized, untimely

mistreat abuse, brutalize, handle roughly, harm, ill-treat, ill-use, injure, knock about (*Inf.*), maltreat, manhandle, maul, misuse, molest, rough up, wrong

mistress concubine, doxy (*Archaic*), fancy woman (*Sl.*), girlfriend, inamorata, kept woman, ladylove (*Rare*), lover, paramour

mistrust 1. *v.* apprehend, beware, be wary of, distrust, doubt, fear, have doubts about, suspect **2.** *n.* apprehension, distrust, doubt, dubiety, fear, misgiving, scepticism, suspicion, uncertainty, wariness

mistrustful apprehensive, cautious, chary, cynical, distrustful, doubtful, dubious, fearful, hesitant, leery (*Sl.*), sceptical, suspicious, uncertain, wary

misty bleary, blurred, cloudy, dark, dim, foggy, fuzzy, hazy, indistinct, murky, nebulous, obscure, opaque, overcast, unclear, vague

misunderstand get (it) wrong, get the wrong end of the stick (*Inf.*), get the wrong idea (about), misapprehend, misconceive, misconstrue, mishear, misinterpret, misjudge, misread, miss the point (of), mistake

misunderstanding 1. error, false impression, misapprehension, misconception, misconstruction, misinterpretation, misjudgment, misreading, mistake, mix-up, wrong idea **2.** argument, breach, conflict, difference, difficulty, disagreement, discord, dissension, falling-out (*Inf.*), quarrel, rift, rupture, squabble, variance

misunderstood misconstrued, misheard, misinterpreted, misjudged, misread, unappreciated, unrecognized

misuse *n.* **1.** abuse, barbarism, catachresis, corruption, desecration, dissipation, malapropism, misapplication, misemployment, misusage, perversion, profanation, solecism, squandering, waste **2.** abuse, cruel treatment, exploitation, harm, ill-treatment, ill-usage, inhumane treatment, injury, maltreatment, manhandling, mistreatment, rough handling ~*v.* **3.** abuse, corrupt, desecrate, dissipate, misapply, misemploy, pervert, profane, prostitute, squander, waste **4.** abuse, brutalize, exploit, handle roughly, harm, ill-treat, ill-use, maltreat, manhandle, maul, mistreat, molest, wrong

mitigate abate, allay, appease, assuage, blunt, calm, check, diminish, dull, ease, extenuate, lessen, lighten, moderate, modify, mollify, pacify, palliate, placate, quiet, reduce the force of, remit, soften, soothe, subdue, take the edge off, temper, tone down, tranquillize, weaken

mitigation abatement, allaying, alleviation, assuagement, diminution, easement, extenuation, moderation, mollification, palliation, relief, remission

piece of material. **3.** a bevelled surface of a mitre joint. ~*vb.* (*tr.*) **4.** to make a mitre joint between (two pieces of material). **5.** to confer a mitre upon: *a mitred abbot.* —'**mitral** *adj.*

mitre box *n.* an open-ended box with sides slotted to guide a saw in cutting mitre joints.

mitt (mɪt) *n.* **1.** any of various glovelike hand coverings, such as one that does not cover the fingers. **2.** *Baseball.* a large round thickly padded leather mitten worn by the catcher. **3.** (*often pl.*) a slang word for **hand. 4.** *Sl.* a boxing glove.

mitten ('mɪtᵊn) *n.* **1.** a glove having one section for the thumb and a single section for the other fingers. Sometimes shortened to **mitt. 2.** *Sl.* a boxing glove.

mix (mɪks) *vb.* **1.** (*tr.*) to combine or blend (ingredients, liquids, objects, etc.) together into one mass. **2.** (*intr.*) to become or have the capacity to become combined, joined, etc.: *some chemicals do not mix.* **3.** (*tr.*) to form (something) by combining constituents: *to mix cement.* **4.** (*tr.; often foll. by in or into*) to add as an additional element (to a mass or compound): *to mix flour into a batter.* **5.** (*tr.*) to do at the same time: *to mix study and pleasure.* **6.** (*tr.*) to consume (different alcoholic drinks) in close succession. **7.** to come or cause to come into association socially: *Pauline mixed well.* **8.** (*intr.; often foll. by with*) to go together; complement. **9.** (*tr.*) to crossbreed (differing strains of plants or breeds of livestock), esp. more or less at random. **10. mix it.** *Inf.* to cause mischief or trouble, often for a person named: *she tried to mix it for John.* ~*n.* **11.** the act or an instance of mixing. **12.** the result of mixing; mixture. **13.** a mixture of ingredients, esp. one commercially prepared for making a cake, bread, etc. **14.** *Inf.* a state of confusion. ~See also **mix-up.** —'**mixable** *adj.* —**mixed** *adj.*

mixed bag *n. Inf.* something composed of diverse elements, characteristics, people, etc.

mixed blessing *n.* an event, situation, etc., having both advantages and disadvantages.

mixed doubles *pl. n. Tennis.* a doubles game with a man and a woman as partners on each side.

mixed farming *n.* combined arable and livestock farming (on **mixed farms**).

mixed marriage *n.* a marriage between persons of different races or religions.

mixed metaphor *n.* a combination of incongruous metaphors, as *when the Nazi jackboots sing their swan song.*

mixed-up *adj.* in a state of mental confusion.

mixer ('mɪksə) *n.* **1.** a person or thing that mixes. **2.** *Inf.* **a.** a person considered in relation to his ability to mix socially. **b.** a person who creates trouble for others. **3.** a kitchen appliance, usually electrical, used for mixing foods, etc. **4.** a drink such as ginger ale, fruit juice, etc., used in preparing cocktails. **5.** *Electronics.* a device in which two or more input signals are combined to give a single output signal.

mixture ('mɪkstʃə) *n.* **1.** the act of mixing or state of being mixed. **2.** something mixed; a result of mixing. **3.** *Chem.* a substance consisting of two or more substances mixed together without any chemical bonding between them. **4.** *Pharmacol.* a liquid medicine in which an insoluble compound is suspended in the liquid. **5.** *Music.* an organ stop that controls several ranks of pipes. **6.** the mixture of petrol vapour and air in an internal-combustion engine.

mix-up *n.* **1.** a confused condition or situation. **2.** *Inf.*

a fight. ~*vb.* **mix up.** (*tr., adv.*) **3.** to make into a mixture. **4.** to confuse or confound: *Tom mixes John up with Bill.* **5.** (*often passive*) to put (someone) into a state of confusion: *I'm all mixed up.* **6.** (foll. by *in* or *with;* usually passive) to involve in (an activity or group, esp. one that is illegal): *mixed up in the drugs racket.*

mizzenmast or **mizenmast** ('mɪzᵊn‚mɑːst; *Naut.* 'mɪzᵊnməst) *n. Naut.* (on a vessel with three or more masts) the third mast from the bow.

mizzle ('mɪzᵊl) *vb., n.* a dialect word for **drizzle.** —'**mizzly** *adj.*

mk. *Currency. abbrev. for* mark.

mks units *pl. n.* a metric system of units based on the metre, kilogram, and second as the units of length, mass, and time; it forms the basis of the SI units.

ml *symbol for:* **1.** millilitre. **2.** mile.

M.L. *abbrev. for* Medieval Latin.

M.L.A. *abbrev. for:* **1.** Member of the Legislative Assembly. **2.** Modern Language Association (of America).

M.Litt. (in Britain) *abbrev. for* Master of Letters.

Mlle or **Mlle.** *pl.* **Mlles** or **Mlles.** the French equivalent of **Miss**

MLR *abbrev. for* minimum lending rate.

mm *abbrev. for* millimetre.

MM. the French equivalent of **Messrs.**

M.M. *abbrev. for* Military Medal.

Mme or **Mme.** *pl.* **Mmes** or **Mmes.** the French equivalent of **Mrs.**

M.Mus. *abbrev. for* Master of Music.

Mn *the chemical symbol for* manganese.

mnemonic (nɪ'mɒnɪk) *adj.* **1.** aiding or meant to aid one's memory. **2.** of or relating to memory or mnemonics. ~*n.* **3.** something, such as a verse, to assist memory. —**mne'monically** *adv.*

mo (məʊ) *n. Inf.* **1.** *Chiefly Brit.* short for **moment** (sense 1) (esp. in **half a mo**). **2.** *Austral.* short for **moustache.**

Mo *the chemical symbol for* molybdenum.

m.o. or **M.O.** *abbrev. for:* **1.** mail order. **2.** money order.

M.O. *abbrev. for* Medical Officer.

-mo *suffix forming nouns.* (in bookbinding) indicating book size by specifying the number of leaves formed by folding one sheet of paper: *16mo* or *sixteenmo.*

moa ('məʊə) *n.* any of various recently extinct large flightless birds of New Zealand.

moan (məʊn) *n.* **1.** a low prolonged mournful sound expressive of suffering or pleading. **2.** any similar mournful sound, esp. that made by the wind. **3.** *Inf.* a grumble or complaint. ~*vb.* **4.** to utter (words, etc.) in a low mournful manner. **5.** (*intr.*) to make a sound like a moan. **6.** (*usually intr.*) *Inf.* to lament. —'**moaner** *n.* —'**moanful** *adj.*

moat (məʊt) *n.* **1.** a wide water-filled ditch surrounding a fortified place, such as a castle. ~*vb.* **2.** (*tr.*) to surround with or as if with a moat.

mob (mɒb) *n.* **1. a.** a riotous or disorderly crowd of people; rabble. **b.** (*as modifier*): *mob law.* **2.** *Often derog.* a group or class of people, animals, or things. **3.** *Often derog.* the masses. **4.** *Sl.* a gang of criminals. **5.** *Austral. & N.Z.* a large number of anything. **6.** *Austral. & N.Z.* a flock or herd of animals. **7. mobs of.** *Austral. & N.Z. inf.* lots of. ~*vb.* **mobbing, mobbed.** (*tr.*) **8.** to attack in a group resembling a mob. **9.** to surround, esp. in order to acclaim. **10.** *U.S.* to crowd into (a building, etc.).

---

mix *v.* 1. alloy, amalgamate, associate, blend, coalesce, combine, commingle, commix, compound, cross, fuse, incorporate, intermingle, interweave, join, jumble, merge, mingle, put together, unite 2. associate, come together, consort, fraternize, hang out (*Inf.*), hobnob, join, mingle, socialize ~*n.* 3. alloy, amalgam, assortment, blend, combination, compound, fusion, medley, mixture

mixed 1. alloyed, amalgamated, blended, combined, composite, compound, fused, incorporated, joint, mingled, united 2. assorted, cosmopolitan, diverse, diversified, heterogeneous, miscellaneous, motley, varied 3. crossbred, hybrid, interbred, interdenominational, mongrel 4. ambivalent, equivocal, indecisive, uncertain

mixed-up bewildered, confused, distraught, disturbed, maladjusted, muddled, perplexed, puzzled, upset

mixture admixture, alloy, amalgam, amalgamation, association, assortment, blend, brew, combine, composite, compound, concoction, conglomeration, cross, fusion, hotchpotch, jumble, medley, *mélange*, miscellany, mix, potpourri, salmagundi, union, variety

mix-up confusion, disorder, fankle (*Scot.*), jumble, mess, mistake, misunderstanding, muddle, snarl-up (*Brit. inf.*), tangle

mix up 1. blend, combine, commix, mix 2. confound, confuse, muddle 3. bewilder, confuse, disturb, fluster, muddle, perplex, puzzle, throw into confusion, upset 4. embroil, entan-

gle, implicate, involve, rope in

moan *n.* 1. groan, lament, lamentation, sigh, sob, sough, wail, whine 2. *Inf.* beef (*Sl.*), bitch (*Sl.*), complaint, gripe (*Inf.*), grouse, grumble, whine, whinge ~*v.* 3. bemoan, bewail, deplore, grieve, groan, keen, lament, mourn, sigh, sob, sough, whine 4. *Inf.* beef (*Sl.*), bitch (*Sl.*), carp, complain, gripe (*Inf.*), groan, grouse, grumble, moan and groan, whine, whinge

mob *n.* 1. assemblage, body, collection, crowd, drove, flock, gang, gathering, herd, horde, host, mass, multitude, pack, press, swarm, throng 2. class, company, crew (*Inf.*), gang, group, lot, set, troop 3. *canaille*, commonalty, great unwashed (*Inf.*), hoi polloi, masses, rabble, riffraff, scum ~*v.* 4. crowd

mobcap ('mɒb,kæp) n. a woman's large cotton cap with a pouched crown, worn esp. during the 18th century.

mobile ('məʊbaɪl) adj. **1.** having freedom of movement; movable. **2.** changing quickly in expression: a mobile face. **3.** Sociol. (of individuals or social groups) moving within and between classes, occupations, and localities. **4.** (of military forces) able to move freely and quickly. **5.** (postpositive) Inf. having transport available: are you mobile? ~n. **6. a.** a sculpture suspended in midair with delicately balanced parts that are set in motion by air currents. **b.** (as modifier): mobile sculpture. —**mobility** (məʊ'bɪlɪtɪ) n.

mobile home n. living quarters mounted on wheels and capable of being towed by a motor vehicle.

mobilize or **-ise** ('məʊbɪ,laɪz) vb. **1.** to prepare for war or another emergency by organizing (national resources, the armed services, etc.). **2.** (tr.) to organize for a purpose. **3.** (tr.) to put into motion or use. —'**mobi,lizable** or **-isable** adj. —,**mobili'zation** or **-i'sation** n.

mobocracy (mɒ'bɒkrəsɪ) n., pl. **-cies.** **1.** rule or domination by a mob. **2.** the mob that rules.

mobster ('mɒbstə) n. a U.S. slang word for **gangster.**

moccasin ('mɒkəsɪn) n. **1.** a shoe of soft leather, esp. deerskin, worn by North American Indians. **2.** any soft shoe resembling this.

mocha ('mɒkə) n. **1.** a dark brown coffee originally imported from the port of Mocha in Arabia. **2.** a flavouring made from coffee and chocolate. **3.** a soft glove leather, made from goatskin or sheepskin. **4. a.** a dark brown colour. **b.** (as adj.): mocha shoes.

mock (mɒk) vb. **1.** (when intr., often foll. by at) to behave with scorn or contempt (towards); show ridicule (for). **2.** (tr.) to imitate, esp. in fun; mimic. **3.** (tr.) to deceive, disappoint, or delude. **4.** (tr.) to defy or frustrate. ~n. **5.** the act of mocking. **6.** a person or thing mocked. **7.** a counterfeit; imitation. ~adj. (prenominal) **8.** sham or counterfeit. **9.** serving as an imitation or substitute, esp. for practice purposes: a mock battle. ~See also **mock-up.** —'**mocker** n. —'**mocking** adj. —'**mockingly** adv.

mockers ('mɒkəz) n. Inf. **put the mockers on.** to ruin the chances of success of.

mockery ('mɒkərɪ) n., pl. **-eries.** **1.** ridicule, contempt, or derision. **2.** a derisive action or comment. **3.** an imitation or pretence, esp. a derisive one. **4.** a person or thing that is mocked. **5.** a person, thing, or action that is inadequate.

mock-heroic adj. **1.** (of a literary work, esp. a poem) imitating the style of heroic poetry in order to satirize an unheroic subject. ~n. **2.** burlesque imitation of the heroic style.

mockingbird ('mɒkɪŋ,bɜːd) n. any of various American songbirds, noted for their ability to mimic the song of other birds.

mock orange n. **1.** Also called: **syringa.** any shrub of a genus with white fragrant flowers resembling those of the orange. **2.** an Australian shrub with white flowers and dark shiny leaves.

mock turtle soup n. an imitation turtle soup made from the calf's head.

mock-up n. **1.** a working full-scale model of a machine, apparatus, etc., for testing, research, etc. **2.** a layout of printed matter. ~vb. **mock up. 3.** (tr., adv.) to build or make a mock-up of.

mod[1] (mɒd) adj. **1.** of or relating to any fashion in dress regarded as stylish, esp. that of the early 1960s in Britain. ~n. **2.** Brit. a member of a group of teenagers, originally in the mid-1960s, noted for their clothes-consciousness.

mod[2] (mɒd) n. an annual Highland Gaelic meeting with musical and literary competitions.

mod. abbrev. for: **1.** moderate. **2.** moderato. **3.** modern.

M.O.D. (in Britain) abbrev. for Ministry of Defence.

modal ('məʊdəl) adj. **1.** of or relating to mode or manner. **2.** Grammar. (of a verb form or auxiliary verb) expressing a distinction of mood, such as that between possibility and actuality. **3.** characterized by or expressing logical modality. **4.** Metaphysics. of or relating to the form of a thing as opposed to its attributes, substance, etc. **5.** Music. of or relating to a mode. **6.** of or relating to a statistical mode. —**mo'dality** n. —'**modally** adv.

mod cons pl. n. Inf. modern conveniences; the usual installations of a modern house, such as hot water, heating, etc.

mode (məʊd) n. **1.** a manner or way of doing, acting, or existing. **2.** the current fashion or style. **3.** Music. **a.** any of the various scales of notes within one octave, esp. any of the twelve natural diatonic scales taken in ascending order used in plainsong, folksong, and art music until 1600. **b.** (in the music of classical Greece) any of the descending diatonic scales from which the liturgical modes evolved. **c.** either of the two main scale systems in music since 1600: major mode; minor mode. **4.** Logic, linguistics. another name for **mood**[2]. **5.** Philosophy. the form in which a thing or one of its attributes manifests itself. **6.** the predominating value in a set of values as determined from statistical data or by observation.

model ('mɒdəl) n. **1. a.** a representation, usually on a smaller scale, of a device, structure, etc. **b.** (as modifier): a model train. **2. a.** a standard to be imitated. **b.** (as modifier): a model wife. **3.** a representative form, style, or pattern. **4.** a person who poses for a sculptor, painter, or photographer. **5.** a person who wears clothes to display them to prospective buyers; mannequin. **6.** a preparatory sculpture in clay, wax, etc., from which the finished work is copied. **7.** a design or style of a particular product. ~vb. **-elling, -elled** or U.S. **-eling, -eled.** **8.** to make a model (of something or someone). **9.** to form in clay, wax, etc.; mould. **10.** to display (clothing and accessories) as a mannequin. **11.** to plan or create according to a model or models. —'**modeller** or U.S. '**modeler** n.

modem ('məʊdɛm) n. Computers. a device for connecting two computers by a telephone line, consisting of a modulator that converts computer signals into audio signals and a corresponding demodulator.

moderate adj. ('mɒdərɪt). **1.** not extreme or excessive. **2.** not violent; mild or temperate. **3.** of average quality or extent: moderate success. ~n. ('mɒdərɪt). **4.** a person who holds moderate views, esp. in politics. ~vb. ('mɒdə,reɪt). **5.** to become or cause to become less extreme or violent. **6.** (when intr., often foll. by over) to preside over a meeting, discussion, etc. **7.** Physics. to slow down (neutrons), esp. by using a moderator. —'**moderately** adv. —'**moderateness** n.

THESAURUS

around, jostle, overrun, set upon, surround, swarm around **5.** cram into, crowd, crowd into, fill, fill to overflowing, jam, pack

mobile 1. ambulatory, itinerant, locomotive, migrant, motile, movable, moving, peripatetic, portable, travelling, wandering **2.** animated, changeable, ever-changing, expressive

mobilize activate, animate, call to arms, call up, get or make ready, marshal, muster, organize, prepare, put in motion, rally, ready

mock v. **1.** chaff, deride, flout, insult, jeer, laugh at, laugh to scorn, make fun of, poke fun at, ridicule, scoff, scorn, show contempt for, sneer, take the mickey (out of) (Inf.), taunt, tease **2.** ape, burlesque, caricature, counterfeit, imitate, lampoon, mimic, parody, satirize, send up (Brit. inf.), take off (Inf.), travesty **3.** belie, cheat, deceive, delude, disappoint, dupe, elude, fool, let down, mislead

4. defeat, defy, disappoint, foil, frustrate, thwart ~n. **5.** banter, derision, gibe, jeering, mockery, ridicule, scorn, sneer, sneering **6.** Aunt Sally (Brit.), butt, dupe, fool, jest, laughing stock, sport, travesty **7.** counterfeit, fake, forgery, fraud, imitation, phoney (Sl.), sham ~adj. **8.** artificial, bogus, counterfeit, dummy, ersatz, fake, faked, false, feigned, forged, fraudulent, imitation, phoney (Sl.), pretended, pseudo (Inf.), sham, spurious

mockery 1. contempt, contumely, derision, disdain, disrespect, gibes, insults, jeering, ridicule, scoffing, scorn **2.** burlesque, caricature, deception, farce, imitation, lampoon, laughing stock, mimicry, parody, pretence, send-up (Brit. sl.), sham, spoof (Inf.), take-off (Inf.), travesty **3.** apology, disappointment, farce, joke, letdown

mocking contemptuous, contumelious, derisive, derisory, disdainful, disrespectful,

insulting, irreverent, sarcastic, sardonic, satiric, satirical, scoffing, scornful, taunting

model n. **1.** copy, dummy, facsimile, image, imitation, miniature, mock-up, replica, representation **2.** archetype, design, epitome, example, exemplar, gauge, ideal, lodestar, mould, original, paradigm, paragon, pattern, prototype, standard, type **3.** poser, sitter, subject **4.** mannequin **5.** configuration, design, form, kind, mark, mode, style, type, variety, version ~v. **6.** base, carve, cast, design, fashion, form, mould, pattern, plan, sculpt, shape **7.** display, show off, sport (Inf.), wear ~adj. **8.** copy, dummy, facsimile, imitation, miniature **9.** archetypal, exemplary, ideal, illustrative, paradigmatic, perfect, standard, typical

moderate adj. **1.** calm, controlled, cool, deliberate, equable, gentle, judicious, limited, middle-of-the-road, mild, modest, peace-

moderation (ˌmɒdəˈreɪʃən) n. 1. the state or an instance of being moderate. 2. the act of moderating. 3. **in moderation.** within moderate or reasonable limits.

moderato (ˌmɒdəˈrɑːtəʊ) adv. Music. 1. at a moderate tempo. 2. a direction indicating that the tempo specified is to be used with restraint: allegro moderato.

moderator (ˈmɒdəˌreɪtə) n. 1. a person or thing that moderates. 2. Presbyterian Church. a minister appointed to preside over a Church court, synod, or general assembly. 3. a presiding officer at a public or legislative assembly. 4. a material, such as heavy water, used for slowing down neutrons in nuclear reactors. 5. an examiner at Oxford or Cambridge Universities in first public examinations. —ˈmoderˌatorˌship n.

modern (ˈmɒdən) adj. 1. of, involving, or befitting the present or a recent time; contemporary. 2. of, relating to, or characteristic of contemporary styles or schools of art, literature, music, etc., esp. those of an experimental kind. 3. belonging or relating to the period in history from the end of the Middle Ages to the present. ~n. 4. a contemporary person. —moˈdernity or ˈmodernness n. —ˌmoderniˈzation or -iˈsation n. —ˈmodernˌize or -ˌise vb.

Modern English n. the English language since about 1450.

Modern Hebrew n. the official language of Israel; a revived form of ancient Hebrew.

modernism (ˈmɒdəˌnɪzəm) n. 1. modern tendencies, thoughts, etc., or the support of these. 2. something typical of contemporary life or thought. 3. (cap.) R.C. Church. the movement at the end of the 19th and beginning of the 20th centuries that sought to adapt doctrine to modern thought. —ˈmodernist n., adj. —ˌmodernˈistic adj. —ˌmodernˈistically adv.

modest (ˈmɒdɪst) adj. 1. having or expressing a humble opinion of oneself or one's accomplishments or abilities. 2. reserved or shy. 3. not ostentatious or pretentious. 4. not extreme or excessive. 5. decorous or decent. —ˈmodestly adv. —ˈmodesty n.

modicum (ˈmɒdɪkəm) n. a small amount or portion.

modifier (ˈmɒdɪˌfaɪə) n. 1. Also called: **qualifier.** Grammar. a word or phrase that qualifies the sense of another word; for example, the noun alarm is a modifier of clock in alarm clock and the phrase every day is an adverbial modifier of walks in he walks every day. 2. a person or thing that modifies.

▷ Usage. Nouns are frequently used in English to modify other nouns: police officer; chicken farm. They should be used with restraint, however, esp. when the appropriate adjective can be used: lunar research (not moon research); educational system (not education system).

modify (ˈmɒdɪˌfaɪ) vb. -fying, -fied. (mainly tr.) 1. to change the structure, character, intent, etc., of. 2. to make less extreme or uncompromising. 3. Grammar. (of a word or phrase) to bear the relation of modifier to (another word or phrase). 4. Linguistics. to change (a vowel) by umlaut. 5. (intr.) to be or become modified. —ˈmodiˌfiable adj. —ˌmodifiˈcation n.

modish (ˈməʊdɪʃ) adj. in the current fashion or style. —ˈmodishly adv. —ˈmodishness n.

modiste (məʊˈdiːst) n. a fashionable dressmaker or milliner.

modulate (ˈmɒdjʊˌleɪt) vb. 1. (tr.) to change the tone, pitch, or volume of. 2. (tr.) to adjust or regulate the degree of. 3. Music. **a.** to change or cause to change from one key to another. **b.** (often foll. by to) to make or become in tune (with a pitch, key, etc.). 4. Physics, electronics. to superimpose the amplitude, frequency, phase, etc., of a wave or signal onto another wave or signal or onto an electron beam. —ˌmoduˈlation n. —ˈmoduˌlator n.

module (ˈmɒdjuːl) n. 1. a standard unit of measure, esp. one used to coordinate the dimensions of buildings and components. 2. a standard self-contained unit or item, such as an assembly of electronic components, that can be used in combination with other units. 3. Astronautics. any of several self-contained separable units making up a spacecraft or launch vehicle, each of which has one or more specified tasks. —ˈmodular adj.

modulus (ˈmɒdjʊləs) n., pl. -li (-ˌlaɪ). 1. Physics. a coefficient expressing a specified property of a specified substance. 2. Maths. the number by which a logarithm to one base is multiplied to give the corresponding logarithm to another base. 3. Maths. an integer that can be divided exactly into the difference between two other integers: 7 is a modulus of 25 and 11. —ˈmodular adj.

modus operandi Latin. (ˈməʊdəs ˌɒpəˈrændiː) n., pl. **modi operandi** (ˈməʊdiː ˌɒpəˈrændiː). a method of operating.

modus vivendi Latin. (ˈməʊdəs vɪˈvɛndiː) n., pl. **modi vivendi** (ˈməʊdiː vɪˈvɛndiː). a working arrangement between conflicting interests; practical compromise.

mog (mɒg) or **moggy** n. Brit. a slang name for **cat**.

mogul (ˈməʊgʌl, məʊˈgʌl) n. an important or powerful person.

Mogul (ˈməʊgʌl, məʊˈgʌl) n. 1. a member of the Muslim dynasty of Indian emperors established in 1526. 2. a Muslim Indian, Mongol, or Mongolian. ~adj. 3. of or relating to the Moguls or their empire.

M.O.H. (in Britain) abbrev. for Medical Officer of Health.

mohair (ˈməʊˌhɛə) n. 1. Also called: **angora.** the long soft silky hair of the Angora goat. 2. **a.** a fabric made from the yarn of this hair and cotton or wool. **b.** (as modifier): a mohair suit.

Mohammedan (məʊˈhæmɪdən) n., adj. another word (not in Muslim use) for **Muslim**. —Moˈhammedanˌism n.

moiety (ˈmɔɪtɪ) n., pl. -ties. 1. a half. 2. one of two parts or divisions of something.

moil (mɔɪl) Arch. or dialect. ~vb. 1. to moisten or soil or become moist, soiled, etc. 2. (intr.) to toil or drudge (esp. in **toil and moil**). ~n. 3. toil; drudgery. 4. confusion; turmoil.

moire (mwɑː) n. a fabric, usually silk, having a watered effect.

moiré (ˈmwɑːreɪ) adj. 1. having a watered or wavelike pattern. ~n. 2. such a pattern, impressed on fabrics by means of engraved rollers. 3. any fabric having such a pattern; moire.

moist (mɔɪst) adj. 1. slightly damp or wet. 2. saturated with or suggestive of moisture. —**moisten** (ˈmɔɪsən) vb. —ˈmoistly adv. —ˈmoistness n.

THESAURUS

able, reasonable, restrained, sober, steady, temperate 2. average, fair, fairish, fair to middling (Inf.), indifferent, mediocre, medium, middling, ordinary, passable, so-so (Inf.), unexceptional ~v. 3. abate, allay, appease, assuage, calm, control, curb, decrease, diminish, lessen, mitigate, modulate, pacify, play down, quiet, regulate, repress, restrain, soften, soft pedal (Inf.), subdue, tame, temper, tone down 4. arbitrate, chair, judge, mediate, preside, referee, take the chair

moderately fairly, gently, in moderation, passably, quite, rather, reasonably, slightly, somewhat, to a degree, tolerably, to some extent, within limits, within reason

moderation 1. calmness, composure, coolness, equanimity, fairness, judiciousness, justice, justness, mildness, moderateness, reasonableness, restraint, sedateness, temperance 2. **in moderation** moderately, within

limits, within reason

modern contemporary, current, fresh, late, latest, neoteric (Rare), new, newfangled, novel, present, present-day, recent, twentieth-century, up-to-date, up-to-the-minute, with-it (Inf.)

modernize bring into the twentieth century, bring up to date, rejuvenate, remake, remodel, renew, renovate, revamp, update

modest 1. bashful, blushing, coy, demure, diffident, discreet, humble, meek, quiet, reserved, reticent, retiring, self-conscious, self-effacing, shy, simple, unassuming, unpretentious 2. fair, limited, middling, moderate, ordinary, small, unexceptional

modesty bashfulness, coyness, decency, demureness, diffidence, discreetness, humbleness, humility, lack of pretension, meekness, propriety, quietness, reserve, reticence, self-effacement, shyness, simplicity, timidity, unobtrusiveness, unpretentiousness

modicum atom, bit, crumb, dash, drop, fragment, grain, inch, iota, little, mite, ounce, particle, pinch, scrap, shred, small amount, speck, tinge, touch

modification adjustment, alteration, change, modulation, mutation, qualification, refinement, reformation, restriction, revision, variation

modify 1. adapt, adjust, alter, change, convert, recast, redo, refashion, reform, remodel, reorganize, reshape, revise, rework, transform, vary 2. abate, lessen, limit, lower, moderate, qualify, reduce, restrain, restrict, soften, temper, tone down

mogul baron, bashaw, big cheese (Sl.), big gun (Sl.), big noise (Brit. sl.), big shot (Sl.), big wheel (Sl.), lord, magnate, nabob (Inf.), notable, personage, potentate, tycoon, V.I.P.

moist clammy, damp, dampish, dank, dewy, dripping, drizzly, humid, not dry, rainy, soggy, wet, wettish

moisture ('mɔɪstʃə) *n.* water or other liquid diffused as vapour or condensed on or in objects. —**'moistureless** *adj.*

moisturize *or* **-ise** ('mɔɪstʃə,raɪz) *vb.* (*tr.*) to add moisture to (the air, the skin, etc.). —**'moistur,izer** *or* **-,iser** *n.*

moke (məʊk) *n. Brit.* a slang name for **donkey** (sense 1).

mol *Chem. symbol for* mole³.

mol. *abbrev. for:* 1. molecular. 2. molecule.

molar ('məʊlə) *n.* 1. any of the 12 grinding teeth in man. 2. a corresponding tooth in other mammals. ~*adj.* 3. of or relating to any of these teeth. 4. used for or capable of grinding.

molasses (mə'læsɪz) *n.* 1. the thick brown uncrystallized bitter syrup obtained from sugar during refining. 2. the U.S. name for **treacle** (sense 1).

mold (məʊld) *n., vb.* the U.S. spelling of **mould**.

moldboard ('məʊld,bɔːd) *n.* the U.S. spelling of **mouldboard**.

molder ('məʊldə) *vb.* the U.S. spelling of **moulder**.

molding ('məʊldɪŋ) *n.* the U.S. spelling of **moulding**.

moldy ('məʊldɪ) *adj.* the U.S. spelling of **mouldy**.

mole¹ (məʊl) *n. Pathol.* a nontechnical name for **naevus**.

mole² (məʊl) *n.* any small burrowing mammal of a family of Europe, Asia, and North and Central America. They have velvety, typically dark fur and forearms specialized for digging.

mole³ (məʊl) *n.* the basic SI unit of amount of substance; the amount that contains as many elementary entities as there are atoms in 0.012 kilogram of carbon-12. The entity may be an atom, a molecule, an ion, a radical, etc. Symbol: mol

mole⁴ (məʊl) *n.* 1. a breakwater. 2. a harbour protected by a breakwater.

molecular weight *n.* the sum of all the atomic weights (relative atomic masses) of the atoms in a molecule; the ratio of the average mass per molecule of a specified isotopic composition of a substance to 1/12 the mass of an atom of carbon-12. Abbrev.: **mol. wt.**

molecule ('mɒlɪ,kjuːl) *n.* 1. the simplest unit of a chemical compound that can exist, consisting of two or more atoms held together by chemical bonds. 2. a very small particle. —**mo'lecular** *adj.*

molehill ('məʊl,hɪl) *n.* 1. the small mound of earth thrown up by a burrowing mole. 2. **make a mountain out of a molehill.** to exaggerate an unimportant matter out of all proportion.

moleskin ('məʊl,skɪn) *n.* 1. the dark grey dense velvety pelt of a mole, used as a fur. 2. a hard-wearing cotton fabric of twill weave. 3. (*modifier*): *a moleskin waistcoat.*

molest (mə'lɛst) *vb.* (*tr.*) 1. to disturb or annoy by malevolent interference. 2. to accost or attack, esp. with the intention of assaulting sexually. —**molestation** (,məʊlɛ'steɪʃən) *n.* —**mo'lester** *n.*

moll (mɒl) *n. Sl.* 1. the female accomplice of a gangster. 2. a prostitute.

mollah ('mɒlə) *n.* an older spelling of **mullah**.

mollify ('mɒlɪ,faɪ) *vb.* **-fying, -fied.** (*tr.*) 1. to pacify; soothe. 2. to lessen the harshness or severity of. —**'molli,fiable** *adj.* —**,mollifi'cation** *n.* —**'molli,fier** *n.*

mollusc *or U.S.* **mollusk** ('mɒləsk) *n.* any of various invertebrates having a soft unsegmented body and often a shell, secreted by a fold of skin (the mantle). The group includes the gastropods (snails, slugs, etc.), bivalves (clams, mussels, etc.), and cephalopods (cuttlefish, octopuses, etc.). —**molluscan** *or U.S.* **molluskan** (mɒ'lʌskən) *adj., n.*

mollycoddle ('mɒlɪ,kɒdəl) *vb.* 1. (*tr.*) to treat with indulgent care; pamper. ~*n.* 2. a pampered person.

Molotov cocktail ('mɒlə,tɒf) *n.* an elementary incendiary weapon, usually a bottle of petrol with a short delay fuse or wick; petrol bomb.

molt (məʊlt) *vb., n.* the usual U.S. spelling of **moult**. —**'molter** *n.*

molten ('məʊltən) *adj.* 1. liquefied; melted. 2. made by having been melted: *molten casts.* ~*vb.* 3. the past participle of **melt**.

molto ('mɒltəʊ) *adv. Music.* very: *allegro molto; molto adagio.*

mol. wt. *abbrev. for* molecular weight.

molybdenite (mɒ'lɪbdɪ,naɪt) *n.* a soft grey mineral consisting of molybdenum sulphide in hexagonal crystalline form with rhenium as an impurity. Formula: MoS_2.

molybdenum (mɒ'lɪbdɪnəm) *n.* a very hard silvery-white metallic element occurring principally in molybdenite: used in alloys, esp. to harden and strengthen steels. Symbol: Mo; atomic no.: 42; atomic wt.: 95.94.

mom (mɒm) *n. Chiefly U.S.* an informal word for **mother**.

moment ('məʊmənt) *n.* 1. a short indefinite period of time. 2. a specific instant or point in time: *at the moment he came, I was out.* 3. **the moment.** the present point of time: *at the moment it's fine.* 4. import, significance, or value: *a man of moment.* 5. *Physics.* **a.** a tendency to produce motion, esp. rotation about a point or axis. **b.** the product of a physical quantity, such as force or mass, and its distance from a fixed reference point.

momentary ('məʊməntərɪ, -trɪ) *adj.* 1. lasting for only a moment; temporary. 2. occurring or present at each moment. —**'momentarily** *adv.* —**'momentariness** *n.*

moment of truth *n.* 1. a moment when a person or thing is put to the test. 2. the point in a bullfight when the matador is about to kill the bull.

momentous (məʊ'mɛntəs) *adj.* of great significance. —**mo'mentously** *adv.* —**mo'mentousness** *n.*

momentum (məʊ'mɛntəm) *n., pl.* **-ta** (-tə) *or* **-tums.** 1. *Physics.* the product of a body's mass and its velocity. 2. the impetus of a body resulting from its motion. 3. driving power or strength.

momma ('mɒmə) *n. Chiefly U.S.* 1. an informal or childish word for **mother**. 2. *Inf.* a buxom and voluptuous woman.

Mon. *abbrev. for* Monday.

mon- *combining form.* variant of **mono-** before a vowel.

monad ('mɒnæd, 'məʊ-) *n.* 1. (*pl.* **-ads** *or* **-ades** (-ə,diːz)) *Philosophy.* any fundamental singular metaphysical entity, esp. if autonomous. 2. a single-celled organism. 3. an atom, ion, or radical with a valency of one. ~Also called (for senses 1, 2): **monas.** —**monadic** (mɒ'nædɪk) *adj.*

monandrous (mɒ'nændrəs) *adj.* 1. having only one male sexual partner over a period of time. 2. (of plants) having flowers with only one stamen. 3. (of flowers) having only one stamen. —**mo'nandry** *n.*

monarch ('mɒnək) *n.* 1. a sovereign head of state, esp. a king, queen, or emperor, who rules usually by hereditary right. 2. a supremely powerful or pre-eminent person or thing. 3. Also called: **milkweed.** a large migratory orange and black butterfly that feeds on the milkweed plant. —**monarchal** (mɒ'nɑːkəl) *or* **monarchial** (mɒ'nɑːkɪəl) *adj.* —**mo'narchical** *adj.* —**'monarchism** *n.* —**'monarchist** *n., adj.* —,**monar'chistic** *adj.*

monarchy ('mɒnəkɪ) *n., pl.* **-chies.** 1. a form of government in which supreme authority is vested in a single and usually hereditary figure, such as a king. 2. a country reigned over by a monarch.

THESAURUS

moisten bedew, damp, dampen, humidify, lick, moisturize, soak, water, wet

moisture damp, dampness, dankness, dew, humidity, liquid, perspiration, sweat, water, wateriness, wetness

molecule atom, iota, jot, mite, mote, particle, speck

molest 1. abuse, afflict, annoy, badger, beset, bother, bug (*Inf.*), disturb, harass, harry, hector, irritate, persecute, pester, plague, tease, torment, upset, vex, worry 2. abuse, accost, assail, attack, harm, hurt, illtreat, injure, interfere with, maltreat, manhandle

moment 1. flash, instant, jiffy (*Inf.*), minute, no time, second, shake (*Inf.*), split second, tick (*Brit. inf.*), trice, twinkling, two shakes (*Inf.*), two shakes of a lamb's tail (*Inf.*) 2. hour, instant, juncture, point, point in time, stage, time 3. concern, consequence, gravity, import, importance, seriousness, significance, substance, value, weight, weightiness, worth

momentarily briefly, for a moment (little while), minute, second, short time, short while), for an instant, temporarily

momentary brief, ephemeral, evanescent, fleeting, flying, fugitive, hasty, passing, quick, short, short-lived, temporary, transitory

momentous consequential, critical, crucial, decisive, earth-shaking (*Inf.*), fateful, grave, historic, important, of moment, pivotal, serious, significant, vital, weighty

momentum drive, energy, force, impetus, power, propulsion, push, strength, thrust

monarch crowned head, emperor, empress, king, potentate, prince, princess, queen, ruler, sovereign

monastery ('mɒnəstərı) *n.*, *pl.* **-teries.** the residence of a religious community, esp. of monks, living in seclusion from secular society and bound by religious vows. —**monasterial** (ˌmɒnə'stɪərɪəl) *adj.*

monastic (mə'næstɪk) *adj. also* **monastical.** 1. of or relating to monasteries or monks, nuns, etc. 2. resembling this sort of life. ~*n.* 3. a person committed to this way of life, esp. a monk. —**mo'nasti‚cism** *n.*

monatomic (ˌmɒnə'tomɪk) *or* **monoatomic** (ˌmɒnəʊə'tomɪk) *adj. Chem.* 1. (of an element) having or consisting of single atoms. 2. (of a compound or molecule) having only one atom or group that can be replaced in a chemical reaction.

monaural (mɒ'nɔːrəl) *adj.* 1. relating to, having, or hearing with only one ear. 2. another word for **monophonic** (sense 1). —**mon'aurally** *adv.*

Monday ('mʌndɪ) *n.* the second day of the week; first day of the working week.

monecious (mɒ'niːʃəs) *adj.* a variant spelling of **monoecious.**

monetarist ('mʌnɪtərɪst) *n.* a person who advocates regulation of the money supply as a method of controlling the economy of a country. —**'monetarism** *n.*

monetary ('mʌnɪtərɪ, -trı) *adj.* of or relating to money or currency. —**'monetarily** *adv.*

money ('mʌnɪ) *n.*, *pl.* **-eys** *or* **-ies.** 1. a medium of exchange that functions as legal tender. 2. the official currency, in the form of bank notes, coins, etc., issued by a government or other authority. 3. a particular denomination or form of currency: *silver money.* 4. a pecuniary sum or income. 5. an unspecified amount of paper currency or coins: *money to lend.* 6. **for one's money.** in one's opinion. 7. **in the money.** *Inf.* well-off; rich. 8. **one's money's worth.** full value for the money one has paid for something. 9. **put money on.** to place a bet on. ~Related adj.: **pecuniary.**

moneybags ('mʌnɪˌbægz) *n. Sl.* a very rich person.

moneychanger ('mʌnɪˌtʃeɪndʒə) *n.* 1. a person engaged in the business of exchanging currencies or money. 2. *Chiefly U.S.* a machine for dispensing coins.

moneyed *or* **monied** ('mʌnɪd) *adj.* 1. having a great deal of money; rich. 2. arising from or characterized by money.

money-grubbing *adj. Inf.* seeking greedily to obtain money. —**'money-‚grubber** *n.*

moneylender ('mʌnɪˌlɛndə) *n.* a person who lends money at interest as a living. —**'money‚lending** *adj.*, *n.*

moneymaker ('mʌnɪˌmeɪkə) *n.* 1. a person who is intent on accumulating money. 2. a person or thing that is or might be profitable. —**'money‚making** *adj.*, *n.*

money-spinner *n. Inf.* an enterprise, idea, person, or thing that is a source of wealth.

monger ('mʌŋgə) *n.* 1. (*in combination except in archaic use*) a trader or dealer: *ironmonger.* 2. (*in combination*) a promoter of something: *warmonger.* —**'mongering** *n.*, *adj.*

Mongolian (mɒŋ'gəʊlɪən) *adj.* 1. of or relating to Mongolia, a region in Central Asia, its people, or their language. ~*n. also* **Mongol.** 2. a native or inhabitant of Mongolia. 3. the language of Mongolia.

mongolism ('mɒŋgəˌlɪzəm) *n. Pathol.* a chromosomal abnormality resulting in a flat face and mental retardation, short stubby fingers, a vertical fold of skin at the inner edge of the eye, and mental retardation. Also called: **Down's syndrome.** —**'mongol** *n.* —**mon'golian** *adj.* —**'mongoloid** *adj.*, *n.*

Mongoloid ('mɒŋgəˌlɔɪd) *adj.* 1. of or relating to a major racial group of mankind, characterized by yellowish complexion, straight black hair, slanting eyes, short nose, and scanty facial hair, including most of the peoples of Asia, the Eskimos, and the North American Indians. ~*n.* 2. a member of this group.

mongoose ('mɒŋˌguːs) *n.*, *pl.* **-gooses.** any of various small predatory mammals occurring in Africa and from S Europe to SE Asia, typically having a long tail and brindled coat.

mongrel ('mʌŋgrəl) *n.* 1. a plant or animal, esp. a dog, of mixed or unknown breeding. 2. *Derog.* a person of mixed race. ~*adj.* 3. of mixed origin, breeding, character, etc. —**'mongrelism** *n.* —**'mongrelize** *or* **-ise** *vb.* —‚mongreli'zation *or* -i'sation *n.* —**'mongrelly** *adj.*

monied ('mʌnɪd) *adj.* a less common spelling of **moneyed.**

monies ('mʌnɪz) *n.* a plural of **money.**

moniker *or* **monicker** ('mɒnɪkə) *n. Inf.* a person's name or nickname.

monism ('mɒnɪzəm) *n.* 1. *Philosophy.* the doctrine that reality consists of only one basic substance or element, such as mind or matter. Cf. **dualism, pluralism.** 2. the attempt to explain anything in terms of one principle only. —**'monist** *n.*, *adj.* —**mo'nistic** *adj.*

monition (məʊ'nɪʃən) *n.* 1. a warning or caution; admonition. 2. *Ecclesiast.* a formal notice from a bishop or ecclesiastical court requiring a person to refrain from committing a specific offence.

monitor ('mɒnɪtə) *n.* 1. a person or piece of equipment that warns, checks, controls, or keeps a continuous record of something. 2. *Education.* **a.** a senior pupil with various supervisory duties, etc. **b.** a pupil assisting a teacher in classroom organization, etc. 3. a television set used in a studio for viewing or checking a programme being transmitted. 4. any of various large predatory lizards inhabiting warm regions of Africa, Asia, and Australia. 5. (formerly) a small heavily armoured warship used for coastal assault. ~*vb.* 6. to act as a monitor of. 7. (*tr.*) to observe or record (the activity or performance of) (an engine or other device). 8. (*tr.*) to check (the technical quality of) (a radio or television broadcast). —**monitorial** (ˌmɒnɪ'tɔːrɪəl) *adj.* —**'monitor‚ship** *n.* —**'monitress** *fem. n.*

monitory ('mɒnɪtərɪ, -trı) *adj. also* **monitorial.** 1. warning or admonishing. ~*n.*, *pl.* **-ries.** 2. *Rare.* a letter containing a monition.

monk (mʌŋk) *n.* a male member of a religious community bound by vows of poverty, chastity, and obedience. Related adj.: **monastic.** —**'monkish** *adj.*

monkey ('mʌŋkɪ) *n.* 1. any of numerous long-tailed primates excluding lemurs, tarsiers, etc. 2. any primate except man. 3. a naughty or mischievous person, esp. a child. 4. the head of a pile driver (**monkey engine**) or of some similar mechanical device. 5. *U.S. sl.* an addict's dependence on a drug (esp. in **have a monkey on one's back**). 6. *Sl.* a butt of derision; someone made to look a fool (esp. in **make a monkey of**). 7. *Sl.* (esp. in bookmaking) £500. 8. *U.S. sl.* $500. ~*vb.* 9. (*intr.*; usually foll. by *around, with,* etc.) to meddle, fool, or tinker. 10. (*tr.*) *Rare.* to imitate; ape.

THESAURUS

monarchy 1. absolutism, autocracy, despotism, kingship, monocracy, royalism, sovereignty 2. empire, kingdom, principality, realm

monastery abbey, cloister, convent, friary, house, nunnery, priory, religious community

monastic ascetic, austere, celibate, cenobitic, cloistered, cloistral, coenobitic, contemplative, conventual, eremitic, hermit-like, monachal, monkish, recluse, reclusive, secluded, sequestered, withdrawn

monetary budgetary, capital, cash, financial, fiscal, pecuniary

money 1. banknotes, bread (*Sl.*), capital, cash, coin, currency, dough (*Sl.*), filthy lucre (*Facetious*), funds, gelt (*Sl.*), green (*Sl.*), hard cash, legal tender, lolly (*Brit. sl.*), loot (*Inf.*), mazuma (*Sl., chiefly U.S.*), moolah (*Sl.*), pelf (*Contemptuous*), readies (*Inf.*), riches, specie, spondulix (*Sl.*), the ready (*Inf.*), the wherewithal, wealth 2. **in the money** affluent, flush (*Inf.*), in clover (*Inf.*), loaded (*Sl.*), on Easy Street (*Inf.*), prosperous, rich, rolling (*Sl.*), wealthy, well-heeled (*Sl.*), well-off, well-to-do

moneymaking *adj.* gainful, going, lucrative, paying, profitable, remunerative, successful, thriving

mongrel 1. *n.* bigener (*Biol.*), cross, crossbreed, half-breed, hybrid, mixed breed 2. *adj.* bastard, crossbred, half-breed, hybrid, of mixed breed

monitor 1. *n.* guide, invigilator, overseer, prefect (*Brit.*), supervisor, watchdog 2. *v.* check, follow, keep an eye on, keep track of, observe, oversee, record, scan, supervise, survey, watch

monk brother, friar (*loosely*), monastic, religious

monkey *n.* 1. primate, simian 2. devil, imp, mischief maker, rascal, rogue, scamp 3. *Sl.* ass, butt, dupe, fool, laughing stock 4. **make a monkey of** make a fool of, make (someone) a laughing stock, make fun of, make (someone) look foolish (ridiculous, silly), play a trick on, ridicule ~*v.* 5. fiddle, fool, interfere, meddle, mess, play, tamper, tinker, trifle

monkey business 1. carry-on (*Inf.*), clowning, mischief, monkey tricks, pranks, shenanigans (*Inf.*), skylarking (*Inf.*), tomfoolery 2. chicanery, dishonesty, funny business, hanky-panky (*Inf.*), skulduggery (*Inf.*), trickery

monkey business *n. Inf.* mischievous, suspect, or dishonest behaviour or acts.

monkey jacket *n.* a short close-fitting jacket, esp. a waist-length jacket similar to a mess jacket.

monkey nut *n. Brit.* another name for a **peanut**.

monkey puzzle *n.* a South American coniferous tree having branches shaped like a candelabra and stiff sharp leaves. Also called: **Chile pine**.

monkey's wedding *n. S. African inf.* a combination of rain and sunshine.

monkey tricks or *U.S.* **monkey shines** *pl. n. Inf.* mischievous behaviour or acts.

monkey wrench *n.* a wrench with adjustable jaws.

monkfish ('mʌŋk,fɪʃ) *n., pl.* **-fish** or **-fishes**. **1.** any of various angler fishes. **2.** another name for **angel fish** (sense 3).

monkshood ('mʌŋkshʊd) *n.* any of several poisonous N temperate plants that have hooded blue-purple flowers.

mono ('mɒnəʊ) *adj.* **1.** short for **monophonic** (sense 1). ~*n.* **2.** monophonic sound; monophony.

mono- or before a vowel **mon-** combining form. **1.** one; single: *monorail.* **2.** indicating that a chemical compound contains a single specified atom or group: *monoxide.*

monoacid (,mɒnəʊ'æsɪd), **monacid, monoacidic** (,mɒnəʊ'sɪdɪk), or **monacidic** *adj. Chem.* (of a base) capable of reacting with only one molecule of a monobasic acid; having only one hydroxide ion per molecule.

monobasic (,mɒnəʊ'beɪsɪk) *adj. Chem.* (of an acid, such as hydrogen chloride) having only one replaceable hydrogen atom per molecule.

monochromatic (,mɒnəʊkrəʊ'mætɪk) or **monochroic** (,mɒnəʊ'krəʊɪk) *adj.* (of light or other electromagnetic radiation) having only one wavelength.

monochrome ('mɒnə,krəʊm) *n.* **1.** a black-and-white photograph or transparency. **2.** *Photog.* black and white. **3. a.** a painting, drawing, etc., done in a range of tones of a single colour. **b.** the technique or art of this. **4.** (*modifier*) executed in or resembling monochrome: *a monochrome print.* ~Also called (for senses 3, 4): **monotint.** —,mono'**chromic** *adj.* —'mono,**chromist** *n.*

monocle ('mɒnəkəl) *n.* a lens for correcting defective vision of one eye, held in position by the facial muscles. —'**monocled** *adj.*

monocline ('mɒnəʊ,klaɪn) *n.* a fold in stratified rocks in which the strata are inclined in the same direction from the horizontal. —,mono'**clinal** *adj., n.*

monoclinic (,mɒnəʊ'klɪnɪk) *adj. Crystallog.* relating to or belonging to the crystal system characterized by three unequal axes, one pair of which are not at right angles to each other.

monocotyledon (,mɒnəʊ,kɒtɪ'liːdən) *n.* any of various flowering plants having a single embryonic seed leaf, leaves with parallel veins, and flowers with parts in threes: includes grasses, lilies, palms, and orchids. Cf. **dicotyledon.** —,mono,coty'**ledonous** *adj.*

monocracy (mɒ'nɒkrəsɪ) *n., pl.* **-cies.** government by one person. —**monocrat** ('mɒnə,kræt) *n.* —,mono-'**cratic** *adj.*

monocular (mɒ'nɒkjʊlə) *adj.* having or intended for the use of only one eye. —**mo'nocularly** *adv.*

monocycle ('mɒnə,saɪkəl) *n.* another name for **unicycle.**

monody ('mɒnədɪ) *n., pl.* **-dies.** **1.** (in Greek tragedy) an ode sung by a single actor. **2.** any poem of lament for someone's death. **3.** *Music.* a style of composition consisting of a single vocal part, usually with accompaniment. —**monodic** (mɒ'nɒdɪk) *adj.* —'**mono- dist** *n.*

monoecious (mɒ'niːʃəs) *adj.* **1.** (of some flowering plants) having the male and female reproductive organs in separate flowers on the same plant. **2.** (of some animals and lower plants) hermaphrodite.

monogamy (mɒ'nɒgəmɪ) *n.* **1.** the state or practice of having only one husband or wife over a period of time. **2.** *Zool.* the practice of having only one mate. —**mo- 'nogamist** *n.* —**mo'nogamous** *adj.*

monogram ('mɒnə,græm) *n.* a design of one or more letters, esp. initials, on clothing, stationery, etc. —**monogrammatic** (,mɒnəgrə'mætɪk) *adj.*

monograph ('mɒnə,grɑːf) *n.* **1.** a paper, book, or other work concerned with a single subject or aspect of a subject. ~*vb.* (*tr.*) **2.** to write a monograph on. —**monographer** (mɒ'nɒgrəfə) or **mo'nographist** *n.* —,mono-'**graphic** *adj.*

monogyny (mɒ'nɒdʒɪnɪ) *n.* the custom of having only one female sexual partner over a period of time. —**mo- 'nogynous** *adj.*

monolingual (,mɒnəʊ'lɪŋgwəl) *adj.* knowing or expressed in only one language.

monolith ('mɒnəlɪθ) *n.* **1.** a large block of stone or anything that resembles one in appearance, intractability, etc. **2.** a statue, obelisk, column, etc., cut from one block of stone. **3.** a large hollow foundation piece sunk as a caisson and filled with concrete. —,mono'**lithic** *adj.*

monologue ('mɒnə,lɒg) *n.* **1.** a long speech made by one actor in a play, film, etc., esp. when alone. **2.** a dramatic piece for a single performer. **3.** any long speech by one person, esp. when interfering with conversation. —**monologic** (,mɒnə'lɒdʒɪk) or ,mono'**logical** *adj.* —**monologist** ('mɒnə,lɒgɪst) *n.* —**monologize** or **-ise** (mɒ'nɒlədʒaɪz) *vb.*

monomania (,mɒnəʊ'meɪnɪə) *n.* an excessive mental preoccupation with one thing, idea, etc. —,mono'**mani- ,ac** *n.* —**monomaniacal** (,mɒnəʊmə'naɪəkəl) *adj.*

monomer ('mɒnəmə) *n. Chem.* a compound whose molecules can join together to form a polymer. —**mono- meric** (,mɒnə'mɛrɪk) *adj.*

monomial (mɒ'nəʊmɪəl) *n.* **1.** *Maths.* an expression consisting of a single term, such as *5ax.* ~*adj.* **2.** consisting of a single algebraic term.

mononucleosis (,mɒnəʊ,njuːklɪ'əʊsɪs) *n.* **1.** *Pathol.* the presence of a large number of monocytes in the blood. **2.** See **infectious mononucleosis.**

monophonic (,mɒnəʊ'fɒnɪk) *adj.* **1.** Also: **monaural.** (of a system of broadcasting, recording, or reproducing sound) using only one channel between source and loudspeaker. Sometimes shortened to **mono.** Cf. **stereo- phonic.** **2.** *Music.* of or relating to a style of musical composition consisting of a single melodic line.

Monophysite (mɒ'nɒfɪ,saɪt) *n. Christianity.* a person who holds that there is only one nature in the person of Christ, which is primarily divine with human attributes. —**Monophysitic** (,mɒnəʊfɪ'sɪtɪk) *adj.*

monoplane ('mɒnəʊ,pleɪn) *n.* an aeroplane with only one pair of wings. Cf. **biplane.**

monopoly (mə'nɒpəlɪ) *n., pl.* **-lies.** **1.** exclusive control of the market supply of a product or service. **2. a.** an enterprise exercising this control. **b.** the product or service so controlled. **3.** *Law.* the exclusive right granted to a person, company, etc., by the state to purchase, manufacture, use, or sell some commodity or to trade in a specified area. **4.** exclusive control, possession, or use of something. —**mo'nopolist** *n.* —,mo,nopo'**listic** *adj.* —,mo,nopoli'**zation** or **-li'sation** *n.* —**mo'nopo,lize** or **-,lise** *vb.*

Monopoly (mə'nɒpəlɪ) *n. Trademark.* a board game for two to six players who throw dice to advance their tokens, the object being to acquire the property on which their tokens land.

monorail ('mɒnəʊ,reɪl) *n.* a single-track railway, often elevated and with suspended cars.

monosaccharide (,mɒnəʊ'sækə,raɪd) *n.* a simple sugar, such as glucose or fructose, that does not hydrolyse to yield other sugars.

monosodium glutamate (,mɒnəʊ'səʊdɪəm 'gluː:tə- ,meɪt) *n.* a white crystalline substance that has a meaty taste: used as a food additive.

monosyllable ('mɒnə,sɪləbəl) *n.* a word of one syllable, esp. one used as a sentence. —,**monosyl'labic** *adj.*

monotheism ('mɒnəʊθɪ,ɪzəm) *n.* the belief or doctrine that there is only one God. —'**mono,theist** *n., adj.* —,**monothe'istic** *adj.* —,**monothe'istically** *adv.*

monotint ('mɒnə,tɪnt) *n.* another word for **mono- chrome** (senses 3, 4).

monotone ('mɒnə,təʊn) *n.* **1.** a single unvaried pitch

THESAURUS

monolithic colossal, giant, gigantic, huge, immovable, impenetrable, imposing, intractable, massive, monumental, solid, substantial, undifferentiated, undivided, unitary

monologue harangue, lecture, sermon, soliloquy, speech

monopolize control, corner, corner the market in, dominate, engross, exercise or have a monopoly of, hog (*Sl.*), keep to oneself, take over, take up

level in speech, sound, etc. **2.** utterance, etc., without change of pitch. **3.** lack of variety in style, expression, etc. ~*adj.* **4.** unvarying.
monotonous (məˈnɒtənəs) *adj.* **1.** tedious, esp. because of repetition. **2.** in unvarying tone. —**mo'notonously** *adv.* —**mo'notonousness** *n.*
monotony (məˈnɒtənɪ) *n., pl.* **-nies. 1.** wearisome routine; dullness. **2.** lack of variety in pitch or cadence.
monotype (ˈmɒnəˌtaɪp) *n.* **1.** a single print made from a metal or glass plate on which a picture has been painted. **2.** *Biol.* a monotypic genus or species. —**monotypic** (ˌmɒnəʊˈtɪpɪk) *adj.*
Monotype (ˈmɒnəˌtaɪp) *n.* **1.** *Trademark.* a typesetting machine, operated by a keyboard, in which each character is cast individually from hot metal. **2.** type produced on such a machine.
monovalent (ˌmɒnəʊˈveɪlənt) *adj. Chem.* Also: **univalent. a.** having a valency of one. **b.** having only one valency. —ˌ**mono'valence** *or* ˌ**mono'valency** *n.*
monoxide (mɒˈnɒksaɪd) *n.* an oxide that contains one oxygen atom per molecule.
Monseigneur *French.* (mɔ̃sɛˈɲœːr) *n., pl. Messeigneurs.* a title given to French bishops, prelates, and princes.
monsieur (məsˈjɜː) *n., pl.* **messieurs** (mɛˈsjø). a French title of address equivalent to *sir* when used alone or *Mr.* before a name.
Monsignor (mɒnˈsiːnjə) *n., pl.* **-nors** *or* **-nori** (*Italian* -ˈnɔːri). *R.C. Church.* an ecclesiastical title attached to certain offices.
monsoon (mɒnˈsuːn) *n.* **1.** a seasonal wind of S Asia from the southwest in summer and from the northeast in winter. **2.** the rainy season when the SW monsoon blows, from about April to October. **3.** any wind that changes direction with the seasons. —**mon'soonal** *adj.*
mons pubis (ˈmɒnz ˈpjuːbɪs) *n., pl.* **montes pubis** (ˈmɒntiːz). the fatty flesh in human females over the junction of the pubic bones. Also called: **mons veneris.**
monster (ˈmɒnstə) *n.* **1.** an imaginary beast, usually made up of various animal or human parts. **2.** a person, animal, or plant with a marked deformity. **3.** a cruel, wicked, or inhuman person. **4. a.** a very large person, animal, or thing. **b.** (*as modifier*): *a monster cake.*
monstrance (ˈmɒnstrəns) *n. R.C. Church.* a receptacle in which the consecrated Host is exposed for adoration.
monstrosity (mɒnˈstrɒsɪtɪ) *n., pl.* **-ties. 1.** an outrageous or ugly person or thing; monster. **2.** the state or quality of being monstrous.
monstrous (ˈmɒnstrəs) *adj.* **1.** abnormal, hideous, or unnatural in size, character, etc. **2.** (of plants and animals) abnormal in structure. **3.** outrageous, atrocious, or shocking. **4.** huge. **5.** of, relating to, or resembling a monster. —ˈ**monstrously** *adv.* —ˈ**monstrousness** *n.*
montage (mɒnˈtɑːʒ) *n.* **1.** the art or process of composing pictures of miscellaneous elements, such as other pictures or photographs. **2.** such a composition. **3.** a method of film editing by juxtaposition or partial superimposition of several shots to form a single image. **4.** a film sequence of this kind.
montane (ˈmɒnteɪn) *adj.* of or inhabiting mountainous regions.

montbretia (mɒnˈbriːʃə) *n.* any plant of an African genus related to the iris, with ornamental orange flowers.
Montessori method (ˌmɒntɪˈsɔːrɪ) *n.* a method of nursery education in which children are allowed to develop at their own pace through practical play.
month (mʌnθ) *n.* **1.** one of the twelve divisions (**calendar months**) of the calendar year. **2.** a period of time extending from one date to a corresponding date in the next calendar month. **3.** a period of four weeks or of 30 days. **4.** the period of time (**solar month**) taken by the moon to return to the same longitude after one complete revolution around the earth; 27.321 58 days (approximately 27 days, 7 hours, 43 minutes, 4.5 seconds). **5.** the period of time (**sidereal month**) taken by the moon to make one complete revolution around the earth, measured between two successive conjunctions with a particular star; 27.321 66 days (approximately 27 days, 7 hours, 43 minutes, 11 seconds). **6.** Also called: **lunation.** the period of time (**lunar** or **synodic month**) taken by the moon to make one complete revolution around the earth, measured between two successive new moons; 29.530 59 days (approximately 29 days, 12 hours, 44 minutes, 3 seconds).
monthly (ˈmʌnθlɪ) *adj.* **1.** occurring, done, appearing, payable, etc., once every month. **2.** lasting or valid for a month. ~*adv.* **3.** once a month. ~*n., pl.* **-lies. 4.** a book, periodical, magazine, etc., published once a month. **5.** *Inf.* a menstrual period.
monument (ˈmɒnjumənt) *n.* **1.** an obelisk, statue, building, etc., erected in commemoration of a person or event. **2.** a notable building or site, esp. one preserved as public property. **3.** a tomb or tombstone. **4.** a literary or artistic work regarded as commemorative of its creator or a particular period. **5.** *U.S.* a boundary marker. **6.** an exceptional example: *his lecture was a monument of tedium.*
monumental (ˌmɒnjuˈmentəl) *adj.* **1.** like a monument, esp. in large size, endurance, or importance. **2.** of, relating to, or being a monument. **3.** *Inf.* (intensifier): *monumental stupidity.* —ˌ**monu'mentally** *adv.*
moo (muː) *vb.* **1.** (*intr.*) (of a cow, bull, etc.) to make a characteristic deep long sound; low. ~*interj.* **2.** an instance or imitation of this sound.
mooch (muːtʃ) *vb. Sl.* **1.** (*intr.*) to loiter or walk aimlessly. **2.** (*intr.*) to lurk; skulk. **3.** (*tr.*) *Chiefly U.S.* **a.** to cadge. **b.** to steal. —ˈ**moocher** *n.*
mood[1] (muːd) *n.* **1.** a temporary state of mind or temper: *a cheerful mood.* **2.** a sullen or gloomy state of mind, esp. when temporary: *she's in a mood.* **3.** a prevailing atmosphere or feeling. **4. in the mood.** in a favourable state of mind.
mood[2] (muːd) *n.* **1.** *Grammar.* a category of the verb or verbal inflections that expresses semantic and grammatical differences, including such forms as the indicative, subjunctive, and imperative. **2.** *Logic.* one of several forms of a syllogism classified by whether the constituent statements are affirmative, negative, universal, or particular. ~Also called: **mode.**
moody (ˈmuːdɪ) *adj.* **moodier, moodiest. 1.** sullen, sulky, or gloomy. **2.** temperamental or changeable. —ˈ**moodily** *adv.* —ˈ**moodiness** *n.*

THESAURUS

monotonous all the same, boring, colourless, droning, dull, flat, humdrum, plodding, repetitious, repetitive, samey (*Inf.*), soporific, tedious, tiresome, toneless, unchanging, uniform, uninflected, unvaried, wearisome

monotony boredom, colourlessness, dullness, flatness, humdrumness, monotonousness, repetitiveness, repetitiousness, routine, sameness, tediousness, tedium, tiresomeness, uniformity, wearisomeness

monster *n.* **1.** barbarian, beast, bogeyman, brute, demon, devil, fiend, ogre, savage, villain **2.** abortion, freak, lusus naturae, miscreation, monstrosity, mutant, teratism **3.** behemoth, Brobdingnagian, colossus, giant, leviathan, mammoth, titan ~*adj.* **4.** Brobdingnagian, colossal, enormous, gargantuan, giant, gigantic, huge, immense, jumbo (*Inf.*), mammoth, massive, monstrous, stupendous, titanic, tremendous

monstrosity 1. abortion, eyesore, freak, horror, lusus naturae, miscreation, monster, mutant, ogre, teratism **2.** abnormality, atrocity, dreadfulness, evil, frightfulness, heinousness, hellishness, hideousness, horror, loathsomeness, obscenity

monstrous 1. abnormal, dreadful, enormous, fiendish, freakish, frightful, grotesque, gruesome, hellish, hideous, horrendous, horrible, miscreated, obscene, teratoid, terrible, unnatural **2.** atrocious, cruel, devilish, diabolical, disgraceful, egregious, evil, fiendish, foul, heinous, horrifying, infamous, inhuman, intolerable, loathsome, odious, outrageous, satanic, scandalous, shocking, vicious, villainous **3.** colossal, elephantine, enormous, gargantuan, giant, gigantic, great, huge, immense, mammoth, massive, prodigious, stupendous, titanic, towering, tremendous, vast

month four weeks, moon, thirty days

monument 1. cairn, cenotaph, commemoration, gravestone, headstone, marker, mausoleum, memorial, obelisk, pillar, shrine, statue, tombstone **2.** memento, record, remembrance, reminder, testament, token, witness

monumental 1. awe-inspiring, awesome, classic, enduring, enormous, epoch-making, historic, immortal, important, lasting, majestic, memorable, outstanding, prodigious, significant, stupendous, unforgettable **2.** commemorative, cyclopean, funerary, memorial, monolithic, statuary **3.** *Inf.* catastrophic, colossal, egregious, gigantic, great, horrible, immense, indefensible, massive, staggering, terrible, tremendous, unforgivable, whopping (*Inf.*)

mood 1. disposition, frame of mind, humour, spirit, state of mind, temper, tenor, vein **2.** bad temper, blues, depression, doldrums, dumps (*Inf.*), fit of pique, grumps (*Inf.*), low spirits, melancholy, sulk, the sulks **3. in the mood** disposed (towards), eager, fa-

Moog synthesizer (muːg, məʊg) *n. Music, trademark.* an electrophonic instrument operated by a keyboard and pedals, in which a wide range of musical sounds is produced. Often shortened to **synthesizer** or **Moog.**

mooi (mɔɪ) *adj. S. African sl.* pleasing; nice.

moon (muːn) *n.* **1.** the natural satellite of the earth. **2.** the face of the moon as it is seen during its revolution around the earth, esp. at one of its phases: *new moon; full moon.* **3.** any natural satellite of a planet. **4.** moonlight. **5.** something resembling a moon. **6.** a month, esp. a lunar one. **7. once in a blue moon.** very seldom. **8. over the moon.** very excited and happy. ~*vb.* **9.** (when *tr.,* often foll. by *away;* when *intr.,* often foll. by *around*) to be idle in a listless way, as if in love, or to idle (time) away. —'**moonless** *adj.*

moonbeam ('muːn‚biːm) *n.* a ray of moonlight.

mooncalf ('muːn‚kɑːf) *n., pl.* **-calves.** **1.** a born fool; dolt. **2.** a person who idles time away.

moon-faced *adj.* having a round face.

moonlight ('muːn‚laɪt) *n.* **1.** light from the sun received on earth after reflection by the moon. **2.** (*modifier*) illuminated by the moon: *a moonlight walk.* ~*vb.* **-lighting, -lighted. 3.** (*intr.*) *Inf.* to work at a secondary job, esp. at night. —'**moon‚lighter** *n.* —'**moon‚lighting** *n.* —'**moon‚lit** *adj.*

moonlight flit *n.* a hurried departure by night to escape from one's creditors.

moonscape ('muːn‚skeɪp) *n.* the general surface of the moon or a representation of it.

moonshine ('muːn‚ʃaɪn) *n.* **1.** another word for **moonlight** (sense 1). **2.** *U.S.* illegally distilled or smuggled whisky. **3.** foolish talk or thought.

moonshot ('muːn‚ʃɒt) *n.* the launching of a spacecraft, rocket, etc., to the moon.

moonstone ('muːn‚stəʊn) *n.* a gem variety of orthoclase or albite that is white and translucent.

moonstruck ('muːn‚strʌk) *or* **moonstricken** ('muːn‚strɪkən) *adj.* deranged or mad.

moony ('muːnɪ) *adj.* **moonier, mooniest. 1.** *Inf.* dreamy or listless. **2.** of or like the moon.

moor[1] (mʊə, mɔː) *n.* a tract of unenclosed waste ground, usually covered with heather, coarse grass, bracken, and moss.

moor[2] (mʊə, mɔː) *vb.* to secure (a vessel, etc.) with cables, ropes, or anchors, or (of a vessel, etc.) to be secured in this way. —**moorage** ('mʊərɪdʒ) *n.*

Moor (mʊə, mɔː) *n.* a member of a Muslim people of North Africa, of mixed Arab and Berber descent. —'**Moorish** *adj.*

moorhen ('mʊə‚hɛn, 'mɔː-) *n.* **1.** a bird of the rail family, inhabiting ponds, lakes, etc., having a black plumage, red bill, and a red shield above the bill. **2.** the female of the red grouse.

mooring ('mʊərɪŋ, 'mɔː-) *n.* **1.** a place for anchoring a vessel. **2.** a permanent anchor with a floating buoy, to which vessels can moor.

moorings ('mʊərɪŋz, 'mɔː-) *pl. n.* **1.** *Naut.* the ropes, anchors, etc., used in mooring a vessel. **2.** (*sometimes sing.*) something that provides security or stability.

moorland ('mʊələnd) *n. Brit.* an area of moor.

moose (muːs) *n., pl.* **moose.** a large North American deer having large flattened palmate antlers: also occurs in Europe and Asia where it is called an elk.

moot (muːt) *adj.* **1.** subject or open to debate: *a moot point.* ~*vb.* (*tr.*) **2.** to suggest or bring up for debate. **3.** to plead or argue hypothetical cases, as an academic exercise or as training for law students. ~*n.* **4.** a discussion or debate of a hypothetical case or point, held as an academic activity. **5.** (in Anglo-Saxon England) an assembly dealing with local legal and administrative affairs.

mop (mɒp) *n.* **1.** an implement with a wooden handle and a head made of twists of cotton or a piece of synthetic sponge, used for polishing or washing floors, or washing dishes. **2.** something resembling this, such as a tangle of hair. ~*vb.* **mopping, mopped.** (*tr.*) **3.** (often foll. by *up*) to clean or soak up as with a mop.

mope (məʊp) *vb.* (*intr.*) **1.** to be gloomy or apathetic. **2.** to move or act in an aimless way. ~*n.* **3.** a gloomy person. —'**moper** *n.*

moped ('məʊpɛd) *n. Brit.* a light motorcycle not over 50cc.

mopes (məʊps) *pl. n.* **the.** low spirits.

moppet ('mɒpɪt) *n.* a less common word for **poppet** (sense 1).

mop up *vb.* (*tr., adv.*) **1.** to clean with a mop. **2.** *Inf.* to complete (a task, etc.). **3.** *Mil.* to clear (remaining enemy forces) after a battle, as by killing, taking prisoner, etc.

moquette (mɒˈkɛt) *n.* a thick velvety fabric used for carpets, upholstery, etc.

Mor. *abbrev. for* Morocco.

moraine (mɒˈreɪn) *n.* a mass of debris, carried by glaciers and forming ridges and mounds when deposited. —**moˈrainal** *or* **moˈrainic** *adj.*

moral ('mɒrəl) *adj.* **1.** concerned with or relating to human behaviour, esp. the distinction between good and bad or right and wrong behaviour: *moral sense.* **2.** adhering to conventionally accepted standards of conduct. **3.** based on a sense of right and wrong according to conscience: *moral courage; moral law.* **4.** having psychological rather than tangible effects: *moral support.* **5.** having the effects but not the appearance of (victory or defeat): *a moral victory.* **6.** having a strong probability: *a moral certainty.* ~*n.* **7.** the lesson to be obtained from a fable or event. **8.** a concise truth; maxim. **9.** (*pl.*) principles of behaviour in accordance with standards of right and wrong. **10.** *Austral. sl.* a certainty: *a moral to win.* —'**morally** *adv.*

morale (mɒˈrɑːl) *n.* the degree of mental or moral confidence of a person or group.

moralist ('mɒrəlɪst) *n.* **1.** a person who seeks to regulate the morals of others. **2.** a person who lives in accordance with moral principles. —‚**moral'istic** *adj.* —‚**moral'istically** *adv.*

morality (məˈrælɪtɪ) *n., pl.* **-ties. 1.** the quality of being moral. **2.** conformity to conventional standards of moral conduct. **3.** a system of moral principles. **4.** an instruction or lesson in morals. **5.** short for **morality play.**

morality play *n.* a type of drama between the 14th and 16th centuries concerned with the conflict between personified virtues and vices.

moralize *or* **-ise** ('mɒrə‚laɪz) *vb.* **1.** (*intr.*) to make moral pronouncements. **2.** (*tr.*) to interpret or explain in a moral sense. **3.** (*tr.*) to improve the morals of.

THESAURUS

vourable, inclined, interested, in the (right) frame of mind, keen, minded, willing

moody 1. angry, broody, cantankerous, crabbed, crabby, crestfallen, cross, crotchety (*Inf.*), crusty, curt, dismal, doleful, dour, downcast, down in the dumps (*Inf.*), down in the mouth (*Inf.*), frowning, gloomy, glum, huffish, huffy, ill-humoured, ill-tempered, in a huff, in the doldrums, introspective, irascible, irritable, lugubrious, melancholy, miserable, mopish, mopy, morose, offended, out of sorts (*Inf.*), pensive, petulant, piqued, sad, saturnine, short-tempered, splenetic, sulky, sullen, temperamental, testy, touchy, waspish, wounded **2.** capricious, changeable, erratic, faddish, fickle, fitful, flighty, impulsive, inconstant, mercurial, temperamental, unpredictable, unstable, unsteady, volatile

moon *n.* **1.** satellite **2. once in a blue moon**

almost never, hardly ever, rarely, very seldom ~*v.* **3.** daydream, idle, languish, mooch (*Sl.*), mope, waste time

moor[1] fell (*Brit.*), heath, moorland, muir (*Scot.*)

moor[2] anchor, berth, dock, fasten, fix, lash, make fast, secure, tie up

moot 1. *adj.* arguable, at issue, contestable, controversial, debatable, disputable, doubtful, open, open to debate, undecided, unresolved, unsettled **2.** *v.* bring up, broach, introduce, propose, put forward, suggest, ventilate

mop *n.* **1.** sponge, squeegee, swab **2.** mane, shock, tangle, thatch ~*v.* **3.** clean, soak up, sponge, swab, wash, wipe

mop up 1. clean up, mop, soak up, sponge, swab, wash, wipe **2.** *Military* account for, clean out, clear, eliminate, finish off, neutral-

ize, pacify, round up, secure

moral *adj.* **1.** ethical **2.** blameless, chaste, decent, ethical, good, high-minded, honest, honourable, incorruptible, innocent, just, meritorious, noble, principled, proper, pure, right, righteous, upright, upstanding, virtuous ~*n.* **3.** lesson, meaning, message, point, significance **4.** adage, aphorism, apophthegm, epigram, gnome, maxim, motto, proverb, saw, saying

morale confidence, esprit de corps, heart, mettle, self-esteem, spirit, temper

morality 1. chastity, decency, ethicality, ethicalness, goodness, honesty, integrity, justice, principle, rectitude, righteousness, rightness, uprightness, virtue **2.** conduct, ethics, habits, ideals, manners, moral code, morals, mores, philosophy, principles, standards

—ˌmoraliˈzation *or* -iˈsation *n.* —ˈmoralˌizer *or* -ˌiser *n.*

moral philosophy *n.* the branch of philosophy dealing with ethics.

morass (məˈræs) *n.* **1.** a tract of swampy low-lying land. **2.** a disordered or muddled situation or circumstance, esp. one that impedes progress.

moratorium (ˌmɒrəˈtɔːrɪəm) *n., pl.* **-ria** (-rɪə) *or* **-riums. 1.** a legally authorized postponement of the fulfilment of an obligation. **2.** an agreed suspension of activity.

Moravian (məˈreɪvɪən, mɒ-) *adj.* **1.** of or relating to Moravia, its people, or their dialect of Czech. **2.** of or relating to the Moravian Church. **~n. 3.** the Moravian dialect. **4.** a native or inhabitant of Moravia. **5.** a member of the Moravian Church. **—Moˈravianism** *n.*

moray (mɒˈreɪ) *n., pl.* **-rays.** a voracious marine coastal eel marked with brilliant colours.

morbid (ˈmɔːbɪd) *adj.* **1.** having an unusual interest in death or unpleasant events. **2.** gruesome. **3.** relating to or characterized by disease. **—morˈbidity** *n.* **—ˈmorbidly** *adv.* **—ˈmorbidness** *n.*

mordant (ˈmɔːdənt) *adj.* **1.** sarcastic or caustic. **2.** having the properties of a mordant. **3.** pungent. **~n. 4.** a substance used before the application of a dye, possessing the ability to fix colours. **5.** an acid or other corrosive fluid used to etch lines on a printing plate. **—ˈmordancy** *n.* **—ˈmordantly** *adv.*

more (mɔː) *determiner.* **1. a.** the comparative of **much** *or* **many:** *more joy than you know; more sausages.* **b.** *(as pronoun; functioning as sing. or pl.): he has more than she does; even more are dying.* **2. a.** additional; further: *no more bananas.* **b.** *(as pronoun; functioning as sing. or pl.): I can't take any more; more than expected.* **3. more of.** to a greater extent or degree: *we see more of Sue; more of a nuisance.* **~adv. 4.** used to form the comparative of some adjectives and adverbs: *a more believable story; more quickly.* **5.** the comparative of **much:** *people listen to the radio more now.* **6. more or less. a.** as an estimate; approximately. **b.** to an unspecified extent or degree: *the party was ruined, more or less.*

▷ **Usage.** See at **most.**

moreish *or* **morish** (ˈmɔːrɪʃ) *adj. Inf.* (of food) causing a desire for more.

morel (mɒˈrɛl) *n.* an edible fungus in which the mushroom has a pitted cap.

morello (məˈrɛləʊ) *n., pl.* **-los.** a variety of small very dark sour cherry.

moreover (mɔːˈrəʊvə) *sentence connector.* in addition to what has already been said.

mores (ˈmɔːreɪz) *pl. n.* the customs and conventions embodying the fundamental values of a group or society.

morganatic (ˌmɔːɡəˈnætɪk) *adj.* of or designating a marriage between a person of high rank and a person of low rank, by which the latter is not elevated to the higher rank and any issue have no rights to the succession of the higher party's titles, property, etc. **—ˌmorgaˈnatically** *adv.*

morgen (ˈmɔːɡən) *n.* **1.** a South African unit of area, equal to about two acres or 0.8 hectare. **2.** a unit of area, formerly used in Prussia and Scandinavia, equal to about two thirds of an acre.

morgue (mɔːɡ) *n.* **1.** another word for **mortuary. 2.** *Inf.* a room or file containing clippings, etc., used for reference in a newspaper.

moribund (ˈmɒrɪˌbʌnd) *adj.* **1.** near death. **2.** without force or vitality. **—ˌmoriˈbundity** *n.* **—ˈmoriˌbundly** *adv.*

Morisco (məˈrɪskəʊ) *or* **Moresco** (məˈrɛskəʊ) *n., pl.* **-cos** *or* **-coes. 1.** a Spanish Moor. **2.** a morris dance. **~adj. 3.** another word for **Moorish;** see **Moor.**

morish (ˈmɔːrɪʃ) *adj.* a variant spelling of **moreish.**

Mormon (ˈmɔːmən) *n.* **1.** a member of the Church of Jesus Christ of Latter-day Saints, founded in 1830 in New York by Joseph Smith. **2.** a prophet whose supposed revelations were recorded by Joseph Smith in the Book of Mormon. **~adj. 3.** of or relating to the Mormons, their Church, or their beliefs. **—ˈMormonism** *n.*

morn (mɔːn) *n.* a poetic word for **morning.**

mornay (ˈmɔːneɪ) *adj. (often immediately postpositive)* denoting a cheese sauce: *eggs mornay.*

morning (ˈmɔːnɪŋ) *n.* **1.** the first part of the day, ending at noon. **2.** sunrise; daybreak; dawn. **3.** the beginning or early period. **4. the morning after.** *Inf.* the after-effects of excess, esp. a hangover. **5.** *(modifier)* of, used, or occurring in the morning: *morning coffee.*

morning dress *n.* formal day dress for men, comprising a cutaway frock coat (**morning coat**), usually with grey trousers and top hat.

morning-glory *n., pl.* **-ries.** any of various mainly tropical plants of the convolvulus family, with trumpet-shaped blue, pink, or white flowers, which close in late afternoon.

mornings (ˈmɔːnɪŋz) *adv. Inf.* in the morning, esp. regularly, or during every morning.

morning sickness *n. Inf.* nausea occurring shortly after rising: a symptom of pregnancy.

morning star *n.* a planet, usually Venus, seen just before sunrise. Also called: **daystar.**

Moroccan (məˈrɒkən) *adj.* **1.** of or denoting Morocco, a kingdom in NW Africa, or its inhabitants, their customs, etc. **~n. 2.** a native or inhabitant of Morocco.

morocco (məˈrɒkəʊ) *n.* a fine soft leather made from goatskins, used for bookbinding, shoes, etc.

moron (ˈmɔːrɒn) *n.* **1.** a foolish or stupid person. **2.** a person having an intelligence quotient of between 50 and 70. **—moronic** (mɒˈrɒnɪk) *adj.* **—moˈronically** *adv.* **—ˈmoronism** *or* **moˈronity** *n.*

morose (məˈrəʊs) *adj.* ill-tempered or gloomy. **—moˈrosely** *adv.* **—moˈroseness** *n.*

-morph *n. combining form.* indicating shape, form, or structure of a specified kind: *ectomorph.* **—ˈmorphic** *or* **-morphous** *adj. combining form.* **—ˈmorphy** *n. combining form.*

morpheme (ˈmɔːfiːm) *n. Linguistics.* a speech element having a meaning or grammatical function that cannot be subdivided into further such elements. **—morˈphemic** *adj.* **—morˈphemically** *adv.*

morphine (ˈmɔːfiːn) *or* **morphia** (ˈmɔːfɪə) *n.* an alkaloid extracted from opium: used in medicine as an anaesthetic and sedative.

morphology (mɔːˈfɒlədʒɪ) *n.* **1.** the branch of biology concerned with the form and structure of organisms. **2.** the form and structure of words in a language. **3.** the study of linguistic forms and structures. **4.** the form and structure of anything. **—morphologic** (ˌmɔːfəˈlɒdʒɪk) *or* **ˌmorphoˈlogical** *adj.* **—ˌmorphoˈlogically** *adv.* **—morˈphologist** *n.*

morris dance (ˈmɒrɪs) *n.* any of various old English folk dances usually performed by men (**morris men**) adorned with bells and often representing characters from folk tales. Often shortened to **morris. —morris dancing** *n.*

morrow (ˈmɒrəʊ) *n. (usually preceded by the)* *Arch.* or *poetic.* **1.** the next day. **2.** the period following a speci-

---

THESAURUS

morals behaviour, conduct, ethics, habits, integrity, manners, morality, mores, principles, scruples, standards

moratorium freeze, halt, postponement, respite, standstill, stay, suspension

morbid 1. brooding, ghoulish, gloomy, grim, melancholy, pessimistic, sick, sombre, unhealthy, unwholesome 2. dreadful, ghastly, grisly, gruesome, hideous, horrid, macabre 3. ailing, deadly, diseased, infected, malignant, pathological, sick, sickly, unhealthy, unsound

more 1. *adj.* added, additional, extra, fresh, further, new, other, spare, supplementary 2. *adv.* better, further, longer, to a greater extent

moreover additionally, also, as well, besides, further, furthermore, in addition, into the bargain, likewise, to boot, too, what is more, withal (*Literary*)

morgue mortuary

moribund 1. at death's door, breathing one's last, doomed, dying, fading fast, failing, (having) one foot in the grave, *in extremis,* near death, near the end, on one's deathbed, on one's last legs 2. at a standstill, declining, forceless, obsolescent, on its last legs, on the way out, stagnant, stagnating, standing still, waning, weak

morning a.m., break of day, dawn, day-

break, forenoon, morn (*Poetic*), morrow (*Archaic*), sunrise

moron ass, blockhead, bonehead (*Sl.*), cretin, dimwit (*Inf.*), dolt, dope (*Sl.*), dummy (*Sl.*), dunce, dunderhead, fool, halfwit, idiot, imbecile, mental defective, muttonhead (*Sl.*), numskull, simpleton, thickhead

morose blue, churlish, crabbed, crabby, cross, crusty, depressed, dour, down, down in the dumps (*Inf.*), gloomy, glum, grouchy (*Inf.*), gruff, ill-humoured, ill-natured, ill-tempered, in a bad mood, low, melancholy, moody, mournful, perverse, pessimistic, saturnine, sour, sulky, sullen, surly, taciturn

fied event. **3.** the morning.

Morse code (mɔːs) *n.* a telegraph code used internationally for transmitting messages. Letters, numbers, etc., are represented by groups of shorter dots and longer dashes, or by groups of the corresponding sounds.

morsel ('mɔːsəl) *n.* **1.** a small slice or mouthful of food. **2.** a small piece; bit.

mortal ('mɔːt'l) *adj.* **1.** (of living beings, esp. human beings) subject to death. **2.** of or involving life or the world. **3.** ending in or causing death; fatal: *a mortal blow.* **4.** deadly or unrelenting: *a mortal enemy.* **5.** of or like the fear of death: *mortal terror.* **6.** great or very intense: *mortal pain.* **7.** conceivable or possible: *there was no mortal reason to go.* **8.** *Sl.* long and tedious: *for three mortal hours.* ~*n.* **9.** a mortal being. **10.** *Inf.* a person: *a mean mortal.* —'**mortally** *adv.*

mortality (mɔː'tælɪtɪ) *n., pl.* **-ties. 1.** the condition of being mortal. **2.** great loss of life, as in war or disaster. **3.** the number of deaths in a given period. **4.** mankind; humanity.

mortal sin *n. Theol.* a sin regarded as involving total loss of grace.

mortar ('mɔːtə) *n.* **1.** a mixture of cement or lime or both with sand and water, used as a bond between bricks or stones or as a covering on a wall. **2.** a cannon having a short barrel and relatively wide bore that fires low-velocity shells in high trajectories. **3.** a vessel, usually bowl-shaped, in which substances are pulverized with a pestle. ~*vb.* (*tr.*) **4.** to join (bricks or stones) or cover (a wall) with mortar. **5.** to fire on with mortars.

mortarboard ('mɔːtə,bɔːd) *n.* **1.** a black tasselled academic cap with a flat square top. **2.** a small square board with a handle on the underside for carrying mortar.

mortgage ('mɔːgɪdʒ) *n.* **1.** a conditional conveyance of property, esp. real property, as security for the repayment of a loan. **2.** the deed effecting such a transaction. ~*vb.* (*tr.*) **3.** to convey (property) by mortgage. **4.** *Inf.* to pledge. —'**mortgageable** *adj.* —,**mortga'gee** *n.* —**mortgagor** (,mɔːgɪ'dʒɔː) *or* '**mortgager** *n.*

mortice ('mɔːtɪs) *n.,vb.* a variant spelling of **mortise.**

mortician (mɔː'tɪʃən) *n. U.S.* another word for **undertaker.**

mortify ('mɔːtɪ,faɪ) *vb.* **-fying, -fied. 1.** (*tr.*) to humiliate or cause to feel shame. **2.** (*tr.*) *Christianity.* to subdue and bring under control by disciplinary exercises, etc. **3.** to cause or undergo tissue death or gangrene. —,**mortifi'cation** *n.* —'**morti,fier** *n.*

mortise *or* **mortice** ('mɔːtɪs) *n.* **1.** a slot or recess cut into a piece of wood, stone, etc., to receive a matching projection (tenon) of another piece, or a mortise lock. ~*vb.* (*tr.*) **2.** to cut a slot or recess in (a piece of wood, etc.). **3.** to join (two pieces of wood, etc.) by means of a mortise and tenon.

mortise lock *n.* a lock set into a mortise in a door so that the mechanism of the lock is enclosed by the door.

mortmain ('mɔːt,meɪn) *n. Law.* the state or condition of lands, etc., held inalienably, as by an ecclesiastical or other corporation.

mortuary ('mɔːtʃʊərɪ) *n., pl.* **-aries. 1.** Also called: **morgue.** a building where dead bodies are kept before cremation or burial. ~*adj.* **2.** of or relating to death or burial.

mosaic (mə'zeɪɪk) *n.* **1.** a design or decoration made up of small pieces of coloured glass, stone, etc. **2.** the process of making a mosaic. **3. a.** a mottled yellowing that occurs in the leaves of plants affected with any of various virus diseases. **b.** Also called: **mosaic disease.** any of the diseases, such as **tobacco mosaic,** that produce this discoloration. **4.** a light-sensitive surface on a television camera tube, consisting of a large number of granules of photoemissive material. —**mosaicist** (mə'zeɪɪsɪst) *n.*

Mosaic (məʊ'zeɪɪk) *adj.* of or relating to Moses or the laws and traditions ascribed to him.

moschatel (,mɒskə'tɛl) *n.* a small N temperate plant with greenish-white musk-scented flowers. Also called: **townhall clock, five-faced bishop.**

mosey ('məʊzɪ) *vb.* (*intr.*) *U.S. sl.* (often foll. by *along* or *on*) to amble.

Moslem ('mɒzləm) *n., pl.* **-lems** *or* **-lem,** *adj.* a variant spelling of **Muslim.**

mosque (mɒsk) *n.* a Muslim place of worship.

mosquito (mə'skiːtəʊ) *n., pl.* **-toes** *or* **-tos.** any dipterous insect of the family *Culicidae:* the females have a long proboscis adapted for piercing the skin of man and animals to suck their blood.

mosquito net *or* **netting** *n.* a fine curtain or net to keep mosquitoes out.

moss (mɒs) *n.* **1.** any of a class of plants, typically growing in dense mats on trees, rocks, moist ground, etc. **2.** a clump or growth of any of these plants. **3.** any of various similar but unrelated plants, such as Spanish moss and reindeer moss. **4.** *Chiefly Scot.* a peat bog or swamp. —'**mossiness** *n.* —'**moss,like** *adj.* —'**mossy** *adj.*

moss rose *n.* a variety of rose that has a mossy stem and calyx and fragrant pink flowers.

moss stitch *n.* a knitting stitch made up of alternate plain and purl stitches.

mosstrooper ('mɒs,truːpə) *n.* a raider in the border country of England and Scotland in the mid-17th century.

most (məʊst) *determiner.* **1. a.** a great majority of; nearly all: *most people like eggs.* **b.** (*as pronoun; functioning as sing. or pl.*): *most of them don't know; most of it is finished.* **2. the most. a.** the superlative of **many** and **much:** *you have the most money; the most apples.* **b.** (*as pronoun*): *the most he can afford is two pounds.* **3. at (the) most.** at the maximum: *that girl is four at the most.* **4. make the most of.** to use to the best advantage: *she makes the most of her accent.* ~*adv.* **5. the most.** used to form the superlative of some adjectives and adverbs: *the most beautiful daughter of all.* **6.** the superlative of **much:** *people welcome a drink most after work.* **7.** (intensifier): *a most absurd story.*

▷ **Usage.** The meanings of *most* and *mostly* should not be confused. In *she was most affected by the news, most* is equivalent to *very* and is generally acceptable. In *she was mostly affected by the news,* the implication is that there was something else, in addition to the news, which affected her, although less so. *More* and *most* should also be distinguished when used in comparisons. *More* applies to cases involving two persons, objects, etc., *most* to cases involving three or more: *John is the more intelligent of the two; he is the most intelligent of the students.*

-most *suffix.* (*forming the superlative degree of some adjectives and adverbs*): *hindmost; uppermost.*

mostly ('məʊstlɪ) *adv.* **1.** almost entirely; chiefly. **2.** on many or most occasions; usually.

Most Reverend *n.* a courtesy title applied to Angli-

THESAURUS

morsel bit, bite, crumb, fraction, fragment, grain, mouthful, nibble, part, piece, scrap, segment, slice, snack, soupçon, taste, titbit

mortal *adj.* **1.** corporeal, earthly, ephemeral, human, impermanent, passing, sublunary, temporal, transient, worldly **2.** deadly, death-dealing, destructive, fatal, killing, lethal, murderous, terminal **3.** bitter, deadly, implacable, irreconcilable, out-and-out, remorseless, sworn, to the death, unrelenting **4.** agonizing, awful, dire, enormous, extreme, grave, great, intense, severe, terrible ~*n.* **5.** being, body, earthling, human, human being, individual, man, person, woman

mortality 1. ephemerality, humanity, impermanence, temporality, transience **2.** bloodshed, carnage, death, destruction, fatal-

ity, killing, loss of life

mortification 1. abasement, annoyance, chagrin, discomfiture, dissatisfaction, embarrassment, humiliation, loss of face, shame, vexation **2.** abasement, chastening, control, denial, discipline, subjugation **3.** *Medical* corruption, festering, gangrene, necrosis, putrescence

mortified 1. abashed, affronted, annoyed, ashamed, chagrined, chastened, confounded, crushed, deflated, discomfited, displeased, embarrassed, given a showing up (*Inf.*), humbled, humiliated, made to eat humble pie (*Inf.*), put down, put out (*Inf.*), put to shame, rendered speechless, shamed, vexed **2.** abased, chastened, conquered, controlled, crushed, disciplined, subdued **3.** *Of flesh* decayed, gangrenous, necrotic, rotted

mortify 1. abase, abash, affront, annoy, chagrin, chasten, confound, crush, deflate, disappoint, discomfit, displease, embarrass, humble, humiliate, make (someone) eat humble pie (*Inf.*), put down, put to shame, shame, take (someone) down a peg (*Inf.*), vex **2.** abase, chasten, control, deny, discipline, subdue **3.** *Of flesh* become gangrenous, corrupt, deaden, die, fester, gangrene, necrose, putrefy

mortuary funeral parlour, morgue

mostly above all, almost entirely, as a rule, chiefly, customarily, for the most part, generally, largely, mainly, most often, on the whole, particularly, predominantly, principally, usually

can archbishops and Roman Catholic bishops.

mot (məʊ) n. short for **bon mot.**

M.O.T. (in Britain) abbrev. for: **1.** Ministry of Transport (Industries). **2.** the M.O.T. test or test certificate.

mote (məʊt) n. a tiny speck.

motel (məʊ'tɛl) n. a roadside hotel for motorists.

motet (məʊ'tɛt) n. a polyphonic choral composition used as an anthem in the Roman Catholic service.

moth (mɒθ) n. any of numerous insects that typically have stout bodies with antennae of various shapes (but not clubbed), including large brightly coloured species, such as hawk moths, and small inconspicuous types, such as the clothes moths. Cf. **butterfly** (sense 1). —**'mothy** adj.

mothball ('mɒθ,bɔːl) n. **1.** a small ball of camphor or naphthalene used to repel clothes moths in stored clothing, etc. **2. put in mothballs.** to postpone work on (a project, activity, etc.). ~vb. (tr.) **3.** to prepare (a ship) for a long period of storage by sealing with plastic. **4.** to postpone work on (a project, activity, etc.).

moth-eaten adj. **1.** decayed, decrepit, or outdated. **2.** eaten away by or as if by moths.

mother ('mʌðə) n. **1. a.** a female who has given birth to offspring. **b.** (as modifier): a mother bird. **2.** (often cap., esp. as a term of address) a person's own mother. **3.** a female substituting in the function of a mother. **4.** (often cap.) Chiefly arch. a term of address for an old woman. **5. a.** motherly qualities, such as maternal affection: it appealed to the mother in her. **b.** (as modifier): mother love. **c.** (in combination): mothercraft. **6. a.** a female or thing that creates, nurtures, protects, etc., something. **b.** (as modifier): mother church; mother earth. **7.** a title given to certain members of female religious orders. **8.** (modifier) native or innate: mother wit. ~vb. (tr.) **9.** to give birth to or produce. **10.** to nurture, protect, etc. as a mother. —**'motherless** adj. —**'motherly** adj.

Mother Carey's chicken ('kɛərɪz) n. any of various small petrels typically having dark plumage and paler underparts. Also called: **stormy petrel, storm petrel.**

mother country n. **1.** the original country of colonists or settlers. **2.** a person's native country.

Mother Goose n. the imaginary author of a collection of nursery rhymes.

motherhood ('mʌðə,hʊd) n. **1.** the state of being a mother. **2.** the qualities characteristic of a mother.

Mothering Sunday ('mʌðərɪŋ) n. Brit. the fourth Sunday in Lent, when mothers traditionally receive presents from their children. Also called: **Mother's Day.**

mother-in-law n., pl. **mothers-in-law.** the mother of one's wife or husband.

motherland ('mʌðə,lænd) n. a person's native country.

mother lode n. Mining. the principal lode in a system.

mother-of-pearl n. a hard iridescent substance that forms the inner layer of the shells of certain molluscs, such as the oyster. It is used to make buttons, etc. Also called: **nacre.**

Mother's Day n. **1.** U.S. & Canad. the second Sunday in May, observed as a day in honour of mothers. **2.** See **Mothering Sunday.**

mother superior n., pl. **mother superiors** or **mothers superior.** the head of a community of nuns.

mother tongue n. **1.** the language first learned by a child. **2.** a language from which another has evolved.

mothproof ('mɒθ,pruːf) adj. **1.** (esp. of clothes) chemically treated so as to repel clothes moths. ~vb. **2.** (tr.) to make (clothes, etc.) mothproof.

motif (məʊ'tiːf) n. **1.** a distinctive idea, esp. a theme elaborated on in a piece of music, literature, etc. **2.** Also called: **motive.** a recurring shape in a design.

motion ('məʊʃən) n. **1.** the process of continual change in the physical position of an object; movement. **2.** a movement or action, esp. of part of the human body; a gesture. **3. a.** the capacity for movement. **b.** a manner of movement, esp. walking; gait. **4.** a mental impulse. **5.** a formal proposal to be discussed and voted on in a debate, meeting, etc. **6.** Law. an application made to a judge or court for an order or ruling necessary to the conduct of legal proceedings. **7.** Brit. **a.** the evacuation of the bowels. **b.** excrement. **8. a.** part of a moving mechanism. **b.** the action of such a part. **9. go through the motions. a.** to act or perform the task (of doing something) mechanically or without sincerity. **b.** to mimic the action (of something) by gesture. **10. in motion.** operational or functioning (often in **set in motion, set the wheels in motion**). ~vb. **11.** (when tr., may take a clause as object or an infinitive) to signal or direct (a person) by a movement or gesture. —**'motionless** adj.

motion picture n. a U.S. term for **film.**

motivate ('məʊtɪ,veɪt) vb. (tr.) to give incentive to. —**,moti'vation** n.

motive ('məʊtɪv) n. **1.** the reason for a certain course of action, whether conscious or unconscious. **2.** a variant spelling of **motif.** ~adj. **3.** of or causing motion: a motive force. **4.** of or acting as a motive; motivating. ~vb. (tr.) **5.** to motivate. —**'motiveless** adj.

motive power n. **1.** any source of energy used to produce motion. **2.** the means of supplying power to an engine, vehicle, etc.

mot juste French. (mo 'ʒyst) n., pl. **mots justes** (mo 'ʒyst). the appropriate word or expression.

motley ('mɒtlɪ) adj. **1.** made up of elements of varying type, quality, etc. **2.** multicoloured. ~n. **3.** a motley collection. **4.** the particoloured attire of a jester.

motocross ('məʊtə,krɒs) n. a motorcycle race across rough ground.

motor ('məʊtə) n. **1. a.** the engine, esp. an internal-combustion engine, of a vehicle. **b.** (as modifier): a motor scooter. **2.** Also called: **electric motor.** a machine that converts electrical energy into mechanical energy. **3.** any device that converts another form of energy into mechanical energy to produce motion. **4. a.** Chiefly Brit. a car. **b.** (as modifier): motor spares. ~adj. **5.** producing or causing motion. **6.** Physiol. **a.** of or relating to nerves or neurons that carry impulses that cause muscles to contract. **b.** of or relating to movement or to muscles that induce movement. ~vb. **7.** (intr.) to travel by car. **8.** (tr.) Brit. to transport by car. —**,motori'zation** or **i'sation** n. —**'motor,ize** or **-,ise** vb.

motorbicycle ('məʊtə,baɪsɪkəl) n. **1.** a motorcycle. **2.** a moped.

motorbike ('məʊtə,baɪk) n. a less formal name for **motorcycle.**

motorboat ('məʊtə,bəʊt) n. any boat powered by a motor.

motorcade ('məʊtə,keɪd) n. a parade of cars.

THESAURUS

moth-eaten antiquated, decayed, decrepit, dilapidated, obsolete, outdated, outworn, ragged, seedy, shabby, stale, tattered, threadbare, worn-out

mother n. **1.** dam, ma (Inf.), mater, mom (U.S. inf.), mum (Brit. inf.), mummy (Brit. inf.), old lady (Inf.), old woman (Inf.) ~adj. **2.** connate, inborn, innate, native, natural ~v. **3.** bear, bring forth, give birth to, produce **4.** care for, cherish, nurse, nurture, protect, raise, rear, tend **5.** baby, fuss over, indulge, pamper, spoil

motherly affectionate, caring, comforting, fond, gentle, kind, loving, maternal, protective, sheltering, tender, warm

mother wit brains, common sense, gumption (Brit. inf.), horse sense, judgment, native intelligence, savvy (Sl.)

motion n. **1.** action, change, flow, kinesics,

locomotion, mobility, motility, move, movement, passage, passing, progress, travel **2.** gesticulation, gesture, sign, signal, wave **3.** proposal, proposition, recommendation, submission, suggestion **4. in motion** afoot, functioning, going, in progress, moving, on the go (Inf.), on the move (Inf.), operational, travelling, under way, working ~v. **5.** beckon, direct, gesticulate, gesture, nod, signal, wave

motionless at a standstill, at rest, calm, fixed, frozen, halted, immobile, inanimate, inert, lifeless, paralysed, standing, static, stationary, still, stock-still, transfixed, unmoved, unmoving

motivate actuate, arouse, bring, cause, draw, drive, give incentive to, impel, induce, inspire, inspirit, instigate, lead, move, persuade, prompt, provoke, set on, stimulate, stir, trigger

motivation **1.** ambition, desire, drive, hunger, inspiration, interest, wish **2.** impulse, incentive, incitement, inducement, inspiration, instigation, motive, persuasion, reason, spur, stimulus

motive **1.** n. cause, design, ground(s), incentive, incitement, inducement, influence, inspiration, intention, mainspring, motivation, object, occasion, purpose, rationale, reason, spur, stimulus, thinking **2.** adj. activating, driving, impelling, motivating, moving, operative, prompting

motley **1.** assorted, disparate, dissimilar, diversified, heterogeneous, mingled, miscellaneous, mixed, unlike, varied **2.** chequered, multicoloured, particoloured, polychromatic, polychrome, polychromous, rainbow, variegated

motorcar ('məʊtəˌkɑː) n. 1. a more formal word for **car**. 2. a self-propelled electric railway car.

motorcycle ('məʊtəˌsaɪkˀl) n. 1. Also called: **motorbike**. a two-wheeled vehicle that is driven by a petrol engine. ~vb. (intr.) 2. to ride on a motorcycle. —'motorˌcyclist n.

motorist ('məʊtərɪst) n. a driver of a car.

motorman ('məʊtəmən) n., pl. -men. 1. the driver of an electric train. 2. the operator of a motor.

motor scooter n. a light motorcycle with small wheels and an enclosed engine. Often shortened to **scooter**.

motor vehicle n. a road vehicle driven esp. by an internal-combustion engine.

motorway ('məʊtəˌweɪ) n. Brit. a main road for fast-moving traffic, having separate carriageways for vehicles travelling in opposite directions.

Motown ('məʊˌtaʊn) n. music combining rhythm and blues and pop, or gospel rhythms and modern ballad harmony.

M.O.T. test n. (in Britain) a compulsory annual test of the roadworthiness of motor vehicles over a certain age.

mottle ('mɒtˀl) vb. 1. (tr.) to colour with streaks or blotches of different shades. ~n. 2. a mottled appearance, as of the surface of marble.

motto ('mɒtəʊ) n., pl. -toes or -tos. 1. a short saying expressing the guiding maxim or ideal of a family, organization, etc., esp. when part of a coat of arms. 2. a verse or maxim contained in a paper cracker. 3. a quotation prefacing a book or chapter of a book.

moue French. (mu) n. a pouting look.

mould¹ or U.S. **mold** (məʊld) n. 1. a shaped cavity used to give a definite form to fluid or plastic material. 2. a frame on which something may be constructed. 3. something shaped in or made on a mould. 4. shape, form, design, or pattern. 5. specific nature, character, or type. ~vb. (tr.) 6. to make in a mould. 7. to shape or form, as by using a mould. 8. to influence or direct: to mould opinion. 9. to cling to: the skirt moulds her figure. 10. Metallurgy. to make (a material) into a mould used in casting. —'mouldable or U.S. 'moldable adj. —'moulder or U.S. 'molder n.

mould² or U.S. **mold** (məʊld) n. 1. a coating or discoloration caused by various fungi that develop in a damp atmosphere on the surface of food, fabrics, etc. 2. any of the fungi that cause this growth. ~vb. 3. to become or cause to become covered with this growth. ~Also called: **mildew**.

mould³ or U.S. **mold** (məʊld) n. loose soil, esp. when rich in organic matter.

mouldboard or U.S. **moldboard** ('məʊldˌbɔːd) n. the curved blade of a plough, which turns over the furrow.

moulder or U.S. **molder** ('məʊldə) vb. (often foll. by away) to crumble or cause to crumble, as through decay.

moulding or U.S. **molding** ('məʊldɪŋ) n. 1. Archit. a. a shaped outline, esp. one used on cornices, etc. b. a shaped strip made of wood, stone, etc. 2. something moulded.

mouldy or U.S. **moldy** ('məʊldɪ) adj. -dier, -diest. 1. covered with mould. 2. stale or musty, esp. from age or lack of use. 3. Sl. boring; dull. —'mouldiness or U.S. 'moldiness n.

moult or U.S. **molt** (məʊlt) vb. 1. (of birds, mammals, arthropods, etc.) to shed (feathers, hair, or cuticle). ~n. 2. the periodic process of moulting. —'moulter or U.S. 'molter n.

mound (maʊnd) n. 1. a raised mass of earth, debris, etc. 2. any heap or pile. 3. a small natural hill. 4. an artificial ridge of earth, stone, etc., as used for defence. ~vb. 5. (often foll. by up) to gather into a mound; heap. 6. (tr.) to cover or surround with a mound: to mound a grave.

mount¹ (maʊnt) vb. 1. to go up (a hill, stairs, etc.); climb. 2. to get up on (a horse, a platform, etc.). 3. (intr.; often foll. by up) to increase; accumulate: excitement mounted. 4. (tr.) to fix onto a backing, setting, or support: to mount a photograph; to mount a slide. 5. (tr.) to provide with a horse for riding, or to place on a horse. 6. (of male animals) to climb onto (a female animal) for copulation. 7. (tr.) to prepare (a play, etc.) for production. 8. (tr.) to plan and organise (a campaign, etc.). 9. (tr.) to prepare (a skeleton, etc.) for exhibition as a specimen. 10. (tr.) to place or carry (weapons) in such a position that they can be fired. 11. **mount guard**. See **guard**. ~n. 12. a backing, setting, or support onto which something is fixed. 13. the act or manner of mounting. 14. a horse for riding. 15. a slide used in microscopy. —'mountable adj. —'mounter n.

mount² (maʊnt) n. a mountain or hill: used in literature and (when cap.) in proper names: Mount Everest.

mountain ('maʊntɪn) n. 1. a. a natural upward projection of the earth's surface, higher and steeper than a hill. b. (as modifier): mountain scenery. c. (in combination): a mountaintop. 2. a huge heap or mass: a mountain of papers. 3. anything of great quantity or size. 4. a surplus of a commodity, esp. in the European Economic Community: a butter mountain.

mountain ash n. 1. any of various trees, such as the European mountain ash or rowan, having clusters of small white flowers and bright red berries. 2. any of several Australian eucalyptus trees, such as Eucalyptus regnans.

mountain cat n. any of various wild feline mammals, such as the bobcat, lynx, or puma.

mountaineer (ˌmaʊntɪ'nɪə) n. 1. a person who climbs mountains. 2. a person living in a mountainous area. ~vb. (intr.) to climb mountains. —ˌmountain'eering n.

mountain goat n. any wild goat inhabiting mountainous regions.

mountain lion n. another name for **puma**.

mountainous ('maʊntɪnəs) adj. 1. of or relating to mountains: a mountainous region. 2. like a mountain, esp. in size or impressiveness.

mountain sickness n. nausea and shortness of breath caused by climbing to high altitudes.

mountebank ('maʊntɪˌbæŋk) n. 1. (formerly) a person who sold quack medicines in public places. 2. a charlatan; fake. ~vb. 3. (intr.) to play the mountebank. —ˌmounte'bankery n.

mounted ('maʊntɪd) adj. 1. riding horses: mounted police. 2. provided with a support, backing, etc.

Mountie or **Mounty** ('maʊntɪ) n., pl. **Mounties**. Inf. a member of the Royal Canadian Mounted Police.

mounting ('maʊntɪŋ) n. another word for **mount¹** (sense 12).

mounting-block n. a block of stone formerly used to aid a person when mounting a horse.

mourn (mɔːn) vb. 1. to feel or express sadness for the death or loss of (someone or something). 2. (intr.) to observe the customs of mourning, as by wearing black. —'mourner n.

THESAURUS

mottled blotchy, brindled, chequered, dappled, flecked, freckled, marbled, piebald, pied, speckled, spotted, stippled, streaked, tabby, variegated

motto adage, byword, cry, formula, gnome, maxim, precept, proverb, rule, saw, saying, slogan, watchword

mould¹ n. 1. cast, die, form, matrix, pattern, shape 2. brand, build, configuration, construction, cut, design, fashion, form, format, frame, kind, line, make, pattern, shape, structure, style 3. calibre, character, ilk, kidney, kind, nature, quality, sort, stamp, type ~v. 4. carve, cast, construct, create, fashion, forge, form, make, model, sculpt, shape, stamp, work 5. affect, control, direct, form,

influence, make, shape

mould² blight, fungus, mildew, mouldiness, mustiness

mouldy bad, blighted, decaying, fusty, mildewed, musty, rotten, rotting, spoiled, stale

mound 1. bing (Scot.), drift, heap, pile, stack 2. bank, dune, embankment, hill, hillock, knoll, rise 3. Archaeology barrow, tumulus 4. bulwark, earthwork, motte (History), rampart

mount v. 1. ascend, clamber up, climb, escalade, go up, make one's way up, scale 2. bestride, climb onto, climb up on, get astride, get (up) on, jump on 3. arise, ascend, rise, soar, tower 4. accumulate, build, escalate,

grow, increase, intensify, multiply, pile up, swell 5. display, frame, set, set off 6. exhibit, get up (Inf.), prepare, produce, put on, stage 7. Military deliver, launch, prepare, ready, set in motion, stage 8. emplace, fit, install, place, position, put in place, set up ~n. 9. backing, base, fixture, foil, frame, mounting, setting, stand, support 10. horse, steed (Literary)

mountain 1. alp, ben (Scot.), elevation, eminence, fell (Brit.), height, mount, peak 2. abundance, heap, mass, mound, pile, stack, ton

mountainous 1. alpine, high, highland, rocky, soaring, steep, towering, upland 2. daunting, enormous, gigantic, great, huge,

mournful ('mɔːnful) *adj.* **1.** evoking grief; sorrowful. **2.** gloomy; sad. —'**mournfully** *adv.* —'**mournfulness** *n.*

mourning ('mɔːnɪŋ) *n.* **1.** the act or feelings of one who mourns; grief. **2.** the conventional symbols of grief, such as the wearing of black. **3.** the period of time during which a death is officially mourned. ~*adj.* **4.** of or relating to mourning. —'**mourningly** *adv.*

mourning band *n.* a piece of black material, esp. an armband, worn to indicate mourning.

mouse *n.* (maʊs), *pl.* **mice** (maɪs). **1.** any of numerous small long-tailed rodents that are similar to but smaller than rats. See also **harvest mouse, dormouse.** **2.** any of various related rodents, such as the jumping mouse. **3.** a quiet, timid, or cowardly person. **4.** *Sl.* a black eye. ~*vb.* (maʊz). **5.** to stalk and catch (mice, etc.). **6.** (*intr.*) to go about stealthily. —'**mouse,like** *adj.*

mouser ('maʊzə, 'maʊsə) *n.* a cat or other animal that is used to catch mice.

mousetrap ('maʊs,træp) *n.* **1.** any trap for catching mice, esp. one with a spring-loaded metal bar that is released by the taking of the bait. **2.** *Brit. inf.* cheese of indifferent quality.

moussaka or **mousaka** (muˈsɑːkə) *n.* a dish originating in the Balkan States, consisting of meat, aubergines, and tomatoes, topped with cheese sauce.

mousse (muːs) *n.* **1.** a light creamy dessert made with eggs, cream, fruit, etc., set with gelatine. **2.** a similar dish made from fish or meat.

mousseline (*French* musˈlin) *n.* **1.** a fine fabric made of rayon or silk. **2.** a type of fine glass.

moustache or *U.S.* **mustache** (məˈstɑːʃ) *n.* **1.** the unshaved growth of hair on the upper lip. **2.** a similar growth of hair or bristles (in animals). **3.** a mark like a moustache. —**mous'tached** or *U.S.* **mus'tached** *adj.*

mousy or **mousey** ('maʊsɪ) *adj.* **mousier, mousiest. 1.** resembling a mouse, esp. in colour. **2.** shy or ineffectual. **3.** infested with mice. —'**mousily** *adv.* —'**mousiness** *n.*

mouth *n.* (maʊθ), *pl.* **mouths** (maʊðz). **1.** the opening through which many animals take in food and issue vocal sounds. **2.** the system of organs surrounding this opening, including the lips, tongue, teeth, etc. **3.** the visible part of the lips on the face. **4.** a person regarded as a consumer of food: *four mouths to feed.* **5.** a particular manner of speaking: *a foul mouth.* **6.** *Inf.* boastful, rude, or excessive talk: *he is all mouth.* **7.** the point where a river issues into a sea or lake. **8.** the opening of a container, such as a jar. **9.** the opening of a cave, tunnel, volcano, etc. **10.** that part of the inner lip of a horse on which the bit acts. **11.** a pout; grimace. **12. by word of mouth.** orally rather than by written means. **13. down in** or **at the mouth.** in low spirits. ~*vb.* (maʊð). **14.** to speak or say (something) insincerely, esp. in public. **15.** (*tr.*) to form (words) with movements of the lips but without speaking. **16.** (*tr.*) to take (something) into the mouth or to move (something) around inside the mouth. **17.** (*intr.*; usually foll. by *at*) to make a grimace. —**mouther** ('maʊðə) *n.*

mouthful ('maʊθ,ful) *n., pl.* -**fuls. 1.** as much as is held in the mouth at one time. **2.** a small quantity, as of food.

3. a long word or phrase that is difficult to say.

mouth organ *n.* another name for **harmonica.**

mouthpiece ('maʊθ,piːs) *n.* **1.** the part of a wind instrument into which the player blows. **2.** the part of a telephone receiver into which a person speaks. **3.** the part of a container forming its mouth. **4.** a person who acts as a spokesman, as for an organization. **5.** a publication expressing the official views of an organization.

mouthwash ('maʊθ,wɒʃ) *n.* a medicated solution for gargling and cleansing the mouth.

movable or **moveable** ('muːvəbəl) *adj.* **1.** able to be moved; not fixed. **2.** (esp. of Easter) varying in date from year to year. **3.** (usually spelt **moveable**) *Law.* denoting or relating to personal property as opposed to realty. ~*n.* **4.** (*often pl.*) a movable article, esp. a piece of furniture. —,**mova'bility,** ,**movea'bility** or '**movableness,** '**moveableness** *n.* —'**movably** or '**moveably** *adv.*

move (muːv) *vb.* **1.** to go or take from one place to another; change in position. **2.** (*usually intr.*) to change (one's dwelling, place of business, etc.). **3.** to be or cause to be in motion; stir. **4.** (*intr.*) (of machines, etc.) to work or operate. **5.** (*tr.*) to cause (to do something); prompt. **6.** (*intr.*) to begin to act: *move soon or we'll lose the order.* **7.** (*intr.*) to associate oneself with a specified social circle: *to move in exalted spheres.* **8.** (*intr.*) to make progress. **9.** (*tr.*) to arouse affection, pity, or compassion in; touch. **10.** (in board games) to change the position of (a piece) or (of a piece) to change position. **11.** (of merchandise) to be disposed of by being bought. **12.** (when *tr., often takes a clause as object*; when *intr.,* often foll. by *for*) to suggest (a proposal) formally, as in debating or parliamentary procedure. **13.** (*intr.*; usually foll. by *on* or *along*) to go away or to another place; leave. **14.** to cause (the bowels) to evacuate or (of the bowels) to be evacuated. ~*n.* **15.** the act of moving; movement. **16.** one of a sequence of actions, usually part of a plan; manoeuvre. **17.** the act of moving one's residence, place of business, etc. **18.** (in board games) **a.** a player's turn to move his piece. **b.** a manoeuvre of a piece. **19. get a move on.** *Inf.* **a.** to get started. **b.** to hurry up. **20. on the move.** *Inf.* **a.** travelling from place to place. **b.** advancing; succeeding. **c.** very active; busy.

move in *vb.* (*mainly adv.*) **1.** (*also prep.*) Also (when *prep.*): **move into.** to occupy or take possession of (a new residence, place of business, etc.). **2.** (*intr.*; often foll. by *on*) *Inf.* to creep close (to), as in preparing to capture. **3.** (*intr.*; often foll. by *on*) *Inf.* to try to gain power or influence (over).

movement ('muːvmənt) *n.* **1. a.** the act, process, or result of moving. **2.** the manner of moving. **3. a.** a group of people with a common ideology. **b.** the organized action of such a group. **4.** a trend or tendency. **5.** the driving and regulating mechanism of a watch or clock. **6.** (*often pl.*) a person's location and activities during a specific time. **7. a.** the evacuation of the bowels. **b.** the matter evacuated. **8.** *Music.* a principal self-contained section of a symphony, sonata, etc. **9.** tempo or pace, as in music or literature. **10.** *Fine arts.* the appearance of motion in painting, sculpture, etc. **11.** *Prosody.* the rhythmical structure of verse. **12.** a posi-

hulking, immense, mammoth, mighty, monumental, ponderous, prodigious

mourn bemoan, bewail, deplore, grieve, keen, lament, miss, rue, sorrow, wail, wear black, weep

mournful 1. afflicting, calamitous, deplorable, distressing, grievous, lamentable, melancholy, painful, piteous, plaintive, sad, sorrowful, tragic, unhappy, woeful **2.** brokenhearted, cheerless, desolate, disconsolate, downcast, funereal, gloomy, grief-stricken, grieving, heartbroken, heavy, heavy-hearted, joyless, lugubrious, melancholy, rueful, sad, sombre, unhappy, woeful

mourning 1. bereavement, grief, grieving, keening, lamentation, weeping, woe **2.** black, sackcloth and ashes, weeds, widow's weeds

mouth *n.* **1.** chops (*Sl.*), gob (*Sl.*), jaws, lips, maw, trap (*Sl.*), yap (*Sl.*) **2.** *Inf.* boasting, braggadocio, bragging, empty talk, gas (*Sl.*), hot air (*Sl.*), idle talk **3.** *Inf.* backchat (*Inf.*), cheek (*Inf.*), impudence, insolence, lip (*Sl.*),

rudeness, sauce (*Inf.*) **4.** aperture, cavity, crevice, door, entrance, gateway, inlet, lips, opening, orifice, rim **5.** face, grimace, *moue,* pout, wry face **6. down in** or **at the mouth** blue, crestfallen, dejected, depressed, disheartened, dispirited, down, downcast, down in the dumps (*Inf.*), in low spirits, melancholy, sad, unhappy

mouthful bit, bite, drop, forkful, little, morsel, sample, sip, spoonful, sup, swallow, taste

mouthpiece 1. agent, delegate, representative, spokesman, spokeswoman **2.** journal, organ, periodical, publication

movable detachable, mobile, not fixed, portable, portative, transferable, transportable

move 1. advance, budge, change position, drift, go, march, proceed, progress, shift, stir, walk **2.** carry, change, shift, switch, transfer, transport, transpose **3.** change residence, flit (*Scot., & northern English dialect*), go away, leave, migrate, move house, quit, relocate,

remove **4.** activate, drive, impel, motivate, operate, propel, push, set going, shift, shove, start, turn **5.** actuate, affect, agitate, cause, excite, give rise to, impel, impress, incite, induce, influence, inspire, instigate, lead, make an impression on, motivate, persuade, prompt, rouse, stimulate, touch, urge **6.** advocate, propose, put forward, recommend, suggest, urge ~*n.* **7.** act, action, deed, manoeuvre, measure, motion, movement, ploy, shift, step, stratagem, stroke, turn **8.** change of address, flit (*Scot., & northern English dialect*), flitting (*Scot., & northern English dialect*), migration, relocation, removal, shift, transfer **9. get a move on** get cracking (*Inf.*), get going (*Inf.*), hurry (up), make haste, speed up, step on it (*Inf.*), stir oneself **10. on the move** *Inf.* **a.** in transit, journeying, moving, on the road (*Inf.*), on the run, on the wing, travelling, under way, voyaging **b.** active, advancing, astir, going forward, moving, progressing, stirring, succeeding

tional change by one or a number of military units. **13.** a change in the market price of a security or commodity.

mover (ˈmuːvə) *n.* **1.** *Inf.* a person, business, idea, etc., that is advancing or progressing. **2.** a person or thing that moves. **3.** a person who moves a proposal, as in a debate. **4.** *U.S.* a removal firm or a person who works for one.

movie (ˈmuːvɪ) *n. U.S.* **a.** an informal word for **film** (sense 1). **b.** (*as modifier*): *movie ticket.*

moving (ˈmuːvɪŋ) *adj.* **1.** arousing or touching the emotions. **2.** changing or capable of changing position. **3.** causing motion. —ˈ**movingly** *adv.*

moving staircase *or* **stairway** *n.* less common terms for **escalator.**

mow (məʊ) *vb.* **mowing, mowed, mowed** *or* **mown. 1.** to cut down (grass, crops, etc.), with a hand implement or machine. **2.** (*tr.*) to cut the growing vegetation of (a field, lawn, etc.). —ˈ**mower** *n.*

mow down *vb.* (*tr., adv.*) to kill in large numbers, esp. by gunfire.

mown (məʊn) *vb.* the past participle of **mow.**

mp *or* **m.p.** *Music. abbrev. for* mezzo piano: moderately soft.

M.P. *abbrev. for:* **1.** (in Britain, Canada, etc.) Member of Parliament. **2.** (in Britain) Metropolitan Police. **3.** Military Police. **4.** Mounted Police.

m.p. *abbrev. for* melting point.

m.p.g. *abbrev. for* miles per gallon.

m.p.h. *abbrev. for* miles per hour.

M.Phil. *or* **M.Ph.** *abbrev. for* Master of Philosophy.

Mr. (ˈmɪstə) *n., pl.* **Messrs.** (ˈmɛsəz). a title used before a man's name or before some office that he holds: *Mr. Jones; Mr. President.*

Mrs. (ˈmɪsɪz) *n., pl.* **Mrs.** *or* **Mesdames.** a title used before the name or names of a married woman.

MS. *or* **ms.** *pl.* **MSS.** *or* **mss.** *abbrev. for* manuscript.

M.S. *abbrev. for:* **1.** Master of Surgery. **2.** (on gravestones, etc.) memoriae sacrum. **3.** multiple sclerosis.

Ms. (mɪz, məs) *n.* a title substituted for **Mrs.** or **Miss** to avoid making a distinction between married and unmarried women.

M.Sc. *abbrev. for* Master of Science.

M.S.C. (in Britain) *abbrev. for* Manpower Services Commission.

MSG *abbrev. for* monosodium glutamate.

Msgr. *abbrev. for* Monsignor.

M.S.T. *abbrev. for* Mountain Standard Time.

Mt. *or* **mt.** *abbrev. for:* **1.** mount: *Mt. Everest.* **2.** Also: **mtn.** mountain.

M.Tech. *abbrev. for* Master of Technology.

mu (mjuː) *n.* the 12th letter in the Greek alphabet (Μ, μ).

much (mʌtʃ) *determiner.* **1. a.** (*usually used with a negative*) a great quantity or degree of: *there isn't much honey left.* **b.** (*as pronoun*): *much has been learned from this.* **2. a bit much.** *Inf.* rather excessive. **3. make much of. a.** (*used with a negative*) to make sense of: *he couldn't make much of her babble.* **b.** to give importance to: *she made much of this fact.* **c.** to pay flattering attention to: *the reporters made much of the film star.* **4. not much of.** not to any appreciable degree or extent: *he's not much of an actor really.* **5. not up to much.** *Inf.* of a low standard: *this beer is not up to much.* ~*adv.* **6.** considerably: *they're much better now.* **7.** practically; nearly (esp. in **much the same**). **8.** (*usually used with a negative*) often; a great deal: *it doesn't happen much in this country.* **9.** (**as**) **much as.** even though; although: *much as I'd like to, I can't come.* ~See also **more, most.**

mucilage (ˈmjuːsɪlɪdʒ) *n.* **1.** a sticky preparation, such as gum or glue, used as an adhesive. **2.** a complex glutinous carbohydrate secreted by certain plants. —**mucilaginous** (ˌmjuːsɪˈlædʒɪnəs) *adj.*

muck (mʌk) *n.* **1.** farmyard dung or decaying vegetable matter. **2.** an organic soil rich in humus and used as a fertilizer. **3.** dirt or filth. **4.** *Sl., chiefly Brit.* trash. **5. make a muck of.** *Sl., chiefly Brit.* to ruin or spoil. ~*vb.* (*tr.*) **6.** to spread manure upon (fields, etc.). **7.** to soil or pollute. **8.** (usually foll. by *up*) *Brit. sl.* to ruin or spoil. **9.** (often foll. by *out*) to clear muck from. —ˈ**mucky** *adj.*

muck about *vb. Brit. sl.* **1.** (*intr.*) to waste time; misbehave. **2.** (when *intr.*, foll. by *with*) to interfere with, annoy, or waste the time of.

muck in *vb.* (*intr., adv.*) *Brit. sl.* to share duties, work, etc. (with other people).

muckrake (ˈmʌkˌreɪk) *vb.* (*intr.*) to seek out and expose scandal, esp. concerning public figures. —ˈ**muckˌraker** *n.* —ˈ**muckˌraking** *n.*

mucksweat (ˈmʌkˌswɛt) *n. Brit. inf.* profuse sweat or a state of profuse sweating.

mucous membrane *n.* a mucus-secreting membrane that lines body cavities or passages that are open to the external environment.

mucus (ˈmjuːkəs) *n.* the slimy protective secretion of the mucous membranes. —**muˈcosity** *n.* —ˈ**mucous** *adj.*

mud (mʌd) *n.* **1.** a fine-grained soft wet deposit that occurs on the ground after rain, at the bottom of ponds, etc. **2.** *Inf.* slander or defamation. **3. clear as mud.** not at all clear. **4. here's mud in your eye.** *Inf.* a humorous drinking toast. **5.** (**someone's**) **name is mud.** *Inf.* (someone) is disgraced. **6. throw** (*or* **sling**) **mud at.** *Inf.* slander; vilify. ~*vb.* **mudding, mudded. 7.** (*tr.*) to soil or cover with mud.

mud bath *n.* **1.** a medicinal bath in heated mud. **2.** a dirty or muddy occasion, state, etc.

muddle (ˈmʌdᵊl) *vb.* (*tr.*) **1.** (often foll. by *up*) to mix up (objects, items, etc.). **2.** to confuse. **3.** *U.S.* to mix or stir (alcoholic drinks, etc.). ~*n.* **4.** a state of physical or mental confusion. —**muddler** (ˈmʌdlə) *n.*

muddleheaded (ˌmʌdᵊlˈhɛdɪd) *adj.* mentally confused or vague. —ˌ**muddleˈheadedness** *n.*

muddle through *vb.* (*intr., adv.*) *Chiefly Brit.* to succeed in spite of lack of organization.

muddy (ˈmʌdɪ) *adj.* **-dier, -diest. 1.** covered or filled with mud. **2.** not clear or bright: *muddy colours.* **3.** cloudy: *a muddy liquid.* **4.** (esp. of thoughts) confused or vague. ~*vb.* **-dying, -died. 5.** to become or cause to become muddy. —ˈ**muddily** *adv.* —ˈ**muddiness** *n.*

mud flat *n.* a tract of low muddy land that is covered at high tide and exposed at low tide.

mudguard (ˈmʌdˌgɑːd) *n.* a curved part of a motor-

THESAURUS

movement 1. act, action, activity, advance, agitation, change, development, displacement, exercise, flow, gesture, manoeuvre, motion, move, moving, operation, progress, progression, shift, steps, stir, stirring, transfer 2. campaign, crusade, drive, faction, front, group, grouping, organization, party 3. current, drift, flow, swing, tendency, trend 4. action, innards (*Inf.*), machinery, mechanism, workings, works 5. *Music* division, part, passage, section 6. beat, cadence, measure, metre, pace, rhythm, swing, tempo

moving 1. affecting, arousing, emotional, emotive, exciting, impelling, impressive, inspiring, pathetic, persuasive, poignant, stirring, touching 2. mobile, motile, movable, portable, running, unfixed 3. dynamic, impelling, inspirational, motivating, propelling, stimulating, stimulative

mow crop, cut, scythe, shear, trim

mow down butcher, cut down, cut to pieces, massacre, shoot down, slaughter

much 1. *adj.* abundant, a lot of, ample, considerable, copious, great, plenteous, plenty of, sizeable, substantial 2. *adv.* a great deal, a lot, considerably, decidedly, exceedingly, frequently, greatly, indeed, often, regularly 3. *n.* a good deal, a great deal, a lot, an appreciable amount, heaps (*Inf.*), loads (*Inf.*), lots (*Inf.*), plenty

muck 1. dung, manure, ordure 2. dirt, filth, gunge (*Inf.*), gunk (*Inf.*), mire, mud, ooze, scum, sewage, slime, sludge 3. **make a muck of** *Sl.* botch, bungle, make a mess of, mar, mess up, muff, ruin, screw up (*Inf.*), spoil

muck up botch, bungle, make a mess of, make a muck of (*Sl.*), mar, mess up, muff, ruin, screw up (*Inf.*), spoil

mud clay, dirt, mire, ooze, silt, sludge

muddle *v.* 1. confuse, disarrange, disorder, disorganize, jumble, make a mess of, mess, mix up, scramble, spoil, tangle 2. befuddle, bewilder, confound, confuse, daze, disorient, perplex, stupefy ~*n.* 3. chaos, clutter, confusion, daze, disarray, disorder, disorganization, fankle (*Scot.*), jumble, mess, mix-up, perplexity, plight, predicament, tangle

muddled 1. chaotic, confused, disarrayed, disordered, disorganized, higgledy-piggledy (*Inf.*), jumbled, messy, mixed-up, scrambled, tangled 2. at sea, befuddled, bewildered, confused, dazed, disoriented, perplexed, stupefied, vague 3. confused, incoherent, loose, muddleheaded, unclear, woolly

muddy *adj.* 1. bespattered, boggy, clarty (*Scot., & northern English dialect*), dirty, grimy, marshy, miry, mucky, mud-caked, quaggy, soiled, swampy 2. blurred, dingy, dull, flat, lustreless, smoky, unclear, washed-out 3. cloudy, dirty, foul, impure, opaque, turbid 4. confused, fuzzy, hazy, indistinct, muddled, unclear, vague, woolly ~*v.* 5. begrime, bespatter, cloud, dirty, smear, smirch, soil

cycle, bicycle, etc., attached above the wheels to reduce the amount of water or mud thrown up by them. U.S. name: **fender.**

mudpack ('mʌd,pæk) n. a cosmetic astringent paste containing fuller's earth.

mudslinging ('mʌd,slɪŋɪŋ) n. casting malicious slurs on an opponent, esp. in politics. —'**mud,slinger** n.

muesli ('mju:zlɪ) n. a mixture of rolled oats, nuts, fruit, etc., eaten with milk.

muezzin (mu:'ɛzɪn) n. Islam. the official of a mosque who calls the faithful to prayer from the minaret.

muff[1] (mʌf) n. an open-ended cylinder of fur or cloth into which the hands are placed for warmth.

muff[2] (mʌf) vb. **1.** to perform (an action) awkwardly. **2.** (tr.) to bungle (a shot, catch, etc.). ~n. **3.** any unskilful play, esp. a dropped catch. **4.** any bungled action. **5.** a bungler.

muffin ('mʌfɪn) n. **1.** Brit. a thick round baked yeast roll, usually toasted and served with butter. **2.** U.S. a small cup-shaped sweet bread roll, usually eaten hot with butter.

muffin man n. Brit. (formerly) an itinerant seller of muffins.

muffle ('mʌfəl) vb. (tr.) **1.** (often foll. by up) to wrap up (the head) in a scarf, cloak, etc., esp. for warmth. **2.** to deaden (a sound or noise), esp. by wrapping. **3.** to prevent (the expression of something) by (someone). ~n. **4.** something that muffles. **5.** a kiln with an inner chamber for firing porcelain, enamel, etc.

muffler ('mʌflə) n. **1.** a thick scarf, collar, etc. **2.** the U.S. name for **silencer** (sense 1).

mufti ('mʌftɪ) n., pl. -**tis.** civilian dress, esp. as worn by a person who normally wears a military uniform.

mug[1] (mʌg) n. **1.** a drinking vessel with a handle, usually cylindrical and made of earthenware. **2.** Also called: **mugful.** the quantity held by a mug or its contents.

mug[2] (mʌg) n. **1.** Sl. a person's face or mouth. **2.** Sl. a gullible person; esp. one who is swindled easily. **3.** a **mug's game.** a worthless activity. ~vb. **mugging, mugged. 4.** (tr.) Inf. to attack or rob (someone) violently. —'**mugger** n.

muggins ('mʌgɪnz) n. **1.** Brit. sl. a simpleton. **2.** a card game.

muggy ('mʌgɪ) adj. -**gier, -giest.** (of weather, air, etc.) unpleasantly warm and humid. —'**mugginess** n.

mug up vb. (adv.) Brit. sl. to study (a subject) hard, esp. for an exam.

Muhammadan or **Muhammedan** (mʊ'hæmədən) n., adj. another word (not in Muslim use) for **Muslim.**

mukluk ('mʌklʌk) n. a soft boot, usually of sealskin, worn by Eskimos.

mulatto (mju:'lætəʊ) n., pl. -**tos** or -**toes. 1.** a person having one Negro and one White parent. ~adj. **2.** of a light brown colour; tawny.

mulberry ('mʌlbərɪ, -brɪ) n., pl. -**ries. 1.** a tree having edible blackberry-like fruit, such as the white mulberry, the leaves of which are used to feed silkworms. **2.** the fruit of any of these trees. **3.** any of several similar or related trees. **4.** a dark purple colour.

mulch (mʌltʃ) n. **1.** half-rotten vegetable matter, peat, etc., used to prevent soil erosion or enrich the soil. ~vb. **2.** (tr.) to cover (the surface of land) with mulch.

mulct (mʌlkt) vb. (tr.) **1.** to cheat or defraud. **2.** to fine (a person). ~n. **3.** a fine or penalty.

mule[1] (mju:l) n. **1.** the sterile offspring of a male donkey and a female horse, used as a beast of burden. **2.** any hybrid animal: a mule canary. **3.** Also called: **spinning mule.** a machine that spins cotton into yarn and

winds the yarn on spindles. **4.** Inf. an obstinate or stubborn person.

mule[2] (mju:l) n. a backless shoe or slipper.

muleteer (,mju:lɪ'tɪə) n. a person who drives mules.

mulish ('mju:lɪʃ) adj. stubborn; obstinate. —'**mulishly** adv. —'**mulishness** n.

mull[1] (mʌl) vb. (tr.) (often foll. by over) to study or ponder.

mull[2] (mʌl) vb. (tr.) to heat (wine, ale, etc.) with sugar and spices.

mull[3] (mʌl) n. Scot. a promontory.

mullah, mulla ('mʌlə, 'mʊlə), or **mollah** n. a Muslim scholar, teacher, or religious leader: also used as a title of respect.

mullet ('mʌlɪt) n. any of various teleost food fishes such as the grey mullet or red mullet.

mulligatawny (,mʌlɪgə'tɔ:nɪ) n. a curry-flavoured soup of Anglo-Indian origin, made with meat stock.

mullion ('mʌlɪən) n. **1.** a vertical member between the casements or panes of a window. ~vb. **2.** (tr.) to furnish (a window, etc.) with mullions. —'**mullioned** adj.

multangular (mʌl'tæŋgjʊlə) or **multiangular** adj. having many angles.

multi- combining form. **1.** many or much: multimillion. **2.** more than one: multistorey.

multifarious (,mʌltɪ'fɛərɪəs) adj. having many parts of great variety. —,**multi'fariously** adv. —,**multi'fariousness** n.

multiflora rose (,mʌltɪ'flɔ:rə) n. an Asian climbing shrubby rose having clusters of small fragrant flowers.

multiform ('mʌltɪ,fɔ:m) adj. having many forms. —**multiformity** (,mʌltɪ'fɔ:mɪtɪ) n.

multilateral (,mʌltɪ'lætərəl, -'lætrəl) adj. **1.** of or involving more than two nations or parties: a multilateral pact. **2.** having many sides. —,**multi'laterally** adv.

multilingual (,mʌltɪ'lɪŋgwəl) adj. **1.** able to speak more than two languages. **2.** written or expressed in more than two languages.

multimedia (,mʌltɪ'mi:dɪə) pl. n. the combined use of media such as television, slides, etc.

multimillionaire (,mʌltɪ,mɪljə'nɛə) n. a person with a fortune of several million pounds, dollars, etc.

multinational (,mʌltɪ'næʃənəl) adj. (of a large business company) operating in several countries.

multiparous (mʌl'tɪpərəs) adj. (of certain species of mammal) producing many offspring at one birth.

multiple ('mʌltɪpəl) adj. **1.** having or involving more than one part, individual, etc. **2.** Electronics, U.S. (of a circuit) having a number of conductors in parallel. ~n. **3.** the product of a given number or polynomial and any other one: 6 is a multiple of 2. —'**multiply** adv.

multiple-choice adj. having a number of possible given answers out of which the correct one must be chosen.

multiple personality n. Psychiatry. a mental disorder in which an individual's personality appears to have become separated into two or more distinct personalities. Nontechnical name: **split personality.**

multiple sclerosis n. a chronic progressive disease of the central nervous system, resulting in speech and visual disorders, tremor, muscular incoordination, partial paralysis, etc.

multiplex ('mʌltɪ,plɛks) n. **1.** Telecomm. **a.** the use of a common communications channel for sending two or more messages or signals. **b.** (as modifier): a multiplex transmitter. ~adj. **2.** a less common word for **multiple.**

multiplicand (,mʌltɪplɪ'kænd) n. a number to be multi-

multicellular adj.
multicoloured adj.
multidimensional adj.

multidirectional adj.
multifaceted adj.
multihull n.

multinuclear adj.
multipurpose adj.
multiracial adj.

THESAURUS

muffle 1. cloak, conceal, cover, disguise, envelop, hood, mask, shroud, swaddle, swathe, wrap up **2.** deaden, dull, gag, hush, muzzle, quieten, silence, soften, stifle, suppress

muffled dim, dull, faint, indistinct, muted, stifled, strangled, subdued, suppressed

mug[1] beaker, cup, flagon, jug, pot, tankard, toby jug

mug[2] chump (Inf.) gull (Archaic), easy or

soft touch (Sl.), fool, innocent, mark (Sl.), muggins (Brit. sl.), simpleton, sucker (Sl.)

muggy clammy, close, damp, humid, moist, oppressive, sticky, stuffy, sultry

mug up bone up (Inf. chiefly U.S.), burn the midnight oil (Inf.), cram (Inf.), get up (Inf.), study, swot (Brit. inf.)

mull consider, contemplate, deliberate, examine, meditate, muse on, ponder, reflect on, review, ruminate, study, think about,

think over, turn over in one's mind, weigh

multifarious different, diverse, diversified, legion, manifold, many, miscellaneous, multiform, multiple, multitudinous, numerous, sundry, varied, variegated

multiple collective, manifold, many, multitudinous, numerous, several, sundry, various

plied by another number. the **multiplier.**

multiplication (ˌmʌltɪplɪˈkeɪʃən) n. **1.** a mathematical operation, the inverse of division, in which the product of two or more numbers or quantities is calculated. Usually written $a \times b$, $a.b$, ab. **2.** the act of multiplying or state of being multiplied. **3.** the act or process in animals, plants, or people, of reproducing or breeding.

multiplication sign n. the symbol $\times$, placed between numbers to be multiplied.

multiplication table n. one of a group of tables giving the results of multiplying two numbers together.

multiplicity (ˌmʌltɪˈplɪsɪtɪ) n., pl. **-ties. 1.** a large number or great variety. **2.** the state of being multiple.

multiply (ˈmʌltɪˌplaɪ) vb. **-plying, -plied. 1.** to increase or cause to increase in number, quantity, or degree. **2.** (tr.) to increase (one number) by another number using multiplication. **3.** (intr.) to increase in number by reproduction. —ˈmultiˌpliable or ˈmultiˌplicable adj. —ˈmultiˌplier n.

multistage (ˈmʌltɪˌsteɪdʒ) adj. **1.** (of a rocket or missile) having several stages, each of which can be jettisoned after it has burnt out. **2.** (of a turbine, compressor, or supercharger) having more than one rotor. **3.** (of any process or device) having more than one stage.

multistorey (ˌmʌltɪˈstɔːrɪ) adj. **1.** (of a building) having many storeys. —n. **2.** a multistorey car park.

multitude (ˈmʌltɪˌtjuːd) n. **1.** a large gathering of people. **2. the.** the common people. **3.** a large number. **4.** the state or quality of being numerous. —ˌmultiˈtudinous adj.

mum[1] (mʌm) n. Chiefly Brit. an informal word for **mother.**

mum[2] (mʌm) adj. **1.** keeping information, etc., to oneself; silent. ~n. **2. mum's the word.** (interj.) silence or secrecy is to be observed.

mum[3] (mʌm) vb. **mumming, mummed.** (intr.) to act in a mummer's play.

mumble (ˈmʌmbəl) vb. **1.** to utter indistinctly, as with the mouth partly closed. **2.** Rare. to chew (food) ineffectually. ~n. **3.** an indistinct or low utterance or sound. —ˈmumbler n. —ˈmumblingly adv.

mumbo jumbo (ˈmʌmbəʊ) n., pl. **mumbo jumbos. 1.** foolish religious reverence, ritual, or incantation. **2.** meaningless or unnecessarily complicated language. **3.** an object of superstitious awe or reverence.

mu meson (mjuː) n. a former name for **muon.**

mummer (ˈmʌmə) n. **1.** one of a group of masked performers in a folk play or mime. **2.** Humorous or derog. an actor.

mummery (ˈmʌmərɪ) n., pl. **-meries. 1.** a performance by mummers. **2.** hypocritical or ostentatious ceremony.

mummy[1] (ˈmʌmɪ) n., pl. **-mies. 1.** an embalmed or preserved body, esp. as prepared for burial in ancient Egypt. **2.** a mass of pulp. **3.** a dark brown pigment. —ˌmummifiˈcation n. —ˈmummiˌfy vb.

mummy[2] (ˈmʌmɪ) n., pl. **-mies.** Chiefly Brit. a child's word for **mother.**

mumps (mʌmps) n. **1.** an acute contagious viral disease of the parotid salivary glands, characterized by swelling of the affected parts, fever, and pain beneath the ear. **2.** sulks. —ˈmumpish adj.

mun. abbrev. for municipal.

munch (mʌntʃ) vb. to chew (food, etc.) steadily, esp. with a crunching noise.

mundane (ˈmʌndeɪn, mʌnˈdeɪn) adj. **1.** everyday, ordinary, or banal. **2.** relating to the world or worldly matters. —ˈmundanely adv. —ˈmundaneness n.

municipal (mjuːˈnɪsɪpəl) adj. of or relating to a town, city, or borough or its local government. —muˌnicipaliˈzation or -iˈsation n. —muˈnicipaˌlize or -ise vb. —muˈnicipally adv.

municipality (mjuːˌnɪsɪˈpælɪtɪ) n., pl. **-ties. 1.** a city, town, or district enjoying local self-government. **2.** the governing body of such a unit.

munificent (mjuːˈnɪfɪsənt) adj. **1.** (of a person) generous; bountiful. **2.** (of a gift, etc.) liberal. —muˈnificence n. —muˈnificently adv.

muniments (ˈmjuːnɪmənts) pl. n. Law. the title deeds and other documentary evidence relating to the title to land.

munitions (mjuːˈnɪʃənz) pl. n. (sometimes sing.) military equipment and stores, esp. ammunition.

muon (ˈmjuːɒn) n. a positive or negative elementary particle with a mass 207 times that of an electron. It was originally called the **mu meson.**

mural (ˈmjʊərəl) n. **1.** a large painting on a wall. ~adj. **2.** of or relating to a wall. —ˈmuralist n.

murder (ˈmɜːdə) n. **1.** the unlawful premeditated killing of one human being by another. Cf. **manslaughter. 2.** Inf. something dangerous, difficult, or unpleasant: driving around London is murder. **3. cry blue murder.** Inf. to make or cause an outcry. **4. get away with murder.** Inf. to escape censure; do as one pleases. ~vb. (mainly tr.) **5.** (also intr.) to kill (someone) unlawfully with premeditation or during the commission of a crime. **6.** to kill brutally. **7.** Inf. to destroy; ruin. **8.** Inf. to defeat completely; beat decisively: the home team murdered their opponents. —ˈmurderer n. —ˈmurderess fem. n. —ˈmurderous adj. —ˈmurderously adv. —ˈmurderousness n.

murk or **mirk** (mɜːk) n. **1.** gloomy darkness. ~adj. **2.** an archaic variant of **murky.**

murky or **mirky** (ˈmɜːkɪ) adj. **murkier, murkiest** or **mirkier, mirkiest. 1.** gloomy or dark. **2.** cloudy or impenetrable as with smoke or fog. —ˈmurkily or ˈmirkily adv. —ˈmurkiness or ˈmirkiness n.

murmur (ˈmɜːmə) n. **1.** a continuous low indistinct sound, as of distant voices. **2.** an indistinct utterance: a murmur of satisfaction. **3.** a complaint; grumble: he made no murmur at my suggestion. **4.** Med. any abnormal soft blowing sound heard usually over the chest (**heart murmur**). ~vb. **5.** to utter (something) in a murmur. **6.** (intr.) to complain. —ˈmurmurer n. —ˈmurmuringly adv. —ˈmurmurous adj.

murrain (ˈmʌrɪn) n. **1.** any plaguelike disease in cattle. **2.** Arch. a plague.

mus. abbrev. for: **1.** museum. **2.** music. **3.** musical.

Mus.B. or **Mus.Bac.** abbrev. for Bachelor of Music.

muscat (ˈmʌskət, -kæt) n. **1.** any of various grapevines that produce sweet white grapes used for making wine

---

or raisins. **2.** another name for **muscatel.**

muscatel (ˌmʌskəˈtɛl) or **muscadel** n. **1.** Also called: **muscat.** a rich sweet wine made from muscat grapes. **2.** the grape or raisin from a muscat vine.

muscle (ˈmʌsəl) n. **1.** a tissue composed of bundles of elongated cells capable of contraction and relaxation to produce movement in an organ or part. **2.** an organ composed of muscle tissue. **3.** strength or force. ~vb. **4.** (intr.; often foll. by in, on, etc.) Inf. to force one's way (in). —ˈmusclely adj.

muscle-bound adj. **1.** having overdeveloped and inelastic muscles. **2.** lacking flexibility.

muscleman (ˈmʌsəlˌmæn) n., pl. **-men.** **1.** a man with highly developed muscles. **2.** a henchman employed by a gangster, etc., to intimidate or use violence upon victims.

Muscovite (ˈmʌskəˌvaɪt) n. **1.** a native or inhabitant of Moscow. ~adj. **2.** an archaic word for **Russian.**

Muscovy duck (ˈmʌskəvɪ) or **musk duck** n. a large crested widely domesticated South American duck, having a greenish-black plumage with white markings and a large red caruncle on the bill.

muscular (ˈmʌskjʊlə) adj. **1.** having well-developed muscles; brawny. **2.** of, relating to, or consisting of muscle. —**muscularity** (ˌmʌskjʊˈlærɪtɪ) n. —**muscularly** adv.

muscular dystrophy n. a genetic disease characterized by progressive deterioration and wasting of muscle fibres.

musculature (ˈmʌskjʊlətʃə) n. **1.** the arrangement of muscles in an organ or part. **2.** the total muscular system of an organism.

Mus.D. or **Mus.Doc.** abbrev. for Doctor of Music.

muse[1] (mjuːz) vb. **1.** (when intr., often foll. by on or about) to reflect (about) or ponder (on), usually in silence. **2.** (intr.) to gaze thoughtfully. ~n. **3.** a state of abstraction.

muse[2] (mjuːz) n. (often preceded by the) a goddess that inspires a creative artist, esp. a poet.

Muse (mjuːz) n. Greek myth. any of nine sister goddesses, each of whom was regarded as the protectress of a different art or science.

museum (mjuːˈzɪəm) n. a building where objects of historical, artistic, or scientific interest are exhibited and preserved.

museum piece n. **1.** an object of sufficient age or interest to be kept in a museum. **2.** Inf. a person or thing regarded as antiquated.

mush[1] (mʌʃ) n. **1.** a soft pulpy mass or consistency. **2.** U.S. a thick porridge made from corn meal. **3.** Inf. cloying sentimentality.

mush[2] (mʌʃ) interj. **1.** an order to dogs in a sled team to start up or go faster. ~n. **2.** a journey with such a sled.

mushroom (ˈmʌʃruːm, -rʊm) n. **1. a.** the fleshy spore-producing body of any of various fungi, typically consisting of a cap at the end of a stem. Some species, such as the field mushroom, are edible. Cf. **toadstool. b.** (as modifier): mushroom soup. **2. a.** something resembling a mushroom in shape or rapid growth. **b.** (as modifier): mushroom growth. ~vb. (intr.) **3.** to grow rapidly: demand mushroomed overnight. **4.** to assume a mushroom-like shape.

mushroom cloud n. the large mushroom-shaped cloud produced by a nuclear explosion.

mushy (ˈmʌʃɪ) adj. **mushier, mushiest.** **1.** soft and pulpy. **2.** Inf. excessively sentimental or emotional. —ˈmushily adv. —ˈmushiness n.

music (ˈmjuːzɪk) n. **1.** an art form consisting of sequences of sounds in time, esp. tones of definite pitch organized melodically, harmonically and rhythmically. **2.** the sounds so produced, esp. by singing or musical instruments. **3.** written or printed music, such as a score or set of parts. **4.** any sequence of sounds perceived as pleasing or harmonious. **5. face the music.** Inf. to ac-

cept the consequences of one's actions.

musical (ˈmjuːzɪkəl) adj. **1.** of, relating to, or used in music. **2.** harmonious; melodious: musical laughter. **3.** talented in or fond of music. **4.** involving or set to music. ~n. **5.** Also called: **musical comedy.** a light romantic play or film having dialogue interspersed with songs and dances. —**musically** adv. —ˌmusiˈcality n.

musical box or **music box** n. a mechanical instrument that plays tunes by means of pins on a revolving cylinder striking the tuned teeth of a comblike metal plate.

musical chairs n. a party game in which players walk around chairs while music is played, there being one less chair than players. Whenever the music stops, the player who fails to find a chair is eliminated.

music centre n. a single hi-fi unit containing a turntable, amplifier, radio and cassette player.

music hall n. Chiefly Brit. **1.** a variety entertainment consisting of songs, comic turns, etc. U.S. name: **vaudeville. 2.** a theatre at which such entertainments are staged.

musician (mjuːˈzɪʃən) n. a person who plays or composes music, esp. as a profession. —**muˈsicianly** adj. —**muˈsicianship** n.

musicology (ˌmjuːzɪˈkɒlədʒɪ) n. the scholarly study of music. —**musicological** (ˌmjuːzɪkəˈlɒdʒɪkəl) adj. —ˌmusiˈcologist n.

musk (mʌsk) n. **1.** a strong-smelling glandular secretion of the male musk deer, used in perfumery. **2.** a similar substance produced by certain other animals, such as the civet and otter, or manufactured synthetically. **3.** a North American plant which has yellow flowers and was formerly cultivated for its musky scent. **4.** the smell of musk or a similar heady smell. **5.** (modifier) containing or resembling musk: musk oil.

musk deer n. a small central Asian mountain deer. The male secretes musk.

musk duck n. **1.** another name for **Muscovy duck. 2.** a duck inhabiting swamps, lakes, and streams in Australia. The male emits a musky odour.

muskellunge (ˈmʌskəˌlʌndʒ) or **maskinonge** (ˈmæskəˌnɒndʒ) n., pl. **-lunges, -nonges** or **-lunge, -nonge.** a large North American freshwater game fish, related to the pike. Often shortened (informally) to **musky** or **muskie.**

musket (ˈmʌskɪt) n. a long-barrelled muzzle-loading shoulder gun used between the 16th and 18th centuries by infantry soldiers. —ˌmuskeˈteer n. —ˈmusketry n.

muskmelon (ˈmʌskˌmɛlən) n. **1.** any of several varieties of the melon, such as the cantaloupe and honeydew. **2.** the fruit of any of these melons, having ribbed or warty rind and sweet yellow, white, or green flesh with a musky aroma.

musk ox n. a large bovid mammal, having a dark shaggy coat, short legs, and widely spaced downward-curving horns: now confined to the tundras of Canada and Greenland.

muskrat (ˈmʌskˌræt) n., pl. **-rats** or **-rat.** **1.** a North American beaver-like amphibious rodent, closely related to but larger than the voles. **2.** the brown fur of this animal. ~Also called: **musquash.**

musk rose n. a Mediterranean rose, cultivated for its white musk-scented flowers.

musky (ˈmʌskɪ) adj. **muskier, muskiest.** resembling the smell of musk; having a heady or pungent sweet aroma. —ˈmuskiness n.

Muslim (ˈmʊzlɪm, ˈmʌz-) or **Moslem** n., pl. **-lims** or **-lim. 1.** a follower of the religion of Islam. ~adj. **2.** of or relating to Islam, its doctrines, culture, etc. ~Also (but not in Muslim use): **Mohammedan, Muhammadan.** —ˈMuslimism or ˈMoslemism n.

muslin (ˈmʌzlɪn) n. a fine plain-weave cotton fabric.

musquash (ˈmʌskwɒʃ) n. another name for **muskrat,** esp. the fur.

THESAURUS

muscle n. **1.** muscle tissue, sinew, tendon, thew **2.** brawn, clout (Sl.), force, forcefulness, might, potency, power, stamina, strength, sturdiness, weight ~v. **3. muscle in** Inf. butt in, elbow one's way in, force one's way in, impose oneself

muscular athletic, beefy (Inf.), brawny, husky (Inf.), lusty, powerful, powerfully built,

robust, sinewy, stalwart, strapping, strong, sturdy, vigorous, well-knit

muse be in a brown study, be lost in thought, brood, cogitate, consider, contemplate, deliberate, dream, meditate, mull over, ponder, reflect, ruminate, speculate, think, think over, weigh

mushroom v. boom, burgeon, expand,

flourish, grow rapidly, increase, luxuriate, proliferate, shoot up, spread, spring up, sprout

musical dulcet, euphonious, harmonious, lilting, lyrical, melodic, melodious, sweet-sounding, tuneful

muss (mʌs) *U.S. inf.* ~*vb.* **1.** (*tr.*; often foll. by *up*) to make untidy; rumple. ~*n.* **2.** a state of disorder; muddle. —**'mussy** *adj.*

mussel ('mʌsəl) *n.* **1.** any of various marine bivalves, esp. the edible mussel, having a dark slightly elongated shell and living attached to rocks, etc. **2.** any of various freshwater bivalves, attached to rocks, sand, etc., having a flattened oval shell (a source of mother-of-pearl).

Mussulman ('mʌsəlmən) *n. pl.* -**mans.** an archaic word for **Muslim.**

must[1] (mʌst; *unstressed* məst, məs) *vb.* (takes an infinitive without *to* or an implied infinitive) used as an auxiliary: **1.** to express obligation or compulsion: *you must pay your dues.* In this sense, *must* does not form a negative. If used with a negative infinitive it indicates obligatory prohibition. **2.** to indicate necessity: *I must go to the bank tomorrow.* **3.** to indicate the probable correctness of a statement: *he must be there by now.* **4.** to indicate inevitability: *all good things must come to an end.* **5.** to express resolution: **a.** on the part of the speaker: *I must finish this.* **b.** on the part of another or others: *let him get drunk if he must.* **6.** (used emphatically) to express conviction or certainty on the part of the speaker: *you must be joking.* **7.** (foll. by *away*) used with an implied verb of motion to express compelling haste: *I must away.* ~*n.* **8.** an essential or necessary thing: *a safety belt in a car is a must these days.*

must[2] (mʌst) *n.* the pressed juice of grapes or other fruit ready for fermentation.

mustachio (məˈstɑːʃɪˌəʊ) *n., pl.* -**chios.** (*often pl.*) Often *humorous.* a moustache, esp. when bushy or elaborately shaped. —**mus'tachioed** *adj.*

mustang ('mʌstæŋ) *n.* a small breed of horse, often wild or half wild, found in the southwestern U.S.

mustard ('mʌstəd) *n.* **1.** any of several Eurasian plants, esp. black mustard and white mustard, having yellow flowers and slender pods: cultivated for their pungent seeds. **2.** a paste made from the powdered seeds of any of these plants and used as a condiment. **3.** a brownish-yellow colour. **4.** *Sl.* zest or enthusiasm.

mustard and cress *n.* seedlings of white mustard and garden cress, used in salads, etc.

mustard gas *n.* an oily liquid vesicant compound used in chemical warfare. Its vapour causes blindness and burns.

mustard plaster *n. Med.* a mixture of powdered black mustard seeds applied to the skin for its counterirritant effects.

muster ('mʌstə) *vb.* **1.** to call together (numbers of men) for duty, inspection, etc., or (of men) to assemble in this way. **2. muster in** *or* **out.** *U.S.* to enlist into or discharge from military service. **3.** (*tr.*; sometimes foll. by *up*) to summon or gather: *to muster one's arguments; to muster up courage.* **4.** *Austral. & N.Z.* to round up (stock). ~*n.* **5.** an assembly of military personnel for duty, etc. **6.** a collection, assembly, or gathering. **7.** *Austral. & N.Z.* the act of rounding up stock. **8. pass muster.** to be acceptable.

musth *or* **must** (mʌst) *n.* (often preceded by *in*) a state of frenzied sexual excitement in the males of certain large mammals, esp. elephants.

musty ('mʌstɪ) *adj.* -**tier, -tiest.** **1.** smelling or tasting old, stale, or mouldy. **2.** old-fashioned, dull, or hackneyed: *musty ideas.* —**'mustily** *adv.* —**'mustiness** *n.*

mutable ('mjuːtəbəl) *adj.* able to or tending to change. —ˌmuta'bility *or* 'mutableness *n.* —'mutably *adv.*

mutant ('mjuːtənt) *n.* **1.** Also called: **mutation.** an animal, organism, or gene that has undergone mutation. ~*adj.* **2.** of, undergoing, or resulting from mutation.

mutation (mjuːˈteɪʃən) *n.* **1.** the act or process of mutating; change; alteration. **2.** a change or alteration. **3.** a change in the chromosomes or genes of a cell which may affect the structure and development of the resultant offspring. **4.** another word for **mutant** (sense 1). **5.** a physical characteristic of an individual resulting from this type of chromosomal change. **6.** *Phonetics.* **a.** (in Germanic languages) another name for **umlaut.** **b.** (in Celtic languages) a phonetic change in certain initial consonants caused by a preceding word. —**mu'tate** *vb.* —**mu'tational** *adj.* —**mu'tationally** *adv.*

mute (mjuːt) *adj.* **1.** not giving out sound or speech; silent. **2.** unable to speak; dumb. **3.** unspoken or unexpressed. **4.** *Law.* (of a person arraigned on indictment) refusing to answer a charge. **5.** another word for **plosive.** **6.** (of a letter in a word) silent. ~*n.* **7.** a person who is unable to speak. **8.** *Law.* a person who refuses to plead. **9.** any of various devices used to soften the tone of stringed or brass instruments. **10.** *Phonetics.* a plosive consonant. **11.** a silent letter. **12.** an actor in a dumb-show. **13.** a hired mourner. ~*vb.* (*tr.*) **14.** to reduce the volume of (a musical instrument) by means of a mute, soft pedal, etc. **15.** to subdue the strength of (a colour, tone, lighting, etc.). —**'mutely** *adv.* —**'muteness** *n.*

mute swan *n.* a Eurasian swan with a pure white plumage and an orange-red bill.

mutilate ('mjuːtɪˌleɪt) *vb.* (*tr.*) to damage or maim, esp. by depriving of a limb, essential part, etc. —ˌmuti'lation *n.* —'muti,lative *adj.* —'muti,lator *n.*

mutiny ('mjuːtɪnɪ) *n., pl.* -**nies.** **1.** open rebellion against constituted authority, esp. by seamen or soldiers against their officers. ~*vb.* -**nying, -nied.** **2.** (*intr.*) to engage in mutiny. —ˌmuti'neer *n.* —'mutinous *adj.*

mutism ('mjuːˌtɪzəm) *n.* **1.** the state of being mute. **2.** *Psychiatry.* **a.** a refusal to speak. **b.** the lack of development of speech.

mutt (mʌt) *n. Sl.* **1.** an inept, ignorant, or stupid person. **2.** a mongrel dog; cur.

mutter ('mʌtə) *vb.* **1.** to utter (something) in a low and indistinct tone. **2.** (*intr.*) to grumble or complain. **3.** (*intr.*) to make a low continuous murmuring sound. ~*n.* **4.** a muttered sound or complaint. —'mutterer *n.*

mutton ('mʌtən) *n.* **1.** the flesh of sheep, esp. of mature sheep, used as food. **2. mutton dressed (up) as lamb.** an older person, thing, or idea dressed up to look young or new. —'muttony *adj.*

mutton chop *n.* a piece of mutton from the loin.

muttonchops ('mʌtənˌtʃɒps) *pl. n.* side whiskers trimmed in the shape of chops.

mutual ('mjuːtʃʊəl) *adj.* **1.** experienced or expressed by each of two or more people about the other; reciprocal: *mutual distrust.* **2.** *Inf.* common to or shared by both: *a mutual friend.* —**mutuality** (ˌmjuːtjʊˈælɪtɪ) *n.* —'mutually *adv.*

mutual insurance *n.* a system of insurance by which all policyholders become company members under contract to pay premiums into a common fund out of which claims are paid.

THESAURUS

muster *v.* **1.** assemble, call together, call up, collect, come together, congregate, convene, convoke, enrol, gather, group, marshal, meet, mobilize, rally, round up, summon ~*n.* **2.** assemblage, assembly, collection, concourse, congregation, convention, convocation, gathering, meeting, mobilization, rally, roundup **3. pass muster** be *or* come up to scratch, be acceptable, fill the bill (*Inf.*), make the grade, measure up, qualify

musty **1.** airless, dank, decayed, frowsty, fusty, mildewed, mildewy, mouldy, old, smelly, stale, stuffy **2.** ancient, antediluvian, antiquated, banal, clichéd, dull, hackneyed, hoary, moth-eaten, obsolete, old-fashioned, stale, threadbare, trite, worn-out

mutability alteration, change, evolution,

metamorphosis, transition, variation, vicissitude

mutation 1. alteration, change, deviation, evolution, metamorphosis, modification, transfiguration, transformation, variation **2.** anomaly, deviant, mutant

mute 1. *adj.* aphasiac, aphasic, aphonic, dumb, mum, silent, speechless, unexpressed, unspeaking, unspoken, voiceless, wordless **2.** *v.* dampen, deaden, lower, moderate, muffle, soften, soft-pedal, subdue, tone down, turn down

mutilate 1. amputate, butcher, cripple, cut to pieces, cut up, damage, disable, disfigure, dismember, hack, injure, lacerate, lame, maim, mangle **2.** adulterate, bowdlerize, butcher, censor, cut, damage, distort, expurgate, hack, mar, spoil

mutinous bolshie (*Brit. inf.*), contuma-

cious, disobedient, insubordinate, insurgent, rebellious, refractory, revolutionary, riotous, seditious, subversive, turbulent, ungovernable, unmanageable, unruly

mutiny 1. *n.* defiance, disobedience, insubordination, insurrection, rebellion, refusal to obey orders, resistance, revolt, revolution, riot, rising, strike, uprising **2.** *v.* be insubordinate, defy authority, disobey, rebel, refuse to obey orders, resist, revolt, rise up, strike

mutter complain, grouch, grouse, grumble, mumble, murmur, rumble

mutual common, communal, correlative, interactive, interchangeable, interchanged, joint, reciprocal, reciprocated, requited, returned, shared

Muzak ('mju:zæk) n. Trademark. recorded light music played in shops, restaurants, factories, etc.

muzzle ('mʌzəl) n. 1. the projecting part of the face, usually the jaws and nose, of animals such as the dog and horse. 2. a guard or strap fitted over an animal's nose and jaws to prevent it biting or eating. 3. the front end of a gun barrel. ~vb. (tr.) 4. to prevent from being heard or noticed. 5. to put a muzzle on (an animal). —'muzzler n.

muzzle-loader n. a firearm receiving its ammunition through the muzzle. —'muzzle-,loading adj.

muzzy ('mʌzɪ) adj. -zier, -ziest. 1. blurred or hazy. 2. confused or befuddled. —'muzzily adv. —'muzziness n.

M.V.O. (in Britain) abbrev. for Member of the Royal Victorian Order.

MW 1. symbol for megawatt. 2. Radio. abbrev. for medium wave.

Mx Physics. symbol for maxwell.

my (maɪ) determiner. 1. of, belonging to, or associated with the speaker or writer (me): my own ideas. 2. used in various forms of address: my lord. ~interj. 3. an exclamation of surprise, awe, etc.: my, how you've grown!

mycelium (maɪ'si:lɪəm) n., pl. -lia (-lɪə). the vegetative body of fungi: a mass of branching filaments (hyphae). —my'celial adj.

Mycenaean (,maɪsɪ'ni:ən) adj. 1. of or relating to ancient Mycenae, a city in S Greece, or its inhabitants. 2. of or relating to the Aegean civilization of Mycenae (1400 to 1100 B.C.)

myeloma (,maɪə'ləʊmə) n. a usually malignant tumour of the bone marrow.

myna, mynah, or **mina** ('maɪnə) n. any of various tropical Asian starlings, some of which can mimic human speech.

Mynheer (mə'nɪə) n. a Dutch title of address equivalent to Sir when used alone or to Mr. before a name.

myocardium (,maɪəʊ'kɑ:dɪəm) n., pl. -dia (-dɪə). the muscular tissue of the heart. —,myo'cardial adj.

myopia (maɪ'əʊpɪə) n. inability to see distant objects clearly because the images are focused in front of the retina; short-sightedness. —myopic (maɪ'ɒpɪk) adj. —my'opically adv.

myosotis (,maɪə'səʊtɪs) n. any plant of the genus Myosotis. See forget-me-not.

myriad ('mɪrɪəd) adj. 1. innumerable. ~n. 2. a large indefinite number. 3. Arch. ten thousand.

myriapod ('mɪrɪə,pɒd) n. 1. any of a group of terrestrial arthropods having a long segmented body and many walking limbs, such as the centipedes and millipedes. ~adj. 2. of, relating to, or belonging to this group.

Myrmidon ('mɜ:mɪ,dɒn, -dən) n. 1. Greek myth. one of a race of people who were led against Troy by Achilles. 2. (often not cap.) a follower or henchman.

myrrh (mɜ:) n. 1. any of several trees and shrubs of Africa and S Asia that exude an aromatic resin. 2. the resin obtained from such a plant, used in perfume, incense, and medicine.

myrtle ('mɜ:təl) n. an evergreen shrub or tree, esp. a S European shrub with pink or white flowers and aromatic blue-black berries.

myself (maɪ'sɛlf) pron. 1. a. the reflexive form of I or me. b. (intensifier): I myself know of no answer. 2. (preceded by a copula) my usual self: I'm not myself today. 3. Not standard. used instead of I or me in compound noun phrases: John and myself are voting together.

▷ **Usage.** The use of myself for I or me is often the result of an attempt to be elegant or correct. However, careful users of English only employ myself when it follows I or me in the same clause: I cut myself, but he gave it to me (not myself). The same is true of the other reflexives. This rule does permit constructions such as he wrote it himself (unassisted) and he himself wrote it (without an intermediary), but these are only to be used to reinforce a previous reference to the same individual.

mysterious (mɪ'stɪərɪəs) adj. 1. characterized by or indicative of mystery. 2. puzzling, curious. —mys'teriously adv. —mys'teriousness n.

mystery[1] ('mɪstərɪ, -trɪ) n., pl. -teries. 1. an unexplained or inexplicable event, phenomenon, etc. 2. a person or thing that arouses curiosity or suspense because of an unknown, obscure, or enigmatic quality. 3. the state or quality of being obscure, inexplicable, or enigmatic. 4. a story, film, etc., which arouses suspense and curiosity because of facts concealed. 5. Theol. any truth that is divinely revealed but otherwise unknowable. 6. Christianity. a sacramental rite, such as the Eucharist, or (when pl.) the consecrated elements of the Eucharist. 7. (often pl.) any rites of certain ancient Mediterranean religions. 8. short for mystery play.

mystery[2] ('mɪstərɪ) n., pl. -teries. Arch. 1. a trade, occupation, or craft. 2. a guild of craftsmen.

mystery play n. (in the Middle Ages) a type of drama based on the life of Christ. Cf. miracle play.

mystery tour n. an excursion to an unspecified destination.

mystic ('mɪstɪk) n. 1. a person who achieves mystical experience or an apprehension of divine mysteries ~adj. 2. another word for mystical.

mystical ('mɪstɪkəl) adj. 1. relating to or characteristic of mysticism. 2. Theol. having a divine or sacred significance that surpasses human apprehension. 3. having occult or metaphysical significance. —'mystically adv.

mysticism ('mɪstɪ,sɪzəm) n. 1. belief in or experience of a reality surpassing normal human understanding or experience. 2. a system of contemplative prayer and spirituality aimed at achieving direct intuitive experience of the divine. 3. obscure or confused belief or thought.

mystify ('mɪstɪ,faɪ) vb. -fying, -fied. (tr.) 1. to confuse, bewilder, or puzzle. 2. to make obscure. —,mystifi'cation n.

mystique (mɪ'sti:k) n. an aura of mystery, power, and awe that surrounds a person or thing.

myth (mɪθ) n. 1. a. a story about superhuman beings of an earlier age, usually of how natural phenomena, social customs, etc., came into existence. b. another word for mythology (senses 1, 3). 2. a fictitious or unproven person or thing.

myth. abbrev. for: 1. mythological. 2. mythology.

mythical ('mɪθɪkəl) adj. 1. of or relating to myth. 2. imaginary or fictitious. —'mythically adv.

mythology (mɪ'θɒlədʒɪ) n., pl. -gies. 1. a body of myths, esp. one associated with a particular culture, institution, person, etc. 2. a body of stories about a person, institution, etc. 3. myths collectively. 4. the study of myths. —mythological (,mɪθə'lɒdʒɪkəl) adj. —my'thologist n. —my'tholo,gize or -,gise vb.

myxoedema or U.S. **myxedema** (,mɪksɪ'di:mə) n. a disease resulting from underactivity of the thyroid gland characterized by puffy eyes, face, and hands and mental sluggishness. See also cretinism.

myxomatosis (,mɪksəmə'təʊsɪs) n. an infectious and usually fatal viral disease of rabbits characterized by swelling of the mucous membranes and formation of skin tumours.

THESAURUS

muzzle n. 1. jaws, mouth, nose, snout 2. gag, guard ~v. 3. censor, choke, curb, gag (Inf.), restrain, silence, stifle, suppress

myopic near-sighted, short-sighted

mysterious abstruse, arcane, baffling, concealed, covert, cryptic, curious, dark, enigmatic, furtive, hidden, impenetrable, incomprehensible, inexplicable, inscrutable, insoluble, mystical, mystifying, obscure, perplexing, puzzling, recondite, secret, secretive, sphinxlike, strange, uncanny, unfathomable, unknown, veiled, weird

mystery conundrum, enigma, problem, puzzle, question, riddle, secrecy, secret

mystic, mystical abstruse, arcane, cabalistic, cryptic, enigmatical, esoteric, hidden, inscrutable, metaphysical, mysterious, nonrational, occult, otherworldly, paranormal, preternatural, supernatural, transcendental

mystify baffle, bamboozle (Inf.), beat (Sl.), befog, bewilder, confound, confuse, elude, escape, perplex, puzzle, stump

myth 1. allegory, fable, fairy story, fiction, folk tale, legend, parable, saga, story, tradition 2. delusion, fancy, fantasy, figment, illusion, imagination, superstition, tall story

mythical 1. allegorical, chimerical, fabled, fabulous, fairy-tale, legendary, mythological, storied 2. fabricated, fanciful, fantasy, fictitious, imaginary, invented, made-up, make-believe, nonexistent, pretended, unreal, untrue

mythology folklore, folk tales, legend, lore, mythos, myths, stories, tradition

N

n *or* **N** (ɛn) *n., pl.* **n's, N's,** *or* **Ns. 1.** the 14th letter of the English alphabet. **2.** a speech sound represented by this letter.

n[1] *symbol for:* **1.** neutron. **2.** *Optics.* index of refraction. **3.** nano-.

n[2] (ɛn) *determiner.* an indefinite number (of): *there are n objects in a box.*

N *symbol for:* **1.** Also: **kt.** *Chess.* knight. **2.** newton(s). **3.** *Chem.* nitrogen. **4.** North. **5.** noun.

n. *abbrev. for:* **1.** neuter. **2.** new. **3.** nominative. **4.** noon. **5.** note. **6.** noun. **7.** number.

N. *abbrev. for:* **1.** National(ist). **2.** Navy. **3.** New. **4.** Norse.

Na *the chemical symbol for* sodium.

N.A. *abbrev. for* North America.

NAAFI ('næfɪ) *n.* **1.** *acronym for* Navy, Army, and Air Force Institutes: an organization providing canteens, shops, etc., for British military personnel at home or overseas. **2.** a canteen, shop, etc., run by this organization.

nab (næb) *vb.* **nabbing, nabbed.** (*tr.*) *Inf.* **1.** to arrest (a criminal, etc.). **2.** to seize suddenly; snatch.

nabob ('neɪbɒb) *n.* **1.** *Inf.* a rich or important man. **2.** (formerly) a European who made a fortune in India. **3.** another name for a **nawab.**

nacre ('neɪkə) *n.* the technical name for **mother-of-pearl.** —'**nacred** *adj.*

nadir ('neɪdɪə, 'næ-) *n.* **1.** the point on the celestial sphere directly below an observer and diametrically opposite the zenith. **2.** the lowest point; depths.

nae (neɪ) *or* **na** (nɑː) a Scot. word for **no**[1] *or* **not.**

naevus *or U.S.* **nevus** ('niːvəs) *n., pl.* **-vi** (-vaɪ). any pigmented blemish on the skin; birthmark or mole. —'**naevoid** *adj.*

nag[1] (næg) *vb.* **nagging, nagged. 1.** to scold or annoy constantly. **2.** (when *intr.,* often foll. by *at*) to be a constant source of discomfort or worry (to). ~*n.* **3.** a person, esp. a woman, who nags. —'**nagger** *n.*

nag[2] (næg) *n.* **1.** *Often derog.* a horse. **2.** a small riding horse.

naiad ('naɪæd) *n., pl.* **-ads** *or* **-ades** (-əˌdiːz). **1.** *Greek myth.* a nymph dwelling in a lake, river, spring, or fountain. **2.** the aquatic larva of the dragonfly, mayfly, and related insects. **3.** Also called: **water nymph.** a submerged aquatic plant, having narrow leaves and small flowers.

naïf (nɑːˈiːf) *adj., n.* a less common word for **naive.**

nail (neɪl) *n.* **1.** a fastening device, usually made of metal, having a point at one end and a head at the other. **2.** anything resembling such a device in function or shape. **3.** the horny plate covering part of the dorsal surface of the fingers or toes. **4.** the claw of a mammal, bird, or reptile. **5.** a unit of length, formerly used for measuring cloth, equal to two and a quarter inches. **6. hit the nail on the head.** to do or say something correct or telling. **7. on the nail.** *Inf.* (of payments) at once. ~*vb.* (*tr.*) **8.** to attach with or as if with nails. **9.** *Inf.* to arrest, catch, or seize. **10.** *Inf.* to hit or bring down, as with a shot. **11.** *Inf.* to expose or detect (a lie or liar). **12.** to fix (one's eyes, attention, etc.) on. **13.** to stud with nails. —'**nailer** *n.*

nailfile ('neɪlˌfaɪl) *n.* a small file of metal or of board coated with emery, used to trim the nails.

nail polish *or* **varnish** *or esp. U.S.* **enamel** *n.* a quick-drying cosmetic lacquer applied to colour the nails or make them shiny or esp. both.

nail set *n.* a punch for driving the head of a nail below or flush with the surrounding surface.

naive, naïve (nɑːˈiːv, naɪˈiːv), *or* **naïf** *adj.* **1.** having or expressing innocence and credulity; ingenuous. **2.** lacking developed powers of reasoning or criticism: *a naive argument.* —**na**'**ively, na**'**ïvely,** *or* **na**'**ïfly** *adv.* —**na**'**iveness, na**'**ïveness,** *or* **na**'**ïfness** *n.*

naiveté, naïveté (ˌnɑːiːvˈteɪ), *or* **naivety** (naɪˈiːvtɪ) *n.* **1.** the state or quality of being naive. **2.** a naive act or statement.

naked ('neɪkɪd) *adj.* **1.** having the body unclothed; undressed. **2.** having no covering; exposed: *a naked flame.* **3.** with no qualification or concealment: *the naked facts.* **4.** unaided by any optical instrument (esp. in **the naked eye**). **5.** with no protection or shield. **6.** (usually foll. by *of*) destitute: *naked of weapons.* **7.** (of animals) lacking hair, feathers, scales, etc. **8.** *Law.* **a.** unsupported by authority: *a naked contract.* **b.** lacking some essential condition to render valid; incomplete. —'**nakedly** *adv.* —'**nakedness** *n.*

NALGO ('nælgəʊ) *n. acronym for* National and Local Government Officers' Association.

namby-pamby (ˌnæmbɪˈpæmbɪ) *adj.* **1.** sentimental or prim in a weak insipid way. **2.** clinging, feeble, or spineless. ~*n., pl.* **-bies. 3.** a person who is namby-pamby.

name (neɪm) *n.* **1.** a word or term by which a person or thing is commonly and distinctively known. **2.** mere outward appearance as opposed to fact: *he was ruler in name only.* **3.** a word or phrase descriptive of character, usually abusive: *to call a person names.* **4.** reputation, esp., if unspecified, good reputation: *he's made quite a name for himself.* **5. a.** a famous person or thing: *a name in the advertising world.* **b.** *Chiefly U.S.* (as modifier): *a name product.* **6. in the name of. a.** for the sake of. **b.** by the authority of. **7. name of the game.** *Chiefly U.S.* **a.** anything that is significant or important. **b.** normal conditions, circumstances, etc.: *in gambling, losing money's the name of the game.* **8. to one's name.** belonging to one: *I haven't a penny to my name.* ~*vb.* (*tr.*) **9.** to give a name to. **10.** to refer to by name; cite: *he named three French poets.* **11.** to fix or specify: *they have named a date for the meeting.* **12.** to appoint or nominate: *he was named Journalist of the Year.* **13. name names.** to cite people, esp. in order to blame or accuse them. **14. name the day.** to choose the day for one's wedding. —'**namable** *or* '**nameable** *adj.*

THESAURUS

nadir bottom, depths, lowest point, minimum, rock bottom, zero

nag[1] **1.** *v.* annoy, badger, berate, chivvy, goad, harass, harry, henpeck, irritate, pester, plague, provoke, scold, torment, upbraid, vex, worry **2.** *n.* harpy, scold, shrew, tartar, termagant, virago

nag[2] hack, horse, jade, plug (*U.S.*)

nagging continuous, critical, distressing, irritating, painful, persistent, scolding, shrewish, worrying

nail *v.* attach, beat, fasten, fix, hammer, join, pin, secure, tack

naive **1.** artless, candid, childlike, confiding, frank, guileless, ingenuous, innocent, jejune, natural, open, simple, trusting, unaffected, unpretentious, unsophisticated, unworldly **2.** callow, credulous, gullible, green (*Inf.*), unsuspicious

naiveté **1.** artlessness, candour, frankness, guilelessness, inexperience, ingenuousness, innocence, naturalness, openness, simplicity **2.** callowness, credulity, gullibility

naked **1.** bare, denuded, disrobed, divested, exposed, in one's birthday suit (*Inf.*), in the altogether (*Inf.*), in the buff (*Inf.*), nude, starkers (*Inf.*), stripped, unclothed, unconcealed, uncovered, undraped, undressed **2.** blatant, evident, manifest, open, overt, patent, plain, simple, stark, unadorned, undisguised, unexaggerated, unmistakable, unqualified, unvarnished **3.** defenceless, helpless, insecure, unarmed, unguarded, unprotected, vulnerable

nakedness **1.** baldness, bareness, nudity, undress **2.** openness, plainness, simplicity, starkness

namby-pamby anaemic, colourless, feeble, insipid, mawkish, prim, prissy (*Inf.*), sentimental, spineless, vapid, weak, wishy-washy (*Inf.*)

name *n.* **1.** appellation, cognomen, denomination, designation, epithet, handle (*Sl.*), moniker (*Inf.*), nickname, sobriquet, term, title **2.** distinction, eminence, esteem, fame, honour, note, praise, renown, repute **3.** character, credit, reputation ~*v.* **4.** baptize, call, christen, denominate, dub, entitle, label, style, term **5.** appoint, choose, cite, classify, commission, designate, identify, mention, nominate, select, specify

named **1.** baptized, called, christened, denominated, dubbed, entitled, known as, labelled, styled, termed **2.** appointed, chosen, cited, classified, commissioned, designated, identified, mentioned, nominated, picked, se-

name day *n. R.C. Church.* the feast day of a saint whose name one bears.

name-dropping *n. Inf.* the practice of referring frequently to famous people, esp. as though they were intimate friends, in order to impress others. —**'name-,dropper** *n.*

nameless ('neɪmlɪs) *adj.* **1.** without a name. **2.** indescribable: *a nameless horror seized him.* **3.** too unpleasant or disturbing to be mentioned: *nameless atrocities.* —**'namelessness** *n.*

namely ('neɪmlɪ) *adv.* that is to say.

nameplate ('neɪm,pleɪt) *n.* a small panel on or next to the door of a room or building, bearing the occupant's name and profession.

namesake ('neɪm,seɪk) *n.* a person or thing named after another, or with the same name as another.

nancy *or* **nancy boy** ('nænsɪ) *n.* an effeminate or homosexual boy or man.

nankeen (næŋ'kiːn) *or* **nankin** ('nænkɪn) *n.* **1.** a hardwearing buff-coloured cotton fabric. **2.** a pale greyish-yellow colour.

nanny ('nænɪ) *n., pl.* -**nies. 1.** a nurse or nursemaid for children. **2.** a child's word for **grandmother.**

nanny goat *n.* a female goat.

nano- *combining form.* denoting 10^{-9}: *nanosecond.* Symbol: n

nap[1] (næp) *vb.* **napping, napped.** (*intr.*) **1.** to sleep for a short while; doze. **2.** to be inattentive or off guard (esp. in **catch someone napping**). ~*n.* **3.** a short light sleep; doze.

nap[2] (næp) *n.* **1. a.** the raised fibres of velvet or similar cloth. **b.** the direction in which these fibres lie. **2.** any similar downy coating. ~*vb.* **napping, napped. 3.** (*tr.*) to raise the nap of (velvet, etc.) by brushing.

nap[3] (næp) *n.* **1.** Also called: **napoleon.** a card game similar to whist, usually played for stakes. **2.** a call in this game, undertaking to win all five tricks. **3.** *Horse racing.* a tipster's choice for a certain winner. **4. nap hand.** a position in which there is a very good chance of success if a risk is taken. ~*vb.* **napping, napped.** (*tr.*) **5.** *Horse racing.* to name (a horse) as likely to win a race.

napalm ('neɪpɑːm, 'næ-) *n.* **1.** a thick and highly incendiary liquid, usually consisting of petrol gelled with aluminium soaps, used in fire bombs, flame throwers, etc. ~*vb.* **2.** (*tr.*) to attack with napalm.

nape (neɪp) *n.* the back of the neck.

naphtha ('næfθə, 'næp-) *n.* a distillation product from coal tar or petroleum: used as a solvent and in petrol.

naphthalene ('næfθə,liːn, 'næp-) *n.* a white crystalline hydrocarbon with a characteristic penetrating odour, used in mothballs and in dyes, explosives, etc. Formula: $C_{10}H_8$. —**naphthalic** (næf'θælɪk, næp-) *adj.*

napkin ('næpkɪn) *n.* **1.** Also called: **table napkin.** a usually square piece of cloth or paper used while eating to protect the clothes, wipe the mouth, etc.; serviette. **2.** *Rare.* a small piece of cloth. **3.** a more formal name for **nappy. 4.** a less common term for **sanitary towel.**

napoleon (nə'pəʊlɪən) *n.* **1.** a former French gold coin worth 20 francs. **2.** *Cards.* the full name for **nap**[3].

nappy ('næpɪ) *n., pl.* -**pies.** *Brit.* a piece of soft towelling material wrapped around a baby in order to absorb its excrement. Also called: **napkin.** U.S. name: **diaper.**

narcissism ('nɑːsɪ,sɪzəm) *or* **narcism** ('nɑːsɪzəm) *n.* **1.** an exceptional interest in or admiration for oneself, esp. one's physical appearance. **2.** sexual satisfaction derived from contemplation of one's own physical endowments. —**'narcissist** *n.* —,**narcis'sistic** *adj.*

narcissus (nɑː'sɪsəs) *n., pl.* -**cissuses** *or* -**cissi** (-'sɪsaɪ). a plant of a Eurasian genus whose yellow, orange, or white flowers have a crown surrounded by spreading segments.

narco- *or sometimes before a vowel* **narc-** *combining form.* indicating numbness or torpor: *narcolepsy.*

narcosis (nɑː'kəʊsɪs) *n.* unconsciousness induced by narcotics or general anaesthetics.

narcotic (nɑː'kɒtɪk) *n.* **1.** any of a group of drugs, such as opium and morphine, that produce numbness and stupor. **2.** anything that relieves pain or induces sleep, mental numbness, etc. ~*adj.* **3.** of or relating to narcotics or narcotics addicts. **4.** of or relating to narcosis. —**nar'cotically** *adv.*

nard (nɑːd) *n.* **1.** another name for **spikenard. 2.** any of several plants whose aromatic roots were formerly used in medicine.

nark (nɑːk) *Brit. & N.Z. sl.* ~*n.* **1.** an informer or spy: *copper's nark.* **2.** someone who complains in an irritating or whining manner. ~*vb.* **3.** (*tr.*) to annoy, upset, or irritate. **4.** (*intr.*) to inform or spy, esp. for the police. **5.** (*intr.*) to complain irritatingly.

narrate (nə'reɪt) *vb.* **1.** to tell (a story); relate. **2.** to speak in accompaniment of (a film, etc.). —**nar'ratable** *adj.* —**nar'rator** *n.*

narration (nə'reɪʃən) *n.* **1.** the act or process of narrating. **2.** a narrated account or story.

narrative ('nærətɪv) *n.* **1.** an account or story, as of events, experiences, etc. **2.** the part of a literary work, etc., that relates events. **3.** the process or technique of narrating. ~*adj.* **4.** telling a story: *a narrative poem.* **5.** of or relating to narration: *narrative art.*

narrow ('nærəʊ) *adj.* **1.** small in breadth, esp. in comparison to length. **2.** limited in range or extent. **3.** limited in outlook. **4.** limited in means or resources. **5.** barely adequate or successful (esp. in **a narrow escape**). **6.** painstakingly thorough: *a narrow scrutiny.* **7.** *Phonetics.* another word for **tense**[1]. ~*vb.* **8.** to make or become narrow; limit; restrict. ~*n.* **9.** a narrow place, esp. a pass or strait. —**'narrowly** *adv.* —**'narrowness** *n.*

narrow boat *n.* a long bargelike boat with a beam of 2.1 metres (7 feet), used on canals.

narrow gauge *n.* **1.** a smaller distance between the lines of a railway than the standard gauge of 56½ inches. ~*adj.* **narrow-gauge. 2.** of or denoting a railway with a narrow gauge.

narrow-minded *adj.* having a biased or illiberal viewpoint; bigoted, intolerant, or prejudiced. —,**narrow-'mindedness** *n.*

narrows ('nærəʊz) *pl. n.* a narrow part of a strait, river, current, etc.

narwhal, narwal ('nɑːwəl), *or* **narwhale** ('nɑː,weɪl) *n.* an arctic toothed whale having a black-spotted whitish skin and, in the male, a long spiral tusk.

N.A.S. *abbrev. for* National Association of Schoolmasters.

NASA ('næsə) *n.* (in the U.S.) *acronym for* National Aeronautics and Space Administration.

THESAURUS

nameless 1. anonymous, innominate, undesignated, unnamed, untitled **2.** incognito, obscure, undistinguished, unheard-of, unknown, unsung **3.** abominable, horrible, indescribable, ineffable, inexpressible, unmentionable, unspeakable, unutterable

namely i.e., specifically, that is to say, to wit, viz.

nap[1] **1.** *v.* catnap, doze, drop off (*Inf.*), drowse, nod, nod off (*Inf.*), rest, sleep, snooze (*Inf.*) **2.** *n.* catnap, forty winks (*Inf.*), rest, shuteye (*Sl.*), siesta, sleep

nap[2] down, fibre, grain, pile, shag, weave

narcissism egotism, self-admiration, self-love, vanity

narcotic 1. *n.* anaesthetic, analgesic, anodyne, drug, opiate, painkiller, sedative, tranquillizer **2.** *adj.* analgesic, calming, dulling,

hypnotic, Lethean, numbing, painkilling, sedative, somnolent, soporific, stupefacient, stupefactive, stupefying

narrate chronicle, describe, detail, recite, recount, rehearse, relate, repeat, report, set forth, tell, unfold

narration description, explanation, reading, recital, rehearsal, relation, storytelling, telling, voice-over (*in film*)

narrative account, chronicle, detail, history, report, statement, story, tale

narrator annalist, author, bard, chronicler, commentator, raconteur, reciter, relater, reporter, storyteller, writer

narrow *adj.* **1.** circumscribed, close, confined, constricted, contracted, cramped, incapacious, limited, meagre, near, pinched, restricted, scanty, straitened, tight **2.** biased, bigoted, dogmatic, illiberal, intolerant,

narrow-minded, partial, prejudiced, reactionary, small-minded **3.** attenuated, fine, slender, slim, spare, tapering, thin **4.** exclusive, select **5.** *Inf.* avaricious, close (*Inf.*), mean, mercenary, niggardly, ungenerous ~*v.* **6.** circumscribe, constrict, diminish, limit, reduce, simplify, straiten, tighten

narrowly 1. barely, by a whisker *or* hair's-breadth, just, only just, scarcely **2.** carefully, closely, painstakingly, scrutinizingly

narrow-minded biased, bigoted, conservative, hidebound, illiberal, insular, intolerant, opinionated, parochial, petty, prejudiced, provincial, reactionary, short-sighted, small-minded, strait-laced

narrows channel, gulf, passage, sound, straits

nasal ('neɪzᵊl) adj. 1. of the nose. 2. *Phonetics.* pronounced with the soft palate lowered allowing air to escape via the nasal cavity. ~n. 3. a nasal speech sound, such as English *m, n,* or *ng.* —**nasality** (neɪˈzælɪtɪ) n. —ˈ**nasally** adv.

nasalize or **-lise** ('neɪzᵊˌlaɪz) vb. (tr.) to pronounce nasally. —ˌ**nasaliˈzation** or **-liˈsation** n.

nascent ('næsᵊnt, 'neɪ-) adj. starting to grow or develop; being born. —ˈ**nascence** or ˈ**nascency** n.

naso- combining form. nose: *nasopharynx.*

nasturtium (nəˈstɜːʃəm) n. a plant having round leaves and yellow, red, or orange trumpet-shaped spurred flowers.

nasty ('nɑːstɪ) adj. **-tier, -tiest.** 1. unpleasant or repugnant. 2. dangerous or painful: *a nasty wound.* 3. spiteful or ill-natured. —ˈ**nastily** adv. —ˈ**nastiness** n.

nat. abbrev. for: 1. national. 2. native. 3. natural.

natal ('neɪtᵊl) adj. of or relating to birth.

nation ('neɪʃən) n. 1. an aggregation of people or peoples of one or more cultures, races, etc., organized into a single state: *the Canadian nation.* 2. a community of persons not constituting a state but bound by common descent, language, history, etc. —ˈ**nation,hood** n.

national ('næʃənᵊl) adj. 1. of or relating to a nation as a whole. 2. characteristic of a particular nation: *the national dress of Poland.* ~n. 3. a citizen or subject. 4. a national newspaper. —ˈ**nationally** adv.

national anthem n. a patriotic song adopted by a nation for use on public occasions.

national assistance n. the former name for **supplementary benefit.**

national debt n. the total financial obligations incurred by a nation's central government.

national insurance n. (in Britain) state insurance based on weekly contributions from employees and employers and providing payments to the unemployed, the sick, the retired, etc., as well as medical services.

nationalism ('næʃənəˌlɪzəm) n. 1. a sentiment based on common cultural characteristics that binds a population and often produces a policy of national independence. 2. loyalty to one's country; patriotism. 3. exaggerated or fanatical devotion to a national community. —ˈ**nationalist** n., adj. —ˌ**nationalˈistic** adj.

nationality (ˌnæʃəˈnælɪtɪ) n., pl. **-ties.** 1. the fact of being a citizen of a particular nation. 2. a body of people sharing common descent, history, language, etc.; a nation. 3. a national group: *30 different nationalities are found in this city.* 4. national character. 5. the fact of being a nation; national status.

nationalize or **-lise** ('næʃənəˌlaɪz) vb. (tr.) 1. to put (an industry, resources, etc.) under state control. 2. to make national in character or status. 3. a less common word for **naturalize.** —ˌ**nationaliˈzation** or **-liˈsation** n.

national park n. an area of land controlled by the state in order to preserve its natural beauty, wildlife, etc.

national service n. Chiefly Brit. compulsory military service.

National Trust n. an organization concerned with the preservation of historic buildings and areas of the countryside of great beauty.

nationwide ('neɪʃən,waɪd) adj. covering or available to the whole of a nation; national.

native ('neɪtɪv) adj. 1. relating or belonging to a person by virtue of conditions existing at birth: *a native language.* 2. natural or innate: *native wit.* 3. born in a specified place: *a native Indian.* 4. (when postpositive, foll. by to) originating in: *kangaroos are native to Australia.* 5. relating to the indigenous inhabitants of a country: *the native art of the New Guinea Highlands.* 6. (of metals) found naturally in the elemental form; not chemically combined as in an ore. 7. unadulterated by civilization, artifice, or adornment; natural. 8. Arch. related by birth or race. ~n. 9. (usually foll. by of) a person born in a particular place: *a native of Geneva.* 10. (usually foll. by of) a species of animal or plant originating in a particular place. 11. a member of an indigenous people of a country, esp. a non-White people, as opposed to colonial immigrants. —ˈ**natively** adv. —ˈ**nativeness** n.

nativity (nəˈtɪvɪtɪ) n., pl. **-ties.** birth or origin.

Nativity (nəˈtɪvɪtɪ) n. 1. the birth of Christ. 2. the feast of Christmas as a commemoration of this. 3. a. an artistic representation of the circumstances of the birth of Christ. b. (as modifier): *a nativity play.*

NATO ('neɪtəʊ) n. acronym for North Atlantic Treaty Organization: an international organization established (1949) for purposes of collective security.

NATSOPA (ˌnætˈsəʊpə) n. acronym for National Society of Operative Printers, Graphical and Media Personnel.

natter ('nætə) Chiefly Brit. inf. ~vb. 1. (intr.) to talk idly and at length; chatter. ~n. 2. prolonged idle chatter.

natty ('nætɪ) adj. **-tier, -tiest.** Inf. smart in appearance or dress; spruce; dapper. —ˈ**nattily** adv. —ˈ**nattiness** n.

natural ('nætʃrəl) adj. 1. of, existing in, or produced by nature: *natural science; natural cliffs.* 2. in accordance with human nature. 3. as is normal or to be expected: *the natural course of events.* 4. not acquired; innate: *a natural gift for sport.* 5. being so through innate qualities: *a natural leader.* 6. not supernatural or strange: *natural phenomena.* 7. genuine or spontaneous. 8. lifelike: *she looked more natural without make-up.* 9. not affected by man; wild: *in the natural state this animal is not ferocious.* 10. born out of wedlock. 11. not adopted but rather related by blood: *her natural parents.* 12. *Music.* a. not sharp or flat. b. (postpositive) denoting a note that is neither sharp nor flat. c. (of a key or scale) containing no sharps or flats. 13. based on the principles and findings of human reason rather than on revelation: *natural religion.* ~n. 14. Inf. a person or thing regarded as certain to qualify for success, selection, etc.: *the horse was a natural for first place.* 15. Music. a. an accidental cancelling a previous sharp or flat. Also called (U.S.): **cancel.** Usual symbol: ♮ b. a note affected by this accidental. 16. Obs. an imbecile; idiot. —ˈ**naturally** adv. —ˈ**naturalness** n.

natural gas n. a gaseous mixture, consisting mainly of methane, trapped below ground; used extensively as a fuel.

natural history n. 1. the study of animals and plants

THESAURUS

nastiness 1. defilement, dirtiness, filth, filthiness, foulness, impurity, pollution, squalor, uncleanliness 2. indecency, licentiousness, obscenity, pollution, porn (Inf.), pornography, ribaldry, smuttiness 3. disagreeableness, malice, meanness, offensiveness, spitefulness, unpleasantness

nasty 1. dirty, disagreeable, disgusting, filthy, foul, horrible, loathsome, malodorous, mephitic, nauseating, noisome, objectionable, obnoxious, odious, offensive, polluted, repellent, repugnant, sickening, unappetizing, unpleasant, vile 2. blue, foul, gross, impure, indecent, lascivious, lewd, licentious, obscene, pornographic, ribald, smutty 3. abusive, annoying, bad-tempered, despicable, disagreeable, distasteful, malicious, mean, spiteful, unpleasant, vicious, vile 4. bad, critical, dangerous, painful, serious, severe

nation commonwealth, community, country, people, population, race, realm, society, state, tribe

national adj. 1. civil, countrywide, governmental, nationwide, public, state, widespread 2. domestic, internal, social ~n. 3. citizen, inhabitant, native, resident, subject

nationalism allegiance, chauvinism, fealty, jingoism, loyalty, nationality, patriotism

nationality birth, ethnic group, nation, race

nationwide countrywide, general, national, overall, widespread

native adj. 1. built-in, congenital, endemic, hereditary, inborn, inbred, indigenous, ingrained, inherent, inherited, innate, instinctive, intrinsic, inveterate, natal, natural 2. genuine, original, real 3. domestic, home, home-grown, home-made, indigenous, local, mother, vernacular 4. aboriginal, autochthonous ~n. 5. aborigine, autochthon, citizen, countryman, dweller, inhabitant, national, resident

nativity 1. birth, delivery, parturition 2. crèche, manger scene

natter 1. v. blather, blether, chatter, gabble, gossip, jabber, jaw (Sl.), palaver, prate, prattle, talk, talk idly, witter (Inf.) 2. n. blather, blether, chat, chinwag (Brit. inf.), chitchat, confabulation, conversation, gab (Inf.), gabble, gossip, jabber, jaw (Sl.), palaver, prattle, talk

natty chic, dapper, elegant, fashionable, neat, smart, snazzy (Inf.), spruce, stylish, trim, well-dressed, well-turned-out

natural 1. common, everyday, legitimate, logical, normal, ordinary, regular, typical, usual 2. characteristic, congenital, essential, inborn, indigenous, inherent, innate, instinctive, intuitive, natal, native 3. artless, candid, frank, genuine, ingenuous, open, real, simple, spontaneous, unaffected, unpretentious, unsophisticated, unstudied 4. organic, plain, pure, unbleached, unmixed, unpolished, unrefined, whole

in the wild state. **2.** the sum of these phenomena in a given place or at a given time: *the natural history of Iran.* —**natural historian** *n.*

naturalism ('nætʃrə,lɪzəm) *n.* **1.** a movement, esp. in art and literature, advocating detailed realistic and factual description. **2.** the belief that all religious truth is based not on revelation but rather on the study of natural causes and processes. **3.** *Philosophy.* a scientific account of the world in terms of causes and natural forces. **4.** action or thought caused by natural instincts.

naturalist ('nætʃrəlɪst) *n.* **1.** a person who is versed in or interested in botany or zoology. **2.** a person who advocates or practises naturalism.

naturalistic (,nætʃrə'lɪstɪk) *adj.* **1.** of or reproducing nature in effect or characteristics. **2.** of or characteristic of naturalism. **3.** of naturalists. —,**natural'istically** *adv.*

naturalize *or* **-lise** ('nætʃrə,laɪz) *vb.* **1.** (*tr.*) to give citizenship to (a person of foreign birth). **2.** to be or cause to be adopted in another place, as a word, custom, etc. **3.** (*tr.*) to introduce (a plant or animal from another region) and cause it to adapt to local conditions. **4.** (*intr.*) (of a plant or animal) to adapt successfully to a foreign environment. **5.** (*tr.*) to make natural or more lifelike. —,**naturali'zation** *or* **-li'sation** *n.*

naturally ('nætʃrəlɪ) *adv.* **1.** in a natural way. **2.** instinctively. **3.** of course; surely.

natural number *n.* any of the positive integers 1, 2, 3, 4,...

natural philosophy *n.* physical science, esp. physics. —**natural philosopher** *n.*

natural resources *pl. n.* naturally occurring materials such as coal, fertile land, etc.

natural science *n.* the sciences that are involved in the study of the physical world and its phenomena, including biology, physics, chemistry, and geology.

natural selection *n.* a process resulting in the survival of those individuals from a population of animals or plants that are best adapted to the prevailing environmental conditions.

nature ('neɪtʃə) *n.* **1.** fundamental qualities; identity or essential character. **2.** (*often cap.*) the whole system of the existence, forces, and events of all physical life that are not controlled by man. **3.** plant and animal life, as distinct from man. **4.** a wild primitive state untouched by man. **5.** natural unspoilt countryside. **6.** disposition or temperament. **7.** desires or instincts governing behaviour. **8.** the normal biological needs of the body. **9.** sort; character. **10. against nature.** unnatural or immoral. **11. by nature.** essentially or innately. **12. call of nature.** *Inf.* the need to urinate or defecate. **13. from nature.** using natural models in drawing, painting, etc. **14. in** (*or* **of**) **the nature of.** essentially the same as; by way of.

nature trail *n.* a path through countryside of particular interest to naturalists.

naught (nɔːt) *n.* **1.** *Arch. or literary.* nothing; ruin or failure. **2.** a variant spelling (esp. U.S.) of **nought.** **3. set at naught.** to disregard or scorn; disdain. ~*adv.* **4.** *Arch. or literary.* not at all: *it matters naught.* ~*adj.* **5.** *Obs.* worthless, ruined, or wicked.

naughty ('nɔːtɪ) *adj.* **-tier, -tiest. 1.** (esp. of children) mischievous or disobedient. **2.** mildly indecent; titillating. —'**naughtily** *adv.* —'**naughtiness** *n.*

nausea ('nɔːzɪə, -sɪə) *n.* **1.** the sensation that precedes vomiting. **2.** a feeling of revulsion.

nauseate ('nɔːzɪ,eɪt, -sɪ-) *vb.* **1.** (*tr.*) to arouse feelings of disgust or revulsion in. **2.** to feel or cause to feel sick. —,**nause'ation** *n.*

nauseous ('nɔːzɪəs, -sɪəs) *adj.* **1.** causing nausea. **2.** distasteful; repulsive.

nautical ('nɔːtɪkəl) *adj.* of or involving ships, navigation, or seamen. —'**nautically** *adv.*

nautical mile *n.* Also called: **international nautical mile, air mile.** a unit of length, used esp. in navigation, equal to 1852 metres (6076.103 feet).

nautilus ('nɔːtɪləs) *n., pl.* **-luses** *or* **-li** (-,laɪ). any of a genus of cephalopod molluscs, esp. the pearly nautilus.

naval ('neɪvəl) *adj.* **1.** of, characteristic of, or having a navy. **2.** of or relating to ships; nautical.

nave[1] (neɪv) *n.* the central space in a church, extending from the narthex to the chancel and often flanked by aisles.

nave[2] (neɪv) *n.* the central block or hub of a wheel.

navel ('neɪvəl) *n.* **1.** the scar in the centre of the abdomen, usually forming a slight depression, where the umbilical cord was attached. Technical name: **umbilicus. 2.** a central part or point.

navel orange *n.* a sweet orange that has at its apex a navel-like depression enclosing an underdeveloped secondary fruit.

navigable ('nævɪgəbəl) *adj.* **1.** wide, deep, or safe enough to be sailed through: *a navigable channel.* **2.** capable of being steered: *a navigable raft.* —,**naviga'bility** *n.* —'**navigably** *adv.*

navigate ('nævɪ,geɪt) *vb.* **1.** to direct or plot the path or position of (a ship, an aircraft, etc.). **2.** (*tr.*) to travel over, through, or on in a boat, aircraft, etc. **3.** *Inf.* to direct (oneself) carefully or safely: *he navigated his way to the bar.* **4.** (of a passenger in a motor vehicle) to give directions to the driver; point out the route. —'**navi,gator** *n.*

navigation (,nævɪ'geɪʃən) *n.* **1.** the skill or process of plotting a route and directing a ship, aircraft, etc., along it. **2.** the act or practice of navigating: *dredging made navigation of the river possible.* —,**navi'gational** *adj.*

navvy ('nævɪ) *n., pl.* **-vies.** *Brit. inf.* a labourer on a building site, excavations, etc.

navy ('neɪvɪ) *n., pl.* **-vies. 1.** the warships and auxiliary vessels of a nation or ruler. **2.** (*often cap.*) the branch of a country's armed services comprising such ships, their crews, and all their supporting services. **3.** short for **navy blue. 4.** *Arch. or literary.* a fleet of ships.

navy blue *n.* a dark greyish-blue colour.

nawab (nə'wɑːb) *n.* (formerly) a Muslim ruling prince or powerful landowner in India.

nay (neɪ) **1.** (*sentence substitute*) a word for **no**[1]: archaic or dialectal except in voting by voice. ~*n.* **2.** a person who votes in the negative. ~*adv.* **3.** (*sentence modifier*) *Arch.* an emphatic form of **no**[1].

Nazarene (,næzə'riːn) *n.* **1.** an early name for a **Christian** (Acts 24:5) or (when preceded by *the*) for **Jesus Christ. 2.** a member of one of several groups of Jewish-Christians found principally in Syria. ~*adj.* **3.** of Nazareth in N Israel, or the Nazarenes.

Nazi ('nɑːtsɪ) *n., pl.* **-zis. 1.** a member of the National Socialist German Workers' Party, which seized political

---

THESAURUS

naturalism factualism, realism, verisimilitude

naturalist l. biologist, botanist, ecologist, zoologist 2. factualist, realist

naturalize acclimate, acclimatize, acculturate, accustom, adapt, adopt, domesticate, enfranchise, familiarize, grant citizenship, habituate

naturally l. *adv.* as anticipated, customarily, genuinely, informally, normally, simply, spontaneously, typically, unaffectedly, unpretentiously 2. *interj.* absolutely, as a matter of course, certainly, of course

nature l. attributes, character, complexion, constitution, essence, features, make-up, quality, traits 2. category, description, kind, sort, species, style, type, variety 3. cosmos, creation, earth, environment, universe, world 4. disposition, humour, mood, outlook,

temper, temperament 5. country, countryside, landscape, natural history, scenery

naturist nudist

naughty l. annoying, bad, disobedient, exasperating, fractious, impish, misbehaved, mischievous, perverse, playful, refractory, roguish, sinful, teasing, wayward, wicked, worthless 2. bawdy, blue, improper, lewd, obscene, off-colour, ribald, risqué, smutty, vulgar

nausea l. biliousness, qualm(s), queasiness, retching, sickness, squeamishness, vomiting 2. abhorrence, aversion, disgust, loathing, repugnance, revulsion

nauseate disgust, horrify, offend, repel, repulse, revolt, sicken

nautical marine, maritime, naval, oceanic, seafaring, seagoing, yachting

naval marine, maritime, nautical, oceanic

navel l. bellybutton (*Inf.*), omphalos (*Literary*), umbilicus 2. central point, centre, hub, middle

navigable l. clear, negotiable, passable, traversable, unobstructed 2. controllable, dirigible, sailable, steerable

navigate con (*Nautical*), cross, cruise, direct, drive, guide, handle, journey, manoeuvre, pilot, plan, plot, sail, skipper, steer, voyage

navigation cruising, helmsmanship, pilotage, sailing, seamanship, steering, voyaging

navigator mariner, pilot, seaman

navvy labourer

navy argosy (*Archaic*), armada, fleet, flotilla, warships

control in Germany in 1933 under Adolf Hitler. **2.** *Derog.* anyone who thinks or acts like a Nazi. ~*adj.* **3.** characteristic of or relating to the Nazis. —**Nazism** ('nɑːtsɪzəm) or **Naziism** ('nɑːtsɪːzəm) *n.*

Nb *the chemical symbol for* niobium.

NB, N.B., *or* **n.b.** *abbrev. for* nota bene.

N.B. *abbrev. for* New Brunswick.

N.C.B. *Brit. abbrev. for* National Coal Board.

N.C.O. *abbrev. for* noncommissioned officer.

n.d. *abbrev. for* no date.

Nd *the chemical symbol for* neodymium.

N.D.P. (in Canada) *abbrev. for* New Democratic Party.

N.D.T. *Canad. abbrev. for* Newfoundland Daylight Time.

Ne *the chemical symbol for* neon.

NE *abbrev. for* northeast(ern).

N.E. *abbrev. for* New England.

ne- *combining form.* variant of **neo-,** esp. before a vowel: *Nearctic.*

Neanderthal man (nɪ'ændə,tɑːl) *n.* a type of primitive man occuring throughout much of Europe in late Palaeolithic times.

neap (niːp) *adj.* **1.** of, relating to, or constituting a neap tide. ~*n.* **2.** short for **neap tide.**

Neapolitan (,nɪə'pɒlɪtən) *n.* **1.** a native or inhabitant of Naples. ~*adj.* **2.** of or relating to Naples.

neap tide *n.* either of the tides that occur at the first or last quarter of the moon when the attractions of the sun and moon almost balance and produce the smallest rise in tidal level. Cf. **spring tide** (sense 1).

near (nɪə) *prep.* **1.** at or to a place or time not far away from; close to. ~*adv.* **2.** at or to a place or time not far away; close by. **3.** short for **nearly:** *I was damn near killed.* ~*adj.* **4.** (*postpositive*) at or in a place not far away. **5.** (*prenominal*) only just successful or only just failing: *a near escape.* ~*vb.* **6.** to come or draw close (to). ~*n.* **7.** Also called: **nearside. a.** the left side of a horse, vehicle, etc. **b.** (*as modifier*): *the near foreleg.* —**'nearness** *n.*

nearby *adj.* ('nɪə,baɪ), *adv.* (,nɪə'baɪ) not far away; close at hand.

nearly ('nɪəlɪ) *adv.* **1.** almost. **2. not nearly.** nowhere near: *not nearly enough.* **3.** closely: *the person most nearly concerned.*

nearside ('nɪə,saɪd) *n.* **1.** (usually preceded by *the*) *Chiefly Brit.* **a.** the side of a vehicle, etc., nearer the kerb. **b.** (*as modifier*): *the nearside door.* **2. a.** the left side of an animal, etc. **b.** (*as modifier*): *the nearside flank.*

near-sighted (,nɪə'saɪtɪd) *adj.* relating to or suffering from myopia. —**,near-'sightedly** *adv.*

neat (niːt) *adj.* **1.** clean, tidy, and orderly. **2.** liking or insisting on order and cleanliness. **3.** smoothly or competently done; efficient: *a neat job.* **4.** pat or slick: *his excuse was suspiciously neat.* **5.** (of alcoholic drinks,

etc.) undiluted. **6.** (of language) concise and well-phrased. **7.** *Sl., chiefly U.S.* pleasing; admirable; excellent. —**'neatly** *adv.* —**'neatness** *n.*

neaten ('niːtən) *vb.* (*tr.*) to make neat; tidy.

neath *or* **'neath** (niːθ) *prep. Arch.* short for **beneath.**

N.E.B. *abbrev. for:* **1.** New English Bible. **2.** National Enterprise Board.

nebula ('nɛbjʊlə) *n., pl.* **-lae** (-,liː) *or* **-las.** **1.** *Astron.* a diffuse cloud of particles and gases visible either as a hazy patch of light or an irregular dark region. **2.** *Pathol.* opacity of the cornea. —**'nebular** *adj.*

nebulous ('nɛbjʊləs) *adj.* **1.** lacking definite form, shape, or content; vague or amorphous. **2.** of stars. **3.** *Rare.* misty or hazy. —**'nebulousness** *n.* —,**nebu'losity** *n.*

necessaries ('nɛsɪsərɪz) *pl. n.* (*sometimes sing.*) what is needed, esp. money or provisions.

necessarily ('nɛsɪsərɪlɪ, ,nɛsɪ'sɛrɪlɪ) *adv.* **1.** as an inevitable or natural consequence. **2.** as a certainty: *he won't necessarily come.*

necessary ('nɛsɪsərɪ) *adj.* **1.** needed to achieve a certain desired result; required. **2.** inevitable: *the necessary consequences of your action.* **3.** *Logic.* **a.** (of a proposition) true or false by the meaning of the words, so that a denial would be a contradiction. **b.** (of a condition) required to be fulfilled to assure the truth of a proposition, etc. Cf. **sufficient** (sense 2). **4.** *Rare.* compelled, as by necessity or law; not free.

necessitarianism (nɪ,sɛsɪ'tɛərɪə,nɪzəm) *n. Philosophy.* the belief that human actions and choices are causally determined and cannot be willed. —**ne,cessi'tarian** *n., adj.*

necessitate (nɪ'sɛsɪ,teɪt) *vb.* (*tr.*) **1.** to cause as an unavoidable result. **2.** (*usually passive*) to compel or require (someone to do something).

necessitous (nɪ'sɛsɪtəs) *adj.* very needy; destitute; poverty-stricken.

necessity (nɪ'sɛsɪtɪ) *n., pl.* **-ties.** **1.** (*sometimes pl.*) something needed; prerequisite: *necessities of life.* **2.** a condition or set of circumstances that inevitably requires a certain result: *it is a matter of necessity to wear formal clothes when meeting the Queen.* **3.** the state or quality of being obligatory or unavoidable. **4.** urgent requirement, as in an emergency. **5.** poverty or want. **6.** *Rare.* compulsion through laws of nature; fate. **7. of necessity.** inevitably.

neck (nɛk) *n.* **1.** the part of an organism connecting the head with the body. **2.** the part of a garment around the neck. **3.** something resembling a neck in shape or position: *the neck of a bottle.* **4.** *Anat.* a constricted portion of an organ or part. **5.** a narrow strip of land; peninsula or isthmus. **6.** a strait or channel. **7.** the part of a violin, cello, etc., that extends from the body to the tuning pegs and supports the fingerboard. **8.** a solid block of lava from an extinct volcano, exposed after erosion of the

THESAURUS

near *adj.* **1.** adjacent, adjoining, alongside, at close quarters, beside, bordering, close, close by, contiguous, nearby, neighbouring, nigh, touching **2.** approaching, forthcoming, imminent, impending, in the offing, looming, near-at-hand, next, on the cards (*Inf.*) **3.** akin, allied, attached, connected, dear, familiar, intimate, related **4.** *Inf.* close-fisted, mean, miserly, niggardly, parsimonious, stingy, tightfisted, ungenerous

nearby 1. *adj.* adjacent, adjoining, convenient, handy, neighbouring **2.** *adv.* at close quarters, close at hand, not far away, within reach

nearly *adv.* about, all but, almost, approaching, approximately, as good as, closely, just about, not quite, practically, roughly, virtually, well-nigh

nearness 1. accessibility, availability, closeness, contiguity, handiness, juxtaposition, propinquity, proximity, vicinity **2.** immediacy, imminence **3.** dearness, familiarity, intimacy **4.** *Inf.* meanness, niggardliness, parsimony, stinginess

near-sighted myopic, short-sighted

near thing close shave (*Inf.*), narrow escape, near miss

neat 1. accurate, dainty, fastidious, methodical, nice, orderly, shipshape, smart, spick-and-span, spruce, straight, systematic, tidy, trim, uncluttered **2.** adept, adroit, agile, apt, clever, deft, dexterous, efficient, effortless, elegant, expert, graceful, handy, nimble, practised, precise, skilful, stylish, well-judged **3.** *Of alcoholic drinks* pure, straight, undiluted, unmixed

neatly 1. accurately, daintily, fastidiously, methodically, nicely, smartly, sprucely, systematically, tidily **2.** adeptly, adroitly, agilely, aptly, cleverly, deftly, dexterously, efficiently, effortlessly, elegantly, expertly, gracefully, handily, nimbly, precisely, skilfully, stylishly

neatness 1. accuracy, daintiness, fastidiousness, methodicalness, niceness, nicety, orderliness, smartness, spruceness, straightness, tidiness, trimness **2.** adeptness, adroitness, agility, aptness, cleverness, deftness, dexterity, efficiency, effortlessness, elegance, expertness, grace, gracefulness, handiness, nimbleness, preciseness, precision, skilfulness, skill, style, stylishness

nebulous ambiguous, amorphous, cloudy, confused, dim, hazy, imprecise, indefinite, indeterminate, indistinct, misty, murky, obscure, shadowy, shapeless, uncertain, unclear, unformed, vague

necessarily accordingly, automatically, axiomatically, by definition, certainly, compulsorily, consequently, incontrovertibly, ineluctably, inevitably, inexorably, irresistibly, naturally, *nolens volens*, of course, of necessity, perforce, undoubtedly, willy-nilly

necessary 1. compulsory, *de rigueur*, essential, imperative, indispensable, mandatory, needed, needful, obligatory, required, requisite, vital **2.** certain, fated, inescapable, inevitable, inexorable, unavoidable

necessitate call for, coerce, compel, constrain, demand, force, impel, make necessary, oblige, require

necessities essentials, fundamentals, indispensables

necessity 1. demand, exigency, indispensability, need, needfulness, requirement **2.** desideratum, essential, fundamental, necessary, need, prerequisite, requirement, requisite, *sine qua non*, want **3.** destitution, extremity, indigence, need, penury, poverty, privation **4.** compulsion, destiny, fate, inevitability, inexorableness, obligation

surrounding rock. **9.** the length of a horse's head and neck taken as an approximate distance by which one horse beats another in a race: *to win by a neck.* **10.** *Archit.* the narrow band at the top of the shaft of a column. **11.** *Sl.* impudence or cheek. **12. get it in the neck.** *Inf.* to be reprimanded or punished severely. **13. neck and neck.** absolutely level in a race or competition. **14. neck of the woods.** *Inf.* area: *a quiet neck of the woods.* **15. neck or nothing.** at any cost. **16. save one's** *or* **someone's neck.** *Inf.* to escape from or help someone else to escape from a difficult or dangerous situation. **17. stick one's neck out.** *Inf.* to risk criticism, ridicule, etc., by speaking one's mind. ~*vb.* **18.** (*intr.*) *Inf.* to kiss or fondle (someone or one another) passionately. —'**necker** *n.*

neckband ('nɛk,bænd) *n.* a band around the neck of a garment as finishing, decoration, or a base for a collar.

neckcloth ('nɛk,klɒθ) *n.* a large ornamental usually white cravat worn formerly by men.

neckerchief ('nɛkətʃɪf, -,tʃiːf) *n.* a piece of ornamental cloth, often square, worn round the neck.

necklace ('nɛklɪs) *n.* a chain, band, or cord, often bearing beads, pearls, jewels, etc., worn around the neck as an ornament, esp. by women.

neckline ('nɛk,laɪn) *n.* the shape or position of the upper edge of a dress, blouse, etc.

necktie ('nɛk,taɪ) *n.* the U.S. name for **tie** (sense 10).

neckwear ('nɛk,wɛə) *n.* articles of clothing, such as ties, scarves, etc., worn round the neck.

necro- *or before a vowel* **necr-** *combining form.* indicating death, a dead body, or dead tissue: *necrosis.*

necromancy ('nɛkrəʊ,mænsɪ) *n.* **1.** the art of supposedly conjuring up the dead, esp. in order to obtain from them knowledge of the future. **2.** black magic; sorcery. —'**necro,mancer** *n.* —,**necro'mantic** *adj.*

necrophilia (,nɛkrəʊ'fɪlɪə) *n.* sexual attraction for or sexual intercourse with dead bodies. Also called: **necromania, necrophilism.** —**necrophile** ('nɛkrəʊ,faɪl) *n.* —,**necro'philic** *adj.*

necropolis (nɛ'krɒpəlɪs) *n., pl.* **-lises** *or* **-leis** (-,leɪs). a burial site or cemetery.

necropsy ('nɛkrɒpsɪ) *or* **necroscopy** (nɛ'krɒskəpɪ) *n., pl.* **-sies** *or* **-pies.** another name for **autopsy.**

necrosis (nɛ'krəʊsɪs) *n.* **1.** the death of one or more cells in the body, usually within a localized area, as from an interruption of the blood supply. **2.** death of plant tissue due to disease, frost, etc. —**necrotic** (nɛ'krɒtɪk) *adj.*

nectar ('nɛktə) *n.* **1.** a sugary fluid produced in the nectaries of flowers and collected by bees. **2.** *Classical myth.* the drink of the gods. Cf. **ambrosia** (sense 1). **3.** any delicious drink. —'**nectarous** *adj.*

nectarine ('nɛktərɪn) *n.* **1.** a variety of peach tree. **2.** the fruit of this tree, which has a smooth skin.

N.E.D.C. *abbrev. for* National Economic Development Council. Also: (inf.) **Neddy** ('nɛdɪ).

neddy ('nɛdɪ) *n., pl.* **-dies.** a child's word for a **donkey** (sense 1).

née *or* **nee** (neɪ) *adj.* indicating the maiden name of a married woman: *Mrs. Bloggs née Blandish.*

need (niːd) *vb.* **1.** to be in want of: *to need money.* **2.** (*tr.*) to be obliged: *to need to do more work.* **3.** (takes an infinitive without *to*) used as an auxiliary to express necessity or obligation and does not add *-s* when used with he, she, it, and singular nouns: *need he go?* **4.** (*intr.*) *Arch.* to be essential to: *there needs no reason for this.* ~*n.* **5.** the fact or an instance of feeling the lack of something: *he has need of a new coat.* **6.** a requirement: *the need for vengeance.* **7.** necessity or obligation: *no need to be frightened.* **8.** distress: *a friend in need.* **9.** poverty or destitution.

needful ('niːdfʊl) *adj.* **1.** necessary; required. **2.** *Arch.* poverty-stricken. ~*n.* **3. the needful.** what is necessary, esp. money. —'**needfulness** *n.*

needle ('niːdəl) *n.* **1.** a pointed slender piece of metal with a hole in it through which thread is passed for sewing. **2.** a somewhat larger rod with a point at one end, used in knitting. **3.** a similar instrument with a hook at one end for crocheting. **4.** another name for **stylus** (sense 3). **b.** a small thin pointed device used to transmit the vibrations from a gramophone record to the pickup. **5.** *Med.* the long hollow pointed part of a hypodermic syringe, which is inserted into the body. **6.** *Surgery.* a pointed instrument, often curved, for suturing, puncturing, or ligating. **7.** a long narrow stiff leaf in which water loss is greatly reduced: *pine needles.* **8.** any slender sharp spine. **9.** a pointer on the scale of a measuring instrument. **10.** short for **magnetic needle.** **11.** a sharp pointed instrument used in engraving. **12.** anything long and pointed, such as an obelisk. **13.** *Inf.* **a.** anger or intense rivalry, esp. in a sporting encounter. **b.** (*as modifier*): *a needle match.* **14. have** *or* **get the needle (to).** *Brit. sl.* to feel dislike, nervousness, or annoyance (for): *she got the needle after he had refused her invitation.* ~*vb.* **15.** (*tr.*) *Inf.* to goad or provoke, as by constant criticism. **16.** (*tr.*) to sew, embroider, or prick (fabric) with a needle.

needlecord ('niːdəl,kɔːd) *n.* a corduroy fabric with narrow ribs.

needlepoint ('niːdəl,pɔɪnt) *n.* embroidery done on canvas with various stitches so as to resemble tapestry.

needless ('niːdlɪs) *adj.* not required; unnecessary. —'**needlessly** *adv.* —'**needlessness** *n.*

needle time *n. Chiefly Brit.* the limited time allocated by a radio channel to the broadcasting of music from records.

needlewoman ('niːdəl,wʊmən) *n., pl.* **-women.** a woman who does needlework; seamstress.

needlework ('niːdəl,wɜːk) *n.* sewing and embroidery.

needs (niːdz) *adv.* (preceded or foll. by *must*) of necessity: *we must needs go.*

needy ('niːdɪ) *adj.* **needier, neediest. a.** in need; poverty-stricken. **b.** (*as n.*): *the needy.*

ne'er (nɛə) *adv.* a poetic contraction of **never.**

ne'er-do-well *n.* **1.** an improvident, irresponsible, or lazy person. ~*adj.* **2.** useless; worthless: *your ne'er-do-well schemes.*

nefarious (nɪ'fɛərɪəs) *adj.* evil; wicked; sinful. —**ne'fariously** *adv.* —**ne'fariousness** *n.*

neg. *abbrev. for* negative(ly).

negate (nɪ'geɪt) *vb.* (*tr.*) **1.** to nullify; invalidate. **2.** to contradict. —**ne'gator** *or* **ne'gater** *n.*

negation (nɪ'geɪʃən) *n.* **1.** the opposite or absence of something. **2.** a negative thing or condition. **3.** the act of negating. **4.** *Logic.* a proposition that is the denial of another proposition and is true only if the original propo-

---

THESAURUS

necromancy black art, black magic, demonology, divination, enchantment, magic, sorcery, thaumaturgy (*Rare*), voodoo, witchcraft, witchery, wizardry

necropolis burial ground, cemetery, churchyard, God's acre, graveyard

need *v.* **1.** call for, demand, have occasion to *or* for, lack, miss, necessitate, require, want ~*n.* **2.** longing, requisite, want, wish **3.** deprivation, destitution, distress, extremity, impecuniousness, inadequacy, indigence, insufficiency, lack, neediness, paucity, penury, poverty, privation, shortage **4.** emergency, exigency, necessity, obligation, urgency, want **5.** demand, desideratum, essential, requirement, requisite

needed called for, desired, lacked, necessary, required, wanted

needful essential, indispensable, necessary, needed, required, requisite, stipulated, vital

needle *v.* aggravate (*Inf.*), annoy, bait, goad, harass, irk, irritate, nag, nettle, pester, prick, prod, provoke, rile, ruffle, spur, sting, taunt

needless causeless, dispensable, excessive, expendable, gratuitous, groundless, nonessential, pointless, redundant, superfluous, uncalled-for, undesired, unnecessary, unwanted, useless

needlework embroidery, fancywork, needlecraft, sewing, stitching, tailoring

needy deprived, destitute, disadvantaged, impecunious, impoverished, indigent, on the breadline (*Inf.*), penniless, poor, poverty-stricken, underprivileged

nefarious abominable, atrocious, base, criminal, depraved, detestable, dreadful, evil, execrable, foul, heinous, horrible, infamous, infernal, iniquitous, monstrous, odious, opprobrious, shameful, sinful, vicious, vile, villainous, wicked

negate **1.** abrogate, annul, cancel, countermand, invalidate, neutralize, nullify, repeal, rescind, retract, reverse, revoke, void, wipe out **2.** contradict, deny, disallow, disprove, gainsay, oppose, refute

negation **1.** antithesis, antonym, contradiction, contrary, converse, counterpart, denial, disavowal, disclaimer, inverse, opposite, rejection, renunciation, reverse **2.** opposition, proscription, refusal, repudiation, veto **3.** cancellation, neutralization, nullification **4.** blank, nonexistence, nothingness, nullity, vacuity, void

sition is false. **5.** *Computers.* another name for **inversion.**

negative ('nɛgətɪv) *adj.* **1.** expressing a refusal or denial: *a negative answer.* **2.** lacking positive qualities, such as enthusiasm or optimism. **3.** showing opposition or resistance. **4.** measured in a direction opposite to that regarded as positive. **5.** *Biol.* indicating movement or growth away from a stimulus: *negative geotropism.* **6.** *Med.* indicating absence of the disease or condition for which a test was made. **7.** another word for **minus** (senses 3b, 4). **8.** *Physics.* **a.** (of an electric charge) having the same polarity as the charge of an electron. **b.** (of a body, system, ion, etc.) having a negative electric charge; having an excess of electrons. **9.** short for **electronegative.** **10.** of or relating to a photographic negative. **11.** *Logic.* (of a proposition) denying the truth of the predicate. ~*n.* **12.** a statement or act of denial or refusal. **13.** a negative thing. **14.** *Photog.* a piece of photographic film or a plate, previously exposed and developed, showing an image that, in black-and-white photography, has a reversal of tones. **15.** *Physics.* a negative object, such as a terminal or a plate in a voltaic cell. **16.** a sentence or other linguistic element with a negative meaning, as the English word *not.* **17.** a quantity less than zero. **18.** *Logic.* a proposition that denies the truth of the predicate. **19. in the negative.** indicating denial or refusal. ~*vb.* (*tr.*) **20.** to deny; negate. **21.** to show to be false; disprove. **22.** to refuse consent to or approval of: *the proposal was negatived.* —**'negatively** *adv.* —**'negativeness** *or* ,**nega'tivity** *n.*

negativism ('nɛgətɪv,ɪzəm) *n.* **1.** a tendency to be unconstructively critical. **2.** any sceptical or derisive system of thought. —**'negativist** *n., adj.*

neglect (nɪ'glɛkt) *vb.* (*tr.*) **1.** to fail to give due care, attention, or time to: *to neglect a child.* **2.** to fail (to do something) through carelessness: *he neglected to tell her.* **3.** to disregard. ~*n.* **4.** lack of due care or attention; negligence: *the child starved through neglect.* **5.** the act or an instance of neglecting or the state of being neglected.

neglectful (nɪ'glɛktful) *adj.* (when *postpositive,* foll. by *of*) careless; heedless.

negligee, negligée, *or* **negligé** ('nɛglɪ,ʒeɪ) *n.* **1.** a woman's light dressing gown, esp. one that is lace-trimmed. **2.** any informal attire.

negligent ('nɛglɪdʒənt) *adj.* **1.** lacking attention, care, or concern; neglectful. **2.** careless or nonchalant. —**'negligence** *n.* —**'negligently** *adv.*

negligible ('nɛglɪdʒəbəl) *adj.* so small, unimportant, etc., as to be not worth considering. —**'negligibly** *adv.*

negotiable (nɪ'gəʊʃəbəl) *adj.* **1.** able to be negotiated. **2.** (of a bill of exchange, promissory note, etc.) legally transferable in title from one party to another. —**ne,gotia'bility** *n.*

negotiate (nɪ'gəʊʃɪ,eɪt) *vb.* **1.** to talk (with others) to achieve (an agreement, etc.). **2.** (*tr.*) to succeed in passing round or over. **3.** (*tr.*) *Finance.* **a.** to transfer (a negotiable commercial paper) by endorsement to another in return for value received. **b.** to sell (financial assets). **c.** to arrange for (a loan). —**ne,goti'ation** *n.* —**ne'goti,ator** *n.*

Negress ('niːgrɪs) *n.* a female Negro.

Negrillo (nɪ'grɪləʊ) *n., pl.*-**los** *or* -**loes.** a member of a dwarfish Negro race of central and southern Africa.

negritude ('niːgrɪ,tjuːd, 'nɛg-) *n.* **1.** the fact of being a Negro. **2.** awareness and cultivation of the Negro heritage, values, and culture.

Negro ('niːgrəʊ) *n., pl.* -**groes.** **1.** a member of any of the dark-skinned indigenous peoples of Africa and their descendants elsewhere. ~*adj.* **2.** relating to or characteristic of Negroes. —**'Negroism** *n.*

Negroid ('niːgrɔɪd) *adj.* **1.** denoting, relating to, or belonging to one of the major racial groups of mankind, characterized by brown-black skin, crisp or woolly hair, a broad flat nose, and full lips. ~*n.* **2.** a member of this racial group.

negus ('niːgəs) *n., pl.* -**guses.** a hot drink of port and lemon juice, usually spiced and sweetened.

neigh (neɪ) *n.* **1.** the high-pitched cry of a horse. ~*vb.* **2.** to make or utter with a sound like a neigh.

neighbour *or U.S.* **neighbor** ('neɪbə) *n.* **1.** a person who lives near or next to another. **2. a.** a person or thing near or next to another. **b.** (*as modifier*): *neighbour states.* ~*vb.* **3.** (when *intr.,* often foll. by *on*) to be or live close to. —**'neighbouring** *adj.*

neighbourhood *or U.S.* **neighborhood** ('neɪbə,hʊd) *n.* **1.** the immediate environment; surroundings. **2.** a district where people live. **3.** the people in a particular area. **4. in the neighbourhood of.** approximately. **5.** *Maths.* the set of all points whose distance from a given point is less than a specified value. **6.** (*modifier*) living or situated in and serving the needs of a local area: *a neighbourhood community worker.*

neighbourly *or U.S.* **neighborly** ('neɪbəlɪ) *adj.* kind, friendly, or sociable, as befits a neighbour. —**'neighbourliness** *or U.S.* **'neighborliness** *n.*

neither ('naɪðə, 'niːðə) *determiner.* **1. a.** not one nor the other (of two). **b.** (*as pronoun*): *neither can win.* ~*conj.* **2.** (*coordinating*) **a.** (used preceding alternatives joined by *nor*) not: *neither John nor Mary nor Joe went.* **b.** another word for **nor** (sense 2). ~*adv.* (*sentence modifier*) **3.** *Not standard.* another word for **either** (sense 4).

▷ **Usage.** A verb following a compound subject that uses *neither...(nor)* should be in the singular if both subjects are in the singular: *neither Jack nor John has done the work.* Where the subjects are different in number, the verb usually agrees with the subject nearest to it: *neither they nor Jack was able to come.* It may be considered preferable to rephrase the sentence in order to avoid this construction.

nelson ('nɛlsən) *n.* any wrestling hold in which a wrestler places his arm or arms under his opponent's arm or arms from behind and exerts pressure with his palms on the back of his opponent's neck.

nematode ('nɛmə,təʊd) *n.* any of a class of unsegmented worms having a tough outer cuticle, including the hookworm and filaria. Also called: **nematode worm, roundworm.**

Nemesis ('nɛmɪsɪs) *n., pl.* -**ses** (-,siːz). **1.** *Greek myth.* the goddess of retribution and vengeance. **2.** (*sometimes not cap.*) any agency of retribution and vengeance.

THESAURUS

negative *adj.* **1.** contradictory, contrary, denying, dissenting, opposing, recusant, refusing, rejecting, resisting **2.** annulling, counteractive, invalidating, neutralizing, nullifying **3.** antagonistic, colourless, contrary, cynical, gloomy, jaundiced, neutral, pessimistic, uncooperative, unenthusiastic, uninterested, unwilling, weak ~*n.* **4.** contradiction, denial, refusal

negativeness, negativity 1. contradiction, contradictoriness, contrariness, denial, dissent, opposition, recusancy, refusal, rejection, resistance **2.** antagonism, colourlessness, contrariness, cynicism, gloom, neutrality, pessimism, uncooperativeness, uninterestedness, unwillingness, weakness

neglect *v.* **1.** contemn, disdain, disregard, ignore, leave alone, overlook, pass by, rebuff, scorn, slight, spurn **2.** be remiss, evade, forget, let slide, omit, pass over, procrastinate, shirk, skimp ~*n.* **3.** disdain, disregard, disre-

spect, heedlessness, inattention, indifference, slight, unconcern **4.** carelessness, default, dereliction, failure, forgetfulness, laxity, laxness, neglectfulness, negligence, oversight, remissness, slackness, slovenliness

neglected 1. abandoned, derelict, overgrown **2.** disregarded, unappreciated, underestimated, undervalued

negligence carelessness, default, dereliction, disregard, failure, forgetfulness, heedlessness, inadvertence, inattention, inattentiveness, indifference, laxity, laxness, neglect, omission, oversight, remissness, shortcoming, slackness, thoughtlessness

negligent careless, cursory, disregardful, forgetful, heedless, inadvertent, inattentive, indifferent, neglectful, nonchalant, offhand, regardless, remiss, slack, thoughtless, unmindful, unthinking

negligible imperceptible, inconsequential, insignificant, minor, minute, petty, small, trifling, trivial, unimportant

negotiable debatable, discussable, discussible, transactional, transferable, variable

negotiate 1. adjudicate, arbitrate, arrange, bargain, conciliate, confer, consult, contract, deal, debate, discuss, handle, manage, mediate, parley, settle, transact, work out **2.** clear, cross, get over, get past, get round, pass, pass through, surmount

negotiation arbitration, bargaining, debate, diplomacy, discussion, mediation, transaction

neighbourhood community, confines, district, environs, locale, locality, precincts, proximity, purlieus, quarter, region, surroundings, vicinity

neighbouring abutting, adjacent, adjoining, bordering, connecting, contiguous, near, nearby, nearest, next, surrounding

neo- *or sometimes before a vowel* **ne-** *combining form.* **1.** (*sometimes cap.*) new, recent, or a modern form: *neoclassicism.* **2.** (*usually cap.*) the most recent subdivision of a geological period: *Neogene.*

neoclassicism (ˌniːəʊˈklæsɪˌsɪzəm) *n.* **1.** a late 18th- and early 19th-century style in architecture and art, based on classical models. **2.** *Music.* a movement of the 1920s that sought to avoid the emotionalism of late romantic music. —**neoclassical** (ˌniːəʊˈklæsɪkəl) *or* ˌneoˈclassic *adj.*

neodymium (ˌniːəʊˈdɪmɪəm) *n.* a toxic silvery-white metallic element of the lanthanide series. Symbol: Nd; atomic no.: 60; atomic wt.: 144.24.

Neolithic (ˌniːəˈlɪθɪk) *n.* **1.** the cultural period that was characterized by primitive farming and the use of polished stone and flint tools and weapons. *~adj.* **2.** relating to this period.

neologism (nɪˈbləˌdʒɪzəm) *or* **neology** *n., pl.* **-gisms** *or* **-gies.** **1.** a newly coined word, or a phrase or familiar word used in a new sense. **2.** the practice of using or introducing neologisms. —**neˈologist** *n.*

neon (ˈniːɒn) *n.* **1.** a colourless odourless rare gaseous element occurring in trace amounts in the atmosphere: used in illuminated signs and lights. Symbol: Ne; atomic no.: 10; atomic wt.: 20.179. **2.** (*modifier*) of or illuminated by neon: *neon sign.*

neon lamp *n.* a glass bulb or tube containing neon at low pressure that gives a pink or red glow when a voltage is applied.

neophyte (ˈniːəʊˌfaɪt) *n.* **1.** a person newly converted to a religious faith. **2.** a novice in a religious order. **3.** a beginner.

Nepali (nɪˈpɔːlɪ) *or* **Nepalese** (ˌnɛpəˈliːz) *n.* **1.** the official language of Nepal, also spoken in parts of India. **2.** a native or inhabitant of Nepal. *~adj.* **3.** of or relating to Nepal, its inhabitants, or their language.

nephew (ˈnɛvjuː, ˈnɛf-) *n.* a son of one's sister or brother.

nephritis (nɪˈfraɪtɪs) *n.* inflammation of a kidney.

nephro- *or before a vowel* **nephr-** *combining form.* kidney or kidneys: *nephritis.*

ne plus ultra *Latin.* (ˈneɪ ˈpluːs ˈʊltrɑː) *n.* the extreme or perfect point or state.

nepotism (ˈnɛpəˌtɪzəm) *n.* favouritism shown to relatives or close friends by those with power. —**ˈnepotist** *n.*

Neptune[1] (ˈnɛptjuːn) *n.* the Roman god of the sea. Greek counterpart: **Poseidon.**

Neptune[2] (ˈnɛptjuːn) *n.* the eighth planet from the sun, having two satellites, Triton and Nereid.

neptunium (nɛpˈtjuːnɪəm) *n.* a silvery metallic element synthesized in the production of plutonium and occurring in trace amounts in uranium ores. Symbol: Np; atomic no.: 93; half-life of most stable isotope, ^{237}Np: 2.14 × 10^{6} years.

N.E.R.C. *abbrev. for* Natural Environment Research Council.

nervate (ˈnɜːveɪt) *adj.* (of leaves) having veins.

nerve (nɜːv) *n.* **1.** any of the cordlike bundles of fibres that conduct impulses between the brain or spinal cord and another part of the body. **2.** bravery or steadfastness. **3. lose one's nerve.** to become timid, esp. failing to perform some audacious act. **4.** *Inf.* effrontery; impudence. **5.** muscle or sinew (often in **strain every nerve**). **6.** a vein in a leaf or an insect's wing. *~vb.* (*tr.*) **7.** to give courage to (oneself); steel (oneself). **8.** to provide with nerve or nerves.

nerve cell *n.* another name for **neuron.**

nerve centre *n.* **1.** a group of nerve cells associated with a specific function. **2.** a principal source of control over any complex activity.

nerve gas *n.* any of various poisonous gases that have a paralysing effect on the central nervous system that can be fatal.

nerveless (ˈnɜːvlɪs) *adj.* **1.** calm and collected. **2.** listless or feeble. —**ˈnervelessly** *adv.*

nerve-racking *or* **nerve-wracking** *adj.* very distressing, exhausting, or harrowing.

nerves (nɜːvz) *pl. n. Inf.* **1.** the imagined source of emotional control: *my nerves won't stand it.* **2.** anxiety, tension, or imbalance: *she's all nerves.* **3. get on one's nerves.** to irritate or upset one.

nervous (ˈnɜːvəs) *adj.* **1.** very excitable or sensitive; highly strung. **2.** (often foll. by *of*) apprehensive or worried. **3.** of or containing nerves: *nervous tissue.* **4.** affecting the nerves or nervous tissue: *a nervous disease.* **5.** *Arch.* vigorous or forceful. —**ˈnervously** *adv.* —**ˈnervousness** *n.*

nervous breakdown *n.* (*not in technical use*) a psychiatric illness characterized by irritability, depression, fatigue, insomnia, and nonspecific or ill-defined physical complaints.

nervous system *n.* the sensory and control apparatus of animals, consisting of a network of nerve cells (see **neuron**).

nervy (ˈnɜːvɪ) *adj.* **nervier, nerviest.** **1.** *Brit. inf.* tense or apprehensive. **2.** having or needing bravery or endurance. **3.** *U.S. inf.* brash or cheeky. **4.** *Arch.* muscular; sinewy.

ness (nɛs) *n. Arch.* a promontory or headland.

-ness *suffix forming nouns chiefly from adjectives and participles.* indicating state, condition, or quality: *greatness; selfishness.*

nest (nɛst) *n.* **1.** a place or structure in which birds, fishes, etc., lay eggs or give birth to young. **2.** a number of animals of the same species occupying a common habitat: *an ants' nest.* **3.** a place fostering something undesirable: *a nest of thievery.* **4.** a cosy or secluded place. **5.** a set of things, usually of graduated sizes, designed to fit together: *a nest of tables.* *~vb.* **6.** (*intr.*) to make or inhabit a nest. **7.** (*intr.*) to hunt for birds' nests. **8.** (*tr.*) to place in a nest. **9.** *Computers.* to position data within other data at different ranks or levels so that the different levels of data can be used or accessed recursively. —**ˈnest‚like** *adj.*

nest egg *n.* **1.** a fund of money kept in reserve; savings. **2.** a natural or artificial egg left in a nest to induce hens to lay their eggs in it.

nestle (ˈnɛsəl) *vb.* **1.** (*intr.*; often foll. by *up* or *down*) to snuggle, settle, or cuddle closely. **2.** (*intr.*) to be in a sheltered position; lie snugly. **3.** (*tr.*) to shelter or place snugly or partly concealed, as in a nest.

nestling (ˈnɛstlɪŋ, ˈnɛslɪŋ) *n.* **a.** a young bird not yet fledged. **b.** (*as modifier*): *a nestling thrush.*

net[1] (nɛt) *n.* **1.** an openwork fabric of string, wire, etc.; mesh. **2.** a device made of net, used to protect or enclose things or to trap animals. **3.** a thin light mesh fabric used for curtains, etc. **4.** a plan, strategy, etc., intended to trap or ensnare: *the murderer slipped through the police net.* **5.** *Tennis, badminton, etc.* **a.** a strip of net that divides the playing area into two equal parts. **b.** a shot that hits the net. **6.** the goal in soccer, hockey, etc. **7.** (often pl.) *Cricket.* **a.** a pitch surrounded by netting, used for practice. **b.** a practice session in a net. **8.** another word for **network** (sense 2). *~vb.* **netting, netted.** **9.** (*tr.*) to ensnare. **10.** (*tr.*) to shelter or surround with a net. **11.** (*intr.*) *Tennis, badminton, etc.* to hit a shot into the net. **12.** to make a net out of (rope, string, etc.).

net[2] *or* **nett** (nɛt) *adj.* **1.** remaining after all deductions,

---

THESAURUS

nerve *n.* **1.** bottle (*Brit. sl.*), bravery, coolness, courage, daring, determination, endurance, energy, fearlessness, firmness, force, fortitude, gameness, grit (*Inf.*), guts (*Inf.*), hardihood, intrepidity, mettle, might, pluck, resolution, spirit, spunk (*Inf.*), steadfastness, vigour, will **2.** *Inf.* audacity, boldness, brass (*Inf.*), brazenness, cheek (*Inf.*), effrontery, gall, impertinence, impudence, insolence, sauce (*Inf.*), temerity *~v.* **3.** brace, embolden, encourage, fortify, hearten, invigorate, steel, strengthen

nerve-racking annoying, difficult, distressing, frightening, harassing, harrowing, maddening, stressful, tense, trying, worrying

nerves anxiety, fretfulness, imbalance, nervousness, strain, stress, tension

nervous agitated, anxious, apprehensive, edgy, excitable, fearful, fidgety, flustered, hesitant, highly strung, hysterical, jittery (*Inf.*), jumpy, nervy (*Inf.*), neurotic, on edge, ruffled, shaky, tense, timid, timorous, uneasy, uptight (*Inf.*), weak, worried

nervous breakdown breakdown, collapse, crack-up (*Inf.*), nervous disorder, neurasthenia (*Obsolete*)

nervousness agitation, anxiety, disquiet, excitability, fluster, perturbation, tension, timidity, touchiness, tremulousness, worry

nest **1.** den, haunt, hideaway, refuge, resort, retreat, snuggery **2.** breeding-ground, den, hotbed

nest egg cache, deposit, fund(s), reserve, savings, store

nestle cuddle, curl up, huddle, nuzzle, snuggle

nestling **1.** chick, fledgling **2.** babe, babe in arms, baby, infant, suckling

as for taxes, expenses, losses, etc.: *net profit.* Cf. **gross** (sense 2). **2.** (of weight) after deducting tare. **3.** final; conclusive (esp. in **net result**). ~*n.* **4.** net income, profits, weight, etc. ~*vb.* **netting, netted. 5.** (*tr.*) to yield or earn as clear profit.

netball ('nɛt,bɔːl) *n.* a team game similar to basketball played mainly by women.

nether ('nɛðə) *adj.* below, beneath, or underground: *nether regions.*

nethermost ('nɛðə,məʊst) *determiner.* **the.** farthest down; lowest.

nether world *n.* **1.** the underworld. **2.** hell. ~Also called: **nether regions.**

net profit *n.* gross profit minus all operating costs not included in the calculation of gross profit, esp. wages, overheads, and depreciation.

nett (nɛt) *adj., n., vb.* a variant spelling of **net**[2].

netting ('nɛtɪŋ) *n.* any netted fabric or structure.

nettle ('nɛtəl) *n.* **1.** a plant having serrated leaves with stinging hairs and greenish flowers. **2.** any of various other plants with stinging hairs or spines. **3.** any of various plants that resemble nettles, such as the dead-nettle. **4. grasp the nettle.** to attempt something with boldness and courage. ~*vb.* (*tr.*) **5.** to bother; irritate. **6.** to sting as a nettle does.

nettle rash *n.* a skin condition characterized by itchy red or whitish raised patches, usually caused by an allergy. Also called: **urticaria.**

network ('nɛt,wɜːk) *n.* **1.** an interconnected group or system: *a network of shops.* **2.** a system of intersecting lines, roads, veins, etc. **3.** another name for **net**[1] (sense 1) or **netting. 4.** *Radio & TV.* a group of broadcasting stations that all transmit the same programme simultaneously. **5.** *Electronics.* a system of interconnected components or circuits. ~*vb.* **6.** *Radio & TV.* to broadcast over a network.

neural ('njʊərəl) *adj.* of or relating to a nerve or the nervous system. —**'neurally** *adv.*

neuralgia (njʊˈrældʒə) *n.* severe spasmodic pain along the course of one or more nerves. —**neu'ralgic** *adj.*

neuritis (njʊˈraɪtɪs) *n.* inflammation of a nerve or nerves, often accompanied by pain and loss of function in the affected part. —**neuritic** (njʊˈrɪtɪk) *adj.*

neuro- *or before a vowel* **neur-** *combining form.* indicating a nerve or the nervous system: *neurology.*

neurology (njʊˈrɒlədʒɪ) *n.* the study of the anatomy, physiology, and diseases of the nervous system. —**neurological** (ˌnjʊərəˈlɒdʒɪkəl) *adj.*

neuron ('njʊərɒn) *or* **neurone** ('njʊərəʊn) *n.* a cell specialized to conduct nerve impulses: consists of a cell body, axon, and dendrites. Also called: **nerve cell.** —**neuronic** (njʊˈrɒnɪk) *adj.*

neurosis (njʊˈrəʊsɪs) *n., pl.* **-ses** (-siːz) a relatively mild mental disorder, characterized by hysteria, anxiety, or obsessive behaviour.

neurosurgery (ˌnjʊərəʊˈsɜːdʒərɪ) *n.* the branch of surgery concerned with the nervous system. —**neuro'surgical** *adj.*

neurotic (njʊˈrɒtɪk) *adj.* **1.** of or afflicted by neurosis. ~*n.* **2.** a person who is afflicted with a neurosis or who

tends to be emotionally unstable. —**neu'rotically** *adv.* —**neu'roticism** *n.*

neuter ('njuːtə) *adj.* **1.** *Grammar.* **a.** denoting or belonging to a gender of nouns which do not specify the sex of their referents. **b.** (*as n.*): *German "Mädchen" (meaning "girl") is a neuter.* **2.** (of animals and plants) having nonfunctional, underdeveloped, or absent reproductive organs. **3.** giving no indication of sex. ~*n.* **4.** a sexually underdeveloped female insect, such as a worker bee. **5.** a castrated animal. ~*vb.* **6.** (*tr.*) to castrate (an animal).

neutral ('njuːtrəl) *adj.* **1.** not siding with any party to a war or dispute. **2.** of or belonging to a neutral party, country, etc. **3.** of no distinctive quality or type. **4.** (of a colour) **a.** having no hue; achromatic. **b.** dull, but harmonizing with most other colours. **5.** a less common term for **neuter** (sense 2). **6.** *Chem.* neither acidic nor alkaline. **7.** *Physics.* having zero charge or potential. **8.** *Phonetics.* (of a vowel) articulated with the tongue relaxed in mid-central position: *"about" begins with a neutral vowel.* ~*n.* **9.** a neutral person, nation, etc. **10.** a citizen of a neutral state. **11.** the position of the controls of a gearbox that leaves the transmission disengaged. —**'neutrally** *adv.*

neutrality (njuːˈtrælɪtɪ) *n.* **1.** the state of being neutral. **2.** the condition of being chemically or electrically neutral.

neutralize *or* **-ise** ('njuːtrə,laɪz) *vb.* (*mainly tr.*) **1.** (*also intr.*) to render or become neutral by counteracting, mixing, etc. **2.** to make or become electrically or chemically neutral. **3.** to exclude (a country) from warfare or alliances by international agreement: *the great powers neutralized Belgium in the 19th century.* —**,neutrali'zation** *or* **-i'sation** *n.* —**'neutral,izer** *or* **-,iser** *n.*

neutrino (njuːˈtriːnəʊ) *n., pl.* **-nos.** *Physics.* a stable elementary particle with zero rest mass and spin $\frac{1}{2}$ that travels at the speed of light.

neutron ('njuːtrɒn) *n.* *Physics.* a neutral elementary particle with approximately the same mass as a proton. In the nucleus of an atom it is stable but when free it decays.

never ('nɛvə) *adv., sentence substitute.* **1.** at no time; not ever. **2.** certainly not; by no means; in no case. ~*interj.* **3.** Also: **well I never!** surely not! ▷ **Usage.** In good usage, *never* is not used with simple past tenses to mean *not* (*I was asleep at midnight, so I did not see* (not *never saw*) *her go*).

nevermore (ˌnɛvəˈmɔː) *adv. Literary.* never again.

never-never *Inf.* ~*n.* **1.** *Brit.* the hire-purchase system of buying. **2.** *Austral.* remote desert country. ~*adj.* **3.** imaginary; idyllic (esp. in **never-never land**).

nevertheless (ˌnɛvəðəˈlɛs) *sentence connector.* in spite of that; however; yet.

new (njuː) *adj.* **1. a.** recently made or brought into being. **b.** (*as n.*): *the new.* **2.** of a kind never before existing; novel: *a new concept in marketing.* **3.** recently discovered: *a new comet.* **4.** markedly different from what was before: *the new liberalism.* **5.** (often foll. by *to* or *at*) recently introduced (to); inexperienced (in) or unaccustomed (to): *new to this neighbourhood.* **6.** (*cap. in*

THESAURUS

net[1] **1.** *n.* lacework, lattice, mesh, netting, network, openwork, reticulation, tracery, web **2.** *v.* bag, capture, catch, enmesh, ensnare, entangle, nab (*Inf.*), trap

net[2], **nett** *adj.* **1.** after taxes, clear, final, take-home **2.** closing, conclusive, final ~*v.* **3.** accumulate, bring in, clear, earn, gain, make, realize, reap

nether basal, below, beneath, bottom, inferior, lower, under, underground

nether world Avernus, Hades, hell, infernal regions, nether regions, underworld

nettle annoy, chafe, exasperate, fret, goad, harass, incense, irritate, pique, provoke, ruffle, sting, tease, vex

nettled aggrieved, angry, annoyed, chafed, cross, exasperated, galled, goaded, harassed, huffy, incensed, irritable, irritated, peeved, peevish, piqued, provoked, put out, riled, ruffled, stung, teased, touchy, vexed

network arrangement, channels, circuitry, complex, convolution, grid, grill, inter-

connections, labyrinth, maze, mesh, net, nexus, organization, plexus, structure, system, tracks, web

neurosis abnormality, affliction, derangement, deviation, instability, maladjustment, mental disturbance, mental illness, obsession, phobia, psychological *or* emotional disorder

neurotic abnormal, anxious, compulsive, deviant, disordered, distraught, disturbed, maladjusted, manic, nervous, obsessive, overwrought, unhealthy, unstable

neuter *v.* castrate, doctor (*Inf.*), dress, emasculate, fix (*Inf.*), geld, spay

neutral **1.** disinterested, dispassionate, even-handed, impartial, indifferent, nonaligned, nonbelligerent, noncombatant, noncommittal, nonpartisan, sitting on the fence, unaligned, unbiased, uncommitted, undecided, uninvolved, unprejudiced **2.** achromatic, colourless, dull, expressionless, indeterminate, indistinct, indistinguishable, intermedi-

ate, toneless, undefined

neutrality detachment, disinterestedness, impartiality, nonalignment, noninterference, noninterventionism, noninvolvement, nonpartisanship

neutralize cancel, compensate for, counteract, counterbalance, frustrate, invalidate, negate, nullify, offset, undo

never-ending boundless, ceaseless, constant, continual, continuous, eternal, everlasting, incessant, interminable, nonstop, perpetual, persistent, relentless, unbroken, unceasing, unchanging, uninterrupted, unremitting

never-never hire-purchase (*Brit.*), H.P. (*Brit.*)

nevertheless but, even so, however, nonetheless, notwithstanding, regardless, still, yet

names or titles) more or most recent of things with the same name: *the New Testament.* **7.** *(prenominal)* fresh; additional: *send some new troops.* **8.** (often foll. by *to*) unknown: *this is new to me.* **9.** (of a cycle) beginning or occurring again: *a new year.* **10.** *(prenominal)* (of crops) harvested early. **11.** changed, esp. for the better: *she returned a new woman.* **12.** up-to-date; fashionable. **13. turn over a new leaf.** to make a fresh start. *~adv.* (*usually in combination*) **14.** recently, freshly: *new-laid eggs.* **15.** anew; again. —'**newish** *adj.* —'**newness** *n.*

newborn ('njuː,bɔːn) *adj.* **1.** recently or just born. **2.** (of hope, faith, etc.) reborn.

newcomer ('njuː,kʌmə) *n.* a person who has recently arrived or started to participate in something.

newel ('njuːəl) *n.* **1.** the central pillar of a winding staircase, esp. one that is made of stone. **2.** Also called: **newel post.** the post at the top or bottom of a flight of stairs that supports the handrail.

newfangled ('njuː'fæŋgəld) *adj.* newly come into existence or fashion, esp. excessively modern.

New Jerusalem *n. Christianity.* heaven.

newly ('njuːlɪ) *adv.* **1.** recently. **2.** again; anew: *newly raised hopes.* **3.** in a new manner; differently: *a newly arranged hairdo.*

newlywed ('njuːlɪ,wɛd) *n.* (*often pl.*) a recently married person.

new maths *n.* an approach to mathematics in which the basic principles of set theory are introduced at an elementary level.

new moon *n.* the moon when it appears as a narrow waxing crescent.

news (njuːz) *n. (functioning as sing.)* **1.** important or interesting recent happenings. **2.** information about such events, as in the mass media. **3. the.** a presentation, such as a radio broadcast, of information of this type. **4.** interesting or important information not previously known. **5.** a person, fashion, etc., widely reported in the mass media: *she is news in the film world.* —'**newsless** *adj.*

newsagent ('njuːz,eɪdʒənt) or *U.S.* **newsdealer** *n. Brit.* a shopkeeper who sells newspapers, stationery, etc.

newscast ('njuːz,kɑːst) *n.* a radio or television broadcast of the news. —'**news,caster** *n.*

news conference *n.* another term for **press conference.**

news flash *n.* a brief item of important news, often interrupting a radio or television programme.

newsletter ('njuːz,lɛtə) *n.* **1.** Also called: **news-sheet.** a printed periodical bulletin circulated to members of a group. **2.** *History.* a written or printed account of the news.

newspaper ('njuːz,peɪpə) *n.* a weekly or daily publication consisting of folded sheets and containing articles on the news, features, reviews, and advertisements. Often shortened to **paper.**

newspeak ('njuː,spiːk) *n.* the language of bureaucrats and politicians, regarded as deliberately ambiguous and misleading.

newsprint ('njuːz,prɪnt) *n.* an inexpensive wood-pulp paper used for newspapers.

newsreel ('njuːz,riːl) *n.* a short film with a commentary presenting current events.

newsstand ('njuːz,stænd) *n.* a portable stand or stall from which newspapers are sold.

newsworthy ('njuːz,wɜːðɪ) *adj.* sufficiently interesting to be reported in a news bulletin, etc.

newsy ('njuːzɪ) *adj.* **newsier, newsiest.** full of news,

esp. gossipy or personal news.

newt (njuːt) *n.* any of various small semiaquatic amphibians having a long slender body and tail and short feeble legs.

New Testament *n.* a collection of writings composed soon after Christ's death and added to the Jewish writings of the Old Testament to make up the Christian Bible.

newton ('njuːtən) *n.* the derived SI unit of force that imparts an acceleration of 1 metre per second per second to a mass of 1 kilogram. Symbol: N

new town *n. Brit.* a town planned as a complete unit and built with government sponsorship, esp. to accommodate overspill population.

New World *n.* **the.** the Americas; the western hemisphere.

New Year *n.* the first day or days of the year in various calendars, usually a holiday.

New Year's Day *n.* January 1, celebrated as a holiday in many countries. Often shortened to (U.S. inf.) **New Year's.**

New Year's Eve *n.* the evening of Dec. 31. See also Hogmanay.

next (nɛkst) *adj.* **1.** immediately following: *the next patient to be examined.* **2.** immediately adjoining: *the next room.* **3.** closest to in degree: *the next-best thing.* **4. the next (Sunday) but one.** the (Sunday) after the next. *~adv.* **5.** at a time immediately to follow: *the patient to be examined next.* **6. next to. a.** adjacent to: *the house next to ours.* **b.** following in degree: *next to your mother, who do you love most?* **c.** almost: *next to impossible.* *~prep.* **7.** *Arch.* next to.

next door *adj.* (**next-door** when prenominal), *adv.* at or to the adjacent house, flat, etc.

next of kin *n.* a person's closest relative.

nexus ('nɛksəs) *n., pl.* **nexus.** **1.** a means of connection; link; bond. **2.** a connected group or series.

NF or **N.F.** (in Britain) *abbrev. for* National Front.

Nfld. or **NF.** *abbrev. for* Newfoundland.

N.F.U. (in Britain) *abbrev. for* National Farmers' Union.

N.G. *abbrev. for:* **1.** Also: **NG** (in the U.S.) National Guard. **2.** New Guinea. **3.** Also: **ng** no good.

N.G.A. *abbrev. for* National Graphical Association.

N.H.S. (in Britain) *abbrev. for* National Health Service.

Ni *the chemical symbol for* nickel.

N.I. *abbrev. for:* **1.** (in Britain) National Insurance. **2.** Northern Ireland.

nib (nɪb) *n.* **1.** the writing point of a pen, esp. an insertable tapered metal part. **2.** a point, tip, or beak. **3.** (*pl.*) crushed cocoa beans. *~vb.* **nibbing, nibbed.** (*tr.*) **4.** to provide with a nib. **5.** to sharpen the nib of.

nibble ('nɪbəl) *vb.* (when *intr.*, often foll. by *at*) **1.** (esp. of animals) to take small repeated bites (of). **2.** to take dainty or tentative bites: *to nibble at a cake.* **3.** to bite (at) gently. *~n.* **4.** a small mouthful. **5.** an instance of nibbling. —'**nibbler** *n.*

nibs (nɪbz) *pl.* **n. his nibs.** *Sl.* a mock title used of someone in authority.

nice (naɪs) *adj.* **1.** pleasant: *a nice day.* **2.** kind or friendly: *a nice gesture of help.* **3.** subtle or discriminating: *a nice point in the argument.* **4.** precise; skilful: *a nice fit.* **5.** *Now rare.* fastidious; respectable: *he was not too nice about his methods.* **6.** *Obs.* **a.** foolish or ignorant. **b.** delicate. **c.** shy; modest. **d.** wanton. —'**nicely** *adv.* —'**niceness** *n.* —'**nicish** *adj.*

THESAURUS

new 1. advanced, contemporary, current, different, fresh, latest, modern, modernistic, modish, newfangled, novel, original, recent, topical, ultramodern, unfamiliar, unknown, unused, unusual, up-to-date, virgin **2.** added, extra, more, supplementary **3.** altered, changed, improved, modernized, redesigned, renewed, restored

newcomer alien, arrival, beginner, foreigner, immigrant, incomer, novice, outsider, settler, stranger

newfangled contemporary, fashionable, gimmicky, modern, new, new-fashioned, novel, recent

newly anew, freshly, just, lately, latterly, recently

news account, advice, bulletin, communiqué, disclosure, dispatch, exposé, gossip, hearsay, information, intelligence, leak, news flash, release, report, revelation, rumour, scandal, statement, story, tidings, word

newsworthy arresting, important, interesting, notable, noteworthy, remarkable, significant, stimulating

next *adj.* **1.** consequent, ensuing, following, later, subsequent, succeeding **2.** adjacent, adjoining, closest, nearest, neighbouring *~adv.* **3.** afterwards, closely, following, later, subse-

quently, thereafter

next world afterlife, afterworld, heaven, hereafter, nirvana, paradise

nibble 1. *n.* bite, crumb, morsel, peck, snack, soupçon, taste, titbit **2.** *v.* bite, eat, gnaw, munch, nip, peck, pick at

nice 1. agreeable, amiable, attractive, charming, commendable, courteous, delightful, friendly, good, kind, likable, pleasant, pleasurable, polite, prepossessing, refined, well-mannered **2.** dainty, fine, neat, tidy, trim **3.** accurate, careful, critical, delicate, discriminating, exact, exacting, fastidious, fine, meticulous, precise, rigorous, scrupulous, strict, subtle **4.** cultured, genteel, refined, re-

nicety ('naısıtı) *n., pl.* **-ties.** **1.** a subtle point: *a nicety of etiquette.* **2.** (*usually pl.*) a refinement or delicacy: *the niceties of first-class travel.* **3.** subtlety, delicacy, or precision. **4. to a nicety.** with precision.

niche (nıtʃ, niːʃ) *n.* **1.** a recess in a wall, esp. one that contains a statue, etc. **2.** a position particularly suitable for the person occupying it: *he found his niche in politics.* **3.** *Ecology.* the status of a plant or animal within its community, which determines its activities, relationships with other organisms, etc. ~*vb.* **4.** (*tr.*) to place (a statue) in a niche; ensconce (oneself).

nick (nık) *n.* **1.** a small notch or indentation. **2.** *Brit. sl.* a prison or police station. **3. in good nick.** in good condition. **4. in the nick of time.** just in time. ~*vb.* **5.** (*tr.*) to chip or cut. **6.** *Sl., chiefly Brit.* **a.** to steal. **b.** to arrest. **7.** (*intr.; often foll. by off*) *Austral. inf.* to depart rapidly. **8. nick (someone) for.** *U.S. sl.* to defraud (someone) to the extent of. **9.** to divide and reset (the tail muscles of a horse) to give the tail a high carriage. **10.** (*tr.*) to guess, catch, etc., exactly.

nickel ('nıkəl) *n.* **1.** a malleable silvery-white metallic element that is corrosion-resistant: used in alloys, in electroplating, and as a catalyst in organic synthesis. Symbol: Ni; atomic no.: 28; atomic wt.: 58.71. **2.** a U.S. and Canadian coin worth five cents. ~*vb.* **-elling, -elled** *or U.S.* **-eling, -eled.** **3.** (*tr.*) to plate with nickel.

nickelodeon (ˌnıkəˈləʊdıən) *n. U.S.* **1.** an early form of jukebox. **2.** (formerly) a Pianola, esp. one operated by inserting a five-cent piece.

nickel plate *n.* a thin layer of nickel deposited on a surface, usually by electrolysis.

nickel silver *n.* any of various white alloys containing copper, zinc, and nickel: used in making tableware, etc. Also called: **German silver.**

nicker[1] ('nıkə) *vb.* (*intr.*) **1.** (of a horse) to neigh softly. **2.** to snigger.

nicker[2] ('nıkə) *n., pl.* **-er.** *Brit. sl.* a pound sterling.

nicknack ('nık,næk) *n.* a variant spelling of **knickknack.**

nickname ('nık,neım) *n.* **1.** a familiar, pet, or derisory name given to a person, animal, or place. **2.** a shortened or familiar form of a person's name: *Joe is a nickname for Joseph.* ~*vb.* **3.** (*tr.*) to call by a nickname.

nicotine ('nıkə,tiːn) *n.* a colourless oily acrid toxic liquid that turns yellowish-brown in air and light: the principal alkaloid in tobacco. —**nicotinic** (ˌnıkəˈtınık) *adj.*

nictitate ('nıktı,teıt) *or* **nictate** ('nıkteıt) *vb.* a technical word for **blink.** —ˌ**nicti'tation** *or* **nic'tation** *n.*

nictitating membrane *n.* (in reptiles, birds, and some mammals) a thin fold of skin beneath the eyelid that can be drawn across the eye.

niece (niːs) *n.* a daughter of one's sister or brother.

niff (nıf) *Brit. sl.* ~*n.* **1.** a bad smell. ~*vb.* **2.** to stink. —**'niffy** *adj.*

nifty ('nıftı) *adj.* **-tier, -tiest.** *Inf.* **1.** pleasing, apt, or stylish. **2.** quick; agile. —**'niftily** *adv.* —**'niftiness** *n.*

niggard ('nıgəd) *n.* **1.** a stingy person. ~*adj. Arch.* **2.** miserly.

niggardly ('nıgədlı) *adj.* **1.** stingy. **2.** meagre: *a niggardly salary.* ~*adv.* **3.** stingily; grudgingly. —**'niggardliness** *n.*

nigger ('nıgə) *Derog.* ~*n.* **1.** another name for a Negro. **2.** a member of any dark-skinned race. **3. nigger in the woodpile.** a hidden snag.

niggle ('nıgəl) *vb.* **1.** (*intr.*) to find fault continually. **2.** (*intr.*) to be preoccupied with details; fuss. **3.** (*tr.*) to irritate; worry.

nigh (naı) *adj., adv., prep.* an archaic, poetic, or dialect word for **near.**

night (naıt) *n.* **1.** the period of darkness that occurs each 24 hours, as distinct from day. **2.** (*modifier*) of, occurring, working, etc., at night: *a night nurse.* **3.** this period considered as a unit: *four nights later they left.* **4.** the period between sunset and retiring to bed; evening. **5.** the time between bedtime and morning. **6.** the weather at night: *a clear night.* **7.** the activity or experience of a person during a night. **8.** (*sometimes cap.*) any evening designated for a special observance or function. **9.** nightfall or dusk. **10.** a state or period of gloom, ignorance, etc. **11. make a night of it.** to celebrate for most of the night. ~Related adj.: **nocturnal.**

nightcap ('naıt,kæp) *n.* **1.** a cloth cap formerly worn in bed. **2.** a bedtime drink.

nightclub ('naıt,klʌb) *n.* a place of entertainment open until late at night, usually offering food, drink, a floor show, dancing, etc.

nightdress ('naıt,drɛs) *n. Brit.* a loose dress worn in bed by women. Also called: **nightgown, nightie.**

nightfall ('naıt,fɔːl) *n.* the approach of darkness; dusk.

nightgown ('naıt,gaʊn) *n.* **1.** another name for **nightdress.** **2.** a man's nightshirt.

nightie *or* **nighty** ('naıtı) *n., pl.* **nighties.** *Inf.* short for **nightdress** *or* **nightgown.**

nightingale ('naıtıŋ,geıl) *n.* a brownish European songbird with a broad reddish-brown tail: well known for its musical song, usually heard at night.

nightjar ('naıt,dʒɑː) *n.* any of a family of nocturnal birds which have large eyes and feed on insects.

night-light *n.* a dim light burning at night, esp. for children.

nightlong ('naıt,lɒŋ) *adj., adv.* throughout the night.

nightly ('naıtlı) *adj.* **1.** happening or relating to each night. **2.** happening at night. ~*adv.* **3.** at night or each night.

nightmare ('naıt,mɛə) *n.* **1.** a terrifying or deeply distressing dream. **2. a.** an event or condition resembling a terrifying dream. **b.** (*as modifier*): *a nightmare drive.* **3.** a thing that is feared. **4.** (formerly) an evil spirit sup-

---

THESAURUS

spectable, virtuous, well-bred

nicely 1. acceptably, agreeably, amiably, attractively, charmingly, commendably, courteously, delightfully, kindly, likably, pleasantly, pleasingly, pleasurably, politely, prepossessingly, well 2. daintily, finely, neatly, tidily, trimly 3. accurately, carefully, critically, delicately, exactingly, exactly, fastidiously, finely, meticulously, precisely, rigorously, scrupulously, strictly, subtly 4. genteelly, respectably, virtuously

niceness 1. agreeableness, amiability, attractiveness, charm, courtesy, delightfulness, friendliness, good manners, goodness, kindness, likableness, pleasantness, pleasurableness, politeness, refinement 2. daintiness, fineness, neatness, tidiness, trimness 3. accuracy, care, carefulness, criticalness, delicacy, discrimination, exactingness, exactitude, exactness, fastidiousness, fineness, meticulosity, meticulousness, preciseness, precision, rigorousness, rigour, scrupulosity, scrupulousness, strictness, subtleness, subtlety 4. gentility, good breeding, refinement, respectability, virtue

nicety 1. accuracy, exactness, fastidiousness, finesse, meticulousness, minuteness, precision 2. daintiness, delicacy, discrimina-

tion, distinction, nuance, refinement, subtlety

niche 1. alcove, corner, hollow, nook, opening, recess 2. calling, pigeonhole (*Inf.*), place, position, slot (*Inf.*), vocation

nick chip, cut, damage, dent, mark, notch, scar, score, scratch, snick

nickname diminutive, epithet, familiar name, handle (*Sl.*), label, pet name, moniker (*Inf.*), sobriquet

niggard cheapskate (*Inf.*), cheeseparer, churl, miser, penny-pincher (*Inf.*), screw (*Sl.*), Scrooge, skinflint

niggardliness 1. avarice, avariciousness, closeness, covetousness, frugality, grudgingness, meanness, mercenariness, miserliness, nearness (*Inf.*), parsimony, penuriousness, sordidness, sparingness, stinginess, thrift, tightfistedness, ungenerousness 2. beggarliness, inadequacy, insufficiency, meagreness, meanness, miserableness, paltriness, scantiness, skimpiness, smallness, wretchedness

niggardly 1. avaricious, close, covetous, frugal, grudging, mean, mercenary, miserly, near (*Inf.*), parsimonious, penurious, Scroogelike, sordid, sparing, stinging, stingy, tightfisted, ungenerous 2. beggarly, inad-

equate, insufficient, meagre, mean, miserable, paltry, scanty, skimpy, small, wretched

niggle 1. carp, cavil, criticize, find fault, fuss 2. annoy, irritate, rankle, worry

niggling 1. cavilling, finicky, fussy, insignificant, minor, nit-picking (*Inf.*), pettifogging, petty, piddling (*Inf.*), quibbling, trifling, unimportant 2. gnawing, irritating, persistent, troubling, worrying

night dark, darkness, dead of night, hours of darkness, night-time, night watches

night and day all the time, ceaselessly, constantly, continually, continuously, day in, day out, endlessly, incessantly, interminably, unremittingly

nightfall crepuscule, dusk, eve (*Archaic*), evening, eventide, gloaming, sundown, sunset, twilight, vespers

nightly *adv./adj.* 1. each night, every night, night after night, nights (*Inf.*) ~*adv.* 2. after dark, at night, by night, in the night, nights (*Inf.*), nocturnally ~*adj.* 3. night-time, nocturnal

nightmare 1. bad dream, hallucination, incubus, succubus 2. horror, ordeal, torment, trial, tribulation

posed to harass or suffocate sleeping people. —'**night-marish** adj.

nights (naɪts) adv. Inf. at night, esp. regularly: he works nights.

night safe n. a safe built into the outside wall of a bank, in which customers can deposit money at times when the bank is closed.

night school n. an educational institution that holds classes in the evening.

nightshade ('naɪt,ʃeɪd) n. any of various solanaceous plants, such as deadly nightshade and black nightshade.

nightshirt ('naɪt,ʃɜːt) n. a loose knee-length or longer shirtlike garment worn in bed by men.

nightspot ('naɪt,spɒt) n. an informal word for **nightclub**.

night-time n. the time from sunset to sunrise; night as distinct from day.

night watch n. 1. a watch or guard kept at night, esp. for security. 2. the period of time the watch is kept. 3. a night watchman.

night watchman n. 1. Also called: **night watch**. a person who keeps guard at night on a factory, public building, etc. 2. Cricket. a batsman sent in to bat to play out time when a wicket has fallen near the end of a day's play.

nihilism ('naɪɪ,lɪzəm) n. 1. a complete denial of all established authority and institutions. 2. Philosophy. an extreme form of scepticism that systematically rejects all values, belief in existence, etc. 3. a revolutionary doctrine of destruction for its own sake. 4. the practice of terrorism. —'**nihilist** n., adj. —,**nihil'istic** adj.

nil (nɪl) n. another word for **nothing**.

nilgai ('nɪlgaɪ) or **nilghau** ('nɪlgaʊ) n., pl. -**gai**, -**gais** or -**ghau**, -**ghaus**. a large Indian antelope, the male of which has small horns.

nimble ('nɪmb°l) adj. 1. agile, quick, and neat in movement. 2. alert; acute. —'**nimbleness** n. —'**nimbly** adv.

nimbus ('nɪmbəs) n., pl. **bi** (-baɪ) or **buses**. 1. a. a dark grey rain-bearing cloud. b. (in combination): cumulonimbus clouds. 2. a. an emanation of light surrounding a saint or deity. b. a representation of this emanation. 3. a surrounding aura.

nincompoop ('nɪnkəm,puːp, 'nɪŋ-) n. a stupid person; fool; idiot.

nine (naɪn) n. 1. the cardinal number that is the sum of one and eight. 2. a numeral, 9, IX, etc., representing this number. 3. something representing, represented by, or consisting of nine units, such as a playing card with nine symbols on it. 4. Also: **nine o'clock**. nine hours after noon or midnight: the play starts at nine. 5. **dressed (up) to the nines**. Inf. elaborately dressed. 6. **999** (in Britain) the telephone number of the emergency services. 7. **nine to five**. normal office hours: a nine-to-five job. ~determiner. 8. a. amounting to nine: nine days. b. (as pronoun): nine of the ten are ready. —**ninth** adj.

nine-days wonder n. something that arouses great interest but only for a short period.

ninefold ('naɪn,fəʊld) adj. 1. equal to or having nine times as many or as much. 2. composed of nine parts. ~adv. 3. by nine times as much.

ninepins ('naɪn,pɪnz) n. (functioning as sing.) 1. the game of skittles. 2. (sing.) one of the pins used in this game.

nineteen (,naɪn'tiːn) n. 1. the cardinal number that is the sum of ten and nine. 2. a numeral, 19, XIX, etc., representing this number. 3. something represented by, representing, or consisting of 19 units. 4. **talk nineteen to the dozen**. to talk incessantly. ~determiner. 5. a. amounting to nineteen: nineteen pictures. b. (as pro-

noun): only nineteen voted. —,**nine'teenth** adj.

nineteenth hole n. Golf, sl. the bar in a golf clubhouse.

ninety ('naɪntɪ) n., pl. -**ties**. 1. the cardinal number that is the product of ten and nine. 2. a numeral, 90, XC, etc., representing this number. 3. something represented by, representing, or consisting of 90 units. ~determiner. 4. a. amounting to ninety: ninety times. b. (as pronoun): at least ninety are missing. —'**ninetieth** adj.

ninny ('nɪnɪ) n., pl. -**nies**. a dull-witted person.

niobium (naɪ'əʊbɪəm) n. a ductile white superconductive metallic element that occurs principally in the black mineral columbite and tantalite. Symbol: Nb; atomic no.: 41; atomic wt.: 92.906. Former name: **columbium**.

nip[1] (nɪp) vb. **nipping**, **nipped**. (mainly tr.) 1. to compress, as between a finger and the thumb; pinch. 2. (often foll. by off) to remove by clipping, biting, etc. 3. (when intr., often foll. by at) to give a small sharp bite (to): the dog nipped at his heels. 4. (esp. of the cold) to affect with a stinging sensation. 5. to harm through cold: the frost nipped the young plants. 6. Also: **nip in the bud**. to check or destroy the growth of. 7. (intr.; foll. by along, up, out, etc.) Brit. inf. to hurry; dart. 8. Sl., chiefly U.S. to snatch. 9. a pinch, snip, etc. 10. severe frost or cold: the first nip of winter. 11. **put the nips in (to)**. Austral. & N.Z. sl. to try to borrow money (from). 12. Arch. a taunting remark. 13. **nip and tuck**. U.S. neck and neck.

nip[2] (nɪp) n. 1. a small drink of spirits; dram. ~vb. **nipping**, **nipped**. 2. to drink spirits, esp. habitually in small amounts.

nipper ('nɪpə) n. 1. a person or thing that nips. 2. the large pincer-like claw of a lobster, crab, etc. 3. Inf., chiefly Brit. a small child.

nippers ('nɪpəz) pl. n. an instrument or tool, such as a pair of pliers, for snipping or squeezing.

nipple ('nɪp°l) n. 1. the small conical projection in the centre of each breast, which in women contains the outlet of the milk ducts. 2. something resembling a nipple in shape or function. 3. Also called: **grease nipple**. a small drilled bush, usually screwed into a bearing, through which grease is introduced.

nippy ('nɪpɪ) adj. -**pier**, -**piest**. 1. biting, sharp, or chilly. 2. Brit. inf. a. quick; nimble; active. b. (of a motor vehicle) small and relatively powerful. 3. (of dogs) inclined or quick to bite. —'**nippily** adv.

nirvana (nɪə'vɑːnə, nɜː-) n. Buddhism, Hinduism. final release from the cycle of reincarnation attained by extinction of all desires and individual existence, culminating (in Buddhism) in absolute blessedness, or (in Hinduism) in absorption into Brahman.

Nissen hut ('nɪs°n) n. a military shelter of semicircular cross section, made of corrugated steel sheet.

nit[1] (nɪt) n. 1. the egg of a louse, usually adhering to human hair. 2. the larva of a louse.

nit[2] (nɪt) n. Inf., chiefly Brit. short for **nitwit**.

nit-picking Inf. ~n. 1. a concern with insignificant details, esp. with the intention of finding fault. ~adj. 2. showing such a concern; fussy. —'**nit-,picker** n.

nitrate ('naɪtreɪt) n. 1. any salt or ester of nitric acid. 2. a fertilizer containing nitrate salts. ~vb. 3. (tr.) to treat with nitric acid or a nitrate. 4. to convert or be converted into a nitrate. —**ni'tration** n.

nitre or U.S. **niter** ('naɪtə) n. another name for **potassium nitrate**.

nitric ('naɪtrɪk) adj. of or containing nitrogen.

nitric acid n. a colourless corrosive liquid important in the manufacture of fertilizers, explosives, and many

---

THESAURUS

nil duck, love, naught, nihil, none, nothing, zero

nimble active, agile, alert, brisk, deft, dexterous, lively, nippy (Brit. inf.), proficient, prompt, quick, quick-witted, ready, smart, sprightly, spry, swift

nimbleness adroitness, agility, alacrity, alertness, dexterity, finesse, grace, lightness, nippiness (Brit. inf.), skill, smartness, sprightliness, spryness

nimbly actively, acutely, agilely, alertly, briskly, deftly, dexterously, easily, fast, fleetly, proficiently, promptly, quickly, quick-

wittedly, readily, sharply, smartly, speedily, spryly, swiftly

nimbus ambience, atmosphere, aura, aureole, cloud, corona, glow, halo, irradiation

nincompoop blockhead, dimwit (Inf.), dolt, dunce, fool, idiot, ninny, nitwit, noodle, numskull, simpleton

nip[1] v. 1. bite, catch, clip, compress, grip, nibble, pinch, snag, snap, snip, squeeze, tweak, twitch 2. check, frustrate, thwart

nip[2] n. dram, draught, drop, finger, mouthful, peg (Brit.), portion, shot (Inf.), sip, snifter

(Inf.), soupçon, sup, swallow, taste

nipper 1. claw, pincer 2. Inf. baby, boy, child, girl, infant, kid (Inf.), little one, tot

nipple breast, dug, mamilla, pap, papilla, teat, tit, udder

nippy 1. biting, chilly, nipping, sharp, stinging 2. Brit. inf. active, agile, fast, nimble, quick, spry

nit-picking captious, carping, cavilling, finicky, fussy, hairsplitting, pedantic, pettifogging, quibbling

other chemicals. Formula: HNO₃. Former name: **aqua fortis.**

nitrify ('naɪtrɪˌfaɪ) *vb.* **-fying, -fied.** (*tr.*) **1.** to treat or cause to react with nitrogen. **2.** to treat (soil) with nitrates. **3.** (of nitrobacteria) to convert (ammonium compounds) into nitrates by oxidation. —**'nitriˌfiable** *adj.*

nitro- *or before a vowel* **nitr-** *combining form.* **1.** indicating that a chemical compound contains a nitro group, -NO₂: *nitrobenzene.* **2.** indicating that a chemical compound is a nitrate ester: *nitrocellulose.*

nitrogen ('naɪtrədʒən) *n.* a colourless odourless relatively unreactive gaseous element that forms 78 per cent of the air and is an essential constituent of proteins and nucleic acids. Symbol: N; atomic no.: 7; atomic wt.: 14.0067. —**nitrogenous** (-'trɒdʒ-) *adj.*

nitrogen cycle *n.* the natural circulation of nitrogen by living organisms. Nitrates in the soil, derived from dead organic matter by bacterial action, are absorbed and synthesized into complex organic compounds by plants and reduced to nitrates again when the plants and the animals feeding on them die and decay.

nitrogen fixation *n.* **1.** the conversion of atmospheric nitrogen into nitrogen compounds by soil bacteria in the root nodules of legumes, and by certain algae. **2.** a process in which atmospheric nitrogen is converted into a nitrogen compound, used esp. for fertilizer.

nitroglycerin (ˌnaɪtrəʊ'glɪsərɪn) *or* **nitroglycerine** (ˌnaɪtrəʊ'glɪsəˌriːn) *n.* a pale yellow viscous explosive liquid made from glycerol and nitric and sulphuric acids. Formula: CH₂NO₃CHNO₃CH₂NO₃. Also called: **trinitroglycerin.**

nitrous ('naɪtrəs) *adj.* of, derived from, or containing nitrogen, esp. in a low valency state.

nitrous oxide *n.* a colourless gas with a sweet smell: used as an anaesthetic in dentistry. Formula: N₂O. Also called: **laughing gas.**

nitty ('nɪtɪ) *adj.* **-tier, -tiest.** infested with nits.

nitty-gritty ('nɪtɪ'grɪtɪ) *n.* **the.** *Sl.* the basic facts of a matter, situation, etc.; the core.

nitwit ('nɪtˌwɪt) *n.* a foolish or dull person.

NNE *abbrev. for* north-northeast.

NNW *abbrev. for* north-northwest.

no¹ (nəʊ) *sentence substitute.* **1.** used to express denial, disagreement, refusal, etc. ~*adv.* **2.** (*sentence modifier*) used to emphasize a negative statement, esp. when disagreeing: *no you can't.* ~*n., pl.* **noes** *or* **nos.** **3.** an answer or vote of *no.* **4.** (*often pl.*) a person who votes in the negative. **5. the noes have it.** there is a majority of votes in the negative. **6. not take no for an answer.** to continue in a course of action, etc., despite refusals.

no² (nəʊ) *determiner.* **1.** not any, not a, or not one: *there's no money left; no card in the file.* **2.** not at all: *she's no youngster.* **3.** (foll. by comparative adjectives and adverbs) not: *no less than forty men; no taller than a child.*

No¹ *or* **Noh** (nəʊ) *n., pl.* **No** *or* **Noh.** the stylized classic drama of Japan, developed in the 15th century or earlier, using music, dancing, and themes from religious stories or myths.

No² *the chemical symbol for* nobelium.

No. *abbrev. for:* **1.** north(ern). **2.** Also: **no.** (*pl.* **Nos., nos.**) number.

n.o. *Cricket. abbrev. for* not out.

nob (nɒb) *n. Sl., chiefly Brit.* a person of wealth or social distinction.

no-ball *n.* **1.** *Cricket.* an illegal ball, as for overstepping the crease, for which the batting side scores a run unless the batsman hits the ball, in which case he can only be out by being run out. **2.** *Rounders.* an illegal ball, esp. one bowled too high or too low. ~*interj.* **3.** *Cricket, rounders.* a call by the umpire indicating a no-ball.

nobble ('nɒbəl) *vb.* (*tr.*) *Brit. sl.* **1.** to disable (a racehorse), esp. with drugs. **2.** to win over or outwit (a person) by underhand means. **3.** to steal. **4.** to grab. **5.** to kidnap.

nobelium (nəʊ'biːlɪəm) *n.* a transuranic element produced artificially from curium. Symbol: No; atomic no.: 102; half-life of most stable isotope, ²⁵⁵No: 180 seconds (approx.).

Nobel prize (nəʊ'bɛl) *n.* an annual prize awarded since 1901 for outstanding contributions to chemistry, physics, physiology and medicine, literature, economics, and peace.

nobility (nəʊ'bɪlɪtɪ) *n., pl.* **-ties.** **1.** a privileged class whose titles are conferred by descent or royal decree. **2.** the quality of being good; dignity: *nobility of mind.* **3.** (in the British Isles) the class of people holding the title of dukes, marquesses, earls, viscounts, or barons and their feminine equivalents; peerage.

noble ('nəʊbəl) *adj.* **1.** of or relating to a hereditary class with special status, often derived from a feudal period. **2.** of or characterized by high moral qualities; magnanimous: *a noble deed.* **3.** having dignity or eminence; illustrious. **4.** imposing; magnificent: *a noble avenue of trees.* **5.** superior; excellent: *a noble strain of horses.* **6.** *Chem.* **a.** (of certain elements) chemically unreactive. **b.** (of certain metals, esp. copper, silver, and gold) resisting oxidation. ~*n.* **7.** a person belonging to a privileged class whose status is usually indicated by a title. **8.** (in the British Isles) a person holding the title of duke, marquess, earl, viscount, or baron, or a feminine equivalent. **9.** a former Brit. gold coin having the value of one third of a pound. —**'nobleness** *n.* —**'nobly** *adv.*

nobleman ('nəʊbəlmən) *or* (*fem.*) **noblewoman** *n., pl.* **-men** *or* **-women** a person of noble rank, title, or status; peer; aristocrat.

noblesse oblige (nəʊ'blɛs əʊ'bliːʒ) *n. Often ironic.* the supposed obligation of nobility to be honourable and generous.

nobody ('nəʊbədɪ) *pron.* **1.** no person; no-one. ~*n., pl.* **-bodies.** **2.** an insignificant person.
▷ **Usage.** See at **everyone.**

nock (nɒk) *n.* **1.** a notch on an arrow that fits on the bowstring. **2.** either of the grooves at each end of a bow that hold the bowstring. ~*vb.* (*tr.*) **3.** to fit (an arrow) on a bowstring.

no-claim bonus *n.* a reduction on an insurance premium, esp. one covering a motor vehicle, if no claims have been made within a specified period. Also called: **no-claims bonus.**

nocturnal (nɒk'tɜːnəl) *adj.* **1.** of, used during, occurring in, or relating to the night. **2.** (of animals) active at night. **3.** (of plants) having flowers that open at night and close by day. —ˌ**noctur'nality** *n.* —**noc'turnally** *adv.*

nocturne ('nɒktɜːn) *n.* **1.** a short, lyrical piece of music, esp. one for the piano. **2.** a painting of a night scene.

nod (nɒd) *vb.* **nodding, nodded.** **1.** to lower and raise (the head) briefly, as to indicate agreement, etc. **2.** (*tr.*) to express by nodding: *she nodded approval.* **3.** (*intr.*) (of flowers, trees, etc.) to sway or bend forwards and back. **4.** (*intr.*) to let the head fall forward through drowsiness; be almost asleep: *the old lady sat nodding by the fire.* **5.** (*intr.*) to be momentarily careless: *even Homer sometimes nods.* ~*n.* **6.** a quick down-and-up movement of the head, as in assent, command, etc. See also: **nod off.** —**'noddingly** *adv.*

THESAURUS

nitty-gritty basics, brass tacks (*Inf.*), core, crux, essence, essentials, facts, fundamentals, gist, heart of the matter, reality, substance

nitwit dimwit (*Inf.*), dummy (*Sl.*), fool, halfwit, nincompoop, ninny, simpleton

nob big shot (*Sl.*), bigwig (*Sl.*), fat cat (*U.S. sl.*), nabob (*Inf.*), toff (*Brit. sl.*)

nobble 1. disable, handicap, incapacitate, weaken 2. bribe, get at, influence, intimidate, outwit, win over 3. filch, knock off (*Sl.*), nick (*Sl.*), pilfer, pinch (*Inf.*), purloin, snitch (*Sl.*), steal, swipe (*Sl.*) 4. get hold of, grab, take

nobility 1. aristocracy, elite, high society,

lords, nobles, patricians, peerage, ruling class, upper class 2. dignity, eminence, excellence, grandeur, greatness, illustriousness, loftiness, magnificence, majesty, nobleness, stateliness, sublimity, superiority, worthiness 3. honour, incorruptibility, integrity, uprightness, virtue

noble *n.* 1. aristocrat, lord, nobleman, peer ~*adj.* 2. aristocratic, blue-blooded, gentle (*Archaic*), highborn, lordly, patrician, titled 3. august, dignified, distinguished, elevated, eminent, excellent, grand, great, imposing, impressive, lofty, splendid, stately 4. gener-

ous, honourable, magnanimous, upright, virtuous, worthy

nobody 1. no-one 2. cipher, lightweight (*Inf.*), menial, nonentity, nothing (*Inf.*)

nocturnal night, nightly, night-time, of the night

nod *v.* 1. acknowledge, bob, bow, dip, duck, gesture, indicate, salute, signal 2. agree, assent, concur, show agreement 3. be sleepy, doze, droop, drowse, nap, sleep, slump ~*n.* 4. acknowledgment, beck, gesture, greeting, indication, salute, sign, signal

noddle ('nɒdəl) *n. Inf., chiefly Brit.* the head or brains: *use your noddle!*

noddy ('nɒdɪ) *n., pl.* **-dies.** 1. any of several tropical terns, typically having a dark plumage. 2. a fool or dunce.

node (nəud) *n.* 1. a knot, swelling, or knob. 2. the point on a plant stem from which the leaves or lateral branches grow. 3. *Physics.* a point of zero or minimum displacement in a standing wave. 4. Also called: **crunode.** *Maths.* a point at which two branches of a curve intersect. 5. *Maths., linguistics.* one of the objects of which a graph or a tree consists. 6. *Astron.* either of the two points at which the orbit of a body intersects the plane of the ecliptic. 7. *Anat.* any natural bulge or swelling, such as those along the course of a lymphatic vessel (**lymph node**). —'**nodal** *adj.*

nod off *vb. (intr., adv.) Inf.* to fall asleep.

nodule ('nɒdjuːl) *n.* 1. a small knot, lump, or node. 2. any of the knoblike outgrowths on the roots of clover and other legumes that contain bacteria involved in nitrogen fixation. 3. a small rounded lump of rock or mineral substance, esp. in a matrix of different rock material. —'**nodular,** '**nodulose,** *or* '**nodulous** *adj.*

Noel *or* **Noël** (nəu'ɛl) *n.* (in carols, etc.) another word for **Christmas.**

nog *or* **nogg** (nɒg) *n.* 1. Also called: **flip.** a drink, esp. an alcoholic one, containing beaten egg. 2. *East Anglian dialect.* strong local beer.

noggin ('nɒgɪn) *n.* 1. a small quantity of spirits. 2. a small mug. 3. an informal word for **head.**

no-go area *n.* a district in a town that is barricaded off, usually by a paramilitary organization, which the police, army, etc., can only enter by force.

noise (nɔɪz) *n.* 1. a sound, esp. one that is loud or disturbing. 2. loud shouting; clamour; din. 3. any undesired electrical disturbance in a circuit, etc. 4. **make a noise.** to talk a great deal or complain (about). ~*vb.* 5. (*tr.;* usually foll. by *abroad* or *about*) to spread (news, gossip, etc.).

noiseless ('nɔɪzlɪs) *adj.* making little or no sound. —'**noiselessly** *adv.* —'**noiselessness** *n.*

noisome ('nɔɪsəm) *adj.* 1. (esp. of smells) offensive. 2. harmful or noxious. —'**noisomeness** *n.*

noisy ('nɔɪzɪ) *adj.* **noisier, noisiest.** 1. making a loud or constant noise. 2. full of or characterized by noise. —'**noisily** *adv.* —'**noisiness** *n.*

nomad ('nəumæd) *n.* 1. a member of a people or tribe who move from place to place to find pasture and food. 2. a wanderer. —**no'madic** *adj.* —'**nomadism** *n.*

no-man's-land *n.* 1. land between boundaries, esp. an unoccupied zone between opposing forces. 2. an unowned or unclaimed piece of land. 3. an ambiguous area of activity.

nom de plume ('nɒm də 'pluːm) *n., pl.* **noms de plume.** another term for **pen name.**

nomenclature (nəu'mɛnklətʃə; *U.S.* 'nəumən,kleɪtʃər) *n.* the terminology used in a particular science, art, activity, etc.

nominal ('nɒmɪnəl) *adj.* 1. in name only; theoretical: *the nominal leader.* 2. minimal in comparison with real worth; token: *a nominal fee.* 3. of, constituting, or giving a name. 4. *Grammar.* of or relating to a noun or noun phrase. ~*n.* 5. *Grammar.* a noun, noun phrase, or syntactically similar structure. —'**nominally** *adv.*

nominalism ('nɒmɪnə,lɪzəm) *n.* the philosophical theory that a general word, such as *dog,* is merely a name and does not denote a real object, the general idea "dog". —'**nominalist** *n.*

nominal value *n.* another name for **par value.**

nominate *vb.* ('nɒmɪ,neɪt). (*mainly tr.*) 1. to propose as a candidate, esp. for an elective office. 2. to appoint to an office or position. 3. (*intr.*) *Austral.* to stand as a candidate in an election. —,**nomi'nation** *n.* —'**nomi,nator** *n.*

nominative ('nɒmɪnətɪv) *adj.* 1. *Grammar.* denoting a case of nouns and pronouns in inflected languages that is used esp. to identify the subject of a finite verb. 2. appointed rather than elected to a position, office, etc. ~*n.* 3. *Grammar.* **a.** the nominative case. **b.** a word or speech element in the nominative case. —**nominatival** (,nɒmɪnə'taɪvəl) *adj.*

nominee (,nɒmɪ'niː) *n.* a person who is nominated to an office or as a candidate.

-nomy *n. combining form.* indicating a science or the laws governing a certain field of knowledge: *agronomy; economy.* —'**nomic** *adj. combining form.*

non- *prefix.* 1. indicating negation: *nonexistent.* 2. indicating refusal or failure: *noncooperation.* 3. indicating exclusion from a specified class: *nonfiction.* 4. indicating lack or absence: *nonobjective; nonevent.*

nonage ('nəunɪdʒ) *n.* 1. *Law.* the state of being under any of various ages at which a person may legally enter into certain transactions, such as marrying, etc. 2. any period of immaturity.

nonagenarian (,nəunədʒɪ'nɛərɪən) *n.* 1. a person who is from 90 to 99 years old. ~*adj.* 2. of, relating to, or denoting a nonagenarian.

nonagon ('nɒnə,gɒn) *n.* a polygon having nine sides. —**nonagonal** (nɒn'ægənəl) *adj.*

nonaligned (,nɒnə'laɪnd) *adj.* (of states, etc.) not part of a major alliance or power bloc. —,**nona'lignment** *n.*

nonce (nɒns) *n.* the present time or occasion (now only in **for the nonce**).

nonce word *n.* a word coined for a single occasion.

nonchalant ('nɒnʃələnt) *adj.* casually unconcerned or

nonacceptance *n.*	noncommunist *n adj.*	noncooperation *n.*	nondrinker *n.*
nonalcoholic *adj.*	noncompetitive *adj.*	noncreative *adj.*	nondriver *n.*
nonappearance *n.*	noncompliance *n.*	noncriminal *adj.*	nonearning *adj.*
nonattendance *n.*	nonconclusive *adj.*	noncritical *adj.*	noneffective *adj.*
nonbelligerent *adj.*	nonconductor *n.*	noncultivated *adj.*	nonessential *adj. n.*
nonbreakable *adj.*	nonconsecutive *adj.*	nondelivery *n.*	nonethical *adj.*
noncentral *adj.*	noncontagious *adj.*	nondemocratic *adj.*	nonexchangeable *adj.*
nonChristian *adj. n.*	noncontributing *adj.*	nondenominational *adj.*	nonexistence *n.*
noncommercial *adj.*	noncontroversial *adj.*	nondepartmental *adj.*	nonexistent *adj.*
noncommissioned *adj.*	nonconventional *adj.*	nondetachable *adj.*	nonexplosive *adj.*
noncummunicant *n.*	nonconversant *adj.*	nondiscriminating *adj.*	nonfatal *adj.*
noncommunicative *adj.*	nonconvertible *adj.*	nondivisible *adj.*	nonfreezing *adj.*

THESAURUS

noggin 1. gill, quarter-pint 2. cup, dram, mug, nip, tot 3. *Inf.* block (*Inf.*), bonce (*Brit. sl.*), conk (*Sl.*), dome (*Sl.*), head, napper (*Sl.*), noddle (*Inf.*), nut (*Sl.*)

no go futile, hopeless, impossible, not on (*Inf.*), vain

noise 1. *n.* babble, blare, clamour, clatter, commotion, cry, din, fracas, hubbub, outcry, pandemonium, racket, row, sound, talk, tumult, uproar 2. *v.* advertise, bruit (*Archaic*), circulate, gossip, publicize, repeat, report, rumour

noiseless hushed, inaudible, mute, muted, quiet, silent, soundless, still

noisy boisterous, cacophonous, chattering, clamorous, deafening, ear-splitting, loud, ob-

streperous, piercing, riotous, strident, tumultuous, turbulent, uproarious, vociferous

nomad drifter, itinerant, migrant, rambler, rover, vagabond, wanderer

nomadic itinerant, migrant, migratory, pastoral, peripatetic, roaming, roving, travelling, vagrant, wandering

nom de plume alias, assumed name, nom de guerre, pen name, pseudonym

nomenclature classification, codification, locution, phraseology, taxonomy, terminology, vocabulary

nominal 1. formal, ostensible, pretended, professed, puppet, purported, self-styled, so-called, *soi-disant,* supposed, theoretical, titular 2. inconsiderable, insignificant, minimal,

small, symbolic, token, trifling, trivial

nominate appoint, assign, choose, commission, designate, elect, elevate, empower, name, present, propose, recommend, select, submit, suggest, term

nomination appointment, choice, designation, election, proposal, recommendation, selection, suggestion

nominee aspirant, candidate, contestant, entrant, favourite, protégé, runner

nonaligned impartial, neutral, uncommitted, undecided

nonchalance calm, composure, cool (*Sl.*), equanimity, imperturbability, indifference, sang-froid, self-possession, unconcern

indifferent; uninvolved. —**'nonchalance** *n.*

non-com ('nɒn,kɒm) *n.* short for **noncommissioned officer.**

noncombatant (nɒn'kɒmbətənt) *n.* **1.** a civilian in time of war. **2.** a member of the armed forces whose duties do not include fighting, such as a chaplain or surgeon.

noncommissioned officer (,nɒnkə'mɪʃənd) *n.* a person holding a military rank, such as sergeant or corporal, that involves the exercise of authority but does not carry a commission: noncommissioned officers are appointed from the ranks.

noncommittal (,nɒnkə'mɪt^əl) *adj.* not involving or revealing commitment to any particular opinion or course of action.

non compos mentis Latin. ('nɒn 'kɒmpəs 'mɛntɪs) *adj.* mentally incapable of managing one's own affairs; of unsound mind.

nonconformist (,nɒnkən'fɔːmɪst) *n.* a person who does not conform to generally accepted patterns of behaviour or thought. —**,noncon'formity** or **,noncon'formism** *n.*

Nonconformist (,nɒnkən'fɔːmɪst) *n.* **1.** a member of a Protestant denomination that dissents from an Established Church, esp. the Church of England. ~*adj.* **2.** of, relating to, or denoting Nonconformists. —**,Noncon-'formity** or **,Noncon'formism** *n.*

noncontributory (,nɒnkən'trɪbjutərɪ) *adj.* denoting an insurance or pension scheme for employees, the premiums of which are paid entirely by the employer.

nondescript ('nɒndɪ,skrɪpt) *adj.* **1.** having no outstanding features. ~*n.* **2.** a nondescript person or thing.

none (nʌn) *pron.* (*functioning as sing. or pl.*) **1.** not any of a particular class: *none of my letters has arrived.* **2.** no-one; nobody: *there were none to tell the tale.* **3.** not any (of): *none of it looks edible.* **4. none other.** no other person: *none other than the Queen herself.* **5. none the.** (*foll. by a comparative adj.*) in no degree: *she was none the worse for her ordeal.* **6. none too.** not very: *he was none too pleased.*

▷ **Usage.** See at **everyone.**

nonentity (nɒn'ɛntɪtɪ) *n., pl.* **-ties. 1.** an insignificant person or thing. **2.** a nonexistent thing. **3.** the state of not existing; nonexistence.

nones (nəʊnz) *n.* (*functioning as sing. or pl.*) **1.** (in the Roman calendar) the ninth day before the ides of each month: the seventh day of March, May, July, and October, and the fifth of each other month. **2.** *Chiefly R.C. Church.* the fifth of the seven canonical hours of the divine office, originally fixed at the ninth hour of the day, about 3 p.m.

nonesuch or **nonsuch** ('nʌn,sʌtʃ) *n. Arch.* a matchless person or thing; nonpareil.

nonetheless (,nʌnðə'lɛs) *sentence connector.* despite that; however; nevertheless.

nonevent (,nɒnɪ'vɛnt) *n.* a disappointing or insignificant occurrence, esp. one predicted to be important.

nonferrous (nɒn'fɛrəs) *adj.* **1.** denoting any metal other than iron. **2.** not containing iron.

nonflammable (nɒn'flæməb^əl) *adj.* incapable of burning or not easily set on fire.

nonintervention (,nɒnɪntə'vɛnʃən) *n.* refusal to intervene, esp. the abstention by a state from intervening in the affairs of other states or in its own internal disputes.

nonmetal (nɒn'mɛt^əl) *n.* any of a number of chemical elements that have acidic oxides and are poor conductors of heat and electricity. —**,nonme'tallic** *adj.*

nonmoral (nɒn'mɒrəl) *adj.* not involving morality or ethics; neither moral nor immoral.

nonpareil ('nɒnpərəl, ,nɒnpə'reɪl) *n.* a person or thing that is unsurpassed or unmatched; peerless example.

nonplus (nɒn'plʌs) *vb.* **-plussing, -plussed** or *U.S.* **-plusing, -plused. 1.** (*tr.*) to put at a loss; confound. ~*n., pl.* **-pluses. 2.** a state of utter perplexity prohibiting action or speech.

nonproliferation (,nɒnprə,lɪfər'eɪʃən) *n.* **a.** limitation of the production or spread of something, esp. nuclear or chemical weapons. **b.** (*as modifier*): *a nonproliferation treaty.*

nonrepresentational (,nɒnrɛprɪzɛn'teɪʃən^əl) *adj. Art.* another word for **abstract.**

nonsense ('nɒnsəns) *n.* **1.** something that has or makes no sense; unintelligible language; drivel. **2.** conduct or action that is absurd. **3.** foolish behaviour: *she'll stand no nonsense.* **4. no-nonsense.** businesslike. **5.** things of little or no value; trash. ~*interj.* **6.** an exclamation of disagreement. —**nonsensical** (nɒn'sɛnsɪk^əl) *adj.* —**non'sensically** *adv.* —**non'sensicalness** or **non,sensi'cality** *n.*

non sequitur ('nɒn 'sɛkwɪtə) *n.* **1.** a statement having little or no relevance to what preceded it. **2.** *Logic.* a conclusion that does not follow from the premisses.

nonstarter (nɒn'stɑːtə) *n.* **1.** a horse that fails to run in a race for which it has been entered. **2.** a person or thing that has little chance of success.

nonstick ('nɒn'stɪk) *adj.* (of saucepans, etc.) coated with a substance that prevents food sticking to them.

nonstop ('nɒn'stɒp) *adj., adv.* without making a stop: *a nonstop flight.*

nonfunctional *adj.*	**nonmigratory** *adj.*	**nonpoisonous** *adj.*	**nonsectarian** *adj.*
nonhuman *adj.*	**nonmilitant** *adj.*	**nonporous** *adj.*	**nonselective** *adj.*
noninfectious *adj.*	**nonnavigable** *adj.*	**nonracial** *adj.*	**nonskilled** *adj.*
noninflammable *adj.*	**nonnegotiable** *adj.*	**nonreader** *n.*	**nonslip** *adj.*
nonintellectual *adj.*	**nonnuclear** *adj.*	**nonrecognition** *n.*	**nonstructural** *adj.*
nonintoxicating *adj.*	**nonoperative** *adj.*	**nonrecoverable** *adj.*	**nonswimmer** *n.*
nonirritant *adj. n.*	**nonparticipating** *adj.*	**nonregistered** *adj.*	**nontechnical** *adj.*
nonlethal *adj.*	**nonpaying** *adj.*	**nonrepresentative** *adj.*	**nontoxic** *adj.*
nonlinear *adj.*	**nonpayment** *n.*	**nonresident** *n. adj.*	**nontransferable** *adj.*
nonmagnetic *adj.*	**nonpermanent** *adj.*	**nonrestricted** *adj.*	**nonvenomous** *adj.*
nonmalignant *adj.*	**nonpermeable** *adj.*	**nonreturnable** *adj.*	**nonverbal** *adj.*
nonmember *n.*	**nonplaying** *adj.*	**nonscheduled** *adj.*	**nonviolent** *adj.*

THESAURUS

nonchalant airy, apathetic, blasé, calm, careless, casual, collected, cool, detached, dispassionate, indifferent, insouciant, offhand, unconcerned, unemotional, unperturbed

noncombatant civilian, neutral, non-belligerent

noncommittal ambiguous, careful, cautious, circumspect, discreet, equivocal, evasive, guarded, indefinite, neutral, politic, reserved, tactful, temporizing, tentative, unrevealing, vague, wary

non compos mentis crazy, deranged, insane, mentally ill, of unsound mind

nonconformist dissenter, dissentient, eccentric, heretic, iconoclast, individualist, maverick, protester, radical, rebel

nondescript characterless, common or garden (*Inf.*), commonplace, dull, featureless, indeterminate, mousy, ordinary, unclassifiable, unclassified, undistinguished, unex-

ceptional, uninspiring, uninteresting, unmemorable, unremarkable, vague

none nil, nobody, no-one, no part, not a bit, not any, nothing, not one, zero

nonentity cipher, lightweight (*Inf.*), mediocrity, nobody, small fry, unimportant person

nonessential dispensable, excessive, expendable, extraneous, inessential, peripheral, superfluous, unimportant, unnecessary

nonetheless despite that, even so, however, in spite of that, nevertheless, yet

nonexistent chimerical, fancied, fictional, hallucinatory, hypothetical, illusory, imaginary, imagined, insubstantial, legendary, missing, mythical, unreal

nonplus astonish, astound, baffle, bewilder, confound, confuse, discomfit, disconcert, discountenance, dismay, dumbfound, embarrass, mystify, perplex, puzzle, stump, stun, take aback

nonsense absurdity, balderdash, blather, bombast, bunk (*Inf.*), claptrap (*Inf.*), double Dutch (*Brit. inf.*), drivel, fatuity, folly, foolishness, gibberish, inanity, jest, ludicrousness, ridiculousness, rot, rubbish, senselessness, silliness, stuff, stupidity, trash, twaddle, waffle (*Brit. inf.*)

nonsensical absurd, crazy, foolish, inane, incomprehensible, irrational, ludicrous, meaningless, ridiculous, senseless, silly

nonstop 1. *adj.* ceaseless, constant, continuous, direct, endless, incessant, interminable, relentless, steady, unbroken, unending, unfaltering, uninterrupted, unremitting **2.** *adv.* ceaselessly, constantly, continuously, directly, endlessly, incessantly, interminably, relentlessly, steadily, unbrokenly, unendingly, unfalteringly, uninterruptedly, unremit-

nonsuch (ˈnʌnˌsʌtʃ) n. a variant spelling of **nonesuch**.

nonsuit (nɒnˈsjuːt) n. **1.** *Law.* an order of a judge dismissing a suit when the plaintiff fails to show he has a good cause of action or fails to produce any evidence. ~vb. **2.** (tr.) to order the dismissal of the suit of (a person).

non-U (nɒnˈjuː) adj. *Brit. inf.* (esp. of language) not characteristic of or used by the upper class.

nonunion (nɒnˈjuːnjən) adj. **1.** not belonging or related to a trade union: *nonunion workers.* **2.** not favouring or employing union labour: *a nonunion shop.* **3.** not produced by union labour.

nonvoter (nɒnˈvəʊtə) n. **1.** a person who does not vote. **2.** a person not eligible to vote.

noodle[1] (ˈnuːdəl) n. (*often pl.*) a ribbon-like strip of pasta.

noodle[2] (ˈnuːdəl) n. **1.** *U.S.* a slang word for **head. 2.** a simpleton.

nook (nʊk) n. **1.** a corner or narrow recess, as in a room. **2.** a secluded or sheltered place.

noon (nuːn) n. **1.** the middle of the day; 12 o'clock. **2.** *Poetic.* the most important part; culmination.

no-one *or* **no one** *pron.* no person; nobody.
▷ Usage. See at **everyone.**

noose (nuːs) n. **1.** a loop in the end of a rope, such as a lasso or hangman's halter, usually tied with a slipknot. **2.** something that restrains or traps. **3. put one's head in a noose.** to bring about one's own downfall. ~vb. (tr.) **4.** to secure in or as if in a noose. **5.** to make a noose of or in.

no-par adj. (of securities) without a par value.

nor (nɔː; *unstressed* nə) conj. (*coordinating*) **1.** (used to join alternatives, the first of which is preceded by *neither*) and not: *neither measles nor mumps.* **2.** (foll. by a verb) (and) not...either: *they weren't talented—nor were they particularly funny.* **3.** *Poetic.* neither: *nor wind nor rain.*

Nor. abbrev. for: **1.** Norman. **2.** north. **3.** Norway. **4.** Norwegian.

Nordic (ˈnɔːdɪk) adj. of or belonging to a subdivision of the Caucasoid race typified by the tall blond blue-eyed long-headed inhabitants of Scandinavia.

Norfolk jacket (ˈnɔːfək) n. a man's single-breasted belted jacket with one or two chest pockets and a box pleat down the back.

norm (nɔːm) n. **1.** an average level of achievement or performance, as of a group. **2.** a standard of achievement or behaviour that is required, desired, or designated as normal.

normal (ˈnɔːməl) adj. **1.** usual; regular; common; typical: *the normal level.* **2.** constituting a standard: *if we take this as normal.* **3.** *Psychol.* **a.** being within certain limits of intelligence, ability, etc. **b.** conforming to the conventions of one's group. **4.** (of laboratory animals) maintained in a natural state for purposes of comparison with animals treated with drugs, etc. **5.** *Chem.* (of a solution) containing a number of grams equal to the equivalent weight of the solute in each litre of solvent. **6.** *Geom.* another word for **perpendicular** (sense 1). ~n. **7.** the usual, average, or typical state, degree, form, etc. **8.** anything that is normal. **9.** *Geom.* a perpendicular line or plane. —**normality** (nɔːˈmælɪtɪ) *or esp. U.S.* ˈ**normalcy** n.

normalize *or* **-ise** (ˈnɔːməˌlaɪz) vb. (tr.) **1.** to bring or make into the normal state. **2.** to bring into conformity with a standard. **3.** to heat (steel) above a critical temperature and allow it to cool in air to relieve internal stresses; anneal. —ˌ**normaliˈzation** *or* **-iˈsation** n.

normally (ˈnɔːməlɪ) adv. **1.** as a rule; usually; ordinarily. **2.** in a normal manner.

Norman (ˈnɔːmən) n. **1.** (in the Middle Ages) a member of the people of Normandy in N France, descended from the 10th-century Scandinavian conquerors of the country and the native French. **2.** a native or inhabitant of Normandy. **3.** another name for **Norman French.** ~adj. **4.** of or characteristic of the Normans or their dialect of French. **5.** of or characteristic of Normandy. **6.** denoting or having the style of Romanesque architecture used in Britain from the Norman Conquest until the 12th century, characterized by the rounded arch, massive masonry walls, etc.

Norman French n. the medieval Norman and English dialect of Old French.

normative (ˈnɔːmətɪv) adj. implying, creating, or prescribing a norm or standard, as in language: *normative grammar.*

Norn (nɔːn) n. **1.** *Norse myth.* any of the three virgin goddesses of fate. **2.** the medieval Norse language of the Orkneys, Shetlands, and parts of N Scotland.

Norse (nɔːs) adj. **1.** of ancient and medieval Scandinavia or its inhabitants. **2.** of or characteristic of Norway. ~n. **3. a.** the N group of Germanic languages, spoken in Scandinavia. **b.** any one of these languages, esp. in their ancient or medieval forms. **4. the Norse.** (*functioning as pl.*) **a.** the Norwegians. **b.** the Vikings.

Norseman (ˈnɔːsmən) n., pl. **men.** another name for a **Viking.**

north (nɔːθ) n. **1.** one of the four cardinal points of the compass, at 0° or 360°, that is 90° from east and west and 180° from south. **2.** the direction along a meridian towards the North Pole. **3.** the direction in which a compass needle points; magnetic north. **4. the north.** (*often cap.*) any area lying in or towards the north. ~adj. **5.** in, towards, or facing the north. **6.** (esp. of the wind) from the north. ~adv. **7.** in, to, or towards the north.

North (nɔːθ) n. **the. 1.** the northern area of England, generally regarded as reaching the southern boundaries of Yorkshire, Derbyshire, and Cheshire. **2.** (in the U.S.) the states north of the Mason-Dixon Line that were known as the Free States during the Civil War. **3.** the northern part of North America, esp. Alaska and the Yukon. ~adj. **4.** of or denoting the northern part of a specified country, area, etc.

Northants. (nɔːˈθænts) abbrev. for Northamptonshire.

North Country n. (usually preceded by *the*) another name for **North** (sense 1).

northeast (ˌnɔːθˈiːst; *Naut.* ˌnɔːrˈiːst) n. **1.** the point of the compass or direction midway between north and east. **2.** (*often cap.;* usually preceded by *the*) any area lying in or towards this direction. ~adj. *also* **northeastern. 3.** (*sometimes cap.*) of or denoting the northeastern part of a specified country, area, etc.: *northeast Lincolnshire.* **4.** in, towards, or facing the northeast. **5.** (esp. of the wind) from the northeast. ~adv. **6.** in, to, towards, or (esp. of the wind) from the northeast. —ˌ**north-ˈeasterly** adj., adv. —ˌ**north'easternmost** adj. —ˌ**north-ˈeastward** adv.

Northeast (ˌnɔːθˈiːst) n. (usually preceded by *the*) the northeastern part of England, esp. Northumberland and Durham.

northeaster (ˌnɔːθˈiːstə; *Naut.* ˌnɔːrˈiːstə) n. a strong wind or storm from the northeast.

northerly (ˈnɔːðəlɪ) adj. **1.** of or situated in the north. ~adv., adj. **2.** towards the north. **3.** from the north: *a northerly wind.* ~n., pl. **-lies. 4.** a wind from the north. —ˈ**northerliness** n.

northern (ˈnɔːðən) adj. **1.** in or towards the north. **2.** (esp. of winds) proceeding from the north. **3.** (*sometimes cap.*) of or characteristic of the north or North.

Northerner (ˈnɔːðənə) n. (*sometimes not cap.*) a native or inhabitant of the north of any specified region, esp. England, the U.S., or the far north of Canada.

northern hemisphere n. (*often caps.*) that half of the globe lying north of the equator.

northern lights pl. n. another name for **aurora borealis.**

tingly, without stopping

nook alcove, cavity, corner, cranny, crevice, cubbyhole, hide-out, inglenook (*Brit.*), niche, opening, recess, retreat

noon high noon, midday, noonday, noontide, noontime, twelve noon

norm average, benchmark, criterion, mean, measure, model, pattern, rule, standard, type, yardstick

normal 1. accustomed, acknowledged, average, common, conventional, habitual, natural, ordinary, popular, regular, routine, run-of-the-mill, standard, typical, usual **2.** rational, reasonable, sane, well-adjusted

normality 1. accustomedness, averageness, commonness, commonplaceness, conventionality, habitualness, naturalness, ordinariness, popularity, regularity, routineness,

typicality, usualness **2.** adjustment, balance, rationality, reason, sanity

normally as a rule, commonly, habitually, ordinarily, regularly, typically, usually

north 1. adj. Arctic, boreal, northerly, northern, polar **2.** adv. northerly, northward(s)

Northman ('nɔːθmən) *n., pl.* **-men.** another name for a **Viking.**

north-northeast *n.* **1.** the point on the compass or the direction midway between north and northeast. ~*adj., adv.* **2.** in, from, or towards this direction.

north-northwest *n.* **1.** the point on the compass or the direction midway between northwest and north. ~*adj., adv.* **2.** in, from, or towards this direction.

North Pole *n.* **1.** the northernmost point on the earth's axis, at a latitude of 90°N, characterized by very low temperatures. **2.** Also called: **north celestial pole.** *Astron.* the point of intersection of the earth's extended axis and the northern half of the celestial sphere.

North Star *n.* **the.** another name for **Polaris.**

northward ('nɔːθwəd; *Naut.* 'nɔːðəd) *adj.* **1.** moving, facing, or situated towards the north. ~*n.* **2.** the northward part, direction, etc. ~*adv. also* **northwards. 3.** towards the north.

northwest (ˌnɔːθ'wɛst; *Naut.* ˌnɔː'wɛst) *n.* **1.** the point of the compass or direction midway between north and west. **2.** (*often cap.;* usually preceded by *the*) any area lying in or towards this direction. ~*adj. also* **northwestern. 3.** (*sometimes cap.*) of or denoting the northwestern part of a specified country, area, etc.: *northwest Greenland.* ~*adj., adv.* **4.** in, to, towards, or (*esp.* of the wind) from the northwest. —ˌ**north'westerly** *adj., adv.* —ˌ**north'westernmost** *adj.* —ˌ**north'westward** *adj.*

Northwest (ˌnɔːθ'wɛst) *n.* (usually preceded by *the*) the northwestern part of England, esp. Lancashire and the Lake District.

northwester (ˌnɔːθ'wɛstə; *Naut.* ˌnɔː'wɛstə) *n.* a strong wind or storm from the northwest.

Norwegian (nɔː'wiːdʒən) *adj.* **1.** of or characteristic of Norway, its language, or its people. ~*n.* **2.** any of the various North Germanic languages of Norway. **3.** a native or inhabitant of Norway.

Nos. *or* **nos.** *abbrev. for* numbers.

nose (nəuz) *n.* **1.** the organ of smell and entrance to the respiratory tract, consisting of a prominent structure divided into two hair-lined air passages. **2.** the sense of smell itself: in animals, the ability to follow trails by scent (esp. in **a good nose**). **3.** instinctive skill in discovering things (sometimes in **follow one's nose**): *he had a nose for good news stories.* **4.** any part resembling a nose in form or function, such as a nozzle or spout. **5.** the forward part of a vehicle, aircraft, etc. **6.** narrow margin of victory (in **(win) by a nose**). **7. cut off one's nose to spite one's face.** to carry out a vengeful action that hurts oneself more than another. **8. keep one's nose clean.** to stay out of trouble. **9. keep one's nose to the grindstone.** to work hard and continuously. **10. lead by the nose.** to control; dominate. **11. look down one's nose at.** *Inf.* to be disdainful of. **12. pay through the nose.** *Inf.* to pay an exorbitant price. **13. on the nose.** *Sl.* **a.** (in horse-race betting) to win only: *I bet twenty pounds on the nose on that horse.* **b.** *Chiefly U.S.* precisely; exactly. **c.** *Austral.* bad or bad-smelling. **14. with one's nose in the air.** haughtily. **15. put someone's nose out of joint.** *Inf.* to thwart or offend someone. **16. rub someone's nose in it.** *Inf.* to remind someone unkindly of a shortcoming. **17. turn up one's nose (at).** *Inf.* to behave disdainfully (towards). ~*vb.* **18.** (*tr.*) (esp. of horses, dogs, etc.) to rub, touch, or sniff with the nose; nuzzle. **19.** to smell or sniff. **20.** (*intr.;* usually foll. by *after* or *for*) to search (for) by or as if by scent. **21.** to move or cause to move forwards slowly and carefully: *we nosed the car into the garage.* **22.** (*intr.;* foll. by *into, around, about,* etc.) to pry or snoop (into) or meddle (in).

—'**noseless** *adj.* —'**nose,like** *adj.*

nosebag ('nəuz,bæg) *n.* a bag, fastened around the head of a horse and covering the nose, in which feed is placed.

noseband ('nəuz,bænd) *n.* the detachable part of a horse's bridle that goes around the nose.

nosebleed ('nəuz,bliːd) *n.* bleeding from the nose as the result of injury, etc.

nose dive *n.* **1.** a sudden plunge with the nose or front pointing downwards, esp. of an aircraft. **2.** *Inf.* a sudden drop or sharp decline: *prices took a nose dive.* ~*vb.* **nose-dive.** (*intr.*) **3.** to perform or cause to perform a nose dive.

nosegay ('nəuz,geɪ) *n.* a small bunch of flowers; posy.

nosh (nɒʃ) *Sl.* ~*n.* **1.** food or a meal. ~*vb.* **2.** to eat. —'**nosher** *n.*

nostalgia (nɒ'stældʒə, -dʒɪə) *n.* **1.** a yearning for past circumstances, events, etc. **2.** the evocation of this emotion, as in a book, film, etc. **3.** homesickness. —**nos'talgic** *adj.* —**nos'talgically** *adv.*

nostril ('nɒstrɪl) *n.* either of the two external openings of the nose.

nostrum ('nɒstrəm) *n.* **1.** a patent or quack medicine. **2.** a favourite remedy.

nosy *or* **nosey** ('nəuzɪ) *adj.* **nosier, nosiest.** *Inf.* prying or inquisitive. —'**nosily** *adv.* —'**nosiness** *n.*

nosy parker *n. Inf., chiefly Brit.* a prying person.

not (nɒt) *adv.* **1. a.** used to negate the sentence, phrase, or word that it modifies: *I will not stand for it.* **b.** (in combination): *they cannot go.* **2. not that.** (*conj.*) Also (arch.): **not but what.** which is not to say or suppose that: *I expect to lose the game—not that I mind.* ~ **3.** *sentence substitute.* used to indicate denial or refusal: *certainly not.*

nota bene *Latin.* ('nəutə 'biːnɪ) *vb.* (*imperative*) note well; take note. *Abbrevs.:* **NB, N.B., nb, n.b.**

notable ('nəutəbəl) *adj.* **1.** worthy of being noted or remembered; remarkable; distinguished. ~*n.* **2.** a notable person. —ˌ**nota'bility** *n.* —'**notably** *adv.*

notary ('nəutərɪ) *n., pl.* **-ries. 1.** a notary public. **2.** (formerly) a clerk licensed to prepare legal documents. **3.** *Arch.* a clerk or secretary. —**notarial** (nəu'tɛərɪəl) *adj.* —'**notary,ship** *n.*

notary public *n., pl.* **notaries public.** a public official, usually a solicitor, who is legally authorized to administer oaths, attest and certify certain documents, etc.

notation (nəu'teɪʃən) *n.* **1.** any series of signs or symbols used to represent quantities or elements in a specialized system, such as music or mathematics. **2.** the act or process of notating. **3.** a note or record. —**no'tational** *adj.*

notch (nɒtʃ) *n.* **1.** a V-shaped cut or indentation; nick. **2.** a nick made in a tally stick. **3.** *U.S.* a narrow gorge. **4.** *Inf.* a step or level (esp. in **a notch above**). ~*vb.* (*tr.*). **5.** to cut or make a notch. **6.** to record with or as if with a notch. **7.** (usually foll. by *up*) *Inf.* to score or achieve: *the team notched up its fourth win.*

note (nəut) *n.* **1.** a brief record in writing, esp. a jotting for future reference. **2.** a brief informal letter. **3.** a formal written communication, esp. from one government to another. **4.** a short written statement giving any kind of information. **5.** a critical comment, explanatory statement, or reference in a book. **6.** short for **bank note. 7.** a characteristic atmosphere: *a note of sarcasm.* **8.** a distinctive vocal sound, as of a species of bird or animal. **9.** any of a series of graphic signs representing the pitch and duration of a musical sound. **10.** Also called (esp. U.S.): **tone.** *Chiefly Brit.* a musical sound of definite

---

THESAURUS

nose dive dive, drop, plummet, plunge

nosegay bouquet, posy

nosh 1. *n.* aliment, chow (*Inf.*), comestibles, eats (*Sl.*), fare, food, grub (*Sl.*), meal, repast, scoff (*Sl.*), sustenance, viands, victuals 2. *v.* consume, eat, scoff (*Sl.*)

nostalgia homesickness, longing, pining, regret, regretfulness, remembrance, reminiscence, wistfulness, yearning

nostalgic homesick, longing, regretful, sentimental, wistful

nostrum cure, cure-all, drug, elixir, medicine, panacea, patent medicine, potion, quack medicine, remedy, sovereign cure, specific, treatment

nosy, nosey curious, eavesdropping, inquisitive, interfering, intrusive, meddlesome, prying, snooping (*Inf.*)

notability 1. celebrity, distinction, eminence, esteem, fame, renown 2. celebrity, dignitary, notable, personage, V.I.P., worthy

notable 1. *adj.* celebrated, conspicuous, distinguished, eminent, evident, extraordinary, famous, manifest, marked, memorable, noteworthy, noticeable, notorious, outstanding, pre-eminent, pronounced, rare, remarkable, renowned, striking, uncommon, unusual, well-known 2. *n.* celebrity, dignitary, notability, personage, V.I.P., worthy

notably conspicuously, distinctly, especially, markedly, noticeably, outstandingly, particularly, remarkably, signally, strikingly, uncommonly

notation 1. characters, code, script, signs, symbols, system 2. jotting, notating, note, noting, record

notch *n.* 1. cleft, cut, incision, indentation, mark, nick, score 2. *Inf.* cut (*Inf.*), degree, grade, level, step ~*v.* 3. cut, indent, mark, nick, score, scratch

notch up achieve, gain, make, register, score

fundamental frequency or pitch. **11.** *Chiefly Brit.* a key on a piano, organ, etc. **12.** a sound used as a signal or warning: *the note to retreat was sounded.* **13.** short for **promissory note. 14.** *Arch. or poetic.* a melody. **15. of note. a.** distinguished or famous. **b.** important: *nothing of note.* **16. strike the right (or a false) note.** to behave appropriately (or inappropriately). **17. take note.** (often foll. by *of*) to pay attention (to). ~*vb.* (*tr.; may take a clause as object*) **18.** to notice; perceive. **19.** to pay close attention to: *they noted every movement.* **20.** to make a written note of: *she noted the date in her diary.* **21.** to remark upon: *I note that you do not wear shoes.* **22.** to write down (music, a melody, etc.) in notes. **23.** a less common word for **annotate.** —'**noteless** *adj.*

notebook ('nəʊtˌbʊk) *n.* a book for recording notes or memoranda.

noted ('nəʊtɪd) *adj.* **1.** celebrated; famous. **2.** of special significance; noticeable. —'**notedly** *adv.*

notepaper ('nəʊtˌpeɪpə) *n.* paper for writing letters; writing paper.

noteworthy ('nəʊtˌwɜːðɪ) *adj.* worthy of notice; notable. —'**note,worthiness** *n.*

nothing ('nʌθɪŋ) *pron.* **1.** (*indefinite*) no thing; not anything: *I can give you nothing.* **2.** no part or share: *to have nothing to do with this crime.* **3.** a matter of no importance: *it doesn't matter, it's nothing.* **4.** indicating the absence of anything perceptible; nothingness. **5.** indicating the absence of meaning, value, worth, etc.: *to amount to nothing.* **6.** zero quantity; nought. **7. be nothing to. a.** not to concern or be significant to (someone). **b.** to be not nearly as good, etc., as. **8. have** *or* **be nothing to do with.** to have no connection with. **9. nothing but.** no more than; only. **10. nothing doing.** *Inf.* an expression of dismissal, refusal, etc. **11. nothing if not.** at the very least; certainly. **12. nothing less than** *or* **nothing short of.** downright; truly. **13. there's nothing to it.** it is very simple, easy, etc. **14. think nothing of. a.** to regard as easy. **b.** to have a very low opinion of. **15. stop at nothing.** to do anything; be ruthless. ~*adv.* **16.** in no way; not at all: *he looked nothing like his brother.* ~*n.* **17.** *Inf.* a person or thing of no importance or significance. **18. sweet nothings.** words of endearment or affection.

▷ **Usage.** *Nothing* always takes a singular verb in careful usage, although a plural verb is often heard in informal speech in sentences such as *nothing but books were on the shelf.*

nothingness ('nʌθɪŋnɪs) *n.* **1.** the state of being nothing; nonexistence. **2.** absence of consciousness or life. **3.** complete insignificance. **4.** something that is worthless.

notice ('nəʊtɪs) *n.* **1.** observation; attention: *to escape notice.* **2. take notice.** to pay attention. **3. take no notice of.** to ignore or disregard. **4.** a warning; announcement. **5.** a displayed placard or announcement giving information. **6.** advance notification of intention to end an arrangement, contract, etc., as of employment (esp.

in **give notice**). **7. at short notice.** with notification only a little in advance. **8.** *Chiefly Brit.* dismissal from employment. **9.** favourable, interested, or polite attention: *she was beneath his notice.* **10.** a theatrical or literary review: *the play received very good notices.* ~*vb.* **11.** to become aware of; perceive; note. **12.** (*tr.*) to point out or remark upon. **13.** (*tr.*) to pay polite or interested attention to. **14.** (*tr.*) to acknowledge (an acquaintance, etc.).

noticeable ('nəʊtɪsəb^əl) *adj.* easily seen or detected; perceptible. —'**noticeably** *adv.*

notice board *n. Brit.* a board on which notices, advertisements, bulletins, etc., are displayed. U.S. name: **bulletin board.**

notifiable ('nəʊtɪˌfaɪəb^əl) *adj.* denoting certain infectious diseases, outbreaks of which must be reported to the public health authorities.

notification (ˌnəʊtɪfɪ'keɪʃən) *n.* **1.** the act of notifying. **2.** a formal announcement. **3.** something that notifies; a notice.

notify ('nəʊtɪˌfaɪ) *vb.* **-fying, -fied.** (*tr.*) **1.** to tell. **2.** *Chiefly Brit.* to make known; announce. —'**noti,fier** *n.*

notion ('nəʊʃən) *n.* **1.** a vague idea; impression. **2.** an idea, concept, or opinion. **3.** an inclination or whim.

notional ('nəʊʃən^əl) *adj.* **1.** expressing or consisting of ideas. **2.** characteristic of a notion, esp. in being speculative or abstract. **3.** *Grammar.* **a.** (of a word) having lexical meaning. **b.** another word for **semantic.** —'**notionally** *adv.*

notorious (nəʊ'tɔːrɪəs) *adj.* **1.** well-known for some bad or unfavourable quality, deed, etc.; infamous. **2.** *Rare.* generally known or widely acknowledged. —**notoriety** (ˌnəʊtə'raɪɪtɪ) *n.* —**no'toriously** *adv.*

not proven ('pruːv^ən) *adj.* (*postpositive*) a third verdict available to Scottish courts, returned when there is insufficient evidence against the accused to convict.

Notts. (nɒts) *abbrev. for* Nottinghamshire.

notwithstanding (ˌnɒtwɪθ'stændɪŋ) *prep.* **1.** (*often immediately postpositive*) in spite of; despite. ~*conj.* **2.** (*subordinating*) although. ~ **3.** *sentence connector.* nevertheless.

nougat ('nuːgɑː) *n.* a hard chewy pink or white sweet containing chopped nuts, cherries, etc.

nought (nɔːt) *n. also* **naught, ought, aught. 1.** another name for **zero**: used esp. in numbering. ~*n., adj., adv.* **2.** a variant spelling of **naught.**

noughts and crosses *n.* a game in which two players, one using a nought, "O", the other a cross, "X", alternately mark squares formed by two pairs of crossed lines, the winner being the first to get three of his symbols in a row. U.S. terms: **tick-tack-toe, crisscross.**

noun (naʊn) *n.* **a.** a word or group of words that refers to a person, place, or thing. **b.** (*as modifier*): *a noun phrase.* Abbrev.: **n.** —'**nounal** *adj.*

nourish ('nʌrɪʃ) *vb.* (*tr.*) **1.** to provide with the materials necessary for life and growth. **2.** to encourage (an

---

THESAURUS

note *n.* **1.** annotation, comment, communication, epistle, gloss, jotting, letter, memo, memorandum, message, minute, record, remark, reminder **2.** indication, mark, sign, symbol, token **3.** heed, notice, observation, regard **4.** celebrity, character, consequence, distinction, eminence, fame, prestige, renown, reputation ~*v.* **5.** denote, designate, indicate, mark, mention, notice, observe, perceive, record, register, remark, see, take note

notebook commonplace book, diary, exercise book, jotter, journal, memorandum book, notepad, record book

noted acclaimed, celebrated, conspicuous, distinguished, eminent, famous, illustrious, notable, notorious, prominent, recognized, renowned, well-known

notes impressions, jottings, outline, record, report, sketch

noteworthy exceptional, extraordinary, important, notable, outstanding, remarkable, significant, unusual

nothing bagatelle, cipher, emptiness, naught, nobody, nonentity, nonexistence, nothingness, nought, nullity, trifle, void, zero

nothingness 1. nihility, nonbeing, non-

existence, nullity, oblivion **2.** insignificance, unimportance, worthlessness

notice *v.* **1.** detect, discern, distinguish, heed, mark, mind, note, observe, perceive, remark, see, spot ~*n.* **2.** cognizance, consideration, heed, note, observation, regard **3.** advice, announcement, communication, instruction, intelligence, intimation, news, notification, order, warning **4.** advertisement, comment, criticism, poster, review, sign **5.** attention, civility, respect

noticeable appreciable, clear, conspicuous, distinct, evident, manifest, observable, obvious, perceptible, plain, striking, unmistakable

notification advice, alert, announcement, declaration, information, intelligence, message, notice, notifying, publication, statement, telling, warning

notify acquaint, advise, alert, announce, apprise, declare, inform, publish, tell, warn

notion 1. apprehension, belief, concept, conception, idea, impression, inkling, judgment, knowledge, opinion, sentiment, understanding, view **2.** caprice, desire, fancy, impulse, inclination, whim, wish

notional abstract, conceptual, fanciful, hypothetical, ideal, imaginary, speculative, theoretical, unreal, visionary

notoriety dishonour, disrepute, infamy, obloquy, opprobrium, scandal

notorious 1. dishonourable, disreputable, infamous, opprobrious, scandalous **2.** blatant, flagrant, glaring, obvious, open, overt, patent, undisputed

notoriously 1. dishonourably, disreputably, infamously, opprobriously, scandalously **2.** blatantly, flagrantly, glaringly, notably, obviously, openly, overtly, particularly, patently, spectacularly, undisputedly

notwithstanding although, despite, however, nevertheless, nonetheless, though, yet

nourish 1. attend, feed, furnish, nurse, nurture, supply, sustain, tend **2.** comfort, cultivate, encourage, foster, maintain, promote, support

nourishing alimentative, beneficial, healthful, health-giving, nutritious, nutritive, wholesome

idea, etc.); foster: *to nourish resentment.* —'**nourisher** *n.* —'**nourishingly** *adv.*

nourishment ('nʌrıʃmənt) *n.* **1.** the act or state of nourishing. **2.** a substance that nourishes; food.

nous (naʊs) *n.* **1.** *Metaphysics.* mind or reason, esp. when regarded as the principle governing all things. **2.** *Brit. sl.* common sense.

nouveau riche *French.* (nuvo 'riʃ) *n., pl. nouveaux riches* (nuvo 'riʃ). (often preceded by *the*) a person who has acquired wealth recently and is regarded as vulgarly ostentatious or lacking in social graces.

Nov. *abbrev. for* November.

nova ('nəʊvə) *n., pl.* **-vae** (-viː) *or* **-vas.** a faint variable star that undergoes an explosion and fast increase of luminosity, decreasing to its original luminosity in months or years.

novel[1] ('nɒvəl) *n.* **1.** an extended fictional work in prose dealing with character, action, thought, etc., esp. in the form of a story. **2. the.** the literary genre represented by novels. —,**novel'istic** *adj.*

novel[2] ('nɒvəl) *adj.* of a kind not seen before; fresh; new; original: *a novel suggestion.* —'**novelly** *adv.*

novelette (,nɒvə'lɛt) *n.* **1.** an extended prose narrative or short novel. **2.** a novel that is regarded as slight, trivial, or sentimental. **3.** a short piece of lyrical music, esp. one for the piano. —,**nove'lettish** *adj.*

novelist ('nɒvəlɪst) *n.* a writer of novels.

novella (nəʊ'vɛlə) *n., pl.* **-las** *or* **-le** (-leɪ). **1.** a short narrative tale, esp. one having a satirical point, such as those in Boccaccio's *Decameron.* **2.** a short novel.

novelty ('nɒvəltɪ) *n., pl.* **-ties. 1. a.** the quality of being new and interesting. **b.** (*as modifier*): *novelty value.* **2.** a new or unusual experience. **3.** (*often pl.*) a small usually cheap new ornament or trinket.

November (nəʊ'vɛmbə) *n.* the eleventh month of the year, consisting of 30 days.

novice ('nɒvɪs) *n.* **1.** a person who is new to or inexperienced in a certain task, situation, etc.; beginner; tyro. **2.** a probationer in a religious order. **3.** a sportsman, esp. an oarsman, who has not won a recognized prize, performed to an established level, etc.

novitiate *or* **noviciate** (nəʊ'vɪʃɪt, -,eɪt) *n.* **1.** the state of being a novice, esp. in a religious order, or the period for which this lasts. **2.** the part of a religious house where the novices live.

now (naʊ) *adv.* **1.** at or for the present time. **2.** immediately. **3.** in these times; nowadays. **4.** given the present circumstances: *now we'll have to stay to the end.* **5.** (preceded by *just*) very recently: *he left just now.* **6.** (often preceded by *just*) very soon: *he is leaving just now.* **7.** (**every**) **now and again** *or* **then.** occasionally; on and off. **8. now now!** (*interj.*) an exclamation used to rebuke or pacify someone. ∼*conj.* **9.** (*subordinating; often foll. by that*) seeing that: *now you're in charge, things will be better.* ∼ **10.** *sentence connector.* **a.** used as a hesitation word: *now, I can't really say.* **b.** used for emphasis: *now listen to this.* **c.** used at the end of a command: *run along, now.* ∼*n.* **11.** the present time: *now is the time to go.*

nowadays ('naʊə,deɪz) *adv.* in these times.

noway ('nəʊ,weɪ) *adv. Sl.* not at all.

Nowel *or* **Nowell** (nəʊ'ɛl) *n.* an archaic spelling of **Noel.**

nowhere ('nəʊwɛə) *adv.* **1.** in, at, or to no place; not anywhere. **2. get nowhere (fast).** *Inf.* to fail completely to make any progress. **3. nowhere near.** far from; not nearly. ∼*n.* **4.** a nonexistent or insignificant place. **5. middle of nowhere.** a completely isolated place.

nowt (naʊt) *n. Northern Brit.* a dialect word for **nothing.**

noxious ('nɒkʃəs) *adj.* poisonous or harmful. —'**noxiously** *adv.* —'**noxiousness** *n.*

nozzle ('nɒzəl) *n.* a projecting pipe or spout from which

fluid is discharged.

Np *the chemical symbol for* neptunium.

N.S. *abbrev. for:* **1.** New Style (method of reckoning dates). **2.** Nova Scotia.

N.S.P.C.C. *abbrev. for* National Society for the Prevention of Cruelty to Children.

N.S.T. *Canad. abbrev. for* Newfoundland Standard Time.

N.S.W. *abbrev. for* New South Wales.

N.T. *abbrev. for:* **1.** National Trust. **2.** New Testament. **3.** Northern Territory. **4.** no trumps.

-n't *contraction of* not: used as an enclitic after *be* and *have* when they function as main verbs and after auxiliary verbs or verbs operating syntactically as auxiliaries: *can't; don't; isn't.*

nth (ɛnθ) *adj.* **1.** *Maths.* of or representing an unspecified ordinal number, usually the greatest in a series: *the nth power.* **2.** *Inf.* being the last or most extreme of a long series: *for the nth time.* **3. to the nth degree.** *Inf.* to the utmost extreme.

nu (njuː) *n.* the 13th letter in the Greek alphabet (N, ν), a consonant.

nuance (njuː'ɑːns, 'njuːɑːns) *n.* a subtle difference in colour, meaning, tone, etc.

nub (nʌb) *n.* **1.** a small lump or protuberance. **2.** a small piece or chunk. **3.** the point or gist: *the nub of a story.* —'**nubbly** *or* '**nubby** *adj.*

nubile ('njuːbaɪl) *adj.* (of a girl) **1.** ready or suitable for marriage by virtue of age or maturity. **2.** sexually attractive. —**nubility** (njuː'bɪlɪtɪ) *n.*

nuclear ('njuːklɪə) *adj.* **1.** of or involving the nucleus of an atom: *nuclear fission.* **2.** *Biol.* of, relating to, or contained within the nucleus of a cell: *a nuclear membrane.* **3.** of, forming, or resembling any other kind of nucleus. **4.** of or operated by energy from fission or fusion of atomic nuclei: *a nuclear weapon.* **5.** involving or possessing nuclear weapons: *nuclear war.*

nuclear bomb *n.* a bomb whose force is due to uncontrolled nuclear fusion or nuclear fission.

nuclear energy *n.* energy released during a nuclear reaction as a result of fission or fusion. Also called: **atomic energy.**

nuclear family *n. Sociol., anthropol.* a primary social unit consisting of parents and their offspring.

nuclear fission *n.* the splitting of an atomic nucleus into approximately equal parts, either spontaneously or as a result of the impact of a particle usually with an associated release of energy. Sometimes shortened to **fission.**

nuclear fusion *n.* a reaction in which two nuclei combine to form a nucleus with the release of energy. Sometimes shortened to **fusion.**

nuclear physics *n.* the branch of physics concerned with the structure and behaviour of the nucleus and the particles of which it consists.

nuclear reactor *n.* a device in which a nuclear reaction is maintained and controlled for the production of nuclear energy. Sometimes shortened to **reactor.**

nucleate ('njuːklɪɪt, -,eɪt) *adj.* **1.** having a nucleus. ∼*vb.* **2.** to form a nucleus.

nuclei ('njuːklɪ,aɪ) *n.* the plural of **nucleus.**

nucleic acid (njuː'kliːɪk, -'kleɪ-) *n. Biochem.* any of a group of complex compounds with a high molecular weight that are vital constituents of all living cells.

nucleo- *or before a vowel* **nucle-** *combining form.* **1.** nucleus or nuclear. **2.** nucleic acid.

nucleonics (,njuːklɪ'ɒnɪks) *n.* (*functioning as sing.*) the branch of physics concerned with the applications of nuclear energy. —,**nucle'onic** *adj.* —,**nucle'onically** *adv.*

nucleus ('njuːklɪəs) *n., pl.* **-clei** (-klɪ,aɪ) *or* **-cleuses. 1.** a central or fundamental thing around which others are

---

THESAURUS

nourishment aliment, diet, food, nutriment, nutrition, sustenance, viands, victuals

nouveau riche arriviste, new-rich, parvenu, upstart

novel 1. *adj.* different, fresh, innovative, new, original, rare, singular, strange, uncommon, unfamiliar, unusual **2.** *n.* fiction, narrative, romance, story, tale

novelty 1. freshness, innovation, newness, oddity, originality, strangeness, surprise, un-

familiarity, uniqueness **2.** bagatelle, bauble, curiosity, gadget, gewgaw, gimcrack, gimmick, knick-knack, memento, souvenir, trifle, trinket

novice amateur, apprentice, beginner, convert, learner, neophyte, newcomer, novitiate, probationer, proselyte, pupil, tyro

now 1. at once, immediately, instanter (*Law*), instantly, presently (*Scot. & U.S.*), promptly, straightaway **2.** any more, at the

moment, nowadays, these days **3. now and then** *or* **again** at times, from time to time, infrequently, intermittently, occasionally, on and off, once in a while, on occasion, sometimes, sporadically

nowadays any more, at the moment, in this day and age, now, these days, today

grouped; core. **2.** a centre of growth or development; basis: *the nucleus of an idea.* **3.** *Biol.* a spherical or ovoid cellular organelle that is responsible for growth and reproduction of the cell. **4.** *Astron.* the central portion in the head of a comet, consisting of small solid particles of ice and frozen gases. **5.** *Physics.* the positively charged dense region at the centre of an atom, composed of protons and neutrons, about which electrons orbit. **6.** *Chem.* a fundamental group of atoms in a molecule serving as the base structure for related compounds.

nude (njuːd) *adj.* **1.** completely undressed. **2.** having no covering; bare; exposed. **3.** *Law.* **a.** lacking some essential legal requirement. **b.** (of a contract, etc.) made without consideration and void unless under seal. ~*n.* **4.** the state of being naked (esp. in **in the nude**). **5.** a naked figure, esp. in painting, sculpture, etc. —'**nudely** *adv.* —'**nudity** *n.*

nudge (nʌdʒ) *vb.* (*tr.*) **1.** to push (someone) gently, esp. with the elbow, to get attention; jog. **2.** to push slowly or lightly: *as I drove out, I just nudged the gatepost.* ~*n.* **3.** a gentle poke or push. —'**nudger** *n.*

nudism ('njuːdɪzəm) *n.* the practice of nudity, esp. for reasons of health, etc. —'**nudist** *n.*

nuisance ('njuːsəns) *n.* **1. a.** a person or thing that causes annoyance or bother. **b.** (*as modifier*): *nuisance value.* **2.** *Law.* something unauthorized that is obnoxious or injurious to the community at large or to an individual, esp. in relation to his ownership of property.

N.U.J. *abbrev. for* National Union of Journalists.

null (nʌl) *adj.* **1.** without legal force; invalid; (esp. in **null and void**). **2.** without value or consequence; useless. **3.** lacking distinction; characterless. **4.** nonexistent; amounting to nothing. **5.** *Maths.* **a.** quantitatively zero. **b.** relating to zero. **c.** (of a set) having no members. **6.** *Physics.* involving measurement in which conditions are adjusted so that an instrument has a zero reading, as with a Wheatstone bridge.

nullify ('nʌlɪˌfaɪ) *vb.* -**fying,** -**fied.** (*tr.*) **1.** to render legally void or of no effect. **2.** to render ineffective or useless; cancel out. —ˌnullifi'cation *n.*

nullity ('nʌlɪtɪ) *n., pl.* -**ties.** **1.** the state of being null. **2.** a null or legally invalid act or instrument. **3.** something null, ineffective, characterless, etc.

N.U.M. *abbrev. for* National Union of Mineworkers.

num. *abbrev. for:* **1.** number. **2.** numeral.

Num. *Bible. abbrev. for* Numbers.

numb (nʌm) *adj.* **1.** deprived of feeling through cold, shock, etc. **2.** unable to move; paralysed. ~*vb.* **3.** (*tr.*) to make numb; deaden, shock, or paralyse. —'**numbly** *adv.* —'**numbness** *n.*

number ('nʌmbə) *n.* **1.** a concept of quantity that is or can be derived from a single unit, the sum of a collection of units, or zero. Every number occupies a unique position in a sequence, enabling it to be used in counting. See also **cardinal number, ordinal number.** **2.** the symbol used to represent a number; numeral. **3.** a numeral or string of numerals used to identify a person or thing: *a telephone number.* **4.** the person or thing so identified or designated: *she was number seven in the race.* **5.** sum or quantity: *a large number of people.* **6.** one of a series, as of a magazine; issue. **7. a.** a self-contained piece of pop or jazz music. **b.** a self-contained part of an opera or other musical score. **8.** a group of people, esp.

an exclusive group: *he was not one of our number.* **9.** *Sl.* a person, esp. a sexually attractive girl: *who's that nice little number?* **10.** *Inf.* an admired article: *that little number is by Dior.* **11.** a grammatical category for the variation in form of nouns, pronouns, and any words agreeing with them, depending on how many persons or things are referred to. **12. any number of.** several or many. **13. by numbers.** *Mil.* (of a drill procedure, etc.) performed step by step, each move being made on the call of a number. **14. get** *or* **have someone's number.** *Chiefly U.S. inf.* to discover a person's true character or intentions. **15. one's number is up.** *Brit. inf.* one is finished; one is dead or ruined. **16. without** *or* **beyond number.** innumerable. ~*vb.* (*mainly tr.*) **17.** to assign a number to. **18.** to add up to; total. **19.** (*also intr.*) to list (items) one by one; enumerate. **20.** (*also intr.*) to put or be put into a group, category, etc.: *they were numbered among the worst hit.* **21.** to limit the number of: *his days were numbered.*

numberless ('nʌmbəlɪs) *adj.* **1.** too many to be counted; countless. **2.** not containing numbers.

number one *n.* **1.** an informal phrase for **oneself, myself,** etc.: *to look after number one.* ~*adj.* **2.** first in importance, urgency, quality, etc.: *number one priority.*

numberplate ('nʌmbəˌpleɪt) *n.* a plate mounted on the front and back of a motor vehicle bearing the registration number. Usual U.S. term: **license plate.**

Number Ten *n.* 10 Downing Street, the British prime minister's official London residence.

numbskull ('nʌmˌskʌl) *n.* a variant spelling of **numskull.**

numeral ('njuːmərəl) *n.* **1.** a symbol or group of symbols used to express a number: for example, *6* (*Arabic*), *VI* (*Roman*), *110* (*binary*). ~*adj.* **2.** of, consisting of, or denoting a number.

numerate *adj.* ('njuːmərɪt) **1.** able to use numbers, esp. in arithmetical operations. ~*vb.* ('njuːməˌreɪt). **2.** (*tr.*) to read (a numerical expression). **3.** a less common word for **enumerate.** —**numeracy** ('njuːmərəsɪ) *n.*

numerator ('njuːməˌreɪtə) *n.* **1.** *Maths.* the dividend of a fraction: the numerator of 7/8 is 7. **2.** a person or thing that numbers; enumerator. Cf. **denominator.**

numerical (njuːˈmɛrɪkəl) *or* **numeric** *adj.* **1.** of, relating to, or denoting a number or numbers. **2.** measured or expressed in numbers: *numerical value.* —**nu'merically** *adv.*

numerous ('njuːmərəs) *adj.* **1.** being many. **2.** consisting of many parts: *a numerous collection.* —'**numerously** *adv.* —'**numerousness** *n.*

numismatics (ˌnjuːmɪzˈmætɪks) *n.* (*functioning as sing.*) the study or collection of coins, medals, etc. Also called: **numismatology** (ˌnjuːmɪzməˈtɒlədʒɪ). —ˌnumis-'matic *adj.* —ˌnumis'matically *adv.*

numskull *or* **numbskull** ('nʌmˌskʌl) *n.* a stupid person; dolt; blockhead.

nun (nʌn) *n.* a female member of a religious order. —'**nunhood** *n.* —'**nunlike** *adj.*

nuncio ('nʌnʃɪˌəʊ, -sɪ-) *n., pl.* -**cios.** *R.C. Church.* a diplomatic representative of the Holy See.

nunnery ('nʌnərɪ) *n., pl.* -**neries.** the convent or religious house of a community of nuns.

NUPE ('njuːpɪ) *n. acronym for* National Union of Public Employees.

THESAURUS

nucleus basis, centre, core, focus, heart, kernel, nub, pivot

nude au naturel, bare, disrobed, exposed, in one's birthday suit (*Inf.*), in the altogether (*Inf.*), in the buff (*Inf.*), naked, starkers (*Inf.*), stark-naked, stripped, unclad, unclothed, uncovered, undraped, undressed

nudge v. bump, dig, elbow, jog, poke, prod, push, shove, touch

nudity bareness, nakedness, undress

nugget chunk, clump, hunk, lump, mass, piece

nuisance annoyance, bore, bother, inconvenience, infliction, irritation, offence, pest, plague, problem, trouble, vexation

null characterless, ineffectual, inoperative, invalid, nonexistent, null and void, powerless, useless, vain, valueless, void, worthless

nullify abolish, abrogate, annul, bring to naught, cancel, counteract, countervail, invalidate, negate, neutralize, quash, render null and void, repeal, rescind, revoke, veto, void

nullity characterlessness, ineffectualness, invalidity, nonexistence, powerlessness, uselessness, valuelessness, voidness, worthlessness

numb 1. *adj.* benumbed, dead, deadened, frozen, immobilized, insensible, insensitive, paralysed, stupefied, torpid, unfeeling **2.** *v.* benumb, deaden, dull, freeze, immobilize, paralyse, stun, stupefy

number *n.* **1.** character, count, digit, figure, integer, numeral, sum, total, unit **2.** aggregate, amount, collection, company, crowd, horde, many, multitude, quantity, throng **3.** copy, edition, imprint, issue, print-

ing ~v. **4.** account, add, calculate, compute, count, enumerate, include, reckon, tell, total

numbered categorized, contained, counted, designated, fixed, included, limited, limited in number, specified, totalled

numberless countless, endless, infinite, innumerable, multitudinous, myriad, unnumbered, untold

numbness deadness, dullness, insensibility, insensitivity, paralysis, stupefaction, torpor, unfeelingness

numeral character, cipher, digit, figure, integer, number, symbol

numerous abundant, copious, many, plentiful, profuse, several

nunnery abbey, cloister, convent, house, monastery

nuptial ('nʌpʃəl, -tʃəl) adj. 1. relating to marriage; conjugal: nuptial vows. 2. Zool. of or relating to mating: the nuptial flight of a queen bee. —'**nuptially** adv.

nuptials ('nʌpʃəlz, -tʃəlz) pl. n. (sometimes sing.) a marriage ceremony; wedding.

N.U.R. abbrev. for National Union of Railwaymen.

nurse (nɜːs) n. 1. a person, often a woman, who is trained to tend the sick and infirm, assist doctors, etc. 2. short for **nursemaid**. 3. a woman employed to breast-feed another woman's child; wet nurse. 4. a worker in a colony of social insects that takes care of the larvae. ~vb. (mainly tr.) 5. (also intr.) to tend (the sick). 6. (also intr.) to feed (a baby) at the breast. 7. to try to cure (an ailment). 8. to clasp fondly: she nursed the child in her arms. 9. to look after (a child) as one's employment. 10. to harbour; preserve: to nurse a grudge. 11. to give special attention to, esp. in order to promote good will: to nurse a difficult constituency. 12. Billiards. to keep (the balls) together for a series of cannons.

nursemaid ('nɜːs,meɪd) or **nurserymaid** n. a woman employed to look after someone else's children. Often shortened to **nurse**.

nursery ('nɜːsrɪ) n., pl. -**ries**. 1. a room in a house set apart for children. 2. a place where plants, young trees, etc., are grown commercially. 3. an establishment providing for babies and young children; crèche. 4. anywhere serving to foster or nourish new ideas, etc. 5. Also called: **nursery cannon**. Billiards. a series of cannons with the three balls adjacent to a cushion, esp. near a corner pocket. **b.** a cannon in such a series.

nurseryman ('nɜːsrɪmən) n., pl. -**men**. a person who owns or works in a nursery in which plants are grown.

nursery rhyme n. a short traditional verse or song for children, such as Little Jack Horner.

nursery school n. a school for young children, usually from three to five years old.

nursery slopes pl. n. gentle slopes used by beginners in skiing.

nursery stakes n. a race for two-year-old horses.

nursing home n. a private hospital or residence for aged or infirm persons.

nursing officer n. (in Britain) the official name for **matron** (sense 4).

nurture ('nɜːtʃə) n. 1. the act or process of promoting the development, etc., of a child. 2. something that nourishes. ~vb. (tr.) 3. to feed or support. 4. to educate or train. —'**nurturable** adj. —'**nurturer** n.

N.U.S. abbrev. for: 1. National Union of Seamen. 2. National Union of Students.

nut (nʌt) n. 1. a dry one-seeded indehiscent fruit that usually possesses a woody wall. 2. (not in technical use) any similar fruit, such as the walnut, having a hard shell and an edible kernel. 3. the edible kernel of such a fruit. 4. Sl. an eccentric or mad person. 5. a slang word for the **head**. 6. **do one's nut**. Brit. sl. to be extremely angry. 7. **off one's nut**. Sl. mad or foolish. 8. a person or thing that presents difficulties (esp. in a **tough nut to crack**). 9. a small metallic block, usually hexagonal or square, with an internal screw thread enabling it to be fitted onto a bolt. 10. Also called (U.S.): **frog**. Music. **a.** the ridge at the upper end of the fingerboard of a violin, cello, etc., over which the strings pass to the tuning pegs. **b.** the end of a violin bow that is held by the player. 11. a small usually gingery biscuit. 12. Brit. a small piece of coal. ~See also **nuts**. ~vb. **nutting, nutted**. 13. (intr.) to gather nuts.

N.U.T. abbrev. for National Union of Teachers.

nutcase ('nʌt,keɪs) n. Sl. an insane or very foolish person.

nutcracker ('nʌt,krækə) n. 1. (often pl.) a device for cracking the shells of nuts. 2. either an Old World bird or a North American bird (**Clark's nutcracker**) having

speckled plumage and feeding on nuts, seeds, etc.

nuthatch ('nʌt,hætʃ) n. a songbird having strong feet and bill, and feeding on insects, seeds, and nuts.

nutmeg ('nʌt,mɛg) n. 1. an East Indian evergreen tree cultivated in the tropics for its hard aromatic seed. See also **mace²**. 2. the seed of this tree, used as a spice.

nutria ('njuːtrɪə) n. another name for **coypu**, esp. the fur.

nutrient ('njuːtrɪənt) n. 1. any of the mineral substances that are absorbed by the roots of plants. 2. any substance that nourishes an animal. ~adj. 3. providing or contributing to nourishment.

nutriment ('njuːtrɪmənt) n. any material providing nourishment. —**nutrimental** (,njuːtrɪ'mɛntəl) adj.

nutrition (njuː'trɪʃən) n. 1. a process in animals and plants involving the intake and assimilation of nutrient materials. 2. the act or process of nourishing. 3. the study of nutrition, esp. in humans. —**nu'tritional** adj. —**nu'tritionist** n.

nutritious (njuː'trɪʃəs) adj. nourishing. —**nu'tritiously** adv. —**nu'tritiousness** n.

nutritive ('njuːtrɪtɪv) adj. 1. providing nourishment. 2. of, concerning, or promoting nutrition. ~n. 3. a nutritious food.

nuts (nʌts) adj. 1. a slang word for **insane**. 2. (foll. by about or on) Sl. extremely fond (of) or enthusiastic (about). ~interj. 3. Sl. an expression of contempt, refusal, or defiance.

nuts and bolts pl. n. Inf. the essential or practical details.

nutshell ('nʌt,ʃɛl) n. 1. the shell around the kernel of a nut. 2. **in a nutshell**. in essence; briefly.

nutter ('nʌtə) n. Brit. sl. a mad or eccentric person.

nutty ('nʌtɪ) adj. -**tier**, -**tiest**. 1. containing nuts. 2. resembling nuts. 3. a slang word for **insane**. 4. (foll. by over or about) Inf. extremely enthusiastic (about). —'**nuttiness** n.

nux vomica ('nʌks 'vɒmɪkə) n. 1. an Indian tree with orange-red berries containing poisonous seeds. 2. any of the seeds of this tree, which contain strychnine and other poisonous alkaloids. 3. a medicine manufactured from the seeds of this tree, formerly used as a heart stimulant.

nuzzle ('nʌzəl) vb. 1. to push or rub gently with the nose or snout. 2. (intr.) to nestle; lie close. 3. (tr.) to dig out with the snout.

NW abbrev. for northwest(ern).

N.W.T. abbrev. for Northwest Territories (of Canada).

N.Y. abbrev. for New York (city or state).

nylon ('naɪlɒn) n. 1. a class of synthetic polyamide materials made by copolymerizing dicarboxylic acids with diamines. Nylon monofilaments are used for bristles, etc., and nylon fibres can be spun into yarn. 2. yarn or cloth made of nylon, used for clothing, stockings, etc.

nylons ('naɪlɒnz) pl. n. stockings made of nylon.

nymph (nɪmf) n. 1. Myth. a spirit of nature envisaged as a beautiful maiden. 2. Chiefly poetic. a beautiful young woman. 3. the larva of insects such as the dragonfly: resembles the adult, apart from having underdeveloped wings and reproductive organs, and develops without a pupal stage. —'**nymphal** or **nymphean** ('nɪmfɪən) adj. —'**nymphlike** adj.

nymphet ('nɪmfɪt) n. a young girl who is sexually precocious and desirable.

nympho ('nɪmfəʊ) n., pl. -**phos**. Inf. short for **nymphomaniac** (see **nymphomania**).

nymphomania (,nɪmfə'meɪnɪə) n. an abnormally intense and persistent desire in a woman for sexual intercourse. —,**nympho'maniac** n., adj.

N.Z. or **N. Zeal.** abbrev. for New Zealand.

THESAURUS

nuptial adj. bridal, conjugal, connubial, hymeneal (Poetic), marital, matrimonial, wedded, wedding

nuptials espousal (Archaic), marriage, matrimony, wedding

nurse v. 1. care for, look after, minister to, tend, treat 2. breast-feed, feed, nourish, nurture, suckle, wet-nurse 3. Fig. cherish, cultivate, encourage, foster, harbour, keep alive, preserve, promote, succour, support

nurture n. 1. diet, food, nourishment 2. development, discipline, education, instruction, rearing, training, upbringing ~v. 3. feed, nourish, nurse, support, sustain, tend 4. bring up, cultivate, develop, discipline, educate, instruct, rear, school, train

nut 1. kernel, seed, stone 2. Sl. brain, head, mind, reason, senses 3. Sl. crackpot (Inf.), crank (Inf.), eccentric, loony (Sl.), lunatic, madman, maniac, nutcase (Sl.)

nutrition food, nourishment, nutriment, sustenance

nutritious alimental, alimentative, beneficial, healthful, health-giving, invigorating, nourishing, nutritive, strengthening, wholesome

nuts bananas (Brit. sl.), batty (Sl.), crazy (Inf.), demented, deranged, eccentric, insane, irrational, loony (Sl.), loopy (Inf.), mad, nutty (Sl.)

O

o *or* **O** (əʊ) *n., pl.* **o's, O's,** *or* **Os. 1.** the 15th letter and fourth vowel of the English alphabet. **2.** any of several speech sounds represented by this letter, as in *code, pot, cow,* or *form.* **3.** another name for **nought.**

O¹ *symbol for:* **1.** *Chem.* oxygen. **2.** a human blood type of the ABO group. **3.** Old.

O² (əʊ) *interj.* **1.** a variant of **oh. 2.** an exclamation introducing an invocation, entreaty, wish, etc.: *O God! O for the wings of a dove!*

o. *abbrev. for:* **1.** octavo. **2.** old. **3.** only. **4.** order. **5.** *Pharmacol.* pint.

O. *abbrev. for:* **1.** Ocean. **2.** octavo. **3.** old.

o' (ə) *prep. Inf. or arch.* shortened form of **of:** *a cup o' tea.*

O'- *prefix.* (in surnames of Irish Gaelic origin) descendant of: *O'Corrigan.*

oaf (əʊf) *n.* a stupid or loutish person. —**'oafish** *adj.* —**'oafishness** *n.*

oak (əʊk) *n.* **1.** any deciduous or evergreen tree or shrub having acorns as fruits and lobed leaves. **2. a.** the wood of any of these trees, used as building timber and for making furniture. **b.** (*as modifier*): *an oak table.* **3.** any of various trees that resemble the oak, such as the poison oak. **4.** anything made of oak, esp. a heavy outer door to a set of rooms in an Oxford college. **5.** the leaves of an oak tree, worn as a garland.

oak apple *or* **gall** *n.* any of various brownish round galls on oak trees, containing the larva of certain wasps.

Oaks (əʊks) *n.* **the.** a horse race for fillies held annually at Epsom since 1779: one of the classics of English flat-racing.

oakum (ˈəʊkəm) *n.* loose fibre obtained by unravelling old rope, used esp. for caulking seams in wooden ships.

O.A.P. *abbrev. for* old age pension *or* pensioner.

oar (ɔː) *n.* **1.** a long shaft of wood for propelling a boat by rowing, having a broad blade that is dipped into and pulled against the water. **2.** short for **oarsman. 3. put one's oar in.** to interfere or interrupt. ~*vb.* **4.** to row or propel with or as if with oars. —**'oarless** *adj.* —**'oar-ˌlike** *adj.*

oarsman (ˈɔːzmən) *n., pl.* **-men.** a man who rows, esp. one who rows in a racing boat. —**'oarsman,ship** *n.*

OAS *abbrev. for:* **1.** Organization of American States. **2.** *Organisation de l'Armée Secrète;* an organization which opposed Algerian independence by acts of terrorism.

oasis (əʊˈeɪsɪs) *n., pl.* **-ses** (-siːz). **1.** a fertile patch in a desert occurring where the water table approaches or reaches the ground surface. **2.** a refuge; haven.

oast (əʊst) *n. Chiefly Brit.* **1.** a kiln for drying hops. **2.** Also called: **oast house.** a building containing such kilns, usually having a conical or pyramidal roof.

oat (əʊt) *n.* **1.** an erect annual grass grown in temperate regions for its edible seed. **2.** (*usually pl.*) the seeds or fruits of this grass. **3.** any of various other grasses such as the wild oat. **4.** *Poetic.* a flute made from an oat

straw. **5. feel one's oats.** *U.S. inf.* **a.** to feel exuberant. **b.** to feel self-important. **6. sow one's (wild) oats.** to indulge in adventure or promiscuity during youth.

oatcake (ˈəʊtˌkeɪk) *n.* a brittle unleavened cake of oatmeal.

oath (əʊθ) *n., pl.* **oaths** (əʊðz). **1.** a solemn pronouncement to affirm the truth of a statement or to pledge a person to some course of action. **2.** the form of such a pronouncement. **3.** an irreverent or blasphemous expression, esp. one involving the name of a deity; curse. **4. on, upon,** *or* **under oath. a.** under the obligation of an oath. **b.** *Law.* having sworn to tell the truth, usually with one's hand on the Bible. **5. my oath.** *Austral. sl.* certainly; yes indeed. **6. take an oath.** to declare formally with a pledge, esp. before giving evidence.

oatmeal (ˈəʊtˌmiːl) *n.* **1.** meal ground from oats, used for making porridge, oatcakes, etc. **2. a.** a greyish-yellow colour. **b.** (*as adj.*): *an oatmeal coat.*

OAU *abbrev. for* Organization of African Unity.

ob. *abbrev. for:* **1.** (on tombstones, etc.) obiit. **2.** obiter. **3.** oboe.

ob- *prefix.* inverse or inversely: *obovate.*

O.B. *Brit. abbrev. for:* **1.** Old Boy. **2.** outside broadcast.

obbligato *or* **obligato** (ˌɒblɪˈɡɑːtəʊ) *Music.* ~*adj.* **1.** not to be omitted in performance. ~*n.,pl.* **-tos** *or* **-ti** (-tiː). **2.** an essential part in a score: *with oboe obbligato.*

obdurate (ˈɒbdjʊrɪt) *adj.* **1.** not easily moved by feelings or supplication; hard-hearted. **2.** impervious to persuasion. —**'obduracy** *or* **'obdurateness** *n.* —**'obdurately** *adv.*

O.B.E. *abbrev. for* Officer of the Order of the British Empire (a Brit. title).

obedient (əˈbiːdɪənt) *adj.* obeying or willing to obey. —o'**bedience** *n.* —o'**bediently** *adv.*

obeisance (əʊˈbeɪsəns, əʊˈbiː-) *n.* **1.** an attitude of deference or homage. **2.** a gesture expressing obeisance. —o'**beisant** *adj.* —o'**beisantly** *adv.*

obelisk (ˈɒbɪlɪsk) *n.* **1.** a stone pillar having a square or rectangular cross section and sides that taper towards a pyramidal top. **2.** *Printing.* another name for **dagger** (sense 2). —ˌobe'**liscal** *adj.* —ˌobe'**liskoid** *adj.*

obese (əʊˈbiːs) *adj.* excessively fat or fleshy; corpulent. —o'**besity** *or* o'**beseness** *n.*

obey (əˈbeɪ) *vb.* **1.** to carry out (instructions or orders); comply with (demands). **2.** to behave or act in accordance with (one's feelings, whims, etc.). —o'**beyer** *n.*

obfuscate (ˈɒbfʌsˌkeɪt) *vb.* (*tr.*) **1.** to obscure or darken. **2.** to perplex or bewilder. —ˌobfus'**cation** *n.* —ˌobfus'**catory** *adj.*

obituary (əˈbɪtjʊərɪ) *n., pl.* **-aries.** a published announcement of a death, often accompanied by a short biography of the dead person. —o'**bituarist** *n.*

obj. *abbrev. for:* **1.** *Grammar.* object(ive). **2.** objection.

THESAURUS

oaf blockhead, bonehead (*Sl.*), booby, brute, clod, dolt, dullard, dummy (*Sl.*), dunce, fool, galoot (*Sl.*), gawk, goon, gorilla (*Inf.*), halfwit, idiot, imbecile, lout, lummox (*Inf.*), moron, nincompoop, sap (*Sl.*), simpleton

oafish blockish, Boeotian, boneheaded (*Sl.*), bovine, brutish, dense, dim, dim-witted (*Inf.*), doltish, dull, dumb (*Inf., chiefly U.S.*), heavy, loutish, lubberly, lumbering, moronic, obtuse, slow on the uptake (*Inf.*), stupid, thick

oasis *Fig.* haven, island, refuge, resting place, retreat, sanctuary, sanctum

oath 1. affirmation, avowal, bond, pledge, promise, sworn statement, vow, word 2. blasphemy, curse, cuss (*Inf.*), expletive, imprecation, malediction, profanity, strong language, swearword

obdurate adamant, callous, dogged, firm,

fixed, hard, hard-hearted, harsh, immovable, implacable, indurate (*Rare*), inexorable, inflexible, iron, mulish, obstinate, perverse, pig-headed, proof against persuasion, relentless, stiff-necked, stubborn,· unbending, unfeeling, unimpressible, unrelenting, unshakable, unyielding

obedience accordance, acquiescence, agreement, compliance, conformability, deference, docility, dutifulness, duty, observance, respect, reverence, submission, submissiveness, subservience, tractability

obedient acquiescent, amenable, biddable, compliant, deferential, docile, duteous, dutiful, law-abiding, observant, regardful, respectful, submissive, subservient, tractable, under control, well-trained, yielding

obelisk column, monolith, monument, needle, pillar, shaft

obese corpulent, Falstaffian, fat, fleshy, gross, heavy, outsize, overweight, paunchy, plump, podgy, portly, roly-poly, rotund, stout, tubby, well-upholstered (*Inf.*)

obesity bulk, corpulence, *embonpoint*, fatness, fleshiness, grossness, overweight, portliness, stoutness, tubbiness, weight problem

obey 1. abide by, act upon, adhere to, be ruled by, carry out, comply, conform, discharge, do what is expected, embrace, execute, follow, fulfil, heed, keep, mind, observe, perform, respond, serve 2. bow to, come to heel, do what one is told, get into line, give in, give way, knuckle under (*Inf.*), submit, surrender (to), take orders from, toe the line, yield

object[1] ('ɒbdʒɪkt) *n.* **1.** a tangible and visible thing. **2.** a person or thing seen as a focus for feelings, thought, etc. **3.** an aim or objective. **4.** *Inf.* a ridiculous or pitiable person, spectacle, etc. **5.** *Philosophy.* that towards which cognition is directed, esp. the external world as opposed to the ego. **6.** *Grammar.* a noun, pronoun, or noun phrase whose referent is the recipient of the action of a verb. See also **direct object, indirect object. 7.** *Grammar.* a noun, pronoun, or noun phrase that is governed by a preposition. **8. no object.** not a hindrance or obstacle: *money is no object.*

object[2] (əb'dʒɛkt) *vb.* **1.** (*tr.; takes a clause as object*) to state as an objection. **2.** (*intr.; often foll. by to*) to raise or state an objection (to); present an argument (against).

objectify (əb'dʒɛktɪˌfaɪ) *vb.* **-fying, -fied.** (*tr.*) to represent concretely; present as an object. —**ob,jectifi-'cation** *n.*

objection (əb'dʒɛkʃən) *n.* **1.** an expression or feeling of opposition or dislike. **2.** a cause for such an expression or feeling. **3.** the act of objecting.

objectionable (əb'dʒɛkʃənəbəl) *adj.* unpleasant, offensive, or repugnant. —**ob,jectiona'bility** or **ob'jection-ableness** *n.* —**ob'jectionably** *adv.*

objective (əb'dʒɛktɪv) *adj.* **1.** existing independently of perception; being a material object as opposed to a concept, idea, etc. **2.** undistorted by emotion or personal bias. **3.** of or relating to actual and external phenomena as opposed to thoughts, feelings, etc. **4.** *Med.* (of disease symptoms) perceptible to persons other than the individual affected. **5.** *Grammar.* denoting a case of nouns and pronouns, esp. in languages having only two cases, that is used to identify the direct object of a finite verb or preposition. See also **accusative. 6.** of or relating to a goal or aim. ~*n.* **7.** the object of one's endeavours; goal; aim. **8.** an actual phenomenon; reality. **9.** *Grammar.* the objective case. **10.** Also called: **object glass.** *Optics.* the lens or combination of lenses nearest to the object in an optical instrument. ~**Abbrev.: obj.** Cf. **subjective.** —**objectival** (ˌɒbdʒɛk'taɪvəl) *adj.* —**ob'jectively** *adv.* —**ob'jectiveness** or ˌ**objec'tivity** *n.*

object lesson *n.* a practical demonstration of some principle or ideal.

objet d'art French. (ɔbʒɛ 'da:r) *n., pl.* **objets d'art** (ɔbʒɛ 'da:r). a small object considered to be of artistic worth.

objurgate ('ɒbdʒəˌgeɪt) *vb.* (*tr.*) to scold or reprimand. —ˌ**objur'gation** *n.* —**'objur,gator** *n.* —**objurgatory** (ɒb-'dʒɜ:gətərɪ, -trɪ) *adj.*

oblate ('ɒbleɪt) *adj.* having an equatorial diameter of greater length than the polar diameter: *the earth is an oblate sphere.* Cf. **prolate.** —**'oblately** *adv.*

oblation (ɒ'bleɪʃən) *n. Christianity.* **1.** the offering of the Eucharist to God. **2.** any offering made for religious

or charitable purposes. —**oblatory** ('ɒblətərɪ, -trɪ) or **ob'lational** *adj.*

obligate ('ɒblɪˌgeɪt) *vb.* **1.** to compel, constrain, or oblige morally or legally. **2.** (in the U.S.) to bind (property, funds, etc.) as security. ~*adj.* **3.** compelled, bound, or restricted. **4.** *Biol.* able to exist under only one set of environmental conditions. —**'obligable** *adj.* —**ob-'ligative** *adj.* —**'obli,gator** *n.*

obligation (ˌɒblɪ'geɪʃən) *n.* **1.** a moral or legal requirement; duty. **2.** the act of obligating or the state of being obligated. **3.** *Law.* **a.** a written contract containing a penalty. **b.** an instrument acknowledging indebtedness to secure the repayment of money borrowed. **4.** a person or thing to which one is bound morally or legally. **5.** a service or favour for which one is indebted. —ˌ**obli-'gational** *adj.*

obligato (ˌɒblɪ'gɑ:təʊ) *adj., n. Music.* a variant spelling of **obbligato.**

obligatory (ɒ'blɪgətərɪ, -trɪ) *adj.* **1.** required to be done, obtained, possessed, etc. **2.** of the nature of or constituting an obligation. —**ob'ligatorily** *adv.*

oblige (ə'blaɪdʒ) *vb.* **1.** (*tr.; often passive*) to bind or constrain (someone to do something) by legal, moral, or physical means. **2.** (*tr.; usually passive*) to make indebted or grateful to (someone) by doing a favour. **3.** to do a service or favour to (someone): *she obliged the guest with a song.* —**o'bliger** *n.*

obliging (ə'blaɪdʒɪŋ) *adj.* ready to do favours; agreeable; kindly. —**o'bligingly** *adv.* —**o'bligingness** *n.*

oblique (ə'bli:k) *adj.* **1.** at an angle; slanting; sloping. **2.** *Geom.* **a.** (of lines, planes, etc.) neither perpendicular nor parallel to one another or to another line, plane, etc. **b.** not related to or containing a right angle. **3.** indirect or evasive. **4.** *Grammar.* denoting any case of nouns, pronouns, etc., other than the nominative and vocative. **5.** *Biol.* having asymmetrical sides or planes: *an oblique leaf.* ~*n.* **6.** something oblique, esp. a line. **7.** another name for **solidus** (sense 1). ~*vb.* (*intr.*) **8.** to take or have an oblique direction. **9.** (of a military formation) to move forward at an angle. —**o'bliquely** *adv.* —**o'bliqueness** *n.* —**obliquity** (ə'blɪkwɪtɪ) *n.*

oblique angle *n.* an angle that is not a right angle or any multiple of a right angle.

obliterate (ə'blɪtəˌreɪt) *vb.* (*tr.*) to destroy every trace of; wipe out completely. —**o,blite'ration** *n.* —**o'blitera-tive** *adj.* —**o'bliter,ator** *n.*

oblivion (ə'blɪvɪən) *n.* **1.** the condition of being forgotten or disregarded. **2.** *Law.* amnesty; pardon.

oblivious (ə'blɪvɪəs) *adj.* (usually foll. by *of*) unaware or forgetful. —**ob'liviously** *adv.* —**ob'liviousness** *n.*

oblong ('ɒbˌlɒŋ) *adj.* **1.** having an elongated, esp. rectangular, shape. ~*n.* **2.** a figure or object having this shape.

THESAURUS

object[1] *n.* **1.** article, body, entity, fact, item, phenomenon, reality, thing **2.** aim, butt, focus, recipient, target, victim **3.** design, end, end in view, end purpose, goal, idea, intent, intention, motive, objective, point, purpose, reason

object[2] *v.* argue against, demur, expostulate, oppose, protest, raise objections, take exception

objection cavil, censure, counterargument, demur, doubt, exception, niggle (*Inf.*), opposition, protest, remonstrance, scruple

objectionable abhorrent, deplorable, disagreeable, dislikable, displeasing, distasteful, exceptionable, indecorous, insufferable, intolerable, noxious, obnoxious, offensive, regrettable, repugnant, unacceptable, undesirable, unpleasant, unseemly, unsociable

objective 1. *adj.* detached, disinterested, dispassionate, equitable, even-handed, fair, impartial, impersonal, judicial, just, open-minded, unbiased, uncoloured, unemotional, uninvolved, unprejudiced **2.** *n.* aim, ambition, aspiration, design, end, end in view, goal, intention, mark, object, purpose, target

objectively disinterestedly, dispassionately, even-handedly, impartially, with an open mind, with objectivity *or* impartiality, without fear or favour

objectivity detachment, disinterest, disinterestedness, dispassion, equitableness, impartiality, impersonality

obligation 1. accountability, accountableness, burden, charge, compulsion, duty, liability, must, onus, requirement, responsibility, trust **2.** agreement, bond, commitment, contract, debt, engagement, promise, understanding **3. under an obligation** beholden, duty-bound, grateful, honour-bound, indebted, in (someone's) debt, obligated, obliged, owing a favour, thankful

obligatory binding, coercive, compulsory, *de rigueur*, enforced, essential, imperative, mandatory, necessary, required, requisite, unavoidable

oblige 1. bind, coerce, compel, constrain, force, impel, make, necessitate, obligate, require **2.** accommodate, benefit, do (someone) a favour *or* a kindness, favour, gratify, indulge, please, put oneself out for, serve

obliged 1. appreciative, beholden, grateful, gratified, indebted, in (someone's) debt, thankful **2.** bound, compelled, forced, required, under an obligation, under compulsion, without any option

obliging accommodating, agreeable, amiable, civil, complaisant, considerate, cooperative, courteous, eager to please, friendly, good-natured, helpful, kind, polite, willing

oblique 1. angled, aslant, at an angle, inclined, slanted, slanting, sloped, sloping, tilted **2.** backhanded, circuitous, circumlocutory, evasive, implied, indirect, roundabout, sidelong

obliquely 1. aslant, aslope, at an angle, diagonally, slantwise **2.** circuitously, evasively, in a roundabout manner *or* way, indirectly, not in so many words

obliterate annihilate, blot out, cancel, delete, destroy, destroy root and branch, efface, eradicate, erase, expunge, extirpate, root out, wipe off the face of the earth, wipe out

obliteration annihilation, deletion, effacement, elimination, eradication, erasure, expunction, extirpation, wiping (blotting, rooting, sponging) out

oblivion 1. abeyance, disregard, forgetfulness, insensibility, neglect, obliviousness, unawareness, unconsciousness, (waters of) Lethe **2.** blackness, darkness, eclipse, extinction, limbo, nothingness, obscurity, void

oblivious blind, careless, deaf, disregardful, forgetful, heedless, ignorant, inattentive, insensible, neglectful, negligent, regardless, unaware, unconcerned, unconscious, unmindful, unobservant

obloquy (ˈɒbləkwɪ) n., pl. **-quies.** 1. defamatory or censorious statements, esp. when directed against one person. 2. disgrace brought about by public abuse.

obnoxious (əbˈnɒkʃəs) adj. 1. extremely unpleasant. 2. Obs. exposed to harm, injury, etc. —obˈnoxiously adv. —obˈnoxiousness n.

oboe (ˈəʊbəʊ) n. 1. a woodwind instrument consisting of a conical tube fitted with a mouthpiece having a double reed. It has a penetrating nasal tone. 2. a person who plays this instrument in an orchestra. ~Arch. form: hautboy. —ˈoboist n.

obs. abbrev. for: 1. observation. 2. obsolete.

obscene (əbˈsiːn) adj. 1. offensive or outrageous to accepted standards of decency or modesty. 2. Law. (of publications, etc.) having a tendency to deprave or corrupt. 3. disgusting; repellent. —obˈscenely adv. —obscenity (-ˈsɛn-) n.

obscure (əbˈskjʊə) adj. 1. unclear. 2. indistinct, vague, or indefinite. 3. inconspicuous or unimportant. 4. hidden, secret, or remote. 5. (of a vowel) reduced to a neutral vowel (ə). 6. gloomy, dark, clouded, or dim. ~vb. (tr.) 7. to make unclear, vague, or hidden. 8. to cover or cloud over. 9. Phonetics. to pronounce (a vowel) so that it becomes a neutral sound represented by (ə). —obscuration (ˌɒbskjʊˈreɪʃən) n. —obˈscurely adv. —obˈscureness n. —obˈscurity n.

obsequies (ˈɒbsɪkwɪz) pl. n., sing. **-quy.** funeral rites.

obsequious (əbˈsiːkwɪəs) adj. 1. obedient or attentive in an ingratiating or servile manner. 2. Now rare. submissive or compliant. —obˈsequiously adv. —obˈsequiousness n.

observance (əbˈzɜːvəns) n. 1. recognition of or compliance with a law, custom, practice, etc. 2. a ritual, ceremony, or practice, esp. of a religion. 3. observation or attention. 4. the degree of strictness of a religious order in following its rule. 5. Arch. respectful or deferential attention.

observant (əbˈzɜːvənt) adj. 1. paying close attention to detail; watchful or heedful. 2. adhering strictly to rituals, ceremonies, laws, etc. —obˈservantly adv.

observation (ˌɒbzəˈveɪʃən) n. 1. the act of observing or the state of being observed. 2. a comment or remark. 3. detailed examination of phenomena prior to analysis, diagnosis, or interpretation: the patient was under observation. 4. the facts learned from observing. 5. Navigation. a. a sight taken with an instrument to determine the position of an observer relative to that of a given heavenly body. b. the data so taken. —ˌobserˈvational adj. —ˌobserˈvationally adv.

observatory (əbˈzɜːvətərɪ, -trɪ) n., pl. **-ries.** 1. an institution or building specially designed and equipped for observing meteorological and astronomical phenomena. 2. any building or structure providing an extensive view of its surroundings.

observe (əbˈzɜːv) vb. 1. (tr.; may take a clause as object) to see; perceive; notice: we have observed that you steal. 2. (when tr., may take a clause as object) to watch (something) carefully; pay attention to (something). 3. to make observations of (something), esp. scientific ones. 4. (when intr., usually foll. by on or upon; when tr., may take a clause as object) to make a comment or remark: the speaker observed that times had changed. 5. (tr.) to abide by, keep, or follow (a custom, tradition, etc.). —obˈservable adj. —obˈservableness n. —obˈserver n.

obsess (əbˈsɛs) vb. (tr.) to preoccupy completely; haunt. —obˈsessive adj. —obˈsessiveness n.

obsession (əbˈsɛʃən) n. 1. Psychiatry. a persistent idea or impulse, esp. one associated with anxiety and mental illness. 2. a persistent preoccupation, idea, or feeling. 3. the act of obsessing or the state of being obsessed. —obˈsessional adj. —obˈsessionally adv.

obsidian (ɒbˈsɪdɪən) n. a dark glassy volcanic rock formed by very rapid solidification of lava.

obsolescent (ˌɒbsəˈlɛsənt) adj. becoming obsolete or out of date. —ˌobsoˈlescence n.

obsolete (ˈɒbsəˌliːt, ˌɒbsəˈliːt) adj. 1. out of use or practice; not current. 2. out of date; unfashionable or outmoded. 3. Biol. (of parts, organs, etc.) vestigial; rudimentary. —ˈobsoˌletely adv. —ˈobsoˌleteness n.

obstacle (ˈɒbstəkəl) n. 1. a person or thing that opposes or hinders something. 2. Brit. a fence or hedge used in show jumping.

obstetric (ɒbˈstɛtrɪk) or **obstetrical** adj. of or relating to childbirth or obstetrics. —obˈstetrically adv.

obstetrician (ˌɒbstɛˈtrɪʃən) n. a physician who special-

THESAURUS

obnoxious abhorrent, abominable, detestable, disagreeable, disgusting, dislikable, foul, hateable, hateful, horrid, insufferable, loathsome, nasty, nauseating, objectionable, odious, offensive, repellent, reprehensible, repugnant, repulsive, revolting, sickening, unpleasant

obscene 1. bawdy, blue, coarse, dirty, disgusting, Fescennine (Rare), filthy, foul, gross, immodest, immoral, improper, impure, indecent, lewd, licentious, loose, offensive, pornographic, prurient, ribald, salacious, scabrous, shameless, smutty, suggestive, unchaste, unwholesome 2. Fig. atrocious, evil, heinous, loathsome, outrageous, shocking, sickening, vile, wicked

obscenity 1. bawdiness, blueness, coarseness, dirtiness, filthiness, foulness, grossness, immodesty, impurity, lewdness, licentiousness, pornography, prurience, salacity, smuttiness, suggestiveness, vileness 2. four-letter word, impropriety, indecency, indelicacy, profanity, smut, swearword, vulgarism 3. abomination, affront, atrocity, blight, evil, offence, outrage, vileness, wrong

obscure adj. 1. abstruse, ambiguous, arcane, concealed, confusing, cryptic, deep, doubtful, enigmatic, esoteric, hazy, hidden, incomprehensible, indefinite, intricate, involved, mysterious, occult, opaque, recondite, unclear, vague 2. blurred, clouded, cloudy, dim, dusky, faint, gloomy, indistinct, murky, obfuscated, shadowy, shady, sombre, tenebrous, unlit, veiled 3. humble, inconspicuous, inglorious, little-known, lowly, minor, nameless, out-of-the-way, remote, undistinguished, unheard-of, unhonoured, unimportant, unknown, unnoted, unseen, unsung ~v. 4. conceal, cover, disguise, hide, muddy, obfuscate, screen, throw a veil over, veil 5. adumbrate, bedim, befog, block, block out, blur, cloak, cloud, darken, dim, dull, eclipse, mask, overshadow, shade, shroud

obscurity 1. abstruseness, ambiguity, complexity, impenetrableness, incomprehensibility, intricacy, reconditeness, vagueness 2. darkness, dimness, dusk, duskiness, gloom, haze, haziness, indistinctness, murkiness, shadowiness, shadows 3. inconspicuousness, ingloriousness, insignificance, lowliness, namelessness, nonrecognition, unimportance

observable apparent, appreciable, clear, detectable, discernible, evident, noticeable, obvious, open, patent, perceivable, perceptible, recognizable, visible

observance 1. adherence to, attention, carrying out, celebration, compliance, discharge, fulfilment, heeding, honouring, notice, observation, performance 2. ceremonial, ceremony, custom, fashion, form, formality, practice, rite, ritual, service, tradition

observant alert, attentive, eagle-eyed, heedful, mindful, obedient, perceptive, quick, sharp-eyed, submissive, vigilant, watchful, wide-awake

observation 1. attention, cognition, consideration, examination, experience, information, inspection, knowledge, monitoring, notice, review, scrutiny, study, surveillance, watching 2. annotation, comment, finding, note, obiter dictum, opinion, pronouncement, reflection, remark, thought, utterance

observe 1. detect, discern, discover, espy, note, notice, perceive, see, spot, witness 2. contemplate, keep an eye on (Inf.), keep under observation, look at, monitor, pay attention to, regard, scrutinize, study, survey, view, watch 3. animadvert, comment, declare, mention, note, opine, remark, say, state 4. abide by, adhere to, comply, conform to, follow, fulfil, heed, honour, keep, mind, obey, perform, respect 5. celebrate, commemorate, keep, remember, solemnize

observer beholder, bystander, commentator, eyewitness, looker-on, onlooker, spectator, spotter, viewer, watcher, witness

obsess bedevil, be on one's mind, be uppermost in one's thoughts, consume, dominate, engross, grip, haunt, monopolize, plague, possess, preoccupy, prey on one's mind, rule, torment

obsessed beset, dominated, gripped, hagridden, haunted, hung up on (Sl., chiefly U.S.), immersed in, infatuated, in the grip of, preoccupied, troubled

obsession bee in one's bonnet (Inf.), complex, enthusiasm, fetish, fixation, hangup (Inf.), idée fixe, infatuation, mania, phobia, preoccupation, ruling passion, thing (Inf.)

obsessive besetting, compulsive, consuming, fixed, gripping, haunting, tormenting, unforgettable

obsolescent ageing, declining, dying out, not with it (Inf.), on the decline, on the wane, on the way out, past its prime, waning

obsolete anachronistic, ancient, antediluvian, antiquated, antique, archaic, bygone, dated, démodé, discarded, disused, extinct, musty, old, old-fashioned, old hat, out, outmoded, out of date, out of fashion, out of the ark (Inf.), outworn, passé, superannuated, vieux jeu

obstacle bar, barrier, check, difficulty, hindrance, hitch, hurdle, impediment, interference, interruption, obstruction, snag, stumbling block

izes in obstetrics.

obstetrics (ɒb'stɛtrɪks) *n.* (*functioning as sing.*) the branch of medicine concerned with childbirth and the treatment of women before and after childbirth.

obstinate ('ɒbstɪnɪt) *adj.* 1. adhering fixedly to a particular opinion, attitude, course of action, etc. 2. self-willed or headstrong. 3. difficult to subdue or alleviate; persistent: *an obstinate fever.* —'**obstinacy** *n.* —'**obstinately** *adv.*

obstreperous (əb'strɛpərəs) *adj.* noisy or rough, esp. in resisting restraint or control. —**ob'streperously** *adv.* —**ob'streperousness** *n.*

obstruct (əb'strʌkt) *vb.* (*tr.*) 1. to block (a road, passageway, etc.) with an obstacle. 2. to make (progress or activity) difficult. 3. to impede or block a clear view of. —**ob'structer** or **ob'structor** *n.* —**ob'structive** *adj.*, *n.* —**ob'structively** *adv.* —**ob'structiveness** *n.*

obstruction (əb'strʌkʃən) *n.* 1. a person or thing that obstructs. 2. the act or an instance of obstructing. 3. delay of business, esp. in a legislature by means of procedural devices. 4. *Sport.* the act of unfairly impeding an opposing player. —**ob'structional** *adj.* —**ob'structionally** *adv.*

obstructionist (əb'strʌkʃənɪst) *n.* a person who deliberately obstructs business, etc., esp. in a legislature. —**ob'structionism** *n.*

obtain (əb'teɪn) *vb.* 1. (*tr.*) to gain possession of; acquire; get. 2. (*intr.*) to be customary, valid, or accepted: *a new law obtains in this case.* —**ob'tainable** *adj.* —**ob,taina'bility** *n.* —**ob'tainer** *n.* —**ob'tainment** *n.*

obtrude (əb'truːd) *vb.* 1. to push (oneself, one's opinions, etc.) on others in an unwelcome way. 2. (*tr.*) to push out or forward. —**ob'truder** *n.* —**obtrusion** (əb'truːʒən) *n.*

obtrusive (əb'truːsɪv) *adj.* 1. obtruding or tending to obtrude. 2. sticking out; protruding; noticeable. —**ob'trusively** *adv.* —**ob'trusiveness** *n.*

obtuse (əb'tjuːs) *adj.* 1. mentally slow or emotionally insensitive. 2. *Maths.* (of an angle) lying between 90° and 180°. 3. not sharp or pointed. 4. indistinctly felt, heard, etc.; dull: *obtuse pain.* 5. (of a leaf or similar flat part) having a rounded or blunt tip. —**ob'tusely** *adv.* —**ob'tuseness** *n.*

obverse ('ɒbvɜːs) *adj.* 1. facing or turned towards the observer. 2. forming or serving as a counterpart. 3. (of leaves) narrower at the base than at the top. ~*n.* 4. a counterpart or complement. 5. *Logic.* a proposition formed from another proposition whose subject is the same as in the original but whose predicate is the contradictory of the original and whose quality is changed, as in *No x is a non-y* inferred from *Every x is a y.* 6. the side of a coin that bears the main design or device. —**ob'versely** *adv.*

obviate ('ɒbvɪˌeɪt) *vb.* (*tr.*) to do away with. —ˌ**obvi'ation** *n.*

obvious ('ɒbvɪəs) *adj.* 1. easy to see or understand; evident. 2. exhibiting motives, feelings, intentions, etc., clearly or without subtlety. 3. naive or unsubtle: *the play was rather obvious.* —'**obviously** *adv.* —'**obviousness** *n.*

O.C. *abbrev. for* Officer Commanding.

o/c *abbrev. for* overcharge.

ocarina (ˌɒkə'riːnə) *n.* an egg-shaped wind instrument with a protruding mouthpiece and six to eight finger holes, producing an almost pure tone.

occasion (ə'keɪʒən) *n.* 1. (sometimes foll. by *of*) the time of a particular happening or event. 2. (sometimes foll. by *for*) a reason or cause (to do or be something); grounds: *there was no occasion to complain.* 3. an opportunity (to do something); chance. 4. a special event, time, or celebration: *the party was quite an occasion.* 5. **on occasion.** every so often. 6. **rise to the occasion.** to have the courage, wit, etc., to meet the special demands of a situation. 7. **take occasion.** to avail oneself of an opportunity (to do something). ~*vb.* 8. (*tr.*) to bring about, esp. incidentally or by chance.

occasional (ə'keɪʒənəl) *adj.* 1. taking place from time to time; not frequent or regular. 2. of, for, or happening on special occasions. 3. serving as an occasion (for something). —**oc'casionally** *adv.*

occident ('ɒksɪdənt) *n.* a literary or formal word for west. Cf. **orient**.

Occident ('ɒksɪdənt) *n.* (usually preceded by *the*) 1. the countries of Europe and America. 2. the western hemisphere. —ˌ**Occi'dental** *adj.*

occiput ('ɒksɪˌpʌt) *n.*, *pl.* **occiputs** or **occipita** (ɒk-'sɪpɪtə). the back part of the head or skull. —**oc'cipital** *adj.*

occlude (ə'kluːd) *vb.* 1. (*tr.*) to block or stop up (a passage or opening); obstruct. 2. (*tr.*) to prevent the passage of. 3. (*tr.*) *Chem.* (of a solid) to incorporate (a substance) by absorption or adsorption. 4. *Meteorol.* to form an occluded front. 5. *Dentistry.* to produce occlusion, as in chewing. —**oc'cludent** *adj.*

occluded front *n. Meteorol.* the line or plane occurring where the cold front of a depression has overtaken the warm front, raising the warm sector from ground level. Also called: **occlusion.**

occlusion (ə'kluːʒən) *n.* 1. the act of occluding or the state of being occluded. 2. *Meteorol.* another term for **occluded front.** 3. *Dentistry.* the normal position of the teeth when the jaws are closed. —**oc'clusive** *adj.*

occult *adj.* (ɒ'kʌlt, 'ɒkʌlt). 1. **a.** of or characteristic of mystical or supernatural phenomena or influences. **b.** (*as n.*): *the occult.* 2. beyond ordinary human under-

---

THESAURUS

obstinacy doggedness, firmness, inflexibility, intransigence, mulishness, obduracy, perseverance, persistence, pertinacity, pigheadedness, resoluteness, stubbornness, tenacity, wilfulness

obstinate contumacious, determined, dogged, firm, headstrong, immovable, inflexible, intractable, intransigent, mulish, opinionated, persistent, pertinacious, perverse, pig-headed, recalcitrant, refractory, self-willed, steadfast, strong-minded, stubborn, tenacious, unyielding, wilful

obstreperous boisterous, clamorous, disorderly, loud, noisy, out of control, out of hand, rackety, rambunctious (*Inf.*), rampaging, raucous, restive, riotous, rip-roaring (*Inf.*), roistering, roisterous, rough, rowdy, stroppy (*Brit. sl.*), tempestuous, tumultuous, turbulent, uncontrolled, undisciplined, unmanageable, unruly, uproarious, vociferous, wild

obstruct arrest, bar, barricade, block, bring to a standstill, check, choke, clog, cumber, curb, cut off, frustrate, get in the way of, hamper, hamstring, hide, hinder, hold up, impede, inhibit, interfere with, interrupt, mask, obscure, prevent, restrict, retard, shield, shut off, slow down, stop, thwart, trammel

obstruction bar, barricade, barrier, blockage, check, difficulty, hindrance, impediment, snag, stop, stoppage, trammel

obstructive awkward, blocking, delaying, hindering, inhibiting, preventative, restrictive, stalling, uncooperative, unhelpful

obtain 1. achieve, acquire, attain, come by, earn, gain, get, get hold of, get one's hands on, procure, secure 2. be in force, be prevalent, be the case, exist, hold, prevail, stand

obtainable achievable, at hand, attainable, available, on tap (*Inf.*), procurable, ready, realizable, to be had

obtrusive 1. forward, importunate, interfering, intrusive, meddling, nosy, officious, prying, pushy (*Inf.*) 2. noticeable, obvious, prominent, protruding, protuberant, sticking out

obtrusively blatantly, bluntly, boldly, crassly, importunately, obviously, officiously, pushily

obtuse 1. boneheaded (*Sl.*), dense, dopey (*Sl.*), dull, dull-witted, dumb (*Inf., chiefly U.S.*), heavy, imperceptive, insensitive, muttonheaded (*Sl.*), retarded, slow, slow on the uptake (*Inf.*), stolid, stupid, thick, thick-skinned, uncomprehending, unintelligent 2. blunt, rounded

obvious apparent, clear, clear as a bell, conspicuous, distinct, evident, indisputable, manifest, much in evidence, noticeable, open, overt, palpable, patent, perceptible, plain, plain as the nose on your face (*Inf.*), pronounced, recognizable, right under one's nose (*Inf.*), self-evident, self-explanatory, staring one in the face (*Inf.*), sticking out a mile (*Inf.*), straightforward, transparent, unconcealed, undeniable, undisguised, unmistakable, unsubtle, visible

obviously certainly, clearly, distinctly, manifestly, of course, palpably, patently, plainly, undeniably, unmistakably, unquestionably, without doubt

occasion *n.* 1. chance, convenience, incident, moment, occurrence, opening, opportunity, time 2. affair, celebration, event, experience, occurrence 3. call, cause, excuse, ground(s), inducement, influence, justification, motive, prompting, provocation, reason ~*v.* 4. bring about, cause, create, effect, elicit, engender, evoke, generate, give rise to, induce, influence, inspire, lead to, move, originate, persuade, produce, prompt, provoke

occasional casual, desultory, incidental, infrequent, intermittent, irregular, odd, rare, sporadic, uncommon

occasionally at intervals, at times, (every) now and then, every so often, from time to time, irregularly, now and again, off and on, on and off, once in a while, on occasion, periodically, sometimes

standing. **3.** secret or esoteric. ~*vb.* (ɒˈkʌlt). **4.** *Astron.* (of a celestial body) to hide (another celestial body) from view by occultation or (of a celestial body) to become hidden by occultation. **5.** to hide or become hidden or shut off from view. **6.** (*intr.*) (of lights, esp. in lighthouses) to shut off at regular intervals. —**ocˈcultness** *n.* —ˈoccul₁tism *n.* —ˈoccultist *n.*

occupancy (ˈɒkjupənsɪ) *n., pl.* **-cies. 1.** the act of occupying; possession of a property. **2.** *Law.* the possession and use of property by or without agreement and without any claim to ownership. **3.** *Law.* the act of taking possession of unowned property, esp. land, with the intent of thus acquiring ownership. **4.** the condition or fact of being an occupant, esp. a tenant. **5.** the period of time during which one is an occupant, esp. of property.

occupant (ˈɒkjupənt) *n.* **1.** a person, thing, etc., holding a position or place. **2.** *Law.* a person who has possession of something, esp. an estate, house, etc.; tenant. **3.** *Law.* a person who acquires by occupancy the title to something previously without an owner.

occupation (₁ɒkjuˈpeɪʃən) *n.* **1.** a person's regular work or profession; job. **2.** any activity on which time is spent by a person. **3.** the act of occupying or the state of being occupied. **4.** the control of a country by a foreign military power. **5.** the period of time that a nation, place, or position is occupied. **6.** (*modifier*) for the use of the occupier of a particular property: *occupation road.* —₁occuˈpational *adj.*

occupational therapy *n. Med.* the therapeutic use of crafts, hobbies, etc., esp. in the rehabilitation of emotionally disturbed patients.

occupier (ˈɒkju₁paɪə) *n.* **1.** *Brit.* a person who is in possession or occupation of a house or land. **2.** a person or thing that occupies.

occupy (ˈɒkju₁paɪ) *vb.* **-pying, -pied.** (*tr.*) **1.** to live or be established in (a house, flat, office, etc.). **2.** (*often passive*) to keep (a person) busy or engrossed. **3.** (*often passive*) to take up (time or space). **4.** to take and hold possession of, esp. as a demonstration: *students occupied the college buildings.* **5.** to fill or hold (a position or rank).

occur (əˈkɜː) *vb.* **-curring, -curred.** (*intr.*) **1.** to happen; take place; come about. **2.** to be found or be present; exist. **3.** (foll. by *to*) to be realized or thought of (by); suggest itself (to).

▷ **Usage.** In careful English, *occur* and *happen* are not used of prearranged events: *the wedding took place* (not *occurred* or *happened*) *in the afternoon.*

occurrence (əˈkʌrəns) *n.* **1.** something that occurs; a happening; event. **2.** the act or an instance of occurring: *a crime of frequent occurrence.* —ocˈcurrent *adj.*

ocean (ˈəʊʃən) *n.* **1.** a very large stretch of sea, esp. one of the five oceans of the world, the Atlantic, Pacific, Indian, Arctic, and Antarctic. **2.** the body of salt water covering approximately 70 per cent of the earth's surface. **3.** a huge quantity or expanse: *an ocean of replies.* **4.** *Literary.* the sea. —**oceanic** (₁əʊʃɪˈænɪk) *adj.*

ocean-going *adj.* (of a ship, boat, etc.) suited for travel on the open ocean.

oceanography (₁əʊʃəˈnɒɡrəfɪ, ₁əʊʃɪə-) *n.* the branch of science dealing with the physical and biological features of the sea. —₁oceanˈographer *n.* —**oceanographic** (₁əʊʃənəˈɡræfɪk, ₁əʊʃɪə-) or ₁oceanoˈgraphical *adj.*

ocelot (ˈɒsɪ₁lɒt, ˈəʊ-) *n.* a feline mammal inhabiting Central and South America and having a dark-spotted buff-brown coat.

och (ɒx) *interj. Scot., Irish.* an expression of surprise, contempt, or disagreement.

ochre or *U.S.* **ocher** (ˈəʊkə) *n.* **1.** any of various natural earths containing ferric oxide, silica, and alumina: used as yellow or red pigments. **2. a.** a moderate yellow-orange to orange colour. **b.** (*as adj.*): *an ochre dress.* ~*vb.* **3.** (*tr.*) to colour with ochre. —**ochreous** (ˈəʊkrɪəs, ˈəʊkərəs), **ochrous** (ˈəʊkrəs), **ochry** (ˈəʊkərɪ, ˈəʊkrɪ) or *U.S.* ˈ**ocherous,** ˈ**ochery** *adj.*

o'clock (əˈklɒk) *adv.* **1.** used after a number from one to twelve to indicate the hour of the day or night. **2.** used after a number to indicate direction or position relative to the observer, twelve o'clock being directly ahead and other positions being obtained by comparisons with a clock face.

OCR *abbrev. for* optical character reader *or* recognition.

oct. *abbrev. for* octavo.

Oct. *abbrev. for* October.

oct- *combining form.* a variant of **octo-** before a vowel.

octa- *combining form.* a variant of **octo-.**

octagon (ˈɒktə₁ɡɒn) or **octangle** *n.* a polygon having eight sides. —ocˈtagonal *adj.*

octahedron (₁ɒktəˈhiːdrən) *n., pl.* **-drons** or **-dra** (-drə). a solid figure having eight plane faces.

octal notation or **octal** (ˈɒktəl) *n. Computers.* a number system having a base 8, one octal digit being equivalent to a group of three bits.

octane (ˈɒkteɪn) *n.* a liquid hydrocarbon found in petroleum. Formula: C_8H_{18}.

octane number or **rating** *n.* a measure of the antiknock quality of a petrol expressed as a percentage.

octave (ˈɒktɪv) *n.* **1. a.** the interval between two musical notes one of which has twice the pitch of the other and lies eight notes away from it counting inclusively along the diatonic scale. **b.** one of these two notes, esp. the one of higher pitch. **c.** (*as modifier*): *an octave leap.* **2.** *Prosody.* a rhythmic group of eight lines of verse. **3.** (ˈɒkteɪv). **a.** a feast day and the seven days following. **b.** the final day of this period. **4.** the eighth of eight basic positions in fencing. **5.** any set or series of eight. ~*adj.* **6.** consisting of eight parts.

octavo (ɒkˈteɪvəʊ) *n., pl.* **-vos. 1.** a book size resulting from folding a sheet of paper of a specified size to form eight leaves: *demi-octavo.* Often written: **8vo, 8°. 2.** a book of this size.

octet (ɒkˈtɛt) *n.* **1.** any group of eight, esp. singers or musicians. **2.** a piece of music composed for such a group. **3.** *Prosody.* another word for **octave** (sense 2). **4.** *Chem.* a stable group of eight electrons. ~Also (for senses 1, 2, 3): **octette.**

octo-, octa-, or *before a vowel* **oct-** *combining form.* eight: *octosyllabic; octagon.*

October (ɒkˈtəʊbə) *n.* the tenth month of the year, consisting of 31 days.

Octobrist (ɒkˈtəʊbrɪst) *n.* a member of a Russian political party favouring the constitutional reforms granted in a manifesto issued by Nicholas II in Oct. 1905.

octogenarian (₁ɒktəʊdʒɪˈnɛərɪən) or **octogenary** (ɒkˈtɒdʒɪnərɪ) *n., pl.* **-narians** or **-naries. 1.** a person who is between 80 and 90 years old. ~*adj.* **2.** of or relating to an octogenarian.

octopus (ˈɒktəpəs) *n., pl.* **-puses. 1.** a cephalopod mollusc having a soft oval body with eight long suckered ten-

---

THESAURUS

occult abstruse, arcane, cabbalistic, concealed, esoteric, hidden, invisible, magical, mysterious, mystic, mystical, obscure, preternatural, recondite, secret, supernatural, unknown, unrevealed, veiled

occultism black magic, diabolism, magic, sorcery, supernaturalism, the black arts, witchcraft

occupant addressee, denizen, holder, incumbent, indweller, inhabitant, inmate, lessee, occupier, resident, tenant, user

occupation 1. activity, business, calling, craft, employment, job, line (of work), post, profession, pursuit, trade, vocation, walk of life, work **2.** control, holding, occupancy, possession, residence, tenancy, tenure, use **3.**

conquest, foreign rule, invasion, seizure, subjugation

occupied 1. busy, employed, engaged, hard at it (*Inf.*), tied up (*Inf.*), working **2.** engaged, full, in use, taken, unavailable **3.** full, inhabited, lived-in, peopled, settled, tenanted

occupy 1. *Often passive* absorb, amuse, busy, divert, employ, engage, engross, entertain, hold the attention of, immerse, interest, involve, keep busy or occupied, monopolize, preoccupy, take up, tie up **2.** be established in, be in residence in, dwell in, ensconce oneself in, establish oneself in, inhabit, live in, own, possess, reside in, stay in (*Scot.*), tenant **3.** cover, fill, hold, permeate, pervade, take up, use, utilize **4.** capture, garrison, hold, in

vade, keep, overrun, seize, take over, take possession of

occur 1. arise, befall, betide, chance, come about, come off (*Inf.*), come to pass (*Archaic*), crop up (*Inf.*), eventuate, happen, materialize, result, take place, turn up (*Inf.*) **2.** appear, be found, be met with, be present, develop, exist, manifest itself, obtain, show itself **3.** *With* **to** come to mind, come to one, cross one's mind, dawn on, enter one's head, spring to mind, strike one, suggest (offer, present) itself

occurrence 1. adventure, affair, circumstance, episode, event, happening, incident, instance, proceeding, transaction **2.** appearance, development, existence, manifestation, materialization

tacles and occurring at the sea bottom. **2.** a powerful influential organization, etc., with far-reaching effects, esp. harmful ones.

OCTU ('ɒktuː) n. Brit. acronym for Officer Cadets Training Unit.

ocular ('ɒkjʊlə) adj. **1.** of or relating to the eye. ~n. **2.** another name for **eyepiece.** —'**ocularly** adv.

O.D. abbrev. for: **1.** Also: **o.d.** Mil. olive drab. **2.** Officer of the Day. **3.** Also: **O/D** Banking. **a.** on demand. **b.** overdrawn. **4.** outside diameter. **5.** ordnance datum. **6.** Also: **o/d** overdose.

odalisque or **odalisk** ('ɒdəlɪsk) n. a female slave or concubine.

odd (ɒd) adj. **1.** unusual or peculiar in appearance, character, etc. **2.** occasional, incidental, or random: odd jobs. **3.** leftover or additional: odd bits of wool. **4. a.** not divisible by two. **b.** represented or indicated by a number that is not divisible by two: graphs are on odd pages. Cf. **even**[1] (sense 7). **5.** being part of a matched pair or set when the other or others are missing: an odd sock. **6.** (in combination). used to designate an indefinite quantity more than the quantity specified in round numbers: fifty-odd pounds. **7.** out-of-the-way. **8. odd man out.** a person or thing excluded from others forming a group, unit, etc. ~n. **9.** Golf. **a.** one stroke more than the score of one's opponent. **b.** a handicap of one stroke. **10.** a thing or person that is odd in sequence or number. —'**oddly** adv. —'**oddness** n.

oddity ('ɒdɪtɪ) n., pl. **-ties. 1.** an odd person or thing. **2.** an odd quality or characteristic. **3.** the condition of being odd.

oddment ('ɒdmənt) n. **1.** (often pl.) an odd piece or thing; leftover. **2.** Printing. any individual part of a book excluding the main text.

odds (ɒdz) pl. n. **1.** (foll. by on or against) the probability, expressed as a ratio, that a certain event will take place: the odds against the outsider are a hundred to one. **2.** the amount, expressed as a ratio, by which the wager of one better is greater than that of another: he was offering odds of five to one. **3.** the likelihood that a certain state of affairs will be so: the odds are that he is drunk. **4.** an equalizing allowance, esp. one given to a weaker side in a contest. **5.** the advantage that one contender is judged to have over another. **6.** Brit. a significant difference (esp. in **it makes no odds**). **7. at odds.** on bad terms. **8. give** or **lay odds.** to offer a bet with favourable odds. **9. take odds.** to accept such a bet. **10. over the odds. a.** Brit. more than is expected, necessary, etc. **b.** Austral. & N.Z. unfair or excessive. **11. what's the odds?** Brit. inf. what difference does it make?

odds and ends pl. n. miscellaneous items or articles.

odds-on adj. **1.** (of a chance, horse, etc.) rated at even money or less to win. **2.** regarded as more or most likely to win, succeed, happen, etc.

ode (əʊd) n. **1.** a lyric poem, typically addressed to a particular subject, with lines of varying lengths and complex rhythms. **2.** (formerly) a poem meant to be sung.

odious ('əʊdɪəs) adj. offensive; repugnant. —'**odiousness** n.

odium ('əʊdɪəm) n. **1.** the dislike accorded to a hated person or thing. **2.** hatred; repugnance.

odometer (ɒ'dɒmɪtə, əʊ-) n. the usual U.S. name for **mileometer.** —o'**dometry** n.

odontology (ˌɒdɒn'tɒlədʒɪ) n. the branch of science concerned with the anatomy, development, and diseases of teeth. —**odontological** (ɒˌdɒntə'lɒdʒɪkəl) adj.

—ˌodon'**tologist** n.

odoriferous (ˌəʊdə'rɪfərəs) adj. having or emitting an odour, esp. a fragrant one. —ˌodor'**iferously** adv. —ˌodor'**iferousness** n.

odour or U.S. **odor** ('əʊdə) n. **1.** the property of a substance that gives it a characteristic scent or smell. **2.** a pervasive quality about something: an odour of dishonesty. **3.** repute or regard (in **in good odour, in bad odour**). **4.** Arch. a sweet-smelling fragrance. —'**odourless** or U.S. '**odorless** adj.

Odyssey ('ɒdɪsɪ) n. **1.** a Greek epic poem, attributed to Homer, describing the ten-year homeward wanderings of Odysseus after the fall of Troy. **2.** (often not cap.) any long eventful journey. —**Odyssean** (ˌɒdɪ'siːən) adj.

OE, O.E., or **OE.** abbrev. for Old English (language).

O.E.C.D. abbrev. for Organization for Economic Cooperation and Development.

oedema or **edema** (ɪ'diːmə) n., pl. **-mata** (-mətə). **1.** Pathol. an excessive accumulation of serous fluid in the intercellular spaces of tissue. **2.** Bot. an abnormal swelling in a plant caused by parenchyma or an accumulation of water in the tissues. —**oedematous, edematous** (ɪ'dɛmətəs) or **oe'dema,tose, e'dema,tose** adj.

Oedipus complex ('iːdɪpəs) n. Psychoanal. the usually unconscious desire of a child, esp. a male child, to possess sexually the parent of the opposite sex while excluding the parent of the same sex. —'**oedipal** or ˌoedi-'**pean** adj.

o'er (ɔː, əʊə) prep., adv. a poetic contraction of **over.**

oesophagus or U.S. **esophagus** (iː'sɒfəgəs) n., pl. **-gi** (-ˌgaɪ). the part of the alimentary canal between the pharynx and the stomach; gullet. —**oesophageal** or U.S. **esophageal** (iːˌsɒfə'dʒiːəl) adj.

oestrogen ('iːstrədʒən, 'ɛstrə-) or U.S. **estrogen** n. any of several hormones that induce oestrus, stimulate changes in the female reproductive organs, and promote development of female secondary sexual characteristics. —**oestrogenic** (ˌiːstrə'dʒɛnɪk, ˌɛstrə-) or U.S. **estrogenic** (ˌɛstrə'dʒɛnɪk, ˌiːstrə-) adj. —ˌoestro-'**genically** or U.S. ˌestro'**genically** adv.

oestrus ('iːstrəs, 'ɛstrəs) or U.S. **estrus** n. a regularly occurring period of sexual receptivity in most female mammals, except humans, during which ovulation occurs and copulation can take place; heat. —'**oestrous** or U.S. '**estrous** adj.

of (ɒv; unstressed əv) prep. **1.** used with a verbal noun or gerund to link it with a following noun that is either the subject or the object of the verb embedded in the gerund: the breathing of a fine swimmer (subject); the breathing of clean air (object). **2.** used to indicate possession, origin, or association: the house of my sister; to die of hunger. **3.** used after words or phrases expressing quantities: a pint of milk. **4.** constituted by, containing, or characterized by: a family of idiots; a rod of iron; a man of some depth. **5.** used to indicate separation, as in time or space: within a mile of the town; within ten minutes of the beginning of the concert. **6.** used to mark apposition: the city of Naples; a speech on the subject of archaeology. **7.** about; concerning: speak to me of love. **8.** used in passive constructions to indicate the agent: he was beloved of all. **9.** Inf. used to indicate a day or part of a period of time when some activity habitually occurs: I go to the pub of an evening. **10.** U.S. before the hour of: a quarter of nine.
▷ **Usage.** See at **off.**

OF, O.F., or **OF.** abbrev. for Old French (language).

THESAURUS

off (ɒf) *prep.* **1.** used to indicate actions in which contact is absent, as between an object and a surface: *to lift a cup off the table.* **2.** used to indicate the removal of something that is appended to or in association with something else: *to take the tax off potatoes.* **3.** out of alignment with: *we are off course.* **4.** situated near to or leading away from: *just off the High Street.* **5.** not inclined towards: *I've gone off you.* ~*adv.* **6.** (*particle*) so as to deactivate or disengage: *turn off the radio.* **7.** (*particle*) **a.** so as to get rid of: *sleep off a hangover.* **b.** so as to be removed from, esp. as a reduction: *he took ten per cent off.* **8.** spent away from work or other duties: *take the afternoon off.* **9. a.** on a trip, journey, or race: *I saw her off at the station.* **b.** (*particle*) so as to be completely absent, used up, or exhausted: *this stuff kills off all vermin.* **10.** out from the shore or land: *the ship stood off.* **11. a.** out of contact; at a distance: *the ship was 10 miles off.* **b.** out of the present location: *the girl ran off.* **12.** away in the future: *August is less than a week off.* **13.** (*particle*) so as to be no longer taking place: *the match has been rained off.* **14.** (*particle*) removed from contact with something, as clothing from the body: *the girl took all her clothes off.* **15. off and on.** occasionally; intermittently: *he comes here off and on.* **16. off with.** (*interj.*) a command or an exhortation to remove or cut off (something specified): *off with his head; off with that coat.* ~*adj.* **17.** not on; no longer operative: *the off position on the dial.* **18.** (*postpositive*) not taking place; cancelled or postponed: *the meeting is off.* **19.** in a specified condition regarding money, provisions, etc.: *well off; how are you off for bread?* **20.** unsatisfactory or disappointing: *his performance was rather off; an off year for good tennis.* **21.** (*postpositive*) in a condition as specified: *I'd be better off without this job.* **22.** (*postpositive*) no longer on the menu: *haddock is off.* **23.** (*postpositive*) (of food or drink) having gone bad, sour, etc.: *this milk is off.* ~*n.* **24.** *Cricket.* **a.** the part of the field on that side of the pitch to which the batsman presents his bat when taking strike. **b.** (*in combination*): a fielding position in this part of the field: *mid-off.* **c.** (*as modifier*): *the off stump.*
▷ **Usage.** In educated usage, *off* is not followed by *from* or *of: he stepped off* (not *off of*) *the platform.* Careful writers also avoid using the word in the place of *from: they bought apples from* (rather than *off*) *the man.*

off. *abbrev. for:* **1.** offer. **2.** office. **3.** officer. **4.** official.

offal ('ɒfəl) *n.* **1.** the edible internal parts of an animal, such as the heart, liver, and tongue. **2.** dead or decomposing organic matter. **3.** refuse; rubbish.

offbeat ('ɒf,biːt) *n.* **1.** *Music.* any of the normally unaccented beats in a bar, such as the second and fourth beats in a bar of four-four time. ~*adj.* **2. a.** unusual, unconventional, or eccentric. **b.** (*as n.*): *he liked the offbeat in music.*

off chance *n.* **1.** a slight possibility. **2. on the off** chance. with the hope: *on the off chance of getting the job.*

off colour *adj.* (**off-colour** *when prenominal*). **1.** *Chiefly Brit.* slightly ill; unwell. **2.** indecent or indelicate; risqué.

off cut *n.* a piece of paper, wood, etc., remaining after the main pieces have been cut; remnant.

offence *or U.S.* **offense** (ə'fɛns) *n.* **1.** a violation or breach of a law, rule, etc. **2.** any public wrong or crime. **3.** annoyance, displeasure, or resentment. **4. give offence (to).** to cause annoyance or displeasure (to). **5. take offence.** to feel injured, humiliated, or offended. **6.** a source of annoyance, displeasure, or anger. **7.** attack; assault. **8.** *Arch.* injury or harm. —of'fenceless *or U.S.* of'fenseless *adj.*

offend (ə'fɛnd) *vb.* **1.** to hurt the feelings, sense of dignity, etc., of (a person, etc.). **2.** (*tr.*) to be disagreeable to; disgust: *the smell offended him.* **3.** (*intr. except in archaic uses*) to break (a law). —of'fender *n.*

offensive (ə'fɛnsɪv) *adj.* **1.** unpleasant or disgusting, as to the senses. **2.** causing anger or annoyance; insulting. **3.** for the purpose of attack rather than defence. ~*n.* **4.** (usually preceded by *the*) an attitude or position of aggression. **5.** an assault, attack, or military initiative, esp. a strategic one. —of'fensively *adv.* —of'fensiveness *n.*

offer ('ɒfə) *vb.* **1.** to present (something, someone, oneself, etc.) for acceptance or rejection. **2.** (*tr.*) to present as part of a requirement: *she offered English as a second subject.* **3.** (*tr.*) to provide or make accessible: *this stream offers the best fishing.* **4.** (*intr.*) to present itself: *if an opportunity should offer.* **5.** (*tr.*) to show or express willingness or the intention (to do something). **6.** (*tr.*) to put forward (a proposal, opinion, etc.) for consideration. **7.** (*tr.*) to present for sale. **8.** (*tr.*) to propose as payment; bid or tender. **9.** (when *tr.*, often foll. by *up*) to present (a prayer, sacrifice, etc.) as or during an act of worship. **10.** (*tr.*) to show readiness for: *to offer battle.* **11.** (*intr.*) to make a proposal of marriage. ~*n.* **12.** something, such as a proposal or bid, that is offered. **13.** the act of offering or the condition of being offered. **14.** a proposal of marriage. **15. on offer.** for sale at a reduced price. —'offerer *or* 'offeror *n.*

offering ('ɒfərɪŋ) *n.* **1.** something that is offered. **2.** a contribution to the funds of a religious organization. **3.** a sacrifice, as of an animal, to a deity.

offertory ('ɒfətərɪ) *n., pl.* -**tories.** *Christianity.* **1.** the oblation of the bread and wine at the Eucharist. **2.** the offerings of the worshippers at this service. **3.** the prayers said or sung while the worshippers' offerings are being brought to the altar during the **offertory procession.**

offhand (ˌɒf'hænd) *adj. also* **offhanded,** *adv.* **1.** without preparation or warning; impromptu. **2.** without care, thought, attention, or consideration: *an offhand manner.* —ˌoff'handedly *adv.* —ˌoff'handedness *n.*

THESAURUS

off *adj.* **1.** absent, cancelled, finished, gone, inoperative, postponed, unavailable **2.** bad, below par, disappointing, disheartening, displeasing, low-quality, mortifying, poor, quiet, slack, substandard, unrewarding, unsatisfactory **3.** bad, decomposed, high, mouldy, rancid, rotten, sour, turned ~*adv.* **4.** apart, aside, away, elsewhere, out

off and on (every) now and again, every once in a while, from time to time, intermittently, now and then, occasionally, on and off, sometimes, sporadically

offbeat bizarre, Bohemian, eccentric, far-out (*Sl.*), freaky (*Sl.*), idiosyncratic, kinky (*Sl.*), novel, oddball (*Chiefly U.S. inf.*), outré, strange, uncommon, unconventional, unorthodox, unusual, way-out (*Inf.*), weird

off colour ill, not up to par, off form, out of sorts, peaky, poorly (*Inf.*), queasy, run down, sick, under the weather (*Inf.*), unwell, washed out

offence 1. breach of conduct, crime, delinquency, fault, lapse, misdeed, misdemeanour, peccadillo, sin, transgression, trespass, wrong, wrongdoing **2.** affront, displeasure, harm, hurt, indignity, injury, injustice, insult, outrage, put-down (*Sl.*), slight, snub **3.** anger,

annoyance, displeasure, hard feelings, huff, indignation, ire (*Literary*), needle (*Sl.*), pique, resentment, umbrage, wounded feelings, wrath **4. take offence** be disgruntled, be offended, get riled, go into a huff, resent, take the huff, take the needle (*Brit. sl.*), take umbrage

offend 1. affront, annoy, disgruntle, displease, fret, gall, give offence, hurt (someone's) feelings, insult, irritate, miff (*Inf.*), outrage, pain, pique, provoke, put (someone's) back up (*Inf.*), rile, slight, snub, tread on (someone's) toes (*Inf.*), upset, vex, wound **2.** be disagreeable to, disgust, make (someone) sick, nauseate, repel, repulse, sicken, turn (someone) off (*Sl.*)

offended affronted, disgruntled, displeased, huffy, in a huff, miffed (*Inf.*), outraged, pained, piqued, put out (*Inf.*), resentful, smarting, stung, upset

offender criminal, culprit, delinquent, lawbreaker, malefactor, miscreant, sinner, transgressor, wrongdoer

offensive *adj.* **1.** abusive, annoying, detestable, discourteous, displeasing, disrespectful, embarrassing, impertinent, insolent, insulting, irritating, objectionable, rude,

uncivil, unmannerly **2.** abominable, detestable, disagreeable, disgusting, grisly, loathsome, nasty, nauseating, noisome, obnoxious, odious, repellent, revolting, sickening, unpalatable, unpleasant, unsavoury, vile **3.** aggressive, attacking, invading ~*n.* **4.** attack, drive, onslaught, push (*Inf.*) **5. on the offensive** advancing, aggressive, attacking, invading, invasive, on the warpath (*Inf.*)

offer *v.* **1.** bid, extend, give, hold out, proffer, put on the market, put under the hammer, put up for sale, tender **2.** afford, furnish, make available, place at (someone's) disposal, present, provide, show **3.** advance, extend, move, propose, put forth, put forward, submit, suggest **4.** be at (someone's) service, come forward, offer one's services, volunteer ~*n.* **5.** attempt, bid, endeavour, essay, overture, proposal, proposition, submission, suggestion, tender

offering contribution, donation, gift, oblation (*in religious contexts*), present, sacrifice, subscription, widow's mite

offhand 1. *adj.* abrupt, aloof, brusque, careless, casual, cavalier, couldn't-care-less, curt, glib, informal, offhanded, perfunctory, take-it-or-leave-it (*Inf.*), unceremonious, un-

office ('ɒfɪs) n. **1. a.** a room or rooms in which business, professional duties, clerical work, etc., are carried out. **b.** (as modifier): office furniture; an office boy. **2.** (often pl.) the building or buildings in which the work of an organization, such as a business, is carried out. **3.** a commercial or professional business: the architect's office approved the plans. **4.** the group of persons working in an office: it was a happy office until she came. **5.** (cap. when part of a name) (in Britain) a department of the national government: the Home Office. **6.** (cap. when part of a name) (in the U.S.) **a.** a governmental agency, esp. of the Federal government. **b.** a subdivision of such an agency: Office of Science and Technology. **7. a.** a position of trust, responsibility, or duty, esp. in a government or organization: to seek office. **b.** (in combination): an office-holder. **8.** duty or function: the office of an administrator. **9.** (often pl.) a minor task or service: domestic offices. **10.** (often pl.) an action performed for another, usually a beneficial action: through his good offices. **11.** a place where tickets, information, etc., can be obtained: a ticket office. **12.** Christianity. **a.** (often pl.) a ceremony or service, prescribed by ecclesiastical authorities, esp. one for the dead. **b.** R.C. Church. the official daily service. **13.** (pl.) the parts of a house or estate where work is done, goods are stored, etc. **14.** Brit. a euphemistic term for **lavatory**. **15. the office.** a hint or signal. **16. in** (or **out**) **of office.** (of a government) in (or out) of power.

officer ('ɒfɪsə) n. **1.** a person in the armed services who holds a position of responsibility, authority, and duty. **2.** a member of a police force, esp. a constable; policeman. **3.** a person authorized to serve as master or mate of a vessel. **4.** a person appointed or elected to a position of responsibility or authority in a government, society, etc. **5.** a government official: a customs officer. **6.** (in the Order of the British Empire) a member of the grade below commander. ~vb. (tr.) **7.** to furnish with officers. **8.** to act as an officer over (some section, group, organization, etc.).

official (ə'fɪʃəl) adj. **1.** of or relating to an office, its administration, or its duration. **2.** sanctioned by, recognized by, or derived from authority: an official statement. **3.** having a formal ceremonial character: an official dinner. ~n. **4.** a person who holds a position in an organization, government department, etc., esp. a subordinate position. —of'ficially adv.

officialdom (ə'fɪʃəldəm) n. **1.** the outlook or behaviour of officials, esp. those rigidly adhering to regulations; bureaucracy. **2.** officials or bureaucrats collectively.

officialese (ə,fɪʃə'liːz) n. language characteristic of official documents, esp. when verbose or pedantic.

Official Receiver n. an officer appointed by the Department of Trade and Industry to receive the income and manage the estate of a bankrupt. See also **receiver**.

officiate (ə'fɪʃɪ,eɪt) vb. (intr.) **1.** to hold the position, responsibility, or function of an official. **2.** to conduct a religious or other ceremony. —of,fici'ation n. —of'fici,ator n.

officious (ə'fɪʃəs) adj. **1.** unnecessarily or obtrusively ready to offer advice or services. **2.** Diplomacy. informal or unofficial. —of'ficiously adv. —of'ficiousness n.

offing ('ɒfɪŋ) n. **1.** the part of the sea that can be seen from the shore. **2. in the offing.** likely to occur soon.

offish ('ɒfɪʃ) adj. Inf. aloof or distant in manner. —'offishly adv. —'offishness n.

off key adj. (**off-key** when prenominal) adv. **1.** Music. **a.** not in the correct key. **b.** out of tune. **2.** out of keeping; discordant.

off-licence n. Brit. **1.** a shop, counter, etc., where alcoholic drinks are sold for consumption elsewhere. U.S. equivalent: **package store. 2.** a licence permitting such sales.

off line adj. (**off-line** when prenominal). **1.** of or concerned with a part of a computer system not connected to the central processing unit but controlled by a computer storage device. Cf. **on line. 2.** disconnected from a computer; switched off.

off-load vb.(tr.) to get rid of (something unpleasant), as by delegation to another.

off-peak adj. of or relating to services as used outside periods of intensive use.

off-putting adj. Brit. inf. disconcerting or disturbing.

off season adj. (**off-season** when prenominal). **1.** denoting or occurring during a period of little activity in a trade or business. ~adv. **2.** in an off-season period.

offset n. ('ɒf,sɛt). **1.** something that counterbalances or compensates for something else. **2. a.** a printing method in which the impression is made onto an intermediate surface, such as a rubber blanket, which transfers it to the paper. **b.** (modifier) relating to, involving, or printed by offset: offset letterpress. **3.** another name for **setoff. 4.** Bot. a short runner in certain plants that produces roots and shoots at the tip. **5.** a ridge projecting from a range of hills or mountains. **6.** a narrow horizontal or sloping surface formed where a wall is reduced in thickness towards the top. **7.** Surveying. a measurement of distance to a point at right angles to a survey line. ~vb. (,ɒf'sɛt), **-setting, -set. 8.** (tr.) to counterbalance or compensate for. **9.** (tr.) to print (text, etc.) using the offset process. **10.** (tr.) to construct an offset in (a wall). **11.** (intr.) to project or develop as an offset.

offshoot ('ɒf,ʃuːt) n. **1.** a shoot or branch growing from the main stem of a plant. **2.** something that develops or derives from a principal source or origin.

offshore (,ɒf'ʃɔː) adj., adv. from, away from, or at some distance from the shore.

offside ('ɒf'saɪd) adj., adv. **1.** Sport. (in football, etc.) in a position illegally ahead of the ball when it is played. ~n. **2.** (usually preceded by the) Chiefly Brit. **a.** the side of a vehicle, etc., nearest the centre of the road. **b.** (as modifier): the offside passenger door.

offspring ('ɒf,sprɪŋ) n. **1.** the immediate descendant or descendants of a person, animal, etc.; progeny. **2.** a product, outcome, or result.

off-the-peg adj. (of clothing) ready to wear; not produced especially for the person buying.

oft (ɒft) adv. short for **often** (archaic or poetic except in combinations such as **oft-repeated** and **oft-recurring**).

often ('ɒfən) adv. **1.** frequently or repeatedly; much of the time. Archaic equivalents: **'often,times, 'oft,times. 2. as often as not.** quite frequently. **3. every so often.** at regular intervals. **4. more often than not.** in more than half the instances. ~adj. **5.** Arch. repeated; frequent.

ogee ('əʊdʒiː) n. Archit. **1.** Also called: **talon.** a mould-

---

concerned, uninterested **2.** adv. ad lib, extempore, just like that (Inf.), off the cuff (Inf.), off the top of one's head (Inf.), without preparation

office 1. appointment, business, capacity, charge, commission, duty, employment, function, obligation, occupation, place, post, responsibility, role, service, situation, station, trust, work **2.** Plural advocacy, aegis, aid, auspices, backing, favour, help, intercession, intervention, mediation, patronage, recommendation, referral, support, word

officer agent, appointee, bureaucrat, dignitary, executive, functionary, office-holder, official, public servant, representative

official 1. adj. accredited, authentic, authoritative, authorized, bona fide, certified, endorsed, ex cathedra, ex officio, formal, legitimate, licensed, proper, sanctioned, straight from the horse's mouth (Inf.) **2.** n.

agent, bureaucrat, executive, functionary, office bearer, officer, representative

officiate chair, conduct, emcee (Inf.), manage, oversee, preside, serve, superintend

officious bustling, dictatorial, forward, impertinent, inquisitive, interfering, intrusive, meddlesome, meddling, mischievous, obtrusive, opinionated, overbusy, overzealous, pragmatical (Rare), pushy (Inf.), self-important

offing in the offing close at hand, coming up, hovering, imminent, in prospect, in the immediate future, in the wings, on the horizon, on the way

off-load disburden, discharge, dump, get rid of, jettison, shift, take off, transfer, unburden, unload, unship

off-putting daunting, discomfiting, disconcerting, discouraging, dismaying, dispiriting, disturbing, formidable, frustrating, in-

timidating, unnerving, unsettling, upsetting

offset 1. v. balance out, cancel out, compensate for, counteract, counterbalance, counterpoise, countervail, make up for, neutralize **2.** n. balance, compensation, counterbalance, counterweight, equipoise

offshoot adjunct, appendage, branch, by-product, development, limb, outgrowth, spin-off, sprout

offspring child, children, descendant, descendants, family, fry, heir, heirs, issue, kids (Inf.), progeny, scion, seed, spawn, successor, successors, young

often again and again, frequently, generally, many a time, much, oft (Poetic), oftentimes (Archaic), ofttimes (Archaic), over and over again, repeatedly, time after time, time and again

ing having a cross section in the form of a letter S. **2.** Also called: **ogee arch.** a pointed arch having an S-shaped curve on both sides.

ogle ('əʊgəl) *vb.* **1.** to look at (someone, esp. a woman) amorously. **2.** (*tr.*) to stare or gape at. ~*n.* **3.** a flirtatious or lewd look. —**'ogler** *n.*

ogre ('əʊgə) *n.* **1.** (in folklore) a giant, usually given to eating human flesh. **2.** any monstrous or cruel person. —**'ogreish** *adj.* —**'ogress** *fem. n.*

oh (əʊ) *interj.* an exclamation expressive of surprise, pain, pleasure, etc.

OHG, O.H.G. *or* **OHG.** *abbrev. for* Old High German.

ohm (əʊm) *n.* the derived SI unit of electric resistance; the resistance between two points on a conductor when a constant potential difference of 1 volt between them produces a current of 1 ampere. Symbol: Ω —**'ohmage** *n.*

O.H.M.S. (in Britain and the Commonwealth) *abbrev. for* On Her (*or* His) Majesty's Service.

oil (ɔɪl) *n.* **1.** any of a number of viscous liquids with a smooth sticky feel. They are usually flammable, insoluble in water, soluble in organic solvents, and are obtained from plants and animals, from mineral deposits, and by synthesis. See also **essential oil. 2. a.** another name for **petroleum. b.** (*as modifier*): *an oil engine; an oil rig.* **3. a.** any of a number of substances usually derived from petroleum and used for lubrication. **b.** (*in combination*): *an oilcan.* **c.** (*as modifier*): *an oil pump.* **4.** a fraction of petroleum used as a fuel in domestic heating, marine engines, etc. Also called: **fuel oil. 5.** *Brit.* **a.** paraffin, esp. when used as a domestic fuel. **b.** (*as modifier*): *an oil lamp.* **6.** any substance of a consistency resembling that of oil: *oil of vitriol.* **7.** the solvent, usually linseed oil, with which pigments are mixed to make artists' paints. **8. a.** (*often pl.*) oil colour or paint. **b.** (*as modifier*): *an oil painting.* **9.** an oil painting. **10.** *Austral. & N.Z. sl.* facts or news. **11. strike oil. a.** to discover petroleum while drilling for it. **b.** *Inf.* to become very rich or successful. ~*vb.* (*tr.*) **12.** to lubricate, smear, polish, etc., with oil or an oily substance. **13. oil one's tongue.** *Inf.* to speak flatteringly or glibly. **14.** *Inf.* to bribe (esp. in **oil someone's palm**). **15. oil the wheels.** to make things run smoothly. **16. well oiled.** drunk. —**'oil-,like** *adj.* —**'oiler** *n.* —**'oilman** *n.*

oil cake *n.* stock feed consisting of compressed cubes made from the residue of the crushed seeds of oil-bearing crops such as linseed.

oilcloth ('ɔɪl,klɒθ) *n.* **1.** waterproof material made by treating one side of a cotton fabric with a drying oil, or a synthetic resin. **2.** another name for **linoleum.**

oilfield ('ɔɪl,fiːld) *n.* an area containing reserves of petroleum, esp. one that is already being exploited.

oilfired ('ɔɪl,faɪəd) *adj.* (of central heating, etc.) using oil as fuel.

oil painting *n.* **1.** a picture painted with oil paints. **2.** the art or process of painting with oil paints. **3.** *Inf.* a person or thing regarded as good-looking (esp. in **she's no oil painting**).

oil rig *n.* See **rig** (sense 6).

oilskin ('ɔɪl,skɪn) *n.* **1. a.** a cotton fabric treated with oil and pigment to make it waterproof. **b.** (*as modifier*): *an oilskin hat.* **2.** (*often pl.*) a protective outer garment of this fabric.

oil slick *n.* a mass of floating oil covering an area of water.

oil well *n.* a boring into the earth or sea bed for the extraction of petroleum.

oily ('ɔɪlɪ) *adj.* **oilier, oiliest. 1.** soaked in or smeared with oil or grease. **2.** consisting of, containing, or resembling oil. **3.** flatteringly servile or obsequious. —**'oilily** *adv.* —**'oiliness** *n.*

oink (ɔɪŋk) *interj.* an imitation or representation of the grunt of a pig or the cry of a goose.

ointment ('ɔɪntmənt) *n.* **1.** a fatty or oily medicated preparation applied to the skin to heal or protect. **2.** a similar substance used as a cosmetic.

O.K. (,əʊ'keɪ) *Inf.* **1.** *sentence substitute.* an expression of approval or agreement. ~*adj.* (*usually postpositive*), *adv.* **2.** in good or satisfactory condition. ~*vb.* **O.K.ing** (,əʊ'keɪɪŋ), **O.K.ed** (,əʊ'keɪd). **3.** (*tr.*) to approve or endorse. ~*n., pl.* **O.K.s. 4.** approval or agreement. ~Also: **okay.**

okapi (əʊ'kɑːpɪ) *n., pl.* **-pis** *or* **-pi.** a ruminant mammal of the forests of central Africa, having a reddish-brown coat with horizontal white stripes on the legs and small horns.

okay (,əʊ'keɪ) *adj., adv., vb., n., sentence substitute.* a variant spelling of **O.K.**

okra ('əʊkrə) *n.* **1.** an annual plant of the Old World tropics, with yellow-and-red flowers and edible oblong sticky green pods. **2.** the pod of this plant, eaten in soups, stews, etc.

old (əʊld) *adj.* **1.** having lived or existed for a relatively long time: *an old man; an old tradition; an old house.* **2. a.** of or relating to advanced years or a long life: *old age.* **b. the old.** old people. **c. old and young.** people of all ages. **3.** decrepit or senile. **4.** worn with age or use: *old clothes; an old car.* **5. a.** (*postpositive*) having lived or existed for a specified period: *a child who is six years old.* **b.** (*in combination*): *a six-year-old child.* **c.** (*as n. in combination*): *a six-year-old.* **6.** (*cap. when part of a name or title*) earlier or earliest of two or more things with the same name: *the old edition; the Old Testament.* **7.** (*cap. when part of a name*) designating the form of a language in which the earliest known records are written: *Old English.* **8.** (*prenominal*) familiar through long acquaintance or repetition: *an old friend; an old excuse.* **9.** practised; hardened: *old in cunning.* **10.** (*prenominal*) (often preceded by *good*) cherished; dear: used as a term of affection or familiarity: *good old George.* **11.** *Inf.* (with any of several nouns) used as a familiar form of address to a person: *old thing; old bean; old stick.* **12.** skilled through long experience (esp. in **an old hand**). **13.** out-of-date; unfashionable. **14.** remote or distant in origin or time of origin: *an old culture.* **15.** (*prenominal*) former; previous: *my old house was small.* **16. a.** (*prenominal*) established for a relatively long time: *an old member.* **b.** (*in combination*): old-established. **17.** sensible, wise, or mature: *old beyond one's years.* **18.** (*intensifier*) (esp. in **a good old time, any old thing, any old how,** etc.). **19. good old days.** an earlier period of time regarded as better than the present. **20. little old.** indicating affection, esp. humorous affection. **21. the old one** (*or* **gentleman**). *Inf.* a jocular name for **Satan.** ~*n.* **22.** an earlier or past time (esp. in **of old**): *in days of old.* —**'oldish** *adj.* —**'oldness** *n.*

old age pension *n.* another name for **retirement pension.** —**old age pensioner** *n.*

Old Bailey ('beɪlɪ) *n.* the Central Criminal Court of England.

THESAURUS

ogre bogey, bogeyman, bugbear, demon, devil, giant, monster, spectre

oil *v.* grease, lubricate

ointment balm, cerate, cream, embrocation, emollient, liniment, lotion, salve, unguent

O.K., okay 1. *adj.* acceptable, accurate, adequate, all right, approved, convenient, correct, fair, fine, good, in order, middling, not bad (*Inf.*), passable, permitted, satisfactory, so-so (*Inf.*), tolerable **2.** *n.* agreement, approbation, sanction, assent, authorization, consent, endorsement, go-ahead (*Inf.*), green light, permission, sanction, say-so (*Inf.*), seal of approval **3.** *v.* agree to, approve, authorize, consent to, endorse, give one's consent to, give the go-ahead to (*Inf.*), give the green light to, give the thumbs up to, pass, rubber-stamp (*Inf.*), sanction, say yes to **4.** *interj.* agreed, all right, right, very good, very well, yes

old 1. advanced in years, aged, ancient, decrepit, elderly, full of years, getting on (*Inf.*), grey, grey-haired, grizzled, hoary, mature, over the hill (*Inf.*), past one's prime, patriarchal, senescent, senile, venerable **2.** antediluvian, antiquated, antique, cast-off, crumbling, dated, decayed, done, hackneyed, obsolete, old-fashioned, outdated, outmoded, out of date, passé, stale, superannuated, timeworn, unfashionable, unoriginal, worn-out **3.** aboriginal, antique, archaic, bygone, early, immemorial, of old, of yore, olden (*Archaic*), original, primeval, primitive, primordial, pristine, remote **4.** age-old, experienced, familiar, hardened, long-established, of long

standing, practised, skilled, time-honoured, traditional, versed, veteran, vintage **5.** earlier, erstwhile, ex-, former, one-time, previous, quondam

old age advancing years, age, agedness, Anno Domini (*Inf.*), autumn *or* evening of one's life, declining years, dotage, senescence, senility

old-fashioned ancient, antiquated, archaic, behind the times, corny (*Sl.*), dated, dead, démodé, fusty, musty, not with it (*Inf.*), obsolescent, obsolete, oldfangled, (old-)fogyish, old hat, old-time, outdated, outmoded, out of date, out of style, out of the ark (*Inf.*), passé, past, square (*Inf.*), superannuated, unfashionable

old boy n. 1. (sometimes caps.) Brit. a male ex-pupil of a school. 2. Inf., chiefly Brit. a. a familiar name used to refer to a man. b. an old man. —**old girl** (fem.) n.

old country n. the country of origin of an immigrant or an immigrant's ancestors.

olden ('əʊldən) adj. an archaic or poetic word for **old** (often in **in olden days** and **in olden times**).

Old English n. 1. Also called: **Anglo-Saxon**. the English language from the time of the earliest Saxon settlements in the fifth century A.D. to about 1100. Abbrev.: **OE**. 2. Printing. a Gothic typeface commonly used in England up to the 18th century.

Old English sheepdog n. a breed of large sheepdog with a profuse shaggy coat.

old-fashioned adj. 1. belonging to, characteristic of, or favoured by former times; outdated: old-fashioned ideas. 2. favouring or adopting the dress, manners, fashions, etc., of a former time. 3. N. English dialect. old for one's age: an old-fashioned child. ~n. 4. a cocktail containing spirit, bitters, fruit, etc.

Old French n. the French language in its earliest forms, from about the 9th century up to about 1400. Abbrev.: **OF**.

old guard n. 1. a group that works for a long-established or old-fashioned cause or principle. 2. the conservative element in a political party or other group.

old hat adj. (postpositive) old-fashioned or trite.

Old High German n. a group of West Germanic dialects that eventually developed into modern German; High German up to about 1200. Abbrev.: **OHG**.

oldie ('əʊldɪ) n. Inf. an old joke, song, film, person, etc.

old lady n. an informal term for **mother** or **wife**.

old maid n. 1. a woman regarded as unlikely ever to marry; spinster. 2. Inf. a prim, fastidious, or excessively cautious person. 3. a card game in which players try to avoid holding the unpaired card at the end of the game. —ˌold-ˈmaidish adj.

old man n. 1. an informal term for **father** or **husband**. 2. (sometimes caps.) Inf. a man in command, such as an employer, foreman, or captain of a ship. 3. Sometimes facetious. an affectionate term used in addressing a man. 4. Also called: **southernwood**. an aromatic shrubby wormwood of S Europe, having drooping yellow flowers. 5. Christianity. the unregenerate aspect of human nature.

old master n. 1. one of the great European painters of the period 1500 to 1800. 2. a painting by one of these.

old moon n. a phase of the moon lying between last quarter and new moon, when it appears as a waning crescent.

Old Nick n. Inf. a jocular name for **Satan**.

old rose n. a. a greyish-pink colour. b. (as adj.): old-rose gloves.

Old Saxon n. the Saxon dialect of Low German up to about 1200, from which modern Low German is derived. Abbrev.: **OS**.

old school n. 1. Chiefly Brit. one's former school. 2. a group of people favouring traditional ideas or conservative practices.

old school tie n. 1. Brit. a distinctive tie that indicates which school the wearer attended. 2. the attitudes, loyalties, values, etc., associated with British public schools.

Old Testament n. the collection of books comprising the sacred Scriptures of the Hebrews; the first part of the Christian Bible.

old-time adj. (prenominal) of or relating to a former time; old-fashioned: old-time dancing.

old wives' tale n. a belief passed on by word of mouth as a piece of traditional wisdom.

old woman n. 1. an informal term for **mother** or **wife**. 2. a timid, fussy, or cautious person. —**old womanish** adj.

Old World n. that part of the world that was known before the discovery of the Americas; the eastern hemisphere.

old-world adj. of or characteristic of former times,

esp., in Europe, quaint or traditional. —ˌold-ˈworldly adv.

oleaginous (ˌəʊlɪˈædʒɪnəs) adj. 1. resembling or having the properties of oil. 2. containing or producing oil.

oleander (ˌəʊlɪˈændə) n. a poisonous evergreen Mediterranean shrub or tree with fragrant white, pink, or purple flowers. Also called: **rosebay**.

oleo- combining form. oil: oleomargarine.

O level n. Brit. 1. a. the basic level of the General Certificate of Education. b. (as modifier): O level maths. 2. a pass in a particular subject at O level: he has eight O levels.

olfactory (ɒlˈfæktərɪ, -trɪ) adj. 1. of or relating to the sense of smell. ~n., pl. -ries. 2. (usually pl.) an organ or nerve concerned with the sense of smell.

oligarch ('ɒlɪˌgɑːk) n. a member of an oligarchy.

oligarchy ('ɒlɪˌgɑːkɪ) n., pl. -chies. 1. government by a small group of people. 2. a state or organization so governed. 3. a small body of individuals ruling such a state. 4. Chiefly U.S. a small clique of private citizens who exert a strong influence on government. —ˌoliˈgarchic or ˌoliˈgarchical adj.

oligo- or before a vowel **olig-** combining form. indicating a few or little: oligopoly.

Oligocene ('ɒlɪgəʊˌsiːn, ɒˈlɪg-) adj. 1. of, denoting, or formed in the third epoch of the Tertiary period. ~n. 2. (preceded by the) the Oligocene epoch or rock series.

olio ('əʊlɪˌəʊ) n., pl. **olios**. 1. a dish of many different ingredients. 2. a miscellany or potpourri.

olive ('ɒlɪv) n. 1. an evergreen oleaceous tree of the Mediterranean region having white fragrant flowers and edible black fruits. 2. the fruit of this plant, eaten as a relish and used as a source of olive oil. 3. the wood of the olive tree, used for ornamental work. 4. a. a yellow-green colour. b. (as adj.): an olive coat. ~adj. 5. of, relating to, or made of the olive tree, its wood, or its fruit.

olive branch n. 1. a branch of an olive tree used to symbolize peace. 2. any offering of peace or conciliation.

olive green n. a. a colour that is greener, stronger, and brighter than olive; deep yellowish-green. b. (as adj.): an olive-green coat.

olive oil n. a pale yellow oil pressed from ripe olive fruits and used in cooking, medicine, etc.

olivine ('ɒlɪˌviːn, ˌɒlɪˈviːn) n. any of a group of hard glassy olive-green minerals consisting of magnesium iron silicate in crystalline form.

-ology n. combining form. see **-logy**.

Olympiad (əˈlɪmpɪˌæd) n. 1. a staging of the modern Olympic Games. 2. the four-year period between consecutive celebrations of the Olympic Games; a unit of ancient Greek chronology dating back to 776 B.C. 3. an international contest in chess, bridge, etc.

Olympian (əˈlɪmpɪən) adj. 1. of or relating to Mount Olympus or to the classical Greek gods. 2. majestic or godlike in manner or bearing. 3. of or relating to ancient Olympia, a plain in Greece, or its inhabitants. ~n. 4. a god of Mount Olympus. 5. an inhabitant of ancient Olympia. 6. Chiefly U.S. a competitor in the Olympic Games.

Olympic (əˈlɪmpɪk) adj. 1. of or relating to the Olympic Games. 2. of or relating to ancient Olympia.

Olympic Games n. (functioning as sing. or pl.) 1. the greatest Panhellenic festival, held every fourth year in honour of Zeus at ancient Olympia, consisting of games and festivities. 2. Also called: **the Olympics**. the modern revival of these games, consisting of international athletic and sporting contests held every four years in a selected country.

O.M. abbrev. for Order of Merit (a Brit. title).

-oma n. combining form. indicating a tumour: glaucoma.

ombudsman ('ɒmbʊdzmən) n., pl. -men. an official who investigates citizens' complaints against the government or its servants. Also called (Brit.): **Parliamentary Commissioner**.

omega ('əʊmɪgə) n. 1. the 24th and last letter of the Greek alphabet (Ω, ω). 2. the ending or last of a series.

THESAURUS

old man elder, elder statesman, father, gaffer, grandfather, greybeard, O.A.P. (Brit.), old codger (Inf.), old stager, oldster (Inf.), old-timer (U.S.), patriarch, senior citizen

old-time ancient, antique, bygone, former, old-fashioned, past, vintage

old-world archaic, ceremonious, chivalrous, courtly, gallant, old-fashioned, picturesque, quaint, traditional

omelette *or esp. U.S.* **omelet** ('ɒmlɪt) *n.* a savoury or sweet dish of beaten eggs cooked in fat.

omen ('əumən) *n.* **1.** a phenomenon or occurrence regarded as a sign of future happiness or disaster. **2.** prophetic significance. ~*vb.* **3.** (*tr.*) to portend.

omicron (əu'maikrɒn, 'ɒmikrɒn) *n.* the 15th letter in the Greek alphabet (O, *o*).

ominous ('ɒminəs) *adj.* **1.** foreboding evil. **2.** serving as or having significance as an omen. —'**ominously** *adv.* —'**ominousness** *n.*

omission (əu'miʃən) *n.* **1.** something that has been omitted or neglected. **2.** the act of omitting or the state of having been omitted. —o'**missive** *adj.* —o'**missiveness** *n.*

omit (əu'mit) *vb.* **omitting, omitted.** (*tr.*) **1.** to neglect to do or include. **2.** to fail (to do something). —**omissible** (əu'misibəl) *adj.* —o'**mitter** *n.*

omni- *combining form.* all or everywhere: *omnipresent.*

omnibus ('ɒmni,bʌs, -bəs) *n., pl.* -**buses.** **1.** a less common word for **bus.** **2.** Also called: **omnibus volume.** a collection of works by one author or several works on a similar topic, reprinted in one volume. ~*adj.* **3.** (*prenominal*) of, dealing with, or providing for many different things or cases.

omnifarious (,ɒmni'fɛəriəs) *adj.* of many or all varieties or forms. —,**omni'fariously** *adv.* —,**omni'fariousness** *n.*

omnipotent (ɒm'nipətənt) *adj.* **1.** having very great or unlimited power. ~*n.* **2. the Omnipotent.** an epithet for God. —**om'nipotence** *n.* —**om'nipotently** *adv.*

omnipresent (,ɒmni'prɛzənt) *adj.* (esp. of a deity) present in all places at the same time. —,**omni'presence** *n.*

omniscient (ɒm'nisiənt) *adj.* **1.** having infinite knowledge or understanding. **2.** having very great or seemingly unlimited knowledge. —**om'niscience** *n.* —**om'nisciently** *adv.*

omnivorous (ɒm'nivərəs) *adj.* **1.** eating any type of food indiscriminately. **2.** taking in or assimilating everything, esp. with the mind. —**om'nivorously** *adv.* —**om'nivorousness** *n.* —'**omni,vore** *n.*

on (ɒn) *prep.* **1.** in contact or connection with the surface of; at the upper surface of: *an apple on the ground; a mark on the table cloth.* **2.** attached to: *a puppet on a string.* **3.** carried with: *I've no money on me.* **4.** in the immediate vicinity of; close to or along the side of: *a house on the sea.* **5.** within the time limits of a day or date: *he arrived on Thursday.* **6.** being performed upon or relayed through the medium of: *what's on the television?* **7.** at the occasion of: *on his retirement.* **8.** used to indicate support, subsistence, contingency, etc.: *he lives on bread.* **9. a.** regularly taking (a drug): *she's on the pill.* **b.** addicted to: *he's on heroin.* **10.** by means of (something considered as a mode of transport) (esp. in **on foot, on horseback,** etc.). **11.** in the process or course of: *on a journey; on strike.* **12.** concerned with or relating to: *a programme on archaeology.* **13.** used to indicate the basis or grounds, as of a statement or action: *I have it on good authority.* **14.** against: used to indicate opposition: *they marched on the city at dawn.* **15.** used to indicate a meeting or encounter: *he crept up on her.* **16.** (used with an adj. preceded by *the*) indicating the manner or way in which an action is carried out: *on the sly; on the cheap.* ~*adv.* (*often used as a particle*) **17.** in the position or state required for the commencement or sustained continuation, as of a mechanical operation: *the radio's been on all night.* **18. a.** attached to, surrounding, or placed in contact with something: *the girl had nothing on.* **b.** taking place: *what's on tonight?* **19.**

in a manner indicating continuity, persistence, etc.: *don't keep on about it; the play went on all afternoon.* **20.** in a direction towards something, esp. forwards: *we drove on towards London; march on!* **21. on and off.** intermittently; from time to time. **22. on and on.** without ceasing; continually. ~*adj.* **23.** functioning; operating: *the on position on a radio.* **24.** (*postpositive*) *Inf.* **a.** staked or wagered as a bet: *ten pounds on that horse.* **b.** performing, as on stage, etc.: *I'm on in five minutes.* **c.** definitely taking place: *the match is on for Friday.* **d.** charged to: *the drinks are on me.* **e.** tolerable or practicable: *your plan just isn't on.* **25. on at.** *Inf.* nagging: *she was always on at her husband.* **26.** *Cricket.* (of a bowler) bowling. ~*n.* **27.** *Cricket.* **a.** (*modifier*) relating to or denoting the leg side of a cricket field or pitch: *an on drive.* **b.** (*in combination*) used to designate certain fielding positions on the leg side: *mid-on.*

-on *suffix forming nouns.* **1.** (in physics) indicating an elementary particle or quantum: *electron; photon.* **2.** (in chemistry) indicating an inert gas: *neon; radon.*

onager ('ɒnədʒə) *n., pl.* -**gri** (-,grai) *or* -**gers.** **1.** a Persian variety of the wild ass. **2.** an ancient war engine for hurling stones, etc.

onanism ('əunə,nizəm) *n.* **1.** the withdrawal of the penis from the vagina before ejaculation. **2.** masturbation. —'**onanist** *n.* —,**onan'istic** *adj.*

O.N.C. (in Britain) *abbrev. for* Ordinary National Certificate.

once (wʌns) *adv.* **1.** one time; on one occasion or in one case. **2.** at some past time: *I could speak French once.* **3.** by one step or degree (of relationship): *a cousin once removed.* **4.** (*in conditional clauses, negatives, etc.*) ever; at all: *if you once forget it.* **5.** multiplied by one. **6. once and away. a.** conclusively. **b.** occasionally. **7. once and for all.** conclusively; for the last time. **8. once in a while.** occasionally; now and then. **9. once or twice** *or* **once and again.** a few times. **10. once upon a time.** used to begin fairy tales and children's stories. ~*conj.* **11.** (*subordinating*) as soon as; if ever: *once you begin, you'll enjoy it.* ~*n.* **12.** one occasion or case: *you may do it, this once.* **13. all at once. a.** suddenly. **b.** simultaneously. **14. at once. a.** immediately. **b.** simultaneously. **15. for once.** this time, if (or but) at no other time.

once-over *n. Inf.* **1.** a quick examination or appraisal. **2.** a quick but comprehensive piece of work. **3.** a violent beating or thrashing. ~*Esp.* (for all senses) in **give (a person or thing) the** (or **a**) **once-over.**

oncoming ('ɒn,kʌmiŋ) *adj.* **1.** coming nearer in space or time; approaching. ~*n.* **2.** the approach or onset: *the oncoming of winter.*

O.N.D. (in Britain) *abbrev. for* Ordinary National Diploma.

one (wʌn) *determiner.* **1. a.** single; lone; not two or more. **b.** (*as pronoun*): *one is enough for now; one at a time.* **c.** (*in combination*): *one-eyed.* **2. a.** distinct from all others; only; unique: *one girl in a million.* **b.** (*as pronoun*): *one of a kind.* **3. a.** a specified (person, item, etc.) as distinct from another or others of its kind: *raise one hand and then the other.* **b.** (*as pronoun*): *which one is correct?* **4.** a certain, indefinite, or unspecified (time); some: *one day you'll be sorry.* **5.** *Inf.* an emphatic word for **a** or **an:** *it was one hell of a fight.* **6.** a certain (person): *one Miss Jones was named.* **7. (all) in one.** combined; united. **8. all one. a.** all the same. **b.** of no consequence: *it's all one to me.* **9. at one.** (often foll. by *with*) in a state of agreement or harmony. **10. be made one.** to become married. **11. many a one.** many people. **12. neither one thing nor the other.** indefinite, undecided, or mixed. **13. never a one.** none. **14. one and all.** every-

omen augury, foreboding, foretoken, indication, portent, premonition, presage, prognostic, prognostication, sign, straw in the wind, warning, writing on the wall

ominous baleful, dark, fateful, foreboding, inauspicious, menacing, minatory, portentous, premonitory, sinister, threatening, unpromising, unpropitious

omission default, exclusion, failure, forgetfulness, gap, lack, leaving out, neglect, noninclusion, oversight

omit disregard, drop, eliminate, exclude, fail, forget, give (something) a miss (*Inf.*), leave out, leave (something) undone, let

(something) slide, miss (out), neglect, overlook, pass over, skip

omnipotence divine right, invincibility, mastery, sovereignty, supremacy, supreme power, undisputed sway

omnipotent all-powerful, almighty, supreme

on and off discontinuously, (every) now and again, fitfully, from time to time, intermittently, now and then, off and on, on occasion, sometimes, spasmodically

once 1. at one time, formerly, in the old days, in the past, in times gone by, in times past, long ago, once upon a time, previously

2. **at once a.** directly, forthwith, immediately, instantly, now, right away, straight away, straightway (*Archaic*), this (very) minute, without delay, without hesitation **b.** at *or* in one go (*Inf.*), at the same time, simultaneously, together 3. **once and for all** conclusively, decisively, finally, for all time, for good, for the last time, permanently, positively, with finality 4. **once in a while** at intervals, at times, every now and then, from time to time, now and again, occasionally, once in a blue moon (*Inf.*), on occasion, sometimes

one, without exception. **15. one by one.** one at a time; individually. **16. one or two.** a few. **17. one way and another.** on balance. **18. one with another.** on average. ~*pron.* **19.** an indefinite person regarded as typical of every person: *one can't say any more than that.* **20.** any indefinite person: used as the subject of a sentence to form an alternative grammatical construction to that of the passive voice: *one can catch fine trout in this stream.* **21.** *Arch.* an unspecified person: *one came to him.* ~*n.* **22.** the smallest whole number and the first cardinal number; unity. **23.** a numeral (1, I, i, etc.) representing this number. **24.** *Inf.* a joke or story (esp. in **the one about**). **25.** something representing, represented by, or consisting of one unit. **26.** Also: **one o'clock.** one hour after noon or midnight. **27.** a blow or setback (esp. in **one in the eye for**). **28. the Holy One** *or* **the One above.** God. **29. the Evil one.** Satan. ~Related prefixes: **mono-, uni-.**
▷ **Usage.** Where the pronoun *one* is repeated, as in *one might think one would be unwise to say that, he* is sometimes substituted: *one might think he would be unwise to say that.* Careful writers avoid *one* followed by *he,* however, because of possible ambiguity: *he* in this case could refer either to the same person as *one* or to some other person.

-one *suffix forming nouns.* indicating that a chemical compound is a ketone: *acetone.*

one-armed bandit *n. Inf.* a fruit machine operated by pulling down a lever at one side.

one-horse *adj.* **1.** drawn by or using one horse. **2.** (*prenominal*) *Inf.* small or obscure: *a one-horse town.*

oneness ('wʌnnɪs) *n.* **1.** the state or quality of being one; singleness. **2.** the state of being united; agreement. **3.** uniqueness. **4.** sameness.

one-night stand *n.* **1.** a performance given only once at any one place. **2.** *Inf.* a sexual encounter lasting only one evening or night.

one-off *n. Brit.* **a.** something that is carried out or made only once. **b.** (*as modifier*): *a one-off job.* Also: **one-shot.**

onerous ('ɒnərəs, 'əʊ-) *adj.* **1.** laborious or oppressive. **2.** *Law.* (of a contract, etc.) having or involving burdens or obligations. —**'onerously** *adv.* —**'onerousness** *n.*

oneself (wʌn'sɛlf) *pron.* **1. a.** the reflexive form of *one.* **b.** (*intensifier*): *one doesn't do that oneself.* **2.** (*preceded by a copula*) one's normal or usual self: *one doesn't feel oneself after such an experience.*

one-sided *adj.* **1.** considering or favouring only one side of a matter, problem, etc. **2.** having all the advantage on one side. **3.** larger or more developed on one side. **4.** having, existing on, or occurring on one side only. —**,one-'sidedly** *adv.* —**,one-'sidedness** *n.*

one-time *adj.* (*prenominal*) at some time in the past; former.

one-to-one *adj.* **1.** (of two or more things) corresponding exactly. **2.** *Maths.* involving the pairing of each member of one set with only one member of another set, without remainder.

one-track *adj.* **1.** *Inf.* obsessed with one idea, subject, etc. **2.** having or consisting of a single track.

one-up *adj. Inf.* having an advantage or lead over someone or something. —**one-'upman,ship** *n.*

one-way *adj.* **1.** moving or allowing travel in one direction only: *one-way traffic.* **2.** entailing no reciprocal obligation, action, etc.: *a one-way agreement.*

ongoing ('ɒn,ɡəʊɪŋ) *adj.* **1.** actually in progress: *ongoing projects.* **2.** continually moving forward; developing.

onion ('ʌnjən) *n.* **1.** an alliaceous plant having greenish-white flowers: cultivated for its rounded edible bulb. **2.** the bulb of this plant, consisting of concentric layers of white succulent leaf bases with a pungent odour and taste. **3. know one's onions.** *Brit. sl.* to be fully acquaint-

ed with a subject. —**'oniony** *adj.*

onionskin ('ʌnjən,skɪn) *n.* a glazed translucent paper.

on line *adj.* (**on-line** *when prenominal*). of or concerned with a peripheral device that is directly connected to and controlled by the central processing unit of a computer. Cf. **off line.**

onlooker ('ɒn,lʊkə) *n.* a person who observes without taking part. —**'on,looking** *adj.*

only ('əʊnlɪ) *adj.* (*prenominal*) **1. the.** being single or very few in number: *the only men left in town were too old to bear arms.* **2.** (of a child) having no siblings. **3.** unique by virtue of being superior to anything else; peerless. **4. one and only. a.** (*adj.*) incomparable; unique. **b.** (*as n.*) the object of all one's love: *you are my one and only.* ~*adv.* **5.** without anyone or anything else being included; alone: *you have one choice only; only a genius can do that.* **6.** merely or just: *it's only Henry.* **7.** no more or no greater than: *we met only an hour ago.* **8.** used in conditional clauses introduced by *if* to emphasize the impossibility of the condition ever being fulfilled: *if I had only known, this would never have happened.* **9.** not earlier than; not...until: *I only found out yesterday.* **10. if only** *or* **if...only.** an expression used to introduce a wish, esp. one felt to be unrealizable. **11. only if.** never...except when. **12. only too. a.** (*intensifier*): *he was only too pleased to help.* **b.** most regrettably (esp. in **only too true**). **13.** *sentence connector.* but; however: used to introduce an exception or condition: *play outside: only don't go into the street.*
▷ **Usage.** In informal English, *only* is often used as a sentence connector: *it would have been possible, only he was not present at the time.* This use is avoided in careful usage, esp. in formal contexts: *it would have been possible had he been present.*

o.n.o. *abbrev. for* or near(est) offer.

onomatopoeia (,ɒnə,mætə'piːə) *n.* **1.** the formation of words whose sound is imitative of the sound of the noise or action designated, such as *hiss.* **2.** the use of such words for poetic or rhetorical effect. —**,ono,mato'poeic** *or* **onomatopoetic** (,ɒnə,mætəpəʊ'ɛtɪk) *adj.* —**,ono,mato'poeically** *or* **,ono,matopo'etically** *adv.*

onrush ('ɒn,rʌʃ) *n.* a forceful forward rush or flow.

onset ('ɒn,sɛt) *n.* **1.** an attack; assault. **2.** a start; beginning.

onshore ('ɒn'ʃɔː) *adj., adv.* **1.** towards the land: *an onshore gale.* **2.** on land; not at sea.

onslaught ('ɒn,slɔːt) *n.* a violent attack.

Ont. *abbrev. for* Ontario.

Ontarian (ɒn'tɛərɪən) *or* **Ontarioan** (ɒn'tɛərɪ,əʊən) *adj.* **1.** of or denoting Ontario, a province of central Canada. ~*n.* **2.** a native or inhabitant of Ontario.

onto *or* **on to** ('ɒntʊ; *unstressed* 'ɒntə) *prep.* **1.** to a position that is on: *step onto the train.* **2.** having become aware of (something illicit or secret): *the police are onto us.* **3.** into contact with: *get onto the factory.*
▷ **Usage.** *Onto* is generally accepted as a word in its own right. *On to* is still used, however, where *on* is considered to be part of the verb: *he moved on to the next platform* as contrasted with *he jumped onto the next platform.*

ontology (ɒn'tɒlədʒɪ) *n.* **1.** *Philosophy.* the branch of metaphysics that deals with the nature of being. **2.** *Logic.* the set of entities presupposed by a theory. —**,onto'logical** *adj.* —**,onto'logically** *adv.*

onus ('əʊnəs) *n., pl.* **onuses.** a responsibility, task, or burden.

onward ('ɒnwəd) *adj.* **1.** directed or moving forwards, onwards, etc. ~*adv.* **2.** Also: **onwards.** ahead; forward.

-onym *n. combining form.* indicating a name or word: *pseudonym.*

onyx ('ɒnɪks) *n.* **1.** a variety of chalcedony with alter-

---

THESAURUS

one-horse backwoods, inferior, minor, obscure, petty, quiet, sleepy, slow, small, small-time (*Inf.*), tinpot (*Brit. inf.*), unimportant

onerous backbreaking, burdensome, crushing, demanding, difficult, exacting, exhausting, exigent, formidable, grave, hard, heavy, laborious, oppressive, responsible, taxing, weighty

one-sided biased, coloured, discriminatory, inequitable, lopsided, partial, partisan, prejudiced, unequal, unfair, unjust

one-time erstwhile, ex-, former, late, previous, quondam, sometime

onlooker bystander, eyewitness, looker-on, observer, spectator, viewer, watcher, witness

only 1. *adv.* at most, barely, exclusively, just, merely, purely, simply **2.** *adj.* exclusive, individual, lone, one and only, single, sole, solitary, unique

onomatopoeic echoic, imitative, onomatopoetic

onset 1. assault, attack, charge, onrush, onslaught **2.** beginning, inception, kick-off (*Inf.*), outbreak, start

onslaught assault, attack, blitz, charge, offensive, onrush, onset

onus burden, liability, load, obligation, responsibility, task

nating black and white parallel bands, used as a gemstone. **2.** a variety of calcite used as an ornamental stone; onyx marble.

oodles ('uːdəlz) *pl. n. Inf.* great quantities: *oodles of money.*

oolite ('əʊəˌlaɪt) *n.* any sedimentary rock, esp. limestone, consisting of tiny spherical concentric grains within a fine matrix. —**oolitic** (ˌəʊə'lɪtɪk) *adj.*

oomiak *or* **oomiac** ('uːmɪˌæk) *n.* other words for **umiak.**

oompah ('uːmˌpɑː) *n.* a representation of the sound made by a deep brass instrument, esp. in military band music.

oomph (ʊmf) *n. Inf.* **1.** enthusiasm, vigour, or energy. **2.** sex appeal.

oops (ʊps, uːps) *interj.* an exclamation of surprise or of apology as when someone drops something or makes a mistake.

ooze[1] (uːz) *vb.* **1.** (*intr.*) to flow or leak out slowly, as through pores or small holes. **2.** to exude or emit (moisture, etc.). **3.** (*tr.*) to overflow with: *to ooze charm.* **4.** (*intr.; often foll. by *away*) to disappear or escape gradually. ~*n.* **5.** a slow flowing or leaking. **6.** an infusion of vegetable matter, such as oak bark, used in tanning.

ooze[2] (uːz) *n.* **1.** a soft thin mud found at the bottom of lakes and rivers. **2.** a fine-grained marine deposit consisting of the hard parts of planktonic organisms. **3.** muddy ground, esp. of bogs. —**'oozy** *adj.*

op. *abbrev. for:* **1.** opera. **2.** operation. **3.** opposite. **4.** opus. **5.** operator. **6.** optical.

o.p. *or* **O.P.** *abbrev. for* out of print.

O.P. *abbrev. for* Ordo Praedictatorum (the Dominicans).

opacity (əʊ'pæsɪtɪ) *n., pl.* **-ties.** **1.** the state or quality of being opaque. **2.** the degree to which something is opaque. **3.** an opaque object or substance. **4.** obscurity of meaning; unintelligibility.

opal ('əʊpəl) *n.* an amorphous form of hydrated silicon dioxide that is colourless or of variable colour and transparent or translucent. Some varieties are used as gemstones. —**'opal-,like** *adj.*

opalescent (ˌəʊpə'lɛsənt) *adj.* having or emitting an iridescence like that of an opal. —ˌ**opal'escence** *n.* —ˌ**opa-'lesce** *vb.* (*intr.*).

opaline ('əʊpəˌlaɪn) *adj.* **1.** opalescent. ~*n.* **2.** an opaque or semiopaque whitish glass.

opaque (əʊ'peɪk) *adj.* **1.** not transmitting light; not transparent or translucent. **2.** not reflecting light; lacking lustre or shine; dull. **3.** hard to understand; unintelligible. **4.** unintelligent; dense. ~*n.* **5.** *Photog.* an opaque pigment used to block out areas on a negative. ~*vb.* **opaquing, opaqued.** (*tr.*) **6.** to make opaque. **7.** *Photog.* to block out areas using an opaque. —o'**paque-ly** *adv.* —o'**paqueness** *n.*

op. cit. (in textual annotations) *abbrev. for* opere citato.

OPEC ('əʊpɛk) *n. acronym for* Organization of Petroleum-Exporting Countries.

open ('əʊpən) *adj.* **1.** not closed or barred. **2.** affording free passage, access, view, etc.; not blocked or obstructed. **3.** not sealed, fastened, or wrapped. **4.** having the interior part accessible: *an open drawer.* **5.** extended, expanded, or unfolded: *an open flower.* **6.** ready for business. **7.** able to be obtained; available: *the position is no longer open.* **8.** unobstructed by buildings, trees, etc.: *open countryside.* **9.** free to all to join, enter, use, visit, etc.: *an open competition.* **10.** unengaged or unoccupied: *the doctor has an hour open for you to call.* **11.** (of a season or period) not restricted for purposes of hunting game or quarry of various kinds. **12.** not decided or finalized: *an open question.* **13.** ready to entertain new ideas; not biased or prejudiced. **14.** unreserved or candid. **15.** liberal or generous: *an open hand.* **16.** extended or eager to receive (esp. in **with open arms**). **17.** exposed to view; blatant: *open disregard of the law.* **18.** liable or susceptible: *you will leave yourself open to attack.* **19.** (of climate or seasons) free from frost; mild. **20.** free from navigational hazards, such as ice, sunken ships, etc. **21.** without barriers to prevent absconding: *an open prison.* **22.** having large or numerous spacing or apertures: *open ranks.* **23.** full of small openings or gaps; porous: *an open texture.* **24.** *Music.* **a.** (of a string) not stopped with the finger. **b.** (of a pipe, such as an organ pipe) not closed at either end. **c.** (of a note) played on such a string or pipe. **25.** *Commerce.* in operation; active: *an open account.* **26.** (of a cheque) not crossed. **27.** (of a return ticket) not specifying a date for travel. **28.** *Sport.* (of a goal, court, etc.) unguarded or relatively unprotected. **29.** (of a wound) exposed to the air. **30.** (esp. of the large intestine) free from obstruction. **31.** undefended and of no military significance: *an open city.* **32.** *Phonetics.* **a.** denoting a vowel pronounced with the lips relatively wide apart. **b.** denoting a syllable that does not end in a consonant, as in *pa.* **33.** *Maths.* (of a set) containing points whose neighbourhood consists of other points of the same set. ~*vb.* **34.** to move from a closed or fastened position: *to open a window.* **35.** (when *intr.*, foll by *on* or *onto*) to render accessible or unobstructed: *to open a road; to open a parcel.* **36.** (*intr.*) to come into or appear in view: *the lake opened before us.* **37.** to extend or unfold: *to open a newspaper.* **38.** to disclose or uncover or be disclosed or uncovered: *to open one's heart.* **39.** to cause (the mind) to become receptive or (of the mind) to become receptive. **40.** to operate: *to open a shop.* **41.** (when *intr.*, sometimes foll. by *out*) to make or become less compact or dense in structure: *to open ranks.* **42.** to set or be set in action; start: *to open the batting.* **43.** (*tr.*) to arrange for (a bank account, etc.), usually by making an initial deposit. **44.** to turn to a specified point in (a book, etc.): *open at page one.* **45.** *Law.* to make the opening statement in (a case before a court of law). **46.** (*intr.*) *Cards.* to bet, bid, or lead first on a hand. ~*n.* **47.** (often prec. by *the*) any wide or unobstructed space or expanse, esp. of land or water. **48.** See **open air. 49.** *Sport.* a competition which all may enter. **50. bring** (or **come**) **into the open.** to make (or become) evident or public. —'**openable** *adj.* —'**openly** *adv.* —'**openness** *n.* —'**opener** *n.*

open air *n.* **a.** the place or space where the air is unenclosed; the outdoors. **b.** (*as modifier*): *an open-air concert.*

open-and-shut *adj.* easily decided or solved; obvious: *an open-and-shut case.*

opencast mining ('əʊpənˌkɑːst) *n. Brit.* mining by excavating from the surface. Also called (*esp. U.S.*): **strip mining** or *Austral. & N.Z.* **open cut mining.**

open-ended *adj.* without definite limits, as of duration or amount: *an open-ended contract.*

THESAURUS

ooze **1.** *v.* bleed, discharge, drain, dribble, drip, drop, emit, escape, exude, filter, leach, leak, overflow with, percolate, seep, strain, sweat, weep **2.** *n.* alluvium, mire, muck, mud, silt, slime, sludge

opaque **1.** clouded, cloudy, dim, dull, filmy, hazy, impenetrable, lustreless, muddied, muddy, murky, obfuscated, turbid **2.** abstruse, baffling, cryptic, difficult, enigmatic, incomprehensible, obscure, unclear, unfathomable, unintelligible

open *adj.* **1.** agape, ajar, expanded, extended, gaping, revealed, spread out, unbarred, unclosed, uncovered, unfastened, unfolded, unfurled, unlocked, unobstructed, unsealed, yawning **2.** airy, bare, clear, exposed, extensive, free, navigable, not built-up, passable, rolling, spacious, sweeping, uncluttered, uncrowded, unenclosed, unfenced, unsheltered, wide, wide-open **3.** accessible, available, free, general, nondiscriminatory, public, unconditional, unengaged, unoccupied, unqualified, unrestricted, vacant **4.** apparent, avowed, barefaced, blatant, clear, conspicuous, downright, evident, flagrant, frank, manifest, noticeable, obvious, overt, plain, unconcealed, undisguised, visible **5.** arguable, debatable, moot, undecided, unresolved, unsettled, up in the air, yet to be decided **6.** disinterested, free, impartial, objective, receptive, unbiased, uncommitted, unprejudiced **7.** *With* **to** an easy target for, at the mercy of, defenceless against, disposed, exposed, liable, susceptible, vulnerable **8.** artless, candid, fair, frank, guileless, honest, ingenuous, innocent, natural, sincere, transparent, unreserved **9.** filigree, fretted, holey, honeycombed, lacy, loose, openwork, porous, spongy **10.** bounteous, bountiful, generous, liberal, munificent **11.** exposed, undefended, unfortified, unprotected ~*v.* **12.** begin, begin business, commence, get *or* start the ball rolling, inaugurate, initiate, kick off (*Inf.*), launch, put up one's plate, set in motion, set up shop, start **13.** clear, crack, throw wide, unbar, unblock, unclose, uncork, uncover, undo, unfasten, unlock, unseal, untie, unwrap **14.** expand, spread (out), unfold, unfurl, unroll **15.** come apart, crack, rupture, separate, split **16.** disclose, divulge, exhibit, explain, lay bare, pour out, show, uncover

open-air alfresco, outdoor

open-handed bountiful, free, generous, lavish, liberal, munificent, unstinting

open-eyed *adj.* **1.** with the eyes wide open, as in amazement. **2.** watchful; alert.

open-handed *adj.* generous. —**,open-'handedly** *adv.*

open-hearted *adj.* **1.** kindly and warm. **2.** disclosing intentions and thoughts clearly; candid. —**,open-'heartedness** *n.*

open-heart surgery *n.* surgical repair of the heart during which the blood circulation is often maintained mechanically.

opening ('ɔʊpənɪŋ) *n.* **1.** the act of making or becoming open. **2.** a vacant or unobstructed space, esp. one that will serve as a passageway; gap. **3.** *Chiefly U.S.* a tract in a forest in which trees are scattered or absent. **4.** the first part or stage of something. **5. a.** the first performance of something, esp. a theatrical production. **b.** (*as modifier*): *the opening night.* **6.** a specific or formal sequence of moves at the start of any of certain games, esp. chess or draughts. **7.** an opportunity or chance. **8.** *Law.* the preliminary statement made by counsel to the court or jury.

opening time *n. Brit.* the time at which pubs can legally start selling alcoholic drinks.

open letter *n.* a letter, esp. one of protest, addressed to a person but also made public, as through the press.

open-minded *adj.* having a mind receptive to new ideas, arguments, etc.; unprejudiced. —**,open-'minded-ness** *n.*

open-mouthed *adj.* **1.** having an open mouth, esp. in surprise. **2.** greedy or ravenous. **3.** clamorous or vociferous.

open-plan *adj.* having no or few dividing walls between areas: *an open-plan office floor.*

open secret *n.* something that is supposed to be secret but is widely known.

open sesame *n.* a very successful means of achieving a result.

Open University *n. Brit.* **the.** a university founded in 1969 for mature students studying by television and radio lectures, correspondence courses, local counselling, and summer schools.

open verdict *n.* a finding by a coroner's jury of death without stating the cause.

opera[1] ('ɒpərə, 'ɒprə) *n.* **1.** an extended dramatic work in which music constitutes a dominating feature. **2.** the branch of music or drama represented by such works. **3.** the score, libretto, etc., of an opera. **4.** a theatre where opera is performed.

opera[2] ('ɒpərə) *n.* a plural of **opus.**

operable ('ɒpərəbəl, 'ɒprə-) *adj.* **1.** capable of being treated by a surgical operation. **2.** capable of being operated. **3.** capable of being put into practice. —**,opera'bility** *n.* —**'operably** *adv.*

opera glasses *pl. n.* small low-powered binoculars used by audiences in theatres, etc.

opera hat *n.* a collapsible top hat operated by a spring.

operate ('ɒpə,reɪt) *vb.* **1.** to function or cause to function. **2.** (*tr.*) to control the functioning of. **3.** to manage, direct, run, or pursue (a business, system, etc.). **4.** to perform a surgical operation upon (a person or animal). **5.** (*intr.*) to produce a desired effect. **6.** (*tr.;* usually foll. by *on*) to treat or process in a particular or specific way. **7.** (*intr.*) to conduct military or naval operations. **8.** (*intr.*) to deal in securities on a stock exchange.

operatic (,ɒpə'rætɪk) *adj.* **1.** of or relating to opera. **2.** histrionic or exaggerated. —**,oper'atically** *adv.*

operating theatre *n.* a room in which surgical operations are performed.

operation (,ɒpə'reɪʃən) *n.* **1.** the act, process, or manner of operating. **2.** the state of being in effect, in action, or operative (esp. in **in** or **into operation**). **3.** a process, method, or series of acts, esp. of a practical or mechanical nature. **4.** *Surgery.* any manipulation of the body or one of its organs or parts to repair damage, arrest the progress of a disease, remove foreign matter, etc. **5. a.** a military or naval action, such as a campaign, manoeuvre, etc. **b.** (*cap. and prenominal when part of a name*): *Operation Crossbow.* **6.** *Maths.* any procedure, such as addition, in which one or more numbers or quantities are operated upon according to specific rules. **7.** a commercial or financial transaction.

operational (,ɒpə'reɪʃənəl) *adj.* **1.** of or relating to an operation. **2.** in working order and ready for use. **3.** *Mil.* capable of, needed in, or actually involved in operations. —**,oper'ationally** *adv.*

operations research *n.* the analysis of problems in business and industry involving quantitative techniques. Also: **operational research.**

operative ('ɒpərətɪv) *adj.* **1.** in force, effect, or operation. **2.** exerting force or influence. **3.** producing a desired effect; significant: *the operative word.* **4.** of or relating to a surgical procedure. ~*n.* **5.** a worker, esp. one with a special skill. **6.** *U.S.* a private detective. —**'operatively** *adv.* —**'operativeness** *or* **,opera'tivity** *n.*

operator ('ɒpə,reɪtə) *n.* **1.** a person who operates a machine, instrument, etc., esp. a telephone switchboard. **2.** a person who owns or operates an industrial or commercial establishment. **3.** a speculator, esp. one who operates on currency or stock markets. **4.** *Inf.* a person who manipulates affairs and other people. **5.** *Maths.* any symbol, term, letter, etc., used to indicate or express a specific operation or process, such as ∫ (the integral operator).

operculum (əʊ'pɜːkjʊləm) *n., pl.* **-la** (-lə) *or* **-lums. 1.** *Zool.* **a.** the hard bony flap covering the gill slits in fishes. **b.** the bony plate in certain gastropods covering the opening of the shell when the body is withdrawn. **2.** *Biol. & Bot.* any other covering or lid in various organisms. —**o'percular** *or* **operculate** (əʊ'pɜːkjʊlɪt, -,leɪt) *adj.*

operetta (,ɒpə'rɛtə) *n.* a type of comic or lighthearted opera. —**,oper'ettist** *n.*

ophthalmia (ɒf'θælmɪə) *n.* inflammation of the eye, often including the conjunctiva.

ophthalmic (ɒf'θælmɪk) *adj.* of or relating to the eye.

ophthalmic optician *n.* See **optician.**

ophthalmo- *or before a vowel* **ophthalm-** *combining form.* indicating the eye or the eyeball.

ophthalmology (,ɒfθæl'mɒlədʒɪ) *n.* the branch of medicine concerned with the eye and its diseases. —**,ophthal'mologist** *n.* —**ophthalmological** (ɒf,θælmə-'lɒdʒɪkəl) *adj.*

ophthalmoscope (ɒf'θælmə,skəʊp) *n.* an instrument for examining the interior of the eye. —**ophthalmoscopic** (ɒf,θælmə'skɒpɪk) *adj.*

-opia *n. combining form.* indicating a visual defect or condition: *myopia.* —**-opic** *adj. combining form.*

opiate *n.* ('əʊpɪɪt). **1.** any of various narcotic drugs containing opium. **2.** any other narcotic or sedative

---

THESAURUS

opening *n.* **1.** aperture, breach, break, chink, cleft, crack, fissure, gap, hole, interstice, orifice, perforation, rent, rupture, slot, space, split, vent **2.** break (*Inf.*), chance, look-in (*Inf.*), occasion, opportunity, place, vacancy **3.** beginning, birth, commencement, dawn, inauguration, inception, initiation, kickoff (*Inf.*), launch, launching, onset, outset, start ~*adj.* **4.** beginning, commencing, early, first, inaugural, initial, initiatory, introductory, maiden, primary

openly 1. candidly, face to face, forthrightly, frankly, plainly, straight from the shoulder (*Inf.*), unhesitatingly, unreservedly **2.** blatantly, brazenly, flagrantly, in full view, in public, publicly, shamelessly, unabashedly, unashamedly, wantonly, without pretence

open-minded broad, broad-minded,

catholic, dispassionate, enlightened, free, impartial, liberal, reasonable, receptive, tolerant, unbiased, undogmatic, unprejudiced

operate 1. act, be in action, function, go, perform, run, work **2.** be in charge of, handle, manage, manoeuvre, use, work **3.** perform surgery

operation 1. action, affair, course, exercise, motion, movement, performance, procedure, process, use, working **2. in operation** effective, functioning, going, in action, in force, operative **3.** activity, agency, effect, effort, force, influence, instrumentality, manipulation **4.** affair, business, deal, enterprise, proceeding, transaction, undertaking **5.** assault, campaign, exercise, manoeuvre **6.** surgery

operational functional, going, in work-

ing order, operative, prepared, ready, usable, viable, workable, working

operative *adj.* **1.** active, current, effective, efficient, functional, functioning, in force, in operation, operational, serviceable, standing, workable **2.** crucial, important, indicative, influential, key, relevant, significant ~*n.* **3.** artisan, employee, hand, labourer, machinist, mechanic, worker

operator 1. conductor, driver, handler, mechanic, operative, practitioner, skilled employee, technician, worker **2.** administrator, contractor, dealer, director, manager, speculator, trader **3.** *Inf.* Machiavellian, machinator, manipulator, mover, punter, shyster (*Sl., chiefly U.S.*), smart aleck (*Inf.*), wheeler-dealer (*Inf.*), wirepuller, worker

drug. **3.** something that soothes, deadens, or induces sleep. ~*adj.* ('əʊpiit). **4.** containing or consisting of opium. **5.** inducing relaxation; soporific. ~*vb.* ('əʊpi‚eit). (*tr.*) *Rare.* **6.** to treat with an opiate. **7.** to dull or deaden.

opine (əʊ'pain) *vb.* (when *tr.*, *usually takes a clause as object*) to hold or express an opinion: *he opined that it was a mistake.*

opinion (ə'pinjən) *n.* **1.** judgment or belief not founded on certainty or proof. **2.** the prevailing or popular feeling or view: *public opinion.* **3.** evaluation, impression, or estimation of the value or worth of a person or thing. **4.** an evaluation or judgment given by an expert: *a medical opinion.* **5.** the advice given by counsel on a case submitted to him for his view on the legal points involved. **6. a matter of opinion.** a point open to question. **7. be of the opinion (that).** to believe (that).

opinionated (ə'pinjə‚neitid) *adj.* holding obstinately and unreasonably to one's own opinions; dogmatic. —o'pinion‚atedly *adv.* —o'pinion‚atedness *n.*

opinionative (ə'pinjə‚neitiv) *adj. Rare.* **1.** of or relating to opinion. **2.** another word for **opinionated.** —o'pinion‚atively *adv.* —o'pinion‚ativeness *n.*

opinion poll *n.* another term for a **poll** (sense 3).

opium ('əʊpiəm) *n.* **1.** an addictive narcotic drug extracted from the seed capsules of the opium poppy: used in medicine as an analgesic and hypnotic. **2.** something having a tranquillizing or stupefying effect.

opossum (ə'pɒsəm) *or* **possum** *n., pl.* **-sums** *or* **-sum.** **1.** a thick-furred marsupial, esp. the **common opossum** of North and South America, having an elongated snout and a hairless prehensile tail. **2.** *Austral. & N.Z.* any of various similar animals, esp. a phalanger: Usually shortened to **possum.**

opp. *abbrev. for:* **1.** opposed. **2.** opposite.

opponent (ə'pəʊnənt) *n.* **1.** a person who opposes another in a contest, battle, etc. **2.** *Anat.* an opponent muscle. ~*adj.* **3.** opposite, as in position. **4.** *Anat.* (of a muscle) bringing two parts into opposition. **5.** opposing; contrary. —op'ponency *n.*

opportune ('ɒpə‚tjuːn) *adj.* **1.** occurring at a time that is suitable or advantageous. **2.** fit or suitable for a particular purpose or occurrence. —'oppor‚tunely *adv.* —'oppor‚tuneness *n.*

opportunist (‚ɒpə'tjuːnist) *n.* **1.** a person who adapts his actions, responses, etc., to take advantage of opportunities, circumstances, etc. ~*adj.* **2.** taking advantage of opportunities and circumstances in this way. —‚oppor'tunism *n.* —‚opportun'istic *adj.*

opportunity (‚ɒpə'tjuːniti) *n., pl.* **-ties.** **1.** a favourable, appropriate, or advantageous combination of circumstances. **2.** a chance or prospect.

opposable (ə'pəʊzəbəl) *adj.* **1.** capable of being op-

posed. **2.** Also: **apposable.** (of the thumb of primates, esp. man) capable of being moved into a position facing the other digits so as to be able to touch the ends of each. **3.** capable of being placed opposite something else. —op'posably *adv.* —op‚posa'bility *n.*

oppose (ə'pəʊz) *vb.* **1.** (*tr.*) to fight against, counter, or resist strongly. **2.** (*tr.*) to be hostile or antagonistic to; be against. **3.** (*tr.*) to place or set in opposition; contrast or counterbalance. **4.** (*tr.*) to place opposite or facing. **5.** (*intr.*) to be or act in opposition. —op'poser *n.* —op'posingly *adv.* —oppositive (ə'pɒzitiv) *adj.*

opposite ('ɒpəzit, -sit) *adj.* **1.** situated or being on the other side or at each side of something between. **2.** facing or going in contrary directions: *opposite ways.* **3.** diametrically different in character, tendency, belief, etc. **4.** *Bot.* **a.** (of leaves) arranged in pairs on either side of the stem. **b.** (of parts of a flower) arranged opposite the middle of another part. **5.** *Maths.* (of a side in a triangle) facing a specified angle. Abbrev.: **opp.** ~*n.* **6.** a person or thing that is opposite; antithesis. ~*prep.* **7.** Also: **opposite to.** facing; corresponding to (something on the other side of a division). **8.** as a co-star with: *she played opposite Olivier.* ~*adv.* **9.** on opposite sides: *she lives opposite.* —'oppositely *adv.* —'oppositeness *n.*

opposite number *n.* a person holding an equivalent and corresponding position on another side or situation.

opposition (‚ɒpə'zɪʃən) *n.* **1.** the act of opposing or the state of being opposed. **2.** hostility, unfriendliness, or antagonism. **3.** a person or group antagonistic or opposite in aims to another. **4. a.** (usually preceded by *the*) a political party or group opposed to the ruling party or government. **b.** (*cap. as part of a name, esp. in Britain and Commonwealth countries*): *Her Majesty's Loyal Opposition.* **c. in opposition.** (of a political party) opposing the government. **5.** a position facing or opposite another. **6.** something that acts as an obstacle to some course or progress. **7.** *Astron.* the position of an outer planet or the moon when it is in line with the earth as seen from the sun and is approximately at its nearest to the earth. **8.** *Astrol.* an exact aspect of 180° between two planets, etc., an orb of 8° being allowed. **9.** *Logic.* the relation between propositions having the same subject and predicate but differing in quality, quantity, or both, as with *all men are wicked; no men are wicked; some men are not wicked.* —‚oppo'sitional *adj.* —‚oppo'sitionist *n.* —‚oppo'sitionless *adj.*

oppress (ə'prɛs) *vb.* (*tr.*) **1.** to subjugate by cruelty, force, etc. **2.** to afflict or torment. **3.** to lie heavy on (the mind, etc.). —op'pressingly *adv.* —op'pression *n.* —op'pressor *n.*

oppressive (ə'prɛsiv) *adj.* **1.** cruel, harsh, or tyrannical. **2.** heavy, constricting, or depressing. —op'pressively *adv.* —op'pressiveness *n.*

THESAURUS

opinion 1. assessment, belief, conception, conjecture, estimation, feeling, idea, impression, judgment, mind, notion, persuasion, point of view, sentiment, theory, view **2. be of the opinion** be convinced, believe, be under the impression, conclude, consider, hold, judge, reckon, suppose, surmise, think **3. matter of opinion** debatable point, matter of judgment, moot point, open question, open to debate, up to the individual

opinionated adamant, biased, bigoted, bull-headed, cocksure, dictatorial, doctrinaire, dogmatic, inflexible, obdurate, obstinate, overbearing, pig-headed, prejudiced, self-assertive, single-minded, stubborn, uncompromising

opponent adversary, antagonist, challenger, competitor, contestant, disputant, dissentient, enemy, foe, opposer, rival, the opposition

opportune advantageous, appropriate, apt, auspicious, convenient, favourable, felicitous, fit, fitting, fortunate, happy, lucky, proper, propitious, seasonable, suitable, timely, well-timed

opportunism expediency, exploitation, Machiavellianism, making hay while the sun shines (*Inf.*), pragmatism, realism, *Realpolitik*, striking while the iron is hot (*Inf.*), trimming, unscrupulousness

opportunity break (*Inf.*), chance, convenience, hour, look-in (*Inf.*), moment, occasion, opening, scope, time

oppose 1. bar, check, combat, confront, contradict, counter, counterattack, defy, face, fight, fly in the face of, hinder, obstruct, prevent, resist, speak against, stand up to, take a stand against, take issue with, take on, thwart, withstand **2.** compare, contrast, counterbalance, match, pit *or* set against, play off

opposed against, antagonistic, anti (*Inf.*), antipathetic, antithetical, at daggers drawn, clashing, conflicting, contrary, dissentient, hostile, incompatible, inimical, in opposition, opposing, opposite

opposing antagonistic, antipathetic, clashing, combatant, conflicting, contrary, enemy, hostile, incompatible, irreconcilable, opposed, opposite, rival, warring

opposite *adj.* **1.** corresponding, facing, fronting **2.** adverse, antagonistic, antithetical, conflicting, contradictory, contrary, contrasted, diametrically opposed, different, differing, diverse, hostile, inconsistent, inimical, irreconcilable, opposed, reverse, unlike ~*n.* **3.** antithesis, contradiction, contrary, converse, inverse, reverse, the other extreme, the other side of the coin (*Inf.*)

opposition 1. antagonism, competition,

contrariety, counteraction, disapproval, hostility, obstruction, obstructiveness, prevention, resistance, unfriendliness **2.** antagonist, competition, foe, opponent, other side, rival

oppress 1. afflict, burden, depress, dispirit, harass, lie *or* weigh heavy upon, sadden, take the heart out of, torment, vex **2.** abuse, crush, harry, maltreat, overpower, overwhelm, persecute, rule with an iron hand, subdue, subjugate, suppress, trample underfoot, tyrannize over, wrong

oppressed abused, browbeaten, burdened, disadvantaged, downtrodden, enslaved, harassed, henpecked, maltreated, misused, prostrate, slave, subject, troubled, tyrannized, underprivileged

oppression abuse, brutality, calamity, cruelty, hardship, harshness, injury, injustice, iron hand, maltreatment, misery, persecution, severity, subjection, suffering, tyranny

oppressive 1. brutal, burdensome, cruel, despotic, grinding, harsh, heavy, inhuman, onerous, overbearing, overwhelming, repressive, severe, tyrannical, unjust **2.** airless, close, heavy, muggy, overpowering, stifling, stuffy, suffocating, sultry, torrid

oppressor autocrat, bully, despot, harrier, intimidator, iron hand, persecutor,

opprobrious (ə'prəʊbrɪəs) *adj.* **1.** expressing scorn, disgrace, or contempt. **2.** shameful or infamous. —**op'probriously** *adv.* —**op'probriousness** *n.*

opprobrium (ə'prəʊbrɪəm) *n.* **1.** the state of being abused or scornfully criticized. **2.** reproach or censure. **3.** a cause of disgrace or ignominy.

oppugn (ə'pjuːn) *vb.* (*tr.*) to call into question; dispute. —**op'pugner** *n.*

opt (ɒpt) *vb.* (when *intr.*, foll. by *for*) to show preference (for) or choose (to do something). ~See also **opt out.**

opt. *abbrev. for:* **1.** *Grammar.* optative. **2.** optical. **3.** optician. **4.** optimum. **5.** optional.

optative ('ɒptətɪv) *adj.* **1.** indicating or expressing choice or wish. **2.** *Grammar.* denoting a mood of verbs in Greek and Sanskrit expressing a wish. ~*n.* **3.** *Grammar.* **a.** the optative mood. **b.** a verb in this mood.

optic ('ɒptɪk) *adj.* **1.** of or relating to the eye or vision. **2.** a less common word for **optical.** ~*n.* **3.** an informal word for **eye.** **4.** *Brit., trademark.* a device attached to an inverted bottle for dispensing measured quantities of liquid.

optical ('ɒptɪkəl) *adj.* **1.** of, relating to, producing, or involving light. **2.** of or relating to the eye or to the sense of sight; optic. **3.** (esp. of a lens) aiding vision or correcting a visual disorder. —**'optically** *adv.*

optical character reader *n.* a computer peripheral device enabling letters, numbers, or other characters usually printed on paper to be optically scanned and input to a storage device, such as magnetic tape. The device uses the process of **optical character recognition.** Abbrev. (for both *reader* and *recognition*): **OCR.**

optician (ɒp'tɪʃən) *n.* a general name used to refer to: **a.** an **ophthalmic optician.** one qualified to examine the eyes and prescribe and supply spectacles and contact lenses. **b. a dispensing optician.** one who supplies and fits spectacle frames and lenses, but is not qualified to examine the eyes.

optics ('ɒptɪks) *n.* (*functioning as sing.*) the branch of science concerned with vision and the generation, nature, propagation, and behaviour of electromagnetic light.

optimism ('ɒptɪˌmɪzəm) *n.* **1.** the tendency to expect the best in all things. **2.** hopefulness; confidence. **3.** the doctrine of the ultimate triumph of good over evil. **4.** the philosophical doctrine that this is the best of all possible worlds. ~Cf. **pessimism.** —**'optimist** *n.* —ˌopti'mistic *or* ˌopti'mistical *adj.* —ˌopti'mistically *adv.*

optimum ('ɒptɪməm) *n., pl.* -**ma** (-mə) *or* -**mums.** **1.** a condition, degree, amount, or compromise that produces the best possible result. ~*adj.* **2.** most favourable or advantageous; best: *optimum conditions.*

option ('ɒpʃən) *n.* **1.** the act or an instance of choosing or deciding. **2.** the power or liberty to choose. **3.** the right, obtained by a fee, to purchase or sell property, esp. shares or commodities, at a specified time in the future at a fixed price. **4.** see **local option.** **5.** something chosen; choice. **6. keep** (*or* **leave**) **one's options open.** not to commit oneself. **7. soft option.** an easy alternative.

optional ('ɒpʃənəl) *adj.* possible but not compulsory; left to personal choice. —**'optionally** *adv.*

opt out *vb.* (*intr., adv.; often foll. by of*) to choose not to be involved (in) or part (of).

opulent ('ɒpjʊlənt) *adj.* **1.** having or indicating wealth. **2.** abundant or plentiful. —**'opulence** *or* **'opulency** *n.* —**'opulently** *adv.*

opus ('əʊpəs) *n., pl.* **opuses** *or* **opera** ('ɒpərə). **1.** an artistic composition, esp. a musical work. **2.** (*often cap.*) (usually followed by a number) a musical composition by a particular composer, generally catalogued in order of publication: *Beethoven's opus 61.* Abbrev.: **op.**

or[1] (ɔː; *unstressed* ə) *conj.* (*coordinating*) **1.** used to join alternatives. **2.** used to join rephrasings of the same thing: *twelve, or a dozen.* **3.** used to join two alternatives when the first is preceded by *either* or *whether*: *either yes or no.* **4. one or two, four or five,** *etc.* a few. **5. or else.** otherwise; if not. **6.** a poetic word for **either** or **whether,** as the first element in correlatives, with *or* also preceding the second alternative.

▷ **Usage.** See at **either** and **neither.**

or[2] (ɔː) *adj.* (*usually postpositive*) *Heraldry.* of the metal gold.

-or[1] *suffix forming nouns from verbs.* a person or thing that does what is expressed by the verb: *actor; conductor; generator; sailor.*

-or[2] *suffix forming nouns.* **1.** indicating state, condition, or activity: *terror; error.* **2.** the U.S. spelling of **-our.**

O.R. *abbrev. for:* **1.** Official Receiver. **2.** operational research.

oracle ('ɒrəkəl) *n.* **1.** a prophecy revealed through the medium of a priest or priestess at the shrine of a god. **2.** a shrine at which an oracular god is consulted. **3.** an agency through which a prophecy is transmitted. **4.** any person or thing believed to indicate future action with infallible authority.

Oracle ('ɒrəkəl) *n. Trademark.* (in Britain) the ITV teletext service.

oracular (ɒ'rækjʊlə) *adj.* **1.** of or relating to an oracle. **2.** wise and prophetic. **3.** mysterious or ambiguous. —**o'racularly** *adv.*

oral ('ɔːrəl, 'ɒrəl) *adj.* **1.** spoken or verbal. **2.** relating to, affecting, or for use in the mouth: *an oral thermometer.* **3.** denoting a drug to be taken by mouth: *an oral contraceptive.* **4.** of, relating to, or using spoken words. **5.** *Psychoanal.* relating to a stage of psychosexual development during which the child's interest is concentrated on the mouth. ~*n.* **6.** an examination in which the questions and answers are spoken rather than written. —**'orally** *adv.*

orange ('ɒrɪndʒ) *n.* **1.** any of several citrus trees, esp. **sweet orange** and the Seville orange, cultivated in warm regions for their round edible fruit. **2. a.** the fruit of any of these trees, having a yellowish-red bitter rind and segmented juicy flesh. **b.** (*as modifier*): *orange peel.* **3.** the hard wood of any of these trees. **4.** any of a group of colours, such as that of the skin of an orange, that lie between red and yellow in the visible spectrum. **5.** a dye or pigment producing these colours. **6.** orange cloth or clothing: *dressed in orange.* **7.** any of several trees or herbaceous plants that resemble the orange, such as mock orange. ~*adj.* **8.** of the colour orange.

orangeade (ˌɒrɪndʒ'eɪd) *n.* an effervescent orange-flavoured drink.

orange blossom *n.* the flowers of the orange tree, traditionally worn by brides.

Orangeman ('ɒrɪndʒmən) *n., pl.* -**men.** a member of a society founded as a secret order in Ireland (1795) to uphold Protestantism.

orangery ('ɒrɪndʒərɪ, -dʒrɪ) *n., pl.* -**eries.** a building, such as a greenhouse, in which orange trees are grown.

orange stick *n.* a small stick used to clean the fingernails and cuticles.

orangewood ('ɒrɪndʒˌwʊd) *n.* **a.** the hard fine-grained yellowish wood of the orange tree. **b.** (*as modifier*): *an orangewood table.*

orang-utan (ɔːˌræŋuː'tæn, ˌɔːræŋ'uːtæn) *or* **orangoutang** (ɔːˌræŋuː'tæŋ, ˌɔːræŋ'uːtæŋ) *n.* a large anthro-

---

THESAURUS

scourge, slave-driver, taskmaster, tormentor, tyrant

opt (for) choose, decide (on), elect, exercise one's discretion (in favour of), go for (*Inf.*), make a selection, plump for, prefer

optimistic 1. disposed to take a favourable view, idealistic, seen through rose-coloured spectacles, Utopian 2. assured, bright, buoyant, buoyed up, cheerful, confident, encouraged, expectant, hopeful, positive, sanguine

optimum *adj.* A1 (*Inf.*), best, choicest, flawless, highest, ideal, most favourable *or*

advantageous, optimal, peak, perfect, superlative

option alternative, choice, election, preference, selection

optional discretionary, elective, extra, noncompulsory, open, possible, up to the individual, voluntary

opulence 1. affluence, easy circumstances, easy street (*Inf.*), fortune, lavishness, luxuriance, luxury, plenty, prosperity, riches, richness, sumptuousness, wealth 2. abundance, copiousness, cornucopia, fullness, profusion, richness, superabundance

opulent 1. affluent, lavish, luxurious, mon-

eyed, prosperous, rich, sumptuous, wealthy, well-heeled (*Sl.*), well-off, well-to-do 2. abundant, copious, lavish, luxuriant, plentiful, profuse, prolific

opus composition, creation, *oeuvre*, piece, production, work

oracle 1. augur, Cassandra, prophet, seer, sibyl, soothsayer 2. answer, augury, divination, divine utterance, prediction, prognostication, prophecy, revelation, vision 3. adviser, authority, guru, high priest, horse's mouth, mastermind, mentor, pundit, source, wizard

oral spoken, verbal, viva voce, vocal

poid ape of the forests of Sumatra and Borneo, with shaggy reddish-brown hair and strong arms. Sometimes shortened to **orang.**

oration (ɔːˈreɪʃən) *n.* **1.** a formal public declaration or speech. **2.** any rhetorical, lengthy, or pompous speech.

orator (ˈɒrətə) *n.* **1.** a public speaker, esp. one versed in rhetoric. **2.** a person given to lengthy or pompous speeches. **3.** *Obs.* the plaintiff in a cause of action in chancery.

oratorio (ˌɒrəˈtɔːrɪəʊ) *n.*, *pl.* **-rios.** a dramatic but unstaged musical composition for soloists, chorus, and orchestra, based on a religious theme.

oratory¹ (ˈɒrətərɪ, -trɪ) *n.* **1.** the art of public speaking. **2.** rhetorical skill or style. —**ˌoraˈtorical** *adj.*

oratory² (ˈɒrətərɪ, -trɪ) *n.*, *pl.* **-ries.** a small room or secluded place, set apart for private prayer.

orb (ɔːb) *n.* **1.** (in regalia) an ornamental sphere surmounted by a cross. **2.** a sphere; globe. **3.** *Poetic.* another word for **eye. 4.** *Obs. or poetic.* **a.** a celestial body, esp. the earth or sun. **b.** the orbit of a celestial body. ~*vb.* **5.** to make or become circular or spherical. **6.** (*tr.*) an archaic word for **encircle.**

orbicular (ɔːˈbɪkjʊlə), **orbiculate,** *or* **orbiculated** *adj.* **1.** circular or spherical. **2.** (of a leaf or similar flat part) circular or nearly circular. —**orbicularity** (ɔːˌbɪkjʊˈlærɪtɪ) *n.* —**orˈbicularly** *adv.*

orbit (ˈɔːbɪt) *n.* **1.** *Astron.* the curved path followed by a planet, satellite, etc., in its motion around another celestial body. **2.** a range or field of action or influence; sphere. **3.** the bony cavity containing the eyeball; eye socket. **4.** *Zool.* **a.** the skin surrounding the eye of a bird. **b.** the hollow in which lies the eye or eyestalk of an insect. **5.** *Physics.* the path of an electron around the nucleus of an atom. ~*vb.* **6.** to move around (a body) in a curved path. **7.** (*tr.*) to send (a satellite, spacecraft, etc.) into orbit. **8.** (*intr.*) to move in or as if in an orbit. —**ˈorbital** *adj.* —**ˈorbitally** *adv.*

Orcadian (ɔːˈkeɪdɪən) *n.* **1.** a native or inhabitant of the Orkneys. ~*adj.* **2.** of or relating to the Orkneys.

orchard (ˈɔːtʃəd) *n.* **1.** an area of land devoted to the cultivation of fruit trees. **2.** a collection of fruit trees especially cultivated.

orchestra (ˈɔːkɪstrə) *n.* **1.** a large group of musicians, esp. one whose members play a variety of different instruments. **2.** a group of musicians, each playing the same type of instrument. **3.** Also called: **orchestra pit.** the space reserved for musicians in a theatre, immediately in front of or under the stage. **4.** *Chiefly U.S.* the stalls in a theatre. **5.** (in ancient Greek theatre) the semicircular space in front of the stage. —**orchestral** (ɔːˈkɛstrəl) *adj.*

orchestrate (ˈɔːkɪˌstreɪt) *vb.* (*tr.*) **1.** to score or arrange a piece of music for orchestra. **2.** to arrange, organize, or build up for special effect. —**ˌorchesˈtration** *n.* —**ˈorchesˌtrator** *n.*

orchid (ˈɔːkɪd) *n.* a terrestrial or epiphytic plant having flowers of unusual shapes and beautiful colours, usually with one petal larger than the other two. The flowers are specialized for pollination by certain insects.

ordain (ɔːˈdeɪn) *vb.* (*tr.*) **1.** to consecrate (someone) as a priest; confer holy orders upon. **2.** (*may take a clause as object*) to decree, appoint, or predestine irrevocably. **3.** (*may take a clause as object*) to order, establish, or enact with authority. —**orˈdainer** *n.* —**orˈdainment** *n.*

ordeal (ɔːˈdiːl) *n.* **1.** a severe or trying experience. **2.** *History.* a method of trial in which the innocence of an accused person was determined by subjecting him to physical danger, esp. by fire or water.

order (ˈɔːdə) *n.* **1.** a state in which all components or elements are arranged logically, comprehensibly, or naturally. **2.** an arrangement or disposition of things in succession; sequence: *alphabetical order.* **3.** an established or customary method or state, esp. of society. **4.** a peaceful or harmonious condition of society: *order reigned in the streets.* **5.** (*often pl.*) a class, rank, or hierarchy: *the lower orders.* **6.** *Biol.* any of the taxonomic groups into which a class is divided and which contains one or more families. **7.** an instruction that must be obeyed; command. **8. a.** a commission or instruction to produce or supply something in return for payment. **b.** the commodity produced or supplied. **c.** (*as modifier*): *order form.* **9.** a procedure followed by an assembly, meeting, etc. **10.** (*cap. when part of a name*) a body of people united in a particular aim or purpose. **11.** Also called: **religious order.** (*usually cap.*) a group of persons who bind themselves by vows in order to devote themselves to the pursuit of religious aims. **12.** (*often pl.*) another name for **holy orders. 13.** *History.* a society of knights constituted as a fraternity, such as the Knights Templars. **14. a.** a group of people holding a specific honour for service or merit, conferred on them by a sovereign or state. **b.** the insignia of such a group. **15. a.** any of the five major classical styles of architecture classified by the style of columns and entablatures used. **b.** any style of architecture. **16.** *Ecclesiast.* **a.** the sacrament by which bishops, priests, etc., have their offices conferred upon them. **b.** any of the degrees into which the ministry is divided. **c.** the office of an ordained Christian minister. **17.** *Maths.* **a.** the number of times a function must be differentiated to obtain a given derivative. **b.** the order of the highest derivative in a differential equation. **c.** the number of rows or columns in a determinant or square matrix. **d.** the number of members of a finite group. **18.** *Mil.* (often preceded by *the*) the dress, equipment, or formation directed for a particular purpose or undertaking: *battle order.* **19. a tall order.** something difficult, demanding, or exacting. **20. in order. a.** in sequence. **b.** properly arranged. **c.** appropriate or fitting. **21. in order to.** (*prep.*, foll. by an infinitive) so that it is possible to: *to eat in order to live.* **22. in order that.** (*conj.*) with the purpose that; so that. **23. keep order.** to maintain or enforce order. **24. of** *or* **in the order of.** having an approximately specified size or quantity. **25. on order.** having been ordered but not having been delivered. **26. out of order. a.** not in sequence. **b.** not working. **c.** not following the rules or customary procedure. **27. to order. a.** according to a buyer's specifications. **b.** on request or demand. ~*vb.* **28.** (*tr.*) to give a command to (a person or animal to do or be something). **29.** to request (something) to be supplied or made, esp. in return for payment. **30.** (*tr.*) to instruct or command to move, go, etc. (to a specified place): *they ordered her into the house.* **31.** (*tr.*; *may take a clause as object*) to authorize; prescribe: *the doctor ordered a strict diet.* **32.** (*tr.*) to arrange, regulate, or dispose (articles, etc.) in their proper places. **33.** (of fate) to will; ordain. ~*interj.* **34.** an exclamation demanding that orderly behaviour be restored. —**ˈorderer** *n.*

THESAURUS

oration address, declamation, discourse, harangue, homily, lecture, speech, spiel (*Inf.*)

orator Cicero, declaimer, lecturer, public speaker, rhetorician, speaker, spellbinder, spieler (*Inf.*)

oratorical bombastic, Ciceronian, declamatory, eloquent, grandiloquent, highflown, magniloquent, rhetorical, silver-tongued, sonorous

oratory declamation, elocution, eloquence, grandiloquence, public speaking, rhetoric, speechifying, speech-making, spieling (*Inf.*)

orb ball, circle, globe, ring, round, sphere

orbit *n.* **1.** circle, circumgyration, course, cycle, ellipse, path, revolution, rotation, track, trajectory **2.** *Fig.* ambit, compass, course, domain, influence, range, reach,

scope, sphere, sphere of influence, sweep ~*v.* **3.** circle, circumnavigate, encircle, revolve around

orchestrate **1.** arrange, score **2.** arrange, concert, coordinate, integrate, organize, present, put together, set up, stage-manage

ordain **1.** anoint, appoint, call, consecrate, destine, elect, frock, invest, nominate **2.** fate, foreordain, intend, predestine, predetermine **3.** decree, dictate, enact, enjoin, fix, lay down, legislate, order, prescribe, pronounce, rule, set, will

ordeal affliction, agony, anguish, nightmare, suffering, test, torture, trial, tribulation(s), trouble(s)

order *n.* **1.** arrangement, harmony, method, neatness, orderliness, organization, pattern, plan, propriety, regularity, symmetry,

system, tidiness **2.** arrangement, array, categorization, classification, codification, disposal, disposition, grouping, layout, line, line-up, ordering, placement, progression, sequence, series, setup (*Inf.*), structure, succession **3. in order a.** arranged, in sequence, neat, orderly, shipshape, tidy **b.** acceptable, appropriate, called for, correct, fitting, O.K. (*Inf.*), right, suitable **4. out of order a.** broken-down, bust (*Sl.*), gone haywire (*Inf.*), gone phut (*Inf.*), in disrepair, inoperative, kaput (*Inf.*), nonfunctional, not working, on the blink (*Sl.*), out of commission, U/S (*Inf.*), wonky (*Brit. sl*) **b.** improper, indecorous, not cricket (*Inf.*), not done, not on (*Inf.*), out of place, out of turn, uncalled-for, wrong **5.** calm, control, discipline, law, law and order, peace, quiet, tranquillity **6.** caste, class, degree, grade, hierarchy, pecking or-

order in council *n.* (in Britain) a decree of the Cabinet, usually made under the authority of a statute: in theory a decree of the sovereign and Privy Council.

orderly ('ɔːdəlɪ) *adj.* **1.** in order, properly arranged, or tidy. **2.** obeying or appreciating method, system, and arrangement. **3.** *Mil.* of or relating to orders: *an orderly book.* ~*adv.* **4.** according to custom or rule. ~*n., pl.* **-lies.** **5.** *Med.* a male hospital attendant. **6.** *Mil.* a junior rank detailed to carry orders for a more senior officer. —'**orderliness** *n.*

Order of Merit *n. Brit.* an order conferred on civilians and servicemen for eminence in any field.

order paper *n.* a list indicating the order in which business is to be conducted, esp. in Parliament.

ordinal ('ɔːdɪnəl) *adj.* **1.** denoting a certain position in a sequence of numbers. **2.** of, relating to, or characteristic of an order in biological classification. ~*n.* **3.** short for **ordinal number.** **4.** a book containing the forms of services for the ordination of ministers. **5.** *R.C. Church.* a service book.

ordinal number *n.* a number denoting order, quality, or degree in a group, such as *first, second, third.* Sometimes shortened to **ordinal.**

ordinance ('ɔːdɪnəns) *n.* an authoritative regulation, decree, law or practice.

ordinarily ('ɔːdənrɪlɪ, 'ɔːdə,nerɪlɪ) *adv.* in ordinary, normal, or usual practice; usually; normally.

ordinary ('ɔːdənrɪ) *adj.* **1.** of common or established type or occurrence. **2.** familiar, everyday, or unexceptional. **3.** uninteresting or commonplace. **4.** having regular or *ex officio* jurisdiction: *an ordinary judge.* **5.** *Maths.* (of a differential equation) containing two variables only and derivatives of one of the variables with respect to the other. ~*n., pl.* **-naries.** **6.** a common or average situation, amount, or degree (esp. in **out of the ordinary**). **7.** a normal or commonplace person or thing. **8.** *Civil law.* a judge who exercises jurisdiction in his own right. **9.** (*usually cap.*) an ecclesiastic, esp. a bishop, holding an office to which certain jurisdictional powers are attached. **10.** *R.C. Church.* **a.** the parts of the Mass that do not vary from day to day. **b.** a prescribed form of divine service, esp. the Mass. **11.** the U.S. name for **penny-farthing.** **12.** *Heraldry.* any of several conventional figures, such as the bend, and the cross, commonly charged upon shields. **13.** *History.* a clergyman who visited condemned prisoners. **14.** *Brit. obs.* **a.** a meal provided regularly at a fixed price. **b.** the inn, etc., providing such meals. **15. in ordinary.** *Brit.* (used esp. in titles) in regular service or attendance: *physician in ordinary to the sovereign.*

Ordinary level *n. Brit.* See **O level.**

ordinary rating *n.* a rank in the Royal Navy comparable to that of a private in the army.

ordinary seaman *n.* a seaman of the lowest rank, being insufficiently experienced to be an able-bodied seaman.

ordinary shares *pl. n. Brit.* shares representing part of the capital issued by a company and entitling their holders to a variable dividend according to the profitability of the company and to a claim on net assets. U.S. equivalent: **common stock.** Cf. **preference shares.**

ordinate ('ɔːdɪnɪt) *n.* the vertical or *y*-coordinate of a point in a two-dimensional system of Cartesian coordinates. Cf. **abscissa.**

ordination (,ɔːdɪ'neɪʃən) *n.* **1. a.** the act of conferring holy orders. **b.** the reception of holy orders. **2.** the condition of being ordained or regulated. **3.** an arrangement or order.

ordnance ('ɔːdnəns) *n.* **1.** cannon or artillery. **2.** military supplies; munitions. **3. the.** a department of an army or government dealing with military supplies.

ordnance datum *n.* mean sea level calculated from observation taken at Newlyn, Cornwall, and used as the official basis for height calculation on British maps. Abbrev.: **O.D.**

Ordnance Survey *n.* the official map-making body of the British or Irish government.

Ordovician (,ɔːdəʊ'vɪʃən) *adj.* **1.** of, denoting, or formed in the second period of the Palaeozoic era, between the Cambrian and Silurian periods. ~*n.* **2. the.** the Ordovician period or rock system.

ordure ('ɔːdjʊə) *n.* excrement; dung.

ore (ɔː) *n.* any naturally occurring mineral or aggregate of minerals from which economically important constituents, esp. metals, can be extracted.

oregano (,ɒrɪ'gɑːnəʊ) *n.* **1.** a Mediterranean variety of wild marjoram (*Origanum vulgare*), with pungent leaves. **2.** the dried powdered leaves of this plant, used to season food.

organ ('ɔːgən) *n.* **1. a.** Also called: **pipe organ.** a large complex musical keyboard instrument in which sound is produced by means of a number of pipes arranged in sets or stops, supplied with air from a bellows. **b.** (*as modifier*): *organ stop; organ loft.* **2.** any instrument, such as a harmonium, in which sound is produced in this way. **3.** a fully differentiated structural and functional unit, such as a kidney or a root, in an animal or plant. **4.** an agency or medium of communication, esp. a periodical issued by a specialist group or party. **5.** an instrument with which something is done or accomplished. **6.** a euphemistic word for **penis.**

organdie or esp. U.S. **organdy** ('ɔːgəndɪ) *n., pl.* **-dies.** a fine and slightly stiff cotton fabric used for dresses, etc.

organic (ɔː'gænɪk) *adj.* **1.** of, relating to, or derived from living plants and animals. **2.** of or relating to animal or plant constituents or products having a carbon basis. **3.** of or relating to one or more organs of an animal or plant. **4.** of, relating to, or belonging to the class of chemical compounds that are formed from carbon: *an organic compound.* **5.** constitutional in the structure of something; fundamental; integral. **6.** of or characterized by the coordination of integral parts; organized. **7.** of or relating to the essential constitutional laws regulating the government of a state: *organic law.* **8.** of, relating to, or grown with the use of fertilizers or pesticides deriving from animal or vegetable matter. ~*n.* **9.** any substance, such as a fertilizer or pesticide, that is derived from animal or vegetable matter. —**or'ganically** *adv.*

organism ('ɔːgə,nɪzəm) *n.* **1.** any living animal or plant, including any bacterium or virus. **2.** anything resembling a living creature in structure, behaviour, etc.

THESAURUS

der (*Inf.*), position, rank, status **7.** breed, cast, class, family, genre, genus, ilk, kind, sort, species, subclass, taxonomic group, tribe, type **8.** behest, command, decree, dictate, direction, directive, injunction, instruction, law, mandate, ordinance, precept, regulation, rule, say-so (*Inf.*), stipulation **9.** application, booking, commission, request, requisition, reservation **10.** association, brotherhood, community, company, fraternity, guild, league, lodge, organization, sect, sisterhood, society, sodality, union ~*v.* **11.** adjure, bid, charge, command, decree, direct, enact, enjoin, instruct, ordain, prescribe, require **12.** apply for, authorize, book, call for, contract for, engage, prescribe, request, reserve, send away for **13.** adjust, align, arrange, catalogue, class, classify, conduct, control, dispose, group, lay out, manage, marshal, neaten, organize, put to rights, regulate, set in order, sort out, systematize, tabulate, tidy

orderly *adj.* **1.** businesslike, in apple-pie

order (*Inf.*), in order, methodical, neat, regular, scientific, shipshape, systematic, systematized, tidy, trim, well-organized, well-regulated **2.** controlled, decorous, disciplined, law-abiding, nonviolent, peaceable, quiet, restrained, well-behaved

ordinarily as a rule, commonly, customarily, generally, habitually, in general, in the general run (of things), in the usual way, normally, usually

ordinary 1. accustomed, common, customary, established, everyday, habitual, humdrum, normal, prevailing, quotidian, regular, routine, settled, standard, stock, typical, usual, wonted **2.** common or garden (*Inf.*), conventional, familiar, homespun, household, humble, modest, plain, prosaic, run-of-the-mill, simple, unmemorable, unpretentious, unremarkable, workaday **3.** average, commonplace, fair, indifferent, inferior, mean, mediocre, pedestrian, second-rate, stereotyped, undistinguished, unexceptional,

uninspired, unremarkable **4. out of the ordinary** atypical, distinguished, exceptional, exciting, extraordinary, high-calibre, imaginative, important, impressive, inspired, noteworthy, outstanding, rare, remarkable, significant, special, striking, superior, uncommon, unusual

organ 1. device, implement, instrument, tool **2.** element, member, part, process, structure, unit **3.** agency, channel, forum, journal, means, medium, mouthpiece, newspaper, paper, periodical, publication, vehicle, voice

organic 1. animate, biological, biotic, live, living, natural **2.** integrated, methodical, ordered, organized, structured, systematic **3.** anatomical, constitutional, fundamental, inherent, innate, integral, structural

organism animal, being, body, creature, entity, living thing, structure

—ˌorgan'ismal or ˌorgan'ismic adj. —ˌorgan'ismally adv.

organist ('ɔːgənɪst) n. a person who plays the organ.

organization or **-isation** (ˌɔːgənaɪ'zeɪʃən) n. **1.** the act of organizing or the state of being organized. **2.** an organized structure or whole. **3.** a business or administrative concern united and constructed for a particular end. **4.** a body of administrative officials, as of a government department, etc. **5.** order, tidiness, or system; method. —ˌorgani'zational or -i'sational adj.

organize or **-ise** ('ɔːgə,naɪz) vb. **1.** to form (parts or elements of something) into a structured whole; coordinate. **2.** (tr.) to arrange methodically or in order. **3.** (tr.) to provide with an organic structure. **4.** (tr.) to enlist (the workers) (of a factory, etc.) in a trade union. **5.** (intr.) to join or form an organization or trade union. **6.** (tr.) Inf. to put (oneself) in an alert and responsible frame of mind. —'orga,nizer or -iser n.

organza (ɔː'gænzə) n. a thin stiff fabric of silk, cotton, nylon, rayon, etc.

orgasm ('ɔːgæzəm) n. **1.** the most intense point during sexual excitement. **2.** Rare. intense or violent excitement. —or'gasmic or or'gastic adj.

orgy ('ɔːdʒɪ) n., pl. -gies. **1.** a wild gathering marked by promiscuous sexual activity, excessive drinking, etc. **2.** an act of immoderate or frenzied indulgence. **3.** (often pl.) secret religious rites of Dionysus, Bacchus, etc., marked by drinking, dancing, and songs. —ˌorgi'astic adj.

oriel ('ɔːrɪəl) n. a bay window, esp. one that is supported by one or more brackets or corbels. Also called: **oriel window**.

orient n. ('ɔːrɪənt). **1.** Poetic. another word for **east**. Cf. **occident**. **2.** Arch. the eastern sky or the dawn. **3. a.** the iridescent lustre of a pearl. **b.** (as modifier): orient pearls. **4.** a pearl of high quality. —adj. ('ɔːrɪənt). **5.** Now chiefly poetic. oriental. **6.** Arch. (of the sun, stars, etc.) rising. ~vb. ('ɔːrɪ,ɛnt). **7.** to adjust or align (oneself or something else) according to surroundings or circumstances. **8.** (tr.) to position or set (a map, etc.) with reference to the compass or other specific directions. **9.** (tr.) to build (a church) with the chancel end facing in an easterly direction.

▷ **Usage.** See at **orientate**.

Orient ('ɔːrɪənt) n. (usually preceded by the) **1.** the countries east of the Mediterranean. **2.** the eastern hemisphere.

oriental (ˌɔːrɪ'ɛntəl) adj. another word for **eastern**.

Oriental (ˌɔːrɪ'ɛntəl) adj. **1.** (sometimes not cap.) of or relating to the Orient. **2.** of or denoting a region consisting of southeastern Asia from India to Borneo, Java, and the Philippines. ~n. **3.** (sometimes not cap.) an inhabitant, esp. a native, of the Orient.

orientate ('ɔːrɪɛn,teɪt) vb. another word for **orient** (senses 7,8,9).

▷ **Usage.** Careful users avoid orientate as an unnecessary back formation from orientation, since orient has the same range of meanings. Nevertheless, there can be little doubt that either form is acceptable. The excessive use of orientate and orientation in such phrases as orientation course (preparatory course), profits-orientated systems (those geared to producing high profits), and student-orientated lectures (lectures written with students in mind) is frowned on in careful usage as jargon.

orientation (ˌɔːrɪɛn'teɪʃən) n. **1.** the act or process of orienting or the state of being oriented. **2.** positioning with relation to the compass or other specific directions. **3.** the adjustment or alignment of oneself or one's ideas to surroundings or circumstances. **4.** Also called: **orientation course.** Chiefly U.S. **a.** a course, lecture, etc., introducing a new situation or environment. **b.** (as modifier): an orientation talk. **5.** Psychol. the knowledge of one's own temporal, social, and practical circumstances. **6.** the siting of a church on an east-west axis. —ˌorien'tational adj.

orienteering (ˌɔːrɪɛn'tɪərɪŋ) n. a sport in which contestants race on foot over a course consisting of checkpoints found with the aid of a map and a compass.

orifice ('ɒrɪfɪs) n. Chiefly technical. an opening or mouth into a cavity; vent; aperture.

orig. abbrev. for: **1.** origin. **2.** original(ly).

origami (ˌɒrɪ'gɑːmɪ) n. the art or process, originally Japanese, of paper folding.

origin ('ɒrɪdʒɪn) n. **1.** a primary source; derivation. **2.** the beginning of something; first part. **3.** (often pl.) ancestry or parentage; birth; extraction. **4.** Anat. **a.** the end of a muscle, opposite its point of insertion. **b.** the beginning of a nerve or blood vessel or the site where it first starts to branch out. **5.** Maths. **a.** the point of intersection of coordinate axes or planes. **b.** the point whose coordinates are all zero.

original (ə'rɪdʒɪnəl) adj. **1.** of or relating to an origin or beginning. **2.** fresh and unusual; novel. **3.** able to think of or carry out new ideas or concepts. **4.** being that from which a copy, translation, etc., is made. ~n. **5.** the first and genuine form of something, from which others are derived. **6.** a person or thing used as a model in art or literature. **7.** a person whose way of thinking is unusual or creative. **8.** the first form or occurrence of something. —o,rigi'nality n. —o'riginally adv.

original sin n. Theol. a state of sin held to be innate in mankind as the descendants of Adam.

originate (ə'rɪdʒɪ,neɪt) vb. **1.** to come or bring into being. **2.** (intr.) U.S. (of a bus, train, etc.) to begin its journey at a specified point. —o,rigi'nation n. —o'rigi,nator n.

oriole ('ɔːrɪ,əʊl) n. **1.** a tropical Old World songbird, such as the golden oriole, having a long pointed bill and a mostly yellow-and-black plumage. **2.** an American songbird, esp. the Baltimore oriole, with a typical male plum-

---

THESAURUS

organization 1. assembling, assembly, construction, coordination, disposal, formation, forming, formulation, making, management, methodology, organizing, planning, regulation, running, standardization, structuring 2. arrangement, chemistry, composition, configuration, conformation, constitution, design, format, framework, grouping, make-up, method, organism, pattern, plan, structure, system, unity, whole 3. association, body, combine, company, concern, confederation, consortium, corporation, federation, group, institution, league, outfit (Inf.), syndicate

organize arrange, be responsible for, catalogue, classify, codify, constitute, construct, coordinate, dispose, establish, form, frame, get going (Inf.), get together (Sl.), group, lay the foundations of, lick into shape, look after, marshal, pigeonhole, put in order, put together, run, see to (Inf.), set up, shape, straighten out, systematize, tabulate, take care of

orgy 1. bacchanal, bacchanalia, debauch, revel, revelry, Saturnalia 2. binge (Inf.), bout, excess, indulgence, overindulgence, splurge, spree, surfeit

orientation 1. bearings, coordination, direction, location, position, sense of direction 2. acclimatization, adaptation, adjustment, assimilation, breaking in, familiarization, introduction, settling in

orifice aperture, cleft, hole, mouth, opening, perforation, pore, rent, vent

origin 1. base, basis, cause, derivation, fons et origo, font (Poetic), fountain, fountainhead, occasion, provenance, root, roots, source, spring, wellspring 2. beginning, birth, commencement, creation, dawning, early stages, emergence, foundation, genesis, inauguration, inception, launch, origination, outset, start 3. ancestry, beginnings, birth, descent, extraction, family, heritage, lineage, parentage, pedigree, stirps, stock

original adj. 1. aboriginal, autochthonous, commencing, earliest, early, embryonic, first, infant, initial, introductory, opening, primary, primitive, primordial, pristine, rudimentary, starting 2. creative, fertile, fresh, imaginative, ingenious, innovative, innovatory, inventive, new, novel, resourceful, seminal, unconventional, unprecedented, untried, unusual 3. archetypal, authentic, first, first-hand, genuine, master, primary, prototypical ~n. 4. archetype, master, model, paradigm, pattern, precedent, prototype, standard, type 5. anomaly, card (Inf.), case (Inf.), character, eccentric, nonconformist, oddity, queer fish (Brit. inf.), weirdo (Inf.)

originality boldness, break with tradition, cleverness, creativeness, creative spirit, creativity, daring, freshness, imagination, imaginativeness, individuality, ingenuity, innovation, innovativeness, inventiveness, new ideas, newness, novelty, resourcefulness, unconventionality, unorthodoxy

originally at first, at the outset, at the start, by origin (birth, derivation), first, initially, in the beginning, in the first place, to begin with

originate 1. arise, be born, begin, come, derive, emanate, emerge, flow, issue, proceed, result, rise, spring, start, stem 2. bring about, conceive, create, develop, discover, evolve, form, formulate, generate, give birth to, inaugurate, initiate, institute, introduce, invent, launch, pioneer, produce, set in motion, set up

originator architect, author, creator, father, founder, generator, innovator, inventor, maker, mother, pioneer, prime mover

age of black with either orange or yellow.

Orion (əˈraɪən) n. a constellation containing two first magnitude stars (Betelgeuse and Rigel) and a distant low density emission nebule (the **Orion Nebula**).

orison (ˈɒrɪzən) n. Literary. another word for **prayer**[1].

Orlon (ˈɔːlɒn) n. Trademark. a crease-resistant acrylic fibre or fabric used for clothing, etc.

ormolu (ˈɔːməˌluː) n. **1. a.** a gold-coloured alloy of copper, tin, or zinc used to decorate furniture, etc. **b.** (as modifier): an ormolu clock. **2.** gold prepared for gilding.

ornament n. (ˈɔːnəmənt). **1.** anything that enhances the appearance of a person or thing. **2.** decorations collectively: she was totally without ornament. **3.** a small decorative object. **4.** something regarded as a source of pride or beauty. **5.** Music. any of several decorations, such as the trill, etc. ~vb. (ˈɔːnəˌment.) (tr.) **6.** to decorate with or as if with ornaments. **7.** to serve as an ornament to.— ˌornaˈmental adj. — ˌornamenˈtation n.

ornate (ɔːˈneɪt) adj. **1.** heavily or elaborately decorated. **2.** (of style in writing, etc.) over-embellished; flowery. —orˈnately adv. —orˈnateness n.

ornitho- or before a vowel **ornith-** combining form. bird or birds.

ornithology (ˌɔːnɪˈθɒlədʒɪ) n. the study of birds. —ornithological (ˌɔːnɪθəˈlɒdʒɪkəl) adj. —ˌornithoˈlogically adv. —ˌorniˈthologist n.

orotund (ˈɒrəʊˌtʌnd) adj. **1.** (of the voice) resonant; booming. **2.** (of speech or writing) bombastic; pompous.

orphan (ˈɔːfən) n. **1. a.** a child, one or both of whose parents are dead. **b.** (as modifier): an orphan child. ~vb. **2.** (tr.) to deprive of one or both parents.

orphanage (ˈɔːfənɪdʒ) n. **1.** an institution for orphans and abandoned children. **2.** the state of being an orphan.

Orphic (ˈɔːfɪk) adj. **1.** of or relating to Orpheus or Orphism, a mystery religion of ancient Greece. **2.** (sometimes not cap.) mystical or occult. —ˈOrphically adv.

orrery (ˈɒrərɪ) n., pl. **-ries.** a mechanical model of the solar system in which the planets can be moved at the correct relative velocities around the sun.

orris or **orrice** (ˈɒrɪs) n. **1.** any of various irises that have fragrant rhizomes. **2.** Also: **orrisroot.** the rhizome of such a plant, prepared and used as perfume.

ortho- or before a vowel **orth-** combining form. **1.** straight or upright: orthorhombic. **2.** perpendicular or at right angles: orthogonal. **3.** correct or right: orthodontics. **4.** (often in italics) denoting an organic compound containing a benzene ring with substituents attached to adjacent carbon atoms (the 1,2- positions). **5.** denoting an oxyacid regarded as the highest hydrated form of the anhydride or a salt of such an acid: orthophosphoric acid. **6.** denoting a diatomic substance in which the spins of the two atoms are parallel: orthohydrogen.

orthodontics (ˌɔːθəʊˈdɒntɪks) or **orthodontia** (ˌɔːθəʊˈdɒntɪə) n. the branch of dentistry concerned with preventing or correcting irregularities of the teeth. —ˌorthoˈdontic adj. —ˌorthoˈdontist n.

orthodox (ˈɔːθəˌdɒks) adj. **1.** conforming with established standards, as in religion, behaviour, or attitudes. **2.** conforming to the Christian faith as established by the early Church. —ˈorthoˌdoxy n.

Orthodox (ˈɔːθəˌdɒks) adj. **1.** of or relating to the Orthodox Church of the East. **2.** (sometimes not cap.) of or relating to Orthodox Judaism.

orthography (ɔːˈθɒɡrəfɪ) n., pl. **-phies. 1.** a writing system. **2. a.** spelling considered to be correct. **b.** the principles underlying spelling. **3.** the study of spelling. —or-

ˈthographer or orˈthographist n. —ˌorthoˈgraphic adj.

orthopaedics or U.S. **orthopedics** (ˌɔːθəˈpiːdɪks) n. (functioning as sing.) **1.** the branch of surgery concerned with disorders of the spine and joints and the repair of deformities of these parts. **2. dental orthopaedics.** another name for **orthodontics.** —ˌorthoˈpaedic or U.S. ˌorthoˈpedic adj. —ˌorthoˈpaedist or U.S. ˌorthoˈpedist n.

ortolan (ˈɔːtələn) n. **1.** a brownish Old World bunting regarded as a delicacy. **2.** any of various other small birds eaten as delicacies, esp. the bobolink.

Os the chemical symbol for osmium.

O.S. abbrev. for: **1.** Old Style. **2.** Ordinary Seaman. **3.** (in Britain) Ordnance Survey. **4.** outsize. **5.** Also **OS.** Old Saxon (language).

Oscar (ˈɒskə) n. any of several small gold statuettes awarded annually in the United States for outstanding achievements in films.

oscillate (ˈɒsɪˌleɪt) vb. **1.** (intr.) to move or swing from side to side regularly. **2.** (intr.) to waver between opinions, courses of action, etc. **3.** Physics. to undergo or produce oscillation. —ˈosciˈllation n. —ˈosciˌlator n.

oscilloscope (ɒˈsɪləˌskəʊp) n. an instrument for producing a representation of a rapidly changing quantity on the screen of a cathode-ray tube.

oscular (ˈɒskjʊlə) adj. **1.** Zool. of or relating to a mouth-like aperture, esp. of a sponge. **2.** of or relating to the mouth or to kissing.

osculate (ˈɒskjʊˌleɪt) vb. **1.** Usually humorous. to kiss. **2.** (intr.) (of an organism) to be intermediate between two taxonomic groups. **3.** Geom. to touch in osculation.

osier (ˈəʊzɪə) n. **1.** any of various willow trees, whose flexible branches or twigs are used for making baskets, etc. **2.** a twig or branch from such a tree. **3.** any of several North American dogwoods, esp. the red osier.

-osis suffix forming nouns. **1.** indicating a process or state: metamorphosis. **2.** indicating a diseased condition: tuberculosis. **3.** indicating the formation or development of something: fibrosis.

Osmanli (ɒzˈmænlɪ) adj. **1.** of or relating to the Ottoman Empire. ~n. **2.** (pl. **-lis**) (formerly) a subject of the Ottoman Empire.

osmium (ˈɒzmɪəm) n. a very hard brittle bluish-white metal, the heaviest known element, occurring with platinum and alloyed with iridium in osmiridium. Symbol: Os; atomic no.: 76; atomic wt.: 190.2.

osmosis (ɒzˈməʊsɪs, ɒs-) n. **1.** the passage of solvent molecules from a less concentrated to a more concentrated solution through a semipermeable membrane until both solutions are of the same concentration. **2.** diffusion through any membrane or porous barrier, as in dialysis. —**osmotic** (ɒzˈmɒtɪk, ɒs-) adj. —osˈmotically adv.

osprey (ˈɒsprɪ, -preɪ) n. **1.** a large broad-winged fish-eating diurnal bird of prey, with a dark back and whitish head and underparts. Often called in U.S.: **fish hawk. 2.** any of the feathers of various other birds, used esp. as trimming for hats.

osseous (ˈɒsɪəs) adj. consisting of or containing bone, bony. —ˈosseously adv.

ossify (ˈɒsɪˌfaɪ) vb. **-fying, -fied. 1.** to convert or be converted into bone. **2.** (intr.) (of habits, attitudes, etc.) to become inflexible. —ˈossiˌfier n. —ˌossifiˈcation n.

ostensible (ɒˈstɛnsɪbəl) adj. **1.** apparent; seeming. **2.** pretended. —osˌtensiˈbility n. —osˈtensibly adv.

ostensive (ɒˈstɛnsɪv) adj. **1.** obviously or manifestly demonstrative. **2.** (of a definition) giving examples of ob-

---

THESAURUS

ornament n. **1.** accessory, adornment, bauble, decoration, embellishment, frill, furbelow, garnish, gewgaw, knick-knack, trimming, trinket **2.** flower, honour, jewel, leading light, pride, treasure ~v. **3.** adorn, beautify, bedizen (Archaic), brighten, deck, decorate, dress up, embellish, festoon, garnish, gild, grace, prettify, prink, trim

ornamental attractive, beautifying, decorative, embellishing, for show, showy

ornamentation adornment, decoration, elaboration, embellishment, embroidery, frills, ornateness

ornate aureate, baroque, beautiful, bedecked, busy, convoluted, decorated, elabo-

rate, elegant, fancy, florid, flowery, fussy, high-wrought, ornamented, overelaborate, rococo

orthodox accepted, approved, conformist, conventional, correct, customary, doctrinal, established, official, received, sound, traditional, true, well-established

orthodoxy authenticity, authoritativeness, authority, conformism, conformity, conventionality, devotion, devoutness, faithfulness, inflexibility, received wisdom, soundness, traditionalism

oscillate fluctuate, seesaw, sway, swing, vacillate, vary, vibrate, waver

oscillation fluctuation, instability, see-

sawing, swing, vacillation, variation, wavering

ossify fossilize, freeze, harden, indurate (Rare), petrify, solidify, stiffen

ostensible alleged, apparent, avowed, exhibited, manifest, outward, plausible, pretended, professed, purported, seeming, so-called, specious, superficial, supposed

ostensibly apparently, for the ostensible purpose of, on the face of it, on the surface, professedly, seemingly, supposedly, to all intents and purposes

jects to which a word or phrase is properly applied. **3.** a less common word for **ostensible.** —**os'tensively** adv.

ostentation (ˌɒstɛn'teɪʃən) n. pretentious, showy, or vulgar display. —ˌosten'tatious adj. —ˌosten'tatiously adv.

osteo- or before a vowel **oste-** combining form. indicating bone or bones.

osteoarthritis (ˌɒstɪəʊɑː'θraɪtɪs) n. chronic inflammation of the joints, esp. those that bear weight, with pain and stiffness. —**osteoarthritic** (ˌɒstɪəʊɑː'θrɪtɪk) adj., n.

osteomyelitis (ˌɒstɪəʊˌmaɪɪ'laɪtɪs) n. inflammation of bone marrow, caused by infection.

osteopathy (ˌɒstɪ'ɒpəθɪ) n. a system of healing based on the manipulation of bones or other parts of the body. —**osteopathic** (ˌɒstɪə'pæθɪk) adj. —ˌosteo'pathically adv. —'osteoˌpath n.

ostler ('ɒslə) or **hostler** n. Arch. a stableman, esp. one at an inn.

ostracize or **-ise** ('ɒstrəˌsaɪz) vb. (tr.) **1.** to exclude or banish (a person) from a particular group, society, etc. **2.** (in ancient Greece) to punish by temporary exile. —'ostracism n. —'ostraˌcizable or **-isable** adj. —'ostraˌcizer or **-iser** n.

ostrich ('ɒstrɪtʃ) n., pl. **-triches** or **-trich. 1.** a fast-running flightless African bird that is the largest living bird, with stout two-toed feet and dark feathers, except on the naked head, neck, and legs. **2. American ostrich.** another name for **rhea. 3.** a person who refuses to recognize the truth, reality, etc.

O.T. abbrev. for: **1.** occupational therapy. **2.** Old Testament. **3.** overtime.

O.T.C. (in Britain) abbrev. for: Officers' Training Corps.

other ('ʌðə) determiner. **1. a.** (when used before a singular noun, usually preceded by the) the remaining (one or ones in a group of which one or some have been specified): I'll read the other sections of the paper later. **b. the other.** (as pronoun; functioning as sing.): one walks while the other rides. **2.** (a) different (one or ones from that or those already specified or understood): no other man but you. **3.** additional; further: there are no other possibilities. **4.** (preceded by every) alternate; two: it buzzes every other minute. **5. other than. a.** apart from; besides: a lady other than his wife. **b.** different from: he couldn't be other than what he is. Archaic form: **other from. 6. no other.** Arch. nothing else: I can do no other. **7. or other.** (preceded by a phrase or word with some) used to add vagueness to the preceding pronoun, noun, or noun phrase: he's somewhere or other. **8. other things being equal.** conditions being the same or unchanged. **9. the other day, night,** etc. a few days, nights, etc., ago. **10. the other thing.** an unexpressed alternative. ~pron. **11.** another: show me one other. **12.** (pl.) additional or further ones. **13.** (pl.) other people or things. **14. the others.** the remaining ones (of a group). ~adv. **15.** (usually used with a negative and foll. by than) otherwise; differently: they couldn't behave other than they do. —'otherness n.

otherwise ('ʌðəˌwaɪz) **1.** sentence connector. or else; if not, then: go home — otherwise your mother will worry. ~adv. **2.** differently: I wouldn't have thought otherwise. **3.** in other respects: an otherwise hopeless situation. ~adj. **4.** (predicative) of an unexpected nature; different: the facts are otherwise. ~pron. **5.** something different in outcome: success or otherwise.

otherworldly (ˌʌðə'wɜːldlɪ) adj. **1.** of or relating to the spiritual or imaginative world. **2.** impractical or unworldly. —ˌother'worldliness n.

otic ('əʊtɪk, 'ɒtɪk) adj. of or relating to the ear.

otiose ('əʊtɪˌəʊs, -ˌəʊz) adj. **1.** serving no useful purpose: otiose language. **2.** Rare. indolent; lazy. —**otiosity** (ˌəʊtɪ'ɒsɪtɪ) or 'otioseness n.

otitis (əʊ'taɪtɪs) n. inflammation of the ear.

oto- or before a vowel **ot-** combining form. indicating the ear.

otter ('ɒtə) n., pl. **-ters** or **-ter. 1.** a freshwater carnivorous mammal, esp. the **Eurasian otter,** typically having smooth fur, a streamlined body, and webbed feet. **2.** the fur of this animal. **3.** a type of fishing tackle consisting of a weighted board to which hooked and baited lines are attached.

ottoman ('ɒtəmən) n., pl. **-mans. 1. a.** a low padded seat, usually armless, sometimes in the form of a chest. **b.** a cushioned footstool. **2.** a corded fabric.

Ottoman ('ɒtəmən) or **Othman** ('ɒθmən) adj. **1.** History. of or relating to the Ottomans or the Ottoman Empire. **2.** denoting or relating to the Turkish language. ~n., pl. **-mans. 3.** a member of a Turkish people in the late 13th century.

O.U. abbrev. for: **1.** the Open University. **2.** Oxford University.

oubliette (ˌuːblɪ'ɛt) n. a dungeon, the only entrance to which is through the top.

ouch (aʊtʃ) interj. an exclamation of sharp sudden pain.

ought[1] (ɔːt) vb. (foll. by to; takes an infinitive or implied infinitive) used as an auxiliary **1.** to indicate duty or obligation: you ought to pay. **2.** to express prudent expediency: you ought to see him. **3.** (usually with reference to future time) to express probability or expectation: you ought to finish this by Friday. **4.** to express a desire or wish on the part of the speaker: you ought to come next week.

▷ **Usage.** In careful English, ought is not used with did or had. I ought not to do it, not I didn't ought to do it; I ought not to have done it, not I hadn't ought to have done it.

ought[2] (ɔːt) n., adv. a variant spelling of **aught.**

ought[3] (ɔːt) n. a less common word for **nought** (zero).

Ouija ('wiːdʒə) n. Trademark. a board on which are marked the letters of the alphabet. Answers to questions are spelt out by a pointer and are supposedly formed by spirits.

ounce (aʊns) n. **1.** a unit of weight equal to one sixteenth of a pound (avoirdupois). Abbrev.: **oz. 2.** a unit of weight equal to one twelfth of a Troy or Apothecaries' pound; 1 ounce is equal to 480 grains. **3.** short for **fluid ounce. 4.** a small portion or amount.

our (aʊə) determiner. **1.** of, belonging to, or associated in some way with us: our best vodka; our parents are good to us. **2.** belonging to or associated with all people or people in general: our nearest planet is Venus. **3.** a formal word for my used by editors or other writers, and monarchs.

-our suffix forming nouns. indicating state, condition, or activity: behaviour; labour.

ours (aʊəz) pron. **1.** something or someone belonging to or associated with us: ours have blue tags. **2. of ours.** belonging to or associated with us.

ourself (aʊə'sɛlf) pron. Arch. a variant of **myself,** formerly used by monarchs or editors.

ourselves (aʊə'sɛlvz) pron. **1. a.** the reflexive form of we or us. **b.** (intensifier): we ourselves will finish it. **2.** (preceded by a copula) our usual selves: we are ourselves when we're together. **3.** Not standard. used instead of we or us in compound noun phrases: other people and ourselves.

▷ **Usage.** See at **myself.**

-ous suffix forming adjectives. **1.** having or full of: dangerous; spacious. **2.** (in chemistry) indicating that an element is chemically combined in the lower of two possible valence states: ferrous. Cf. **-ic** (sense 2).

ousel ('uːzəl) n. a variant spelling of **ouzel.**

oust (aʊst) vb. (tr.) **1.** to eject; expel. **2.** Property law. to deprive (a person) of the possession of land, etc.

out (aʊt) adv. **1.** (often used as a particle) at or to a

THESAURUS

ostentation affectation, boasting, display, exhibitionism, flamboyance, flashiness, flaunting, flourish, pageantry, parade, pomp, pretension, pretentiousness, show, showiness, showing off (Inf.), swank (Inf.), vaunting, window-dressing

ostentatious boastful, conspicuous, crass, dashing, extravagant, flamboyant, flash (Inf.), flashy, flaunted, gaudy, loud, obtrusive, pompous, pretentious, showy, swanky (Inf.), vain, vulgar

ostracism avoidance, banishment, boycott, cold-shouldering, exclusion, exile, expulsion, isolation, rejection

ostracize avoid, banish, blackball, blacklist, boycott, cast out, cold-shoulder, exclude, excommunicate, exile, expatriate, expel, give (someone) the cold shoulder, reject, send to Coventry, shun

other adj. **1.** added, additional, alternative, auxiliary, extra, further, more, spare, supplementary **2.** contrasting, different, dissimilar, distinct, diverse, remaining, separate, unrelated, variant

otherwise adv. **1.** if not, or else, or then **2.** any other way, contrarily, differently

ounce atom, crumb, drop, grain, iota, particle, scrap, shred, speck, trace, whit

point beyond the limits of some location; outside: *get out at once.* **2.** (*particle*) out of consciousness: *she passed out.* **3.** (*particle*) used to indicate a burst of activity as indicated by the verb: *fever broke out.* **4.** (*particle*) used to indicate obliteration of an object: *the graffiti was painted out.* **5.** (*particle*) used to indicate an approximate drawing or description: *chalk out.* **6.** on sale or on view to the public: *the book is being brought out next May.* **7.** (of a young woman) in or into polite society: *Lucinda had a fabulous party when she came out.* **8.** (of a jury) withdrawn to consider a verdict in private. **9.** (*particle*) used to indicate exhaustion or extinction: *the sugar's run out; put the light out.* **10.** (*particle*) used to indicate a goal or object achieved at the end of the action specified by the verb: *he worked it out.* **11.** (*preceded by a superlative*) existing: *the friendliest dog out.* **12.** an expression in signalling, radio, etc., to indicate the end of a transmission. **13.** **out of. a.** at or to a point outside: *out of his reach.* **b.** away from; not in: *stepping out of line; out of focus.* **c.** because of; motivated by: *out of jealousy.* **d.** from (a material or source): *made out of plastic.* **e.** not or no longer having any of (a substance, material, etc.): *we're out of sugar.* ~*adj.* (*postpositive*). **14.** not or not any longer worth considering: *that plan is out.* **15.** not allowed: *smoking on duty is out.* **16.** (*also prenominal*) not in vogue; unfashionable. **17.** (of a fire or light) no longer burning or providing illumination. **18.** not working: *the radio's out.* **19.** unconscious: *he was out for two minutes.* **20.** not in; not at home. **21.** desirous of or intent on (something or doing something): *I'm out for as much money as I can get.* **22.** Also: **out on strike.** on strike. **23.** *Sport.* denoting the state in which a player is caused to discontinue active participation, esp. in some specified role. **24.** used up; exhausted: *our supplies are completely out.* **25.** worn into holes: *out at the elbows.* **26.** inaccurate, deficient, or discrepant: *out by six pence.* **27.** not in office or authority. **28.** completed or concluded, as of time: *before the year is out.* ~*prep.* **29.** out of; out through: *he ran out the door.* ~*interj.* **30. a.** an exclamation of dismissal, reproach, etc. **b.** (in wireless telegraphy) an expression used to signal that the speaker is signing off. **31. out with it.** a command to make something known immediately, without missing any details. ~*n.* **32.** *Chiefly U.S.* a method of escape from a place, difficult situation, etc. **33.** *Baseball.* an instance of causing a batter to be out by fielding. **34. ins and outs.** See **in** (sense 26). ~*vb.* **35.** (*tr.*) to put or throw out. **36.** (*intr.*) to be made known or effective despite efforts to the contrary (esp. in the **truth will out**).

out- *prefix.* **1.** excelling or surpassing in a particular action: *outlast; outlive.* **2.** indicating an external location or situation away from the centre: *outpost; outpatient.* **3.** indicating emergence, an issuing forth, etc.: *outcrop; outgrowth.* **4.** indicating the result of an action: *outcome.*

outage ('aʊtɪdʒ) *n.* **1.** a quantity of goods missing or lost after storage or shipment. **2.** a period of power failure, machine stoppage, etc.

out-and-out *adj.* (*prenominal*) thoroughgoing; complete.

outback ('aʊt,bæk) *n. Austral.* **a.** the remote bush country of Australia. **b.** (*as modifier*): *outback life.*

outboard ('aʊt,bɔːd) *adj.* **1.** (of a boat's engine) portable, with its own propeller, and designed to be attached externally to the stern. **2.** in a position away from, or further away from, the centre line of a vessel or aircraft, esp. outside the hull or fuselage. ~*adv.* **3.** away from the centre line of a vessel or aircraft, esp. outside the hull or fuselage. ~*n.* **4.** an outboard motor.

outbreak ('aʊt,breɪk) *n.* a sudden, violent, or spontaneous occurrence, esp. of disease or strife.

outbuilding ('aʊt,bɪldɪŋ) *n.* a building separate from a main building; outhouse.

outburst ('aʊt,bɜːst) *n.* **1.** a sudden and violent expression of emotion. **2.** an explosion or eruption.

outcast ('aʊt,kɑːst) *n.* **1.** a person who is rejected or excluded from a social group. **2.** a vagabond or wanderer. **3.** anything thrown out or rejected. ~*adj.* **4.** rejected, abandoned, or discarded; cast out.

outcaste ('aʊt,kɑːst) *n.* **1.** a person who has been expelled from a caste. **2.** a person having no caste. ~*vb.* **3.** (*tr.*) to cause (someone) to lose his caste.

outclass (,aʊt'klɑːs) *vb.* (*tr.*) **1.** to surpass in class, quality, etc. **2.** to defeat easily.

outcome ('aʊt,kʌm) *n.* something that follows from an action or situation; result; consequence.

outcrop *n.* ('aʊt,krɒp). **1.** part of a rock formation or mineral vein that appears at the surface of the earth. **2.** an emergence; appearance. ~*vb.* (,aʊt'krɒp), **-cropping, -cropped. 3.** (*intr.*) (of rock strata, mineral veins, etc.) to protrude through the surface of the earth.

outcry *n.* ('aʊt,kraɪ), *pl.* **-cries. 1.** a widespread or vehement protest. **2.** clamour; uproar. ~*vb.* (,aʊt'kraɪ), **-crying, -cried. 3.** (*tr.*) to cry louder or make more noise than (someone or something).

outdated (,aʊt'deɪtɪd) *adj.* old-fashioned or obsolete.

outdo (,aʊt'duː) *vb.* **-doing, -did, -done.** (*tr.*) to surpass or exceed in performance.

outdoor ('aʊt'dɔː) *adj.* (*prenominal*) Also: **out-of-door.** taking place, existing, or intended for use in the open air: *outdoor games; outdoor clothes.*

outdoors (,aʊt'dɔːz) *adv.* **1.** Also: **out-of-doors.** in the open air; outside. ~*n.* **2.** the world outside habitation.

outer ('aʊtə) *adj.* (*prenominal*) **1.** being or located on the outside; external. **2.** further from the middle or central part. ~*n.* **3.** *Archery.* **a.** the white outermost ring on a target. **b.** a shot that hits this ring. **4.** *Austral.* the unsheltered part of the spectator area at a sports ground. **5. on the outer.** *Austral. & N.Z.* excluded or neglected.

outermost ('aʊtə,məʊst) *adj.* furthest from the centre or middle; outmost.

outer space *n.* any region of space beyond the atmosphere of the earth.

outfall ('aʊt,fɔːl) *n.* the end of a river, sewer, drain, etc., from which it discharges.

outact *vb.*	outdrink *vb.*	outnumber *vb.*	outreach *vb.*
outbid *vb.*	outface *vb.*	outpace *vb.*	outrun *vb.*
outbox *vb.*	outfight *vb.*	outperform *vb.*	outsell *vb.*
outdare *vb.*	outlast *vb.*	outplay *vb.*	outshine *vb.*
outdistance *vb.*	outmatch *vb.*	outrange *vb.*	outstare *vb.*

THESAURUS

out *adj.* **1.** impossible, not allowed, not on (*Inf.*), ruled out, unacceptable **2.** abroad, absent, away, elsewhere, gone, not at home, outside **3.** antiquated, behind the times, dated, dead, démodé, old-fashioned, old hat, passé, square (*Inf.*), unfashionable **4.** at an end, cold, dead, doused, ended, exhausted, expired, extinguished, finished, used up

out-and-out absolute, complete, consummate, downright, dyed-in-the-wool, outright, perfect, thoroughgoing, total, unmitigated, unqualified, utter

outbreak burst, epidemic, eruption, explosion, flare-up, flash, outburst, rash, spasm, upsurge

outburst access, attack, discharge, eruption, explosion, fit of temper, flare-up, gush,

outbreak, outpouring, paroxysm, spasm, storm, surge

outcast *n.* castaway, derelict, displaced person, exile, leper, pariah, *persona non grata*, refugee, reprobate, untouchable, vagabond, wretch

outclass be a cut above (*Inf.*), beat, eclipse, exceed, excel, leave *or* put in the shade, leave standing (*Inf.*), outdistance, outdo, outrank, outshine, outstrip, overshadow, surpass

outcome aftereffect, aftermath, conclusion, consequence, end, end result, issue, payoff (*Inf.*), result, upshot

outcry clamour, commotion, complaint, cry, exclamation, howl, hue and cry, hullaballoo, noise, outburst, protest, scream, screech, uproar, yell

outdated antiquated, antique, archaic, behind the times (*Inf.*), démodé, obsolete, old-fashioned, outmoded, out of date, out of style, passé, unfashionable

outdistance leave behind, leave standing (*Inf.*), lose, outrun, outstrip, shake off

outdo beat, be one up on, best, eclipse, exceed, excel, get the better of, go one better than (*Inf.*), outclass, outdistance, outfox, outjockey, outmanoeuvre, outshine, outsmart (*Inf.*), overcome, surpass, top, transcend

outdoor alfresco, open-air, out-of-door(s), outside

outer exposed, exterior, external, outlying, outside, outward, peripheral, remote, superficial, surface

outfield (ˈaʊtˌfiːld) n. 1. Cricket. the area of the field relatively far from the pitch; the deep. Cf. **infield**. 2. Baseball. **a.** the area of the playing field beyond the lines connecting first, second, and third bases. **b.** the positions of the left fielder, centre fielder, and right fielder taken collectively. 3. Agriculture. farm land most distant from the farmstead. —ˈoutˌfielder n.

outfit (ˈaʊtˌfɪt) n. 1. a set of articles or equipment for a particular task, etc. 2. a set of clothes, esp. a carefully selected one. 3. Inf. any group or association regarded as a cohesive unit, such as a military company, etc. ~vb. **-fitting, -fitted**. 4. to furnish or be furnished with an outfit, equipment, etc. —ˈoutˌfitter n.

outflank (ˌaʊtˈflæŋk) vb. (tr.) 1. to go around the flank of (an opposing army, etc.). 2. to get the better of.

outflow (ˈaʊtˌfləʊ) n. 1. anything that flows out, such as liquid, money, etc. 2. the amount that flows out. 3. the act or process of flowing out.

outfox (ˌaʊtˈfɒks) vb. (tr.) to surpass in guile or cunning.

outgoing (ˈaʊtˌgəʊɪŋ) adj. 1. departing; leaving. 2. retiring from office. 3. friendly and sociable. ~n. 4. the act of going out.

outgrow (ˌaʊtˈgrəʊ) vb. **-growing, -grew, -grown**. (tr.) 1. to grow too large for (clothes, shoes, etc.). 2. to lose (a habit, idea, reputation, etc.) in the course of development or time. 3. to grow larger or faster than.

outgrowth (ˈaʊtˌgrəʊθ) n. 1. a thing growing out of a main body. 2. a development, result, or consequence. 3. the act of growing out.

outhouse (ˈaʊtˌhaʊs) n. a building near to, but separate from, a main building; outbuilding.

outing (ˈaʊtɪŋ) n. a short outward and return journey; trip; excursion.

outlandish (aʊtˈlændɪʃ) adj. 1. grotesquely unconventional in appearance, habits, etc. 2. Arch. foreign. —ˈoutˈlandishly adv. —ˈoutˈlandishness n.

outlaw (ˈaʊtˌlɔː) n. 1. (formerly) a person excluded from the law and deprived of its protection. 2. any fugitive from the law, esp. a habitual transgressor. ~vb. (tr.) 3. to put (a person) outside the law and deprive of its protection. 4. to ban. —ˈoutˌlawry n.

outlay n. (ˈaʊtˌleɪ). 1. an expenditure of money, effort, etc. ~vb. (ˌaʊtˈleɪ), **-laying, -laid**. 2. (tr.) to spend (money, etc.).

outlet (ˈaʊtlɛt, -lɪt) n. 1. an opening or vent permitting escape or release. 2. **a.** a market for a product or service. **b.** a commercial establishment retailing the goods of a particular producer or wholesaler. 3. a channel that drains a body of water. 4. a point in a wiring system from which current can be taken to supply electrical devices.

outline (ˈaʊtˌlaɪn) n. 1. a preliminary or schematic plan, draft, etc. 2. (usually pl.) the important features of a theory, work, etc. 3. the line by which an object or figure is or appears to be bounded. 4. **a.** a drawing or manner of drawing consisting only of external lines. **b.** (as modifier): an outline map. ~vb. (tr.) 5. to draw or display the outline of. 6. to give the main features or general idea of.

outlive (ˌaʊtˈlɪv) vb. (tr.) 1. to live longer than (someone). 2. to live beyond a date or period: he outlived the century. 3. to live through (an experience).

outlook (ˈaʊtˌlʊk) n. 1. a mental attitude or point of view. 2. the probable or expected condition or outcome of something: the weather outlook. 3. the view from a place. 4. view or prospect. 5. the act or state of looking out.

outlying (ˈaʊtˌlaɪɪŋ) adj. distant or remote from the main body or centre, as of a town or region.

outmanoeuvre or U.S. **outmaneuver** (ˌaʊtməˈnuːvə) vb. (tr.) to secure a strategic advantage over by skilful manoeuvre.

outmoded (ˌaʊtˈməʊdɪd) adj. no longer fashionable or widely accepted. —ˌoutˈmodedly adv. —ˌoutˈmodedness n.

out of date adj. (**out-of-date** when prenominal), adv. no longer valid, current, or fashionable; outmoded.

out-of-doors adv., adj. (postpositive) in the open air; outside. Also: **outdoors**.

out of pocket adj. (**out-of-pocket** when prenominal). 1. (postpositive) having lost money, as in a commercial enterprise. 2. without money to spend. 3. (prenominal) (of expenses) unbudgeted and paid for in cash.

out-of-the-way adj. (prenominal) 1. distant from more populous areas. 2. uncommon or unusual.

outpatient (ˈaʊtˌpeɪʃənt) n. a non-resident hospital patient. Cf. **inpatient**.

outport (ˈaʊtˌpɔːt) n. 1. Chiefly Brit. a subsidiary port built in deeper water than the original port. 2. Canad. a small fishing village of Newfoundland.

outpost (ˈaʊtˌpəʊst) n. 1. Mil. **a.** a position stationed at a distance from the area occupied by a major formation. **b.** the troops assigned to such a position. 2. an outlying settlement or position.

output (ˈaʊtˌpʊt) n. 1. the act of production or manufacture. 2. the amount produced, as in a given period: a weekly output. 3. the material produced, manufactured, etc. 4. Electronics. **a.** the power, voltage, or current delivered by a circuit or component. **b.** the point at which the signal is delivered. 5. the power, energy, or work produced by an engine or a system. 6. Computers. **a.** the information produced by a computer. **b.** the operations and devices involved in producing this information. 7. (modifier) of or relating to electronic or computer out-

---

THESAURUS

outfit n. 1. accoutrements, clothes, costume, ensemble, garb, gear, get-up (Inf.), kit, rigout (Inf.), suit, togs (Inf.), trappings 2. Inf. clique, company, corps, coterie, crew, firm, galère, group, organization, set, setup (Inf.), squad, team, unit ~v. 3. accoutre, appoint, equip, fit out, furnish, kit out, provision, stock, supply, turn out

outfitter clothier, costumier, couturier, dressmaker, haberdasher (U.S.), modiste, tailor

outflow discharge, drainage, ebb, effluence, efflux, effusion, emanation, emergence, gush, jet, outfall, outpouring, rush, spout

outgoing 1. departing, ex-, former, last, leaving, past, retiring, withdrawing 2. approachable, communicative, cordial, demonstrative, easy, expansive, extrovert, friendly, genial, gregarious, informal, open, sociable, sympathetic, unreserved, warm

outgoings costs, expenditure, expenses, outlay, overheads

outing excursion, expedition, jaunt, pleasure trip, spin (Inf.), trip

outlandish alien, barbarous, bizarre, eccentric, exotic, fantastic, far-out (Sl.), foreign, freakish, grotesque, outré, preposterous, queer, strange, unheard-of, weird

outlaw 1. n. bandit, brigand, desperado, fugitive, highwayman, marauder, outcast, pariah, robber 2. v. ban, banish, bar, condemn, disallow, embargo, exclude, forbid, interdict, make illegal, prohibit, proscribe, put a price on (someone's) head

outlay n. cost, disbursement, expenditure, expenses, investment, outgoings, spending

outlet 1. avenue, channel, duct, egress, exit, means of expression, opening, orifice, release, safety valve, vent, way out 2. market, shop, store

outline n. 1. draft, drawing, frame, framework, layout, lineament(s), plan, rough, skeleton, sketch, tracing 2. bare facts, main features, recapitulation, résumé, rough idea, rundown, summary, synopsis, thumbnail sketch 3. configuration, contour, delineation, figure, form, profile, shape, silhouette ~v. 4. adumbrate, delineate, draft, plan, rough out, sketch (in), summarize, trace

outlook 1. angle, attitude, frame of mind, perspective, point of view, slant, standpoint, viewpoint, views 2. expectations, forecast, future, prospect 3. aspect, panorama, prospect, scene, view, vista

outlying backwoods, distant, far-flung, outer, out-of-the-way, peripheral, provincial, remote

outmoded anachronistic, antediluvian, antiquated, antique, archaic, behind the times (Inf.), bygone, dated, démodé, fossilized, obsolescent, obsolete, olden (Archaic), oldfangled, old-fashioned, old-time, out, out of date, out of style, outworn, passé, square (Inf.), superannuated, superseded, unfashionable, unusable

out of date antiquated, archaic, dated, discarded, elapsed, expired, extinct, invalid, lapsed, obsolete, old-fashioned, outmoded, outworn, passé, stale, superannuated, superseded, unfashionable

out-of-the-way 1. distant, far-flung, inaccessible, isolated, lonely, obscure, off the beaten track, outlying, remote, secluded, unfrequented 2. abnormal, curious, exceptional, extraordinary, odd, outlandish, out of the ordinary, peculiar, strange, uncommon, unusual

out of work idle, jobless, laid off, on the dole (Brit.), out of a job, redundant, unemployed

outpouring cascade, debouchment, deluge, effluence, efflux, effusion, emanation, flow, flux, outflow, spate, spurt, stream, torrent

output achievement, manufacture, outturn (Rare), product, production, productivity, yield

put: *output signal.* ~*vb.* **8.** *Computers.* to put out; supply.

outrage ('aut,reɪdʒ) *n.* **1.** a wantonly vicious or cruel act. **2.** a gross violation of decency, morality, honour, etc. **3.** profound indignation, anger, or hurt, caused by such an act. ~*vb.* (*tr.*) **4.** to cause profound indignation, anger, or resentment in. **5.** to offend grossly. **6.** to commit an act of wanton viciousness, cruelty, or indecency on. **7.** a euphemistic word for **rape**¹.

outrageous (aut'reɪdʒəs) *adj.* **1.** being or having the nature of an outrage. **2.** grossly offensive to decency, authority, etc. **3.** violent or unrestrained in behaviour or temperament. **4.** extravagant or immoderate. —**out'rageously** *adv.* —**out'rageousness** *n.*

outrank (,aut'ræŋk) *vb.* (*tr.*) **1.** to be of higher rank than. **2.** to take priority over.

outré *French.* (u'tre) *adj.* deviating from what is usual or proper.

outrider ('aut,raɪdə) *n.* **1.** a person who goes in advance to investigate, discover a way, etc.; scout. **2.** a person who rides in front of or beside a carriage, esp. as an attendant or guard. **3.** *U.S.* a mounted herdsman.

outrigger ('aut,rɪgə) *n.* **1.** a framework for supporting a pontoon outside and parallel to the hull of a boat to provide stability. **2.** a boat equipped with such a framework, esp. one of the canoes of the South Pacific. **3.** any projecting framework attached to a boat, aircraft, building, etc., to act as a support.

outright ('aut,raɪt) *adj.* (*prenominal*) **1.** without qualifications or limitations: *outright ownership.* **2.** complete; total. **3.** straightforward; direct. ~*adv.* **4.** without restrictions. **5.** without reservation or concealment: *ask outright.* **6.** instantly: *he was killed outright.*

outset ('aut,sɛt) *n.* a start; beginning (esp. in **from** (or **at**) **the outset**).

outside *prep.* (,aut'saɪd). **1.** (sometimes foll. by *of*) on or to the exterior of: *outside the house.* **2.** beyond the limits of. **3.** apart from; other than: *no-one knows outside you.* ~*adj.* ('aut,saɪd). **4.** (*prenominal*) situated on the exterior: *an outside lavatory.* **5.** remote; unlikely. **6.** not a member of. **7.** the greatest possible or probable (prices, odds, etc.). ~*adv.* (,aut'saɪd). **8.** outside a specified thing or place; out of doors. **9.** *Sl.* not in prison. ~*n.* ('aut,saɪd). **10.** the external side or surface. **11.** the external appearance or aspect. **12.** (of a pavement, etc.) the side nearest the road or away from a wall. **13.** *Sport.* an outside player, as in football. **14.** (*pl.*) the outer sheets of a ream of paper. **15.** *Canad.* (in the north) the settled parts of Canada. **16. at the outside.** *Inf.* at the most or at the greatest extent: *two days at the outside.*

▷ **Usage.** In careful usage, *outside* and *inside* are preferred to *outside of* and *inside of: she waits outside* (not *outside of*) *the school.*

outside broadcast *n. Radio, television.* a broadcast not made from a studio.

outsider (,aut'saɪdə) *n.* **1.** a person or thing excluded from or not a member of a set, group, etc. **2.** a contestant, esp. a horse, thought unlikely to win in a race. **3.** *Canad.* a person who does not live in the arctic regions.

outsize ('aut,saɪz) *adj.* **1.** Also: **outsized.** very large or larger than normal. ~*n.* **2.** something outsize, such as a garment or person. **3.** (*modifier*) relating to or dealing in outsize clothes: *an outsize shop.*

outskirts ('aut,skɜːts) *pl. n.* (*sometimes sing.*) outlying or bordering areas, districts, etc., as of a city.

outsmart (,aut'smɑːt) *vb.* (*tr.*) *Inf.* to get the better of; outwit.

outspan *S. African.* ~*n.* ('aut,spæn). **1.** an area on a farm kept available for travellers to rest and refresh animals, etc. **2.** the act of unharnessing or unyoking. ~*vb.* ('aut'spæn), **-spanning, -spanned. 3.** to unharness or unyoke (animals).

outspoken (,aut'spəukən) *adj.* **1.** candid or bold in speech. **2.** said or expressed with candour or boldness.

outspread *vb.* (,aut'sprɛd), **-spreading, -spread. 1.** to spread out. ~*adj.* ('aut'sprɛd). **2.** spread or stretched out. **3.** scattered or diffused widely. ~*n.* ('aut,sprɛd). **4.** a spreading out.

outstanding (,aut'stændɪŋ) *adj.* **1.** superior; excellent. **2.** prominent, remarkable, or striking. **3.** unsettled, unpaid, or unresolved. **4.** (of shares, bonds, etc.) issued and sold. **5.** projecting or jutting upwards or outwards.

outstay (,aut'steɪ) *vb.* (*tr.*) **1.** to stay longer than. **2.** to stay too long. **3. outstay one's welcome.** See **overstay** (sense 2).

outstretch (,aut'strɛtʃ) *vb.* (*tr.*) **1.** to extend or expand; stretch out. **2.** to stretch or extend beyond.

outstrip (,aut'strɪp) *vb.* **-stripping, -stripped.** (*tr.*) **1.** to surpass in a sphere of activity, competition, etc. **2.** to be or grow greater than. **3.** to go faster than and leave behind.

outvote (,aut'vəut) *vb.* (*tr.*) to defeat by a majority of votes.

outward ('autwəd) *adj.* **1.** of or relating to what is apparent or superficial. **2.** of or relating to the outside of the body. **3.** belonging or relating to the external, as opposed to the mental, spiritual, or inherent. **4.** of, relating to, or directed towards the outside or exterior. **5. the outward man. a.** *Theol.* the body as opposed to the soul. **b.** *Facetious.* clothing. ~*adv.* **6.** (of a ship) away from port. **7.** Also: **outwards.** towards the outside; away. ~*n.* **8.** the outward part; exterior. —**'outwardly** *adv.* —**'outwardness** *n.* —**'outwards** *adv.*

outweigh (,aut'weɪ) *vb.* (*tr.*) **1.** to prevail over; overcome. **2.** to be more important or significant than. **3.** to be heavier than.

outwit (,aut'wɪt) *vb.* **-witting, -witted.** (*tr.*) to get the better of by cunning or ingenuity.

THESAURUS

outrage *n.* **1.** atrocity, barbarism, enormity, evil, inhumanity **2.** abuse, affront, desecration, indignity, injury, insult, offence, profanation, rape, ravishing, shock, violation, violence **3.** anger, fury, hurt, indignation, resentment, shock, wrath ~*v.* **4.** affront, incense, infuriate, madden, make one's blood boil, offend, scandalize, shock **5.** abuse, defile, desecrate, injure, insult, maltreat, rape, ravage, ravish, violate

outrageous **1.** abominable, atrocious, barbaric, beastly, egregious, flagrant, heinous, horrible, infamous, inhuman, iniquitous, nefarious, scandalous, shocking, unspeakable, villainous, violent, wicked **2.** disgraceful, excessive, exorbitant, extravagant, immoderate, offensive, preposterous, scandalous, shocking, steep (*Inf.*), unreasonable

outright *adj.* **1.** absolute, arrant, complete, consummate, downright, out-and-out, perfect, pure, thorough, thoroughgoing, total, unconditional, undeniable, unmitigated, unqualified, utter, wholesale **2.** definite, direct, flat, straightforward, unequivocal, unqualified ~*adv.* **3.** absolutely, completely, explicitly, openly, overtly, straightforwardly, thoroughly, to the full, without hesitation, without restraint **4.** at once, cleanly, immediately, instantaneously, instantly, on the spot, straight away, there and then, without more ado

outset beginning, commencement, early days, inauguration, inception, kickoff (*Inf.*), onset, opening, start, starting point

outshine be head and shoulders above, be superior to, eclipse, leave *or* put in the shade, outclass, outdo, outstrip, overshadow, surpass, top, transcend, upstage

outside *adj.* **1.** exterior, external, extramural, extraneous, extreme, out, outdoor, outer, outermost, outward, surface **2.** distant, faint, marginal, negligible, remote, slight, slim, small, unlikely ~*n.* **3.** exterior, façade, face, front, skin, surface, topside

outsider alien, foreigner, incomer, interloper, intruder, newcomer, nonmember, odd man out, outlander, stranger

outskirts borders, boundary, edge, environs, faubourgs, periphery, purlieus, suburbia, suburbs, vicinity

outspoken abrupt, blunt, candid, direct, explicit, forthright, frank, free, free-spoken, open, plain-spoken, round, unceremonious, undissembling, unequivocal, unreserved

outspread **1.** *adj.* expanded, extended, fanlike, fanned out, flared, open, opened up, outstretched, unfolded, unfurled, wide-open

2. *v.* expand, extend, fan out, open, open wide, outstretch, spread out, unfold, unfurl

outstanding **1.** celebrated, distinguished, eminent, excellent, exceptional, great, important, impressive, meritorious, pre-eminent, special, superior, superlative, well-known **2.** arresting, conspicuous, eye-catching, marked, memorable, notable, noteworthy, prominent, salient, signal, striking **3.** due, ongoing, open, owing, payable, pending, remaining, uncollected, unpaid, unresolved, unsettled

outward *adj.* apparent, evident, exterior, external, noticeable, observable, obvious, ostensible, outer, outside, perceptible, superficial, surface, visible

outwardly apparently, as far as one can see, externally, officially, on the face of it, on the surface, ostensibly, professedly, seemingly, superficially, to all appearances, to all intents and purposes, to the eye

outweigh cancel (out), compensate for, eclipse, make up for, outbalance, overcome, override, predominate, preponderate, prevail over, take precedence over, tip the scales

outwit cheat, circumvent, deceive, defraud, dupe, get the better of, gull (*Archaic*),

outwork n. ('aʊt,wɜːk). **1.** (often pl.) defences which lie outside main defensive works. **2.** work done away from the factory, etc., by which it has been commissioned. ~vb. (,aʊt'wɜːk), **-working, -worked** or **-wrought.** (tr.) **3.** to work better, harder, etc., than. **4.** to work out to completion. —'**out,worker** n.

ouzel or **ousel** ('uːzəl) n. **1.** Also called: **water ouzel.** other names for **dipper** (sense 2). **2.** an archaic name for the (European) **blackbird.**

ouzo ('uːzəʊ) n. a strong aniseed-flavoured spirit from Greece.

ova ('əʊvə) n. the plural of **ovum.**

oval ('əʊvəl) adj. **1.** having the shape of an ellipse or ellipsoid. ~n. **2.** anything that is oval in shape, such as a sports ground. **3.** Austral. **a.** an Australian Rules ground. **b.** any sports field. —'**ovally** adv. —'**ovalness** or **ovality** (əʊ'vælɪtɪ) n.

ovary ('əʊvərɪ) n., pl. **-ries. 1.** either of the two female reproductive organs, which produce ova and secrete oestrogen hormones. **2.** the corresponding organ in vertebrate and invertebrate animals. **3.** Bot. the hollow basal region of a carpel containing one or more ovules. —**ovarian** (əʊ'vɛərɪən) adj.

ovate ('əʊveɪt) adj. **1.** shaped like an egg. **2.** (esp. of a leaf) shaped like the longitudinal section of an egg, with the broader end at the base. —'**ovately** adv.

ovation (əʊ'veɪʃən) n. **1.** an enthusiastic reception, esp. one of prolonged applause. **2.** a victory procession less glorious than a triumph awarded to a Roman general. —o'**vational** adj.

oven ('ʌvən) n. **1.** an enclosed heated compartment or receptacle for baking or roasting food. **2.** a similar device, usually lined with a refractory material, used for drying substances, firing ceramics, heat-treating, etc. —'**oven-,like** adj.

over ('əʊvə) prep. **1.** directly above; on the top of; via the top or upper surface of: over one's head. **2.** on or to the other side of: over the river. **3.** during; through or throughout (a period of time). **4.** in or throughout all parts of: to travel over England. **5.** throughout the whole extent of: over the racecourse. **6.** above; in preference to. **7.** by the agency of (an instrument of telecommunication): over the radio. **8.** more than: over a century ago. **9.** on the subject of; about: an argument over nothing. **10.** while occupied in: discussing business over golf. **11.** having recovered from the effects of. **12. over and above.** added to; in addition to. ~adv. **13.** in a state, condition, situation, or position that is placed or put over something: to climb over. **14.** (particle) so as to cause to fall: knocking over a policeman. **15.** at or to a point across intervening space, water, etc. **16.** throughout a whole area: the world over. **17.** (particle) from be-

ginning to end, usually cursorily: to read a document over. **18.** throughout a period of time: stay over for this week. **19.** (esp. in signalling and radio) it is now your turn to speak, act, etc. **20.** more than is expected or usual: not over well. **21. over again.** once more. **22. over against. a.** opposite to. **b.** contrasting with. **23. over and over.** (often followed by **again**) repeatedly. **24. over the odds.** in addition, esp. when not expected. ~adj. **25.** (postpositive) finished; no longer in progress. ~adv., adj. **26.** remaining; surplus (often in **left over**). ~n. **27.** Cricket. a set of six balls (eight in Australia) bowled by a bowler from the same end of the pitch.

over- prefix. **1.** excessive or excessively; beyond an agreed or desirable limit: overcharge; overdue. **2.** indicating superior rank: overseer. **3.** indicating location or movement above: overhang. **4.** indicating movement downwards: overthrow.

overage (,əʊvər'eɪdʒ) adj. beyond a specified age.

overall adj. ('əʊvər,ɔːl). **1.** (prenominal) from one end to the other. **2.** (prenominal) including or covering everything: the overall cost. ~adv. (,əʊvər'ɔːl). **3.** in general; on the whole. ~n. ('əʊvər,ɔːl). **4.** Brit. a protective work garment usually worn over ordinary clothes. **5.** (pl.) hard-wearing work trousers with a bib and shoulder-straps or jacket attached.

overarm ('əʊvər,ɑːm) adj. **1.** Sport, esp. cricket. bowled, thrown, or performed with the arm raised above the shoulder. ~adv. **2.** with the arm raised above the shoulder.

overawe (,əʊvər'ɔː) vb. (tr.) to subdue, restrain, or overcome by affecting with a feeling of awe.

overbalance vb. (,əʊvə'bæləns). **1.** to lose or cause to lose balance. **2.** (tr.) another word for **outweigh.** ~n. ('əʊvə,bæləns). **3.** excess of weight, value, etc.

overbear (,əʊvə'bɛə) vb. **-bearing, -bore, -borne. 1.** (tr.) to dominate or overcome. **2.** (tr.) to press or bear down with weight or physical force. **3.** to produce or bear (fruit, etc.) excessively.

overbearing (,əʊvə'bɛərɪŋ) adj. **1.** domineering or dictatorial in manner or action. **2.** of particular or overriding importance or significance. —,**over'bearingly** adv.

overblown (,əʊvə'bləʊn) adj. **1.** overdone or excessive. **2.** bombastic; turgid: overblown prose. **3.** (of flowers) past the stage of full bloom.

overboard ('əʊvə,bɔːd) adv. **1.** from on board a vessel into the water. **2. go overboard.** Inf. **a.** to be extremely enthusiastic. **b.** to go to extremes. **3. throw overboard.** to reject or abandon.

overcast adj. ('əʊvə,kɑːst). **1.** covered over or obscured, esp. by clouds. **2.** Meteorol. (of the sky) cloud-covered. **3.** gloomy or melancholy. **4.** sewn over by overcasting. ~vb. (,əʊvə'kɑːst). **5.** to make or become

overabundance n.	overcapacity n.	overcook vb.	overeager adj.
overact vb.	overcareful adj.	overcostly adj.	overeat vb.
overactive adj.	overcautious adj.	overcritical adj.	overeducate vb.
overaggressive adj.	overcivil adj.	overcrowd vb.	overembellish vb.
overambitious adj.	overcommon adj.	overcurious adj.	overemotional adj.
overanxious adj.	overcompensate vb.	overdecorative vb.	overemphasis n.
overapprehensive adj.	overcomplacency n.	overdependence n.	overemphasize vb.
overassertive adj.	overcomplicate vb.	overdependent adj.	overenthusiasm n.
overbid vb.	overconcern n.	overdetailed adj.	overenthusiastic adj.
overbid n.	overconfident adj.	overdevelop vb.	overexcitable adj.
overbold adj.	overconscientious adj.	overdiligent adj.	overexert vb.
overbook vb.	overconsiderate adj.	overdramatize vb.	overexpand vb.

THESAURUS

make a fool or monkey of, outfox, outjockey, outmanoeuvre, outsmart (Inf.), outthink, put one over on (Inf.), run rings round (Inf.), swindle, take in (Inf.)

outworn abandoned, antiquated, behind the times (Inf.), defunct, discredited, disused, exhausted, hackneyed, obsolete, outdated, outmoded, out of date, overused, rejected, stale, superannuated, threadbare, tired, worn-out

oval adj. egg-shaped, ellipsoidal, elliptical, ovate, oviform, ovoid

ovation acclaim, acclamation, applause, cheering, cheers, clapping, laudation, plaudits, tribute

over adj. **1.** accomplished, ancient history (Inf.), at an end, by, bygone, closed, complet-

ed, concluded, done (with), ended, finished, gone, past, settled, up (Inf.) ~adj./adv. **2.** beyond, extra, in addition, in excess, left over, remaining, superfluous, surplus, unused ~prep. **3.** above, on, on top of, superior to, upon **4.** above, exceeding, in excess of, more than ~adv. **5.** above, aloft, on high, overhead **6. over and above** added to, as well as, besides, in addition to, let alone, not to mention, on top of, plus **7. over and over (again)** ad nauseam, again and again, frequently, often, repeatedly, time and again

overact exaggerate, ham or ham up (Inf.), overdo, overplay

overall 1. adj. all-embracing, blanket, complete, comprehensive, general, global, inclusive, long-range, long-term, total, um-

brella **2.** adv. generally speaking, in general, in (the) large, in the long term, on the whole

overawe abash, alarm, browbeat, cow, daunt, frighten, intimidate, scare, terrify

overbalance capsize, keel over, lose one's balance, lose one's footing, overset, overturn, slip, take a tumble, tip over, topple over, tumble, turn turtle, upset

overbearing arrogant, autocratic, bossy (Inf.), cavalier, despotic, dictatorial, dogmatic, domineering, haughty, high-handed, imperious, lordly, magisterial, officious, oppressive, overweening, peremptory, supercilious, superior, tyrannical

overclouded or gloomy. **6.** to sew (an edge, as of a hem) with long stitches passing successively over the edge. ~*n.* (ˈəʊvəˌkɑːst). **7.** a covering, as of clouds or mist. **8.** *Meteorol.* the state of the sky when it is cloud-covered.

overcharge *vb.* (ˌəʊvəˈtʃɑːdʒ). **1.** to charge too much. **2.** (*tr.*) to fill or load beyond capacity. **3.** *Literary.* another word for **exaggerate**. ~*n.* (ˈəʊvəˌtʃɑːdʒ). **4.** an excessive price or charge. **5.** an excessive load.

overcoat (ˈəʊvəˌkəʊt) *n.* a warm heavy coat worn over the outer clothes in cold weather.

overcome (ˌəʊvəˈkʌm) *vb.* **-coming, -came, -come. 1.** (*tr.*) to get the better of in a conflict. **2.** (*often passive*) to render incapable or powerless by laughter, sorrow, exhaustion, etc. **3.** (*tr.*) to surmount obstacles, objections, etc. **4.** (*intr.*) to be victorious.

overdo (ˌəʊvəˈduː) *vb.* **-doing, -did, -done.** (*tr.*) **1.** to take or carry too far; do to excess. **2.** to exaggerate, overelaborate, or overplay. **3.** to cook or bake too long. **4. overdo it, things,** *etc.* to overtax one's strength, capacity, etc.

overdose *n.* (ˈəʊvəˌdəʊs). **1.** (esp. of drugs) an excessive dose. ~*vb.* (ˌəʊvəˈdəʊs). **2.** (*tr.*) to give an excessive dose to. —ˌover'dosage *n.*

overdraft (ˈəʊvəˌdrɑːft) *n.* **1.** a withdrawal of money in excess of the credit balance on a bank account. **2.** the amount of money withdrawn thus.

overdraw (ˌəʊvəˈdrɔː) *vb.* **-drawing, -drew, -drawn. 1.** to draw on (a bank account) in excess of the credit balance. **2.** (*tr.*) to exaggerate in describing or telling.

overdress *vb.* (ˌəʊvəˈdrɛs). **1.** to dress (oneself or another) too elaborately or finely. ~*n.* (ˈəʊvəˌdrɛs). **2.** a dress that may be worn over a jumper, blouse, etc.

overdrive *n.* (ˈəʊvəˌdraɪv). **1.** a very high gear in a motor vehicle used at high speeds to reduce wear. ~*vb.* (ˌəʊvəˈdraɪv), **-driving, -drove, -driven. 2.** (*tr.*) to drive too hard or too far; overwork or overuse.

overdue (ˌəʊvəˈdjuː) *adj.* past the time specified, required, or preferred for arrival, occurrence, payment, etc.

overestimate *vb.* (ˌəʊvərˈɛstɪˌmeɪt). **1.** (*tr.*) to estimate too highly. ~*n.* (ˌəʊvərˈɛstɪmɪt). **2.** an estimate that is too high. —ˌover,esti'mation *n.*

overflow *vb.* (ˌəʊvəˈfləʊ), **-flowing, -flowed, -flown. 1.** to flow or run over (a limit, brim, etc.). **2.** to fill or be filled beyond capacity so as to spill or run over. **3.** (*intr.*; usually foll. by *with*) to be filled with happiness, tears, etc. **4.** (*tr.*) to spread or cover over; flood or inundate. ~*n.* (ˈəʊvəˌfləʊ). **5.** overflowing matter, esp. liquid. **6.** any outlet that enables surplus liquid to be discharged or drained off. **7.** the amount by which a limit, capacity, etc., is exceeded.

overgrow (ˌəʊvəˈgrəʊ) *vb.* **-growing, -grew, -grown. 1.** (*tr.*) to grow over or across (an area, path, etc.). **2.** (*tr.*) to choke or supplant by a stronger growth. **3.** (*tr.*) to grow too large for. **4.** (*intr.*) to grow beyond normal size. —ˈoverˌgrowth *n.*

overhang *vb.* (ˌəʊvəˈhæŋ), **-hanging, -hung. 1.** to project or extend beyond (a surface, building, etc.). **2.** (*tr.*) to hang or be suspended over. **3.** (*tr.*) to menace, threaten, or dominate. ~*n.* (ˈəʊvəˌhæŋ). **4.** a formation, object, etc., that extends beyond or hangs over something, such as an outcrop of rock overhanging a mountain face. **5.** the amount or extent of projection.

overhaul *vb.* (ˌəʊvəˈhɔːl). (*tr.*) **1.** to examine carefully for faults, necessary repairs, etc. **2.** to make repairs or adjustments to (a car, machine, etc.). **3.** to overtake. ~*n.* (ˈəʊvəˌhɔːl). **4.** a thorough examination and repair.

overhead *adj.* (ˈəʊvəˌhɛd). **1.** situated or operating above head height or some other reference level. **2.** (*prenominal*) inclusive: *the overhead price included meals.* ~*adv.* (ˌəʊvəˈhɛd). **3.** over or above head height, esp. in the sky. ~*n.* (ˈəʊvəˌhɛd). **4. a.** a stroke in racket games played from above head height. **b.** (*as modifier*): *an overhead smash.* **5.** (*modifier*) of, concerned with, or resulting from overheads: *overhead costs.*

overheads (ˈəʊvəˌhɛdz) *pl. n.* business expenses, such as rent, that are not directly attributable to any depart-

overexpenditure *n.*	**overindulgence** *n.*	**overmodest** *adj.*	**oversensitive** *adj.*
overfamiliar *adj.*	**overinfluence** *vb.*	**overparticular** *adj.*	**oversimplify** *vb.*
overfanciful *adj.*	**overinsistent** *adj.*	**overpay** *vb.*	**oversleep** *vb.*
overfeed *vb.*	**overinsure** *vb.*	**overpopulate** *vb.*	**overstock** *vb.*
overfill *vb.*	**overintense** *adj.*	**overpopulation** *n.*	**overstretch** *vb.*
overfish *vb.*	**overladen** *adj.*	**overprice** *vb.*	**overstrict** *adj.*
overfly *vb.*	**overlarge** *adj.*	**overproduce** *vb.*	**overtire** *vb.*
overfond *adj.*	**overlavish** *adj.*	**overproduction** *n.*	**overtop** *vb.*
overfull *adj.*	**overleap** *vb.*	**overprotect** *vb.*	**overtrump** *vb.*
overgenerous *adj.*	**overload** *vb.*	**overproud** *adj.*	**overuse** *vb. n.*
overhasty *adj.*	**overload** *n.*	**overripe** *adj.*	**overvalue** *vb.*
overindulge *vb.*	**overmany** *adj.*	**overscrupulous** *adj.*	**overzealous** *adj.*

THESAURUS

overcast clouded, clouded over, cloudy, darkened, dismal, dreary, dull, grey, hazy, leaden, lowering, murky, sombre, sunless, threatening

overcharge 1. cheat, clip (*Sl.*), diddle (*Inf.*), do (*Sl.*), fleece, rip off (*Sl.*), rook (*Sl.*), short-change, sting (*Inf.*), surcharge **2.** burden, oppress, overburden, overload, overtask, overtax, strain, surfeit **3.** *Literary* embellish, embroider, exaggerate, hyperbolize, lay it on thick (*Inf.*), overstate

overcome **1.** *v.* beat, best, be victorious, come out on top (*Inf.*), conquer, crush, defeat, get the better of, lick (*Inf.*), master, overpower, overthrow, overwhelm, prevail, render incapable (helpless, powerless), rise above, subdue, subjugate, surmount, survive, triumph over, vanquish, weather, worst **2.** *adj.* affected, at a loss for words, bowled over (*Inf.*), overwhelmed, speechless, swept off one's feet, unable to continue, visibly moved

overconfident brash, cocksure, foolhardy, hubristic, overweening, presumptuous, riding for a fall (*Inf.*), uppish (*Brit. inf.*)

overcritical captious, carping, cavilling, fault-finding, hairsplitting, hard to please, hypercritical, nit-picking (*Inf.*), overparticular, pernickety (*Inf.*)

overcrowded choked, congested, crammed full, jam-packed, like the Black

Hole of Calcutta, overloaded, overpopulated, packed (out), swarming

overdo 1. be intemperate, belabour, carry too far, do to death (*Inf.*), exaggerate, gild the lily, go overboard (*Inf.*), go to extremes, lay it on thick (*Inf.*), not know when to stop, overindulge, overplay, overreach, overstate, overuse, overwork, run riot **2. overdo it** bite off more than one can chew, burn the candle at both ends (*Inf.*), drive oneself, fatigue, go too far, have too many irons in the fire, overburden, overload, overtax one's strength, overtire, overwork, strain *or* overstrain oneself, wear oneself out

overdone 1. beyond all bounds, exaggerated, excessive, fulsome, immoderate, inordinate, overelaborate, preposterous, too much, undue, unnecessary **2.** burnt, burnt to a cinder, charred, dried up, overcooked, spoiled

overdue behindhand, behind schedule, behind time, belated, late, long delayed, not before time (*Inf.*), owing, tardy, unpunctual

overeat binge (*Inf.*), eat like a horse (*Inf.*), gorge, gormandize, guzzle, make a pig of oneself (*Inf.*), overindulge, pack away (*Sl.*), pig away (*Sl.*), stuff, stuff oneself

overemphasize belabour, blow up out of all proportion, lay too much stress on, make a big thing of (*Inf.*), make a mountain

out of a molehill (*Inf.*), make something out of nothing, make too much of, overdramatize, overstress

overflow *v.* **1.** bubble (brim, fall, pour, run, slop, well) over, discharge, pour out, run with, shower, spill, spray, surge **2.** cover, deluge, drown, flood, inundate, soak, submerge, swamp ~*n.* **3.** discharge, flash flood, flood, flooding, inundation, overabundance, spill, spilling over, surplus

overflowing abounding, bountiful, brimful, copious, plentiful, profuse, rife, superabundant, swarming, teeming, thronged

overhang *v.* beetle, bulge, cast a shadow, extend, impend, jut, loom, project, protrude, stick out, threaten

overhaul *v.* **1.** check, do up (*Inf.*), examine, inspect, recondition, re-examine, repair, restore, service, survey ~*n.* **2.** check, checkup, examination, going-over (*Inf.*), inspection, reconditioning, service ~*v.* **3.** catch up with, draw level with, get ahead of, overtake, pass

overhead 1. *adv.* above, aloft, atop, in the sky, on high, skyward, up above, upward **2.** *adj.* aerial, overhanging, roof, upper

overheads burden, oncosts, operating cost(s), running cost(s)

ment or product and can therefore be assigned only arbitrarily.

overhear (ˌəʊvəˈhɪə) vb. **-hearing, -heard.** (tr.) to hear (a person, remark, etc.) without the knowledge of the speaker.

overjoy (ˌəʊvəˈdʒɔɪ) vb. (tr.) to give great delight to.

overkill (ˈəʊvəˌkɪl) n. **1.** the capability to deploy more weapons, esp. nuclear weapons, than is necessary to ensure military advantage. **2.** any capacity or treatment that is greater than that required.

overland (ˈəʊvəˌlænd) adj. (prenominal), adv. **1.** over or across land. ~vb. **2.** Austral. to drive (animals) overland. —ˈover,lander n.

overlap vb. (ˌəʊvəˈlæp), **-lapping, -lapped. 1.** (of two things) to extend or lie partly over (each other). **2.** to cover and extend beyond (something). **3.** (intr.) to coincide partly in time, subject, etc. ~n. (ˈəʊvəˌlæp). **4.** a part that overlaps or is overlapped. **5.** the amount, length, etc., overlapping. **6.** Geol. the horizontal extension of the lower beds in a series of rock strata beyond the upper beds.

overlay vb. (ˌəʊvəˈleɪ), **-laying, -laid.** (tr.) **1.** to lay or place over or upon something else. **2.** (often foll. by with) to cover, overspread, or conceal with. **3.** (foll. by with) to cover a surface with an applied decoration: ebony overlaid with silver. **4.** to achieve the correct printing pressure all over (a forme or plate) by adding to the appropriate areas of the packing. ~n. (ˈəʊvəˌleɪ). **5.** something that is laid over something else; covering. **6.** an applied decoration or layer, as of gold leaf. **7.** a transparent sheet giving extra details to a map or diagram over which it is designed to be placed. **8.** Printing. material, such as paper, used to overlay a forme or plate.

overleaf (ˌəʊvəˈliːf) adv. on the other side of the page.

overlook vb. (ˌəʊvəˈlʊk). (tr.) **1.** to fail to notice or take into account. **2.** to disregard deliberately or indulgently. **3.** to afford a view of from above: the house overlooks the bay. **4.** to rise above. **5.** to look at carefully. **6.** to cast the evil eye upon (someone). ~n. (ˈəʊvəˌlʊk). U.S. **7.** a high place affording a view. **8.** an act of overlooking.

overmuch (ˌəʊvəˈmʌtʃ) adv., adj. **1.** too much; very much. ~n. **2.** an excessive amount.

overnight adv. (ˌəʊvəˈnaɪt). **1.** for the duration of the night. **2.** in or as if in the course of one night; suddenly: the situation changed overnight. ~adj. (ˈəʊvəˌnaɪt). (usually prenominal) **3.** done in, occurring in, or lasting the night: an overnight stop. **4.** staying for one night. **5.** for use during a single night. **6.** occurring in or as if in the course of one night; sudden: an overnight victory.

overpass n. (ˈəʊvəˌpɑːs). **1.** another name for **flyover** (sense 1). ~vb. (ˌəʊvəˈpɑːs), **-passing, -passed, -past.** (tr.) Now rare. **1.** to pass over, through, or across. **2.** to exceed. **3.** to go beyond. **4.** to ignore.

overplay (ˌəʊvəˈpleɪ) vb. **1.** (tr.) to exaggerate the importance of. **2.** to act or behave in an exaggerated man-

ner. **3. overplay one's hand.** to overestimate the worth or strength of one's position.

overpower (ˌəʊvəˈpaʊə) vb. (tr.) **1.** to conquer or subdue by superior force. **2.** to have such a strong effect on as to make helpless or ineffective. **3.** to supply with more power than necessary. —ˌoverˈpowering adj.

overprint vb. (ˌəʊvəˈprɪnt). **1.** (tr.) to print (additional matter or another colour) on a sheet of paper. ~n. (ˈəʊvəˌprɪnt). **2.** additional matter or another colour printed onto a previously printed sheet. **3.** additional matter applied to a finished postage stamp by printing, stamping, etc.

overrate (ˌəʊvəˈreɪt) vb. (tr.) to assess too highly.

overreach (ˌəʊvəˈriːtʃ) vb. **1.** (tr.) to defeat or thwart (oneself) by attempting to do or gain too much. **2.** (tr.) to aim for but miss by going too far. **3.** to get the better of (a person) by trickery. **4.** (tr.) to reach beyond or over. **5.** (intr.) to reach or go too far. **6.** (intr.) (of a horse) to strike the back of a forefoot with the edge of the opposite hind foot.

overreact (ˌəʊvərɪˈækt) vb. (intr.) to react excessively to something. —ˌoverreˈaction n.

override (ˌəʊvəˈraɪd) vb. **-riding, -rode, -ridden.** (tr.) **1.** to set aside or disregard with superior authority or power. **2.** to supersede or annul. **3.** to dominate or vanquish by or as if by trampling down. **4.** to extend or pass over, esp. to overlap. **5.** to ride (a horse, etc.) too hard. **6.** to ride over.

overriding adj. taking precedence.

overrule (ˌəʊvəˈruːl) vb. (tr.) **1.** to disallow the arguments of (a person) by the use of authority. **2.** to rule or decide against (an argument, decision, etc.). **3.** to prevail over, dominate, or influence. **4.** to exercise rule over.

overrun vb. (ˌəʊvəˈrʌn), **-running, -ran, -run. 1.** (tr.) to swarm or spread over rapidly. **2.** to run over (something); overflow. **3.** to extend or run beyond a limit. **4.** (intr.) (of an engine) to run with a closed throttle at a speed dictated by that of the vehicle it drives. **5.** (tr.) to print (a book, journal, etc.) in a greater quantity than ordered. **6.** (tr.) Printing. to transfer (set type) from one column, line, or page, to another. **7.** (tr.) Arch. to run faster than. ~n. (ˈəʊvəˌrʌn). **8.** the act or an instance of overrunning. **9.** the amount or extent of overrunning. **10.** the number of copies of a publication in excess of the quantity ordered.

overseas adv. (ˌəʊvəˈsiːz). **1.** beyond the sea; abroad. ~adj. (ˈəʊvəˈsiːz). **2.** of, to, in, from, or situated in countries beyond the sea. **3.** Also: **oversea** (ˌəʊvəˈsiː). of or relating to passage over the sea. ~n. (ˌəʊvəˈsiːz). **4.** (functioning as sing.) Inf. a foreign country or foreign countries collectively.

oversee (ˌəʊvəˈsiː) vb. **-seeing, -saw, -seen.** (tr.) **1.** to watch over and direct; supervise. **2.** to watch secretly or accidentally. **3.** Arch. to scrutinize; inspect. —ˈover,seer n.

THESAURUS

overindulge be immoderate or intemperate, drink or eat too much, have a binge (Inf.), live it up (Inf.), make a pig of oneself (Inf.), overdo it

overindulgence excess, immoderation, intemperance, overeating, surfeit

overjoyed delighted, deliriously happy, elated, euphoric, happy as a lark, in raptures, joyful, jubilant, on cloud nine (Inf.), only too happy, over the moon (Inf.), rapturous, thrilled, tickled pink, transported

overlay 1. v. adorn, blanket, cover, inlay, laminate, ornament, overspread, superimpose, veneer **2.** n. adornment, appliqué, covering, decoration, ornamentation, veneer

overload burden, encumber, oppress, overburden, overcharge, overtax, saddle (with), strain, weigh down

overlook 1. disregard, fail to notice, forget, ignore, leave out of consideration, leave undone, miss, neglect, omit, pass, slight, slip up on **2.** blink at, condone, disregard, excuse, forgive, let bygones be bygones, let one off with, let pass, let ride, make allowances for, pardon, turn a blind eye to, wink at **3.** afford a view of, command a view of, front on to,

give upon, have a view of, look over or out on

overly exceedingly, excessively, immoderately, inordinately, over, too, unduly, very much

overpower beat, conquer, crush, defeat, get the upper hand over, immobilize, knock out, master, overcome, overthrow, overwhelm, quell, subdue, subjugate, vanquish

overpowering compelling, extreme, forceful, invincible, irrefutable, irresistible, nauseating, overwhelming, powerful, sickening, strong, suffocating, telling, unbearable, uncontrollable

overrate assess too highly, exaggerate, make too much of, overestimate, overpraise, overprize, oversell, overvalue, rate too highly, think or expect too much of, think too highly of

overreach 1. overreach oneself be hoist with one's own petard, bite off more than one can chew, defeat one's own ends, go too far, have one's schemes rebound (backfire, boomerang) on one, try to be too clever **2.** cheat, circumvent, deceive, defraud, dupe, gull (Archaic), outsmart (Inf.), outwit, swindle, trick, victimize

override annul, cancel, countermand, disregard, ignore, nullify, outweigh, overrule, quash, reverse, ride roughshod over, set aside, supersede, take no account of, trample underfoot, upset, vanquish

overriding cardinal, compelling, determining, dominant, final, major, number one, overruling, paramount, pivotal, predominant, prevailing, primary, prime, ruling, supreme, ultimate

overrule 1. alter, annul, cancel, countermand, disallow, invalidate, make null and void, outvote, override, overturn, recall, repeal, rescind, reverse, revoke, rule against, set aside, veto **2.** bend to one's will, control, direct, dominate, govern, influence, prevail over, sway

overrun 1. cut to pieces, invade, massacre, occupy, overwhelm, put to flight, rout, swamp **2.** choke, infest, inundate, overflow, overgrow, permeate, ravage, spread like wildfire, spread over, surge over, swarm over **3.** exceed, go beyond, overshoot, run over or on

overseer boss (Inf.), chief, foreman, gaffer (Inf.), manager, master, super (Inf.), superintendent, superior, supervisor

overshadow (ˌəʊvəˈʃædəʊ) *vb.* (*tr.*) **1.** to render insignificant or less important in comparison. **2.** to cast a shadow or gloom over.

overshoe (ˈəʊvəˌʃuː) *n.* a protective shoe worn over an ordinary shoe.

overshoot (ˌəʊvəˈʃuːt) *vb.* **-shooting, -shot. 1.** to shoot or go beyond (a mark or target). **2.** (of an aircraft) to fly or taxi too far along a runway. **3.** (*tr.*) to pass swiftly over or down over, as water over a wheel.

overshot (ˈəʊvəˌʃɒt) *adj.* **1.** having or designating an upper jaw that projects beyond the lower jaw. **2.** (of a water wheel) driven by a flow of water that passes over the wheel.

oversight (ˈəʊvəˌsaɪt) *n.* **1.** an omission or mistake, esp. one made through failure to notice something. **2.** supervision.

overspend (ˌəʊvəˈspɛnd) *vb.* **-spending, -spent. 1.** to spend in excess of (one's desires or what one can afford). **2.** (*tr.; usually passive*) to wear out; exhaust.

overspill *n.* (ˈəʊvəˌspɪl). **1. a.** something that spills over or is in excess. **b.** (*as modifier*): *overspill population.* ~*vb.* (ˌəʊvəˈspɪl), **-spilling, -spilt** *or* **-spilled. 2.** (*intr.*) to overflow.

overstate (ˌəʊvəˈsteɪt) *vb.* (*tr.*) to state too strongly; exaggerate or overemphasize. —ˌover'statement *n.*

overstay (ˌəʊvəˈsteɪ) *vb.* (*tr.*) **1.** to stay beyond the time, limit, or duration of. **2. overstay** *or* **outstay one's welcome.** to stay (at a party etc.), longer than pleases the host.

overstep (ˌəʊvəˈstɛp) *vb.* **-stepping, -stepped.** (*tr.*) to go beyond (a certain or proper limit).

oversubscribe (ˌəʊvəsəbˈskraɪb) *vb.* (*tr.; often passive*) to subscribe or apply for in excess of available supply.

overt (ˈəʊvɜːt) *adj.* **1.** open to view; observable. **2.** *Law.* open; deliberate.

overtake (ˌəʊvəˈteɪk) *vb.* **-taking, -took, -taken. 1.** *Chiefly Brit.* to move past (another vehicle or person) travelling in the same direction. **2.** (*tr.*) to pass or do better than, after catching up with. **3.** (*tr.*) to come upon suddenly or unexpectedly: *night overtook him.* **4.** (*tr.*) to catch up with; draw level with.

overtax (ˌəʊvəˈtæks) *vb.* (*tr.*) **1.** to tax too heavily. **2.** to impose too great a strain on.

overthrow *vb.* (ˌəʊvəˈθrəʊ), **-throwing, -threw, -thrown. 1.** (*tr.*) to effect the downfall or destruction of (a ruler, institution, etc.), esp. by force. **2.** (*tr.*) to throw or turn over. **3.** to throw (something, esp. a ball) too far. ~*n.* (ˈəʊvəˌθrəʊ). **4.** downfall; destruction. **5.** *Cricket.* **a.** a ball thrown back too far by a fielder. **b.** a run scored because of this.

overtime *n.* (ˈəʊvəˌtaɪm). **1. a.** work at a regular job done in addition to regular working hours. **b.** (*as modifier*): *overtime pay.* **2.** the rate of pay established for such work. **3.** time in excess of a set period. **4.** *Sport, U.S.* extra time. ~*adv.* (ˈəʊvəˌtaɪm). **5.** beyond the regular or stipulated time. ~*vb.* (ˌəʊvəˈtaɪm). **6.** (*tr.*) to exceed the required time for (a photographic exposure, etc.).

overtone (ˈəʊvəˌtəʊn) *n.* **1.** (*often pl.*) additional meaning or nuance: *overtones of despair.* **2.** *Music, acoustics.* any of the tones, with the exception of the fundamental, that constitute a musical sound and contribute to its quality.

overture (ˈəʊvəˌtjʊə) *n.* **1.** *Music.* **a.** a piece of orchestral music that is played at the beginning of an opera or oratorio, often containing the main musical themes of the work. **b.** a one-movement orchestral piece, usually having a descriptive or evocative title. **2.** (*often pl.*) a proposal, act, or gesture initiating a relationship, negotiation, etc. **3.** something that introduces what follows. ~*vb.* (*tr.*) **4.** to make or present an overture to. **5.** to introduce with an overture.

overturn *vb.* (ˌəʊvəˈtɜːn). **1.** to turn or cause to turn from an upright or normal position. **2.** (*tr.*) to overthrow or destroy. ~*n.* (ˈəʊvəˌtɜːn). **3.** the act of overturning or the state of being overturned.

overweening (ˌəʊvəˈwiːnɪŋ) *adj.* **1.** (of a person) excessively arrogant or presumptuous. **2.** (of opinions, appetites, etc.) excessive; immoderate. —ˌover'weening-ness *n.*

overweight *adj.* (ˌəʊvəˈweɪt). **1.** weighing more than is usual, allowed, or healthy. ~*n.* (ˈəʊvəˌweɪt). **2.** extra or excess weight. ~*vb.* (ˌəʊvəˈweɪt). (*tr.*) **3.** to give too much emphasis or consideration to. **4.** to add too much weight to. **5.** to weigh down.

overwhelm (ˌəʊvəˈwɛlm) *vb.* (*tr.*) **1.** to overpower the thoughts, emotions, or senses of. **2.** to overcome with irresistible force. **3.** to cover over or bury completely. **4.** to weigh or rest upon overpoweringly. —ˌover'whelm-ing *adj.*

overwork *vb.* (ˌəʊvəˈwɜːk). (*mainly tr.*) **1.** (*also intr.*) to work too hard or too long. **2.** to use too much: *to overwork an excuse.* **3.** to decorate the surface of. ~*n.* (ˈəʊvəˌwɜːk). **4.** excessive or excessively tiring work.

overwrought (ˌəʊvəˈrɔːt) *adj.* **1.** full of nervous tension; agitated. **2.** too elaborate; fussy: *an overwrought style.* **3.** (*often postpositive* and foll. by *with*) with the surface decorated or adorned.

ovi- *or* **ovo-** *combining form.* egg or ovum: *oviform; ovoviviparous.*

oviduct (ˈɒvɪˌdʌkt, ˈəʊ-) *n.* the tube through which ova are conveyed from an ovary. Also called (in mammals):

THESAURUS

overshadow 1. dominate, dwarf, eclipse, excel, leave *or* put in the shade, outshine, outweigh, render insignificant by comparison, rise above, steal the limelight from, surpass, take precedence over, throw into the shade, tower above **2.** adumbrate, becloud, bedim, cloud, darken, dim, obfuscate, obscure, veil **3.** blight, cast a gloom upon, mar, ruin, spoil, take the edge off, take the pleasure *or* enjoyment out of, temper

oversight 1. blunder, carelessness, delinquency, error, fault, inattention, lapse, laxity, mistake, neglect, omission, slip **2.** administration, care, charge, control, custody, direction, handling, inspection, keeping, management, superintendence, supervision, surveillance

overt apparent, manifest, observable, obvious, open, patent, plain, public, unconcealed, undisguised, visible

overtake 1. catch up with, do better than, draw level with, get past, leave behind, outdistance, outdo, outstrip, overhaul, pass **2.** befall, catch unprepared, come upon, engulf, happen, hit, overwhelm, strike, take by surprise

overthrow *v.* **1.** abolish, beat, bring down, conquer, crush, defeat, depose, dethrone, do away with, master, oust, overcome, overpower, overwhelm, subdue, subjugate, topple, unseat, vanquish **2.** bring to

ruin, demolish, destroy, knock down, level, overturn, put an end to, raze, ruin, subvert, upend, upset ~*n.* **3.** defeat, deposition, destruction, dethronement, discomfiture, disestablishment, displacement, dispossession, downfall, end, fall, ousting, prostration, rout, ruin, subjugation, subversion, suppression, undoing, unseating

overtone association, connotation, flavour, hint, implication, innuendo, intimation, nuance, sense, suggestion, undercurrent

overture 1. *Often plural* advance, approach, conciliatory move, invitation, offer, opening move, proposal, proposition, signal, tender **2.** *Music* introduction, opening, prelude

overturn 1. capsize, keel over, knock over *or* down, overbalance, reverse, spill, tip over, topple, tumble, upend, upset, upturn **2.** abolish, annul, bring down, countermand, depose, destroy, invalidate, overthrow, repeal, rescind, reverse, set aside, unseat

overweening 1. arrogant, cavalier, cocksure, cocky, conceited, egotistical, haughty, high and mighty (*Inf.*), high-handed, insolent, lordly, opinionated, pompous, presumptuous, proud, self-confident, supercilious, uppish (*Brit. inf.*), vain, vainglorious **2.** blown up out of all proportion, excessive, extravagant, immoderate

overweight *adj.* ample, bulky, chubby,

chunky, corpulent, fat, fleshy, gross, heavy, hefty, huge, massive, obese, on the plump side, outsize, plump, podgy, portly, stout, tubby (*Inf.*), well-padded (*Inf.*), well-upholstered (*Inf.*)

overwhelm 1. bury, crush, deluge, engulf, flood, inundate, snow under, submerge, swamp **2.** bowl over (*Inf.*), confuse, devastate, knock (someone) for six (*Inf.*), overcome, overpower, prostrate, render speechless, stagger **3.** crush, cut to pieces, destroy, massacre, overpower, overrun, rout

overwhelming breathtaking, crushing, devastating, invincible, irresistible, overpowering, shattering, stunning, towering, uncontrollable, vast, vastly superior

overwork be a slave-driver *or* hard taskmaster to, burden, burn the midnight oil, drive into the ground, exhaust, exploit, fatigue, oppress, overstrain, overtax, overuse, prostrate, strain, sweat (*Inf.*), wear out, weary, work one's fingers to the bone

overwrought 1. agitated, beside oneself, distracted, excited, frantic, in a state (tizzy, twitter) (*Inf.*), keyed up, on edge, overexcited, overworked, stirred, strung up (*Inf.*), tense, uptight (*Inf.*), worked up (*Inf.*), wound up (*Inf.*) **2.** baroque, busy, contrived, florid, flowery, fussy, overdone, overelaborate, overembellished, overornate, rococo

Fallopian tube. —**oviducal** (ˌɒvɪˈdjuːkəl, ˌəʊ-) or ˌovi-ˈductal adj.

oviform (ˈəʊvɪˌfɔːm) adj. Biol. shaped like an egg.

oviparous (əʊˈvɪpərəs) adj. (of fishes, reptiles, birds, etc.) producing eggs that hatch outside the body of the mother. Cf. **viviparous** (sense 1). —**oviparity** (ˌəʊvɪ-ˈpærɪtɪ) n. —o**ʹviparously** adv.

ovoid (ˈəʊvɔɪd) adj. 1. egg-shaped. ~n. 2. something that is ovoid.

ovulate (ˈɒvjʊˌleɪt) vb. (intr.) to produce or discharge eggs from an ovary. —ˌo**vuʹlation** n.

ovule (ˈɒvjuːl) n. 1. a small body in seed-bearing plants that contains the egg cell and develops into the seed after fertilization. 2. Zool. an immature ovum. —**ʹovular** adj.

ovum (ˈəʊvəm) n., pl. **ova** (ˈəʊvə). an unfertilized female gamete; egg cell.

owe (əʊ) vb. (mainly tr.) 1. to be under an obligation to pay (someone) to the amount of. 2. (intr.) to be in debt: he still owes for his house. 3. (often foll. by to) to have as a result (of). 4. to feel the need or obligation to do, give, etc. 5. to hold or maintain in the mind or heart (esp. in **owe a grudge**).

owing (ˈəʊɪŋ) adj. 1. (postpositive) owed; due. 2. **owing to.** (prep.) because of or on account of.

▷ **Usage.** See at **due.**

owl (aʊl) n. 1. a nocturnal bird of prey having large front-facing eyes, a small hooked bill, soft feathers, and a short neck. 2. any of various breeds of owl-like fancy domestic pigeon. 3. a person who looks or behaves like an owl, esp. in having a solemn manner. —**ʹowlish** adj.

own (əʊn) determiner. (preceded by a possessive) 1. a. (intensifier): John's own idea. b. (as pronoun): I'll use my own. 2. on behalf of oneself or in relation to oneself: he is his own worst enemy. 3. **come into one's own. a.** to fulfil one's potential. **b.** to receive what is due to one. 4. **get one's own back.** Inf. to have revenge. 5. **hold one's own.** to maintain one's situation or position, esp. in spite of opposition or difficulty. 6. **on one's own. a.** without help. **b.** by oneself; alone. ~vb. 7. (tr.) to have as one's possession. 8. (when intr., often foll. by up, to, or up to) to confess or admit; acknowledge. 9. (tr.; takes a clause as object) Now rare. to concede: I own that you are right. —**ʹowner** n. —**ʹowner**ˌ**ship** n.

ox (ɒks) n., pl. **oxen.** 1. an adult castrated male of any domesticated species of cattle used for draught work and meat. 2. any bovine mammal, esp. any of the domestic cattle.

oxalic acid (ɒkˈsælɪk) n. a colourless poisonous crystalline acid found in many plants: used as a bleach and a cleansing agent for metals. Formula: $(COOH)_2$.

oxbow (ˈɒksˌbəʊ) n. 1. a U-shaped piece of wood fitted under and around the neck of a harnessed ox and attached to the yoke. 2. Also called: **oxbow lake.** a small curved lake lying on the flood plain of a river and constituting the remnant of a former meander.

Oxbridge (ˈɒksˌbrɪdʒ) n. a. the British universities of Oxford and Cambridge, esp. considered as ancient and prestigious academic institutions, bastions of privilege and superiority, etc. b. (as modifier): Oxbridge arrogance.

oxen (ˈɒksən) n. the plural of **ox.**

oxeye (ˈɒksˌaɪ) n. 1. a Eurasian composite plant having daisy-like flower heads with yellow rays and dark centres. 2. any of various North American plants having daisy-like flowers. 3. **oxeye daisy.** a type of hardy perennial chrysanthemum.

Oxfam (ˈɒksˌfæm) n. acronym for Oxford Committee for Famine Relief.

oxidation (ˌɒksɪˈdeɪʃən) n. a. the act or process of oxidizing. b. (as modifier): an oxidation state. —ˌoxiˈdational adj. —ˈoxiˌdative adj. —ˈoxiˌdate vb.

oxide (ˈɒksaɪd) n. 1. any compound of oxygen with another element. 2. any organic compound in which an oxygen atom is bound to two alkyl groups; an ether.

oxidize or **-ise** (ˈɒksɪˌdaɪz) vb. 1. to undergo or cause to undergo a chemical reaction with oxygen, as in formation of an oxide. 2. to form a layer of metal oxide, as in rusting. 3. to lose or cause to lose hydrogen atoms. 4. to undergo a decrease in the number of electrons. —ˌoxidiˈzation or **-iʹsation** n.

Oxon. (ˈɒksɒn) abbrev. for: 1. (in degree titles, etc.) of Oxford. 2. Oxfordshire.

Oxonian (ɒkˈsəʊnɪən) adj. 1. of or relating to Oxford or Oxford University. ~n. 2. a member of Oxford University. 3. an inhabitant or native of Oxford.

oxtail (ˈɒksˌteɪl) n. the skinned tail of an ox, used esp. in soups and stews.

oxtongue (ˈɒksˌtʌŋ) n. 1. any of various Eurasian composite plants having oblong bristly leaves and clusters of dandelion-like flowers. 2. any of various other plants having bristly tongue-shaped leaves. 3. the tongue of an ox, braised or boiled as food.

oxy-¹ combining form. denoting something sharp; acute: oxytone.

oxy-² combining form. containing or using oxygen: oxyacetylene.

oxyacetylene (ˌɒksɪəˈsɛtɪˌliːn) n. a. a mixture of oxygen and acetylene; used in a blowpipe for cutting or welding metals at high temperatures. b. (as modifier): an oxyacetylene burner.

oxygen (ˈɒksɪdʒən) n. a. a colourless odourless highly reactive gaseous element: the most abundant element in the earth's crust. Symbol: O; atomic no.: 8; atomic wt.: 15.9994. b. (as modifier): an oxygen mask. —**oxygenic** (ˌɒksɪˈdʒɛnɪk) or **oxygenous** (ɒkˈsɪdʒɪnəs) adj.

oxygenate (ˈɒksɪdʒɪˌneɪt), **oxygenize** or **-ise** vb. to enrich or be enriched with oxygen: to oxygenate blood. —ˌoxygenˈation n. —ˌoxygenˈizable or **-ʹisable** adj. —**ʹoxygeˌnizer** or **-iser** n.

oxyhaemoglobin (ˌɒksɪˌhiːməʊˈgləʊbɪn) n. Biochem. the bright red product formed when oxygen from the lungs combines with haemoglobin in the blood.

oxymoron (ˌɒksɪˈmɔːrɒn) n., pl. **-mora** (-ˈmɔːrə). Rhetoric. an epigrammatic effect, by which contradictory terms are used in conjunction: beautiful tyrant.

oyster (ˈɔɪstə) n. 1. a. an edible marine bivalve mollusc having a rough irregularly shaped shell and occurring on the sea bed, mostly in coastal waters. b. (as modifier): oyster farm; oyster knife. 2. any of various similar and related molluscs, such as the pearl oyster and the saddle oyster. 3. the oyster-shaped piece of dark meat in the hollow of the pelvic bone of a fowl. 4. something from which advantage, delight, profit, etc., may be derived: the world is his oyster. 5. Inf. a very uncommunicative person. ~vb. 6. (intr.) to dredge for, gather, or raise oysters.

oystercatcher (ˈɔɪstəˌkætʃə) n. a shore bird having a black or black-and-white plumage and a long stout laterally compressed red bill.

oz or **oz.** abbrev. for ounce.

ozone (ˈəʊzəʊn, əʊˈzəʊn) n. 1. a colourless gas with a chlorine-like odour, formed by an electric discharge in oxygen: a strong oxidizing agent, used in bleaching, sterilizing water, purifying air, etc. Formula: O_3. 2. Inf. clean bracing air, as found at the seaside. —**ozonic** (əʊ-ˈzɒnɪk) or **ozonous** adj.

owe be beholden to, be in arrears, be in debt, be obligated or indebted, be under an obligation to

owing adj. due, outstanding, overdue, owed, payable, unpaid, unsettled

own adj. 1. individual, particular, personal, private 2. **on one's own** alone, by oneself, by one's own efforts, independently, isolated, left to one's own devices, off one's own bat, on one's tod (Brit. sl.), singly, (standing) on one's own two feet, unaided, unassisted 3. **hold one's own** compete, keep going, keep one's end up, keep one's head above water, maintain one's position ~v. 4. be in possession of, be responsible for, enjoy, have, hold, keep, possess, retain 5. **own up (to)** admit, come clean (about) (Inf.), confess, make a clean breast of, tell the truth (about) 6. acknowledge, admit, allow, allow to be valid, avow, concede, confess, disclose, go along with (Inf.), grant, recognize

owner holder, landlord, lord, master, mistress, possessor, proprietor, proprietress, proprietrix

ownership dominion, possession, proprietary rights, proprietorship, right of possession, title

P

p or **P** (piː) n., pl. **p's, P's,** or **Ps.** 1. the 16th letter of the English alphabet. 2. a speech sound represented by this letter. 3. **mind one's p's and q's.** to be careful to use polite or suitable language.

p symbol for: 1. (in Britain) penny or pence. 2. Music. piano: an instruction to play quietly. 3. Physics. pico-. 4. Physics. **a.** momentum. **b.** proton. **c.** pressure.

P symbol for: 1. Chem. phosphorus. 2. Physics. **a.** pressure. **b.** power. **c.** parity. **d.** poise. 3. (on road signs) parking. 4. Chess. pawn. 5. (of a medicine or drug) available only from a chemist's shop, but not requiring a prescription to obtain it.

p. abbrev. for: 1. (pl. **pp.**) page. 2. part. 3. participle. 4. past. 5. per. 6. Currency. a. peseta. **b.** peso. 7. pint. 8. pipe. 9. population. 10. post 11. pro

pa (paː) n. an informal word for **father.**

Pa the chemical symbol for protactinium.

P.A. abbrev. for: 1. personal assistant. 2. Mil. Post Adjutant. 3. power of attorney. 4. press agent. 5. Press Association. 6. private account. 7. public-address system. 8. publicity agent. 9. Publishers Association. 10. purchasing agent.

p.a. abbrev. for per annum.

pabulum ('pæbjʊləm) n. Rare. 1. food. 2. food for thought.

pace[1] (peɪs) n. 1. **a.** a single step in walking. **b.** the distance covered by a step. 2. a measure of length equal to the average length of a stride, approximately 3 feet. 3. speed of movement, esp. of walking or running. 4. rate or style of proceeding at some activity: to live at a fast pace. 5. manner or action of stepping, walking, etc.; gait. 6. any of the manners in which a horse or other quadruped walks or runs. 7. a manner of moving, sometimes developed in the horse, in which the two legs on the same side are moved at the same time. 8. **put (someone) through his paces.** to test the ability of (a person). 9. **keep pace with.** to proceed at the same speed as. 10. **set the pace.** to determine the rate at which a group runs or walks or proceeds at some other activity. ~vb. 11. (tr.) to set or determine the pace for, as in a race. 12. (often foll. by about, up and down, etc.) to walk with regular slow or fast paces, as in boredom, agitation, etc.: to pace the room. 13. (tr.; often foll. by out) to measure by paces: to pace out the distance. 14. (intr.) to walk with slow regular strides. 15. (intr.) (of a horse) to move at the pace (the specially developed gait).

pace[2] ('peɪsɪ; Latin 'paːkɛ) prep. with due deference to: used to acknowledge politely someone who disagrees.

pacemaker ('peɪs,meɪkə) n. 1. a person, horse, vehicle, etc., used in a race or speed trial to set the pace. 2. a person, organization, etc., regarded as being the leader in a particular activity. 3. Also called: **cardiac pacemaker.** a small area of specialized tissue within the wall of the heart whose spontaneous electrical activity initiates and controls the heartbeat. 4. Also called: **artificial pacemaker.** an electronic device to assume the functions of the natural cardiac pacemaker.

pachyderm ('pækɪ,dɜːm) n. any very large thick-skinned mammal, such as an elephant, rhinoceros, or hippopotamus. —,pachy'dermatous adj.

pacific (pə'sɪfɪk) adj. 1. tending or conducive to peace; conciliatory. 2. not aggressive. 3. free from conflict; peaceful. —pa'cifically adv.

Pacific (pə'sɪfɪk) n. 1. **the.** short for **Pacific Ocean,** the world's largest and deepest ocean. ~adj. 2. of or relating to the Pacific Ocean or its islands.

pacifier ('pæsɪ,faɪə) n. 1. a person or thing that pacifies. 2. U.S. a baby's dummy or teething ring.

pacifism ('pæsɪ,fɪzəm) n. 1. the belief that violence of any kind is unjustifiable and that one should not participate in war, etc. 2. the belief that international disputes can be settled by arbitration rather than war. —'pacifist n., adj.

pacify ('pæsɪ,faɪ) vb. **-fying, -fied.** (tr.) 1. to calm the anger or agitation of; mollify. 2. to restore to peace or order. —'pacifiable adj. —,pacifi'cation n.

pack[1] (pæk) n. 1. **a.** a bundle or load, esp. one carried on the back. **b.** (as modifier): a pack animal. 2. a collected amount of anything. 3. a complete set of similar things, esp. a set of 52 playing cards. 4. a group of animals of the same kind, esp. hunting animals: a pack of hounds. 5. any group or band that associates together, esp. for criminal purposes. 6. any group or set regarded dismissively: a pack of fools; a pack of lies. 7. Rugby. the forwards of a team. 8. the basic organizational unit of Cub Scouts and Brownies. 9. a small package, carton, or container, used to retail commodities, esp. foodstuffs, cigarettes, etc. 10. short for **pack ice.** 11. the quantity of something, such as food, packaged for preservation. 12. Med. a sheet or blanket, either damp or dry, for wrapping about the body, esp. for its soothing effect. 13. Austral. & N.Z. another name for **rucksack.** 14. Also called: **face pack.** a cream treatment that cleanses and tones the skin. 15. a parachute folded and ready for use. 16. **go to the pack.** Austral. & N.Z. inf. to fall into a worse state or condition. 17. Computers. another name for **deck** (sense 5). ~vb. 18. to place or arrange (articles) in (a container), such as clothes in a suitcase. 19. (tr.) to roll up into a bundle. 20. (when passive, often foll. by out) to press tightly together; cram: the audience packed into the foyer; the hall was packed out. 21. to form (snow, ice, etc.) into a hard compact mass or (of snow, etc.) to become compacted. 22. (tr.) to press in or cover tightly. 23. (tr.) to load (a horse, donkey, etc.) with a burden. 24. (often foll. by off or away) to send away or go away, esp. hastily. 25. (tr.) to seal (a joint) by inserting a layer of compressible material between the faces. 26. (tr.) Med. to treat with a pack. 27. (tr.) Sl. to be capable of inflicting (a blow, etc.): he packs a mean punch. 28. (tr.) U.S. inf. to carry or wear habitually: he packs a gun. 29. (tr.; often foll. by in, into, to, etc.) U.S. & N.Z. to carry (goods, etc.), esp. on the back. 30. **send packing.** Inf. to dismiss peremptorily. ~See also **pack in, pack up.** —'packable adj.

pack[2] (pæk) vb. (tr.) to fill (a legislative body, committee, etc.) with one's own supporters: to pack a jury.

package ('pækɪdʒ) n. 1. any wrapped or boxed object or group of objects. 2. **a.** a proposition, offer, or thing for sale in which separate items are offered together as a unit. **b.** (as modifier): a package holiday; a package deal. 3. the act or process of packing or packaging. 4. Computers. a set of programs designed for a specific type of problem. 5. the usual U.S. word for **packet** (sense 1). ~vb. (tr.) 6. to wrap in or put into a package. 7. to design and produce a package for (retail goods). 8. to group (separate items) together as a single unit. —'packager n.

▰ THESAURUS ▰

pace n. 1. gait, measure, step, stride, tread, walk 2. clip (Inf.), lick (Inf.), momentum, motion, movement, progress, rate, speed, tempo, time, velocity ~v. 3. march, patrol, pound, stride, walk back and forth, walk up and down 4. count, determine, mark out, measure, step

pacific 1. appeasing, conciliatory, diplomatic, irenic, pacificatory, peacemaking, placatory, propitiatory 2. dovelike, dovish, friendly, gentle, mild, nonbelligerent, nonviolent, pacifist, peaceable, peace-loving 3.

at peace, calm, halcyon, peaceful, placid, quiet, serene, smooth, still, tranquil, unruffled

pacifist conchie (Inf.), conscientious objector, dove, passive resister, peace lover, peacemonger, peacenik (Inf.), satyagrahi

pack n. 1. back pack, bale, bundle, burden, fardel (Archaic), kit, kitbag, knapsack, load, package, packet, parcel, rucksack, truss 2. assemblage, band, bunch, collection, company, crew, crowd, deck, drove, flock, gang, group, herd, lot, mob, set, troop ~v. 3. batch,

bundle, burden, load, package, packet, store, stow 4. charge, compact, compress, cram, crowd, fill, jam, mob, press, ram, stuff, tamp, throng, wedge 5. With off bundle out, dismiss, hustle out, send someone about his business, send away, send packing (Inf.)

package n. 1. box, carton, container, packet, parcel 2. amalgamation, combination, entity, unit, whole ~v. 3. batch, box,

packet ('pækıt) *n.* **1.** a small or medium-sized container of cardboard, paper, etc., often together with its contents: *a packet of biscuits.* Usual U.S. word: **package. 2.** a small package; parcel. **3.** Also called: **packet boat.** a boat that transports mail, passengers, goods, etc., on a fixed short route. **4.** *Sl.* a large sum of money: *to cost a packet.* ~*vb.* **5.** (*tr.*) to wrap up in a packet or as a packet.

packhorse ('pæk,hɔːs) *n.* a horse used to transport goods, equipment, etc.

pack ice *n.* a large area of floating ice, consisting of pieces that have become massed together.

pack in *vb.* (*tr., adv.*) *Brit. & N.Z. inf.* to stop doing (something) (often in **pack it in**).

packing ('pækıŋ) *n.* **1. a.** material used to cushion packed goods. **b.** (*as modifier*): *a packing needle.* **2.** the packaging of foodstuffs. **3.** any substance or material used to make joints watertight or gastight.

packsaddle ('pæk,sædəl) *n.* a saddle hung with packs, equipment, etc., used on a pack animal.

packthread ('pæk,θrɛd) *n.* a strong twine for sewing or tying up packages.

pack up *vb.* (*adv.*) **1.** to put (things) away in a proper or suitable place. **2.** *Inf.* to give up (an attempt) or stop doing (something). **3.** (*intr.*) (of an engine, etc.) to fail to operate; break down.

pact (pækt) *n.* an agreement or compact between two or more parties, nations, etc.

pad[1] (pæd) *n.* **1.** a thick piece of soft material used to make something comfortable, give it shape, or protect it. **2.** Also called: **stamp pad, ink pad.** a block of firm absorbent material soaked with ink for transferring to a rubber stamp. **3.** Also called: **notepad, writing pad.** a number of sheets of paper fastened together along one edge. **4.** a flat piece of stiff material used to back a piece of blotting paper. **5. a.** the fleshy cushion-like underpart of the foot of a cat, dog, etc. **b.** any of the parts constituting such a structure. **6.** any of various level surfaces or flat-topped structures, such as a launch pad. **7.** the large flat floating leaf of the waterlily. **8.** *Sl.* a person's residence. ~*vb.* **padding, padded.** (*tr.*) **9.** to line, stuff, or fill out with soft material, esp. in order to protect or shape. **10.** (often foll. by *out*) to inflate with irrelevant or false information: *to pad out a story.*

pad[2] (pæd) *vb.* **padding, padded.** **1.** (*intr.*; often foll. by *along, up,* etc.) to walk with a soft or muffled tread. **2.** (when *intr.*, often foll. by *around*) to travel (a route, etc.) on foot, esp. at a slow pace; tramp: *to pad around the country.* ~*n.* **3.** a dull soft sound, esp. of footsteps.

padded cell *n.* a room, esp. one in a mental hospital, with padded surfaces in which violent inmates are placed.

padding ('pædıŋ) *n.* **1.** any soft material used to pad clothes, etc. **2.** superfluous material put into a speech or written work to pad it out; waffle. **3.** inflated or false entries in a financial account, esp. an expense account.

paddle[1] ('pædəl) *n.* **1.** a short light oar with a flat blade at one or both ends, used without a rowlock. **2.** Also called: **float.** a blade of a water wheel or paddle wheel. **3.** a period of paddling: *to go for a paddle upstream.* **4. a.** a paddle wheel used to propel a boat. **b.** (*as modifier*): *a paddle steamer.* **5.** any of various instruments shaped like a paddle and used for beating, mixing, etc. **6.** a table-tennis bat. **7.** the flattened limb of a seal, turtle, etc., specialized for swimming. ~*vb.* **8.** to propel (a ca-

noe, etc.) with a paddle. **9. paddle one's own canoe. a.** to be self-sufficient. **b.** to mind one's own business. **10.** (*tr.*) to stir or mix with or as if with a paddle. **11.** to row (a boat) steadily, but not at full pressure. **12.** (*intr.*) to swim with short rapid strokes, like a dog. **13.** *U.S. inf.* to spank. —'**paddler** *n.*

paddle[2] ('pædəl) *vb.* (*mainly intr.*) **1.** to walk or play barefoot in shallow water, mud, etc. **2.** to dabble the fingers, hands, or feet in water. **3.** to walk unsteadily, like a baby. **4.** (*tr.*) *Arch.* to fondle with the fingers. ~*n.* **5.** the act of paddling in water. —'**paddler** *n.*

paddle wheel *n.* a large wheel fitted with paddles, turned by an engine to propel a vessel.

paddock ('pædək) *n.* **1.** a small enclosed field, usually near a house or stable. **2.** (in horse racing) the enclosure in which horses are paraded and mounted before a race. **3.** *Austral. & N.Z.* any area of fenced land.

paddy[1] ('pædı) *n., pl.* -**dies.** **1.** Also called: **paddy field.** a field planted with rice. **2.** rice as a growing crop or when harvested but not yet milled.

paddy[2] ('pædı) *n., pl.* -**dies.** *Brit. inf.* a fit of temper.

padlock ('pæd,lɒk) *n.* **1.** a detachable lock having a hinged or sliding shackle, which can be used to secure a door, lid, etc., by passing the shackle through rings or staples. ~*vb.* **2.** (*tr.*) to fasten as with a padlock.

padre ('pɑːdrı) *n. Inf.* (*sometimes cap.*) **1.** father: used to address or refer to a priest. **2.** a chaplain to the armed forces.

paean *or U.S.* (*sometimes*) **pean** ('piːən) *n.* **1.** a hymn sung in ancient Greece in thanksgiving to a deity. **2.** any song of praise. **3.** enthusiastic praise: *the film received a paean from the critics.*

paediatrician *or U.S.* **pediatrician** (,piːdɪə'trɪʃən) *n.* a medical practitioner who specializes in paediatrics.

paediatrics *or U.S.* **pediatrics** (,piːdɪ'ætrɪks) *n.* the branch of medical science concerned with children and their diseases. —,**paedi'atric** *or U.S.* ,**pedi'atric** *adj.*

paedo-, pedo- *or before a vowel* **paed-, ped-** *combining form.* indicating a child or children: *paedophilia.*

paedophilia (,piːdəʊ'fɪlɪə) *n.* the condition of being sexually attracted to children. —**paedophile** ('piːdəʊ,faɪl) *or* ,**paedo'philiac** *n., adj.*

paella (paɪ'ɛlə) *n., pl.* -**las** (-ləz). **1.** a Spanish dish made from rice, shellfish, chicken, and vegetables. **2.** the pan in which a paella is cooked.

pagan ('peɪgən) *n.* **1.** a member of a group professing any religion other than Christianity, Judaism, or Islam. **2.** a person without any religion; heathen. ~*adj.* **3.** of or relating to pagans. **4.** heathen; irreligious. —'**pagandom** *n.* —'**paganish** *adj.* —'**paganism** *n.*

page[1] (peɪdʒ) *n.* **1.** one side of one of the leaves of a book, newspaper, etc. or the written or printed matter it bears. **2.** such a leaf considered as a unit. **3.** an episode, phase, or period: *a glorious page in the revolution.* ~*vb.* **4.** (*tr.*) another word for **paginate.**

page[2] (peɪdʒ) *n.* **1.** a boy employed to run errands, carry messages, etc., for the guests in a hotel, club, etc. **2.** a youth in attendance at official functions or ceremonies, esp. weddings. **3.** *Medieval history.* **a.** a boy in training for knighthood in personal attendance on a knight. **b.** a youth in the personal service of a person of rank. ~*vb.* (*tr.*) **4.** to call out the name of a person, esp. by a loudspeaker system, so as to give him a message. **5.** to act as a page to or attend as a page.

THESAURUS

pack, packet, parcel (up), wrap, wrap up

packed brimful, chock-a-block, chock-full, congested, cram-full, crammed, crowded, filled, full, hoatching (*Scot.*), jammed, jam-packed, loaded *or* full to the gunwales, overflowing, overloaded, packed like sardines, seething, swarming

packet 1. bag, carton, container, package, parcel, poke (*Dialect*), wrapper, wrapping **2.** *Sl.* a bob or two (*Brit. inf.*), bomb (*Brit. sl.*), bundle (*Sl.*), fortune, king's ransom (*Inf.*), lot(s), mint, pile (*Inf.*), pot(s) (*Inf.*), pretty penny (*Inf.*), tidy sum (*Inf.*)

pack in 1. attract, cram, draw, fill to capacity, squeeze in **2.** *Brit. inf.* cease, chuck (*Inf.*), desist, give up *or* over, jack in, leave off, stop

pack up 1. put away, store, tidy up **2.** *Inf.*

call it a day (*Inf.*), finish, give up, pack in (*Brit. inf.*) **3.** break down, conk out (*Inf.*), fail, give out, stall, stop

pact agreement, alliance, arrangement, bargain, bond, compact, concord, concordat, contract, convention, covenant, deal, league, protocol, treaty, understanding

pad *n.* **1.** buffer, cushion, protection, stiffening, stuffing, wad **2.** block, jotter, notepad, tablet, writing pad **3.** foot, paw, sole **4.** *Sl.* apartment, flat, hang-out (*Inf.*), home, place, quarters, room ~*v.* **5.** cushion, fill, line, pack, protect, shape, stuff **6.** *Often with* out amplify, augment, eke, elaborate, fill out, flesh out, inflate, lengthen, protract, spin out, stretch

padding 1. filling, packing, stuffing, wadding **2.** hot air (*Inf.*), prolixity, verbiage, verbosity, waffle (*Inf.*), wordiness

paddle[1] **1.** *n.* oar, scull, sweep **2.** *v.* oar, propel, pull, row, scull

paddle[2] dabble, plash, slop, splash (about), stir, wade

pagan 1. *n.* Gentile, heathen, idolater, infidel, polytheist, unbeliever **2.** *adj.* Gentile, heathen, heathenish, idolatrous, infidel, irreligious, polytheistic

page[1] *n.* **1.** folio, leaf, sheet, side **2.** chapter, episode, epoch, era, event, incident, period, phase, point, stage, time ~*v.* **3.** foliate, number, paginate

page[2] **1.** *n.* attendant, bellboy (*U.S.*), footboy, pageboy, servant, squire **2.** *v.* announce, call, call out, preconize, seek, send for, summon

pageant ('pædʒənt) n. 1. an elaborate colourful display portraying scenes from history, etc. 2. any magnificent or showy display, procession, etc.

pageantry ('pædʒəntrɪ) n., pl. **-ries.** 1. spectacular display or ceremony. 2. Arch. pageants collectively.

pageboy ('peɪdʒ,bɔɪ) n. 1. a smooth medium-length hair style with the ends of the hair curled under. 2. a less common word for **page².**

paginate ('pædʒɪ,neɪt) vb. (tr.) to number the pages of (a book, manuscript, etc.) in sequence. —,**pagi'nation** n.

pagoda (pə'gəʊdə) n. an Indian or Far Eastern temple, esp. a tower, usually pyramidal and having many storeys.

paid (peɪd) vb. 1. the past tense or past participle of **pay¹.** 2. **put paid to.** Chiefly Brit. to end or destroy: breaking his leg put paid to his hopes of running in the Olympics.

pail (peɪl) n. 1. a bucket, esp. one made of wood or metal. 2. Also called: **pailful.** the quantity that fills a pail.

pain (peɪn) n. 1. the sensation of acute physical hurt or discomfort caused by injury, illness, etc. 2. emotional suffering or mental distress. 3. **on pain of.** subject to the penalty of. 4. Also called: **pain in the neck.** Inf. a person or thing that is a nuisance. ~vb. (tr.) 5. to cause (a person) hurt, grief, anxiety, etc. 6. Inf. to annoy; irritate. —'**painless** adj.

pained (peɪnd) adj. having or expressing pain or distress, esp. mental or emotional distress.

painful ('peɪnfʊl) adj. 1. causing pain; distressing: a painful duty. 2. affected with pain. 3. tedious or difficult. 4. Inf. extremely bad. —'**painfully** adv. —'**painfulness** n.

painkiller ('peɪn,kɪlə) n. 1. an analgesic drug or agent. 2. anything that relieves pain.

pains (peɪnz) pl. n. 1. care or trouble (esp. in **take pains, be at pains to**). 2. labour pains.

painstaking ('peɪnz,teɪkɪŋ) adj. extremely careful, esp. as to fine detail. —'**pains,takingly** adv. —'**pains-,takingness** n.

paint (peɪnt) n. 1. a substance used for decorating or protecting a surface, esp. a mixture consisting of a solid pigment suspended in a liquid that dries to form a hard coating. 2. a dry film of paint on a surface. 3. Inf. face make-up, such as rouge. 4. short for **greasepaint.** ~vb. 5. to make (a picture) of (a figure, landscape, etc.) with paint applied to a surface such as canvas. 6. to coat (a surface, etc.) with paint, as in decorating. 7. (tr.) to apply (liquid, etc.) onto (a surface): she painted the cut with antiseptic. 8. (tr.) to apply make-up onto (the face, lips, etc.). 9. (tr.) to describe vividly in words. 10. **paint the town red.** Inf. to celebrate uninhibitedly. —'**painty** adj.

paintbrush ('peɪnt,brʌʃ) n. a brush used to apply paint.

painted lady n. a migratory butterfly with pale brownish-red mottled wings.

painter¹ ('peɪntə) n. 1. a person who paints surfaces as a trade. 2. an artist who paints pictures. —'**painterly** adj.

painter² ('peɪntə) n. a line attached to the bow of a boat

for tying it up.

painting ('peɪntɪŋ) n. 1. the art of applying paints to canvas, etc. 2. a picture made in this way. 3. the act of applying paint to a surface.

pair (pɛə) n., pl. **pairs** or inf. **pair.** 1. two identical or similar things matched for use together: a pair of socks. 2. two persons, animals, things, etc., used or grouped together: a pair of horses; a pair of scoundrels. 3. an object considered to be two identical or similar things joined together: a pair of trousers. 4. two people joined in love or marriage. 5. a male and a female animal of the same species kept for breeding purposes. 6. Parliament. **a.** two opposed members who both agree not to vote on a specified motion. **b.** the agreement so made. 7. two playing cards of the same rank or denomination. 8. one member of a matching pair: I can't find the pair to this glove. ~vb. 9. (often foll. by off) to arrange or fall into groups of twos. 10. to group or be grouped in matching pairs. 11. to join or be joined in marriage; mate or couple. 12. (when tr., usually passive) Parliament. to form or cause to form a pair.

▷ **Usage.** Like other collective nouns, pair takes a singular or a plural verb according to whether it is seen as a unit or as a collection of two things: the pair of cuff links was gratefully received; that pair (the two of them) are on very good terms.

paisley ('peɪzlɪ) n. 1. a pattern of small curving shapes with intricate detailing. 2. a soft fine wool fabric traditionally printed with this pattern. 3. a shawl made of this fabric, popular in the late 19th century. 4. (modifier) of or decorated with this pattern: a paisley scarf.

pajamas (pə'dʒɑːməz) pl. n. the U.S. spelling of **pyjamas.**

Paki ('pækɪ) n. Brit. sl. derog. a Pakistani immigrant residing in Britain.

Pakistani (,pɑːkɪ'stɑːnɪ) adj. 1. of or relating to Pakistan, a country in the Indian subcontinent. ~n. 2. a native or inhabitant of Pakistan.

pal (pæl) Inf. ~n. 1. a close friend; comrade. ~vb. **palling, palled.** 2. (intr.; usually foll. by with) to associate as friends.

palace ('pælɪs) n. (cap. when part of a name) 1. the official residence of a reigning monarch. 2. the official residence of various high-ranking people, as of an archbishop. 3. a large and richly furnished building resembling a royal palace.

paladin ('pælədɪn) n. 1. one of the legendary twelve peers of Charlemagne's court. 2. a knightly champion.

palaeo-, before a vowel **palae-** or esp. U.S. **paleo-, pale-** combining form. old, ancient, or prehistoric: palaeography.

Palaeocene ('pælɪəʊ,siːn) adj. 1. of, denoting, or formed in the first epoch of the Tertiary period. ~n. 2. **the.** the Palaeocene epoch or rock series.

palaeography (,pælɪ'ɒgrəfɪ) n. 1. the study of the handwritings of the past, and often the manuscripts, etc., so that they may be dated, read, etc. 2. a handwriting of the past. —**palae'ographer** n. —**palaeographic** (,pælɪəʊ'græfɪk) or ,**palaeo'graphical** adj.

Palaeolithic (,pælɪəʊ'lɪθɪk) n. 1. the period of the

pageant display, extravaganza, parade, procession, ritual, show, spectacle, tableau

pageantry display, drama, extravagance, glamour, glitter, grandeur, magnificence, parade, pomp, show, showiness, spectacle, splash (Inf.), splendour, state, theatricality

pain n. 1. ache, cramp, discomfort, hurt, irritation, pang, smarting, soreness, spasm, suffering, tenderness, throb, throe (Rare), trouble, twinge 2. affliction, agony, anguish, bitterness, distress, grief, heartache, misery, suffering, torment, torture, tribulation, woe, wretchedness 3. Inf. aggravation, annoyance, bore, bother, drag (Sl.), headache (Inf.), irritation, nuisance, pain in the neck (Inf.), pest, vexation ~v. 4. ail, chafe, discomfort, harm, hurt, inflame, injure, smart, sting, throb 5. afflict, aggrieve, agonize, cut to the quick, disquiet, distress, grieve, hurt, sadden, torment, torture, vex, worry, wound 6. Inf. annoy, exasperate, gall, harass, irritate, rile, vex

pained aggrieved, anguished, distressed,

hurt, injured, miffed (Inf.), offended, reproachful, stung, unhappy, upset, worried, wounded

painful 1. afflictive, disagreeable, distasteful, distressing, grievous, saddening, unpleasant 2. aching, agonizing, excruciating, harrowing, hurting, inflamed, raw, smarting, sore, tender, throbbing 3. arduous, difficult, hard, laborious, severe, tedious, troublesome, trying, vexatious 4. Inf. awful, dire, dreadful, excruciating, extremely bad, terrible

painfully alarmingly, clearly, deplorably, distressingly, dreadfully, excessively, markedly, sadly, unfortunately, woefully

painkiller anaesthetic, analgesic, anodyne, drug, palliative, remedy, sedative

painless easy, effortless, fast, no trouble, pain-free, quick, simple, trouble-free

pains 1. assiduousness, bother, care, diligence, effort, industry, labour, special attention, trouble 2. birth-pangs, childbirth, contractions, labour

painstaking assiduous, careful, consci-

entious, diligent, earnest, exacting, hardworking, industrious, meticulous, persevering, punctilious, scrupulous, sedulous, strenuous, thorough, thoroughgoing

paint n. 1. colour, colouring, dye, emulsion, pigment, stain, tint 2. Inf. cosmetics, face (Inf.), greasepaint, make-up, maquillage, war paint (Inf.) ~v. 3. catch a likeness, delineate, depict, draw, figure, picture, portray, represent, sketch 4. apply, coat, colour, cover, daub, decorate, slap on (Inf.) 5. bring to life, capture, conjure up a vision, depict, describe, evoke, make one see, portray, put graphically, recount, tell vividly 6. **paint the town red** Inf. celebrate, go on a binge (Inf.), go on a spree, go on the town, live it up (Inf.), make merry, make whoopee (Inf.), revel

pair 1. n. brace, combination, couple, doublet, duo, match, matched set, span, twins, two of a kind, twosome, yoke 2. v. bracket, couple, join, marry, match, match up, mate, pair off, put together, team, twin, wed, yoke

emergence of primitive man and the manufacture of un-polished chipped stone tools, about 2.5 million to 3 million years ago. ~*adj.* **2.** (*sometimes not cap.*) of or relating to this period.

palaeontology (ˌpælɪɒnˈtɒlədʒɪ) *n.* the study of fossils to determine the structure and evolution of extinct animals and plants and the age and conditions of deposition of the rock strata in which they are found. —**palaeontological** (ˌpælɪˌɒntəˈlɒdʒɪkəl) *adj.* —ˌpalaeonˈtologist *n.*

Palaeozoic (ˌpælɪəʊˈzəʊɪk) *adj.* **1.** of, denoting, or relating to an era of geological time that began with the Cambrian period and lasted until the end of the Permian period. ~*n.* **2. the.** the Palaeozoic era.

palanquin *or* **palankeen** (ˌpælənˈkiːn) *n.* a covered litter, formerly used in the Orient, carried on the shoulders of four men.

palatable (ˈpælətəbəl) *adj.* pleasant, acceptable, or satisfactory. —ˌpalataˈbility *or* ˈpalatableness *n.* —ˈpalatably *adv.*

palatal (ˈpælətəl) *adj.* **1.** Also: **palatine.** of or relating to the palate. **2.** *Phonetics.* of, relating to, or denoting a speech sound articulated with the blade of the tongue touching the hard palate. ~*n.* **3.** Also called: **palatine.** the bony plate that forms the palate. **4.** *Phonetics.* a palatal speech sound, such as (j). —ˈpalatally *adv.*

palate (ˈpælɪt) *n.* **1.** the roof of the mouth, separating the oral and nasal cavities. See **hard palate, soft palate.** **2.** the sense of taste: *she had no palate for the wine.* **3.** relish or enjoyment.

palatial (pəˈleɪʃəl) *adj.* of, resembling, or suitable for a palace; sumptuous. —**paˈlatially** *adv.*

palatine[1] (ˈpælətaɪn) *adj.* **1.** (of an individual) possessing royal prerogatives in a territory. **2.** of or relating to a count palatine, county palatine, palatinate, or palatine. **3.** of or relating to a palace. ~*n.* **4.** *Feudal history.* the lord of a palatinate. **5.** any of various important officials at the late Roman, Merovingian, or Carolingian courts.

palatine[2] (ˈpælətaɪn) *adj.* **1.** of the palate. ~*n.* **2.** either of two bones forming the hard palate.

palaver (pəˈlɑːvə) *n.* **1.** tedious or time-consuming business, esp. when of a formal nature: *all the palaver of filling in forms.* **2.** confused talk and activity; hubbub. **3.** (often used humorously) a conference. **4.** *Now rare.* talk intended to flatter or persuade. ~*vb.* **5.** (*intr.*) (often used humorously) to have a conference. **6.** (*intr.*) to talk confusedly. **7.** (*tr.*) to flatter or cajole.

pale[1] (peɪl) *adj.* **1.** lacking brightness or colour: *pale morning light.* **2.** (of a colour) whitish. **3.** dim or wan: *the pale stars.* **4.** feeble: *a pale effort.* ~*vb.* **5.** to make or become pale or paler; blanch. **6.** (*intr.*; often foll. by *before*) to lose superiority (in comparison to): *her beauty paled before that of her hostess.* —ˈpalely *adv.* —ˈpaleness *n.* —ˈpalish *adj.*

pale[2] (peɪl) *n.* **1.** a wooden post or strip used as an upright member in a fence. **2.** an enclosing barrier, esp. a fence made of pales. **3.** an area enclosed by a pale. **4.** *Heraldry.* a vertical stripe, usually in the centre of a shield. **5. beyond the pale.** outside the limits of social convention.

paleface (ˈpeɪlˌfeɪs) *n.* a derogatory term for a White person, said to have been used by North American Indians.

paleo- *or before a vowel* **pale-** *combining form.* variants (esp. U.S.) of **palaeo-**.

Palestinian (ˌpælɪˈstɪnɪən) *adj.* **1.** of or relating to Palestine, a former country in the Middle East. ~*n.* **2.** a native or inhabitant of this area. **3.** a descendant of an inhabitant of this area, displaced when Israel became a state.

palette *or* **pallet** (ˈpælɪt) *n.* **1.** a flat piece of wood, plastic, etc., used by artists as a surface on which to mix their paints. **2.** the range of colours characteristic of a particular artist, painting, or school of painting: *a restricted palette.*

palette knife *n.* a spatula with a thin flexible blade used in painting and cookery.

palfrey (ˈpɔːlfrɪ) *n. Arch.* a light saddle horse, esp. ridden by women.

palindrome (ˈpælɪnˌdrəʊm) *n.* a word or phrase the letters of which, when taken in reverse order, read the same: *able was I ere I saw Elba.* —**palindromic** (ˌpælɪnˈdrɒmɪk) *adj.*

paling (ˈpeɪlɪŋ) *n.* **1.** a fence made of pales. **2.** pales collectively. **3.** a single pale. **4.** the act of erecting pales.

palisade (ˌpælɪˈseɪd) *n.* **1.** a strong fence made of stakes driven into the ground, esp. for defence. **2.** one of the stakes used in such a fence. ~*vb.* **3.** (*tr.*) to enclose with a palisade.

pall[1] (pɔːl) *n.* **1.** a cloth covering, usually black, spread over a coffin or tomb. **2.** a coffin, esp. during the funeral ceremony. **3.** a dark heavy covering; shroud: *the clouds formed a pall over the sky.* **4.** a depressing or oppressive atmosphere: *her bereavement cast a pall on the party.* **5.** *Heraldry.* a Y-shaped bearing. **6.** *Christianity.* a small square linen cloth with which the chalice is covered at the Eucharist. ~*vb.* **7.** (*tr.*) to cover or depress with a pall.

pall[2] (pɔːl) *vb.* **1.** (*intr.*; often foll. by *on*) to become boring, insipid, or tiresome (to): *history classes palled on me.* **2.** to cloy or satiate, or become cloyed or satiated.

palladium (pəˈleɪdɪəm) *n.* a ductile malleable silvery-white element of the platinum metal group: used as a catalyst and, alloyed with gold, in jewellery, etc. Symbol: Pd; atomic no.: 46; atomic wt.: 106.4.

pallbearer (ˈpɔːlˌbeərə) *n.* a person who carries or escorts the coffin at a funeral.

pallet[1] (ˈpælɪt) *n.* a straw-filled mattress or bed.

pallet[2] (ˈpælɪt) *n.* **1.** an instrument with a handle and a flat, sometimes flexible, blade used by potters for shaping. **2.** a portable platform for storing and moving goods. **3.** *Horology.* the locking lever that engages and disengages to give impulses to the balance. **4.** a variant spelling of **palette** (sense 1). **5.** *Music.* a flap valve that opens to admit air to the wind chest of an organ.

palliasse *or* **paillasse** (ˈpælɪˌæs, ˌpælɪˈæs) *n.* a straw-filled mattress; pallet.

palliate (ˈpælɪˌeɪt) *vb.* (*tr.*) **1.** to lessen the severity of (pain, disease, etc.) without curing; alleviate. **2.** to cause (an offence, etc.) to seem less serious; extenuate. —ˌpalliˈation *n.* —ˈpalliˌator *n.*

palliative (ˈpælɪətɪv) *adj.* **1.** relieving without curing. ~*n.* **2.** something that palliates, such as a sedative drug. —ˈpalliatively *adv.*

pallid (ˈpælɪd) *adj.* lacking colour, brightness, or vigour: *a pallid complexion; a pallid performance.* —ˈpallidly *adv.* —ˈpallidness *or* palˈlidity *n.*

pall-mall (ˈpælˈmæl) *n. Obs.* **1.** a game in which a ball is driven by a mallet along an alley and through an iron ring. **2.** the alley itself.

pallor (ˈpælə) *n.* a pale condition, esp. when unnatural: *fear gave his face a deathly pallor.*

pally (ˈpælɪ) *adj.* **-lier, -liest.** *Inf.* on friendly terms.

palm[1] (pɑːm) *n.* **1.** the inner part of the hand from the wrist to the base of the fingers. **2.** a linear measure based on the breadth or length of a hand, equal to three to four inches (7.5 to 10 centimetres) or seven to ten inches (17.5 to 25 centimetres) respectively. **3.** the part of a glove that covers the palm. **4. a.** one side of the blade of an oar. **b.** the face of the fluke of an anchor. **5.** a flattened part of the antlers of certain deer. **6. in the palm of one's hand.** at one's mercy or command. ~*vb.* (*tr.*) **7.** to conceal in or about the hand, as in sleight-of-hand tricks, etc. ~See also **palm off.** —**palmar** (ˈpælmə) *adj.*

palm[2] (pɑːm) *n.* **1.** any treelike plant of a tropical and subtropical family having a straight unbranched trunk crowned with large pinnate or palmate leaves. **2.** a leaf or branch of any of these trees, a symbol of victory, success, etc. **3.** merit or victory. —**palmaceous** (pælˈmeɪʃəs) *adj.*

THESAURUS

palatable 1. appetizing, delectable, delicious, luscious, mouthwatering, savoury, tasty, toothsome 2. acceptable, agreeable, attractive, enjoyable, fair, pleasant, satisfactory

palate 1. appetite, heart, stomach, taste 2.

appreciation, enjoyment, gusto, liking, relish, zest

palatial de luxe, grand, grandiose, illustrious, imposing, luxurious, magnificent, majestic, opulent, plush (*Inf.*), regal, spacious, splendid, stately, sumptuous

pale *adj.* 1. anaemic, ashen, ashy, bleached,

bloodless, colourless, faded, light, pallid, pasty, sallow, wan, washed-out, white, whitish 2. dim, faint, feeble, inadequate, poor, thin, weak ~*v.* 3. become pale, blanch, go white, lose colour, whiten 4. decrease, dim, diminish, dull, fade, grow dull, lessen, lose lustre

pall *v.* become dull *or* tedious, bore, cloy,

palmate ('pælmeɪt, -mɪt) *or* **palmated** *adj.* **1.** shaped like an open hand: *palmate antlers.* **2.** *Bot.* having five lobes that spread out from a common point: *palmate leaves.* **3.** (of most water birds) having three toes connected by a web.

palmetto (pæl'mɛtəʊ) *n., pl.* **-tos** *or* **-toes.** any of several small chiefly tropical palms with fan-shaped leaves.

palmistry ('pɑːmɪstrɪ) *n.* the process or art of telling fortunes, etc., by the configuration of lines and bumps on a person's hand. Also called: **chiromancy.** —'palmist *n.*

palm off *vb.* (*tr., adv.,* often foll. by *on*) **1.** to offer, sell or spend fraudulently: *to palm off a counterfeit coin.* **2.** to divert in order to be rid of: *I palmed the unwelcome visitor off on John.*

palm oil *n.* an oil obtained from the fruit of certain palms, used as an edible fat and in soap, etc.

Palm Sunday *n.* the Sunday before Easter commemorating Christ's triumphal entry into Jerusalem.

palmy ('pɑːmɪ) *adj.* **palmier, palmiest.** **1.** prosperous, flourishing, or luxurious: *a palmy life.* **2.** covered with, relating to, or resembling palms.

palomino (ˌpælə'miːnəʊ) *n., pl.* **-nos.** a golden horse with a white mane and tail.

palpable ('pælpəbᵊl) *adj.* **1.** (*usually prenominal*) easily perceived by the senses or the mind; obvious: *a palpable lie.* **2.** capable of being touched; tangible. —ˌpalpa'bil-ity *n.* —'palpably *adv.*

palpate ('pælpeɪt) *vb.* (*tr.*) *Med.* to examine (an area of the body) by the sense of touch. —pal'pation *n.*

palpitate ('pælpɪˌteɪt) *vb.* (*intr.*) **1.** (of the heart) to beat rapidly. **2.** to flutter or tremble. —'palpitant *adj.* —ˌpalpi'tation *n.*

palsy ('pɔːlzɪ) *n., pl.* **-sies.** **1.** *Pathol.* paralysis, esp. of a specified type: *cerebral palsy.* ~*vb.* **-sying, -sied.** (*tr.*) **2.** to paralyse. —'palsied *adj.*

paltry ('pɔːltrɪ) *adj.* **-trier, -triest.** **1.** insignificant; meagre. **2.** worthless or petty. —'paltrily *adv.* —'paltri-ness *n.*

pampas ('pæmpəz) *n.* (*often functioning as pl.*) **a.** the extensive grassy plains of temperate South America, esp. in Argentina. **b.** (*as modifier*): *pampas dwellers.* —**pampean** ('pæmpɪən, pæm'piːən) *adj.*

pampas grass ('pæmpəs, -pɑːz) *n.* any of various large South American grasses, widely cultivated for their large feathery silver-coloured flower branches.

pamper ('pæmpə) *vb.* (*tr.*) **1.** to treat with affectionate and usually excessive indulgence; coddle; spoil. **2.** *Arch.* to feed to excess. —'pamperer *n.*

pamphlet ('pæmflɪt) *n.* **1.** a brief publication generally having a paper cover; booklet. **2.** a brief treatise, often on a subject of current interest, in pamphlet form.

pamphleteer (ˌpæmflɪ'tɪə) *n.* **1.** a person who writes or issues pamphlets. ~*vb.* **2.** (*intr.*) to write or issue pamphlets.

pan¹ (pæn) *n.* **1. a.** a wide metal vessel used in cooking. **b.** (*in combination*): *saucepan.* **2.** Also called: **panful.** the amount such a vessel will hold. **3.** any of various similar vessels used in industry, etc. **4.** a dish used esp. by gold prospectors for separating gold from gravel by washing and agitating. **5.** either of the two dishlike receptacles on a balance. **6.** Also called: **lavatory pan.** *Brit.* the bowl of a lavatory. **7. a.** a natural or artificial depression in the ground where salt can be obtained by the evaporation of brine. **b.** a natural depression containing water or mud. **8.** a small cavity containing priming powder in the locks of old guns. **9.** a hard substratum of soil. ~*vb.* **panning, panned.** **10.** (when *tr.,* often foll. by *off* or *out*) to wash (gravel) in a pan to separate particles of (valuable minerals) from it. **11.** (*intr.;* often foll. by *out*) (of gravel, etc.) to yield valuable minerals by this process. **12.** (*tr.*) *Inf.* to criticize harshly: *the critics panned his new play.* ~See also **pan out.**

pan² (pæn) *vb.* **panning, panned.** **1.** to move (a film camera) or (of a film camera) to be moved so as to follow a moving object or obtain a panoramic effect. ~*n.* **2.** the act of panning.

pan- *combining form.* **1.** all or every: *panchromatic.* **2.** including or relating to all parts or members: *Pan-American; pantheistic.*

panacea (ˌpænə'sɪə) *n.* a remedy for all diseases or ills. —ˌpana'cean *adj.*

panache (pə'næʃ, -'nɑːʃ) *n.* **1.** a dashing manner; swagger: *he rides with panache.* **2.** a plume on a helmet.

Pan-American *adj.* of, relating to, or concerning North, South, and Central America collectively or the advocacy of political or economic unity among American countries. —'Pan-A'mericanism *n.*

pancake ('pæn,keɪk) *n.* **1.** a thin flat cake made from batter and fried on both sides. **2.** a stick or flat cake of compressed make-up. **3.** Also called: **pancake landing.** an aircraft landing made by levelling out a few feet from the ground and then dropping onto it. ~*vb.* **4.** to cause (an aircraft) to make a pancake landing or (of an aircraft) to make a pancake landing.

Pancake Day *n.* another name for **Shrove Tuesday.** See **Shrovetide.**

pancreas ('pæŋkrɪəs) *n.* a large elongated glandular organ, situated behind the stomach, that secretes insulin and pancreatic juice. —**pancreatic** (ˌpæŋkrɪ'ætɪk) *adj.*

panda ('pændə) *n.* **1.** Also called: **giant panda.** a large black-and-white herbivorous bearlike mammal, related to the raccoons and inhabiting the bamboo forests of China. **2. lesser** or **red panda.** a closely related smaller animal resembling a raccoon of the mountain forests of S Asia, having a reddish-brown coat and ringed tail.

panda car *n. Brit.* a police patrol car.

pandemic (pæn'dɛmɪk) *adj.* **1.** (of a disease) affecting persons over a wide geographical area; extensively epidemic. ~*n.* **2.** a pandemic disease.

pandemonium (ˌpændɪ'məʊnɪəm) *n.* **1.** wild confusion; uproar. **2.** a place of uproar and chaos.

pander ('pændə) *vb.* **1.** (*intr.;* foll. by *to*) to give gratification (to weaknesses or desires). **2.** (*arch. when tr.*) to act as a go-between in a sexual intrigue (for). ~*n. also* **panderer.** **3.** a person who caters for vulgar desires. **4.** a person who procures a sexual partner for another; pimp.

pandit ('pʌndɪt; *spelling pron.* 'pændɪt) *n. Hinduism.* a variant spelling of **pundit.**

p. & p. *Brit. abbrev. for* postage and packing.

THESAURUS

glut, jade, satiate, sicken, surfeit, tire, weary

palm¹ **1.** hand, mitt (*Sl.*), paw (*Inf.*) **2. in the palm of one's hand** at one's mercy, in one's clutches (control, power) **3. grease someone's palm** *Sl.* bribe, buy, corrupt, fix (*Inf.*), give a backhander (*Sl.*), induce, influence, pay off (*Inf.*), square, suborn

palm² *Fig.* bays, crown, fame, glory, honour, laurels, merit, prize, success, triumph, trophy, victory

palm off **1.** *With* **on** *or* **with** fob off, foist off, pass off **2.** *With* **on** foist on, force upon, impose upon, take advantage of, thrust upon, unload upon

palmy flourishing, fortunate, glorious, golden, halcyon, happy, joyous, luxurious, prosperous, thriving, triumphant

palpable **1.** apparent, blatant, clear, conspicuous, evident, manifest, obvious, open, patent, plain, unmistakable, visible **2.** concrete, material, real, solid, substantial, tangible, touchable

palpitate beat, flutter, pitapat, pitter-patter, pound, pulsate, pulse, quiver, shiver, throb, tremble, vibrate

palsied arthritic, atonic (*Pathol.*), crippled, debilitated, disabled, helpless, paralysed, paralytic, rheumatic, sclerotic, shaking, shaky, spastic, trembling

palter **1.** be evasive, deceive, double-talk, equivocate, fudge, hedge, mislead, prevaricate, shuffle, tergiversate, trifle **2.** bargain, barter, chaffer, dicker (*Chiefly U.S.*), haggle, higgle

paltry base, beggarly, contemptible, derisory, despicable, inconsiderable, insignificant, low, meagre, mean, Mickey Mouse (*Sl.*), minor, miserable, petty, picayune (*U.S.*), piddling (*Inf.*), pitiful, poor, puny, slight, small, sorry, trifling, trivial, twopenny-halfpenny (*Brit. inf.*), unimportant, worthless, wretched

pamper baby, cater to one's every whim, coddle, cosset, fondle, gratify, humour, indulge, mollycoddle, pet, spoil

pamphlet booklet, brochure, circular, folder, leaflet, tract

pan¹ *n.* **1.** container, pot, saucepan, vessel ~*v.* **2.** look for, search for, separate, sift out, wash **3.** *Inf.* censure, criticize, flay, hammer (*Brit.*), knock (*Inf.*), roast (*Inf.*), rubbish (*Inf.*), slam (*Sl.*), slate (*Inf.*), throw brickbats at (*Inf.*)

pan² *v.* follow, move, scan, sweep, swing, track, traverse

panacea catholicon, cure-all, elixir, nostrum, sovereign remedy, universal cure

panache a flourish, brio, dash, élan, flair, flamboyance, spirit, style, swagger, verve

pandemonium babel, bedlam, chaos, clamour, commotion, confusion, din, hubbub, hue and cry, hullabaloo, racket, ruckus (*Inf.*), ruction (*Inf.*), rumpus, tumult, turmoil, uproar

pane (peɪn) *n.* **1.** a sheet of glass in a window or door. **2.** a panel of a window, door, wall, etc. **3.** a flat section or face, as of a cut diamond.

panegyric (ˌpænɪˈdʒɪrɪk) *n.* a formal public commendation; eulogy. —ˌpaneˈgyrical *adj.* —ˌpaneˈgyrically *adv.* —ˌpaneˈgyrist *n.* —**panegyrize** *or* **-rise** (ˈpænɪdʒɪˌraɪz) *vb.*

panel (ˈpænəl) *n.* **1.** a flat section of a wall, door, etc. **2.** any distinct section of something, esp. of a car body. **3.** a piece of material inserted in a skirt, etc. **4. a.** a group of persons selected to act as a team in a quiz, to discuss a topic before an audience, etc. **b.** (*as modifier*): *a panel game.* **5.** *Law.* **a.** a list of persons summoned for jury service. **b.** the persons on a jury. **6.** *Scot. law.* a person accused of a crime. **7. a.** a thin board used as a surface or backing for an oil painting. **b.** a painting done on such a surface. **8.** any picture with a length much greater than its breadth. **9.** *Brit.* (formerly) **a.** a list of patients insured under the National Health Insurance Scheme. **b.** a list of medical practitioners available for consultation by these patients. ~*vb.* **-elling, -elled** *or U.S.* **-eling, -eled**. (*tr.*) **10.** to furnish or decorate with panels. **11.** *Law.* **a.** to empanel (a jury). **b.** (in Scotland) to bring (a person) to trial; indict.

panelling *or U.S.* **paneling** (ˈpænəlɪŋ) *n.* **1.** panels collectively, as on a wall or ceiling. **2.** material used for making panels.

panellist *or U.S.* **panelist** (ˈpænəlɪst) *n.* a member of a panel, esp. on radio or television.

pang (pæŋ) *n.* a sudden brief sharp feeling, as of loneliness, physical pain, or hunger.

pangolin (pæŋˈgəʊlɪn) *n.* a mammal of tropical Africa, S Asia, and Indonesia, having a scaly body and a long snout for feeding on ants and termites. Also called: **scaly anteater.**

panic (ˈpænɪk) *n.* **1.** a sudden overwhelming feeling of terror or anxiety, esp. one affecting a whole group of people. **2.** (*modifier*) of or resulting from such terror: *panic measures.* **3.** (*modifier*) for use in an emergency: *panic stations; panic button.* ~*vb.* **-icking, -icked. 4.** to feel or cause to feel panic. —**'panicky** *adj.*

panicle (ˈpænɪkəl) *n.* a compound raceme, as in the oat. —**'panicled** *adj.* —**paniculate** (pəˈnɪkjʊˌleɪt, -lɪt) *adj.*

panic-stricken *or* **panic-struck** *adj.* affected by panic.

panjandrum (pænˈdʒændrəm) *n.* a pompous self-important man.

pannier (ˈpænɪə) *n.* **1.** a large basket, esp. one of a pair slung over a beast of burden. **2.** one of a pair of bags slung either side of the back wheel of a motor cycle, etc. **3.** (esp. in the 18th century) **a.** a hooped framework to distend a woman's skirt. **b.** one of two puffed out loops of material worn drawn back onto the hips.

panoply (ˈpænəplɪ) *n., pl.* **-plies. 1.** a complete or magnificent array. **2.** the entire equipment of a warrior. —**'panoplied** *adj.*

panorama (ˌpænəˈrɑːmə) *n.* **1.** an extensive unbroken view in all directions. **2.** a wide or comprehensive survey of a subject. **3.** a large extended picture of a scene, unrolled before spectators a part at a time so as to appear continuous. —**panoramic** (ˌpænəˈræmɪk) *adj.* —ˌpanoˈramically *adv.*

pan out *vb.* (*intr., adv.*) *Inf.* to work out; result.

pansy (ˈpænzɪ) *n., pl.* **-sies. 1.** a garden plant having flowers with rounded velvety petals, white, yellow, or purple in colour. **2.** *Sl.* an effeminate or homosexual man or boy.

pant (pænt) *vb.* **1.** to breathe with noisy deep gasps, as when out of breath from exertion. **2.** to say (something) while breathing thus. **3.** (*intr.; often foll. by for*) to have a frantic desire (for). **4.** (*intr.*) to throb rapidly. ~*n.* **5.** the act or an instance of panting. **6.** a short deep gasping noise.

pantaloon (ˌpæntəˈluːn) *n.* **1.** (in pantomime) an absurd old man, the butt of the clown's tricks. **2.** (*usually cap.*) (in commedia dell'arte) a lecherous old merchant dressed in pantaloons.

pantaloons (ˌpæntəˈluːnz) *pl. n.* **1.** (formerly) men's tight-fitting trousers fastened below the calf or under the shoe. **2.** *Inf.* any trousers, esp. baggy ones.

pantechnicon (pænˈtɛknɪkən) *n. Brit.* **1.** a large van, esp. one used for furniture removals. **2.** a warehouse where furniture is stored.

pantheism (ˈpænθɪˌɪzəm) *n.* **1.** the doctrine that regards God as identical with the material universe or the forces of nature. **2.** readiness to worship all gods. —**'pantheist** *n.* —**panthe'istic** *or* **panthe'istical** *adj.* —ˌpanthe'istically *adv.*

pantheon (ˈpænθɪən) *n.* **1.** (esp. in ancient Greece or Rome) a temple to all the gods. **2.** all the gods of a religion. **3.** a building commemorating a nation's dead heroes.

panther (ˈpænθə) *n., pl.* **-thers** *or* **-ther. 1.** another name for **leopard** (sense 1), esp. the black variety (**black panther**). **2.** *U.S.* any of various related animals, esp. the puma.

panties (ˈpæntɪz) *pl. n.* a pair of women's or children's underpants.

pantihose (ˈpæntɪˌhəʊz) *n.* a less common word for **tights.**

pantile (ˈpænˌtaɪl) *n.* a roofing tile, with an S-shaped cross section, so that the downward curve of one tile overlaps the upward curve of the next.

panto (ˈpæntəʊ) *n., pl.* **-tos.** *Brit. inf.* short for **pantomime.**

panto- *or before a vowel* **pant-** *combining form.* all: *pantisocracy; pantograph; pantomime.*

pantograph (ˈpæntəˌɡrɑːf) *n.* **1.** an instrument consisting of pivoted levers for copying drawings, maps, etc., to any scale. **2.** a sliding type of current collector, esp. a diamond-shaped frame mounted on a train roof in contact with an overhead wire. —**pantographic** (ˌpæntəˈgræfɪk) *adj.*

pantomime (ˈpæntəˌmaɪm) *n.* **1.** (in Britain) a kind of play performed at Christmas time characterized by farce, music, lavish sets, stock roles, and topical jokes. **2.** a theatrical entertainment in which words are replaced by gestures and bodily actions. **3.** action without words as a means of expression. **4.** *Inf., chiefly Brit.* a confused or farcical situation. ~*vb.* **5.** another word for **mime.** —**pantomimic** (ˌpæntəˈmɪmɪk) *adj.* —**pantomimist** (ˈpæntəˌmaɪmɪst) *n.*

pantry (ˈpæntrɪ) *n., pl.* **-tries.** a small room in which provisions, cooking utensils, etc., are kept; larder.

pants (pænts) *pl. n.* **1.** *Brit.* an undergarment covering the body from the waist to the thighs or knees. **2.** the usual U.S. name for **trousers. 3. bore, scare,** etc., **the pants off.** *Inf.* to bore, scare, etc., extremely.

panzer (ˈpænzə; *German* ˈpantsər) *n.* **1.** (*modifier*) of or relating to the fast mechanized armoured units employed by the German army in World War II: *a panzer attack.* **2.** a vehicle belonging to a panzer unit, esp. a tank. **3.** (*pl.*) armoured troops.

THESAURUS

pang ache, agony, anguish, discomfort, distress, gripe, pain, prick, spasm, stab, sting, stitch, throe (*Rare*), twinge, wrench

panic *n.* 1. agitation, alarm, consternation, dismay, fear, fright, horror, hysteria, scare, terror ~*v.* 2. become hysterical, be terror-stricken, go to pieces (*Inf.*), lose one's bottle (*Sl.*), lose one's nerve, overreact 3. alarm, put the wind up (someone) (*Inf.*), scare, startle, terrify, unnerve

panicky afraid, agitated, distressed, fearful, frantic, frenzied, frightened, hysterical, in a flap (*Inf.*), in a tizzy (*Inf.*), jittery (*Inf.*), nervous, windy (*Sl.*), worked up, worried

panic-stricken *or* **panic-struck** aghast, agitated, alarmed, ap-

palled, fearful, frenzied, frightened, frightened out of one's wits, frightened to death, horrified, horror-stricken, hysterical, in a cold sweat (*Inf.*), panicky, petrified, scared, scared stiff, startled, terrified, terror-stricken, unnerved

panoply array, attire, dress, garb, get-up (*Inf.*), insignia, raiment (*Archaic*), regalia, show, trappings, turnout

panorama 1. bird's-eye view, prospect, scenery, scenic view, view, vista 2. overall picture, overview, perspective, survey

panoramic all-embracing, bird's-eye, comprehensive, extensive, far-reaching, general, inclusive, overall, scenic, sweeping, wide

pant *v.* 1. blow, breathe, gasp, heave, huff, palpitate, puff, throb, wheeze 2. *Fig.* ache, covet, crave, desire, hanker after, hunger, long, pine, set one's heart on, sigh, thirst, want, yearn ~*n.* 3. gasp, huff, puff, wheeze

panting *adj.* 1. breathless, gasping, out of breath, out of puff, puffed, puffed out, puffing, short of breath, winded 2. agog, all agog, anxious, champing at the bit (*Inf.*), eager, impatient, raring to go

pants 1. *Brit.* boxer shorts, briefs, drawers, knickers, panties, underpants, Y-fronts 2. *U.S.* slacks, trousers

pap[1] (pæp) *n.* **1.** any soft or semiliquid food esp. for babies or invalids; mash. **2.** worthless or oversimplified ideas, etc.; drivel. **3.** *S. African.* maize porridge.

pap[2] (pæp) *n.* **1.** *Arch. or N Brit. dialect.* a nipple or teat. **2.** something resembling a breast, such as one of a pair of rounded hilltops.

papa (pə'pɑː) *n. Arch.* an informal word for **father.**

papacy ('peɪpəsɪ) *n., pl.* **-cies. 1.** the office or term of office of a pope. **2.** the system of government in the Roman Catholic Church in which the pope is head.

papal ('peɪpəl) *adj.* of or relating to the pope or the papacy. —'**papally** *adv.*

papaw *or* **pawpaw** ('pɔː,pɔː) *n.* **1.** Also called: **custard apple. a.** a bush or small tree of Central North America, having small fleshy edible fruit. **b.** the fruit of this tree. **2.** another name for **papaya.**

papaya (pə'paɪə) *n.* **1.** a West Indian evergreen tree with a crown of large dissected leaves and large green hanging fruit. **2.** the fruit of this tree, having a yellow sweet edible pulp and small black seeds. ~Also called: **pawpaw.**

paper ('peɪpə) *n.* **1.** a substance made from cellulose fibres derived from rags, wood, etc., and formed into flat thin sheets suitable for writing on, decorating walls, wrapping, etc. **2.** a single piece of such material, esp. if written or printed on. **3.** (*usually pl.*) documents for establishing the identity of the bearer. **4.** (*pl.*) Also called: **ship's papers.** official documents relating to a ship. **5.** (*pl.*) collected diaries, letters, etc. **6.** See **newspaper** or **wallpaper. 7.** *Government.* See **white paper, green paper. 8.** a lecture or treatise on a specific subject. **9.** a short essay. **10. a.** a set of examination questions. **b.** the student's answers. **11.** *Theatre sl.* a free ticket. **12. on paper.** in theory, as opposed to fact. ~*adj.* **13.** made of paper: *paper cups do not last long.* **14.** thin like paper: *paper walls.* **15.** (*prenominal*) existing only in theory: *paper expenditure.* **16.** taking place in writing: *paper battles.* ~*vb.* **17.** to cover (walls) with wallpaper. **18.** (*tr.*) to cover or furnish with paper. **19.** (*tr.*) *Theatre sl.* to fill (a performance, etc.) by giving away free tickets (esp. in **paper the house**). ~See also **paper over.** —'**paperer** *n.* —'**papery** *adj.*

paperback ('peɪpə,bæk) *n.* **1.** a book or edition with covers made of flexible card. ~*adj.* **2.** of or denoting a paperback or publication of paperbacks. ~*vb.* **3.** (*tr.*) to publish a paperback edition of a book.

paperboy ('peɪpə,bɔɪ) *n.* a boy employed to deliver newspapers, etc. —'**paper,girl** *fem. n.*

paper chase *n.* a cross-country run in which a runner lays a trail of paper for others to follow.

paperclip ('peɪpə,klɪp) *n.* a clip for holding sheets of paper together; esp. one of bent wire.

paperhanger ('peɪpə,hæŋə) *n.* a person who hangs wallpaper as an occupation.

paperknife ('peɪpə,naɪf) *n., pl.* **-knives.** a knife with a comparatively blunt blade for opening sealed envelopes, etc.

paper money *n.* paper currency issued by the government or the central bank as legal tender and which circulates as a substitute for specie.

paper over *vb.* (*tr., adv.*) to conceal (something controversial or unpleasant).

paperweight ('peɪpə,weɪt) *n.* a small heavy object to prevent loose papers from scattering.

paperwork ('peɪpə,wɜːk) *n.* clerical work, such as the writing of reports or letters.

papier-mâché (,pæpjeɪ'mæʃeɪ) *n.* **1.** a hard strong substance made of paper pulp or layers of paper mixed with paste, size, etc., and moulded when moist. ~*adj.* **2.** made of papier-mâché.

papilla (pə'pɪlə) *n., pl.* **-lae** (-liː). **1.** the small projection of tissue at the base of a hair, tooth, or feather. **2.** any similar protuberance. —**pa'pillary,** '**papillate,** *or* '**papillose** *adj.*

papist ('peɪpɪst) *n., adj.* (*often cap.*) *Usually disparaging.* another term for **Roman Catholic.** —**pa'pistical** *or* **pa'pistic** *adj.* —'**papistry** *n.*

papoose (pə'puːs) *n.* an American Indian baby.

paprika ('pæprɪkə, pæ'priː-) *n.* **1.** a mild powdered seasoning made from a sweet variety of red pepper. **2.** the fruit or plant from which this seasoning is obtained.

Pap test *or* **smear** *n. Med.* an examination of stained cells in a smear taken of bodily secretions, esp. from the uterus, for detection of cancer.

papyrus (pə'paɪrəs) *n., pl.* **-ri** (-raɪ) *or* **-ruses. 1.** a tall aquatic plant of S Europe and N and central Africa. **2.** a kind of paper made from the stem pith of this plant, used by the ancient Egyptians, Greeks, and Romans. **3.** an ancient document written on this paper.

par (pɑː) *n.* **1.** an accepted standard, such as an average (esp. in **up to par**). **2.** a state of equality (esp. in **on a par with**). **3.** *Finance.* the established value of the unit of one national currency in terms of the unit of another. **4.** *Commerce.* **a.** See **par value. b.** equality between the current market value of a share, bond, etc., and its face value, indicated by **at par;** **above** (*or* **below**) **par** indicates that the market value is above (or below) face value. **5.** *Golf.* a standard score for a hole or course that a good player should make: *par for the course was 72.* ~*adj.* **6.** average or normal. **7.** (*usually prenominal*) of or relating to par: *par value.*

par. *abbrev. for:* **1.** paragraph. **2.** parallel. **3.** parenthesis. **4.** parish.

para ('pærə) *n. Inf.* **1.** a parachutist, esp. a soldier. **2.** paragraph.

para-[1] *or before a vowel* **par-** *prefix.* **1.** beside; near: *parameter.* **2.** beyond: *parapsychology.* **3.** resembling: *paratyphoid fever.* **4.** defective; abnormal: *paranoia.* **5.** (*usually in italics*) denoting that an organic compound contains a benzene ring with substituents attached to atoms that are directly opposite (the 1,4- positions): *para-cresol.* **6.** denoting an isomer, polymer, or compound related to a specified compound: *paraldehyde.* **7.** denoting the form of a diatomic substance in which the spins of the two constituent atoms are antiparallel: *parahydrogen.*

para-[2] *combining form.* indicating an object that acts as a protection against something: *parachute; parasol.*

parable ('pærəbəl) *n.* **1.** a short story that uses familiar events to illustrate a religious or ethical situation. **2.** any of the stories of this kind told by Jesus Christ.

parabola (pə'ræbələ) *n.* a conic section formed by the intersection of a cone by a plane parallel to its side.

parabolic[1] (,pærə'bɒlɪk) *adj.* of, relating to, or shaped like a parabola.

parabolic[2] (,pærə'bɒlɪk) *or* **parabolical** *adj.* of or like a parable. —,**para'bolically** *adv.*

paracetamol (,pærə'siːtə,mɒl, -'sɛtə-) *n.* a mild analgesic drug.

parachute ('pærə,ʃuːt) *n.* **1.** a device used to retard the fall of a person or package from an aircraft, consisting of a large fabric canopy connected to a harness. ~*vb.* **2.** (of troops, supplies, etc.) to land or cause to land by parachute from an aircraft. —'**para,chutist** *n.*

parade (pə'reɪd) *n.* **1.** an ordered, esp. ceremonial, march or procession, as of troops being reviewed. **2.** Also called: **parade ground.** a place where military formations regularly assemble. **3.** a visible show or display: *to make a parade of one's grief.* **4.** a public promenade or street of shops. **5.** a successive display of things or people. **6. on parade.** exhibiting oneself. ~*vb.*

THESAURUS

pap 1. baby food, mash, mush, pulp **2.** drivel, rubbish, trash, trivia
paper *n.* **1.** *Often plural* certificate, deed, documents, instrument, record **2.** *Plural* archive, diaries, documents, dossier, file, letters, records **3.** daily, gazette, journal, news, newspaper, organ, rag (*Inf.*) **4.** analysis, article, assignment, composition, critique, dissertation, essay, examination, monograph, report, script, study, thesis, treatise **5. on paper** ideally, in the abstract, in theory, theoretically ~*adj.* **6.** cardboard, disposable,

flimsy, insubstantial, paper-thin, papery, thin ~*v.* **7.** cover with paper, hang, line, paste up, wallpaper
papery flimsy, fragile, frail, insubstantial, light, lightweight, paperlike, paper-thin, thin
par *n.* **1.** average, level, mean, median, norm, standard, usual **2.** balance, equal footing, equality, equilibrium, equivalence, parity **3. above par** excellent, exceptional, first-rate (*Inf.*), outstanding, superior **4. below par a.** below average, inferior, lacking, not up to scratch (*Inf.*), poor, second-rate, substand-

ard, wanting **b.** not oneself, off colour (*Chiefly Brit.*), off form, poorly (*Inf.*), sick, under the weather (*Inf.*), unfit, unhealthy **5. par for the course** average, expected, ordinary, predictable, standard, typical, usual **6. on a par** equal, much the same, the same, well-matched **7. up to par** acceptable, adequate, good enough, passable, satisfactory, up to scratch (*Inf.*), up to the mark

parable allegory, exemplum, fable, lesson, moral tale, story

7. (when *intr.*, often foll. by *through* or *along*) to walk or march, esp. in a procession. **8.** (*tr.*) to exhibit or flaunt: *he was parading his medals.* **9.** (*tr.*) to cause to assemble in formation, as for a military parade. **10.** (*intr.*) to walk about in a public place. **—pa'rader** *n.*

paradigm ('pærə,daɪm) *n.* **1.** the set of all the inflected forms of a word. **2.** a pattern or model. **—paradigmatic** (,pærədɪg'mætɪk) *adj.*

paradise ('pærə,daɪs) *n.* **1.** heaven as the ultimate abode or state of the righteous. **2.** *Islam.* the sensual garden of delights that the Koran promises the faithful after death. **3.** Also called: **limbo.** (according to some theologians) the intermediate abode or state of the just prior to the Resurrection of Jesus. **4.** the Garden of Eden. **5.** any place or condition that fulfils all one's desires or aspirations. **6.** a park in which foreign animals are kept. **—paradisiacal** (,pærədɪ'saɪəkəl), **paradisiac** (,pærə'dɪsɪ,æk), *or* **paradisaical** (,pærədɪ'seɪɪkəl) *adj.*

paradox ('pærə,dɒks) *n.* **1.** a seemingly absurd or self-contradictory statement that is or may be true: *religious truths are often expressed in paradox.* **2.** a self-contradictory proposition, such as *I am always a liar.* **3.** a person or thing exhibiting apparently contradictory characteristics. **4.** an opinion that conflicts with common belief. **—para'doxical** *adj.* **—para'doxically** *adv.*

paraffin ('pærəfɪn) *n.* **1.** Also called: **paraffin oil,** (esp. U.S.) **kerosene.** a liquid mixture consisting mainly of alkane hydrocarbons, used as an aircraft fuel, in domestic heaters, and as a solvent. **2.** Also called: **paraffin wax.** a white insoluble odourless waxlike solid distilled from petroleum, used in candles, waterproof paper, and as a sealing agent. **3.** See **liquid paraffin.** ~*vb.* (*tr.*) **4.** to treat with paraffin.

paragon ('pærəgən) *n.* a model of excellence; pattern: *a paragon of virtue.*

paragraph ('pærə,grɑːf, -,græf) *n.* **1.** one of a number of blocks into which a text is subdivided in order to separate ideas, etc., usually marked by the beginning of a new line, indention, etc. **2.** *Printing.* the character ¶, used to indicate the beginning of a new paragraph. **3.** a short article, etc., in a newspaper. ~*vb.* (*tr.*) **4.** to form into paragraphs. **5.** to express or report in a paragraph. **—paragraphic** (,pærə'græfɪk) *adj.*

parakeet *or* **parrakeet** ('pærə,kiːt) *n.* any of numerous small long-tailed parrots.

parallax ('pærə,læks) *n.* **1.** an apparent change in the position of an object resulting from a change in position of the observer. **2.** *Astron.* the angle subtended at a celestial body, esp. a star, by the radius of the earth's orbit. **—parallactic** (,pærə'læktɪk) *adj.*

parallel ('pærə,lɛl) *adj.* (when *postpositive*, usually foll. by *to*) **1.** separated by an equal distance at every point; never touching or intersecting: *parallel walls.* **2.** corresponding; similar: *parallel situations.* **3.** *Music.* Also: **consecutive.** (of two or more parts or melodies) moving in similar motion but keeping the same interval apart throughout: *parallel fifths.* **4.** *Grammar.* denoting syntactic constructions in which the constituents of one construction correspond to those of the other. **5.** *Computers.* operating on several items of information, instructions, etc., simultaneously. ~*n.* **6.** *Maths.* one of a set of

parallel lines, planes, etc. **7.** an exact likeness. **8.** a comparison. **9.** Also called: **parallel of latitude.** any of the imaginary lines around the earth parallel to the equator, designated by degrees of latitude. **10. a.** a configuration of two or more electrical components connected between two points in a circuit so that the same voltage is applied to each (esp. in **in parallel**). Cf. **series** (sense 6). **b.** (*as modifier*): *a parallel circuit.* **11.** *Printing.* the character (‖) used as a reference mark. ~*vb.* **-leling, -leled.** (*tr.*) **12.** to make parallel. **13.** to supply a parallel to. **14.** to be a parallel to or correspond with: *your experience parallels mine.*

parallel bars *n.* *Gymnastics.* a pair of wooden bars on uprights used for various exercises.

parallelepiped (,pærə,lɛlə'paɪpɛd) *or* **parallelepipedon** (,pærə,lɛlɪ'paɪpɪdən) *n.* a geometric solid whose six faces are parallelograms.

parallelism ('pærə,lɛlɪzəm) *n.* **1.** the state of being parallel. **2.** *Grammar.* the use of parallel constructions. **3.** *Philosophy.* the doctrine that mental and physical processes are concomitant but not causally connected.

parallelogram (,pærə'lɛlə,græm) *n.* a quadrilateral whose opposite sides are parallel and equal in length.

paralyse *or* U.S. **-lyze** ('pærə,laɪz) *vb.* (*tr.*) **1.** *Pathol.* to affect with paralysis. **2.** *Med.* to render (a part of the body) insensitive to pain, touch, etc. **3.** to make immobile; transfix. **—,paraly'sation** *or* U.S. **-ly'zation** *n.* **—'para,lyser** *or* U.S. **-,lyzer** *n.*

paralysis (pə'rælɪsɪs) *n., pl.* **-ses** (-,siːz) **1.** *Pathol.* **a.** impairment or loss of voluntary muscle function or of sensation (**sensory paralysis**) in a part or area of the body. **b.** a disease characterized by such impairment or loss; palsy. **2.** cessation or impairment of activity: *paralysis of industry by strikes.*

paralytic (,pærə'lɪtɪk) *adj.* **1.** of, relating to, or of the nature of paralysis. **2.** afflicted with or subject to paralysis. **3.** *Brit. inf.* drunk. ~*n.* **4.** a person afflicted with paralysis.

paramedical (,pærə'mɛdɪkəl) *adj.* of or designating a person, such as a laboratory technician, who supplements the work of the medical profession. **—'para,medic** *n.*

parameter (pə'ræmɪtə) *n.* **1.** an arbitrary constant that determines the specific form of a mathematical expression, such as a and b in $y = ax^2 + b$. **2.** a characteristic constant of a statistical population, such as its variance or mean. **3.** *Inf.* any constant or limiting factor: *a designer must work within the parameters of budget and practicality.* **—parametric** (,pærə'mɛtrɪk) *adj.*

paramilitary (,pærə'mɪlɪtərɪ, -trɪ) *adj.* denoting or relating to a group of personnel with military structure functioning either as a civil force or in support of military forces.

paramount ('pærə,maʊnt) *adj.* of the greatest importance or significance. **—'para,mountcy** *n.* **—'para,mountly** *adv.*

paramour ('pærə,mʊə) *n.* **1.** *Now usually derog.* a lover, esp. adulterous. **2.** an archaic word for **beloved.**

parang ('pɑːræŋ) *n.* a Malay short stout straight-edged knife used in Borneo.

paranoia (,pærə'nɔɪə) *n.* **1.** a mental disorder characterized by any of several types of delusions, as of gran-

---

THESAURUS

parade *n.* **1.** array, cavalcade, ceremony, column, march, pageant, procession, review, spectacle, train **2.** array, display, exhibition, flaunting, ostentation, pomp, show, spectacle, vaunting ~*v.* **3.** defile, march, process **4.** air, brandish, display, exhibit, flaunt, make a show of, show, show off (*Inf.*), strut, swagger, vaunt

paradise 1. City of God, divine abode, Elysian fields, garden of delights (*Islam*), heaven, heavenly kingdom, Olympus (*Poetic*), Promised Land, Zion **2.** Eden, Garden of Eden **3.** bliss, delight, felicity, heaven, seventh heaven, utopia

paradox absurdity, ambiguity, anomaly, contradiction, enigma, inconsistency, mystery, oddity, puzzle

paradoxical absurd, ambiguous, baffling, confounding, contradictory, enigmatic, equivocal, illogical, impossible, improbable, inconsistent, puzzling, riddling

paragon apotheosis, archetype, criterion, cynosure, epitome, exemplar, ideal, jewel, masterpiece, model, nonesuch (*Archaic*), nonpareil, paradigm, pattern, prototype, quintessence, standard

paragraph clause, item, notice, part, passage, portion, section, subdivision

parallel *adj.* **1.** aligned, alongside, coextensive, equidistant, side by side **2.** akin, analogous, complementary, correspondent, corresponding, like, matching, resembling, similar, uniform ~*n.* **3.** analogue, complement, corollary, counterpart, duplicate, equal, equivalent, likeness, match, twin **4.** analogy, comparison, correlation, correspondence, likeness, parallelism, resemblance, similarity ~*v.* **5.** agree, be alike, chime with, compare, complement, conform, correlate, correspond, equal, keep pace (with), match

paralyse 1. cripple, debilitate, disable, in-

capacitate, lame **2.** anaesthetize, arrest, benumb, freeze, halt, immobilize, numb, petrify, stop dead, stun, stupefy, transfix

paralysis 1. immobility, palsy, paresis (*Pathol.*) **2.** arrest, breakdown, halt, shutdown, stagnation, standstill, stoppage

paralytic *adj.* **1.** crippled, disabled, immobile, immobilized, incapacitated, lame, numb, palsied, paralysed **2.** *Inf.* canned (*Sl.*), drunk, inebriated, intoxicated, legless (*Inf.*), pie-eyed (*Sl.*), plastered (*Sl.*), sloshed (*Sl.*), smashed (*Sl.*), stewed (*Sl.*), stoned (*Sl.*)

parameter constant, criterion, framework, guideline, limit, limitation, restriction, specification

paramount capital, cardinal, chief, dominant, eminent, first, foremost, main, outstanding, predominant, pre-eminent, primary, prime, principal, superior, supreme

deur or persecution. **2.** *Inf.* intense fear or suspicion, esp. when unfounded. —**'para,noid** *or* **paranoiac** (,pærə'nɔɪik) *adj., n.*

paranormal (,pærə'nɔːməl) *adj.* beyond normal explanation.

parapet ('pærəpit, -,pɛt) *n.* **1.** a low wall or railing along the edge of a balcony, roof, etc. **2.** another word for **breastwork.**

paraphernalia (,pærəfə'neiliə) *pl. n.* (*sometimes functioning as sing.*) **1.** miscellaneous articles or equipment. **2.** *Law.* (formerly) articles of personal property given to a married woman by her husband and regarded in law as her possessions.

paraphrase ('pærə,freiz) *n.* **1.** an expression of a statement or text in other words. ~*vb.* **2.** to put into other words; restate. —**paraphrastic** (,pærə'fræstik) *adj.*

paraplegia (,pærə'pliːdʒə) *n. Pathol.* paralysis of the lower half of the body, usually as the result of disease or injury of the spine. —**,para'plegic** *adj., n.*

parapsychology (,pærəsai'kɒlədʒi) *n.* the study of mental phenomena, such as telepathy, which are beyond the scope of normal physical explanation.

Paraquat ('pærə,kwɒt) *n. Trademark.* a yellow extremely poisonous weedkiller.

parasite ('pærə,sait) *n.* **1.** an animal or plant that lives in or on another (the host) from which it obtains nourishment. **2.** a person who habitually lives at the expense of others; sponger. —**parasitic** (,pærə'sitik) *or* **,para'sitical** *adj.* —**,para'sitically** *adv.* —**'parasi,tism** *n.*

parasol ('pærə,sɒl) *n.* an umbrella used for protection against the sun; sunshade.

parathion (,pærə'θaiɒn) *n.* a toxic oil used as an insecticide.

paratroops ('pærə,truːps) *pl. n.* troops trained and equipped to be dropped by parachute into a battle area. Also called: **paratroopers.**

paratyphoid fever (,pærə'taifɔid) *n.* a disease resembling but less severe than typhoid fever, caused by bacteria of the genus *Salmonella.*

par avion *French.* (par a'vjɔ̃) by aeroplane: used in labelling mail sent by air.

parboil ('paː,bɔil) *vb.* (*tr.*) **1.** to boil until partially cooked. **2.** to subject to uncomfortable heat.

parcel ('paːsəl) *n.* **1.** something wrapped up: package. **2.** a group of people or things having some common characteristic. **3.** a quantity of some commodity offered for sale; lot. **4.** a distinct portion of land. ~*vb.* -**celling,** -**celled** *or U.S.* -**celing, -celed.** (*tr.*) **5.** (often foll. by *up*) to make a parcel of; wrap up. **6.** (often foll. by *out*) to divide (up) into portions.

parch (paːtʃ) *vb.* **1.** to deprive or be deprived of water; dry up: *the sun parches the fields.* **2.** (*tr.; usually passive*) to make very thirsty. **3.** (*tr.*) to roast (corn, etc.) lightly.

parchment ('paːtʃmənt) *n.* **1.** the skin of certain animals, such as sheep, treated to form a durable material, as for manuscripts. **2.** a manuscript, etc., made of this material. **3.** a type of stiff yellowish paper resembling parchment.

pard (paːd) *n. Arch.* a leopard or panther.

pardon ('paːdən) *vb.* (*tr.*) **1.** to excuse or forgive (a person) for (an offence, mistake, etc.): *to pardon someone;*

to pardon a fault. ~*n.* **2.** forgiveness. **3. a.** release from punishment for an offence. **b.** the warrant granting such release. **4.** a Roman Catholic indulgence. ~*interj.* **5.** Also: **pardon me; I beg your pardon. a.** sorry; excuse me. **b.** what did you say? —**'pardonable** *adj.* —**'pardonably** *adv.*

pardoner ('paːdənə) *n.* (before the Reformation) a person licensed to sell ecclesiastical indulgences.

pare (pɛə) *vb.* (*tr.*) **1.** to peel (the outer layer) from (something). **2.** to cut the edges from (the nails). **3.** to decrease bit by bit. —**'parer** *n.*

paregoric (,pærɪ'gɒrik) *n.* a medicine consisting of opium, benzoic acid, and camphor, formerly widely used to relieve diarrhoea and coughing.

parent ('pɛərənt) *n.* **1.** a father or mother. **2.** a person acting as a father or mother; guardian. **3.** *Rare.* an ancestor. **4.** a source or cause. **5.** an organism or organization that has produced one or more organisms similar to itself. **6.** *Physics, chem.* a precursor, such as a nucleus or compound, of a derived entity. —**pa'rental** *adj.* —**'parenthood** *n.*

parentage ('pɛərəntidʒ) *n.* **1.** ancestry. **2.** derivation from a particular origin. **3.** a less common word for **parenthood.**

parent company *n.* a company that owns a number of subsidiary companies.

parenthesis (pə'rɛnθisis) *n., pl.* -**ses** (-,siːz). **1.** a phrase, often explanatory or qualifying, inserted into a passage with which it is not grammatically connected, and marked off by brackets, dashes, etc. **2.** Also called: **bracket.** either of a pair of characters, (), used to enclose such a phrase or as a sign of aggregation in mathematical or logical expressions. **3.** an interlude; interval. **4. in parenthesis.** inserted as a parenthesis. —**parenthetic** (,pærən'θɛtik) *or* **,paren'thetical** *adj.* —**,paren'thetically** *adv.*

parenthesize *or* -**sise** (pə'rɛnθi,saiz) *vb.* (*tr.*) **1.** to place in parentheses. **2.** to insert as a parenthesis. **3.** to intersperse (a speech, writing, etc.) with parentheses.

parent teacher association *n.* a social group of the parents of children at a school and their teachers formed in order to foster better understanding between them and to organize fund-raising activities on behalf of the school.

par excellence *French.* (par ɛksɛ'lãːs; *English* paːr 'ɛksələns) to a degree of excellence; beyond comparison.

parfait (paː'fei) *n.* a rich frozen dessert made from eggs and cream, etc.

pariah (pə'raiə; 'pæriə) *n.* **1.** a social outcast. **2.** (formerly) a member of a low caste in South India.

parietal (pə'raiɪtəl) *adj.* **1.** *Anat., biol.* of or forming the walls of a bodily cavity: *the parietal bones of the skull.* **2.** of or relating to the side of the skull. **3.** (of plant ovaries) having ovules attached to the walls. **4.** *U.S.* living or having authority within a college. ~*n.* **5.** a parietal bone.

pari-mutuel (,pæri'mjuːtjuəl) *n., pl.* **pari-mutuels** *or* **paris-mutuels** (,pæri'mjuːtjuəlz) a system of betting in which those who have bet on the winners of a race share in the total amount wagered less a percentage for the management.

paring ('pɛəriŋ) *n.* (*often pl.*) something pared or cut off.

THESAURUS

paraphernalia accoutrements, apparatus, appurtenances, baggage, belongings, clobber (*Brit. sl.*), effects, equipage, equipment, gear, impedimenta, material, stuff, tackle, things, trappings

paraphrase 1. *n.* interpretation, rehash, rendering, rendition, rephrasing, restatement, rewording, translation, version **2.** *v.* express in other words *or* one's own words, interpret, rehash, render, rephrase, restate, reword

parasite bloodsucker (*Inf.*), cadger, drone (*Brit.*), hanger-on, leech, scrounger (*Inf.*), sponger (*Inf.*), sponger (*Inf.*)

parasitic, parasitical bloodsucking (*Inf.*), cadging, leechlike, scrounging (*Inf.*), sponging (*Inf.*)

parcel *n.* **1.** bundle, carton, pack, package, packet **2.** band, batch, bunch, collection,

company, crew, crowd, gang, group, lot, pack **3.** piece of land, plot, property, tract ~*v.* **4.** *Often with* up do up, pack, package, tie up, wrap **5.** *Often with* out allocate, allot, apportion, carve up, deal out, dispense, distribute, divide, dole out, mete out, portion, share out, split up

parch blister, burn, dehydrate, desiccate, dry up, evaporate, make thirsty, scorch, sear, shrivel, wither

parched arid, dehydrated, dried out *or* up, drouthy (*Scot.*), dry, scorched, shrivelled, thirsty, waterless, withered

parching *adj.* baking, blistering, burning, dry, drying, hot, roasting (*Inf.*), scorching, searing, sweltering, withering

pardon 1. *v.* absolve, acquit, amnesty, condone, exculpate, excuse, exonerate, forgive, free, let off (*Inf.*), liberate, overlook, release,

remit, reprieve **2.** *n.* absolution, acquittal, allowance, amnesty, condonation, discharge, excuse, exoneration, forgiveness, grace, indulgence, mercy, release, remission, reprieve

pardonable allowable, condonable, excusable, forgivable, minor, not serious, permissible, understandable, venial

parent 1. begetter, father, guardian, mother, procreator, progenitor, sire **2.** architect, author, cause, creator, forerunner, origin, originator, prototype, root, source, wellspring

parentage ancestry, birth, derivation, descent, extraction, family, line, lineage, origin, paternity, pedigree, race, stirps, stock

pariah exile, leper, outcast, outlaw, undesirable, unperson, untouchable

parish ('pærɪʃ) *n.* **1.** a subdivision of a diocese, having its own church and a clergyman. **2.** the churchgoers of such a subdivision. **3.** (in England and, formerly, Wales) the smallest unit of local government. **4.** (in Louisiana) a county. **5.** (in Quebec and New Brunswick, Canada) a subdivision of a county. **6.** the people living in a parish. **7. on the parish.** *History.* receiving parochial relief.

parish clerk *n.* a person designated to assist in various church duties.

parish council *n. Brit.* the administrative body of a parish. See **parish** (sense 3).

parishioner (pə'rɪʃənə) *n.* a member of a particular parish.

parish register *n.* a book in which the births, baptisms, marriages, and deaths in a parish are recorded.

parity ('pærɪtɪ) *n., pl.* **-ties. 1.** equality of rank, pay, etc. **2.** close or exact analogy or equivalence. **3.** *Finance.* the amount of a foreign currency equivalent to a specific sum of domestic currency. **4.** equality between prices of commodities or securities in two separate markets. **5.** *Physics.* **a.** a property of a physical system characterized by the behaviour of the sign of its wave function when reflected in space. The wave function either remains unchanged (**even parity**) or changes in sign (**odd parity**). **b.** a quantum number describing this property, equal to +1 for even parity systems and –1 for odd parity systems. Symbol: *P* **6.** *Maths.* a relationship between two integers. If both are odd or both even they have the same parity; if one is odd and one even they have different parity.

park (pɑːk) *n.* **1.** a large area of land preserved in a natural state for recreational use by the public. **2.** a piece of open land in a town with public amenities. **3.** a large area of land forming a private estate. **4.** *U.S.* a playing field or sports stadium. **5. the park.** *Brit. inf.* a soccer pitch. **6.** a gear selector position on the automatic transmission of a motor vehicle that acts as a parking brake. **7.** the area in which the equipment and supplies of a military formation are assembled. ~*vb.* **8.** to stop and leave (a vehicle) temporarily. **9.** to manoeuvre (a motor vehicle) into a space for it to be left: *try to park without hitting the kerb.* **10.** (*tr.*) *Inf.* to leave or put somewhere: *park yourself in front of the fire.* **11.** *Mil.* to arrange equipment in a park. **12.** (*tr.*) to enclose in or as a park.

parka ('pɑːkə) *n.* a warm knee-length weatherproof coat, often with a hood, originally worn by Eskimos.

parkin ('pɑːkɪn) *n. Brit.* moist spicy ginger cake usually containing oatmeal.

parking meter *n.* a timing device, usually coin-operated, that indicates how long a vehicle may be left parked.

parking ticket *n.* a summons served for a parking offence.

Parkinson's disease ('pɑːkɪnsənz) *n.* a progressive chronic disorder of the central nervous system characterized by impaired muscular coordination and tremor. Also called: **parkinsonism.**

Parkinson's law *n.* the notion, expressed facetiously as a law of economics, that work expands to fill the time available.

parkland ('pɑːk,lænd) *n.* grassland with scattered trees.

parky ('pɑːkɪ) *adj.* **parkier, parkiest.** (*usually postpositive*) *Brit. inf.* (of the weather) chilly; cold.

Parl. *abbrev. for:* **1.** Parliament. **2.** Also: **parl.** parliamentary.

parlance ('pɑːləns) *n.* a particular manner of speaking, esp. when specialized; idiom: *political parlance.*

parley ('pɑːlɪ) *n.* **1.** a discussion, esp. between enemies under a truce to decide terms of surrender, etc. ~*vb.* **2.** (*intr.*) to discuss, esp. with an enemy.

parliament ('pɑːləmənt) *n.* **1.** an assembly of the representatives of a political nation or people, often the supreme legislative authority. **2.** any legislative or deliberative assembly, conference, etc.

Parliament ('pɑːləmənt) *n.* **1.** the highest legislative authority in Britain, consisting of the House of Commons, which exercises effective power, the House of Lords, and the sovereign. **2.** a similar legislature in another country or state. **3.** any of the assemblies of such a body created by a general election and royal summons and dissolved before the next election.

parliamentarian (,pɑːləmɛn'tɛərɪən) *n.* **1.** an expert in parliamentary procedures. ~*adj.* **2.** of or relating to a parliament.

parliamentary (,pɑːlə'mɛntərɪ) *adj.* (*sometimes cap.*) **1.** of or proceeding from a parliament or Parliament: *a parliamentary decree.* **2.** conforming to the procedures of a parliament or Parliament: *parliamentary conduct.* **3.** having a parliament or Parliament.

parlour *or U.S.* **parlor** ('pɑːlə) *n.* **1.** *Old-fashioned.* a living room, esp. one kept tidy for the reception of visitors. **2.** a small room for guests away from the public rooms in an inn, club, etc. **3.** *Chiefly U.S. & N.Z.* a room or shop equipped as a place of business: *a billiard parlor.* **4.** a building equipped for milking cows in.

parlous ('pɑːləs) *Arch.* ~*adj.* **1.** dangerous or difficult. **2.** cunning. ~*adv.* **3.** extremely. —'**parlously** *adv.*

Parmesan cheese (,pɑːmɪ'zæn) *n.* a hard dry cheese used grated, esp. on pasta dishes and soups.

parochial (pə'rəʊkɪəl) *adj.* **1.** narrow in outlook or scope; provincial. **2.** of or relating to a parish. —**pa'rochialism** *n.* —**pa'rochially** *adv.*

parody ('pærədɪ) *n., pl.* **-dies. 1.** a musical, literary, or other composition that mimics the style of another composer, author, etc., in a humorous or satirical way. **2.** something so badly done as to seem an intentional mockery; travesty. ~*vb.* **-dying, -died. 3.** (*tr.*) to make a parody of. —**parodic** (pə'rɒdɪk) *or* **pa'rodical** *adj.* —'**parodist** *n.*

parole (pə'rəʊl) *n.* **1. a.** the freeing of a prisoner before his sentence has expired, on the condition that he is of good behaviour. **b.** the duration of such conditional release. **2.** a promise given by a prisoner, as to be of good behaviour if granted liberty or partial liberty. **3.** *Linguistics.* language as manifested in the individual speech acts of particular speakers. **4. on parole.** conditionally released from detention. ~*vb.* (*tr.*) **5.** to place (a person) on parole. —**parolee** (pərəʊ'liː) *n.*

parotid (pə'rɒtɪd) *adj.* **1.** relating to, denoting, or near either of the salivary glands below and in front of each ear. ~*n.* **2.** Also **parotid gland.** either of these glands.

parotitis (,pærə'taɪtɪs) *n.* inflammation of the parotid gland. See also **mumps.**

-parous *adj. combining form.* giving birth to: *oviparous.*

paroxysm ('pærək,sɪzəm) *n.* **1.** an uncontrollable outburst: *a paroxysm of giggling.* **2.** *Pathol.* **a.** a sudden attack or recurrence of a disease. **b.** any fit or convulsion. —,**parox'ysmal** *adj.*

parquet ('pɑːkeɪ, -kɪ) *n.* **1.** a floor covering of pieces of hardwood fitted in a decorative pattern; parquetry. **2.**

THESAURUS

parish church, churchgoers, community, congregation, flock, fold, parishioners

parity 1. consistency, equality, equal terms, equivalence, par, parallelism, quits (*Inf.*), uniformity, unity **2.** affinity, agreement, analogy, conformity, congruity, correspondence, likeness, resemblance, sameness, similarity, similitude

park 1. *n.* estate, garden, grounds, parkland, pleasure garden, recreation ground, woodland **2.** *v.* leave, manoeuvre, position, station

parley 1. *n.* colloquy, confab (*Inf.*), conference, council, dialogue, discussion, meeting, palaver, powwow, talk(s) **2.** *v.* confabulate, confer, deliberate, discuss, negotiate, pala-

ver, powwow, speak, talk

parliament 1. assembly, congress, convocation, council, diet, legislature, senate, talking shop (*Inf.*) **2. Parliament** Houses of Parliament, Mother of Parliaments, the House, the House of Commons and the House of Lords, Westminster

parliamentary congressional, deliberative, governmental, lawgiving, lawmaking, legislative

parlour best room, drawing room, front room, lounge, reception room, sitting room

parlous chancy (*Inf.*), dangerous, desperate, difficult, dire, hairy (*Sl.*), hazardous, perilous, risky

parochial insular, inward-looking, limit-

ed, narrow, narrow-minded, parish-pump, petty, provincial, restricted, small-minded

parodist burlesquer, caricaturist, humorist, impressionist, ironist, lampooner, mimic, mocker, pasquinader, satirist

parody *n.* **1.** burlesque, caricature, imitation, lampoon, satire, send-up (*Brit. inf.*), skit, spoof (*Inf.*), takeoff (*Inf.*) **2.** apology, caricature, farce, mockery, travesty ~*v.* **3.** burlesque, caricature, do a takeoff of (*Inf.*), lampoon, mimic, poke fun at, satirize, send up (*Brit. inf.*), spoof (*Inf.*), take off (*Inf.*), travesty

paroxysm attack, convulsion, eruption, fit, flare-up (*Inf.*), outburst, seizure, spasm

Also called: **parquet floor.** a floor so covered. **3.** *U.S.* the stalls of a theatre. ~*vb.* (*tr.*) **4.** to cover a floor with parquet.

parquetry ('pɑːkɪtrɪ) *n.* a geometric pattern of inlaid pieces of wood, esp. as used to cover a floor.

parr (pɑː) *n., pl.* **parrs** or **parr.** a salmon up to two years of age.

parrakeet ('pærə,kiːt) *n.* a variant spelling of **parakeet.**

parricide ('pærɪ,saɪd) *n.* **1.** the act of killing either of one's parents. **2.** a person who kills his or her parent. —,parri'cidal *adj.*

parrot ('pærət) *n.* **1.** any of several related tropical and subtropical birds having a short hooked bill, bright plumage, and an ability to mimic sounds. **2.** a person who repeats or imitates the words or actions of another. ~*vb.* **3.** (*tr.*) to repeat or imitate without understanding.

parrot fever or **disease** *n.* another name for **psittacosis.**

parry ('pærɪ) *vb.* **-rying, -ried. 1.** to ward off (an attack, etc.) by blocking or deflecting, as in fencing. **2.** (*tr.*) to evade (questions, etc.), esp. adroitly. ~*n., pl.* **-ries. 3.** an act of parrying. **4.** a skilful evasion, as of a question.

parse (pɑːz) *vb. Grammar.* to assign constituent structure to (a sentence or the words in a sentence).

parsec ('pɑː,sɛk) *n.* a unit of astronomical distance equivalent to 3.0857 × 10^{16} metres or 3.262 light-years.

Parsee ('pɑːsiː) *n.* an adherent of a Zoroastrian religion, the practitioners of which were driven out of Persia by the Muslims in the eighth century A.D. It is now found chiefly in western India. —'**Parseeism** *n.*

parsimony ('pɑːsɪmənɪ) *n.* extreme care in spending; niggardliness. —**parsimonious** (,pɑːsɪ'məʊnɪəs) *adj.* —,parsi'moniously *adv.*

parsley ('pɑːslɪ) *n.* **1.** a S European umbelliferous plant, widely cultivated for its curled aromatic leaves, which are used in cooking. **2.** any of various similar and related plants, such as fool's-parsley and cow parsley.

parsnip ('pɑːsnɪp) *n.* **1.** an umbelliferous plant cultivated for its long whitish root. **2.** the root of this plant, eaten as a vegetable.

parson ('pɑːsən) *n.* **1.** a parish priest in the Church of England. **2.** any clergyman.

parsonage ('pɑːsənɪdʒ) *n.* the residence of a parson, as provided by the parish.

parson's nose *n.* the fatty extreme end portion of the tail of a fowl when cooked.

part (pɑːt) *n.* **1.** a piece or portion of a whole. **2.** an integral constituent of something: *dancing is part of what we teach.* **3.** an amount less than the whole; bit: *they only recovered part of the money.* **4.** one of several equal divisions: *mix two parts flour to one part water.* **5.** an actor's role in a play. **6.** a person's proper role or duty: *everyone must do his part.* **7.** (*often pl.*) region; area: *you're well-known in these parts.* **8.** *Anat.* any portion of a larger structure. **9.** a component that can be replaced in a machine, etc. **10.** the U.S. word for **parting**

(sense 1). **11.** *Music.* one of a number of separate melodic lines which is assigned to one or more instrumentalists or singers. **12. for the most part.** generally. **13. for one's part.** as far as one is concerned. **14. in part.** to some degree; partly. **15. of many parts.** having many different abilities. **16. on the part of.** on behalf of. **17. part and parcel.** an essential ingredient. **18. play a part. a.** to pretend to be what one is not. **b.** to have something to do with; be instrumental. **19. take in good part.** to respond to (teasing, etc.) with good humour. **20. take part in.** to participate in. **21. take someone's part.** to support one person in an argument, etc. ~*vb.* **22.** to divide or separate from one another; take or come apart: *to part the curtains; the seams parted when I washed the dress.* **23.** to go away or cause to go away from one another: *the couple parted amicably.* **24.** (*intr.;* foll. by *from*) to leave; say goodbye to. **25.** (*intr.;* foll. by *with*) to relinquish, esp. reluctantly: *I couldn't part with my teddy bear.* **26.** (*tr.,* foll. by *from*) to cause to relinquish, esp. reluctantly: *he's not easily parted from his cash.* **27.** (*intr.*) to split; separate: *the path parts here.* **28.** (*tr.*) to arrange (the hair) in such a way that a line of scalp is left showing. **29.** (*intr.*) a euphemism for **die**^{1}. **30.** (*intr.*) *Arch.* to depart. ~*adv.* **31.** to some extent; partly.

part. *abbrev. for:* **1.** participle. **2.** particular.

partake (pɑː'teɪk) *vb.* **-taking, -took, -taken.** (*mainly intr.*) **1.** (foll. by *in*) to have a share; participate. **2.** (foll. by *of*) to take or receive a portion, esp. of food or drink. **3.** (foll. by *of*) to suggest or have some of the quality (of): *music partaking of sadness.* —**par'taker** *n.*

parterre (pɑː'tɛə) *n.* **1.** a formally patterned flower garden. **2.** the pit of a theatre.

parthenogenesis (,pɑːθɪnəʊ'dʒɛnɪsɪs) *n.* a type of reproduction, occurring in some insects and flowers, in which the unfertilized ovum develops directly into a new individual. —**parthenogenetic** (,pɑːθɪ,nəʊdʒɪ'nɛtɪk) *adj.*

Parthian shot ('pɑːθɪən) *n.* a hostile remark or gesture delivered while departing.

partial ('pɑːʃəl) *adj.* **1.** relating to only a part; not general or complete: *a partial eclipse.* **2.** biased: *a partial judge.* **3.** (*postpositive;* foll. by *to*) having a particular liking (for). **4.** *Maths.* designating or relating to an operation in which only one of a set of independent variables is considered at a time. ~*n.* **5.** Also called: **partial tone.** *Music & acoustics.* any of the component tones of a single musical sound. **6.** *Maths.* a partial derivative. —,parti'ality *n.* —'**partially** *adv.* —'**partialness** *n.*

partial derivative *n.* the derivative of a function of two or more variables with respect to one of the variables, the other or others being considered constant. Written ∂f/∂x.

participate (pɑː'tɪsɪ,peɪt) *vb.* (*intr.;* often foll. by *in*) to take part, be or become actively involved, or share (in). —**par'ticipant** *adj., n.* —**par,tici'pation** or **par'ticipance** *n.* —**par'tici,pator** *n.* —**par,tici'patory** *adj.*

THESAURUS

parrot *n.* **1.** *Fig.* copycat (*Inf.*), imitator, (little) echo, mimic **2. parrot-fashion** *Inf.* by rote, mechanically, mindlessly ~*v.* **3.** copy, echo, imitate, mimic, reiterate, repeat

parry 1. block, deflect, fend off, hold at bay, rebuff, repel, repulse, stave off, ward off **2.** avoid, circumvent, dodge, duck (*Inf.*), evade, fence, fight shy of, shun, sidestep

parsimonious cheeseparing, close, close-fisted, frugal, grasping, mean, mingy (*Brit. inf.*), miserable, miserly, near (*Inf.*), niggardly, penny-pinching (*Inf.*), penurious, saving, scrimpy, skinflinty, sparing, stingy, stinting, tightfisted

parsimony frugality, meanness, minginess (*Brit. inf.*), miserliness, nearness (*Inf.*), niggardliness, penny-pinching (*Inf.*), stinginess, tightness

parson churchman, clergyman, cleric, divine, ecclesiastic, incumbent, man of God, man of the cloth, minister, pastor, preacher, priest, rector, reverend (*Inf.*), vicar

part *n.* **1.** bit, fraction, fragment, lot, particle, piece, portion, scrap, section, sector, segment, share, slice **2.** branch, component, constituent, department, division, element, in-

gredient, limb, member, module, organ, piece, unit **3.** behalf, cause, concern, faction, interest, party, side **4.** bit, business, capacity, charge, duty, function, involvement, office, place, responsibility, role, say, share, task, work **5.** *Theat.* character, lines, role **6.** *Often plural* airt (*Scot.*), area, district, neck of the woods (*Inf.*), neighbourhood, quarter, region, territory, vicinity **7. for the most part** chiefly, generally, in the main, largely, mainly, mostly, on the whole, principally **8. in good part** cheerfully, cordially, good-naturedly, well, without offence **9. in part** a little, in some measure, partially, partly, slightly, somewhat, to a certain extent, to some degree **10. on the part of** for the sake of, in support of, in the name of, on behalf of **11. take part in** associate oneself with, be instrumental in, be involved in, have a hand in, join in, partake in, participate in, play a part in, put one's twopence-worth in, take a hand in ~*v.* **12.** break, cleave, come apart, detach, disconnect, disjoin, dismantle, disunite, divide, rend, separate, sever, split, tear **13.** break up, depart, go, go away, go (their) separate ways, leave, part company, quit, say goodbye, separate, split up, take one's leave, with-

draw **14. part with** abandon, discard, forgo, give up, let go of, relinquish, renounce, sacrifice, surrender, yield

partake 1. *With* in engage, enter into, participate, share, take part **2.** *With* of consume, eat, receive, share, take **3.** *With* of evince, evoke, have the quality of, show, suggest

partial 1. fragmentary, imperfect, incomplete, limited, uncompleted, unfinished **2.** biased, discriminatory, influenced, interested, one-sided, partisan, predisposed, prejudiced, tendentious, unfair, unjust **3. be partial to** be fond of, be keen on, be taken with, care for, have a liking (soft spot, weakness) for

partiality 1. bias, favouritism, partisanship, predisposition, preference, prejudice **2.** affinity, fondness, inclination, liking, love, penchant, predilection, predisposition, preference, proclivity, taste, weakness

partially fractionally, halfway, incompletely, in part, moderately, not wholly, partly, piecemeal, somewhat, to a certain extent or degree

participant associate, contributor,

participle ('pɑːtɪsɪpəl) *n.* a nonfinite form of verbs, in English and other languages, used adjectivally and in the formation of certain compound tenses. See also **present participle, past participle.** —**participial** (ˌpɑːtɪ'sɪpɪəl) *adj.* —ˌparti'cipially *adv.*

particle ('pɑːtɪkəl) *n.* **1.** an extremely small piece of matter; speck. **2.** a very tiny amount; iota: *it doesn't make a particle of difference.* **3.** a function word, esp. (in certain languages) a word belonging to an uninflected class having grammatical function: up *is sometimes regarded as an adverbial particle.* **4.** a common affix, such as *re-, un-,* or *-ness.* **5.** *Physics.* a body with finite mass that can be treated as having negligible size, and internal structure. **6.** See **elementary particle.**

parti-coloured ('pɑːtɪˌkʌləd) *adj.* having different colours in different parts; variegated.

particular (pə'tɪkjʊlə) *adj.* **1.** (*prenominal*) of or belonging to a single or specific person, thing, category, etc.; specific; special: *the particular demands of the job.* **2.** (*prenominal*) exceptional or marked: *a matter of particular importance.* **3.** (*prenominal*) relating to or providing specific details or circumstances: *a particular account.* **4.** exacting or difficult to please, esp. in details; fussy. **5.** (of the solution of a differential equation) obtained by giving specific values to the arbitrary constants in a general equation. **6.** *Logic.* (of a proposition) affirming or denying something about only some members of a class of objects, as in *some men are not wicked.* Cf. **universal** (sense 9.). ~*n.* **7.** a separate distinct item that helps to form a generalization: opposed to *general.* **8.** (*often pl.*) an item of information; detail: *complete in every particular.* **9.** *Logic.* a particular proposition. **10.** **in particular.** especially or exactly. —**par'ticularly** *adv.*

particularity (pəˌtɪkjʊ'lærɪtɪ) *n., pl.* -**ties.** **1.** (*often pl.*) a specific circumstance: *the particularities of the affair.* **2.** great attentiveness to detail; fastidiousness. **3.** the quality of being precise: *a description of great particularity.* **4.** the state or quality of being particular as opposed to general; individuality.

particularize *or* -**ise** (pə'tɪkjʊləˌraɪz) *vb.* **1.** to treat in detail; give details (about). **2.** (*tr.*) to apply to a particular case. —parˌticulari'zation *or* -i'sation *n.*

parting ('pɑːtɪŋ) *n.* **1.** *Brit.* the line of scalp showing when sections of hair are combed in opposite directions. U.S. equivalent: **part. 2.** the act of separating or the state of being separated. **3. a.** a departure or leave-taking, esp. one causing a final separation. **b.** (*as modifier*): *a parting embrace.* **4.** a place or line of separation or division. **5.** a euphemism for **death.** ~*adj.* (*prenominal*) **6.** *Literary.* departing: *the parting day.* **7.** serving to divide or separate.

partisan *or* **partizan** (ˌpɑːtɪ'zæn, 'pɑːtɪˌzæn) *n.* **1.** an adherent or devotee of a cause, party, etc. **2.** a member of an armed resistance group within occupied territory. ~*adj.* **3.** of, relating to, or characteristic of a partisan. **4.** excessively devoted to one party, faction, etc.; one-sided. —ˌparti'sanship *or* ˌparti'zanship *n.*

partition (pɑː'tɪʃən) *n.* **1.** a division into parts; separation. **2.** something that separates, such as a large screen dividing a room in two. **3.** a part or share. **4.** *Property law.* a division of property, esp. realty, among joint owners. ~*vb.* (*tr.*) **5.** (often foll. by *off*) to separate or apportion into sections: *to partition a room off with a large screen.* **6.** *Property law.* to divide (property, esp. realty) among joint owners. —**par'titioner** *or* **par'titionist** *n.*

partitive ('pɑːtɪtɪv) *adj.* **1.** *Grammar.* indicating that a noun involved in a construction refers only to a part of what it otherwise refers to. The phrase *some of the butter* is a partitive construction. **2.** serving to separate or divide into parts. ~*n.* **3.** *Grammar.* a partitive linguistic element or feature. —**'partitively** *adv.*

partly ('pɑːtlɪ) *adv.* not completely.

partner ('pɑːtnə) *n.* **1.** an ally or companion: *a partner in crime.* **2.** a member of a partnership. **3.** one of a pair of dancers or players on the same side in a game: *my bridge partner.* **4.** either member of a married couple. ~*vb.* **5.** to be or cause to be a partner (of).

partnership ('pɑːtnəˌʃɪp) *n.* **1. a.** a contractual relationship between two or more persons carrying on a joint business venture. **b.** the deed creating such a relationship. **c.** the persons associated in such a relationship. **2.** the state or condition of being a partner.

part of speech *n.* a class of words sharing important syntactic or semantic features; a group of words in a language that may occur in similar positions or fulfil similar functions in a sentence. The chief parts of speech in English are noun, pronoun, adjective, determiner, adverb, verb, preposition, conjunction, and interjection.

partook (pɑː'tʊk) *vb.* the past tense of **partake.**

partridge ('pɑːtrɪdʒ) *n., pl.* -**tridges** *or* -**tridge.** any of various small Old World game birds of the pheasant family, esp. the common or European partridge.

parts (pɑːts) *pl. n.* **1.** personal abilities or talents: *a man of many parts.* **2. private parts.** *Euphemistic.* external genital regions.

part song *n.* **1.** a song composed in harmonized parts. **2.** (*in more technical usage*) a piece of choral music in which the topmost part carries the melody.

part-time *adj.* **1.** for less than the entire time appropriate to an activity: *a part-time job.* ~*adv.* **2.** on a part-time basis: *he works part time.* ~Cf. **full-time.** —**part-'timer** *n.*

parturient (pɑː'tjʊərɪənt) *adj.* **1.** of or relating to childbirth. **2.** giving birth. **3.** producing a new idea, etc. —**par'turiency** *n.*

parturition (ˌpɑːtjʊ'rɪʃən) *n.* the act or process of giving birth.

party ('pɑːtɪ) *n., pl.* -**ties. 1. a.** a social gathering for pleasure, often held as a celebration. **b.** (*as modifier*): *party spirit.* **c.** (*in combination*): *partygoer.* **2.** a group of people associated in some activity: *a rescue party.* **3. a.** (*often cap.*) a group of people organized together to further a common political aim, etc. **b.** (*as modifier*): *party politics.* **4.** a person, esp. one entering into a contract. **5.** the person or persons taking part in legal proceedings: *a party to the action.* ~*adj.* **6.** *Heraldry.* (of a

---

member, partaker, participator, party, shareholder

participate be a participant, be a party to, engage in, enter into, get in on the act, have a hand in, join in, partake, perform, share, take part

participation assistance, contribution, involvement, joining in, partaking, partnership, sharing in, taking part

particle atom, bit, crumb, grain, iota, jot, mite, molecule, mote, piece, scrap, shred, speck, tittle, whit

particular *adj.* **1.** distinct, exact, express, peculiar, precise, special, specific **2.** especial, exceptional, marked, notable, noteworthy, remarkable, singular, uncommon, unusual **3.** blow-by-blow, circumstantial, detailed, itemized, minute, painstaking, precise, selective, thorough **4.** choosy (*Inf.*), critical, dainty, demanding, discriminating, exacting, fastidious, finicky, fussy, meticulous, nice (*Rare*), overnice, pernickety (*Inf.*), picky (*Inf.*) ~*n.* **5.** *Usually plural* circumstance, detail, fact, feature, item, specification **6. in particular** distinctly, especially, ex-

actly, expressly, particularly, specifically

particularly **1.** decidedly, especially, exceptionally, markedly, notably, outstandingly, peculiarly, singularly, surprisingly, uncommonly, unusually **2.** distinctly, especially, explicitly, expressly, in particular, specifically

parting *n.* **1.** adieu, departure, farewell, going, goodbye, leave-taking, valediction **2.** breaking, detachment, divergence, division, partition, rift, rupture, separation, split ~*adj.* **3.** departing, farewell, final, last, valedictory

partisan *n.* **1.** adherent, backer, champion, devotee, disciple, follower, stalwart, supporter, upholder, votary ~*adj.* **2.** biased, factional, interested, one-sided, partial, prejudiced, sectarian, tendentious ~*n.* **3.** guerrilla, irregular, resistance fighter, underground fighter ~*adj.* **4.** guerrilla, irregular, resistance, underground

partition *n.* **1.** dividing, division, segregation, separation, severance, splitting **2.** barrier, divider, room divider, screen, wall **3.** allotment, apportionment, distribution, por-

tion, rationing out, share ~*v.* **4.** apportion, cut up, divide, parcel out, portion, section, segment, separate, share, split up, subdivide **5.** divide, fence off, screen, separate, wall off

partly halfway, incompletely, in part, in some measure, not fully, partially, relatively, slightly, somewhat, to a certain degree *or* extent, up to a certain point

partner **1.** accomplice, ally, associate, bedfellow, collaborator, colleague, companion, comrade, confederate, copartner, helper, mate, participant, team-mate **2.** bedfellow, consort, helpmate, husband, mate, spouse, wife

partnership **1.** companionship, connection, cooperation, copartnership, fellowship, interest, participation, sharing **2.** alliance, association, combine, company, conglomerate, cooperative, corporation, firm, house, society, union

parts 1. ability, accomplishments, attributes, calibre, capabilities, endowments, faculties, genius, gifts, intellect, intelligence, talents **2.** bits and pieces, components, spare parts, spares

shield) divided vertically into two colours, metals, or furs.

party line *n.* **1.** a telephone line serving two or more subscribers. **2.** the policies or dogma of a political party, etc.

party wall *n. Property law.* a wall separating two properties or pieces of land and over which each of the adjoining owners has certain rights.

par value *n.* the value imprinted on the face of a share certificate or bond and used to assess dividend, capital ownership, or interest.

parvenu *or (fem.)* **parvenue** ('pɑːvəˌnjuː) *n.* **1.** a person who, having risen socially or economically, is considered to be an upstart. ~*adj.* **2.** of or characteristic of a parvenu.

pas (pɑː) *n., pl.* **pas.** a dance step or movement, esp. in ballet.

pascal ('pæskəl) *n.* the derived SI unit of pressure; the pressure exerted on an area of 1 square metre by a force of 1 newton; equivalent to 10 dynes per square centimetre or 1.45×10^{-4} pound per square inch. Symbol: Pa

Pasch (pɑːsk, pæsk) *n.* an archaic name for **Passover** or **Easter.** —'**Paschal** *adj.*

pas de deux (*French* pɑ də 'dø) *n., pl.* **pas de deux.** *Ballet.* a sequence for two dancers.

pasha *or* **pacha** ('pɑːʃə, 'pæʃə) *n.* (formerly) a high official of the Ottoman Empire or the modern Egyptian kingdom: placed after a name when used as a title.

pasqueflower ('pɑːskˌflaʊə) *n.* **1.** a small purple-flowered plant of N and Central Europe and W Asia. **2.** any of several related North American plants.

pass (pɑːs) *vb.* **1.** to go onwards or move by or past (a person, thing, etc.). **2.** to run, extend, or lead through, over, or across (a place): *the route passes through the city.* **3.** to go through or cause to go through (an obstacle or barrier): *to pass a needle through cloth.* **4.** to move or cause to move onwards or over: *he passed his hand over her face.* **5.** (*tr.*) to go beyond or exceed: *this victory passes all expectation.* **6.** to gain or cause to gain an adequate mark or grade in (an examination, course, etc.). **7.** (often foll. by *away* or *by*) to elapse or allow to elapse: *we passed the time talking.* **8.** (*intr.*) to take place or happen: *what passed at the meeting?* **9.** to speak or exchange or be spoken or exchanged: *angry words passed between them.* **10.** to spread or cause to spread: *we passed the news round the class.* **11.** to transfer or exchange or be transferred or exchanged: *the bomb passed from hand to hand.* **12.** (*intr.*) to undergo change or transition: *to pass from joy to despair.* **13.** (when *tr.*, often foll. by *down*) to transfer or be transferred by inheritance: *the house passed to the younger son.* **14.** to agree to or be agreed to by a legislative body, etc.: *the assembly passed 10 resolutions.* **15.** (*tr.*) (of a legislative measure) to undergo (a procedural stage) and be agreed: *the bill passed the committee stage.* **16.** (when *tr.*, often foll. by *on* or *upon*) to pronounce (judgment, findings, etc.): *the court passed sentence.* **17.** to

go or allow to go without comment or censure: *the insult passed unnoticed.* **18.** (*intr.*) to opt not to exercise a right, as by not answering a question or not making a bid or a play in card games. **19.** to discharge (urine, etc.) from the body. **20.** (*intr.*) to come to an end or disappear: *his anger soon passed.* **21.** (*intr.*; usually foll. by *for* or *as*) to be likely to be mistaken for (someone or something else): *you could easily pass for your sister.* **22.** (*intr.*; foll. by *away, on,* or *over*) a euphemism for **die**[1]. **23.** *Sport.* to hit, kick, or throw (the ball, etc.) to another player. **24. bring to pass.** *Arch.* to cause to happen. **25. come to pass.** *Arch.* to happen. ~*n.* **26.** the act of passing. **27.** a route through a range of mountains where there is a gap between peaks. **28.** a permit, licence, or authorization to do something without restriction. **29. a.** a document allowing entry to and exit from a military installation. **b.** a document authorizing leave of absence. **30.** *Brit.* **a.** the passing of a college or university examination to a satisfactory standard but not as high as honours. **b.** (*as modifier*): *a pass degree.* **31.** a dive, sweep, or bombing or landing run by an aircraft. **32.** a motion of the hand or of a wand as part of a conjuring trick. **33.** *Inf.* an attempt to invite sexual intimacy. **34.** a state of affairs, esp. a bad one (esp. in **a pretty pass**). **35.** *Sport.* the transfer of a ball, etc., from one player to another. **36.** *Fencing.* a thrust or lunge. **37.** *Bridge, etc.* the act of passing (making no bid). ~*interj.* **38.** *Bridge, etc.* a call indicating that a player has no bid to make. ~See also **pass off, pass out,** etc.

pass. *abbrev. for:* **1.** passive. **2.** passenger. **3.** passage.

passable ('pɑːsəbəl) *adj.* **1.** adequate, fair, or acceptable. **2.** (of an obstacle) capable of being crossed. **3.** (of currency) valid for circulation. **4.** (of a proposed law) able to be enacted. —'**passableness** *n.* —'**passably** *adv.*

passage ('pæsɪdʒ) *n.* **1.** a channel, opening, etc., through or by which a person may pass. **2.** *Music.* a section or division of a piece, movement, etc. **3.** a way, as in a hall or lobby. **4.** a section of a written work, speech, etc. **5.** a journey, esp. by ship. **6.** the act or process of passing from one place, condition, etc., to another: *passage of a gas through a liquid.* **7.** the permission, right, or freedom to pass: *to be denied passage through a country.* **8.** the enactment of a law by a legislative body. **9.** *Rare.* an exchange, as of blows, words, etc.

passageway ('pæsɪdʒˌweɪ) *n.* a way, esp. one in or between buildings; passage.

passbook ('pɑːsˌbʊk) *n.* **1.** a book for keeping a record of withdrawals from and payments into a building society. **2.** another name for **bankbook.** **3.** *S. African.* an official document to identify the bearer, his race, residence, and employment.

passé ('pɑːseɪ, 'pæseɪ) *adj.* **1.** out-of-date: *passé ideas.* **2.** past the prime; faded: *a passé society beauty.*

passenger ('pæsɪndʒə) *n.* **1. a.** a person travelling in a car, train, boat, etc., not driven by him. **b.** (*as modifier*):

THESAURUS

party 1. at-home, bash (*Inf.*), celebration, do (*Inf.*), festivity, function, gathering, get-together (*Inf.*), knees-up (*Brit. inf.*), rave-up (*Brit. sl.*), reception, shindig (*Sl.*), social, social gathering, soirée **2.** band, body, bunch (*Inf.*), company, crew, detachment (*Military*), gang, gathering, group, squad, team, unit **3.** alliance, association, cabal, clique, coalition, combination, confederacy, coterie, faction, grouping, league, set, side **4.** individual, person, somebody, someone **5.** *Law* contractor (*Law*), defendant, litigant, participant, plaintiff

pass[1] *v.* **1.** depart, elapse, flow, go, go by or past, lapse, leave, move, move onwards, proceed, roll, run **2.** beat, exceed, excel, go beyond, outdistance, outdo, outstrip, surmount, surpass, transcend **3.** answer, come up to scratch (*Inf.*), do, get through, graduate, pass muster, qualify, succeed, suffice, suit **4.** beguile, devote, employ, experience, fill, occupy, spend, suffer, undergo, while away **5.** befall, come up, develop, fall out, happen, occur, take place **6.** convey, deliver, exchange, give, hand, kick, let have, reach, send, throw, transfer, transmit **7.** accept, adopt, approve,

authorize, decree, enact, establish, legislate, ordain, ratify, sanction, validate **8.** declare, deliver, express, pronounce, utter **9.** disregard, ignore, miss, neglect, not heed, omit, overlook, skip (*Inf.*) **10.** defecate, discharge, eliminate, empty, evacuate, excrete, expel, void **11.** blow over, cease, die, disappear, dissolve, dwindle, ebb, end, evaporate, expire, fade, go, melt away, terminate, vanish, wane **12.** *With* **for** *or* **as** be accepted as, be mistaken for, be regarded as, be taken for, impersonate, serve as

pass[2] *n.* **1.** canyon, col, defile, gap, gorge, ravine **2.** authorization, identification, licence, passport, permission, permit, safe-conduct, ticket, warrant **3.** *Inf.* advances, approach, overture, play (*Inf.*), proposition, suggestion **4.** condition, juncture, pinch, plight, predicament, situation, stage, state, state of affairs, straits **5.** feint, jab, lunge, push, swing, thrust

passable 1. acceptable, adequate, admissible, allowable, all right, average, fair, fair enough, mediocre, middling, moderate, not too bad, ordinary, presentable, so-so (*Inf.*), tolerable, unexceptional **2.** clear, crossable,

navigable, open, traversable, unobstructed

passage 1. avenue, channel, course, lane, opening, path, road, route, thoroughfare, way **2.** corridor, doorway, entrance, entrance hall, exit, hall, hallway, lobby, passageway, vestibule **3.** clause, excerpt, extract, paragraph, piece, quotation, reading, section, sentence, text, verse **4.** crossing, journey, tour, trek, trip, voyage **5.** advance, change, conversion, flow, motion, movement, passing, progress, progression, transit, transition **6.** allowance, authorization, freedom, permission, right, safe-conduct, visa, warrant **7.** acceptance, enactment, establishment, legalization, legislation, passing, ratification

pass away croak (*Sl.*), decease, depart (this life), die, expire, pass on, pass over, peg out (*Inf.*), shuffle off this mortal coil, snuff it (*Inf.*)

pass by 1. go past, leave, move past, pass **2.** disregard, miss, neglect, not choose, overlook, pass over

a passenger seat. **2.** *Chiefly Brit.* a member of a group or team who is not participating fully in the work.

passe-partout (ˌpæspɑːˈtuː) *n.* **1.** a mounting for a picture in which strips of gummed paper bind together the glass, picture and backing. **2.** the gummed paper used for this. **3.** a mat on which a photograph, etc., is mounted. **4.** something that secures entry everywhere, esp. a master key.

passer-by *n., pl.* **passers-by.** a person that is passing or going by, esp. on foot.

passerine (ˈpæsəˌraɪn, -ˌriːn) *adj.* **1.** of, relating to, or belonging to an order of birds characterized by the perching habit: includes the larks, finches, starlings, etc. ~*n.* **2.** any bird belonging to this order.

passim *Latin.* (ˈpæsɪm) *adv.* here and there; throughout: used to indicate that what is referred to occurs frequently in the work cited.

passing (ˈpɑːsɪŋ) *adj.* **1.** transitory or momentary: *a passing fancy.* **2.** cursory or casual in action or manner: *a passing reference.* ~*adv., adj. Arch.* **3.** to an extreme degree: *the events were passing strange.* ~*n.* **4.** a place where or means by which one may pass, cross, ford, etc. **5.** a euphemistic word for **death. 6. in passing.** by the way; incidentally.

passion (ˈpæʃən) *n.* **1.** ardent love or affection. **2.** intense sexual love. **3.** a strong affection or enthusiasm for an object, concept, etc.: *a passion for poetry.* **4.** any strongly felt emotion, such as love, hate, envy, etc. **5.** the object of an intense desire, ardent affection, or enthusiasm. **6.** an outburst expressing intense emotion: *he burst into a passion of sobs.* **7.** the sufferings and death of a Christian martyr. —**ˈpassional** *adj.* —**ˈpassionless** *adj.*

Passion (ˈpæʃən) *n.* **1.** the sufferings of Christ from the Last Supper to his death on the cross. **2.** any of the four Gospel accounts of this. **3.** a musical setting of this: *the St. Matthew Passion.*

passionate (ˈpæʃənɪt) *adj.* **1.** manifesting or exhibiting intense sexual feeling or desire. **2.** capable of, revealing, or characterized by intense emotion. **3.** easily roused to anger; quick-tempered. —**ˈpassionately** *adv.*

passionflower (ˈpæʃənˌflaʊə) *n.* any plant of a tropical American genus cultivated for their red, yellow, greenish, or purple showy flowers: some species have edible fruit.

passion fruit *n.* the edible fruit of any of various passionflowers, esp. granadilla.

Passion play *n.* a play depicting the Passion of Christ.

passive (ˈpæsɪv) *adj.* **1.** not active or not participating perceptibly in an activity, organization, etc. **2.** unresisting and receptive to external forces; submissive. **3.** affected or acted upon by an external object or force. **4.** *Grammar.* denoting a voice of verbs in sentences in which the grammatical subject is the recipient of the action described by the verb, as *was broken* in the sentence *The glass was broken by a boy.* **5.** *Chem.* (of a substance, esp. a metal) apparently chemically unreactive. **6.** *Electronics, telecomm.* **a.** capable only of attenuating a signal: *a passive network.* **b.** not capable of amplifying a signal or controlling a function: *a passive communications satellite.* **7.** *Finance.* (of a bond, share, debt, etc.) yielding no interest. ~*n.* **8.** *Grammar.* **a.** the passive voice. **b.** a passive verb. —**ˈpassively** *adv.* —**ˈpassiveness** *or* **pasˈsivity** *n.*

passive resistance *n.* resistance to a government, law, etc., without violence, as by fasting, demonstrating, or refusing to cooperate.

passkey (ˈpɑːsˌkiː) *n.* **1.** any of various keys, esp. a latchkey. **2.** another term for **master key** or **skeleton key.**

pass off *vb.* (*adv.*) **1.** to be or cause to be accepted in a false character: *he passed the fake diamonds off as real.* **2.** (*intr.*) to come to a gradual end; disappear: *eventually the pain passed off.* **3.** (*intr.*) to take place: *the meeting passed off without disturbance.* **4.** (*tr.*) to set aside or disregard: *I managed to pass off his insult.*

pass out *vb.* (*adv.*) **1.** (*intr.*) *Inf.* to become unconscious; faint. **2.** (*intr.*) *Brit.* (esp. of an officer cadet) to qualify for a military commission, etc. **3.** (*tr.*) to distribute.

pass over *vb.* **1.** (*tr., adv.*) to take no notice of; disregard: *they passed me over in the last round of promotions.* **2.** (*intr., prep.*) to disregard (something bad or embarrassing).

Passover (ˈpɑːsˌəʊvə) *n.* an eight-day Jewish festival celebrated in commemoration of the passing over or sparing of the Israelites in Egypt (Exodus 12).

passport (ˈpɑːspɔːt) *n.* **1.** an official document issued by a government, identifying an individual, granting him permission to travel abroad, and requesting the protection of other governments for him. **2.** a quality, asset, etc., that gains a person admission or acceptance.

pass up *vb.* (*tr., adv.*) *Inf.* to refuse or reject: *I won't pass up this opportunity.*

password (ˈpɑːsˌwɜːd) *n.* **1.** a secret word, phrase, etc., that ensures admission by proving identity, membership, etc. **2.** an action, quality, etc., that gains admission or acceptance.

past (pɑːst) *adj.* **1.** completed, finished, and no longer in existence: *past happiness.* **2.** denoting or belonging to the time that has elapsed at the present moment: *the past history of the world.* **3.** denoting a specific unit of time that immediately precedes the present one: *the past month.* **4.** (*prenominal*) denoting a person who has held an office or position; former: *a past president.* **5.** *Grammar.* denoting any of various tenses of verbs that are used in describing actions, events, or states that have been begun or completed at the time of utterance. ~*n.* **6. the past.** the period of time that has elapsed: *forget the past.* **7.** the history, experience, or background of a nation, person, etc. **8.** an earlier period of someone's life, esp. one regarded as disreputable. **9.** *Grammar.* **a.** a past tense. **b.** a verb in a past tense. ~*adv.* **10.** at a time before the present; ago: *three years past.* **11.** on or onwards: *I greeted him but he just walked past.* ~*prep.* **12.** beyond in time: *it's past midnight.* **13.** beyond in place or position: *the library is past the church.* **14.** moving beyond: *he walked past me.* **15.** beyond or above the reach, limit, or scope of: *his foolishness is past comprehension.* **16. past it.** *Inf.* unable to perform the tasks one could do when one was younger. **17. not put it past someone.** to consider a person capable of (something).

passenger fare, hitchhiker, pillion rider, rider, traveller

passer-by bystander, onlooker, witness

passing *adj.* **1.** brief, ephemeral, fleeting, momentary, short, short-lived, temporary, transient, transitory **2.** casual, cursory, glancing, hasty, quick, shallow, short, slight, superficial **3. in passing** accidentally, by the bye, by the way, en passant, incidentally, on the way ~*n.* **4.** death, decease, demise, end, finish, loss, termination

passion **1.** animation, ardour, eagerness, emotion, excitement, feeling, fervour, fire, heat, intensity, joy, rapture, spirit, transport, warmth, zeal, zest **2.** adoration, affection, ardour, attachment, concupiscence, desire, fondness, infatuation, itch, keenness, love, lust **3.** bug (*Inf.*), craving, craze, enthusiasm, fancy, fascination, idol, infatuation, mania, obsession **4.** anger, fit, flare-up (*Inf.*), frenzy,

fury, indignation, ire, outburst, paroxysm, rage, resentment, storm, vehemence, wrath

passionate **1.** amorous, ardent, aroused, desirous, erotic, hot, loving, lustful, sensual, sexy (*Inf.*), wanton **2.** animated, ardent, eager, emotional, enthusiastic, excited, fervent, fervid, fierce, frenzied, heartfelt, impassioned, impetuous, impulsive, intense, strong, vehement, warm, wild, zealous **3.** choleric, excitable, fiery, hot-headed, hot-tempered, irascible, irritable, peppery, quick-tempered, stormy, tempestuous, violent

passive acquiescent, compliant, docile, enduring, inactive, inert, lifeless, long-suffering, nonviolent, patient, quiescent, receptive, resigned, submissive, unassertive, uninvolved, unresisting

pass off **1.** counterfeit, fake, feign, make a pretence of, palm off **2.** come to an end, die

away, disappear, fade out, vanish **3.** emit, evaporate, give off, send forth, vaporize **4.** be completed, go off, happen, occur, take place, turn out **5.** dismiss, disregard, ignore, pass by, wink at

pass out **1.** *Inf.* become unconscious, black out (*Inf.*), drop, faint, flake out (*Inf.*), keel over (*Inf.*), lose consciousness, swoon (*Literary*) **2.** deal out, distribute, dole out, hand out

pass over disregard, forget, ignore, not dwell on, omit, overlook, pass by, take no notice of

pass up decline, forgo, give (something) a miss (*Inf.*), ignore, let go, let slip, miss, neglect, refuse, reject

password countersign, key word, open sesame, signal, watchword

past *adj.* **1.** accomplished, completed, done, elapsed, ended, extinct, finished, forgotten,

pasta ('pæstə) *n.* any of several variously shaped edible preparations made from a flour and water dough, such as spaghetti.

paste (peist) *n.* 1. a mixture of a soft or malleable consistency, such as toothpaste. 2. an adhesive made from water and flour or starch, used for joining pieces of paper, etc. 3. a preparation of food, such as meat, that has been pounded to a creamy mass, for spreading on bread, etc. 4. any of various sweet doughy confections: *almond paste*. 5. dough, esp. for making pastry. 6. **a.** a hard shiny glass used for making imitation gems. **b.** an imitation gem made of this glass. 7. the combined ingredients of porcelain. ~*vb.* (*tr.*) 8. (often foll. by *on* or *onto*) to attach as by using paste: *he pasted posters onto the wall.* 9. (usually foll. by *with*) to cover (a surface) with paper, etc.: *he pasted the wall with posters.* 10. *Sl.* to thrash or beat; defeat.

pasteboard ('peist,bɔːd) *n.* 1. a stiff board formed from layers of paper or pulp pasted together. ~*adj.* 2. flimsy or fake.

pastel ('pæstəl, pæ'stɛl) *n.* 1. **a.** a substance made of ground pigment bound with gum. **b.** a crayon of this. **c.** a drawing done in such crayons. 2. the medium or technique of pastel drawing. 3. a pale delicate colour. ~*adj.* 4. (of a colour) pale; delicate: *pastel blue.* —'**pastelist** or '**pastellist** *n.*

pastern ('pæstən) *n.* the part of a horse's foot between the fetlock and the hoof.

paste-up *n. Printing.* a sheet of paper or board on which are pasted artwork, proofs, etc., for photographing prior to making a plate.

pasteurization or **-isation** (,pæstəraɪ'zeɪʃən, -stjə-, ,pɑː-) *n.* the process of heating beverages, such as milk, beer, wine, or cider, or solid foods, such as cheese or crab meat, to destroy harmful microorganisms.

pasteurize or **-ise** ('pæstə,raɪz, -stjə-, 'pɑː-) *vb.* (*tr.*) to subject (milk, beer, etc.) to pasteurization. —'**pasteurizer** or **-iser** *n.*

pastiche (pæ'stiːʃ) or **pasticcio** (pæ'stiːtʃəʊ) *n.* 1. a work of art that mixes styles, materials, etc. 2. a work of art in the style of another artist.

pastille or **pastil** ('pæstɪl) *n.* 1. a small flavoured or medicated lozenge. 2. an aromatic substance burnt to fumigate the air.

pastime ('pɑːs,taɪm) *n.* an activity or entertainment which makes time pass pleasantly.

past master *n.* 1. a person with talent for, or experience in, a particular activity. 2. a person who has held the office of master in a guild, etc.

pastor ('pɑːstə) *n.* 1. a clergyman or priest in charge of a congregation. 2. a person who exercises spiritual guidance over a number of people. 3. a S Asian starling having a black head and wings and a pale pink body. —'**pastor,ship** *n.*

pastoral ('pɑːstərəl) *adj.* 1. of, characterized by, or depicting rural life, scenery, etc. 2. (of a literary work) dealing with an idealized form of rural existence. 3. (of land) used for pasture. 4. of or relating to a clergyman or priest in charge of a congregation or his duties as such. 5. of or relating to shepherds, their work, etc. ~*n.* 6. a literary work or picture portraying rural life, esp. in an idealizing way. 7. *Music.* a variant spelling of **pastorale**. 8. *Ecclesiast.* **a.** a letter from a clergyman to the people under his charge. **b.** the letter of a bishop to the clergy or people of his diocese. **c.** Also called: **pastoral staff.** the crosier carried by a bishop. —'**pastoralism** *n.* —'**pastorally** *adv.*

pastorale (,pæstə'rɑːl) *n., pl.* **-rales** or **-rali** (*Italian* -'rɑːli). *Music.* 1. a composition evocative of rural life, sometimes with a droning accompaniment. 2. a musical

play based on a rustic story.

pastoralist ('pɑːstərəlɪst) *n. Austral.* a grazier raising sheep, cattle, etc., on a large scale.

pastorate ('pɑːstərɪt) *n.* 1. the office or term of office of a pastor. 2. a body of pastors.

past participle *n.* a participial form of verbs used to modify a noun that is logically the object of a verb, also used in certain compound tenses and passive forms of the verb.

past perfect *Grammar.* ~*adj.* 1. denoting a tense of verbs used in relating past events where the action had already occurred at the time of the action of a main verb that is itself in a past tense. In English this is a compound tense formed with *had* plus the past participle. ~*n.* 2. **a.** the past perfect tense. **b.** a verb in this tense.

pastry ('peɪstrɪ) *n., pl.* **-tries.** 1. a dough of flour, water, and fat. 2. baked foods, such as tarts, made with this dough. 3. an individual cake or pastry pie.

pasturage ('pɑːstjʊərɪdʒ) *n.* 1. the business of grazing cattle. 2. another word for **pasture.**

pasture ('pɑːstʃə) *n.* 1. land covered with grass or herbage and grazed by or suitable for grazing by livestock. 2. the grass or herbage growing on it. ~*vb.* 3. (*tr.*) to cause (livestock) to graze or (of livestock) to graze (a pasture).

pasty[1] ('peɪstɪ) *adj.* **pastier, pastiest.** 1. of or like the colour, texture, etc., of paste. 2. (esp. of the complexion) pale or unhealthy-looking. —'**pastily** *adv.* —'**pastiness** *n.*

pasty[2] ('pæstɪ) *n., pl.* **pasties.** a round of pastry folded over a filling of meat, vegetables, etc.

pat[1] (pæt) *vb.* **patting, patted.** 1. to hit (something) lightly with the palm of the hand or some other flat surface: *to pat a ball.* 2. to slap (a person or animal) gently, esp. on the back, as an expression of affection, congratulation, etc. 3. (*tr.*) to shape, smooth, etc., with a flat instrument or the palm. 4. (*intr.*) to walk or run with light footsteps. 5. **pat (someone) on the back.** *Inf.* to congratulate. ~*n.* 6. a light blow with something flat. 7. a gentle slap. 8. a small mass of something: *a pat of butter.* 9. the sound of patting. 10. **pat on the back.** *Inf.* a gesture or word indicating approval.

pat[2] (pæt) *adv.* 1. Also: **off pat.** exactly or fluently memorized: *he recited it pat.* 2. opportunely or aptly. 3. **stand pat. a.** *Chiefly U.S.* to refuse to abandon a belief, decision, etc. **b.** (in poker, etc.) to play without adding new cards to the hand dealt. ~*adj.* 4. exactly right; apt: *a pat reply.* 5. too exactly fitting; glib: *a pat answer to a difficult problem.* 6. exactly right: *a pat hand in poker.*

pat. *abbrev. for* patent(ed).

patch (pætʃ) *n.* 1. a piece of material used to mend a garment, etc., or to make patchwork, a sewn-on pocket, etc. 2. **a.** a small plot of land. **b.** its produce: *a patch of cabbages.* 3. *Med.* **a.** a protective covering for an injured eye. **b.** any protective dressing. 4. an imitation beauty spot made of black silk, etc., worn esp. in the 18th century. 5. an identifying piece of fabric worn on the shoulder of a uniform. 6. a small contrasting section: *a patch of cloud in the blue sky.* 7. a scrap; remnant. 8. **not a patch on.** not nearly as good as. 9. **strike** or **hit a bad patch.** to have a difficult time. ~*vb.* (*tr.*) 10. to mend or supply (a garment, etc.) with a patch or patches. 11. to put together or produce with patches. 12. (of material) to serve as a patch to. 13. (often foll. by *up*) to mend hurriedly or in a makeshift way. 14. (often foll. by *up*) to make (up) or settle (a quarrel, etc.). 15. to connect (electric circuits) together temporarily. —'**patcher** *n.*

gone, over, over and done with, spent 2. ancient, bygone, early, erstwhile, foregoing, former, late, long-ago, olden, preceding, previous, prior, quondam, recent ~*n.* 3. **the past** antiquity, days gone by, days of yore, former times, good old days, history, long ago, olden days, old times, times past, yesteryear (*Literary*) 4. background, experience, history, life, past life ~*adv.* 5. across, beyond, by, on, over ~*prep.* 6. after, beyond, farther than, later than, outside, over, subsequent to

paste 1. *n.* adhesive, cement, glue, gum,

mucilage 2. *v.* cement, fasten, fix, glue, gum, stick

pastel *adj.* delicate, light, muted, pale, soft, soft-hued

pastiche blend, farrago, gallimaufry, hotchpotch, medley, *mélange*, miscellany, mixture, motley

pastille cough drop, jujube, lozenge, tablet, troche (*Medical*)

pastime activity, amusement, distraction, diversion, entertainment, game, hobby, leisure, play, recreation, relaxation, sport

past master ace (*Inf.*), artist, dab hand

(*Brit. inf.*), expert, old hand, virtuoso, wizard

pastor churchman, clergyman, divine, ecclesiastic, minister, parson, priest, rector, vicar

pastoral *adj.* 1. Arcadian, bucolic, country, georgic (*Literary*), idyllic, rural, rustic, simple 2. clerical, ecclesiastical, ministerial, priestly

pasture grass, grassland, grazing, grazing land, lea (*Poetic*), meadow, pasturage, shieling (*Scot.*)

pat *v.* 1. caress, dab, fondle, pet, slap, stroke, tap, touch ~*n.* 2. clap, dab, light blow, slap,

patchwork ('pætʃˌwɜːk) n. 1. needlework done by sewing pieces of different materials together. 2. something made up of various parts.

patchy ('pætʃɪ) adj. **patchier, patchiest.** 1. irregular in quality, occurrence, intensity, etc.: a patchy essay. 2. having or forming patches. —'**patchily** adv. —'**patchiness** n.

pate (peɪt) n. the head, esp. with reference to baldness or (in facetious use) intelligence.

pâté ('pæteɪ) n. 1. a spread of finely minced liver, poultry, etc., served usually as an hors d'oeuvre. 2. a savoury pie.

pâté de foie gras (French pɑte də fwa 'grɑ) n., pl. **pâtés de foie gras** (French pɑte). a smooth rich paste made from the liver of a specially fattened goose.

patella (pə'tɛlə) n., pl. **-lae** (-liː). Anat. a small flat triangular bone in front of and protecting the knee joint. Nontechnical name: **kneecap.** —pa'**tellar** adj.

paten ('pætən) n. a plate, usually made of silver or gold, esp. for the bread in the Eucharist.

patent ('peɪtənt, 'pætənt) n. 1. **a.** a government grant to an inventor assuring him the sole right to make, use, and sell his invention for a limited period. **b.** a document conveying such a grant. 2. an invention, privilege, etc., protected by a patent. 3. **a.** an official document granting a right. **b.** any right granted by such a document. ~adj. 4. open or available for inspection (esp. in letters **patent, patent writ**). 5. ('peɪtənt). obvious: their scorn was patent to everyone. 6. concerning protection, appointment, etc., of or by a patent or patents. 7. proprietary. 8. (esp. of a bodily passage or duct) being open or unobstructed. ~vb. (tr.) 9. to obtain a patent for. 10. to grant by a patent. —'**patentable** adj. —ˌpaten'**tee** n. —ˌpaten'**tor** n.

patent leather ('peɪtənt) n. leather processed with lacquer to give a hard glossy surface.

patently ('peɪtəntlɪ) adv. obviously.

patent medicine ('peɪtənt) n. a medicine with a patent, available without a prescription.

Patent Office n. a government department that issues patents.

pater ('peɪtə) n. Brit. sl. another word for **father:** now chiefly used facetiously.

paternal (pə'tɜːnəl) adj. 1. relating to or characteristic of a father; fatherly. 2. (prenominal) related through the father: his paternal grandfather. 3. inherited or derived from the male parent. —pa'**ternally** adv.

paternity (pə'tɜːnɪtɪ) n. 1. **a.** the fact or state of being a father. **b.** (as modifier): a paternity suit was filed against the man. 2. descent or derivation from a father. 3. authorship or origin.

Paternoster (ˌpætə'nɒstə) n. (sometimes not cap.) R.C. Church. 1. the Lord's Prayer, esp. in Latin. 2. the recital of this as an act of devotion.

path (pɑːθ) n., pl. **paths** (pɑːðz). 1. a road or way, esp. a narrow trodden track. 2. a surfaced walk, as through a garden. 3. the course or direction in which something moves: the path of a whirlwind. 4. a course of conduct: the path of virtue. —'**pathless** adj.

path. abbrev. for: 1. pathological. 2. pathology.

-path suffix forming nouns. 1. denoting a person suffering from a specified disease or disorder: neuropath. 2. denoting a practitioner of a particular method of treatment: osteopath.

pathetic (pə'θɛtɪk) adj. 1. evoking or expressing pity, sympathy, etc. 2. distressingly inadequate: a pathetic fire flickered in the hearth. 3. Brit. sl. uninteresting; worthless. 4. Obs. of or affecting the feelings. —pa'**thetically** adv.

pathetic fallacy n. (in literature) the presentation of nature, etc., as possessing human feelings.

patho- or before a vowel **path-** combining form. disease: pathology.

pathogen ('pæθəˌdʒɛn) n. any agent that can cause disease. —ˌpatho'**genic** adj.

pathological (ˌpæθə'lɒdʒɪkəl) or **pathologic** adj. 1. of or relating to pathology. 2. relating to, involving, or caused by disease. 3. Inf. compulsively motivated: a pathological liar. —ˌpatho'**logically** adv.

pathology (pə'θɒlədʒɪ) n., pl. **-gies.** 1. the branch of medicine concerned with the cause, origin, and nature of disease, including the changes occurring as a result of disease. 2. the manifestations of disease, esp. changes occurring in tissues or organs. —pa'**thologist** n.

pathos ('peɪθɒs) n. 1. the quality or power, esp. in literature or speech, of arousing feelings of pity, sorrow, etc. 2. a feeling of sympathy or pity.

pathway ('pɑːθˌweɪ) n. 1. another word for **path.** 2. Biochem. a chain of reactions associated with a particular metabolic process.

-pathy n. combining form. 1. indicating feeling or perception: telepathy. 2. indicating disease: psychopathy. 3. indicating a method of treating disease: osteopathy. —'**-pathic** adj. combining form.

patience ('peɪʃəns) n. 1. tolerant and even-tempered perseverance. 2. the capacity for calmly enduring pain, trying situations, etc. 3. Brit. any of various card games for one player only. U.S. word: **solitaire.**

patient ('peɪʃənt) adj. 1. enduring trying circumstances with even temper. 2. tolerant; understanding. 3. capable of accepting delay with equanimity. 4. persevering or diligent: a patient worker. ~n. 5. a person who is receiving medical care. —'**patiently** adv.

patina ('pætɪnə) n. 1. a film formed on the surface of a metal, esp. the green oxidation of bronze or copper. 2. any fine layer on a surface: a patina of frost. 3. the sheen on a surface caused by long handling.

patio ('pætɪˌəʊ) n., pl. **-os.** 1. an open inner courtyard, esp. one in a Spanish or Spanish-American house. 2. an area adjoining a house, esp. one that is paved.

patois ('pætwɑː; French pa'twa) n., pl. **patois** ('pætwɑːz; French pa'twa). a regional dialect of a language, usually considered substandard.

pat. pend. abbrev. for patent pending.

patri- combining form. father: patricide; patriarch.

patrial ('peɪtrɪəl) n. Brit. a person who has rights of nationality by virtue of the birth of a parent or grandparents.

patriarch ('peɪtrɪˌɑːk) n. 1. the male head of a tribe or family. 2. a very old or venerable man. 3. Bible. **a.** any of a number of persons regarded as the fathers of the human race. **b.** any of the three ancestors of the Hebrew

---

THESAURUS

stroke, tap **3.** cake, dab, lump, portion, small piece

patch n. 1. piece of material, reinforcement **2.** bit, scrap, shred, small piece, spot, stretch **3.** area, ground, land, plot, tract ~v. **4.** cover, fix, mend, reinforce, repair, sew up **5.** With up bury the hatchet, conciliate, make friends, placate, restore, settle, settle differences, smooth

patchwork confusion, hash, hotchpotch, jumble, medley, mishmash, mixture, pastiche

patchy bitty, erratic, fitful, irregular, random, sketchy, spotty, uneven, variable, varying

patent 1. adj. apparent, blatant, clear, conspicuous, downright, evident, flagrant, glaring, indisputable, manifest, obvious, open, palpable, transparent, unconcealed, unequivocal, unmistakable **2.** n. copyright, invention, licence

paternal 1. benevolent, concerned, fatherlike, fatherly, protective, solicitous, vigilant **2.** patrilineal, patrimonial

paternity 1. fatherhood, fathership **2.** descent, extraction, family, lineage, parentage **3.** authorship, derivation, origin, source

path 1. footpath, footway, pathway, towpath, track, trail, walkway (Chiefly U.S.) **2.** avenue, course, direction, passage, procedure, road, route, track, walk, way

pathetic 1. affecting, distressing, heartbreaking, heart-rending, melting, moving, pitiable, plaintive, poignant, sad, tender, touching **2.** deplorable, feeble, inadequate, lamentable, meagre, miserable, paltry, petty, pitiful, poor, puny, sorry, wet (Brit. inf.), woeful **3.** Sl. crummy (Sl.), rubbishy, trashy, uninteresting, useless, worthless

pathfinder discoverer, explorer, guide, pioneer, scout, trailblazer

pathless impassable, impenetrable, trackless, uncharted, unexplored, untrodden, waste, wild

pathos pitiableness, pitifulness, plaintiveness, poignancy, sadness

patience 1. calmness, composure, cool (Sl.), equanimity, even temper, forbearance, imperturbability, restraint, serenity, sufferance, tolerance, toleration **2.** constancy, diligence, endurance, fortitude, long-suffering, perseverance, persistence, resignation, stoicism, submission

patient adj. 1. calm, composed, enduring, long-suffering, persevering, persistent, philosophical, quiet, resigned, self-possessed, serene, stoical, submissive, uncomplaining, untiring **2.** accommodating, even-tempered, forbearing, forgiving, indulgent, lenient, mild, tolerant, understanding ~n. **3.** case, invalid, sick person, sufferer

people: Abraham, Isaac, or Jacob. **c.** any of Jacob's twelve sons, regarded as the ancestors of the twelve tribes of Israel. **4.** *Early Christian Church.* the bishop of one of several principal sees, esp. those of Rome, Antioch, and Alexandria. **5.** *Eastern Orthodox.* the bishops of the four ancient principal sees of Constantinople, Antioch, Alexandria, and Jerusalem, and also of Russia, Rumania, and Serbia. **6.** *R.C. Church.* **a.** a title given to the Pope. **b.** a title given to a number of bishops, esp. of the Uniat Churches, indicating their rank as immediately below that of the Pope. **7.** the oldest or most venerable member of a group, community, etc. **8.** a person regarded as the founder of a community, tradition, etc. —ˌpatri'archal *adj.*

patriarchate ('peɪtrɪˌɑːkɪt) *n.* the office, jurisdiction, province, or residence of a patriarch.

patriarchy ('peɪtrɪˌɑːkɪ) *n., pl.* **-chies.** **1.** a form of social organization in which a male is the head of the family and descent, kinship, and title are traced through the male line. **2.** any society governed by such a system.

patrician (pəˈtrɪʃən) *n.* **1.** a member of the hereditary aristocracy of ancient Rome. **2.** (in medieval Europe) a member of the upper class in numerous Italian republics and German free cities. **3.** an aristocrat. **4.** a person of refined conduct, tastes, etc. ~*adj.* **5.** (esp. in ancient Rome) of, relating to, or composed of patricians. **6.** aristocratic.

patricide ('pætrɪˌsaɪd) *n.* **1.** the act of killing one's father. **2.** a person who kills his father. —ˌpatri'cidal *adj.*

patrimony ('pætrɪmənɪ) *n., pl.* **-nies.** **1.** an inheritance from one's father or other ancestor. **2.** the endowment of a church. —**patrimonial** (ˌpætrɪˈməʊnɪəl) *adj.*

patriot ('peɪtrɪət, 'pæt-) *n.* a person who vigorously supports his country and its way of life. —**patriotic** (ˌpætrɪˈɒtɪk) *adj.* —ˌpatri'otically *adv.* —**patriotism** ('pætrɪəˌtɪzəm) *n.*

patrol (pəˈtrəʊl) *n.* **1.** the action of going round a town, etc., at regular intervals for purposes of security or observation. **2.** a person or group that carries out such an action. **3.** a military detachment with the mission of security or the destruction of enemy forces. **4.** a division of a troop of Scouts or Guides. ~*vb.* **-trolling, -trolled. 5.** to engage in a patrol of (a place). —pa'**troller** *n.*

patron ('peɪtrən) *n.* **1.** a person who sponsors or aids artists, charities, etc.; protector or benefactor. **2.** a customer of a shop, hotel, etc., esp. a regular one. **3.** See **patron saint.**

patronage ('pætrənɪdʒ) *n.* **1. a.** the support given or custom brought by a patron. **b.** the position of a patron. **2.** (in politics) **a.** the practice of making appointments to office, granting contracts, etc. **b.** the favours, etc., so distributed. **3. a.** a condescending manner. **b.** any kindness done in a condescending way.

patronize *or* **-ise** ('pætrəˌnaɪz) *vb.* **1.** to behave or treat in a condescending way. **2.** to act as a patron by sponsoring or bringing trade to. —'**patron,izer** *or* ˌ-**iser** *n.* —'**patron,izingly** *or* -ˌ**isingly** *adv.*

patron saint *n.* a saint regarded as the particular guardian of a country, person, etc.

patronymic (ˌpætrəˈnɪmɪk) *adj.* **1.** (of a name) derived from the name of its bearer's father. ~*n.* **2.** a patronymic name.

patter[1] ('pætə) *vb.* **1.** (*intr.*) to walk or move with quick soft steps. **2.** (*intr.*) to strike with or make a quick succession of light tapping sounds. ~*n.* **3.** a quick succession of light tapping sounds, as of feet: *the patter of mice.*

patter[2] ('pætə) *n.* **1.** the glib rapid speech of comedians, etc. **2.** quick idle talk; chatter. **3.** the jargon of a particular group, etc.; lingo. ~*vb.* **4.** to speak glibly and rapidly. **5.** to repeat (prayers, etc.) in a mechanical or perfunctory manner.

pattern ('pætən) *n.* **1.** an arrangement of repeated or corresponding parts, decorative motifs, etc. **2.** a decorative design: *a paisley pattern.* **3.** a style: *various patterns of cutlery.* **4.** a plan or diagram used as a guide in making something: *a paper pattern for a dress.* **5.** a standard way of moving, acting, etc.: *traffic patterns.* **6.** a model worthy of imitation: *a pattern of kindness.* **7.** a representative sample. **8.** a wooden or metal shape or model used in a foundry to make a mould. ~*vb.* (*tr.*). **9.** (often foll. by *after* or *on*) to model. **10.** to arrange as or decorate with a pattern.

patty ('pætɪ) *n., pl.* **-ties.** **1.** a small cake of minced food. **2.** a small pie.

paucity ('pɔːsɪtɪ) *n.* **1.** insufficiency; dearth. **2.** smallness of number; fewness.

Pauline ('pɔːlaɪn) *adj.* relating to Saint Paul or his doctrines.

paunch (pɔːntʃ) *n.* **1.** the belly or abdomen, esp. when protruding. ~*vb.* (*tr.*). **2.** to stab in the stomach; disembowel. —'**paunchy** *adj.* —'**paunchiness** *n.*

pauper ('pɔːpə) *n.* **1.** a person who is extremely poor. **2.** (formerly) a person supported by public charity. —'**pauperism** *n.*

pause (pɔːz) *vb.* (*intr.*) **1.** to cease an action temporarily. **2.** to hesitate; delay: *she replied without pausing.* ~*n.* **3.** a temporary stop or rest, esp. in speech or action; short break. **4.** *Prosody.* another word for **caesura.** **5.** Also called: **fermata.** *Music.* a continuation of a note or rest beyond its normal length. Usual symbol: ⌢ **6.** **give pause (to).** to cause to hesitate.

pavane *or* **pavan** (pəˈvɑːn, 'pævən) *n.* **1.** a slow and stately dance of the 16th and 17th centuries. **2.** music for or in the rhythm of this dance.

pave (peɪv) *vb.* (*tr.*) **1.** to cover (a road, etc.) with a firm surface suitable for travel, as with paving stones or concrete. **2.** to serve as the material for a pavement or other hard layer: *bricks paved the causeway.* **3.** (often foll. by *with*) to cover with a hard layer (of): *shelves paved with marble.* **4.** to prepare or make easier (esp. in **pave the way**). —'**paver** *n.*

THESAURUS

patriot chauvinist, flag-waver (*Inf.*), jingo, lover of one's country, loyalist, nationalist

patriotic chauvinistic, flag-waving (*Inf.*), jingoistic, loyal, nationalistic

patriotism flag-waving (*Inf.*), jingoism, love of one's country, loyalty, nationalism

patrol *n.* **1.** guarding, policing, protecting, rounds, safeguarding, vigilance, watching **2.** garrison, guard, patrolman, sentinel, watch, watchman ~*v.* **3.** cruise, guard, inspect, keep guard, keep watch, make the rounds, police, pound, range, safeguard, walk the beat

patron 1. advocate, angel (*Inf.*), backer, benefactor, champion, defender, friend, guardian, helper, philanthropist, protector, sponsor, supporter **2.** buyer, client, customer, frequenter, habitué, shopper

patronage 1. aid, assistance, backing, benefaction, championship, encouragement, help, promotion, sponsorship, support **2.** business, clientele, commerce, custom, trade, trading, traffic **3.** condescension, deigning, disdain, patronizing, stooping

patronize 1. be lofty with, look down on, talk down to, treat as inferior, treat condescendingly, treat like a child **2.** assist, back, befriend, foster, fund, help, maintain, promote, sponsor, subscribe to, support **3.** be a customer or client of, buy from, deal with, do business with, frequent, shop at, trade with

patronizing condescending, contemptuous, disdainful, gracious, haughty, lofty, snobbish, stooping, supercilious, superior, toffee-nosed (*Sl.*)

patter[1] *v.* **1.** scurry, scuttle, skip, tiptoe, trip, walk lightly **2.** beat, pat, pelt, pitapat, pitter-patter, rat-a-tat, spatter, tap ~*n.* **3.** pattering, pitapat, pitter-patter, tapping

patter[2] *n.* **1.** line, monologue, pitch, spiel (*Inf.*) **2.** chatter, gabble, jabber, nattering, prattle, yak (*Sl.*) **3.** argot, cant, jargon, lingo (*Inf.*), patois, slang, vernacular ~*v.* **4.** babble, blab, chatter, hold forth, jabber, prate, rattle off, rattle on, spiel (*Inf.*), spout (*Inf.*), tattle

pattern *n.* **1.** arrangement, decoration, decorative design, design, device, figure, motif, ornament **2.** arrangement, method, order, orderliness, plan, sequence, system **3.** kind, shape, sort, style, type, variety **4.** design, diagram, guide, instructions, original, plan, stencil, template **5.** archetype, criterion, cynosure, example, exemplar, guide, model, norm, original, paradigm, paragon, prototype, sample, specimen, standard ~*v.* **6.** copy, emulate, follow, form, imitate, model, mould, order, shape, style **7.** decorate, design, trim

paucity dearth, deficiency, fewness, insufficiency, lack, meagreness, paltriness, poverty, rarity, scantiness, scarcity, shortage, slenderness, slightness, smallness, sparseness, sparsity

paunch abdomen, beer-belly (*Sl.*), belly, corporation (*Brit. inf.*), pot, potbelly

pauper bankrupt, beggar, down-and-out, have-not, indigent, insolvent, mendicant, poor person

pause 1. *v.* break, cease, delay, deliberate, desist, discontinue, halt, have a breather (*Inf.*), hesitate, interrupt, rest, stop briefly, take a break, wait, waver **2.** *n.* break, breather (*Inf.*), caesura, cessation, delay, discontinuance, gap, halt, hesitation, interlude, intermission, interruption, interval, let-up (*Inf.*), lull, respite, rest, stay, stoppage, wait

pave asphalt, concrete, cover, flag, floor, macadamize, surface, tar, tile

pavement ('peɪvmənt) n. 1. a hard-surfaced path for pedestrians alongside and a little higher than a road. U.S. word: **sidewalk**. 2. the material used in paving.

pavilion (pə'vɪljən) n. 1. Brit. a building at a sports ground, esp. a cricket pitch, in which players change, etc. 2. a summerhouse or other decorative shelter. 3. a building or temporary structure, esp. one that is open and ornamental, for housing exhibitions, etc. 4. a large ornate tent, esp. one with a peaked top, as used by medieval armies. 5. one of a set of buildings that together form a hospital or other large institution. ~vb. (tr.) Literary. 6. to place as in a pavilion: pavilioned in splendour. 7. to provide with a pavilion or pavilions.

paving ('peɪvɪŋ) n. 1. a paved surface; pavement. 2. material used for a pavement.

pavlova (pæv'ləʊvə) n. a meringue cake topped with whipped cream and fruit.

paw (pɔː) n. 1. any of the feet of a four-legged mammal, bearing claws or nails. 2. Inf. a hand, esp. one that is large, clumsy, etc. ~vb. 3. to scrape or contaminate with the paws or feet. 4. (tr.) Inf. to touch or caress in a clumsy, rough, or overfamiliar manner.

pawl (pɔːl) n. a pivoted lever shaped to engage with a ratchet wheel to prevent motion in a particular direction.

pawn[1] (pɔːn) vb. (tr.) 1. to deposit (an article) as security for the repayment of a loan, esp. from a pawnbroker. 2. to stake: to pawn one's honour. ~n. 3. an article deposited as security. 4. the condition of being so deposited (esp. in **in pawn**). 5. a person or thing that is held as a security. 6. the act of pawning. —'pawnage n.

pawn[2] (pɔːn) n. 1. a chess piece of the lowest theoretical value. 2. a person, group, etc., manipulated by another.

pawnbroker ('pɔːn,brəʊkə) n. a dealer licensed to lend money at a specified rate of interest on the security of movable personal property, which can be sold if the loan is not repaid within a specified period. —'pawn,broking n.

pawnshop ('pɔːn,ʃɒp) n. the premises of a pawnbroker.

pawpaw ('pɔː,pɔː) n. another name for **papaw** or **papaya**.

pax (pæks) n. 1. Chiefly R.C. Church. a. the kiss of peace. b. a small metal or ivory plate, formerly used to convey the kiss of peace from the celebrant at Mass to those attending it. ~interj. 2. Brit. school sl. a call signalling an end to hostilities or claiming immunity from the rules of a game.

P.A.X. Brit. abbrev. for private automatic exchange.

pay (peɪ) vb. **paying, paid.** 1. to discharge (a debt, obligation, etc.) by giving or doing something: he paid his creditors. 2. (when intr., often foll. by for) to give (money, etc.) to (a person) in return for goods or services: they pay their workers well; they pay by the hour. 3. to give or afford (a person, etc.) a profit or benefit: it pays one to be honest. 4. (tr.) to give or bestow (a compliment, regards, attention, etc.). 5. (tr.) to make (a visit or call). 6. (intr.; often foll. by for) to give compensation or make amends. 7. (tr.) to yield a return of: the shares pay 15 per cent. 8. Austral. inf. to acknowledge or accept (something) as true, just, etc. 9. **pay one's way. a.** to contribute one's share of expenses. **b.** to remain solvent without outside help. ~n. 10. **a.** a money given in return for work or services; a salary or wage. **b.** (as modifier): a pay slip; pay claim. 11. paid employment (esp.

in **in the pay of**). 12. (modifier) Chiefly U.S. requiring the insertion of money before or during use: a pay phone. 13. (modifier) rich enough in minerals to be profitably worked: pay gravel. ~See also **pay back, pay for,** etc. —'payer n.

payable ('peɪəbəl) adj. 1. (often foll. by on) to be paid: payable on the third of each month. 2. that is capable of being paid. 3. capable of being profitable. 4. (of a debt, etc.) imposing an obligation on the debtor to pay, esp. at once.

pay back vb. (tr., adv.) 1. to retaliate against: to pay someone back for an insult. 2. to give or do (something equivalent) in return for a favour, insult, etc. 3. to repay (a loan, etc.).

pay bed n. a bed in a hospital for which the user has paid as a private patient.

P.A.Y.E. (in Britain and New Zealand) abbrev. for pay as you earn; a system by which income tax levied on wage and salary earners is paid by employers directly to the government.

payee (peɪ'iː) n. the person to whom a cheque, money order, etc., is made out.

pay for vb. (prep.) 1. to make (payment) (for). 2. (intr.) to suffer or be punished, as for a mistake, wrong decision, etc.

paying guest n. a euphemism for **lodger**.

payload ('peɪ,ləʊd) n. 1. that part of a cargo earning revenue. 2. **a.** the passengers, cargo, or bombs carried by an aircraft. **b.** the equipment carried by a rocket, satellite, or spacecraft. 3. the explosive power of a warhead, bomb, etc., carried by a missile or aircraft.

paymaster ('peɪ,mɑːstə) n. an official of a government, business, etc., responsible for the payment of wages and salaries.

payment ('peɪmənt) n. 1. the act of paying. 2. a sum of money paid. 3. something given in return; punishment or reward.

pay off vb. 1. (tr., adv.) to pay all that is due in wages, etc., and discharge from employment. 2. (tr., adv.) to pay the complete amount of (a debt, bill, etc.). 3. (intr., adv.) to turn out to be profitable, effective, etc.: the gamble paid off. 4. (tr., adv. or intr., prep.) to take revenge on (a person) or for (a wrong done): to pay someone off for an insult. 5. (tr., adv.) Inf. to give a bribe to. ~n. **payoff.** 6. the final settlement, esp. in retribution. 7. Inf. the climax, consequence, or outcome of events, a story, etc. 8. the final payment of a debt, salary, etc. 9. the time of such a payment. 10. Inf. a bribe.

payola (peɪ'əʊlə) n. Inf. 1. a bribe given to secure special treatment, esp. to a disc jockey to promote a commercial product. 2. the practice of paying or receiving such bribes.

pay out vb. (adv.) 1. to distribute (money, etc.); disburse. 2. (tr.) to release (a rope) gradually, hand over hand.

payroll ('peɪ,rəʊl) n. 1. a list of employees, specifying the salary or wage of each. 2. the total of these amounts or the actual money equivalent.

pay up vb. (adv.) to pay (money) promptly, in full, or on demand.

Pb the chemical symbol for lead.

P.C. abbrev. for: 1. Parish Council(lor). 2. (in Britain) Police Constable. 3. (in Britain) Privy Council(lor). 4. (in Canada) Progressive Conservative.

THESAURUS

paw v. grab, handle roughly, manhandle, maul, molest

pawn[1] 1. v. deposit, gage (Archaic), hazard, hock (Inf., chiefly U.S.), mortgage, pledge, pop (Inf.), stake, wager 2. n. assurance, bond, collateral, gage, guarantee, guaranty, pledge, security

pawn[2] n. cat's-paw, creature, dupe, instrument, plaything, puppet, stooge (Sl.), tool, toy

pay v. 1. clear, compensate, cough up (Inf.), discharge, foot, give, honour, liquidate, meet, offer, recompense, reimburse, remit, remunerate, render, requite, reward, settle, square up 2. be advantageous, benefit, be worthwhile, repay, serve 3. bestow, extend, give, grant, present, proffer, render 4. Often with for answer for, atone, be punished, compensate, get one's deserts, make

amends, suffer, suffer the consequences 5. bring in, produce, profit, return, yield 6. be profitable, be remunerative, make a return, make money, provide a living 7. avenge oneself for, get even with (Inf.), get revenge on, pay back, punish, reciprocate, repay, requite, settle a score ~n. 8. allowance, compensation, earnings, emoluments, fee, hire, income, payment, recompense, reimbursement, remuneration, reward, salary, stipend, takings, wages

payable due, mature, obligatory, outstanding, owed, owing, receivable, to be paid

pay back 1. get even with (Inf.), get one's own back, reciprocate, recompense, retaliate, settle a score 2. refund, reimburse, repay, return, settle up, square

payment 1. defrayal, discharge, outlay,

paying, remittance, settlement 2. advance, deposit, instalment, portion, premium, remittance 3. fee, hire, remuneration, reward, wage

pay off 1. discharge, dismiss, fire, lay off, let go, sack (Inf.) 2. clear, discharge, liquidate, pay in full, settle, square 3. be effective (profitable, successful), succeed, work 4. get even with (Inf.), pay back, retaliate, settle a score 5. Inf. bribe, buy off, corrupt, get at, grease the palm of (Sl.), oil (Inf.), suborn

pay out 1. cough up (Inf.), disburse, expend, fork out or over or up (Sl.), lay out (Inf.), shell out (Inf.), spend 2. get even with (Inf.), pay back, retaliate, settle a score

p.c. *abbrev. for:* **1.** per cent. **2.** postcard.

Pd *the chemical symbol for* palladium.

pd. *abbrev. for* paid.

p.d. *abbrev. for:* **1.** Also: **P.D.** per diem. **2.** potential difference.

P.D.S.A. (in Britain) *abbrev. for* People's Dispensary for Sick Animals.

P.D.T. (in the U.S. and Canada) *abbrev. for* Pacific Daylight Time.

P.E. *abbrev. for:* **1.** physical education. **2.** potential energy. **3.** Presiding Elder. **4.** Also: **p.e.** printer's error. **5.** *Statistics.* probable error. **6.** Protestant Episcopal.

pea (piː) *n.* **1.** an annual climbing plant with small white flowers and long green pods containing edible green seeds: cultivated in temperate regions. **2.** the seed of this plant, eaten as a vegetable. **3.** any of several other leguminous plants, such as the sweet pea.

peace (piːs) *n.* **1. a.** the state existing during the absence of war. **b.** (*as modifier*): *peace negotiations.* **2.** (*often cap.*) a treaty marking the end of a war. **3.** a state of harmony between people or groups. **4.** law and order within a state: *a breach of the peace.* **5.** absence of mental anxiety (often in **peace of mind**). **6.** a state of stillness, silence, or serenity. **7. at peace. a.** in a state of harmony or friendship. **b.** in a state of serenity. **c.** dead: *the old lady is at peace now.* **8. hold** or **keep one's peace.** to keep silent, esp. about something secret. **9. keep the peace.** to maintain law and order. ~*vb.* **10.** (*intr.*) *Obs. except as an imperative.* to be or become silent or still.

peaceable ('piːsəbəl) *adj.* **1.** inclined towards peace. **2.** tranquil; calm. —'**peaceableness** *n.* —'**peaceably** *adv.*

peaceful ('piːsfʊl) *adj.* **1.** not in a state of war or disagreement. **2.** calm; tranquil. **3.** of, relating to, or in accord with a time of peace. **4.** inclined towards peace. —'**peacefully** *adv.* —'**peacefulness** *n.*

peacemaker ('piːsˌmeɪkə) *n.* a person who establishes peace, esp. between others. —'**peace**ˌ**making** *n.*

peace offering *n.* **1.** something given to an adversary in the hope of procuring or maintaining peace. **2.** *Judaism.* a sacrificial meal shared between the offerer and Jehovah.

peace pipe *n.* a long decorated pipe smoked by North American Indians, esp. as a token of peace. Also called: **calumet.**

peacetime ('piːsˌtaɪm) *n.* **a.** a period without war; time of peace. **b.** (*as modifier*): *a peacetime agreement.*

peach[1] (piːtʃ) *n.* **1.** a small tree with pink flowers and rounded edible fruit: cultivated in temperate regions. **2.** the soft juicy fruit of this tree, which has a downy reddish-yellow skin, yellowish-orange sweet flesh, and a single stone. **3.** a pinkish-yellow to orange colour. **4.** *Inf.* a person or thing that is especially pleasing.

peach[2] (piːtʃ) *vb.* (*intr.*) *Sl.* to inform against (an accomplice).

peach melba *n.* a dessert made of halved peaches, vanilla ice cream, and raspberries.

peachy ('piːtʃɪ) *adj.* **peachier, peachiest. 1.** of or like a peach, esp. in colour or texture. **2.** *Inf.* excellent; fine. —'**peachiness** *n.*

peacock ('piːˌkɒk) *n., pl.* **-cocks** or **-cock. 1.** a male peafowl, having a crested head and a very large fan-like tail marked with blue and green eyelike spots. **2.** a vain strutting person. ~*vb.* **3.** to display (oneself) proudly. —'**pea**ˌ**cockish** *adj.* —'**pea**ˌ**hen** *fem. n.*

pea green *n., adj.* (**pea-green** *when prenominal*). **a.** a yellowish-green colour. **b.** (*as adj.*): *a pea-green teapot.*

pea jacket or **peacoat** ('piːˌkəʊt) *n.* a sailor's short heavy woollen overcoat.

peak[1] (piːk) *n.* **1.** a pointed end, edge, or projection: *the peak of a roof.* **2.** the pointed summit of a mountain. **3.** a mountain with a pointed summit. **4.** the point of greatest development, strength, etc.: *the peak of his career.* **5. a.** a sharp increase followed by a sharp decrease: *a voltage peak.* **b.** the maximum value of this quantity. **c.** (*as modifier*): *peak voltage.* **6.** Also called: **visor.** a projecting piece on the front of some caps. **7.** *Naut.* **a.** the extreme forward (**forepeak**) or aft (**afterpeak**) parts of the hull. **b.** (of a fore-and-aft quadrilateral sail) the after uppermost corner. **c.** the after end of a gaff. ~*vb.* **8.** (*tr.*) *Naut.* to set (a gaff) or tilt (oars) vertically. **9.** to form or reach or cause to form or reach a peak.

peak[2] (piːk) *vb.* (*intr.*) to become wan, emaciated, or sickly. —'**peaky** or '**peakish** *adj.*

peaked (piːkt) *adj.* having a peak; pointed.

peak load *n.* the maximum load on an electrical power-supply system.

peal (piːl) *n.* **1.** a loud prolonged usually reverberating sound, as of bells, thunder or laughter. **2.** *Bell-ringing.* a series of changes rung in accordance with specific rules. **3.** (*not in technical usage*) the set of bells in a belfry. ~*vb.* **4.** (*intr.*) to sound with a peal or peals. **5.** (*tr.*) to give forth loudly and sonorously. **6.** (*tr.*) to ring (bells) in peals.

peanut ('piːˌnʌt) *n.* **a.** a leguminous plant of tropical America widely cultivated for its edible seeds. **b.** the edible nutlike seed of this plant, used for food and as a source of oil. Also called: **groundnut, monkey nut.**

peanut butter *n.* a brownish oily paste made from peanuts.

peanuts ('piːˌnʌts) *n. Sl.* a trifling amount of money.

pear (pɛə) *n.* **1.** a widely cultivated tree, having white flowers and edible fruits. **2.** the sweet gritty-textured juicy fruit of this tree, which has a globular base and tapers towards the apex. **3.** the wood of this tree, used for making furniture.

pearl (pɜːl) *n.* **1.** a hard smooth lustrous typically rounded structure occurring on the inner surface of the shell of a clam or oyster around an invading particle such as a sand grain; much valued as a gem. **2.** any artificial gem resembling this. **3.** See **mother-of-pearl. 4.** a person or thing that is like a pearl, esp. in beauty or value. **5. a.** pale greyish-white colour, often with a bluish tinge. ~*adj.* **6.** of, made of, or set with pearl or mother-of-pearl. **7.** having the shape or colour of a pearl. ~*vb.* **8.** (*tr.*) to set with or as if with pearls. **9.** to shape into or assume a pearl-like form or colour. **10.** (*intr.*) to dive or search for pearls.

pearl barley *n.* barley ground into small round grains, used esp. in soups and stews.

pearly ('pɜːlɪ) *adj.* **pearlier, pearliest. 1.** resembling a pearl, esp. in lustre. **2.** decorated with pearls or mother-of-pearl. ~*n., pl.* **pearlies.** *Brit.* **3.** a London costermonger or the wife of one who wears on ceremonial occasions a traditional dress of dark clothes covered with pearl buttons. **4.** (*pl.*) the clothes or the buttons themselves. —'**pearliness** *n.*

Pearly Gates *pl. n. Inf.* the entrance to heaven.

pearly king or (*fem.*) **pearly queen** *n.* the London costermonger whose ceremonial clothes display the most lavish collection of pearl buttons.

peasant ('pɛzənt) *n.* **1.** a member of a class of low social status that depends on either cottage industry or agricultural labour as a means of subsistence. **2.** *Inf.* a person who lives in the country; rustic. **3.** *Inf.* an uncouth or uncultured person.

peasantry ('pɛzəntrɪ) *n.* peasants as a class.

THESAURUS

peace 1. accord, agreement, amity, concord, harmony **2.** armistice, cessation of hostilities, conciliation, pacification, treaty, truce **3.** calm, composure, contentment, placidity, relaxation, repose, serenity **4.** calm, calmness, hush, peacefulness, quiet, quietude, repose, rest, silence, stillness, tranquillity

peaceable 1. amiable, amicable, conciliatory, dovish, friendly, gentle, inoffensive, mild, nonbelligerent, pacific, peaceful, peace-loving, placid, unwarlike **2.** balmy, calm, peaceful, quiet, restful, serene, still, tranquil, undisturbed

peaceful 1. amicable, at peace, free from strife, friendly, harmonious, nonviolent, on friendly or good terms, without hostility **2.** calm, gentle, placid, quiet, restful, serene, still, tranquil, undisturbed, unruffled, untroubled **3.** conciliatory, irenic, pacific, peaceable, peace-loving, placatory, unwarlike

peacemaker appeaser, arbitrator, conciliator, mediator, pacifier, peacemonger

peak *n.* **1.** aiguille, apex, brow, crest, pinnacle, point, summit, tip, top **2.** acme, apogee, climax, crown, culmination, high point, maximum point, *ne plus ultra*, zenith ~*v.* **3.** be at its height, climax, come to a head, culminate, reach its highest point, reach the zenith

peal 1. *n.* blast, carillon, chime, clamour, clang, clap, crash, resounding, reverberation, ring, ringing, roar, rumble, sound, tintinnabulation **2.** *v.* chime, crack, crash, resonate, resound, reverberate, ring, roar, roll, rumble, sound, tintinnabulate, toll

peasant 1. churl (*Archaic*), countryman, hind (*Archaic*), rustic, son of the soil, swain (*Archaic*) **2.** *Inf.* boor, churl, country bumpkin, lout, provincial, yokel

pease (pi:z) *n., pl.* **pease.** *Arch. or dialect.* another word for **pea.**

peasecod *or* **peascod** ('pi:z,kɒd) *n. Arch.* the pod of a pea plant.

pease pudding *n. Chiefly Brit.* a dish of split peas that have been soaked and boiled.

peashooter ('pi:,ʃu:tə) *n.* a tube through which dried peas are blown, used as a toy weapon.

peasouper ('pi:,su:pə) *n.* **1.** *Inf., chiefly Brit.* dense dirty yellowish fog. **2.** *Canad.* a disparaging name for a French Canadian.

peat (pi:t) *n.* **a.** a compact brownish deposit of partially decomposed vegetable matter saturated with water: found in uplands and bogs and used as a fuel (when dried) and as a fertilizer. **b.** (*as modifier*): *peat bog.* —'**peaty** *adj.*

peat moss *n.* any of various mosses, esp. sphagnum, that grow in wet places and decay to form peat. See also **sphagnum.**

pebble ('pɛbəl) *n.* **1.** a small smooth rounded stone, esp. one worn by the action of water. **2. a.** a transparent colourless variety of rock crystal, used for making certain lenses. **b.** such a lens. **3.** (*modifier*) *Inf.* (of a lens or of spectacles) thick, with a high degree of magnification or distortion. **4. a.** a grainy irregular surface, esp. on leather. **b.** leather having such a surface. ~*vb.* **5.** to cover with pebbles. **6.** (*tr.*) to impart a grainy surface to (leather). —'**pebbly** *adj.*

pebble dash *n. Brit.* a finish for external walls consisting of small stones embedded in plaster.

pecan (pɪ'kæn, 'pi:kən) *n.* **1.** a hickory tree of the southern U.S. having deeply furrowed bark and edible nuts. **2.** the smooth oval nut of this tree, which has a sweet oily kernel.

peccadillo (,pɛkə'dɪləʊ) *n., pl.* **-los** *or* **-loes.** a petty sin or fault.

peccary ('pɛkərɪ) *n., pl.* **-ries** *or* **-ry.** either of two pig-like mammals of forests of southern North America, Central and South America.

peck[1] (pɛk) *n.* **1.** a unit of dry measure equal to 8 quarts or one quarter of a bushel. **2.** a container used for measuring this quantity. **3.** a large quantity or number.

peck[2] (pɛk) *vb.* **1.** (when *intr.*, sometimes foll. by *at*) to strike with the beak or with a pointed instrument. **2.** (*tr.*; sometimes foll. by *out*) to dig (a hole, etc.) by pecking. **3.** (*tr.*) (of birds) to pick up (corn, worms, etc.) by pecking. **4.** (*intr.*; often foll. by *at*) to nibble or pick (at one's food). **5.** *Inf.* to kiss (a person) quickly and lightly. **6.** (*intr.*; foll. by *at*) to nag. ~*n.* **7.** a quick light blow, esp. from a bird's beak. **8.** a mark made by such a blow. **9.** *Inf.* a quick light kiss.

pecker ('pɛkə) *n. Brit. sl.* good spirits (esp. in **keep one's pecker up**).

peckish ('pɛkɪʃ) *adj. Inf., chiefly Brit.* feeling slightly hungry.

pectin ('pɛktɪn) *n. Biochem.* any of the acidic polysaccharides that occur in ripe fruit and vegetables: used in the manufacture of jams because of their ability to solidify to a gel. —'**pectic** *or* '**pectinous** *adj.*

pectoral ('pɛktərəl) *adj.* **1.** of or relating to the chest, breast, or thorax: *pectoral fins.* **2.** worn on the breast or chest: *a pectoral medallion.* ~*n.* **3.** a pectoral organ or part, esp. a muscle or fin. **4.** a medicine for disorders of the chest or lungs. **5.** anything worn on the chest or

breast for decoration or protection. —'**pectorally** *adv.*

pectoral fin *n.* either of a pair of fins, situated just behind the head in fishes, that help to control the direction of movement during locomotion.

peculate ('pɛkjʊ,leɪt) *vb.* to appropriate or embezzle (public money, etc.). —,**pecu'lation** *n.* —'**pecu,lator** *n.*

peculiar (pɪ'kju:lɪə) *adj.* **1.** strange or unusual; odd: *a peculiar idea.* **2.** distinct from others; special. **3.** (*postpositive;* foll. by *to*) belonging characteristically or exclusively (to): *peculiar to North America.* —**pe'culiarly** *adv.*

peculiarity (pɪ,kju:lɪ'ærɪtɪ) *n., pl.* **-ties. 1.** a strange or unusual habit or characteristic. **2.** a distinguishing trait, etc., that is characteristic of a particular person; idiosyncrasy. **3.** the state or quality of being peculiar.

pecuniary (pɪ'kju:nɪərɪ) *adj.* **1.** of or relating to money. **2.** *Law.* (of an offence) involving a monetary penalty. —**pe'cuniarily** *adv.*

-ped *or* **-pede** *n. combining form.* foot or feet: *quadruped; centipede.*

pedagogue *or U.S.* (*sometimes*) **pedagog** ('pɛdə,gɒg) *n.* **1.** a teacher or educator. **2.** a pedantic or dogmatic teacher. —,**peda'gogic** *or* ,**peda'gogical** *adj.* —,**peda'gogically** *adv.*

pedagogy ('pɛdə,gɒgɪ, -,gɒdʒɪ, -,gəʊdʒɪ) *n.* the principles, practice, or profession of teaching.

pedal[1] ('pɛdəl) *n.* **1. a.** any foot-operated lever, esp. one of the two levers that drive the chainwheel of a bicycle, the foot-brake, clutch control, or accelerator of a car, one of the levers on an organ controlling deep bass notes, or one of the levers on a piano used to mute or sustain tone. **b.** (*as modifier*): *a pedal cycle.* ~*vb.* **-alling, -alled** *or U.S.* **-aling, -aled. 2.** to propel (a bicycle, etc.) by operating the pedals. **3.** (*intr.*) to operate the pedals of an organ, piano, etc. **4.** to work (pedals of any kind).

pedal[2] ('pi:dəl) *adj.* of or relating to the foot or feet.

pedant ('pɛdənt) *n.* **1.** a person who relies too much on academic learning or who is concerned chiefly with insignificant detail. **2.** *Arch.* a schoolmaster or teacher. —**pedantic** (pɪ'dæntɪk) *adj.* —**pe'dantically** *adv.*

pedantry ('pɛdəntrɪ) *n., pl.* **-ries.** the habit or an instance of being a pedant, esp. in the display of useless knowledge or minute observance of petty rules or details.

peddle ('pɛdəl) *vb.* **1.** to go from place to place selling (goods, esp. small articles). **2.** (*tr.*) to sell (illegal drugs, esp. narcotics). **3.** (*tr.*) to advocate (ideas, etc.) insistently: *to peddle a new philosophy.*

pederasty *or* **paederasty** ('pɛdə,ræstɪ) *n.* homosexual relations between men and boys. —'**pede,rast** *or* '**paede,rast** *n.* —,**peder'astic** *or* ,**paeder'astic** *adj.*

pedestal ('pɛdɪstəl) *n.* **1.** a base that supports a column, statue, etc. **2.** a position of eminence or supposed superiority (esp. in **place, put,** *or* **set on a pedestal**).

pedestrian (pɪ'dɛstrɪən) *n.* **1. a.** a person travelling on foot; walker. **b.** (*as modifier*): *a pedestrian precinct.* ~*adj.* **2.** dull; commonplace: *a pedestrian style of writing.*

pedestrian crossing *n. Brit.* a path across a road marked as a crossing for pedestrians.

pedestrianize *or* **-ise** (pɪ'dɛstrɪə,naɪz) *vb.* (*tr.*) to convert (a street, etc.) into an area for the use of pedestrians only. —**pe,destriani'zation** *or* **-i'sation** *n.*

THESAURUS

peccadillo error, indiscretion, infraction, lapse, misdeed, misdemeanour, petty offence, slip, trifling fault

peck *v./n.* bite, dig, hit, jab, kiss, nibble, pick, poke, prick, strike, tap

peculiar 1. abnormal, bizarre, curious, eccentric, exceptional, extraordinary, far-out (*Sl.*), freakish, funny, odd, offbeat, outlandish, out-of-the-way, quaint, queer, singular, strange, uncommon, unconventional, unusual, weird **2.** appropriate, characteristic, distinct, distinctive, distinguishing, endemic, idiosyncratic, individual, local, particular, personal, private, restricted, special, specific, unique

peculiarity 1. abnormality, bizarreness, eccentricity, foible, freakishness, idiosyncrasy, mannerism, oddity, odd trait, queerness,

quirk **2.** attribute, characteristic, distinctiveness, feature, mark, particularity, property, quality, singularity, speciality, trait

pedagogue dogmatist, dominie (*Scot.*), educator, instructor, master, mistress, pedant, schoolmaster, schoolmistress, teacher

pedant casuist, doctrinaire, dogmatist, hairsplitter, literalist, nit-picker (*Inf.*), pedagogue, pettifogger, precisian, quibbler, scholastic, sophist

pedantic abstruse, academic, bookish, didactic, donnish, erudite, formal, fussy, hairsplitting, nit-picking (*Inf.*), overnice, particular, pedagogic, pompous, precise, priggish, punctilious, scholastic, schoolmasterly, sententious, stilted

pedantry bookishness, finicality, hairsplitting, overnicety, pedagogism, pettifog-

gery, pomposity, punctiliousness, quibbling, sophistry, stuffiness

peddle flog (*Sl.*), hawk, huckster, market, push (*Inf.*), sell, sell door to door, trade, vend

pedestal 1. base, dado (*Architect.*), foot, foundation, mounting, pier, plinth, socle, stand, support **2. put on a pedestal** apotheosize, deify, dignify, ennoble, exalt, glorify, idealize, worship

pedestrian 1. *n.* footslogger, foot-traveller, walker **2.** *adj.* banal, boring, commonplace, dull, flat, humdrum, mediocre, mundane, ordinary, plodding, prosaic, run-of-the-mill, unimaginative, uninspired, uninteresting

pedi- *combining form.* indicating the foot: *pedicure.*

pediculosis (pɪˌdɪkjʊˈləʊsɪs) *n. Pathol.* the state of being infested with lice. **—pediculous** (pɪˈdɪkjʊləs) *adj.*

pedicure (ˈpɛdɪˌkjʊə) *n.* treatment of the feet, either by a medical expert or a cosmetician.

pedigree (ˈpɛdɪˌgriː) *n.* **1. a.** the line of descent of a pure-bred animal. **b.** (*as modifier*): *a pedigree bull.* **2.** a document recording this. **3.** a genealogical table, esp. one indicating pure ancestry. **—ˈpediˌgreed** *adj.*

pediment (ˈpɛdɪmənt) *n.* a low-pitched gable, esp. one that is triangular as used in classical architecture. **—ˌpediˈmental** *adj.*

pedlar *or esp. U.S.* **peddler** (ˈpɛdlə) *n.* a person who peddles; hawker.

pedo- *or before a vowel* **ped-** *combining form.* a U.S. spelling of **paedo-.**

pedometer (pɪˈdɒmɪtə) *n.* a device that records the number of steps taken in walking and hence the distance travelled.

peduncle (pɪˈdʌŋkəl) *n.* **1.** the stalk of a plant bearing an inflorescence or solitary flower. **2.** *Anat. & pathol.* any stalklike structure. **—peduncular** (pɪˈdʌŋkjʊlə) *or* **pedunculate** (pɪˈdʌŋkjʊlɪt, -ˌleɪt) *adj.*

pee (piː) *Sl.* ~*vb.* **peeing, peed. 1.** (*intr.*) to urinate. ~*n.* **2.** urine. **3.** the act of urinating.

peek (piːk) *vb.* **1.** (*intr.*) to glance quickly or furtively. ~*n.* **2.** such a glance.

peel[1] (piːl) *vb.* **1.** (*tr.*) to remove (the skin, rind, etc.) of (a fruit, egg, etc.). **2.** (*intr.*) (of paint, etc.) to be removed from a surface, esp. by weathering. **3.** (*intr.*) (of a surface) to lose its outer covering of paint, etc., esp. by weathering. **4.** (*intr.*) (of a person or part of the body) to shed skin in flakes or (of skin) to be shed in flakes, esp. as a result of sunburn. **5.** (*intr.; often foll. by off*) *Sl.* to undress. **6. keep one's eyes peeled** (*or* **skinned**). to keep a sharp lookout. ~*n.* **7.** the skin or rind of a fruit, etc. ~See also **peel off. —ˈpeeler** *n.*

peel[2] (piːl) *n. Brit.* a fortified tower of the 16th century on the borders of Scotland.

peeling (ˈpiːlɪŋ) *n.* a strip of skin, rind, bark, etc., that has been peeled off: *a potato peeling.*

peel off *vb.* (*adv.*) **1.** to remove or be removed by peeling. **2.** (*intr.*) (of an aircraft) to turn away as by banking, and leave a formation.

peen (piːn) *n.* **1.** the end of a hammer head opposite the striking face, often rounded or wedge-shaped. ~*vb.* **2.** (*tr.*) to strike with the peen of a hammer or a stream of metal shot.

peep[1] (piːp) *vb.* (*intr.*) **1.** to look furtively or secretly, as through a small aperture or from a hidden place. **2.** to appear partially or briefly: *the sun peeped through the clouds.* ~*n.* **3.** a quick or furtive look. **4.** the first appearance: *the peep of dawn.* **—ˈpeeper** *n.*

peep[2] (piːp) *vb.* (*intr.*) **1.** (esp. of young birds) to utter shrill small noises. **2.** to speak in a weak voice. ~*n.* **3.** a peeping sound.

Peeping Tom *n.* a man who furtively observes women undressing; voyeur.

peepshow (ˈpiːpˌʃəʊ) *n.* a box with a peephole through which a series of pictures can be seen.

peer[1] (pɪə) *n.* **1.** a member of a nobility; nobleman. **2.** a person who holds any of the five grades of the British nobility: duke, marquess, earl, viscount, and baron. See also **life peer. 3.** a person who is an equal in social standing, rank, age, etc.: *to be tried by one's peers.*

peer[2] (pɪə) *vb.* (*intr.*) **1.** to look intently with or as if with difficulty: *to peer into the distance.* **2.** to appear partially or dimly: *the sun peered through the fog.*

peerage (ˈpɪərɪdʒ) *n.* **1.** the whole body of peers; aristocracy. **2.** the position, rank, or title of a peer. **3.** (esp. in the British Isles) a book listing the peers and giving their genealogy.

peeress (ˈpɪərɪs) *n.* **1.** the wife or widow of a peer. **2.** a woman holding the rank of a peer in her own right.

peer group *n.* a social group composed of individuals of approximately the same age.

peerless (ˈpɪəlɪs) *adj.* having no equals; matchless.

peeve (piːv) *Inf.* ~*vb.* **1.** (*tr.*) to irritate; vex; annoy. ~*n.* **2.** something that irritates; vexation.

peevish (ˈpiːvɪʃ) *adj.* fretful or irritable. **—ˈpeevishly** *adv.* **—ˈpeevishness** *n.*

peewit *or* **pewit** (ˈpiːwɪt) *n.* another name for **lapwing.**

peg (pɛg) *n.* **1.** a small cylindrical pin or dowel used to join two parts together. **2.** a pin pushed or driven into a surface: used to mark scores, define limits, support coats, etc. **3.** any of several pins on a violin, etc., which can be turned so as to tune strings wound around them. **4.** Also called: **clothes peg.** *Brit.* a split or hinged pin for fastening wet clothes to a line to dry. U.S. equivalent: **clothespin. 5.** *Brit.* a small drink of wine or spirits. **6.** an opportunity or pretext for doing something: *a peg on which to hang a theory.* **7.** *Inf.* a level of self-esteem, importance, etc. (esp. in **come** *or* **take down a peg**). **8.** *Inf.* See **peg leg. 9. off the peg.** *Chiefly Brit.* (of clothes) ready-to-wear, as opposed to tailor-made. ~*vb.* **pegging, pegged. 10.** (*tr.*) to knock or insert a peg into. **11.** (*tr.*) to secure with pegs: *to peg a tent.* **12.** (*tr.*) to mark (a score) with pegs, as in some card games. **13.** (*tr.*) *Inf.* to throw (stones, etc.) at a target. **14.** (*intr.; foll. by away, along,* etc.) *Chiefly Brit.* to work steadily: *he pegged away at his job for years.* **15.** (*tr.*) to stabilize (the price of a commodity, an exchange rate, etc.).

pegboard (ˈpɛgˌbɔːd) *n.* **1.** a board having a pattern of holes into which small pegs can be fitted, used for playing certain games or keeping a score. **2.** another name for **solitaire** (sense 1). **3.** hardboard perforated by a pattern of holes in which articles may be hung, as for display.

peg leg *n. Inf.* **1.** an artificial leg, esp. one made of wood. **2.** a person with an artificial leg.

peg out *vb.* (*adv.*) **1.** (*intr.*) *Inf.* to collapse or die. **2.** *Cribbage.* (*intr.*) to score the point that wins the game. **3.** (*tr.*) to mark or secure with pegs: *to peg out one's claims to a piece of land.*

P.E.I. *abbrev. for* Prince Edward Island.

peignoir (ˈpeɪnwɑː) *n.* a woman's dressing gown.

pejorative (pɪˈdʒɒrətɪv, ˈpiːdʒər-) *adj.* **1.** (of words, expressions, etc.) having an unpleasant or disparaging connotation. ~*n.* **2.** a pejorative word, etc. **—peˈjoratively** *adv.*

peke (piːk) *n. Inf.* a Pekingese dog.

Pekingese (ˌpiːkɪŋˈiːz) *or* **Pekinese** (ˌpiːkəˈniːz) *n.* **1.** (*pl.* **-ese**) a small breed of pet dog with a profuse straight coat, curled plumed tail, and short wrinkled muzzle. **2.** the dialect of Mandarin Chinese spoken in Peking. **3.** (*pl.* **-ese**) a native or inhabitant of Peking. ~*adj.* **4.** of or

---

THESAURUS

pedigree 1. *n.* ancestry, blood, breed, derivation, descent, extraction, family, family tree, genealogy, heritage, line, lineage, race, stemma, stirps, stock **2.** *adj.* full-blooded, purebred, thoroughbred

peek 1. *v.* glance, keek (*Scot.*), look, peep, peer, snatch a glimpse, sneak a look, spy, squinny, take *or* have a gander (*Inf.*), take a look **2.** *n.* blink, gander (*Inf.*), glance, glim (*Scot.*), glimpse, keek (*Scot.*), look, look-see (*Sl.*), peep

peel 1. *v.* decorticate, desquamate, flake off, pare, scale, skin, strip off **2.** *n.* epicarp, exocarp, peeling, rind, skin

peep[1] *v.* **1.** keek (*Scot.*), look from hiding, look surreptitiously, peek, peer, sneak a look, spy, steal a look **2.** appear briefly, emerge, peer out, show partially ~*n.* **3.** gander (*Inf.*),

glim (*Scot.*), glimpse, keek (*Scot.*), look, look-see (*Sl.*), peek

peep[2] *v./n.* cheep, chirp, chirrup, pipe, squeak, tweet, twitter

peephole aperture, chink, crack, crevice, fissure, hole, keyhole, opening, pinhole, slit, spyhole

peer[1] *n.* **1.** aristocrat, baron, count, duke, earl, lord, marquess, marquis, noble, nobleman, viscount **2.** coequal, compeer, equal, fellow, like, match

peer[2] *v.* **1.** gaze, inspect, peep, scan, scrutinize, snoop, spy, squinny, squint **2.** appear, become visible, emerge, peep out

peerage aristocracy, lords and ladies, nobility, peers, titled classes

peerless beyond compare, excellent, incomparable, matchless, nonpareil, outstanding, second to none, superlative, unequalled,

unique, unmatched, unparalleled, unrivalled, unsurpassed

peeved annoyed, exasperated, galled, irked, irritated, nettled, piqued, put out, riled, sore, upset, vexed

peevish acrimonious, cantankerous, captious, childish, churlish, crabbed, cross, crotchety (*Inf.*), crusty, fractious, fretful, grumpy, ill-natured, ill-tempered, irritable, pettish, petulant, querulous, ratty (*Brit. sl.*), short-tempered, snappy, splenetic, sulky, sullen, surly, testy, touchy, waspish, whingeing (*Inf.*)

peg *v.* **1.** attach, fasten, fix, join, make fast, secure **2.** *With along* or *away* apply oneself to, beaver away (*Brit. inf.*), keep at it, keep going, keep on, persist, plod along, plug away at (*Inf.*), stick to it, work at, work away **3.** *Of prices, etc.* control, fix, freeze, limit, set

relating to Peking or its inhabitants.

Peking man (piː'kɪŋ) n. an early type of man, of the Lower Palaeolithic age, remains of which were found in a cave near Peking.

pekoe ('piːkəʊ) n. a high-quality tea made from the downy tips of the young buds of the tea plant.

pelargonium (ˌpɛlɑ'gəʊnɪəm) n. any plant of a chiefly southern African genus having circular or lobed leaves and red, pink, or white aromatic flowers: includes many cultivated geraniums.

pelf (pɛlf) n. Contemptuous. money or wealth; lucre.

pelican ('pɛlɪkən) n. any aquatic bird of a tropical and warm water family. They have a long straight flattened bill, with a distensible pouch for engulfing fish.

pelican crossing n. a type of road crossing with a pedestrian-operated traffic-light system.

pelisse (pɛ'liːs) n. 1. a fur-trimmed cloak. 2. a loose coat, usually fur-trimmed, worn esp. by women in the early 19th century.

pellagra (pə'leɪgrə, -'læ-) n. Pathol. a disease caused by a dietary deficiency of niacin, characterized by scaling of the skin, inflammation of the mouth, diarrhoea, mental impairment, etc. —**pel'lagrous** adj.

pellet ('pɛlɪt) n. 1. a small round ball, esp. of compressed matter. 2. a. an imitation bullet used in toy guns. b. a piece of small shot. 3. a stone ball formerly used in a catapult. 4. Ornithol. a mass of undigested food that is regurgitated by birds of prey. 5. a small pill. ~vb. (tr.) 6. to strike with pellets. 7. to make or form into pellets.

pell-mell ('pɛl'mɛl) adv. 1. in a confused headlong rush: the hounds ran pell-mell into the yard. 2. in a disorderly manner: the things were piled pell-mell in the room. ~adj. 3. disordered; tumultuous: a pell-mell rush for the exit. ~n. 4. disorder; confusion.

pellucid (pɛ'luːsɪd) adj. 1. transparent or translucent. 2. extremely clear in style and meaning. —**pel'lucidly** adv. —ˌpellu'cidity or pel'lucidness n.

pelmet ('pɛlmɪt) n. an ornamental drapery or board fixed above a window to conceal the curtain rail.

pelota (pə'ləʊtə) n. any of various games played in Spain, Spanish America, SW France, etc., by two players who use a basket strapped to their wrists to propel a ball against a specially marked wall.

pelt[1] (pɛlt) vb. 1. (tr.) to throw (missiles, etc.) at (a person, etc.). 2. (tr.) to hurl (insults, etc.) at (a person, etc.). 3. (intr.; foll. by along, etc.) to hurry. 4. (intr.) to rain heavily. ~n. 5. a blow. 6. speed (esp. in at full pelt).

pelt[2] (pɛlt) n. 1. the skin of a fur-bearing animal, esp. when it has been removed from the carcass. 2. the hide of an animal, stripped of hair.

pelvis ('pɛlvɪs) n., pl. **-vises** or **-ves** (-viːz). 1. the large funnel-shaped structure at the lower end of the trunk of most vertebrates. 2. Also called: **pelvic girdle**. the bones that form this structure. 3. any anatomical cavity or structure shaped like a funnel or cup. —**'pelvic** adj.

pen[1] (pɛn) n. 1. an implement for writing or drawing using ink, formerly consisting of a sharpened and split quill, and now of a metal nib attached to a holder. See also **ballpoint, fountain pen**. 2. the writing end of such an implement; nib. 3. style of writing. 4. **the pen.** writing as an occupation. ~vb. **penning, penned.** 5. (tr.) to write or compose.

pen[2] (pɛn) n. 1. an enclosure in which domestic animals are kept. 2. any place of confinement. 3. a dock for servicing submarines, esp. having a bombproof roof. ~vb. **penning, penned** or **pent.** 4. (tr.) to enclose in a pen.

pen[3] (pɛn) n. U.S. inf. short for **penitentiary.**

pen[4] (pɛn) n. a female swan.

Pen. abbrev. for Peninsula.

P.E.N. (pɛn) abbrev. for International Association of Poets, Playwrights, Editors, Essayists, and Novelists.

penal ('piːnəl) adj. 1. of, relating to, constituting, or prescribing punishment. 2. used or designated as a place of punishment: a penal institution. —**'penally** adv.

penal code n. the codified body of the laws that relate to crime and its punishment.

penalize or **-ise** ('piːnəˌlaɪz) vb. (tr.) 1. to impose a penalty on (someone), as for breaking a law or rule. 2. to inflict a disadvantage on. 3. Sport. to award a free stroke, point, or penalty against (a player or team). 4. to declare (an act) legally punishable. —ˌpenali'zation or -i'sation n.

penalty ('pɛnəltɪ) n., pl. **-ties.** 1. a legal or official punishment, such as a term of imprisonment. 2. some other form of punishment, such as a fine or forfeit for not fulfilling a contract. 3. loss, suffering, or other unfortunate result of one's own action, error, etc. 4. Sport, games, etc. a handicap awarded against a player or team for illegal play, such as a free shot at goal by the opposing team.

penalty box n. 1. Also called: **penalty area.** Soccer. a rectangular area in front of the goal, within which a penalty is awarded for a foul by the defending team. 2. Ice hockey. a bench for players serving time penalties.

penance ('pɛnəns) n. 1. voluntary self-punishment to atone for a sin, crime, etc. 2. a feeling of regret for one's wrongdoings. 3. Christianity. a punishment usually consisting of prayer, fasting, etc., imposed by church authority as a condition of absolution. 4. R.C. Church. a sacrament in which repentant sinners are absolved on condition of confession of their sins to a priest and of performing a penance. ~vb. 5. (tr.) (of ecclesiastical authorities) to impose a penance upon (a sinner).

pence (pɛns) n. the plural of **penny.**

▷ Usage. Since the decimalization of British currency and the introduction of the abbreviation p, as in 10p, 85p, etc., the abbreviation has tended to replace pence in speech, as in 4p (ˌfɔː'piː), etc.

penchant ('pɒntʃɒnt; French pɑ̃ʃɑ̃) n. strong inclination or liking; bent or taste.

pencil ('pɛnsəl) n. 1. a thin cylindrical instrument used for writing, drawing, etc., consisting of a central rod of graphite encased in wood and sharpened. 2. something similar in shape or function: a styptic pencil. 3. a narrow set of lines or rays, such as light rays, diverging from or converging to a point. 4. Rare. an artist's individual style. 5. a type of artist's brush. ~vb. **-cilling, -cilled** or U.S. **-ciling, -ciled.** (tr.) 6. to draw, colour, or write with a pencil. 7. to mark with a pencil. —**'penciller** or U.S. **'penciler** n.

pend (pɛnd) vb. (intr.) to await judgment or settlement.

pendant ('pɛndənt) n. 1. a. an ornament that hangs from a piece of jewellery. b. a necklace with such an ornament. 2. a hanging light, esp. a chandelier. 3. a carved ornament that is suspended from a ceiling or roof. ~adj. 4. a variant spelling of **pendent.**

pendent ('pɛndənt) adj. 1. dangling. 2. jutting. 3. (of a grammatical construction) incomplete. 4. a less common word for **pending.** ~n. 5. a variant spelling of **pendant.** —**'pendency** n. —**'pendently** adv.

pending ('pɛndɪŋ) prep. 1. while waiting for. ~adj. (postpositive) 2. not yet decided, confirmed, or finished. 3. imminent: these developments have been pending for some time.

pendragon (pɛn'drægən) n. a supreme war chief or leader of the ancient Britons.

pendulous ('pɛndjʊləs) adj. hanging downwards, esp. so as to swing from side to side. —**'pendulously** adv.

pendulum ('pɛndjʊləm) n. 1. a body mounted so that it

THESAURUS

pelt v. 1. assail, batter, beat, belabour, bombard, cast, hurl, pepper, pummel, shower, sling, strike, thrash, throw, wallop (Inf.) 2. belt (Sl.), career, charge, dash, hurry, run fast, rush, shoot, speed, tear, whiz (Inf.) 3. bucket down (Inf.), pour, rain cats and dogs (Inf.), rain hard, teem

pen[1] v. commit to paper, compose, draft, draw up, jot down, write

pen[2] 1. n. cage, coop, enclosure, fold, hutch, sty 2. v. cage, confine, coop up, enclose,

fence in, hedge, hem in, hurdle, mew (up), shut up or in

penal corrective, disciplinary, penalizing, punitive, retributive

penalize award a penalty against (Sport), correct, discipline, handicap, impose a penalty on, inflict a handicap on, punish, put at a disadvantage

penalty disadvantage, fine, forfeit, forfeiture, handicap, mulct, price, punishment, retribution

penance 1. atonement, mortification,

penalty, punishment, reparation, sackcloth and ashes 2. **do penance** accept punishment, atone, make amends, make reparation, mortify oneself, show contrition, suffer

penchant affinity, bent, bias, disposition, fondness, inclination, leaning, liking, partiality, predilection, predisposition, proclivity, proneness, propensity, taste, tendency, turn

pending awaiting, forthcoming, hanging fire, imminent, impending, in the balance, in the offing, undecided, undetermined, unsettled, up in the air

can swing freely under the influence of gravity. **2.** such a device used to regulate a clock mechanism. **3.** something that changes fairly regularly: *the pendulum of public opinion.*

peneplain *or* **peneplane** ('piːnɪˌpleɪn) *n.* a relatively flat land surface produced by erosion.

penetrate ('penɪˌtreɪt) *vb.* **1.** to find or force a way into or through (something); pierce; enter. **2.** to diffuse through (a substance, etc.); permeate. **3.** (*tr.*) to see through: *their eyes could not penetrate the fog.* **4.** (*tr.*) (of a man) to insert the penis into the vagina of (a woman). **5.** (*tr.*) to grasp the meaning of (a principle, etc.). **6.** (*intr.*) to be understood: *his face lit up as the new idea penetrated.* —**'penetrable** *adj.* —ˌpenetra'bility *n.* —'pene,trator *n.*

penetrating ('penɪˌtreɪtɪŋ) *adj.* tending to or able to penetrate: *a penetrating mind; a penetrating voice.* —'pene,tratingly *adv.*

penetration (ˌpenɪ'treɪʃən) *n.* **1.** the act or an instance of penetrating. **2.** the ability or power to penetrate. **3.** keen insight or perception. **4.** *Mil.* an offensive manoeuvre that breaks through an enemy's defensive position.

pen friend *n.* another name for **pen pal.**

penguin ('peŋgwɪn) *n.* a flightless marine bird of cool southern, esp. Antarctic, regions: they have wings modified as flippers, webbed feet, and feathers lacking barbs.

penicillin (ˌpenɪ'sɪlɪn) *n.* an antibiotic with powerful action against bacteria: obtained from the fungus *Penicillium.*

peninsula (pɪ'nɪnsjʊlə) *n.* a narrow strip of land projecting into a sea or lake from the mainland. —**pen'insular** *adj.*

penis ('piːnɪs) *n., pl.* **-nises** *or* **-nes** (-niːz). the male organ of copulation in higher vertebrates, also used for urine excretion in many mammals. —**penile** ('piːnaɪl) *adj.*

penitent ('penɪtənt) *adj.* **1.** feeling regret for one's sins; repentant. ~*n.* **2.** a person who is penitent. **3.** *Christianity.* **a.** a person who repents his sins and seeks forgiveness for them. **b.** *R.C. Church.* a person who confesses his sins and submits to a penance. —**'penitence** *n.* —ˌpeni'tential *adj.* —**'penitently** *adv.*

penitentiary (ˌpenɪ'tenʃərɪ) *n., pl.* **-ries.** **1.** (in the U.S.) a state prison. **2.** *R.C. Church.* **a.** a cardinal who presides over a tribunal that decides all matters affecting the sacrament of penance. **b.** this tribunal itself. ~*adj.* **3.** (of an offence) punishable by imprisonment in a penitentiary.

penknife ('pen,naɪf) *n., pl.* **-knives.** a small knife with one or more blades that fold into the handle; pocketknife.

penman ('penmən) *n., pl.* **-men.** **1.** a person skilled in handwriting. **2.** a person who writes by hand in a specified way: *a bad penman.* **3.** an author. **4.** *Rare.* a scribe.

penmanship ('penmənˌʃɪp) *n.* style or technique of writing by hand.

pen name *n.* an author's pseudonym. Also called: **nom de plume.**

pennant ('penənt) *n.* **1.** a type of pennon, esp. one flown from vessels as identification or for signalling. **2.** *Chiefly U.S. & Austral.* **a.** a flag serving as an emblem of championship in certain sports. **b.** (*as modifier*): *pennant cricket.*

penniless ('penɪlɪs) *adj.* very poor; almost totally without money. —**'pennilessly** *adv.* —**'pennilessness** *n.*

pennon ('penən) *n.* **1.** a long flag, often tapering and divided at the end, originally a knight's personal flag. **2.** a small tapering or triangular flag borne on a ship or boat. **3.** a poetic word for **wing.**

penny ('penɪ) *n., pl.* **pennies** *or* **pence** (pens). **1.** Also called: **new penny.** *Brit.* a bronze coin having a value equal to one hundredth of a pound. Abbrev.: **p.** **2.** *Brit.* (before 1971) a bronze or copper coin having a value equal to one twelfth of a shilling. Symbol: **d.** **3.** (*pl.* **pennies**). *U.S. & Canad.* a cent. **4.** a coin of similar value, as used in several other countries. **5.** (*used with a negative*) *Inf., chiefly Brit.* the least amount of money: *I don't have a penny.* **6. a pretty penny.** *Inf.* a considerable sum of money. **7. spend a penny.** *Brit. inf.* to urinate. **8. the penny dropped.** *Inf., chiefly Brit.* the explanation of something was finally realized.

Penny Black *n.* the first adhesive postage stamp, issued in Britain in 1840.

penny-dreadful *n., pl.* **-fuls.** *Brit. inf.* a cheap, often lurid book or magazine.

penny-farthing *n. Brit.* an early type of bicycle with a large front wheel and a small rear wheel, the pedals being on the front wheel.

penny-pincher *n. Inf.* a person who is excessively careful with money. —**'penny-,pinching** *n., adj.*

pennyroyal (ˌpenɪ'rɔɪəl) *n.* **1.** a Eurasian plant with hairy leaves and small mauve flowers, yielding an aromatic oil used in medicine. **2.** a similar and related plant of E North America.

pennyweight ('penɪˌweɪt) *n.* a unit of weight equal to 24 grains or one twentieth of an ounce (Troy).

penny-wise *adj.* **1.** greatly concerned with saving small sums of money. **2. penny-wise and pound-foolish.** careful about trifles but wasteful in large ventures.

pennywort ('penɪˌwɜːt) *n.* **1.** a Eurasian rock plant with whitish-green tubular flowers and rounded leaves. **2.** a marsh plant of Europe and North Africa, having circular leaves and greenish-pink flowers. **3.** any of various other plants with rounded penny-like leaves.

pennyworth ('penɪˌwɜːθ) *n.* **1.** the amount that can be bought for a penny. **2.** a small amount: *he hasn't got a pennyworth of sense.*

penology (piː'nɒlədʒɪ) *n.* **1.** the branch of the social sciences concerned with the punishment of crime. **2.** the science of prison management. —**penological** (ˌpiːnə'lɒdʒɪkəl) *adj.* —**pe'nologist** *n.*

pen pal *n.* a person with whom one exchanges letters, often a person in another country whom one has not met. Also called: **pen friend.**

penpusher ('pen,pʊʃə) *n.* a person who writes a lot, esp. a clerk involved with boring paperwork. —**'pen,pushing** *adj., n.*

pension¹ ('penʃən) *n.* **1.** a regular payment made by the state to people over a certain age to enable them to subsist without having to work. **2.** a regular payment made by an employer to former employees after they retire. **3.** any regular payment made by way of patronage, or in recognition of merit, service, etc.: *a pension paid to a disabled soldier.* ~*vb.* **4.** (*tr.*) to grant a pension to. —**'pensionable** *adj.* —**'pensionary** *adj.* —**'pensioner** *n.*

pension² *French.* (pã'sjɔ̃) *n.* (in France and some other countries) a relatively cheap boarding house.

pension off *vb.* (*tr., adv.*) **1.** to cause to retire from a

---

THESAURUS

penetrate 1. bore, enter, go through, perforate, pierce, prick, probe, stab **2.** diffuse, enter, get in, infiltrate, permeate, pervade, seep, suffuse **3.** *Fig.* affect, become clear, be understood, come across, get through to, impress, touch **4.** *Fig.* comprehend, decipher, discern, fathom, figure out (*Inf.*), get to the bottom of, grasp, understand, unravel, work out

penetrating 1. biting, carrying, harsh, intrusive, pervasive, piercing, pungent, sharp, shrill, stinging, strong **2.** *Fig.* acute, astute, critical, discerning, discriminating, incisive, intelligent, keen, perceptive, perspicacious, profound, quick, sagacious, searching, sharp, sharp-witted, shrewd

penetration 1. entrance, entry, incision, inroad, invasion, perforation, piercing, puncturing **2.** acuteness, astuteness, discernment, insight, keenness, perception, perspicacity, sharpness, shrewdness, wit

penitence compunction, contrition, regret, remorse, repentance, ruefulness, self-reproach, shame, sorrow

penitent *adj.* abject, apologetic, atoning, conscience-stricken, contrite, regretful, remorseful, repentant, rueful, sorrowful, sorry

penmanship calligraphy, chirography, fist (*Inf.*), hand, handwriting, longhand, script, writing

pen name allonym, nom de plume, pseudonym

pennant banderole, banner, burgee (*Nautical*), ensign, flag, jack, pennon, streamer

penniless bankrupt, broke (*Inf.*), cleaned out (*Sl.*), destitute, impecunious, impoverished, indigent, moneyless, necessitous, needy, on one's uppers, penurious, poor, poverty-stricken, ruined, skint (*Brit. sl.*), stony-broke (*Brit. sl.*), strapped (*U.S. sl.*), without a penny to one's name

penny-pinching *adj.* cheeseparing, close, frugal, mean, mingy (*Brit. inf.*), miserly, near (*Inf.*), niggardly, scrimping, Scrooge-like, stingy, tightfisted

pennyworth bit, crumb, jot, little, mite, modicum, particle, scrap, small amount, tittle

pension allowance, annuity, benefit, superannuation

pensioner O.A.P., retired person, senior citizen

job and pay a pension to. **2.** to discard, because of age: *to pension off submarines.*

pensive ('pɛnsɪv) *adj.* **1.** deeply or seriously thoughtful, often with a tinge of sadness. **2.** expressing or suggesting pensiveness. —'**pensively** *adv.* —'**pensiveness** *n.*

pent (pɛnt) *vb.* a past tense of **pen**[2].

penta- *combining form.* five: *pentagon; pentameter.*

pentacle ('pɛntəkəl) *n.* **1.** Also called: **pentagram, pentangle.** a star-shaped figure with five points. **2.** such a figure used by the Pythagoreans, black magicians, etc.

pentagon ('pɛntə,gɒn) *n.* a polygon having five sides. —**pentagonal** (pɛn'tægənəl) *adj.*

Pentagon ('pɛntə,gɒn) *n.* **1.** the five-sided building in Arlington, Virginia, that houses the headquarters of the U.S. armed forces. **2.** the military leadership of the U.S.

pentameter (pɛn'tæmɪtə) *n.* **1.** a verse line consisting of five metrical feet. **2.** (in classical prosody) a verse line consisting of two dactyls, one stressed syllable, two dactyls, and a final stressed syllable. ~*adj.* **3.** designating a verse line consisting of five metrical feet.

Pentateuch ('pɛntə,tjuːk) *n.* the first five books of the Old Testament. —**,Penta'teuchal** *adj.*

pentathlon (pɛn'tæθlən) *n.* an athletic contest consisting of five different events.

pentatonic scale (,pɛntə'tɒnɪk) *n. Music.* any of several scales consisting of five notes.

Pentecost ('pɛntɪ,kɒst) *n.* **1.** a Christian festival occurring on Whit Sunday commemorating the descent of the Holy Ghost on the apostles. **2.** *Judaism.* the Jewish harvest festival occurring on the fiftieth day after the second day of Passover.

Pentecostal (,pɛntɪ'kɒstəl) *adj.* **1.** (*usually prenominal*) of or relating to any of various Christian groups that emphasize the charismatic aspects of Christianity and adopt a fundamental attitude to the Bible. **2.** of or relating to Pentecost or the influence of the Holy Ghost. ~*n.* **3.** a member of a Pentecostal Church. —,**Pente'costalist** *n., adj.*

penthouse ('pɛnt,haʊs) *n.* **1.** a flat or maisonette built onto the top floor or roof of a block of flats. **2.** a construction on the roof of a building, esp. one used to house machinery, etc. **3.** a shed built against a building, esp. one that has a sloping roof.

pent-up *adj.* not released; repressed: *pent-up emotions.*

penult ('pɛnʌlt, pɪ'nʌlt) *n.* the last syllable but one in a word.

penultimate (pɪ'nʌltəmɪt) *adj.* **1.** next to the last. ~*n.* **2.** anything next to last, esp. a penult.

penumbra (pɪ'nʌmbrə) *n., pl.* **-brae** (-briː) *or* **-bras.** **1.** a fringe region of half shadow resulting from the partial obstruction of light by an opaque object. **2.** *Astron.* the lighter and outer region of a sunspot. **3.** *Painting.* the area in which light and shade blend. —**pe'numbral** *adj.*

penurious (pɪ'njʊərɪəs) *adj.* **1.** niggardly with money. **2.** lacking money or means. **3.** scanty. —**pe'nuriously** *adv.* —**pe'nuriousness** *n.*

penury ('pɛnjʊrɪ) *n.* **1.** extreme poverty. **2.** extreme scarcity.

peon[1] ('piːən, 'piːɒn) *n.* **1.** a Spanish-American farm labourer or unskilled worker. **2.** (formerly in Spanish America) a debtor compelled to work off his debts. **3.** any very poor person. —'**peonage** *n.*

peon[2] (pjuːn, 'piːun, 'piːɒn) *n.* (in India, Ceylon, etc., esp. formerly) **1.** a messenger or attendant, esp. in an office. **2.** a native policeman. **3.** a foot soldier.

peony ('piːənɪ) *n., pl.* **-nies.** **1.** any of a genus of shrubs and plants of Eurasia and North America, having large

pink, red, white, or yellow flowers. **2.** the flower of any of these plants.

people ('piːpəl) *n.* (*usually functioning as pl.*) **1.** persons collectively or in general. **2.** a group of persons considered together: *blind people.* **3.** (*pl.* **peoples**) the persons living in and sharing the same nationality: *the French people.* **4.** one's family: *he took her home to meet his people.* **5.** persons loyal to someone powerful: *the king's people accompanied him in exile.* **6.** the **people. a.** the mass of persons without special distinction, privileges, etc. **b.** the body of persons in a country, etc., esp. those entitled to vote. ~*vb.* **7.** (*tr.*) to provide with or as if with people or inhabitants.

▷ **Usage.** See at **person.**

pep (pɛp) *n.* **1.** high spirits, energy, or vitality. ~*vb.* **pepping, pepped. 2.** (*tr.; usually foll. by up*) to liven by imbuing with new vigour. —'**peppy** *adj.*

pepper ('pɛpə) *n.* **1.** a woody climbing plant, *Piper nigrum,* of the East Indies, having small black berry-like fruits. **2.** the dried fruit of this plant, which is ground to produce a sharp hot condiment. See also **black pepper, white pepper. 3.** any of various other plants of the genus *Piper.* **4.** Also called: **capsicum.** any of various tropical plants, the fruits of which are used as a vegetable and a condiment. See also **sweet pepper, red pepper, cayenne pepper. 5.** the fruit of any of these capsicums, which has a mild or pungent taste. **6.** the condiment made from the fruits of any of these plants. ~*vb.* (*tr.*) **7.** to season with pepper. **8.** to sprinkle liberally; dot: *his prose was peppered with alliteration.* **9.** to pelt with small missiles.

pepper-and-salt *adj.* **1.** (of cloth, etc.) marked with a fine mixture of black and white. **2.** (of hair) streaked with grey.

peppercorn ('pɛpə,kɔːn) *n.* **1.** the small dried berry of the pepper plant (*Piper nigrum*). **2.** something trifling.

peppercorn rent *n.* a rent that is very low or nominal.

pepper mill *n.* a small hand mill used to grind peppercorns.

peppermint ('pɛpə,mɪnt) *n.* **1.** a temperate mint plant with purple or white flowers and downy leaves, which yield a pungent oil. **2.** the oil from this plant, which is used as a flavouring. **3.** a sweet flavoured with peppermint.

peppery ('pɛpərɪ) *adj.* **1.** flavoured with or tasting of pepper. **2.** quick-tempered; irritable. **3.** full of bite and sharpness: *a peppery speech.* —'**pepperiness** *n.*

pep pill *n. Inf.* a tablet containing a stimulant drug.

pepsin ('pɛpsɪn) *n.* an enzyme produced in the stomach, which, when activated by acid, splits proteins into peptones.

pep talk *n. Inf.* an enthusiastic talk designed to increase confidence, production, cooperation, etc.

peptic ('pɛptɪk) *adj.* **1.** of, relating to, or promoting digestion. **2.** of, relating to, or caused by pepsin or the action of the digestive juices.

peptic ulcer *n. Pathol.* an ulcer of the mucous membrane lining those parts of the alimentary tract exposed to digestive juices, including the oesophagus, the stomach, and the duodenum.

per (pɜː; *unstressed* pə) *determiner.* **1.** for every: *three pence per pound.* ~*prep.* **2.** (esp. in some Latin phrases) by; through. **3. as per.** according to: *as per specifications.* **4. as per usual.** *Inf.* as usual.

per- *prefix.* **1.** indicating that a chemical compound contains a high proportion of a specified element: *peroxide.* **2.** indicating that a chemical element is in a higher than usual state of oxidation: *permanganate.*

pensive blue (*Inf.*), cogitative, contemplative, dreamy, grave, in a brown study (*Inf.*), meditative, melancholy, mournful, musing, preoccupied, reflective, ruminative, sad, serious, sober, solemn, sorrowful, thoughtful, wistful

pent-up bottled up, bridled, checked, constrained, curbed, held back, inhibited, repressed, smothered, stifled, suppressed

penurious 1. cheeseparing, close, closefisted, frugal, grudging, mean, miserly, near (*Inf.*), niggardly, parsimonious, skimping, stingy, tightfisted, ungenerous 2. destitute, impecunious, impoverished, indigent, needy,

penniless, poor, poverty-stricken 3. beggarly, deficient, inadequate, meagre, miserable, miserly, paltry, poor, scanty

penury 1. beggary, destitution, indigence, need, pauperism, poverty, privation, straitened circumstances, want 2. dearth, deficiency, lack, paucity, scantiness, scarcity, shortage, sparseness

people *n.* 1. human beings, humanity, humans, mankind, men and women, mortals, persons 2. citizens, clan, community, family, folk, inhabitants, nation, population, public, race, tribe 3. commonalty, crowd, general public, grass roots, hoi polloi, masses, mob,

multitude, plebs (*Brit. sl.*), populace, rabble, rank and file, the herd ~*v.* 4. colonize, inhabit, occupy, populate, settle

pepper *v.* 1. flavour, season, spice 2. bespeckle, dot, fleck, spatter, speck, sprinkle, stipple, stud 3. bombard, pelt, riddle, scatter, shower

peppery 1. fiery, highly seasoned, hot, piquant, pungent, spicy 2. choleric, hottempered, irascible, irritable, quicktempered, snappish, testy, touchy, waspish 3. astringent, biting, caustic, incisive, sarcastic, sharp, stinging, trenchant

peradventure (pərəd'vɛntʃə, ˌpɜːr-) *Arch.* ~*adv.* **1.** by chance; perhaps. ~*n.* **2.** chance or doubt.

perambulate (pə'ræmbjuˌleɪt) *vb.* **1.** to walk about (a place). **2.** (*tr.*) to walk round in order to inspect. —**perˌambu'lation** *n.* —**perambulatory** (pə'ræmbjulə-tərɪ, -trɪ) *adj.*

perambulator (pə'ræmbjuˌleɪtə) *n.* a formal word for **pram.**

per annum (pər 'ænəm) *adv.* every year or by the year.

percale (pə'keɪl, -'kɑːl) *n.* a close-textured woven cotton fabric, used esp. for sheets.

per capita (pə 'kæpɪtə) *adj., adv.* of or for each person.

perceive (pə'siːv) *vb.* **1.** to become aware of (something) through the senses; recognize or observe. **2.** (*tr.; may take a clause as object*) to come to comprehend; grasp. —**per'ceivable** *adj.* —**per'ceivably** *adv.* —**per'ceiver** *n.*

per cent (pə 'sɛnt) *adv.* **1.** Also: **per centum.** in or for every hundred. ~*n. also* **percent.** **2.** a percentage or proportion. **3.** (*often pl.*) securities yielding a rate of interest as specified: *he bought three percents.*

percentage (pə'sɛntɪdʒ) *n.* **1.** proportion or rate per hundred parts. **2.** *Commerce.* the interest, tax, commission, or allowance on a hundred items. **3.** any proportion in relation to the whole. **4.** *Inf.* profit or advantage.

percentile (pə'sɛntaɪl) *n.* one of 99 actual or notional values of a variable dividing its distribution into 100 groups with equal frequencies. Also called (in the U.S.): **centile.**

perceptible (pə'sɛptəbəl) *adj.* able to be perceived; noticeable or recognizable. —**perˌcepti'bility** *n.* —**per'ceptibly** *adv.*

perception (pə'sɛpʃən) *n.* **1.** the act or the effect of perceiving. **2.** insight or intuition gained by perceiving. **3.** the ability or capacity to perceive. **4.** the process by which an organism detects and interprets information from the external world by means of the sensory receptors. —**per'ceptional** *adj.* —**perceptual** (pə'sɛptjʊəl) *adj.*

perceptive (pə'sɛptɪv) *adj.* **1.** quick at perceiving; observant. **2.** perceptual. **3.** able to perceive. —**per'ceptively** *adv.* —**ˌpercep'tivity** *or* **per'ceptiveness** *n.*

perch[1] (pɜːtʃ) *n.* **1.** a pole, branch, or other resting place above ground on which a bird roosts. **2.** a similar resting place for a person or thing. **3.** another name for **rod** (sense 7). ~*vb.* **4.** (usually foll. by *on*) to alight, rest, or cause to rest on or as if on a perch: *the bird perched on the branch; the cap was perched on his head.* —'**percher** *n.*

perch[2] (pɜːtʃ) *n., pl.* **perch** *or* **perches.** **1.** any of a family of freshwater spiny-finned teleost fishes of Europe and North America: valued as food and game fishes. **2.** any of various similar or related fishes.

perchance (pə'tʃɑːns) *adv. Arch. or poetic.* **1.** perhaps; possibly. **2.** by chance; accidentally.

percipient (pə'sɪpɪənt) *adj.* **1.** able to perceive. **2.** perceptive. ~*n.* **3.** a person who perceives. —**per'cipience** *n.* —**per'cipiently** *adv.*

percolate *vb.* ('pɜːkəˌleɪt). **1.** to cause (a liquid) to pass through a fine mesh, porous substance, etc. or (of a liquid) to pass through a fine mesh, etc.; trickle: *rain percolated through the roof.* **2.** to permeate; penetrate gradually: *water percolated the road.* **3.** to make (coffee) or (of coffee) to be made in a percolator. ~*n.*

('pɜːkəlɪt, -ˌleɪt). **4.** a product of percolation. —**percolable** ('pɜːkələbəl) *adj.* —ˌperco'lation *n.*

percolator ('pɜːkəˌleɪtə) *n.* a kind of coffeepot in which boiling water is forced up through a tube and filters down through the coffee grounds into a container.

percussion (pə'kʌʃən) *n.* **1.** the act, an instance, or an effect of percussing. **2.** *Music.* the family of instruments in which sound arises from the striking of materials with sticks or hammers. **3.** *Music.* instruments of this family constituting a section of an orchestra, etc. **4.** *Med.* the act of percussing a body surface. **5.** the act of exploding a percussion cap. —**per'cussive** *adj.* —**per'cussively** *adv.* —**per'cussiveness** *n.*

percussion cap *n.* a detonator consisting of a paper or thin metal cap containing material that explodes when struck.

percussion instrument *n.* any of various musical instruments that produce a sound when their resonating surfaces are struck directly, as with a stick or mallet, or by leverage action.

percussionist (pə'kʌʃənɪst) *n. Music.* a person who plays any of several percussion instruments.

perdition (pə'dɪʃən) *n.* **1.** *Christianity.* **a.** final and irrevocable spiritual ruin. **b.** this state as one that the wicked are said to be destined to endure forever. **2.** another word for **hell.** **3.** *Arch.* utter ruin or destruction.

peregrinate ('pɛrɪɡrɪˌneɪt) *vb.* **1.** (*intr.*) to travel or wander about from place to place; voyage. **2.** (*tr.*) to travel through (a place). —ˌperegri'nation *n.* —'peregriˌnator *n.*

peregrine falcon *n.* a falcon occurring in most parts of the world, having a dark plumage on the back and wings and lighter underparts.

peremptory (pə'rɛmptərɪ) *adj.* **1.** urgent or commanding: *a peremptory ring on the bell.* **2.** not able to be remitted or debated; decisive. **3.** dogmatic. **4.** *Law.* **a.** admitting of no denial or contradiction; precluding debate. **b.** obligatory rather than permissive. —**per'emptorily** *adv.* —**per'emptoriness** *n.*

perennial (pə'rɛnɪəl) *adj.* **1.** lasting throughout the year or through many years. **2.** everlasting; perpetual. ~*n.* **3.** a woody or herbaceous plant that continues its growth for at least three years. —**per'ennially** *adv.*

perfect *adj.* ('pɜːfɪkt). **1.** having all essential elements. **2.** unblemished; faultless: *a perfect gemstone.* **3.** correct or precise: *perfect timing.* **4.** utter or absolute: *a perfect stranger.* **5.** excellent in all respects: *a perfect day.* **6.** *Maths.* exactly divisible into equal integral or polynomial roots: *36 is a perfect square.* **7.** *Bot.* **a.** (of flowers) having functional stamens and pistils. **b.** (of plants) having all parts present. **8.** *Grammar.* denoting a tense of verbs used in describing an action that has been completed. In English this is formed with *have* or *has* plus the past participle. **9.** *Music.* **a.** of or relating to the intervals of the unison, fourth, fifth, and octave. **b.** (of a cadence) ending on the tonic chord, giving a feeling of conclusion. Also: **final.** ~*n.* ('pɜːfɪkt). **10.** *Grammar.* **a.** the perfect tense. **b.** a verb in this tense. ~*vb.* (*tr.*) (pə'fɛkt). **11.** to make perfect; improve to one's satisfaction: *he is in Paris to perfect his French.* **12.** to make fully accomplished. —**per'fecter** *n.* —'**perfectly** *adv.* —'**perfectness** *n.*

▷ Usage. See at **unique.**

THESAURUS

perceive 1. be aware of, behold, descry, discern, discover, distinguish, espy, make out, note, notice, observe, recognize, remark, see, spot 2. appreciate, apprehend, comprehend, conclude, deduce, feel, gather, get (*Inf.*), grasp, know, learn, realize, see, sense, understand

perceptible apparent, appreciable, clear, conspicuous, detectable, discernible, distinct, evident, noticeable, observable, obvious, palpable, perceivable, recognizable, tangible, visible

perception apprehension, awareness, conception, consciousness, discernment, feeling, grasp, idea, impression, insight, notion, observation, recognition, sensation, sense, taste, understanding

perceptive acute, alert, astute, aware,

discerning, insightful, intuitive, observant, penetrating, percipient, perspicacious, quick, responsive, sensitive, sharp

perch 1. *n.* branch, pole, post, resting place, roost 2. *v.* alight, balance, land, rest, roost, settle, sit on

perchance by chance, for all one knows, haply (*Archaic*), maybe, mayhap (*Archaic*), peradventure (*Archaic*), perhaps, possibly, probably

percipient alert, alive, astute, aware, discerning, discriminating, intelligent, penetrating, perceptive, perspicacious, quick-witted, sharp, wide-awake

percolate drain, drip, exude, filter, filtrate, leach, ooze, penetrate, perk (*of coffee, inf.*), permeate, pervade, seep, strain, transfuse

percussion blow, brunt, bump, clash, collision, concussion, crash, impact, jolt, knock, shock, smash, thump

peremptory 1. absolute, binding, categorical, commanding, compelling, decisive, final, imperative, incontrovertible, irrefutable, obligatory, undeniable 2. arbitrary, assertive, authoritative, autocratic, bossy (*Inf.*), dictatorial, dogmatic, domineering, high-handed, imperious, intolerant, overbearing

perennial 1. abiding, chronic, constant, continual, continuing, enduring, incessant, inveterate, lasting, lifelong, persistent, recurrent, unchanging 2. ceaseless, deathless, eternal, everlasting, immortal, imperishable, never-ending, permanent, perpetual, unceasing, undying, unfailing, uninterrupted

perfectible (pəˈfɛktəbəl) *adj.* capable of becoming or being made perfect. —**perˌfectiˈbility** *n.*

perfection (pəˈfɛkʃən) *n.* **1.** the act of perfecting or the state or quality of being perfect. **2.** the highest degree of a quality, etc. **3.** an embodiment of perfection.

perfectionism (pəˈfɛkʃəˌnɪzəm) *n.* **1.** *Philosophy.* the doctrine that man can attain perfection in this life. **2.** the demand for the highest standard of excellence. —**perˈfectionist** *n.*

perfect participle *n.* another name for **past participle.**

perfect pitch *n.* another name (not in technical usage) for **absolute pitch** (sense 1).

perfidious (pəˈfɪdɪəs) *adj.* guilty, treacherous, or faithless; deceitful. —**perˈfidiously** *adv.* —**perˈfidiousness** *n.* —**ˈperfidy** *n.*

perforate *vb.* (ˈpɜːfəˌreɪt). **1.** to make a hole or holes in (something). **2.** (*tr.*) to punch rows of holes between (stamps, etc.) for ease of separation. ~*adj.* (ˈpɜːfərɪt). **3.** *Biol.* pierced by small holes: *perforate shells.* **4.** *Philately.* perforated. —**perforable** (ˈpɜːfərəbəl) *adj.* —ˈperfoˌrator *n.*

perforation (ˌpɜːfəˈreɪʃən) *n.* **1.** the act of perforating or the state of being perforated. **2.** a hole or holes made in something. **3. a.** a method of making individual stamps, etc. easily separable by punching holes along their margins. **b.** the holes punched in this way. Abbrev.: **perf.**

perforce (pəˈfɔːs) *adv.* by necessity; unavoidably.

perform (pəˈfɔːm) *vb.* **1.** to carry out (an action). **2.** (*tr.*) to fulfil: *to perform someone's request.* **3.** to present or enact (a play, concert, etc.): *the group performed Hamlet.* —**perˈformable** *adj.* —**perˈformer** *n.*

performance (pəˈfɔːməns) *n.* **1.** the act, process, or art of performing. **2.** an artistic or dramatic production: *last night's performance was terrible.* **3.** manner or quality of functioning: *a machine's performance.* **4.** *Inf.* mode of conduct or behaviour, esp. when distasteful: *what did you mean by that performance at the restaurant?* **5.** *Inf.* any tiresome procedure: *the performance of preparing to go out in the snow.*

perfume *n.* (ˈpɜːfjuːm). **1.** a mixture of alcohol and fragrant essential oils extracted from flowers, etc., or made synthetically. **2.** a scent or odour, esp. a fragrant one. ~*vb.* (pəˈfjuːm). **3.** (*tr.*) to impart a perfume to.

perfumer (pəˈfjuːmə) *n.* a person who makes or sells perfume.

perfumery (pəˈfjuːmərɪ) *n., pl.* **-eries. 1.** a place where perfumes are sold. **2.** a factory where perfumes are made. **3.** the process of making perfumes. **4.** perfumes in general.

perfunctory (pəˈfʌŋktərɪ) *adj.* **1.** done superficially,

only as a matter of routine. **2.** dull or indifferent. —**perˈfunctorily** *adv.* —**perˈfunctoriness** *n.*

pergola (ˈpɜːɡələ) *n.* a horizontal trellis or framework, supported on posts, that carries climbing plants.

perhaps (pəˈhæps; *informal* præps) *adv.* **1. a.** possibly; maybe. **b.** (*as sentence modifier*): *he'll arrive tomorrow, perhaps.* ~*sentence substitute.* **2.** it may happen, be so, etc.; maybe.

peri- *prefix.* **1.** enclosing, encircling, or around: *pericardium; pericarp.* **2.** near or adjacent: *perihelion.*

perianth (ˈpɛrɪˌænθ) *n.* the outer part of a flower, consisting of the calyx and corolla.

pericardium (ˌpɛrɪˈkɑːdɪəm) *n., pl.* **-dia** (-dɪə). the membranous sac enclosing the heart. —ˌperiˈcardial *or* ˌperiˈcardiac *adj.*

perigee (ˈpɛrɪˌdʒiː) *n.* the point in its orbit around the earth when the moon or a satellite is nearest the earth. —ˌperiˈgean *adj.*

perihelion (ˌpɛrɪˈhiːlɪən) *n., pl.* **-lia** (-lɪə). the point in its orbit when a planet or comet is nearest the sun.

peril (ˈpɛrɪl) *n.* exposure to risk or harm; danger or jeopardy. —ˈperilous *adj.*

perimeter (pəˈrɪmɪtə) *n.* **1.** *Maths.* **a.** the curve or line enclosing a plane area. **b.** the length of this curve or line. **2. a.** any boundary around something. **b.** (*as modifier*): *a perimeter fence.* **3.** a medical instrument for measuring the field of vision. —**perimetric** (ˌpɛrɪˈmɛtrɪk) *adj.*

perineum (ˌpɛrɪˈniːəm) *n., pl.* **-nea** (-ˈniːə). **1.** the region of the body between the anus and the genital organs. **2.** the surface of the human trunk between the thighs. —ˌperiˈneal *adj.*

period (ˈpɪərɪəd) *n.* **1.** a portion of time of indefinable length: *he spent a period away from home.* **2. a.** a portion of time specified in some way: *Picasso's blue period.* **b.** (*as modifier*): *period costume.* **3.** a nontechnical name for **menstruation.** See **menstruate. 4.** *Geol.* a unit of geological time during which a system of rocks is formed: *the Jurassic period.* **5.** a division of time, esp. of the academic day. **6.** *Physics, maths.* the time taken to complete one cycle of a regularly recurring phenomenon; the reciprocal of frequency. Symbol: *T.* **7.** *Astron.* **a.** the time required by a body to make one complete rotation on its axis. **b.** the time interval between two successive maxima or minima of light variation of a variable star. **8.** *Chem.* one of the horizontal rows of elements in the periodic table. Each period starts with an alkali metal and ends with a rare gas. **9.** another term (esp. U.S.) for **full stop. 10.** a complete sentence, esp. one with several clauses. **11.** a completion or end.

periodic (ˌpɪərɪˈɒdɪk) *adj.* **1.** happening or recurring at intervals; intermittent. **2.** of, relating to, or resembling a period. **3.** having or occurring in repeated periods or cy-

perfect *adj.* **1.** absolute, complete, completed, consummate, entire, finished, full, out-and-out, sheer, unadulterated, unalloyed, unmitigated, utter, whole **2.** blameless, excellent, faultless, flawless, ideal, immaculate, impeccable, pure, splendid, spotless, sublime, superb, superlative, supreme, unblemished, unmarred, untarnished **3.** accurate, close, correct, exact, faithful, precise, right, spot-on (*Brit. inf.*), strict, true, unerring **4.** accomplished, adept, experienced, expert, finished, masterly, polished, practised, skilful, skilled ~*v.* **5.** accomplish, achieve, carry out, complete, consummate, effect, finish, fulfil, perform, realize **6.** ameliorate, cultivate, develop, elaborate, hone, improve, polish, refine

perfection **1.** accomplishment, achievement, achieving, completion, consummation, evolution, fulfilment, realization **2.** completeness, exactness, excellence, exquisiteness, faultlessness, integrity, maturity, perfectness, precision, purity, sublimity, superiority, wholeness **3.** acme, crown, ideal, paragon

perfectionist formalist, precisian, precisionist, purist, stickler

perfectly **1.** absolutely, altogether, completely, consummately, entirely, fully, quite, thoroughly, totally, utterly, wholly **2.** admirably, exquisitely, faultlessly, flawlessly,

ideally, impeccably, superbly, superlatively, supremely, to perfection, wonderfully

perfidious corrupt, deceitful, dishonest, disloyal, double-dealing, double-faced, faithless, false, recreant (*Archaic*), traitorous, treacherous, treasonous, two-faced, unfaithful, untrustworthy

perfidy betrayal, deceit, disloyalty, double-dealing, duplicity, faithlessness, falsity, infidelity, perfidiousness, treachery, treason

perforate bore, drill, hole, honeycomb, penetrate, pierce, punch, puncture

perform **1.** accomplish, achieve, act, bring about, carry out, complete, comply with, discharge, do, effect, execute, fulfil, function, observe, pull off, satisfy, transact, work **2.** act, appear as, depict, enact, play, present, produce, put on, render, represent, stage

performance **1.** accomplishment, achievement, act, carrying out, completion, conduct, consummation, discharge, execution, exploit, feat, fulfilment, work **2.** acting, appearance, exhibition, gig (*Inf.*), interpretation, play, portrayal, presentation, production, representation, show **3.** action, conduct, efficiency, functioning, operation, practice, running, working **4.** *Inf.* act, behaviour, both-

er, business, carry-on (*Brit. inf.*), fuss, pother, rigmarole, to-do

performer actor, actress, artiste, play-actor, player, Thespian, trouper

perfume aroma, attar, balminess, bouquet, cologne, essence, fragrance, incense, odour, redolence, scent, smell, sweetness

perfunctory automatic, careless, cursory, heedless, inattentive, indifferent, mechanical, negligent, offhand, routine, sketchy, slipshod, slovenly, stereotyped, superficial, unconcerned, unthinking, wooden

perhaps as the case may be, conceivably, feasibly, for all one knows, it may be, maybe, perchance (*Archaic*), possibly

peril danger, exposure, hazard, insecurity, jeopardy, menace, pitfall, risk, uncertainty, vulnerability

perilous chancy (*Inf.*), dangerous, exposed, fraught with danger, hairy (*Sl.*), hazardous, parlous (*Archaic*), precarious, risky, threatening, unsafe, unsure, vulnerable

perimeter ambit, border, borderline, boundary, bounds, circumference, confines, edge, limit, margin, periphery

period **1.** interval, season, space, span, spell, stretch, term, time, while **2.** aeon, age, course, cycle, date, days, epoch, era, generation, season, stage, term, time, years

cles. —**peri'odically** adv. —**periodicity** (ˌpɪərɪə'dɪsɪtɪ) n.

periodical (ˌpɪərɪ'ɒdɪkəl) n. **1.** a publication issued at regular intervals, usually monthly or weekly. ~adj. **2.** of or relating to such publications. **3.** published at regular intervals. **4.** periodic or occasional.

periodic law n. the principle that the chemical properties of the elements are periodic functions of their atomic weights or, more accurately, of their atomic numbers.

periodic table n. a table of the elements, arranged in order of increasing atomic number, based on the periodic law.

peripatetic (ˌpɛrɪpə'tɛtɪk) adj. **1.** itinerant. **2.** Brit. employed in two or more educational establishments and travelling from one to another: a peripatetic football coach. ~n. **3.** a peripatetic person. —**ˌperipa'tetically** adv.

Peripatetic (ˌpɛrɪpə'tɛtɪk) adj. **1.** of or relating to the teachings of Aristotle, who used to teach philosophy while walking about the Lyceum in ancient Athens. ~n. **2.** a student of Aristotelianism.

peripheral (pə'rɪfərəl) adj. **1.** not relating to the most important part of something; incidental. **2.** of or relating to a periphery. **3.** Anat. of, relating to, or situated near the surface of the body: a peripheral nerve. —**pe'ripherally** adv.

peripheral device or **unit** n. Computers. any device, such as a card punch, line printer, etc., concerned with input/output, storage, etc. Often shortened to **peripheral.**

periphery (pə'rɪfərɪ) n., pl. **-eries. 1.** the outermost boundary of an area. **2.** the outside surface of something.

periphrasis (pə'rɪfrəsɪs) n., pl. **-rases** (-rəˌsiːz). **1.** a roundabout way of expressing something; circumlocution. **2.** an expression of this kind.

periscope ('pɛrɪˌskəup) n. any of a number of optical instruments that enable the user to view objects that are not in the direct line of vision, such as one in a submarine for looking above the surface of the water. They have a system of mirrors or prisms to reflect the light. —**periscopic** (ˌpɛrɪ'skɒpɪk) adj.

perish ('pɛrɪʃ) vb. **1.** (intr.) to be destroyed or die, esp. in an untimely way. **2.** (tr. sometimes foll. by with or from) to cause to suffer: we were perished with cold. **3.** to rot or cause to rot: leather perishes if exposed to bad weather. ~ **4. do a perish.** Austral. inf. to die or come near to dying of thirst or starvation.

perishable ('pɛrɪʃəbl) adj. **1.** liable to rot. ~n. **2.** (often pl.) a perishable article, esp. food. —**ˌperisha'bility** or **'perishableness** n.

perishing ('pɛrɪʃɪŋ) adj. **1.** Inf. (of weather, etc.) extremely cold. **2.** Sl. (intensifier qualifying something undesirable): you perishing blighter! —**'perishingly** adv.

peristalsis (ˌpɛrɪ'stælsɪs) n., pl. **-ses** (-siːz). Physiol. the succession of waves of involuntary muscular contraction of various bodily tubes, esp. of the alimentary tract, where it effects transport of food and waste products. —**ˌperi'staltic** adj.

peritoneum (ˌpɛrɪtə'niːəm) n., pl. **-nea** (-'niːə) or **-neums.** a serous sac that lines the walls of the abdominal cavity and covers the viscera. —**ˌperito'neal** adj.

peritonitis (ˌpɛrɪtə'naɪtɪs) n. inflammation of the peritoneum.

periwig ('pɛrɪˌwɪg) n. a wig, such as a peruke.

periwinkle¹ ('pɛrɪˌwɪŋkəl) n. any of various edible marine gastropods having a spirally coiled shell. Often shortened to **winkle.**

periwinkle² ('pɛrɪˌwɪŋkəl) n. any of several Eurasian evergreen plants having trailing stems and blue flowers.

perjure ('pɜːdʒə) vb. (tr.) Criminal law. to render (oneself) guilty of perjury. —**'perjurer** n.

perjury ('pɜːdʒərɪ) n., pl. **-juries.** Criminal law. the offence committed by a witness in judicial proceedings who, having been lawfully sworn, wilfully gives false evidence. —**perjurious** (pɜː'dʒuərɪəs) adj.

perk¹ (pɜːk) vb. (intr.) Inf. (of coffee) to percolate.

perk² (pɜːk) n. Brit. inf. short for **perquisite.**

perk up vb. (adv.) **1.** to make or become more cheerful, hopeful, or lively. **2.** to rise or cause to rise briskly: the dog's ears perked up. **3.** (tr.) to make smarter in appearance: she perked up her outfit with a bright scarf.

perky ('pɜːkɪ) adj. **perkier, perkiest. 1.** jaunty; lively. **2.** confident; spirited. —**'perkily** adv. —**'perkiness** n.

perm¹ (pɜːm) Inf. ~n. **1.** short for **permanent wave.** ~vb. (tr.) **2.** to give (hair) a permanent wave.

perm² (pɜːm) n. Inf. short for **permutation** (sense 4).

permafrost ('pɜːməˌfrɒst) n. ground that is permanently frozen.

permanent ('pɜːmənənt) adj. **1.** existing or intended to exist for an indefinite period: a permanent structure. **2.** not expected to change; not temporary: a permanent condition. —**'permanence** or **'permanency** n. —**'permanently** adv.

permanent wave n. a series of waves or curls made in the hair by application of heat or chemicals, lasting several months. Often shortened to **perm.**

permanent way n. Chiefly Brit. the track of a railway, including the sleepers, rails, etc.

permanganate (pə'mæŋgəˌneɪt, -nɪt) n. a salt of an acid containing manganese.

permeable ('pɜːmɪəbəl) adj. capable of being permeated, esp. by liquids. —**ˌpermea'bility** n. —**'permeably** adv.

permeate ('pɜːmɪˌeɪt) vb. **1.** to penetrate or pervade (a substance, area, etc.): a lovely smell permeated the room. **2.** to pass through or cause to pass through by osmosis or diffusion: to permeate a membrane. —**ˌperme'ation** n. —**'permeative** adj. —**'permeˌator** n.

Permian ('pɜːmɪən) adj. **1.** of, denoting, or formed in the last period of the Palaeozoic era, between the Carboniferous and Triassic periods. ~n. **2. the.** the Permian period or rock system.

permissible (pə'mɪsəbəl) adj. permitted; allowable. —**ˌperˌmissi'bility** n. —**per'missibly** adv.

permission (pə'mɪʃən) n. authorization to do something.

permissive (pə'mɪsɪv) adj. **1.** tolerant; lenient: permissive parents. **2.** indulgent in matters of sex: a permissive society. **3.** granting permission. —**per'missively** adv. —**per'missiveness** n.

permit vb. (pə'mɪt), **-mitting, -mitted. 1.** (tr.) to grant permission to do something: you are permitted to smoke.

THESAURUS

periodic at fixed intervals, cyclic, cyclical, every once in a while, every so often, infrequent, intermittent, occasional, periodical, recurrent, regular, repeated, seasonal, spasmodic, sporadic

periodical n. journal, magazine, monthly, organ, paper, publication, quarterly, review, serial, weekly

perish 1. be killed, be lost, decease, die, expire, lose one's life, pass away **2.** be destroyed, collapse, decline, disappear, fall, go under, vanish **3.** decay, decompose, disintegrate, moulder, rot, waste, wither

perishable decaying, decomposable, destructible, easily spoilt, liable to rot, shortlived, unstable

perjure (oneself) bear false witness, commit perjury, forswear, give false testimony, lie under oath, swear falsely

perjured deceitful, false, forsworn, lying,

mendacious, perfidious, traitorous, treacherous, untrue, untruthful

perjury bearing false witness, false oath, false statement, false swearing, forswearing, giving false testimony, lying under oath, oath breaking, violation of an oath, wilful falsehood

perk up brighten, buck up (Inf.), cheer up, liven up, look up, pep up, rally, recover, recuperate, revive, take heart

permanence constancy, continuance, continuity, dependability, durability, duration, endurance, finality, fixedness, fixity, immortality, indestructibility, lastingness, perdurability (Rare), permanency, perpetuity, stability, survival

permanent abiding, constant, durable, enduring, everlasting, fixed, immutable, imperishable, indestructible, invariable, lasting, long-lasting, perennial, perpetual, persistent,

stable, steadfast, unchanging, unfading

permeate charge, diffuse throughout, fill, filter through, imbue, impregnate, infiltrate, pass through, penetrate, percolate, pervade, saturate, seep through, soak through, spread throughout

permissible acceptable, admissible, allowable, all right, authorized, kosher (Inf.), lawful, legal, legit (Sl.), legitimate, licit, O.K. (Inf.), permitted, proper, sanctioned

permission allowance, approval, assent, authorization, consent, dispensation, freedom, go-ahead (Inf.), green light, leave, liberty, licence, permit, sanction, sufferance, tolerance

permissive acquiescent, easy-going, forbearing, free, indulgent, latitudinarian, lax, lenient, liberal, open-minded, tolerant

2. (*tr.*) to consent to or tolerate: *she will not permit him to come.* **3.** (when *intr.*, often foll. by *of;* when *tr.*, often foll. by an infinitive) to allow the possibility (of): *the passage permits of two interpretations; his work permits him to relax nowadays.* ~*n.* ('pɜːmɪt). **4.** an official document granting authorization; licence. **5.** permission. —**per'mitter** *n.*

permutation (ˌpɜːmjuˈteɪʃən) *n.* **1.** *Maths.* **a.** an ordered arrangement of the numbers, terms, etc., of a set into specified groups: *the permutations of a, b, and c, taken two at a time, are ab, ba, ac, ca, bc, cb.* **b.** a group formed in this way. **2.** a combination of items, etc., made by reordering. **3.** an alteration; transformation. **4.** a fixed combination for selections of results on football pools. Usually shortened to **perm.** —ˌpermuˈtational *adj.*

pernicious (pəˈnɪʃəs) *adj.* **1.** wicked or malicious: *pernicious lies.* **2.** causing grave harm; deadly. —**perˈni-ciously** *adv.* —**perˈniciousness** *n.*

pernicious anaemia *n.* a form of anaemia characterized by lesions of the spinal cord, weakness, sore tongue, diarrhoea, etc.: associated with inadequate absorption of vitamin B_{12}.

pernickety (pəˈnɪkɪtɪ) *adj. Inf.* **1.** excessively precise; fussy. **2.** (of a task) requiring close attention.

peroration (ˌpɛrəˈreɪʃən) *n.* the conclusion of a speech or discourse, in which points made previously are summed up.

peroxide (pəˈrɒksaɪd) *n.* **1.** short for **hydrogen peroxide**, esp. when used for bleaching hair. **2.** any of a class of metallic oxides, such as sodium peroxide, Na_2O_2. **3.** (*not in technical usage*) any of certain dioxides, such as manganese peroxide, MnO_2, that resemble peroxides in their formula. **4.** any of a class of organic compounds whose molecules contain two oxygen atoms bound together. **5.** (*modifier*) of, relating to, bleached with, or resembling peroxide: *a peroxide blonde.* ~*vb.* **6.** (*tr.*) to bleach (the hair) with peroxide.

perpendicular (ˌpɜːpənˈdɪkjʊlə) *adj.* **1.** at right angles. **2.** denoting, relating to, or having the style of Gothic architecture used in England during the 14th and 15th centuries, characterized by tracery having vertical lines. **3.** upright; vertical. ~*n.* **4.** *Geom.* a line or plane perpendicular to another. **5.** any instrument used for indicating the vertical line through a given point. —**perpen-dicularity** (ˌpɜːpənˌdɪkjʊˈlærɪtɪ) *n.* —ˌperpenˈdicularly *adv.*

perpetrate ('pɜːpɪˌtreɪt) *vb.* (*tr.*) to perform or be responsible for (a deception, crime, etc.). —ˌperpeˈtra-tion *n.* —'perpeˌtrator *n.*

perpetual (pəˈpɛtjʊəl) *adj.* **1.** (*usually prenominal*) eternal; permanent. **2.** (*usually prenominal*) seemingly ceaseless because often repeated: *your perpetual complaints.* —perˈpetually *adv.*

perpetual motion *n.* motion of a hypothetical mechanism that continues indefinitely without any external source of energy. It is impossible in practice because of friction.

perpetuate (pəˈpɛtjʊˌeɪt) *vb.* (*tr.*) to cause to continue: *to perpetuate misconceptions.* —perˌpetuˈation *n.*

perpetuity (ˌpɜːpɪˈtjuːɪtɪ) *n., pl.* **-ties. 1.** eternity. **2.** the state of being perpetual. **3.** *Property law.* a limitation preventing the absolute disposal of an estate for longer than the period allowed by law. **4.** an annuity that is payable indefinitely. **5. in perpetuity.** for ever.

perplex (pəˈplɛks) *vb.* (*tr.*) **1.** to puzzle; bewilder; confuse. **2.** to complicate: *to perplex an issue.* —**perplexedly** (pəˈplɛksɪdlɪ, -ˈplɛkstlɪ) *adv.* —**perˈplex-ingly** *adv.*

perplexity (pəˈplɛksɪtɪ) *n., pl.* **-ties. 1.** the state of being perplexed. **2.** the state of being intricate or complicated. **3.** something that perplexes.

perquisite ('pɜːkwɪzɪt) *n.* **1.** an incidental benefit gained from a certain type of employment, such as the use of a company car. **2.** a customary benefit received in addition to a regular income. **3.** a customary tip. **4.** something expected or regarded as an exclusive right. ~Often shortened (informal) to **perk.**

perry ('pɛrɪ) *n., pl.* **-ries.** wine made of pears, similar in taste to cider.

per se ('pɜː 'seɪ) *adv.* by or in itself; intrinsically.

persecute ('pɜːsɪˌkjuːt) *vb.* (*tr.*) **1.** to oppress, harass, or maltreat, esp. because of race, religion, etc. **2.** to bother persistently. —ˌperseˈcution *n.* —'perseˌcutive *adj.* —'perseˌcutor *n.*

perseverance (ˌpɜːsɪˈvɪərəns) *n.* **1.** continued steady belief or efforts; persistence. **2.** *Christian Theol.* continuance in a state of grace.

persevere (ˌpɜːsɪˈvɪə) *vb.* (*intr.*; often foll. by *in*) to show perseverance.

Persian ('pɜːʃən) *adj.* **1.** of or relating to ancient Persia or modern Iran, their inhabitants, or their languages. ~*n.* **2.** a native, citizen, or inhabitant of modern Iran; an Iranian. **3.** the language of Iran or Persia in any of its ancient or modern forms.

Persian cat *n.* a long-haired variety of domestic cat.

Persian lamb *n.* **1.** a black loosely curled fur from the karakul lamb. **2.** a karakul lamb.

persiflage ('pɜːsɪˌflɑːʒ) *n.* light frivolous conversation, style, or treatment; friendly teasing.

persimmon (pɜːˈsɪmən) *n.* **1.** any of several tropical trees, typically having hard wood and large orange-red fruit. **2.** the sweet fruit of any of these trees, which is edible when completely ripe.

persist (pəˈsɪst) *vb.* (*intr.*) **1.** (often foll. by *in*) to continue steadfastly or obstinately despite opposition. **2.** to continue without interruption: *the rain persisted*

THESAURUS

permit 1. *v.* admit, agree, allow, authorize, consent, empower, enable, endorse, endure, give leave *or* permission, grant, let, license, sanction, suffer, tolerate, warrant **2.** *n.* authorization, liberty, licence, pass, passport, permission, sanction, warrant

permutation alteration, change, shift, transformation, transmutation, transposition

pernicious bad, baleful, baneful (*Archaic*), damaging, dangerous, deadly, deleterious, destructive, detrimental, evil, fatal, harmful, hurtful, injurious, maleficent, malevolent, malicious, malign, malignant, noisome, noxious, offensive, pestilent, poisonous, ruinous, venomous, wicked

pernickety 1. careful, carping, difficult to please, exacting, fastidious, finicky, fussy, hairsplitting, nice, nit-picking (*Inf.*), overprecise, painstaking, particular, punctilious **2.** detailed, exacting, fiddly, fine, tricky

peroration closing remarks, conclusion, recapitulation, recapping (*Inf.*), reiteration, summing-up

perpendicular at right angles to, on end, plumb, straight, upright, vertical

perpetrate be responsible for, bring about, carry out, commit, do, effect, enact, execute, inflict, perform, wreak

perpetual 1. abiding, endless, enduring,

eternal, everlasting, immortal, infinite, lasting, never-ending, perennial, permanent, sempiternal (*Literary*), unchanging, undying, unending **2.** ceaseless, constant, continual, continuous, endless, incessant, interminable, never-ending, perennial, persistent, recurrent, repeated, unceasing, unfailing, uninterrupted, unremitting

perpetuate continue, eternalize, immortalize, keep alive, keep going, keep up, maintain, preserve, sustain

perplex 1. baffle, befuddle, beset, bewilder, confound, confuse, dumbfound, mix up, muddle, mystify, nonplus, puzzle, stump **2.** complicate, encumber, entangle, involve, jumble, mix up, snarl up, tangle, thicken

perplexing baffling, bewildering, complex, complicated, confusing, difficult, enigmatic, hard, inexplicable, intricate, involved, knotty, labyrinthine, mysterious, mystifying, paradoxical, puzzling, strange, taxing, thorny, unaccountable, weird

perplexity 1. bafflement, bewilderment, confusion, incomprehension, mystification, puzzlement, stupefaction **2.** complexity, difficulty, inextricability, intricacy, involvement, obscurity **3.** difficulty, dilemma, enigma, fix (*Inf.*), knotty problem, mystery, paradox, puzzle, snarl

perquisite benefit, bonus, dividend, extra, fringe benefit, perk (*Inf.*), plus

persecute 1. afflict, distress, dragoon, harass, hound, hunt, ill-treat, injure, maltreat, martyr, molest, oppress, pursue, torment, torture, victimize **2.** annoy, badger, bait, bother, pester, tease, vex, worry

perseverance constancy, dedication, determination, diligence, doggedness, endurance, indefatigability, persistence, pertinacity, purposefulness, resolution, sedulity, stamina, steadfastness, tenacity

persevere be determined *or* resolved, carry on, continue, endure, go on, hang on, hold fast, hold on (*Inf.*), keep going, keep on *or* at, maintain, persist, plug away (*Inf.*), pursue, remain, stand firm, stick at *or* to

persist 1. be resolute, continue, hold on (*Inf.*), insist, persevere, stand firm **2.** abide, carry on, continue, endure, keep up, last, linger, remain

persistence constancy, determination, diligence, doggedness, endurance, grit, indefatigability, perseverance, pertinacity, pluck, resolution, stamina, steadfastness, tenacity, tirelessness

throughout the night. —**per'sister** *n.*

persistent (pə'sɪstənt) *adj.* 1. showing persistence. 2. incessantly repeated; unrelenting: *your persistent questioning.* 3. (of plant parts) remaining attached to the plant after the normal time of withering. 4. *Zool.* (of parts normally present only in young stages) present in the adult. —**per'sistence** *n.* —**per'sistently** *adv.*

person ('pɜːsən) *n., pl.* **persons.** 1. an individual human being. 2. the body of a human being: *guns hidden on his person.* 3. a grammatical category into which pronouns and forms of verbs are subdivided depending on whether they refer to the speaker, the person addressed, or some other individual, thing, etc. 4. a human being or a corporation recognized in law as having certain rights and obligations. 5. **in person.** actually present: *the author will be there in person.*

▷ **Usage.** *People* is the word usually used to refer to more than one individual: *there were a hundred people at the reception. Persons* is rarely used, except in official English: *several persons were interviewed.*

-person *suffix of nouns.* sometimes used instead of *-man* and *-woman* or *-lady: chairperson.*

persona (pɜː'səʊnə) *n., pl.* **-nae** (-niː). 1. (*often pl.*) a character in a play, novel, etc. 2. (in Jungian psychology) the mechanism that conceals a person's true thoughts and feelings, esp. in adaptation to the outside world.

personable ('pɜːsənəbəl) *adj.* pleasant in appearance and personality. —**'personableness** *n.* —**'personably** *adv.*

personage ('pɜːsənɪdʒ) *n.* 1. an important or distinguished person. 2. another word for **person.** 3. *Rare.* a figure in literature, history, etc.

persona grata *Latin.* (pɜː'səʊnə 'grɑːtə) *n., pl.* **personae gratae** (pɜː'səʊniː 'grɑːtiː). an acceptable person, esp. a diplomat.

personal ('pɜːsənəl) *adj.* 1. of or relating to the private aspects of a person's life: *personal letters.* 2. (*prenominal*) of or relating to a person's body, its care, or its appearance: *personal hygiene.* 3. (*prenominal*) belonging to or intended for a particular person and no one else: *for your personal use.* 4. (*prenominal*) undertaken by an individual: *a personal appearance by a celebrity.* 5. referring to or involving a person's individual personality, intimate affairs, etc., esp. in an offensive way: *personal remarks; don't be so personal.* 6. having the attributes of an individual conscious being: *a personal God.* 7. of, relating to, or denoting grammatical person. 8. *Law.* of or relating to moveable property, as money, etc.

personal column *n.* a newspaper column containing personal messages and advertisements.

personality (ˌpɜːsə'nælɪtɪ) *n., pl.* **-ties.** 1. *Psychol.* the sum total of all the behavioural and mental characteristics by means of which an individual is recognized as being unique. 2. the distinctive character of a person that makes him socially attractive: *a salesman needs a lot of personality.* 3. a well-known person in a certain field, such as entertainment. 4. a remarkable person. 5. (*often pl.*) a personal remark.

personalize *or* **-ise** ('pɜːsənəˌlaɪz) *vb.* (*tr.*) 1. to endow with personal or individual qualities. 2. to mark (stationery, clothing, etc.) with a person's initials, name, etc. 3. to take (a remark, etc.) personally. 4. another word for **personify.** —ˌ**personali'zation** *or* **-i'sation** *n.*

personally ('pɜːsənəlɪ) *adv.* 1. without the help or intervention of others: *I'll attend to it personally.* 2. (*sentence modifier*) in one's own opinion or as regards oneself: *personally, I hate onions.* 3. as if referring to oneself: *to take the insults personally.* 4. as a person: *we like him personally, but professionally he's incompetent.*

persona non grata *Latin.* (pɜː'səʊnə nɒn 'grɑːtə) *n., pl.* **personae non gratae** (pɜː'səʊni: nɒn 'grɑːtiː). 1. an unacceptable or unwelcome person. 2. a diplomat who is not acceptable to the government to whom he is accredited.

personate ('pɜːsəˌneɪt) *vb.* (*tr.*) 1. to act the part of (a character in a play); portray. 2. *Criminal law.* to assume the identity of (another person) with intent to deceive. —ˌ**person'ation** *n.* —**'personative** *adj.* —**'person,ator** *n.*

personification (pɜːˌsɒnɪfɪ'keɪʃən) *n.* 1. the attribution of human characteristics to things, abstract ideas, etc. 2. the representation of an abstract quality or idea in the form of a person, creature, etc., as in art and literature. 3. a person or thing that personifies. 4. a person or thing regarded as an embodiment of a quality: *he is the personification of optimism.*

personify (pɜː'sɒnɪˌfaɪ) *vb.* **-fying, -fied.** (*tr.*) 1. to attribute human characteristics to (a thing or abstraction). 2. to represent (an abstract quality) in human or animal form. 3. (of a person or thing) to represent (an abstract quality), as in art. 4. to be the embodiment of. —**per'soni,fier** *n.*

personnel (ˌpɜːsə'nel) *n.* 1. the people employed in an organization or for a service. 2. **a.** the department that interviews, appoints, or keeps records of employees. **b.** (*as modifier*): *a personnel officer.*

perspective (pə'spektɪv) *n.* 1. a way of regarding situations, facts, etc., and judging their relative importance. 2. the proper or accurate point of view or the ability to see it; objectivity: *try to get some perspective on your troubles.* 3. the theory or art of suggesting three dimensions on a two-dimensional surface, in order to recreate the dimensions and spatial relationships that objects or a scene in recession present to the eye. 4. the appearance of objects, buildings, etc., relative to each other, as determined by their distance from the viewer, or the effects of this distance on their appearance. —**per'spectively** *adv.*

Perspex ('pɜːspeks) *n. Trademark.* any of various clear acrylic resins.

perspicacious (ˌpɜːspɪ'keɪʃəs) *adj.* acutely perceptive or discerning. —ˌ**perspi'caciously** *adv.* —ˌ**perspi'caciousness** *or* **perspicacity** (ˌpɜːspɪ'kæsɪtɪ) *n.*

perspicuous (pə'spɪkjʊəs) *adj.* (of speech or writing) easily understood; lucid. —**per'spicuously** *adv.* —**per'spicuousness** *or* **perspicuity** (ˌpɜːspɪ'kjuːɪtɪ) *n.*

perspiration (ˌpɜːspə'reɪʃən) *n.* 1. the salty fluid se-

THESAURUS

persistent 1. assiduous, determined, dogged, enduring, fixed, immovable, indefatigable, obdurate, obstinate, persevering, pertinacious, resolute, steadfast, steady, stubborn, tenacious, tireless, unflagging 2. constant, continual, continuous, endless, incessant, interminable, never-ending, perpetual, relentless, repeated, unrelenting, unremitting

person 1. being, body, human, human being, individual, living soul, soul 2. **in person** bodily, in the flesh, oneself, personally

persona assumed role, character, façade, face, front, mask, part, personality, public face, role

personable affable, agreeable, amiable, attractive, charming, good-looking, handsome, likable, nice, pleasant, pleasing, presentable, winning

personage big noise (*Brit. sl.*), big shot (*Sl.*), celebrity, dignitary, luminary, notable, personality, public figure, somebody, V.I.P., well-known person, worthy

personal 1. exclusive, individual, inti-

mate, own, particular, peculiar, private, privy, special 2. bodily, corporal, corporeal, exterior, material, physical 3. derogatory, disparaging, insulting, nasty, offensive, pejorative, slighting

personality 1. character, disposition, identity, individuality, make-up, nature, psyche, temper, temperament, traits 2. attraction, attractiveness, character, charisma, charm, dynamism, likableness, magnetism, pleasantness 3. celebrity, famous name, household name, notable, personage, star, well-known face, well-known person

personally 1. alone, by oneself, independently, in person, in the flesh, on one's own, solely 2. for oneself, for one's part, from one's own viewpoint, in one's own view 3. individualistically, individually, privately, specially, subjectively

personate act, depict, do (*Inf.*), enact, feign, imitate, impersonate, play-act, portray, represent

personification embodiment, image, incarnation, likeness, portrayal, recreation,

representation, semblance

personify body forth, embody, epitomize, exemplify, express, image (*Rare*), incarnate, mirror, represent, symbolize, typify

personnel employees, helpers, human resources, liveware, members, men and women, people, staff, workers, work force

perspective 1. angle, attitude, broad view, context, frame of reference, objectivity, outlook, overview, proportion, relation, relative importance, relativity, way of looking 2. outlook, panorama, prospect, scene, view, vista

perspicacious acute, alert, astute, aware, clear-sighted, clever, discerning, keen, observant, penetrating, perceptive, percipient, sagacious, sharp, sharp-witted, shrewd

perspicacity acumen, acuteness, discernment, discrimination, insight, keenness, penetration, perceptiveness, percipience, perspicaciousness, perspicuity, sagaciousness, sagacity, sharpness, shrewdness, wit

creted by the sweat glands of the skin. **2.** the act of secreting this fluid. —**perspiratory** (pə'spaɪərətərɪ) *adj.*

perspire (pə'spaɪə) *vb.* to secrete or exude (perspiration) through the pores of the skin. —**per'spiringly** *adv.*

persuade (pə'sweɪd) *vb.* (*tr.; may take a clause as object or an infinitive*) **1.** to induce, urge, or prevail upon successfully: *he finally persuaded them to buy it.* **2.** to cause to believe; convince: *even with the evidence, the police were not persuaded.* —**per'suadable** *or* **per'suasible** *adj.* —**per,suada'bility** *or* **per,suasi'bility** *n.* —**per'suader** *n.*

persuasion (pə'sweɪʒən) *n.* **1.** the act of persuading or of trying to persuade. **2.** the power to persuade. **3.** a strong belief. **4.** an established creed or belief, esp. a religious one. **5.** a sect, party, or faction.

persuasive (pə'sweɪsɪv) *adj.* having the power or tending to persuade: *a persuasive salesman.* —**per'suasively** *adv.* —**per'suasiveness** *n.*

pert (pɜːt) *adj.* **1.** saucy, impudent, or forward. **2.** jaunty: *a pert little bow.* **3.** *Obs.* clever or brisk. —**'pertly** *adv.* —**'pertness** *n.*

pertain (pə'teɪn) *vb.* (*intr.; often foll. by to*) **1.** to have reference or relevance. **2.** to be appropriate. **3.** to belong (to) or be a part (of).

pertinacious (,pɜːtɪ'neɪʃəs) *adj.* **1.** doggedly resolute in purpose or belief; unyielding. **2.** stubbornly persistent. —**,perti'naciously** *adv.* —**pertinacity** (,pɜːtɪ'næsɪtɪ) *or* **,perti'naciousness** *n.*

pertinent ('pɜːtɪnənt) *adj.* relating to the matter at hand; relevant. —**'pertinence** *or* **'pertinency** *n.* —**'pertinently** *adv.*

perturb (pə'tɜːb) *vb.* (*tr.; often passive*) **1.** to disturb the composure of; trouble. **2.** to throw into disorder. **3.** *Physics, astron.* to cause (a planet, electron, etc.) to undergo a perturbation. —**per'turbable** *adj.* —**per'turbingly** *adv.*

perturbation (,pɜːtə'beɪʃən) *n.* **1.** the act of perturbing or the state of being perturbed. **2.** a cause of disturbance. **3.** *Physics.* a secondary influence on a system that modifies simple behaviour, such as the effect of the other electrons on one electron in an atom. **4.** *Astron.* a small continuous deviation in the orbit of a planet or comet, due to the attraction of neighbouring planets.

peruke (pə'ruːk) *n.* a wig for men in the 17th and 18th centuries. Also called: **periwig.**

peruse (pə'ruːz) *vb.* (*tr.*) **1.** to read or examine with care; study. **2.** to browse or read in a leisurely way. —**pe'rusal** *n.* —**pe'ruser** *n.*

pervade (pɜː'veɪd) *vb.* (*tr.*) to spread through or throughout, esp. subtly or gradually; permeate. —**per'vader** *n.* —**pervasion** (pɜː'veɪʒən) *n.* —**pervasive** (pɜː'veɪsɪv) *adj.* —**per'vasively** *adv.* —**per'vasiveness** *n.*

perverse (pə'vɜːs) *adj.* **1.** deliberately deviating from what is regarded as normal, good, or proper. **2.** persistently holding to what is wrong. **3.** wayward or contrary; obstinate. —**per'versely** *adv.* —**per'verseness** *or* **per'versity** *n.*

perversion (pə'vɜːʃən) *n.* **1.** any abnormal means of obtaining sexual satisfaction. **2.** the act of perverting or the state of being perverted. **3.** a perverted form or usage.

pervert *vb.* (pə'vɜːt). (*tr.*) **1.** to use wrongly or badly. **2.** to interpret wrongly or badly; distort. **3.** to lead into deviant or perverted beliefs or behaviour; corrupt. **4.** to debase. ~*n.* ('pɜːvɜːt). **5.** a person who practises sexual perversion. —**per'verted** *adj.* —**per'verter** *n.* —**per'vertible** *adj.* —**per'versive** *adj.*

pervious ('pɜːvɪəs) *adj.* **1.** able to be penetrated; permeable. **2.** receptive to new ideas, etc.; open-minded. —**'perviously** *adv.* —**'perviousness** *n.*

peseta (pə'seɪtə; *Spanish* pe'seta) *n.* the standard monetary unit of Spain, divided into 100 céntimos.

pesky ('pɛskɪ) *adj.* **peskier, peskiest.** *U.S. inf.* troublesome. —**'peskily** *adv.* —**'peskiness** *n.*

peso ('peɪsəʊ; *Spanish* 'peso) *n., pl.* **-sos** (-səʊz; *Spanish* -sos). the standard monetary unit of Argentina, Bolivia, Colombia, Cuba, the Dominican Republic, Mexico, the Philippines, and Uruguay.

pessary ('pɛsərɪ) *n., pl.* **-ries.** *Med.* **1.** a device for inserting into the vagina, either as a support for the uterus or (**diaphragm pessary**) as a contraceptive. **2.** a vaginal suppository.

pessimism ('pɛsɪ,mɪzəm) *n.* **1.** the tendency to expect the worst in all things. **2.** the doctrine of the ultimate triumph of evil over good. **3.** the doctrine that this is the worst of all possible worlds. —**'pessimist** *n.* —**,pessi'mistic** *adj.* —**,pessi'mistically** *adv.*

pest (pɛst) *n.* **1.** a person or thing that annoys, esp. by

---

THESAURUS

perspiration exudation, moisture, sweat, wetness

perspire be damp, be wet, drip, exude, glow, pour with sweat, secrete, sweat, swelter

persuade **1.** actuate, advise, allure, bring round (*Inf.*), coax, counsel, entice, impel, incite, induce, influence, inveigle, prevail upon, prompt, sway, talk into, urge, win over **2.** cause to believe, convert, convince, satisfy

persuasion **1.** blandishment, cajolery, conversion, enticement, exhortation, inducement, influencing, inveiglement, wheedling **2.** cogency, force, persuasiveness, potency, power, pull (*Inf.*) **3.** belief, certitude, conviction, credo, creed, faith, firm belief, fixed opinion, opinion, tenet, views **4.** camp, cult, denomination, faction, party, school, school of thought, sect, side

persuasive cogent, compelling, convincing, credible, effective, eloquent, forceful, impelling, impressive, inducing, influential, logical, moving, plausible, sound, telling, touching, valid, weighty, winning

pertain appertain, apply, be appropriate, bear on, befit, belong, be part of, be relevant, concern, refer, regard, relate

pertinacious bull-headed, determined, dogged, headstrong, inflexible, intractable, mulish, obdurate, obstinate, persevering, persistent, perverse, pig-headed, relentless, resolute, self-willed, strong-willed, stubborn, tenacious, unyielding, wilful

pertinent admissible, *ad rem*, applicable, apposite, appropriate, apropos, apt, fit, fitting, germane, material, pat, proper, relevant, suitable, to the point, to the purpose

pertness audacity, brashness, brass

(*Inf.*), bumptiousness, cheek (*Inf.*), cheekiness, cockiness, effrontery, forwardness, impertinence, impudence, insolence, presumption, rudeness, sauciness

perturb **1.** agitate, alarm, bother, discompose, disconcert, discountenance, disquiet, disturb, fluster, ruffle, trouble, unsettle, upset, vex, worry **2.** confuse, disarrange, disorder, muddle, unsettle

perturbed agitated, alarmed, anxious, disconcerted, disquieted, disturbed, fearful, flurried, flustered, ill at ease, nervous, restless, shaken, troubled, uncomfortable, uneasy, upset, worried

perusal browse, check, examination, inspection, look through, read, scrutiny, study

peruse browse, check, examine, inspect, look through, read, run one's eye over, scan, scrutinize, study

pervade affect, charge, diffuse, extend, fill, imbue, infuse, overspread, penetrate, percolate, permeate, spread through, suffuse

pervasive common, extensive, general, inescapable, omnipresent, permeating, pervading, prevalent, rife, ubiquitous, universal, widespread

perverse **1.** abnormal, contradictory, contrary, delinquent, depraved, deviant, disobedient, froward, improper, incorrect, miscreant, rebellious, refractory, troublesome, unhealthy, unmanageable, unreasonable **2.** contrary, contumacious, cross-grained, dogged, headstrong, intractable, intransigent, obdurate, wilful, wrong-headed **3.** contrary, mulish, obstinate, pig-headed, stubborn, unyielding, wayward **4.** cantankerous, churlish, crabbed, cross, fractious, ill-natured, ill-

tempered, peevish, petulant, spiteful, stroppy (*Brit. sl.*), surly

perversion **1.** aberration, abnormality, debauchery, depravity, deviation, immorality, kink (*Brit. sl.*), kinkiness (*Sl.*), unnaturalness, vice, vitiation, wickedness **2.** corruption, distortion, falsification, misinterpretation, misrepresentation, misuse, twisting

perversity contradictoriness, contradictoriness, contrariness, contumacy, frowardness, intransigence, obduracy, refractoriness, waywardness, wrong-headedness

pervert *v.* **1.** abuse, distort, falsify, garble, misconstrue, misinterpret, misrepresent, misuse, twist, warp **2.** corrupt, debase, debauch, degrade, deprave, desecrate, initiate, lead astray, subvert ~*n.* **3.** debauchee, degenerate, deviant, weirdo (*Sl.*)

perverted aberrant, abnormal, corrupt, debased, debauched, depraved, deviant, distorted, evil, immoral, impaired, kinky (*Sl.*), misguided, sick, twisted, unhealthy, unnatural, vicious, vitiated, warped, wicked

pessimism cynicism, dejection, depression, despair, despondency, distrust, gloom, gloominess, gloomy outlook, glumness, hopelessness, melancholy

pessimist cynic, defeatist, doomster, gloom merchant (*Inf.*), kill-joy, melancholic, misanthrope, prophet of doom, wet blanket (*Inf.*), worrier

pessimistic bleak, cynical, dark, dejected, depressed, despairing, despondent, distrustful, downhearted, fatalistic, foreboding, gloomy, glum, hopeless, melancholy, misanthropic, morose, resigned, sad

imposing itself when it is not wanted; nuisance. **2.** any organism that damages crops, or injures or irritates livestock or man. **3.** *Rare.* an epidemic disease.

pester ('pɛstə) *vb.* (*tr.*) to annoy or nag continually. —'**pesterer** *n.*

pesticide ('pɛstɪˌsaɪd) *n.* a chemical used for killing pests, esp. insects. —ˌpesti'**cidal** *adj.*

pestiferous (pɛ'stɪfərəs) *adj.* **1.** *Inf.* troublesome; irritating. **2.** breeding, carrying, or spreading infectious disease. **3.** corrupting; pernicious.

pestilence ('pɛstɪləns) *n.* **1. a.** any epidemic of a deadly infectious disease, such as the plague. **b.** such a disease. **2.** an evil influence.

pestilent ('pɛstɪlənt) *adj.* **1.** annoying; irritating. **2.** highly destructive morally or physically; pernicious. **3.** likely to cause epidemic or infectious disease. —'**pestilently** *adv.* —**pestilential** (ˌpɛstɪ'lɛnʃəl) *adj.* —ˌpesti'**lentially** *adv.*

pestle ('pɛsəl) *n.* **1.** a club-shaped instrument for mixing or grinding substances in a mortar. **2.** a tool for pounding or stamping. ~*vb.* **3.** to pound (a substance or object) with or as if with a pestle.

pet[1] (pɛt) *n.* **1.** a tame animal kept for companionship, amusement, etc. **2.** a person who is fondly indulged; favourite: *teacher's pet.* ~(*modifier*) **3.** kept as a pet: *a pet dog.* **4.** of or for pet animals: *pet food.* **5.** particularly cherished: *a pet hatred.* **6.** showing fondness: *a pet name.* ~*vb.* **petting, petted. 7.** (*tr.*) to treat (a person, animal, etc.) as a pet; pamper. **8.** (*tr.*) to pat or fondle (an animal, child, etc.). **9.** (*intr.*) *Inf.* (of two people) to caress each other in an erotic manner. —'**petter** *n.*

pet[2] (pɛt) *n.* a fit of sulkiness, esp. at what is felt to be a slight; pique.

Pet. *Bible.* abbrev. for Peter.

petal ('pɛtəl) *n.* any of the separate parts of the corolla of a flower: often brightly coloured. —'**petaline** *adj.* —'**petal-,like** *adj.* —'**petalled** *adj.*

petard (pɪ'tɑːd) *n.* **1.** (formerly) a device containing explosives used to breach a wall, doors, etc. **2. hoist with one's own petard.** being the victim of one's own schemes, etc.

peter ('piːtə) *vb.* (*intr.*; foll. by *out* or *away*) to fall (off) in volume, intensity, etc., and finally cease.

Peter Pan *n.* a youthful, boyish, or immature man.

petersham ('piːtəʃəm) *n.* **1.** a thick corded ribbon used to stiffen belts, etc. **2.** a heavy woollen fabric used for coats, etc. **3.** a kind of overcoat made of such fabric.

pethidine ('pɛθɪˌdiːn) *n.* a white crystalline water-soluble drug used as an analgesic. Also called: (esp U.S.) **meperidine.**

petiole ('pɛtɪˌəʊl) *n.* **1.** the stalk by which a leaf is attached to the plant. **2.** *Zool.* a slender stalk or stem, as between the thorax and abdomen of ants. —**petiolate** ('pɛtɪəˌleɪt) *adj.*

petit ('pɛtɪ) *adj.* (*prenominal*) *Chiefly law.* of lesser importance; small.

petit bourgeois ('pɛtɪ 'bʊəʒwɑː) *n., pl.* **petits bourgeois** ('pɛtɪ 'bʊəʒwɑːz). **1.** Also called: **petite bourgeoisie, petty bourgeoisie.** the section of the middle class with the lowest social status, as shopkeepers, lower clerical staff, etc. **2.** a member of this stratum. ~*adj.* **3.** of,

relating to, or characteristic of the petit bourgeois, esp. indicating a sense of self-righteousness and conformity to established standards of behaviour.

petite (pə'tiːt) *adj.* (of women) small, delicate, and dainty.

petit four ('pɛtɪ 'fɔː) *n., pl.* **petits fours** ('pɛtɪ 'fɔːz). any of various very small fancy cakes and biscuits.

petition (pɪ'tɪʃən) *n.* **1.** a written document signed by a large number of people demanding some form of action from a government or other authority. **2.** any formal request to a higher authority; entreaty. **3.** *Law.* a formal application in writing made to a court asking for some specific judicial action: *a petition for divorce.* **4.** the action of petitioning. ~*vb.* **5.** (*tr.*) to address or present a petition to (a person in authority, government, etc.): *to petition Parliament.* **6.** (*intr.*; foll by *for*) to seek by petition: *to petition for a change in the law.* —**pe'titionary** *adj.* —**pe'titioner** *n.*

petit mal ('pɛtɪ 'mæl) *n.* a mild form of epilepsy characterized by periods of impairment or loss of consciousness for up to 30 seconds. Cf. **grand mal.**

petit point ('pɛtɪ 'pɔɪnt) *n.* **1.** a small diagonal needlepoint stitch used for fine detail. **2.** work done with such stitches.

petrel ('pɛtrəl) *n.* any of a family of oceanic birds having a hooked bill and tubular nostrils: includes albatrosses, storm petrels, and shearwaters.

petrify ('pɛtrɪˌfaɪ) *vb.* **-fying, -fied. 1.** (*tr.; often passive*) to convert (organic material) into a fossilized form by impregnation with dissolved minerals so that the original appearance is preserved. **2.** to make or become dull, unresponsive, etc.; deaden. **3.** (*tr.; often passive*) to stun or daze with horror, fear, etc. —ˌpetri'**faction** or ˌpetrifi'**cation** *n.* —'**petri,fier** *n.*

petro- or before a vowel **petr-** combining form. **1.** indicating stone or rock: *petrology.* **2.** indicating petroleum, its products, etc.: *petrochemical.*

petrochemical (ˌpɛtrəʊ'kɛmɪkəl) *n.* **1.** any substance, such as acetone or ethanol, obtained from petroleum. ~*adj.* **2.** of, concerned with, or obtained from petrochemicals or related to petrochemistry. —ˌpetro-'**chemistry** *n.*

petrodollar ('pɛtrəʊˌdɒlə) *n.* money earned by a country by the exporting of petroleum.

petrol ('pɛtrəl) *n.* any one of various volatile flammable liquid mixtures of hydrocarbons, obtained from petroleum and used as a solvent and a fuel for internal-combustion engines. U.S. name: **gasoline.**

petrolatum (ˌpɛtrə'leɪtəm) *n.* a translucent gelatinous substance obtained from petroleum; used as a lubricant and in medicine as an ointment base. Also called: **petroleum jelly.**

petroleum (pə'trəʊliəm) *n.* a dark-coloured thick flammable crude oil occurring in sedimentary rocks, consisting mainly of hydrocarbons. Fractional distillation separates the crude oil into petrol, paraffin, diesel oil, lubricating oil, etc. Fuel oil, paraffin wax, asphalt, and carbon black are extracted from the residue.

petroleum jelly *n.* another name for **petrolatum.**

petrol station *n. Brit.* another term for **filling station.**

petticoat ('pɛtɪˌkəʊt) *n.* **1.** a woman's underskirt. **2.**

THESAURUS

pest 1. annoyance, bane, bore, bother, irritation, nuisance, pain (*Inf.*), pain in the neck (*Inf.*), thorn in one's flesh, trial, vexation **2.** bane, blight, bug, curse, epidemic, infection, pestilence, plague, scourge

pester annoy, badger, bedevil, bother, bug (*Inf.*), chivvy, disturb, drive one up the wall (*Sl.*), fret, get at, get on someone's nerves, harass, harry, hassle (*Inf.*), irk, nag, pick on, plague, ride (*Inf.*), torment, worry

pestilence 1. Black Death, epidemic, pandemic, plague, visitation **2.** affliction, bane, blight, cancer, canker, curse, scourge

pestilent 1. annoying, bothersome, galling, irksome, irritating, plaguy (*Inf.*), tiresome, vexing **2.** corrupting, deleterious, destructive, detrimental, evil, harmful, injurious, pernicious, ruinous, vicious **3.** catching, contagious, contaminated, diseased, disease-ridden, infected, infectious, plague-ridden, tainted

pestilential 1. annoying, dangerous, deleterious, destructive, detrimental, evil, foul, harmful, hazardous, injurious, pernicious, ruinous, troublesome **2.** catching, contagious, contaminated, deadly, disease-ridden, infectious, malignant, noxious, pestiferous, poisonous, venomous

pet[1] *n.* **1.** apple of one's eye, blue-eyed boy (*Inf.*), darling, favourite, idol, jewel, treasure ~*adj.* **2.** cherished, dearest, dear to one's heart, favoured, favourite, particular, preferred, special **3.** domesticated, house, house-broken, house-trained (*Brit.*), tame, trained ~*v.* **4.** baby, coddle, cosset, mollycoddle, pamper, spoil **5.** caress, fondle, pat, stroke **6.** *Inf.* canoodle (*Sl.*), cuddle, kiss, neck (*Inf.*), smooch (*Sl.*), snog (*Brit. sl.*)

pet[2] bad mood, huff, ill temper, miff (*Inf.*), paddy (*Brit. inf.*), paddywhack (*Brit. inf.*), pique, pout, sulk, sulks, tantrum, temper

peter out come to nothing, die out, dwindle, ebb, evaporate, fade, fail, give out, run dry, run out, stop, taper off, wane

petition 1. *n.* address, appeal, application, entreaty, invocation, memorial, plea, prayer, request, round robin, solicitation, suit, supplication **2.** *v.* adjure, appeal, ask, beg, beseech, call upon, crave, entreat, plead, pray, press, solicit, sue, supplicate, urge

petrified 1. fossilized, ossified, rocklike **2.** aghast, appalled, dazed, dumbfounded, frozen, horrified, numb, scared stiff, shocked, speechless, stunned, stupefied, terrified, terror-stricken

petrify 1. calcify, fossilize, harden, set, solidify, turn to stone **2.** amaze, appal, astonish, astound, confound, dumbfound, horrify, immobilize, paralyse, stun, stupefy, terrify, transfix

Inf. **a.** a humorous or mildly disparaging name for a woman. **b.** (*as modifier*): *petticoat politics.*

pettifogger ('pɛtɪ,fɒgə) *n.* **1.** a lawyer who conducts unimportant cases, esp. one who resorts to trickery. **2.** any person who quibbles. —'**petti,foggery** *n.* —'**petti,fog** *vb.* (*intr.*) -**fogging, -fogged.** —'**petti,fogging** *adj.*

pettish ('pɛtɪʃ) *adj.* peevish; petulant. —'**pettishly** *adv.* —'**pettishness** *n.*

petty ('pɛtɪ) *adj.* -**tier, -tiest.** **1.** trivial; trifling: *petty details.* **2.** narrow-minded, mean: *petty spite.* **3.** minor or subordinate in rank: *petty officialdom.* **4.** *Law.* a variant of **petit.** —'**pettily** *adv.* —'**pettiness** *n.*

petty cash *n.* a small cash fund for minor incidental expenses.

petty jury *n.* a group of 12 persons picked to weigh evidence in and decide the issue of a trial in court. Also called: **petit jury.**

petty officer *n.* a noncommissioned officer in a naval service comparable in rank to a sergeant in an army or marine corps.

petulant ('pɛtjʊlənt) *adj.* irritable, impatient, or sullen in a peevish or capricious way. —'**petulance** *or* '**petulancy** *n.* —'**petulantly** *adv.*

petunia (pɪ'tjuːnɪə) *n.* any plant of a tropical American genus: cultivated for their colourful funnel-shaped flowers.

pew (pjuː) *n.* **1.** (in a church) **a.** one of several long benchlike seats with backs, used by the congregation. **b.** an enclosed compartment reserved for the use of a family or other small group. **2.** *Brit. inf.* a seat (esp. in **take a pew**).

pewter ('pjuːtə) *n.* **1. a.** any of various alloys containing tin, lead, and sometimes copper and antimony. **b.** (*as modifier*): *pewter ware; a pewter tankard.* **2.** plate or kitchen utensils made from pewter. —'**pewterer** *n.*

pF *abbrev. for* picofarad.

pH *n.* potential of hydrogen; a measure of the acidity or alkalinity of a solution. Pure water has a pH of 7, acid solutions have a pH less than 7, and alkaline solutions a pH greater than 7.

phaeton ('feɪtən) *n.* a light four-wheeled horse-drawn carriage with or without a top.

phago- *or before a vowel* **phag-** *combining form.* eating, consuming, or destroying: *phagocyte.*

phagocyte ('fægə,saɪt) *n.* a cell or protozoan that engulfs particles, such as microorganisms. —**phagocytic** (,fægə'sɪtɪk) *adj.*

phalanger (fə'lændʒə) *n.* any of various Australasian arboreal marsupials, having dense fur and a long tail. Also called (in Australia): **possum.**

phalanx ('fælæŋks) *n., pl.* **phalanxes** *or* **phalanges** (fæ-'lændʒiːz). **1.** an ancient Greek and Macedonian battle formation of hoplites presenting long spears from behind a wall of overlapping shields. **2.** any closely ranked unit or mass of people: *the police formed a phalanx to protect the embassy.* **3.** a number of people united for a common purpose. **4.** any of the bones of the fingers or toes. **5.** *Bot.* a bundle of stamens.

phallic ('fælɪk) *adj.* **1.** of, relating to, or resembling a phallus: *a phallic symbol.* **2.** *Psychoanal.* relating to a stage of psychosexual development during which the child's interest is concentrated on the genital organs. **3.** of or relating to phallicism.

phallus ('fæləs) *n., pl.* **-li** (-laɪ) *or* **-luses.** **1.** another word for **penis.** **2.** an image of the male sexual organ, esp. as a symbol of reproductive power.

phantasm ('fæntæzəm) *n.* **1.** a phantom. **2.** an illusory perception of an object, person, etc. —**phan'tasmal** *or* **phan'tasmic** *adj.*

phantasmagoria (,fæntæzmə'gɔːrɪə) *or* **phantasmagory** (fæn'tæzməgərɪ) *n.* **1.** *Psychol.* a shifting medley of real or imagined figures, as in a dream. **2.** *Films.* a sequence of pictures made to vary in size rapidly. **3.** a shifting scene composed of different elements. —**phantasmagoric** (,fæntæzmə'gɒrɪk) *or* **phantasma'gorical** *adj.*

phantasy ('fæntəsɪ) *n., pl.* -**sies.** an archaic spelling of **fantasy.**

phantom ('fæntəm) *n.* **1. a.** an apparition or spectre. **b.** (*as modifier*): *a phantom army marching through the sky.* **2.** the visible representation of something abstract, esp. as in a dream or hallucination: *phantoms of evil haunted his sleep.* **3.** something apparently unpleasant or horrific that has no material form.

Pharaoh ('fɛərəʊ) *n.* the title of the ancient Egyptian kings. —**Pharaonic** (fɛə'rɒnɪk) *adj.*

Pharisaic (,færɪ'seɪɪk) *or* **Pharisaical** *adj.* **1.** *Judaism.* of, relating to, or characteristic of the Pharisees or Pharisaism. **2.** (*often not cap.*) righteously hypocritical. —,**Phari'saically** *adv.*

Pharisee ('færɪ,siː) *n.* **1.** a member of an ancient Jewish sect teaching strict observance of Jewish traditions. **2.** (*often not cap.*) a self-righteous or hypocritical person.

pharmaceutical (,fɑːmə'sjuːtɪkəl) *or* **pharmaceutic** *adj.* of or relating to drugs or pharmacy. —,**pharma-'ceutically** *adv.*

pharmaceutics (,fɑːmə'sjuːtɪks) *n.* **1.** (*functioning as sing.*) another term for **pharmacy** (sense 1). **2.** pharmaceutical remedies.

pharmacist ('fɑːməsɪst) *n.* a person qualified to prepare and dispense drugs.

pharmaco- *combining form.* indicating drugs: *pharmacology.*

pharmacology (,fɑːmə'kɒlədʒɪ) *n.* the science or study of drugs, including their characteristics, action, and uses. —**pharmacological** (,fɑːməkə'lɒdʒɪkəl) *adj.* —,**pharmaco'logically** *adv.* —,**pharma'cologist** *n.*

pharmacopoeia *or U.S.* (*sometimes*) **pharmacopeia** (,fɑːməkə'piːə) *n.* an authoritative book containing a list of medicinal drugs with their uses, preparation, dosages, formulas, etc. —,**pharmaco'poeial** *adj.*

pharmacy ('fɑːməsɪ) *n., pl.* -**cies.** **1.** Also: **pharmaceutics.** the practice or art of preparing and dispensing drugs. **2.** a dispensary.

pharyngitis (,færɪn'dʒaɪtɪs) *n.* inflammation of the pharynx.

pharynx ('færɪŋks) *n., pl.* **pharynges** (fæ'rɪndʒiːz) *or* **pharynxes.** the part of the alimentary canal between the mouth and the oesophagus. —**pharyngeal** (,færɪn-'dʒiːəl) *adj.*

phase (feɪz) *n.* **1.** any distinct or characteristic period or stage in a sequence of events: *there were two phases to the resolution.* **2.** *Astron.* one of the recurring shapes of the portion of the moon or an inferior planet illuminated by the sun. **3.** *Physics.* the fraction of a cycle of a periodic quantity that has been completed at a specific reference time, expressed as an angle. **4.** *Physics.* a particular stage in a periodic process or phenomenon. **5. in phase.** (of two waveforms) reaching corresponding phases at the same time. **6. out of phase.** (of two waveforms) not in phase. **7.** *Chem.* a distinct state of matter characterized by homogeneous composition and properties and the possession of a clearly defined boundary. **8.** *Zool.* a variation in the normal form of an animal, esp. a colour variation, brought about by seasonal or geographical change. ~*vb.* (*tr.*) **9.** (*often passive*) to execute, arrange, or introduce gradually or in stages: *the withdrawal was phased over several months.* **10.** (sometimes foll. by *with*) to cause (a part, process, etc.) to function or coincide with (another part, etc.): *he tried to phase the intake and output of the machine; he phased the intake with the output.* **11.** *Chiefly U.S.* to arrange (processes, goods, etc.) to be supplied or executed when required. —'**phasic** *adj.*

phase in *vb.* (*tr., adv.*) to introduce in a gradual or cau-

---

THESAURUS

petty 1. contemptible, inconsiderable, inessential, inferior, insignificant, little, measly (*Inf.*), negligible, paltry, piddling (*Inf.*), slight, small, trifling, trivial, unimportant 2. cheap, grudging, mean, mean-minded, shabby, small-minded, spiteful, stingy, ungenerous 3. inferior, junior, lesser, lower, minor, secondary, subordinate

petulance bad temper, crabbiness, ill humour, irritability, peevishness, pettish-ness, pique, pouts, querulousness, spleen, sulkiness, sullenness, waspishness

petulant bad-tempered, captious, cavilling, crabbed, cross, crusty, fault-finding, fretful, ill-humoured, impatient, irritable, moody, peevish, perverse, pouting, querulous, snappish, sour, sulky, sullen, ungracious, waspish

phantom 1. apparition, eidolon, ghost, phantasm, revenant, shade (*Literary*), spec-tre, spirit, spook (*Inf.*), wraith 2. chimera, figment, figment of the imagination, hallucination, illusion, vision

pharisee canter, dissembler, dissimulator, fraud, humbug, hypocrite, phoney (*Sl.*), pietist, whited sepulchre

phase aspect, chapter, condition, development, juncture, period, point, position, stage, state, step, time

tious manner: *the legislation was phased in over two years.*

phase out *vb.* (*tr., adv.*) **1.** to discontinue or withdraw gradually. ~*n.* **phase-out. 2.** Chiefly U.S. the action or an instance of phasing out: *a phase-out of conventional forces.*

-phasia *n. combining form.* indicating speech disorder of a specified kind: *aphasia.* —**phasic** *adj. and n. combining form.*

Ph.D. *abbrev. for* Doctor of Philosophy. Also: **D.Phil.**

pheasant ('fɛzənt) *n.* **1.** any of various long-tailed gallinaceous birds, having a brightly-coloured plumage in the male: native to Asia but introduced elsewhere. **2.** any of various other related birds, including the quails and partridges. **3.** U.S. any of several other gallinaceous birds, esp. the ruffed grouse.

pheno- *or before a vowel* **phen-** *combining form.* **1.** showing or manifesting: *phenotype.* **2.** indicating that a molecule contains benzene rings: *phenobarbitone.*

phenobarbitone (ˌfiːnəʊ'bɑːbɪˌtəʊn) *or* **phenobarbital** (ˌfiːnəʊ'bɑːbɪtəl) *n.* a white crystalline derivative of barbituric acid used as a sedative for treating insomnia and epilepsy.

phenol ('fiːnɒl) *n.* **1.** Also called: **carbolic acid.** a white crystalline derivative of benzene, used as an antiseptic and disinfectant and in the manufacture of resins, explosives, and pharmaceuticals. Formula: C_6H_5OH. **2.** *Chem.* any of a class of organic compounds whose molecules contain one or more hydroxyl groups bound directly to a carbon atom in an aromatic ring. —**phenolic** *adj.*

phenomena (fɪ'nɒmɪnə) *n.* a plural of **phenomenon.**

phenomenal (fɪ'nɒmɪnəl) *adj.* **1.** of or relating to a phenomenon. **2.** extraordinary; outstanding; remarkable: *a phenomenal achievement.* **3.** *Philosophy.* known or perceived by the senses rather than the mind. —**phenomenally** *adv.*

phenomenalism (fɪ'nɒmɪnəˌlɪzəm) *n.* **1.** the theory that only phenomena are real and can be known. **2.** the tendency to think about things as phenomena only. —**phenomenalist** *n., adj.*

phenomenon (fɪ'nɒmɪnən) *n., pl.* **-ena** (-ɪnə) *or* **-enons. 1.** anything that can be perceived as an occurrence or fact by the senses. **2.** any remarkable occurrence or person. **3.** *Philosophy.* **a.** the object of perception, experience, etc. **b.** (in the writings of Kant (1724–1804), German philosopher) a thing as it appears, as distinguished from its real nature as a thing-in-itself.

▷ **Usage.** Although *phenomena* is often treated as if it were singular, correct usage is to employ *phenomenon* with a singular construction and *phenomena* with a plural: *that is an interesting phenomenon* (not *phenomena*); *several new phenomena were recorded in his notes.*

phenyl ('fiːnaɪl, 'fɛnɪl) *n.* (*modifier*) of, containing, or consisting of the monovalent group C_6H_5, derived from benzene: *a phenyl group.*

phew (fjuː) *interj.* an exclamation of relief, surprise, disbelief, weariness, etc.

phi (faɪ) *n., pl.* **phis.** the 21st letter in the Greek alphabet, Φ, φ.

phial ('faɪəl) *n.* a small bottle for liquids, etc.; vial.

Phil. *abbrev. for:* **1.** Philippians. **2.** Philippines. **3.** Philadelphia.

philadelphus (ˌfɪlə'dɛlfəs) *n.* any of a N temperate genus of shrubs cultivated for their strongly scented showy

flowers. See also **mock orange.**

philander (fɪ'lændə) *vb.* (*intr.,* often foll. by *with*) (of a man) to flirt with women. —**phi'lanederer** *n.*

philanthropy (fɪ'lænθrəpɪ) *n., pl.* **-pies. 1.** the practice of performing charitable or benevolent actions. **2.** love of mankind in general. —ˌ**philan'thropic** *adj.* —**phi'lanthropist** *or* **philanthrope** ('fɪlən,θrəʊp) *n.*

philately (fɪ'lætəlɪ) *n.* the collection and study of postage stamps. —**philatelic** (ˌfɪlə'tɛlɪk) *adj.* —ˌ**phila'telically** *adv.* —**phi'latelist** *n.*

-phile *or* **-phil** *n. combining form.* indicating a person or thing having a fondness for something specified: *bibliophile.*

philharmonic (ˌfɪlhɑː'mɒnɪk, ˌfɪlə-) *adj.* **1.** fond of music. **2.** (*cap. when part of a name*) denoting an orchestra, choir, society, etc., devoted to music. ~*n.* **3.** (*cap. when part of a name*) a specific philharmonic choir, orchestra, or society.

philhellene (fɪl'hɛliːn) *n.* **1.** a lover of Greece and Greek culture. **2.** *European history.* a supporter of the cause of Greek national independence. —**philhellenic** (ˌfɪlhɛ'liːnɪk) *adj.*

-philia *n. combining form.* **1.** indicating a tendency towards: *haemophilia.* **2.** indicating an abnormal liking for: *necrophilia.* —**philiac** *n. combining form.* —**philous** *or* **-philic** *adj. combining form.*

philippic (fɪ'lɪpɪk) *n.* a bitter or impassioned speech of denunciation; invective.

Philippine ('fɪlɪˌpiːn) *n., adj.* another name for **Filipino.**

Philistine ('fɪlɪˌstaɪn) *n.* **1.** a person who is hostile towards culture, the arts, etc.; a smug boorish person. **2.** a member of the non-Semitic people who inhabited ancient Philistia, a country on the coast of SW Palestine. ~*adj.* **3.** (*sometimes not cap.*) boorishly uncultured. **4.** of or relating to the ancient Philistines. —**Philistinism** ('fɪlɪstɪˌnɪzəm) *n.*

Phillips screw ('fɪlɪps) *n. Trademark.* a screw with a cross-shaped slot.

philo- *or before a vowel* **phil-** *combining form.* indicating a love of: *philology; philanthropic.*

philology (fɪ'lɒlədʒɪ) *n.* (no longer in scholarly use) **1.** comparative and historical linguistics. **2.** the scientific analysis of written records and literary texts. **3.** the study of literature. —**philological** (ˌfɪlə'lɒdʒɪkəl) *adj.* —ˌ**philo'logically** *adv.* —**phi'lologist** *or* **phi'loologer** *n.*

philos. *abbrev. for:* **1.** philosopher. **2.** philosophical.

philosopher (fɪ'lɒsəfə) *n.* **1.** a student or adherent of a particular philosophy. **2.** a person of philosophical temperament, esp. one who is patient, wise, and stoical. **3.** (formerly) an alchemist or devotee of occult science.

philosopher's stone *n.* a stone or substance thought by alchemists to be capable of transmuting base metals into gold.

philosophize *or* **-phise** (fɪ'lɒsəˌfaɪz) *vb.* **1.** (*intr.*) to make philosophical pronouncements and speculations. **2.** (*tr.*) to explain philosophically. —**phi'loso,phizer** *or* **-,phiser** *n.*

philosophy (fɪ'lɒsəfɪ) *n., pl.* **-phies. 1.** the rational investigation of being, knowledge, and right conduct. **2.** a system or school of thought: *the philosophy of Descartes.* **3.** the basic principles of a discipline: *the philosophy of law.* **4.** any system of belief, values, or tenets. **5.** a personal outlook or viewpoint. **6.** serenity of temper. —ˌ**philo'sophical** *adj.*

THESAURUS

phase out close, deactivate, dispose of gradually, ease off, eliminate, pull out, remove, replace, run down, taper off, terminate, wind down, wind up (*Inf.*), withdraw

phenomenal exceptional, extraordinary, fantastic, marvellous, miraculous, outstanding, prodigious, remarkable, sensational, singular, uncommon, unique, unparalleled, unusual, wondrous

phenomenon 1. circumstance, episode, event, fact, happening, incident, occurrence **2.** exception, marvel, miracle, nonpareil, prodigy, rarity, sensation, sight, spectacle, wonder

philander coquet, court, dally, flirt, fool around (*Inf.*), toy, trifle, womanize (*Inf.*)

philanderer Casanova, dallier, Don

Juan, flirt, gallant, gay dog, ladies' man, lady-killer (*Inf.*), Lothario, playboy, stud (*Sl.*), trifler, wolf (*Inf.*), womanizer (*Inf.*)

philanthropic alms-giving, altruistic, beneficent, benevolent, benignant, charitable, eleemosynary, gracious, humane, humanitarian, kind, kind-hearted, munificent, public-spirited

philanthropist alms-giver, altruist, benefactor, contributor, donor, giver, humanitarian, patron

philanthropy alms-giving, altruism, beneficence, benevolence, benignity, bounty, brotherly love, charitableness, charity, generosity, humanitarianism, kind-heartedness, liberality, munificence, open-handedness, patronage, public-spiritedness

philistine 1. *n.* barbarian, boor, bourgeois, Goth, ignoramus, lout, lowbrow, vulgarian, yahoo **2.** *adj.* anti-intellectual, boorish, bourgeois, crass, ignorant, lowbrow, tasteless, uncultivated, uncultured, uneducated, unrefined

philosopher dialectician, logician, metaphysician, sage, seeker after truth, theorist, thinker, wise man

philosophical, philosophic 1. abstract, erudite, learned, logical, rational, sagacious, theoretical, thoughtful, wise **2.** calm, collected, composed, cool, impassive, imperturbable, patient, resigned, serene, stoical, tranquil, unruffled

philosophy 1. aesthetics, knowledge, logic, metaphysics, rationalism, reason, rea-

philtre or U.S. **philter** ('fɪltə) n. a drink supposed to arouse desire.

phlebitis (flɪ'baɪtɪs) n. inflammation of a vein. —**phlebitic** (flɪ'bɪtɪk) adj.

phlebo- or before a vowel **phleb-** combining form. indicating a vein: phlebotomy.

phlegm (flɛm) n. 1. the viscid mucus secreted by the walls of the respiratory tract. 2. Arch. one of the four bodily humours. 3. apathy; stolidity. 4. imperturbability; coolness. —'**phlegmy** adj.

phlegmatic (flɛg'mætɪk) or **phlegmatical** adj. 1. having a stolid or unemotional disposition. 2. not easily excited. —**phleg'matically** adv.

phloem ('fləʊɛm) n. tissue in higher plants that conducts synthesized food substances to all parts of the plant.

phlogiston (flɒ'dʒɪstən, -tən) n. Chem. a hypothetical substance formerly thought to be present in all combustible materials.

phlox (flɒks) n., pl. **phlox** or **phloxes.** any of a chiefly North American genus of plants cultivated for their clusters of white, red, or purple flowers.

-phobe n. combining form. indicating one that fears or hates: xenophobe. —**-phobic** adj. combining form.

phobia ('fəʊbɪə) n. a compelling fear or dread, esp. of a particular object or situation. —'**phobic** adj.

-phobia n. combining form. indicating an extreme abnormal fear of or aversion to: acrophobia; claustrophobia. —**-phobic** adj. combining form.

Phoenician (fɪ'nɪʃən, -'niː∫ən) n. 1. a member of an ancient Semitic people of NW Syria. 2. the extinct language of this people. ~adj. 3. of or relating to Phoenicia, the Phoenicians, or their language.

phoenix or U.S. **phenix** ('fiːnɪks) n. 1. a legendary Arabian bird said to set fire to itself and rise anew from the ashes every 500 years. 2. a person or thing of surpassing beauty or quality.

phone (fəʊn) n., vb. Inf. short for **telephone.**

-phone combining form. 1. (forming nouns) indicating a device giving off sound: telephone. 2. (forming adjectives) speaking a particular language: Francophone. —**-phonic** adj. combining form.

phone-in n. **a.** a radio or television programme in which listeners' or viewers' questions, comments, etc., are telephoned to the studio and broadcast live as part of a discussion. **b.** (as modifier): a phone-in programme.

phoneme ('fəʊniːm) n. Linguistics. one of the set of speech sounds in any given language that serve to distinguish one word from another. —**phonemic** (fə'niːmɪk) adj.

phonemics (fə'niːmɪks) n. (functioning as sing.) that aspect of linguistics concerned with the classification and analysis of the phonemes of a language. —**pho'nemicist** n.

phonetic (fə'nɛtɪk) adj. 1. of or relating to phonetics. 2. denoting any perceptible distinction between one speech sound and another. 3. conforming to pronunciation: phonetic spelling. —**pho'netically** adv.

phonetics (fə'nɛtɪks) n. (functioning as sing.) the science concerned with the study of speech processes, including the production, perception, and analysis of speech sounds. —**phonetician** (ˌfəʊnɪ'tɪʃən) or **phonetist** ('fəʊnɪtɪst) n.

phoney or **phony** ('fəʊnɪ) Sl. ~adj. **-nier, -niest.** 1. not genuine; fake. 2. (of a person) insincere or pretentious. ~n., pl. **-neys** or **-nies.** 3. an insincere or pretentious person. 4. something that is not genuine; a fake. —'**phoneyness** or '**phoniness** n.

phono- or before a vowel **phon-** combining form. indicating a sound or voice: phonograph; phonology.

phonograph ('fəʊnəˌgrɑːf, -ˌgræf) n. 1. an early form of gramophone capable of recording and reproducing sound on wax cylinders. 2. the usual U.S. word for **gramophone.**

phonology (fə'nɒlədʒɪ) n., pl. **-gies.** 1. the study of the sound system of a language or of languages in general. 2. such a sound system. —**phonological** (ˌfəʊnə'lɒdʒɪkəl, ˌfɒn-) adj. —ˌphono'logically adv. —pho'nologist n.

-phony n. combining form. indicating a specified type of sound: cacophony; euphony. —**-phonic** adj. combining form.

phooey ('fuːɪ) interj. Inf. an exclamation of scorn, contempt, etc.

-phore n. combining form. indicating one that bears or produces: semaphore. —**-phorous** adj. combining form.

phosphate ('fosfeɪt) n. 1. any salt or ester of any phosphoric acid. 2. (often pl.) any of several chemical fertilizers containing phosphorous compounds. —**phosphatic** (fos'fætɪk) adj.

phospho- or before a vowel **phosph-** combining form. containing phosphorus: phosphoric.

phosphor ('fosfə) n. a substance capable of emitting light when irradiated with particles or electromagnetic radiation.

phosphoresce (ˌfosfə'rɛs) vb. (intr.) to exhibit phosphorescence.

phosphorescence (ˌfosfə'rɛsəns) n. 1. Physics. a fluorescence that persists after the bombarding radiation producing it has stopped. 2. the light emitted in phosphorescence. 3. the emission of light in which insufficient heat is evolved to cause fluorescence. Cf. **fluorescence.** —ˌphospho'rescent adj.

phosphoric (fos'forɪk) adj. of or containing phosphorus in the pentavalent state.

phosphorous ('fosfərəs) adj. of or containing phosphorus in the trivalent state.

phosphorous acid n. 1. Also called: **orthophosphorous acid.** a white or yellowish hygroscopic crystalline dibasic acid. 2. any oxyacid of phosphorus containing less oxygen than the corresponding phosphoric acid.

phosphorus ('fosfərəs) n. 1. an allotropic nonmetallic element occurring in phosphates and living matter. Ordinary phosphorus is a toxic flammable phosphorescent white solid; the red form is less reactive and nontoxic: used in matches, pesticides, and alloys. The radioisotope **phosphorus-32 (radiophosphorus),** with a half-life of 14.3 days, is used in radiotherapy and as a tracer. Symbol: P; atomic no.: 15; atomic wt.: 30.974. 2. Rare. another name for a **phosphor.**

photo ('fəʊtəʊ) n., pl. **-tos.** Inf. short for **photograph.**

photo- combining form. 1. of, relating to, or produced by light: photosynthesis. 2. indicating a photographic process: photolithography.

photocopier ('fəʊtəʊˌkopɪə) n. an instrument using light-sensitive photographic materials to reproduce written, printed, or graphic work.

photocopy ('fəʊtəʊˌkopɪ) n., pl. **-copies.** 1. a photographic reproduction of written, printed, or graphic work. ~vb. **-copying, -copied.** 2. to reproduce (written, printed, or graphic work) on photographic material.

photoelectric (ˌfəʊtəʊɪ'lɛktrɪk) adj. of or concerned with electric or electronic effects caused by light or other electromagnetic radiation. —**photoelectricity** (ˌfəʊtəʊɪlɛk'trɪsɪtɪ) n.

photoengraving (ˌfəʊtəʊɪn'greɪvɪŋ) n. 1. a photomechanical process for producing letterpress printing plates. 2. a plate made by this process. 3. a print made from such a plate. —ˌphotoen'grave vb. (tr.)

photo finish n. 1. a finish of a race in which contestants are so close that a photograph is needed to decide the result. 2. Inf. any race or competition in which the

---

THESAURUS

soning, thinking, thought, wisdom 2. attitude to life, basic idea, beliefs, convictions, doctrine, ideology, principle, tenets, thinking, values, viewpoint, Weltanschauung, worldview 3. composure, coolness, dispassion, equanimity, resignation, restraint, self-possession, serenity, stoicism

phlegmatic apathetic, bovine, cold, dull, frigid, heavy, impassive, indifferent, lethargic, listless, lymphatic, matter-of-fact, placid, sluggish, stoical, stolid, undemonstrative, un-

emotional, unfeeling

phobia aversion, detestation, dislike, distaste, dread, fear, hatred, horror, irrational fear, loathing, obsession, overwhelming anxiety, repulsion, revulsion, terror, thing (Inf.)

phone n. 1. blower (Inf.), telephone 2. bell (Brit. sl.), buzz (Inf.), call, ring, tinkle (Brit. inf.) ~v. 3. buzz (Inf.), call, get on the blower (Inf.), give someone a bell (Brit. sl.), give someone a buzz (Inf.), give someone a call, give someone a ring, give someone a tinkle

(Brit. inf.), make a call, ring, ring up, telephone

phoney 1. adj. affected, assumed, bogus, counterfeit, fake, false, forged, imitation, pseudo (Inf.), put-on, sham, spurious, trick 2. n. counterfeit, fake, faker, forgery, fraud, humbug, impostor, pretender, pseud (Sl.), sham

winners are separated by a very small margin.

photoflash ('fəʊtəʊˌflæʃ) n. another name for **flashbulb**.

photoflood ('fəʊtəʊˌflʌd) n. a highly incandescent tungsten lamp used for indoor photography, television, etc.

photogenic (ˌfəʊtə'dʒɛnɪk) adj. **1.** (esp. of a person) having a general facial appearance that looks attractive in photographs. **2.** Biol. producing or emitting light. —ˌphoto'genically adv.

photograph ('fəʊtəˌgrɑːf, -ˌgræf) n. **1.** an image of an object, person, scene, etc., in the form of a print or slide recorded by a camera. Often (informal) shortened to **photo**. ~vb. **2.** to take photographs of (an object, person, scene, etc.).

photographic (ˌfəʊtə'græfɪk) adj. **1.** of or relating to photography. **2.** like a photograph in accuracy or detail. **3.** (of a person's memory) able to retain facts, appearances, etc., in precise detail. —ˌphoto'graphically adv.

photography (fə'tɒgrəfɪ) n. **1.** the process of recording images on sensitized material by the action of light, x-rays, etc. **2.** the art, practice, or occupation of taking photographs. —pho'tographer n.

photogravure (ˌfəʊtəʊgrə'vjʊə) n. **1.** any of various methods in which an intaglio plate for printing is produced by the use of photography. **2.** matter printed from such a plate.

photolithography (ˌfəʊtəʊlɪ'θɒgrəfɪ) n. **1.** a lithographic printing process using photographically made plates. Often shortened to **photolitho**. **2.** Electronics. a process used in the manufacture of semiconductor devices and printed circuits in which a particular pattern is transferred from a photograph onto a substrate. —ˌphotoli'thographer n.

photometer (fəʊ'tɒmɪtə) n. an instrument used in photometry, usually one that compares the illumination produced by a particular light source with that produced by a standard source.

photometry (fəʊ'tɒmɪtrɪ) n. **1.** the measurement of the intensity of light. **2.** the branch of physics concerned with such measurements. —pho'tometrist n.

photomontage (ˌfəʊtəʊmɒn'tɑːʒ) n. **1.** the technique of producing a composite picture by combining several photographs. **2.** the composite picture so produced.

photon ('fəʊtɒn) n. a quantum of electromagnetic radiation with energy equal to the product of the frequency of the radiation and the Planck constant.

photosensitive (ˌfəʊtəʊ'sɛnsɪtɪv) adj. sensitive to electromagnetic radiation, esp. light. —ˌphotoˌsensi'tivity n. —ˌphoto'sensitize or -tise vb. (tr.)

Photostat ('fəʊtəʊˌstæt) n. **1.** Trademark. a machine or process used to make photographic copies of written, printed, or graphic matter. **2.** any copy made by such a machine. ~vb. **3.** to make a Photostat copy. —ˌphoto'static adj.

photosynthesis (ˌfəʊtəʊ'sɪnθɪsɪs) n. (in plants) the synthesis of organic compounds from carbon dioxide and water using light energy absorbed by chlorophyll. —ˌphoto'synthesize or -sise vb. —photosynthetic (ˌfəʊtəʊsɪn'θɛtɪk) adj. —ˌphotosyn'thetically adv.

phototropism (ˌfəʊtəʊ'trəʊpɪzəm) n. the growth response of plant parts to the stimulus of light. —ˌphoto'tropic adj.

phrasal verb ('freɪzəl) n. a phrase that consists of a verb plus an adverbial or prepositional particle, esp. one the meaning of which cannot be deduced from the constituents: "take in" meaning "deceive" is a phrasal verb.

phrase (freɪz) n. **1.** a group of words forming together a syntactic constituent of a sentence but (in English) not containing a finite verb. Cf. **clause** (sense 1). **2.** an idiomatic or original expression. **3.** manner or style of speech or expression. **4.** Music. a small group of notes forming a coherent unit of melody. ~vb. (tr.) **5.** Music. to divide (a melodic line, part, etc.) into musical phrases,

esp. in performance. **6.** to express orally or in a phrase. —'phrasal adj.

phraseology (ˌfreɪzɪ'ɒlədʒɪ) n., pl. **-gies**. **1.** the manner in which words or phrases are used. **2.** a set of phrases used by a particular group of people. —**phraseological** (ˌfreɪzɪə'lɒdʒɪkəl) adj.

phrenetic (frɪ'nɛtɪk) adj. an obsolete spelling of **frenetic**. —phre'netically adv.

phrenology (frɪ'nɒlədʒɪ) n. (formerly) the branch of science concerned with determination of the strength of the faculties by the shape and size of the skull overlying the parts of the brain thought to be responsible for them. —**phrenological** (ˌfrɛnə'lɒdʒɪkəl) adj. —phre'nologist n.

phthisis ('θaɪsɪs, 'fθaɪ-, 'taɪ-) n. Rare. any disease that causes wasting of the body, esp. pulmonary tuberculosis.

phut (fʌt) Inf. ~n. **1.** a representation of a dull heavy sound. ~adv. **2.** to go phut. to break down or collapse.

phylactery (fɪ'læktərɪ) n., pl. **-teries**. **1.** Judaism. either of two small leather cases containing strips of parchment inscribed with religious texts, worn by Jewish men during morning prayer. **2.** a reminder. **3.** Arch. an amulet or charm.

-phyll or **-phyl** n. combining form. leaf: chlorophyll.

phyllo- or before a vowel **phyll-** combining form. leaf: phyllopod.

phylo- or before a vowel **phyl-** combining form. tribe; race; phylum: phylogeny.

phylum ('faɪləm) n., pl. **-la** (-lə). **1.** a major taxonomic division of the animals and plants that contain one or more classes. **2.** a group of related language families or linguistic stocks.

phys. abbrev. for: **1.** physical. **2.** physician. **3.** physics. **4.** physiological. **5.** physiology.

physic ('fɪzɪk) n. **1.** Rare. a medicine, esp. a cathartic. **2.** Arch. the art or skill of healing. ~vb. **-icking, -icked**. (tr.) Arch. **3.** to treat (a patient) with medicine.

physical ('fɪzɪkəl) adj. **1.** of or relating to the body, as distinguished from the mind or spirit. **2.** of, relating to, or resembling material things or nature: the physical universe. **3.** of or concerned with matter and energy. **4.** of or relating to physics. —'physically adv.

physical education n. training and practice in sports, gymnastics, etc. Abbrev.: **PE**

physical geography n. the branch of geography that deals with the natural features of the earth's surface.

physical jerks pl. n. Sl. See **jerk**[1] (sense 6).

physical science n. any of the sciences concerned with nonliving matter, such as physics, chemistry, astronomy, and geology.

physical therapy n. another term for **physiotherapy**.

physician (fɪ'zɪʃən) n. **1.** a person legally qualified to practise medicine, esp. other than surgery; doctor of medicine. **2.** Arch. any person who treats diseases; healer.

physicist ('fɪzɪsɪst) n. a person versed in or studying physics.

physics ('fɪzɪks) n. (functioning as sing.) **1.** the branch of science concerned with the properties of matter and energy and the relationships between them. It is based on mathematics and traditionally includes mechanics, optics, electricity and magnetism, acoustics, and heat. Modern physics, based on quantum theory, includes atomic, nuclear, particle, and solid-state studies. **2.** physical properties of behaviour: the physics of the electron. **3.** Arch. natural science.

physio- or before a vowel **phys-** combining form. **1.** of or relating to nature or natural functions: physiology. **2.** physical: physiotherapy.

physiognomy (ˌfɪzɪ'ɒnəmɪ) n. **1.** a person's features considered as an indication of personality. **2.** the art or

---

THESAURUS

photograph **1.** n. image, likeness, photo (Inf.), picture, print, shot, slide, snap (Inf.), snapshot, transparency **2.** v. capture on film, film, get a shot of, record, shoot, snap (Inf.), take, take a picture of, take (someone's) picture

photographic accurate, cinematic, detailed, exact, faithful, filmic, graphic, lifelike, minute, natural, pictorial, precise, realistic, retentive, visual, vivid

phrase **1.** n. expression, group of words, idiom, locution, motto, remark, saying, tag, utterance, way of speaking **2.** v. couch, express, formulate, frame, present, put, put into words, say, term, utter, voice, word

phraseology choice of words, diction, expression, idiom, language, parlance, phrase, phrasing, speech, style, syntax, wording

physical **1.** bodily, carnal, corporal, corporeal, earthly, fleshly, incarnate, mortal, somatic, unspiritual **2.** material, natural, palpable, real, sensible, solid, substantial, tangible, visible

physician doc (Inf.), doctor, doctor of medicine, general practitioner, G.P., healer, M.D., medic (Inf.), medical practitioner, medico (Inf.), sawbones (Sl.), specialist

practice of judging character from facial features. **3.** the outward appearance of something. —**physiognomic** (ˌfɪzɪəˈnɒmɪk) or ˌphysiog'nomical adj. —ˌphysiog'nomically adv. —ˌphysi'ognomist n.

physiography (ˌfɪzɪˈɒɡrəfɪ) n. another name for **physical geography**. —**physi'ographer** n. —**physiographic** (ˌfɪzɪəˈɡræfɪk) or ˌphysio'graphical adj.

physiology (ˌfɪzɪˈɒlədʒɪ) n. **1.** the branch of science concerned with the functioning of organisms. **2.** the processes and functions of all or part of an organism. —ˌphysi'ologist n. —**physiological** (ˌfɪzɪəˈlɒdʒɪkəl) adj. —ˌphysio'logically adv.

physiotherapy (ˌfɪzɪəʊˈθɛrəpɪ) n. the treatment of disease, injury, etc. by physical means, such as massage or exercises, rather than by drugs. —ˌphysio'therapist n.

physique (fɪˈziːk) n. the general appearance of the body with regard to size, shape, muscular development, etc.

-phyte n. combining form. indicating a plant of a specified type or habitat: lithophyte. —**-phytic** adj. combining form.

phyto- or before a vowel **phyt-** combining form. indicating a plant or vegetation: phytogenesis.

pi[1] (paɪ) n., pl. **pis. 1.** the 16th letter in the Greek alphabet (Π, π). **2.** Maths. a transcendental number, fundamental to mathematics, that is the ratio of the circumference of a circle to its diameter. Approximate value: 3.141 592... ; symbol: π

pi[2] or **pie** (paɪ) n., pl. **pies. 1.** a jumbled pile of printer's type. **2.** a jumbled mixture. ~vb. **piing, pied** or **pieing, pied.** (tr.) **3.** to spill and mix (set type) indiscriminately. **4.** to mix up.

pia mater (ˈpaɪə ˈmeɪtə) n. the innermost of the three membranes (see **meninges**) that cover the brain and spinal cord.

pianissimo (pɪəˈnɪsɪˌməʊ) adj., adv. Music. to be performed very quietly. Symbol: pp

pianist (ˈpɪənɪst) n. a person who plays the piano.

piano[1] (pɪˈænəʊ) n., pl. **-anos.** a musical stringed instrument played by depressing keys that cause hammers to strike the strings and produce audible vibrations.

piano[2] (ˈpjɑːnəʊ) adj., adv. Music. to be performed softly.

piano accordion (pɪˈænəʊ) n. an accordion in which the right hand plays a piano-like keyboard. See **accordion.** —**piano accordionist** n.

pianoforte (pɪˌænəʊˈfɔːtɪ) n. the full name for **piano**[1].

Pianola (pɪəˈnəʊlə) n. Trademark. a type of mechanical piano in which the keys are depressed by air pressure, this air flow being regulated by perforations in a paper roll.

piazza (pɪˈætsə; Italian ˈpjattsa) n. **1.** a large open square in an Italian town. **2.** Chiefly Brit. a covered passageway or gallery.

pibroch (ˈpiːbrɒk; Gaelic ˈpiːbrɒx) n. a piece of music for Scottish bagpipes, consisting of a theme and variations.

pica (ˈpaɪkə) n. **1.** Also called: **em, pica em.** a printer's unit of measurement, equal to 12 points or 0.166 ins. **2.** (formerly) a size of printer's type equal to 12 point.

picador (ˈpɪkəˌdɔː) n. Bullfighting. a horseman who pricks the bull with a lance to weaken it.

picaresque (ˌpɪkəˈrɛsk) adj. of or relating to a type of fiction in which the hero, a rogue, goes through a series of episodic adventures.

picayune (ˌpɪkəˈjuːn) adj. also **picayunish.** U.S. **1.** Inf. of small value or importance. **2.** Inf. mean; petty. ~n. **3.** the half real, an old Spanish-American coin. **4.** U.S. any coin of little value, esp. a five-cent piece.

piccalilli (ˈpɪkəˌlɪlɪ) n. a pickle of mixed vegetables in a mustard sauce.

piccanin (ˈpɪkəˌnɪn) n. S. African inf. a Black African child.

piccaninny or **pickaninny** (ˌpɪkəˈnɪnɪ) n. a small Negro or Aboriginal child.

piccolo (ˈpɪkəˌləʊ) n., pl. **-los.** a woodwind instrument, an octave higher than the flute.

pick[1] (pɪk) vb. **1.** to choose (something) deliberately or carefully, as from a number; select. **2.** to pluck or gather (fruit, berries, or crops) from (a tree, bush, field, etc.). **3.** (tr.) to remove loose particles from (the teeth, the nose, etc.). **4.** (esp. of birds) to nibble or gather (corn, etc.). **5.** (tr.) to pierce, dig, or break up (a hard surface) with a pick. **6.** (tr.) to form (a hole, etc.) in this way. **7.** (when intr., foll. by at) to nibble (at) fussily or without appetite. **8.** to separate (strands, fibres, etc.), as in weaving. **9.** (tr.) to provoke (an argument, fight, etc.) deliberately. **10.** (tr.) to steal (money or valuables) from (a person's pocket). **11.** (tr.) to open (a lock) with an instrument other than a key. **12.** to pluck the strings of (a guitar, banjo, etc.). **13.** (tr.) to make (one's way) carefully on foot: they picked their way through the rubble. **14. pick and choose.** to select fastidiously, fussily, etc. **15. pick someone's brains.** Inf. to obtain information or ideas from someone. ~n. **16.** freedom or right of selection (esp. in **take one's pick**). **17.** a person, thing, etc. that is chosen first or preferred: the pick of the bunch. **18.** the act of picking. **19.** the amount of a crop picked at one period or from one area. ~ See also **pick off, pick on,** etc. —'**picker** n.

pick[2] (pɪk) n. **1.** a tool with a handle carrying a long steel head curved and tapering to a point at one or both ends, used for loosening soil, breaking rocks, etc. **2.** any of various tools used for picking, such as an ice pick or toothpick.

pickaback (ˈpɪkəˌbæk) n., adv. another word for **piggyback.**

pickaxe or U.S. **pickax** (ˈpɪkˌæks) n. **1.** a large pick or mattock. ~vb. **2.** to use a pickaxe on (earth, rocks, etc.).

picket (ˈpɪkɪt) n. **1.** a pointed stake that is driven into the ground to support a fence, etc. **2.** an individual or group standing outside an establishment to make a protest, to dissuade or prevent employees or clients from entering, etc. **3.** a small detachment of troops positioned to give early warning of attack. ~vb. **4.** to post or serve as pickets at (a factory, embassy, etc.). **5.** to guard (a main body or place) by using or acting as a picket. **6.** (tr.) to fasten (a horse or other animal) to a picket. **7.** (tr.) to fence (an area, etc.) with pickets. —'**picketer** n.

picket fence n. a fence consisting of pickets driven into the ground.

picket line n. a line of people acting as pickets.

pickings (ˈpɪkɪŋz) pl. n. (sometimes sing.) money, profits, etc. acquired easily; spoils.

pickle (ˈpɪkəl) n. **1.** (often pl.) vegetables, such as onions, etc., preserved in vinegar, brine, etc. **2.** any food preserved in this way. **3.** a liquid or marinade, such as spiced vinegar, for preserving vegetables, meat, fish, etc. **4.** U.S. a cucumber that has been preserved and flavoured in a pickling solution, as brine or vinegar. **5.** Inf. an awkward or difficult situation: to be in a pickle. **6.** Brit. inf. a mischievous child. ~vb. (tr.) **7.** to preserve in a pickling liquid. **8.** to immerse (a metallic object) in a liquid, such as an acid, to remove surface scale. —'**pickler** n.

pickled (ˈpɪkəld) adj. **1.** preserved in a pickling liquid. **2.** Inf. intoxicated; drunk.

pick-me-up n. Inf. a tonic or restorative, esp. a special drink taken as a stimulant.

pick off vb. (tr., adv.) to aim at and shoot one by one.

pick on vb. (intr., prep.) to select for something unpleasant, esp. in order to bully or blame.

THESAURUS

physique body, build, constitution, figure, form, frame, make-up, shape, structure

pick v. 1. choose, decide upon, elect, fix upon, hand-pick, mark out, opt for, select, settle upon, sift out, single out, sort out 2. collect, cull, cut, gather, harvest, pluck, pull 3. have no appetite, nibble, peck at, play or toy with, push the food round the plate 4. foment, incite, instigate, provoke, start 5. break into, break open, crack, force, jemmy, open, prise open 6. **pick one's way** be tentative, find or

make one's way, move cautiously, tread carefully, work through ~n. 7. choice, choosing, decision, option, preference, selection 8. choicest, crème de la crème, elect, elite, flower, pride, prize, the best, the cream, the tops (Sl.)

picket n. 1. pale, paling, palisade, peg, post, stake, stanchion, upright 2. demonstrator, picketer, protester 3. guard, lookout, patrol, scout, sentinel, sentry, spotter, vedette (Military), watch ~v. 4. blockade, boycott,

demonstrate 5. corral (U.S.), enclose, fence, hedge in, palisade, pen in, rail in, shut in, wall in

pickle n. 1. Inf. bind (Inf.), difficulty, dilemma, fix (Inf.), hot water (Inf.), jam (Inf.), predicament, quandary, scrape (Inf.), spot (Inf.), tight spot 2. Brit. inf. little horror, mischief, mischief maker, monkey, naughty child, rascal ~v. 3. cure, keep, marinade, preserve, steep

pick-me-up bracer (Inf.), drink, pick-up

pick out *vb.* (*tr., adv.*) **1.** to select for use or special consideration, etc., as from a group. **2.** to distinguish (an object from its surroundings), as in painting: *she picked out the woodwork in white.* **3.** to recognize (a person or thing): *we picked out his face among the crowd.* **4.** to distinguish (sense or meaning) as from a mass of detail or complication. **5.** to play (a tune) tentatively, as by ear.

pickpocket ('pɪk,pɒkɪt) *n.* a person who steals from the pockets of others in public places.

pick-up *n.* **1.** the light balanced arm of a gramophone that carries the wires from the cartridge to the preamplifier. **2.** an electromagnetic transducer that converts vibrations into electric signals. **3.** another name for **cartridge** (sense 2). **4.** a small truck with an open body used for light deliveries. **5.** *Inf.* an ability to accelerate rapidly: *this car has good pick-up.* **6.** *Inf.* a casual acquaintance, usually for a sexual liaison. **7.** *Inf.* a stop to collect passengers, goods, etc. **b.** the people or things collected. **8.** *Inf.* an improvement. **9.** *Sl.* a pick-me-up. ~*vb.* **pick up.** (*adv.*) **10.** (*tr.*) to gather up in the hand or hands. **11.** (*tr.*) to obtain casually, incidentally, etc. **12.** (*intr.*) to improve in health, condition, activity, etc.: *the market began to pick up.* **13.** (*tr.*) to learn gradually or as one goes along. **14.** (*tr.*) to collect or give a lift to (passengers, goods, etc.). **15.** (*tr.*) *Inf.* to become acquainted with, esp. with a view to having sexual relations. **16.** (*tr.*) *Sl.* to arrest. **17.** to increase (speed). **18.** (*tr.*) to receive (electrical signals, a radio signal, sounds, etc.).

picky ('pɪkɪ) *adj.* **pickier, pickiest.** *Inf.* fussy; finicky. —'**pickily** *adv.* —'**pickiness** *n.*

picnic ('pɪknɪk) *n.* **1.** a trip or excursion on which people bring food to be eaten in the open air. **2. a.** any informal meal eaten outside. **b.** (*as modifier*): *a picnic lunch.* **3.** *Inf.* an easy or agreeable task. ~*vb.* **-nicking, -nicked. 4.** (*intr.*) to eat or take part in a picnic. —'**picnicker** *n.*

pico- *prefix.* denoting 10^{-12}: *picofarad.* Symbol: p

picot ('pi:kəʊ) *n.* any of a pattern of small loops, as on lace.

picric acid ('pɪkrɪk) *n.* a toxic sparingly soluble crystalline yellow acid; 2,4,6-trinitrophenol: used as a dye, antiseptic, and explosive.

Pict (pɪkt) *n.* a member of a pre-Celtic people of N Britain. —'**Pictish** *adj.*

pictograph ('pɪktə,grɑːf) *n.* **1.** a picture or symbol standing for a word or group of words, as in written Chinese. **2.** a chart on which symbols are used to represent values. ~Also called: **pictogram.** —**pictographic** (,pɪktə'græfɪk) *adj.* —**pictography** (pɪk'tɒgrəfɪ) *n.*

pictorial (pɪk'tɔːrɪəl) *adj.* **1.** relating to, consisting of, or expressed by pictures. **2.** (of language, style, etc.) suggesting a picture; vivid; graphic. ~*n.* **3.** a magazine, newspaper, etc., containing many pictures. —**pic'torially** *adv.*

picture ('pɪktʃə) *n.* **1. a.** a visual representation of something, such as a person or scene, produced on a surface, as in a photograph, painting, etc. **b.** (*as modifier*): *picture gallery; picture postcard.* **2.** a mental image: *a clear picture of events.* **3.** a verbal description, esp. one that is vivid. **4.** a situation considered as an observable scene: *the political picture.* **5.** a person or thing resembling another: *he was the picture of his father.* **6.** a person, scene, etc., typifying a particular state: *the picture of despair.* **7.** the image on a television screen. **8.** a motion picture; film. **9. the pictures.** *Chiefly Brit.* a cinema or film show. **10. in the picture.** informed about a situation. ~*vb.* (*tr.*) **11.** to visualize or imagine. **12.** to describe or depict, esp. vividly. **13.** (*often passive*) to put in a picture or make a picture of: *they were pictured sitting on the rocks.*

picture card *n.* another name for **court card.**

picture moulding *n.* **1.** the edge around a framed picture. **2.** Also called: **picture rail.** the moulding or rail near the top of a wall from which pictures are hung.

picture palace *n. Brit., old-fashioned.* another name for **cinema.**

picturesque (,pɪktʃə'rɛsk) *adj.* **1.** visually pleasing, esp. in being striking or quaint: *a picturesque view.* **2.** (of language) graphic; vivid. —**pictur'esquely** *adv.* —,**pictur'esqueness** *n.*

picture window *n.* a large window having a single pane of glass, usually facing a view.

piddle ('pɪdᵊl) *vb.* **1.** (*intr.*) *Inf.* to urinate. **2.** (when *tr.*, often foll. by *away*) to spend (one's time) aimlessly; fritter. —'**piddler** *n.*

piddling ('pɪdlɪŋ) *adj. Inf.* petty; trifling; trivial.

pidgin ('pɪdʒɪn) *n.* a language made up of elements of two or more other languages and used for contacts, esp. trading contacts, between the speakers of other languages.

pidgin English *n.* a pidgin in which one of the languages involved is English.

pie¹ (paɪ) *n.* **1.** a baked sweet or savoury filling in a pastry-lined dish, often covered with a pastry crust. **2. have a finger in the pie.** to have a share in something. **3. pie in the sky.** *Inf.* illusory hope of some future good.

pie² (paɪ) *n.* an archaic or dialect name for **magpie.**

pie³ (paɪ) *n. Printing.* a variant spelling of **pi².**

piebald ('paɪ,bɔːld) *adj.* **1.** marked in two colours, esp. black and white. ~*n.* **2.** a black-and-white horse.

piece (piːs) *n.* **1.** an amount or portion forming a separate mass or structure; bit: *a piece of wood.* **2.** a small part, item, or amount forming part of a whole, esp. when broken off or separated: *a piece of bread.* **3.** a length by which a commodity is sold, esp. cloth, wallpaper, etc. **4.** an instance or occurrence: *a piece of luck.* **5.** an example or specimen of a style or type: *a beautiful piece of Dresden.* **6.** *Inf.* an opinion or point of view: *to state one's piece.* **7.** a literary, musical, or artistic composition. **8.** a coin: *fifty-pence piece.* **9.** a small object used in playing certain games: *chess pieces.* **10.** a firearm or cannon. **11.** any chessman other than a pawn. **12.** *N Brit. dialect.* a packed lunch taken to work. **13. give someone a piece of one's mind.** *Inf.* to criticize or censure a person frankly. **14. go to pieces. a.** (of a person) to lose control of oneself; have a breakdown. **b.** (of a building, organization, etc.) to disintegrate. **15. nasty piece of work.** *Brit. inf.* a cruel or mean person. **16. of a piece.** of the same kind; alike. **17. piece of cake.** *Brit. inf.* something easily obtained or achieved. ~*vb.* (*tr.*) **18.** (often foll. by *together*) to fit or assemble piece by piece. **19.** (often foll. by *up*) to patch or make up (a gar-

---

THESAURUS

(*Sl.*), refreshment, restorative, roborant, shot in the arm (*Inf.*), stimulant, tonic

pick on badger, bait, blame, bully, goad, hector, tease, torment

pick out 1. choose, cull, hand-pick, select, separate the sheep from the goats, single out, sort out **2.** discriminate, distinguish, make distinct, make out, notice, perceive, recognize, tell apart

pick-up *n.* **1.** acceleration, response, revving (*Inf.*), speed-up **2.** change for the better, gain, improvement, rally, recovery, revival, strengthening, upswing, upturn

pick up *v.* **1.** gather, grasp, hoist, lift, raise, take up, uplift **2.** buy, come across, find, garner, happen upon, obtain, purchase, score (*Sl.*) **3.** gain, gain ground, get better, improve, make a comeback (*Inf.*), mend, perk up, rally, recover, take a turn for the better **4.** call for, collect, get, give someone a lift, go to get, uplift (*Scot.*) **5.** acquire, get the

hang of (*Inf.*), learn, master **6.** *Sl.* apprehend, arrest, bust (*Inf.*), collar (*Inf.*), do (*Sl.*), nab (*Inf.*), nick (*Brit. sl.*), pinch (*Inf.*), pull in (*Brit. sl.*), run in (*Sl.*), take into custody

picnic 1. excursion, fête champêtre, outdoor meal, outing **2.** *Inf.* child's play (*Inf.*), cinch (*Sl.*), piece of cake (*Brit. inf.*), pushover (*Sl.*), snap (*Inf.*), walkover (*Inf.*)

pictorial expressive, graphic, illustrated, picturesque, representational, scenic, striking, vivid

picture *n.* **1.** delineation, drawing, effigy, engraving, illustration, image, likeness, painting, photograph, portrait, portrayal, print, representation, similitude, sketch **2.** account, depiction, description, image, impression, re-creation, report **3.** carbon copy, copy, dead ringer (*Sl.*), double, duplicate, image, likeness, living image, lookalike, replica, ringer (*Sl.*), spit (*Inf.*), spit and image (*Inf.*), spitting image (*Inf.*), twin **4.** archetype,

embodiment, epitome, essence, living example, perfect example, personification **5.** film, flick (*Sl.*), motion picture, movie (*U.S. inf.*) ~*v.* **6.** conceive of, envision, image, see, see in the mind's eye, visualize **7.** delineate, depict, describe, draw, illustrate, paint, photograph, portray, render, represent, show, sketch

picturesque attractive, beautiful, charming, colourful, graphic, pretty, quaint, scenic, striking, vivid

piddling derisory, fiddling, insignificant, little, measly (*Inf.*), Mickey Mouse (*Sl.*), paltry, petty, piffling, puny, trifling, trivial, unimportant, useless, worthless

piebald black and white, brindled, dappled, flecked, mottled, pied, speckled, spotted

ment, etc.) by adding pieces.

pièce de résistance *French*. (pjɛs də rezis'tã:s) *n*. **1.** the principal or most outstanding item in a series. **2.** the main dish of a meal.

piece goods *pl. n*. goods, esp. fabrics, made in standard widths and lengths.

piecemeal ('pi:s‚mi:l) *adv*. **1.** by degrees; bit by bit; gradually. **2.** in or into pieces. ~*adj*. **3.** fragmentary or unsystematic: *a piecemeal approach*.

piece of eight *n., pl.* **pieces of eight.** a former Spanish coin worth eight reals; peso.

piecework ('pi:s‚wɜːk) *n*. work paid for according to the quantity produced.

pie chart *n*. a circular graph divided into sectors proportional to the magnitudes of the quantities represented.

pied (paɪd) *adj*. having markings of two or more colours.

pied-à-terre *French*. (pjeta'tɛːr) *n., pl.* **pieds-à-terre** (pjeta'tɛːr). a flat or other lodging for occasional use.

pier (pɪə) *n*. **1.** a structure with a deck that is built out over water, and used as a landing place, promenade, etc. **2.** a pillar that bears heavy loads. **3.** the part of a wall between two adjacent openings. **4.** another name for **buttress.**

pierce (pɪəs) *vb. (mainly tr.)* **1.** to form or cut (a hole) in (something) as with a sharp instrument. **2.** to thrust into sharply or violently: *the thorn pierced his heel.* **3.** to force (a way, route, etc.) through (something). **4.** (of light, etc.) to shine through or penetrate (darkness). **5.** (*also intr.*) to discover or realize (something) suddenly or (of an idea, etc.) to become suddenly apparent. **6.** (of sounds or cries) to sound sharply through (the silence, etc.). **7.** to move or affect deeply or sharply: *the cold pierced their bones.* **8.** (*intr.*) to penetrate: *piercing cold.* —'**piercer** *n*. —'**piercing** *adj*. —'**piercingly** *adv*.

pier glass *n*. a tall narrow mirror, designed to hang on the wall between windows.

Pierrot ('pɪərəʊ; *French* pjɛ'ro) *n*. **1.** a male character from French pantomime with a whitened face, white costume, and pointed hat. **2.** (*usually not cap.*) a clown so made up.

pietism ('paɪ‚tɪzəm) *n*. exaggerated or affected piety. —'**pietist** *n*. —‚**pie'tistic** *or* ‚**pie'tistical** *adj*.

piety ('paɪɪtɪ) *n., pl.* **-ties.** **1.** dutiful devotion to God and observance of religious principles. **2.** the quality of being pious. **3.** a pious action, saying, etc. **4.** *Now rare.* devotion and obedience to parents or superiors.

piezoelectric effect (paɪ‚iːzəʊɪ'lɛktrɪk) *or* **piezoelectricity** (paɪ‚iːzəʊɪlɛk'trɪsɪtɪ) *n. Physics.* **a.** the production of electricity or electric polarity by applying a mechanical stress to certain crystals. **b.** the converse effect in which stress is produced in a crystal as a result of an applied potential difference. —**pi‚ezoe'lectrically** *adv*.

piffle ('pɪfəl) *n. Inf*. **1.** nonsense. ~*vb*. **2.** (*intr.*) to talk or behave feebly.

pig (pɪg) *n*. **1.** any artiodactyl mammal of an African and Eurasian family, esp. the domestic pig, typically having a long head with a movable snout and a thick bristle-covered skin. **2.** *Inf*. a dirty, greedy, or bad-mannered person. **3.** the meat of swine; pork. **4.** *Derog*. a slang word for **policeman. 5. a.** a mass of metal, cast into a simple shape. **b.** the mould used. **6.** *Brit. inf.* something that is difficult or unpleasant. **7. a pig in a poke.** something bought or received without prior sight or knowledge. **8. make a pig of oneself.** *Inf*. to overindulge oneself. ~*vb*. **pigging, pigged. 9.** (*intr.*) (of a sow) to give birth. **10.** (*intr.*) Also: **pig it.** *Inf*. to live in squalor. **11.** (*tr.*) *Inf*. to devour (food) greedily.

pigeon ('pɪdʒɪn) *n*. **1.** any of numerous related birds having a heavy body, small head, short legs, and long pointed wings. **2.** *Sl*. a victim or dupe. **3.** *Brit. inf.* concern or responsibility (often in **it's his, her,** etc., **pigeon**).

pigeonhole ('pɪdʒɪn‚həʊl) *n*. **1.** a small compartment for papers, letters, etc., as in a bureau. **2.** a hole or recess in a dovecote for pigeons to nest in. ~*vb*. (*tr.*) **3.** to put aside or defer. **4.** to classify or categorize.

pigeon-toed *adj*. having the toes turned inwards.

piggery ('pɪgərɪ) *n., pl.* **-geries. 1.** a place where pigs are kept. **2.** great greediness.

piggish ('pɪgɪʃ) *adj*. **1.** like a pig, esp. in appetite or manners. **2.** *Inf., chiefly Brit.* obstinate or mean. —'**piggishly** *adv*. —'**piggishness** *n*.

piggy ('pɪgɪ) *n., pl.* **-gies. 1.** a child's word for a pig. **2.** a child's word for toe. ~*adj.*-**gier, -giest. 3.** another word for **piggish.**

piggyback ('pɪgɪ‚bæk) *or* **pickaback** ('pɪkə‚bæk) *n*. **1. a.** a ride on the back and shoulders of another person. **b.** (*as modifier*): *a piggyback ride.* ~*adv*. **2.** on the back and shoulders of another person.

piggy bank *n*. a child's coin bank shaped like a pig with a slot for coins.

pig-headed *adj*. stupidly stubborn. —'**pig-‚headedly** *adv*. —'**pig-‚headedness** *n*.

pig iron *n*. crude iron produced in a blast furnace and poured into moulds.

piglet ('pɪglɪt) *n*. a young pig.

pigment ('pɪgmənt) *n*. **1.** a substance occurring in plant or animal tissue and producing a characteristic colour. **2.** any substance used to impart colour. **3.** a powder that is mixed with a liquid to give a paint, ink, etc. —'**pigmentary** *adj*.

pigmentation (‚pɪgmən'teɪʃən) *n*. **1.** coloration in plants, animals, or man caused by the presence of pigments. **2.** the deposition of pigment in animals, plants, or man.

Pigmy ('pɪgmɪ) *n., pl.* **-mies.** a variant spelling of **Pygmy.**

pignut ('pɪg‚nʌt) *n*. **a.** the bitter nut of any of several North American hickory trees. **b.** any of the trees bearing such a nut. ~Also called: **hognut.**

pigpen ('pɪg‚pɛn) *n*. another word for **pigsty.**

THESAURUS

piece *n*. **1.** allotment, bit, chunk, division, fraction, fragment, length, morsel, mouthful, part, portion, quantity, scrap, section, segment, share, shred, slice **2.** case, example, instance, occurrence, sample, specimen, stroke **3.** article, bit (*Sl.*), composition, creation, item, production, study, work, work of art **4. go to pieces** break down, crack up (*Inf.*), crumple, disintegrate, fall apart, lose control, lose one's head **5. in pieces** broken, bust (*Inf.*), damaged, disintegrated, in bits, in smithereens, ruined, shattered, smashed **6. of a piece** alike, analogous, consistent, identical, of the same kind, similar, the same, uniform ~*v*. **7.** *Often with* **together** assemble, compose, fix, join, mend, patch, repair, restore, unite

pièce de résistance *chef-d'oeuvre*, jewel, masterpiece, masterwork, showpiece

piecemeal 1. *adv*. at intervals, bit by bit, by degrees, by fits and starts, fitfully, intermittently, little by little, partially, slowly **2.** *adj*. fragmentary, intermittent, interrupted, partial, patchy, spotty, unsystematic

pied dappled, flecked, irregular, motley, mottled, multicoloured, parti-coloured, pie-

bald, spotted, streaked, varicoloured, variegated

pier *n*. **1.** jetty, landing place, promenade, quay, wharf **2.** buttress, column, pile, piling, pillar, post, support, upright

pierce 1. bore, drill, enter, penetrate, perforate, prick, probe, puncture, run through, spike, stab, stick into, transfix **2.** comprehend, discern, discover, fathom, grasp, realize, see, understand **3.** *Fig*. affect, cut, cut to the quick, excite, hurt, move, pain, rouse, sting, stir, strike, thrill, touch, wound

piercing 1. *Usually of sound* ear-splitting, high-pitched, loud, penetrating, sharp, shattering, shrill **2.** alert, aware, keen, penetrating, perceptive, perspicacious, probing, quick-witted, searching, sharp, shrewd **3.** *Usually of weather* arctic, biting, bitter, cold, freezing, frosty, keen, nipping, nippy, numbing, raw, wintry **4.** acute, agonizing, excruciating, exquisite, fierce, intense, painful, powerful, racking, severe, sharp, shooting, stabbing

piety devotion, devoutness, dutifulness, duty, faith, godliness, grace, holiness, pious-

ness, religion, reverence, sanctity, veneration

pig 1. boar, grunter, hog, piggy, piglet, porker, shoat, sow, swine **2.** *Inf*. animal, beast, boor, brute, glutton, greedy guts (*Sl.*), guzzler, hog (*Inf.*), slob (*Sl.*), sloven, swine

pigeon 1. bird, culver (*Archaic*), cushat, dove, squab **2.** *Sl*. dupe, fall guy (*Inf.*), gull (*Archaic*), mug (*Sl.*), sitting duck, sucker (*Sl.*), victim **3.** *Brit. inf.* baby (*Sl.*), business, concern, lookout (*Inf.*), responsibility, worry

pigeonhole *n*. **1.** compartment, cubbyhole, cubicle, locker, niche, place, section **2.** *Inf*. category, class, classification, slot (*Inf.*) ~*v*. **3.** defer, file, postpone, put off, shelve **4.** catalogue, characterize, classify, codify, compartmentalize, label, slot (*Inf.*), sort

pig-headed bull-headed, contrary, cross-grained, dense, froward, inflexible, mulish, obstinate, perverse, self-willed, stiff-necked, stubborn, stupid, unyielding, wilful, wrong-headed

pigment colorant, colour, colouring, colouring matter, dye, dyestuff, paint, stain, tincture, tint

pigskin ('pɪg,skɪn) n. 1. the skin of the domestic pig. 2. leather made of this skin. 3. U.S. inf. a football. ~adj. 4. made of pigskin.

pigsty ('pɪg,staɪ) or U.S. **pigpen** n., pl. -sties. 1. a pen for pigs; sty. 2. Brit. an untidy place.

pigswill ('pɪg,swɪl) n. waste food or other edible matter fed to pigs. Also called: **pig's wash.**

pigtail ('pɪg,teɪl) n. 1. a bunch of hair or one of two bunches on either side of the face, worn loose or plaited. 2. a twisted roll of tobacco.

pike¹ (paɪk) n., pl. **pike** or **pikes.** 1. any of several large predatory freshwater teleost fishes having a broad flat snout, strong teeth, and an elongated body covered with small scales. 2. any of various similar fishes.

pike² (paɪk) n. 1. a medieval weapon consisting of a metal spearhead joined to a long pole. 2. a point or spike. ~vb. 3. (tr.) to pierce using a pike. —'**pikeman** n.

pike³ (paɪk) n. N English dialect. a pointed or conical hill.

pikestaff ('paɪk,stɑːf) n. the wooden handle of a pike.

pilaster (pɪ'læstə) n. a shallow rectangular column attached to the face of a wall. —pi'**lastered** adj.

pilchard ('pɪltʃəd) n. a European food fish of the herring family, with a rounded body covered with large scales.

pile¹ (paɪl) n. 1. a collection of objects laid on top of one another; heap; mound. 2. Inf. a large amount of money (esp. in **make a pile**). 3. (often pl.) Inf. a large amount: a pile of work. 4. a less common word for **pyre.** 5. a large building or group of buildings. 6. Physics. a structure of uranium and a moderator used for producing atomic energy; nuclear reactor. ~vb. 7. (often foll. by up) to collect or be collected into or as if into a pile: snow piled up in the drive. 8. (intr.; foll. by in, into, off, out, etc.) to move in a group, esp. in a hurried or disorganized manner: to pile off the bus. 9. **pile it on.** Inf. to exaggerate. ~See also **pile up.**

pile² (paɪl) n. 1. a long column of timber, concrete, or steel, driven into the ground as a foundation for a structure. ~vb. (tr.) 2. to drive (piles) into the ground. 3. to support (a structure) with piles.

pile³ (paɪl) n. 1. the yarns in a fabric that stand up or out from the weave, as in carpeting, velvet, etc. 2. soft fine hair, fur, wool, etc.

pile-driver n. a machine that drives piles into the ground.

piles (paɪlz) pl. n. a nontechnical name for **haemorrhoids.**

pile up vb. (adv.) 1. to gather or be gathered in a pile. 2. Inf. to crash or cause to crash. ~n. **pile-up.** 3. Inf. a multiple collision of vehicles.

pilfer ('pɪlfə) vb. to steal (minor items), esp. in small quantities. —'**pilferage** n. —'**pilferer** n.

pilgrim ('pɪlgrɪm) n. 1. a person who undertakes a journey to a sacred place. 2. any wayfarer.

pilgrimage ('pɪlgrɪmɪdʒ) n. 1. a journey to a shrine or other sacred place. 2. a journey or long search made for exalted or sentimental reasons. ~vb. 3. (intr.) to make a pilgrimage.

Pilgrim Fathers or **Pilgrims** pl. n. **the.** the English Puritans who sailed on the Mayflower to New England, where they founded Plymouth Colony in SE Massachusetts (1620).

pill (pɪl) n. 1. a small spherical or ovoid mass of a medicinal substance, intended to be swallowed whole. 2.

the. (sometimes cap.) Inf. an oral contraceptive. 3. something unpleasant that must be endured (esp. in **bitter pill to swallow**). 4. Sl. a ball or disc. 5. Sl. an unpleasant or boring person. ~vb. 6. (tr.) to give pills to.

pillage ('pɪlɪdʒ) vb. 1. to rob (a town, village, etc.) of (booty or spoils). ~n. 2. the act of pillaging. 3. something obtained by pillaging; booty. —'**pillager** n.

pillar ('pɪlə) n. 1. an upright structure of stone, brick, metal, etc. that supports a superstructure. 2. something resembling this in shape or function: a pillar of smoke. 3. a prominent supporter: a pillar of the Church. 4. **from pillar to post.** from one place to another.

pillar box n. Brit. a red pillar-shaped public letter box situated on a pavement.

pillbox ('pɪl,bɒks) n. 1. a box for pills. 2. a small enclosed fortified emplacement, made of reinforced concrete. 3. a small round hat.

pillion ('pɪljən) n. 1. a seat or place behind the rider of a motorcycle, scooter, horse, etc. ~adv. 2. on a pillion: to ride pillion.

pillory ('pɪlərɪ) n., pl. -ries. 1. a wooden framework into which offenders were formerly locked by the neck and wrists and exposed to public abuse and ridicule. 2. exposure to public scorn or abuse. ~vb. -rying, -ried. (tr.) 3. to expose to public scorn or ridicule. 4. to punish by putting in a pillory.

pillow ('pɪləʊ) n. 1. a cloth case stuffed with feathers, foam rubber, etc., used to support the head, esp. during sleep. 2. Also called: **cushion.** a padded cushion or board on which pillow lace is made using bobbins. 3. anything like a pillow in shape or function. ~vb. 4. (tr.) to rest (one's head) on or as if on a pillow. 5. (tr.) to serve as a pillow for.

pillowcase ('pɪləʊ,keɪs) or **pillowslip** ('pɪləʊ,slɪp) n. a removable washable cover of cotton, linen, nylon, etc., for a pillow.

pilot ('paɪlət) n. 1. a person who is qualified to operate an aircraft or spacecraft in flight. 2. a. a person who is qualified to steer or guide a ship into or out of a port, river mouth, etc. b. (as modifier): a pilot ship. 3. a person who steers a ship. 4. a person who acts as a leader or guide. 5. Machinery. a guide used to assist in joining two mating parts together. 6. an experimental programme on radio or television. 7. (modifier) used in or serving as a test or trial: a pilot project. 8. (modifier) serving as a guide: a pilot beacon. ~vb. (tr.) 9. to act as pilot of. 10. to control the course of. 11. to guide or lead (a project, people, etc.). —'**pilotage** n.

pilot house n. Naut. an enclosed structure on the bridge of a vessel from which it can be navigated; a wheelhouse.

pilot lamp n. a small light in an electric circuit or device that lights when the current is on.

pilot light n. 1. a small auxiliary flame that ignites the main burner of a gas appliance. 2. a small electric light used as an indicator.

pilot officer n. the most junior commissioned rank in the British Royal Air Force and in certain other air forces.

pilule ('pɪljuːl) n. a small pill. —'**pilular** adj.

pimento (pɪ'mɛntəʊ) n., pl. -tos. another name for **allspice** or **pimiento.**

pimiento (pɪ'mjɛntəʊ, -'mɛn-) n., pl. -tos. a Spanish

THESAURUS

pile¹ n. 1. accumulation, assemblage, assortment, collection, heap, hoard, mass, mound, mountain, stack, stockpile 2. Inf. bomb (Brit. sl.), fortune, mint, money, packet (Sl.), pot, tidy sum (Inf.), wealth 3. Often plural. Inf. a lot, great deal, ocean, oodles (Inf.), quantity, stacks 4. building, edifice, erection, structure ~v. 5. accumulate, amass, assemble, collect, gather, heap, hoard, load up, mass, stack, store 6. charge, crowd, crush, flock, flood, jam, pack, rush, stream
pile² beam, column, foundation, pier, piling, pillar, post, support, upright
pile³ down, fibre, filament, fur, hair, nap, plush, shag, surface
piles haemorrhoids
pile-up accident, collision, crash, multiple collision, smash, smash-up (Inf.)

pilfer appropriate, embezzle, filch, knock off (Sl.), lift (Inf.), nick (Brit. sl.), pinch (Inf.), purloin, rifle, rob, snaffle (Brit. inf.), snitch (Sl.), steal, swipe (Sl.), take, thieve, walk off with
pilgrim crusader, hajji, palmer, traveller, wanderer, wayfarer
pilgrimage crusade, excursion, expedition, hajj, journey, mission, tour, trip
pill 1. bolus, capsule, pellet, pilule, tablet 2. **the pill** oral contraceptive 3. Sl. bore, drag (Sl.), nuisance, pain (Inf.), pain in the neck (Inf.), pest, trial
pillage v. 1. depredate (Rare), despoil, freeboot, loot, maraud, plunder, raid, ransack, ravage, reive (Dialect), rifle, rob, sack, spoil (Archaic), spoliate, strip ~n. 2. depredation, devastation, marauding, plunder, rap-

ine, robbery, sack, spoliation 3. booty, loot, plunder, spoils

pillar 1. column, pier, pilaster, piling, post, prop, shaft, stanchion, support, upright 2. leader, leading light (Inf.), mainstay, rock, supporter, tower of strength, upholder, worthy

pillory v. brand, cast a slur on, denounce, expose to ridicule, heap or pour scorn on, hold up to shame, lash; show up, stigmatize

pilot 1. n. airman, aviator, captain, conductor, coxswain, director, flier, guide, helmsman, leader, navigator, steersman 2. v. conduct, control, direct, drive, fly, guide, handle, lead, manage, navigate, operate, shepherd, steer 3. adj. experimental, model, test, trial

pepper with a red fruit used as a vegetable. Also called: **pimento.**

pimp (pɪmp) n. 1. a man who solicits for a prostitute or brothel. 2. a man who procures sexual gratification for another; procurer; pander. ~vb. 3. (intr.) to act as a pimp.

pimpernel ('pɪmpə,nɛl, -nəl) n. any of several plants, such as the scarlet pimpernel, typically having small star-shaped flowers.

pimple ('pɪmpəl) n. a small round usually inflamed swelling of the skin. —'**pimpled** adj. —'**pimply** adj. —'**pimpliness** n.

pin (pɪn) n. 1. a short stiff straight piece of wire pointed at one end and either rounded or having a flattened head at the other: used mainly for fastening pieces of cloth, paper, etc. 2. short for **cotter pin, hairpin, rolling pin,** or **safety pin.** 3. an ornamental brooch, esp. a narrow one. 4. a badge worn fastened to the clothing by a pin. 5. something of little or no importance (esp. in **not care** or **give a pin (for)**). 6. a peg or dowel. 7. anything resembling a pin in shape, function, etc. 8. (in various bowling games) a usually club-shaped wooden object set up in groups as a target. 9. Also called: **safety pin.** a clip on a hand grenade that prevents its detonation until removed or released. 10. Naut. the sliding closure for a shackle. 11. Music. a metal tuning peg on a piano. 12. Surgery. a metal rod, esp. of stainless steel, for holding together adjacent ends of broken or fractured bones during healing. 13. Chess. a position in which a piece is pinned against a more valuable piece or the king. 14. Golf. the flagpole marking the hole on a green. 15. (usually pl.) Inf. legs. ~vb. **pinning, pinned.** (tr.) 16. to attach, hold, or fasten with or as if with a pin or pins. 17. to transfix with a pin, spear, etc. 18. (foll. by on) Inf. to place (the blame for something): he pinned the charge on his accomplice. 19. Chess. to cause (an enemy piece) to be effectively immobilized since moving it would reveal a check or expose a more valuable piece to capture. ~See also **pin down.**

pinafore ('pɪnə,fɔ:) n. 1. Chiefly Brit. an apron, esp. one with a bib. 2. Also called: **pinafore dress.** a dress with a sleeveless bodice or bib top, worn over a jumper or blouse.

pince-nez ('pæns,neɪ, 'pɪns-; French pĕs'ne) n., pl. **pince-nez.** eyeglasses that are held in place only by means of a clip over the bridge of the nose.

pincers ('pɪnsəz) pl. n. 1. Also called: **pair of pincers.** a gripping tool consisting of two hinged arms with handles at one end and, at the other, curved bevelled jaws that close on the workpiece. 2. the pair or pairs of jointed grasping appendages in lobsters and certain other arthropods.

pinch (pɪntʃ) vb. 1. to press (something, esp. flesh) tightly between two surfaces, esp. between a finger and thumb. 2. to confine, squeeze, or painfully press (toes, fingers, etc.) because of lack of space: these shoes pinch. 3. (tr.) to cause stinging pain to: the cold pinched his face. 4. (tr.) to make thin or drawn-looking, as from grief, lack of food, etc. 5. (usually foll. by on) to provide (oneself or another person) with meagre allowances, amounts, etc. 6. **pinch pennies.** to live frugally because of meanness or to economize. 7. (usually foll. by off, out, or back) to remove the tips of (buds, shoots, etc.) to correct or encourage growth. 8. (tr.) Inf. to steal or take without asking. 9. (tr.) Inf. to arrest. ~n. 10. a squeeze or sustained nip. 11. the quantity of a substance, such as salt, that can be taken between a thumb and finger. 12. a very small quantity. 13. (usually preceded by the)

sharp, painful, or extreme stress, need, etc.: the pinch of poverty. 14. Sl. a robbery. 15. Sl. a police raid or arrest. 16. **at a pinch.** if absolutely necessary.

pinchbeck ('pɪntʃ,bɛk) n. 1. an alloy of copper and zinc, used as imitation gold. 2. a spurious or cheap imitation. ~adj. 3. made of pinchbeck. 4. sham or cheap.

pincushion ('pɪn,kuʃən) n. a small well-padded cushion in which pins are stuck ready for use.

pin down vb. (tr., adv.) 1. to force (someone) to make a decision or carry out a promise. 2. to define clearly: he had a vague suspicion that he couldn't quite pin down. 3. to confine to a place.

pine[1] (paɪn) n. 1. an evergreen resinous coniferous tree of the N hemisphere, with long needle-shaped leaves (**pine needle**) and brown cones. 2. the wood of any of these trees. —'**piny** or '**piney** adj.

pine[2] (paɪn) vb. 1. (intr.; often foll. by for or an infinitive) to feel great longing or desire; yearn. 2. (intr.; often foll. by away) to become ill or thin through worry, longing, etc.

pineal gland or **body** n. a pea-sized organ situated at the base of the brain. Technical names: **epiphysis, epiphysis cerebri.**

pineapple ('paɪn,æpəl) n. 1. a tropical American plant cultivated for its large fleshy edible fruit. 2. the fruit of this plant, consisting of an inflorescence clustered around a fleshy axis and surmounted by a tuft of leaves. 3. Mil. sl. a hand grenade.

pine cone n. the seed-producing structure of a pine tree. See **cone** (sense 3a).

ping (pɪŋ) n. 1. a short high-pitched resonant sound, as of a bullet striking metal or a sonar echo. ~vb. 2. (intr.) to make such a noise. —'**pinger** n.

Ping-Pong ('pɪŋ,pɒŋ) n. Trademark. another name for **table tennis.** Also called: **ping pong.**

pinhead ('pɪn,hɛd) n. 1. the head of a pin. 2. something very small. 3. Sl. a stupid person. —'**pin,headed** adj. —'**pin,headedness** n.

pinhole ('pɪn,həʊl) n. a small hole made with or as if with a pin.

pinion[1] ('pɪnjən) n. 1. Chiefly poetic. a bird's wing. 2. the part of a bird's wing including the flight feathers. ~vb. (tr.) 3. to hold or bind (the arms) of (a person) so as to restrain or immobilize him. 4. to confine or shackle. 5. to make (a bird) incapable of flight by removing the flight feathers.

pinion[2] ('pɪnjən) n. a cogwheel that engages with a larger wheel or rack.

pink[1] (pɪŋk) n. 1. a pale reddish colour. 2. pink cloth or clothing: dressed in pink. 3. any of various Old World plants, such as the garden pink, cultivated for their fragrant flowers. See also **carnation** (sense 1). 4. the flower of any of these plants. 5. the highest or best degree, condition, etc. (esp. in **in the pink**). 6. **a.** a huntsman's scarlet coat. **b.** a huntsman who wears a scarlet coat. ~adj. 7. of the colour pink. 8. Brit. inf. left wing. 9. (of a huntsman's coat) scarlet or red. ~vb. 10. (intr.) another word for **knock** (sense 7). —'**pinkish** adj. —'**pinkness** n. —'**pinky** adj.

pink[2] (pɪŋk) vb. (tr.) 1. to prick lightly with a sword, etc. 2. to decorate (leather, etc.) with a perforated or punched pattern. 3. to cut with pinking shears.

pinkie or **pinky** ('pɪŋkɪ) n., pl. **-ies.** U.S., Scot. the little finger.

pinking shears pl. n. scissors with a serrated edge on one or both blades, producing a wavy edge to material cut, thus preventing fraying.

THESAURUS

pimple boil, papule (Pathol.), plook (Scot.), pustule, spot, swelling

pin v. 1. affix, attach, fasten, fix, join, secure 2. fix, hold down, hold fast, immobilize, pinion, press, restrain

pinch v. 1. compress, grasp, nip, press, squeeze, tweak 2. chafe, confine, cramp, crush, hurt, pain 3. afflict, be stingy, distress, economize, oppress, pinch pennies, press, scrimp, skimp, spare, stint 4. Inf. filch, knock off (Sl.), lift (Inf.), nick (Brit. sl.), pilfer, purloin, rob, snaffle (Brit. inf.), snatch, snitch (Sl.), steal, swipe (Sl.) 5. Inf. apprehend, arrest, bust (Inf.), collar (Inf.), do (Sl.), nab (Inf.), nick (Brit. sl.), pick up (Sl.), pull in

(Brit. sl.), run in (Sl.), take into custody ~n. 6. nip, squeeze, tweak 7. bit, dash, jot, mite, small quantity, soupçon, speck, taste 8. crisis, difficulty, emergency, exigency, hardship, necessity, oppression, pass, plight, predicament, pressure, strait, stress

pinched careworn, drawn, gaunt, haggard, peaky, starved, thin, worn

pin down 1. compel, constrain, force, make, press, pressurize 2. designate, determine, home in on, identify, locate, name, pinpoint, specify 3. bind, confine, constrain, fix, hold, hold down, immobilize, nail down, tie down

pine 1. Often with **for** ache, carry a torch

for, covet, crave, desire, hanker, hunger for, long, lust after, sigh, thirst for, wish, yearn 2. decay, decline, droop, dwindle, fade, flag, languish, peak, sicken, sink, waste, weaken, wilt, wither

pinion v. bind, chain, confine, fasten, fetter, immobilize, manacle, pin down, shackle, tie

pink[1] 1. n. acme, best, height, peak, perfection, summit 2. adj. flesh, flushed, reddish, rose, roseate, rosy, salmon

pink[2] incise, notch, perforate, prick, punch, scallop, score

pin money *n.* **1.** an allowance by a husband to his wife for personal expenditure. **2.** money saved or earned for incidental expenses.

pinnace ('pınıs) *n.* any of various kinds of ship's tender.

pinnacle ('pınəkəl) *n.* **1.** the highest point, esp. of fame, success, etc. **2.** a towering peak, as of a mountain. **3.** a slender upright structure in the form of a spire on the top of a buttress, gable, or tower. ~*vb.* (*tr.*) **4.** to set as on a pinnacle. **5.** to furnish with a pinnacle or pinnacles. **6.** to crown with a pinnacle.

pinnate ('pıneıt, 'pınıt) *adj.* **1.** like a feather in appearance. **2.** (of compound leaves) having the leaflets growing opposite each other in pairs on either side of the stem. —'**pinnately** *adv.* —**pin'nation** *n.*

pinny ('pını) *n., pl.* -**nies.** a child's or informal name for **pinafore.**

pinpoint ('pın,pɔınt) *vb.* (*tr.*) **1.** to locate or identify exactly: *to pinpoint a problem; to pinpoint a place on a map.* ~*n.* **2.** an insignificant or trifling thing. **3.** the point of a pin. **4.** (*modifier*) exact: *a pinpoint aim.*

pinprick ('pın,prık) *n.* **1.** a slight puncture made by or as if by a pin. **2.** a small irritation. ~*vb.* **3.** (*tr.*) to puncture with or as if with a pin.

pins and needles *n. Inf.* **1.** a tingling sensation in the fingers, toes, legs, etc., caused by the return of normal blood circulation after its temporary impairment. **2. on pins and needles.** in a state of anxious suspense.

pinstripe ('pın,straıp) *n.* (in textiles) a very narrow stripe in fabric or the fabric itself.

pint (paınt) *n.* **1.** a unit of liquid measure of capacity equal to one eighth of a gallon. 1 Brit. pint is equal to 0.568 litre, 1 U.S. pint to 0.473 litre. **2.** a unit of dry measure of capacity equal to one half of a quart. 1 U.S. dry pint is equal to one sixty-fourth of a U.S. bushel or 0.5506 litre. **3.** a measure having such a capacity. **4.** *Brit. inf.* **a.** a pint of beer. **b.** a drink of beer: *he's gone out for a pint.*

pinta ('paıntə) *n.* an informal word for **pint,** esp. of milk.

pintail ('pın,teıl) *n., pl.* -**tails** *or* -**tail.** a greyish-brown duck with a pointed tail.

pintle ('pıntəl) *n.* **1.** a pin or bolt forming the pivot of a hinge. **2.** the link bolt, hook, or pin on a vehicle's towing bracket. **3.** the needle or plunger of the injection valve of an oil engine.

pinto ('pıntəʊ) *U.S.* ~*adj.* **1.** marked with patches of white; piebald. ~*n., pl.* -**tos.** **2.** a pinto horse.

pint-size *or* **pint-sized** *adj. Inf.* very small.

pin tuck *n.* a narrow, ornamental fold, esp. used on shirt fronts and dress bodices.

pin-up *n.* **1.** *Inf.* **a.** a picture of a sexually attractive person, esp. when partially or totally undressed. **b.** (*as modifier*): *a pin-up magazine.* **2.** *Sl.* a person who has appeared in such a picture. **3.** a photograph of a famous personality.

pinwheel ('pın,wi:l) *n.* another name for a **Catherine wheel** (sense 1).

pion ('paıɒn) *or* **pi meson** *n. Physics.* a meson having a positive or negative charge and a rest mass 273 times that of the electron, or no charge and a rest mass 264 times that of the electron.

pioneer (,paıə'nıə) *n.* **1. a.** a colonist, explorer, or settler of a new land, region, etc. **b.** (*as modifier*): *a pioneer wagon.* **2.** an innovator or developer of something new. **3.** *Mil.* a member of an infantry group that digs entrenchments, makes roads, etc. ~*vb.* **4.** to be a pioneer (in or of something). **5.** (*tr.*) to initiate, prepare, or open up: *to pioneer a medical programme.*

pious ('paıəs) *adj.* **1.** having or expressing reverence for a god or gods; religious; devout. **2.** marked by reverence. **3.** marked by false reverence; sanctimonious. **4.** sacred; not secular. —'**piously** *adv.* —'**piousness** *n.*

pip¹ (pıp) *n.* **1.** the seed of a fleshy fruit, such as an apple or pear. **2.** any of the segments marking the surface of a pineapple.

pip² (pıp) *n.* **1.** a short high-pitched sound, a sequence of which can act as a time signal, esp. on radio. **2.** a radar blip. **3. a.** a device, such as a spade, diamond, heart, or club on a playing card. **b.** any of the spots on dice or dominoes. **4.** *Inf.* the emblem worn on the shoulder by junior officers in the British Army, indicating their rank. ~*vb.* **pipping, pipped.** **5.** (of a young bird) **a.** (*intr.*) to chirp; peep. **b.** to pierce (the shell of its egg) while hatching. **6.** (*intr.*) to make a short high-pitched sound.

pip³ (pıp) *n.* **1.** a contagious disease of poultry characterized by the secretion of thick mucus in the mouth and throat. **2.** *Facetious sl.* a minor human ailment. **3.** *Brit. sl.* a bad temper or depression (esp. in **give (someone) the pip).** ~*vb.* **pipping, pipped.** **4.** *Brit. sl.* to be or cause to be annoyed or depressed.

pip⁴ (pıp) *vb.* **pipping, pipped.** (*tr.*) *Brit. sl.* **1.** to wound, esp. with a gun. **2.** to defeat (a person), esp. when his success seems certain (often in **pip at the post**). **3.** to blackball or ostracize.

pipe¹ (paıp) *n.* **1.** a long tube of metal, plastic, etc. used to convey water, oil, gas, etc. **2.** a long tube or case. **3.** an object made in various shapes and sizes, consisting of a small bowl with an attached tubular stem, in which tobacco or other substances are smoked. **4.** Also called: **pipeful.** the amount of tobacco that fills the bowl of a pipe. **5.** *Zool., bot.* any of various hollow organs, such as the respiratory passage of certain animals. **6. a.** any musical instrument whose sound production results from the vibration of an air column in a simple tube. **b.** any of the tubular devices on an organ. **7. the pipes.** bagpipes. **8.** a shrill voice or sound, as of a bird. **9. a.** a boatswain's pipe. **b.** the sound it makes. **10.** (*pl.*) *Inf.* the respiratory tract or vocal cords. **11.** *Metallurgy.* a conical hole in the head of an ingot. **12.** a cylindrical vein of rich ore. **13.** Also called: **volcanic pipe.** a vertical cylindrical passage in a volcano through which molten lava is forced during eruption. **14. put that in your pipe and smoke it.** *Inf.* accept that fact if you can. ~*vb.* **15.** to play (music) on a pipe. **16.** (*tr.*) to summon or lead by a pipe: *to pipe the dancers.* **17.** to utter (something) shrilly. **18. a.** to signal orders to (the crew) by a boatswain's pipe. **b.** (*tr.*) to signal the arrival or departure of: *to pipe the admiral aboard.* **19.** (*tr.*) to convey (water, gas, etc.) by a pipe or pipes. **20.** (*tr.*) to provide with pipes. **21.** (*tr.*) to trim (an article, esp. of clothing) with piping. **22.** to force cream or icing, etc., through a shaped nozzle to decorate food. ~See also **pipe down, pipe up.**

pipe² (paıp) *n.* **1.** a large cask for wine, oil, etc. **2.** a measure of capacity for wine equal to four barrels or 105 Brit. gallons. **3.** a cask holding this quantity with its contents.

pipeclay ('paıp,kleı) *n.* **1.** a fine white pure clay, used in the manufacture of tobacco pipes and pottery and for whitening leather and similar materials. ~*vb.* **2.** (*tr.*) to whiten with pipeclay.

pipe cleaner *n.* a short length of thin wires twisted so as to hold tiny tufts of yarn: used to clean the stem of a tobacco pipe.

pipe down *vb.* (*intr., adv.*) *Sl.* to stop talking, making noise, etc.

pipe dream *n.* a fanciful or impossible plan or hope.

pipeline ('paıp,laın) *n.* **1.** a long pipe used to transport oil, natural gas, etc. **2.** a medium of communication, esp. a private one. **3. in the pipeline.** in the process of being completed, delivered, or produced. ~*vb.* (*tr.*) **4.** to convey by pipeline. **5.** to supply with a pipeline.

THESAURUS

pinnacle 1. acme, apex, apogee, crest, crown, eminence, height, meridian, peak, summit, top, vertex, zenith 2. belfry, cone, needle, obelisk, pyramid, spire, steeple

pinpoint define, distinguish, get a fix on, home in on, identify, locate, spot

pint ale, beer, jar (*Brit. inf.*), jug (*Brit. inf.*)

pint-size diminutive, little, midget, miniature, pocket, small, tiny, wee

pioneer *n.* 1. colonist, colonizer, explorer, frontiersman, settler 2. developer, founder,

founding father, innovator, leader, trailblazer ~*v.* 3. create, develop, discover, establish, initiate, instigate, institute, invent, launch, lay the groundwork, map out, open up, originate, prepare, show the way, start, take the lead

pious 1. dedicated, devoted, devout, God-fearing, godly, holy, religious, reverent, righteous, saintly, spiritual 2. goody-goody, holier-than-thou, hypocritical, pietistic, re-

ligiose, sanctimonious, self-righteous, unctuous

pipe *n.* 1. conduit, conveyor, duct, hose, line, main, passage, pipeline, tube 2. briar, clay, meerschaum 3. fife, horn, tooter, whistle, wind instrument ~*v.* 4. cheep, peep, play, sing, sound, tootle, trill, tweet, twitter, warble, whistle 5. bring in, channel, conduct, convey, siphon, supply, transmit

pipe down belt up (*Sl.*), be quiet, hold one's tongue, hush, quieten down, shush, shut

pipe organ *n.* another name for **organ** (the musical instrument).

piper ('paɪpə) *n.* **1.** a person who plays a pipe or bagpipes. **2. pay the piper and call the tune.** to bear the cost of an undertaking and control it.

pipette (pɪ'pɛt) *n.* a slender glass tube for transferring or measuring out known volumes of liquid.

pipe up *vb.* (*intr., adv.*) **1.** to commence singing or playing a musical instrument: *the band piped up.* **2.** to speak up, esp. in a shrill voice.

piping ('paɪpɪŋ) *n.* **1.** pipes collectively, as in the plumbing of a house. **2.** a cord of icing, whipped cream, etc., often used to decorate desserts and cakes. **3.** a thin strip of covered cord or material, used to edge hems, etc. **4.** the sound of a pipe or bagpipes. **5.** the art or technique of playing a pipe or bagpipes. **6.** a shrill voice or sound, esp. a whistling sound. ~*adj.* **7.** making a shrill sound. **8. piping hot.** extremely hot.

pipit ('pɪpɪt) *n.* any of various songbirds, esp. the **meadow pipit,** having brownish speckled plumage and a long tail.

pippin ('pɪpɪn) *n.* any of several varieties of eating apple.

pipsqueak ('pɪp,skwiːk) *n. Inf.* a person or thing that is insignificant or contemptible.

piquant ('piːkənt, -kɑːnt) *adj.* **1.** having an agreeably pungent or tart taste. **2.** lively or stimulating to the mind. —'**piquancy** or '**piquantness** *n.* —'**piquantly** *adv.*

pique (piːk) *n.* **1.** a feeling of resentment or irritation, as from having one's pride wounded. ~*vb.* **piquing, piqued.** (*tr.*) **2.** to cause to feel resentment or irritation. **3.** to excite or arouse. **4.** (foll. by *on* or *upon*) to pride or congratulate (oneself).

piqué ('piːkeɪ) *n.* a close-textured fabric of cotton, silk, or spun rayon woven with lengthwise ribs.

piquet (pɪ'kɛt, -'keɪ) *n.* a card game for two people played with a reduced pack.

piracy ('paɪrəsɪ) *n., pl.* -**cies.** **1.** *Brit.* robbery on the seas. **2.** a felony, such as robbery or hijacking, committed aboard a ship or aircraft. **3.** the unauthorized use or appropriation of patented or copyrighted material, ideas, etc.

piranha or **piraña** (pɪ'rɑːnjə) *n.* any of various small freshwater voracious fishes of tropical America, having strong jaws and sharp teeth.

pirate ('paɪrɪt) *n.* **1.** a person who commits piracy. **2. a.** a vessel used by pirates. **b.** (*as modifier*): *a pirate ship.* **3.** a person who uses or appropriates literary, artistic, or other work of someone else illicitly. **4. a.** a person or group of people who broadcast illegally. **b.** (*as modifier*): *a pirate radio station.* ~*vb.* **5.** (*tr.*) to use, appropriate, or reproduce (artistic work, ideas, etc.) illicitly. —**piratic** (paɪ'rætɪk) or **pi'ratical** *adj.* —**pi'ratically** *adv.*

pirouette (,pɪru'ɛt) *n.* **1.** a body spin, esp. in dancing, on the toes or the ball of the foot. ~*vb.* **2.** (*intr.*) to perform a pirouette.

piscatorial (,pɪskə'tɔːrɪəl) or **piscatory** ('pɪskətərɪ) *adj.* **1.** of or relating to fish, fishing, or fishermen. **2.** devoted to fishing. —,**pisca'torially** *adv.*

Pisces ('paɪsiːz, 'pɪ-) *n., Latin genitive* **Piscium** ('pɪsɪəm). **1.** *Astron.* a faint extensive zodiacal constellation lying between Aquarius and Aries on the ecliptic. **2.** *Astrol.* Also called: the **Fishes.** the twelfth sign of the zodiac. The sun is in this sign between about Feb. 19 and March 20. **3. a.** a taxonomic group that comprises all fishes. See **fish** (sense 1). **b.** a taxonomic group that comprises the bony fishes only.

pisci- *combining form.* fish: *pisciculture.*

pisciculture ('pɪsɪ,kʌltʃə) *n.* the rearing and breeding of fish under controlled conditions. —,**pisci'cultural** *adj.* —,**pisci'culturist** *n., adj.*

piscine ('pɪsaɪn) *adj.* of, relating to, or resembling a fish.

pish (pʃ, pɪʃ) *interj.* **1.** an exclamation of impatience or contempt. ~*vb.* **2.** to make this exclamation at (someone or something).

piss (pɪs) *Taboo sl.* ~*vb.* **1.** (*intr.*) to urinate. **2.** (*tr.*) to discharge as or in one's urine: *to piss blood.* ~*n.* **3.** an act of urinating. **4.** urine.

pissed (pɪst) *adj. Brit. taboo sl.* drunk.

piss off *vb.* (*adv.*) *Taboo sl.* **1.** (*tr.; often passive*) to annoy, irritate, or disappoint. **2.** (*intr.*) *Chiefly Brit.* to go away; depart, often used to dismiss a person.

pistachio (pɪ'stɑːʃɪ,əʊ) *n., pl.* -**os.** **1.** a tree of the Mediterranean region and W Asia, with small hard-shelled nuts. **2.** Also called: **pistachio nut.** the nut of this tree, having an edible green kernel. **3.** the sweet flavour of the pistachio nut, used in ice creams, etc. ~*adj.* **4.** of a yellowish-green colour.

piste (piːst) *n.* a slope or course for skiing.

pistil ('pɪstɪl) *n.* the female reproductive part of a flower, consisting of one or more separate or fused carpels.

pistillate ('pɪstɪlɪt, -,leɪt) *adj.* (of plants) **1.** having pistils but no anthers. **2.** having or producing pistils.

pistol ('pɪstəl) *n.* **1.** a short-barrelled handgun. **2. hold a pistol to a person's head.** to threaten a person in order to force him to do what one wants. ~*vb.* -**tolling, -tolled** or *U.S.* -**toling, -toled. 3.** (*tr.*) to shoot with a pistol.

pistol-whip *vb.* -**whipping, -whipped.** (*tr.*) *U.S.* to beat or strike with a pistol barrel.

piston ('pɪstən) *n.* a disc or cylindrical part that slides to and fro in a hollow cylinder. In an internal-combustion engine it is attached by a pivoted connecting rod to a crankshaft or flywheel, thus converting reciprocating motion into rotation.

pit[1] (pɪt) *n.* **1.** a large, usually deep opening in the ground. **2. a.** a mine or excavation, esp. for coal. **b.** the shaft in a mine. **c.** (*as modifier*): *pit pony; pit prop.* **3.** a concealed danger or difficulty. **4. the pit.** hell. **5.** Also called: **orchestra pit.** the area that is occupied by the orchestra in a theatre, located in front of the stage. **6.** an enclosure for fighting animals or birds. **7.** *Anat.* **a.** a small natural depression on the surface of a body, organ, or part. **b.** the floor of any natural bodily cavity: *the pit of the stomach.* **8.** *Pathol.* a small indented scar at the site of a former pustule; pockmark. **9.** a working area at the side of a motor-racing track for servicing or refuelling vehicles. **10.** *U.S.* a section on the floor of a commodity exchange devoted to a special line of trading. **11.** the ground floor of the auditorium of a theatre. **12.** another word for **pitfall** (sense 2). ~*vb.* **pitting, pitted. 13.** (*tr.; often foll. by against*) to match in opposition, esp. as antagonists. **14.** to mark or become marked with pits. **15.** (*tr.*) to place or bury in a pit.

pit[2] (pɪt) *Chiefly U.S.* ~*n.* **1.** the stone of a cherry, etc. ~*vb.* **pitting, pitted.** (*tr.*) **2.** to extract the stone from (a fruit).

pitapat ('pɪtə,pæt) *adv.* **1.** with quick light taps. ~*vb.* -**patting, -patted. 2.** (*intr.*) to make quick light taps. ~*n.* **3.** such taps.

pitch[1] (pɪtʃ) *vb.* **1.** to hurl or throw (something); cast;

THESAURUS

pipe dream castle in the air, chimera, daydream, delusion, dream, fantasy, notion, reverie, vagary

pipeline 1. conduit, conveyor, duct, line, passage, pipe, tube 2. **in the pipeline** brewing, coming, getting ready, in process, in production, on the way, under way

piquancy 1. bite (*Inf.*), edge, flavour, kick (*Inf.*), pungency, relish, sharpness, spice, spiciness, tang, zest 2. colour, excitement, interest, pep, pizazz (*Sl.*), raciness, spirit, vigour, vitality, zip (*Inf.*)

piquant 1. biting, highly-seasoned, peppery, pungent, savoury, sharp, spicy, stinging, tangy, tart, with a kick (*Inf.*), zesty 2. in-teresting, lively, provocative, racy, salty, scintillating, sparkling, spirited, stimulating

pique *n.* 1. annoyance, displeasure, grudge, huff, hurt feelings, irritation, miff (*Inf.*), offence, resentment, umbrage, vexation, wounded pride ~*v.* 2. affront, annoy, displease, gall, get (*Inf.*), incense, irk, irritate, miff (*Inf.*), mortify, nettle, offend, peeve (*Inf.*), provoke, put out, put someone's nose out of joint (*Inf.*), rile, sting, vex, wound 3. arouse, excite, galvanize, goad, kindle, provoke, rouse, spur, stimulate, stir, whet 4. *With* **on** or **upon** *Of oneself* congratulate, flatter, plume, preen, pride

piracy buccaneering, freebooting, hijacking, infringement, plagiarism, rapine, rob-bery at sea, stealing, theft

pirate *n.* 1. buccaneer, corsair, filibuster, freebooter, marauder, raider, rover, sea robber, sea rover, sea wolf 2. cribber (*Inf.*), infringer, plagiarist, plagiarizer ~*v.* 3. appropriate, borrow, copy, crib (*Inf.*), lift (*Inf.*), plagiarize, poach, reproduce, steal

pit *n.* 1. abyss, cavity, chasm, coal mine, crater, dent, depression, dimple, excavation, gulf, hole, hollow, indentation, mine, pockmark, pothole, trench ~*v.* 2. *Often with* **against** match, oppose, put in opposition, set against 3. dent, dint, gouge, hole, indent, mark, nick, notch, pockmark, scar

fling. **2.** (*usually tr.*) to set up (a camp, tent, etc.). **3.** (*tr.*) to set the level, character, or slope of. **4.** (*intr.*) to slope downwards. **5.** (*intr.*) to fall forwards or downwards. **6.** (*intr.*) (of a vessel) to alternatively dip and raise its bow and stern. **7.** (*tr.*; foll. by *up*) *Cricket.* to bowl (a ball) so that it bounces near the batsman. **8.** (*intr.*) (of a missile, aircraft, etc.) to deviate from a stable flight attitude by movement of the longitudinal axis about the lateral axis. **9.** (*tr.*) (in golf, etc.) to hit (a ball) steeply into the air. **10.** (*tr.*) *Music.* **a.** to sing or play accurately (a note, interval, etc.). **b.** (*usually passive*) (of a wind instrument) to specify or indicate its basic key or harmonic series by its size, manufacture, etc. ~*n.* **11.** the degree of elevation or depression. **12. a.** the angle of descent of a downward slope. **b.** such a slope. **13.** the extreme height or depth. **14.** a section of a route up a slope between two belay points. **15.** the degree of slope of a roof. **16.** the distance between corresponding points on adjacent members of a body of regular form, esp. the distance between teeth on a gearwheel or between threads on a screw thread. **17.** the pitching motion of a ship, missile, etc. **18.** *Music.* **a.** the auditory property of a note that is conditioned by its frequency relative to other notes: *high pitch; low pitch.* **b.** an absolute frequency assigned to a specific note, fixing the relative frequencies of all other notes. **19.** *Cricket.* the rectangular area between the stumps, 22 yards long and 10 feet wide; the wicket. **20.** the act or manner of pitching a ball, as in cricket, etc. **21.** *Chiefly Brit.* a vendor's station, esp. on a pavement. **22.** *Sl.* a persuasive sales talk, esp. one routinely repeated. **23.** *Chiefly Brit.* (in many sports) the field of play. **24.** Also called: **pitch shot.** *Golf.* an approach shot in which the ball is struck in a high arc. **25. queer someone's pitch.** *Brit. inf.* to upset the plans of another. ~See also **pitch in, pitch into.**

pitch² (pɪtʃ) *n.* **1.** any of various heavy dark viscid substances obtained as a residue from the distillation of tars. **2.** any of various similar substances, such as asphalt, occurring as natural deposits. **3.** crude turpentine obtained as sap from pine trees. ~*vb.* **4.** (*tr.*) to apply pitch to (something).

pitch-black *adj.* **1.** extremely dark; unlit: *the room was pitch-black.* **2.** of a deep black colour.

pitchblende ('pɪtʃ,blɛnd) *n.* a blackish mineral that occurs in veins, frequently associated with silver: the principal source of uranium and radium.

pitch-dark *adj.* extremely or completely dark.

pitched battle *n.* **1.** a battle ensuing from the deliberate choice of time and place. **2.** any fierce encounter, esp. one with large numbers.

pitcher¹ ('pɪtʃə) *n.* a large jug, usually rounded with a narrow neck and often of earthenware, used mainly for holding water.

pitcher² ('pɪtʃə) *n.* *Baseball.* the player on the fielding team who pitches the ball to the batter.

pitcher plant *n.* any of various insectivorous plants, having leaves modified to form pitcher-like organs that attract and trap insects, which are then digested.

pitchfork ('pɪtʃ,fɔːk) *n.* **1.** a long-handled fork with two long curved tines for tossing hay. ~*vb.* (*tr.*) **2.** to use a pitchfork on (something). **3.** to thrust (someone) unwillingly into a position.

pitch in *vb.* (*intr., adv.*) **1.** to cooperate or contribute. **2.** to begin energetically.

pitch into *vb.* (*intr., prep.*) **1.** to assail physically or verbally. **2.** to get on with doing (something).

pitch pine *n.* **1.** any of various coniferous trees of North America: valued as a source of turpentine and pitch. **2.** the wood of any of these trees.

pitch pipe *n.* a small pipe that sounds a note or notes of standard frequency. It is used for establishing the correct starting note for unaccompanied singing.

pitchy ('pɪtʃɪ) *adj.* **pitchier, pitchiest. 1.** full of or covered with pitch. **2.** resembling pitch. —'**pitchiness** *n.*

piteous ('pɪtɪəs) *adj.* exciting or deserving pity. —'**piteously** *adv.* —'**piteousness** *n.*

pitfall ('pɪt,fɔːl) *n.* **1.** an unsuspected difficulty or danger. **2.** a trap in the form of a concealed pit, designed to catch men or wild animals.

pith (pɪθ) *n.* **1.** the soft fibrous tissue lining the inside of the rind in fruits such as the orange. **2.** the essential or important part, point, etc. **3.** weight; substance. **4.** *Bot.* the central core of unspecialized cells surrounded by conducting tissue in stems. **5.** the soft central part of a bone, feather, etc. ~*vb.* (*tr.*) **6.** to kill (animals) by severing the spinal cord. **7.** to remove the pith from (a plant).

pithead ('pɪt,hɛd) *n.* the top of a mine shaft and the buildings, hoisting gear, etc., around it.

pith helmet *n.* a lightweight hat made of the pith of the sola, an E Indian swamp plant, that protects the wearer from the sun. Also called: **topee, topi.**

pithy ('pɪθɪ) *adj.* **pithier, pithiest. 1.** terse and full of meaning or substance. **2.** of, resembling, or full of pith. —'**pithily** *adv.* —'**pithiness** *n.*

pitiable ('pɪtɪəbᵊl) *adj.* exciting or deserving pity or contempt. —'**pitiableness** *n.* —'**pitiably** *adv.*

pitiful ('pɪtɪfʊl) *adj.* **1.** arousing or deserving pity. **2.** arousing or deserving contempt. **3.** *Arch.* full of pity or compassion. —'**pitifully** *adv.* —'**pitifulness** *n.*

pitiless ('pɪtɪlɪs) *adj.* having or showing little or no pity or mercy. —'**pitilessly** *adv.* —'**pitilessness** *n.*

piton ('piːtɒn) *n.* *Mountaineering.* a metal spike that may be driven into a crevice and used to secure a rope, etc.

pittance ('pɪtᵊns) *n.* a small amount or portion, esp. a meagre allowance of money.

pitter-patter ('pɪtə,pætə) *n.* **1.** the sound of light rapid taps or pats, as of raindrops. ~*vb.* **2.** (*intr.*) to make such a sound. ~*adv.* **3.** with such a sound.

pituitary (pɪ'tjuːɪtərɪ) *n., pl.* **-taries. 1.** See **pituitary gland.** ~*adj.* **2.** of or relating to the pituitary gland.

pituitary gland *or* **body** *n.* the master endocrine gland, attached by a stalk to the base of the brain. Its two lobes secrete hormones affecting skeletal growth, development of the sex glands, and the functioning of the other endocrine glands.

pity ('pɪtɪ) *n., pl.* **pities. 1.** sympathy or sorrow felt for the sufferings of another. **2. have** (*or* **take**) **pity on.** to have sympathy or show mercy for. **3.** something that causes regret. **4.** an unfortunate chance: *what a pity you can't come.* ~*vb.* **pitying, pitied. 5.** to feel pity (for). —'**pityingly** *adv.*

THESAURUS

pitch *v.* **1.** bung (*Brit. sl.*), cast, chuck (*Inf.*), fling, heave, hurl, launch, lob (*Inf.*), sling, throw, toss **2.** erect, fix, locate, place, plant, put up, raise, settle, set up, station **3.** flounder, lurch, make heavy weather, plunge, roll, toss, wallow, welter **4.** dive, drop, fall headlong, stagger, topple, tumble ~*n.* **5.** angle, cant, dip, gradient, incline, slope, steepness, tilt **6.** degree, height, highest point, level, point, summit **7.** harmonic, modulation, sound, timbre, tone **8.** line, patter, sales talk, spiel (*Inf.*) **9.** field of play, ground, park (*Brit. inf.*), sports field

pitch-black dark, ebony, inky, jet, jet-black, pitch-dark, raven, sable, unlit

pitch in **1.** chip in (*Inf.*), contribute, co-operate, do one's bit, help, join in, lend a hand, participate **2.** begin, fall to, get busy, get cracking (*Inf.*), plunge into, set about, set to, tackle

piteous affecting, deplorable, distressing,

doleful, grievous, heartbreaking, heart-rending, lamentable, miserable, mournful, moving, pathetic, pitiable, pitiful, plaintive, poignant, sad, sorrowful, woeful, wretched

pitfall **1.** catch, danger, difficulty, drawback, hazard, peril, snag, trap **2.** deadfall, downfall, pit, snare, trap

pith **1.** core, crux, essence, gist, heart, heart of the matter, kernel, marrow, meat, nub, point, quintessence, salient point, the long and the short of it **2.** consequence, depth, force, import, importance, matter, moment, power, significance, strength, substance, value, weight

pithy brief, cogent, compact, concise, epigrammatic, expressive, finely honed, forceful, laconic, meaningful, pointed, short, succinct, terse, to the point, trenchant

pitiful **1.** deplorable, distressing, grievous, heartbreaking, heart-rending, lamentable, miserable, pathetic, piteous, pitiable, sad,

woeful, wretched **2.** abject, base, beggarly, contemptible, despicable, inadequate, insignificant, low, mean, miserable, paltry, scurvy, shabby, sorry, vile, worthless

pitiless brutal, callous, cold-blooded, cold-hearted, cruel, hardhearted, harsh, heartless, implacable, inexorable, inhuman, merciless, relentless, ruthless, uncaring, unfeeling, unmerciful, unsympathetic

pittance allowance, chicken feed (*Sl.*), drop, mite, modicum, peanuts (*Sl.*), portion, ration, slave wages, trifle

pity *n.* **1.** charity, clemency, commiseration, compassion, condolence, fellow feeling, forbearance, kindness, mercy, sympathy, tenderness, understanding **2.** crime (*Inf.*), crying shame, misfortune, regret, sad thing, shame, sin **3. take pity on** feel compassion for, forgive, have mercy on, melt, pardon, put out of one's misery, relent, reprieve, show mercy, spare ~*v.* **4.** bleed for, commis-

più (pjuː) *adv. Music.* (*in combination*) more (quickly, etc.): *più allegro.*

pivot ('pɪvət) *n.* **1.** a short shaft or pin supporting something that turns; fulcrum. **2.** the end of a shaft or arbor that terminates in a bearing. **3.** a person or thing upon which progress, success, etc., depends. **4.** the person or position from which a military formation takes its reference when altering position, etc. ~*vb.* **5.** (*tr.*) to mount on or provide with a pivot or pivots. **6.** (*intr.*) to turn on or as if on a pivot.

pivotal ('pɪvətəl) *adj.* **1.** of, involving, or acting as a pivot. **2.** of crucial importance.

pix[1] (pɪks) *pl. n. Inf.* photographs; prints.

pix[2] (pɪks) *n.* a less common spelling of **pyx**.

pixie *or* **pixy** ('pɪksɪ) *n., pl.* **pixies.** (in folklore) a fairy or elf.

pizza ('piːtsə) *n.* a dish of Italian origin consisting of a baked disc of dough covered with cheese and tomatoes, etc.

pizzicato (ˌpɪtsɪ'kɑːtəʊ) *Music.* ~*adj., adv.* **1.** (in music for the violin family) to be plucked with the finger. ~*n.* **2.** this style or technique of playing.

pl. *abbrev. for:* **1.** place. **2.** plate. **3.** plural.

Pl. (in street names) *abbrev. for* Place.

P.L.A. *abbrev. for* Port of London Authority.

placable ('plækəbəl) *adj.* easily placated or appeased. —ˌplaca'bility *n.*

placard ('plækɑːd) *n.* **1.** a notice for public display; poster. **2.** a small plaque or card. ~*vb.* (*tr.*) **3.** to post placards on or in. **4.** to advertise by placards. **5.** to display as a placard.

placate (plə'keɪt) *vb.* (*tr.*) to pacify or appease. —**pla'cation** *n.* —**pla'catory** *adj.*

place (pleɪs) *n.* **1.** a particular point or part of space or of a surface, esp. that occupied by a person or thing. **2.** a geographical point, such as a town, city, etc. **3.** a position or rank in a sequence or order. **4.** an open square lined with houses in a city or town. **5.** space or room. **6.** a house or living quarters. **7.** any building or area set aside for a specific purpose. **8.** a passage in a book, play, film, etc.: *to lose one's place.* **9.** proper, right, or customary surroundings (esp. in **out of place, in place**). **10.** right, prerogative, or duty: *it is your place to give a speech.* **11.** appointment, position, or job: *a place at college.* **12.** position, condition, or state: *if I were in your place.* **13. a.** a space or seat, as at a dining table. **b.** (*as modifier*): *place mat.* **14.** *Maths.* the relative position of a digit in a number. **15.** any of the best times in a race. **16.** *Horse racing.* **a.** *Brit.* the first, second, or third position at the finish. **b.** *U.S.* the first or usually the second position at the finish. **c.** (*as modifier*): *a place bet.* **17. all over the place.** in disorder or disarray. **18. give place (to).** to make room (for) or be superseded (by). **19. go places.** *Inf.* **a.** to travel. **b.** to become successful. **20. in place of.** a. instead of; in lieu of: *go in place of my sister.* **b.** in exchange for: *he gave her it in place of her ring.* **21. know one's place.** to be aware of one's inferior position. **22. pride of place.** the highest or foremost position. **23. put someone in his** (*or* **her**) **place.** to humble someone who is arrogant, conceited, forward, etc. **24. take one's place.** to take up one's usual or specified position. **25. take the place of.** to be a substitute for. **26.**

take place. to happen or occur. ~*vb.* (*mainly tr.*) **27.** to put or set in a particular or appropriate place. **28.** to find or indicate the place of. **29.** to identify or classify by linking with an appropriate context: *to place a face.* **30.** to regard or view as being: *to place prosperity above sincerity.* **31.** to make (an order, bet, etc.). **32.** to find a home or job for (someone). **33.** to appoint to an office or position. **34.** (often foll. by *with*) to put under the care (of). **35.** to direct or aim carefully. **36.** (*passive*) *Brit.* to cause (a racehorse, greyhound, athlete, etc.) to arrive in first, second, third, or sometimes fourth place. **37.** (*intr.*) *U.S.* (of a racehorse, greyhound, etc.) to finish among the first three in a contest, esp. in second position. **38.** to invest (funds). **39.** to insert (an advertisement) in a newspaper, journal, etc.

placebo (plə'siːbəʊ) *n., pl.* **-bos** *or* **-boes.** **1.** *Med.* an inactive substance administered to a patient who insists on receiving medication or who would benefit by the psychological deception. **2.** something said or done to please or humour another. **3.** *R.C. Church.* a traditional name for the vespers of the office for the dead.

place kick *Football.* ~*n.* **1.** a kick in which the ball is placed in position before it is kicked. ~*vb.* **place-kick. 2.** to kick (a ball) in this way.

placement ('pleɪsmənt) *n.* **1.** the act of placing or the state of being placed. **2.** arrangement or position. **3.** the process of finding employment.

placenta (plə'sɛntə) *n., pl.* **-tas** *or* **-tae** (-tiː). **1.** the vascular organ formed in the uterus of most mammals during pregnancy, consisting of both maternal and embryonic tissues and providing oxygen and nutrients for the foetus. **2.** *Bot.* the part of the ovary of flowering plants to which the ovules are attached. —**pla'cental** *adj.*

placer ('plæsə) *n.* **a.** surface sediment containing particles of gold or some other valuable mineral. **b.** (*in combination*): *placer-mining.*

place setting *n.* the cutlery, crockery, and glassware laid for one person at a dining table.

placid ('plæsɪd) *adj.* having a calm appearance or nature. —**placidity** (plə'sɪdɪtɪ) *or* **'placidness** *n.* —**'placidly** *adv.*

placket ('plækɪt) *n. Dressmaking.* **1.** a piece of cloth sewn in under a closure with buttons, zips, etc. **2.** the closure itself.

plagiarize *or* **-ise** ('pleɪdʒəˌraɪz) *vb.* to appropriate (ideas, passages, etc.) from (another work or author). —**plagia,rism** *n.* —**'plagia,rizer** *or* **-iser** *n.*

plague (pleɪg) *n.* **1.** any widespread and usually highly contagious disease with a high fatality rate. **2.** an infectious disease of rodents, esp. rats, transmitted to man by the bite of the rat flea. **3.** See **bubonic plague. 4.** something that afflicts or harasses. **5.** *Inf.* an annoyance or nuisance. **6.** a pestilence, affliction, or calamity on a large scale, esp. when regarded as sent by God. ~*vb.* **plaguing, plagued.** (*tr.*) **7.** to afflict or harass. **8.** to bring down a plague upon. **9.** *Inf.* to annoy. —**'plaguer** *n.*

plaguy *or* **plaguey** ('pleɪgɪ) *Inf.* ~*adj.* **1.** disagreeable or vexing. ~*adv.* **2.** disagreeably or annoyingly. —**'plaguily** *adv.*

plaice (pleɪs) *n., pl.* **plaice** *or* **plaices. 1.** a European flatfish having an oval brown body marked with red or

---

THESAURUS

erate with, condole with, feel for, feel sorry for, grieve for, have compassion for, sympathize with, weep for

pivot *n.* 1. axis, axle, fulcrum, spindle, swivel 2. centre, focal point, heart, hinge, hub, kingpin ~*v.* 3. revolve, rotate, spin, swivel, turn, twirl 4. be contingent, depend, hang, hinge, rely, revolve round, turn

pixie brownie, elf, fairy, sprite

placard advertisement, *affiche*, bill, poster, public notice, sticker

placate appease, assuage, calm, conciliate, humour, mollify, pacify, propitiate, satisfy, soothe, win over

place *n.* 1. area, location, locus, point, position, site, situation, spot, station, venue, whereabouts 2. city, district, hamlet, locale, locality, neighbourhood, quarter, region, town, vicinity, village 3. grade, position, rank, station, status 4. appointment, berth (*Inf.*), billet (*Inf.*), employment, job, position,

post 5. abode, apartment, domicile, dwelling, flat, home, house, manor, mansion, pad (*Sl.*), property, residence, seat 6. accommodation, room, space, stead 7. affair, charge, concern, duty, function, prerogative, responsibility, right, role 8. **in place of** as an alternative to, as a substitute for, in exchange for, in lieu of, instead of, taking the place of 9. **put (someone) in his place** bring down, cut down to size, humble, humiliate, make (someone) eat humble pie, make (someone) swallow his pride, mortify, take down a peg (*Inf.*) 10. **take place** befall, betide, come about, come to pass (*Archaic*), go on, happen, occur, transpire (*Inf.*) ~*v.* 11. bung (*Inf.*), deposit, dispose, establish, fix, install, lay, locate, plant, position, put, rest, set, settle, situate, stand, station, stick (*Inf.*) 12. arrange, class, classify, grade, group, order, rank, sort 13. associate, identify, know, put one's finger on, recognize, remember, set in context 14. allo-

cate, appoint, assign, charge, commission, entrust, give

placid calm, collected, composed, cool, equable, even, even-tempered, gentle, halcyon, imperturbable, mild, peaceful, quiet, self-possessed, serene, still, tranquil, undisturbed, unexcitable, unmoved, unruffled, untroubled

plagiarize appropriate, borrow, crib (*Inf.*), infringe, lift (*Inf.*), pirate, steal, thieve

plague *n.* 1. contagion, disease, epidemic, infection, pandemic, pestilence 2. *Fig.* affliction, bane, blight, calamity, cancer, curse, evil, scourge, torment, trial 3. *Inf.* aggravation (*Inf.*), annoyance, bother, irritant, nuisance, pain (*Inf.*), pest, problem, thorn in one's flesh, vexation ~*v.* 4. afflict, annoy, badger, bedevil, bother, disturb, fret, harass, harry, hassle (*Inf.*), haunt, molest, pain, persecute, pester, tease, torment, torture, trouble, vex

orange spots and valued as a food fish. **2.** *U.S.* any of various other related fishes.

plaid (plæd) *n.* **1.** a long piece of cloth of a tartan pattern, worn over the shoulder as part of Highland costume. **2. a.** a crisscross weave or cloth. **b.** (*as modifier*): *a plaid scarf.*

Plaid Cymru (ˌplaɪd ˈkʌmrɪ) *n.* the Welsh nationalist party.

plain (pleɪn) *adj.* **1.** flat or smooth; level. **2.** not complicated; clear: *the plain truth.* **3.** not difficult; simple or easy: *a plain task.* **4.** honest or straightforward. **5.** lowly, esp. in social rank or education. **6.** without adornment or show: *a plain coat.* **7.** (of fabric) without pattern or of simple untwilled weave. **8.** not attractive. **9.** not mixed; simple: *plain vodka.* **10.** *Knitting.* of or done in plain. ~*n.* **11.** a level or almost level tract of country. **12.** a simple stitch in knitting. ~*adv.* **13.** (intensifier): *just plain tired.* —ˈplainly *adv.* —ˈplainness *n.*

plain chocolate *n.* chocolate with a slightly bitter flavour and dark colour.

plain clothes *pl. n.* **a.** ordinary clothes, as distinguished from uniform, as worn by a police detective on duty. **b.** (*as modifier*): *a plain-clothes policeman.*

plain flour *n.* flour to which no raising agent has been added.

plain sailing *n.* **1.** *Inf.* smooth or easy progress. **2.** *Naut.* sailing in a body of water that is unobstructed; clear sailing.

plainsong (ˈpleɪnˌsɒŋ) *n.* the style of unison unaccompanied vocal music used in the medieval Church, esp. in Gregorian chant.

plain-spoken *adj.* candid; frank; blunt.

plaint (pleɪnt) *n.* **1.** *Arch.* a complaint or lamentation. **2.** *Law.* a statement in writing of grounds of complaint made to a court of law.

plaintiff (ˈpleɪntɪf) *n.* a person who brings a civil action in a court of law.

plaintive (ˈpleɪntɪv) *adj.* expressing melancholy; mournful. —ˈplaintively *adv.* —ˈplaintiveness *n.*

plait (plæt) *n.* **1.** a length of hair, etc., that has been plaited. **2.** a rare spelling of **pleat.** ~*vb.* **3.** (*tr.*) to intertwine (strands or strips) in a pattern.

plan (plæn) *n.* **1.** a detailed scheme, method, etc., for attaining an objective. **2.** (*sometimes pl.*) a proposed, usually tentative idea for doing something. **3.** a drawing to scale of a horizontal section through a building taken at a given level. **4.** an outline, sketch, etc. ~*vb.* **planning, planned. 5.** to form a plan (for) or make plans (for). **6.** (*tr.*) to make a plan of (a building). **7.** (*tr.; takes a clause as object or an infinitive*) to have in mind as a purpose; intend.

planar (ˈpleɪnə) *adj.* **1.** of or relating to a plane. **2.** lying in one plane; flat.

planchette (plɑːnˈʃɛt) *n.* a heart-shaped board on wheels with a pencil attached that writes messages under supposed spirit guidance.

plane¹ (pleɪn) *n.* **1.** *Maths.* a flat surface in which a straight line joining any two of its points lies entirely on that surface. **2.** a level surface. **3.** a level of existence, attainment, etc. **4. a.** short for **aeroplane. b.** an aerofoil or supporting surface of an aircraft. ~*adj.* **5.** level or flat. **6.** *Maths.* lying entirely in one plane. ~*vb.* (*intr.*) **7.** to glide. **8.** (of a boat) to rise partly and skim over the water when moving at a certain speed.

plane² (pleɪn) *n.* **1.** a tool with a steel blade set obliquely in a wooden or iron body, for smoothing timber surfaces, cutting grooves, etc. **2.** a flat tool, usually metal, for smoothing the surface of clay or plaster in a mould. ~*vb.* **3.** (*tr.*) to smooth or cut (timber, etc.) using a plane. **4.** (*tr.; often foll. by off*) to remove using a plane.

plane³ (pleɪn) *n.* a tree with ball-shaped heads of fruit and leaves with pointed lobes.

planet (ˈplænɪt) *n.* **1.** Also called: **major planet.** any of the nine celestial bodies, Mercury, Venus, earth, Mars, Jupiter, Saturn, Uranus, Neptune, or Pluto, that revolve around the sun in elliptical orbits. **2.** any celestial body revolving around a star. **3.** *Astrol.* any of the planets of the solar system, excluding the earth but including the sun and moon, each thought to rule one or sometimes two signs of the zodiac. —ˈplanetary *adj.*

planetarium (ˌplænɪˈtɛərɪəm) *n., pl.* **-iums** *or* **-ia** (-ɪə). **1.** an instrument for simulating the apparent motions of the sun, moon, and planets by projecting images of these bodies onto a domed ceiling. **2.** a building in which such an instrument is housed. **3.** a model of the solar system.

planetoid (ˈplænɪˌtɔɪd) *n.* another name for **asteroid** (sense 1). —ˌplaneˈtoidal *adj.*

plank (plæŋk) *n.* **1.** a stout length of sawn timber. **2.** something that supports or sustains. **3.** *Chiefly U.S.* one of the policies in a political party's programme. **4. walk the plank.** to be forced by pirates, etc., to walk to one's death off the end of a plank jutting out from the side of a ship. ~*vb.* **5.** (*tr.*) to cover or provide with planks.

planking (ˈplæŋkɪŋ) *n.* a number of planks.

plankton (ˈplæŋktən) *n.* the organisms inhabiting the surface layer of a sea or lake, consisting of small drifting plants and animals.

plano- *or sometimes before a vowel* **plan-** *combining form.* indicating flatness or planeness: *plano-concave.*

plant (plɑːnt) *n.* **1.** any living organism that typically synthesizes its food from inorganic substances, lacks specialized sense organs, and has no powers of locomotion. **2.** such an organism that is smaller than a shrub or tree; a herb. **3.** a cutting, seedling, or similar structure, esp. when ready for transplantation. **4. a.** a factory or works. **b.** specialized mechanical apparatus: *generating plant.* **5.** *Inf.* a thing positioned secretly for discovery by another, esp. in order to incriminate an innocent person. ~*vb.* (*tr.*) **6.** (often foll. by *out*) to set (seeds, crops, etc.) into (ground) to grow. **7.** to place firmly in position. **8.** to establish; found. **9.** (foll. by *with*) to stock or furnish. **10.** to implant in the mind. **11.** *Sl.* to deliver (a blow). **12.** *Sl.* to position or hide, esp. in order to deceive or observe. **13.** *Austral.* to hide or secrete, esp. for some illegal purpose. —ˈplantable *adj.*

plantain¹ (ˈplæntɪn) *n.* any of various N temperate plants, esp. the great plantain, which has a rosette of broad leaves and a slender spike of small greenish flowers.

plantain² (ˈplæntɪn) *n.* a large tropical plant with a green-skinned banana-like fruit which is eaten as a staple food in many tropical regions.

plantation (plænˈteɪʃən) *n.* **1.** an estate, esp. in tropical countries, where cash crops such as rubber, oil palm, etc., are grown on a large scale. **2.** a group of cultivated trees or plants. **3.** (formerly) a colony or group of settlers.

planter (ˈplɑːntə) *n.* **1.** the owner or manager of a plan-

---

THESAURUS

plain *adj.* 1. apparent, clear, comprehensible, distinct, evident, legible, lucid, manifest, obvious, patent, transparent, unambiguous, understandable, unmistakable, visible 2. artless, blunt, candid, direct, downright, forthright, frank, guileless, honest, ingenuous, open, outspoken, sincere, straightforward 3. common, commonplace, everyday, frugal, homely, lowly, modest, ordinary, simple, unaffected, unpretentious, workaday 4. austere, bare, basic, discreet, modest, muted, pure, restrained, severe, simple, Spartan, stark, unadorned, unembellished, unornamented, unpatterned, unvarnished 5. illfavoured, not beautiful, not striking, ordinary, ugly, unalluring, unattractive, unlovely, unprepossessing 6. even, flat, level, plane, smooth ~*n.* 7. flatland, grassland, lowland,

open country, plateau, prairie, steppe, tableland

plain-spoken blunt, candid, direct, downright, explicit, forthright, frank, open, outright, outspoken, straightforward, unequivocal

plaintive disconsolate, doleful, griefstricken, grievous, heart-rending, melancholy, mournful, pathetic, piteous, pitiful, rueful, sad, sorrowful, wistful, woebegone, woeful

plan *n.* 1. contrivance, design, device, idea, method, plot, procedure, programme, project, proposal, proposition, scenario, scheme, strategy, suggestion, system 2. blueprint, chart, delineation, diagram, drawing, illustration, layout, map, representation, scale drawing, sketch ~*v.* 3. arrange, concoct, contrive, design, devise, draft, formulate,

frame, invent, organize, outline, plot, prepare, represent, scheme, think out 4. aim, contemplate, envisage, foresee, intend, mean, propose, purpose

plane *n.* 1. flat surface, level surface 2. condition, degree, footing, level, position, stratum 3. aeroplane, aircraft, jet ~*adj.* 4. even, flat, flush, horizontal, level, plain, regular, smooth, uniform ~*v.* 5. glide, sail, skate, skim, volplane

plant *n.* 1. bush, flower, herb, shrub, vegetable, weed 2. factory, foundry, mill, shop, works, yard 3. apparatus, equipment, gear, machinery ~*v.* 4. implant, put in the ground, scatter, seed, set out, sow, transplant 5. establish, fix, found, imbed, insert, institute, lodge, root, set, settle

tation. **2.** a machine designed for rapid and efficient planting of seeds. **3.** a colonizer or settler. **4.** a decorative pot for house plants.

plantigrade ('plænti₁greid) *adj.* **1.** walking with the entire sole of the foot touching the ground, as man and bears. ~*n.* **2.** a plantigrade animal.

plaque (plæk, plɑːk) *n.* **1.** an ornamental or commemorative inscribed tablet. **2.** a small flat brooch or badge. **3.** *Pathol.* any small abnormal patch on or within the body. **4.** Also called: **dental plaque.** a filmy deposit on teeth consisting of mucus, bacteria, food, etc.

plash (plæʃ) *n., vb.* a less common word for **splash.** —'**plashy** *adj.*

-plasm *n. combining form.* (in biology) indicating the material forming cells: *protoplasm.* —**-plasmic** *adj. combining form.*

plasma ('plæzmə) *or* **plasm** ('plæzəm) *n.* **1.** the clear yellowish fluid portion of blood or lymph in which the corpuscles and cells are suspended. **2.** Also called: **blood plasma.** a sterilized preparation of such fluid, taken from the blood, for use in transfusions. **3.** a former name for **protoplasm** or **cytoplasm. 4.** *Physics.* a hot ionized gas containing positive ions and electrons. **5.** a green variety of chalcedony. —**plasmatic** (plæz'mætɪk) *or* '**plasmic** *adj.*

-plast *n. combining form.* indicating a living cell or particle of living matter: *protoplast.*

plaster ('plɑːstə) *n.* **1.** a mixture of lime, sand, and water that is applied to a wall or ceiling as a soft paste that hardens when dry. **2.** *Brit.* an adhesive strip of material for dressing a cut, wound, etc. **3.** short for **mustard plaster** or **plaster of Paris.** ~*vb.* **4.** to coat (a wall, ceiling, etc.) with plaster. **5.** (*tr.*) to apply like plaster: *she plastered make-up on her face.* **6.** (*tr.*) to cause to lie flat or to adhere. **7.** (*tr.*) to apply a plaster cast to. **8.** (*tr.*) *Sl.* to strike or defeat with great force. —'**plasterer** *n.*

plasterboard ('plɑːstə₁bɔːd) *n.* a thin rigid board, in the form of a layer of plaster compressed between two layers of fibreboard, used to form or cover walls, etc.

plastered ('plɑːstəd) *adj. Sl.* intoxicated; drunk.

plaster of Paris *n.* **1.** a white powder that sets to a hard solid when mixed with water, used for making sculptures and casts, as an additive for lime plasters, and for making casts for setting broken limbs. **2.** the hard plaster produced when this powder is mixed with water.

plastic ('plæstɪk) *n.* **1.** any one of a large number of synthetic materials that have a polymeric structure and can be moulded when soft and then set. Plastics are used in the manufacture of many articles and in coatings, artificial fibres, etc. ~*adj.* **2.** made of plastic. **3.** easily influenced; impressionable. **4.** capable of being moulded or formed. **5. a.** of moulding or modelling: *the plastic arts.* **b.** produced or apparently produced by moulding: *the plastic draperies of Giotto's figures.* **6.** having the power to form or influence: *the plastic forces of the imagination.* **7.** *Biol.* able to change, develop, or grow: *plastic tissues.* **8.** *Sl.* superficially attractive yet unoriginal or artificial: *plastic food.* —'**plastically** *adv.* —**plasticity** (plæ'stɪsɪtɪ) *n.*

-plastic *adj. combining form.* growing or forming.

plastic bomb *n.* a bomb consisting of an adhesive jelly-like explosive fitted around a detonator.

Plasticine ('plæstɪ₁siːn) *n. Trademark.* a soft coloured material used, esp. by children, for modelling.

plasticize *or* **-cise** ('plæstɪ₁saɪz) *vb.* to make or become plastic, as by the addition of a plasticizer. —₁**plastici'zation** *or* **-ci'sation** *n.*

plasticizer *or* **-ciser** ('plæstɪ₁saɪzə) *n.* any of a number of substances added to materials. Their uses include softening and improving the flexibility of plastics and preventing dried paint coatings from becoming too brittle.

plastic surgery *n.* the branch of surgery concerned with therapeutic or cosmetic repair or reformation of missing, injured, or malformed tissues or parts. —**plastic surgeon** *n.*

plate (pleit) *n.* **1. a.** a shallow usually circular dish made of porcelain, earthenware, glass, etc., on which food is served. **b.** (*as modifier*): *a plate ᵔᵃᶜᵏ* ?. **2. a.** Also called: **plateful.** the contents of a plate **b.** *Austral. & N.Z.* a plate of cakes, sandwiches, etc., brought by a guest to a party: *everyone was asked to bring a plate.* **3.** an entire course of a meal: *a cold plate.* **4.** any shallow receptacle, esp. for receiving a collection in church. **5.** flat metal of uniform thickness obtained by rolling, usually having a thickness greater than about three millimetres. **6.** a thin coating of metal on another metal, as produced by electrodeposition. **7.** metal or metalware that has been coated in this way: *Sheffield plate.* **8.** dishes, cutlery, etc., made of gold or silver. **9.** a sheet of metal, plastic, rubber, etc., having a printing surface produced by a process such as stereotyping. **10.** a print taken from such a sheet or from a woodcut. **11.** a thin flat sheet of a substance, such as metal or glass. **12.** a small piece of metal, plastic, etc. designed to bear an inscription and to be fixed to another surface. **13.** armour made of overlapping or articulated pieces of thin metal. **14.** *Photog.* a sheet of glass, or sometimes metal, coated with photographic emulsion on which an image can be formed by exposure to light. **15.** a device for straightening teeth. **16.** an informal word for **denture. 17.** *Anat.* any flat platelike structure. **18. a.** a cup awarded to the winner of a sporting contest, esp. a horse race. **b.** a race or contest for such a prize. **19.** any of the rigid layers of the earth's lithosphere. **20.** *Electronics. Chiefly U.S.* the anode in an electronic valve. **21.** a horizontal timber joist that supports rafters. **22.** a light horseshoe for flat racing. **23.** Also called: **Communion plate.** *R.C. Church.* a flat plate held under the chin of a communicant in order to catch any fragments of the consecrated Host. **24.** **on a plate.** acquired without trouble: *he was handed the job on a plate.* **25. on one's plate.** waiting to be done or dealt with. ~*vb.* (*tr.*) **26.** to coat (a metal) with a thin layer of other metal by electrolysis, etc. **27.** to cover with metal plates, as for protection. **28.** *Printing.* to make a stereotype or electrotype from (type or another plate). **29.** to form (metal) into plate, esp. by rolling.

plateau ('plætəʊ) *n., pl.* **-eaus** *or* **-eaux** (-əʊz). **1.** a wide mainly level area of elevated land. **2.** a relatively long period of stability; levelling off: *the rising prices reached a plateau.*

plated ('pleitid) *adj.* **a.** coated with a layer of metal. **b.** (*in combination*): *goldplated.*

plate glass *n.* glass formed into a thin sheet by rolling, used for windows, etc.

platelayer ('pleit₁leiə) *n. Brit.* a workman who lays and maintains railway track. U.S. equivalent: **trackman.**

platelet ('pleitlit) *n.* a minute particle occurring in the blood of vertebrates and involved in the clotting of the blood.

platen ('plætən) *n.* **1.** a flat plate in a printing press that presses the paper against the type. **2.** the roller on a typewriter, against which the keys strike.

platform ('plætfɔːm) *n.* **1.** a raised floor or other horizontal surface. **2.** a raised area at a railway station, from which passengers have access to the trains. **3.** See **drilling platform. 4.** the declared principles, aims, etc., of a political party. **5. a.** the thick raised sole of some shoes. **b.** (*as modifier*): *platform shoes.* **6.** a vehicle or level place on which weapons are mounted and fired.

platform ticket *n.* a ticket for admission to railway platforms but not for travel.

plating ('pleitiŋ) *n.* **1.** a coating or layer of material, esp. metal. **2.** a layer or covering of metal plates.

platinum ('plætɪnəm) *n.* a ductile malleable silvery-

THESAURUS

plaque badge, brooch, cartouche, medal, medallion, panel, plate, slab, tablet

plaster *n.* **1.** gypsum, mortar, plaster of Paris, stucco **2.** adhesive plaster, bandage, dressing, Elastoplast (*Trademark*), sticking plaster ~*v.* **3.** bedaub, besmear, coat, cover, daub, overlay, smear, spread

plastic *adj.* **1.** compliant, docile, easily influenced, impressionable, malleable, manageable, pliable, receptive, responsive, trac-

table **2.** ductile, fictile, flexible, mouldable, pliable, pliant, soft, supple **3.** *Sl.* artificial, false, meretricious, phoney (*Inf.*), pseudo (*Inf.*), sham, specious, spurious, superficial, synthetic

plate *n.* **1.** dish, platter, trencher (*Archaic*) **2.** course, dish, helping, portion, serving **3.** layer, panel, sheet, slab **4.** illustration, lithograph, print ~*v.* **5.** anodize, coat, cover, elec-

troplate, face, gild, laminate, nickel, overlay, platinize, silver

plateau 1. highland, mesa, table, tableland, upland **2.** level, levelling off, stability, stage

platform 1. dais, podium, rostrum, stage, stand **2.** manifesto, objective(s), party line, policy, principle, programme, tenet(s)

white metallic element, very resistant to heat and chemicals: used in jewellery, laboratory apparatus, electrical contacts, dentistry, electroplating, and as a catalyst. Symbol: Pt; atomic no.: 78; atomic wt.: 195.09.

platitude ('plætɪˌtjuːd) *n.* **1.** a trite, dull, or obvious remark. **2.** staleness or insipidity of thought or language; triteness. —ˌplati'tudinous *adj.*

Platonic (plə'tɒnɪk) *adj.* **1.** of or relating to Plato or his teachings. **2.** (*often not cap.*) free from physical desire: *Platonic love.* —Pla'tonically *adv.*

Platonism ('pleɪtəˌnɪzəm) *n.* **1.** the teachings of Plato, ?427–?347 B.C., Greek philosopher, and his followers. **2.** the philosophical theory that the meanings of general words are real entities (forms) and describe particular objects, etc., by virtue of some relationship of these to the form. —'Platonist *n.*

platoon (plə'tuːn) *n.* **1.** *Mil.* a subdivision of a company comprising one or more sections of an army formation. **2.** a group of people sharing a common activity, etc.

platteland ('plɑtəˌlɑnt) *n.* **the.** (in South Africa) the area outside the cities and chief towns.

platter ('plætə) *n.* a large shallow usually oval dish or plate.

platy- *combining form.* indicating something flat, as **platyhelminth**, the flatworm.

platypus ('plætɪpəs) *n., pl.* **-puses.** See **duck-billed platypus.**

plaudit ('plɔːdɪt) *n.* (*usually pl.*) **1.** an expression of enthusiastic approval. **2.** a round of applause.

plausible ('plɔːzəbəl) *adj.* **1.** apparently reasonable, valid, truthful, etc.: *a plausible excuse.* **2.** apparently trustworthy or believable: *a plausible speaker.* —ˌplausi'bility *or* 'plausibleness *n.* —'plausibly *adv.*

play (pleɪ) *vb.* **1.** to occupy oneself in (a sport or diversion). **2.** (*tr.*) to contend against (an opponent) in a sport or game: *Ed played Tony at chess and lost.* **3.** to fulfil or cause to fulfil (a particular role) in a team game: *he plays in the defence.* **4.** (*intr.*; often foll. by *about* or *around*) to behave carelessly, esp. in a way that is unconsciously cruel or hurtful: *to play about with a young girl's affections.* **5.** (when *intr.*; often foll. by *at*) to perform or act the part (of) in or as in a dramatic production. **6.** to perform (a dramatic production). **7. a.** to have the ability to perform on (a musical instrument): *David plays the harp.* **b.** to perform as specified: *he plays out of tune.* **8.** (*tr.*) **a.** to reproduce (a piece of music, note, etc.) on an instrument. **b.** to perform works by: *to play Brahms.* **9.** to discharge or cause to discharge: *he played the water from the hose onto the garden.* **10.** to cause (a radio, etc.) to emit sound. **11.** to move freely, quickly, or irregularly: *lights played on the scenery.* **12.** (*tr.*) *Stock Exchange.* to speculate or operate aggressively for gain in (a market). **13.** (*tr.*) *Angling.* to attempt to tire (a hooked fish) by alternately letting out and reeling in line. **14.** to put (a card, counter, piece, etc.) into play.

15. to gamble. **16. play fair** (*or* **false**). (often foll. by *with*) to prove oneself fair (or unfair) in one's dealings. **17. play by ear.** See **ear**[1]. **18. play for time.** to delay the outcome of some activity so as to gain time to one's own advantage. **19. play into the hands of.** to act directly to the advantage of (an opponent). **20. play the game.** to act in accordance with acknowledged principles. ~*n.* **21.** a dramatic composition written for performance by actors on a stage, etc.; drama. **22.** the performance of a dramatic composition. **23. a.** games, exercise, or other activity undertaken for pleasure, esp. by children. **b.** (*in combination*): *playroom.* **c.** (*as modifier*): *a play group.* **24.** conduct: *fair play.* **25.** the playing of a game or the period during which a game is in progress: *rain stopped play.* **26.** *U.S.* a manoeuvre in a game: *a brilliant play.* **27.** the situation of a ball, etc., that is within the declared area and being played according to the rules (in **in play**, **out of play**). **28.** gambling. **29.** activity or operation: *the play of the imagination.* **30.** freedom of movement: *too much play in the rope.* **31.** light, free, or rapidly shifting motion: *the play of light on the water.* **32.** fun, jest, or joking: *I only did it in play.* **33. make a play for.** *Inf.* to make an obvious attempt to gain. ~See **play along**, **playback**, etc. —'playable *adj.*

play along *vb.* (*adv.*) **1.** (*intr.*; usually foll. by *with*) to cooperate (with), esp. as a temporary measure. **2.** (*tr.*) to manipulate as if in a game, esp. for one's own advantage: *he played the widow along until she gave him her money.*

playback ('pleɪˌbæk) *n.* **1.** the act or process of reproducing a recording, esp. on magnetic tape. **2.** the part of a tape recorder serving to or used for reproducing recorded material. ~*vb.* **play back.** (*adv.*) **3.** to reproduce (recorded material) on (a magnetic tape) by means of a tape recorder.

playbill ('pleɪˌbɪl) *n.* **1.** a poster or bill advertising a play. **2.** the programme of a play.

playboy ('pleɪˌbɔɪ) *n.* a man, esp. one of private means, who devotes himself to the pleasures of nightclubs, female company, etc.

play down *vb.* (*tr., adv.*) to make little or light of; minimize the importance of.

player ('pleɪə) *n.* **1.** a person who participates in or is skilled at some game or sport. **2.** a person who plays a game or sport professionally. **3.** a person who plays a musical instrument. **4.** an actor.

player piano *n.* a mechanical piano; Pianola.

playful ('pleɪful) *adj.* **1.** full of high spirits and fun: *a playful kitten.* **2.** good-natured and humorous: *a playful remark.* —'playfully *adv.*

playgoer ('pleɪˌgəʊə) *n.* a person who goes to theatre performances, esp. frequently.

playground ('pleɪˌgraʊnd) *n.* **1.** an outdoor area for children's play, esp. one having swings, slides, etc., or ad-

<hr>

THESAURUS

platitude **1.** banality, bromide, cliché, commonplace, hackneyed saying, inanity, stereotype, trite remark, truism **2.** banality, dullness, inanity, insipidity, triteness, triviality, vapidity, verbiage

platitudinous banal, clichéd, commonplace, corny (*Sl.*), hack, hackneyed, overworked, set, stale, stereotyped, stock, tired, trite, truistic, vapid, well-worn

platoon company, group, outfit (*Inf.*), patrol, squad, squadron, team

platter charger, dish, plate, salver, tray, trencher (*Archaic*)

plaudit *Usually plural* acclaim, acclamation, applause, approbation, approval, clapping, commendation, congratulation, hand, kudos, ovation, praise, round of applause

plausible believable, colourable, conceivable, credible, fair-spoken, glib, likely, persuasive, possible, probable, reasonable, smooth, smooth-talking, smooth-tongued, specious, tenable

play *v.* **1.** amuse oneself, caper, engage in games, entertain oneself, frisk, frolic, gambol, have fun, revel, romp, sport, trifle **2.** be in a team, challenge, compete, contend against, participate, rival, take on, take part,

vie with **3.** act, act the part of, execute, impersonate, perform, personate, portray, represent, take the part of **4.** bet, chance, gamble, hazard, punt (*Brit.*), risk, speculate, take, wager **5. play ball** *Inf.* collaborate, cooperate, go along, play along, reciprocate, respond, show willing **6. play by ear** ad lib, extemporize, improvise, rise to the occasion, take it as it comes **7. play for time** delay, drag one's feet (*Inf.*), filibuster, hang fire, procrastinate, stall, temporize **8. play the fool** act the goat (*Inf.*), clown, clown around, horse around (*Inf.*), lark (about) (*Inf.*), mess about, monkey around, skylark (*Inf.*) **9. play the game** *Inf.* conform, follow the rules, go along with, keep in step, play by the rules, play fair, toe the line ~*n.* **10.** comedy, drama, dramatic piece, entertainment, farce, masque, performance, piece, radio play, show, stage show, television drama, tragedy **11.** amusement, caper, diversion, entertainment, frolic, fun, gambol, game, jest, pastime, prank, recreation, romp, sport **12.** gambling, gaming **13.** action, activity, elbowroom, exercise, give (*Inf.*), latitude, leeway, margin, motion, movement, operation, range, room, scope, space, sweep, swing **14.** action, activity, employment, function, op-

eration, transaction, working **15.** foolery, fun, humour, jest, joking, lark (*Inf.*), prank, sport, teasing

play around dally, fool around, mess around, philander, take lightly, trifle, womanize

playboy gay dog, ladies' man, lady-killer (*Inf.*), lover boy (*Sl.*), man about town, philanderer, pleasure seeker, rake, roué, socialite, womanizer

play down gloss over, make light of, make little of, minimize, set no store by, softpedal (*Inf.*), underplay, underrate

player **1.** competitor, contestant, participant, sportsman, sportswoman, team member **2.** actor, actress, entertainer, performer, Thespian, trouper **3.** artist, instrumentalist, musician, music maker, performer, virtuoso

playful **1.** cheerful, coltish, frisky, frolicsome, gay, impish, joyous, kittenish, larkish (*Inf.*), lively, merry, mischievous, puckish, rollicking, spirited, sportive, sprightly, vivacious **2.** arch, coy, flirtatious, good-natured, humorous, jesting, jokey, joking, roguish, teasing, tongue-in-cheek, waggish

joining a school. **2.** a place popular as a sports or holiday resort.

playgroup ('pleɪˌgruːp) *n.* another name for **playschool.**

playhouse ('pleɪˌhaʊs) *n.* **1.** a theatre. **2.** *U.S.* a small house for children to play in.

playing field *n. Chiefly Brit.* a field or open space used for sport.

playmate ('pleɪˌmeɪt) *or* **playfellow** *n.* a friend or partner in play or recreation.

play off *vb.* (*adv.; usually foll. by against*) to manipulate as if in playing a game: *to play one person off against another.* **2.** (*intr.*) to take part in a play-off. ~*n.* **play-off.** **3.** *Sport.* an extra contest to decide the winner when competitors are tied. **4.** *Chiefly U.S.* a contest or series of games to determine a championship.

play on *vb.* (*intr.*) **1.** (*adv.*) to continue to play. **2.** (*prep.*) Also: **play upon.** to exploit or impose upon (the feelings or weakness of another).

play on words *n.* another term for **pun.**

playpen ('pleɪˌpɛn) *n.* a small enclosure, usually portable, in which a young child can be left to play in safety.

playschool ('pleɪˌskuːl) *n.* an informal nursery group for preschool children. Also called: **playgroup.**

plaything ('pleɪˌθɪŋ) *n.* **1.** a toy. **2.** a person regarded or treated as a toy.

playtime ('pleɪˌtaɪm) *n.* a time for play or recreation, esp. the school break.

play up *vb.* (*adv.*) **1.** (*tr.*) to highlight: *to play up one's best features.* **2.** *Brit. inf.* to behave irritatingly (towards). **3.** (*intr.*) *Brit. inf.* (of a machine, etc.) to function erratically: *the car is playing up again.* **4. play up to. a.** to support (another actor) in a performance. **b.** *Inf.* to try to gain favour with, by flattery.

playwright ('pleɪˌraɪt) *n.* a person who writes plays.

plaza ('plɑːzə) *n.* **1.** an open space or square, esp. in Spain. **2.** *Chiefly U.S.* a modern complex of shops, buildings, and parking areas.

PLC *abbrev. for* Public Limited Company.

plea (pliː) *n.* **1.** an earnest entreaty or request. **2. a.** *Law.* something alleged by or on behalf of a party to legal proceedings in support of his claim or defence. **b.** *Criminal law.* the answer made by an accused to the charge: *a plea of guilty.* **c.** (formerly in England) a suit or action at law.

plead (pliːd) *vb.* **pleading, pleaded, plead** (plɛd), *or* **pled.** **1.** (when *intr.,* often foll. by *with*) to appeal earnestly or humbly (to). **2.** (*tr.; may take a clause as object*) to give as an excuse: *to plead ignorance.* **3.** *Law.* to declare oneself to be (guilty or not guilty) in answer to the charge. **4.** *Law.* to advocate (a case) in a court of law. **5.** (*intr.*) *Law.* **a.** to file pleadings. **b.** to address a court as an advocate. —'**pleadable** *adj.* —'**pleader** *n.*

pleadings ('pliːdɪŋz) *pl. n. Law.* the formal written statements presented alternately by the plaintiff and defendant in a lawsuit.

pleasant ('plɛzənt) *adj.* **1.** giving or affording pleasure; enjoyable. **2.** having pleasing or agreeable manners, appearance, habits, etc. **3.** *Obs.* merry and lively. —'**pleasantly** *adv.*

pleasantry ('plɛzəntrɪ) *n., pl.* **-ries. 1.** (*often pl.*) an agreeable or amusing remark, etc., often one made in order to be polite: *they exchanged pleasantries.* **2.** an agreeably humorous manner or style.

please (pliːz) *vb.* **1.** to give satisfaction, pleasure, or contentment to (a person). **2.** to be the will of or have the will (to): *if it pleases you; the court pleases.* **3. if you please.** if you will or wish, sometimes used in ironic exclamation. **4. pleased with.** happy because of. **5. please oneself.** to do as one likes. ~*adv.* **6.** (*sentence modifier*) used in making polite requests, pleading, etc. **7. yes please.** a polite formula for accepting an offer, invitation, etc. —'**pleasedly** ('pliːzɪdlɪ) *adv.*

pleasing ('pliːzɪŋ) *adj.* giving pleasure; likeable or gratifying. —'**pleasingly** *adv.*

pleasurable ('plɛʒərəbəl) *adj.* enjoyable, agreeable, or gratifying. —'**pleasurably** *adv.*

pleasure ('plɛʒə) *n.* **1.** an agreeable or enjoyable sensation or emotion: *the pleasure of hearing good music.* **2.** something that gives enjoyment: *his garden was his only pleasure.* **3. a.** amusement, recreation, or enjoyment. **b.** (*as modifier*): *a pleasure ground.* **4.** *Euphemistic.* sexual gratification: *he took his pleasure of her.* **5.** a person's preference. ~*vb.* **6.** (when *intr.,* often foll. by *in*) *Arch.* to give pleasure to or take pleasure (in).

pleat (pliːt) *n.* **1.** any of various types of fold formed by doubling back fabric, etc., and pressing, stitching, or steaming into place. ~*vb.* **2.** (*tr.*) to arrange (material, part of a garment, etc.) in pleats.

pleb (plɛb) *n.* **1.** short for **plebeian. 2.** *Brit. sl.* a common vulgar person.

plebeian (plə'biːən) *adj.* **1.** of or characteristic of the common people, esp. those of ancient Rome. **2.** lacking refinement; philistine or vulgar: *plebeian tastes.* ~*n.* **3.** one of the common people, esp. one of the Roman plebs. **4.** a person who is coarse, vulgar, etc. —**ple'beianism** *n.*

plebiscite ('plɛbɪˌsaɪt, -sɪt) *n.* **1.** a direct vote by the electorate of a state, region, etc., on some question of usually national importance. **2.** any expression of public opinion on some matter. ~See also **referendum.** —**plebiscitary** (plə'bɪsɪtərɪ) *adj.*

plectrum ('plɛktrəm) *or* **plectron** ('plɛktrən) *n., pl.* **-tra** (-trə), **-trums** *or* **-tra, -trons.** any implement for plucking a string, such as a small piece of plastic, wood, etc., used to strum a guitar.

pled (plɛd) *vb. U.S. or* (*esp. in legal usage*) *Scot.* a past tense or past participle of **plead.**

pledge (plɛdʒ) *n.* **1.** a formal or solemn promise or agreement. **2. a.** collateral for the payment of a debt or the performance of an obligation. **b.** the condition of being collateral (esp. in **in pledge**). **3.** a token: *the gift is a pledge of their sincerity.* **4.** an assurance of support or

---

THESAURUS

playmate chum (*Inf.*), companion, comrade, friend, neighbour, pal (*Inf.*), playfellow

play on *or* **upon** abuse, capitalize on, exploit, impose on, milk, profit by, take advantage of, trade on, turn to account, utilize

plaything amusement, bauble, game, gewgaw, gimcrack, pastime, toy, trifle, trinket

play up 1. accentuate, bring to the fore, call attention to, emphasize, highlight, magnify, point up, stress, turn the spotlight on, underline **2.** *Brit. inf.* be painful, be sore, bother, give one gyp (*Brit. sl.*), give one trouble, hurt, pain, trouble **3.** *Brit. inf.* be awkward, be bolshie (*Brit. inf.*), be cussed (*Inf.*), be disobedient, be stroppy (*Brit. sl.*), give trouble, misbehave **4.** *Brit. inf.* be on the blink (*Sl.*), be wonky (*Brit. sl.*), malfunction, not work properly **5. play up to** *Inf.* bootlick (*Inf.*), butter up, curry favour, fawn, flatter, get in with, ingratiate oneself, suck up to (*Inf.*), toady

play with 1. amuse oneself with, flirt with, string along, toy with, trifle with **2.** fiddle with, fidget with, fool around, interfere with, jiggle, mess about, waggle, wiggle

playwright dramatist, dramaturge, dramaturgist

plea 1. appeal, begging, entreaty, intercession, overture, petition, prayer, request, suit, supplication **2.** *Law* action, allegation, cause, suit **3.** apology, claim, defence, excuse, explanation, extenuation, justification, pretext, vindication

plead 1. appeal (to), ask, beg, beseech, crave, entreat, implore, importune, petition, request, solicit, supplicate **2.** adduce, allege, argue, assert, maintain, put forward, use as an excuse

pleasant 1. acceptable, agreeable, amusing, delectable, delightful, enjoyable, fine, gratifying, lovely, nice, pleasing, pleasurable, refreshing, satisfying, welcome **2.** affable, agreeable, amiable, charming, cheerful, cheery, congenial, engaging, friendly, genial, good-humoured, likeable, nice

pleasantry badinage, banter, bon mot, good-natured remark, jest, joke, quip, sally, witticism

please 1. amuse, charm, cheer, content, delight, entertain, give pleasure to, gladden, gratify, humour, indulge, rejoice, satisfy, suit,

tickle, tickle pink **2.** be inclined, choose, desire, like, opt, prefer, see fit, want, will, wish

pleased chuffed (*Brit. sl.*), contented, delighted, euphoric, glad, gratified, happy, in high spirits, over the moon (*Inf.*), pleased as punch (*Inf.*), satisfied, thrilled, tickled, tickled pink

pleasing agreeable, amiable, amusing, attractive, charming, delightful, engaging, enjoyable, entertaining, gratifying, likable, pleasurable, polite, satisfying, winning

pleasure 1. amusement, bliss, comfort, contentment, delectation, delight, diversion, ease, enjoyment, gladness, gratification, happiness, joy, recreation, satisfaction, solace **2.** choice, command, desire, inclination, mind, option, preference, purpose, will, wish

plebeian 1. *adj.* base, coarse, common, ignoble, low, lowborn, lower-class, mean, non-U (*Brit. inf.*), proletarian, uncultivated, unrefined, vulgar, working-class **2.** *n.* commoner, common man, man in the street, peasant, pleb (*Brit. sl.*), prole (*Sl.*), proletarian

goodwill, conveyed by drinking a toast: *we drank a pledge to their success.* **5.** a person who binds himself, as by becoming bail or surety for another. **6. take** *or* **sign the pledge.** to make a vow to abstain from alcoholic drink. ~*vb.* **7.** to promise formally or solemnly. **8.** (*tr.*) to bind by or as if by a pledge: *they were pledged to secrecy.* **9.** to give or offer (one's word, freedom, property, etc.) as a guarantee, as for the repayment of a loan. **10.** to drink a toast to (a person, cause, etc.). —'**pledgable** *adj.* —'**pledger** *or* '**pledgor** *n.*

-plegia *n. combining form.* indicating a specified type of paralysis: *paraplegia.* —**plegic** *adj. and n. combining form.*

Pleiocene ('plaiəu,si:n) *adj., n.* a variant spelling of **Pliocene.**

Pleistocene ('plaistə,si:n) *adj.* **1.** of, denoting, or formed in the first epoch of the Quaternary period. It was characterized by extensive glaciations of the N hemisphere and the evolutionary development of man. ~*n.* **2. the Pleistocene.** the Pleistocene epoch or rock series.

plenary ('pli:nəri, 'plɛn-) *adj.* **1.** full, unqualified, or complete: *plenary powers; plenary indulgence.* **2.** (of assemblies, councils, etc.) attended by all the members. —'**plenarily** *adv.*

plenipotentiary (,plɛnipə'tɛnʃəri) *adj.* **1.** (esp. of a diplomatic envoy) invested with or possessing full authority. **2.** conferring full authority. **3.** (of power or authority) full; absolute. ~*n., pl.* **-aries.** **4.** a person invested with full authority to transact business, esp. a diplomat authorized to represent a country. See also **envoy**[1] (sense 1).

plenitude ('plɛni,tju:d) *n.* **1.** abundance. **2.** the condition of being full or complete.

plenteous ('plɛntiəs) *adj.* **1.** ample; abundant: *a plenteous supply of food.* **2.** producing or yielding abundantly: *a plenteous grape harvest.* —'**plenteously** *adv.* —'**plenteousness** *n.*

plentiful ('plɛntiful) *adj.* **1.** ample; abundant. **2.** having or yielding an abundance: *a plentiful year.* —'**plentifully** *adv.* —'**plentifulness** *n.*

plenty ('plɛnti) *n., pl.* **-ties.** **1.** (often foll. by *of*) a great number, amount, or quantity; lots: *plenty of time; there are plenty of cars on display here.* **2.** ample supplies or resources: *the age of plenty.* **3. in plenty.** existing in abundance: *food in plenty.* ~*determiner.* **4. a.** very many; ample: *plenty of people believe in ghosts.* **b.** (as pronoun): *that's plenty, thanks.* ~*adv.* **5.** *Inf.* fully or abundantly: *the coat was plenty big enough.*

plenum ('pli:nəm) *n., pl.* **-nums** *or* **-na** (-nə). **1.** an enclosure containing gas at a higher pressure than the surrounding environment. **2.** a fully attended meeting. **3.** (esp. in the philosophy of the Stoics) space regarded as filled with matter.

pleonasm ('pli:ə,næzəm) *n. Rhetoric.* **1.** the use of more words than necessary or an instance of this, such as *a tiny little child.* **2.** a word or phrase that is superfluous. —,**pleo'nastic** *adj.*

plethora ('plɛθərə) *n.* **1.** superfluity or excess; over-abundance. **2.** *Pathol., obs.* a condition caused by dilation of superficial blood vessels, characterized esp. by a reddish face. —**plethoric** (plɛ'θɒrik) *adj.*

pleura ('pluərə) *n., pl.* **pleurae** ('pluəri:). the thin transparent membrane enveloping the lungs and lining the walls of the thoracic cavity. —'**pleural** *adj.*

pleurisy ('pluərisi) *n.* inflammation of the pleura, characterized by pain that is aggravated by deep breathing or coughing. —**pleuritic** (plu'ritik) *adj., n.*

pleuro- *or before a vowel* **pleur-** *combining form.* **1.** of or relating to the side. **2.** indicating the pleura.

plexus ('plɛksəs) *n., pl.* **-uses** *or* **-us.** **1.** any complex network of nerves, blood vessels, or lymphatic vessels. **2.** an intricate network or arrangement.

pliable ('plaiəb'l) *adj.* easily moulded, bent, influenced, or altered. —,**plia'bility** *or* '**pliableness** *n.* —'**pliably** *adv.*

pliant ('plaiənt) *adj.* **1.** easily bent; supple: *a pliant young tree.* **2.** adaptable; yielding readily to influence; compliant. —'**pliancy** *n.* —'**pliantly** *adv.*

pliers ('plaiəz) *pl. n.* a gripping tool consisting of two hinged arms usually with serrated jaws.

plight[1] (plait) *n.* a condition of extreme hardship, danger, etc.

plight[2] (plait) *vb.* (*tr.*) **1.** to promise formally or pledge (allegiance, support, etc.). **2. plight one's troth.** to make a promise, esp. of marriage. ~*n.* **3.** *Arch. or Brit. dialect.* a solemn promise, esp. of engagement; pledge. —'**plighter** *n.*

plimsoll *or* **plimsole** ('plimsəl) *n. Brit.* a light rubber-soled canvas shoe worn for various sports. Also called: **gym shoe.**

Plimsoll line ('plimsəl) *n.* a line on the outside of merchant ships, showing the water level to which they may be legally loaded.

plinth (plinθ) *n.* **1.** the rectangular slab or block that forms the lowest part of the base of a column, pedestal, or pier. **2.** Also called: **plinth course.** the lowest part of the wall of a building, esp. one that is formed of a course of stone or brick. **3.** a flat block on either side of a door frame, where the architrave meets the skirting.

Pliocene *or* **Pleiocene** ('plaiəu,si:n) *adj.* **1.** of, denoting, or formed in the last epoch of the Tertiary period, during which many modern mammals appeared. ~*n.* **2. the Pliocene.** the Pliocene epoch or rock series.

plissé ('pli:sei, 'plis-) *n.* **1.** fabric with a wrinkled finish, achieved by treatment involving caustic soda: *cotton plissé.* **2.** such a finish on a fabric.

P.L.O. *abbrev. for* Palestine Liberation Organization.

plod (plɒd) *vb.* **plodding, plodded.** **1.** to make (one's way) or walk along (a path, etc.) with heavy usually slow steps. **2.** (*intr.*) to work slowly and perseveringly. ~*n.* **3.** the act of plodding. —'**plodder** *n.* —'**ploddingly** *adv.*

-ploid *adj. and n. combining form.* indicating a specific multiple of a single set of chromosomes: *diploid.* —**ploidy** *n. combining form.*

plonk[1] (plɒŋk) *vb.* **1.** (often foll. by *down*) to drop or be dropped heavily: *he plonked the money on the table.* ~*n.* **2.** the act or sound of plonking.

plonk[2] (plɒŋk) *n. Inf.* alcoholic drink, usually wine, esp. of inferior quality.

plop (plɒp) *n.* **1.** the characteristic sound made by an object dropping into water without a splash. ~*vb.* **plopping, plopped.** **2.** to fall or cause to fall with the sound of a plop: *the stone plopped into the water.* ~*interj.* **3.** an exclamation imitative of this sound: *to go plop.*

plosive ('pləusiv) *Phonetics.* ~*adj.* **1.** accompanied by plosion. ~*n.* **2.** a plosive consonant; stop.

plot[1] (plɒt) *n.* **1.** a secret plan to achieve some purpose, esp. one that is illegal or underhand. **2.** the story or plan

---

THESAURUS

pledge *n.* **1.** assurance, covenant, oath, promise, undertaking, vow, warrant, word, word of honour **2.** bail, bond, collateral, deposit, earnest, gage, guarantee, pawn, security, surety **3.** health, toast ~*v.* **4.** contract, engage, give one's oath (word, word of honour), promise, swear, undertake, vouch, vow **5.** bind, engage, gage (*Archaic*), guarantee, mortgage, plight **6.** drink the health of, drink to, toast

plenteous **1.** abundant, ample, bounteous (*Literary*), bountiful, copious, generous, inexhaustible, infinite, lavish, liberal, overflowing, plentiful, profuse **2.** bumper, fertile, fruitful, luxuriant, plentiful, productive, prolific

plentiful **1.** abundant, ample, bounteous (*Literary*), bountiful, complete, copious, generous, inexhaustible, infinite, lavish, liberal,

overflowing, plenteous, profuse **2.** bumper, fertile, fruitful, luxuriant, plenteous, productive, prolific

plenty **1.** abundance, enough, fund, good deal, great deal, heap(s) (*Inf.*), lots (*Inf.*), mass, masses, mine, mountain(s), oodles (*Inf.*), pile(s) (*Inf.*), plethora, quantities, quantity, stack(s), store, sufficiency, volume **2.** abundance, affluence, copiousness, fertility, fruitfulness, luxury, opulence, plenitude, plenteousness, plentifulness, profusion, prosperity, wealth

plethora excess, glut, overabundance, profusion, superabundance, superfluity, surfeit, surplus

pliable **1.** bendable, bendy, ductile, flexible, limber, lithe, malleable, plastic, pliant, supple **2.** adaptable, compliant, docile, easily

led, impressionable, influenceable, manageable, persuadable, pliant, receptive, responsive, susceptible, tractable, yielding

pliant **1.** bendable, bendy, ductile, flexible, lithe, plastic, pliable, supple **2.** adaptable, biddable, compliant, easily led, impressionable, influenceable, manageable, persuadable, pliable, susceptible, tractable, yielding

plight *n.* case, circumstances, condition, difficulty, dilemma, extremity, hole (*Sl.*), jam (*Inf.*), perplexity, pickle (*Inf.*), predicament, scrape (*Inf.*), situation, spot (*Inf.*), state, straits, trouble

plod **1.** clump, drag, lumber, slog, stomp (*Inf.*), tramp, tread, trudge **2.** drudge, grind (*Inf.*), grub, labour, peg away, persevere, plough through, plug away (*Inf.*), slog, soldier on, toil

of a play, novel, etc. **3.** *Mil.* a graphic representation of an individual or tactical setting that pinpoints an artillery target. **4.** *Chiefly U.S.* a diagram or plan. ~*vb.* **plotting, plotted. 5.** to plan secretly (something illegal, revolutionary, etc.); conspire. **6.** (*tr.*) to mark (a course, as of a ship or aircraft) on a map. **7.** (*tr.*) to make a plan or map of. **8. a.** to locate and mark (points) on a graph by means of coordinates. **b.** to draw (a curve) through these points. **9.** (*tr.*) to construct the plot of (a literary work, etc.). —'**plotter** *n.*

plot² (plɒt) *n.* a small piece of land: *a vegetable plot.*

plough *or esp. U.S.* **plow** (plaʊ) *n.* **1.** an agricultural implement with sharp-blades for cutting or turning over the earth. **2.** any of various similar implements, such as a device for clearing snow. **3.** ploughed land. **4. put one's hand to the plough.** to perform a task. ~*vb.* **5.** to till (the soil, etc.) with a plough. **6.** to make (furrows or grooves) in (something) with or as if with a plough. **7.** (when *intr.*, usually foll. by *through*) to move (through something) in the manner of a plough. **8.** (*intr.*; foll. by *through*) to work at slowly or perseveringly. **9.** (*intr.*) *Brit. sl.* to fail an examination. —'**plougher** *or esp. U.S.* '**plower** *n.*

Plough *or esp. U.S.* **Plow** (plaʊ) *n.* **the.** the group of the seven brightest stars in the constellation Ursa Major. Also called: **Charles's Wain.** Usual U.S. name: the **Big Dipper.**

ploughman *or esp. U.S.* **plowman** ('plaʊmən) *n., pl.* **-men.** a man who ploughs, esp. using horses.

ploughshare *or esp. U.S.* **plowshare** ('plaʊˌʃɛə) *n.* the horizontal pointed cutting blade of a mouldboard plough.

plover ('plʌvə) *n.* **1.** any of a family of shore birds, typically having a round head, straight bill, and large pointed wings. **2. green plover.** another name for **lapwing.**

plow (plaʊ) *n., vb.* the usual U.S. spelling of **plough.** —'**plower** *n.*

ploy (plɔɪ) *n.* **1.** a manoeuvre or tactic in a game, conversation, etc. **2.** any business, job, hobby, etc., with which one is occupied: *angling is his latest ploy.* **3.** *Chiefly Brit.* a frolic, escapade, or practical joke.

P.L.P. (in Britain) *abbrev. for* Parliamentary Labour Party.

P.L.R. *abbrev. for* Public Lending Right.

pluck (plʌk) *vb.* **1.** (*tr.*) to pull off (feathers, fruit, etc.) from (a fowl, tree, etc.). **2.** (when *intr.*, foll. by *at*) to pull or tug. **3.** (*tr.*; foll. by *off, away,* etc.) *Arch.* to pull (something) forcibly or violently (from something or someone). **4.** (*tr.*) to sound (the strings) of (a musical instrument) with the fingers, a plectrum, etc. **5.** (*tr.*) *Sl.* to fleece or swindle. ~*n.* **6.** courage, usually in the face of difficulties or hardship. **7.** a sudden pull or tug. **8.** the heart, liver, and lungs, esp. of an animal used for food. —'**plucker** *n.*

pluck up *vb.* (*tr., adv.*) **1.** to pull out; uproot. **2.** to muster (courage, one's spirits, etc.).

plucky ('plʌkɪ) *adj.* **pluckier, pluckiest.** having or showing courage in the face of difficulties, danger, etc. —'**pluckily** *adv.* —'**pluckiness** *n.*

plug (plʌg) *n.* **1.** a piece of wood, cork, or other material, used to stop up holes or waste pipes or as a wedge for taking a screw or nail. **2.** a device usually having three pins to which the terminals of a flex are attached: used to make an electrical connection when inserted into a socket. **3.** Also called: **volcanic plug.** a mass of solidified magma filling the neck of an extinct volcano. **4.** See **sparking plug. 5. a.** a cake of pressed or twisted tobacco, esp. for chewing. **b.** a small piece of such a cake. **6.** *Inf.* a favourable mention of a product, show, etc., as on television. ~*vb.* **plugging, plugged. 7.** (*tr.*) to stop up or secure (a hole, gap, etc.) with or as if with a plug. **8.** (*tr.*) to insert or use (something) as a plug: *to plug a finger into one's ear.* **9.** (*tr.*) *Inf.* to make favourable and often-repeated mentions of (a song, product, show, etc.), as on television. **10.** (*tr.*) *Sl.* to shoot: *he plugged six rabbits.* **11.** (*tr.*) *Sl.* to punch. **12.** (*intr.*; foll. by *along, away,* etc.) *Inf.* to work steadily or persistently. —'**plugger** *n.*

plug in *vb.* (*tr., adv.*) to connect (an electrical appliance, etc.) with a power source by means of an electrical plug.

plum (plʌm) *n.* **1.** a small rosaceous tree with an edible oval fruit that is purple, yellow, or green and contains an oval stone. **2.** the fruit of this tree. **3.** a raisin, as used in a cake or pudding. **4.** a dark reddish-purple colour. **5.** *Inf.* **a.** something of a superior or desirable kind, such as a financial bonus. **b.** (*as modifier*): *a plum job.* —'**plum-ˌlike** *adj.*

plumage ('pluːmɪdʒ) *n.* the layer of feathers covering the body of a bird.

plumb (plʌm) *n.* **1.** a weight, usually of lead, suspended at the end of a line and used to determine water depth or verticality. **2.** the perpendicular position of a freely suspended plumb line (esp. in **out of plumb, off plumb**). ~*adv. also* **plum. 3.** vertical or perpendicular. **4.** *Inf., chiefly U.S.* (intensifier): *plumb idiotic.* **5.** *Inf.* exactly; precisely. ~*vb.* **6.** (*tr.*; often foll. by *up*) to test the alignment of or adjust to the vertical with a plumb line. **7.** (*tr.*) to experience (the worst extremes of): *to plumb the depths of despair.* **8.** (*tr.*) to understand or master (something obscure): *to plumb a mystery.* **9.** to connect or join (a device, such as a tap, etc.) to a waterpipe or drainage system. —'**plumbable** *adj.*

plumber ('plʌmə) *n.* a person who installs and repairs pipes, fixtures, etc., for water, drainage, and gas.

plumbing ('plʌmɪŋ) *n.* **1.** the trade or work of a plumber. **2.** the pipes, fixtures, etc., used in a water, drainage, or gas installation. **3.** the act or procedure of using a plumb.

plumb line *n.* a string with a metal weight, or **plumb bob,** at one end that, when suspended, points directly towards the earth's centre of gravity and so is used to determine verticality, depth, etc.

plume (pluːm) *n.* **1.** a feather, esp. one that is large or ornamental. **2.** a feather or cluster of feathers worn esp. formerly as a badge or ornament in a headband, hat, etc. **3.** *Biol.* any feathery part. **4.** something that resembles a plume: *a plume of smoke.* **5.** a token or decoration of honour; prize. ~*vb.* (*tr.*) **6.** to adorn with feathers or plumes. **7.** (of a bird) to clean or preen (itself or its feathers). **8.** (foll. by *on* or *upon*) to pride or congratulate (oneself). —'**plume-ˌlike** *adj.*

plummet ('plʌmɪt) *vb.* **1.** (*intr.*) to drop down; plunge. ~*n.* **2.** the weight on a plumb line; plumb bob. **3.** a lead plumb used by anglers.

plummy ('plʌmɪ) *adj.* **-mier, -miest. 1.** of, full of, or resembling plums. **2.** *Brit. inf.* (of speech) deep, refined, and somewhat drawling. **3.** *Brit. inf.* choice; desirable.

plump¹ (plʌmp) *adj.* **1.** well filled out or rounded; chub-

plot¹ *n.* **1.** cabal, conspiracy, covin (*Law*), intrigue, machination, plan, scheme, stratagem **2.** action, narrative, outline, scenario, story, story line, subject, theme, thread ~*v.* **3.** cabal, collude, conspire, contrive, hatch, intrigue, machinate, manoeuvre, plan, scheme **4.** calculate, chart, compute, draft, draw, locate, map, mark, outline **5.** brew, conceive, concoct, contrive, cook up (*Inf.*), design, devise, frame, hatch, imagine, lay, project

plot² *n.* allotment, area, ground, lot, parcel, patch, tract

plough *v.* **1.** break ground, cultivate, dig, furrow, ridge, till, turn over **2.** *Usually with* **through** cut, drive, flounder, forge, plod, plunge, press, push, stagger, surge, wade **3.** *With* **into** bulldoze, career, crash, hurtle, plunge, shove, smash

pluck¹ *n.* backbone, boldness, bottle (*Brit. sl.*), bravery, courage, determination, grit, guts (*Inf.*), hardihood, heart, intrepidity, mettle, nerve, resolution, spirit, spunk (*Inf.*)

pluck² *v.* **1.** collect, draw, gather, harvest, pick, pull out or off **2.** catch, clutch, jerk, pull at, snatch, tug, tweak, yank **3.** finger, pick, plunk, strum, thrum, twang

plucky bold, brave, courageous, daring, doughty, game, gritty, gutsy (*Sl.*), hardy, heroic, intrepid, mettlesome, spirited, spunky (*Inf.*), undaunted, unflinching, valiant

plug *n.* **1.** bung, cork, spigot, stopper, stopple **2.** cake, chew, pigtail, quid, twist, wad **3.** *Inf.* advert (*Brit. inf.*), advertisement, good word, hype (*Sl.*), mention, publicity, puff, push ~*v.* **4.** block, bung, choke, close, cork, cover, fill, pack, seal, stop, stopper, stopple, stop up, stuff **5.** *Inf.* advertise, build up, hype

(*Sl.*), mention, promote, publicize, puff, push, write up **6.** *Sl.* gun down, pick off, pop, pot, put a bullet in, shoot **7.** *With* **along** *or* **away** *Inf.* drudge, grind (*Inf.*), labour, peg away, plod, slog, toil

plum *Fig.* **1.** *n.* bonus, cream, find, pick, prize, treasure **2.** *adj.* best, choice, first-class, prize

plumb *n.* **1.** lead, plumb bob, plummet, weight ~*adv.* **2.** perpendicularly, up and down, vertically **3.** bang, exactly, precisely, slap, spot-on (*Brit. inf.*) ~*v.* **4.** delve, explore, fathom, gauge, go into, measure, penetrate, probe, search, sound, unravel

plume **1.** *n.* aigrette, crest, feather, pinion, quill **2.** *v. With* **on** *or* **upon** congratulate oneself, pat oneself on the back, pique oneself, preen oneself, pride oneself

by: *a plump turkey.* **2.** bulging; full: *a plump wallet.*
~*vb.* **3.** (often foll. by *up* or *out*) to make or become
plump: *to plump up a pillow.* —'**plumply** *adv.*
—'**plumpness** *n.*

plump² (plʌmp) *vb.* **1.** (often foll. by *down, into,* etc.) to
drop or fall suddenly and heavily. **2.** (*intr.;* foll. by *for*)
to give support (to) or make a choice (of) one out of a
group or number. ~*n.* **3.** a heavy abrupt fall or the
sound of this. ~*adv.* **4.** suddenly or heavily. **5.** straight
down; directly: *the helicopter landed plump in the middle of the field.* ~*adj., adv.* **6.** in a blunt, direct, or decisive manner.

plum pudding *n. Brit.* a boiled or steamed pudding
made with flour, suet, sugar, and dried fruit.

plumy ('plu:mɪ) *adj.* **plumier, plumiest.** **1.** plumelike;
feathery. **2.** consisting of, covered, or adorned with
feathers.

plunder ('plʌndə) *vb.* **1.** to steal (valuables, goods, sacred items, etc.) from (a town, church, etc.) by force,
esp. in time of war; loot. **2.** (*tr.*) to rob or steal (choice
or desirable things) from (a place): *to plunder an orchard.* ~*n.* **3.** anything taken by plundering; booty. **4.**
the act of plundering; pillage. —'**plunderer** *n.*

plunge (plʌndʒ) *vb.* **1.** (usually foll. by *into*) to thrust or
throw (something, oneself, etc.): *they plunged into the
sea.* **2.** to throw or be thrown into a certain condition:
the room was plunged into darkness. **3.** (usually foll. by
into) to involve or become involved deeply (in). **4.**
(*intr.*) to move or dash violently or with great speed or
impetuosity. **5.** (*intr.*) to descend very suddenly or
steeply: *the ship plunged in heavy seas; a plunging neckline.* **6.** (*intr.*) *Inf.* to speculate or gamble recklessly, for
high stakes, etc. ~*n.* **7.** a leap or dive. **8.** *Inf.* a swim;
dip. **9.** a pitching or tossing motion. **10. take the
plunge.** *Inf.* to resolve to do something dangerous or
irrevocable.

plunger ('plʌndʒə) *n.* **1.** a rubber suction cup used to
clear a blocked drain, etc. **2.** a device or part of a machine that has a plunging or thrusting motion; piston. **3.**
Inf. a reckless gambler.

plunk (plʌŋk) *vb.* **1.** to pluck (the strings) of (a banjo,
etc.) or (of such an instrument) to give forth a sound
when plucked. **2.** (often foll. by *down*) to drop or be
dropped, esp. heavily or suddenly. ~*n.* **3.** the act or
sound of plunking.

pluperfect (plu:'pɜːfɪkt) *adj., n. Grammar.* another
term for **past perfect.**

plural ('plʊərəl) *adj.* **1.** containing, involving, or composed of more than one. **2.** denoting a word indicating
that more than one referent is being referred to or described. ~*n.* **3.** *Grammar.* **a.** the plural number. **b.** a
plural form. —'**plurally** *adv.*

pluralism ('plʊərə,lɪzəm) *n.* **1.** the holding by a single
person of more than one ecclesiastical benefice or office; plurality. **2.** *Sociol.* a theory of society as several
autonomous but interdependent groups. **3.** the existence
in a society of groups having distinctive ethnic origin,
cultural forms, religions, etc. **4.** *Philosophy.* the doctrine
that reality consists of several basic substances or elements. —'**pluralist** *n., adj.* —,**plural'istic** *adj.*

plurality (plʊə'rælɪtɪ) *n., pl.* -**ties.** **1.** the state of being
plural. **2.** *Maths.* a number greater than one. **3.** a large
number. **4.** the greater number; majority. **5.** another
word for **pluralism** (sense 1).

pluralize *or* -**ise** ('plʊərə,laɪz) *vb.* **1.** (*intr.*) to hold
more than one ecclesiastical benefice or office at the
same time. **2.** to make or become plural.

pluri- *combining form.* denoting several.

plus (plʌs) *prep.* **1.** increased by the addition of: *four
plus two.* **2.** with or with the addition of: *a good job, plus
a new car.* ~*adj.* **3.** (*prenominal*) indicating or involving
addition: *a plus sign.* **4.** another word for **positive**
(senses 7, 8). **5.** on the positive part of a scale or coordinate axis: *a value of +x.* **6.** involving advantage: *a plus
factor.* **7.** (*postpositive*) *Inf.* having a value above that
which is stated: *she had charm plus.* **8.** (*postpositive*)
slightly above a specified standard: *he received a B+
grade for his essay.* ~*n.* **9.** Also called: **plus sign.** the
symbol +, indicating addition or positive quantity. **10.** a
positive quantity. **11.** *Inf.* something positive or to the
good. **12.** a gain, surplus, or advantage.
▷ **Usage.** *Plus, together with,* and *along with* do not create compound subjects in the way that *and* does: the
number of the verb depends on that of the subject to
which *plus, together with,* or *along with* are added: *this
task, plus all the others,* was (not *were*) *undertaken by
the government.*

plus fours *pl. n.* men's baggy knickerbockers reaching
below the knee, now only worn for golf, etc.

plush (plʌʃ) *n.* **1.** a fabric with a cut pile that is longer
and softer than velvet. ~*adj.* **2.** Also: **plushy.** *Inf.* lavishly appointed; rich; costly. —'**plushly** *adv.*

Pluto ('plu:təʊ) *n.* the second smallest planet and the
farthest known from the sun.

plutocracy (plu:'tɒkrəsɪ) *n., pl.* -**cies.** **1.** the rule of society by the wealthy. **2.** a state or government characterized by the rule of the wealthy. **3.** a class that exercises power by virtue of its wealth. —**plutocratic**
(,plu:tə'krætɪk) *adj.* —,**pluto'cratically** *adv.*

plutocrat ('plu:tə,kræt) *n.* a member of a plutocracy.

plutonic (plu:'tɒnɪk) *adj.* (of igneous rocks) derived
from magma that has cooled and solidified below the
surface of the earth.

plutonium (plu:'təʊnɪəm) *n.* a highly toxic metallic
transuranic element. It occurs in trace amounts in uranium ores and is produced in a nuclear reactor by neutron bombardment of uranium-238. The most stable isotope, **plutonium-239,** readily undergoes fission and is
used as a reactor fuel. Symbol: Pu; atomic no.: 94; half-
life of ^{239}Pu: 24 360 years.

pluvial ('plu:vɪəl) *adj.* **1.** of, characterized by, or due to
the action of rain; rainy. ~*n.* **2.** *Geol.* a period of persistent heavy rainfall.

ply¹ (plaɪ) *vb.* **plying, plied.** (*mainly tr.*) **1.** to carry on,
pursue, or work at (a job, trade, etc.). **2.** to manipulate
or wield (a tool, etc.). **3.** to sell (goods, wares, etc.) esp.
at a regular place. **4.** (usually foll. by *with*) to provide
(with) or subject (to) repeatedly or persistently: *he plied
us with drink; he plied the speaker with questions.* **5.**
(*intr.*) to work at steadily or diligently. **6.** (*also intr.*)
(esp. of a ship, etc.) to travel regularly along (a route) or
in (an area): *to ply the trade routes.*

ply² (plaɪ) *n., pl.* **plies.** **1. a.** a layer, fold, or thickness, as
of yarn. **b.** (*in combination*): *four-ply.* **2.** a thin sheet of
wood glued to other similar sheets to form plywood. **3.**
one of the strands twisted together to make rope, etc.

Plymouth Brethren ('plɪməð) *n.* a religious sect
founded about 1827, strongly Puritanical in outlook and
having no organized ministry.

plywood ('plaɪ,wʊd) *n.* a structural board consisting of
thin layers of wood glued together under pressure, with
the grain of one layer at right angles to the grain of the
adjoining layer.

Pm *the chemical symbol for* promethium.

p.m. *or* **P.M.** *abbrev. for:* **1.** (indicating the time from
midday to midnight) post meridiem. **2.** post-mortem
(examination).

P.M. *abbrev. for:* **1.** Prime Minister. **2.** Past Master
(of a fraternity). **3.** Paymaster. **4.** Postmaster. **5.** *Mil.*
Provost Marshal.

P.M.G. *abbrev. for:* **1.** Paymaster General. **2.** Postmaster General.

PMS *abbrev. for* premenstrual syndrome.

THESAURUS

plump *adj.* beefy (*Inf.*), burly, buxom,
chubby, corpulent, dumpy, fat, fleshy, full,
obese, podgy, portly, roly-poly, rotund, round,
stout, tubby, well-covered, well-upholstered
(*Inf.*)

plunder **1.** *v.* despoil, devastate, loot, pillage, raid, ransack, ravage, rifle, rob, sack,
spoil, steal, strip **2.** *n.* booty, ill-gotten gains,
loot, pillage, prey, prize, rapine, spoils, swag
(*Sl.*)

plunge *v.* **1.** cast, descend, dip, dive, douse,
drop, fall, go down, immerse, jump, nose-
dive, pitch, plummet, sink, submerge, swoop,
throw, tumble **2.** career, charge, dash, hurtle,
lurch, rush, tear ~*n.* **3.** descent, dive, drop,
fall, immersion, jump, submersion, swoop

plus **1.** *prep.* added to, and, coupled with,
with, with the addition of **2.** *adj.* added, additional, extra, positive, supplementary **3.** *n.*
Inf. advantage, asset, benefit, bonus, extra,
gain, good point, perk (*Inf.*), surplus

plush costly, de luxe, lavish, luxurious,

luxury, opulent, palatial, rich, ritzy (*Sl.*),
sumptuous

plutocrat capitalist, Croesus, Dives, fat
cat (*Sl.*), magnate, millionaire, moneybags
(*Sl.*), rich man, tycoon

ply **1.** carry on, exercise, follow, practise,
pursue, work at **2.** employ, handle, manipulate, swing, utilize, wield **3.** assail, beset, besiege, bombard, harass, importune, press,
urge

PMT *abbrev. for* premenstrual tension.

pneumatic (njʊ'mætɪk) *adj.* **1.** of or concerned with air, gases, or wind. **2.** (of a machine or device) operated by compressed air or by a vacuum. **3.** containing compressed air: *a pneumatic tyre.* **4.** (of the bones of birds) containing air spaces which reduce their weight as an adaptation to flying. ~*n.* **5.** a pneumatic tyre. —**pneu-'matically** *adv.*

pneumatics (njʊ'mætɪks) *n.* (*functioning as sing.*) the branch of physics concerned with the mechanical properties of gases, esp. air.

pneumoconiosis (ˌnjuːməʊˌkəʊnɪ'əʊsɪs) *or* **pneumonoconiosis** (ˌnjuːmənəʊˌkəʊnɪ'əʊsɪs) *n.* any disease of the lungs or bronchi caused by the inhalation of metallic or mineral particles.

pneumonia (njuː'məʊnɪə) *n.* inflammation of one or both lungs, in which the air sacs (alveoli) become filled with liquid. —**pneumonic** (njuː'mɒnɪk) *adj.*

po (pəʊ) *n., pl.* **pos.** *Brit.* an informal word for **chamber pot.**

Po *the chemical symbol for* polonium.

P.O. *abbrev. for:* **1.** Post Office. **2.** Personnel Officer. **3.** petty officer. **4.** Pilot Officer. **5.** Also: **p.o.** postal order.

poach[1] (pəʊtʃ) *vb.* **1.** to catch (game, fish, etc.) illegally by trespassing on private property. **2.** to encroach on or usurp (another person's rights, duties, etc.) or steal (an idea, employee, etc.). **3.** *Tennis, badminton, etc.* to take or play (shots that should belong to one's partner). **4.** to break up (land) into wet muddy patches, as by riding over it. —**'poacher** *n.*

poach[2] (pəʊtʃ) *vb.* to simmer (eggs, fish, etc.) very gently in water, milk, stock, etc. —**'poacher** *n.*

pock (pɒk) *n.* **1.** any pustule resulting from an eruptive disease, esp. from smallpox. **2.** another word for **pockmark.** —**'pocky** *adj.*

pocket ('pɒkɪt) *n.* **1.** a small bag or pouch in a garment for carrying small articles, money, etc. **2.** any bag or pouch or anything resembling this. **3.** *S. African.* a bag or sack of vegetables or fruit. **4.** a cavity in the earth, etc., such as one containing ore. **5.** a small enclosed or isolated area: *a pocket of resistance.* **6.** any of the six holes with pouches or nets let into the corners and sides of a billiard table. **7. in one's pocket.** under one's control. **8. in or out of pocket.** having made a profit or loss. **9. line one's pockets.** to make money, esp. by dishonesty when in a position of trust. **10.** (*modifier*) small: *a pocket edition.* ~*vb.* (*tr.*) **11.** to put into one's pocket. **12.** to take surreptitiously or unlawfully; steal. **13.** (*usually passive*) to confine in or as if in a pocket. **14.** *Billiards, etc.* to drive (a ball) into a pocket. —**'pocketless** *adj.*

pocketbook ('pɒkɪtˌbʊk) *n.* *Chiefly U.S.* a small bag or case for money, papers, etc.

pocket borough *n.* (before the Reform Act of 1832) an English borough constituency controlled by one person or family who owned the land.

pocketful ('pɒkɪtˌfʊl) *n., pl.* **-fuls.** as much as a pocket will hold.

pocketknife ('pɒkɪtˌnaɪf) *n., pl.* **-knives.** a small knife with one or more blades that fold into the handle; penknife.

pocket money *n.* **1.** *Brit.* a small weekly sum of money given to children by parents as an allowance. **2.** money for day-to-day spending, incidental expenses, etc.

pockmark ('pɒkˌmɑːk) *n.* **1.** Also called: **pock.** a pitted scar left on the skin after the healing of a smallpox or similar pustule. **2.** any pitting of a surface that resembles or suggests such scars. ~*vb.* **3.** (*tr.*) to scar or pit with pockmarks.

poco ('pəʊkəʊ; *Italian* 'pɔːko) *or* **un poco** *adj., adv.* *Music.* (*in combination*) a little; to a small degree.

pod (pɒd) *n.* **1. a.** the fruit of any leguminous plant, consisting of a long two-valved case that contains seeds. **b.** the seed case as distinct from the seeds. **2.** any similar fruit. **3.** a streamlined structure attached to an aircraft and used to house a jet engine, fuel tank, armament, etc. ~*vb.* **podding, podded.** **4.** (*tr.*) to remove the pod from.

-pod *or* **-pode** *n. combining form.* indicating a certain type or number of feet: *arthropod; tripod.*

podgy ('pɒdʒɪ) *adj.* **podgier, podgiest.** **1.** short and fat; chubby. **2.** (of the face, arms, etc.) unpleasantly chubby and pasty looking. —**'podgily** *adv.* —**'podginess** *n.*

podium ('pəʊdɪəm) *n., pl.* **-diums** *or* **-dia** (-dɪə). **1.** a small raised platform used by lecturers, conductors, etc. **2.** a plinth that supports a colonnade or wall. **3.** a low wall surrounding the arena of an ancient amphitheatre. **4.** *Zool.* any footlike organ, such as the tube foot of a starfish.

poem ('pəʊɪm) *n.* **1.** a composition in verse, usually characterized by words chosen for their sound and suggestive power as well as for their sense, and using such techniques as metre, rhyme, and alliteration. **2.** a literary composition that is not in verse but exhibits the intensity of imagination and language common to it: *a prose poem.* **3.** anything resembling a poem in beauty, effect, etc.

poesy ('pəʊɪzɪ) *n., pl.* **-sies.** **1.** an archaic word for **poetry.** **2.** *Poetic.* the art of writing poetry.

poet ('pəʊɪt) *or* (*sometimes when fem.*) **poetess** *n.* **1.** a person who writes poetry. **2.** a person with great imagination and creativity.

poetaster (ˌpəʊɪ'tæstə, -'teɪ-) *n.* a writer of inferior verse.

poetic (pəʊ'etɪk) *or* **poetical** *adj.* **1.** of poetry. **2.** characteristic of poetry, as in being elevated, sublime, etc. **3.** characteristic of a poet. **4.** recounted in verse. —**po'etically** *adv.*

poetic justice *n.* fitting retribution.

poetic licence *n.* justifiable departure from conventional rules of form, fact, etc., as in poetry.

poet laureate *n., pl.* **poets laureate.** *Brit.* the poet appointed as court poet of Britain who is given a lifetime post in the Royal Household.

poetry ('pəʊɪtrɪ) *n.* **1.** literature in metrical form; verse. **2.** the art or craft of writing verse. **3.** poetic qualities, spirit, or feeling in anything. **4.** anything resembling poetry in rhythm, beauty, etc.

po-faced *adj.* wearing a disapproving stern expression.

pogo stick ('pəʊgəʊ) *n.* a stout pole with a handle at the top, steps for the feet and a spring at the bottom, so that the user can spring up, down, and along on it.

pogrom ('pɒgrəm) *n.* an organized persecution or extermination of an ethnic group, esp. of Jews.

poignant ('pɔɪnjənt, -nənt) *adj.* **1.** sharply distressing or painful to the feelings. **2.** to the point; cutting or piercing: *poignant wit.* **3.** keen or pertinent in mental appeal: *a poignant subject.* **4.** pungent in smell. —**'poignancy** *or* **'poignance** *n.* —**'poignantly** *adv.*

poinsettia (pɔɪn'setɪə) *n.* a shrub of Mexico and Central America, widely cultivated for its showy scarlet bracts, which resemble petals.

point (pɔɪnt) *n.* **1.** a dot or tiny mark. **2.** a location, spot, or position. **3.** any dot used in writing or printing, such as a decimal point or a full stop. **4.** the sharp tapered end of a pin, knife, etc. **5.** *Maths.* **a.** a geometric element having no dimensions whose position is located by means of its coordinates. **b.** a location: *point of in-*

THESAURUS

poach appropriate, encroach, hunt *or* fish illegally, infringe, intrude, plunder, rob, steal, steal game, trespass

pocket *n.* **1.** bag, compartment, hollow, pouch, receptacle, sack ~*adj.* **2.** abridged, compact, concise, little, miniature, pint-size(d) (*Inf.*), portable, potted (*Inf.*), small ~*v.* **3.** appropriate, filch, help oneself to, lift (*Inf.*), pilfer, purloin, snaffle (*Brit. inf.*), steal, take **4.** accept, bear, brook, endure, put up with (*Inf.*), stomach, swallow, take, tolerate

pod *n./v.* hull, husk, shell, shuck

podgy chubby, chunky, dumpy, fat, fleshy,

plump, roly-poly, rotund, short and fat, squat, stout, stubby, stumpy, tubby

podium dais, platform, rostrum, stage

poem lyric, ode, rhyme, song, sonnet, verse

poet bard, lyricist, maker (*Archaic*), rhymer, versifier

poetic elegiac, lyric, lyrical, metrical, rhythmical, songlike

poetry metrical composition, poems, poesy (*Archaic*), rhyme, rhyming, verse

poignancy **1.** emotion, emotionalism,

evocativeness, feeling, pathos, piteousness, plaintiveness, sadness, sentiment, tenderness **2.** bitterness, intensity, keenness, piquancy, pungency, sharpness

poignant **1.** affecting, agonizing, bitter, distressing, heartbreaking, heart-rending, intense, moving, painful, pathetic, sad, touching, upsetting **2.** acute, biting, caustic, keen, penetrating, piercing, pointed, sarcastic, severe **3.** acrid, piquant, pungent, sharp, stinging, tangy

flection. **6.** a small promontory. **7.** a specific condition or degree. **8.** a moment: *at that point he left the room.* **9.** a reason, aim, etc.: *the point of this exercise is to train new teachers.* **10.** an essential element in an argument: *I take your point.* **11.** a suggestion or tip. **12.** a detail or item. **13.** a characteristic, physical attribute, etc.: *he has his good points.* **14.** a distinctive characteristic or quality of an animal, esp. one used as a standard in judging livestock. **15.** (*often pl.*) any of the extremities, such as the tail, ears, or feet, of a domestic animal. **16.** a single unit for measuring or counting, as in scoring of a game. **17.** *Printing.* a unit of measurement equal to one twelfth of a pica. There are approximately 72 points to the inch. **18.** *Finance.* a unit of value used to quote security and commodity prices and their fluctuations. **19.** *Navigation.* **a.** one of the 32 marks on the compass indicating direction. **b.** the angle of 11°15′ between two adjacent marks. **20.** *Cricket.* a fielding position at right angles to the batsman on the off side and relatively near the pitch. **21.** either of the two electrical contacts that make or break the current flow in the distributor of an internal-combustion engine. **22.** *Brit.* (*often pl.*) a junction of railway tracks in which a pair of rails can be moved so that a train can be directed onto either of two lines. U.S. equivalent: **switch.** **23.** (*often pl.*) a piece of ribbon, cord, etc., with metal tags at the end: used during the 16th and 17th centuries to fasten clothing. **24.** *Brit.* an informal name for **socket** (sense 2). **25.** the position of the body of a pointer or setter when it discovers game. **26.** *Boxing.* a mark awarded for a scoring blow, knockdown, etc. **27.** any diacritic used in a writing system, esp. in a phonetic transcription, to indicate modifications of vowels or consonants. **28.** *Jewellery.* a unit of weight equal to 0.01 carat. **29.** the act of pointing. **30. at** (*or* **on**) **the point of.** at the moment immediately before: *on the point of leaving the room.* **31. beside the point.** irrelevant. **32. case in point.** a specific or relevant instance. **33. make a point of. a.** to make (something) one's regular habit. **b.** to do (something) because one thinks it important. **34. not to put too fine a point on it.** to speak plainly and bluntly. **35. score points off.** to gain an advantage at someone else's expense. **36. stretch a point.** to make a concession or exception. **37. to the point.** relevant. **38. up to a point.** not completely. ~*vb.* **39.** (usually foll. by *at* or *to*) to indicate the location or direction of by or as by extending (a finger or other pointed object) towards it: *he pointed to the front door; don't point that gun at me.* **40.** (*intr.;* usually foll. by *at* or *to*) to indicate or identify a specific person or thing among several: *all evidence pointed to Donald as the murderer.* **41.** (*tr.*) to direct or face in a specific direction: *point me in the right direction.* **42.** (*tr.*) to sharpen or taper. **43.** (*intr.*) (of gun dogs) to indicate the place where game is lying by standing rigidly with the muzzle turned in its direction. **44.** (*tr.*) to finish or repair the joints of (brickwork, masonry, etc.) with mortar or cement. **45.** (*tr.*) *Music.* to mark (a psalm text) with vertical lines to indicate the points at which the music changes during chanting. **46.** (*tr.*) *Phonetics.* to provide (a letter or letters) with diacritics. **47.** (*tr.*) to provide (a Hebrew or similar text) with vowel points. ~See also **point out.**

point-blank *adj.* **1. a.** aimed or fired horizontally at a target without making allowance for the drop in the course of the projectile. **b.** permitting such aim or fire without loss of accuracy: *at point-blank range.* **2.** aimed or fired at nearly zero range. **3.** plain or blunt: *a point-blank question.* ~*adv.* **4.** directly or straight. **5.** plainly or bluntly.

point duty *n.* the stationing of a policeman or traffic warden at a road junction to control and direct traffic.

pointed ('pɔɪntɪd) *adj.* **1.** having a point. **2.** cutting or incisive: *a pointed wit.* **3.** obviously directed at a particular person: *pointed criticism.* **4.** emphasized or made conspicuous: *pointed ignorance.* **5.** (of an arch or style of architecture) Gothic. —'**pointedly** *adv.*

pointer ('pɔɪntə) *n.* **1.** a person or thing that points. **2.** an indicator on a measuring instrument. **3.** a long rod or cane used by a lecturer to point to parts of a map, blackboard, etc. **4.** one of a breed of large swift hunting dogs, usually white with black, liver, or lemon markings. **5.** a helpful piece of information.

pointillism ('pwænti,lizəm) *n.* the technique of painting elaborated from impressionism, in which dots of unmixed colour are juxtaposed on a white ground so that from a distance they fuse in the viewer's eye into appropriate intermediate tones. —'**pointillist** *n., adj.*

pointing ('pɔɪntɪŋ) *n.* the act or process of repairing or finishing joints in brickwork, masonry, etc., with mortar.

pointless ('pɔɪntlɪs) *adj.* **1.** without a point. **2.** without meaning, relevance, or force. **3.** *Sport.* without a point scored. —'**pointlessly** *adv.*

point of no return *n.* **1.** a point at which an irreversible commitment must be made to an action, progression, etc. **2.** a point in a journey at which, if one continues, supplies will be insufficient for a return to the starting place.

point of order *n., pl.* **points of order.** a question raised in a meeting as to whether the rules governing procedures are being breached.

point of view *n., pl.* **points of view.** **1.** a position from which someone or something is observed. **2.** a mental viewpoint or attitude.

point out *vb.* (*tr., adv.*) to indicate or specify.

point-to-point *n. Brit.* a steeplechase organized by a recognized hunt or other body, usually restricted to amateurs riding horses that have been regularly used in hunting.

poise (pɔɪz) *n.* **1.** composure or dignity of manner. **2.** physical balance. **3.** equilibrium; stability. **4.** the position of hovering. ~*vb.* **5.** to be or cause to be balanced or suspended. **6.** (*tr.*) to hold, as in readiness: *to poise a lance.*

poison ('pɔɪz⁰n) *n.* **1.** any substance that can impair function or otherwise injure the body. **2.** something that destroys, corrupts, etc. **3.** a substance that retards a chemical reaction or the activity of a catalyst. **4.** a substance that absorbs neutrons in a nuclear reactor and thus slows down the reaction. ~*vb.* (*tr.*) **5.** to give poison to (a person or animal) esp. with intent to kill. **6.** to

---

THESAURUS

point *n.* **1.** dot, full stop, mark, period, speck, stop **2.** location, place, position, site, spot, stage, station **3.** apex, end, nib, prong, sharp end, spike, spur, summit, tine, tip, top **4.** bill, cape, foreland, head, headland, ness (*Archaic*), promontory **5.** circumstance, condition, degree, extent, position, stage **6.** instant, juncture, moment, time, very minute **7.** aim, design, end, goal, intent, intention, motive, object, objective, purpose, reason, use, usefulness, utility **8.** burden, core, crux, drift, essence, gist, heart, import, main idea, marrow, matter, meaning, nub, pith, proposition, question, subject, text, theme, thrust **9.** aspect, detail, facet, feature, instance, item, nicety, particular **10.** aspect, attribute, characteristic, peculiarity, property, quality, respect, side, trait **11.** score, tally, unit **12. beside the point** immaterial, incidental, inconsequential, irrelevant, not to the purpose, off the subject, out of the way, pointless, unimportant, without connection **13. to the point** applicable, appropriate, apropos, apt, brief, fitting, germane, pertinent, pithy, pointed,

relevant, short, suitable, terse ~*v.* **14.** bespeak, call attention to, denote, designate, direct, indicate, show, signify **15.** aim, bring to bear, direct, level, train **16.** barb, edge, sharpen, taper, whet

point-blank 1. *adj.* abrupt, blunt, categorical, direct, downright, explicit, express, plain, straight-from-the-shoulder, unreserved **2.** *adv.* bluntly, brusquely, candidly, directly, explicitly, forthrightly, frankly, openly, plainly, straight, straightforwardly

pointed 1. acicular, acuminate, acute, barbed, cuspidate, edged, mucronate, sharp **2.** accurate, acute, biting, cutting, incisive, keen, penetrating, pertinent, sharp, telling, trenchant

pointer 1. guide, hand, indicator, needle **2.** advice, caution, hint, information, recommendation, suggestion, tip, warning

pointless absurd, aimless, fruitless, futile, inane, ineffectual, irrelevant, meaningless, nonsensical, senseless, silly, stupid, unavailing, unproductive, unprofitable, useless, vague, vain, worthless

point of view 1. angle, orientation, outlook, perspective, position, standpoint **2.** approach, attitude, belief, judgment, opinion, slant, view, viewpoint, way of looking at it

point out allude to, bring up, call attention to, identify, indicate, mention, remind, reveal, show, specify

poise 1. *n.* aplomb, assurance, calmness, composure, cool (*Sl.*), coolness, dignity, elegance, equanimity, equilibrium, grace, presence, presence of mind, sang-froid, savoir-faire, self-possession, serenity **2.** *v.* balance, float, hang, hang in midair, hang suspended, hold, hover, position, support, suspend

poised 1. calm, collected, composed, dignified, graceful, nonchalant, self-confident, self-possessed, serene, suave, together (*Inf.*), unruffled, urbane **2.** all set, in the wings, on the brink, prepared, ready, standing by, waiting

add poison to. **7.** to taint or infect with or as if with poison. **8.** (foll. by *against*) to turn (a person's mind) against: *he poisoned her mind against me.* **9.** to retard or stop (a chemical or nuclear reaction) by the action of a poison. —'**poisoner** *n.*

poison ivy *n.* any of several North American shrubs or climbing plants that cause an itching rash on contact.

poisonous ('pɔɪzənəs) *adj.* **1.** having the effects or qualities of a poison. **2.** capable of killing or inflicting injury. **3.** corruptive or malicious. —'**poisonously** *adv.* —'**poisonousness** *n.*

poison-pen letter *n.* a letter written in malice, usually anonymously, and intended to abuse, frighten, or insult the recipient.

poke[1] (pəʊk) *vb.* **1.** (*tr.*) to jab or prod, as with the elbow, a stick, etc. **2.** (*tr.*) to make (a hole) by or as by poking. **3.** (when *intr.*, often foll. by *at*) to thrust (at). **4.** (*tr.*) *Inf.* to hit with the fist; punch. **5.** (usually foll. by *in*, *through*, etc.) to protrude or cause to protrude: *don't poke your arm out of the window.* **6.** (*tr.*) to stir (a fire, etc.) by poking. **7.** (*intr.*) to meddle or intrude. **8.** (*intr.*; often foll. by *about* or *around*) to search or pry. **9. poke fun at.** to ridicule. **10. poke one's nose into.** to interfere with or meddle in. ~*n.* **11.** a jab or prod. **12.** *Inf.* a blow with one's fist; punch.

poke[2] (pəʊk) *n.* **1.** *Dialect.* a pocket or bag. **2. a pig in a poke.** See **pig.**

poker[1] ('pəʊkə) *n.* a metal rod, usually with a handle, for stirring a fire.

poker[2] ('pəʊkə) *n.* a card game of bluff and skill in which bets are made on the hands dealt, the highest-ranking hand winning the pool.

poker face *n. Inf.* a face without expression, as that of a poker player attempting to conceal the value of his cards. —'**poker-,faced** *adj.*

pokerwork ('pəʊkə,wɜːk) *n.* the art of producing pictures or designs on wood by charring it with a heated tool.

poky *or* **pokey** ('pəʊkɪ) *adj.* **pokier, pokiest. 1.** (esp. of rooms) small and cramped. **2.** *Inf.* without speed or energy; slow. —'**pokily** *adv.* —'**pokiness** *n.*

Pol. *abbrev. for:* **1.** Poland. **2.** Polish.

polar ('pəʊlə) *adj.* **1.** at, near, or relating to either of the earth's poles or the area inside the Arctic or Antarctic Circles: *polar regions.* **2.** having or relating to a pole or poles. **3.** pivotal or guiding in the manner of the Pole Star. **4.** directly opposite, as in tendency or character. **5.** *Chem.* (of a molecule) having an uneven distribution of electrons and thus a permanent dipole moment: *water has polar molecules.*

polar bear *n.* a white carnivorous bear of coastal regions of the North Pole.

polar circle *n.* a term for either the **Arctic Circle** or **Antarctic Circle.**

Polaris (pə'lɑːrɪs) *n.* **1.** Also called: the **Pole Star,** the **North Star.** the brightest star in the constellation Ursa Minor, situated slightly less than 1° from the north celestial pole. **2.** a type of U.S. two-stage intermediate-range ballistic missile, usually fired by a submerged submarine.

polarity (pəʊ'lærɪtɪ) *n., pl.* **-ties. 1.** the condition of having poles. **2.** the condition of a body or system in which it has opposing physical properties, esp. magnetic poles or electric charge. **3.** the particular state of a part that has polarity: *an electrode with positive polarity.* **4.** the state of having or expressing two directly opposite tendencies, opinions, etc.

polarization *or* **-isation** (,pəʊləraɪ'zeɪʃən) *n.* **1.** the condition of having or giving polarity. **2.** *Physics.* the

phenomenon in which waves of light or other radiation are restricted to certain directions of vibration.

polarize *or* **-ise** ('pəʊlə,raɪz) *vb.* to acquire or cause to acquire polarity or polarization. —'**polar,izer** *or* -,**iser** *n.*

Polaroid ('pəʊlə,rɔɪd) *Trademark.* ~*n.* **1.** a type of plastic sheet that can polarize a transmitted beam of normal light because it is composed of long parallel molecules. It only transmits plane-polarized light if these molecules are parallel to the plane of polarization. **2. Polaroid Land Camera.** any of several types of camera yielding a finished print by means of a special developing and processing technique that occurs inside the camera and takes only a few seconds.

polder ('pəʊldə, 'pɒl-) *n.* a stretch of land reclaimed from the sea or a lake, esp. in the Netherlands.

pole[1] (pəʊl) *n.* **1.** a long slender usually round piece of wood, metal, or other material. **2.** the piece of timber on each side of which a pair of carriage horses are hitched. **3.** another name for **rod** (sense 7). **4. under bare poles.** *Naut.* (of a sailing vessel) with no sails set. **5. up the pole.** *Brit. & Austral. inf.* **a.** slightly mad. **b.** mistaken; on the wrong track. ~*vb.* **6.** (*tr.*) to strike or push with a pole. **7.** (*tr.*) **a.** to set out (an area of land or garden) with poles. **b.** to support (a crop, such as hops) on poles. **8.** to punt (a boat).

pole[2] (pəʊl) *n.* **1.** either of the two antipodal points where the earth's axis of rotation meets the earth's surface. See also **North Pole, South Pole. 2.** *Physics.* **a.** either of the two regions at the extremities of a magnet to which the lines of force converge. **b.** either of two points at which there are opposite electric charges, as at the terminals of a battery. **3.** *Biol.* either end of the axis of a cell, spore, ovum, or similar body. **4.** either of two mutually exclusive or opposite actions, opinions, etc. **5. poles apart** (*or* **asunder**). having widely divergent opinions, tastes, etc.

Pole (pəʊl) *n.* a native, inhabitant, or citizen of Poland or a speaker of Polish.

poleaxe *or U.S.* **poleax** ('pəʊl,æks) *n.* **1.** another term for a battle-axe or a butcher's axe. ~*vb.* **2.** (*tr.*) to hit or fell with or as if with a poleaxe.

polecat ('pəʊl,kæt) *n., pl.* **-cats** *or* **-cat. 1.** a dark brown musteline mammal of Europe, Asia, and N Africa, that is closely related to but larger than the weasel and gives off an unpleasant smell. **2.** *U.S.* a nontechnical name for **skunk.**

polemic (pə'lɛmɪk) *adj. also* **polemical. 1.** of or involving dispute or controversy. ~*n.* **2.** an argument or controversy, esp. over a doctrine, belief, etc. **3.** a person engaged in such controversy. —**po'lemically** *adv.* —**po'lemicist** (pə'lɛmɪsɪst) *n.*

polemics (pə'lɛmɪks) *n.* (*functioning as sing.*) the art or practice of dispute or argument, as in attacking or defending a doctrine or belief.

pole star *n.* a guiding principle, rule, etc.

Pole Star *n.* **the.** the star closest to the N celestial pole at any particular time. At present this is Polaris, but it will eventually be replaced owing to precession of the earth's axis.

pole vault *n.* **1. the.** a field event in which competitors attempt to clear a high bar with the aid of an extremely flexible long pole. ~*vb.* **pole-vault. 2.** (*intr.*) to perform a pole vault or compete in the pole vault. —'**pole-,vaulter** *n.*

police (pə'liːs) *n.* **1.** (often preceded by *the*) the organized civil force of a state, concerned with maintenance of law and order. **2.** (*functioning as pl.*) the members of such a force collectively. **3.** any organized body with a

---

THESAURUS

poison *n.* **1.** bane, toxin, venom **2.** bane, blight, cancer, canker, contagion, contamination, corruption, malignancy, miasma, virus ~*v.* **3.** adulterate, contaminate, envenom, give (someone) poison, infect, kill, murder, pollute **4.** corrupt, defile, deprave, pervert, subvert, taint, undermine, vitiate, warp ~*adj.* **5.** deadly, lethal, poisonous, toxic, venomous

poisonous 1. baneful (*Archaic*), deadly, fatal, lethal, mephitic, mortal, noxious, toxic, venomous, virulent **2.** baleful, baneful (*Archaic*), corruptive, evil, malicious, noxious, pernicious, pestiferous, pestilential, vicious

poke *v.* **1.** butt, dig, elbow, hit, jab, nudge, prod, punch, push, shove, stab, stick, thrust **2.** butt in, interfere, intrude, meddle, nose, peek, poke one's nose into (*Inf.*), pry, snoop (*Inf.*), tamper **3. poke fun at** chaff, jeer, make a mock of, make fun of, mock, rib (*Inf.*), ridicule, send up (*Brit. inf.*), take the mickey (*Inf.*), tease ~*n.* **4.** butt, dig, hit, jab, nudge, prod, punch, thrust

poky confined, cramped, incommodious, narrow, small, tiny

polar 1. Antarctic, Arctic, cold, extreme, freezing, frozen, furthest, glacial, icy, terminal **2.** beacon-like, cardinal, guiding, leading, pivotal **3.** antagonistic, antipodal, antithetical, contradictory, contrary, diametric, opposed, opposite

polarity ambivalence, contradiction, contrariety, dichotomy, duality, opposition, paradox

pole[1] bar, mast, post, rod, shaft, spar, staff, standard, stick

pole[2] **1.** antipode, extremity, limit, terminus **2. poles apart** at opposite ends of the earth, at opposite extremes, incompatible, irreconcilable, miles apart, widely separated, worlds apart

similar function: *security police.* ~*vb.* (*tr.*) **4.** to regulate, control, or keep in order by means of a police or similar force. **5.** to observe or record the activity or enforcement of: *a committee was set up to police the new agreement on picketing.*

police dog *n.* a dog, often an Alsatian, trained to help the police, as in tracking.

policeman (pə'liːsmən) *or* (*fem.*) **policewoman** *n.*, *pl.* **-men** *or* **-women.** a member of a police force, esp. one holding the rank of constable.

police state *n.* a state or country in which a repressive government maintains control through the police.

police station *n.* the office or headquarters of the police force of a district.

policy[1] ('pɒlɪsɪ) *n.*, *pl.* **-cies.** **1.** a plan of action adopted or pursued by an individual, government, party, business, etc. **2.** wisdom, shrewdness, or sagacity. **3.** *Scot.* (*sometimes pl.*) the improved grounds surrounding a country house.

policy[2] ('pɒlɪsɪ) *n.*, *pl.* **-cies.** a document containing a contract of insurance. —**'policy,holder** *n.*

polio ('pəʊlɪəʊ) *n.* short for **poliomyelitis.**

poliomyelitis (,pəʊlɪəʊ,maɪə'laɪtɪs) *n.* an acute infectious viral disease, esp. affecting children. In its paralytic form the brain and spinal cord are involved, causing paralysis and wasting of muscle. Also called: **infantile paralysis.**

polish ('pɒlɪʃ) *vb.* **1.** to make or become smooth and shiny by rubbing, esp. with wax or an abrasive. **2.** (*tr.*) to make perfect or complete. **3.** to make or become elegant or refined. ~*n.* **4.** a finish or gloss. **5.** the act of polishing. **6.** a substance used to produce a shiny, often protective surface. **7.** elegance or refinement, esp. in style, manner, etc. —**'polisher** *n.*

Polish ('pəʊlɪʃ) *adj.* **1.** of, relating to, or characteristic of Poland, its people, or their language. ~*n.* **2.** the official language of Poland. **3. the Polish.** (*functioning as pl.*) the people of Poland or Polish speakers collectively.

polished ('pɒlɪʃt) *adj.* **1.** accomplished: *a polished actor.* **2.** impeccably or professionally done: *a polished performance.* **3.** (of rice) having had the outer husk removed by milling.

polish off *vb.* (*tr., adv.*) *Inf.* **1.** to finish or process completely. **2.** to dispose of or kill.

polish up *vb.* (*adv.*) **1.** to make or become smooth and shiny by polishing. **2.** (when *intr.*, foll. by *on*) to study or practise until adept at; improve: *he's polishing up on his German.*

Politburo ('pɒlɪt,bjʊərəʊ) *n.* **1.** the executive and policy-making committee of a Communist Party. **2.** the supreme policy-making authority in most Communist countries.

polite (pə'laɪt) *adj.* **1.** showing a great regard for others, as in manners, speech, etc.; courteous. **2.** cultivated or refined: *polite society.* **3.** elegant or polished: *polite letters.* —**po'litely** *adv.* —**po'liteness** *n.*

politic ('pɒlɪtɪk) *adj.* **1.** artful or shrewd; ingenious. **2.** crafty or unscrupulous; cunning. **3.** wise or prudent, esp. in ·statesmanship: *a politic choice.* **4.** an archaic word for **political.** See **body politic.** —**'politicly** *adv.*

political (pə'lɪtɪkəl) *adj.* **1.** of or relating to the state, government, public administration, etc. **2. a.** of or relating to government policy-making as distinguished from administration or law. **b.** of or relating to the civil aspects of government as distinguished from the military. **3.** of, dealing with, or relating to politics: *a political person.* **4.** of or relating to the parties and the partisan aspects of politics. **5.** organized with respect to government: *a political unit.* —**po'litically** *adv.*

political prisoner *n.* someone imprisoned for holding or expressing particular political beliefs.

political science *n.* the study of the state, government, and politics: one of the social sciences. —**political scientist** *n.*

politician (,pɒlɪ'tɪʃən) *n.* **1.** a person actively engaged in politics, esp. a full-time professional member of a deliberative assembly. **2.** a person who is experienced or skilled in government or administration; statesman. **3.** *Disparaging, chiefly U.S.* a person who engages in politics out of a wish for personal gain.

politicize *or* **-ise** (pə'lɪtɪ,saɪz) *vb.* **1.** (*tr.*) to render political in tone, interest, or awareness. **2.** (*intr.*) to participate in political discussion or activity. —**po,litici'zation** *or* **-i'sation** *n.*

politics ('pɒlɪtɪks) *n.* **1.** (*functioning as sing.*) the art and science of directing and administrating states and other political units; government. **2.** (*functioning as sing.*) the complex or aggregate of relationships of men in society, esp. those relationships involving authority or power. **3.** (*functioning as pl.*) political activities or affairs: *party politics.* **4.** (*functioning as sing.*) the business or profession of politics. **5.** (*functioning as sing. or pl.*) any activity concerned with the acquisition of power, etc.: *company politics are frequently vicious.* **6.** manoeuvres or factors leading up to or influencing (something): *the politics of the decision.* **7.** (*functioning as pl.*) opinions, sympathies, etc., with respect to politics: *his conservative politics.*

polity ('pɒlɪtɪ) *n.*, *pl.* **-ties.** **1.** a form of government or organization of a society, etc.; constitution. **2.** a politically organized society, etc. **3.** the management of public affairs. **4.** political organization.

polka ('pɒlkə) *n.*, *pl.* **-kas.** **1.** a 19th-century Bohemian dance with three steps and a hop, in fast duple time. **2.** a piece of music composed for this dance. ~*vb.* **-kaing,** **-kaed.** **3.** (*intr.*) to dance a polka.

polka dot *n.* one of a pattern of small circular regularly spaced spots on a fabric.

poll (pəʊl) *n.* **1.** the casting, recording, or counting of votes in an election; a voting. **2.** the result of such a voting: *a heavy poll.* **3.** Also called: **opinion poll. a.** a canvassing of a representative sample of people on some question in order to determine the general opinion. **b.** the results of such a canvassing. **4.** any counting or enumeration, esp. for taxation or voting purposes. **5.** the back part of the head of an animal. ~*vb.* (*mainly tr.*) **6.** to receive (a vote or quantity of votes): *he polled 10 000 votes.* **7.** to receive, take, or record the votes of: *he polled the whole town.* **8.** to canvass (a person, group, area, etc.) as part of a survey of opinion. **9.** (*sometimes intr.*) to cast (a vote) in an election. **10.** to clip or shear. **11.** to remove or cut short the horns of (cattle).

pollack *or* **pollock** ('pɒlək) *n.*, *pl.* **-lacks, -lack** *or* **-locks,**

police *n.* **1.** boys in blue (*Inf.*), constabulary, fuzz (*Sl.*), law enforcement agency, police force, the law (*Inf.*), the Old Bill (*Sl.*) ~*v.* **2.** control, guard, keep in order, keep the peace, patrol, protect, regulate, watch **3.** *Fig.* check, monitor, observe, oversee, supervise

policeman bobby (*Inf.*), bogey (*Sl.*), constable, cop (*Sl.*), copper (*Sl.*), fuzz (*Sl.*), gendarme (*Sl.*), officer, peeler (*Obsolete Brit. sl.*), pig (*Sl.*), rozzer (*Sl.*)

policy **1.** action, approach, code, course, custom, guideline, line, plan, practice, procedure, programme, protocol, rule, scheme, stratagem, theory **2.** discretion, good sense, prudence, sagacity, shrewdness, wisdom

polish *v.* **1.** brighten, buff, burnish, clean, furbish, rub, shine, smooth, wax **2.** brush up, correct, cultivate, emend, enhance, finish, improve, perfect, refine, touch up ~*n.* **3.** brightness, brilliance, finish, glaze, gloss, lustre, sheen, smoothness, sparkle, veneer **4.** varnish, wax **5.** *Fig.* class (*Inf.*), elegance, finesse, finish, grace, politesse, refinement, style, suavity, urbanity

polished **1.** bright, burnished, furbished, glassy, gleaming, glossy, shining, slippery, smooth **2.** *Fig.* accomplished, civilized, courtly, cultivated, elegant, finished, genteel, polite, refined, sophisticated, urbane, well-bred **3.** adept, expert, faultless, fine, flawless, impeccable, masterly, outstanding, professional, skilful, superlative

polish off **1.** consume, down, eat up, finish, put away, shift (*Inf.*), swill, wolf **2.** bump off (*Inf.*), dispose of, do away with, do in (*Sl.*), eliminate, get rid of, kill, liquidate, murder

polite **1.** affable, civil, complaisant, courteous, deferential, gracious, mannerly, obliging, respectful, well-behaved, well-mannered **2.** civilized, courtly, cultured, elegant, genteel, polished, refined, urbane, well-bred

politic **1.** artful, astute, canny, crafty, cunning, designing, ingenious, intriguing, Machiavellian, scheming, shrewd, sly, subtle, unscrupulous **2.** advisable, diplomatic, discreet, expedient, in one's best interests, judicious, prudent, sagacious, sensible, tactful, wise

politician legislator, Member of Parliament, M.P., office bearer, politico (*Inf., chiefly U.S.*), public servant, statesman

politics **1.** affairs of state, civics, government, government policy, political science, polity, statecraft, statesmanship **2.** Machiavellianism, machination, power struggle, Realpolitik

poll *n.* **1.** figures, returns, tally, vote, voting **2.** ballot, canvass, census, count, Gallup Poll, (public) opinion poll, sampling, survey ~*v.* **3.** register, tally **4.** ballot, canvass, interview, question, sample, survey

-lock. a gadoid food fish that has a projecting lower jaw and occurs in northern seas.

pollard ('pɒləd) *n.* **1.** an animal, such as a sheep or deer, that has either shed its horns or antlers or has had them removed. **2.** a tree that has had its branches cut back to encourage a more bushy growth. ~*vb.* **3.** (*tr.*) to convert into a pollard; poll.

pollen ('pɒlən) *n.* a substance produced by the anthers of seed-bearing plants, consisting of numerous fine grains containing the male gametes. —**pollinic** (pə-'lɪnɪk) *adj.*

pollen count *n.* a measure of the pollen present in the air over a 24-hour period, often published to enable sufferers from hay fever to predict the severity of their attacks.

pollinate ('pɒlɪˌneɪt) *vb.* (*tr.*) to transfer pollen from the anthers to the stigma of (a flower). —ˌpolli'nation *n.* —'polliˌnator *n.*

polling booth *n.* a semienclosed space in which a voter stands to mark a ballot paper during an election.

polling station *n.* a building, such as a school, designated as the place to which voters go during an election in order to cast their votes.

pollster ('pəʊlstə) *n.* a person who conducts opinion polls.

pollutant (pə'luːtənt) *n.* a substance that pollutes, esp. a chemical produced as a waste product of an industrial process.

pollute (pə'luːt) *vb.* (*tr.*) **1.** to contaminate, as with poisonous or harmful substances. **2.** to make morally corrupt. **3.** to desecrate. —**pol'luter** *n.* —**pol'lution** *n.*

polo ('pəʊləʊ) *n.* **1.** a game similar to hockey played on horseback using long-handled mallets (**polo sticks**) and a wooden ball. **2.** short for **water polo**. **3.** Also called: **polo neck. a.** a collar on a garment, worn rolled over to fit closely round the neck. **b.** a garment, esp. a sweater, with such a collar.

polonaise (ˌpɒlə'neɪz) *n.* **1.** a ceremonial marchlike dance in three-four time from Poland. **2.** a piece of music composed for or in the rhythm of this dance. **3.** a woman's costume with a tight bodice and an overskirt drawn back to show a decorative underskirt.

polonium (pə'ləʊnɪəm) *n.* a very rare radioactive element that occurs in trace amounts in uranium ores. Symbol: Po; atomic no.: 84; half-life of most stable isotope, ^{208}Po: 103 years.

poltergeist ('pɒltəˌgaɪst) *n.* a spirit believed to manifest its presence by noises and acts of mischief, such as throwing furniture about.

poltroon (pɒl'truːn) *n.* an abject or contemptible coward.

poly ('pɒlɪ) *n.*, *pl.* **polys.** *Inf.* short for **polytechnic.**

poly- *combining form.* **1.** more than one; many or much: *polyhedron.* **2.** having an excessive or abnormal number or amount: *polyphagia.*

polyandry ('pɒlɪˌændrɪ) *n.* **1.** the practice or condition of being married to more than one husband at the same time. **2.** the practice in animals of a female mating with more than one male during one breeding season. **3.** the condition in flowers of having a large indefinite number of stamens. —ˌpoly'androus *adj.*

polyanthus (ˌpɒlɪ'ænθəs) *n.*, *pl.* **-thuses.** any of several hybrid garden primroses with brightly coloured flowers.

polychromatic (ˌpɒlɪkrəʊ'mætɪk), **polychromic** (ˌpɒlɪ'krəʊmɪk), *or* **polychromous** *adj.* **1.** having various or changing colours. **2.** (of light or other radiation) containing radiation with more than one wavelength. —**polychromatism** (ˌpɒlɪ'krəʊməˌtɪzəm) *n.*

polyester ('pɒlɪˌɛstə) *n.* any of a large class of synthetic materials that are polymers containing recurring -COO- groups: used as plastics, textile fibres, and adhesives.

polyethylene (ˌpɒlɪ'ɛθɪˌliːn) *n.* another name (esp. U.S.) for **polythene.**

polygamy (pə'lɪgəmɪ) *n.* **1.** the practice of being married to more than one woman at the same time. **2.** the condition of having male, female, and hermaphrodite flowers on the same plant or on separate plants of the same species. **3.** the practice in male animals of having more than one mate during one breeding season. —**po-**

'lygamist *n.* —**po'lygamous** *adj.* —**po'lygamously** *adv.*

polyglot ('pɒlɪˌglɒt) *adj.* **1.** having a command of many languages. **2.** written in or containing many languages. ~*n.* **3.** a person with a command of many languages. **4.** a book, esp. a Bible, containing several versions of the same text written in various languages. **5.** a mixture of languages.

polygon ('pɒlɪˌgɒn) *n.* a closed plane figure consisting of three or more straight sides that connect three or more points, none of the sides intersecting. Specific polygons are named according to the number of sides, such as triangle, pentagon, etc. —**polygonal** (pə'lɪgənəl) *adj.* —**po'lygonally** *adv.*

polygraph ('pɒlɪˌgraːf, -ˌgræf) *n.* **1.** an instrument for the simultaneous recording of several involuntary physiological activities, including pulse rate and perspiration, used esp. as a lie detector. **2.** a device for producing copies of written matter.

polygyny (pə'lɪdʒənɪ) *n.* **1.** the practice in animals of a male mating with more than one female during one breeding season. **2.** the condition in flowers of having many styles. —**po'lygynous** *adj.*

polyhedron (ˌpɒlɪ'hiːdrən) *n.*, *pl.* **-drons** *or* **-dra** (-drə). a solid figure consisting of four or more plane faces (all polygons), pairs of which meet along an edge, three or more edges meeting at a vertex. Specific polyhedrons are named according to the number of faces, such as tetrahedron, icosahedron, etc. —ˌpoly'hedral *adj.*

polymath ('pɒlɪˌmæθ) *n.* a person of great and varied learning. —**polymathy** (pə'lɪməθɪ) *n.*

polymer ('pɒlɪmə) *n.* a naturally occurring or synthetic compound, such as starch or Perspex, that has large molecules made up of many relatively simple repeated units. —**polymerism** (pə'lɪməˌrɪzəm, 'pɒlɪmə-) *n.*

polymeric (ˌpɒlɪ'mɛrɪk) *adj.* of, concerned with, or being a polymer: *a polymeric compound.*

polymerization *or* **-isation** (pəˌlɪməraɪ'zeɪʃən, ˌpɒl-ɪməraɪ-) *n.* the act or process of forming a polymer or copolymer. —**'polymerˌize** *or* **-ise** (*or* pə'lɪməˌraɪz) *vb.*

polymorphous (ˌpɒlɪ'mɔːfəs) *or* **polymorphic** *adj.* **1.** having, taking, or passing through many different forms or stages. **2.** exhibiting or undergoing polymorphism.

Polynesian (ˌpɒlɪ'niːʒən, -ʒɪən) *adj.* **1.** of or relating to Polynesia, a group of Pacific islands, or to its people, or any of their languages. ~*n.* **2.** a member of the people that inhabit Polynesia, generally of Caucasoid features with light skin and wavy hair. **3.** a branch of the Malayo-Polynesian family of languages, including Maori and Hawaiian.

polynomial (ˌpɒlɪ'nəʊmɪəl) *adj.* **1.** of, consisting of, or referring to two or more names or terms. ~*n.* **2. a.** a mathematical expression consisting of a sum of terms each of which is the product of a constant and one or more variables raised to a positive or zero integral power. **b.** Also called: **multinomial.** any mathematical expression consisting of the sum of a number of terms. **3.** *Biol.* a taxonomic name consisting of more than two terms, such as *Parus major minor* in which *minor* designates the subspecies.

polyp ('pɒlɪp) *n.* **1.** *Zool.* one of the two forms of individual that occur in coelenterates. It usually has a hollow cylindrical body with a ring of tentacles around the mouth. **2.** Also called: **polypus.** *Pathol.* a small growth arising from the surface of a mucous membrane. —'polypous *or* 'polypoid *adj.*

polyphonic (ˌpɒlɪ'fɒnɪk) *adj.* **1.** *Music.* composed of relatively independent parts; contrapuntal. **2.** many-voiced. **3.** *Phonetics.* denoting a polyphone. —ˌpoly'phonically *adv.*

polyphony (pə'lɪfənɪ) *n.*, *pl.* **-nies. 1.** polyphonic style of composition or a piece of music utilizing it. **2.** the use of polyphones in a writing system. —**po'lyphonous** *adj.* —**po'lyphonously** *adv.*

polystyrene (ˌpɒlɪ'staɪriːn) *n.* a synthetic thermoplastic material obtained by polymerizing styrene; used as a white rigid foam (**expanded polystyrene**) for insulating and packing and as a glasslike material in light fittings.

polysyllable ('pɒlɪˌsɪləbəl) *n.* a word consisting of more than two syllables. —**polysyllabic** (ˌpɒlɪsɪ'læbɪk) *adj.*

THESAURUS

pollute 1. adulterate, befoul, contaminate, dirty, foul, infect, make filthy, mar, poison, soil, spoil, stain, taint 2. besmirch, corrupt, debase, debauch, defile, deprave, desecrate, dishonour, profane, sully, violate

pollution adulteration, contamination, corruption, defilement, dirtying, foulness, impurity, taint, uncleanness, vitiation

—₁polysyl'labically *adv.*

polytechnic (₁poli'tɛknɪk) *n.* **1.** *Brit.* a college offering advanced courses in many fields at and below degree standard. ~*adj.* **2.** of or relating to technical instruction and training.

polytheism ('polɪθiː₁ɪzəm, ₁polɪ'θiː₁ɪzəm) *n.* the worship of or belief in more than one god. —₁polythe'istic *adj.* —₁polythe'istically *adv.*

polythene ('polɪ₁θiːn) *n.* any one of various light thermoplastic materials made from ethylene with properties depending on the molecular weight of the polymer. Also called (esp. U.S.): **polyethylene.**

polyunsaturated (₁polɪʌn'sætʃʊ₁reɪtɪd) *adj.* of or relating to a class of animal and vegetable fats, the molecules of which consist of long carbon chains with many double bonds.

polyurethane (₁polɪ'jʊərə₁θeɪn) *n.* a class of synthetic materials commonly used as a foam for insulation and packing.

polyvinyl chloride (₁polɪ'vaɪnɪl, -'vaɪnəl) *n.* the full name of **PVC.**

pomace ('pʌmɪs) *n.* **1.** the pulpy residue of apples or similar fruit after crushing and pressing, as in cidermaking. **2.** any pulpy substance left after crushing, mashing, etc.

pomade (pə'mɑːd) *n.* **1.** a perfumed oil or ointment put on the hair, as to make it smooth and shiny. ~*vb.* **2.** (*tr.*) to put pomade on. —Also: **pomatum.**

pomander (pəʊ'mændə) *n.* **1.** a mixture of aromatic substances in a sachet or an orange, formerly carried as scent or as a protection against disease. **2.** a container for such a mixture.

pomegranate ('pomɪ₁grænɪt, 'pom₁grænɪt) *n.* **1.** an Asian shrub or small tree cultivated in semitropical regions for its edible fruit. **2.** the many-chambered globular fruit of this tree, which has tough reddish rind, juicy red pulp, and many seeds.

Pomeranian (₁pomə'reɪnɪən) *adj.* **1.** of or relating to Pomerania, a region in N central Europe. ~*n.* **2.** a breed of toy dog with a long thick straight coat, related to the Spitz.

pomfret *or* **pomfret-cake** ('pʌmfrɪt, 'pom-) *n.* a small black rounded confection of liquorice. Also called: **Pontefract cake.**

pommel ('pʌməl, 'pom-) *n.* **1.** the raised part on the front of a saddle. **2.** a knob at the top of a sword or similar weapon. ~*vb.* **-melling, -melled** *or U.S.* **-meling, -meled.** 3. a less common word for **pummel.**

pommy ('pomɪ) *n.*, *pl.* **-mies.** (*sometimes cap.*) *Sl.* a mildly offensive word used by Australians and New Zealanders for a British person. Sometimes shortened to **pom.**

pomp (pomp) *n.* **1.** stately or magnificent display; ceremonial splendour. **2.** vain display, esp. of dignity or importance. **3.** *Obs.* a procession or pageant.

pom-pom ('pompom) *n.* an automatic rapid-firing cannon, esp. a type of antiaircraft cannon used in World War II. Also called: **pompom.**

pompon ('pompon) *or* **pompom** *n.* **1.** a ball of tufted silk, wool, feathers, etc., worn on a hat for decoration. **2. a.** the small globelike flower head of certain varieties of dahlia and chrysanthemum. **b.** (*as modifier*): *pompon dahlia.*

pompous ('pompəs) *adj.* **1.** exaggeratedly or ostentatiously dignified or self-important. **2.** ostentatiously lofty in style: *a pompous speech.* **3.** *Rare.* characterized by ceremonial pomp or splendour. —'pompously *adv.* —pomposity (pom'positɪ) *or* 'pompousness *n.*

ponce (pons) *Sl.*, *chiefly Brit.* ~*n.* **1.** a man given to ostentatious or effeminate display. **2.** another word for **pimp.** ~*vb.* **3.** (*intr.*; often foll. by *around* or *about*) to act like a ponce.

poncho ('pontʃəʊ) *n.*, *pl.* **-chos.** a cloak of a kind originally worn in South America, made of a rectangular or circular piece of cloth with a hole in the middle for the head.

pond (pond) *n.* a pool of still water, often artificially created.

ponder ('pondə) *vb.* (when *intr.*, sometimes foll. by *on* or *over*) to give thorough or deep consideration (to); meditate (upon). —'ponderable *adj.*

ponderous ('pondərəs) *adj.* **1.** heavy; huge. **2.** (esp. of movement) lacking ease or lightness; lumbering or graceless. **3.** dull or laborious: *a ponderous oration.* —'ponderously *adv.* —'ponderousness *or* **ponderosity** (₁pondə'rositɪ) *n.*

pondok ('pondok) *or* **pondokie** *n. Derog.* (in southern Africa) a crudely made house built of tin sheet, reeds, etc.

pondweed ('pond₁wiːd) *n.* **1.** any of various water plants of the genus *Potamogeton,* which grow in ponds and slow streams. **2.** Also called: **waterweed.** *Brit.* any of various water plants, such as mare's-tail, that have thin or much divided leaves.

pong (pon) *Brit. inf.* ~*n.* **1.** a disagreeable or offensive smell; stink. ~*vb.* **2.** (*intr.*) to stink.

pongee (pon'dʒiː, 'pondʒiː) *n.* **1.** a thin plain-weave silk fabric from China or India, left in its natural colour. **2.** a cotton or rayon fabric similar to this.

poniard ('ponjəd) *n.* **1.** a small dagger with a slender blade. ~*vb.* **2.** (*tr.*) to stab with a poniard.

pontiff ('pontɪf) *n.* a former title of the pagan high priest at Rome, later used of popes and occasionally of other bishops, and now confined to the pope.

pontifical (pon'tɪfɪkəl) *adj.* **1.** of, relating to, or characteristic of a pontiff. **2.** having an excessively authoritative manner; pompous. ~*n.* **3.** *R.C. Church, Church of England.* a book containing the prayers and ritual instructions for ceremonies restricted to a bishop. —pon'tifically *adv.*

pontificate *vb.* (pon'tɪfɪ₁keɪt). (*intr.*) **1.** to speak or behave in a pompous or dogmatic manner. **2.** to serve or officiate at a Pontifical Mass. ~*n.* (pon'tɪfɪkɪt). **3.** the office or term of office of a pope.

pontoon[1] (pon'tuːn) *n.* **a.** a watertight float or vessel used where buoyancy is required in water, as in supporting a bridge, in salvage work, or where a temporary or mobile structure is required in military operations. **b.** (*as modifier*): *a pontoon bridge.*

pontoon[2] (pon'tuːn) *n.* a gambling game in which players try to obtain card combinations better than the banker's but never worth more than 21 points. Also called: **twenty-one** (esp. U.S.). **vingt-et-un.**

pony ('pəʊnɪ) *n.*, *pl.* **-nies.** **1.** any of various breeds of small horse, usually under 14.2 hands. **2.** a small drinking glass, esp. for liqueurs. **3.** anything small of its kind. **4.** *Brit. sl.* a sum of £25, esp. in bookmaking. **5.** Also called: **trot.** *U.S. sl.* a translation used by students, often illicitly; crib.

ponytail ('pəʊnɪ₁teɪl) *n.* a hair style for girls in which the hair is pulled tightly into a band at the back of the head into a loose hanging fall.

pony trekking *n.* the act of riding ponies cross-country, esp. as a pastime.

poodle ('puːdəl) *n.* an intelligent breed of dog, with curly hair, which is generally clipped from ribs to tail.

poof (puf, puːf) *or* **poove** (puːv) *n. Brit. sl.* a male homosexual.

THESAURUS

pomp 1. ceremony, flourish, grandeur, magnificence, pageant, pageantry, parade, solemnity, splendour, state 2. display, grandiosity, ostentation, pomposity, show, vainglory

pomposity 1. affectation, airs, arrogance, flaunting, grandiosity, haughtiness, pompousness, portentousness, presumption, pretension, pretentiousness, self-importance, vainglory, vanity 2. bombast, fustian, grandiloquence, loftiness, magniloquence, rant, turgidity

pompous 1. affected, arrogant, bloated, grandiose, imperious, magisterial, ostentatious, overbearing, pontifical, portentous, pretentious, puffed up, self-important, showy, supercilious, vainglorious 2. boastful, bombastic, flatulent, fustian, grandiloquent, high-flown, inflated, magniloquent, orotund, overblown, turgid, windy

pond dew pond, duck pond, fish pond, lochan (*Scot.*), millpond, pool, small lake, tarn

ponder brood, cerebrate, cogitate, consider, contemplate, deliberate, examine, excogitate, give thought to, meditate, mull over, muse, puzzle over, reflect, ruminate, study, think, weigh

ponderous 1. bulky, cumbersome, cumbrous, heavy, hefty, huge, massive, unwieldy, weighty 2. awkward, clumsy, elephantine, graceless, heavy-footed, laborious, lumbering 3. dreary, dull, heavy, laboured, lifeless, long-winded, pedantic, pedestrian, plodding, prolix, stilted, stodgy, tedious, verbose

pontificate declaim, dogmatize, expound, hold forth, lay down the law, pontify, preach, pronounce, sound off

pooh (pu:) *interj.* an exclamation of disdain, contempt, or disgust.

pooh-pooh ('pu:'pu:) *vb.* (*tr.*) to express disdain or scorn for; dismiss or belittle.

pool[1] (pu:l) *n.* 1. a small body of still water, usually fresh; small pond. 2. a small isolated collection of spilt liquid, puddle: *a pool of blood.* 3. a deep part of a stream or river where the water runs very slowly. 4. an underground accumulation of oil or gas. 5. See **swimming pool.**

pool[2] (pu:l) *n.* 1. any communal combination of resources, funds, etc.: *a typing pool.* 2. the combined stakes of the betters in many gambling games; kitty. 3. *Commerce.* a group of producers who agree to establish and maintain output levels and high prices, each member of the group being allocated a maximum quota. 4. *Finance, chiefly U.S.* a joint fund organized by security-holders for speculative or manipulative purposes on financial markets. 5. any of various billiard games in which the object is to pot all the balls with the cue ball, esp. that played with 15 coloured and numbered balls, popular in the U.S.; pocket billiards. ~*vb.* (*tr.*) 6. to combine (investments, money, interests, etc.) into a common fund, as for a joint enterprise. 7. *Commerce.* to organize a pool of (enterprises).

pools (pu:lz) *pl. n. Brit.* an organized nationwide principally postal gambling pool betting on the result of football matches. Also called: **football pools.**

poop[1] (pu:p) *Naut.* ~*n.* 1. a raised structure at the stern of a vessel, esp. a sailing ship. 2. Also called: **poop deck.** a raised deck at the stern of a ship. ~*vb.* 3. (*tr.*) (of a wave or sea) to break over the stern of (a vessel). 4. (*intr.*) (of a vessel) to ship a wave or sea over the stern, esp. repeatedly.

poop[2] (pu:p) *vb. U.S. sl.* 1. (*tr.; usually passive*) to cause to become exhausted; tire: *he was pooped after the race.* 2. (*intr.; usually foll. by out*) to give up or fail: *he pooped out of the race.*

poor (puǝ, pɔ:) *adj.* 1. lacking financial or other means of subsistence; needy. 2. characterized by or indicating poverty: *the country had a poor economy.* 3. scanty or inadequate: *a poor salary.* 4. (when *postpositive*, usually foll. by *in*) badly supplied (with resources, etc.): *a region poor in wild flowers.* 5. inferior. 6. contemptible or despicable. 7. disappointing or disagreeable: *a poor play.* 8. (*prenominal*) deserving of pity; unlucky: *poor John is ill again.* —'**poorness** *n.*

poorhouse ('puǝ,haus, 'pɔ:-) *n.* (formerly) a publicly maintained institution offering accommodation to the poor.

poor law *n. English history.* a law providing for the relief or support of the poor from parish funds.

poorly ('puǝlı, 'pɔ:-) *adv.* 1. badly. ~*adj.* 2. (usually *postpositive*) *Inf.* in poor health; rather ill.

poor White *n. Often offens.* **a.** a poverty-stricken and underprivileged White person, esp. in the southern U.S. and South Africa. **b.** (*as modifier*): *poor White trash.*

pop[1] (pɒp) *vb.* **popping, popped.** 1. to make or cause to make a light sharp explosive sound. 2. to burst open with such a sound. 3. (*intr.*; often foll. by *in, out,* etc.) *Inf.* to come (to) or go (from) rapidly or suddenly. 4. (*intr.*) (esp. of the eyes) to protrude: *her eyes popped with amazement.* 5. to shoot at (a target) with a firearm. 6. (*tr.*) to place with a sudden movement: *she popped some tablets into her mouth.* 7. (*tr.*) *Inf.* to pawn: *he popped his watch yesterday.* 8. **pop the question.** *Inf.* to propose

marriage. ~*n.* 9. a light sharp explosive sound; crack. 10. *Inf.* a flavoured nonalcoholic carbonated beverage. ~*adv.* 11. with a popping sound. ~See also **pop off.**

pop[2] (pɒp) *n.* 1. **a.** music of general appeal, esp. among young people, that originated as a distinctive genre in the 1950s. It is generally characterized by a heavy rhythmic element and the use of electrical amplification. **b.** (*as modifier*): *a pop group.* 2. *Inf.* a piece of popular or light classical music. ~*adj.* 3. *Inf.* short for **popular.**

pop[3] (pɒp) *n.* 1. an informal word for **father.** 2. *Inf.* a name used in addressing an old man.

pop. *abbrev. for:* 1. popular(ly). 2. population.

P.O.P. *abbrev. for* Post Office Preferred (size of envelopes, etc.).

pop art *n.* a movement in modern art that imitates the methods, styles, and themes of popular culture and mass media, such as comic strips, advertising, and science fiction.

popcorn ('pɒp,kɔ:n) *n.* 1. a variety of maize having hard pointed kernels that puff up when heated. 2. the puffed edible kernels of this plant.

pope (pǝup) *n.* 1. (*often cap.*) the bishop of Rome as head of the Roman Catholic Church. 2. *Eastern Orthodox Churches.* a title sometimes given to a parish priest or to the Greek Orthodox patriarch of Alexandria. —'**popedom** *n.*

popery ('pǝupǝrɪ) *n.* a derogatory name for **Roman Catholicism.**

popeyed ('pɒp,aɪd) *adj.* 1. having bulging prominent eyes. 2. staring in astonishment.

popgun ('pɒp,gʌn) *n.* a toy gun that fires a pellet or cork by means of compressed air.

popinjay ('pɒpɪn,dʒeɪ) *n.* 1. a conceited, foppish, or excessively talkative person. 2. an archaic word for **parrot.** 3. the figure of a parrot used as a target.

popish ('pǝupɪʃ) *adj. Derog.* belonging to or characteristic of Roman Catholicism.

poplar ('pɒplǝ) *n.* 1. a tree of N temperate regions, having triangular leaves, flowers borne in catkins, and light soft wood. 2. *U.S.* the tulip tree.

poplin ('pɒplɪn) *n.* a strong fabric, usually of cotton, in plain weave with fine ribbing.

pop off *vb.* (*intr., adv.*) *Inf.* 1. to depart suddenly or unexpectedly. 2. to die, esp. suddenly.

poppadom *or* **poppadum** ('pɒpǝdǝm) *n.* a thin round crisp Indian bread, fried or roasted and served with curry, etc.

popper ('pɒpǝ) *n.* 1. a person or thing that pops. 2. *Brit.* an informal name for **press stud.** 3. *Chiefly U.S.* a container for cooking popcorn in.

poppet ('pɒpɪt) *n.* 1. a term of affection for a small child or sweetheart. 2. Also called: **poppet valve.** a mushroom-shaped valve that is lifted from its seating by applying an axial force to its stem. 3. *Naut.* a temporary supporting brace for a vessel hauled on land.

popping crease *n. Cricket.* a line four feet in front of and parallel with the bowling crease, at or behind which the batsman stands.

poppy ('pɒpɪ) *n., pl.* **-pies.** 1. any of a numerous genus of plants having red, orange, or white flowers and a milky sap. 2. any of several similar or related plants, such as the California poppy and Welsh poppy. 3. any of the drugs, such as opium, that are obtained from these plants. 4. an artificial red poppy flower worn to mark

---

THESAURUS

pooh-pooh belittle, brush aside, deride, disdain, dismiss, disregard, make little of, play down, scoff, scorn, slight, sneer, sniff at, spurn, turn up one's nose at (*Inf.*)

pool[1] 1. lake, mere, pond, puddle, splash, tarn 2. swimming bath, swimming pool

pool[2] *n.* 1. collective, combine, consortium, group, syndicate, team, trust 2. bank, funds, jackpot, kitty, pot, stakes ~*v.* 3. amalgamate, combine, join forces, league, merge, put together, share

poor 1. badly off, broke (*Inf.*), destitute, hard up (*Inf.*), impecunious, impoverished, indigent, in need, in want, necessitous, needy, on one's beam-ends, on one's uppers, on the rocks, penniless, penurious, poverty-stricken, skint (*Brit. sl.*), stony-broke (*Brit.*

sl.) 2. deficient, exiguous, inadequate, incomplete, insufficient, lacking, meagre, miserable, niggardly, pitiable, reduced, scanty, skimpy, slight, sparse, straitened 3. below par, faulty, feeble, inferior, low-grade, mediocre, rotten (*Inf.*), rubbishy, second-rate, shabby, shoddy, sorry, substandard, unsatisfactory, valueless, weak, worthless 4. bad, bare, barren, depleted, exhausted, fruitless, impoverished, infertile, sterile, unfruitful, unproductive 5. hapless, ill-fated, luckless, miserable, pathetic, pitiable, unfortunate, unhappy, unlucky, wretched 6. humble, insignificant, lowly, mean, modest, paltry, plain, trivial

poorly 1. *adv.* badly, crudely, inadequately, incompetently, inexpertly, inferiorly, in-

sufficiently, meanly, shabbily, unsatisfactorily, unsuccessfully 2. *adj. Inf.* ailing, below par, ill, indisposed, off colour, out of sorts, rotten (*Inf.*), seedy (*Inf.*), sick, under the weather (*Inf.*), unwell

pop *v.* 1. bang, burst, crack, explode, go off, report, snap 2. *Often with* **in, out,** *etc. Inf.* appear, call, come *or* go suddenly, drop in (*Inf.*), leave quickly, nip in (*Brit. inf.*), nip out (*Brit. inf.*), visit 3. *Esp. of eyes* bulge, protrude, stick out 4. insert, push, put, shove, slip, stick, thrust, tuck ~*n.* 5. bang, burst, crack, explosion, noise, report 6. *Inf.* fizzy drink, lemonade, soda water, soft drink

pope Bishop of Rome, Holy Father, pontiff, Vicar of Christ

Remembrance Sunday.

poppycock ('pɒpɪˌkɒk) *n. Inf.* nonsense.

popsy ('pɒpsɪ) *n., pl.* **-sies.** *Old-fashioned Brit. sl.* an attractive young woman.

populace ('pɒpjʊləs) *n.* (*sometimes functioning as pl.*) **1.** local inhabitants. **2.** the common people; masses.

popular ('pɒpjʊlə) *adj.* **1.** widely favoured or admired. **2.** favoured by an individual or limited group: *I'm not very popular with her.* **3.** prevailing among the general public; common: *popular discontent.* **4.** appealing to or comprehensible to the layman: *a popular lecture on physics.* —**popularity** (ˌpɒpjʊˈlærɪtɪ) *n.* —**popularly** *adv.*

popular front *n.* (*often cap.*) any of the left-wing groups or parties that were organized from 1935 onwards to oppose the spread of fascism.

popularize *or* **-ise** ('pɒpjʊləˌraɪz) *vb.* (*tr.*) **1.** to make popular. **2.** to make or cause to become easily understandable or acceptable. —ˌ**populariˈzation** *or* **-iˈsation** *n.* —**popularˌizer** *or* -ˌ**iser** *n.*

populate ('pɒpjʊˌleɪt) *vb.* (*tr.*) **1.** (*often passive*) to live in; inhabit. **2.** to provide a population for; colonize to people.

population (ˌpɒpjʊˈleɪʃən) *n.* **1.** (*sometimes functioning as pl.*) all the persons inhabiting a specified place. **2.** the number of such inhabitants. **3.** (*sometimes functioning as pl.*) all the people of a particular class in a specific area: *the Chinese population of San Francisco.* **4.** the act or process of providing a place with inhabitants; colonization. **5.** *Ecology.* a group of individuals of the same species inhabiting a given area. **6.** *Astron.* either of two main groups of stars classified according to age and location. **7.** *Statistics.* the entire aggregate of individuals or items from which samples are drawn.

populous ('pɒpjʊləs) *adj.* containing many inhabitants. —ˈ**populously** *adv.* —ˈ**populousness** *n.*

porcelain ('pɔːslɪn) *n.* **1.** a more or less translucent ceramic material, the principal ingredients being kaolin and petuntse (hard paste) or other clays, bone ash, etc. **2.** an object made of this or such objects collectively. **3.** (*modifier*) of, relating to, or made from this material: *a porcelain cup.* —**porcelianeous** (ˌpɔːsəˈleɪnɪəs) *adj.*

porch (pɔːtʃ) *n.* **1.** a low structure projecting from the doorway of a house and forming a covered entrance. **2.** *U.S.* a veranda.

porcine ('pɔːsaɪn) *adj.* of or characteristic of pigs.

porcupine ('pɔːkjʊˌpaɪn) *n.* any of various large rodents that have a body covering of protective spines or quills. —ˈ**porcuˌpinish** *adj.* —ˈ**porcuˌpiny** *adj.*

pore[1] (pɔː) *vb.* (*intr.*) **1.** (foll. by *over*) to make a close intent examination or study (of): *he pored over the documents for several hours.* **2.** (foll. by *over, on,* or *upon*) to think deeply (about). **3.** (foll. by *over, on,* or *upon*) *Rare.* to gaze fixedly (upon).

pore[2] (pɔː) *n.* **1.** any small opening in the skin or outer surface of an animal. **2.** any other small hole, such as a space in a rock, etc.

pork (pɔːk) *n.* the flesh of pigs used as food.

porker ('pɔːkə) *n.* a pig, esp. a young one, fattened to provide meat.

pork pie *n.* a pie filled with minced seasoned pork.

porky ('pɔːkɪ) *adj.* **porkier, porkiest. 1.** characteristic of pork. **2.** *Inf.* fat; obese.

porn (pɔːn) *or* **porno** *n. Inf.* short for **pornography.**

pornography (pɔːˈnɒgrəfɪ) *n.* **1.** writings, pictures, films, etc., designed to stimulate sexual excitement. **2.** the production of such material. —Sometimes (informal) shortened to **porn** (pɔːn) *or* **porno** ('pɔːnəʊ). —**porˈnographer** *n.* —**pornographic** (ˌpɔːnəˈgræfɪk) *adj.* —ˌ**pornoˈgraphically** *adv.*

porous ('pɔːrəs) *adj.* **1.** able to absorb water, air, or other fluids. **2.** *Biol., geol.* having pores. —**porously** *adv.* —**porosity** (pɔːˈrɒsɪtɪ) *or* **ˈporousness** *n.*

porphyria (pɔːˈfɪrɪə) *n.* a hereditary disease of body metabolism, producing abdominal pain, mental confusion, etc.

porphyry ('pɔːfɪrɪ) *n., pl.* **-ries. 1.** a reddish-purple rock consisting of large crystals of feldspar in a finer groundmass of feldspar, hornblende, etc. **2.** any igneous rock with large crystals embedded in a finer groundmass of minerals. —ˌ**porphyˈritic** *adj.*

porpoise ('pɔːpəs) *n., pl.* **-poise** *or* **-poises.** any of various small cetacean mammals having a blunt snout and many teeth.

porridge ('pɒrɪdʒ) *n.* **1.** a dish made from oatmeal or another cereal, cooked in water or milk to a thick consistency. **2.** *Sl.* a term of imprisonment.

porringer ('pɒrɪndʒə) *n.* a small dish, often with a handle, for soup, porridge, etc.

port[1] (pɔːt) *n.* a town or place alongside navigable water with facilities for the loading and unloading of ships.

port[2] (pɔːt) *n.* **1.** Also called (formerly): **larboard.** the left side of an aircraft or vessel when facing the nose or bow. Cf. **starboard.** ~*vb.* **2.** to turn or be turned towards the port.

port[3] (pɔːt) *n.* a sweet fortified dessert wine.

port[4] (pɔːt) *vb.* (*tr.*) *Mil.* to carry (a rifle, etc.) in a position diagonally across the body with the muzzle near the left shoulder.

Port. *abbrev. for:* **1.** Portugal. **2.** Portuguese.

portable ('pɔːtəb[l]) *adj.* **1.** able to be carried or moved easily, esp. by hand. ~*n.* **2.** an article that can be readily carried by hand, such as a tape recorder, typewriter, etc. —ˌ**portaˈbility** *n.* —ˈ**portably** *adv.*

portage ('pɔːtɪdʒ) *n.* **1.** the act of carrying; transport. **2.** the cost of carrying or transporting. **3.** the transporting of boats, supplies, etc., overland between navigable waterways. **4.** the route used for such transport. ~*vb.* **5.** to transport (boats, supplies, etc.) thus.

portal ('pɔːt[ə]l) *n.* an entrance, gateway, or doorway, esp. one that is large and impressive.

portcullis (pɔːtˈkʌlɪs) *n.* an iron or wooden grating suspended vertically in grooves in the gateway of a castle or town and able to be lowered so as to bar the entrance.

portend (pɔːˈtɛnd) *vb.* (*tr.*) to give warning of; foreshadow.

portent ('pɔːtɛnt) *n.* **1.** a sign of a future event; omen. **2.** momentous or ominous significance: *a cry of dire portent.* **3.** a marvel.

portentous (pɔːˈtɛntəs) *adj.* **1.** of momentous or omi-

THESAURUS

populace commonalty, crowd, general public, hoi polloi, inhabitants, masses, mob, multitude, people, rabble, throng

popular 1. accepted, approved, celebrated, famous, fashionable, favoured, favourite, in, in demand, in favour, liked, sought-after, well-liked **2.** common, conventional, current, general, prevailing, prevalent, public, standard, stock, ubiquitous, universal, widespread

popularity acceptance, acclaim, adoration, approval, celebrity, currency, esteem, fame, favour, idolization, lionization, recognition, regard, renown, reputation, repute, vogue

popularize disseminate, familiarize, give currency to, give mass appeal, make available to all, simplify, spread, universalize

popularly commonly, conventionally, customarily, generally, ordinarily, regularly, traditionally, universally, usually, widely

populate colonize, inhabit, live in, occupy, people, settle

population citizenry, community, denizens, folk, inhabitants, natives, people, populace, residents, society

populous crowded, heavily populated, overpopulated, packed, populated, swarming, teeming, thronged

pore[1] *v.* brood, contemplate, dwell on, examine, go over, peruse, ponder, read, scrutinize, study

pore[2] *n.* hole, opening, orifice, outlet, stoma

pornographic blue, dirty, filthy, indecent, lewd, obscene, offensive, prurient, salacious, smutty

pornography dirt, erotica, filth, indecency, obscenity, porn (*Inf.*), porno (*Inf.*), smut

porous absorbent, absorptive, penetrable, permeable, pervious, spongy

port *Nautical* anchorage, harbour, haven, roads, roadstead, seaport

portable compact, convenient, easily carried, handy, light, lightweight, manageable, movable, portative

portend adumbrate, augur, bespeak, betoken, bode, foreshadow, foretell, foretoken, forewarn, harbinger, herald, indicate, omen, point to, predict, presage, prognosticate, promise, threaten, warn of

portent augury, foreboding, foreshadowing, forewarning, harbinger, indication, omen, premonition, presage, presentiment, prognostic, prognostication, sign, threat, warning

portentous 1. alarming, crucial, fateful, important, menacing, minatory, momentous, ominous, significant, sinister, threatening **2.** amazing, astounding, awe-inspiring, extraordinary, miraculous, phenomenal, prodigious, remarkable **3.** bloated, elephantine, heavy, pompous, ponderous, pontifical, self-important, solemn

porter · positive

769

porter ('pɔːtə) n. 1. a man employed to carry luggage, parcels, supplies, etc., at a railway station or hotel. 2. *U.S.* a railway employee who waits on passengers, esp. in a sleeper. —'**porterage** n.

porter[2] ('pɔːtə) n. 1. *Chiefly Brit.* a person in charge of a gate or door; doorman or gatekeeper. 2. a person employed as a caretaker and doorkeeper who also answers enquiries. 3. a person in charge of the maintenance of a building, esp. a block of flats.

porter[3] ('pɔːtə) n. *Brit.* a dark sweet ale brewed from black malt.

porterhouse ('pɔːtə,haus) n. 1. Also called: **porterhouse steak.** a thick choice steak of beef cut from the middle ribs or sirloin. 2. (formerly) a place in which porter, beer, etc., and sometimes chops and steaks, were served.

portfolio (pɔːt'fəuliəu) n., pl. **-os.** 1. a flat case, esp. of leather, used for carrying maps, drawings, etc. 2. such a case used for carrying ministerial or state papers. 3. the responsibilities or role of the head of a government department: *the portfolio for foreign affairs.* 4. **Minister without portfolio.** a cabinet minister who is not responsible for any government department. 5. a list of financial assets, such as shares, bonds, bills of exchange, etc.

porthole ('pɔːt,həul) n. 1. a small aperture in the side of a vessel to admit light and air, fitted with a watertight cover. Sometimes shortened to **port.** 2. an opening in a wall or parapet through which a gun can be fired.

portico ('pɔːtɪkəu) n., pl. **-coes** or **-cos.** 1. a covered entrance to a building; porch. 2. a covered walkway in the form of a roof supported by columns or pillars, esp. one built on to the exterior of a building.

portion ('pɔːʃən) n. 1. a part of a whole. 2. a part allotted or belonging to a person or group. 3. an amount of food served to one person; helping. 4. *Law.* **a.** a share of property, esp. one coming to a child from the estate of his parents. **b.** a dowry. 5. a person's lot or destiny. ~vb. (tr.) 6. to divide up; share out. 7. to give a share to (a person). —'**portionless** adj.

portly ('pɔːtlɪ) adj. **-lier, -liest.** 1. stout or corpulent. 2. *Arch.* stately; impressive. —'**portliness** n.

portmanteau (pɔːt'mæntəu) n., pl. **-teaus** or **-teaux** (-təuz). 1. a large travelling case made of stiff leather, esp. one hinged at the back so as to open out into two compartments. 2. (modifier) embodying several uses or qualities: *the heroine is a portmanteau figure of all the virtues.*

portmanteau word n. another name for **blend** (sense 7).

portrait ('pɔːtrɪt, -treɪt) n. 1. a painting or other likeness of an individual, esp. of the face. 2. a verbal description, esp. of a person's character. —'**portraitist** n.

portraiture ('pɔːtrɪtʃə) n. 1. the practice or art of making portraits. 2. **a.** a portrait. **b.** portraits collectively. 3. a verbal description.

portray (pɔː'treɪ) vb. (tr.) 1. to make a portrait of. 2. to depict in words. 3. to play the part of (a character) in a play or film. —'**por'trayal** n. —'**por'trayer** n.

Portuguese (,pɔːtjʊ'giːz) n. 1. the official language of Portugal and Brazil; it belongs to the Romance group of the Indo-European family. 2. (pl. **-guese**) a native, citizen, or inhabitant of Portugal. ~adj. 3. of Portugal, its inhabitants, or their language.

Portuguese man-of-war n. any of several large hydrozoans having an aerial float and long stinging tentacles. Sometimes shortened to **man-of-war.**

pose[1] (pəuz) vb. 1. to assume or cause to assume a physical attitude, as for a photograph or painting. 2. (intr.; often foll. by *as*) to present oneself (as something one is not). 3. (intr.) to affect an attitude in order to impress others. 4. (tr.) to put forward or ask: *to pose a question.* 5. *Sl.* to adopt a particular style of appearance and stand or strut around, esp. in bars, discotheques, etc., in order to attract attention. ~n. 6. a physical attitude, esp. one deliberately adopted for an artist or photographer. 7. a mode of behaviour that is adopted for effect.

pose[2] (pəuz) vb. (tr.) *Rare.* to puzzle or baffle.

poser[1] ('pəuzə) n. a person who poses.

poser[2] ('pəuzə) n. a baffling or insoluble question.

poseur (pəu'zɜː) n. a person who strikes an attitude or assumes a pose in order to impress others.

posh (pɒʃ) adj. *Inf., chiefly Brit.* 1. smart, elegant, or fashionable. 2. upper-class or genteel.

position (pə'zɪʃən) n. 1. place, situation, or location: *he took up a position to the rear.* 2. the appropriate or customary location: *the telescope is in position for use.* 3. the manner in which a person or thing is placed; arrangement. 4. *Mil.* an area or point occupied for tactical reasons. 5. point of view; stand: *what's your position on this issue?* 6. social status, esp. high social standing. 7. a post of employment; job. 8. the act of positing a fact or viewpoint. 9. something posited, such as an idea. 10. *Sport.* the part of a field or playing area where a player is placed or where he generally operates. 11. *Music.* the vertical spacing or layout of the written notes in a chord. 12. (in classical prosody) the situation in which a short vowel may be regarded as long, that is, when it occurs before two or more consonants. 13. *Finance.* the market commitment of an investor in securities or a trader in commodities: *a short position.* 14. **in a position.** (foll. by an infinitive) able (to). ~vb. (tr.) 15. to put in the proper or appropriate place; locate. 16. *Sport.* to place (oneself or another player) in a particular part of a field or playing area. —**po'sitional** adj.

positive ('pɒzɪtɪv) adj. 1. expressing certainty or affirmation: *a positive answer.* 2. possessing actual or specific qualities; real: *a positive benefit.* 3. tending to emphasize what is good or laudable; constructive: *he takes a very positive attitude when correcting pupils' mistakes.* 4. tending towards progress or improvement. 5. *Philosophy.* of or relating to positivism. 6. (prenominal) *Inf.* (intensifier): *a positive delight.* 7. *Maths.* having a value greater than zero: *a positive number.* 8. *Maths.* **a.** measured in a direction opposite to that regarded as negative. **b.** having the same magnitude as but opposite sense to an equivalent negative quantity. 9. *Grammar.* denoting the usual form of an adjective as opposed to its comparative or superlative form. 10. *Physics.* **a.** (of an electric charge) having an opposite polarity to the charge of an electron and the same polarity as the charge of a proton. **b.** (of a body, system, ion, etc.) having a positive electric charge. 11. *Med.* (of the results of an examination or test) indicating the presence of a suspected disorder or organism. ~n. 12. something that is

---

THESAURUS

porter[1] baggage attendant, bearer, carrier

porter[2] caretaker, concierge, doorman, gatekeeper, janitor

portion n. 1. bit, fraction, fragment, morsel, part, piece, scrap, section, segment 2. allocation, allotment, allowance, division, lot, measure, parcel, quantity, quota, ration, share 3. helping, piece, serving 4. cup, destiny, fate, fortune, lot, luck ~v. 5. allocate, allot, apportion, assign, deal, distribute, divide, divvy up (Inf.), dole out, parcel out, partition, share out

portrait 1. image, likeness, painting, photograph, picture, portraiture, representation, sketch 2. account, characterization, depiction, description, portrayal, profile, thumbnail sketch, vignette

portray 1. delineate, depict, draw, figure, illustrate, limn, paint, picture, render, represent, sketch 2. characterize, depict, describe, paint a mental picture of, put in words 3. act the part of, play, represent

portrayal characterization, delineation, depiction, description, impersonation, interpretation, performance, picture, rendering, representation

pose v. 1. arrange, model, position, sit, sit for 2. Often with **as** feign, impersonate, masquerade as, pass oneself off as, pretend to be, profess to be, sham 3. affect, attitudinize, posture, put on airs, show off (Inf.), strike an attitude 4. advance, posit, present, propound, put, put forward, set, state, submit ~n. 5. attitude, bearing, mien (Literary), position, posture, stance 6. act, affectation, air, attitudinizing, façade, front, mannerism, masquerade, posturing, pretence, role

poser brain-teaser (Inf.), conundrum, enigma, knotty point, problem, puzzle, question, riddle, tough one, vexed question

position n. 1. area, bearings, locale, locality, location, place, point, post, reference, site, situation, spot, station, whereabouts 2. arrangement, attitude, disposition, pose, posture, stance 3. angle, attitude, belief, opinion, outlook, point of view, slant, stance, standpoint, view, viewpoint 4. circumstances, condition, pass, plight, predicament, situation, state, strait(s) 5. caste, class, consequence, importance, place, prestige, rank, reputation, standing, station, stature, status 6. berth (Inf.), billet (Inf.), capacity, duty, employment, function, job, occupation, office, place, post, role, situation ~v. 7. arrange, array, dispose, fix, lay out, locate, place, put, set, settle, stand, stick (Inf.)

positive. **13.** *Maths.* a quantity greater than zero. **14.** *Photog.* a print or slide showing a photographic image whose colours or tones correspond to those of the original subject. **15.** *Grammar.* the positive degree of an adjective or adverb. **16.** a positive object, such as a terminal or plate in a voltaic cell. —**'positively** *adv.* —**'positiveness** *n.*

positivism ('pɒzɪtɪ,vɪzəm) *n.* **1.** a philosophical system that bases knowledge on perception. **2.** the philosophical system of Auguste Comte, in which the importance of positive science is stressed, esp. that of sociology over religion and metaphysics. **3.** the quality of being definite, certain, etc. —**'positivist** *n., adj.*

positron ('pɒzɪ,trɒn) *n. Physics.* the antiparticle of the electron, having the same mass but an equal and opposite charge.

poss. *abbrev. for:* **1.** possession. **2.** possessive. **3.** possible. **4.** possibly.

posse ('pɒsɪ) *n.* **1.** *U.S.* short for **posse comitatus,** the able-bodied men of a district forming a group upon whom the sheriff may call for assistance in maintaining law and order. **2.** (in W Canada), a troop of trained horses and riders who perform at stampedes. **3.** *Law.* possibility (esp. in **in posse**).

possess (pə'zɛs) *vb.* (*tr.*) **1.** to have as one's property; own. **2.** to have as a quality, characteristic, etc.: *to possess good eyesight.* **3.** to have knowledge of: *to possess a little French.* **4.** to gain control over or dominate: *whatever possessed you to act so foolishly?* **5.** (foll. by *of*) to cause to be the owner or possessor: *I am possessed of the necessary information.* **6.** to have sexual intercourse with. **7.** *Now rare.* to maintain (oneself or one's feelings) in a certain state or condition: *possess yourself in patience until I tell you the news.* —**pos'sessor** *n.* —**pos'sessory** *adj.*

possessed (pə'zɛst) *adj.* **1.** (foll. by *of*) owning or having. **2.** (*usually postpositive*) under the influence of a powerful force, such as a spirit or strong emotion. **3.** a less common word for **self-possessed**.

possession (pə'zɛʃən) *n.* **1.** the act of possessing or state of being possessed: *in possession of the crown.* **2.** anything that is owned or possessed. **3.** (*pl.*) wealth or property. **4.** the state of being controlled by or as if by evil spirits. **5.** the occupancy of land, property, etc., whether or not accompanied by ownership: *to take possession of a house.* **6.** a territory subject to a foreign state: *colonial possessions.* **7.** *Sport.* control of the ball, puck, etc., as exercised by a player or team: *he got possession in his own half.*

possessive (pə'zɛsɪv) *adj.* **1.** of or relating to possession. **2.** having or showing an excessive desire to possess or dominate: *a possessive mother.* **3.** *Grammar.* **a.** another word for **genitive.** **b.** denoting an inflected form of a noun or pronoun used to convey the idea of possession, association, etc., as *my* or *Harry's.* ~*n.* **4.** *Grammar.* **a.** the possessive case. **b.** a word or speech element in the possessive case. —**pos'sessively** *adv.* —**pos'sessiveness** *n.*

possible ('pɒsɪbəl) *adj.* **1.** capable of existing, taking place, or proving true without contravention of any natural law. **2.** capable of being achieved: *it is not possible to finish in three weeks.* **3.** having potential: *the idea is a possible money-spinner.* **4.** feasible but less than probable: *it is possible that man will live on Mars.* —,**pos'sibility** *n.*

possibly ('pɒsɪblɪ) *sentence substitute, adv.* **1. a.** perhaps or maybe. **b.** (*as sentence modifier*): *possibly he'll come.* ~*adv.* **2.** by any chance; at all: *he can't possibly come.*

possum ('pɒsəm) *n.* **1.** another name for **opossum.** **2. play possum.** to pretend to be dead, asleep, etc., in order to deceive an opponent.

post[1] (pəʊst) *n.* **1.** a length of wood, metal, etc., fixed upright to serve as a support, marker, point of attachment, etc. **2.** *Horse racing.* **a.** either of two upright poles marking the beginning (**starting post**) and end (**winning post**) of a racecourse. **b.** the finish of a horse race. ~*vb.* (*tr.*) **3.** (sometimes foll. by *up*) to fasten or put up (a notice) in a public place. **4.** to announce by or as if by means of a poster: *to post banns.* **5.** to publish (a name) on a list. **6.** to denounce publicly; brand.

post[2] (pəʊst) *n.* **1.** a position to which a person is appointed or elected; appointment; job. **2.** a position to which a person, such as a sentry, is assigned for duty. **3.** a permanent military establishment. **4.** *Brit.* either of two military bugle calls (**first post** and **last post**) giving notice of the time to retire for the night. ~*vb.* **5.** (*tr.*) to assign to or station at a particular place or position. **6.** *Chiefly Brit.* to transfer to a different unit or ship on taking up a new appointment, etc.

post[3] (pəʊst) *n.* **1.** *Chiefly Brit.* letters, packages, etc., that are transported and delivered by the Post Office; mail. **2.** *Chiefly Brit.* a single collection or delivery of mail. **3.** *Brit.* an official system of mail delivery. **4.** (formerly) any of a series of stations furnishing relays of men and horses to deliver mail over a fixed route. **5.** a rider who carried mail between such stations. **6.** *Brit.* a postbox or post office: *take this to the post.* **7.** any of various book sizes, esp. 5¼ by 8¼ inches (**post octavo**). **8. by return of post.** by the next mail in the opposite direction. ~*vb.* **9.** (*tr.*) *Chiefly Brit.* to send by post. U.S. word: **mail. 10.** (*tr.*) *Book-keeping.* **a.** to enter (an item) in a ledger. **b.** (often foll. by *up*) to compile or enter all paper items in (a ledger). **11.** (*tr.*) to inform of the latest news. **12.** (*intr.*) (formerly) to travel with relays of post horses. **13.** *Arch.* to travel or dispatch with speed; hasten. ~*adv.* **14.** with speed; rapidly. **15.** (formerly) by means of post horses.

post- *prefix.* **1.** after in time or sequence; following; subsequent: *postgraduate.* **2.** behind; posterior to: *postorbital.*

postage ('pəʊstɪdʒ) *n.* the charge for delivering a piece of mail.

postage stamp *n.* **1.** a printed paper label with a gummed back for attaching to mail as an official indication that the required postage has been paid. **2.** a mark

---

THESAURUS

positive **1.** absolute, actual, affirmative, categorical, certain, clear, clear-cut, conclusive, concrete, decisive, definite, direct, explicit, express, firm, incontrovertible, indisputable, real, unequivocal, unmistakable **2.** assured, certain, confident, convinced, sure **3.** assertive, cocksure, decided, dogmatic, emphatic, firm, forceful, opinionated, peremptory, resolute, stubborn **4.** beneficial, constructive, effective, efficacious, forward-looking, helpful, practical, productive, progressive, useful **5.** *Inf.* absolute, complete, consummate, out-and-out, perfect, rank, thorough, thoroughgoing, unmitigated, utter

positively absolutely, assuredly, categorically, certainly, definitely, emphatically, firmly, surely, undeniably, unequivocally, unmistakably, unquestionably, with certainty, without qualification

possess **1.** be blessed with, be born with, be endowed with, enjoy, have, have to one's name, hold, own **2.** acquire, control, dominate, hold, occupy, seize, take over, take possession of **3.** bewitch, consume, control, dominate, enchant, fixate, influence, mes-

merize, obsess, put under a spell

possessed bedevilled, berserk, bewitched, consumed, crazed, cursed, demented, enchanted, frenetic, frenzied, hag-ridden, haunted, maddened, obsessed, raving, under a spell

possession **1.** control, custody, hold, occupancy, occupation, ownership, proprietorship, tenure, title **2.** *Plural* assets, belongings, chattels, effects, estate, goods and chattels, property, things, wealth **3.** colony, dominion, protectorate, province, territory

possessive acquisitive, controlling, covetous, dominating, domineering, grasping, jealous, overprotective, selfish

possibility **1.** feasibility, likelihood, plausibility, potentiality, practicability, workableness **2.** chance, hazard, hope, liability, likelihood, odds, probability, prospect, risk **3.** *Often plural* capabilities, potential, potentiality, promise, prospects, talent

possible **1.** conceivable, credible, hypothetical, imaginable, likely, potential **2.** attainable, doable, feasible, on (*Inf.*), practicable, realizable, viable, within reach, work-

able **3.** hopeful, likely, potential, probable, promising

possibly **1.** God willing, haply (*Archaic*), maybe, mayhap (*Archaic*), peradventure (*Archaic*), perchance (*Archaic*), perhaps **2.** at all, by any chance, by any means, in any way

post[1] **1.** *n.* column, newel, pale, palisade, picket, pillar, pole, shaft, stake, standard, stock, support, upright **2.** *v.* advertise, affix, announce, display, make known, pin up, proclaim, promulgate, publicize, publish, put up, stick up

post[2] **1.** appointment, assignment, berth (*Inf.*), billet (*Inf.*), employment, job, office, place, position, situation **2.** beat, place, position, station ~*v.* **3.** assign, establish, locate, place, position, put, situate, station

post[3] *n.* **1.** collection, delivery, mail, postal service ~*v.* **2.** dispatch, mail, send, transmit **3.** advise, brief, fill in on, inform, notify, report to

printed on an envelope, etc., serving the same function.

postal ('pəʊstəl) *adj.* of or relating to a Post Office or to the mail-delivery service. —**'postally** *adv.*

postal code *n.* another name for **postcode.**

postal order *n.* a written order for the payment of a sum of money, to a named payee, obtainable and payable at a post office.

postbag ('pəʊst,bæg) *n.* **1.** *Chiefly Brit.* another name for **mailbag. 2.** the mail received by a magazine, radio programme, public figure, etc.

postbox ('pəʊst,bɒks) *n. Chiefly Brit.* a box into which mail is put for collection.

postcard ('pəʊst,kɑːd) *n.* a card, often bearing a photograph, picture, etc., on one side, (**picture postcard**), for sending a message by post without an envelope. Also called (U.S.): **postal card.**

post chaise *n.* a closed four-wheeled horse-drawn coach used as a rapid means for transporting mail and passengers in the 18th and 19th centuries.

postcode ('pəʊst,kəʊd) *n.* a code of letters and digits used as part of a postal address to aid the sorting of mail. Also called: **postal code.** U.S. name: **zip code.**

postdate (pəʊst'deɪt) *vb.* (*tr.*) **1.** to write a future date on (a document, etc.), as on a cheque to prevent it being paid until then. **2.** to assign a date to (an event, period, etc.) that is later than its previously assigned date of occurrence. **3.** to be or occur at a later date than.

poster ('pəʊstə) *n.* **1.** a placard or bill posted in a public place as an advertisement. **2.** a person who posts bills.

poste restante ('pəʊst rɪ'stænt) *n.* **1.** an address on mail indicating that it should be kept at a specified post office until collected by the addressee. **2.** the mail-delivery service or post-office department that handles mail having this address. ~U.S. and Canadian equivalent: **general delivery.**

posterior (pɒ'stɪərɪə) *adj.* **1.** situated at the back of or behind something. **2.** coming after or following another in a series. **3.** coming after in time. ~*n.* **4.** the buttocks; rump. —**pos'teriorly** *adv.*

posterity (pɒ'stɛrɪtɪ) *n.* **1.** future or succeeding generations. **2.** all of one's descendants.

postern ('pɒstən) *n.* a back door or gate, esp. one that is for private use.

post-free *adv., adj.* **1.** *Brit.* with the postage prepaid; postpaid. **2.** free of postal charge.

postgraduate (pəʊst'grædjʊɪt) *n.* a student who has obtained a degree from a university, etc., and is pursuing studies for a more advanced qualification. ~Also (U.S.): **graduate.**

posthaste ('pəʊst'heɪst) *adv.* **1.** with great haste. ~*n.* **2.** *Arch.* great haste.

posthumous ('pɒstjʊməs) *adj.* **1.** happening or continuing after one's death. **2.** (of a book, etc.) published after the author's death. **3.** (of a child) born after the father's death. —**'posthumously** *adv.*

postilion *or* **postillion** (pɒ'stɪljən) *n.* a person who rides the near horse of the leaders in order to guide a team of horses drawing a coach.

postimpressionism (,pəʊstɪm'prɛʃə,nɪzəm) *n.* a movement in painting in France at the end of the 19th century which rejected the naturalism and momentary effects of impressionism but adapted its use of pure colour to paint subjects with greater subjective emotion. —,**postim'pressionist** *n., adj.*

postman ('pəʊstmən) *or* (*fem.*) **postwoman** *n., pl.* -**men** *or* -**women.** a person who carries and delivers mail as a profession.

postmark ('pəʊst,mɑːk) *n.* any mark stamped on mail by postal officials, such as a simple obliteration, date mark, or indication of route.

postmaster ('pəʊst,mɑːstə) *or* (*fem.*) **postmistress** *n.* an official in charge of a local post office.

postmaster general *n., pl.* **postmasters general.** the executive head of the postal service in certain countries.

postmeridian (,pəʊstmə'rɪdɪən) *adj.* after noon; in the afternoon or evening.

post meridiem ('pəʊst mə'rɪdɪəm) the full form of **p.m.**

postmortem (pəʊst'mɔːtəm) *adj.* **1.** (*prenominal*) occurring after death. ~*n.* **2.** analysis or study of a recent event: *a postmortem on a game of chess.* **3.** In full **postmortem examination.** dissection and examination of a dead body to determine the cause of death.

post-obit (pəʊst'əʊbɪt, -'ɒbɪt) *Chiefly law.* ~*n.* **1.** a bond given by a borrower, payable after the death of a specified person, esp. one given to a moneylender by an expectant heir promising to repay when his interest falls into possession. ~*adj.* **2.** taking effect after death.

post office *n.* a building or room where postage stamps are sold and other postal business is conducted.

Post Office *n.* a government department or authority in many countries responsible for postal services and often telecommunications.

postoperative (pəʊst'ɒpərətɪv) *adj.* of or occurring in the period following a surgical operation.

postpaid ('pəʊst'peɪd) *adv., adj.* with the postage prepaid.

postpone (pəʊst'pəʊn, pə'spəʊn) *vb.* (*tr.*) **1.** to put off or delay until a future time. **2.** to put behind in order of importance; defer. —**post'ponable** *adj.* —**post'ponement** *n.* —**post'poner** *n.*

postpositive (pəʊst'pɒzɪtɪv) *adj.* **1.** (of an adjective or other modifier) placed after the word modified, either immediately after, as in *two men abreast,* or as part of a complement, as in *those men are bad.* ~*n.* **2.** a postpositive modifier.

postscript ('pəʊs,skrɪpt) *n.* **1.** a message added at the end of a letter, after the signature. **2.** any supplement, as to a document or book.

postulant ('pɒstjʊlənt) *n.* a person who makes a request or application, esp. a candidate for admission to a religious order.

postulate *vb.* ('pɒstjʊ,leɪt) (*tr.; may take a clause as object*) **1.** to assume to be true or existent; take for granted. **2.** to ask, demand, or claim. **3.** to nominate (a person) to a post or office subject to approval by a higher authority. ~*n.* ('pɒstjʊlɪt) **4.** something taken as self-evident or assumed as the basis of an argument. **5.** a prerequisite. **6.** a fundamental principle. **7.** *Logic, maths.* an unproved statement that should be taken for granted: used as an initial premiss in a process of reasoning. —,**postu'lation** *n.*

posture ('pɒstʃə) *n.* **1.** a position or attitude of the limbs or body. **2.** a characteristic manner of bearing the body: *good posture.* **3.** the disposition of the parts of a visible object. **4.** a mental attitude. **5.** a state or condition. **6.** a false or affected attitude; pose. ~*vb.* **7.** to assume or cause to assume a bodily attitude. **8.** (*intr.*) to assume an affected posture; pose. —**'postural** *adj.* —**'posturer** *n.*

posy ('pəʊzɪ) *n., pl.* **-sies. 1.** a small bunch of flowers. **2.** *Arch.* a brief motto or inscription, esp. one on a trinket or a ring.

pot¹ (pɒt) *n.* **1.** a container, usually round and deep and often having a handle and lid, used for cooking and other domestic purposes. **2.** the amount that a pot will hold; potful. **3.** a large mug or tankard. **4.** *Austral.* any of various measures used for serving beer. **5.** the money or stakes in the pool in gambling games. **6.** a wicker trap for catching fish, esp. crustaceans: *a lobster pot.* **7.** *Billiards, etc.* a shot by which a ball is pocketed. **8.** a chamberpot, esp. a small one designed for a baby or toddler. **9.** *Sl.* a prize or trophy. **10.** *Chiefly Brit.* In full **chimneypot.** a short pipe on the top of a chimney. **11.** See **flowerpot. 12.** See **potbelly. 13. go to pot.** to go to

THESAURUS

poster advertisement, *affiche,* announcement, bill, notice, placard, public notice, sticker

posterity 1. children, descendants, family, heirs, issue, offspring, progeny, scions, seed **2.** future, future generations, succeeding generations

postmortem *n.* analysis, autopsy, dissection, examination, necropsy

postpone adjourn, defer, delay, hold

over, put back, put off, shelve, suspend, table

postponement adjournment, deferment, deferral, delay, moratorium, respite, stay, suspension

postscript addition, afterthought, afterword, appendix, P.S., supplement

postulate advance, assume, hypothesize, posit, predicate, presuppose, propose, put forward, suppose, take for granted, theorize

posture *n.* **1.** attitude, bearing, carriage,

disposition, mien (*Literary*), pose, position, set, stance **2.** circumstance, condition, mode, phase, position, situation, state **3.** attitude, disposition, feeling, frame of mind, inclination, mood, outlook, point of view, stance, standpoint ~*v.* **4.** affect, attitudinize, do for effect, make a show, pose, put on airs, show off (*Inf.*), try to attract attention

ruin. ~*vb.* **potting, potted.** (*mainly tr.*) **14.** to put or preserve (meat, etc.) in a pot. **15.** to plant (a cutting, seedling, etc.) in soil in a flowerpot. **16.** to cause (a baby or toddler) to use or sit on a pot. **17.** to shoot (game) for food rather than for sport. **18.** (*also intr.*) to shoot casually or without careful aim. **19.** *Billiards, etc.* to pocket (a ball). **20.** *Inf.* to capture or win.

pot² (pɒt) *n. Sl.* cannabis used as a drug in any form.

potable ('pəʊtəbəl) *adj.* drinkable. —ˌpota'bility *n.*

potage *French.* (pɔ'taːʒ; *English* pəʊ'tɑːʒ) *n.* any thick soup.

potash ('pɒtˌæʃ) *n.* potassium chemically combined in certain compounds: *chloride of potash.*

potassium (pə'tæsɪəm) *n.* a light silvery element of the alkali metal group that is highly reactive and rapidly oxidizes in air. Symbol: K; atomic no.: 19; atomic wt.: 39.102. —po'tassic *adj.*

potassium nitrate *n.* a colourless or white crystalline compound used in gunpowders, pyrotechnics, fertilizers, and as a preservative. Formula: KNO_3. Also called: **saltpetre, nitre.**

potation (pəʊ'teɪʃən) *n.* **1.** the act of drinking. **2.** a drink or draught, esp. of alcoholic drink.

potato (pə'teɪtəʊ) *n., pl.* **-toes.** **1. a.** a plant of South America widely cultivated for its edible tubers. **b.** the starchy oval tuber of this plant, which has a brown or red skin and is cooked and eaten as a vegetable. **2.** any of various similar plants, esp. the sweet potato. **3. hot potato.** *Sl.* a delicate or awkward matter.

potato beetle *n.* another name for the **Colorado beetle.**

potato crisp *n.* (*usually pl.*) another name for **crisp** (sense 10).

potbelly ('pɒtˌbɛlɪ) *n., pl.* **-lies.** **1.** a protruding or distended belly. **2.** a person having such a belly. —'pot,bellied *adj.*

potboiler ('pɒtˌbɔɪlə) *n. Inf.* an artistic work of little merit produced quickly to make money.

pot-bound *adj.* (of a pot plant) having grown to fill all the available root space and therefore lacking room for continued growth.

poteen (pɒ'tiːn) *n.* (in Ireland) illicit spirit, often distilled from potatoes.

potent ('pəʊtənt) *adj.* **1.** possessing great strength; powerful. **2.** (of arguments, etc.) persuasive or forceful. **3.** influential or authoritative. **4.** tending to produce violent physical or chemical effects: *a potent poison.* **5.** (of a male) capable of having sexual intercourse. —'potently *adv.* —'potency *or* 'potence *n.*

potentate ('pəʊtənˌteɪt) *n.* a ruler or monarch.

potential (pə'tɛnʃəl) *adj.* **1. a.** possible but not yet actual. **b.** (*prenominal*) capable of being or becoming: latent. **2.** *Grammar.* (of a verb) expressing possibility, as English *may* and *might.* ~*n.* **3.** latent but unrealized ability: *Jones has great potential as a sales manager.* **4.** *Grammar.* a potential verb or verb form. —po'tentially *adv.*

potential difference *n.* the difference in electric potential between two points in an electric field; the work that has to be done in transferring unit positive charge from one point to the other, measured in volts. Abbrev.: **p.d.**

potentiality (pəˌtɛnʃɪ'ælɪtɪ) *n., pl.* **-ties.** **1.** latent or inherent capacity for growth, fulfilment, etc. **2.** a person or thing that possesses this.

potful ('pɒtˌfʊl) *n.* the amount held by a pot.

pother ('pɒðə) *n.* **1.** a commotion, fuss, or disturbance. **2.** a choking cloud of smoke, dust, etc. ~*vb.* **3.** to make or be troubled or upset.

potherb ('pɒtˌhɜːb) *n.* any plant having leaves, flowers, stems, etc., that are used in cooking.

pothole ('pɒtˌhəʊl) *n.* **1.** *Geog.* **a.** a deep hole in lime-

stone areas resulting from action by running water. **b.** a circular hole in the bed of a river produced by abrasion. **2.** a deep hole produced in a road surface by wear or weathering.

potholing ('pɒtˌhəʊlɪŋ) *n. Brit.* a sport in which participants explore underground caves. —'pot,holer *n.*

pothook ('pɒtˌhʊk) *n.* **1.** a curved or S-shaped hook used for suspending a pot over a fire. **2.** a long hook used for lifting hot pots, lids, etc. **3.** an S-shaped mark, often made by children when learning to write.

pothunter ('pɒtˌhʌntə) *n.* **1.** a person who hunts for profit without regard to the rules of sport. **2.** *Inf.* a person who enters competitions for the sole purpose of winning prizes.

potion ('pəʊʃən) *n.* a drink, esp. of medicine, poison, or some supposedly magic beverage.

potluck ('pɒt'lʌk) *n. Inf.* **1.** whatever food happens to be available without special preparation. **2.** a choice dictated by lack of alternative (esp. in **take potluck**).

potpourri (ˌpəʊ'pʊərɪ) *n., pl.* **-ris.** **1.** a collection of mixed flower petals dried and preserved in a pot to scent the air. **2.** a collection of unrelated items; miscellany. **3.** a medley of popular tunes.

pot roast *n.* meat cooked slowly in a covered pot with very little water.

potsherd ('pɒtˌʃɜːd) *or* **potshard** ('pɒtˌʃɑːd) *n.* a broken fragment of pottery.

pot shot *n.* **1.** a chance shot taken casually, hastily, or without careful aim. **2.** a shot fired to kill game in disregard of the rules of sport. **3.** a shot fired at quarry within easy range.

pottage ('pɒtɪdʒ) *n.* a thick soup.

potted ('pɒtɪd) *adj.* **1.** placed or grown in a pot. **2.** cooked or preserved in a pot: *potted shrimps.* **3.** *Inf.* abridged: *a potted version of a novel.*

potter¹ ('pɒtə) *n.* a person who makes pottery.

potter² ('pɒtə) *or esp. U.S.* **putter** *Chiefly Brit. vb.* **1.** (*intr.; often foll. by about or around*) to busy oneself in a desultory though agreeable manner. **2.** (*intr.; often foll. by along or about*) to move with little energy or direction: *to potter about town.* **3.** (*tr.; usually foll. by away*) to waste (time): *to potter the day away.* —'potterer *or esp. U.S.* 'putterer *n.*

Potteries ('pɒtərɪz) *pl. n.* **the.** a region of W central England, in Staffordshire, in which the china industries are concentrated.

potter's wheel *n.* a device with a horizontal rotating disc, on which clay is moulded by hand.

pottery ('pɒtərɪ) *n., pl.* **-teries.** **1.** articles made from earthenware and baked in a kiln. **2.** a place where such articles are made. **3.** the craft or business of making such articles.

potting shed ('pɒtɪŋ) *n.* a building in which plants are grown in flowerpots before being planted outside.

potty¹ ('pɒtɪ) *adj.* **-tier, -tiest.** *Brit. inf.* **1.** foolish or slightly crazy. **2.** trivial or insignificant. —'pottiness *n.*

potty² ('pɒtɪ) *n., pl.* **-ties.** a child's word for **chamber pot.**

pouch (paʊtʃ) *n.* **1.** a small flexible baglike container: *a tobacco pouch.* **2.** a saclike structure in any of various animals, such as the cheek fold in rodents. **3.** *Anat.* any sac, pocket, or pouchlike cavity. **4.** a Scot. word for **pocket.** ~*vb.* **5.** (*tr.*) to place in or as if in a pouch. **6.** to arrange or become arranged in a pouchlike form. **7.** (*tr.*) (of certain birds and fishes) to swallow. —'pouchy *adj.*

pouf *or* **pouffe** (puːf) *n.* **1.** a large solid cushion used as a seat. **2. a.** a woman's hair style, fashionable esp. in the 18th century, in which the hair is piled up in rolled puffs. **b.** a pad set in the hair to make such puffs. **3.** (puf, puːf) *Brit. sl.* less common spellings of **poof.**

poulterer ('pəʊltərə) *or* **poultryman** ('pəʊltrɪmən) *n.,* *pl.* **-terers** *or* **-trymen.** 1. a person who rears domestic fowls for their eggs or meat. 2. a dealer in poultry.

poultice ('pəʊltɪs) *n. Med.* a local moist and often heated application for the skin used to improve the circulation, treat inflamed areas, etc.

poultry ('pəʊltrɪ) *n.* domestic fowls collectively.

pounce (paʊns) *vb.* 1. (*intr.;* often foll. by *on* or *upon*) to spring or swoop, as in capturing prey. ~*n.* 2. the act of pouncing; a spring or swoop. 3. the claw of a bird of prey. —'**pouncer** *n.*

pound[1] (paʊnd) *vb.* 1. (when *intr.,* often foll. by *on* or *at*) to strike heavily and often. 2. (*tr.*) to beat to a pulp; pulverize. 3. (*tr.;* foll. by *out*) to produce, as by typing heavily. 4. to walk or move with heavy steps or thuds. 5. (*intr.*) to throb heavily. ~*n.* 6. the act of pounding. —'**pounder** *n.*

pound[2] (paʊnd) *n.* 1. an avoirdupois unit of weight that is divided into 16 ounces and is equal to 0.453 592 kilograms. Abbrev.: **lb.** 2. a troy unit of weight divided into 12 ounces equal to 0.373 242 kilograms. 3. **a.** the standard monetary unit of the United Kingdom, divided into 100 pence. Official name: **pound sterling. b.** (*as modifier*): *a pound note.* 4. the standard monetary unit of various other countries, including Cyprus, Egypt, Ireland, Israel, and Malta. 5. Also called: **pound Scots.** a former Scottish monetary unit originally worth an English pound but later declining in value to 1 shilling 8 pence.

pound[3] (paʊnd) *n.* 1. an enclosure for keeping officially removed vehicles or distrained goods or animals, esp. stray dogs. 2. a place where people are confined. 3. a trap for animals. ~*vb.* 4. (*tr.*) to confine in or as if in a pound; impound, imprison, or restrain.

poundage ('paʊndɪdʒ) *n.* 1. a charge of so much per pound of weight. 2. a charge of so much per pound sterling. 3. a weight expressed in pounds.

-pounder ('paʊndə) *n.* (*in combination*) 1. something weighing a specified number of pounds: *a 200-pounder.* 2. something worth a specified number of pounds: *a ten-pounder.* 3. a gun that discharges a shell weighing a specified number of pounds: *a two-pounder.*

pour (pɔː) *vb.* 1. to flow or cause to flow in a stream. 2. (*tr.*) to emit in a profuse way. 3. (*intr.;* often foll. by *down*) Also: **pour with rain.** to rain heavily. 4. (*intr.*) to move together in large numbers; swarm. 5. (*intr.*) to serve tea, coffee, etc.: *shall I pour?* 6. **it never rains but it pours.** events, esp. unfortunate ones, come in rapid succession. 7. **pour cold water on.** *Inf.* to discourage or disparage. 8. **pour oil on troubled waters.** to calm a quarrel, etc. ~*n.* 9. a pouring, downpour, etc. —'**pourer** *n.*

pourboire *French.* (pur'bwaːr) *n.* a tip; gratuity.

pout (paʊt) *vb.* 1. to thrust out (the lips), as when sullen, or (of the lips) to be thrust out. 2. (*intr.*) to swell out; protrude. 3. (*tr.*) to utter with a pout. ~*n.* 4. (*sometimes* **the pouts.**) a fit of sullenness. 5. the act or state of pouting. —'**poutingly** *adv.*

pouter ('paʊtə) *n.* 1. a person or thing that pouts. 2. a breed of domestic pigeon with a large crop capable of being greatly puffed out.

poverty ('pɒvətɪ) *n.* 1. the condition of being without

adequate food, money, etc. 2. scarcity: *a poverty of wit.* 3. a lack of elements conducive to fertility in soil.

poverty-stricken *adj.* suffering from extreme poverty.

poverty trap *n.* the situation of being unable to raise one's living standard because one is dependent on state benefits which are reduced if one gains any extra income.

pow (paʊ) *interj.* an exclamation imitative of a collision, explosion, etc.

P.O.W. *abbrev. for* prisoner of war.

powder ('paʊdə) *n.* 1. a substance in the form of tiny loose particles. 2. preparations in this form, such as gunpowder, face powder, or soap powder. ~*vb.* 3. to turn into powder; pulverize. 4. (*tr.*) to cover or sprinkle with or as if with powder. —'**powderer** *n.* —'**powdery** *adj.*

powder horn *n.* a powder flask consisting of the hollow horn of an animal.

powder keg *n.* 1. a small barrel to hold gunpowder. 2. a potential source of violence, disaster, etc.

powder puff *n.* a soft pad of fluffy material used for applying cosmetic powder to the skin.

powder room *n.* a ladies' cloakroom.

power ('paʊə) *n.* 1. ability to do something. 2. (*often pl.*) a specific ability, capacity, or faculty. 3. political, financial, social, etc., force or influence. 4. control or dominion or a position of control, dominion, or authority. 5. a state or other political entity with political, industrial, or military strength. 6. a person or group that exercises control, influence, or authority: *he's a power in the state.* 7. a prerogative, privilege, or liberty. 8. legal authority to act for another. 9. **a.** a military force. **b.** military potential. 10. *Maths.* **a.** the value of a number or quantity raised to some exponent. **b.** another name for **exponent** (sense 4). 11. *Physics, engineering.* a measure of the rate of doing work expressed as the work done per unit time. It is measured in watts, horsepower, etc. 12. **a.** the rate at which electrical energy is fed into or taken from a device or system. It is measured in watts. **b.** (*as modifier*): *a power amplifier.* 13. the ability to perform work. 14. **a.** mechanical energy as opposed to manual labour. **b.** (*as modifier*): *a power tool.* 15. a particular form of energy: *nuclear power.* 16. **a.** a measure of the ability of a lens or optical system to magnify an object. **b.** another word for **magnification.** 17. *Inf.* a large amount: *a power of good.* 18. **in one's power.** (*often foll. by an infinitive*) able or allowed (to). 19. **in** (**someone's**) **power.** under the control of (someone). 20. **the powers that be.** established authority. ~*vb.* (*tr.*) 21. to give or provide power to. 22. to fit (a machine) with a motor or engine.

power cut *n.* a temporary interruption or reduction in the supply of electrical power.

powerful ('paʊəful) *adj.* 1. having great power. 2. extremely effective or efficient: *a powerful drug.* ~*adv.* 3. *Dialect.* very: *he ran powerful fast.* —'**powerfully** *adv.* —'**powerfulness** *n.*

powerhouse ('paʊə,haʊs) *n.* 1. an electrical generat-

THESAURUS

pounce 1. *v.* ambush, attack, bound onto, dash at, drop, fall upon, jump, leap at, snatch, spring, strike, swoop, take by surprise, take unawares 2. *n.* assault, attack, bound, jump, leap, spring, swoop

pound[1] 1. batter, beat, belabour, clobber (*Sl.*), hammer, pelt, pummel, strike, thrash, thump 2. bray (*Dialect*), bruise, comminute, crush, powder, pulverize, triturate 3. din into, drub into, drum into, hammer into 4. *With out* bang, beat, hammer, thump 5. clomp, march, stomp (*Inf.*), thunder, tramp 6. beat, palpitate, pitapat, pulsate, pulse, throb

pound[2] *n.* compound, enclosure, pen, yard

pour 1. decant, let flow, spill, splash 2. course, emit, flow, gush, run, rush, spew, spout, stream 3. bucket down (*Inf.*), come down in torrents, rain, rain cats and dogs (*Inf.*), rain hard *or* heavily, sheet, teem 4. crowd, stream, swarm, teem, throng

pout 1. *v.* glower, look petulant, look sullen, lower, make a *moue*, mope, pull a long face, purse one's lips, sulk, turn down the corners

of one's mouth 2. *n.* glower, long face, *moue*, sullen look

poverty 1. beggary, destitution, distress, hand-to-mouth existence, hardship, indigence, insolvency, necessitousness, necessity, need, pauperism, penniless, penury, privation, want 2. dearth, deficiency, insufficiency, lack, paucity, scarcity, shortage 3. aridity, bareness, barrenness, deficiency, infertility, meagreness, poorness, sterility, unfruitfulness

poverty-stricken bankrupt, beggared, broke (*Inf.*), destitute, distressed, impecunious, impoverished, indigent, needy, on one's beam-ends, on one's uppers, penniless, penurious, poor, skint (*Brit. sl.*), stony-broke (*Brit. sl.*)

powder *n.* 1. dust, fine grains, loose particles, pounce, talc ~*v.* 2. crush, granulate, grind, pestle, pound, pulverize 3. cover, dredge, dust, scatter, sprinkle, strew

powdery chalky, crumbling, crumbly, dry, dusty, fine, friable, grainy, granular,

loose, pulverized, sandy

power 1. ability, capability, capacity, competence, competency, faculty, potential 2. brawn, energy, force, forcefulness, intensity, might, muscle, potency, strength, vigour, weight 3. ascendancy, authority, command, control, dominance, domination, dominion, influence, mastery, rule, sovereignty, supremacy, sway 4. authority, authorization, licence, prerogative, privilege, right, warrant

powerful 1. energetic, mighty, potent, robust, stalwart, strapping, strong, sturdy, vigorous 2. authoritative, commanding, controlling, dominant, influential, prevailing, puissant, sovereign, supreme 3. cogent, compelling, convincing, effective, effectual, forceful, forcible, impressive, persuasive, telling, weighty

powerfully forcefully, forcibly, hard, mightily, strongly, vigorously, with might and main

ing station or plant. **2.** a forceful or powerful person or thing.

powerless ('pauǝlıs) *adj.* without power or authority. —'**powerlessly** *adv.* —'**powerlessness** *n.*

power of attorney *n.* **1.** legal authority to act for another person in certain specified matters. **2.** the document conferring such authority.

power point *n.* an electrical socket mounted on or recessed into a wall.

power station *n.* an electrical generating station.

powwow ('pau,wau) *n.* **1.** a talk, conference, or meeting. **2.** a magical ceremony of certain North American Indians. **3.** (among certain North American Indians) a medicine man. **4.** a meeting of North American Indians. ~*vb.* **5.** (*intr.*) to hold a powwow.

pox (pɒks) *n.* **1.** any disease characterized by the formation of pustules on the skin that often leave pockmarks when healed. **2.** (usually preceded by *the*) an informal name for **syphilis. 3. a pox on (someone** *or* **something).** (*interj.*) *Arch.* an expression of intense disgust or aversion.

pp *or* **pp. 1.** *abbrev. for* per procurationem: by proxy; for and on behalf of. **2.** *symbol for* pianissimo. See **p**

pp. *abbrev. for* pages.

p.p. *abbrev. for:* **1.** parcel post. **2.** past participle. **3.** prepaid. **4.** post paid. **5.** by delegation to. **6.** (on prescriptions) post prandium: after a meal.

ppd. *abbrev. for:* **1.** postpaid. **2.** prepaid.

ppr. *or* **p.pr.** *abbrev. for* present participle.

P.P.S. *abbrev. for:* **1.** parliamentary private secretary. **2.** Also: **p.p.s.** post postscriptum: after postscript; additional postscript.

P.Q. *abbrev. for:* **1.** (in Canada) Parti Quebecois. **2.** Province of Quebec.

Pr *the chemical symbol for* praseodymium.

pr. *abbrev. for:* **1.** (*pl.* **prs.**) pair. **2.** paper. **3.** price. **4.** pronoun. **5.** power.

P.R. *abbrev. for:* **1.** proportional representation. **2.** public relations. **3.** Puerto Rico.

practicable ('præktɪkǝbǝl) *adj.* **1.** capable of being done; feasible. **2.** usable. —,**practica'bility** *or* '**practicableness** *n.* —'**practicably** *adv.*

▷ Usage. See at **practical.**

practical ('præktɪkǝl) *adj.* **1.** of, involving, or concerned with experience or actual use; not theoretical. **2.** of or concerned with ordinary affairs, work, etc. **3.** adapted or adaptable for use. **4.** of, involving, or trained by practice. **5.** being such for all general purposes; virtual. ~*n.* **6.** an examination in a practical subject. —,**practi'cality** *or* '**practicalness** *n.* —'**practically** *adv.*

▷ Usage. In careful usage, a distinction is made between *practical* and *practicable. Practical* refers to a person, idea, project, etc., as being more concerned with or relevant to practice than theory: *he is a very practical person; the idea had no practical application. Practicable* refers to a project or idea as being capable of being done or put into effect: *the plan was expensive, yet practicable.*

practical joke *n.* a prank or trick usually intended to make the victim appear foolish. —**practical joker** *n.*

practice ('præktɪs) *n.* **1.** a usual or customary action: *it was his practice to rise at six.* **2.** repetition of an activity in order to achieve mastery and fluency. **3.** the condition of having mastery of a skill or activity through repetition (esp. in **in practice, out of practice**). **4.** the exercise of a profession: *he set up practice as a lawyer.* **5.** the act of doing something: *he put his plans into practice.* **6.** the established method of conducting proceedings in a court of law. ~*vb.* **7.** the U.S. spelling of **practise.**

practise *or* U.S. **practice** ('præktɪs) *vb.* **1.** to do or cause to do repeatedly in order to gain skill. **2.** (*tr.*) to do (something) habitually or frequently: *they practise ritual murder.* **3.** to observe or pursue (something): *to practise Christianity.* **4.** to work at (a profession, etc.): *he practises medicine.* **5.** (foll. by *on* or *upon*) to take advantage of (someone, someone's credulity, etc.).

practitioner (præk'tɪʃǝnǝ) *n.* **1.** a person who practises a profession or art. **2.** *Christian Science.* a person authorized to practise spiritual healing.

praetor *or* **pretor** ('priːtǝ, -tɔː) *n.* (in ancient Rome) any of several senior magistrates ranking just below the consuls. —**prae'torian** *or* **pre'torian** *adj.,* *n.* —'**praetorship** *or* '**pretorship** *n.*

pragmatic (præg'mætɪk) *adj.* **1.** advocating behaviour that is dictated more by practical consequences than by theory. **2.** *Philosophy.* of pragmatism. **3.** involving everyday or practical business. **4.** of or concerned with the affairs of a state or community. **5.** *Rare.* meddlesome; officious. Also (for senses 3, 5): **pragmatical.** —**prag,mati'cality** *n.* —**prag'matically** *adv.*

pragmatism ('prægmǝ,tɪzǝm) *n.* **1.** a philosophical movement holding that practical consequences are the criterion of knowledge, meaning, and value. **2.** the condition of being pragmatic. —'**pragmatist** *n., adj.*

prairie ('prɛǝrɪ) *n.* (*often pl.*) a treeless grassy plain of the central U.S. and S Canada.

prairie dog *n.* any of several rodents that live in large complex burrows in the prairies of North America. Also called: **prairie marmot.**

praise (preɪz) *n.* **1.** the act of expressing commendation, admiration, etc. **2.** the rendering of homage and gratitude to a deity. **3. sing someone's praises.** to commend someone highly. ~*vb.* (*tr.*) **4.** to express commendation, admiration, etc., for. **5.** to proclaim the glorious attributes of (a deity) with homage and thanksgiving. —'**praiser** *n.*

praiseworthy ('preɪz,wɜːðɪ) *adj.* deserving of praise; commendable. —'**praise,worthily** *adv.* —'**praise,worthiness** *n.*

praline ('prɑːliːn) *n.* **1.** a confection of nuts with caramelized sugar. **2.** Also called: **sugared almond.** a sweet consisting of an almond encased in sugar.

pram (præm) *n. Brit.* a cotlike four-wheeled carriage for a baby. U.S. term: **baby carriage.**

prance (prɑːns) *vb.* **1.** (*intr.*) to swagger or strut. **2.** (*intr.*) to caper, gambol, or dance about. **3.** (*intr.*) (of a horse) to move with high lively springing steps. **4.** (*tr.*) to cause to prance. ~*n.* **5.** the act or an instance of prancing. —'**prancer** *n.* —'**prancingly** *adv.*

THESAURUS

powerless 1. debilitated, disabled, etiolated, feeble, frail, helpless, impotent, incapable, incapacitated, ineffectual, infirm, paralysed, prostrate, weak **2.** defenceless, dependent, disenfranchised, disfranchised, ineffective, subject, tied, unarmed, vulnerable

practicability advantage, feasibility, operability, possibility, practicality, use, usefulness, value, viability, workability

practicable achievable, attainable, doable, feasible, performable, possible, viable, within the realm of possibility, workable

practical 1. applied, efficient, empirical, experimental, factual, functional, pragmatic, realistic, utilitarian **2.** businesslike, down-to-earth, everyday, hard-headed, matter-of-fact, mundane, ordinary, realistic, sensible, workaday **3.** doable, feasible, practicable, serviceable, sound, useful, workable **4.** accomplished, efficient, experienced, profi-

cient, qualified, seasoned, skilled, trained, veteran, working

practically 1. all but, almost, basically, close to, essentially, fundamentally, in effect, just about, nearly, to all intents and purposes, very nearly, virtually, well-nigh **2.** clearly, matter-of-factly, rationally, realistically, reasonably, sensibly, unsentimentally, with common sense

practice 1. custom, habit, method, mode, praxis, routine, rule, system, tradition, usage, use, usual procedure, way, wont **2.** discipline, drill, exercise, preparation, rehearsal, repetition, study, training, work-out **3.** action, application, effect, exercise, experience, operation, use **4.** business, career, profession, vocation, work

practise 1. discipline, drill, exercise, go over, go through, polish, prepare, rehearse, repeat, study, train, warm up, work out **2.** apply, carry out, do, follow, live up to, observe,

perform, put into practice **3.** carry on, engage in, ply, pursue, specialize in, undertake, work at

practised able, accomplished, experienced, expert, proficient, qualified, seasoned, skilled, trained, versed

pragmatic businesslike, down-to-earth, efficient, hard-headed, matter-of-fact, practical, realistic, sensible, utilitarian

praise *n.* **1.** acclaim, acclamation, accolade, applause, approbation, approval, cheering, commendation, compliment, congratulation, encomium, eulogy, good word, kudos, laudation, ovation, panegyric, plaudit, tribute **2.** adoration, devotion, glory, homage, thanks, worship ~*v.* **3.** acclaim, admire, applaud, approve, cheer, compliment, congratulate, cry up, eulogize, extol, honour, laud, pay tribute to, sing the praises of **4.** adore, bless, exalt, give thanks to, glorify, magnify (*Archaic*), pay homage to, worship

prang (præŋ) *Chiefly Brit. inf.* ~*n.* **1.** an accident or crash in an aircraft, car, etc. **2.** an aircraft bombing raid. ~*vb.* **3.** to crash or damage (an aircraft, car, etc.). **4.** to damage (a town, etc.) by bombing.

prank (præŋk) *n.* a mischievous trick or joke. —**'prankish** *adj.* —**'prankster** *n.*

praseodymium (ˌpreɪzɪəʊ'dɪmɪəm) *n.* a malleable ductile silvery-white element of the lanthanide series of metals. Symbol: Pr; atomic no.: 59; atomic wt.: 140.91.

prate (preɪt) *vb.* **1.** (*intr.*) to talk idly and at length; chatter. **2.** (*tr.*) to utter in an idle or empty way. ~*n.* **3.** idle or trivial talk; chatter. —**'prater** *n.* —**'pratingly** *adv.*

prattle ('prætᵊl) *vb.* **1.** (*intr.*) to talk in a foolish or childish way; babble. **2.** (*tr.*) to utter in a foolish or childish way. ~*n.* **3.** foolish or childish talk. —**'prattler** *n.* —**'prattlingly** *adv.*

prawn (prɔːn) *n.* **1.** any of various small edible marine decapod crustaceans having a slender flattened body with a long tail and two pairs of pincers. **2. come the raw prawn (with).** *Austral. inf.* to attempt to deceive (someone). —**'prawner** *n.*

praxis ('præksɪs) *n., pl.* **praxises** *or* **praxes** ('præksiːz). **1.** the practice of a field of study, as opposed to the theory. **2.** a practical exercise. **3.** accepted practice or custom.

pray (preɪ) *vb.* **1.** (when *intr.*, often foll. by *for;* when *tr.*, *usually takes a clause as object*) to utter prayers (to God or other object of worship). **2.** (when *tr.*, *usually takes a clause as object or an infinitive*) to beg or implore: *she prayed to be allowed to go.* ~*interj.* **3.** *Arch.* I beg you; please: *pray, leave us alone.*

prayer[1] (prɛə) *n.* **1.** a personal communication or petition addressed to a deity, esp. in the form of supplication, adoration, praise, contrition, or thanksgiving. **2.** a similar personal communication that does not involve adoration, addressed to beings closely associated with a deity, such as saints. **3.** the practice of praying: *prayer is our solution to human problems.* **4.** (*often pl.*) a form of devotion spent mainly or wholly praying: *morning prayers.* **5.** (*cap. when part of a recognized name*) a form of words used in praying: *the Lord's Prayer.* **6.** an object or benefit prayed for. **7.** an earnest request or entreaty. —**'prayerful** *adj.*

prayer[2] ('preɪə) *n.* a person who prays.

prayer book (prɛə) *n.* a book containing the prayers used at church services or recommended for private devotions.

prayer rug (prɛə) *n.* the small carpet on which a Muslim kneels and prostrates himself while saying his prayers. Also called: **prayer mat.**

prayer wheel (prɛə) *n.* *Buddhism.* (esp. in Tibet) a wheel or cylinder inscribed with or containing prayers, each revolution of which is counted as an uttered prayer, so that such prayers can be repeated by turning it.

praying mantis *or* **mantid** *n.* another name for **mantis.**

pre- *prefix.* before in time, position, etc.: *predate; preeminent.*

preach (priːtʃ) *vb.* **1.** to make known (religious truth) or give religious or moral instruction or exhortation in (sermons). **2.** to advocate (a virtue, action, etc.), esp. in a moralizing way.

preacher ('priːtʃə) *n.* a person who preaches, esp. a Protestant clergyman.

preamble (priː'æmbᵊl) *n.* **1.** a preliminary or introductory statement, esp. attached to a statute setting forth its purpose. **2.** a preliminary event, fact, etc. —**preambular** (priː'æmbjʊlə), **preambulatory** (priː'æmbjʊlətərɪ, -trɪ), *or* **pre'ambulary** *adj.*

prebend ('prɛbənd) *n.* **1.** the stipend assigned by a cathedral or collegiate church to a canon or member of the chapter. **2.** the land, tithe, or other source of such a stipend. **3.** a less common word for **prebendary. 4.** *Church of England.* the office of a prebendary. —**prebendal** (prɪ'bɛndᵊl) *adj.*

prebendary ('prɛbəndərɪ, -drɪ) *n., pl.* **-daries. 1.** a canon or member of the chapter of a cathedral or collegiate church who holds a prebend. **2.** *Church of England.* an honorary canon with the title of prebendary.

Precambrian *or* **Pre-Cambrian** (priː'kæmbrɪən) *adj.* **1.** of, denoting, or formed in the earliest geological era, which lasted for about 4000 000 000 years before the Cambrian period. ~*n.* **2. the Precambrian.** the Precambrian era.

precarious (prɪ'kɛərɪəs) *adj.* **1.** liable to failure or catastrophe; insecure; perilous. **2.** *Arch.* dependent on another's will. —**pre'cariously** *adv.* —**pre'cariousness** *n.*

precaution (prɪ'kɔːʃən) *n.* **1.** an action taken to avoid a dangerous or undesirable event. **2.** caution practised beforehand; circumspection. —**pre'cautionary** *adj.*

precede (prɪ'siːd) *vb.* **1.** to go or be before (someone or something) in time, place, rank, etc. **2.** (*tr.*) to preface or introduce.

precedence ('prɛsɪdəns) *or* **precedency** *n.* **1.** the act of preceding or the condition of being precedent. **2.** the ceremonial order or priority to be observed on formal occasions: *the officers are seated according to precedence.* **3.** a right to preferential treatment: *I take precedence over you.*

precedent *n.* ('prɛsɪdənt). **1.** *Law.* a judicial decision that serves as an authority for deciding a later case. **2.** an example or instance used to justify later similar occurrences. ~*adj.* (prɪ'siːdᵊnt, 'prɛsɪdənt). **3.** preceding.

precentor (prɪ'sɛntə) *n.* **1.** a cleric who directs the choral services in a cathedral. **2.** a person who leads a congregation or choir in the sung parts of church services. —**precentorial** (ˌpriːsɛn'tɔːrɪəl) *adj.* —**pre'centorˌship** *n.*

precept ('priːsɛpt) *n.* **1.** a rule or principle for action.

preaccept *vb.*
preadapt *vb.*
preadolescent *n. adj.*
preadvertise *vb.*
prearrange *vb.*
prearrangement *n.*
precheck *vb.*
pre-Christian *adj.*
preclassical *adj.*
precollege *adj.*
preconviction *n.*
precook *vb.*
pre-engagement *n.*
pre-exist *vb.*
pre-existence *n.*
prefreeze *vb.*
preheat *vb.*
premenstrual *adj.*
prepack *vb.*
prepackage *vb.*
preprandial *adj.*
prerecord *vb.*
pre-Reformation *adj.*
preschool *adj.*
preselect *vb.*
preshrink *vb.*
presurgical *adj.*
prewar *adj.*

THESAURUS

praiseworthy admirable, commendable, creditable, estimable, excellent, exemplary, fine, honourable, laudable, meritorious, worthy

prance 1. bound, caper, cavort, dance, frisk, gambol, jump, leap, romp, skip, spring 2. parade, show off (*Inf.*), stalk, strut, swagger, swank (*Inf.*)

prank antic, caper, escapade, frolic, jape, lark (*Inf.*), practical joke, skylarking (*Inf.*), trick

prattle babble, blather, blether, chatter, clack, drivel, gabble, jabber, patter, rattle on, run on, twitter, witter (*Inf.*)

pray 1. offer a prayer, recite the rosary, say one's prayers 2. adjure, ask, beg, beseech, call upon, crave, cry for, entreat, implore, importune, invoke, petition, plead, request, solicit, sue, supplicate, urge

prayer 1. communion, devotion, invocation, litany, orison, supplication 2. appeal, entreaty, petition, plea, request, suit, supplication

preach 1. address, deliver a sermon, evangelize, exhort, orate 2. admonish, advocate, exhort, harangue, lecture, moralize, sermonize, urge

preacher clergyman, evangelist, minister, missionary, parson, revivalist

preamble exordium, foreword, introduction, opening statement *or* remarks, overture, preface, prelude, proem, prolegomenon

precarious chancy (*Inf.*), dangerous, dicey (*Sl.*), dodgy (*Brit. inf.*), doubtful, dubious, hairy (*Sl.*), hazardous, insecure, perilous, risky, shaky, slippery, touch and go, tricky, uncertain, unreliable, unsafe, unsettled, unstable, unsteady, unsure

precaution 1. insurance, preventative measure, protection, provision, safeguard, safety measure 2. anticipation, care, caution, circumspection, foresight, forethought, providence, prudence, wariness

precede antecede, antedate, come first, forerun, go ahead of, go before, head, herald, introduce, lead, pave the way, preface, take precedence, usher

precedence antecedence, lead, preeminence, preference, primacy, priority, rank, seniority, superiority, supremacy

precedent *n.* antecedent, authority, criterion, example, exemplar, instance, model, paradigm, pattern, previous example, prototype, standard

preceding above, aforementioned, aforesaid, anterior, earlier, foregoing, former, past, previous, prior

2. a guide or rule for morals; maxim. **3.** a direction, esp. for a technical operation. **4.** *Law.* **a.** a writ or warrant. **b.** (in England) an order to collect money under a rate. —**pre'ceptive** *adj.*

preceptor (prɪ'sɛptə) *n. Rare.* a tutor or instructor. —**preceptorial** (ˌprɪːsɛp'tɔːrɪəl) *or* **pre'ceptoral** *adj.* —**pre'ceptress** *fem. n.*

precession (prɪ'sɛʃən) *n.* **1.** the act of preceding. **2.** the motion of a spinning body, such as a top, gyroscope, or planet, in which it wobbles so that the axis of rotation sweeps out a cone. —**pre'cessional** *adj.* —**pre'cessionally** *adv.*

precinct ('priːsɪŋkt) *n.* **1. a.** an enclosed area or building marked by a fixed boundary such as a wall. **b.** such a boundary. **2.** a limited area, esp. of thought. **3.** an area in a town, often closed to traffic, that is designed or reserved for a particular activity: *a shopping precinct.* **4.** *U.S.* **a.** a district of a city for administrative or police purposes. **b.** a polling district.

precincts ('priːsɪŋkts) *pl. n.* the surrounding region or area.

preciosity (ˌprɛʃɪ'ɒsɪtɪ) *n., pl.* **-ties.** fastidiousness or affectation.

precious ('prɛʃəs) *adj.* **1.** beloved; dear; cherished. **2.** very costly or valuable. **3.** very fastidious or affected, as in speech, manners, etc. —**'preciously** *adv.* —**'preciousness** *n.*

precious metal *n.* gold, silver, or platinum.

precious stone *n.* any of certain rare minerals, such as diamond, ruby, or opal, that are highly valued as gemstones.

precipice ('prɛsɪpɪs) *n.* **1.** the steep sheer face of a cliff or crag. **2.** the cliff or crag itself. —**'precipiced** *adj.*

precipitant (prɪ'sɪpɪtənt) *adj.* **1.** hasty or impulsive; rash. **2.** rushing or falling rapidly or without heed. **3.** abrupt or sudden. ~*n.* **4.** *Chem.* a substance that causes a precipitate to form. —**pre'cipitance** *or* **pre'cipitancy** *n.*

precipitate *vb.* (prɪ'sɪpɪˌteɪt). **1.** (*tr.*) to cause to happen too soon; bring on. **2.** to throw or fall from or as from a height. **3.** to cause (moisture) to condense and fall as snow, rain, etc., or (of moisture, rain, etc.) to condense and fall thus. **4.** *Chem.* to undergo or cause to undergo a process in which a dissolved substance separates from solution as a fine suspension of solid particles. ~*adj.* (prɪ'sɪpɪtɪt). **5.** rushing ahead. **6.** done rashly or with undue haste. **7.** sudden and brief. ~*n.* (prɪ'sɪpɪtɪt). **8.** *Chem.* a precipitated solid. —**pre'cipitable** *adj.* —**pre,cipita'bility** *n.* —**pre'cipitately** *adv.* —**pre'cipiˌtator** *n.*

precipitation (prɪˌsɪpɪ'teɪʃən) *n.* **1.** *Meteorol.* **a.** rain, snow, sleet, dew, etc., formed by condensation of water vapour in the atmosphere. **b.** the deposition of these on the earth's surface. **2.** the formation of a chemical precipitate. **3.** the act of precipitating or the state of being

precipitated. **4.** rash or undue haste.

precipitous (prɪ'sɪpɪtəs) *adj.* **1.** resembling a precipice. **2.** very steep. **3.** hasty or precipitate. —**pre'cipitously** *adv.* —**pre'cipitousness** *n.*

precis *or* **précis** ('preɪsiː) *n., pl.* **precis** *or* **précis** ('preɪsiːz). **1.** a summary of a text; abstract. ~*vb.* **2.** (*tr.*) to make a précis of.

precise (prɪ'saɪs) *adj.* **1.** strictly correct in amount or value: *a precise sum.* **2.** particular: *this precise location.* **3.** using or operating with total accuracy: *precise instruments.* **4.** strict in observance of rules, standards, etc.: *a precise mind.* —**pre'cisely** *adv.* —**pre'ciseness** *n.*

precision (prɪ'sɪʒən) *n.* **1.** the quality of being precise; accuracy. **2.** (*modifier*) characterized by a high degree of exactness: *precision grinding.* —**pre'cisionism** *n.* —**pre'cisionist** *n.*

preclude (prɪ'kluːd) *vb.* (*tr.*) **1.** to exclude or debar. **2.** to make impossible, esp. beforehand. —**preclusion** (prɪ'kluːʒən) *n.* —**preclusive** (prɪ'kluːsɪv) *adj.*

precocious (prɪ'kəʊʃəs) *adj.* **1.** ahead in development, such as the mental development of a child. **2.** *Bot.* flowering or ripening early. —**pre'cociously** *adv.* —**pre'cociousness** *or* **precocity** (prɪ'kɒsɪtɪ) *n.*

precognition (ˌpriːkɒg'nɪʃən) *n. Psychol.* the alleged ability to foresee future events. —**precognitive** (priː'kɒgnɪtɪv) *adj.*

preconceive (ˌpriːkən'siːv) *vb.* (*tr.*) to form an idea beforehand. —**preconception** (ˌpriːkən'sɛpʃən) *n.*

precondition (ˌpriːkən'dɪʃən) *n.* **1.** a necessary or required condition; prerequisite. ~*vb.* **2.** (*tr.*) *Psychol.* to present two stimuli to (an organism) consecutively and repeatedly so that they become associated.

precursor (prɪ'kɜːsə) *n.* **1.** a person or thing that precedes and announces someone or something to come. **2.** a predecessor.

precursory (prɪ'kɜːsərɪ) *or* **precursive** *adj.* **1.** serving as a precursor. **2.** preliminary.

pred. *abbrev. for* predicate.

predacious *or* **predaceous** (prɪ'deɪʃəs) *adj.* (of animals) habitually hunting and killing other animals for food. —**pre'daciousness, pre'daceousness,** *or* **predacity** (prɪ'dæsɪtɪ) *n.*

predate (priː'deɪt) *vb.* (*tr.*) **1.** to affix a date to (a document, paper, etc.) that is earlier than the actual date. **2.** to assign a date to (an event, period, etc.) that is earlier than the actual or previously assigned date of occurrence. **3.** to be or occur at an earlier date than; precede in time.

predator ('prɛdətə) *n.* **1.** any carnivorous animal. **2.** a predatory person or thing.

predatory ('prɛdətərɪ) *adj.* **1.** *Zool.* another word for **predacious.** **2.** of or characterized by plundering, robbing, etc. —**'predatorily** *adv.* —**'predatoriness** *n.*

THESAURUS

precept 1. behest, canon, command, commandment, decree, direction, instruction, law, mandate, order, ordinance, principle, regulation, rule, statute **2.** axiom, byword, guideline, maxim, motto, principle, rule, saying

precinct 1. bound, boundary, confine, enclosure, limit **2.** area, district, quarter, section, sector, zone

precincts borders, bounds, confines, district, environs, limits, milieu, neighbourhood, purlieus, region, surrounding area

precious 1. adored, beloved, cherished, darling, dear, dearest, favourite, idolized, loved, prized, treasured, valued **2.** choice, costly, dear, expensive, exquisite, fine, high-priced, inestimable, invaluable, priceless, prized, rare, recherché, valuable **3.** affected, alembicated, artificial, chichi, fastidious, overnice, overrefined, twee (*Brit. inf.*)

precipice bluff, brink, cliff, cliff face, crag, height, rock face, sheer drop, steep

precipitate *v.* **1.** accelerate, advance, bring on, dispatch, expedite, further, hasten, hurry, press, push forward, quicken, speed up, trigger **2.** cast, discharge, fling, hurl, launch, let fly, send forth, throw ~*adj.* **3.** breakneck, headlong, plunging, rapid, rush-

ing, swift, violent **4.** frantic, harum-scarum, hasty, heedless, hurried, ill-advised, impetuous, impulsive, indiscreet, madcap, precipitous, rash, reckless **5.** abrupt, brief, quick, sudden, unexpected, without warning

precipitous 1. abrupt, dizzy, falling sharply, high, perpendicular, sheer, steep **2.** abrupt, careless, harum-scarum, hasty, heedless, hurried, ill-advised, precipitate, rash, reckless, sudden

précis 1. *n.* abridgment, abstract, *aperçu,* compendium, condensation, digest, outline, résumé, rundown, sketch, summary, synopsis **2.** *v.* abridge, abstract, compress, condense, outline, shorten, summarize, sum up

precise 1. absolute, accurate, actual, clear-cut, correct, definite, exact, explicit, express, fixed, literal, particular, specific, strict, unequivocal **2.** careful, ceremonious, exact, fastidious, finicky, formal, inflexible, meticulous, nice, particular, prim, punctilious, puritanical, rigid, scrupulous, stiff, strict

precisely absolutely, accurately, bang, correctly, exactly, just, just so, literally, neither more nor less, plumb (*Inf.*), slap (*Inf.*), smack (*Inf.*), square, squarely, strictly

precision accuracy, care, correctness, definiteness, exactitude, exactness, fidelity,

meticulousness, nicety, particularity, preciseness, rigour

preclude check, debar, exclude, forestall, hinder, inhibit, make impossible, make impracticable, obviate, prevent, prohibit, put a stop to, restrain, rule out, stop

precocious advanced, ahead, bright, developed, forward, quick, smart

preconception bias, notion, preconceived idea *or* notion, predisposition, prejudice, prepossession, presumption, presupposition

precondition essential, must, necessity, prerequisite, requirement, *sine qua non*

precursor 1. forerunner, harbinger, herald, messenger, usher, vanguard **2.** antecedent, forebear, forerunner, originator, pioneer, predecessor

precursory antecedent, introductory, preceding, prefatory, preliminary, preparatory, previous, prior

predatory 1. carnivorous, hunting, predacious, rapacious, raptorial, ravening **2.** despoiling, greedy, marauding, pillaging, plundering, rapacious, ravaging, thieving, voracious, vulturine, vulturous

predecease (ˌpriːdɪˈsiːs) vb. to die before (some other person).

predecessor ('priːdɪˌsɛsə) n. 1. a person who precedes another, as in an office. 2. something that precedes something else. 3. an ancestor.

predestinate vb. (priːˈdɛstɪˌneɪt). 1. (tr.) another word for **predestine**. ~adj. (priːˈdɛstɪnɪt, -ˌneɪt). 2. predestined.

predestination (priːˌdɛstɪˈneɪʃən) n. 1. Christian theol. a. the act of God foreordaining every event from eternity. b. the doctrine or belief, esp. associated with Calvin, that the final salvation of some of mankind is foreordained from eternity by God. 2. the act of predestining or the state of being predestined.

predestine (priːˈdɛstɪn) or **predestinate** vb. (tr.) 1. to determine beforehand. 2. Christian theol. (of God) to decree from eternity (any event, esp. the final salvation of individuals).

predetermine (ˌpriːdɪˈtɜːmɪn) vb. (tr.) 1. to determine beforehand. 2. to influence or bias. —ˌprede'terminable adj. —ˌprede'terminate adj. —ˌprede,termi'nation n.

predicable ('prɛdɪkəbəl) adj. 1. capable of being predicated or asserted. ~n. 2. a quality that can be predicated. 3. Logic. any of the five general forms of attribution, namely genus, species, differentia, property, and accident. —ˌpredica'bility n.

predicament (prɪˈdɪkəmənt) n. 1. a perplexing, embarrassing, or difficult situation. 2. ('prɛdɪkəmənt). Logic. a logical category.

predicant ('prɛdɪkənt) adj. 1. of or relating to preaching. ~n. 2. a member of a religious order founded for preaching, esp. a Dominican.

predicate vb. ('prɛdɪˌkeɪt). (mainly tr.) 1. (also intr.; when tr., may take a clause as object) to declare or affirm. 2. to imply or connote. 3. (foll. by on or upon) Chiefly U.S. to base (a proposition, argument, etc.). 4. Logic. to assert (a property or condition) of the subject of a proposition. ~n. ('prɛdɪkɪt). 5. Grammar. the part of a sentence in which something is asserted or denied of the subject of a sentence. 6. Logic. a term, property, or condition that is affirmed or denied concerning the subject of a proposition. ~adj. ('prɛdɪkɪt). 7. of or relating to something that has been predicated. —ˌpredi'cation n. —'predicative adj.

predict (prɪˈdɪkt) vb. (tr.; may take a clause as object) to state or make a declaration about in advance; foretell. —pre'dictable adj. —preˌdicta'bility n. —pre'dictably adv. —pre'dictor n.

prediction (prɪˈdɪkʃən) n. 1. the act of predicting. 2. something predicted; a forecast.

predikant (ˌprɛdɪˈkænt) n. a minister in the Dutch Reformed Church, esp. in South Africa.

predilection (ˌpriːdɪˈlɛkʃən) n. a predisposition, preference, or bias.

predispose (ˌpriːdɪˈspəʊz) vb. (tr.) (often foll. by to or towards) to incline or make (someone) susceptible to something beforehand. —ˌpredis'posal n. —ˌpredispo'sition n.

predominant (prɪˈdɒmɪnənt) adj. 1. superior in power, influence, etc., over others. 2. prevailing. —pre'dominance n. —pre'dominantly adv.

predominate vb. (prɪˈdɒmɪˌneɪt). 1. (intr.; often foll. by over) to have power, influence, or control. 2. (intr.) to prevail or preponderate. ~adj. (prɪˈdɒmɪnɪt). 3. another word for **predominant**. —pre'dominately adv. —pre,domi'nation n.

pre-eminent (prɪˈɛmɪnənt) adj. extremely eminent or distinguished; outstanding. —pre-'eminence n. —pre-'eminently adv.

pre-empt (prɪˈɛmpt) vb. 1. (tr.) to acquire in advance of or to the exclusion of others; appropriate. 2. (tr.) Chiefly U.S. to occupy (public land) in order to acquire a prior right to purchase. 3. (intr.) Bridge. to make a high opening bid, often on a weak hand, to shut out opposition bidding. —pre-'emptive adj. —pre-'emptor n.

pre-emption (prɪˈɛmpʃən) n. 1. Law. the purchase of or right to purchase property in preference to others. 2. International law. the right of a government to intercept and seize property of the subjects of another state while in transit, esp. in time of war.

preen (priːn) vb. 1. (of birds) to maintain (feathers) in a healthy condition by arrangement, cleaning, and other contact with the bill. 2. to dress or array (oneself) carefully; primp. 3. (usually foll. by on) to pride or congratulate (oneself). —'preener n.

pref. abbrev. for: 1. preface. 2. prefatory. 3. preference. 4. preferred. 5. prefix.

prefab ('priːˌfæb) n. a building that is prefabricated, esp. a small house.

prefabricate (priːˈfæbrɪˌkeɪt) vb. (tr.) to manufacture sections of (a building) so that they can be easily transported to and rapidly assembled on a building site. —pre,fabri'cation n.

preface ('prɛfɪs) n. 1. a statement written as an introduction to a literary or other work, typically explaining its scope, intention, method, etc.; foreword. 2. anything introductory. ~vb. (tr.) 3. to furnish with a preface. 4. to serve as a preface to. —'prefacer n.

prefatory ('prɛfətərɪ, -trɪ) or **prefatorial** (ˌprɛfəˈtɔːrɪəl) adj. of or serving as a preface; introductory.

prefect ('priːfɛkt) n. 1. (in France, Italy, etc.) the chief administrative officer in a department. 2. (in France, etc.) the head of a police force. 3. Brit. a schoolchild ap-

---

THESAURUS

predecessor 1. antecedent, forerunner, precursor, previous (former, prior) job holder 2. ancestor, antecedent, forebear, forefather

predestination destiny, doom, election (Theology), fate, foreordainment, foreordination, lot, necessity, predetermination

predestine doom, fate, foreordain, mean, predestinate, predetermine, pre-elect, preordain

predetermined agreed, arranged in advance, cut and dried (Inf.), decided beforehand, fixed, prearranged, preplanned, set, settled, set up

predicament corner, dilemma, emergency, fix (Inf.), hole (Sl.), jam (Inf.), mess, pickle (Inf.), pinch, plight, quandary, scrape (Inf.), situation, spot (Inf.), state

predicate 1. affirm, assert, aver, avouch, avow, contend, declare, maintain, proclaim, state 2. connote, imply, indicate, intimate, signify, suggest 3. With on or upon base, build, establish, found, ground, postulate, rest

predict augur, divine, forebode, forecast, foresee, foretell, portend, presage, prognosticate, prophesy, soothsay

predictable anticipated, calculable, certain, expected, foreseeable, foreseen, likely, reliable, sure, sure-fire (Inf.)

prediction augury, divination, forecast,

prognosis, prognostication, prophecy, soothsaying

predilection bias, fancy, fondness, inclination, leaning, liking, love, partiality, penchant, predisposition, preference, proclivity, proneness, propensity, taste, tendency, weakness

predispose affect, bias, dispose, incline, induce, influence, lead, make (one) of a mind to, prejudice, prepare, prime, prompt, sway

predisposed agreeable, amenable, given to, inclined, liable, minded, prone, ready, subject, susceptible, willing

predisposition bent, bias, disposition, inclination, likelihood, penchant, potentiality, predilection, proclivity, proneness, propensity, susceptibility, tendency, willingness

predominance ascendancy, control, dominance, dominion, edge, greater number, hold, leadership, mastery, paramountcy, preponderance, supremacy, sway, upper hand, weight

predominant ascendant, capital, chief, controlling, dominant, important, leading, main, paramount, preponderant, prevailing, prevalent, primary, prime, principal, prominent, ruling, sovereign, superior, supreme

predominate be most noticeable, carry weight, get the upper hand, hold sway, outweigh, overrule, overshadow, preponderate,

prevail, reign, rule, tell

pre-eminence distinction, excellence, paramountcy, predominance, prestige, prominence, renown, superiority, supremacy, transcendence

pre-eminent chief, consummate, distinguished, excellent, foremost, incomparable, matchless, outstanding, paramount, peerless, predominant, renowned, superior, supreme, transcendent, unequalled, unrivalled, unsurpassed

pre-eminently above all, by far, conspicuously, eminently, emphatically, exceptionally, far and away, incomparably, inimitably, matchlessly, notably, par excellence, particularly, second to none, signally, singularly, strikingly, superlatively, supremely

pre-empt acquire, anticipate, appropriate, arrogate, assume, seize, take over, usurp

preen 1. Of birds clean, plume 2. array, deck out, doll up (Sl.), dress up, prettify, primp, prink, spruce up, titivate, trim 3. **preen oneself (on)** congratulate oneself, pique oneself, plume oneself, pride oneself

preface 1. n. exordium, foreword, introduction, preamble, preliminary, prelude, proem, prolegomenon, prologue 2. v. begin, introduce, launch, lead up to, open, precede, prefix

pointed to a position of limited power over his fellows. **4.** (in ancient Rome) any of several magistrates or military commanders. **5.** *R.C. Church.* one of two senior masters in a Jesuit school or college. —**prefectorial** (ˌpriːfɛkˈtɔːrɪəl) *adj.*

prefecture (ˈpriːfɛkˌtjʊə) *n.* **1.** the office, position, or area of authority of a prefect. **2.** the official residence of a prefect in France, etc.

prefer (prɪˈfɜː) *vb.* **-ferring, -ferred. 1.** (when *tr., may take a clause as object or an infinitive*) to like better or value more highly: *I prefer to stand.* **2.** *Law.* (esp. of the police) to put (charges) before a court, magistrate, etc., for consideration and judgment. **3.** (*tr.; often passive*) to advance in rank over another or others; promote.

preferable (ˈprɛfərəbəl) *adj.* preferred or more desirable. —**ˈpreferably** *adv.*

preference (ˈprɛfərəns, ˈprɛfrəns) *n.* **1.** the act of preferring. **2.** something or someone preferred. **3.** *International trade.* the granting of favour or precedence to particular foreign countries, as by levying differential tariffs.

preference shares *pl. n. Brit.* fixed interest shares issued by a company and giving their holders a prior right over ordinary shareholders to payment of dividend and to repayment of capital if the company is liquidated. U.S. name: **preferred stock.** Cf. **ordinary shares.**

preferential (ˌprɛfəˈrɛnʃəl) *adj.* **1.** showing or resulting from preference. **2.** giving, receiving, or originating from preference in international trade. —**ˌpreferˈentially** *adv.*

preferment (prɪˈfɜːmənt) *n.* **1.** the act of promoting to a higher position, office, etc. **2.** the state of being preferred for promotion or social advancement. **3.** the act of preferring.

prefigure (priːˈfɪgə) *vb.* (*tr.*) **1.** to represent or suggest in advance. **2.** to imagine beforehand. —**ˌprefiguˈration** *n.* —**preˈfigurement** *n.*

prefix *n.* (ˈpriːfɪks). **1.** *Grammar.* an affix that precedes the stem to which it is attached, as for example *un-* in *unhappy.* Cf. **suffix** (sense 1). **2.** something coming or placed before. ~*vb.* (priːˈfɪks, ˈpriːfɪks). (*tr.*) **3.** to put or place before. **4.** *Grammar.* to add (a morpheme) as a prefix to the beginning of a word. —**prefixion** (priːˈfɪkʃən) *n.*

pregnant (ˈprɛgnənt) *adj.* **1.** carrying a foetus or foetuses within the womb. **2.** full of meaning or significance. **3.** inventive or imaginative. **4.** prolific or fruitful. —**ˈpregnancy** *n.* —**ˈpregnantly** *adv.*

prehensile (prɪˈhɛnsaɪl) *adj.* adapted for grasping, esp. by wrapping around a support: *a prehensile tail.* —**prehensility** (ˌpriːhɛnˈsɪlɪtɪ) *n.*

prehistoric (ˌpriːhɪˈstɒrɪk) *or* **prehistorical** *adj.* of or relating to man's development before the appearance of the written word. —**ˌprehisˈtorically** *adv.* —**preˈhistory** *n.*

prejudge (priːˈdʒʌdʒ) *vb.* (*tr.*) to judge beforehand, esp. without sufficient evidence.

prejudice (ˈprɛdʒʊdɪs) *n.* **1.** an opinion formed beforehand, esp. an unfavourable one based on inadequate facts. **2.** the act or condition of holding such opinions. **3.** intolerance of or dislike for people of a specific race, religion, etc. **4.** disadvantage or injury resulting from prejudice. **5. in** (*or* **to**) **the prejudice of.** to the detriment of. **6. without prejudice.** *Law.* without dismissing or detracting from an existing right or claim. ~*vb.* (*tr.*) **7.** to cause to be prejudiced. **8.** to disadvantage or injure by prejudice.

prejudicial (ˌprɛdʒʊˈdɪʃəl) *adj.* causing prejudice; damaging. —**ˌprejuˈdicially** *adv.*

prelacy (ˈprɛləsɪ) *n., pl.* **-cies. 1.** Also called: **prelature** (ˈprɛlɪtʃə). **a.** the office or status of a prelate. **b.** prelates collectively. **2.** *Often derog.* government of the Church by prelates.

prelate (ˈprɛlɪt) *n.* a Church dignitary of high rank, such as a cardinal, bishop, or abbot. —**prelatic** (prɪˈlætɪk) *or* **preˈlatical** *adj.*

preliminaries (prɪˈlɪmɪnərɪz) *pl. n.* the full word for **prelims.**

preliminary (prɪˈlɪmɪnərɪ) *adj.* **1.** (*usually prenominal*) occurring before or in preparation; introductory. ~*n., pl.* **-naries. 2.** a preliminary event or occurrence. **3.** an eliminating contest held before the main competition. —**preˈliminarily** *adv.*

prelims (ˈpriːlɪmz, prəˈlɪmz) *pl. n.* **1.** Also called: **front matter.** the pages of a book, such as the title page and contents, before the main text. **2.** the first public examinations taken for the bachelor's degree in some universities. **3.** (in Scotland) the school examinations taken before public examinations.

prelude (ˈprɛljuːd) *n.* **1. a.** a piece of music that precedes a fugue, or forms the first movement of a suite, or an introduction to an act in an opera, etc. **b.** (esp. for piano) a self-contained piece of music. **2.** an introduction or preceding event, occurrence, etc. ~*vb.* **3.** to serve as a prelude to (something). **4.** (*tr.*) to introduce by a prelude. —**preˈludial** *adj.* —**prelusion** (prɪˈljuːʒən) *n.*

premarital (priːˈmærɪtəl) *adj.* (esp. of sexual relations) occurring before marriage.

premature (ˌprɛməˈtjʊə, ˈprɛməˌtjʊə) *adj.* **1.** occurring or existing before the normal or expected time. **2.** impulsive or hasty: *a premature judgment.* **3.** (of an infant) born before the end of the full period of gestation. —**ˌpremaˈturely** *adv.*

premeditate (prɪˈmɛdɪˌteɪt) *vb.* to plan or consider (something, such as a violent crime) beforehand. —**preˌmediˈtation** *n.* —**preˈmediˌtator** *n.*

THESAURUS

prefer 1. adopt, be partial to, choose, desire, elect, fancy, favour, go for, incline towards, like better, opt for, pick, plump for, select, single out, wish, would rather, would sooner **2.** file, lodge, place, present, press, put forward **3.** advance, aggrandize, elevate, move up, promote, raise, upgrade

preferable best, better, choice, chosen, favoured, more desirable, more eligible, superior, worthier

preferably as a matter of choice, by choice, first, in or for preference, much rather, much sooner, rather, sooner, willingly

preference 1. choice, desire, election, favourite, first choice, option, partiality, pick, predilection, selection, top of the list **2.** advantage, favoured treatment, favouritism, first place, precedence, pride of place, priority

preferential advantageous, better, favoured, partial, partisan, privileged, special, superior

preferment advancement, dignity, elevation, exaltation, promotion, rise, upgrading

pregnancy gestation, gravidity

pregnant 1. big *or* heavy with child, enceinte, expectant, expecting (*Inf.*), gravid, in the club (*Brit. sl.*), in the family way (*Inf.*), in the pudding club (*Sl.*), preggers (*Brit. inf.*),

with child **2.** charged, eloquent, expressive, loaded, meaningful, pointed, significant, suggestive, telling, weighty **3.** creative, imaginative, inventive, original, seminal **4.** abounding in, abundant, fecund, fertile, fraught, fruitful, full, productive, prolific, replete, rich in, teeming

prehistoric 1. earliest, early, primeval, primitive, primordial **2.** ancient, antediluvian, antiquated, archaic, out of date, out of the ark (*Inf.*)

prejudge anticipate, forejudge, jump to conclusions, make a hasty assessment, presume, presuppose

prejudice *n.* **1.** bias, jaundiced eye, partiality, preconceived notion, preconception, prejudgment, warp **2.** bigotry, chauvinism, discrimination, injustice, intolerance, narrow-mindedness, racism, sexism, unfairness **3.** damage, detriment, disadvantage, harm, hurt, impairment, loss, mischief ~*v.* **4.** bias, colour, distort, influence, jaundice, poison, predispose, prepossess, slant, sway, warp **5.** damage, harm, hinder, hurt, impair, injure, mar, spoil, undermine

prejudiced biased, bigoted, conditioned, discriminatory, influenced, intolerant, jaundiced, narrow-minded, one-sided, opinionated, partial, partisan, prepossessed, unfair

prejudicial counterproductive, damag-

ing, deleterious, detrimental, disadvantageous, harmful, hurtful, inimical, injurious, undermining, unfavourable

preliminary 1. *adj.* exploratory, first, initial, initiatory, introductory, opening, pilot, precursory, prefatory, preparatory, prior, qualifying, test, trial **2.** *n.* beginning, first round, foundation, groundwork, initiation, introduction, opening, preamble, preface, prelims, prelude, preparation, start

prelude beginning, commencement, curtain-raiser, exordium, foreword, intro (*Inf.*), introduction, overture, preamble, preface, preliminary, preparation, proem, prolegomenon, prologue, start

premature 1. abortive, early, embryonic, forward, green, immature, incomplete, predeveloped, raw, undeveloped, unfledged, unripe, unseasonable, untimely **2.** *Fig.* hasty, ill-considered, ill-timed, impulsive, inopportune, overhasty, precipitate, previous (*Inf.*), rash, too soon, untimely

prematurely 1. before one's time, too early, too soon, untimely **2.** at half-cock, half-cocked, overhastily, precipitately, rashly, too hastily, too soon

premeditated aforethought, calculated, conscious, considered, contrived, deliberate, intended, intentional, planned, prepense, studied, wilful

premenstrual tension or **syndrome** (priː-ˈmɛnstrʊəl) n. nervous tension that may be experienced as a result of hormonal changes in the days before a menstrual period. Abbrevs.: **PMT, PMS**.

premier (ˈprɛmjə) n. **1.** another name for **prime minister**. **2.** any of the heads of governments of the Canadian provinces and the Australian states. **3.** Austral. a team that wins a premiership. ~adj. (prenominal) **4.** first in importance, rank, etc. **5.** first in occurrence; earliest.

premiere (ˈprɛmɪˌɛə, ˈprɛmɪə) n. **1.** the first public performance of a film, play, opera, etc. **2.** the leading lady in a theatre company. ~vb. **3.** (tr.) to give a premiere of: the show will be premiered on Broadway.

premise (prɪˈmaɪz, ˈprɛmɪs) vb. (when tr., may take a clause as object) to state or assume (a proposition) as a premiss in an argument, etc.

premises (ˈprɛmɪsɪz) pl. n. **1.** a piece of land together with its buildings, esp. considered as a place of business. **2.** Law. (in a deed, etc.) the matters referred to previously; the aforesaid.

premiss or **premise** (ˈprɛmɪs) n. **1.** a statement from which a conclusion can logically be drawn. **2.** Logic. either of the two propositions of a syllogism.

premium (ˈpriːmɪəm) n. **1.** an amount paid in addition to a standard rate, price, wage, etc.; bonus. **2.** the amount paid or payable, usually in regular instalments, for an insurance policy. **3.** the amount above nominal or par value at which something sells. **4.** an offer of something free or at a reduced price as an inducement to buy a commodity or service. **5.** a prize given to the winner of a competition. **6.** U.S. an amount sometimes charged for a loan of money in addition to the interest. **7.** great value or regard: to put a premium on someone's services. **8. at a premium. a.** in great demand, usually because of scarcity. **b.** above par.

Premium Savings Bonds pl. n. (in Britain) bonds issued by the Treasury since 1956 for purchase by the public. No interest is paid but there is a monthly draw for cash prizes of various sums. Also called: **premium bonds**.

premonition (ˌprɛməˈnɪʃən) n. **1.** an intuition of a future, usually unwelcome, occurrence; foreboding. **2.** an early warning of a future event. —**premonitory** (prɪˈmɒnɪtərɪ) adj.

preoccupy (priːˈɒkjʊˌpaɪ) vb. -**pying**, -**pied**. (tr.) **1.** to engross the thoughts or mind of. **2.** to occupy before or in advance of another. —**preˌoccuˈpation** n.

preordain (ˌpriːɔːˈdeɪn) vb. (tr.) to ordain, decree, or appoint beforehand.

prep (prɛp) n. Inf. short for **preparation** (sense 5) or (chiefly U.S.) **preparatory school**.

prep. abbrev. for: **1.** preparation. **2.** preparatory. **3.** preposition.

preparation (ˌprɛpəˈreɪʃən) n. **1.** the act or process of preparing. **2.** the state of being prepared; readiness. **3.** (often pl.) a measure done in order to prepare for something; provision: to make preparations for something. **4.** something that is prepared, esp. a medicine. **5.** (esp. in a boarding school) **a.** homework. **b.** the period reserved for this. Usually shortened to **prep. 6.** Music. **a.** the anticipation of a dissonance so that the note producing it in one chord is first heard in the preceding chord as a consonance. **b.** a note so employed.

preparatory (prɪˈpærətərɪ) adj. **1.** serving to prepare. **2.** introductory. **3.** occupied in preparation. **4. preparatory to.** before: a drink preparatory to eating. —**preˈparatorily** adv.

preparatory school n. **1.** (in Britain) a private school, usually single-sex and for children between the ages of 6 and 13, generally preparing pupils for public school. **2.** (in the U.S.) a private secondary school preparing pupils for college. ~Often shortened to **prep school**.

prepare (prɪˈpɛə) vb. **1.** to make ready or suitable in advance for some use, event, etc.: to prepare a meal; to prepare to go. **2.** to put together using parts or ingredients; construct. **3.** (tr.) to equip or outfit, as for an expedition. **4.** (tr.) Music. to soften the impact of (a dissonant note) by the use of preparation. **5. be prepared.** (foll. by an infinitive) to be willing and able: I'm not prepared to reveal these figures. —**preˈparer** n.

prepay (priːˈpeɪ) vb. -**paying**, -**paid**. (tr.) to pay for in advance. —**preˈpayable** adj.

prepense (prɪˈpɛns) adj. (postpositive) (usually in legal contexts) premeditated (esp. in **malice prepense**).

preponderant (prɪˈpɒndərənt) adj. greater in weight, force, influence, etc. —**preˈponderance** n. —**preˈponderantly** adv.

preponderate (prɪˈpɒndəˌreɪt) vb. (intr.) **1.** (often foll. by over) to be more powerful, important, numerous, etc., (than). **2.** to be of greater weight than something else. —**preˌponderˈation** n.

preposition (ˌprɛpəˈzɪʃən) n. a word or group of words used before a noun or pronoun to relate it grammatically or semantically to some other constituent of a sentence. —**ˌprepoˈsitional** adj. —**ˌprepoˈsitionally** adv.
▷ **Usage.** The practice of ending a sentence with a preposition (they are the people I hate talking to) has been much condemned, but careful users avoid it only where it would be stylistically clumsy.

prepossess (ˌpriːpəˈzɛs) vb. (tr.) **1.** to preoccupy or engross mentally. **2.** to influence in advance, esp., to make a favourable impression on beforehand. —**ˌprepos'session** n.

prepossessing (ˌpriːpəˈzɛsɪŋ) adj. creating a favourable impression; attractive.

THESAURUS

premeditation deliberation, design, determination, forethought, intention, malice aforethought, planning, plotting, prearrangement, predetermination, purpose

premier n. **1.** chancellor, head of government, P.M., prime minister ~adj. **2.** arch, chief, first, foremost, head, highest, leading, main, primary, prime, principal, top **3.** earliest, first, inaugural, initial, original

premiere debut, first night, first performance, first showing, opening

premises building, establishment, place, property, site

premiss, premise argument, assertion, assumption, ground, hypothesis, postulate, postulation, presupposition, proposition, supposition, thesis

premium 1. bonus, boon, bounty, fee, percentage (Inf.), perk (Brit. inf.), perquisite, prize, recompense, remuneration, reward **2.** appreciation, regard, stock, store, value **3. at a premium** beyond one's means, costly, expensive, hard to come by, in great demand, in short supply, like gold dust, not to be had for love or money, rare, scarce, valuable

premonition apprehension, feeling, feeling in one's bones, foreboding, forewarning, funny feeling (Inf.), hunch, idea, intuition, misgiving, omen, portent, presage, presentiment, sign, suspicion, warning

preoccupation 1. absence of mind, absent-mindedness, absorption, abstraction, brown study, daydreaming, engrossment, immersion, inattentiveness, musing, oblivion, pensiveness, prepossession, reverie, woolgathering **2.** bee in one's bonnet, concern, fixation, hang-up (Inf.), hobbyhorse, idée fixe, obsession, pet subject

preoccupied absent-minded, absorbed, abstracted, caught up in, distracted, distrait, engrossed, faraway, heedless, immersed, in a brown study, intent, lost in, lost in thought, oblivious, rapt, taken up, unaware, wrapped up

preparation 1. development, getting ready, groundwork, preparing, putting in order **2.** alertness, anticipation, expectation, foresight, precaution, preparedness, provision, readiness, safeguard **3.** Often plural arrangement, measure, plan, provision **4.** composition, compound, concoction, medicine, mixture, tincture **5.** homework, prep (Inf.), revision, schoolwork, study, swotting (Inf.)

preparatory 1. basic, elementary, introductory, opening, prefatory, preliminary, preparative, primary **2. preparatory to** before, in advance of, in anticipation of, in preparation for, prior to

prepare 1. adapt, adjust, anticipate, arrange, coach, dispose, form, groom, make provision, make ready, plan, practise, prime, put in order, train, warm up **2.** brace, fortify, gird, ready, steel, strengthen **3.** assemble, concoct, construct, contrive, draw up, fashion, fix up, get up (Inf.), make, produce, put together, turn out **4.** accoutre, equip, fit, fit out, furnish, outfit, provide, supply

prepared 1. all set, arranged, fit, in order, in readiness, planned, primed, ready, set **2.** able, disposed, inclined, minded, of a mind, predisposed, willing

preparedness alertness, fitness, order, preparation, readiness

preponderance ascendancy, bulk, dominance, domination, dominion, extensiveness, greater numbers, greater part, lion's share, mass, power, predominance, prevalence, superiority, supremacy, sway, weight

preponderant ascendant, dominant, extensive, foremost, greater, important, larger, paramount, predominant, prevailing, prevalent, significant

prepossessed biased, inclined, partial, partisan, predisposed, prejudiced

prepossessing alluring, amiable, appealing, attractive, beautiful, bewitching,

preposterous (prɪ'pɒstərəs) *adj.* contrary to nature, reason, or sense; absurd; ridiculous. —**pre'posterously** *adv.* —**pre'posterousness** *n.*

prep school *n. Inf.* See **preparatory school.**

prepuce ('priːpjuːs) *n.* **1.** the retractable fold of skin covering the tip of the penis. Nontechnical name: **foreskin. 2.** a similar fold of skin covering the tip of the clitoris.

Pre-Raphaelite (ˌpriː'ræfəˌlaɪt) *n.* **1.** a member of the **Pre-Raphaelite Brotherhood,** an association of painters and writers founded in 1848 to revive the fidelity to nature and the vivid realistic colour considered typical of Italian painting before Raphael. ~*adj.* **2.** of, in the manner of, or relating to Pre-Raphaelite painting and painters. —ˌ**Pre-'Raphael,itism** *n.*

prerequisite (priː'rɛkwɪzɪt) *adj.* **1.** required as a prior condition. ~*n.* **2.** something required as a prior condition.

prerogative (prɪ'rɒgətɪv) *n.* **1.** an exclusive privilege or right exercised by a person or group of people holding a particular office or hereditary rank. **2.** any privilege or right. **3.** a power, privilege, or immunity restricted to a sovereign or sovereign government. ~*adj.* **4.** having or able to exercise a prerogative.

pres. *abbrev. for:* **1.** present (time). **2.** presidential. **Pres.** *abbrev. for* President.

presage *n.* ('prɛsɪdʒ). **1.** an intimation or warning of something about to happen; portent; omen. **2.** a sense of what is about to happen; foreboding. ~*vb.* ('prɛsɪdʒ, prɪ'seɪdʒ). **3.** (*tr.*) to have a presentiment of. **4.** (*tr.*) to give a forewarning of; portend. —**pre'sageful** *adj.* —**pre'sager** *n.*

presbyopia (ˌprɛzbɪ'əʊpɪə) *n.* a progressively diminishing ability of the eye to focus, noticeable from middle to old age, caused by loss of elasticity of the crystalline lens. —**presbyopic** (ˌprɛzbɪ'ɒpɪk) *adj.*

presbyter ('prɛzbɪtə) *n.* **1. a.** an elder of a congregation in the early Christian Church. **b.** (in some Churches having episcopal politics) an official who is subordinate to a bishop and has administrative and sacerdotal functions. **2.** (in some hierarchical Churches) another name for **priest. 3.** (in the Presbyterian Church) an elder. —ˌ**presby'terial** *adj.*

presbyterian (ˌprɛzbɪ'tɪərɪən) *adj.* **1.** of or designating Church government by presbyters or lay elders. ~*n.* **2.** an upholder of this type of Church government. —ˌ**presby'terianism** *n.*

Presbyterian (ˌprɛzbɪ'tɪərɪən) *adj.* **1.** of or relating to any of various Protestant Churches governed by presbyters or lay elders and adhering to various modified forms of Calvinism. ~*n.* **2.** a member of a Presbyterian Church. —ˌ**Presby'terianism** *n.*

presbytery ('prɛzbɪtərɪ) *n., pl.* **-teries. 1.** *Presbyterian Church.* **a.** a local Church court. **b.** the congregations within the jurisdiction of any such court. **2.** the part of a church east of the choir, in which the main altar is situated; a sanctuary. **3.** presbyters or elders collectively. **4.** *R.C. Church.* the residence of a parish priest.

prescience ('prɛsɪəns) *n.* knowledge of events before they take place; foreknowledge. —**'prescient** *adj.*

prescribe (prɪ'skraɪb) *vb.* **1.** to lay down as a rule or directive. **2.** *Med.* to recommend or order the use of (a drug or other remedy). —**pre'scriber** *n.*

prescription (prɪ'skrɪpʃən) *n.* **1. a.** written instructions from a physician to a pharmacist stating the form, dosage, strength, etc., of a drug to be issued to a specific patient. **b.** the drug or remedy prescribed. **2.** written instructions for an optician on the proper grinding of lenses for spectacles. **3.** the act of prescribing. **4.** something that is prescribed. **5.** a long-established custom or a claim based on one. **6.** *Law.* **a.** the uninterrupted possession of property over a stated time, after which a right or title is acquired (**positive prescription**). **b.** the barring of adverse claims to property, etc., after a specified time has elapsed, allowing the possessor to acquire title (**negative prescription**).

prescriptive (prɪ'skrɪptɪv) *adj.* **1.** making or giving directions, rules, or injunctions. **2.** sanctioned by longstanding custom. **3.** based upon legal prescription: *a prescriptive title.* —**pre'scriptively** *adv.* —**pre'scriptiveness** *n.*

presence ('prɛzəns) *n.* **1.** the state or fact of being present. **2.** immediate proximity. **3.** personal appearance or bearing, esp. of a dignified nature. **4.** an imposing or dignified personality. **5.** an invisible spirit felt to be nearby. **6.** *Obs.* assembly or company.

presence of mind *n.* the ability to remain calm and act constructively during times of crisis.

present¹ ('prɛzənt) *adj.* **1.** (*prenominal*) in existence at the time at which something is spoken or written. **2.** (*postpositive*) being in a specified place, thing, etc.: *the murderer is present in this room.* **3.** (*prenominal*) now being dealt with or under discussion: *the present author.* **4.** *Grammar.* denoting a tense of verbs used when the action or event described is occurring at the time of utterance or when the speaker does not wish to make any explicit temporal reference. **5.** *Arch.* instant: *present help is at hand.* ~*n.* **6. the present.** the time being; now. **7.** *Grammar.* **a.** the present tense. **b.** a verb in this tense. **8. at present.** now. **9. for the present.** for the time being; temporarily.

present² *vb.* (prɪ'zɛnt). (*tr.*) **1.** to introduce (a person) to another, esp. to someone of higher rank. **2.** to introduce to the public: *to present a play.* **3.** to show; exhibit: *he presented a brave face to the world.* **4.** to bring or suggest to the mind: *to present a problem.* **5.** to award: *to present a prize; to present a university with a foundation scholarship.* **6.** to offer formally: *to present one's compliments.* **7.** to hand over for action or settlement: *to present a bill.* **8.** to depict in a particular manner: *the actor presented Hamlet as a very young man.* **9.** to salute someone with (one's weapon) (usually in **present arms**). **10.** to aim (a weapon). **11.** to nominate (a clergyman) to a bishop for institution to a benefice in his diocese. **12.** to lay (a charge, etc.) before a court, magistrate, etc., for consideration or trial. **13.** to bring a formal charge or accusation against (a person); indict. **14. present onself.** to appear, esp. at a specific time and place. ~*n.* ('prɛzənt). **15.** a gift. —**pre'senter** *n.*

THESAURUS

captivating, charming, engaging, fair, fascinating, fetching, good-looking, handsome, inviting, likable, lovable, magnetic, pleasing, striking, taking, winning

preposterous absurd, asinine, bizarre, crazy, excessive, exorbitant, extravagant, extreme, foolish, impossible, incredible, insane, irrational, laughable, ludicrous, monstrous, nonsensical, out of the question, outrageous, ridiculous, senseless, shocking, unreasonable, unthinkable

prerequisite 1. *adj.* called for, essential, imperative, indispensable, mandatory, necessary, needful, obligatory, of the essence, required, requisite, vital 2. *n.* condition, essential, imperative, must, necessity, precondition, qualification, requirement, requisite, *sine qua non*

prerogative advantage, authority, birthright, choice, claim, droit, due, exemption, immunity, liberty, perquisite, privilege, right, sanction, title

prescient clairvoyant, discerning, divinatory, divining, far-sighted, foresighted, mantic, perceptive, prophetic, psychic

prescribe appoint, assign, command, decree, define, dictate, direct, enjoin, fix, impose, lay down, ordain, order, require, rule, set, specify, stipulate

prescript command, dictate, dictum, direction, directive, edict, instruction, law, mandate, order, ordinance, precept, regulation, requirement, rule

prescription 1. direction, formula, instruction, recipe 2. drug, medicine, mixture, preparation, remedy

prescriptive authoritarian, dictatorial, didactic, dogmatic, legislating, preceptive, rigid

presence 1. attendance, being, companionship, company, existence, habitation, inhabitance, occupancy, residence 2. closeness, immediate circle, nearness, neighbourhood, propinquity, proximity, vicinity 3. air, appearance, aspect, aura, bearing, carriage, comportment, demeanour, ease, mien (*Liter-*

ary), personality, poise, self-assurance 4. apparition, ghost, manifestation, revenant, shade (*Literary*), spectre, spirit, supernatural being, wraith

presence of mind alertness, aplomb, calmness, composure, cool (*Sl.*), coolness, imperturbability, level-headedness, phlegm, quickness, sang-froid, self-assurance, self-command, self-possession, wits

present¹ *adj.* 1. contemporary, current, existent, existing, extant, immediate, instant, present-day 2. accounted for, at hand, available, here, in attendance, near, nearby, ready, there, to hand ~*n.* 3. here and now, now, present moment, the time being, this day and age, today 4. **at present** at the moment, just now, now, nowadays, right now 5. **for the present** for a while, for the moment, for the time being, in the meantime, not for long, provisionally, temporarily

present² *v.* 1. acquaint with, introduce, made known 2. demonstrate, display, exhibit, give, mount, put before the public, put on,

presentable (prɪ'zɛntəbəl) adj. 1. fit to be presented or introduced to other people. 2. fit to be displayed or offered. —**pre'sentableness** or **pre,senta'bility** n. —**pre'sentably** adv.

presentation (,prɛzən'teɪʃən) n. 1. the act of presenting or state of being presented. 2. the manner of presenting; delivery. 3. a. an offering, as of a gift. b. (as modifier): a presentation copy of a book. 4. a performance or representation, as of a play. 5. the formal introduction of a person, as or at court; debut. 6. the act or right of nominating a clergyman to a benefice. —,**presen'tational** adj.

present-day n. (modifier) of the modern day; current: I don't like present-day fashions.

presentiment (prɪ'zɛntɪmənt) n. a sense of something about to happen; premonition.

presently ('prɛzəntlɪ) adv. 1. in a short while; soon. 2. Chiefly Scot. & U.S. at the moment. 3. an archaic word for immediately.

present participle ('prɛzənt) n. a participial form of verbs used adjectivally when the action it describes is contemporaneous with that of the main verb of a sentence and also used in the formation of certain compound tenses. In English this form ends in -ing.

present perfect ('prɛzənt) adj., n. Grammar. another term for perfect (senses 8, 10).

presents ('prɛzənts) pl. n. Law. used in a deed or document to refer to itself: know all men by these presents.

preservative (prɪ'zɜːvətɪv) n. 1. something that preserves, esp. a chemical added to foods. ~adj. 2. tending or intended to preserve.

preserve (prɪ'zɜːv) vb. (mainly tr.) 1. to keep safe from danger or harm; protect. 2. to protect from decay or dissolution; maintain: to preserve old buildings. 3. to maintain possession of; keep up: to preserve a facade of indifference. 4. to prevent from decomposition or chemical change. 5. to prepare (food), as by salting, so that it will resist decomposition. 6. to make preserves of (fruit, etc.). 7. to rear and protect (game) in restricted places for hunting or fishing. 8. (intr.) to maintain protection for game in preserves. ~n. 9. something that preserves or is preserved. 10. a special domain: archaeology is the preserve of specialists. 11. (usually pl.) fruit, etc., prepared by cooking with sugar. 12. areas where game is reared for private hunting or fishing. —**pre'servable** adj. —**preservation** (,prɛzə'veɪʃən) n. —**pre'server** n.

preside (prɪ'zaɪd) vb. (intr.) 1. to sit in or hold a position of authority, as over a meeting. 2. to exercise authority; control.

presidency ('prɛzɪdənsɪ) n., pl. **-cies.** 1. the office, dignity, or term of a president. 2. (often cap.) the office of president of a republic, esp. of the President of the U.S.

president ('prɛzɪdənt) n. 1. (often cap.) the head of state of a republic, esp. of the U.S. 2. (in the U.S.) the chief executive officer of a company, corporation, etc. 3. a person who presides over an assembly, meeting, etc.

4. the chief executive officer of certain establishments of higher education. —**presidential** (,prɛzɪ'dɛnʃəl) adj. —,**presi'dentially** adv. —**'president,ship** n.

presidium (prɪ'sɪdɪəm) n. 1. (often cap.) (in Communist countries) a permanent committee of a larger body, such as a legislature, that acts for it when it is recessed. 2. a collective presidency.

press[1] (prɛs) vb. 1. to apply or exert weight, force, or steady pressure on: he pressed the button on the camera. 2. (tr.) to squeeze or compress so as to alter in shape. 3. to apply heat or pressure to (clothing) so as to smooth out creases. 4. to make (objects) from soft material by pressing with a mould, etc., esp. to make gramophone records from plastic. 5. (tr.) to clasp; embrace. 6. (tr.) to extract or force out (juice) by pressure (from). 7. (tr.) to force or compel. 8. to importune (a person) insistently: they pressed for an answer. 9. to harass or cause harassment. 10. (tr.) to plead or put forward strongly: to press a claim. 11. (intr.) to be urgent. 12. (tr.; usually passive) to have little of: we're hard pressed for time. 13. (when intr., often foll. by on or forward) to hasten or advance or cause to hasten or advance in a forceful manner. 14. (tr.) Arch. to trouble or oppress. ~n. 15. any machine that exerts pressure to form, shape, or cut materials or to extract liquids, compress solids, or hold components together while an adhesive joint is formed. 16. See printing press. 17. the art or process of printing. 18. to (the) press. to be printed: when is this book going to press? 19. a. the press. news media collectively, esp. newspapers. b. (as modifier): press relations. 20. the opinions and reviews in the newspapers, etc.: the play received a poor press. 21. the act of pressing or state of being pressed. 22. the act of crowding or pushing together. 23. a closely packed throng; crowd. 24. a cupboard, esp. a large one used for storing clothes or linen. 25. a wood or metal clamp to prevent tennis rackets, etc., from warping when not in use.

press[2] (prɛs) vb. (tr.) 1. to recruit (men) by forcible measures for military service. 2. to use for a purpose other than intended, (esp. in **press into service**). ~n. 3. recruitment into military service by forcible measures, as by a press gang.

press agent n. a person employed to obtain favourable publicity, such as notices in newspapers, for an organization, actor, etc.

press conference n. an interview for press reporters given by a politician, film star, etc.

press gallery n. an area for newspaper reporters, esp. in a legislative assembly.

press gang n. 1. (formerly) a detachment of men used to press civilians for service in the navy or army. ~vb. **press-gang.** (tr.) 2. to force (a person) to join the navy or army by a press gang. 3. to induce (a person) to perform a duty by forceful persuasion.

pressing ('prɛsɪŋ) adj. 1. demanding immediate attention. 2. persistent or importunate. ~n. 3. a large

---

THESAURUS

show, stage 3. adduce, advance, declare, expound, extend, hold out, introduce, offer, pose, produce, proffer, put forward, raise, recount, relate, state, submit, suggest, tender 4. award, bestow, confer, donate, entrust, furnish, give, grant, hand over, offer, proffer, put at (someone's) disposal ~n. 5. benefaction, boon, bounty, donation, endowment, favour, gift, grant, gratuity, largess, offering, prezzie (Inf.)

presentable acceptable, becoming, decent, fit to be seen, good enough, not bad (Inf.), O.K. (Inf.), passable, proper, respectable, satisfactory, suitable, tolerable

presentation 1. award, bestowal, conferral, donation, giving, investiture, offering 2. appearance, arrangement, delivery, exposition, production, rendition, staging, submission 3. demonstration, display, exhibition, performance, production, representation, show 4. coming out, debut, introduction, launch, launching, reception

presentiment anticipation, apprehension, expectation, fear, feeling, foreboding, forecast, forethought, hunch, intuition, misgiving, premonition, presage

presently anon (Archaic), before long, by and by, in a minute, in a moment, in a short while, pretty soon (Inf.), shortly, soon

preservation conservation, defence, keeping, maintenance, perpetuation, protection, safeguarding, safekeeping, safety, salvation, security, storage, support, upholding

preserve v. 1. care for, conserve, defend, guard, keep, protect, safeguard, save, secure, shelter, shield 2. continue, keep, keep up, maintain, perpetuate, retain, sustain, uphold 3. conserve, keep, put up, save, store ~n. 4. area, domain, field, realm, specialism, sphere 5. Often plural confection, confiture, conserve, jam, jelly, marmalade, sweetmeat 6. game reserve, reservation, reserve, sanctuary

preside administer, be at the head of, be in authority, chair, conduct, control, direct, govern, head, lead, manage, officiate, run, supervise

press v. 1. bear down on, compress, condense, crush, depress, force down, jam, mash, push, reduce, squeeze, stuff 2. calender, finish, flatten, iron, mangle, put the creases in, smooth, steam 3. clasp, crush,

embrace, encircle, enfold, fold in one's arms, hold close, hug, squeeze 4. compel, constrain, demand, enforce, enjoin, force, insist on 5. beg, entreat, exhort, implore, importune, petition, plead, pressurize, sue, supplicate, urge 6. afflict, assail, beset, besiege, disquiet, harass, plague, torment, trouble, vex, worry 7. be pressed be hard put, be pushed (hurried, rushed), be short of 8. cluster, crowd, flock, gather, hasten, herd, hurry, mill, push, rush, seethe, surge, swarm, throng ~n. 9. the press a. Fleet Street, fourth estate, journalism, news media, newspapers, the papers b. columnists, correspondents, gentlemen of the press, journalists, newsmen, photographers, pressmen, reporters 10. bunch, crowd, crush, flock, herd, horde, host, mob, multitude, pack, push (Inf.), swarm, throng 11. bustle, demand, hassle (Inf.), hurry, pressure, strain, stress, urgency

pressing burning, constraining, crucial, exigent, high-priority, imperative, important, importunate, serious, urgent, vital

specified number of gramophone records produced at one time from a master record. —**'pressingly** adv.

press stud n. a fastening device consisting of one part with a projecting knob that snaps into a hole on another like part, used esp. on clothing.

press-up n. an exercise in which the body is alternately raised from and lowered to the floor by the arms only, the trunk being kept straight. Also called (U.S.): **push-up**.

pressure ('prɛʃə) n. 1. the state of pressing or being pressed. 2. the exertion of force by one body on the surface of another. 3. a moral force that compels: *to bring pressure to bear*. 4. urgent claims or demands: *to work under pressure*. 5. a burdensome condition that is hard to bear: *the pressure of grief*. 6. the force applied to a unit area of a surface, usually measured in pascals, millibars, torrs, or atmospheres. 7. short for **blood pressure**. ~vb. 8. (tr.) Chiefly U.S. to constrain or compel, as by moral force. 9. another word for **pressurize**.

pressure cooker n. a strong hermetically sealed pot in which food may be cooked quickly under pressure at a temperature above the normal boiling point of water. —**'pressure-,cook** vb.

pressure group n. a group of people who seek to exert pressure on legislators, public opinion, etc., in order to promote their own ideas or welfare.

pressurize or **-ise** ('prɛʃə,raɪz) vb. (tr.) 1. to increase the pressure in (an enclosure, such as an aircraft cabin) in order to maintain approximately atmospheric pressure when the external pressure is low. 2. to increase pressure on (a fluid). —**,pressuri'zation** or **-i'sation** n.

Prestel ('prɛstɛl) n. Trademark. (in Britain) the Post Office public viewdata service.

prestidigitation (,prɛstɪ,dɪdʒɪ'teɪʃən) n. another name for **sleight of hand**. —**,presti'digi,tator** n.

prestige (prɛ'stiːʒ) n. 1. high status or reputation achieved through success, influence, wealth, etc.; renown. 2. a. the power to impress; glamour. b. (modifier): *a prestige car*. —**prestigious** (prɛ'stɪdʒəs) adj.

presto ('prɛstəʊ) adj., adv. 1. Music. to be played very fast. ~adv. 2. immediately (esp. in **hey presto**). ~n., pl. **-tos**. 3. Music. a passage directed to be played very quickly.

prestressed concrete (priː'strɛst) n. concrete that contains steel wires that are stretched to counteract the stresses that will occur under load.

presumably (prɪ'zjuːməblɪ) adv. (sentence modifier) one supposes that: *presumably he won't see you, if you're leaving tomorrow*.

presume (prɪ'zjuːm) vb. 1. (when tr., often takes a clause as object) to take (something) for granted; as-

sume. 2. (when tr., often foll. by an infinitive) to dare (to do something): *do you presume to copy my work?* 3. (intr.; foll. by on or upon) to rely or depend: *don't presume on his agreement*. 4. (intr.; foll. by on or upon) to take advantage of: *don't presume upon his good nature too far*. 5. Law. to take as proved until contrary evidence is produced. —**presumedly** (prɪ'zjuːmɪdlɪ) adv.

presumption (prɪ'zʌmpʃən) n. 1. the act of presuming. 2. bold or insolent behaviour. 3. a belief or assumption based on reasonable evidence. 4. a basis on which to presume. 5. Law. an inference of the truth of a fact from other facts proved. —**pre'sumptive** adj.

presumptuous (prɪ'zʌmptjʊəs) adj. characterized by presumption or tending to presume; bold; forward. —**pre'sumptuously** adv. —**pre'sumptuousness** n.

presuppose (,priːsə'pəʊz) vb. (tr.) 1. to take for granted. 2. to require as a necessary prior condition. —**presupposition** (,priːsʌpə'zɪʃən) n.

pretence or U.S. **pretense** (prɪ'tɛns) n. 1. the act of pretending. 2. a false display; affectation. 3. a claim, esp. a false one, to a right, title, or distinction. 4. make-believe. 5. a pretext.

pretend (prɪ'tɛnd) vb. 1. (when tr., usually takes a clause as object or an infinitive) to claim or allege (something untrue). 2. (tr.; may take a clause as object or an infinitive) to make believe, as in a play: *you pretend to be Ophelia*. 3. (intr.; foll. by to) to present a claim, esp. a dubious one: *to pretend to the throne*. 4. (intr.; foll. by to) Obs. to aspire as a candidate or suitor (for).

pretender (prɪ'tɛndə) n. 1. a person who pretends or makes false allegations. 2. a person who mounts a claim, as to a throne or title.

pretension (prɪ'tɛnʃən) n. 1. (often pl.) a false claim, esp. to merit, worth, or importance. 2. a specious or unfounded allegation; pretext. 3. the quality of being pretentious.

pretentious (prɪ'tɛnʃəs) adj. 1. making claim to distinction or importance, esp. undeservedly. 2. ostentatious. —**pre'tentiously** adv. —**pre'tentiousness** n.

preterite or esp. U.S. **preterit** ('prɛtərɪt) Grammar. ~n. 1. a tense of verbs used to relate past action, formed in English by inflection of the verb, as *jumped*, *swam*. 2. a verb in this tense. ~adj. 3. denoting this tense.

preternatural (,priːtə'nætʃrəl) adj. 1. beyond what is ordinarily found in nature; abnormal. 2. another word for **supernatural**. —**,preter'naturally** adv.

pretext ('priːtɛkst) n. 1. a fictitious reason given in order to conceal the real one. 2. a pretence.

prettify ('prɪtɪ,faɪ) vb. **-fying**, **-fied**. (tr.) Often ironical.

THESAURUS

pressure 1. compressing, compression, crushing, force, heaviness, squeezing, weight 2. coercion, compulsion, constraint, force, influence, obligation, power, sway 3. adversity, affliction, burden, demands, difficulty, distress, exigency, hassle (Inf.), heat, hurry, load, press, strain, stress, urgency

prestige authority, cachet, celebrity, credit, distinction, eminence, esteem, fame, honour, importance, influence, kudos, regard, renown, reputation, standing, stature, status, weight

prestigious celebrated, eminent, esteemed, exalted, great, illustrious, important, imposing, impressive, influential, prominent, renowned, reputable, respected

presumably apparently, doubtless, doubtlessly, in all likelihood, in all probability, it would seem, likely, most likely, on the face of it, probably, seemingly

presume 1. assume, believe, conjecture, infer, posit, postulate, presuppose, suppose, surmise, take for granted, take it, think 2. dare, go so far, have the audacity, make bold, make so bold, take the liberty, undertake, venture 3. bank on, count on, depend, rely, trust

presumption 1. assurance, audacity, boldness, brass (Inf.), brass neck (Inf.), cheek (Inf.), effrontery, forwardness, gall (Inf.), impudence, insolence, nerve (Inf.), presumptuousness, temerity 2. anticipation,

assumption, belief, conjecture, guess, hypothesis, opinion, premiss, presupposition, supposition, surmise 3. basis, chance, grounds, likelihood, plausibility, probability, reason

presumptive 1. assumed, believed, expected, hypothetical, inferred, supposed, understood 2. believable, conceivable, credible, likely, plausible, possible, probable, reasonable

presumptuous arrogant, audacious, bigheaded (Inf.), bold, conceited, foolhardy, forward, insolent, overconfident, overfamiliar, overweening, presuming, pushy (Inf.), rash, too big for one's boots, uppish (Brit. inf.)

presuppose accept, assume, consider, imply, posit, postulate, presume, suppose, take as read, take for granted, take it

presupposition assumption, belief, hypothesis, preconceived idea, preconception, premiss, presumption, supposition, theory

pretence 1. acting, charade, deceit, deception, fabrication, fakery, faking, falsehood, feigning, invention, make-believe, sham, simulation, subterfuge, trickery 2. affectation, appearance, artifice, display, façade, posing, posturing, show, veneer 3. claim, cloak, colour, cover, excuse, façade, garb, guise, mask, masquerade, pretext, ruse, semblance, show, veil, wile

pretend 1. affect, allege, assume, counterfeit, dissemble, dissimulate, fake, falsify, feign, impersonate, make out, pass oneself off as, profess, put on, sham, simulate 2. act, imagine, make believe, make up, play, play the part of, suppose 3. allege, aspire, claim, lay claim, profess, purport

pretended alleged, avowed, bogus, counterfeit, fake, false, feigned, fictitious, imaginary, ostensible, phoney (Sl.), pretend (Inf.), professed, pseudo (Inf.), purported, sham, so-called, spurious

pretender aspirant, claimant, claimer

pretension 1. aspiration, assertion, assumption, claim, demand, pretence, profession 2. affectation, airs, conceit, hypocrisy, ostentation, pomposity, pretentiousness, self-importance, show, showiness, snobbery, snobbishness, vainglory, vanity

pretentious affected, assuming, bombastic, conceited, exaggerated, extravagant, flaunting, grandiloquent, grandiose, highfalutin (Inf.), high-flown, high-sounding, hollow, inflated, magniloquent, mannered, ostentatious, overambitious, pompous, puffed up, showy, snobbish, specious, vainglorious

pretext affectation, alleged reason, appearance, cloak, cover, device, excuse, guise, mask, ploy, pretence, red herring, ruse, semblance, show, simulation, veil

to make pretty; embellish. —**,prettifi'cation** n. —**'pretti,fier** n.

pretty ('prɪtɪ) adj. **-tier, -tiest. 1.** pleasing or appealing in a delicate or graceful way. **2.** dainty, neat, or charming. **3.** Inf., often ironical. excellent, grand, or fine: here's a pretty mess! **4.** commendable; good of its kind: he replied with a pretty wit. **5.** Inf. effeminate; foppish. **6.** Arch. or Scot. vigorous or brave. **7. a pretty penny.** Inf. a large sum of money. **8. sitting pretty.** Inf. in a favourable or satisfactory state. ~n., pl. **-ties. 9.** a pretty person or thing. ~adv. **10.** Inf. fairly; somewhat. **11.** Inf. very. ~vb. **-tying, -tied. 12.** (tr.; often foll. by up) to make pretty; adorn. —**'prettily** adv. —**'prettiness** n.

▷ **Usage.** The use of pretty as an adverb meaning fairly or quite is accepted informal usage but is avoided in formal contexts by careful writers of English: the profit was fairly (not pretty) large that year.

pretty-pretty adj. Inf. excessively or ostentatiously pretty.

pretzel ('prɛtsəl) n. a brittle savoury biscuit, in the form of a knot or stick, eaten esp. in Germany.

prevail (prɪ'veɪl) vb. (intr.) **1.** (often foll. by over or against) to prove superior; gain mastery: skill will prevail. **2.** to be the most important feature; be prevalent. **3.** to exist widely; be in force. **4.** (often foll. by on or upon) to succeed in persuading or inducing. —**pre'vailer** n.

prevailing (prɪ'veɪlɪŋ) adj. **1.** generally accepted; widespread: the prevailing opinion. **2.** most frequent; predominant: the prevailing wind is from the north. —**pre'vailingly** adv.

prevalent ('prɛvələnt) adj. **1.** widespread or current. **2.** superior in force or power; predominant. —**'prevalence** n. —**'prevalently** adv.

prevaricate (prɪ'værɪ,keɪt) vb. (intr.) to speak or act falsely or evasively with intent to deceive. —**pre,vari-'cation** n. —**pre'vari,cator** n.

prevent (prɪ'vɛnt) vb. **1.** (tr.) to keep from happening, esp. by taking precautionary action. **2.** (tr.; often foll. by from) to keep (someone from doing something). **3.** (intr.) to interpose or act as a hindrance. **4.** (tr.) Arch. to anticipate or precede. —**pre'ventable** or **pre'ventible** adj. —**pre'ventably** or **pre'ventibly** adv. —**pre'venter** n. —**pre'vention** n.

preventive (prɪ'vɛntɪv) adj. **1.** tending or intended to prevent or hinder. **2.** Med. tending to prevent disease; prophylactic. **3.** (in Britain) of, relating to, or belonging to the customs and excise service or the coastguard. ~n. **4.** something that serves to prevent or hinder. **5.** Med. any drug or agent that tends to prevent disease. Also (for senses 1, 2, 4, 5) **preventative** (prɪ'vɛntətɪv). —**pre'ventively** or **pre'ventatively** adv.

preview ('priː,vjuː) n. **1.** an advance view or sight. **2.** an advance showing before public presentation of a film, art exhibition, etc., usually before an invited audience. ~vb. **3.** (tr.) to view in advance.

previous ('priːvɪəs) adj. **1.** (prenominal) existing or coming before something else. **2.** (postpositive) Inf. taking place or done too soon; premature. **3. previous to.** before. —**'previously** adv. —**'previousness** n.

prey (preɪ) n. **1.** an animal hunted or captured by another for food. **2.** a person or thing that becomes the victim of a hostile person, influence, etc. **3. bird** or **beast of prey.** a bird or animal that preys on others for food. **4.** an archaic word for **booty.** ~vb. (intr.; often foll. by on or upon) **5.** to hunt food by killing other animals. **6.** to make a victim (of others), as by profiting at their expense. **7.** to exert a depressing or obsessive effect (on the mind, spirits, etc.). —**'preyer** n.

price (praɪs) n. **1.** the sum in money or goods for which anything is or may be bought or sold. **2.** the cost at which anything is obtained. **3.** the cost of bribing a person. **4.** a sum of money offered as a reward for a capture or killing. **5.** value or worth, esp. high worth. **6.** Gambling. another word for **odds. 7. at any price.** whatever the price or cost. **8. at a price.** at a high price. **9. what price (something)?** what are the chances of (something) happening now? ~vb. (tr.) **10.** to fix the price of. **11.** to discover the price of. **12. price out of the market.** to charge so highly for as to prevent the sale, hire, etc., of. —**'pricer** n.

price control n. the establishment and maintenance of maximum price levels for basic goods and services by a government.

price-fixing n. Chiefly U.S. **1.** the setting of prices by agreement among producers and distributors. **2.** another name for **price control** or **resale price maintenance.**

priceless ('praɪslɪs) adj. **1.** of inestimable worth; invaluable. **2.** Inf. extremely amusing or ridiculous. —**'pricelessly** adv. —**'pricelessness** n.

pricey or **pricy** ('praɪsɪ) adj. **pricier, priciest.** an informal word for **expensive.**

prick (prɪk) vb. (mainly tr.) **1. a.** to make (a small hole) in (something) by piercing lightly with a sharp point. **b.** to wound in this manner. **2.** (intr.) to cause or have a piercing or stinging sensation. **3.** to cause to feel a sharp

THESAURUS

pretty adj. **1.** appealing, attractive, beautiful, bonny, charming, comely, cute, fair, good-looking, graceful, lovely, personable **2.** bijou, dainty, delicate, elegant, fine, neat, nice, pleasing, tasteful, trim ~adv. **3.** Inf. fairly, kind of (Inf.), moderately, quite, rather, reasonably, somewhat

prevail 1. be victorious, carry the day, gain mastery, overcome, overrule, prove superior, succeed, triumph, win **2.** abound, be current (prevalent, widespread), exist generally, obtain, predominate, preponderate **3.** Often with **on** or **upon** bring round, convince, dispose, incline, induce, influence, persuade, prompt, sway, talk into, win over

prevailing 1. common, current, customary, established, fashionable, general, in style, in vogue, ordinary, popular, prevalent, set, usual, widespread **2.** dominant, influential, main, operative, predominating, preponderating, principal, ruling

prevalence 1. acceptance, commonness, common occurrence, currency, frequency, pervasiveness, popularity, profusion, regularity, ubiquity, universality **2.** ascendancy, hold, mastery, predominance, preponderance, primacy, rule, sway

prevalent 1. accepted, common, commonplace, current, customary, established, everyday, extensive, frequent, general, habitual, popular, rampant, rife, ubiquitous, universal, usual, widespread **2.** ascendant, compelling, dominant, governing, powerful, predominant, prevailing, successful, superior

prevaricate beat about the bush, beg the question, cavil, deceive, dodge, equivocate, evade, give a false colour to, hedge, lie, palter, quibble, shift, shuffle, stretch the truth, tergiversate

prevarication cavilling, deceit, deception, equivocation, evasion, falsehood, falsification, lie, misrepresentation, pretence, quibbling, tergiversation, untruth

prevent anticipate, avert, avoid, balk, bar, block, check, counteract, defend against, foil, forestall, frustrate, hamper, head off, hinder, impede, inhibit, intercept, nip in the bud, obstruct, obviate, preclude, restrain, stave off, stop, thwart, ward off

prevention 1. anticipation, avoidance, deterrence, elimination, forestalling, obviation, precaution, preclusion, prophylaxis, safeguard, thwarting **2.** bar, check, deterrence, frustration, hindrance, impediment, interruption, obstacle, obstruction, stoppage

preventive, preventative adj. **1.** hampering, hindering, impeding, obstructive **2.** counteractive, deterrent, inhibitory, precautionary, prophylactic, protective, shielding ~n. **3.** block, hindrance, impediment, obstacle, obstruction **4.** deterrent, neutralizer, prevention, prophylactic, protection, protective, remedy, safeguard, shield

previous 1. antecedent, anterior, earlier, erstwhile, ex-, foregoing, former, one-time, past, preceding, prior, quondam, sometime **2.** Inf. ahead of oneself, precipitate, premature, too early, too soon, untimely

previously at one time, a while ago, before, beforehand, earlier, formerly, heretofore, hitherto, in advance, in anticipation, in days or years gone by, in the past, once, then, until now

prey n. **1.** game, kill, quarry **2.** dupe, fall guy (Inf.), mark, mug (Sl.), target, victim ~v. **3.** devour, eat, feed upon, hunt, live off, seize **4.** blackmail, bleed (Inf.), bully, exploit, intimidate, take advantage of, terrorize, victimize **5.** burden, distress, hang over, haunt, oppress, trouble, weigh down, weigh heavily, worry

price n. **1.** amount, asking price, assessment, bill, charge, cost, damage (Inf.), estimate, expenditure, expense, face value, fee, figure, outlay, payment, rate, valuation, value, worth **2.** consequences, cost, penalty, sacrifice, toll **3.** bounty, compensation, premium, recompense, reward **4. at any price** anyhow, cost what it may, expense no object, no matter what the cost, regardless, whatever the cost **5. beyond price** inestimable, invaluable, of incalculable value, precious, priceless, treasured, without price ~v. **6.** assess, cost, estimate, evaluate, put a price on, rate, value

priceless 1. beyond price, cherished, costly, dear, expensive, incalculable, incomparable, inestimable, invaluable, irreplaceable, precious, prized, rare, rich, treasured, worth a king's ransom **2.** Inf. absurd, a hoot (Brit. inf.), amusing, a scream (Inf.), comic, droll, funny, hilarious, killing (Inf.), rib-tickling, ridiculous, riotous, side-splitting

emotional pain: *knowledge of such poverty pricked his conscience.* **4.** to puncture something. **5.** to outline by dots or punctures. **6.** (*also intr.; usually foll. by up*) to rise or raise erect: *the dog pricked his ears up.* **7.** (usually foll. by *out* or *off*) to transplant (seedlings) into a larger container. **8.** *Arch.* to urge on, esp. to spur a horse on. **9. prick up one's ears.** to listen attentively. ~*n.* **10.** the act of pricking or the sensation of being pricked. **11.** a mark made by a sharp point; puncture. **12.** a sharp emotional pain: *a prick of conscience.* **13.** a taboo slang word for **penis. 14.** *Sl., derog.* an obnoxious or despicable person. **15.** an instrument or weapon with a sharp point. **16.** the track of an animal, esp. a hare. **17. kick against the pricks.** to hurt oneself by struggling against something in vain. —'**pricker** *n.*

prickle ('prɪkəl) *n.* **1.** *Bot.* a pointed process arising from the outer layer of a stem, leaf, etc., and containing no woody tissue. Cf. **thorn. 2.** a pricking or stinging sensation. ~*vb.* **3.** to feel or cause to feel a stinging sensation. **4.** (*tr.*) to prick, as with a thorn.

prickly ('prɪklɪ) *adj.* **-lier, -liest. 1.** having or covered with prickles. **2.** stinging. **3.** irritable. **4.** full of difficulties: *a prickly problem.* —'**prickliness** *n.*

prickly heat *n.* a nontechnical name for **miliaria.**

prickly pear *n.* **1.** any of various tropical cacti having flattened or cylindrical spiny joints and oval fruit that is edible in some species. **2.** the fruit of any of these plants.

pride (praɪd) *n.* **1.** a feeling of honour and self-respect; a sense of personal worth. **2.** excessive self-esteem; conceit. **3.** a source of pride. **4.** satisfaction or pleasure in one's own or another's success, achievements, etc. (esp. in **take (a) pride in**). **5.** the better or superior part of something. **6.** the most flourishing time. **7.** a group (of lions). **8.** courage; spirit. **9.** *Arch.* pomp or splendour. **10. pride of place.** the most important position. ~*vb.* **11.** (*tr.; foll. by on* or *upon*) to take pride in (oneself) for. —'**prideful** *adj.* —'**pridefully** *adv.*

prie-dieu (priː'djɜː) *n.* a piece of furniture consisting of a low surface for kneeling upon and a narrow front surmounted by a rest, for use when praying.

priest (priːst) *or* (*fem.*) **priestess** *n.* **1.** a person ordained to act as a mediator between God and man in administering the sacraments, preaching, etc. **2.** (in episcopal Churches) a minister in the second grade of the hierarchy of holy orders, ranking below a bishop but above a deacon. **3.** a minister of any religion. **4.** an official who offers sacrifice on behalf of the people and performs other religious ceremonies. ~*vb.* **5.** (*tr.*) to make a priest; ordain. —'**priest,hood** *n.* —'**priest,like** *adj.* —'**priestly** *adj.*

prig (prɪg) *n.* a person who is smugly self-righteous and narrow-minded. —'**priggery** *or* '**priggishness** *n.* —'**priggish** *adj.* —'**priggishly** *adv.*

prim (prɪm) *adj.* **primmer, primmest. 1.** affectedly proper, precise, or formal. ~*vb.* **primming, primmed. 2.** (*tr.*) to make prim. **3.** to purse (the mouth) primly or (of the mouth) to be so pursed. —'**primly** *adv.*

—'**primness** *n.*

prima ballerina ('priːmə) *n.* a leading female ballet dancer.

primacy ('praɪməsɪ) *n., pl.* **-cies. 1.** the state of being first in rank, grade, etc. **2.** *Ecclesiast.* the office, rank, or jurisdiction of a primate, senior bishop, or pope.

prima donna ('priːmə 'dɒnə) *n., pl.* **prima donnas. 1.** a leading female operatic star. **2.** *Inf.* a temperamental person.

prima facie ('praɪmə 'feɪʃɪ) *adv.* at first sight; as it seems at first.

primal ('praɪməl) *adj.* **1.** first or original. **2.** chief or most important.

primarily ('praɪmərəlɪ) *adv.* **1.** principally; chiefly; mainly. **2.** at first; originally.

primary ('praɪmərɪ) *adj.* **1.** first in importance, degree, rank, etc. **2.** first in position or time, as in a series. **3.** fundamental; basic. **4.** being the first stage; elementary. **5.** (*prenominal*) of or relating to the education of children up to the age of 11. **6.** (of the flight feathers of a bird's wing) growing from the manus. **7. a.** being the part of an electric circuit, such as a transformer, in which a changing current induces a current in a neighbouring circuit: *a primary coil.* **b.** (of a current) flowing in such a circuit. **8. a.** (of a product) consisting of a natural raw material; unmanufactured. **b.** (of production or industry) involving the extraction or winning of such products. **9.** (of Latin, Greek, or Sanskrit tenses) referring to present or future time. **10.** *Geol., obs.* relating to the Palaeozoic or earlier eras. ~*n., pl.* **-ries. 11.** a person or thing that is first in rank, occurrence, etc. **12.** (in the U.S.) a preliminary election in which the voters of a state or region choose a party's convention delegates, nominees for office, etc. Full name: **primary election. 13.** See **primary colour. 14.** any of the flight feathers growing from the manus of a bird's wing. **15.** a primary coil, winding, inductance, or current in an electric circuit. **16.** *Astron.* a celestial body around which one or more specified secondary bodies orbit: *the sun is the primary of the earth.*

primary accent *or* **stress** *n. Linguistics.* the strongest accent in a word or breath group, as that on the first syllable of *agriculture.*

primary colour *n.* **1.** any of the colours red, green, or blue. An equal mixture of the three gives white light. **2.** any one of the colours magenta, yellow, or cyan. An equal mixture of the three produces a black pigment. **3.** any one of the colours red, yellow, green, blue, black, or white. Any colour can be regarded as formed from a mixture of two or more of these.

primary school *n.* **1.** (in England and Wales) a school for children below the age of 11. It is usually divided into an infant and a junior section. **2.** (in Scotland) a school for children below the age of 12. **3.** (in the U.S.) a school equivalent to the first three or four grades of elementary school.

primate[1] ('praɪmeɪt) *n.* **1.** any placental mammal of the order *Primates,* typically having flexible hands, good

THESAURUS

prick *v.* **1.** bore, jab, lance, perforate, pierce, pink, punch, puncture, stab **2.** bite, itch, prickle, smart, sting, tingle **3.** cut, distress, grieve, move, pain, stab, touch, trouble, wound **4.** *Usually with* **up** point, raise, rise, stand erect ~*n.* **5.** cut, gash, hole, perforation, pinhole, puncture, wound **6.** gnawing, pang, prickle, smart, spasm, sting, twinge

prickle *n.* **1.** barb, needle, point, spike, spine, spur, thorn **2.** chill, formication, goose flesh, paraesthesia (*Medical*), pins and needles (*Inf.*), smart, tickle, tingle, tingling ~*v.* **3.** itch, smart, sting, tingle, twitch **4.** jab, nick, prick, stick

prickly 1. barbed, brambly, briery, bristly, spiny, thorny **2.** crawling, itchy, pricking, prickling, scratchy, sharp, smarting, stinging, tingling **3.** bad-tempered, cantankerous, edgy, fractious, grumpy, irritable, peevish, pettish, petulant, ratty (*Brit. sl.*), shirty (*Sl.*), snappish, stroppy (*Brit. sl.*), tetchy, touchy, waspish **4.** complicated, difficult, intricate, involved, knotty, thorny, ticklish, tricky, troublesome, trying

pride *n.* **1.** amour-propre, dignity, honour,

self-esteem, self-respect, self-worth **2.** arrogance, bigheadedness (*Inf.*), conceit, egotism, haughtiness, hauteur, hubris, loftiness, morgue, presumption, pretension, pretentiousness, self-importance, self-love, smugness, snobbery, superciliousness, vainglory, vanity **3.** boast, gem, jewel, pride and joy, prize, treasure **4.** delight, gratification, joy, pleasure, satisfaction **5.** best, choice, cream, elite, flower, glory, pick ~*v.* **6.** be proud of, boast, brag, congratulate oneself, crow, exult, flatter oneself, glory in, pique, plume, preen, revel in, take pride, vaunt

priest churchman, clergyman, cleric, curate, divine, ecclesiastic, father, father confessor, holy man, man of God, man of the cloth, minister, padre (*Inf.*), vicar

priestly canonical, clerical, ecclesiastic, hieratic, pastoral, priestlike, sacerdotal

prig goody-goody (*Inf.*), Holy Joe (*Inf.*), Holy Willie (*Inf.*), Mrs Grundy, old maid (*Inf.*), pedant, prude, puritan, stuffed shirt (*Inf.*)

priggish goody-goody (*Inf.*), holier-than-thou, narrow-minded, pedantic, prim, pru-

dish, puritanical, self-righteous, self-satisfied, smug, starchy (*Inf.*), stiff, stuffy

prim demure, fastidious, formal, fussy, old-maidish (*Inf.*), particular, precise, priggish, prissy (*Inf.*), proper, prudish, puritanical, schoolmarmish (*Brit. inf.*), starchy (*Inf.*), stiff, strait-laced

prima donna diva, leading lady, star

primarily 1. above all, basically, chiefly, especially, essentially, for the most part, fundamentally, generally, mainly, mostly, on the whole, principally **2.** at first, at *or* from the start, first and foremost, initially, in the beginning, in the first place, originally

primary 1. best, capital, cardinal, chief, dominant, first, greatest, highest, leading, main, paramount, prime, principal, top **2.** aboriginal, earliest, initial, original, primal, primeval, primitive, primordial, pristine **3.** basic, beginning, elemental, essential, fundamental, radical, ultimate, underlying **4.** elementary, introductory, rudimentary, simple

eyesight, and, in the higher apes, a highly developed brain: includes lemurs, apes, and man. ~*adj.* **2.** of, relating to, or belonging to the order *Primates.* —**primatial** (praɪˈmeɪʃəl) *adj.*

primate² (ˈpraɪmeɪt) *n.* **1.** another name for an **archbishop. 2. Primate of all England.** the Archbishop of Canterbury. **3. Primate of England.** the Archbishop of York.

prime (praɪm) *adj.* **1.** (*prenominal*) first in quality or value; first-rate. **2.** (*prenominal*) fundamental; original. **3.** (*prenominal*) first in importance; chief. **4.** *Maths.* **a.** having no factors except itself or one: $x^2 + x + 3$ is a prime polynomial. **b.** (foll. by *to*) having no common factors (with): *20 is prime to 21.* **5.** *Finance.* having the best credit rating: *prime investments.* ~*n.* **6.** the time when a thing is at its best. **7.** a period of power, vigour, etc. (esp. in **the prime of life**). **8.** *Maths.* short for **prime number. 9.** *Chiefly R.C. Church.* the second of the seven canonical hours of the divine office, originally fixed for the first hour of the day, at sunrise. **10.** the first of eight basic positions from which a parry or attack can be made in fencing. ~*vb.* **11.** to prepare (something). **12.** (*tr.*) to apply a primer, such as paint or size, to (a surface). **13.** (*tr.*) to fill (a pump) with its working fluid before starting, in order to expel air from it before starting. **14.** (*tr.*) to increase the quantity of fuel in the float chamber of (a carburettor) in order to facilitate the starting of an engine. **15.** (*tr.*) to insert a primer into (a gun, mine, etc.) preparatory to detonation or firing. **16.** (*tr.*) to provide with facts beforehand; brief. —**ˈprimely** *adv.* —**ˈprimeness** *n.*

prime meridian *n.* the 0° meridian from which the other meridians are calculated, usually taken to pass through Greenwich.

prime minister *n.* **1.** the head of a parliamentary government. **2.** the chief minister of a sovereign or a state.

prime number *n.* an integer that cannot be factorized into other integers but is only divisible by itself or 1, such as 2, 3, 7, and 11.

primer¹ (ˈpraɪmə) *n.* an introductory text, such as a school textbook.

primer² (ˈpraɪmə) *n.* **1.** a person or thing that primes. **2.** a device, such as a tube containing explosive, for detonating the main charge in a gun, mine, etc. **3.** a substance, such as paint, applied to a surface as a base, sealer, etc.

primeval or **primaeval** (praɪˈmiːvəl) *adj.* of or belonging to the first ages of the world. —**priˈmevally** or **priˈmaevally** *adv.*

priming (ˈpraɪmɪŋ) *n.* **1.** something used to prime. **2.** a substance used to ignite an explosive charge.

primitive (ˈprɪmɪtɪv) *adj.* **1.** of or belonging to the beginning; original. **2.** characteristic of an early state, esp. in being crude or uncivilized: *a primitive dwelling.* **3.** *Anthropol.* denoting a preliterate and nonindustrial social system. **4.** *Biol.* of, relating to, or resembling an early stage in development: *primitive amphibians.* **5.** showing the characteristics of primitive painters; untrained, childlike, or naive. **6.** *Geol.* of or denoting rocks formed in or before the Palaeozoic era. **7.** denoting a word from which another word is derived, as for example *hope,* from which *hopeless* is derived. **8.** *Protestant theol.* of or associated with a group that breaks away from a sect, denomination, or Church in order to return to what is regarded as the original simplicity of the Gospels. ~*n.* **9.** a primitive person or thing. **10. a.** an artist whose work does not conform to traditional standards of Western

painting, such as a painter from an African civilization. **b.** a painter of the pre-Renaissance era in European painting. **c.** a painter of any era whose work appears childlike or untrained. **11.** a work by such an artist. **12.** a word from which another word is derived. **13.** *Maths.* a curve or other form from which another is derived. —**ˈprimitively** *adv.* —**ˈprimitiveness** *n.*

primogenitor (ˌpraɪməʊˈdʒɛnɪtə) *n.* **1.** a forefather; ancestor. **2.** an earliest parent or ancestor, as of a race.

primogeniture (ˌpraɪməʊˈdʒɛnɪtʃə) *n.* **1.** the state of being a first-born. **2.** *Law.* the right of an eldest son to succeed to the estate of his ancestor to the exclusion of all others. —**primogenitary** (ˌpraɪməʊˈdʒɛnɪtərɪ) *adj.*

primordial (praɪˈmɔːdɪəl) *adj.* **1.** existing at or from the beginning; primeval. **2.** constituting an origin; fundamental. **3.** *Biol.* relating to an early stage of development. —**priˈmordiality** *n.* —**priˈmordially** *adv.*

primp (prɪmp) *vb.* to dress (oneself), esp. in fine clothes; prink.

primrose (ˈprɪmˌrəʊz) *n.* **1.** any of various temperate plants of the genus *Primula,* esp. a European variety which has pale yellow flowers. **2.** short for **evening primrose. 3.** Also called: **primrose yellow.** a light yellow, sometimes with a greenish tinge. ~*adj.* **4.** of or abounding in primroses. **5.** of the colour primrose.

primrose path *n.* (often preceded by *the*) a pleasurable way of life.

primula (ˈprɪmjʊlə) *n.* any plant of the N temperate genus *Primula,* having white, yellow, pink, or purple funnel-shaped flowers with five spreading petals: includes the primrose, oxlip, cowslip, and polyanthus.

Primus (ˈpraɪməs) *n. Trademark.* a portable paraffin cooking stove, used esp. by campers. Also called: **Primus stove.**

prince (prɪns) *n.* **1.** (in Britain) a son of the sovereign or of one of the sovereign's sons. **2.** a nonreigning male member of a sovereign family. **3.** the monarch of a small territory that was at some time subordinate to an emperor or king. **4.** any monarch. **5.** a nobleman in various countries, such as Italy and Germany. **6.** an outstanding member of a specified group: *a merchant prince.* —**ˈprincedom** *n.* —**ˈprinceˌlike** *adj.*

princeling (ˈprɪnslɪŋ) *n.* **1.** a young prince. **2.** Also called: **princelet.** the ruler of an insignificant territory.

princely (ˈprɪnslɪ) *adj.* **-lier, -liest. 1.** generous or lavish. **2.** of or characteristic of a prince. ~*adv.* **3.** in a princely manner. —**ˈprinceliness** *n.*

Prince of Wales *n.* the eldest son and heir apparent of the British sovereign.

princess (prɪnˈsɛs) *n.* **1.** (in Britain) a daughter of the sovereign or of one of the sovereign's sons. **2.** a nonreigning female member of a sovereign family. **3.** the wife and consort of a prince. **4.** *Arch.* a female sovereign.

princess royal *n.* the eldest daughter of a British or (formerly) a Prussian sovereign.

principal (ˈprɪnsɪpəl) *adj.* (*prenominal*) **1.** first in importance, rank, value, etc. **2.** denoting capital or property as opposed to interest, etc. ~*n.* **3.** a person who is first in importance or directs some event, organization, etc. **4.** *Law.* **a.** a person who engages another to act as his agent. **b.** an active participant in a crime. **c.** the person primarily liable to fulfil an obligation. **5.** the head of a school or other educational institution. **6.** (in the British civil service) an officer of the grade below that of secretary. **7.** *Finance.* **a.** capital or property, as contrasted with income. **b.** the original amount of a debt on which interest is calculated. **8.** a main roof truss or rafter. **9.** *Music.* either of two types of open diapason organ stops. —**'principally** *adv.* —**'principal,ship** *n.*

principal boy *n.* the leading male role in a pantomime, played by a woman.

principality (ˌprɪnsɪ'pælɪtɪ) *n., pl.* **-ties. 1.** a territory ruled by a prince or from which a prince draws his title. **2.** the authority of a prince.

principal parts *pl. n. Grammar.* the main inflected forms of a verb, from which all other inflections may be deduced.

principle ('prɪnsɪpəl) *n.* **1.** a standard or rule of personal conduct. **2.** a set of such moral rules: *a man of principle.* **3.** a fundamental or general truth. **4.** the essence of something. **5.** a source; origin. **6.** a law concerning a natural phenomenon or the behaviour of a system: *the principle of the conservation of mass.* **7.** *Chem.* a constituent of a substance that gives the substance its characteristics. **8. in principle.** in theory. **9. on principle.** because of or in demonstration of a principle.

prink (prɪŋk) *vb.* **1.** to dress (oneself, etc.) finely; deck out. **2.** (*intr.*) to preen oneself.

print (prɪnt) *vb.* **1.** to reproduce (text, pictures, etc.), esp. in large numbers, by applying ink to paper or other material. **2.** to produce or reproduce (a manuscript, data, etc.) in print, as for publication. **3.** to write (letters, etc.) in the style of printed matter. **4.** to mark or indent (a surface) by pressing (something) onto it. **5.** to produce a photographic print from (a negative). **6.** (*tr.*) to fix in the mind or memory. **7.** (*tr.*) to make (a mark) by applying pressure. ~*n.* **8.** printed matter such as newsprint. **9.** a printed publication such as a book. **10. in print. a.** in printed or published form. **b.** (of a book, etc.) offered for sale by the publisher. **11. out of print.** no longer available from a publisher. **12.** a design or picture printed from an engraved plate, wood block, or other medium. **13.** printed text, esp. with regard to the typeface: *small print.* **14.** a positive photographic image produced from a negative image on film. **15. a.** a fabric with a printed design. **b.** (*as modifier*): *a print dress.* **16. a.** a mark made by pressing something onto a surface. **b.** a stamp, die, etc., that makes such an impression. **17.** See **fingerprint.** ~See also **print out.** —**'printable** *adj.*

printed circuit *n.* an electronic circuit in which certain components and the connections between them are formed by etching a metallic coating or by electrodeposition on one or both sides of a thin insulating board.

printer ('prɪntə) *n.* **1.** a person or business engaged in printing. **2.** a machine or device that prints. **3.** *Computers.* an output device for printing results on paper.

printer's devil *n.* an apprentice or errand boy in a printing establishment.

printing ('prɪntɪŋ) *n.* **1.** the business or art of producing printed matter. **2.** printed text. **3.** Also called: **impression.** all the copies of a book, etc., printed at one time. **4.** a form of writing in which letters resemble printed letters.

printing press *n.* any of various machines used for printing.

print out *vb.* (*tr., adv.*) **1.** (of a computer output device) to produce (printed information). ~*n.* **print-out. 2.** such printed information.

prior[1] ('praɪə) *adj.* **1.** (*prenominal*) previous. **2. prior**

to. before; until.

prior[2] ('praɪə) *n.* **1.** the superior of a community in certain religious orders. **2.** the deputy head of a monastery or abbey, immediately below the abbot. —**'priorate** *n.* —**'prioress** *fem. n.*

priority (praɪ'ɒrɪtɪ) *n., pl.* **-ties. 1.** the condition of being prior; antecedence; precedence. **2.** the right of precedence over others. **3.** something given specified attention: *my first priority.*

priory ('praɪərɪ) *n., pl.* **-ories.** a religious house governed by a prior, sometimes being subordinate to an abbey.

prise *or* **prize** (praɪz) *vb.* (*tr.*) **1.** to force open by levering. **2.** to extract or obtain with difficulty: *they had to prise the news out of him.*

prism ('prɪzəm) *n.* **1.** a transparent polygonal solid, often having triangular ends and rectangular sides, for dispersing light into a spectrum or for reflecting light: used in binoculars, periscopes, etc. **2.** *Maths.* a polyhedron having parallel bases and sides that are parallelograms.

prismatic (prɪz'mætɪk) *adj.* **1.** of or produced by a prism. **2.** exhibiting bright spectral colours: *prismatic light.* —**pris'matically** *adv.*

prison ('prɪzn) *n.* **1.** a public building used to house convicted criminals and accused persons awaiting trial. **2.** any place of confinement.

prisoner ('prɪznə) *n.* **1.** a person kept in custody as a punishment for a crime, while awaiting trial, or for some other reason. **2.** a person confined by any of various restraints: *we are all prisoners of time.* **3. take (someone) prisoner.** to capture and hold (someone) as a prisoner.

prisoner of war *n.* a person, esp. a serviceman, captured by an enemy in time of war. Abbrev.: **P.O.W.**

prissy ('prɪsɪ) *adj.***-sier, -siest.** *Inf.* fussy and prim, esp. in a prudish way. —**'prissily** *adv.* —**'prissiness** *n.*

pristine ('prɪstaɪn, -tiːn) *adj.* **1.** of or involving the earliest period, state, etc.; original. **2.** pure; uncorrupted.

privacy ('praɪvəsɪ, 'prɪvəsɪ) *n., pl.* **-cies. 1.** the condition of being private. **2.** secrecy.

private ('praɪvɪt) *adj.* **1.** not widely or publicly known: *they had private reasons for the decision.* **2.** confidential; secret: *a private conversation.* **3.** not for general or public use: *a private bathroom.* **4.** (*prenominal*) individual; special: *my own private recipe.* **5.** (*prenominal*) having no public office, rank, etc.: *a private man.* **6.** (*prenominal*) denoting a soldier of the lowest military rank. **7. in private.** in secret. ~*n.* **8.** a soldier of the lowest rank in many armies and marine corps. —**'privately** *adv.*

private bill *n.* a bill presented to Parliament or Congress on behalf of a private individual, corporation, etc.

private company *n.* a limited company that does not issue shares for public subscription and whose owners do not enjoy an unrestricted right to transfer their shareholdings. Cf. **public company.**

privateer (ˌpraɪvə'tɪə) *n.* **1.** an armed privately owned vessel commissioned for war service by a government. **2.** Also called: **privateersman.** a member of the crew of a privateer. ~*vb.* **3.** (*intr.*) to serve as a privateer.

private eye *n. Inf.* a private detective.

private income *n.* an income from sources other

THESAURUS

principally above all, chiefly, especially, first and foremost, for the most part, in the main, mainly, mostly, particularly, predominantly, primarily

principle 1. assumption, axiom, canon, criterion, dictum, doctrine, dogma, ethic, formula, fundamental, golden rule, law, maxim, moral law, precept, proposition, rule, standard, truth, verity **2.** attitude, belief, code, credo, ethic, morality, opinion, tenet **3.** conscience, integrity, morals, probity, rectitude, scruples, sense of duty, sense of honour, uprightness **4. in principle** ideally, in essence, in theory, theoretically

print *v.* **1.** engrave, go to press, impress, imprint, issue, mark, publish, put to bed (*Inf.*), run off, stamp ~*n.* **2.** book, magazine, newspaper, newsprint, periodical, printed matter, publication, typescript **3. in print a.** in black and white, on paper, on the streets,

out, printed, published **b.** available, current, in the shops, obtainable, on the market, on the shelves **4. out of print** no longer published, o.p., unavailable, unobtainable **5.** copy, engraving, photo (*Inf.*), photograph, picture, reproduction **6.** characters, face, font (*Chiefly U.S.*), fount, lettering, letters, type, typeface

priority first concern, greater importance, precedence, pre-eminence, preference, prerogative, rank, right of way, seniority, superiority, supremacy, the lead

priory abbey, cloister, convent, monastery, nunnery, religious house

prison can (*Sl.*), choky (*Sl.*), clink (*Sl.*), confinement, cooler (*Sl.*), dungeon, gaol, glasshouse (*Military inf.*), jail, jug (*Sl.*), lockup, penal institution, penitentiary (*U.S.*), quod (*Sl.*), stir (*Sl.*)

prisoner 1. con (*Sl.*), convict, jailbird, lag

(*Sl.*) **2.** captive, detainee, hostage, internee

privacy 1. isolation, privateness, retirement, retreat, seclusion, separateness, sequestration, solitude **2.** clandestineness, concealment, confidentiality, secrecy

private *adj.* **1.** clandestine, closet, confidential, hush-hush (*Inf.*), in camera, inside, off the record, privy (*Archaic*), secret, unofficial **2.** exclusive, individual, intimate, own, particular, personal, reserved, special **3.** independent, nonpublic **4.** concealed, isolated, not overlooked, retired, secluded, secret, separate, sequestered, solitary, withdrawn **5. in private** behind closed doors, confidentially, in camera, in secret, personally, privately ~*n.* **6.** enlisted man (*U.S.*), private soldier, squaddy (*Inf.*), tommy (*Brit. inf.*), Tommy Atkins (*Brit. inf.*)

than employment, such as investment. Also called: **private means.**

private member *n.* a member of a legislative assembly not having an appointment in the government.

private member's bill *n.* a parliamentary bill sponsored by a Member of Parliament who is not a government minister.

private parts or **privates** ('praɪvɪts) *pl. n.* euphemistic terms for **genitals.**

private school *n.* a school under the financial and managerial control of a private body, accepting mostly fee-paying pupils.

privation (praɪ'veɪʃən) *n.* **1.** loss or lack of the necessities of life, such as food and shelter. **2.** hardship resulting from this. **3.** the state of being deprived.

privative ('prɪvətɪv) *adj.* **1.** causing privation. **2.** expressing lack or negation, as for example the English suffix -*less* and prefix *un*-. —**'privatively** *adv.*

privatize or **-ise** ('praɪvɪ,taɪz) *vb.* (*tr.*) to take into, or return to, private ownership, a company or concern that has previously been owned by the state. —**'privati,zation** or **-i,sation** *n.*

privet ('prɪvɪt) *n.* **a.** any of a genus of shrubs, esp. one having oval dark green leaves, white flowers, and purplish-black berries. **b.** (*as modifier*): *a privet hedge.*

privilege ('prɪvɪlɪdʒ) *n.* **1.** a benefit, immunity, etc., granted under certain conditions. **2.** the advantages and immunities enjoyed by a small usually powerful group or class, esp. to the disadvantage of others: *one of the obstacles to social harmony is privilege.* **3.** *U.S. stock exchange.* a speculative contract permitting its purchaser to make optional purchases or sales of securities at a specified time over a limited period. ~*vb.* (*tr.*) **4.** to bestow a privilege or privileges upon. **5.** (foll. by *from*) to free or exempt.

privileged ('prɪvɪlɪdʒd) *adj.* **1.** enjoying or granted as a privilege or privileges. **2.** *Law.* **a.** not actionable as a libel or slander. **b.** (of a communication, document, etc.) that a witness cannot be compelled to divulge.

privy ('prɪvɪ) *adj.* **privier, priviest. 1.** (*postpositive; foll.* by *to*) participating in the knowledge of something secret. **2.** *Arch.* secret, hidden, etc. ~*n., pl.* **privies. 3.** a small lavatory, esp. an outhouse. **4.** *Law.* a person in privity with another. —**'privily** *adv.*

privy council *n.* **1.** the council of state of a monarch, esp. formerly. **2.** *Arch.* a secret council.

Privy Council *n.* **1.** the private council of the British sovereign, consisting of all current and former ministers of the Crown and other distinguished subjects, all of whom are appointed for life. **2.** (in Canada), a ceremonial body of advisors of the Governor General, the chief of them being the Federal cabinet ministers. —**Privy Councillor** *n.*

privy purse *n.* (*often cap.*) **1.** an allowance voted by Parliament for the private expenses of the monarch. **2.** an official of the royal household responsible for dealing with the monarch's private expenses. Full name: **Keeper of the Privy Purse.**

privy seal *n.* (*often cap.*) (in Britain) a seal affixed to certain documents issued by royal authority: of less importance than the great seal.

prize[1] (praɪz) *n.* **1. a.** a reward or honour for having won a contest, competition, etc. **b.** (*as modifier*): *prize jockey; prize essay.* **2.** something given to the winner of any game of chance, lottery, etc. **3.** something striven for.

4. any valuable property captured in time of war, esp. a vessel.

prize[2] (praɪz) *vb.* (*tr.*) to esteem greatly; value highly.

prizefight ('praɪz,faɪt) *n.* a boxing match for a prize or purse. —**'prize,fighter** *n.* —**'prize,fighting** *n.*

pro[1] (prəʊ) *adv.* **1.** in favour of a motion, issue, course of action, etc. ~*prep.* **2.** in favour of. ~*n., pl.* **pros. 3.** (*usually pl.*) an argument or vote in favour of a proposal or motion.

pro[2] (prəʊ) *n., pl.* **pros,** *adj. Inf.* **1.** short for **professional. 2.** a professional prostitute.

P.R.O. *abbrev. for:* **1.** Public Records Office. **2.** public relations officer.

pro-[1] *prefix.* **1.** in favour of; supporting: *pro-Chinese.* **2.** acting as a substitute for: *proconsul; pronoun.*

pro-[2] *prefix.* before in time or position; anterior; forward: *prognathous.*

probability (,prɒbə'bɪlɪtɪ) *n., pl.* **-ties. 1.** the condition of being probable. **2.** an event or other thing that is probable. **3.** *Statistics.* a measure of the relative frequency or likelihood of occurrence. Values are derived from a theoretical distribution or from observations.

probable ('prɒbəbəl) *adj.* **1.** likely to be or to happen but not necessarily so. **2.** most likely: *the probable cause of the accident.* ~*n.* **3.** a person who is probably to be chosen for a team, event, etc.

probably ('prɒbəblɪ) *adv.* **1.** (*sentence modifier*) in all likelihood or probability: *I'll probably see you tomorrow.* ~ **2.** *sentence substitute.* I believe such a thing may be the case.

probate ('prəʊbɪt, -beɪt) *n.* **1.** the process of officially proving the validity of a will. **2.** the official certificate stating a will to be genuine and conferring on the executors power to administer the estate. **3.** (*modifier*) relating to probate: *a probate court.* ~*vb.* **4.** (*tr.*) *Chiefly U.S.* to establish officially the validity of (a will).

probation (prə'beɪʃən) *n.* **1.** a system of dealing with offenders by placing them under the supervision of a probation officer. **2. on probation. a.** under the supervision of a probation officer. **b.** undergoing a test period. **3.** a trial period, as for a teacher. —**pro'bational** or **pro'bationary** *adj.*

probationer (prə'beɪʃənə) *n.* a person on probation.

probation officer *n.* an officer of a court who supervises offenders placed on probation and assists and befriends them.

probe (prəʊb) *vb.* **1.** (*tr.*) to search into closely. **2.** to examine (something) with or as if with a probe. ~*n.* **3.** something that probes or tests. **4.** *Surgery.* a slender instrument for exploring a wound, sinus, etc. **5.** a thorough inquiry, such as one by a newspaper into corrupt practices. **6.** *Electronics.* a lead connecting to or containing a monitoring circuit used for testing. **7.** anything which provides or acts as a coupling, esp. a flexible tube extended from an aircraft to link it with another so that it can refuel. **8.** See **space probe.** —**'probeable** *adj.* —**'prober** *n.*

probity ('prəʊbɪtɪ) *n.* confirmed integrity.

problem ('prɒbləm) *n.* **1. a.** any thing, matter, person, etc., that is difficult to deal with. **b.** (*as modifier*): *a problem child.* **2.** a puzzle, question, etc., set for solution. **3.** *Maths.* a statement requiring a solution usually by means of several operations or constructions. **4.** (*modifier*) designating a literary work that deals with difficult moral questions: *a problem play.*

THESAURUS

privilege advantage, benefit, birthright, claim, concession, due, entitlement, franchise, freedom, immunity, liberty, prerogative, right, sanction

privileged 1. advantaged, elite, entitled, favoured, honoured, indulged, powerful, ruling, special **2.** allowed, empowered, exempt, free, granted, licensed, sanctioned, vested **3.** *Of information* confidential, exceptional, inside, not for publication, off the record, privy, special

prize[1] *n.* **1.** accolade, award, honour, premium, reward, trophy **2.** haul, jackpot, purse, stakes, windfall, winnings **3.** aim, ambition, conquest, desire, gain, goal, hope **4.** booty, capture, loot, pickings, pillage, plunder, spoil(s), trophy ~*adj.* **5.** award-winning, best,

champion, first-rate, outstanding, top, top-notch (*Inf.*), winning

prize[2] *v.* appreciate, cherish, esteem, hold dear, regard highly, set store by, treasure, value

probability chance(s), expectation, liability, likelihood, likeliness, odds, presumption, prospect

probable apparent, credible, feasible, likely, most likely, odds-on, on the cards, ostensible, plausible, possible, presumable, presumed, reasonable, seeming

probably as likely as not, doubtless, in all likelihood, in all probability, likely, maybe, most likely, perchance (*Archaic*), perhaps, possibly, presumably

probation apprenticeship, examination,

initiation, novitiate, test, trial, trial period

probe *v.* **1.** examine, explore, go into, investigate, look into, query, scrutinize, search, sift, sound, test, verify **2.** explore, feel around, poke, prod ~*n.* **3.** detection, examination, exploration, inquest, inquiry, investigation, research, scrutiny, study

problem *n.* **1.** can of worms (*Inf.*), complication, difficulty, dilemma, disagreement, dispute, disputed point, doubt, hard nut to crack (*Inf.*), point at issue, predicament, quandary, trouble **2.** brain-teaser (*Inf.*), conundrum, enigma, poser, puzzle, question, riddle ~*adj.* **3.** delinquent, difficult, intractable, uncontrollable, unmanageable, unruly

problematic (ˌprɒbləˈmætɪk) *or* **problematical**
adj. **1.** having the nature of a problem; uncertain; questionable. **2.** *Logic.* (of a proposition or judgment) that may or may not be true. —ˌproblemˈatically *adv.*

proboscis (prəʊˈbɒsɪs) *n., pl.* -**cises** *or* -**cides** (-sɪˌdiːz). **1.** a long flexible prehensile trunk or snout, as of an elephant. **2.** the elongated mouthparts of certain insects. **3.** any similar organ. **4.** *Inf., facetious.* a person's nose.

procedure (prəˈsiːdʒə) *n.* **1.** a way of acting or progressing, esp. an established method. **2.** the established form of conducting the business of a legislature, the enforcement of a legal right, etc. **3.** *Computers.* another name for **subroutine.** —proˈcedural *adj.* —proˈcedurally *adv.*

proceed (prəˈsiːd) *vb.* (*intr.*) **1.** (often foll. by *to*) to advance or carry on, esp. after stopping. **2.** (often foll. by *with*) to continue: *he proceeded with his reading.* **3.** (often foll. by *against*) to institute or carry on a legal action. **4.** to originate; arise: *evil proceeds from the heart.* —proˈceeder *n.*

proceeding (prəˈsiːdɪŋ) *n.* **1.** an act or course of action. **2. a.** a legal action. **b.** any step taken in a legal action. **3.** (*pl.*) the minutes of the meetings of a society, etc. **4.** (*pl.*) legal action; litigation. **5.** (*pl.*) the events of an occasion.

proceeds (ˈprəʊsiːdz) *pl. n.* **1.** the profit or return derived from a commercial transaction, investment, etc. **2.** the result, esp. the total sum, accruing from some undertaking.

process (ˈprəʊsɛs) *n.* **1.** a series of actions which produce a change or development: *the process of digestion.* **2.** a method of doing or producing something. **3.** progress or course of time. **4. in the process of.** during or in the course of. **5. a.** a summons commanding a person to appear in court. **b.** the whole proceedings in an action at law. **6.** a natural outgrowth or projection of a part or organism. **7.** (*modifier*) relating to the general preparation of a printing forme or plate by the use, at some stage, of photography. ~*vb.* (*tr.*) **8.** to subject to a routine procedure; handle. **9.** to treat or prepare by a special method: *to process cheese.* **10. a.** to institute legal proceedings against. **b.** to serve a process on. **11.** *Photog.* **a.** to develop, rinse, fix, wash, and dry (exposed film, etc.). **b.** to produce final prints or slides from (undeveloped film). **12.** *Computers.* to perform operations on (data) according to programmed instructions in order to obtain the required information.

procession (prəˈsɛʃən) *n.* **1.** the act of proceeding in a regular formation. **2.** a group of people or things moving forwards in an orderly, regular, or ceremonial manner. **3.** the emanation of the Holy Spirit. ~*vb.* **4.** (*intr.*) *Rare.* to go in procession.

processional (prəˈsɛʃənəl) *adj.* **1.** of or suitable for a procession. ~*n.* **2.** *Christianity.* **a.** a book containing the prayers, hymns, etc., prescribed for processions. **b.** a hymn, etc., used in a procession.

processor (ˈprəʊsɛsə) *n.* **1.** *Computers.* another name for **central processing unit. 2.** a person or thing that carries out a process.

process-server *n.* a sheriff's officer who serves legal documents such as writs for appearance in court.

proclaim (prəˈkleɪm) *vb.* (*tr.*) **1.** (*may take a clause as object*) to announce publicly. **2.** (*may take a clause as object*) to indicate plainly. **3.** to praise or extol. —proclamation (ˌprɒkləˈmeɪʃən) *n.* —**proclamatory** (prəˈklæmətərɪ) *adj.* —proˈclaimer *n.*

proclivity (prəˈklɪvɪtɪ) *n., pl.* -**ties.** a tendency or inclination.

procrastinate (prəʊˈkræstɪˌneɪt, prə-) *vb.* (*usually intr.*) to put off (an action) until later; delay. —proˌcrastiˈnation *n.* —proˈcrastiˌnator *n.*

procreate (ˈprəʊkrɪˌeɪt) *vb.* **1.** to beget or engender (offspring). **2.** (*tr.*) to bring into being. —ˌprocreˈation *n.* —ˈprocreant *or* ˈprocreˌative *adj.* —ˈprocreˌator *n.*

Procrustean (prəʊˈkrʌstɪən) *adj.* designed to produce conformity by ruthless methods.

proctor (ˈprɒktə) *n.* **1.** a member of the staff of certain universities having duties including the enforcement of discipline. **2.** (formerly) an agent, esp. one engaged to conduct another's case in a court. **3.** *Church of England.* one of the elected representatives of the clergy in Convocation. —**proctorial** (prɒkˈtɔːrɪəl) *adj.*

procurator (ˈprɒkjʊˌreɪtə) *n.* **1.** (in ancient Rome) a civil official of the emperor's administration, often employed as the governor of a minor province. **2.** *Rare.* a person engaged by another to manage his affairs. —**procuracy** (ˈprɒkjʊrəsɪ) *or* ˈprocuˌratorship *n.* —**procuratorial** (ˌprɒkjʊrəˈtɔːrɪəl) *adj.*

procurator fiscal *n.* (in Scotland) a legal officer who performs the functions of public prosecutor and coroner.

procure (prəˈkjʊə) *vb.* **1.** (*tr.*) to obtain or acquire; secure. **2.** to obtain (women or girls) to act as prostitutes. —proˈcurable *adj.* —proˈcurement, proˈcural, *or* ˌprocuˈration *n.*

procurer (prəˈkjʊərə) *n.* a person who procures, esp. a man who procures women as prostitutes.

prod (prod) *vb.* **prodding, prodded. 1.** to poke or jab with or as if with a pointed object. **2.** (*tr.*) to rouse to action. ~*n.* **3.** the act or an instance of prodding. **4.** a sharp object. **5.** a stimulus or reminder. —ˈprodder *n.*

prodigal (ˈprɒdɪɡəl) *adj.* **1.** recklessly wasteful or extravagant, as in disposing of goods or money. **2.** lavish: *prodigal of compliments.* ~*n.* **3.** a person who spends lavishly or squanders money. —ˌprodiˈgality *n.* —ˈprodigally *adv.*

prodigious (prəˈdɪdʒəs) *adj.* **1.** vast in size, extent, power, etc. **2.** wonderful or amazing. —proˈdigiously *adv.* —proˈdigiousness *n.*

THESAURUS

problematic chancy (*Inf.*), debatable, doubtful, dubious, enigmatic, moot, open to doubt, problematical, puzzling, questionable, tricky, uncertain, unsettled

procedure action, conduct, course, custom, form, formula, method, modus operandi, operation, performance, plan of action, policy, practice, process, routine, scheme, step, strategy, system, transaction

proceed 1. advance, carry on, continue, get going, get on with, get under way with, go ahead, go on, make a start, move on, press on, progress, set in motion 2. arise, come, derive, emanate, ensue, flow, follow, issue, originate, result, spring, stem

proceeding 1. act, action, course of action, deed, measure, move, occurrence, procedure, process, step, undertaking, venture 2. *Plural* account, affairs, annals, archives, business, dealings, doings, matters, minutes, records, report, transactions

proceeds earnings, gain, income, produce, products, profit, receipts, returns, revenue, takings, yield

process *n.* 1. action, course, course of action, manner, means, measure, method, mode, operation, performance, practice, procedure, proceeding, system, transaction

2. advance, course, development, evolution, formation, growth, movement, progress, progression, stage, step, unfolding 3. *Law* action, case, suit, trial ~*v.* 4. deal with, dispose of, fulfil, handle, take care of 5. alter, convert, prepare, refine, transform, treat

procession 1. cavalcade, column, cortege, file, march, motorcade, parade, train 2. course, cycle, run, sequence, series, string, succession, train

proclaim advertise, affirm, announce, blaze (abroad), blazon (abroad), circulate, declare, enunciate, give out, herald, indicate, make known, profess, promulgate, publish, shout from the housetops (*Inf.*), show, trumpet

proclamation announcement, declaration, decree, edict, manifesto, notice, notification, promulgation, pronouncement, pronunciamento, publication

procrastinate adjourn, be dilatory, dally, defer, delay, drag one's feet (*Inf.*), gain time, play a waiting game, play for time, postpone, prolong, protract, put off, retard, stall, temporize

procure acquire, appropriate, buy, come by, earn, effect, find, gain, get, get hold of, lay hands on, manage to get, obtain, pick up,

purchase, secure, win

prod *v.* 1. dig, drive, elbow, jab, nudge, poke, prick, propel, push, shove 2. egg on, goad, impel, incite, motivate, move, prompt, rouse, spur, stimulate, stir up, urge ~*n.* 3. boost, dig, elbow, jab, nudge, poke, push, shove 4. goad, poker, spur, stick 5. boost, cue, prompt, reminder, signal, stimulus

prodigal *adj.* 1. excessive, extravagant, immoderate, improvident, intemperate, profligate, reckless, spendthrift, squandering, wanton, wasteful 2. bounteous, bountiful, copious, exuberant, lavish, luxuriant, profuse, sumptuous, superabundant, teeming ~*n.* 3. big spender, profligate, spendthrift, squanderer, wastrel

prodigality 1. abandon, dissipation, excess, extravagance, immoderation, intemperance, profligacy, recklessness, squandering, wantonness, waste, wastefulness 2. abundance, amplitude, bounteousness, bounty, copiousness, cornucopia, exuberance, horn of plenty, lavishness, luxuriance, plenteousness, plenty, profusion, richness, sumptuousness

prodigious 1. colossal, enormous, giant, gigantic, huge, immeasurable, immense, inordinate, mammoth, massive, monstrous, monumental, stupendous, tremendous, vast

prodigy ('prɒdɪdʒɪ) n., pl -gies. 1. a person, esp. a child, of unusual or marvellous talents. 2. anything that is a cause of wonder. 3. something monstrous or abnormal.

produce vb. (prə'dju:s). 1. to bring (something) into existence; yield. 2. to make: she produced a delicious dinner. 3. (tr.) to give birth to. 4. (tr.) to present to view: to produce evidence. 5. to bring before the public: he produced a film last year. 6. (tr.) Geom. to extend (a line). ~n. ('prɒdju:s). 7. anything produced; a product. 8. agricultural products collectively: farm produce. —pro'ducible adj. —pro,duci'bility n.

producer (prə'dju:sə) n. 1. a person or thing that produces. 2. Brit. a person responsible for the artistic direction of a play. 3. U.S. a person who organizes the stage production of a play, including the finance, management, etc. 4. Econ. a person or business enterprise that generates goods or services for sale. Cf. **consumer** (sense 1). 5. Chem. an apparatus or plant for making producer gas.

product ('prɒdʌkt) n. 1. something produced by effort, or some mechanical or industrial process. 2. the result of some natural process. 3. a result or consequence. 4. Maths. the result of the multiplication of two or more numbers, quantities, etc.

production (prə'dʌkʃən) n. 1. the act of producing. 2. anything that is produced; a product. 3. the amount produced or the rate at which it is produced. 4. Econ. the creation or manufacture of goods and services with exchange value. 5. any work created as a result of literary or artistic effort. 6. the presentation of a play, opera, etc. 7. Brit. the artistic direction of a play. 8. (modifier) manufactured by mass-production: a production model of a car. —pro'ductional adj.

productive (prə'dʌktɪv) adj. 1. producing or having the power to produce; fertile. 2. yielding favourable results. 3. Econ. a. producing goods and services that have exchange value: productive assets. b. relating to such production: the productive processes of an industry. 4. (postpositive; foll. by of) resulting in: productive of good results. —pro'ductively adv. —productivity (,prɒdʌk-'tɪvɪtɪ) or pro'ductiveness n.

proem ('prəʊɛm) n. an introduction or preface, such as to a work of literature. —proemial (prəʊ'i:mɪəl) adj.

Prof. abbrev. for Professor.

profane (prə'feɪn) adj. 1. having or indicating contempt, irreverence, or disrespect for a divinity or something sacred. 2. not designed for religious purposes; secular. 3. not initiated into the inner mysteries or sacred rites. 4. coarse or blasphemous: profane language. ~vb. (tr.) 5. to treat (something sacred) with irreverence. 6. to put to an unworthy use. —profanation (,prɒfə'neɪʃən) n. —profanatory (prə'fænətərɪ, -trɪ) adj. —pro'faner n. —pro'fanely adv. —pro'faneness n.

profanity (prə'fænɪtɪ) n., pl. -ties. 1. the state or quality of being profane. 2. vulgar or irreverent action, speech, etc.

profess (prə'fɛs) vb. 1. to affirm or acknowledge: to profess ignorance; to profess a belief in God. 2. (tr.) to claim (something), often insincerely or falsely: to profess to be a skilled driver. 3. to receive or be received into a religious order, as by taking vows. —pro'fessed adj.

profession (prə'fɛʃən) n. 1. an occupation requiring special training in the liberal arts or sciences, esp. one of the three learned professions, law, theology, or medicine. 2. the body of people in such an occupation. 3. an avowal; declaration. 4. Also called: **profession of faith**. a declaration of faith in a religion, esp. as made on entering the Church or an order belonging to it.

professional (prə'fɛʃənəl) adj. 1. of, suitable for, or engaged in as a profession. 2. engaging in an activity as a means of livelihood. 3. a. extremely competent in a job, etc. b. (of a piece of work or anything performed) produced with competence or skill. 4. undertaken or performed by people who are paid. ~n. 5. a person who belongs to one of the professions. 6. a person who engages for his livelihood in some activity also pursued by amateurs. 7. a person who engages in an activity with great competence. 8. an expert player of a game who gives instruction, esp. to members of a club by whom he is hired. —pro'fessionally adv. —pro'fessiona,lism n.

professor (prə'fɛsə) n. 1. Also called (esp. in the U.S.): **full professor**. the principal teacher in a field of learning at a university or college; a holder of a university chair. 2. Chiefly U.S. any teacher in a university or college. 3. a person who professes his opinions, beliefs, etc. —professorial (,prɒfɪ'sɔ:rɪəl) adj. —,profes'sorially adv. —,profes'soriate or pro'fessorship. n.

proffer ('prɒfə) vb. 1. (tr.) to offer for acceptance. ~n. 2. the act of proffering.

proficient (prə'fɪʃənt) adj. 1. having great facility (in an art, occupation, etc.); skilled. ~n. 2. an expert. —pro'ficiency n. —pro'ficiently adv.

profile ('prəʊfaɪl) n. 1. a side view or outline of an ob-

THESAURUS

2. abnormal, amazing, astounding, exceptional, extraordinary, fabulous, fantastic (Inf.), flabbergasting (Inf.), impressive, marvellous, miraculous, phenomenal, remarkable, staggering, startling, striking, stupendous, unusual, wonderful

prodigy 1. child genius, genius, mastermind, talent, whiz (Inf.), whiz kid (Inf.), wizard, wonder child, wunderkind 2. marvel, miracle, one in a million, phenomenon, rare bird (Inf.), sensation, wonder 3. abnormality, curiosity, freak, grotesque, monster, monstrosity, mutation, spectacle

produce v. 1. compose, construct, create, develop, fabricate, invent, make, manufacture, originate, put together, turn out 2. afford, bear, beget, breed, bring forth, deliver, engender, furnish, give, render, supply, yield 3. bring about, cause, effect, generate, give rise to, make for, occasion, provoke, set off 4. advance, bring forward, bring to light, demonstrate, exhibit, offer, present, put forward, set forth, show 5. direct, do, exhibit, mount, present, put before the public, put on, show, stage 6. Geometry extend, lengthen, prolong, protract ~n. 7. crop, fruit and vegetables, greengrocery, harvest, product, yield

producer 1. director, impresario, régisseur 2. farmer, grower, maker, manufacturer

product 1. artefact, commodity, concoction, creation, goods, invention, merchandise, produce, production, work 2. consequence, effect, fruit, issue, legacy, offshoot, outcome, result, returns, spin-off, upshot, yield

production 1. assembly, construction, creation, fabrication, formation, making, manufacture, manufacturing, origination, preparation, producing 2. direction, management, presentation, staging

productive 1. creative, dynamic, energetic, fecund, fertile, fruitful, generative, inventive, plentiful, producing, prolific, rich, teeming, vigorous 2. advantageous, beneficial, constructive, effective, fruitful, gainful, gratifying, profitable, rewarding, useful, valuable, worthwhile

productivity abundance, mass production, output, production, productive capacity, productiveness, work rate, yield

profane adj. 1. disrespectful, godless, heathen, idolatrous, impious, impure, irreligious, irreverent, pagan, sacrilegious, sinful, ungodly, wicked 2. lay, secular, temporal, unconsecrated, unhallowed, unholy, unsanctified, worldly 3. abusive, blasphemous, coarse, crude, filthy, foul, obscene, vulgar ~v. 4. abuse, commit sacrilege, contaminate, debase, defile, desecrate, misuse, pervert, pollute, prostitute, violate, vitiate

profanity abuse, blasphemy, curse, cursing, execration, foul language, four-letter word, impiety, imprecation, irreverence, malediction, obscenity, profaneness, sacrilege, swearing, sword

profess 1. acknowledge, admit, affirm, announce, assert, asseverate, aver, avow, certify, confess, confirm, declare, maintain, own, proclaim, state, vouch 2. act as if, allege, call oneself, claim, dissemble, fake, feign, let on, make out, pretend, purport, sham

professed 1. avowed, certified, confirmed, declared, proclaimed, self-acknowledged, self-confessed 2. alleged, apparent, ostensible, pretended, purported, self-styled, so-called, soi-disant, supposed, would-be

professedly 1. allegedly, apparently, by one's own account, falsely, ostensibly, purportedly, supposedly, under the pretext of 2. admittedly, avowedly, by open declaration, confessedly

profession 1. business, calling, career, employment, line, line of work, métier, occupation, office, position, sphere, vocation, walk of life 2. acknowledgment, affirmation, assertion, attestation, avowal, claim, confession, declaration, statement, testimony, vow

professional 1. adj. ace (Inf.), adept, competent, crack (Sl.), efficient, experienced, expert, finished, masterly, polished, practised, proficient, qualified, skilled, slick, trained 2. n. adept, authority, dab hand (Brit. inf.), expert, maestro, master, past master, pro (Inf.), specialist, virtuoso, wizard

professor don (Brit.), fellow (Brit.), head of faculty, prof (Inf.)

proficiency ability, accomplishment, aptitude, competence, dexterity, expertise, expertness, facility, knack, know-how (Inf.), mastery, skilfulness, skill, talent

proficient able, accomplished, adept, apt, capable, clever, competent, conversant, efficient, experienced, expert, gifted, masterly, qualified, skilful, skilled, talented, trained, versed

ject, esp. of a human head. **2. keep a low profile.** to behave so as to avoid publicity or notice. **3.** a short biographical sketch. **4.** a graph or table representing the extent to which a person, field, or object exhibits various tested characteristics: *a population profile.* **5.** a vertical section of soil or rock showing the different layers. **6.** the outline of the shape of a river valley either from source to mouth (**long profile**) or at right angles to the flow of the river (**cross profile**). ~*vb.* **7.** (*tr.*) to draw, write, or make a profile of. —**profilist** ('prəʊfɪlɪst) *n.*

profit ('prɒfɪt) *n.* **1.** (*often pl.*) excess of revenues over outlays and expenses in a business enterprise. **2.** the monetary gain derived from a transaction. **3.** income derived from property or an investment, as contrasted with capital gains. **4.** *Econ.* the income accruing to a successful entrepreneur and held to be the motivating factor of a capitalist economy. **5.** a gain, benefit, or advantage. ~*vb.* **6.** to gain or cause to gain profit. —'**profitable** *adj.* —'**profiter** *n.* —'**profitless** *adj.*

profit and loss *n. Book-keeping.* an account compiled at the end of a financial year showing that year's revenue and expense items and indicating gross and net profit or loss.

profiteer (ˌprɒfɪ'tɪə) *n.* **1.** a person who makes excessive profits, esp. by charging exorbitant prices for goods in short supply. ~*vb.* **2.** (*intr.*) to make excessive profits.

profit-sharing *n.* a system in which a portion of the net profit of a business is distributed to its employees, usually in proportion to their wages or their length of service.

profligate ('prɒflɪgɪt) *adj.* **1.** shamelessly immoral or debauched. **2.** wildly extravagant or wasteful. ~*n.* **3.** a profligate person. —**profligacy** ('prɒflɪgəsɪ) *n.* —'**profligately** *adv.*

pro forma *Latin.* ('prəʊ 'fɔːmə) *adj.* **1.** prescribing a set form or procedure. ~*adv.* **2.** performed in a set manner.

profound (prə'faʊnd) *adj.* **1.** penetrating deeply into subjects or ideas: *a profound mind.* **2.** showing or requiring great knowledge or understanding: *a profound treatise.* **3.** situated at or extending to a great depth. **4.** stemming from the depths of one's nature: *profound regret.* **5.** intense or absolute: *profound silence.* **6.** thoroughgoing; extensive: *profound changes.* ~*n.* **7.** *Arch. or literary.* a great depth; abyss. —**pro'foundly** *adv.* —**profundity** (prə'fʌndɪtɪ) *n.*

profuse (prə'fjuːs) *adj.* **1.** plentiful or abundant: *profuse compliments.* **2.** (*often foll. by in*) free or generous in the giving (of): *profuse in thanks.* —**pro'fusely** *adv.*

—**pro'fuseness** *or* **pro'fusion** *n.*

progenitor (prəʊ'dʒenɪtə) *n.* **1.** a direct ancestor. **2.** an originator or founder.

progeny ('prɒdʒɪnɪ) *n., pl.* -**nies.** **1.** the immediate descendant or descendants of a person, animal, etc. **2.** a result or outcome.

progesterone (prəʊ'dʒestəˌrəʊn) *n.* a steroid hormone, secreted mainly by the corpus luteum in the ovary, that prepares and maintains the uterus for pregnancy.

prognosis (prɒg'nəʊsɪs) *n., pl.* -**noses** (-'nəʊsiːz). **1.** *Med.* a prediction of the course or outcome of a disease. **2.** any prediction. —**prognostic** (-'nɒs-) *adj.*

prognosticate (prɒg'nɒstɪˌkeɪt) *vb.* **1.** to foretell (future events); prophesy. **2.** (*tr.*) to foreshadow or portend. —**progˌnosti'cation** *n.* —**prog'nosticative** *adj.* —**prog'nostiˌcator** *n.*

program *or* (*sometimes*) **programme** ('prəʊgræm) *n.* **1.** a sequence of coded instructions fed into a computer, enabling it to perform specified logical and arithmetical operations on data. ~*vb.* -**grams,** -**gramming,** -**grammed** *or* -**grammes,** -**gramming,** -**grammed.** **2.** (*tr.*) to feed a program into (a computer). **3.** (*tr.*) to arrange (data) in a suitable form so that it can be processed by a computer. **4.** (*intr.*) to write a program. —'**programmer** *n.*

programmable *or* **programable** (prəʊ'græməbəl) *adj.* capable of being programmed.

programme *or* U.S. **program** ('prəʊgræm) *n.* **1.** a written or printed list of the events, performers, etc., in a public performance. **2.** a performance presented at a scheduled time, esp. on radio or television. **3.** a specially arranged selection of things to be done: *what's the programme for this afternoon?* **4.** a plan, schedule, or procedure. **5.** a syllabus or curriculum. ~*vb.* -**gramming,** -**grammed** *or* U.S. -**graming,** -**gramed.** **6.** to design or schedule (something) as a programme. ~*n., vb.* **7.** *Computers.* a variant spelling of **program.** —ˌprogram-'matic *adj.*

programming language *n.* a language system by which instructions to a computer are coded, using a set of characters that are mutually comprehensible to user and computer.

progress *n.* ('prəʊgres). **1.** movement forwards, esp. towards a place or objective. **2.** satisfactory development or advance. **3.** advance towards completion or perfection. **4.** (*modifier*) of or relating to progress: *a progress report.* **5.** (*formerly*) a stately royal journey. **6. in progress.** taking place. ~*vb.* (prə'gres). **7.** (*intr.*) to move forwards or onwards. **8.** to move towards or bring nearer to completion or perfection.

THESAURUS

profile *n.* **1.** contour, drawing, figure, form, outline, portrait, shape, side view, silhouette, sketch **2.** biography, characterization, character sketch, sketch, thumbnail sketch, vignette **3.** analysis, chart, diagram, examination, graph, review, study, survey, table

profit *n.* **1.** *Often plural* bottom line, earnings, emoluments, gain, percentage (*Inf.*), proceeds, receipts, return, revenue, surplus, takings, winnings, yield **2.** advancement, advantage, avail, benefit, gain, good, interest, use, value ~*v.* **3.** aid, avail, benefit, be of advantage to, better, contribute, gain, help, improve, promote, serve, stand in good stead **4.** capitalize on, cash in on (*Sl.*), exploit, learn from, make capital of, make good use of, make the most of, put to good use, reap the benefit of, take advantage of, turn to advantage *or* account, use, utilize **5.** clean up (*Inf.*), clear, earn, gain, make a good thing of (*Inf.*), make a killing (*Inf.*), make money

profitable **1.** commercial, cost-effective, fruitful, gainful, lucrative, money-making, paying, remunerative, rewarding, worthwhile **2.** advantageous, beneficial, fruitful, productive, rewarding, serviceable, useful, valuable, worthwhile

profiteer **1.** *n.* exploiter, racketeer **2.** *v.* exploit, fleece, make a quick buck (*Sl.*), make someone pay through the nose, overcharge, racketeer, sting (*Inf.*)

profligate *adj.* **1.** abandoned, corrupt, debauched, degenerate, depraved, dissipated, dissolute, immoral, iniquitous, libertine, licentious, loose, promiscuous, shameless, unprincipled, vicious, vitiated, wanton, wicked, wild **2.** extravagant, immoderate, improvident, prodigal, reckless, spendthrift, squandering, wasteful ~*n.* **3.** debauchee, degenerate, dissipater, libertine, rake, reprobate, roué **4.** prodigal, spendthrift, squanderer, waster, wastrel

profound **1.** abstruse, deep, discerning, erudite, learned, penetrating, philosophical, recondite, sagacious, sage, serious, skilled, subtle, thoughtful, weighty, wise **2.** abysmal, bottomless, cavernous, deep, fathomless, yawning **3.** abject, acute, deeply felt, extreme, great, heartfelt, heartrending, hearty, intense, keen, sincere **4.** absolute, complete, consummate, exhaustive, extensive, extreme, far-reaching, intense, out-and-out, pronounced, thoroughgoing, total, utter

profoundly abjectly, acutely, deeply, extremely, from the bottom of one's heart, greatly, heartily, intensely, keenly, seriously, sincerely, thoroughly, very

profuse **1.** abundant, ample, bountiful, copious, luxuriant, overflowing, plentiful, prolific, teeming **2.** excessive, extravagant, exuberant, fulsome, generous, immoderate, lavish, liberal, open-handed, prodigal, unstinting

profusion abundance, bounty, copiousness, cornucopia, excess, extravagance, exuberance, glut, lavishness, luxuriance, multi-

tude, oversupply, plenitude, plethora, prodigality, quantity, riot, superabundance, superfluity, surplus, wealth

progeny breed, children, descendants, family, issue, lineage, offspring, posterity, race, scions, seed, stock, young

programme *n.* **1.** agenda, curriculum, line-up, list, listing, list of players, order of events, order of the day, plan, schedule, syllabus **2.** broadcast, performance, presentation, production, show **3.** design, order of the day, plan, plan of action, procedure, project, scheme ~*v.* **4.** arrange, bill, book, design, engage, formulate, itemize, lay on, line up, list, map out, plan, prearrange, schedule, work out

progress *n.* **1.** advance, course, movement, onward course, passage, progression, way **2.** advance, advancement, amelioration, betterment, breakthrough, development, gain, gaining ground, growth, headway, improvement, increase, progression, promotion, step forward **3. in progress** being done, going on, happening, occurring, proceeding, taking place, under way ~*v.* **4.** advance, come on, continue, cover ground, forge ahead, gain ground, gather way, get on, go forward, make headway, make one's way, make strides, move on, proceed, travel **5.** advance, ameliorate, better, blossom, develop, gain, grow, improve, increase, mature

progression (prə'grɛʃən) n. 1. the act of progressing; advancement. 2. the act or an instance of moving from one thing in a sequence to the next. 3. *Maths.* a sequence of numbers in which each term differs from the succeeding term by a constant relation. See also **arithmetic progression, geometric progression.** 4. *Music.* movement from one note or chord to the next. —**pro-'gressional** adj. —**pro'gressionally** adv.

progressive (prə'grɛsɪv) adj. 1. of or relating to progress. 2. progressing by steps or degrees. 3. (*often cap.*) favouring or promoting political or social reform: *a progressive policy.* 4. denoting an educational system that allows flexibility in learning procedures, based on activities determined by the needs and capacities of the individual child. 5. (esp. of a disease) advancing in severity, complexity, or extent. 6. (of a dance, card game, etc.) involving a regular change of partners. 7. denoting an aspect of verbs in some languages, including English, used to express continuous activity: *a progressive aspect of the verb "to walk" is "is walking".* ~n. 8. a person who advocates progress, as in education, politics, etc. 9. a. the progressive aspect of a verb. b. a verb in this aspect. —**pro'gressively** adv. —**pro'gressiveness** n. —**pro'gressivism** n. —**pro'gressivist** n.

prohibit (prə'hɪbɪt) vb. (tr.) 1. to forbid by law or other authority. 2. to hinder or prevent. —**pro'hibiter** or **pro-'hibitor** n.

prohibition (ˌprəʊɪ'bɪʃən) n. 1. the act of prohibiting or state of being prohibited. 2. an order or decree that prohibits. 3. (*sometimes cap.*) (esp. in the U.S.) a policy of legally forbidding the manufacture, sale, or consumption of alcoholic beverages. 4. *Law.* a writ from a superior court forbidding an inferior court to determine a matter outside its jurisdiction. —ˌprohi'bitionary adj. —ˌprohi-'bitionist n.

Prohibition (ˌprəʊɪ'bɪʃən) n. the period (1920–33) when the manufacture, sale, and transportation of intoxicating liquors was banned in the U.S. —ˌProhi'bitionist n.

prohibitive (prə'hɪbɪtɪv) or **prohibitory** (prə'hɪbɪtərɪ) adj. 1. prohibiting or tending to prohibit. 2. (esp. of prices) tending or designed to discourage sale or purchase. —**pro'hibitively** adv. —**pro'hibitiveness** n.

project n. ('prɒdʒɛkt). 1. a proposal, scheme, or design. 2. a. a task requiring considerable or concerted effort, such as one by students. b. the subject of such a task. ~vb. (prə'dʒɛkt). 3. (tr.) to propose or plan. 4. (tr.) to throw forwards. 5. to jut or cause to jut out. 6. (tr.) to transport in the imagination: *to project oneself into the future.* 7. to make a prediction based on known data and observations. 8. (tr.) to cause (an image) to appear on a surface. 9. to cause (one's voice) to be heard clearly at a distance. 10. *Psychol.* a. (intr.) (esp. of a child) to believe that others share one's subjective mental life. b. to impute to others (one's hidden desires). 11. (tr.) *Geom.* to draw a projection of. 12. (intr.) to communicate effectively, esp. to a large gathering.

projectile (prə'dʒɛktaɪl) n. 1. an object thrown forwards. 2. any self-propelling missile, esp. a rocket. 3. any object that can be fired from a gun, such as a shell. ~adj. 4. designed to be hurled forwards. 5. projecting forwards.

projection (prə'dʒɛkʃən) n. 1. the act of projecting or the state of being projected. 2. a part that juts out. 3. in map making, the representation on a plane of all or part of the earth's surface or of the celestial sphere. 4. the representation of a line, figure, or solid on a given plane as it would be seen from a particular direction or in accordance with an accepted set of rules. 5. a scheme or plan. 6. a prediction based on known evidence and observations. 7. a. the process of showing film on a screen. b. the images shown. 8. *Psychol.* a. the belief that others share one's subjective mental life. b. the process of projecting one's own hidden desires and impulses. —**pro-'jectional** adj. —**pro'jective** adj.

projectionist (prə'dʒɛkʃənɪst) n. a person responsible for the operation of film projection machines.

projector (prə'dʒɛktə) n. 1. an optical instrument that projects an enlarged image of individual slides. Full name: **slide projector.** 2. an optical instrument in which a film is wound past a lens so that the frames can be viewed as a continuously moving sequence. Full name: **film** or **cine projector.** 3. a device for projecting a light beam. 4. a person who devises projects.

prolapse ('prəʊlæps, prəʊ'læps) *Pathol.* ~n. 1. Also: **prolapsus** (prəʊ'læpsəs). the sinking or falling down of an organ or part. ~vb. (intr.) 2. (of an organ, etc.) to sink from its normal position.

prolate ('prəʊleɪt) adj. having a polar diameter of greater length than the equatorial diameter. Cf. **oblate.** —'prolately adv.

prole (prəʊl) n. *Derog. sl., chiefly Brit.* a member of the proletariat; proletarian.

proletariat (ˌprəʊlɪ'tɛərɪət) n. 1. all wage-earners collectively. 2. the lower or working class. 3. (in Marxist theory) the class of wage-earners, esp. industrial workers, in a capitalist society, whose only possession of significant material value is their labour. 4. (in ancient Rome) the lowest class of citizens, who had no property. —ˌprole'tarian adj.,n.

proliferate (prə'lɪfəˌreɪt) vb. 1. to grow or reproduce (new parts, cells, etc.) rapidly. 2. to grow or increase rapidly. —pro,lifer'ation n. —pro'liferative adj.

prolific (prə'lɪfɪk) adj. 1. producing fruit, offspring, etc., in abundance. 2. producing constant or successful results. 3. (often foll. by *in* or *of*) rich or fruitful. —**pro-'lifically** adv. —**pro'lificness** or **pro'lificacy** n.

prolix ('prəʊlɪks, prəʊ'lɪks) adj. 1. (of a speech, book, etc.) so long as to be boring. 2. long-winded. —**pro'lixity** n. —**pro'lixly** adv.

prologue or U.S. (often) **prolog** ('prəʊlɒg) n. 1. the prefatory lines introducing a play or speech. 2. a preliminary act or event. 3. (in early opera) a. an introductory scene in which a narrator summarizes the main action of the work. b. a brief independent play preceding the opera, esp. one in honour of a patron. ~vb. -loguing,

---

═THESAURUS═

progression 1. advance, advancement, furtherance, gain, headway, movement forward, progress 2. chain, course, cycle, order, sequence, series, string, succession

progressive 1. accelerating, advancing, continuing, continuous, developing, escalating, growing, increasing, intensifying, ongoing 2. advanced, avant-garde, dynamic, enlightened, enterprising, forward-looking, go-ahead, liberal, modern, radical, reformist, revolutionary, up-and-coming

prohibit 1. ban, debar, disallow, forbid, interdict, outlaw, proscribe, veto 2. constrain, hamper, hinder, impede, make impossible, obstruct, preclude, prevent, restrict, rule out, stop

prohibited banned, barred, forbidden, not allowed, proscribed, taboo, verboten, vetoed

prohibition 1. constraint, exclusion, forbiddance, interdiction, negation, obstruction, prevention, restriction 2. ban, bar, disallowance, embargo, injunction, interdict, proscription, veto

prohibitive 1. forbidding, prohibiting, proscriptive, repressive, restraining, restrictive, suppressive 2. *Esp. of prices* beyond one's means, excessive, exorbitant, extortionate, high-priced, preposterous, sky-high, steep (*Inf.*)

project n. 1. activity, assignment, design, enterprise, job, occupation, plan, programme, proposal, scheme, task, undertaking, venture, work ~v. 2. contemplate, contrive, design, devise, draft, frame, map out, outline, plan, propose, purpose, scheme 3. cast, discharge, fling, hurl, launch, make carry, propel, shoot, throw, transmit 4. beetle, bulge, extend, jut, overhang, protrude, stand out, stick out 5. calculate, estimate, extrapolate, forecast, gauge, predetermine, predict, reckon

projectile bullet, missile, rocket, shell

projection 1. bulge, eaves, jut, ledge, overhang, protrusion, protuberance, ridge, shelf, sill 2. blueprint, diagram, map, outline, plan, representation 3. calculation, computation, estimate, estimation, extrapolation, forecast, prediction, reckoning

proletarian 1. adj. cloth-cap (*Inf.*), common, plebeian, working-class 2. n. commoner, Joe Bloggs (*Brit. inf.*), man of the people, pleb (*Sl.*), plebeian, prole (*Sl.*), worker

proletariat commonalty, commoners, hoi polloi, labouring classes, lower classes, lower orders, plebs, proles (*Sl.*), the common people, the great unwashed (*Derogatory*), the herd, the masses, the rabble, wage-earners, working class

proliferate breed, burgeon, escalate, expand, grow rapidly, increase, multiply, mushroom, run riot, snowball

proliferation build-up, concentration, escalation, expansion, extension, increase, intensification, multiplication, spread, step-up (*Inf.*)

prolific abundant, bountiful, copious, fecund, fertile, fruitful, generative, luxuriant, productive, profuse, rank, rich, teeming

prologue exordium, foreword, introduction, preamble, preface, preliminary, prelude, proem

-logued *or U.S.* **-loging, -loged.** **4.** (*tr.*) to introduce with a prologue.

prolong (prə'lɒŋ) *vb.* (*tr.*) to lengthen; extend. **—prolongation** (ˌprəʊlɒŋ'geɪʃən) *n.*

prom (prɒm) *n.* **1.** *Brit.* short for **promenade** or **promenade concert.** **2.** *U.S. inf.* a formal dance held at a high school or college.

PROM (prɒm) *n. Computers.* acronym for Programmable Read Only Memory.

promenade (ˌprɒmə'nɑːd) *n.* **1.** *Chiefly Brit.* a public walk, esp. at a seaside resort. **2.** a leisurely walk, esp. one in a public place for pleasure or display. **3.** a marchlike step in dancing. **4.** a marching sequence in a square or country dance. ~*vb.* **5.** to take a promenade in or through (a place). **6.** (*intr.*) *Dancing.* to perform a promenade. **7.** (*tr.*) to display or exhibit (someone or oneself) on or as if on a promenade. **—ˌprome'nader** *n.*

promenade concert *n.* a concert at which some of the audience stand rather than sit.

promethium (prə'miːθɪəm) *n.* a radioactive element of the lanthanide series artificially produced by the fission of uranium. Symbol: Pm; atomic no.: 61; half-life of most stable isotope, ¹⁴⁵Pm: 17.7 years.

prominent ('prɒmɪnənt) *adj.* **1.** jutting or projecting outwards. **2.** standing out from its surroundings; noticeable. **3.** widely known; eminent. **—'prominence** *n.* **—'prominently** *adv.* **—'prominentness** *n.*

promiscuous (prə'mɪskjʊəs) *adj.* **1.** indulging in casual and indiscriminate sexual relationships. **2.** consisting of a number of dissimilar parts or elements mingled indiscriminately. **3.** indiscriminate in selection. **4.** casual or heedless. **—pro'miscuously** *adv.* **—promiscuity** (ˌprɒmɪ'skjuːɪtɪ) *or* **pro'miscuousness** *n.*

promise ('prɒmɪs) *vb.* **1.** (often foll. by *to;* when *tr.,* may take a clause as object or an infinitive) to give an assurance of (something to someone): *I promise that I will come.* **2.** (*tr.*) to undertake to give (something to someone): *he promised me a car for my birthday.* **3.** (when *tr.,* takes an infinitive) to cause one to expect that one is likely (to be or do something): *she promises to be a fine soprano.* **4.** (*usually passive*) *Obs.* to betroth: *I'm promised to Bill.* **5.** (*tr.*) to assure (someone) of the authenticity or inevitability of something: *there'll be trouble, I promise you.* ~*n.* **6.** an assurance given by one person to another agreeing or guaranteeing to do or not to do something. **7.** indication of forthcoming excellence: *a writer showing considerable promise.* **8.** the thing of which an assurance is given. **—'promiser** *or* (*Law*) **'promisor** *n.* **—'promisee** *n.*

Promised Land *n.* **1.** *Old Testament.* the land of Canaan, promised by God to Abraham and his descendants as their heritage (Genesis 12:7). **2.** *Christianity.* heaven. **3.** any longed-for place where one expects to find greater happiness.

promising ('prɒmɪsɪŋ) *adj.* showing promise of future success. **—'promisingly** *adv.*

promissory note *n. Commerce.* a document containing a signed promise to pay a stated sum of money to a specified person at a designated date or on demand. Also called: **note, note of hand.**

promontory ('prɒmǝntǝrɪ, -trɪ) *n., pl.* **-ries.** **1.** a high point of land, esp. of rocky coast, that juts out into the sea. **2.** *Anat.* any of various projecting structures.

promote (prə'məʊt) *vb.* (*tr.*) **1.** to encourage the progress or existence of. **2.** to raise to a higher rank, status, etc. **3.** to advance (a pupil or student) to a higher course, class, etc. **4.** to work for: *to promote reform.* **5.** to encourage the sale of (a product) by advertising or securing financial support. **—pro'motable** *adj.* **—pro'motion** *n.* **—pro'motional** *adj.* **—pro'motive** *adj.*

promoter (prə'məʊtə) *n.* **1.** a person or thing that promotes. **2.** a person who helps to organize, develop, or finance an undertaking. **3.** a person who organizes and finances a sporting event, esp. a boxing match.

prompt (prɒmpt) *adj.* **1.** performed or executed without delay. **2.** quick or ready to act or respond. ~*adv.* **3.** *Inf.* punctually. ~*vb.* **4.** (*tr.*) to urge or induce (someone to do something). **5.** to remind (an actor, singer, etc.) of lines forgotten during a performance. **6.** (*tr.*) to refresh the memory of. **7.** (*tr.*) to give rise to by suggestion: *his affairs will prompt discussion.* ~*n.* **8.** *Commerce.* **a.** the time limit allowed for payment of the debt incurred by purchasing on credit. **b.** Also called: **prompt note.** a memorandum sent to a purchaser to remind him of the time limit and the sum due. **9.** anything that serves to remind. **—'prompti,tude** *n.* **—'promptly** *adv.* **—'promptness** *n.*

prompter ('prɒmptə) *n.* **1.** a person offstage who reminds the actors of forgotten lines or cues. **2.** a person, thing, etc., that prompts.

THESAURUS

prolong carry on, continue, delay, drag out, draw out, extend, lengthen, make longer, perpetuate, protract, spin out, stretch

promenade *n.* **1.** boulevard, esplanade, parade, prom, public walk, walkway **2.** airing, constitutional, saunter, stroll, turn, walk ~*v.* **3.** perambulate, saunter, stretch one's legs, stroll, take a walk, walk **4.** flaunt, parade, strut, swagger

prominence **1.** cliff, crag, crest, elevation, headland, height, high point, hummock, mound, pinnacle, projection, promontory, rise, rising ground, spur **2.** bulge, jutting, projection, protrusion, protuberance, swelling **3.** conspicuousness, markedness, outstandingness, precedence, salience, specialness, top billing, weight **4.** celebrity, distinction, eminence, fame, greatness, importance, name, notability, pre-eminence, prestige, rank, reputation, standing

prominent **1.** bulging, jutting, projecting, protruding, protrusive, protuberant, standing out **2.** conspicuous, easily seen, eye-catching, in the foreground, noticeable, obtrusive, obvious, outstanding, pronounced, remarkable, salient, striking, to the fore, unmistakable **3.** celebrated, chief, distinguished, eminent, famous, foremost, important, leading, main, noted, outstanding, popular, pre-eminent, renowned, respected, top, well-known, well-thought-of

promiscuous **1.** abandoned, debauched, dissipated, dissolute, fast, immoral, lax, libertine, licentious, loose, of easy virtue, profligate, unbridled, unchaste, wanton, wild **2.** chaotic, confused, disordered, diverse, heterogeneous, ill-assorted, indiscriminate, intermingled, intermixed, jumbled, mingled, miscellaneous, mixed, motley **3.** careless, casual, haphazard, heedless, indifferent, indiscriminate, irregular, irresponsible, random, slovenly, uncontrolled, uncritical, undiscriminating, unfastidious, unselective

promise *v.* **1.** assure, contract, cross one's heart, engage, give an undertaking, give one's word, guarantee, pledge, plight, stipulate, swear, take an oath, undertake, vouch, vow, warrant **2.** augur, bespeak, betoken, bid fair, denote, give hope of, hint at, hold a probability, hold out hopes of, indicate, lead one to expect, look like, seem likely to, show signs of, suggest ~*n.* **3.** assurance, bond, commitment, compact, covenant, engagement, guarantee, oath, pledge, undertaking, vow, word, word of honour **4.** ability, aptitude, capability, capacity, flair, potential, talent

promising **1.** auspicious, bright, encouraging, favourable, full of promise, hopeful, likely, propitious, reassuring, rosy **2.** able, gifted, likely, rising, talented, up-and-coming

promontory cape, foreland, head, headland, ness (*Archaic*), point, spur

promote **1.** advance, aid, assist, back, boost, contribute to, develop, encourage, forward, foster, further, help, nurture, stimulate, support **2.** aggrandize, dignify, elevate, exalt, honour, kick upstairs (*Inf.*), prefer, raise, upgrade **3.** advocate, call attention to, champion, endorse, espouse, popularize, push for, recommend, speak for, sponsor, support, urge, work for **4.** advertise, beat the drum for (*Inf.*), hype (*Sl.*), plug (*Inf.*), publicize, puff, push, sell

promotion **1.** advancement, aggrandizement, elevation, ennoblement, exaltation, honour, move up, preferment, rise, upgrading **2.** advancement, advocacy, backing, boosting, cultivation, development, encouragement, espousal, furtherance, progress, support **3.** advertising, advertising campaign, ballyhoo (*Inf.*), hard sell, hype (*Sl.*), media hype (*Sl.*), plugging (*Inf.*), propaganda, publicity, puffery (*Inf.*), pushing

prompt *adj.* **1.** early, immediate, instant, instantaneous, on time, punctual, quick, rapid, speedy, swift, timely, unhesitating **2.** alert, brisk, eager, efficient, expeditious, quick, ready, responsive, smart, willing ~*adv.* **3.** *Inf.* exactly, on the dot, promptly, punctually, sharp ~*v.* **4.** cause, impel, incite, induce, inspire, instigate, motivate, move, provoke, spur, stimulate, urge **5.** assist, cue, help out, jog the memory, prod, refresh the memory, remind **6.** call forth, cause, elicit, evoke, give rise to, occasion, provoke ~*n.* **7.** cue, help, hint, jog, jolt, prod, reminder, spur, stimulus

prompter **1.** autocue, idiot board (*Sl.*), Teleprompter (*Trademark*) **2.** agitator, catalyst, gadfly, inspirer, instigator, moving spirit, prime mover

prompting assistance, encouragement, hint, incitement, influence, jogging, persuasion, pressing, pressure, prodding, pushing, reminder, reminding, suggestion, urging

promptly at once, by return, directly, immediately, instantly, on the dot, on time, pronto (*Inf.*), punctually, quickly, speedily, swiftly, unhesitatingly

promptness alacrity, alertness, briskness, dispatch, eagerness, haste, promptitude, punctuality, quickness, readiness, speed, swiftness, willingness

promulgate ('promǝl,geit) vb. (tr.) **1.** to put into effect (a law, decree, etc.), esp. by formal proclamation. **2.** to announce officially. **3.** to make widespread. —,**promul'gation** n. —'**promul,gator** n.

pron. abbrev. for: **1.** pronominal. **2.** pronoun. **3.** pronounced. **4.** pronunciation.

prone (prǝun) adj. **1.** lying flat or face downwards; prostrate. **2.** sloping or tending downwards. **3.** having an inclination to do something. —'**pronely** adv. —'**proneness** n.

-prone adj. combining form. liable or disposed to suffer: accident-prone.

prong (proŋ) n. **1.** a sharply pointed end of an instrument, such as on a fork. **2.** any pointed projecting part. ~vb. **3.** (tr.) to prick or spear with or as if with a prong. —**pronged** adj.

pronominal (prǝu'nominǝl) adj. relating to or playing the part of a pronoun. —**pro'nominally** adv.

pronoun ('prǝu,naun) n. one of a class of words that serves to replace a noun or noun phrase that has already been or is about to be mentioned in the sentence or context. Abbrev.: **pron.**

pronounce (prǝ'nauns) vb. **1.** to utter or articulate (a sound or sounds). **2.** (tr.) to utter (words) in the correct way. **3.** (tr.; may take a clause as object) to proclaim officially: I now pronounce you man and wife. **4.** (when tr., may take a clause as object) to declare as one's judgment: to pronounce the death sentence upon someone. —**pro'nounceable** adj. —**pro'nouncer** n.

pronounced (prǝ'naunst) adj. **1.** strongly marked or indicated. **2.** (of a sound) articulated with vibration of the vocal cords; voiced. —**pronouncedly** (prǝ'naunsidli) adv.

pronouncement (prǝ'naunsmǝnt) n. **1.** an official or authoritative announcement. **2.** the act of declaring or uttering formally.

pronto ('prontǝu) adv. U.S. inf. at once.

pronunciation (prǝ,nʌnsi'eiʃǝn) n. **1.** the act, instance, or manner of pronouncing sounds. **2.** the supposedly correct manner of pronouncing sounds in a given language. **3.** a phonetic transcription of a word.

proof (pru:f) n. **1.** any evidence that establishes or helps to establish the truth, validity, quality, etc., of something. **2.** Law. the whole body of evidence upon which the verdict of a court is based. **3.** Maths., logic. a sequence of steps or statements that establishes the truth of a proposition. **4.** the act of testing the truth of something (esp. in **put to the proof**). **5.** Scot. law. trial before a judge without a jury. **6.** Printing. a trial impression made from composed type for the correction of errors. **7.** (in engraving, etc.) a print made by an artist or under his supervision for his own satisfaction before he hands the plate over to a professional printer. **8.** Photog. a trial print from a negative. **9. a.** the alcoholic strength of proof spirit. **b.** the strength of a liquor as measured on a scale in which the strength of proof spirit is 100 degrees. ~adj. **10.** (usually postpositive; foll. by against) impervious (to): the roof is proof against rain. **11.** having the alcoholic strength of proof spirit. **12.** of proved impenetrability: proof armour. ~vb. **13.** (tr.) to take a proof from (type matter, a plate, etc.). **14.** to

proofread (text) or inspect (a print, etc.), as for approval. **15.** to render (something) proof, esp. to waterproof.

-proof adj. combining form. impervious to; resisting the effects of: waterproof.

proofread ('pru:f,ri:d) vb. **-reading, -read** (-,rɛd). to read (copy or printer's proofs) and mark errors to be corrected. —'**proof,reader** n.

proof spirit n. (in Britain) a mixture of alcohol and water or an alcoholic beverage that contains 49.28 per cent of alcohol by weight, 57.1 per cent by volume at 60°F (15.6°C): used as a standard of alcoholic liquids.

prop[1] (prop) vb. **propping, propped.** (tr.; often foll. by up) **1.** to support with a rigid object, such as a stick. **2.** (usually also foll. by against) to place or lean. **3.** to sustain or support. ~n. **4.** something that gives rigid support, such as a stick. **5.** In full **clothes prop.** a long wooden pole with a forked end used to raise a line of washing into the breeze. **6.** a person or thing giving support, as of a moral nature. **7.** Rugby. either of the forwards at either end of the front row of a scrum.

prop[2] (prop) n. short for **property** (sense 8).

prop[3] (prop) n. an informal word for **propeller.**

prop. abbrev. for: **1.** proper(ly). **2.** property. **3.** proposition. **4.** proprietor.

propaganda (,propǝ'gændǝ) n. **1.** the organized dissemination of information, allegations, etc., to assist or damage the cause of a government, movement, etc. **2.** such information, allegations, etc. —**propa'gandism** n. —,**propa'gandist** n., adj.

propagate ('propǝ,geit) vb. **1.** Biol. to reproduce or cause to reproduce; breed. **2.** Horticulture. (tr.) to produce (plants) by layering, grafting, cuttings, etc. **3.** (tr.) to promulgate. **4.** Physics. to transmit, esp. in the form of a wave: to propagate sound. **5.** (tr.) to transmit (characteristics) from one generation to the next. —,**propa'gation** n. —,**propa'gational** adj. —'**propagative** adj. —'**propa,gator** n.

propane ('prǝupein) n. a flammable gaseous alkane found in petroleum and used as a fuel. Formula: $CH_3CH_2CH_3$.

propel (prǝ'pɛl) vb. **-pelling, -pelled.** (tr.) to impel, drive, or cause to move forwards. —**pro'pellant** or **pro'pellent** n.

propeller (prǝ'pɛlǝ) n. **1.** a device having blades radiating from a central hub that is rotated to produce thrust to propel a ship, aircraft, etc. **2.** a person or thing that propels.

propensity (prǝ'pɛnsiti) n., pl. **-ties. 1.** a natural tendency. **2.** Obs. partiality.

proper ('propǝ) adj. **1.** (usually prenominal) appropriate or usual: in its proper place. **2.** suited to a particular purpose: use the proper knife to cut the bread. **3.** correct in behaviour. **4.** vigorously or excessively moral. **5.** up to a required or regular standard. **6.** (immediately postpositive) (of an object, quality, etc.) referred to so as to exclude anything not directly connected with it: his claim is connected with the deed proper. **7.** (postpositive; foll. by to) belonging to or characteristic of a person or thing. **8.** (prenominal) Brit. inf. (intensifier): I felt a proper fool. **9.** (usually postpositive) (of heraldic colours) considered correct for the natural colour of the ob-

promulgate advertise, announce, broadcast, circulate, communicate, declare, decree, disseminate, issue, make known, make public, notify, proclaim, promote, publish, spread

prone 1. face down, flat, horizontal, lying down, procumbent, prostrate, recumbent, supine 2. apt, bent, disposed, given, inclined, liable, likely, predisposed, subject, susceptible, tending

prong point, projection, spike, tine, tip

pronounce 1. accent, articulate, enunciate, say, sound, speak, stress, utter, vocalize, voice 2. affirm, announce, assert, declare, decree, deliver, judge, proclaim

pronounced broad, clear, conspicuous, decided, definite, distinct, evident, marked, noticeable, obvious, striking, strong, unmistakable

pronouncement announcement, declaration, decree, dictum, edict, judgment, manifesto, notification, proclamation, prom-

ulgation, pronunciamento, statement

pronunciation accent, accentuation, articulation, diction, elocution, enunciation, inflection, intonation, speech, stress

proof n. 1. attestation, authentication, certification, confirmation, corroboration, demonstration, evidence, substantiation, testimony, verification 2. As in **put to the proof** assay, examination, experiment, ordeal, scrutiny, test, trial 3. Printing galley, galley proof, page proof, pull, slip, trial impression, trial print ~adj. 4. impenetrable, impervious, repellent, resistant, strong, tight, treated 5. be **proof against** hold out against, resist, stand firm against, stand up to, withstand

prop v. 1. bolster, brace, buttress, hold up, maintain, shore, stay, support, sustain, truss, uphold 2. lean, rest, set, stand ~n. 3. brace, buttress, mainstay, stanchion, stay, support, truss

propaganda advertising, agitprop, ballyhoo (Inf.), brainwashing, disinformation,

hype (Sl.), information, newspeak, promotion, publicity

propagate 1. beget, breed, engender, generate, increase, multiply, procreate, produce, proliferate, reproduce 2. broadcast, circulate, diffuse, disseminate, make known, proclaim, promote, promulgate, publicize, publish, spread, transmit

propagation 1. breeding, generation, increase, multiplication, procreation, proliferation, reproduction 2. circulation, communication, diffusion, dissemination, distribution, promotion, promulgation, spread, spreading, transmission

propel drive, force, impel, launch, push, send, set in motion, shoot, shove, start, thrust

propensity aptness, bent, bias, disposition, inclination, leaning, liability, penchant, predisposition, proclivity, proneness, susceptibility, tendency, weakness

ject depicted: *three martlets proper.* **10.** *Arch.* pleasant or good. **11. good and proper.** *Inf.* thoroughly. ~*n.* **12.** the parts of the Mass that vary according to the particular day or feast on which the Mass is celebrated. —'**properly** *adv.* —'**properness** *n.*

proper fraction *n.* a fraction in which the numerator has a lower absolute value than the denominator, as ½ or $x/(3 + x^2)$.

proper noun *or* **name** *n.* the name of a person, place, or object, as for example *Iceland, Patrick,* or *Uranus.*

propertied ('propətid) *adj.* owning land or property.

property ('propəti) *n., pl.* **-ties.** **1.** something of value, either tangible, such as land, or intangible, such as copyrights. **2.** *Law.* the right to possess, use, and dispose of anything. **3.** possessions collectively. **4. a.** land or real estate. **b.** (*as modifier*): *property rights.* **5.** *Chiefly Austral.* a ranch or station. **6.** a quality or characteristic attribute, such as the density or strength of a material. **7.** *Logic.* an attribute that is not essential to a species but is common and peculiar to it. **8.** any movable object used on the set of a stage play or film. Usually shortened to **prop.**

prophecy ('profisi) *n., pl.* **-cies.** **1. a.** a message of divine truth revealing God's will. **b.** the act of uttering such a message. **2.** a prediction or guess. **3.** the charismatic endowment of a prophet.

prophesy ('profi,sai) *vb.* **-sying, -sied.** **1.** to foretell (something) by or as if by divine inspiration. **2.** (*intr.*) *Arch.* to give instructions in religious subjects. —'**prophe,siable** *adj.* —'**prophe,sier** *n.*

prophet ('profit) *n.* **1.** a person who speaks by divine inspiration, esp. one through whom a divinity expresses his will. **2.** a person who predicts the future: *a prophet of doom.* **3.** a spokesman for a movement, doctrine, etc. —'**prophetess** *fem. n.*

Prophet ('profit) *n.* **the. 1.** the principal designation of Mohammed as the founder of Islam. **2.** a name for Joseph Smith as founder of the Mormon Church.

prophetic (prə'fetik) *adj.* **1.** of or relating to a prophet or prophecy. **2.** of the nature of a prophecy; predictive. —pro'**phetically** *adv.*

prophylactic (,profi'læktik) *adj.* **1.** protecting from or preventing disease. **2.** protective or preventive. ~*n.* **3.** a prophylactic drug or device. **4.** *Chiefly U.S.* another name for **condom.**

propinquity (prə'piŋkwiti) *n.* **1.** nearness in place or time. **2.** nearness in relationship.

propitiate (prə'pifi,eit) *vb.* (*tr.*) to appease or make well disposed; conciliate. —pro'**pitiable** *adj.* —pro,pi'ti'ation *n.* —pro'**pitiative** *adj.* —pro'**piti,ator** *n.*

propitious (prə'pifəs) *adj.* **1.** favourable or auspicious. **2.** gracious or favourably inclined. —pro'**pitiously** *adv.* —pro'**pitiousness** *n.*

propjet ('prop,dʒet) *n.* another name for **turboprop.**

proponent (prə'pəunənt) *n.* a person who argues in favour of something or puts forward a proposal, etc.

proportion (prə'pɔːʃən) *n.* **1.** relative magnitude or ex-

tent; ratio. **2.** correct or desirable relationship between parts; symmetry. **3.** a part considered with respect to the whole. **4.** (*pl.*) dimensions or size: *a building of vast proportions.* **5.** a share or quota. **6.** a relationship that maintains a constant ratio between two variable quantities: *prices increase in proportion to manufacturing costs.* **7.** *Maths.* a relationship between four numbers or quantities in which the ratio of the first pair equals the ratio of the second pair. ~*vb.* (*tr.*) **8.** to adjust in relative amount, size, etc. **9.** to cause to be harmonious in relationship of parts. —pro'**portionable** *adj.* —pro-'**portionably** *adv.* —pro'**portionment** *n.*

proportional (prə'pɔːʃənəl) *adj.* **1.** of, involving, or being in proportion. ~*n.* **2.** *Maths.* an unknown term in a proportion: *in a/b = c/x, x is the fourth proportional.* —pro,portion'ality *n.* —pro'**portionally** *adv.*

proportional representation *n.* representation of parties in an elective body in proportion to the votes they win. Abbrev.: **P.R.**

proportionate *adj.* (prə'pɔːʃənit). **1.** being in proper proportion. ~*vb.* (prə'pɔːʃə,neit). **2.** (*tr.*) to make proportionate. —pro'**portionately** *adv.*

proposal (prə'pəuzəl) *n.* **1.** the act of proposing. **2.** something proposed, as a plan. **3.** an offer, esp. of marriage.

propose (prə'pəuz) *vb.* **1.** (when *tr., may take a clause as object*) to put forward (a plan, etc.) for consideration. **2.** (*tr.*) to nominate, as for a position. **3.** (*tr.*) to intend (to do something): *I propose to leave town now.* **4.** (*tr.*) to announce the drinking of (a toast) to. **5.** (*intr.; often foll. by to*) to make an offer of marriage. —pro'**posable** *adj.* —pro'**poser** *n.*

proposition (,propə'ziʃən) *n.* **1.** a proposal for consideration. **2.** *Logic.* a statement in which the predicate affirms or denies something about the subject, or which affirms a relation between objects, and is either true or false. **3.** *Maths.* a statement or theorem, usually containing its proof. **4.** *Inf.* **a.** a person or matter to be dealt with: *he's a difficult proposition.* **b.** an invitation to engage in sexual intercourse. ~*vb.* **5.** (*tr.*) to propose a plan, deal, etc., to, esp. to engage in sexual intercourse. —,**propo'sitional** *adj.*

propound (prə'paund) *vb.* (*tr.*) **1.** to put forward for consideration. **2.** *English law.* to produce (a will or similar instrument) to the proper court or authority for its validity to be established. —pro'**pounder** *n.*

proprietary (prə'praiitəri) *adj.* **1.** of or belonging to property or proprietors. **2.** privately owned and controlled. **3.** *Med.* denoting a drug manufactured and distributed under a trade name. ~*n., pl.* **-taries. 4.** *Med.* a proprietary drug. **5.** a proprietor or proprietors collectively. **6. a.** right to property. **b.** property owned. **7.** (in Colonial America) an owner of a **proprietary colony,** a colony which was granted by the Crown to a particular person or group. —pro'**prietarily** *adv.*

proprietor (prə'praiitə) *n.* **1.** an owner of a business. **2.** a person enjoying exclusive right of ownership to some property. —pro'**prietress** *or* pro'**prietrix** *fem. n.*

THESAURUS

proper **1.** appropriate, apt, becoming, befitting, fit, fitting, legitimate, meet (*Archaic*), right, suitable, suited **2.** *comme il faut*, decent, decorous, *de rigueur*, genteel, gentlemanly, ladylike, mannerly, polite, punctilious, refined, respectable, seemly **3.** accepted, accurate, conventional, correct, established, exact, formal, orthodox, precise, right **4.** characteristic, individual, own, particular, peculiar, personal, respective, special, specific

property **1.** assets, belongings, building(s), capital, chattels, effects, estate, goods, holdings, house(s), means, possessions, resources, riches, wealth **2.** acres, estate, freehold, holding, land, real estate, real property, realty, title **3.** ability, attribute, characteristic, feature, hallmark, idiosyncrasy, mark, peculiarity, quality, trait, virtue

prophecy augury, divination, forecast, foretelling, prediction, prognosis, prognostication, revelation, second sight, soothsaying, vaticination (*Rare*)

prophesy augur, divine, forecast, foresee, foretell, forewarn, predict, presage,

prognosticate, soothsay, vaticinate (*Rare*)

prophet augur, Cassandra, clairvoyant, diviner, forecaster, oracle, prognosticator, prophesier, seer, sibyl, soothsayer

prophetic augural, divinatory, fatidic (*Rare*), foreshadowing, mantic, oracular, predictive, presaging, prescient, prognostic, sibylline, vatic (*Rare*)

propitious **1.** advantageous, auspicious, bright, encouraging, favourable, fortunate, full of promise, happy, lucky, opportune, promising, prosperous, rosy, timely **2.** benevolent, benign, favourably inclined, friendly, gracious, kind, well-disposed

proportion **1.** distribution, ratio, relationship, relative amount **2.** agreement, balance, congruity, correspondence, harmony, symmetry **3.** amount, cut (*Inf.*), division, fraction, measure, part, percentage, quota, segment, share **4.** *Plural* amplitude, breadth, bulk, capacity, dimensions, expanse, extent, magnitude, measurements, range, scope, size, volume

proportional, proportionate

balanced, commensurate, comparable, compatible, consistent, correspondent, corresponding, equitable, equivalent, even, in proportion, just

proposal bid, design, motion, offer, overture, plan, presentation, proffer, programme, project, proposition, recommendation, scheme, suggestion, tender, terms

propose **1.** advance, come up with, present, proffer, propound, put forward, submit, suggest, tender **2.** introduce, invite, name, nominate, present, put up, recommend **3.** aim, design, have every intention, have in mind, intend, mean, plan, purpose, scheme **4.** ask for someone's hand (in marriage), offer marriage, pay suit, pop the question (*Inf.*)

proposition **1.** *n.* motion, plan, programme, project, proposal, recommendation, scheme, suggestion **2.** *v.* accost, make an improper suggestion, make an indecent proposal, solicit

propound advance, advocate, contend, lay down, postulate, present, propose, put forward, set forth, submit, suggest

propriety (prə'praɪətɪ) n., pl. **-ties.** 1. the quality or state of being appropriate or fitting. 2. conformity to the prevailing standard of behaviour, speech, etc. 3. (pl.) **the proprieties.** the standards of behaviour considered correct by polite society.

propulsion (prə'pʌlʃən) n. 1. the act of propelling or the state of being propelled. 2. a propelling force. —**propulsive** (prə'pʌlsɪv) or **pro'pulsory** adj.

pro rata ('prəʊ 'rɑːtə) in proportion.

prorogue (prə'rəʊg) vb. to discontinue the meetings of (a legislative body) without dissolving it. —**prorogation** (ˌprəʊrə'geɪʃən) n.

prosaic (prəʊ'zeɪɪk) adj. 1. lacking imagination. 2. having the characteristics of prose. —**pro'saically** adv.

proscenium (prə'siːnɪəm) n., pl. **-nia** (-nɪə) or **-niums.** 1. the arch or opening separating the stage from the auditorium together with the area immediately in front of the arch. 2. (in ancient theatres) the stage itself.

proscribe (prəʊ'skraɪb) vb. (tr.) 1. to condemn or prohibit. 2. to outlaw; banish; exile. —**pro'scriber** n. —**proscription** (prəʊ'skrɪpʃən) n.

prose (prəʊz) n. 1. spoken or written language distinguished from poetry by its lack of a marked metrical structure. 2. a passage set for translation into a foreign language. 3. commonplace or dull discourse, expression, etc. 4. (modifier) written in prose. 5. (modifier) matter-of-fact. ~vb. 6. to write (something) in prose. 7. (intr.) to speak or write in a tedious style. —**'prose-ˌlike** adj.

prosecute ('prɒsɪˌkjuːt) vb. 1. (tr.) to bring a criminal action against (a person). 2. (intr.) a. to seek redress by legal proceedings. b. to institute or conduct a prosecution. 3. (tr.) to practise (a profession or trade). 4. (tr.) to continue to do (a task, etc.). —**'prose,cutable** adj. —**'prose,cutor** n.

prosecution (ˌprɒsɪ'kjuːʃən) n. 1. the act of prosecuting or the state of being prosecuted. 2. a. the institution and conduct of legal proceedings against a person. b. the proceedings brought in the name of the Crown to put an accused on trial. 3. the lawyers acting for the Crown to put the case against a person. 4. the following up or carrying on of something begun.

proselyte ('prɒsɪˌlaɪt) n. 1. a person newly converted to a religious faith, esp. a gentile converted to Judaism. ~vb. 2. a less common word for **proselytize.** —**proselytism** ('prɒsɪlɪˌtɪzəm) n. —**proselytic** (ˌprɒsɪ'lɪtɪk) adj.

proselytize or **-ise** ('prɒsɪlɪˌtaɪz) vb. to convert (someone) from one religious faith to another. —**proselyt,izer** or **-,iser** n.

prosody ('prɒsədɪ) n. 1. the study of poetic metre and of the art of versification. 2. a system of versification.

3. the patterns of stress and intonation in a language. —**prosodic** (prə'sɒdɪk) adj. —**'prosodist** n.

prospect n. ('prɒspɛkt). 1. (sometimes pl.) a probability of future success. 2. a view or scene. 3. a mental outlook. 4. expectation, or what one expects. 5. a prospective buyer, project, etc. 6. a survey or observation. 7. Mining. a. a known or likely deposit of ore. b. the location of a deposit of ore. c. the yield of mineral obtained from a sample of ore. ~vb. (prə'spɛkt). 8. (when intr., often foll. by for) to explore (a region) for gold or other valuable minerals. 9. (tr.) to work (a mine) to discover its profitability. 10. (intr.; often foll. by for) to search (for). —**pro'spector** n.

prospective (prə'spɛktɪv) adj. 1. looking towards the future. 2. (prenominal) expected or likely. —**pro'spectively** adv.

prospectus (prə'spɛktəs) n., pl. **-tuses.** 1. a formal statement giving details of a forthcoming event, such as the issue of shares. 2. a brochure giving details of courses, as at a school.

prosper ('prɒspə) vb. (usually intr.) to thrive, succeed, etc., or cause to thrive, etc., in a healthy way.

prosperity (prɒ'spɛrɪtɪ) n., pl. **-ities.** the condition of prospering; success or wealth.

prosperous ('prɒspərəs) adj. 1. flourishing; prospering. 2. wealthy. —**'prosperously** adv. —**'prosperousness** n.

prostaglandin (ˌprɒstə'glændɪn) n. any of a group of hormone-like compounds found in all mammalian tissues, which stimulate the muscles and affect the nervous system.

prostate ('prɒsteɪt) n. 1. Also called: **prostate gland.** a gland in male mammals that surrounds the neck of the bladder and secretes a liquid constituent of the semen. ~adj. 2. Also: **prostatic** (prɒ'stætɪk). of the prostate gland.

prosthesis ('prɒsθɪsɪs) n., pl. **-ses** (-ˌsiːz). Surgery. a. the replacement of a missing bodily part with an artificial substitute. b. an artificial part such as a limb, eye, or tooth. —**prosthetic** (prɒs'θɛtɪk) adj. —**pros'thetically** adv.

prostitute ('prɒstɪˌtjuːt) n. 1. a woman who engages in sexual intercourse for money. 2. a man who engages in such activity, esp. in homosexual practices. 3. a person who offers his talent for unworthy purposes. ~vb. (tr.) 4. to offer (oneself or another) in sexual intercourse for money. 5. to offer for unworthy purposes. —**prosti'tution** n. —**'prosti,tutor** n.

prostrate adj. ('prɒstreɪt). 1. lying face downwards, as in submission. 2. exhausted physically or emotionally. 3. helpless or defenceless. ~vb. (prɒ'streɪt). (tr.) 4.

THESAURUS

proprietor, proprietress deed holder, freeholder, landlady, landlord, landowner, owner, possessor, titleholder

propriety 1. appropriateness, aptness, becomingness, correctness, fitness, rightness, seemliness, suitableness 2. breeding, courtesy, decency, decorum, delicacy, etiquette, good form, good manners, manners, modesty, politeness, protocol, punctilio, rectitude, refinement, respectability, seemliness 3. **the proprieties** accepted conduct, amenities, civilities, etiquette, niceties, rules of conduct, social code, social conventions, social graces, the done thing

propulsion drive, impetus, impulse, impulsion, momentum, motive power, power, pressure, propelling force, push, thrust

prosaic banal, boring, commonplace, dry, dull, everyday, flat, hackneyed, humdrum, matter-of-fact, mundane, ordinary, pedestrian, routine, stale, tame, trite, unimaginative, uninspiring, vapid, workaday

proscribe 1. ban, boycott, censure, condemn, damn, denounce, doom, embargo, forbid, interdict, prohibit, reject 2. attaint (Archaic), banish, blackball, deport, exclude, excommunicate, exile, expatriate, expel, ostracize, outlaw

proscription 1. ban, boycott, censure, condemnation, damning, denunciation, dooming, embargo, interdict, prohibition, rejection 2. attainder (Archaic), banishment,

deportation, ejection, eviction, exclusion, excommunication, exile, expatriation, expulsion, ostracism, outlawry

prosecute 1. Law arraign, bring action against, bring suit against, bring to trial, do (Sl.), indict, litigate, prefer charges, put in the dock, put on trial, seek redress, sue, summon, take to court, try 2. carry on, conduct, direct, discharge, engage in, manage, perform, practise, work at 3. carry through, continue, follow through, persevere, persist, pursue, see through

prospect n. 1. anticipation, calculation, contemplation, expectation, future, hope, odds, opening, outlook, plan, presumption, probability, promise, proposal, thought 2. landscape, outlook, panorama, perspective, scene, sight, spectacle, view, vision, vista 3. **in prospect** in sight, in store, in the offing, in the wind, in view, on the cards, on the horizon, planned, projected 4. Sometimes plural chance, likelihood, possibility ~v. 5. explore, go after, look for, search, seek, survey

prospective about to be, anticipated, approaching, awaited, coming, destined, eventual, expected, forthcoming, future, hoped-for, imminent, intended, likely, looked-for, possible, potential, soon-to-be, -to-be, to come

prospectus announcement, catalogue, conspectus, list, outline, plan, programme, scheme, syllabus, synopsis

prosper advance, be fortunate, bloom, do well, fare well, flourish, flower, get on, grow rich, make good, make it (Inf.), progress, succeed, thrive

prosperity affluence, boom, ease, fortune, good fortune, good times, life of luxury, life of Riley (Inf.), luxury, plenty, prosperousness, riches, success, the good life, wealth, well-being

prosperous 1. blooming, booming, doing well, flourishing, fortunate, lucky, on the up and up (Brit.), palmy, prospering, successful, thriving 2. affluent, in clover (Inf.), in the money (Inf.), moneyed, opulent, rich, wealthy, well-heeled (Sl.), well-off, well-to-do 3. advantageous, auspicious, bright, favourable, good, profitable, promising, propitious, timely

prostitute 1. n. bawd (Archaic), brass (Sl.), call girl, camp follower, cocotte, courtesan, fallen woman, fille de joie, harlot, hooker (U.S. sl.), hustler (Sl.), loose woman, moll (Sl.), pro (Sl.), streetwalker, strumpet, tart (Inf.), trollop, white slave, whore 2. v. cheapen, debase, degrade, demean, devalue, misapply, pervert, profane

prostitution harlotry, harlot's trade, Mrs. Warren's profession, streetwalking, the game (Sl.), the oldest profession, vice, whoredom

to cast (oneself) down, as in submission. **5.** to lay or throw down flat. **6.** to make helpless. **7.** to make exhausted. —**pros'tration** n.

prosy ('prəʊzɪ) adj. **prosier, prosiest. 1.** of the nature of or similar to prose. **2.** dull, tedious, or long-winded. —**'prosily** adv. —**'prosiness** n.

Prot. abbrev. for: **1.** Protestant. **2.** Protectorate.

protactinium (ˌprəʊtækˈtɪnɪəm) n. a toxic radioactive element that occurs in uranium ores and is produced by neutron irradiation of thorium. Symbol: Pa; atomic no.: 91; half-life of most stable isotope, [231]Pa: 32 500 years.

protagonist (prəʊˈtægənɪst) n. **1.** the principal character in a play, story, etc. **2.** a supporter, esp. when important or respected, of a cause, party, etc. —**pro'tagonism** n.

protea ('prəʊtɪə) n. a shrub of tropical and southern Africa, having flowers with coloured bracts arranged in showy heads.

protean (prəʊˈtiːən, ˈprəʊtɪən) adj. readily taking on various shapes or forms; variable.

protect (prəˈtɛkt) vb. (tr.) **1.** to defend from trouble, harm, etc. **2.** Econ. to assist (domestic industries) by the imposition of protective tariffs on imports. **3.** Commerce. to provide funds in advance to guarantee payment of (a note, etc.).

protection (prəˈtɛkʃən) n. **1.** the act of protecting or the condition of being protected. **2.** something that protects. **3. a.** the imposition of duties on imports, for the protection of domestic industries against overseas competition, etc. **b.** Also called: **protectionism.** the system or theory of such restrictions. **4.** Inf. **a.** Also called: **protection money.** money demanded by gangsters for freedom from molestation. **b.** freedom from molestation purchased in this way. —**pro'tection₁ism** n. —**pro'tectionist** n.

protective (prəˈtɛktɪv) adj. **1.** giving or capable of giving protection. **2.** Econ. of or intended for protection of domestic industries. —**pro'tectively** adv. —**pro'tectiveness** n.

protector (prəˈtɛktə) n. **1.** a person or thing that protects. **2.** History. a person who exercised royal authority during the minority, absence, or incapacity of the monarch. —**pro'tectress** fem. n.

Protector (prəˈtɛktə) n. short for **Lord Protector,** the title borne by Oliver Cromwell (1653–58) and by Richard Cromwell (1658–59) as heads of state during the period known as the Protectorate.

protectorate (prəˈtɛktərɪt) n. **1. a.** a territory largely controlled by but not annexed to a stronger state. **b.** the relation of a protecting state to its protected territory. **2.** the office or period of office of a protector.

protégé or (fem.) **protégée** ('prəʊtɪˌʒeɪ) n. a person who is protected and aided by the patronage of another.

protein ('prəʊtiːn) n. any of a large group of nitrogenous compounds of high molecular weight that are essential constituents of all living organisms.

—**₁protein'aceous, pro'teinic,** or **pro'teinous** adj.

pro tempore Latin. ('prəʊ ˈtɛmpərɪ) for the time being. Often shortened to **pro tem** ('prəʊ ˈtɛm).

protest n. ('prəʊtɛst). **1. a.** public, often organized, manifestation of dissent. **b,** (as modifier): a protest march. **2.** a formal or solemn objection. **3.** a formal notarial statement drawn up on behalf of a creditor and declaring that the debtor has dishonoured a bill of exchange, etc. **4.** the act of protesting. ~vb. (prəˈtɛst). **5.** (when intr., foll. by against, at, about, etc.; when tr., may take a clause as object) to make a strong objection (to something, esp. a supposed injustice or offence). **6.** (when tr., may take a clause as object) to assert in a formal or solemn manner. —**pro'testant** adj., n. —**pro'tester** n. —**pro'testingly** adv.

Protestant ('prɒtɪstənt) n. **a.** an adherent of Protestantism. **b.** (as modifier): the Protestant Church.

protestation (ˌprɒtɛsˈteɪʃən) n. **1.** the act of protesting. **2.** a strong declaration.

protium ('prəʊtɪəm) n. the most common isotope of hydrogen, having a mass number of 1.

proto- or sometimes before a vowel **prot-** combining form. **1.** first: protomartyr. **2.** primitive or original: prototype. **3.** first in a series of chemical compounds: protoxide.

protocol ('prəʊtəˌkɒl) n. **1.** the formal etiquette and procedure for state and diplomatic ceremonies. **2.** a record of an agreement, esp. in international negotiations, etc. **3. a.** an amendment to a treaty or convention. **b.** an annex appended to a treaty to deal with subsidiary matters.

proton ('prəʊtɒn) n. a stable, positively charged elementary particle, found in atomic nuclei in numbers equal to its atomic number.

protoplasm ('prəʊtəˌplæzəm) n. Biol. the living contents of a cell: a complex translucent colourless colloidal substance. —**₁proto'plasmic, ₁proto'plasmal,** or **₁protoplas'matic** adj.

prototype ('prəʊtəˌtaɪp) n. **1.** an original model from which improved types can be made or that has analogies at a later period. **2.** a person or thing that serves as an example of a type. **3.** Biol. the ancestral or primitive form of a species. —**₁proto'typal, prototypic** (ˌprəʊtəˈtɪpɪk), or **₁proto'typical** adj.

protozoan (ˌprəʊtəˈzəʊən) n., pl. **-zoa** (-ˈzəʊə). **1.** Also **protozoon.** any minute invertebrate of a phylum including amoebas and foraminifers. ~adj. also **protozoic. 2.** of or belonging to this group.

protract (prəˈtrækt) vb. (tr.) **1.** to lengthen or extend (a speech, etc.). **2.** (of a muscle) to draw, thrust, or extend (a part, etc.) forwards. **3.** to plot using a protractor and scale. —**protractedly** (prəʊˈtræktɪdlɪ) adv. —**pro'traction** n.

protractor (prəˈtræktə) n. **1.** an instrument for measuring or drawing angles on paper, usually a flat semicircular transparent plastic sheet graduated in degrees. **2.**

THESAURUS

prostrate adj. **1.** abject, bowed low, flat, horizontal, kowtowing, procumbent, prone **2.** at a low ebb, dejected, depressed, desolate, drained, exhausted, fagged out (Inf.), fallen, inconsolable, overcome, spent, worn out **3.** brought to one's knees, defenceless, disarmed, helpless, impotent, overwhelmed, paralysed, powerless, reduced ~v. **4.** Of oneself abase, bend the knee to, bow before, bow down to, cast oneself before, cringe, fall at (someone's) feet, fall on one's knees before, grovel, kneel, kowtow, submit **5.** bring low, crush, depress, disarm, lay low, overcome, overthrow, overturn, overwhelm, paralyse, reduce, ruin **6.** drain, exhaust, fag out (Inf.), fatigue, sap, tire, wear out, weary

protagonist 1. central character, hero, heroine, lead, leading character, principal **2.** advocate, champion, exponent, leader, mainstay, moving spirit, prime mover, standard-bearer, supporter

protean changeable, ever-changing, many-sided, mercurial, multiform, mutable, polymorphous, variable, versatile, volatile

protect care for, chaperon, cover, cover up for, defend, foster, give sanctuary, guard, harbour, keep, keep safe, look after, mount or stand guard over, preserve, safeguard, save, screen, secure, shelter, shield, support, take under one's wing, watch over

protection 1. aegis, care, charge, custody, defence, guardianship, guarding, preservation, protecting, safeguard, safekeeping, safety, security **2.** armour, barrier, buffer, bulwark, cover, guard, refuge, safeguard, screen, shelter, shield

protective careful, covering, defensive, fatherly, insulating, jealous, maternal, motherly, paternal, possessive, protecting, safeguarding, sheltering, shielding, vigilant, warm, watchful

protector advocate, benefactor, bodyguard, champion, counsel, defender, guard, guardian, guardian angel, knight in shining armour, patron, safeguard, tower of strength

protégé, protégée charge, dependant, discovery, pupil, student, ward

protest n. **1.** complaint, declaration, demur, demurral, disapproval, dissent, formal complaint, objection, outcry, protestation, remonstrance ~v. **2.** complain, cry out, demonstrate, demur, disagree, disapprove, expostulate, express disapproval, kick (against) (Inf.), object, oppose, remonstrate, say no to, take exception **3.** affirm, argue, assert, asseverate, attest, avow, contend, declare, insist, maintain, profess, testify, vow

protestation 1. complaint, disagreement, dissent, expostulation, objection, outcry, protest, remonstrance, remonstration **2.** affirmation, asseveration, avowal, declaration, oath, pledge, profession, vow

protester agitator, demonstrator, dissenter, dissident, protest marcher, rebel

protocol 1. code of behaviour, conventions, courtesies, customs, decorum, etiquette, formalities, good form, manners, politesse, propriety, rules of conduct **2.** agreement, compact, concordat, contract, convention, covenant, pact, treaty

prototype archetype, example, first, mock-up, model, norm, original, paradigm, pattern, precedent, standard, type

protract continue, drag on or out, draw out, extend, keep going, lengthen, prolong, spin out, stretch out

protracted dragged out, drawn-out, extended, interminable, lengthy, long, long-drawn-out, never-ending, overlong, prolonged, spun out, time-consuming

Anat. a former term for **extensor.**

protrude (prə'truːd) *vb.* **1.** to thrust forwards or outwards. **2.** to project or cause to project. **—pro'trusion** *n.* **—pro'trusive** *adj.*

protuberant (prə'tjuːbərənt) *adj.* swelling out; bulging. **—pro'tuberance** *or* **pro'tuberancy** *n.* **—pro'tuberantly** *adv.*

proud (praud) *adj.* **1.** (foll. by *of,* an infinitive, or a clause) pleased or satisfied, as with oneself, one's possessions, achievements, etc. **2.** feeling honoured or gratified by some distinction. **3.** having an inordinately high opinion of oneself; haughty. **4.** characterized by or proceeding from a sense of pride: *a proud moment.* **5.** stately or distinguished. **6.** bold or fearless. **7.** (of a surface, edge, etc.) projecting or protruding. **8.** (of animals) restive or excited, often sexually. *~adv.* **9. do (someone) proud. a.** to entertain (a person) on a grand scale: *they did us proud at the hotel.* **b.** to honour (a person): *his honesty did him proud.* **—'proudly** *adv.* **—'proudness** *n.*

proud flesh *n.* a mass of tissue formed around a healing wound.

Prov. *abbrev. for:* **1.** Provençal. **2.** *Bible.* Proverbs. **3.** Province. **4.** Provost.

prove (pruːv) *vb.* **proving, proved; proved** *or* **proven.** (*mainly tr.*) **1.** (*may take a clause as object or an infinitive*) to demonstrate the truth or validity of, esp. by using an established sequence of procedures. **2.** to establish the quality of, esp. by experiment. **3.** *Law.* to establish the genuineness of (a will). **4.** to show (oneself) able or courageous. **5.** (*copula*) to be found (to be): *this has proved useless.* **6.** (*intr.*) (of dough) to rise in a warm place before baking. **—'provable** *adj.* **—,prova'bility** *n.* **—'provably** *adv.*

proven ('pruːvən, 'prəʊ-) *vb.* **1.** a past participle of **prove. 2.** See **not proven.** *~adj.* **3.** tried; tested: *a proven method.*

provenance ('provinəns) *n.* a place of origin, as of a work of art.

Provençal (,provon'saːl; *French* prɔvã'sal) *adj.* **1.** denoting or characteristic of Provence, a former province of SE France, its inhabitants, their dialect of French, or their Romance language. *~n.* **2.** a language of Provence, closely related to French and Italian, belonging to the Romance group of the Indo-European family. **3.** a native or inhabitant of Provence.

provender ('provində) *n.* **1.** fodder for livestock. **2.** food in general.

proverb ('provɜːb) *n.* **1.** a short memorable saying embodying some commonplace fact. **2.** a person or thing exemplary of a characteristic: *Antarctica is a proverb for extreme cold.* **3.** *Ecclesiast.* a wise saying providing guidance.

proverbial (prə'vɜːbɪəl) *adj.* **1.** (*prenominal*) commonly or traditionally referred to as an example of some peculiarity, characteristic, etc. **2.** of, embodied in, or resembling a proverb. **—pro'verbially** *adv.*

provide (prə'vaɪd) *vb.* (*mainly tr.*) **1.** to furnish or supply. **2.** to afford; yield: *this meeting provides an opportunity to talk.* **3.** (*intr.;* often foll. by *for* or *against*) to take careful precautions: *he provided against financial ruin by wise investment.* **4.** (*intr.;* foll. by *for*) to supply means of support (to): *he provides for his family.* **5.** (of a person, law, etc.) to state as a condition; stipulate. **6.** to confer and induct into ecclesiastical offices. **—pro'vider** *n.*

providence ('providəns) *n.* **1. a.** God's foreseeing protection and care of his creatures. **b.** such protection and care as manifest by some other force. **2.** a manifestation of such care and guidance. **3.** the foresight or care exercised by a person in the management of his affairs.

Providence ('providəns) *n.* God, esp. as showing foreseeing care of his creatures.

provident ('provident) *adj.* **1.** providing for future needs. **2.** exercising foresight in the management of one's affairs. **3.** characterized by foresight. **—'providently** *adv.*

providential (,provi'denʃəl) *adj.* characteristic of or presumed to proceed from or as if from divine providence. **—,provi'dentially** *adv.*

providing (prə'vaɪdɪŋ) *or* **provided** *conj.* (*subordinating;* sometimes foll. by *that*) on the condition or understanding (that): *I'll play, providing you pay me.*

province ('provins) *n.* **1.** a territory governed as a unit of a country or empire. **2.** (*pl.;* usually preceded by *the*) those parts of a country lying outside the capital and other large cities and regarded as outside the mainstream of sophisticated culture. **3.** an area of learning, activity, etc. **4.** the extent of a person's activities or office. **5.** an ecclesiastical territory, having an archbishop or metropolitan at its head. **6.** an administrative and territorial subdivision of a religious order. **7.** *History.* a region of the Roman Empire outside Italy ruled by a governor from Rome.

provincial (prə'vinʃəl) *adj.* **1.** of or connected with a province. **2.** characteristic of or connected with the provinces. **3.** having attitudes and opinions supposedly common to people living in the provinces; unsophisticated; limited. **4.** *N.Z.* denoting a football team representing a province, one of the historical administrative areas of New Zealand. *~n.* **5.** a person lacking the sophistications of city life; rustic or narrow-minded individual. **6.** a person coming from or resident in a province or the provinces. **7.** the head of an ecclesiastical province. **8.** the head of a territorial subdivision of a religious order. **—pro'vincia,lism** *n.* **—provinciality** (prə,vinʃi'æliti) *n.*

THESAURUS

protrude bulge, come through, extend, jut, obtrude, point, pop (*of eyes*), project, shoot out, stand out, start (from), stick out

protrusion bulge, bump, jut, lump, outgrowth, projection, protuberance, swelling

protuberance bulge, bump, excrescence, knob, lump, outgrowth, process, projection, prominence, protrusion, swelling, tumour

protuberant beetling, bulbous, bulging, gibbous, jutting, popping (*of eyes*), prominent, protruding, protrusive, proud (*Dialect*), swelling, swollen

proud 1. appreciative, content, contented, glad, gratified, honoured, pleased, satisfied, self-respecting, well-pleased **2.** arrogant, boastful, conceited, disdainful, egotistical, haughty, high and mighty (*Inf.*), imperious, lordly, narcissistic, orgulous (*Archaic*), overbearing, presumptuous, self-important, self-satisfied, snobbish, snooty (*Inf.*), stuck-up (*Inf.*), supercilious, toffee-nosed (*Sl.*), vain **3.** exalted, glorious, gratifying, illustrious, memorable, pleasing, red-letter, rewarding, satisfying **4.** august, distinguished, eminent, grand, great, illustrious, imposing, magnificent, majestic, noble, splendid, stately

provable attestable, demonstrable, evincible, testable, verifiable

prove 1. ascertain, attest, authenticate,

bear out, confirm, corroborate, demonstrate, determine, establish, evidence, evince, justify, show, show clearly, substantiate, verify **2.** analyse, assay, check, examine, experiment, put to the test, put to trial, test, try **3.** be found to be, come out, end up, result, turn out

proverb adage, aphorism, apophthegm, byword, dictum, gnome, maxim, saw, saying

proverbial accepted, acknowledged, archetypal, axiomatic, conventional, current, customary, famed, famous, legendary, notorious, self-evident, time-honoured, traditional, typical, unquestioned, well-known

provide 1. accommodate, cater, contribute, equip, furnish, outfit, provision, stock up, supply **2.** add, afford, bring, give, impart, lend, present, produce, render, serve, yield **3.** *With* **for** *or* **against** anticipate, arrange for, forearm, get ready, make arrangements, make plans, plan ahead, plan for, prepare for, take measures, take precautions **4.** *With* **for** care for, keep, look after, maintain, support, sustain, take care of **5.** determine, lay down, require, specify, state, stipulate

providence 1. destiny, divine intervention, fate, fortune, God's will, predestination **2.** care, caution, discretion, far-sightedness, foresight, forethought, perspicacity, presence of mind, prudence

provident canny, careful, cautious, dis-

creet, economical, equipped, far-seeing, far-sighted, forearmed, foresighted, frugal, prudent, sagacious, shrewd, thrifty, vigilant, well-prepared, wise

providential fortuitous, fortunate, happy, heaven-sent, lucky, opportune, timely, welcome

provider 1. benefactor, donor, giver, source, supplier **2.** breadwinner, earner, mainstay, supporter, wage earner

providing, provided *conj.* as long as, contingent upon, given, if and only if, in case, in the event, on condition, on the assumption, subject to, upon these terms, with the proviso, with the understanding

province 1. colony, county, department, dependency, district, division, domain, region, section, territory, tract, zone **2.** *Fig.* area, business, capacity, charge, concern, duty, employment, field, function, line, orbit, part, pigeon (*Brit. inf.*), post, responsibility, role, sphere

provincial *adj.* **1.** country, home-grown, homespun, local, rural, rustic **2.** insular, inward-looking, limited, narrow, narrow-minded, parish-pump, parochial, small-minded, small-town (*U.S.*), uninformed, unsophisticated, upcountry *~n.* **3.** country cousin, rustic, yokel

—**pro'vincially** adv.
provision (prə'vɪʒən) n. 1. the act of supplying food, etc. 2. something that is supplied. 3. preparations (esp. in **make provision for**). 4. (pl.) food and other necessities, as for an expedition. 5. a condition or stipulation incorporated in a document; proviso. 6. the conferring of and induction into ecclesiastical offices. ~vb. 7. (tr.) to supply with provisions. —**pro'visioner** n.
provisional (prə'vɪʒənəl) adj. subject to later alteration; temporary or conditional: a provisional decision. —**pro-'visionally** adv.
Provisional (prə'vɪʒənəl) adj. 1. designating one of the two factions of the IRA and Sinn Fein that have existed since a split in late 1969. The Provisional movement advocates terrorism to achieve Irish unity. ~n. 2. Also called: **Provo**. a member of the Provisional IRA or Sinn Fein.
proviso (prə'vaɪzəu) n., pl. **-sos** or **-soes**. 1. a clause in a document or contract that embodies a condition or stipulation. 2. a condition or stipulation.
provisory (prə'vaɪzərɪ) adj. 1. containing a proviso; conditional. 2. provisional. 3. making provision. —**pro'visorily** adv.
provocation (ˌprɒvə'keɪʃən) n. 1. the act of provoking or inciting. 2. something that causes indignation, anger, etc.
provocative (prə'vɒkətɪv) adj. serving or intended to provoke or incite, esp. to anger or sexual desire: a provocative woman; a provocative remark. —**pro'vocatively** adv.
provoke (prə'vəuk) vb. (tr.) 1. to anger or infuriate. 2. to incite or stimulate. 3. to promote (anger, indignation, etc.) in a person. 4. to cause; bring about: the accident provoked an inquiry. —**pro'vokingly** adv.
provost ('prɒvəst) n. 1. the head of certain university colleges or schools. 2. the principal magistrate of a Scottish burgh. 3. Church of England. the senior dignitary of one of the more recent cathedral foundations. 4. R.C. Church. a. the head of a cathedral chapter. b. (formerly) the member of a monastic community second in authority under the abbot. 5. (in medieval times) an overseer, steward, or bailiff.
provost marshal (prə'vəu) n. the officer in charge of military police in a camp or city.
prow (prau) n. the bow of a vessel.
prowess ('prauɪs) n. 1. outstanding or superior skill or ability. 2. bravery or fearlessness, esp. in battle.
prowl (praul) vb. 1. (when intr., often foll. by around or about) to move stealthily around (a place) as if in search of prey or plunder. ~n. 2. the act of prowling. 3. **on the prowl. a.** moving around stealthily. **b.** pursuing members of the opposite sex. —**'prowler** n.
prox. abbrev. for proximo (next month).

proximate ('prɒksɪmɪt) adj. 1. next or nearest in space or time. 2. very near; close. 3. immediately preceding or following in a series. 4. a less common word for **approximate**. —**'proximately** adv.
proximity (prɒk'sɪmɪtɪ) n. 1. nearness in space or time. 2. nearness or closeness in a series.
proximo ('prɒksɪməu) adv. Now rare except when abbreviated in formal correspondence. in or during the next or coming month: a letter of the seventh proximo. Abbrev.: **prox.** Cf. **instant, ultimo**.
proxy ('prɒksɪ) n., pl. **proxies.** 1. a person authorized to act on behalf of someone else; agent: to vote by proxy. 2. the authority, esp. in the form of a document, given to a person to act on behalf of someone else.
prude (pru:d) n. a person who affects or shows an excessively modest, prim, or proper attitude, esp. regarding sex. —**'prudish** adj. —**'prudishly** adv. —**'prudery** n.
prudence ('pru:dəns) n. 1. caution in practical affairs; discretion. 2. care taken in the management of one's resources. 3. consideration for one's own interests. 4. the quality of being prudent.
prudent ('pru:dənt) adj. 1. discreet or cautious in managing one's activities; circumspect. 2. practical and careful in providing for the future. 3. exercising good judgment. —**'prudently** adv.
prudential (pru:'dɛnʃəl) adj. 1. characterized by or resulting from prudence. 2. exercising sound judgment. —**pru'dentially** adv.
prune[1] (pru:n) n. 1. a purplish-black partially dried fruit of any of several varieties of plum tree. 2. Sl., chiefly Brit. a dull or foolish person. 3. **prunes and prisms.** denoting an affected and mincing way of speaking.
prune[2] (pru:n) vb. 1. to remove (dead or superfluous twigs, branches, etc.) from (a tree, shrub, etc.), esp. by cutting off. 2. to remove (anything undesirable or superfluous) from (a book, etc.). —**'prunable** adj. —**'pruner** n.
prurient ('pruərɪənt) adj. 1. unusually or morbidly interested in sexual thoughts or practices. 2. exciting lustfulness. —**'prurience** n. —**'pruriently** adv.
pruritus (pruə'raɪtəs) n. Pathol. any intense sensation of itching. —**pruritic** (pruə'rɪtɪk) adj.
prussic acid ('prʌsɪk) n. the extremely poisonous aqueous solution of hydrogen cyanide.
pry (praɪ) vb. **prying, pried.** 1. (intr.; often foll. by into) to make an impertinent or uninvited inquiry (about a private matter, topic, etc.). ~n., pl. **pries.** 2. the act of prying. 3. a person who pries.
P.S. abbrev. for: 1. Passenger Steamer. 2. Police Sergeant. 3. Also: **p.s.** postscript. 4. private secretary. 5. prompt side.

THESAURUS

provision 1. accoutrement, catering, equipping, fitting out, furnishing, providing, supplying, victualling 2. arrangement, plan, prearrangement, precaution, preparation 3. Fig. agreement, clause, condition, demand, proviso, requirement, specification, stipulation, term
provisional conditional, contingent, interim, limited, pro tem, provisory, qualified, stopgap, temporary, tentative, transitional
provisions comestibles, eatables, eats (Sl.), edibles, fare, food, foodstuff, groceries, grub (Sl.), provender, rations, stores, supplies, sustenance, viands, victuals
proviso clause, condition, limitation, provision, qualification, requirement, reservation, restriction, rider, stipulation, strings
provocation 1. casus belli, cause, grounds, incitement, inducement, instigation, justification, motivation, reason, stimulus 2. affront, annoyance, challenge, dare, grievance, indignity, injury, insult, offence, red rag, taunt, vexation
provocative 1. aggravating (Inf.), annoying, challenging, disturbing, galling, goading, incensing, insulting, offensive, outrageous, provoking, stimulating 2. alluring, arousing, erotic, exciting, inviting, seductive, sexy (Inf.), stimulating, suggestive, tantalizing, tempting

provoke 1. affront, aggravate (Inf.), anger, annoy, chafe, enrage, exasperate, gall, get on one's nerves, incense, infuriate, insult, irk, irritate, madden, make one's blood boil, offend, pique, put out, rile, try one's patience, vex 2. bring about, bring on or down, call forth, cause, draw forth, elicit, evoke, excite, fire, generate, give rise to, incite, induce, inflame, inspire, instigate, kindle, lead to, motivate, move, occasion, precipitate, produce, promote, prompt, rouse, stimulate, stir
provoking aggravating (Inf.), annoying, exasperating, galling, irking, irksome, irritating, maddening, obstructive, offensive, tiresome, vexatious, vexing
prow bow(s), fore, forepart, front, head, nose, sharp end (Jocular), stem
prowess 1. ability, accomplishment, adeptness, adroitness, aptitude, attainment, command, dexterity, excellence, expertise, expertness, facility, genius, mastery, skill, talent 2. boldness, bravery, courage, daring, dauntlessness, doughtiness, fearlessness, gallantry, hardihood, heroism, intrepidity, mettle, valiance, valour
prowl cruise, hunt, lurk, move stealthily, nose around, patrol, range, roam, rove, scavenge, skulk, slink, sneak, stalk, steal
proximity adjacency, closeness, contiguity, juxtaposition, nearness, neighbourhood,

propinquity, vicinity
proxy agent, attorney, delegate, deputy, factor, representative, substitute, surrogate
prude Grundy, old maid (Inf.), prig, puritan, schoolmarm (Brit. inf.)
prudence 1. canniness, care, caution, circumspection, common sense, discretion, good sense, heedfulness, judgment, judiciousness, sagacity, vigilance, wariness, wisdom 2. careful budgeting, economizing, economy, far-sightedness, foresight, forethought, frugality, good management, husbandry, planning, precaution, preparedness, providence, saving, thrift
prudent 1. canny, careful, cautious, circumspect, discerning, discreet, judicious, politic, sagacious, sage, sensible, shrewd, vigilant, wary, wise 2. canny, careful, economical, far-sighted, frugal, provident, sparing, thrifty
prudery Grundyism, old-maidishness (Inf.), overmodesty, priggishness, primness, prudishness, puritanicalness, squeamishness, starchiness (Inf.), strictness, stuffiness
prudish demure, narrow-minded, old-maidish (Inf.), overmodest, overnice, priggish, prim, prissy (Inf.), proper, puritanical, schoolmarmish (Brit. inf.), squeamish, starchy (Inf.), strait-laced, stuffy, Victorian

Ps. *or* **Psa.** *Bible. abbrev. for* Psalm(s).

psalm (saːm) *n.* **1.** (*often cap.*) any of the sacred songs that constitute a book (Psalms) of the Old Testament. **2.** a musical setting of one of these. **3.** any sacred song. —'**psalmic** *adj.* —'**psalmist** *n.*

psalmody ('saːmədɪ, 'sæl-) *n., pl.* **-dies.** **1.** the act of singing psalms or hymns. **2.** the art of setting psalms to music. —'**psalmodist** *n.* —**psalmodic** (saː'mɒdɪk, sæl-) *adj.*

Psalter ('sɔːltə) *n.* **1.** another name for the Book of Psalms, esp. in the version in the Book of Common Prayer. **2.** a translation, musical, or metrical version of the Psalms. **3.** a book containing a version of Psalms.

psaltery ('sɔːltərɪ) *n., pl.* **-teries.** *Music.* an ancient stringed instrument similar to the lyre, but having a trapezoidal sounding board over which the strings are stretched.

psephology (sɛ'fɒlədʒɪ) *n.* the statistical and sociological study of elections. —**psephological** (ˌsɛfə'lɒdʒɪkəl) *adj.* —ˌpsepho'logically *adv.* —**pse'phologist** *n.*

pseud (sjuːd) *n.* **1.** *Sl.* a false or pretentious person. ~*adj.* **2.** another word for **pseudo.**

pseudo ('sjuːdəʊ) *adj. Inf.* not genuine.

pseudo- *or sometimes before a vowel* **pseud-** *combining form.* **1.** false, pretending, or inauthentic: *pseudointellectual.* **2.** having a close resemblance to: *pseudopodium.*

pseudonym ('sjuːdə,nɪm) *n.* a fictitious name adopted, esp. by an author. —ˌpseudo'nymity *n.* —**pseudonymous** (sjuː'dɒnɪməs) *adj.*

pshaw (pʃɔː) *interj. Becoming rare.* an exclamation of disgust, impatience, disbelief, etc.

psi (psaɪ) *n.* the 23rd letter of the Greek alphabet (Ψ, ψ), a composite consonant, transliterated as *ps.*

psittacosis (ˌsɪtə'kəʊsɪs) *n.* a viral disease of parrots and other birds that can be transmitted to man, in whom it produces pneumonia. Also called: **parrot fever.**

psoriasis (sə'raɪəsɪs) *n.* a skin disease characterized by the formation of reddish spots and patches covered with silvery scales. —**psoriatic** (ˌsɔːrɪ'ætɪk) *adj.*

psst (pst) *interj.* an exclamation of beckoning, esp. one made surreptitiously.

P.S.T. (in the U.S. & Canada) *abbrev. for* Pacific Standard Time.

P.S.V. *abbrev. for* public service vehicle.

psych *or* **psyche** (saɪk) *vb.* (*tr.*) *Inf.* **1.** to psychoanalyse. **2.** (often foll. by *out*) **a.** to guess correctly the intentions of (another). **b.** to analyse (a problem, etc.) psychologically. **3.** to intimidate or frighten. **4.** (usually foll. by *up*) to prepare (oneself) for an action, performance, etc.

psyche ('saɪkɪ) *n.* the human mind or soul.

psychedelic (ˌsaɪkɪ'dɛlɪk) *adj.* **1.** relating to or denoting new or altered perceptions or sensory experiences, as through the use of hallucinogenic drugs. **2.** denoting any of the drugs, esp. LSD, that produce these effects. **3.** *Inf.* (of painting, fabric design, etc.) having the vivid colours and complex patterns popularly associated with the visual effects of psychedelic states. —ˌpsyche'delically *adv.*

psychiatry (saɪ'kaɪətrɪ) *n.* the branch of medicine concerned with the diagnosis and treatment of mental disorders. —**psychiatric** (ˌsaɪkɪ'ætrɪk) *or* ˌpsychi'atrical *adj.* —ˌpsychi'atrically *adv.* —**psy'chiatrist** *n.*

psychic ('saɪkɪk) *adj.* **1. a.** outside the possibilities defined by natural laws, as mental telepathy. **b.** (of a person) sensitive to forces not recognized by natural laws. **2.** mental as opposed to physical. ~*n.* **3.** a person who is sensitive to parapsychological forces or influences. —'**psychical** *adj.* —'**psychically** *adv.*

psycho ('saɪkəʊ) *n., pl.* **-chos,** *adj.* a slang word for **psychopath** or **psychopathic.**

psycho- *or sometimes before a vowel* **psych-** *combining form.* indicating the mind or psychological or mental processes: *psychology; psychosomatic.*

psychoanalyse *or esp. U.S.* **-lyze** (ˌsaɪkəʊ'ænə,laɪz) *vb.* (*tr.*) to examine or treat (a person) by psychoanalysis.

psychoanalysis (ˌsaɪkəʊə'nælɪsɪs) *n.* a method of studying the mind and treating mental and emotional disorders based on revealing and investigating the role of the unconscious mind. —**psychoanalyst** (ˌsaɪkəʊ-'ænəlɪst) *n.* —**psychoanalytic** (ˌsaɪkəʊ,ænə'lɪtɪk) *or* ˌpsycho,ana'lytical *adj.* —ˌpsycho,ana'lytically *adv.*

psychogenic (ˌsaɪkəʊ'dʒɛnɪk) *adj. Psychol.* (esp. of disorders or symptoms) of mental, rather than organic, origin. —ˌpsycho'genically *adv.*

psychokinesis (ˌsaɪkəʊkɪ'niːsɪs, -kaɪ-) *n.* (in parapsychology) alteration of the state of an object supposedly by mental influence alone.

psychological (ˌsaɪkə'lɒdʒɪkəl) *adj.* **1.** of or relating to psychology. **2.** of or relating to the mind or mental activity. **3.** having no real or objective basis; arising in the mind: *his backaches are all psychological.* **4.** affecting the mind. —ˌpsycho'logically *adv.*

psychological moment *n.* the most appropriate time for producing a desired effect.

psychological warfare *n.* the military application of psychology, esp. to the manipulation of morale in time of war.

psychologize *or U.S.* **-gise** (saɪ'kɒlə,dʒaɪz) *vb.* (*intr.*) **1.** to make interpretations of mental processes. **2.** to carry out investigation in psychology.

psychology (saɪ'kɒlədʒɪ) *n., pl.* **-gies.** **1.** the scientific study of all forms of human and animal behaviour. **2.** *Inf.* the mental make-up of an individual that causes him to think or act in the way he does. —**psy'chologist** *n.*

psychopath ('saɪkəʊ,pæθ) *n.* a person afflicted with a personality disorder characterized by a tendency to commit antisocial and sometimes violent acts and a failure to feel guilt for such acts. —ˌpsycho'pathic *adj.* —ˌpsycho'pathically *adv.*

psychopathology (ˌsaɪkəʊpə'θɒlədʒɪ) *n.* the scientific study of mental disorders. —**psychopathological** (ˌsaɪkəʊ,pæθə'lɒdʒɪkəl) *adj.*

psychopathy (saɪ'kɒpəθɪ) *n.* any mental disorder or disease.

psychosis (saɪ'kəʊsɪs) *n., pl.* **-choses** (-'kəʊsiːz). any form of severe mental disorder in which the individual's contact with reality becomes highly distorted. —**psychotic** (-'kɒt-) *adj.*

psychosomatic (ˌsaɪkəʊsə'mætɪk) *adj.* of disorders, such as stomach ulcers, thought to be caused or aggravated by psychological stress.

psychotherapy (ˌsaɪkəʊ'θɛrəpɪ) *or* **psychotherapeutics** (ˌsaɪkəʊ,θɛrə'pjuːtɪks) *n.* the use of psychological (as opposed to physical) methods to treat mental disorders. —ˌpsycho,thera'peutic *adj.* —ˌpsycho,thera-'peutically *adv.* —ˌpsycho'therapist *n.*

Pt *the chemical symbol for* platinum.

THESAURUS

prune clip, cut, cut back, dock, lop, pare down, reduce, shape, shorten, snip, trim

pry be a busybody, be inquisitive, be nosy (*Inf.*), ferret about, interfere, intrude, meddle, nose into, peep, peer, poke, poke one's nose in *or* into (*Inf.*), snoop (*Inf.*)

prying curious, eavesdropping, impertinent, inquisitive, interfering, intrusive, meddlesome, meddling, nosy (*Inf.*), snooping (*Inf.*), snoopy (*Inf.*), spying

psalm chant, hymn, paean, song of praise

pseudo *adj.* artificial, bogus, counterfeit, ersatz, fake, false, imitation, mock, not genuine, phoney (*Sl.*), pretended, quasi-, sham, spurious

pseudonym alias, assumed name, false name, incognito, nom de guerre, nom de

plume, pen name, professional name, stage name

psyche anima, essential nature, individuality, inner man, innermost self, mind, personality, pneuma (*Philos.*), self, soul, spirit, subconscious, true being

psychiatrist analyst, headshrinker (*Sl.*), psychoanalyser, psychoanalyst, psychologist, psychotherapist, shrink (*Sl.*), therapist

psychic **1.** clairvoyant, extrasensory, mystic, occult, preternatural, supernatural, telekinetic, telepathic **2.** mental, psychogenic, psychological, spiritual

psychological **1.** cerebral, cognitive, intellectual, mental **2.** all in the mind, emotional, imaginary, irrational, psychosomatic,

subconscious, subjective, unconscious, unreal

psychology **1.** behaviourism, science of mind, study of personality **2.** *Inf.* attitude, mental make-up, mental processes, thought processes, way of thinking, what makes one tick

psychopath insane person, lunatic, madman, maniac, mental case, nutcase (*Sl.*), nutter (*Brit. sl.*), psychotic, sociopath

psychotic *adj.* certifiable, demented, deranged, insane, lunatic, mad, mental, *non compos mentis,* off one's chump (head, rocker, trolley) (*Sl.*), psychopathic, unbalanced

pt. *abbrev. for:* **1.** part. **2.** patient. **3.** payment. **4.** pint. **5.** point. **6.** port. **7.** preterite.

Pt. (in place names) *abbrev. for:* **1.** Point. **2.** Port.

p.t. *abbrev. for:* **1.** past tense. **2.** pro tempore.

P.T. *abbrev. for:* **1.** physical therapy. **2.** physical training. **3.** postal telegraph.

P.T.A. *abbrev. for:* **1.** Parent-Teacher Association. **2.** (in Britain) Passenger Transport Authority.

ptarmigan ('tɑːmɪgən) *n., pl.* **-gans** *or* **-gan.** any of several arctic and subarctic grouse, esp. one which has a white winter plumage.

ptero- *combining form.* a wing, or a part resembling a wing: *pterodactyl.*

pterodactyl (ˌterəˈdæktɪl) *n.* an extinct flying reptile having membranous wings supported on an elongated fourth digit.

P.T.O. *or* **p.t.o.** *abbrev. for* please turn over.

Ptolemaic (ˌtɒlɪˈmeɪɪk) *adj.* **1.** of or relating to Ptolemy, the 2nd-century A.D. Greek astronomer, or to his conception of the universe. **2.** of or relating to the Macedonian dynasty that ruled Egypt from the death of Alexander the Great (323 B.C.) to the death of Cleopatra (30 B.C.).

ptomaine *or* **ptomain** ('təʊmeɪn) *n.* any of a group of amines formed by decaying organic matter.

pty. *Chiefly Austral. abbrev. for* proprietary.

Pu *the chemical symbol for* plutonium.

pub (pʌb) *Inf.* ~*n.* **1.** *Chiefly Brit.* a building with a bar and one or more public rooms licensed for the sale and consumption of alcoholic drink, often also providing light meals. Formal name: **public house.** **2.** *Austral. & N.Z.* a hotel. ~*vb.* **pubbing, pubbed. 3.** (*intr.*) to visit a pub or pubs (esp. in **go pubbing**).

pub. *abbrev. for:* **1.** public. **2.** publication. **3.** published. **4.** publisher. **5.** publishing.

pub-crawl *Sl., chiefly Brit.* ~*n.* **1.** a drinking tour of a number of pubs or bars. ~*vb.* **2.** (*intr.*) to make such a tour.

puberty ('pjuːbətɪ) *n.* the period at the beginning of adolescence when the sex glands become functional. Also called: **pubescence.** —'**pubertal** *adj.*

pubes ('pjuːbiːz) *n., pl.* **pubes** ('pjuːbiːz). **1.** the region above the external genital organs, covered with hair from the time of puberty. **2.** pubic hair. **3.** the pubic bones. **4.** the plural of **pubis.**

pubescent (pjuːˈbesənt) *adj.* **1.** arriving or arrived at puberty. **2.** (of certain plants and animals or their parts) covered with a layer of fine short hairs or down. —**pu-'bescence** *n.*

pubic ('pjuːbɪk) *adj.* of or relating to the pubes or pubis: *pubic hair.*

pubis ('pjuːbɪs) *n., pl.* **-bes** (-biːz). one of the three sections of the hipbone that forms part of the pelvis.

public ('pʌblɪk) *adj.* **1.** of or concerning the people as a whole. **2.** open to all: *public gardens.* **3.** performed or made openly: *public proclamation.* **4.** (*prenominal*) well-known: *a public figure.* **5.** (*usually prenominal*) maintained at the expense of, serving, or for the use of a community: *a public library.* **6.** open, acknowledged, or notorious: *a public scandal.* **7. go public.** (of a private company) to issue shares for subscription by the public. ~*n.* **8.** the community or people in general. **9.** a section of the community grouped because of a common interest, activity, etc.: *the racing public.* —'**publicly** *adv.*

public-address system *n.* a system of microphones, amplifiers, and loudspeakers for increasing the sound level, used in auditoriums, public gatherings, etc. Sometimes shortened to **PA system.**

publican ('pʌblɪkən) *n.* **1.** (in Britain) a person who keeps a public house. **2.** (in ancient Rome) a public contractor, esp. one who farmed the taxes of a province.

publication (ˌpʌblɪˈkeɪʃən) *n.* **1.** the act or process of publishing a printed work. **2.** any printed work offered for sale or distribution. **3.** the act or an instance of making information public.

public company *n.* a limited company whose shares may be purchased by the public and traded freely on the open market and whose share capital is not less than a statutory minimum. Cf. **private company.**

public convenience *n.* a public lavatory.

public enemy *n.* a notorious person, such as a criminal, who is regarded as a menace to the public.

public house *n.* **1.** *Brit.* the formal name for a **pub. 2.** *U.S.* an inn, tavern, or small hotel.

publicist ('pʌblɪsɪst) *n.* **1.** a person who publicizes something, esp. a press or publicity agent. **2.** a journalist. **3.** *Rare.* a person learned in public or international law.

publicity (pʌˈblɪsɪtɪ) *n.* **1. a.** the technique or process of attracting public attention to people, products, etc., as by the use of the mass media. **b.** (*as modifier*): *a publicity agent.* **2.** public interest aroused by such a technique or process. **3.** information used to draw public attention to people, products, etc. **4.** the state of being public.

publicize *or* **-ise** ('pʌblɪˌsaɪz) *vb.* (*tr.*) to bring to public notice; advertise.

public lending right *n.* the right of authors to receive payment when their books are borrowed from public libraries.

public prosecutor *n. Law.* an official in charge of prosecuting important cases.

public relations *n.* **1. a.** the practice of creating, promoting, or maintaining good will and a favourable image among the public towards an institution, public body, etc. **b.** the professional staff employed for this purpose. Abbrev.: **P.R. c.** the techniques employed. **d.** (*as modifier*): *the public relations industry.* **2.** the relationship between an organization and the public.

public school *n.* **1.** (in England and Wales) a private independent fee-paying secondary school. **2.** in certain Canadian provinces, a public elementary school as distinguished from a separate school. **3.** any school that is part of a free local educational system.

public sector *n.* the part of an economy which consists of state-owned institutions, including nationalized industries and services provided by local authorities.

public servant *n.* **1.** an elected or appointed holder of a public office. **2.** *Austral. & N.Z.* a civil servant.

public-spirited *adj.* having or showing active interest in the good of the community.

public utility *n.* an enterprise concerned with the provision to the public of essentials, such as electricity or water. Also called (in the U.S.): **public-service corporation.**

publish ('pʌblɪʃ) *vb.* **1.** to produce and issue (printed matter) for distribution and sale. **2.** (*intr.*) to have one's written work issued for publication. **3.** (*tr.*) to announce formally or in public. **4.** (*tr.*) to communicate (defamatory matter) to someone other than the person defamed: *to publish a libel.* —'**publishable** *adj.*

publisher ('pʌblɪʃə) *n.* **1.** a company or person engaged in publishing periodicals, books, music, etc. **2.**

THESAURUS

pub *or* **public house** alehouse (*Archaic*), bar, boozer (*Inf.*), inn, local (*Brit. inf.*), roadhouse, tavern

puberty adolescence, awkward age, juvenescence, pubescence, teenage, teens, young adulthood

public *adj.* **1.** civic, civil, common, general, national, popular, social, state, universal, widespread **2.** accessible, communal, community, free to all, not private, open, open to the public, unrestricted **3.** acknowledged, exposed, in circulation, known, notorious, obvious, open, overt, patent, plain, published, recognized **4.** important, prominent, respected, well-known ~*n.* **5.** citizens, commonalty, community, country, electorate, everyone,

hoi polloi, masses, multitude, nation, people, populace, population, society, voters **6.** audience, buyers, clientele, followers, following, patrons, supporters, those interested, trade **7. in public** *coram populo*, for all to see, in full view, openly, publicly

publication 1. advertisement, airing, announcement, appearance, broadcasting, declaration, disclosure, dissemination, notification, proclamation, promulgation, publishing, reporting **2.** book, booklet, brochure, handbill, issue, leaflet, magazine, newspaper, pamphlet, periodical

publicity advertising, attention, ballyhoo (*Sl.*), boost, build-up, hype (*Sl.*), plug (*Inf.*),

press, promotion, public notice, puff, puffery (*Inf.*)

publicize advertise, beat the drum for (*Inf.*), bring to public notice, broadcast, give publicity to, hype (*Sl.*), make known, play up, plug (*Inf.*), promote, puff, push, spotlight, spread about, write up

public-spirited altruistic, charitable, community-minded, generous, humanitarian, philanthropic, unselfish

publish 1. bring out, issue, print, produce, put out **2.** advertise, announce, broadcast, circulate, communicate, declare, disclose, distribute, divulge, impart, leak, proclaim, promulgate, publicize, reveal, spread

U.S. the proprietor of a newspaper.

puce (pju:s) *n., adj.* (of) a colour varying from deep red to dark purplish-brown.

puck[1] (pʌk) *n.* a small disc of hard rubber used in ice hockey.

puck[2] (pʌk) *n.* a mischievous or evil spirit. —'**puckish** *adj.*

pucker ('pʌkə) *vb.* **1.** to gather (a soft surface such as the skin) into wrinkles, or (of such a surface) to be so gathered. ~*n.* **2.** a wrinkle, crease, or irregular fold.

pudding ('pudɪŋ) *n.* **1.** a sweetened usually cooked dessert made in many forms and of various ingredients. **2.** a savoury dish, usually consisting partially of pastry or batter: *steak-and-kidney pudding.* **3.** the dessert course in a meal. **4.** a sausage-like mass of meat, oatmeal, etc., stuffed into a prepared skin or bag and boiled. —'**puddingy** *adj.*

puddle ('pʌdəl) *n.* **1.** a small pool of water, esp. of rain. **2.** a small pool of any liquid. **3.** a worked mixture of wet clay and sand that is impervious to water and is used to line a pond or canal. ~*vb.* (*tr.*) **4.** to make (clay, etc.) into puddle. **5.** to subject (iron) to puddling. —'**puddler** *n.* —'**puddly** *adj.*

puddling ('pʌdlɪŋ) *n.* a process for converting pig iron into wrought iron by heating it with ferric oxide in a furnace and stirring it to oxidize the carbon.

pudendum (pju:'dɛndəm) *n., pl.* **-da** (-də). (*often pl.*) the human external genital organs collectively, esp. of a female. —**pu'dendal** *or* **pudic** ('pju:dɪk) *adj.*

pudgy ('pʌdʒɪ) *adj.* **pudgier, pudgiest.** a variant spelling (esp. U.S.) of **podgy.** —'**pudgily** *adv.* —'**pudginess** *n.*

puerile ('pjʊəraɪl) *adj.* **1.** exhibiting silliness; immature; trivial. **2.** of or characteristic of a child. —'**puerilely** *adv.* —**puerility** (pjʊə'rɪlɪtɪ) *n.*

puerperal (pju:'ɜːpərəl) *adj.* of or occurring during the period following childbirth.

puerperal fever *n.* a serious, formerly widespread, form of blood poisoning caused by infection contracted during childbirth.

puff (pʌf) *n.* **1.** a short quick gust or emission, as of wind, smoke, etc. **2.** the amount of wind, smoke, etc., released in a puff. **3.** the sound made by a puff. **4.** an instance of inhaling and expelling the breath as in smoking. **5.** a light aerated pastry usually filled with cream, jam, etc. **6.** a powder puff. **7.** exaggerated praise, as of a book, product, etc., esp. through an advertisement. **8.** a piece of clothing fabric gathered up so as to bulge in the centre while being held together at the edges. **9.** a cylindrical roll of hair pinned in place in a coiffure. **10.** U.S. name for **quilt** (sense 1). **11.** one's breath (esp. in **out of puff**). **12.** *Sl.* a male homosexual. ~*vb.* **13.** to blow or breathe or cause to blow or breathe in short quick draughts. **14.** (*tr.*; often foll. by *out*; usually passive) to cause to be out of breath. **15.** to take draws at (a cigarette, etc.). **16.** to move with or by the emission of puffs: *the steam train puffed up the incline.* **17.** (often foll. by *up, out,* etc.) to swell, as with air, pride, etc. **18.** (*tr.*) to praise with exaggerated empty words, often in advertising. **19.** (*tr.*) to apply (powder, dust, etc.) to (something). —'**puffy** *adj.*

puff adder *n.* a large venomous African viper that inflates its body when alarmed.

puffball ('pʌf,bɔːl) *n.* any of various fungi having a round fruiting body that discharges a cloud of brown spores when mature.

puffin ('pʌfɪn) *n.* any of various northern diving birds, having a black-and-white plumage and a brightly coloured vertically flattened bill.

puff pastry *or U.S.* **puff paste** *n.* a dough used for making a rich flaky pastry.

puff-puff *n. Brit.* a children's name for a steam locomotive or railway train.

pug[1] (pʌg) *n.* a small compact breed of dog with a smooth coat, lightly curled tail, and a short wrinkled nose. —'**puggish** *adj.*

pug[2] (pʌg) *n.* a slang name for **boxer** (sense 1).

pugilism ('pju:dʒɪ,lɪzəm) *n.* the art, practice, or profession of fighting with the fists; boxing. —'**pugilist** *n.* —,**pugi'listic** *adj.* —,**pugi'listically** *adv.*

pugnacious (pʌg'neɪʃəs) *adj.* readily disposed to fight; belligerent. —**pug'naciously** *adv.* —**pugnacity** (pʌg-'næsɪtɪ) *n.*

pug nose *n.* a short stubby upturned nose. —'**pug-,nosed** *adj.*

puissance ('pju:ɪsəns, 'pwi:sɑːns) *n.* **1.** a competition in showjumping that tests a horse's ability to jump large obstacles. **2.** *Arch. or poetic.* power.

puissant ('pju:ɪsənt) *adj. Arch. or poetic.* powerful. —'**puissantly** *adv.*

puke (pju:k) *Sl.* ~*vb.* **1.** to vomit (matter). ~*n.* **2.** the act of vomiting. **3.** the matter vomited.

pukka *or* **pucka** ('pʌkə) *adj. Anglo-Indian.* properly or perfectly done, constructed, etc.; good; genuine.

pulchritude ('pʌlkrɪ,tju:d) *n. Formal or literary.* physical beauty. —,**pulchri'tudinous** *adj.*

pule (pju:l) *vb.* (*intr.*) to cry plaintively; whimper. —'**puler** *n.*

pull (pul) *vb.* (*mainly tr.*) **1.** (*also intr.*) to exert force on (an object) so as to draw it towards the source of the force. **2.** to remove; extract: *to pull a tooth.* **3.** to strip of feathers, hair, etc.; pluck. **4.** to draw the entrails from (a fowl). **5.** to rend or tear. **6.** to strain (a muscle or tendon). **7.** (usually foll. by *off*) *Inf.* to bring about: *to pull off a million-pound deal.* **8.** *Inf.* (often foll. by *on*) to draw out (a weapon) for use: *he pulled a knife on his attacker.* **9.** *Inf.* to attract: *the pop group pulled a crowd.* **10.** (*intr.*; usually foll. by *on* or *at*) to drink or inhale deeply: *to pull at one's pipe.* **11.** to make (a grimace): *to pull a face.* **12.** (*also intr.*; foll. by *away, out, over,* etc.) to move (a vehicle) or (of a vehicle) to be moved in a specified manner. **13.** (*intr.*) to possess or exercise the power to move: *this car doesn't pull well on hills.* **14.** *Printing.* to take (a proof) from type. **15.** *Golf, baseball, etc.* to hit (a ball) so that it veers away from the direction in which the player intended to hit it. **16.** *Cricket.* to hit (a ball pitched straight or on the off side) to the leg side. **17.** (*also intr.*) to row (a boat) or take a stroke of (an oar) in rowing. **18.** (of a rider) to restrain (a horse), esp. to prevent it from winning a race. **19. pull a fast one.** *Sl.* to play a sly trick. **20. pull apart** *or* **to pieces.** to criticize harshly. **21. pull (one's) punches. a.** *Boxing.* to restrain the force of one's blows. **b.** *Inf.* to restrain the force of one's criticisms or actions. **22. pull one's weight.** *Inf.* to do a fair share of a task. **23. pull strings.** *Brit. inf.* to exercise personal influence. **24. pull (someone's) leg.** *Inf.* to make fun of or tease (someone). ~*n.* **25.** an act or an instance of pulling or being pulled. **26.** the force or effort used in pulling: *the pull of the moon affects the tides.* **27.** the act or an instance of taking in drink or smoke. **28.** *Printing.* a proof taken from type: *the first pull was smudged.* **29.** something used for pulling, such as a handle. **30.** *Inf.* special advantage or influence: *his uncle is chairman of the company, so he has quite a lot of pull.* **31.** *Inf.* the power to attract attention or support. **32.** a period of rowing. **33.** a single stroke of an oar in rowing. **34.** the act of pulling the ball in golf, cricket, etc. **35.** the act of reining in a horse. ~See also **pull down, pull in,** etc. —'**puller** *n.*

THESAURUS

pudding afters (*Brit. inf.*), dessert, last course, pud (*Inf.*), second course, sweet

puerile babyish, childish, foolish, immature, inane, infantile, irresponsible, jejune, juvenile, naive, petty, ridiculous, silly, trivial, weak

puff *n.* **1.** blast, breath, draught, emanation, flurry, gust, whiff **2.** drag (*Inf.*), pull, smoke **3.** bulge, bunching, swelling **4.** advertisement, commendation, favourable mention, good word, plug (*Inf.*), sales talk ~*v.* **5.** blow, breathe, exhale, gasp, gulp, pant, wheeze **6.** drag (*Sl.*), draw, inhale, pull at *or* on, smoke,

suck **7.** *Usually with* **up** bloat, dilate, distend, expand, inflate, swell **8.** hype (*Sl.*), overpraise, plug (*Inf.*), praise, promote, publicize, push

puffed 1. done in (*Inf.*), exhausted, gasping, out of breath, panting, short of breath, spent, winded **2. puffed up** bigheaded (*Inf.*), full of oneself, high and mighty (*Inf.*), proud, swollen-headed, too big for one's boots

puffy bloated, distended, enlarged, inflamed, inflated, puffed up, swollen

pugilism boxing, fighting, prizefighting,

the noble art *or* science, the prize ring, the ring

pugilist boxer, bruiser (*Inf.*), fighter, prizefighter, pug (*Sl.*)

pugnacious aggressive, antagonistic, argumentative, bellicose, belligerent, choleric, combative, contentious, disputatious, hot-tempered, irascible, irritable, petulant, quarrelsome

pull *v.* **1.** drag, draw, haul, jerk, tow, trail, tug, yank **2.** cull, draw out, extract, gather, pick, pluck, remove, take out, uproot, weed **3.** dislocate, rend, rip, sprain, strain, stretch,

pull down *vb.* (*tr., adv.*) to destroy or demolish: *the old houses were pulled down.*

pullet ('pʊlɪt) *n.* a young hen of the domestic fowl, less than one year old.

pulley ('pʊlɪ) *n.* **1.** a wheel with a grooved rim in which a rope can run in order to change the direction of a force applied to the rope, etc. **2.** a number of such wheels pivoted in parallel in a block, used to raise heavy loads. **3.** a wheel with a flat, convex, or grooved rim mounted on a shaft and driven by or driving a belt passing around it.

pull in *vb.* (*adv.*) **1.** (*intr.*; often foll. by *to*) to reach a destination: *the train pulled in at the station.* **2.** (*intr.*) Also: **pull over.** (of a motor vehicle) **a.** to draw in to the side of the road. **b.** to stop (at a café, lay-by, etc.). **3.** (*tr.*) to attract: *his appearance will pull in the crowds.* **4.** (*tr.*) Brit. sl. to arrest. **5.** (*tr.*) to earn or gain (money). ~*n.* **pull-in. 6.** Brit. a roadside café, esp. for lorry drivers.

Pullman ('pʊlmən) *n., pl.* **-mans.** a luxurious railway coach. Also called: **Pullman car.**

pull off *vb.* (*tr.*) **1.** to remove (clothing) forcefully. **2.** (*adv.*) to succeed in performing (a difficult feat).

pull out *vb.* (*adv.*) **1.** (*tr.*) to extract. **2.** (*intr.*) to depart: *the train pulled out of the station.* **3.** Mil. to withdraw or be withdrawn: *the troops were pulled out of the ruined city.* **4.** (*intr.*) (of a motor vehicle) **a.** to draw away from the side of the road. **b.** to draw out from behind another vehicle to overtake. **5.** (*intr.*) to abandon a position or situation. **6.** (foll. by *of*) to level out (from a dive). ~*n.* **pull-out. 7.** an extra leaf of a book that folds out. **8.** a removable section of a magazine, etc.

pullover ('pʊl,əʊvə) *n.* a garment, esp. a sweater, that is pulled on over the head.

pull through *vb.* to survive or recover or cause to survive or recover, esp. after a serious illness or crisis. Also: **pull round.**

pull together *vb.* **1.** (*intr., adv.*) to cooperate, or work harmoniously. **2. pull oneself together.** Inf. to regain one's self-control or composure.

pull up *vb.* (*adv.*) **1.** (*tr.*) to remove by the roots. **2.** (often foll. by *with* or *on*) to move level (with) or ahead (of), esp. in a race. **3.** to stop: *the car pulled up suddenly.* **4.** (*tr.*) to rebuke.

pulmonary ('pʌlmənərɪ, 'pʊl-) *adj.* **1.** of or affecting the lungs. **2.** having lungs or lunglike organs.

pulp (pʌlp) *n.* **1.** soft or fleshy plant tissue, such as the succulent part of a fleshy fruit. **2.** a moist mixture of cellulose fibres, as obtained from wood, from which paper is made. **3.** U.S. a magazine or book containing trite or sensational material, and usually printed on cheap rough paper. **4.** Dentistry. the soft innermost part of a tooth, containing nerves and blood vessels. **5.** any soft soggy mass. **6.** Mining. pulverized ore. ~*vb.* **7.** to reduce (a material) to pulp or (of a material) to be reduced to pulp. **8.** (*tr.*) to remove the pulp from (fruit, etc.). —'**pulpy** *adj.*

pulpit ('pʊlpɪt) *n.* **1.** a raised platform, usually surrounded by a barrier, set up in churches as the appointed place for preaching, etc. **2.** a medium for expressing an opinion, such as a newspaper column. **3.** (usually preceded by *the*) **a.** the preaching of the Christian message. **b.** the clergy or their influence.

pulpwood ('pʌlp,wʊd) *n.* pine, spruce, or any other soft wood used to make paper.

pulsar ('pʌl,sɑː) *n.* any of a number of very small stars first discovered in 1967, which rotate fast emitting regular pulses of polarized radiation.

pulsate (pʌl'seɪt) *vb.* (*intr.*) **1.** to expand and contract with a rhythmical beat; throb. **2.** Physics. to vary in intensity, magnitude, etc. **3.** to quiver or vibrate. —**pul'sative** ('pʌlsətɪv) *adj.* —**pul'sation** *n.* —**pul'sator** *n.* —**pulsatory** ('pʌlsətərɪ) *adj.*

pulse¹ (pʌls) *n.* **1.** Physiol. **a.** the rhythmical contraction and expansion of an artery at each beat of the heart. **b.** a single such pulsation. **2.** Physics, electronics. **a.** a transient sharp change in some quantity normally constant in a system. **b.** one of a series of such transient disturbances, usually recurring at regular intervals. **3. a.** a recurrent rhythmical series of beats, vibrations, etc. **b.** any single beat, wave, etc., in such a series. **4.** bustle, vitality, or excitement: *the pulse of a city.* **5. keep one's finger on the pulse.** to be well-informed about current events, opinions, etc. ~*vb.* **6.** (*intr.*) to beat, throb, or vibrate. —**pulseless** *adj.*

pulse² (pʌls) *n.* **1.** the edible seeds of any of several leguminous plants, such as peas, beans, and lentils. **2.** the plant producing any of these.

pulverize *or* **-ise** ('pʌlvə,raɪz) *vb.* **1.** to reduce (a substance) to fine particles, as by grinding, or (of a substance) to be so reduced. **2.** (*tr.*) to destroy completely. —'**pulver,izable** *or* **-,isable** *adj.* —,**pulveri'zation** *or* **-i'sation** *n.* —'**pulver,izer** *or* **-,iser** *n.*

puma ('pjuːmə) *n.* a large American feline mammal that resembles a lion, having a plain greyish-brown coat and long tail. Also called: **cougar, mountain lion.**

pumice ('pʌmɪs) *n.* **1.** Also called: **pumice stone.** a light porous volcanic rock used for scouring and, in powdered form, as an abrasive and for polishing. ~*vb.* **2.** to rub or polish with pumice. —**pumiceous** (pjuː'mɪʃəs) *adj.*

pummel ('pʌməl) *vb.* **-melling, -melled** *or U.S.* **-meling, -meled.** (*tr.*) to strike repeatedly with or as if with the fists. Also (less common): **pommel.**

pump¹ (pʌmp) *n.* **1.** any device for compressing, driving, raising, or reducing the pressure of a fluid, esp. by means of a piston or set of rotating impellers. ~*vb.* **2.** (when *tr.*, usually foll. by *from, out,* etc.) to raise or drive (air, liquid, etc., esp. into or from something) with a pump. **3.** (*tr.*; usually foll. by *in* or *into*) to supply in large amounts: *to pump capital into a project.* **4.** (*tr.*) to deliver (bullets, etc.) repeatedly. **5.** to operate (something, esp. a handle) in the manner of a pump or (of something) to work in this way: *to pump the pedals of a bicycle.* **6.** (*tr.*) to obtain (information) from (a person) by persistent questioning. **7.** (*intr.*; usually foll. by *from* or *out of*) (of liquids) to flow freely in large spurts: *oil pumped from the fissure.*

pump² (pʌmp) *n.* **1.** a low-cut low-heeled shoe without fastenings, worn esp. for dancing. **2.** a type of shoe with a rubber sole, used in games such as tennis; plimsoll.

pumpernickel ('pʌmpə,nɪkəl) *n.* a slightly sour black bread, originating in Germany, made of coarse rye flour.

pumpkin ('pʌmpkɪn) *n.* **1.** any of several creeping plants of the genus *Cucurbita.* **2.** the large round fruit of

---

THESAURUS

tear, wrench **4.** *Inf.* attract, draw, entice, lure, magnetize **5. pull apart** *or* **to pieces** attack, criticize, find fault, flay, lay into, pan (*Inf.*), pick holes in, run down, slam (*Sl.*), slate (*Inf.*) **6. pull oneself together** *Inf.* buck up (*Inf.*), get a grip on oneself, get over it, regain composure, snap out of it (*Inf.*) **7. pull strings** *Brit. inf.* influence, pull wires (*U.S.*), use one's influence **8. pull someone's leg** *Inf.* chaff, have (someone) on, joke, make fun of, poke fun at, rag, rib (*Inf.*), tease, twit ~*n.* **9.** jerk, tug, twitch, yank **10.** attraction, drawing power, effort, exertion, force, forcefulness, influence, lure, magnetism, power **11.** *Inf.* advantage, clout (*Inf.*), influence, leverage, muscle, weight **12.** drag (*Inf.*), inhalation, puff

pull down bulldoze, demolish, destroy, raze, remove

pull in 1. arrive, come in, draw in, draw up, reach, stop **2.** attract, bring in, draw **3.**

Brit. sl. arrest, bust (*Inf.*), collar (*Inf.*), nab (*Inf.*), nail (*Inf.*), pinch (*Inf.*), run in (*Sl.*), take into custody **4.** clear, earn, gain, gross, make, net, pocket, take home

pull off 1. detach, doff, remove, rip off, tear off, wrench off **2.** accomplish, bring off, carry out, manage, score a success, secure one's object, succeed

pull out abandon, depart, evacuate, leave, quit, rat on, retreat, stop participating, withdraw

pull through come through, get better, get over, pull round, rally, recover, survive, weather

pull up 1. dig out, lift, raise, uproot **2.** brake, come to a halt, halt, reach a standstill, stop **3.** admonish, carpet (*Inf.*), castigate, dress down (*Inf.*), rebuke, reprimand, reprove, take to task, tell off (*Inf.*), tick off (*Inf.*)

pulp *n.* **1.** flesh, marrow, soft part **2.** mash,

mush, pap, paste, pomace, semiliquid, semisolid, triturate ~*v.* **3.** crush, mash, pulverize, squash, triturate ~*adj.* **4.** cheap, lurid, mushy (*Inf.*), rubbishy, sensational, trashy

pulse 1. *n.* beat, beating, oscillation, pulsation, rhythm, stroke, throb, throbbing, vibration **2.** *v.* beat, pulsate, throb, tick, vibrate

pulverize 1. bray, comminute, crush, granulate, grind, levigate (*Chem.*), mill, pestle, pound, triturate **2.** *Fig.* annihilate, crush, defeat, demolish, destroy, flatten, smash, vanquish, wreck

pump *v.* **1.** *With* **out** bail out, drain, draw off, drive out, empty, force out, siphon **2.** *With* **up** blow up, dilate, inflate **3.** drive, force, inject, pour, push, send, supply **4.** cross-examine, give (someone) the third degree, grill (*Inf.*), interrogate, probe, question closely, quiz, worm out of

any of these plants, which has a thick orange rind, pulpy flesh, and numerous seeds.

pun (pʌn) n. **1.** the use of words to exploit ambiguities and innuendoes for humorous effect; a play on words. An example is: *"Ben Battle was a soldier bold, And used to war's alarms: But a cannonball took off his legs, So he laid down his arms."* (Thomas Hood). ~vb. **punning, punned. 2.** (intr.) to make puns.

punch[1] (pʌntʃ) vb. **1.** to strike at, esp. with a clenched fist. **2.** (tr.) Western U.S. to herd or drive (cattle), esp. for a living. **3.** (tr.) to poke with a stick, etc. ~n. **4.** a blow with the fist. **5.** Inf. point or vigour: *his arguments lacked punch.* —**'puncher** n.

punch[2] (pʌntʃ) n. **1.** a tool or machine for piercing holes in a material. **2.** a tool or machine used for stamping a design on something or shaping it by impact. **3.** the solid die of a punching machine. **4.** Computers. a device for making holes in a card or paper tape. ~vb. **5.** (tr.) to pierce, cut, stamp, shape, or drive with a punch.

punch[3] (pʌntʃ) n. any mixed drink containing fruit juice and, usually, alcoholic liquor, generally hot and spiced.

Punch (pʌntʃ) n. the main character in the traditional children's puppet show **Punch and Judy.**

punchball ('pʌntʃ,bɔːl) n. **1.** Also called (U.S.): **punching bag.** a stuffed or inflated ball or bag, either suspended or supported by a flexible rod, that is punched for exercise, esp. boxing training. **2.** U.S. a game resembling baseball.

punch-drunk adj. **1.** demonstrating or characteristic of the behaviour of a person who has suffered repeated blows to the head, esp. a professional boxer. **2.** dazed; stupefied.

Punchinello (,pʌntʃi'nɛləʊ) n., pl. **-los** or **-loes. 1.** a clown from Italian puppet shows, the prototype of Punch. **2.** (sometimes not cap.) any grotesque or absurd character.

punch line n. the culminating part of a joke, funny story, etc., that gives it its point.

punch-up n. Brit. sl. a fight or brawl.

punchy ('pʌntʃi) adj. **punchier, punchiest. 1.** an informal word for **punch-drunk. 2.** Inf. incisive or forceful. —**'punchily** adv. —**'punchiness** n.

punctate ('pʌŋkteɪt) adj. having or marked with minute spots or depressions. —**punc'tation** n.

punctilio (pʌŋk'tɪlɪ,əʊ) n., pl. **-os. 1.** strict attention to minute points of etiquette. **2.** a petty formality or fine point of etiquette.

punctilious (pʌŋk'tɪliəs) adj. **1.** paying scrupulous attention to correctness in etiquette. **2.** attentive to detail. —**punc'tiliously** adv. —**punc'tiliousness** n.

punctual ('pʌŋktjʊəl) adj. **1.** arriving or taking place at an arranged time. **2.** (of a person) having the characteristic of always keeping to arranged times. **3.** Obs. precise; exact. **4.** Maths. consisting of or confined to a point. —,**punctu'ality** n. —**'punctually** adv.

punctuation (,pʌŋktjʊ'eɪʃən) n. **1.** the use of symbols not belonging to the alphabet of a writing system to indicate aspects of the intonation and meaning not otherwise conveyed in the written language. **2.** the symbols used for this purpose.

punctuation mark n. any of the signs used in punctuation, such as a comma.

puncture ('pʌŋktʃə) n. **1.** a small hole made by a sharp object. **2.** a perforation and loss of pressure in a pneumatic tyre. **3.** the act of puncturing or perforating. ~vb. **4.** (tr.) to pierce (a hole) in (something) with a sharp object. **5.** to cause (something pressurized, esp. a tyre) to lose pressure by piercing, or (of a tyre, etc.) to collapse in this way. **6.** (tr.) to depreciate (a person's self-esteem, pomposity, etc.).

pundit or **pandit** ('pʌndɪt) n. **1.** a self-appointed expert. **2.** (formerly) a learned person. **3.** a Brahman learned in Sanskrit and, esp. in Hindu religion, philosophy or law.

pungent ('pʌndʒənt) adj. **1.** having an acrid smell or sharp bitter flavour. **2.** (of wit, satire, etc.) biting; caustic. **3.** Biol. ending in a sharp point. —**'pungency** n. —**'pungently** adv.

punish ('pʌnɪʃ) vb. **1.** to force (someone) to undergo a penalty for some crime or misdemeanour. **2.** (tr.) to inflict punishment for (some crime, etc.). **3.** (tr.) to treat harshly, esp. as by overexertion: *to punish a horse.* **4.** (tr.) Inf. to consume in large quantities: *to punish the bottle.* —**'punishable** adj. —**'punisher** n. —**'punishingly** adv.

punishment ('pʌnɪʃmənt) n. **1.** a penalty for a crime or offence. **2.** the act of punishing or state of being punished. **3.** Inf. rough treatment.

punitive ('pjuːnɪtɪv) or **punitory** ('pjuːnɪtərɪ) adj. relating to, involving, or with the intention of inflicting punishment: *a punitive expedition.* —**'punitively** adv.

punk (pʌŋk) n. **1.** an inferior or worthless person or thing. **2.** a follower or practitioner of punk rock, esp. one wearing worthless articles such as safety pins for decoration. **3.** worthless articles collectively. **4.** short for **punk rock. 5.** Obs. a young male homosexual; catamite. **6.** Obs. a prostitute. ~adj. **7.** rotten or worthless. **8.** denoting punk rock.

punk rock n. rock music in a style of the late 1970s, characterized by offensive lyrics and aggressive performance. —**punk rocker** n.

punnet ('pʌnɪt) n. Chiefly Brit. a small basket for fruit.

punster ('pʌnstə) n. a person who is fond of making puns, esp. one who makes a tedious habit of this.

punt[1] (pʌnt) n. **1.** an open flat-bottomed boat with square ends, propelled by a pole. ~vb. **2.** to propel (a boat, esp. a punt) by pushing with a pole on the bottom of a river, etc.

punt[2] (pʌnt) n. **1.** a kick in certain sports, such as rugby, in which the ball is released and kicked before it hits the ground. ~vb. **2.** to kick (a ball, etc.) using a punt.

punt[3] (pʌnt) Chiefly Brit. ~vb. **1.** (intr.) to gamble; bet. ~n. **2.** a gamble or bet, esp. against the bank, as in rou-

---

THESAURUS

pun double entendre, equivoque, paronomasia (Rhetoric), play on words, quip, witticism

punch[1] v. **1.** bash (Inf.), biff (Sl.), bop (Inf.), box, clout (Inf.), hit, plug (Sl.), pummel, slam, slug, smash, sock (Sl.), strike, wallop (Inf.) ~n. **2.** bash (Inf.), biff (Sl.), blow, bop (Inf.), clout (Inf.), hit, jab, knock, plug (Sl.), sock (Sl.), thump, wallop (Inf.) **3.** Inf. bite, drive, effectiveness, force, forcefulness, impact, point, verve, vigour

punch[2] v. bore, cut, drill, perforate, pierce, pink, prick, puncture, stamp

punch-drunk befuddled, confused, dazed, groggy (Inf.), in a daze, knocked silly, punchy (Inf.), reeling, slaphappy (Inf.), staggering, stupefied, unsteady, woozy (Inf.)

punctilio 1. exactitude, finickiness, meticulousness, particularity, precision, punctiliousness, scrupulousness, strictness **2.** convention, delicacy, distinction, fine point, formality, nicety, particular, refinement

punctilious careful, ceremonious, conscientious, exact, finicky, formal, fussy, meticulous, nice, particular, precise, proper, scrupulous, strict

punctual early, exact, in good time, on the dot, on time, precise, prompt, punctilious, seasonable, strict, timely

punctuality promptitude, promptness, readiness, regularity

punctuate 1. break, interject, interrupt, intersperse, pepper, sprinkle **2.** accentuate, emphasize, lay stress on, mark, point up, stress, underline

puncture n. **1.** break, cut, damage, hole, leak, nick, opening, perforation, rupture, slit **2.** flat, flat tyre ~v. **3.** bore, cut, nick, penetrate, perforate, pierce, prick, rupture **4.** deflate, go down, go flat **5.** deflate, discourage, disillusion, flatten, humble, take down a peg (Inf.)

pundit buff (Inf.), maestro, one of the cognoscenti, (self-appointed) authority or expert

pungent 1. acid, acrid, aromatic, bitter, highly flavoured, hot, peppery, piquant, seasoned, sharp, sour, spicy, stinging, strong, tangy, tart **2.** acrimonious, acute, barbed, biting, caustic, cutting, incisive, keen, mordant, penetrating, piercing, poignant, pointed, sar-

castic, scathing, sharp, stinging, stringent, telling, trenchant

punish 1. beat, castigate, chasten, chastise, correct, discipline, flog, give a lesson to, give (someone) the works (Sl.), lash, penalize, rap someone's knuckles, scourge, sentence, slap someone's wrist, whip **2.** abuse, batter, give (someone) a going over (Inf.), harm, hurt, injure, knock about, maltreat, manhandle, misuse, oppress, rough up

punishable blameworthy, chargeable, convictable, criminal, culpable, indictable

punishing arduous, backbreaking, burdensome, demanding, exhausting, grinding, gruelling, hard, strenuous, taxing, tiring, uphill, wearing

punishment 1. chastening, chastisement, comeuppance (Sl.), correction, discipline, just deserts, penalty, penance, punitive measures, retribution, sanction, what for (Inf.) **2.** Inf. abuse, beating, hard work, maltreatment, manhandling, pain, rough treatment, slave labour, torture, victimization

punitive in reprisal, in retaliation, punitory, retaliative, retaliatory, revengeful, vindictive

lette, or on horses. **3.** Also called: **punter.** a person who bets. **4. take a punt at.** *Austral. inf.* to make an attempt at.

punter ('pʌntə) *n.* **1.** one who gambles or bets. **2.** *Inf.* any person. **3.** a person who punts a boat. **4.** a person who punts a ball. **5.** *Inf.* a customer or client, esp. a prostitute's client.

puny ('pju:nɪ) *adj.* **-nier, -niest. 1.** small and weakly. **2.** paltry; insignificant. —'**puniness** *n.*

pup (pʌp) *n.* **1. a. a** young dog; puppy. **b.** the young of various other animals, such as the seal. **2. in pup.** (of a bitch) pregnant. **3.** *Inf., chiefly Brit.* a conceited young man (esp. in **young pup**). **4.** *Inf.* a worthless purchase (esp. in **be sold a pup**). ~*vb.* **pupping, pupped. 5.** (of dogs, seals, etc.) to give birth to (young).

pupa ('pju:pə) *n., pl.* **-pae** (-pi:) *or* **-pas.** an insect at the immobile nonfeeding stage of development between larva and adult, when many internal changes occur. —'**pupal** *adj.*

pupil¹ ('pju:pɪl) *n.* **1.** a student who is taught by a teacher. **2.** *Civil & Scot. law.* a boy under 14 or a girl under 12 who is in the care of a guardian. —'**pupillage** *or U.S.* '**pupilage** *n.* —'**pupillary** *adj.*

pupil² ('pju:pɪl) *n.* the dark circular aperture at the centre of the iris of the eye, through which light enters. —'**pupillary** *adj.*

puppet ('pʌpɪt) *n.* **1. a.** a small doll or figure moved by strings attached to its limbs or by the hand inserted in its cloth body. **b.** (*as modifier*): *a puppet theatre.* **2. a.** a person, state, etc., that appears independent but is controlled by another. **b.** (*as modifier*): *a puppet government.* —'**puppetry** *n.*

puppeteer (,pʌpɪ'tɪə) *n.* a person who manipulates puppets.

puppy ('pʌpɪ) *n., pl.* **-pies. 1.** a young dog; pup. **2.** *Inf., contemptuous.* a brash or conceited young man; pup. —'**puppy,hood** *n.* —'**puppyish** *adj.*

puppy fat *n.* fatty tissue in a child or adolescent, usually disappearing with age.

purblind ('pɜ:,blaɪnd) *adj.* **1.** partly or nearly blind. **2.** lacking in insight or understanding; obtuse.

purchase ('pɜ:tʃɪs) *vb.* (*tr.*) **1.** to obtain (goods, etc.) by payment. **2.** to obtain by effort, sacrifice, etc.: *to purchase one's freedom.* **3.** to draw or lift (a load) with mechanical apparatus. ~*n.* **4.** something that is purchased. **5.** the act of buying. **6.** acquisition of an estate by any lawful means other than inheritance. **7.** a tackle or lever used in moving a heavy load. **8.** a firm foothold, grasp, etc., as for climbing something. —'**purchasable** *adj.* —'**purchaser** *n.*

purdah ('pɜ:də) *n.* **1.** the custom in some Muslim and Hindu communities of keeping women in seclusion, with clothing that conceals them completely when they go out. **2.** a screen in a Hindu house used to keep the women out of view.

pure (pjuə) *adj.* **1.** not mixed with any extraneous or dissimilar materials, elements, etc. **2.** free from tainting or polluting matter: *pure water.* **3.** free from moral taint or defilement: *pure love.* **4.** (*prenominal*) (intensifier): *a pure coincidence.* **5.** (of a subject, etc.) studied in its theoretical aspects rather than for its practical applications: *pure mathematics.* **6.** (of a vowel) pronounced with more or less unvarying quality without any glide. **7.** (of a consonant) not accompanied by another consonant. **8.** of unmixed descent. **9.** *Genetics, biol.* breeding true; homozygous. **10.** *Philosophy.* independent of empirical concepts: *pure reason.* —'**purely** *adv.* —'**pureness** *n.*

purebred *adj.* ('pjuə'brɛd). **1.** denoting a pure strain obtained through many generations of controlled breeding. ~*n.* ('pjuə,brɛd). **2.** a purebred animal.

purée ('pjuəreɪ) *n.* **1.** a smooth thick pulp of sieved fruit, vegetables, meat, or fish. ~*vb.* **-réeing, -réed. 2.** (*tr.*) to make (cooked foods) into a purée.

purgative ('pɜ:gətɪv) *Med.* ~*n.* **1.** a drug or agent for purging the bowels. ~*adj.* **2.** causing evacuation of the bowels. —'**purgatively** *adv.*

purgatory ('pɜ:gətərɪ) *n.* **1.** *Chiefly R.C. Church.* a state or place in which the souls of those who have died in a state of grace are believed to undergo a limited amount of suffering to expiate their venial sins. **2.** a place or condition of suffering or torment, esp. one that is temporary. —,**purga'torial** *adj.*

purge (pɜ:dʒ) *vb.* **1.** (*tr.*) to rid (something) of (impure elements). **2.** (*tr.*) to rid (a state, political party, etc.) of (dissident people). **3.** (*tr.*) **a.** to empty (the bowels) by evacuation of faeces. **b.** to cause (a person) to evacuate his bowels. **4. a.** to clear (a person) of a charge. **b.** to free (oneself) of guilt, as by atonement. **5.** (*intr.*) to be purified. ~*n.* **6.** the act or process of purging. **7.** the elimination of opponents or dissidents from a state, political party, etc. **8.** a purgative drug or agent. —'**purger** *n.*

purify ('pjuərɪ,faɪ) *vb.* **-fying, -fied. 1.** to free (something) of contaminating or debasing matter. **2.** (*tr.*) to free (a person, etc.) from sin or guilt. **3.** (*tr.*) to make clean, as in a ritual. —,**purifi'cation** *n.* —**purificatory** ('pjuərɪfɪ,keɪtərɪ) *adj.* —'**puri,fier** *n.*

purism ('pjuə,rɪzəm) *n.* insistence on traditional canons of correctness of form or purity of style or content. —'**purist** *adj., n.* —**pu'ristic** *adj.*

puritan ('pjuərɪtən) *n.* **1.** a person who adheres to strict moral or religious principles, esp. one opposed to luxury and sensual enjoyment. ~*adj.* **2.** characteristic of a puritan. —'**puritan,ism** *n.*

Puritan ('pjuərɪtən) (in the late 16th and 17th centuries) ~*n.* **1.** any of the extreme English Protestants who wished to purify the Church of England of most of its ceremony and other aspects that they deemed to be Catho-

---

THESAURUS

punt *v.* **1.** back, bet, gamble, lay, stake, wager ~*n.* **2.** bet, gamble, stake, wager **3.** backer, better, gambler, punter

punter *n.* **1.** backer, better, gambler, punt **2.** *Inf.* bloke (*Brit. inf.*), fellow, guy (*Inf.*), man in the street, person **3.** *Inf.* client, customer

puny 1. diminutive, dwarfish, feeble, frail, little, pint-sized (*Inf.*), pygmy, sickly, stunted, tiny, underfed, undersized, undeveloped, weak, weakly **2.** inconsequential, inferior, insignificant, minor, paltry, petty, piddling (*Inf.*), trifling, trivial, worthless

pup *or* **puppy** *Fig.* braggart, cub, jackanapes, popinjay, whelp, whippersnapper, young dog

pupil beginner, catechumen, disciple, learner, neophyte, novice, scholar, schoolboy, schoolgirl, student, tyro

puppet 1. doll, marionette **2.** *Fig.* cat's-paw, creature, dupe, figurehead, gull (*Archaic*), instrument, mouthpiece, pawn, stooge, tool

purchasable 1. bribable, corrupt, corruptible, dishonest, having one's price, unscrupulous, venal **2.** available, for sale, in stock, obtainable, on sale, on the market, to be had

purchase *v.* **1.** acquire, buy, come by, gain, get, get hold of, invest in, make a purchase, obtain, pay for, pick up, procure, secure, shop for **2.** achieve, attain, earn, gain, realize, win ~*n.* **3.** acquisition, asset, buy, gain, investment, possession, property **4.** advantage, edge, foothold, footing, grasp, grip, hold, influence, lever, leverage, support, toehold

purchaser buyer, consumer, customer, vendee (*Law*)

pure 1. authentic, clear, flawless, genuine, natural, neat, perfect, real, simple, straight, true, unalloyed, unmixed **2.** clean, disinfected, germ-free, immaculate, pasteurized, sanitary, spotless, sterile, sterilized, unadulterated, unblemished, uncontaminated, unpolluted, untainted, wholesome **3.** blameless, chaste, guileless, honest, immaculate, innocent, maidenly, modest, true, uncorrupted, undefiled, unspotted, unstained, unsullied, upright, virgin, virginal, virtuous **4.** absolute, complete, mere, sheer, thorough, unmitigated, unqualified, utter **5.** abstract, academic, philosophical, speculative, theoretical

purely absolutely, completely, entirely, exclusively, just, merely, only, plainly, simply, solely, totally, wholly

purgatory *As used informally* agony, hell (*Inf.*), hell on earth, misery, murder (*Inf.*), the rack, torment, torture

purge *v.* **1.** clean out, dismiss, do away with, eject, eradicate, expel, exterminate, get rid of, kill, liquidate, oust, remove, rid of, rout out, sweep out, wipe out **2.** absolve, cleanse, clear, exonerate, expiate, forgive, pardon, purify, wash ~*n.* **3.** cleanup, crushing, ejection, elimination, eradication, expulsion, liquidation, reign of terror, removal, suppression, witch hunt **4.** aperient (*Medical*), cathartic, dose of salts, emetic, enema, laxative, physic (*Rare*), purgative (*Medical*)

purify 1. clarify, clean, cleanse, decontaminate, disinfect, filter, fumigate, refine, sanitize, wash **2.** absolve, cleanse, exculpate, exonerate, lustrate, redeem, sanctify, shrive

purist classicist, formalist, pedant, precisian, stickler

puritan 1. *n.* fanatic, moralist, pietist, prude, rigorist, zealot **2.** *adj.* ascetic, austere, hidebound, intolerant, moralistic, narrow, narrow-minded, prudish, puritanical, severe, strait-laced, strict

lic. ~*adj.* **2.** of or relating to the Puritans. —**'Puritan-,ism** *n.*

puritanical (,pjʊərɪ'tænɪkəl) *or* **puritanic** *adj.* **1.** *Usually disparaging.* strict in moral or religious outlook, esp. in shunning sensual pleasures. **2.** (*sometimes cap.*) of or relating to a puritan or the Puritans. —,**puri'tani-cally** *adv.*

purity ('pjʊərɪtɪ) *n.* the state or quality of being pure.

purl[1] (pɜːl) *n.* **1.** a knitting stitch made by doing a plain stitch backwards. **2.** a decorative border, as of lace. **3.** gold or silver wire thread. ~*vb.* **4.** to knit in purl stitch. **5.** to edge (something) with a purl.

purl[2] (pɜːl) *vb.* **1.** (*intr.*) (of a stream, etc.) to flow with a gentle swirling or rippling movement and a murmuring sound. ~*n.* **2.** a swirling movement of water; eddy. **3.** a murmuring sound, as of a shallow stream.

purlieu ('pɜːljuː) *n.* **1.** *English history.* land on the edge of a forest once included within the bounds of the royal forest but later separated although still subject to some of the forest laws. **2.** (*usually pl.*) a neighbouring area; outskirts. **3.** (*often pl.*) a place one frequents; haunt.

purlin *or* **purline** ('pɜːlɪn) *n.* a horizontal beam that provides intermediate support for the common rafters of a roof construction.

purloin (pɜː'lɔɪn) *vb.* to steal. —**pur'loiner** *n.*

purple ('pɜːpəl) *n.* **1.** a colour between red and blue. **2.** a dye or pigment producing such a colour. **3.** cloth of this colour, often used to symbolize royalty or nobility. **4.** (usually preceded by *the*) high rank; nobility. **5. a.** the official robe of a cardinal. **b.** the rank of a cardinal as signified by this. ~*adj.* **6.** of the colour purple. **7.** (of writing) excessively elaborate or full of imagery: *purple prose.* —**'purpleness** *n.* —**'purplish** *adj.* —**'purply** *adj.*

purple heart *n.* **1.** any of several tropical American trees. **2.** *Inf., chiefly Brit.* a heart-shaped purple tablet consisting mainly of amphetamine.

Purple Heart *n.* a decoration awarded to members of the U.S. Armed Forces for a wound received in action.

purport *vb.* (pɜː'pɔːt). (*tr.*) **1.** to claim to be (true, official, etc.) by manner or appearance, esp. falsely. **2.** to signify or imply. ~*n.* ('pɜːpɔːt). **3.** meaning; significance. **4.** object; intention.

purpose ('pɜːpəs) *n.* **1.** the reason for which anything is done, created, or exists. **2.** a fixed design or idea that is the object of an action or other effort. **3.** determination: *a man of purpose.* **4.** practical advantage or use: *to work to good purpose.* **5.** that which is relevant (esp. in **to** *or* **from the purpose**). **6.** *Arch.* purport. **7. on purpose.** intentionally. ~*vb.* **8.** (*tr.*) to intend or determine to do (something). —**'purposeful** *adj.* —**'purposeless** *adj.*

purpose-built *adj.* made to serve a specific purpose.

purposely ('pɜːpəslɪ) *adv.* on purpose.

purposive ('pɜːpəsɪv) *adj.* **1.** having or indicating conscious intention. **2.** serving a purpose; useful. —**'purpos-**

ively *adv.* —**'purposiveness** *n.*

purr (pɜː) *vb.* **1.** (*intr.*) (esp. of cats) to make a low vibrant sound, usually considered as expressing pleasure, etc. **2.** (*tr.*) to express (pleasure, etc.) by this sound. ~*n.* **3.** a purring sound.

purse (pɜːs) *n.* **1.** a small bag or pouch for carrying money, esp. coins. **2.** *U.S.* a woman's handbag. **3.** anything resembling a small bag or pouch in form or function. **4.** wealth; funds; resources. **5.** a sum of money that is offered, esp. as a prize. ~*vb.* **6.** (*tr.*) to contract (the mouth, lips, etc.) into a small rounded shape.

purser ('pɜːsə) *n.* an officer aboard a ship or aircraft who keeps the accounts and attends to the welfare of the passengers.

purse strings *pl. n.* control of expenditure (esp. in **hold** *or* **control the purse strings**).

purslane ('pɜːslɪn) *n.* a plant with fleshy leaves used (esp. formerly) in salads and as a potherb.

pursuance (pə'sjuːəns) *n.* the carrying out or pursuing of an action, plan, etc.

pursuant (pə'sjuːənt) *adj.* **1.** (*usually postpositive; often foll. by* to) *Chiefly law.* in agreement or conformity. **2.** *Arch.* pursuing. —**pur'suantly** *adv.*

pursue (pə'sjuː) *vb.* -**suing, -sued.** (*mainly tr.*) **1.** (*also intr.*) to follow (a fugitive, etc.) in order to capture or overtake. **2.** to follow closely or accompany: *ill health pursued her.* **3.** to seek or strive to attain (some desire, etc.). **4.** to follow the precepts of (a plan, policy, etc.). **5.** to apply oneself to (studies, interests, etc.). **6.** to follow persistently or seek to become acquainted with. **7.** to continue to discuss or argue (a point, subject, etc.). —**pur'suer** *n.*

pursuit (pə'sjuːt) *n.* **1. a.** the act of pursuing. **b.** (*as modifier*): *a pursuit plane.* **2.** an occupation or pastime. **3.** (in cycling) a race in which the riders set off at intervals along the track and attempt to overtake each other.

pursuivant ('pɜːsɪvənt) *n.* **1.** the lowest rank of heraldic officer. **2.** *History.* a state or royal messenger. **3.** *History.* a follower or attendant.

pursy ('pɜːsɪ) *adj.* **1.** short-winded. **2.** *Arch.* fat; overweight.

purulent ('pjʊərʊlənt) *adj.* of, relating to, or containing pus. —**'purulence** *n.* —**'purulently** *adv.*

purvey (pə'veɪ) *vb.* (*tr.*) **1.** to sell or provide (commodities, esp. foodstuffs) on a large scale. **2.** to publish (lies, scandal, etc.). —**pur'veyor** *n.*

purview ('pɜːvjuː) *n.* **1.** scope of operation. **2.** breadth or range of outlook. **3.** *Law.* the body of a statute, containing the enacting clauses.

pus (pʌs) *n.* the yellow or greenish fluid product of inflammation.

push (pʊʃ) *vb.* **1.** (when *tr.*, often foll. by *off, away*, etc.) to apply steady force to in order to move. **2.** to thrust (one's way) through something, such as a crowd. **3.** (*tr.*) to encourage or urge (a person) to some action, decision, etc. **4.** (when *intr.*, often foll. by *for*) to be an advocate

---

THESAURUS

puritanical ascetic, austere, bigoted, disapproving, fanatical, forbidding, narrow, narrow-minded, prim, proper, prudish, puritan, rigid, severe, stiff, strait-laced, strict, stuffy

purity 1. brilliance, clarity, cleanliness, cleanness, clearness, faultlessness, fineness, genuineness, immaculateness, pureness, untaintedness, wholesomeness 2. blamelessness, chasteness, chastity, decency, guilelessness, honesty, innocence, integrity, piety, rectitude, sincerity, virginity, virtue, virtuousness

purport v. 1. allege, assert, claim, declare, maintain, pose as, pretend, proclaim, profess 2. betoken, convey, denote, express, imply, import, indicate, intend, mean, point to, signify, suggest ~n. 3. bearing, drift, gist, idea, implication, import, meaning, significance, spirit, tendency, tenor 4. aim, design, intent, intention, object, objective, plan, purpose

purpose n. 1. aim, design, function, idea, intention, object, point, principle, reason 2. aim, ambition, aspiration, design, desire, end, goal, hope, intention, object, objective, plan, project, scheme, target, view, wish 3.

constancy, determination, firmness, persistence, resolution, resolve, single-mindedness, steadfastness, tenacity, will 4. advantage, avail, benefit, effect, gain, good, outcome, profit, result, return, use, utility 5. **on purpose** by design, deliberately, designedly, intentionally, knowingly, purposely, wilfully, wittingly ~v. 6. aim, aspire, commit oneself, contemplate, decide, design, determine, have a mind to, intend, make up one's mind, mean, meditate, plan, propose, resolve, set one's sights on, think to, work towards

purposeful decided, deliberate, determined, firm, fixed, positive, resolute, resolved, settled, single-minded, steadfast, strong-willed, tenacious, unfaltering

purposeless aimless, empty, goalless, motiveless, needless, pointless, senseless, uncalled-for, unnecessary, useless, vacuous, wanton

purposely by design, calculatedly, consciously, deliberately, designedly, expressly, intentionally, knowingly, on purpose, wilfully, with intent

purse n. 1. money-bag, pouch, wallet 2. coffers, exchequer, funds, means, money, resources, treasury, wealth, wherewithal 3.

award, gift, present, prize, reward ~v. 4. close, contract, press together, pucker, tighten, wrinkle

pursuance bringing about, carrying out, discharge, doing, effecting, execution, following, performance, prosecution, pursuing

pursue 1. accompany, attend, chase, dog, follow, give chase to, go after, harass, harry, haunt, hound, hunt, hunt down, plague, run after, shadow, stalk, tail, track 2. aim for, aspire to, desire, have as one's goal, purpose, seek, strive for, try for, work towards 3. adhere to, carry on, continue, cultivate, hold to, keep on, maintain, persevere in, persist in, proceed, see through 4. apply oneself, carry on, conduct, engage in, perform, ply, practise, prosecute, tackle, wage, work at 5. chase after, court, make up to (*Inf.*), pay attention to, pay court to, set one's cap at, woo

pursuit 1. chase, hunt, hunting, inquiry, quest, search, seeking, tracking, trail, trailing 2. activity, hobby, interest, line, occupation, pastime, pleasure, vocation

purvey 1. cater, deal in, furnish, provide, provision, retail, sell, supply, trade in, victual 2. communicate, make available, pass on, publish, retail, spread, transmit

or promoter (of): *to push for acceptance of one's theories*. **5.** (*tr.*) to use one's influence to help (a person): *to push one's own candidate*. **6.** to bear upon (oneself or another person) in order to achieve better results, etc. **7.** (*tr.*) to rely too much on: *to push one's luck*. **8.** *Cricket, etc.* to hit (a ball) with a stiff pushing stroke. **9.** (*tr.*) *Inf.* to sell (narcotic drugs) illegally. **10.** (*intr.*; foll. by *out, into*, etc.) to extend: *the cliffs pushed out to the sea.* ~*n.* **11.** the act of pushing; thrust. **12.** a part or device that is pressed to operate some mechanism. **13.** *Inf.* drive, energy, etc. **14.** *Inf.* a special effort or attempt to advance, as of an army: *to make a push.* **15.** *Austral. sl.* a group, gang, or clique. **16.** *Cricket, etc.* a stiff pushing stroke. **17. at a push.** *Inf.* with difficulty; only just. **18. the push.** *Sl., chiefly Brit.* dismissal, esp. from employment. ~See also **push off, push through.**

push-bike *n. Brit.* an informal name for **bicycle.**

push button *n.* **1.** an electrical switch operated by pressing a button, which closes or opens a circuit. **2.** (*modifier*) **push-button. a.** operated by a push button: *a push-button radio.* **b.** initiated as simply as by pressing a button: *push-button warfare.*

pushchair ('puʃ,tʃɛə) *n. Brit.* a chair-shaped carriage for a small child. U.S. word: **stroller.** Austral. words: **pusher, stroller.**

pusher ('puʃə) *n.* **1.** *Inf.* a person who sells illegal drugs. **2.** *Inf.* an aggressively ambitious person. **3.** a person or thing that pushes. **4.** *Austral.* the usual name for **pushchair.**

pushing ('puʃɪŋ) *adj.* **1.** enterprising or aggressively ambitious. **2.** impertinently self-assertive. ~*adv.* **3.** almost or nearly (a certain age, speed, etc.): *pushing fifty.* —'**pushingly** *adv.*

push off *vb.* (*adv.*) **1.** Also: **push out.** to move into open water, as by being cast off from a mooring. **2.** (*intr.*) *Inf.* to go away; leave.

pushover ('puʃ,əuvə) *n. Sl.* **1.** something that is easily achieved. **2.** a person, team, etc., that is easily taken advantage of or defeated.

push-start *vb.* (*tr.*) **1.** to start (a motor vehicle) by pushing it while it is in gear, thus turning the engine. ~*n.* **2.** this process.

push through *vb.* (*tr.*) to compel to accept: *the bill was pushed through Parliament.*

pushy ('puʃɪ) *adj.* **pushier, pushiest.** *Inf.* **1.** offensively assertive. **2.** aggressively or ruthlessly ambitious. —'**pushily** *adv.* —'**pushiness** *n.*

pusillanimous (,pjuːsɪ'lænɪməs) *adj.* characterized by a lack of courage or determination. —**pusillanimity** (,pjuːsɪlə'nɪmɪtɪ) *n.* —,pusil'lanimously *adv.*

puss (pus) *n.* **1.** an informal name for a **cat. 2.** *Sl.* a girl or woman. **3.** an informal name for a **hare.**

pussy[1] ('pusɪ) *n., pl.* **pussies. 1.** Also called: **puss, pussycat** ('pusɪ,kæt). an informal name for a **cat. 2.** a furry catkin. **3.** *Taboo sl.* the female pudenda.

pussy[2] ('pʌsɪ) *adj.* **-sier, -siest.** containing or full of pus.

pussyfoot ('pusɪ,fut) *vb.* (*intr.*) *Inf.* **1.** to move about

stealthily or warily like a cat. **2.** to avoid committing oneself.

pussy willow ('pusɪ) *n.* a willow tree with silvery silky catkins.

pustulate *vb.* ('pʌstjʊ,leɪt). **1.** to form or cause to form into pustules. ~*adj.* ('pʌstjʊlɪt). **2.** covered with pustules. —,pustu'lation *n.*

pustule ('pʌstjuːl) *n.* **1.** a small inflamed elevated area of skin containing pus. **2.** any spot resembling a pimple. —**pustular** ('pʌstjʊlə) *adj.*

put (put) *vb.* **putting, put.** (*mainly tr.*) **1.** to cause to be (in a position or place): *to put a book on the table.* **2.** to cause to be (in a state, relation, etc.): *to put one's things in order.* **3.** (foll. by *to*) to cause (a person) to experience or suffer: *to put to death.* **4.** to set or commit (to an action, task, or duty), esp. by force: *he put him to work.* **5.** to render or translate: *to put into English.* **6.** to set (words) in a musical form (esp. in **put to music**). **7.** (foll. by *at*) to estimate: *he put the distance at fifty miles.* **8.** (foll. by *to*) to utilize: *he put his knowledge to use.* **9.** (foll. by *to*) to couple a female animal (with a male) for breeding: *the farmer put his heifer to the bull.* **10.** to express: *to put it bluntly.* **11.** to make (an end or limit): *he put an end to the proceedings.* **12.** to present for consideration; propose: *he put the question to the committee.* **13.** to invest (money) in or expend (time, energy, etc.) on: *he put five thousand pounds into the project.* **14.** to impart: *to put zest into a party.* **15.** to throw or cast. **16. not know where to put oneself.** to feel embarrassed. **17. put paid to.** to destroy utterly. **18. stay put.** to remain in one place; remain stationary. ~*n.* **19.** a throw, esp. in putting the shot. **20.** Also called: **put option.** *Stock Exchange.* an option to sell a stated number of securities at a specified price during a limited period. ~See also **put about, put across,** etc.

put about *vb.* (*adv.*) **1.** *Naut.* to change course. **2.** (*tr.*) to make widely known: *he put about the news of the air disaster.* **3.** (*tr.; usually passive*) to disconcert or disturb.

put across *vb.* (*tr.*) **1.** (*adv.*) to communicate in a comprehensible way: *he couldn't put things across very well.* **2. put one across.** *Inf.* to get (someone) to believe a claim, excuse, etc., by deception: *they put one across their teacher.*

put aside *or* **by** *vb.* (*tr., adv.*) **1.** to move (an object, etc.) to one side, esp. in rejection. **2.** to save: *to put money aside for a rainy day.* **3.** to disregard: *let us put aside our differences.*

putative ('pjuːtətɪv) *adj.* **1.** (*prenominal*) commonly regarded as being: *the putative father.* **2.** (*prenominal*) considered to exist or have existed; inferred. —'**putatively** *adv.*

put away *vb.* (*tr., adv.*) **1.** to return (something) to the proper place. **2.** to save: *to put away money for the future.* **3.** to lock up in a prison, mental institution, etc.: *they put him away for twenty years.* **4.** to eat or drink, esp. in large amounts. **5.** to put to death, because of old

---

THESAURUS

push *v.* **1.** depress, drive, poke, press, propel, ram, shove, thrust **2.** elbow, jostle, make or force one's way, move, shoulder, shove, squeeze, thrust **3.** egg on, encourage, expedite, hurry, impel, incite, persuade, press, prod, speed (up), spur, urge **4.** advertise, boost, cry up, hype (*Sl.*), make known, plug (*Inf.*), promote, propagandize, publicize, puff **5.** browbeat, coerce, constrain, dragoon, encourage, exert influence on, influence, oblige ~*n.* **6.** butt, jolt, nudge, poke, prod, shove, thrust **7.** *Inf.* ambition, determination, drive, dynamism, energy, enterprise, get-up-and-go (*Inf.*), go (*Inf.*), gumption (*Inf.*), initiative, vigour, vitality **8.** *Inf.* advance, assault, attack, charge, effort, offensive, onset, thrust **9. the push** *Sl.* discharge, dismissal, marching orders (*Inf.*), one's books (*Inf.*), one's cards, the boot (*Sl.*), the sack (*Inf.*)

pushed *Often with* **for** hurried, in difficulty, pressed, rushed, short of, tight, under pressure, up against it (*Inf.*)

pushing **1.** ambitious, determined, driving, dynamic, enterprising, go-ahead, on the go, purposeful, resourceful **2.** assertive, bold, brash, bumptious, forward, impertinent, in-

trusive, presumptuous, pushy (*Inf.*), self-assertive

push off beat it (*Sl.*), depart, get lost (*Inf.*), go away, hit the road (*Sl.*), launch, leave, light out (*Inf.*), make oneself scarce (*Inf.*), shove off (*Inf.*), take off (*Inf.*)

pushover **1.** child's play (*Inf.*), cinch (*Sl.*), doddle (*Brit. sl.*), picnic (*Inf.*), piece of cake (*Brit. inf.*), walkover (*Inf.*) **2.** chump (*Inf.*), easy or soft mark, easy game (*Inf.*), mug (*Sl.*), soft touch (*Inf.*), stooge (*Sl.*), sucker (*Sl.*), walkover (*Inf.*)

pushy aggressive, ambitious, bold, brash, bumptious, forceful, loud, obnoxious, obtrusive, offensive, officious, presumptuous, pushing, self-assertive

pusillanimous chicken-hearted, cowardly, craven, faint-hearted, fearful, feeble, gutless (*Inf.*), lily-livered, recreant (*Archaic*), spineless, timid, timorous, weak, yellow (*Inf.*)

put **1.** bring, deposit, establish, fix, lay, place, position, rest, set, settle, situate **2.** commit, condemn, consign, doom, enjoin, impose, inflict, levy, subject **3.** assign, constrain, employ, force, induce, make, oblige,

require, set, subject to **4.** express, phrase, pose, set, state, utter, word **5.** advance, bring forward, forward, offer, posit, present, propose, set before, submit, tender **6.** cast, fling, heave, hurl, lob, pitch, throw, toss

put across *or* **over** communicate, convey, explain, get across, get through, make clear, make oneself understood, spell out

put aside *or* **by** **1.** cache, deposit, keep in reserve, lay by, salt away, save, squirrel away, stockpile, store, stow away **2.** bury, discount, disregard, forget, ignore

putative alleged, assumed, commonly believed, imputed, presumed, presumptive, reported, reputed, supposed

put away **1.** put back, replace, return to (its) place, tidy away **2.** deposit, keep, lay in, put by, save, set aside, store away **3.** certify, commit, confine, institutionalize, lock up **4.** consume, devour, eat up, gobble, gulp down, wolf down **5.** destroy, do away with, put down, put out of its misery, put to sleep

age or illness: *the dog had to be put away.*

put back *vb.* (*tr., adv.*) **1.** to return to its former place. **2.** to move to a later time: *the wedding was put back a fortnight.* **3.** to impede the progress of: *the strike put back production.*

put down *vb.* (*tr., adv.*) **1.** to make a written record of. **2.** to repress: *to put down a rebellion.* **3.** to consider: *they put him down for an ignoramus.* **4.** to attribute: *I put the mistake down to inexperience.* **5.** to put (an animal) to death, because of old age or illness. **6.** to table on the agenda: *the MPs put down a motion on the increase in crime.* **7.** *Sl.* to reject or humiliate. ~*n.* **put-down. 8.** a cruelly critical remark.

put forward *vb.* (*tr., adv.*) **1.** to propose; suggest. **2.** to offer the name of; nominate.

put in *vb.* (*adv.*) **1.** (*intr.*) *Naut.* to bring a vessel into port. **2.** (often foll. by *for*) to apply (for a job, etc.). **3.** (*tr.*) to submit: *he put in his claims form.* **4.** to intervene with (a remark) during a conversation. **5.** (*tr.*) to devote (time, effort, etc.): *he put in three hours overtime last night.* **6.** *N.Z.* (*tr.*) to establish or appoint, esp. in relation to a farm: *he put in a manager.* **7.** (*tr.*) *Cricket.* to cause to bat: *England won the toss and put the visitors in to bat.*

put off *vb.* **1.** (*tr., adv.*) to postpone: *they have put off the dance until tomorrow.* **2.** (*tr., adv.*) to evade (a person) by postponement or delay: *they tried to put him off, but he came anyway.* **3.** (*tr., adv.*) to disconcert: *he was put off by her appearance.* **4.** (*tr., prep.*) to cause to lose interest in: *the accident put him off driving.*

put on *vb.* (*tr., mainly adv.*) **1.** to clothe oneself in. **2.** (*usually passive*) to adopt (an attitude or feeling) insincerely: *his misery was just put on.* **3.** to present (a play, show, etc.). **4.** to add: *she put on weight.* **5.** to cause (an electrical device) to function. **6.** (*also prep.*) to wager (money) on a horse race, game, etc. **7.** (*also prep.*) to impose: *to put a tax on cars.* **8.** *Cricket.* to cause (a bowler) to bowl.

put out *vb.* (*tr., adv.*) **1.** (*often passive*) **a.** to annoy; anger. **b.** to disturb; confuse. **2.** to extinguish (a fire, light, etc.). **3.** to poke forward: *to put out one's tongue.* **4.** to be a source of inconvenience to: *I hope I'm not putting you out.* **5.** to publish; broadcast: *the authorities put out a leaflet.* **6.** to render unconscious. **7.** to dislocate: *he put out his shoulder in the accident.* **8.** to give out (work to be done) at different premises. **9.** to lend (money) at interest. **10.** *Cricket.* to dismiss (a player or team).

put over *vb.* (*tr., adv.*) **1.** *Inf.* to communicate (facts, information, etc.). **2.** *Chiefly U.S.* to postpone. **3. put (a fast) one over on.** *Inf.* to get (someone) to believe a claim, excuse, etc., by deception: *he put one over on his boss.*

putrefy ('pjuːtrɪˌfaɪ) *vb.* **-fying, -fied.** (of organic matter) to decompose or rot with an offensive smell. —**putrefaction** (ˌpjuːtrɪˈfækʃən) *n.* —ˌputreˈfactive *or* putrefacient (ˌpjuːtrɪˈfeɪʃənt) *adj.*

putrescent (pjuːˈtrɛsənt) *adj.* **1.** becoming putrid; rotting. **2.** characterized by or undergoing putrefaction. —puˈtrescence *n.*

putrid ('pjuːtrɪd) *adj.* **1.** (of organic matter) in a state of decomposition: *putrid meat.* **2.** morally corrupt. **3.** sickening; foul: *a putrid smell.* **4.** *Inf.* deficient in quality

or value: *a putrid film.* —**puˈtridity** *or* ˈputridness *n.* —ˈputridly *adv.*

Putsch *German.* (pʊtʃ) *n.* a violent and sudden uprising; political revolt.

putt (pʌt) *Golf.* ~*n.* **1.** a stroke on the green with a putter to roll the ball into or near the hole. ~*vb.* **2.** to strike (the ball) in this way.

puttee *or* **putty** ('pʌtɪ) *n., pl.* **-tees** *or* **-ties.** (*often pl.*) a strip of cloth worn wound around the leg from the ankle to the knee, esp. as part of a uniform in World War I.

putter[1] ('pʌtə) *n. Golf.* **1.** a club with a short shaft for putting, usually having a solid metal head. **2.** a golfer who putts: *he is a good putter.*

putter[2] ('pʌtə) *vb.* the usual U.S. spelling of **potter**[2]. —ˈputterer *n.*

put through *vb.* (*tr., mainly adv.*) **1.** to carry out to a conclusion: *he put through his plan.* **2.** (*also prep.*) to organize the processing of: *she put through his application to join the organization.* **3.** to connect by telephone. **4.** to make (a telephone call).

putting green ('pʌtɪŋ) *n.* **1.** (on a golf course) the area of closely mown grass at the end of a fairway where the hole is. **2.** an area of smooth grass with several holes for putting games.

putty ('pʌtɪ) *n., pl.* **-ties. 1.** a stiff paste made of whiting and linseed oil that is used to fix glass into frames and to fill cracks in woodwork, etc. **2.** any substance with a similar function or appearance. **3.** a mixture of lime and water with sand or plaster of Paris used on plaster as a finishing coat. **4.** (*as modifier*): *a putty knife.* **5.** a person who is easily influenced: *he's putty in her hands.* **6.** a colour varying from greyish-yellow to greyish-brown. ~*vb.* **-tying, -tied. 7.** (*tr.*) to fix, fill, or coat with putty.

put up *vb.* (*adv., mainly tr.*) **1.** to build; erect: *to put up a statue.* **2.** to accommodate or be accommodated at: *can you put me up for tonight?* **3.** to increase (prices). **4.** to submit (a plan, case, etc.). **5.** to offer: *to put a house up for sale.* **6.** to give: *to put up a good fight.* **7.** to provide (money) for: *they put up five thousand for the new project.* **8.** to preserve or can (jam, etc.). **9.** to pile up (long hair) on the head in any of several styles. **10.** (*also intr.*) to nominate or be nominated as a candidate: *he put up for president.* **11.** *Arch.* to sheathe (a weapon) into its holder: *put up your sword!* **12. put up to.** **a.** to inform or instruct (a person) about (tasks, duties, etc.). **b.** to incite to. **13. put up with.** (*intr.*) *Inf.* to endure; tolerate. ~*adj.* **put-up. 14.** dishonestly or craftily prearranged (esp. in **put-up job**).

put upon *vb.* (*intr., prep., usually passive*) **1.** to presume on (a person's generosity, good nature, etc.): *he's always being put upon.* **2.** to impose hardship on: *he was sorely put upon.*

puzzle ('pʌzəl) *vb.* **1.** to perplex or be perplexed. **2.** (*intr.;* foll. by *over*) to ponder about the cause of: *he puzzled over her absence.* **3.** (*tr.;* usually foll. by *out*) to solve by mental effort: *he puzzled out the meaning.* ~*n.* **4.** a person or thing that puzzles. **5.** a problem that cannot be easily solved. **6.** the state of being puzzled. **7.** a toy, game, or question presenting a problem that requires skill or ingenuity for its solution. —ˈpuzzlement *n.* —ˈpuzzler *n.* —ˈpuzzlingly *adv.*

THESAURUS

put down 1. enter, inscribe, log, record, set down, take down, transcribe, write down **2.** crush, quash, quell, repress, silence, stamp out, suppress **3.** *With* to ascribe, attribute, impute, set down **4.** destroy, do away with, put away, put out of its misery, put to sleep **5.** *Sl.* condemn, crush, deflate, dismiss, disparage, humiliate, mortify, reject, shame, slight, snub

put forward advance, introduce, move, nominate, present, press, proffer, propose, recommend, submit, suggest, tender

put off 1. defer, delay, hold over, postpone, put back, reschedule **2.** abash, confuse, discomfit, disconcert, dismay, distress, nonplus, perturb, rattle (*Inf.*), throw (*Inf.*), unsettle **3.** discourage, dishearten, dissuade

put on 1. change into, don, dress, get dressed in, slip into **2.** affect, assume, fake, feign, make believe, play-act, pretend, sham,

simulate **3.** do, mount, present, produce, show, stage **4.** add, gain, increase by **5.** back, bet, lay, place, wager

put out 1. anger, annoy, confound, disturb, exasperate, harass, irk, irritate, nettle, perturb, provoke, vex **2.** blow out, douse, extinguish, quench, smother, snuff out, stamp out **3.** bother, discomfit, discommode, discompose, disconcert, discountenance, disturb, embarrass, impose upon, incommode, inconvenience, put on the spot, trouble, upset **4.** bring out, broadcast, circulate, issue, make known, make public, publish, release

putrefy corrupt, decay, decompose, deteriorate, go bad, rot, spoil, stink, taint

putrescent decaying, decomposing, going bad, rotting, stinking

putrid bad, contaminated, corrupt, decayed, decomposed, fetid, foul, off, putrefied,

rancid, rank, reeking, rotten, rotting, spoiled, stinking, tainted

put through accomplish, achieve, bring off, carry through, conclude, do, effect, execute, manage, pull off, realize

put up 1. build, construct, erect, fabricate, raise **2.** accommodate, board, entertain, give one lodging, house, lodge, take in **3.** float, nominate, offer, present, propose, put forward, recommend, submit **4.** advance, give, invest, pay, pledge, provide, supply **5. put up to** egg on, encourage, goad, incite, instigate, prompt, put the idea into one's head, urge **6. put up with** *Inf.* abide, bear, brook, endure, lump (*Inf.*), pocket, stand, stand for, stomach, suffer, swallow, take, tolerate

put-upon abused, beset, exploited, harried, imposed upon, inconvenienced, overworked, put-out, saddled, taken advantage of, taken for a fool, taken for granted, troubled

PVC *abbrev. for* polyvinyl chloride; a synthetic thermoplastic material made by polymerizing vinyl chloride. The flexible forms are used in insulation, shoes, etc. Rigid PVC is used for moulded articles.

P.W. *abbrev. for* policewoman.

pyaemia *or* **pyemia** (paɪˈiːmɪə) *n.* blood poisoning characterized by pus-forming microorganisms in the blood. —**py'aemic** *or* **py'emic** *adj.*

pye-dog *or* **pie-dog** *n.* an ownerless half-wild Asian dog.

pygmy *or* **pigmy** (ˈpɪɡmɪ) *n., pl.* **-mies. 1.** an abnormally undersized person. **2.** something that is a very small example of its type. **3.** a person of little importance or significance. **4.** (*modifier*) very small. —**pygmaean** *or* **pygmean** (pɪɡˈmiːən) *adj.*

Pygmy *or* **Pigmy** (ˈpɪɡmɪ) *n., pl.* **-mies.** a member of one of the dwarf peoples of Equatorial Africa, noted for their hunting and forest culture.

pyjamas *or U.S.* **pajamas** (pəˈdʒɑːməz) *pl. n.* **1.** loose-fitting nightclothes comprising a jacket or top and trousers. **2.** full loose-fitting ankle-length trousers worn by either sex in various Eastern countries.

pylon (ˈpaɪlən) *n.* **1.** a large vertical steel tower-like structure supporting high-tension electrical cables. **2.** a post or tower for guiding pilots or marking a turning point in a race. **3.** a streamlined aircraft structure for attaching an engine pod, etc., to the main body of the aircraft. **4.** a monumental gateway, such as one at the entrance to an ancient Egyptian temple.

pyo- *or before a vowel* **py-** *combining form.* denoting pus: *pyosis.*

pyorrhoea *or esp. U.S.* **pyorrhea** (ˌpaɪəˈrɪə) *n. Pathol.* **1.** any condition characterized by a discharge of pus. **2.** See **pyorrhoea alveolaris.**

pyorrhoea alveolaris (ˌælvɪəˈlɑːrɪs) *n. Dentistry.* inflammation of the gums characterized by the discharge of pus and loosening of the teeth.

pyramid (ˈpɪrəmɪd) *n.* **1.** a huge masonry construction that has a square base and, as in the case of the ancient Egyptian royal tombs, four sloping triangular sides. **2.** an object or structure resembling such a construction. **3.** *Maths.* a solid having a polygonal base and triangular sides that meet in a common vertex. **4.** *Crystallography.* a crystal form in which three planes intersect all three axes of the crystal. **5.** *Finance.* a group of enterprises containing a series of holding companies structured so that the top holding company controls the entire group with a relatively small proportion of the total capital invested. **6.** (*pl.*) a game similar to billiards. ~*vb.* **7.** to build up or be arranged in the form of a pyramid. **8.** *Finance.* to form (companies) into a pyramid. —**pyramidal** (pɪˈræmɪdəl), **pyra'midical,** *or* **pyra'midic** *adj.* —**py'ramidally** *or* **pyra'midically** *adv.*

pyramid selling *n.* a practice adopted by some manufacturers of advertising for distributors and selling them batches of goods. The first distributors then advertise for more distributors who are sold subdivisions of the original batches at an increased price. This process continues until the final distributors are left with a stock that is unsaleable except at a loss.

pyre (paɪə) *n.* a pile of wood or other combustible material, esp. one for cremating a corpse.

pyrethrum (paɪˈriːθrəm) *n.* **1.** any of several cultivated Eurasian chrysanthemums with white, pink, red, or purple flowers. **2.** any insecticide prepared from the dried flowers of any of these plants.

pyretic (paɪˈrɛtɪk) *adj. Pathology.* of, relating to, or characterized by fever.

Pyrex (ˈpaɪrɛks) *n. Trademark.* **a.** any of a variety of glasses that have low coefficients of expansion, making them suitable for heat-resistant glassware used in cookery and chemical apparatus. **b.** (*as modifier*): *a Pyrex dish.*

pyrite (ˈpaɪraɪt) *n.* a yellow mineral consisting of iron sulphide in cubic crystalline form. It occurs in all types of rocks and veins, associated with various metals, and is used mainly in the manufacture of sulphuric acid and paper. Formula: FeS_2. Also called: **iron pyrites, pyrites.** —**pyritic** (paɪˈrɪtɪk) *or* **py'ritous** *adj.*

pyrites (paɪˈraɪtiːz) *n., pl.* **-tes. 1.** another name for **pyrite. 2.** any of a number of other disulphides of metals, esp. of copper and tin.

pyro- *or before a vowel* **pyr-** *combining form.* **1.** denoting fire or heat: *pyromania; pyrometer.* **2.** *Chem.* denoting a new substance obtained by heating another: *pyroboric acid is obtained by heating boric acid.* **3.** *Mineralogy.* **a.** having a property that changes upon the application of heat. **b.** having a flame-coloured appearance: *pyroxylin.*

pyrography (paɪˈrɒɡrəfɪ) *n., pl.* **-phies. 1.** the art or process of burning designs on wood or leather with heated tools or a fire flame. **2.** a design made by this process. —**py'rographer** *n.*

pyromania (ˌpaɪrəʊˈmeɪnɪə) *n. Psychiatry.* the uncontrollable impulse and practice of setting things on fire. —**pyro'mani.ac** *n.*

pyrotechnics (ˌpaɪrəʊˈtɛknɪks) *n.* **1.** (*functioning as sing.*) the art of making fireworks. **2.** (*functioning as sing. or pl.*) a firework display. **3.** (*functioning as sing. or pl.*) brilliance of display, as in the performance of music. —**pyro'technic** *or* **pyro'technical** *adj.*

Pyrrhic victory *n.* a victory in which the victor's losses are as great as those of the defeated. Also called: **Cadmean victory.**

Pythagoras' theorem (paɪˈθæɡərəs) *n.* the theorem that in a right-angled triangle the square of the length of the hypotenuse equals the sum of the squares of the other two sides.

python (ˈpaɪθən) *n.* any of a family of large nonvenomous snakes of Africa, S Asia, and Australia. They reach a length of more than 20 feet and kill their prey by constriction. —**pythonic** (paɪˈθɒnɪk) *adj.*

pythoness (ˈpaɪθənɛs) *n.* a woman, such as Apollo's priestess at Delphi, believed to be possessed by an oracular spirit.

pyx *or* **pix** (pɪks) *n.* **1.** Also called: **pyx chest.** the chest in which coins from the British mint are placed to be tested for weight, etc. **2.** *Christianity.* any receptacle in which the Eucharistic Host is kept.

THESAURUS

puzzle *v.* **1.** baffle, beat (*Sl.*), bewilder, confound, confuse, flummox, mystify, nonplus, perplex, stump **2.** ask oneself, brood, cudgel or rack one's brains, mull over, muse, ponder, study, think about, think hard, wonder **3.** *Usually with* out clear up, crack, crack the code, decipher, figure out, find the key, get it, get the answer, resolve, see, solve, sort out, think through, unravel, work out ~*n.* **4.** brain-teaser (*Inf.*), conundrum, enigma, labyrinth, maze, mystery, paradox, poser, problem, question, question mark, riddle **5.** bafflement, bewilderment, confusion, difficulty, dilemma, perplexity, quandary, uncertainty

puzzled at a loss, at sea, baffled, beaten, bewildered, clueless, confused, doubtful, flummoxed, in a fog, lost, mixed up, mystified, nonplussed, perplexed, stuck, stumped, without a clue

puzzlement bafflement, bewilderment, confusion, disorientation, doubt, doubtfulness, mystification, perplexity, questioning, surprise, uncertainty, wonder

puzzling abstruse, ambiguous, baffling, bewildering, beyond one, enigmatic, full of surprises, hard, incomprehensible, inexplicable, involved, knotty, labyrinthine, misleading, mystifying, perplexing, unaccountable, unclear, unfathomable

pygmy *n.* **1.** dwarf, homunculus, Lilliputian, manikin, midget, shrimp (*Inf.*), Tom Thumb **2.** cipher, lightweight (*Inf.*), mediocrity, nobody, nonentity, pipsqueak (*Inf.*), small fry ~*adj.* **3.** baby, diminutive, dwarf, dwarfish, elfin, Lilliputian, midget, miniature, minuscule, pocket, pygmean, small, stunted, tiny, undersized, wee

Q

q *or* **Q** (kjuː) *n., pl.* **q's, Q's,** *or* **Qs. 1.** the 17th letter of the English alphabet. **2.** a speech sound represented by this letter.

Q *symbol for:* **1.** *Chess.* queen. **2.** question. **3.** *Physics.* heat.

q. *abbrev. for:* **1.** quart. **2.** quarter. **3.** quarterly. **4.** query. **5.** question. **6.** quire.

Q. *abbrev. for:* **1.** quartermaster. **2.** (*pl.* **Qq., qq.**) Also: **q.** quarto. **3.** Quebec. **4.** Queen. **5.** question. **6.** *Electronics.* Q factor.

Q.A.R.A.N.C. *abbrev. for* Queen Alexandra's Royal Army Nursing Corps.

Q.B. *abbrev. for* Queen's Bench.

Q.C. *abbrev. for* Queen's Counsel.

Q.E.D. *abbrev. for* quod erat demonstrandum.

Qld. *abbrev. for* Queensland.

Q.M. *abbrev. for* Quartermaster.

Q.M.G. *abbrev. for* Quartermaster General.

qr. *pl.* **qrs.** *abbrev. for:* **1.** quarter. **2.** quarterly. **3.** quire.

qt. *pl.* **qt.** *or* **qts.** *abbrev. for* quart.

q.t. *Inf.* **1.** *abbrev. for* quiet. **2. on the q.t.** secretly.

qua (kweɪ, kwɑː) *prep.* in the capacity of; by virtue of being.

quack¹ (kwæk) *vb.* (*intr.*) **1.** (of a duck) to utter a harsh guttural sound. **2.** to make a noise like a duck. ~*n.* **3.** the sound made by a duck.

quack² (kwæk) *n.* **1. a.** an unqualified person who claims medical knowledge or other skills. **b.** (*as modifier*): *a quack doctor.* **2.** *Sl., chiefly Austral.* a doctor; physician or surgeon. ~*vb.* **3.** (*intr.*) to act in the manner of a quack. —**'quackery** *n.* —**'quackish** *adj.*

quad¹ (kwɒd) *n. Inf.* short for quadrangle.

quad² (kwɒd) *n. Inf.* short for quadruplet.

Quadragesima (ˌkwɒdrə'dʒɛsɪmə) *n.* Also called: **Quadragesima Sunday.** the first Sunday in Lent.

quadrangle ('kwɒdˌræŋɡəl) *n.* **1.** *Geom.* a plane figure consisting of four points connected by four lines, esp. a rectangle or square. **2.** a rectangular courtyard, esp. one having buildings on all four sides. **3.** the building surrounding such a courtyard. —**quadrangular** (kwɒ'dræŋɡjʊlə) *adj.*

quadrant ('kwɒdrənt) *n.* **1.** *Geom.* **a.** a quarter of the circumference of a circle. **b.** the area enclosed by two perpendicular radii of a circle. **c.** any of the four sections into which a plane is divided by two coordinate axes. **2.** a piece of a mechanism in the form of a quarter circle. **3.** an instrument formerly used in astronomy and navigation for measuring the altitudes of stars. —**quadrantal** (kwɒ'dræntəl) *adj.*

quadraphonics *or* **quadrophonics** (ˌkwɒdrə'fɒnɪks) *n.* (*functioning as sing.*) a system of sound recording and reproduction that uses four independent loudspeakers to give directional sources of sound. —ˌ**quadra'phonic** *or* ˌ**quadro'phonic** *adj.*

quadrate *n.* ('kwɒdrɪt, -reɪt). **1.** a cube, square, or a square or cubelike object. **2.** one of a pair of bones of the upper jaw of fishes, amphibians, reptiles, and birds. ~*adj.* ('kwɒdrɪt, -reɪt). **3.** of or relating to this bone. **4.** square or rectangular. ~*vb.* (kwɒ'dreɪt). **5.** (*tr.*) to make square or rectangular. **6.** (often foll. by *with*) to conform or cause to conform.

quadratic (kwɒ'drætɪk) *Maths.* ~*n.* **1.** Also called: **quadratic equation.** an equation containing one or more terms in which the variable is raised to the power of two, but no terms in which it is raised to a higher power. ~*adj.* **2.** of or relating to the second power.

quadrature ('kwɒdrətʃə) *n.* **1.** *Maths.* the process of determining a square having an area equal to that of a given figure or surface. **2.** the process of making square or dividing into squares. **3.** *Astron.* a configuration in which two celestial bodies form an angle of 90° with a third body. **4.** *Electronics.* the relationship between two waves that are 90° out of phase.

quadrennial (kwɒ'drɛnɪəl) *adj.* **1.** occurring every four years. **2.** lasting four years. ~*n.* **3.** a period of four years. —**quad'rennially** *adv.*

quadri- *or before a vowel* **quadr-** *combining form.* four: *quadrilateral.*

quadrilateral (ˌkwɒdrɪ'lætərəl) *adj.* **1.** having or formed by four sides. ~*n.* **2.** Also called: **tetragon.** a polygon having four sides.

quadrille¹ (kwɒ'drɪl) *n.* **1.** a square dance for four couples. **2.** a piece of music for such a dance.

quadrillion (kwɒ'drɪljən) *n.* **1.** (in Britain and Germany) the number represented as one followed by 24 zeros (10^{24}). U.S. word: **septillion. 2.** (in the U.S. and France) the number represented as one followed by 15 zeros (10^{15}). ~*determiner.* **3.** amounting to this number: *a quadrillion atoms.* —**quad'rillionth** *adj.*

quadriplegia (ˌkwɒdrɪ'pliːdʒɪə) *n.* paralysis of all four limbs. Also called: **tetraplegia.** —**quadriplegic** (ˌkwɒdrɪ'pliːdʒɪk) *adj.*

quadruped ('kwɒdruˌpɛd) *n.* **1.** an animal, esp. a mammal, that has all four limbs specialized for walking. ~*adj.* **2.** having four feet. —**quadrupedal** (kwɒ'druːpɪdəl) *adj.*

quadruple ('kwɒdrupəl, kwɒ'druːpəl) *vb.* **1.** to multiply by four or increase fourfold. ~*adj.* **2.** four times as much or as many; fourfold. **3.** consisting of four parts. **4.** *Music.* having four beats in each bar. ~*n.* **5.** a quantity or number four times as great as another. —**'quadruply** *adv.*

quadruplet ('kwɒdruplɪt, kwɒ'druːplɪt) *n.* **1.** one of four offspring born at one birth. **2.** a group of four similar things. **3.** *Music.* a group of four notes to be played in a time value of three.

quadruplicate *adj.* (kwɒ'druːplɪkɪt). **1.** fourfold or quadruple. ~*vb.* (kwɒ'druːplɪˌkeɪt). **2.** to multiply or be multiplied by four. ~*n.* (kwɒ'druːplɪkɪt). **3.** a group or set of four things.

quaestor ('kwiːstə) *or U.S.* (*sometimes*) **questor** ('kwɛstə) *n.* any of several magistrates of ancient Rome, usually a financial administrator. —**quaestorial** (kwɛ'stɔːrɪəl) *adj.*

quaff (kwɒf) *vb.* to drink heartily or in one draught. —**'quaffer** *n.*

quagga ('kwæɡə) *n., pl.* **-gas** *or* **-ga.** a recently extinct member of the horse family of southern Africa: it had zebra-like stripes on the head and shoulders.

quagmire ('kwæɡˌmaɪə) *n.* **1.** a soft wet area of land that gives way under the feet; bog. **2.** an awkward, complex, or embarrassing situation.

quail¹ (kweɪl) *n., pl.* **quails** *or* **quail.** any of various small Old World game birds having rounded bodies and small tails.

quail² (kweɪl) *vb.* (*intr.*) to shrink back with fear; cower.

quaint (kweɪnt) *adj.* **1.** attractively unusual, esp. in an old-fashioned style. **2.** odd or inappropriate. —**'quaintly** *adv.* —**'quaintness** *n.*

quake (kweɪk) *vb.* (*intr.*) **1.** to shake or tremble with or as with fear. **2.** to convulse or quiver, as from instability. ~*n.* **3.** a quaking. **4.** *Inf.* an earthquake. —**'quaky** *adj.*

THESAURUS

quack 1. *n.* charlatan, fake, fraud, humbug, impostor, mountebank, phoney (*Sl.*), pretender, quacksalver (*Archaic*) **2.** *adj.* counterfeit, fake, fraudulent, phoney (*Sl.*), pretended, sham

quagmire 1. bog, fen, marsh, mire, morass, quicksand, slough, swamp **2.** difficulty, dilemma, entanglement, fix (*Inf.*), imbroglio,

impasse, jam (*Inf.*), muddle, pass, pickle (*Inf.*), pinch, plight, predicament, quandary, scrape (*Inf.*)

quail blanch, blench, cower, cringe, droop, faint, falter, flinch, have cold feet (*Inf.*), quake, recoil, shake, shrink, shudder, tremble

quaint 1. bizarre, curious, droll, eccentric,

fanciful, fantastic, odd, old-fashioned, original, peculiar, queer, singular, strange, unusual, whimsical **2.** antiquated, antique, artful, charming, gothic, ingenious, old-fashioned, old-world, picturesque

quake convulse, move, pulsate, quail, quiv-

Quaker ('kweɪkə) n. 1. a member of the Society of Friends, a Christian sect founded by George Fox about 1650. Quakers reject sacraments, ritual, and formal ministry, and have promoted many causes for social reform. ~adj. 2. of the Society of Friends or its beliefs or practices. —'**Quakeress** fem. n. —'**Quakerish** adj. —'**Quakerism** n.

qualification (ˌkwɒlɪfɪ'keɪʃən) n. 1. an ability, quality, or attribute, esp. one that fits a person to perform a particular job or task. 2. a condition that modifies or limits; restriction. 3. a qualifying or being qualified.

qualified ('kwɒlɪˌfaɪd) adj. 1. having the abilities, qualities, attributes, etc., necessary to perform a particular job or task. 2. limited, modified, or restricted; not absolute.

qualify ('kwɒlɪˌfaɪ) vb. -fying, -fied. 1. to provide or be provided with the abilities or attributes necessary for a task, office, duty, etc.: his degree qualifies him for the job. 2. (tr.) to make less strong, harsh, or violent; moderate or restrict. 3. (tr.) to modify or change the strength or flavour of. 4. (tr.) Grammar. another word for **modify**. 5. (tr.) to attribute a quality to; characterize. 6. (intr.) to progress to the final stages of a competition, as by winning preliminary contests. —'**quali,fiable** adj. —'**quali,fier** n.

qualitative ('kwɒlɪtətɪv) adj. involving or relating to distinctions based on quality or qualities. —'**qualitatively** adv.

qualitative analysis n. See **analysis** (sense 4).

quality ('kwɒlɪtɪ) n., pl. -ties. 1. a distinguishing characteristic or attribute. 2. the basic character or nature of something. 3. a feature of personality. 4. degree or standard of excellence, esp. a high standard. 5. (formerly) high social status or the distinction associated with it. 6. musical tone colour; timbre. 7. Logic. the characteristic of a proposition that makes it affirmative or negative. 8. Phonetics. the distinctive character of a vowel, determined by the configuration of the mouth, tongue, etc. 9. (modifier) having or showing excellence or superiority: a quality product.

quality control n. control of the relative quality of a manufactured product, usually by statistical sampling techniques.

qualm (kwɑːm) n. 1. a sudden feeling of sickness or nausea. 2. a pang of doubt, esp. concerning moral conduct; scruple. 3. a sudden sensation of misgiving. —'**qualmish** adj.

quandary ('kwɒndrɪ) n., pl. -ries. a difficult situation; predicament; dilemma.

quango ('kwæŋgəʊ) n., pl. -gos. acronym for quasi-autonomous national government organization or quasi-autonomous non-governmental organization.

quantify ('kwɒntɪˌfaɪ) vb. -fying, -fied. (tr.) 1. to discover or express the quantity of. 2. Logic. to specify the quantity of (a term) by using a quantifier, such as all, some, or no. —'**quantifiable** adj. —,**quantifi'cation** n.

quantitative ('kwɒntɪtətɪv) or **quantitive** adj. 1. involving or relating to considerations of amount or size. 2. capable of being measured. 3. Prosody. of a metrical system that is based on the length of syllables. —'**quantitatively** or '**quantitively** adv.

quantitative analysis n. See **analysis** (sense 4).

quantity ('kwɒntɪtɪ) n., pl. -ties. 1. a. a specified or definite amount, number, etc. b. (as modifier): a quantity estimate. 2. the aspect of anything that can be measured, weighed, counted, etc. 3. a large amount. 4. Maths. an entity having a magnitude that is denoted by a constant, a variable, or a combination of both. 5. Physics. a specified magnitude or amount. 6. Logic. the characteristic of a proposition that makes it universal or particular. 7. Prosody. the relative duration of a syllable or the vowel in it.

quantity surveyor n. a person who estimates the cost of the materials and labour necessary for a construction job.

quantum ('kwɒntəm) n., pl. -ta (-tə). 1. Physics. a. the smallest quantity of some physical property that a system can possess according to the quantum theory. b. a particle with such a unit of energy. 2. amount or quantity, esp. a specific amount. ~adj. 3. of or designating a major breakthrough or sudden advance: a quantum leap forward.

quantum mechanics n. the branch of mechanics, based on the quantum theory, used for interpreting the behaviour of elementary particles and atoms, which do not obey Newtonian mechanics.

quantum theory n. a theory concerning the behaviour of physical systems based on the idea that they can only possess certain properties, such as energy and angular momentum, in discrete amounts (quanta).

quarantine ('kwɒrənˌtiːn) n. 1. a period of isolation or detention, esp. of persons or animals arriving from abroad, to prevent the spread of disease. 2. the place where such detention is enforced. 3. any period or state of enforced isolation. ~vb. 4. (tr.) to isolate in or as if in quarantine.

quark (kwɑːk) n. Physics. any of four or more hypothetical elementary particles postulated to be fundamental units of all baryons and mesons.

quarrel ('kwɒrəl) n. 1. an angry disagreement; argument. 2. a cause of dispute; grievance. ~vb. -relling, -relled or U.S. -reling, -reled. (intr.; often foll. by with) 3. to engage in a disagreement or dispute; argue. 4. to find fault; complain. —'**quarreller** n.

quarrelsome ('kwɒrəlsəm) adj. inclined to quarrel or disagree; belligerent.

quarry[1] ('kwɒrɪ) n., pl. -ries. 1. an open surface excavation for the extraction of building stone, slate, marble, etc. 2. a copious source, esp. of information. ~vb. -rying, -ried. 3. to extract (stone, etc.) from or as if from a quarry. 4. (tr.) to excavate a quarry in. 5. to obtain (something) diligently and laboriously.

quarry[2] ('kwɒrɪ) n., pl. -ries. 1. an animal, etc. that is hunted, esp. by other animals; prey. 2. anything pursued.

quarry tile n. an unglazed floor tile.

quart (kwɔːt) n. 1. a unit of liquid measure equal to a quarter of a gallon or two pints. 1 U.S. quart (0.946 litre)

THESAURUS

er, rock, shake, shiver, shudder, throb, totter, tremble, vibrate, waver, wobble

qualification 1. ability, accomplishment, aptitude, attribute, capability, capacity, eligibility, endowment(s), fitness, quality, skill, suitability, suitableness 2. allowance, caveat, condition, criterion, exception, exemption, limitation, modification, objection, prerequisite, proviso, requirement, reservation, restriction, stipulation

qualified 1. able, accomplished, adept, capable, certificated, competent, efficient, equipped, experienced, expert, fit, knowledgeable, licensed, practised, proficient, skilful, talented, trained 2. bounded, circumscribed, conditional, confined, contingent, equivocal, guarded, limited, modified, provisional, reserved, restricted

qualify 1. capacitate, certify, commission, condition, empower, endow, equip, fit, ground, permit, prepare, ready, sanction, train 2. abate, adapt, assuage, circumscribe, diminish, ease, lessen, limit, mitigate, moderate, modify, modulate, reduce, regulate, re-

strain, restrict, soften, temper, vary 3. characterize, describe, designate, distinguish, modify, name

quality 1. aspect, attribute, characteristic, condition, feature, mark, peculiarity, property, trait 2. character, constitution, description, essence, kind, make, nature, sort 3. calibre, distinction, excellence, grade, merit, position, pre-eminence, rank, standing, status, superiority, value, worth 4. Obsolete aristocracy, gentry, nobility, ruling class, upper class

qualm 1. anxiety, apprehension, compunction, disquiet, doubt, hesitation, misgiving, regret, reluctance, remorse, scruple, twinge or pang of conscience, uncertainty, uneasiness 2. agony, attack, nausea, pang, queasiness, sickness, spasm, throe (Rare), twinge

quandary bewilderment, cleft stick, delicate situation, difficulty, dilemma, doubt, embarrassment, impasse, perplexity, plight, predicament, puzzle, strait, uncertainty

quantity 1. aggregate, allotment, amount, lot, number, part, portion, quota, sum, total 2.

bulk, capacity, expanse, extent, greatness, length, magnitude, mass, measure, size, volume

quarrel n. 1. affray, altercation, argument, brawl, breach, broil, commotion, contention, controversy, difference (of opinion), disagreement, discord, disputation, dispute, dissension, dissidence, disturbance, feud, fight, fracas, fray, misunderstanding, row, scrap (Inf.), spat, squabble, strife, tiff, tumult, vendetta, wrangle ~v. 2. altercate, argue, bicker, brawl, clash, differ, disagree, dispute, fall out (Inf.), fight, row, spar, squabble, wrangle 3. carp, cavil, complain, decry, disapprove, find fault, object to, take exception to

quarrelsome argumentative, belligerent, cat-and-dog (Inf.), choleric, combative, contentious, cross, disputatious, fractious, ill-tempered, irascible, irritable, peevish, petulant, pugnacious, querulous

quarry aim, game, goal, objective, prey, prize, victim

is equal to 0.8326 U.K. quart. 1 U.K. quart (1.136 litres) is equal to 1.2009 U.S. quarts. **2.** a unit of dry measure equal to 2 pints or one eighth of a peck.

quarter ('kwɔːtə) n. **1.** one of four equal parts of an object, quantity, etc. **2.** the fraction equal to one divided by four (1/4). **3.** U.S., Canad., etc. a 25-cent piece. **4.** a unit of weight equal to a quarter of a hundredweight. 1 U.S. quarter is equal to 25 pounds; 1 Brit. quarter is equal to 28 pounds. **5.** a quarter-hour. **6.** a fourth part of a year; three months. **7.** Astron. **a.** one fourth of the moon's period of revolution around the earth. **b.** either of two phases of the moon when half of the lighted surface is visible. **8.** Inf. a unit of weight equal to a quarter of a pound or 4 ounces. **9.** Brit. a unit of capacity for grain, etc., usually equal to 8 U.K. bushels. **10.** Sport. one of the four periods into which certain games are divided. **11.** Naut. the part of a vessel's side towards the stern. **12.** a region or district of a town or city: the Spanish quarter. **13.** a region, direction, or point of the compass. **14.** (sometimes pl.) an unspecified person or group of people: to get word from the highest quarter. **15.** mercy or pity, as shown to a defeated opponent (esp. in **ask for** or **give quarter**). **16.** any of the four limbs, including the adjacent parts, of a quadruped or bird. **17.** Heraldry. one of four quadrants into which a shield may be divided. ~vb. **18.** (tr.) to divide into four equal parts. **19.** (tr.) to divide into any number of parts. **20.** (tr.) (esp. formerly) to dismember (a human body). **21.** to billet or be billeted in lodgings, esp. (of military personnel) in civilian lodgings. **22.** (intr.) (of hounds) to range over an area of ground in search of game or the scent of quarry. **23.** (intr.) Naut. (of the wind) to blow onto a vessel's quarter. **24.** (tr.) Heraldry. **a.** to divide (a shield) into four separate bearings. **b.** to place (one set of arms) in diagonally opposite quarters to another. ~adj. **25.** being or consisting of one of four equal parts. ~See also **quarters**.

quarter day n. any of four days in the year when certain payments become due. In England, Wales, and Ireland these are Lady Day, Midsummer Day, Michaelmas, and Christmas. In Scotland they are Candlemas, Whit Sunday, Lammas, and Martinmas.

quarterdeck ('kwɔːtə,dɛk) n. Naut. the after part of the weather deck of a ship, traditionally the deck for official or ceremonial use.

quarterfinal (,kwɔːtə'faɪnəl) n. the round before the semifinal in a competition.

quartering ('kwɔːtərɪŋ) n. **1.** Mil. the allocation of accommodation to service personnel. **2.** Heraldry. **a.** the marshalling of several coats of arms on one shield, usually representing intermarriages. **b.** any coat of arms marshalled in this way.

quarterlight ('kwɔːtə,laɪt) n. Brit. a small pivoted window in the door of a car for ventilation.

quarterly ('kwɔːtəlɪ) adj. **1.** occurring, done, paid, etc., at intervals of three months. **2.** of, relating to, or consisting of a quarter. ~n., pl. **-lies. 3.** a periodical issued every three months. ~adv. **4.** once every three months.

quartermaster ('kwɔːtə,mɑːstə) n. **1.** an officer responsible for accommodation, food, and equipment in a military unit. **2.** a rating in the navy, usually a petty officer, with particular responsibility for navigational duties.

quartern ('kwɔːtən) n. **1.** a fourth part of certain weights or measures. **2.** Also called: **quartern loaf.** Brit. **a.** a type of loaf 4 inches square. **b.** any loaf weighing 1600 g.

quarters ('kwɔːtəz) pl. n. **1.** accommodation, esp. as provided for military personnel. **2.** the stations assigned to crew members of a warship: general quarters.

quarter sessions n. (formerly) a criminal court held four times a year before justices of the peace or a re-

corder, empowered to try all but the most serious offences.

quarterstaff ('kwɔːtə,stɑːf) n., pl. **-staves** (-,steɪvz). a stout iron-tipped wooden staff about 6ft. long, formerly used as a weapon.

quartet or **quartette** (kwɔː'tɛt) n. **1.** a group of four singers or instrumentalists or a piece of music composed for such a group. **2.** any group of four.

quartile ('kwɔːtaɪl) n. **1.** Statistics. one of three values of a variable dividing its distribution into four groups with equal frequencies. ~adj. **2.** Statistics. of a quartile. **3.** Astrol. denoting an aspect of two heavenly bodies when their longitudes differ by 90°.

quarto ('kwɔːtəʊ) n., pl. **-tos.** a book size resulting from folding a sheet of paper into four leaves or eight pages.

quartz (kwɔːts) n. a hard glossy mineral consisting of silicon dioxide in crystalline form. It occurs as colourless rock crystal and as several impure coloured varieties including agate, chalcedony, flint, and amethyst. Formula: SiO_2.

quartzite ('kwɔːtsaɪt) n. **1.** a sandstone composed of quartz. **2.** a very hard rock consisting of intergrown quartz crystals.

quartz timepiece n. a watch or clock that is operated by a vibrating quartz crystal.

quasar ('kweɪzɑː, -sɑː) n. any of a class of quasi-stellar objects that are powerful sources of radio waves and other forms of energy. Many have large red shifts which imply distances of several thousand million light years.

quash (kwɒʃ) vb. (tr.) **1.** to subdue forcefully and completely. **2.** to annul or make void (a law, etc.). **3.** to reject (an indictment, etc.) as invalid.

quasi- combining form. **1.** almost but not really; seemingly: a quasi-religious cult. **2.** resembling but not actually being; so-called: a quasi-scholar.

quassia ('kwɒʃə) n. **1.** any of a genus of tropical American trees having bitter bark and wood. **2.** the wood of this tree or a bitter compound extracted from it, formerly used as a tonic and vermifuge, now used in insecticides.

quaternary (kwə'tɜːnərɪ) adj. **1.** consisting of fours or by fours. **2.** fourth in a series. **3.** Chem. containing or being an atom bound to four other atoms or groups. ~n., pl. **-naries. 4.** the number four or a set of four.

Quaternary (kwə'tɜːnərɪ) adj. **1.** of or denoting the most recent period of geological time, which succeeded the Tertiary period one million years ago. ~n. **2. the.** the Quaternary period or rock system.

quatrain ('kwɒtreɪn) n. a stanza or poem of four lines.

quatrefoil ('kætrə,fɔɪl) n. **1.** a leaf composed of four leaflets. **2.** Archit. a carved ornament having four foils arranged about a common centre.

quattrocento (,kwætrəʊ'tʃɛntəʊ) n. the 15th century, esp. in reference to Renaissance Italian art and literature.

quaver ('kweɪvə) vb. **1.** to say or sing (something) with a trembling voice. **2.** (intr.) (esp. of the voice) to quiver or tremble. **3.** (intr.) Rare. to sing or play trills. ~n. **4.** Music. a note having the time value of an eighth of a semibreve. Usual U.S. name: **eighth note. 5.** a tremulous sound or note. —'**quaverer** n. —'**quaveringly** adv.

quay (kiː) n. a wharf, typically one built parallel to the shoreline.

Que. abbrev. for Quebec.

quean (kwiːn) n. **1.** Arch. **a.** a boisterous impudent woman. **b.** a prostitute. **2.** Scot. an unmarried girl.

queasy ('kwiːzɪ) adj. **-sier, -siest. 1.** having the feeling that one is about to vomit; nauseous. **2.** feeling or causing uneasiness. —'**queasily** adv. —'**queasiness** n.

Quebecker or **Quebecer** (kwɪ'bɛkə, kə'bɛkə) n. a native or inhabitant of Quebec.

THESAURUS

quarter n. **1.** area, direction, district, locality, location, neighbourhood, part, place, point, position, province, region, side, spot, station, territory, zone **2.** clemency, compassion, favour, forgiveness, leniency, mercy, pity ~v. **3.** accommodate, billet, board, house, install, lodge, place, post, put up, station

quarters abode, accommodation, barracks, billet, cantonment (Military), cham-

bers, digs (Inf.), domicile, dwelling, habitation, lodging, lodgings, post, residence, rooms, shelter, station

quash 1. beat, crush, destroy, extinguish, extirpate, overthrow, put down, quell, quench, repress, squash, subdue, suppress **2.** annul, cancel, declare null and void, invalidate, nullify, overrule, overthrow, rescind, reverse, revoke, set aside, void

quasi- 1. almost, apparently, partly, seem-

ingly, supposedly **2.** apparent, fake, mock, near, nominal, pretended, pseudo-, seeming, semi-, sham, so-called, synthetic, virtual, would-be

quaver 1. v. flicker, flutter, oscillate, pulsate, quake, quiver, shake, shudder, thrill, tremble, trill, twitter, vibrate, waver **2.** n. break, quiver, shake, sob, throb, tremble, trembling, tremor, trill, vibration, warble

queen (kwi:n) *n.* **1.** the wife of a king. **2.** a female sovereign who is the official ruler or head of state. **3.** a woman or a thing personified as a woman considered the best or most important of her kind: *the queen of ocean liners.* **4.** *Inf.* a male homosexual. **5.** the only fertile female in a colony of bees, ants, etc. **6.** a playing card bearing the picture of a queen. **7.** the most powerful chess piece, able to move in a straight line in any direction or diagonally. ~*vb.* **8.** *Chess.* to promote (a pawn) to a queen when it reaches the eighth rank. **9.** (*tr.*) to crown as queen. **10.** (*intr.*) to reign as queen. **11. queen it.** (often foll. by *over*) *Inf.* to behave in an overbearing manner. —'**queenly** *adj.*

Queen-Anne *n.* **1.** a style of furniture popular in England about 1700–20 and in America about 1720–70, characterized by the use of curves, walnut veneer, and the cabriole leg. ~*adj.* **2.** in or of this style. **3.** of a style of architecture popular in early 18th-century England, characterized by red-brick construction with classical ornamentation.

Queen Anne's lace *n.* another name for the **wild carrot.**

queen consort *n.* the wife of a reigning king.

queen dowager *n.* the widow of a king.

queen mother *n.* the widow of a former king who is also the mother of the reigning sovereign.

queen post *n.* one of a pair of vertical posts that connect the tie beam of a truss to the principal rafters.

Queen's Bench *n.* (in England when the sovereign is female) one of the divisions of the High Court of Justice.

Queensberry rules ('kwi:nzbərɪ) *pl. n.* **1.** the code of rules followed in modern boxing. **2.** *Inf.* gentlemanly conduct, esp. in a dispute.

Queen's Counsel *n.* **1.** (in England when the sovereign is female) a barrister appointed Counsel to the Crown on the recommendation of the Lord Chancellor. **2.** (in Canada) an honorary title which may be bestowed by the government on lawyers with long experience.

Queen's English *n.* (when the British sovereign is female) standard Southern British English.

queen's evidence *n. English law.* (when the sovereign is female) evidence given for the Crown against his former associates in crime by an accomplice (esp. in **turn queen's evidence**). U.S. equivalent: **state's evidence.**

queen's highway *n.* **1.** (in Britain when the sovereign is female) any public road or right of way. **2.** (in Canada), a main road maintained by the provincial government.

queer (kwɪə) *adj.* **1.** differing from the normal or usual; odd or strange. **2.** dubious; shady. **3.** faint, giddy, or queasy. **4.** *Inf.* homosexual. **5.** *Inf.* eccentric or slightly mad. **6.** *Sl.* worthless or counterfeit. ~*n.* **7.** *Inf.* a homosexual. ~*vb.* (*tr.*) *Inf.* **8.** to spoil or thwart (esp. in **queer someone's pitch**). **9.** to put in a difficult position. —'**queerly** *adv.* —'**queerness** *n.*

queer street *n.* (*sometimes cap.*) *Inf.* a difficult situation, such as debt or bankruptcy (in **in queer street**).

quell (kwɛl) *vb.* (*tr.*) **1.** to suppress (rebellion, etc.); sub-

due. **2.** to overcome or allay. —'**queller** *n.*

quench (kwɛntʃ) *vb.* (*tr.*) **1.** to satisfy (one's thirst, desires, etc.); slake. **2.** to put out (a fire, etc.); extinguish. **3.** to put down; suppress; subdue. **4.** to cool (hot metal) by plunging it into cold water. —'**quenchable** *adj.* —'**quencher** *n.*

quern (kwɜ:n) *n.* a stone hand mill for grinding corn.

querulous ('kwɛrʊləs, 'kwɛrjʊ-) *adj.* **1.** inclined to make whining or peevish complaints. **2.** characterized by or proceeding from a complaining fretful attitude or disposition. —'**querulously** *adv.* —'**querulousness** *n.*

query ('kwɪərɪ) *n., pl.* **-ries.** **1.** a question, esp. one expressing doubt. **2.** a question mark. ~*vb.* **-rying, -ried.** (*tr.*) **3.** to express uncertainty, doubt, or an objection concerning (something). **4.** to put a question to (a person); ask.

quest (kwɛst) *n.* **1.** a looking for or seeking; search. **2.** (in medieval romance) an expedition by a knight or knights to accomplish some task, such as finding the Holy Grail. **3.** the object of a search; a goal or target. ~*vb.* (*mainly intr.*) **4.** (foll. by *for* or *after*) to go in search (of). **5.** (of dogs, etc.) to search for game. **6.** (*also tr.*) *Arch.* to seek or pursue. —'**quester** *n.* —'**questingly** *adv.*

question ('kwɛstʃən) *n.* **1.** a form of words addressed to a person in order to elicit information or evoke a response; interrogative sentence. **2.** a point at issue: *it's only a question of time until she dies.* **3.** a difficulty or uncertainty. **4. a.** an act of asking. **b.** an investigation into some problem. **5.** a motion presented for debate. **6. put the question.** to require members of a deliberative assembly to vote on a motion presented. **7.** *Law.* a matter submitted to a court or other tribunal. **8. beg the question. a.** to avoid giving a direct answer by posing another question. **b.** to assume the truth of that which is intended to be proved. **9. beyond (all) question.** beyond (any) dispute or doubt. **10. call in** or **into question. a.** to make (something) the subject of disagreement. **b.** to cast doubt upon the validity, truth, etc., of (something). **11. in question.** under discussion: *this is the man in question.* **12. out of the question.** beyond consideration; unthinkable or impossible. **13. pop the question.** *Inf.* to ask a girl to marry one. **14. put to the question.** (formerly) to interrogate by torture. ~*vb.* (*mainly tr.*) **15.** to put a question or questions to (a person); interrogate. **16.** to make (something) the subject of dispute. **17.** to express uncertainty about the validity, truth, etc., of (something); doubt. —'**questioner** *n.*

questionable ('kwɛstʃənəbəl) *adj.* **1.** (esp. of a person's morality or honesty) admitting of some doubt; dubious. **2.** of disputable value or authority. —'**questionableness** *n.* —'**questionably** *adv.*

question mark *n.* **1.** the punctuation mark **?**, used at the end of questions and in other contexts where doubt or ignorance is implied. **2.** this mark used for any other purpose, as to draw attention to a possible mistake.

question master *n. Brit.* the chairman of a radio or television quiz or panel game.

questionnaire (ˌkwɛstʃə'nɛə, ˌkɛs-) *n.* a set of questions on a form, submitted to a number of people in or-

---

THESAURUS

queen 1. consort, monarch, ruler, sovereign 2. diva, doyenne, ideal, idol, mistress, model, perfection, prima donna, star

queenly grand, imperial, majestic, noble, regal, royal, stately

queer *adj.* 1. abnormal, anomalous, atypical, curious, disquieting, droll, eerie, erratic, extraordinary, funny, odd, outlandish, *outré*, peculiar, remarkable, singular, strange, uncanny, uncommon, unconventional, unnatural, unorthodox, unusual, weird 2. doubtful, dubious, fishy (*Inf.*), irregular, mysterious, puzzling, questionable, shady (*Inf.*), suspicious 3. dizzy, faint, giddy, light-headed, queasy, reeling, uneasy 4. crazy, demented, eccentric, idiosyncratic, irrational, mad, odd, touched, unbalanced, unhinged ~*v.* 5. botch, endanger, harm, impair, imperil, injure, jeopardize, mar, ruin, spoil, thwart, wreck

quell 1. conquer, crush, defeat, extinguish, overcome, overpower, put down, quash, squelch, stamp out, stifle, subdue, suppress, vanquish 2. allay, alleviate, appease, as-

suage, calm, compose, deaden, dull, mitigate, moderate, mollify, pacify, quiet, silence, soothe

quench 1. check, crush, destroy, douse, end, extinguish, put out, smother, snuff out, squelch, stifle, suppress 2. allay, appease, cool, sate, satiate, satisfy, slake

querulous cantankerous, captious, carping, censorious, complaining, critical, cross, discontented, dissatisfied, fault-finding, fretful, grouchy (*Inf.*), grumbling, hard to please, irascible, irritable, murmuring, peevish, petulant, plaintive, sour, testy, touchy, waspish, whining

query *v.* 1. ask, enquire, question 2. challenge, disbelieve, dispute, distrust, doubt, mistrust, suspect ~*n.* 3. demand, doubt, hesitation, inquiry, objection, problem, question, reservation, scepticism, suspicion

quest *n.* adventure, crusade, enterprise, expedition, exploration, hunt, journey, mission, pilgrimage, pursuit, search, voyage

question *v.* 1. ask, catechize, cross-

examine, enquire, examine, grill (*Inf.*), interrogate, interview, investigate, probe, pump (*Inf.*), quiz, sound out 2. call into question, cast doubt upon, challenge, controvert, disbelieve, dispute, distrust, doubt, impugn, mistrust, oppose, query, suspect ~*n.* 3. examination, inquiry, interrogation, investigation 4. argument, confusion, contention, controversy, debate, difficulty, dispute, doubt, dubiety, misgiving, problem, query, uncertainty 5. issue, motion, point, point at issue, proposal, proposition, subject, theme, topic 6. **in question** at issue, in doubt, open to debate, under discussion 7. **out of the question** impossible, inconceivable, not to be thought of, unthinkable

questionable arguable, controversial, controvertible, debatable, disputable, doubtful, dubious, dubitable, equivocal, fishy (*Inf.*), moot, paradoxical, problematical, shady (*Inf.*), suspect, suspicious, uncertain, unproven, unreliable

der to collect statistical information.

question time n. (in parliamentary bodies of the British type) the time set aside each day for questions to government ministers.

queue (kjuː) *Chiefly Brit.* ~n. **1.** a line of people, vehicles, etc., waiting for something. ~vb. **queuing, queued.** **2.** (*intr.*, often foll. by *up*) to form or remain in a line while waiting. ~*U.S.* word: **line.**

quibble ('kwɪbəl) vb. (intr.) **1.** to make trivial objections. **2.** *Arch.* to play on words; pun. ~n. **3.** a trivial objection or equivocation, esp. one used to avoid an issue. **4.** *Arch.* a pun. —'**quibbler** n. —'**quibblingly** adv.

quiche (kiːʃ) n. an open savoury tart with an egg custard filling to which bacon, onion, cheese, etc., are added.

quick (kwɪk) adj. **1.** performed or occurring during a comparatively short time: *a quick move.* **2.** lasting a short time; brief. **3.** accomplishing something in a time that is shorter than normal: *a quick worker.* **4.** characterized by rapidity of movement; fast. **5.** immediate or prompt. **6.** (*postpositive*) eager or ready to perform (an action): *quick to criticize.* **7.** responsive to stimulation; alert; lively. **8.** eager or enthusiastic for learning. **9.** easily excited or aroused. **10.** nimble in one's movements or actions; deft: *quick fingers.* **11.** *Arch.* **a.** alive; living. **b.** (*as n.*) living people (esp. in **the quick and the dead**). **12. quick with child.** *Arch.* pregnant. ~n. **13.** any area of sensitive flesh, esp. that under a toenail or fingernail. **14.** the most important part (of a thing). **15. cut (someone) to the quick.** to hurt (a person's) feelings deeply. ~adv. *Inf.* **16.** in a rapid manner; swiftly. **17.** soon: *I hope he comes quick.* ~interj. **18.** a command to perform an action immediately. —'**quickly** adv. —'**quickness** n.

quick-change artist n. an actor or entertainer who undertakes several rapid changes of costume during his performance.

quicken ('kwɪkən) vb. **1.** to make or become faster; accelerate. **2.** to impart to or receive vigour, enthusiasm, etc.: *science quickens man's imagination.* **3.** to make or become alive; revive. **4. a.** (of an unborn foetus) to begin to show signs of life. **b.** (of a pregnant woman) to reach the stage of pregnancy at which movements can be felt.

quick-freeze vb. **-freezing, -froze, -frozen.** (tr.) to preserve (food) by subjecting it to rapid refrigeration at temperatures of 0°C or lower.

quickie ('kwɪkɪ) n. *Inf.* **1.** Also called (esp. Brit.): **quick one.** a speedily consumed alcoholic drink. **2.** anything made or done rapidly.

quicklime ('kwɪk,laɪm) n. lime, or calcium oxide, which gives off much heat in combining with water; unslaked lime.

quicksand ('kwɪk,sænd) n. a deep mass of loose wet sand that sucks anything on top of it inextricably into it.

quickset ('kwɪk,sɛt) *Chiefly Brit.* ~n. **1. a.** a plant or cutting, esp. of hawthorn, set so as to form a hedge. **b.** such plants or cuttings collectively. **2.** a hedge composed of such plants. ~adj. **3.** composed of such plants.

quicksilver ('kwɪk,sɪlvə) n. **1.** another name for **mercury** (sense 1). ~adj. **2.** rapid or unpredictable in movement or change.

quickstep ('kwɪk,stɛp) n. **1.** a modern ballroom dance in rapid quadruple time. **2.** a piece of music composed for or in the rhythm of this dance. ~vb. **-stepping, -stepped. 3.** (intr.) to perform this dance.

quick-tempered adj. readily roused to anger; irascible.

quick time n. *Mil.* the normal marching rate of 120 paces to the minute.

quick-witted adj. having a keenly alert mind, esp. as used to avert danger, make effective reply, etc. —,**quick-'wittedly** adv. —,**quick-'wittedness** n.

quid[1] (kwɪd) n. a piece of tobacco, suitable for chewing.

quid[2] (kwɪd) n., pl. **quid.** *Brit.* a slang word for **pound** (sterling).

quiddity ('kwɪdɪtɪ) n., pl. **-ties. 1.** the essential nature of something. **2.** a petty or trifling distinction; quibble.

quid pro quo ('kwɪd prəʊ 'kwəʊ) n., pl. **quid pro quos. 1.** a reciprocal exchange. **2.** something given in compensation, esp. an advantage or object given in exchange for another.

quiescent (kwɪ'ɛsənt) adj. quiet, inactive, or dormant. —**qui'escence** or **qui'escency** n. —**qui'escently** adv.

quiet ('kwaɪət) adj. **1.** characterized by an absence of noise. **2.** calm or tranquil: *the sea is quiet tonight.* **3.** free from activities, distractions, etc.; untroubled: *a quiet life.* **4.** private; not public; secret: *a quiet word with someone.* **5.** free from anger, impatience, or other extreme emotion. **6.** free from pretentiousness; modest or reserved: *quiet humour.* **7.** *Astron.* (of the sun) exhibiting a very low number of sunspots, solar flares, etc.; inactive. ~n. **8.** the state of being silent, peaceful, or untroubled. **9. on the quiet.** without other people knowing. ~vb. **10.** a less common word for **quieten.** —'**quietly** adv. —'**quietness** n.

quieten ('kwaɪətən) vb. *Chiefly Brit.* **1.** (often foll. by *down*) to make or become calm, silent, etc. **2.** (tr.) to allay (fear, doubts, etc.).

quietism ('kwaɪə,tɪzəm) n. a form of religious mysticism originating in Spain in the late 17th century, requiring complete passivity to God's will. —'**quietist** n., adj.

quietude ('kwaɪə,tjuːd) n. the state or condition of being quiet, peaceful, calm, or tranquil.

quietus (kwaɪ'iːtəs, -'eɪtəs) n., pl. **-tuses. 1.** anything that serves to quash, eliminate, or kill. **2.** a release from life; death. **3.** the discharge or settlement of debts, duties, etc.

THESAURUS

queue chain, concatenation, file, line, order, progression, sequence, series, string, succession, train

quibble 1. *v.* carp, cavil, equivocate, evade, pretend, prevaricate, shift, split hairs **2.** *n.* artifice, cavil, complaint, criticism, duplicity, equivocation, evasion, nicety, niggle, objection, pretence, prevarication, protest, quirk, shift, sophism, subterfuge, subtlety

quick 1. active, brief, brisk, cursory, expeditious, express, fast, fleet, hasty, headlong, hurried, perfunctory, prompt, rapid, speedy, sudden, swift **2.** agile, alert, animated, energetic, flying, keen, lively, nimble, spirited, sprightly, spry, vivacious, winged **3.** able, acute, adept, adroit, all there (*Inf.*), apt, astute, bright, clever, deft, dexterous, discerning, intelligent, nimble-witted, perceptive, quick on the uptake (*Inf.*), quick-witted, receptive, sharp, shrewd, skilful, smart **4.** abrupt, curt, excitable, hasty, impatient, irascible, irritable, passionate, petulant, testy, touchy **5.** *Archaic* alive, animate, existing, live, living, viable

quicken 1. accelerate, dispatch, expedite, hasten, hurry, impel, precipitate, speed **2.** activate, animate, arouse, energize, excite, galvanize, incite, inspire, invigorate, kindle, refresh, reinvigorate, resuscitate, revitalize, revive, rouse, stimulate, strengthen, vitalize, vivify

quickly abruptly, at a rate of knots (*Inf.*), at *or* on the double, at speed, briskly, expeditiously, fast, hastily, hell for leather, hurriedly, immediately, instantly, posthaste, promptly, quick, rapidly, soon, speedily, swiftly, with all speed

quick-tempered choleric, excitable, fiery, hot-tempered, impatient, impulsive, irascible, irritable, petulant, quarrelsome, shrewish, splenetic, testy, waspish

quick-witted alert, astute, clever, keen, perceptive, sharp, shrewd, smart

quid pro quo compensation, equivalent, exchange, interchange, reprisal, retaliation, substitution, tit for tat

quiescent calm, dormant, in abeyance, inactive, latent, motionless, peaceful, placid, quiet, resting, serene, silent, smooth, still, tranquil, unagitated, undisturbed, unmoving, unruffled

quiet adj. **1.** dumb, hushed, inaudible, low, low-pitched, noiseless, peaceful, silent, soft, soundless **2.** calm, contented, gentle, mild, motionless, pacific, peaceful, placid, restful, serene, smooth, tranquil, untroubled **3.** isolated, private, retired, secluded, secret, sequestered, undisturbed, unfrequented **4.** conservative, modest, plain, restrained, simple, sober, subdued, unassuming, unobtrusive, unpretentious **5.** collected, docile, even-tempered, gentle, imperturbable, meek, mild, phlegmatic, reserved, retiring, sedate, shy, unexcitable ~n. **6.** calmness, ease, peace, quietness, repose, rest, serenity, silence, stillness, tranquillity

quieten v. allay, alleviate, appease, assuage, blunt, calm, compose, deaden, dull, hush, lull, mitigate, mollify, muffle, mute, palliate, quell, quiet, shush (*Inf.*), silence, soothe, stifle, still, stop, subdue, tranquillize

quietly 1. confidentially, dumbly, in a low voice *or* whisper, in an undertone, inaudibly, in hushed tones, in silence, mutely, noiselessly, privately, secretly, silently, softly, without talking **2.** calmly, contentedly, dispassionately, meekly, mildly, patiently, placidly, serenely, undemonstratively **3.** coyly, demurely, diffidently, humbly, modestly, unassumingly, unobtrusively, unostentatiously, unpretentiously

quietness calm, calmness, hush, peace, placidity, quiescence, quiet, quietude, repose, rest, serenity, silence, still, stillness, tranquillity

quiff (kwɪf) *n. Brit.* a tuft of hair brushed up above the forehead.

quill (kwɪl) *n.* **1. a.** any of the large stiff feathers of the wing or tail of a bird. **b.** the long hollow part of a feather; calamus. **2.** Also called: **quill pen.** a feather made into a pen for writing. **3.** any of the stiff hollow spines of a porcupine or hedgehog. **4.** a device, formerly a crow's feather, for plucking a harpsichord string. **5.** a small roll of bark, esp. one of dried cinnamon. **6.** a bobbin or spindle. **7.** a fluted fold, as in a ruff. ~*vb.* (*tr.*) **8.** to wind (thread, etc.) onto a spool or bobbin. **9.** to make or press fluted folds in (a ruff, etc.).

quilt (kwɪlt) *n.* **1.** a cover for a bed, consisting of a soft filling sewn between two layers of material, usually with crisscross seams. **2.** a bedspread. **3.** anything resembling a quilt. ~*vb.* (*tr.*) **4.** to stitch together (two pieces of fabric) with (a thick padding or lining) between them. **5.** to create (a garment, etc.) in this way. **6.** to pad with material. —**'quilter** *n.*

quilting ('kwɪltɪŋ) *n.* **1.** material for quilts. **2.** the act of making a quilt. **3.** quilted work.

quin (kwɪn) *n. Brit. inf.* short for **quintuplet** (sense 1). *U.S.* word: **quint.**

quince (kwɪns) *n.* **1.** a small widely cultivated Asian tree with edible pear-shaped fruits. **2.** the fruit of this tree, much used in preserves.

quincentenary (ˌkwɪnsɛn'tiːnərɪ) *n., pl.* **-naries.** a 500th anniversary. —**quincentennial** (ˌkwɪnsɛn'tɛnɪəl) *adj., n.*

quincunx ('kwɪnkʌŋks) *n.* a group of five objects arranged in the shape of a rectangle with one at each of the four corners and the fifth in the centre. —**quincuncial** (kwɪn'kʌnʃəl) *adj.*

quinine (kwɪ'niːn; *U.S.* 'kwaɪnaɪn) *n.* a bitter crystalline alkaloid extracted from cinchona bark, the salts of which are used as a tonic, analgesic, etc., and in malaria therapy.

Quinquagesima (ˌkwɪŋkwə'dʒɛsɪmə) *n.* the Sunday preceding Lent. Also called: **Quinquagesima Sunday.**

quinquennial (kwɪn'kwɛnɪəl) *adj.* **1.** occurring once every five years or over a period of five years. ~*n.* **2.** a fifth anniversary. —**quin'quennially** *adv.*

quinquereme (ˌkwɪŋkwɪ'riːm) *n.* an ancient Roman galley with five banks of oars.

quinsy ('kwɪnzɪ) *n.* inflammation of the tonsils and surrounding tissues with the formation of abscesses.

quintal ('kwɪntəl) *n.* **1.** a unit of weight equal to (esp. in Britain) 112 pounds or (esp. in U.S.) 100 pounds. **2.** a unit of weight equal to 100 kilograms.

quintessence (kwɪn'tɛsəns) *n.* **1.** the most typical representation of a quality, state, etc. **2.** an extract of a substance containing its principle in its most concentrated form. **3.** (in ancient philosophy) ether, the fifth essence or element, which was thought to be the constituent matter of the heavenly bodies and latent in all things. —**quintessential** (ˌkwɪntɪ'sɛnʃəl) *adj.* —ˌquintes'sentially *adv.*

quintet or **quintette** (kwɪn'tɛt) *n.* **1.** a group of five singers or instrumentalists or a piece of music composed for such a group. **2.** any group of five.

quintillion (kwɪn'tɪljən) *n., pl.* **-lions** or **-lion.** **1.** (in Britain and Germany) the number represented as one followed by 30 zeros (10^{30}). *U.S.* word: **nonillion.** **2.** (in the U.S. and France) the number represented as one followed by 18 zeros (10^{18}). *Brit.* word: **trillion.** —**quin'tillionth** *adj.*

quintuple ('kwɪntjʊpəl, kwɪn'tjuːpəl) *vb.* **1.** to multiply by five. ~*adj.* **2.** five times as much or as many; five-

fold. **3.** consisting of five parts. ~*n.* **4.** a quantity or number five times as great as another.

quintuplet ('kwɪntjʊplɪt, kwɪn'tjuːplɪt) *n.* **1.** one of five offspring born at one birth. **2.** a group of five similar things. **3.** *Music.* a group of five notes to be played in a time value of three or four.

quip (kwɪp) *n.* **1.** a sarcastic remark. **2.** a witty saying. **3.** *Arch.* another word for quibble. ~*vb.* **quipping, quipped.** **4.** (*intr.*) to make a quip. —**'quipster** *n.*

quire (kwaɪə) *n.* **1.** a set of 24 or 25 sheets of paper. **2.** four sheets of paper folded to form 16 pages. **3.** a set of all the sheets in a book.

quirk (kwɜːk) *n.* **1.** a peculiarity of character; mannerism or foible. **2.** an unexpected twist or turn: *a quirk of fate.* **3.** a continuous groove in an architectural moulding. **4.** a flourish, as in handwriting. —**'quirkiness** *n.* —**'quirky** *adj.*

quisling ('kwɪzlɪŋ) *n.* a traitor who aids an occupying enemy force; collaborator.

quit (kwɪt) *vb.* **quitting, quit** or **quitted.** **1.** to desist or cease from (something or doing something). **2.** (*tr.*) to depart from; leave. **3.** to resign; give up (a job). **4.** to release one's grasp upon. **5.** (*tr.*) to pay off (a debt). **6.** (*tr.*) *Arch.* to conduct or acquit (oneself); comport (oneself). ~*adj.* **7.** (*usually predicative;* foll. by *of*) free (from); released (from). —**'quitter** *n.*

▷ **Usage.** Some users of English have felt that *quit* in the sense of *leave* is informal, but this use is quite standard at all levels of language. Careful users do not use *quit* to mean *cease* (*he never quit moaning*) because this is felt to be an Americanism.

quite (kwaɪt) *adv.* **1.** completely or absolutely: *you're quite right.* **2.** (*not used with a negative*) somewhat: *she's quite pretty.* **3.** in actuality; truly. **4. quite a** or **an.** (*not used with a negative*) of an exceptional, considerable, or noticeable kind: *quite a girl.* **5. quite something.** a remarkable or noteworthy thing or person. ~*sentence substitute.* **6.** Also: **quite so.** an expression used to indicate agreement.

▷ **Usage.** See at **very.**

quitrent ('kwɪt,rɛnt) *n.* (formerly) a rent payable by a freeholder or copyholder to his lord in lieu of services.

quits (kwɪts) *adj.* (*postpositive*) *Inf.* **1.** on an equal footing; even. **2. call it quits.** to agree to end a dispute, contest, etc., agreeing that honours are even.

quittance ('kwɪtəns) *n.* **1.** release from debt or other obligation. **2.** a receipt or other document certifying this.

quiver[1] ('kwɪvə) *vb.* **1.** (*intr.*) to shake with a tremulous movement; tremble. ~*n.* **2.** the state, process, or noise of shaking or trembling. —**'quivery** *adj.*

quiver[2] ('kwɪvə) *n.* a case for arrows.

quixotic (kwɪk'sɒtɪk) *adj.* preoccupied with an unrealistically optimistic or chivalrous approach to life; impractically idealistic. —**quix'otically** *adv.*

quiz (kwɪz) *n., pl.* **quizzes.** **1. a.** an entertainment in which the knowledge of the players is tested by a series of questions. **b.** (*as modifier*): *a quiz programme.* **2.** any set of quick questions designed to test knowledge. **3.** an investigation by close questioning. **4.** *Obs.* a practical joke. **5.** *Obs.* a puzzling individual. **6.** *Obs.* a person who habitually looks quizzically at others. ~*vb.* **quizzing, quizzed.** (*tr.*) **7.** to investigate by close questioning; interrogate. **8.** *U.S. inf.* to test the knowledge of (a student or class). **9.** (*tr.*) *Obs.* to look quizzically at, esp. through a small monocle. —**'quizzer** *n.*

quizzical ('kwɪzɪkəl) *adj.* questioning and mocking or supercilious. —**'quizzically** *adv.*

THESAURUS

quilt bedspread, comforter (*U.S.*), counterpane, coverlet, duvet, eiderdown

quintessence core, distillation, essence, extract, gist, heart, kernel, lifeblood, marrow, pith, soul, spirit

quip *n.* badinage, *bon mot*, gibe, jest, joke, pleasantry, repartee, retort, riposte, sally, wisecrack (*Inf.*), witticism

quirk aberration, caprice, characteristic, eccentricity, fancy, fetish, foible, habit, *idée fixe,* idiosyncrasy, kink, mannerism, oddity, peculiarity, singularity, trait, vagary, whim

quisling betrayer, collaborator, fifth columnist, Judas, renegade, traitor, turncoat

quit *v.* **1.** abandon, abdicate, decamp, depart, desert, exit, forsake, go, leave, pull out, relinquish, renounce, resign, retire, surrender, take off (*Inf.*), withdraw **2.** abandon, cease, conclude, discontinue, drop, end, give up, halt, stop, suspend ~*adj.* **3.** absolved, acquitted, clear, discharged, exculpated, exempt, exonerated, free, released, rid of

quite **1.** absolutely, completely, considerably, entirely, fully, in all respects, largely, perfectly, precisely, totally, wholly, without reservation **2.** fairly, moderately, rather, reasonably, relatively, somewhat, to a certain extent, to some degree **3.** in fact, in reality,

in truth, really, truly

quiver **1.** *v.* agitate, convulse, oscillate, palpitate, pulsate, quake, quaver, shake, shiver, shudder, tremble, vibrate **2.** *n.* convulsion, oscillation, palpitation, pulsation, shake, shiver, shudder, spasm, throb, tic, tremble, tremor, vibration

quiz **1.** *n.* examination, investigation, questioning, test **2.** *v.* ask, catechize, examine, grill (*Inf.*), interrogate, investigate, pump (*Inf.*), question

quod (kwɒd) *n. Chiefly Brit.* a slang word for jail.

quoin (kɔɪn, kwɔɪn) *n.* **1.** an external corner of a wall. **2.** a stone forming the external corner of a wall. **3.** another name for **keystone**. **4.** *Printing.* a wedge or an expanding device used to lock type up in a chase. **5.** a wedge used for any of various other purposes.

quoit (kɔɪt) *n.* a ring of iron, plastic, etc., used in the game of quoits.

quoits (kɔɪts) *pl. n. (usually functioning as sing.)* a game in which quoits are tossed at a stake in the ground in attempts to encircle it.

quondam ('kwɒndæm) *adj. (prenominal)* of an earlier time; former.

quorum ('kwɔ:rəm) *n.* a minimum number of members in an assembly, etc., required to be present before any business can be transacted.

quota ('kwəʊtə) *n.* **1.** the proportional share or part that is due from, due to, or allocated to a person or group. **2.** a prescribed number or quantity, as of items to be imported or students admitted to a college, etc.

quotation (kwəʊ'teɪʃən) *n.* **1.** a phrase or passage from a book, etc., remembered and spoken, esp. to support a point. **2.** the act or habit of quoting. **3.** *Commerce.* a statement of the current market price of a security or commodity. **4.** an estimate of costs submitted to a contractor to a prospective client. **5.** *Printing.* a quadrat used to fill up spaces.

quotation mark *n.* either of the punctuation marks used to begin or end a quotation, respectively " and " or ' and '

quote (kwəʊt) *vb.* **1.** to recite a quotation. **2.** *(tr.)* to put quotation marks round (a phrase, etc.). **3.** *Stock Exchange.* to state (a current market price) of (a security or commodity). ~*n.* **4.** an informal word for **quotation**. **5.** *(often pl.)* an informal word for **quotation mark**. ~*interj.* **6.** an expression used to indicate that the words that follow it form a quotation. —'**quotable** *adj.*

quoth (kwəʊθ) *vb. Arch.* (used with all pronouns except *thou* and *you*, and with nouns) said.

quotidian (kwəʊ'tɪdɪən) *adj.* **1.** (esp. of fever) recurring daily. **2.** commonplace. ~*n.* **3.** a fever characterized by attacks that recur daily.

quotient ('kwəʊʃənt) *n.* **1. a.** the result of the division of one number or quantity by another. **b.** the integral part of the result of division. **2.** a ratio of two numbers or quantities to be divided.

q.v. (denoting a cross-reference) *abbrev. for* quod vide.

THESAURUS

---

quota allocation, allowance, assignment, cut (*Inf.*), part, portion, proportion, ration, share, slice, whack (*Inf.*)

quotation 1. citation, cutting, excerpt, extract, passage, quote (*Inf.*), reference, selection **2.** *Commerce* bid price, charge, cost, estimate, figure, price, quote (*Inf.*), rate, tender

quote adduce, attest, cite, detail, extract, instance, name, paraphrase, proclaim, recall, recite, recollect, refer to, repeat, retell

R

r *or* **R** (ɑː) *n., pl.* **r's, R's** *or* **Rs.** **1.** the 18th letter of the English alphabet. **2.** a speech sound represented by this letter.

R *symbol for:* **1.** *Chem.* radical. **2.** *Currency.* **a.** rand. **b.** rupee. **3.** Réaumur (scale). **4.** *Physics, electronics.* resistance. **5.** roentgen *or* röntgen. **6.** *Chess.* rook. **7.** Royal. **8.** *Chem.* gas constant.

R. *abbrev. for:* **1.** rabbi. **2.** rector. **3.** Regiment. **4.** Regina: Queen. **5.** Republican. **6.** Rex: King. **7.** River. **8.** Royal.

R. *or* **r.** *abbrev. for:* **1.** radius. **2.** railway. **3.** registered (trademark). **4.** right. **5.** river. **6.** road. **7.** rouble.

Ra *the chemical symbol for* radium.

R.A. *abbrev. for:* **1.** rear admiral. **2.** *Astron.* right ascension. **3.** (in Britain) Royal Academician *or* Academy. **4.** (in Britain) Royal Artillery.

R.A.A.F. *abbrev. for* Royal Australian Air Force.

rabbet (ˈræbɪt) *n., vb.* another word for **rebate**².

rabbi (ˈræbaɪ) *n., pl.* **-bis.** **1.** the chief religious minister of a synagogue; the spiritual leader of a Jewish congregation. **2.** Also: **rabbin** (ˈræbɪn). a scholar learned in Jewish Law, esp. one authorized to teach it. —**rabbinical** (rəˈbɪnɪkəl) *or* **rab'binic** *adj.*

rabbit (ˈræbɪt) *n., pl.* **-bits** *or* **-bit.** **1.** any of various common gregarious burrowing mammals of Europe and North Africa. They are closely related and similar to hares but are smaller and have shorter ears. **2.** the fur of such an animal. **3.** *Brit. inf.* a poor performer at a game or sport. ~*vb.* (*intr.*) **4.** to hunt or shoot rabbits. **5.** (often foll. by *on* or *away*) *Brit. sl.* to talk inconsequentially; chatter.

rabbit punch *n.* a short sharp blow to the back of the neck that can cause loss of consciousness or even death. Austral. name: **rabbit killer.**

rabble (ˈræbəl) *n.* **1.** a disorderly crowd; mob. **2. the.** *Contemptuous.* the common people.

rabble-rouser *n.* a person who manipulates the passions of the mob; demagogue. —**'rabble-,rousing** *adj., n.*

Rabelaisian (ˌræbəˈleɪzɪən, -ʒən) *adj.* **1.** of, relating to, or resembling the work of François Rabelais (?1494-1553), French writer, esp. by broad, often bawdy humour and sharp satire. ~*n.* **2.** a student or admirer of Rabelais. —**Rabe'laisianism** *n.*

rabid (ˈræbɪd, ˈreɪ-) *adj.* **1.** relating to or having rabies. **2.** zealous; fanatical; violent; raging. —**rabidity** (rəˈbɪdɪtɪ) *or* **rabidness** *n.* —**'rabidly** *adv.*

rabies (ˈreɪbiːz) *n. Pathol.* an acute infectious viral disease of the nervous system transmitted by the saliva of infected animals, esp. dogs. —**rabic** (ˈræbɪk) *or* **rabietic** (ˌreɪbɪˈɛtɪk) *adj.*

R.A.C. *abbrev. for:* **1.** Royal Automobile Club. **2.** Royal Armoured Corps.

raccoon *or* **racoon** (rəˈkuːn) *n., pl.* **-coons** *or* **-coon.** **1.** an omnivorous mammal, esp. the **North American raccoon,** inhabiting forests of North and Central America. Raccoons have a pointed muzzle, long tail, and greyish-black fur with black bands around the tail and across the face. **2.** the fur of the raccoon.

race¹ (reɪs) *n.* **1.** a contest of speed, as in running, etc. **2.** any competition or rivalry. **3.** rapid or constant onward movement: *the race of time.* **4.** a rapid current of water, esp. one through a narrow channel that has a tidal range greater at one end than the other. **5.** a channel of a stream, esp. one for conducting water to or from a

water wheel for energy: *a mill race.* **6. a.** a channel or groove that contains ball bearings or roller bearings. **b.** the inner or outer cylindrical ring in a ball bearing or roller bearing. **7.** *Austral. & N.Z.* a narrow passage or enclosure in a sheep yard through which sheep pass individually, as to a sheep dip. **8.** *Austral.* a wire tunnel through which footballers pass from the changing room onto a football field. **9.** *Arch.* the span or course of life. ~*vb.* **10.** to engage in a contest of speed with (another). **11.** to engage in a race, esp. as a profession: *to race pigeons.* **12.** to move or go as fast as possible. **13.** to run (an engine, propeller, etc.) or (of an engine, propeller, etc.) to run at high speed, esp. after reduction of the load or resistance.

race² (reɪs) *n.* **1.** a group of people of common ancestry, distinguished from others by physical characteristics, such as hair type, colour of skin, stature, etc. **2. the human race.** human beings collectively. **3.** a group of animals or plants having common characteristics that distinguish them from other members of the same species, usually forming a geographically isolated group; subspecies. **4.** a group of people sharing the same interests, characteristics, etc.: *the race of authors.*

racecourse (ˈreɪsˌkɔːs) *n.* a long broad track, over which horses are raced. Also called (esp. U.S.): **racetrack.**

racehorse (ˈreɪsˌhɔːs) *n.* a horse specially bred for racing.

raceme (rəˈsiːm) *n.* an inflorescence in which the flowers are borne along the main stem. —**'race,mose** *adj.*

race meeting *n.* a prearranged fixture for racing horses (or greyhounds) over a set course.

race relations *n.* **1.** (*functioning as pl.*) the relations between members of two or more human races, esp. within a single community. **2.** (*functioning as sing.*) the branch of sociology concerned with such relations.

race riot *n.* a riot among members of different races in the same community.

races (ˈreɪsɪz) *pl. n.* **the.** a series of contests of speed between horses (or greyhounds) over a set course.

racetrack (ˈreɪsˌtræk) *n.* **1.** a circuit or course, esp. an oval one, used for motor racing, etc. **2.** the usual U.S. word for a **racecourse.**

racial (ˈreɪʃəl) *adj.* **1.** denoting or relating to the division of the human species into races on grounds of physical characteristics. **2.** characteristic of any such group. —**'racially** *adv.*

racialism (ˈreɪʃəˌlɪzəm) *or* **racism** *n.* **1.** the belief that races have distinctive cultural characteristics determined by hereditary factors and that this endows some races with an intrinsic superiority. **2.** abusive or aggressive behaviour towards members of another race on the basis of such a belief. —**'racialist** *or* **'racist** *n., adj.*

rack¹ (ræk) *n.* **1.** a framework for holding, carrying, or displaying a specific load or object. **2.** a toothed bar designed to engage a pinion to form a mechanism that will adjust the position of something. **3.** (preceded by *the*) an instrument of torture that stretched the body of the victim. **4.** a cause or state of mental or bodily stress, suffering, etc. (esp. in **on the rack**). **5.** *U.S.* (in pool, snooker, etc.) **a.** the triangular frame used to arrange the balls for the opening shot. **b.** the balls so grouped. Brit. equivalent: **frame.** ~*vb.* (*tr.*) **6.** to torture on the rack. **7.** to cause great suffering to: *guilt racked his conscience.* **8.** to strain or shake (something) violently: *the storm*

---

racked the town. **9.** to place or arrange in or on a rack. **10.** to move (parts of machinery or a mechanism) using a toothed rack. **11.** to raise (rents) exorbitantly. **12.** *Austral. sl.* **rack off.** go away. **13. rack one's brains.** to strain in mental effort. —'**racker** *n.*

rack² (ræk) *n.* destruction; wreck (obs. except in **go to rack and ruin**).

rack³ *or* **wrack** (ræk) *n.* **1.** a group of broken clouds moving in the wind. ~*vb.* **2.** (*intr.*) (of clouds) to be blown along by the wind.

rack⁴ (ræk) *vb.* (*tr.*) to clear (wine, beer, etc.) as by siphoning it off from the dregs.

rack-and-pinion *n.* **1.** a device for converting rotary into linear motion and vice versa, in which a gearwheel (the pinion) engages with a flat toothed bar (the rack). ~*adj.* **2.** (of a type of steering gear in motor vehicles) having a track rod with a rack along part of its length that engages with a pinion attached to the steering column.

racket¹ ('rækɪt) *n.* **1.** a noisy disturbance or loud commotion; clamour; din. **2.** an illegal enterprise carried on for profit, such as extortion, fraud, etc. **3.** *Sl.* a business or occupation: *what's your racket?* **4.** *Music.* a medieval woodwind instrument of deep bass pitch. ~*vb.* **5.** (*intr.*; often foll. by *about*) *Now rare.* to go about gaily or noisily, in search of pleasure, etc. —'**rackety** *adj.*

racket² *or* **racquet** ('rækɪt) *n.* **1.** a bat consisting of an open network of strings stretched in an oval frame with a handle, used to strike a tennis-ball, etc. **2.** a snowshoe shaped like a tennis racket. ~*vb.* **3.** (*tr.*) to strike (a ball, etc.) with a racket.

racketeer (ˌrækɪˈtɪə) *n.* **1.** a person engaged in illegal enterprises for profit. ~*vb.* **2.** (*intr.*) to operate an illegal enterprise. —ˌ**racket'eering** *n.*

rackets ('rækɪts) *n.* (*functioning as sing.*) **a.** a game similar to squash played in a four-walled court by two or four players using rackets and a small hard ball. **b.** (*as modifier*): *a rackets court.*

rack railway *n.* a steep mountain railway having a middle rail fitted with a rack that engages a pinion on the locomotive to provide traction. Also called: **cog railway.**

rack-rent *n.* **1.** a high rent that annually equals the value of the property upon which it is charged. **2.** any extortionate rent. ~*vb.* **3.** to charge an extortionate rent for. —'**rack-,renter** *n.*

raconteur (ˌrækɒnˈtɜː) *n.* a person skilled in telling stories.

racoon (rəˈkuːn) *n., pl.* **-coons** *or* **-coon.** a variant spelling of **raccoon.**

racquet ('rækɪt) *n.* a variant spelling of **racket².**

racy ('reɪsɪ) *adj.* **racier, raciest.** **1.** (of a person's manner, literary style, etc.) having a distinctively lively and spirited quality. **2.** having a characteristic or distinctive flavour: *a racy wine.* **3.** suggestive; slightly indecent; risqué. —'**racily** *adv.* —'**raciness** *n.*

RADA ('rɑːdə) *n.* (in Britain) *acronym for* Royal Academy of Dramatic Art.

radar ('reɪdɑː) *n.* **1.** a method for detecting the position and velocity of a distant object. A narrow beam of extremely high-frequency radio pulses is transmitted and reflected by the object back to the transmitter. The direction of the reflected beam and the time between transmission and reception of a pulse determine the position of the object. **2.** the equipment used in such detection.

radar trap *n.* a device using radar to detect motorists who exceed the speed limit.

raddle ('rædºl) *vb.* (*tr.*) *Chiefly Brit.* to paint (the face) with rouge.

radial ('reɪdɪəl) *adj.* **1.** (of lines, etc.) emanating from a common central point; arranged like the radii of a circle. **2.** of, like, or relating to a radius or ray. **3.** short for **radial-ply.** **4.** *Anat.* of or relating to the radius or forearm. **5.** *Astron.* (of velocity) in a direction along the line of sight of a celestial object and measured by means of the red shift (or blue shift) of the spectral lines of the object. ~*n.* **6.** a radial part or section. —'**radially** *adv.*

radial-ply *adj.* (of a motor tyre) having the fabric cords in the outer casing running radially to enable the sidewalls to be flexible.

radian ('reɪdɪən) *n.* an SI unit of plane angle; the angle between two radii of a circle that cut off on the circumference an arc equal in length to the radius. 1 radian is equivalent to 57.296 degrees. Abbrev. **rad.**

radiant ('reɪdɪənt) *adj.* **1.** sending out rays of light; bright; shining. **2.** characterized by health, happiness, etc.: *a radiant smile.* **3.** emitted or propagated by or as radiation; radiated: *radiant heat.* **4.** *Physics.* (of a physical quantity in photometry) evaluated by absolute energy measurements: *radiant flux.* ~*n.* **5.** a point or object that emits radiation, esp. the part of a heater that gives out heat. **6.** *Astron.* the point in space from which a meteor shower appears to emanate. —'**radiance** *or* '**radiancy** *n.* —'**radiantly** *adv.*

radiant energy *n.* energy that is emitted or propagated in the form of particles or electromagnetic radiation.

radiate *vb.* ('reɪdɪˌeɪt). **1.** Also: **eradiate.** to emit (heat, light, or other forms of radiation) or (of heat, light, etc.) to be emitted as radiation. **2.** (*intr.*) (of lines, beams, etc.) to spread out from a centre or be arranged in a radial pattern. **3.** (*tr.*) (of a person) to show (happiness, etc.) to a great degree. ~*adj.* ('reɪdɪɪt, -ˌeɪt). **4.** having rays; radiating. **5.** (of a capitulum) consisting of ray flowers. **6.** (of animals) showing radial symmetry. —'**radiative** *adj.*

radiation (ˌreɪdɪˈeɪʃən) *n.* **1.** *Physics.* **a.** the emission or transfer of radiant energy as particles, electromagnetic waves, sound, etc. **b.** the particles, etc., emitted, esp. the particles and gamma rays emitted in nuclear decay. **2.** Also called: **radiation therapy.** *Med.* treatment using a radioactive substance. **3.** the act, state, or process of radiating or being radiated. —ˌ**radi'ational** *adj.*

radiation sickness *n.* *Pathol.* illness caused by overexposure of the body to ionizing radiations from radioactive material or x-rays.

radiator ('reɪdɪˌeɪtə) *n.* **1.** a device for heating a room, building, etc., consisting of a series of pipes through which hot water or steam passes. **2.** a device for cooling an internal-combustion engine, consisting of a metal honeycomb through which water passes. **3.** *Electronics.* the part of an aerial or transmission line that radiates electromagnetic waves.

radical ('rædɪkəl) *adj.* **1.** of, relating to, or characteristic of the basic or inherent constitution of a person or thing; fundamental: *a radical fault.* **2.** concerned with or tending to concentrate on fundamental aspects of a matter; searching or thoroughgoing: *radical thought.* **3.** favouring or tending to produce extreme or fundamental changes in political, economic, or social conditions, institutions, etc.: *a radical party.* **4.** of or arising from the root or the base of the stem of a plant: *radical leaves.* **5.** *Maths.* of, relating to, or containing roots of numbers or quantities. **6.** *Linguistics.* of or relating to the root of a word. ~*n.* **7.** a person who favours extreme or fundamental change in existing institutions or in political, social, or economic conditions. **8.** *Maths.* a root of a number or quantity, such as $^3\sqrt{5}$, $\sqrt{x}$. **9.** *Chem.* **a.** an atom or group of atoms containing at least one unpaired electron

---

THESAURUS

rack *n.* **1.** frame, framework, stand, structure **2.** affliction, agony, anguish, misery, pain, pang, persecution, suffering, torment, torture ~*v.* **3.** afflict, agonize, crucify, distress, excruciate, harass, harrow, oppress, pain, torment, torture **4.** force, pull, shake, strain, stress, stretch, tear, wrench

racket **1.** babel, ballyhoo (*Inf.*), clamour, commotion, din, disturbance, fuss, hubbub, hullabaloo, noise, outcry, pandemonium, row, shouting, tumult, uproar **2.** criminal activity, fraud, illegal enterprise, scheme **3.** *Sl.* business, game (*Inf.*), line, occupation

racy **1.** animated, buoyant, energetic, entertaining, exciting, exhilarating, heady, lively, sparkling, spirited, stimulating, vigorous, zestful **2.** distinctive, piquant, pungent, rich, sharp, spicy, strong, tangy, tart, tasty **3.** bawdy, blue, broad, immodest, indecent, indelicate, naughty, near the knuckle (*Inf.*), off colour, risqué, smutty, spicy (*Inf.*), suggestive

radiance **1.** brightness, brilliance, effulgence, glare, gleam, glitter, glow, incandescence, light, luminosity, lustre, resplendence, shine **2.** delight, gaiety, happiness, joy, pleas-ure, rapture, warmth

radiant **1.** beaming, bright, brilliant, effulgent, gleaming, glittering, glorious, glowing, incandescent, luminous, lustrous, resplendent, shining, sparkling, sunny **2.** beaming, beatific, blissful, delighted, ecstatic, gay, glowing, happy, joyful, joyous, rapturous

radiate **1.** diffuse, disseminate, emanate, emit, give off *or* out, gleam, glitter, pour, scatter, send out, shed, shine, spread **2.** branch out, diverge, issue, spread out

radiation emanation, emission, rays

and existing for a brief period before reacting to produce a stable molecule. Also called: **free radical. b.** another name for **group** (sense 9). **10.** *Linguistics.* another word for **root**[1] (sense 8). —**'radica,lism** *or* **'radicalness** *n.* —**'radically** *adv.*

radical sign *n.* the symbol $\sqrt{}$ placed before a number or quantity to indicate the extraction of a root, esp. a square root. The value of a higher root is indicated by a raised digit in front of the symbol, as in $^3\sqrt{}$.

radicle ('rædɪk³l) *n.* **1.** *Bot.* **a.** the part of the embryo of seed-bearing plants that develops into the main root. **b.** a very small root or rootlike part. **2.** *Anat.* any bodily structure resembling a rootlet, esp. one of the smallest branches of a vein or nerve. **3.** *Chem.* a variant spelling of **radical** (sense 9).

radii ('reɪdɪ,aɪ) *n.* a plural of **radius.**

radio ('reɪdɪəʊ) *n., pl.* **os. 1.** the use of electromagnetic waves, lying in the radio-frequency range, for broadcasting, two-way communications, etc. **2.** an electronic device designed to receive, demodulate, and amplify radio signals from broadcasting stations, etc. **3.** the broadcasting, content, etc., of radio programmes: *he thinks radio is poor these days.* **4.** the occupation or profession concerned with any aspect of the broadcasting of radio programmes. **5.** short for **radiotelegraph, radiotelegraphy,** or **radiotelephone. 6.** (*modifier*) **a.** of, relating to, or sent by radio signals: *a radio station.* **b.** of, concerned with, using, or operated by radio frequencies: *radio spectrum.* ~*vb.* **-oing, -oed. 7.** to transmit (a message, etc.) to (a person, etc.) by means of radio waves. ~Also called (esp. Brit.): **wireless.**

radio- *combining form.* **1.** denoting radio, broadcasting, or radio frequency: *radiogram.* **2.** indicating radioactivity or radiation: *radiochemistry.*

radioactive (,reɪdɪəʊ'æktɪv) *adj.* exhibiting, using, or concerned with radioactivity. —**,radio'actively** *adv.*

radioactivity (,reɪdɪəʊæk'tɪvɪtɪ) *n.* the spontaneous emission of alpha, beta, and gamma radiation from atomic nuclei.

radio astronomy *n.* a branch of astronomy in which the radio telescope is used to detect and analyse radio signals received on earth from radio sources in space.

radiocarbon (,reɪdɪəʊ'kɑːbən) *n.* a radioactive isotope of carbon, esp. carbon-14. See **carbon.**

radiochemistry (,reɪdɪəʊ'kemɪstrɪ) *n.* the chemistry of radioactive elements and their compounds. —**,radio-'chemical** *adj.* —**,radio'chemist** *n.*

radio frequency *n.* **1. a.** any frequency that lies in the range 10 kilohertz to 300 000 megahertz and can be used for broadcasting. Abbrev.: **rf, RF. b.** (*as modifier*): *a radio-frequency amplifier.* **2.** the frequency transmitted by a particular radio system.

radiogram ('reɪdɪəʊ,græm) *n.* **1.** *Brit.* a unit comprising a radio and gramophone. **2.** a message transmitted by radiotelegraphy. **3.** another name for **radiograph.**

radiograph ('reɪdɪəʊ,grɑːf) *n.* an image produced on a specially sensitized photographic film or plate by radiation, usually by x-rays or gamma-rays.

radiography (,reɪdɪ'ɒgrəfɪ) *n.* the production of radiographs of opaque objects for use in medicine, surgery, industry, etc. —**,radi'ographer** *n.* —**radiographic** (,reɪdɪəʊ'græfɪk) *adj.* —**,radio'graphically** *adv.*

radioisotope (,reɪdɪəʊ'aɪsətəʊp) *n.* a radioactive isotope. —**radioisotopic** (,reɪdɪəʊ,aɪsə'tɒpɪk) *adj.*

radiology (,reɪdɪ'ɒlədʒɪ) *n.* the use of x-rays and radioactive substances in the diagnosis and treatment of disease. —**,radi'ologist** *n.*

radioscopy (,reɪdɪ'ɒskəpɪ) *n.* examination of a person, object, etc. by means of a device consisting of a fluorescent screen and an x-ray source. —**radioscopic** (,reɪdɪəʊ'skɒpɪk) *adj.* —**,radio'scopically** *adv.*

radiosonde ('reɪdɪəʊ,sɒnd) *n.* an airborne instrument to send meteorological information back to earth by radio.

radiotelegraphy (,reɪdɪəʊtɪ'legrəfɪ) *n.* a type of telegraphy in which messages (usually in Morse code) are transmitted by radio waves. —**,radio'tele,graph** *n.*

radiotelephone (,reɪdɪəʊ'telɪ,fəʊn) *n.* **1.** a device for communications by means of radio waves rather than by transmitting along wires or cables. ~*vb.* **2.** to tele-

phone (a person) by radiotelephone. —**radiotelephonic** (,reɪdɪəʊ,telɪ'fɒnɪk) *adj.* —**radiotelephony** (,reɪdɪəʊtɪ'lefənɪ) *n.*

radio telescope *n.* an instrument used in radio astronomy to pick up and analyse radio waves from space and also to transmit radio waves.

radiotherapy (,reɪdɪəʊ'θerəpɪ) *n.* the treatment of disease by means of alpha or beta particles emitted from an implanted or ingested radioisotope, or by means of a beam of high-energy radiation. —**radiotherapeutic** (,reɪdɪəʊ,θerə'pjuːtɪk) *adj.* —**,radio'therapist** *n.*

radish ('rædɪʃ) *n.* **1.** any of a genus of plants of Europe and Asia, with petals arranged like a cross, cultivated for their edible roots. **2.** the root of this plant, which has a pungent taste and is eaten raw in salads.

radium ('reɪdɪəm) *n.* **a.** a highly radioactive luminescent white element of the alkaline earth group of metals. It occurs in pitchblende and other uranium ores. Symbol: Ra; atomic no.: 88; half-life of most stable isotope, ^{226}Ra: 1620 years. **b.** (*as modifier*): *radium needle.*

radius ('reɪdɪəs) *n., pl.* **-dii** (-dɪ,aɪ) *or* **-diuses. 1.** a straight line joining the centre of a circle or sphere to any point on the circumference or surface. **2.** the length of this line, usually denoted by the symbol *r.* **3.** *Anat.* the outer, slightly shorter of the two bones of the human forearm, extending from the elbow to the wrist. **4.** a corresponding bone in other vertebrates. **5.** any of the veins of an insect's wing. **6.** a group of ray flowers, occurring in such plants as the daisy. **7. a.** any radial or radiating part, such as a spoke. **b.** (*as modifier*): *a radius arm.* **8.** a circular area of a size indicated by the length of its radius: *the police stopped every lorry within a radius of four miles.* **9.** the operational limit of a ship, aircraft, etc.

radon ('reɪdɒn) *n.* a colourless radioactive element of the rare gas group, the most stable isotope of which, radon-222, is a decay product of radium. Symbol: Rn; atomic no.: 86; half-life of ^{222}Rn: 3.82 days.

RAF (*Not standard* ræf) *or* **R.A.F.** *abbrev. for* Royal Air Force.

raffia *or* **raphia** ('ræfɪə) *n.* **1.** a palm tree, native to Madagascar, that has large plumelike leaves, the stalks of which yield a useful fibre. **2.** the fibre obtained from this plant, used for weaving, etc. **3.** any of several related palms or the fibre obtained from them.

raffish ('ræfɪʃ) *adj.* **1.** careless or unconventional in dress, manners, etc.; rakish. **2.** tawdry; flashy; vulgar. —**'raffishly** *adv.* —**'raffishness** *n.*

raffle ('ræf³l) *n.* **1.** a lottery in which the prizes are goods rather than money. **b.** (*as modifier*): *a raffle ticket.* ~*vb.* **2.** (*tr.; often foll. by off*) to dispose of (goods) in a raffle. —**'raffler** *n.*

raft (rɑːft) *n.* **1.** a buoyant platform of logs, planks, etc., used as a vessel or moored platform. **2.** a thick slab of reinforced concrete laid over soft ground to provide a foundation for a building. ~*vb.* **3.** to convey on or travel by raft, or make a raft from.

rafter ('rɑːftə) *n.* any one of a set of parallel sloping beams that form the framework of a roof.

rag[1] (ræg) *n.* **1. a.** a small piece of cloth, such as one torn from a discarded garment, or such pieces of cloth collectively. **b.** (*as modifier*): *a rag doll.* **2.** a fragmentary piece of any material; scrap; shred. **3.** *Inf.* a newspaper esp. one considered as worthless, sensational, etc. **4.** *Inf.* an item of clothing. **5.** *Inf.* a handkerchief. **6.** *Brit. sl., esp. naval.* a flag or ensign. **7. chew the rag.** *Sl.* to argue or grumble.

rag[2] (ræg) *vb.* **ragging, ragged.** (*tr.*) **1.** to draw attention facetiously and persistently to the shortcomings of (a person). **2.** *Brit.* to play rough practical jokes on. ~*n.* **3.** *Brit.* a boisterous practical joke. **4.** (in British universities, etc.) **a.** a period in which various events are organized to raise money for charity. **b.** (*as modifier*): *rag day.*

rag[3] (ræg) *Jazz.* ~*n.* **1.** a piece of ragtime music. ~*vb.* **ragging, ragged. 2.** (*tr.*) to compose or perform in ragtime.

ragamuffin ('rægə,mʌfɪn) *n.* a ragged unkempt person, esp. a child.

rag-and-bone man *n. Brit.* a man who buys and sells

THESAURUS

radical *adj.* **1.** basic, constitutional, deep-seated, essential, fundamental, innate, native, natural, organic, profound, thorough-going **2.** complete, entire, excessive, extreme, extremist, fanatical, revolutionary, severe, sweeping, thorough, violent ~*n.* **3.** extremist, fanatic, militant, revolutionary

raffle draw, lottery, sweep, sweepstake

discarded clothing, etc. U.S. equivalent: **junkman.**

ragbag ('ræg,bæg) n. 1. a bag for storing odd rags. 2. a confused assortment; jumble.

rage (reidʒ) n. 1. intense anger; fury. 2. violent movement or action, esp. of the sea, wind, etc. 3. great intensity of hunger or other feelings. 4. a fashion or craze (esp. **in all the rage**). 5. N.Z. & Austral. sl. a dance or party. ~vb. (intr.) 6. to feel or exhibit intense anger. 7. (esp. of storms, fires, etc.) to move or surge with great violence. 8. (esp. of a disease) to spread rapidly and uncontrollably.

ragged ('rægid) adj. 1. (of clothes) worn to rags; tattered. 2. (of a person) dressed in tattered clothes. 3. having a neglected or unkempt appearance: ragged weeds. 4. having a rough or uneven surface or edge; jagged. 5. uneven or irregular: a ragged beat; a ragged shout. —'**raggedly** adv. —'**raggedness** n. —'**raggedy** adj.

ragged robin n. a plant related to the carnation family and native to Europe and Asia, that has pink or white flowers with ragged petals.

raglan ('ræglən) n. 1. a coat, jumper, etc. with sleeves that continue to the collar instead of having armhole seams. ~adj. 2. cut in this design: a raglan sleeve.

ragout (ræ'gu:) n. 1. a richly seasoned stew of meat and vegetables. ~vb. -**gouting** (-'gu:iŋ), -**gouted** (-'gu:d). 2. (tr.) to make into a ragout.

ragtag ('ræg,tæg) n. Derog. the common people; rabble (esp. in **ragtag and bobtail**).

ragtime ('ræg,taim) n. a style of jazz piano music, developed by Scott Joplin around 1900, having a two-four rhythm base and a syncopated melody.

rag trade n. Inf. the clothing business.

ragwort ('ræg,wɜ:t) n. any of several European plants of the composite family, that have yellow daisy-like flowers.

raid (reid) n. 1. a sudden surprise attack. 2. an attempt by speculators to force down commodity prices by rapid selling. ~vb. 3. to make a raid against (a person, thing, etc.). —'**raider** n.

rail[1] (reil) n. 1. a horizontal bar of wood, etc., supported by vertical posts, functioning as a fence, barrier, etc. 2. a horizontal bar fixed to a wall on which to hang things: a picture rail. 3. a horizontal framing member in a door. 4. short for **railing**. 5. one of a pair of parallel bars laid on a track, roadway, etc., that serve as a guide and running surface for the wheels of a train, tramcar, etc. 6. a. short for **railway**. b. (as modifier): rail transport. 7. Naut. a trim for finishing the top of a bulwark. 8. **off the rails. a.** into or in a state of disorder. **b.** eccentric or mad. ~vb. (tr.) 9. to provide with a rail or railings. 10. (usually foll. by in or off) to fence (an area) with rails.

rail[2] (reil) vb. (intr.; foll. by at or against) to complain bitterly or vehemently. —'**railer** n.

rail[3] (reil) n. any of various small cranelike wading marsh birds with short wings and neck, long legs, and dark plumage.

railhead ('reil,hed) n. 1. a terminal of a railway. 2. the farthest point reached by completed track on an unfinished railway.

railing ('reiliŋ) n. 1. a fence, balustrade, or barrier that consists of rails supported by posts. 2. rails collectively or material for making rails.

raillery ('reiləri) n., pl. -**leries.** 1. light-hearted satire or ridicule; banter. 2. a bantering remark.

railroad ('reil,rəud) n. 1. the usual U.S. word for **railway.** ~vb. 2. (tr.) Inf. to force (a person) into (an action) with haste or by unfair means.

railway ('reil,wei) or U.S. **railroad** n. 1. a permanent track composed of a line of parallel metal rails fixed to sleepers, for transport of passengers and goods in trains. 2. any track for the wheels of a vehicle to run on: a cable railway. 3. the entire equipment, rolling stock, buildings, property, and system of tracks used in such a transport system. 4. the organization responsible for operating a railway network. 5. (modifier) of, relating to, or used on a railway: a railway engine.

raiment ('reimənt) n. Arch. or poetic. attire; clothing.

rain (rein) n. 1. a. precipitation from clouds in the form of drops of water, formed by the condensation of water vapour in the atmosphere. b. a fall of rain; shower. c. (in combination): a raindrop. 2. a large quantity of anything falling rapidly or in quick succession: a rain of abuse. 3. (come) **rain or shine.** regardless of the weather or circumstances. 4. **right as rain.** Brit. inf. perfectly all right. ~vb. 5. (intr.; with it as subject) to be the case that rain is falling. 6. (often with it as subject) to fall or cause to fall like rain. 7. (tr.) to bestow in large measure: to rain abuse on someone. 8. **rain cats and dogs.** Inf. to rain heavily; pour. 9. **rained off.** cancelled or postponed on account of rain. U.S. term: **rained out.** —'**rainless** adj. —'**rainy** adj.

rainbow ('rein,bəu) n. 1. a. a bow-shaped display in the sky of the colours of the spectrum, caused by the refraction and reflection of the sun's rays through rain. b. (as modifier): a rainbow pattern. 2. an illusory hope: to chase rainbows.

rainbow trout n. a freshwater trout of North American origin, marked with many black spots and two longitudinal red stripes.

raincoat ('rein,kəut) n. a coat worn for protection against rain.

rainfall ('rein,fɔ:l) n. 1. precipitation in the form of raindrops. 2. Meteorol. the amount of precipitation in a specified place and time.

rainforest ('rein,fɒrist) n. dense forest found in tropical areas of heavy rainfall.

rains (reinz) pl. n. **the.** the season of heavy rainfall, esp. in the tropics.

rain shadow n. the relatively dry area on the leeward side of high ground in the path of rain-bearing winds.

rainwater ('rein,wɔ:tə) n. pure water from rain (as distinguished from spring water, tap water, etc., which may contain minerals and impurities).

rainy day n. a future time of need, esp. financial.

raise (reiz) vb. (mainly tr.) 1. to move or elevate to a higher position or level; lift. 2. to set or place in an upright position. 3. to construct, build, or erect: to raise a barn. 4. to increase in amount, size, value, etc.: to raise prices. 5. to increase in degree, strength, intensity, etc.: to raise one's voice. 6. to advance in rank or status; promote. 7. to arouse or awaken from sleep or death. 8. to stir up or incite; activate: to raise a mutiny. 9. **raise Cain** (or **the devil, hell, the roof,** etc.). to create a disturbance, esp. by making a great noise. 10. to give rise to; cause or provoke: to raise a smile. 11. to put forward for consideration: to raise a question. 12. to cause to assemble or gather together: to raise an army. 13. to grow

---

THESAURUS

ragbag 1. confusion, hotchpotch, jumble, medley, miscellany, mixture, omnium-gatherum, potpourri 2. Inf. frump, scarecrow (Inf.), scruff (Inf.), slattern, sloven, slut, trollop

rage n. 1. agitation, anger, frenzy, fury, high dudgeon, ire, madness, mania, obsession, passion, rampage, raving, vehemence, violence, wrath 2. craze, enthusiasm, fad (Inf.), fashion, latest thing, mode, style, vogue ~v. 3. be beside oneself, be furious, blow one's top, blow up (Inf.), chafe, foam at the mouth, fret, fume, rant and rave, rave, seethe, storm, throw a fit (Inf.) 4. be at its height, be uncontrollable, rampage, storm, surge

ragged 1. contemptible, down at heel, frayed, in holes, in rags, in tatters, mean, poor, rent, scraggy, shabby, shaggy, tattered,

tatty, threadbare, torn, unkempt, worn-out 2. crude, jagged, notched, poor, rough, rugged, serrated, uneven, unfinished 3. broken, desultory, disorganized, fragmented, irregular, uneven

raging beside oneself, boiling mad (Inf.), doing one's nut (Brit. sl.), enraged, fit to be tied (Sl.), fizzing (Scot.), foaming at the mouth, frenzied, fuming, furious, incensed, infuriated, mad, raving, seething

rags 1. castoffs, old clothes, tattered clothing, tatters 2. **in rags** down at heel, out at elbow, ragged, seedy, shabby, tattered

raid 1. n. attack, break-in, descent, foray, hit-and-run attack, incursion, inroad, invasion, irruption, onset, sally, seizure, sortie, surprise attack 2. v. assault, attack, break into, descend on, fall upon, forage (Military), foray, invade, pillage, plunder, reive (Dia-

lect), rifle, sack, sally forth, swoop down upon

raider attacker, forager (Military), invader, marauder, plunderer, reiver (Dialect), robber, thief

railing balustrade, barrier, fence, paling, rails

rain n. 1. cloudburst, deluge, downpour, drizzle, fall, precipitation, raindrops, rainfall, showers 2. deluge, flood, hail, shower, spate, stream, torrent, volley ~v. 3. bucket down (Inf.), come down in buckets (Inf.), drizzle, fall, pour, rain cats and dogs (Inf.), shower, teem 4. deposit, drop, fall, shower, sprinkle 5. bestow, lavish, pour, shower

rainy damp, drizzly, showery, wet

or cause to grow: *to raise a crop.* **14.** to bring up; rear: *to raise a family.* **15.** to cause to be heard or known; utter or express: *to raise a shout.* **16.** to bring to an end; remove: *to raise a siege.* **17.** to cause (bread, etc.) to rise, as by the addition of yeast. **18.** *Poker.* to bet more than (the previous player). **19.** *Bridge.* to bid (one's partner's suit) at a higher level. **20.** *Naut.* to cause (something) to seem to rise above the horizon by approaching: *we raised land after 20 days.* **21.** to establish radio communications with: *we raised Moscow last night.* **22.** to obtain (money, funds, etc.). **23.** to bring (a surface, a design, etc.) into relief; cause to project. **24.** to cause (a blister, etc.) to form on the skin. **25.** *Maths.* to multiply (a number) by itself a specified number of times: *8 is 2 raised to the power 3.* **26. raise an eyebrow** *or* **one's eyebrows.** to look quizzical or surprised. **27. raise one's glass (to).** to drink a toast (to). **28. raise one's hat.** *Old-fashioned.* to take one's hat briefly off one's head as a greeting or mark of respect. ~*n.* **29.** the act or an instance of raising. **30.** *Chiefly U.S.* an increase, esp. in salary, wages, etc.; rise. —**'raisable** *or* **'raiseable** *adj.*

raisin ('reɪzən) *n.* a dried grape. —**'raisiny** *adj.*

raison d'être *French.* (rezɔ̃ 'dɛtr) *n., pl.* **raisons d'être** (rezɔ̃ 'dɛtr). reason or justification for existence.

raj (rɑːdʒ) *n.* **1.** (in India) government; rule. **2.** (*cap.* and preceded by *the*) the British government in India before 1947.

rajah *or* **raja** ('rɑːdʒə) *n.* **1.** (in India, formerly) a ruler: sometimes used as a title preceding a name. **2.** a Malayan or Javanese prince or chieftain.

rake[1] (reɪk) *n.* **1.** a hand implement consisting of a row of teeth set in a headpiece attached to a long shaft and used for gathering hay, straw, etc., or for smoothing loose earth. **2.** any of several mechanical farm implements equipped with rows of teeth or rotating wheels mounted with tines and used to gather hay, straw, etc. **3.** any of various implements similar in shape or function. **4.** the act of raking. ~*vb.* **5.** to scrape, gather, or remove (leaves, refuse, etc.) with a rake. **6.** to level or prepare (a surface) with a rake. **7.** (*tr.*; sometimes foll. by *out*) to clear (ashes, etc.) from (a fire). **8.** (*tr.*; foll. by *up* or *together*) to gather (items or people) with difficulty, as from a scattered area or limited supply. **9.** (*tr.*; often foll. by *through, over,* etc.) to search or examine carefully. **10.** (when *intr.*, foll. by *against, along,* etc.) to scrape or graze: *the ship raked the side of the quay.* **11.** (*tr.*) to direct (gunfire) along the length of (a target): *machine-guns raked the column.* **12.** (*tr.*) to sweep (one's eyes) along the length of (something); scan. ~See also **rake in, rake-off,** etc. —**'raker** *n.*

rake[2] (reɪk) *n.* a dissolute man, esp. one in fashionable society; roué.

rake[3] (reɪk) *vb.* (*mainly intr.*) **1.** to incline from the vertical by a perceptible degree, esp. (of a ship's mast) towards the stern. **2.** (*tr.*) to construct with a backward slope. ~*n.* **3.** the degree to which an object, such as a ship's mast, inclines from the perpendicular, esp. towards the stern. **4.** *Theatre.* the slope of a stage from the back towards the footlights. **5.** the angle between the working face of a cutting tool and a plane perpendicular to the surface of the workpiece.

rake in *vb.* (*tr., adv.*) *Inf.* to acquire (money) in large amounts.

rake-off *Sl.* ~*n.* **1.** a share of profits, esp. one that is illegal or given as a bribe. ~*vb.* **rake off.** **2.** (*tr., adv.*) to take or receive (such a share of profits).

rake up *vb.* (*tr., adv.*) to revive, discover, or bring to light (something forgotten): *to rake up an old quarrel.*

rakish[1] ('reɪkɪʃ) *adj.* dissolute; profligate. —**'rakishly** *adv.* —**'rakishness** *n.*

rakish[2] ('reɪkɪʃ) *adj.* **1.** dashing; jaunty: *a hat set at a rakish angle.* **2.** *Naut.* (of a ship or boat) having lines suggestive of speed.

rallentando (ˌrælɛn'tændəʊ) *adj., adv. Music.* becoming slower. Also: **ritardando.**

rally[1] ('rælɪ) *vb.* **-lying, -lied.** **1.** to bring (a group, unit, etc.) into order, as after dispersal, or (of such a group) to reform and come to order. **2.** (when *intr.*, foll. by *to*) to organize (supporters, etc.) for a common cause or (of such people) to come together for a purpose. **3.** to summon up (one's strength, spirits, etc.) or (of a person's health, strength, or spirits) to revive or recover. **4.** (*intr.*) *Stock Exchange.* to increase sharply after a decline. **5.** (*intr.*) *Tennis, squash, etc.* to engage in a rally. ~*n., pl.* **-lies.** **6.** a large gathering of people for a common purpose. **7.** a marked recovery of strength or spirits, as during illness. **8.** a return to order after dispersal or rout, as of troops, etc. **9.** *Stock Exchange.* a sharp increase in price or trading activity after a decline. **10.** *Tennis, squash, etc.* an exchange of several shots before one player wins the point. **11.** a type of motoring competition over public roads. —**'rallier** *n.*

rally[2] ('rælɪ) *vb.* **-lying, -lied.** to mock or ridicule (someone) in a good-natured way; chaff; tease.

rally round *vb.* (*intr.*) to come to the aid of (someone); offer moral or practical support.

ram (ræm) *n.* **1.** an uncastrated adult male sheep. **2.** a piston or moving plate, esp. one driven hydraulically or pneumatically. **3.** the falling weight of a pile driver. **4.** short for **battering ram.** **5.** a pointed projection in the stem of an ancient warship for puncturing the hull of enemy ships. **6.** a warship equipped with a ram. ~*vb.* **ramming, rammed.** **7.** (*tr.*; usually foll. by *into*) to force or drive, as by heavy blows: *to ram a post into the ground.* **8.** (of a moving object) to crash with force (against another object) or (of two moving objects) to collide in this way. **9.** (*tr.*; often foll. by *in* or *down*) to stuff or cram (something into a hole, etc.). **10.** (*tr.*; foll. by *onto, against,* etc.) to thrust violently: *he rammed the books onto the desk.* **11.** (*tr.*) *Sl.* to instil (knowledge, etc.) into a person, esp. by repetition (esp. in **ram (something) down someone's throat**). **12.** (*tr.*) to drive (a charge) into a firearm. —**'rammer** *n.*

Ram (ræm) *n.* **the.** the constellation Aries, the first sign of the zodiac.

RAM (ræm) *n. Computers. acronym for* random access memory.

R.A.M. *abbrev. for* Royal Academy of Music.

ramble ('ræmbəl) *vb.* (*intr.*) **1.** to stroll about freely, as for relaxation, with no particular direction. **2.** (of paths, streams, etc.) to follow a winding course; meander. **3.** to grow or develop in a random fashion. **4.** (of speech, writing, etc.) to lack organization. ~*n.* **5.** a leisurely stroll, esp. in the countryside.

raise l. build, construct, elevate, erect, exalt, heave, hoist, lift, move up, promote, put up, rear, set upright, uplift 2. advance, aggravate, amplify, augment, boost, enhance, enlarge, escalate, exaggerate, heighten, hike (up) (*Inf.*), increase, inflate, intensify, jack up, magnify, put up, reinforce, strengthen 3. advance, aggrandize, elevate, exalt, prefer, promote, upgrade 4. activate, arouse, awaken, cause, evoke, excite, foment, foster, incite, instigate, kindle, motivate, provoke, set on foot, stir up, summon up, whip up 5. bring about, cause, create, engender, give rise to, occasion, originate, produce, provoke, start 6. advance, bring up, broach, introduce, moot, put forward, suggest 7. assemble, collect, form, gather, get, levy, mass, mobilize, muster, obtain, rally, recruit 8. breed, bring up, cultivate, develop, grow, nurture, produce, propagate, rear 9. abandon, end, give

up, lift, relieve, relinquish, remove, terminate

rake[1] *v.* l. collect, gather, remove, scrape up 2. break up, harrow, hoe, scour, scrape, scratch 3. *With* **up** *or* **together** assemble, collect, dig up, dredge up, gather, scrape together 4. comb, examine, hunt, ransack, scan, scour, scrutinize, search 5. graze, scrape, scratch 6. enfilade, pepper, sweep

rake[2] *n.* debauchee, dissolute man, lecher, libertine, playboy, profligate, rakehell (*Archaic*), roué, sensualist, voluptuary

rakish[2] breezy, dapper, dashing, debonair, devil-may-care, flashy, jaunty, natty (*Inf.*), raffish, smart, snazzy (*Inf.*), sporty

rally *v.* l. bring *or* come to order, reassemble, re-form, regroup, reorganize, unite ~*n.* 2. regrouping, reorganization, reunion, stand ~*v.* 3. assemble, bond together, bring *or* come together, collect, convene, gather, get

together, marshal, mobilize, muster, organize, round up, summon, unite ~*n.* 4. assembly, conference, congregation, convention, convocation, gathering, mass meeting, meeting, muster ~*v.* 5. come round, get better, get one's second wind, improve, perk up, pick up, pull through, recover, recuperate, regain one's strength, revive, take a turn for the better ~*n.* 6. comeback (*Inf.*), improvement, recovery, recuperation, renewal, resurgence, revival, turn for the better

ram *v.* l. butt, collide with, crash, dash, drive, force, hit, impact, run into, slam, smash, strike 2. beat, cram, crowd, drum, force, hammer, jam, pack, pound, stuff, tamp, thrust

ramble *v.* l. amble, drift, perambulate, peregrinate, range, roam, rove, saunter, straggle, stravaig (*Scot.*), stray, stroll, traipse (*Inf.*), walk, wander 2. meander, snake, twist

rambler ('ræmblə) n. 1. a weak-stemmed plant that straggles over other vegetation. 2. a person who rambles, esp. one who takes country walks. 3. a person who lacks organization in his speech or writing.

rambunctious (ræm'bʌŋkʃəs) adj. Inf. boisterous; unruly. —**ram'bunctiousness** n.

R.A.M.C. abbrev. for Royal Army Medical Corps.

ramekin or **ramequin** ('ræmɪkɪn) n. 1. a savoury dish made from a cheese mixture baked in a fireproof dish. 2. the dish itself.

ramification (ˌræmɪfɪ'keɪʃən) n. 1. the act or process of ramifying or branching out. 2. an offshoot or subdivision. 3. a structure of branching parts.

ramify ('ræmɪˌfaɪ) vb. -fying, -fied. 1. to divide into branches or branchlike parts. 2. (intr.) to develop complicating consequences.

ramose ('reɪməʊs, ræ'məʊs) or **ramous** ('reɪməs) adj. having branches. —**'ramosely** or **'ramously** adv. —**ramosity** (ræ'mɒsɪtɪ) n.

ramp (ræmp) n. 1. a sloping floor, path, etc., that joins two surfaces at different levels. 2. a movable stairway by which passengers enter and leave an aircraft. 3. the act of ramping. 4. Brit. sl. a swindle, esp. one involving exorbitant prices. ~vb. (intr.) 5. (often foll. by about or around) (esp. of animals) to rush around in a wild excited manner. 6. to act in a violent or threatening manner (esp. in ramp and rage).

rampage vb. (ræm'peɪdʒ). 1. (intr.) to rush about in a violent or agitated fashion. ~n. ('ræmpeɪdʒ, ræm'peɪdʒ). 2. angry or destructive behaviour. 3. **on the rampage.** behaving violently or destructively. —**ram'pageous** adj. —**ram'pageously** adv. —**ram'pager** n.

rampant ('ræmpənt) adj. 1. unrestrained or violent in behaviour, etc. 2. growing or developing unchecked. 3. (postpositive) Heraldry. (of a beast) standing on the hind legs, the right foreleg raised above the left. 4. (of an arch) having one abutment higher than the other. —**'rampancy** n. —**'rampantly** adv.

rampart ('ræmpɑːt) n. 1. the surrounding embankment of a fort, often including any walls, etc., that are built on the bank. 2. any defence or bulwark. ~vb. 3. (tr.) to provide with a rampart; fortify.

ramrod ('ræmˌrɒd) n. 1. a rod for cleaning the barrel of a rifle, etc. 2. a rod for ramming in the charge of a muzzle-loading firearm.

ramshackle ('ræmˌʃækəl) adj. (esp. of buildings) rickety, shaky, or derelict.

ran (ræn) vb. the past tense of **run**.

R.A.N. abbrev. for Royal Australian Navy.

ranch (rɑːntʃ) n. 1. a large tract of land, esp. one in North America, together with the necessary personnel, buildings, and equipment, for rearing livestock, esp. cattle. 2. a. any large farm for the rearing of a particular kind of livestock or crop: a mink ranch. b. the buildings, land, etc., connected with it. ~vb. 3. (intr.) to run a ranch. —**'rancher** n.

rancid ('rænsɪd) adj. 1. (of food) having an unpleasant stale taste or smell as the result of decomposition. 2. (of a taste or smell) rank or sour; stale. —**'rancidness** or **rancidity** (ræn'sɪdɪtɪ) n.

rancour or U.S. **rancor** ('ræŋkə) n. malicious resentfulness or hostility; spite. —**'rancorous** adj. —**'rancorously** adv.

rand (rænd, rɒnt) n. the standard monetary unit of the Republic of South Africa, divided into 100 cents.

Rand (rænd) n. **the.** short for Witwatersrand, an area in South Africa rich in mineral deposits, esp. gold.

R & D abbrev. for research and development.

random ('rændəm) adj. 1. lacking any definite plan or prearranged order; haphazard: a random selection. 2. Statistics. a. (of a variable) having several possible experimental values any one of which is uncertain and depends on chance. b. (of a sampling process) carried out so that each member of the population has an equal probability of being selected. ~n. 3. **at random.** not following any prearranged order. —**'randomly** adv. —**'randomness** n.

random access n. another name for **direct access**.

randy ('rændɪ) adj. **randier, randiest. 1.** Sl., chiefly Brit. sexually eager or lustful. 2. Chiefly Scot. lacking any sense of propriety; reckless. ~n., pl. **randies. 3.** Chiefly Scot. a rude or reckless person. —**'randily** adv. —**'randiness** n.

ranee ('rɑːnɪ) n. a variant spelling of **rani**.

rang (ræŋ) vb. the past tense of **ring²**.

▷ Usage. See at **ring²**.

range (reɪndʒ) n. 1. the limits within which a person or thing can function effectively: the range of vision. 2. the limits within which any fluctuation takes place: a range of values. 3. a. the maximum effective distance of a projectile fired from a weapon. b. the distance between a target and a weapon. 4. an area set aside for shooting practice or rocket testing. 5. the total distance which a ship, aircraft, or land vehicle is capable of covering without taking on fresh fuel: the range of this car is about 160 miles. 6. Maths. a. (of a function) the set of functional values. b. (of a variable) the set of values that a variable can take. 7. U.S. a. an extensive tract of open land on which livestock can graze. b. (as modifier): range cattle. 8. the geographical region in which a species of plant or animal normally grows or lives. 9. a rank, row, or series of items. 10. a series or chain of mountains. 11. a large stove with burners and one or more ovens, usually heated by solid fuel. 12. the act or process of ranging. ~vb. 13. to establish or be situated in a line, row, or series. 14. (tr.; often reflexive, foll. by with) to put into a specific category; classify: she ranges herself with the angels. 15. (foll. by on) to aim or point (a telescope, gun, etc.) or (of a gun, telescope, etc.) to be pointed or aimed. 16. to establish the distance of (a target) from (a weapon). 17. (intr.) (of a gun or missile) to have a specified range. 18. (when intr., foll. by over) to wander about (in) an area; roam (over). 19. (intr., foll. by over) (of an animal or plant) to live or grow in its normal habitat. 20. (tr.) to put (cattle) to graze on a range. 21. (intr.) to fluctuate within specific limits. 22. (intr.) to extend or run in a specific direction. 23. (intr.) Naut. (of a vessel) to swing back and forth while at anchor. 24. (tr.) to make (lines of printers' type) level or even at the margin.

THESAURUS

and turn, wind, zigzag **3**. babble, chatter, digress, expatiate, maunder, rabbit on (Brit. sl.), rattle on, wander, witter on (Inf.) ~n. **4**. excursion, hike, perambulation, peregrination, roaming, roving, saunter, stroll, tour, traipse (Inf.), trip, walk

rambler drifter, hiker, roamer, rover, stroller, walker, wanderer, wayfarer

rambling 1. circuitous, desultory, diffuse, digressive, disconnected, discursive, disjointed, incoherent, irregular, long-winded, periphrastic, prolix, wordy **2**. irregular, sprawling, spreading, straggling, trailing

ramification 1. branch, development, divarication, division, excrescence, extension, forking, offshoot, outgrowth, subdivision **2**. complication, consequence, development, result, sequel, upshot

ramify 1. branch, divaricate, divide, fork, separate, split up **2**. become complicated, multiply, thicken

ramp grade, gradient, incline, inclined plane, rise, slope

rampage v. **1**. go berserk, rage, run amuck, run riot, run wild, storm, tear ~n. **2**. destruction, frenzy, fury, rage, storm, tempest, tumult, uproar, violence **3. on the rampage** amuck, berserk, destructive, out of control, raging, rampant, riotous, violent, wild

rampant 1. aggressive, dominant, excessive, flagrant, on the rampage, out of control, out of hand, outrageous, raging, rampaging, riotous, unbridled, uncontrollable, ungovernable, unrestrained, vehement, violent, wanton, wild **2**. epidemic, exuberant, luxuriant, prevalent, profuse, rank, rife, spreading like wildfire, unchecked, uncontrolled, unrestrained, widespread **3**. Heraldry erect, rearing, standing, upright

rampart barricade, bastion, breastwork, bulwark, defence, earthwork, embankment, fence, fort, fortification, guard, parapet, security, stronghold, wall

ramshackle broken-down, crumbling, decrepit, derelict, dilapidated, flimsy, jerrybuilt, rickety, shaky, tottering, tumbledown, unsafe, unsteady

rancid bad, fetid, foul, frowsty, fusty, off, putrid, rank, rotten, sour, stale, strong-smelling, tainted

random 1. accidental, adventitious, aimless, arbitrary, casual, chance, desultory, fortuitous, haphazard, hit or miss, incidental, indiscriminate, purposeless, spot, stray, unplanned, unpremeditated **2. at random** accidentally, adventitiously, aimlessly, arbitrarily, by chance, casually, haphazardly, indiscriminately, irregularly, purposelessly, randomly, unsystematically, willy-nilly

range n. **1**. amplitude, area, bounds, compass, confines, distance, extent, field, latitude, limits, orbit, parameters (Inf.), province, purview, radius, reach, scope, span, sphere, sweep **2**. chain, file, line, rank, row, sequence, series, string, tier **3**. assort-

rangefinder ('reɪndʒˌfaɪndə) n. an instrument for determining the distance of an object from the observer, esp. in order to sight a gun or focus a camera.

ranger ('reɪndʒə) n. 1. *Brit.* an official in charge of a royal forest, park, etc. 2. *Orig. U.S.* a person employed to patrol a State or national park. *Brit.* equivalent: **warden**. 3. *U.S.* one of a body of armed troops employed to police a State or district: *a Texas ranger.* 4. (in the U.S.) a commando specially trained in making raids. 5. a person who wanders about; a rover.

Ranger *or* **Ranger Guide** ('reɪndʒə) n. *Brit.* a member of the senior branch of the Guides.

rangy ('reɪndʒɪ) adj. **rangier, rangiest.** 1. having long slender limbs. 2. adapted to wandering or roaming. 3. allowing considerable freedom of movement; spacious. —**'rangily** adv. —**'ranginess** n.

rani *or* **ranee** ('rɑːnɪ) n. a queen or princess; the wife of a rajah.

rank¹ (ræŋk) n. 1. a position, esp. an official one, within a social organization: *the rank of captain.* 2. high social or other standing; status. 3. a line or row of people or things: *a taxi rank.* 4. a line of soldiers drawn up abreast of each other. 5. any of the eight horizontal rows of squares on a chessboard. 6. *Music.* a set of organ pipes controlled by the same stop. 7. **break ranks.** *Mil.* to fall out of line, esp. when under attack. 8. **close ranks.** to maintain discipline or solidarity. 9. **pull rank.** to get one's own way by virtue of one's superior position or rank. 10. **rank and file. a.** the ordinary soldiers, excluding the officers. **b.** the great mass or majority of any group, as opposed to the leadership. **c.** (*modifier*) rank-and-file support. ~vb. 11. (tr.) to arrange (people or things) in rows or lines; range. 12. to accord or be accorded a specific position in an organization or group. 13. *U.S.* to take precedence or surpass in rank.

rank² (ræŋk) adj. 1. showing vigorous and profuse growth: *rank weeds.* 2. highly offensive or disagreeable, esp. in smell or taste. 3. (*prenominal*) complete or absolute; utter: *a rank outsider.* 4. coarse or vulgar; gross: *his language was rank.* —**'rankly** adv. —**'rankness** n.

rankle ('ræŋkəl) vb. (intr.) to cause severe and continuous irritation, anger, or bitterness; fester.

ransack ('rænsæk) vb. (tr.) 1. to search through every part of (a house, box, etc.); examine thoroughly. 2. to plunder; pillage. —**'ransacker** n.

ransom ('rænsəm) n. 1. the release of captured prisoners, property, etc., on payment of a stipulated price. 2. the price demanded or stipulated for such a release. 3. **hold to ransom. a.** to keep (prisoners, etc.) in confinement until payment for their release is received. **b.** to attempt to force (a person) to comply with one's demands. 4. **a king's ransom.** a very large amount of money or valuables. ~vb. (tr.) 5. to pay a stipulated price

and so obtain the release of (prisoners, property, etc.). 6. to set free (prisoners, property, etc.) upon receiving the payment demanded. 7. to redeem; rescue: *Christ ransomed men from sin.* —**'ransomer** n.

rant (rænt) vb. 1. to utter (something) in loud, violent, or bombastic tones. ~n. 2. loud, declamatory, or extravagant speech; bombast. —**'ranter** n. —**'rantingly** adv.

R.A.O.C. *abbrev. for* Royal Army Ordnance Corps.

rap¹ (ræp) vb. **rapping, rapped.** 1. to strike (a fist, stick, etc.) against (something) with a sharp quick blow; knock. 2. (intr.) to make a sharp loud sound, esp. by knocking. 3. (tr.; foll. by *out*) to put (forth) in sharp rapid speech; utter in an abrupt fashion: *to rap out orders.* 4. (intr.) *U.S. sl.* to talk, esp. volubly. 5. **rap over the knuckles.** to reprimand. ~n. 6. a sharp quick blow or the sound produced by such a blow. 7. *U.S. sl.* voluble talk; chatter. 8. **beat the rap.** *U.S. sl.* to escape punishment or be acquitted of a crime. 9. **take the rap.** *Sl.* to suffer the punishment for a crime, whether guilty or not.

rap² (ræp) n. (*used with a negative*) the least amount (esp. in **not to care a rap**).

rapacious (rə'peɪʃəs) adj. 1. practising pillage or rapine. 2. greedy or grasping. 3. (of animals, esp. birds) subsisting by catching living prey. —**ra'paciously** adv. —**rapacity** (rə'pæsɪtɪ) *or* **ra'paciousness** n.

rape¹ (reɪp) n. 1. *Criminal law.* the offence of forcing a woman to submit to sexual intercourse against her will. 2. the act of despoiling a country in warfare. 3. any violation or abuse: *the rape of justice.* 4. *Arch.* abduction: *the rape of the Sabine women.* ~vb. (*mainly tr.*) 5. *Criminal law.* to commit rape upon (a person). 6. *Arch.* to carry off by force; abduct. —**'rapist** n.

rape² (reɪp) n. a Eurasian plant that is cultivated for its seeds, **rapeseed,** which yield a useful oil, **rape oil,** and as a fodder plant. Also called: **colza, cole.**

rapid ('ræpɪd) adj. 1. (of an action) performed or occurring during a short interval of time; quick. 2. acting or moving quickly; fast: *a rapid worker.* —**'rapidly** adv. —**rapidity** (rə'pɪdɪtɪ) *or* **'rapidness** n.

rapids ('ræpɪdz) pl. n. part of a river where the current is very fast and turbulent.

rapier ('reɪpɪə) n. 1. a long narrow two-edged sword with a guarded hilt, used as a thrusting weapon, popular in the 16th and 17th centuries. 2. a smaller single-edged 18th-century sword, used principally in France.

rapine ('ræpaɪn) n. the seizure of property by force; pillage.

rapport (ræ'pɔː) n. (often foll. by *with*) a sympathetic relationship or understanding.

rapprochement *French.* (raprɔʃ'mɑ̃) n. a resumption of friendly relations, esp. between two countries.

rapscallion (ræp'skæljən) n. a disreputable person;

THESAURUS

ment, class, collection, gamut, kind, lot, order, selection, series, sort, variety ~v. 4. align, arrange, array, dispose, draw up, line up, order 5. arrange, bracket, catalogue, categorize, class, classify, file, grade, group, pigeonhole, rank 6. aim, align, direct, level, point, train 7. cruise, explore, ramble, roam, rove, straggle, stray, stroll, sweep, traverse, wander 8. extend, fluctuate, go, reach, run, stretch, vary between

rank¹ n. 1. caste, class, classification, degree, dignity, division, echelon, grade, level, nobility, order, position, quality, sort, standing, station, status, stratum, type 2. column, file, formation, group, line, range, row, series, tier ~v. 3. align, arrange, array, class, classify, dispose, grade, line up, locate, marshal, order, position, range, sort

rank² 1. abundant, dense, exuberant, flourishing, lush, luxuriant, productive, profuse, strong-growing, vigorous 2. bad, disagreeable, disgusting, fetid, foul, fusty, gamy, mephitic, musty, noisome, noxious, off, offensive, pungent, putrid, rancid, revolting, stale, stinking, strong-smelling 3. absolute, arrant, blatant, complete, downright, egregious, excessive, extravagant, flagrant, glaring, gross, rampant, sheer, thorough, total, undisguised, unmitigated, utter 4. abusive, atrocious, coarse, crass, filthy, foul, gross, indecent,

nasty, obscene, outrageous, scurrilous, shocking, vulgar

rank and file 1. lower ranks, men, other ranks, private soldiers, soldiers, troops 2. body, general public, majority, mass, masses

rankle anger, annoy, chafe, embitter, fester, gall, get one's goat (*Inf.*), irk, irritate, rile

ransack 1. comb, explore, go through, rake, rummage, scour, search, turn inside out 2. despoil, gut, loot, pillage, plunder, raid, ravage, rifle, sack, strip

ransom n. 1. deliverance, liberation, redemption, release, rescue 2. money, payment, payoff, price ~v. 3. buy (someone) out (*Inf.*), buy the freedom of, deliver, liberate, obtain *or* pay for the release of, redeem, release, rescue, set free

rant 1. v. bellow, bluster, cry, declaim, rave, roar, shout, spout (*Inf.*), vociferate, yell 2. n. bluster, bombast, diatribe, fanfaronade (*Rare*), harangue, philippic, rhetoric, tirade, vociferation

rapacious avaricious, extortionate, grasping, greedy, insatiable, marauding, plundering, predatory, preying, ravenous, usurious, voracious, wolfish

rapacity avarice, avidity, cupidity, graspingness, greed, greediness, insatiableness, predatoriness, rapaciousness, ravenousness,

usury, voraciousness, voracity, wolfishness

rape n. 1. outrage, ravishment, sexual assault, violation 2. depredation, despoilment, despoliation, pillage, plundering, rapine, sack, spoliation 3. abuse, defilement, desecration, maltreatment, perversion, violation ~v. 4. outrage, ravish, sexually assault, violate 5. despoil, loot, pillage, plunder, ransack, sack, spoliate

rapid brisk, expeditious, express, fast, fleet, flying, hasty, hurried, precipitate, prompt, quick, speedy, swift

rapidity alacrity, briskness, celerity, dispatch, expedition, fleetness, haste, hurry, precipitateness, promptitude, promptness, quickness, rush, speed, speediness, swiftness, velocity

rapidly at speed, briskly, expeditiously, fast, hastily, hurriedly, in a hurry, in a rush, in haste, like a shot, precipitately, promptly, quickly, speedily, swiftly, with dispatch

rapport affinity, bond, empathy, harmony, interrelationship, link, relationship, sympathy, understanding

rapprochement détente, reconcilement, reconciliation, restoration of harmony, reunion, softening

rascal or rogue.

rapt (ræpt) *adj.* **1.** totally absorbed; engrossed; spellbound, esp. through or as if through emotion: *rapt with wonder.* **2.** characterized by or proceeding from rapture: *a rapt smile.* —**'raptly** *adv.*

raptorial (ræp'tɔːrɪəl) *adj. Zool.* **1.** (of the feet of birds) adapted for seizing prey. **2.** of or relating to birds of prey.

rapture ('ræptʃə) *n.* **1.** the state of mind resulting from feelings of high emotion; joyous ecstasy. **2.** (*often pl.*) an expression of ecstatic joy. **3.** *Arch.* the act of transporting a person from one sphere of existence to another. ~*vb.* **4.** (*tr.*) *Arch. or literary.* to enrapture. —**'rapturous** *adj.*

rare[1] (rɛə) *adj.* **1.** not widely known; not frequently used or experienced; uncommon or unusual: *a rare word.* **2.** not widely distributed; not generally occurring: *a rare herb.* **3.** (of a gas, esp. the atmosphere at high altitudes) having a low density; thin; rarefied. **4.** uncommonly great; extreme: *kind to a rare degree.* **5.** exhibiting uncommon excellence: *rare skill.* —**'rareness** *n.*

rare[2] (rɛə) *adj.* (of meat, esp. beef) undercooked.

rarebit ('rɛəbɪt) *n.* another term for **Welsh rabbit.**

rare earth *n.* **1.** any oxide of a lanthanide. **2.** Also called: **rare-earth element.** any element of the lanthanide series.

rarefied ('rɛərɪˌfaɪd) *adj.* **1.** exalted in nature or character; lofty: *a rarefied spiritual existence.* **2.** current within only a small group. **3.** thin: *air rarefied at altitude.*

rarefy ('rɛərɪˌfaɪ) *vb.* **-fying, -fied.** to make or become rarer or less dense; thin out. —**'rareˌfiable** *adj.* —**'rareˌfier** *n.*

rarely ('rɛəlɪ) *adv.* **1.** hardly ever; seldom. **2.** to an unusual degree; exceptionally. **3.** *Brit. dialect.* uncommonly well; excellently: *he did rarely at market yesterday.*

raring ('rɛərɪŋ) *adj.* ready; willing; enthusiastic (esp. in **raring to go).**

rarity ('rɛərɪtɪ) *n., pl.* **-ties. 1.** a rare person or thing, esp. something valued because it is uncommon. **2.** the state of being rare.

rascal ('rɑːskəl) *n.* **1.** a disreputable person; villain. **2.** a mischievous or impish rogue. **3.** an affectionate or mildly reproving term, esp. for a child: *you little rascal.* **4.** *Obs.* a person of lowly birth. ~*adj.* **5.** (*prenominal*) *Obs.* **a.** belonging to the rabble. **b.** dishonest; knavish. —**ras'cality** *n.* —**'rascally** *adj.*

rase (reɪz) *vb.* a variant spelling of **raze.** —**'raser** *n.*

rash[1] (ræʃ) *adj.* **1.** acting without due thought; impetuous. **2.** resulting from excessive haste or impetuosity: *a rash word.* —**'rashly** *adv.* —**'rashness** *n.*

rash[2] (ræʃ) *n.* **1.** *Pathol.* any skin eruption. **2.** a series of unpleasant and unexpected occurrences: *a rash of forest fires.*

rasher ('ræʃə) *n.* a thin slice of bacon or ham.

rasp (rɑːsp) *n.* **1.** a harsh grating noise. **2.** a coarse file with rows of raised teeth. ~*vb.* **3.** (*tr.*) to scrape or rub (something) roughly, esp. with a rasp; abrade. **4.** to utter with or make a harsh grating noise. **5.** to irritate

(one's nerves); grate (upon). —**'rasper** *n.* —**'raspish** *adj.* —**'rasping** *adj.*

raspberry ('rɑːzbərɪ, -brɪ) *n., pl.* **-ries. 1.** a prickly rosaceous shrub of North America and Europe, that has pinkish-white flowers and typically red berry-like fruits (drupelets). See also **bramble. 2. a.** the fruit of any such plant. **b.** (*as modifier*): *raspberry jelly.* **3. a.** a dark purplish-red colour. **b.** (*as adj.*): *a raspberry dress.* **4.** a spluttering noise made with the tongue and lips to express contempt (esp. in **blow a raspberry**).

Rastafarian (ˌræstəˈfɛərɪən) *n.* **1.** a member of a Jamaican cult that regards Ras Tafari, the former emperor of Ethiopia, Haile Selassie, as God. ~*adj.* **2.** of, characteristic of, or relating to the Rastafarians. —**'Rasta** *adj., n.*

rat (ræt) *n.* **1.** any of numerous long-tailed Old World rodents, that are similar to but larger than mice and are now distributed all over the world. **2.** *Inf.* a person who deserts his friends or associates, esp. in time of trouble. **3.** *Inf.* a worker who works during a strike; blackleg; scab. **4.** *Sl.* a despicable person. **5. smell a rat.** to have suspicions of some treacherous practice. **6. have or be rats.** *Austral. sl.* to be mad or eccentric. ~*vb.* **ratting, ratted. 7.** (*intr.;* usually foll. by *on*) **a.** to divulge secret information (about); betray the trust (of). **b.** to default (on); abandon. **8.** to hunt and kill rats.

rata ('rɑːtə) *n.* a New Zealand tree with red flowers.

ratable *or* **rateable** ('reɪtəbəl) *adj.* **1.** able to be rated or evaluated. **2.** *Brit.* (of property, etc.) liable to payment of rates. —**ˌrata'bility** *or* **ˌratea'bility** *n.* —**'ratably** *or* **'rateably** *adv.*

ratable value *or* **rateable value** *n. Brit.* a fixed value assigned to a property by a local authority, on the basis of which variable annual rates are charged.

ratafia (ˌrætəˈfiə) *or* **ratafee** (ˌrætəˈfiː) *n.* **1.** any liqueur made from fruit or from brandy with added fruit. **2.** a flavouring essence made from almonds. **3.** *Chiefly Brit.* Also called: **ratafia biscuit.** a small macaroon flavoured with almonds.

ratan (ræ'tæn) *n.* a variant spelling of **rattan.**

ratatat-tat ('rætəˌtæt'tæt) *or* **ratatat** ('rætə'tæt) *n.* the sound of knocking on a door.

ratatouille (ˌrætəˈtwiː) *n.* a vegetable casserole made of tomatoes, aubergines, peppers, etc., fried in oil and stewed slowly.

ratchet ('rætʃɪt) *n.* **1.** a device in which a toothed rack or wheel is engaged by a pawl to permit motion in one direction only. **2.** the toothed rack or wheel forming part of such a device.

rate[1] (reɪt) *n.* **1.** a quantity or amount considered in relation to or measured against another quantity or amount: *a rate of 70 miles an hour.* **2.** a price or charge with reference to a standard or scale: *rate of interest.* **3.** a charge made per unit for a commodity, service, etc. **4.** See **rates. 5.** the relative speed of progress or change of something variable; pace: *the rate of production has doubled.* **6. a.** relative quality; class or grade. **b.** (*in combination*): *first-rate ideas.* **7. at any rate.** in any case; at all events; anyway. ~*vb.* (*mainly tr.*) **8.** (*also intr.*) to assign or receive a position on a scale of relative

rapt 1. absorbed, carried away, engrossed, enthralled, entranced, fascinated, gripped, held, intent, preoccupied, spellbound **2.** bewitched, blissful, captivated, charmed, delighted, ecstatic, enchanted, enraptured, rapturous, ravished, transported

rapture beatitude, bliss, cloud nine (*Inf.*), delectation, delight, ecstasy, enthusiasm, euphoria, exaltation, felicity, happiness, joy, ravishment, rhapsody, seventh heaven, spell, transport

rapturous blissful, delighted, ecstatic, enthusiastic, euphoric, exalted, happy, in seventh heaven, joyful, joyous, on cloud nine (*Inf.*), overjoyed, over the moon (*Inf.*), ravished, rhapsodic, transported

rare 1. exceptional, few, infrequent, out of the ordinary, recherché, scarce, singular, sparse, sporadic, strange, thin on the ground, uncommon, unusual **2.** admirable, choice, excellent, exquisite, extreme, fine, great, incomparable, peerless, superb, superlative **3.** invaluable, precious, priceless, rich

rarely 1. almost never, hardly, hardly ever, infrequently, little, once in a blue moon, once in a while, only now and then, on rare occasions, scarcely ever, seldom **2.** exceptionally, extraordinarily, finely, notably, remarkably, singularly, uncommonly, unusually

rarity 1. curio, curiosity, find, gem, one-off, pearl, treasure **2.** infrequency, scarcity, shortage, singularity, sparseness, strangeness, uncommonness, unusualness **3.** choiceness, excellence, exquisiteness, fineness, incomparableness, incomparableness, peerlessness, quality, superbness **4.** invaluableness, preciousness, pricelessness, richness, value, worth

rascal blackguard, caitiff (*Archaic*), devil, disgrace, good-for-nothing, imp, knave (*Archaic*), miscreant, ne'er-do-well, rake, rapscallion, reprobate, rogue, scallywag (*Inf.*), scamp, scoundrel, varmint (*Inf.*), villain, wastrel, wretch

rash[1] adventurous, audacious, brash, careless, foolhardy, harebrained, harum-scarum, hasty, headlong, headstrong, heedless, helter-skelter, hot-headed, ill-advised, illconsidered, impetuous, imprudent, impulsive, incautious, indiscreet, injudicious, madcap, precipitate, premature, reckless, thoughtless, unguarded, unthinking, unwary, venturesome

rash[2] **1.** eruption, outbreak **2.** epidemic, flood, outbreak, plague, series, spate, succession, wave

rashness adventurousness, audacity, brashness, carelessness, foolhardiness, hastiness, heedlessness, indiscretion, precipitation, recklessness, temerity, thoughtlessness

rasp *n.* **1.** grating, grinding, scrape, scratch ~*v.* **2.** abrade, excoriate, file, grind, rub, sand, scour, scrape **3.** grate (upon), irk, irritate, jar (upon), rub (someone) up the wrong way, set one's teeth on edge, wear upon

rasping *or* **raspy** creaking, croaking, croaky, grating, gravelly, gruff, harsh, hoarse, husky, jarring, rough, scratchy

values; rank: *he is rated fifth in the world.* **9.** to estimate the value of; evaluate: *we rate your services highly.* **10.** to be worthy of; deserve: *this hotel does not rate four stars.* **11.** to consider; regard: *I rate him among my friends.* **12.** *Brit.* to assess the value of (property) for the purpose of local taxation.
▷ **Usage.** The use of the verb *rate* alone with the sense of thinking highly of something is avoided in careful usage: *the clients do not think highly of* (not *do not rate*) *the new system.*

rate[2] ('reɪt) *vb.* (*tr.*) to scold or criticize severely; rebuke harshly.

ratepayer ('reɪt,peɪə) *n. Brit.* a person who pays local rates, esp. a householder.

rates (reɪts) *pl. n. Brit.* a tax on property levied by a local authority.

rather ('rɑːðə) *adv.* (*in senses 1-4, not used with a negative*) **1.** relatively or fairly; somewhat: *it's rather dull.* **2.** to a significant or noticeable extent; quite: *she's rather pretty.* **3.** to a limited extent or degree: *I rather thought that was the case.* **4.** with better or more just cause: *this text is rather to be deleted than rewritten.* **5.** more readily or willingly; sooner: *I would rather not see you tomorrow.* ~*sentence connector.* **6.** on the contrary: *it's not cold. Rather, it's very hot.* ~*sentence substitute.* ('rɑː'ðɜː) **7.** an expression of strong affirmation: *Is it worth seeing? Rather!*
▷ **Usage.** Both *would* and *had* are used with *rather* in sentences such as *I would rather* (or *had rather*) *go to the film than to the play. Had rather* is less common and now widely regarded as slightly old-fashioned.

ratify ('rætɪ,faɪ) *vb.* **-fying, -fied.** (*tr.*) to give formal approval or consent to. —'**rati,fiable** *n.* —,**ratifi'cation** *n.* —'**rati,fier** *n.*

rating[1] ('reɪtɪŋ) *n.* **1.** a classification according to order or grade; ranking. **2.** an ordinary seaman. **3.** *Sailing.* a handicap assigned to a racing boat based on its dimensions, draught, etc. **4.** the estimated financial or credit standing of a business enterprise or individual. **5.** *Radio, television, etc.* a figure based on statistical sampling indicating what proportion of the total audience tune in to a specific programme.

rating[2] ('reɪtɪŋ) *n.* a sharp scolding or rebuke.

ratio ('reɪʃɪəʊ) *n., pl.* **-tios. 1.** a relationship that indicates the extent to which one class of objects exists compared to another: *the ratio of boys to girls.* **2.** *Maths.* a quotient of two numbers or quantities. See also **proportion** (sense 6).

ratiocinate (,rætɪ'ɒsɪ,neɪt) *vb.* (*intr.*) to think or argue logically and methodically; reason. —,**rati,oci'nation** *n.* —,**rati'oci,native** *adj.* —,**rati'oci,nator** *n.*

ration ('ræʃən) *n.* **1. a.** a fixed allowance of food, provisions, etc., esp. a statutory one for civilians in time of scarcity or soldiers in time of war. **b.** (*as modifier*): *a ration book.* **2.** a sufficient or adequate amount: *you've had your ration of television for today.* ~*vb.* (*tr.*) **3.** (often foll. by *out*) to distribute (provisions), esp. to an army. **4.** to restrict the distribution or consumption of (a commodity) by (people): *the government has rationed sugar.*

rational ('ræʃənəl) *adj.* **1.** using reason or logic in think-

ing out a problem. **2.** in accordance with the principles of logic or reason; reasonable. **3.** of sound mind; sane: *the patient seemed quite rational.* **4.** endowed with the capacity to reason: *man is a rational being.* **5. a.** *Maths.* (of an expression, equation, etc.) containing no variable either in irreducible radical form or raised to a fractional power. **b.** (*as n.*): a rational. —'**rationally** *adv.* —'**rationalness** *n.* —,**ratio'nality** *n.*

rationale (,ræʃə'nɑːl) *n.* a reasoned exposition, esp. one defining the fundamental reasons for an action, etc.

rationalism ('ræʃənə,lɪzəm) *n.* **1.** the doctrine that reason is the proper basis for regulating morals, conduct, etc. **2.** *Philosophy.* the doctrine that knowledge is acquired by reason without regard to experience. **3.** *Theol.* the doctrine that human reason, rather than divine revelation, is the basis for establishing religious truth. —'**rationalist** *n.* —,**rational'istic** *adj.* —,**rational'istically** *adv.*

rationalize *or* **-ise** ('ræʃənə,laɪz) *vb.* **1.** to justify (one's actions) with plausible reasons, esp. after the event. **2.** to apply logic or reason to (something). **3.** (*tr.*) to eliminate unnecessary equipment, etc. from (a factory, etc.), in order to make it more efficient. **4.** (*tr.*) *Maths.* to eliminate radicals without changing the value of (an expression) or the roots of (an equation). —,**rationali'zation** *or* **-i'sation** *n.* —'**rational,izer** *or* **-,iser** *n.*

rational number *n.* any real number of the form a/b, where a and b are integers and b is not zero, as 7 or 7/3.

rations ('ræʃənz) *pl. n.* (*sometimes sing.*) a fixed daily allowance of food, esp. to military personnel or when supplies are limited.

ratline *or* **ratlin** ('rætlɪn) *n. Naut.* any of a series of light lines tied across the shrouds of a sailing vessel for climbing aloft.

rat race *n.* a continual routine of hectic competitive activity: *working in the City is a real rat race.*

ratsbane ('ræts,beɪn) *n.* rat poison, esp. arsenic oxide.

rattan *or* **ratan** (ræ'tæn) *n.* **1.** a climbing palm having tough stems used for wickerwork and canes. **2.** the stems of such a plant collectively. **3.** a stick made from one of these stems.

ratter ('rætə) *n.* **1.** a dog or cat that catches and kills rats. **2.** another word for **rat** (sense 3).

rattle ('rætəl) *vb.* **1.** to make a rapid succession of short sharp sounds, as of loose pellets colliding when shaken in a container. **2.** to shake with such a sound. **3.** to send, move, drive, etc., with such a sound: *the car rattled along the country road.* **4.** (*intr.*; foll. by *on*) to chatter idly: *he rattled on about his work.* **5.** (*tr.*, foll. by *off, out,* etc.) to recite perfunctorily or rapidly. **6.** (*tr.*) *Inf.* to disconcert; make frightened or anxious. ~*n.* **7.** a rapid succession of short sharp sounds. **8.** a baby's toy filled with small pellets that rattle when shaken. **9.** a series of loosely connected horny segments on the tail of a rattlesnake, vibrated to produce a rattling sound. **10.** any of various European scrophulariaceous plants having a capsule in which the seeds rattle, such as the **red rattle** and the **yellow rattle. 11.** idle chatter. —'**rattly** *adj.*

rattlesnake ('rætəl,sneɪk) *n.* any of the venomous New World snakes such as the **black** or **timber rattlesnake**

THESAURUS

rate *n.* **1.** degree, percentage, proportion, ratio, relation, scale, standard **2.** charge, cost, dues, duty, fee, figure, hire, price, tariff, tax, toll **3.** gait, measure, pace, speed, tempo, time, velocity **4.** class, classification, degree, grade, position, quality, rank, rating, status, value, worth **5. at any rate** anyhow, anyway, at all events, in any case, nevertheless ~*v.* **6.** adjudge, appraise, assess, class, classify, consider, count, esteem, estimate, evaluate, grade, measure, rank, reckon, regard, value, weigh **7.** be entitled to, be worthy of, deserve, merit **8.** *Sl.* admire, esteem, respect, think highly of, value

rather 1. a bit, a little, fairly, kind of (*Inf.*), moderately, pretty (*Inf.*), quite, relatively, slightly, somewhat, sort of (*Inf.*), to some degree, to some extent **2.** a good bit, noticeably, significantly, very **3.** instead, more readily, more willingly, preferably, sooner

ratify affirm, approve, authenticate, authorize, bear out, bind, certify, confirm,

consent to, corroborate, endorse, establish, sanction, sign, uphold, validate

rating class, classification, degree, designation, estimate, evaluation, grade, order, placing, position, rank, rate, standing, status

ratio arrangement, correlation, correspondence, equation, fraction, percentage, proportion, rate, relation, relationship

ration *n.* **1.** allotment, allowance, dole, helping, measure, part, portion, provision, quota, share **2.** *Plural* commons (*Brit.*), food, provender, provisions, stores, supplies ~*v.* **3.** **With out** allocate, allot, apportion, deal, distribute, dole, give out, issue, measure out, mete, parcel out **4.** budget, conserve, control, limit, restrict, save

rational 1. enlightened, intelligent, judicious, logical, lucid, realistic, reasonable, sagacious, sane, sensible, sound, wise **2.** cerebral, cognitive, ratiocinative, reasoning, thinking **3.** all there (*Inf.*), balanced, *compos*

mentis, in one's right mind, lucid, normal, of sound mind, sane

rationale exposition, grounds, logic, motivation, philosophy, principle, *raison d'être*, reasons, theory

rationalize 1. account for, excuse, explain away, extenuate, justify, make allowance for, make excuses for, vindicate **2.** apply logic to, elucidate, reason out, resolve, think through **3.** make cuts, make more efficient, streamline, trim

rattle *v.* **1.** bang, clatter, jangle **2.** bounce, jar, jiggle, jolt, jounce, shake, vibrate **3.** *With on* blether, cackle, chatter, gabble, gibber, jabber, prate, prattle, rabbit on (*Brit. sl.*), run on, witter (*Inf.*), yak (away) (*Sl.*) **4.** *Inf.* discomfit, discompose, disconcert, discountenance, disturb, faze (*U.S. inf.*), frighten, perturb, put (someone) off his stride, put (someone) out of countenance, scare, shake, upset **5.** *With off* list, recite, reel off, rehearse, run through, spiel off (*Inf.*)

belonging to the family of pit vipers. They have a series of loose horny segments on the tail that are vibrated to produce a buzzing or whirring sound. Also (*Inf.*): '**rattler.**

rattletrap ('ræt_əl_ətræp) *n*. *Inf.* a broken-down old vehicle, esp. an old car.

rattling ('rætlɪŋ) *adv*. *Inf.* (intensifier qualifying something good, fine, etc.): *a rattling good lunch.*

ratty ('rætɪ) *adj*. -**tier**, -**tiest**. **1**. *Brit. & N.Z. sl.* irritable; annoyed. **2**. *Sl.* (of the hair) straggly, unkempt, or greasy. **3**. *U.S. sl.* shabby; dilapidated. **4**. *Austral. sl.* mad, eccentric, or odd. **5**. of, like, or full of rats. —'**rattily** *adv*. —'**rattiness** *n*.

raucous ('rɔːkəs) *adj*. (of voices, cries, etc.) harshly or hoarsely loud. —'**raucously** *adv*. —'**raucousness** *n*.

raunchy ('rɔːntʃɪ) *adj*. **chier**, **chiest**. *U.S. sl.* **1**. lecherous or smutty. **2**. slovenly; dirty. —'**raunchiness** *n*.

ravage ('rævɪdʒ) *vb*. **1**. to cause extensive damage to. ~*n*. **2**. (*often pl.*) destructive action: *the ravages of time.* —'**ravager** *n*.

rave (reɪv) *vb*. **1**. to utter (something) in a wild or incoherent manner, as when delirious. **2**. (*intr.*) to speak in an angry uncontrolled manner. **3**. (*intr.*) (of the sea, wind, etc.) to rage or roar. **4**. (*intr.*; foll. by *over* or *about*) *Inf.* to write or speak (about) with great enthusiasm. **5**. (*intr.*) *Brit. sl.* to enjoy oneself wildly or uninhibitedly. ~*n*. **6**. *Inf.* **a**. enthusiastic or extravagant praise. **b**. (*as modifier*): *a rave review.* **7**. Also called: **rave-up**. *Brit. sl.* a party.

ravel ('ræv^əl) *vb*. -**elling**, -**elled** or *U.S.* -**eling**, -**eled**. **1**. to tangle (threads, fibres, etc.) or (of threads, etc.) to become entangled. **2**. (often foll. by *out*) to tease or draw out (the fibres of a fabric) or (of a fabric) to fray out in loose ends; unravel. **3**. (*tr.*; usually foll. by *out*) to disentangle or resolve: *to ravel out a complicated story.* ~*n*. **4**. a tangle or complication. —'**raveller** *n*. —'**ravelly** *adj*.

raven ('reɪv^ən) *n*. **1**. a large passerine bird of the crow family, having a large straight bill, long wedge-shaped tail, and black plumage. **2. a.** a shiny black colour. **b**. (*as adj.*): *raven hair.*

ravening ('rævənɪŋ) *adj*. (of animals) voracious; predatory. —'**raveningly** *adv*.

ravenous ('rævənəs) *adj*. **1**. famished; starving. **2**. rapacious; voracious. —'**ravenously** *adv*. —'**ravenousness** *n*.

ravine (rə'viːn) *n*. a deep narrow steep-sided valley.

raving ('reɪvɪŋ) *adj*. **1. a**. delirious; frenzied. **b**. (*as adv.*): *raving mad.* **2**. *Inf.* (intensifier): *a raving beauty.* —'**ravingly** *adv*.

ravioli (ˌrævɪ'əʊlɪ) *n*. small squares of pasta containing a savoury mixture of meat, cheese, etc.

ravish ('rævɪʃ) *vb*. (*tr.*) **1**. (*often passive*) to enrapture. **2**. to rape. **3**. *Arch.* to carry off by force. —'**ravisher** *n*. —'**ravishment** *n*.

ravishing ('rævɪʃɪŋ) *adj*. delightful; lovely; entrancing. —'**ravishingly** *adv*.

raw (rɔː) *adj*. **1**. (of food) not cooked. **2**. (*prenominal*) in an unfinished, natural, or unrefined state; not treated by manufacturing or other processes: *raw materials.* **3**.

(of the skin, a wound, etc.) having the surface exposed or abraded, esp. painfully. **4**. (of edge of material) unhemmed; liable to fray. **5**. ignorant, inexperienced, or immature: *a raw recruit.* **6**. (*prenominal*) not selected or modified: *raw statistics.* **7**. frank or realistic: *a raw picture of a marriage.* **8**. (of spirits) undiluted. **9**. *Chiefly U.S.* coarse, vulgar, or obscene. **10**. (of the weather) harshly cold and damp. **11**. *Inf.* unfair; unjust (esp. in **a raw deal**). ~*n*. **12. the raw**. *Brit. inf.* a sensitive point: *his criticism touched me on the raw.* **13. in the raw. a**. *Inf.* without clothes; naked. **b**. in a natural or unmodified state. —'**rawish** *adj*. —'**rawly** *adv*. —'**rawness** *n*.

rawboned ('rɔː'bəʊnd) *adj*. having a lean bony physique.

rawhide ('rɔːˌhaɪd) *n*. **1**. untanned hide. **2**. a whip or rope made of strips cut from such a hide.

ray[1] (reɪ) *n*. **1**. a narrow beam of light; gleam. **2**. a slight indication: *a ray of solace.* **3**. *Maths.* a straight line extending from a point. **4**. a thin beam of electromagnetic radiation or particles. **5**. any of the bony or cartilaginous spines of the fin of a fish that form the support for the soft part of the fin. **6**. any of the arms or branches of a starfish. ~*vb*. **7**. (of an object) to emit (light) in rays or (of light) to issue in the form of rays. **8**. (*intr.*) (of lines, etc.) to extend in rays or on radiating paths. **9**. (*tr.*) to adorn (an ornament, etc.) with rays or radiating lines. —'**rayless** *adj*.

ray[2] (reɪ) *n*. any of various marine selachian fishes typically having a flattened body, greatly enlarged winglike pectoral fins, gills on the undersurface of the fins, and a long whiplike tail.

ray[3] (reɪ) *n*. *Music.* (in tonic solfa) the second degree of any major scale; supertonic.

rayon ('reɪɒn) *n*. **1**. any of a number of textile fibres made from wood pulp or other forms of cellulose. **2**. any fabric made from such a fibre. **3**. (*modifier*): *a rayon shirt.*

raze or **rase** (reɪz) *vb*. (*tr.*) **1**. to demolish (buildings, etc.) completely (esp. in **raze to the ground**). **2**. to delete; erase. **3**. *Arch.* to graze. —'**razer** or '**raser** *n*.

razor ('reɪzə) *n*. **1**. a sharp implement used esp. for shaving the face. **2. on a razor's edge** or **razor-edge**. in an acute dilemma. ~*vb*. **3**. (*tr.*) to cut or shave with a razor.

razorbill ('reɪzəˌbɪl) or **razor-billed auk** *n*. a common auk of the North Atlantic, having a thick laterally compressed bill with white markings.

razzle-dazzle ('ræz^əl'dæz^əl) or **razzmatazz** ('ræzmə-'tæz) *n*. *Sl.* **1**. noisy or showy fuss or activity. **2**. a spree or frolic.

Rb the chemical symbol for rubidium.

R.C. *abbrev. for*: **1**. Red Cross. **2**. Roman Catholic.

R.C.A. *abbrev. for*: **1**. Radio Corporation of America. **2**. Royal College of Art.

R.C.A.F. *abbrev. for* Royal Canadian Air Force.

R.C.M. *abbrev. for* Royal College of Music.

R.C.M.P. *abbrev. for* Royal Canadian Mounted Police.

R.C.N. *abbrev. for*: **1**. Royal Canadian Navy. **2**. Royal College of Nursing.

R.C.P. *abbrev. for* Royal College of Physicians.

THESAURUS

raucous grating, harsh, hoarse, husky, loud, noisy, rasping, rough, strident

ravage **1**. *v*. demolish, desolate, despoil, destroy, devastate, gut, lay waste, leave in ruins, loot, pillage, plunder, ransack, raze, ruin, sack, shatter, spoil, wreak havoc on, wreck **2**. *n*. *Often plural* damage, demolition, depredation, desolation, destruction, devastation, havoc, pillage, plunder, rapine, ruin, ruination, spoliation, waste

rave *v*. **1**. babble, be delirious, fume, go mad, rage, rant, roar, run amuck, splutter, storm, talk wildly, thunder **2**. *With about Inf.* be delighted by, be mad about (*Inf.*), be wild about (*Inf.*), cry up, enthuse, gush, praise, rhapsodize ~*n*. **3**. *Inf.* acclaim, applause, encomium, praise **4**. *Also* **rave-up** *Brit. sl.* affair, bash (*Inf.*), blow-out (*Sl.*), celebration, do (*Inf.*), party **5**. *Brit. sl.* craze, fad, fashion, vogue ~*adj*. **6**. *Inf.* ecstatic, enthusiastic, excellent, favourable, laudatory

ravenous **1**. famished, starved, starving,

very hungry **2**. avaricious, covetous, devouring, ferocious, gluttonous, grasping, greedy, insatiable, insatiate, predatory, rapacious, ravening, voracious, wolfish

ravine canyon, clough (*Dialect*), defile, flume, gap (*U.S.*), gorge, gulch (*U.S.*), gully, linn (*Scot.*), pass

raving berserk, crazed, crazy, delirious, frantic, frenzied, furious, hysterical, insane, irrational, mad, out of one's mind, rabid, raging, wild

ravish **1**. captivate, charm, delight, enchant, enrapture, entrance, fascinate, overjoy, spellbind, transport **2**. abuse, outrage, rape, sexually assault, violate

ravishing beautiful, bewitching, charming, dazzling, delightful, enchanting, entrancing, gorgeous, lovely, radiant, stunning (*Inf.*)

raw **1**. bloody (*of meat*), fresh, natural, uncooked, undressed, unprepared **2**. basic, coarse, crude, green, natural, organic, rough, unfinished, unprocessed, unrefined, unripe,

untreated **3**. abraded, chafed, grazed, open, scratched, sensitive, skinned, sore, tender **4**. callow, green, ignorant, immature, inexperienced, new, undisciplined, unpractised, unseasoned, unskilled, untrained, untried **5**. bare, blunt, brutal, candid, frank, naked, plain, realistic, unembellished, unvarnished **6**. biting, bitter, bleak, chill, chilly, cold, damp, freezing, harsh, piercing, unpleasant, wet

ray **1**. bar, beam, flash, gleam, shaft **2**. flicker, glimmer, hint, indication, scintilla, spark, trace

raze **1**. bulldoze, demolish, destroy, flatten, knock down, level, pull down, remove, ruin, tear down, throw down **2**. delete, efface, erase, expunge, extinguish, extirpate, obliterate, rub out, scratch out, strike out, wipe out

R.C.S. *abbrev. for:* **1.** Royal College of Science. **2.** Royal College of Surgeons. **3.** Royal Corps of Signals.

rd. *abbrev. for:* **1.** rod (unit of length). **2.** road. **3.** round. **4.** *Physics.* rutherford.

Rd. *abbrev. for* Road.

re¹ (reɪ, riː) *n. Music.* an alternative spelling of **ray³**.

re² (riː) *prep.* with reference to.

▷ **Usage.** *Re,* in contexts such as *re your letter, your remarks have been noted* or *he spoke to me re your complaint,* is common in business. In general English *with reference to* is preferable in the former case and *about* or *concerning* in the latter. The use of *re* is often restricted to the letter heading.

Re the chemical symbol for rhenium.

R.E. *abbrev. for* Royal Engineers.

re- *prefix.* **1.** indicating return to a previous condition, withdrawal, etc.: *rebuild; renew.* **2.** indicating repetition of an action: *remarry.*

▷ **Usage.** Verbs with *re-* indicate repetition or restoration. It is unnecessary to add an adverb such as *back* or *again: This must not occur again* (not *recur again*).

reach (riːtʃ) *vb.* **1.** *(tr.)* to arrive at or get to (a place, person, etc.) in the course of movement or action: *to reach the office.* **2.** to extend as far as (a point or place): *to reach the ceiling; can you reach?* **3.** *(tr.)* to come to (a certain condition or situation): *to reach the point of starvation.* **4.** *(intr.)* to extend in influence or operation: *the Roman conquest reached throughout England.* **5.** *(tr.) Inf.* to pass or give (something to a person) with the outstretched hand. **6.** *(intr.; foll. by out, for,* or *after)* to make a movement (towards), as if to grasp or touch. **7.** *(tr.)* to make contact or communication with (someone): *we tried to reach him all day.* **8.** *(tr.)* to strike, esp. in fencing or boxing. **9.** *(tr.)* to amount to (a certain sum): *to reach five million.* **10.** *(intr.) Naut.* to sail on a tack with the wind on or near abeam. ~*n.* **11.** the act of reaching. **12.** the extent or distance of reaching: *within reach.* **13.** the range of influence, power, jurisdiction, etc. **14.** an open stretch of water, esp. on a river. **15.** *Naut.* the direction or distance sailed by a vessel on one tack. —**'reachable** *adj.* —**'reacher** *n.*

reach-me-down *n.* **1.** another name for **hand-me-down.** **2.** a ready-made garment.

react (rɪ'ækt) *vb.* **1.** *(intr.,* foll. by *to, upon,* etc.) (of a person or thing) to act in response to another person, a stimulus, etc. **2.** *(intr.,* foll. by *against)* to act in an opposing or contrary manner. **3.** *(intr.) Physics.* to exert an equal force in the opposite direction to an acting force. **4.** *Chem.* to undergo or cause to undergo a chemical reaction. —**re'active** *adj.*

reactance (rɪ'æktəns) *n.* the opposition to the flow of alternating current by the capacitance or inductance of an electrical circuit.

reaction (rɪ'ækʃən) *n.* **1.** a response to some foregoing action or stimulus. **2.** the reciprocal action of two things acting together. **3.** opposition to change, esp. political change, or a desire to return to a former system. **4.** a response indicating a person's feelings or emotional attitude. **5.** *Med.* **a.** any effect produced by the action of a drug. **b.** any effect produced by a substance (allergen) to which a person is allergic. **6.** *Chem.* a process that involves changes in the structure and energy content of atoms, molecules, or ions. **7.** the equal but opposite force produced when any force is applied to a body or system. —**re'actional** *adj.*

reactionary (rɪ'ækʃənərɪ, -ʃənrɪ) *or* **reactionist** *adj.* **1.** of, relating to, or characterized by reaction, esp. against radical political or social change. ~*n.* **2.** a person opposed to radical change. —**re'actionism** *n.*

reactivate (rɪ'æktɪˌveɪt) *vb. (tr.)* to make (something) active again. —**re,acti'vation** *n.*

reactor (rɪ'æktə) *n.* **1.** *Chem.* a substance, such as a reagent, that undergoes a reaction. **2.** short for **nuclear reactor.** **3.** a vessel in which a chemical reaction takes place. **4.** a coil of low resistance and high inductance that introduces reactance into a circuit. **5.** *Med.* a person sensitive to a particular drug or agent.

read (riːd) *vb.* **reading, read** (rɛd). **1.** to comprehend the meaning of (something written or printed) by looking at and interpreting the written or printed characters. **2.** *(when tr.,* often foll. by *out)* to look at, interpret, and speak aloud (something written or printed). **3.** *(tr.)* to interpret the significance or meaning of through scrutiny and recognition: *to read a map.* **4.** *(tr.)* to interpret or understand the meaning of (signs, characters, etc.) other than by visual means: *to read Braille.* **5.** *(tr.)* to have sufficient knowledge of (a language) to understand the written or printed word. **6.** *(tr.)* to discover or make out the true nature or mood of: *to read someone's mind.* **7.** to interpret or understand (something read) in a specified way: *I read this speech as satire.* **8.** *(tr.)* to adopt as a reading in a particular passage: *for "boon" read "bone".* **9.** *(intr.)* to have or contain a certain form or wording: *the sentence reads as follows.* **10.** to undertake a course of study in (a subject): *to read history.* **11.** to gain knowledge by reading: *he read about the war.* **12.** *(tr.)* to register, indicate, or show: *the meter reads 100.* **13.** *(tr.)* to put into a specified condition by reading: *to read a child to sleep.* **14.** *(tr.)* to hear and understand, esp. when using a two-way radio: *we are reading you loud and clear.* **15.** *Computers.* to obtain (data) from a storage device, such as magnetic tape. **16. read a lesson** *(or* lecture). *Inf.* to censure or reprimand. **17. read between the lines.** *Inf.* to perceive or deduce a meaning that is hidden or implied. ~*n.* **18.** matter suitable for reading: *this book is a very good read.* **19.** the act or a spell of reading. ~See also **read into, read out,** etc.

readable ('riːdəbl) *adj.* **1.** (of handwriting, etc.) able to be read or deciphered; legible. **2.** (of style of writing) interesting, easy, or pleasant to read. —**,reada'bility** *or* **'readableness** *n.* —**'readably** *adv.*

reader ('riːdə) *n.* **1.** a person who reads. **2.** *Chiefly Brit.* a senior lecturer at a university. **3. a.** a book that is part of a planned series for those learning to read. **b.** a standard textbook, esp. for foreign-language learning. **4.** a person who reads aloud in public. **5.** a person who

readapt *vb.*	**reallocate** *vb.*	**reappraise** *vb.*	**rebind** *vb.*
readdress *vb.*	**reallocation** *n.*	**rearrange** *vb.*	**reborn** *adj.*
readjust *vb.*	**reappear** *vb.*	**rearrangement** *n.*	**rebroadcast** *vb.*
readmission *n.*	**reappearance** *n.*	**reassemble** *vb.*	**rebuild** *vb.*
readmit *vb.*	**reapplication** *n.*	**reassess** *vb.*	**reburial** *n.*
readopt *vb.*	**reapply** *vb.*	**reassessment** *n.*	**rebury** *vb.*
reaffirm *vb.*	**reappoint** *vb.*	**reassign** *vb.*	**recalculate** *vb.*
reaffirmation *n.*	**reappointment** *n.*	**reattempt** *vb.*	**recast** *vb.*
realign *vb.*	**reapportion** *vb.*	**reawaken** *vb.*	**recharge** *vb.*
realignment *n.*	**reappraisal** *n.*	**rebid** *vb.*	**recheck** *vb.*

THESAURUS

reach *v.* **1.** arrive at, attain, get as far as, get to, land at, make **2.** contact, extend to, get (a) hold of, go as far as, grasp, stretch to, touch **3.** amount to, arrive at, attain, climb to, come to, drop, fall, move, rise, sink **4.** *Inf.* hand, hold out, pass, stretch **5.** communicate with, contact, establish contact with, find, get, get hold of, get in touch with, get through to, make contact with ~*n.* **6.** ambit, capacity, command, compass, distance, extension, extent, grasp, influence, jurisdiction, mastery, power, range, scope, spread, stretch, sweep

react 1. acknowledge, answer, reply, respond **2.** act, behave, conduct oneself, function, operate, proceed, work

reaction 1. acknowledgment, answer, feedback, reply, response **2.** compensation, counteraction, counterbalance, counterpoise, recoil **3.** conservatism, counter-revolution, obscurantism, the right

reactionary 1. *adj.* blimpish, conservative, counter-revolutionary, obscurantist, rightist **2.** *n.* Colonel Blimp, conservative, counter-revolutionary, die-hard, obscurantist, rightist, right-winger

read 1. glance at, look at, peruse, pore over, refer to, run one's eye over, scan, study **2.** announce, declaim, deliver, recite, speak, utter **3.** comprehend, construe, decipher, discover, interpret, perceive the meaning of, see, understand **4.** display, indicate, record, register, show

readable 1. clear, comprehensible, decipherable, intelligible, legible, plain, understandable **2.** easy to read, enjoyable, entertaining, enthralling, gripping, interesting, pleasant, worth reading

reads and assesses the merit of manuscripts submitted to a publisher. **6.** a proofreader. **7.** short for **lay reader.**

readership ('riːdəˌʃɪp) n. all the readers collectively of a particular publication or author: a readership of five million.

reading ('riːdɪŋ) n. **1. a.** the act of a person who reads. **b.** (as modifier): a reading room. **2. a.** ability to read. **b.** (as modifier): a child of reading age. **3.** any matter that can be read; written or printed text. **4.** a public recital or rendering of a literary work. **5.** the form of a particular word or passage in a given text, esp. where more than one version exists. **6.** an interpretation, as of a piece of music, a situation, or something said or written. **7.** knowledge gained from books: a person of little reading. **8.** a measurement indicated by a gauge, dial, scientific instrument, etc. **9.** Parliamentary procedure. **a.** the formal recital of the body or title of a bill in a legislative assembly in order to begin one of the stages of its passage. **b.** one of the three stages in the passage of a bill through a legislative assembly. **10.** the formal recital of something written, esp. a will.

read into (riːd) vb. (tr., prep.) to discern in or infer from a statement (meanings not intended by the speaker or writer).

read out (riːd) vb. (adv.) **1.** (tr.) to read (something) aloud. **2.** (tr.) U.S. to expel (someone) from a political party or other society. **3.** to retrieve information from a computer memory or storage device. ~n. **read-out. 4. a.** the act of retrieving information from a computer memory or storage device. **b.** the information retrieved.

read up (riːd) vb. (adv.; when intr., often foll. by on) to acquire information about (a subject) by reading intensively.

read-write head ('riːd'raɪt) n. Computers. an electromagnet that can both read and write information on a magnetic tape or disk.

ready ('rɛdɪ) adj. **readier, readiest. 1.** in a state of completion or preparedness, as for use or action. **2.** willing or eager: ready helpers. **3.** prompt or rapid: a ready response. **4.** (prenominal) quick in perceiving; intelligent: a ready mind. **5.** (postpositive) (foll. by to) on the point (of) or liable (to): ready to collapse. **6.** (postpositive) conveniently near (esp. in **ready to hand**). **7. make** or **get ready.** to prepare (oneself or something) for use or action. ~n. **8.** Inf. cash available for immediate use. Also called: **ready money. 9. at** or **to the ready. a.** (of a rifle) in the position adopted prior to aiming and firing. **b.** poised for use or action: with pen at the ready. —'readily adv. —'readiness n.

ready-made adj. **1.** made for purchase and immediate use by any customer. **2.** extremely convenient or ideally suited: a ready-made solution. **3.** unoriginal or conventional: ready-made phrases. ~n. **4.** a ready-made article, esp. a garment.

ready reckoner n. a table of numbers used to facilitate simple calculations, esp. one for working out interest, etc.

reagent (riː'eɪdʒənt) n. a substance for use in a chemical reaction, esp. for use in chemical synthesis and analysis.

real[1] (rɪəl) adj. **1.** existing or occurring in the physical world; not imaginary, fictitious, or theoretical; actual. **2.** (prenominal) true; actual; not false: the real reason. **3.** (prenominal) deserving the name; rightly so called: a real friend. **4.** not artificial or simulated; genuine: real fur. **5.** Philosophy. existent or relating to actual existence (as opposed to nonexistent, potential, contingent, or apparent). **6.** (prenominal) Econ. (of prices, incomes, etc.) considered in terms of purchasing power rather than nominal currency value. **7.** (prenominal) denoting or relating to immovable property such as land and tenements: real estate. **8.** Maths. involving or containing real numbers; nonimaginary. The real part of a complex number z is usually written Re z. **9.** Inf. (intensifier): a real genius. ~n. **10. the real.** that which exists in fact; reality. **11. for real.** Sl. not as a test or trial; in earnest. —'realness n.

real[2] (reɪ'ɑːl) n., pl. **reals** or **reales** (Spanish re'ales). a former small Spanish or Spanish-American silver coin.

real estate n. land, including the buildings or improvements on it and its natural assets, as minerals, timber, etc.

realism ('rɪəˌlɪzəm) n. **1.** awareness or acceptance of the physical universe, events, etc., as they are, as opposed to the abstract or ideal. **2.** a style of painting and sculpture that seeks to represent the familiar or typical in real life. **3.** any similar style in other arts, esp. literature. **4.** Philosophy. the theory that things named by general words, including universals, have a real existence independent of their names. **5.** Philosophy. the theory that physical objects continue to exist whether they are perceived or not. —'realist n.

reality (rɪ'ælɪtɪ) n., pl. **-ties. 1.** the state of things as they are or appear to be, rather than as one might wish them to be. **2.** something that is real. **3.** the state of being real. **4.** Philosophy. **a.** that which exists, independent of human awareness. **b.** the totality of facts. **5. in reality.** actually; in fact.

rechristen vb.	**reconnect** vb.	**redirect** vb.	**re-elect** vb.
recirculate vb.	**reconnection** n.	**redirection** n.	**re-election** n.
reclassification n.	**reconquer** vb.	**rediscover** vb.	**re-enact** vb.
reclassify vb.	**reconquest** n.	**rediscovery** n.	**re-enactment** n.
reclothe vb.	**reconvene** vb.	**redraft** n.	**re-enforce** vb.
recommence vb.	**recross** vb.	**redraft** vb.	**re-enforcement** n.
recommencement n.	**redecorate** vb.	**redraw** vb.	**re-enter** vb.
recompose vb.	**redevelop** vb.	**re-edit** vb.	**re-equip** vb.
reconfirm vb.	**redeveloper** n.	**re-educate** vb.	**re-erect** vb.
reconfirmation n.	**redevelopment** n.	**re-education** n.	**re-examine** vb.

THESAURUS

readily 1. cheerfully, eagerly, freely, gladly, promptly, quickly, voluntarily, willingly, with good grace, with pleasure **2.** at once, easily, effortlessly, in no time, quickly, right away, smoothly, speedily, straight away, unhesitatingly, without delay, without demur, without difficulty, without hesitation

readiness 1. fitness, maturity, preparation, preparedness, ripeness **2.** aptness, eagerness, gameness (Inf.), inclination, keenness, willingness **3.** adroitness, dexterity, ease, facility, handiness, promptitude, promptness, quickness, rapidity, skill **4. in readiness** all set, at or on hand, at the ready, fit, prepared, primed, ready, set, waiting, waiting in the wings

reading 1. examination, inspection, perusal, review, scrutiny, study **2.** homily, lecture, lesson, performance, recital, rendering, rendition, sermon **3.** conception, construction, grasp, impression, interpretation, treatment, understanding, version **4.** book-learning, edification, education, erudition, knowledge,

learning, scholarship

ready adj. **1.** all set, arranged, completed, fit, in readiness, organized, prepared, primed, ripe, set **2.** agreeable, apt, disposed, eager, game (Inf.), glad, happy, inclined, keen, minded, predisposed, prone, willing **3.** acute, adroit, alert, apt, astute, bright, clever, deft, dexterous, expert, handy, intelligent, keen, perceptive, prompt, quick, quick-witted, rapid, resourceful, sharp, skilful, smart **4.** about, close, in danger of, liable, likely, on the brink of, on the point of, on the verge of **5.** accessible, at or on hand, at one's fingertips, at the ready, available, close to hand, convenient, handy, near, on call, on tap (Inf.), present ~n. **6. at the ready** in readiness, poised, prepared, ready for action, waiting ~v. **7.** arrange, equip, fit out, get ready, make ready, order, organize, prepare, set

real absolute, actual, authentic, bona fide, certain, essential, existent, factual, genuine, heartfelt, honest, intrinsic, legitimate, posi-

tive, right, rightful, sincere, true, unaffected, unfeigned, valid, veritable

realistic 1. businesslike, common-sense, down-to-earth, hard-headed, level-headed, matter-of-fact, practical, pragmatic, rational, real, sensible, sober, unromantic, unsentimental **2.** authentic, faithful, genuine, graphic, lifelike, natural, naturalistic, representational, true, true to life, truthful

reality 1. actuality, authenticity, certainty, corporeality, fact, genuineness, materiality, realism, truth, validity, verisimilitude, verity **2. in reality** actually, as a matter of fact, in actuality, in fact, in point of fact, in truth, really

realization 1. appreciation, apprehension, awareness, cognizance, comprehension, conception, consciousness, grasp, imagination, perception, recognition, understanding **2.** accomplishment, achievement, carrying-out, completion, consummation, ef-

realize *or* **-ise** ('rɪə,laɪz) *vb.* **1.** (when *tr.*, *may take a clause as object*) to become conscious or aware of (something). **2.** (*tr.*, *often passive*) to bring (a plan, ambition, etc.) to fruition. **3.** (*tr.*) to give (a drama or film) the appearance of reality. **4.** (*tr.*) (of goods, property, etc.) to sell for or make (a certain sum): *this table realized £800*. **5.** (*tr.*) to convert (property or goods) into cash. **6.** (*tr.*) (of a musicologist or performer) to reconstruct (a composition) from an incomplete set of parts. —'real,izable *or* -,isable *adj.* —'real,izably *or* -,isably *adv.* —,reali'zation *or* -i'sation *n.* —'real,izer *or* -,iser *n.*

really ('rɪəlɪ) *adv.* **1.** in reality; in actuality; assuredly: *it's really quite harmless.* **2.** truly; genuinely: *really beautiful.* ~*interj.* **3.** an exclamation of dismay, disapproval, doubt, surprise, etc. **4. not really?** an exclamation of surprise or polite doubt.
▷ *Usage.* See at **very.**

realm (rɛlm) *n.* **1.** a royal domain; kingdom: *peer of the realm.* **2.** a field of interest, study, etc.: *the realm of the occult.*

real property *n.* immoveable property, esp. freehold land.

real tennis *n.* an ancient form of tennis played in a four-walled indoor court.

real-time *adj.* denoting or relating to a data-processing system in which a computer is on-line to a source of data and processes the data as it is generated.

realty ('rɪəltɪ) *n.* another term for **real property.**

ream (riːm) *n.* **1.** a number of sheets of paper, formerly 480 sheets (**short ream**), now 500 sheets (**long ream**) or 516 sheets (**printer's ream** or **perfect ream**). One ream is equal to 20 quires. **2.** (*often pl.*) *Inf.* a large quantity, esp. of written matter: *he wrote reams.*

reap (riːp) *vb.* **1.** to cut or harvest (a crop) from (a field). **2.** (*tr.*) to gain or get (something) as a reward for or result of some action or enterprise. —'reapable *adj.*

reaper ('riːpə) *n.* **1.** a person who reaps or a machine for reaping. **2. the grim reaper.** death.

rear[1] (rɪə) *n.* **1.** the back or hind part. **2.** the area or position that lies at the back: *a garden at the rear of the house.* **3.** the section of a military force farthest from the front. **4.** an informal word for **buttocks. 5. bring up the rear.** to be at the back in a procession, race, etc. **6. in the rear.** at the back. **7.** (*modifier*) of or in the rear: *the rear side.*

rear[2] (rɪə) *vb.* **1.** (*tr.*) to care for and educate (children) until maturity; raise. **2.** (*tr.*) to breed (animals) or grow (plants, etc.). **3.** (*tr.*) to place or lift (a ladder, etc.) upright. **4.** (*tr.*) to erect (a monument, building, etc.). **5.** (*intr.*; often foll. by *up*) (esp. of horses) to lift the front legs in the air and stand nearly upright. **6.** (*intr.*; often foll. by *up* or *over*) (esp. of tall buildings) to rise high; tower. **7.** (*intr.*) to start with anger, resentment, etc. —'rearer *n.*

rear admiral *n.* an officer holding flag rank in any of certain navies junior to a vice admiral.

rearguard ('rɪə,gɑːd) *n.* **1.** a detachment detailed to protect the rear of a military formation, esp. in retreat. **2.** an entrenched or conservative element, as in a political party. **3.** (*modifier*) of, relating to, or characteristic of a rearguard: *a rearguard action.*

rear light *or* **lamp** *n.* a red light, usually one of a pair, attached to the rear of a motor vehicle. U.S. names: **taillight, tail lamp.**

rearm (riːˈɑːm) *vb.* **1.** to arm again. **2.** (*tr.*) to equip (an army, etc.) with better weapons. —reˈarmament *n.*

rearmost ('rɪə,məʊst) *adj.* nearest the rear; coming last.

rear-view mirror *n.* a mirror on a motor vehicle enabling the driver to see traffic behind him.

rearward ('rɪəwəd) *adj., adv.* **1.** Also (for adv. only): **rearwards.** towards or in the rear. ~*n.* **2.** a position in the rear, esp. the rear division of a military formation.

reason ('riːzən) *n.* **1.** the faculty of rational argument, deduction, judgment, etc. **2.** sound mind; sanity. **3.** a cause or motive, as for a belief, action, etc. **4.** an argument in favour or a justification for something. **5.** *Philosophy.* intellect, as opposed to sensibility. **6.** *Logic.* a premiss of an argument, esp. the minor premiss. **7. by reason of.** because of. **8. in** *or* **within reason.** within moderate or justifiable bounds. **9. it stands to reason.** it is logical or obvious. **10. listen to reason.** to be persuaded peaceably. **11. reasons of State.** political justifications for an immoral act. ~*vb.* **12.** (when *tr.*, *takes a clause as object*) to think logically or draw (logical conclusions) from facts or premisses. **13.** (*intr.*, usually foll. by *with*) to seek to persuade by reasoning. **14.** (*tr.*, often foll. by *out*) to work out or resolve (a problem) by reasoning. —'reasoner *n.*
▷ *Usage.* Careful users of English avoid the expression *the reason is because...* since *the reason is...* and *because* mean the same thing. *Because* should be replaced by *that: the reason is that...*

reasonable ('riːzənəbəl) *adj.* **1.** showing reason or sound judgment. **2.** having the ability to reason. **3.** hav-

refloat *vb.*	**reinfect** *vb.*	**relearn** *vb.*	**remodel** *vb.*
refocus *vb.*	**reinfection** *n.*	**relet** *vb.*	**rename** *vb.*
refurnish *vb.*	**reinsert** *vb.*	**relight** *vb.*	**renegotiable** *adj.*
reglaze *vb.*	**reinsertion** *n.*	**reload** *vb.*	**renegotiate** *vb.*
regrade *vb.*	**reinterpret** *vb.*	**relocate** *vb.*	**renegotiation** *n.*
regrow *vb.*	**reinterpretation** *n.*	**relocation** *n.*	**renumber** *vb.*
regrowth *n.*	**reinvestigate** *vb.*	**remarriage** *n.*	**reoccupation** *n.*
reheel *vb.*	**reinvestigation** *n.*	**remarry** *vb.*	**reoccupy** *vb.*
rehouse *vb.*	**rekindle** *vb.*	**rematch** *n.*	**reopen** *vb.*
reimpose *vb.*	**relay** *vb.*	**remeasure** *vb.*	**reorder** *vb. n.*

THESAURUS

fectuation, fulfilment

realize 1. appreciate, apprehend, be cognizant of, become aware of, become conscious of, catch on (*Inf.*), comprehend, conceive, grasp, imagine, recognize, take in, twig (*Brit. inf.*), understand **2.** accomplish, actualize, bring about, bring off, bring to fruition, carry out *or* through, complete, consummate, do, effect, effectuate, fulfil, make concrete, make happen, perform, reify **3.** acquire, bring *or* take in, clear, earn, gain, get, go for, make, net, obtain, produce, sell for

really absolutely, actually, assuredly, categorically, certainly, genuinely, in actuality, indeed, in fact, in reality, positively, surely, truly, undoubtedly, verily, without a doubt

realm 1. country, domain, dominion, empire, kingdom, land, monarchy, principality, province, state **2.** area, branch, department, field, orbit, province, region, sphere, territory, world, zone

reap acquire, bring in, collect, cut, derive, gain, garner, gather, get, harvest, obtain, win

rear[1] **1.** *n.* back, back end, end, rearguard, stern, tail, tail end **2.** *adj.* aft, after (*Nautical*), back, following, hind, hindmost, last

rear[2] *v.* **1.** breed, bring up, care for, cultivate, educate, foster, grow, nurse, nurture, raise, train **2.** elevate, hoist, hold up, lift, raise, set upright **3.** build, construct, erect, fabricate, put up **4.** loom, rise, soar, tower

reason *n.* **1.** apprehension, brains, comprehension, intellect, judgment, logic, mentality, mind, ratiocination, rationality, reasoning, sanity, sense(s), sound mind, soundness, understanding **2.** aim, basis, cause, design, end, goal, grounds, impetus, incentive, inducement, intention, motive, object, occasion, purpose, target, warrant, why and wherefore (*Inf.*) **3.** apologia, apology, argument, case, defence, excuse, explanation, exposition, ground, justification, rationale, vindication **4.** bounds, limits, moderation, propriety, reasonableness, sense, sensibleness, wisdom **5. in** *or* **within reason** in moderation, proper, reasonable, sensible, warrant-

able, within bounds, within limits ~*v.* **6.** conclude, deduce, draw conclusions, infer, make out, ratiocinate, resolve, solve, syllogize, think, work out **7.** *With* **with** argue, bring round (*Inf.*), debate, dispute, dissuade, expostulate, move, persuade, prevail upon, remonstrate, show (someone) the error of his ways, talk into *or* out of, urge, win over

reasonable 1. advisable, arguable, believable, credible, intelligent, judicious, justifiable, logical, plausible, practical, rational, reasoned, sane, sensible, sober, sound, tenable, well-advised, well thought-out, wise **2.** acceptable, average, equitable, fair, fit, honest, inexpensive, just, moderate, modest, O.K. (*Inf.*), proper, right, tolerable, within reason

reasoned clear, judicious, logical, sensible, systematic, well expressed, well presented, well thought-out

ing modest or moderate expectations. **4.** moderate in price. **5.** fair; average: *reasonable weather.* —'**reasonably** *adv.* —'**reasonableness** *n.*

reasoning ('ri:zənɪŋ) *n.* **1.** the act or process of drawing conclusions from facts, evidence, etc. **2.** the arguments, proofs, etc., so adduced.

reassure (ˌri:ə'ʃuə) *vb.* (*tr.*) **1.** to relieve (someone) of anxieties; restore confidence to. **2.** to insure again. —ˌreas'surance *n.* —ˌreas'surer *n.* —ˌreas'suringly *adv.*

rebate[1] *n.* ('ri:beɪt). **1.** a refund of a fraction of the amount payable; discount. ~*vb.* (rɪ'beɪt) (*tr.*) **2.** to deduct (a part) of a payment from (the total). **3.** *Arch.* to reduce. —re'**batable** *or* re'**bateable** *adj.* —'**rebater** *n.*

rebate[2] ('ri:beɪt, 'ræbɪt) *or* **rabbet** *n.* **1.** a recess, groove, or step, of rectangular section, cut along the edge of a piece of timber to receive a mating piece. ~*vb.* (*tr.*) **2.** to cut a rebate in (timber, etc.). **3.** to join (pieces of timber) using a rebate.

rebec *or* **rebeck** ('ri:bɛk) *n.* a medieval stringed instrument resembling the violin but having a lute-shaped body.

rebel *vb.* (rɪ'bɛl), **-belling, -belled.** (*intr.*, often foll. by *against*) **1.** to resist or rise up against a government or authority, esp. by force of arms. **2.** to dissent from an accepted moral code or convention of behaviour, etc. **3.** to show repugnance (towards). ~*n.* ('rɛbəl). **4. a.** a person who rebels. **b.** (*as modifier*): *a rebel soldier.* **5.** a person who dissents from some accepted moral code or convention of behaviour, etc.

rebellion (rɪ'bɛljən) *n.* **1.** organized opposition to a government or other authority. **2.** dissent from an accepted moral code or convention of behaviour, etc.

rebellious (rɪ'bɛljəs) *adj.* **1.** showing a tendency towards rebellion. **2.** (of a problem, etc.) difficult to overcome; refractory. —re'**belliously** *adv.* —re'**belliousness** *n.*

rebirth (ri:'bɜ:θ) *n.* **1.** a revival or renaissance: *the rebirth of learning.* **2.** a second or new birth.

rebound *vb.* (rɪ'baund). (*intr.*) **1.** to spring back, as from a sudden impact. **2.** to misfire, esp. so as to hurt the perpetrator. ~*n.* ('ri:baund). **3.** the act or an instance of rebounding. **4. on the rebound. a.** in the act of

springing back. **b.** *Inf.* in a state of recovering from rejection, etc.: *he married her on the rebound from an unhappy love affair.*

rebuff (rɪ'bʌf) *vb.* (*tr.*) **1.** to snub, reject, or refuse (help, sympathy, etc.). **2.** to beat back (an attack); repel. ~*n.* **3.** a blunt refusal or rejection; snub.

rebuke (rɪ'bju:k) *vb.* **1.** (*tr.*) to scold or reprimand (someone). ~*n.* **2.** a reprimand or scolding. —re'**bukable** *adj.* —re'**buker** *n.* —re'**bukingly** *adv.*

rebus ('ri:bəs) *n., pl.* -**buses.** **1.** a puzzle consisting of pictures representing syllables and words; the word *hear* might be represented by H and a picture of an ear. **2.** a heraldic device that is a pictorial representation of the name of the bearer.

rebut (rɪ'bʌt) *vb.* **-butting, -butted.** (*tr.*) to refute or disprove, esp. by offering a contrary contention or argument. —re'**buttable** *adj.* —re'**buttal** *n.*

rec. *abbrev. for:* **1.** receipt. **2.** recipe. **3.** record.

recalcitrant (rɪ'kælsɪtrənt) *adj.* **1.** not susceptible to control; refractory. ~*n.* **2.** a recalcitrant person. —re'**calcitrance** *n.*

recall (rɪ'kɔ:l) *vb.* (*tr.*) **1.** (*may take a clause as object*) to bring back to mind; recollect; remember. **2.** to order to return. **3.** to revoke or take back. **4.** to cause (one's thoughts, attention, etc.) to return from a reverie or digression. ~*n.* **5.** the act of recalling or state of being recalled. **6.** revocation or cancellation. **7.** the ability to remember things; recollection. **8.** *Mil.* (formerly) a signal to call back troops, etc. **9.** *U.S.* the process by which elected officials may be deprived of office by popular vote. —re'**callable** *adj.*

recant (rɪ'kænt) *vb.* to repudiate or withdraw (a former belief or statement), esp. formally in public. —**recantation** (ˌri:kæn'teɪʃən) *n.* —re'**canter** *n.*

recap *vb.* ('ri:ˌkæp, ri:'kæp), **-capping, -capped,** *n.* ('ri:ˌkæp). *Inf.* short for **recapitulate** *or* **recapitulation.** —re'**cappable** *adj.*

recapitulate (ˌri:kə'pɪtjuˌleɪt) *vb.* **1.** to restate the main points of (an argument, speech, etc.). **2.** (*tr.*) (of an animal) to repeat (stages of its evolutionary development) during the embryonic stages of its life. —ˌreca-'pitulative *or* ˌreca'pitulatory *adj.*

recapitulation (ˌri:kəˌpɪtjʊ'leɪʃən) *n.* **1.** the act of

reorganization *n.*	**repot** *vb.*	**reshuffle** *vb. n.*	**retrain** *vb.*
reorganize *vb.*	**reprice** *vb.*	**respray** *vb.*	**retrial** *n.*
reorganizer *n.*	**reread** *vb.*	**respray** *n.*	**retry** *vb.*
repack *vb.*	**reroute** *vb.*	**restart** *vb. n.*	**returf** *vb.*
repackage *vb.*	**resalable** *or*	**restring** *vb.*	**retype** *vb.*
repaint *vb.*	**resaleable** *adj.*	**restructure** *vb.*	**reupholster** *vb.*
repaper *vb.*	**reschedule** *vb.*	**restyle** *vb.*	**reusable** *adj.*
rephrase *vb.*	**reseal** *vb.*	**rethink** *vb.*	**reuse** *vb. n.*
replan *vb.*	**resettle** *vb.*	**rethink** *n.*	**revisit** *vb.*
replant *vb.*	**resettlement** *n.*	**retie** *vb.*	**rewrap** *vb.*

THESAURUS

reasoning 1. analysis, cogitation, deduction, logic, ratiocination, reason, thinking, thought **2.** argument, case, exposition, hypothesis, interpretation, proof, train of thought

reassure bolster, buoy up, cheer up, comfort, encourage, hearten, inspirit, put *or* set one's mind at rest, relieve (someone) of anxiety, restore confidence to

rebel *v.* **1.** man the barricades, mutiny, resist, revolt, rise up, take to the streets, take up arms **2.** come out against, defy, disobey, dissent, refuse to obey **3.** flinch, recoil, show repugnance, shrink, shy away ~*n.* **4.** insurgent, insurrectionary, mutineer, resistance fighter, revolutionary, revolutionist, secessionist **5.** apostate, dissenter, heretic, nonconformist, schismatic ~*adj.* **6.** insubordinate, insurgent, insurrectionary, mutinous, rebellious, revolutionary

rebellion 1. insurgence, insurgency, insurrection, mutiny, resistance, revolt, revolution, rising, uprising **2.** apostasy, defiance, disobedience, dissent, heresy, insubordination, nonconformity, schism

rebellious 1. contumacious, defiant, disaffected, disloyal, disobedient, disorderly, insubordinate, insurgent, insurrectionary, in-

tractable, mutinous, rebel, recalcitrant, revolutionary, seditious, turbulent, ungovernable, unruly **2.** difficult, incorrigible, obstinate, recalcitrant, refractory, resistant, unmanageable

rebirth new beginning, regeneration, reincarnation, renaissance, renascence, renewal, restoration, resurgence, resurrection, revitalization, revival

rebound *v.* **1.** bounce, recoil, resound, return, ricochet, spring back **2.** backfire, boomerang, misfire, recoil ~*n.* **3.** bounce, comeback, kickback, repercussion, return, ricochet

rebuff 1. *v.* brush off (*Sl.*), check, cold-shoulder, cut, decline, deny, discourage, put off, refuse, reject, repulse, resist, slight, snub, spurn, turn down **2.** *n.* brushoff (*Sl.*), check, cold shoulder, defeat, denial, discouragement, opposition, refusal, rejection, repulse, slight, snub, thumbs down

rebuke 1. *v.* admonish, bawl out (*Inf.*), berate, blame, carpet (*Inf.*), castigate, censure, chide, dress down (*Inf.*), haul (someone) over the coals (*Inf.*), lecture, reprehend, reprimand, reproach, reprove, scold, take to task, tear (someone) off a strip (*Inf.*), tell off (*Inf.*), tick off (*Inf.*), upbraid **2.** *n.* admonition,

blame, castigation, censure, dressing down (*Inf.*), lecture, reprimand, reproach, reproof, reproval, row, telling-off (*Inf.*), ticking-off (*Inf.*), tongue-lashing, wigging (*Brit. sl.*)

recalcitrant contrary, contumacious, defiant, disobedient, insubordinate, intractable, obstinate, refractory, stubborn, uncontrollable, ungovernable, unmanageable, unruly, unwilling, wayward, wilful

recall *v.* **1.** bring *or* call to mind, call *or* summon up, evoke, look *or* think back to, mind (*Dialect*), recollect, remember, reminisce about **2.** abjure, annul, call back, call in, cancel, countermand, nullify, repeal, rescind, retract, revoke, take back, withdraw ~*n.* **3.** annulment, cancellation, nullification, recision, repeal, rescindment, rescission, retraction, revocation, withdrawal **4.** memory, recollection, remembrance

recant abjure, apostatize, deny, disavow, disclaim, disown, forswear, recall, renounce, repudiate, retract, revoke, take back, unsay, withdraw

recapitulate epitomize, go over again, outline, recap (*Inf.*), recount, reiterate, repeat, restate, review, run over, run through again, summarize, sum up

recapitulating, esp. summing up, as at the end of a speech. **2.** Also called: **palingenesis.** *Biol.* the apparent repetition in the embryonic development of an animal of the changes that occurred during its evolutionary history. **3.** *Music.* the repeating of earlier themes, esp. in the final section of a movement in sonata form.

recapture (riː'kæptʃə) *vb.* (*tr.*) **1.** to capture or take again. **2.** to recover, renew, or repeat (a lost or former ability, sensation, etc.). ~*n.* **3.** the act of recapturing or fact of being recaptured.

recce ('rɛkɪ) *n., vb.,* **-ceing, -ced** *or* **-ceed.** a slang word for **reconnaissance** or **reconnoitre.**

recd. *or* **rec'd.** *abbrev. for* received.

recede (rɪ'siːd) *vb.* (*intr.*) **1.** to withdraw from a point or limit; go back: *the tide receded.* **2.** to become more distant: *hopes of rescue receded.* **3.** to slope backwards: *apes have receding foreheads.* **4. a.** (of a man's hair) to cease to grow at the temples and above the forehead. **b.** (of a man) to start to go bald in this way. **5.** to decline in value. **6.** (usually foll. by *from*) to draw back or retreat, as from a promise.

receipt (rɪ'siːt) *n.* **1.** a written acknowledgment by a receiver of money, goods, etc., that payment or delivery has been made. **2.** the act of receiving or fact of being received. **3.** (*usually pl.*) an amount or article received. **4.** *Obs.* another word for **recipe.** ~*vb.* **5.** (*tr.*) to acknowledge payment of (a bill), as by marking it.

receivable (rɪ'siːvəbəl) *adj.* **1.** suitable for or capable of being received, esp. as payment or legal tender. **2.** (of a bill, etc.) awaiting payment: *accounts receivable.* ~*n.* **3.** (*usually pl.*) the part of the assets of a business represented by accounts due for payment.

receive (rɪ'siːv) *vb.* (*mainly tr.*) **1.** to take (something offered) into one's hand or possession. **2.** to have (an honour, blessing, etc.) bestowed. **3.** to accept delivery or transmission of (a letter, etc.). **4.** to be informed of (news). **5.** to hear and consent to or acknowledge (a confession, etc.). **6.** (of a container) to take or hold (a substance, commodity, or certain amount). **7.** to support or sustain (the weight of something); bear. **8.** to apprehend or perceive (ideas, etc.). **9.** to experience, undergo, or meet with: *to receive a crack on the skull.* **10.** (*also intr.*) to be at home to (visitors). **11.** to greet or welcome (guests), esp. in formal style. **12.** to admit (a person) to a place, society, condition, etc.: *he was received into the priesthood.* **13.** to accept or acknowledge (a precept or principle) as true or valid. **14.** to convert (incoming radio signals) into sounds, pictures, etc., by means of a receiver. **15.** (*also intr.*) *Tennis., etc.* to play at the other end from the server. **16.** (*also intr.*) to partake of (the Christian Eucharist). **17.** (*intr.*) *Chiefly Brit.* to buy and sell stolen goods.

Received Pronunciation *n.* the accent of standard Southern British English. Abbrev.: **RP**

receiver (rɪ'siːvə) *n.* **1.** a person who receives something; recipient. **2.** a person appointed by a court to manage property pending the outcome of litigation, during the infancy of the owner, or after the owner has been declared bankrupt or insane. **3.** *Chiefly Brit.* a person who receives stolen goods knowing that they have been stolen. **4.** the equipment in a telephone, radio, or television that receives incoming electrical signals or modulated radio waves and converts them into the original audio or video signals. **5.** the detachable part of a telephone that is held to the ear. **6.** *Chem.* a vessel in which the distillate is collected during distillation.

receivership (rɪ'siːvəˌʃɪp) *n. Law.* **1.** the office or function of a receiver. **2.** the condition of being administered by a receiver.

recent ('riːsənt) *adj.* having appeared, happened, or been made not long ago; modern, fresh, or new. —'recently *adv.* —'recentness *or* 'recency *n.*

Recent ('riːsənt) *adj., n. Geol.* of or formed in the second epoch of the Quaternary period, extending from the close of the Pleistocene and including the present. Also called: **Holocene.**

receptacle (rɪ'sɛptəkəl) *n.* **1.** an object that holds something; container. **2.** *Bot.* **a.** the enlarged or modified tip of the flower stalk that bears the parts of the flower. **b.** the part of lower plants that bears the reproductive organs or spores.

reception (rɪ'sɛpʃən) *n.* **1.** the act of receiving or state of being received. **2.** the manner in which something, such as a guest or a new idea, is received: *a cold reception.* **3.** a formal party for guests, such as after a wedding. **4.** an area in an office, hotel, etc., where visitors or guests are received and appointments or reservations dealt with. **5.** short for **reception room. 6.** the quality or fidelity of a received radio broadcast: *the reception was poor.*

receptionist (rɪ'sɛpʃənɪst) *n.* a person employed in an office, surgery, etc., to receive clients, patients, or guests, arrange appointments, etc.

reception room *n.* **1.** a room in a private house suitable for entertaining guests. **2.** a room in a hotel suitable for receptions, etc.

receptive (rɪ'sɛptɪv) *adj.* **1.** able to apprehend quickly. **2.** tending to receive new ideas or suggestions favourably. **3.** able to hold or receive. —re'ceptively *adv.* —receptivity (ˌriːsɛp'tɪvɪtɪ) *or* re'ceptiveness *n.*

recess *n.* (rɪ'sɛs, 'riːsɛs). **1.** a space, such as a niche or alcove, set back or indented. **2.** (*often pl.*) a secluded or secret place: *recesses of the mind.* **3.** a cessation of business, such as the closure of Parliament during a vacation. **4.** *Anat.* a small cavity or depression in a bodily organ. **5.** *U.S.* a break between classes at a school. ~*vb.* (rɪ'sɛs). **6.** (*tr.*) to place or set (something) in a recess. **7.** (*tr.*) to build a recess in (a wall, etc.).

recession (rɪ'sɛʃən) *n.* **1.** a temporary depression in economic activity or prosperity. **2.** the withdrawal of the clergy and choir in procession after a church service. **3.** the act of receding. **4.** a part of a building, wall, etc., that recedes.

recessional (rɪ'sɛʃənəl) *adj.* **1.** of or relating to recession. ~*n.* **2.** a hymn sung as the clergy and choir withdraw after a church service.

recessive (rɪ'sɛsɪv) *adj.* **1.** tending to recede or go back. **2.** *Genetics.* **a.** (of a gene) capable of producing its characteristic phenotype in the organism only when its allele is identical. **b.** (of a character) controlled by such a gene. Cf. **dominant** (sense 4). **3.** *Linguistics.* (of stress) tending to be placed on or near the initial syllable of a polysyllabic word. ~*n.* **4.** *Genetics.* a recessive gene or character. —re'cessively *adv.* —re'cessiveness *n.*

recherché (rə'ʃɛəʃeɪ) *adj.* **1.** known only to connoisseurs; choice or rare. **2.** studiedly refined or elegant.

recidivism (rɪ'sɪdɪˌvɪzəm) *n.* habitual relapse into crime. —re'cidivist *n., adj.* —reˌcidi'vistic *or* re'cidivous *adj.*

recipe ('rɛsɪpɪ) *n.* **1.** a list of ingredients and directions for making something, esp. when preparing food. **2.**

THESAURUS

recede 1. abate, draw back, ebb, fall back, go back, regress, retire, retreat, retrogress, return, subside, withdraw 2. decline, diminish, dwindle, fade, lessen, shrink, sink, wane

receipt 1. acknowledgment, counterfoil, proof of purchase, sales slip, stub, voucher 2. acceptance, delivery, receiving, reception, recipience 3. *Plural* gains, gate, income, proceeds, profits, return, takings

receive 1. accept, accept delivery of, acquire, be given, be in receipt of, collect, derive, get, obtain, pick up, take 2. apprehend, be informed of, be told, gather, hear, perceive 3. bear, be subjected to, encounter, experience, go through, meet with, suffer, sustain, undergo 4. accommodate, admit, be at

home to, entertain, greet, meet, take in, welcome

recent contemporary, current, fresh, late, latter, latter-day, modern, new, novel, present-day, up-to-date, young

recently currently, freshly, lately, newly, not long ago, of late

receptacle container, holder, repository

reception 1. acceptance, admission, receipt, receiving, recipience 2. acknowledgment, greeting, reaction, recognition, response, treatment, welcome 3. do (*Inf.*), entertainment, function, levee, party, soirée

receptive 1. alert, bright, perceptive, quick on the uptake (*Inf.*), responsive, sensitive 2. accessible, amenable, approachable, favourable, friendly, hospitable, interested,

open, open-minded, open to suggestions, susceptible, sympathetic, welcoming

recess 1. alcove, bay, cavity, corner, depression, hollow, indentation, niche, nook, oriel 2. *Plural* bowels, depths, heart, innards (*Inf.*), innermost parts, penetralia, reaches, retreats, secret places 3. break, cessation of business, closure, holiday, intermission, interval, respite, rest, vacation

recession decline, depression, downturn, slump

recipe 1. directions, ingredients, instructions, receipt (*Obsolete*) 2. formula, method, modus operandi, prescription, procedure, process, programme, technique

Med. (formerly) a medical prescription. **3.** a method for achieving some desired objective: *a recipe for success.*
recipient (rɪˈsɪpɪənt) *n.* **1.** a person who or thing that receives. *~adj.* **2.** receptive. **—reˈcipience** *or* **reˈcipiency** *n.*
reciprocal (rɪˈsɪprəkəl) *adj.* **1.** of, relating to, or designating something given by each of two people, countries, etc., to the other; mutual: *reciprocal trade.* **2.** given or done in return: *a reciprocal favour.* **3.** (of a pronoun) indicating that action is given and received by each subject; for example, *each other* in they started to shout at each other. **4.** *Maths.* of or relating to a number or quantity divided into one. *~n.* **5.** something that is reciprocal. **6.** Also called: **inverse.** *Maths.* a number or quantity that when multiplied by a given number or quantity gives a product of one: *the reciprocal of 2 is 0.5.* **—re₁ciproˈcality** *n.* **—reˈciprocally** *adv.*
reciprocate (rɪˈsɪprə₁keɪt) *vb.* **1.** to give or feel in return. **2.** to move or cause to move backwards and forwards. **3.** (*intr.*) to be correspondent or equivalent. **—re₁ciproˈcation** *n.* **—reˈciprocative** *or* **reˈcipro₁catory** *adj.* **—reˈcipro₁cator** *n.*
reciprocity (₁rɛsɪˈprɒsɪtɪ) *n.* **1.** reciprocal action or relation. **2.** a mutual exchange of commercial or other privileges.
recital (rɪˈsaɪtəl) *n.* **1.** a musical performance by a soloist. **2.** the act of reciting or repeating something learned or prepared. **3.** an account, narration, or description. **4.** (*often pl.*) *Law.* the preliminary statement in a deed showing the reason for its existence and explaining the operative part. **—reˈcitalist** *n.*
recitation (₁rɛsɪˈteɪʃən) *n.* **1.** the act of reciting from memory, esp. a formal reading of verse before an audience. **2.** something recited.
recitative (₁rɛsɪtəˈtiːv) *n.* a passage in a musical composition, esp. the narrative parts in an oratorio, reflecting the natural rhythms of speech.
recite (rɪˈsaɪt) *vb.* **1.** to repeat (a poem, etc.) aloud from memory before an audience. **2.** (*tr.*) to give a detailed account of. **3.** (*tr.*) to enumerate (examples, etc.). **—reˈcitable** *adj.* **—reˈciter** *n.*
reck (rɛk) *vb. Arch.* (*used mainly with a negative*) **1.** to mind or care about (something): *to reck nought.* **2.** (*usually impersonal*) to concern or interest (someone).
reckless (ˈrɛklɪs) *adj.* having or showing no regard for danger or consequences; heedless; rash: *a reckless driver.* **—ˈrecklessly** *adv.* **—ˈrecklessness** *n.*
reckon (ˈrɛkən) *vb.* **1.** to calculate or ascertain by calculating; compute. **2.** (*tr.*) to include; count as part of a set or class. **3.** (*usually passive*) to consider or regard: *he is reckoned clever.* **4.** (when *tr.*, takes a clause as object) to think or suppose; be of the opinion: *I reckon you don't know.* **5.** (*intr.*, foll. by *with*) to settle accounts (with). **6.** (*intr.*, foll. by *with* or *without*) to take into account or fail to take into account: *they reckoned without John.* **7.** (*intr.*, foll. by *on* or *upon*) to rely or depend: *I reckon on your support.* **8. to be reckoned with.** of con-

siderable importance or influence.
▷ **Usage.** Some senses of *reckon* are considered informal. The usage *I reckon on your support* is avoided in formal contexts, while in the sentence *It will snow tonight, I reckon,* the words *believe, suppose, think,* or *imagine* are preferred.
reckoner (ˈrɛkənə) *n.* any of various devices or tables used to facilitate reckoning, esp. a ready reckoner.
reckoning (ˈrɛkənɪŋ) *n.* **1.** the act of counting or calculating. **2.** settlement of an account or bill. **3.** a bill or account. **4.** retribution for one's actions (esp. in **day of reckoning**). **5.** *Navigation.* short for **dead reckoning.**
reclaim (rɪˈkleɪm) *vb.* (*tr.*) **1.** to regain possession of. **2.** to convert (desert, marsh, etc.) into land suitable for growing crops. **3.** to recover (useful substances) from waste products. **4.** to convert (someone) from sin, folly, vice, etc. *~n.* **5.** the act of reclaiming or state of being reclaimed. **—reˈclaimable** *adj.* **—reˈclaimant** *or* **reˈclaimer** *n.* **—reclamation** (₁rɛkləˈmeɪʃən) *n.*
recline (rɪˈklaɪn) *vb.* to rest in a leaning position. **—reˈclinable** *adj.* **—reclination** (₁rɛklɪˈneɪʃən) *n.* **—reˈcliner** *n.*
recluse (rɪˈkluːs) *n.* **1.** a person who lives in seclusion, esp. to devote himself to prayer and religious meditation; a hermit. *~adj.* **2.** solitary; retiring. **—reclusion** (rɪˈkluːʒən) *n.* **—reˈclusive** *adj.*
recognition (₁rɛkəgˈnɪʃən) *n.* **1.** the act of recognizing or fact of being recognized. **2.** acceptance or acknowledgment of a claim, duty, etc. **3.** a token of thanks. **4.** formal acknowledgment of a government or of the independence of a country. **—recognitive** (rɪˈkɒgnɪtɪv) *or* **reˈcognitory** *adj.*
recognizance *or* **recognisance** (rɪˈkɒgnɪzəns) *n. Law.* **a.** a bond entered into before a court or magistrate by which a person binds himself to do a specified act, as to appear in court on a stated day, keep the peace, or pay a debt. **b.** a monetary sum pledged to the performance of such an act. **—reˈcognizant** *or* **reˈcognisant** *adj.*
recognize *or* **-ise** (ˈrɛkəgˌnaɪz) *vb.* (*tr.*) **1.** to perceive (a person or thing) to be the same as or belong to the same class as something previously seen or known; know again. **2.** to accept or be aware of (a fact, problem, etc.): *to recognize necessity.* **3.** to acknowledge formally (a government) or the independence of (a country). **4.** *U.S.* to grant (a person) the right to speak in a deliberative body. **5.** to give a token of thanks for (a service rendered, etc.). **6.** to acknowledge formally (a claim, etc.). **7.** to show approval or appreciation of (something good). **8.** to acknowledge or greet (a person). **—ˈrecog₁nizable** *or* **-isable** *adj.* **—₁recog₁nizaˈbility** *or* **-isaˈbility** *n.* **—ˈrecog₁nizably** *or* **-isably** *adv.* **—ˈrecog₁nizer** *or* **-iser** *n.*
recoil *vb.* (rɪˈkɔɪl). (*intr.*) **1.** to jerk back, as from an impact or violent thrust. **2.** (often foll. by *from*) to draw back in fear, horror, or disgust. **3.** (foll. by *on* or *upon*) to go wrong, esp. so as to hurt the perpetrator. **4.** (of an

reciprocal alternate, complementary, correlative, corresponding, equivalent, exchanged, give-and-take, interchangeable, interdependent, mutual, reciprocative, reciprocatory
reciprocate 1. barter, exchange, feel in return, interchange, reply, requite, respond, return, return the compliment, swap, trade 2. be equivalent, correspond, equal, match
recital account, description, detailing, enumeration, narration, narrative, performance, reading, recapitulation, recitation, rehearsal, relation, rendering, repetition, statement, story, tale, telling
recitation lecture, narration, passage, performance, piece, reading, recital, rendering, telling
recite declaim, deliver, describe, detail, do one's party piece (*Inf.*), enumerate, itemize, narrate, perform, recapitulate, recount, rehearse, relate, repeat, speak, tell
reckless careless, daredevil, devil-may-care, foolhardy, harebrained, harum-scarum, hasty, headlong, heedless, ill-advised, imprudent, inattentive, incautious, indiscreet, irresponsible, madcap, mindless, negligent, over-

venturesome, precipitate, rash, regardless, thoughtless, wild
reckon 1. add up, calculate, compute, count, enumerate, figure, number, tally, total 2. account, appraise, consider, count, deem, esteem, estimate, evaluate, gauge, hold, judge, look upon, rate, regard, think of 3. assume, believe, be of the opinion, conjecture, expect, fancy, guess (*Inf.*), imagine, suppose, surmise, think 4. *With* with cope, deal, face, handle, settle accounts, treat 5. *With* with anticipate, bargain for, bear in mind, be prepared for, expect, foresee, plan for, take cognizance of, take into account 6. *With on or* upon bank, calculate, count, depend, hope for, rely, take for granted, trust in 7. **to be reckoned with** consequential, considerable, important, influential, powerful, significant, strong, weighty
reckoning 1. adding, addition, calculation, computation, count, counting, estimate, summation, working 2. account, bill, charge, due, score, settlement 3. doom, judgment, last judgment, retribution
reclaim get *or* take back, recapture, recover, redeem, reform, regain, regenerate,

reinstate, rescue, restore, retrieve, salvage
recline be recumbent, lay (something) down, lean, lie (down), loll, lounge, repose, rest, sprawl, stretch out
recluse 1. *n.* anchoress, anchorite, ascetic, eremite, hermit, monk, solitary 2. *adj.* cloistered, isolated, reclusive, retiring, secluded, sequestered, solitary, withdrawn
recognition 1. detection, discovery, identification, recall, recollection, remembrance 2. acceptance, acknowledgment, admission, allowance, appreciation, avowal, awareness, cognizance, concession, confession, notice, perception, realization, respect, understanding 3. acknowledgment, appreciation, approval, gratitude, greeting, honour, salute
recognize 1. identify, know, know again, make out, notice, place, recall, recollect, remember, spot 2. accept, acknowledge, admit, allow, appreciate, avow, be aware of, concede, confess, grant, own, perceive, realize, respect, see, understand 3. acknowledge, appreciate, approve, greet, honour, salute

atom, etc.) to change momentum as a result of the emission of a particle. ~*n*. (rɪ'kɔɪl, 'riːkɔɪl). **5. a.** the backward movement of a gun when fired. **b.** the distance moved. **6.** the motion acquired by an atom, etc. as a result of its emission of a particle. **7.** the act of recoiling. —**re'coiler** *n*.

recollect (ˌrɛkə'lɛkt) *vb.* (when *tr.*, often takes a clause as object) to recall from memory; remember. —ˌ**recol-** '**lection** *n*. —ˌ**recol'lective** *adj*. —ˌ**recol'lectively** *adv*.

recommend (ˌrɛkə'mɛnd) *vb.* (*tr.*) **1.** (may take a clause as object or an infinitive) to advise as the best course or choice; counsel. **2.** to praise or commend: *to recommend a new book*. **3.** to make attractive or advisable: *the trip has little to recommend it*. **4.** *Arch.* to entrust (a person or thing) to someone else's care; commend. —ˌ**recom'mendable** *adj*. —ˌ**recommen'da-tion** *n*. —ˌ**recom'mender** *n*. —ˌ**recom'mendatory** *adj*.

recompense ('rɛkəmˌpɛns) *vb.* **1.** (*tr.*) to pay or reward for service, work, etc. **2.** (*tr.*) to compensate for loss, injury, etc. ~*n*. **3.** compensation for loss, injury, etc. **4.** reward, remuneration, or repayment. —'**rec-**omˌ**pensable** *adj*. —'**recomˌpenser** *n*.

reconcile ('rɛkənˌsaɪl) *vb.* (*tr.*) **1.** (often passive; usually foll. by *to*) to make (oneself or another) no longer opposed; cause to acquiesce in something unpleasant: *she reconciled herself to poverty*. **2.** to become friendly with (someone) after estrangement or to re-establish friendly relations between (two or more people). **3.** to settle (a quarrel). **4.** to make (two apparently conflicting things) compatible or consistent with each other. **5.** to reconsecrate (a desecrated church, etc.). —'**recon-**ˌ**cilement** *n*. —'**reconˌciler** *n*. —**reconciliation** (ˌrɛkənˌsɪlɪ'eɪʃən) *n*. —**reconciliatory** (ˌrɛkən'sɪlɪətərɪ, -trɪ) *adj*.

recondite (rɪ'kɒndaɪt, 'rɛkənˌdaɪt) *adj*. **1.** requiring special knowledge; abstruse. **2.** dealing with abstruse or profound subjects. —**re'conditely** *adv*. —**re'condite-ness** *n*.

recondition (ˌriːkən'dɪʃən) *vb.* (*tr.*) to restore to good condition or working order: *to recondition an engine*. —ˌ**recon'ditioner** *n*.

reconnaissance (rɪ'kɒnɪsəns) *n*. **1.** the act of reconnoitring. **2.** the process of obtaining information about the position, etc., of an enemy. **3.** a preliminary inspection of an area of land.

reconnoitre or U.S. **reconnoiter** (ˌrɛkə'nɔɪtə) *vb.* **1.** to survey or inspect (an enemy's position, region of land, etc.). ~*n*. **2.** the act or process of reconnoitring; a reconnaissance. —ˌ**recon'noitrer** or U.S. ˌ**recon'noiter-er** *n*.

reconsider (ˌriːkən'sɪdə) *vb.* to consider (something) again, with a view to changing one's policy or course of action. —ˌ**reconˌsider'ation** *n*.

reconstitute (riː'kɒnstɪˌtjuːt) *vb.* (*tr.*) **1.** to restore (food, etc.) to its former or natural state, as by the addition of water to a concentrate. **2.** to reconstruct; form again. —**reconstituent** (ˌriːkən'stɪtjuənt) *adj., n.* —ˌ**reconsti'tution** *n*.

reconstruct (ˌriːkən'strʌkt) *vb.* (*tr.*) **1.** to construct or form again; rebuild. **2.** to form a picture of (a crime, past event, etc.) by piecing together evidence. —ˌ**re-**con'**structible** *adj*. —ˌ**recon'struction** *n*. —ˌ**recon-** '**structive** or ˌ**recon'structional** *adj*. —ˌ**recon'struct-** or *n*.

record *n*. ('rɛkɔːd). **1.** an account in permanent form, esp. in writing, preserving knowledge or information. **2.** a written account of some transaction that serves as legal evidence of the transaction. **3.** a written official report of the proceedings of a court of justice or legislative body. **4.** anything serving as evidence or as a memorial: *the First World War is a record of human folly*. **5.** (often pl.) information or data on a specific subject collected methodically over a long period: *weather records*. **6. a.** the best or most outstanding amount, rate, height, etc., ever attained, as in some field of sport: *a world record*. **b.** (as modifier): *a record time*. **7.** the sum of one's recognized achievements, career, or performance. **8.** a list of crimes of which an accused person has previously been convicted. **9. have a record.** to be a known criminal. **10.** Also called: **gramophone record, disc.** a thin disc of a plastic material upon which sound has been recorded. **11.** the markings made by a recording instrument such as a seismograph. **12.** *Computers.* a group of data or piece of information preserved as a unit in machine-readable form. **13. for the record.** for the sake of strict factual accuracy. **14. go on record.** to state one's views publicly. **15. off the record.** confidential or confidentially. **16. on record. a.** stated in a public document. **b.** publicly known. **17. set** or **put the record straight.** to correct an error. ~*vb.* (rɪ'kɔːd). (mainly *tr.*) **18.** to set down in some permanent form so as to preserve the true facts of: *to record the minutes of a meeting*. **19.** to contain or serve to relate (facts, information, etc.). **20.** to indicate, show, or register: *his face recorded his disappointment*. **21.** to remain as or afford evidence of: *these ruins record the life of the Romans in Britain*. **22.** (also intr.) to make a recording of (music, speech, etc.) for reproduction, esp. on a record-player or tape recorder, or for later broadcasting. **23.** (also intr.) (of an instrument) to register or indicate (information) on a scale: *the barometer recorded a low pressure*. —**re'cordable** *adj*.

recorded delivery *n*. a Post Office service by which an official record of posting and delivery is obtained for a letter or package.

recorder (rɪ'kɔːdə) *n*. **1.** a person who records, such as

---

THESAURUS

recoil *v.* **1.** jerk back, kick, react, rebound, resile, spring back **2.** balk at, draw back, falter, flinch, quail, shrink, shy away **3.** backfire, boomerang, go wrong, misfire, rebound ~*n.* **4.** backlash, kick, reaction, rebound, repercussion

recollect call to mind, mind (*Dialect*), place, recall, remember, reminisce, summon up

recollection impression, memory, mental image, recall, remembrance, reminiscence

recommend 1. advance, advise, advocate, counsel, enjoin, exhort, propose, put forward, suggest, urge **2.** approve, commend, endorse, praise, put in a good word for, speak well of, vouch for **3.** make attractive (acceptable, appealing, interesting)

recommendation 1. advice, counsel, proposal, suggestion, urging **2.** advocacy, approbation, approval, blessing, commendation, endorsement, favourable mention, good word, plug (*Inf.*), praise, reference, sanction, testimonial

reconcile 1. accept, accommodate, get used, make the best of, put up with (*Inf.*), resign, submit, yield **2.** appease, bring to terms, conciliate, make peace between, pacify, placate, propitiate, re-establish friendly relations, restore harmony between, re-

unite **3.** adjust, compose, harmonize, patch up, put to rights, rectify, resolve, settle, square

reconciliation 1. appeasement, conciliation, détente, pacification, propitiation, rapprochement, reconcilement, reunion, understanding **2.** accommodation, adjustment, compromise, harmony, rectification, settlement

recondite abstruse, arcane, cabbalistic, concealed, dark, deep, difficult, esoteric, hidden, involved, mysterious, mystical, obscure, occult, profound, secret

recondition do up (*Inf.*), fix up (*Inf.*, chiefly U.S.), overhaul, remodel, renew, renovate, repair, restore, revamp

reconnaissance exploration, inspection, investigation, observation, patrol, recce (*Sl.*), reconnoitring, scan, scouting, scrutiny, survey

reconnoitre explore, get the lie of the land, inspect, investigate, make a reconnaissance (of), observe, patrol, recce (*Sl.*), scan, scout, scrutinize, see how the land lies, spy out, survey

reconsider change one's mind, have second thoughts, reassess, re-evaluate, re-examine, rethink, review, revise, take another look at, think again, think better of, think over, think twice

reconstruct 1. reassemble, rebuild, recreate, re-establish, reform, regenerate, remake, remodel, renovate, reorganize, restore **2.** build up, build up a picture of, deduce, piece together

record *n.* **1.** account, annals, archives, chronicle, diary, document, entry, file, journal, log, memoir, memorandum, memorial, minute, register, report **2.** documentation, evidence, memorial, remembrance, testimony, trace, witness **3.** background, career, curriculum vitae, history, performance, track record (*Inf.*) **4.** album, disc, EP, forty-five, gramophone record, LP, platter (*U.S. sl.*), recording, release, single **5. off the record** confidential, confidentially, in confidence, in private, not for publication, private, sub rosa, under the rose, unofficial, unofficially ~*v.* **6.** chalk up (*Inf.*), chronicle, document, enrol, enter, inscribe, log, minute, note, preserve, put down, put on file, put on record, register, report, set down, take down, transcribe, write down **7.** contain, give evidence of, indicate, read, register, say, show **8.** cut, lay down (*Sl.*), make a recording of, put on wax (*Inf.*), tape, tape-record, video, video-tape, wax (*Inf.*)

an official or historian. **2.** something that records, esp. an apparatus that provides a permanent record of experiments, etc. **3.** short for **tape recorder. 4.** *Music.* a wind instrument of the flute family, blown through a fipple in the mouth end, having a reedlike quality of tone. **5.** (in England) a barrister or solicitor of at least ten years' standing appointed to sit as a part-time judge in the crown court. —**re'corder,ship** *n.*

recording (rɪ'kɔːdɪŋ) *n.* **1. a.** the act or process of making a record, esp. of sound on a gramophone record or magnetic tape. **b.** (*as modifier*): *recording studio.* **2.** the record or tape so produced. **3.** something that has been recorded, esp. a radio or television programme.

record-player *n.* a machine, often a small or portable one, for playing gramophone records.

recount (rɪ'kaʊnt) *vb.* (*tr.*) to tell the story or details of; narrate. —**re'countal** *n.*

re-count *vb.* (riː'kaʊnt). **1.** to count (votes, etc.) again. ~*n.* ('riː,kaʊnt). **2.** a second or further count, esp. of votes in an election.

recoup (rɪ'kuːp) *vb.* **1.** to regain or make good (a financial or other loss). **2.** (*tr.*) to reimburse or compensate (someone), as for a loss. **3.** *Law.* to keep back (something due), having rightful claim to do so. ~*n.* **4.** *Rare.* the act of recouping; recoupment. —**re'coupable** *adj.* —**re'coupment** *n.*

recourse (rɪ'kɔːs) *n.* **1.** the act of resorting to a person, course of action, etc., in difficulty (esp. in **have recourse to**). **2.** a person, organization, or course of action that is turned to for help, etc. **3.** the right to demand payment, esp. from the drawer or endorser of a bill of exchange or other negotiable instrument when the person accepting it fails to pay. **4. without recourse.** a qualified endorsement on such a negotiable instrument, by which the endorser protects himself from liability to subsequent holders.

recover (rɪ'kʌvə) *vb.* **1.** (*tr.*) to find again or obtain the return of (something lost). **2.** to regain (loss of money, time, etc.). **3.** (of a person) to regain (health, spirits, composure, etc.). **4.** to regain (a former and better condition): *industry recovered after the war.* **5.** *Law.* **a.** (*tr.*) to gain (something) by the judgment of a court of law: *to recover damages.* **b.** (*intr.*) to succeed in a lawsuit. **6.** (*tr.*) to obtain (useful substances) from waste. **7.** (*intr.*) (in fencing, rowing, etc.) to make a recovery. —**re'coverable** *adj.* —**re,covera'bility** *n.* —**re'coverer** *n.*

recovery (rɪ'kʌvərɪ) *n.*, *pl.* **-eries. 1.** the act or process of recovering, esp. from sickness, a shock, or a setback. **2.** restoration to a former or better condition. **3.** the regaining of something lost. **4.** the extraction of useful substances from waste. **5.** the retrieval of a space capsule after a spaceflight. **6.** *Law.* the obtaining of a right, etc., by the judgment of a court. **7.** *Fencing.* a return to the position of guard after making an attack. **8.** *Swimming, rowing, etc.* the action of bringing the arm, oar, etc., forward for another stroke. **9.** *Golf.* a stroke played from the rough or a bunker to the fairway or green.

recreant ('rɛkrɪənt) *Arch.* ~*adj.* **1.** cowardly; fainthearted. **2.** disloyal. ~*n.* **3.** a disloyal or cowardly person. —**'recreance** or **'recreancy** *n.* —**'recreantly** *adv.*

recreate ('rɛkrɪ,eɪt) *vb. Rare.* to amuse (oneself or someone else). —**'recreative** *adj.* —**'recreatively** *adv.*

—**'recre,ator** *n.*

re-create (,riːkrɪ'eɪt) *vb.* to create anew; reproduce. —,**re-cre'ation** *n.* —,**re-cre'ator** *n.*

recreation (,rɛkrɪ'eɪʃən) *n.* **1.** refreshment of health or spirits by relaxation and enjoyment. **2.** an activity that promotes this. **3. a.** an interval of free time between school lessons. **b.** (*as modifier*): *recreation period.* —,**recre'ational** *adj.*

recriminate (rɪ'krɪmɪ,neɪt) *vb.* (*intr.*) to return an accusation against someone or engage in mutual accusations. —**re'criminative** or **re'criminatory** *adj.* —**re'crimi,nator** *n.* —**re,crimi'nation** *n.*

recrudesce (,riːkruː'dɛs) *vb.* (*intr.*) (of a disease, trouble, etc.) to break out or appear again after a period of dormancy. —,**recru'descence** *n.*

recruit (rɪ'kruːt) *vb.* **1. a.** to enlist (men) for military service. **b.** to raise or strengthen (an army, etc.) by enlistment. **2.** (*tr.*) to enrol or obtain (members, support, etc.). **3.** to furnish or be furnished with a fresh supply; renew. **4.** *Arch.* to recover (health, spirits, etc.). ~*n.* **5.** a newly joined member of a military service. **6.** any new member or supporter. —**re'cruitable** *adj.* —**re'cruiter** *n.* —**re'cruitment** *n.*

rectal ('rɛktəl) *adj.* of or relating to the rectum. —**'rectally** *adv.*

rectangle ('rɛk,tæŋgəl) *n.* a parallelogram having four right angles. —**rec'tangular** *adj.*

recti- or before a vowel **rect-** *combining form.* straight or right: *rectangle.*

rectifier ('rɛktɪ,faɪə) *n.* **1.** an electronic device that converts an alternating current to a direct current. **2.** *Chem.* an apparatus for condensing a hot vapour to a liquid in distillation; condenser. **3.** a thing or person that rectifies.

rectify ('rɛktɪ,faɪ) *vb.* **-fying, -fied.** (*tr.*) **1.** to put right; correct; remedy. **2.** to separate (a substance) from a mixture or refine (a substance) by fractional distillation. **3.** to convert (alternating current) into direct current. **4.** *Maths.* to determine the length of (a curve). —**'recti,fiable** *adj.* —,**rectifi'cation** *n.*

rectilinear (,rɛktɪ'lɪnɪə) or **rectilineal** *adj.* **1.** in, moving in, or characterized by a straight line. **2.** consisting of, bounded by, or formed by a straight line. —,**recti-'linearly** or ,**recti'lineally** *adv.*

rectitude ('rɛktɪ,tjuːd) *n.* **1.** moral or religious correctness. **2.** correctness of judgment.

recto ('rɛktəʊ) *n.*, *pl.* **-tos. 1.** the front of a sheet of printed paper. **2.** the right-hand pages of a book. Cf. **verso** (sense 1b).

rector ('rɛktə) *n.* **1.** *Church of England.* a clergyman in charge of a parish in which, as its incumbent, he would formerly have been entitled to the whole of the tithes. **2.** *R.C. Church.* a cleric in charge of a college, religious house, or congregation. **3.** *Protestant Episcopal Church.* a clergyman in charge of a parish. **4.** *Chiefly Brit.* the head of certain schools, colleges, or universities. **5.** (in South Africa) a prinicipal of an Afrikaans university. —**'rectorate** *n.* —**rectorial** (rɛk'tɔːrɪəl) *adj.* —**'rectorship** *n.*

rectory ('rɛktərɪ) *n.*, *pl.* **-ries. 1.** the official house of a rector. **2.** *Church of England.* the office and benefice of a rector.

THESAURUS

recorder annalist, archivist, chronicler, clerk, diarist, historian, registrar, scorekeeper, scorer, scribe

recording cut (*Inf.*), disc, gramophone record, record, tape, video

recount delineate, depict, describe, detail, enumerate, give an account of, narrate, portray, recite, rehearse, relate, repeat, report, tell, tell the story of

recourse alternative, appeal, choice, expedient, option, refuge, remedy, resort, resource, way out

recover 1. find again, get back, make good, recapture, reclaim, recoup, redeem, regain, repair, repossess, restore, retake, retrieve, take back, win back **2.** bounce back, come round, convalesce, feel oneself again, get back on one's feet, get better, get well, heal, improve, mend, pick up, pull through, rally, recuperate, regain one's health *or*

strength, revive, take a turn for the better

recovery 1. convalescence, healing, improvement, mending, rally, recuperation, return to health, revival, turn for the better **2.** amelioration, betterment, improvement, rally, rehabilitation, restoration, revival, upturn **3.** recapture, reclamation, redemption, repair, repossession, restoration, retrieval

recreation amusement, distraction, diversion, enjoyment, entertainment, exercise, fun, hobby, leisure activity, pastime, play, pleasure, refreshment, relaxation, relief, sport

recrimination bickering, counterattack, countercharge, mutual accusation, name-calling, quarrel, retaliation, retort, squabbling

recruit *v.* **1.** draft, enlist, enrol, impress, levy, mobilize, muster, raise, strengthen **2.** engage, enrol, gather, obtain, procure, pros-

elytize, round up, take on, win (over) **3.** augment, build up, refresh, reinforce, renew, replenish, restore, strengthen, supply ~*n.* **4.** apprentice, beginner, convert, greenhorn (*Inf.*), helper, initiate, learner, neophyte, novice, proselyte, rookie (*Inf.*), trainee, tyro

rectify 1. adjust, amend, correct, emend, fix, improve, make good, mend, put right, redress, reform, remedy, repair, right, square **2.** *Chem.* distil, purify, refine, separate

rectitude 1. correctness, decency, equity, goodness, honesty, honour, incorruptibility, integrity, justice, morality, principle, probity, righteousness, scrupulousness, uprightness, virtue **2.** accuracy, correctness, exactness, justice, precision, rightness, soundness, verity

rectum ('rɛktəm) n., pl. **-tums** or **-ta** (-tə). the lower part of the alimentary canal, between the sigmoid flexure of the colon and the anus.

recumbent (rɪ'kʌmbənt) adj. **1.** lying down; reclining. **2.** (of an organ) leaning or resting against another organ. —**re'cumbence** or **re'cumbency** n. —**re'cumbently** adv.

recuperate (rɪ'ku:pə,reit, -'kju:-) vb. **1.** (intr.) to recover from illness or exhaustion. **2.** to recover (money, etc.). —**re,cuper'ation** n. —**re'cuperative** adj. —**re'cuper,ator** n.

recur (rɪ'kɜ:) vb. **-curring, -curred.** (intr.) **1.** to happen again. **2.** (of a thought, etc.) to come back to the mind. **3.** (of a problem, etc.) to come up again. **4.** Maths. (of a digit or group of digits) to be repeated an infinite number of times at the end of a decimal. —**recurrence** (rɪ'kʌrəns) n. —**re'current** adj. —**re'currently** or **re'curringly** adv.

recusant ('rɛkjuzənt) n. **1.** (in 16th to 18th century England) a Roman Catholic who did not attend the services of the Church of England. **2.** any person who refuses to submit to authority. ~adj. **3.** (formerly, of Catholics) refusing to attend services of the Church of England. **4.** refusing to submit to authority. —'**recusance** or '**recusancy** n.

recycle (ri:'saikəl) vb. (tr.) **1.** to pass (a substance) through a system again for further treatment or use. **2.** to reclaim for further use: to recycle water. ~n. **3.** the repetition of a fixed sequence of events.

red (rɛd) n. **1.** any of a group of colours, such as that of a ripe tomato or fresh blood. **2.** a pigment or dye of or producing these colours. **3.** red cloth or clothing: dressed in red. **4.** a red ball in snooker, etc. **5.** (in roulette) one of two colours on which players may place even bets. **6. in the red.** Inf. in debt. **7. see red.** Inf. to become very angry. ~adj. **redder, reddest. 8.** of the colour red. **9.** reddish in colour or having parts or marks that are reddish: red deer. **10.** having the face temporarily suffused with blood, being a sign of anger, shame, etc. **11.** (of the eyes) bloodshot. **12.** (of the hands) stained with blood. **13.** bloody or violent: red revolution. **14.** (of wine) made from black grapes and coloured by their skins. ~vb. **redding, redded. 15.** another word for **redden.** —'**redness** n. —'**reddish** adj.

Red (rɛd) Inf. ~adj. **1.** Communist, Socialist, or Soviet. **2.** radical, leftist, or revolutionary. ~n. **3.** a member or supporter of a Communist or Socialist Party or a national of the Soviet Union. **4.** a radical leftist or revolutionary.

red admiral n. a butterfly of temperate Europe and Asia, having black wings with red and white markings.

red blood cell n. another name for **erythrocyte.**

red-blooded adj. Inf. vigorous; virile. —,**red-'bloodedness** n.

redbreast ('rɛd,brɛst) n. any of various birds having a red breast, esp. the Old World robin.

redbrick ('rɛd,brɪk) n. (modifier) denoting, relating to, or characteristic of a provincial British university of relatively recent foundation.

red card n. Soccer. a piece of red pasteboard displayed by a referee to indicate that a player has been sent off.

red carpet n. **1.** a strip of red carpeting laid for important dignitaries to walk on. **2. a.** deferential treatment accorded to a person of importance. **b.** (as modifier): a red-carpet reception.

redcoat ('rɛd,kəʊt) n. **1.** (formerly) a British soldier. **2.** Canad. inf. another name for **Mountie.**

Red Crescent n. the emblem of the Red Cross Society in a Muslim country.

Red Cross n. **1.** an international humanitarian organization (**Red Cross Society**) formally established by the Geneva Convention of 1864. **2.** the emblem of this organization, consisting of a red cross on a white background.

redcurrant ('rɛd'kʌrənt) n. **1.** a N temperate shrub having greenish flowers and small edible rounded red berries. **2. a.** the fruit of this shrub. **b.** (as modifier): redcurrant jelly.

red deer n. a large deer formerly widely distributed in the woodlands of Europe and Asia. The coat is reddish brown in summer and the short tail is surrounded by a patch of light-coloured hair.

redden ('rɛdən) vb. **1.** to make or become red. **2.** (intr.) to flush with embarrassment, anger, etc.

redeem (rɪ'di:m) vb. (tr.) **1.** to recover possession or ownership of by payment of a price or service; regain. **2.** to convert (bonds, shares, etc.) into cash. **3.** to pay off (a loan, etc.). **4.** to recover (something pledged, mortgaged, or pawned). **5.** to convert (paper money) into bullion or specie. **6.** to fulfil (a promise, pledge, etc.). **7.** to exchange (coupons, etc.) for goods. **8.** to reinstate in someone's estimation or good opinion: he redeemed himself by his altruistic action. **9.** to make amends for. **10.** to recover from captivity, esp. by a money payment. **11.** Christianity. (of Christ as Saviour) to free (men) from sin by death on the Cross. —**re'deemer** n. —**re'deemable** or **re'demptible** adj.

redeeming (rɪ'di:mɪŋ) adj. serving to compensate for faults or deficiencies.

redemption (rɪ'dɛmpʃən) n. **1.** the act or process of redeeming. **2.** the state of being redeemed. **3.** Christianity. **a.** deliverance from sin through the incarnation, sufferings, and death of Christ. **b.** atonement for guilt. —**re'demptional, re'demptive,** or **re'demptory** adj. —**re'demptively** adv.

Red Ensign n. the ensign of the British Merchant Navy, having the Union Jack on a red background at the upper corner of the vertical edge alongside the hoist. It was also the national flag of Canada until 1965.

redeploy (,ri:dɪ'plɔɪ) vb. to assign new positions or tasks to (labour, troops, etc.). —,**rede'ployment** n.

redfish ('rɛd,fɪʃ) n., pl. **-fish** or **-fishes. 1.** a male salmon that has recently spawned. **2.** Canad. another name for **kokanee.**

red flag n. **1.** a symbol of socialism, communism, or revolution. **2.** an object or event likely to arouse anger.

red-handed adj. (postpositive) in the act of committing a crime or doing something wrong or shameful (esp. in **catch red-handed**). —,**red-'handedly** adv. —,**red-'handedness** n.

red hat n. the broad-brimmed crimson hat given to cardinals as the symbol of their rank.

redhead ('rɛd,hɛd) n. a person with red hair. —'**red,headed** adj.

red herring n. **1.** anything that diverts attention

THESAURUS

recuperate convalesce, get back on one's feet, get better, improve, mend, pick up, recover, regain one's health

recur 1. come again, come and go, come back, happen again, persist, reappear, repeat, return, revert **2.** be remembered, come back, haunt one's thoughts, return to mind, run through one's mind

recurrent continued, cyclical, frequent, habitual, periodic, recurring, regular, repeated, repetitive

recycle reclaim, reprocess, reuse, salvage, save

red adj. **1.** cardinal, carmine, cherry, coral, crimson, gules (Heraldry), maroon, pink, rose, ruby, scarlet, vermeil, vermilion, wine **2.** bay, carroty, chestnut, flame-coloured, flaming, foxy, reddish, sandy, titian **3.** blushing, embarrassed, florid, flushed, rubicund, shamefaced, suffused **4.** blooming, glowing,

healthy, roseate, rosy, ruddy **5.** bloodshot, inflamed, red-rimmed **6.** bloodstained, bloody, ensanguined (Literary), gory, sanguine ~n. **7.** colour, redness **8. in the red** Inf. bankrupt, in arrears, in debt, in deficit, in deficit, insolvent, on the rocks, overdrawn, owing money, showing a loss **9. see red** Inf. be or get very angry, be beside oneself with rage (Inf.), become enraged, blow one's top, boil, go mad (Inf.), go off one's head (Sl.), lose one's rag (Sl.), lose one's temper, seethe

redden blush, colour (up), crimson, flush, go red, suffuse

redeem 1. buy back, reclaim, recover, recover possession of, regain, repossess, repurchase, retrieve, win back **2.** cash (in), change, exchange, trade in **3.** abide by, acquit, adhere to, be faithful to, carry out, discharge, fulfil, hold to, keep, keep faith with, make good, meet, perform, satisfy **4.** absolve,

rehabilitate, reinstate, restore to favour **5.** atone for, compensate for, defray, make amends for, make good, make up for, offset, outweigh, redress, save **6.** buy the freedom of, deliver, emancipate, extricate, free, liberate, pay the ransom of, ransom, rescue, save, set free

redemption 1. reclamation, recovery, repossession, repurchase, retrieval **2.** discharge, exchange, fulfilment, performance, quid pro quo, trade-in **3.** amends, atonement, compensation, expiation, reparation **4.** deliverance, emancipation, liberation, ransom, release, rescue, salvation

red-handed (in) flagrante delicto, in the act, with one's fingers or hand in the till (Inf.)

from a topic or line of inquiry. **2.** a dried and smoked herring.

red-hot *adj.* **1.** (esp. of metal) heated to the temperature at which it glows red. **2.** extremely hot. **3.** keen, excited, or eager. **4.** furious; violent: *red-hot anger.* **5.** very recent or topical: *red-hot information.*

red-hot poker *n.* a liliaceous plant: widely cultivated for its showy spikes of red or yellow flowers.

Red Indian *n., adj.* another name for **American Indian.**

redistribution (ˌriːdɪstrɪ'bjuːʃən) *n.* **1.** the act or an instance of distributing again. **2.** a revision of the number of seats in the Canadian House of Commons allocated to each province, made every ten years on the basis of a new census.

red lead (lɛd) *n.* a bright-red poisonous insoluble oxide of lead.

red-letter day *n.* a memorably important or happy occasion.

red light *n.* **1.** a signal to stop, esp. a red traffic signal. **2.** a danger signal. **3. a.** a red lamp hanging outside a house indicating that it is a brothel. **b.** (*as modifier*): *a red-light district.*

red meat *n.* any meat that is dark in colour, esp. beef and lamb. Cf. **white meat.**

redo (riː'duː) *vb.* **doing, did, done.** (*tr.*) **1.** to do over again. **2.** *Inf.* to redecorate, esp. thoroughly: *we redid the house last summer.*

redolent ('rɛdəʊlənt) *adj.* **1.** having a pleasant smell; fragrant. **2.** (*postpositive; foll. by of or with*) having the odour or smell (of): *a room redolent of flowers.* **3.** (*postpositive; foll. by of or with*) reminiscent or suggestive (of): *a picture redolent of the 18th century.* —'**redolence** *or* '**redolency** *n.* —'**redolently** *adv.*

redouble (rɪ'dʌbəl) *vb.* **1.** to make or become much greater in intensity, number, etc.: *to redouble one's efforts.* **2.** to send back (sounds) or (of sounds) to be sent back. **3.** *Bridge.* to double (an opponent's double). ~*n.* **4.** the act of redoubling.

redoubt (rɪ'daʊt) *n.* **1.** a temporary earthwork built inside a permanent fort as a last defensive position. **2.** any isolated fortified stronghold.

redoubtable (rɪ'daʊtəbəl) *adj.* **1.** to be feared; formidable. **2.** worthy of respect. —re'**doubtableness** *n.* —re'**doubtably** *adv.*

redound (rɪ'daʊnd) *vb.* **1.** (*intr.; foll. by to*) to have an advantageous or disadvantageous effect (on): *brave deeds redound to your credit.* **2.** (*intr.; foll. by on or upon*) to recoil or rebound. **3.** (*tr.*) *Arch.* to reflect; bring: *his actions redound dishonour upon him.*

red pepper *n.* **1.** any of several varieties of the pepper plant cultivated for their hot pungent red podlike fruits. **2.** the fruit of any of these plants. **3.** the ripe red fruit of the sweet pepper. **4.** another name for **cayenne pepper.**

redpoll ('rɛdˌpɒl) *n.* either of two widely distributed types of finches, having a greyish-brown plumage with a red crown and pink breast.

red rag *n.* a provocation; something that infuriates.

redress (rɪ'drɛs) *vb.* (*tr.*) **1.** to put right (a wrong), esp. by compensation; make reparation for. **2.** to correct or adjust (esp. in **redress the balance**). **3.** to make compensation to (a person) for a wrong. ~*n.* **4.** the act or an instance of setting right a wrong; remedy or cure. **5.** compensation, amends, or reparation for a wrong, injury, etc. —re'**dressable** *or* re'**dressible** *adj.* —re'**dresser** *or* re'**dressor** *n.*

Red River cart *n. Canad. history.* a strongly-built, two-wheeled, ox- or horse-drawn cart used in W Canada.

red salmon *n.* any salmon having reddish flesh, esp.

the sockeye salmon.

redshank ('rɛdˌʃæŋk) *n.* any of various large common European sandpipers, esp. the **spotted redshank,** having red legs.

red shift *n.* a shift in the spectral lines of a stellar spectrum towards the red end of the visible region relative to the wavelength of these lines in the terrestrial spectrum.

redskin ('rɛdˌskɪn) *n.* an informal name for an **American Indian.**

red squirrel *n.* a reddish-brown squirrel, inhabiting woodlands of Europe and parts of Asia.

redstart ('rɛdˌstɑːt) *n.* **1.** a European songbird of the thrush family: the male has a black throat, orange-brown tail and breast, and grey back. **2.** a North American warbler.

red tape *n.* obstructive official routine or procedure; time-consuming bureaucracy.

reduce (rɪ'djuːs) *vb.* (*mainly tr.*) **1.** (*also intr.*) to make or become smaller in size, number, etc. **2.** to bring into a certain state, condition, etc.: *to reduce a forest to ashes.* **3.** (*also intr.*) to make or become slimmer; lose or cause to lose excess weight. **4.** to impoverish (esp. in **in reduced circumstances**). **5.** to bring into a state of submission to one's authority; subjugate: *the whole country was reduced after three months.* **6.** to bring down the price of (a commodity). **7.** to lower the rank or status of; demote: *reduced to the ranks.* **8.** to set out systematically as an aid to understanding; simplify: *his theories have been reduced in a treatise.* **9.** *Maths.* to modify or simplify the form of (an expression or equation), esp. by substitution of one term by another. **10.** to thin out (paint) by adding oil, turpentine, etc. **11.** (*also intr.*) *Chem.* **a.** to undergo or cause to undergo a chemical reaction with hydrogen. **b.** to lose or cause to lose oxygen atoms. **c.** to undergo or cause to undergo an increase in the number of electrons. **12.** *Photog.* to lessen the density of (a negative or print). **13.** *Surgery.* to manipulate or reposition (a broken or displaced bone, organ, or part) back to its normal site. —re'**ducible** *adj.* —reˌduci'**bility** *n.* —re'**ducibly** *adv.*

reduction (rɪ'dʌkʃən) *n.* **1.** the act or process or an instance of reducing. **2.** the state or condition of being reduced. **3.** the amount by which something is reduced. **4.** a form of an original resulting from a reducing process, such as a copy on a smaller scale. **5.** *Maths.* **a.** the process of converting a fraction into its decimal form. **b.** the process of dividing out the common factors in the numerator and denominator of a fraction. —re'**ductional** *or* re'**ductive** *adj.*

reductionism (rɪ'dʌkʃəˌnɪzəm) *n.* **1.** the analysis of complex things, data, etc., into less complex constituents. **2.** *Often disparaging.* any theory or method that holds that a complex idea, system, etc., can be completely understood in terms of its simpler parts or components. —re'**ductionist** *n.* —reˌduction'**istic** *adj.*

redundant (rɪ'dʌndənt) *adj.* **1.** surplus to requirements; unnecessary or superfluous. **2.** verbose or tautological. **3.** deprived of one's job because it is no longer necessary. —re'**dundancy** *n.* —re'**dundantly** *adv.*

reduplicate *vb.* (rɪ'djuːplɪˌkeɪt) **1.** to make or become double; repeat. **2.** to repeat (a sound or syllable) in a word or (of a sound or syllable) to be repeated. ~*adj.* (rɪ'djuːplɪkɪt) **3.** doubled or repeated. **4.** (of petals or sepals) having the margins curving outwards. —re'**duplicative** *adj.* —reˌdupli'**cation** *n.*

redwing ('rɛdˌwɪŋ) *n.* a small European thrush having a speckled breast, reddish flanks, and brown back.

redwood ('rɛdˌwʊd) *n.* a giant coniferous tree of coastal regions of California, having reddish fibrous bark and durable timber.

THESAURUS

redound **1.** conduce, contribute, effect, lead to, militate for, tend **2.** accrue, come back, ensue, rebound, recoil, reflect, result

redress *v.* **1.** compensate for, make amends (reparation, restitution) for, make up for, pay for, put right, recompense for **2.** adjust, amend, balance, correct, ease, even up, mend, put right, rectify, reform, regulate, relieve, remedy, repair, restore the balance, square ~*n.* **3.** aid, assistance, correction, cure, ease, help, justice, rectification, relief, remedy, satisfaction **4.** amends, atonement,

compensation, payment, quittance, recompense, reparation, requital, restitution

reduce **1.** abate, abridge, contract, curtail, cut down, debase, decrease, depress, dilute, diminish, impair, lessen, lower, moderate, shorten, slow down, tone down, truncate, turn down, weaken, wind down **2.** bankrupt, break, impoverish, pauperize, ruin **3.** bring, bring to the point of, conquer, drive, force, master, overpower, subdue, vanquish **4.** be *or* go on a diet, diet, lose weight, shed weight, slenderize (*Chiefly U.S.*), slim, trim **5.** bring

down the price of, cheapen, cut, discount, lower, mark down, slash **6.** break, bring low, degrade, demote, downgrade, humble, humiliate, lower in rank, lower the status of, take down a peg (*Inf.*)

redundant **1.** de trop, excessive, extra, inessential, inordinate, supererogatory, superfluous, supernumerary, surplus, unnecessary, unwanted **2.** diffuse, padded, periphrastic, pleonastic, prolix, repetitious, tautological, verbose, wordy

re-echo (riː'ɛkəʊ) *vb.* **-oing, -oed. 1.** to echo (a sound that is already an echo); resound. **2.** (*tr.*) to repeat like an echo.

reed (riːd) *n.* **1.** any of various widely distributed tall grasses that grow in swamps and shallow water and have jointed hollow stalks. **2.** the stalk, or stalks collectively, of any of these plants, esp. as used for thatching. **3.** *Music.* **a.** a thin piece of cane or metal inserted into the tubes of certain wind instruments, which sets in vibration the air column inside the tube. **b.** a wind instrument or organ pipe that sounds by means of a reed. **4.** one of the several vertical parallel wires on a loom that may be moved upwards to separate the warp threads. **5.** a small semicircular architectural moulding. **6.** an archaic word for **arrow. 7. broken reed.** a weak, unreliable, or ineffectual person. ~*vb.* (*tr.*) **8.** to fashion into or supply with reeds or reeding. **9.** to thatch using reeds.

reed bunting *n.* a common European bunting that has a brown streaked plumage with, in the male, a black head.

reedy ('riːdɪ) *adj.* **reedier, reediest. 1.** (of a place) abounding in reeds. **2.** of or like a reed. **3.** having a tone like a reed instrument; shrill or piping. —**'reediness** *n.*

reef[1] (riːf) *n.* **1.** a ridge of rock, sand, coral, etc., the top of which lies close to the surface of the sea. **2.** a vein of ore, esp. one of gold-bearing quartz. **3.** (*caps.*) **the. a.** the Great Barrier Reef in Australia. **b.** the Witwatersrand in South Africa, a gold-bearing ridge.

reef[2] (riːf) *Naut.* ~*n.* **1.** the part gathered in when sail area is reduced, as in a high wind. ~*vb.* **2.** to reduce the area of (sail) by taking in a reef. **3.** (*tr.*) to shorten or bring inboard (a spar).

reefer ('riːfə) *n.* **1.** *Naut.* a person who reefs, such as a midshipman. **2.** a man's short double-breasted jacket. **3.** *Sl.* a hand-rolled cigarette containing cannabis.

reef knot *n.* a knot consisting of two overhand knots turned opposite ways. Also called: **square knot.**

reek (riːk) *vb.* **1.** (*intr.*) to give off or emit a strong unpleasant odour; smell or stink. **2.** (*intr.;* often foll. by *of*) to be permeated (by): *the letter reeks of subservience.* **3.** (*tr.*) to treat with smoke; fumigate. **4.** (*tr.*) *Chiefly dialect.* to give off or emit (smoke, fumes, etc.). ~*n.* **5.** a strong offensive smell; stink. **6.** *Chiefly dialect.* smoke or steam; vapour. —**'reeky** *adj.*

reel[1] (riːl, rɪəl) *n.* **1.** any of various cylindrical objects or frames that turn on an axis and onto which film, tape, wire, etc., may be wound. U.S. equivalent: **spool. 2.** *Angling.* a device for winding, casting, etc., consisting of a revolving spool with a handle, attached to a fishing rod. ~*vb.* (*tr.*) **3.** to wind (cotton, thread, etc.) onto a reel. **4.** (foll. by *in, out,* etc.) to wind or draw with a reel: *to reel in a fish.* —**'reelable** *adj.* —**'reeler** *n.*

reel[2] (riːl, rɪəl) *vb.* (mainly intr.) **1.** to sway, esp. under the shock of a blow or through dizziness or drunkenness. **2.** to whirl about or have the feeling of whirling about: *his brain reeled.* ~*n.* **3.** a staggering or swaying motion or sensation.

reel[3] (riːl, rɪəl) *n.* **1.** any of various lively Scottish dances for a fixed number of couples who combine in square and circular formations. **2.** a piece of music composed for or in the rhythm of this dance.

reel off *vb.* (*tr., adv.*) to recite or write fluently and without apparent effort.

re-entry (riː'ɛntrɪ) *n., pl.* **-tries. 1.** the act of retaking possession of land, etc. **2.** the return of a spacecraft into the earth's atmosphere.

reeve[1] (riːv) *n.* **1.** *English history.* the local representative of the king in a shire until the early 11th century. **2.** (in medieval England) a manorial steward who supervised the daily affairs of the manor. **3.** *Canad. government.* a president of a local council, esp. in a rural area. **4.** (formerly) a minor local official in England and the U.S.

reeve[2] (riːv) *vb.* **reeving, reeved** *or* **rove.** (*tr.*) *Naut.* **1.** to pass (a rope or cable) through an eye or other narrow opening. **2.** to fasten by passing through or around something.

ref (rɛf) *n.* an informal shortening of **referee.**

ref. *abbrev. for:* **1.** referee. **2.** reference. **3.** reformed.

refection (rɪ'fɛkʃən) *n.* refreshment with food and drink.

refectory (rɪ'fɛktərɪ, -trɪ) *n., pl.* **-ries.** a dining hall in a religious or academic institution.

refectory table *n.* a long narrow dining table supported by two trestles.

refer (rɪ'fɜː) *vb.* **-ferring, -ferred.** (often foll. by *to*). **1.** (*intr.*) to make mention (of); allude (to). **2.** (*tr.*) to direct the attention of (someone) for information, facts, etc.: *the reader is referred to Chomsky, 1965.* **3.** (*intr.*) to seek information (from): *he referred to his notes.* **4.** (*intr.*) to be relevant (to); pertain or relate (to). **5.** (*tr.*) to assign or attribute: *Cromwell referred his victories to God.* **6.** (*tr.*) to hand over for consideration, reconsideration, or decision: *to refer a complaint to another department.* **7.** (*tr.*) to hand back to the originator as unacceptable or unusable. **8.** (*tr.*) *Brit.* to fail (a student) in an examination. **9. refer to drawer.** a request by a bank that the payee consult the drawer concerning a cheque payable by that bank. **10.** (*tr.*) to direct (a patient) for treatment to another doctor, usually a specialist. —**referable** ('rɛfərəb°l) *or* **referrable** (rɪ'fɜːrəb°l) *adj.* —**re'ferral** *n.* —**re'ferrer** *n.*

▷ **Usage.** The common practice of adding *back* to *refer* is tautologous, since this meaning is already contained in the *re-* of *refer: this refers to* (not *back to*) *what has already been said.* However, when *refer* is used in the sense of passing a document or question for further consideration to the person from whom it was received, it may be appropriate to say *he referred the matter back.*

referee (,rɛfə'riː) *n.* **1.** a person to whom reference is made, esp. for an opinion, information, or a decision. **2.** the umpire or judge in any of various sports, esp. football and boxing. **3.** a person who is willing to testify to the character or capabilities of someone. **4.** *Law.* a person appointed by a court to report on a matter. ~*vb.* **-eeing, -eed. 5.** to act as a referee (in); preside (over).

reference ('rɛfərəns, 'rɛfrəns) *n.* **1.** the act or an instance of referring. **2.** something referred, esp. proceedings submitted to a referee in law. **3.** a direction of the attention to a passage elsewhere or to another book, etc. **4.** a book or passage referred to. **5.** a mention or allusion: *this book contains several references to the Civil War.* **6.** the relation between a word or phrase and the object or idea to which it refers. **7. a.** a source of information or facts. **b.** (*as modifier*): *a reference book; a reference library.* **8.** a written testimonial regarding one's character or capabilities. **9.** a person referred to for such a testimonial. **10. a.** (foll. by *to*) relation or delimitation, esp. to or by membership of a specific group: *without reference to sex or age.* **b.** (*as modifier*): *a reference group.* **11. terms of reference.** the specific limits of responsibility that determine the activities of an investigating body, etc. ~*vb.* (*tr.*) **12.** to furnish or compile a list of references for (a publication, etc.). **13.** to make a reference to; refer to. ~*prep.* **14.** *Business jargon.* with reference to: *reference your letter of the 9th inst.* Abbrev.: **re** —**referential** (,rɛfə'rɛnʃəl) *adj.*

referendum (,rɛfə'rɛndəm) *n., pl.* **-dums** *or* **-da** (-də). **1.** submission of an issue of public importance to the direct vote of the electorate. **2.** a vote on such a measure.

THESAURUS

reek *v.* **1.** hum (*Sl.*), pong (*Brit. inf.*), smell, smell to high heaven, stink **2.** be characterized by, be permeated by, be redolent of **3.** *Dialect* fume, give off smoke *or* fumes, smoke, steam ~*n.* **4.** effluvium, fetor, mephitis, odour, pong (*Brit. inf.*), smell, stench, stink **5.** *Dialect* exhalation, fumes, smoke, steam, vapour

reel 1. falter, lurch, pitch, rock, roll, stagger, stumble, sway, totter, waver, wobble **2.** go round and round, revolve, spin, swim, swirl, twirl, whirl

refer 1. advert, allude, bring up, cite, hint, invoke, make mention of, make reference, mention, speak of, touch on **2.** direct, guide, point, recommend, send **3.** apply, consult, go, have recourse to, look up, seek information from, turn to **4.** apply, be directed to, belong, be relevant to, concern, pertain, relate **5.** accredit, ascribe, assign, attribute, credit, impute, put down to **6.** commit, consign, deliver, hand over, pass on, submit, transfer, turn over

referee 1. *n.* adjudicator, arbiter, arbitrator, judge, ref (*Inf.*), umpire **2.** *v.* adjudicate, arbitrate, judge, umpire

reference 1. allusion, citation, mention, note, quotation, remark **2.** applicability, bearing, concern, connection, consideration, regard, relation, respect **3.** certification, character, credentials, endorsement, good word, recommendation, testimonial

referendum plebiscite, popular vote, public vote

~See also **plebiscite**.

refill vb. (riːˈfɪl). **1.** to fill (something) again. ~n. (ˈriːfɪl). **2.** a replacement for a consumable substance in a permanent container. **3.** a second or subsequent filling. —**reˈfillable** adj.

refine (rɪˈfaɪn) vb. **1.** to make or become free from impurities or foreign matter; purify. **2.** (tr.) to separate (a mixture) into pure constituents, as in an oil refinery. **3.** to make or become elegant or polished. **4.** (intr.; often foll. by on or upon) to enlarge or improve (upon) by making subtle or fine distinctions. **5.** (tr.) to make (language) more subtle or polished. —**reˈfinable** adj. —**reˈfiner** n.

refined (rɪˈfaɪnd) adj. **1.** not coarse or vulgar; genteel, elegant, or polite. **2.** freed from impurities; purified.

refinement (rɪˈfaɪnmənt) n. **1.** the act of refining or the state of being refined. **2.** a fine or delicate point or distinction; a subtlety. **3.** fineness or precision of thought, expression, manners, etc. **4.** an improvement to a piece of equipment, etc.

refinery (rɪˈfaɪnərɪ) n., pl. **-eries.** a factory for the purification of some crude material, such as sugar, oil, etc.

refit vb. (riːˈfɪt), **-fitting, -fitted. 1.** to make or be made ready for use again by repairing, re-equipping, or resupplying. ~n. (ˈriːˌfɪt). **2.** a repair or re-equipping, as of a ship, for further use. —**reˈfitment** n.

reflation (riːˈfleɪʃən) n. **1.** an increase in economic activity. **2.** an increase in the supply of money and credit designed to cause such economic activity. ~Cf. **inflation** (sense 2).

reflect (rɪˈflɛkt) vb. **1.** to undergo or cause to undergo a process in which light, other electromagnetic radiation, sound, particles, etc., are thrown back after impinging on a surface. **2.** (of a mirror, etc.) to form an image of (something) by reflection. **3.** (tr.) to show or express in one's behaviour, attitude, etc.: his tactics reflect his desire for power. **4.** (intr.; usually foll. by on) to think, meditate, or ponder. **5.** (intr.; often foll. by on or upon) to cast dishonour or honour, credit or discredit, etc. (on). —**reˈflectingly** adv.

reflection or **reflexion** (rɪˈflɛkʃən) n. **1.** the act of reflecting or the state of being reflected. **2.** something reflected or the image so produced, as by a mirror. **3.** careful or long consideration or thought. **4.** attribution of discredit or blame. **5.** Maths. a transformation in which the direction of one axis is reversed. **6.** Anat. the bending back of a structure or part upon itself. —**reˈflectional** or **reˈflexional** adj.

reflective (rɪˈflɛktɪv) adj. **1.** characterized by quiet thought or contemplation. **2.** capable of reflecting: a reflective surface. **3.** produced by reflection. —**reˈflectively** adv.

reflector (rɪˈflɛktə) n. **1.** a person or thing that reflects. **2.** a surface or object that reflects light, sound, heat, etc.

reflex n. (ˈriːflɛks). **1. a.** an immediate involuntary response, such as coughing or blinking, evoked by a given stimulus. **b.** (as modifier): a reflex action. See also **reflex arc. 2. a.** a mechanical action to a particular situation, involving no conscious decision. **b.** (as modifier): a reflex response. **3.** a reflection; an image produced by or as if by reflection. ~adj. (ˈriːflɛks). **4.** Maths. (of an angle) between 180° and 360°. **5.** (prenominal) turned, reflected, or bent backwards. ~vb. (rɪˈflɛks). **6.** (tr.) to bend, turn, or reflect backwards. —**reˈflexible** adj. —reˌflexiˈbility n.

reflexive (rɪˈflɛksɪv) adj. **1.** denoting a class of pronouns that refer back to the subject of a sentence or clause. Thus, in that man thinks a great deal of himself, the pronoun himself is reflexive. **2.** denoting a verb used transitively with the reflexive pronoun as its direct object, as in to dress oneself. **3.** Physiol. of or relating to a reflex. ~n. **4.** a reflexive pronoun or verb. —**reˈflexively** adv. —**reˈflexiveness** or **reflexivity** (ˌriːflɛkˈsɪvɪtɪ) n.

reform (rɪˈfɔːm) vb. **1.** (tr.) to improve (an existing institution, law, etc.) by alteration or correction of abuses. **2.** to give up or cause to give up a reprehensible habit or immoral way of life. ~n. **3.** an improvement or change for the better, esp. as a result of correction of legal or political abuses or malpractices. **4.** a principle, campaign, or measure aimed at achieving such change. **5.** improvement of morals or behaviour. —**reˈformable** adj. —**reˈformative** adj. —**reˈformer** n.

reformation (ˌrɛfəˈmeɪʃən) n. **1.** the act or an instance of reforming or the state of being reformed. **2.** (usually cap.) a religious and political movement of 16th-century Europe that began as an attempt to reform the Roman Catholic Church and resulted in the establishment of the Protestant Churches. —ˌreforˈmational adj.

reformatory (rɪˈfɔːmətərɪ, -trɪ) n., pl. **-ries. 1.** Also called: **reform school.** (formerly) a place of instruction where young offenders were sent for corrective training. ~adj. **2.** having the purpose or function of reforming.

Reformed (rɪˈfɔːmd) adj. **1.** of or designating a Protestant Church, esp. the Calvinist. **2.** of or designating Reform Judaism.

refract (rɪˈfrækt) vb. **1.** to cause or undergo refraction. **2.** (tr.) to measure the amount of refraction of (the eye, a lens, etc.). —**reˈfractable** adj. —**reˈfractive** adj. —**reˈfractor** n.

refraction (rɪˈfrækʃən) n. **1.** Physics. the change in direction of a propagating wave, such as light or sound, in passing from one medium to another in which it has a different velocity. **2.** the amount by which a wave is refracted. **3.** the ability of the eye to refract light. —**reˈfractional** adj.

refractory (rɪˈfræktərɪ) adj. **1.** unmanageable or obstinate. **2.** Med. not responding to treatment. **3.** Physiol. (of a nerve or muscle) incapable of responding to stimulation. **4.** (of a material) able to withstand high temperatures without fusion or decomposition. ~n., pl. **-ries. 5.** a material, such as fireclay, that is able to withstand high temperatures. —**reˈfractorily** adv. —**reˈfractoriness** n.

refrain¹ (rɪˈfreɪn) vb. (intr.; usually foll. by from) to abstain (from action); forbear. —**reˈfrainer** n. —**reˈfrainment** n.

refrain² (rɪˈfreɪn) n. **1.** a regularly recurring melody, such as the chorus of a song. **2.** a much repeated saying or idea.

refrangible (rɪˈfrændʒɪbəl) adj. capable of being refracted. —reˌfrangiˈbility or reˈfrangibleness n.

refresh (rɪˈfrɛʃ) vb. **1.** (usually tr. or reflexive) to make or become fresh or vigorous, as through rest, drink, or food; revive or reinvigorate. **2.** (tr.) to enliven (something worn or faded), as by adding new decorations. **3.** to pour cold water over previously blanched and drained food. **4.** (tr.) to stimulate (the memory, etc.). **5.** (tr.) to replenish, as with new equipment or stores. —**reˈfresher** n. —**reˈfreshing** adj.

THESAURUS

refine 1. clarify, cleanse, distil, filter, process, purify, rarefy **2.** civilize, cultivate, elevate, hone, improve, perfect, polish, temper

refined 1. civil, civilized, courtly, cultivated, cultured, elegant, genteel, gentlemanly, gracious, ladylike, polished, polite, sophisticated, urbane, well-bred, well-mannered **2.** cultured, delicate, discerning, discriminating, exact, fastidious, fine, nice, precise, punctilious, sensitive, sublime, subtle **3.** clarified, clean, distilled, filtered, processed, pure, purified

refinement 1. clarification, cleansing, distillation, filtering, processing, purification, rarefaction, rectification **2.** fine point, fine tuning, nicety, nuance, subtlety **3.** civility, civilization, courtesy, courtliness, cultivation,

culture, delicacy, discrimination, elegance, fastidiousness, fineness, finesse, finish, gentility, good breeding, good manners, grace, graciousness, polish, politeness, politesse, precision, sophistication, style, taste, urbanity

reflect 1. echo, give back, imitate, mirror, reproduce, return, throw back **2.** bear out, bespeak, communicate, demonstrate, display, evince, exhibit, express, indicate, manifest, reveal, show **3.** cogitate, consider, contemplate, deliberate, meditate, mull over, muse, ponder, ruminate, think, wonder

reflection 1. counterpart, echo, image, mirror image **2.** cerebration, cogitation, consideration, contemplation, deliberation, idea, impression, meditation, musing, observation,

opinion, pondering, rumination, study, thinking, thought, view **3.** aspersion, censure, criticism, derogation, imputation, reproach, slur

reform v. **1.** ameliorate, amend, better, correct, emend, improve, mend, rebuild, reclaim, reconstitute, reconstruct, rectify, regenerate, rehabilitate, remodel, renovate, reorganize, repair, restore, revolutionize **2.** get back on the straight and narrow (Inf.), go straight (Inf.), mend one's ways, turn over a new leaf ~n. **3.** amelioration, amendment, betterment, correction, improvement, rectification, rehabilitation, renovation

refrain¹ v. abstain, avoid, cease, desist, do without, eschew, forbear, give up, leave off, renounce, stop

refresh 1. brace, breathe new life into,

refreshment (rɪ'freʃmənt) n. **1.** the act of refreshing or the state of being refreshed. **2.** (pl.) snacks and drinks served as a light meal.

refrigerant (rɪ'frɪdʒərənt) n. **1.** a fluid capable of changes of phase at low temperatures: used as the working fluid of a refrigerator. **2.** a cooling substance, such as ice or solid carbon dioxide. **3.** Med. an agent that provides a sensation of coolness or reduces fever. ~adj. **4.** causing cooling or freezing.

refrigerate (rɪ'frɪdʒə‚reɪt) vb. to make or become frozen or cold, esp. for preservative purposes; chill or freeze. —**re‚friger'ation** n. —**re'frigerative** or **re'frigeratory** adj.

refrigerator (rɪ'frɪdʒə‚reɪtə) n. a chamber in which food, drink, etc., are kept cool. Informal name: **fridge.**

reft (reft) vb. a past tense and past participle of **reave.**

refuel (ri:'fju:əl) vb. **-elling, -elled** or U.S. **-eling, -eled.** to supply or be supplied with fresh fuel.

refuge ('refju:dʒ) n. **1.** shelter or protection, as from the weather or danger. **2.** any place, person, action, or thing that offers protection, help, or relief.

refugee (‚refju'dʒi:) n. **a.** a person who has fled from some danger or problem, esp. political persecution. **b.** (as modifier): a refugee camp. —‚**refu'geeism** n.

refulgent (rɪ'fʌldʒənt) adj. Literary. shining, brilliant, or radiant. —**re'fulgence** or **re'fulgency** n. —**re'fulgently** adv.

refund vb. (rɪ'fʌnd). (tr.) **1.** to give back (money, etc.), as when an article purchased is unsatisfactory. **2.** to reimburse (a person). ~n. ('ri:‚fʌnd). **3.** return of money to a purchaser or the amount so returned. —**re'fundable** adj. —**re'funder** n.

refurbish (ri:'fɜ:bɪʃ) vb. (tr.) to renovate, re-equip, or restore. —**re'furbishment** n.

refusal (rɪ'fju:zəl) n. **1.** the act or an instance of refusing. **2.** the opportunity to reject or accept; option.

refuse[1] (rɪ'fju:z) vb. **1.** (tr.) to decline to accept (something offered): to refuse promotion. **2.** to decline to give or grant (something) to (a person, etc.). **3.** (when tr., takes an infinitive) to express determination not (to do something); decline: he refuses to talk about it. **4.** (of a horse) to be unwilling to take (a jump). —**re'fusable** adj. —**re'fuser** n.

refuse[2] ('refju:s) n. **a.** anything thrown away; waste; rubbish. **b.** (as modifier): a refuse collection.

refute (rɪ'fju:t) vb. (tr.) to prove (a statement, theory, charge, etc.) of (a person) to be false or incorrect; disprove. —**refutable** ('refjutəb'l, rɪ'fju:-) adj. —‚**refu'tation** n. —**re'futably** adv. —**re'futer** n.

▷ **Usage.** Refute is often used incorrectly as a synonym of deny. In careful usage, however, to deny something is to state that it is untrue; to refute something is to assemble evidence in order to prove it untrue: all he could do was deny the allegations since he was unable to refute them.

regain (rɪ'geɪn) vb. (tr.) **1.** to take or get back; recover. **2.** to reach again. —**re'gainer** n.

regal ('ri:g'l) adj. of, relating to, or befitting a king or queen; royal. —**'regally** adv. —**re'gality** n.

regale (rɪ'geɪl) vb. (tr., usually foll. by with) **1.** to give delight or amusement to: he regaled them with stories. **2.** to provide with choice or abundant food or drink. ~n. **3.** Arch. **a.** a feast. **b.** a delicacy of food or drink. —**re'galement** n.

regalia (rɪ'geɪlɪə) n. (pl., sometimes functioning as sing.) **1.** the ceremonial emblems or robes of royalty, high office, an order, etc. **2.** any splendid or special clothes; finery.

regard (rɪ'gɑ:d) vb. **1.** to look closely or attentively at (something or someone); observe steadily. **2.** (tr.) to hold (a person or thing) in respect, admiration, or affection: we regard your work very highly. **3.** (tr.) to look upon or consider in a specified way: she regarded her brother as her responsibility. **4.** (tr.) to relate to; concern; have a bearing on. **5.** to take notice of or pay attention to (something); heed: he has never regarded the conventions. **6. as regards.** (prep.) in respect of; concerning. ~n. **7.** a gaze; look. **8.** attention; heed: he spends without regard to his bank balance. **9.** esteem, affection, or respect. **10.** reference, relation, or connection (esp. in **with regard to** or **in regard to**). **11.** (pl.) good wishes or greetings (esp. in **with kind regards,** used at the close of a letter).

regarding (rɪ'gɑ:dɪŋ) prep. in respect of; on the subject of.

regardless (rɪ'gɑ:dlɪs) adj. **1.** (usually foll. by of) taking no regard or heed; heedless. ~adv. **2.** in spite of everything; disregarding drawbacks. —**re'gardlessly** adv. —**re'gardlessness** n.

regatta (rɪ'gætə) n. an organized series of races of yachts, rowing boats, etc.

regency ('ri:dʒənsɪ) n., pl. **-cies. 1.** government by a regent. **2.** the office of a regent. **3.** a territory under the jurisdiction of a regent.

Regency ('ri:dʒənsɪ) n. (preceded by the) **1.** (in Britain) the period (1811-20) of the regency of the Prince of Wales (later George IV). **2.** (in France) the period (1715-23) of the regency of Philip, Duke of Orleans. ~adj. **3.** characteristic of or relating to the Regency periods or to the styles of architecture, art, etc., produced in them.

regenerate vb. (rɪ'dʒenə‚reɪt). **1.** to undergo or cause to undergo moral, spiritual, or physical renewal or invigoration. **2.** to form or be formed again; come or bring into existence once again. **3.** to replace (lost or damaged tissues or organs) by new growth, or to cause (such tissues) to be replaced. **4.** (tr.) Electronics. to use positive feedback to improve the demodulation and amplification of a signal. ~adj. (rɪ'dʒenərɪt). **5.** morally, spiritually, or physically renewed or reborn. —**re'generacy** n. —**re'generative** adj. —**re'generatively** adv. —**re'gener‚ator** n. —**re‚gener'ation** n.

THESAURUS

cheer, cool, enliven, freshen, inspirit, reanimate, reinvigorate, rejuvenate, revitalize, revive, revivify, stimulate **2.** brush up (Inf.), jog, prod, prompt, renew, stimulate **3.** renew, renovate, repair, replenish, restore, top up

refreshing bracing, cooling, different, fresh, inspiriting, invigorating, new, novel, original, revivifying, stimulating, thirst-quenching

refreshment 1. enlivenment, freshening, reanimation, renewal, renovation, repair, restoration, revival, stimulation **2.** Plural drinks, food and drink, snacks, titbits

refrigerate chill, cool, freeze, keep cold

refuge asylum, bolt hole, harbour, haven, hide-out, protection, resort, retreat, sanctuary, security, shelter

refugee displaced person, émigré, escapee, exile, fugitive, runaway

refund 1. v. give back, make good, pay back, reimburse, repay, restore, return **2.** n. reimbursement, repayment, return

refurbish clean up, do up (Inf.), fix up (Inf., chiefly U.S.), mend, overhaul, re-equip, refit, remodel, renovate, repair, restore, revamp, set to rights, spruce up

refusal 1. defiance, denial, knockback

(Sl.), negation, no, rebuff, rejection, repudiation, thumbs down **2.** choice, consideration, opportunity, option

refuse[1] v. decline, deny, reject, repel, repudiate, say no, spurn, turn down, withhold

refute confute, counter, discredit, disprove, give the lie to, negate, overthrow, prove false, rebut, silence

regain 1. get back, recapture, recoup, recover, redeem, repossess, retake, retrieve, take back, win back **2.** get back to, reach again, reattain, return to

regal fit for a king or queen, kingly, magnificent, majestic, noble, princely, proud, queenly, royal, sovereign

regard v. **1.** behold, eye, gaze at, look closely at, mark, notice, observe, remark, scrutinize, view, watch **2.** account, adjudge, believe, consider, deem, esteem, estimate, hold, imagine, judge, look upon, rate, see, suppose, think, treat, value, view **3.** apply to, be relevant to, concern, have a bearing on, have to do with, interest, pertain to, relate to **4.** attend, heed, listen to, mind, note, pay attention to, respect, take into consideration, take notice of ~n. **5.** attention, heed, mind, notice **6.** account, affection, attachment,

care, concern, consideration, deference, esteem, honour, love, note, reputation, repute, respect, store, sympathy, thought **7.** aspect, detail, feature, item, matter, particular, point, respect **8.** gaze, glance, look, scrutiny, stare **9.** bearing, concern, connection, reference, relation, relevance **10.** Plural best wishes, compliments, devoirs, good wishes, greetings, respects, salutations

regarding about, apropos, as regards, as to, concerning, in or with regard to, in re, in respect of, in the matter of, on the subject of, re, respecting, with reference to

regardless 1. adj. disregarding, heedless, inattentive, inconsiderate, indifferent, neglectful, negligent, rash, reckless, remiss, unconcerned, unmindful **2.** adv. anyway, come what may, despite everything, for all that, in any case, in spite of everything, nevertheless, no matter what, nonetheless

regenerate breathe new life into, change, inspirit, invigorate, reawaken, reconstruct, re-establish, reinvigorate, rejuvenate, renew, renovate, reproduce, restore, revive, revivify, uplift

regent ('ri:dʒənt) n. **1.** the ruler or administrator of a country during the minority, absence, or incapacity of its monarch. **2.** U.S. a member of the governing board of certain schools and colleges. ~adj. **3.** (usually postpositive) acting or functioning as a regent: a queen regent. —'regental adj. —'regent,ship n.

reggae ('rɛgeɪ) n. a type of West Indian popular music having four beats to the bar, the upbeat being strongly accented.

regicide ('rɛdʒɪ,saɪd) n. **1.** the killing of a king. **2.** a person who kills a king. —,regi'cidal adj.

regime or **régime** (reɪ'ʒi:m) n. **1.** a system of government or a particular administration: a fascist regime. **2.** a social system or order. **3.** Med. another word for **regimen** (sense 1).

regimen ('rɛdʒɪ,mɛn) n. **1.** Also called: **regime**. Med. a systematic course of therapy, often including a recommended diet. **2.** administration or rule.

regiment n. ('rɛdʒɪmənt). **1.** an army unit usually containing a number of subunits, such as batteries or squadrons. **2.** a large number in regular or organized groups. ~vb. ('rɛdʒɪ,mɛnt). (tr.) **3.** to force discipline or order on, esp. in a domineering manner. **4.** to organize into a regiment. **5.** to form into organized groups. —,regi'mental adj. —,regi'mentally adv. —,regimen'tation n.

regimentals (,rɛdʒɪ'mɛntəlz) pl. n. **1.** the uniform and insignia of a regiment. **2.** military dress.

Regina (rɪ'dʒaɪnə) n. queen: now used chiefly in documents, inscriptions, etc. Cf. **Rex**.

region ('ri:dʒən) n. **1.** any large, indefinite, and continuous part of a surface or space. **2.** an area considered as a unit for geographical, functional, social, or cultural reasons. **3.** an administrative division of a country, or a Canadian province. **4.** a realm or sphere of activity or interest. **5.** range, area, or scope: in what region is the price likely to be? **6.** a division or part of the body: the lumbar region. —'regional adj. —'regionally adv.

register ('rɛdʒɪstə) n. **1.** an official or formal list recording names, events, or transactions. **2.** the book in which such a list is written. **3.** an entry in such a list. **4.** a recording device that accumulates data, totals sums of money, etc.: a cash register. **5.** a movable plate that controls the flow of air into a furnace, chimney, room, etc. **6.** Music. **a.** the timbre characteristic of a certain manner of voice production. **b.** any of the stops on an organ as classified in respect of its tonal quality: the flute register. **7.** Printing. the exact correspondence of lines of type, etc., on the two sides of a printed sheet of paper. **8.** a form of a language associated with a particular social situation or subject matter. **9.** the act or an instance of registering. ~vb. **10.** (tr.) to enter or cause someone to enter (an event, person's name, ownership, etc.) on a register. **11.** to show or be shown on a scale or other measuring instrument: the current didn't register on the meter. **12.** to show or be shown in a person's face, bearing, etc.: his face registered surprise. **13.** (intr.) Inf. to have an effect; make an impression: her uncle's death did not register. **14.** to send (a letter, package, etc.) by registered post. **15.** (tr.) Printing. to adjust (a printing press, forme, etc.) to ensure that the printed matter is in register. —'registerer n. —'registrable adj.

registered post n. **1.** a Post Office service by which compensation is paid for loss or damage to mail for which a registration fee has been paid. **2.** mail sent by this service.

registrar (,rɛdʒɪ'strɑ:) n. **1.** a person who keeps official records. **2.** an administrative official responsible for student records, enrolment procedure, etc., in a school,

college, or university. **3.** Brit. a hospital doctor senior to a houseman but junior to a consultant. **4.** Austral. & N.Z. the chief medical administrator of a large hospital. **5.** Chiefly U.S. a person employed by a company to maintain a register of its security issues. —'registrar,ship n.

registration (,rɛdʒɪ'streɪʃən) n. **1. a.** the act of registering or state of being registered. **b.** (as modifier): a registration number. **2.** an entry in a register. **3.** a group of people, such as students, who register at a particular time. **4.** Austral. **a.** a tax payable by the owner of a motor vehicle. **b.** the period paid for.

registration plate n. N.Z. & Austral. the numberplate of a vehicle.

registry ('rɛdʒɪstrɪ) n., pl. **-tries**. **1.** a place where registers are kept. **2.** the registration of a ship's country of origin: a ship of Liberian registry. **3.** another word for **registration**.

registry office n. Brit. a government office where civil marriages are performed and births, marriages, and deaths are recorded.

regnant ('rɛgnənt) adj. **1.** (postpositive) reigning. **2.** prevalent; current. —'regnancy n.

regress vb. (rɪ'grɛs). **1.** (intr.) to return or revert, as to a former place, condition, or mode of behaviour. **2.** (tr.) Statistics. to measure the extent to which (a dependent variable) is associated with one or more independent variables. ~n. ('ri:grɛs). **3.** movement in a backward direction; retrogression. —re'gressor n. —re'gressive adj.

regression (rɪ'grɛʃən) n. **1.** Psychol. the adoption by an adult of behaviour more appropriate to a child. **2.** Statistics. **a.** the measure of the association between one variable (the dependent variable) and other variables (the independent variables). **b.** (as modifier): regression curve. **3.** the act of regressing.

regret (rɪ'grɛt) vb. **-gretting, -gretted**. (tr.) **1.** (may take a clause as object or an infinitive) to feel sorry, repentant, or upset about. **2.** to bemoan or grieve the death or loss of. ~n. **3.** a sense of repentance, guilt, or sorrow. **4.** a sense of loss or grief. **5.** (pl.) a polite expression of sadness, esp. in a formal refusal of an invitation. —re'gretful adj. —re'gretfully adv. —re'gretfulness n. —re'grettable adj. —re'grettably adv.

regular ('rɛgjulə) adj. **1.** normal, customary, or usual. **2.** according to a uniform principle, arrangement, or order. **3.** occurring at fixed or prearranged intervals: a regular call on a customer. **4.** following a set rule or normal practice; methodical or orderly. **5.** symmetrical in appearance or form; even: regular features. **6.** (prenominal) organized, elected, conducted, etc., in a proper or officially prescribed manner. **7.** (prenominal) officially qualified or recognized: he's not a regular doctor. **8.** (prenominal) (intensifier): a regular fool. **9.** U.S. inf. likable, dependable, or nice: a regular guy. **10.** denoting or relating to the personnel or units of the permanent military services: a regular soldier. **11.** (of flowers) having any of their parts, esp. petals, alike in size, etc.; symmetrical. **12.** Grammar. following the usual pattern of formation in a language. **13.** Maths. **a.** (of a polygon) equilateral and equiangular. **b.** (of a polyhedron) having identical regular polygons as faces. **c.** (of a prism) having regular polygons as bases. **d.** (of a pyramid) having a regular polygon as a base and the altitude passing through the centre of the base. **14.** Bot. (of a flower) having radial symmetry. **15.** (postpositive) subject to the rule of an established religious order or community: canons regular. ~n. **16.** a professional long-term serviceman in a military unit. **17.** Inf. a person who does something regularly, such as attending a theatre. **18.** a

---

regime administration, establishment, government, leadership, management, reign, rule, system

regiment v. bully, control, discipline, order, organize, regulate, systematize

region **1.** area, country, district, division, expanse, land, locality, part, place, province, quarter, section, sector, territory, tract, zone **2.** domain, field, province, realm, sphere, world **3.** area, locality, neighbourhood, range, scope, vicinity

regional district, local, parochial, provincial, sectional, zonal

register n. **1.** annals, archives, catalogue, chronicle, diary, file, ledger, list, log, memorandum, record, roll, roster, schedule ~v. **2.** catalogue, check in, chronicle, enlist, enrol, enter, inscribe, list, note, record, set down, sign on or up, take down **3.** be shown, bespeak, betray, display, exhibit, express, indicate, manifest, mark, read, record, reflect, reveal, say, show **4.** Inf. come home, dawn on, get through, have an effect, impress, make an impression, sink in, tell

regress backslide, degenerate, deteriorate, ebb, fall away or off, fall back, go back, lapse, lose ground, recede, relapse, retreat,

retrogress, return, revert, wane

regret 1. v. bemoan, be upset, bewail, deplore, feel remorse for, feel sorry for, grieve, lament, miss, mourn, repent, rue, weep over **2.** n. bitterness, compunction, contrition, disappointment, grief, lamentation, pang of conscience, penitence, remorse, repentance, ruefulness, self-reproach, sorrow

regrettable deplorable, disappointing, distressing, ill-advised, lamentable, pitiable, sad, shameful, unfortunate, unhappy, woeful, wrong

member of a religious order or congregation, as contrasted with a secular. —**ˈreguˈlarity** n. —**ˈregularly** adv. —**ˈregularˌize** or **-ˌise** vb.

regulate (ˈrɛgjuˌleɪt) vb. (tr.) **1.** to adjust (the amount of heat, sound, etc.) as required; control. **2.** to adjust (an instrument or appliance) so that it operates correctly. **3.** to bring into conformity with a rule, principle, or usage. —**ˈreguˌlative** or **ˈreguˌlatory** adj. —**ˈreguˌlatively** adv.

regulation (ˌrɛgjuˈleɪʃən) n. **1.** the act or process of regulating. **2.** a rule, principle, or condition that governs procedure or behaviour. **3.** (modifier) as required by official rules: regulation uniform. **4.** (modifier) normal; usual; conforming to accepted standards: a regulation haircut.

regulator (ˈrɛgjuˌleɪtə) n. **1.** a person or thing that regulates. **2.** the mechanism by which the speed of a timepiece is regulated. **3.** any of various mechanisms or devices, such as a governor valve, for controlling fluid flow, pressure, temperature, etc.

regurgitate (rɪˈgɜːdʒɪˌteɪt) vb. **1.** to vomit forth (partially digested food). **2.** (of some birds and animals) to bring back to the mouth (undigested or partly digested food to feed the young). **3.** (intr.) to be cast up or out, esp. from the mouth. —**reˈgurgitant** n., adj. —**reˌgurgiˈtation** n.

rehabilitate (ˌriːəˈbɪlɪˌteɪt) vb. (tr.) **1.** to help (a physically or mentally disabled person or an ex-prisoner) to readapt to society or a new job, as by vocational guidance, retraining, or therapy. **2.** to restore to a former position or rank. **3.** to restore the good reputation of. —ˌrehaˈbilitative adj. —ˌrehaˌbiliˈtation n.

rehash (riːˈhæʃ) vb. **1.** (tr.) to rework, reuse, or make over (old or already used material). ~n. **2.** something consisting of old, reworked, or reused material.

rehearse (rɪˈhɜːs) vb. **1.** to practise (a play, concert, etc.), in preparation for public performance. **2.** (tr.) to run through; recount; recite: he rehearsed the grievances of the committee. **3.** (tr.) to train or drill (a person) for public performance. —**reˈhearsal** n. —**reˈhearser** n.

Reich (raɪk) n. **1.** the Holy Roman Empire (962–1806) (**First Reich**). **2.** the Hohenzollern empire in Germany from 1871 to 1918 (**Second Reich**). **3.** the Nazi dictatorship in Germany from 1933–45 (**Third Reich**).

reign (reɪn) n. **1.** the period during which a monarch is the official ruler of a country. **2.** a period during which a person or thing is dominant or powerful: the reign of violence. ~vb. (intr.) **3.** to exercise the power and authority of a sovereign. **4.** to be accorded the rank and title of a sovereign without having ruling authority. **5.** to predominate; prevail: darkness reigns. **6.** (usually present participle) to be the most recent winner of a contest, etc.: the reigning champion.

reimburse (ˌriːɪmˈbɜːs) vb. (tr.) to repay or compensate (someone) for (money already spent, losses, damages, etc.). —ˌreimˈbursable adj. —ˌreimˈbursement n. —ˌreimˈburser n.

rein (reɪn) n. **1.** (often pl.) one of a pair of long straps, usually connected together and made of leather, used to control a horse. **2.** a similar device used to control a very young child. **3.** any form or means of control: to take up the reins of government. **4.** the direction in which a rider turns (in **on a left rein**). **5.** something that restrains, controls, or guides. **6.** **give (a) free rein.** to allow considerable freedom; remove restraints. **7.** **keep a tight rein on.** to control carefully; limit: we have to keep a tight rein on expenditure. ~vb. **8.** (tr.) to check, restrain, hold back, or halt with or as if with reins. **9.** to control or guide (a horse) with a rein or reins: they reined left. ~See also **rein in**.

reincarnation (ˌriːɪnkɑːˈneɪʃən) n. **1.** the belief that on the death of the body the soul transmigrates to or is born again in another body. **2.** the incarnation or embodiment of a soul in a new body after it has left the old one at physical death. **3.** embodiment again in a new form, as of a principle or idea. —ˌreincarˈnationist n., adj.

reindeer (ˈreɪnˌdɪə) n., pl. **-deer** or **-deers**. a large deer, having large branched antlers in the male and female and inhabiting the arctic regions. It also occurs in North America, where it is known as a caribou.

reinforce (ˌriːɪnˈfɔːs) vb. (tr.) **1.** to give added strength or support to. **2.** to give added emphasis to; stress or increase: his rudeness reinforced my determination. **3.** to give added support to (a military force) by providing more men, supplies, etc. —ˌreinˈforcement n.

reinforced concrete n. concrete with steel bars, mesh, etc., embedded in it to enable it to withstand tensile and shear stresses.

rein in vb. (adv.) to stop (a horse) by pulling on the reins.

reins (reɪnz) pl. n. Arch. the kidneys or loins.

reinstate (ˌriːɪnˈsteɪt) vb. (tr.) to restore to a former rank or condition. —ˌreinˈstatement n. —ˌreinˈstator n.

reiterate (riːˈɪtəˌreɪt) vb. (tr.; may take a clause as object) to say or do again or repeatedly. —reˌiterˈation n. —reˈiterative adj. —reˈiteratively adv.

reject vb. (rɪˈdʒɛkt). (tr.) **1.** to refuse to accept, use, believe, etc. **2.** to throw out as useless or worthless; discard. **3.** to rebuff (a person). **4.** (of an organism) to fail to accept (a foreign tissue graft or organ transplant). ~n. (ˈriːdʒɛkt). **5.** something rejected as imperfect, unsatisfactory, or useless. —reˈjecter or reˈjector n. —reˈjection n. —reˈjective adj.

rejig (riːˈdʒɪg) vb. **-jigging, -jigged.** (tr.) **1.** to re-equip (a factory or plant). **2.** Inf. to rearrange. —reˈjigger n.

rejoice (rɪˈdʒɔɪs) vb. (when tr., takes a clause as object or an infinitive; when intr., often foll. by in) to feel or express great joy or happiness. —reˈjoicer n.

THESAURUS

regular 1. common, commonplace, customary, daily, everyday, habitual, normal, ordinary, routine, typical, unvarying, usual **2.** consistent, constant, established, even, fixed, steady, systematic, uniform **3.** dependable, efficient, formal, methodical, orderly, standardized, steady, systematic **4.** balanced, even, flat, level, smooth, straight, symmetrical, uniform **5.** approved, bona fide, classic, correct, established, formal, official, orthodox, prevailing, proper, sanctioned, standard, time-honoured, traditional

regulate adjust, administer, arrange, balance, conduct, control, direct, fit, govern, guide, handle, manage, moderate, modulate, monitor, order, organize, oversee, rule, run, settle, superintend, supervise, systematize, tune

regulation n. **1.** adjustment, administration, arrangement, control, direction, governance, government, management, modulation, supervision, tuning **2.** commandment, decree, dictate, direction, edict, law, order, ordinance, precept, procedure, requirement, rule, standing order, statute ~adj. **3.** customary, mandatory, normal, official, prescribed,

required, standard, usual

rehabilitate 1. adjust, redeem, reform, reintegrate, save **2.** clear, convert, fix up, make good, mend, rebuild, recondition, reconstitute, reconstruct, re-establish, reinstate, reinvigorate, renew, renovate, restore

rehearsal 1. drill, going-over, practice, practice session, preparation, reading, rehearsing, run-through **2.** account, catalogue, description, enumeration, list, narration, recital, recounting, relation, telling

rehearse 1. act, drill, go over, practise, prepare, ready, recite, repeat, run through, study, train, try out **2.** delineate, depict, describe, detail, enumerate, go over, list, narrate, recite, recount, relate, review, run through, spell out, tell, trot out (Inf.)

reign n. **1.** ascendancy, command, control, dominion, empire, hegemony, influence, monarchy, power, rule, sovereignty, supremacy, sway ~v. **2.** administer, be in power, command, govern, hold sway, influence, occupy or sit on the throne, rule, wear the crown, wield the sceptre **3.** be rampant, be rife, be supreme, hold sway, obtain, predominate, prevail

rein n. **1.** brake, bridle, check, control, curb, harness, hold, restraint, restriction **2.** **give (a) free rein (to)** free, give a free hand, give carte blanche, give (someone) his head, give way to, indulge, let go, remove restraints ~v. **3.** bridle, check, control, curb, halt, hold, hold back, limit, restrain, restrict, slow down

reincarnation metempsychosis, rebirth, transmigration of souls

reinforce augment, bolster, buttress, emphasize, fortify, harden, increase, prop, shore up, stiffen, strengthen, stress, supplement, support, toughen, underline

reinforcement 1. addition, amplification, augmentation, enlargement, fortification, increase, strengthening, supplement **2.** brace, buttress, prop, shore, stay, support **3.** Plural additional or fresh troops, auxiliaries, reserves, support

reinstate bring back, recall, re-establish, rehabilitate, replace, restore, return

reject 1. v. cast aside, decline, deny, despise, disallow, discard, eliminate, exclude, jettison, jilt, rebuff, refuse, renounce, repel, repudiate, repulse, say no to, scrap, spurn, throw away or out, turn down, veto **2.** n. castoff, discard, failure, flotsam, second

rejoin¹ (riː'dʒɔɪn) vb. **1.** to come again into company with (someone or something). **2.** (tr.) to put or join together again; reunite.

rejoin² (rɪ'dʒɔɪn) vb. (tr.) **1.** to answer or reply. **2.** Law. to answer (a plaintiff's reply).

rejoinder (rɪ'dʒɔɪndə) n. **1.** a reply or response to a question or remark. **2.** Law. (in pleading) the answer made by a defendant to the plaintiff's reply.

rejuvenate (rɪ'dʒuːvɪˌneɪt) vb. (tr.) **1.** to give new youth, restored vitality, or youthful appearance to. **2.** (usually passive) Geog. to cause (a river) to begin eroding more vigorously to a new lower base level. —reˌjuve'nation n. —re'juveˌnator n.

relapse (rɪ'læps) vb. (intr.) **1.** to lapse back into a former state or condition, esp. one involving bad habits. **2.** to become ill again after apparent recovery. ~n. **3.** the act or an instance of relapsing. **4.** the return of ill health after an apparent or partial recovery. —re'lapser n.

relate (rɪ'leɪt) vb. **1.** (tr.) to tell or narrate (a story, etc.). **2.** (often foll. by to) to establish association (between two or more things) or (of something) to have relation or reference (to something else). **3.** (intr.; often foll. by to) to form a sympathetic or significant relationship (with other people, things, etc.). —re'latable adj. —re'later n.

▷ Usage. Relate is frequently applied to personal relationships, as in sense 3, but this usage is vague and is avoided by careful speakers and writers.

related (rɪ'leɪtɪd) adj. **1.** connected; associated. **2.** connected by kinship or marriage. —re'latedness n.

relation (rɪ'leɪʃən) n. **1.** the state or condition of being related or the manner in which things are related. **2.** connection by blood or marriage; kinship. **3.** a person who is connected by blood or marriage; relative. **4.** reference or regard (esp. in **in** or **with relation to**). **5.** the position, association, connection, or status of one person or thing with regard to another. **6.** the act of relating or narrating. **7.** an account or narrative. **8.** Law. the statement of grounds of complaint made by a relator. **9. a.** Maths. an association, such as equality or inequality, between two numbers, quantities, expressions, etc. **b.** Logic. an association between things, as in John is the son of James.

relations (rɪ'leɪʃənz) pl. n. **1.** social, political, or personal connections or dealings between or among individuals, groups, nations, etc. **2.** family or relatives. **3.** Euphemistic. sexual intercourse.

relationship (rɪ'leɪʃənˌʃɪp) n. **1.** the state of being connected or related. **2.** association by blood or marriage; kinship. **3.** the mutual dealings, connections, or feelings that exist between two countries, people, etc. **4.** an emotional or sexual affair or liaison.

relative ('rɛlətɪv) adj. **1.** having meaning or significance only in relation to something else; not absolute. **2.** (prenominal) (of a scientific quantity) being measured or stated relative to some other substance or measurement: relative density. **3.** (prenominal) comparative or respective: the relative qualities of speed and accuracy. **4.** (postpositive; foll. by to) in proportion (to); corre-

sponding (to): earnings relative to production. **5.** Grammar. denoting or belonging to a class of words that function as subordinating conjunctions in introducing relative clauses such as who, which, and that. Cf. **demonstrative. 6.** Grammar. denoting or relating to a clause (**relative clause**) that modifies a noun or pronoun occurring earlier in the sentence. **7.** (of a musical key or scale) having the same key signature as another key or scale. ~n. **8.** a person who is related by blood or marriage; relation. **9.** a relative pronoun, clause, or grammatical construction. —'relatively adv. —'relativeness n.

relative atomic mass n. another name for **atomic weight.**

relativity (ˌrɛlə'tɪvɪtɪ) n. **1.** either of two theories developed by Albert Einstein. The **special theory of relativity,** proposed in 1905, deals with space, time, and the uniform motion of frames of reference, relative to each other. It also assumes that the velocity of light is independent of an observer's velocity. The **general theory of relativity,** proposed in 1916, extends the special theory to include relative motion between accelerated frames of reference. Both theories contain the idea of a space-time continuum and that mass and energy are equivalent. **2.** the state or quality of being relative.

relax (rɪ'læks) vb. **1.** to make (muscles, a grip, etc.) less tense or rigid or (of muscles and the like) to become looser or less rigid. **2.** (intr.) to take rest, as from work or effort. **3.** to lessen the force of (effort, concentration) or (of effort) to become diminished. **4.** to make (rules or discipline) less rigid or strict or (of rules, etc.) to diminish in severity. **5.** (intr.) (of a person) to become less formal; unbend. —**relaxedly** (rɪ'læksɪdlɪ) adv. —re'laxer n.

relaxant (rɪ'læksənt) n. **1.** Med. a drug or agent that relaxes, esp. one that relaxes tense muscles. ~adj. **2.** of or tending to produce relaxation.

relaxation (ˌriːlæk'seɪʃən) n. **1.** rest or refreshment, as after work or effort; recreation. **2.** a form of rest or recreation: his relaxation is cricket. **3.** a partial lessening of a punishment, duty, etc. **4.** the act of relaxing or state of being relaxed. **5.** Physics. the return of a system to equilibrium after a displacement from this state.

relay n. ('riːleɪ). **1.** a person or team of people relieving others, as on a shift. **2.** a fresh team of horses posted along a route to relieve others. **3.** the act of relaying or process of being relayed. **4.** short for **relay race. 5.** an automatic device that controls a valve, switch, etc., by means of an electric motor, solenoid, or pneumatic mechanism. **6.** Electronics. an electrical device in which a small change in current or voltage controls the switching on or off of circuits. **7.** Radio. **a.** a combination of a receiver and transmitter designed to receive radio signals and retransmit them. **b.** (as modifier): a relay station. ~vb. (rɪ'leɪ). (tr.) **8.** to carry or spread (news or information) by relays. **9.** to supply or replace with relays. **10.** to retransmit (a signal) by means of a relay. **11.** Brit. to broadcast (a performance) by sending out signals through a transmitting station.

THESAURUS

rejection brushoff (Sl.), denial, dismissal, elimination, exclusion, rebuff, refusal, renunciation, repudiation, thumbs down, veto

rejoice be glad (happy, overjoyed), celebrate, delight, exult, glory, joy, jump for joy, make merry, revel, triumph

rejoicing celebration, cheer, delight, elation, exultation, festivity, gaiety, gladness, happiness, joy, jubilation, merrymaking, revelry, triumph

relapse v. **1.** backslide, degenerate, fail, fall back, lapse, regress, retrogress, revert, slip back, weaken **2.** deteriorate, fade, fail, sicken, sink, weaken, worsen ~n. **3.** backsliding, fall from grace, lapse, recidivism, regression, retrogression, reversion **4.** deterioration, recurrence, setback, turn for the worse, weakening, worsening

relate 1. chronicle, describe, detail, give an account of, impart, narrate, present, recite, recount, rehearse, report, set forth, tell **2.** ally, associate, connect, coordinate, correlate, couple, join, link **3.** appertain, apply, bear upon, be relevant to, concern, have ref-

erence to, have to do with, pertain, refer

related 1. accompanying, affiliated, agnate, akin, allied, associated, cognate, concomitant, connected, correlated, interconnected, joint, linked **2.** agnate, akin, cognate, consanguineous, kin, kindred

relation 1. affiliation, affinity, consanguinity, kindred, kinship, propinquity, relationship **2.** kin, kinsman, kinswoman, relative **3.** application, bearing, bond, comparison, connection, correlation, interdependence, link, pertinence, reference, regard, similarity, tie-in **4.** account, description, narration, narrative, recital, recounting, report, story, tale

relations 1. affairs, associations, communications, connections, contact, dealings, interaction, intercourse, liaison, meetings, rapport, relationship, terms **2.** clan, family, kin, kindred, kinsmen, relatives, tribe

relationship affair, association, bond, communications, conjunction, connection, correlation, exchange, kinship, liaison, link, parallel, proportion, rapport, ratio, similarity, tie-up

relative adj. **1.** allied, associated, comparative, connected, contingent, corresponding, dependent, proportionate, reciprocal, related, respective **2.** applicable, apposite, appropriate, appurtenant, apropos, germane, pertinent, relevant **3.** With to corresponding to, in proportion to, proportional to ~n. **4.** connection, kinsman, kinswoman, member of one's or the family, relation

relatively comparatively, in or by comparison, rather, somewhat, to some extent

relax 1. abate, diminish, ease, ebb, lessen, let up, loosen, lower, mitigate, moderate, reduce, relieve, slacken, weaken **2.** be or feel at ease, calm, laze, let oneself go (Inf.), let one's hair down (Inf.), loosen up, put one's feet up, rest, soften, take it easy (Inf.), take one's ease, tranquillize, unbend, unwind

relaxation 1. amusement, enjoyment, entertainment, fun, leisure, pleasure, recreation, refreshment, rest **2.** abatement, diminution, easing, lessening, let-up (Inf.), moderation, reduction, slackening, weakening

relay n. **1.** relief, shift, turn **2.** communica-

relay race *n.* a race between two or more teams of contestants in which each contestant covers a specified portion of the distance.

release (rɪˈliːs) *vb.* (*tr.*) **1.** to free (a person or animal) from captivity or imprisonment. **2.** to free (someone) from obligation or duty. **3.** to free (something) from (one's grip); let fall. **4.** to issue (a record, film, or book) for sale or circulation. **5.** to make (news or information) known or allow (news, etc.) to be made known. **6.** *Law.* to relinquish (a right, claim, or title) in favour of someone else. ~*n.* **7.** the act of freeing or state of being freed. **8.** the act of issuing for sale or publication. **9.** something issued for sale or public showing, esp. a film or a record: *a new release from Bob Dylan.* **10.** a news item, etc., made available for publication, broadcasting, etc. **11.** *Law.* the surrender of a claim, right, title, etc., in favour of someone else. **12.** a control mechanism for starting or stopping an engine. —**reˈleaser** *n.*

relegate (ˈrɛlɪˌgeɪt) *vb.* (*tr.*) **1.** to move to a position of less authority, importance, etc.; demote. **2.** (*usually passive*) *Chiefly Brit.* to demote (a football team) to a lower division. **3.** to assign or refer (a matter) to another. **4.** (foll. by *to*) to banish or exile. **5.** to assign (something) to a particular group or category. —**ˈreleˌgatable** *adj.* —ˌ**releˈgation** *n.*

relent (rɪˈlɛnt) *vb.* (*intr.*) **1.** to change one's mind about some decision, esp. a harsh one; become more mild or amenable. **2.** (of the pace or intensity of something) to slacken. **3.** (of the weather) to become more mild.

relentless (rɪˈlɛntlɪs) *adj.* **1.** (of an enemy, etc.) implacable; inflexible; inexorable. **2.** (of pace or intensity) sustained; unremitting. —**reˈlentlessly** *adv.* —**reˈlentlessness** *n.*

relevant (ˈrɛlɪvənt) *adj.* having direct bearing on the matter in hand; pertinent. —**ˈrelevance** *or* **ˈrelevancy** *n.* —**ˈrelevantly** *adv.*

reliable (rɪˈlaɪəb°l) *adj.* able to be trusted; dependable. —**reˌliaˈbility** *or* **reˈliableness** *n.* —**reˈliably** *adv.*

reliance (rɪˈlaɪəns) *n.* **1.** dependence, confidence, or trust. **2.** something or someone upon which one relies. —**reˈliant** *adj.* —**reˈliantly** *adv.*

relic (ˈrɛlɪk) *n.* **1.** something that has survived from the past, such as an object or custom. **2.** something treasured for its past associations; keepsake. **3.** (*usually pl.*) a remaining part or fragment. **4.** *R.C. Church, Eastern Church.* part of the body of a saint or his belongings, venerated as holy. **5.** *Inf.* an old or old-fashioned person or thing. **6.** (*pl.*) *Arch.* the remains of a dead person; corpse.

relict (ˈrɛlɪkt) *n.* **1.** *Ecology.* **a.** a group of animals or plants that exists as a remnant of a formerly widely distributed group. **b.** (*as modifier*): *a relict fauna.* **2.** *Geol.* a mountain, lake, glacier, etc., that is a remnant of a preexisting formation after a destructive process has occurred. **3.** an archaic word for **widow**. **4.** an archaic word for **relic**.

relief (rɪˈliːf) *n.* **1.** a feeling of cheerfulness or optimism that follows the removal of anxiety, pain, or distress. **2.** deliverance from or alleviation of anxiety, pain, etc. **3.**

a. help or assistance, as to the poor or needy. **b.** (*as modifier*): *relief work.* **4.** a diversion from monotony. **5.** a person who replaces another at some task or duty. **6.** a bus, plane, etc., that carries additional passengers when a scheduled service is full. **7.** a road (**relief road**) carrying traffic round an urban area; bypass. **8. a.** the act of freeing a beleaguered town, fortress, etc.: *the relief of Mafeking.* **b.** (*as modifier*): *a relief column.* **9.** Also called: **relievo, rilievo.** *Sculpture, archit.* **a.** the projection of forms or figures from a flat ground, so that they are partly or wholly free of it. **b.** a piece of work of this kind. **10.** a printing process that employs raised surfaces from which ink is transferred to the paper. **11.** any vivid effect resulting from contrast: *comic relief.* **12.** variation in altitude in an area; difference between highest and lowest level. **13.** *Law.* redress of a grievance or hardship: *to seek relief through the courts.* **14. on relief.** *U.S.* (of people) in receipt of government aid because of personal need.

relieve (rɪˈliːv) *vb.* (*tr.*) **1.** to bring alleviation of (pain, distress, etc.) to (someone). **2.** to bring aid or assistance to (someone in need, etc.). **3.** to take over the duties or watch of (someone). **4.** to bring aid or a relieving force to (a besieged town, etc.). **5.** to free (someone) from an obligation. **6.** to make (something) less unpleasant, arduous, or monotonous. **7.** to bring into relief or prominence, as by contrast. **8.** (foll. by *of*) *Inf.* to take from: *the thief relieved him of his watch.* **9. relieve oneself.** to urinate or defecate. —**reˈlievable** *adj.* —**reˈlieved** *adj.* —**reˈliever** *n.*

religion (rɪˈlɪdʒən) *n.* **1.** belief in, worship of, or obedience to a supernatural power or powers considered to be divine or to have control of human destiny. **2.** any formal or institutionalized expression of such belief: *the Christian religion.* **3.** the attitude and feeling of one who believes in a transcendent controlling power or powers. **4.** *Chiefly R.C. Church.* the way of life entered upon by monks and nuns: *to enter religion.* **5.** something of overwhelming importance to a person: *football is his religion.*

religious (rɪˈlɪdʒəs) *adj.* **1.** of, relating to, or concerned with religion. **2. a.** pious; devout; godly. **b.** (*as collective n.*, preceded by *the*): *the religious.* **3.** appropriate to or in accordance with the principles of a religion. **4.** scrupulous, exact, or conscientious. **5.** *Christianity.* of or relating to a way of life dedicated to religion and defined by a monastic rule. ~*n.* **6.** *Christianity.* a monk or nun. —**reˈligiously** *adv.* —**reˈligiousness** *n.*

relinquish (rɪˈlɪŋkwɪʃ) *vb.* (*tr.*) **1.** to give up (a task, struggle, etc.); abandon. **2.** to surrender or renounce (a claim, right, etc.). **3.** to release; let go. —**reˈlinquisher** *n.* —**reˈlinquishment** *n.*

reliquary (ˈrɛlɪkwərɪ) *n., pl.* **-quaries.** a receptacle or repository for relics, esp. relics of saints.

relish (ˈrɛlɪʃ) *vb.* (*tr.*) **1.** to savour or enjoy (an experience) to the full. **2.** to anticipate eagerly; look forward to. **3.** to enjoy the taste or flavour of (food, etc.); savour. ~*n.* **4.** liking or enjoyment, as of something eaten or experienced (esp. in **with relish**). **5.** pleasurable anticipa-

---

THESAURUS

tion, dispatch, message, transmission ~*v.* **3.** broadcast, carry, communicate, hand on, pass on, send, spread, transmit

release *v.* **1.** deliver, discharge, disengage, drop, emancipate, extricate, free, let go, let out, liberate, loose, manumit, set free, turn loose, unchain, undo, unfasten, unfetter, unloose, unshackle, untie **2.** absolve, acquit, dispense, excuse, exempt, exonerate, let go, let off **3.** break, circulate, disseminate, distribute, issue, launch, make known, make public, present, publish, put out, unveil ~*n.* **4.** acquittal, deliverance, delivery, discharge, emancipation, freedom, liberation, liberty, manumission, relief **5.** absolution, acquittance, dispensation, exemption, exoneration, let-off (*Inf.*) **6.** announcement, issue, offering, proclamation, publication

relent 1. acquiesce, be merciful, capitulate, change one's mind, come round, forbear, give in, give quarter, give way, have pity, melt, show mercy, soften, unbend, yield **2.** die down, drop, ease, fall, let up, relax, slacken, slow, weaken

relentless 1. cruel, fierce, grim, hard, harsh, implacable, inexorable, inflexible, merciless, pitiless, remorseless, ruthless, uncompromising, undeviating, unforgiving, unrelenting, unstoppable, unyielding **2.** incessant, nonstop, persistent, punishing, sustained, unabated, unbroken, unfaltering, unflagging, unrelenting, unrelieved, unremitting, unstoppable

relevant admissible, *ad rem*, applicable, apposite, appropriate, appurtenant, apt, fitting, germane, material, pertinent, proper, related, relative, significant, suited, to the point, to the purpose

reliable certain, dependable, faithful, honest, predictable, regular, responsible, safe, sound, stable, sure, tried and true, true, trustworthy, trusty, unfailing, upright

relic fragment, keepsake, memento, remembrance, remnant, scrap, souvenir, survival, token, trace, vestige

relief 1. abatement, alleviation, assuagement, balm, comfort, cure, deliverance, ease, easement, mitigation, palliation, release, remedy, solace **2.** aid, assistance, help, succour, support, sustenance **3.** break, breather (*Inf.*), diversion, let-up (*Inf.*), refreshment, relaxation, remission, respite, rest

relieve 1. abate, alleviate, appease, assuage, calm, comfort, console, cure, diminish, dull, ease, mitigate, mollify, palliate, relax, salve, soften, solace, soothe **2.** aid, assist, bring aid to, help, succour, support, sustain **3.** give (someone) a break *or* rest, stand in for, substitute for, take over from, take the place of **4.** deliver, discharge, disembarrass, disencumber, exempt, free, release, unburden **5.** break, brighten, interrupt, let up on (*Inf.*), lighten, slacken, vary

religious 1. churchgoing, devotional, devout, divine, doctrinal, faithful, god-fearing, godly, holy, pious, pure, reverent, righteous, sacred, scriptural, sectarian, spiritual, theological **2.** conscientious, exact, faithful, fastidious, meticulous, punctilious, rigid, rigorous, scrupulous, unerring, unswerving

tion: *he didn't have much relish for the idea.* **6.** an appetizing or spicy food added to a main dish to enhance its flavour. **7.** an appetizing taste or flavour. **8.** a zestful trace or touch: *there was a certain relish in all his writing.* —**'relishable** *adj.*

relive (riː'lɪv) *vb.* (*tr.*) to experience (a sensation, event, etc.) again, esp. in the imagination. —**re'livable** *adj.*

relocate (ˌriːləʊ'keɪt) *vb.* (esp. of a business or an employee) to move to a new location. —ˌrelo'cation *n.*

reluctance (rɪ'lʌktəns) *or* **reluctancy** *n.* **1.** lack of eagerness or willingness; disinclination. **2.** *Physics.* a measure of the resistance of a closed magnetic circuit to a magnetic flux.

reluctant (rɪ'lʌktənt) *adj.* not eager; unwilling; disinclined. —**re'luctantly** *adv.*

rely (rɪ'laɪ) *vb.* **-lying, -lied.** (*intr.;* foll. by *on* or *upon*) **1.** to be dependent (on): *he relies on his charm.* **2.** to have trust or confidence (in): *you can rely on us.*

remain (rɪ'meɪn) *vb.* (*mainly intr.*) **1.** to stay behind or in the same place: *to remain at home.* **2.** (*copula*) to continue to be: *to remain cheerful.* **3.** to be left, as after use, consumption, the passage of time, etc. **4.** to be left to be done, said, etc.: *it remains to be pointed out.*

remainder (rɪ'meɪndə) *n.* **1.** a part or portion that is left, as after use, subtraction, expenditure, the passage of time, etc.: *the remainder of the milk.* **2.** *Maths.* **a.** the amount left over when one quantity cannot be exactly divided by another: *for 10 ÷ 3, the remainder is 1.* **b.** another name for **difference** (sense 7). **3.** *Property law.* a future interest in property; an interest in a particular estate that will pass to one at some future date, as on the death of the current possessor. **4.** a number of copies of a book left unsold when demand ceases, which are sold at a reduced price. ~*vb.* **5.** (*tr.*) to sell (copies of a book) as a remainder.

remains (rɪ'meɪnz) *pl. n.* **1.** any pieces, fragments, etc., that are left unused or still extant, as after use, consumption, the passage of time: *archaeological remains.* **2.** the body of a dead person; corpse. **3.** Also called: **literary remains.** the unpublished writings of an author at the time of his death.

remand (rɪ'mɑːnd) *vb.* (*tr.*) **1.** *Law.* (of a court or magistrate) to send (a prisoner or accused person) back into custody. **2.** to send back. ~*n.* **3.** the sending of a prisoner or accused person back into custody to await trial. **4.** the act of remanding or state of being remanded. **5. on remand.** in custody or on bail awaiting trial. —**re'mandment** *n.*

remand home *or* **centre** *n.* (in England) an institution to which juvenile offenders are sent for detention while awaiting appearance before a court.

remark (rɪ'mɑːk) *vb.* **1.** (when *intr.,* often foll. by *on* or *upon;* when *tr.,* may take a clause as object) to pass a casual comment (about); reflect in informal speech or writing. **2.** (*tr.; may take a clause as object*) to perceive; observe; notice. ~*n.* **3.** a brief casually expressed thought or opinion. **4.** notice, comment, or observation: *the event passed without remark.* **5.** a mark in the mar-

gin of an engraved plate to indicate the stage of production. —**re'marker** *n.*

remarkable (rɪ'mɑːkəbəl) *adj.* **1.** worthy of note or attention: *a remarkable achievement.* **2.** unusual, striking, or extraordinary: *a remarkable sight.* —**re'markableness** *n.* —**re'markably** *adv.*

REME ('riːmiː) *n.* acronym for Royal Electrical and Mechanical Engineers.

remedial (rɪ'miːdɪəl) *adj.* **1.** affording a remedy; curative. **2.** denoting or relating to special teaching for backward and slow learners: *remedial education.* —**re'medially** *adv.*

remedy ('rɛmɪdɪ) *n., pl.* **-dies. 1.** (usually foll. by *for* or *against*) any drug or agent that cures a disease or controls its symptoms. **2.** (usually foll. by *for* or *against*) anything that serves to cure defects, improve conditions, etc.: *a remedy for industrial disputes.* **3.** the legally permitted variation from the standard weight or quality of coins. ~*vb.* (*tr.*) **4.** to relieve or cure (a disease, illness, etc.) by a remedy. **5.** to put to rights (a fault, error, etc.); correct. —**remediable** (rɪ'miːdɪəbəl) *adj.* —**re'mediably** *adv.* —**'remediless** *adj.*

remember (rɪ'mɛmbə) *vb.* **1.** to become aware of (something forgotten) again; bring back to one's consciousness. **2.** to retain (an idea, intention, etc.) in one's conscious mind: *remember to do one's shopping.* **3.** (*tr.*) to give money, etc., to (someone), as in a will or in tipping. **4.** (*tr.;* foll. by *to*) to mention (a person's name) to another person, as by way of greeting: *remember me to your mother.* **5.** (*tr.*) to mention (a person) favourably, as in prayer. **6.** (*tr.*) to commemorate (a person, event, etc.): *to remember the dead of the wars.* **7. remember oneself.** to recover one's good manners after a lapse. —**re'memberer** *n.*

remembrance (rɪ'mɛmbrəns) *n.* **1.** the act of remembering or state of being remembered. **2.** something that is remembered; reminiscence. **3.** a memento or keepsake. **4.** the extent in time of one's power of recollection. **5.** the act of honouring some past event, person, etc.

Remembrance Day *n.* **1.** (in Britain) another name for **Remembrance Sunday. 2.** (in Canada) a statutory holiday observed on November 11 in memory of the dead of both World Wars.

remind (rɪ'maɪnd) *vb.* (*tr.;* usually foll. by *of; may take a clause as object or an infinitive*) to cause (a person) to remember (something or to do something); put (a person) in mind (of something): *remind me to phone home; flowers remind me of holidays.* —**re'minder** *n.* —**re'mindful** *adj.*

reminisce (ˌrɛmɪ'nɪs) *vb.* (*intr.*) to talk or write about old times, past experiences, etc.

reminiscence (ˌrɛmɪ'nɪsəns) *n.* **1.** the act of recalling or narrating past experiences. **2.** (*often pl.*) some past experience, event, etc., that is recalled. **3.** an event, phenomenon, or experience that reminds one of something else. **4.** *Philosophy.* the doctrine that the mind has seen

---

THESAURUS

relish *v.* **1.** appreciate, delight in, enjoy, fancy, like, look forward to, luxuriate in, prefer, revel in, savour, taste ~*n.* **2.** appetite, appreciation, enjoyment, fancy, fondness, gusto, liking, love, partiality, penchant, predilection, stomach, taste, zest **3.** appetizer, condiment, sauce, seasoning **4.** flavour, piquancy, savour, smack, spice, tang, taste, trace

reluctance aversion, backwardness, disinclination, dislike, disrelish, distaste, hesitancy, indisposition, loathing, repugnance, unwillingness

reluctant averse, backward, disinclined, grudging, hesitant, indisposed, loath, recalcitrant, slow, unenthusiastic, unwilling

rely bank, be confident of, be sure of, bet, count, depend, have confidence in, lean, reckon, repose trust in, swear by, trust

remain abide, be left, cling, continue, delay, dwell, endure, go on, last, linger, persist, prevail, rest, stand, stay, stay behind, stay put (*Inf.*), survive, tarry, wait

remainder balance, dregs, excess, leavings, relic, remains, remnant, residue, resid-

uum, rest, surplus, trace, vestige(s)

remaining abiding, extant, lasting, left, lingering, outstanding, persisting, residual, surviving, unfinished

remains **1.** balance, crumbs, debris, detritus, dregs, fragments, leavings, leftovers, oddments, odds and ends, pieces, relics, remainder, remnants, residue, rest, scraps, traces, vestiges **2.** body, cadaver, carcass, corpse

remark *v.* **1.** animadvert, comment, declare, mention, observe, pass comment, reflect, say, state **2.** espy, heed, make out, mark, note, notice, observe, perceive, regard, see, take note *or* notice of ~*n.* **3.** assertion, comment, declaration, observation, opinion, reflection, statement, thought, utterance, word **4.** acknowledgment, attention, comment, consideration, heed, mention, notice, observation, recognition, regard, thought

remarkable conspicuous, distinguished, extraordinary, famous, impressive, miraculous, notable, noteworthy, odd, outstanding, phenomenal, pre-eminent, prominent, rare,

signal, singular, strange, striking, surprising, uncommon, unusual, wonderful

remedy *n.* **1.** antidote, counteractive, cure, medicament, medicine, nostrum, panacea, physic (*Rare*), relief, restorative, specific, therapy, treatment **2.** antidote, corrective, countermeasure, panacea, redress, relief, solution ~*v.* **3.** alleviate, assuage, control, cure, ease, heal, help, mitigate, palliate, relieve, restore, soothe, treat **4.** ameliorate, correct, fix, put right, rectify, redress, reform, relieve, repair, set to rights, solve

remember bear in mind, call to mind, call up, commemorate, keep in mind, look back (on), recall, recognize, recollect, reminisce, retain, summon up, think back

remind awaken memories of, bring back to, bring to mind, call to mind, call up, jog one's memory, make (someone) remember, prompt, put in mind, refresh one's memory

reminiscence anecdote, memoir, memory, recall, recollection, reflection, remembrance, retrospection, review

the universal forms of all things in a previous disembodied existence.

reminiscent (ˌrɛmɪˈnɪsənt) adj. 1. (postpositive; foll. by of) stimulating memories (of) or comparisons (with). 2. characterized by reminiscence. 3. (of a person) given to reminiscing. —ˌreminˈiscently adv.

remiss (rɪˈmɪs) adj. (postpositive) 1. lacking in care or attention to duty; negligent. 2. lacking in energy. —reˈmissly adv. —reˈmissness n.

remission (rɪˈmɪʃən) or **remittal** (rɪˈmɪtəl) n. 1. the act of remitting or state of being remitted. 2. a reduction of the term of a sentence of imprisonment, as for good conduct. 3. forgiveness for sin. 4. discharge or release from penalty, obligation, etc. 5. lessening of intensity; abatement, as in the symptoms of a disease. 6. Rare. the act of sending a remittance. —reˈmissive adj. —reˈmissively adv.

remit vb. (rɪˈmɪt). **-mitting, -mitted.** (mainly tr.) 1. (also intr.) to send (payment, etc.), as for goods or service, esp. by post. 2. Law. (esp. of an appeal court) to send back (a case) to an inferior court for further consideration. 3. to cancel or refrain from exacting (a penalty or punishment). 4. (also intr.) to relax (pace, intensity, etc.) or (of pace) to slacken or abate. 5. to postpone; defer. 6. Arch. to pardon or forgive (crime, sins, etc.). ~n. (ˈriːmɪt, rɪˈmɪt). 7. area of authority (of a committee, etc.). 8. Law. the transfer of a case from one court or jurisdiction to another. 9. the act of remitting. —reˈmittable adj. —reˈmitter n.

remittance (rɪˈmɪtəns) n. 1. payment for goods or services received or as an allowance, esp. when sent by post. 2. the act of remitting.

remittent (rɪˈmɪtənt) adj. (of the symptoms of a disease) characterized by periods of diminished severity. —reˈmittence n. —reˈmittently adv.

remnant (ˈrɛmnənt) n. 1. (often pl.) a part left over after use, processing, etc. 2. a surviving trace or vestige: a remnant of imperialism. 3. a piece of material from the end of a roll. ~adj. 4. remaining; left over.

remonstrance (rɪˈmɒnstrəns) n. 1. the act of remonstrating. 2. a protest or reproof, esp. a petition protesting against something.

remonstrate (ˈrɛmənˌstreɪt) vb. (intr.) (usually foll. by with, against, etc.) to argue in protest or objection: to remonstrate with the government. —ˌremonˈstration n. —remonstrative (rɪˈmɒnstrətɪv) adj. —ˈremonˌstrator n.

remorse (rɪˈmɔːs) n. 1. a sense of deep regret and guilt for some misdeed. 2. compunction; pity; compassion. —reˈmorseful adj. —reˈmorsefully adv. —reˈmorse-

fulness n. —reˈmorseless adj.

remote (rɪˈməʊt) adj. 1. located far away; distant. 2. far from society, or civilization; out-of-the-way. 3. distant in time. 4. distantly related or connected: a remote cousin. 5. slight or faint (esp. in not the remotest idea). 6. (of a person's manner) aloof or abstracted. —reˈmotely adv. —reˈmoteness n.

remote control n. control of a system or activity from a distance, usually by means of radio, ultrasonic, or electrical signals. —reˌmote-conˈtrolled adj.

remould vb. (ˌriːˈməʊld). 1. (tr.) to mould again. ~n. (ˈriːˌməʊld). 2. another name for retread (tyre).

removal (rɪˈmuːvəl) n. 1. the act of removing or state of being removed. 2. a. a change of residence. b. (as modifier): a removal company. 3. dismissal from office.

remove (rɪˈmuːv) vb. (mainly tr.) 1. to take away and place elsewhere. 2. to dismiss (someone) from office. 3. to do away with; abolish; get rid of. 4. Euphemistic. to assassinate; kill. 5. (intr.) Formal. to change the location of one's home or place of business. ~n. 6. the act of removing, esp. (formal) a removal of one's residence or place of work. 7. the degree of difference: only one remove from madness. 8. Brit. (in certain schools) a class or form. —reˈmovable adj. —reˌmovaˈbility n. —reˈmover n.

remunerate (rɪˈmjuːnəˌreɪt) vb. (tr.) to reward or pay for work, service, etc. —reˌmunerˈation n. —reˈmunerable adj. —reˈmunerative adj. —reˈmuneratively adv. —reˈmunerˌator n.

renaissance (rəˈneɪsəns; U.S. also ˈrɛnəˌsɒns) or **renascence** n. a revival or rebirth, esp. of culture and learning.

Renaissance (rəˈneɪsəns; U.S. also ˈrɛnəˌsɒns) n. 1. the. the great revival of art, literature, and learning in Europe in the 14th, 15th, and 16th centuries. 2. the spirit, culture, art, science, and thought of this period. ~adj. 3. of, characteristic of, or relating to the Renaissance, its culture, etc.

renal (ˈriːnəl) adj. of, relating to, resembling, or situated near the kidney.

renascent (rɪˈnæsənt, -ˈneɪ-) adj. becoming active or vigorous again; reviving: renascent nationalism. —reˈnascence n.

rend (rɛnd) vb. **rending, rent.** 1. to tear with violent force or to be torn in this way; rip. 2. (tr.) to tear or pull (one's clothes, etc.), esp. as a manifestation of rage or grief. 3. (tr.) (of a noise or cry) to disturb (the silence) with a shrill or piercing tone. —ˈrendible adj.

render (ˈrɛndə) vb. (tr.) 1. to present or submit (accounts, etc.) for payment, etc. 2. to give or provide (aid,

---

THESAURUS

reminiscent evocative, redolent, remindful, similar, suggestive

remiss careless, culpable, delinquent, derelict, dilatory, forgetful, heedless, inattentive, indifferent, lackadaisical, lax, neglectful, negligent, regardless, slack, slipshod, sloppy (Inf.), slothful, slow, tardy, thoughtless, unmindful

remission 1. absolution, acquittal, amnesty, discharge, excuse, exemption, exoneration, forgiveness, indulgence, pardon, release, reprieve 2. abatement, abeyance, alleviation, amelioration, decrease, diminution, ebb, lessening, let-up (Inf.), lull, moderation, reduction, relaxation, respite, suspension

remit v. 1. dispatch, forward, mail, post, send, transmit 2. cancel, desist, forbear, halt, repeal, rescind, stop 3. abate, alleviate, decrease, diminish, dwindle, ease up, fall away, mitigate, moderate, reduce, relax, sink, slacken, soften, wane, weaken 4. defer, delay, postpone, put off, shelve, suspend ~n. 5. authorization, brief, guidelines, instructions, orders, terms of reference

remittance allowance, consideration, fee, payment

remnant balance, bit, end, fragment, hangover, leftovers, piece, remainder, remains, residue, residuum, rest, rump, scrap, shred, survival, trace, vestige

remonstrate argue, challenge, complain, dispute, dissent, expostulate, object, protest, take exception, take issue

remorse anguish, bad or guilty conscience, compassion, compunction, contrition, grief, guilt, pangs of conscience, penitence, pity, regret, repentance, ruefulness, self-reproach, shame, sorrow

remorseful apologetic, ashamed, chastened, conscience-stricken, contrite, guilt-ridden, guilty, penitent, regretful, repentant, rueful, sad, self-reproachful, sorrowful, sorry

remorseless 1. inexorable, relentless, unrelenting, unremitting, unstoppable 2. callous, cruel, hard, hardhearted, harsh, implacable, inhumane, merciless, pitiless, ruthless, savage, uncompassionate, unforgiving, unmerciful

remote 1. backwoods, distant, far, far-away, far-off, godforsaken, inaccessible, isolated, lonely, off the beaten track, outlying, out-of-the-way, secluded 2. alien, extraneous, extrinsic, foreign, immaterial, irrelevant, outside, removed, unconnected, unrelated 3. doubtful, dubious, faint, implausible, inconsiderable, meagre, negligible, outside, poor, slender, slight, slim, small, unlikely 4. abstracted, aloof, cold, detached, distant, faraway, indifferent, introspective, introverted, removed, reserved, standoffish, unapproachable, uncommunicative, uninterested, uninvolved, withdrawn

removal 1. abstraction, dislodgment, dismissal, displacement, dispossession, ejection, elimination, eradication, erasure, expulsion, expunction, extraction, purging, stripping,

subtraction, taking off, uprooting, withdrawal 2. departure, flitting (Scot., & northern English dialect), move, relocation, transfer

remove 1. abolish, abstract, amputate, carry off or away, delete, depose, detach, dethrone, discharge, dislodge, dismiss, displace, do away with, doff, efface, eject, eliminate, erase, expel, expunge, extract, get rid of, move, oust, purge, relegate, shed, strike out, take away, take off, take out, throw out, transfer, transport, unseat, wipe out, withdraw 2. depart, flit (Scot., & northern English dialect), move, move away, quit, relocate, shift, transfer, transport, vacate 3. Fig. assassinate, bump off (Sl.), dispose of, do away with, do in (Sl.), eliminate, execute, get rid of, kill, liquidate, murder

remuneration compensation, earnings, emolument, fee, income, indemnity, pay, payment, profit, recompense, reimbursement, reparation, repayment, retainer, return, reward, salary, stipend, wages

remunerative gainful, lucrative, moneymaking, paying, profitable, recompensing, rewarding, rich, worthwhile

renaissance, renascence awakening, new birth, new dawn, reappearance, reawakening, rebirth, re-emergence, regeneration, renewal, restoration, resurgence, resurrection, revival

charity, a service, etc.). **3.** to show (obedience), as expected. **4.** to give or exchange, as by way of return or requital: *to render blow for blow.* **5.** to cause to become: *grief had rendered him simple-minded.* **6.** to deliver (a verdict or opinion) formally. **7.** to portray or depict (something), as in painting, music, or acting. **8.** to translate (something). **9.** (sometimes foll. by *up*) to yield or give: *the tomb rendered up its secret.* **10.** (often foll. by *back*) to return (something); give back. **11.** to cover the surface of (brickwork, etc.) with a coat of plaster. **12.** (often foll. by *down*) to extract (fat) from (meat) by melting. ~*n.* **13.** a first thin coat of plaster applied to a surface. **14.** one who or that which renders. —'**renderable** *adj.* —'**renderer** *n.* —'**rendering** *n.*

rendezvous ('rɒndɪ,vuː) *n., pl.* -**vous** (-,vuːz). **1.** a meeting or appointment to meet at a specified time and place. **2.** a place where people meet. ~*vb.* **3.** to meet at a specified time or place.

rendition (rɛn'dɪʃən) *n.* **1.** a performance of a musical composition, dramatic role, etc. **2.** a translation. **3.** the act of rendering.

renegade ('rɛnɪ,geɪd) *n.* **1. a.** a person who deserts his cause or faith for another; traitor. **b.** (*as modifier*): *a renegade priest.* **2.** any outlaw or rebel.

renege *or* **renegue** (rɪ'niːg, -'neɪg) *vb.* **1.** (*intr.; often* foll. by *on*) to go back (on one's promise, etc.). ~*vb., n.* **2.** *Cards.* other words for **revoke** (senses 2, 3). —re'**neger** *or* re'**neguer** *n.*

renew (rɪ'njuː) *vb.* (*mainly tr.*) **1.** to take up again. **2.** (*also intr.*) to begin (an activity) again; recommence. **3.** to restate or reaffirm (a promise, etc.). **4.** (*also intr.*) to make (a lease, etc.) valid for a further period. **5.** to regain or recover (vigour, strength, activity, etc.). **6.** to restore to a new or fresh condition. **7.** to replace (an old or worn-out part or piece). **8.** to replenish (a supply, etc.). —re'**newable** *adj.* —re'**newal** *n.* —re'**newer** *n.*

rennet ('rɛnɪt) *n.* **1.** the membrane lining the fourth stomach of a young calf. **2.** a substance prepared esp. from the stomachs of calves and used for curdling milk in making cheese.

renounce (rɪ'naʊns) *vb.* **1.** (*tr.*) to give up formally (a claim or right): *to renounce a title.* **2.** (*tr.*) to repudiate: *to renounce Christianity.* **3.** (*tr.*) to give up (some habit, etc.) voluntarily: *to renounce one's old ways.* **4.** (*intr.*) *Cards.* to fail to follow suit because one has no more cards of the suit led. ~*n.* **5.** *Cards.* a failure to follow suit. —re'**nouncement** *n.* —re'**nouncer** *n.*

renovate ('rɛnə,veɪt) *vb.* (*tr.*) **1.** to restore (something) to good condition. **2.** to revive or refresh (one's spirits, health, etc.). —,**reno'vation** *n.* —'**reno,vative** *adj.* —'**reno,vator** *n.*

renown (rɪ'naʊn) *n.* widespread reputation, esp. of a good kind; fame. —re'**nowned** *adj.*

rent[1] (rɛnt) *n.* **1.** a payment made periodically by a tenant to a landlord or owner for the occupation or use of land, buildings, etc. **2.** *Econ.* the return derived from the cultivation of land in excess of production costs. **3.** for

rent. *Chiefly U.S.* available for use and occupation subject to the payment of rent. ~*vb.* **4.** (*tr.*) to grant (a person) the right to use one's property in return for periodic payments. **5.** (*tr.*) to occupy or use (property) in return for periodic payments. **6.** (*intr.*; often foll. by *at*) to be let or rented (for a specified rental). —'**rentable** *adj.* —'**renter** *n.*

rent[2] (rɛnt) *n.* **1.** a slit or opening made by tearing or rending. **2.** a breach or division. ~*vb.* **3.** the past tense or past participle of **rend.**

rental ('rɛntəl) *n.* **1. a.** the amount paid by a tenant as rent. **b.** an income derived from rents received. **2.** property available for renting. ~*adj.* **3.** of or relating to rent.

rentier *French.* (rɑ̃'tje) *n.* a person whose income consists primarily of fixed unearned amounts, such as rent or interest.

renunciation (rɪ,nʌnsɪ'eɪʃən) *n.* **1.** the act or an instance of renouncing. **2.** a formal declaration renouncing something. —re'**nunciative** *or* re'**nunciatory** *adj.*

rep[1] *or* **repp** (rɛp) *n.* a silk, wool, rayon, or cotton fabric with a transversely corded surface. —**repped** *adj.*

rep[2] (rɛp) *n. Theatre.* short for **repertory company.**

rep[3] (rɛp) *n.* **1.** short for **representative** (sense 2). **2.** *N.Z. inf.* a rugby player selected to represent his district.

repair[1] (rɪ'pɛə) *vb.* (*tr.*) **1.** to restore (something damaged or broken) to good condition or working order. **2.** to heal (a breach or division) in (something): *to repair a broken marriage.* **3.** to make amends for (a mistake, injury, etc.). ~*n.* **4.** the act, task, or process of repairing. **5.** a part that has been repaired. **6.** state or condition: *in good repair.* —re'**pairable** *adj.* —re'**pairer** *n.*

repair[2] (rɪ'pɛə) *vb.* (*intr.*) **1.** (usually foll. by *to*) to go (to a place). **2.** (usually foll. by *to*) to have recourse (to) for help, etc.: *to repair to one's lawyer.* ~*n.* **3.** a haunt or resort.

reparable ('rɛpərəbəl, 'rɛprə-) *adj.* able to be repaired, recovered, or remedied. —'**reparably** *adv.*

reparation (,rɛpə'reɪʃən) *n.* **1.** the act or process of making amends. **2.** (*usually pl.*) compensation exacted as an indemnity from a defeated nation by the victors. **3.** the act or process of repairing or state of having been repaired. —**reparative** (rɪ'pærətɪv) *or* re'**paratory** *adj.*

repartee (,rɛpɑː'tiː) *n.* **1.** a sharp, witty, or aphoristic remark made as a reply. **2.** skill in making sharp witty replies.

repast (rɪ'pɑːst) *n.* a meal or the food provided at a meal: *a light repast.*

repatriate *vb.* (riː'pætrɪ,eɪt). **1.** (*tr.*) to send back (a person) to the country of his birth or citizenship. ~*n.* (riː'pætrɪɪt). **2.** a person who has been repatriated. —re,**patri'ation** *n.*

repay (rɪ'peɪ) *vb.* -**paying, -paid. 1.** to pay back (money, etc.) to (a person); refund or reimburse. **2.** to make a return for (something): *to repay kindness.* —re'**payable**

adj. —**re'payment** *n.*

repeal (rɪ'piːl) *vb.* (*tr.*) **1.** to annul or rescind officially: revoke: *these laws were repealed.* ~*n.* **2.** an instance or the process of repealing; annulment. —**re'pealable** *adj.* —**re'pealer** *n.*

repeat (rɪ'piːt) *vb.* **1.** (when *tr., may take a clause as object*) to do or experience (something) again once or several times, esp. to say or write (something) again. **2.** (*intr.*) to occur more than once: *the last figure repeats.* **3.** (*tr.; may take a clause as object*) to reproduce (the words, sounds, etc.) uttered by someone else; echo. **4.** (*tr.*) to utter (a poem, etc.) from memory; recite. **5.** (*intr.*) (of food) to be tasted again after ingestion as the result of belching. **6.** (*tr.; may take a clause as object*) to tell to another person (the secrets imparted to one by someone else). **7.** (*intr.*) (of a clock) to strike the hour or quarter-hour just past. **8.** (*intr.*) *U.S.* to vote (illegally) more than once in a single election. **9. repeat oneself.** to say or do the same thing more than once, esp. so as to be tedious. ~*n.* **10. a.** the act or an instance of repeating. **b.** (*as modifier*): *a repeat performance.* **11.** a word, action, etc., that is repeated. **12.** an order made out for goods, etc., that duplicates a previous order. **13.** *Radio, television.* a broadcast of a programme, film, etc., which has been broadcast before. **14.** *Music.* a passage that is an exact restatement of the passage preceding it. —**re'peatable** *adj.*

repeater (rɪ'piːtə) *n.* **1.** a person or thing that repeats. **2.** Also called: **repeating firearm.** a firearm capable of discharging several shots without reloading. **3.** a timepiece which strikes the hour or quarter-hour just past, when a spring is pressed. **4.** *Electrical engineering.* a device that amplifies or augments incoming electrical signals and retransmits them.

repel (rɪ'pɛl) *vb.* **-pelling, -pelled.** (*mainly tr.*) **1.** to force or drive back (something or somebody). **2.** (*also intr.*) to produce a feeling of aversion or distaste in (someone or something); be disgusting (to). **3.** to be effective in keeping away, controlling, or resisting: *a spray that repels flies.* **4.** to have no affinity for; fail to mix with or absorb: *water and oil repel each other.* **5.** to disdain to accept (something); turn away from or spurn: *she repelled his advances.* —**re'pellent** *adj.* —**re'peller** *n.* —**re'pellingly** *adv.*

▷ Usage. See at **repulse.**

repent (rɪ'pɛnt) *vb.* to feel remorse (for); be contrite (about); show penitence (for). —**re'pentance** *n.* —**re'penter** *n.*

repercussion (ˌriːpə'kʌʃən) *n.* **1.** (*often pl.*) a result or consequence of an action or event: *the repercussions of the war are still felt.* **2.** recoil after impact; rebound. **3.** a reflection, esp. of sound; echo or reverberation. —ˌ**reper'cussive** *adj.*

repertoire ('rɛpə,twɑː) *n.* **1.** all the works collectively that a company, actor, etc., is competent to perform. **2.**

the entire stock of things available in a field or of a kind.

repertory ('rɛpətərɪ, -trɪ) *n., pl.* **-ries.** **1.** the entire stock of things available in a field or of a kind; repertoire. **2.** a building or place where a stock of things is kept; repository. **3.** short for **repertory company.** —ˌ**reper'torial** *adj.*

repertory company *n.* a theatrical company that performs plays from a repertoire. U.S. name: **stock company.**

repetition (ˌrɛpɪ'tɪʃən) *n.* **1.** the act or an instance of repeating; reiteration. **2.** a thing, word, action, etc., that is repeated. **3.** a replica or copy. —ˌ**repe'titious** *or* **re'petitive** *adj.*

repine (rɪ'paɪn) *vb.* (*intr.*) to be fretful or low-spirited through discontent.

replace (rɪ'pleɪs) *vb.* (*tr.*) **1.** to take the place of; supersede. **2.** to substitute a person or thing for (another); put in place of: *to replace an old pair of shoes.* **3.** to restore to its rightful place. —**re'placeable** *adj.* —**re'placer** *n.*

replacement (rɪ'pleɪsmənt) *n.* **1.** the act or process of replacing. **2.** a person or thing that replaces another.

replay *n.* ('riː,pleɪ). **1.** Also called: **action replay.** a showing again of a sequence of action in slow motion immediately after it happens. **2.** a rematch. ~*vb.* (riː-'pleɪ). **3.** to play again (a record, sporting contest, etc.).

replenish (rɪ'plɛnɪʃ) *vb.* (*tr.*) **1.** to make full or complete again by supplying what has been used up. **2.** to put fresh fuel on (a fire). —**re'plenisher** *n.* —**re'plenishment** *n.*

replete (rɪ'pliːt) *adj.* (*usually postpositive*) **1.** (often foll. by *with*) copiously supplied (with); abounding (in). **2.** having one's appetite completely or excessively satisfied; gorged; satiated. —**re'pletely** *adv.* —**re'pleteness** *n.* —**re'pletion** *n.*

replica ('rɛplɪkə) *n.* an exact copy or reproduction, esp. on a smaller scale.

replicate *vb.* ('rɛplɪ,keɪt). (*mainly tr.*) **1.** (*also intr.*) to make or be a copy of; reproduce. **2.** to fold (something) over on itself; bend back. ~*adj.* ('rɛplɪkɪt). **3.** folded back on itself: *a replicate leaf.* —ˌ**repli'cation** *n.* —'**replicative** *adj.*

reply (rɪ'plaɪ) *vb.* **-plying, -plied.** (*mainly intr.*) **1.** to make answer (to) in words or writing or by an action; respond. **2.** (*tr.; takes a clause as object*) to say (something) in answer to: *he replied that he didn't want to come.* **3.** *Law.* to answer a defendant's plea. **4.** to return (a sound); echo. ~*n., pl.* **-plies.** **5.** an answer; response. **6.** the answer made by a plaintiff or petitioner to a defendant's case. —**re'plier** *n.*

report (rɪ'pɔːt) *n.* **1.** an account prepared after investigation and published or broadcast. **2.** a statement made widely known; rumour: *according to report, he is not dead.* **3.** an account of the deliberations of a committee, body, etc.: *a report of parliamentary proceedings.* **4.** *Brit.* a statement on the progress of each schoolchild. **5.**

THESAURUS

repeal 1. *v.* abolish, abrogate, annul, cancel, countermand, declare null and void, invalidate, nullify, recall, rescind, reverse, revoke, set aside, withdraw **2.** *n.* abolition, abrogation, annulment, cancellation, invalidation, nullification, rescinding, rescindment, rescission, revocation, withdrawal

repeat 1. *v.* duplicate, echo, iterate, quote, recapitulate, recite, redo, rehearse, reiterate, relate, renew, replay, reproduce, rerun, reshow, restate, retell **2.** *n.* duplicate, echo, recapitulation, reiteration, repetition, replay, reproduction, rerun, reshowing

repeatedly again and again, frequently, many a time and oft, many times, often, over and over, time after time, time and (time) again

repel 1. beat off, check, confront, decline, drive off, fight, hold off, keep at arm's length, oppose, parry, put to flight, rebuff, refuse, reject, repulse, resist, ward off **2.** disgust, give one the creeps (*Inf.*), make one shudder, make one sick, nauseate, offend, put one off, revolt, sicken, turn one off (*Inf.*), turn one's stomach

repellent 1. abhorrent, abominable, discouraging, disgusting, distasteful, hateful, horrid, loathsome, nauseating, noxious, ob-

noxious, odious, offensive, off-putting (*Brit. inf.*), repugnant, repulsive, revolting, sickening **2.** impermeable, proof, repelling, resistant

repent atone, be ashamed, be contrite, be sorry, deplore, feel remorse, lament, regret, relent, reproach oneself, rue, see the error of one's ways, show penitence, sorrow

repentance compunction, contrition, grief, guilt, penitence, regret, remorse, sackcloth and ashes, self-reproach, sorriness, sorrow

repentant apologetic, ashamed, chastened, contrite, penitent, regretful, remorseful, rueful, self-reproachful, sorry

repercussion backlash, consequence, echo, rebound, recoil, result, reverberation, side effect

repetition duplication, echo, iteration, reappearance, recapitulation, recital, recurrence, redundancy, rehearsal, reiteration, relation, renewal, repeat, repetitiousness, replication, restatement, return, tautology

repetitive boring, dull, mechanical, monotonous, recurrent, samey (*Inf.*), tedious, unchanging, unvaried

repine brood, complain, fret, grieve,

grumble, lament, languish, moan, mope, murmur, sulk

replace follow, oust, put back, reestablish, reinstate, restore, stand in lieu of, substitute, succeed, supersede, supplant, supply, take over from, take the place of

replacement double, fill-in, proxy, stand-in, substitute, successor, surrogate, understudy

replenish fill, furnish, make up, provide, refill, reload, renew, replace, restock, restore, stock, supply, top up

replete abounding, brimful, brimming, charged, chock-full, crammed, filled, full, full to bursting, full up, glutted, gorged, jammed, jam-packed, sated, satiated, stuffed, teeming, well-provided, well-stocked

replica carbon copy, copy, duplicate, facsimile, imitation, model, reproduction

reply 1. *v.* acknowledge, answer, come back, counter, echo, make answer, react, reciprocate, rejoin, respond, retaliate, retort, return, riposte, write back **2.** *n.* acknowledgment, answer, comeback (*Inf.*), counter, echo, reaction, reciprocation, rejoinder, response, retaliation, retort, return, riposte

a written account of a case decided at law. **6.** comment on a person's character or actions; reputation: *he is of good report here.* **7.** a sharp loud noise, esp. one made by a gun. ~*vb.* (when *tr.*, *may take a clause as object;* when *intr.*, often foll. by *on*) **8.** to give an account (of); describe. **9.** to give an account of the results of an investigation (into): *to report on housing conditions.* **10.** (of a committee, legislative body, etc.) to make a formal report on (a bill). **11.** (*tr.*) to complain about (a person), esp. to a superior. **12.** to present (oneself) or be present at an appointed place or for a specific purpose: *report to the manager's office.* **13.** (*intr.*) to say or show that one is (in a certain state): *to report fit.* **14.** (*intr.*) to act as a reporter. **15.** *Law.* to take down in writing details of (the proceedings of a court of law, etc.) as a record or for publication. —**re′portable** *adj.* —**re′portedly** *adv.*

reported speech *n.* another term for **indirect speech.**

reporter (rɪ′pɔːtə) *n.* **1.** a person who reports, esp. one employed to gather news for a newspaper or broadcasting organization. **2.** a person authorized to report the proceedings of a legislature.

repose[1] (rɪ′pəʊz) *n.* **1.** a state of quiet restfulness; peace or tranquillity. **2.** dignified calmness of manner; composure. ~*vb.* **3.** to lie or lay down at rest. **4.** (*intr.*) to lie when dead, as in the grave. **5.** (*intr.*; foll. by *on, in,* etc.) *Formal.* to be based (on): *your plan reposes on a fallacy.* —**re′posal** *n.* —**reposedly** (rɪ′pəʊzɪdlɪ) *adv.* —**re′poser** *n.* —**re′poseful** *adj.* —**re′posefully** *adv.*

repose[2] (rɪ′pəʊz) *vb.* (*tr.*) **1.** to put (trust) in a person or thing. **2.** to place or put (an object) somewhere. —**re′posal** *n.*

repository (rɪ′pɒzɪtərɪ, -trɪ) *n., pl.* **-ries. 1.** a place or container in which things can be stored for safety. **2.** a place where things are kept for exhibition; museum. **3.** a place of burial; sepulchre. **4.** a person to whom a secret is entrusted; confidant.

repossess (ˌriːpə′zɛs) *vb.* (*tr.*) to take back possession of (property), esp. for nonpayment of money due under a hire-purchase agreement. —**repossession** (ˌriːpə′zɛʃən) *n.* —**repos′sessor** *n.*

reprehend (ˌrɛprɪ′hɛnd) *vb.* (*tr.*) to find fault with; criticize. —**repre′hender** *n.* —**reprehensory** (ˌrɛprɪ′hɛnsərɪ) *adj.* —**repre′hension** *n.*

reprehensible (ˌrɛprɪ′hɛnsəb[ə]l) *adj.* open to criticism or rebuke; blameworthy. —**repre′hensi′bility** *n.* —**repre′hensibly** *adv.*

represent (ˌrɛprɪ′zɛnt) *vb.* (*tr.*) **1.** to stand as an equivalent of; correspond to. **2.** to act as a substitute or proxy (for). **3.** to act as or be the authorized delegate or agent for (a person, country, etc.): *an M.P. represents his constituency.* **4.** to serve or use as a means of ex-

pressing: *letters represent the sounds of speech.* **5.** to exhibit the characteristics of; exemplify; typify: *romanticism in music is represented by Beethoven.* **6.** to present an image of through the medium of a picture or sculpture; portray. **7.** to bring clearly before the mind. **8.** to set forth in words; state or explain. **9.** to describe as having a specified character or quality: *he represented her as a saint.* **10.** to act out the part of on stage; portray. —**repre′sentable** *adj.* —**repre**ˌ**senta′bility** *n.*

representation (ˌrɛprɪzɛn′teɪʃən) *n.* **1.** the act or an instance of representing or the state of being represented. **2.** anything that represents, such as a verbal or pictorial portrait. **3.** anything that is represented, such as an image brought clearly to mind. **4.** the principle by which delegates act for a constituency. **5.** a body of representatives. **6.** an instance of acting for another in a particular capacity, such as executor. **7.** a dramatic production or performance. **8.** (*often pl.*) a statement of facts, true or alleged, esp. one set forth by way of remonstrance or expostulation. —**represen′tational** *adj.*

representative (ˌrɛprɪ′zɛntətɪv) *n.* **1.** a person or thing that represents another. **2.** a person who represents and tries to sell the products or services of a firm. **3.** a typical example. **4.** a person representing a constituency in a deliberative, legislative, or executive body, esp. (*cap.*) a member of the **House of Representatives** (the lower house of Congress). ~*adj.* **5.** serving to represent; symbolic. **6.** exemplifying a class or kind; typical. **7.** acting as deputy or proxy for another. **8.** representing a constituency or the whole people in the process of government: *a representative council.* **9.** of or relating to the political representation of the people: *representative government.* **10.** of or relating to a mental picture or representation. —**repre′sentatively** *adv.* —**repre′sentativeness** *n.*

repress (rɪ′prɛs) *vb.* (*tr.*) **1.** to keep (feelings, etc.) under control; suppress or restrain. **2.** to put into a state of subjugation: *to repress a people.* **3.** *Psychol.* to banish (unpleasant thoughts) from one's conscious mind. —**re′presser** *or* **re′pressor** *n.* —**re′pressible** *adj.* —**re′pression** *n.* —**re′pressive** *adj.*

reprieve (rɪ′priːv) *vb.* (*tr.*) **1.** to postpone or remit the punishment of (a person, esp. one condemned to death). **2.** to give temporary relief to (a person or thing), esp. from otherwise irrevocable harm. ~*n.* **3.** a postponement or remission of punishment. **4.** a warrant granting a postponement. **5.** a temporary relief from pain or harm; respite. —**re′prievable** *adj.* —**re′priever** *n.*

reprimand (′rɛprɪˌmɑːnd) *n.* **1.** a reproof or formal admonition; rebuke. ~*vb.* **2.** (*tr.*) to admonish or rebuke, esp. formally. —**repri′mandingly** *adv.*

THESAURUS

report *n.* **1.** account, announcement, article, communication, communiqué, declaration, description, detail, dispatch, information, message, narrative, news, note, paper, piece, recital, record, relation, statement, story, summary, tale, tidings, version, word, write-up **2.** gossip, hearsay, rumour, talk **3.** character, esteem, fame, regard, reputation, repute **4.** bang, blast, boom, crack, crash, detonation, discharge, explosion, noise, reverberation, sound ~*v.* **5.** air, announce, bring word, broadcast, circulate, communicate, cover, declare, describe, detail, document, give an account of, inform of, mention, narrate, note, notify, pass on, proclaim, publish, recite, record, recount, relate, relay, state, tell, write up **6.** appear, arrive, be present, clock in *or* on, come, present oneself, show up (*Inf.*), turn up

reporter announcer, correspondent, hack (*Derogatory*), journalist, newscaster, newshound (*Inf.*), newspaperman, newspaperwoman, pressman, writer

repose[1] *n.* **1.** ease, inactivity, peace, quiet, quietness, quietude, relaxation, respite, rest, restfulness, sleep, slumber, stillness, tranquillity **2.** aplomb, calmness, composure, dignity, equanimity, peace of mind, poise, self-possession, serenity, tranquillity ~*v.* **3.** lay down, lie, lie down, lie upon, recline, relax, rest, rest upon, sleep, slumber, take it easy

(*Inf.*), take one's ease

reprehensible bad, blameworthy, censurable, condemnable, culpable, delinquent, discreditable, disgraceful, errant, erring, ignoble, objectionable, opprobrious, remiss, shameful, unworthy

represent **1.** act for, be, betoken, correspond to, equal, equate with, express, mean, serve as, speak for, stand for, substitute for, symbolize **2.** embody, epitomize, exemplify, personify, symbolize, typify **3.** delineate, denote, depict, describe, designate, evoke, express, illustrate, outline, picture, portray, render, reproduce, show, sketch **4.** describe as, make out to be, pass off as, pose as, pretend to be **5.** act, appear as, assume the role of, enact, exhibit, perform, play the part of, produce, put on, show, stage

representation **1.** account, delineation, depiction, description, illustration, image, likeness, model, narration, narrative, picture, portrait, portrayal, relation, resemblance, sketch **2.** body of representatives, committee, delegates, delegation, embassy **3.** exhibition, performance, play, production, show, sight, spectacle **4.** *Often plural* account, argument, explanation, exposition, expostulation, remonstrance, statement

representative *n.* **1.** agent, commercial traveller, rep, salesman, traveller **2.** archetype, embodiment, epitome, exemplar,

personification, type, typical example **3.** agent, commissioner, councillor, delegate, depute (*Scot.*), deputy, member, member of parliament, M.P., proxy, spokesman, spokeswoman ~*adj.* **4.** archetypal, characteristic, emblematic, evocative, exemplary, illustrative, symbolic, typical **5.** chosen, delegated, elected, elective

repress bottle up, chasten, check, control, crush, curb, hold back, hold in, inhibit, keep in check, master, muffle, overcome, overpower, quash, quell, restrain, silence, smother, stifle, subdue, subjugate, suppress, swallow

repression authoritarianism, censorship, coercion, constraint, control, despotism, domination, inhibition, restraint, subjugation, suppression, tyranny

repressive absolute, authoritarian, coercive, despotic, dictatorial, harsh, oppressive, severe, tough, tyrannical

reprieve *v.* **1.** grant a stay of execution to, let off the hook (*Sl.*), pardon, postpone *or* remit the punishment of **2.** abate, allay, alleviate, mitigate, palliate, relieve, respite ~*n.* **3.** abeyance, amnesty, deferment, pardon, postponement, remission, stay of execution, suspension **4.** abatement, alleviation, let-up (*Inf.*), mitigation, palliation, relief, respite

reprimand **1.** *n.* admonition, blame, castigation, censure, dressing-down (*Inf.*), flea

reprint *n.* ('ri:ˌprɪnt). **1.** a reproduction in print of any matter already published. **2.** a reissue of a printed work using the same type, plates, etc., as the original. ~*vb.* (ri:'prɪnt). **3.** (*tr.*) to print again. —**re'printer** *n.*

reprisal (rɪ'praɪzəl) *n.* **1.** the act or an instance of retaliation in any form. **2.** (*often pl.*) retaliatory action against an enemy in wartime. **3.** (formerly) the forcible seizure of the property or subjects of one nation by another.

reproach (rɪ'prəʊtʃ) *vb.* (*tr.*) **1.** to impute blame to (a person) for an action or fault; rebuke. ~*n.* **2.** the act of reproaching. **3.** rebuke or censure; reproof. **4.** disgrace or shame: *to bring reproach upon one's family* **5. above or beyond reproach.** perfect; beyond criticism. —**re'proachable** *adj.* —**re'proacher** *n.* —**re'proachful** *adj.* —**re'proachingly** *adv.*

reprobate ('rɛprəʊˌbeɪt) *adj.* **1.** morally unprincipled; depraved. **2.** *Christianity.* condemned to eternal punishment in hell. ~*n.* **3.** an unprincipled, depraved, or damned person. **4.** a disreputable or roguish person. ~*vb.* (*tr.*) **5.** to disapprove of; condemn. **6.** (of God) to condemn to eternal punishment in hell. —**reprobacy** ('rɛprəbəsɪ) *n.* —**'repro,bater** *n.* —,**repro'bation** *n.*

reproduce (ˌri:prə'dju:s) *vb.* (*mainly tr.*) **1.** to make a copy, representation, or imitation of; duplicate. **2.** (*also intr.*) *Biol.* to undergo or cause to undergo a process of reproduction. **3.** to produce again; bring back into existence again; re-create. **4.** (*intr.*) to come out (well, badly, etc.), when copied. —,**repro'ducer** *n.* —,**repro'ducible** *adj.* —,**repro'ducibly** *adv.* —,**repro,duci'bility** *n.*

reproduction (ˌri:prə'dʌkʃən) *n.* **1.** *Biol.* any of various processes, either sexual or asexual, by which an animal or plant produces one or more individuals similar to itself. **2. a.** an imitation or facsimile of a work of art. **b.** (*as modifier*): *a reproduction portrait.* **3.** the act or process of reproducing. —,**repro'ductive** *adj.*

reprography (rɪ'prɒgrəfɪ) *n.* the art or process of copying, reprinting, or reproducing printed material. —**reprographic** (ˌrɛprə'græfɪk) *adj.* —,**repro'graphically** *adv.*

reproof (rɪ'pru:f) *n.* an act or expression of rebuke or censure. Also: **reproval** (rɪ'pru:vəl).

reprove (rɪ'pru:v) *vb.* (*tr.*) to rebuke or scold. —**re'provable** *adj.* —**re'prover** *n.* —**re'provingly** *adv.*

reptile ('rɛptaɪl) *n.* **1.** any of the cold-blooded vertebrates characterized by lungs, an outer covering of horny scales or plates, and young produced in eggs, such as the tortoises, turtles, snakes, lizards, and crocodiles. **2.** a grovelling insignificant person: *you miserable little reptile!* ~*adj.* **3.** creeping, crawling, or squirming. —**reptilian** (rɛp'tɪlɪən) *n., adj.*

republic (rɪ'pʌblɪk) *n.* **1.** a form of government in which the people or their elected representatives possess the supreme power. **2.** a political or national unit possessing such a form of government. **3.** a constitutional form in which the head of state is an elected or nominated president.

republican (rɪ'pʌblɪkən) *adj.* **1.** of, resembling, or relating to a republic. **2.** supporting or advocating a republic. ~*n.* **3.** a supporter or advocate of a republic. —**re'publica,nism** *n.*

Republican (rɪ'pʌblɪkən) *adj.* **1.** of, belonging to, or relating to a Republican Party. ~*n.* **2.** a member or supporter of a Republican Party.

repudiate (rɪ'pju:dɪˌeɪt) *vb.* (*tr.*) **1.** to reject the authority or validity of; refuse to accept or ratify. **2.** to refuse to acknowledge or pay (a debt). **3.** to cast off or disown (a son, lover, etc.). —**re'pudiable** *adj.* —**re,pudi'ation** *n.* —**re'pudiative** *adj.* —**re'pudi,ator** *n.*

repugnant (rɪ'pʌgnənt) *adj.* **1.** repellent to the senses; causing aversion. **2.** distasteful; offensive; disgusting. **3.** contradictory; inconsistent or incompatible. —**re'pugnance** *or* **re'pugnancy** *n.* —**re'pugnantly** *adv.*

repulse (rɪ'pʌls) *vb.* (*tr.*) **1.** to drive back or ward off (an attacking force); repel; rebuff. **2.** to reject with coldness or discourtesy: *she repulsed his advances.* ~*n.* **3.** the act or an instance of driving back or warding off; rebuff. **4.** a cold discourteous rejection or refusal. —**re'pulser** *n.*

▷ **Usage.** The verbs *repulse* and *repel* share the meaning of physically driving back or away, but they can be carefully distinguished in other senses. Although the related adjective *repulsive* has the meaning of causing feelings of disgust, *repulse* does not mean to drive away by arousing disgust. Instead, *repel* is normally used in this sense, and *repulse* is used when the required meaning is to reject coldly or drive away with discourtesy.

repulsion (rɪ'pʌlʃən) *n.* **1.** a feeling of disgust or aversion. **2.** *Physics.* a force separating two objects, such as the force between two like electric charges.

repulsive (rɪ'pʌlsɪv) *adj.* **1.** causing or occasioning repugnance; loathsome; disgusting or distasteful. **2.** tending to repel, esp. by coldness and discourtesy. **3.** *Physics.* concerned with, producing, or being a repulsion. —**re'pulsively** *adv.* —**re'pulsiveness** *n.*

reputable ('rɛpjutəbəl) *adj.* **1.** having a good reputation; honoured, trustworthy, or respectable. **2.** (of words) acceptable as good usage; standard. —**'reputableness** *n.* —**'reputably** *adv.*

reputation (ˌrɛpju'teɪʃən) *n.* **1.** the estimation in which a person or thing is generally held; opinion. **2.** a high opinion generally held about a person or thing; esteem. **3.** notoriety or fame, esp. for some specified characteristic.

repute (rɪ'pju:t) *vb.* **1.** (*tr.; usually passive*) to consider (a person or thing) to be as specified: *he is reputed to be rich.* ~*n.* **2.** public estimation; reputation: *a writer of little repute.*

reputed (rɪ'pju:tɪd) *adj.* (*prenominal*) generally reckoned or considered; supposed: *the reputed writer of two epic poems.* —**re'putedly** *adv.*

THESAURUS

in one's ear (*Inf.*), lecture, rebuke, reprehension, reproach, reproof, row, talking-to (*Inf.*), telling-off (*Inf.*), ticking-off (*Inf.*), tonguelashing, wigging (*Brit. sl.*) **2. v.** admonish, blame, castigate, censure, check, chide, dress down (*Inf.*), give (someone) a row (*Inf.*), haul over the coals (*Inf.*), lecture, rap over the knuckles (*Inf.*), rebuke, reprehend, reproach, reprove, scold, send one away with a flea in one's ear (*Inf.*), take to task, tell off (*Inf.*), tick off (*Inf.*), tongue-lash, upbraid

reprisal an eye for an eye, counterstroke, requital, retaliation, retribution, revenge, vengeance

reproach 1. v. abuse, blame, censure, chide, condemn, criticize, defame, discredit, disparage, find fault with, rebuke, reprehend, reprimand, reprove, scold, take to task, upbraid **2. n.** abuse, blame, blemish, censure, condemnation, contempt, disapproval, discredit, disgrace, dishonour, disrepute, ignominy, indignity, obloquy, odium, opprobrium, scorn, shame, slight, slur, stain, stigma

reproachful abusive, admonitory, castigatory, censorious, condemnatory, contemptuous, critical, disappointed, disapproving, fault-finding, reproving, scolding, upbraiding

reproduce 1. copy, duplicate, echo, emulate, imitate, match, mirror, parallel, print, recreate, repeat, replicate, represent, transcribe **2.** breed, generate, multiply, procreate, produce young, proliferate, propagate, spawn

reproduction 1. breeding, generation, increase, multiplication, procreation, proliferation, propagation **2.** copy, duplicate, facsimile, imitation, picture, print, replica

reproof admonition, blame, castigation, censure, chiding, condemnation, criticism, dressing-down (*Inf.*), rebuke, reprehension, reprimand, reproach, reproval, scolding, ticking-off (*Inf.*), tongue-lashing, upbraiding

reprove abuse, admonish, berate, blame, censure, check, chide, condemn, rebuke, reprehend, reprimand, scold, take to task, tell off (*Inf.*), tick off (*Inf.*), upbraid

repudiate abandon, abjure, cast off, cut off, deny, desert, disavow, discard, disclaim, disown, forsake, reject, renounce, rescind, retract, reverse, revoke, turn one's back on, wash one's hands of

repugnance abhorrence, antipathy, aversion, disgust, dislike, disrelish, distaste, hatred, loathing, reluctance, repulsion, revulsion

repugnant 1. abhorrent, abominable, disgusting, distasteful, foul, hateful, horrid, loathsome, nauseating, objectionable, obnoxious, odious, offensive, repellent, revolting, sickening, vile **2.** adverse, antagonistic, antipathetic, averse, contradictory, hostile, incompatible, inconsistent, inimical, opposed

repulsive abhorrent, abominable, disagreeable, disgusting, distasteful, forbidding, foul, hateful, hideous, horrid, loathsome, nauseating, objectionable, obnoxious, odious, offensive, repellent, revolting, sickening, ugly, unpleasant, vile

reputable creditable, estimable, excellent, good, honourable, honoured, legitimate, of good repute, reliable, respectable, trustworthy, upright, well-thought-of, worthy

reputation character, credit, distinction, esteem, estimation, fame, honour, name, opinion, renown, repute, standing, stature

repute celebrity, distinction, esteem, estimation, fame, name, renown, reputation, standing, stature

reputed accounted, alleged, believed,

request (rɪ'kwɛst) vb. (tr.) **1.** to express a desire for, esp. politely; ask for or demand: *to request a bottle of wine.* ~n. **2.** the act or an instance of requesting, esp. in the form of a written statement, etc.; petition or solicitation. **3. by request.** in accordance with someone's desire. **4. in request.** in demand; popular: *he is in request all over the world.* **5. on request.** on the occasion of a demand or request: *application forms are available on request.* —re'quester n.

request stop n. a point on a route at which a bus, etc., will stop only if signalled to do so. U.S. equivalent: **flag stop.**

Requiem ('rɛkwɪ,ɛm) n. **1.** R.C. Church. a Mass celebrated for the dead. **2.** a musical setting of this Mass. **3.** any piece of music composed or performed as a memorial to a dead person.

require (rɪ'kwaɪə) vb. (mainly tr.; may take a clause as object or an infinitive) **1.** to have need of; depend upon; want. **2.** to impose as a necessity; make necessary: *this work requires precision.* **3.** (also intr.) to make formal request (for); insist upon. **4.** to call upon or oblige (a person) authoritatively; order or command: *to require someone to account for his actions.* —re'quirer n.

requirement (rɪ'kwaɪəmənt) n. **1.** something demanded or imposed as an obligation. **2.** a thing desired or needed. **3.** the act or an instance of requiring.

requisite ('rɛkwɪzɪt) adj. **1.** absolutely essential; indispensable. ~n. **2.** something indispensable; necessity. —'requisitely adv. —'requisiteness n.

requisition (,rɛkwɪ'zɪʃən) n. **1.** a request or demand, esp. an authoritative or formal one. **2.** an official form on which such a demand is made. **3.** the act of taking something over, esp. temporarily for military or public use. ~vb. (tr.) **4.** to demand and take for use, esp. by military or public authority. **5.** (may take an infinitive) to require (someone) formally to do (something): *to requisition a soldier to drive an officer's car.* —,requisi'tionary adj. —,requi'sitioner or ,requi'sitionist n.

requite (rɪ'kwaɪt) vb. (tr.) to make return to (a person for a kindness or injury); repay with a similar action. —re'quitable adj. —re'quitement n. —re'quiter n. —re'quital n.

reredos ('rɪədɒs) n. a screen or wall decoration at the back of an altar.

rerun vb. (ri:'rʌn), **-running, -ran.** (tr.) **1.** to broadcast or put on (a film, etc.) again. **2.** to run (a race, etc.) again. ~n. ('ri:,rʌn). **3.** a film, etc., that is broadcast again; repeat. **4.** a race that is run again.

rescind (rɪ'sɪnd) vb. (tr.) to annul or repeal. —re'scindable adj. —re'scinder n. —re'scindment n.

rescission (rɪ'sɪʒən) n. the act of rescinding.

rescript ('ri:,skrɪpt) n. **1.** (in ancient Rome) a reply by the emperor to a question on a point of law. **2.** any official announcement or edict; a decree. **3.** something rewritten.

rescue ('rɛskju:) vb. **-cuing, -cued.** (tr.) **1.** to bring (someone or something) out of danger, etc.; deliver or save. **2.** to free (a person) from legal custody by force. **3.** Law. to seize (goods) by force. ~n. **4. a.** the act or an instance of rescuing. **b.** (as modifier): *a rescue party.* **5.** the forcible removal of a person from legal custody. **6.** Law. the forcible seizure of goods or property. —'rescuer n.

research (rɪ'sɜːtʃ) n. **1.** systematic investigation to establish facts or collect information on a subject. ~vb. **2.** to carry out investigations into (a subject, problem, etc.). —re'searchable adj. —re'searcher n.

resection (rɪ'sɛkʃən) n. **1.** Surgery. excision of part of a bone, organ, or other part. **2.** Surveying. a method of fixing the position of a point by making angular observations to three fixed points. —re'sectional adj.

resemble (rɪ'zɛmbəl) vb. (tr.) to possess some similarity to; be like. —re'semblance n. —re'sembler n.

resent (rɪ'zɛnt) vb. (tr.) to feel bitter, indignant, or aggrieved at. —re'sentful adj. —re'sentment n.

reservation (,rɛzə'veɪʃən) n. **1.** the act or an instance of reserving. **2.** something reserved, esp. accommodation or a seat. **3.** (often pl.) a stated or unstated qualification of opinion that prevents one's wholehearted acceptance of a proposal, etc. **4.** an area of land set aside, esp. (in the U.S. and Canada) for American Indian peoples. **5.** Brit. the strip of land between the two carriageways of a dual carriageway. **6.** the act or process of keeping back, esp. for oneself; withholding. **7.** Law. a right or interest retained by the grantor in property dealings.

reserve (rɪ'zɜːv) vb. (tr.) **1.** to keep back or set aside, esp. for future use or contingency; withhold. **2.** to keep for oneself; retain: *I reserve the right to question these men later.* **3.** to obtain or secure by advance arrangement: *I have reserved two tickets for tonight's show.* **4.** to delay delivery of (a judgment). ~n. **5. a.** something kept back or set aside, esp. for future use or contingency. **b.** (as modifier): *a reserve stock.* **6.** the state or condition of being reserved: *I have plenty in reserve.* **7.** a tract of land set aside for a special purpose: *a nature reserve.* **8.** Austral. a public park. **9.** Sport. a substitute. **10.** (often pl.) **a.** a part of an army not committed to immediate action in a military engagement. **b.** that part of a nation's armed services not in active service. **11.** coolness or formality of manner; restraint, silence, or reticence. **12.** Finance. liquid assets or a portion of capital not invested or a portion of profits not distributed by a bank or business enterprise and held to meet future liabilities, or contingencies. **13. without reserve.** without reservations; fully. —re'servable adj. —re'server n.

considered, deemed, estimated, held, ostensible, putative, reckoned, regarded, rumoured, said, seeming, supposed, thought

reputedly allegedly, apparently, ostensibly, seemingly, supposedly

request 1. v. appeal for, apply for, ask (for), beg, beseech, call for, demand, desire, entreat, petition, pray, put in for, requisition, seek, solicit, sue for, supplicate **2.** n. appeal, application, asking, begging, call, demand, desire, entreaty, petition, prayer, requisition, solicitation, suit, supplication

require 1. crave, depend upon, desire, have need of, lack, miss, need, stand in need of, want, wish **2.** ask, beg, beseech, bid, call upon, command, compel, constrain, demand, direct, enjoin, exact, insist upon, instruct, oblige, order, request **3.** call for, demand, involve, necessitate, take

required called for, compulsory, demanded, essential, mandatory, necessary, needed, obligatory, prescribed, recommended, requisite, set, unavoidable, vital

requirement demand, desideratum, essential, lack, must, necessity, need, precondition, prerequisite, qualification, requisite, sine qua non, specification, stipulation, want

requisite 1. adj. called for, essential, indispensable, mandatory, necessary, needed, needful, obligatory, prerequisite, required,

vital **2.** n. condition, desideratum, essential, must, necessity, need, precondition, prerequisite, requirement, sine qua non

requisition n. **1.** application, call, demand, request, summons **2.** appropriation, commandeering, occupation, seizure, takeover ~v. **3.** apply for, call for, demand, put in for, request **4.** appropriate, commandeer, occupy, seize, take over, take possession of

rescind abrogate, annul, cancel, countermand, declare null and void, invalidate, overturn, quash, recall, repeal, retract, reverse, revoke, set aside, void

rescue 1. v. deliver, extricate, free, get out, liberate, recover, redeem, release, salvage, save, save the life of, set free **2.** n. deliverance, extrication, liberation, recovery, redemption, release, relief, salvage, salvation, saving

research 1. n. analysis, delving, examination, experimentation, exploration, factfinding, groundwork, inquiry, investigation, probe, scrutiny, study **2.** v. analyse, consult the archives, do tests, examine, experiment, explore, investigate, look into, make inquiries, probe, scrutinize, study

resemblance affinity, analogy, closeness, comparability, comparison, conformity, correspondence, counterpart, facsimile, image, kinship, likeness, parallel, parity,

sameness, semblance, similarity, similitude

resemble bear a resemblance to, be like, be similar to, duplicate, echo, favour (Inf.), look like, mirror, parallel, put one in mind of, remind one of, take after

resent be angry about, bear a grudge about, begrudge, be in a huff about, be offended by, dislike, feel bitter about, grudge, harbour a grudge against, have hard feelings about, object to, take amiss, take as an insult, take exception to, take offence at, take umbrage at

resentful aggrieved, angry, bitter, embittered, exasperated, grudging, huffish, huffy, hurt, in a huff, incensed, indignant, in high dudgeon, irate, jealous, miffed (Inf.), offended, peeved (Inf.), piqued, put out, revengeful, unforgiving, wounded

resentment anger, animosity, bitterness, displeasure, fury, grudge, huff, hurt, ill feeling, ill will, indignation, ire, irritation, malice, pique, rage, rancour, umbrage, vexation, wrath

reservation 1. condition, demur, doubt, hesitancy, proviso, qualification, scepticism, scruple, stipulation **2.** enclave, homeland, preserve, reserve, sanctuary, territory, tract

reserve v. **1.** conserve, hang on to, hoard, hold, husband, keep, keep back, lay up, preserve, put by, retain, save, set aside, stock-

reserved (rɪ'zɜːvd) *adj.* **1.** set aside for use by a particular person. **2.** cool or formal in manner; restrained or reticent. **3.** destined; fated: *a man reserved for greatness.* —**reservedly** (rɪ'zɜːvɪdlɪ) *adv.* —**re'servedness** *n.*

reserve price *n. Brit.* the minimum price acceptable to the owner of property being auctioned. Cf. **upset price.**

reservist (rɪ'zɜːvɪst) *n.* one who serves in the reserve formations of a nation's armed forces.

reservoir ('rɛzə,vwɑː) *n.* **1.** a natural or artificial lake or large tank used for collecting and storing water for community use. **2.** *Biol.* a cavity in an organism containing fluid. **3.** a place where a great stock of anything is accumulated. **4.** a large supply of something: *a reservoir of talent.*

reside (rɪ'zaɪd) *vb.* (*intr.*) *Formal.* **1.** to live permanently (in a place); have one's home (in): *he resides in London.* **2.** (of things, qualities, etc.) to be inherently present (in); be vested (in): *political power resides in military strength.* —**re'sider** *n.*

residence ('rɛzɪdəns) *n.* **1.** the place in which one resides; abode or home. **2.** a large imposing house; mansion. **3.** the fact of residing in a place or a period of residing. **4.** the state of being officially present (esp. in **in residence**).

residency ('rɛzɪdənsɪ) *n., pl.* -**cies. 1.** a variant of **residence. 2.** *U.S.* the period, during which a physician undergoes specialized training. **3.** (in India, formerly) the official house of the governor general at the court of a native prince.

resident ('rɛzɪdənt) *n.* **1.** a person who resides in a place. **2.** (esp. formerly) a representative of the British government in a British protectorate. **3.** (in India, formerly) a representative of the British governor general at the court of a native prince. **4.** a bird or animal that does not migrate. **5.** *U.S.* a physician who lives in the hospital while undergoing specialist training after completing his internship. ~*adj.* **6.** living in a place; residing. **7.** living or staying at a place in order to discharge a duty, etc. **8.** (of qualities, etc.) existing or inherent (in). **9.** (of birds and animals) not in the habit of migrating. —**'resident,ship** *n.*

residential (,rɛzɪ'dɛnʃəl) *adj.* **1.** suitable for or allocated for residence: *a residential area.* **2.** relating to residence. —,**resi'dentially** *adv.*

residual (rɪ'zɪdjuəl) *adj.* **1.** of, relating to, or designating a residue or remainder; remaining; left over. **2.** *U.S.* of or relating to the payment of residuals. ~*n.* **3.** something left over as a residue; remainder. **4.** *Statistics.* **a.** the difference between the mean of a set of observations and one particular observation. **b.** the difference between the numerical value of one particular observation and the theoretical result. **5.** (*often pl.*) *U.S.* payment made to an actor or actress for subsequent use of film in which the actor or actress appears. —**re'sidually** *adv.*

residuary (rɪ'zɪdjuərɪ) *adj.* **1.** of, relating to, or constituting a residue; residual. **2.** *Law.* entitled to the residue of an estate after payment of debts and distribution of specific gifts.

residue ('rɛzɪ,djuː) *n.* **1.** matter remaining after something has been removed. **2.** *Law.* what is left of an estate after the discharge of debts and distribution of specific gifts.

residuum (rɪ'zɪdjuəm) *n., pl.* -**ua** (-juə). a more formal word for **residue.**

resign (rɪ'zaɪn) *vb.* **1.** (when *intr.,* often foll. by *from*) to give up tenure of (a job, office, etc.). **2.** (*tr.*) to reconcile (oneself) to; yield: *to resign oneself to death.* **3.** (*tr.*) to give up (a right, claim, etc.); relinquish. —**re'signer** *n.*

resignation (,rɛzɪg'neɪʃən) *n.* **1.** the act of resigning. **2.** a formal document stating one's intention to resign. **3.** a submissive unresisting attitude; passive acquiescence.

resigned (rɪ'zaɪnd) *adj.* characteristic of or proceeding from an attitude of resignation; acquiescent or submissive. —**resignedly** (rɪ'zaɪnɪdlɪ) *adv.* —**re'signedness** *n.*

resilient (rɪ'zɪlɪənt) *adj.* **1.** (of an object) capable of regaining its original shape or position after bending, stretching, or other deformation; elastic. **2.** (of a person) recovering easily and quickly from illness, hardship, etc. —**re'silience** *or* **re'siliency** *n.* —**re'siliently** *adv.*

resin ('rɛzɪn) *n.* **1.** Also called: **rosin.** any of a group of solid or semisolid amorphous compounds that are obtained directly from certain plants as exudations. **2.** any of a large number of synthetic, usually organic, materials that have a polymeric structure, esp. such a substance in a raw state before it is moulded or treated with plasticizer, etc. ~*vb.* **3.** (*tr.*) to treat or coat with resin. —**'resinous** *adj.* —**'resinously** *adv.* —**'resinousness** *n.*

resist (rɪ'zɪst) *vb.* **1.** to stand firm (against); not yield (to); fight (against). **2.** (*tr.*) to withstand the deleterious action of; be proof against: *to resist corrosion.* **3.** (*tr.*) to oppose; refuse to accept or comply with: *to resist arrest.* **4.** (*tr.*) to refrain from, esp. in spite of temptation (esp. in **cannot resist (something)**). ~*n.* **5.** a substance used to protect something, esp. a coating that prevents corrosion. —**re'sister** *n.* —**re'sistible** *adj.* —**re,sisti'bility** *n.* —**re'sistibly** *adv.* —**re'sistless** *adj.*

resistance (rɪ'zɪstəns) *n.* **1.** the act or an instance of resisting. **2.** the capacity to withstand something, esp. the body's natural capacity to withstand disease. **3. a.** the opposition to a flow of electric current through a circuit component, medium, or substance. It is measured in ohms. Symbol: R **b.** (*as modifier*): *a resistance thermometer.* **4.** any force that tends to retard or oppose motion: *air resistance; wind resistance.* **5.** *Physics.* the magnitude of the real part of the acoustic or mechanical impedance. **6. line of least resistance.** the easiest, but not necessarily the best or most honourable, course of action. **7.** See **passive resistance.** —**re'sistant** *adj., n.*

THESAURUS

pile, store, withhold **2.** bespeak, book, engage, prearrange, pre-engage, retain, secure **3.** defer, delay, keep back, postpone, put off, withhold ~*n.* **4.** backlog, cache, capital, fund, hoard, reservoir, savings, stock, stockpile, store, supply **5.** park, preserve, reservation, sanctuary, tract **6.** aloofness, constraint, coolness, formality, modesty, reluctance, reservation, restraint, reticence, secretiveness, shyness, silence, taciturnity ~*adj.* **7.** alternate, auxiliary, extra, secondary, spare, substitute

reserved 1. booked, engaged, held, kept, restricted, retained, set aside, spoken for, taken **2.** aloof, cautious, close-mouthed, cold, cool, demure, formal, modest, prim, restrained, reticent, retiring, secretive, shy, silent, standoffish, taciturn, unapproachable, uncommunicative, undemonstrative, unforthcoming, unresponsive, unsociable **3.** bound, destined, fated, intended, meant, predestined

reservoir 1. basin, lake, pond, tank **2.** container, holder, receptacle, repository, store, tank **3.** accumulation, fund, pool, reserves, source, stock, stockpile, store, supply

reshuffle 1. *n.* change, interchange, realignment, rearrangement, redistribution,

regrouping, reorganization, restructuring, revision, shake-up (*Inf.*) **2.** *v.* change around, change the line-up of, interchange, realign, rearrange, redistribute, regroup, reorganize, restructure, revise, shake up (*Inf.*)

reside 1. abide, dwell, hang out (*Inf.*), have one's home, inhabit, live, lodge, remain, settle, sojourn, stay **2.** abide, be intrinsic to, be vested, consist, dwell, exist, inhere, lie, rest with

residence 1. abode, domicile, dwelling, habitation, home, house, household, lodging, pad (*Sl.*), place, quarters **2.** hall, manor, mansion, palace, seat, villa **3.** occupancy, occupation, sojourn, stay, tenancy

resident 1. *n.* citizen, denizen, indweller, inhabitant, local, lodger, occupant, tenant **2.** *adj.* dwelling, inhabiting, living, local, neighbourhood, settled

residue balance, dregs, excess, extra, leftovers, remainder, remains, remnant, residuum, rest, surplus

resign 1. abandon, abdicate, cede, forgo, forsake, give in one's notice, give up, hand over, leave, quit, relinquish, renounce, surrender, turn over, vacate, yield **2. resign oneself** accept, acquiesce, bow, give in, give up, reconcile, submit, yield

resignation 1. abandonment, abdication, departure, leaving, notice, relinquishment, renunciation, retirement, surrender **2.** acceptance, acquiescence, compliance, endurance, forbearing, fortitude, nonresistance, passivity, patience, submission, sufferance

resigned acquiescent, compliant, long-suffering, patient, stoical, subdued, submissive, unprotesting, unresisting

resilient 1. bouncy, elastic, flexible, plastic, pliable, rubbery, springy, supple, whippy **2.** bouncy, buoyant, hardy, irrepressible, quick to recover, strong, tough

resist 1. battle, be proof against, check, combat, confront, contend with, counteract, countervail, curb, defy, dispute, fight back, hinder, hold out against, oppose, put up a fight (against), refuse, repel, stand up to, struggle against, thwart, weather, withstand **2.** abstain from, avoid, forbear, forgo, keep from, leave alone, prevent oneself from, refrain from, refuse, turn down

resistance battle, combat, contention, counteraction, defiance, fight, fighting, hindrance, impediment, intransigence, obstruction, opposition, refusal, struggle

Resistance (rɪˈzɪstəns) *n.* **the.** an illegal organization fighting for national liberty in a country under enemy occupation.

resistor (rɪˈzɪstə) *n.* an electrical component designed to introduce a known value of resistance into a circuit.

resit (riːˈsɪt) *vb.* **-sitting, -sat.** (*tr.*) **1.** to sit (an examination) again. ~*n.* **2.** an examination which one must sit again.

resoluble (rɪˈzɒljubəl, ˈrɛzəl-) *or* **resolvable** *adj.* able to be resolved or analysed. —**re,solu'bility, re,solva'bility** *or* **re'solubleness, re'solvableness** *n.*

resolute (ˈrɛzə,luːt) *adj.* **1.** firm in purpose or belief; steadfast. **2.** characterized by resolution; determined: *a resolute answer.* —**'reso,lutely** *adv.* —**'reso,luteness** *n.*

resolution (ˌrɛzəˈluːʃən) *n.* **1.** the act or an instance of resolving. **2.** firmness or determination. **3.** something resolved or determined; decision. **4.** a formal expression of opinion by a meeting. **5.** a judicial decision on some matter; verdict; judgment. **6.** the act of separating something into its constituent parts or elements. **7.** *Med.* subsidence of the symptoms of a disease, esp. the disappearance of inflammation without pus. **8.** *Music.* the process in harmony whereby a dissonant note or chord is followed by a consonant one. **9.** *Physics.* the ability of a microscope or telescope to produce separate images of closely placed objects. —**,reso'lutioner** *or* **,reso'lutionist** *n.*

resolve (rɪˈzɒlv) *vb.* (*mainly tr.*) **1.** (*takes a clause as object or an infinitive*) to decide or determine firmly. **2.** to express (an opinion) formally, esp. by a vote. **3.** (*also intr.; usually foll. by into*) to separate or cause to separate (into) (constituent parts). **4.** (*usually reflexive*) to change, alter: *the ghost resolved itself into a tree.* **5.** to make up the mind of; cause to decide: *the tempest resolved him to stay at home.* **6.** to find the answer or solution to. **7.** to explain away or dispel: *to resolve a doubt.* **8.** to bring to an end; conclude: *to resolve an argument.* **9.** *Med.* to cause (an inflammation) to subside, esp. without the formation of pus. **10.** *Music.* (*also intr.*) to follow (a dissonant note or chord) by one producing a consonance. **11.** *Physics.* to distinguish between (separate parts) of (an image) as in a microscope, telescope, or other optical instrument. ~*n.* **12.** something determined or decided; resolution: *he had made a resolve to work all day.* **13.** firmness of purpose; determination: *nothing can break his resolve.* —**re'solvable** *adj.* —**re,solva'bility** *n.* —**re'solver** *n.*

resolved (rɪˈzɒlvd) *adj.* fixed in purpose or intention; determined. —**resolvedly** (rɪˈzɒlvɪdlɪ) *adv.* —**re'solvedness** *n.*

resonance (ˈrɛzənəns) *n.* **1.** the condition or quality of being resonant. **2.** sound produced by a body vibrating in sympathy with a neighbouring source of sound. **3.** the condition of a body or system when it is subjected to a periodic disturbance of the same frequency as the natural frequency of the body or system. **4.** amplification of speech sounds by sympathetic vibration in the bone structure of the head and chest, resounding in the cavities of the nose, mouth, and pharynx. **5.** *Electronics.* the condition of an electrical circuit when the frequency is such that the capacitive reactance is just balanced by the inductive reactance, leading to relatively large alternating currents. **6.** *Med.* the sound heard when tapping a hollow bodily structure, esp. the chest or abdomen. **7.** *Chem.* the phenomenon in which the electronic structure of a molecule can be represented by two or more hypothetical structures involving single, double, and triple chemical bonds. **8.** *Physics.* the condition of a system in which there is a sharp maximum probability for the absorption of electromagnetic radiation or capture of particles.

resonant (ˈrɛzənənt) *adj.* **1.** resounding or re-echoing. **2.** producing resonance: *resonant walls.* **3.** full of, or intensified by, resonance: *a resonant voice.* —**'resonantly** *adv.*

resonate (ˈrɛzəˌneɪt) *vb.* **1.** to resound or cause to resound; reverberate. **2.** *Chem., electronics.* to exhibit or cause to exhibit resonance. —**,reso'nation** *n.* —**'reso,nator** *n.*

resort (rɪˈzɔːt) *vb.* (*intr.*) **1.** (*usually foll. by to*) to have recourse (to) for help, use, etc.: *to resort to violence.* **2.** to go, esp. often or habitually: *to resort to the beach.* ~*n.* **3.** a place to which many people go for recreation, etc.: *a holiday resort.* **4.** the use of something as a means, help, or recourse. **5. last resort.** the last possible course of action open to one. —**re'sorter** *n.*

resound (rɪˈzaʊnd) *vb.* (*intr.*) **1.** to ring or echo with sound; reverberate. **2.** to make a prolonged echoing noise: *the trumpet resounded.* **3.** (*of sounds*) to echo or ring. **4.** to be widely famous: *his fame resounded throughout India.* —**re'sounding** *adj.* —**re'soundingly** *adv.*

resource (rɪˈzɔːs, -ˈsɔːs) *n.* **1.** capability, ingenuity, and initiative; quick-wittedness: *a man of resource.* **2.** (*often pl.*) a source of economic wealth, esp. of a country or business enterprise. **3.** a supply or source of aid or support; something resorted to in time of need. **4.** a means of doing something; expedient. —**re'sourceless** *adj.*

resourceful (rɪˈzɔːsful, -ˈsɔːs-) *adj.* ingenious, capable, and full of initiative. —**re'sourcefully** *adv.* —**re'sourcefulness** *n.*

respect (rɪˈspɛkt) *n.* **1.** an attitude of deference, admiration, or esteem; regard. **2.** the state of being honoured or esteemed. **3.** a detail, point, or characteristic: *they differ in some respects.* **4.** reference or relation (esp. in **in respect of, with respect to**). **5.** polite or kind regard; consideration: *respect for people's feelings.* **6.** (*often pl.*) an expression of esteem or regard (esp. in **pay one's respects**). ~*vb.* (*tr.*) **7.** to have an attitude of esteem towards: *to respect one's elders.* **8.** to pay proper attention to; not violate: *to respect Swiss neutrality.* **9.** *Arch.* to concern or refer to. —**re'specter** *n.*

THESAURUS

resistant 1. hard, impervious, insusceptible, proof against, strong, tough, unaffected by, unyielding 2. antagonistic, combative, defiant, dissident, hostile, intractable, intransigent, opposed, recalcitrant, unwilling

resolute bold, constant, determined, dogged, firm, fixed, inflexible, obstinate, persevering, purposeful, relentless, set, staunch, steadfast, strong-willed, stubborn, tenacious, unbending, undaunted, unflinching, unshakable, unshaken, unwavering

resolution 1. boldness, constancy, courage, dedication, determination, doggedness, earnestness, energy, firmness, fortitude, obstinacy, perseverance, purpose, relentlessness, resoluteness, resolve, sincerity, staunchness, staying power, steadfastness, stubbornness, tenacity, willpower 2. aim, decision, declaration, determination, intent, intention, judgment, motion, purpose, resolve, verdict 3. answer, end, finding, outcome, settlement, solution, solving, sorting out, unravelling, upshot, working out

resolve v. 1. agree, conclude, decide, design, determine, fix, intend, make up one's mind, purpose, settle, undertake 2. answer, clear up, crack, elucidate, fathom, find the

solution to, work out 3. banish, clear up, dispel, explain, remove 4. analyse, anatomize, break down, clear, disentangle, disintegrate, dissect, dissolve, liquefy, melt, reduce, separate, solve, split up, unravel 5. alter, change, convert, metamorphose, transform, transmute ~n. 6. conclusion, decision, design, intention, objective, project, purpose, resolution, undertaking 7. boldness, courage, determination, earnestness, firmness, resoluteness, resolution, steadfastness, willpower

resort v. 1. avail oneself of, bring into play, employ, exercise, fall back on, have recourse to, look to, make use of, turn to, use, utilize 2. frequent, go, haunt, head for, repair, visit ~n. 3. haunt, holiday centre, refuge, retreat, spot, tourist centre, watering place (Brit.) 4. alternative, chance, course, expedient, hope, possibility, recourse, reference

resound echo, fill the air, re-echo, resonate, reverberate, ring

resounding booming, echoing, full, powerful, resonant, reverberating, rich, ringing, sonorous, sounding, vibrant

resource 1. ability, capability, cleverness, ingenuity, initiative, inventiveness, quick-wittedness, resourcefulness, talent 2.

hoard, reserve, source, stockpile, supply 3. appliance, contrivance, course, device, expedient, means, resort

resourceful able, bright, capable, clever, creative, imaginative, ingenious, inventive, quick-witted, sharp, talented

resources assets, capital, funds, holdings, materials, means, money, property, reserves, riches, supplies, wealth, wherewithal

respect n. 1. admiration, appreciation, approbation, consideration, deference, esteem, estimation, honour, recognition, regard, reverence, veneration 2. aspect, characteristic, detail, facet, feature, matter, particular, point, sense, way 3. bearing, connection, reference, regard, relation 4. Plural compliments, devoirs, good wishes, greetings, regards, salutations ~v. 5. admire, adore, appreciate, defer to, esteem, have a good or high opinion of, honour, look up to, recognize, regard, revere, reverence, set store by, show consideration for, think highly of, value, venerate 6. abide by, adhere to, attend, comply with, follow, heed, honour, notice, obey, observe, pay attention to, regard, show consideration for

respectable (rɪ'spɛktəbəl) *adj.* **1.** having or deserving the respect of other people; estimable; worthy. **2.** having good social standing or reputation. **3.** having socially or conventionally acceptable morals, etc.: *a respectable woman.* **4.** relatively or fairly good; considerable: *a respectable salary.* —re₁specta'bility *n.* —re'spectably *adv.*

respectful (rɪ'spɛktfʊl) *adj.* full of, showing, or giving respect. —re'spectfully *adv.* —re'spectfulness *n.*

respecting (rɪ'spɛktɪŋ) *prep.* concerning; regarding.

respective (rɪ'spɛktɪv) *adj.* belonging or relating separately to each of several people or things; several: *we took our respective ways home.* —re'spectiveness *n.*

respectively (rɪ'spɛktɪvlɪ) *adv.* (in listing a number of items or attributes that refer to another list) separately in the order given: *he gave Janet and John a cake and a chocolate respectively.*

respiration (₁rɛspə'reɪʃən) *n.* **1.** the process in living organisms of taking in oxygen from the surroundings and giving out carbon dioxide. **2.** the chemical breakdown of complex organic substances that takes place in the cells and tissues of animals and plants, during which energy is released and carbon dioxide produced. —respiratory ('rɛspərətərɪ, -trɪ) *or* ₁respi'rational *adj.*

respirator ('rɛspə₁reɪtə) *n.* **1.** an apparatus for providing long-term artificial respiration. **2.** a device worn over the mouth and nose to prevent inhalation of noxious fumes or to warm cold air before it is breathed.

respire (rɪ'spaɪə) *vb.* **1.** to inhale and exhale (air); breathe. **2.** *(intr.)* to undergo the process of respiration.

respite ('rɛspɪt, -paɪt) *n.* **1.** a pause from exertion; interval of rest. **2.** a temporary delay. **3.** a temporary stay of execution; reprieve. ~*vb.* **4.** *(tr.)* to grant a respite to; reprieve.

resplendent (rɪ'splɛndənt) *adj.* having a brilliant or splendid appearance. —re'splendence *or* re'splendency *n.* —re'splendently *adv.*

respond (rɪ'spɒnd) *vb.* **1.** to state or utter (something) in reply. **2.** *(intr.)* to act in reply; react: *to respond by issuing an invitation.* **3.** *(intr.;* foll. by *to)* to react favourably: *this patient will respond to treatment.* **4.** an archaic word for **correspond.** ~*n.* **5.** *Archit.* a pilaster or an engaged column that supports an arch or a lintel. **6.** *Christianity.* a choral anthem chanted in response to a lesson read. —re'spondence *or* re'spondency *n.* —re'sponder *n.*

respondent (rɪ'spɒndənt) *n.* **1.** *Law.* a person against whom a petition is brought. ~*adj.* **2.** a less common word for **responsive.**

response (rɪ'spɒns) *n.* **1.** the act of responding; reply or reaction. **2.** *Bridge.* a bid replying to a partner's bid or double. **3.** *(usually pl.) Christianity.* a short sentence or phrase recited or sung in reply to the officiant at a church service. **4.** *Electronics.* the ratio of the output to the input level of an electrical device. **5.** any glandular, muscular, or electrical reactions that arise from stimulation of the nervous system. —re'sponseless *adj.*

responsibility (rɪ₁spɒnsə'bɪlɪtɪ) *n., pl.* **-ties. 1.** the state or position of being responsible. **2.** a person or thing for which one is responsible.

responsible (rɪ'spɒnsəbəl) *adj.* **1.** *(postpositive;* usually foll. by *for)* having control or authority (over). **2.** *(postpositive;* foll. by *to)* being accountable for one's actions and decisions (to): *responsible to one's commanding officer.* **3.** (of a position, duty, etc.) involving decision and accountability. **4.** (often foll. by *for)* being the agent or cause (of some action): *responsible for a mistake.* **5.** able to take rational decisions without supervision; accountable for one's own actions. **6.** able to meet financial obligations; of sound credit. —re'sponsibleness *n.* —re'sponsibly *adv.*

responsive (rɪ'spɒnsɪv) *adj.* **1.** reacting or replying quickly or favourably, as to a suggestion, initiative, etc. **2.** (of an organism) reacting to a stimulus. —re'sponsively *adv.* —re'sponsiveness *n.*

rest[1] (rɛst) *n.* **1. a.** relaxation from exertion or labour. **b.** *(as modifier): a rest period.* **2.** repose; sleep. **3.** any relief or refreshment, as from worry. **4.** calm; tranquillity. **5.** death regarded as repose: *eternal rest.* **6.** cessation from motion. **7. at rest. a.** not moving. **b.** calm. **c.** dead. **d.** asleep. **8.** a pause or interval. **9.** a mark in a musical score indicating a pause of specific duration. **10.** *Prosody.* a pause at the end of a line; caesura. **11.** to put pastry in a cool place to allow the gluten to contract. **12.** a shelter or lodging: *a seaman's rest.* **13.** a thing or place on which to put something for support or to steady it. **14.** *Billiards.* any of various special sticks used as supports for difficult shots. **15. lay to rest.** to bury (a dead person). **16. set (someone's mind) at rest.** to reassure or settle. ~*vb.* **17.** to take or give rest, as by sleeping, lying down, etc. **18.** to place or position (oneself, etc.) for rest or relaxation. **19.** *(tr.)* to place or position for support or steadying: *to rest one's elbows on the table.* **20.** *(intr.)* to be at ease; be calm. **21.** to cease from motion or exertion. **22.** *(intr.)* to remain without further attention or action: *let the matter rest.* **23.** (of one's eyes) to be directed: *her eyes rested on the child.* **24.** to depend; base; rely: *the whole argument rests on one crucial fact.* **25.** *(intr.;* foll. by *with, on, upon,* etc.) to be a responsibility (of): *it rests with us to apportion blame.* **26.** *Law.* to finish the introduction of evidence in (a case). **27. rest on one's laurels.** to depend on one's past achievements for power, merit, etc. **28. rest on one's oars.** to stop doing anything for a time. —'rester *n.*

rest[2] (rɛst) *n.* (usually preceded by *the)* **1.** something left or remaining; remainder. **2.** the others: *the rest of the world.* ~*vb.* **3.** *(copula)* to continue to be (as specified); remain: *rest assured.*

restaurant ('rɛstə₁rɒŋ, 'rɛstrɒŋ) *n.* a commercial establishment where meals are prepared and served to customers.

restaurant car *n. Brit.* a railway coach in which meals are served. Also called: **dining car.**

restaurateur (₁rɛstərə'tɜː) *n.* a person who owns or

---

respectable 1. admirable, decent, decorous, dignified, estimable, good, honest, honourable, proper, reputable, respected, upright, venerable, worthy 2. ample, appreciable, considerable, decent, fair, fairly good, goodly, presentable, reasonable, sizable, substantial, tidy (*Inf.*), tolerable

respective corresponding, individual, own, particular, personal, relevant, separate, several, specific, various

respite 1. break, breather (*Inf.*), breathing space, cessation, halt, hiatus, intermission, interruption, interval, let-up (*Inf.*), lull, pause, recess, relaxation, relief, rest 2. adjournment, delay, moratorium, postponement, reprieve, stay, suspension

respond acknowledge, act in response, answer, come back, counter, react, reciprocate, rejoin, reply, retort, return

response acknowledgment, answer, comeback (*Inf.*), counterblast, feedback, reaction, rejoinder, reply, retort, return, riposte

responsibility 1. accountability, amenability, answerability, care, charge, duty,

liability, obligation, onus, trust 2. authority, importance, power 3. blame, burden, culpability, fault, guilt 4. conscientiousness, dependability, level-headedness, maturity, rationality, reliability, sensibleness, soberness, stability, trustworthiness

responsible 1. at the helm, carrying the can (*Inf.*), in authority, in charge, in control 2. accountable, amenable, answerable, bound, chargeable, duty-bound, liable, subject, under obligation 3. authoritative, decision-making, executive, high, important 4. at fault, culpable, guilty, to blame 5. adult, conscientious, dependable, level-headed, mature, rational, reliable, sensible, sober, sound, stable, trustworthy

responsive alive, awake, aware, forthcoming, impressionable, open, perceptive, quick to react, reactive, receptive, sensitive, sharp, susceptible, sympathetic

rest[1] *n.* 1. calm, doze, forty winks (*Inf.*), idleness, inactivity, leisure, lie-down, motionlessness, nap, refreshment, relaxation, relief, repose, siesta, sleep, slumber, snooze (*Inf.*), somnolence, standstill, stillness, tranquillity 2. **at rest** asleep, at a standstill, at peace,

calm, dead, motionless, peaceful, resting, sleeping, still, stopped, tranquil, unmoving 3. break, breather (*Inf.*), breathing space, cessation, halt, holiday, interlude, intermission, interval, lull, pause, stop, time off, vacation 4. haven, lodging, refuge, retreat, shelter 5. base, holder, prop, shelf, stand, support, trestle ~*v.* 6. be at ease, be calm, doze, have a snooze (*Inf.*), have forty winks (*Inf.*), idle, laze, lie down, lie still, nap, put one's feet up, refresh oneself, relax, sit down, sleep, slumber, snooze (*Inf.*), take a nap, take it easy (*Inf.*), take one's ease 7. be supported, lay, lean, lie, prop, recline, repose, sit, stand, stretch out 8. break off, cease, come to a standstill, desist, discontinue, halt, have a break, knock off (*Inf.*), stay, stop, take a breather (*Inf.*) 9. base, be based, be founded, depend, found, hang, hinge, lie, rely, reside, turn

rest[2] 1. *n.* balance, excess, leftovers, others, remainder, remains, remnants, residue, residuum, rump, surplus 2. *v.* be left, continue being, go on being, keep, remain, stay

runs a restaurant.

rest-cure *n.* a rest taken as part of a course of medical treatment, so as to relieve stress, anxiety, etc.

restful ('restful) *adj.* **1.** giving or conducive to rest. **2.** being at rest; tranquil; calm. —'**restfully** *adv.* —'**restfulness** *n.*

restitution (ˌrɛstɪ'tjuːʃən) *n.* **1.** the act of giving back something that has been lost or stolen. **2.** *Law.* compensating for loss or injury by reverting as far as possible to the original position. **3.** the return of an object or system to its original state, esp. after elastic deformation. —'**resti,tutive** or '**resti,tutory** *adj.*

restive ('restɪv) *adj.* **1.** restless, nervous, or uneasy. **2.** impatient of control or authority. —'**restively** *adv.* —'**restiveness** *n.*

restless ('restlɪs) *adj.* **1.** unable to stay still or quiet. **2.** ceaselessly active or moving: *the restless wind.* **3.** worried; anxious; uneasy. **4.** not restful; without repose: *a restless night.* —'**restlessly** *adv.* —'**restlessness** *n.*

restoration (ˌrɛstə'reɪʃən) *n.* **1.** the act of restoring to a former or original condition, place, etc. **2.** the giving back of something lost, stolen, etc. **3.** something restored, replaced, or reconstructed. **4.** a model or representation of an extinct animal, etc. **5.** (*usually cap.*) *Brit. history.* the re-establishment of the monarchy in 1660 or the reign of Charles II (1660–85).

restorative (rɪ'stɒrətɪv) *adj.* **1.** tending to revive or renew health, spirits, etc. ~*n.* **2.** anything that restores or revives, esp. a drug.

restore (rɪ'stɔː) *vb.* (*tr.*) **1.** to return (something) to its original or former condition. **2.** to bring back to health, good spirits, etc. **3.** to return (something lost, stolen, etc.) to its owner. **4.** to reintroduce or re-enforce: *to restore discipline.* **5.** to reconstruct (an extinct animal, etc.). —**re'storable** *adj.* —**re'storer** *n.*

restrain (rɪ'streɪn) *vb.* (*tr.*) **1.** to hold (someone) back from some action, esp. by force. **2.** to deprive (someone) of liberty, as by imprisonment. **3.** to limit or restrict. —**re'strainable** *adj.* —**restrainedly** (rɪ'streɪnɪdlɪ) *adv.* —**re'strainer** *n.*

restraint (rɪ'streɪnt) *n.* **1.** the ability to control or moderate one's impulses, passions, etc. **2.** the act of restraining or the state of being restrained. **3.** something that restrains; restriction.

restrict (rɪ'strɪkt) *vb.* (often foll. by *to*) to confine or keep within certain, often specified, limits or selected bounds.

restriction (rɪ'strɪkʃən) *n.* **1.** something that restricts;

a restrictive measure, law, etc. **2.** the act of restricting or the state of being restricted. —**re'strictionist** *n., adj.*

restrictive practice (rɪ'strɪktɪv) *n. Brit.* **1.** a trading agreement against the public interest. **2.** a practice of a union or other group tending to limit the freedom of other workers or employers.

rest room *n. U.S.* a room in a public building with toilets, washbasins, and, sometimes, couches.

result (rɪ'zʌlt) *n.* **1.** something that ensues from an action, policy, etc.; outcome; consequence. **2.** a number, quantity, or value obtained by solving a mathematical problem. **3.** *U.S.* a decision of a legislative body. **4. a.** (often *pl.*) the final score or outcome of a sporting contest. **b.** in some sports, a win, as opposed to a draw or tie. ~*vb.* (*intr.*) **5.** (often foll. by *from*) to be the outcome or consequence (of). **6.** (foll. by *in*) to issue or terminate (in a specified way, etc.); end: *to result in tragedy.*

resultant (rɪ'zʌltənt) *adj.* **1.** that results; resulting. ~*n.* **2.** *Maths., physics.* a single vector that is the vector sum of two or more other vectors.

resume (rɪ'zjuːm) *vb.* **1.** to begin again or go on with (something interrupted). **2.** (*tr.*) to occupy again, take back, or recover: *to resume one's seat; resume the presidency.* **3.** *Arch.* to summarize; make a résumé of. —**re'sumable** *adj.* —**re'sumer** *n.*

résumé ('rezjʊˌmeɪ) *n.* a short descriptive summary, as of events, etc.

resumption (rɪ'zʌmpʃən) *n.* the act of resuming or beginning again. —**re'sumptive** *adj.* —**re'sumptively** *adv.*

resurgent (rɪ'sɜːdʒənt) *adj.* rising again, as to new life, vigour, etc.: *resurgent nationalism.* —**re'surgence** *n.*

resurrect (ˌrɛzə'rɛkt) *vb.* **1.** to rise or raise from the dead; bring or be brought back to life. **2.** (*tr.*) to bring back into use or activity; revive. **3.** (*tr.*) *Facetious.* (formerly) to exhume and steal (a body) from its grave.

resurrection (ˌrɛzə'rɛkʃən) *n.* **1.** a supposed act or instance of a dead person coming back to life. **2.** belief in the possibility of this as part of a religious or mystical system. **3.** the condition of those who have risen from the dead: *we shall all live in the resurrection.* **4.** (usually *cap.*) *Christian theol.* the rising again of Christ from the tomb three days after his death. **5.** (usually *cap.*) the rising again from the dead of all men at the Last Judgment. —ˌresur'rectional or ˌresur'rectionary *adj.*

resurrectionist (ˌrɛzə'rɛkʃənɪst) *n.* **1.** *Facetious.* (for-

---

THESAURUS

restful calm, calming, comfortable, languid, pacific, peaceful, placid, quiet, relaxed, relaxing, serene, sleepy, soothing, tranquil, tranquillizing, undisturbed, unhurried

restitution amends, compensation, indemnification, indemnity, recompense, redress, refund, reimbursement, remuneration, reparation, repayment, requital, restoration, return, satisfaction

restive agitated, edgy, fidgety, fractious, fretful, ill at ease, impatient, jittery (*Inf.*), jumpy, nervous, on edge, recalcitrant, refractory, restless, uneasy, unquiet, unruly

restless 1. active, bustling, changeable, footloose, hurried, inconstant, irresolute, moving, nomadic, roving, transient, turbulent, unsettled, unstable, unsteady, wandering 2. agitated, anxious, disturbed, edgy, fidgeting, fidgety, fitful, fretful, ill at ease, jumpy, nervous, on edge, restive, sleepless, tossing and turning, troubled, uneasy, unquiet, unruly, unsettled, worried

restlessness 1. activity, bustle, hurry, hurry-scurry, inconstancy, instability, movement, transience, turbulence, turmoil, unrest, unsettledness 2. agitation, ants in one's pants (*Sl.*), anxiety, disquiet, disturbance, edginess, fitfulness, fretfulness, heebie-jeebies (*Sl.*), inquietude, insomnia, jitters (*Inf.*), jumpiness, nervousness, restiveness, uneasiness, worriedness

restoration 1. reconstruction, recovery, refreshment, refurbishing, rehabilitation, rejuvenation, renewal, renovation, repair, revitalization, revival 2. recovery, re-

establishment, reinstallation, reinstatement, replacement, restitution, return

restore 1. fix, mend, rebuild, recondition, reconstruct, recover, refurbish, rehabilitate, renew, renovate, repair, retouch, set to rights, touch up 2. bring back to health, build up, reanimate, refresh, rejuvenate, revitalize, revive, revivify, strengthen 3. bring back, give back, hand back, recover, re-establish, reinstate, replace, return, send back 4. reconstitute, re-enforce, reimpose, reinstate, reintroduce

restrain 1. bridle, check, confine, constrain, contain, control, curb, curtail, debar, govern, hamper, handicap, harness, hinder, hold, hold back, inhibit, keep, keep under control, limit, muzzle, prevent, repress, restrict, subdue, suppress 2. arrest, bind, chain, confine, detain, fetter, hold, imprison, jail, lock up, manacle, pinion, tie up

restrained 1. calm, controlled, mild, moderate, muted, reasonable, reticent, self-controlled, soft, steady, temperate, undemonstrative 2. discreet, quiet, subdued, tasteful, unobtrusive

restraint 1. coercion, command, compulsion, confines, constraint, control, curtailment, grip, hindrance, hold, inhibition, limitation, moderation, prevention, restriction, self-control, self-discipline, self-possession, self-restraint, suppression 2. arrest, bondage, bonds, captivity, chains, confinement, detention, fetters, imprisonment, manacles, pinions, straitjacket 3. ban, bridle, check, curb,

embargo, interdict, limit, limitation, rein, taboo

restrict bound, circumscribe, confine, contain, cramp, demarcate, hamper, handicap, hem in, impede, inhibit, keep within bounds *or* limits, limit, regulate, restrain

restriction check, condition, confinement, constraint, containment, control, curb, demarcation, handicap, inhibition, limitation, regulation, restraint, rule, stipulation

result *n.* 1. conclusion, consequence, decision, development, effect, end, event, fruit, issue, outcome, product, reaction, sequel, termination, upshot ~*v.* 2. appear, arise, derive, develop, emanate, ensue, eventuate, flow, follow, happen, issue, spring, stem, turn out 3. *With* in culminate, end, finish, terminate, wind up (*Inf.*)

resume 1. begin again, carry on, continue, go on, proceed, recommence, reinstitute, reopen, restart, take up *or* pick up where one left off 2. assume again, occupy again, reoccupy, take back, take up again

resumption carrying on, continuation, fresh outbreak, new beginning, re-establishment, renewal, reopening, restart, resurgence

resurrect breathe new life into, bring back, raise from the dead, reintroduce, renew, restore to life, revive

resurrection comeback (*Inf.*), raising *or* rising from the dead, reappearance, rebirth, renaissance, renascence, renewal, restoration, resurgence, resuscitation, return, return from the dead, revival

merly) a body-snatcher. **2.** a person who believes in the Resurrection.

resuscitate (rɪˈsʌsɪˌteɪt) *vb.* (*tr.*) to restore to consciousness; revive. —**reˌsusciˈtation** *n.* —**reˈsuscitative** *adj.* —**reˈsusciˌtator** *n.*

retail (ˈriːteɪl) *n.* **1.** the sale of goods individually or in small quantities to consumers. Cf. **wholesale.** ~*adj.* **2.** of, relating to, or engaged in such selling: *retail prices.* ~*adv.* **3.** in small amounts or at a retail price. ~*vb.* **4.** to sell or be sold in small quantities to consumers. **5.** (rɪˈteɪl). (*tr.*) to relate (gossip, scandal, etc.) in detail. —ˈ**retailer** *n.*

retain (rɪˈteɪn) *vb.* (*tr.*) **1.** to keep in one's possession. **2.** to be able to hold or contain: *soil that retains water.* **3.** (of a person) to be able to remember (information, etc.) without difficulty. **4.** to hold in position. **5.** to keep for one's future use, as by paying a retainer or nominal charge. **6.** *Law.* to engage the services of (a barrister) by payment of a preliminary fee. —**reˈtainable** *adj.* —**reˌtainaˈbility** *or* **reˈtainableness** *n.* —**reˈtainment** *n.*

retainer (rɪˈteɪnə) *n.* **1.** *History.* a supporter or dependant of a person of rank. **2.** a servant, esp. one who has been with a family for a long time. **3.** a clip, frame, or similar device that prevents a part of a machine, etc., from moving. **4.** a fee paid in advance to secure first option on the services of a barrister, jockey, etc. **5.** a reduced rent paid for a flat, etc., to reserve it for future use.

retaining wall *n.* a wall constructed to hold back earth, loose rock, etc. Also called: **revetment.**

retake *vb.* (riːˈteɪk), **-taking, -took, -taken.** (*tr.*) **1.** to take back or capture again: *to retake a fortress.* **2.** *Films.* to shoot (a scene) again. **3.** to tape (a recording) again. ~*n.* (ˈriːˌteɪk). **4.** *Films.* a rephotographed scene. **5.** a retaped recording. —**reˈtaker** *n.*

retaliate (rɪˈtælɪˌeɪt) *vb.* (*intr.*) **1.** to take retributory action, esp. by returning some injury or wrong in kind. **2.** to cast (accusations) back upon a person. —**reˌtaliˈation** *n.* —**reˈtaliative** *or* **reˈtaliatory** *adj.*

retard (rɪˈtɑːd) *vb.* (*tr.*) to delay or slow down (the progress or speed) of (something). —ˌ**retarˈdation** *n.* —**reˈtardingly** *adv.*

retarded (rɪˈtɑːdɪd) *adj.* underdeveloped, usually mentally and esp. having an IQ of 70 to 85.

retch (retʃ, riːtʃ) *vb.* **1.** (*intr.*) to undergo an involuntary spasm of ineffectual vomiting. ~*n.* **2.** an involuntary spasm of ineffectual vomiting.

retention (rɪˈtenʃən) *n.* **1.** the act of retaining or state of being retained. **2.** the capacity to hold or retain liquid, etc. **3.** the capacity to remember. **4.** *Pathol.* the abnormal holding within the body of urine, faeces, etc. —**reˈtentive** *adj.*

reticent (ˈretɪsənt) *adj.* not communicative; not saying all that one knows; taciturn; reserved. —ˈ**reticence** *n.* —ˈ**reticently** *adv.*

reticulate *adj.* (rɪˈtɪkjulɪt), *also* **reticular** (rɪˈtɪkjulə). **1.** in the form of a network or having a network of parts: *a reticulate leaf.* ~*vb.* (rɪˈtɪkjuˌleɪt). **2.** to form or be formed into a net. —**reˈticulately** *adv.*

—**reˌticuˈlation** *n.*

reticule (ˈretɪˌkjuːl) *n.* (formerly) a woman's small bag or purse, usually with a drawstring and made of net, beading, brocade, etc.

retina (ˈretɪnə) *n.*, *pl.* **-nas** *or* **-nae** (-ˌniː). the light-sensitive membrane forming the inner lining of the posterior wall of the eyeball. —ˈ**retinal** *adj.*

retinue (ˈretɪˌnjuː) *n.* a body of aides and retainers attending an important person.

retire (rɪˈtaɪə) *vb.* (*mainly intr.*) **1.** (*also tr.*) to give up or to cause (a person) to give up his work, esp. on reaching pensionable age. **2.** to go away, as into seclusion, for recuperation, etc. **3.** to go to bed. **4.** to recede or disappear: *the sun retired behind the clouds.* **5.** to withdraw from a sporting contest, esp. because of injury. **6.** (*also tr.*) to pull back (troops, etc.) from battle or (of troops, etc.) to fall back. **7.** (*tr.*) to remove (money, bonds, shares, etc.) from circulation. —**reˈtirement** *n.* —reˈtirer *n.* —**reˈtired** *adj.*

retirement pension *n. Brit.* a weekly payment made by the government to a retired man over 65 or a woman over 60.

retiring (rɪˈtaɪərɪŋ) *adj.* shunning contact with others; shy; reserved. —**reˈtiringly** *adv.*

retort[1] (rɪˈtɔːt) *vb.* **1.** (when *tr.*, takes a clause as object) to utter (something) quickly, wittily, or angrily, in response. **2.** to use (an argument) against its originator. ~*n.* **3.** a sharp, angry, or witty reply. **4.** an argument used against its originator. —**reˈtorter** *n.*

retort[2] (rɪˈtɔːt) *n.* **1.** a glass vessel with a long tapering neck that is bent down, used for distillation. **2.** a vessel used for heating ores in the production of metals or heating coal to produce gas. ~*vb.* **3.** (*tr.*) to heat in a retort.

retouch (riːˈtʌtʃ) *vb.* (*tr.*) **1.** to restore, correct, or improve (a painting, make-up, etc.) with new touches. **2.** *Photog.* to alter (a negative or print) by painting over blemishes or adding details. ~*n.* **3.** the art or practice of retouching. **4.** a detail that is the result of retouching. **5.** a photograph, painting, etc., that has been retouched. —**reˈtoucher** *n.*

retrace (rɪˈtreɪs) *vb.* (*tr.*) **1.** to go back over (one's steps, a route, etc.) again. **2.** to go over (a past event) in the mind; recall. **3.** to go over (a story, account, etc.) from the beginning.

retract (rɪˈtrækt) *vb.* **1.** (*tr.*) to draw in (a part or appendage): *a snail can retract its horns; to retract the landing gear of an aircraft.* **2.** to withdraw (a statement, opinion, charge, etc.) as invalid or unjustified. **3.** to go back on (a promise or agreement). —**reˈtractable** *or* **reˈtractible** *adj.* —**reˈtraction** *n.* —**reˈtractive** *adj.*

retractile (rɪˈtræktaɪl) *adj.* capable of being drawn in: *the retractile claws of a cat.* —**retractility** (ˌriːtrækˈtɪlɪtɪ) *n.*

retread *vb.* (riːˈtred), **-treading, -treaded. 1.** (*tr.*) to remould (a used pneumatic tyre) to give it new treads. ~*n.* (ˈriːˌtred). **2.** Also called: **remould.** a used pneumatic tyre that has been remoulded to give it new treads. **3.** *N.Z. sl.* a pensioner who has resumed employment, esp. in the same profession as formerly.

retreat (rɪˈtriːt) *vb.* (*mainly intr.*) **1.** *Mil.* to withdraw

---

THESAURUS

resuscitate breathe new life into, bring round, bring to life, give artificial respiration to, give the kiss of life (*Inf.*), quicken, reanimate, renew, rescue, restore, resurrect, revitalize, revive, revivify, save

retain 1. absorb, contain, detain, grasp, grip, hang *or* hold onto, hold, hold back, hold fast, keep, keep possession of, maintain, preserve, reserve, restrain, save 2. bear in mind, impress on the memory, keep in mind, memorize, recall, recollect, remember 3. commission, employ, engage, hire, pay, reserve

retainer 1. attendant, dependant, domestic, flunky, footman, lackey, servant, supporter, valet, vassal 2. advance, deposit, fee

retaliate even the score, exact retribution, get back at (*Inf.*), get even with (*Inf.*), get one's own back (*Inf.*), give as good as one gets (*Inf.*), give one a taste of one's own medicine, give tit for tat, make reprisal, pay one back in one's own coin, reciprocate, return like for like, strike back, take an eye for

an eye, take revenge, wreak vengeance

retaliation an eye for an eye, a taste of one's own medicine, counterblow, counterstroke, reciprocation, repayment, reprisal, requital, retribution, revenge, tit for tat, vengeance

retard arrest, brake, check, clog, decelerate, defer, delay, detain, encumber, handicap, hinder, hold back *or* up, impede, obstruct, set back, slow down, stall

retch be sick, disgorge, gag (*Sl.*), heave, puke (*Sl.*), regurgitate, spew, throw up (*Inf.*), vomit

reticence quietness, reserve, restraint, secretiveness, silence, taciturnity, uncommunicativeness, unforthcomingness

reticent close-mouthed, mum, quiet, reserved, restrained, secretive, silent, taciturn, tight-lipped, uncommunicative, unforthcoming, unspeaking

retire 1. be pensioned off, (be) put out to grass (*Inf.*), give up work, stop working 2. absent oneself, betake oneself, depart, exit, go

away, leave, remove, withdraw 3. go to bed, go to one's room, go to sleep, hit the sack (*Sl.*), kip down (*Brit. sl.*), turn in (*Inf.*) 4. decamp, ebb, fall back, give ground, give way, pull back, pull out, recede, retreat, withdraw

retirement loneliness, obscurity, privacy, retreat, seclusion, solitude, withdrawal

retiring bashful, coy, demure, diffident, humble, meek, modest, quiet, reclusive, reserved, reticent, self-effacing, shrinking, shy, timid, timorous, unassertive, unassuming

retouch brush up, correct, finish, improve, recondition, renovate, restore, touch up

retract 1. draw in, pull back, pull in, reel in, sheathe 2. abjure, cancel, deny, disavow, disclaim, disown, recall, recant, renounce, repeal, repudiate, rescind, reverse, revoke, take back, unsay, withdraw 3. back out of, go back on, renege on

or retire in the face of or from action with an enemy. **2.** to retire or withdraw, as to seclusion or shelter. **3.** (of a person's features) to slope back; recede. **4.** (*tr.*) *Chess.* to move (a piece) back. ~*n.* **5.** the act of retreating or withdrawing. **6.** *Mil.* **a.** a withdrawal or retirement in the face of the enemy. **b.** a bugle call signifying withdrawal or retirement. **7.** retirement or seclusion. **8.** a place to which one may retire for religious contemplation. **9.** a period of seclusion, esp. for religious contemplation. **10.** an institution for the care and treatment of the mentally ill, infirm, elderly, etc.

retrench (rɪ'trentʃ) *vb.* **1.** to reduce (costs); economize. **2.** (*tr.*) to shorten, delete, or abridge. —**re'trenchment** *n.*

retribution (ˌrɛtrɪ'bjuːʃən) *n.* **1.** the act of punishing or taking vengeance for wrongdoing, sin, or injury. **2.** punishment or vengeance. —**retributive** (rɪ'trɪbjʊtɪv) *or* re-'tributory *adj.* —**re'tributively** *adv.*

retrieve (rɪ'triːv) *vb.* (*mainly tr.*) **1.** to get or fetch back again; recover. **2.** to bring back to a more satisfactory state; revive. **3.** to rescue or save. **4.** to recover or make newly available (stored information) from a computer system. **5.** (*also intr.*) (of dogs) to find and fetch (shot game, etc.). **6.** *Tennis, etc.* to return successfully (a shot difficult to reach). **7.** to recall; remember. ~*n.* **8.** the act of retrieving. **9.** the chance of being retrieved. —**re'trievable** *adj.* —**re'trieval** *n.*

retriever (rɪ'triːvə) *n.* **1.** one of a breed of large hunting dogs that can be trained to retrieve game. **2.** any dog used to retrieve shot game. **3.** a person or thing that retrieves.

retro- *prefix.* **1.** back or backwards: *retroactive.* **2.** located behind: *retrochoir.*

retroactive (ˌrɛtrəʊ'æktɪv) *adj.* **1.** applying or referring to the past: *retroactive legislation.* **2.** effective from a date or for a period in the past. —**ˌretro'actively** *adv.* —**ˌretroac'tivity** *n.*

retrochoir ('rɛtrəʊˌkwaɪə) *n.* the space in a large church or cathedral behind the high altar.

retrofire ('rɛtrəʊˌfaɪə) *n.* **1.** the act of firing a retrorocket. **2.** the moment at which it is fired.

retrograde ('rɛtrəʊˌɡreɪd) *adj.* **1.** moving or bending backwards. **2.** (esp. of order) reverse or inverse. **3.** tending towards an earlier worse condition; declining or deteriorating. **4.** *Astron.* **a.** occurring or orbiting in a direction opposite to that of the earth's motion around the sun. Cf. **direct** (sense 18). **b.** occurring or orbiting in a direction around a planet opposite to the planet's rotational direction. **c.** appearing to move in a clockwise direction due to the rotational period exceeding the period of revolution around the sun: *Venus has retrograde rotation.* ~*vb.* (*intr.*) **5.** to move in a retrograde direction; retrogress. —**ˌretrogra'dation** *n.* —'**retroˌgradely** *adv.*

retrogress (ˌrɛtrəʊ'ɡrɛs) *vb.* (*intr.*) **1.** to go back to an earlier, esp. worse, condition; degenerate or deteriorate. **2.** to move backwards; recede. —**ˌretro'gression** *n.* —ˌretro'gressive *adj.* —ˌretro'gressively *adv.*

retrorocket ('rɛtrəʊˌrɒkɪt) *n.* a small auxiliary rocket engine on a larger rocket, missile, or spacecraft, that produces thrust in the opposite direction to the direction of flight in order to decelerate. Often shortened to **retro.**

retrospect ('rɛtrəʊˌspɛkt) *n.* the act of surveying things past (often in **in retrospect**). —**ˌretro'spection** *n.*

retrospective (ˌrɛtrəʊ'spɛktɪv) *adj.* **1.** looking or directed backwards, esp. in time; characterized by retrospection. **2.** applying to the past; retroactive. ~*n.* **3.** an exhibition of an artist's life's work. —**ˌretro'spectively** *adv.*

retroussé (rə'truːseɪ) *adj.* (of a nose) turned up.

retsina (rɛt'siːnə) *n.* a Greek wine flavoured with resin.

return (rɪ'tɜːn) *vb.* **1.** (*intr.*) to come back to a former place or state. **2.** (*tr.*) to give, take, or carry back; replace or restore. **3.** (*tr.*) to repay or recompense, esp. with something of equivalent value: *return the compliment.* **4.** (*tr.*) to earn or yield (profit or interest) as an income from an investment or venture. **5.** (*intr.*) to come back or revert in thought or speech: *I'll return to that later.* **6.** (*intr.*) to recur or reappear: *the symptoms have returned.* **7.** to answer or reply. **8.** (*tr.*) to vote into office; elect. **9.** (*tr.*) *Law.* (of a jury) to deliver or render (a verdict). **10.** (*tr.*) to submit (a report, etc.) about (someone or something) to someone in authority. **11.** (*tr.*) *Cards.* to lead back (the suit led by one's partner). **12.** (*tr.*) *Ball games.* to hit, throw, or play (a ball) back. **13. return thanks.** (of Christians) to say grace before a meal. ~*n.* **14.** the act or an instance of coming back. **15.** something that is given or sent back, esp. unsatisfactory merchandise or a theatre ticket for resale. **16.** the act or an instance of putting, sending, or carrying back; replacement or restoration. **17.** (*often pl.*) the yield or profit from an investment or venture. **18.** the act or an instance of reciprocation or repayment (esp. in **in return for**). **19.** a recurrence or reappearance. **20.** an official report, esp. of the financial condition of a company. **21. a.** a form (a **tax return**) on which a statement of one's taxable income is made. **b.** the statement itself. **22.** (*often pl.*) a statement of the votes counted at an election. **23.** an answer or reply. **24.** *Brit.* Also called: **return ticket.** a ticket entitling a passenger to travel to his destination and back. **25.** *Archit.* a part of a building that forms an angle with the façade. **26.** *Law.* a report by a bailiff or other officer on the outcome of a formal document such as a writ, summons, etc. **27.** *Cards.* a lead of a card in the suit that one's partner has previously led. **28.** *Ball games.* the act of playing or throwing a ball, etc., back. **29.** (*modifier*) of, relating to, or characterized by a return: *a return visit.* **30. by return (of post).** *Brit.* by the next post. **31. many happy returns (of the day).** a conventional birthday greeting. —**re'turnable** *adj.* —**re'turner** *n.*

returning officer *n.* (in Britain, Canada, Australia, etc.) an official in charge of conducting an election.

return ticket *n. Brit.* a ticket entitling a passenger to travel to his destination and back.

reunify (riː'juːnɪˌfaɪ) *vb.* **-fying, -fied.** (*tr.*) to bring together again (something, esp. a country previously divided). —**ˌreunifi'cation** *n.*

reunion (riː'juːnjən) *n.* **1.** the act of coming together again. **2.** the state or condition of having been brought together again. **3.** a gathering of relatives, friends, or former associates.

Reuters ('rɔɪtəz) *n.* a private news agency in London that distributes news to member newspapers. It was founded by Baron Paul Julius von Reuter, a 19th-century telegrapher.

rev (rɛv) *Inf.* ~*n.* **1.** revolution per minute. ~*vb.* **revving, revved. 2.** (often foll. by *up*) to increase the speed of revolution of (an engine).

rev. *abbrev. for:* **1.** revenue. **2.** reverse(d). **3.** review.

THESAURUS

retreat *v.* **1.** back away, depart, draw back, ebb, fall back, give ground, go back, leave, pull back, recede, recoil, retire, shrink, turn tail, withdraw ~*n.* **2.** departure, ebb, evacuation, flight, retirement, withdrawal **3.** asylum, den, haunt, haven, hideaway, privacy, refuge, resort, retirement, sanctuary, seclusion, shelter

retrench curtail, cut, cut back, decrease, diminish, economize, husband, lessen, limit, make economies, pare, prune, reduce, save, tighten one's belt, trim

retrenchment contraction, cost-cutting, curtailment, cut, cutback, economy, pruning, reduction, rundown, tightening one's belt

retribution an eye for an eye, compensation, justice, Nemesis, punishment, reckon-ing, recompense, redress, repayment, reprisal, requital, retaliation, revenge, reward, satisfaction, vengeance

retrieve fetch back, get back, recall, recapture, recoup, recover, redeem, regain, repair, repossess, rescue, restore, salvage, save, win back

retrospect afterthought, hindsight, recollection, re-examination, remembrance, reminiscence, review, survey

return *v.* **1.** come back, come round again, go back, reappear, rebound, recoil, recur, repair, retreat, revert, turn back **2.** carry back, convey, give back, put back, re-establish, reinstate, remit, render, replace, restore, send, send back, take back, transmit **3.** give back, pay back, reciprocate, recompense, refund, reimburse, repay, requite **4.** bring in, earn, make, net, repay, yield **5.** answer, come back (with), communicate, rejoin, reply, respond, retort **6.** choose, elect, pick, vote in **7.** announce, arrive at, bring in, come to, deliver, render, report, submit ~*n.* **8.** homecoming, reappearance, rebound, recoil, recrudescence, recurrence, retreat, reversion **9.** re-establishment, reinstatement, replacement, restoration **10.** advantage, benefit, gain, income, interest, proceeds, profit, revenue, takings, yield **11.** compensation, reciprocation, recompense, reimbursement, reparation, repayment, requital, retaliation, reward **12.** account, form, list, report, statement, summary **13.** answer, comeback (*Inf.*), rejoinder, reply, response, retort, riposte

4. revise(d). **5.** revision. **6.** revolution. **7.** revolving.

Rev. *abbrev. for:* **1.** *Bible.* Revelation (of Saint John the Divine). **2.** Reverend.

revamp (riː'væmp) *vb.* (*tr.*) **1.** to patch up or renovate; repair or restore. ~*n.* **2.** something that has been renovated or revamped. **3.** the act or process of revamping.

Revd. *abbrev. for* Reverend.

reveal (rɪ'viːl) *vb.* (*tr.*) **1.** (*may take a clause as object or an infinitive*) to disclose (a secret); divulge. **2.** to expose to view or show (something concealed). **3.** (of God) to disclose (divine truths). ~*n.* **4.** *Archit.* the vertical side of an opening in a wall, esp. the side of a window or door between the frame and the front of the wall. —**re-**'**vealable** *adj.* —**re**'**vealer** *n.* —**re**'**vealingly** *adv.* —**re-**'**vealment** *n.*

reveille (rɪ'vælɪ) *n.* **1.** a signal, given by a bugle, drum, etc., to awaken soldiers or sailors in the morning. **2.** the hour at which this takes place.

revel ('rɛvəl) *vb.* **-elling, -elled** or *U.S.* **-eling, -eled.** (*intr.*) **1.** (foll. by *in*) to take pleasure or wallow: *to revel in success.* **2.** to take part in noisy festivities; make merry. ~*n.* **3.** (*often pl.*) an occasion of noisy merrymaking. —'**reveller** *n.* —'**revelry** *n.*

revelation (ˌrɛvə'leɪʃən) *n.* **1.** the act or process of disclosing something previously secret or obscure, esp. something true. **2.** a fact disclosed or revealed, esp. in a dramatic or surprising way. **3.** *Christianity.* God's disclosure of his own nature and his purpose for mankind. —ˌreve'lational *adj.*

Revelation (ˌrɛvə'leɪʃən) *n.* (*often pl.*) the last book of the New Testament, containing visionary descriptions of heaven, and of the end of the world. Also called: the **Apocalypse,** the **Revelation of Saint John the Divine.**

revenge (rɪ'vɛndʒ) *n.* **1.** the act of retaliating for wrongs or injury received; vengeance. **2.** something done as a means of vengeance. **3.** the desire to take vengeance. **4.** a return match, regarded as a loser's opportunity to even the score. ~*vb.* (*tr.*) **5.** to inflict equivalent injury or damage for (injury received). **6.** to take vengeance for (oneself or another); avenge. —**re-**'**vengeful** *adj.* —**re**'**venger** *n.* —**re**'**vengingly** *adv.*

revenue ('rɛvɪˌnjuː) *n.* **1.** the income accruing from taxation to a government. **2. a.** a government department responsible for the collection of government revenue. **b.** (*as modifier*): *revenue men.* **3.** the gross income from a business enterprise, investment, etc. **4.** a particular item of income. **5.** a source of income.

reverberate (rɪ'vɜːbəˌreɪt) *vb.* **1.** (*intr.*) to resound or re-echo. **2.** to reflect or be reflected many times. **3.** (*intr.*) to rebound or recoil. **4.** (*intr.*) (of the flame or heat in a reverberatory furnace) to be deflected onto the metal or ore on the hearth. **5.** (*tr.*) to heat, melt, or refine (a metal or ore) in a reverberatory furnace. —**re-**'**verberative** *adj.* —**re**'**verberantly** *adv.* —**re**ˌ**verber**'**ation** *n.*

revere (rɪ'vɪə) *vb.* (*tr.*) to be in awe of and respect deeply; venerate.

reverence ('rɛvərəns) *n.* **1.** a feeling or attitude of profound respect, usually reserved for the sacred or divine.

2. an outward manifestation of this feeling, esp. a bow or act of obeisance. **3.** the state of being revered or commanding profound respect. ~*vb.* **4.** (*tr.*) to revere or venerate.

Reverence ('rɛvərəns) *n.* (preceded by *Your* or *His*) a title sometimes used to address or refer to a Roman Catholic priest.

reverend ('rɛvərənd) *adj.* **1.** worthy of reverence. **2.** relating to or designating a clergyman. ~*n.* **3.** *Inf.* a clergyman.

Reverend ('rɛvərənd) *adj.* a title of respect for a clergyman. Abbrev.: **Rev.** or **Revd.**

▷ **Usage.** *Reverend* with a surname alone (*Reverend Smith*), as a term of address ("*Yes, Reverend*"), or in the salutation of a letter (*Dear Rev. Mr. Smith*) are all considered to be wrong usage. Preferred are (*the*) *Reverend John Smith* or *Reverend Mr. Smith* and *Dear Mr. Smith.*

reverent ('rɛvərənt, 'rɛvrənt) *adj.* feeling, expressing, or characterized by reverence. —ˌreve'rential *adj.* —'reverently *adv.*

reverie ('rɛvərɪ) *n., pl.* **-eries. 1.** an act or state of absent-minded daydreaming: *to fall into a reverie.* **2.** a piece of instrumental music suggestive of a daydream. **3.** *Arch.* a fanciful or visionary notion; daydream.

revers (rɪ'vɪə) *n., pl.* **-vers** (-'vɪəz). (*usually pl.*) the turned-back lining of part of a garment, esp. of a lapel or cuff.

reverse (rɪ'vɜːs) *vb.* (*mainly tr.*) **1.** to turn or set in an opposite direction, order, or position. **2.** to change into something different or contrary; alter completely: *reverse one's policy.* **3.** (*also intr.*) to move or cause to move backwards or in an opposite direction: *to reverse a car.* **4.** to run (machinery, etc.) in the opposite direction to normal. **5.** to turn inside out. **6.** *Law.* to revoke or set aside (a judgment, decree, etc.); annul. **7. reverse the charge(s).** to make a telephone call at the recipient's expense. ~*n.* **8.** the opposite or contrary of something. **9.** the back or rear side of something. **10.** a change to an opposite position, state, or direction. **11.** a change for the worse; setback or defeat. **12. a.** the mechanism or gears by which machinery, a vehicle, etc., can be made to reverse its direction. **b.** (*as modifier*): *reverse gear.* **13.** the side of a coin bearing a secondary design. **14. a.** printed matter in which normally black or coloured areas, esp. lettering, appear white, and vice versa. **b.** (*as modifier*): *reverse plates.* **15. in reverse.** in an opposite or backward direction. **16. the reverse of.** emphatically not; not at all: *he was the reverse of polite when I called.* ~*adj.* **17.** opposite or contrary in direction, position, order, nature, etc.; turned backwards. **18.** back to front; inverted. **19.** operating or moving in a manner contrary to that which is usual. **20.** denoting or relating to a mirror image. —**re**'**versal** *n.* —**re**'**versely** *adv.* —**re**'**verser** *n.*

reversible (rɪ'vɜːsəbəl) *adj.* **1.** capable of being reversed: *a reversible decision.* **2.** capable of returning to an original condition. **3.** *Chem., physics.* capable of assuming or producing either of two possible states and

---

THESAURUS

reveal 1. announce, betray, broadcast, communicate, disclose, divulge, give away, give out, impart, leak, let on, let out, let slip, make known, make public, proclaim, publish, tell **2.** bare, bring to light, display, exhibit, expose to view, lay bare, manifest, open, show, uncover, unearth, unmask, unveil

revel *v.* **1.** *With* **in** bask, crow, delight, gloat, indulge, joy, lap up, luxuriate, rejoice, relish, savour, take pleasure, thrive on, wallow **2.** carouse, celebrate, go on a spree, live it up (*Inf.*), make merry, paint the town red (*Inf.*), push the boat out (*Brit. inf.*), rave (*Brit. sl.*), roister, whoop it up (*Inf.*) ~*n.* **3.** *Often plural* bacchanal, carousal, carouse, celebration, debauch, festivity, gala, jollification, merrymaking, party, saturnalia, spree

revelation announcement, betrayal, broadcasting, communication, disclosure, discovery, display, exhibition, exposé, exposition, exposure, giveaway, leak, manifestation, news, proclamation, publication, telling, uncovering, unearthing, unveiling

reveller carouser, celebrator, merry-maker, partygoer, pleasure-seeker, roisterer

revelry carousal, carouse, celebration, debauch, debauchery, festivity, fun, jollification, jollity, merrymaking, party, roistering, saturnalia, spree

revenge 1. *n.* an eye for an eye, reprisal, requital, retaliation, retribution, satisfaction, vengeance, vindictiveness **2.** *v.* avenge, even the score for, get one's own back for (*Inf.*), make reprisal for, repay, requite, retaliate, take an eye for an eye for, take revenge for, vindicate

revenue gain, income, interest, proceeds, profits, receipts, returns, rewards, takings, yield

reverberate echo, rebound, recoil, re-echo, resound, ring, vibrate

revere adore, be in awe of, defer to, exalt, have a high opinion of, honour, look up to, put on a pedestal, respect, reverence, think highly of, venerate, worship

reverence 1. *n.* admiration, adoration, awe, deference, devotion, high esteem, homage, honour, respect, veneration, worship **2.**

v. admire, adore, be in awe of, hold in awe, honour, pay homage to, respect, revere, venerate, worship

reverent adoring, awed, decorous, deferential, devout, humble, loving, meek, pious, respectful, reverential, solemn, submissive

reverse *v.* **1.** invert, transpose, turn back, turn over, turn round, turn upside down, upend **2.** alter, annul, cancel, change, countermand, declare null and void, invalidate, negate, overrule, overset, overthrow, overturn, quash, repeal, rescind, retract, revoke, set aside, undo, upset **3.** back, backtrack, back up, go backwards, move backwards, retreat ~*n.* **4.** antithesis, contradiction, contrary, converse, inverse, opposite **5.** back, flip side, other side, rear, underside, verso, wrong side **6.** adversity, affliction, blow, check, defeat, disappointment, failure, hardship, misadventure, misfortune, mishap, repulse, reversal, setback, trial, vicissitude ~*adj.* **7.** back to front, backward, contrary, converse, inverse, inverted, opposite

changing from one to the other: *a reversible reaction*. **4.** (of a fabric or garment) woven, printed, or finished so that either side may be used as the outer side. ~*n*. **5.** a reversible garment, esp. a coat. —**re₁versi'bility** *n*. —**re'versibly** *adv*.

reversing light *n*. a light on the rear of a motor vehicle to provide illumination when the vehicle is being reversed.

reversion (rɪ'vɜːʃən) *n*. **1.** a return to an earlier condition, practice, or belief; act of reverting. **2.** *Biol*. the return of individuals, organs, etc., to a more primitive condition or type. **3.** *Property law*. **a.** an interest in an estate that reverts to the grantor or his heirs at the end of a period, esp. at the end of the life of a grantee. **b.** an estate so reverting. **c.** the right to succeed to such an estate. **4.** the benefit payable on the death of a life-insurance policyholder. —**re'versionary** *or* **re'versional** *adj*.

revert (rɪ'vɜːt) *vb*. (*intr*., foll. by *to*). **1.** to go back to a former practice, condition, belief, etc.: *he reverted to his old wicked ways*. **2.** to take up again or come back to a former topic. **3.** *Biol*. (of individuals, organs, etc.) to return to a more primitive, earlier, or simpler condition or type. **4.** *Property law*. (of an estate or interest in land) to return to its former owner or his heirs. **5. revert to type.** to resume characteristics that were thought to have disappeared. —**re'verter** *n*. —**re'vertible** *adj*.

review (rɪ'vjuː) *vb*. (*mainly tr*.) **1.** to look at or examine again: *to review a situation*. **2.** to look back upon (a period of time, sequence of events, etc.); remember: *he reviewed his achievements with pride*. **3.** to inspect, esp. formally or officially: *the general reviewed his troops*. **4.** *Law*. to re-examine (a decision) judicially. **5.** to write a critical assessment of (a book, film, play, concert, etc.), esp. as a profession. ~*n*. **6.** Also called: **reviewal.** the act or an instance of reviewing. **7.** a general survey or report: *a review of the political situation*. **8.** a critical assessment of a book, film, play, concert, etc., esp. one printed in a newspaper or periodical. **9.** a publication containing such articles. **10.** a second consideration; re-examination. **11.** a retrospective survey. **12.** a formal or official inspection. **13.** a U.S. word for **revision** (sense 2). **14.** *Law*. judicial re-examination of a case, esp. by a superior court. **15.** a less common spelling of **revue.** —**re'viewer** *n*.

revile (rɪ'vaɪl) *vb*. to use abusive or scornful language against (someone or something). —**re'vilement** *n*. —**re'viler** *n*. —**re'vilingly** *adv*.

revise (rɪ'vaɪz) *vb*. **1.** (*tr*.) to change or amend: *to revise one's opinion*. **2.** *Brit*. to reread (a subject or notes on it) so as to memorize it, esp. for an examination. **3.** (*tr*.) to prepare a new version or edition of (a previously printed work). ~*n*. **4.** the act, process, or result of revising; revision. —**re'visal** *n*. —**re'viser** *n*.

Revised Version *n*. a revision of the Authorized Version of the Bible by two committees of British scholars,

the New Testament being published in 1881 and the Old in 1885.

revision (rɪ'vɪʒən) *n*. **1.** the act or process of revising. **2.** *Brit*. the process of rereading a subject or notes on it, esp. for an examination. **3.** a corrected or new version of a book, article, etc. —**re'visional** *or* **re'visionary** *adj*.

revisory (rɪ'vaɪzərɪ) *adj*. of, relating to, or having the power to revise.

revitalize *or* **-lise** (riː'vaɪtə₁laɪz) *vb*. (*tr*.) to restore vitality or animation to.

revival (rɪ'vaɪvəl) *n*. **1.** the act or an instance of reviving or the state of being revived. **2.** an instance of returning to life or consciousness; restoration of vigour or vitality. **3.** a renewed use, acceptance of, or interest in (past customs, styles, etc.): *the Gothic revival*. **4.** a new production of a play that has not been recently performed. **5.** a reawakening of faith. **6.** an evangelistic meeting or meetings intended to effect such a reawakening in those present.

revive (rɪ'vaɪv) *vb*. **1.** to bring or be brought back to life, consciousness, or strength: *revived by a drop of whisky*. **2.** to give or assume new vitality; flourish again or cause to flourish again. **3.** to make or become operative or active again: *the youth movement was revived*. **4.** to bring or come back to mind. **5.** (*tr*.) *Theatre*. to mount a new production of (an old play). —**re'vivable** *adj*. —**re₁viva'bility** *n*. —**re'viver** *n*.

revivify (rɪ'vɪvɪ₁faɪ) *vb*. **-fying, -fied.** (*tr*.) to give new life or spirit to. —**re₁vivifi'cation** *n*.

revoke (rɪ'vəʊk) *vb*. **1.** (*tr*.) to take back or withdraw; cancel; rescind. **2.** (*intr*.) *Cards*. to break a rule by failing to follow suit when able to do so. ~*n*. **3.** *Cards*. the act of revoking. —**₁revo'cation** *n*. —**re'voker** *n*.

revolt (rɪ'vəʊlt) *n*. **1.** a rebellion or uprising against authority. **2. in revolt.** in the process or state of rebelling. ~*vb*. **3.** (*intr*.) to rise up in rebellion against authority. **4.** (*usually passive*) to feel or cause to feel revulsion, disgust, or abhorrence.

revolting (rɪ'vəʊltɪŋ) *adj*. **1.** causing revulsion; nauseating, disgusting, or repulsive. **2.** *Inf*. unpleasant or nasty. —**re'voltingly** *adv*.

revolution (₁revə'luːʃən) *n*. **1.** the overthrow or repudiation of a regime or political system by the governed. **2.** (in Marxist theory) the inevitable, violent transition from one system of production in a society to the next. **3.** a far-reaching and drastic change, esp. in ideas, methods, etc. **4. a.** movement in or as if in a circle. **b.** one complete turn in such a circle: *33 revolutions per minute*. **5. a.** the orbital motion of one body, such as a planet, around another. **b.** one complete turn in such motion. **6.** a cycle of successive events or changes.

revolutionary (₁revə'luːʃənərɪ) *n*., *pl*. **-aries. 1.** a person who advocates or engages in revolution. ~*adj*. **2.** relating to or characteristic of a revolution. **3.** advocating or engaged in revolution. **4.** radically new or different: *a revolutionary method of making plastics*.

THESAURUS

revert backslide, come back, go back, hark back, lapse, recur, regress, relapse, resume, return, take up where one left off

review *v*. **1.** go over again, look at again, reassess, recapitulate, reconsider, re-evaluate, re-examine, rethink, revise, run over, take another look at, think over **2.** call to mind, look back on, recall, recollect, reflect on, remember, summon up **3.** assess, criticize, discuss, evaluate, examine, give one's opinion of, inspect, judge, read through, scrutinize, study, weigh, write a critique of ~*n*. **4.** analysis, examination, report, scrutiny, study, survey **5.** commentary, critical assessment, criticism, critique, evaluation, judgment, notice, study **6.** journal, magazine, periodical **7.** another look, fresh look, reassessment, recapitulation, reconsideration, re-evaluation, re-examination, rethink, retrospect, revision, second look **8.** *Military* display, inspection, march past, parade, procession

reviewer arbiter, commentator, connoisseur, critic, essayist, judge

revise **1.** alter, amend, change, correct, edit, emend, modify, reconsider, redo, re-examine, revamp, review, rework, rewrite,

update **2.** go over, memorize, reread, run through, study, swot up (*Brit. inf.*)

revision 1. alteration, amendment, change, correction, editing, emendation, modification, re-examination, review, rewriting, updating **2.** homework, memorizing, rereading, studying, swotting (*Brit. inf.*)

revival awakening, quickening, reanimation, reawakening, rebirth, recrudescence, renaissance, renascence, renewal, restoration, resurgence, resurrection, resuscitation, revitalization, revivification

revive animate, awaken, breathe new life into, bring back to life, bring round, cheer, come round, comfort, invigorate, quicken, rally, reanimate, recover, refresh, rekindle, renew, renovate, restore, resuscitate, revitalize, rouse, spring up again

revoke abolish, abrogate, annul, call back, cancel, countermand, declare null and void, disclaim, invalidate, negate, nullify, quash, recall, recant, renounce, repeal, repudiate, rescind, retract, reverse, set aside, take back, withdraw

revolt *n*. **1.** defection, insurgency, insurrection, mutiny, putsch, rebellion, revolution, rising, sedition, uprising ~*v*. **2.** defect, muti-

ny, rebel, resist, rise, take to the streets, take up arms (against) **3.** disgust, give one the creeps (*Sl.*), make one's flesh creep, nauseate, offend, repel, repulse, shock, sicken, turn off (*Inf.*), turn one's stomach

revolting abhorrent, abominable, appalling, disgusting, distasteful, foul, horrible, horrid, loathsome, nasty, nauseating, nauseous, noisome, obnoxious, obscene, offensive, repellent, repugnant, repulsive, shocking, sickening

revolution *n*. **1.** coup, coup d'état, insurgency, mutiny, putsch, rebellion, revolt, rising, uprising **2.** drastic *or* radical change, innovation, metamorphosis, reformation, sea change, shift, transformation, upheaval **3.** circle, circuit, cycle, gyration, lap, orbit, rotation, round, spin, turn, wheel, whirl

revolutionary *n*. **1.** insurgent, insurrectionary, insurrectionist, mutineer, rebel, revolutionist ~*adj*. **2.** extremist, insurgent, insurrectionary, mutinous, radical, rebel, seditious, subversive **3.** avant-garde, different, drastic, experimental, fundamental, innovative, new, novel, progressive, radical, thoroughgoing

Revolutionary (ˌrɛvəˈluːʃənərɪ) *adj.* **1.** *Chiefly U.S.* of or relating to the War of American Independence (1775-83). **2.** of or relating to any of various other Revolutions, esp. the **Russian Revolution** (1917) or the **French Revolution** (1789).

revolutionize *or* **-ise** (ˌrɛvəˈluːʃəˌnaɪz) *vb.* (*tr.*) **1.** to bring about a radical change in: *science has revolutionized civilization.* **2.** to inspire or infect with revolutionary ideas: *they revolutionized the common soldiers.* **3.** to cause a revolution in (a country, etc.). —ˌrevoˈlutionˌizer *or* -ˌiser *n.*

revolve (rɪˈvɒlv) *vb.* **1.** to move or cause to move around a centre or axis; rotate. **2.** (*intr.*) to occur periodically or in cycles. **3.** to consider or be considered. **4.** (*intr.*; foll. by *around* or *about*) to be centred or focused (upon): *Juliet's thoughts revolved around Romeo.* —reˈvolvable *adj.*

revolver (rɪˈvɒlvə) *n.* a pistol having a revolving multichambered cylinder that allows several shots to be discharged without reloading.

revolving door *n.* a door that rotates about a vertical axis, esp. one with four leaves at right angles to each other, thereby excluding draughts.

revue *or* **review** (rɪˈvjuː) *n.* a light entertainment consisting of topical sketches, songs, dancing, etc.

revulsion (rɪˈvʌlʃən) *n.* **1.** a sudden violent reaction in feeling, esp. one of extreme loathing. **2.** the act or an instance of drawing back or recoiling from something. **3.** the diversion of disease from one part of the body to another by cupping, counterirritants, etc.

reward (rɪˈwɔːd) *n.* **1.** something given in return for a deed or service rendered. **2.** a sum of money offered, esp. for help in finding a criminal or for the return of lost or stolen property. **3.** profit or return. ~*vb.* **4.** (*tr.*) to give (something) to (someone), esp. in gratitude for a service rendered; recompense. —reˈwardless *adj.*

rewarding (rɪˈwɔːdɪŋ) *adj.* giving personal satisfaction; gratifying.

rewind *vb.* (riːˈwaɪnd), **-winding, -wound. 1.** (*tr.*) to wind back, esp. a film or tape onto the original reel. ~*n.* (ˈriːˌwaɪnd, riːˈwaɪnd). **2.** something rewound. **3.** the act of rewinding. —reˈwinder *n.*

rewire (riːˈwaɪə) *vb.* (*tr.*) to provide (a house, engine, etc.) with new wiring. —reˈwiring *adj.*

reword (riːˈwɜːd) *vb.* (*tr.*) to alter the wording of; express differently.

rewrite *vb.* (riːˈraɪt), **-writing, -wrote, -written.** (*tr.*) **1.** to write (material) again, esp. changing the words or form. ~*n.* (ˈriːˌraɪt). **2.** something rewritten.

Rex (rɛks) *n.* king: part of the official title of a king, now used chiefly in documents, legal proceedings, on coins, etc. Cf. **Regina.**

Rexine (ˈrɛksiːn) *n. Trademark.* a form of artificial leather.

Reynard *or* **Renard** (ˈrɛnəd, ˈrɛnɑːd) *n.* a name for a fox, used in fables, etc.

RF *abbrev. for* radio frequency.

R.F.C. *abbrev. for* Rugby Football Club.

R.G.S. *abbrev. for* Royal Geographical Society.

Rh 1. *the chemical symbol for* rhodium. **2.** *abbrev. for* rhesus (esp. in **Rh factor**).

r.h. *or* **R.H.** *abbrev. for* right hand.

rhabdomancy (ˈræbdəˌmænsɪ) *n.* divination for water or mineral ore by means of a rod or wand. —ˈrhabdoˌmantist *or* ˈrhabdoˌmancer *n.*

rhapsodize *or* **-ise** (ˈræpsəˌdaɪz) *vb.* **1.** to speak or write (something) with extravagant enthusiasm. **2.** (*intr.*) to recite or write rhapsodies. —ˈrhapsodist *n.*

rhapsody (ˈræpsədɪ) *n., pl.* **-dies. 1.** *Music.* a composition, free in structure and highly emotional in character. **2.** an expression of ecstatic enthusiasm. **3.** (in ancient

Greece) an epic poem or part of an epic recited by a rhapsodist. **4.** a literary work composed in an intense or exalted style. **5.** rapturous delight or ecstasy. —ˈrhapˈsodic *adj.*

rhea (ˈrɪə) *n.* either of two large fast-running flightless birds inhabiting the open plains of S South America. They are similar to but smaller than the ostrich.

Rhenish (ˈrɛnɪʃ, ˈriː-) *adj.* **1.** of or relating to the River Rhine or the lands adjacent to it. ~*n.* **2.** another word for **hock** (the wine).

rhenium (ˈriːnɪəm) *n.* a dense silvery-white metallic element that has a high melting point. Symbol: Re; atomic no.: 75; atomic wt.: 186.2.

rheostat (ˈrɪəˌstæt) *n.* a variable resistance, usually a coil of wire with a terminal at one end and a sliding contact that moves along the coil to tap off the current. —ˌrheoˈstatic *adj.*

rhesus factor *n.* See **Rh factor.**

rhesus monkey *n.* a macaque monkey of S Asia.

rhetoric (ˈrɛtərɪk) *n.* **1.** the study of the technique of using language effectively. **2.** the art of using speech to persuade, influence, or please; oratory. **3.** excessive ornamentation and contrivance in spoken or written discourse; bombast. **4.** speech or discourse that pretends to significance but lacks true meaning: *mere rhetoric.* —rheˈtorical *adj.* —rheˈtorically *adv.*

rhetorical question *n.* a question to which no answer is required: used esp. for dramatic effect. An example is *Who knows?* (with the implication *Nobody knows*).

rheum (ruːm) *n.* a watery discharge from the eyes or nose. —ˈrheumy *adj.*

rheumatic (ruːˈmætɪk) *adj.* **1.** of, relating to, or afflicted with rheumatism. ~*n.* **2.** a person afflicted with rheumatism. —rheuˈmatically *adv.*

rheumatic fever *n.* a disease characterized by inflammation and pain in the joints.

rheumatics (ruːˈmætɪks) *n. Inf.* rheumatism.

rheumatism (ˈruːməˌtɪzəm) *n.* any painful disorder of joints, muscles, or connective tissue.

rheumatoid (ˈruːməˌtɔɪd) *or* **rheumatoidal** *adj.* (of symptoms) resembling rheumatism.

rheumatoid arthritis *n.* a chronic disease characterized by inflammation and swelling of joints (esp. in the hands, wrists, knees, and feet), muscle weakness, and fatigue.

Rh factor *n.* an antigen commonly found in human blood: the terms **Rh positive** and **Rh negative** are used to indicate its presence or absence. It may cause a haemolytic reaction, esp. during pregnancy or following transfusion of blood that does not contain this antigen. Full name: **rhesus factor.**

rhinal (ˈraɪnəl) *adj.* of or relating to the nose.

rhinestone (ˈraɪnˌstəʊn) *n.* an imitation gem made of paste.

rhino (ˈraɪnəʊ) *n., pl.* **-nos** *or* **-no.** short for **rhinoceros.**

rhinoceros (raɪˈnɒsərəs, -ˈnɒsrəs) *n., pl.* **-oses** *or* **-os.** any of several mammals constituting a family of SE Asia and Africa and having either one horn, like the **Indian rhinoceros,** or two horns, like the African **white rhinoceros.** They have a very thick skin and a massive body.

rhizome (ˈraɪzəʊm) *n.* a thick horizontal underground stem whose buds develop into new plants. Also called: **rootstock, rootstalk.** —**rhizomatous** (raɪˈzɒmətəs, -ˈzəʊ-) *adj.*

rho (rəʊ) *n., pl.* **rhos.** the 17th letter in the Greek alphabet (P, ρ).

Rhodes scholarship (rəʊdz) *n.* one of 72 scholarships founded by Cecil Rhodes, (1853-1902), English statesman, awarded annually to Commonwealth and U.S.

THESAURUS

revolve 1. circle, go round, gyrate, orbit, rotate, spin, turn, twist, wheel, whirl **2.** consider, deliberate, meditate, mull over, ponder, reflect, ruminate, study, think about, think over, turn over (in one's mind)

revulsion abhorrence, abomination, aversion, detestation, disgust, distaste, loathing, recoil, repugnance, repulsion

reward *n.* **1.** benefit, bonus, bounty, compensation, gain, honour, merit, payment, premium, prize, profit, recompense, remunera-

tion, repayment, requital, return, wages **2.** comeuppance (*Sl.*), desert, just deserts, punishment, requital, retribution ~*v.* **3.** compensate, honour, make it worth one's while, pay, recompense, remunerate, repay, requite

rewarding advantageous, beneficial, edifying, enriching, fruitful, fulfilling, gainful, gratifying, pleasing, productive, profitable, remunerative, satisfying, valuable, worthwhile

rhetoric 1. eloquence, oratory **2.** bom-

bast, fustian, grandiloquence, hot air (*Inf.*), hyperbole, magniloquence, pomposity, rant, verbosity, wordiness

rhetorical 1. bombastic, declamatory, flamboyant, flashy, florid, flowery, grandiloquent, high-flown, high-sounding, hyperbolic, magniloquent, oratorical, pompous, pretentious, showy, silver-tongued, verbose, windy **2.** linguistic, oratorical, stylistic, verbal

students to study at Oxford University. —**Rhodes scholar** *n.*

rhodium (ˈrəʊdɪəm) *n.* a hard silvery-white element of the platinum metal group. Used as an alloying agent to harden platinum and palladium. Symbol: Rh; atomic no.: 45; atomic wt.: 102.90.

rhododendron (ˌrəʊdəˈdɛndrən) *n.* any of various shrubs native to S Asia but widely cultivated in N temperate regions. They are mostly evergreen and have clusters of showy red, purple, pink, or white flowers.

rhombohedron (ˌrɒmbəʊˈhiːdrən) *n.* a six-sided prism whose sides are parallelograms.

rhomboid (ˈrɒmbɔɪd) *n.* **1.** a parallelogram having adjacent sides of unequal length. ∼*adj. also* **rhomˈboidal. 2.** having such a shape.

rhombus (ˈrɒmbəs) *n., pl.* **-buses** *or* **-bi** (-baɪ). an oblique-angled parallelogram having four equal sides. Also called: **rhomb.** —**ˈrhombic** *adj.*

R.H.S. *abbrev. for:* **1.** Royal Historical Society. **2.** Royal Horticultural Society. **3.** Royal Humane Society.

rhubarb (ˈruːbɑːb) *n.* **1.** any of several temperate and subtropical plants, esp. **common garden rhubarb,** which has long green and red acid-tasting edible leafstalks, usually eaten sweetened and cooked. **2.** the leafstalks of this plant. **3.** a related plant of central Asia, having a bitter-tasting underground stem that can be dried and used as a laxative or astringent. **4.** *U.S. sl.* a heated discussion or quarrel. ∼*interj., n., vb.* **5.** the noise made by actors to simulate conversation, esp. by repeating the word *rhubarb.*

rhumba (ˈrʌmbə, ˈrʊm-) *n., pl.* **-bas.** a variant spelling of **rumba.**

rhyme *or* **rime** (raɪm) *n.* **1.** identity of the terminal sounds in lines of verse or in words. **2.** a word that is identical to another in its terminal sound: *"while" is a rhyme for "mile".* **3.** a piece of poetry, esp. having corresponding sounds at the ends of the lines. **4. rhyme or reason.** sense, logic, or meaning. ∼*vb.* **5.** to use (a word) or (of a word) to be used so as to form a rhyme. **6.** to render (a subject) into rhyme. **7.** to compose (verse) in a metrical structure. ∼*See also* **eye rhyme.** —**ˈrhymeless** *or* **ˈrimeless** *adj.*

rhymester, rimester (ˈraɪmstə), **rhymer,** *or* **rimer** (ˈraɪmə) *n.* a poet, esp. one considered to be mediocre; poetaster or versifier.

rhyming slang *n.* slang in which a word is replaced by another word or phrase that rhymes with it; e.g., *apples and pears* meaning *stairs.*

rhythm (ˈrɪðəm) *n.* **1. a.** the arrangement of the durations and accents on the notes of a melody, usually laid out into regular groups (**bars**) of beats. **b.** any specific arrangement of such groupings; time: *quadruple rhythm.* **2.** (in poetry) **a.** the arrangement of words into a sequence of stressed and unstressed or long and short syllables. **b.** any specific sequence of arrangement; metre. **3.** (in painting, sculpture, etc.) a harmonious sequence or pattern of masses alternating with voids, of light alternating with shade, of alternating colours, etc. **4.** any sequence of regularly recurring functions or events, such as certain physiological functions of the body. —**ˈrhythmical** *or* **ˈrhythmic** *adj.* —**ˈrhythmically** *adv.*

rhythm-and-blues *n.* any of various kinds of popular music derived from or influenced by the blues. Abbrev.: **R & B**

rhythm method *n.* a method of contraception by restricting sexual intercourse to those days in a woman's menstrual cycle when conception is considered least likely to occur.

rialto (rɪˈæltəʊ) *n., pl.* **-tos.** a market or exchange.

rib[1] (rɪb) *n.* **1.** any of the 24 elastic arches of bone that together form the chest wall in man. All are attached behind to the thoracic part of the spinal column. **2.** the corresponding bone in other vertebrates. **3.** a cut of meat including one or more ribs. **4.** a part or element similar in function or appearance to a rib, esp. a structural member or a ridge. **5.** a structural member in an aerofoil that extends from the leading edge to the trailing edge. **6.** a projecting moulding or band on the underside of a vault or ceiling. **7.** one of a series of raised rows in knitted fabric. **8.** a raised ornamental line on the spine of a book where the stitching runs across it. **9.** any of the transverse stiffening timbers or joists forming the frame of a ship's hull. **10.** any of the larger veins of a leaf. **11.** a vein of ore in rock. **12.** a projecting ridge of a mountain; spur. ∼*vb.* **ribbing, ribbed.** (*tr.*) **13.** to furnish or support with a rib or ribs. **14.** to mark with or form into ribs or ridges. **15.** to knit plain and purl stitches alternately in order to make raised rows in (knitting). —**ˈribless** *adj.*

rib[2] (rɪb) *vb.* **ribbing, ribbed.** (*tr.*) *Inf.* to tease or ridicule.

R.I.B.A. *abbrev.* for Royal Institute of British Architects.

ribald (ˈrɪbəld) *adj.* **1.** coarse, obscene, or licentious, usually in a humorous or mocking way. ∼*n.* **2.** a ribald person. —**ˈribaldry** *n.*

riband *or* **ribband** (ˈrɪbənd) *n.* a ribbon, esp. one awarded for some achievement.

ribbing (ˈrɪbɪŋ) *n.* **1.** a framework or structure of ribs. **2.** a pattern of ribs in woven or knitted material. **3.** *Inf.* teasing.

ribbon (ˈrɪbən) *n.* **1.** a narrow strip of fine material, esp. silk, used for trimming, tying, etc. **2.** something resembling a ribbon; a long strip. **3.** a long thin flexible band of metal used as a graduated measure, spring, etc. **4.** a long narrow strip of ink-impregnated cloth for making the impression of type characters on paper in a typewriter, etc. **5.** (*pl.*) ragged strips or shreds (esp. in **torn to ribbons**). **6.** a small strip of coloured cloth signifying membership of an order or award of military decoration, prize, etc. ∼*vb.* (*tr.*) **7.** to adorn with a ribbon or ribbons. **8.** to mark with narrow ribbon-like marks.

ribbon development *n. Brit.* the building of houses in a continuous row along a main road.

riboflavin *or* **riboflavine** (ˌraɪbəʊˈfleɪvɪn) *n.* a vitamin of the B complex that occurs in green vegetables, milk, fish, egg yolk, liver, and kidney. Also called: **vitamin B₂.**

ribonucleic acid (ˌraɪbəʊnjuːˈkliːɪk, -ˈkleɪ-) *n.* the full name of **RNA.**

rice (raɪs) *n.* **1.** an erect grass that grows in East Asia on wet ground and has yellow oblong edible grains that become white when polished. **2.** the grain of this plant. ∼*vb.* **3.** (*tr.*) *U.S.* to sieve (potatoes or other vegetables) to a coarse mashed consistency.

rice paper *n.* **1.** a thin edible paper made from the straw of rice, on which macaroons and similar cakes are baked. **2.** a thin delicate Chinese paper made from the **rice-paper plant,** the pith of which is pared and flattened into sheets.

rich (rɪtʃ) *adj.* **1. a.** well supplied with wealth, property, etc.; owning much. **b.** (*as collective n.*): *the rich.* **2.** (when *postpositive,* usually foll. by *in*) having an abundance of natural resources, minerals, etc.: *a land rich in metals.* **3.** producing abundantly; fertile: *rich soil.* **4.** (when *postpositive,* foll. by *in* or *with*) well supplied (with desirable qualities); abundant (in): *a country rich with cultural interest.* **5.** of great worth or quality: *a rich collection of antiques.* **6.** luxuriant or prolific: *a rich growth of weeds.* **7.** expensively elegant, elaborate, or fine; costly: *a rich display.* **8.** (of food) having a large proportion of flavoursome or fatty ingredients. **9.** having a full-bodied flavour: *a rich ruby port.* **10.** (of a smell) pungent or fragrant. **11.** (of colour) intense or vivid; deep: *a rich red.* **12.** (of sound or a voice) full, mellow, or resonant. **13.** (of a fuel-air mixture) containing a relatively high proportion of fuel. **14.** very amusing or ridiculous: *a rich joke.* ∼*n.* **15.** See **riches.** —**ˈrichness** *n.*

▌THESAURUS▐

rhyme *n.* **1.** ode, poem, poetry, song, verse **2. rhyme or reason** logic, meaning, method, plan, sense ∼*v.* **3.** chime, harmonize, sound like

rhythm accent, beat, cadence, flow, lilt, measure (*Prosody*), metre, movement, pattern, periodicity, pulse, swing, tempo, time

rhythmic, rhythmical cadenced, flowing, harmonious, lilting, melodious, metrical, musical, periodic, pulsating, throbbing

ribald bawdy, blue, broad, coarse, earthy, filthy, gross, indecent, licentious, naughty, near the knuckle (*Inf.*), obscene, off colour, Rabelaisian, racy, risqué, rude, scurrilous, smutty, vulgar

rich 1. affluent, filthy rich (*Inf.*), flush (*Inf.*), loaded (*Sl.*), made of money (*Inf.*), moneyed, opulent, propertied, prosperous, rolling (*Sl.*), stinking rich (*Inf.*), wealthy, well-heeled (*Sl.*), well-off, well-to-do **2.** abounding, full, productive, well-endowed, well-provided, well-stocked, well-supplied **3.** abounding, abundant, ample, copious, exuberant, fecund, fertile, fruitful, full, lush, luxurious, plenteous, plentiful, productive, prolific **4.** beyond price, costly, elaborate, elegant, expensive, exquisite, fine, gorgeous, lavish, palatial, precious,

riches ('rɪtʃɪz) *pl. n.* wealth; an abundance of money, valuable possessions, or property.

Richter scale ('rɪktə) *n.* a scale for expressing the intensity of an earthquake, ranging from 0 to over 8.

rick[1] (rɪk) *n.* **1.** a large stack of hay, corn, etc., built in a regular-shaped pile, esp. with a thatched top. ~*vb.* **2.** (*tr.*) to stack into ricks.

rick[2] (rɪk) *n.* **1.** a wrench or sprain, as of the back. ~*vb.* **2.** (*tr.*) to wrench or sprain (a joint, limb, the back, etc.)

rickets ('rɪkɪts) *n.* a disease mainly of children, characterized by softening of developing bone, and hence bow legs, caused by a deficiency of vitamin D.

rickettsia (rɪ'kɛtsɪə) *n., pl.* **-siae** (-sɪ,iː) *or* **-sias.** any of a group of parasitic microorganisms, that live in the tissues of ticks, mites, etc. and cause disease when transmitted to man. —**rick'ettsial** *adj.*

rickety ('rɪkɪtɪ) *adj.* **1.** (of a structure, piece of furniture, etc.) likely to collapse or break. **2.** feeble. **3.** resembling or afflicted with rickets. —'**ricketiness** *n.*

rickrack *or* **ricrac** ('rɪk,ræk) *n.* a zigzag braid used for trimming.

rickshaw ('rɪkʃɔː) *or* **ricksha** ('rɪkʃə) *n.* **1.** Also called: **jinrikisha.** a small two-wheeled passenger vehicle drawn by one or two men, used in parts of Asia. **2.** Also called: **trishaw.** a similar vehicle with three wheels, propelled by a man pedalling as on a tricycle.

ricochet ('rɪkə,ʃeɪ, 'rɪkə,ʃɛt) *vb.* **-cheting** (-,ʃeɪŋ), **-cheted** (-,ʃeɪd) *or* **-chetting** (-,ʃɛtɪŋ), **-chetted** (-,ʃɛtɪd). **1.** (*intr.*) (esp. of a bullet) to rebound from a surface, usually with a whining or zipping sound. ~*n.* **2.** the motion or sound of a rebounding object, esp. a bullet.

R.I.C.S. *abbrev. for* Royal Institution of Chartered Surveyors.

rid (rɪd) *vb.* **ridding, rid** *or* **ridded.** (*tr.*) **1.** (foll. by *of*) to relieve from something disagreeable or undesirable; make free (of). **2. get rid of.** to relieve or free oneself of (something unpleasant or undesirable).

riddance ('rɪdəns) *n.* the act of getting rid of something; removal (esp. in **good riddance**).

ridden ('rɪdən) *vb.* **1.** the past participle of **ride.** ~*adj.* **2.** (*in combination*) afflicted or dominated by something specified: *disease-ridden.*

riddle[1] ('rɪdəl) *n.* **1.** a question, puzzle, or verse so phrased that ingenuity is required for elucidation of the answer or meaning. **2.** a person or thing that puzzles, perplexes, or confuses. ~*vb.* **3.** to solve, explain, or interpret (a riddle). **4.** (*intr.*) to speak in riddles. —'**riddler** *n.*

riddle[2] ('rɪdəl) *vb.* (*tr.*) **1.** (usually foll. by *with*) to pierce or perforate with numerous holes: *riddled with bullets.* **2.** to put through a sieve; sift. ~*n.* **3.** a sieve, esp. a coarse one used for sand, grain, etc. —'**riddler** *n.*

ride (raɪd) *vb.* **riding, rode, ridden. 1.** to sit on and control the movements of (a horse or other animal). **2.** (*tr.*) to sit on and propel (a bicycle or similar vehicle). **3.** (*intr.*; often foll. by *on* or *in*) to be carried along or travel on or in a vehicle: *she rides to work on the bus.* **4.** (*tr.*) to travel over or traverse: *they rode the countryside in search of shelter.* **5.** (*tr.*) to take part in by riding: *to ride a race.* **6.** (*tr.*) to travel through or be carried across (sea, sky, etc.): *the small boat rode the waves; the moon was riding high.* **7.** (*tr.*) *U.S.* to cause to be carried: *to ride someone out of town.* **8.** (*intr.*) to be supported as if floating: *the candidate rode to victory on his new policies.* **9.** (*intr.*) (of a vessel) to lie at anchor. **10.** (*tr.*) (of

a vessel) to be attached to (an anchor). **11.** (*tr.*) (esp. of a male animal) to copulate with; mount. **12.** (*tr.*; *usually passive*) to tyrannize over or dominate: *ridden by fear.* **13.** (*tr.*) *Inf.* to persecute, esp. by constant or petty criticism: *don't ride me so hard.* **14.** (*intr.*) *Inf.* to continue undisturbed: *let it ride.* **15.** (*intr.*; often foll. by *on*) (of a bet) to remain placed: *let your winnings ride on the same number.* **16. ride roughshod over.** to act with complete disregard (for). **17. ride for a fall.** to act in such a way as to invite disaster. **18. ride again.** *Inf.* to return to a former activity or scene. **19. riding high.** confident, popular, and successful. ~*n.* **20.** a journey or outing on horseback or in a vehicle. **21.** a path specially made for riding on horseback. **22.** transport in a vehicle; lift: *can you give me a ride to the station?* **23.** a device or structure, such as a roller coaster at a fairground, in which people ride for pleasure or entertainment. **24. take for a ride.** *Inf.* **a.** to cheat, swindle, or deceive. **b.** to take (someone) away in a car and murder him. ~*See* also **ride out, ride up.** —'**ridable** *or* '**rideable** *adj.*

ride out *vb.* (*tr., adv.*) to endure successfully; survive (esp. in **ride out the storm**).

rider ('raɪdə) *n.* **1.** a person or thing that rides. **2.** an additional clause, amendment, or stipulation added to a document, esp. (in Britain) a legislative bill at its third reading. **3.** *Brit.* a statement made by a jury in addition to its verdict, such as a recommendation for mercy. **4.** *Maths.* a problem arising out of a theorem. **5.** any of various objects or devices resting on or strengthening something else. —'**riderless** *adj.*

ride up *vb.* (*intr., adv.*) to work away from the proper position: *her new skirt rode up.*

ridge (rɪdʒ) *n.* **1.** a long narrow raised land formation with sloping sides. **2.** any long narrow raised strip or elevation, as on a fabric or in ploughed land. **3.** *Anat.* any elongated raised margin or border on a bone, tissue etc. **4. a.** the top of a roof at the junction of two sloping sides. **b.** (*as modifier*): *a ridge tile.* **5.** *Meteorol.* an elongated area of high pressure, esp. an extension of an anticyclone. Cf. **trough** (sense 4). ~*vb.* **6.** to form into a ridge or ridges. —'**ridge,like** *adj.* —'**ridgy** *adj.*

ridgepole ('rɪdʒ,pəʊl) *n.* **1.** a timber along the ridge of a roof, to which the rafters are attached. **2.** the horizontal pole at the apex of a tent.

ridicule ('rɪdɪ,kjuːl) *n.* **1.** language or behaviour intended to humiliate or mock. ~*vb.* **2.** (*tr.*) to make fun of or mock.

ridiculous (rɪ'dɪkjʊləs) *adj.* worthy of or exciting ridicule; absurd, preposterous, laughable, or contemptible. —ri'**diculousness** *n.*

riding[1] ('raɪdɪŋ) *n.* **1. a.** the art or practice of horsemanship. **b.** (*as modifier*): *a riding school.* **2.** a track for riding.

riding[2] ('raɪdɪŋ) *n.* (*cap. when part of a name*) any of the three former administrative divisions of Yorkshire: **North Riding, East Riding,** and **West Riding**

riding crop *n.* a short whip with a handle at one end for opening gates.

riesling ('riːzlɪŋ, 'raɪz-) *n.* **1.** a dry white wine from the Rhine valley in Germany and from certain districts in Austria, Hungary, and Yugoslavia. **2.** the grape used to make this wine.

rife (raɪf) *adj.* (*postpositive*) **1.** of widespread occurrence; current. **2.** very plentiful; abundant. **3.** (foll. by *with*) rich or abounding (in): *a garden rife with flowers.* —'**rifely** *adv.* —'**rifeness** *n.*

THESAURUS

priceless, splendid, sumptuous, superb, valuable **5.** creamy, delicious, fatty, flavoursome, full-bodied, heavy, highly-flavoured, juicy, luscious, savoury, spicy, succulent, sweet, tasty **6.** bright, deep, gay, intense, strong, vibrant, vivid, warm **7.** deep, dulcet, full, mellifluous, mellow, resonant **8.** amusing, comical, funny, hilarious, humorous, laughable, ludicrous, ridiculous, risible, side-splitting

riches abundance, affluence, assets, fortune, gold, money, opulence, plenty, property, resources, richness, substance, treasure, wealth

richly 1. elaborately, elegantly, expensively, exquisitely, gorgeously, lavishly, luxuriously, opulently, palatially, splendidly, sumptuously **2.** amply, appropriately, fully, in full

measure, properly, suitably, thoroughly, well

rid 1. clear, deliver, disabuse, disburden, disembarrass, disencumber, free, make free, purge, relieve, unburden **2. get rid of** dispense with, dispose of, do away with, dump, eject, eliminate, expel, jettison, remove, shake off, throw away *or* out, unload, weed out

riddle brain-teaser (*Inf.*), Chinese puzzle, conundrum, enigma, mystery, poser, problem, puzzle, rebus

ride *v.* **1.** control, handle, manage, sit on **2.** be borne (carried, supported), float, go, journey, move, progress, sit, travel **3.** dominate, enslave, grip, haunt, oppress, tyrannize over ~*n.* **4.** drive, jaunt, journey, lift, outing, spin (*Inf.*), trip, whirl (*Inf.*)

ridicule 1. *n.* banter, chaff, derision, gibe, irony, jeer, laughter, mockery, raillery, sarcasm, satire, scorn, sneer, taunting **2.** *v.* banter, caricature, chaff, deride, humiliate, jeer, lampoon, laugh at, laugh out of court, laugh to scorn, make a fool of, make fun of, make one a laughing stock, mock, parody, poke fun at, pooh-pooh, satirize, scoff, send up (*Brit. inf.*), sneer, take the mickey out of (*Inf.*), taunt

ridiculous absurd, comical, contemptible, derisory, farcical, foolish, funny, hilarious, incredible, laughable, ludicrous, nonsensical, outrageous, preposterous, risible, silly, stupid, unbelievable

riffle ('rɪfəl) vb. 1. (when intr., often foll. by through) to flick rapidly through (pages of a book, etc.). 2. to shuffle (cards) by halving the pack and flicking the corners together. 3. to make or become a riffle. ~n. 4. U.S. a. a rapid in a stream. b. a rocky shoal causing a rapid. c. a ripple on water. 5. Mining. a contrivance on the bottom of a sluice, containing grooves for trapping particles of gold. 6. the act or an instance of riffling.

riffraff ('rɪf,ræf) n. (sometimes functioning as pl.) worthless people, esp. collectively; rabble.

rifle¹ ('raɪfəl) n. 1. a. a firearm having a long barrel with a spirally grooved interior, which imparts to the bullet spinning motion and thus greater accuracy over a longer range. b. (as modifier): rifle fire. 2. (formerly) a large cannon with a rifled bore. 3. one of the grooves in a rifled bore. 4. (pl.) a. a unit of soldiers equipped with rifles. b. (cap. as part of a name): the King's Own Rifles. ~vb. (tr.) 5. to make spiral grooves inside the barrel of (a gun).

rifle² ('raɪfəl) vb. (tr.) 1. to search (a house, safe, etc.) and steal from it; ransack. 2. to steal and carry off: to rifle goods. —'rifler n.

rifling ('raɪflɪŋ) n. 1. the cutting of spiral grooves on the inside of a firearm's barrel. 2. the series of grooves so cut.

rift (rɪft) n. 1. a gap or space made by cleaving or splitting. 2. Geol. a fault produced by tension on either side of the fault plane. 3. a gap between two cloud masses; break or chink. 4. a break in friendly relations between people, nations, etc. ~vb. 5. to burst or cause to burst open; split.

rift valley n. a long narrow valley resulting from the subsidence of land between two faults.

rig (rɪg) vb. **rigging, rigged.** (tr.) 1. Naut. to equip (a vessel, mast, etc.) with (sails, rigging, etc.). 2. Naut. to set up or prepare ready for use. 3. to put the components of (an aircraft, etc.) into their correct positions. 4. to manipulate in a fraudulent manner, esp. for profit: to rig prices. ~n. 5. Naut. the distinctive arrangement of the sails, masts, etc., of a vessel. 6. the installation used in drilling for and exploiting petroleum and natural gas deposits: an oil rig. 7. apparatus or equipment. 8. U.S. an articulated lorry. ~See also **rig out, rig up.**

-rigged adj. (in combination) (of a sailing vessel) having a rig of a certain kind: ketch-rigged; schooner-rigged.

rigging ('rɪgɪŋ) n. 1. the shrouds, stays, etc., of a vessel. 2. the bracing wires, struts, and lines of a biplane, etc. 3. any form of lifting gear.

right (raɪt) adj. 1. in accordance with accepted standards of moral or legal behaviour, justice, etc.: right conduct. 2. correct or true: the right answer. 3. appropriate, suitable, or proper: the right man for the job. 4. most favourable or convenient: the right time to act. 5. in a satisfactory condition: things are right again now. 6. indicating or designating the correct time: the clock is right. 7. correct in opinion or judgment. 8. sound in mind or body. 9. (usually prenominal) of, designating, or located near the side of something or someone that faces east when the front is turned towards the north. 10. (usually prenominal) worn on a right hand, foot, etc. 11. (sometimes cap.) of, designating, belonging to, or relat-

ing to the political or intellectual right (see sense 34). 12. (sometimes cap.) conservative: the right wing of the party. 13. Geom. a. formed by or containing a line or plane perpendicular to another line or plane. b. having the axis perpendicular to the base: a right circular cone. c. straight: a right line. 14. relating to or designating the side of cloth worn or facing outwards. 15. in one's right mind. sane. 16. the right side of. a. in favour with: you'd better stay on the right side of him. b. younger than: she's still on the right side of fifty. ~adv. 17. in accordance with correctness or truth: to guess right. 18. in the appropriate manner: do it right next time! 19. in a straight line: right to the top. 20. in the direction of the east from the point of view of a person or thing facing north. 21. absolutely or completely: he went right through the floor. 22. without delay: I'll be right over. 23. exactly or precisely: right here. 24. in a manner consistent with a legal or moral code: do right by me. 25. in accordance with propriety; fittingly: it serves you right. 26. to good or favourable advantage: it all came out right in the end. 27. (esp. in religious titles) most or very: right reverend. 28. **right, left, and centre.** on all sides. 29. **she'll be right.** Austral. & N.Z. inf. that's all right; not to worry. ~n. 30. any claim, title, etc., that is morally just or legally granted as allowable or due to a person: I know my rights. 31. anything that accords with the principles of legal or moral justice. 32. the fact or state of being in accordance with reason, truth, or accepted standards (esp. in **in the right**). 33. the right side, direction, position, area, or part: the right of the army. 34. (often cap. and preceded by the) the supporters or advocates of social, political, or economic conservatism or reaction. 35. Boxing. a. a punch with the right hand. b. the right hand. 36. Finance. (often pl.) the privilege of a company's shareholders to subscribe for new issues of the company's shares on advantageous terms. 37. **by right** (or **rights**). properly: by rights you should be in bed. 38. **in one's own right.** having a claim or title oneself rather than through marriage or other connection. 39. **to rights.** consistent with justice or orderly arrangement: he put the matter to rights. ~vb. (mainly tr.) 40. (also intr.) to restore to or attain a normal, esp. an upright, position: the raft righted in a few seconds. 41. to make (something) accord with truth or facts. 42. to restore to an orderly state or condition. 43. to compensate for or redress (esp. in **right a wrong**). ~interj. 44. an expression of agreement or compliance. —'rightable adj. —'righter n. —'rightness n.

right angle n. 1. the angle between two perpendicular lines; an angle of 90°. 2. **at right angles.** perpendicular or perpendicularly. —'right-,angled adj.

right-angled triangle n. a triangle one angle of which is a right angle. U.S. name: **right triangle.**

right away adv. without delay.

righteous ('raɪtʃəs) adj. 1. a. characterized by, proceeding from, or in accordance with accepted standards of morality, justice, or uprightness: a righteous man. b. (as n.): the righteous. 2. morally justifiable or right: righteous indignation. —'righteously adv. —'righteousness n.

THESAURUS

riffraff canaille, dregs of society, hoi polloi, rabble, ragtag and bobtail, scum, undesirables

rifle v. burgle, despoil, go through, gut, loot, pillage, plunder, ransack, rob, rummage, sack, strip

rift 1. breach, break, chink, cleavage, cleft, crack, cranny, crevice, fault, fissure, flaw, fracture, gap, opening, space, split 2. alienation, breach, difference, disagreement, division, estrangement, falling out (Inf.), quarrel, schism, separation, split

rig v. 1. accoutre, equip, fit out, furnish, kit out, outfit, provision, supply, turn out 2. arrange, doctor, engineer, fake, falsify, fiddle with (Inf.), fix (Inf.), gerrymander, juggle, manipulate, tamper with, trump up ~n. 3. accoutrements, apparatus, equipage, equipment, fitments, fittings, fixtures, gear, machinery, outfit, tackle

right adj. 1. equitable, ethical, fair, good,

honest, honourable, just, lawful, moral, proper, righteous, true, upright, virtuous 2. accurate, admissible, authentic, correct, exact, factual, genuine, precise, satisfactory, sound, spot-on (Brit. inf.), true, unerring, valid, veracious 3. advantageous, appropriate, becoming, comme il faut, convenient, deserved, desirable, done, due, favourable, fit, fitting, ideal, opportune, proper, propitious, rightful, seemly, suitable 4. all there (Inf.), balanced, compos mentis, fine, fit, healthy, in good health, in the pink, lucid, normal, rational, reasonable, sane, sound, unimpaired, up to par, well 5. conservative, reactionary, Tory 6. absolute, complete, out-and-out, real, thorough, thoroughgoing, utter ~adv. 7. accurately, aright, correctly, exactly, factually, genuinely, precisely, truly 8. appropriately, aptly, befittingly, fittingly, properly, satisfactorily, suitably 9. directly, immediately, instantly, promptly, quickly, straight, straightaway, without delay 10. bang, exactly, precisely, slap-bang (Inf.), squarely 11. absolute-

ly, all the way, altogether, completely, entirely, perfectly, quite, thoroughly, totally, utterly, wholly 12. ethically, fairly, honestly, honourably, justly, morally, properly, righteously, virtuously 13. advantageously, beneficially, favourably, for the better, fortunately, to advantage, well ~n. 14. authority, business, claim, due, freedom, interest, liberty, licence, permission, power, prerogative, privilege, title 15. equity, good, goodness, honour, integrity, justice, lawfulness, legality, morality, propriety, reason, rectitude, righteousness, truth, uprightness, virtue 16. **by rights** equitably, in fairness, justly, properly 17. **to rights** arranged, in order, straight, tidy ~v. 18. compensate for, correct, fix, put right, rectify, redress, repair, settle, set upright, sort out, straighten, vindicate

right away at once, directly, forthwith, immediately, instantly, now, promptly, right off, straightaway, straight off (Inf.), this instant, without delay, without hesitation

rightful (ˈraɪtfʊl) *adj.* **1.** in accordance with what is right. **2.** (*prenominal*) having a legally or morally just claim: *the rightful owner.* **3.** (*prenominal*) held by virtue of a legal or just claim: *my rightful property.* —ˈrightfully *adv.*

right-hand *adj.* (*prenominal*) **1.** of, located on, or moving towards the right: *a right-hand bend.* **2.** for use by the right hand. **3. right-hand man.** one's most valuable assistant.

right-handed *adj.* **1.** using the right hand with greater skill or ease than the left. **2.** performed with the right hand. **3.** made for use by the right hand. **4.** turning from left to right. —ˌright-ˈhandedness *n.*

rightist (ˈraɪtɪst) *adj.* **1.** of, tending towards, or relating to the political right or its principles. ~*n.* **2.** a person who supports or belongs to the political right. —ˈrightism *n.*

rightly (ˈraɪtlɪ) *adv.* **1.** in accordance with the true facts. **2.** in accordance with principles of justice or morality. **3.** with good reason: *he was rightly annoyed with her.* **4.** properly or suitably. **5.** (*used with a negative*) *Inf.* with certainty (usually in **I don't rightly know**).

right-minded *adj.* holding opinions or principles that accord with what is right or with the opinions of the speaker.

right of way *n., pl.* **rights of way. 1.** the right of one vehicle or vessel to take precedence over another, as laid down by law or custom. **2. a.** the legal right of someone to pass over another's land, acquired by grant or by long usage. **b.** the path used by this right. **3.** *U.S.* the strip of land over which a power line, road, etc., extends.

Right Reverend *adj.* a title of respect for a bishop, esp. an Anglican bishop.

rightward (ˈraɪtwəd) *adj.* **1.** situated on or directed towards the right. ~*adv.* **2.** to the right —ˈrightwards *adv.*

right whale *n.* a large whalebone whale which is grey or black, has a large head and no dorsal fin, and is hunted as a source of whalebone and oil.

right wing *n.* **1.** (*often cap.*) the conservative faction of an assembly, party, etc. **2.** the part of an army or field of battle on the right from the point of view of one facing the enemy. **3. a.** the right-hand side of the field of play from the point of view of a team facing its opponent's goal. **b.** a player positioned in this area in any of various games. ~*adj.* **right-wing. 4.** of, belonging to, or relating to the right wing. —ˈright-ˈwinger *n.*

rigid (ˈrɪdʒɪd) *adj.* **1.** physically inflexible or stiff: *a rigid piece of plastic.* **2.** rigorously strict: *rigid rules.* —ˈrigidly *adv.* —riˈgidity *n.*

rigmarole (ˈrɪgməˌrəʊl) *or* **rigamarole** (ˈrɪgəməˌrəʊl) *n.* **1.** any long complicated procedure. **2.** a set of incoherent or pointless statements.

rigor mortis (ˈrɪgə ˈmɔːtɪs) *n. Pathol.* the stiffness of joints and muscular rigidity of a dead body.

rigorous (ˈrɪgərəs) *adj.* **1.** harsh, strict, or severe: *rigorous discipline.* **2.** severely accurate: *rigorous bookkeeping.* **3.** (*esp. of weather*) extreme or harsh. **4.** *Maths., logic.* logically valid or correct. —ˈrigorously *adv.*

rigour *or U.S.* **rigor** (ˈrɪgə) *n.* **1.** harsh but just treatment or action. **2.** a severe or cruel circumstance: *the rigours of famine.* **3.** strictness, harshness, or severity of character. **4.** strictness in judgment or conduct.

rig out *vb.* **1.** (*tr., adv.; often foll. by with*) to equip or fit out (with): *his car is rigged out with gadgets.* **2.** to dress or be dressed: *rigged out smartly.* ~*n.* **rigout. 3.**

Inf. a person's clothing or costume, esp. a bizarre outfit.

rig up *vb.* (*tr., adv.*) to erect or construct, esp. as a temporary measure: *cameras were rigged up to televise the event.*

rile (raɪl) *vb.* (*tr.*) **1.** *Inf.* to annoy or anger. **2.** *U.S.* to agitate (water, etc.).

rill (rɪl) *n.* **1.** a brook or stream. **2.** a small channel or gulley, such as one formed during soil erosion. **3.** Also **rille.** one of many winding cracks on the moon.

rim (rɪm) *n.* **1.** the raised edge of an object, esp. of something more or less circular such as a cup or crater. **2.** the peripheral part of a wheel, to which the tyre is attached. **3.** *Basketball.* the hoop from which the net is suspended. ~*vb.* **rimming, rimmed.** (*tr.*) **4.** to put a rim on (a pot, cup, wheel, etc.).

rime[1] (raɪm) *n.* **1.** frost formed by the freezing of water droplets in fog onto solid objects. ~*vb.* **2.** (*tr.*) to cover with rime or something resembling rime. —ˈrimy *adj.*

rime[2] (raɪm) *n.* a variant spelling of **rhyme.**

rind (raɪnd) *n.* **1.** a hard outer layer or skin on bacon, cheese, etc. **2.** the outer layer of a fruit or of the spore-producing body of certain fungi. **3.** the outer layer of the bark of a tree.

rinderpest (ˈrɪndəˌpɛst) *n.* an acute contagious viral disease of cattle, characterized by severe inflammation of the intestinal tract and diarrhoea.

ring[1] (rɪŋ) *n.* **1.** a circular band of a precious metal often set with gems and worn upon the finger as an adornment or as a token of engagement or marriage. **2.** any object or mark that is circular in shape. **3.** a circular path or course: *to run around in a ring.* **4.** a group of people or things standing or arranged so as to form a circle: *a ring of spectators.* **5.** an enclosed space, usually circular in shape, where circus acts are performed. **6.** a square raised platform, marked off by ropes, in which contestants box or wrestle. **7. the ring.** the sport of boxing. **8. throw one's hat in the ring.** to announce one's intention to be a candidate or contestant. **9.** a group of people, usually illegal, cooperating for the purpose of controlling the market in antiques, etc. **10.** (*esp. at county fairs*) an enclosure where horses, cattle, and other livestock are paraded and auctioned. **11.** an area reserved for betting at a racecourse. **12.** a circular strip of bark cut from a tree or branch. **13.** a single turn in a spiral. **14.** *Geom.* the area of space lying between two concentric circles. **15.** *Maths.* a set that is subject to two binary operations, addition and multiplication, such that the set is a commutative group under addition and is closed under multiplication, this latter operation being associative. **16.** Also called: **annual ring.** *Bot.* a ring indicating one year's growth, seen in the cross section of stems and roots of woody plants. **17.** *Chem.* a closed loop of atoms in a molecule. **18.** one of the system of circular bands orbiting the planet Saturn. **19. to run rings around.** *Inf.* to outclass completely. ~*vb.* **ringing, ringed.** (*tr.*) **20.** to surround with, or as if with, or form a ring. **21.** to mark a bird with a ring or clip for subsequent identification. **22.** to fit a ring in the nose of (a bull, pig, etc.) so that it can be led easily. **23. to ringbark.** —**ringed** *adj.*

ring[2] (rɪŋ) *vb.* **ringing, rang, rung. 1.** to emit or cause to emit a resonant sound, characteristic of certain metals when struck. **2.** to cause (a bell, etc.) to emit a ringing sound by striking it once or repeatedly or (of a bell) to emit such a sound. **3. a.** (*tr.*) to cause (a large bell) to emit a ringing sound by pulling on a rope that is attached to a wheel on which the bell swings back and forth, being sounded by a clapper inside it. **b.** (*intr.*) (of a bell) to sound by being swung in this way. **4.** (*intr.*) (of a building, place, etc.) to be filled with sound: *the church rang*

---

righteous blameless, equitable, ethical, fair, good, honest, honourable, just, law-abiding, moral, pure, upright, virtuous

righteousness blamelessness, equity, ethicalness, faithfulness, goodness, honesty, honour, integrity, justice, morality, probity, purity, rectitude, uprightness, virtue

rigid adamant, austere, exact, fixed, harsh, inflexible, intransigent, invariable, rigorous, set, severe, stern, stiff, strict, stringent, unalterable, unbending, uncompromising, undeviating, unrelenting, unyielding

rigorous 1. austere, challenging, demanding, exacting, firm, hard, harsh, inflexible,

rigid, severe, stern, strict, stringent, tough **2.** accurate, conscientious, exact, meticulous, nice, painstaking, precise, punctilious, scrupulous, thorough **3.** bad, bleak, extreme, harsh, inclement, inhospitable, severe

rigour 1. asperity, austerity, firmness, hardness, hardship, harshness, inflexibility, ordeal, privation, rigidity, sternness, strictness, stringency, suffering, trial **2.** accuracy, conscientiousness, exactitude, exactness, meticulousness, preciseness, precision, punctiliousness, thoroughness

rig-out apparel, clobber (*Brit. sl.*), clothing, costume, dress, garb, gear (*Sl.*), get-up

(*Inf.*), habit, outfit, raiment, togs

rig out 1. accoutre, equip, fit, furnish, kit out, outfit, set up **2.** array, attire, clothe, costume, dress, kit out

rig up arrange, assemble, build, cobble together, construct, erect, fix up, improvise, put together, put up, set up, throw together

rim border, brim, brink, circumference, edge, lip, margin, verge

rind crust, epicarp, husk, integument, outer layer, peel, skin

with singing. **5.** (*intr.; foll. by for*) to call by means of a bell, etc.: *to ring for the butler.* **6.** Also: **ring up.** *Chiefly Brit.* to call (a person) by telephone. **7.** (*tr.*) to strike or tap (a coin) in order to assess its genuineness by the sound produced. **8.** (*intr.*) (of the ears) to have or give the sensation of humming or ringing. **9. ring a bell.** to bring something to the mind or memory: *that rings a bell.* **10. ring down the curtain. a.** to lower the curtain at the end of a theatrical performance. **b.** (*foll. by on*) to put an end (to). **11. ring false.** to give the impression of being false. **12. ring the bell. a.** to do, say, or be the right thing. **b.** to reach the pinnacle of success. **13. ring the changes.** to vary the manner or performance of an action that is often repeated. **14. ring true.** to give the impression of being true. ~*n.* **15.** the act of or a sound made by ringing. **16.** a sound produced by or suggestive of a bell. **17.** any resonant or metallic sound: *the ring of trumpets.* **18.** *Inf., chiefly Brit.* a telephone call. **19.** the complete set of bells in a tower or belfry: *a ring of eight bells.* **20.** an inherent quality or characteristic: *his explanation has the ring of sincerity.* ~See also **ring in**, etc.

▷ **Usage.** *Rang* and *sang* are the correct forms of the past tenses of *ring* and *sing*, although *rung* and *sung* are still heard informally and dialectically: *he rung (rang) the bell.*

ringdove ('rɪŋˌdʌv) *n.* **1.** another name for **wood pigeon**. **2.** an Old World turtledove, having a black band around the neck.

ring finger *n.* the third finger, esp. of the left hand, on which a wedding ring is worn.

ring in *vb.* (*adv.*) **1.** (*intr.*) *Chiefly Brit.* to report to someone by telephone. **2.** (*tr.*) to accompany the arrival of with bells (esp. in **ring in the new year**). ~*n.* **ring-in**. **3.** *Austral. & N.Z. sl.* a person or thing that is not normally a member of a particular group; outsider.

ringleader ('rɪŋˌliːdə) *n.* a person who leads a riot or mutiny.

ringlet ('rɪŋlɪt) *n.* **1.** a lock of hair hanging down in a spiral curl. **2.** a butterfly that occurs in S Europe and has dark brown wings marked with small black-and-white eyespots. —**'ringleted** *adj.*

ring main *n.* a domestic electrical supply in which outlet sockets are connected to the mains supply through a continuous closed circuit (**ring circuit**).

ringmaster ('rɪŋˌmɑːstə) *n.* the master of ceremonies in a circus.

ring off *vb.* (*intr., adv.*) *Chiefly Brit.* to terminate a telephone conversation by replacing the receiver; hang up.

ring out *vb.* (*adv.*) **1.** (*tr.*) to accompany the departure of with bells (esp. in **ring out the old year**). **2.** (*intr.*) to send forth a loud resounding noise.

ring road *n.* a main road that bypasses a town or town centre. U.S. names: **belt**, **beltway**.

ringside ('rɪŋˌsaɪd) *n.* **1.** the row of seats nearest a boxing or wrestling ring. **2. a.** any place affording a close uninterrupted view. **b.** (*as modifier*): *a ringside seat.*

ring up *vb.* (*adv.*) **1.** *Chiefly Brit.* to make a telephone call (to). **2.** (*tr.*) to record on a cash register. **3. ring up the curtain. a.** to begin a theatrical performance. **b.** (often foll. by *on*) to make a start (on).

ringworm ('rɪŋˌwɜːm) *n.* any of various fungal infections of the skin or nails, often appearing as itching circular patches. Also called: **tinea**.

rink (rɪŋk) *n.* **1.** an expanse of ice for skating on, esp. one that is artificially prepared and under cover. **2.** an area for roller skating on. **3.** a building or enclosure for ice skating or roller skating. **4.** *Bowls.* a strip of the green on which a game is played. **5.** *Curling.* the strip of ice on which the game is played. **6.** (in bowls and curling) the players on one side in a game.

rinse (rɪns) *vb.* (*tr.*) **1.** to remove soap from (clothes, etc.) by applying clean water in the final stage in washing. **2.** to wash lightly, esp. without using soap. **3.** to give a light tint to (hair). ~*n.* **4.** the act or an instance of rinsing. **5.** *Hairdressing.* a liquid preparation put on the hair when wet to give a tint to it: *a blue rinse.* —**'rinser** *n.*

riot ('raɪət) *n.* **1. a.** a disturbance made by an unruly mob or (in law) three or more persons. **b.** (*as modifier*): *a riot shield.* **2.** unrestrained revelry. **3.** an occasion of boisterous merriment. **4.** *Sl.* a person who occasions boisterous merriment. **5.** a dazzling display: *a riot of colour.* **6.** *Hunting.* the indiscriminate following of any scent by hounds. **7.** *Arch.* wanton lasciviousness. **8. run riot. a.** to behave without restraint. **b.** (of plants) to grow profusely. ~*vb.* **9.** (*intr.*) to take part in a riot. **10.** (*intr.*) to indulge in unrestrained revelry. **11.** (*tr.; foll. by away*) to spend (time or money) in wanton or loose living. —**'rioter** *n.*

riotous ('raɪətəs) *adj.* **1.** proceeding from or of the nature of riots or rioting. **2.** characterized by wanton revelry: *riotous living.* **3.** characterized by unrestrained merriment: *riotous laughter.* —**'riotously** *adv.* —**'riotousness** *n.*

rip[1] (rɪp) *vb.* **ripping, ripped. 1.** to tear or be torn violently or roughly. **2.** (*intr.*) *Inf.* to move violently or precipitously. **3.** (*intr., foll. by into*) *Inf.* to pour violent abuse (on). **4.** (*tr.*) to saw or split (wood) in the direction of the grain. **5. let rip.** to act or speak without restraint. ~*n.* **6.** a tear or split. **7.** short for **ripsaw**. ~See also **rip off**.

rip[2] (rɪp) *n.* **1.** a stretch of turbulent water. **2.** a strong current, esp. one in an estuary.

rip[3] (rɪp) *n. Inf., arch.* **1.** a debauched person. **2.** an old worn-out horse.

R.I.P. *abbrev. for* requiescat *or* requiescant in pace: may he, she, *or* they rest in peace.

riparian (raɪˈpɛərɪən) *adj.* **1.** of, inhabiting, or situated on the bank of a river. **2.** denoting or relating to the legal rights of the owner of land on a river bank, such as fishing. ~*n.* **3.** *Property law.* a person who owns land on a river bank.

ripcord ('rɪpˌkɔːd) *n.* **1.** a cord that when pulled opens a parachute from its pack. **2.** a cord on the gas bag of a balloon that when pulled enables gas to escape and the balloon to descend.

ripe (raɪp) *adj.* **1.** (of fruit, grain, etc.) mature and ready to be eaten or used. **2.** mature enough to be eaten or used: *ripe cheese.* **3.** fully developed in mind or body. **4.** resembling ripe fruit, esp. in redness or fullness: *a ripe complexion.* **5.** (*postpositive; foll. by for*) ready or eager (to undertake or undergo an action). **6.** (*postpositive; foll. by for*) suitable: *the time is not yet ripe.* **7.** mature in judgment or knowledge. **8.** advanced but healthy (esp. in **a ripe old age**). —**'ripely** *adv.* —**'ripeness** *n.*

ripen ('raɪpən) *vb.* to make or become ripe.

rip off *vb.* **1.** (*tr.*) to tear roughly (from). **2.** (*adv.*) *Sl.* to steal from or cheat (someone). ~*n.* **rip-off. 3.** *Sl.* a grossly overpriced article. **4.** *Sl.* the act of stealing or cheating.

THESAURUS

ring[1] *n.* **1.** band, circle, circuit, halo, hoop, loop, round **2.** arena, circus, enclosure, rink **3.** association, band, cabal, cartel, cell, circle, clique, combine, coterie, crew (*Inf.*), gang, group, junto, knot, mob, organization, syndicate ~*v.* **4.** circumscribe, encircle, enclose, encompass, gird, girdle, hem in, seal off, surround

ring[2] *v.* **1.** chime, clang, peal, resonate, resound, reverberate, sound, toll **2.** buzz (*Inf.*), call, phone, telephone ~*n.* **3.** chime, knell, peal **4.** buzz (*Inf.*), call, phone call

rinse **1.** *v.* bathe, clean, cleanse, dip, splash, wash, wash out, wet **2.** *n.* bath, dip, splash, wash, wetting

riot *n.* **1.** anarchy, commotion, confusion, disorder, disturbance, donnybrook, fray, law-lessness, mob violence, quarrel, row, street fighting, strife, tumult, turbulence, turmoil, uproar **2.** boisterousness, carousal, excess, festivity, frolic, high jinks, jollification, merrymaking, revelry, romp **3.** display, extravaganza, flourish, show, splash **4. run riot a.** be out of control, break *or* cut loose, go wild, let oneself go, raise hell, rampage, throw off all restraint **b.** grow like weeds, grow profusely, luxuriate, spread like wild-fire ~*v.* **5.** fight in the streets, go on the rampage, raise an uproar, rampage, run riot, take to the streets **6.** carouse, cut loose, frolic, go on a binge *or* spree, make merry, paint the town red (*Inf.*), revel, roister, romp

riotous 1. anarchic, disorderly, insubordinate, lawless, mutinous, rampageous, rebel-lious, refractory, rowdy, tumultuous, ungovernable, unruly, uproarious, violent **2.** boisterous, loud, luxurious, noisy, orgiastic, rambunctious (*Inf.*), roisterous, rollicking, saturnalian, side-splitting, unrestrained, uproarious, wanton, wild

ripe 1. fully developed, fully grown, mature, mellow, ready, ripened, seasoned **2.** accomplished, complete, finished, in readiness, perfect, prepared, ready **3.** auspicious, favourable, ideal, opportune, right, suitable, timely

ripen burgeon, come of age, come to fruition, develop, get ready, grow ripe, make ripe, mature, prepare, season

riposte (rɪˈpɒst, rɪˈpəʊst) n. 1. a swift sharp reply in speech or action. 2. *Fencing.* a counterattack made immediately after a successful parry. ~vb. 3. (*intr.*) to make a riposte.

ripple (ˈrɪpəl) n. 1. a slight wave or undulation on the surface of water. 2. a small wave or undulation in fabric, hair, etc. 3. a sound reminiscent of water flowing quietly in ripples: *a ripple of laughter.* 4. *Electronics.* an oscillation of small amplitude superimposed on a steady value. 5. *U.S.* a small rapid. ~vb. 6. (*intr.*) to form ripples or flow with an undulating motion. 7. (*tr.*) to stir up (water) so as to form ripples. 8. (*tr.*) to make ripple marks. 9. (*intr.*) (of sounds) to rise and fall gently. —ˈrippler n. —ˈripply adj.

rip-roaring adj. *Inf.* characterized by excitement, intensity, or boisterous behaviour.

ripsaw (ˈrɪpˌsɔː) n. a handsaw for cutting along the grain of timber.

rise (raɪz) vb. **rising, rose, risen.** (*mainly intr.*) 1. to get up from a lying, sitting, kneeling, or prone position. 2. to get out of bed, esp. to begin one's day: *he always rises early.* 3. to move from a lower to a higher position or place. 4. to ascend or appear above the horizon: *the sun is rising.* 5. to increase in height or level: *the water rose above the normal level.* 6. to attain higher rank, status, or reputation: *he will rise in the world.* 7. to be built or erected: *those blocks of flats are rising fast.* 8. to appear: *new troubles rose to afflict her.* 9. to increase in strength, degree, etc.: *the wind is rising.* 10. to increase in amount or value: *house prices are always rising.* 11. to swell up: *dough rises.* 12. to become erect, stiff, or rigid: *the hairs on his neck rose in fear.* 13. (of one's stomach or gorge) to manifest or feel nausea. 14. to revolt: *the people rose against their oppressors.* 15. to slope upwards: *the ground rises beyond the lake.* 16. to be resurrected. 17. to originate: *that river rises in the mountains.* 18. (of a session of a court, legislative assembly, etc.) to come to an end. 19. *Angling.* (of fish) to come to the surface of the water. 20. (often foll. by *to*) *Inf.* to respond (to teasing, etc.). ~n. 21. the act or an instance of rising. 22. an increase in height. 23. an increase in rank, status, or position. 24. an increase in amount, cost, or value. 25. an increase in degree or intensity. 26. *Brit.* an increase in salary or wages. U.S. word: **raise.** 27. the vertical height of a step or of a flight of stairs. 28. the vertical height of a roof above the walls or columns. 29. *Angling.* the act or instance of fish coming to the surface of the water to take flies, etc. 30. the beginning, origin, or source. 31. a piece of rising ground; incline. 32. **get a rise out of.** *Sl.* to provoke an angry or petulant reaction from. 33. **give rise to.** to cause the development of.

riser (ˈraɪzə) n. 1. a person who rises, esp. from bed: *an early riser.* 2. the vertical part of a stair. 3. a vertical pipe, esp. one within a building.

risible (ˈrɪzɪbəl) adj. 1. having a tendency to laugh. 2. causing laughter; ridiculous. —ˌrisiˈbility n. —ˈrisibly adv.

rising (ˈraɪzɪŋ) n. 1. a rebellion; revolt. 2. the leaven used to make dough rise in baking. ~adj. (*prenominal*) 3. increasing in rank, status, or reputation: *a rising young*

politician. 4. growing up to adulthood: *the rising generation.* 5. *Inf.* approaching: *he's rising 50.*

rising damp n. capillary movement of moisture from the ground into the walls of buildings, resulting in damage up to a level of 3 feet.

risk (rɪsk) n. 1. the possibility of incurring misfortune or loss. 2. *Insurance.* **a.** chance of a loss or other event on which a claim may be filed. **b.** the type of such an event, such as fire or theft. **c.** the amount of the claim should such an event occur. **d.** a person or thing considered with respect to the characteristics that may cause an insured event to occur. 3. **take** *or* **run a risk.** to proceed in an action without regard to the possibility of danger involved. ~vb. (*tr.*) 4. to expose to danger or loss. 5. to act in spite of the possibility of (injury or loss): *to risk a fall in climbing.* —ˈrisky adj.

risotto (rɪˈzɒtəʊ) n. a dish of rice cooked in stock and served variously with tomatoes, cheese, chicken, etc.

risqué (ˈrɪskeɪ) adj. bordering on impropriety or indecency: *a risqué joke.*

rissole (ˈrɪsəʊl) n. a mixture of minced cooked meat coated in egg and breadcrumbs, often covered with pastry, and fried.

ritardando (ˌrɪtɑːˈdændəʊ) adj., adv. another word for **rallentando.** Abbrev.: **rit.**

rite (raɪt) n. 1. a formal act prescribed or customary in religious ceremonies: *the rite of baptism.* 2. a particular body of such acts, esp. of a particular Christian Church: *the Latin rite.* 3. a Christian Church: *the Greek rite.*

ritual (ˈrɪtjʊəl) n. 1. the prescribed or established form of a religious or other ceremony. 2. such prescribed forms in general or collectively. 3. stereotyped activity or behaviour. 4. any formal act, institution, or procedure that is followed consistently: *the ritual of the law.* ~adj. 5. of or characteristic of religious, social, or other rituals. —ˈritually adv.

ritualism (ˈrɪtjʊəˌlɪzəm) n. 1. exaggerated emphasis on the importance of rites and ceremonies. 2. the study of rites and ceremonies, esp. magical or religious ones. —ˈritualist n. —ˌritualˈistic adj. —ˌritualˈistically adv.

ritzy (ˈrɪtsɪ) adj. **ritzier, ritziest.** *Sl.* luxurious or elegant. —ˈritzily adv. —ˈritziness n.

rival (ˈraɪvəl) n. 1. **a.** a person, organization, team, etc., that competes with another for the same object or in the same field. **b.** (*as modifier*): *rival suitors.* ~vb. **-valling, -valled** *or U.S.* **-valing, -valed.** (*tr.*) 2. to be the equal or near equal of: *an empire that rivalled Rome.* 3. to try to equal or surpass.

rivalry (ˈraɪvəlrɪ) n., pl. **-ries.** 1. the act of rivalling. 2. the state of being a rival or rivals.

rive (raɪv) vb. **riving, rived, rived** *or* **riven** (ˈrɪvən). (*usually passive*) 1. to split asunder: *a tree riven by lightning.* 2. to tear apart: *riven to shreds.*

river (ˈrɪvə) n. 1. **a.** a large natural stream of fresh water flowing along a definite course, usually into the sea, being fed by tributary streams. **b.** (*as modifier*): *river traffic.* **c.** (*in combination*): *riverside; riverbed.* Related adj.: **fluvial.** 2. any abundant stream or flow: *a river of blood.* 3. **sell down the river.** *Inf.* to betray. —ˈriverless adj.

THESAURUS

riposte 1. *n.* answer, comeback (*Inf.*), rejoinder, repartee, reply, response, retort, return, sally 2. *v.* answer, come back, reciprocate, rejoin, reply, respond, retort, return

rise *v.* 1. arise, get out of bed, get to one's feet, get up, rise and shine, stand up, surface 2. arise, ascend, climb, enlarge, go up, grow, improve, increase, intensify, levitate, lift, mount, move up, soar, swell, wax 3. advance, be promoted, climb the ladder, get on, get somewhere, go places (*Inf.*), progress, prosper, work one's way up 4. appear, become apparent, crop up, emanate, emerge, eventuate, flow, happen, issue, occur, originate, spring, turn up 5. mount the barricades, mutiny, rebel, resist, revolt, take up arms 6. ascend, climb, get steeper, go uphill, mount, slope upwards ~n. 7. advance, ascent, climb, improvement, increase, upsurge, upswing, upturn, upward turn 8. advancement, aggrandizement, climb, progress, promotion 9. acclivity, ascent, elevation, hillock, incline,

rising ground, upward slope 10. increment, pay increase, raise (*U.S.*) 11. **give rise to** bring about, bring on, cause, effect, produce, provoke, result in

risk 1. *n.* chance, danger, gamble, hazard, jeopardy, peril, possibility, speculation, uncertainty, venture 2. *v.* chance, dare, endanger, expose to danger, gamble, hazard, imperil, jeopardize, put in jeopardy, take a chance on, venture

risky chancy (*Inf.*), dangerous, dicey (*Sl.*), dodgy (*Brit. inf.*), fraught with danger, hazardous, perilous, precarious, touch-and-go, tricky, uncertain, unsafe

rite act, ceremonial, ceremony, communion, custom, form, formality, liturgy, mystery, observance, ordinance, practice, procedure, ritual, sacrament, service, solemnity, usage

ritual *n.* 1. ceremonial, ceremony, communion, liturgy, mystery, observance, rite, sacrament, service, solemnity 2. convention,

custom, form, formality, habit, ordinance, practice, prescription, procedure, protocol, red tape, routine, stereotype, usage ~adj. 3. ceremonial, ceremonious, conventional, customary, formal, habitual, prescribed, procedural, routine, stereotyped

rival *n.* 1. adversary, antagonist, challenger, competitor, contender, contestant, emulator, opponent 2. compeer, equal, equivalent, fellow, match, peer ~adj. 3. competing, competitive, conflicting, emulating, opposed, opposing ~v. 4. be a match for, bear comparison with, come up to, compare with, compete, contend, emulate, equal, match, measure up to, oppose, seek to displace, vie with

rivalry antagonism, competition, competitiveness, conflict, contention, contest, duel, emulation, opposition, struggle, vying

rivet ('rɪvɪt) *n.* **1.** a short metal pin for fastening two or more pieces together, having a head at one end, the other end being hammered flat after being passed through holes in the pieces. ~*vb.* **2.** to join by riveting. **3.** to hammer in order to form into a head. **4.** (*often passive*) to cause to be fixed, as in fascinated attention, horror, etc.: *to be riveted to the spot.* —'**riveter** *n.*

rivulet ('rɪvjʊlɪt) *n.* a small stream.

rly. *abbrev. for* railway.

R.M. *abbrev. for:* **1.** Royal Mail. **2.** Royal Marines. **3.** (in Canada) Rural Municipality.

rm. *abbrev. for:* **1.** ream. **2.** room.

R.M.A. *abbrev. for* Royal Military Academy (Sandhurst).

Rn *the chemical symbol for* radon.

R.N. *abbrev. for:* **1.** Royal Navy. **2.** (in Canada) Registered Nurse.

RNA *n. Biochem.* ribonucleic acid; any of a group of nucleic acids, present in all living cells, that play an essential role in the synthesis of proteins.

R.N.A.S. *abbrev. for:* **1.** Royal Naval Air Service(s). **2.** Royal Naval Air Station.

R.N.L.I. *abbrev. for* Royal National Lifeboat Institution.

roach (rəʊtʃ) *n., pl.* **roaches** *or* **roach.** a European freshwater food fish having a deep compressed body and reddish ventral and tail fins.

road (rəʊd) *n.* **1. a.** an open way, usually surfaced with tarmac or concrete, providing passage from one place to another. **b.** (*as modifier*): *road traffic; a road sign.* **c.** (*in combination*): *the roadside.* **2. a.** a street. **b.** (*cap. as part of a name*): *London Road.* **3.** *Brit.* one of the tracks of a railway. **4.** a way, path, or course: *the road to fame.* **5.** (*often pl.*) Also called: **roadstead.** *Naut.* a partly sheltered anchorage. **6.** a drift or tunnel in a mine, esp. a level one. **7. hit the road.** *Sl.* to start or resume travelling. **8. on the road. a.** travelling about. **b.** leading a wandering life. **9. take (to) the road.** to begin a journey or tour. **10. one for the road.** *Inf.* a last alcoholic drink before leaving. —'**roadless** *adj.*

roadblock ('rəʊd‚blɒk) *n.* a barrier set up across a road by the police or military, in order to stop a fugitive, inspect traffic, etc.

road-fund licence *n. Brit.* a licence showing that the tax payable in respect of a motor vehicle has been paid.

road hog *n. Inf.* a selfish or aggressive driver.

roadholding ('rəʊd‚həʊldɪŋ) *n.* the extent to which a motor vehicle is stable and does not skid, esp. on sharp bends or wet roads.

roadhouse ('rəʊd‚haʊs) *n.* a pub, restaurant, etc., that is situated at the side of a road.

road show *n.* **1.** *Radio.* a live programme, usually with some audience participation, transmitted from a radio van taking a particular show on the road. **2.** a group of entertainers on tour.

roadstead ('rəʊd‚stɛd) *n. Naut.* another word for **road** (sense 5).

roadster ('rəʊdstə) *n.* **1.** *Arch.* an open car, esp. one seating only two. **2.** a kind of bicycle.

road test *n.* **1.** a test to ensure that a vehicle is roadworthy, esp. after repair or servicing, by driving it on roads. ~*vb.* **road-test.** (*tr.*) **2.** to test a vehicle in this way.

roadway ('rəʊd‚weɪ) *n.* **1.** the surface of a road. **2.** the part of a road that is used by vehicles.

road works *pl. n.* repairs to a road or cable under a road, esp. when forming a hazard or obstruction to traffic.

roadworthy ('rəʊd‚wɜːðɪ) *adj.* (of a motor vehicle) mechanically sound; fit for use on the roads. —'**road‚worthiness** *n.*

roam (rəʊm) *vb.* **1.** to travel or walk about with no fixed purpose or direction. ~*n.* **2.** the act of roaming. —'**roamer** *n.*

roan (rəʊn) *adj.* **1.** (of a horse) having a bay (**red roan**), chestnut (**strawberry roan**), or black (**blue roan**) coat sprinkled with white hairs. ~*n.* **2.** a horse having such a coat. **3.** a soft sheepskin leather used in bookbinding, etc.

roar (rɔː) *vb.* (*mainly intr.*) **1.** (of lions and other animals) to utter characteristic loud growling cries. **2.** (*also tr.*) (of people) to utter (something) with a loud deep cry, as in anger or triumph. **3.** to laugh in a loud hearty unrestrained manner. **4.** (of horses) to breathe with laboured rasping sounds. **5.** (of the wind, waves, etc.) to blow or break loudly and violently, as during a storm. **6.** (of a fire) to burn fiercely with a roaring sound. **7.** (*tr.*) to bring (oneself) into a certain condition by roaring: *to roar oneself hoarse.* ~*n.* **8.** a loud deep cry, uttered by a person or crowd, esp. in anger or triumph. **9.** a prolonged loud cry of certain animals, esp. lions. **10.** any similar noise made by a fire, the wind, waves, an engine, etc. —'**roarer** *n.*

roaring ('rɔːrɪŋ) *adj.* **1.** *Inf.* very brisk and profitable (esp. in **a roaring trade**). ~*adv.* **2.** noisily or boisterously (esp. in **roaring drunk**). ~*n.* **3.** a loud prolonged cry. —'**roaringly** *adv.*

roast (rəʊst) *vb.* (*mainly tr.*) **1.** to cook (meat or other food) by dry heat, usually with added fat and esp. in an oven. **2.** to brown or dry (coffee, etc.) by exposure to heat. **3.** *Metallurgy.* to heat (an ore) in order to produce a concentrate that is easier to smelt. **4.** to heat (oneself or something) to an extreme degree, as when sunbathing, etc. **5.** (*intr.*) to be excessively and uncomfortably hot. **6.** *Inf.* to criticize severely. ~*n.* **7.** something that has been roasted, esp. meat. —'**roaster** *n.*

rob (rɒb) *vb.* **robbing, robbed. 1.** to take something from (someone) illegally, as by force. **2.** (*tr.*) to plunder (a house, etc.). **3.** (*tr.*) to deprive unjustly: *to be robbed of an opportunity.* —'**robber** *n.*

robbery ('rɒbərɪ) *n., pl.* **-beries. 1.** *Criminal law.* the stealing of property from a person by using or threatening to use force. **2.** the act or an instance of robbing.

robe (rəʊb) *n.* **1.** any loose flowing garment, esp. the official vestment of a peer, judge, or academic. **2.** a dressing gown or bathrobe. ~*vb.* **3.** to put a robe, etc., on (oneself or someone else).

robin ('rɒbɪn) *n.* **1.** Also called: **robin redbreast.** a small Old World songbird related to the thrushes. The male has a brown back, orange-red breast and face, and grey underparts. **2.** a North American thrush similar to but larger than the Old World robin.

Robin Hood *n.* a legendary English outlaw of the reign of Richard I, who lived in Sherwood Forest and robbed the rich to give to the poor.

robot ('rəʊbɒt) *n.* **1.** any automated machine programmed to perform specific mechanical functions in the manner of a man. **2.** (*modifier*) automatic: *a robot pilot.* **3.** a person who works or behaves like a machine. **4.** *S. African.* a set of traffic lights. —'**robotism** *or* '**ro‚botry** *n.* —'**robot-‚like** *adj.*

robust (rəʊ'bʌst, 'rəʊbʌst) *adj.* **1.** strong in constitution. **2.** sturdily built: *a robust shelter.* **3.** requiring or suited to physical strength: *a robust sport.* **4.** (esp. of wines) having a full-bodied flavour. **5.** rough or boisterous. **6.** (of thought, intellect, etc.) straightforward. —ro'**bustly** *adv.* —ro'**bustness** *n.*

THESAURUS

road 1. avenue, course, direction, highway, lane, motorway, path, pathway, roadway, route, street, thoroughfare, track, way **2.** *Nautical* anchorage, roadstead

roam drift, meander, peregrinate, prowl, ramble, range, rove, stravaig (*Scot.*), stray, stroll, travel, walk, wander

roar *v.* **1.** bawl, bay, bellow, clamour, crash, cry, howl, rumble, shout, thunder, vociferate, yell **2.** guffaw, hoot, laugh heartily, split one's sides (*Inf.*) ~*n.* **3.** bellow, clamour, crash, cry, howl, outcry, rumble, shout, thunder, yell **4.** belly laugh (*Inf.*), guffaw, hoot

rob bereave, burgle, cheat, con (*Sl.*), defraud, deprive, despoil, dispossess, do out of (*Inf.*), gyp (*Sl.*), hold up, loot, pillage, plunder, raid, ransack, rifle, rip off (*Inf.*), sack, strip, swindle

robber bandit, brigand, burglar, cheat, con man (*Inf.*), fraud, highwayman, looter, pirate, plunderer, raider, stealer, swindler, thief

robbery burglary, depredation, embezzlement, filching, fraud, hold-up, larceny, pillage, plunder, raid, rapine, rip-off (*Inf.*), spoliation, stealing, stick-up (*U.S. sl.*), swindle, theft, thievery

robe *n.* **1.** costume, gown, habit, vestment **2.** bathrobe, dressing gown, housecoat, peignoir, wrapper ~*v.* **3.** apparel (*Archaic*), attire, clothe, drape, dress, garb

robot android, automaton, machine, mechanical man

robust 1. able-bodied, athletic, brawny, fit, hale, hardy, healthy, hearty, husky (*Inf.*), in fine fettle, in good health, lusty, muscular, powerful, rude, rugged, sinewy, sound, staunch, stout, strapping, strong, sturdy,

robustious (rəʊ'bʌstʃəs) *adj. Arch.* **1.** rough; boisterous. **2.** strong, robust, or stout. —**ro'bustiously** *adv.* —**ro'bustiousness** *n.*

roc (rɒk) *n.* (in Arabian legend) a bird of enormous size and power.

R.O.C. *abbrev. for* Royal Observer Corps.

rochet ('rɒtʃɪt) *n.* a white surplice with tight sleeves, worn by bishops, abbots, and certain other Church dignitaries.

rock[1] (rɒk) *n.* **1.** *Geol.* any aggregate of minerals that makes up part of the earth's crust. It may be unconsolidated, such as a sand, clay, or mud, or consolidated, such as granite, limestone, or coal. **2.** any hard mass of consolidated mineral matter, such as a boulder. **3.** *U.S., Austral.* a stone. **4.** a person or thing suggesting a rock, esp. in being dependable, unchanging, or providing firm foundation. **5.** *Brit.* a hard sweet, typically a long brightly coloured peppermint-flavoured stick, sold esp. in holiday resorts. **6.** *Sl.* a jewel, esp. a diamond. **7. on the rocks. a.** in a state of ruin or destitution. **b.** (of drinks, esp. whisky) served with ice.

rock[2] (rɒk) *vb.* **1.** to move or cause to move from side to side or backwards and forwards. **2.** to reel or sway or cause (someone) to reel or sway, as with a violent shock or emotion. **3.** (*tr.*) to shake or move (something) violently. **4.** (*intr.*) to dance in the rock-and-roll style. **5. rock the boat.** to create a disturbance. ~*n.* **6.** a rocking motion. **7.** short for **rock-and-roll. 8.** Also called: **rock music.** any of various styles of pop music having a heavy beat, derived from rock-and-roll. —**'rockingly** *adv.*

Rock (rɒk) *n.* **the.** an informal name for Gibraltar, at the Western end of the Mediterranean.

rock-and-roll *or* **rock-'n'-roll** *n.* **1. a.** a type of pop music originating in the 1950s as a blend of rhythm-and-blues and country-and-western. **b.** (*as modifier*): *the rock-and-roll era.* **2.** dancing performed to such music, with exaggerated body movements stressing the beat. ~*vb.* **3.** (*intr.*) to perform this dance. —**'rock-and-'roller** *or* **'rock-'n'-'roller** *n.*

rock bottom *n.* **a.** the lowest possible level. **b.** (*as modifier*): *rock-bottom prices.*

rock-bound *adj.* hemmed in or encircled by rocks. Also (*poetic*): **rock-girt.**

rock cake *n.* a small cake containing dried fruit and spice, with a rough surface supposed to resemble a rock.

rock crystal *n.* a pure transparent colourless quartz, used in electronic and optical equipment.

rock dove *or* **pigeon** *n.* a common dove from which domestic and feral pigeons are descended.

rocker ('rɒkə) *n.* **1.** any of various devices that transmit or operate with a rocking motion. **2.** another word for **rocking chair. 3.** either of two curved supports on the legs of a chair on which it may rock. **4. a.** an ice skate with a curved blade. **b.** the curve itself. **5.** *Brit.* a member of a group of teenagers in the mid-1960s who characteristically wore leather jackets and rode powerful motorcycles. **6. off one's rocker.** *Sl.* crazy.

rockery ('rɒkərɪ) *n., pl.* **-eries.** a garden constructed with rocks, esp. one where alpine plants are grown.

rocket ('rɒkɪt) *n.* **1.** a self-propelling device, esp. a cylinder containing a mixture of solid explosives, used as a firework, distress signal, etc. **2. a.** any vehicle propelled by a rocket engine, esp. one used to carry a spacecraft, etc. **b.** (*as modifier*): *rocket launcher.* **3.** *Brit. inf.* a severe reprimand (esp. in **get a rocket**). ~*vb.* **4.** (*tr.*) to propel (a missile, spacecraft, etc.) by means of a rocket. **5.** (*intr.; foll. by off, away, etc.*) to move off at high speed. **6.** (*intr.*) to rise rapidly: *he rocketed to the top.*

rocketry ('rɒkɪtrɪ) *n.* the science and technology of the design, operation, maintenance, and launching of rockets.

rock garden *n.* a garden featuring rocks or rockeries.

rocking chair *n.* a chair set on curving supports so that the sitter may rock backwards and forwards.

rocking horse *n.* a toy horse mounted on a pair of rockers on which a child can rock to and fro in a seesaw movement.

rock plant *n.* any plant that grows on rocks or in rocky ground.

rock rabbit *n. S. African.* another name for **dassie.** See **hyrax.**

rock salmon *n. Brit.* any of several coarse fishes when used as food, esp. the dogfish.

rock salt *n.* sodium chloride occurring in sedimentary beds and dried salt lakes: an important source of table salt.

rocky[1] ('rɒkɪ) *adj.* **rockier, rockiest. 1.** consisting of or abounding in rocks: *a rocky shore.* **2.** unyielding: *rocky determination.* **3.** hard like rock: *rocky muscles.* —**'rockiness** *n.*

rocky[2] ('rɒkɪ) *adj.* **rockier, rockiest. 1.** weak or unstable. **2.** *Inf.* (of a person) dizzy; nauseated. —**'rockily** *adv.* —**'rockiness** *n.*

rococo (rə'kəʊkəʊ) *n.* (*often cap.*) **1.** a style of architecture and decoration that originated in France in the early 18th century, characterized by elaborate but graceful ornamentation. **2.** an 18th-century style of music characterized by prettiness and extreme use of ornamentation. **3.** any florid or excessively ornamental style. ~*adj.* **4.** denoting, being in, or relating to the rococo. **5.** florid or excessively elaborate.

rod (rɒd) *n.* **1.** a slim cylinder of metal, wood, etc. **2.** a switch or bundle of switches used to administer corporal punishment. **3.** any of various staffs of insignia or office. **4.** power, esp. of a tyrannical kind: *a dictator's iron rod.* **5.** a straight slender shoot, stem, or cane of a woody plant. **6.** See **fishing rod. 7.** Also called: **pole, perch. a.** a unit of length equal to 5½ yards. **b.** a unit of square measure equal to 30¼ square yards. **7.** *Surveying.* another name (esp. U.S.) for **staff** (sense 8). **9.** Also called: **retinal rod.** any of the elongated cylindrical cells in the retina of the eye, which are sensitive to dim light but not to colour. **10.** any rod-shaped bacterium. **11.** *U.S.* a slang name for **pistol. 12.** short for **hot rod.** —**'rod,like** *adj.*

rode (rəʊd) *vb.* the past tense of **ride.**

rodent ('rəʊdənt) *n.* **a.** any of the relatively small placental mammals having constantly growing incisor teeth specialized for gnawing. The group includes rats, mice, squirrels, etc. **b.** (*as modifier*): *rodent characteristics.* —**'rodent-,like** *adj.*

rodeo ('rəʊdɪ,əʊ) *n., pl.* **-os.** *Chiefly U.S.* **1.** a display of the skills of cowboys, including bareback riding, etc. **2.** the rounding up of cattle for branding, etc. **3.** an enclosure for cattle that have been rounded up.

rodomontade (,rɒdəmɒn'teɪd, -'tɑːd) *Literary.* ~*n.* **1. a.** boastful words or behaviour. **b.** (*as modifier*): *rodomontade behaviour.* ~*vb.* **2.** (*intr.*) to boast or rant.

roe[1] (rəʊ) *n.* **1.** Also called: **hard roe.** the ovary of a female fish filled with mature eggs. **2.** Also called: **soft roe.** the testis of a male fish filled with mature sperm.

roe[2] (rəʊ) *n., pl.* **roes** *or* **roe.** short for **roe deer.**

roe deer *n.* a small graceful deer of woodlands of Europe and Asia. The antlers are small and the summer coat is reddish-brown.

rogation (rəʊ'geɪʃən) *n.* (*usually pl.*) *Christianity.* a solemn supplication, esp. in a form of ceremony prescribed by the Church.

Rogation Days *pl. n.* April 25 (the **Major Rogation**) and the Monday, Tuesday, and Wednesday before Ascension Day, observed by Christians as days of solemn supplication and marked by processions and special prayers.

roger ('rɒdʒə) *interj.* **1.** (used in signalling, telecommunications, etc.) message received and understood. **2.** an expression of agreement.

rogue (rəʊg) *n.* **1.** a dishonest or unprincipled person, esp. a man. **2.** *Often jocular.* a mischievous or wayward person, often a child. **3.** any inferior or defective speci-

---

THESAURUS

tough, vigorous, well **2.** boisterous, coarse, earthy, indecorous, raw, roisterous, rollicking, rough, rude, unsubtle **3.** commonsensical, down-to-earth, hard-headed, practical, pragmatic, realistic, sensible, straightforward

rock[1] **1.** boulder, stone **2.** anchor, bulwark,

cornerstone, foundation, mainstay, protection, support, tower of strength

rock[2] **1.** lurch, pitch, reel, roll, sway, swing, toss, wobble **2.** astonish, astound, daze, dumbfound, jar, set one back on one's heels (*Inf.*), shake, shock, stagger, stun, surprise

rocky **1.** boulder-strewn, craggy, pebbly,

rough, rugged, stony **2.** adamant, firm, flinty, hard, rocklike, rugged, solid, steady, tough, unyielding

rod bar, baton, birch, cane, dowel, mace, pole, sceptre, shaft, staff, stick, switch, wand

men, esp. a defective crop plant. **4.** *Arch.* a vagrant. **5. a.** an animal of vicious character that leads a solitary life. **b.** (*as modifier*): *a rogue elephant.* ~*vb.* **6.** (*tr.*) to remove (plants) from the main crop. —'**roguish** *adj.*

roguery ('rəʊgərɪ) *n., pl.* -**gueries. 1.** behaviour characteristic of a rogue. **2.** a roguish or mischievous act.

rogues' gallery *n.* a collection of portraits of known criminals kept by the police for identification purposes.

roister ('rɔɪstə) *vb.* (*intr.*) **1.** to engage in noisy or unrestrained merrymaking. **2.** to brag, bluster, or swagger. —'**roisterer** *n.* —'**roisterous** *adj.* —'**roisterously** *adv.*

role *or* **rôle** (rəʊl) *n.* **1.** a part or character in a play, film, etc., to be played by an actor or actress. **2.** *Psychol.* the part played by a person in a particular social setting, influenced by his expectation of what is appropriate. **3.** usual function: *what is his role in the organization?*

roll (rəʊl) *vb.* **1.** to move or cause to move along by turning over and over. **2.** to move or cause to move along on wheels or rollers. **3.** to flow or cause to flow onwards in an undulating movement. **4.** (*intr.*) (of animals, etc.) to turn onto the back and roll. **5.** (*intr.*) to extend in undulations: *the hills roll down to the sea.* **6.** (*intr.; usually foll. by around*) to move or occur in cycles. **7.** (*intr.*) (of a planet, the moon, etc.) to revolve in an orbit. **8.** (*intr.; foll. by on, by,* etc.) to pass or elapse: *the years roll by.* **9.** to rotate or cause to rotate wholly or partially: *to roll one's eyes.* **10.** to curl, cause to curl, or admit of being curled, so as to form a ball, tube, or cylinder. **11.** to make or form by shaping into a ball, tube, or cylinder: *to roll a cigarette.* **12.** (often foll. by *out*) to spread or cause to spread out flat or smooth under or as if under a roller: *to roll pastry.* **13.** to emit or utter with a deep prolonged reverberating sound: *the thunder rolled continuously.* **14.** to trill or cause to be trilled: *to roll one's r's.* **15.** (*intr.*) (of a vessel, aircraft, rocket, etc.) to turn from side to side around the longitudinal axis. **16.** to cause (an aircraft) to execute a roll or (of an aircraft) to execute a roll (sense 35). **17.** (*intr.*) to walk with a swaying gait, as when drunk. **18.** *Chiefly U.S.* to throw (dice). **19.** (*intr.*) to operate or begin to operate: *the presses rolled.* **20.** *Inf.* to make progress: *let the good times roll.* **21.** (*tr.*) *Sl., chiefly U.S. & N.Z.* to rob (a helpless person). **22. start the ball rolling.** *Inf.* to open or initiate (an action, discussion, etc.). ~*n.* **23.** the act or an instance of rolling. **24.** anything rolled up in a cylindrical form: *a roll of newspaper.* **25.** an official list or register, esp. of names: *an electoral roll.* **26.** a rounded mass: *rolls of flesh.* **27.** a cylinder used to flatten something; roller. **28.** a small cake of bread for one person. **29.** a flat pastry or cake rolled up with a meat (**sausage roll**), jam (**jam roll**), or other filling. **30.** a swell or undulation on a surface: *the roll of the hills.* **31.** a swaying, rolling, or unsteady movement or gait. **32.** a deep prolonged reverberating sound: *the roll of thunder.* **33.** a trilling sound; trill. **34.** a very rapid beating of the sticks on a drum. **35.** a flight manoeuvre in which an aircraft makes one complete rotation about its longitudinal axis without loss of height or change in direction. **36.** *Sl.* an act of sexual intercourse or petting (esp. in **a roll in the hay**). **37.** *U.S. sl.* an amount of money, esp. a wad of paper money. **38. strike off the roll(s). a.** to expel from membership. **b.** to debar (a solicitor) from practising, usually because of dishonesty. ~See also **roll in, roll on,** etc.

roll call *n.* the reading aloud of an official list of names, those present responding when their names are read out.

rolled gold *n.* a metal, such as brass, coated with a thin layer of gold. Also called (U.S.): **filled gold.**

roller ('rəʊlə) *n.* **1.** a cylinder having an absorbent surface and a handle, used for spreading paint. **2.** Also called: **garden roller.** a heavy cast-iron cylinder on an axle to which a handle is attached; used for flattening lawns. **3.** a long heavy wave of the sea, advancing towards the shore. **4.** a hardened cylinder of precision-ground steel that forms one of the rolling components of a roller bearing or of a linked driving chain. **5.** a cylinder fitted on pivots, used to enable heavy objects to be easily moved. **6.** *Printing.* a cylinder, usually of hard rubber, used to ink a plate before impression. **7.** any of various other cylindrical devices that rotate about a cylinder, used for any of various purposes. **8.** a small cylinder onto which a woman's hair may be rolled to make it curl. **9.** *Med.* a bandage consisting of a long strip of muslin rolled tightly into a cylindrical form before application. **10.** any of various Old World birds, such as the **European roller**, that have a blue, green, and brown plumage, a slightly hooked bill, and an erratic flight. **11.** (*often cap.*) a variety of tumbler pigeon. **12.** a person or thing that rolls. **13.** short for **steamroller.**

roller coaster *n.* (at a fair, etc.) a narrow railway with open carriages that run over sharp bends and steep inclines. Also called: **big dipper.**

roller skate *n.* **1.** a device having straps for fastening to a shoe and four small wheels that enable the wearer to glide swiftly over a floor. ~*vb.* **roller-skate. 2.** (*intr.*) to move on roller skates. —**roller skater** *n.*

roller towel *n.* a towel with the two ends sewn together, hung on a roller.

rollick ('rɒlɪk) *vb.* **1.** (*intr.*) to behave in a carefree or boisterous manner. ~*n.* **2.** a boisterous or carefree escapade. —'**rollicking** *adj.*

roll in *vb.* (*mainly intr.*) **1.** (*adv.*) to arrive in abundance or in large numbers. **2.** (*adv.*) *Inf.* to arrive at one's destination. **3. be rolling in.** (*prep.*) *Sl.* to abound or luxuriate in (wealth, money, etc.).

rolling ('rəʊlɪŋ) *adj.* **1.** having gentle rising and falling slopes: *rolling country.* **2.** reverberating: *rolling thunder.* **3.** that may be turned up or down: *a rolling hat brim.* **4.** *Sl.* extremely rich. ~*adv.* **5.** *Sl.* swaying or staggering (in **rolling drunk**).

rolling mill *n.* **1.** a mill or factory where ingots of heated metal are passed between rollers to produce sheets or bars of a required cross section and form. **2.** a machine having rollers that may be used for this purpose.

rolling pin *n.* a cylinder with handles at both ends used for rolling dough, pastry, etc., out flat.

rolling stock *n.* the wheeled vehicles collectively used on a railway, including the locomotives, passenger coaches, etc.

rolling stone *n.* a restless or wandering person.

rollmop ('rəʊlˌmɒp) *n.* a herring fillet rolled, usually around onion slices, and pickled in spiced vinegar.

rollneck ('rəʊlˌnɛk) *adj.* **1.** (of a garment) having a high neck that may be rolled over. ~*n.* **2.** a rollneck sweater or other garment.

roll on *vb.* **1.** *Brit.* used to express the wish that an eagerly anticipated event or date will come quickly: *roll on Saturday.* ~*adj.* **roll-on. 2.** (of a deodorant, etc.) dispensed by means of a revolving ball fitted into the neck of the container. ~*n.* **3.** a woman's foundation garment, made of elasticized material and having no fastenings.

roll-top desk *n.* a desk having a slatted wooden panel that can be pulled down over the writing surface when not in use.

roll up *vb.* (*adv.*) **1.** to form or cause to form a cylindrical shape. **2.** (*tr.*) to wrap (an object) round on itself or on an axis: *to roll up a map.* **3.** (*intr.*) *Inf.* to arrive, esp. in a vehicle. **4.** *Austral.* to assemble; congregate.

THESAURUS

rogue blackguard, charlatan, cheat, con man (*Inf.*), crook (*Inf.*), deceiver, devil, fraud, knave (*Archaic*), mountebank, ne'er-do-well, rapscallion, rascal, reprobate, scamp, scoundrel, sharper, swindler, villain

role 1. character, impersonation, part, portrayal, representation **2.** capacity, duty, function, job, part, position, post, task

roll *v.* **1.** elapse, flow, go past, go round, gyrate, pass, pivot, reel, revolve, rock, rotate, run, spin, swivel, trundle, turn, twirl, undulate, wheel, whirl **2.** bind, coil, curl, enfold,

entwine, envelop, furl, swathe, twist, wind, wrap **3.** even, flatten, level, press, smooth, spread **4.** boom, drum, echo, grumble, resound, reverberate, roar, rumble, thunder **5.** billow, lurch, reel, rock, sway, swing, toss, tumble, wallow, welter **6.** lumber, lurch, reel, stagger, swagger, sway, waddle ~*n.* **7.** cycle, gyration, reel, revolution, rotation, run, spin, turn, twirl, undulation, wheel, whirl **8.** ball, bobbin, cylinder, reel, scroll, spool **9.** annals, catalogue, census, chronicle, directory, index, inventory, list, record, register, roster,

schedule, scroll, table **10.** billowing, lurching, pitching, rocking, rolling, swell, tossing, undulation, wallowing, waves **11.** boom, drumming, growl, grumble, resonance, reverberation, roar, rumble, thunder

rollicking *adj.* boisterous, carefree, cavorting, devil-may-care, exuberant, frisky, frolicsome, hearty, jaunty, jovial, joyous, lively, merry, playful, rip-roaring (*Inf.*), romping, spirited, sportive, sprightly, swashbuckling

~n. **roll-up. 5.** *Austral.* the number attending a meeting, etc.

roly-poly ('rəʊlɪ'pəʊlɪ) *adj.* **1.** plump, buxom, or rotund. ~*n., pl.* **-lies. 2.** *Brit.* a strip of suet pastry spread with jam, fruit, or a savoury mixture, rolled up, and baked or steamed.

ROM (rom) *n. Computers. acronym for* read only memory.

rom. *Printing. abbrev. for* roman (type).

Rom. *abbrev. for:* **1.** Roman. **2.** Romance (languages). **3.** *Bible.* Romans.

roman ('rəʊmən) *adj.* **1.** of, relating to, or denoting a vertical style of printing type: the usual form of type for most printed matter. Cf. **italic.** ~*n.* **2.** roman type.

Roman ('rəʊmən) *adj.* **1.** of or relating to Rome or its inhabitants in ancient or modern times. **2.** of or relating to Roman Catholicism or the Roman Catholic Church. ~*n.* **3.** a citizen or inhabitant of ancient or modern Rome.

Roman alphabet *n.* the alphabet evolved by the ancient Romans for the writing of Latin, derived ultimately from the Phoenicians. The alphabet serves for writing most of the languages of W Europe.

Roman candle *n.* a firework that produces a continuous shower of sparks punctuated by coloured balls of fire.

Roman Catholic *adj.* **1.** of or relating to the Roman Catholic Church. ~*n.* **2.** a member of this Church. ~Often shortened to **Catholic.** —**Roman Catholicism** *n.*

Roman Catholic Church *n.* the Christian Church over which the pope presides, with administrative headquarters in the Vatican. Also called: **Catholic Church, Church of Rome.**

romance *n.* (rə'mæns, 'rəʊmæns). **1.** a love affair. **2.** love, esp. romantic love idealized for its purity or beauty. **3.** a spirit of or inclination for adventure or mystery. **4.** a mysterious, exciting, sentimental, or nostalgic quality, esp. one associated with a place. **5.** a narrative in verse or prose, written in a vernacular language in the Middle Ages, dealing with adventures of chivalrous heroes. **6.** any similar narrative work dealing with events and characters remote from ordinary life. **7.** a story, novel, film, etc., dealing with love, usually in an idealized or sentimental way. **8.** an extravagant, absurd, or fantastic account. **9.** a lyrical song or short instrumental composition having a simple melody. ~*vb.* (rə'mæns). **10.** *(intr.)* to tell, invent, or write extravagant or romantic fictions. **11.** *(intr.)* to tell extravagant or improbable lies. —**ro'mancer** *n.*

Romance (rə'mæns, 'rəʊmæns) *adj.* **1.** denoting, relating to, or belonging to the languages derived from Latin, including Italian, Spanish, Portuguese, French, and Rumanian. **2.** denoting a word borrowed from a Romance language. ~*n.* **3.** this group of languages.

Romanesque (ˌrəʊmə'nɛsk) *adj.* **1.** denoting or having the style of architecture used in W and S Europe from the 9th to the 12th century, characterized by the rounded arch and massive-masonry wall construction. **2.** denoting a corresponding style in painting, sculpture, etc.

Roman nose *n.* a nose having a high prominent bridge.

Roman numerals *pl. n.* the letters used by the Romans for the representation of cardinal numbers, still used occasionally today. The integers are represented by the following letters: I (= 1), V (= 5), X (= 10), L (= 50), C (= 100), D (= 500), and M (= 1000). VI = 6 (V + I), but IV = 4 (V − I).

romantic (rəʊ'mæntɪk) *adj.* **1.** of, relating to, imbued with, or characterized by romance. **2.** evoking or given to thoughts and feelings of love, esp. idealized or sentimental love: *a romantic setting.* **3.** impractical, visionary, or idealistic: *a romantic scheme.* **4.** *Often euphemistic.* imaginary or fictitious: *a romantic account*

of one's war service. **5.** *(often cap.)* of or relating to a movement in European art, music, and literature in the late 18th and early 19th centuries, characterized by an emphasis on feeling and content rather than order and form. ~*n.* **6.** a person who is romantic, as in being idealistic, amorous, or soulful. **7.** a person whose tastes in art, literature, etc., lie mainly in romanticism. **8.** *(often cap.)* a poet, composer, etc., of the romantic period or whose main inspiration is romanticism. —**ro'mantically** *adv.*

romanticism (rəʊ'mæntɪˌsɪzəm) *n.* **1.** *(often cap.)* the theory, practice, and style of the romantic art, music, and literature of the late 18th and early 19th centuries, usually opposed to classicism. **2.** romantic attitudes, ideals, or qualities. —**ro'manticist** *n.*

romanticize *or* **-cise** (rəʊ'mæntɪˌsaɪz) *vb.* **1.** *(intr.)* to think or act in a romantic way. **2.** *(tr.)* to interpret according to romantic precepts. **3.** to make or become romantic, as in style. —**ro,mantici'zation** *or* **-ci'sation** *n.*

Romany *or* **Rommany** ('rɒmənɪ, 'rəʊ-) *n., pl.* **-nies. 1. a.** another name for a **Gypsy. b.** *(as modifier):* Romany customs. **2.** the language of the Gypsies, belonging to the Indic branch of the Indo-European family.

Romeo ('rəʊmɪəʊ) *n., pl.* **-os.** an ardent male lover.

romp (rɒmp) *vb.* *(intr.)* **1.** to play or run about wildly, boisterously, or joyfully. **2. romp home** *(or* **in).** to win a race, etc., easily. ~*n.* **3.** a noisy or boisterous game or prank. **4.** *Arch.* a playful or boisterous child, esp. a girl. **5.** an easy victory. —'**rompingly** *adv.*

rompers ('rɒmpəz) *pl. n.* **1.** a one-piece baby garment consisting of trousers and a bib with straps. **2.** *N.Z.* a type of costume worn by schoolgirls for games and gymnastics.

rondeau ('rɒndəʊ) *n., pl.* **-deaux** (-dəʊ, -dəʊz). a poem consisting of 13 or 10 lines with two rhymes and having the opening words of the first line used as an unrhymed refrain.

rondo ('rɒndəʊ) *n., pl.* **-dos.** a piece of music in which a refrain is repeated between episodes: often constitutes the form of the last movement of a sonata or concerto.

rone (rəʊn) *n. Scot.* a drainpipe for carrying rainwater from a roof.

rood (ruːd) *n.* **1. a.** a crucifix, esp. one set on a beam or screen at the entrance to the chancel of a church. **b.** *(as modifier):* rood screen. **2.** the Cross on which Christ was crucified. **3.** a unit of area equal to one quarter of an acre or 0.10117 hectares. **4.** a unit of area equal to one square rod.

roof (ruːf) *n., pl.* **roofs** (ruːfs, ruːvz). **1. a.** a structure that covers or forms the top of a building. **b.** *(in combination):* the rooftop. **c.** *(as modifier):* a roof garden. **2.** the top covering of a vehicle, oven, or other structure: *the roof of a car.* **3.** *Anat.* any structure that covers an organ or part: *the roof of the mouth.* **4.** a highest or topmost point or part: *Mount Everest is the roof of the world.* **5.** a house or other shelter: *a poor man's roof.* **6. hit** *(or* **raise** *or* **go through) the roof.** *Inf.* to get extremely angry. ~*vb.* **7.** *(tr.)* to provide or cover with a roof or rooflike part. —'**roofer** *n.* —'**roofless** *adj.*

roof garden *n.* a garden on a flat roof of a building.

roofing ('ruːfɪŋ) *n.* **1.** material used to construct a roof. **2.** the act of constructing a roof.

roof rack *n.* a rack attached to the roof of a motor vehicle for carrying luggage, skis, etc.

rooftree ('ruːfˌtriː) *n.* another name for **ridgepole.**

rook¹ (rʊk) *n.* **1.** a large Eurasian passerine bird, with a black plumage and a whitish base to its bill. **2.** *Sl.* a swindler or cheat, esp. one who cheats at cards. ~*vb.* **3.** *(tr.) Sl.* to overcharge, swindle, or cheat.

rook² (rʊk) *n.* a chess piece that may move any number of unoccupied squares in a straight line, horizontally or vertically. Also called: **castle.**

THESAURUS

roly-poly buxom, chubby, fat, overweight, plump, podgy, pudgy, rotund, rounded, tubby

romance *n.* **1.** affair, *affaire (du coeur)*, affair of the heart, amour, attachment, intrigue, liaison, love affair, passion, relationship **2.** adventure, charm, colour, excitement, exoticness, fascination, glamour, mystery, nostalgia, sentiment **3.** fairy tale, fantasy, fiction, idyll, legend, love story, melodra-

ma, novel, story, tale, tear-jerker (*Inf.*) **4.** absurdity, exaggeration, fabrication, fairy tale, falsehood, fiction, flight of fancy, invention, lie, tall story (*Inf.*), trumped-up story ~*v.* **5.** exaggerate, fantasize, let one's imagination run away with one, lie, make up stories, stretch the truth, tell stories

romantic *adj.* **1.** amorous, fond, lovey-dovey, loving, mushy (*Inf.*), passionate, sentimental, sloppy (*Inf.*), soppy (*Brit. inf.*), ten-

der **2.** charming, colourful, exciting, exotic, fascinating, glamorous, mysterious, nostalgic, picturesque **3.** dreamy, high-flown, idealistic, impractical, quixotic, starry-eyed, unrealistic, utopian, visionary, whimsical **4.** chimerical, exaggerated, extravagant, fabulous, fairy-tale, fanciful, fantastic, fictitious, idyllic, imaginary, imaginative, improbable, legendary, made-up, unrealistic, wild ~*n.* **5.** Don Quixote, dreamer, idealist, romancer,

rookery ('rokərı) n., pl. **-eries. 1.** a group of nesting rooks. **2.** a clump of trees containing rooks' nests. **3.** a group of breeding birds of certain other species, esp. penguins.

rookie ('roki) n. Inf. a newcomer, esp. a raw recruit in the army.

room (ru:m, rom) n. **1.** space or extent, esp. unoccupied or unobstructed space for a particular purpose: *is there room to pass?* **2.** an area within a building enclosed by a floor, a ceiling, and walls or partitions. **3.** (functioning as sing. or pl.) the people present in a room: *the whole room was laughing.* **4.** (foll. by for) opportunity or scope: *room for manoeuvre.* ~vb. **5.** (intr.) to occupy or share a room or lodging: *where does he room?* —'roomer n. —'room,ful n.

rooming house n. U.S. a house having self-contained furnished rooms or flats for renting.

roommate ('ru:m,meit, 'rom-) n. a person with whom one shares a room or lodging.

room service n. service in a hotel providing meals, etc., in guests' rooms.

roomy ('ru:mı, 'romı) adj. **roomier, roomiest.** spacious. —'roomily adv. —'roominess n.

roost (ru:st) n. **1.** a place, perch, branch, etc., where birds, esp. domestic fowl, rest or sleep. **2.** a temporary place to rest or stay. **3. rule the roost.** to be in charge or dominate. ~vb. **4.** (intr.) to rest or sleep on a roost. **5.** (intr.) to settle down or stay. **6. come home to roost.** to have unfavourable repercussions.

rooster ('ru:stə) n. Chiefly U.S. the male of the domestic fowl; a cock.

root[1] (ru:t) n. **1. a.** the organ of a higher plant that anchors the rest of the plant in the ground and absorbs water and mineral salts from the soil. **b.** (loosely) any of the branches of such an organ. **2.** any plant part, such as a tuber, that is similar to a root in function or appearance. **3.** the essential part or nature of something: *your analysis strikes at the root of the problem.* **4.** Anat. the embedded portion of a tooth, nail, hair, etc. **5.** origin or derivation. **6.** (pl.) a person's sense of belonging in a community, place, etc., esp. the one in which he was born or brought up. **7.** Bible. a descendant. **8.** Linguistics. the form of a word that remains after removal of all affixes. **9.** Maths. a quantity that when multiplied by itself a certain number of times equals a given quantity: *3 is a cube root of 27.* **10.** Also called: **solution.** Maths. a number that when substituted for the variable satisfies a given equation. **11.** Music. (in harmony) the note forming the foundation of a chord. **12.** Austral. taboo sl. sexual intercourse. **13. root and branch.** (adv.) entirely; utterly. ~Related adj.: **radical.** ~vb. **14.** (intr.) Also: **take root.** to establish a root and begin to grow. **15.** (intr.) Also: **take root.** to become established, embedded, or effective. **16.** (tr.) to embed with or as if with a root or roots. **17.** Austral. taboo sl. to have sexual intercourse (with). ~See also **root out.** —'rooter n. —'root,like adj. —'rooty adj. —'rootiness n.

root[2] (ru:t) vb. (intr.) **1.** (of a pig) to burrow in or dig up the earth in search of food, using the snout. **2.** (foll. by about, around, in, etc.) Inf. to search vigorously but unsystematically. —'rooter n.

root canal n. the passage in the root of a tooth through which its nerves and blood vessels enter the pulp cavity.

root crop n. a crop, as of turnips or beets, cultivated for the food value of its roots.

root for vb. (intr., prep.) U.S. Inf. to give support to (a contestant, team, etc.), as by cheering.

rootle ('ru:t^əl) vb. (intr.) Brit. another word for **root**[2].

rootless ('ru:tlɪs) adj. having no roots, esp. (of a person) having no ties with a particular place.

root mean square n. the square root of the average of the squares of a set of numbers or quantities: *the root mean square of* 1, 2, *and* 4 is $\sqrt{} = \sqrt{7}$. Abbrev.: **rms**

root out vb. (tr., adv.) to remove or eliminate completely: *we must root out inefficiency.*

rootstock ('ru:t,stɒk) n. **1.** another name for **rhizome. 2.** another name for **stock** (sense 7). **3.** Biol. a basic structure from which offshoots have developed.

rope (rəop) n. **1. a.** a fairly thick cord made of intertwined hemp or other fibres or of wire or other strong material. **b.** (as modifier): *a rope ladder.* **2.** a row of objects fastened to form a line: *a rope of pearls.* **3.** a quantity of material wound in the form of a cord. **4.** filament or strand, esp. of something viscous or glutinous: *a rope of slime.* **5. the rope. a.** a rope halter used for hanging. **b.** death by hanging. **6. give (someone) enough rope to hang himself** or **plenty of rope.** to allow (a person) to accomplish his own downfall by his own foolish acts. **7. know the ropes.** to have a thorough understanding of a particular sphere of activity. **8. on the ropes. a.** Boxing. driven against the ropes enclosing the ring by an opponent's attack. **b.** in a hopeless position. ~vb. **9.** (tr.) to bind or fasten with or as if with a rope. **10.** (tr.; usually foll. by off) to enclose or divide by means of a rope. **11.** (when intr., foll. by up) Mountaineering. to tie (climbers) together with a rope.

rope in vb. (tr., adv.) **1.** Brit. to persuade to take part in some activity. **2.** U.S. to trick or entice into some activity.

ropewalk ('rəop,wɔ:k) n. a long narrow usually covered path or shed where ropes are made.

ropy ('rəopı) adj. **ropier, ropiest. 1.** Also: **ropey.** Brit. inf. inferior. **2.** (of a viscous or sticky substance) forming strands. **3.** resembling a rope. —'ropily adv. —'ropiness n.

Roquefort ('rɒkfɔ:) n. a blue-veined cheese with a strong flavour, made from ewe's and goat's milk.

rorqual ('rɔ:kwəl) n. any of several whalebone whales that have a dorsal fin and a series of grooves along the throat and chest. Also called: **finback.**

Rorschach test ('rɔ:ʃɑ:k) n. Psychol. a personality test consisting of a number of unstructured ink blots presented for interpretation.

rosaceous (rəo'zeıʃəs) adj. **1.** of or belonging to the Rosaceae, a family of plants typically having white, yellow, pink, or red five-petalled flowers. The family includes the rose, strawberry, blackberry, and many fruit trees. **2.** like a rose, pink-, or rose-coloured.

rosary ('rəozərı) n., pl. **-saries. 1.** R.C. Church. **a.** a series of prayers counted on a string of beads, usually five or 15 decades of Aves, each decade beginning with a Paternoster and ending with a Gloria. **b.** a string of 55 or 165 beads used to count these prayers as they are recited. **2.** (in other religions) a similar string of beads used in praying. **3.** an archaic word for a **garland** (of flowers, etc.).

rose[1] (rəoz) n. **1. a.** a shrub or climbing plant having prickly stems, compound leaves, and fragrant flowers. **b.** (in combination): *rosebush.* **2.** the flower of any of these plants. **3.** any of various similar plants, such as the Christmas rose. **4.** a purplish-pink colour. **5. a.** a cut for a gemstone, having a hemispherical faceted crown and a flat base. **b.** a gem so cut. **6.** a perforated cap fitted to a

---

THESAURUS

rook bilk, cheat, clip (Sl.), defraud, diddle (Inf.), do (Sl.), fleece, gyp (Sl.), mulct, overcharge, rip off (Sl.), sting (Inf.), swindle

room 1. allowance, area, capacity, compass, elbowroom, expanse, extent, latitude, leeway, margin, play, range, scope, space, territory, volume **2.** apartment, chamber, office **3.** chance, occasion, opportunity, scope

roomy ample, broad, capacious, commodious, extensive, generous, large, sizable, spacious, wide

root n. **1.** radicle, radix, rhizome, stem, tuber **2.** base, beginnings, bottom, cause, core, crux, derivation, essence, foundation, fountainhead, fundamental, germ, heart, mainspring, nub, nucleus, occasion, origin, seat, seed, source, starting point **3.** Plural birthplace, cradle, family, heritage, home, origins, sense of belonging **4. root and branch** completely, entirely, finally, radically, thoroughly, totally, to the last man, utterly, wholly, without exception ~v. **5.** anchor, become established, become settled, embed, entrench, establish, fasten, fix, ground, implant, moor, set, stick, take root

rooted confirmed, deep, deeply felt, deepseated, entrenched, established, firm, fixed, ingrained, radical, rigid

root out 1. Also **root up** abolish, cut out, destroy, dig up by the roots, do away with, efface, eliminate, eradicate, erase, extermi-nate, extirpate, get rid of, remove, tear out by the roots, uproot, weed out **2.** bring to light, dig out, discover, dredge up, produce, turn up, unearth

rope n. **1.** cable, cord, hawser, line, strand **2. the rope** capital punishment, halter, hanging, lynching, noose **3. know the ropes** be an old hand, be experienced, be knowledgeable, know all the ins and outs, know one's way around, know the score (Inf.), know what's what ~v. **4.** bind, fasten, hitch, lash, lasso, moor, pinion, tether, tie

rope in drag in, engage, enlist, inveigle, involve, persuade, talk into

watering can or hose, causing the water to issue in a spray. **7.** a design or decoration shaped like a rose; ro-sette. **8. bed of roses.** a situation of ease and luxury. **9. under the rose.** in secret; privately; sub rosa. ~*vb.* **10.** (*tr.*) to make rose-coloured; cause to blush or redden. —'rose,like *adj.*

rose² ('rəʊz) *vb.* the past tense of **rise.**

rosé ('rəʊzeɪ) *n.* any pink wine, made either by remov-ing the skins of red grapes after only a little colour has been extracted or by mixing red and white wines.

roseate ('rəʊzɪ,eɪt) *adj.* **1.** of the colour rose or pink. **2.** excessively or idealistically optimistic.

rosebay ('rəʊz,beɪ) *n.* **1.** *U.S.* any of several rhododen-drons. **2. rosebay willowherb.** a perennial plant that has spikes of deep pink flowers and is widespread in N temperate regions. **3.** another name for **oleander.**

rosebud ('rəʊz,bʌd) *n.* **1.** the bud of a rose. **2.** *Literary.* a pretty young woman.

rose-coloured *adj.* **1.** of the colour rose; rosy. **2.** ex-cessively optimistic. **3. see through rose-coloured glas-ses** (*or* **spectacles**). to view in an excessively optimistic light.

rosemary ('rəʊzmərɪ) *n., pl.* **-maries.** an aromatic European shrub widely cultivated for its grey-green evergreen leaves, which are used in cookery and in the manufacture of perfumes. It is the traditional flower of remembrance.

rose of Sharon ('ʃærən) *n.* a creeping shrub native to SE Europe but widely cultivated, having large yellow flowers. Also called: **Aaron's beard.**

rosette (rəʊ'zɛt) *n.* **1.** a decoration resembling a rose, esp. an arrangement of ribbons in a rose-shaped design worn as a badge or presented as a prize. **2.** another name for **rose window. 3.** *Bot.* a circular cluster of leaves growing from the base of a stem.

rose-water *n.* **1.** scented water made by the distilla-tion of rose petals or by impregnation with oil of roses. **2.** (*modifier*) elegant or delicate, esp. excessively so.

rose window *n.* a circular window, esp. one that has ornamental tracery radiating from the centre to form a symmetrical roselike pattern. Also called: **wheel win-dow, rosette.**

rosewood ('rəʊz,wʊd) *n.* the hard dark wood of any of various tropical trees. It has a roselike scent and is used in cabinetwork.

rosin ('rɒzɪn) *n.* **1.** Also called: **colophony.** a translucent brittle amber substance produced in the distillation of crude turpentine oleoresin and used in making varnish-es, printing inks, and sealing waxes and for treating the bows of stringed instruments. **2.** another name for **resin** (sense 1). ~*vb.* **3.** (*tr.*) to treat or coat with rosin. —'rosiny *adj.*

ROSPA ('rɒspə) *n.* (in Britain) *acronym for* Royal Soci-ety for the Prevention of Accidents.

roster ('rɒstə) *n.* **1.** a list or register, esp. one showing the order of people enrolled for duty. ~*vb.* **2.** (*tr.*) to place on a roster.

rostrum ('rɒstrəm) *n., pl.* **-trums** *or* **-tra** (-trə). **1.** any platform on which public speakers stand to address an audience. **2.** a platform in front of an orchestra on which the conductor stands. **3.** another word for **ram**

(sense 5). **4.** the prow of an ancient Roman ship. **5.** *Biol.* a beak or beaklike part. —'rostral *adj.*

rosy ('rəʊzɪ) *adj.* **rosier, rosiest. 1.** of the colour rose or pink. **2.** having a healthy pink complexion: *rosy cheeks.* **3.** optimistic, esp. excessively so: *a rosy view of social improvements.* **4.** resembling or abounding in roses. —'rosily *adv.* —'rosiness *n.*

rot (rɒt) *vb.* **rotting, rotted. 1.** to decay or cause to de-cay as a result of bacterial or fungal action. **2.** (*intr.; usually foll. by off or away*) to crumble (off) or break (away), as from decay or long use. **3.** (*intr.*) to become weak or depressed through inertia, confinement, etc.; languish: *rotting in prison.* **4.** to become or cause to be-come morally degenerate. ~*n.* **5.** the process of rotting or the state of being rotten. **6.** something decomposed. Related *adj.*: **putrid. 7.** short for **dry rot. 8.** *Pathol.* any putrefactive decomposition of tissues. **9.** a condition in plants characterized by decay of tissues, caused by bac-teria, fungi, etc. **10.** *Vet. science.* a contagious fungal disease of sheep. **11.** (*also interj.*) nonsense; rubbish.

rota ('rəʊtə) *n. Chiefly Brit.* a register of names showing the order in which people take their turn to perform cer-tain duties.

rotary ('rəʊtərɪ) *adj.* **1.** operating by rotation. **2.** turn-ing; revolving. ~*n., pl.* **-ries. 3.** a part of a machine that rotates about an axis. **4.** *U.S. & Canad.* another term for **roundabout** (sense 2).

Rotary Club *n.* any of the local clubs that form **Rota-ry International,** an international association of profes-sional and business men founded in the U.S. in 1905 to promote community service. —**Rotarian** (rəʊ'tɛərɪən) *n., adj.*

rotate *vb.* (rəʊ'teɪt). **1.** to turn or cause to turn around an axis; revolve or spin. **2.** to follow or cause to follow a set sequence. ~*adj.* ('rəʊteɪt). **3.** *Bot.* designating a co-rolla the petals of which radiate like the spokes of a wheel. —**ro'tatable** *adj.* —**ro'tation** *n.*

rote (rəʊt) *n.* **1.** a habitual or mechanical routine or pro-cedure. **2. by rote.** by repetition; by heart (often in **learn by rote**).

rotgut ('rɒt,gʌt) *n. Facetious sl.* alcoholic drink, esp. spirits, of inferior quality.

rotisserie (rəʊ'tɪsərɪ) *n.* **1.** a rotating spit on which meat, poultry, etc., can be cooked. **2.** a shop or restau-rant where meat is roasted to order.

rotor ('rəʊtə) *n.* **1.** the rotating member of a machine or device, such as the revolving arm of the distributor of an internal-combustion engine. **2.** a system of rotating parts, esp. the assembly of aerofoils of a helicopter.

rotovator ('rəʊtə,veɪtə) *n.* a mechanical cultivator with rotary blades. —'roto,vate *vb.*

rotten ('rɒtən) *adj.* **1.** decomposing, decaying, or putrid. **2.** breaking up, esp. through age or hard use: *rotten iron-work.* **3.** morally corrupt. **4.** disloyal or treacherous. **5.** *Inf.* unpleasant: *rotten weather.* **6.** *Inf.* unsatisfactory or poor: *rotten workmanship.* —'rottenly *adv.* —'rotten-ness *n.*

rotter ('rɒtə) *n. Sl., chiefly Brit.* a worthless, unpleasant, or despicable person.

rotund (rəʊ'tʌnd) *adj.* **1.** rounded or spherical in shape. **2.** plump. **3.** sonorous or grandiloquent. —**ro'tundity** *n.*

THESAURUS

roster agenda, catalogue, inventory, list, listing, register, roll, rota, schedule, scroll, ta-ble

rostrum dais, platform, podium, stage

rosy 1. pink, red, roseate, rose-coloured **2.** blooming, blushing, fresh, glowing, healthy-looking, reddish, roseate, rubicund, ruddy **3.** auspicious, bright, cheerful, encouraging, fa-vourable, hopeful, optimistic, promising, re-assuring, roseate, rose-coloured, sunny

rot *v.* **1.** corrode, corrupt, crumble, decay, decompose, degenerate, deteriorate, disinte-grate, fester, go bad, moulder, perish, putre-fy, spoil, taint **2.** decline, degenerate, deterio-rate, languish, waste away, wither away ~*n.* **3.** blight, canker, corrosion, corruption, de-cay, decomposition, deterioration, disinte-gration, mould, putrefaction, putrescence **4.** balderdash, bosh (*Inf.*), bunk (*Inf.*), bunkum, claptrap (*Inf.*), codswallop (*Brit. sl.*), drivel, flapdoodle (*Sl.*), guff (*Sl.*), hogwash, moon-shine, nonsense, poppycock (*Inf.*), rubbish,

stuff and nonsense, tommyrot, tosh (*Inf.*), twaddle

rotary gyratory, revolving, rotating, rota-tional, rotatory, spinning, turning

rotate 1. go round, gyrate, pirouette, pivot, reel, revolve, spin, swivel, turn, wheel **2.** al-ternate, follow in sequence, interchange, switch, take turns

rotation 1. gyration, orbit, pirouette, reel, revolution, spin, spinning, turn, turning, wheel **2.** alternation, cycle, interchanging, sequence, succession, switching

rotten 1. bad, corroded, corrupt, crum-bling, decayed, decaying, decomposed, de-composing, disintegrating, festering, fetid, foul, mouldering, mouldy, perished, putres-cent, putrid, rank, sour, stinking, tainted, un-sound **2.** bent (*Sl.*), corrupt, crooked (*Inf.*), deceitful, degenerate, dishonest, dishonour-able, disloyal, faithless, immoral, mercenary, perfidious, treacherous, untrustworthy, ve-nal, vicious **3.** *Inf.* base, contemptible, despic-

able, dirty, disagreeable, filthy, mean, nasty, scurrilous, unpleasant, vile, wicked **4.** *Inf.* bad, deplorable, disappointing, regrettable, unfortunate, unlucky **5.** *Inf.* crummy (*Sl.*), ill-considered, ill thought-out, inadequate, infe-rior, lousy (*Sl.*), low-grade, poor, punk, ropy (*Inf.*), sorry, substandard, unacceptable, un-satisfactory **6.** *Inf.* bad, below par, ill, off col-our, poorly (*Inf.*), ropy (*Inf.*), rough (*Inf.*), sick, under the weather (*Inf.*), unwell

rotter bad lot, blackguard, blighter (*Brit. inf.*), bounder (*Inf.*), cad (*Brit. inf.*), cur, louse (*Sl.*), rat (*Sl.*), stinker (*Sl.*), swine

rotund 1. bulbous, globular, orbicular, round, rounded, spherical **2.** chubby, corpu-lent, fat, fleshy, heavy, obese, plump, podgy, portly, roly-poly, rounded, stout, tubby **3.** full, grandiloquent, magniloquent, orotund, reso-nant, rich, round, sonorous

—**ro'tundly** adv.
rotunda (rəʊ'tʌndə) n. a circular building or room, esp. one that has a dome.
rouble or **ruble** ('ruːbəl) n. the standard monetary unit of the Soviet Union.
roué ('ruːeɪ) n. a debauched or lecherous man; rake.
rouge (ruːʒ) n. **1.** a red powder or cream, used as a cosmetic for adding redness to the cheeks. **2.** Canad. football. a score of one point gained by the kicking team when the defending team fails to run a kickoff or a punt back from their own end zone. ~vb. (tr.) **3.** to apply rouge to. **4.** to score a rouge.
rough (rʌf) adj. **1.** (of a surface) not smooth; uneven or irregular. **2.** (of ground) covered with scrub, boulders, etc. **3.** denoting or taking place on uncultivated ground: rough grazing. **4.** shaggy or hairy. **5.** turbulent: a rough sea. **6.** (of performance or motion) uneven; irregular: a rough engine. **7.** (of behaviour or character) rude, coarse, or violent. **8.** harsh or sharp: rough words. **9.** Inf. severe or unpleasant: a rough lesson. **10.** (of work, etc.) requiring physical rather than mental effort. **11.** Inf. ill: he felt rough after an evening of heavy drinking. **12.** unfair: rough luck. **13.** harsh or grating to the ear. **14.** without refinement, luxury, etc. **15.** not perfected in any detail; rudimentary: rough workmanship; rough justice. **16.** not prepared or dressed: rough gemstones. **17.** (of a guess, etc.) approximate. **18.** having the sound of h; aspirated. **19. rough on.** Inf., chiefly Brit. **a.** severe towards. **b.** unfortunate for (a person). **20. the rough side of one's tongue.** harsh words; a rebuke. ~n. **21.** rough ground. **22.** a sketch or preliminary piece of artwork. **23.** unfinished or crude state (esp. in **in the rough**). **24. the rough.** Golf. the part of the course bordering the fairways where the grass is untrimmed. **25.** Inf. a violent person; thug. **26.** the unpleasant side of something (esp. in **take the rough with the smooth**). ~adv. **27.** roughly. **28. sleep rough.** to spend the night in the open; be without shelter. ~vb. **29.** (tr.) to make rough; roughen. **30.** (tr.; foll. by out, in, etc.) to prepare (a sketch, report, etc.) in preliminary form. **31. rough it.** Inf. to live without the usual comforts of life. ~See also **rough up.** —'**roughish** adj. —'**roughly** adv. —'**roughness** n.
roughage ('rʌfɪdʒ) n. **1.** the coarse indigestible constituents of food, which provide bulk to the diet and aid digestion. **2.** any rough material.
rough-and-ready adj. **1.** crude, unpolished, or hastily prepared, but sufficient for the purpose. **2.** (of a person) without formality or refinement.
rough-and-tumble n. **1.** a fight or scuffle without rules. ~adj. **2.** characterized by disorderliness and disregard for rules.
roughcast ('rʌf,kɑːst) n. **1.** a coarse plaster used to cover the surface of an external wall. **2.** any rough or preliminary form, model, etc. ~adj. **3.** covered with roughcast. ~vb. **-casting, -cast.** **4.** to apply roughcast to (a wall, etc.). **5.** to prepare in rough. —'**rough,caster** n.
rough diamond n. **1.** an unpolished diamond. **2.** an intrinsically trustworthy or good person with uncouth manners or dress.
rough-dry adj. **1.** (of clothes or linen) dried ready for pressing. ~vb. **-drying, -dried.** **2.** (tr.) to dry (clothes, etc.) without ironing them.
roughen ('rʌfən) vb. to make or become rough.

rough-hew vb. **-hewing, -hewed; -hewed** or **-hewn.** (tr.) to cut or shape roughly without finishing the surface.
roughhouse ('rʌf,haʊs) n. Sl. rough, disorderly, or noisy behaviour.
roughneck ('rʌf,nɛk) n. Sl. **1.** a rough or violent person; thug. **2.** a worker in an oil-drilling operation.
roughshod ('rʌf,ʃɒd) adj. **1.** (of a horse) shod with rough-bottomed shoes to prevent sliding. ~adv. **2. ride roughshod over.** to treat harshly and without consideration.
rough up vb. (tr., adv.) **1.** to treat violently; beat up. **2.** to cause (feathers, hair, etc.) to stand up by rubbing against the grain.
roulette (ruː'lɛt) n. **1.** a gambling game in which a ball is dropped onto a spinning horizontal wheel divided into numbered slots, with players betting on the slot into which the ball will fall. **2.** a toothed wheel for making a line of perforations. **3.** a curve generated by a point on one curve rolling on another. ~vb. (tr.) **4.** to use a roulette on (something), as in engraving, making stationery, etc.
round (raʊnd) adj. **1.** having a flat circular shape, as a hoop. **2.** having the shape of a ball. **3.** curved; not angular. **4.** involving or using circular motion. **5.** (prenominal) complete: a round dozen. **6.** Maths. **a.** forming or expressed by a whole number, with no fraction. **b.** expressed to the nearest ten, hundred, or thousand: in round figures. **7.** (of a sum of money) considerable. **8.** fully depicted or developed, as a character in a book. **9.** (of sound) full and sonorous. **10.** (of pace) brisk; lively. **11.** (prenominal) (of speech) candid; unmodified: a round assertion. **12.** (of a vowel) pronounced with rounded lips. ~n. **13.** a round shape or object. **14. in the round. a.** in full detail. **b.** Theatre. with the audience all round the stage. **15.** a session, as of a negotiation: a round of talks. **16.** a series: a giddy round of parties. **17. the daily round.** the usual activities of one's day. **18.** a stage of a competition: he was eliminated in the first round. **19.** (often pl.) a series of calls: a milkman's round. **20.** a playing of all the holes on a golf course. **21.** a single turn of play by each player, as in a card game. **22.** one of a number of periods in a boxing, wrestling, or other match. **23.** a single discharge by a gun. **24.** a bullet or other charge of ammunition. **25.** a number of drinks bought at one time for a group of people. **26.** a single slice of bread. **27.** a general outburst of applause, etc. **28.** movement in a circle. **29.** Music. a partsong in which the voices follow each other at equal intervals at the same pitch. **30.** a sequence of bells rung in order of treble to tenor. **31.** a cut of beef from the thigh. **32. go or make the rounds. a.** to go from place to place, as in making social calls. **b.** (of information, rumour, etc.) to be passed around, so as to be generally known. ~prep., adv. **33.** a less formal word for **around.** **34. all year round.** throughout the year. ~vb. **35.** to make or become round. **36.** (tr.) to encircle; surround. **37.** to move or cause to move with turning motion: to round a bend. **38.** (tr.) **a.** to pronounce (a speech sound) with rounded lips. **b.** to purse (the lips). ~See also **round down, round off,** etc. —'**roundish** adj. —'**roundness** n.
▷ Usage. See **around.**

THESAURUS

rough adj. **1.** broken, bumpy, craggy, irregular, jagged, rocky, rugged, stony, uneven **2.** bristly, bushy, coarse, dishevelled, disordered, fuzzy, hairy, shaggy, tangled, tousled, uncut, unshaven, unshorn **3.** agitated, boisterous, choppy, inclement, squally, stormy, tempestuous, turbulent, wild **4.** bearish, bluff, blunt, brusque, churlish, coarse, curt, discourteous, ill-bred, ill-mannered, impolite, inconsiderate, indelicate, loutish, rude, unceremonious, uncivil, uncouth, uncultured, ungracious, unmannerly, unpolished, unrefined, untutored **5.** boisterous, cruel, curt, drastic, extreme, hard, harsh, nasty, rowdy, severe, sharp, tough, unfeeling, unjust, unpleasant, violent **6.** Inf. below par, ill, not a hundred per cent (Inf.), off colour, poorly (Inf.), ropy (Inf.), rotten (Inf.), sick, under the weather (Inf.), unwell, upset **7.** cacophonous, discordant, grating, gruff, harsh, husky, inharmoni-

ous, jarring, rasping, raucous, unmusical **8.** arduous, austere, hard, rugged, spartan, tough, uncomfortable, unpleasant, unrefined **9.** basic, crude, cursory, formless, hasty, imperfect, incomplete, quick, raw, rough-and-ready, rough-hewn, rudimentary, shapeless, sketchy, unfinished, unpolished, unrefined, untutored **10.** crude, raw, rough-hewn, uncut, undressed, unhewn, unpolished, unprocessed, unwrought **11.** amorphous, approximate, estimated, foggy, general, hazy, imprecise, inexact, sketchy, vague ~n. **12.** draft, mock-up, outline, preliminary sketch, suggestion **13.** Inf. bruiser, bully boy, roughneck (Sl.), rowdy, ruffian, thug, tough ~v. **14. rough out** adumbrate, block out, delineate, draft, outline, plan, sketch, suggest **15. rough up** bash up (Sl.), batter, beat up, do over (Sl.), knock about, maltreat, manhandle, mistreat, thrash

rough-and-tumble 1. n. affray (Law), brawl, donnybrook, dust-up, (Inf.), fight, fracas, melee, punch-up (Brit. sl.), roughhouse (Sl.), scrap (Inf.), scuffle, struggle **2.** adj. boisterous, disorderly, haphazard, indisciplined, irregular, rough, rowdy, scrambled, scrambling

round adj. **1.** annular, ball-shaped, bowed, bulbous, circular, curved, curvilinear, cylindrical, discoid, disc-shaped, globular, orbicular, ring-shaped, rotund, rounded, spherical **2.** complete, entire, full, solid, unbroken, undivided, whole **3.** ample, bounteous, bountiful, considerable, generous, great, large, liberal, substantial **4.** ample, fleshy, full, full-fleshed, plump, roly-poly, rotund, rounded **5.** full, mellifluous, orotund, resonant, rich, rotund, sonorous **6.** blunt, candid, direct, frank, outspoken, plain, straightforward, unmodified ~n. **7.** ball, band, circle, disc, globe, orb,

roundabout ('raʊndə‚baʊt) n. 1. Brit. a revolving circular platform provided with wooden animals, seats, etc., on which people ride for amusement; merry-go-round. 2. a road junction in which traffic streams circulate around a central island. U.S. name: **traffic circle.** ~adj. 3. indirect; devious. ~adv., prep. **round about.** 4. on all sides: spectators standing round about. 5. approximately: at round about 5 o'clock.

round dance n. 1. a dance in which the dancers form a circle. 2. a ballroom dance, such as the waltz, in which couples revolve.

round down vb. (tr., adv.) to lower (a number) to the nearest whole number or ten, hundred, or thousand below it.

roundel ('raʊndəl) n. 1. a form of rondeau consisting of three stanzas each of three lines with a refrain after the first and the third. 2. a circular mark of red, white, and blue on British military aircraft. 3. a small circular window, medallion, etc. 4. a round plate of armour used to protect the armpit. 5. another word for **roundelay.**

roundelay ('raʊndɪ‚leɪ) n. 1. Also called: **roundel.** a slow medieval dance performed in a circle. 2. a song in which a line or phrase is repeated as a refrain.

rounders ('raʊndəz) n. Brit. a ball game in which players run between bases after hitting the ball, scoring a **rounder** if they run round all four before the ball is retrieved.

Roundhead ('raʊnd‚hɛd) n. English history. a supporter of Parliament against Charles I during the Civil War.

roundhouse ('raʊnd‚haʊs) n. 1. U.S. a building in which railway locomotives are serviced, radial tracks being fed by a central turntable. 2. U.S. Boxing sl. a swinging punch or style of punching. 3. an obsolete word for **jail.** 4. Obs. a cabin on the quarter-deck of a sailing ship.

roundly ('raʊndlɪ) adv. 1. frankly, bluntly, or thoroughly: to be roundly criticized. 2. in a round manner or so as to be round.

round off vb. (tr., adv.) 1. (often foll. by with) to complete, esp. agreeably: we rounded off the evening with a brandy. 2. to make less jagged.

round on vb. (intr., prep.) to attack or reply to (someone) with sudden irritation or anger.

round robin n. 1. a petition or protest having the signatures in a circle to disguise the order of signing. 2. U.S. a tournament in which each player plays against every other player.

round-shouldered adj. denoting a faulty posture characterized by drooping shoulders and a slight forward bending of the back.

round table n. a. a meeting of parties or people on equal terms for discussion. b. (as modifier): a round-table conference.

Round Table n. the. 1. (in Arthurian legend) the table of King Arthur, shaped so that his knights could sit around it without any having precedence. 2. Arthur and his knights collectively. 3. one of an organization of clubs of young business and professional men who meet in order to further charitable work.

round-the-clock adj. (or as adv. **round the clock**) throughout the day and night.

round trip n. a trip to a place and back again, esp. returning by a different route.

roundup ('raʊnd‚ʌp) n. 1. the act of gathering together livestock, esp. cattle, so that they may be branded, counted, or sold. 2. Inf. any similar act of bringing together: a roundup of today's news. ~vb. **round up.** (tr., adv.) 3. to gather together: to round ponies up. 4. to raise (a number) to the nearest whole number or ten, hundred, or thousand above it.

roundworm ('raʊnd‚wɜːm) n. a nematode worm that is a common intestinal parasite of man and pigs.

rouse (raʊz) vb. 1. to bring (oneself or another person) out of sleep, unconsciousness, etc., or (of a person) to come to consciousness in this way. 2. (tr.) to provoke: to rouse someone's anger. 3. **rouse oneself.** to become energetic. 4. to start or cause to start from cover: to rouse game birds. 5. (intr.; foll. by on) Austral. to scold or rebuke. —'rouser n.

roustabout ('raʊstə‚baʊt) n. an unskilled labourer on an oil rig.

rout[1] (raʊt) n. 1. an overwhelming and disorderly defeat. 2. a noisy rabble. 3. Law. a group of three or more people proceeding to commit an illegal act. 4. Arch. a large party or social gathering. ~vb. 5. (tr.) to defeat and cause to flee in confusion.

rout[2] (raʊt) vb. 1. to dig over or turn up (something), esp. (of an animal) with the snout; root. 2. (tr.; usually foll. by out or up) to find by searching. 3. (tr.; usually foll. by out) to drive out: they routed him out of bed at midnight. 4. (tr.; often foll. by out) to hollow or gouge out. 5. (intr.) to search, poke, or rummage.

route (ruːt) n. 1. the choice of roads taken to get to a place. 2. a regular journey travelled. ~vb. (tr.) 3. to plan the route of; send by a particular route.

routemarch ('ruːt‚mɑːtʃ) n. 1. Mil. a long training march. 2. Inf. any long exhausting walk.

routine (ruː'tiːn) n. 1. a usual or regular method of procedure, esp. one that is unvarying. 2. Computers. a program or part of a program performing a specific function: an input routine. 3. a set sequence of dance steps. 4. Inf. a hackneyed or insincere speech. ~adj. 5. relating to or characteristic of routine. —rou'tinely adv. —rou'tinism n.

roux (ruː) n. a mixture of equal amounts of fat and flour, heated, blended, and used as a basis for sauces.

rove[1] (rəʊv) vb. 1. to wander about (a place) with no fixed direction; roam. 2. (tr.) (of the eyes) to look around; wander. ~n. 3. the act of roving.

rove[2] (rəʊv) vb. a past tense or past participle of **reeve**[2].

rover ('rəʊvə) n. 1. a person who roves. 2. Archery. a mark selected at random for use as a target. 3. Australian Rules football. a player without a fixed position who, with the ruckmen, forms the ruck.

row[1] (rəʊ) n. 1. an arrangement of persons or things in a line: a row of chairs. 2. Chiefly Brit. a street, esp. a narrow one lined with identical houses. 3. a line of seats, as in a cinema, theatre, etc. 4. Maths. a horizontal linear arrangement of numbers, quantities, or terms. 5. a horizontal rank of squares on a chessboard or draughtboard. 6. **in a row.** in succession; one after the other: he won two gold medals in a row. 7. **a hard row to hoe.** a difficult task or assignment.

row[2] (rəʊ) vb. 1. to propel (a boat) by using oars. 2. (tr.) to carry (people, goods, etc.) in a rowing boat. 3. to be propelled by means of (oars or oarsmen). 4. (intr.) to take part in the racing of rowing boats as a sport. 5. (tr.) to race against in a boat propelled by oars: Oxford row Cambridge every year. ~n. 6. an act, instance, pe-

---

THESAURUS

ring, sphere 8. bout, cycle, sequence, series, session, succession 9. division, lap, level, period, session, stage, turn 10. ambit, beat, circuit, compass, course, routine, schedule, series, tour, turn 11. bullet, cartridge, discharge, shell, shot ~v. 12. bypass, circle, circumnavigate, encircle, flank, go round, skirt, turn

roundabout adj. circuitous, circumlocutory, devious, discursive, evasive, indirect, meandering, oblique, periphrastic, tortuous

round off bring to a close, cap, close, complete, conclude, crown, finish off, put the finishing touch to, settle

round up assemble, bring together, collect, drive, gather, group, herd, marshal, muster, rally

rouse 1. arouse, awaken, call, get up, rise, wake, wake up 2. agitate, anger, animate, arouse, bestir, disturb, excite, exhilarate, galvanize, get going, incite, inflame, instigate, move, provoke, startle, stimulate, stir, whip up

rousing brisk, electrifying, exciting, exhilarating, inflammatory, inspiring, lively, moving, spirited, stimulating, stirring, vigorous

rout 1. n. beating, debacle, defeat, disorderly retreat, drubbing, headlong flight, hiding (Inf.), licking (Inf.), overthrow, overwhelming defeat, ruin, shambles, thrashing 2. v. beat, chase, conquer, crush, cut to pieces, defeat, destroy, dispel, drive off, drub, lick (Inf.), overpower, overthrow, put to flight, put to rout, scatter, thrash, throw back in confusion, worst

route 1. n. avenue, beat, circuit, course, direction, itinerary, journey, passage, path, road, round, run, way 2. v. convey, direct, dispatch, forward, send, steer

routine n. 1. custom, formula, grind (Inf.), groove, method, order, pattern, practice, procedure, programme, usage, way, wont 2. Inf. act, bit (Inf.), line, performance, piece, spiel (Inf.) ~adj. 3. conventional, customary, everyday, familiar, habitual, normal, ordinary, standard, typical, usual, wonted, workaday 4. boring, clichéd, dull, hackneyed, humdrum, predictable, run-of-the-mill, tedious, tiresome, unimaginative, uninspired, unoriginal

riod, or distance of rowing. **7.** an excursion in a rowing boat. —**'rower** n.

row³ (raʊ) Inf. ~n. **1.** a noisy quarrel. **2.** a noisy disturbance: *we couldn't hear the music for the row next door.* **3.** a reprimand. ~vb. **4.** (*intr.;* often foll. by *with*) to quarrel noisily. **5.** (*tr.*) Arch. to reprimand.

rowan ('rəʊən, 'raʊ-) n. another name for the (European) **mountain ash.**

rowdy ('raʊdɪ) adj. **-dier, -diest. 1.** tending to create noisy disturbances; rough, loud, or disorderly: *a rowdy gang of football supporters.* ~n., pl. **-dies. 2.** a person who behaves in such a fashion. —**'rowdily** adv. —**'rowdiness** or **'rowdyism** n.

rowel ('raʊəl) n. **1.** a small spiked wheel attached to a spur. **2.** Vet. science. a piece of leather inserted under the skin of a horse to cause a discharge. ~vb. **-elling, -elled** or U.S. **-eling, -eled.** (*tr.*) **3.** to goad (a horse) using a rowel. **4.** Vet. science. to insert a rowel in (the skin of a horse) to cause a discharge.

rowing boat ('rəʊɪŋ) n. Chiefly Brit. a small pleasure boat propelled by one or more pairs of oars. Usual U.S. word: **rowboat.**

rowlock ('rɒlək) n. a swivelling device attached to the gunwale of a boat that holds an oar in place. Usual U.S. word: **oarlock.**

royal ('rɔɪəl) adj. **1.** of, relating to, or befitting a king, queen, or other monarch; regal. **2.** (*prenominal; often cap.*) established by, chartered by, under the patronage of, or in the service of royalty: *the Royal Society of St. George.* **3.** being a member of a royal family. **4.** above the usual or normal in standing, size, quality, etc. **5.** Inf. unusually good or impressive; first-rate. **6.** Naut. just above the topgallant (in **royal mast**). ~n. **7.** Naut. a sail set next above the topgallant, on a royal mast. **8.** a size of printing paper, 20 by 25 inches. **9.** Also: **royal stag.** a stag with antlers having 12 or more branches. —**'royally** adv.

Royal Air Force n. the airforce of Great Britain. Abbrevs.: **RAF, R.A.F.**

royal blue n., adj. **a.** a deep blue colour. **b.** (*as adj.*): *a royal-blue carpet.*

royalist ('rɔɪəlɪst) n. **1.** a supporter of a monarch or monarchy, esp. during the English Civil War. **2.** Inf. an extreme reactionary: *an economic royalist.* ~adj. also **royalistic. 3.** of or relating to royalists. —**'royalism** n.

royal jelly n. a substance secreted by the pharyngeal glands of worker bees and fed to all larvae when very young and to larvae destined to become queens throughout their development.

Royal Marines pl. n. Brit. a corps of soldiers specially trained in amphibious warfare.

Royal Navy n. the navy of Great Britain. Abbrev.: **R.N.**

royal palm n. any of several palm trees of tropical America, having a tall trunk with a tuft of feathery pinnate leaves.

royalty ('rɔɪəltɪ) n., pl. **-ties. 1.** the rank, power, or position of a king or queen. **2. a.** royal persons collectively. **b.** one who belongs to the royal family. **3.** any quality characteristic of a monarch. **4.** a percentage of the revenue from the sale of a book, performance of a theatrical work, use of a patented invention or of land, etc., paid to the author, inventor, or proprietor.

royal warrant n. an authorization to a tradesman to supply goods to a royal household.

rozzer ('rɒzə) n. Sl. a policeman.

r.p.m. abbrev. for: **1.** revolutions per minute. **2.** resale price maintenance.

R.R. abbrev. for: **1.** Right Reverend. **2.** Canad. & U.S. rural route.

r-RNA abbrev. for ribosomal RNA.

R.S. (in Britain) abbrev. for Royal Society.

R.S.A. abbrev. for: **1.** Republic of South Africa. **2.** Royal Scottish Academy. **3.** Royal Scottish Academician. **4.** Royal Society of Arts. **5.** (in New Zealand) Returned Services Association.

RSFSR abbrev. for Russian Soviet Federated Socialist Republic.

R.S.M. abbrev. for: **1.** regimental sergeant major. **2.** Royal School of Music. **3.** Royal Society of Medicine.

R.S.P.C.A. (in Britain) abbrev. for Royal Society for the Prevention of Cruelty to Animals.

R.S.V. abbrev. for Revised Standard Version (of the Bible).

R.S.V.P. abbrev. for répondez s'il vous plaît: please reply.

Rt. Hon. abbrev. for Right Honourable.

Ru the chemical symbol for ruthenium.

R.U. abbrev. for Rugby Union.

rub (rʌb) vb. **rubbing, rubbed. 1.** to apply pressure and friction to (something) with a backward and forward motion. **2.** to move (something) with pressure along, over, or against (a surface). **3.** to chafe or fray. **4.** (*tr.*) to bring into a certain condition by rubbing: *rub it clean.* **5.** (*tr.*) to spread with pressure, esp. in order to cause to be absorbed: *she rubbed ointment into his back.* **6.** (*tr.*) to mix (fat) into flour with the fingertips, as in making pastry. **7.** (foll. by *off, out, away,* etc.) to remove or be removed by rubbing: *the mark would not rub off the chair.* **8.** Bowls. (of a bowl) to be slowed or deflected by an uneven patch on the green. **9.** (*tr.;* often foll. by *together*) to move against each other with pressure and friction (esp. in **rub one's hands,** often a sign of glee, keen anticipation, or satisfaction, and **rub noses,** a greeting among Eskimos). **10. rub (someone's) nose in (something).** to harp insistently on (something distasteful or distressing to a person). **11. rub (up) the wrong way.** to arouse anger (in); annoy. **12. rub shoulders with.** to mix with socially. ~n. **13.** the act of rubbing. **14.** (preceded by *the*) an obstacle or difficulty (esp. in **there's the rub**). **15.** something that hurts the feelings or annoys; cut; rebuke. **16.** Bowls. an uneven patch in the green. ~See also **rub along, rub down,** etc.

rub along vb. (*intr., adv.*) Brit. **1.** to continue in spite of difficulties. **2.** to maintain an amicable relationship; not quarrel.

rubato (ru:'bɑːtəʊ) Music. ~n., pl. **-tos. 1.** flexibility of tempo in performance. ~adj., adv. **2.** to be played with a flexible tempo.

rubber¹ ('rʌbə) n. **1.** Also called: **India rubber, gum elastic, caoutchouc.** a cream to dark brown elastic material obtained by coagulating and drying the latex from certain plants, esp. the rubber tree. **2.** any of a large variety of elastomers produced from natural rubber or by synthetic means. **3.** Chiefly Brit. a piece of rubber used for erasing something written; eraser. **4.** a cloth, pad, etc., used for polishing. **5.** a person who rubs something in order to smooth, polish, or massage. **6.** (often pl.) Chiefly U.S. a rubberized waterproof article, such as a mackintosh or overshoe. **7.** Sl. a male contraceptive; condom. **8.** (*modifier*) made of or producing rubber: *a rubber ball; a rubber factory.* —**'rubbery** adj.

rubber² ('rʌbə) n. **1.** Bridge, whist, etc. **a.** a match of three games. **b.** the deal that wins such a match. **2.** a series of matches or games in any of various sports.

rubber band n. a continuous loop of thin rubber, used to hold papers, etc., together. Also called: **elastic band.**

rubberize or **-ise** ('rʌbəˌraɪz) vb. (*tr.*) to coat or impregnate with rubber.

rubberneck ('rʌbəˌnɛk) Sl. ~n. **1.** a person who

THESAURUS

row¹ bank, column, file, line, queue, range, rank, sequence, series, string, tier

row² n. **1.** altercation, brawl, commotion, controversy, dispute, disturbance, falling-out (*Inf.*), fracas, fray, fuss, noise, quarrel, racket, ruckus (*Inf.*), ruction (*Inf.*), rumpus, scrap (*Inf.*), shouting match (*Inf.*), slanging match (*Brit.*), squabble, tiff, trouble, tumult, uproar **2.** castigation, dressing-down (*Inf.*), flea in one's ear (*Inf.*), lecture, reprimand, reproof, rollicking (*Brit. inf.*), talking-to (*Inf.*), telling-off (*Inf.*), ticking-off (*Inf.*), tongue-lashing

~v. **3.** argue, brawl, dispute, fight, scrap (*Inf.*), squabble, wrangle

rowdy **1.** adj. boisterous, disorderly, loud, loutish, noisy, obstreperous, rough, unruly, uproarious, wild **2.** n. brawler, hooligan, lout, rough (*Inf.*), ruffian, tearaway (*Brit.*), tough, troublemaker, yahoo

royal **1.** imperial, kinglike, kingly, monarchical, princely, queenly, regal, sovereign **2.** august, grand, impressive, magnificent, majestic, splendid, stately, superb, superior

rub v. **1.** abrade, caress, chafe, clean, fray, grate, knead, massage, polish, scour, scrape, shine, smooth, stroke, wipe **2.** apply, put, smear, spread **3. rub up the wrong way** anger, annoy, bug (*Inf.*), get one's goat (*Inf.*), get under one's skin (*Inf.*), irk, irritate, peeve (*Inf.*), vex ~n. **4.** caress, kneading, massage, polish, shine, stroke, wipe **5.** catch, difficulty, drawback, hindrance, hitch, impediment, obstacle, problem, snag, trouble

stares or gapes inquisitively. **2.** a sightseer or tourist. ~*vb.* **3.** (*intr.*) to stare in a naive or foolish manner.

rubber plant *n.* **1.** a plant with glossy leathery leaves that grows as a tall tree in India and Malaya but is cultivated as a house plant in Europe and North America. **2.** any of several tropical trees, the sap of which yields crude rubber.

rubber stamp *n.* **1.** a device used for imprinting dates, etc., on forms, invoices, etc. **2.** automatic authorization of a payment, proposal, etc. **3.** a person who makes such automatic authorizations; a cipher or person of little account. ~*vb.* **rubber-stamp.** (*tr.*) **4.** to imprint (forms, invoices, etc.) with a rubber stamp. **5.** *Inf.* to approve automatically.

rubbing (ˈrʌbɪŋ) *n.* an impression taken of an incised or raised surface by laying paper over it and rubbing with wax, graphite, etc.

rubbish (ˈrʌbɪʃ) *n.* **1.** worthless, useless, or unwanted matter. **2.** discarded or waste matter; refuse. **3.** foolish words or speech; nonsense. ~*vb.* **4.** (*tr.*) *Inf.* to criticize; attack verbally. —ˈ**rubbishy** *adj.*

rubble (ˈrʌbəl) *n.* **1.** fragments of broken stones, bricks, etc. **2.** debris from ruined buildings. **3.** Also called: **rubblework.** masonry constructed of broken pieces of rock, stone, etc. —ˈ**rubbly** *adj.*

rub down *vb.* (*adv.*) **1.** to dry or clean (a horse, athlete, oneself, etc.) vigorously, esp. after exercise. **2.** to make or become smooth by rubbing. **3.** (*tr.*) to prepare (a surface) for painting by rubbing it with sandpaper. ~*n.* **rubdown.** **4.** the act of rubbing down.

rubella (ruːˈbɛlə) *n.* a mild contagious viral disease, somewhat similar to measles, characterized by cough, sore throat, and skin rash. Also called: **German measles.**

Rubicon (ˈruːbɪkən) *n.* **1.** a stream in N Italy: in ancient times the boundary between Italy and Cisalpine Gaul. By leading his army across it and marching on Rome in 49 B.C., Julius Caesar committed himself to civil war with the senatorial party. **2.** (*sometimes not cap.*) a point of no return. **3.** a penalty in piquet by which the score of a player who fails to reach 100 points in six hands is added to his opponent's. **4. cross** (*or* **pass**) **the Rubicon.** to commit oneself irrevocably to some course of action.

rubicund (ˈruːbɪkənd) *adj.* of a reddish colour; ruddy; rosy. —**rubicundity** (ˌruːbɪˈkʌndɪtɪ) *n.*

rubidium (ruːˈbɪdɪəm) *n.* a soft highly reactive radioactive element of the alkali metal group. It is used in electronic valves, photocells, and special glass. Symbol: Rb; atomic no.: 37; atomic wt.: 85.47; half-life of [87]Rb: 5 × 10[11] years. —**ruˈbidic** *adj.*

rub in *vb.* (*tr., adv.*) **1.** to spread with pressure, esp. in order to cause to be absorbed. **2.** *Inf.* to harp on (something distasteful to a person).

ruble (ˈruːbəl) *n.* a variant spelling of **rouble.**

rub off *vb.* **1.** to remove or be removed by rubbing. **2.** (*intr.*; often foll. by *on* or *onto*) to have an effect through close association or contact: *her crude manners have rubbed off on you.*

rub out *vb.* (*tr., adv.*) **1.** to remove or be removed with a rubber. **2.** *U.S. sl.* to murder.

rubric (ˈruːbrɪk) *n.* **1.** a title, heading, or initial letter in a book, manuscript, or section of a legal code, esp. one printed or painted in red ink or in some similarly distinguishing manner. **2.** a set of rules of conduct or procedure. **3.** a set of directions for the conduct of Christian church services, often printed in red in a prayerbook or missal. —ˈ**rubrical** *adj.* —ˈ**rubrically** *adv.*

ruby (ˈruːbɪ) *n., pl.* **-bies. 1.** a deep red transparent precious variety of corundum: used as a gemstone, in lasers, and for bearings and rollers in watchmaking. **2. a.** the deep-red colour of a ruby. **b.** (*as adj.*): *ruby lips.* **3. a.** something resembling, made of, or containing a ruby. **b.** (*as modifier*): *ruby necklace.* **4.** (*modifier*) denoting a fortieth anniversary: *our ruby wedding.*

ruche (ruːʃ) *n.* a strip of pleated or frilled lawn, lace, etc., used to decorate blouses, dresses, etc.

ruck[1] (rʌk) *n.* **1.** a large number or quantity; mass, esp. of undistinguished people or things. **2.** (in a race) a group of competitors who are well behind the leaders. **3.** *Rugby.* a loose scrummage or maul for the ball. **4.** *Australian Rules football.* a group of three players who follow the ball closely. ~*vb.* **5.** (*intr.*) *Rugby.* to try to win the ball by mauling and scrummaging.

ruck[2] (rʌk) *n.* **1.** a wrinkle, crease, or fold. ~*vb.* **2.** (usually foll. by *up*) to become or make wrinkled, creased, or puckered.

rucksack (ˈrʌkˌsæk) *n.* a large bag, usually having two straps, carried on the back and often used to carry camping equipment, etc. Also called: **back pack.**

ruction (ˈrʌkʃən) *n.* *Inf.* an uproar; noisy or quarrelsome disturbance.

rudder (ˈrʌdə) *n.* **1.** *Naut.* a pivoted vertical vane that projects into the water at the stern and can be used to steer a vessel. **2.** a vertical control surface attached to the rear of the fin used to steer an aircraft. **3.** anything that guides or directs. —ˈ**rudderless** *adj.*

ruddy (ˈrʌdɪ) *adj.* **-dier, -diest. 1.** (of the complexion) having a healthy reddish colour. **2.** coloured red or pink: *a ruddy sky.* ~*adv., adj. Inf., chiefly Brit.* **3.** (intensifier) bloody; damned: *a ruddy fool.* —ˈ**ruddily** *adv.* —ˈ**ruddiness** *n.*

rude (ruːd) *adj.* **1.** insulting or uncivil; discourteous; impolite. **2.** lacking refinement; coarse or uncouth. **3.** vulgar or obscene: *a rude joke.* **4.** roughly or crudely made: *we made a rude shelter on the island.* **5.** rough or harsh in sound, appearance, or behaviour. **6.** humble or lowly. **7.** (*prenominal*) robust or sturdy: *in rude health.* **8.** (*prenominal*) approximate or imprecise: *a rude estimate.* —ˈ**rudely** *adv.* —ˈ**rudeness** *or* ˈ**rudery** *n.*

rudiment (ˈruːdɪmənt) *n.* **1.** (*often pl.*) the first principles or elementary stages of a subject. **2.** (*often pl.*) a partially developed version of something. **3.** *Biol.* an organ or part in an embryonic or vestigial state. —ˌ**rudiˈmentary** *adj.*

rue[1] (ruː) *vb.* **ruing, rued. 1.** to feel sorrow, remorse, or regret for (one's own wrongdoing, past events, etc.). ~*n.* **2.** *Arch.* sorrow, pity, or regret. —ˈ**ruer** *n.*

rue[2] (ruː) *n.* an aromatic Eurasian shrub with small yellow flowers and evergreen leaves which yield an acrid volatile oil, formerly used medicinally as a narcotic and stimulant. Archaic name: **herb of grace.**

rueful (ˈruːfʊl) *adj.* **1.** feeling or expressing sorrow or regret: *a rueful face.* **2.** inspiring sorrow or pity. —ˈ**ruefully** *adv.* —ˈ**ruefulness** *n.*

ruff[1] (rʌf) *n.* **1.** a circular pleated or fluted collar of lawn, muslin, etc., worn by both men and women in the 16th and 17th centuries. **2.** a natural growth of long or coloured hair or feathers around the necks of certain animals or birds. **3.** an Old World shore bird of the sandpiper family, the male of which has a large erectile ruff of feathers in the breeding season. —ˈ**ruff,like** *adj.*

ruff[2] (rʌf) *n. Cards.* **1.** (*also vb.*) another word for **trump**[1]. **2.** an old card game similar to whist.

ruffian (ˈrʌfɪən) *n.* a violent or lawless person; hoodlum. —ˈ**ruffianism** *n.* —ˈ**ruffianly** *adj.*

◗◖ T H E S A U R U S ◗◖

rubbish 1. debris, dregs, dross, flotsam and jetsam, garbage, junk, litter, lumber, offal, offscourings, refuse, scrap, trash, waste **2.** balderdash, bosh (*Inf.*), bunkum, claptrap (*Inf.*), codswallop (*Brit. sl.*), drivel, flapdoodle (*Sl.*), gibberish, guff (*Sl.*), havers (*Scot.*), hogwash, moonshine, nonsense, piffle (*Inf.*), poppycock (*Inf.*), rot, stuff and nonsense, tommyrot, tosh (*Inf.*), twaddle

rub out cancel, delete, efface, erase, expunge, obliterate, remove, wipe out

ruddy 1. blooming, blushing, florid, flushed, fresh, glowing, healthy, red, reddish, rosy, rosy-cheeked, rubicund, sanguine, sun-

burnt **2.** crimson, pink, red, reddish, roseate, ruby, scarlet

rude 1. abrupt, abusive, blunt, brusque, cheeky, churlish, curt, discourteous, disrespectful, ill-mannered, impertinent, impolite, impudent, inconsiderate, insolent, insulting, offhand, peremptory, short, uncivil, unmannerly **2.** barbarous, boorish, brutish, coarse, crude, graceless, gross, ignorant, illiterate, loutish, low, oafish, obscene, rough, savage, scurrilous, uncivilised, uncouth, uncultured, uneducated, ungracious, unpolished, unrefined, untutored, vulgar **3.** artless, crude, inartistic, inelegant, makeshift, primitive, raw,

rough, rough-hewn, roughly-made, simple **4.** abrupt, harsh, sharp, startling, sudden, unpleasant, violent

rudimentary basic, early, elementary, embryonic, fundamental, immature, initial, introductory, primary, primitive, undeveloped, vestigial

rudiments basics, beginnings, elements, essentials, first principles, foundation, fundamentals

rueful conscience-stricken, contrite, dismal, doleful, grievous, lugubrious, melancholy, mournful, penitent, pitiable, pitiful, plaintive, regretful, remorseful, repentant,

ruffle ('rʌfəl) *vb.* **1.** to make, be, or become irregular or rumpled: *a breeze ruffling the water.* **2.** to annoy, irritate, or be annoyed or irritated. **3.** (*tr.*) to make into a ruffle; pleat. **4.** (of a bird) to erect (its feathers) in anger, display, etc. **5.** (*tr.*) to flick (cards, pages, etc.) rapidly. ~*n.* **6.** an irregular or disturbed surface. **7.** a strip of pleated material used as a trim. **8.** *Zool.* another name for **ruff**[1] (sense 2). **9.** annoyance or irritation.

rufous ('ru:fəs) *adj.* reddish brown.

rug (rʌg) *n.* **1.** a floor covering, smaller than a carpet and made of thick wool or of other material, such as an animal skin. **2.** *Chiefly Brit.* a blanket, esp. one used for travellers. **3. pull the rug out from under.** to betray, expose, or leave defenceless.

ruga ('ru:gə) *n., pl.* **-gae** (-dʒi:). (*usually pl.*) *Anat.* a fold, wrinkle, or crease.

rugby *or* **rugby football** ('rʌgbɪ) *n.* **1.** a form of football played with an oval ball in which the handling and carrying of the ball is permitted. Also called: **rugger**. See also **rugby league, rugby union**. **2.** (in Canada) football.

rugby league *n.* a form of rugby football played between teams of 13 players, professionalism being allowed.

rugby union *n.* a form of rugby football played only by amateurs, in teams of 15.

rugged ('rʌgɪd) *adj.* **1.** having an uneven or jagged surface. manners. **2.** rocky or steep: *rugged scenery.* **3.** (of the face) strong-featured or furrowed. **4.** rough, severe, or stern in character. **5.** without refinement or culture: *rugged manners.* **6.** involving hardship; harsh: *he leads a rugged life in the mountains.* **7.** difficult or hard: *a rugged test.* **8.** *Chiefly U.S.* sturdy or strong; robust. —**'ruggedly** *adv.* —**'ruggedness** *n.*

rugger ('rʌgə) *n. Chiefly Brit.* an informal name for **rugby**.

ruin ('ru:ɪn) *n.* **1.** a destroyed or decayed building or town. **2.** the state of being destroyed or decayed. **3.** loss of wealth, position, etc., or something that causes such loss; downfall. **4.** something that is severely damaged: *his life was a ruin.* **5.** a person who has suffered a downfall, bankruptcy, etc. **6.** *Arch.* loss of her virginity by a woman outside marriage. ~*vb.* **7.** (*tr.*) to bring to ruin; destroy. **8.** (*tr.*) to injure or spoil: *the town has been ruined with tower blocks.* **9.** (*intr.*) *Arch. or poetic.* to fall into ruins; collapse. **10.** (*tr.*) *Arch.* to seduce and abandon (a woman).

ruination (,ru:ɪ'neɪʃən) *n.* **1.** the act of ruining or the state of being ruined. **2.** something that causes ruin.

ruinous ('ru:ɪnəs) *adj.* causing, tending to cause, or characterized by ruin or destruction. —**'ruinously** *adv.* —**'ruinousness** *n.*

rule (ru:l) *n.* **1.** an authoritative regulation or direction concerning method or procedure, as for a court of law, legislative body, game, or other activity: *judges' rules; play according to the rules.* **2.** the exercise of governmental authority or control: *the rule of Caesar.* **3.** the period of time in which a monarch or government has power: *his rule lasted 100 days.* **4.** a customary form or procedure: *he made a morning swim his rule.* **5.** (usually preceded by *the*) the common order of things: *violence was the rule rather than the exception.* **6.** a prescribed method or procedure for solving a mathematical problem. **7.** any of various devices with a straight edge for guiding or measuring; ruler: *a carpenter's rule.* **8.** *Printing.* **a.** a printed or drawn character in the form of a long thin line. **b.** another name for **dash**[1] (sense 12): *en rule; em rule.* **c.** a strip of metal used to print such a line. **9.** *Christianity.* a systematic body of prescriptions followed by members of a religious order. **10.** *Law.* an order by a court or judge. **11. as a rule.** normally or ordinarily. ~*vb.* **12.** to exercise governing or controlling authority over (a people, political unit, individual, etc.). **13.** (when *tr.,* often takes a clause as object) to decide authoritatively; decree: *the chairman ruled against the proposal.* **14.** (*tr.*) to mark with straight parallel lines or one straight line. **15.** (*tr.*) to restrain or control. **16.** (*intr.*) to be customary or prevalent: *chaos rules in this school.* **17.** (*intr.*) to be pre-eminent or superior: *football rules in the field of sport.* **18. rule the roost** (*or* **roast**). to be pre-eminent; be in charge. —**'rulable** *adj.*

rule of thumb *n.* **a.** a rough and practical approach, based on experience, rather than theory. **b.** (*as modifier*): *a rule-of-thumb decision.*

rule out *vb.* (*tr., adv.*) **1.** to dismiss from consideration. **2.** to make impossible; preclude.

ruler ('ru:lə) *n.* **1.** a person who rules or commands. **2.** Also called: **rule.** a strip of wood, metal, or other material, having straight edges, used for measuring and drawing straight lines.

ruling ('ru:lɪŋ) *n.* **1.** a decision of someone in authority, such as a judge. **2.** one or more parallel ruled lines. ~*adj.* **3.** controlling or exercising authority. **4.** predominant.

rum[1] (rʌm) *n.* spirit made from sugar cane.

rum[2] (rʌm) *adj.* **rummer, rummest.** *Brit. sl.* strange; peculiar; odd. —**'rumly** *adv.* —**'rumness** *n.*

rum[3] (rʌm) *n.* short for **rummy.**

Rumanian (ru:'meɪnɪən) *or* **Romanian** *n.* **1.** the official language of Rumania, in SE Europe. **2.** a native, citizen, or inhabitant of Rumania. ~*adj.* **3.** relating to, denoting, or characteristic of Rumania, its people, or their language.

rumba *or* **rhumba** ('rʌmbə, 'rʊm-) *n.* **1.** a rhythmic

sad, self-reproachful, sorrowful, sorry, woebegone, woeful

ruffian bruiser (*Inf.*), brute, bully, bully boy, hoodlum, hooligan, miscreant, rascal, rogue, rough (*Inf.*), roughneck (*Sl.*), rowdy, scoundrel, thug, tough, villain, wretch

ruffle **1.** derange, disarrange, discompose, dishevel, disorder, mess up, rumple, tousle, wrinkle **2.** agitate, annoy, confuse, disconcert, disquiet, disturb, fluster, harass, irritate, nettle, peeve (*Inf.*), perturb, put out, rattle (*Inf.*), shake up (*Inf.*), stir, torment, trouble, unsettle, upset, vex, worry

rugged **1.** broken, bumpy, craggy, difficult, irregular, jagged, ragged, rocky, rough, stark, uneven **2.** furrowed, leathery, lined, rough-hewn, strong-featured, weatherbeaten, weathered, worn, wrinkled **3.** austere, crabbed, dour, gruff, hard, harsh, rough, rude, severe, sour, stern, surly **4.** barbarous, blunt, churlish, crude, graceless, rude, uncouth, uncultured, unpolished, unrefined **5.** arduous, demanding, difficult, exacting, hard, harsh, laborious, rigorous, stern, strenuous, taxing, tough, trying, uncompromising **6.** beefy (*Inf.*), brawny, burly, hale, hardy, husky (*Inf.*), muscular, robust, strong, sturdy, tough, vigorous, well-built

ruin *n.* **1.** bankruptcy, breakdown, collapse, crackup (*Inf.*), crash, damage, decay, defeat, destitution, destruction, devastation, disinte-

gration, disrepair, dissolution, downfall, failure, fall, havoc, insolvency, nemesis, overthrow, ruination, subversion, the end, undoing, Waterloo, wreck, wreckage ~*v.* **2.** bankrupt, break, bring down, bring to nothing, bring to ruin, crush, defeat, demolish, destroy, devastate, impoverish, lay in ruins, lay waste, overthrow, overturn, overwhelm, pauperize, raze, shatter, smash, wreak havoc upon, wreck **3.** botch, damage, disfigure, injure, make a mess of, mangle, mar, mess up, spoil

ruinous **1.** baleful, baneful (*Archaic*), calamitous, catastrophic, crippling, deadly, deleterious, destructive, devastating, dire, disastrous, extravagant, fatal, immoderate, injurious, murderous, noxious, pernicious, shattering, wasteful, withering **2.** broken-down, decrepit, derelict, dilapidated, in ruins, ramshackle, ruined

rule *n.* **1.** axiom, canon, criterion, decree, direction, guide, guideline, law, maxim, order, ordinance, precept, principle, regulation, ruling, standard, tenet **2.** administration, ascendancy, authority, command, control, direction, domination, dominion, empire, government, influence, jurisdiction, leadership, mastery, power, regime, reign, supremacy, sway **3.** condition, convention, custom, form, habit, order *or* way of things, practice, procedure, routine, wont **4.** course, formula,

method, policy, procedure, way **5. as a rule** customarily, for the most part, generally, mainly, normally, on the whole, ordinarily, usually ~*v.* **6.** administer, be in authority, be in power, be number one (*Inf.*), command, control, direct, dominate, govern, guide, hold sway, lead, manage, preside over, regulate, reign, wear the crown **7.** adjudge, adjudicate, decide, decree, determine, establish, find, judge, lay down, pronounce, resolve, settle **8.** be customary (pre-eminent, prevalent, superior), hold sway, obtain, predominate, preponderate, prevail

rule out ban, debar, dismiss, eliminate, exclude, forbid, leave out, obviate, preclude, prevent, prohibit, proscribe, reject

ruler **1.** commander, controller, crowned head, emperor, empress, governor, head of state, king, leader, lord, monarch, potentate, prince, princess, queen, sovereign **2.** measure, rule, straight edge, yardstick

ruling *n.* **1.** adjudication, decision, decree, finding, judgment, pronouncement, resolution, verdict ~*adj.* **2.** commanding, controlling, dominant, governing, leading, regnant, reigning, upper **3.** chief, current, dominant, main, predominant, pre-eminent, preponderant, prevailing, prevalent, principal, regnant, supreme

and syncopated Cuban dance in duple time. **2.** a ballroom dance derived from this. **3.** a piece of music composed for or in the rhythm of this dance.

rumble ('rʌmbəl) *vb.* **1.** to make or cause to make a deep resonant sound: *thunder rumbled in the sky.* **2.** to move with such a sound: *the train rumbled along.* **3.** (*tr.*) to utter with a rumbling sound: *he rumbled an order.* **4.** (*tr.*) *Brit. sl.* to find out about (someone or something): *the police rumbled their plans.* **5.** (*intr.*) *U.S. sl.* to be involved in a gang fight. ~*n.* **6.** a deep resonant sound. **7.** a widespread murmur of discontent. **8.** *U.S. & N.Z. sl.* a gang fight. —'**rumbler** *n.* —'**rumblingly** *adv.*

rumbustious (rʌm'bʌstjəs) *adj.* boisterous or unruly. —**rum'bustiously** *adv.* —**rum'bustiousness** *n.*

ruminant ('ruːmɪnənt) *n.* **1.** any of a suborder of artiodactyl mammals which chew the cud and have a stomach of four compartments. The suborder includes deer, antelopes, cattle, sheep, and goats. **2.** any other animal that chews the cud, such as a camel. ~*adj.* **3.** of, relating to, or belonging to this suborder. **4.** (of members of this suborder and related animals, such as camels) chewing the cud; ruminating. **5.** meditating or contemplating in a slow quiet way. —'**ruminantly** *adv.*

ruminate ('ruːmɪˌneɪt) *vb.* **1.** (of ruminants) to chew (the cud). **2.** (when *intr.,* often foll. by *upon, on,* etc.) to meditate or ponder (upon). —ˌrumi'**nation** *n.* —'**ruminative** *adj.* —'**ruminatively** *adv.* —'**rumiˌnator** *n.*

rummage ('rʌmɪdʒ) *vb.* **1.** (when *intr.,* often foll. by *through*) to search (through) while looking for something, often causing disorder. ~*n.* **2.** an act of rummaging. **3.** a jumble of articles. —'**rummager** *n.*

rummage sale *n.* **1.** the U.S. term for **jumble sale.** **2.** *U.S.* a sale of unclaimed property.

rummy ('rʌmɪ) *or* **rum** *n.* a card game based on collecting sets and sequences.

rumour *or U.S.* **rumor** ('ruːmə) *n.* **1. a.** information, often a mixture of truth and untruth, passed around verbally. **b.** (*in combination*): *a rumour-monger.* **2.** gossip or hearsay. ~*vb.* **3.** (*tr.; usually passive*) to pass around or circulate in the form of a rumour: *it is rumoured that the Queen is coming.*

rump (rʌmp) *n.* **1.** the hindquarters of a mammal, not including the legs. **2.** the rear part of a bird's back, nearest to the tail. **3.** a person's buttocks. **4.** Also called: **rump steak.** a cut of beef from behind the loin. **5.** an inferior remnant. —'**rumpless** *adj.*

rumple ('rʌmpəl) *vb.* **1.** to make or become crumpled or dishevelled. ~*n.* **2.** a wrinkle, fold, or crease. —'**rumply** *adj.*

rumpus ('rʌmpəs) *n., pl.* **-puses.** a noisy, confused, or disruptive commotion.

run (rʌn) *vb.* **running, ran, run. 1.** (*intr.*) **a.** (of a two-legged creature) to move on foot at a rapid pace so that both feet are off the ground for part of each stride. **b.** (of a four-legged creature) to move at a rapid gait. **2.** (*tr.*) to pass over (a distance, route, etc.) in running: *to run a mile.* **3.** (*intr.*) to run in or finish a race as specified, esp. in a particular position: *John is running third.* **4.** (*tr.*) to perform as by running: *to run an errand.* **5.** (*tr.*) to bring into a specified state by running: *to run oneself to a standstill.* **6.** (*tr.*) to track down or hunt (an animal): *to run a fox to earth.* **7.** (*tr.*) to set (animals) loose on (a field or tract of land) so as to graze freely: *he ran stock on that pasture last year.* **8.** (*intr.; often foll. by over, round,* or *up*) to make a short trip or brief visit: *I'll run over this afternoon.* **9.** to move quickly and easily on wheels by rolling, or in any of certain other ways: *a sledge running over snow.* **10.** to move or cause to move with a specified result: *to run a ship aground; run into a tree.* **11.** (often foll. by *over*) to move or pass or cause to move or pass quickly: *to run one's eyes over a page.* **12.** (*tr.; foll. by into, out of, through,* etc.) to force, thrust, or drive: *she ran a needle into her finger.* **13.** (*tr.*) to drive or maintain and operate (a vehicle). **14.** (*tr.*) to give a lift to (someone) in a vehicle: *he ran her to the station.* **15.** to ply or cause to ply between places on a route: *the bus runs from Piccadilly to Golders Green.* **16.** to function or cause to function: *the engine is running smoothly.* **17.** (*tr.*) to manage: *to run a company.* **18.** to extend or

continue or cause to extend or continue in a particular direction, for a particular duration or distance, etc.: *the road runs north; the play ran for two years.* **19.** (*intr.*) *Law.* to have legal force or effect: *the lease runs for two more years.* **20.** (*tr.*) to be subjected to, be affected by, or incur: *to run a risk; run a temperature.* **21.** (*intr.; often foll. by to*) to be characterized (by); tend or incline: *to run to fat.* **22.** (*intr.*) to recur persistently or be inherent: *red hair runs in my family.* **23.** to cause or allow (liquids) to flow or (of liquids) to flow: *the well has run dry.* **24.** (*intr.*) to melt and flow: *the wax grew hot and began to run.* **25.** *Metallurgy.* **a.** to melt or fuse. **b.** (*tr.*) to cast (molten metal): *to run lead into ingots.* **26.** (*intr.*) (of waves, tides, rivers, etc.) to rise high, surge, or be at a specified height: *a high sea was running that night.* **27.** (*intr.*) to be diffused: *the colours in my dress ran when I washed it.* **28.** (*intr.*) (of stitches) to unravel or come undone or (of a garment) to have stitches unravel or come undone. **29.** (*intr.*) (of growing creepers, etc.) to trail, spread, or climb: *ivy running over a cottage wall.* **30.** (*intr.*) to spread or circulate quickly: *a rumour ran through the town.* **31.** (*intr.*) to be stated or reported: *his story runs as follows.* **32.** to publish or print or be published or printed in a newspaper, magazine, etc.: *they ran his story in the next issue.* **33.** (often foll. by *for*) *Chiefly U.S.* to be a candidate or present as a candidate for political or other office: *Jones is running for president.* **34.** (*tr.*) to get past or through: *to run a blockade.* **35.** (*tr.*) to deal in (arms, etc.), esp. by importing illegally: *he runs guns for the rebels.* **36.** *Naut.* to sail (a vessel, esp. a sailing vessel) or (of such a vessel) to be sailed with the wind coming from astern. **37.** (*intr.*) (of fish) to migrate upstream from the sea, esp. in order to spawn. **38.** (*tr.*) *Cricket.* to score (a run or number of runs) by hitting the ball and running between the wickets. **39.** (*tr.*) *Billiards, etc.* to make (a number of successful shots) in sequence. **40.** (*tr.*) *Golf.* to hit (the ball) so that it rolls along the ground. **41.** (*tr.*) *Bridge.* to cash (all one's winning cards in a long suit) successively. ~*n.* **42.** an act, instance, or period of running. **43.** a gait, pace, or motion faster than a walk: *she went off at a run.* **44.** a distance covered by running or a period of running: *a run of ten miles.* **45.** an instance or period of travelling in a vehicle, esp. for pleasure: *to go for a run in the car.* **46.** free and unrestricted access: *we had the run of the house.* **47. a.** a period of time during which a machine, computer, etc., operates. **b.** the amount of work performed in such a period. **48.** a continuous or sustained period: *a run of good luck.* **49.** a continuous sequence of performances: *the play had a good run.* **50.** *Cards.* a sequence of winning cards in one suit: *a run of spades.* **51.** tendency or trend: *the run of the market.* **52.** type, class, or category: *the usual run of graduates.* **53.** (usually foll. by *on*) a continuous and urgent demand: *a run on the dollar.* **54.** a series of unravelled stitches, esp. in tights; ladder. **55.** the characteristic pattern or direction of something: *the run of the grain on wood.* **56. a.** a period during which water or other liquid flows. **b.** the amount of such a flow. **57.** a pipe, channel, etc., through which water or other liquid flows. **58.** *U.S.* a small stream. **59.** a steeply inclined course, esp. a snow-covered one used for skiing. **60.** an enclosure for domestic fowls or other animals: *a chicken run.* **61.** (esp. in Australia and New Zealand) a tract of land for grazing livestock. **62.** the migration of fish upstream in order to spawn. **63.** *Mil.* **a.** a mission in a warplane. **b.** Also called: **bombing run.** an approach by a bomber to a target. **64.** the movement of an aircraft along the ground during takeoff or landing. **65.** *Music.* a rapid scalelike passage of notes. **66.** *Cricket.* a score of one, normally achieved by both batsmen running from one end of the wicket to the other after one of them has hit the ball. **67.** *Baseball.* an instance of a batter touching all four bases safely, thereby scoring. **68.** *Golf.* the distance that a ball rolls after hitting the ground. **69. a run for (one's) money.** *Inf.* **a.** a close competition. **b.** pleasure derived from an activity. **70. in the long run.** as the eventual outcome of a series of events, etc. **71. in the short run.** as the immediate outcome of a series of events, etc. **72. on the run. a.** escaping from arrest; fugitive. **b.** in rapid flight; retreating:

THESAURUS

ruminate brood, chew over, cogitate, consider, contemplate, deliberate, meditate, mull over, muse, ponder, reflect, revolve, think, turn over in one's mind

rumour 1. *n.* bruit (*Archaic or U.S.*), buzz, canard, gossip, hearsay, news, report, story, talk, tidings, whisper, word **2.** *v.* bruit (*Archaic or U.S.*), circulate, gossip, noise abroad,

pass around, publish, put about, report, say, tell, whisper

the enemy is on the run. **c.** hurrying from place to place. **73. the runs.** *Sl.* diarrhoea. ~See also **run across, run along,** etc.

runabout ('rʌnə,baʊt) *n.* **1.** a small light vehicle or aeroplane. ~*vb.* **run about. 2.** (*intr., adv.*) to move busily from place to place.

run across *vb.* (*intr., prep.*) to meet unexpectedly; encounter by chance.

run along *vb.* (*intr., adv.*) (often said patronizingly) to go away; leave.

run away *vb.* (*intr., adv.*) **1.** to take flight; escape. **2.** to go away; depart. **3.** (of a horse) to gallop away uncontrollably. **4. run away with. a.** to abscond or elope with: *he ran away with his boss's daughter.* **b.** to make off with; steal. **c.** to escape from the control of: *his enthusiasm ran away with him.* **d.** to win easily or be assured of victory in (a competition): *he ran away with the race.* ~*n.* **runaway. 5. a.** a person or animal that runs away. **b.** (*as modifier*): *a runaway horse.* **6.** the act or an instance of running away. **7.** (*modifier*) rising rapidly, as prices: *runaway inflation.* **8.** (*modifier*) (of a race, victory, etc.) easily won.

run down *vb.* (*mainly adv.*) **1.** to allow (an engine, etc.) to lose power gradually and cease to function or (of an engine, etc.) to do this. **2.** to decline or reduce in number or size: *the firm ran down its sales force.* **3.** (*tr., usually passive*) to tire, sap the strength of, or exhaust: *he was thoroughly run down.* **4.** (*tr.*) to criticize adversely; decry. **5.** (*tr.*) to hit and knock to the ground with a moving vehicle. **6.** (*tr.*) *Naut.* to collide with and cause to sink. **7.** (*tr.*) to pursue and find or capture: *to run down a fugitive.* **8.** (*tr.*) to read swiftly or perfunctorily: *he ran down their list of complaints.* ~*adj.* **run-down. 9.** tired; exhausted. **10.** worn-out, shabby, or dilapidated. ~*n.* **rundown. 11.** a brief review, résumé, or summary. **12.** the process of a mechanism coming gradually to a standstill after the power is removed. **13.** a reduction in number or size.

rune (ruːn) *n.* **1.** any of the characters of an ancient Germanic alphabet, in use, esp. in Scandinavia, from the 3rd century A.D. to the end of the Middle Ages. **2.** any obscure piece of writing using mysterious symbols. **3.** a kind of Finnish poem or a stanza in such a poem. —'**runic** *adj.*

rung[1] (rʌŋ) *n.* **1.** one of the bars or rods that form the steps of a ladder. **2.** a crosspiece between the legs of a chair, etc. **3.** *Naut.* a spoke on a ship's wheel or a handle projecting from the periphery. —'**rungless** *adj.*

rung[2] (rʌŋ) *vb.* the past participle of **ring**[2]. ▷ **Usage.** See at **ring**[2].

run in *vb.* (*adv.*) **1.** to run (an engine) gently, usually when it is new. **2.** (*tr.*) to insert or include. **3.** (*intr.*) (of an aircraft) to approach a point or target. **4.** (*tr.*) *Sl.* to take into custody; arrest. ~*n.* **run-in. 5.** *Inf.* an argument or quarrel. **6.** *Printing.* matter inserted in an existing paragraph.

run into *vb.* (*prep.; mainly intr.*) **1.** (*also tr.*) to collide with or cause to collide with: *her car ran into a tree.* **2.** to encounter unexpectedly. **3.** (*also tr.*) to be beset by: *the project ran into financial difficulties.* **4.** to extend to; be of the order of: *debts running into thousands.*

runnel ('rʌnᵊl) *n. Literary.* a small stream.

runner ('rʌnə) *n.* **1.** a person who runs, esp. an athlete. **2.** a messenger for a bank, etc. **3.** a person engaged in the solicitation of business. **4.** a person on the run; fugitive. **5. a.** a person or vessel engaged in smuggling. **b.** (*in combination*): *a gun-runner.* **6.** a person who operates, manages, or controls something. **7. a.** either of the strips of metal or wood on which a sledge runs. **b.** the blade of an ice skate. **8.** a roller or guide for a sliding component. **9.** *Bot.* **a.** Also called: **stolon.** a slender horizontal stem, as of the strawberry, that grows along the surface of the soil and propagates by producing roots and shoots at the nodes or tip. **b.** a plant that propagates in this way. **10.** a strip of lace, linen, etc., placed across a table or dresser for protection and decoration. **11.** another word for **rocker** (on a rocking chair).

runner bean *n.* a climbing bean plant with long green edible pods.

runner-up *n., pl.* **runners-up.** a contestant finishing a race or competition in second place.

running ('rʌnɪŋ) *adj.* **1.** maintained continuously; incessant: *running commentary.* **2.** (*postpositive*) without interruption; consecutive: *he lectured for two hours running.* **3.** denoting or relating to the scheduled operation of a public vehicle: *the running time of a train.* **4.** accomplished at a run: *a running jump.* **5.** moving or slipping easily, as a rope or a knot. **6.** (of a wound, etc.) discharging pus. **7.** prevalent; current: *running prices.* **8.** repeated or continuous: *a running design.* **9.** (of plants, plant stems, etc.) creeping along the ground. **10.** flowing: *running water.* **11.** (of handwriting) having the letters run together. ~*n.* **12.** management or organization: *the running of a company.* **13.** operation or mainte-

---

THESAURUS

run *v.* **1.** bolt, career, dart, dash, gallop, hare (*Brit. inf.*), hasten, hie, hotfoot, hurry, jog, leg it (*Inf.*), lope, race, rush, scamper, scramble, scud, scurry, speed, sprint **2.** abscond, beat a retreat, beat it (*Sl.*), bolt, clear out, cut and run (*Inf.*), decamp, depart, escape, flee, leg it (*Inf.*), make a run for it, make off, scarper (*Brit. sl.*), show a clean pair of heels, skedaddle (*Inf.*), take flight, take off (*Inf.*), take to one's heels **3.** course, glide, go, move, pass, roll, skim, slide **4.** bear, carry, convey, drive, give a lift to, manoeuvre, operate, propel, transport **5.** go, operate, ply **6.** function, go, operate, perform, tick, work **7.** administer, be in charge of, boss (*Inf.*), carry on, conduct, control, coordinate, direct, head, lead, look after, manage, mastermind, operate, oversee, own, regulate, superintend, supervise, take care of **8.** continue, extend, go, last, lie, proceed, range, reach, stretch **9.** cascade, discharge, flow, go, gush, issue, leak, move, pour, proceed, spill, spout, stream **10.** dissolve, fuse, go soft, liquefy, melt, turn to liquid **11.** be diffused, bleed, lose colour, mix, spread **12.** come apart, come undone, ladder, tear, unravel **13.** be current, circulate, climb, creep, go round, spread, trail **14.** display, feature, print, publish **15.** be a candidate, challenge, compete, contend, put oneself up for, stand, take part **16.** bootleg, deal in, ship, smuggle, sneak, traffic in **17. run for it** abscond, bolt, cut and run (*Inf.*), do a bunk (*Brit. inf.*), escape, flee, fly, make a break for it, make off, scarper (*Brit. sl.*), scram (*Inf.*), show a clean pair of heels, skedaddle (*Inf.*), take flight, take off

~*n.* **18.** dash, gallop, jog, race, rush, spurt **19.** drive, excursion, jaunt, journey, joy ride (*Inf.*), lift, outing, ride, round, spin (*Inf.*), trip **20.** chain, course, cycle, passage, period, round, season, sequence, series, spell, streak, stretch, string **21.** category, class, kind, order, sort, type, variety **22.** application, demand, pressure, rush **23.** ladder, rip, snag, tear **24.** course, current, direction, drift, flow, motion, movement, passage, path, progress, stream, tendency, tenor, tide, trend, way **25.** coop, enclosure, pen **26. in the long run** at the end of the day, eventually, in the end, in the final analysis, in time, ultimately, when all is said and done **27. on the run a.** at liberty, escaping, fugitive, in flight, on the lam (*U.S. sl.*), on the loose **b.** defeated, falling back, fleeing, in flight, in retreat, retreating, running away **c.** at speed, hastily, hurriedly, hurrying, in a hurry, in a rush, in haste

run across bump into, chance upon, come across, come upon, encounter, meet, meet with, run into

runaway *n.* **1.** absconder, deserter, escapee, escaper, fugitive, refugee, truant ~*adj.* **2.** escaped, fleeing, fugitive, loose, out of control, uncontrolled, wild **3.** easily won, easy, effortless

run away 1. abscond, beat it (*Sl.*), bolt, clear out, cut and run (*Inf.*), decamp, do a bunk (*Brit. inf.*), escape, flee, make a run for it, run off, scarper (*Brit. sl.*), scram (*Inf.*), show a clean pair of heels, skedaddle (*Inf.*), take flight, take off, take to one's heels **2. With away a.** abduct, abscond, elope **b.** abscond, make off, pinch (*Inf.*), run off, snatch,

steal **c.** romp home, walk it (*Inf.*), win by a mile (*Inf.*), win easily, win hands down

rundown briefing, outline, précis, recap (*Inf.*), résumé, review, run-through, sketch, summary, synopsis

run-down 1. below par, debilitated, drained, enervated, exhausted, fatigued, out of condition, peaky, tired, under the weather (*Inf.*), unhealthy, weak, weary, worn-out **2.** broken-down, decrepit, dilapidated, dingy, ramshackle, seedy, shabby, tumble-down, worn-out

run down 1. curtail, cut, cut back, decrease, drop, pare down, reduce, trim **2.** debilitate, exhaust, sap the strength of, tire, undermine the health of, weaken **3.** belittle, criticize adversely, decry, defame, denigrate, disparage, knock (*Inf.*), revile, speak ill of, vilify **4.** hit, knock down, knock over, run into, run over, strike

run in 1. break in, run gently **2.** *Sl.* apprehend, arrest, bust (*Inf.*), collar (*Inf.*), jail, nab (*Inf.*), pick up, pinch (*Inf.*), pull in (*Brit. sl.*), take into custody, take to jail, throw in jail

run into 1. bump into, collide with, crash into, dash against, hit, ram, strike **2.** be beset by, be confronted by, bump into, chance upon, come across, come upon, encounter, meet, meet with, run across

runner 1. athlete, harrier, jogger, miler, sprinter **2.** courier, dispatch bearer, errand boy, messenger **3.** offshoot, shoot, sprig, sprout, stem, stolon (*Bot.*), tendril

nance: *the running of a machine.* **14.** competition or competitive situation (in **in the running, out of the running**). **15. make the running.** to set the pace in a competition or race.

running board *n.* a ledge beneath the doors of certain old cars.

running head *or* **title** *n. Printing.* a heading printed at the top of every page of a book.

running repairs *pl. n.* repairs that do not, or do not greatly, interrupt operations.

runny (ˈrʌnɪ) *adj.* **-nier, -niest. 1.** tending to flow; liquid. **2.** (of the nose) exuding mucus.

run off *vb.* (*adv.*) **1.** (*intr.*) to depart in haste. **2.** (*tr.*) to produce quickly, as copies on a duplicating machine. **3.** to drain (liquid) or (of liquid) to be drained. **4.** (*tr.*) to decide (a race) by a run-off. **5. run off with. a.** to steal; purloin. **b.** to elope with. ~*n.* **run-off. 6.** an extra race to decide the winner after a tie. **7.** *N.Z.* grazing land for store cattle. **8.** that portion of rainfall that runs into streams as surface water rather than being absorbed by the soil. **9.** the overflow of a liquid from a container.

run-of-the-mill *adj.* ordinary, average, or undistinguished in quality, character, or nature.

run on *vb.* (*adv.*) **1.** (*intr.*) to continue without interruption. **2.** to handwrite with linked-up characters. **3.** *Printing.* to compose text matter without indention or paragraphing. ~*n.* **run-on. 4.** *Printing.* **a.** text matter composed without indenting. **b.** an additional quantity required in excess of the originally stated amount, whilst the job is being produced. **5. a.** a word added at the end of a dictionary entry whose meaning can be easily inferred from the definition of the headword. **b.** (*as modifier*): *a run-on entry.*

run out *vb.* (*adv.*) **1.** (*intr.; often foll. by of*) to exhaust (a supply of something) or (of a supply) to become exhausted. **2. run out on.** *Inf.* to desert or abandon. **3.** (*tr.*) *Cricket.* to dismiss (a running batsman) by breaking the wicket with the ball, or with the ball in the hand, while he is out of his ground. ~*n.* **run-out. 4.** *Cricket.* dismissal of a batsman by running him out.

run over *vb.* **1.** (*tr., adv.*) to knock down (a person) with a moving vehicle. **2.** (*intr.*) to overflow the capacity of (a container). **3.** (*intr., prep.*) to examine hastily or make a rapid survey of. **4.** (*intr., prep.*) to exceed (a limit): *we've run over our time.*

runt (rʌnt) *n.* **1.** the smallest and weakest young animal in a litter, esp. the smallest piglet in a litter. **2.** *Derog.* an undersized or inferior person. **3.** a large pigeon, originally bred for eating. —ˈ**runtish** *adj.* —ˈ**runty** *adj.* —ˈ**runtiness** *n.*

run through *vb.* **1.** (*tr., adv.*) to pierce with a sword or other weapon. **2.** (*intr., prep.*) to exhaust (money) by wasteful spending. **3.** (*intr., prep.*) to practise or rehearse: *let's run through the plan.* **4.** (*intr., prep.*) to examine hastily. ~*n.* **run-through. 5.** a practice or rehearsal. **6.** a brief survey.

run to *vb.* (*intr., prep.*) to be sufficient for: *my income doesn't run to luxuries.*

run up *vb.* (*tr., adv.*) **1.** to amass; incur: *to run up debts.* **2.** to make by sewing together quickly. **3.** to hoist: *to run up a flag.* ~*n.* **run-up. 4.** an approach run by an athlete for a long jump, pole vault, etc. **5.** a preliminary or preparatory period: *the run-up to the election.*

runway (ˈrʌnˌweɪ) *n.* **1.** a hard level roadway from which aircraft take off and on which they land. **2.** *Forestry, North American.* a chute for sliding logs down. **3.** a narrow ramp extending from the stage into the audience in a theatre, etc.

rupee (ruːˈpiː) *n.* the standard monetary unit of India, Pakistan, Sri Lanka, the Maldive Islands, Mauritius, the Seychelles, and Nepal.

rupture (ˈrʌptʃə) *n.* **1.** the act of breaking or bursting or the state of being broken or burst. **2.** a breach of peaceful or friendly relations. **3.** *Pathol.* **a.** the breaking or tearing of a bodily structure or part. **b.** another word for **hernia.** ~*vb.* **4.** to break or burst. **5.** to be affected with a rupture or hernia. **6.** to undergo a breach in relations or friendship. —ˈ**rupturable** *adj.*

rural (ˈrʊərəl) *adj.* **1.** of, relating to, or characteristic of the country or country life. **2.** living in the country. **3.** of, relating to, or associated with farming. ~Cf. **urban.** —ˈ**ruralism** *n.* —ˈ**ruralist** *n.* —ru**ˈrality** *n.* —ˈ**rurally** *adv.*

rural dean *n. Chiefly Brit.* a clergyman having authority over a group of parishes.

rural district *n.* (*formerly*), a rural division of a county.

ruse (ruːz) *n.* an action intended to mislead, deceive, or trick; stratagem.

rush¹ (rʌʃ) *vb.* **1.** to hurry or cause to hurry; hasten. **2.** (*tr.*) to make a sudden attack upon (a fortress, position, person, etc.). **3.** (when *intr.*, often foll. by *at, in,* or *into*) to proceed or approach in a reckless manner. **4. rush one's fences.** to proceed with precipitate haste. **5.** (*intr.*) to come, flow, swell, etc., quickly or suddenly: *tears rushed to her eyes.* **6.** *Sl.* to charge (somebody) an exorbitant price. **7.** (*tr.*) *U.S.* to make a concerted effort to secure the agreement, participation, etc., of (a person). **8.** (*tr.*) *Rugby.* (of a pack) to move (the ball) forwards by short kicks and runs. ~*n.* **9.** the act or condition of rushing. **10.** a sudden surge towards someone or something: *a gold rush.* **11.** a sudden demand. **12.** (*usually pl.*) (in film-making) the initial prints of a scene before editing. ~*adj.* (*prenominal*) **13.** requiring speed or urgency: *a rush job.* **14.** characterized by much movement, business, etc.: *a rush period.* —ˈ**rusher** *n.*

rush² (rʌʃ) *n.* **1.** an annual or perennial plant growing in wet places and typically having grasslike cylindrical leaves and small green or brown flowers. **2.** something valueless; a trifle; straw: *not worth a rush.* **3.** short for **rush light.** —ˈ**rush,like** *adj.* —ˈ**rushy** *adj.*

rush hour *n.* a period at the beginning and end of the working day when large numbers of people are travelling to or from work.

rush light *or* **candle** *n.* a narrow candle, formerly in

THESAURUS

running *adj.* **1.** constant, continuous, incessant, in succession, on the trot (*Inf.*), perpetual, together, unbroken, unceasing, uninterrupted **2.** flowing, moving, streaming ~*n.* **3.** administration, charge, conduct, control, coordination, direction, leadership, management, organization, regulation, superintendency, supervision **4.** functioning, maintenance, operation, performance, working **5.** competition, contention, contest

run off 1. bolt, clear out, cut and run (*Inf.*), decamp, escape, flee, make off, run away, scarper (*Brit. sl.*), show a clean pair of heels, skedaddle (*Inf.*), take flight, take to one's heels **2.** churn out (*Inf.*), duplicate, print, produce **3.** bleed, drain, flow away, siphon, tap **4.** *With* **with a.** lift (*Inf.*), make off, pinch (*Inf.*), purloin, run away, steal, swipe (*Sl.*) **b.** abscond, elope, run away

run-of-the-mill average, common, commonplace, fair, mediocre, middling, modest, ordinary, passable, tolerable, undistinguished, unexceptional, unexciting, unimpressive

run out 1. be exhausted, cease, close,

come to a close, dry up, end, expire, fail, finish, give out, peter out, terminate **2.** *With* **of** be cleaned out, be out of, exhaust one's supply of, have no more of, have none left, have no remaining **3.** *With* **on** *Inf.* abandon, desert, forsake, leave high and dry, leave holding the baby, leave in the lurch, rat, run away from

run over 1. hit, knock down, knock over, run down, strike **2.** brim over, overflow, spill, spill over **3.** check, examine, go over, go through, rehearse, reiterate, review, run through, survey

run through 1. pierce, spit, stab, stick, transfix **2.** blow (*Sl.*), dissipate, fritter away, spend like water, squander, throw away, waste **3.** go over, practise, read, rehearse, run over **4.** check, examine, go through, look over, review, run over, survey

rupture *n.* **1.** breach, break, burst, cleavage, cleft, crack, fissure, fracture, rent, split, tear **2.** altercation, breach, break, bust-up (*Inf.*), contention, disagreement, disruption, dissolution, estrangement, falling-out (*Inf.*), feud, hostility, quarrel, rift, schism, split **3.**

Medical hernia ~*v.* **4.** break, burst, cleave, crack, fracture, puncture, rend, separate, sever, split, tear **5.** break off, cause a breach, come between, disrupt, dissever, divide, split

rural agrarian, agricultural, Arcadian, bucolic, countrified, country, pastoral, rustic, sylvan, upcountry

ruse artifice, blind, deception, device, dodge, hoax, imposture, manoeuvre, ploy, sham, stratagem, subterfuge, trick, wile

rush *v.* **1.** accelerate, bolt, career, dart, dash, dispatch, expedite, fly, hasten, hotfoot, hurry, hustle, lose no time, make haste, make short work of, press, push, quicken, race, run, scramble, scurry, shoot, speed, speed up, sprint, tear ~*n.* **2.** charge, dash, dispatch, expedition, haste, hurry, race, scramble, speed, surge, swiftness, urgency ~*v.* **3.** attack, capture, charge, overcome, storm, take by storm ~*n.* **4.** assault, charge, onslaught, push, storm, surge ~*adj.* **5.** brisk, cursory, emergency, expeditious, fast, hasty, hurried, prompt, quick, rapid, swift, urgent

use, made of the pith of various types of rush dipped in tallow.

rusk (rʌsk) *n.* **1.** a kind of light biscuit. **2.** a light bread dough, sweet or plain, baked twice until it is brown, hard, and crisp.

Russ. *abbrev. for* Russia(n).

russet ('rʌsɪt) *n.* **1.** brown with a yellowish or reddish tinge. **2.** a rough homespun fabric, reddish-brown in colour, formerly in use for clothing. **3.** any of various apples with rough brownish-red skins. ~*adj.* **4.** *Arch.* simple; homely; rustic: *a russet life.* **5.** of the colour russet: *russet hair.* —'**russet-,like** *adj.* —'**russety** *adj.*

Russian ('rʌʃən) *n.* **1.** the official language of the Soviet Union: an Indo-European language belonging to the East Slavonic branch. **2.** a native or inhabitant of Russia or the Soviet Union. ~*adj.* **3.** of, relating to, or characteristic of Russia or the Soviet Union, its people, or their language.

Russian roulette *n.* **1.** an act of bravado in which each person in turn spins the cylinder of a revolver loaded with only one cartridge and presses the trigger with the barrel against his own head. **2.** any foolish or potentially suicidal undertaking.

Russo- ('rʌsəʊ-) *combining form.* Russia or Russian: *Russo-Japanese.*

rust (rʌst) *n.* **1.** a reddish-brown oxide coating formed on iron or steel by the action of oxygen and moisture. **2.** Also called: **rust fungus.** *Plant pathol.* **a.** a fungus which is parasitic on cereal plants, conifers, etc. **b.** any of various plant diseases characterized by reddish-brown discoloration of the leaves and stem, esp. that caused by the rust fungi. **3. a.** a strong brown colour, sometimes with a reddish or yellowish tinge. **b.** (*as adj.*): *a rust carpet.* **4.** any corrosive or debilitating influence, esp. lack of use. ~*vb.* **5.** to become coated with a layer of rust. **6.** to deteriorate or cause to deteriorate through some debilitating influence or lack of use: *he allowed his talent to rust over the years.* —'**rustless** *adj.*

rustic ('rʌstɪk) *adj.* **1.** of, characteristic of, or living in the country; rural. **2.** having qualities ascribed to country life or people; simple; unsophisticated: *rustic pleasures.* **3.** crude, awkward, or uncouth. **4.** made of untrimmed branches: *a rustic seat.* **5.** (of masonry, etc.) having a rough or irregular surface and chamfered or recessed joints. ~*n.* **6.** a person who comes from or lives in the country. **7.** an unsophisticated, simple, or clownish person from the country. **8.** Also called: **rusticwork.** brick or stone having a rough finish. —'**rustically** *adv.* —**rusticity** (rʌ'stɪsɪtɪ) *n.*

rusticate ('rʌstɪ,keɪt) *vb.* **1.** to banish or retire to the country. **2.** to make or become rustic in style, etc. **3.** (*tr.*) to construct (brickwork or masonry) in a rustic manner. **4.** (*tr.*) *Brit.* to send down from university for a

specified time as a punishment. —,**rusti'cation** *n.* —'**rusti,cator** *n.*

rustle[1] ('rʌsəl) *vb.* **1.** to make or cause to make a low crisp whispering or rubbing sound, as of dry leaves or paper. **2.** to move with such a sound. ~*n.* **3.** such a sound or sounds.

rustle[2] ('rʌsəl) *vb. U.S.* **1.** to steal (cattle, horses, etc.). **2.** *Inf.* to move swiftly and energetically. —'**rustler** *n.*

rustle up *vb.* (*tr., adv.*) **1.** to prepare (a meal, etc.) rapidly, esp. at short notice. **2.** to forage for and obtain.

rustproof ('rʌst,pruːf) *adj.* treated against rusting.

rusty ('rʌstɪ) *adj.* **rustier, rustiest.** **1.** covered with, affected by, or consisting of rust: *a rusty machine.* **2.** of the colour rust. **3.** discoloured by age: *a rusty coat.* **4.** (of the voice) tending to croak. **5.** old-fashioned in appearance: *a rusty old gentleman.* **6.** impaired in skill or knowledge by inaction or neglect. **7.** (of plants) affected by the rust fungus. —'**rustily** *adv.* —'**rustiness** *n.*

rut[1] (rʌt) *n.* **1.** a groove or furrow in a soft road, caused by wheels. **2.** a narrow or predictable way of life; dreary or undeviating routine (esp. in **in a rut**). ~*vb.* **rutting, rutted.** **3.** (*tr.*) to make a rut in. —'**rutty** *adj.*

rut[2] (rʌt) *n.* **1.** a recurrent period of sexual excitement and reproductive activity in certain male ruminants. ~*vb.* **rutting, rutted.** **2.** (*intr.*) (of male ruminants) to be in a period of sexual excitement and activity.

ruthenium (ruː'θiːnɪəm) *n.* a hard brittle white element of the platinum metal group. It is used to harden platinum and palladium. Symbol: Ru; atomic no.: 44; atomic wt.: 101.07.

rutherford ('rʌðəfəd) *n.* a unit of activity equal to the quantity of a radioactive nuclide required to produce one million disintegrations per second. Abbrev.: rd.

ruthless ('ruːθlɪs) *adj.* feeling or showing no mercy; hard-hearted. —'**ruthlessly** *adv.* —'**ruthlessness** *n.*

ruttish ('rʌtɪʃ) *adj.* **1.** (of an animal) in a condition of rut. **2.** lascivious or salacious. —'**ruttishly** *adv.* —'**ruttishness** *n.*

R.V. *abbrev. for* Revised Version (of the Bible).

Rwy. *or* **Ry.** *abbrev. for* railway.

rye (raɪ) *n.* **1.** a tall hardy widely cultivated annual grass having bristly flower spikes and light brown grain. **2.** the grain of this grass, used in making flour and whisky, and as a livestock food. **3.** Also called: **rye whiskey.** whisky distilled from rye.

rye bread *n.* any of various breads made entirely or partly from rye flour, often with caraway seeds.

rye-grass *n.* any of various grasses native to Europe, N Africa, and Asia, and widely cultivated as forage crops. They have flattened flower spikes and hairless leaves.

THESAURUS

rust *n.* **1.** corrosion, oxidation ~*v.* **2.** corrode, oxidize ~*n.* **3.** blight, mildew, mould, must, rot ~*v.* **4.** atrophy, decay, decline, deteriorate, go stale, stagnate, tarnish

rustic *adj.* **1.** Arcadian, bucolic, countrified, country, pastoral, rural, sylvan, upcountry **2.** artless, homely, homespun, plain, simple, unaffected, unpolished, unrefined, unsophisticated **3.** awkward, boorish, churlish, cloddish, clodhopping (*Inf.*), clownish, coarse, crude, graceless, loutish, lumpish, maladroit, rough, uncouth, uncultured, unmannerly ~*n.* **4.** boor, bumpkin, clod, clodhopper (*Inf.*), clown, country boy, country

cousin, countryman, countrywoman, hillbilly, Hodge, peasant, son of the soil, swain (*Archaic*), yokel

rustle **1.** *v.* crackle, crepitate, crinkle, susurrate (*Literary*), swish, whish, whisper, whoosh **2.** *n.* crackle, crepitation, crinkling, susurration *or* susurrus (*Literary*), rustling, whisper

rusty **1.** corroded, oxidized, rust-covered, rusted **2.** chestnut, coppery, reddish, reddish-brown, russet, rust-coloured **3.** cracked, creaking, croaking, croaky, hoarse **4.** ancient, antiquated, antique, dated, old-fashioned, outmoded, out of date, passé **5.** de-

ficient, impaired, not what it was, out of practice, sluggish, stale, unpractised, weak

rut *n.* **1.** furrow, gouge, groove, indentation, pothole, score, track, trough, wheelmark **2.** dead end, groove, habit, humdrum existence, pattern, routine, system ~*v.* **3.** cut, furrow, gouge, groove, hole, indent, mark, score

ruthless adamant, barbarous, brutal, callous, cruel, ferocious, fierce, hard, hard-hearted, harsh, heartless, inexorable, inhuman, merciless, pitiless, relentless, remorseless, savage, severe, stern, unfeeling, unmerciful, unpitying, unrelenting, without pity

S

s or **S** (ɛs) n., pl. **s's, S's,** or **Ss. 1.** the 19th letter of the English alphabet. **2.** a speech sound represented by this letter, either voiceless, as in *sit,* or voiced, as in *dogs.* **3. a.** something shaped like an S. **b.** (*in combination*): *an S-bend in a road.*

S *symbol for:* **1.** Society. **2.** South. **3.** *Chem.* sulphur. **4.** *Physics.* **a.** entropy. **b.** siemens. **5.** *Physics.* strangeness.

s. *abbrev. for:* **1.** second (of time). **2.** shilling. **3.** singular. **4.** son. **5.** succeeded.

S. *abbrev. for:* **1.** sabbath. **2.** (*pl.* **SS**) Saint. **3.** Saturday. **4.** Saxon. **5.** *Currency.* schilling. **6.** school. **7.** September. **8.** Signor. **9.** Sunday.

-s¹ or **-es** *suffix.* forming the plural of most nouns: *boys; boxes.*

-s² or **-es** *suffix.* forming the third person singular present indicative tense of verbs: *he runs.*

-'s *suffix.* **1.** forming the possessive singular of nouns and some pronouns: *man's; one's.* **2.** forming the possessive plural of nouns whose plurals do not end in *-s: children's.* **3.** forming the plural of numbers, letters, or symbols: *20's.* **4.** *Inf.* contraction of *is* or *has: it's gone.* **5.** *Inf.* contraction of *us* with *let: let's.* **6.** *Inf.* contraction of *does* in some questions: *what's he do?*

-s' *suffix.* forming the possessive of plural nouns ending in the sound *s* or *z* and of some singular nouns: *girls'; for goodness' sake.*

S.A. *abbrev. for:* **1.** Salvation Army. **2.** South Africa. **3.** South America. **4.** South Australia.

Sabbatarian (ˌsæbəˈtɛərɪən) n. **1.** a person advocating the strict religious observance of Sunday. **2.** a person who observes Saturday as the Sabbath. ~*adj.* **3.** of the Sabbath or its observance. —**ˌSabbaˈtarianism** n.

Sabbath (ˈsæbəθ) n. **1.** the seventh day of the week, Saturday, devoted to worship and rest from work in Judaism and in certain Christian Churches. **2.** Sunday, observed by Christians as the day of worship and rest. **3.** (*not cap.*) a period of rest. **4.** Also called: **sabbat, witches' Sabbath.** a midnight meeting for practitioners of witchcraft or devil worship.

sabbatical (səˈbætɪkəl) *adj.* **1.** denoting a period of leave granted to university staff, teachers, etc., esp. originally every seventh year: *a sabbatical year.* ~*n.* **2.** any sabbatical period.

Sabbatical (səˈbætɪkəl) *adj.* of, relating to, or appropriate to the Sabbath as a day of rest and religious observance.

S.A.B.C. *abbrev. for* South African Broadcasting Corporation.

Sabine (ˈsæbaɪn) n. **1.** a member of an ancient people who lived in central Italy. ~*adj.* **2.** of or relating to this people or their language.

sable (ˈseɪbəl) n., pl. **-bles** or **-ble. 1.** a marten of N Asian forests, with dark brown luxuriant fur. **2. a.** the highly valued fur of this animal. **b.** (*as modifier*): *a sable coat.* **3. American sable.** the brown, slightly less valuable fur of the American marten. **4.** a dark brown to yellowish-brown colour. ~*adj.* **5.** of the colour of sable fur. **6.** black; dark. **7.** (*usually postpositive*) *Heraldry.* of the colour black.

sabot (ˈsæbəʊ) n. **1.** a shoe made from a single block of wood. **2.** a shoe with a wooden sole and a leather or cloth upper. **3.** *Austral.* a small yacht with a shortened bow.

sabotage (ˈsæbəˌtɑːʒ) n. **1.** the deliberate destruction, disruption, or damage of equipment, a public service, etc., as by enemy agents, dissatisfied employees, etc. **2.** any similar action. ~*vb.* **3.** (*tr.*) to destroy or disrupt, esp. by secret means.

saboteur (ˌsæbəˈtɜː) n. a person who commits sabotage.

sabre or *U.S.* **saber** (ˈseɪbə) n. **1.** a stout single-edged cavalry sword, having a curved blade. **2.** a sword used in fencing, having a narrow V-shaped blade. ~*vb.* **3.** (*tr.*) to injure or kill with a sabre.

sac (sæk) n. a pouch, bag, or pouchlike part in an animal or plant. —**saccate** (ˈsækɪt, -eɪt) *adj.* —**ˈsacˌlike** *adj.*

saccharin (ˈsækərɪn) n. a very sweet white crystalline slightly soluble powder used as a nonfattening sweetener.

saccharine (ˈsækəˌriːn) *adj.* **1.** excessively sweet; sugary: *a saccharine smile.* **2.** of the nature of or containing sugar or saccharin.

saccharo- or *before a vowel* **sacchar-** *combining form.* sugar.

sacerdotal (ˌsæsəˈdəʊtəl) *adj.* of, relating to, or characteristic of priests. —**ˌsacerˈdotaˌlism** n. —**ˌsacerˈdotally** *adv.*

sachem (ˈseɪtʃəm) n. *U.S.* a leader of a political party or organization.

sachet (ˈsæʃeɪ) n. **1.** a small sealed envelope, usually made of plastic, for containing shampoo, etc. **2. a.** a small soft bag containing perfumed powder, placed in drawers to scent clothing. **b.** the powder contained in such a bag.

sack¹ (sæk) n. **1.** a large bag made of coarse cloth, thick paper, etc., used as a container. **2.** Also called: **sackful.** the amount contained in a sack. **3.** Also called: **sacque** (sæk). **a.** a woman's full loose hip-length jacket. **b.** a woman's loose tube-shaped dress. **4.** a slang word for bed. **5. the sack.** *Inf.* dismissal from employment. **6. hit the sack.** *Sl.* to go to bed. ~*vb.* (*tr.*) **7.** *Inf.* to dismiss from employment. **8.** to put into a sack or sacks. —**ˈsackˌlike** *adj.*

sack² (sæk) n. **1.** the plundering of a place by an army or mob. ~*vb.* **2.** (*tr.*) to plunder and partially destroy (a place). —**ˈsacker** n.

sack³ (sæk) n. *Arch. except in trademarks.* any dry white wine from SW Europe.

sackbut (ˈsækˌbʌt) n. a medieval form of trombone.

sackcloth (ˈsækˌklɒθ) n. **1.** coarse cloth such as sacking. **2.** garments made of such cloth, worn formerly to indicate mourning. **3. sackcloth and ashes.** a public display of extreme grief.

sacking (ˈsækɪŋ) n. coarse cloth used for making sacks, woven from flax, hemp, jute, etc.

sacrament (ˈsækrəmənt) n. **1.** an outward sign combined with a prescribed form of words and regarded as conferring grace upon those who receive it. The Protestant sacraments are baptism and the Lord's Supper. In the Roman Catholic and Eastern Churches they are baptism, penance, confirmation, the Eucharist, holy orders, matrimony, and extreme unction. **2.** (*often cap.*) the Eucharist. **3.** the consecrated elements of the Eucharist, esp. the bread. **4.** something regarded as possessing a sacred significance. **5.** a pledge.

sacred (ˈseɪkrɪd) *adj.* **1.** exclusively devoted to a deity or to some religious ceremony or use. **2.** worthy of or regarded with reverence, awe, or respect. **3.** connected

---

THESAURUS

sabotage 1. *v.* cripple, damage, destroy, disable, disrupt, incapacitate, sap the foundations of, subvert, throw a spanner in the works (*Inf.*), undermine, vandalize, wreck 2. *n.* damage, destruction, disruption, subversion, treachery, treason, wrecking

sack¹ 1. *v.* axe (*Inf.*), discharge, dismiss, fire (*Inf.*), give (someone) his cards, give (someone) his marching orders, give (someone) the boot (*Sl.*), kick out (*Inf.*) 2. *n.* **the sack**

discharge, dismissal, termination of employment, the axe (*Inf.*), the boot (*Sl.*), the chop (*Brit. sl.*), the push (*Sl.*)

sack² 1. *v.* demolish, depredate (*Rare*), despoil, destroy, devastate, lay waste, loot, maraud, pillage, plunder, raid, ravage, rifle, rob, ruin, spoil, strip 2. *n.* depredation, despoliation, destruction, devastation, looting, pillage, plunder, plundering, rape, rapine, ravage, ruin, waste

sackcloth and ashes compunction, contrition, grief, hair shirt, mortification, mourning, penitence, remorse, repentance

sacred 1. blessed, consecrated, divine, hallowed, holy, revered, sanctified, venerable 2. inviolable, inviolate, invulnerable, protected, sacrosanct, secure 3. holy, religious, solemn

with or intended for religious use: *sacred music*. **4. sa-cred to.** dedicated to. —**'sacredly** *adv*. —**'sacredness** *n*.

sacred cow *n. Inf.* a person, custom, etc., held to be beyond criticism.

sacrifice ('sækrɪ,faɪs) *n*. **1.** a surrender of something of value as a means of gaining something more desirable or of preventing some evil. **2.** a ritual killing of a person or animal with the intention of propitiating or pleasing a deity. **3.** a symbolic offering of something to a deity. **4.** the person, animal, or object killed or offered. **5.** loss entailed by giving up or selling something at less than its value. **6.** *Chess.* the act or an instance of sacrificing a piece. ~*vb*. **7.** to make a sacrifice (of). **8.** *Chess.* to permit or force one's opponent to capture a piece freely, as in playing a gambit: *he sacrificed his queen and checkmated his opponent on the next move*. —**'sacri-,ficer** *n*. —**sacrificial** (,sækrɪ'fɪʃəl) *adj*.

sacrilege ('sækrɪlɪdʒ) *n*. **1.** the misuse or desecration of anything regarded as sacred or as worthy of extreme respect. **2.** the act or an instance of taking anything sacred for secular use. —**sacrilegist** (,sækrɪ'liːdʒɪst) *n*. —,**sacri'legious** *adj*. —,**sacri'legiously** *adv*.

sacristan ('sækrɪstən) *or* **sacrist** ('sækrɪst, 'seɪ-) *n*. **1.** a person who has charge of the contents of a church. **2.** a less common word for **sexton**.

sacristy ('sækrɪstɪ) *n., pl.* **-ties.** a room attached to a church or chapel where the sacred vessels, etc., are kept.

sacrosanct ('sækrəʊ,sæŋkt) *adj*. very sacred or holy. —,**sacro'sanctity** *n*.

sacrum ('seɪkrəm) *n., pl.* **-cra** (-krə). the large wedge-shaped bone, consisting of five fused vertebrae, in the lower part of the back. —**'sacral** *adj*.

sad (sæd) *adj.* **sadder, saddest. 1.** feeling sorrow; unhappy. **2.** causing, suggestive, or expressive of such feelings: *a sad story*. **3.** unfortunate; shabby: *her clothes were in a sad state*. —**'sadly** *adv*. —**'sadness** *n*.

sadden ('sædən) *vb*. to make or become sad.

saddle ('sædəl) *n*. **1.** a seat for a rider, usually made of leather, placed on a horse's back and secured with a girth under the belly. **2.** a similar seat on a bicycle, tractor, etc. **3.** a back pad forming part of the harness of a packhorse. **4.** anything that resembles a saddle in shape, position, or function. **5.** a cut of meat, esp. mutton, consisting of both loins. **6.** the part of a horse or similar animal on which a saddle is placed. **7.** the part of the back of a domestic chicken that is nearest to the tail. **8.** Also called: **saddleback.** a pass or ridge that slopes gently between two peaks. **9. in the saddle.** in a position of control. ~*vb*. **10.** (sometimes foll. by *up*) to put a saddle on (a horse). **11.** (*intr.*) to mount into the saddle. **12.** (*tr.*) to burden: *I didn't ask to be saddled with this job*. —**'saddle-,like** *adj*.

saddleback ('sædəl,bæk) *n*. a marking resembling a saddle on the backs of various animals. —**'saddle-,backed** *adj*.

saddlebag ('sædəl,bæg) *n*. a pouch or small bag attached to the saddle of a horse, bicycle, etc.

saddle horse *n*. a lightweight horse kept for riding only.

saddler ('sædlə) *n*. a person who makes, deals in, or re-pairs saddles and other leather equipment for horses.

saddlery ('sædlərɪ) *n., pl.* **-dleries. 1.** saddles, harness, and other leather equipment for horses collectively. **2.** the business, work, or place of work of a saddler.

saddle soap *n*. a soft soap containing neat's-foot oil used to preserve and clean leather.

saddletree ('sædəl,triː) *n*. the frame of a saddle.

Sadducee ('sædjʊ,siː) *n. Judaism.* a member of an ancient Jewish sect that was opposed to the Pharisees, denying the resurrection of the dead and the validity of oral tradition. —,**Saddu'cean** *adj*.

sadhu *or* **saddhu** ('sɑːduː) *n*. a Hindu wandering holy man.

sadism ('seɪdɪzəm) *n*. the gaining of pleasure or sexual gratification from the infliction of pain and mental suffering on another person. Cf. **masochism.** —**'sadist** *n*. —**sadistic** (sə'dɪstɪk) *adj*. —**sa'distically** *adv*.

sadomasochism (,seɪdəʊ'mæsə,kɪzəm) *n*. the combination of sadistic and masochistic elements in one person. —,**sadomaso'chistic** *adj*.

s.a.e. *abbrev. for* stamped addressed envelope.

safari (sə'fɑːrɪ) *n., pl.* **-ris. 1.** an overland journey or hunting expedition, esp. in Africa. **2.** the people, animals, etc., that go on the expedition.

safari park *n*. an enclosed park in which lions and other wild animals are kept in the open and can be viewed by the public in cars, etc.

safe (seɪf) *adj*. **1.** affording security or protection from harm: *a safe place*. **2.** (*postpositive*) free from danger, etc.: *you'll be safe here*. **3.** secure from risk: *a safe investment*. **4.** worthy of trust: *a safe companion*. **5.** tending to avoid controversy or risk: *a safe player*. **6.** not dangerous: *water safe to drink*. **7. on the safe side.** as a precaution. ~*adv*. **8.** in a safe condition: *the children are safe in bed now*. **9. play safe.** to act in a way least likely to cause danger, controversy, or defeat. ~*n*. **10.** a strong container, usually of metal and provided with a secure lock, for storing money or valuables. **11.** a container for storing food. —**'safely** *adv*. —**'safeness** *n*.

safe-conduct *n*. **1.** a document giving official permission to travel through a region, esp. in time of war. **2.** the protection afforded by such a document.

safe-deposit *or* **safety-deposit** *n*. **a.** a place with facilities for the safe storage of money. **b.** (*as modifier*): *a safe-deposit box*.

safeguard ('seɪf,gɑːd) *n*. **1.** a person or thing that ensures protection against danger, injury, etc. **2.** a safe-conduct. ~*vb*. **3.** (*tr.*) to protect.

safety ('seɪftɪ) *n., pl.* **-ties. 1.** the quality of being safe. **2.** freedom from danger or risk of injury. **3.** a contrivance designed to prevent injury. **4.** *American football.* Also called: **safetyman.** the defensive player furthest back in the field.

safety belt *n*. **1.** another name for **seat belt. 2.** a belt or strap worn by a person working at a great height to prevent him from falling.

safety curtain *n*. a curtain made of fireproof material that can be lowered to separate the auditorium and stage in a theatre to prevent the spread of a fire.

safety lamp *n*. an oil-burning miner's lamp in which

THESAURUS

sacrifice 1. *v.* forego, forfeit, give up, immolate, let go, lose, offer, offer up, surrender **2.** *n.* burnt offering, destruction, hecatomb, immolation, loss, oblation, renunciation, surrender

sacrilege blasphemy, desecration, heresy, impiety, irreverence, mockery, profanation, profaneness, profanity, violation

sad 1. blue, cheerless, dejected, depressed, disconsolate, dismal, doleful, down, downcast, down in the dumps (*Inf.*), down in the mouth (*Inf.*), gloomy, glum, grief-stricken, grieved, heavy-hearted, low, low-spirited, lugubrious, melancholy, mournful, pensive, sick at heart, sombre, triste (*Archaic*), unhappy, wistful, woebegone **2.** calamitous, dark, depressing, disastrous, dismal, grievous, heart-rending, lachrymose, moving, pathetic, pitiable, pitiful, poignant, sorry, tearful, tragic, upsetting **3.** bad, deplorable, dismal, distressing, grave, lamentable, miserable, regrettable, serious, shabby, sorry, to

be deplored, unfortunate, unhappy, unsatisfactory, wretched

sadden bring tears to one's eyes, cast a gloom upon, cast down, dash, deject, depress, desolate, dispirit, distress, grieve, make blue, make one's heart bleed, upset

saddle *v.* burden, charge, encumber, load, lumber (*Brit. inf.*), task, tax

sadistic barbarous, brutal, cruel, fiendish, perverse, perverted, ruthless, vicious

sadness bleakness, cheerlessness, dejection, depression, despondency, dolefulness, dolour (*Poetic*), gloominess, grief, heavy heart, melancholy, misery, mournfulness, poignancy, sorrow, sorrowfulness, the blues, the dumps (*Inf.*), unhappiness

safe 1. free from harm, guarded, impregnable, in safety, intact, O.K. *or* okay (*Inf.*), out of danger, out of harm's way, protected, safe and sound, secure, undamaged, unharmed, unhurt, unscathed **2.** harmless, innocuous, nonpoisonous, nontoxic, pure, tame,

unpolluted, wholesome **3.** cautious, circumspect, conservative, dependable, discreet, on the safe side, prudent, realistic, reliable, sure, tried and true, trustworthy, unadventurous **4.** certain, impregnable, risk-free, riskless, secure, sound ~*n.* **5.** coffer, deposit box, repository, safe-deposit box, strongbox, vault

safeguard 1. *v.* defend, guard, look after, preserve, protect, screen, shield, watch over **2.** *n.* aegis, armour, bulwark, convoy, defence, escort, guard, protection, security, shield, surety

safely in one piece, in safety, safe and sound, securely, with impunity, without risk, with safety

safety assurance, cover, immunity, impregnability, protection, refuge, sanctuary, security, shelter

the flame is surrounded by a metal gauze to prevent it from igniting combustible gas.

safety match *n.* a match that will light only when struck against a specially prepared surface.

safety pin *n.* a spring wire clasp with a covering catch, made so as to shield the point when closed.

safety razor *n.* a razor with a guard over the blade or blades to prevent accidental cutting of the skin.

safety valve *n.* 1. a valve in a pressure vessel that allows fluid to escape at excess pressure. 2. a harmless outlet for emotion, etc.

safflower ('sæflauə) *n.* 1. a thistle-like Eurasian annual plant having large heads of orange-yellow flowers and yielding a dye and an oil used in paints, medicines, etc. 2. a red dye used for cotton and for colouring foods and cosmetics.

saffron ('sæfrən) *n.* 1. an Old World crocus having purple or white flowers with orange stigmas. 2. the dried stigmas of this plant, used to flavour or colour food. 3. **meadow saffron.** another name for **autumn crocus.** 4. an orange to orange-yellow colour.

sag (sæg) *vb.* (*mainly intr.*) **sagging, sagged.** 1. (*also tr.*) to sink or cause to sink in parts, as under weight or pressure: *the bed sags in the middle.* 2. to fall in value: *prices sagged to a new low.* 3. to hang unevenly. 4. (of courage, etc.) to weaken. ~*n.* 5. the act or an instance of sagging: *a sag in profits.* 6. *Naut.* the extent to which a vessel's keel sags at the centre. —'**saggy** *adj.*

saga ('sɑ:gə) *n.* 1. any of several medieval prose narratives written in Iceland and recounting the exploits of a hero or a family. 2. any similar heroic narrative. 3. a series of novels about several generations or members of a family. 4. *Inf.* a series of events or a story stretching over a long period.

sagacious (sə'geɪʃəs) *adj.* having or showing sagacity; wise. —**sa'gaciously** *adv.* —**sagacity** (-'gæs-) *n.*

sage[1] (seɪdʒ) *n.* 1. a man revered for his profound wisdom. ~*adj.* 2. profoundly wise or prudent. —'**sagely** *adv.* —'**sageness** *n.*

sage[2] (seɪdʒ) *n.* 1. a perennial Mediterranean plant having grey-green leaves and purple, blue, or white flowers. 2. the leaves of this plant, used in cooking for flavouring. 3. short for **sagebrush.**

sagebrush ('seɪdʒ,brʌʃ) *n.* any of a genus of aromatic plants of W North America, having silver-green leaves and large clusters of small white flowers.

Sagittarius (,sædʒɪ'tɛərɪəs) *n.,* *Latin genitive* **Sagittarii** (,sædʒɪ'tɛərɪ,aɪ). 1. *Astron.* a S constellation. 2. *Astrol.* the ninth sign of the zodiac. The sun is in this sign between Nov. 22 and Dec. 21. —**Sagittarian** (,sædʒɪ-'tɛərɪən) *adj.*

sago ('seɪgəʊ) *n.* a starchy cereal obtained from the powdered pith of a palm (**sago palm**), used for puddings and as a thickening agent.

sahib ('sɑ:hɪb) *n.* (in India) a form of address placed after a man's name, used as a mark of respect.

said (sɛd) *adj.* 1. (*prenominal*) (in contracts, etc.) aforesaid. ~*vb.* 2. the past tense or past participle of **say.**

sail (seɪl) *n.* 1. an area of fabric, usually Terylene or nylon (formerly canvas), with fittings for holding it in any suitable position to catch the wind, used for propelling certain kinds of vessels, esp. over water. 2. a voyage on such a vessel: *a sail down the river.* 3. a vessel with sails or such vessels collectively: *to travel by sail.* 4. a ship's sails collectively. 5. something resembling a sail in shape, position, or function, such as the part of a windmill that is turned by the wind. 6. **in sail.** having the sail set. 7. **make sail. a.** to run up the sail or to run up more sail. **b.** to begin a voyage. 8. **set sail. a.** to embark on a voyage by ship. **b.** to hoist sail. 9. **under sail. a.** with sail hoisted. **b.** under way. ~*vb.* (*mainly intr.*) 10. to travel in a boat or ship: *we sailed to Le Havre.* 11. to begin a voyage: *we sail at 5 o'clock.* 12. (of a vessel) to

move over the water. 13. (*tr.*) to manoeuvre or navigate a vessel: *he sailed the schooner up the channel.* 14. (*tr.*) to sail over: *she sailed the Atlantic single-handed.* 15. (often foll. by *over, through,* etc.) to move fast or effortlessly: *we sailed through customs.* 16. to move along smoothly; glide. 17. (often foll. by *in* or *into*) *Inf.* **a.** to begin (something) with vigour. **b.** to make an attack (on) violently. —'**sailable** *adj.* —'**sailless** *adj.*

sailcloth ('seɪl,klɒθ) *n.* 1. any of various fabrics from which sails are made. 2. a canvas-like cloth used for clothing, etc.

sailer ('seɪlə) *n.* a vessel, with specified sailing characteristics: *a good sailer.*

sailfish ('seɪl,fɪʃ) *n., pl.* **-fish** *or* **-fishes.** any of several large game fishes of warm and tropical seas. They have an elongated upper jaw and a long sail-like dorsal fin.

sailor ('seɪlə) *n.* 1. any member of a ship's crew, esp. one below the rank of officer. 2. a person who sails, esp. with reference to the likelihood of his becoming seasick: *a good sailor.*

sainfoin ('sænfɔɪn) *n.* a Eurasian perennial plant, widely grown as a forage crop, having pale pink flowers and curved pods.

saint (seɪnt; *unstressed* sənt) *n.* 1. a person who after death is formally recognized by a Christian Church as having attained a specially exalted place in heaven entitling him to veneration. 2. a person of exceptional holiness. 3. (*pl.*) *Bible.* the collective body of those who are righteous in God's sight. ~*vb.* 4. (*tr.*) to recognize formally as a saint. —'**sainthood** *n.* —'**saintlike** *adj.*

Saint Bernard ('bɜ:nəd) *n., usually abbreviated to* **St. Bernard.** a large breed of dog with a dense red-and-white coat, often used as a rescue dog in mountainous areas.

sainted ('seɪntɪd) *adj.* 1. canonized. 2. like a saint in character or nature. 3. hallowed or holy.

Saint John's wort ('dʒɒnz) *n., usually abbreviated to* **St. John's wort.** any of a genus of shrubs or herbaceous plants, having yellow flowers.

Saint Leger ('ledʒə) *n., usually abbreviated to* **St. Leger. the.** an annual horse race run at Doncaster, England, since 1776.

saintly ('seɪntlɪ) *adj.* like, relating to, or suitable for a saint. —'**saintlily** *adv.* —'**saintliness** *n.*

Saint Vitus's dance ('vaɪtəsɪz) *n., usually abbreviated to* **St. Vitus's dance.** *Pathol.* a nontechnical name for **chorea.**

saithe (seɪθ) *n. Brit.* another name for **coalfish.**

sake[1] (seɪk) *n.* 1. benefit or interest (esp. in **for** (**some-one's** *or* **one's own**) **sake**). 2. the purpose of obtaining or achieving (esp. in **for the sake of** (**something**)). 3. used in various exclamations of impatience, urgency, etc.: *for heaven's sake.*

sake[2], **saké,** *or* **saki** ('sɑ:kɪ) *n.* a Japanese alcoholic drink made of fermented rice.

salaam (sə'lɑ:m) *n.* 1. a Muslim form of salutation consisting of a deep bow with the right palm on the forehead. 2. a salutation signifying peace. ~*vb.* 3. to make a salaam (to).

salacious (sə'leɪʃəs) *adj.* 1. having an excessive interest in sex. 2. (of books, etc.) erotic, bawdy, or lewd. —**sa'laciously** *adv.* —**sa'laciousness** *or* **salacity** (sə-'læsɪtɪ) *n.*

salad ('sæləd) *n.* 1. a dish of raw vegetables, such as lettuce, tomatoes, etc., served as a separate course with cold meat, eggs, etc., or as part of a main course. 2. any dish of cold vegetables or fruit served with a dressing: *potato salad.* 3. any green vegetable or herb used in such a dish.

salad days *pl. n.* a period of youth and inexperience.

salad dressing *n.* a sauce for salad, such as oil and vinegar or mayonnaise.

THESAURUS

sage 1. *adj.* acute, canny, discerning, intelligent, judicious, learned, perspicacious, politic, prudent, sagacious, sapient, sensible, wise 2. *n.* authority, elder, expert, guru, man of learning, master, Nestor, philosopher, pundit, savant, Solomon, Solon, wise man

sail *v.* 1. cast *or* weigh anchor, embark, get under way, hoist the blue peter, put to sea, set sail 2. captain, cruise, go by water, navigate, pilot, ride the waves, skipper, steer,

voyage 3. drift, float, fly, glide, scud, shoot, skim, skirr, soar, sweep, wing 4. *Inf. With* **in** *or* **into** assault, attack, begin, belabour, fall upon, get going, get to work on, lambaste, set about, tear into (*Inf.*)

sailor hearty (*Inf.*), Jack Tar, lascar, leatherneck (*Sl.*), marine, mariner, matelot (*Sl.*), navigator, salt, sea dog, seafarer, seafaring man, seaman, tar (*Inf.*)

saintly angelic, beatific, blameless, bless-

ed, devout, full of good works, god-fearing, godly, holy, pious, religious, righteous, sainted, saintlike, sinless, virtuous, worthy'

sake 1. account, advantage, behalf, benefit, consideration, gain, good, interest, profit, regard, respect, welfare, wellbeing 2. aim, cause, end, motive, objective, principle, purpose, reason

salamander ('sælə,mændə) n. 1. any of various amphibians of central and S Europe. They have an elongated body, and only return to water to breed. 2. *Chiefly U.S.* any amphibian with a tail, as the newt. 3. a mythical reptilian creature supposed to live in fire. 4. an elemental fire-inhabiting being.

salami (sə'lɑːmɪ) n. a highly seasoned type of sausage, usually flavoured with garlic.

salaried ('sælərɪd) adj. earning or yielding a salary: *a salaried worker; salaried employment.*

salary ('sælərɪ) n., pl. **-ries.** 1. a fixed payment made by an employer, often monthly, for professional or office work. Cf. **wage.** ~vb. **-rying, -ried.** 2. (tr.) to pay a salary to.

sale (seɪl) n. 1. the exchange of goods, property, or services for an agreed sum of money or credit. 2. the amount sold. 3. the opportunity to sell: *there was no sale for luxuries.* 4. **a.** an event at which goods are sold at reduced prices, usually to clear old stocks. **b.** (as modifier): *sale bargains.* 5. an auction.

saleable or U.S. **salable** ('seɪləbəl) adj. fit for selling or capable of being sold. **—,salea'bility** or U.S. ,**sala'bility** n.

sale of work n. a sale of articles, often handmade, the proceeds of which benefit a charity or charities.

saleroom ('seɪl,ruːm) n. *Chiefly Brit.* a room where objects are displayed for sale, esp. by auction.

salesman ('seɪlzmən) n., pl. **-men.** 1. Also called: **salesperson** or fem. **saleswoman, salesgirl.** a person who sells merchandise or services in a shop. 2. short for **travelling salesman.**

salesmanship ('seɪlzmən,ʃɪp) n. 1. the technique of, skill, or ability in selling. 2. the work of a salesman.

sales talk or **pitch** n. an argument or other persuasion used in selling.

Salic law ('sælɪk) n. *History.* 1. the code of laws of the Salian Franks and other Germanic tribes. 2. a law excluding women from succession to the throne in certain countries, such as France and Spain.

salicylic acid (,sælɪ'sɪlɪk) n. a white crystalline substance with a sweet taste and bitter aftertaste, used in the manufacture of aspirin, and as a fungicide.

salient ('seɪlɪənt) adj. 1. conspicuous or striking: *a salient feature.* 2. projecting outwards at an angle of less than 180°. 3. (esp. of animals) leaping. ~n. 4. Mil. a projection of the forward line into enemy-held territory. 5. a salient angle. —**'salience** or **'saliency** n. —**'saliently** adv.

saline ('seɪlaɪn) adj. 1. of, consisting of, or containing common salt: *a saline taste.* 2. Med. of or relating to a saline. 3. of, consisting of, or containing any chemical salt, esp. sodium chloride. ~n. 4. Med. a solution of sodium chloride and water. —**salinity** (sə'lɪnɪtɪ) n.

saliva (sə'laɪvə) n. the secretion of salivary glands, consisting of a clear usually slightly acid aqueous fluid of variable composition. —**salivary** (sə'laɪvərɪ) adj.

salivate ('sælɪ,veɪt) vb. 1. (intr.) to secrete saliva, esp. an excessive amount. 2. (tr.) to cause (an animal, etc.) to produce saliva, as by the administration of mercury. —,**sali'vation** n.

Salk vaccine (sɔːlk) n. a vaccine against poliomyelitis.

sallow[1] ('sæləʊ) adj. 1. (esp. of human skin) of an unhealthy pale or yellowish colour. ~vb. 2. (tr.) to make sallow. —**'sallowish** adj. —**'sallowness** n.

sallow[2] ('sæləʊ) n. 1. any of several small willow trees, esp. the common sallow, which has large catkins that appear before the leaves. 2. a twig or the wood of any of these trees. —**'sallowy** adj.

sally ('sælɪ) n., pl. **-lies.** 1. a sudden sortie, esp. by troops. 2. a sudden outburst or emergence into action or expression. 3. an excursion. 4. a jocular retort. ~vb. **-lying, -lied.** 5. to make a sudden violent sortie.

6. (often foll. by *forth*) to go out on an expedition, etc. 7. to come or set out in an energetic manner. 8. to rush out suddenly.

Sally Lunn (lʌn) n. a flat round cake made from a sweet yeast dough.

salmagundi (,sælmə'gʌndɪ) n. 1. a mixed salad dish of cooked meats, eggs, beetroot, etc., popular in 18th-century England. 2. a miscellany.

salmon ('sæmən) n., pl. **-ons** or **-on.** 1. a soft-finned fish of the Atlantic and the Pacific, which is an important food fish. Salmon occur in cold and temperate waters and many species migrate to fresh water to spawn. 2. Austral. any of several unrelated fish. —**'salmo,noid** adj.

salmonella (,sælmə'nɛlə) n., pl. **-lae** (-,liː). any of a genus of rod-shaped aerobic bacteria including many species causing food poisoning.

salmon ladder n. a series of steps designed to enable salmon to move upstream to their breeding grounds.

salon ('sælɒn) n. 1. a room in a large house in which guests are received. 2. an assembly of guests in a fashionable household, esp. a gathering of major literary, artistic, and political figures. 3. a commercial establishment in which hairdressers, etc., carry on their businesses. 4. **a.** a hall for exhibiting works of art. **b.** such an exhibition, esp. one showing the work of living artists.

saloon (sə'luːn) n. 1. Also called: **saloon bar.** *Brit.* another word for **lounge** (sense 5). 2. a large public room on a passenger ship. 3. any large public room used for a purpose: *a dancing saloon.* 4. U.S. a place where alcoholic drink is sold and consumed. 5. a closed two-door or four-door car with four to six seats. U.S. name: **sedan.**

salopette (,sælə'pɛt) n. a garment worn for skiing, consisting of quilted trousers held up by shoulder straps.

salsify ('sælsɪfɪ) n., pl. **-fies.** 1. Also called: **oyster plant, vegetable oyster.** a Mediterranean plant having grasslike leaves, purple flower heads, and a long white edible taproot. 2. the root of this plant, which tastes of oysters and is eaten as a vegetable.

SALT (sɔːlt) n. acronym for Strategic Arms Limitation Talks or Treaty.

salt (sɔːlt) n. 1. a white powder or colourless crystalline solid, consisting mainly of sodium chloride and used for seasoning and preserving food. 2. (modifier) preserved in, flooded with, containing, or growing in salt or salty water: *salt pork.* 3. Chem. any of a class of crystalline solid compounds that are formed from, or can be regarded as formed from, an acid and a base. 4. liveliness or pungency: *his wit added salt to the discussion.* 5. dry or laconic wit. 6. an experienced sailor. 7. short for **saltcellar.** 8. **rub salt into someone's wounds.** to make someone's pain, shame, etc., even worse. 9. **salt of the earth.** a person or group of people regarded as the finest of their kind. 10. **with a grain** (or **pinch**) **of salt.** with reservations. ~vb. (tr.) 12. to season or preserve with salt. 13. to scatter salt over (an iced road, etc.) to melt the ice. 14. to add zest to. 15. (often foll. by *down* or *away*) to preserve or cure with salt. 16. Chem. to treat with salt. 17. to give a false appearance of value to, esp. to introduce valuable ore fraudulently into (a mine, sample, etc.). ~adj. 18. not sour, sweet, or bitter; salty. ~See also **salt away, salts.** —'**salt,like** adj. —'**saltness** n.

salt away or **down** vb. (tr., adv.) to hoard or save (money, valuables, etc.).

saltcellar ('sɔːlt,sɛlə) n. 1. a small container for salt used at the table. 2. Brit. inf. either of the two hollows formed above the collarbones.

salt lick n. 1. a place where wild animals go to lick salt deposits. 2. a block of salt given to domestic animals to lick. 3. Austral. & N.Z. a soluble cake of minerals used to supplement the diet of farm animals.

THESAURUS

salary earnings, emolument, income, pay, remuneration, stipend
sale 1. deal, disposal, marketing, selling, transaction, vending 2. buyers, consumers, customers, demand, market, outlet, purchasers 3. **for sale** available, in stock, obtainable, on offer, on sale, on the market
salient arresting, conspicuous, important, jutting, marked, noticeable, outstanding, projecting, prominent, pronounced, protruding,

remarkable, signal, striking
sallow anaemic, bilious, jaundiced-looking, pale, pallid, pasty, sickly, unhealthy, wan, yellowish
sally v. 1. erupt, go forth, issue, rush, set out, surge ~n. 2. Military foray, incursion, offensive, raid, sortie, thrust 3. Fig. bon mot, crack (Inf.), jest, joke, quip, retort, riposte, smart remark, wisecrack (Inf.), witticism 4. escapade, excursion, frolic, jaunt, trip

salt n. 1. flavour, relish, savour, seasoning, taste 2. **with a grain** or **pinch of salt** cynically, disbelievingly, doubtfully, sceptically, suspiciously, with reservations 3. Fig. Attic wit, bite, dry humour, liveliness, piquancy, punch, pungency, sarcasm, sharpness, wit, zest, zip (Inf.) 4. mariner, sailor, sea dog, seaman, tar (Inf.) ~adj. 5. brackish, briny, saline, salted, salty

saltpetre or U.S. **saltpeter** (ˌsɔːltˈpiːtə) n. another name for **potassium nitrate.**

salts (sɔːlts) pl. n. **1.** Med. any of various mineral salts, such as magnesium sulphate, for use as a cathartic. **2.** short for **smelling salts.**

saltwater ('sɔːlt,wɔːtə) adj. of or inhabiting salt water, esp. the sea: saltwater fishes.

salty ('sɔːltɪ) adj. **saltier, saltiest. 1.** of, tasting of, or containing salt. **2.** (esp. of humour) sharp. **3.** relating to life at sea. —'**saltiness** n.

salubrious (səˈluːbrɪəs) adj. conducive or favourable to health. —sa'**lubriously** adv. —salubrity (səˈluːbrɪtɪ) n.

Saluki (səˈluːkɪ) n. a tall breed of hound with a smooth coat and long fringes on the ears and tail.

salutary ('sæljʊtərɪ) adj. **1.** promoting or intended to promote an improvement: a salutary warning. **2.** promoting or intended to promote health. —'**salutarily** adv.

salutation (ˌsæljʊˈteɪʃən) n. **1.** an act, phrase, gesture, etc., that serves as a greeting. **2.** a form of words used as an opening to a speech or letter, such as Dear Sir.

salute (səˈluːt) vb. **1.** (tr.) to address or welcome with friendly words or gestures of respect, such as bowing. **2.** (tr.) to acknowledge with praise: we salute your gallantry. **3.** Mil. to pay formal respect, as by presenting arms or raising the right arm. ~n. **4.** the act of saluting. **5.** a formal military gesture of respect. —sa'**luter** n.

salvage ('sælvɪdʒ) n. **1.** the act, process, or business of rescuing vessels or their cargoes from loss at sea. **2. a.** the act of saving any goods or property in danger of damage or destruction. **b.** (as modifier): a salvage operation. **3.** the goods or property so saved. **4.** compensation paid for the salvage of a vessel or its cargo. **5.** the proceeds from the sale of salvaged goods. ~vb. (tr.) **6.** to save or rescue (goods or property) from fire, shipwreck, etc. **7.** to gain (something beneficial) from a failure. —'**salvageable** adj. —'**salvager** n.

salvation (sælˈveɪʃən) n. **1.** the act of preserving or the state of being preserved from harm. **2.** a person or thing that is the means of preserving from harm. **3.** Christian theol. deliverance by redemption from the power of sin.

Salvation Army n. a Christian body founded in 1865 by William Booth and organized on quasi-military lines for evangelism and social work among the poor.

salve (sælv, sɑːv) n. **1.** an ointment for wounds, etc. **2.** anything that heals or soothes. ~vb. (tr.) **3.** to apply salve to (a wound, etc.). **4.** to soothe, comfort, or appease.

salver ('sælvə) n. a tray, esp. one of silver, on which food, letters, visiting cards, etc., are presented.

salvia ('sælvɪə) n. any of a genus of herbaceous plants or small shrubs, such as the sage, grown for their medicinal or culinary properties or for ornament.

salvo ('sælvəʊ) n., pl. **-vos** or **-voes. 1.** a discharge of fire from weapons in unison, esp. on a ceremonial occasion. **2.** concentrated fire from many weapons, as in a naval battle. **3.** an outburst, as of applause.

sal volatile (vɒˈlætɪlɪ) n. Also called: **spirits of ammonia.** a solution of ammonium carbonate in alcohol and aqueous ammonia, used as smelling salts.

SAM (sæm) n. acronym for surface-to-air missile.

Sam. Bible. abbrev. for Samuel.

samara (səˈmɑːrə) n. a dry winged one-seeded fruit: occurs in the ash, maple, etc. Also called: **key fruit.**

Samaritan (səˈmærɪtən) n. **1.** a native or inhabitant of

Samaria, a kingdom in ancient Palestine. **2.** short for **Good Samaritan. 3.** a member of a voluntary organization (**the Samaritans**) whose aim is to help people in distress or despair.

samarium (səˈmɛərɪəm) n. a silvery metallic element of the lanthanide series used in carbon-arc lighting, as a doping agent in laser crystals, and as a neutron-absorber. Symbol: Sm; atomic no.: 62; atomic wt.: 150.35.

same (seɪm) adj. (usually preceded by the) **1.** being the very one: she is wearing the same hat. **2. a.** being the one previously referred to. **b.** (as n.): a note received about same. **3. a.** identical in kind, quantity, etc.: two girls of the same age. **b.** (as n.): we'd like the same. **4.** unchanged in character or nature: his attitude is the same as ever. **5. all the same. a.** Also: **just the same.** nevertheless; yet. **b.** immaterial: it's all the same to me. ~adv. **6.** in an identical manner. —'**sameness** n.

▷ **Usage.** The use of same exemplified in if you send us your order for the materials, we will deliver same tomorrow is common in business and official English. In general English, however, this use of the word is avoided: may I borrow your book? I'll return it (not same) tomorrow.

samite ('sæmaɪt) n. a heavy fabric of silk, often woven with gold or silver threads, used in the Middle Ages.

samizdat (Russian səmizˈdat) n. (in the Soviet Union) **a.** a system of clandestine printing and distribution of banned literature. **b.** (as modifier): a samizdat publication.

samoosa (səˈmuːsə) n., pl. **-sas.** S. African. a small spiced meat pasty.

samovar ('sæmə,vɑː) n. (esp. in Russia) a metal urn for making tea, in which the water is usually heated by an inner container.

Samoyed (for 1 & 2, ˌsæməˈjɛd, for 3, səˈmɔɪɛd) n. **1.** (pl. **-yed** or **-yeds**) a member of a people who live chiefly in the area of the N Urals: related to the Finns. **2.** the language of this people. **3.** a white or cream breed of dog having a dense coat and a tightly curled tail.

samp (sæmp) n. S. African. crushed maize used for porridge.

sampan ('sæmpæn) n. a small skiff, widely used in the Orient, that is propelled by oars.

samphire ('sæm,faɪə) n. **1.** an umbelliferous plant of Eurasian coasts, having fleshy divided leaves and clusters of small white flowers. **2. golden samphire.** a Eurasian coastal plant with fleshy leaves and yellow flower heads. **3.** any of several other plants of coastal areas.

sample ('sɑːmpəl) n. **1. a.** a small part of anything, intended as representative of the whole. **b.** (as modifier): a sample bottle. **2.** Also called: **sampling.** Statistics. a set of individuals or items selected at random from a population and analysed to test hypotheses about the population. ~vb. **3.** (tr.) to take a sample or samples of.

sampler ('sɑːmplə) n. **1.** a person who takes samples. **2.** a piece of embroidery in which many different stitches are used.

Samson ('sæmsən) n. **1.** a judge of Israel, who performed herculean feats of strength until he was betrayed by his mistress Delilah (Judges 13–16). **2.** any man of outstanding physical strength.

samurai ('sæmʊ,raɪ) n., pl. **-rai. 1.** the Japanese warrior or caste from the 11th to the 19th centuries. **2.** a member of this aristocratic caste.

THESAURUS

salty 1. brackish, briny, over-salted, saline, salt, salted **2.** colourful, humorous, lively, piquant, pungent, racy, sharp, snappy (Inf.), spicy, tangy, tart, witty, zestful

salubrious beneficial, good for one, healthful, health-giving, healthy, invigorating, salutary, wholesome

salutary 1. advantageous, beneficial, good, good for one, helpful, practical, profitable, timely, useful, valuable **2.** healthful, healthy, salubrious

salutation address, greeting, obeisance, salute, welcome

salute v. **1.** accost, acknowledge, address, doff one's cap to, greet, hail, kiss, pay one's respects to, salaam, welcome **2.** acknowledge, honour, pay tribute or homage to, pres-

ent arms, recognize, take one's hat off to (Inf.) ~n. **3.** address, greeting, kiss, obeisance, recognition, salaam, salutation, tribute

salvage v. glean, recover, redeem, rescue, restore, retrieve, save

salvation deliverance, escape, lifeline, preservation, redemption, rescue, restoration, saving

same adj. **1.** aforementioned, aforesaid, selfsame, very **2.** alike, corresponding, duplicate, equal, equivalent, identical, indistinguishable, interchangeable, synonymous, twin **3.** changeless, consistent, constant, invariable, unaltered, unchanged, unfailing, uniform, unvarying **4. all the same a.** after all, anyhow, be that as it may, in any event,

just the same, nevertheless, nonetheless, still **b.** immaterial, not worth mentioning, of no consequence, unimportant

sameness identicalness, identity, indistinguishability, lack of variety, likeness, monotony, oneness, predictability, repetition, resemblance, similarity, standardization, tedium, uniformity

sample 1. n. cross section, example, exemplification, illustration, indication, instance, model, pattern, representative, sign, specimen **2.** v. experience, inspect, partake of, taste, test, try **3.** adj. illustrative, pilot, representative, specimen, test, trial

sanatorium (ˌsænəˈtɔːrɪəm) *or U.S.* **sanitarium** *n.*, *pl.* **-riums** *or* **-ria** (-rɪə). **1.** an institution for the medical care and recuperation of persons who are chronically ill. **2.** *Brit.* a room as in a boarding school where sick pupils may be treated in isolation.

sanctify (ˈsæŋktɪˌfaɪ) *vb.* **-fying, -fied.** (*tr.*) **1.** to make holy. **2.** to free from sin. **3.** to sanction (an action or practice) as religiously binding: *to sanctify a marriage.* **4.** to declare or render (something) productive of or conductive to holiness or grace. —ˌsanctifiˈcation *n.* —ˈsanctiˌfier *n.*

sanctimonious (ˌsæŋktɪˈməʊnɪəs) *adj.* affecting piety or making a display of holiness. —ˌsanctiˈmoniously *adv.* —ˌsanctiˈmoniousness *or* ˈsanctiˌmony *n.*

sanction (ˈsæŋkʃən) *n.* **1.** authorization. **2.** aid or encouragement. **3.** something, such as an ethical principle, that imparts binding force to a rule, oath, etc. **4.** the penalty laid down in a law for contravention of its provisions. **5.** (*often pl.*) a coercive measure, esp. one taken by one or more states against another guilty of violating international law. ~*vb.* (*tr.*) **6.** to give authority to. **7.** to confirm.

sanctity (ˈsæŋktɪtɪ) *n.*, *pl.* **-ties.** **1.** the condition of being sanctified; holiness. **2.** anything regarded as sanctified or holy.

sanctuary (ˈsæŋktjʊərɪ) *n.*, *pl.* **-aries.** **1.** a holy place. **2.** a consecrated building or shrine. **3.** *Old Testament.* **a.** the Israelite temple at Jerusalem. **b.** the tabernacle in which the Ark was enshrined. **4.** the chancel, or that part of a sacred building surrounding the main altar. **5. a.** a sacred building where fugitives were formerly entitled to immunity from arrest or execution. **b.** the immunity so afforded. **6.** a place of refuge. **7.** a place, protected by law, where animals can live and breed without interference.

sanctum (ˈsæŋktəm) *n.*, *pl.* **-tums** *or* **-ta** (-tə). **1.** a sacred or holy place. **2.** a room or place of total privacy.

Sanctus (ˈsæŋktəs) *n.* **1.** *Liturgy.* the hymn that occurs immediately after the preface in the celebration of the Eucharist. **2.** a musical setting of this.

sand (sænd) *n.* **1.** loose material consisting of rock or mineral grains, esp. rounded grains of quartz. **2.** (*often pl.*) a sandy area, esp. on the seashore or in a desert. **3.** a greyish-yellow colour. **4.** the grains of sandlike material in an hourglass. **5.** *U.S. inf.* courage. **6. the sands are running out.** time is passing quickly. ~*vb.* **7.** (*tr.*) to smooth or polish the surface of with sandpaper or sand. **8.** (*tr.*) to sprinkle or cover with or as if with sand. **9.** to fill or cause to fill with sand: *the channel sanded up.* —ˈsandˌlike *adj.*

sandal (ˈsænd°l) *n.* **1.** a light shoe consisting of a sole held on the foot by thongs, straps, etc. **2.** a strap passing over the instep or around the ankle to keep a low shoe on the foot. **3.** another name for **sandalwood.** —ˈsandalled *adj.*

sandalwood (ˈsænd°lˌwʊd) *or* **sandal** *n.* **1.** any of a genus of evergreen trees, esp. the **white sandalwood,** of S Asia and Australia, having hard light-coloured heartwood. **2.** the wood of any of these trees, which is used for carving, is burned as incense, and yields an aromatic oil used in perfumery. **3.** any of various similar trees or their wood, esp. a leguminous tree of SE Asia having dark red wood used as a dye.

sandbag (ˈsændˌbæg) *n.* **1.** a sack filled with sand used for protection against gunfire, floodwater, etc., or as ballast in a balloon, etc. **2.** a bag filled with sand and used as a weapon. ~*vb.* **bagging, bagged.** (*tr.*) **3.** to protect or strengthen with sandbags. **4.** to hit with or as if with a sandbag. —ˈsandˌbagger *n.*

sand bar *n.* a ridge of sand in a river or sea, built up by the action of tides, etc., and often exposed at low tide.

sandblast (ˈsændˌblɑːst) *n.* **1.** a jet of sand blown from

a nozzle under air or steam pressure. ~*vb.* **2.** (*tr.*) to clean or decorate (a surface) with a sandblast. —ˈsandˌblaster *n.*

sandboy (ˈsændˌbɔɪ) *n.* **happy** (*or* **jolly**) **as a sandboy.** very happy; high-spirited.

sand castle *n.* a mass of sand moulded into a castle-like shape, esp. as made by a child on the seashore.

sander (ˈsændə) *n.* **1.** a power-driven tool for smoothing surfaces by rubbing with an abrasive disc. **2.** a person who uses such a device.

sanderling (ˈsændəlɪŋ) *n.* a small sandpiper that frequents sandy shores.

sandman (ˈsændˌmæn) *n.*, *pl.* **-men.** (in folklore) a magical person supposed to put children to sleep by sprinkling sand in their eyes.

sand martin *n.* a small brown European songbird with white underparts: it nests in tunnels bored in sand, river banks, etc.

sandpaper (ˈsændˌpeɪpə) *n.* **1.** a strong paper coated with sand or other abrasive material for smoothing and polishing. ~*vb.* **2.** (*tr.*) to polish or grind (a surface) with or as if with sandpaper.

sandpiper (ˈsændˌpaɪpə) *n.* **1.** any of numerous N hemisphere shore birds having a long slender bill and legs and cryptic plumage. **2.** any other bird of the family which includes snipes and woodcocks.

sandpit (ˈsændˌpɪt) *n.* **1.** a shallow pit or container holding sand for children to play in. **2.** a pit from which sand is extracted.

sandshoes (ˈsændˌʃuːz) *pl. n.* light canvas shoes with rubber soles.

sandstone (ˈsændˌstəʊn) *n.* any of a group of common sedimentary rocks consisting of sand grains consolidated with such materials as quartz, haematite, and clay minerals.

sandstorm (ˈsændˌstɔːm) *n.* a strong wind that whips up clouds of sand, esp. in a desert.

sandwich (ˈsænwɪdʒ, -wɪtʃ) *n.* **1.** two or more slices of bread, usually buttered, with a filling of meat, cheese, etc. **2.** anything that resembles a sandwich in arrangement. ~*vb.* (*tr.*) **3.** to insert tightly between two other things. **4.** to put into a sandwich. **5.** to place between two dissimilar things.

sandwich board *n.* one of two connected boards that are hung over the shoulders in front of and behind a person to display advertisements.

sandwich course *n.* any of several courses consisting of alternate periods of study and industrial work.

sandwich man *n.* a man who carries sandwich boards.

sandy (ˈsændɪ) *adj.* **sandier, sandiest.** **1.** consisting of, containing, or covered with sand. **2.** (esp. of hair) reddish-yellow. **3.** resembling sand in texture. —ˈsandiness *n.*

sand yacht *n.* a wheeled boat with sails, built to be propelled over sand by the wind.

sane (seɪn) *adj.* **1.** free from mental disturbance. **2.** having or showing reason or sound sense. —ˈsanely *adv.* —ˈsaneness *n.*

sang (sæŋ) *vb.* the past tense of **sing.**
▷ *Usage.* See at **ring².**

sang-froid (French sɑ̃ ˈfrwa) *n.* composure; self-possession.

sangoma (sæŋˈgəʊmə) *n.*, *pl.* **-mas.** *S. African.* a witchdoctor.

Sangraal (sæŋˈgreɪl), **Sangrail** *or* **Sangreal** (ˈsæŋgrɪəl) *n.* another name for the **Holy Grail.**

sangria (sæŋˈgriːə) *n.* a Spanish drink of red wine, sugar, and orange or lemon juice, sometimes laced with brandy.

sanguinary (ˈsæŋgwɪnərɪ) *adj.* **1.** accompanied by

THESAURUS

sanctify absolve, anoint, bless, cleanse, consecrate, hallow, purify, set apart
sanctimonious canting, false, goody-goody (*Inf.*), holier-than-thou, hypocritical, pharisaical, pi (*Brit. sl.*), pietistic, pious, self-righteous, self-satisfied, smug, Tartuffian *or* Tartufian, too good to be true, unctuous
sanction *n.* **1.** allowance, approbation, approval, authority, authorization, backing, confirmation, countenance, endorsement, O.K. *or* okay (*Inf.*), ratification, stamp *or* seal

of approval, support **2.** *Often plural* ban, boycott, coercive measures, embargo, penalty ~*v.* **3.** allow, approve, authorize, back, countenance, endorse, lend one's name to, permit, support, vouch for **4.** confirm, ratify, warrant

sanctity **1.** devotion, godliness, goodness, grace, holiness, piety, purity, religiousness, righteousness, sanctitude, spirituality **2.** inviolability, sacredness, solemnity

sanctuary **1.** altar, church, Holy of

Holies, sanctum, shrine, temple **2.** asylum, haven, protection, refuge, retreat, shelter **3.** conservation area, national park, nature reserve, reserve

sane **1.** all there (*Inf.*), compos mentis, in one's right mind, in possession of all one's faculties, lucid, mentally sound, normal, of sound mind, rational **2.** balanced, judicious, level-headed, moderate, reasonable, sensible, sober, sound

much bloodshed. **2.** bloodthirsty. **3.** consisting of or stained with blood. —**'sanguinarily** *adv.* —**'sanguinariness** *n.*

sanguine ('sæŋgwɪn) *adj.* **1.** cheerful and confident; optimistic. **2.** (esp. of the complexion) ruddy in appearance. **3.** blood-red. ~*n.* **4.** a red pencil containing ferric oxide, used in drawing. —**'sanguinely** *adv.* —**'sanguineness** *n.*

Sanhedrin ('sænɪdrɪn) *n. Judaism.* the supreme judicial, ecclesiastical, and administrative council of the Jews in New Testament times.

sanitary ('sænɪtərɪ) *adj.* **1.** of or relating to health and measures for the protection of health. **2.** free from dirt, germs, etc.; hygienic. —**sanitarian** (,sænɪ'tɛərɪən) *n.* —**'sanitariness** *n.*

sanitary towel *or esp. U.S.* **napkin** *n.* an absorbent pad worn externally by women during menstruation to absorb the menstrual flow.

sanitation (,sænɪ'teɪʃən) *n.* the study and use of practical measures for the preservation of public health.

sanity ('sænɪtɪ) *n.* **1.** the state of being sane. **2.** good sense or soundness of judgment.

sank (sæŋk) *vb.* the past tense of **sink.**

sans (sænz) *prep.* an archaic word for **without.**

Sans. *or* **Sansk.** *abbrev. for* Sanskrit.

sans-culotte (,sænzkju'lɒt) *n.* **1.** (during the French Revolution) **a.** (originally) a revolutionary of the poorer class. **b.** (later) any revolutionary. **2.** any revolutionary extremist.

Sanskrit ('sænskrɪt) *n.* an ancient language of India. It is the oldest recorded member of the Indic branch of the Indo-European family of languages. Although it is used only for religious purposes, it is one of the official languages of India. —**San'skritic** *adj.*

sans serif *or* **sanserif** (sæn'sɛrɪf) *n.* a style of printer's typeface in which the characters have no serifs.

Santa ('sæntə) *n. Inf.* short for **Santa Claus.**

Santa Claus ('sæntə ,klɔːz) *n.* the legendary patron saint of children, commonly identified as Saint Nicholas, who brings presents to children on Christmas Eve. Also called: **Father Christmas.**

sap¹ (sæp) *n.* **1.** a solution of mineral salts, sugars, etc., that circulates in a plant. **2.** any vital body fluid. **3.** energy; vigour. **4.** *Sl.* a gullible person. ~*vb.* **sapping, sapped.** (*tr.*) **5.** to drain of sap.

sap² (sæp) *n.* **1.** a deep and narrow trench used to approach or undermine an enemy position. ~*vb.* **sapping, sapped. 2.** to undermine (a fortification, etc.) by digging saps. **3.** (*tr.*) to weaken.

sapid ('sæpɪd) *adj.* **1.** having a pleasant taste. **2.** agreeable or engaging. —**sapidity** (sə'pɪdɪtɪ) *n.*

sapient ('seɪpɪənt) *adj. Often used ironically.* wise or sagacious. —**'sapience** *n.* —**'sapiently** *adv.*

sapling ('sæplɪŋ) *n.* **1.** a young tree. **2.** *Literary.* a youth.

saponify (sə'pɒnɪ,faɪ) *vb.* **-fying, -fied.** *Chem.* **1.** to undergo or cause to undergo a process in which a fat is converted into a soap by treatment with alkali. **2.** to undergo or cause to undergo a reaction in which an ester is converted to an acid and an alcohol as a result of treatment with an alkali. —**sa,ponifi'cation** *n.*

sapper ('sæpə) *n.* **1.** a soldier who digs trenches, etc. **2.** (in the British Army) a private of the Royal Engineers.

Sapphic ('sæfɪk) *adj.* **1.** *Prosody.* denoting a metre associated with Sappho, 6th-century B.C. Greek poetess. **2.** of or relating to Sappho or her poetry. **3.** of or denoting a lesbian relationship. ~*n.* **4.** *Prosody.* a verse, line, or stanza written in the Sapphic form.

sapphire ('sæfaɪə) *n.* **1. a.** any precious corundum gemstone that is not red, esp. the highly valued transparent blue variety. **b.** (*as modifier*): *a sapphire ring.* **2.** the

blue colour of sapphire. **3.** (*modifier*) denoting a forty-fifth anniversary: *our sapphire wedding.*

sappy ('sæpɪ) *adj.* **-pier, -piest. 1.** (of plants) full of sap. **2.** full of energy or vitality.

sapro- *or before a vowel* **sapr-** *combining form.* indicating dead or decaying matter: *saprogenic.*

saprophyte ('sæprəʊ,faɪt) *n.* any plant, esp. a fungus, that lives and feeds on dead organic matter. —**saprophytic** (,sæprəʊ'fɪtɪk) *adj.*

saraband *or* **sarabande** ('særə,bænd) *n.* **1.** a decorous 17th-century courtly dance. **2.** *Music.* a piece of music composed for or in the rhythm of this dance, in slow triple time.

Saracen ('særəsən) *n.* **1.** *History.* a member of one of the nomadic Arabic tribes, esp. of the Syrian desert. **2. a.** a Muslim, esp. one who opposed the crusades. **b.** (in later use) any Arab. ~*adj.* **3.** of or relating to Arabs of either of these periods, regions, or types. —**Saracenic** (,særə'sɛnɪk) *adj.*

sarcasm ('sɑːkæzəm) *n.* **1.** mocking or ironic language intended to convey scorn or insult. **2.** the use or tone of such language.

sarcastic (sɑː'kæstɪk) *adj.* **1.** characterized by sarcasm. **2.** given to the use of sarcasm. —**sar'castically** *adv.*

sarco- *or before a vowel* **sarc-** *combining form.* indicating flesh: *sarcoma.*

sarcoma (sɑː'kəʊmə) *n. Pathol.* a usually malignant tumour arising from connective tissue. —**sar'comatous** *adj.*

sarcophagus (sɑː'kɒfəgəs) *n., pl.* **-gi** (-,gaɪ) *or* **-guses.** a stone or marble coffin or tomb, esp. one bearing sculpture or inscriptions.

sard (sɑːd) *or* **sardius** ('sɑːdɪəs) *n.* a red or brown variety of chalcedony.

sardine (sɑː'diːn) *n., pl.* **-dine** *or* **-dines. 1.** any of various small food fishes of the herring family, esp. a young pilchard. **2. like sardines.** very closely crowded together.

sardonic (sɑː'dɒnɪk) *adj.* characterized by irony, mockery, or derision. —**sar'donically** *adv.*

sardonyx ('sɑːdənɪks) *n.* a variety of chalcedony with alternating reddish-brown and white parallel bands.

sargassum (sɑː'gæsəm) *n.* a floating brown seaweed having ribbon-like fronds containing air sacs, esp. abundant in the **Sargasso Sea** in the N Atlantic.

sarge (sɑːdʒ) *n. Inf.* sergeant.

sari ('sɑːrɪ) *n., pl.* **-ris.** the traditional dress of women of India, Pakistan, etc., consisting of a very long piece of cloth swathed around the body.

sarong (sə'rɒŋ) *n.* a skirtlike garment worn by men and women in the Malay Archipelago, Sri Lanka, etc.

sarsaparilla (,sɑːsəpə'rɪlə) *n.* **1.** any of a genus of tropical American prickly climbing plants having large aromatic roots and heart-shaped leaves. **2.** the dried roots of any of these plants, formerly used in medicine to treat psoriasis, etc. **3.** a nonalcoholic drink prepared from these roots.

sartorial (sɑː'tɔːrɪəl) *adj.* of or relating to a tailor or to tailoring. —**sar'torially** *adv.*

sash¹ (sæʃ) *n.* a long piece of ribbon, etc., worn around the waist or over one shoulder, as a symbol of rank.

sash² (sæʃ) *n.* **1.** a frame that contains the panes of a window or door. **2.** a complete frame together with panes of glass. ~*vb.* **3.** (*tr.*) to furnish (a house, etc.) with a sash, sashes, or sash windows.

sash cord *n.* a strong cord connecting a sash weight to a sliding sash.

sash window *n.* a window consisting of two sashes placed one above the other so that they can be slid past each other.

THESAURUS

sanguine 1. animated, assured, buoyant, cheerful, confident, hopeful, in good heart, lively, optimistic, spirited **2.** florid, red, rubicund, ruddy

sanitary clean, germ-free, healthy, hygienic, salubrious, unpolluted, wholesome

sanity 1. mental health, normality, rationality, reason, right mind (*Inf.*), saneness, stability **2.** common sense, good sense, judiciousness, level-headedness, rationality, sense, soundness of judgment

sap¹ *n.* **1.** animating force, essence, life-blood, vital fluid **2.** *Inf.* charlie (*Brit. inf.*), chump (*Inf.*), drip (*Inf.*), fool, gull (*Archaic*), idiot, jerk (*Sl.*), muggins (*Brit. sl.*), nincompoop, ninny, nitwit, noddy, noodle, Simple Simon, simpleton, twit (*Inf.*), weakling, wet (*Inf.*)

sap² *v.* bleed, deplete, devitalize, drain, enervate, erode, exhaust, rob, undermine, weaken, wear down

sarcasm bitterness, causticness, con-

tempt, cynicism, derision, irony, mockery, mordancy, satire, scorn, sneering

sarcastic acerbic, acrimonious, backhanded, biting, caustic, contemptuous, cutting, cynical, derisive, disparaging, ironical, mocking, mordant, sardonic, sarky (*Brit. inf.*), satirical, sharp, sneering, taunting

sardonic bitter, cynical, derisive, dry, ironical, jeering, malevolent, malicious, malignant, mocking, mordant, sarcastic, wry

sasquatch ('sæs,kwætʃ) *n.* (in Canadian folklore) in British Columbia, a hairy beast or manlike monster said to leave huge footprints.

sassafras ('sæsə,fræs) *n.* **1.** an aromatic deciduous tree of North America, having three-lobed leaves and dark blue fruits. **2.** the aromatic dried root bark of this tree, used as a flavouring, and yielding **sassafras oil. 3.** *Austral.* any of several unrelated trees having a similar fragrant bark.

Sassenach ('sæsə,næx) *n. Scot. & occasionally Irish.* an English person.

sat (sæt) *vb.* the past tense or past participle of **sit.**

Sat. *abbrev. for:* **1.** Saturday. **2.** Saturn.

Satan ('seitən) *n.* the devil, adversary of God, and tempter of mankind: sometimes identified with Lucifer (Luke 4:5-8).

satanic (sə'tænik) *adj.* **1.** of or relating to Satan. **2.** supremely evil or wicked. **—sa'tanically** *adv.*

Satanism ('seitə,nizəm) *n.* **1.** the worship of Satan. **2.** a form of such worship which includes blasphemous parodies of Christian prayers, etc. **3.** a satanic disposition. **—'Satanist** *n., adj.*

S.A.T.B. *abbrev. for* soprano, alto, tenor, bass: a combination of voices in choral music.

satchel ('sætʃəl) *n.* a rectangular bag, usually made of leather or cloth and provided with a shoulder strap, used for carrying school books. **—'satchelled** *adj.*

sate (seit) *vb.* (*tr.*) **1.** to satisfy (a desire or appetite) fully. **2.** to supply beyond capacity or desire.

sateen (sæ'ti:n) *n.* a glossy linen or cotton fabric that resembles satin.

satellite ('sætə,lait) *n.* **1.** a celestial body orbiting around a planet or star: *the earth is a satellite of the sun.* **2.** a man-made device orbiting around the earth, moon, or another planet transmitting to earth scientific information or used for communication. **3.** a country or political unit under the domination of a foreign power. **4.** a subordinate area that is dependent upon a larger adjacent town. **5.** (*modifier*) **a.** of or relating to a satellite: *satellite communications.* **b.** dependent upon another: *a satellite nation.*

satiable ('seiʃiəbəl) *adj.* capable of being satiated. **—,satia'bility** *n.* **—'satiably** *adv.*

satiate ('seiʃi,eit) *vb.* (*tr.*) **1.** to fill or supply beyond capacity or desire. **2.** to supply to capacity. **—,sati'ation** *n.*

satiety (sə'taiiti) *n.* the state of being satiated.

satin ('sætin) *n.* **1.** a fabric of silk, rayon, etc., closely woven to show much of the warp, giving a smooth glossy appearance. **2.** (*modifier*) like satin in texture: *a satin finish.* **—'satiny** *adj.*

satinwood ('sætin,wud) *n.* **1.** a tree that occurs in the East Indies and has hard wood with a satiny texture. **2.** the wood of this tree, used in veneering, marquetry, etc.

satire ('sætaiə) *n.* **1.** a novel, play, etc., in which topical issues, folly, or evil are held up to scorn by means of ridicule. **2.** the genre constituted by such works. **3.** the use

of ridicule, irony, etc., to create such an effect. **—sa-'tirical** *adj.*

satirist ('sætərist) *n.* **1.** a person who writes satire. **2.** a person given to the use of satire.

satirize *or* **-rise** ('sætə,raiz) *vb.* to deride (a person or thing) by means of satire. **—,satiri'zation** *or* **-ri'sation** *n.*

satisfaction (,sætis'fækʃən) *n.* **1.** the act of satisfying or state of being satisfied. **2.** the fulfilment of a desire. **3.** the pleasure obtained from such fulfilment. **4.** a source of fulfilment. **5.** compensation for a wrong done or received. **6.** *R.C. Church, Church of England.* the performance of a penance. **7.** *Christianity.* the atonement for sin by the death of Christ.

satisfactory (,sætis'fæktəri) *adj.* **1.** adequate or suitable; acceptable. **2.** giving satisfaction. **3.** constituting or involving atonement or expiation for sin. **—,satis-'factorily** *adv.*

satisfy ('sætis,fai) *vb.* **-fying, -fied.** (*mainly tr.*) **1.** (*also intr.*) to fulfil the desires or needs of (a person). **2.** to provide amply for (a need or desire). **3.** to convince. **4.** to dispel (a doubt). **5.** to make reparation to or for. **6.** to discharge or pay off (a debt) to (a creditor). **7.** to fulfil the requirements of; comply with: *you must satisfy the terms of your lease.* **8.** *Maths.* **a.** to reduce (an equation or set of equations) to an identity, following substitution: $x = 3$ satisfies $x^2 - 4x + 3 = 0$. **b.** to fulfil conditions of (a theorem, inequality, etc.). **—'satis,fiable** *adj.* **—'satis,fying** *adj.* **—'satis,fyingly** *adv.*

satrap ('sætrəp) *n.* **1.** (in ancient Persia) a provincial governor. **2.** a subordinate ruler.

satsuma (sæt'su:mə) *n.* **1.** a small citrus tree cultivated, esp. in Japan, for its edible fruit. **2.** the fruit of this tree, which has easily separable segments.

saturate *vb.* ('sætʃə,reit). **1.** to fill, soak, or imbue totally. **2.** to make (a chemical compound, solution, etc.) saturated or (of a compound, etc.) to become saturated. **3.** (*tr.*) *Mil.* to bomb or shell heavily. *~adj.* ('sætʃərit, -,reit). **4.** saturated.

saturation (,sætʃə'reiʃən) *n.* **1.** the act of saturating or the state of being saturated. **2.** *Chem.* the state of a chemical compound, solution, or vapour when it is saturated. **3.** *Meteorol.* the state of the atmosphere when it can hold no more water vapour at its particular temperature and pressure. **4.** the attribute of a colour that enables an observer to judge its proportion of pure chromatic colour.

Saturday ('sætədi) *n.* the seventh and last day of the week: the Jewish Sabbath.

Saturn[1] ('sætɜ:n) *n.* the Roman god of agriculture and vegetation.

Saturn[2] ('sætɜ:n) *n.* **1.** the sixth planet from the sun, around which revolve planar concentric rings (**Saturn's rings**) consisting of small frozen particles. **2.** the alchemical name for lead.[2] **—Saturnian** (sæ'tɜ:niən) *adj.*

Saturnalia (,sætə'neiliə) *n., pl.* **-lia** *or* **-lias. 1.** an ancient Roman festival celebrated in December: renowned for its general merrymaking. **2.** (*sometimes not cap.*) a

---

━━━━━━━━━━━ THESAURUS ━━━━━━━━━━━

Satan Apollyon, Beelzebub, Lord of the Flies, Lucifer, Mephistopheles, Old Nick, Prince of Darkness, The Devil, The Evil One

satanic accursed, black, demoniac, demoniacal, demonic, devilish, diabolic, evil, fiendish, hellish, infernal, inhuman, iniquitous, malevolent, malignant, wicked

satellite *n.* **1.** communications satellite, moon, sputnik **2.** *Fig.* attendant, dependant, follower, hanger-on, lackey, minion, parasite, retainer, sidekick (*Sl.*), sycophant, vassal *~adj.* **3.** *Fig.* client, dependent, puppet, subordinate, tributary, vassal

satiate 1. cloy, glut, gorge, jade, nauseate, overfill, stuff **2.** sate, satisfy, slake, surfeit

satire burlesque, caricature, irony, lampoon, parody, pasquinade, raillery, ridicule, sarcasm, send-up (*Brit. inf.*), skit, spoof (*Inf.*), takeoff (*Inf.*), travesty, wit

satirical, satiric biting, bitter, burlesque, caustic, censorious, cutting, cynical, incisive, ironical, mocking, mordant, pungent, Rabelaisian, sarcastic, sardonic, taunting

satirize abuse, burlesque, censure, criticize, deride, hold up to ridicule, lampoon, lash, parody, ridicule, send up (*Brit. inf.*), take off (*Inf.*), travesty

satisfaction 1. comfort, complacency, content, contentedness, contentment, ease, enjoyment, gratification, happiness, peace of mind, pleasure, pride, repletion, satiety, well-being **2.** achievement, appeasing, assuaging, fulfilment, gratification, resolution, settlement **3.** amends, atonement, compensation, damages, indemnification, justice, recompense, redress, reimbursement, remuneration, reparation, requital, restitution, settlement, vindication

satisfactory acceptable, adequate, all right, average, competent, fair, good enough, passable, sufficient, suitable, up to standard, up to the mark

satisfied at ease, complacent, content, contented, convinced, easy in one's mind, happy, like the cat that swallowed the canary (*Inf.*), pacified, positive, smug, sure

satisfy 1. appease, assuage, content, fill,

gratify, indulge, mollify, pacify, please, quench, sate, satiate, slake, surfeit **2.** answer, be enough (adequate, sufficient), come up to expectations, do, fill the bill (*Inf.*), fulfil, meet, qualify, serve, serve the purpose, suffice **3.** assure, convince, dispel (someone's) doubts, persuade, put (someone's) mind at rest, quiet, reassure **4.** answer, comply with, discharge, fulfil, meet, pay (off), settle, square up **5.** atone, compensate, indemnify, make good, make reparation for, recompense, remunerate, requite, reward

satisfying cheering, convincing, filling, gratifying, pleasing, pleasurable, satisfactory

saturate douse, drench, drook (*Scot.*), imbue, impregnate, ret (*used of flax, etc.*), soak, souse, steep, suffuse, waterlog, wet through

saturated drenched, dripping, droukit (*Scot.*), soaked, soaked to the skin, soaking (wet), sodden, sopping (wet), wet through, wringing wet

period or occasion of wild revelry. —ˌSatur'nalian adj.

saturnine ('sætəˌnaɪn) adj. **1.** having a gloomy temperament. **2.** Arch. **a.** of or relating to lead. **b.** having lead poisoning. —'satur‚ninely adv.

satyr ('sætə) n. **1.** Greek myth. one of a class of sylvan deities, represented as goatlike men who drank and danced in the train of Dionysus and chased the nymphs. **2.** a man who has strong sexual desires. **3.** any of various butterflies, having dark wings often marked with eyespots. —**satyric** (sə'tɪrɪk) adj.

sauce (sɔːs) n. **1.** any liquid or semiliquid preparation eaten with food to enhance its flavour. **2.** anything that adds piquancy. **3.** U.S. stewed fruit. **4.** U.S. dialect. vegetables eaten with meat. **5.** Inf. impudent language or behaviour. ~vb. (tr.) **6.** to prepare (food) with sauce. **7.** to add zest to. **8.** Inf. to be saucy to.

saucepan ('sɔːspən) n. a metal or enamel pan with a long handle and often a lid, used for cooking food.

saucer ('sɔːsə) n. **1.** a small round dish on which a cup is set. **2.** any similar dish. —'saucerful n.

saucy ('sɔːsɪ) adj. **-cier, -ciest. 1.** impertinent. **2.** pert; sprightly: a saucy hat. —'saucily adv. —'sauciness n.

sauerkraut ('sauəˌkraut) n. finely shredded and pickled cabbage.

sauger ('sɔːgə) n. a small North American pikeperch with a spotted dorsal fin: valued as a food and game fish.

sault (suː) n. Canad. a waterfall or rapids.

sauna ('sɔːnə) n. **1.** an invigorating bath originating in Finland in which the bather is subjected to hot steam, usually followed by a cold plunge. **2.** the place in which such a bath is taken.

saunter ('sɔːntə) vb. **1.** (intr.) to walk in a casual manner; stroll. ~n. **2.** a leisurely pace or stroll. —'saunterer n.

-saur or **-saurus** n. combining form. lizard: dinosaur.

saurian ('sɔːrɪən) adj. **1.** of or resembling a lizard. ~n. **2.** a former name for **lizard.**

sausage ('sɒsɪdʒ) n. **1.** finely minced meat, esp. pork or beef, mixed with fat, cereal, and seasonings (**sausage meat**), and packed into a tube-shaped animal intestine or synthetic casing. **2.** Scot. sausage meat. **3.** an object shaped like a sausage. **4. not a sausage.** nothing at all.

sausage roll n. Brit. a roll of sausage meat in pastry.

sauté ('səuteɪ) vb. **-téing** or **-téeing, -téed. 1.** to fry (food) quickly in a little fat. ~n. **2.** a dish of sautéed food, esp. meat that is browned and then cooked in a sauce. ~adj. **3.** sautéed until lightly brown: sauté potatoes.

Sauternes (səu'tɜːn) n. a sweet white wine from the Sauternes district of southern Bordeaux.

savage ('sævɪdʒ) adj. **1.** wild; untamed: savage beasts. **2.** ferocious in temper: a savage dog. **3.** uncivilized; crude: savage behaviour. **4.** (of peoples) nonliterate or primitive: a savage tribe. **5.** (of terrain) rugged and uncultivated. ~n. **6.** a member of a nonliterate society, esp. one regarded as primitive. **7.** a fierce or vicious person or animal. ~vb. (tr.) **8.** to criticize violently. **9.**

to attack ferociously and wound. —'savagely adv. —'savageness n.

savagery ('sævɪdʒrɪ) n., pl. **-ries. 1.** an uncivilized condition. **2.** a savage act or nature. **3.** savages collectively.

savanna or **savannah** (sə'vænə) n. open grasslands, usually with scattered bushes or trees, characteristic of much of tropical Africa.

savant ('sævənt) n. a man of great learning; sage. —'savante fem. n.

save[1] (seɪv) vb. **1.** (tr.) to rescue, preserve, or guard (a person or thing) from danger or harm. **2.** to avoid the spending, waste, or loss of (money, possessions, etc.). **3.** (tr.) Theol. to deliver from sin; redeem. **4.** (often foll. by up) to set aside or reserve (money, goods, etc.) for future use. **5.** (tr.) to treat with care so as to avoid or lessen wear or degeneration. **6.** (tr.) to prevent the necessity for; obviate the trouble of. **7.** (tr.) Soccer, hockey, etc. to prevent (a goal) by stopping (a struck ball or puck). ~n. **8.** Soccer, hockey, etc. the act of saving a goal. —'savable or 'saveable adj. —'saver n.

save[2] (seɪv) Arch. ~prep. **1.** (often foll. by for) Also: **saving.** with the exception of. ~conj. **2.** but.

save as you earn n. (in Britain) a savings scheme operated by the government, in which monthly contributions earn tax-free interest. Abbrev.: **S.A.Y.E.**

saveloy ('sævɪˌlɔɪ) n. a smoked sausage made from salted pork, coloured red with saltpetre.

saving ('seɪvɪŋ) adj. **1.** tending to save or preserve. **2.** redeeming or compensating (esp. in **saving grace**). **3.** thrifty or economical. **4.** Law. denoting or relating to an exception or reservation: a saving clause in an agreement. ~n. **5.** preservation or redemption. **6.** economy or avoidance of waste. **7.** reduction in cost or expenditure. **8.** anything saved. **9.** (pl.) money saved for future use. ~prep. **10.** with the exception of. ~conj. **11.** except. —'savingly adv.

saviour or U.S. **savior** ('seɪvjə) n. a person who rescues another person or a thing from danger or harm.

Saviour or U.S. **Savior** ('seɪvjə) n. Christianity. Jesus Christ regarded as the saviour of men from sin.

savoir-faire ('sævwɑː'fɛə; French savwar'fɛːr) n. the ability to do the right thing in any situation.

savory ('seɪvərɪ) n., pl. **-vories. 1.** any of numerous aromatic plants, including the **winter savory** and **summer savory,** of the Mediterranean region, having narrow leaves and white, pink, or purple flowers. **2.** the leaves of any of these plants, used as a potherb.

savour or U.S. **savor** ('seɪvə) n. **1.** the quality in a substance that is perceived by the sense of taste or smell. **2.** a specific taste or smell: the savour of lime. **3.** a slight but distinctive quality or trace. **4.** the power to excite interest: the savour of wit has been lost. ~vb. **5.** (intr.: often foll. by of) to possess the taste or smell (of). **6.** (intr.: often foll. by of) to have a suggestion (of). **7.** (tr.) to season. **8.** (tr.) to taste or smell, esp. appreciatively. **9.** (tr.) to relish or enjoy. —'savourless or U.S. 'savorless adj.

savoury or U.S. **savory** ('seɪvərɪ) adj. **1.** attractive to

---

THESAURUS

sauce n. backchat (Inf.), brass (Inf.), cheek (Inf.), cheekiness, disrespectfulness, impertinence, impudence, insolence, lip (Sl.), nerve (Inf.), rudeness

sauciness backchat (Inf.), brass (Inf.), brazenness, cheek (Inf.), flippancy, impertinence, impudence, insolence, lip (Sl.), pertness, rudeness, sauce (Inf.)

saucy 1. cheeky (Inf.), disrespectful, flip (Inf.), flippant, forward, fresh (Inf.), impertinent, impudent, insolent, pert, presumptuous, rude, smart-alecky (Inf.) 2. dashing, gay, jaunty, natty (Inf.), perky, rakish, sporty

saunter 1. v. amble, dally, linger, loiter, meander, mosey (Inf.), ramble, roam, rove, stravaig (Scot. & Northern English dialect), stroll, take a stroll, tarry, wander 2. n. airing, amble, constitutional, promenade, ramble, stroll, turn, walk

savage adj. 1. feral, rough, rugged, uncivilized, uncultivated, undomesticated, untamed, wild 2. barbarous, beastly, bestial, bloodthirsty, bloody, brutal, brutish, cruel, devilish, diabolical, ferocious, fierce, harsh, inhuman, merciless, murderous, pitiless, rav-

ening, ruthless, sadistic, vicious 3. in a state of nature, nonliterate, primitive, rude, unspoilt ~n. 4. aboriginal, aborigine, autochthon, barbarian, heathen, indigene, native, primitive 5. barbarian, bear, boor, roughneck (Sl.), yahoo, yobbo (Brit. sl.) 6. beast, brute, fiend, monster ~v. 7. attack, lacerate, mangle, maul, tear into (Inf.)

savagery barbarity, bestiality, bloodthirstiness, brutality, cruelty, ferocity, fierceness, inhumanity, ruthlessness, sadism, viciousness

save 1. bail (someone) out, come to (someone's) rescue, deliver, free, liberate, recover, redeem, rescue, salvage, set free 2. be frugal, be thrifty, collect, economize, gather, hide away, hoard, hold, husband, keep, keep up one's sleeve (Inf.), lay by, put aside for a rainy day, put by, reserve, retrench, salt away, set aside, store, tighten one's belt (Inf.), treasure up 3. conserve, guard, keep safe, look after, preserve, protect, safeguard, screen, shield, take care of 4. hinder, obviate, prevent, rule out, spare

saving 1. adj. compensatory, extenuating,

qualifying, redeeming 2. n. bargain, discount, economy, reduction

savings fund, nest egg, provision for a rainy day, reserves, resources, store

saviour defender, deliverer, friend in need, Good Samaritan, guardian, knight in shining armour, liberator, preserver, protector, rescuer, salvation

Saviour Our or The Christ, Jesus, Messiah, Redeemer

savoir-faire accomplishment, address, diplomacy, discretion, finesse, poise, social graces, social know-how (Inf.), tact, urbanity

savour n. 1. flavour, piquancy, relish, smack, smell, tang, taste 2. distinctive quality, excitement, flavour, interest, salt, spice, zest ~v. 3. Often with of bear the hallmarks, be indicative, be suggestive, partake, show signs, smack, suggest, verge on 4. appreciate, delight in, enjoy, enjoy to the full, gloat over, like, luxuriate in, partake, relish, revel in, smack one's lips over

the sense of taste or smell. **2.** salty or spicy: *a savoury dish.* **3.** pleasant. **4.** respectable. ~*n.*, *pl.* **-vouries. 5.** *Chiefly Brit.* a savoury dish served as an hors d'oeuvre or dessert. —'**savouriness** *or U.S.* '**savoriness** *n.*

savoy (sə'vɔɪ) *n.* a cultivated variety of cabbage having a compact head and wrinkled leaves.

savvy ('sævɪ) *Sl.* ~*vb.* -**vying, -vied. 1.** to understand or get the sense of (an idea, etc.). ~*n.* **2.** comprehension. ~*adj.* **-vier, -viest. 3.** *Chiefly U.S.* shrewd.

saw[1] (sɔː) *n.* **1.** any of various hand tools for cutting wood, metal, etc., having a blade with teeth along one edge. **2.** any of various machines or devices for cutting by use of a toothed blade, such as a power-driven toothed band of metal. ~*vb.* **sawing, sawed; sawed** *or* **sawn. 3.** to cut with a saw. **4.** to form by sawing. **5.** to cut as if wielding a saw: *to saw the air.* **6.** to move (an object) from side to side as if moving a saw. —'**sawer** *n.* —'**saw**ˌ**like** *adj.*

saw[2] (sɔː) *vb.* the past tense of **see**[1].

saw[3] (sɔː) *n.* a wise saying, maxim, or proverb.

sawbones ('sɔːˌbəʊnz) *n.*, *pl.* -**bones** *or* -**boneses.** *Sl.* a surgeon or doctor.

sawdust ('sɔːˌdʌst) *n.* particles of wood formed by sawing.

sawfish ('sɔːˌfɪʃ) *n.*, *pl.* -**fish** *or* -**fishes.** a sharklike ray of subtropical coastal waters, having a serrated bladelike mouth.

sawhorse ('sɔːˌhɔːs) *n.* a stand for timber during sawing.

sawmill ('sɔːˌmɪl) *n.* an industrial establishment where timber is sawn into planks, etc.

sawn (sɔːn) *vb.* a past participle of **saw**[1].

sawn-off *adj.* (*prenominal*) (of a shotgun) having the barrel cut short, mainly to facilitate concealment of the weapon.

sawyer ('sɔːjə) *n.* a person who saws timber for a living.

sax (sæks) *n.* *Inf.* short for **saxophone.**

saxifrage ('sæksɪˌfreɪdʒ) *n.* a plant having small white, yellow, purple, or pink flowers.

Saxon ('sæksən) *n.* **1.** a member of a West Germanic people who raided and settled parts of S Britain in the fifth and sixth centuries A.D. **2.** a native or inhabitant of Saxony, in Germany. **3. a.** the Low German dialect of Saxony. **b.** any of the West Germanic dialects spoken by the ancient Saxons. ~*adj.* **4.** of or characteristic of the ancient Saxons, the Anglo-Saxons, or their descendants. **5.** of or characteristic of Saxony, its inhabitants, or their Low German dialect.

saxophone ('sæksəˌfəʊn) *n.* a keyed wind instrument of mellow tone colour, used mainly in jazz and dance music. Often shortened to **sax.** —**saxophonic** (ˌsæksə-'fɒnɪk) *adj.* —**saxophonist** (sæk'sɒfənɪst) *n.*

say (seɪ) *vb.* **saying, said.** (*mainly tr.*) **1.** to speak, pronounce, or utter. **2.** (*also intr.*) to express (an idea, etc.) in words; tell. **3.** (*also intr.*; *may take a clause as object*) to state (an opinion, fact, etc.) positively. **4.** to recite: *to say grace.* **5.** (*may take a clause as object*) to report or allege: *they say we shall have rain today.* **6.** (*may take a clause as object*) to suppose: *let us say that he is lying.* **7.** (*may take a clause as object*) to convey by means of artistic expression. **8.** to make a case for: *there is much to be said for it.* **9. go without saying.** to be so obvious as to need no explanation. **10. I say!** *Chiefly Brit. inf.* an exclamation of surprise. **11. not to say.** even. **12. that is to say.** in other words. **13. to say the least.** at the very least. ~*adv.* **14.** approximately: *there were, say, 20 people present.* **15.** for example: *choose a number, say, four.* ~*n.* **16.** the right or chance to speak: *let him have his say.* **17.** authority, esp. to influence a decision: *he has*

a lot of say. **18.** a statement of opinion: *you've had your say.* ~*interj.* **19.** *U.S. inf.* an exclamation to attract attention or express surprise. —'**sayer** *n.*

S.A.Y.E. *abbrev. for* save as you earn.

saying ('seɪɪŋ) *n.* a maxim, adage, or proverb.

Sb *the chemical symbol for* antimony.

Sc *the chemical symbol for* scandium.

s.c. *Printing. abbrev. for* small capitals.

S.C. *abbrev. for:* **1.** *Austral. & N.Z.* School Certificate. **2.** Signal Corps. **3.** *Canad.* Social Credit.

scab (skæb) *n.* **1.** the dried crusty surface of a healing skin wound or sore. **2.** a contagious disease of sheep resembling mange, caused by a mite. **3.** a fungal disease of plants characterized by crusty spots on the fruits, leaves, etc. **4.** *Derog.* **a.** Also called: **blackleg.** a person who refuses to support a trade union's actions. esp. strikes. **b.** (*as modifier*): *scab labour.* **5.** a despicable person. ~*vb.* (*intr.*) **scabbing, scabbed. 6.** to become covered with a scab. **7.** to replace a striking worker.

scabbard ('skæbəd) *n.* a holder for a bladed weapon such as a sword or bayonet.

scabby ('skæbɪ) *adj.* -**bier, -biest. 1.** *Pathol.* having an area of the skin covered with scabs. **2.** *Pathol.* having scabies. **3.** *Inf.* despicable. —'**scabbily** *adv.* —'**scabbiness** *n.*

scabies ('skeɪbiːz) *n.* a contagious skin infection caused by a mite, characterized by intense itching and inflammation.

scabious[1] ('skeɪbɪəs) *adj.* **1.** having or covered with scabs. **2.** of, relating to, or resembling scabies.

scabious[2] ('skeɪbɪəs) *n.* any of a genus of plants of the Mediterranean region, having blue, red, or whitish dome-shaped flower heads.

scabrous ('skeɪbrəs) *adj.* **1.** roughened because of small projections. **2.** indecent or salacious: *scabrous humour.* **3.** difficult to deal with. —'**scabrously** *adv.*

scaffold ('skæfəld) *n.* **1.** a temporary framework that is used to support workmen and materials during the erection, repair, etc., of a building. **2.** a raised wooden platform on which plays are performed, tobacco, etc., is dried, or (esp. formerly) criminals are executed. ~*vb.* (*tr.*) **3.** to provide with a scaffold. **4.** to support by means of a scaffold. —'**scaffolder** *n.*

scaffolding ('skæfəldɪŋ) *n.* **1.** a scaffold or system of scaffolds. **2.** the building materials used to make scaffolds.

scalar ('skeɪlə) *n.* **1.** a variable quantity, such as time or temperature, that has magnitude but not direction. ~*adj.* **2.** having magnitude but not direction.

scalawag ('skælə,wæg) *n.* a variant spelling of **scallywag.**

scald (skɔːld) *vb.* **1.** to burn or be burnt with or as if with hot liquid or steam. **2.** (*tr.*) to subject to the action of boiling water, esp. so as to sterilize. **3.** (*tr.*) to heat (a liquid) almost to boiling point. ~*n.* **4.** the act or result of scalding. **5.** an abnormal condition in plants, caused by exposure to excessive sunlight, gases, etc. —'**scalder** *n.*

scale[1] (skeɪl) *n.* **1.** any of the numerous plates, made of various substances, covering the bodies of fishes. **2. a.** any of the horny or chitinous plates covering a part or the entire body of certain reptiles and mammals. **b.** any of the numerous minute structures covering the wings of lepidoptera. **3.** a thin flat piece or flake. **4.** a thin flake of dead epidermis shed from the skin. **5.** a specialized leaf or bract, esp. the protective covering of a bud or the dry membranous bract of a catkin. **6.** See **scale insect. 7.** any oxide formed on a metal when heated. **8.** tartar formed on the teeth. ~*vb.* **9.** (*tr.*) to remove the scales

---

or coating from. **10.** to peel off or cause to peel off in flakes or scales. **11.** (*intr.*) to shed scales. **12.** to cover or become covered with scales, incrustation, etc.

scale² (skeɪl) *n.* **1.** (*often pl.*) a machine or device for weighing. **2.** one of the pans of a balance. **3. tip the scales. a.** to exercise a decisive influence. **b.** (foll. by *at*) to amount in weight (to). ~*vb.* (*tr.*) **4.** to weigh with or as if with scales.

scale³ (skeɪl) *n.* **1.** a sequence of marks at regular intervals, used as a reference in making measurements. **2.** a measuring instrument having such a scale. **3. a.** the ratio between the size of something real and that of a representation of it. **b.** (*as modifier*): *a scale model.* **4.** a line, numerical ratio, etc., for showing this ratio. **5.** a progressive or graduated table of things, wages, etc.: *a wage scale for carpenters.* **6.** an established standard. **7.** a relative degree or extent: *he entertained on a grand scale.* **8.** *Music.* a group of notes taken in ascending or descending order, esp. within the compass of one octave. **9.** *Maths.* the notation of a given number system: *the decimal scale.* ~*vb.* **10.** to climb to the top of (a height) by or as if by a ladder. **11.** (*tr.*) to make or draw (a model, etc.) according to a particular ratio of proportionate reduction. **12.** (*tr.;* usually foll. by *up* or *down*) to increase or reduce proportionately in size, etc. **13.** (*intr.*) *Austral. inf.* to ride on public transport without paying a fare. —'**scaly** *adj.*

scale inscet *n.* a small insect which typically lives and feeds on plants and secretes a protective scale around itself. Many species are pests.

scalene ('skeɪliːn) *adj.* **1.** *Maths.* (of a triangle) having all sides of unequal length. **2.** *Anat.* of or relating to any of the scalenus muscles.

scallion ('skæljən) *n.* any of various onions, such as the spring onion, that have a small bulb and long leaves and are eaten in salads.

scallop ('skɒləp, 'skæl-) *n.* **1.** any of various marine bivalves having a fluted fan-shaped shell. **2.** the edible adductor muscle of certain of these molluscs. **3.** either of the shell valves of any of these molluscs. **4.** a scallop shell in which fish, esp. shellfish, is cooked and served. **5.** one of a series of curves along an edge. **6.** the shape of a scallop shell used as the badge of a pilgrim, esp. in the Middle Ages. **7.** *Chiefly Austral.* a slice of potato fried in batter. ~*vb.* **8.** (*tr.*) to decorate (an edge) with scallops. **9.** to bake (food) in a scallop shell or similar dish. —'**scalloper** *n.* —'**scalloping** *n.*

scallywag ('skælɪˌwæg) *n. Inf.* a scamp; rascal. ~Also: **scalawag, scallawag.**

scalp (skælp) *n.* **1.** *Anat.* the skin and subcutaneous tissue covering the top of the head. **2.** (among North American Indians) a part of this removed as a trophy from a slain enemy. **3.** a trophy or token signifying conquest. **4.** *Scot. dialect.* a projection of bare rock from vegetation, etc. ~*vb.* (*tr.*) **5.** to cut the scalp from. **6.** *Inf., chiefly U.S.* to purchase and resell (securities) quickly so as to make several small profits. **7.** *Inf.* to buy (tickets) cheaply and resell at an inflated price. —'**scalper** *n.*

scalpel ('skælpəl) *n.* a surgical knife with a short thin blade.

scamp¹ (skæmp) *n.* **1.** an idle mischievous person. **2.** a mischievous child. —'**scampish** *adj.*

scamp² (skæmp) *vb.* a less common word for **skimp.** —'**scamper** *n.*

scamper ('skæmpə) *vb.* **1.** (*intr.*) to run about playfully. ~*n.* **2.** the act of scampering.

scampi ('skæmpɪ) *n.* (*functioning as sing. or pl.*) large prawns, usually eaten fried in batter.

scan (skæn) *vb.* **scanning, scanned. 1.** (*tr.*) to scrutinize minutely. **2.** (*tr.*) to glance at quickly. **3.** (*tr.*) *Prosody.* to read or analyse (verse) according to the rules of metre and versification. **4.** (*intr.*) *Prosody.* to conform to the rules of metre and versification. **5.** (*tr.*) *Electronics.* to move a beam of light, electrons, etc., in a predetermined pattern over (a surface or region) to obtain information, esp. to reproduce a television image. **6.** (*tr.*) to examine data stored on (magnetic tape, etc.), usually in order to retrieve information. **7.** to examine or search (a prescribed region) by systematically varying the direction of a radar or sonar beam. ~*n.* **8.** the act or an instance of scanning. —'**scannable** *adj.*

scandal ('skændəl) *n.* **1.** a disgraceful action or event: *his negligence was a scandal.* **2.** censure or outrage arising from an action or event. **3.** a person whose conduct causes reproach or disgrace. **4.** malicious talk, esp. gossip. **5.** *Law.* a libellous action or statement. —'**scandalous** *adj.* —'**scandalously** *adv.*

scandalize *or* **-ise** ('skændə,laɪz) *vb.* (*tr.*) to shock, as by improper behaviour. —,**scandali'zation** *or* **-i'sation** *n.*

scandalmonger ('skændəl,mʌŋgə) *n.* a person who spreads or enjoys scandal, gossip, etc.

Scandinavian (,skændɪ'neɪvɪən) *adj.* **1.** of or characteristic of Scandinavia, (Norway, Sweden, Denmark, and Iceland), its inhabitants, or their languages. ~*n.* **2.** a native or inhabitant of Scandinavia. **3.** the group of Germanic languages, consisting of Swedish, Danish, Norwegian, Icelandic, and Faeroese.

scandium ('skændɪəm) *n.* a rare silvery-white metallic element occurring in minute quantities in numerous minerals. Symbol: Sc; atomic no.: 21; atomic wt.: 44.96.

scanner ('skænə) *n.* **1.** a person or thing that scans. **2.** a device, usually electronic, used to measure or sample the distribution of some quantity or condition in a particular system, region, or area. **3.** an aerial or similar device designed to transmit or receive signals, esp. radar signals, inside a given solid angle of space.

scansion ('skænʃən) *n.* the analysis of the metrical structure of verse.

scant (skænt) *adj.* **1.** scarcely sufficient: *he paid her scant attention.* **2.** (*prenominal*) bare: *a scant ten inches.* **3.** (*postpositive;* foll. by *of*) having a short supply (of). ~*vb.* (*tr.*) **4.** to limit in size or quantity. **5.** to provide with a limited supply of. **6.** to treat in an inadequate manner. ~*adv.* **7.** scarcely; barely. —'**scantly** *adv.*

scanty ('skæntɪ) *adj.* **scantier, scantiest. 1.** limited; barely enough. **2.** inadequate. **3.** lacking fullness. —'**scantily** *adv.* —'**scantiness** *n.*

scape *or* **'scape** (skeɪp) *vb., n.* an archaic word for **escape.**

-scape *suffix forming nouns.* indicating a scene or view of something: *seascape.*

scapegoat ('skeɪp,gəʊt) *n.* **1.** a person made to bear the blame for others. **2.** *Bible.* a goat symbolically laden with the sins of the Israelites and sent into the wilderness.

scapegrace ('skeɪp,greɪs) *n.* a mischievous person.

THESAURUS

scale¹ *n.* **1.** calibration, degrees, gamut, gradation, graduated system, graduation, hierarchy, ladder, pecking order (*Inf.*), progression, ranking, register, seniority system, sequence, series, spectrum, spread, steps **2.** proportion, ratio **3.** degree, extent, range, reach, scope, way ~*v.* **4.** ascend, clamber, climb, escalade, mount, surmount **5.** adjust, proportion, prorate (*Chiefly U.S.*), regulate

scale² *n.* flake, lamina, layer, plate, squama (*Biol.*)

scaly flaky, furfuraceous (*Medical*), scabrous, scurfy, squamous *or* squamose (*Biol.*), squamulose

scamp devil, imp, knave (*Archaic*), mischief-maker, monkey, prankster, rascal, rogue, scallywag (*Inf.*), scapegrace, tyke (*Inf.*), wretch

scamper dart, dash, fly, hasten, hie (*Archaic*), hurry, romp, run, scoot, scurry, scuttle, sprint

scan check, con (*Archaic*), examine, glance over, investigate, look one up and down, look through, run one's eye over, run over, scour, scrutinize, search, size up (*Inf.*), skim, survey, sweep, take stock of

scandal 1. crime, crying shame (*Inf.*), disgrace, embarrassment, offence, sin, wrongdoing **2.** calumny, defamation, detraction, discredit, disgrace, dishonour, ignominy, infamy, obloquy, offence, opprobrium, reproach, shame **3.** abuse, aspersion, backbiting, dirt, dirty linen (*Inf.*), gossip, rumours, skeleton in the cupboard, slander, talk, tattle

scandalize affront, appal, cause a few raised eyebrows (*Inf.*), disgust, horrify, offend, outrage, shock

scandalous 1. atrocious, disgraceful, disreputable, highly improper, infamous, monstrous, odious, opprobrious, outrageous, shameful, shocking, unseemly **2.** defamatory, gossiping, libellous, scurrilous, slanderous, untrue

scant bare, barely sufficient, deficient, inadequate, insufficient, limited, little, minimal, sparse

scanty bare, deficient, exiguous, inadequate, insufficient, meagre, narrow, poor, restricted, scant, short, skimpy, slender, sparing, sparse, thin

scapegoat fall guy (*Inf.*), whipping boy

scapula ('skæpjʊlə) *n., pl.* **-lae** (-liː) *or* **-las.** either of two large flat triangular bones, one on each side of the back part of the shoulder in man. Nontechnical name: **shoulder blade.**

scapular ('skæpjʊlə) *adj.* **1.** *Anat.* of or relating to the scapula. ~*n.* **2.** part of the monastic habit worn by members of many Christian religious orders, consisting of a piece of woollen cloth worn over the shoulders, and hanging down to the ankles. **3.** two small rectangular pieces of cloth joined by tapes passing over the shoulders and worn in token of affiliation to a religious order. **4.** any of the small feathers of a bird that lie along the shoulder. ~Also called (for senses 2 and 3): **scapulary.**

scar[1] (skɑː) *n.* **1.** any mark left on the skin or other tissue following the healing of a wound, etc. **2.** a permanent change in a person's character resulting from emotional distress. **3.** the mark on a plant indicating the former point of attachment of a part. **4.** a mark of damage. ~*vb.* **scarring, scarred. 5.** to mark or become marked with a scar. **6.** (*intr.*) to heal leaving a scar.

scar[2] (skɑː) *n.* a bare craggy rock formation.

scarab ('skærəb) *n.* **1.** any scarabaeid beetle, esp. the **sacred scarab,** regarded by the ancient Egyptians as divine. **2.** the scarab as represented on amulets, etc.

scarce (skɛəs) *adj.* **1.** rarely encountered. **2.** insufficient to meet the demand. **3. make oneself scarce.** *Inf.* to go away. ~*adv.* **4.** *Arch. or literary.* scarcely. —'**scarceness** *n.*

scarcely ('skɛəslı) *adv.* **1.** hardly at all. **2.** *Often used ironically.* probably or definitely not: *that is scarcely justification for your actions.*

▷ **Usage.** See at **hardly.**

scarcity ('skɛəsıtı) *n., pl.* **-ties. 1.** inadequate supply. **2.** rarity or infrequent occurrence.

scare (skɛə) *vb.* **1.** to fill or become filled with fear or alarm. **2.** (*tr.; often foll. by* away *or* off) to drive (away) by frightening. ~*n.* **3.** a sudden attack of fear or alarm. **4.** a period of general fear or alarm. —'**scarer** *n.*

scarecrow ('skɛəˌkrəʊ) *n.* **1.** an object, usually in the shape of a man, made out of sticks and old clothes to scare birds away from seeds, etc. **2.** a person or thing that appears frightening. **3.** *Inf.* an untidy-looking person.

scaremonger ('skɛəˌmʌŋgə) *n.* a person who delights in spreading rumours of disaster. —'**scareˌmongering** *n.*

scarf[1] (skɑːf) *n., pl.* **scarfs** *or* **scarves** (skɑːvz). a rectangular, triangular, or long narrow piece of cloth worn around the head, neck, or shoulders for warmth or decoration.

scarf[2] (skɑːf) *n., pl.* **scarfs. 1.** Also called: **scarf joint, scarfed joint.** a lapped joint between two pieces of timber made by notching the ends and strapping or gluing the two pieces together. **2.** the end of a piece of timber shaped to form such a joint. **3.** *Whaling.* an incision made along a whale before stripping off the blubber. ~*vb.* (*tr.*) **4.** to join (two pieces of timber) by means of a scarf. **5.** to make a scarf on (a piece of timber). **6.** to cut a scarf in (a whale).

scarify ('skɛərıˌfaı, 'skærı-) *vb.* **-fying, -fied.** (*tr.*) **1.** *Surgery.* to make tiny punctures or superficial incisions in (the skin or other tissue), as for inoculating. **2.** *Agriculture.* to break up and loosen (soil) to a shallow depth. **3.** to wound with harsh criticism. —ˌ**scarifiˈcation** *n.* —'**scariˌfier** *n.*

scarlatina (ˌskɑːləˈtiːnə) *n.* the technical name for **scarlet fever.**

scarlet ('skɑːlıt) *n.* **1.** a vivid orange-red colour. **2.** cloth or clothing of this colour. ~*adj.* **3.** of the colour scarlet. **4.** sinful or immoral.

scarlet fever *n.* an acute communicable disease characterized by fever, strawberry-coloured tongue, and a rash starting on the neck and chest and spreading to the abdomen and limbs. Technical name: **scarlatina.**

scarp (skɑːp) *n.* **1.** a steep slope, esp. one formed by erosion or faulting. **2.** *Fortifications.* the side of a ditch cut nearest to a rampart. ~*vb.* **3.** (*tr.; often passive*) to wear or cut so as to form a steep slope.

scarper ('skɑːpə) *Brit. sl.* ~*vb.* **1.** (*intr.*) to depart in haste. ~*n.* **2.** a hasty departure.

scarves (skɑːvz) *n.* a plural of **scarf**[1].

scary ('skɛərı) *adj.* **scarier, scariest.** *Inf.* **1.** causing fear or alarm. **2.** timid.

scat[1] (skæt) *vb.* **scatting, scatted.** (*intr.; usually imperative*) *Inf.* to go away in haste.

scat[2] (skæt) *n.* **1.** a type of jazz singing characterized by improvised vocal sounds instead of words. ~*vb.* **scatting, scatted. 2.** (*intr.*) to sing jazz in this way.

scathe (skeıð) *vb.* (*tr.*) **1.** *Rare.* to attack with severe criticism. **2.** *Arch. or dialect.* to injure. ~*n.* **3.** *Arch. or dialect.* harm.

scathing ('skeıðıŋ) *adj.* **1.** harshly critical; scornful. **2.** damaging. —'**scathingly** *adv.*

scatology (skæ'tɒlədʒı) *n.* **1.** the scientific study of excrement, esp. in medicine and in palaeontology. **2.** obscenity or preoccupation with obscenity, esp. in the form of references to excrement. —**scatological** (ˌskætə'lɒdʒıkəl) *adj.*

scatter ('skætə) *vb.* **1.** (*tr.*) to throw about in various directions. **2.** to separate and move or cause to move in various directions. **3.** to deviate or cause to deviate in many directions, as in the refraction of light. ~*n.* **4.** the act of scattering. **5.** a substance or a number of objects scattered about. —'**scatterer** *n.*

scatterbrain ('skætəˌbreın) *n.* a person who is incapable of serious thought or concentration. —'**scatterˌbrained** *adj.*

scatty ('skætı) *adj.* **-tier, -tiest.** *Brit. inf.* empty-headed or thoughtless. —'**scattily** *adv.* —'**scattiness** *n.*

scavenge ('skævındʒ) *vb.* **1.** to search for (anything usable) among discarded material. **2.** (*tr.*) to purify (a molten metal) by bubbling a suitable gas through it. **3.** to clean up filth from (streets, etc.).

scavenger ('skævındʒə) *n.* **1.** a person who collects things discarded by others. **2.** any animal that feeds on decaying organic matter. **3.** a person employed to clean the streets. —'**scavengery** *n.*

Sc.D. *abbrev. for* Doctor of Science.

S.C.E. *abbrev. for* Scottish Certificate of Education.

scenario (sı'nɑːrıˌəʊ) *n., pl.* **-narios.** a summary of the plot of a play, etc., including information about its characters, scenes, etc.

scene (siːn) *n.* **1.** the place where an action or event, real or imaginary, occurs. **2.** the setting for the action of a play, novel, etc. **3.** an incident or situation, real or imaginary, esp. as described or represented. **4. a.** a subdivision of an act of a play, in which the setting is fixed. **b.** a single event, esp. a significant one, in a play. **5.** *Films.* a shot or series of shots that constitutes a unit of the action. **6.** the backcloths, etc., for a play or film set. **7.** the prospect of a place, landscape, etc. **8.** a display of emotion. **9.** *Inf.* the environment for a specific activity: *the fashion scene.* **10.** *Inf.* interest or chosen occupation: *classical music is not my scene.* **11.** *Rare.* the stage. **12. behind the scenes.** out of public view.

THESAURUS

scar 1. *n.* blemish, cicatrix, injury, mark, wound **2.** *v.* brand, damage, disfigure, mark, traumatize

scarce at a premium, deficient, few, few and far between, infrequent, in short supply, insufficient, rare, seldom met with, uncommon, unusual, wanting

scarcely 1. barely, hardly, only just, scarce (*Archaic*) **2.** by no means, definitely not, hardly, not at all, on no account, under no circumstances

scarcity dearth, deficiency, infrequency, insufficiency, lack, paucity, poverty, rareness, shortage, undersupply, want

scare 1. *v.* affright (*Archaic*), alarm, daunt, dismay, frighten, give (someone) a fright, give (someone) a turn (*Inf.*), intimidate, panic, put the wind up (someone) (*Inf.*), shock, startle, terrify, terrorize **2.** *n.* alarm, alert, fright, panic, shock, start, terror

scared fearful, frightened, panicky, panic-stricken, petrified, shaken, startled, terrified

scathing belittling, biting, brutal, caustic, critical, cutting, harsh, mordant, sarcastic, scornful, searing, trenchant, withering

scatter 1. broadcast, diffuse, disseminate, fling, litter, shower, sow, spread, sprinkle, strew **2.** disband, dispel, disperse, dissipate, disunite, put to flight, separate

scatterbrain bird-brain (*Inf.*), butterfly, featherbrain, flibbertigibbet, grasshopper mind, madcap

scattering few, handful, scatter, smatter, smattering, sprinkling

scenario master plan, outline, résumé, rundown, scheme, sequence of events, sketch, story line, summary, synopsis

scene 1. display, exhibition, pageant, picture, representation, show, sight, spectacle, tableau **2.** area, locality, place, position, setting, site, situation, spot, whereabouts **3.** backdrop, background, location, *mise en scène*, set, setting **4.** act, division, episode, incident, part, stage **5.** carry-on (*Brit. inf.*),

scenery (ˈsiːnərɪ) *n., pl.* **-eries. 1.** the natural features of a landscape. **2.** *Theatre.* the painted backcloths, etc., used to represent a location in a theatre or studio.

scenic (ˈsiːnɪk) *adj.* **1.** of or relating to natural scenery. **2.** having beautiful natural scenery: *a scenic drive.* **3.** of or relating to the stage or stage scenery. **4.** (in painting, etc.) representing a scene. —**ˈscenically** *adv.*

scent (sɛnt) *n.* **1.** a distinctive smell, esp. a pleasant one. **2.** a smell left in passing, by which a person or animal may be traced. **3.** a trail, clue, or guide. **4.** an instinctive ability for detecting. **5.** another word (esp. Brit.) for **perfume.** ~*vb.* **6.** (*tr.*) to recognize by or as if by the smell. **7.** (*tr.*) to have a suspicion of: *I scent foul play.* **8.** (*tr.*) to fill with odour or fragrance. **9.** (*intr.*) (of hounds, etc.) to hunt by the sense of smell. **10.** to smell (at): *the dog scented the air.*

sceptic *or U.S.* **skeptic** (ˈskɛptɪk) *n.* **1.** a person who habitually doubts the authenticity of accepted beliefs. **2.** a person who mistrusts people, ideas, etc., in general. **3.** a person who doubts the truth of religion. —**ˈsceptical** *or U.S.* **ˈskeptical** *adj.* —**ˈsceptically** *or U.S.* **ˈskeptically** *adv.* —**ˈscepticism** *or U.S.* **ˈskepticism** *n.*

sceptre *or U.S.* **scepter** (ˈsɛptə) *n.* **1.** a ceremonial staff held by a monarch as the symbol of authority. **2.** imperial authority; sovereignty. —**ˈsceptred** *or U.S.* **ˈsceptered** *adj.*

schedule (ˈʃɛdjuːl; *also, esp. U.S.* ˈskɛdʒʊəl) *n.* **1.** a plan of procedure for a project. **2.** a list of items: *a schedule of fixed prices.* **3.** a list of times; timetable. **4.** a list of tasks to be performed, esp. within a set period. **5.** *Law.* a list or inventory. ~*vb.* (*tr.*) **6.** to make a schedule of or place in a schedule. **7.** to plan to occur at a certain time.

schema (ˈskiːmə) *n., pl.* **-mata** (-mətə). **1.** a plan, diagram, or scheme. **2.** (in the philosophy of Kant) a rule or principle that enables the understanding to unify experience. **3.** *Logic.* **a.** a syllogistic figure. **b.** a representation of the form of an inference.

schematic (skɪˈmætɪk) *adj.* **1.** of or relating to the nature of a diagram, plan, or schema. ~*n.* **2.** a schematic diagram, esp. of an electrical circuit, etc. —**scheˈmatically** *adv.*

schematize *or* **-ise** (ˈskiːməˌtaɪz) *vb.* (*tr.*) to form into or arrange in a scheme. —**ˌschematiˈzation** *or* **-iˈsation** *n.* —**ˈschemaˌtism** *n.*

scheme (skiːm) *n.* **1.** a systematic plan for a course of action. **2.** a systematic arrangement of parts. **3.** a secret plot. **4.** a chart, diagram, or outline. **5.** an astrological diagram giving the aspects of celestial bodies. **6.** *Chiefly Brit.* a plan formally adopted by a commercial enterprise or governmental body, as for pensions, etc. ~*vb.* **7.** (*tr.*) to devise a system for. **8.** to form intrigues (for) in an underhand manner. —**ˈschemer** *n.*

scheming (ˈskiːmɪŋ) *adj.* **1.** given to making plots; cunning. ~*n.* **2.** intrigues.

scherzo (ˈskɛətsəʊ) *n., pl.* **-zos** *or* **-zi** (-tsiː). a brisk lively movement, developed from the minuet, with a contrastive middle section (a trio).

schilling (ˈʃɪlɪŋ) *n.* **1.** the standard monetary unit of Austria. **2.** an old German coin of low denomination.'

schism (ˈsɪzəm, ˈskɪz-) *n.* **1.** the division of a group into opposing factions. **2.** the factions so formed. **3.** division within or separation from an established Church, not necessarily involving differences in doctrine. —**schisˈmatic** *or* **schisˈmatical** *adj.*

schist (ʃɪst) *n.* any metamorphic rock that can be split into thin layers.

schizo (ˈskɪtsəʊ) *Inf.* ~*adj.* **1.** schizophrenic. ~*n., pl.* **-os. 2.** a schizophrenic person.

schizo- *or before a vowel* **schiz-** *combining form.* indicating a cleavage, split, or division: *schizophrenia.*

schizoid (ˈskɪtsɔɪd) *adj.* **1.** of or characteristic of schizophrenia. **2.** of or characteristic of a personality that is inwardly directed. ~*n.* **3.** a person who has a schizoid personality.

schizophrenia (ˌskɪtsəʊˈfriːnɪə) *n.* any of a group of psychotic disorders characterized by progressive deterioration of the personality, withdrawal from reality, hallucinations, emotional instability, etc. —ˌ**schizoˈphrenic** *adj., n.*

schmaltz *or* **schmalz** (ʃmælts, ʃmɔːlts) *n. Sl.* excessive sentimentality, esp. in music. —**ˈschmaltzy** *adj.*

schnapps *or* **schnaps** (ʃnæps) *n.* **1.** a Dutch spirit distilled from potatoes. **2.** (in Germany) any strong spirit.

schnitzel (ˈʃnɪtsəl) *n.* a thin slice of meat, esp. veal.

schnorkle (ˈʃnɔːkəl) *n.* a less common variant of **snorkel.**

scholar (ˈskɒlə) *n.* **1.** a learned person, esp. in the humanities. **2.** a person, esp. a child, who studies; pupil. **3.** a student receiving a scholarship. —**ˈscholarly** *adj.* —**ˈscholarliness** *n.*

scholarship (ˈskɒləˌʃɪp) *n.* **1.** academic achievement; learning. **2. a.** financial aid provided for a scholar because of academic merit. **b.** the position of a student who gains this financial aid. **c.** (*as modifier*): *a scholarship student.* **3.** the qualities of a scholar.

scholastic (skəˈlæstɪk) *adj.* **1.** of or befitting schools, scholars, or education. **2.** pedantic or precise. **3.** (*often cap.*) characteristic of or relating to the medieval Schoolmen. ~*n.* **4.** a student or pupil. **5.** a person who is given to logical subtleties. **6.** (*often cap.*) a disciple or adherent of scholasticism; Schoolman. **7.** a Jesuit student who is undergoing a period of probation prior to commencing his theological studies. —**schoˈlastically** *adv.*

scholasticism (skəˈlæstɪˌsɪzəm) *n.* (*sometimes cap.*) the system of philosophy, theology, and teaching that dominated medieval western Europe and was based on the writings of the Church Fathers and Aristotle.

school[1] (skuːl) *n.* **1. a.** an institution or building at which children and young people receive education. **b.** (*as modifier*): *school day.* **c.** (*in combination*): *schoolwork.* **2.** any educational institution or building. **3.** a faculty or department specializing in a particular subject: *a law school.* **4.** the staff and pupils of a school. **5.** the period of instruction in a school or one session of this: *he stayed after school to do extra work.* **6.** a place or sphere of activity that instructs: *the school of hard knocks.* **7.** a body of people or pupils adhering to a certain set of principles, doctrines, or methods. **8.** a group of artists, writers, etc., linked by the same style, teachers, or aims. **9.** a style of life: *a gentleman of the old school.* **10.** *Austral. & N.Z.* a group assembled for a common purpose, esp. gambling or drinking. ~*vb.* (*tr.*) **11.** to train or educate in or as in a school. **12.** to discipline or control.

THESAURUS

commotion, confrontation, display of emotion, exhibition, fuss, performance, row, tantrum, to-do, upset **6.** landscape, panorama, prospect, view, vista **7.** *Inf.* arena, business, environment, field of interest, milieu, world

scenery 1. landscape, surroundings, terrain, view, vista **2.** *Theatre.* backdrop, décor, flats, *mise en scène,* set, setting, stage set

scent *n.* **1.** aroma, bouquet, fragrance, odour, perfume, redolence, smell **2.** spoor, track, trail ~*v.* **3.** be on the track *or* trail of, detect, discern, get wind of, nose out, recognize, sense, smell, sniff, sniff out

scented aromatic, fragrant, perfumed, sweet-smelling

sceptic agnostic, cynic, disbeliever, doubter, doubting Thomas, Pyrrhonist, scoffer

sceptical cynical, disbelieving, doubtful, doubting, dubious, hesitating, incredulous, mistrustful, questioning, quizzical, scoffing, unbelieving, unconvinced

scepticism cynicism, disbelief, doubt, incredulity, Pyrrhonism, suspicion

schedule 1. *n.* agenda, calendar, catalogue, inventory, itinerary, list, list of appointments, plan, programme, timetable **2.** *v.* appoint, arrange, be due, book, organize, plan, programme, time

scheme *n.* **1.** contrivance, course of action, design, device, plan, programme, project, proposal, strategy, system, tactics, theory **2.** arrangement, blueprint, chart, codification, diagram, disposition, draft, layout, outline, pattern, schedule, schema, system **3.** conspiracy, dodge, game (*Inf.*), intrigue, machinations, manoeuvre, plot, ploy, ruse, shift, stratagem, subterfuge ~*v.* **4.** contrive, design, devise, frame, imagine, lay plans, plan, project, work out **5.** collude, conspire, intrigue, machinate, manoeuvre, plot, wheel and deal (*Inf.*)

scheming artful, calculating, conniving, cunning, deceitful, designing, duplicitous, foxy, Machiavellian, slippery, sly, tricky, underhand, wily

schism breach, break, discord, disunion, division, rift, rupture, separation, splintering, split

scholar 1. academic, bookworm, egghead (*Inf.*), intellectual, man of letters, savant **2.** disciple, learner, pupil, schoolboy, schoolgirl, student

scholarly academic, bookish, erudite, intellectual, learned, lettered

scholarship 1. accomplishments, attainments, book-learning, education, erudition, knowledge, learning, lore **2.** bursary, exhibition, fellowship

scholastic 1. academic, bookish, learned, lettered, literary, scholarly **2.** pedagogic, pedantic, precise

school² (skuːl) n. 1. a group of fish or other aquatic animals that swim together. ~vb. 2. (intr.) to form such a group.

schoolboy ('skuːlˌbɔɪ) or (fem.) **schoolgirl** n. a child attending school.

schoolhouse ('skuːlˌhaʊs) n. 1. a building used as a school. 2. a house attached to a school.

schooling ('skuːlɪŋ) n. 1. education, esp. when received at school. 2. the process of teaching or being taught in a school. 3. the training of an animal, esp. of a horse for dressage.

schoolman ('skuːlmən) n., pl. -men. (sometimes cap.) a scholar versed in the learning of the **Schoolmen**, the masters in the universities of the Middle Ages who were versed in scholasticism.

schoolmarm ('skuːlˌmɑːm) n. Inf. 1. a woman schoolteacher. 2. any woman considered to be prim or old-fashioned. —'**school**ˌ**marmish** adj.

schoolmaster ('skuːlˌmɑːstə) or (fem.) **schoolmistress** n. 1. a person who teaches in or runs a school. 2. a person or thing that acts as an instructor.

Schools (skuːlz) pl. n. 1. **the.** the medieval Schoolmen collectively. 2. (at Oxford University) a. the University building in which examinations are held. b. Inf. the Second Public Examination for the degree of Bachelor of Arts.

schoolteacher ('skuːlˌtiːtʃə) n. a person who teaches in a school.

school year n. 1. a twelve-month period, usually of three terms, during which pupils remain in the same class. 2. the time during this period when the school is open.

schooner ('skuːnə) n. 1. a sailing vessel with at least two masts, with lower sails rigged fore-and-aft. 2. Brit. a large glass for sherry. 3. U.S., Austral. a large glass for beer.

schottische (ʃɒˈtiːʃ) n. 1. a 19th-century German dance resembling a slow polka. 2. a piece of music composed for or in the manner of this dance.

schuss (ʃʊs) Skiing. ~n. 1. a straight high-speed downhill run. ~vb. 2. (intr.) to perform a schuss.

schwa or **shwa** (ʃwɑː) n. 1. a central vowel represented in the International Phonetic Alphabet by (ə). The sound occurs in unstressed syllables in English, as in around and sofa. 2. the symbol (ə) used to represent this sound.

sci. abbrev. for: 1. science. 2. scientific.

sciatic (saɪˈætɪk) adj. 1. Anat. of or relating to the hip or the hipbone. 2. of or afflicted with sciatica.

sciatica (saɪˈætɪkə) n. a form of neuralgia characterized by intense pain along the body's longest nerve (**sciatic nerve**), extending from the back of the thigh down to the calf of the leg.

science ('saɪəns) n. 1. the systematic study of the nature and behaviour of the material and physical universe, based on observation, experiment, and measurement. 2. the knowledge so obtained or the practice of obtaining it. 3. any particular branch of this knowledge: the applied sciences. 4. any body of knowledge organized in a systematic manner. 5. skill or technique. 6. Arch. knowledge.

science fiction n. a. a literary genre that makes imaginative use of scientific knowledge. b. (as modifier): a science fiction writer.

scientific (ˌsaɪənˈtɪfɪk) adj. 1. (prenominal) of, derived from, or used in science: scientific equipment. 2. (pre-

nominal) occupied in science: scientific manpower. 3. conforming with the methods used in science. —ˌ**scien**-'**tifically** adv.

scientist ('saɪəntɪst) n. a person who studies or practises any of the sciences or who uses scientific methods.

sci-fi ('saɪˈfaɪ) n. short for **science fiction**.

scilicet ('sɪlɪˌsɛt) adv. namely: used esp. in explaining a text that is obscure or supplying a missing word.

scimitar ('sɪmɪtə) n. an oriental sword with a curved blade.

scintilla (sɪnˈtɪlə) n. Rare. a minute amount; hint, trace, or particle.

scintillate ('sɪntɪˌleɪt) vb. (mainly intr.) 1. (also tr.) to give off (sparks); sparkle. 2. to be animated or brilliant. 3. Physics. to give off flashes of light as a result of the impact of photons. —'**scintillant** adj. —ˌ**scintil**'**lation** n.

scintillation counter n. an instrument for detecting and measuring the intensity of high-energy radiation. It consists of a phosphor with which particles collide producing flashes of light that are converted into pulses of electric current that are counted by electronic equipment.

sciolism ('saɪəˌlɪzəm) n. Rare. the practice of opinionating on subjects of which one has only superficial knowledge. —'**sciolist** n. —ˌ**scio**'**listic** adj.

scion ('saɪən) n. 1. a descendant or young member of a family. 2. a shoot of a plant used to form a graft.

scissors ('sɪzəz) pl. n. 1. Also called: **pair of scissors**. a cutting instrument used for cloth, hair, etc., having two crossed pivoted blades that cut by a shearing action. 2. a wrestling hold in which a wrestler wraps his legs round his opponent's body or head and squeezes. 3. any gymnastic feat in which the legs cross and uncross in a scissor-like movement.

sclera ('sklɪərə) n. the firm white fibrous membrane that forms the outer covering of the eyeball. Also called: **sclerotic.** —**scle**'**ritis** n.

sclero- or before a vowel **scler-** combining form. 1. indicating hardness: sclerosis. 2. of the sclera: sclerotomy.

sclerosis (sklɪəˈrəʊsɪs) n., pl. -ses (-siːz). 1. Pathol. a hardening or thickening of organs, tissues, or vessels from inflammation, degeneration, or (esp. on the inner walls of arteries) deposition of fatty plaques. 2. the hardening of a plant cell wall or tissue.

sclerotic (sklɪəˈrɒtɪk) adj. 1. of or relating to the sclera. 2. of, relating to, or having sclerosis. ~n. 3. another name for **sclera**.

scoff¹ (skɒf) vb. 1. (intr.; often foll. by at) to speak contemptuously (about); mock. 2. (tr.) Obs. to regard with derision. ~n. 3. an expression of derision. 4. an object of derision. —'**scoffer** n.

scoff² (skɒf) Sl., chiefly Brit. ~vb. 1. to eat (food) fast and greedily. ~n. 2. food or rations.

scold (skəʊld) vb. 1. to find fault with or reprimand (a person) harshly. 2. (intr.) to use harsh or abusive language. ~n. 3. a person, esp. a woman, who constantly finds fault. —'**scolder** n. —'**scolding** n.

scollop ('skɒləp) n., vb. a variant spelling of **scallop.**

sconce¹ (skɒns) n. 1. a bracket fixed to a wall for holding candles or lights. 2. a flat candlestick with a handle.

sconce² (skɒns) n. a small protective fortification, such as an earthwork.

scone (skəʊn, skɒn) n. a light plain doughy cake made from flour with very little fat, cooked in an oven or (esp. originally) on a griddle.

THESAURUS

school n. 1. academy, alma mater, college, department, discipline, faculty, institute, institution, seminary 2. adherents, circle, class, clique, denomination, devotees, disciples, faction, followers, following, group, pupils, sect, set 3. creed, faith, outlook, persuasion, school of thought, stamp, way of life ~v. 4. coach, discipline, drill, educate, indoctrinate, instruct, prepare, prime, train, tutor, verse

schooling 1. book-learning, education, formal education, teaching, tuition 2. coaching, drill, grounding, guidance, instruction, preparation, training

schoolteacher dominie (Scot.), instructor, pedagogue, schoolmarm (Inf.), schoolmaster, schoolmistress

science 1. body of knowledge, branch of knowledge, discipline 2. art, skill, technique

scientific accurate, controlled, exact, mathematical, precise, systematic

scintillate coruscate, flash, give off sparks, gleam, glint, glisten, glitter, sparkle, twinkle

scintillating animated, bright, brilliant, dazzling, ebullient, exciting, glittering, lively, sparkling, stimulating, witty

scoff belittle, deride, despise, flout, gibe, jeer, knock (Inf.), laugh at, make light of, make sport of, mock, poke fun at, pooh-pooh, revile, ridicule, scorn, scout (Archaic), sneer, taunt, twit

scold 1. v. bawl out (Inf.), berate, blame,

bring (someone) to book, castigate, censure, chide, find fault with, give (someone) a dressing-down (row, talking-to) (Inf.), go on at (Inf.), haul (someone) over the coals (Inf.), have (someone) on the carpet (Inf.), lecture, nag, rate, rebuke, remonstrate with, reprimand, reproach, reprove, take (someone) to task, tell off (Inf.), tick off (Inf.), upbraid, vituperate 2. n. nag, shrew, termagant (Rare), Xanthippe

scolding dressing-down (Inf.), (good) talking-to (Inf.), lecture, piece of one's mind (Inf.), rebuke, row, telling-off (Inf.), ticking-off (Inf.), tongue-lashing, wigging (Brit. sl.)

scoop (sku:p) n. **1.** a utensil used as a shovel or ladle, esp. a small shovel with deep sides and a short handle, used for taking up flour, etc. **2.** a utensil with a long handle and round bowl used for dispensing liquids, etc. **3.** anything that resembles a scoop in action, such as the bucket on a dredge. **4.** a utensil used for serving mashed potatoes, ice cream, etc. **5.** a spoonlike surgical instrument for extracting foreign matter, etc., from the body. **6.** the quantity taken up by a scoop. **7.** the act of scooping, dredging, etc. **8.** a hollow cavity. **9.** *Sl.* a large quick gain, as of money. **10.** a news story reported in one newspaper, etc., before all the others. ~*vb.* (*mainly tr.*) **11.** (often foll. by *up*) to take up and remove (an object or substance) with or as if with a scoop. **12.** (often foll. by *out*) to hollow out with or as if with a scoop. **13.** to make (a large sudden profit). **14.** to beat (rival newspapers, etc.) in uncovering a news item. —'**scooper** n. —'**scoop·ful** n.

scoot (sku:t) *vb.* **1.** to go or cause to go quickly or hastily; dart or cause to dart off or away. ~*n.* **2.** the act of scooting.

scooter ('sku:tə) n. **1.** a child's vehicle consisting of a low footboard mounted between two small wheels with a handlebar. **2.** See **motor scooter.**

scope (skəʊp) n. **1.** opportunity for exercising the faculties or abilities. **2.** range of view or grasp. **3.** the area covered by an activity, topic, etc.: *the scope of his thesis was vast.* **4.** *Naut.* slack left in an anchor cable. **5.** *Logic.* the part of a formula that follows a quantifier or an operator. **6.** *Inf.* short for **telescope, microscope, oscilloscope,** etc. **7.** *Arch.* purpose.

-scope n. combining form. indicating an instrument for observing or detecting: *microscope.* —**scopic** adj. combining form.

scopolamine (skə'pɒlə,mi:n) n. a colourless viscous liquid alkaloid extracted from certain plants, such as henbane: used in preventing travel sickness and as a sedative and truth serum. Also called: **hyoscine.**

-scopy n. combining form. indicating a viewing or observation: *microscopy.*

scorbutic (skɔ:'bju:tɪk) or **scorbutical** adj. of or having scurvy. —**scor'butically** adv.

scorch (skɔ:tʃ) *vb.* **1.** to burn or become burnt, esp. so as to affect the colour, taste, etc. **2.** to wither or parch or cause to wither from exposure to heat. **3.** (*intr.*) *Inf.* to be very hot: *it is scorching outside.* **4.** (*tr.*) *Inf.* to criticize harshly. ~*n.* **5.** a slight burn. **6.** a mark caused by the application of too great heat. **7.** *Horticulture.* a mark on fruit, etc., caused by pests or insecticides. —'**scorching** adj.

scorcher ('skɔ:tʃə) n. **1.** a person or thing that scorches. **2.** something caustic. **3.** *Inf.* a very hot day. **4.** *Brit. inf.* something remarkable.

score (skɔ:) n. **1.** a numerical record of a competitive game or match. **2.** the total number of points made by a side or individual in a game. **3.** the act of scoring, esp. a point or points. **4.** **the score.** *Inf.* the actual situation. **5.** a group or set of twenty: *three score years and ten.* **6.** (*usually pl.; foll. by of*) lots: *I have scores of things to do.* **7.** *Music.* **a.** the printed form of a composition in which the instrumental or vocal parts appear on separate staves vertically arranged on large pages (**full score**) or in a condensed version, usually for piano (**short score**) or voices and piano (**vocal score**). **b.** the incidental music for a film or play. **c.** the songs, music, etc., for a stage or film musical. **8.** a mark or notch, esp. one made in keeping a tally. **9.** an account of amounts due. **10.** an amount recorded as due. **11.** a reason: *the book was rejected on the score of length.* **12.** a grievance. **13. a.** a line marking a division or boundary. **b.** (*as modifier*): *score line.* **14. settle** or **pay off a score. a.** to avenge a wrong. **b.** to repay a debt. ~*vb.* **15.** to gain (a point or points) in a game or contest. **16.** (*tr.*) to make a total score of. **17.** to keep a record of the score (of). **18.** (*tr.*) to be worth (a certain amount) in a game. **19.** (*tr.*) to record by making notches in. **20.** to make (cuts, lines, etc.) in or on. **21.** (*intr.*) *Sl.* to obtain something desired, esp. to purchase an illegal drug. **22.** (*intr.*) *Sl.* (of men) to be successful in seducing a person. **23.** (*tr.*) **a.** to arrange (a piece of music) for specific instruments or voices. **b.** to write the music for (a film, play, etc.). **24.** to achieve (success or an advantage): *your idea scored with the boss.* —'**scorer** n.

scoreboard ('skɔ:,bɔ:d) n. *Sport, etc.* a board for displaying the score of a game or match.

scorecard ('skɔ:,kɑ:d) n. **1.** a card on which scores are recorded, as in golf. **2.** a card identifying the players in a sports match, esp. cricket.

score off *vb.* (*intr., prep.*) to gain an advantage at someone else's expense.

scoria ('skɔ:rɪə) n., pl. **-riae** (-rɪ,i:). **1.** a mass of solidified lava containing many cavities. **2.** refuse obtained from smelted ore.

scorn (skɔ:n) n. **1.** open contempt for a person or thing. **2.** an object of contempt or derision. ~*vb.* **3.** to treat with contempt or derision. **4.** (*tr.*) to reject with contempt. —'**scorner** n. —'**scornful** adj. —'**scornful·ly** adv.

Scorpio ('skɔ:pɪ,əʊ) n. **1.** Also called: **Scorpius.** *Astron.* a large S constellation. **2.** *Astrol.* the eighth sign of the zodiac. The sun is in this sign between about Oct. 23 and Nov. 21.

scorpion ('skɔ:pɪən) n. **1.** an arachnid of warm dry regions, having a segmented body with a long tail terminating in a venomous sting. **2. false scorpion.** a small nonvenomous arachnid that superficially resembles the scorpion but lacks the long tail. **3.** *Bible.* a barbed scourge (I Kings 12:11).

Scorpion ('skɔ:pɪən) n. **the.** the constellation Scorpio, the eighth sign of the zodiac.

Scot (skɒt) n. **1.** a native or inhabitant of Scotland. **2.** a member of a tribe of Celtic raiders from northern Ireland who eventually settled in N Britain during the 5th and 6th centuries.

Scot. abbrev. for: **1.** Scotch (whisky). **2.** Scotland. **3.** Scottish.

scotch (skɒtʃ) *vb.* (*tr.*) **1.** to put an end to; crush: *bad weather scotched our plans.* **2.** *Obs.* to cut or score. ~*n.* **3.** *Arch.* a gash. **4.** a line marked down, as for hopscotch.

THESAURUS

scoop n. **1.** dipper, ladle, spoon **2.** exclusive, exposé, inside story, revelation, sensation ~v. **3.** *Often with* **up** clear away, gather up, lift, pick up, remove, sweep up *or* away, take up **4.** bail, dig, dip, empty, excavate, gouge, hollow, ladle, scrape, shovel

scope area, capacity, compass, confines, elbowroom, extent, field of reference, freedom, latitude, liberty, opportunity, orbit, outlook, purview, range, reach, room, space, span, sphere

scorch blacken, blister, burn, char, parch, roast, sear, shrivel, singe, wither

scorching baking, boiling, broiling, burning, fiery, flaming, red-hot, roasting, searing, sizzling, sweltering, torrid, tropical, unbearably hot

score n. **1.** grade, mark, outcome, points, record, result, total **2. the score** *Inf.* the facts, the reality, the setup (*Inf.*), the situation, the truth **3.** *Plural* a flock, a great number, an army, a throng, crowds, droves, hosts, hundreds, legions, lots, masses, millions, multitudes, myriads, swarms, very many **4.** account, basis, cause, ground, grounds, reason **5.** a bone to pick, grievance, grudge, injury, injustice, wrong **6. pay off old scores** avenge, get even with (*Inf.*), get one's own back (*Inf.*), give an eye for an eye, give like for like *or* tit for tat, give (someone) a taste of his own medicine, pay (someone) back (in his own coin), repay, requite, retaliate **7.** account, amount due, bill, charge, debt, obligation, reckoning, tab (*U.S. inf.*), tally, total ~v. **8.** achieve, amass, chalk up (*Inf.*), gain, make, notch up (*Inf.*), win **9.** count, keep a tally of, keep count, record, register, tally **10.** crosshatch, cut, deface, gouge, graze, indent, mar, mark, nick, notch, scrape, scratch, slash **11.** *With* **out** *or* **through** cancel, cross out, delete, obliterate, put a line through, strike out **12.** *Music* adapt, arrange, orchestrate, set **13.** gain an advantage, go down well with (someone), impress, make a hit (*Inf.*), make an impact *or* impression, make a point, put oneself across, triumph

score off be one up on (*Inf.*), get the better of, have the laugh on, humiliate, make a fool of, make (someone) look silly, worst

scorn 1. n. contempt, contemptuousness, contumely, derision, despite, disdain, disparagement, mockery, sarcasm, scornfulness, slight, sneer **2.** v. be above, consider beneath one, contemn, curl one's lip at, deride, disdain, flout, hold in contempt, look down on, make fun of, reject, scoff at, scout (*Archaic*), slight, sneer at, spurn, turn up one's nose at (*Inf.*)

scornful contemptuous, contumelious, defiant, derisive, disdainful, haughty, insolent, insulting, jeering, mocking, sarcastic, sardonic, scathing, scoffing, slighting, sneering, supercilious, withering

scornfully contemptuously, disdainfully, dismissively, scathingly, slightingly, with a sneer, with contempt, with disdain, witheringly, with lip curled

Scotch[1] (skɒtʃ) *adj.* **1.** another word for **Scottish**. ~*n.* **2.** the Scots or their language.
▷ **Usage.** In the north of England and in Scotland, *Scotch* is not used outside fixed expressions such as *Scotch whisky*. The use of *Scotch* for *Scots* or *Scottish* is otherwise felt to be incorrect, esp. when applied to persons.

Scotch[2] (skɒtʃ) *n.* Also called: **Scotch whisky.** whisky distilled from fermented malted barley and made in Scotland.

Scotch broth *n. Brit.* a thick soup made from beef stock, vegetables, and pearl barley.

Scotch egg *n. Brit.* a hard-boiled egg enclosed in a layer of sausage meat, covered in egg and crumbs, and fried.

Scotch mist *n.* **1.** a heavy wet mist. **2.** drizzle.

Scotch terrier *n.* another name for **Scottish terrier.**

scot-free *adv., adj.* (*predicative*) without harm, loss, or penalty.

Scotland Yard ('skɒtlənd) *n.* the headquarters of the police force of metropolitan London. Official name: **New Scotland Yard.**

Scots (skɒts) *adj.* **1.** of or characteristic of Scotland, its people, their English dialect, or their Gaelic language. ~*n.* **2.** any of the English dialects spoken or written in Scotland.

Scotsman ('skɒtsmən) *n., pl.* **-men.** a native or inhabitant of Scotland. —**'Scotswoman** *fem. n.*

Scots pine *or* **Scotch pine** *n.* **1.** a coniferous tree of Europe and W and N Asia, having blue-green needle-like leaves and brown cones with a small prickle on each scale. **2.** the wood of this tree.

Scotticism ('skɒtɪˌsɪzəm) *n.* a Scottish idiom, word, etc.

Scottie *or* **Scotty** ('skɒtɪ) *n., pl.* **-ties.** **1.** See **Scottish terrier. 2.** *Inf.* a Scotsman.

Scottish ('skɒtɪʃ) *adj.* of, relating to, or characteristic of Scotland, its people, their Gaelic language, or their English dialect.

Scottish terrier *n.* a small long-haired breed of terrier, usually with a black coat.

scoundrel ('skaundrəl) *n.* a worthless or villainous person.

scour[1] (skauə) *vb.* **1.** to clean or polish (a surface) by washing and rubbing. **2.** to remove dirt from or have the dirt removed from. **3.** (*tr.*) to clear (a channel) by the force of water. **4.** (*tr.*) to remove by or as if by rubbing. **5.** (*tr.*) to cause (livestock) to purge their bowels. ~*n.* **6.** the act of scouring. **7.** the place scoured, esp. by running water. **8.** something that scours, such as a cleansing agent. **9.** (*often pl.*) prolonged diarrhoea in livestock, esp. cattle. —**'scourer** *n.*

scour[2] (skauə) *vb.* **1.** to range over (territory), as in making a search. **2.** to move swiftly or energetically over (territory).

scourge (skɜːdʒ) *n.* **1.** a whip used for inflicting punishment or torture. **2.** a means of inflicting punishment or suffering. **3.** a person who harasses or causes destruction. ~*vb.* (*tr.*) **4.** to whip. **5.** to punish severely. —**'scourger** *n.*

scouse (skaus) *n. Liverpool dialect.* a stew made from left-over meat.

Scouse (skaus) *Brit. inf.* ~*n.* **1.** a person who comes from Liverpool. **2.** the dialect spoken by such a person. ~*adj.* **3.** of or from Liverpool.

scout[1] (skaut) *n.* **1.** a person, ship, or aircraft sent out to gain information. **2.** *Mil.* a person or unit despatched to reconnoitre the position of the enemy, etc. **3.** the act or an instance of scouting. **4.** (esp. at Oxford University) a college servant. **5.** (in Britain) a patrolman of a motoring organization. **6.** *Inf.* a fellow. ~*vb.* **7.** to examine or observe (anything) in order to obtain information. **8.** (*tr.*; sometimes foll. by *out* or *up*) to seek. **9.** (*intr.*, foll. by *about* or *around*) to go in search (for). —**'scouter** *n.*

scout[2] (skaut) *vb. Arch.* to reject (a person, etc.) with contempt.

Scout (skaut) *n.* (*sometimes not cap.*) a boy or (in the U.S.) a girl who is a member of a worldwide movement (the **Scout Association**) founded as the Boy Scouts in England in 1908 by Lord Baden-Powell. British female counterpart: **Guide.** —**'Scouting** *n.*

Scouter ('skautə) *n.* the leader of a troop of Scouts. Also called (esp. formerly): **Scoutmaster.**

scow (skau) *n.* an unpowered barge used for freight, etc.; lighter.

scowl (skaul) *vb.* **1.** (*intr.*) to contract the brows in a threatening or angry manner. ~*n.* **2.** a gloomy or threatening expression. —**'scowler** *n.*

scrabble ('skræbᵊl) *vb.* **1.** (*intr.*; often foll. by *about* or *at*) to scrape (at) or grope (for), as with hands or claws. **2.** to struggle (with). **3.** (*intr.*; often foll. by *for*) to struggle to gain possession. **4.** to scribble. ~*n.* **5.** the act or an instance of scrabbling. **6.** scribble. **7.** a disorderly struggle. —**'scrabbler** *n.*

Scrabble ('skræbᵊl) *n. Trademark.* a game in which words are formed in a pattern similar to a crossword puzzle.

scrag (skræg) *n.* **1.** a thin or scrawny person or animal. **2.** the lean end of a neck of veal or mutton. **3.** *Inf.* the neck of a human being. ~*vb.* **scragging, scragged. 4.** (*tr.*) *Inf.* to wring the neck of.

scraggly ('skræglɪ) *adj.* **-glier, -gliest.** untidy or irregular.

scraggy ('skrægɪ) *adj.* **-gier, -giest. 1.** lean or scrawny. **2.** rough; unkempt. —**'scraggily** *adv.* —**'scragginess** *n.*

scram (skræm) *vb.* **scramming, scrammed.** (*intr.*; often imperative) *Inf.* to go away hastily.

scramble ('skræmbᵊl) *vb.* **1.** (*intr.*) to climb, crawl, or proceed hurriedly. **2.** (*intr.*; often foll. by *for*) to compete with others, esp. in a disordered manner. **3.** (*intr.*; foll. by *through*) to deal with hurriedly. **4.** (*tr.*) to throw together in a haphazard manner. **5.** (*tr.*) to collect in a hurried or disorganized manner. **6.** (*tr.*) to cook (eggs that have been whisked up with milk) in a pan containing a little melted butter. **7.** *Mil.* to order (a crew or aircraft) to take off immediately or (of a crew or aircraft) to take off immediately. **8.** (*tr.*) to render (speech) unintelligible during transmission by means of an electronic scrambler. ~*n.* **9.** the act of scrambling. **10.** a climb or trek over difficult ground. **11.** a disorderly struggle, esp. to gain possession. **12.** *Mil.* an immediate preparation for action, as of crew, aircraft, etc. **13.** *Brit.* a motorcycle rally in which competitors race across rough open ground.

scrambler ('skræmblə) *n.* an electronic device that renders speech unintelligible during transmission.

scrap[1] (skræp) *n.* **1.** a small piece of something larger; fragment. **2.** an extract from something written. **3. a.** waste material or used articles, esp. metal, often collected and reprocessed. **b.** (*as modifier*): *scrap iron.* **4.** (*pl.*) pieces of discarded food. ~*vb.* **scrapping, scrapped.** (*tr.*) **5.** to discard as useless.

scrap[2] (skræp) *Inf.* ~*n.* **1.** a fight or argument. ~*vb.* **scrapping, scrapped. 2.** (*intr.*) to quarrel or fight.

THESAURUS

Scots Caledonian, Scottish

scoundrel blackguard, caitiff (*Archaic*), cheat, dastard (*Archaic*), good-for-nothing, heel (*Sl.*), incorrigible, knave (*Archaic*), miscreant, ne'er-do-well, rascal, reprobate, rogue, rotter (*Sl.*), scamp, scapegrace, vagabond, villain, wretch

scour[1] abrade, buff, burnish, clean, cleanse, flush, furbish, polish, purge, rub, scrub, wash, whiten

scour[2] beat, comb, forage, go over with a fine-tooth comb, hunt, look high and low, rake, ransack, search

scourge *n.* **1.** affliction, bane, curse, infliction, misfortune, penalty, pest, plague, punishment, terror, torment, visitation **2.** cat,

cat-o'-nine-tails, lash, strap, switch, thong, whip ~*v.* **3.** beat, belt, cane, castigate, chastise, discipline, flog, horsewhip, lash, lather (*Inf.*), leather, punish, take a strap to, tan (someone's) hide (*Sl.*), thrash, trounce, wallop (*Inf.*), whale, whip **4.** afflict, curse, excoriate, harass, plague, terrorize, torment

scout *v.* **1.** case (*Sl.*), check out, investigate, make a reconnaissance, observe, probe, reconnoitre, see how the land lies, spy, spy out, survey, watch **2.** *Often with* **out, up,** *or* **around** cast around for, ferret out, hunt for, look for, rustle up, search for, search out, seek, track down ~*n.* **3.** advance guard, escort, lookout, outrider, precursor, reconnoitrer, vanguard **4.** recruiter, talent scout

scowl 1. *v.* frown, glower, look daggers at, lower **2.** *n.* black look, dirty look, frown, glower

scramble *v.* **1.** clamber, climb, crawl, move with difficulty, push, scrabble, struggle, swarm **2.** contend, hasten, jockey for position, jostle, look lively *or* snappy (*Inf.*), make haste, push, run, rush, strive, vie ~*n.* **3.** climb, trek **4.** commotion, competition, confusion, free-for-all (*Inf.*), hassle (*Inf.*), hustle, melee, muddle, race, rat race, rush, struggle, tussle

scrap[1] *n.* **1.** atom, bit, bite, crumb, fragment, grain, iota, mite, modicum, morsel, mouthful, part, particle, piece, portion, sliver, snatch, snippet, trace **2.** junk, off cuts,

scrapbook ('skræp,bʊk) n. a book or album of blank pages in which to mount newspaper cuttings, pictures, etc.

scrape (skreɪp) vb. 1. to move (a rough or sharp object) across (a surface), esp. to smooth or clean. 2. (tr., often foll. by *away* or *off*) to remove (a layer) by rubbing. 3. to produce a harsh or grating sound by rubbing against (a surface, etc.). 4. (tr.) to injure or damage by rough contact: *to scrape one's knee.* 5. (intr.) to be very economical (esp. in **scrimp and scrape**). 6. (intr.) to draw the foot backwards in making a bow. 7. **bow and scrape.** to behave with excessive humility. 8. **scrape acquaintance with.** to contrive an acquaintance with. ~n. 9. the act of scraping. 10. a scraped place. 11. a harsh or grating sound. 12. *Inf.* an awkward or embarrassing predicament. 13. *Inf.* a conflict or struggle. —'**scraper** n.

scrape through vb. (adv.) 1. (intr.) to manage or survive with difficulty. 2. to succeed in with difficulty or by a narrow margin.

scrape together or **up** vb. (tr., adv.) to collect with difficulty: *to scrape together money for a new car.*

scrappy ('skræpɪ) adj. **-pier, -piest.** fragmentary; disjointed. —'**scrappily** adv.

scratch (skrætʃ) vb. 1. to mark or cut (the surface of something) with a rough or sharp instrument. 2. (often foll. by *at, out, off,* etc.) to scrape (the surface of something), as with claws, nails, etc. 3. to scrape (the surface of the skin) with the nails, as to relieve itching. 4. to chafe or irritate (a surface, esp. the skin). 5. to make or cause to make a grating sound. 6. (tr.; sometimes foll. by *out*) to erase by or as if by scraping. 7. (tr.) to write or draw awkwardly. 8. (intr.; sometimes foll. by *along*) to earn a living, manage, etc., with difficulty. 9. to withdraw (an entry) from a race, (U.S.) election, etc. ~n. 10. the act of scratching. 11. a slight injury. 12. a mark made by scratching. 13. a slight grating sound. 14. (in a handicap sport) a competitor or the status of a competitor who has no allowance. 15. **a.** the line from which competitors start in a race. **b.** (formerly) a line drawn on the floor of a prize ring at which the contestants stood to begin fighting. 16. *Billiards, etc.* a lucky shot. 17. **from scratch.** *Inf.* from the very beginning. 18. **up to scratch.** (*usually used with a negative*) *Inf.* up to standard. ~adj. 19. *Sport.* (of a team) assembled hastily. 20. (in a handicap sport) with no allowance or penalty. 21. *Inf.* rough or haphazard. —'**scratcher** n. —'**scratchy** adj.

scrawl (skrɔːl) vb. 1. to write or draw (words, etc.) carelessly or hastily. ~n. 2. careless or scribbled writing or drawing. —'**scrawly** adj.

scrawny ('skrɔːnɪ) adj. **scrawnier, scrawniest.** 1. very thin and bony. 2. meagre or stunted. —'**scrawnily** adv. —'**scrawniness** n.

scream (skriːm) vb. 1. to utter or emit (a sharp piercing cry or similar sound), esp. as of fear, pain, etc. 2. (intr.) to laugh wildly. 3. (intr.) to speak, shout, or behave in a wild manner. 4. (tr.) to bring (oneself) into a specified state by screaming: *she screamed herself hoarse.* 5. (intr.) to be extremely conspicuous: *the colours in the room screamed.* ~n. 6. a sharp piercing cry or sound, esp. one denoting fear or pain. 7. *Inf.* a person

or thing that causes great amusement.

scree (skriː) n. an accumulation of rock fragments at the foot of a cliff or hillside, often forming a sloping heap.

screech[1] (skriːtʃ) n. 1. a shrill or high-pitched sound or cry. ~vb. 2. to utter with or produce a screech. —'**screecher** n. —'**screechy** adj.

screech[2] (skriːtʃ) n. *Canad. sl.* 1. a dark rum. 2. any strong cheap drink.

screech owl n. 1. a small North American owl having a reddish-brown or grey plumage. 2. *Brit.* any owl that utters a screeching cry.

screed (skriːd) n. 1. a long or prolonged speech or piece of writing. 2. a strip of wood, plaster, or metal placed on a surface to act as a guide to the thickness of the cement or plaster coat to be applied. 3. a mixture of cement, sand, and water applied to a concrete slab, etc., to give a smooth surface finish.

screen (skriːn) n. 1. a light movable frame, panel, or partition serving to shelter, divide, hide, etc. 2. anything that serves to shelter, protect, or conceal. 3. a frame containing a mesh that is placed over a window to keep out insects. 4. a decorated partition, esp. in a church around the choir. 5. a sieve. 6. the wide end of a cathode-ray tube, esp. in a television set, on which a visible image is formed. 7. a white or silvered surface, placed in front of a projector to receive the enlarged image of a film or of slides. 8. **the screen.** the film industry or films collectively. 9. *Photog.* a plate of ground glass in some types of camera on which the image of a subject is focused. 10. men or ships deployed around and ahead of a larger military formation to warn of attack. ~vb. (tr.) 11. (sometimes foll. by *off*) to shelter, protect, or conceal. 12. to sieve or sort. 13. to test or check (an individual or group) so as to determine suitability for a task, etc. 14. to examine for the presence of a disease, weapons, etc. 15. to provide with a screen or screens. 16. to project (a film) onto a screen, esp. for public viewing. —'**screenable** adj. —'**screener** n.

screenplay ('skriːn,pleɪ) n. the script for a film, including instructions for sets and camera work.

screen process n. a method of printing using a fine mesh of silk, nylon, etc., treated with an impermeable coating except in the areas through which ink is subsequently forced onto the paper behind. Also called: **silk-screen printing.**

screw (skruː) n. 1. a device used for fastening materials together, consisting of a threaded shank that has a slotted head by which it may be rotated so as to cut its own thread. 2. a threaded cylindrical rod that engages with a similarly threaded cylindrical hole. 3. a thread in a cylindrical hole corresponding with that on the screw with which it is designed to engage. 4. anything resembling a screw in shape or spiral form. 5. a twisting movement of or resembling that of a screw. 6. Also called: **screw-back.** *Billiards, etc.* a stroke in which the cue ball moves backward after striking the object ball. 7. another name for **propeller** (sense 1). 8. *Sl.* a prison guard. 9. *Brit. sl.* salary, wages, or earnings. 10. *Brit.* a small amount of salt, tobacco, etc., in a twist of paper. 11. *Sl.* a person who is mean with money. 12. *Sl.* an old or worthless horse. 13. (*often pl.*) *Sl.* force or compul-

---

THESAURUS

waste 3. **on the scrap heap** discarded, ditched (*Sl.*), jettisoned, put out to grass (*Inf.*), redundant, written off 4. *Plural* bits, leavings, leftovers, remains, scrapings ~v. 5. abandon, break up, demolish, discard, dispense with, ditch (*Sl.*), drop, get rid of, jettison, junk (*Inf.*), shed, throw away or out, throw on the scrapheap, toss out, write off

scrap[2] 1. *n.* argument, battle, brawl, disagreement, dispute, dust-up (*Inf.*), fight, quarrel, row, scuffle, set-to (*Inf.*), squabble, tiff, wrangle 2. *v.* argue, bicker, come to blows, fall out (*Inf.*), fight, have a shouting match (*Inf.*), have words, row, squabble, wrangle

scrape *v.* 1. abrade, bark, graze, rub, scratch, scuff, skin 2. grate, grind, rasp, scratch, screech, set one's teeth on edge, squeak 3. clean, erase, file, remove, rub, scour 4. pinch, save, scrimp, skimp, stint 5. **scrape by, in, through** barely make it, cut it

fine (*Inf.*), get by (*Inf.*), have a close shave (*Inf.*), struggle ~n. 6. *Inf.* awkward or embarrassing situation, difficulty, dilemma, distress, fix (*Inf.*), mess, plight, predicament, pretty pickle (*Inf.*), tight spot (*Inf.*), trouble

scrappy bitty, disjointed, fragmentary, incomplete, perfunctory, sketchy, thrown together

scratch *v.* 1. claw, cut, damage, etch, grate, graze, incise, lacerate, make a mark on, mark, rub, score, scrape 2. annul, cancel, delete, eliminate, erase, pull out, stand down, strike off, withdraw ~n. 3. blemish, claw mark, gash, graze, laceration, mark, scrape 4. **up to scratch** acceptable, adequate, capable, competent, satisfactory, sufficient, up to snuff (*Inf.*), up to standard ~adj. 5. haphazard, hastily prepared, impromptu, improvised, rough, rough-and-ready

scrawl doodle, scrabble, scratch, scribble, squiggle

scream *v.* 1. bawl, cry, holler (*Inf.*), screech, shriek, shrill, sing out, squeal, yell 2. *Fig.* be conspicuous, clash, jar, shriek ~n. 3. howl, outcry, screech, shriek, wail, yell, yelp 4. *Inf.* card (*Inf.*), caution (*Inf.*), character (*Inf.*), comedian, comic, entertainer, hoot (*Brit. inf.*), joker, laugh, riot (*Sl.*), sensation, wit

screech cry, scream, shriek, squawk, squeal, yelp

screen *v.* 1. cloak, conceal, cover, hide, mask, shade, shroud, shut out, veil 2. defend, guard, protect, safeguard, shelter, shield 3. cull, evaluate, examine, filter, gauge, grade, process, riddle, scan, sieve, sift, sort, vet 4. broadcast, present, put on, show ~n. 5. awning, canopy, cloak, concealment, cover, guard, hedge, mantle, shade, shelter, shield, shroud 6. mesh, net, partition, room divider

sion (esp. in **put the screws on**). **14.** *Taboo sl.* sexual intercourse. **15. have a screw loose.** *Sl.* to be insane. ~*vb.* **16.** (*tr.*) to rotate (a screw or bolt) so as to drive it into or draw it out of a material. **17.** (*tr.*) to cut a screw thread in (a rod or hole) with a tap or die or on a lathe. **18.** to turn or cause to turn in the manner of a screw. **19.** (*tr.*) to attach or fasten with a screw or screws. **20.** (*tr.*) *Inf.* to take advantage of; cheat. **21.** (*tr.*; often foll. by *up*) *Inf.* to distort or contort: *he screwed his face into a scowl*. **22.** (*tr.*) *Inf.* to coerce or force. **23.** *Taboo sl.* to have sexual intercourse (with). **24.** (*tr.*) *Inf.* to burgle. **25. have one's head screwed on the right way.** *Inf.* to be sensible. ~See also **screw up**. —**'screwer** *n.*

screwball ('skruː,bɔːl) *U.S. sl.* ~*n.* **1.** an odd or eccentric person. ~*adj.* **2.** odd; eccentric.

screwdriver ('skruː,draɪvə) *n.* **1.** a tool used for turning screws, usually having a steel shank with a flattened square-cut tip that fits into a slot in the head of the screw. **2.** an alcoholic beverage consisting of orange juice and vodka.

screwed (skruːd) *adj.* **1.** fastened by a screw or screws. **2.** having spiral grooves like a screw. **3.** twisted or distorted. **4.** *Brit. sl.* drunk.

screw top *n.* a bottle top that screws onto the bottle, allowing the bottle to be resealed after use. —**'screw-top** *adj.*

screw up *vb.* (*tr.*, *adv.*) **1.** to twist out of shape or distort. **2.** to summon up: *to screw up one's courage*. **3.** *Inf.* to mishandle or bungle.

screwy ('skruːɪ) *adj.* **screwier**, **screwiest.** *Inf.* odd, crazy, or eccentric.

scribble ('skrɪbəl) *vb.* **1.** to write or draw in a hasty or illegible manner. **2.** to make meaningless or illegible marks (on). **3.** *Derog. or facetious.* to write poetry, novels, etc. ~*n.* **4.** hasty careless writing or drawing. **5.** meaningless or illegible marks. —**'scribbler** *n.* —**'scribbly** *adj.*

scribe (skraɪb) *n.* **1.** a person who copies documents, esp. a person who made handwritten copies before the invention of printing. **2.** a clerk or public copyist. **3.** *Bible.* a recognized scholar and teacher of the Jewish Law. ~*vb.* **4.** to score a line on (a surface) with a pointed instrument, as in metalworking. —**'scribal** *adj.*

scrim (skrɪm) *n.* a fine open-weave fabric, used in the theatre to create the illusion of a solid wall.

scrimmage ('skrɪmɪdʒ) *n.* **1.** a rough or disorderly struggle. **2.** *American football.* the period of a game from the time the ball goes into play to the time it is declared dead. ~*vb.* **3.** (*intr.*) to engage in a scrimmage. **4.** (*tr.*) to put (the ball) into a scrimmage. —**'scrimmager** *n.*

scrimp (skrɪmp) *vb.* **1.** (when *intr.*, sometimes foll. by *on*) to be very sparing in the use (of) (esp. in **scrimp and scrape**). **2.** (*tr.*) to treat meanly: *he is scrimping his children*. —**'scrimpy** *adj.* —**'scrimpiness** *n.*

scrip (skrɪp) *n.* **1.** a written certificate, list, etc. **2.** a small scrap, esp. of paper with writing on it. **3.** *Finance.* **a.** a certificate representing a claim to part of a share of stock. **b.** the shares issued by a company (**scrip** or **bonus issue**) without charge and distributed among existing shareholders.

script (skrɪpt) *n.* **1.** handwriting as distinguished from print. **2.** the letters, characters, or figures used in writing by hand. **3.** any system or style of writing. **4.** written copy for the use of performers in films and plays. **5.** *Law.* an original or principal document. **6.** an answer paper in an examination. ~*vb.* **7.** (*tr.*) to write a script (for).

scripture ('skrɪptʃə) *n.* a sacred, solemn, or authorita-

tive book or piece of writing. —**'scriptural** *adj.*

Scripture ('skrɪptʃə) *n.* **1.** Also called: **Holy Scripture, Holy Writ, the Scriptures.** *Christianity.* the Old and New Testaments. **2.** any book or body of writings, esp. when regarded as sacred by a particular religious group.

scriptwriter ('skrɪpt,raɪtə) *n.* a person who prepares scripts, esp. for a film. —**'script,writing** *n.*

scrivener ('skrɪvnə) *n. Arch.* **1.** a person who writes out deeds, etc. **2.** a notary.

scrofula ('skrɒfjʊlə) *n. Pathol.* (*no longer in technical use*) tuberculosis of the lymphatic glands. Also called (formerly): (the) **king's evil.** —**'scrofulous** *adj.*

scroll (skrəʊl) *n.* **1.** a roll of parchment, etc., usually inscribed with writing. **2.** an ancient book in the form of a roll of parchment, papyrus, etc. **3.** a decorative carving or moulding resembling a scroll. ~*vb.* **4.** (*tr.*) to saw into scrolls. **5.** to roll up like a scroll.

Scrooge (skruːdʒ) *n.* a mean or miserly person.

scrotum ('skrəʊtəm) *n.*, *pl.* **-ta** (-tə) *or* **-tums.** the pouch of skin containing the testes in most mammals. —**'scrotal** *adj.*

scrounge (skraʊndʒ) *vb. Inf.* **1.** (when *intr.*, sometimes foll. by *around*) to search in order to acquire (something) without cost. **2.** to obtain or seek to obtain (something) by begging. —**'scrounger** *n.*

scrub[1] (skrʌb) *vb.* **scrubbing, scrubbed. 1.** to rub (a surface, etc.) hard, with or as if with a brush, soap, and water, in order to clean it. **2.** to remove (dirt) by rubbing with a brush, etc., and water. **3.** (*intr.*; foll. by *up*) (of a surgeon) to wash the hands and arms thoroughly before operating. **4.** (*tr.*) to purify (a gas) by removing impurities. **5.** (*tr.*) *Inf.* to delete or cancel. ~*n.* **6.** the act of or an instance of scrubbing.

scrub[2] (skrʌb) *n.* **1. a.** vegetation consisting of stunted trees, bushes, and other plants growing in an arid area. **b.** (*as modifier*): *scrub vegetation*. **2.** an area of arid land covered with such vegetation. **3. a.** an animal of inferior breeding or condition. **b.** (*as modifier*): *a scrub bull*. **4.** a small person. **5.** anything stunted or inferior. **6.** *Sport, U.S.* **a.** a player not in the first team. **b.** a team composed of such players. **7. the scrub.** *Austral. inf.* a remote or uncivilized place. ~*adj.* (*prenominal*) **8.** small or inferior. **9.** *Sport, U.S.* **a.** (of a player) not in the first team. **b.** (of a team) composed of such players.

scrubber ('skrʌbə) *n.* **1.** a person or thing that scrubs. **2.** an apparatus for purifying a gas. **3.** *Derog. sl.* a promiscuous girl.

scrubby ('skrʌbɪ) *adj.* **-bier, -biest. 1.** covered with or consisting of scrub. **2.** (of trees, etc.) stunted in growth. **3.** *Brit. inf.* messy.

scruff (skrʌf) *n.* the nape of the neck (esp. in **by the scruff of the neck**).

scruffy ('skrʌfɪ) *adj.* **scruffier, scruffiest.** unkempt or shabby.

scrum (skrʌm) *n.* **1.** *Rugby.* the act or method of restarting play when the two opposing packs of forwards group together with heads down and arms interlocked and push to gain ground while the scrum half throws the ball in and the hookers attempt to scoop it out to their own team. **2.** *Inf.* a disorderly struggle. ~*vb.* **scrumming, scrummed. 3.** (*intr.*; usually foll. by *down*) *Rugby.* to form a scrum.

scrum half *n. Rugby.* **1.** a player who puts in the ball at scrums and tries to get it away to his three-quarter backs. **2.** this position in a team.

scrummage ('skrʌmɪdʒ) *n.*, *vb.* **1.** *Rugby.* another word for **scrum. 2.** a variant of **scrimmage.**

scrump (skrʌmp) *vb. Brit. dialect.* to steal (apples) from

---

screw *v.* **1.** tighten, turn, twist, work in **2.** contort, contract, crumple, distort, pucker, wrinkle **3.** *Inf.* bring pressure to bear on, coerce, constrain, force, hold a knife to (someone's) throat, oppress, pressurize, put the screws on (*Inf.*), squeeze **4.** *Inf.* Often with **out of** bleed, extort, extract, wrest, wring

scribble *v.* dash off, doodle, jot, pen, scratch, scrawl, write

scribe amanuensis, clerk, copyist, notary (*Archaic*), penman (*Rare*), scrivener (*Archaic*), secretary, writer

script **1.** calligraphy, hand, handwriting, letters, longhand, penmanship, writing **2.**

book, copy, dialogue, libretto, lines, manuscript, text, words

Scripture Holy Bible, Holy Scripture, Holy Writ, The Bible, The Book of Books, The Good Book, The Gospels, The Scriptures, The Word, The Word of God

scroll inventory, list, parchment, roll

Scrooge meanie (*Inf.*), miser, moneygrubber (*Inf.*), niggard, penny-pincher (*Inf.*), skinflint, tightwad (*U.S. sl.*)

scrounge beg, bum (*Inf., chiefly U.S.*), cadge, forage for, freeload (*U.S. sl.*), hunt around (for), sorn (*Scot.*), sponge (*Inf.*), wheedle

scrounger cadger, freeloader (*U.S. sl.*), parasite, sorner (*Scot.*), sponger (*Inf.*)

scrub *v.* **1.** clean, cleanse, rub, scour **2.** *Inf.* abandon, abolish, call off, cancel, delete, discontinue, do away with, drop, forget about, give up

scruffy disreputable, draggletailed (*Archaic*), frowzy, ill-groomed, mangy, messy, ragged, run-down, scrubby (*Brit. inf.*), seedy, shabby, slatternly, slovenly, sluttish, squalid, tattered, ungroomed, unkempt, untidy

an orchard or garden.

scrumptious ('skrʌmpʃəs) *adj. Inf.* very pleasing; delicious. —'**scrumptiously** *adv.*

scrumpy ('skrʌmpɪ) *n.* a rough dry cider, brewed esp. in the West Country of England.

scrunch (skrʌntʃ) *vb.* 1. to crumple or crunch or to be crumpled or crunched. ~*n.* 2. the act or sound of scrunching.

scruple ('skru:pəl) *n.* 1. a doubt or hesitation as to what is morally right in a certain situation. 2. *Arch.* a very small amount. 3. a unit of weight equal to 20 grains (1.296 grams). ~*vb.* 4. (*obs. when tr.*) to have doubts (about), esp. from a moral compunction.

scrupulous ('skru:pjʊləs) *adj.* 1. characterized by careful observation of what is morally right. 2. very careful or precise. —'**scrupulously** *adv.* —'**scrupulousness** *n.*

scrutinize *or* **-nise** ('skru:tɪˌnaɪz) *vb.* (*tr.*) to examine carefully or in minute detail. —'**scrutiˌnizer** *or* **-ˌniser** *n.*

scrutiny ('skru:tɪnɪ) *n., pl.* **-nies.** 1. close or minute examination. 2. a searching look. 3. (in the early Christian Church) a formal testing that catechumens had to undergo before being baptized.

scuba ('skju:bə) *n.* an apparatus used in skindiving, consisting of a cylinder or cylinders containing compressed air attached to a breathing apparatus.

scud (skʌd) *vb.* **scudding, scudded.** (*intr.*) 1. (esp. of clouds) to move along swiftly and smoothly. 2. *Naut.* to run before a gale. ~*n.* 3. the act of scudding. 4. **a.** a formation of low ragged clouds driven by a strong wind beneath rain-bearing clouds. **b.** a sudden shower or gust of wind.

scuff (skʌf) *vb.* 1. to drag (the feet) while walking. 2. to scratch (a surface) or (of a surface) to become scratched. 3. (*tr.*) *U.S.* to poke at (something) with the foot. ~*n.* 4. the act or sound of scuffing. 5. a rubbed place caused by scuffing. 6. a backless slipper.

scuffle ('skʌfəl) *vb.* (*intr.*) 1. to fight in a disorderly manner. 2. to move by shuffling. ~*n.* 3. a disorderly struggle. 4. the sound made by scuffling.

scull (skʌl) *n.* 1. a single oar moved from side to side over the stern of a boat to propel it. 2. one of a pair of short-handled oars, both of which are pulled by one oarsman. 3. a racing shell propelled by a single oarsman pulling two oars. 4. an act, instance, period, or distance of sculling. ~*vb.* 5. to propel (a boat) with a scull. —'**sculler** *n.*

scullery ('skʌlərɪ) *n., pl.* **-leries.** *Chiefly Brit.* a small room or part of a kitchen where kitchen utensils are kept and pans are washed.

scullion ('skʌljən) *n.* 1. a mean or despicable person. 2. *Arch.* a servant employed to work in a kitchen.

sculpt (skʌlpt) *vb.* 1. a variant of **sculpture.** 2. (*intr.*) to practise sculpture. ~Also: **sculp.**

sculptor ('skʌlptə) *or* (*fem.*) **sculptress** *n.* a person who practises sculpture.

sculpture ('skʌlptʃə) *n.* 1. the art of making figures or designs in relief or the round by carving wood, moulding plaster, etc., or casting metals, etc. 2. works or a work made in this way. 3. ridges or indentations as on a shell, formed by natural processes. ~*vb.* (*mainly tr.*) 4. (*also intr.*) to carve, cast, or fashion (stone, bronze, etc.) three-dimensionally. 5. to portray (a person, etc.) by means of sculpture. 6. to form in the manner of sculpture. 7. to decorate with sculpture. —'**sculptural** *adj.*

scum (skʌm) *n.* 1. a layer of impure matter that forms on the surface of a liquid, often as the result of boiling or fermentation. 2. the greenish film of algae and similar vegetation surface of a stagnant pond. 3. the skin of oxides or impurities on the surface of a molten metal. 4. waste matter. 5. a worthless person or group of people. ~*vb.* **scumming, scummed.** 6. (*tr.*) to remove scum from. 7. (*intr.*) *Rare.* to form a layer of or become covered with scum. —'**scummy** *adj.*

scumble ('skʌmbəl) *vb.* 1. (in painting and drawing) to soften or blend (an outline or colour) with an upper coat of opaque colour, applied very thinly. 2. to produce an effect of broken colour on doors, panelling, etc. by exposing coats of paint below the top coat. ~*n.* 3. the upper layer of colour applied in this way.

scunner ('skʌnə) *Dialect, chiefly Scot.* ~*vb.* 1. (*intr.*) to feel aversion. 2. (*tr.*) to produce a feeling of aversion in. ~*n.* 3. a strong aversion (often in **take a scunner**). 4. an object of dislike.

scupper[1] ('skʌpə) *n. Naut.* a drain or spout allowing water on the deck of a vessel to flow overboard.

scupper[2] ('skʌpə) *vb.* (*tr.*) *Brit. sl.* to overwhelm, ruin, or disable.

scurf (skɜːf) *n.* 1. another name for **dandruff.** 2. flaky or scaly matter adhering to or peeling off a surface. —'**scurfy** *adj.*

scurrilous ('skʌrɪləs) *adj.* 1. grossly or obscenely abusive or defamatory. 2. characterized by gross or obscene humour. —**scurrility** (skə'rɪlɪtɪ) *n.* —'**scurrilously** *adv.*

scurry ('skʌrɪ) *vb.* **-rying, -ried.** 1. to move about hurriedly. 2. (*intr.*) to whirl about. ~*n., pl.* **-ries.** 3. the act or sound of scurrying. 4. a brisk light whirling movement, as of snow.

scurvy ('skɜːvɪ) *n.* 1. a disease caused by a lack of vitamin C, characterized by anaemia, spongy gums, and bleeding beneath the skin. ~*adj.* **-vier, -viest.** 2. mean or despicable. —'**scurvily** *adv.* —'**scurviness** *n.*

scut (skʌt) *n.* the short tail of animals such as the deer and rabbit.

scuttle[1] ('skʌtəl) *n.* 1. See **coal scuttle.** 2. *Dialect, chiefly Brit.* a shallow basket for carrying vegetables, etc. 3. the part of a motorcar body lying immediately behind the bonnet.

scuttle[2] ('skʌtəl) *vb.* 1. (*intr.*) to run or move about with short hasty steps. ~*n.* 2. a hurried pace or run.

scuttle[3] ('skʌtəl) *vb.* 1. (*tr.*) *Naut.* to cause (a vessel) to sink by opening the seacocks or making holes in the bottom. 2. (*tr.*) to give up (hopes, plans, etc.). ~*n.* 3. *Naut.* a small hatch or its cover.

Scylla ('sɪlə) *n.* 1. *Greek myth.* a sea nymph transformed into a sea monster believed to drown sailors navigating the Straits of Messina. Cf. **Charybdis.** 2. **between Scylla and Charybdis.** in a predicament in which avoidance of either of two dangers means exposure to the other.

scythe (saɪð) *n.* 1. a long-handled implement for cutting grass, etc., having a curved sharpened blade that moves in a plane parallel to the ground. ~*vb.* 2. (*tr.*) to cut (grass, etc.) with a scythe.

SDP *abbrev. for* Social Democratic Party.

Se *the chemical symbol for* selenium.

SE *abbrev. for* southeast(ern).

sea (si:) *n.* 1. **a.** (usually preceded by *the*) the mass of salt water on the earth's surface as differentiated from the land. Related adjs.: **marine, maritime. b.** (*as modifi-*

THESAURUS

scruple 1. *v.* balk at, be loath, be reluctant, demur, doubt, falter, have misgivings about, have qualms about, hesitate, stick at, think twice about, vacillate, waver 2. *n.* caution, compunction, difficulty, doubt, hesitation, misgiving, perplexity, qualm, reluctance, second thoughts, squeamishness, twinge of conscience, uneasiness

scrupulous careful, conscientious, exact, fastidious, honourable, meticulous, minute, moral, nice, painstaking, precise, principled, punctilious, rigorous, strict, upright

scrutinize analyse, dissect, examine, explore, inquire into, inspect, investigate, peruse, pore over, probe, scan, search, sift, study

scrutiny analysis, close study, examination, exploration, inquiry, inspection, investigation, perusal, search, sifting, study

scuffle 1. *v.* clash, come to blows, contend, exchange blows, fight, grapple, jostle, struggle, tussle 2. *n.* affray (*Law*), brawl, commotion, disturbance, fight, fray, ruck (*Sl.*), ruckus (*Inf.*), ruction (*Inf.*), rumpus, scrap (*Inf.*), set-to (*Inf.*), tussle

sculpture *v.* carve, chisel, cut, fashion, form, hew, model, mould, sculp, sculpt, shape

scum 1. algae, crust, dross, film, froth, impurities, offscourings, scruff 2. *Fig. canaille,* dregs of society, lowest of the low, rabble, ragtag and bobtail, riffraff, rubbish, trash (*Chiefly U.S.*)

scurrility abusiveness, billingsgate, coarseness, grossness, indecency, infamousness, invective, obloquy, obscenity, offensiveness, scurrilousness, vituperation

scurrilous abusive, coarse, defamatory, foul, foul-mouthed, gross, indecent, infamous, insulting, low, obscene, offensive, Rabelaisian, ribald, salacious, scabrous, scandalous, slanderous, vituperative, vulgar

scurry 1. *v.* dart, dash, fly, hurry, race, scamper, scoot, scud, scuttle, skim, sprint, whisk 2. *n.* bustle, flurry, scampering, whirl

scuttle bustle, hare (*Brit. inf.*), hasten, hurry, run, rush, scamper, scoot, scramble, scud, scurry, scutter (*Brit. inf.*)

er): **sea air. 2.** (*cap. when part of place name*) **a.** one of the smaller areas of ocean: *the Irish Sea.* **b.** a large inland area of water: *the Caspian Sea.* **3.** turbulence or swell: *heavy seas.* **4.** (*cap. when part of a name*) *Astron.* any of many huge dry plains on the surface of the moon: *Sea of Serenity.* See also **mare**². **5.** anything resembling the sea in size or apparent limitlessness. **6. at sea. a.** on the ocean. **b.** in a state of confusion. **7. go to sea.** to become a sailor. **8. put (out) to sea.** to embark on a sea voyage.

sea anchor *n. Naut.* any device, such as a bucket, dragged in the water to slow a vessel.

sea anemone *n.* any of various coelenterates having a polypoid body with oral rings of tentacles.

sea bird *n.* a bird such as a gull, that lives on the sea.

seaboard ('siː,bɔːd) *n. Chiefly U.S.* land bordering on the sea.

seaborne ('siː,bɔːn) *adj.* **1.** carried on or by the sea. **2.** transported by ship.

sea breeze *n.* a wind blowing from the sea to the land, esp. during the day when the land surface is warmer.

seacoast ('siː,kəust) *n.* land bordering on the sea; coast.

sea cow *n.* **1.** a dugong or manatee. **2.** an archaic name for **walrus.**

sea dog *n.* an experienced or old sailor.

seafarer ('siː,fɛərə) *n.* **1.** a traveller who goes by sea. **2.** a sailor.

seafaring ('siː,fɛərɪŋ) *adj.* (*prenominal*) **1.** travelling by sea. **2.** working as a sailor. ~*n.* **3.** the act of travelling by sea. **4.** the work of a sailor.

seafood ('siː,fuːd) *n.* edible saltwater fish or shellfish.

sea-girt *adj. Literary.* surrounded by the sea.

seagoing ('siː,gəuɪŋ) *adj.* intended for or used at sea.

sea green *n., adj.* (of) a moderate green colour, sometimes with a bluish or yellowish tinge.

sea gull *n.* **1.** a popular name for the **gull** (the bird). **2.** *N.Z. inf.* a casual dock worker.

sea horse *n.* **1.** a marine teleost fish of temperate and tropical waters, having a bony-plated body, a prehensile tail, and a horselike head and swimming in an upright position. **2.** an archaic name for the **walrus.** **3.** a fabled sea creature with the tail of a fish and the front parts of a horse.

sea kale *n.* a European coastal plant with broad fleshy leaves and white flowers: cultivated for its edible asparagus-like shoots. Cf. **kale.**

seal¹ (siːl) *n.* **1.** a device impressed on a piece of wax, etc., fixed to a letter, etc., as a mark of authentication. **2.** a stamp, ring, etc., engraved with a device to form such an impression. **3.** a substance, esp. wax, so placed over an envelope, etc., that it must be broken before the object can be opened or used. **4.** any substance or device used to close or fasten tightly. **5.** a small amount of water contained in the trap of a drain to prevent the passage of foul smells. **6.** anything that gives a pledge or confirmation. **7.** a token; sign: *seal of death.* **8.** a decorative stamp sold in aid of charity. **9.** *R.C. Church.* Also called: **seal of confession.** the obligation never to reveal anything said in confession. **10. set one's seal on** (*or* **to**). **a.** to mark with one's sign or seal. **b.** to endorse. ~*vb.* (*tr.*) **11.** to affix a seal to, as proof of authenticity, etc. **12.** to stamp with or as if with a seal. **13.** to approve or authorize. **14.** (sometimes foll. by *up*) to close or secure with or as if with a seal: *to seal one's lips.* **15.** (foll. by *off*) to enclose (a place) with a fence, etc. **16.** to decide irrevocably. **17.** to close tightly so as to render airtight or watertight. **18.** to subject (the outside of meat, etc.) to fierce heat so as to retain the juices during cooking. **19.** to paint (a porous material) with a nonporous coating. **20.** *Austral.* to cover (a road) with bitumen, asphalt, tarmac, etc. —'**sealable** *adj.*

seal² (siːl) *n.* **1.** a fish-eating mammal with four flippers which is aquatic but comes on shore to breed. **2.** sealskin. ~*vb.* **3.** (*intr.*) to hunt for seals. —'**sealer** *n.* —'**seal-,like** *adj.*

sealant ('siːlənt) *n.* **1.** any substance, such as wax, used for sealing documents, bottles, or the like. **2.** any of a number of substances used for waterproofing wood, etc.

sea legs *pl. n. Inf.* **1.** the ability to maintain one's balance on board ship. **2.** the ability to resist seasickness.

sea level *n.* the level of the surface of the sea with respect to the land, taken to be the mean level between high and low tide.

sealing wax *n.* a hard material made of shellac, turpentine, and pigment that softens when heated.

sea lion *n.* any of various large eared seals, such as the **Californian sea lion,** of the N Pacific, often used as a performing animal.

Sea Lord *n.* (in Britain) either of the two serving naval officers (**First** and **Second Sea Lords**) who sit on the admiralty board of the Ministry of Defence.

seal ring *n.* another term for **signet ring.**

sealskin ('siːl,skɪn) *n.* **a.** the skin or pelt of a fur seal, esp. when dressed with the outer hair removed and the underfur dyed dark brown. **b.** (*as modifier*): *a sealskin coat.*

seam (siːm) *n.* **1.** the line along which pieces of fabric, etc., are joined, esp. by stitching. **2.** a ridge or line made by joining two edges. **3.** a stratum of coal, ore, etc. **4.** a linear indentation, such as a wrinkle or scar. **5.** (*modifier*) *Cricket.* of or relating to a style of bowling in which the bowler utilizes the stitched seam round the ball in order to make it swing in flight and after touching the ground: *a seam bowler.* **6. bursting at the seams.** full to overflowing. ~*vb.* **7.** (*tr.*) to join or sew together by or as if by a seam. **8.** to mark or become marked with or as if with a seam or wrinkle. —'**seamer** *n.* —'**seamless** *adj.*

seaman ('siːmən) *n., pl.* -**men.** **1.** a naval rating trained in seamanship. **2.** a man who serves as a sailor. **3.** a person skilled in seamanship. —'**seamanly** *adj., adv.* —'**seaman-,like** *adj.*

seamanship ('siːmən,ʃɪp) *n.* skill in and knowledge of the work of navigating, maintaining, and operating a vessel.

seamstress ('sɛmstrɪs) *or* **sempstress** ('sɛmpstrɪs) *n.* a woman who sews and makes clothes, esp. professionally.

seamy ('siːmɪ) *adj.* **seamier, seamiest.** showing the least pleasant aspect; sordid. —'**seaminess** *n.*

seance ('seɪɒns) *n.* a meeting at which spiritualists attempt to receive messages from the spirits of the dead.

seaplane ('siː,pleɪn) *n.* any aircraft that lands on and takes off from water.

seaport ('siː,pɔːt) *n.* **1.** a port or harbour accessible to seagoing vessels. **2.** a town or city located at such a place.

sear (sɪə) *vb.* (*tr.*) **1.** to scorch or burn the surface of. **2.** to brand with a hot iron. **3.** to cause to wither. **4.** *Rare.* to make unfeeling. ~*adj.* **5.** *Poetic.* dried up.

search (sɜːtʃ) *vb.* **1.** to look through (a place, etc.) thoroughly in order to find someone or something. **2.** (*tr.*) to examine (a person) for concealed objects. **3.** to look at or examine (something) closely: *to search one's conscience.* **4.** (*tr.*; foll. by *out*) to discover by investigation. **5.** *Surgery.* to probe (a wound, etc.). **6.** *Arch.* to penetrate. **7. search me.** *Inf.* I don't know. ~*n.* **8.** the act or an instance of searching. **9.** the examination of a vessel by the right of search. **10. right of search.** *International law.* the right possessed by the warships of a belligerent state to search merchant vessels to ascertain whether ship or cargo is liable to seizure. —'**searchable** *adj.* —'**searcher** *n.*

THESAURUS

sea *n.* **1.** main, ocean, the briny (*Inf.*), the deep, the drink (*Inf.*), the waves **2.** *Fig.* abundance, expanse, mass, multitude, plethora, profusion, sheet, vast number **3. at sea** adrift, astray, at a loss, at sixes and sevens, baffled, bewildered, confused, disoriented, lost, mystified, puzzled, upset ~*adj.* **4.** aquatic, briny, marine, maritime, ocean, oceangoing, oceanic, pelagic, salt, saltwater, seagoing

seafaring marine, maritime, nautical, naval, oceanic

seal *v.* **1.** close, cork, enclose, fasten, make airtight, plug, secure, shut, stop, stopper, stop up, waterproof **2.** assure, attest, authenticate, confirm, establish, ratify, stamp, validate **3.** clinch, conclude, consummate, finalize, settle, shake hands on (*Inf.*) **4. With off** board up, fence off, isolate, put out of bounds, quarantine, segregate ~*n.* **5.** assurance, attestation, authentication, confirmation, imprimatur, insignia, notification, ratification, stamp

seam *n.* **1.** closure, joint, suture (*Surgery*) **2.** layer, lode, stratum, vein **3.** furrow, line, ridge, scar, wrinkle

search *v.* **1.** cast around, check, comb, examine, explore, ferret, frisk (*Inf.*), go over with a fine-tooth comb, inquire, inspect, investigate, leave no stone unturned, look, look high and low, probe, pry, ransack, rifle

searching ('sɜːtʃɪŋ) *adj.* keenly penetrating: *a searching look.* —**'searchingly** *adv.*

searchlight ('sɜːtʃˌlaɪt) *n.* 1. a device that projects a powerful beam of light in a particular direction. 2. the beam of light produced by such a device.

search warrant *n.* a written order issued by a justice of the peace authorizing a constable to enter and search premises for stolen goods, etc.

Sea Scout *n.* a Scout belonging to any of a number of Scout troops whose main activities are canoeing, sailing, etc.

seashell ('siːˌʃɛl) *n.* the empty shell of a marine mollusc.

seashore ('siːˌʃɔː) *n.* 1. land bordering on the sea. 2. *Law.* the land between the marks of high and low water.

seasick ('siːˌsɪk) *adj.* suffering from nausea and dizziness caused by the motion of a ship at sea. —**'sea,sickness** *n.*

seaside ('siːˌsaɪd) *n.* **a.** any area bordering on the sea, esp. one regarded as a resort. **b.** (*as modifier*): *a seaside hotel.*

season ('siːzən) *n.* 1. one of the four equal periods into which the year is divided by the equinoxes and solstices. These periods (spring, summer, autumn, and winter) have characteristic weather conditions, and occur at opposite times of the year in the N and S hemispheres. 2. a period of the year characterized by particular conditions or activities: *the rainy season.* 3. the period during which any particular species of animal, bird, or fish is legally permitted to be caught or killed: *open season on red deer.* 4. any definite or indefinite period. 5. any of the major periods into which the ecclesiastical calendar is divided, such as Lent or Easter. 6. fitting or proper time. 7. **in good season.** early enough. 8. **in season. a.** (of game) permitted to be killed. **b.** (of fresh food) readily available. **c.** (of some female mammals) sexually receptive. **d.** appropriate. ~*vb.* 9. (*tr.*) to add herbs, salt, pepper, or spice to (food). 10. (*tr.*) to add zest to. 11. (in the preparation of timber) to undergo or cause to undergo seasoning. 12. (*tr.; usually passive*) to make or become experienced: *seasoned troops.* 13. (*tr.*) to mitigate or temper. —**'seasoner** *n.*

seasonable ('siːzənəbəl) *adj.* 1. suitable for the season: *a seasonable Christmas scene of a snow-covered village.* 2. taking place at the appropriate time. —**'seasonableness** *n.* —**'seasonably** *adv.*

seasonal ('siːzənəl) *adj.* of, relating to, or occurring at a certain season or certain seasons of the year: *seasonal labour.* —**'seasonally** *adv.*

seasoning ('siːzənɪŋ) *n.* 1. something that enhances the flavour of food, such as salt or herbs. 2. the processing of timber until it has a moisture content suitable for the purposes for which it is to be used.

season ticket *n.* a ticket for a series of events, number of journeys, etc., within a limited time, usually obtained at a reduced rate.

seat (siːt) *n.* 1. a piece of furniture designed for sitting on, such as a chair or sofa. 2. the part of a chair, bench, etc., on which one sits. 3. a place to sit, esp. one that requires a ticket: *I have two seats for the film tonight.* 4. the buttocks. 5. the part of a garment covering the buttocks. 6. the part or area serving as the base of an object. 7. the part or surface on which the base of an object rests. 8. the place or centre in which something is located: *a seat of government.* 9. a place of abode, esp. a country mansion. 10. a membership or the right to membership in a legislative or similar body. 11. *Chiefly Brit.* a parliamentary constituency. 12. the manner in

which a rider sits on a horse. ~*vb.* 13. (*tr.*) to bring to or place on a seat. 14. (*tr.*) to provide with seats. 15. (*tr.; often passive*) to place or centre: *the ministry is seated in the capital.* 16. (*tr.*) to set firmly in place. 17. (*tr.*) to fix or install in a position of power. 18. (*intr.*) (of garments) to sag in the area covering the buttocks: *your thin skirt has seated badly.* —**'seater** *n.*

seat belt *n.* 1. Also called: **safety belt.** a belt or strap worn in a car to restrain forward motion in the event of a collision. 2. a similar belt or strap worn in an aircraft at takeoff and landing.

SEATO ('siːtəʊ) *n. acronym for* South East Asia Treaty Organization; a former anti-Communist defence association for the Far East and the W Pacific (1954–77).

sea trout *n.* a silvery marine variety of the brown trout that migrates to fresh water to spawn.

sea urchin *n.* any echinoderm such as the **edible sea urchin**, having a globular body enclosed in a rigid spiny test and occurring in shallow marine waters.

seaward ('siːwəd) *adv.* 1. Also called: **seawards.** towards the sea. ~*adj.* 2. directed or moving towards the sea. 3. (esp. of a wind) coming from the sea.

seaway ('siːˌweɪ) *n.* 1. a waterway giving access to an inland port. 2. a vessel's progress. 3. a route across the sea.

seaweed ('siːˌwiːd) *n.* any of numerous multicellular marine algae that grow on the seashore, in salt marshes, in brackish water, or submerged in the ocean.

seaworthy ('siːˌwɜːðɪ) *adj.* in a fit condition or ready for a sea voyage. —**'sea,worthiness** *n.*

sebaceous (sɪ'beɪʃəs) *adj.* 1. of or resembling sebum, fat, or tallow. 2. secreting fat.

sebaceous glands *pl. n.* the small glands in the skin that secrete sebum into hair follicles and onto most of the body surface except the soles of the feet and the palms of the hands.

sebum ('siːbəm) *n.* the oily secretion of the sebaceous glands that acts as a lubricant for the hair and skin and provides some protection against bacteria.

sec¹ (sɛk) *adj.* 1. (of wines) dry. 2. (of champagne) of medium sweetness.

sec² (sɛk) *n. Inf.* short for **second²**: *wait a sec.*

sec³ (sɛk) *abbrev. for* secant.

sec. *abbrev. for:* 1. second (of time). 2. secondary. 3. secretary. 4. section. 5. sector.

secant ('siːkənt) *n.* 1. (of an angle) a trigonometric function that in a right-angled triangle is the ratio of the length of the hypotenuse to that of the adjacent side; the reciprocal of cosine. Abbrev.: **sec** 2. a line that intersects a curve.

secateurs ('sɛkətəz) *pl. n. Chiefly Brit.* a small pair of shears for pruning, having a pair of pivoted handles and a single cutting blade that closes against a flat surface.

secede (sɪ'siːd) *vb.* (*intr.; often foll. by from*) (of a person, section, etc.) to make a formal withdrawal of membership, as from a political alliance, etc. —**se'ceder** *n.*

secession (sɪ'sɛʃən) *n.* 1. the act of seceding. 2. (*often cap.*) *Chiefly U.S.* the withdrawal in 1860–61 of 11 Southern states from the Union to form the Confederacy, precipitating the American Civil War. —**se'cession,ism** *n.* —**se'cessionist** *n.*

seclude (sɪ'kluːd) *vb.* (*tr.*) 1. to remove from contact with others. 2. to shut off or screen from view.

secluded (sɪ'kluːdɪd) *adj.* 1. kept apart from the company of others: *a secluded life.* 2. private. —**se'cludedly** *adv.* —**se'cludedness** *n.*

THESAURUS

through, rummage through, scour, scrutinize, seek, sift, turn inside out, turn upside down ~*n.* 2. examination, exploration, going-over (*Inf.*), hunt, inquiry, inspection, investigation, pursuit, quest, researches, rummage, scrutiny 3. **in search of** hunting for, in need of, in pursuit of, looking for, making enquiries concerning, on the lookout for, on the track of, seeking

searching *adj.* close, intent, keen, minute, penetrating, piercing, probing, quizzical, severe, sharp, thorough

seasickness *mal de mer*

season *n.* 1. division, interval, juncture, occasion, opportunity, period, spell, term, time,

time of year ~*v.* 2. colour, enliven, flavour, lace, leaven, pep up, salt, salt and pepper, spice 3. acclimatize, accustom, anneal, discipline, habituate, harden, inure, mature, prepare, toughen, train 4. mitigate, moderate, qualify, temper

seasonable appropriate, convenient, fit, opportune, providential, suitable, timely, welcome, well-timed

seasoned battle-scarred, experienced, hardened, long-serving, mature, old, practised, time-served, veteran, weathered, well-versed

seasoning condiment, dressing, flavouring, relish, salt and pepper, sauce, spice

seat *n.* 1. bench, chair, pew, settle, stall, stool 2. axis, capital, centre, cradle, headquarters, heart, hub, location, place, site, situation, source, station 3. base, bed, bottom, cause, footing, foundation, ground, groundwork 4. abode, ancestral hall, house, mansion, residence 5. chair, constituency, incumbency, membership, place ~*v.* 6. accommodate, cater for, contain, have room *or* capacity for, hold, sit, take 7. deposit, fix, install, locate, place, set, settle, sit

seating accommodation, chairs, places, room, seats

secede apostatize, break with, disaffiliate, leave, pull out, quit, resign, retire, separate,

seclusion (sɪ'klu:ʒən) *n.* **1.** the act of secluding or the state of being secluded. **2.** a secluded place.

second¹ ('sɛkənd) *adj.* (*usually prenominal*) **1. a.** coming directly after the first in numbering or counting order, position, time, etc.; being the ordinal number of *two*: often written 2nd. **b.** (*as n.*): *the second in line.* **2.** graded or ranked between the first and third levels. **3.** alternate: *every second Thursday.* **4.** extra: *a second opportunity.* **5.** resembling a person or event from an earlier period of history: *a second Wagner.* **6.** of lower quality; inferior. **7.** denoting the lowest but one forward ratio of a gearbox in a motor vehicle. **8.** *Music.* denoting a musical part, voice, or instrument subordinate to or lower in pitch than another (the first): *the second violins.* **9.** at **second hand.** by hearsay. ~*n.* **10.** *Brit. education.* an honours degree of the second class, usually further divided into an upper and lower designation. Full term: **second-class honours degree.** **11.** the lowest but one forward ratio of a gearbox in a motor vehicle. **12.** (in boxing, duelling, etc.) an attendant who looks after a competitor. **13.** a speech seconding a motion or the person making it. **14.** *Music.* the interval between one note and another lying next above or below it in the diatonic scale. **15.** (*pl.*) goods of inferior quality. **16.** (*pl.*) *Inf.* a second helping of food. **17.** (*pl.*) the second course of a meal. ~*vb.* (*tr.*) **18.** to give aid or backing to. **19.** (in boxing, etc.) to act as second to (a competitor). **20.** to express formal support for (a motion already proposed). ~*adv.* **21.** Also: **secondly.** in the second place. **22.** ~*sentence connector.* Also: **secondly.** as the second point. —'**seconder** *n.*

▷ **Usage.** See at **important.**

second² ('sɛkənd) *n.* **1. a.** 1/60 of a minute of time. **b.** the basic SI unit of time: the duration of 9 192 631 770 periods of radiation corresponding to the transition between two hyperfine levels of the ground state of caesium-133. Symbol: s **2.** 1/60 of a minute of angle. Symbol:" **3.** a very short period of time.

second³ (sɪ'kɒnd) *vb.* (*tr.*) *Brit.* **1.** to transfer (an employee) temporarily to another branch, etc. **2.** *Mil.* to transfer (an officer) to another post. —se'**condment** *n.*

secondary ('sɛkəndərɪ) *adj.* **1.** one grade or step after the first. **2.** derived from or depending on what is primary or first: *a secondary source.* **3.** below the first in rank, importance, etc. **4.** (*prenominal*) of or relating to the education of young people between the ages of 11 and 18: *secondary education.* **5.** (of the flight feathers of a bird's wing) growing from the ulna. **6. a.** being the part of an electric circuit, such as a transformer or induction coil, in which a current is induced by a changing current in a neighbouring coil: *a secondary coil.* **b.** (of a current) flowing in such a circuit. **7.** *Chem.* **a.** (of an amine) containing the group NH. **b.** (of a salt) derived from a tribasic acid by replacement of two acidic hydrogen atoms with metal atoms. ~*n., pl.* -**aries.** **8.** a person or thing that is secondary. **9.** a subordinate, deputy, or inferior. **10.** a secondary coil, winding, inductance, or current in an electric circuit. **11.** *Ornithol.* any of the flight feathers that grow from the ulna of a bird's wing. **12.** *Astron.* a celestial body that orbits around a specified primary body: *the moon is the secondary of the earth.* **13.** short for **secondary colour.** —'**secondarily** *adv.* —'**secondariness** *n.*

secondary picketing *n.* the picketing by striking workers of a factory, distribution outlet, etc., that supplies goods to or distributes goods from their employer.

second-best *adj.* **1.** next to the best. **2.** come off second best. *Inf.* to be defeated in competition.

second chamber *n.* the upper house of a bicameral legislative assembly.

second childhood *n.* dotage; senility (esp. in **in his, her**, *etc.*, **second childhood**).

second class *n.* **1.** the class or grade next in value, quality, etc., to the first. ~*adj.* (**second-class** *when prenominal*). **2.** of the class or grade next to the best in quality, etc. **3.** shoddy or inferior. **4.** of or denoting the class of accommodation in a hotel or on an aircraft, etc., next in quality and price to first class. **5.** (in Britain) of letters that are handled more slowly than first-class letters. **6.** *Education.* See **second¹** (sense 10). ~*adv.* **7.** by second-class mail, transport, etc.

Second Coming *or* **Advent** *n. Christian theol.* the prophesied return of Christ to earth at the Last Judgment.

second cousin *n.* the child of a first cousin of either of one's parents.

second-degree burn *n. Pathol.* a burn in which blisters appear on the skin.

second floor *n. Brit.* the storey of a building immediately above the first and two floors up from the ground. U.S. term: **third floor.**

second hand *n.* a pointer on the face of a timepiece that indicates the seconds.

second-hand *adj.* **1.** previously owned or used. **2.** not from an original source or experience. **3.** dealing in or selling goods that are not new: *a second-hand car dealer.* ~*adv.* **4.** from a source of previously owned or used goods: *he prefers to buy second-hand.* **5.** not directly: *he got the news second-hand.*

second lieutenant *n.* an officer holding the lowest commissioned rank in the armed forces of certain nations.

secondly ('sɛkəndlɪ) *adv.* another word for **second¹**, usually used to precede the second item in a list of topics.

second nature *n.* a habit, characteristic, etc., long practised or acquired so as to seem innate.

second person *n.* a grammatical category of pronouns and verbs used when referring to or describing the individual or individuals being addressed.

second-rate *adj.* **1.** not of the highest quality; mediocre. **2.** second in importance, etc.

second sight *n.* the alleged ability to foresee the future, see actions taking place elsewhere, etc. —'**second-'sighted** *adj.*

second wind (wɪnd) *n.* **1.** the return of the ability to breathe at a normal rate, esp. following a period of exertion. **2.** renewed ability to continue in an effort.

secrecy ('si:krɪsɪ) *n., pl.* -**cies.** **1.** the state or quality of being secret. **2.** the state of keeping something secret. **3.** the ability or tendency to keep things secret.

secret ('si:krɪt) *adj.* **1.** kept hidden or separate from the knowledge of others. Related adj.: **cryptic.** **2.** known only to initiates: *a secret password.* **3.** hidden from general view or use: *a secret garden.* **4.** able or tending to keep things private or to oneself. **5.** operating without the knowledge of outsiders: *a secret society.* ~*n.* **6.** something kept or to be kept hidden. **7.** something unrevealed; a mystery. **8.** an underlying explanation, reason, etc.: *the secret of success.* **9.** a method, plan, etc., known only to initiates. **10.** *Liturgy.* a prayer said by the celebrant of the Mass after the offertory and before the preface. —'**secretly** *adv.*

THESAURUS

split from, withdraw

secluded cloistered, cut off, isolated, lonely, off the beaten track, out-of-the-way, private, reclusive, remote, retired, sequestered, sheltered, solitary, tucked away, unfrequented

seclusion concealment, hiding, isolation, privacy, remoteness, retirement, retreat, shelter, solitude

second¹ *adj.* **1.** following, next, subsequent, succeeding **2.** additional, alternative, extra, further, other, repeated **3.** inferior, lesser, lower, secondary, subordinate, supporting **4.** double, duplicate, reproduction, twin ~*n.* **5.** assistant, backer, helper, supporter ~*v.* **6.** advance, aid, approve, assist,

back, encourage, endorse, forward, further, give moral support to, go along with, help, promote, support

second² *n.* flash, instant, jiffy (*Inf.*), minute, moment, sec (*Inf.*), split second, tick (*Brit. inf.*), trice, twinkling, twinkling of an eye, two shakes of a lamb's tail (*Inf.*)

secondary **1.** derivative, derived, indirect, resultant, resulting, second-hand **2.** consequential, contingent, inferior, lesser, lower, minor, second-rate, subordinate, unimportant **3.** alternate, auxiliary, backup, extra, relief, reserve, second, subsidiary, supporting

second class *adj.* déclassé, indifferent, inferior, mediocre, outclassed, second-best,

second-rate, undistinguished, uninspiring

second-hand 1. *adj.* handed down, handme-down (*Inf.*), nearly new, reach-me-down (*Inf.*), used **2.** *adv.* at second-hand, indirectly, on the grapevine (*Inf.*)

second in command depute (*Scot.*), deputy, number two, right-hand man, successor designate

secondly in the second place, next, second

second-rate cheap, cheap and nasty (*Inf.*), commonplace, inferior, low-grade, low-quality, mediocre, poor, rubbishy, shoddy, substandard, tacky (*Inf.*), tawdry

secrecy 1. concealment, confidentiality, huggermugger (*Rare*), mystery, privacy, re-

secret agent *n.* a person employed in espionage.

secretariat (ˌsɛkrɪˈtɛərɪət) *n.* **1. a.** an office responsible for the secretarial, clerical, and administrative affairs of a legislative body or international organization. **b.** the staff of such an office. **2.** a body of secretaries. **3.** a secretary's place of work; office. **4.** the position of a secretary.

secretary (ˈsɛkrətrɪ) *n., pl.* **-taries. 1.** a person who handles correspondence, keeps records, and does general clerical work for an individual, organization, etc. **2.** the official manager of the day-to-day business of a society or board. **3.** (in the U.S.) the head of a government administrative department. **4.** (in Britain) See **secretary of state. 5.** Also called (esp. Brit.): **secretaire** (ˌsɛkrɪˈtɛə). an enclosed writing desk, usually having an upper cabinet section. —**secretarial** (ˌsɛkrɪˈtɛərɪəl) *adj.* —'**secretary**ˌship *n.*

secretary bird *n.* a large African long-legged bird of prey having a crest and tail of long feathers and feeding chiefly on snakes.

secretary-general *n., pl.* **secretaries-general.** a chief administrative official, as of the United Nations.

secretary of state *n.* **1.** (in Britain) the head of any of several government departments. **2.** (in the U.S.) the head of the government department in charge of foreign affairs (**State Department**).

secrete[1] (sɪˈkriːt) *vb.* (of a cell, organ, etc.) to synthesize and release (a secretion). —**se**ˈ**cretor** *n.*

secrete[2] (sɪˈkriːt) *vb.* (*tr.*) to put in a hiding place.

secretion (sɪˈkriːʃən) *n.* **1.** a substance that is released from a cell, esp. a glandular cell. **2.** the process involved in producing and releasing such a substance from the cell.

secretive (ˈsiːkrɪtɪv) *adj.* **1.** inclined to secrecy. **2.** another word for **secretory.** —'**secretively** *adv.* —'**secretiveness** *n.*

secretory (sɪˈkriːtərɪ) *adj.* of, relating to, or producing a secretion: *secretory function.*

secret police *n.* a police force that operates relatively secretly to check subversion.

secret service *n.* a government agency or department that conducts intelligence or counterintelligence operations.

sect (sɛkt) *n.* **1.** a subdivision of a larger religious group (esp. the Christian Church as a whole) the members of which have to some extent diverged from the rest by developing deviating beliefs, practices, etc. **2.** *Often disparaging.* **a.** a schismatic religious body. **b.** a religious group regarded as extreme or heretical. **3.** a group of people with a common interest, doctrine, etc..

-sect *vb. combining form.* to cut or divide, esp. into a specified number of parts: *trisect.*

sectarian (sɛkˈtɛərɪən) *adj.* **1.** of, relating to, or characteristic of sects or sectaries. **2.** adhering to a particular sect, faction, or doctrine. **3.** narrow-minded, esp. as a result of rigid adherence to a particular sect. ~*n.* **4.** a member of a sect or faction, esp. one who is intolerant towards other sects, etc. —**sec**ˈ**tarian**ˌism *n.*

section (ˈsɛkʃən) *n.* **1.** a part cut off or separated from the main body of something. **2.** a part or subdivision of a piece of writing, book, etc.: *the sports section of the newspaper.* **3.** one of several component parts. **4.** a dis-

tinct part of a country, community, etc. **5.** *U.S.* an area one mile square. **6.** *N.Z.* a plot of land for building, esp. in a suburban area. **7.** the section of a railway track that is controlled by a particular signal box. **8.** the act or process of cutting or separating by cutting. **9.** *Geom.* **a.** a plane surface formed by cutting through a solid. **b.** the shape or area of such a plane surface. **10.** a thin slice of biological tissue, etc., prepared for examination by microscope. **11.** a segment of an orange or other citrus fruit. **12.** a small military formation. **13.** *Austral. & N.Z.* a fare stage on a bus, tram, etc. **14.** *Music.* **a.** an extended division of a composition or movement: *the development section.* **b.** a division in an orchestra, band, etc., containing instruments belonging to the same class: *the brass section.* **15.** Also called: **signature, gathering.** a folded printing sheet or sheets ready for gathering and binding. ~*vb.* (*tr.*) **16.** to cut or divide into sections. **17.** to cut through so as to reveal a section. **18.** (in drawing, esp. mechanical drawing) to shade so as to indicate sections.

sectional (ˈsɛkʃənəl) *adj.* **1.** composed of several sections. **2.** of or relating to a section. —'**sectiona**ˌ**lize** or **-ise** *vb.* (*tr.*). —'**sectionally** *adv.*

sector (ˈsɛktə) *n.* **1.** a part or subdivision, esp. of a society or an economy: *the private sector.* **2.** *Geom.* either portion of a circle included between two radii and an arc. **3.** a measuring instrument consisting of two graduated arms hinged at one end. **4.** a part or subdivision of an area of military operations. —'**sectoral** *adj.*

secular (ˈsɛkjʊlə) *adj.* **1.** of or relating to worldly as opposed to sacred things. **2.** not concerned with or related to religion. **3.** not within the control of the Church. **4.** (of an education, etc.) having no particular religious affinities. **5.** (of clerics) not bound by religious vows to a monastic or other order. **6.** occurring or appearing once in an age or century. **7.** lasting for a long time. **8.** *Astron.* occurring slowly over a long period of time. ~*n.* **9.** a member of the secular clergy. —**secularity** (ˌsɛkjʊ-ˈlærɪtɪ) *n.* —'**secularly** *adv.*

secularism (ˈsɛkjʊləˌrɪzəm) *n.* **1.** *Philosophy.* a doctrine that rejects religion, esp. in ethics. **2.** the attitude that religion should have no place in civil affairs. —'**secularist** *n.*

secularize or **-rise** (ˈsɛkjʊləˌraɪz) *vb.* (*tr.*) **1.** to change from religious or sacred to secular functions, etc. **2.** to dispense from allegiance to a religious order. **3.** *Law.* to transfer (property) from ecclesiastical to civil possession or use. —ˌ**seculari**ˈ**zation** or **-ri**ˈ**sation** *n.*

secure (sɪˈkjʊə) *adj.* **1.** free from danger, damage, etc. **2.** free from fear, care, etc. **3.** in safe custody. **4.** not likely to fail, become loose, etc. **5.** able to be relied on: *a secure investment.* **6.** *Arch.* overconfident. ~*vb.* **7.** (*tr.*) to obtain: *I will secure some good seats.* **8.** (when *intr.,* often foll. by *against*) to make or become free from danger, fear, etc. **9.** (*tr.*) to make fast or firm. **10.** (when *intr.,* often foll. by *against*) to make or become certain: *this plan will secure your happiness.* **11.** (*tr.*) to assure (a creditor) of payment, as by giving security. **12.** (*tr.*) to make (a military position) safe from attack. **13.** *Naut.* to make (a vessel or its contents) safe or ready by battening down hatches, etc. —**se**ˈ**curable** *adj.* —**se**ˈ**curely** *adv.* —**se**ˈ**curement** *n.* —**se**ˈ**curer** *n.*

THESAURUS

tirement, seclusion, silence, solitude, surreptitiousness **2.** clandestineness, covertness, furtiveness, secretiveness, stealth

secret *adj.* **1.** backstairs, camouflaged, cloak-and-dagger, close, closet (*Inf.*), concealed, conspiratorial, covered, covert, disguised, furtive, hidden, hole-and-corner (*Inf.*), hush-hush (*Inf.*), reticent, shrouded, undercover, underground, under wraps, undisclosed, unknown, unpublished, unrevealed, unseen **2.** abstruse, arcane, cabbalistic, clandestine, classified, cryptic, esoteric, mysterious, occult, recondite **3.** hidden, out-of-the-way, private, retired, secluded, unfrequented, unknown **4.** close, deep, discreet, reticent, secretive, sly, stealthy, underhand ~*n.* **5.** code, confidence, enigma, formula, key, mystery, recipe, skeleton in the cupboard **6. in secret** behind closed doors, by stealth, huggermugger (*Archaic*), in camera, incognito, secretly, slyly, surreptitiously

secrete bury, cache, conceal, cover, disguise, harbour, hide, screen, secure, shroud, stash away (*Inf.*), stow, veil

secretive cagey (*Inf.*), clamlike, close, cryptic, deep, enigmatic, playing one's cards close to one's chest, reserved, reticent, tightlipped, uncommunicative, unforthcoming, withdrawn

secretly behind closed doors, behind (someone's) back, clandestinely, confidentially, covertly, furtively, in camera, in confidence, in one's heart, in one's inmost thoughts, in secret, on the q.t. (*Inf.*), on the sly, privately, quietly, stealthily, surreptitiously, unobserved

sect camp, denomination, division, faction, group, party, school, school of thought, splinter group, wing

sectarian 1. *adj.* bigoted, clannish, cliquish, doctrinaire, dogmatic, exclusive, fac-

tional, fanatic, fanatical, hidebound, insular, limited, narrow-minded, parochial, partisan, rigid **2.** *n.* adherent, bigot, disciple, dogmatist, extremist, fanatic, partisan, true believer, zealot

section *n.* **1.** component, cross section, division, fraction, fragment, instalment, part, passage, piece, portion, sample, segment, slice, subdivision **2.** *Chiefly U.S.* area, department, district, region, sector, zone

sector area, category, district, division, part, quarter, region, stratum, subdivision, zone

secular civil, earthly, laic, laical, lay, nonspiritual, profane, state, temporal, worldly

secure *adj.* **1.** immune, impregnable, out of harm's way, protected, safe, sheltered, shielded, unassailable, undamaged, unharmed **2.** dependable, fast, fastened, firm, fixed, fortified, immovable, stable, steady,

security (sɪˈkjʊərɪtɪ) n., pl. **-ties.** **1.** the state of being secure. **2.** assured freedom from poverty or want: *he needs the security of a permanent job.* **3.** a person or thing that secures, guarantees, etc. **4.** precautions taken to ensure against theft, espionage, etc. **5.** (*often pl.*) **a.** a certificate of creditorship or property carrying the right to receive interest or dividend, such as shares or bonds. **b.** the financial asset represented by such a certificate. **6.** the specific asset that a creditor can claim in the event of default on an obligation. **7.** something given or pledged to secure the fulfilment of a promise or obligation.

Security Council n. an organ of the United Nations established to maintain world peace.

security risk n. a person deemed to be a threat to state security in that he could be open to pressure, have subversive political beliefs, etc.

sedan chair n. a closed chair for one passenger, carried on poles by two bearers, commonly used in the 17th and 18th centuries.

sedate[1] (sɪˈdeɪt) adj. **1.** habitually calm and composed in manner. **2.** sober or decorous. —**se'dately** adv. —**se'dateness** n.

sedate[2] (sɪˈdeɪt) vb. (*tr.*) to administer a sedative to.

sedation (sɪˈdeɪʃən) n. **1.** a state of calm or reduced nervous activity. **2.** the administration of a sedative.

sedative (ˈsɛdətɪv) adj. **1.** having a soothing or calming effect. **2.** of or relating to sedation. ~n. **3.** *Med.* a sedative drug or agent.

sedentary (ˈsɛdəntərɪ) adj. **1.** characterized by or requiring a sitting position: *sedentary work.* **2.** tending to sit about without taking much exercise. **3.** (of animals) moving about very little. **4.** (of birds) not migratory. —**'sedentarily** adv. —**'sedentariness** n.

sedge (sɛdʒ) n. a grasslike plant growing on wet ground and having rhizomes, triangular stems, and minute flowers in spikelets. —**'sedgy** adj.

sedge warbler n. a European songbird of reed beds and swampy areas, having a streaked brownish plumage with white eye stripes.

sediment (ˈsɛdɪmənt) n. **1.** matter that settles to the bottom of a liquid. **2.** material that has been deposited from water, ice, or wind. —**ˌsedi'mentary** adj. —**ˌsedimen'tation** n.

sedition (sɪˈdɪʃən) n. **1.** speech or behaviour directed against the peace of a state. **2.** an offence that tends to undermine the authority of a state. **3.** an incitement to public disorder. —**se'ditionary** n., adj. —**se'ditious** adj.

seduce (sɪˈdjuːs) vb. (*tr.*) **1.** to persuade to engage in sexual intercourse. **2.** to lead astray, as from the right action. **3.** to win over, attract, or lure. —**se'ducer** n. —**se'ducible** adj. —**se'duction** n.

seductive (sɪˈdʌktɪv) adj. tending to seduce or capable of seducing; enticing; alluring. —**se'ductively** adv.

—**se'ductiveness** n.

sedulous (ˈsɛdjʊləs) adj. assiduous; diligent. —**sedulity** (sɪˈdjuːlɪtɪ) or **'sedulousness** n. —**'sedulously** adv.

sedum (ˈsiːdəm) n. a rock plant having thick fleshy leaves and clusters of white, yellow, or pink flowers.

see[1] (siː) vb. **seeing, saw, seen.** **1.** to perceive with the eyes. **2.** (when *tr.*, *may take a clause as object*) to understand: *I explained the problem but he could not see it.* **3.** (*tr.*) to perceive with any or all of the senses: *I hate to see you so unhappy.* **4.** (*tr.*; *may take a clause as object*) to foresee: *I can see what will happen if you don't help.* **5.** (when *tr.*, *may take a clause as object*) to ascertain or find out (a fact): *see who is at the door.* **6.** (when *tr.*, takes a clause as object*; when *intr.*, foll. by *to*) to make sure (of something) or take care (of something): *see that he gets to bed early.* **7.** (when *tr.*, *may take a clause as object*) to consider, deliberate, or decide: *see if you can come next week.* **8.** (*tr.*) to have experience of: *he had seen much unhappiness in his life.* **9.** (*tr.*) to allow to be in a specified condition: *I cannot stand by and see a child in pain.* **10.** (*tr.*) to be characterized by: *this period of history has seen much unrest.* **11.** (*tr.*) to meet or pay a visit to: *to see one's solicitor.* **12.** (*tr.*) to receive: *the Prime Minister will see the deputation now.* **13.** (*tr.*) to frequent the company of: *she is seeing a married man.* **14.** (*tr.*) to accompany: *I saw her to the door.* **15.** (*tr.*) to refer to or look up: *for further information see the appendix.* **16.** (in gambling, esp. in poker) to match (another player's bet) or match the bet of (another player) by staking an equal sum. **17. as far as I can see.** to the best of my judgment. **18. see fit.** (*takes an infinitive*) to consider proper, etc.: *I don't see fit to allow her to come here.* **19. see (someone) hanged** or **damned first.** *Inf.* to refuse absolutely to do what one has been asked. **20. see you, see you later,** or **be seeing you.** an expression of farewell. ~See also **see about, see into,** etc.

see[2] (siː) n. the diocese of a bishop, or the place within it where his cathedral is situated.

see about vb. (*intr.*, *prep.*) **1.** to take care of: *he couldn't see about the matter because he was ill.* **2.** to investigate: *to see about a new car.*

seed (siːd) n. **1.** *Bot.* a mature fertilized plant ovule, consisting of an embryo and its food store surrounded by a protective seed coat (testa). Related adj.: **seminal.** **2.** the small hard seedlike fruit of plants such as wheat. **3.** any propagative part of a plant, such as a tuber, spore, or bulb. **4.** the source, beginning, or germ of anything: *the seeds of revolt.* **5.** *Chiefly Bible.* descendants: *the seed of Abraham.* **6.** an archaic term for **sperm** or **semen.** **7.** *Sport.* a seeded player. **8.** *Chem.* a small crystal added to a supersaturated solution to induce crystallization. **9. go** or **run to seed. a.** (of plants) to produce and shed seeds. **b.** to lose vigour, usefulness, etc. ~vb. **10.** to plant (seeds, grain, etc.) in (soil): *we seeded this field with oats.* **11.** (*intr.*) (of plants) to form or shed seeds.

tight **3.** assured, certain, confident, easy, reassured, sure **4.** absolute, conclusive, definite, in the bag (*Inf.*), reliable, solid, steadfast, tried and true, well-founded ~v. **5.** acquire, come by, gain, get, get hold of, land (*Inf.*), make sure of, obtain, pick up, procure, win possession of **6.** attach, batten down, bolt, chain, fasten, fix, lash, lock, lock up, make fast, moor, padlock, rivet, tie up **7.** assure, ensure, guarantee, insure

security 1. asylum, care, cover, custody, immunity, preservation, protection, refuge, retreat, safekeeping, safety, sanctuary **2.** defence, guards, precautions, protection, safeguards, safety measures, surveillance **3.** assurance, certainty, confidence, conviction, ease of mind, freedom from doubt, positiveness, reliance, sureness **4.** collateral, gage, guarantee, hostage, insurance, pawn, pledge, surety

sedate calm, collected, composed, cool, decorous, deliberate, demure, dignified, earnest, grave, imperturbable, middle-aged, placid, proper, quiet, seemly, serene, serious, slow-moving, sober, solemn, staid, tranquil, unflappable (*Inf.*), unruffled

sedative 1. adj. allaying, anodyne, calmative, calming, lenitive, relaxing, sleep-

inducing, soothing, soporific, tranquillizing **2.** n. anodyne, calmative, downer or down (*Sl.*), narcotic, opiate, sleeping pill, tranquillizer

sedentary desk, desk-bound, inactive, motionless, seated, sitting, torpid

sediment deposit, dregs, grounds, lees, precipitate, residuum, settlings

sedition agitation, disloyalty, incitement to riot, rabble-rousing, subversion, treason

seditious disloyal, dissident, insubordinate, mutinous, rebellious, refractory, revolutionary, subversive, treasonable

seduce 1. betray, corrupt, debauch, deflower, deprave, dishonour, ruin (*Archaic*) **2.** allure, attract, beguile, deceive, decoy, ensnare, entice, inveigle, lead astray, lure, mislead, tempt

seduction 1. corruption, defloration, ruin (*Archaic*) **2.** allure, enticement, lure, snare, temptation

seductive alluring, attractive, beguiling, bewitching, captivating, come-hither (*Inf.*), enticing, flirtatious, inviting, irresistible, provocative, ravishing, sexy (*Inf.*), siren, specious, tempting

seductress Circe, enchantress, *femme fatale,* Lorelei, siren, temptress, vamp (*Inf.*)

see v. **1.** behold, catch a glimpse of, catch

sight of, descry, discern, distinguish, espy, get a load of (*Sl.*), glimpse, heed, identify, lay or clap eyes on (*Inf.*), look, make out, mark, note, notice, observe, perceive, recognize, regard, sight, spot, view, witness **2.** appreciate, catch on (*Inf.*), comprehend, fathom, feel, follow, get, get the drift of, get the hang of (*Inf.*), grasp, know, make out, realize, take in, understand **3.** ascertain, determine, discover, find out, investigate, learn, make enquiries, refer to **4.** ensure, guarantee, make certain, make sure, mind, see to it, take care **5.** consider, decide, deliberate, give some thought to, judge, make up one's mind, mull over, reflect, think over **6.** confer with, consult, encounter, interview, meet, receive, run into, speak to, visit **7.** accompany, attend, escort, lead, show, usher, walk **8.** consort or associate with, court, date (*Inf., chiefly U.S.*), go out with, go steady with (*Inf.*), keep company with, walk out with (*Obsolete*) **9.** anticipate, divine, envisage, foresee, foretell, imagine, picture, visualize

see about 1. attend to, consider, deal with, give some thought to, look after, see to, take care of **2.** investigate, look into, make enquiries

12. (*tr.*) to remove the seeds from (fruit, etc.). **13.** (*tr.*) *Chem.* to add a small crystal to (a supersaturated solution) in order to cause crystallization. **14.** (*tr.*) to scatter certain substances, such as silver iodide, in (clouds) in order to cause rain. **15.** (*tr.*) to arrange (the draw of a tournament) so that outstanding teams or players will not meet in the early rounds. —'**seeder** *n.* —'**seedless** *adj.*

seedbed ('si:d₁bɛd) *n.* **1.** a plot of land in which seedlings are grown before being transplanted. **2.** the place where something develops.

seedling ('si:dlɪŋ) *n.* a plant produced from a seed, esp. a very young plant.

seed pearl *n.* a tiny pearl weighing less than a quarter of a grain.

seed pod *n.* a carpel or pistil enclosing the seeds of a plant, esp. a flowering plant.

seed vessel *n.* *Bot.* a dry fruit, such as a capsule.

seedy ('si:dɪ) *adj.* **seedier, seediest. 1.** shabby in appearance: *seedy clothes.* **2.** (of a plant) at the stage of producing seeds. **3.** *Inf.* not physically fit. —'**seedily** *adv.* —'**seediness** *n.*

seeing ('si:ɪŋ) *n.* **1.** the sense or faculty of sight. **2.** *Astron.* the condition of the atmosphere with respect to observation of stars, planets, etc. ~*conj.* **3.** (*subordinating*; often foll. by *that*) in light of the fact (that).

see into *vb.* (*intr., prep.*) **1.** to examine or investigate. **2.** to discover the true nature of: *I can't see into your thoughts.*

seek (si:k) *vb.* **seeking, sought.** (*mainly tr.*) **1.** (when *intr.*, often foll. by *for* or *after*) to try to find by searching: *to seek a solution.* **2.** (*also intr.*) to try to obtain or acquire: *to seek happiness.* **3.** to attempt (to do something): *I'm only seeking to help.* **4.** (*also intr.*) to enquire about or request (something). **5.** to resort to: *to seek the garden for peace.* —'**seeker** *n.*

seek out *vb.* (*tr., adv.*) to search hard for and find a specific person or thing: *she sought out her friend from amongst the crowd.*

seem (si:m) *vb.* (may take an infinitive) **1.** (*copula*) to appear to the mind or eye; look: *the car seems to be running well.* **2.** to appear to be: *there seems no need for all this nonsense.* **3.** used to diminish the force of a following infinitive to be polite, more noncommittal, etc.: *I can't seem to get through to you.*

seeming ('si:mɪŋ) *adj.* **1.** (*prenominal*) apparent but not actual or genuine. ~*n.* **2.** outward or false appearance. —'**seemingly** *adv.*

seemly ('si:mlɪ) *adj.* **-lier, -liest. 1.** proper or fitting. **2.** *Obs.* pleasing in appearance. ~*adv.* **3.** *Arch.* decorously.

seen (si:n) *vb.* the past participle of **see**[1].

see off *vb.* (*tr., adv.*) **1.** to be present at the departure of (a person making a journey). **2.** *Inf.* to cause to leave or depart, esp. by force.

seep (si:p) *vb.* **1.** (*intr.*) to pass gradually or leak as if through small openings. ~*n.* **2.** a small spring or place where water, oil, etc., has oozed through the ground. —'**seepage** *n.*

seer (sɪə) *n.* **1.** a person who can supposedly see into the future. **2.** a person who professes supernatural powers.

3. a person who sees.

seersucker ('sɪə₁sʌkə) *n.* a light cotton, linen, or other fabric with a crinkled surface and often striped.

seesaw ('si:₁sɔ:) *n.* **1.** a plank balanced in the middle so that two people seated on the ends can ride up and down by pushing on the ground with their feet. **2.** the pastime of riding up and down on a seesaw. **3.** an up-and-down or back-and-forth movement. ~*vb.* **4.** (*intr.*) to move up and down or back and forth in such a manner.

seethe (si:ð) *vb.* **1.** (*intr.*) to boil or to foam as if boiling. **2.** (*intr.*) to be in a state of extreme agitation. **3.** (*tr.*) to soak in liquid. **4.** (*tr.*) *Arch.* to cook by boiling. —'**seethingly** *adv.*

see through *vb.* **1.** (*tr.*) to help out in time of need or trouble. **2.** (*tr., adv.*) to remain with until the end or completion: *let's see the job through.* **3.** (*intr., prep.*) to perceive the true nature of: *I can see through your evasion.* ~*adj.* **see-through. 4.** partly or wholly transparent or translucent, esp. (of clothes) in a titillating way.

segment *n.* ('sɛgmənt). **1.** *Maths.* **a.** a part of a line or curve between two points. **b.** a part of a plane or solid figure cut off by an intersecting line, plane, or planes. **2.** one of several parts or sections into which an object is divided. **3.** *Zool.* any of the parts into which the body or appendages of an annelid or arthropod are divided. **4.** *Linguistics.* a speech sound considered in isolation. ~*vb.* (sɛg'mɛnt). **5.** to cut or divide (a whole object) into segments. —**segmentary** ('sɛgməntərɪ) *adj.* —**seg-**'**mental** *adj.* —₁**segmen**'**tation** *n.*

segregate ('sɛgrɪ₁geɪt) *vb.* **1.** to set or be set apart from others or from the main group. **2.** (*tr.*) to impose segregation on (a racial or minority group). **3.** *Genetics.* to undergo or cause to undergo segregation. —'**segre-**₁**gative** *adj.* —'**segre**₁**gator** *n.*

segregation (₁sɛgrɪ'geɪʃən) *n.* **1.** the act of segregating or state of being segregated. **2.** *Sociol.* the practice or policy of creating separate facilities within the same society for the use of a particular group. **3.** *Genetics.* the separation at meiosis of the two members of any pair of alleles into separate gametes. —₁**segre**'**gational** *adj.* —₁**segre**'**gationist** *n.*

Seidlitz powder *or* **powders** ('sɛdlɪts) *n.* a laxative consisting of two powders, tartaric acid and a mixture of sodium bicarbonate and Rochelle salt.

seigneur (sɛ'njɜ:; *French* sɛ'nœ:r) *n.* a feudal lord, esp. in France. —**sei**'**gneurial** *adj.*

seigneury ('seɪnjərɪ) *n., pl.* **-gneuries.** the estate of a seigneur.

seignior ('seɪnjə) *n.* **1.** a less common name for a **seigneur. 2.** (in England) the lord of a seigniory. —**seigniorial** (seɪ'njɔ:rɪəl) *adj.*

seigniory ('seɪnjərɪ) *or* **signory** ('si:njərɪ) *n., pl.* **-gniories** *or* **-gnories. 1.** less common names for a **seigneury. 2.** (in England) the fee or manor of a seignior; a feudal domain. **3.** the authority of a seignior.

seine (seɪn) *n.* **1.** a large fishing net that hangs vertically in the water by means of floats at the top and weights at the bottom. ~*vb.* **2.** to catch (fish) using this net.

seismic ('saɪzmɪk) *adj.* relating to or caused by earthquakes or artificially produced earth tremors.

seismo- *or before a vowel* **seism-** *combining form.*

THESAURUS

seed 1. egg, egg cell, embryo, germ, grain, kernel, ovule, ovum, spore **2.** beginning, germ, inkling, nucleus, source, start, suspicion **3.** *Fig.* children, descendants, heirs, issue, offspring, progeny, race, scions, spawn, successors **4. go** *or* **run to seed** decay, decline, degenerate, deteriorate, go downhill (*Inf.*), go to pieces, go to pot, go to rack and ruin, go to waste, let oneself go

seedy 1. crummy (*Sl.*), decaying, dilapidated, down at heel, faded, grubby, mangy, manky (*Scot. dialect*), old, run-down, scruffy (*Brit. inf.*), shabby, sleazy, slovenly, squalid, tatty, unkempt, worn **2.** *Inf.* ailing, ill, off colour, out of sorts, poorly (*Inf.*), sickly, under the weather (*Inf.*), unwell

seeing *conj.* as, inasmuch as, in view of the fact that, since

seek 1. be after, follow, go gunning for, go in pursuit (quest, search) of, hunt, inquire, look for, pursue, search for **2.** aim, aspire to,

attempt, endeavour, essay, have a go (*Inf.*), strive, try **3.** ask, beg, entreat, inquire, invite, petition, request, solicit

seem appear, assume, give the impression, have the *or* every appearance of, look, look as if, look to be, pretend, sound like, strike one as being

seemly appropriate, becoming, befitting, *comme il faut*, decent, decorous, fit, fitting, in good taste, meet (*Archaic*), nice, proper, suitable, suited, the done thing

see over inspect, look round, see round, tour

seer augur, predictor, prophet, sibyl, soothsayer

seesaw *v.* alternate, fluctuate, go from one extreme to the other, oscillate, pitch, swing, teeter

seethe 1. boil, bubble, churn, ferment, fizz, foam, froth **2.** be in a state (*Inf.*), be livid (furious, incensed), breathe fire and slaughter,

foam at the mouth, fume, get hot under the collar (*Inf.*), rage, simmer, storm **3.** be alive with, swarm, teem

see through 1. be undeceived by, be wise to, fathom, get to the bottom of, have (someone's) number (*Inf.*), not fall for, penetrate **2. see (something** *or* **someone) through** help out, keep at, persevere (with), persist, see out, stay to the bitter end, stick by, stick out (*Inf.*), support

see to arrange, attend to, be responsible for, do, look after, manage, organize, sort out, take care of, take charge of

segment bit, compartment, division, part, piece, portion, section, slice, wedge

segregate discriminate against, dissociate, isolate, separate, set apart, single out

segregation apartheid (*in South Africa*), discrimination, isolation, separation

earthquake: *seismology.*

seismograph ('saɪzmə,grɑːf) *n.* an instrument that registers and records earthquakes. A **seismogram** is the record from such an instrument. —**seismographic** (,saɪzmə'græfɪk) *adj.* —**seismographer** (saɪz'mɒgrəfə) *n.* —**seis'mography** *n.*

seismology (saɪz'mɒlədʒɪ) *n.* the branch of geology concerned with the study of earthquakes. —**seismologic** (,saɪzmə'lɒdʒɪk) *or* ,**seismo'logical** *adj.* —,**seismo'logically** *adv.* —**seis'mologist** *n.*

seize (siːz) *vb.* (*mainly tr.*) 1. (also *intr.*, foll. by *on*) to take hold of quickly; grab. 2. to grasp mentally, esp. rapidly: *she immediately seized his idea.* 3. to take mental possession of: *alarm seized the crowd.* 4. to take possession of rapidly and forcibly: *the thief seized the woman's purse.* 5. to take legal possession of. 6. to take by force or capture: *the army seized the undefended town.* 7. to take immediate advantage of: *to seize an opportunity.* 8. *Naut.* to bind (two ropes together). 9. (*intr.; often* foll. by *up*) (of mechanical parts) to become jammed, esp. because of excessive heat. —'**seizable** *adj.*

seizure ('siːʒə) *n.* 1. the act or an instance of seizing or the state of being seized. 2. *Pathol.* a sudden manifestation or recurrence of a disease, such as an epileptic convulsion.

seldom ('sɛldəm) *adv.* rarely.

select (sɪ'lɛkt) *vb.* 1. to choose (someone or something) in preference to another or others. ~*adj.* *also* **selected.** 2. chosen in preference to others. 3. of particular quality. 4. limited as to membership or entry: *a select gathering.* —**se'lectness** *n.* —**se'lector** *n.*

select committee *n.* a parliamentary committee set up to study and report on a particular topic.

selection (sɪ'lɛkʃən) *n.* 1. the act or an instance of selecting or the state of being selected. 2. a thing or number of things that have been selected. 3. a range from which something may be selected: *a good selection of clothes.* 4. *Biol.* the process by which certain organisms or characters are reproduced and perpetuated in the species in preference to others.

selective (sɪ'lɛktɪv) *adj.* 1. of or characterized by selection. 2. tending to choose carefully or characterized by careful choice. 3. *Electronics.* occurring at or operating at a particular frequency or band of frequencies. —**se'lectively** *adv.* —**se,lec'tivity** *n.*

selenium (sɪ'liːnɪəm) *n.* a nonmetallic element that exists in several allotropic forms. The common form is a grey crystalline solid that is photoconductive, photovoltaic, and semiconducting: used in photocells, solar cells, and in xerography. Symbol: Se; atomic no.: 34; atomic wt.: 78.96.

self (sɛlf) *n.*, *pl.* **selves** (sɛlvz). 1. distinct identity or character. 2. one's bodily make-up or personal characteristics: *her usual self.* 3. one's own welfare or interests: *he only thinks of self.* 4. an individual's consciousness of his own identity or being. 5. a bird, animal, etc., that is a single colour throughout. ~*pron.* 6. *Not standard.* myself, yourself, etc.: *seats for self and wife.* ~*adj.* 7. the same in colour or material as the rest; matching. 8. *Obs.* the same.

self- *combining form.* 1. of oneself or itself: *self-*

defence. 2. by, to, in, due to, for, or from the self: *self-employed; self-respect.* 3. automatic or automatically: *self-propelled.*

self-abnegation *n.* the denial of one's own interests in favour of the interests of others.

self-absorption *n.* 1. preoccupation with oneself to the exclusion of others. 2. *Physics.* the process in which some of the radiation emitted by a material is absorbed by the material itself.

self-abuse *n.* 1. disparagement or misuse of one's own abilities, etc. 2. a censorious term for **masturbation** (see **masturbate**).

self-addressed *adj.* 1. addressed for return to the sender. 2. directed to oneself: *a self-addressed remark.*

self-aggrandizement *n.* the act of increasing one's own power, importance, etc. —,**self-ag'gran,dizing** *adj.*

self-appointed *adj.* having assumed authority without the agreement of others: *a self-appointed critic.*

self-assertion *n.* the act or an instance of putting forward one's own opinions, etc., esp. in an aggressive or conceited manner. —,**self-as'serting** *adj.* —,**self-as'sertive** *adj.*

self-assurance *n.* confidence in the validity, value, etc., of one's own ideas, opinions, etc. —,**self-as'sured** *adj.*

self-centred *adj.* totally preoccupied with one's own concerns. —,**self-'centredness** *n.*

self-coloured *adj.* 1. having only a single and uniform colour: *a self-coloured dress.* 2. (of cloth, material, etc.) having the natural or original colour.

self-confessed *adj.* according to one's own testimony or admission: *a self-confessed liar.*

self-confidence *n.* confidence in one's own powers, judgment, etc. —,**self-'confident** *adj.* —,**self-'confidently** *adv.*

self-conscious *adj.* 1. unduly aware of oneself as the object of the attention of others. 2. conscious of one's existence. —,**self-'consciously** *adv.* —,**self-'consciousness** *n.*

self-contained *adj.* 1. containing within itself all parts necessary for completeness. 2. (of a flat) having its own kitchen, bathroom, and lavatory not shared by others. 3. able or tending to keep one's feelings, thoughts, etc., to oneself. —,**self-con'tainedness** *n.*

self-control *n.* the ability to exercise restraint or control over one's feelings, emotions, reactions, etc. —,**self-con'trolled** *adj.*

self-deception *or* **self-deceit** *n.* the act or an instance of deceiving oneself. —,**self-de'ceptive** *adj.*

self-defence *n.* 1. the act of defending oneself, one's actions, ideas, etc. 2. boxing as a means of defending the person (esp. in **noble art of self-defence**). 3. *Law.* the right to defend one's person or property against attack or threat of attack. —,**self-de'fensive** *adj.*

self-denial *n.* the denial or sacrifice of one's own desires. —,**self-de'nying** *adj.*

self-determination *n.* 1. the ability to make a decision for oneself without influence from outside. 2. the right of a nation or people to determine its own form of government. —,**self-de'termined** *adj.* —,**self-**

self-absorbed *adj.*	**self-complacent** *adj.*	**self-doubt** *n.*	**self-knowledge** *n.*
self-adhesive *adj.*	**self-consistent** *adj.*	**self-fertilization** *n.*	**self-portrait** *n.*
self-catering *adj.*	**self-content** *n. adj.*	**self-fulfilment** *n.*	**self-proclaimed** *adj.*
self-cleaning *adj.*	**self-defeating** *adj.*	**self-imposed** *adj.*	**self-righting** *adj.*
self-closing *adj.*	**self-delusion** *n.*	**self-inflicted** *adj.*	**self-taught** *adj.*

THESAURUS

seize 1. clutch, collar (*Inf.*), fasten, grab, grasp, grip, lay hands on, snatch, take 2. apprehend, catch, get, grasp 3. abduct, annex, appropriate, arrest, capture, commandeer, confiscate, hijack, impound, take by storm, take captive, take possession of

seizure 1. abduction, annexation, apprehension, arrest, capture, commandeering, confiscation, grabbing, taking 2. attack, convulsion, fit, paroxysm, spasm

seldom hardly ever, infrequently, not often, occasionally, once in a blue moon (*Inf.*), rarely, scarcely ever

select *v.* 1. choose, opt for, pick, prefer, single out, sort out ~*adj.* 2. choice, excellent,

first-class, first-rate, hand-picked, picked, posh (*Inf.*), preferable, prime, rare, recherché, selected, special, superior, top-notch (*Inf.*) 3. cliquish, elite, exclusive, limited, privileged

selection 1. choice, choosing, option, pick, preference 2. anthology, assortment, choice, collection, line-up, medley, miscellany, potpourri, range, variety

selective careful, discerning, discriminating, discriminatory, eclectic, particular

self-assurance assertiveness, confidence, positiveness, self-confidence

self-centred egotistic, inward looking, narcissistic, self-absorbed, selfish, self-

seeking, wrapped up in oneself

self-confidence aplomb, confidence, high morale, nerve, poise, self-assurance, self-reliance, self-respect

self-confident assured, fearless, poised, secure, self-assured, self-reliant, sure of oneself

self-conscious affected, awkward, bashful, diffident, embarrassed, ill at ease, insecure, nervous, out of countenance, shamefaced, sheepish, uncomfortable

self-control restraint, self-discipline, self-mastery, self-restraint, strength of mind *or* will, willpower

de'termining *adj.*

self-discipline *n.* the act of disciplining or power to discipline one's own feelings, desires, etc. —ˌself-'disciplined *adj.*

self-educated *adj.* **1.** educated through one's own efforts without formal instruction. **2.** educated at one's own expense.

self-effacement *n.* the act of making oneself, one's actions, etc., inconspicuous, esp. because of timidity. —ˌself-ef'facing *adj.*

self-employed *adj.* earning one's living in one's own business or through freelance work, rather than as the employee of another. —ˌself-em'ployment *n.*

self-esteem *n.* a good, esp. unduly high, opinion of oneself.

self-evident *adj.* containing its own evidence or proof without need of further demonstration. —ˌself-'evidence *n.* —ˌself-'evidently *adv.*

self-existent *adj. Philosophy.* existing independently of any other being or cause.

self-explanatory *or* **self-explaining** *adj.* understandable without explanation; self-evident.

self-expression *n.* the expression of one's own personality, feelings, etc., as in painting or poetry. —ˌself-ex'pressive *adj.*

self-government *n.* **1.** the government of a country, nation, etc., by its own people. **2.** the state of being self-controlled. —ˌself-'governed *adj.* —ˌself-'governing *adj.*

selfheal ('sɛlf,hiːl) *n.* **1.** a low-growing European herbaceous plant with tightly clustered violet-blue flowers and reputedly having healing powers. **2.** any of several other plants thought to have healing powers.

self-help *n.* the act or state of providing the means to help oneself without relying on the assistance of others.

self-important *adj.* having or showing an unduly high opinion of one's own abilities, importance, etc. —ˌself-im'portantly *adv.* —ˌself-im'portance *n.*

self-improvement *n.* the improvement of one's status, position, education, etc., by one's own efforts.

self-interest *n.* **1.** one's personal interest or advantage. **2.** the act or an instance of pursuing one's own interest. —ˌself-'interested *adj.*

selfish ('sɛlfɪʃ) *adj.* **1.** chiefly concerned with one's own interest, advantage, etc., esp. to the exclusion of the interests of others. **2.** relating to or characterized by self-interest. —'selfishly *adv.* —'selfishness *n.*

self-justification *n.* the act or an instance of justifying or providing excuses for one's own behaviour, etc.

selfless ('sɛlflɪs) *adj.* having little concern for one's own interests. —'selflessly *adv.* —'selflessness *n.*

self-made *adj.* **1.** having achieved wealth, status, etc., by one's own efforts. **2.** made by oneself.

self-opinionated *adj.* **1.** having an unduly high regard for oneself or one's own opinions. **2.** clinging stubbornly to one's own opinions.

self-pity *n.* the act or state of pitying oneself, esp. in an exaggerated or self-indulgent manner. —ˌself-'pitying *adj.* —ˌself-'pityingly *adv.*

self-possessed *adj.* having control of one's emotions, etc. —ˌself-pos'session *n.*

self-preservation *n.* the preservation of oneself from danger or injury.

self-propelled *adj.* (of a vehicle) provided with its own source of tractive power rather than requiring an external means of propulsion. —ˌself-pro'pelling *adj.*

self-raising *adj.* (of flour) having a raising agent, such as bicarbonate of soda, already added.

self-realization *n.* the realization or fulfilment of one's own potential or abilities.

self-regard *n.* **1.** concern for one's own interest. **2.** proper esteem for oneself.

self-reliance *n.* reliance on one's own abilities, decisions, etc. —ˌself-re'liant *adj.*

self-reproach *n.* the act of finding fault with or blaming oneself. —ˌself-re'proachful *adj.*

self-respect *n.* a proper sense of one's own dignity and integrity. —ˌself-re'spectful *or* ˌself-re'specting *adj.*

self-restraint *n.* restraint imposed by oneself on one's own feelings, desires, etc.

self-righteous *adj.* having an exaggerated awareness of one's own virtuousness. —ˌself-'righteously *adv.* —ˌself-'righteousness *n.*

self-sacrifice *n.* the sacrifice of one's own desires, etc., for the sake of duty or for the well-being of others. —ˌself-'sacriˌficing *adj.*

selfsame ('sɛlf,seɪm) *adj.* (*prenominal*) the very same.

self-satisfied *adj.* having or showing a complacent satisfaction with oneself, one's own actions, behaviour, etc. —ˌself-ˌsatis'faction *n.*

self-sealing *adj.* (esp. of an envelope) designed to become sealed with the application of pressure only.

self-service *adj.* **1.** of or denoting a shop, restaurant, etc., where the customer serves himself. ~*n.* **2.** the practice of serving oneself, as in a shop, etc.

self-starter *n.* **1.** an electric motor used to start an internal-combustion engine. **2.** the switch that operates this motor.

self-styled *adj.* (*prenominal*) claiming to be of a specified nature, quality, profession, etc.: *a self-styled expert.*

self-sufficient *or* **self-sufficing** *adj.* **1.** able to provide for or support oneself without the help of others. **2.** *Rare.* having undue confidence in oneself. —ˌself-suf'ficiency *n.* —ˌself-suf'ficiently *adv.*

self-winding *adj.* (of a wrist watch) having a mechanism in which a rotating or oscillating weight rewinds the mainspring.

sell (sɛl) *vb.* **selling, sold. 1.** to dispose of or transfer or be disposed of or transferred to a purchaser in exchange for money or other consideration. **2.** to deal in (objects, property, etc.): *he sells used cars.* **3.** (*tr.*) to give up or surrender for a price or reward: *to sell one's honour.* **4.** to promote or facilitate the sale of (objects, property, etc.): *publicity sells many products.* **5.** to gain acceptance of: *to sell an idea.* **6.** (*intr.*) to be in demand on the market: *these dresses sell well.* **7.** (*tr.*) *Inf.* to deceive. **8. sell down the river.** *Inf.* to betray. **9. sell oneself. a.** to convince someone else of one's potential or worth. **b.** to give up one's moral standards, etc. **10. sell short. a.** *Inf.* to belittle. **b.** *Finance.* to sell securities or goods

self-esteem *amour-propre,* confidence, faith in oneself, pride, self-assurance, self-regard, self-respect, vanity

self-evident axiomatic, clear, incontrovertible, inescapable, manifestly *or* patently true, obvious, undeniable, written all over (something)

self-government autonomy, home rule, independence, self-determination, self-rule, sovereignty

self-important arrogant, conceited, overbearing, pompous, presumptuous, pushy (*Inf.*), strutting, swaggering, swollen-headed

self-indulgence dissipation, excess, extravagance, incontinence, intemperance, self-gratification, sensualism

selfish egoistic, egotistical, egotistic, egotistical, greedy, looking out for number one (*Inf.*), mean, mercenary, narrow, self-centred, self-interested, self-seeking, ungenerous

selfless altruistic, generous, magnanimous, self-denying, self-sacrificing, ungrudging, unselfish

self-possessed collected, confident, cool, cool as a cucumber (*Inf.*), poised, self-assured, sure of oneself, together (*Sl.*), unruffled

self-reliant able to stand on one's own two feet (*Inf.*), capable, independent, self-sufficient

self-respect *amour-propre,* dignity, faith in oneself, morale, one's own image, pride, self-esteem

self-righteous complacent, goody-goody (*Inf.*), holier-than-thou, hypocritical, pharisaic, pi (*Brit. sl.*), pietistic, pious, priggish, sanctimonious, self-satisfied, smug, superior, too good to be true

self-sacrifice altruism, generosity, self-abnegation, self-denial, selflessness

self-satisfaction complacency, contentment, ease of mind, flush of success, glow of achievement, pride, self-approbation, self-approval, smugness

self-satisfied complacent, flushed with success, like a cat that has swallowed the cream *or* the canary, pleased with oneself, proud of oneself, puffed up, self-congratulatory, smug, well-pleased

self-seeking *adj.* acquisitive, calculating, careerist, fortune-hunting, gold-digging, lookin out for number one (*Inf.*), mercenary, on the make (*Sl.*), opportunistic, out for what one can get, self-interested, selfish, self-serving

self-willed cussed (*Inf.*), headstrong, intractable, obstinate, opinionated, pig-headed, refractory, stiff-necked, stubborn, stubborn as a mule, ungovernable, wilful

without owning them in anticipation of buying them before delivery at a lower price. ~*n.* **11.** the act or an instance of selling: *a soft sell.* **12.** *Inf.* a hoax or deception. —**'seller** *n.*

selling race *or* **plate** *n.* a horse race in which the winner must be offered for sale at auction.

sell off *vb.* (*tr., adv.*) to sell (remaining or unprofitable items), esp. at low prices.

Sellotape ('sɛlə,teɪp) *n.* **1.** *Trademark.* a type of adhesive tape. ~*vb.* (*tr.*) **2.** to seal or stick using adhesive tape.

sell out *vb.* (*adv.*) **1.** Also (*chiefly Brit.*): **sell up.** to dispose of (something) completely by selling. **2.** (*tr.*) *Inf.* to betray. ~*n.* **sellout.** **3.** *Inf.* a performance for which all tickets are sold. **4.** a commercial success. **5.** *Inf.* a betrayal.

sell up *vb.* (*adv.*) *Chiefly Brit.* **1.** (*tr.*) to sell all (the possessions) of (a bankrupt debtor) in order to discharge his debts. **2.** (*intr.*) to sell a business.

selvage *or* **selvedge** ('sɛlvɪdʒ) *n.* **1.** the finished nonfraying edge of a length of woven fabric. **2.** a similar strip of material allowed in fabricating a metal or plastic article. —**'selvaged** *adj.*

selves (sɛlvz) *n.* **a.** the plural of **self.** **b.** (*in combination*): *ourselves, yourselves, themselves.*

Sem. *abbrev. for:* **1.** Seminary. **2.** Semitic.

semantic (sɪ'mæntɪk) *adj.* **1.** of or relating to the meanings of different words or symbols. **2.** of or relating to semantics. —**se'mantically** *adv.*

semantics (sɪ'mæntɪks) *n.* (*functioning as sing.*) **1.** the branch of linguistics that deals with the study of meaning. **2.** the study of the relationships between signs and symbols and what they represent. **3.** *Logic.* the principles that determine the truth-values of the formulas in a logical system. —**se'manticist** *n.*

semaphore ('sɛmə,fɔː) *n.* **1.** an apparatus for conveying information by means of visual signals, as with flags, etc. **2.** a system of signalling by holding a flag in each hand and moving the arms to designated positions for each letter of the alphabet. ~*vb.* **3.** to signal (information) by means of semaphore. —**semaphoric** (,sɛmə'fɒrɪk) *adj.*

semblance ('sɛmbləns) *n.* **1.** outward appearance, esp. without any inner substance. **2.** a resemblance.

semen ('siːmɛn) *n.* **1.** the thick whitish fluid containing spermatozoa that is ejaculated from the male genital tract. **2.** another name for **sperm.**

semester (sɪ'mɛstə) *n.* **1.** *Chiefly U.S.* either of two divisions of the academic year. **2.** (in German universities) a session of six months.

semi ('sɛmɪ) *n. Inf.* **1.** *Brit.* short for **semidetached (house). 2.** short for **semifinal.**

semi- *prefix.* **1.** half: *semicircle.* **2.** partially, partly, or almost: *semiprofessional.* **3.** occurring twice in a specified period of time: *semiweekly.*

▷ Usage. See at **bi-.**

semiannual (,sɛmɪ'ænjʊəl) *adj.* **1.** occurring every half-year. **2.** lasting for half a year. —**,semi'annually** *adv.*

semibreve ('sɛmɪ,briːv) *n. Music.* a note, now the longest in common use, having a time value that may be divided by any power of 2 to give all other notes. Usual U.S. name: **whole note.**

semicircle ('sɛmɪ,sɜːkəl) *n.* **1. a.** one half of a circle. **b.** half the circumference of a circle. **2.** anything having the shape or form of half a circle. —**semicircular** (,sɛmɪ'sɜːkjʊlə) *adj.*

semicircular canal *n. Anat.* any of the three looped fluid-filled membranous tubes, at right angles to one another, that comprise the labyrinth of the ear.

semicolon (,sɛmɪ'kəʊlən) *n.* the punctuation mark (;) used to indicate a pause intermediate in value or length between that of a comma and that of a full stop.

semiconductor (,sɛmɪkən'dʌktə) *n.* **1.** a substance, such as germanium or silicon, that has an electrical conductivity that increases with temperature. **2. a.** a device, such as a transistor or integrated circuit, that depends on the properties of such a substance. **b.** (*as modifier*): *a semiconductor diode.*

semiconscious (,sɛmɪ'kɒnʃəs) *adj.* not fully conscious. —**,semi'consciously** *adv.* —**,semi'consciousness** *n.*

semidetached (,sɛmɪdɪ'tætʃt) *adj.* **a.** (of a building) joined to another building on one side by a common wall. **b.** (*as n.*): *they live in a semidetached.*

semifinal (,sɛmɪ'faɪnəl) *n.* **a.** the round before the final in a competition. **b.** (*as modifier*): *the semifinal draw.* —**,semi'finalist** *n.*

seminal ('sɛmɪnəl) *adj.* **1.** potentially capable of development. **2.** highly original and important. **3.** rudimentary or unformed. **4.** of or relating to semen: *seminal fluid.* **5.** *Biol.* of or relating to seed. —**'seminally** *adv.*

seminar ('sɛmɪ,nɑː) *n.* **1.** a small group of students meeting regularly under the guidance of a tutor, professor, etc. **2.** one such meeting or the place in which it is held. **3.** a higher course for postgraduates. **4.** any group or meeting for holding discussions or exchanging information.

seminary ('sɛmɪnərɪ) *n., pl.* **-naries. 1.** an academy for the training of priests, etc. **2.** *Rare.* a private secondary school, esp. for girls. —**,semi'narial** *adj.* —**seminarian** (,sɛmɪ'nɛərɪən) *n.*

semiotics (,sɛmɪ'ɒtɪks) *n.* (*functioning as sing.*) **1.** the study of signs and symbols, esp. the relations between written or spoken signs and their referents in the physical world or the world of ideas. **2.** the scientific study of the symptoms of disease. ~Also called: **semiology.** —**,semi'otic** *adj.*

semipermeable (,sɛmɪ'pɜːmɪəbəl) *adj.* (esp. of a cell membrane) selectively permeable. —**,semi,permea'bility** *n.*

semiprecious (,sɛmɪ'prɛʃəs) *adj.* (of certain stones) having less value than a precious stone.

semiprofessional (,sɛmɪprə'fɛʃənəl) *adj.* **1.** (of a person) engaged in an activity or sport part-time but for pay. **2.** (of an activity or sport) engaged in by semiprofessional people. **3.** of or relating to a person whose activities are professional in some respects. ~*n.* **4.** a semiprofessional person. —**,semipro'fessionally** *adv.*

semiquaver ('sɛmɪ,kweɪvə) *n. Music.* a note having the time value of one-sixteenth of a semibreve. Usual U.S. name: **sixteenth note.**

semirigid (,sɛmɪ'rɪdʒɪd) *adj.* **1.** partly but not wholly rigid. **2.** (of an airship) maintaining shape by means of a main supporting keel and internal gas pressure.

semiskilled (,sɛmɪ'skɪld) *adj.* partly skilled or trained but not sufficiently so to perform specialized work.

semisolid (,sɛmɪ'sɒlɪd) *adj.* having a viscosity and rigidity intermediate between that of a solid and a liquid.

Semite ('siːmaɪt) *n.* a member of the group of peoples who speak a Semitic language, including the Jews and Arabs as well as the ancient Babylonians, Assyrians, and Phoenicians.

Semitic (sɪ'mɪtɪk) *n.* **1.** a branch or subfamily of the Afro-Asiatic family of languages that includes Arabic,

semiagricultural *adj.*	**semidarkness** *n.*	**semiofficial** *adj.*	**semiretired** *adj.*
semiautobiographical *adj.*	**semi-independent** *adj.*	**semipermanent** *adj.*	**semirural** *adj.*
semiautonomous *adj.*	**semi-invalid** *n.*	**semipolitical** *adj.*	**semisweet** *adj.*
semiclassical *adj.*	**seminude** *adj.*	**semiporous** *adj.*	**semitransparent** *adj.*

THESAURUS

sell 1. barter, dispose of, exchange, put up for sale, trade **2.** be in the business of, deal in, handle, hawk, market, merchandise, peddle, retail, stock, trade in, traffic in, vend **3.** gain acceptance for, promote, put across **4.** *Inf. With* **on** convert to, convince of, get (someone) hooked on (*Inf.*), persuade of, talk (someone) into, win (someone) over to **5.** betray, deliver up, give up, sell down the river (*Inf.*), sell out (*Inf.*), surrender

seller agent, dealer, merchant, rep, representative, retailer, salesman, saleswoman, shopkeeper, tradesman, traveller, vendor

selling 1. business, commercial transactions, dealing, trading, traffic **2.** marketing, merchandising, promotion, salesmanship

sell out 1. be out of stock of, dispose of, get rid of, run out of, sell up **2.** *Inf.* betray, break faith with, double-cross (*Inf.*), fail, give away,

play false, rat on, sell down the river (*Inf.*), stab in the back

semblance air, appearance, aspect, bearing, façade, figure, form, front, guise, image, likeness, mask, mien, pretence, resemblance, show, similarity, veneer

semidarkness dusk, gloaming, gloom, half-light, murk, twilight, waning light

Hebrew, Aramaic, and such ancient languages as Phoenician. ~*adj.* **2.** denoting or belonging to this group of languages. **3.** denoting or characteristic of any of the peoples speaking a Semitic language, esp. the Jews or the Arabs. **4.** another word for **Jewish.**

semitone ('sɛmɪˌtəʊn) *n.* an interval denoting the pitch difference between certain adjacent degrees of the diatonic scale (**diatonic semitone**) or between one note and its sharpened or flattened equivalent (**chromatic semitone**); minor second. Also called (U.S.): **half step.** —**semitonic** (ˌsɛmɪ'tɒnɪk) *adj.*

semitrailer (ˌsɛmɪ'treɪlə) *n.* a type of trailer or articulated lorry that has wheels only at the rear, the front end being supported by the towing vehicle.

semitropical (ˌsɛmɪ'trɒpɪkəl) *adj.* partly tropical. —ˌsemi'tropics *pl. n.*

semivowel ('sɛmɪˌvaʊəl) *n. Phonetics.* Also called: **glide.** a vowel-like sound that acts like a consonant. In English and many other languages the chief semivowels are (w) in *well* and (j), represented as *y*, in *yell.*

semolina (ˌsɛmə'liːnə) *n.* the large hard grains of wheat left after flour has been bolted, used for puddings, soups, etc.

sempiternal (ˌsɛmpɪ'tɜːnəl) *adj. Literary.* everlasting; eternal. —ˌsempi'ternally *adv.*

sempre ('sɛmprɪ) *adv. Music.* (preceding a tempo or dynamic marking) always; consistently. It is used to indicate that a specified volume, tempo, etc., is to be sustained throughout a piece or passage.

sempstress ('sɛmpstrɪs) *n.* a rare word for **seamstress.**

S.E.N. (in Britain) *abbrev. for* State Enrolled Nurse.

Sen. *or* **sen.** *abbrev. for:* **1.** senate. **2.** senator. **3.** senior.

senate ('sɛnɪt) *n.* **1.** any legislative body considered to resemble a Senate. **2.** the main governing body at some universities.

Senate ('sɛnɪt) *n.* (*sometimes not cap.*) **1.** the upper chamber of the legislatures of the U.S., Canada, Australia, and many other countries. **2.** the legislative council of ancient Rome.

senator ('sɛnətə) *n.* **1.** (*often cap.*) a member of a Senate or senate. **2.** any legislator. —**senatorial** (ˌsɛnə'tɔːrɪəl) *adj.*

send (sɛnd) *vb.* **sending, sent. 1.** (*tr.*) to cause or order (a person or thing) to be taken, directed, or transmitted to another place: *to send a letter.* **2.** (when *intr.*, foll. by *for;* when *tr.*, *takes an infinitive*) to dispatch a request or command (for something or to do something): *he sent for a bottle of wine.* **3.** (*tr.*) to direct or cause to go to a place or point: *his blow sent the champion to the floor.* **4.** (*tr.*) to bring to a state or condition: *this noise will send me mad.* **5.** (*tr.*; often foll. by *forth, out,* etc.) to cause to issue: *his cooking sent forth a lovely smell from the kitchen.* **6.** (*tr.*) to cause to happen or come: *misery sent by fate.* **7.** to transmit (a message) by radio. **8.** (*tr.*) *Sl.* to move to excitement or rapture: *this music really sends me.* ~*n.* **9.** another word for **swash** (sense 4). —'**sendable** *adj.* —'**sender** *n.*

send down *vb.* (*tr., adv.*) **1.** *Brit.* to expel from a university. **2.** to send to prison.

sendoff ('sɛndˌɒf) *n. Inf.* **1.** a demonstration of good wishes to a person about to set off on a journey, etc. ~*vb.* **send off.** (*tr., adv.*) **2.** to cause to depart. **3.** *Soccer, rugby, etc.* (of the referee) to dismiss (a player) from the field of play for some offence. **4.** *Inf.* to give a sendoff to.

send up *Sl.* ~*vb.* (*tr., adv.*) **1.** to send to prison. **2.** *Brit.* to make fun of, esp. by doing an imitation or parody

of. ~*n.* **send-up. 3.** *Brit.* a parody or imitation.

senescent (sɪ'nɛsənt) *adj.* **1.** growing old. **2.** characteristic of old age. —**se'nescence** *n.*

seneschal ('sɛnɪʃəl) *n.* **1.** a steward of the household of a medieval prince or nobleman. **2.** *Brit.* a cathedral official.

senile ('siːnaɪl) *adj.* **1.** of or characteristic of old age. **2.** mentally or physically weak or infirm on account of old age. —**senility** (sɪ'nɪlɪtɪ) *n.*

senior ('siːnjə) *adj.* **1.** higher in rank or length of service. **2.** older in years: *senior citizens.* **3.** of or relating to maturity or old age: *senior privileges.* **4.** *Education.* **a.** of or designating more advanced or older pupils. **b.** of or relating to a secondary school. **c.** *U.S.* denoting a student in the last year of school or university. ~*n.* **5.** a senior person. **6.** a senior pupil, student, etc.

Senior ('siːnjə) *adj. Chiefly U.S.* being the older: used to distinguish the father from the son: *Charles Parker, Senior.* Abbrev.: **Sr., Sen.**

senior aircraftman *n.* a rank in the Royal Air Force comparable to that of a private in the army, though not the lowest rank in the Royal Air Force.

senior citizen *n. Brit., Austral. & N.Z., euphemistic.* an elderly person.

senior common room *n.* (in British universities, colleges, etc.) a common room for the use of academic staff.

seniority (ˌsiːnɪ'ɒrɪtɪ) *n., pl.* **-ties. 1.** the state of being senior. **2.** precedence in rank, etc., due to senior status.

senior service *n. Brit.* the Royal Navy.

senna ('sɛnə) *n.* **1.** any of a genus of tropical plants having typically yellow flowers and long pods. **2. senna leaf.** the dried leaflets of any of these plants, used as a cathartic and laxative. **3. senna pods.** the dried fruits of any of these plants, used as a cathartic and laxative.

sennight *or* **se'nnight** ('sɛnaɪt) *n.* an archaic word for **week.**

señor (sɛ'njɔː; *Spanish* se'ɲor) *n., pl.* **-ñors** *or* **-ñores** (*Spanish* -'ɲores). a Spaniard: a title of address equivalent to *Mr.* when placed before a name or *sir* when used alone.

señora (sɛ'njɔːrə; *Spanish* se'ɲora) *n., pl.* **-ras** (-rəz; *Spanish* -ras). a married Spanish woman: a title of address equivalent to *Mrs.* when placed before a name or *madam* when used alone.

señorita (ˌsɛnjɔː'riːtə; *Spanish* ˌseɲo'rita) *n., pl.* **-tas** (-təz; *Spanish* -tas). an unmarried Spanish woman: a title of address equivalent to *Miss* when placed before a name or *madam* or *miss* when used alone.

sensation (sɛn'seɪʃən) *n.* **1.** the power of perceiving through the senses. **2.** a physical experience resulting from the stimulation of one of the sense organs. **3.** a general feeling or awareness: *a sensation of fear.* **4.** a state of widespread public excitement: *his announcement caused a sensation.* **5.** anything that causes such a state: *your speech was a sensation.*

sensational (sɛn'seɪʃənəl) *adj.* **1.** causing or intended to cause intense feelings, esp. of curiosity, horror, etc.: *sensational disclosures in the press.* **2.** *Inf.* extremely good: *a sensational skater.* **3.** of or relating to the faculty of sensation. —**sen'sationally** *adv.*

sensationalism (sɛn'seɪʃənəˌlɪzəm) *n.* **1.** the use of sensational language, etc., to arouse an intense emotional response. **2.** such sensational matter itself. **3.** *Philosophy.* the theory that all knowledge derives from the senses. —**sen'sationalist** *n.* —**sen,sational'istic** *adj.*

sense (sɛns) *n.* **1.** any of the five faculties of sight, hearing, smell, taste, and touch, through which humans and animals perceive the external world. **2.** the ability to

---

THESAURUS

send 1. communicate, consign, convey, direct, dispatch, forward, remit, transmit **2.** cast, deliver, fire, fling, hurl, let fly, propel, shoot **3.** *With* **off, out,** *etc.* broadcast, discharge, emit, exude, give off, radiate **4.** *Sl.* charm, delight, electrify, enrapture, enthrall, excite, intoxicate, move, please, ravish, stir, thrill, titillate, turn (someone) on (*Sl.*) **5. send (someone) packing** discharge, dismiss, give (someone) the bird (*Inf.*), give (someone) the brushoff (*Sl.*), send away, send (someone) about his *or* her business, send (someone) away with a flea in his *or* her ear (*Inf.*)

send for call for, order, request, summon

sendoff departure, farewell, going-away party, leave-taking, start, valediction

senile decrepit, doddering, doting, failing, imbecile, in one's dotage, in one's second childhood

senior *adj.* elder, higher ranking, major (*Brit.*), older, superior

seniority eldership, longer service, precedence, priority, rank, superiority

sensation 1. awareness, consciousness, feeling, impression, perception, sense, tingle **2.** agitation, commotion, crowd puller (*Inf.*),

excitement, furore, hit (*Inf.*), scandal, stir, surprise, thrill, wow (*Sl.*, *chiefly U.S.*)

sensational 1. amazing, astounding, breathtaking, dramatic, electrifying, exciting, hair-raising, horrifying, lurid, melodramatic, revealing, scandalous, sensationalistic, shocking, spectacular, staggering, startling, thrilling, yellow (*of the press*) **2.** *Inf.* excellent, exceptional, fabulous (*Inf.*), first class, impressive, marvellous, mind-blowing (*Inf.*), out of this world (*Inf.*), smashing (*Inf.*), superb

perceive. **3.** a feeling perceived through one of the senses: *a sense of warmth*. **4.** a mental perception or awareness: *a sense of happiness*. **5.** moral discernment: *a sense of right and wrong*. **6.** (*sometimes pl.*) sound practical judgment or intelligence. **7.** reason or purpose: *what is the sense of going out?* **8.** meaning: *what is the sense of this proverb?* **9.** an opinion or consensus. **10.** *Maths.* one of two opposite directions in which a vector can operate. **11. make sense.** to be understandable. **12. take leave of one's senses.** *Inf.* to go mad. ~*vb.* (*tr.*) **13.** to perceive through one or more of the senses. **14.** to apprehend or detect without or in advance of the evidence of the senses. **15.** to understand. **16.** *Computers.* **a.** to test or locate the position of (a part of computer hardware). **b.** to read (data).

senseless ('sɛnslɪs) *adj.* **1.** foolish: *a senseless plan*. **2.** lacking in feeling; unconscious. **3.** lacking in perception. —'**senselessly** *adv.* —'**senselessness** *n.*

sense organ *n.* a structure in animals that is specialized for receiving external stimuli and transmitting them in the form of nervous impulses to the brain.

sensibility (ˌsɛnsɪ'bɪlɪtɪ) *n., pl.* -**ties.** **1.** the ability to perceive or feel. **2.** (*often pl.*) the capacity for responding to emotion, etc. **3.** (*often pl.*) the capacity for responding to aesthetic stimuli. **4.** discernment; awareness. **5.** (*usually pl.*) emotional or moral feelings: *cruelty offends most people's sensibilities*.

sensible ('sɛnsɪbəl) *adj.* **1.** having or showing good sense or judgment. **2.** having the capacity for sensation; sensitive. **3.** capable of being apprehended by the senses. **4.** perceptible to the mind. **5.** having perception; aware. **6.** readily perceived. —'**sensibleness** *n.* —'**sensibly** *adv.*

sensitive ('sɛnsɪtɪv) *adj.* **1.** having the power of sensation. **2.** easily irritated; delicate. **3.** affected by external conditions or stimuli. **4.** easily offended. **5.** of or relating to the senses or the power of sensation. **6.** capable of registering small differences or changes in amounts, etc.: *a sensitive instrument*. **7.** *Photog.* responding readily to light: *a sensitive emulsion*. **8.** *Chiefly U.S.* connected with matters affecting national security. **9.** (of a stock market or prices) quickly responsive to external influences. —'**sensitively** *adv.* —ˌsensi'tivity *n.*

sensitize *or* -**tise** ('sɛnsɪˌtaɪz) *vb.* **1.** to make or become sensitive. **2.** (*tr.*) to render (an individual) sensitive to a drug, etc. **3.** (*tr.*) *Photog.* to make (a material) sensitive to light by coating it with a photographic emulsion often containing special chemicals, such as dyes. —ˌsensiti'zation *or* -ti'sation *n.* —'sensiˌtizer *or* -ˌtiser *n.*

sensor ('sɛnsə) *n.* anything, such as a photoelectric cell, that receives a signal or stimulus and responds to it.

sensory ('sɛnsərɪ) *or* **sensorial** (sɛn'sɔːrɪəl) *adj.* of or relating to the senses or the power of sensation.

sensual ('sɛnsjʊəl) *adj.* **1.** of or relating to any of the senses or sense organs; bodily. **2.** strongly or unduly inclined to gratification of the senses. **3.** tending to arouse the bodily appetites, esp. the sexual appetite. —'**sensually** *adv.*

sensualism ('sɛnsjʊəˌlɪzəm) *n.* **1.** the quality or state of being sensual. **2.** the doctrine that the ability to gratify the senses is the only criterion of goodness.

sensuality (ˌsɛnsjʊ'ælɪtɪ) *n., pl.* -**ties.** **1.** the quality or state of being sensual. **2.** excessive indulgence in sensual pleasures. —**sensualist** ('sɛnsjʊəlɪst) *n.*

sensuous ('sɛnsjʊəs) *adj.* **1.** aesthetically pleasing to the senses. **2.** appreciative of qualities perceived by the senses. **3.** of or derived from the senses. —'**sensuously** *adv.* —'**sensuousness** *n.*

sent (sɛnt) *vb.* the past tense or past participle of **send.**

sentence ('sɛntəns) *n.* **1.** a sequence of words capable of standing alone to make an assertion, ask a question, or give a command, usually consisting of a subject and a predicate. **2.** the judgment formally pronounced upon a person convicted in criminal proceedings, esp. the decision as to what punishment is to be imposed. **3.** *Music.* a passage or division of a piece of music, usually consisting of two or more contrasting musical phrases and ending in a cadence. **4.** *Arch.* a proverb, maxim, or aphorism. ~*vb.* **5.** (*tr.*) to pronounce sentence on (a convicted person) in a court of law. —**sentential** (sɛn'tɛnʃəl) *adj.*

sententious (sɛn'tɛnʃəs) *adj.* **1.** characterized by or full of aphorisms or axioms. **2.** constantly using aphorisms, etc. **3.** tending to indulge in pompous moralizing. —**sen'tentiously** *adv.* —**sen'tentiousness** *n.*

sentient ('sɛntɪənt) *adj.* **1.** having the power of sense perception or sensation; conscious. ~*n.* **2.** *Rare.* a sentient person or thing. —**sentience** ('sɛnʃəns) *n.*

sentiment ('sɛntɪmənt) *n.* **1.** susceptibility to tender or romantic emotion: *she has too much sentiment to be successful*. **2.** (*often pl.*) a thought, opinion, or attitude. **3.** exaggerated or mawkish feeling or emotion. **4.** an expression of response to deep feeling, esp. in art. **5.** a feeling or awareness: *a sentiment of pity*. **6.** a mental attitude determined by feeling: *there is a strong revolutionary sentiment in his country*.

sentimental (ˌsɛntɪ'mɛntəl) *adj.* **1.** tending to indulge the emotions excessively. **2.** making a direct appeal to the emotions, esp. to romantic feelings. **3.** relating to or characterized by sentiment. —ˌsenti'mentaˌlism *n.*

THESAURUS

sense *n.* **1.** faculty, feeling, sensation, sensibility **2.** appreciation, atmosphere, aura, awareness, consciousness, feel, impression, intuition, perception, premonition, presentiment, sentiment **3.** definition, denotation, drift, gist, implication, import, interpretation, meaning, message, nuance, purport, significance, signification, substance **4.** *Sometimes plural* brains (*Inf.*), clear-headedness, cleverness, common sense, discernment, discrimination, gumption (*Brit. inf.*), intelligence, judgment, mother wit, nous (*Brit. sl.*), quickness, reason, sagacity, sanity, sharpness, tact, understanding, wisdom, wit(s) **5.** advantage, good, logic, point, purpose, reason, use, value, worth ~*v.* **6.** appreciate, apprehend, be aware of, discern, divine, feel, get the impression, grasp, have a feeling in one's bones (*Inf.*), have a funny feeling (*Inf.*), have a hunch, just know, notice, observe, perceive, pick up, realize, suspect, understand

senseless **1.** absurd, asinine, crazy, daft (*Inf.*), fatuous, foolish, halfwitted, idiotic, illogical, imbecilic, inane, incongruous, inconsistent, irrational, ludicrous, mad, meaningless, mindless, moronic, nonsensical, pointless, ridiculous, silly, simple, stupid, unintelligent, unreasonable, unwise **2.** anaesthetized, cold, deadened, insensate, insensible, numb, numbed, out, out cold, stunned, unconscious, unfeeling

sensibility **1.** responsiveness, sensitiveness, sensitivity, susceptibility **2.** *Often plural* emotions, feelings, moral sense, sentiments, susceptibilities **3.** appreciation, awareness, delicacy, discernment, insight, intuition, perceptiveness, taste

sensible **1.** canny, discreet, discriminating, down-to-earth, far-sighted, intelligent, judicious, matter-of-fact, practical, prudent, rational, realistic, reasonable, sagacious, sage, sane, shrewd, sober, sound, well-reasoned, well-thought-out, wise **2.** *Usually with of* acquainted with, alive to, aware, conscious, convinced, mindful, observant, sensitive to, understanding **3.** appreciable, considerable, discernable, noticeable, palpable, perceptible, significant, tangible, visible

sensitive **1.** acute, delicate, easily affected, fine, impressionable, keen, perceptive, precise, reactive, responsive, sentient, susceptible **2.** delicate, easily upset (hurt, offended), irritable, temperamental, tender, thin-skinned, touchy, umbrageous (*Rare*)

sensitivity delicacy, reactiveness, reactivity, receptiveness, responsiveness, sensitiveness, susceptibility

sensual **1.** animal, bodily, carnal, epicurean, fleshly, luxurious, physical, unspiritual, voluptuous **2.** erotic, lascivious, lecherous, lewd, libidinous, licentious, lustful, randy (*Sl.*), raunchy (*U.S. sl.*), sexual, sexy (*Inf.*), unchaste

sensuality animalism, carnality, eroticism, lasciviousness, lecherousness, lewdness, libidinousness, licentiousness, prurience, salaciousness, sexiness (*Inf.*), voluptuousness

sensuous epicurean, gratifying, hedonistic, lush, pleasurable, rich, sensory, sumptuous, sybaritic

sentence **1.** *n.* condemnation, decision, decree, doom, judgment, order, pronouncement, ruling, verdict **2.** *v.* condemn, doom, mete out justice to, pass judgment on, penalize

sententious **1.** aphoristic, axiomatic, brief, compact, concise, epigrammatic, gnomic, laconic, pithy, pointed, short, succinct, terse **2.** canting, judgmental, moralistic, pompous, ponderous, preachifying (*Inf.*), sanctimonious

sentiment **1.** emotion, sensibility, softheartedness, tender feeling, tenderness **2.** *Often plural* attitude, belief, feeling, idea, judgment, opinion, persuasion, saying, thought, view, way of thinking **3.** emotionalism, mawkishness, overemotionalism, romanticism, sentimentality, slush (*Inf.*)

sentimental corny (*Sl.*), dewy-eyed, drippy (*Inf.*), emotional, gushy (*Inf.*), impressionable, maudlin, mawkish, mushy (*Inf.*), nostalgic, overemotional, pathetic, romantic, schmaltzy (*Sl.*), simpering, sloppy (*Inf.*), slushy (*Inf.*), soft-hearted, tearful, tearjerking (*Inf.*), tender, touching, weepy (*Inf.*)

—ˌsentiˈmentalist n. —ˌsentiˈmentally adv.

sentimentality (ˌsɛntɪmɛnˈtælɪtɪ) n., pl. **-ties.** 1. the state, quality, or an instance of being sentimental. 2. an act, statement, etc., that is sentimental.

sentimentalize or **-lise** (ˌsɛntɪˈmɛntəˌlaɪz) vb. to make sentimental or behave sentimentally. —ˌsentiˌmentaliˈzation or -liˈsation n.

sentimental value n. the value of an article in terms of its sentimental associations for a particular person.

sentinel (ˈsɛntɪnəl) n. 1. a person, such as a sentry, assigned to keep guard. ~vb. (tr.) 2. to guard as a sentinel. 3. to post as a sentinel.

sentry (ˈsɛntrɪ) n., pl. **-tries.** a soldier who guards or prevents unauthorized access to a place, etc.

sentry box n. a small shelter with an open front in which a sentry may stand to be sheltered from the weather.

sepal (ˈsɛpəl) n. any of the separate parts of the calyx of a flower.

separable (ˈsɛpərəbəl) adj. able to be separated, divided, or parted. —ˌseparaˈbility or ˈseparableness n. —ˈseparably adv.

separate vb. (ˈsɛpəˌreɪt). 1. (tr.) to act as a barrier between: a range of mountains separates the two countries. 2. to part or be parted from a mass or group. 3. (tr.) to discriminate between: to separate the men and the boys. 4. to divide or be divided into component parts. 5. to sever or be severed. 6. (intr.) (of a married couple) to cease living together. ~adj. (ˈsɛprɪt, ˈsɛpərɪt). 7. existing or considered independently: a separate problem. 8. disunited or apart. 9. set apart from the main body or mass. 10. distinct, individual, or particular. 11. solitary or withdrawn. —ˈseparately adv. —ˈseparateness n. —ˈseparative adj. —ˈsepaˌrator n.

separates (ˈsɛprɪts, ˈsɛpərɪts) pl. n. women's outer garments that only cover part of the body; skirts, blouses, jackets, trousers, etc.

separate school n. 1. (in certain Canadian provinces) a school for a large religious minority financed by provincial grants in addition to the education tax. 2. a Roman Catholic school.

separation (ˌsɛpəˈreɪʃən) n. 1. the act of separating or state of being separated. 2. the place or line where a separation is made. 3. a gap that separates. 4. Family law. the cessation of cohabitation between a man and wife, either by mutual agreement or under a decree of a court.

separatist (ˈsɛpərətɪst) n. a. a person who advocates secession from an organization, federation, union, etc. b. (as modifier): a separatist movement. —ˈseparaˌtism n.

Sephardi (sɪˈfɑːdiː) n., pl. **-dim** (-dɪm). Judaism. 1. a Jew of Spanish, Portuguese, or North African descent. 2. the pronunciation of Hebrew used by these Jews, and of Modern Hebrew as spoken in Israel. ~Cf. **Ashkenazi.** —Seˈphardic adj.

sepia (ˈsiːpɪə) n. 1. a dark reddish-brown pigment obtained from the inky secretion of the cuttlefish. 2. a brownish tone imparted to a photograph, esp. an early one. 3. a brownish-grey to dark yellowish-brown colour. 4. a drawing or photograph in sepia. ~adj. 5. of the colour sepia or done in sepia: a sepia print.

sepoy (ˈsiːpɔɪ) n. (formerly) an Indian soldier in the service of the British.

sepsis (ˈsɛpsɪs) n. the presence of pus-forming bacteria in the body.

sept (sɛpt) n. 1. Anthropol. a clan that believes itself to be descended from a common ancestor. 2. a branch of a tribe, esp. in Ireland or Scotland.

Sept. abbrev. for: 1. September. 2. Septuagint.

September (sɛpˈtɛmbə) n. the ninth month of the year, consisting of 30 days.

septennial (sɛpˈtɛnɪəl) adj. 1. occurring every seven years. 2. relating to or lasting seven years.

septet (sɛpˈtɛt) n. 1. Music. a group of seven singers or instrumentalists or a piece of music composed for such a group. 2. a group of seven people or things.

septic (ˈsɛptɪk) adj. 1. of or caused by sepsis. 2. of or caused by putrefaction. ~n. 3. Austral. inf. See **septic tank.** —ˈseptically adv. —**septicity** (sɛpˈtɪsɪtɪ) n.

septicaemia or **septicemia** (ˌsɛptɪˈsiːmɪə) n. any of various diseases caused by microorganisms in the blood. Nontechnical name: **blood poisoning.** —ˌseptiˈcaemic or ˌseptiˈcemic adj.

septic tank n. a tank, usually below ground, for containing sewage to be decomposed by anaerobic bacteria. Also called (in Australia): **septic system.**

septillion (sɛpˈtɪljən) n., pl. **-lions** or **-lion.** 1. (in Britain and Germany) the number represented as one followed by 42 zeros (10^{42}). 2. (in the U.S. and France) the number represented as one followed by 24 zeros (10^{24}). Brit. word: **quadrillion.** —sepˈtillionth adj., n.

septuagenarian (ˌsɛptjʊədʒɪˈnɛərɪən) n. 1. a person who is from 70 to 79 years old. ~adj. 2. being between 70 and 79 years old. 3. of or relating to a septuagenarian.

Septuagint (ˈsɛptjʊəˌdʒɪnt) n. the principal Greek version of the Old Testament, including the Apocrypha, believed to have been translated by 70 or 72 scholars.

septum (ˈsɛptəm) n., pl. **-ta** (-tə). Biol., anat. a dividing partition between two tissues or cavities.

septuple (ˈsɛptjʊpəl) adj. 1. seven times as much or many. 2. consisting of seven parts or members. ~vb. 3. (tr.) to multiply by seven. —**septuplicate** (sɛpˈtjuːplɪkət) n., adj.

sepulchral (sɪˈpʌlkrəl) adj. 1. suggestive of a tomb; gloomy. 2. of or relating to a sepulchre. —seˈpulchrally adv.

sepulchre or U.S. **sepulcher** (ˈsɛpəlkə) n. 1. a burial vault, tomb, or grave. 2. Also called: **Easter sepulchre.** an alcove in some churches in which the Eucharistic elements were kept from Good Friday until Easter. ~vb. 3. (tr.) to bury in a sepulchre.

sepulture (ˈsɛpəltʃə) n. the act of placing in a sepulchre.

sequel (ˈsiːkwəl) n. 1. anything that follows from something else. 2. a consequence. 3. a novel, play, etc., that continues a previously related story.

sequence (ˈsiːkwəns) n. 1. an arrangement of two or more things in a successive order. 2. the successive order of two or more things: chronological sequence. 3. an action or event that follows another or others. 4. a. Cards. a set of three or more consecutive cards, usually of the same suit. b. Bridge. a set of two or more consecutive cards. 5. Music. an arrangement of notes or chords repeated several times at different pitches. 6. Maths. an ordered set of numbers or other mathematical entities in one-to-one correspondence with the integers 1 to n. 7. a section of a film constituting a single continuous uninterrupted episode.

sequential (sɪˈkwɛnʃəl) adj. characterized by or having a regular sequence. —**sequentiality** (sɪˌkwɛnʃɪˈælɪtɪ) n.

THESAURUS

sentimentality bathos, corniness (Sl.), emotionalism, gush (Inf.), mawkishness, mush (Inf.), nostalgia, play on the emotions, romanticism, schmaltz (Sl.), sloppiness (Inf.), slush (Inf.), sob stuff (Inf.), tenderness

sentinel or **sentry** guard, lookout, picket, watch, watchman

separable detachable, distinguishable, divisible, scissile, severable

separate v. 1. break off, cleave, come apart, come away, come between, detach, disconnect, disentangle, disjoin, divide, keep apart, remove, sever, split, sunder, uncouple 2. discriminate between, isolate, put on one side, segregate, single out, sort out 3. bifurcate, break up, disunite, diverge, divorce, es-

trange, go different ways, part, part company, set at variance or at odds, split up ~adj. 4. detached, disconnected, discrete, disjointed, divided, divorced, isolated, unattached, unconnected 5. alone, apart, autonomous, distinct, independent, individual, particular, single, solitary

separated apart, broken up, disassociated, disconnected, disunited, divided, living apart, parted, put asunder, separate, split up, sundered

separately alone, apart, independently, individually, one at a time, one by one, personally, severally, singly

separation 1. break, detachment, disconnection, disengagement, disjunction, dis-

sociation, disunion, division, gap, segregation, severance 2. break-up, divorce, estrangement, farewell, leave-taking, parting, rift, split, split-up

septic festering, infected, poisoned, pussy, putrefactive, putrefying, putrid, toxic

sepulchre burial place, grave, tomb, vault

sequel conclusion, consequence, continuation, development, end, follow-up, issue, outcome, payoff (Inf.), result, upshot

sequence arrangement, chain, course, cycle, order, procession, progression, series, succession

—se'quentially *adv.*

sequential access *n.* a method of reading data from a computer file by reading through the file from the beginning.

sequester (sɪ'kwɛstə) *vb.* (*tr.*) **1.** to remove or separate. **2.** (*usually passive*) to retire into seclusion. **3.** *Law.* to take (property) temporarily out of the possession of its owner, esp. to hold a debtor's goods until his creditors are satisfied. **4.** *International law.* to appropriate (enemy property).

sequestrate (sɪ'kwɛstreɪt) *vb.* (*tr.*) *Law.* a variant of **sequester** (sense 3). —**sequestrator** ('si:kwɛs,treɪtə) *n.*

sequestration (,si:kwɛ'streɪʃən) *n.* **1.** the act of sequestering or state of being sequestered. **2.** *Law.* the sequestering of property. **3.** *Chem.* the effective removal of ions from a solution by coordination with another type of ion or molecule to form complexes.

sequin ('si:kwɪn) *n.* **1.** a small piece of shiny coloured metal foil, usually round, used to decorate garments, etc. **2.** a gold coin formerly minted in Italy. —**'sequined** *adj.*

sequoia (sɪ'kwɔɪə) *n.* either of two giant Californian coniferous trees, the **redwood**, or the **big tree** or **giant sequoia**.

seraglio (sɛ'rɑːlɪˌəʊ) *or* **serail** (sə'raɪ) *n., pl.* **-raglios** *or* **-rails**. **1.** the harem of a Muslim house or palace. **2.** a sultan's palace, esp. in the former Turkish empire.

seraph ('sɛrəf) *n., pl.* **-aphs** *or* **-aphim** (-əfɪm). *Theol.* a member of the highest order of angels in the celestial hierarchies, often depicted as the winged head of a child. —**seraphic** (sɪ'ræfɪk) *adj.*

Serb (sɜːb) *n., adj.* another word for **Serbian**.

Serbian ('sɜːbɪən) *adj.* **1.** of, relating to, or characteristic of Serbia, in Yugoslavia, its people, or their dialect of Serbo-Croatian. ~*n.* **2.** the dialect of Serbo-Croatian spoken in Serbia. **3.** a native or inhabitant of Serbia.

Serbo-Croatian *or* **Serbo-Croat** *n.* **1.** the chief official language of Yugoslavia. The Serbian dialect is usually written in the Cyrillic alphabet, the Croatian in Roman. ~*adj.* **2.** of or relating to this language.

sere (sɪə) *adj.* **1.** *Arch.* dried up. ~*vb., n.* **2.** a rare spelling of **sear**.

serenade (,sɛrɪ'neɪd) *n.* **1.** a piece of music characteristically played outside the house of a woman. **2.** a piece of music suggestive of this. **3.** an extended composition in several movements similar to the modern suite. ~*vb.* **4.** (*tr.*) to play a serenade for (someone). **5.** (*intr.*) to play a serenade. —**sere'nader** *n.*

serendipity (,sɛrən'dɪpɪtɪ) *n.* the faculty of making fortunate discoveries by accident.

serene (sɪ'riːn) *adj.* **1.** peaceful or tranquil; calm. **2.** clear or bright: *a serene sky.* **3.** (*often cap.*) honoured: *His Serene Highness.* —**se'renely** *adv.* —**serenity** (sɪ'rɛnɪtɪ) *n.*

serf (sɜːf) *n.* (esp. in medieval Europe) an unfree person, esp. one bound to the land. —**'serfdom** *or* **'serfhood** *n.*

serge (sɜːdʒ) *n.* **1.** a twill-weave woollen or worsted fabric used for clothing. **2.** a similar twilled cotton, silk, or rayon fabric.

sergeant ('sɑːdʒənt) *n.* **1.** a noncommissioned officer in certain armies, air forces, and marine corps, usually ranking immediately above a corporal. **2. a.** (in Britain) a police officer ranking between constable and inspector. **b.** (in the U.S.) a police officer ranking below a captain. **3.** a court or municipal officer who has ceremonial duties. ~*Also:* **serjeant.** —**sergeancy** ('sɑːdʒənsɪ) *or* **'sergeant,ship** *n.*

sergeant at arms *n.* an officer of a legislative or fraternal body responsible for maintaining internal order.

~*Also:* **sergeant, serjeant at arms.**

sergeant major *n.* the chief administrative noncommissioned officer of a military headquarters. See also **warrant officer.**

Sergt. *abbrev. for* Sergeant.

serial ('sɪərɪəl) *n.* **1.** a novel, play, etc., presented in instalments at regular intervals. **2.** a publication, regularly issued and consecutively numbered. ~*adj.* **3.** of or resembling a series. **4.** published or presented as a serial. **5.** of or relating to such publication or presentation. **6.** *Computers.* of or operating on items of information, etc., in the order in which they occur. **7.** of or using the techniques of serialism. —**'serially** *adv.*

serialize *or* **-lise** ('sɪərɪəˌlaɪz) *vb.* (*tr.*) to publish or present in the form of a serial. —**,seriali'zation** *or* **-li'sation** *n.*

serial number *n.* any of the consecutive numbers assigned to machines, tools, books, etc.

series ('sɪəriːz) *n., pl.* **-ries**. **1.** a group or succession of related things, usually arranged in order. **2.** a set of radio or television programmes having the same characters but different stories. **3.** a set of books having the same format, related content, etc., published by one firm. **4.** a set of stamps, coins, etc., issued at a particular time. **5.** *Maths.* the sum of a finite or infinite sequence of numbers or quantities. **6.** *Electronics.* a configuration of two or more components connected in a circuit so that the same current flows in turn through each of them (esp. in **in series**). Cf. **parallel** (sense 10). **7.** *Geol.* a stratigraphical unit that represents the rocks formed during an epoch.

serif *or* **seriph** ('sɛrɪf) *n. Printing.* a small line at the extremities of a main stroke in a type character.

seriocomic (,sɪərɪəʊ'kɒmɪk) *adj.* mixing serious and comic elements. —**,serio'comically** *adv.*

serious ('sɪərɪəs) *adj.* **1.** grave in nature or disposition: *a serious person.* **2.** marked by deep feeling; sincere: *is he serious or joking?* **3.** concerned with important matters: *a serious conversation.* **4.** requiring effort or concentration: *a serious book.* **5.** giving rise to fear or anxiety: *a serious illness.* —**'seriously** *adv.* —**'seriousness** *n.*

serjeant ('sɑːdʒənt) *n.* a variant spelling of **sergeant.**

sermon ('sɜːmən) *n.* **1. a.** an address of religious instruction or exhortation, often based on a passage from the Bible, esp. one delivered during a church service. **b.** a written version of such an address. **2.** a serious speech, esp. one administering reproof.

Sermon on the Mount *n. Bible.* the first major discourse delivered by Christ (Matthew 5-7).

sero- *combining form.* indicating a serum: *serology.*

serous ('sɪərəs) *adj.* of, producing, or containing serum. —**serosity** (sɪ'rɒsɪtɪ) *n.*

serpent ('sɜːpənt) *n.* **1.** a literary word for **snake**. **2.** *Bible.* a manifestation of Satan as a guileful tempter (Genesis 3:1-5). **3.** a sly or unscrupulous person. **4.** an obsolete wind instrument resembling a snake in shape.

serpentine[1] ('sɜːpənˌtaɪn) *adj.* **1.** of, relating to, or resembling a serpent. **2.** twisting; winding.

serpentine[2] ('sɜːpənˌtaɪn) *n.* any of several secondary minerals, consisting of hydrated magnesium silicate, that are green to black in colour and greasy to the touch.

serrate *adj.* ('sɛrɪt, -eɪt). **1.** (of leaves) having a margin of forward pointing teeth. **2.** having a notched or sawlike edge. ~*vb.* (sɛ'reɪt). **3.** (*tr.*) to make serrate. —**ser'rated** *adj.*

serration (sɛ'reɪʃən) *n.* **1.** the state or condition of being serrated. **2.** a row of toothlike projections on an

---

THESAURUS

sequestered cloistered, isolated, lonely, out-of-the-way, private, quiet, remote, retired, secluded, unfrequented

seraphic angelic, beatific, blissful, celestial, divine, heavenly, holy, pure, sublime

serene 1. calm, composed, imperturbable, peaceful, placid, tranquil, undisturbed, unruffled, untroubled 2. bright, clear, cloudless, fair, halcyon, unclouded

serenity 1. calm, calmness, composure, peace, peacefulness, peace of mind, placidity, quietness, quietude, stillness, tranquillity 2. brightness, clearness, fairness

series arrangement, chain, course, line,

order, progression, run, sequence, set, string, succession, train

serious 1. grave, humourless, long-faced, pensive, sedate, sober, solemn, stern, thoughtful, unsmiling 2. deliberate, determined, earnest, genuine, honest, in earnest, resolute, resolved, sincere 3. crucial, deep, difficult, far-reaching, fateful, grim, important, momentous, no laughing matter, of moment *or* consequence, pressing, significant, urgent, weighty, worrying 4. acute, alarming, critical, dangerous, grave, severe

seriously 1. all joking aside, earnestly, gravely, in all conscience, in earnest, no jok-

ing (*Inf.*), sincerely, solemnly, thoughtfully, with a straight face 2. acutely, badly, critically, dangerously, distressingly, gravely, grievously, severely, sorely

seriousness 1. earnestness, gravity, humourlessness, sedateness, sobriety, solemnity, staidness, sternness 2. danger, gravity, importance, moment, significance, urgency, weight

sermon 1. address, exhortation, homily 2. dressing-down (*Inf.*), harangue, lecture, talking-to (*Inf.*)

edge. **3.** a single notch.

serried ('sɛrɪd) adj. in close or compact formation: serried ranks of troops.

serum ('sɪərəm) n., pl. **-rums** or **-ra** (-rə). **1.** Also called: **blood serum.** blood plasma from which the clotting factors have been removed. **2.** antitoxin obtained from the blood serum of immunized animals. **3.** Physiol., zool. clear watery fluid, esp. that exuded by serous membranes. **4.** a less common word for **whey.**

serum hepatitis n. an acute infectious viral disease characterized by inflammation of the liver, fever and jaundice: transmitted by means of injection with a contaminated needle or transfusion of contaminated blood.

servant ('sɜːvənt) n. **1.** a person employed to work for another, esp. one who performs household duties. **2.** See **public servant.**

serve (sɜːv) vb. **1.** to be in the service of (a person). **2.** to render or be of service to (a person, cause, etc.); help. **3.** to attend to (customers) in a shop, etc. **4.** (tr.) to provide (guests, etc.) with food, drink, etc.: she served her guests with cocktails. **5.** to distribute or provide (food, drink, etc.) for guests, etc.: do you serve coffee? **6.** (tr., sometimes foll. by up) to present (food, drink, etc.) in a specified manner: cauliflower served with cheese sauce. **7.** (tr.) to provide with a regular supply of. **8.** (tr.) to work actively for: to serve the government. **9.** (tr.) to pay homage to: to serve God. **10.** to suit: this will serve my purpose. **11.** (intr.; may take an infinitive) to function: this wood will serve to build a fire. **12.** to go through (a period of service, enlistment, etc.). **13.** (intr.) (of weather, conditions, etc.) to be suitable. **14.** (tr.) Also: **service.** (of a male animal) to copulate with (a female animal). **15.** Tennis, squash, etc. to put (the ball) into play. **16.** (tr.) to deliver (a legal document) to (a person). **17.** (tr.) Naut. to bind (a rope, etc.) with fine cord to protect it from chafing, etc. **18. serve (a person) right.** Inf. to pay back, esp. for wrongful or foolish treatment or behaviour. ~n. **19.** Tennis, squash, etc. short for **service. 20.** Austral. inf. hostile or critical remarks. —'**servable** or '**serveable** adj. —'**server** n.

service ('sɜːvɪs) n. **1.** an act of help or assistance. **2.** an organized system of labour and material aids used to supply the needs of the public: telephone service. **3.** the supply, installation, or maintenance of goods carried out by a dealer. **4.** the state of availability for use by the public (esp. in **into** or **out of service**). **5.** a periodic overhaul made on a car, etc. **6.** the act or manner of serving guests, customers, etc., in a shop, hotel, etc. **7.** a department of public employment and its employees: civil service. **8.** employment in or performance of work for another: in the service of his firm. **9. a.** one of the branches of the armed forces. **b.** (as modifier): service life. **10.** the state or duties of a domestic servant (esp. in **in service**). **11.** the act or manner of serving food. **12.** a set of dishes, cups, etc. for use at table. **13.** public worship carried out according to certain prescribed forms: divine service. **14.** the prescribed form according to which a specific kind of religious ceremony is to be carried out: the burial service. **15.** Tennis, squash, etc. **a.** the act, manner, or right of serving a ball. **b.** the game in which a particular player serves: he has lost his service. **16.** the serving of a writ, summons, etc., upon a person. **17.** (of male animals) the act of mating. **18.** (modifier) of or for the use of servants or employees. **19.** (modifier) serving the public rather than producing goods: service industry. ~vb. (tr.) **20.** to make fit for use. **21.** to supply with assistance. **22.** to overhaul (a car, machine, etc.). **23.** (of a male animal) to mate with (a female). **24.** Brit. to meet interest on (debt).

serviceable ('sɜːvɪsəbəl) adj. **1.** capable of or ready for service. **2.** capable of giving good service. —,**service-**

a'**bility** n. —'**serviceably** adv.

service area n. a place on a motorway providing garage services, restaurants, toilet facilities, etc.

service charge n. a percentage of a bill, as at a hotel, added to the total to pay for service.

serviceman ('sɜːvɪs,mæn, -mən) n., pl. **-men. 1.** a person who serves in the armed services of a country. **2.** a man employed to service and maintain equipment.

service road n. Brit. a narrow road running parallel to a main road and providing access to houses, shops, etc., situated along its length.

services ('sɜːvɪsɪz) pl. n. **1.** work performed for remuneration. **2.** (usually preceded by the) the armed forces. **3.** (sometimes sing.) Econ. commodities, such as banking, that are mainly intangible and usually consumed concurrently with their production. **4.** a system of providing the public with gas, water, etc.

service station n. a place that supplies fuel, oil, etc., for motor vehicles and often carries out repairs, servicing, etc.

service tree n. **1.** Also called: **sorb.** a Eurasian rosaceous tree, cultivated for its white flowers and brown edible apple-like fruits. **2. wild service tree.** a similar and related Eurasian tree.

serviette (,sɜːvɪ'ɛt) n. Chiefly Brit. a small square of cloth or paper used while eating to protect the clothes, etc.

servile ('sɜːvaɪl) adj. **1.** obsequious or fawning in attitude or behaviour. **2.** of or suitable for a slave. **3.** existing in or relating to a state of slavery. **4.** (when postpositive, foll. by to) submitting or obedient. —**servility** (sɜː-'vɪlɪtɪ) n.

serving ('sɜːvɪŋ) n. a portion or helping of food or drink.

servitor ('sɜːvɪtə) n. Arch. a person who serves another.

servitude ('sɜːvɪ,tjuːd) n. **1.** the state or condition of a slave. **2.** the state or condition of being subjected to or dominated by a person or thing. **3.** Law. a burden attaching to an estate for the benefit of an adjoining estate or of some definite person. See also **easement.**

servomechanism ('sɜːvəʊ,mɛkə,nɪzəm) n. a mechanism for converting a small mechanical force into a larger force, esp. for control purposes.

servomotor ('sɜːvəʊ,məʊtə) n. any motor that supplies power to a servomechanism.

sesame ('sɛsəmɪ) n. **1.** a tropical herbaceous plant of the East Indies, cultivated, esp. in India, for its small oval seeds. **2.** the seeds of this plant, used in flavouring bread and yielding an edible oil (**benne oil** or **gingili**).

sessile ('sɛsaɪl) adj. **1.** (of flowers or leaves) having no stalk. **2.** (of animals such as the barnacle) permanently attached. —**sessility** (sɛ'sɪlɪtɪ) n.

session ('sɛʃən) n. **1.** the meeting of a court, legislature, judicial body, etc., for the execution of its function or the transaction of business. **2.** a single continuous meeting of such a body. **3.** a series or period of such meetings. **4.** Education. **a.** the time during which classes are held. **b.** a school or university year. **5.** Presbyterian Church. the body presiding over a local congregation and consisting of the minister and elders. **6.** any period devoted to an activity. —'**sessional** adj.

sestet (sɛ'stɛt) n. **1.** Prosody. the last six lines of a sonnet. **2.** another word for **sextet** (sense 1).

set[1] (sɛt) vb. **setting, set.** (mainly tr.) **1.** to put or place in position or into a specified state or condition: to set someone free. **2.** (also intr.; foll. by to or on) to put or be put (to); apply or be applied: he set fire to the house. **3.** to put into order or readiness for use: to set the table for dinner. **4.** (also intr.) to put, form, or be formed into a jelled, firm, or rigid state: the jelly set in three hours. **5.** (also intr.) to put or be put into a position that will re-

---

THESAURUS

servant attendant, domestic, drudge, help, helper, lackey, maid, menial, retainer, servitor (Archaic), slave, vassal

serve 1. aid, assist, attend to, be in the service of, be of assistance, be of use, help, minister to, oblige, succour, wait on, work for **2.** act, attend, complete, discharge, do, fulfil, go through, observe, officiate, pass, perform **3.** answer, answer the purpose, be acceptable, be adequate, be good enough, content, do, do duty as, do the work of, fill the bill (Inf.), function as, satisfy, suffice, suit **4.** arrange,

deal, deliver, dish up, distribute, handle, present, provide, set out, supply

service n. **1.** advantage, assistance, avail, benefit, help, ministrations, supply, use, usefulness, utility **2.** check, maintenance, overhaul, servicing **3.** business, duty, employ, employment, labour, office, work **4.** ceremony, function, observance, rite, worship ~v. **5.** check, fine tune, go over, maintain, overhaul, recondition, repair, tune (up)

serviceable advantageous, beneficial, convenient, dependable, durable, efficient,

functional, hard-wearing, helpful, operative, practical, profitable, usable, useful, utilitarian

serving n. helping, plateful, portion

servitude bondage, bonds, chains, enslavement, obedience, serfdom, slavery, subjugation, thraldom, thrall, vassalage

session assembly, conference, discussion, get-together (Inf.), hearing, meeting, period, sitting, term

store a normal state: *to set a broken bone.* **6.** to adjust (a clock or other instrument) to a position. **7.** to establish: *we have set the date for our wedding.* **8.** to prescribe (an undertaking, course of study, etc.): *the examiners have set "Paradise Lost".* **9.** to arrange in a particular fashion, esp. an attractive one: *she set her hair.* **10.** Also: **set to music.** to provide music for (a poem or other text to be sung). **11.** Also: **set up.** *Printing.* to arrange or produce (type, film, etc.) from (text or copy). **12.** to arrange (a stage, television studio, etc.) with scenery and props. **13.** to describe (a scene or the background to a literary work, etc.) in words: *his novel is set in Russia.* **14.** to present as a model of good or bad behaviour (esp. in **set an example**). **15.** (foll. by *on* or *by*) to value (something) at a specified price or estimation of worth: *he set a high price on his services.* **16.** (*also intr.*) to give or be given a particular direction: *his course was set to the East.* **17.** (*also intr.*) to rig (a sail) or (of a sail) to be rigged so as to catch the wind. **18.** (*intr.*) (of the sun, moon, etc.) to disappear beneath the horizon. **19.** to leave (dough, etc.) in one place so that it may prove. **20.** to sink (the head of a nail) below the surface surrounding it by using a nail set. **21.** *Computers.* to give (a binary circuit) the value 1, so that it can be operated when required. **22.** (of plants) to produce (fruits, seeds, etc.) after pollination or (of fruits or seeds) to develop after pollination. **23.** to plant (seeds, seedlings, etc.). **24.** to place (a hen) on (eggs) for the purpose of incubation. **25.** (*intr.*) (of a gun dog) to turn in the direction of game. **26.** *Bridge.* to defeat (one's opponents) in their attempt to make a contract. **27.** a dialect word for **sit.** **28. set eyes on.** to see. ~*n.* **29.** the act of setting or the state of being set. **30.** a condition of firmness or hardness. **31.** bearing, carriage, or posture: *the set of a gun dog when pointing.* **32.** the scenery and other props used in a dramatic production. **33.** Also called: **set width.** *Printing.* **a.** the width of the body of a piece of type. **b.** the width of the lines of type in a page or column. **34.** *Psychol.* a temporary bias disposing an organism to react to a stimulus in one way rather than in others. **35.** a seedling, cutting, or similar part that is ready for planting: *onion sets.* **36.** a variant spelling of **sett.** ~*adj.* **37.** fixed or established by authority or agreement: *set hours of work.* **38.** (*usually postpositive*) rigid or inflexible: *she is set in her ways.* **39.** unmoving; fixed: *a set expression on his face.* **40.** conventional, artificial, or stereotyped: *she made her apology in set phrases.* **41.** (*postpositive; foll. by on or upon*) resolute in intention: *he is set upon marrying.* **42.** (of a book, etc.) prescribed for students' preparation for an examination. ~See also **set about, set against,** etc.

set² (sɛt) *n.* **1.** a number of objects or people grouped or belonging together, often having certain features or characteristics in common: *a set of coins.* **2.** a group of people who associate together, etc.: *he's part of the jet set.* **3.** *Maths.* a collection of numbers, objects, etc., that have at least one common property or characteristic: *the set of positive integers.* **4.** any apparatus that receives or transmits television or radio signals. **5.** *Tennis, squash, etc.* one of the units of a match, in tennis, one in which one player or pair of players must win at least six

games. **6. a.** the number of couples required for a formation dance. **b.** a series of figures that make up a formation dance. **7. make a dead set at. a.** to attack by arguing or ridiculing. **b.** (of a woman) to try to gain the affections of (a man). ~*vb.* **setting, set.** **8.** (*intr.*) (in square and country dancing) to perform a sequence of steps while facing towards another dancer. **9.** (*usually tr.*) to divide into sets: *in this school we set our older pupils for English.*

set about *vb.* (*intr., prep.*) **1.** to start or begin. **2.** to attack physically or verbally.

set against *vb.* (*tr., prep.*) **1.** to balance or compare. **2.** to cause to be unfriendly to.

set aside *vb.* (*tr., adv.*) **1.** to reserve for a special purpose. **2.** to discard or quash.

set back *vb.* (*tr., adv.*) **1.** to hinder; impede. **2.** *Inf.* to cost (a person) a specified amount. ~*n.* **setback.** **3.** anything that serves to hinder or impede. **4.** a recession in the upper part of a high building. **5.** a steplike shelf where a wall is reduced in thickness.

set down *vb.* (*tr., adv.*) **1.** to record. **2.** to judge or regard: *he set him down as an idiot.* **3.** (foll. by *to*) to attribute: *his attitude was set down to his illness.* **4.** to rebuke. **5.** to snub. **6.** *Brit.* to allow (passengers) to alight from a bus, etc.

set forth *vb.* (*adv.*) *Formal or arch.* **1.** (*tr.*) to state, express, or utter. **2.** (*intr.*) to start out on a journey.

set in *vb.* (*intr., adv.*) **1.** to become established: *the winter has set in.* **2.** (of wind) to blow or (of current) to move towards shore. ~*adj.* **set-in.** **3.** (of a part) made separately and then added to a larger whole: *a set-in sleeve.*

set off *vb.* (*adv.*) **1.** (*intr.*) to embark on a journey. **2.** (*tr.*) to cause (a person) to act or do something, such as laugh. **3.** (*tr.*) to cause to explode. **4.** (*tr.*) to act as a foil or contrast to: *that brooch sets your dress off well.* **5.** (*tr.*) *Accounting.* to cancel a credit on (one account) against a debit on another. ~*n.* **setoff.** **6.** anything that serves as a counterbalance. **7.** anything that serves to contrast with or enhance something else; foil. **8.** a cross claim brought by a debtor that partly offsets the creditor's claim.

set on *vb.* **1.** (*prep.*) to attack or cause to attack: *they set the dogs on him.* **2.** (*tr., adv.*) to instigate or incite; urge.

set out *vb.* (*adv., mainly tr.*) **1.** to present, arrange, or display. **2.** to give a full account of: *he set out the matter in full.* **3.** to plan or lay out (a garden, etc.). **4.** (*intr.*) to begin or embark on an undertaking, esp. a journey.

set piece *n.* **1.** a work of literature, music, etc., often having a conventional or prescribed theme, intended to create an impressive effect. **2.** a display of fireworks.

setscrew ('sɛt,skru:) *n.* a screw that fits into the boss or hub of a wheel, coupling, cam, etc., and prevents motion of the part relative to the shaft on which it is mounted.

set square *n.* a thin flat piece of plastic, metal, etc., in the shape of a right-angled triangle, used in technical drawing.

sett *or* **set** (sɛt) *n.* **1.** a small rectangular paving block made of stone, such as granite. **2.** the burrow of a badg-

---

THESAURUS

set¹ *v.* **1.** aim, apply, deposit, direct, embed, fasten, fix, install, lay, locate, lodge, mount, park, place, plant, plonk, plump, position, put, rest, seat, situate, station, stick, turn **2.** agree upon, allocate, appoint, arrange, assign, conclude, decide (upon), designate, determine, establish, fix, fix up, name, ordain, regulate, resolve, schedule, settle, specify **3.** arrange, lay, make ready, prepare, spread **4.** adjust, coordinate, rectify, regulate, synchronize **5.** cake, condense, congeal, crystallize, gelatinize, harden, jell, solidify, stiffen, thicken **6.** allot, decree, impose, lay down, ordain, prescribe, specify **7.** decline, dip, disappear, go down, sink, subside, vanish ~*n.* **8.** attitude, bearing, carriage, fit, hang, position, posture, turn **9.** *mise-en-scène,* scene, scenery, setting, stage set, stage setting ~*adj.* **10.** agreed, appointed, arranged, customary, decided, definite, established, firm, fixed, prearranged, predetermined, prescribed, regular, scheduled, settled, usual **11.** artificial, conventional, formal, hackneyed, rehearsed,

routine, standard, stereotyped, stock, traditional, unspontaneous **12.** entrenched, firm, hard and fast, hardened, hidebound, immovable, inflexible, rigid, strict, stubborn **13.** *With* **on** *or* **upon** bent, determined, intent, resolute

set² *n.* **1.** band, circle, class, clique, company, coterie, crew (*Inf.*), crowd, faction, gang, group, outfit (*Inf.*), sect **2.** assemblage, assortment, batch, collection, compendium, coordinated group, kit, outfit, series

set about 1. address oneself to, attack, begin, get cracking (*Inf.*), get down to (*Inf.*), get to work, get weaving (*Inf.*), make a start on, put one's shoulder to the wheel (*Inf.*), roll up one's sleeves, sail into (*Inf.*), set to, start, tackle, take the first step, wade into **2.** assail, assault, belabour, lambaste, sail into (*Inf.*)

set aside 1. keep, keep back, put on one side, reserve, save, select, separate, set apart, single out **2.** abrogate, annul, cancel, discard, dismiss, nullify, overrule, overturn,

quash, reject, render null and void, repudiate, reverse

setback bit of trouble, blow, check, defeat, disappointment, hitch, hold-up, misfortune, rebuff, reverse, upset

set back delay, hinder, hold up, impede, retard, slow

set off 1. depart, embark, leave, sally forth, set out, start out **2.** detonate, explode, ignite, light, set in motion, touch off **3.** bring out the highlights in, enhance, show off, throw into relief

set on assail, assault, attack, fall upon, fly at, go for, incite, instigate, let fly at, pitch into, pounce on, sail into (*Inf.*), set about, sic, spur on, urge

set out 1. arrange, array, describe, detail, display, dispose, elaborate, elucidate, exhibit, explain, expose to view, lay out, present, set forth **2.** begin, embark, get under way, hit the road (*Sl.*), sally forth, set off, start out, take to the road

er. **3. a.** a square in a pattern of tartan. **b.** the pattern itself.

settee (sɛˈtiː) *n.* a seat, for two or more people, with a back and usually with arms.

setter (ˈsɛtə) *n.* any of various breeds of large long-haired gundog trained to point out game by standing rigid.

setting (ˈsɛtɪŋ) *n.* **1.** the surroundings in which something is set. **2.** the scenery, properties, or background used to create the location for a stage play, film, etc. **3.** *Music.* a composition consisting of a certain text and music arranged for it. **4.** the metal mounting and surround of a gem. **5.** the tableware, cutlery, etc., for a single place at table.

settle[1] (ˈsɛtəl) *vb.* **1.** (*tr.*) to put in order: *he settled his affairs before he died*. **2.** to arrange or be arranged in a fixed or comfortable position: *he settled himself by the fire*. **3.** (*intr.*) to come to rest or a halt: *a bird settled on the hedge*. **4.** to take up or cause to take up residence: *the family settled in the country*. **5.** to establish or become established in a way of life, job, etc. **6.** (*tr.*) to migrate to and form a community; colonize. **7.** to make or become quiet, calm, or stable. **8.** to cause (sediment) to sink to the bottom, as in a liquid, or (of sediment) to sink thus. **9.** to subside or cause to subside: *the dust settled*. **10.** (sometimes foll. by *up*) to pay off or account for (a bill, debt, etc.). **11.** (*tr.*) to decide or dispose of: *to settle an argument*. **12.** (*intr.*; often foll. by *on* or *upon*) to agree or fix: *to settle upon a plan*. **13.** (*tr.*; usually foll. by *on* or *upon*) to secure (title, property, etc.) to a person: *he settled his property on his wife*. **14.** to determine (a legal dispute, etc.) by agreement of the parties without resort to court action (esp. in **settle out of court**). —ˈ**settleable** *adj.*

settle[2] (ˈsɛtəl) *n.* a seat, for two or more people, usually made of wood with a high back and arms, and sometimes having a storage space in the boxlike seat.

settle down *vb.* (*adv., mainly intr.*) **1.** (*also tr.*) to make or become quiet and orderly. **2.** (often foll. by *to*) to apply oneself diligently: *please settle down to work*. **3.** to adopt an orderly and routine way of life, esp. after marriage.

settle for *vb.* (*intr., prep.*) to accept or agree to in spite of dispute or dissatisfaction.

settlement (ˈsɛtəlmənt) *n.* **1.** the act or state of settling or being settled. **2.** the establishment of a new region; colonization. **3.** a place newly settled; colony. **4.** a community formed by members of a group, esp. of a religious sect. **5.** a public building used to provide educational and general welfare facilities for persons living in deprived areas. **6.** a subsidence of all or part of a structure. **7.** an agreement reached in matters of finance, business, etc. **8.** *Law.* **a.** a conveyance, usually to trustees, of property to be enjoyed by several persons in succession. **b.** the deed conveying such property.

settler (ˈsɛtlə) *n.* a person who settles in a new country or a colony.

set to *vb.* (*intr., adv.*) **1.** to begin working. **2.** to start fighting. ~*n.* **set-to.** **3.** *Inf.* a brief disagreement or fight.

set up *vb.* (*adv., mainly tr.*) **1.** (*also intr.*) to put into a position of power, etc. **2.** (*also intr.*) to begin or enable (someone) to begin (a new venture), as by acquiring or providing means, etc. **3.** to build or construct: *to set up a shed*. **4.** to raise or produce: *to set up a wail*. **5.** to advance or propose: *to set up a theory*. **6.** to restore the health of: *the sea air will set you up again*. **7.** to establish (a record). **8.** *Inf.* to cause (a person) to be blamed, accused, etc. ~*n.* **setup.** **9.** *Inf.* the way in which anything is organized or arranged. **10.** *Sl. chiefly U.S.* an event, the result of which is prearranged: *it's a setup*. **11.** a prepared arrangement of materials, machines, etc., for a job or undertaking. ~*adj.* **set-up.** **12.** physically well-built.

seven (ˈsɛvən) *n.* **1.** the cardinal number that is the sum of six and one and is a prime number. **2.** a numeral 7, VII, etc., representing this number. **3.** the amount or quantity that is one greater than six. **4.** anything representing, represented by, or consisting of seven units, such as a playing card with seven symbols on it. **5.** Also called: **seven o'clock.** seven hours after noon or midnight. ~*determiner.* **6. a.** amounting to seven: *seven swans a-swimming*. **b.** (*as pronoun*): *you've eaten seven already*. —ˈ**seventh** *adj.*

sevenfold (ˈsɛvənˌfəʊld) *adj.* **1.** equal to or having seven times as many or as much. **2.** composed of seven parts. ~*adv.* **3.** by or up to seven times as many or as much.

sevens (ˈsɛvənz) *n.* a Rugby Union match or competition played with seven players on each side.

seven seas *pl. n.* the oceans of the world considered as the N and S Pacific, the N and S Atlantic, and the Arctic, Antarctic, and Indian Oceans.

seventeen (ˈsɛvənˈtiːn) *n.* **1.** the cardinal number that is the sum of ten and seven and is a prime number. **2.** a numeral 17, XVII, etc., representing this number. **3.** the amount or quantity that is seven more than ten. **4.** something represented by, representing, or consisting of 17 units. ~*determiner.* **5. a.** amounting to seventeen: *seventeen attempts*. **b.** (*as pronoun*): *seventeen were sold.* —ˈ**seven'teenth** *adj.*

seventh heaven *n.* **1.** the final state of eternal bliss. **2.** a state of supreme happiness.

seventy (ˈsɛvəntɪ) *n., pl.* **-ties.** **1.** the cardinal number that is the product of ten and seven. **2.** a numeral 70, LXX, etc., representing this number. **3.** (*pl.*) the numbers 70–79, esp. the 70th to the 79th year of a person's life or of a particular century. **4.** the amount or quantity that is seven times as big as ten. **5.** something represented by, representing, or consisting of 70 units. ~*determiner.* **6. a.** amounting to seventy: *the seventy varieties of fabric*. **b.** (*as pronoun*): *to invite seventy to the wedding.* —ˈ**seventieth** *adj.*

sever (ˈsɛvə) *vb.* **1.** to put or be put apart. **2.** to divide or be divided into parts. **3.** (*tr.*) to break off or dissolve (a tie, relationship, etc.). —ˈ**severable** *adj.* —ˈ**severance** *n.*

several (ˈsɛvrəl) *determiner.* **1. a.** more than a few: *several people objected*. **b.** (*as pronoun; functioning as pl.*): *several of them know.* ~*adj.* **2.** (*prenominal*) various; separate: *the members with their several occupations*. **3.** (*prenominal*) distinct; different: *three several times*. **4.** *Law.* capable of being dealt with separately.

severally (ˈsɛvrəlɪ) *adv. Arch. or literary.* **1.** separately or distinctly. **2.** each in turn.

severance pay *n.* compensation paid by a firm to an employee on the termination of his contract.

severe (sɪˈvɪə) *adj.* **1.** rigorous or harsh in the treatment of others: *a severe parent*. **2.** serious in appearance or manner. **3.** critical or dangerous: *a severe ill-*

THESAURUS

setting backdrop, background, context, frame, locale, location, *mise en scène*, mounting, perspective, scene, scenery, set, site, surround, surroundings

settle 1. adjust, dispose, order, put into order, regulate, set to rights, straighten out, work out **2.** choose, clear up, complete, conclude, decide, dispose of, put an end to, reconcile, resolve **3.** *Often with* **on** *or* **upon** agree, appoint, arrange, choose, come to an agreement, confirm, decide, determine, establish, fix **4.** calm, compose, lull, pacify, quell, quiet, quieten, reassure, relax, relieve, sedate, soothe, tranquillize **5.** alight, bed down, come to rest, descend, land, light, make oneself comfortable **6.** dwell, inhabit, live, make one's home, move to, put down roots, reside, set up home, take up residence

7. colonize, found, people, pioneer, plant, populate **8.** acquit oneself of, clear, discharge, liquidate, pay, quit, square (up) **9.** decline, fall, sink, subside

settlement 1. adjustment, agreement, arrangement, completion, conclusion, confirmation, disposition, establishment, resolution, termination, working out **2.** clearance, clearing, defrayal, discharge, liquidation, payment, satisfaction **3.** colonization, colony, community, encampment, hamlet, outpost, peopling

settler colonist, colonizer, frontiersman, immigrant, pioneer, planter

set-to argument, argy-bargy (*Brit. inf.*), barney (*Inf.*), brush, disagreement, dust-up (*Inf.*), fight, quarrel, row, scrap (*Inf.*), slanging match (*Brit.*), spat, squabble, wrangle

setup arrangement, circumstances, conditions, organization, regime, structure, system

set up 1. arrange, begin, compose, establish, found, initiate, install, institute, make provision for, organize, prearrange, prepare **2.** back, build up, establish, finance, promote, put some beef into (*Inf.*), strengthen, subsidize **3.** assemble, build, construct, elevate, erect, put together, put up, raise

set upon ambush, assail, assault, attack, beat up, fall upon, go for, lay into, mug (*Inf.*), set about, turn on

several *adj.* assorted, different, disparate, distinct, divers (*Archaic*), diverse, indefinite, individual, many, particular, respective, single, some, sundry, various

ness. **4.** causing discomfort by its harshness: *severe weather.* **5.** strictly restrained in appearance: *a severe way of dressing.* **6.** hard to perform or accomplish: *a severe test.* —se'**verely** *adv.* —**severity** (sɪ'vɛrɪtɪ) *n.*

Seville orange (sə'vɪl) *n.* **1.** an orange tree of tropical and semitropical regions: grown for its bitter fruit, which is used to make marmalade. **2.** the fruit of this tree.

Sèvres (*French* 'sɛːvr) *n.* porcelain ware manufactured at Sèvres, near Paris, from 1756, characterized by the use of clear colours and elaborate decorative detail.

sew (səʊ) *vb.* **sewing, sewed; sewn** *or* **sewed. 1.** to join or decorate (pieces of fabric, etc.) by means of a thread repeatedly passed through with a needle. **2.** (*tr.; often foll. by* *on or up*) to attach, fasten, or close by sewing. **3.** (*tr.*) to make (a garment, etc.) by sewing. ~*See also* **sew up.**

sewage ('suːɪdʒ) *n.* waste matter from domestic or industrial establishments that is carried away in sewers or drains.

sewage farm *n.* a place where sewage is treated, esp. for use as manure.

sewer[1] ('suːə) *n.* **1.** a drain or pipe, esp. one that is underground, used to carry away surface water or sewage. ~*vb.* **2.** (*tr.*) to provide with sewers.

sewer[2] ('səʊə) *n.* a person or thing that sews.

sewerage ('suːərɪdʒ) *n.* **1.** an arrangement of sewers. **2.** the removal of surface water or sewage by means of sewers. **3.** another word for **sewage.**

sewing ('səʊɪŋ) *n.* **a.** a piece of cloth, etc., that is sewn or to be sewn. **b.** (*as modifier*): *sewing basket.*

sewing machine *n.* any machine designed to sew material. It is now usually driven by electric motor but is sometimes operated by a foot treadle or by hand.

sewn (səʊn) *vb.* a past participle of **sew.**

sew up *vb.* (*tr., adv.*) **1.** to fasten or mend completely by sewing. **2.** *U.S.* to acquire sole use or control of. **3.** *Inf.* to complete or negotiate successfully: *to sew up a deal.*

sex (sɛks) *n.* **1.** the sum of the characteristics that distinguish organisms on the basis of their reproductive function. **2.** either of the two categories, male or female, into which organisms are placed on this basis. **3.** *Inf.* short for **sexual intercourse. 4.** feelings or behaviour resulting from the urge to gratify the sexual instinct. **5.** sexual matters in general. ~*modifier.* **6.** of or concerning sexual matters: *sex education.* **7.** based on or arising from the difference between the sexes: *sex discrimination.* ~*vb.* **8.** (*tr.*) to ascertain the sex of.

sex- *combining form.* six: *sexcentenary.*

sexagenarian (ˌsɛksədʒɪ'nɛərɪən) *n.* **1.** a person from 60 to 69 years old. ~*adj.* **2.** being from 60 to 69 years old. **3.** of or relating to a sexagenarian.

sex appeal *n.* the quality or power of attracting the opposite sex.

sex chromosome *n.* either of the chromosomes determining the sex of animals.

sexed (sɛkst) *adj.* **1.** (*in combination*) having a specified degree of sexuality: *under-sexed.* **2.** of, relating to, or having sexual differentiation.

sex hormone *n.* an animal hormone affecting development and growth of reproductive organs and related parts.

sexism ('sɛksɪzəm) *n.* discrimination on the basis of sex,

esp. the oppression of women by men. —'**sexist** *n., adj.*

sexless ('sɛkslɪs) *adj.* **1.** having or showing no sexual differentiation. **2.** having no sexual desires. **3.** sexually unattractive.

sex object *n.* someone, esp. a woman, regarded only from the point of view of someone else's sexual desires.

sexology (sɛk'sɒlədʒɪ) *n.* the study of sexual behaviour in human beings. —**sex'ologist** *n.* —**sexological** (ˌsɛksə-'lɒdʒɪkəl) *adj.*

sext (sɛkst) *n. Chiefly R.C. Church.* the fourth of the seven canonical hours of the divine office or the prayers prescribed for it.

sextant ('sɛkstənt) *n.* **1.** an instrument used in navigation and consisting of a telescope through which a sighting of a heavenly body is taken, with protractors for determining its angular distance above the horizon. **2.** a sixth part of a circle.

sextet *or* **sextette** (sɛks'tɛt) *n.* **1.** *Music.* a group of six singers or instrumentalists or a piece of music composed for such a group. **2.** a group of six people or things.

sextillion (sɛks'tɪljən) *n., pl.* **-lions** *or* **-lion. 1.** (in Britain and Germany) the number represented as one followed by 36 zeros (10^{36}). **2.** (in the U.S. and France) the number represented as one followed by 21 zeros (10^{21}).

sexton ('sɛkstən) *n.* a man employed to act as caretaker of a church and often also as a bell-ringer, gravedigger, etc.

sextuple ('sɛkstjʊpəl) *n.* **1.** a quantity or number six times as great as another. ~*adj.* **2.** six times as much or many. **3.** consisting of six parts or members.

sextuplet ('sɛkstjʊplɪt) *n.* **1.** one of six offspring at one birth. **2.** a group of six. **3.** *Music.* a group of six notes played in a time value of four.

sexual ('sɛksjʊəl) *adj.* **1.** of or characterized by sex. **2.** (of reproduction) characterized by the union of male and female gametes. Cf. **asexual** (sense 2). —**sexuality** (ˌsɛksjʊ'ælɪtɪ) *n.* —'**sexually** *adv.*

sexual intercourse *n.* the act of sexual procreation in which the male's erect penis is inserted into the female's vagina; copulation; coitus.

sexy ('sɛksɪ) *adj.* **sexier, sexiest.** *Inf.* provoking or intended to provoke sexual interest: *a sexy dress.* —'**sexily** *adv.* —'**sexiness** *n.*

sf, sf., sfz, *or* **sfz.** *Music. abbrev. for* sforzando.

SF *or* **sf** *abbrev. for* science fiction.

SFA *abbrev. for* Scottish Football Association.

sforzando (sfɔː'tsɑːndəʊ) *or* **sforzato** (sfɔː'tsɑːtəʊ) *Music.* ~*adj., adv.* **1.** to be played with strong initial attack. Abbrev: **sf** ~*n.* **2.** a symbol, mark, etc., indicating this.

Sgt. *abbrev. for* Sergeant.

sh (*spelling pron.* ʃ) *interj.* an exclamation to request silence or quiet.

shabby ('ʃæbɪ) *adj.* **-bier, -biest. 1.** threadbare or dilapidated in appearance. **2.** wearing worn and dirty clothes. **3.** mean or unworthy: *shabby treatment.* **4.** dirty or squalid. —'**shabbily** *adv.* —'**shabbiness** *n.*

shack (ʃæk) *n.* **1.** a roughly built hut. ~*vb.* **2.** See **shack up.**

shackle ('ʃækəl) *n.* **1.** (*often pl.*) a metal ring or fastening, usually part of a pair used to secure a person's wrists or ankles. **2.** (*often pl.*) anything that confines or re-

---

THESAURUS

severe 1. austere, cruel, Draconian, hard, harsh, inexorable, iron-handed, oppressive, pitiless, relentless, rigid, strict, unbending, unrelenting 2. cold, disapproving, dour, flinty, forbidding, grave, grim, serious, sober, stern, strait-laced, tight-lipped, unsmiling 3. acute, bitter, critical, dangerous, distressing, extreme, fierce, grinding, inclement, intense, violent 4. ascetic, austere, chaste, classic, forbidding, functional, plain, restrained, simple, Spartan, unadorned, unembellished, unfussy 5. arduous, demanding, difficult, exacting, fierce, hard, punishing, rigorous, stringent, taxing, tough, unrelenting 6. astringent, biting, caustic, cutting, harsh, satirical, scathing, unsparing

severely 1. harshly, rigorously, sharply, sternly, strictly, with an iron hand, with a rod of iron 2. acutely, badly, critically, dan-

gerously, extremely, gravely, hard, sorely

severity austerity, gravity, hardness, harshness, plainness, rigour, seriousness, severeness, sternness, strictness, stringency, toughness

sex 1. gender 2. *Inf.* coition, coitus, copulation, fornication, going to bed (with someone), intimacy, lovemaking, (sexual) intercourse, sexual relations 3. desire, facts of life, libido, reproduction, sexuality, the birds and the bees (*Inf.*)

sexual 1. carnal, erotic, intimate, of the flesh, sensual, 2. genital, procreative, reproductive, sex, venereal

sexual intercourse carnal knowledge, coition, coitus, commerce (*Archaic*), congress, copulation, coupling, mating, union

sexuality bodily appetites, carnality, desire, eroticism, lust, sensuality, sexiness

(*Inf.*), voluptuousness

sexy arousing, beddable, bedroom, comehither (*Inf.*), cuddly, erotic, flirtatious, inviting, kissable, naughty, provocative, provoking, seductive, sensual, sensuous, slinky, suggestive, titillating, voluptuous

shabby 1. dilapidated, down at heel, faded, frayed, having seen better days, mean, neglected, poor, ragged, run-down, scruffy, seedy, tattered, tatty, the worse for wear, threadbare, worn, worn-out 2. cheap, contemptible, despicable, dirty, dishonourable, ignoble, low, low-down (*Inf.*), mean, rotten (*Inf.*), scurvy, shameful, shoddy, ungentlemanly, unworthy

shack cabin, dump (*Inf.*), hovel, hut, leanto, shanty, shiel (*Scot.*), shieling (*Scot.*).

stricts freedom. **3.** a U-shaped bracket, the open end of which is closed by a bolt (**shackle pin**), used for securing ropes, chains, etc. ~*vb.* (*tr.*) **4.** to confine with or as if with shackles. **5.** to fasten or connect with a shackle. —'**shackler** *n.*

shack up *vb.* (*intr., adv.; usually foll. by with*) *Sl.* to live, esp. with a lover.

shad (ʃæd) *n., pl.* **shad** or **shads.** any of various herring-like food fishes that migrate from the sea to fresh water to spawn.

shade (ʃeɪd) *n.* **1.** relative darkness produced by the blocking out of light. **2.** a place made relatively darker or cooler than other areas by the blocking of light, esp. sunlight. **3.** a position of relative obscurity. **4.** something used to provide a shield or protection from a direct source of light, such as a lampshade. **5.** a darker area indicated in a painting, drawing, etc., by shading. **6.** a colour that varies slightly from a standard colour: *a darker shade of green.* **7.** a slight amount: *a shade of difference.* **8.** *Literary.* a ghost. ~*vb.* (*mainly tr.*) **9.** to screen or protect from heat, light, view, etc. **10.** to make darker or dimmer. **11.** to represent (a darker area) in (a painting, etc.), by means of hatching, etc. **12.** (*also intr.*) to change or cause to change slightly. **13.** to lower (a price). —'**shadeless** *adj.*

shades (ʃeɪdz) *pl. n.* **1.** gathering darkness at nightfall. **2.** *Sl.* sunglasses. **3.** (*often cap; preceded by the*) a literary term for **Hades. 4.** (*foll. by of*) undertones: *shades of my father!*

shading ('ʃeɪdɪŋ) *n.* the graded areas of tone, lines, dots, etc., indicating light and dark in a painting or drawing.

shadow ('ʃædəʊ) *n.* **1.** a dark image or shape cast on a surface by the interception of light rays by an opaque body. **2.** an area of relative darkness. **3.** the dark portions of a picture. **4.** a hint or faint semblance: *beyond a shadow of a doubt.* **5.** a remnant or vestige: *a shadow of one's past self.* **6.** a reflection. **7.** a threatening influence: *a shadow over one's happiness.* **8.** a spectre. **9.** an inseparable companion. **10.** a person who trails another in secret, such as a detective. **11.** *Med.* a dark area on an x-ray film representing an opaque structure or part. **12.** *Arch.* shelter. **13.** (*modifier*) *Brit.* designating a member or members of the main opposition party in Parliament who would hold ministerial office if their party were in power: *shadow cabinet.* ~*vb.* (*tr.*) **14.** to cast a shadow over. **15.** to make dark or gloomy. **16.** to shade from light. **17.** to follow or trail secretly. **18.** (*often foll. by forth*) to represent vaguely. —'**shadower** *n.*

shadow-box *vb.* (*intr.*) *Boxing.* to practise blows and footwork against an imaginary opponent. —'**shadow-,boxing** *n.*

shadowy ('ʃædəʊɪ) *adj.* **1.** dark; shady. **2.** resembling a shadow in faintness. **3.** illusory or imaginary. —'**shadowiness** *n.*

shady ('ʃeɪdɪ) *adj.* **shadier, shadiest. 1.** shaded. **2.** affording or casting a shade. **3.** quiet or concealed. **4.** *Inf.* questionable as to honesty or legality. —'**shadily** *adv.* —'**shadiness** *n.*

shaft (ʃɑːft) *n.* **1.** the long narrow pole that forms the body of a spear, arrow, etc. **2.** something directed at a person in the manner of a missile. **3.** a ray or streak,

esp. of light. **4.** a rod or pole forming the handle of a hammer, golf club, etc. **5.** a revolving rod that transmits motion or power. **6.** one of the two wooden poles by which an animal is harnessed to a vehicle. **7.** *Anat.* the middle part of a long bone. **8.** the middle part of a column or pier, between the base and the capital. **9.** *Archit.* a column that supports a vaulting rib, sometimes one of a set. **10.** a vertical passageway through a building, as for a lift. **11.** a vertical passageway into a mine. **12.** *Ornithol.* the central rib of a feather. **13.** an archaic or literary word for **arrow.** ~*vb.* **14.** *U.S. sl.* to trick or cheat.

shag¹ (ʃæg) *n.* **1.** a matted tangle, esp. of hair, etc. **2.** a napped fabric, usually a rough wool. **3.** shredded coarse tobacco.

shag² (ʃæg) *n.* another name for **cormorant.**

shaggy ('ʃægɪ) *adj.* **-gier, -giest. 1.** having or covered with rough unkempt fur, hair, wool, etc.: *a shaggy dog.* **2.** rough or unkempt. —'**shaggily** *adv.* —'**shagginess** *n.*

shagreen (ʃæ'griːn) *n.* **1.** the rough skin of certain sharks and rays, used as an abrasive. **2.** a rough grainy leather made from certain animal hides.

shah (ʃɑː) *n.* a ruler of certain Middle Eastern countries, esp. formerly Iran. —'**shahdom** *n.*

shake (ʃeɪk) *vb.* **shaking, shook, shaken. 1.** to move or cause to move up and down or back and forth with short quick movements. **2.** to sway or totter or cause to sway or totter. **3.** to clasp or grasp (the hand) of (a person) in greeting, agreement, etc.: *he shook John's hand.* **4. shake hands.** to clasp hands in greeting, agreement, reconciliation, etc. **6.** to bring or come to a specified condition by or as if by shaking: *he shook free and ran.* **7.** (*tr.*) to wave or brandish: *he shook his sword.* **8.** (*tr.; often foll. by up*) to rouse or agitate. **9.** (*tr.*) to undermine or weaken: *the crisis shook his faith.* **10.** to mix (dice) by rattling in a cup or the hand before throwing. **11.** *Austral. sl.* to steal. **12.** (*tr.*) *U.S. inf.* to escape from. **13.** *Music.* to perform a trill on (a note). **14. shake a leg.** *Inf.* to hurry or hasten. **15. shake in one's shoes.** to tremble with fear or apprehension. **16. shake one's head.** to indicate disagreement or disapproval by moving the head from side to side. **17. shake the dust from one's feet.** to depart gladly. ~*n.* **18.** the act or an instance of shaking. **19.** a tremor or vibration. **20. the shakes.** *Inf.* a state of uncontrollable trembling or a condition that causes it, such as a fever. **21.** *Inf.* a very short period of time: *in half a shake.* **22.** a fissure or crack in timber or rock. **23.** an instance of shaking dice before casting. **24.** *Music.* another word for **trill¹** (sense 1). **25.** an informal name for **earthquake. 26.** short for **milk shake. 27. no great shakes.** *Inf.* of no great merit or value. ~See also **shake down, shake off, shake up.** —'**shakable** or '**shakeable** *adj.*

shake down *vb.* (*adv.*) **1.** to fall or settle or cause to fall or settle by shaking. **2.** (*tr.*) *U.S. sl.* to extort money from, esp. by blackmail. **3.** (*tr.*) *Inf., chiefly U.S.* to submit (a vessel, etc.) to a shakedown test. **4.** (*intr.*) to go to bed, esp. to a makeshift bed. ~*n.* **shakedown. 5.** *U.S. sl.* a swindle or act of extortion. **6.** a makeshift bed, esp. of straw, blankets, etc. **7.** *Inf., chiefly U.S.* **a.** a voyage to

shackle *n.* **1.** *Often plural* bond, chain, fetter, gyve (*Archaic*), handcuff, hobble, iron, leg-iron, manacle, rope, tether ~*v.* **2.** bind, chain, fetter, handcuff, hobble, manacle, pinion, put in irons, secure, tether, tie, trammel **3.** constrain, embarrass, encumber, hamper, hamstring, impede, inhibit, limit, obstruct, restrain, restrict, tie (someone's) hands

shade *n.* **1.** coolness, dimness, dusk, gloom, gloominess, obscurity, screen, semidarkness, shadiness, shadow, shadows **2. put into the shade** eclipse, make pale by comparison, outclass, outshine, overshadow **3.** blind, canopy, cover, covering, curtain, screen, shield, veil **4.** colour, hue, stain, tinge, tint, tone **5.** amount, dash, degree, difference, gradation, hint, nuance, semblance, suggestion, suspicion, trace, variety **6.** apparition, ghost, manes, phantom, shadow, spectre, spirit ~*v.* **7.** cast a shadow over, cloud, conceal, cover, darken, dim, hide, mute, obscure, protect, screen, shadow, shield, shut out the light, veil

shadow *n.* **1.** cover, darkness, dimness, dusk, gathering darkness, gloaming, gloom, obscurity, protection, shade, shelter **2.** hint, suggestion, suspicion, trace **3.** ghost, image, phantom, remnant, representation, spectre, vestige **4.** blight, cloud, gloom, sadness ~*v.* **5.** cast a shadow over, darken, overhang, screen, shade, shield **6.** dog, follow, spy on, stalk, tail (*Inf.*), trail

shadowy 1. crepuscular, dark, dim, dusky, gloomy, indistinct, murky, obscure, shaded, shady, tenebrious, tenebrous **2.** dim, dreamlike, faint, ghostly, illusory, imaginary, impalpable, intangible, nebulous, obscure, phantom, spectral, undefined, unreal, unsubstantial, vague, wraithlike

shady 1. bosky (*Literary*), bowery, cool, dim, leafy, shaded, shadowy, umbrageous **2.** *Inf.* crooked, disreputable, dubious, fishy (*Inf.*), questionable, shifty, slippery, suspect, suspicious, unethical, unscrupulous, untrustworthy

shaft 1. handle, pole, rod, shank, stem, upright **2.** beam, gleam, ray, streak **3.** barb, cut, dart, gibe, sting, thrust

shaggy hairy, hirsute, long-haired, rough, unkempt, unshorn

shake *v.* **1.** bump, fluctuate, jar, joggle, jolt, jounce, oscillate, quake, quiver, rock, shiver, shudder, sway, totter, tremble, vibrate, waver, wobble **2.** brandish, flourish, wave **3.** *Often with up* agitate, churn, convulse, rouse, stir **4.** discompose, distress, disturb, frighten, intimidate, move, rattle (*Inf.*), shock, unnerve, upset **5.** impair, pull the rug out from under (*Inf.*), undermine, weaken ~*n.* **6.** agitation, convulsion, disturbance, jar, jerk, jolt, jounce, pulsation, quaking, shiver, shock, shudder, trembling, tremor, vibration **7.** *Inf.* instant, jiffy (*Inf.*), moment, second, tick (*Brit. inf.*), trice

test the performance of a ship or aircraft or to familiarize the crew with their duties. **b.** (*as modifier*): *a shake-down run*.

shake off *vb.* (*adv.*) **1.** to remove or be removed with or as if with a quick movement: *she shook off her depression.* **2.** (*tr.*) to escape from; elude: *they shook off the police.*

shaker ('ʃeɪkə) *n.* **1.** a person or thing that shakes. **2.** a container from which a condiment is shaken. **3.** a container in which the ingredients of alcoholic drinks are shaken together.

Shakespearean *or* **Shakespearian** (ʃeɪk'spɪərɪən) *adj.* **1.** of, relating to, or characteristic of Shakespeare (1564-1616), English dramatist, or his works. **~n.** **2.** a student of or specialist in Shakespeare's works.

shake up *vb.* (*tr., adv.*) **1.** to shake in order to mix. **2.** to reorganize drastically. **3.** to stir. **4.** to restore the shape of (a pillow, etc.). **5.** *Inf.* to shock mentally or physically. **~n.** **shake-up.** **6.** *Inf.* a radical reorganization.

shako ('ʃækəʊ) *n., pl.* **shakos** *or* **shakoes.** a tall usually cylindrical military headdress, having a plume and often a peak.

shaky ('ʃeɪkɪ) *adj.* **shakier, shakiest.** **1.** tending to shake or tremble. **2.** liable to prove defective. **3.** uncertain or questionable: *your arguments are very shaky.* **—'shakily** *adv.* **—'shakiness** *n.*

shale (ʃeɪl) *n.* a dark fine-grained sedimentary rock formed by compression of successive layers of clay. **—'shaly** *adj.*

shale oil *n.* an oil distilled from shales and used as fuel.

shall (ʃæl; *unstressed* ʃəl) *vb. past* **should.** (takes an infinitive without *to* or an implied infinitive) used as an auxiliary: **1.** (esp. with *I* or *we* as subject) to make the future tense: *we shall see you tomorrow.* Cf. **will**[1] (sense 1). **2.** (with *you, he, she, it, they,* or a noun as subject) **a.** to indicate determination on the part of the speaker, as in issuing a threat: *you shall pay for this!* **b.** to indicate compulsion, now esp. in official documents. **c.** to indicate certainty or inevitability: *our day shall come.* **3.** (with *any noun or pronoun as subject, esp. in conditional clauses or clauses expressing doubt*) to indicate nonspecific futurity: *I don't think I shall ever see her again.*
▷ **Usage.** The usual rule given for the use of *shall* and *will* is that where the meaning is one of simple futurity, *shall* is used for the first person of the verb and *will* for the second and third: *I shall go tomorrow; they will be there now.* Where the meaning involves command, obligation, or determination, the positions are reversed: *it shall be done; I will definitely go.* However, *shall* has come to be largely neglected in favour of *will*.

shallot (ʃə'lɒt) *n.* **1.** an alliaceous plant cultivated for its edible bulb. **2.** the bulb of this plant, which divides into small sections and is used in cooking for flavouring.

shallow ('ʃæləʊ) *adj.* **1.** having little depth. **2.** lacking intellectual or mental depth or subtlety. **~n.** **3.** (*often pl.*) a shallow place in a body of water. **~vb.** **4.** to make or become shallow. **—'shallowness** *n.*

sham (ʃæm) *n.* **1.** anything that is not what it appears to be. **2.** something false or fictitious that purports to be genuine. **3.** a person who pretends to be something other than he is. **~adj.** **4.** counterfeit or false. **~vb.**

shamming, shammed. **5.** to assume the appearance of (something); counterfeit: *to sham illness.*

shaman ('ʃæmən) *n.* **1.** a priest of shamanism. **2.** a medicine man of a similar religion, esp. among certain tribes of North American Indians.

shamanism ('ʃæmə,nɪzəm) *n.* **1.** the religion of certain peoples of northern Asia, based on the belief that the world is pervaded by good and evil spirits who can be influenced or controlled only by the shamans. **2.** any similar religion involving forms of spiritualism. **—'shamanist** *n., adj.*

shamble ('ʃæmbəl) *vb.* **1.** (*intr.*) to walk or move along in an awkward or unsteady way. **~n.** **2.** an awkward or unsteady walk.

shambles ('ʃæmbəlz) *n.* (*functioning as sing. or pl.*) **1.** a place of great disorder: *the room was a shambles after the party.* **2.** a place where animals are brought to be slaughtered. **3.** any place of slaughter or execution.

shame (ʃeɪm) *n.* **1.** a painful emotion resulting from an awareness of having done something dishonourable, unworthy, etc. **2.** capacity to feel such an emotion. **3.** ignominy or disgrace. **4.** a person or thing that causes this. **5.** an occasion for regret, disappointment, etc.: *it's a shame you can't come with us.* **6. put to shame. a.** to disgrace. **b.** to surpass totally. **~vb.** (*tr.*) **7.** to cause to feel shame. **8.** to bring shame on. **9.** (often foll. by *into*) to compel through a sense of shame. **~interj.** **10.** *S. African sl.* a general exclamation of delight, sympathy, etc. **—'shamable** *or* **'shameable** *adj.*

shamefaced ('ʃeɪm,feɪst) *adj.* **1.** bashful or modest. **2.** showing a sense of shame. **—shamefacedly** (ʃeɪm-'feɪsɪdlɪ) *adv.*

shameful ('ʃeɪmfʊl) *adj.* causing or deserving shame. **—'shamefulness** *n.*

shameless ('ʃeɪmlɪs) *adj.* **1.** having no sense of shame. **2.** without decency or modesty. **—'shamelessly** *adv.* **—'shamelessness** *n.*

shammy ('ʃæmɪ) *n., pl.* **-mies.** *Inf.* another word for **chamois** (sense 3). Also called: **shammy leather.**

shampoo (ʃæm'puː) *n.* **1.** a preparation of soap or detergent to wash the hair. **2.** a similar preparation for washing carpets, etc. **3.** the process of shampooing. **~vb.** **-pooing, -pooed.** **4.** (*tr.*) to wash (the hair, etc.) with such a preparation.

shamrock ('ʃæm,rɒk) *n.* a plant having leaves divided into three leaflets: the national emblem of Ireland.

shandy ('ʃændɪ) *or U.S.* **shandygaff** ('ʃændɪ,gæf) *n., pl.* **dies** *or* **galfs.** an alcoholic drink made of beer and ginger beer or lemonade.

shanghai ('ʃæŋhaɪ, ʃæŋ'haɪ) *Sl.* **~vb.** **-haiing, -haied.** (*tr.*) **1.** to kidnap (a man or seaman) for enforced service at sea. **2.** to force or trick (someone) into doing something, etc. **3.** *Austral. & N.Z.* to shoot with a catapult. **~n.** **4.** *Austral. & N.Z.* a catapult.

shank (ʃæŋk) *n.* **1.** *Anat.* the shin. **2.** the corresponding part of the leg in other vertebrates. **3.** a cut of meat from the top part of an animal's shank. **4.** the main part of a tool, between the working part and the handle. **5.** the part of a bolt between the thread and the head. **6.** the ring or stem on the back of some buttons. **7.** the stem or long narrow part of a key, hook, spoon handle, nail, etc. **8.** the band of a ring as distinguished from the setting. **9.** the part of a shoe connecting the wide part of

---

THESAURUS

shake off dislodge, elude, get away from, get rid of, get shot of (*Sl.*), give the slip, leave behind, lose, rid oneself of, throw off

shake up agitate, churn (*up*), disturb, mix, overturn, reorganize, shock, stir (*up*), turn upside down, unsettle, upset

shaky **1.** all of a quiver (*Inf.*), faltering, insecure, precarious, quivery, rickety, tottering, trembling, tremulous, unstable, unsteady, weak, wobbly **2.** dubious, questionable, suspect, uncertain, undependable, unreliable, unsound, unsupported

shallow **1.** *adj. Fig.* empty, flimsy, foolish, frivolous, idle, ignorant, meaningless, puerile, simple, skin-deep, slight, superficial, surface, trivial, unintelligent **2.** *n. Often plural* bank, flat, sandbank, sand bar, shelf, shoal

sham **1.** *n.* counterfeit, feint, forgery, fraud, hoax, humbug, imitation, impostor, imposture, phoney (*Sl.*), pretence, pretender,

pseud (*Sl.*), wolf in sheep's clothing **2.** *adj.* artificial, bogus, counterfeit, ersatz, false, feigned, imitation, mock, phoney (*Sl.*), pretended, pseud (*Sl.*), pseudo (*Inf.*), simulated, spurious, synthetic **3.** *v.* affect, assume, counterfeit, fake, feign, imitate, play possum, pretend, put on, simulate

shambles anarchy, chaos, confusion, disarray, disorder, disorganization, havoc, madhouse, mess, muddle

shame *n.* **1.** blot, contempt, degradation, derision, disgrace, dishonour, disrepute, ill repute, infamy, obloquy, odium, opprobrium, reproach, scandal, skeleton in the cupboard, smear **2.** abashment, chagrin, compunction, embarrassment, humiliation, ignominy, loss of face, mortification, shamefacedness **3. put to shame** disgrace, eclipse, outclass, outdo, outstrip, show up, surpass **~v.** **4.** abash, confound, disconcert, disgrace, embarrass, hum-

ble, humiliate, mortify, reproach, ridicule, take (someone) down a peg (*Inf.*) **5.** blot, debase, defile, degrade, discredit, dishonour, smear, stain

shameful **1.** atrocious, base, dastardly, degrading, disgraceful, dishonourable, ignominious, indecent, infamous, low, mean, outrageous, reprehensible, scandalous, unbecoming, unworthy, vile, wicked **2.** blushmaking (*Inf.*), degrading, embarrassing, humiliating, mortifying, shaming

shameless abandoned, audacious, barefaced, brash, brazen, corrupt, depraved, dissolute, flagrant, hardened, immodest, improper, impudent, incorrigible, indecent, insolent, profligate, reprobate, unabashed, unashamed, unblushing, unprincipled, wanton

the sole with the heel. **10.** *Printing.* the body of a piece of type. ~*vb.* **11.** (*intr.*) (of fruits, roots, etc.) to show disease symptoms, esp. discoloration.

shanks's pony or *U.S.* **shanks's mare** ('ʃæŋksɪz) *n.* *Inf.* one's own legs as a means of transportation.

shantung (ʃæn'tʌŋ) *n.* **1.** a heavy silk fabric with a knobbly surface. **2.** a cotton or rayon imitation of this.

shanty[1] ('ʃæntɪ) *n., pl.* **-ties. 1.** a ramshackle hut; crude dwelling. **2.** *Austral. & N.Z.* a public house, esp. an unlicensed one.

shanty[2] ('ʃæntɪ) or **chanty** *n., pl.* **-ties.** a song originally sung by sailors, esp. a rhythmical one forming an accompaniment to work.

shantytown ('ʃæntɪˌtaʊn) *n.* a town or section of a town or city inhabited by very poor people.

shape (ʃeɪp) *n.* **1.** the outward form of an object defined by outline. **2.** the figure or outline of the body of a person. **3.** a phantom. **4.** organized or definite form: *my plans are taking shape.* **5.** the form that anything assumes. **6.** pattern; mould. **7.** *Inf.* condition or state of efficiency: *to be in good shape.* **8. out of shape. a.** in bad physical condition. **b.** bent, twisted, or deformed. **9. take shape.** to assume a definite form. ~*vb.* **10.** (when *intr.,* often foll. by *into* or *up*) to receive or cause to receive shape or form. **11.** (*tr.*) to mould into a particular pattern or form. **12.** (*tr.*) to plan, devise, or prepare: *to shape a plan of action.* —'**shapable** or '**shapeable** *adj.* —'**shaper** *n.*

SHAPE (ʃeɪp) *n.* acronym for Supreme Headquarters Allied Powers Europe.

shapeless ('ʃeɪplɪs) *adj.* **1.** having no definite shape or form: *a shapeless mass.* **2.** lacking a symmetrical or aesthetically pleasing shape: *a shapeless figure.* —'**shapelessness** *n.*

shapely ('ʃeɪplɪ) *adj.* **-lier, -liest.** (esp. of a woman's body or legs) pleasing or attractive in shape. —'**shapeliness** *n.*

shape up *vb.* (*intr., adv.*) *Inf.* **1.** to proceed or develop satisfactorily. **2.** to develop a definite or proper form.

shard (ʃɑːd) or **sherd** *n.* **1.** a broken piece or fragment of a brittle substance, esp. of pottery. **2.** *Zool.* a tough sheath, scale, or shell, esp. the elytra of a beetle.

share[1] (ʃɛə) *n.* **1.** a part or portion of something owned or contributed by a person or group. **2.** (*often pl.*) any of the equal parts, usually of low par value, into which is divided the capital stock of a company. **3. go shares.** *Inf.* to share (something) with another or others. ~*vb.* **4.** (*tr.; often foll. by out*) to divide or apportion, esp. equally. **5.** (when *intr.,* often foll. by *in*) to receive or contribute a portion of: *we can share the cost of the petrol.* **6.** to join with another or others in the use of (something): *can I share your umbrella?* —'**sharable** or '**shareable** *adj.* —'**sharer** *n.*

share[2] (ʃɛə) *n.* short for **ploughshare.**

sharecropper ('ʃɛəˌkrɒpə) *n.* *Chiefly U.S.* a farmer, esp. a tenant farmer, who pays over a proportion of a crop or crops as rent.

shareholder ('ʃɛəˌhəʊldə) *n.* the owner of one or more shares in a company.

shark[1] (ʃɑːk) *n.* any of various usually ferocious fishes, with a long body, two dorsal fins, and rows of sharp teeth. —'**shark,like** *adj.*

shark[2] (ʃɑːk) *n.* a person who preys on or victimizes others, esp. by swindling or extortion.

sharkskin ('ʃɑːkˌskɪn) *n.* a smooth glossy fabric of acetate rayon, used for sportswear, etc.

sharp (ʃɑːp) *adj.* **1.** having a keen edge suitable for cutting. **2.** having an edge or point. **3.** involving a sudden change, esp. in direction: *a sharp bend.* **4.** moving, acting, or reacting quickly, etc.: *sharp reflexes.* **5.** clearly defined. **6.** mentally acute; keen-witted; attentive. **7.** sly or artful: *sharp practice.* **8.** bitter or harsh: *sharp words.* **9.** shrill or penetrating: *a sharp cry.* **10.** having an acrid taste. **11.** keen; biting: *a sharp wind.* **12.** *Music.* **a.** (*immediately postpositive*) denoting a note that has been raised in pitch by one chromatic semitone: *B sharp.* **b.** (of an instrument, voice, etc.) out of tune by being too high in pitch. Cf. **flat**[1] (sense 19). ~*adv.* **13.** in a sharp manner. **14.** exactly: *six o'clock sharp.* **15.** *Music.* **a.** higher than a standard pitch. **b.** out of tune by being too high in pitch: *she sings sharp.* Cf. **flat**[1] (sense 23). ~*n.* **16.** *Music.* **a.** an accidental that raises the pitch of the following note by one chromatic semitone. Usual symbol: ♯ **b.** a note affected by this accidental. Cf. **flat**[1] (sense 29). **17.** a thin needle with a sharp point. **18.** *Inf.* a sharper. ~*vb.* **19.** (*tr.*) *Music.* the usual U.S. word for **sharpen.** —'**sharpish** *adj., adv.* —'**sharply** *adv.* —'**sharpness** *n.*

sharpen ('ʃɑːpən) *vb.* **1.** to make or become sharp or sharper. **2.** *Music.* to raise the pitch of (a note), esp. by one semitone. —'**sharpener** *n.*

sharper ('ʃɑːpə) *n.* a person who cheats or swindles; fraud.

sharp-set *adj.* **1.** set to give an acute cutting angle. **2.** keenly hungry. **3.** keen or eager.

sharp-tongued *adj.* bitter or critical in speech; sarcastic.

sharp-witted *adj.* having or showing a keen intelligence; perceptive. —ˌsharp-'wittedly *adv.* —ˌsharp-'wittedness *n.*

shatter ('ʃætə) *vb.* **1.** to break or be broken into many small pieces. **2.** (*tr.*) to impair or destroy: *his nerves were shattered by the torture.* **3.** (*tr.*) to dumbfound or thoroughly upset: *she was shattered by the news.* —'**shatteringly** *adv.*

shave (ʃeɪv) *vb.* **shaving, shaved; shaved** or **shaven.** (*mainly tr.*) **1.** (*also intr.*) to remove (the beard, hair, etc.) from (the face, head, or body) by scraping the skin with a razor. **2.** to cut or trim very closely. **3.** to reduce to shavings. **4.** to remove thin slices from (wood, etc.) with a sharp cutting tool. **5.** to touch or graze in passing. **6.** *Inf.* to reduce (a price) by a slight amount. ~*n.* **7.** the act or an instance of shaving. **8.** any tool for scraping. **9.** a thin slice or shaving. **10. close shave.** *Inf.* a narrow escape. —'**shavable** or '**shaveable** *adj.*

shaver ('ʃeɪvə) *n.* **1.** a person or thing that shaves. **2.** Also called: **electric razor, electric shaver.** an electrically powered implement for shaving, having rotating blades behind a fine metal comb. **3.** *Inf.* a youngster, esp. a young boy.

Shavian ('ʃeɪvɪən) *adj.* **1.** of or like George Bernard Shaw (1856–1950), Irish dramatist, his works, ideas, etc. ~*n.* **2.** an admirer of Shaw or his works.

shaving ('ʃeɪvɪŋ) *n.* **1.** a thin paring or slice, esp. of wood, that has been shaved from something. ~*modifi-*

THESAURUS

shanty cabin, hovel, hut, lean-to, shack, shed, shiel (*Scot.*), shieling (*Scot.*)

shape *n.* 1. build, configuration, contours, cut, figure, form, lines, make, outline, profile, silhouette 2. frame, model, mould, pattern 3. appearance, aspect, form, guise, likeness, semblance 4. condition, fettle, health, kilter, state, trim ~*v.* 5. create, fashion, form, make, model, mould, produce 6. accommodate, adapt, define, develop, devise, frame, guide, modify, plan, prepare, regulate, remodel

shapeless amorphous, asymmetrical, battered, embryonic, formless, indeterminate, irregular, misshapen, nebulous, undeveloped, unstructured

share 1. *v.* apportion, assign, distribute, divide, go Dutch (*Inf.*), go fifty-fifty (*Inf.*), go halves, parcel out, partake, participate, receive, split, use in common 2. *n.* allotment,

allowance, contribution, cut (*Inf.*), division, due, lot, part, portion, proportion, quota, ration, whack (*Inf.*)

sharp *adj.* 1. acute, cutting, honed, jagged, keen, knife-edged, knifelike, pointed, razor-sharp, serrated, sharpened, spiky 2. abrupt, distinct, extreme, marked, sudden 3. alert, apt, astute, bright, clever, discerning, knowing, long-headed, observant, penetrating, perceptive, quick, quick-witted, ready, subtle 4. artful, crafty, cunning, dishonest, fly (*Sl.*), shrewd, sly, smart, unscrupulous, wily 5. acute, distressing, excruciating, fierce, intense, painful, piercing, severe, shooting, sore, stabbing, stinging, violent 6. clear, clear-cut, crisp, distinct, well-defined 7. *Inf.* chic, classy (*Sl.*), dressy, fashionable, natty (*Inf.*), smart, snappy, stylish 8. acrimonious, barbed, biting, bitter, caustic, cutting, harsh, hurtful, sarcastic, sardonic, scathing, severe,

trenchant, vitriolic 9. acerbic, acid, acrid, burning, hot, piquant, pungent, sour, tart, vinegary ~*adv.* 10. exactly, on the dot, on time, precisely, promptly, punctually 11. abruptly, suddenly, unexpectedly, without warning

sharpen edge, grind, hone, put an edge on, strop, whet

shatter 1. break, burst, crack, crush, crush to smithereens, demolish, explode, implode, pulverize, shiver, smash, split 2. blast, blight, bring to nought, demolish, destroy, disable, exhaust, impair, overturn, ruin, torpedo, wreck 3. break (someone's) heart, crush, devastate, dumbfound, knock the stuffing out of (someone) (*Inf.*), upset

shave *v.* 1. crop, pare, plane, shear, trim 2. brush, graze, touch

er. **2.** used when shaving the face, etc.: *shaving cream.*

shawl (ʃɔːl) *n.* a piece of fabric or knitted or crocheted material worn around the shoulders by women or wrapped around a baby.

she (ʃiː) *pron.* (*subjective*) **1.** refers to a female person or animal: *she is an actress.* **2.** refers to things personified as feminine, such as cars, ships, and nations. **3.** *Austral. & N.Z.* a pronoun often used instead of it, as in **she'll be right** it will be all right. ~*n.* **4.** a female person or animal.

sheaf (ʃiːf) *n., pl.* **sheaves** (ʃiːvz). **1.** a bundle of reaped but unthreshed corn tied with one or two bonds. **2.** a bundle of objects tied together. **3.** the arrows contained in a quiver. ~*vb.* **4.** (*tr.*) to bind or tie into a sheaf.

shear (ʃɪə) *vb.* **shearing, sheared** *or Austral. & N.Z.* **shore; sheared** *or* **shorn.** **1.** (*tr.*) to remove (the fleece or hair) of (sheep, etc.) by cutting or clipping. **2.** to cut or cut through (something) with shears or a sharp instrument. **3.** *Engineering.* to cause (a part, member, etc.) to deform or fracture or (of a part, etc.) to deform or fracture as a result of excess torsion. **4.** (*tr.; often foll. by of*) to strip or divest: *to shear someone of his power.* **5.** (when *intr.,* foll. by *through*) to move through (something) by or as if by cutting. ~*n.* **6.** the act, process, or an instance of shearing. **7.** a shearing of a sheep or flock of sheep: *a sheep of two shears.* **8.** a form of deformation or fracture in which parallel planes in a body slide over one another. **9.** *Physics.* the deformation of a body, part, etc., expressed as the lateral displacement between two points in parallel planes divided by the distance between the planes. **10.** either one of the blades of a pair of shears, scissors, etc. —'**shearer** *n.*

shears (ʃɪəz) *pl. n.* **1. a.** large scissors, as for cutting cloth, jointing poultry, etc. **b.** a large scissor-like and usually hand-held cutting tool with flat blades, as for cutting hedges. **2.** any of various analogous cutting implements.

shearwater (ˈʃɪəˌwɔːtə) *n.* any of several oceanic birds specialized for an aerial or aquatic existence.

sheath (ʃiːθ) *n., pl.* **sheaths** (ʃiːðz). **1.** a case or covering for the blade of a knife, sword, etc. **2.** any similar close-fitting case. **3.** *Biol.* an enclosing or protective structure. **4.** the protective covering on an electric cable. **5.** a figure-hugging dress with a narrow tapering skirt. **6.** another name for **condom.**

sheathe (ʃiːð) *vb.* (*tr.*) **1.** to insert (a knife, sword, etc.) into a sheath. **2.** (esp. of cats) to retract (the claws). **3.** to surface with or encase in a sheath or sheathing.

sheathing (ˈʃiːðɪŋ) *n.* **1.** any material used as an outer layer, as on a ship's hull. **2.** boarding, etc., used to cover a timber frame.

sheave (ʃiːv) *vb.* (*tr.*) to gather or bind into sheaves.

sheaves (ʃiːvz) *n.* the plural of **sheaf.**

shebeen *or* **shebean** (ʃəˈbiːn) *n.* **1.** *Irish, Scot., S. African.* a place where alcoholic drink is sold illegally. **2.** (in South Africa) a place where Black African men engage in social drinking.

shebeen king *or* (*fem.*) **shebeen queen** *n.* (in South Africa) the proprietor of a shebeen.

shed¹ (ʃɛd) *n.* **1.** a small building or lean-to of light construction, used for storage, shelter, etc. **2.** a large roofed structure, esp. one with open sides, used for storage, repairing locomotives, etc. **3.** *Austral.* the building in which sheep are shorn.

shed² (ʃɛd) *vb.* **shedding, shed.** (*mainly tr.*) **1.** to pour forth or cause to pour forth: *to shed tears.* **2.** **shed light on** *or* **upon.** to clarify (a problem, etc.). **3.** to cast off or lose: *the snake shed its skin.* **4.** to repel: *this coat sheds water.* **5.** *N.Z.* to separate or divide a group of sheep: *a good dog can shed his sheep in minutes.* ~*n.* **6.** short for **watershed.** **7.** *N.Z.* the action of separating or dividing a group of sheep: *the old dog was better at the shed than the young one.* —'**shedable** *or* '**sheddable** *adj.*

sheen (ʃiːn) *n.* **1.** a gleaming or glistening brightness; lustre. **2.** *Poetic.* splendid clothing. ~*adj.* **3.** *Rare.* beautiful. —'**sheeny** *adj.*

sheep (ʃiːp) *n., pl.* **sheep.** **1.** any of a genus of ruminant mammals having transversely ribbed horns and a narrow face. **2.** a meek or timid person. **3. separate the sheep from the goats.** to pick out the people who are superior in some respects. —'**sheep,like** *adj.*

sheep-dip *n.* **1.** any of several liquid disinfectants and insecticides in which sheep are immersed. **2.** a deep trough containing such a liquid.

sheepdog (ˈʃiːpˌdɒg) *n.* any of various breeds of dog reared originally for herding sheep. See **Old English sheepdog, Shetland sheepdog.**

sheepfold (ˈʃiːpˌfəʊld) *n.* a pen or enclosure for sheep.

sheepish (ˈʃiːpɪʃ) *adj.* **1.** abashed or embarrassed, esp. through looking foolish. **2.** resembling a sheep in timidity. —'**sheepishly** *adv.* —'**sheepishness** *n.*

sheep's eyes *pl. n. Inf.* amorous or inviting glances.

sheepshank (ˈʃiːpˌʃæŋk) *n.* a knot, hitch, or bend made in a rope to shorten it temporarily.

sheepskin (ˈʃiːpˌskɪn) *n.* **a.** the skin of a sheep, esp. when used for clothing, etc. **b.** (*as modifier*): *a sheepskin coat.*

sheer¹ (ʃɪə) *adj.* **1.** perpendicular; very steep: *a sheer cliff.* **2.** (of textiles) so fine as to be transparent. **3.** (*prenominal*) absolute: *sheer folly.* **4.** *Obs.* bright. ~*adv.* **5.** steeply. **6.** completely or absolutely. —'**sheerly** *adv.* —'**sheerness** *n.*

sheer² (ʃɪə) *vb.* (foll. by *off* or *away* (*from*)). **1.** to deviate or cause to deviate from a course. **2.** (*intr.*) to avoid an unpleasant person, thing, topic, etc. ~*n.* **3.** *Naut.* the position of a vessel relative to its mooring.

sheet¹ (ʃiːt) *n.* **1.** a large rectangular piece of cotton, linen, etc., generally one of a pair used as inner bedclothes. **2. a.** a thin piece of a substance such as paper, glass, or metal, usually rectangular in form. **b.** (*as modifier*): *sheet iron.* **3.** a broad continuous surface: *a sheet of water.* **4.** a newspaper, esp. a tabloid. **5.** a piece of printed paper to be folded into a section for a book. ~*vb.* **6.** (*tr.*) to provide with, cover, or wrap in a sheet.

sheet² (ʃiːt) *n. Naut.* a line or rope for controlling the position of a sail relative to the wind.

sheet anchor *n. Naut.* a large strong anchor for use in emergency.

sheet bend *n.* a knot used esp. for joining ropes of different sizes.

sheeting (ˈʃiːtɪŋ) *n.* fabric from which sheets are made.

sheet lightning *n.* lightning that appears as a broad sheet, caused by the reflection of more distant lightning.

sheet metal *n.* metal in the form of a sheet, the thickness being intermediate between that of plate and that of foil.

sheet music *n.* **1.** the printed or written copy of a short composition or piece. **2.** music in its written or printed form.

sheik *or* **sheikh** (ʃeɪk) *n.* (in Muslim countries) **a.** the head of an Arab tribe, village, etc. **b.** a religious leader. —'**sheikdom** *or* '**sheikhdom** *n.*

sheila (ˈʃiːlə) *n. Austral.* an old-fashioned word for **girl** or **woman.**

shekel (ˈʃɛkəl) *n.* **1.** any of several former coins and units of weight of the Near East. **2.** (*often pl.*) *Inf.* any coin or money.

shelduck (ˈʃɛlˌdʌk) *or* (*masc.*) **sheldrake** (ˈʃɛlˌdreɪk) *n., pl.* **-ducks, -duck** *or* **-drakes, -drake.** any of various large usually brightly coloured gooselike ducks of the Old World.

shelf (ʃɛlf) *n., pl.* **shelves** (ʃɛlvz). **1.** a thin flat plank of wood, metal, etc., fixed horizontally against a wall, etc., for the purpose of supporting objects. **2.** something resembling this in shape or function. **3.** the objects placed on a shelf: *a shelf of books.* **4.** a projecting layer of ice, rock, etc., on land or in the sea. **5. on the shelf.** put aside or abandoned, used esp. of unmarried women considered to be past the age of marriage. —'**shelf,like** *adj.*

shelf life *n.* the length of time a packaged food, etc., will last without deteriorating.

THESAURUS

shed *v.* **1.** afford, cast, diffuse, drop, emit, give, give forth, pour forth, radiate, scatter, shower, spill, throw **2.** cast off, discard, exuviate, moult, slough

sheepish abashed, chagrined, embarrassed, foolish, mortified, self-conscious, shamefaced, silly, uncomfortable

sheer 1. abrupt, headlong (*Archaic*), perpendicular, precipitous, steep **2.** absolute, arrant, complete, downright, out-and-out, pure, rank, thoroughgoing, total, unadulterated, unalloyed, unmitigated, unqualified, utter **3.** *Of fabrics* diaphanous, fine, gauzy, gossamer, seethrough, thin, transparent

sheet 1. coat, film, folio, lamina, layer, leaf, membrane, overlay, pane, panel, piece, plate, slab, stratum, surface, veneer **2.** area, blanket, covering, expanse, stretch, sweep

shell (ʃɛl) *n.* **1.** the protective outer layer of an egg, esp. a bird's egg. **2.** the hard outer covering of many molluscs. **3.** any other hard outer layer, such as the exoskeleton of many arthropods. **4.** the hard outer layer of some fruits, esp. of nuts. **5.** any hard outer case. **6.** a hollow artillery projectile filled with explosive primed to explode either during flight or on impact. **7.** a small-arms cartridge. **8.** a pyrotechnic cartridge designed to explode in the air. **9.** *Rowing.* a very light narrow racing boat. **10.** the external structure of a building, esp. one that is unfinished. **11.** *Physics.* a class of electron orbits in an atom in which the electrons have the same principal quantum number and little difference in their energy levels. **12. come** (*or* **bring**) **out of one's shell.** to become (or help a person to become) less shy and reserved. ∼*vb.* **13.** to divest or be divested of a shell, husk, etc. **14.** to separate or be separated from the ear, husk, etc. **15.** (*tr.*) to bombard with artillery shells. ∼See also **shell out.** —**'shell-less** *adj.* —**'shell-,like** *adj.* —**'shelly** *adj.*

she'll (ʃiːl; *unstressed* ʃɪl) *contraction of* she will *or* she shall.

shellac (ʃə'læk, 'ʃɛlæk) *n.* **1.** a yellowish resin secreted by the lac insect, esp. a commercial preparation of this used in varnishes, polishes, etc. **2.** Also called: **shellac varnish.** a varnish made by dissolving shellac in ethanol or a similar solvent. ∼*vb.* **-lacking, -lacked.** (*tr.*) **3.** to coat (an article, etc.) with a shellac varnish.

shellfire ('ʃɛl,faɪə) *n.* the firing of artillery shells.

shellfish ('ʃɛl,fɪʃ) *n., pl.* **-fish** *or* **-fishes.** any aquatic invertebrate having a shell or shell-like carapace, esp. such an animal used as human food. Examples are crustaceans such as crabs and lobsters and molluscs such as oysters.

shell out *vb.* (*adv.*) *Inf.* to pay out or hand over (money).

shellproof ('ʃɛl,pruːf) *adj.* designed, intended, or able to resist shellfire.

shell shock *n.* loss of sight, etc., resulting from psychological strain during prolonged engagement in warfare. —**'shell-,shocked** *adj.*

Shelta ('ʃɛltə) *n.* a secret language used by some itinerant tinkers in Ireland and parts of Britain, based on Gaelic.

shelter ('ʃɛltə) *n.* **1.** something that provides cover or protection, as from weather or danger. **2.** the protection afforded by such a cover. **3.** the state of being sheltered. ∼*vb.* **4.** (*tr.*) to provide with or protect by a shelter. **5.** (*intr.*) to take cover, as from rain. **6.** (*tr.*) to act as a shelter for. —**'shelterer** *n.*

sheltie *or* **shelty** ('ʃɛltɪ) *n., pl.* **-ties.** another name for **Shetland pony** *or* **Shetland sheepdog.**

shelve¹ (ʃɛlv) *vb.* (*tr.*) **1.** to place on a shelf. **2.** to provide with shelves. **3.** to put aside or postpone from consideration. **4.** to dismiss or cause to retire. —**'shelver** *n.*

shelve² (ʃɛlv) *vb.* (*intr.*) to slope away gradually.

shelves (ʃɛlvz) *n.* the plural of **shelf.**

shelving ('ʃɛlvɪŋ) *n.* **1.** material for making shelves. **2.** a set of shelves; shelves collectively.

shenanigan (ʃɪ'nænɪgən) *n. Inf.* **1.** (*usually pl.*) roguishness; mischief. **2.** an act of treachery; deception.

shepherd ('ʃɛpəd) *n.* **1.** a person employed to tend sheep. Fem. equivalent: **shepherdess. 2.** a person, such as a clergyman, who watches over a group of people. ∼*vb.* (*tr.*) **3.** to guide or watch over in the manner of a shepherd. **4.** *Austral. Rules football, Rugby, etc.* to prevent opponents from tackling (a member of one's

own team) by blocking their path: illegal in Rugby.

shepherd's pie *n. Chiefly Brit.* a baked dish of minced meat covered with mashed potato.

Sheraton ('ʃɛrətən) *adj.* denoting furniture made by or in the style of Thomas Sheraton (1751-1806), English furniture maker, characterized by lightness and elegance.

sherbet ('ʃɜːbət) *n.* **1.** a fruit-flavoured slightly effervescent powder, eaten as a sweet or used to make a drink. **2.** another word (esp. U.S.) for **sorbet** (sense 1).

sherd (ʃɜːd) *n.* another word for **shard.**

sheriff ('ʃɛrɪf) *n.* **1.** (in the U.S.) the chief elected law-enforcement officer in a county. **2.** (in Canada) a municipal official who enforces court orders, escorts convicted criminals to prison, etc. **3.** (in England and Wales) the chief executive officer of the Crown in a county, having chiefly ceremonial duties. **4.** (in Scotland) a judge in any of the sheriff courts.

sheriff court *n.* (in Scotland) a court having jurisdiction to try all but the most serious crimes and to deal with most civil actions.

Sherpa ('ʃɜːpə) *n., pl.* **-pas** *or* **-pa.** a member of a Tibetan people living on the southern slopes of the Himalayas in Nepal, noted as mountaineers.

sherry ('ʃɛrɪ) *n., pl.* **-ries.** a fortified wine, originally only from the Jerez region of southern Spain.

she's (ʃiːz) *contraction of* she is *or* she has.

Shetland pony ('ʃɛtlənd) *n.* a very small sturdy breed of pony with a long shaggy mane and tail.

Shetland sheepdog *n.* a small sheepdog similar in appearance to a collie.

shew (ʃəʊ) *vb.* **shewing, shewed; shewn** *or* **shewed.** an archaic spelling of **show.**

shibboleth ('ʃɪbə,lɛθ) *n.* a custom, phrase, or use of language that distinguishes members of a particular social class, profession, etc., from other people.

shied (ʃaɪd) *vb.* the past tense or past participle of **shy**².

shield (ʃiːld) *n.* **1.** any protection used to intercept blows, missiles, etc., such as a tough piece of armour carried on the arm. **2.** any similar protective device. **3.** *Heraldry.* a pointed stylized shield used for displaying armorial bearings. **4.** anything that resembles a shield in shape, such as a prize in a sports competition. **5.** *Physics.* a structure of concrete, lead, etc., placed around a nuclear reactor. **6.** a broad stable plateau of ancient Precambrian rocks forming the rigid nucleus of a particular continent. **7. the shield.** *N.Z.* the Bledisloe shield, a trophy competed for by provincial rugby teams. ∼*vb.* (*tr.*) **8.** to protect, hide, or conceal (something) from danger or harm. —**'shield,like** *adj.*

Shield (ʃiːld) *n.* **the.** *Canad.* another term for the **Canadian Shield.**

shieling ('ʃiːlɪŋ) *n. Chiefly Scot.* **1.** a temporary shelter used by people tending cattle on high ground. **2.** pasture land for the grazing of cattle in summer.

shift (ʃɪft) *vb.* **1.** to move or cause to move from one place or position to another. **2.** (*tr.*) to change for another or others. **3.** to change (gear) in a motor vehicle. **4.** (*intr.*) (of a sound or set of sounds) to alter in a systematic way. **5.** (*intr.*) to provide for one's needs (esp. in **shift for oneself**). **6.** to remove or be removed, esp. with difficulty: *no detergent can shift these stains.* **7.** *Sl.* to move quickly. ∼*n.* **8.** the act or an instance of shifting. **9.** a group of workers who work for a specific period. **10.** the period of time worked by such a group. **11.** an expedient, contrivance, or artifice. **12.** an underskirt or dress with little shaping. —**'shifter** *n.*

shiftless ('ʃɪftlɪs) *adj.* lacking in ambition or initiative. —**'shiftlessness** *n.*

THESAURUS

shell *n.* 1. carapace, case, husk, pod ∼*v.* 2. husk, shuck 3. attack, barrage, blitz, bomb, bombard, strafe, strike ∼*n.* 4. chassis, frame, framework, hull, skeleton, structure

shelter 1. *v.* cover, defend, guard, harbour, hide, protect, safeguard, seek refuge, shield, take in, take shelter 2. *n.* asylum, cover, covert, defence, guard, haven, protection, refuge, retreat, roof over one's head, safety, sanctuary, screen, security, shiel (*Scot.*), umbrella

sheltered cloistered, conventual, ensconced, hermitic, isolated, protected, quiet, reclusive, retired, screened, secluded, shad-

ed, shielded, withdrawn

shelve defer, dismiss, freeze, hold in abeyance, hold over, lay aside, mothball, pigeonhole, postpone, put aside, put off, put on ice, table (*U.S.*)

shepherd *v.* conduct, convoy, guide, herd, marshal, steer, usher

shield *n.* 1. buckler, escutcheon (*Heraldry*), targe (*Archaic*) 2. aegis, bulwark, cover, defence, guard, protection, rampart, safeguard, screen, shelter, ward (*Archaic*) ∼*v.* 3. cover, defend, guard, protect, safeguard, screen, shelter, ward off

shift *v.* 1. alter, budge, change, displace,

fluctuate, move, move around, rearrange, relocate, remove, reposition, swerve, switch, transfer, transpose, vary, veer 2. *As in* **shift for oneself** assume responsibility, contrive, devise, fend, get along, look after, make do, manage, plan, scheme, take care of ∼*n.* 3. about-turn, alteration, change, displacement, fluctuation, modification, move, permutation, rearrangement, removal, shifting, switch, transfer, veering 4. artifice, contrivance, craft, device, dodge, equivocation, evasion, expedient, move, resource, ruse, stratagem, subterfuge, trick, wile

shifty ('ʃɪftɪ) *adj.* **shiftier, shiftiest.** **1.** given to evasions. **2.** furtive in character or appearance. —'**shiftily** *adv.* —'**shiftiness** *n.*

shillelagh *or* **shillala** (ʃə'leɪlə, -lɪ) *n.* (in Ireland) a stout club or cudgel.

shilling ('ʃɪlɪŋ) *n.* **1.** a British silver or (later) cupronickel coin worth one twentieth of a pound, replaced by the 5p piece in 1970. Abbrev.: **s., sh.** **2.** the standard monetary unit of Kenya, Uganda, the Somali Republic, and Tanzania.

shillyshally ('ʃɪlɪˌʃælɪ) *Inf.* ~*vb.* **-lying, -lied.** **1.** (*intr.*) to be indecisive, esp. over unimportant matters. ~*adv.* **2.** in an indecisive manner. ~*adj.* **3.** indecisive or hesitant. ~*n., pl.* **-lies.** **4.** vacillation. —'**shilly,shallier** *n.*

shim (ʃɪm) *n.* **1.** a thin washer or strip often used with a number of similar washers or strips to adjust a clearance for gears, etc. ~*vb.* **shimming, shimmed.** **2.** (*tr.*) to modify clearance on (a gear, etc.) by use of shims.

shimmer ('ʃɪmə) *vb.* **1.** (*intr.*) to shine with a glistening or tremulous light. ~*n.* **2.** a faint, glistening, or tremulous light. —'**shimmeringly** *adv.* —'**shimmery** *adj.*

shimmy ('ʃɪmɪ) *n., pl.* **-mies.** **1.** an American ragtime dance with much shaking of the hips and shoulders. **2.** abnormal wobbling motion in a motor vehicle, esp. in the front wheels or steering. ~*vb.* **-mying, -mied.** (*intr.*) **3.** to dance the shimmy. **4.** to vibrate or wobble.

shin (ʃɪn) *n.* **1.** the front part of the lower leg. **2.** the front edge of the tibia. **3.** *Chiefly Brit.* a cut of beef, the lower foreleg. ~*vb.* **shinning, shinned.** **4.** (when *intr.*, often foll. by *up*) to climb (a pole, tree, etc.) by gripping with the hands or arms and the legs and hauling oneself up. **5.** (*tr.*) to kick (a person) in the shins.

shinbone ('ʃɪnˌbəʊn) *n.* the nontechnical name for **tibia** (sense 1).

shindig ('ʃɪnˌdɪg) *or* **shindy** ('ʃɪndɪ) *n., pl.* **-digs** *or* **-dies.** *Sl.* **1.** a noisy party, dance, etc. **2.** a quarrel or commotion.

shine (ʃaɪn) *vb.* **shining, shone.** **1.** (*intr.*) to emit light. **2.** (*intr.*) to glow or be bright with reflected light. **3.** (*tr.*) to direct the light of (a lamp, etc.): *he shone the torch in my eyes.* **4.** (*tr.; p.t. & p.p.* **shined**) to cause to gleam by polishing: *to shine shoes.* **5.** (*intr.*) to excel: *she shines at tennis.* **6.** (*intr.*) to appear clearly. ~*n.* **7.** the state or quality of shining; sheen; lustre. **8. come rain or shine.** whatever the weather. **9.** *Inf.* a liking or fancy (esp. in **take a shine to**).

shiner ('ʃaɪnə) *n.* **1.** something that shines, such as a polishing device. **2.** any of numerous small North American freshwater cyprinid fishes. **3.** *Inf.* a black eye. **4.** *N.Z. old-fashioned sl.* a tramp.

shingle[1] ('ʃɪŋgəl) *n.* **1.** a thin rectangular tile, esp. one made of wood, that is laid with others in overlapping rows to cover a roof or a wall. **2.** a woman's short-cropped hair style. **3.** *U.S. inf.* a small signboard fixed outside the office of a doctor, lawyer, etc. ~*vb.* (*tr.*) **4.** to cover (a roof or a wall) with shingles. **5.** to cut (the hair) in a short-cropped style. —'**shingler** *n.*

shingle[2] ('ʃɪŋgəl) *n.* **1.** coarse gravel, esp. the pebbles found on beaches. **2.** a place or area strewn with shingle. —'**shingly** *adj.*

shingles ('ʃɪŋgəlz) *n.* an acute viral disease characterized by inflammation, pain, and skin eruptions along the course of affected nerves. Technical names: **herpes zoster, zoster.**

Shinto ('ʃɪntəʊ) *n.* the religion of Japan, polytheistic in character and incorporating the worship of a number of ethnic divinities. —'**Shintoism** *n.* —'**Shintoist** *n., adj.*

shinty ('ʃɪntɪ) *n., pl.* **-ties.** **1.** a simple form of hockey played with a ball and sticks curved at the lower end. **2.** the stick used in this game.

shiny ('ʃaɪnɪ) *adj.* **shinier, shiniest.** **1.** glossy or polished; bright. **2.** (of clothes or material) worn to a smooth and glossy state, as by continual rubbing. —'**shininess** *n.*

ship (ʃɪp) *n.* **1.** a vessel propelled by engines or sails for navigating on the water, esp. a large vessel. **2.** *Naut.* a large sailing vessel with three or more square-rigged masts. **3.** the crew of a ship. **4.** short for **airship** or **spaceship.** **5. when one's ship comes in** (*or* **home**). when one has become successful. ~*vb.* **shipping, shipped.** **6.** to place, transport, or travel on any conveyance, esp. aboard a ship. **7.** (*tr.*) *Naut.* to take (water) over the side. **8.** to bring or go aboard a vessel: *to ship oars.* **9.** (*tr.; often foll. by off*) *Inf.* to send away: *they shipped the children off to boarding school.* **10.** (*intr.*) to engage to serve aboard a ship: *I shipped aboard a Liverpool liner.* —'**shippable** *adj.*

-ship *suffix forming nouns.* **1.** indicating state or condition: *fellowship.* **2.** indicating rank, office, or position: *lordship.* **3.** indicating craft or skill: *scholarship.*

shipboard ('ʃɪpˌbɔːd) *n.* (*modifier*) taking place, used, or intended for use aboard a ship: *a shipboard encounter.*

shipbuilder ('ʃɪpˌbɪldə) *n.* a person or business engaged in the building of ships. —'**ship,building** *n.*

shipmaster ('ʃɪpˌmɑːstə) *n., pl.* **-masters.** the master or captain of a ship.

shipmate ('ʃɪpˌmeɪt) *n.* a sailor who serves on the same ship as another.

shipment ('ʃɪpmənt) *n.* **1. a.** goods shipped together as part of the same lot: *a shipment of grain.* **b.** (*as modifier*): *a shipment schedule.* **2.** the act of shipping cargo.

ship money *n. English history.* a tax levied to finance the fitting out of warships: abolished 1640.

shipowner ('ʃɪpˌəʊnə) *n.* a person who owns or has shares in a ship or ships.

shipper ('ʃɪpə) *n.* a person or company in the business of shipping freight.

shipping ('ʃɪpɪŋ) *n.* **1. a.** the business of transporting freight, esp. by ship. **b.** (*as modifier*): *a shipping magnate.* **2.** ships collectively: *there is a lot of shipping in the Channel.*

shipshape ('ʃɪpˌʃeɪp) *adj.* **1.** neat; orderly. ~*adv.* **2.** in a neat and orderly manner.

shipwreck ('ʃɪpˌrɛk) *n.* **1.** the partial or total destruction of a ship at sea. **2.** a wrecked ship or part of such a ship. **3.** ruin or destruction: *the shipwreck of all my hopes.* ~*vb.* (*tr.*) **4.** to wreck or destroy (a ship). **5.** to bring to ruin or destruction.

shipwright ('ʃɪpˌraɪt) *n.* an artisan skilled in one or more of the tasks required to build vessels.

shipyard ('ʃɪpˌjɑːd) *n.* a place or facility for the building, maintenance, and repair of ships.

shire (ʃaɪə) *n.* **1. a.** one of the British counties. **b.** (*in combination*): *Yorkshire.* **2.** (in Australia) a rural district having its own local council. **3.** See **shire horse.** **4. the Shires.** the Midland counties of England, famous for hunting, etc.

shire horse *n.* a large heavy breed of carthorse with long hair on the fetlocks.

shirk (ʃɜːk) *vb.* **1.** to avoid discharging (work, a duty, etc.); evade. ~*n.* also **shirker.** **2.** a person who shirks.

shirr (ʃɜː) *vb.* **1.** to gather (fabric) into two or more parallel rows to decorate a dress, blouse, etc., often using elastic thread. **2.** (*tr.*) to bake (eggs) out of their shells. ~*n.* also **shirring.** **3.** a series of gathered rows decorating a dress, blouse, etc.

shirt (ʃɜːt) *n.* **1.** a garment worn on the upper part of the body, esp. by men, usually having a collar and sleeves and buttoning up the front. **2.** short for **nightshirt.** **3. keep your shirt on.** *Inf.* to refrain from losing

---

THESAURUS

shifty contriving, crafty, deceitful, devious, duplicitous, evasive, fly-by-night (*Inf.*), furtive, scheming, slippery, tricky, underhand, unprincipled, untrustworthy, wily

shimmer **1.** *v.* dance, gleam, glisten, phosphoresce, scintillate, twinkle **2.** *n.* diffused light, gleam, glimmer, glow, incandescence, iridescence, lustre, phosphorescence, unsteady light

shine *v.* **1.** beam, emit light, flash, give off light, glare, gleam, glimmer, glisten, glitter, glow, radiate, scintillate, shimmer, sparkle,

twinkle **2.** be conspicuous (distinguished, outstanding, pre-eminent), excel, stand out, stand out in a crowd, star **3.** brush, buff, burnish, polish, rub up ~*n.* **4.** brightness, glare, gleam, lambency, light, luminosity, radiance, shimmer, sparkle **5.** glaze, gloss, lustre, patina, polish, sheen

shining **1.** beaming, bright, brilliant, effulgent, gleaming, glistening, glittering, luminous, radiant, resplendent, shimmering, sparkling **2.** *Fig.* brilliant, celebrated, conspicuous, distinguished, eminent, glorious, il-

lustrious, leading, outstanding, splendid

shiny agleam, bright, burnished, gleaming, glistening, glossy, lustrous, nitid (*Poetic*), polished, satiny, sheeny

shirk avoid, dodge, duck (out of) (*Inf.*), evade, get out of, scrimshank (*Brit. military sl.*), shun, sidestep, skive (*Brit. sl.*), slack

shirker clock-watcher, dodger, gold brick (*U.S. sl.*), idler, malingerer, quitter, scrimshanker (*Brit. military sl.*), shirk, skiver (*Brit. sl.*), slacker

one's temper. **4. put** or **lose one's shirt on.** *Inf.* to bet or lose all one has on (a horse, etc.).

shirting (ˈʃɜːtɪŋ) *n.* fabric used in making men's shirts.

shirtsleeve (ˈʃɜːtˌsliːv) *n.* **1.** the sleeve of a shirt. **2. in one's shirtsleeves.** not wearing a jacket.

shirt-tail *n.* the part of a shirt that extends below the waist.

shirtwaister (ˈʃɜːtˌweɪstə) or *U.S.* **shirtwaist** *n.* a woman's dress with a tailored bodice resembling a shirt.

shirty (ˈʃɜːtɪ) *adj.* **shirtier, shirtiest.** *Sl., chiefly Brit.* bad-tempered or annoyed.

shish kebab (ˈʃiːʃ kəˈbæb) *n.* the full term for **kebab.**

shit (ʃɪt) *vb.* **shitting; shitted** or **shit.** **1.** to defecate. ~*n.* **2.** faeces; excrement. **3.** *Sl.* rubbish; nonsense. ~*interj.* **4.** *Sl.* an exclamation expressing anger, disgust, etc. —ˈ**shitty** *adj.*

shiver[1] (ˈʃɪvə) *vb.* (*intr.*) **1.** to shake or tremble, as from cold or fear. ~*n.* **2.** the act of shivering; a tremulous motion. **3. the shivers.** an attack of shivering, esp. through fear or illness. —ˈ**shiverer** *n.* —ˈ**shivery** *adj.*

shiver[2] (ˈʃɪvə) *vb.* **1.** to break or cause to break into fragments. ~*n.* **2.** a splintered piece.

shoal[1] (ʃəʊl) *n.* **1.** a stretch of shallow water. **2.** a sandbank or rocky area, esp. one that is visible at low water. ~*vb.* **3.** to make or become shallow. **4.** (*intr.*) *Naut.* to sail into shallower water. ~*adj.* also **shoaly.** **5.** a less common word for **shallow.**

shoal[2] (ʃəʊl) *n.* **1.** a large group of fish. **2.** a large group of people or things. ~*vb.* **3.** (*intr.*) to collect together in such a group.

shock[1] (ʃɒk) *vb.* **1.** to experience or cause to experience extreme horror, disgust, surprise, etc.: *the atrocities shocked us.* **2.** to cause a state of shock in (a person). **3.** to come or cause to come into violent contact. ~*n.* **4.** a sudden and violent jarring blow or impact. **5.** something that causes a sudden and violent disturbance in the emotions. **6.** *Pathol.* a state of bodily collapse, as from severe bleeding, burns, fright, etc. **7.** See **electric shock.** —ˈ**shockable** *adj.* —ˌ**shocka'bility** *n.* —ˈ**shocker** *n.*

shock[2] (ʃɒk) *n.* **1.** a number of sheaves set on end in a field to dry. **2.** a pile or stack of unthreshed corn. ~*vb.* **3.** (*tr.*) to set up (sheaves) in shocks.

shock[3] (ʃɒk) *n.* a thick bushy mass, esp. of hair.

shock absorber *n.* any device designed to absorb mechanical shock, esp. one fitted to a motor vehicle to damp the recoil of the road springs.

shocking (ˈʃɒkɪŋ) *adj.* **1.** causing shock, horror, or disgust. **2. shocking pink.** a garish shade of pink. **3.** *Inf.* very bad or terrible: *shocking weather.* —ˈ**shockingly** *adv.*

shockproof (ˈʃɒkˌpruːf) *adj.* capable of absorbing shock without damage.

shock therapy or **treatment** *n.* the treatment of certain psychotic conditions by injecting drugs or by passing an electric current through the brain (**electroconvulsive therapy**) to produce convulsions and coma.

shod (ʃɒd) *vb.* a past participle of **shoe.**

shoddy (ˈʃɒdɪ) *adj.* **-dier, -diest.** **1.** imitating something of better quality. **2.** of poor quality. ~*n.* **3.** a yarn or fabric made from wool waste or clippings. **4.** anything of inferior quality that is designed to simulate superior quality. —ˈ**shoddily** *adv.* —ˈ**shoddiness** *n.*

shoe (ʃuː) *n.* **1. a.** one of a matching pair of coverings shaped to fit the foot, esp. one ending below the ankle, having an upper of leather, plastic, etc., on a sole and heel of heavier material. **b.** (*as modifier*): *shoe cleaner.* **2.** anything resembling a shoe in shape, function, position, etc., such as a horseshoe. **3.** a band of metal or wood on the bottom of the runner of a sledge. **4.** See **brake shoe.** **5. be in (a person's) shoes.** *Inf.* to be in another person's situation. ~*vb.* **shoeing, shod.** (*tr.*) **6.** to furnish with shoes. **7.** to fit (a horse) with horseshoes. **8.** to furnish with a hard cover, such as a metal plate, for protection against friction or bruising.

shoehorn (ˈʃuːˌhɔːn) *n.* a smooth curved implement of horn, metal, plastic, etc., inserted at the heel of a shoe to ease the foot into it.

shoelace (ˈʃuːˌleɪs) *n.* a cord or lace for fastening shoes.

shoe leather *n.* **1.** leather used to make shoes. **2. save shoe leather.** to avoid wearing out shoes, as by taking a bus rather than walking.

shoemaker (ˈʃuːˌmeɪkə) *n.* a person who makes or repairs shoes or boots. —ˈ**shoeˌmaking** *n.*

shoestring (ˈʃuːˌstrɪŋ) *n.* **1.** another word for **shoelace.** **2.** *Inf.* a very small or petty amount of money (esp. in **on a shoestring**).

shoetree (ˈʃuːˌtriː) *n.* a wooden or metal form inserted into a shoe or boot to stretch it or preserve its shape.

shone (ʃɒn; *U.S.* ʃəʊn) *vb.* the past tense or past participle of **shine.**

shoo (ʃuː) *interj.* **1.** go away!: used to drive away unwanted or annoying people, animals, etc. ~*vb.* **shooing, shooed.** **2.** (*tr.*) to drive away by or as if by crying "shoo". **3.** (*intr.*) to cry "shoo".

shook (ʃʊk) *vb.* the past tense of **shake.**

shoot (ʃuːt) *vb.* **shooting, shot.** **1.** (*tr.*) to hit, wound, damage, or kill with a missile fired from a weapon. **2.** to discharge (a missile or missiles) from a weapon. **3.** to fire (a weapon) or (of a weapon) to be fired. **4.** to send out or be sent out as if from a weapon: *he shot questions at her.* **5.** (*intr.*) to move very rapidly. **6.** (*tr.*) to slide or push into or out of a fastening: *to shoot a bolt.* **7.** to emit (a ray of light) or (of a ray of light) to be emitted. **8.** (*tr.*) to go or pass quickly over or through: *to shoot rapids.* **9.** (*intr.*) to hunt game with a gun for sport. **10.** (*tr.*) to pass over (an area) in hunting game. **11.** (*intr.*) (of a plant) to produce (buds, branches, etc.). **12.** to photograph or record (a sequence, etc.). **13.** (*tr.; usually passive*) to variegate or streak, as with colour. **14.** *Soccer, hockey, etc.* to hit or propel (the ball, etc.) towards the goal. **15.** (*tr.*) *Sport, chiefly U.S.* to score (strokes, etc.): *he shot 72 on the first round.* **16.** (*tr.*) to measure the altitude of (a celestial body). **17.** (*often foll. by* up) *Sl.* to inject (someone, esp. oneself) with (a drug, esp. heroin). **18. shoot a line.** *Sl.* **a.** to boast. **b.** to tell a lie. ~*n.* **19.** the act of shooting. **20.** the action or motion of something that is shot. **21.** the first aerial part of a plant to develop from a germinating seed. **22.** any new growth of a plant, such as a bud, etc. **23.** *Chiefly Brit.* a meeting or party organized for hunting game with guns. **24.** an area where game can be hunted with guns. **25.** a steep descent in a stream; rapid. **26. the whole shoot.** *Sl.* everything. ~*interj.* **27.** *U.S.* an exclamation expressing disbelief, scepticism, etc. —ˈ**shooter** *n.*

shooting brake *n. Brit.* another name for **estate car.**

shooting star *n.* an informal name for **meteor.**

shooting stick *n.* a device that resembles a walking stick, having a spike at one end and a folding seat at the other.

shop (ʃɒp) *n.* **1.** a place, esp. a small building, for the retail sale of goods and services. **2.** a place for the performance of a specified type of work; workshop. **3. all over the shop.** *Inf.* **a.** in disarray: *his papers were all over the shop.* **b.** in every direction: *I've searched for it all over the shop.* **4. shut up shop.** to close business at the end of the day or permanently. **5. talk shop.** *Inf.* to discuss one's business, profession, etc., esp. on a social occasion.

THESAURUS

shiver *v.* break, crack, fragment, shatter, smash, smash to smithereens, splinter

shivery chilled, chilly, cold, quaking, quivery, shaking, trembly

shoal sandbank, sand bar, shallow, shelf

shock *v.* **1.** agitate, appal, astound, disgust, disquiet, give (someone) a turn (*Inf.*), horrify, jar, jolt, nauseate, numb, offend, outrage, paralyse, revolt, scandalize, shake, shake out of one's complacency, shake up (*Inf.*), sicken, stagger, stun, stupefy, traumatize, unsettle ~*n.* **2.** blow, bolt from the blue, bombshell, breakdown, collapse, consternation, distress, disturbance, prostration, state of shock, stupefaction, stupor, trauma, turn (*Inf.*), upset **3.** blow, clash, collision, encounter, impact, jarring, jolt

shocking abominable, appalling, atrocious, detestable, disgraceful, disgusting, disquieting, distressing, dreadful, foul, frightful, ghastly, hideous, horrible, horrifying, loathsome, monstrous, nauseating, odious, offensive, outrageous, repulsive, revolting, scandalous, sickening, stupefying, unspeakable

shoddy cheap-jack (*Inf.*), inferior, junky, poor, rubbishy, second-rate, slipshod, tacky (*Inf.*), tatty, tawdry, trashy

shoemaker bootmaker, cobbler, souter (*Scot.*)

shoot[1] *v.* **1.** bag, blast (*Sl.*), bring down, hit, kill, open fire, pick off, plug (*Sl.*), pump full of lead (*Sl.*), zap (*Sl.*) **2.** discharge, emit, fire, fling, hurl, launch, let fly, project, propel **3.** bolt, charge, dart, dash, flash, fly, hurtle, race, rush, scoot, speed, spring, streak, tear, whisk, whiz (*Inf.*)

shoot[2] **1.** *n.* branch, bud, offshoot, scion, slip, sprig, sprout, twig **2.** *v.* bud, burgeon, germinate, put forth new growth, sprout

~*vb.* **shopping, shopped. 6.** (*intr.; often foll. by for*) to visit a shop or shops in search of (goods) with the intention of buying them. **7.** (*tr.*) *Sl., chiefly Brit.* to inform on (someone) to the police. —'**shopping** *n.*

shop around *vb.* (*intr., adv.*) *Inf.* **1.** to visit a number of shops or stores to compare goods and prices. **2.** to consider a number of possibilities before making a choice.

shop assistant *n.* a person who serves in a shop.

shop floor *n.* **1.** the part of a factory housing the machines and men directly involved in production. **2.** workers, esp. factory workers organized in a union.

shopkeeper ('ʃɒpˌkiːpə) *n.* a person who owns or manages a shop or small store. —'**shop,keeping** *n.*

shoplifter ('ʃɒpˌlɪftə) *n.* a person who steals goods from a shop. —'**shop,lifting** *n.*

shopper ('ʃɒpə) *n.* a person who buys goods in a shop.

shopping centre *n.* **1.** the area of a town where most of the shops are situated. **2.** a complex of stores, restaurants, etc. with an adjoining car park.

shopping mall *n. U.S., Canad., & Austral.* a large enclosed shopping centre, often with central heating and air conditioning.

shopping plaza *n. Chiefly U.S. & Canad.* a shopping centre, esp. a small group of stores built as a strip.

shopsoiled ('ʃɒpˌsɔɪld) *adj.* worn, faded, etc., from being displayed in a shop or store.

shop steward *n.* an elected representative of the union workers in a shop, factory, etc.

shoptalk ('ʃɒpˌtɔːk) *n.* conversation concerning one's work, esp. when carried on outside business hours.

shopwalker ('ʃɒpˌwɔːkə) *n. Brit.* a person employed by a departmental store to supervise sales personnel, assist customers, etc.

shore[1] (ʃɔː) *n.* **1.** the land along the edge of a sea, lake, or wide river. Related adj.: **littoral. 2. a.** land, as opposed to water. **b.** (*as modifier*): *shore duty.* **3.** *Law.* the tract of coastal lying between the ordinary marks of high and low water. **4.** (*often pl.*) a country: *his native shores.*

shore[2] (ʃɔː) *n.* **1.** a prop or beam used to support a wall, building, etc. ~*vb.* **2.** (*tr.; often foll. by up*) to make safe with or as if with a shore. —'**shoring** *n.*

shoreline ('ʃɔːˌlaɪn) *n.* the edge of a body of water.

shoreward ('ʃɔːwəd) *adj.* **1.** near or facing the shore. ~*adv.* also **shorewards. 2.** towards the shore.

shorn (ʃɔːn) *vb.* a past participle of **shear.**

short (ʃɔːt) *adj.* **1.** of little length; not long. **2.** of little height; not tall. **3.** of limited duration. **4.** deficient: *the number of places laid at the table was short by four.* **5.** (*postpositive; often foll. by of or on*) lacking (in) or needful (of): *I'm always short of money.* **6.** concise; succinct. **7.** (of drinks) consisting chiefly of a spirit, such as whisky. **8.** *Cricket.* (of a fielding position) near the batsman: *short leg.* **9.** lacking in the power of retentiveness: *a short memory.* **10.** abrupt to the point of rudeness: *the salesgirl was very short with him.* **11.** (of betting odds) almost even. **12.** *Finance.* **a.** not possessing the securities or commodities that have been sold under contract and therefore obliged to make a purchase before the delivery date. **b.** of or relating to such sales, which depend on falling prices for profit. **13.** *Phonetics.* **a.** denoting a vowel of relatively brief temporal duration. **b.** (in popular usage) denoting the qualities of the five English vowels represented orthographically in the words *pat, pet,*

pit, pot, put, and *putt.* **14.** *Prosody.* **a.** denoting a vowel that is phonetically short or a syllable containing such a vowel. **b.** (of a vowel or syllable in verse) not carrying emphasis or accent. **15.** (of pastry) crumbly in texture. **16. caught** *or* **taken short.** having a sudden need to urinate or defecate. **17. short for.** an abbreviation for. **18. short and sweet.** unexpectedly brief. **19. in short supply.** scarce. ~*adv.* **20.** abruptly: *to stop short.* **21.** briefly or concisely. **22.** rudely or curtly. **23. fall short.** not to reach the required mark or standard. **24.** *Finance.* without possessing the securities or commodities at the time of their contractual sale: *to sell short.* **25. go short.** not to have a sufficient amount, etc. **26. short of.** except: *nothing short of a miracle can save him now.* ~*n.* **27.** anything that is short. **28.** a drink consisting of a spirit, often with lime, soda, etc., added. **29.** *Phonetics, prosody.* a short vowel or syllable. **30.** *Finance.* **a.** a short contract or sale. **b.** a short seller. **31.** a short film, usually of a factual nature. **32.** See **short circuit. 33. for short.** *Inf.* as an abbreviation: *he is called Jim for short.* **34. in short. a.** as a summary. **b.** in a few words. ~*vb.* **35.** See **short-circuit.** —'**shortness** *n.*

shortage ('ʃɔːtɪdʒ) *n.* a deficiency or lack in the amount needed, expected, or due; deficit.

shortbread ('ʃɔːtˌbrɛd) *n.* a rich crumbly biscuit made with a large proportion of butter.

shortcake ('ʃɔːtˌkeɪk) *n.* **1.** shortbread. **2.** a dessert made of layers of biscuit or cake filled with fruit and cream.

short-change *vb.* (*tr.*) **1.** to give less than correct change to. **2.** *Sl.* to cheat or swindle.

short circuit *n.* **1.** a faulty or accidental connection between two points of different potential in an electric circuit, establishing a path of low resistance through which an excessive current can flow. ~*vb.* **short-circuit. 2.** to develop or cause to develop a short circuit. **3.** (*tr.*) to bypass (a procedure, etc.). **4.** (*tr.*) to hinder or frustrate (plans, etc.). ~Sometimes (for senses 1, 2) shortened to **short.**

shortcoming ('ʃɔːtˌkʌmɪŋ) *n.* a failing, defect, or deficiency.

short cut *n.* **1.** a route that is shorter than the usual one. **2.** a means of saving time or effort. ~*vb.* **short-cut. -cutting, -cut. 3.** to use a short cut.

shorten ('ʃɔːtən) *vb.* **1.** to make or become short or shorter. **2.** (*tr.*) *Naut.* to reduce the area of (sail). **3.** (*tr.*) to make (pastry, etc.) short, by adding fat to the dough. **4.** *Gambling.* to cause (the odds) to lessen or (of odds) to become less.

shortening ('ʃɔːtənɪŋ) *n.* butter, lard, or other fat, used in a dough, cake mixture, etc., to make the mixture short.

shortfall ('ʃɔːtˌfɔːl) *n.* **1.** failure to meet a goal or a requirement. **2.** the amount of such a failure.

shorthand ('ʃɔːtˌhænd) *n.* **a.** a system of rapid handwriting employing simple strokes and other symbols to represent words or phrases. **b.** (*as modifier*): *a shorthand typist.*

shorthand typist *n Brit.* a person skilled in the use of shorthand and in typing. U.S. name **stenographer.**

short-handed *adj.* lacking the usual or necessary number of assistants, workers, etc.

shorthorn ('ʃɔːtˌhɔːn) *n.* a short-horned breed of cattle with several regional varieties.

short list *Chiefly Brit.* ~*n.* **1.** a list of suitable applicants for a job, post, etc., from which the successful can-

---

THESAURUS

shore 1. *n.* beach, coast, foreshore, lakeside, sands, seaboard (*Chiefly U.S.*), seashore, strand (*Poetic*), waterside **2.** *adj.* littoral

short *adj.* **1.** abridged, brief, compendious, compressed, concise, curtailed, laconic, pithy, sententious, succinct, summary, terse **2.** diminutive, dumpy, little, low, petite, small, squat, wee **3.** brief, fleeting, momentary, short-lived, short-term **4.** *Often with of* deficient, inadequate, insufficient, lacking, limited, low (on), meagre, poor, scant, scanty, scarce, short-handed, slender, slim, sparse, tight, wanting **5.** abrupt, blunt, brusque, crusty, curt, discourteous, gruff, impolite, offhand, sharp, terse, testy, uncivil **6.** direct, straight **7.** *Of pastry* brittle, crisp,

crumbly, friable ~*adv.* **8.** abruptly, by surprise, suddenly, unaware, without warning **9.** weak point

cut short abbreviate, arrest, butt in, curtail, cut in on, dock, halt, interrupt, reduce, stop, terminate **10. fall short** be inadequate, disappoint, fail, fall down on (*Inf.*), not come up to expectations *or* scratch (*Inf.*) **11. in short** briefly, in a nutshell, in a word, in essence, to come to the point, to cut a long story short, to put it briefly **12. short of a.** apart from, except, other than, unless **b.** deficient in, in need of, lacking, low (on), missing, wanting

shortage dearth, deficiency, deficit, failure, inadequacy, insufficiency, lack, leanness, paucity, poverty, scarcity, shortfall, want

shortcoming defect, drawback, failing,

fault, flaw, frailty, imperfection, weakness, weak point

shorten abbreviate, abridge, curtail, cut, cut back, cut down, decrease, diminish, dock, lessen, reduce, trim, turn up

short-sighted 1. myopic, near-sighted **2.** careless, ill-advised, ill-considered, impolitic, impractical, improvident, imprudent, injudicious, unthinking

short-staffed below strength, shorthanded, undermanned, understaffed

short-tempered choleric, fiery, hot-tempered, impatient, irascible, peppery, quick-tempered, ratty (*Brit. sl.*), testy, touchy

didate will be selected. ~*vb.* (*tr.*) **short-list. 2.** to put (someone) on a short list.

short-lived *adj.* living or lasting only for a short time.

shortly ('ʃɔːtlɪ) *adv.* **1.** in a short time; soon. **2.** briefly. **3.** in a curt or rude manner.

shorts (ʃɔːts) *pl. n.* **1.** trousers reaching the top of the thigh, worn by both sexes for sport, etc. **2.** *Chiefly U.S.* men's underpants that usually reach mid-thigh. **3.** short-dated gilt-edged securities. **4.** short-term bonds. **5.** a livestock feed containing a large proportion of bran and wheat germ.

short shrift *n.* **1.** brief and unsympathetic treatment. **2.** (formerly) a brief period allowed to a condemned prisoner to make confession. **3. make short shrift of.** to dispose of quickly.

short-sighted *adj.* **1.** relating to or suffering from myopia. **2.** lacking foresight: *a short-sighted plan.* —,**short-'sightedly** *adv.* —,**short-'sightedness** *n.*

short-tempered *adj.* easily moved to anger.

short-term *adj.* **1.** of, for, or extending over a limited period. **2.** *Finance.* extending over or maturing within a short period of time, usually twelve months: *short-term credit.*

short ton *n.* the full name for **ton**[1] (sense 2).

short wave *n.* **a.** a radio wave with a wavelength in the range 10–100 metres. **b.** (*as modifier*): *a short-wave broadcast.*

short-winded *adj.* **1.** tending to run out of breath, esp. after exertion. **2.** (of speech or writing) terse or abrupt.

shot[1] (ʃɒt) *n.* **1.** the act or an instance of firing a projectile. **2.** (*pl.* **shot**) a solid missile, such as an iron ball or a lead pellet, discharged from a firearm. **3. a.** small round pellets of lead collectively, as used in cartridges. **b.** metal in the form of coarse powder or small pellets. **4.** the distance that a discharged projectile travels or is capable of travelling. **5.** a person who shoots, esp. with regard to his ability: *he is a good shot.* **6.** *Inf.* an attempt. **7.** *Inf.* a guess. **8.** any act of throwing or hitting something, as in certain sports. **9.** the launching of a rocket, etc., esp. to a specified destination: *a moon shot.* **10. a.** a single photograph. **b.** a length of film taken by a single camera without breaks. **11.** *Inf.* an injection, as of a vaccine or narcotic drug. **12.** *Inf.* a glass of alcoholic drink, esp. spirits. **13.** *Sport.* a heavy metal ball used in the shot put. **14. call the shots.** *Sl.* to have control over an organization, etc. **15. have a shot at.** *Inf.* to attempt. **16. like a shot.** very quickly, esp. willingly. **17. shot in the arm.** *Inf.* anything that regenerates, increases confidence or efficiency, etc. **18. shot in the dark.** a wild guess.

shot[2] (ʃɒt) *vb.* **1.** the past tense or past participle of **shoot.** ~*adj.* **2.** (of textiles) woven so as to give a changing colour effect. **3.** streaked with colour.

shotgun ('ʃɒt,gʌn) *n.* **1.** a shoulder firearm with unrifled bore used mainly for hunting small game. ~*adj.* **2.** *Chiefly U.S.* involving coercion or duress: *a shotgun merger.*

shot put *n.* an athletic event in which contestants hurl or put a heavy metal ball or shot as far as possible. —'**shot-,putter** *n.*

should (ʃʊd) *vb.* the past of **shall:** used as an auxiliary verb to indicate that an action is considered by the speaker to be obligatory (*you should go*) or to form the subjunctive mood with *I* or *we* (*I should like to see you*).

▷ **Usage.** *Should* has, as its most common meaning in modern English, the sense *ought to* as in *I should go to the graduation, but I don't see how I can.* However, the older sense of the subjunctive of *shall* is often used with *I* or *we* to indicate a more polite form than *would: I should like to go, but I can't.* In much speech and writing, *should* has been replaced by *would* in contexts of this kind, but it remains in conditional subjunctives: *should* (never *would*) *I go, I should* (or *would*) *wear my black dress.*

shoulder ('ʃəʊldə) *n.* **1.** the part of the vertebrate body where the arm or a corresponding forelimb joins the trunk. **2.** the joint at the junction of the forelimb with the pectoral girdle. **3.** a cut of meat including the upper part of the foreleg. **4.** *Printing.* the flat surface of a piece of type from which the face rises. **5.** the part of a garment that covers the shoulder. **6.** anything that resembles a shoulder in shape or position. **7.** the strip of unpaved land that borders a road. **8. give (someone) the cold shoulder.** *Inf.* **a.** to treat in a cold manner; snub. **b.** to ignore or shun. **9. put one's shoulder to the wheel.** *Inf.* to work very hard. **10. rub shoulders with.** *Inf.* to associate with. **11. shoulder to shoulder. a.** side by side. **b.** in a corporate effort. ~*vb.* **12.** (*tr.*) to bear or carry (a burden, etc.) as if on one's shoulders. **13.** to push (something) with or as if with the shoulder. **14.** (*tr.*) to lift or carry on the shoulders. **15. shoulder arms.** *Mil.* to bring the rifle vertically close to the right side with the muzzle uppermost.

shoulder blade *n.* the nontechnical name for **scapula.**

shoulder strap *n.* a strap over the shoulders, as to hold up a garment or to support a bag, etc.

shout (ʃaʊt) *n.* **1.** a loud cry, esp. to convey emotion or a command. **2.** *Inf.* a round, esp. of drinks. ~*vb.* **3.** to utter (something) in a loud cry. **4.** (*intr.*) to make a loud noise. **5.** (*tr.*) *Austral. & N.Z. inf.* to treat (someone) to (something), esp. a round of drinks. —'**shouter** *n.*

shout down *vb.* (*tr., adv.*) to drown, overwhelm, or silence by talking loudly.

shove (ʃʌv) *vb.* **1.** to give a thrust or push to (a person or thing). **2.** (*tr.*) to give a violent push to. **3.** (*tr.*) *Inf.* to put (something) somewhere: *shove it in the bin.* ~*n.* **4.** the act or an instance of shoving. ~*See also* **shove off.** —'**shover** *n.*

shovel ('ʃʌvəl) *n.* **1.** an instrument for lifting or scooping loose material, such as earth, coal, etc., consisting of a curved blade or a scoop attached to a handle. **2.** any machine or part resembling a shovel in action. **3.** *Also called:* **shovelful.** the amount that can be contained in a shovel. ~*vb.* **-elling, -elled** *or U.S.* **-eling, -eled. 4.** to lift (earth, etc.) with a shovel. **5.** (*tr.*) to clear or dig (a path) with or as if with a shovel. **6.** (*tr.*) to gather, load, or unload in a hurried or careless way. —'**shoveller** *or U.S.* '**shoveler** *n.*

shove off *vb.* (*intr., adv.; often imperative*) **1.** to move from the shore in a boat. **2.** *Inf.* to go away; depart.

show (ʃəʊ) *vb.* **showing, showed; shown** *or* **showed. 1.** to make, be, or become visible or noticeable: *to show one's dislike.* **2.** (*tr.*) to exhibit: *he showed me a picture.* **3.** (*tr.*) to indicate or explain; prove: *to show that the earth moves round the sun.* **4.** (*tr.*) to present (oneself or itself) in a specific character: *to show oneself to be trustworthy.* **5.** (*tr.; foll. by how* and an infinitive) to instruct by demonstration: *show me how to swim.* **6.** (*tr.*) to indicate: *a barometer shows changes in the weather.* **7.** (*tr.*) to grant or bestow: *to show favour to someone.* **8.** (*intr.*) to appear: *to show to advantage.* **9.** to exhibit, display, or offer (goods, etc.) for sale: *three artists were showing at the gallery.* **10.** (*tr.*) to allege, as in a legal

shot *n.* **1.** discharge, lob, pot shot, throw **2.** ball, bullet, lead, pellet, projectile, slug **3.** marksman, shooter **4.** *Inf.* attempt, chance, conjecture, crack (*Inf.*), effort, endeavour, essay, go, guess, opportunity, stab, surmise, try, turn **5. by a long shot** by far, easily, far and away, indubitably, undoubtedly, without doubt **b.** by any means, in any circumstances, on any account **6. have a shot** *Inf.* attempt, have a go (bash (*Inf.*), crack (*Inf.*), stab), tackle, try, try one's luck **7. like a shot** at once, eagerly, immediately, like a flash, quickly, unhesitatingly **8. shot in the arm** *Inf.* boost, encouragement, fillip, impetus, lift, stimulus

shoulder *n.* **1. give (someone) the cold shoulder** cut (*Inf.*), ignore, ostracize, rebuff, shun, snub **2. put one's shoulder to the wheel** *Inf.* apply oneself, buckle down to (*Inf.*), exert oneself, get down to, make every effort, set to work, strive **3. rub shoulders with** *Inf.* associate with, consort with, fraternize with, hobnob with, mix with, socialize with **4. shoulder to shoulder** as one, in co-operation, in partnership, in unity, jointly, side by side, together, united **5. straight from the shoulder** candidly, directly, frankly, man to man, outright, plainly, pulling no punches (*Inf.*), straight, unequivocally, with no holds barred ~*v.* **6.** accept, assume, bear, be responsible for, carry, take on, take upon oneself **7.** elbow, jostle, press, push, shove, thrust

shoulder blade scapula

shout 1. *n.* bellow, call, cry, roar, scream, yell **2.** *v.* bawl, bay, bellow, call (out), cry (out), holler (*Inf.*), hollo, raise one's voice, roar, scream, yell

shout down drown, drown out, overwhelm, silence

shove *v.* crowd, drive, elbow, impel, jostle, press, propel, push, shoulder, thrust

shovel *v.* convey, dredge, heap, ladle, load, move, scoop, shift, spoon, toss

document: *to show cause*. **11.** to present (a film, etc.) or (of a play, etc.) to be presented, as at a theatre or cinema. **12.** (*tr.*) to guide or escort: *please show me to my room.* **13. show in** *or* **out.** to conduct a person into or out of a room or building by opening the door for him. **14.** (*intr.*) *Sl.* to arrive. ~*n.* **15.** a display or exhibition. **16.** a public spectacle. **17.** an ostentatious display. **18.** a theatrical or other entertainment. **19.** a trace or indication. **20.** *Obstetrics.* a discharge of blood at the onset of labour. **21.** *Inf.* a chance (esp. in **give someone a show**). **22.** *Sl., chiefly Brit.* a thing or affair (esp. in **good show, bad show,** etc.). **23. for show.** in order to attract attention. **24. run the show.** *Inf.* to take charge of or manage an affair, business, etc. **25. steal the show.** *Inf.* to draw the most attention or admiration. ~See also **show off, show up.**

show business *n.* the entertainment industry, including theatres, films, television, and radio. Informal term: **show biz.**

showcase ('ʃəʊˌkeɪs) *n.* **1.** a glass case used to display objects in a museum or shop. **2.** a setting in which anything may be displayed to best advantage.

showdown ('ʃəʊˌdaʊn) *n.* **1.** *Inf.* an action that brings matters to a head or acts as a conclusion. **2.** *Poker.* the exposing of the cards in the players' hands at the end of the game.

shower ('ʃaʊə) *n.* **1.** a brief period of rain, hail, sleet, or snow. **2.** a sudden abundant fall or downpour, as of tears, sparks, or light. **3.** a rush: *a shower of praise.* **4.** **a.** a kind of bath in which a person stands upright and is sprayed with water from a nozzle. **b.** the room, booth, etc., containing such a bath. Full name: **shower bath.** **5.** *Brit. sl.* a derogatory term applied to a person or group. **6.** *U.S. & N.Z.* a party held to honour and present gifts to a person, as to a prospective bride. **7.** a large number of particles formed by the collision of a cosmic-ray particle with a particle in the atmosphere. **8.** *N.Z.* a light fabric put over a tea table to protect the food from flies, etc. ~*vb.* **9.** (*tr.*) to sprinkle or spray with or as if with a shower. **10.** (often with *it* as subject) to fall or cause to fall in the form of a shower. **11.** (*tr.*) to give (gifts, etc.) in abundance or present (a person) with (gifts, etc.): *they showered gifts on him.* **12.** (*intr.*) to take a shower. —'**showery** *adj.*

showing ('ʃəʊɪŋ) *n.* **1.** a presentation, exhibition, or display. **2.** manner of presentation.

showjumping ('ʃəʊˌdʒʌmpɪŋ) *n.* the riding of horses in competitions to demonstrate skill in jumping over or between various obstacles. —'**show-ˌjumper** *n.*

showman ('ʃəʊmən) *n., pl.* **-men.** **1.** a person who presents or produces a theatrical show, etc. **2.** a person skilled at presenting anything in an effective manner. —'**showmanship** *n.*

shown (ʃəʊn) *vb.* a past participle of **show.**

show off *vb.* (*adv.*) **1.** (*tr.*) to exhibit or display so as to invite admiration. **2.** (*intr.*) *Inf.* to behave in such a manner as to make an impression. ~*n.* **show-off.** **3.** *Inf.* a person who makes a vain display of himself.

showpiece ('ʃəʊˌpiːs) *n.* **1.** anything displayed or exhibited. **2.** anything prized as a very fine example of its type.

showplace ('ʃəʊˌpleɪs) *n.* a place exhibited or visited for its beauty, historic interest, etc.

showroom ('ʃəʊˌruːm, -ˌrʊm) *n.* a room in which goods for sale, such as cars, are on display.

show up *vb.* (*adv.*) **1.** to reveal or be revealed clearly. **2.** (*tr.*) to expose or reveal the faults or defects of by comparison. **3.** (*tr.*) *Inf.* to put to shame; embarrass. **4.** (*intr.*) *Inf.* to appear or arrive.

showy ('ʃəʊɪ) *adj.* **showier, showiest.** **1.** gaudy or ostentatious. **2.** making an imposing display. —'**showily** *adv.* —'**showiness** *n.*

shrank (ʃræŋk) *vb.* a past tense of **shrink.**

shrapnel ('ʃræpnəl) *n.* **1.** a projectile containing a number of small pellets or bullets exploded before impact. **2.** fragments from this type of shell.

shred (ʃrɛd) *n.* **1.** a long narrow strip or fragment torn or cut off. **2.** a very small piece or amount. ~*vb.* **shredding, shredded** *or* **shred.** **3.** (*tr.*) to tear or cut into shreds. —'**shredder** *n.*

shrew (ʃruː) *n.* **1.** Also called: **shrewmouse.** a small mouse-like long-snouted mammal. **2.** a bad-tempered or mean-spirited woman. —'**shrewish** *adj.*

shrewd (ʃruːd) *adj.* **1.** astute and penetrating, often with regard to business. **2.** artful: *a shrewd politician.* **3.** *Obs.* piercing: *a shrewd wind.* —'**shrewdly** *adv.* —'**shrewdness** *n.*

shriek (ʃriːk) *n.* **1.** a shrill and piercing cry. ~*vb.* **2.** to produce or utter (words, sounds, etc.) in a shrill piercing tone. —'**shrieker** *n.*

shrift (ʃrɪft) *n. Arch.* the act or an instance of shriving or being shriven. ~See also **short shrift.**

shrike (ʃraɪk) *n.* an Old World songbird having a heavy hooked bill and feeding on smaller animals which it sometimes impales on thorns, barbed wire, etc. Also called: **butcherbird.**

shrill (ʃrɪl) *adj.* **1.** sharp and high-pitched in quality. **2.** emitting a sharp high-pitched sound. ~*vb.* **3.** to utter (words, sounds, etc.) in a shrill tone. —'**shrillness** *n.* —'**shrilly** *adv.*

shrimp (ʃrɪmp) *n.* **1.** any of a genus of chiefly marine decapod crustaceans having a slender flattened body with a long tail and a single pair of pincers. **2.** *Inf.* a diminutive person, esp. a child. ~*vb.* **3.** (*intr.*) to fish for shrimps. —'**shrimper** *n.*

shrine (ʃraɪn) *n.* **1.** a place of worship hallowed by association with a sacred person or object. **2.** a container for sacred relics. **3.** the tomb of a saint or other holy person. **4.** a place or site venerated for its association with a famous person or event. **5.** *R.C. Church.* a building, alcove, or shelf arranged as a setting for a statue, picture, etc. of Christ, the Virgin Mary, or a saint. ~*vb.* **6.** short for **enshrine.** —'**shrineˌlike** *adj.*

shrink (ʃrɪŋk) *vb.* **shrinking; shrank** *or* **shrunk; shrunk** *or* **shrunken.** **1.** to contract or cause to contract as from wetness, heat, cold, etc. **2.** to become or cause to become smaller in size. **3.** (*intr.*; often foll. by *from*) **a.** to recoil or withdraw: *to shrink from the sight of blood.* **b.** to feel great reluctance (at). ~*n.* **4.** the act or an instance of shrinking. **5. shrinking violet.** *Inf.* a shy person. **6.** *Sl.* a psychiatrist. —'**shrinkable** *adj.* —'**shrinker** *n.*

THESAURUS

show *v.* **1.** appear, be visible, disclose, display, divulge, evidence, evince, exhibit, indicate, make known, manifest, present, register, reveal, testify to **2.** assert, clarify, demonstrate, elucidate, evince, explain, instruct, point out, present, prove, teach **3.** accompany, attend, conduct, escort, guide, lead **4.** accord, act with, bestow, confer, grant ~*n.* **5.** array, demonstration, display, exhibition, expo (*Inf.*), exposition, fair, manifestation, pageant, pageantry, parade, representation, sight, spectacle, view **6.** affectation, air, appearance, display, illusion, likeness, ostentation, parade, pose, pretence, pretext, profession, semblance **7.** entertainment, presentation, production

showdown breaking point, clash, climax, confrontation, crisis, culmination, exposé, moment of truth

shower *n.* **1.** *Fig.* barrage, deluge, fusillade, plethora, rain, stream, torrent, volley **2.**

Brit. sl. bunch of layabouts, crew, rabble ~*v.* **3.** deluge, heap, inundate, lavish, load, pour, rain, spray, sprinkle

showing *n.* **1.** display, exhibition, presentation, staging **2.** account of oneself, appearance, impression, performance, show, track record **3.** evidence, representation, statement

showman entertainer, impresario, performer, publicist, stage manager

show off **1.** advertise, demonstrate, display, exhibit, flaunt, parade, spread out **2.** boast, brag, make a spectacle of oneself, shoot a line (*Inf.*), swagger

show up **1.** expose, highlight, lay bare, pinpoint, put the spotlight on, reveal, unmask **2.** appear, be conspicuous, be visible, catch the eye, leap to the eye, stand out **3.** *Inf.* embarrass, let down, mortify, put to shame, shame, show in a bad light **4.** *Inf.* appear, arrive, come, make an appearance, put

in an appearance, turn up

shred *n.* **1.** bit, fragment, piece, rag, ribbon, scrap, sliver, snippet, tatter **2.** *Fig.* atom, grain, iota, jot, particle, scrap, trace, whit

shrewd acute, artful, astute, calculated, calculating, canny, clever, crafty, cunning, discerning, discriminating, far-seeing, far-sighted, fly (*Sl.*), intelligent, keen, knowing, long-headed, perceptive, perspicacious, sagacious, sharp, sly, smart, wily

shrewdly artfully, astutely, cannily, cleverly, far-sightedly, knowingly, perceptively, perspicaciously, sagaciously, with all one's wits about one, with consummate skill

shrewdness acumen, acuteness, astuteness, canniness, discernment, grasp, judgment, penetration, perspicacity, quick wits, sagacity, sharpness, smartness

shriek *v./n.* cry, howl, scream, screech, squeal, wail, whoop, yell

shrill acute, ear-piercing, ear-splitting,

shrinkage (ˈʃrɪŋkɪdʒ) n. 1. the act or fact of shrinking. 2. the amount by which anything decreases in size, value, weight, etc.

shrink-wrap vb. **-wrapping, -wrapped.** (tr.) to package a product in a flexible plastic wrapping designed to shrink about its contours to protect and seal it.

shrive (ʃraɪv) vb. **shriving; shrove** or **shrived; shriven** or **shrived.** Chiefly R.C. Church. 1. to hear the confession of (a penitent). 2. (tr.) to impose a penance upon (a penitent) and grant him absolution. 3. (intr.) to confess one's sins to a priest in order to obtain forgiveness. —ˈshriver n.

shrivel (ˈʃrɪvəl) vb. **-elling, -elled** or U.S. **-eling, -eled.** 1. to make or become shrunken and withered. 2. to lose or cause to lose vitality.

shroud (ʃraud) n. 1. a garment or piece of cloth used to wrap a dead body. 2. anything that envelops like a garment: a shroud of mist. 3. a protective covering for a piece of equipment. 4. Naut. one of a pattern of ropes or cables used to stay a mast. ~vb. 5. (tr.) to wrap in a shroud. 6. (tr.) to cover, envelop, or hide. —ˈshroudless adj.

shrove (ʃrəʊv) vb. a past tense of **shrive.**

Shrovetide (ˈʃrəʊvˌtaɪd) n. the Sunday, Monday, and Tuesday before Ash Wednesday, formerly a time when confessions were made for Lent.

shrub (ʃrʌb) n. a woody perennial plant, smaller than a tree, with several major branches arising from near the base of the main stem. —ˈshrub‚like adj.

shrubbery (ˈʃrʌbərɪ) n., pl. **-beries.** 1. a place where a number of shrubs are planted. 2. shrubs collectively.

shrubby (ˈʃrʌbɪ) adj. **-bier, -biest.** 1. consisting of, planted with, or abounding in shrubs. 2. resembling a shrub. —ˈshrubbiness n.

shrug (ʃrʌg) vb. **shrugging, shrugged.** 1. to draw up and drop (the shoulders) abruptly in a gesture expressing indifference, ignorance, etc. ~n. 2. the gesture so made.

shrug off vb. (tr., adv.) 1. to minimize the importance of; dismiss. 2. to get rid of.

shrunk (ʃrʌŋk) vb. a past participle or past tense of **shrink.**

shrunken (ˈʃrʌŋkən) vb. 1. a past participle of **shrink.** ~adj. 2. (usually prenominal) reduced in size.

shudder (ˈʃʌdə) vb. 1. (intr.) to shake or tremble suddenly and violently, as from horror, fear, aversion, etc. ~n. 2. a convulsive shiver. —ˈshudderingly adv. —ˈshuddery adj.

shuffle (ˈʃʌfəl) vb. 1. to walk or move (the feet) with a slow dragging motion. 2. to change the position of (something), esp. in order to deceive others. 3. (tr.) to mix together in a careless manner: he shuffled the papers nervously. 4. to mix up (cards in a pack) to change their order. 5. (intr.) to behave in an evasive or underhand manner. 6. (when intr., often foll. by into or out of) to move or cause to move clumsily: he shuffled out of the door. ~n. 7. the act or an instance of shuffling. 8. a rearrangement: a Cabinet shuffle. 9. a dance or dance step with short dragging movements of the feet. —ˈshuffler n.

shufty (ˈʃʊftɪ, ˈʃʌftɪ) n., pl. **-ties.** Brit. sl. a look; peep.

shun (ʃʌn) vb. **shunning, shunned.** (tr.) to avoid deliberately.

shunt (ʃʌnt) vb. 1. to turn or cause to turn to one side. 2. Railways. to transfer (rolling stock) from track to track. 3. Electronics. to divert or be diverted through a shunt. 4. (tr.) to evade by putting off onto someone else. ~n. 5. the act or an instance of shunting. 6. a railway point. 7. Electronics. a low-resistance conductor connected in parallel across a part of a circuit to provide an alternative path for a known fraction of the current. 8. Med. a channel that bypasses the normal circulation of the blood. 9. Sl. a car crash. —ˈshunter n.

shush (ʃʊʃ) interj. 1. be quiet! hush! ~vb. 2. to silence or calm (someone) by or as if by saying "shush".

shut (ʃʌt) vb. **shutting, shut.** 1. to move (something) so as to cover an aperture: to shut a door. 2. to close (something) by bringing together the parts: to shut a book. 3. (tr.; often foll. by up) to close or lock the doors of: to shut up a house. 4. (tr.; foll. by in, out, etc.) to confine, enclose, or exclude. 5. (tr.) to prevent (a business, etc.) from operating. 6. **shut one's eyes to.** to ignore deliberately. 7. **shut the door on. a.** to refuse to think about. **b.** to render impossible. ~adj. 8. closed or fastened. ~n. 9. the act or time of shutting. ~See also **shutdown, shut-off, shutout, shut up.**

shutdown (ˈʃʌtˌdaʊn) n. 1. the closing of a factory, shop, etc. ~vb. **shut down.** (adv.) 2. to cease or cause to cease operation. 3. (tr.) to close by lowering.

shuteye (ˈʃʌtˌaɪ) n. a slang term for **sleep.**

shut-in n. **a.** Chiefly U.S. a person confined indoors by illness. **b.** (as modifier): a shut-in patient.

shut-off n. 1. a device that shuts something off, esp. a machine control. 2. a stoppage or cessation. ~vb. **shut off.** (tr., adv.) 3. to stem the flow of. 4. to block off the passage through. 5. to isolate or separate.

shutout (ˈʃʌtˌaʊt) n. 1. a less common word for a **lockout.** ~vb. **shut out.** (tr., adv.) 2. to keep out or exclude. 3. to conceal from sight: we planted trees to shut out the view of the road.

shutter (ˈʃʌtə) n. 1. a hinged doorlike cover, often louvred and usually one of a pair, for closing off a window. 2. **put up the shutters.** to close business at the end of the day or permanently. 3. Photog. an opaque shield in a camera that, when tripped, admits light to expose the film or plate for a predetermined period, usually a fraction of a second. 4. Music. one of the louvred covers over the mouths of organ pipes, operated by the swell pedal. 5. a person or thing that shuts. ~vb. (tr.) 6. to close with a shutter or shutters. 7. to equip with a shutter or shutters.

shuttle (ˈʃʌtəl) n. 1. a bobbin-like device used in weaving for passing the weft thread between the warp threads. 2. a small bobbin-like device used to hold the thread in a sewing machine, etc. 3. a bus, train, aircraft, etc., that plies between two points. 4. **a.** the movement between various countries of a diplomat in order to negotiate with rulers who refuse to meet each other. **b.** (as modifier): shuttle diplomacy. 5. Badminton, etc. short for **shuttlecock.** ~vb. 6. to move or cause to move by or as if by a shuttle.

shuttlecock (ˈʃʌtəlˌkɒk) n. 1. a light cone consisting of a cork stub with feathered flights, struck to and fro in badminton and battledore. 2. anything moved to and fro, as in an argument.

shut up vb. (adv.) 1. (tr.) to prevent all access to. 2. (tr.) to confine or imprison. 3. Inf. to cease to talk or make a noise or cause to cease to talk or make a noise: often used in commands.

shy[1] (ʃaɪ) adj. **shyer, shyest** or **shier, shiest.** 1. not at ease in the company of others. 2. easily frightened; tim-

---

THESAURUS

id. **3.** (often foll. by *of*) watchful or wary. **4.** *Inf.* short of. **5.** (*in combination*) showing reluctance or disinclination: *work-shy.* ~*vb.* **shying, shied.** (*intr.*) **6.** to move suddenly, as from fear: *the horse shied at the snake in the road.* **7.** (usually foll. by *off* or *away*) to draw back. ~*n., pl.* **shies. 8.** a sudden movement, as from fear. —'**shyer** *n.* —'**shyly** *adv.* —'**shyness** *n.*

shy² (ʃaɪ) *vb.* **shying, shied. 1.** to throw (something) with a sideways motion. ~*n., pl.* **shies. 2.** a quick throw. **3.** *Inf.* a gibe. **4.** *Inf.* an attempt. —'**shyer** *n.*

Shylock ('ʃaɪˌlɒk) *n.* a heartless or demanding creditor.

si (siː) *n. Music.* a variant of **te.**

Si *the chemical symbol for* silicon.

SI see **SI unit.**

Siamese (ˌsaɪə'miːz) *n., pl.* **-mese. 1.** See **Siamese cat.** ~*adj.* **2.** characteristic of, relating to, or being a Siamese twin. ~*adj., n.* **3.** another word for **Thai.**

Siamese cat *n.* a short-haired breed of cat with a tapering tail, blue eyes, and dark ears, mask, tail, and paws.

Siamese twins *pl. n.* twin babies born joined together at some point, such as at the hips.

sibilant ('sɪbɪlənt) *adj.* **1.** *Phonetics.* relating to or denoting the consonants (s, z, ʃ, ʒ), all pronounced with a characteristic hissing sound. **2.** having a hissing sound. ~*n.* **3.** a sibilant consonant. —'**sibilance** *or* '**sibilancy** *n.* —'**sibilantly** *adv.*

sibling ('sɪblɪŋ) *n.* **a.** a person's brother or sister. **b.** (*as modifier*): *sibling rivalry.*

sibyl ('sɪbɪl) *n.* **1.** (in ancient Greece and Rome) any of a number of women believed to be oracles or prophetesses. **2.** a witch, fortune-teller, or sorceress. —**sibylline** ('sɪbɪˌlaɪn) *adj.*

sic¹ (sɪk) *adv.* so or thus: inserted in brackets in a text to indicate that an odd or questionable reading is in fact accurate.

sic² (sɪk) *vb.* **sicking, sicked.** (*tr.*) **1.** to attack: used only in commands, as to a dog. **2.** to urge (a dog) to attack.

sick (sɪk) *adj.* **1.** inclined or likely to vomit. **2. a.** suffering from ill health. **b.** (*as n.*): *the sick.* **3. a.** of or used by people who are unwell: *sick benefits.* **b.** (*in combination*): *a sickroom.* **4.** deeply affected with a mental or spiritual feeling akin to physical sickness: *sick at heart.* **5.** mentally or spiritually disturbed. **6.** *Inf.* delighting in or catering for the macabre: *sick humour.* **7.** (often foll. by *of*) *Inf.* disgusted or weary: *I am sick of his everlasting laughter.* **8.** (often foll. by *for*) weary with longing: *I am sick for my own country.* **9.** pallid or sickly. **10.** not in working order. ~*n., vb.* **11.** an informal word for **vomit.** —'**sickish** *adj.*

sickbay ('sɪkˌbeɪ) *n.* a room for the treatment of the sick or injured, as on board a ship.

sicken ('sɪkən) *vb.* **1.** to make or become sick, nauseated, or disgusted. **2.** (*intr.*; often foll. by *for*) to show symptoms (of an illness).

sickening ('sɪkənɪŋ) *adj.* **1.** causing sickness or revulsion. **2.** *Inf.* extremely annoying. —'**sickeningly** *adv.*

sickle ('sɪkəl) *n.* an implement for cutting grass, corn, etc., having a curved blade and a short handle.

sick leave *n.* leave of absence from work through illness.

sickle cell anaemia *n.* an inherited form of anae-

mia occurring mainly in Negroes, in which a large number of red blood cells become sickle-shaped.

sickly ('sɪklɪ) *adj.* **-lier, -liest. 1.** disposed to frequent ailments; not healthy; weak. **2.** of or caused by sickness. **3.** (of a smell, taste, etc.) causing revulsion or nausea. **4.** (of light or colour) faint or feeble. **5.** mawkish; insipid. ~*adv.* **6.** in a sick or sickly manner. —'**sickliness** *n.*

sickness ('sɪknɪs) *n.* **1.** an illness or disease. **2.** nausea or queasiness. **3.** the state or an instance of being sick.

side (saɪd) *n.* **1.** a line or surface that borders anything. **2.** *Geom.* **a.** any line segment forming part of the perimeter of a plane geometric figure. **b.** another name for **face** (sense 13). **3.** either of two parts into which an object, surface, area, etc., can be divided: *the right side and the left side.* **4.** either of the two surfaces of a flat object: *the right and wrong side of the cloth.* **5.** a surface or part of an object that extends vertically: *the side of a cliff.* **6.** either half of a human or animal body, esp. the area around the waist: *I have a pain in my side.* **7.** the area immediately next to a person or thing: *he stood at her side.* **8.** a district, point, or direction within an area identified by reference to a central point: *the south side of the city.* **9.** the area at the edge of a room, road, etc. **10.** aspect or part: *look on the bright side.* **11.** one of two or more contesting factions, teams, etc. **12.** a page in an essay, etc. **13.** a position, opinion, etc., held in opposition to another in a dispute. **14.** line of descent: *he gets his brains from his mother's side.* **15.** *Inf.* a television channel. **16.** *Billiards, etc.* spin imparted to a ball by striking it off-centre with the cue. **17.** *Brit. sl.* insolence or pretentiousness: *to put on side.* **18. on one side.** set apart from the rest, as provision for emergencies, etc. **19. on the side. a.** apart from or in addition to the main object. **b.** as a sideline. **20. take sides.** to support one group, opinion, etc., as against another. ~*adj.* **21.** being on one side; lateral. **22.** from or viewed as if from one side. **23.** directed towards one side. **24.** subordinate or incidental: *side road.* ~*vb.* **25.** (*intr.*; usually foll. by *with*) to support or associate oneself with a faction, interest, etc.

side arms *pl. n.* weapons carried on the person, by belt or holster, such as a sword, pistol, etc.

sideboard ('saɪdˌbɔːd) *n.* a piece of furniture intended to stand at the side of a dining room, with drawers, cupboards, and shelves to hold silver, china, linen, etc.

sideboards ('saɪdˌbɔːdz) *pl. n. Brit.* a man's whiskers grown down either side of the face in front of the ears. U.S. term: **sideburns.**

sideburns ('saɪdˌbɜːnz) *pl. n.* another term (esp. U.S.) for **sideboards.**

sidecar ('saɪdˌkɑː) *n.* a small car attached on one side to a motorcycle, the other side being supported by a single wheel.

-sided *adj.* (*in combination*) having a side or sides as specified: *three-sided; many-sided.*

side effect *n.* **1.** any unwanted nontherapeutic effect caused by a drug. **2.** any secondary effect, esp. an undesirable one.

sidekick ('saɪdˌkɪk) *n. Sl., chiefly U.S.* a close friend or follower who accompanies another on adventures, etc.

sidelight ('saɪdˌlaɪt) *n.* **1.** light coming from the side. **2.** a side window. **3.** either of the two navigational running lights used by vessels at night, a red light on the port and a green on the starboard. **4.** *Brit.* either of two small lights on the front of a motor vehicle. **5.** additional

---

▌THESAURUS▐

shy 1. *adj.* backward, bashful, cautious, chary, coy, diffident, distrustful, hesitant, modest, mousy, nervous, reserved, reticent, retiring, self-conscious, self-effacing, shrinking, suspicious, timid, wary **2.** *v. Sometimes with* off *or* away balk, buck, draw back, flinch, quail, rear, recoil, start, swerve, take fright, wince

shyness bashfulness, diffidence, lack of confidence, modesty, mousiness, nervousness, reticence, self-consciousness, timidity, timidness, timorousness

sick 1. green around the gills (*Inf.*), ill, nauseated, puking (*Sl.*), qualmish, queasy **2.** ailing, diseased, feeble, indisposed, laid up (*Inf.*), on the sick list (*Inf.*), poorly (*Inf.*), under the weather (*Inf.*), unwell, weak **3.** *Inf.* black, ghoulish, macabre, morbid, sadistic **4.** *Inf. Often with* of blasé, bored, disgusted, dis-

pleased, fed up, jaded, revolted, satiated, tired, weary

sicken 1. disgust, make one's gorge rise, nauseate, repel, revolt, turn one's stomach **2.** be stricken by, contract, fall ill, go down with (*Brit.*), show symptoms of, take sick

sickening disgusting, distasteful, foul, loathsome, nauseating, nauseous, noisome, offensive, putrid, repulsive, revolting, stomach-turning (*Inf.*), vile

sickly 1. ailing, bilious, bloodless, delicate, faint, feeble, indisposed, infirm, in poor health, lacklustre, languid, pallid, peaky, pining, unhealthy, wan, weak **2.** bilious (*Inf.*), cloying, mawkish, nauseating, revolting (*Inf.*), syrupy (*Inf.*)

sickness 1. nausea, queasiness, (the) collywobbles (*Sl.*), vomiting **2.** affliction, ailment, bug (*Inf.*), complaint, disease, disor-

der, illness, indisposition, infirmity, malady

side *n.* **1.** border, boundary, division, edge, limit, margin, part, perimeter, periphery, rim, sector, verge **2.** aspect, face, facet, flank, hand, part, surface, view **3.** angle, light, opinion, point of view, position, slant, stand, standpoint, viewpoint **4.** camp, cause, faction, party, sect, team **5.** *Brit. sl.* airs, arrogance, insolence, pretentiousness ~*adj.* **6.** flanking, lateral **7.** ancillary, incidental, indirect, lesser, marginal, minor, oblique, roundabout, secondary, subordinate, subsidiary ~*v.* **8.** *Usually with* with ally with, associate oneself with, befriend, favour, go along with (*Inf.*), join with, second, support, take the part of, team up with (*Inf.*)

or incidental information.

sideline ('saɪd,laɪn) n. 1. *Sport.* a line that marks the side boundary of a playing area. 2. a subsidiary interest or source of income. 3. an auxiliary business activity or line of merchandise. ~vb. 4. (tr.) *Chiefly U.S.* to prevent (a player) from taking part in a game.

sidelines ('saɪd,laɪnz) pl. n. 1. *Sport.* the area immediately outside the playing area, where substitute players sit. 2. the peripheral areas of any region, organization, etc.

sidelong ('saɪd,lɒŋ) adj. (prenominal) 1. directed or inclining to one side. 2. indirect or oblique. ~adv. 3. from the side; obliquely.

sidereal (saɪ'dɪərɪəl) adj. 1. of or involving the stars. 2. determined with reference to one or more stars: *the sidereal day.* —si'dereally adv.

sidero- or before a vowel **sider-** combining form. indicating iron: *siderolite.*

side-saddle n. 1. a riding saddle originally designed for women riders in skirts who sit with both legs on the near side of the horse. ~adv. 2. on or as if on a side-saddle.

sideshow ('saɪd,ʃəʊ) n. 1. a small show or entertainment offered in conjunction with a larger attraction, as at a circus or fair. 2. a subordinate event or incident.

sideslip ('saɪd,slɪp) n. 1. a sideways skid, as of a motor vehicle. ~vb. **slipping, slipped.** 2. another name for **slip¹** (sense 11).

sidesman ('saɪdzmən) n., pl. **-men.** *Church of England.* a man elected to help the parish church warden.

side-splitting adj. 1. producing great mirth. 2. (of laughter) uproarious or very hearty.

sidestep ('saɪd,stɛp) vb. **stepping, stepped.** 1. to step aside from or out of the way of (something). 2. (tr.) to dodge or circumvent. ~n. **side step.** 3. a movement to one side, as in dancing, boxing, etc. —'side,stepper n.

sideswipe ('saɪd,swaɪp) n. 1. a glancing blow or hit along or from the side. ~vb. 2. to strike (someone) with such a blow. —'side,swiper n.

sidetrack ('saɪd,træk) vb. 1. to distract or be distracted from a main subject or topic. ~n. 2. *U.S.* a railway siding. 3. a digression.

sidewalk ('saɪd,wɔːk) n. the U.S. word for **pavement.**

sideways ('saɪd,weɪz) adv. 1. moving, facing, or inclining towards one side. 2. from one side; obliquely. 3. with one side forward. ~adj. (prenominal) 4. moving or directed to or from one side. 5. towards or from one side.

side whiskers pl. n. another name for **sideboards.**

siding ('saɪdɪŋ) n. 1. a short stretch of railway track connected to a main line, used to enable trains on the same line to pass. 2. a short railway line giving access to the main line for freight from a factory, etc. 3. *U.S.* material attached to the outside of a building to make it weatherproof.

sidle ('saɪdəl) vb. (intr.) 1. to move in a furtive or stealthy manner. 2. to move along sideways.

SIDS abbrev. for sudden infant death syndrome. See **cot death.**

siege (siːdʒ) n. 1. **a.** the offensive operations carried out to capture a fortified place by surrounding it, and deploying weapons against it. **b.** (as modifier): *siege warfare.* 2. a persistent attempt to gain something. 3. *Obs.* a seat or throne. 4. **lay siege to.** to besiege.

siemens ('siːmənz) n., pl. **siemens.** the derived SI unit of electrical conductance equal to 1 reciprocal ohm. Symbol: S Formerly called: **mho.**

sienna (sɪ'ɛnə) n. 1. a natural earth containing ferric oxide used as a yellowish-brown pigment when untreated (**raw sienna**) or a reddish-brown pigment when roasted (**burnt sienna**). 2. the colour of this pigment.

sierra (sɪ'ɛərə) n. a range of mountains with jagged peaks, esp. in Spain or America. —si'erran adj.

siesta (sɪ'ɛstə) n. a rest or nap, usually taken in the early afternoon, as in hot countries.

sieve (sɪv) n. 1. a device for separating lumps from powdered material, straining liquids, etc., consisting of a container with a mesh or perforated bottom through which the material is shaken or poured. 2. *Inf.* a person who gossips and spreads secrets. ~vb. 3. to pass or cause to pass through a sieve. 4. (tr.; often foll. by *out*) to separate or remove (lumps, materials, etc.) by use of a sieve. —'sieve,like adj.

sift (sɪft) vb. 1. (tr.) to sieve (sand, flour, etc.) in order to remove the coarser particles. 2. to scatter (something) over a surface through a sieve. 3. (tr.) to separate with or as if with a sieve. 4. (tr.) to examine minutely: *to sift evidence.* 5. (intr.) to move as if through a sieve. —'sifter n.

sigh (saɪ) vb. 1. (intr.) to draw in and exhale audibly a deep breath as an expression of weariness, relief, etc. 2. (intr.) to make a sound resembling this. 3. (intr.; often foll. by *for*) to yearn, long, or pine. 4. (tr.) to utter or express with sighing. ~n. 5. the act or sound of sighing. —'sigher n.

sight (saɪt) n. 1. the power or faculty of seeing; vision. Related adj.: **visual.** 2. the act or an instance of seeing. 3. the range of vision: *within sight of land.* 4. point of view; judgment: *in his sight she could do nothing wrong.* 5. a glimpse or view (esp. in **to catch sight of**). 6. anything that is seen. 7. (often pl.) anything worth seeing: *the sights of London.* 8. *Inf.* anything unpleasant or undesirable to see: *his room was a sight!* 9. any of various devices or instruments used to assist the eye in making alignments or directional observations, esp. such a device used in aiming a gun. 10. an observation or alignment made with such a device. 11. **a sight.** *Inf.* a great deal: *she's a sight too good for him.* 12. **a sight for sore eyes.** a person or thing that one is pleased or relieved to see. 13. **at** (or **on**) **sight. a.** as soon as seen. **b.** on presentation: *a bill payable at sight.* 14. **know by sight.** to be familiar with the appearance of without having personal acquaintance. 15. **not by a long sight.** *Inf.* on no account. 16. **set one's sights on.** to have (a specified goal) in mind. 17. **sight unseen.** without having seen the object at issue: *to buy a car sight unseen.* ~vb. 18. (tr.) to see, view, or glimpse. 19. (tr.) **a.** to furnish with a sight or sights. **b.** to adjust the sight of. 20. to aim (a firearm) using the sight. —'sightable adj. —'sighter n.

sighted ('saɪtɪd) adj. 1. not blind. 2. (in combination) having sight of a specified kind: *short-sighted.*

sightless ('saɪtlɪs) adj. 1. blind. 2. invisible. —'sightlessly adv. —'sightlessness n.

sightly ('saɪtlɪ) adj. **-lier, -liest.** pleasing or attractive to see. —'sightliness n.

sight-read ('saɪt,riːd) vb. **-reading, -read** (-,rɛd). to sing or play (music in a printed or written form) without previous preparation. —'sight-,reader n. —'sight,reading n.

sightscreen ('saɪt,skriːn) n. *Cricket.* a large white screen placed near the boundary behind the bowler to help the batsman see the ball.

sightsee ('saɪt,siː) vb. **seeing, saw, seen.** *Inf.* to visit the famous or interesting sights of (a place). —'sight,seer n. —'sight,seeing n.

sigma ('sɪgmə) n. 1. the 18th letter in the Greek alphabet (Σ, σ or, when final, ς), a consonant, transliterated as S. 2. *Maths.* the symbol Σ, indicating summation.

sign (saɪn) n. 1. something that indicates a fact, condition, etc., that is not immediately or outwardly observable. 2. an action or gesture intended to convey information, a command, etc. 3. **a.** a board, placard, etc., displayed in public and intended to inform, warn, etc. **b.**

THESAURUS

sidelong adj. covert, indirect, oblique, sideways

sidestep avoid, bypass, circumvent, dodge, duck (*Inf.*), elude, evade, skip, skirt

sidetrack deflect, distract, divert, lead off the subject

sideways 1. adv. crabwise, edgeways, laterally, obliquely, sidelong, sidewards, to the side 2. adj. oblique, side, sidelong, slanted

siesta catnap, doze, forty winks (*Inf.*), nap, rest, sleep, snooze (*Inf.*)

sieve 1. n. colander, riddle, screen, sifter, strainer, tammy cloth 2. v. bolt, remove, riddle, separate, sift, strain

sift 1. bolt, filter, pan, part, riddle, separate, sieve 2. analyse, examine, fathom, go through, investigate, pore over, probe, screen, scrutinize

sigh v. 1. breathe, complain, grieve, lament, moan, sorrow, sough, suspire (*Archaic*) 2. *Often with* **for** languish, long, mourn, pine, yearn

sight n. 1. eye, eyes, eyesight, seeing, vision 2. appearance, apprehension, eyeshot, field of vision, ken, perception, range of vision, view, viewing, visibility 3. display, exhibition, pageant, scene, show, spectacle, vista 4. *Inf.* blot on the landscape (*Inf.*), eyesore, fright (*Inf.*), mess, monstrosity, spectacle 5. **catch sight of** descry, espy, glimpse, recognize, spot, view ~v. 6. behold, discern, distinguish, make out, observe, perceive, see, spot

(*as modifier*): *a sign painter.* **4.** an arbitrary mark or device that stands for a word, phrase, etc. **5.** a symbol used to indicate a mathematical operation: *a plus sign.* **6.** an indication or vestige: *the house showed no signs of being occupied.* **7.** a portentous or significant event. **8.** the scent or spoor of an animal. **9.** *Med.* any objective evidence of the presence of a disease or disorder. **10.** *Astrol.* See **sign of the zodiac.** ~*vb.* **11.** to write (one's name) as a signature to (a document, etc.) in attestation, confirmation, etc. **12.** (*intr.; often foll. by to*) to make a sign. **13.** to engage or be engaged by written agreement, as a player for a team, etc. **14.** (*tr.*) to outline in gestures a sign over, esp. the sign of the cross. **15.** (*tr.*) to indicate by or as if by a sign; betoken. ~See also **sign away, sign in, sign off,** etc. — **'signable** *adj.* — **'signer** *n.*

signal ('sɪgnəl) *n.* **1.** any sign, gesture, etc., that serves to communicate information. **2.** anything that acts as an incitement to action: *the rise in prices was a signal for rebellion.* **3. a.** a variable parameter, such as a current or electromagnetic wave, by which information is conveyed through an electronic circuit, etc. **b.** the information so conveyed. **c.** (*as modifier*): *a signal generator.* ~*adj.* **4.** distinguished or conspicuous. **5.** used to give or act as a signal. ~*vb.* **-nalling, -nalled** *or U.S.* **-naling, -naled. 6.** to communicate (a message, etc.) to (a person). — **'signaller** *n.*

signal box *n.* **1.** a building containing signal levers for all the railway lines in its section. **2.** a control point for a large area of a railway system.

signalize *or* **-lise** ('sɪgnə,laɪz) *vb.* (*tr.*) **1.** to make noteworthy. **2.** to point out carefully.

signally ('sɪgnəlɪ) *adv.* conspicuously or especially.

signalman ('sɪgnəlmən) *n., pl.* **-men.** a railway employee in charge of the signals and points within a section.

signatory ('sɪgnətərɪ) *n., pl.* **-ries. 1.** a person who has signed a document such as a treaty or an organization, state, etc., on whose behalf such a document has been signed. ~*adj.* **2.** having signed a document, treaty, etc.

signature ('sɪgnɪtʃə) *n.* **1.** the name of a person or a mark or sign representing his name. **2.** the act of signing one's name. **3.** a distinctive mark, characteristic, etc., that identifies a person or thing. **4.** *Music.* See **key signature, time signature. 5.** *Printing.* **a.** a sheet of paper printed with several pages that upon folding will become a section or sections of a book. **b.** such a sheet so folded. **c.** a mark, esp. a letter, printed on the first page of a signature.

signature tune *n. Brit.* a melody used to introduce or identify a television or radio programme, a dance band, a performer, etc.

sign away *vb.* (*tr., adv.*) to dispose of by or as if by signing a document.

signboard ('saɪn,bɔːd) *n.* a board carrying a sign or notice, esp. one used to advertise a product, event, etc.

signet ('sɪgnɪt) *n.* **1.** a small seal, esp. one as part of a finger ring. **2.** a seal used to stamp or authenticate documents. **3.** the impression made by such a seal.

signet ring *n.* a finger ring bearing a signet.

significance (sɪg'nɪfɪkəns) *n.* **1.** consequence or importance. **2.** something expressed or intended. **3.** the state or quality of being significant.

significant (sɪg'nɪfɪkənt) *adj.* **1.** having or expressing a meaning. **2.** having a covert or implied meaning. **3.** important or momentous. **4.** *Statistics.* of or relating to a difference between a result derived from a hypothesis

and its observed value that is too large to be attributed to chance. — **sig'nificantly** *adv.*

significant figures *pl. n.* **1.** the figures of a number that express a magnitude to a specified degree of accuracy: *3.141 59 to four significant figures is 3.142.* **2.** the number of such figures: *3.142 has four significant figures.*

signify ('sɪgnɪ,faɪ) *vb.* **-fying, -fied.** (when *tr., may take a clause as object*) **1.** (*tr.*) to indicate or suggest. **2.** (*tr.*) to imply or portend: *the clouds signified the coming storm.* **3.** (*tr.*) to stand as a symbol, sign, etc. (for). **4.** (*intr.*) to be important. — **,signifi'cation** *n.* — **sig'nificative** *adj.* — **'signi,fier** *n.*

sign in *vb.* (*adv.*) **1.** to sign or cause to sign a register, as at a hotel, club, etc. **2.** to make or become a member, as of a club.

sign language *n.* any system of communication by manual signs or gestures, such as one used by the deaf.

sign off *vb.* (*adv.*) **1.** (*intr.*) to announce the end of a radio or television programme, esp. at the end of a day. **2.** (*tr.*) (of a doctor) to declare unfit for work, because of illness.

sign of the zodiac *n.* any of the twelve equal areas into which the zodiac can be divided, named after the 12 zodiacal constellations. In astrology, it is thought that a person's attitudes to life can be correlated with the sign in which the sun lay at the moment of his birth.

sign on *vb.* (*adv.*) **1.** (*tr.*) to hire or employ. **2.** (*intr.*) to commit oneself to a job, activity, etc. **3.** (*intr.*) *Brit.* to register at an employment agency.

signor *or* **signior** ('siːnjɔː; *Italian* siɲ'ɲoːr) *n., pl.* **-gnors** *or* **-gnori** (*Italian* -'ɲoːri). an Italian man: usually used before a name as a title equivalent to *Mr.*

signora (siːn'jɔːrə; *Italian* siɲ'ɲoːra) *n., pl.* **-ras** *or* **-re** (*Italian* -re). a married Italian woman: a title of address equivalent to *Mrs.* when placed before a name or *madam* when used alone.

signorina (,siːnjɔː'riːnə; *Italian* ,siɲɲo'riːna) *n., pl.* **-nas** *or* **-ne** (*Italian* -ne). an unmarried Italian woman: a title of address equivalent to *Miss* when placed before a name or *madam* or *miss* when used alone.

sign out *vb.* (*adv.*) to sign (one's name) to indicate that one is leaving a place: *he signed out for the evening.*

signpost ('saɪn,pəʊst) *n.* **1.** a post bearing a sign that shows the way, as at a roadside. **2.** something that serves as a clue or indication. ~*vb.* (*tr.; usually passive*) **3.** to mark with signposts. **4.** to indicate direction towards.

sign up *vb.* (*adv.*) to enlist or cause to enlist, as for military service.

Sikh (siːk) *n.* **1.** a member of a Hindu sect, founded in the 16th century, that teaches monotheism and rejects the authority of the Vedas. ~*adj.* **2.** of or relating to the Sikhs or their religious beliefs. — **'Sikh,ism** *n.*

silage ('saɪlɪdʒ) *n.* any crop harvested while green for fodder and kept succulent by partial fermentation in a silo. Also called: **ensilage.**

sild (sɪld) *n.* any of various small young herrings, esp. when prepared and canned in Norway.

silence ('saɪləns) *n.* **1.** the state or quality of being silent. **2.** the absence of sound or noise. **3.** refusal or failure to speak, etc., when expected: *his silence on their promotion was alarming.* **4.** a period of time without noise. **5.** oblivion or obscurity. ~*vb.* (*tr.*) **6.** to bring to silence. **7.** to put a stop to: *to silence all complaint.*

silencer ('saɪlənsə) *n.* **1.** any device designed to reduce noise, esp. the device in the exhaust system of a motor vehicle. *U.S.* name: **muffler. 2.** a device fitted to the

---

THESAURUS

sign *n.* **1.** clue, evidence, gesture, giveaway, hint, indication, manifestation, mark, note, proof, signal, spoor, suggestion, symptom, token, trace, vestige **2.** board, notice, placard, warning **3.** badge, character, cipher, device, emblem, ensign, figure, logo, mark, representation, symbol **4.** augury, auspice, foreboding, forewarning, omen, portent, presage, warning, writing on the wall ~*v.* **5.** autograph, endorse, initial, inscribe, set one's hand to, subscribe **6.** beckon, gesticulate, gesture, indicate, signal, use sign language, wave

signal 1. *n.* beacon, cue, gesture, go-ahead (*Inf.*), green light, indication, indicator, mark, sign, token **2.** *adj.* conspicuous, distin-

guished, eminent, exceptional, extraordinary, famous, memorable, momentous, notable, noteworthy, outstanding, remarkable, significant, striking **3.** *v.* beckon, communicate, gesticulate, gesture, give a sign to, indicate, motion, nod, sign, wave

significance 1. force, implication(s), import, meaning, message, point, purport, sense, signification **2.** consequence, consideration, importance, impressiveness, matter, moment, relevance, weight

significant 1. denoting, eloquent, expressing, expressive, indicative, knowing, meaning, meaningful, pregnant, suggestive **2.** critical, important, material, momentous, noteworthy, serious, vital, weighty

signify 1. announce, be a sign of, betoken, communicate, connote, convey, denote, evidence, exhibit, express, imply, indicate, intimate, matter, mean, portend, proclaim, represent, show, stand for, suggest, symbolize **2.** *Inf.* be of importance *or* significance, carry weight, count, matter

silence *n.* **1.** calm, hush, lull, noiselessness, peace, quiescence, quiet, stillness **2.** dumbness, muteness, reticence, speechlessness, taciturnity, uncommunicativeness ~*v.* **3.** cut off, cut short, deaden, extinguish, gag, muffle, quell, quiet, quieten, stifle, still, strike dumb, subdue, suppress

muzzle of a firearm to deaden the report. **3.** a person or thing that silences.

silent ('saɪlənt) *adj.* **1.** characterized by an absence or near absence of noise or sound: *a silent house.* **2.** tending to speak very little or not at all. **3.** unable to speak. **4.** failing to speak, communicate, etc., when expected: *the witness chose to remain silent.* **5.** not spoken or expressed. **6.** (of a letter) used in the orthography of a word but no longer pronounced in that word: *the "k" in "know" is silent.* **7.** denoting a film that has no accompanying soundtrack. —'**silently** *adv.* —'**silentness** *n.*

silhouette (,sɪluː'ɛt) *n.* **1.** the outline of a solid figure as cast by its shadow. **2.** an outline drawing filled in with black, often a profile portrait cut out of black paper and mounted on a light ground. ~*vb.* **3.** (*tr.*) to cause to appear in silhouette.

silica ('sɪlɪkə) *n.* the dioxide of silicon, occurring naturally as quartz. It is a refractory insoluble material used in the manufacture of glass, ceramics, and abrasives.

siliceous *or* **silicious** (sɪ'lɪʃəs) *adj.* **1.** of, relating to, or containing silica: *a siliceous clay.* **2.** (of plants) growing in soil rich in silica.

silicon ('sɪlɪkən) *n.* a brittle metalloid element that exists in two allotropic forms; occurs principally in sand, quartz, granite, feldspar, and clay. It is usually a grey crystalline solid but is also found as a brown amorphous powder. It is used in transistors, solar cells, and in alloys. Its compounds are widely used in glass manufacture and the building industry. Symbol: Si; atomic no.: 14; atomic wt.: 28.09.

silicon chip *n.* another term for **chip** (sense 7).

silicone ('sɪlɪ,kəʊn) *n. Chem.* **a.** any of a large class of polymeric synthetic materials that usually have resistance to temperature, water, and chemicals, and good insulating and lubricating properties, making them suitable for wide use as oils, water-repellents, resins, etc. **b.** (*as modifier*): *silicone rubber.*

silicosis (,sɪlɪ'kəʊsɪs) *n. Pathol.* a form of pneumoconiosis caused by breathing in tiny particles of silica, quartz, or slate, and characterized by shortness of breath.

silk (sɪlk) *n.* **1.** the very fine soft lustrous fibre produced by a silkworm to make its cocoon. **2. a.** thread or fabric made from this fibre. **b.** (*as modifier*): *a silk dress.* **3.** a garment made of this. **4.** a very fine fibre produced by a spider to build its web, nest, or cocoon. **5.** the tuft of long fine styles on an ear of maize. **6.** *Brit.* **a.** the gown worn by a Queen's (or King's) Counsel. **b.** *Inf.* a Queen's (or King's) Counsel. **c. take silk.** to become a Queen's (or King's) Counsel. —'**silk,like** *adj.*

silken ('sɪlkən) *adj.* **1.** made of silk. **2.** resembling silk in smoothness or gloss. **3.** dressed in silk. **4.** soft and delicate.

silk hat *n.* a man's top hat covered with silk.

silk-screen printing *n.* another name for **screen process.**

silkworm ('sɪlk,wɜːm) *n.* **1.** the larva of the Chinese moth that feeds on the leaves of the mulberry tree: widely cultivated as a source of silk. **2.** any of various similar or related larvae.

silky ('sɪlkɪ) *adj.* **silkier, silkiest. 1.** resembling silk in texture; glossy. **2.** made of silk. **3.** (of a voice, manner, etc.) suave; smooth. **4.** *Bot.* covered with long fine soft hairs: *silky leaves.* —'**silkily** *adv.* —'**silkiness** *n.*

sill (sɪl) *n.* **1.** a shelf at the bottom of a window inside a room. **2.** a horizontal piece along the outside lower member of a window, that throws water clear of the wall below. **3.** the lower horizontal member of a window or door frame. **4.** a horizontal member placed on top of a foundation wall in order to carry a timber framework. **5.** a mass of igneous rock, situated between two layers of older sedimentary rock.

sillabub ('sɪlə,bʌb) *n.* a variant spelling of **syllabub.**

silly ('sɪlɪ) *adj.* **-lier, -liest. 1.** lacking in good sense; ab-

surd. **2.** frivolous, trivial, or superficial. **3.** feeble-minded. **4.** *Inf.* dazed, as from a blow. ~*n.* **5.** (*modifier*) *Cricket.* (of a fielding position) near the batsman's wicket: *silly mid-on.* **6.** Also called: **silly-billy.** *Inf.* a foolish person. —'**silliness** *n.*

silo ('saɪləʊ) *n., pl.* **-los. 1.** a pit, trench, or tower, often cylindrical in shape, in which silage is made and stored. **2.** an underground position in which missile systems are sited for protection.

silt (sɪlt) *n.* **1.** a fine deposit of mud, clay, etc., esp. one in a river or lake. ~*vb.* **2.** (usually foll. by *up*) to fill or become filled with silt; choke. —**sil'tation** *n.* —'**silty** *adj.*

Silurian (saɪ'lʊərɪən) *adj.* **1.** of or formed in the third period of the Palaeozoic era, during which fishes first appeared. ~*n.* **2. the.** the Silurian period or rock system.

silvan ('sɪlvən) *adj.* a variant spelling of **sylvan.**

silver ('sɪlvə) *n.* **1. a.** a ductile malleable brilliant greyish-white element having the highest electrical and thermal conductivity of any metal. It occurs free and in argentite and other ores: used in jewellery, tableware, coinage, electrical contacts, and in electroplating. Symbol: Ag; atomic no.: 47; atomic wt.: 107.870. **b.** (*as modifier*): *a silver coin.* Related adj.: **argent. 2.** coin made of this metal. **3.** cutlery, whether made of silver or not. **4.** any household articles made of silver. **5.** short for **silver medal. 6. a.** a brilliant or light greyish-white colour. **b.** (*as adj.*): *silver hair.* ~*adj.* **7.** well-articulated: *silver speech.* **8.** (*prenominal*) denoting the 25th in a series: *a silver wedding anniversary.* ~*vb.* **9.** (*tr.*) to coat with silver or a silvery substance: *to silver a spoon.* **10.** to become or cause to become silvery in colour. —'**silvering** *n.*

silver birch *n.* a tree of N temperate regions of the Old World, having silvery-white peeling bark.

silverfish ('sɪlvə,fɪʃ) *n., pl.* **-fish** *or* **-fishes. 1.** a silver variety of the goldfish. **2.** any of various other silvery fishes, such as the moonfish. **3.** any of various small primitive wingless insects, that have long antennae and tail appendages and occur in buildings, feeding on food scraps, book bindings, etc.

silver lining *n.* a hopeful aspect of an otherwise desperate or unhappy situation.

silver medal *n.* a medal of silver awarded to a competitor who comes second in a contest or race.

silver plate *n.* **1.** a thin layer of silver deposited on a base metal. **2.** articles, esp. tableware, made of silver plate. ~*vb.* **silver-plate. 3.** (*tr.*) to coat (a metal, object, etc.) with silver, as by electroplating.

silver screen *n.* **the.** *Inf.* **1.** films collectively or the film industry. **2.** the screen onto which films are projected.

silverside ('sɪlvə,saɪd) *n.* **1.** *Brit.* a cut of beef below the aitchbone and above the leg. **2.** a small marine or freshwater teleost fish related to the grey mullets.

silversmith ('sɪlvə,smɪθ) *n.* a craftsman who makes or repairs articles of silver. —'**silver,smithing** *n.*

silverware ('sɪlvə,wɛə) *n.* articles, esp. tableware, made of or plated with silver.

silvery ('sɪlvərɪ) *adj.* **1.** of or having the appearance of silver: *the silvery moon.* **2.** containing or covered with silver. **3.** having a clear ringing sound. —'**silveriness** *n.*

silviculture ('sɪlvɪ,kʌltʃə) *n.* the branch of forestry that is concerned with the cultivation of trees. —,silvi'cultural *adj.* —,silvi'culturist *n.*

simian ('sɪmɪən) *adj.* **1.** of or resembling a monkey or ape. ~*n.* **2.** a monkey or ape.

similar ('sɪmɪlə) *adj.* **1.** showing resemblance in qualities, characteristics, or appearance. **2.** *Geom.* (of two or more figures) having corresponding angles equal and all corresponding sides in the same ratio. —**similarity**

THESAURUS

silent 1. hushed, muted, noiseless, quiet, soundless, still, stilly (*Poetic*) **2.** dumb, mum, mute, nonvocal, not talkative, speechless, struck dumb (*Inf.*), taciturn, tongue-tied, uncommunicative, unspeaking, voiceless, wordless **3.** aphonic (*Phonetics*), implicit, implied, tacit, understood, unexpressed, unpronounced, unspoken

silently as quietly as a mouse (*Inf.*), dumbly, in silence, mutely, noiselessly, quiet-

ly, soundlessly, speechlessly, without a sound, wordlessly

silhouette 1. *n.* delineation, form, outline, profile, shape **2.** *v.* delineate, etch, outline, stand out

silky silken, sleek, smooth, velvety

silly *adj.* **1.** absurd, asinine, brainless, childish, fatuous, foolhardy, foolish, frivolous, giddy, idiotic, immature, imprudent, inane, inappropriate, irresponsible, meaningless,

pointless, preposterous, puerile, ridiculous, senseless, stupid, unwise, witless **2.** *Inf.* benumbed, dazed, groggy (*Inf.*), in a daze, muzzy, stunned, stupefied ~*n.* **3.** *Inf.* clot (*Brit. sl.*), duffer (*Inf.*), goose (*Inf.*), ignoramus, ninny, silly-billy (*Inf.*), simpleton, twit (*Inf.*)

silver 1. *adj.* argent (*Poetic*), pearly, silvered, silvery **2.** *n.* silver plate, silverware

(ˌsɪmɪ'lærɪtɪ) n. —'similarly adv.
▷ **Usage.** Careful writers prefer not to use *similarly* where *correspondingly* would be appropriate: *if our competitors raise their prices, we must correspondingly* (not *similarly*) *make increases in ours.*

simile ('sɪmɪlɪ) n. a figure of speech that expresses the resemblance of one thing to another of a different category, usually introduced by *as* or *like*. Cf. **metaphor.**

similitude (sɪ'mɪlɪˌtjuːd) n. **1.** likeness. **2.** a thing or sometimes a person that is like or the counterpart of another. **3.** *Arch.* a simile or parable.

simmer ('sɪmə) vb. **1.** to cook (food) gently at or just below the boiling point. **2.** (*intr.*) to be about to break out in rage or excitement. ~n. **3.** the act, sound, or state of simmering. —'**simmeringly** adv.

simmer down vb. (adv.) **1.** (*intr.*) *Inf.* to grow calmer, as after intense rage. **2.** (*tr.*) to reduce the volume of (a liquid) by boiling slowly.

simnel cake ('sɪmnəl) n. *Brit.* a fruit cake covered with a layer of marzipan, traditionally eaten in Lent or at Easter.

simony ('saɪmənɪ) n. *Ecclesiast.* the practice, now usually regarded as a sin, of buying or selling spiritual or Church benefits such as pardons, relics, etc. —'**simonist** n.

simoom (sɪ'muːm) or **simoon** (sɪ'muːn) n. a strong suffocating sand-laden wind of the deserts of Arabia and North Africa.

simper ('sɪmpə) vb. **1.** (*intr.*) to smile coyly, affectedly, or in a silly self-conscious way. **2.** (*tr.*) to utter (something) in such a manner. ~n. **3.** a simpering smile; smirk. —'**simperingly** adv.

simple ('sɪmpəl) adj. **1.** easy to understand or do: *a simple problem.* **2.** plain; unadorned: *a simple dress.* **3.** not combined or complex: *a simple mechanism.* **4.** unaffected or unpretentious: *although he became famous, he remained a simple man.* **5.** sincere; frank: *her simple explanation was readily accepted.* **6.** of humble condition or rank: *the peasant was of simple birth.* **7.** feebleminded. **8.** (*prenominal*) without additions or modifications: *the witness told the simple truth.* **9.** (*prenominal*) straightforward: *a simple case of mumps.* **10.** *Chem.* (of a substance) consisting of only one chemical compound. **11.** *Maths.* (of an equation) containing variables to the first power only. **12.** *Biol.* **a.** not divided into parts: *a simple leaf.* **b.** formed from only one ovary: *simple fruit.* **13.** *Music.* relating to or denoting a time where the number of beats per bar may be two, three, or four. ~n. *Arch.* **14.** a simpleton. **15.** a plant having medicinal properties. —**simplicity** (sɪm'plɪsɪtɪ) n.

simple fraction n. a fraction in which the numerator and denominator are both integers. Also called: **common fraction, vulgar fraction.**

simple fracture n. a fracture in which the broken bone does not pierce the skin.

simple interest n. interest paid on the principal alone. Cf. **compound interest.**

simple-minded adj. **1.** stupid; foolish; feeble-minded. **2.** mentally defective. **3.** unsophisticated; artless. —ˌsimple-'mindedly adv. —ˌsimple-'mindedness n.

simple sentence n. a sentence consisting of a single main clause.

simpleton ('sɪmpəltən) n. a foolish or ignorant person.

simplify ('sɪmplɪˌfaɪ) vb. **-fying, -fied.** (*tr.*) **1.** to make less complicated or easier. **2.** *Maths.* to reduce (an equation, fraction, etc.) to its simplest form. —ˌsimplifi'cation n.

simplistic (sɪm'plɪstɪk) adj. **1.** characterized by extreme simplicity. **2.** making unrealistically simple judgments or analyses. —'**simplism** n. —sim'plistically adv.

simply ('sɪmplɪ) adv. **1.** in a simple manner. **2.** merely. **3.** absolutely; altogether: *a simply wonderful holiday.* **4.** (*sentence modifier*) frankly.

simulacrum (ˌsɪmjʊ'leɪkrəm) n., pl. **-cra** (-krə). *Arch.* **1.** any image or representation of something. **2.** a superficial likeness.

simulate vb. ('sɪmjʊˌleɪt). (*tr.*) **1.** to make a pretence of: *to simulate anxiety.* **2.** to reproduce the conditions of (a situation, etc.), as in carrying out an experiment: *to simulate weightlessness.* **3.** to have the appearance of. ~adj. ('sɪmjʊlɪt, -ˌleɪt). **4.** *Arch.* assumed. —ˌsimu'lation n. —'simulative adj.

simulator ('sɪmjʊˌleɪtə) n. **1.** any device that simulates specific conditions for the purposes of research or operator training: *space simulator.* **2.** a person who simulates.

simultaneous (ˌsɪməl'teɪnɪəs) adj. occurring, existing, or operating at the same time. —ˌsimul'taneously adv. —ˌsimul'taneousness or simultaneity (ˌsɪməltə'niːɪtɪ) n.
▷ **Usage.** See at **unique.**

sin[1] (sɪn) n. **1.** *Theol.* **a.** transgression of God's known will or any principle or law regarded as embodying this. **b.** the condition of estrangement from God arising from such transgression. **2.** any serious offence, as against a religious or moral principle. **3.** any offence against a principle or standard. **4. live in sin.** *Inf.* (of an unmarried couple) to live together. ~vb. (*intr.*) **sinning, sinned. 5.** *Theol.* to commit a sin. **6.** (usually foll. by *against*) to commit an offence (against a person, etc.). —'sinner n.

sin[2] *Maths.* abbrev. for sine.

SIN (in Canada) abbrev. for Social Insurance Number.

sin bin n. *Canad. sl.* the penalty box used in ice hockey.

since (sɪns) prep. **1.** during or throughout the period of time after: *since May it has only rained once.* ~conj. (*subordinating*) **2.** (sometimes preceded by *ever*) continuously from or starting from the time when. **3.** seeing that; because. ~adv. **4.** since that time: *I haven't seen him since.*
▷ **Usage.** See at **ago.**

sincere (sɪn'sɪə) adj. **1.** not hypocritical or deceitful; genuine: *sincere regret.* **2.** *Arch.* pure; unmixed. —sin'cerely adv. —sin'cereness or sincerity (sɪn'scrɪtɪ) n.

THESAURUS

similar alike, comparable, congruous, corresponding, in agreement, much the same, resembling, uniform

similarity affinity, agreement, analogy, closeness, comparability, concordance, congruence, correspondence, likeness, point of comparison, relation, resemblance, sameness, similitude

similarly by the same token, correspondingly, in like manner, likewise

simmer v. *Fig.* be angry (agitated, tense, uptight (*Inf.*)), boil, burn, fume, rage, seethe, smart, smoulder

simmer down calm down, collect oneself, contain oneself, control oneself, cool off *or* down, get down off one's high horse (*Inf.*), grow quieter, unwind (*Inf.*)

simple 1. clear, easy, elementary, intelligible, lucid, manageable, plain, straightforward, uncomplicated, understandable, uninvolved 2. classic, clean, natural, plain, Spartan, unadorned, uncluttered, unembellished, unfussy 3. elementary, pure, single, unalloyed, unblended, uncombined, undivided, unmixed 4. artless, childlike, frank,

green, guileless, ingenuous, innocent, naive, natural, sincere, unaffected, unpretentious, unsophisticated 5. bald, basic, direct, frank, honest, naked, plain, sincere, stark, undeniable, unvarnished 6. homely, humble, lowly, modest, rustic, unpretentious 7. brainless, credulous, dense, dumb (*Inf.*), feeble, feeble-minded, foolish, half-witted, moronic, obtuse, shallow, silly, slow, stupid, thick

simple-minded 1. a bit lacking (*Inf.*), addle-brained, backward, brainless, dead from the neck up (*Sl.*), dim-witted, feeble-minded, foolish, idiot, idiotic, moronic, retarded, simple, stupid 2. artless, natural, unsophisticated

simpleton blockhead, booby, dolt, dope (*Sl.*), dullard, dunce, fool, goose (*Inf.*), greenhorn (*Inf.*), idiot, imbecile (*Inf.*), jackass, moron, nincompoop, ninny, numskull, Simple Simon, stupid (*Inf.*), twerp (*Inf.*)

simplicity 1. absence of complications, clarity, clearness, ease, easiness, elementariness, obviousness, straightforwardness 2. clean lines, lack of adornment, modesty, naturalness, plainness, purity, restraint 3.

artlessness, candour, directness, guilelessness, innocence, lack of sophistication, naivety, openness

simplify abridge, decipher, disentangle, facilitate, make intelligible, reduce to essentials, streamline

simply 1. clearly, directly, easily, intelligibly, modestly, naturally, plainly, straightforwardly, unaffectedly, unpretentiously, without any elaboration 2. just, merely, only, purely, solely 3. absolutely, altogether, completely, really, totally, unreservedly, utterly, wholly

simultaneous at the same time, coincident, coinciding, concurrent, contemporaneous, synchronous

simultaneously all together, at the same time, concurrently, in chorus, in concert, in the same breath, in unison, together

sin 1. n. crime, damnation, error, evil, guilt, iniquity, misdeed, offence, sinfulness, transgression, trespass, ungodliness, unrighteousness, wickedness, wrong, wrongdoing 2. v. err, fall, fall from grace, go astray, lapse, offend, transgress, trespass (*Archaic*)

sine (saın) *n.* (of an angle) a trigonometric function that in a right-angled triangle is the ratio of the length of the opposite side to that of the hypotenuse.

sinecure (ˈsaınıˌkjʊə) *n.* **1.** a paid office or post involving minimal duties. **2.** a Church benefice to which no spiritual charge is attached. —ˈsineˌcurism *n.* —ˈsineˌcurist *n.*

sine curve (saın) *n.* a curve of the equation $y = \sin x$. Also called: **sinusoid.**

sine die *Latin.* (ˈsaını ˈdaıı) *adv., adj.* without a day fixed.

sine qua non *Latin.* (ˈsaını kweı ˈnɒn) *n.* an essential requirement.

sinew (ˈsınjuː) *n.* **1.** *Anat.* another name for **tendon. 2.** (*often pl.*) **a.** a source of strength or power. **b.** a literary word for **muscle.** —ˈsinewless *adj.*

sinewy (ˈsınjuı) *adj.* **1.** consisting of or resembling a tendon or tendons. **2.** muscular. **3.** (esp. of language, style, etc.) forceful. **4.** (of meat, etc.) tough. —ˈsinewiness *n.*

sinful (ˈsınful) *adj.* **1.** having committed or tending to commit sin: *a sinful person.* **2.** characterized by or being a sin: *a sinful act.* —ˈsinfully *adv.* —ˈsinfulness *n.*

sing (sıŋ) *vb.* **singing, sang, sung. 1.** to produce or articulate (sounds, words, a song, etc.) with musical intonation. **2.** (when *intr.*, often foll. by *to*) to perform (a song) to the accompaniment (of): *to sing to a guitar.* **3.** (*intr.*; foll. by *of*) to tell a story in song (about): *I sing of a maiden.* **4.** (*intr.*) to perform songs for a living. **5.** (*intr.*) (esp. of certain birds and insects) to utter calls or sounds reminiscent of music. **6.** (when *intr.*, usually foll. by *of*) to tell (something), esp. in verse: *the poet who sings of the Trojan dead.* **7.** (*intr.*) to make a whining, ringing, or whistling sound: *the arrow sang past his ear.* **8.** (*intr.*) (of the ears) to experience a continuous ringing. **9.** (*tr.*) to bring to a given state by singing: *to sing a child to sleep.* **10.** (*intr.*) *Sl.*, chiefly *U.S.* to confess or act as an informer. ~*n.* **11.** *Inf.* an act or performance of singing. ~See also **sing out.** —ˈsingable *adj.* —ˈsinger *n.* —ˈsingingly *adv.*

▷ **Usage.** See at **ring².**

sing. *abbrev. for* singular.

singe (sındʒ) *vb.* **1.** to burn or be burnt superficially; scorch: *to singe one's clothes.* **2.** (*tr.*) to burn the ends of (hair, etc.). **3.** (*tr.*) to expose (a carcass) to flame to remove bristles or hair. ~*n.* **4.** a superficial burn.

Singh (sıŋ) *n.* a title assumed by a Sikh when he becomes a full member of the community.

single (ˈsıŋgəl) *adj.* (*usually prenominal*) **1.** existing alone; solitary: *upon the hill stood a single tower.* **2.** distinct from other things. **3.** composed of one part. **4.** designed or sufficient for one user: *a single bed.* **5.** (*also postpositive*) unmarried. **6.** connected with the condition of being unmarried: *he led a single life.* **7.** (esp. of combat) involving two individuals. **8.** even one: *there wasn't a single person on the beach.* **9.** (of a flower) having only one set or whorl of petals. **10.** single-minded: *a single devotion to duty.* **11.** *Rare.* honest or sincere. ~*n.* **12.** something forming one individual unit. **13.** a gramophone record with a short recording, usually of pop music, on each side. **14.** (*often pl.*) **a.** an unmarried, usually young, person. **b.** (*as modifier*): *singles bar.* **15.** *Cricket.* a hit from which one run is scored. **16. a.**

Brit. a pound note. **b.** *U.S.* a dollar note. **17.** See **single ticket.** ~*vb.* **18.** (*tr.*; usually foll. by *out*) to select from a group of people or things: *he singled him out for special mention.* —ˈsingleness *n.*

single-breasted *adj.* (of a garment) having the fronts overlapping only slightly and with one row of fastenings.

single-decker *n. Brit. inf.* a bus with only one passenger deck.

single entry *n.* **a.** a book-keeping system in which transactions are entered in one account only. **b.** (*as modifier*): *a single-entry account.*

single file *n.* a line of persons, animals, or things ranged one behind the other.

single-handed *adj., adv.* **1.** unaided or working alone: *a single-handed crossing of the Atlantic.* **2.** having or operated by one hand or one person only. —ˌsingle-ˈhandedly *adv.* —ˌsingle-ˈhandedness *n.*

single-lens reflex *n.* See **reflex camera.**

single-minded *adj.* having but one aim or purpose; dedicated. —ˌsingle-ˈmindedly *adv.* —ˌsingle-ˈmindedness *n.*

singles (ˈsıŋgəlz) *pl. n. Tennis, etc.* a match played with one person on each side.

singlestick (ˈsıŋgəlˌstık) *n.* **1.** a wooden stick used instead of a sword for fencing. **2.** fencing with such a stick. **3.** any short heavy stick.

singlet (ˈsıŋglıt) *n. Chiefly Brit.* **1.** a man's sleeveless vest. **2.** a garment worn with shorts by athletes, boxers, etc.

single ticket *n. Brit.* a ticket entitling a passenger to travel only to his destination, without returning.

singleton (ˈsıŋgəltən) *n.* **1.** *Bridge, etc.* an original holding of one card only in a suit. **2.** a single object, etc., distinguished from a pair or group. **3.** *Maths.* a set containing only one member.

singly (ˈsıŋglı) *adv.* **1.** one at a time; one by one. **2.** apart from others; separately; alone.

sing out *vb.* (*tr., adv.*) to call out in a loud voice; shout.

singsong (ˈsıŋˌsɒŋ) *n.* **1.** an accent or intonation that is characterized by an alternately rising and falling rhythm, such as in a person's voice. **2.** *Brit.* an informal session of singing, esp. of popular songs. ~*adj.* **3.** having a monotonous rhythm: *a singsong accent.*

singular (ˈsıŋgjʊlə) *adj.* **1.** remarkable; extraordinary: *a singular feat.* **2.** unusual; odd: *a singular character.* **3.** unique. **4.** denoting a word or an inflected form of a word indicating that one referent is being referred to or described. **5.** *Logic.* (of a proposition) referring to a specific thing or person. ~*n.* **6.** *Grammar.* **a.** the singular number. **b.** a singular form of a word. —ˌsinguˈlarity *n.* —ˈsingularly *adv.*

Sinhalese (ˌsınhəˈliːz) *or* **Singhalese** *n., pl.* -leses *or* -lese. former words for **Sri Lankan.**

sinister (ˈsınıstə) *adj.* **1.** threatening or suggesting evil or harm: *a sinister glance.* **2.** evil or treacherous. **3.** (*usually postpositive*) *Heraldry.* of, on, or starting from the left side from the bearer's point of view. **4.** *Arch.* located on the left side. —ˈsinisterly *adv.* —ˈsinisterness *n.*

sink (sıŋk) *vb.* **sinking, sank** *or* **sunk; sunk** *or* **sunken. 1.** to descend or cause to descend, esp. beneath the surface of a liquid. **2.** (*intr.*) to appear to move down to-

---

THESAURUS

sincere artless, bona fide, candid, earnest, frank, genuine, guileless, heartfelt, honest, natural, no-nonsense, open, real, serious, straightforward, true, unaffected, unfeigned, wholehearted

sincerely earnestly, genuinely, honestly, in all sincerity, in good faith, really, seriously, truly, wholeheartedly

sincerity artlessness, bona fides, candour, frankness, genuineness, good faith, guilelessness, honesty, probity, seriousness, straightforwardness, truth, wholeheartedness

sinecure cushy number (*Sl.*), gravy train (*Sl., chiefly U.S.*), money for jam *or* old rope (*Inf.*), soft job (*Inf.*), soft option

sinful bad, corrupt, criminal, depraved, erring, guilty, immoral, iniquitous, irreligious, morally wrong, ungodly, unholy, unrighteous, wicked

sing 1. carol, chant, chirp, croon, make melody, pipe, trill, vocalize, warble, yodel **2.** *Sl.*, chiefly *U.S.* betray, blow the whistle (on) (*Inf.*), fink (on) (*Sl.*, chiefly *U.S.*), grass (*Brit. sl.*), inform (on), peach (*Sl.*), rat (on), spill the beans (*Inf.*), squeal (*Sl.*), turn in (*Inf.*) **3.** buzz, hum, purr, whine, whistle

singe burn, char, scorch, sear

singer chanteuse (*Fem.*), chorister, crooner, minstrel, songster, vocalist

single *adj.* **1.** distinct, individual, lone, one, only, particular, separate, singular, sole, solitary, unique **2.** free, unattached, unmarried, unwed **3.** exclusive, individual, separate, simple, unblended, uncompounded, undivided, unmixed, unshared ~*v.* **4.** *Usually with* **out** choose, cull, distinguish, fix on, pick, pick on *or* out, put on one side, select, separate, set apart, winnow

single-handed alone, by oneself, inde-

pendently, on one's own, solo, unaided, unassisted, without help

single-minded dedicated, determined, dogged, fixed, monomaniacal, steadfast, stubborn, tireless, undeviating, unswerving, unwavering

singly individually, one at a time, one by one, separately

singular 1. conspicuous, eminent, exceptional, noteworthy, outstanding, prodigious, rare, remarkable, uncommon, unique, unparalleled **2.** atypical, curious, eccentric, extraordinary, odd, out-of-the-way, peculiar, puzzling, queer, strange, unusual **3.** individual, separate, single, sole

sinister dire, disquieting, evil, injurious, malevolent, malign, malignant, menacing, ominous, threatening

wards or descend below the horizon. **3.** (*intr.*) to slope downwards. **4.** (*intr.; often foll. by in or into*) to pass into a specified lower state or condition: *to sink into apathy.* **5.** to make or become lower in volume, pitch, etc. **6.** to make or become lower in value, price, etc. **7.** (*intr.*) to become weaker in health, strength, etc. **8.** (*intr.*) to seep or penetrate. **9.** (*tr.*) to dig, cut, drill, bore, or excavate (a hole, shaft, etc.). **10.** (*tr.*) to drive into the ground: *to sink a stake.* **11.** (*tr.; usually foll. by in or into*) **a.** to invest (money). **b.** to lose (money) in an unwise investment. **12.** (*tr.*) to pay (a debt). **13.** (*intr.*) to become hollow: *his cheeks had sunk during his illness.* **14.** (*tr.*) to hit or propel (a ball) into a hole, pocket, etc.: *he sank a 15-foot putt.* **15. sink or swim.** to take risks where the alternatives are loss or success. ~*n.* **16.** a fixed basin, esp. in a kitchen, made of stone, metal, etc., used for washing. **17.** a place of vice or corruption. **18.** an area of ground below that of the surrounding land, where water collects. **19.** *Physics.* a device by which energy is removed from a system: *a heat sink.* —'**sinkable** *adj.*

sinker ('sɪŋkə) *n.* **1.** a weight attached to a fishing line, net, etc., to cause it to sink in water. **2.** a person who sinks shafts, etc.

sink in *vb.* (*intr., adv.*) to enter or penetrate the mind: *eventually the news sank in.*

sinking fund *n.* a fund accumulated out of a business enterprise's earnings or a government's revenue and invested to repay a long-term debt.

sinless ('sɪnlɪs) *adj.* free from sin or guilt; pure. —'**sinlessly** *adv.* —'**sinlessness** *n.*

Sinn Fein ('ʃɪn 'feɪn) *n.* an Irish republican political movement founded about 1905 and linked to the revolutionary Irish Republican Army. —**Sinn Feiner** *n.* —**Sinn Feinism** *n.*

Sino- *combining form.* Chinese: *Sino-Tibetan; Sinology.*

Sinology (saɪ'nɒlədʒɪ) *n.* the study of Chinese history, language, culture, etc. —**Sinological** (ˌsaɪnə'lɒdʒɪkəl) *adj.* —**Si'nologist** *n.* —**Sinologue** ('saɪnə,lɒg) *n.*

sinter ('sɪntə) *n.* **1.** a whitish porous incrustation, usually consisting of silica, that is deposited from hot springs. **2.** the product of a sintering process. ~*vb.* **3.** (*tr.*) to form large particles, lumps, or masses from (metal powders) by heating or pressure or both.

sinuous ('sɪnjʊəs) *adj.* **1.** full of turns or curves. **2.** devious; not straightforward. **3.** supple. —'**sinuously** *adv.* —**sinuosity** (ˌsɪnjʊ'ɒsɪtɪ) *n.*

sinus ('saɪnəs) *n., pl.* **-nuses.** **1.** *Anat.* **a.** any bodily cavity or hollow space. **b.** a large channel for venous blood, esp. between the brain and the skull. **c.** any of the air cavities in the cranial bones. **2.** *Pathol.* a passage leading to a cavity containing pus.

sinusitis (ˌsaɪnə'saɪtɪs) *n.* inflammation of the membrane lining a sinus, esp. a nasal sinus.

Sion ('saɪən) *n.* a variant spelling of **Zion.**

sip (sɪp) *vb.* **sipping, sipped.** **1.** to drink (a liquid) by taking small mouthfuls. ~*n.* **2.** a small quantity of a liquid taken into the mouth and swallowed. **3.** an act of sipping. —'**sipper** *n.*

siphon *or* **syphon** ('saɪfən) *n.* **1.** a tube placed with one end at a certain level in a vessel of liquid and the other end outside the vessel below this level, so that atmospheric pressure forces the liquid through the tube and out of the vessel. **2.** See **soda siphon.** **3.** *Zool.* any of various tubular organs in different aquatic animals, such as molluscs, through which water passes. ~*vb.* **4.** (*often foll. by off*) to draw off through or as if through a siphon. —'**siphonal** *or* **siphonic** (saɪ'fɒnɪk) *adj.*

sir (sɜː) *n.* **1.** a polite term of address for a man. **2.** *Arch.* a gentleman of high social status.

Sir (sɜː) *n.* **1.** a title of honour placed before the name of a knight or baronet: *Sir Walter Raleigh.* **2.** *Arch.* a title placed before the name of a figure from ancient history.

sire (saɪə) *n.* **1.** a male parent, esp. of a horse or other

domestic animal. **2.** a respectful term of address, now used only in addressing a male monarch. ~*vb.* **3.** (*tr.*) (*esp. of a domestic animal*) to father.

siren ('saɪərən) *n.* **1.** a device for emitting a loud wailing sound, esp. as a warning or signal, consisting of a rotating perforated metal drum through which air or steam is passed under pressure. **2.** (*sometimes cap.*) *Greek myth.* one of several sea nymphs whose singing was believed to lure sailors to destruction on the rocks the nymphs inhabited. **3.** a woman considered to be dangerously alluring or seductive. **4.** an aquatic eel-like salamander of North America, having external gills, no hind limbs, and reduced forelimbs.

Sirius ('sɪrɪəs) *n.* the brightest star in the sky, lying in the constellation Canis Major. Also called: the **Dog Star.**

sirloin ('sɜː,lɔɪn) *n.* a prime cut of beef from the loin, esp. the upper part.

sirocco (sɪ'rɒkəʊ) *n., pl.* **-cos.** a hot oppressive and often dusty wind usually occurring in spring, beginning in N Africa and reaching S Europe.

sirrah ('sɪrə) *n. Arch.* a contemptuous term used in addressing a man or boy.

sis (sɪs) *n. Inf.* short for **sister.**

sisal ('saɪsəl) *n.* **1.** a Mexican agave plant cultivated for its large fleshy leaves, which yield a stiff fibre used for making rope. **2.** the fibre of this plant. ~Also called: **sisal hemp.**

siskin ('sɪskɪn) *n.* **1.** a yellow-and-black Eurasian finch. **2. pine siskin.** a North American finch, having a streaked yellowish-brown plumage.

sissy ('sɪsɪ) *n., pl.* **-sies.** **1.** an effeminate, weak, or cowardly boy or man. ~*adj.* **2.** effeminate, weak, or cowardly. —'**sissyish** *adj.*

sister ('sɪstə) *n.* **1.** a female person having the same parents as another person. **2.** a female person who belongs to the same group, trade union, etc., as another or others. **3.** a senior nurse. **4.** *Chiefly R.C. Church.* a nun or a title given to a nun. **5.** a woman fellow member of a religious body. **6.** (*modifier*) belonging to the same class, fleet, etc., as another or others: *a sister ship.*

sisterhood ('sɪstə,hʊd) *n.* **1.** the state of being related as a sister or sisters. **2.** a religious body or society of sisters.

sister-in-law *n., pl.* **sisters-in-law.** **1.** the sister of one's husband or wife. **2.** the wife of one's brother. **3.** the wife of the brother of one's husband or wife.

sisterly ('sɪstəlɪ) *adj.* of or suitable to a sister, esp. in showing kindness. —'**sisterliness** *n.*

Sisyphean (ˌsɪsɪ'fiːən) *adj.* **1.** relating to Sisyphus, in Greek myth doomed to roll a stone uphill eternally. **2.** actually or seemingly endless and futile.

sit (sɪt) *vb.* **sitting, sat.** (*mainly intr.*) **1.** (*also tr.; when intr., often foll. by down, in, or on*) to adopt a posture in which the body is supported on the buttocks and the torso is more or less upright: *to sit on a chair.* **2.** (*tr.*) to cause to adopt such a posture. **3.** (*of an animal*) to adopt or rest in a posture with the hindquarters lowered to the ground. **4.** (*of a bird*) to perch or roost. **5.** (*of a hen or other bird*) to cover eggs to hatch them. **6.** to be situated or located. **7.** (*of the wind*) to blow from the direction specified. **8.** to adopt and maintain a posture for one's portrait to be painted, etc. **9.** to occupy or be entitled to a seat in some official capacity, as a judge, etc. **10.** (*of a deliberative body*) to be in session. **11.** to remain inactive or unused: *his car sat in the garage.* **12.** (*of a garment*) to fit or hang as specified: *that dress sits well on you.* **13.** to weigh, rest, or lie as specified: *greatness sits easily on him.* **14.** (*tr.*) *Chiefly Brit.* to take (an examination): *he's sitting his bar finals.* **15.** (*usually foll. by for*) *Chiefly Brit.* to be a candidate (for a qualification): *he's sitting for a B.A.* **16.** to keep watch over an invalid, a baby, etc. **17.** (*tr.*) to have seating capacity for. **18. sitting pretty.** *Inf.* well placed financially, socially, etc. **19. sit tight.** *Inf.* to wait patiently. ~See also **sit back, sit**

THESAURUS

sink *v.* **1.** cave in, decline, descend, dip, disappear, droop, drop, drown, ebb, engulf, fall, founder, go down, go under, lower, merge, plummet, plunge, sag, slope, submerge, subside **2.** abate, collapse, drop, fall, lapse, relapse, retrogress, slip, slump, subside **3.** decay, decline, decrease, degenerate, depreciate, deteriorate, die, diminish, dwindle, fade, fail, flag, go downhill (*Inf.*), lessen, weaken,

worsen **4.** bore, dig, drill, drive, excavate, lay, put down **5.** be the ruin of, defeat, destroy, finish, overwhelm, ruin, scupper (*Brit. sl.*), seal the doom of **6.** be reduced to, debase oneself, lower oneself, stoop, succumb

sinless faultless, guiltless, immaculate, innocent, pure, unblemished, uncorrupted, undefiled, unsullied, virtuous, without fault, without sin

sinner evildoer, miscreant, offender, reprobate, transgressor, trespasser (*Archaic*), wrongdoer

sip 1. *v.* sample, sup, taste **2.** *n.* drop, swallow, taste, thimbleful

siren charmer, Circe, *femme fatale*, Lorelei, seductress, temptress, vamp (*Inf.*), witch

down, sit on, etc.

sitar (sɪˈtɑ:) n. a stringed musical instrument, esp. of India, having a long neck, a rounded body, and movable frets. —siˈtarist n.

sit back vb. (intr., adv.) to relax, as when action should be taken: many people just sit back and ignore the problems of today.

sitcom (ˈsɪtˌkɒm) n. an informal term for **situation comedy**.

sit down vb. (adv.) 1. to adopt or cause (oneself or another) to adopt a sitting posture. 2. (intr.; foll. by under) to suffer (insults, etc.) without protests or resistance. ~n. sit-down. 3. a form of civil disobedience in which demonstrators sit down in a public place. 4. See sit-down strike. ~adj. sit-down. 5. (of a meal, etc.) eaten while sitting down at a table.

sit-down strike n. a strike in which workers refuse to leave their place of employment until a settlement is reached.

site (saɪt) n. 1. a. the piece of land where something was, is, or is intended to be located: a building site. b. (as modifier): site office. ~vb. 2. (tr.) to locate or install (something) in a specific place.

sit-in n. 1. a form of civil disobedience in which demonstrators occupy seats in a public place and refuse to move. ~vb. sit in. (intr., adv.) 2. (often foll. by for) to deputize (for). 3. (foll. by on) to take part (in) as a visitor or guest. 4. to organize or take part in a sit-in.

sitkamer (ˈsɪtˌkɑːmə) n. S. African. a sitting room.

sitka spruce n. a tall North American spruce tree having yellowish-green needle-like leaves.

sit on vb. (intr., prep.) 1. to be a member of (a committee, etc.). 2. Inf. to suppress. 3. Inf. to check or rebuke.

sit out vb. (adv.) 1. (tr.) to endure to the end: I sat out the play although it was terrible. 2. (tr.) to remain seated throughout (a dance, etc.).

sitter (ˈsɪtə) n. 1. a person or animal that sits. 2. a person who is posing for his or her portrait to be painted, etc. 3. a broody hen that is sitting on its eggs to hatch them. 4. See baby-sitter.

sitting (ˈsɪtɪŋ) n. 1. a continuous period of being seated: I read his novel at one sitting. 2. such a period in a restaurant, canteen, etc.: dinner will be served in two sittings. 3. the act or period of posing for one's portrait to be painted, etc. 4. a meeting, esp. of an official body, to conduct business. 5. the incubation period of a bird's eggs during which the mother sits on them.

sitting duck n. Inf. a person or thing in a defenceless or precarious position.

sitting room n. a room in a private house or flat used for relaxation and entertainment of guests.

sitting tenant n. a tenant occupying a house, flat, etc.

situate (ˈsɪtjʊˌeɪt) vb. 1. (tr.; often passive) to place. ~adj. 2. (now used esp. in legal contexts) situated.

situation (ˌsɪtjʊˈeɪʃən) n. 1. physical placement, esp. with regard to the surroundings. 2. a. state of affairs. b. a complex or critical state of affairs in a novel, play, etc. 3. social or financial status, position, or circumstances. 4. a position of employment. —ˌsituˈational adj.

▷ **Usage.** Situation is often used in contexts in which it is redundant or imprecise. Typical examples are: the company is in a crisis situation or people in a job situation. In the first example, situation does not add to the meaning and should be omitted. In the second example, it would be clearer and more concise to substitute a phrase such as people at work.

situation comedy n. comedy based on the humorous situations that could arise in day-to-day life.

sit up vb. (adv.) 1. to raise (oneself or another) from a recumbent to an upright posture. 2. (intr.) to remain out of bed and awake, esp. until a late hour. 3. (intr.) Inf. to become suddenly interested: devaluation of the dollar made the money market sit up.

sitz bath (sɪts, zɪts) n. a bath in which the buttocks and hips are immersed in hot water.

SI unit n. any of the units adopted for international use under the Système International d'Unités, now employed for all scientific and most technical purposes. There are seven fundamental units: the metre, kilogram, second, ampere, kelvin, candela, and mole; and two supplementary units: the radian and the steradian. All other units are derived by multiplication or division of these units.

six (sɪks) n. 1. the cardinal number that is the sum of five and one. 2. a numeral, 6, VI, etc., representing this number. 3. something representing, represented by, or consisting of six units, such as a playing card with six symbols on it. 4. Also: six o'clock. six hours after noon or midnight. 5. Cricket. a. a shot that crosses the boundary without bouncing. b. the six runs scored for such a shot. 6. a division of a Brownie Guide or Cub Scout pack. 7. at sixes and sevens. a. in disagreement. b. in a state of confusion. 8. knock (someone) for six. Inf. to upset or overwhelm completely. 9. six of one and half a dozen of the other. a situation in which the alternatives are considered equivalent. ~determiner. 10. a. amounting to six: six nations. b. (as pronoun): set the table for six. —sixth adj.

sixfold (ˈsɪksˌfəʊld) adj. 1. equal to or having six times as many or as much. 2. composed of six parts. ~adv. 3. by or up to six times as many or as much.

sixpence (ˈsɪkspəns) n. a small British cupronickel coin with a face value of six pennies, worth 2½ (new) pence, not minted since 1970.

six-shooter n. U.S. inf. a revolver with six chambers. Also called: six-gun.

sixteen (ˈsɪksˈtiːn) n. 1. the cardinal number that is the sum of ten and six. 2. a numeral, 16, XVI, etc., representing this number. 3. something represented by, representing, or consisting of 16 units. ~determiner. 4. a. amounting to sixteen: sixteen tons. b. (as pronoun): sixteen are known to the police. —ˈsixˈteenth adj.

sixth form n. a. the most senior level in a secondary school to which pupils, usually above the legal leaving age, may proceed to take A levels, retake O levels, etc. b. (as modifier): a sixth-form college. —ˈsixth-ˌformer n.

sixth sense n. any supposed means of perception, such as intuition, other than the five senses of sight, hearing, touch, taste, and smell.

sixty (ˈsɪkstɪ) n., pl. -ties. 1. the cardinal number that is the product of ten and six. 2. a numeral, 60, LX, etc., representing sixty. 3. something represented by, representing, or consisting of 60 units. ~determiner. 4. a. amounting to sixty: sixty soldiers. b. (as pronoun): sixty are dead. —ˈsixtieth adj.

sizable or **sizeable** (ˈsaɪzəbəl) adj. quite large. —ˈsizably or ˈsizeably adv.

size¹ (saɪz) n. 1. the dimensions, amount, or extent of something. 2. large dimensions, etc. 3. one of a series of graduated measurements, as of clothing: she takes size 4 shoes. 4. Inf. state of affairs as summarized: he's bankrupt, that's the size of it. ~vb. 5. to sort according to size. 6. (tr.) to cut to a particular size or sizes. —ˈsizer n.

size² (saɪz) n. 1. Also called: sizing. a thin gelatinous mixture, made from glue, clay, or wax, that is used as a sealer on paper or plaster surfaces. ~vb. 2. (tr.) to treat or coat (a surface) with size.

sized (saɪzd) adj. of a specified size: medium-sized.

size up vb. (adv.) 1. (tr.) Inf. to make an assessment of (a person, problem, etc.). 2. to conform to or make so as to conform to certain specifications of dimension.

sizzle (ˈsɪzəl) vb. (intr.) 1. to make the hissing sound characteristic of frying fat. 2. Inf. to be very hot. 3. Inf. to be very angry. ~n. 4. a hissing sound. —ˈsizzler n.

SJA abbrev. for Saint John's Ambulance (Brigade or Association).

THESAURUS

sit 1. be seated, perch, rest, settle, take a seat, take the weight off one's feet 2. assemble, be in session, convene, deliberate, meet, officiate, preside 3. accommodate, contain, have space for, hold, seat

site 1. n. ground, location, place, plot, position, spot 2. v. install, locate, place, position, set, situate

sitting n. consultation, get-together (Inf.), hearing, meeting, period, session

situation 1. locale, locality, location, place, position, seat, setting, site, spot 2. ball game (Inf.), case, circumstances, condition, kettle of fish (Inf.), plight, state, state of affairs, status quo, the picture (Inf.) 3. rank, sphere, station, status 4. berth (Inf.), employment, job, office, place, position, post

size amount, bigness, bulk, dimensions, extent, greatness, hugeness, immensity, largeness, magnitude, mass, measurement(s), proportions, range, vastness, volume

size up appraise, assess, evaluate, get (something) taped (Brit. inf.), get the measure of, take stock of

sizzle crackle, frizzle, fry, hiss, spit, sputter

skate¹ (skeɪt) *n.* **1.** See **roller skate, ice skate. 2.** the steel blade or runner of an ice skate. **3.** such a blade fitted with straps for fastening to a shoe. **4. get one's skates on.** to hurry. ~*vb.* (*intr.*) **5.** to glide swiftly on skates. **6.** to slide smoothly over a surface. **7. skate on thin ice.** to place oneself in a dangerous situation. —'**skater** *n.*

skate² (skeɪt) *n., pl.* **skate** *or* **skates.** any of a family of large rays of temperate and tropical seas, having two dorsal fins, a short spineless tail, and a long snout.

skateboard ('skeɪt,bɔːd) *n.* **1.** a plank mounted on roller-skate wheels, usually ridden while standing up. ~*vb.* **2.** (*intr.*) to ride on a skateboard. —'**skate,boarder** *n.*

skate over *vb.* (*intr., prep.*) **1.** to cross on or as if on skates. **2.** to avoid dealing with (a matter) fully.

skedaddle (skɪ'dædəl) *Inf.* ~*vb.* **1.** (*intr.*) to run off hastily. ~*n.* **2.** a hasty retreat.

skein (skeɪn) *n.* **1.** a length of yarn, etc., wound in a long coil. **2.** something resembling this, such as a lock of hair. **3.** a flock of geese flying.

skeleton ('skɛlɪtən) *n.* **1.** a hard framework consisting of inorganic material that supports and protects the soft parts of an animal's body: may be internal, as in vertebrates, or external, as in arthropods. **2.** *Inf.* a very thin emaciated person or animal. **3.** the essential framework of any structure, such as a building or leaf. **4.** an outline consisting of bare essentials: *the skeleton of a novel.* **5.** (*modifier*) reduced to a minimum: *a skeleton staff.* **6. skeleton in the cupboard** *or* (*U.S.*) **closet.** a scandalous fact or event in the past that is kept secret. —'**skeletal** *adj.* —'**skeleton-,like** *adj.*

skeleton key *n.* a key with the serrated edge filed down so that it can open numerous locks. Also called: **passkey.**

skeptic ('skɛptɪk) *n., adj.* the usual U.S. spelling of **sceptic.**

sketch (skɛtʃ) *n.* **1.** a rapid drawing or painting. **2.** a brief usually descriptive essay or other literary composition. **3.** a short play, often comic, forming part of a revue. **4.** a short evocative piece of instrumental music. **5.** any brief outline. ~*vb.* **6.** to make (a rough drawing, etc.) (of). **7.** (*tr.; often foll. by out*) to make a brief description of. —'**sketcher** *n.*

sketchbook ('skɛtʃ,bʊk) *n.* **1.** a book of plain paper containing sketches or for making sketches in. **2.** a book of literary sketches.

sketchy ('skɛtʃɪ) *adj.* **sketchier, sketchiest. 1.** existing only in outline. **2.** superficial or slight. —'**sketchily** *adv.* —'**sketchiness** *n.*

skew (skju:) *adj.* **1.** placed in or turning into an oblique position or course. **2.** *Machinery.* having a component that is at an angle to the main axis of an assembly: *a skew bevel gear.* **3.** *Maths.* composed of or being elements that are neither parallel nor intersecting. **4.** (of a statistical distribution) not having equal probabilities above and below the mean. **5.** distorted or biased. ~*n.* **6.** an oblique, slanting, or indirect course or position. ~*vb.* **7.** to take or cause to take an oblique course or direction. **8.** (*intr.*) to look sideways. **9.** (*tr.*) to distort. —'**skewness** *n.*

skewbald ('skju:,bɔːld) *adj.* **1.** marked or spotted in white and any colour except black. ~*n.* **2.** a horse with this marking.

skewer ('skju:ə) *n.* **1.** a long pin for holding meat in position while being cooked, etc. **2.** a similar pin having some other function. ~*vb.* **3.** (*tr.*) to drive a skewer through or fasten with a skewer.

skewwhiff ('skju:'wɪf) *adj.* (*postpositive*) *Brit. inf.* not straight.

ski (ski:) *n., pl.* **skis** *or* **ski. 1. a.** one of a pair of wood,

metal, or plastic runners that are used for gliding over snow. **b.** (*as modifier*): *a ski boot.* **2.** a water-ski. ~*vb.* **skiing; skied** *or* **ski'd. 3.** (*intr.*) to travel on skis. —'**skier** *n.*

skibob ('ski:bɒb) *n.* a vehicle made of two short skis, the forward one having a steering handle and the rear one supporting a low seat, for gliding down snow slopes. —'**skibobber** *n.*

skid (skɪd) *vb.* **skidding, skidded. 1.** to cause (a vehicle) to slide sideways or (of a vehicle) to slide sideways while in motion, esp. out of control. **2.** (*intr.*) to slide without revolving, as the wheel of a moving vehicle after sudden braking. ~*n.* **3.** an instance of sliding, esp. sideways. **4.** a support on which heavy objects may be stored and moved short distances by sliding. **5.** a shoe or drag used to apply pressure to the metal rim of a wheel to act as a brake.

skidoo ('skɪdu:) *Canad.* ~*n.* **1.** a snowmobile. ~*vb.* (*intr.*) **2.** to travel using a snowmobile.

skid row (rəʊ) *or* **skid road** *n. Sl., chiefly U.S.* a dilapidated section of a city inhabited by vagrants, etc.

skiff (skɪf) *n.* any of various small boats propelled by oars, sail, or motor.

ski jump *n.* **1.** a high ramp overhanging a slope from which skiers compete to make the longest jump. ~*vb.* **ski-jump. 2.** (*intr.*) to perform a ski jump. —**ski jumper** *n.*

skilful *or U.S.* **skillful** ('skɪlfʊl) *adj.* **1.** possessing or displaying accomplishment or skill. **2.** involving or requiring accomplishment or skill. —'**skilfully** *or U.S.* '**skillfully** *adv.*

ski lift *n.* a device for carrying skiers up a slope, usually consisting of seats suspended from a moving cable.

skill (skɪl) *n.* **1.** special ability in a sport, etc., esp. ability acquired by training. **2.** something, esp. a trade or technique, requiring special training or manual proficiency. —'**skill-less** *or* '**skilless** *adj.* —**skilled** *adj.*

skillet ('skɪlɪt) *n.* **1.** a small frying pan. **2.** *Chiefly Brit.* a saucepan.

skim (skɪm) *vb.* **skimming, skimmed. 1.** (*tr.*) to remove floating material from the surface of (a liquid), as with a spoon: *to skim milk.* **2.** to glide smoothly or lightly over (a surface). **3.** (*tr.*) to throw (something) in a path over a surface, so as to bounce or ricochet: *to skim stones over water.* **4.** (when *intr.*, usually foll. by *through*) to read (a book) in a superficial manner. ~*n.* **5.** the act or process of skimming. **6.** material skimmed off a liquid, esp. off milk. **7.** any thin layer covering a surface.

skim milk *n.* milk from which the cream has been removed. Also called: **skimmed milk.**

skimp (skɪmp) *vb.* **1.** to be extremely sparing or supply (someone) sparingly. **2.** to perform (work, etc.) carelessly or with inadequate materials.

skimpy ('skɪmpɪ) *adj.* **skimpier, skimpiest. 1.** made of too little material. **2.** excessively thrifty; mean. —'**skimpily** *adv.* —'**skimpiness** *n.*

skin (skɪn) *n.* **1. a.** the tissue forming the outer covering of the vertebrate body: it consists of two layers, the outermost of which may be covered with hair, scales, feathers, etc. **b.** (*as modifier*): *a skin disease.* **2.** any similar covering in a plant or lower animal. **3.** any coating or film, such as one that forms on the surface of a liquid. **4.** the outer covering of a fur-bearing animal, dressed and finished with the hair on. **5.** a container made from animal skin. **6.** the outer covering surface of a vessel, rocket, etc. **7.** a person's skin regarded as his life: *to save one's skin.* **8.** (*often pl.*) *Inf.* (in jazz or pop use) a drum. **9. by the skin of one's teeth.** only just. **10. get under one's skin.** *Inf.* to irritate. **11. no skin off one's nose.** *Inf.* not a matter that affects one adversely. **12. skin and bone.** extremely thin. **13. thick** (*or* **thin**) **skin.** an insensitive (*or* sensitive) nature. ~*vb.* **skin-**

THESAURUS

skeleton *Fig.* bare bones, bones, draft, frame, framework, outline, sketch, structure

sketch 1. *v.* block out, delineate, depict, draft, draw, outline, paint, plot, portray, represent, rough out **2.** *n.* delineation, design, draft, drawing, outline, plan, skeleton

sketchy bitty, cobbled together, crude, cursory, inadequate, incomplete, outline, perfunctory, rough, scrappy, skimpy, slight, superficial, unfinished, vague

skilful able, accomplished, adept, adroit,

apt, clever, competent, dexterous, experienced, expert, handy, masterly, practised, professional, proficient, quick, ready, skilled, trained

skill ability, accomplishment, adroitness, aptitude, art, cleverness, competence, dexterity, experience, expertise, expertness, facility, finesse, handiness, ingenuity, intelligence, knack, proficiency, quickness, readiness, skilfulness, talent, technique

skilled able, accomplished, a dab hand at

(*Brit. inf.*), experienced, expert, masterly, practised, professional, proficient, skilful, trained

skim 1. cream, separate **2.** brush, coast, dart, float, fly, glide, sail, soar **3.** *Usually with* **through** glance, run one's eye over, scan, skip (*Inf.*), thumb *or* leaf through

skimp be mean with, be niggardly, be sparing with, pinch, scamp, scant, scrimp, stint, withhold

ning, skinned. 14. (*tr.*) to remove (the outer covering) from (fruit, etc.). **15.** (*tr.*) to scrape a small piece of skin from (a part of oneself) in falling, etc.: *he skinned his knee.* **16.** (often foll. by *over*) to cover (something) with skin or a skinlike substance or (of something) to become covered in this way. **17.** (*tr.*) *Sl.* to swindle. —'**skinless** *adj.* —'**skin,like** *adj.*

skin-deep *adj.* **1.** superficial; shallow. ~*adv.* **2.** superficially.

skin diving *n.* the sport or activity of underwater swimming using breathing apparatus. —'**skin-,diver** *n.*

skin flick *n.* a film containing much nudity and explicit sex for sensational purposes.

skinflint ('skɪn,flɪnt) *n.* an ungenerous or niggardly person.

skin graft *n.* a piece of skin removed from one part of the body and surgically grafted at the site of a severe burn or similar injury.

skinhead ('skɪn,hɛd) *n. Brit.* one of a gang of boys characterized by closely cropped hair and distinctive clothes.

skinned (skɪnd) *adj.* **1.** stripped of the skin. **2. a.** having a skin as specified. **b.** (*in combination*): *thick-skinned.* **3. keep one's eyes skinned** (*or* **peeled**). to watch carefully.

skinny ('skɪnɪ) *adj.* **-nier, -niest. 1.** lacking in flesh; thin. **2.** consisting of or resembling skin.

skint (skɪnt) *adj.* (*usually postpositive*) *Brit. sl.* without money.

skintight ('skɪn'taɪt) *adj.* (of garments) fitting tightly over the body; clinging.

skip[1] (skɪp) *vb.* **skipping, skipped. 1.** (when *intr.*, often foll. by *over, along, into*, etc.) to spring or move lightly, esp. to move by hopping from one foot to the other. **2.** (*intr.*) to jump over a skipping-rope. **3.** to cause (a stone, etc.) to skim over a surface or (of a stone) to move in this way. **4.** to omit (intervening matter): *he skipped a chapter of the book.* **5.** (*intr.*; foll. by *through*) *Inf.* to read or deal with quickly or superficially. **6. skip it!** *Inf.* it doesn't matter! **7.** (*tr.*) *Inf.* to miss deliberately: *to skip school.* **8.** (*tr.*) *Inf., chiefly U.S.* to leave (a place) in haste: *to skip town.* ~*n.* **9.** a skipping movement or gait. **10.** the act of passing over or omitting.

skip[2] (skɪp) *n.* **1.** a large open container for transporting building materials, etc. **2.** a cage used as a lift in mines, etc.

ski pants *pl. n.* stretch trousers worn for skiing, kept taut by a strap under the foot.

skipper ('skɪpə) *n.* **1.** the captain of any vessel. **2.** the captain of an aircraft. **3.** a leader, as of a sporting team. ~*vb.* **4.** to act as skipper (of).

skipping-rope *n. Brit.* a cord, usually having handles at each end, that is held in the hands and swung round and down so that the holder or others can jump over it.

skirl (skɜːl) *vb.* **1.** *Northern Brit. dialect.* (esp. of a bagpipe) to emit a shrill sound. ~*n.* **2.** the sound of a bagpipe.

skirmish ('skɜːmɪʃ) *n.* **1.** a minor short-lived military engagement. **2.** any brisk clash or encounter. ~*vb.* **3.** (*intr.*; often foll. by *with*) to engage in a skirmish. —'**skirmisher** *n.*

skirt (skɜːt) *n.* **1.** a garment hanging from the waist, worn chiefly by women and girls. **2.** the part of a dress below the waist. **3.** Also called: **apron.** a circular flap, so that around the base of a hovercraft. **4.** the flaps on a saddle. **5.** *Brit.* a cut of beef from the flank. **6.** (*often pl.*) an outlying area. **7. bit of skirt.** *Sl.* a girl or woman. ~*vb.* **8.**

(*tr.*) to form the edge of. **9.** (*tr.*) to provide with a border. **10.** (when *intr.*, foll. by *around, along*, etc.) to pass (by) or be situated (near) the outer edge of (an area, etc.). **11.** (*tr.*) to avoid (a difficulty, etc.): *he skirted the issue.* **12.** *Chiefly Austral.* to trim the ragged edges from (a fleece). —'**skirted** *adj.*

skirting board *n.* a skirting made of wood.

ski stick *or* **pole** *n.* a stick, usually with a metal point, used by skiers to gain momentum and maintain balance.

skit (skɪt) *n.* **1.** a brief satirical theatrical sketch. **2.** a short satirical piece of writing.

ski tow *n.* a device for pulling skiers uphill, usually a motor-driven rope grasped by the skier while riding on his skis.

skittish ('skɪtɪʃ) *adj.* **1.** playful, lively, or frivolous. **2.** difficult to handle or predict. —'**skittishly** *adv.* —'**skittishness** *n.*

skittle ('skɪtəl) *n.* **1.** a wooden or plastic pin, typically widest just above the base. **2.** (*pl., functioning as sing.*) Also called (esp. U.S.): **ninepins.** a bowling game in which players knock over as many skittles as possible by rolling a wooden ball at them. **3. beer and skittles.** *Sl.* amusement.

skive[1] (skaɪv) *vb.* (*tr.*) to shave or remove the surface of (leather). —'**skiver** *n.*

skive[2] (skaɪv) *vb.* (when *intr.*, often foll. by *off*) *Brit. sl.* to evade (work or responsibility). —'**skiver** *n.*

skivvy ('skɪvɪ) *n., pl.* **-vies. 1.** *Chiefly Brit., often contemptuous.* a servant, esp. a female; drudge. **2.** *Austral.* a close-fitting lightweight sweater with long sleeves and a round neck. ~*vb.* **-vying, -vied. 3.** (*intr.*) *Brit.* to work as a skivvy.

skua ('skjuːə) *n.* a predatory aquatic gull-like bird having a dark plumage and long tail.

skulduggery *or U.S.* **skullduggery** (skʌl'dʌgərɪ) *n. Inf.* underhand dealing; trickery.

skulk (skʌlk) *vb.* (*intr.*) **1.** to move stealthily so as to avoid notice. **2.** to lie in hiding; lurk. **3.** to shirk duty or evade responsibilities. ~*n.* **4.** a person who skulks. **5.** *Obs.* a pack of foxes. —'**skulker** *n.*

skull (skʌl) *n.* **1.** the bony skeleton of the head of vertebrates. **2.** *Often derog.* the head regarded as the mind or intelligence: *to have a dense skull.* **3.** a picture of a skull used to represent death or danger.

skull and crossbones *n.* a picture of the human skull above two crossed thigh bones, formerly on the pirate flag, now used as a warning of danger or death.

skullcap ('skʌl,kæp) *n.* **1.** a rounded brimless hat fitting the crown of the head. **2.** the top part of the skull. **3.** any of a genus of perennial plants, that have helmet-shaped flowers.

skunk (skʌŋk) *n., pl.* **skunk** *or* **skunks. 1.** any of various American mammals having a black-and-white coat and bushy tail: they eject an unpleasant-smelling fluid from the anal gland when attacked. **2.** *Inf.* a despicable person.

sky (skaɪ) *n., pl.* **skies. 1.** (*sometimes pl.*) the apparently dome-shaped expanse extending upwards from the horizon that is blue or grey during the day and black at night. **2.** outer space, as seen from the earth. **3.** (*often pl.*) weather, as described by the appearance of the upper air: *sunny skies.* **4.** heaven. **5.** *Inf.* the highest level of attainment: *the sky's the limit.* **6. to the skies.** extravagantly. ~*vb.* **skying, skied. 7.** *Rowing.* to lift (the blade of an oar) too high before a stroke. **8.** (*tr.*) *Inf.* to hit (a ball) high in the air.

THESAURUS

skin *n.* **1.** fell, hide, integument, pelt, tegument **2.** casing, coating, crust, film, husk, membrane, outside, peel, rind **3. by the skin of one's teeth** by a hair's-breadth, by a narrow margin, by a whisker (*Inf.*), narrowly, only just **4. get under one's skin** annoy, grate on, irk, irritate, needle (*Inf.*), nettle, rub up the wrong way ~*v.* **5.** abrade, bark, excoriate, flay, graze, peel, scrape

skinflint miser, niggard, penny-pincher (*Inf.*), Scrooge, tightwad (*U.S. sl.*)

skinny emaciated, lean, scraggy, skeletal, skin-and-bone (*Inf.*), thin, twiggy, undernourished

skip *v.* **1.** bob, bounce, caper, cavort, dance, flit, frisk, gambol, hop, prance, trip **2.** es-

chew, give (something) a miss, leave out, miss out, omit, pass over, skim over **3.** *Inf.* cut (*Inf.*), dog it *or* dog off (*Dialect*), miss, play truant from, twag (*Dialect*)

skirmish 1. *n.* affair, affray (*Law*), battle, brush, clash, combat, conflict, contest, dust-up (*Inf.*), encounter, engagement, fracas, incident, scrap (*Inf.*), scrimmage, set-to (*Inf.*), spat, tussle **2.** *v.* clash, collide, come to blows, scrap (*Inf.*), tussle

skirt *v.* **1.** border, edge, flank, lie alongside **2.** *Often with* **around** *or* **round** avoid, bypass, circumvent, detour, evade, steer clear of ~*n.* **3.** *Often plural* border, edge, fringe, hem, margin, outskirts, periphery, purlieus, rim

skit burlesque, parody, sketch, spoof (*Inf.*), takeoff (*Inf.*), travesty, turn

skittish excitable, fickle, fidgety, frivolous, highly strung, jumpy, lively, nervous, playful, restive

skulk creep, lie in wait, loiter, lurk, pad, prowl, slink, sneak

sky *n.* **1.** azure (*Poetic*), empyrean (*Poetic*), firmament, heavens, upper atmosphere, vault of heaven, welkin (*Archaic*) **2. to the skies** excessively, extravagantly, fulsomely, highly, immoderately, inordinately, profusely

sky blue *n., adj.* (of) a light or pale blue colour.

skydiving ('skaɪˌdaɪvɪŋ) *n.* the sport of parachute jumping, in which participants perform manoeuvres before opening the parachute. —'**sky,dive** *vb.* —'**sky,diver** *n.*

Skye terrier (skaɪ) *n.* a short-legged breed of terrier with long wiry hair and erect ears.

sky-high *adj., adv.* 1. at or to an unprecedented level: *prices rocketed sky-high.* ~*adv.* 2. high into the air. 3. **blow sky-high.** to destroy.

skyjack ('skaɪˌdʒæk) *vb.* (*tr.*) to commandeer an aircraft, usually during flight, forcing the pilot to fly somewhere other than to its scheduled destination.

skylark ('skaɪˌlɑːk) *n.* 1. an Old World lark, noted for singing while hovering at a great height. ~*vb.* 2. (*intr.*) *Inf.* to romp or play jokes.

skylight ('skaɪˌlaɪt) *n.* a window placed in a roof or ceiling to admit daylight. Also called: **fanlight.**

skyline ('skaɪˌlaɪn) *n.* 1. the line at which the earth and sky appear to meet. 2. the outline of buildings, trees, etc., seen against the sky.

skyrocket ('skaɪˌrɒkɪt) *n.* 1. another word for **rocket** (sense 1). ~*vb.* 2. (*intr.*) *Inf.* to rise rapidly, as in price.

skyscraper ('skaɪˌskreɪpə) *n.* a very tall multistorey building.

skyward ('skaɪwəd) *adj.* 1. directed or moving towards the sky. ~*adv.* 2. Also: **skywards.** towards the sky.

slab (slæb) *n.* 1. a broad flat thick piece of wood, stone, or other material. 2. a thick slice of cake, etc. 3. any of the outside parts of a log that are sawn off while the log is being made into planks. 4. *Austral. & N.Z.* **a.** a rough-hewn wooden plank. **b.** (*as modifier*): *a slab hut.* 5. *Inf., chiefly Brit.* an operating or mortuary table. ~*vb.* **slab-bing, slabbed.** (*tr.*) 6. to cut or make into a slab or slabs. 7. to saw slabs from (a log).

slack¹ (slæk) *adj.* 1. not tight, tense, or taut. 2. negligent or careless. 3. (esp. of water, etc.) moving slowly. 4. (of trade, etc.) not busy. 5. *Phonetics.* another term for **lax** (sense 4). ~*adv.* 6. in a slack manner. ~*n.* 7. a part of a rope, etc., that is slack: *take in the slack.* 8. a period of decreased activity. ~*vb.* 9. to neglect (one's duty, etc.). 10. (often foll. by *off*) to loosen. —'**slackly** *adv.* —'**slackness** *n.*

slack² (slæk) *n.* small pieces of coal with a high ash content.

slacken ('slækən) *vb.* (often foll. by *off*) 1. to make or become looser. 2. to make or become slower, less intense, etc.

slacker ('slækə) *n.* a person who evades work or duty; shirker.

slacks (slæks) *pl. n.* informal trousers worn by both sexes.

slack water *n.* the period of still water around the turn of the tide, esp. at low tide.

slag (slæg) *n.* 1. Also called: **cinder.** the fused material formed during the smelting or refining of metals. It usually consists of a mixture of silicates with calcium, phosphorus, sulphur, etc. 2. the mass of rough fragments of rock derived from volcanic lava. 3. a mixture of shale, clay, coal dust, etc., produced during coal-mining. ~*vb.* **slagging, slagged.** 4. to convert into or become slag.

—'**slaggy** *adj.*

slag heap *n.* a hillock of waste matter from coal-mining, etc.

slain (sleɪn) *vb.* the past participle of **slay.**

slake (sleɪk) *vb.* 1. (*tr.*) *Literary.* to satisfy (thirst, desire, etc.). 2. (*tr.*) *Poetic.* to cool or refresh. 3. to undergo or cause to undergo the process in which lime reacts with water to produce calcium hydroxide. 4. (*tr.*) to mix flour, arrowroot, etc., to a thin paste using water. —'**slakable** *or* '**slakeable** *adj.*

slaked lime *n.* another name for **calcium hydroxide.**

slalom ('slɑːləm) *n. Skiing, etc.* a race, esp. one downhill, over a winding course marked by artificial obstacles.

slam¹ (slæm) *vb.* **slamming, slammed.** 1. to cause (a door or window) to close noisily or (of a door, etc.) to close in this way. 2. (*tr.*) to throw (something) down violently. 3. (*tr.*) *Sl.* to criticize harshly. 4. (*intr.*; usually foll. by *into* or *out of*) *Inf.* to go (into or out of a room, etc.) in violent haste or anger. 5. (*tr.*) to strike with violent force. 6. (*tr.*) *Inf.* to defeat easily. ~*n.* 7. the act or noise of slamming.

slam² (slæm) *n.* **a.** the winning of all (**grand slam**) or all but one (**little** *or* **small slam**) of the 13 tricks at bridge or whist. **b.** the bid to do so in bridge.

slander ('slɑːndə) *n.* 1. *Law.* **a.** a defamation in some transient form, as by spoken words, gestures, etc. **b.** a slanderous statement, etc. 2. any defamatory words spoken about a person. ~*vb.* 3. to utter or circulate slander (about). —'**slanderer** *n.* —'**slanderous** *adj.*

slang (slæŋ) *n.* 1. **a.** vocabulary, idiom, etc., that is not appropriate to the standard form of a language or to formal contexts and may be restricted as to social status or distribution. **b.** (*as modifier*): *a slang word.* ~*vb.* 2. to abuse (someone) with vituperative language. —'**slangy** *adj.* —'**slangily** *adv.* —'**slanginess** *n.*

slant (slɑːnt) *vb.* 1. to incline or be inclined at an oblique or sloping angle. 2. to write or present (news, etc.) with a bias. 3. (*intr.*) foll. by *towards*) (of a person's opinions) to be biased. ~*n.* 4. an inclined or oblique line or direction. 5. a way of looking at something. 6. a bias or opinion, as in an article. 7. **on a** (*or* **the**) **slant.** sloping. ~*adj.* 8. oblique, sloping. —'**slanting** *adj.*

slap (slæp) *n.* 1. a sharp blow or smack, as with the open hand, something flat, etc. 2. the sound made by or as if by such a blow. 3. (**a bit of**) **slap and tickle.** *Brit. inf.* sexual play. 4. **a slap in the face.** an insult or rebuff. 5. **a slap on the back.** congratulation. ~*vb.* **slapping, slapped.** 6. (*tr.*) to strike (a person or thing) sharply, as with the open hand or something flat. 7. (*tr.*) to bring down (the hand, etc.) sharply. 8. (when *intr.*, usually foll. by *against*) to strike (something) with or as if with a slap. 9. (*tr.*) *Inf., chiefly Brit.* to apply in large quantities, haphazardly, etc.: *she slapped butter on the bread.* 10. **slap on the back.** to congratulate. ~*adv. Inf.* 11. exactly: *slap on time.* 12. forcibly or abruptly: *to fall slap on the floor.*

slapdash ('slæpˌdæʃ) *adv., adj.* 1. in a careless, hasty, or haphazard manner. ~*n.* 2. slapdash activity or work.

slaphappy ('slæpˌhæpɪ) *adj.* **-pier, -piest.** *Inf.* 1.

THESAURUS

slab chunk, hunk, lump, piece, portion, slice, wedge, wodge (*Brit. inf.*)

slack *adj.* 1. baggy, easy, flaccid, flexible, lax, limp, loose, not taut, relaxed 2. asleep on the job (*Inf.*), easy-going, idle, inactive, inattentive, lax, lazy, neglectful, negligent, permissive, remiss, tardy 3. dull, inactive, quiet, slow, slow-moving, sluggish ~*n.* 4. excess, give (*Inf.*), leeway, looseness, play, room ~*v.* 5. dodge, flag, idle, neglect, relax, shirk, skive (*Brit. sl.*), slacken

slacken (**off**) abate, decrease, diminish, drop off, ease (off), lessen, let up, loosen, moderate, reduce, relax, release, slack off, slow down, tire

slacker dodger, do-nothing, gold brick (*U.S. sl.*), good-for-nothing, idler, loafer, passenger, scrimshanker (*Brit. military sl.*), shirker, skiver (*Brit. sl.*)

slam 1. bang, crash, dash, fling, hurl, smash, throw, thump 2. *Sl.* attack, castigate, criticize, damn, excoriate, lambaste, pan

(*Inf.*), pillory, shoot down (*Inf.*), slate (*Inf.*), vilify

slander 1. *n.* aspersion, backbiting, calumny, defamation, detraction, libel, misrepresentation, muckraking, obloquy, scandal, smear 2. *v.* backbite, blacken (someone's) name, calumniate, decry, defame, detract, disparage, libel, malign, muckrake, slur, smear, traduce, vilify

slanderous abusive, calumnious, damaging, defamatory, libellous, malicious

slang *v.* abuse, berate, call names, hurl insults at, insult, inveigh against, malign, rail against, revile, vilify, vituperate

slant *v.* 1. angle off, bend, bevel, cant, incline, lean, list, shelve, skew, slope, tilt ~*n.* 2. camber, declination, diagonal, gradient, incline, pitch, rake, ramp, slope, tilt ~*v.* 3. angle, bias, colour, distort, twist, weight ~*n.* 4. angle, attitude, bias, emphasis, leaning, one-sidedness, point of view, prejudice, viewpoint

slanting angled, aslant, asymmetrical, at

an angle, bent, canted, cater-cornered (*U.S. inf.*), diagonal, inclined, oblique, on the bias, sideways, slanted, slantwise, sloping, tilted, tilting

slap *n.* 1. bang, blow, clout (*Inf.*), cuff, smack, spank, wallop (*Inf.*), whack 2. **a slap in the face** blow, humiliation, insult, put-down, rebuff, rebuke, rejection, repulse, snub ~*v.* 3. bang, clap, clout (*Inf.*), cuff, hit, spank, strike, whack 4. *Inf.* daub, plaster, plonk, spread ~*adv.* 5. *Inf.* bang, directly, exactly, plumb (*Inf.*), precisely, slap-bang (*Inf.*), smack (*Inf.*)

slapdash careless, clumsy, disorderly, haphazard, hasty, hurried, last-minute, messy, negligent, perfunctory, slipshod, sloppy (*Inf.*), slovenly, thoughtless, thrown-together, untidy

slap down bring to heel, put (someone) in his place, rebuke, reprimand, restrain, squash

cheerfully irresponsible or careless. **2.** dazed or giddy from or as if from repeated blows.

slapstick ('slæp₁stɪk) *n.* **1. a.** comedy characterized by horseplay and physical action. **b.** (*as modifier*): *slapstick humour.* **2.** a pair of paddles formerly used in pantomime to strike a blow with a loud sound but without injury.

slap-up *adj.* (*prenominal*) *Brit. inf.* (esp. of meals) lavish; excellent; first-class.

slash (slæʃ) *vb.* (*tr.*) **1.** to cut or lay about (a person or thing) with sharp sweeping strokes, as with a sword, etc. **2.** to lash with a whip. **3.** to make large gashes in: *to slash tyres.* **4.** to reduce (prices, etc.) drastically. **5.** to criticize harshly. **6.** to slit (the outer fabric of a garment) so that the lining material is revealed. ~*n.* **7.** a sharp, sweeping stroke, as with a sword or whip. **8.** a cut or rent made by such a stroke. **9.** a decorative slit in a garment revealing the lining material. **10.** *North American.* littered wood chips that remain after trees have been cut down. **11.** another name for **solidus** (sense 1). **12.** *Brit. sl.* the act of urinating. —'**slasher** *n.*

slat (slæt) *n.* **1.** a narrow thin strip of wood or metal, as used in a Venetian blind, etc. **2.** a movable or fixed aerofoil attached to the leading edge of an aircraft wing to increase lift.

slate¹ (sleɪt) *n.* **1. a.** a smooth fine-grained metamorphic rock that can be split into thin layers and is used as a roofing and paving material. **b.** (*as modifier*): *a slate tile.* **2.** a roofing tile of slate. **3.** (formerly) a writing tablet of slate. **4.** a dark grey colour. **5.** *U.S.* a list of candidates in an election. **6. clean slate.** a record without dishonour. **7. on the slate.** *Brit. inf.* on credit. ~*vb.* (*tr.*) **8.** to cover (a roof) with slates. **9.** *Chiefly U.S.* to enter (a person's name) on a list, esp. on a political slate. ~*adj.* **10.** of the colour slate. —'**slaty** *adj.*

slate² (sleɪt) *vb.* (*tr.*) *Inf., chiefly Brit.* to criticize harshly. —'**slating** *n.*

slattern ('slætən) *n.* a slovenly woman or girl. —'**slatternly** *adj.* —'**slatternliness** *n.*

slaughter ('slɔːtə) *n.* **1.** the killing of animals, esp. for food. **2.** the savage killing of a person. **3.** the indiscriminate or brutal killing of large numbers of people, as in war. ~*vb.* (*tr.*) **4.** to kill (animals), esp. for food. **5.** to kill in a brutal manner. **6.** to kill indiscriminately or in large numbers. —'**slaughterer** *n.* —'**slaughterous** *adj.*

slaughterhouse ('slɔːtə₁haʊs) *n.* a place where animals are butchered for food; abattoir.

Slav (slɑːv) *n.* a member of any of the peoples of E Europe or Soviet Asia who speak a Slavonic language.

slave (sleɪv) *n.* **1.** a person legally owned by another and having no freedom of action or right to property. **2.** a person who is forced to work for another against his will. **3.** a person under the domination of another person or some habit or influence. **4.** a drudge. **5.** a device that is controlled by or that duplicates the action of another similar device. ~*vb.* **6.** (*intr.*) to work like a slave.

slave-driver *n.* **1.** (esp. formerly) a person forcing slaves to work. **2.** an employer who demands excessively hard work from his employees.

slaver¹ ('sleɪvə) *n.* an owner of or dealer in slaves.

slaver² ('slævə) *vb.* (*intr.*) **1.** to dribble saliva. **2.** (often foll. by *over*) **a.** to fawn or drool (over someone). **b.** to show great desire (for). ~*n.* **3.** saliva dribbling from the mouth. **4.** *Inf.* drivel. —'**slaverer** *n.*

slavery ('sleɪvərɪ) *n.* **1.** the state or condition of being a slave. **2.** the subjection of a person to another person, esp. in being forced into work. **3.** the condition of being subject to some influence or habit. **4.** work done under harsh conditions for low pay.

slavish ('sleɪvɪʃ) *adj.* **1.** of or befitting a slave. **2.** being or resembling a slave. **3.** unoriginal; imitative. —'**slavishly** *adv.*

Slavonic (slə'vɒnɪk) *or* **Slavic** *n.* **1.** a branch of the Indo-European family of languages, usually divided into three subbranches: **South Slavonic** (including Old Church Slavonic, Bulgarian, etc.), **East Slavonic** (including Russian, etc.), and **West Slavonic** (including Polish, Czech, etc.). ~*adj.* **2.** of or relating to this group of languages. **3.** of or relating to the people who speak these languages. —**Sla'vonically** *adv.*

slay (sleɪ) *vb.* **slaying, slew, slain.** (*tr.*) **1.** *Arch. or literary.* to kill, esp. violently. **2.** *Inf.* to impress (someone of the opposite sex). —'**slayer** *n.*

sleazy ('sliːzɪ) *adj.* **-zier, -ziest.** **1.** disreputable: *a sleazy nightclub.* **2.** flimsy, as cloth. —'**sleazily** *adv.* —'**sleaziness** *n.*

sledge¹ (slɛdʒ) *or* (*esp. U.S.*) **sled** (slɛd) *n.* **1.** a vehicle mounted on runners, drawn by horses or dogs, for transporting people or goods, esp. over snow. **2.** a light wooden frame used, esp. by children, for sliding over snow. ~*vb.* **3.** to convey or travel by sledge.

sledge² (slɛdʒ) *n.* short for **sledgehammer.**

sledgehammer ('slɛdʒ₁hæmə) *n.* **1.** a large heavy hammer with a long handle used with both hands for heavy work such as breaking rocks, etc. **2.** (*modifier*) resembling the action of a sledgehammer in power, etc.: *a sledgehammer blow.*

sleek (sliːk) *adj.* **1.** smooth and shiny. **2.** polished in speech or behaviour. **3.** (of an animal or bird) having a shiny healthy coat or feathers. **4.** (of a person) having a prosperous appearance. ~*vb.* (*tr.*) **5.** to make smooth and glossy, as by grooming, etc. **6.** (usually foll. by *over*) to gloss (over). —'**sleekly** *adv.* —'**sleekness** *n.* —'**sleeky** *adj.*

sleep (sliːp) *n.* **1.** a periodic state of physiological rest during which consciousness is suspended. **2.** *Bot.* the nontechnical name for **nyctitropism. 3.** a period spent sleeping. **4.** a state of quiescence or dormancy. **5.** a poetic word for **death.** ~*vb.* **sleeping, slept. 6.** (*intr.*) to be in or as in the state of sleep. **7.** (*intr.*) (of plants) to show nyctitropism. **8.** (*intr.*) to be inactive or quiescent. **9.** (*tr.*) to have sleeping accommodation for (a certain number): *the boat could sleep six.* **10.** (*tr.*; foll. by *away*) to pass (time) sleeping. **11.** (*intr.*) *Poetic.* to be dead. **12. sleep on it.** to give (something) extended consideration, esp. overnight. ~See also **sleep around, sleep in, sleep off,** etc.

sleep around *vb.* (*intr., adv.*) *Inf.* to be sexually promiscuous.

sleeper ('sliːpə) *n.* **1.** a person, animal, or thing that sleeps. **2.** a railway sleeping car or compartment. **3.** *Brit.* one of the blocks supporting the rails on a railway track. **4.** a heavy timber beam, esp. one that is laid horizontally on the ground. **5.** *Chiefly Brit.* a small plain gold circle worn in a pierced ear lobe to prevent the hole from closing up. **6.** *Inf., chiefly U.S.* a person or thing that achieves unexpected success. **7.** a spy planted in advance for future use.

sleep in *vb.* (*intr., adv.*) **1.** *Brit.* to sleep longer than

---

◼◼◼ THESAURUS ◼◼◼

slapstick *n.* buffoonery, farce, horseplay, knockabout comedy

slash *v.* **1.** cut, gash, hack, lacerate, rend, rip, score, slit ~*n.* **2.** cut, gash, incision, laceration, rent, rip, slit ~*v.* **3.** cut, drop, lower, reduce

slashing aggressive, biting, brutal, harsh, savage, searing, vicious

slate *v.* berate, blame, castigate, censure, criticize, haul over the coals (*Inf.*), lambaste, lay into (*Inf.*), pan (*Inf.*), pitch into, rail against, rap (someone's) knuckles (*Inf.*), rebuke, roast (*Inf.*), scold, slam (*Sl.*), slang, take to task, tear (someone) off a strip (*Inf.*)

slaughter *n.* **1.** blood bath, bloodshed, butchery, carnage, extermination, killing, liquidation, massacre, murder, slaying ~*v.* **2.** butcher, destroy, do to death, exterminate,

kill, liquidate, massacre, murder, put to the sword, slay **3.** *Inf.* crush, defeat, hammer (*Inf.*), overwhelm, rout, thrash, trounce, vanquish, wipe the floor with (*Inf.*)

slaughterhouse abattoir, butchery, shambles

slave 1. *n.* bondservant, bondsman, drudge, scullion (*Archaic*), serf, servant, skivvy, slavey (*Brit. inf.*), vassal, villein **2.** *v.* drudge, grind (*Inf.*), skivvy (*Brit.*), slog, toil, work one's fingers to the bone

slavery bondage, captivity, enslavement, serfdom, servitude, subjugation, thraldom, thrall, vassalage

slavish 1. abject, base, cringing, despicable, fawning, grovelling, low, mean, menial, obsequious, servile, submissive, sycophantic **2.** conventional, imitative, second-hand, un-

imaginative, uninspired, unoriginal

slay 1. annihilate, assassinate, butcher, destroy, dispatch, do away with, eliminate, exterminate, kill, massacre, mow down, murder, rub out (*U.S. sl.*), slaughter **2.** *Inf.* amuse, be the death of (*Inf.*), impress, make a hit with (*Inf.*), wow (*Sl., chiefly U.S.*)

sleek glossy, lustrous, shiny, smooth, well-fed, well-groomed

sleep 1. *v.* be in the land of Nod, catnap, doze, drop off (*Inf.*), drowse, hibernate, nod off (*Inf.*), rest in the arms of Morpheus, slumber, snooze (*Inf.*), snore, take a nap, take forty winks (*Inf.*) **2.** *n.* beauty sleep (*Inf.*), dormancy, doze, forty winks (*Inf.*), hibernation, nap, repose, rest, shuteye (*Sl.*), siesta, slumber(s), snooze (*Inf.*)

usual. **2.** to sleep at the place of one's employment.

sleeping bag *n.* a large well-padded bag designed for sleeping in, esp. outdoors.

sleeping car *n.* a railway car fitted with compartments containing bunks for people to sleep in.

sleeping partner *n.* a partner in a business who does not play an active role. Also called: **silent partner.**

sleeping pill *n.* a pill or tablet containing a sedative drug, such as a barbiturate, used to induce sleep.

sleeping policeman *n.* a bump built across roads, esp. in housing estates, to deter motorists from speeding.

sleeping sickness *n.* **1.** Also called: **African sleeping sickness.** an African disease transmitted by the bite of tsetse fly, characterized by fever and sluggishness. **2.** an epidemic viral form of encephalitis characterized by extreme drowsiness. Technical name: **encephalitis lethargica.**

sleepless ('sli:plɪs) *adj.* **1.** without sleep or rest: *a sleepless journey.* **2.** unable to sleep. **3.** always alert. **4.** *Chiefly poetic.* always active or moving. —'**sleeplessly** *adv.* —'**sleeplessness** *n.*

sleep off *vb.* (*tr., adv.*) *Inf.* to lose by sleeping: *to sleep off a hangover.*

sleep out *vb.* (*intr., adv.*) **1.** (esp. of a tramp) to sleep in the open air. **2.** to sleep away from the place of work. ~*n.* **sleep-out. 3.** *Austral.* an area of a verandah partitioned off so that it may be used as a bedroom.

sleepwalk ('sli:p,wɔ:k) *vb.* (*intr.*) to walk while asleep. —'**sleep,walker** *n.* —'**sleep,walking** *n., adj.*

sleep with *vb.* (*intr., prep.*) to have sexual intercourse and (usually) spend the night with. Also: **sleep together.**

sleepy ('sli:pɪ) *adj.* **sleepier, sleepiest. 1.** inclined to or needing sleep. **2.** characterized by or exhibiting drowsiness, etc. **3.** conducive to sleep. **4.** without activity or bustle: *a sleepy town.* —'**sleepily** *adv.* —'**sleepiness** *n.*

sleet (sli:t) *n.* **1.** partly melted falling snow or hail or (esp. U.S.) partly frozen rain. **2.** *Chiefly U.S.* the thin coat of ice that forms when sleet or rain freezes on cold surfaces. ~*vb.* **3.** (*intr.*) to fall as sleet. —'**sleety** *adj.*

sleeve (sli:v) *n.* **1.** the part of a garment covering the arm. **2.** a tubular piece that is shrunk into a cylindrical bore to reduce its bore or to line it with a different material. **3.** a tube fitted externally over two cylindrical parts in order to join them. **4.** a wrapping for a gramophone record. **5.** (**have a few tricks**) **up one's sleeve.** (to have options, etc.) secretly ready. **6. roll up one's sleeves.** to prepare oneself for work, a fight, etc. ~*vb.* **7.** (*tr.*) to provide with a sleeve or sleeves. —'**sleeveless** *adj.* —'**sleeve,like** *adj.*

sleigh (sleɪ) *n.* **1.** another name for **sledge**[1] (sense 1). ~*vb.* **2.** (*intr.*) to travel by sleigh.

sleight (slaɪt) *n. Arch.* **1.** skill; dexterity. **2.** a trick or stratagem. **3.** cunning.

sleight of hand *n.* **1.** manual dexterity used in performing conjuring tricks. **2.** the performance of such tricks.

slender ('slɛndə) *adj.* **1.** of small width relative to length or height. **2.** (esp. of a person's figure) slim and well-formed. **3.** small or inadequate in amount, size, etc.: *slender resources.* **4.** (of hopes, etc.) feeble. **5.** very small: *a slender margin.* —'**slenderly** *adv.* —'**slenderness** *n.*

slept (slɛpt) *vb.* the past tense or past participle of **sleep.**

sleuth (slu:θ) *n.* **1.** an informal word for **detective.** ~*vb.* **2.** (*tr.*) to track or follow.

slew[1] (slu:) *vb.* the past tense of **slay.**

slew[2] *or* **slue** (slu:) *vb.* **1.** to twist or be twisted sideways, esp. awkwardly. **2.** *Naut.* to cause (a mast) to rotate in its step or (of a mast) to rotate in its step. ~*n.* **3.** the act of slewing.

slice (slaɪs) *n.* **1.** a thin flat piece cut from something having bulk: *a slice of pork.* **2.** a share or portion: *a slice of the company's revenue.* **3.** any of various utensils having a broad flat blade and resembling a spatula. **4.** (in golf, tennis, etc.) **a.** the flight of a ball that travels obliquely. **b.** the action of hitting such a shot. **c.** the shot so hit. ~*vb.* **5.** to divide or cut (something) into parts or slices. **6.** (when *intr.*, usually foll. by *through*) to cut in a clean and effortless manner. **7.** (when *intr.*, foll. by *into* or *through*) to move or go (through something) like a knife. **8.** (usually foll. by *off, from, away,* etc.) to cut or be cut (from) a larger piece. **9.** (*tr.*) to remove by use of a slicing implement. **10.** to hit (a ball) with a slice. —'**sliceable** *adj.* —'**slicer** *n.*

slick (slɪk) *adj.* **1.** flattering and glib: *a slick salesman.* **2.** adroitly devised or executed: *a slick show.* **3.** *Inf., chiefly U.S.* shrewd; sly. **4.** *Inf.* superficially attractive: *a slick publication.* **5.** *Chiefly U.S.* slippery. ~*n.* **6.** a slippery area, esp. a patch of oil floating on water. ~*vb.* (*tr.*) **7.** *Chiefly U.S.* to make smooth or sleek. —'**slickly** *adv.* —'**slickness** *n.*

slide (slaɪd) *vb.* **sliding, slid; slid** *or* **slidden. 1.** to move or cause to move smoothly along a surface in continual contact with it: *doors that slide open.* **2.** (*intr.*) to lose grip or balance: *he slid on his back.* **3.** (*intr.;* usually foll. by *into, out of, away from,* etc.) to pass or move unobtrusively: *she slid into the room.* **4.** (*intr.;* usually foll. by *into*) to go (into a specified condition) by degrees, etc.: *he slid into loose living.* **5.** (foll. by *in, into,* etc.) to move (an object) unobtrusively or (of an object) to move in this way: *he slid the gun into his pocket.* **6. let slide.** to allow to deteriorate: *to let things slide.* ~*n.* **7.** the act or an instance of sliding. **8.** a smooth surface, as of ice or mud, for sliding on. **9.** a construction incorporating an inclined smooth slope for sliding down in playgrounds, etc. **10.** a small glass plate on which specimens are mounted for microscopical study. **11.** Also called: **transparency.** a positive photograph on a transparent base, mounted in a frame, that can be viewed by means of a slide projector. **12.** Also called: **hair slide.** *Chiefly Brit.* an ornamental clip to hold hair in place. **13.** *Machinery.* a sliding part or member. **14.** *Music.* **a.** the sliding curved tube of a trombone that is moved in or out. **b.** a portamento. **15.** *Geol.* **a.** the downward movement of a large mass of earth, rocks, etc. **b.** the mass of material involved in this descent. See also **landslide.** —'**slidable** *adj.* —'**slider** *n.*

slide rule *n.* a mechanical calculating device consisting of two strips, one sliding along a central groove in the other, each strip graduated in two or more logarithmic scales of numbers, trigonometric functions, etc.

sliding scale *n.* a variable scale according to which specified wages, prices, etc., fluctuate in response to changes in some other factor.

slight (slaɪt) *adj.* **1.** small in quantity or extent. **2.** of small importance. **3.** slim and delicate. **4.** lacking in strength or substance. ~*vb.* (*tr.*) **5.** to show disregard for (someone); snub. **6.** to devote inadequate attention to (work, duties, etc.). **7.** to treat as unimportant or trifling. ~*n.* **8.** an act or omission indicating supercilious neglect. —'**slightingly** *adv.* —'**slightly** *adv.* —'**slightness** *n.*

THESAURUS

sleepiness doziness, drowsiness, heaviness, lethargy, somnolence, torpor

sleepless 1. disturbed, insomniac, restless, unsleeping, wakeful **2.** alert, unsleeping, vigilant, watchful, wide awake

sleeplessness insomnia, wakefulness

sleepwalker noctambulist, somnambulist

sleepwalking noctambulation, noctambulism, somnambulation, somnambulism

sleepy 1. drowsy, dull, heavy, inactive, lethargic, sluggish, slumbersome, somnolent, torpid **2.** dull, hypnotic, inactive, quiet, sleep-inducing, slow, slumberous, somnolent, soporific

slender 1. lean, narrow, slight, slim, svelte, sylphlike, willowy **2.** inadequate, inconsiderable, insufficient, little, meagre, scanty, small, spare **3.** faint, feeble, flimsy, fragile, poor, remote, slight, slim, tenuous, thin, weak

sleuth detective, dick (*U.S. sl.*), gumshoe (*U.S. sl.*), private eye (*Inf.*), (private) investigator, sleuthhound (*Inf.*), tail (*Inf.*)

slice 1. *n.* cut, helping, piece, portion, segment, share, sliver, wedge **2.** *v.* carve, cut, divide, sever

slick *adj.* **1.** glib, meretricious, plausible, polished, smooth, sophistical, specious **2.** adroit, deft, dextrous, polished, professional, sharp, skilful ~*v.* **3.** make glossy, plaster down, sleek, smarm down (*Brit. inf.*), smooth

slide *v.* **1.** coast, glide, glissade, skim, slip, slither, toboggan, veer **2. let slide** forget, gloss over, ignore, let ride, neglect, pass over, push to the back of one's mind, turn a blind eye to

slight *adj.* **1.** feeble, inconsiderable, insignificant, insubstantial, meagre, minor, modest, negligible, paltry, scanty, small, superficial, trifling, trivial, unimportant, weak **2.** delicate, feeble, fragile, lightly-built, slim, small, spare ~*v.* **3.** affront, cold-shoulder, despise, disdain, disparage, give offence *or* umbrage to, ignore, insult, neglect, scorn, show disrespect for, snub, treat with contempt ~*n.* **4.** affront, contempt, discourtesy, disdain, disregard, disrespect, inattention, in-

slim (slɪm) *adj.* **slimmer, slimmest.** **1.** small in width relative to height or length. **2.** small in amount: *slim chances of success.* ~*vb.* **3.** to make or become slim, esp. by diets and exercise. **4.** to reduce in size: *the workforce was slimmed.* —'**slimly** *adv.* —'**slimmer** *n.* —'**slimness** *n.*

slime (slaɪm) *n.* **1.** soft thin runny mud or filth. **2.** any moist viscous fluid, esp. when noxious or unpleasant. **3.** a mucous substance produced by various organisms, such as fish, slugs, and fungi. ~*vb.* (*tr.*) **4.** to cover with slime.

slimy ('slaɪmɪ) *adj.* **slimier, slimiest.** **1.** characterized by, covered with, secreting, or resembling slime. **2.** offensive or repulsive. **3.** *Chiefly Brit.* characterized by servility.

sling¹ (slɪŋ) *n.* **1.** a simple weapon consisting of a loop of leather, etc., in which a stone is whirled and then let fly. **2.** a rope or strap by which something may be secured or lifted. **3.** *Med.* a wide piece of cloth suspended from the neck for supporting an injured hand or arm. **4.** a loop or band attached to an object for carrying. **5.** the act of slinging. ~*vb.* **slinging, slung.** **6.** (*tr.*) to hurl with or as if with a sling. **7.** to attach a sling or slings to (a load, etc.). **8.** (*tr.*) to carry or hang loosely from or as if from a sling: *to sling washing from the line.* —'**slinger** *n.*

sling² (slɪŋ) *n.* a mixed drink with a spirit base, usually sweetened.

slingback ('slɪŋˌbæk) *n.* a shoe with a strap instead of a full covering for the heel.

slink (slɪŋk) *vb.* **slinking, slunk.** **1.** (*intr.*) to move or act in a furtive manner from or as if from fear, guilt, etc. **2.** (*intr.*) to move in a sinuous alluring manner. **3.** (*tr.*) (of animals, esp. cows) to give birth to prematurely. ~*n.* **4.** an animal, esp. a calf, born prematurely.

slinky ('slɪŋkɪ) *adj.* **slinkier, slinkiest.** *Inf.* **1.** moving in a sinuously graceful or provocative way. **2.** (of clothes, etc.) figure-hugging. —'**slinkily** *adv.* —'**slinkiness** *n.*

slip¹ (slɪp) *vb.* **slipping, slipped.** **1.** to move or cause to move smoothly and easily. **2.** (*tr.*) to place, insert, or convey quickly or stealthily. **3.** (*tr.*) to put on or take off easily or quickly: *to slip on a sweater.* **4.** (*intr.*) to lose balance and slide unexpectedly: *he slipped on the ice.* **5.** to let loose or be let loose. **6.** to be released from (something). **7.** (*tr.*) to let go (mooring or anchor lines) over the side. **8.** (when *intr.,* often foll. by *from* or *out of*) to pass out of (the mind or memory). **9.** (*intr.*) to move or pass swiftly or unperceived: *to slip quietly out of the room.* **10.** (*intr.;* sometimes foll. by *up*) to make a mistake. **11.** Also: **sideslip.** to cause (an aircraft) to slide sideways or (of an aircraft) to slide sideways. **12.** (*intr.*) to decline in health, mental ability, etc. **13.** (*intr.*) (of an intervertebral disc) to become displaced from the normal position. **14.** (*tr.*) to dislocate (a bone). **15.** (of animals) to give birth to (offspring) prematurely. **16.** (*tr.*) to pass (a stitch) from one needle to another without knitting it. **17. a.** (*tr.*) to operate (the clutch of a motor vehicle) so that it partially disengages. **b.** (*intr.*) (of the clutch of a motor vehicle) to fail to engage, esp. as a result of wear. **18. let slip. a.** to allow to escape. **b.** to say unintentionally. ~*n.* **19.** the act or an instance of slipping. **20.** a mistake or oversight: *a slip of the pen.* **21.** a moral lapse or failing. **22.** a woman's sleeveless undergarment, worn as a lining for a dress. **23.** a pillowcase. **24.** See **slipway.** **25.** *Cricket.* **a.** the position of the fielder

who stands a little way behind and to the offside of the wicketkeeper. **b.** the fielder himself. **26.** the relative movement of rocks along a fault plane. **27.** *Metallurgy, crystallog.* the deformation of a metallic crystal caused when one part glides over another part along a plane. **28.** *Austral. & N.Z.* a landslide. **29.** the deviation of a propeller from its helical path through a fluid. **30.** another name for **sideslip** (sense 1). **31. give someone the slip.** to elude or escape from someone. ~See also **slip up.** —'**slippage** *n.* —'**slipless** *adj.* —'**slippingly** *adv.*

slip² (slɪp) *n.* **1.** a narrow piece; strip. **2.** a small piece of paper: *a receipt slip.* **3.** a part of a plant that, when detached from the parent, will grow into a new plant; cutting. **4.** a young slender person: *a slip of a child.* **5.** *Printing.* **a.** a long galley. **b.** a galley proof. ~*vb.* **slipping, slipped.** **6.** (*tr.*) to detach (portions of stem, etc.) from (a plant) for propagation.

slip³ (slɪp) *n.* clay mixed with water to a creamy consistency, used for decorating or patching a ceramic piece.

slipknot ('slɪpˌnɒt) *n.* **1.** Also called: **running knot.** a nooselike knot tied so that it will slip along the rope round which it is made. **2.** a knot that can be easily untied by pulling one free end.

slip-on *adj.* **1.** (of a garment or shoe) made so as to be easily and quickly put on or taken off. ~*n.* **2.** a slip-on garment or shoe.

slipped disc *n. Pathol.* a herniated intervertebral disc, often resulting in pain because of pressure on the spinal nerves.

slipper ('slɪpə) *n.* **1.** a light shoe of some soft material, for wearing around the house. **2.** a woman's evening shoe. ~*vb.* **3.** (*tr.*) *Inf.* to hit or beat with a slipper. —'**slippered** *adj.*

slippery ('slɪpərɪ, -prɪ) *adj.* **1.** causing or tending to cause objects to slip: *a slippery road.* **2.** liable to slip from the grasp, etc. **3.** not to be relied upon: *a slippery character.* **4.** (esp. of a situation) unstable. —'**slipperiness** *n.*

slippery elm *n.* **1.** a North American tree, having notched winged fruits and a mucilaginous inner bark. **2.** the bark of this tree, used medicinally as a demulcent. ~Also called: **red elm.**

slippy ('slɪpɪ) *adj.* **-pier, -piest.** **1.** *Inf.* or *dialect.* another word for **slippery** (senses 1, 2). **2.** *Brit. inf.* alert; quick. —'**slippiness** *n.*

slip road *n. Brit.* a relatively narrow road giving access to a motorway, etc.

slipshod ('slɪpˌʃɒd) *adj.* **1.** (of an action) negligent; careless. **2.** (of a person's appearance) slovenly; down-at-heel.

slip-slop *n. S. African.* a sandal attached to the foot by a thong between the big toe and the next toe.

slipstream ('slɪpˌstriːm) *n.* Also called: **airstream. a.** the stream of air forced backwards by an aircraft propeller. **b.** a stream of air behind any moving object.

slip up *vb.* (*intr., adv.*) **1.** *Inf.* to make a blunder or mistake. ~*n.* **slip-up. 2.** *Inf.* a mistake or mishap.

slipway ('slɪpˌweɪ) *n.* **1.** the sloping area in a shipyard, containing the ways. **2.** the ways on which a vessel is launched.

slit (slɪt) *vb.* **slitting, slit.** (*tr.*) **1.** to make a straight long incision in. **2.** to cut into strips lengthwise. ~*n.* **3.** a long narrow cut. **4.** a long narrow opening. —'**slitter** *n.*

THESAURUS

difference, insult, neglect, rebuff, slap in the face (*Inf.*), snub, (the) cold shoulder

slighting belittling, derogatory, disdainful, disparaging, disrespectful, insulting, offensive, scornful, supercilious, uncomplimentary

slightly a little, marginally, on a small scale, somewhat, to some extent or degree

slim *adj.* 1. lean, narrow, slender, slight, svelte, sylphlike, thin, trim 2. faint, poor, remote, slender, slight ~*v.* 3. diet, lose weight, reduce, slenderize (*Chiefly U.S.*)

slimy 1. clammy, glutinous, miry, mucous, muddy, oozy, viscous 2. creeping, grovelling, obsequious, oily, servile, smarmy (*Brit. inf.*), soapy (*Sl.*), sycophantic, toadying, unctuous

sling *v.* 1. cast, chuck (*Inf.*), fling, heave, hurl, lob (*Inf.*), shy, throw, toss 2. dangle,

hang, suspend, swing

slink creep, prowl, pussyfoot (*Inf.*), skulk, slip, sneak, steal

slip *v.* 1. glide, skate, slide, slither 2. fall, lose one's balance, miss or lose one's footing, skid, trip (over) 3. conceal, creep, hide, insinuate oneself, sneak, steal 4. *Sometimes with* up blunder, boob (*Brit. sl.*), err, go wrong, make a mistake, miscalculate, misjudge, mistake 5. break away from, break free from, disappear, escape, get away, get clear of, take French leave 6. let slip blurt out, come out with (*Inf.*), disclose, divulge, give away, leak, let out (*Inf.*), let the cat out of the bag, reveal ~*n.* 7. bloomer (*Brit. inf.*), blunder, boob (*Brit. sl.*), error, failure, fault, imprudence, indiscretion, mistake, omission, oversight, slip of the tongue, slip-up (*Inf.*) 8.

give (someone) the slip dodge, elude, escape from, evade, get away from, lose (someone), outwit, shake (someone) off

slippery 1. glassy, greasy, icy, lubricious (*Rare*), perilous, skiddy (*Inf.*), slippy (*Inf.*), smooth, unsafe, unstable, unsteady 2. crafty, cunning, devious, dishonest, duplicitous, evasive, false, foxy, shifty, sneaky, treacherous, tricky, two-faced, unpredictable, unreliable, untrustworthy

slipshod careless, loose, slapdash, sloppy (*Inf.*), slovenly, unsystematic, untidy

slit 1. *v.* cut (open), gash, knife, lance, pierce, rip, slash, split open 2. *n.* cut, fissure, gash, incision, opening, rent, split, tear

slither ('slɪðə) vb. 1. to move or slide or cause to move or slide unsteadily, as on a slippery surface. 2. (intr.) to travel with a sliding motion. ~n. 3. a slithering motion. —'**slithery** adj.

sliver ('slɪvə) n. 1. a thin piece that is cut or broken off lengthwise. 2. a loose fibre obtained by carding. ~vb. 3. to divide or be divided into splinters. 4. (tr.) to form (wool, etc.) into slivers. —'**sliverer** n.

slob (slɒb) n. 1. Sl. a stupid or coarse person. 2. Irish. mire.

slobber ('slɒbə) or **slabber** vb. 1. to dribble (saliva, food, etc.) from the mouth. 2. (intr.) to speak or write mawkishly. 3. (tr.) to smear with matter dribbling from the mouth. ~n. 4. liquid or saliva spilt from the mouth. 5. maudlin language or behaviour. —'**slobberer** or '**slabberer** n. —'**slobbery** or '**slabbery** adj.

sloe (sləʊ) n. 1. the small sour blue-black fruit of the blackthorn. 2. another name for **blackthorn**.

sloe-eyed adj. having dark slanted or almond-shaped eyes.

slog (slɒg) vb. **slogging, slogged.** 1. to hit with heavy blows, as in boxing. 2. (intr.) to work hard; toil. 3. (intr.; foll. by down, up, along, etc.) to move with difficulty. 4. Cricket. to take large swipes at the ball. ~n. 5. a tiring walk. 6. long exhausting work. 7. a heavy blow or swipe. —'**slogger** n.

slogan ('sləʊgən) n. 1. a distinctive or topical phrase used in politics, advertising, etc. 2. Scot. history. a Highland battle cry.

sloop (slu:p) n. a single-masted sailing vessel, rigged fore-and-aft.

slop (slɒp) vb. **slopping, slopped.** 1. (when intr., often foll. by about) to cause (liquid) to splash or spill or (of liquid) to splash or spill. 2. (intr.; foll. by along, through, etc.) to tramp (through) mud or slush. 3. (tr.) to feed slop or swill to: to slop the pigs. 4. (tr.) to ladle or serve, esp. clumsily. 5. (intr.; foll. by over) Inf., chiefly U.S. to be unpleasantly effusive. ~n. 6. a puddle of spilled liquid. 7. (pl.) wet feed, esp. for pigs, made from kitchen waste, etc. 8. (pl.) waste food or liquid refuse. 9. (often pl.) Inf. liquid or semiliquid food of low quality. 10. soft mud, snow, etc.

slope (sləʊp) vb. 1. to lie or cause to lie at a slanting or oblique angle. 2. (intr.) (esp. of natural features) to follow an inclined course: many paths sloped down the hillside. 3. (intr.; foll. by off, away, etc.) to go furtively. 4. (tr.) Mil. to hold (a rifle) in the slope position. ~n. 5. an inclined portion of ground. 6. (pl.) hills or foothills. 7. any inclined surface or line. 8. the degree or amount of such inclination. 9. Maths. (of a line) the tangent of the angle between the line and another line parallel to the x-axis. 10. the position adopted for military drill when the rifle is rested on the shoulder. —'**sloper** n. —'**sloping** adj.

slop out vb. (intr., adv.) (of prisoners) to empty chamber pots and collect water for washing.

sloppy ('slɒpɪ) adj. **-pier, -piest.** 1. (esp. of the ground, etc.) wet; slushy. 2. Inf. careless; untidy. 3. Inf. mawkishly sentimental. 4. (of food or drink) watery and unappetizing. 5. splashed with slops. 6. (of clothes) loose; baggy. —'**sloppily** adv. —'**sloppiness** n.

slosh (slɒʃ) n. 1. watery mud, snow, etc. 2. Brit. sl. a heavy blow. 3. the sound of splashing liquid. ~vb. 4. (tr.; foll. by around, on, in, etc.) Inf. to throw or pour (liquid). 5. (when intr., often foll. by about or around) Inf. **a.** to shake or stir (something) in a liquid. **b.** (of a person) to splash (around) in water, etc. 6. (tr.) Brit. sl. to deal a heavy blow to. 7. (usually foll. by about or around) Inf.

to shake (a container of liquid) or (of liquid within a container) to be shaken. —'**sloshy** adj.

sloshed (slɒʃt) adj. Chiefly Brit. sl. drunk.

slot (slɒt) n. 1. an elongated aperture or groove, such as one in a vending machine for inserting a coin. 2. Inf. a place in a series or scheme. ~vb. **slotting, slotted.** 3. (tr.) to furnish with a slot or slots. 4. (usually foll. by in or into) to fit or adjust in a slot. 5. Inf. to situate or be situated in a series. —'**slotter** n.

sloth (sləʊθ) n. 1. any of a family of shaggy-coated arboreal edentate mammals, such as the three-toed sloth or ai or the two-toed sloth or unau, of Central and South America. They are slow-moving, hanging upside down by their long arms and feeding on vegetation. 2. reluctance to exert oneself.

slothful ('sləʊθfʊl) adj. lazy; indolent. —'**slothfully** adv. —'**slothfulness** n.

slot machine n. a machine, esp. one for gambling, activated by placing a coin in a slot.

slouch (slaʊtʃ) vb. 1. (intr.) to sit or stand with a drooping bearing. 2. (intr.) to walk or move with an awkward slovenly gait. 3. (tr.) to cause (the shoulders) to droop. ~n. 4. a drooping carriage. 5. (usually used in negative constructions) Inf., chiefly U.S. & N.Z. an incompetent or slovenly person: he's no slouch at football. —'**slouchy** adj.

slouch hat n. any soft hat with a brim that can be pulled down over the ears, esp. an Australian army hat with the left side of the brim turned up.

slough¹ (slaʊ) n. 1. a hollow filled with mud; bog. 2. (slu:) North American. a large hole where water collects or a marshy inlet. 3. despair or degradation. —'**sloughy** adj.

slough² (slʌf) n. 1. any outer covering that is shed, such as the dead outer layer of the skin of a snake, the cellular debris in a wound, etc. ~vb. 2. (often foll. by off) to shed (a skin, etc.) or (of a skin, etc.) to be shed. —'**sloughy** adj.

slough off (slʌf) vb. (tr., adv.) to cast off (cares, etc.).

sloven ('slʌvən) n. a person who is habitually negligent in appearance, hygiene, or work.

slovenly ('slʌvənlɪ) adj. 1. frequently or habitually unclean or untidy. 2. negligent and careless: slovenly manners. ~adv. 3. in a negligent or slovenly manner. —'**slovenliness** n.

slow (sləʊ) adj. 1. performed or occurring during a comparatively long interval of time. 2. lasting a comparatively long time: a slow journey. 3. characterized by lack of speed: a slow walker. 4. (prenominal) adapted to or productive of slow movement: the slow lane of a motorway. 5. (of a clock, etc.) indicating a time earlier than the correct time. 6. not readily responsive to stimulation: a slow mind. 7. dull or uninteresting: the play was very slow. 8. not easily aroused: a slow temperament. 9. lacking promptness or immediacy: a slow answer. 10. unwilling to perform an action or enter into a state: slow to anger. 11. behind the times. 12. (of trade, etc.) unproductive; slack. 13. (of a fire) burning weakly. 14. (of an oven) cool. 15. Photog. requiring a relatively long time of exposure to produce a given density: a slow lens. 16. Sport. (of a court, track, etc.) tending to reduce the speed of the ball or the competitors. 17. Cricket. (of a bowler, etc.) delivering the ball slowly, usually with spin. ~adv. 18. in a manner characterized by lack of speed; slowly. ~vb. 19. (often foll. by up, down, etc.) to decrease or cause to decrease in speed, efficiency, etc. —'**slowly** adv. —'**slowness** n.

THESAURUS

slither v. glide, skitter, slide, slink, slip, snake, undulate

slog v. 1. hit, hit for six, slosh (Brit. sl.), slug, sock (Sl.), strike, thump, wallop (Inf.) 2. apply oneself to, labour, peg away at, persevere, plod, plough through, slave, toil, tramp, trek, trudge, work ~n. 3. effort, exertion, hike, labour, struggle, tramp, trek, trudge

slogan catchword, jingle, motto, rallying cry

slop v. overflow, slosh (Inf.), spatter, spill, splash, splatter

slope v. 1. drop away, fall, incline, lean, pitch, rise, slant, tilt ~n. 2. brae (Scot.), dec-

lination, declivity, descent, downgrade (Chiefly U.S.), gradient, inclination, incline, ramp, rise, scarp, slant, tilt ~v. 3. **With off, away,** etc. creep, make oneself scarce, skulk, slink, slip, steal

sloping bevelled, cant, inclined, inclining, leaning, oblique, slanting

sloppy 1. sludgy, slushy, splashy, watery, wet 2. Inf. amateurish, careless, clumsy, hit-or-miss (Inf.), inattentive, messy, slipshod, slovenly, unkempt, untidy, weak 3. banal, gushing, mawkish, mushy (Inf.), overemotional, sentimental, slushy (Inf.), soppy (Brit. inf.), trite, wet (Brit. inf.)

slot n. 1. aperture, channel, groove, hole,

slit 2. Inf. niche, opening, place, position, space, time, vacancy ~v. 3. adjust, assign, fit, fit in, insert, pigeonhole

sloth faineance, idleness, inactivity, indolence, inertia, laziness, slackness, slothfulness, sluggishness, torpor

slothful do-nothing (Inf.), fainéant, idle, inactive, indolent, inert, lazy, skiving (Brit. inf.), slack, sluggish, torpid, workshy

slouch v. droop, loll, slump, stoop

slovenly careless, disorderly, heedless, loose, negligent, slack, slapdash, slatternly, slipshod, sloppy (Inf.), unkempt, untidy

slow adj. 1. creeping, dawdling, deliberate, easy, lackadaisical, laggard, lagging, lazy,

slowcoach ('sləu,kəutʃ) n. Brit. inf. a person who moves or works slowly. U.S. equivalent: **slowpoke**.

slow motion n. 1. Films, television, etc. action that appears to have occurred at a slower speed than normal, usually achieved by cranking the film at a faster rate. ~adj. **slow-motion**. 2. of or relating to such action. 3. moving or functioning at considerably less than usual speed.

slowworm ('sləu,wɜːm) n. a Eurasian legless lizard with a brownish-grey snakelike body. Also called: **blindworm**.

sludge (slʌdʒ) n. 1. soft mud, snow, etc. 2. any deposit or sediment. 3. a surface layer of ice that is not frozen solid but has a slushy appearance. 4. (in sewage disposal) the solid constituents of sewage that are removed for subsequent purification. —'**sludgy** adj.

slue (sluː) n., vb. a variant spelling (esp. U.S.) of **slew**².

slug¹ (slʌg) n. 1. any of various terrestrial gastropod molluscs in which the body is elongated and the shell is absent or very much reduced. 2. any of various other invertebrates having a soft slimy body, esp. the larvae of certain sawflies.

slug² (slʌg) n. 1. an fps unit of mass; the mass that will acquire an acceleration of 1 foot per second per second when acted upon by a force of 1 pound. 2. Metallurgy. a metal blank from which small forgings are worked. 3. a bullet. 4. Chiefly U.S. a metal token for use in slot machines, etc. 5. Printing. **a.** a thick strip of type metal that is used for spacing. **b.** a metal strip containing a line of characters as produced by a linotype machine. 6. a draught of alcoholic drink, esp. spirits.

slug³ (slʌg) vb. **slugging, slugged.** 1. to hit very hard and solidly, as in boxing or baseball. 2. (tr.) Austral. & N.Z. inf. to charge (someone) an exorbitant price. ~n. 3. a heavy blow. 4. Austral. & N.Z. inf. an exorbitant price. —'**slugger** n.

sluggard ('slʌgəd) n. 1. a person who is habitually indolent. ~adj. 2. lazy. —'**sluggardly** adj.

sluggish ('slʌgɪʃ) adj. 1. lacking energy; inactive. 2. functioning at below normal rate or level. 3. exhibiting poor response to stimulation. —'**sluggishly** adv. —'**sluggishness** n.

sluice (sluːs) n. 1. Also called: **sluiceway**. a channel that carries a rapid current of water, esp. one that has a sluicegate to control the flow. 2. the body of water controlled by a sluicegate. 3. Mining. an inclined trough for washing ore. 4. an artificial channel through which logs can be floated. ~vb. 5. (tr.) to draw out or drain (water, etc.) from (a pond, etc.) by means of a sluice. 6. (tr.) to wash or irrigate with a stream of water. 7. (tr.) Mining. to wash in a sluice. 8. (tr.) to send (logs, etc.) down a sluice. 9. (intr.; often foll. by away or out) (of water, etc.) to run or flow from or as if from a sluice. 10. (tr.) to provide with a sluice. —'**sluice,like** adj.

slum (slʌm) n. 1. a squalid overcrowded house, etc. 2. (often pl.) a squalid section of a city, characterized by inferior living conditions. 3. (modifier) of or characteristic of slums: slum conditions. ~vb. **slumming, slummed.** (intr.) 4. to visit slums, esp. for curiosity. 5. Also: **slum it.** to suffer conditions below those to which one is accustomed. —'**slummy** adj.

slumber ('slʌmbə) vb. 1. (intr.) to sleep, esp. peacefully. 2. (intr.) to be quiescent or dormant. 3. (tr.; foll. by away) to spend (time) sleeping. ~n. 4. (sometimes pl.) sleep. 5. a dormant or quiescent state. —'**slumberer** n.

slump (slʌmp) vb. (intr.) 1. to sink or fall heavily and suddenly. 2. to relax ungracefully. 3. (of business activity, etc.) to decline suddenly. 4. (of health, interest, etc.) to deteriorate or decline suddenly. ~n. 5. a sudden or marked decline or failure, as in progress or achievement. 6. a decline in commercial activity, prices, etc.; depression. 7. the act of slumping.

slung (slʌŋ) vb. the past tense or past participle of **sling**.

slunk (slʌŋk) vb. the past tense or past participle of **slink**.

slur (slɜː) vb. **slurring, slurred.** (mainly tr.) 1. (often foll. by over) to treat superficially, hastily, or without due deliberation. 2. (also intr.) to pronounce or utter (words, etc.) indistinctly. 3. to speak disparagingly of. 4. Music. to execute (a melodic interval of two or more notes) smoothly, as in legato performance. ~n. 5. an indistinct sound or utterance. 6. a slighting remark. 7. a stain or disgrace, as upon one's reputation. 8. Music. **a.** a performance or execution of a melodic interval of two or more notes in a part. **b.** the curved line (⌢ or ⌣) indicating this.

slurp (slɜːp) Inf. ~vb. 1. to eat or drink (something) noisily. ~n. 2. a sound produced in this way.

slurry ('slʌrɪ) n., pl. **-ries.** a suspension of solid particles in a liquid, as in a mixture of cement, clay, or coal dust with water.

slush (slʌʃ) n. 1. any watery muddy substance, esp. melting snow. 2. Inf. sloppily sentimental language. ~vb. 3. (intr.; often foll. by along) to make one's way through or as if through slush. —'**slushiness** n. —'**slushy** adj.

slush fund n. U.S. a fund for financing political corruption, such as buying votes.

slut (slʌt) n. 1. a dirty slatternly woman. 2. an immoral woman. —'**sluttish** adj. —'**sluttishness** n.

sly (slaɪ) adj. **slyer, slyest** or **slier, sliest.** 1. crafty; artful: a sly dodge. 2. insidious; furtive: a sly manner. 3. roguish: sly humour. ~n. 4. **on the sly.** in a secretive manner. —'**slyly** or '**slily** adv. —'**slyness** n.

Sm the chemical symbol for samarium.

smack¹ (smæk) n. 1. a smell or flavour that is distinctive though faint. 2. a distinctive trace: the smack of corruption. 3. a small quantity, esp. a taste. 4. a slang word for **heroin**. ~vb. (intr.; foll. by of) 5. to have the characteristic smell or flavour (of something): to smack of the sea. 6. to have an element suggestive of (something): his speeches smacked of bigotry.

smack² (smæk) vb. 1. (tr.) to strike or slap smartly, with or as if with the open hand. 2. to strike or send forcibly or loudly or to be struck or sent forcibly or loudly. 3. to open and close (the lips) loudly, esp. to show pleasure. ~n. 4. a sharp resounding slap or blow with something flat, or the sound of such a blow. 5. a loud kiss. 6. a sharp sound made by the lips, as in enjoyment. 7. **have a smack at.** Inf., chiefly Brit. to attempt. 8. **smack in the eye.** Inf., chiefly Brit. a snub or setback. ~adv. 9. Inf. directly; squarely. 10. Inf. sharply and unexpectedly.

smack³ (smæk) n. a sailing vessel, usually sloop-rigged, used in coasting and fishing along the British coast.

THESAURUS

leaden, leisurely, loitering, measured, plodding, ponderous, slow-moving, sluggardly, sluggish, tortoise-like, unhurried 2. backward, behind, behindhand, delayed, dilatory, late, long-delayed, tardy, unpunctual 3. gradual, lingering, long-drawn-out, prolonged, protracted, time-consuming 4. behind the times, boring, conservative, dead, dead-and-alive (Brit.), dull, inactive, one-horse (Inf.), quiet, slack, sleepy, sluggish, stagnant, tame, tedious, uneventful, uninteresting, unproductive, unprogressive, wearisome 5. blockish, bovine, dense, dim, dull, dull-witted, dumb (Inf.), obtuse, retarded, slow on the uptake (Inf.), slow-witted, stupid, thick, unresponsive 6. With up or down averse, disinclined, hesitant, indisposed, loath, reluctant, unwilling ~v. 7. Often with up or down brake, check, curb, decelerate, delay, detain, handicap, hold up, lag, reduce speed, rein in, relax, restrict, re-

tard, slacken (off), spin out

slowly at a snail's pace, at one's leisure, by degrees, gradually, inchmeal, in one's own (good) time, leisurely, ploddingly, steadily, taking one's time, unhurriedly, with leaden steps

sluggish dull, heavy, inactive, indolent, inert, lethargic, lifeless, listless, phlegmatic, slothful, slow, slow-moving, torpid, unresponsive

sluggishness apathy, drowsiness, dullness, heaviness, indolence, inertia, languor, lassitude, lethargy, listlessness, slothfulness, somnolence, stagnation, torpor

slumber v. be inactive, doze, lie dormant, nap, repose, sleep, snooze (Inf.)

slump v. 1. collapse, crash, decline, deteriorate, fall, fall off, go downhill (Inf.), plummet, plunge, reach a new low, sink, slip ~n. 2. collapse, crash, decline, depreciation,

depression, downturn, failure, fall, falling-off, low, recession, reverse, stagnation, trough ~v. 3. bend, droop, hunch, loll, sag, slouch

slur n. affront, aspersion, blot, brand, calumny, discredit, disgrace, innuendo, insinuation, insult, reproach, smear, stain, stigma

slut drab (Archaic), slattern, sloven, trollop

sly adj. 1. artful, astute, clever, conniving, covert, crafty, cunning, devious, foxy, furtive, guileful, insidious, scheming, secret, shifty, stealthy, subtle, underhand, wily 2. arch, impish, knowing, mischievous, roguish ~n. 3. **on the sly** behind (someone's) back, covertly, like a thief in the night, on the q.t. (Inf.), on the quiet, privately, secretly, surreptitiously, underhandedly, under the counter (Inf.)

smack v. 1. box, clap, cuff, hit, pat, slap, sock (Sl.), spank, strike, tap ~n. 2. blow, crack, slap 3. **smack in the eye** blow, rebuff,

smacker (ˈsmækə) *n. Sl.* **1.** a loud kiss; smack. **2.** a pound note or dollar bill.

small (smɔːl) *adj.* **1.** limited in size, number, importance, etc. **2.** of little importance or on a minor scale: *a small business.* **3.** lacking in moral or mental breadth or depth: *a small mind.* **4.** modest or humble: *small beginnings.* **5.** of low or inferior status, esp. socially. **6.** (of a child or animal) young; not mature. **7.** unimportant; trivial: *a small matter.* **8.** of or designating the ordinary modern minuscule letter used in printing and cursive writing. **9.** lacking great strength or force: *a small effort.* **10.** in fine particles: *small gravel.* *~adv.* **11.** into small pieces: *cut it small.* **12.** in a small or soft manner. **13. feel small.** to be humiliated. *~n.* **14.** (often preceded by *the*) an object, person, or group considered to be small: *the small or the large?* **15.** a small slender part, esp. of the back. **16.** (*pl.*) *Inf., chiefly Brit.* items of personal laundry, such as underwear. —ˈ**smallish** *adj.* —ˈ**smallness** *n.*

small beer *n.* **1.** *Inf., chiefly Brit.* people or things of no importance. **2.** *Now rare.* weak beer.

small change *n.* **1.** coins, esp. those of low value. **2.** *Rare.* a person or thing that is not outstanding or important.

small fry *pl. n.* **1.** people or things regarded as unimportant. **2.** young children. **3.** young or small fishes.

smallholding (ˈsmɔːlˌhəʊldɪŋ) *n.* a holding of agricultural land smaller than a small farm. —ˈ**smallˌholder** *n.*

small hours *pl. n.* **the.** the early hours of the morning, after midnight and before dawn.

small intestine *n.* the longest part of the alimentary canal, in which digestion is completed. Cf. **large intestine.**

small-minded *adj.* narrow-minded; petty; intolerant; mean. —ˌ**small-**ˈ**mindedly** *adv.* —ˌ**small-**ˈ**mindedness** *n.*

smallpox (ˈsmɔːlˌpɒks) *n.* a highly contagious viral disease characterized by high fever and a rash changing to pustules, which dry up and form scabs that are cast off, leaving pitted depressions. Technical name: **variola.**

small print *n.* matter in a contract, etc., printed in small type, esp. when considered to be a trap for the unwary.

small-scale *adj.* **1.** of limited size or scope. **2.** (of a map, model, etc.) giving a relatively small representation of something.

small talk *n.* light conversation for social occasions.

small-time *adj. Inf.* insignificant; minor: *a small-time criminal.* —ˈ**small-**ˈ**timer** *n.*

smarm (smɑːm) *vb. Brit. inf.* **1.** (*tr.*; often foll. by *down*) to flatten (the hair, etc.) with grease. **2.** (when *intr.*, foll. by *up to*) to ingratiate oneself (with). —ˈ**smarmy** *adj.*

smart (smɑːt) *adj.* **1.** astute, as in business. **2.** quick, witty, and often impertinent in speech: *a smart talker.* **3.** fashionable; chic: *a smart hotel.* **4.** well-kept; neat. **5.** causing a sharp stinging pain. **6.** vigorous or brisk. *~vb.* (*mainly intr.*) **7.** to feel, cause, or be the source of a sharp stinging physical pain or keen mental distress: *he smarted under their abuse.* **8.** (often foll. by *for*) to suffer a harsh penalty. *~n.* **9.** a stinging pain or feeling. *~adv.* **10.** in a smart manner. —ˈ**smartingly** *adv.* —ˈ**smartly** *adv.* —ˈ**smartness** *n.*

smart aleck (ˈælɪk) *or* **smarty** (ˈsmɑːtɪ) *n., pl.* **smart alecks** *or* **smarties.** *Inf.* an irritatingly oversmart person. —ˈ**smart-**ˌ**alecky** *adj.*

smarten (ˈsmɑːtᵊn) *vb.* (usually foll. by *up*) **1.** (*intr.*) to make oneself neater. **2.** (*tr.*) to make quicker or livelier.

smash (smæʃ) *vb.* **1.** to break into pieces violently and usually noisily. **2.** (when *intr.*, foll. by *against, through, into,* etc.) to throw or crash (against) vigorously, causing shattering: *he smashed the equipment.* **3.** (*tr.*) to hit forcefully and suddenly. **4.** (*tr.*) *Tennis, etc.* to hit (the ball) fast and powerfully, esp. with an overhead stroke. **5.** (*tr.*) to defeat (persons, theories, etc.). **6.** to make or become bankrupt. **7.** (*intr.*) to collide violently; crash. *~n.* **8.** an act, instance, or sound of smashing or the state of being smashed. **9.** a violent collision, esp. of vehicles. **10.** a total failure or collapse, as of a business. **11.** *Tennis, etc.* a fast and powerful overhead stroke. **12.** *Inf.* **a.** something having popular success. **b.** (*in combination*): *smash-hit.* *~adv.* **13.** with a smash. —ˈ**smashable** *adj.*

smashing (ˈsmæʃɪŋ) *adj. Inf., chiefly Brit.* excellent or first-rate: *we had a smashing time.*

smash-up *Inf.* *~n.* **1.** a bad collision, esp of cars. *~vb.* **smash up.** **2.** (*tr., adv.*) to damage to the point of complete destruction: *they smashed the place up.*

smattering (ˈsmætərɪŋ) *n.* **1.** a slight or superficial knowledge. **2.** a small amount. —ˈ**smatteringly** *adv.*

smear (smɪə) *vb.* (*mainly tr.*) **1.** to bedaub or cover with oil, grease, etc. **2.** to rub over or apply thickly. **3.** to rub so as to produce a smudge. **4.** to slander. **5.** (*intr.*) to be or become smeared or dirtied. *~n.* **6.** a dirty mark or smudge. **7. a.** a slanderous attack. **b.** (*as modifier*): *smear tactics.* **8.** a preparation of blood, secretions, etc., smeared onto a glass slide for examination under a microscope. —ˈ**smearer** *n.* —ˈ**smeary** *adj.* —ˈ**smeariness** *n.*

smear test *n. Med.* another name for **Pap test.**

smell (smɛl) *vb.* **smelling, smelt** *or* **smelled.** **1.** (*tr.*) to perceive the scent of (a substance) by means of the olfactory nerves. **2.** (*copula*) to have a specified smell: *the beaches smell of seaweed.* **3.** (*intr.*; often foll. by *of*) to emit an odour (of): *the park smells of flowers.* **4.** (*intr.*) to emit an unpleasant odour. **5.** (*tr.*; often foll. by *out*) to detect through shrewdness or instinct. **6.** (*intr.*) to have or use the sense of smell; sniff. **7.** (*intr.*; foll. by *of*) to give indications (of): *he smells of money.* **8.** (*intr.*; foll. by *around, about,* etc.) to search, investigate, or pry. **9.** (*copula*) to be or seem to be untrustworthy. **10. smell a rat.** *Inf.* to detect something suspicious. *~n.* **11.** that sense (olfaction) by which scents or odours are perceived. Related adj.: **olfactory.** **12.** anything detected by the sense of smell. **13.** a trace or indication. **14.** the act or an instance of smelling. —ˈ**smeller** *n.*

▷ **Usage.** *Smell* in its neutral sense of emitting an odour is followed by an adjective rather than by an adverb: *this flower smells good* (rather than *well*). *Smell* in the

THESAURUS

repulse, setback, slap in the face, snub *~adv.* **4.** *Inf.* directly, exactly, plumb, point-blank, precisely, right, slap (*Inf.*), squarely, straight

small **1.** diminutive, immature, little, mini, miniature, minute, petite, pint-sized (*Inf.*), pocket-sized, puny, slight, tiny, undersized, wee, young **2.** insignificant, lesser, minor, negligible, paltry, petty, trifling, trivial, unimportant **3.** inadequate, inconsiderable, insufficient, limited, meagre, scanty **4.** humble, modest, small-scale, unpretentious **5.** base, grudging, illiberal, mean, narrow, petty, selfish **6. make (someone) feel small** chagrin, disconcert, humble, humiliate, make (someone) look foolish, mortify, put down (*Sl.*), show up (*Inf.*), take down a peg or two (*Inf.*)

small-minded bigoted, envious, grudging, hidebound, intolerant, mean, narrow-minded, petty, rigid, ungenerous

small-time insignificant, minor, no-account (*U.S. inf.*), of no account, of no consequence, petty, unimportant

smart[1] *adj.* **1.** acute, adept, agile, apt, astute, bright, brisk, canny, clever, ingenious, intelligent, keen, nimble, quick, quick-witted, ready, sharp, shrewd **2.** chic, elegant, fashionable, fine, modish, natty (*Inf.*), neat, snappy, spruce, stylish, trim, well turned-out **3.** effective, impertinent, nimble-witted, pointed, ready, saucy, smart-alecky (*Inf.*), witty **4.** brisk, cracking (*Inf.*), jaunty, lively, quick, spanking, spirited, vigorous

smart[2] **1.** *v.* burn, hurt, pain, sting, throb, tingle **2.** *adj.* hard, keen, painful, piercing, resounding, sharp, stinging **3.** *n.* burning sensation, pain, pang, smarting, soreness, sting

smash *v.* **1.** break, collide, crash, crush, demolish, disintegrate, pulverize, shatter, shiver *~n.* **2.** accident, collision, crash, pile-up (*Inf.*), smash-up (*Inf.*) *~v.* **3.** defeat, destroy, lay waste, overthrow, ruin, wreck *~n.* **4.** collapse, defeat, destruction, disaster, downfall, failure, ruin, shattering

smashing excellent, exhilarating, fab (*Sl.*), fabulous (*Inf.*), fantastic (*Inf.*), first-class, first-rate, great (*Inf.*), magnificent, marvellous, out of this world (*Inf.*), sensational, stupendous, super (*Inf.*), superb, superlative, terrific (*Inf.*), wonderful

smattering bit, dash, elements, modicum, rudiments, smatter, sprinkling

smear *v.* **1.** bedaub, bedim, besmirch, blur, coat, cover, daub, dirty, patch, plaster, rub on, smudge, soil, spread over, stain, sully *~n.* **2.** blot, blotch, daub, smudge, splotch, streak *~v.* **3.** asperse, besmirch, blacken, calumniate, drag (someone's) name through the mud (*Inf.*), malign, sully, tarnish, traduce, vilify *~n.* **4.** calumny, defamation, libel, mudslinging, slander, vilification, whispering campaign

smell *n.* **1.** aroma, bouquet, fragrance, odour, perfume, redolence, scent, whiff *~v.* **2.** get a whiff of (*Brit. sl.*), nose, scent, sniff *~n.* **3.** fetor, pong (*Brit. inf.*), stench, stink *~v.* **4.** be malodorous, hum (*Sl.*), pong (*Brit. inf.*), reek, stink, stink to high heaven (*Inf.*), whiff (*Brit. sl.*)

sense of emitting an unpleasant odour is followed by an adverb.

smelling salts *pl. n.* a pungent preparation containing crystals of ammonium carbonate that has a stimulant action when sniffed in cases of faintness, headache, etc.

smelly ('smɛlɪ) *adj.* **smellier, smelliest.** having a strong or nasty smell. —**'smelliness** *n.*

smelt[1] (smɛlt) *vb.* (*tr.*) to extract (a metal) from (an ore) by heating.

smelt[2] (smɛlt) *n.*, *pl.* **smelt** *or* **smelts.** a marine or fresh-water salmonoid food fish having a long silvery body and occurring in temperate and cold northern waters.

smelt[3] (smɛlt) *vb.* a past tense or past participle of **smell.**

smelter ('smɛltə) *n.* **1.** a person engaged in smelting. **2.** Also called: **smeltery.** an industrial plant in which smelting is carried out.

smew (smju:) *n.* a merganser of N Europe and Asia, having a male plumage of white with black markings.

smilax ('smaɪlæks) *n.* **1.** any of a genus of climbing shrubs having slightly lobed leaves, small greenish or yellow flowers, and berry-like fruits: includes the sarsaparilla plant and greenbrier. **2.** a fragile, much branched vine of southern Africa: cultivated for its glossy green foliage.

smile (smaɪl) *n.* **1.** a facial expression characterized by an upturning of the corners of the mouth, usually showing amusement, friendliness, etc. **2.** favour or blessing: *the smile of fortune.* ~*vb.* **3.** (*intr.*) to wear or assume a smile. **4.** (*intr.*; foll. by *at*) **a.** to look (at) with a kindly expression. **b.** to look derisively (at). **c.** to bear (troubles, etc.) patiently. **5.** (*intr.*; foll. by *on* or *upon*) to show approval. **6.** (*tr.*) to express by means of a smile: *she smiled a welcome.* **7.** (*tr.*; often foll. by *away*) to drive away or change by smiling. **8. come up smiling.** to recover cheerfully from misfortune. —**'smiler** *n.* —**'smilingly** *adv.*

smirch (smɜ:tʃ) *vb.* (*tr.*) **1.** to dirty; soil. ~*n.* **2.** the act of smirching or state of being smirched. **3.** a smear or stain.

smirk (smɜ:k) *n.* **1.** a smile expressing scorn, smugness, etc., rather than pleasure. ~*vb.* **2.** (*intr.*) to give such a smile. **3.** (*tr.*) to express with such a smile. —**'smirker** *n.* —**'smirkingly** *adv.*

smite (smaɪt) *vb.* **smiting, smote; smitten** *or* **smit.** (*mainly tr.*) Now *arch.* in most senses. **1.** to strike with a heavy blow. **2.** to damage with or as if with blows. **3.** to affect severely: *smitten with flu.* **4.** to afflict in order to punish. **5.** (*intr.*; foll. by *on*) to strike forcibly or abruptly: *the sun smote down on him.* —**'smiter** *n.*

smith (smɪθ) *n.* **1. a.** a person who works in metal. **b.** (*in combination*): *a silversmith.* **2.** See **blacksmith.**

smithereens (ˌsmɪðəˈriːnz) *pl. n.* little shattered pieces or fragments.

smithy ('smɪðɪ) *n.*, *pl.* **smithies.** a place in which metal, usually iron or steel, is worked by heating and hammering; forge.

smitten ('smɪtən) *vb.* the past participle of **smite.**

smock (smɒk) *n.* **1.** any loose protective garment, worn by artists, laboratory technicians, etc. **2.** a woman's loose blouse-like garment, reaching to below the waist, worn over slacks, etc. **3.** Also called: **smock frock.** a loose protective overgarment decorated with smocking, worn formerly esp. by farm workers. **4.** *Arch.* a woman's loose undergarment. ~*vb.* **5.** to ornament (a garment) with smocking. —**'smock,like** *adj.*

smocking ('smɒkɪŋ) *n.* ornamental needlework used to gather and stitch material in a honeycomb pattern so that the part below the gathers hangs in even folds.

smog (smɒg) *n.* a mixture of smoke and fog. —**'smoggy** *adj.*

smoke (sməʊk) *n.* **1.** the product of combustion, consist-

ing of fine particles of carbon carried by hot gases and air. **2.** any cloud of fine particles suspended in a gas. **3. a.** the act of smoking tobacco, esp. as a cigarette. **b.** the duration of smoking such substances. **4.** *Inf.* a cigarette or cigar. **5.** something with no concrete or lasting substance: *everything turned to smoke.* **6.** a thing or condition that obscures. **7. go** *or* **end up in smoke. a.** to come to nothing. **b.** to burn up vigorously. **c.** to flare up in anger. ~*vb.* **8.** (*intr.*) to emit smoke or the like, sometimes excessively or in the wrong place. **9.** to draw in on (a burning cigarette, etc.) and exhale the smoke. **10.** (*tr.*) to bring (oneself) into a specified state by smoking. **11.** (*tr.*) to subject or expose to smoke. **12.** (*tr.*) to cure (meat, fish, etc.) by treating with smoke. **13.** (*tr.*) to fumigate or purify the air of (rooms, etc.). **14.** (*tr.*) to darken (glass, etc.) by exposure to smoke. ~See also **smoke out.** —**'smokable** *or* **'smokeable** *adj.*

Smoke (sməʊk) *n.* **the.** *Brit.* a slang name for **London.**

smokeless ('sməʊklɪs) *adj.* having or producing little or no smoke: *smokeless fuel.*

smokeless zone *n.* an area designated by the local authority where only smokeless fuels are permitted.

smoke out *vb.* (*tr., adv.*) **1.** to subject to smoke in order to drive out of hiding. **2.** to bring into the open: *they smoked out the plot.*

smoker ('sməʊkə) *n.* **1.** a person who habitually smokes tobacco. **2.** Also called: **smoking compartment.** a compartment of a train where smoking is permitted. **3.** an informal social gathering, as at a club.

smoke screen *n.* **1.** *Mil.* a cloud of smoke produced to obscure movements. **2.** something said or done in order to hide the truth.

smokestack ('sməʊkˌstæk) *n.* a tall chimney that conveys smoke into the air.

smoky ('sməʊkɪ) *adj.* **smokier, smokiest. 1.** emitting or resembling smoke. **2.** emitting smoke excessively or in the wrong place: *a smoky fireplace.* **3.** having the flavour or having been cured by smoking. **4.** made dirty or hazy by smoke. —**'smokily** *adv.* —**'smokiness** *n.*

smolt (sməʊlt) *n.* a young salmon at the stage when it migrates from fresh water to the sea.

smooch (smu:tʃ) *Sl.* ~*vb.* (*intr.*) **1.** Also (*Austral.*): **smoodge.** (of two people) to kiss and cuddle. **2.** *Brit.* to dance very slowly and amorously with one's arms around another person, or (of two people) to dance together in such a way. ~*n.* **3.** the act of smooching.

smooth (smu:ð) *adj.* **1.** without bends or irregularities. **2.** silky to the touch: *smooth velvet.* **3.** lacking roughness of surface; flat. **4.** tranquil or unruffled: *smooth temper.* **5.** lacking obstructions or difficulties. **6. a.** suave or persuasive, esp. as suggestive of insincerity. **b.** (*in combination*): *smooth-tongued.* **7.** (of the skin) free from hair. **8.** of uniform consistency: *smooth batter.* **9.** free from jolts: *smooth driving.* **10.** not harsh or astringent: *a smooth wine.* **11.** having all projections worn away: *smooth tyres.* **12.** *Phonetics.* without preliminary aspiration. **13.** *Physics.* (of a plane, etc.) regarded as being frictionless. ~*adv.* **14.** in a calm or even manner. ~*vb.* (*mainly tr.*) **15.** (*also intr.*; often foll. by *down*) to make or become flattened or without roughness. **16.** (often foll. by *out* or *away*) to take or rub (away) in order to make smooth: *she smoothed out the creases in her dress.* **17.** to make calm; soothe. **18.** to make easier: *smooth his path.* ~*n.* **19.** the smooth part of something. **20.** the act of smoothing. **21.** *Tennis, etc.* the side of a racket on which the binding strings form a continuous line. —**'smoothen** *vb.* —**'smoother** *n.* —**'smoothly** *adv.* —**'smoothness** *n.*

smoothie *or* **smoothy** ('smu:ðɪ) *n.*, *pl.* **smoothies.** *Sl.*, usually *derog.* a person, esp. a man, who is suave or slick, esp. in speech, dress, or manner.

smoothing iron *n.* a former name for **iron** (sense 3).

THESAURUS

smelly evil-smelling, fetid, foul, foul-smelling, high, malodorous, mephitic, noisome, pongy (*Brit. inf.*), putrid, reeking, stinking, strong, strong-smelling, whiffy (*Brit. sl.*)

smirk *n.* grin, leer, simper, smug look, sneer

smitten 1. afflicted, beset, laid low, plagued, struck **2.** beguiled, bewitched, bowled over (*Inf.*), captivated, charmed, en-

amoured, infatuated, swept off one's feet

smoky begrimed, black, caliginous (*Archaic*), grey, grimy, hazy, murky, reeky, smoke-darkened, sooty, thick

smooth *adj.* **1.** even, flat, flush, horizontal, level, plain, plane, unwrinkled **2.** glossy, polished, shiny, silky, sleek, soft, velvety **3.** calm, equable, glassy, mirror-like, peaceful, serene, tranquil, undisturbed, unruffled **4.** agreeable, bland, mellow, mild, pleasant,

soothing **5.** facile, glib, ingratiating, persuasive, silky, slick, smarmy (*Brit. inf.*), suave, unctuous, urbane **6.** easy, effortless, flowing, fluent, frictionless, regular, rhythmic, steady, unbroken, uneventful, uniform, uninterrupted, untroubled, well-ordered ~*v.* **7.** flatten, iron, level, plane, polish, press **8.** allay, alleviate, appease, assuage, calm, ease, extenuate, facilitate, iron out the difficulties of, mitigate, mollify, palliate, pave the way, soften

smooth over vb. (tr.) to ease or gloss over: to smooth over a situation.

smooth-spoken adj. speaking or spoken in a gently persuasive or competent manner.

smooth-tongued adj. suave or persuasive in speech.

smorgasbord ('smɔːgəs,bɔːd) n. a variety of cold or hot savoury dishes served in Scandinavia as hors d'oeuvres or as a buffet meal.

smote (sməʊt) vb. the past tense of **smite**.

smother ('smʌðə) vb. **1.** to suffocate or stifle by cutting off or being cut off from the air. **2.** (tr.) to surround (with) or envelop (in): he smothered her with love. **3.** (tr.) to extinguish (a fire) by covering so as to cut it off from the air. **4.** to be or cause to be suppressed or stifled: smother a giggle. **5.** (tr.) to cook or serve (food) thickly covered with sauce, etc. ~n. **6.** anything, such as a cloud of smoke, that stifles. **7.** a profusion or turmoil. —'**smothery** adj.

smoulder or U.S. **smolder** ('sməʊldə) vb. (intr.) **1.** to burn slowly without flame, usually emitting smoke. **2.** (esp. of anger, etc.) to exist in a suppressed state. **3.** to have strong repressed feelings, esp. anger. ~n. **4.** a smouldering fire.

smudge (smʌdʒ) vb. **1.** to smear or soil or cause to do so. **2.** (tr.) Chiefly U.S. to fill (an area) with smoke in order to drive insects away. ~n. **3.** a smear or dirty mark. **4.** a blurred form or area: that smudge in the distance is a quarry. **5.** Chiefly U.S. a smoky fire for driving insects away or protecting plants from frost. —'**smudgy** adj. —'**smudgily** adv. —'**smudginess** n.

smug (smʌg) adj. **smugger, smuggest.** excessively self-satisfied or complacent. —'**smugly** adv. —'**smugness** n.

smuggle ('smʌgəl) vb. **1.** to import or export (prohibited or dutiable goods) secretly. **2.** (tr.; often foll. by into or out of) to bring or take secretly, as against the law or rules. —'**smuggler** n. —'**smuggling** n.

smut (smʌt) n. **1.** a small dark smudge or stain, esp. one caused by soot. **2.** a speck of soot or dirt. **3.** something obscene or indecent. **4. a.** any of various fungal diseases of flowering plants, esp. cereals, in which black sooty masses of spores cover the affected parts. **b.** any parasitic fungus that causes such a disease. ~vb. **smutting, smutted. 5.** to mark or become marked or smudged, as with soot. **6.** to affect (grain, etc.) or (of grain) to be affected with smut. —'**smutty** adj. —'**smuttily** adv. —'**smuttiness** n.

Sn the chemical symbol for tin.

snack (snæk) n. **1.** a light quick meal eaten between or in place of main meals. **2.** a sip or bite. ~vb. **3.** (intr.) to eat a snack.

snack bar n. a place where light meals or snacks can be obtained, often with a self-service system.

snaffle ('snæfəl) n. **1.** Also called: **snaffle bit.** a simple jointed bit for a horse. ~vb. (tr.) **2.** Brit. inf. to steal or take for oneself. **3.** to equip or control with a snaffle.

snafu (snæ'fuː) U.S. sl., chiefly mil. ~n. **1.** confusion or chaos regarded as the normal state. ~adj. **2.** (postpositive) confused or muddled up, as usual. ~vb. **-fuing, -fued. 3.** (tr.) to throw into chaos.

snag (snæg) n. **1.** a difficulty or disadvantage: the snag is that I have nothing suitable to wear. **2.** a sharp protuberance, such as a tree stump. **3.** a small loop or hole in a fabric caused by a sharp object. **4.** a tree stump in a riverbed that is dangerous to navigation. **5.** Austral. sl. a

sausage. ~vb. **snagging, snagged. 6.** (tr.) to hinder or impede. **7.** (tr.) to tear or catch (fabric). **8.** (intr.) to develop a snag. **9.** (intr.) Chiefly U.S. (of a boat) to strike a snag. **10.** (tr.) to clear (a stretch of water) of snags. **11.** (tr.) U.S. to seize (an opportunity, etc.). —'**snaggy** adj.

snail (sneɪl) n. **1.** any of numerous terrestrial or freshwater gastropod molluscs with a spirally coiled shell, esp. the **garden snail. 2.** any other gastropod with a spirally coiled shell, such as a whelk. **3.** a slow-moving person or animal. —'**snail-,like** adj.

snail's pace n. a very slow or sluggish speed or rate.

snake (sneɪk) n. **1.** a reptile having a scaly cylindrical limbless body, fused eyelids, and a jaw modified for swallowing large prey: includes venomous forms such as cobras and rattlesnakes, large nonvenomous constrictors (boas and pythons), and small harmless types such as the grass snake. **2.** Also: **snake in the grass.** a deceitful or treacherous person. **3.** anything resembling a snake in appearance or action. **4.** a group of currencies, any one of which can only fluctuate within narrow limits, but each can fluctuate more against other currencies. **5.** a tool in the form of a long flexible wire for unblocking drains. ~vb. **6.** (intr.) to glide or move like a snake. **7.** (tr.) to move in or follow (a sinuous course). —'**snake-,like** adj.

snake charmer n. an entertainer, esp. in Asia, who charms or appears to charm snakes by playing music.

snakes and ladders n. (functioning as sing.) a board game in which players move counters along a series of squares by means of dice. A ladder provides a short cut to a square nearer the finish and a snake obliges a player to return to a square nearer the start.

snaky ('sneɪkɪ) adj. **snakier, snakiest. 1.** of or like a snake. **2.** treacherous or insidious. **3.** infested with snakes. **4.** Austral. sl. angry or bad-tempered. —'**snakily** adv. —'**snakiness** n.

snap (snæp) vb. **snapping, snapped. 1.** to break or cause to break suddenly, esp. with a sharp sound. **2.** to make or cause to make a sudden sharp cracking sound. **3.** (intr.) to give way or collapse suddenly, esp. from strain. **4.** to move, close, etc., or cause to move, close, etc., with a sudden sharp sound. **5.** to move or cause to move in a sudden or abrupt way. **6.** (intr.; often foll. by at or up) to seize something suddenly or quickly. **7.** (when intr., often foll. by at) to bite at (something) bringing the jaws rapidly together. **8.** to speak (words) sharply or abruptly. **9.** to take a snapshot of (something). **10.** (tr.) American football. to put (the ball) into play by sending it back from the line of scrimmage. **11. snap one's fingers at. Inf. a.** to dismiss with contempt. **b.** to defy. **12. snap out of it.** Inf. to recover quickly, esp. from depression or anger. ~n. **13.** the act of breaking suddenly or the sound produced by a sudden breakage. **14.** a sudden sharp sound, esp. of bursting, popping, or cracking. **15.** a catch, clasp, or fastener that operates with a snapping sound. **16.** a sudden grab or bite. **17.** a thin crisp biscuit: ginger snaps. **18.** Inf. See **snapshot. 19.** Inf. vigour, liveliness, or energy. **20.** Inf. a task or job that is easy or profitable to do. **21.** a short spell or period, esp. of cold weather. **22.** Brit. a card game in which the word snap is called when two cards of equal value are turned up on the separate piles dealt by each player. **23.** (modifier) done on the spur of the moment: a snap decision. **24.** (modifier) closed or fastened with a snap. ~adv. **25.** with a snap. ~interj. **26. a.** Cards. the word called while playing snap. **b.** an exclamation used to

---

smoothness **1.** evenness, flushness, levelness, regularity, unbrokenness **2.** silkiness, sleekness, smooth texture, softness, velvetiness **3.** calmness, glassiness, placidity, serenity, stillness, unruffled surface **4.** glibness, oiliness, smarminess (Brit. inf.), suavity, urbanity **5.** ease, efficiency, effortlessness, felicity, finish, flow, fluency, polish, rhythm, slickness, smooth running

smother v. **1.** choke, extinguish, snuff, stifle, strangle, suffocate **2.** conceal, hide, keep back, muffle, repress, stifle, suppress **3.** be swimming in, cocoon, cover, envelop, heap, inundate, overwhelm, shower, shroud, surround ~n. **4.** fug (Chiefly Brit.), smog

smoulder Fig. be resentful, boil, burn,

fester, fume, rage, seethe, simmer, smart under

smudge **1.** v. blacken, blur, daub, dirty, mark, smear, smirch, soil **2.** n. blemish, blot, blur, smear, smut, smutch

smug complacent, conceited, holier-than-thou, priggish, self-opinionated, self-righteous, self-satisfied, superior

smuggler bootlegger, contrabandist, gentleman, moonshiner (U.S.), rum-runner, runner, wrecker

snack bite, bite to eat, break, elevenses (Brit. inf.), light meal, nibble, refreshment(s), titbit

snag **1.** n. catch, complication, difficulty, disadvantage, drawback, hitch, inconvenience, obstacle, problem, stumbling block,

the rub **2.** v. catch, hole, rip, tear

snap v. **1.** break, come apart, crack, give way, separate **2.** bite, bite at, catch, grip, nip, seize, snatch **3.** bark, flare out, flash, fly off the handle at (Inf.), growl, jump down (someone's) throat (Inf.), lash out at, retort, snarl, speak sharply **4.** click, crackle, pop **5. snap one's fingers at** cock a snook at (Brit.), defy, flout, pay no attention to, scorn, set at naught, wave two fingers at (Sl.) **6. snap out of it** cheer up, get a grip on oneself, get over, liven up, perk up, pull oneself together (Inf.), recover ~n. **7.** crackle, fillip, flick, pop **8.** bite, grab, nip **9.** Inf. energy, get-up-and-go (Inf.), go (Inf.), liveliness, pizazz (Inf.), vigour, zip (Inf.) ~adj. **10.** abrupt, immediate, instant, on-the-spot, sudden, unpremeditated

draw attention to the similarity of two things. ~See also
snap up. —'**snapless** adj. —'**snappingly** adv.

snapdragon ('snæp‚drægən) n. any of several plants of
the genus *Antirrhinum* having spikes of showy white,
yellow, pink, red, or purplish flowers. Also called: **antirrhinum.**

snap fastener n. another name for **press stud.**

snapper ('snæpə) n., pl. **-per** or **-pers**. **1.** any large
sharp-toothed percoid food fish of warm and tropical
coastal regions. **2.** an Australian sparid food fish that
has a pinkish body covered with blue spots. **3.** a person
or thing that snaps. ~Also (for sense 1, 2): **schnapper.**

snappy ('snæpɪ) adj. **-pier, -piest**. **1.** Also: **snappish**. apt
to speak sharply or irritably. **2.** Also: **snappish**. apt to
snap or bite. **3.** crackling in sound: *a snappy fire*. **4.**
brisk, sharp, or chilly: *a snappy pace*. **5.** smart and fashionable: *a snappy dresser*. **6. make it snappy.** *Sl.* hurry
up! —'**snappily** adv. —'**snappiness** n.

snapshot ('snæp‚ʃot) n. an informal photograph taken
with a simple camera. Often shortened to **snap.**

snap up vb. (tr., adv.) **1.** to avail oneself of eagerly
and quickly: *she snapped up the bargains*. **2.** to interrupt abruptly.

snare[1] (snɛə) n. **1.** a device for trapping birds or small
animals, esp. a flexible loop that is drawn tight around
the prey. **2.** a surgical instrument for removing certain
tumours, consisting of a wire loop that may be drawn
tight around their base to sever them. **3.** anything that
traps or entangles someone or something unawares.
~vb. (tr.) **4.** to catch birds or small animals with a
snare. **5.** to catch or trap in or as if in a snare. —'**snarer** n. —'**snaringly** adv.

snare[2] (snɛə) n. *Music*. a set of gut strings wound with
wire fitted against the lower drumhead of a snare drum.
They produce a rattling sound when the drum is beaten.

snare drum n. *Music*. a cylindrical drum with two
drumheads, the upper of which is struck and the lower
fitted with a snare. See **snare**[2].

snarl[1] (snɑːl) vb. **1.** (intr.) (of an animal) to growl viciously, baring the teeth. **2.** to speak or express (something) viciously. ~n. **3.** a vicious growl or facial expression. **4.** the act of snarling. —'**snarler** n.
—'**snarly** adj.

snarl[2] (snɑːl) n. **1.** a tangled mass of thread, hair, etc.
2. a complicated or confused state or situation. **3.** a knot
in wood. ~vb. **4.** (often foll. by *up*) to be, become, or
make tangled or complicated. **5.** (tr.; often foll. by *up*) to
confuse mentally. **6.** (tr.) to emboss (metal) by hammering on a tool held against the under surface. —'**snarler**
n. —'**snarly** adj.

snarl-up n. *Inf.*, chiefly Brit. a confusion, obstruction,
or tangle, esp. a traffic jam.

snatch (snætʃ) vb. **1.** (tr.) to seize or grasp (something)
suddenly or peremptorily: *he snatched the chocolate*. **2.**
(intr.; usually foll. by *at*) to seize or attempt to seize suddenly. **3.** (tr.) to take hurriedly: *to snatch some sleep*.
4. (tr.) to remove suddenly: *she snatched her hand away*.
5. (tr.) to gain, win, or rescue, esp. narrowly: *they
snatched victory in the closing seconds*. ~n. **6.** an act
of snatching. **7.** a fragment or incomplete part: *snatches
of conversation*. **8.** a brief spell: *snatches of time off*. **9.**
Weightlifting. a lift in which the weight is raised in one
quick motion from the floor to an overhead position. **10.**
Sl., chiefly U.S. an act of kidnapping. **11.** *Brit. sl.* a robbery: *a diamond snatch*. —'**snatcher** n. —'**snatchy**
adj.

snazzy ('snæzɪ) adj. **-zier, -ziest**. *Inf.* (esp. of clothes)

stylishly and often flashily attractive. —'**snazzily** adv.
—'**snazziness** n.

sneak (sniːk) vb. **1.** (intr.; often foll. by *along, off, in,*
etc.) to move furtively. **2.** (intr.) to behave in a cowardly or underhand manner. **3.** (tr.) to bring, take, or put
stealthily. **4.** (intr.) *Inf.*, chiefly Brit. to tell tales (esp. in
schools). **5.** (tr.) *Inf.* to steal. **6.** (intr.; foll. by *off, out,
away*, etc.) *Inf.* to leave unobtrusively. ~n. **7.** a person
who acts in an underhand or cowardly manner, esp. as
an informer. **8. a.** a stealthy act. **b.** (as modifier): *a
sneak attack*. —'**sneaky** adj. —'**sneakily** adv.
—'**sneakiness** n.

sneakers ('sniːkəz) pl. n. Chiefly U.S. canvas shoes with
rubber soles worn informally.

sneaking ('sniːkɪŋ) adj. **1.** acting in a furtive or cowardly way. **2.** secret: *a sneaking desire to marry a millionaire*. **3.** slight but nagging (esp. in **a sneaking suspicion**). —'**sneakingly** adv.

sneak thief n. a person who steals paltry articles
from premises, which he enters through open doors, windows, etc.

sneer (snɪə) n. **1.** a facial expression of scorn or contempt, typically with the upper lip curled. **2.** a scornful
or contemptuous remark or utterance. ~vb. **3.** (intr.)
to assume a facial expression of scorn or contempt. **4.**
to say or utter (something) in a scornful manner.
—'**sneerer** n. —'**sneering** adj., n.

sneeze (sniːz) vb. **1.** (intr.) to expel air from the nose
involuntarily, esp. as the result of irritation of the nasal
mucous membrane. ~n. **2.** the act or sound of sneezing.
—'**sneezer** n. —'**sneezy** adj.

sneeze at vb. (intr., prep.; usually with a negative) *Inf.*
to dismiss lightly: *his offer is not to be sneezed at*.

sneezewood ('sniːz‚wʊd) n. **1.** a South African tree. **2.**
its exceptionally hard wood, used for furniture, gateposts
and railway sleepers.

snick (snɪk) n. **1.** a small cut; notch. **2.** *Cricket*. **a.** a
glancing blow off the edge of the bat. **b.** the ball so hit.
~vb. (tr.) **3.** to cut a small corner or notch in (material,
etc.). **4.** *Cricket*. to hit (the ball) with a snick.

snicker ('snɪkə) n., vb. **1.** another word, esp. U.S., for
snigger. ~vb. **2.** (of a horse) to whinny. —'**snicker-
ingly** adv.

snide (snaɪd) adj. **1.** (of a remark, etc.) maliciously derogatory. **2.** counterfeit. ~n. **3.** *Sl.* sham jewellery.
—'**snideness** n.

sniff (snɪf) vb. **1.** to inhale through the nose, usually in
short rapid audible inspirations, as for clearing a congested nasal passage. **2.** (when intr., often foll. by *at*) to
perceive or attempt to perceive (a smell) by inhaling
through the nose. ~n. **3.** the act or sound of sniffing. **4.**
a smell perceived by sniffing, esp. a faint scent.
—'**sniffer** n. —'**sniffingly** adv.

sniff at vb. (intr., prep.) to express contempt or dislike
for.

sniffle ('snɪfəl) vb. **1.** (intr.) to breathe audibly through
the nose, as when the nasal passages are congested.
~n. **2.** the act, sound, or an instance of sniffling.
—'**sniffler** n.

sniffles ('snɪfəlz) or **snuffles** n. *Inf.* **the.** a cold in
the head.

sniff out vb. (tr., adv.) to detect through shrewdness
or instinct.

sniffy ('snɪfɪ) adj. **-fier, -fiest**. *Inf.* contemptuous or disdainful. —'**sniffily** adv. —'**sniffiness** n.

snifter ('snɪftə) n. **1.** a pear-shaped glass with a bowl

THESAURUS

snappy 1. apt to fly off the handle (*Inf.*),
cross, edgy, hasty, irritable, like a bear with
a sore head (*Inf.*), quick-tempered, snappish,
tart, testy, touchy, waspish **2.** chic, dapper,
fashionable, modish, natty (*Inf.*), smart, stylish, trendy (*Brit. inf.*), up-to-the-minute **3.**
look snappy be quick, buck up (*Inf.*), get a
move on (*Inf.*), get one's skates on, hurry
(up), look lively, make haste

snap up avail oneself of, grab, grasp, nab
(*Inf.*), pounce upon, seize, swoop down on,
take advantage of

snare 1. v. catch, entrap, net, seize,
springe, trap, trepan (*Archaic*), wire **2.** n.
catch, gin, net, noose, pitfall, springe, trap,
wire

snarl[1] v. complain, growl, grumble, mumble, murmur, show its teeth (*of an animal*)

snarl[2] v. Often *with* up complicate, confuse, embroil, enmesh, entangle, entwine,
muddle, ravel, tangle

snarl-up confusion, entanglement, muddle, tangle, (traffic) jam

snatch 1. v. clutch, gain, grab, grasp, grip,
make off with, pluck, pull, rescue, seize, take,
win, wrench, wrest **2.** n. bit, fragment, part,
piece, smattering, snippet, spell

sneak v. **1.** cower, lurk, pad, sidle, skulk,
slink, slip, smuggle, spirit, steal **2.** *Inf.* grass
on (*Brit. inf.*), inform on, peach (*Sl.*), tell on
(*Inf.*), tell tales ~n. **3.** informer, snake in the
grass, telltale ~adj. **4.** clandestine, furtive,

quick, secret, stealthy, surprise

sneaking 1. hidden, private, secret, suppressed, unavowed, unconfessed, undivulged,
unexpressed, unvoiced **2.** intuitive, nagging,
niggling, persistent, uncomfortable, worrying **3.** contemptible, furtive, mean, sly,
sneaky, surreptitious, two-faced, underhand

sneer 1. v. curl one's lip, deride, disdain,
gibe, hold in contempt, hold up to ridicule,
jeer, laugh, look down on, mock, ridicule,
scoff, scorn, sniff at, snigger, turn up one's
nose (*Inf.*) **2.** n. derision, disdain, gibe, jeer,
mockery, ridicule, scorn, snidery, snigger

sniff v. breathe, inhale, smell, snuff, snuffle

that narrows towards the top so that the aroma of brandy or some other liqueur is retained. **2.** *Inf.* a small quantity of alcoholic drink.

snigger ('snɪgə) *n.* **1.** a sly or disrespectful laugh, esp. one partly stifled. ~*vb.* (*intr.*) **2.** to utter such a laugh. —'**sniggeringly** *adv.*

snip (snɪp) *vb.* **snipping, snipped. 1.** to cut or clip with a small quick stroke or a succession of small quick strokes, esp. with scissors or shears. ~*n.* **2.** the act of snipping. **3.** the sound of scissors or shears closing. **4.** Also called: **snipping.** a small piece of anything. **5.** a small cut made by snipping. **6.** *Chiefly Brit.* an informal word for **bargain. 7.** *Inf.* something easily done; cinch.

snipe (snaɪp) *n., pl.* **snipe** or **snipes. 1.** any of a genus of birds, such as the common or Wilson's snipe, of marshes and river banks, having a long straight bill. **2.** a shot, esp. a gunshot, fired from a place of concealment. ~*vb.* **3.** (when *intr.*, often foll. by *at*) to attack (a person or persons) with a rifle from a place of concealment. **4.** (*intr.*; often foll. by *at*) to criticize a person or persons from a position of security. **5.** (*intr.*) to hunt or shoot snipe. —'**sniper** *n.*

snippet ('snɪpɪt) *n.* a small scrap or fragment. —'**snippy** *adj.* —'**snippily** *adv.* —'**snippiness** or '**snippetiness** *n.*

snitch (snɪtʃ) *Sl.* ~*vb.* **1.** (*tr.*) to steal; take, esp. in an underhand way. **2.** (*intr.*) to act as an informer. ~*n.* **3.** an informer.

snivel ('snɪvəl) *vb.* **-elling, -elled** *or U.S.* **-eling, -eled. 1.** (*intr.*) to sniffle as a sign of distress. **2.** to utter (something) tearfully; whine. **3.** (*intr.*) to have a runny nose. ~*n.* **4.** an instance of snivelling. —'**sniveller** *n.* —'**snivelling** *adj., n.*

snob (snɒb) *n.* **1.** a person who strives to associate with those of higher social status and who behaves condescendingly to others. **2.** a person having similar pretensions with regard to his tastes, etc.: *an intellectual snob.* —'**snobbery** *n.* —'**snobbish** *adj.* —'**snobbishly** *adv.*

SNOBOL ('snəʊbɒl) *n.* String Oriented Symbolic Language: a computer-programming language for handling strings of symbols.

snoek (snʊk) *n.* a South African edible marine fish.

snog (snɒg) *Brit. sl.* ~*vb.* **snogging, snogged. 1.** (*intr.*) to kiss and cuddle. ~*n.* **2.** the act of kissing and cuddling.

snood (snuːd) *n.* **1.** a pouchlike hat, often of net, loosely holding a woman's hair at the back. **2.** a headband, esp. one formerly worn by young unmarried women in Scotland.

snook[1] (snuːk) *n., pl.* **snook** or **snooks.** any of a genus of large game fishes of tropical American marine and fresh waters.

snook[2] (snuːk) *n. Brit.* a rude gesture, made by putting one thumb to the nose with the fingers of the hand outstretched (esp. in **cock a snook**).

snooker ('snuːkə) *n.* **1.** a game played on a billiard table with 15 red balls, six balls of other colours, and a white cue ball. The object is to pot the balls in a certain order. **2.** a shot in which the cue ball is left in a position such that another ball blocks the object ball. ~*vb.* (*tr.*) **3.** to leave (an opponent) in an unfavourable position by playing a snooker. **4.** to place (someone) in a difficult situation.

snoop (snuːp) *Inf.* ~*vb.* **1.** (*intr.*; often foll. by *about* or *around*) to pry into the private business of others. ~*n.* **2.** a person who pries into the business of others. **3.** an act or instance of snooping. —'**snooper** *n.* —'**snoopy** *adj.*

snoot (snuːt) *n. Sl.* the nose.

snooty ('snuːtɪ) *adj.* **snootier, snootiest.** *Inf.* **1.** aloof or supercilious. **2.** snobbish: *a snooty restaurant.* —'**snootily** *adv.* —'**snootiness** *n.*

snooze (snuːz) *Inf.* ~*vb.* **1.** (*intr.*) to take a brief light sleep. ~*n.* **2.** a nap. —'**snoozer** *n.* —'**snoozy** *adj.*

snore (snɔː) *vb.* **1.** (*intr.*) to breathe through the mouth and nose while asleep with snorting sounds caused by the soft palate vibrating. ~*n.* **2.** the act or sound of snoring. —'**snorer** *n.*

snorkel ('snɔːkəl) *n.* **1.** a device allowing a swimmer to breathe while face down on the surface of the water, consisting of a bent tube fitting into the mouth and projecting above the surface. **2.** (on a submarine) a retractable vertical device containing air-intake and exhaust pipes for the engines and general ventilation. ~*vb.* **3.** (*intr.*) to swim with a snorkel.

snort (snɔːt) *vb.* **1.** (*intr.*) to exhale forcibly through the nostrils, making a characteristic noise. **2.** (*intr.*) (of a person) to express contempt or annoyance by such an exhalation. **3.** (*tr.*) to utter in a contemptuous or annoyed manner. ~*n.* **4.** a forcible exhalation of air through the nostrils, esp. (of persons) as a noise of contempt. —'**snortingly** *adv.*

snorter ('snɔːtə) *n.* **1.** a person or animal that snorts. **2.** *Brit. sl.* something outstandingly impressive or difficult.

snot (snɒt) *n.* (*usually considered vulgar*) **1.** nasal mucus or discharge. **2.** *Sl.* a contemptible person.

snotty ('snɒtɪ) (*considered vulgar*) ~*adj.* **-tier, -tiest. 1.** dirty with nasal discharge. **2.** *Sl.* contemptible; nasty. **3.** snobbish; conceited. ~*n., pl.* **-ties. 4.** a slang word for **midshipman.** —'**snottily** *adv.* —'**snottiness** *n.*

snout (snaʊt) *n.* **1.** the part of the head of a vertebrate, esp. a mammal, consisting of the nose, jaws, and surrounding region. **2.** the corresponding part of the head of such insects as weevils. **3.** anything projecting like a snout, such as a nozzle. **4.** *Sl.* a person's nose. **5.** *Brit. sl.* a cigarette or tobacco. —'**snouted** *adj.* —'**snoutless** *adj.*

snow (snəʊ) *n.* **1.** precipitation from clouds in the form of flakes of ice crystals formed in the upper atmosphere. **2.** a layer of snowflakes on the ground. **3.** a fall of such precipitation. **4.** anything resembling snow in whiteness, softness, etc. **5.** the random pattern of white spots on a television or radar screen, occurring when the signal is weak. **6.** *Sl.* **a.** cocaine crystals. **b.** heroin in powder form. ~*vb.* **7.** (*intr.*, with *it* as subject) to be the case that snow is falling. **8.** (*tr.*; usually passive, foll. by *over, under, in,* or *up*) to cover or confine with a heavy fall of snow. **9.** (often with *it* as subject) to fall or cause to fall as or like snow. **10.** (*tr.*) *U.S. sl.* to overwhelm with elaborate often insincere talk. **11. be snowed under.** to be overwhelmed, esp. with paperwork. —'**snowless** *adj.* —'**snow,like** *adj.* —'**snowy** *adj.*

snowball ('snəʊ,bɔːl) *n.* **1.** snow pressed into a ball for throwing, as in play. **2.** a drink made of advocaat and lemonade. ~*vb.* **3.** (*intr.*) to increase rapidly in size, importance, etc. **4.** (*tr.*) to throw snowballs at.

snowberry ('snəʊbərɪ) *n., pl.* **-ries. 1.** a shrub cultivated for its small pink flowers and white berries. **2.** Also called: **waxberry.** any of the berries of such a plant.

snow-blind *adj.* temporarily unable to see or having impaired vision because of the intense reflection of sunlight from snow. —**snow blindness** *n.*

snowblower ('snəʊ,bləʊə) *n.* a snow-clearing machine that draws the snow in and blows it away.

snowbound ('snəʊ,baʊnd) *adj.* confined to one place by heavy falls or drifts of snow; snowed-in.

snow bunting *n.* a bunting of northern and arctic regions, having a white plumage with dark markings on the wings, back, and tail.

snowcap ('snəʊ,kæp) *n.* a cap of snow, as on top of a mountain. —'**snow,capped** *adj.*

snowdrift ('snəʊ,drɪft) *n.* a bank of deep snow driven together by the wind.

snowdrop ('snəʊ,drɒp) *n.* an amaryllidaceous plant

THESAURUS

snigger giggle, laugh, smirk, sneer, snicker, titter

snip *v.* **1.** clip, crop, cut, nick, nip off, notch, shave, trim ~*n.* **2.** bit, clipping, fragment, piece, scrap, shred, snippet **3.** *Inf.* bargain, giveaway, good buy

snippet fragment, part, particle, piece, scrap, shred, snatch

snivel blubber, cry, girn (*Dialect*), gripe (*Inf.*), grizzle (*Inf.*), mewl, moan, sniffle, snuffle, weep, whimper, whine, whinge (*Inf.*)

snobbery arrogance, condescension, pretension, pride, side (*Brit. sl.*), snobbishness, snootiness (*Inf.*), uppishness (*Brit. inf.*)

snobbish arrogant, condescending, high and mighty (*Inf.*), high-hat (*Inf., chiefly U.S.*), hoity-toity (*Inf.*), patronizing, pretentious, snooty (*Inf.*), stuck-up (*Inf.*), superior, toffee-nosed (*Sl.*), uppish (*Brit. inf.*)

snoop interfere, poke one's nose in (*Inf.*), pry, spy

snooper busybody, meddler, nosy parker (*Inf.*), Paul Pry, pry, snoop (*Inf.*), stickybeak (*Aust. inf.*)

snooze 1. *v.* catnap, doze, drop off (*Inf.*), drowse, kip (*Brit. sl.*), nap, nod off (*Inf.*), take forty winks (*Inf.*) **2.** *n.* catnap, doze, forty winks (*Inf.*), kip (*Brit. sl.*), nap, siesta

having drooping white bell-shaped flowers that bloom in early spring.

snowfall ('snəʊˌfɔːl) n. **1.** a fall of snow. **2.** Meteorol. the amount of snow received in a specified place and time.

snow fence n. a lath and wire fence put up in winter beside windy roads to prevent snowdrifts.

snowflake ('snəʊˌfleɪk) n. **1.** one of the mass of small thin delicate arrangements of ice crystals that fall as snow. **2.** any of various European amaryllidaceous plants that have white nodding bell-shaped flowers.

snow goose n. a North American goose, having a white plumage with black wing tips.

snow lily n. Canad. another name for **dogtooth violet.**

snow line n. the altitudinal or latitudinal limit of permanent snow.

snowman ('snəʊˌmæn) n., pl. **-men.** a figure resembling a man, made of packed snow.

snowmobile ('snəʊməˌbiːl) n. a motor vehicle for travelling on snow, esp. one with caterpillar tracks and front skis.

snowplough ('snəʊˌplaʊ) n. an implement or vehicle for clearing away snow.

snowshoe ('snəʊˌʃuː) n. **1.** a device to facilitate walking on snow, esp. a racket-shaped frame with a network of thongs stretched across it. ~vb. **shoeing, shoed. 2.** (intr.) to walk or go using snowshoes. —'**snow,shoer** n.

snowstorm ('snəʊˌstɔːm) n. a storm with heavy snow.

SNP abbrev. for Scottish National Party.

snub (snʌb) vb. **snubbing, snubbed.** (tr.) **1.** to insult (someone) deliberately. **2.** to stop or check the motion of (a boat, horse, etc.) by taking turns of a rope around a post. ~n. **3.** a deliberately insulting act or remark. **4.** Naut. an elastic shock absorber attached to a mooring line. ~adj. **5.** short and blunt. See also **snub-nosed.** —'**snubber** n. —'**snubbingly** adv. —'**snubby** adj.

snub-nosed adj. **1.** having a short turned-up nose. **2.** (of a pistol) having an extremely short barrel.

snuff¹ (snʌf) vb. **1.** (tr.) to inhale through the nose. **2.** (when intr., often foll. by at) (esp. of an animal) to examine by sniffing. ~n. **3.** an act or the sound of snuffing. —'**snuffer** n.

snuff² (snʌf) n. **1.** finely powdered tobacco, esp. for sniffing up the nostrils. **2.** a small amount of this. **3. up to snuff.** Inf. **a.** in good health or in good condition. **b.** Chiefly Brit. not easily deceived. ~vb. **4.** (intr.) to use or inhale snuff. —'**snuffer** n. —'**snuffy** adj.

snuff³ (snʌf) vb. (tr.) **1.** (often foll. by out) to extinguish (a light from a candle). **2.** to cut off the charred part of (the wick of a candle, etc.). **3.** (usually foll. by out) Inf. to put an end to. **4. snuff it.** Brit. inf. to die. ~n. **5.** the burned portion of the wick of a candle.

snuffbox ('snʌfˌbɒks) n. a container, often of elaborate ornamental design, for holding small quantities of snuff.

snuffer ('snʌfə) n. **1.** a cone-shaped implement for extinguishing candles. **2.** (pl.) an instrument resembling a pair of scissors for trimming the wick or extinguishing the flame of a candle. **3.** Rare. a person who takes snuff.

snuffle ('snʌfəl) vb. **1.** (intr.) to breathe noisily or with difficulty. **2.** to say or speak in a nasal tone. **3.** (intr.) to snivel. ~n. **4.** an act or the sound of snuffling. **5.** a nasal voice. **6. the snuffles.** a condition characterized by snuffling. —'**snuffly** adj.

snug (snʌg) adj. **snugger, snuggest. 1.** comfortably warm and well-protected; cosy: the children were snug in bed. **2.** small but comfortable: a snug cottage. **3.** well-ordered; compact: a snug boat. **4.** sheltered and secure: a snug anchorage. **5.** fitting closely and comfortably. **6.** offering safe concealment. ~n. **7.** (in Britain and Ireland) one of the bars in certain pubs, offering intimate seating for only a few persons. ~vb. **snugging, snugged. 8.** to make or become comfortable and warm. —'**snugly** adv. —'**snugness** n.

snuggery ('snʌgərɪ) n., pl. **-geries. 1.** a cosy and comfortable place or room. **2.** another name for **snug** (sense 7).

snuggle ('snʌgəl) vb. **1.** (usually intr.; usually foll. by down, up, or together) to nestle into or draw close to (somebody or something) for warmth or from affection. ~n. **2.** the act of snuggling.

so¹ (səʊ) adv. **1.** (foll. by an adjective or adverb and a correlative clause often introduced by that) to such an extent: the river is so dirty that it smells. **2.** (used with a negative; it replaces the first as in an equative comparison) to the same extent as: she is not so old as you. **3.** (intensifier): it's so lovely. **4.** in the state or manner expressed or implied: they're happy and will remain so. **5.** (not used with a negative; foll. by an auxiliary verb or do, have, or be used as main verbs) also: I can speak Spanish and so can you. **6.** Arch. provided that. **7. and so on** or **forth.** and continuing similarly. **8. just so.** arranged with precision. **9. or so.** approximately: fifty or so people came to see me. **10. quite so.** I agree. **11. so be it.** used to express agreement or resignation. **12. so much. a.** a certain degree or amount (of). **b.** a lot (of): it's just so much nonsense. **13. so much for. a.** no more can or need be said about. **b.** used to express contempt for something that has failed. ~conj. (subordinating; often foll. by that) **14.** in order (that): to die so that you might live. **15.** with the consequence (that): he was late home, so that there was trouble. **16. so as.** (takes an infinitive) in order (to): to diet so as to lose weight. ~sentence connector. **17.** in consequence: she wasn't needed, so she left. **18.** thereupon: and so we ended up in France. **19. so what!** Inf. what importance does that have? ~pron. **20.** used to substitute for a clause or sentence, which may be understood: you'll stop because I said so. ~adj. **21.** (used with is, was, etc.) factual: it can't be so. ~interj. **22.** an exclamation of surprise, etc.

▷ **Usage.** Careful writers of formal English consider it poor style to use so as a conjunction, to indicate either purpose (he did it so he could feel happier) or result (he could not do it so he did not try). In the former case in order to should be used instead and in the latter case and so or and therefore would be more acceptable.

so² (səʊ) n. Music. a variant spelling of **soh.**

So. abbrev. for south(ern).

soak (səʊk) vb. **1.** to make, become, or be thoroughly wet or saturated, esp. by immersion in a liquid. **2.** (when intr., usually foll. by in or into) (of a liquid) to penetrate or permeate. **3.** (tr.; usually foll. by in or up) (of a permeable solid) to take in (a liquid) by absorption: the earth soaks up rainwater. **4.** (tr.; foll. by out or out of) to remove by immersion in a liquid: she soaked the stains out of the dress. **5.** Inf. to drink excessively or make or become drunk. **6.** (tr.) Sl. to overcharge. ~n. **7.** the act of immersing in a liquid or the period of immersion. **8.** the liquid in which something may be soaked. **9.** Austral. a natural depression holding rainwater, esp. just beneath the surface of the ground. **10.** Sl. a person who drinks to excess. —'**soaker** n. —'**soakingly** adv.

soakaway ('səʊkəˌweɪ) n. a pit filled with rubble, etc., into which waste water drains.

so-and-so n., pl. **so-and-sos.** Inf. **1.** a person whose name is forgotten or ignored. **2.** Euphemistic. a person or thing regarded as unpleasant: which so-and-so broke my razor?

soap (səʊp) n. **1.** a cleaning agent made by reacting animal or vegetable fats or oils with potassium or sodium hydroxide. Soaps act by emulsifying grease and lowering the surface tension of water, so that it more readily penetrates open materials such as textiles. **2.** any metallic salt of a fatty acid, such as palmitic or stearic acid. **3.** Sl. flattery or persuasive talk (esp. in **soft soap**). **4.** no **soap.** Sl. not possible. ~vb. **5.** (tr.) to apply soap to. **6.** (tr.; often foll. by up) Sl. to flatter. —'**soapless** adj. —'**soap,like** adj.

soapbox ('səʊpˌbɒks) n. **1.** a box or crate for packing soap. **2.** a crate used as a platform for speech-making. **3.** a child's home-made racing cart.

THESAURUS

snub 1. v. cold-shoulder, cut (Inf.), cut dead (Inf.), give (someone) the brush-off (Sl.), give (someone) the cold shoulder, humble, humiliate, mortify, rebuff, shame, slight **2.** n. affront, brush-off (Sl.), humiliation, insult, put-down, slap in the face

snug 1. comfortable, comfy (Inf.), cosy, homely, intimate, sheltered, warm **2.** close, compact, neat, trim

snuggle cuddle, nestle, nuzzle

soak v. **1.** bathe, damp, drench, immerse, infuse, marinate (Cookery), moisten, penetrate, permeate, saturate, steep, wet **2.** With **up** absorb, assimilate, drink in, take up or in

soaking drenched, dripping, drookit (Scot.), saturated, soaked, soaked to the skin, sodden, sopping, streaming, waterlogged, wet through, wringing wet

soap opera *n.* a serialized drama, usually dealing with domestic themes, broadcast on radio or television.

soapstone ('səʊp,stəʊn) *n.* a massive compact variety of talc, used for making tabletops, hearths, ornaments, etc. Also called: **steatite.**

soapsuds ('səʊp,sʌdz) *pl. n.* foam or lather made from soap. —'**soap,sudsy** *adj.*

soapy ('səʊpɪ) *adj.* **soapier, soapiest.** **1.** containing or covered with soap: *soapy water.* **2.** resembling or characteristic of soap. **3.** *Sl.* flattering. —'**soapily** *adv.* —'**soapiness** *n.*

soar (sɔː) *vb.* (*intr.*) **1.** to rise or fly upwards into the air. **2.** (of a bird, aircraft, etc.) to glide while maintaining altitude by the use of ascending air currents. **3.** to rise or increase in volume, size, etc.: *soaring prices.* —'**soarer** *n.* —'**soaringly** *adv.*

sob (sɒb) *vb.* **sobbing, sobbed.** **1.** (*intr.*) to weep with convulsive gasps. **2.** (*tr.*) to utter with sobs. **3.** to cause (oneself) to be in a specified state by sobbing: *to sob oneself to sleep.* ~*n.* **4.** a convulsive gasp made in weeping. —'**sobber** *n.* —'**sobbingly** *adv.*

sober ('səʊbə) *adj.* **1.** not drunk. **2.** not given to excessive indulgence in drink or any other activity. **3.** sedate and rational: *a sober attitude to a problem.* **4.** (of colours) plain and dull or subdued. **5.** free from exaggeration or speculation: *he told us the sober truth.* ~*vb.* **6.** (usually foll. by *up*) to make or become less intoxicated. —'**soberingly** *adv.* —'**soberly** *adv.*

sobriety (səʊ'braɪɪtɪ) *n.* **1.** the state or quality of being sober. **2.** the quality of refraining from excess. **3.** the quality of being serious or sedate.

sobriquet *or* **soubriquet** ('səʊbrɪ,keɪ) *n.* a humorous epithet, assumed name, or nickname.

sob story *n.* a tale of personal distress intended to arouse sympathy.

Soc. *or* **soc.** *abbrev. for:* **1.** socialist. **2.** society.

so-called *adj.* **a.** (*prenominal*) designated or styled by the name or word mentioned, esp. (in the speaker's opinion) incorrectly: *a so-called genius.* **b.** (also used parenthetically after a noun): *these experts, so-called, are no help.*

soccer ('sɒkə) *n.* **a.** a game in which two teams of eleven players try to kick or head a ball into their opponents' goal, only the goalkeeper on either side being allowed to touch the ball with his hands and arms, except in the case of throw-ins. **b.** (*as modifier*): *a soccer player.* Also called: **Association Football.**

sociable ('səʊʃəbəl) *adj.* **1.** friendly or companionable. **2.** (of an occasion) providing the opportunity for friendliness and conviviality. ~*n.* **3.** *Chiefly U.S.* a social. **4.** a type of carriage with two seats facing each other. —,**socia'bility** *n.* —'**sociably** *adv.*

social ('səʊʃəl) *adj.* **1.** living or preferring to live in a community rather than alone. **2.** denoting or relating to human society or any of its subdivisions. **3.** of or characteristic of the behaviour and interaction of persons forming groups. **4.** relating to or having the purpose of promoting companionship, communal activities, etc.: *a social club.* **5.** relating to or engaged in social services: *a social worker.* **6.** relating to or considered appropriate to a certain class of society. **7.** (esp. of certain species of insects) living together in organized colonies: *social bees.* **8.** (of plant species) growing in clumps. ~*n.* **9.** an informal gathering, esp. of an organized group. —'**socially** *adv.*

social anthropology *n.* the branch of anthropology that deals with cultural and social phenomena such as kinship systems or beliefs.

social contract *or* **compact** *n.* (in the theories of Rousseau and others) an agreement, entered into by individuals, that results in the formation of the state, the prime motive being the desire for protection, which entails the surrender of some personal liberties.

Social Credit *n.* **1.** (esp. in Canada) a right-wing Populist political party, movement, or doctrine. **2. Social Credit League.** (in New Zealand) a middle-of-the-road political party, in favour of free enterprise. **3. Social Credit Rally.** (in Canada) a political party formed in 1963 from a splinter group of the Social Credit Party.

social democrat *n.* any socialist who believes in the gradual transformation of capitalism into democratic socialism.

Social Insurance Number *n. Canad.* an identification number issued to individuals by the government in connection with income tax and social insurance.

socialism ('səʊʃə,lɪzəm) *n.* **1.** an economic theory or system in which the means of production, distribution, and exchange are owned by the community collectively, usually through the state. Cf. **capitalism. 2.** any of various social or political theories or movements in which the common welfare is to be achieved through the establishment of a socialist economic system. **3.** (in Marxist theory) a transitional stage in the development of a society from capitalism to communism: characterized by the distribution of income according to work rather than need.

socialite ('səʊʃə,laɪt) *n.* a person who is or seeks to be prominent in fashionable society.

socialize *or* **-lise** ('səʊʃə,laɪz) *vb.* **1.** (*intr.*) to behave in a friendly or sociable manner. **2.** (*tr.*) to prepare for life in society. **3.** (*tr.*) *Chiefly U.S.* to alter or create so as to be in accordance with socialist principles.

social science *n.* the study of society and of the relationship of individual members within society, including economics, history, political science, psychology, anthropology, and sociology. —**social scientist** *n.*

social security *n.* **1.** public provision for the economic welfare of the aged, unemployed, etc., esp. through pensions and other monetary assistance. **2.** (*often cap.*) a government programme designed to provide such assistance.

social services *pl. n.* welfare activities organized by the state and carried out by trained personnel.

social studies *n.* (*functioning as sing.*) the study of how people live and organize themselves in society, embracing geography, history, economics, and other subjects.

social work *n.* any of various social services designed to alleviate the conditions of the poor and aged and to increase the welfare of children. —**social worker** *n.*

society (sə'saɪətɪ) *n., pl.* **-ties. 1.** the totality of social relationships among organized groups of human beings or animals. **2.** a system of human organizations generating distinctive cultural patterns and institutions. **3.** such a system with reference to its mode of social and economic organization or its dominant class: *middle-class society.* **4.** those with whom one has companionship. **5.** an organized group of people associated for some specific purpose or on account of some common interest: *a learned society.* **6. a.** the privileged class of people in a community, esp. as considered superior or fashionable. **b.** (*as modifier*): *a society woman.* **7.** the social life and intercourse of such people: *to enter society.* **8.** companionship: *I enjoy her society.* **9.** *Ecology.* a small community of plants within a larger association. —**so'cietal** *adj.*

THESAURUS

soar 1. ascend, fly, mount, rise, tower, wing 2. climb, escalate, rise, rocket, shoot up

sob *v.* bawl, blubber, boohoo, cry, greet (*Dialect*), howl, shed tears, snivel, weep

sober *adj.* 1. abstemious, abstinent, moderate, on the wagon (*Inf.*), temperate 2. calm, clear-headed, cold, composed, cool, dispassionate, grave, level-headed, lucid, peaceful, practical, rational, realistic, reasonable, sedate, serene, serious, solemn, sound, staid, steady, unexcited, unruffled 3. dark, drab, plain, quiet, severe, sombre, subdued ~*v.* 4. *Usually with* **up** bring (someone) back to earth, calm down, clear one's head, come *or* bring to one's senses, give (someone) pause

for thought, make (someone) stop and think

sobriety 1. abstemiousness, abstinence, moderation, nonindulgence, self-restraint, soberness, temperance 2. calmness, composure, coolness, gravity, level-headedness, reasonableness, restraint, sedateness, seriousness, solemnity, staidness, steadiness

so-called *soi-disant*, alleged, ostensible, pretended, professed, self-styled, supposed

sociability affability, companionability, congeniality, conviviality, cordiality, friendliness, gregariousness, neighbourliness

sociable accessible, affable, approachable, companionable, conversable, convivial, cordial, familiar, friendly, genial, gregarious,

neighbourly, outgoing, social, warm

social *adj.* 1. collective, common, communal, community, general, group, organized, public, societal 2. companionable, friendly, gregarious, neighbourly, sociable ~*n.* 3. do (*Inf.*), gathering, get-together (*Inf.*)

socialize be a good mixer, entertain, fraternize, get about *or* around, get together, go out, mix

society 1. civilization, culture, humanity, mankind, people, population, social order, the community, the general public, the public, the world at large 2. camaraderie, companionship, company, fellowship, friendship 3. association, brotherhood, circle, club, cor-

Society of Friends *n.* the official name for the **Quakers.**

Society of Jesus *n.* the religious order of the Jesuits, founded by Ignatius Loyola.

socio- *combining form.* denoting social or society: *socioeconomic; sociopolitical; sociology.*

socioeconomic (ˌsəʊsɪəʊˌiːkəˈnɒmɪk) *adj.* of, relating to, or involving both economic and social factors. —ˌsocioˌecoˈnomically *adv.*

sociology (ˌsəʊsɪˈɒlədʒɪ) *n.* the study of the development, organization, functioning, and classification of human societies. —**sociological** (ˌsəʊsɪəˈlɒdʒɪkəl) *adj.* —ˌsociˈologist *n.*

sociopolitical (ˌsəʊsɪəʊpəˈlɪtɪkəl) *adj.* of or involving both political and social factors.

sock¹ (sɒk) *n.* **1.** a cloth covering for the foot, reaching to between the ankle and knee and worn inside a shoe. **2.** an insole put in a shoe, as to make it fit better. **3.** a light shoe worn by actors in ancient Greek and Roman comedy. **4. pull one's socks up.** *Brit. inf.* to make a determined effort, esp. in order to regain control of a situation. **5. put a sock in it.** *Brit. sl.* be quiet!

sock² (sɒk) *Sl.* ~*vb.* **1.** (*usually tr.*) to hit with force. **2. sock it to it.** *Sl.* to make a forceful impression on. ~*n.* **3.** a forceful blow.

socket (ˈsɒkɪt) *n.* **1.** a device into which an electric plug can be inserted in order to make a connection in a circuit. **2.** *Chiefly Brit.* such a device mounted on a wall and connected to the electricity supply. **3.** a part with an opening or hollow into which some other part can be fitted. **4.** *Anat.* **a.** a bony hollow into which a part or structure fits: *an eye socket.* **b.** the receptacle of a ball-and-socket joint. ~*vb.* **5.** (*tr.*) to furnish with or place into a socket.

Socratic (sɒˈkrætɪk) *adj. also* **Socratical.** **1.** of or relating to Socrates, his methods, etc. ~*n.* **2.** a person who follows the teachings of Socrates. —**Soˈcratically** *adv.*

Socratic method *n. Philosophy.* the method of instruction by question and answer used by Socrates in order to elicit from his pupils truths he considered to be implicitly known by all rational beings.

sod¹ (sɒd) *n.* **1.** a piece of grass-covered surface soil held together by the roots of the grass; turf. **2.** *Poetic.* the ground. ~*vb.* **sodding, sodded.** **3.** (*tr.*) to cover with sods.

sod² (sɒd) *n. Sl., chiefly Brit.* **1.** a person considered to be obnoxious. **2.** a jocular word for a person. ~*interj.* **3.** a strong exclamation of annoyance. —ˈ**sodding** *adj.*

soda (ˈsəʊdə) *n.* **1.** any of a number of simple inorganic compounds of sodium, such as sodium carbonate (**washing soda**), sodium bicarbonate (**baking soda**), and sodium hydroxide (**caustic soda**). **2.** See **soda water.** **3.** *U.S.* a fizzy drink.

soda bread *n.* a doughy bread leavened with sodium bicarbonate combined with milk and cream of tartar.

soda fountain *n. U.S.* **1.** a counter that serves drinks, snacks, etc. **2.** an apparatus dispensing soda water.

sodality (səʊˈdælɪtɪ) *n., pl.* **-ties.** **1.** *R.C. Church.* a religious society. **2.** fellowship.

soda siphon *n.* a sealed bottle containing and dispensing soda water. The water is forced up a tube reaching to the bottom of the bottle by the pressure of gas above the water.

soda water *n.* an effervescent beverage made by charging water with carbon dioxide under pressure. Sometimes shortened to **soda.**

sodden (ˈsɒdən) *adj.* **1.** completely saturated. **2. a.** dulled, esp. by excessive drinking. **b.** (*in combination*): *a drink-sodden mind.* **3.** doughy, as bread is when improperly cooked. ~*vb.* **4.** to make or become sodden.

—ˈ**soddenness** *n.*

sodium (ˈsəʊdɪəm) *n.* **a.** a very reactive soft silvery-white element of the alkali metal group occurring principally in common salt, Chile saltpetre, and cryolite. It is used in the production of chemicals, in metallurgy, and, alloyed with potassium, as a cooling medium in nuclear reactors. Symbol: Na; atomic no.: 11; atomic wt.: 22.99. **b.** (*as modifier*): *sodium light.*

sodium bicarbonate *n.* a white crystalline soluble compound used in effervescent drinks, baking powders, fire-extinguishers, and in medicine as an antacid; sodium hydrogen carbonate. Formula: $NaHCO_3$. Also called: **bicarbonate of soda, baking soda.**

sodium carbonate *n.* a colourless or white odourless soluble crystalline compound used in the manufacture of glass, ceramics, soap, and paper, and as a cleansing agent. Formula: Na_2CO_3.

sodium chloride *n.* common table salt; a soluble colourless crystalline compound widely used as a seasoning and preservative for food and in the manufacture of chemicals, glass, and soap. Formula: NaCl. Also called: **salt.**

Sodom (ˈsɒdəm) *n.* **1.** *Old Testament.* a city destroyed by God for its wickedness that, with Gomorrah, traditionally typifies depravity (Genesis 19:24). **2.** this city as representing homosexuality. **3.** any place notorious for depravity.

sodomite (ˈsɒdəˌmaɪt) *n.* a person who practises sodomy.

sodomy (ˈsɒdəmɪ) *n.* anal intercourse committed by a man with another man or a woman.

soever (səʊˈɛvə) *adv.* in any way at all: used to emphasize or make less precise a word or phrase, usually in combination with *what, where, when, how,* etc., or else separated by intervening words. Cf. **whatsoever.**

sofa (ˈsəʊfə) *n.* an upholstered seat with back and arms for two or more people.

soft (sɒft) *adj.* **1.** easy to dent, work, or cut without shattering; malleable. **2.** not hard; giving little or no resistance to pressure or weight. **3.** fine, light, smooth, or fluffy to the touch. **4.** gentle; tranquil. **5.** (of music, sounds, etc.) low and pleasing. **6.** (of light, colour, etc.) not excessively bright or harsh. **7.** (of a breeze, climate, etc.) temperate, mild, or pleasant. **8.** slightly blurred; not sharply outlined: *soft focus.* **9.** (of a diet) consisting of easily digestible foods. **10.** kind or lenient, often excessively so. **11.** easy to influence or impose upon. **12.** *Inf.* feeble or silly; simple (often in **soft in the head**). **13.** unable to endure hardship, esp. through pampering. **14.** physically out of condition; flabby: *soft muscles.* **15.** loving; tender: *soft words.* **16.** *Inf.* requiring little exertion; easy: *a soft job.* **17.** *Chem.* (of water) relatively free of mineral salts and therefore easily able to make soap lather. **18.** (of a drug such as cannabis) nonaddictive. **19.** *Phonetics.* (not in technical usage) denoting the consonants *c* and *g* in English when they are pronounced as palatal or alveolar fricatives or affricates (s, dʒ, ʃ, ð, tʃ) before *e* and *i*, rather than as velar stops (k, g). **20.** *Finance, chiefly U.S.* (of prices, a market, etc.) unstable and tending to decline. **21.** (of money or currency) **a.** relatively unstable in exchange value. **b.** in paper rather than coin. **22.** (of radiation, such as x-rays and ultraviolet radiation) having low energy and not capable of deep penetration of materials. **23. soft on or about. a.** gentle, sympathetic, or lenient towards. **b.** feeling affection or infatuation for. ~*adv.* **24.** in a soft manner: *to speak soft.* ~*n.* **25.** a soft object, part, or piece. **26.** *Inf.* See **softy.** ~*interj. Arch.* **27.** quiet! **28.** wait! —ˈ**softly** *adv.* —ˈ**softness** *n.*

soft ball *n. Cookery.* a term used for sugar syrup boiled to a consistency at which it may be rubbed into

---

═══ THESAURUS ═══

poration, fellowship, fraternity, group, guild, institute, league, organization, sisterhood, union **4.** beau monde, elite, gentry, *haut monde*, high society, polite society, the country set, the nobs (*Sl.*), the smart set, the swells (*Inf.*), the toffs (*Brit. sl.*), the top drawer, upper classes, upper crust (*Inf.*)

sodden boggy, drenched, drookit (*Scot.*), marshy, miry, saturated, soaked, soggy, sopping, waterlogged

soft 1. creamy, cushioned, cushiony, doughy, elastic, gelatinous, pulpy, quaggy,

spongy, squashy, swampy, yielding **2.** bendable, ductile (*of metals*), elastic, flexible, impressible, malleable, mouldable, plastic, pliable, supple **3.** downy, feathery, fleecy, flowing, fluid, furry, like a baby's bottom (*Inf.*), rounded, silky, smooth, velvety **4.** balmy, bland, caressing, delicate, diffuse, dim, dimmed, dulcet, faint, gentle, light, low, mellifluous, mellow, melodious, mild, murmured, muted, pale, pastel, pleasing, quiet, restful, shaded, soft-toned, soothing, subdued, sweet, temperate, twilight, understated, whispered

5. compassionate, gentle, kind, pitying, sensitive, sentimental, sympathetic, tender, tenderhearted **6.** easy-going, indulgent, lax, lenient, liberal, overindulgent, permissive, spineless, weak **7.** *Inf.* comfortable, cushy (*Sl.*), easy, undemanding **8.** effeminate, flabby, flaccid, limp, namby-pamby, out of condition, out of training, overindulged, pampered, podgy, weak **9.** *Inf.* a bit lacking (*Inf.*), daft (*Inf.*), feeble-minded, foolish, silly, simple, soft in the head (*Inf.*), soppy (*Brit. inf.*)

balls after dipping in cold water.

soft-boiled *adj.* (of an egg) boiled for a short time so that the yolk is still soft.

soft coal *n.* another name for **bituminous coal.**

soft drink *n.* a nonalcoholic drink.

soften ('sɒfən) *vb.* to make or become soft or softer. —'**softener** *n.*

soft furnishings *pl. n. Brit.* curtains, hangings, rugs, etc.

softhearted (‚sɒft'hɑːtɪd) *adj.* easily moved to pity. —‚**soft'heartedly** *adv.* —‚**soft'heartedness** *n.*

soft palate *n.* the posterior fleshy portion of the roof of the mouth.

soft-pedal *vb.* **-alling, -alled** *or U.S.* **-aling, -aled.** (*tr.*) **1.** to mute the tone of (a piano) by depressing the soft pedal. **2.** *Inf.* to make (something, esp. something unpleasant) less obvious by deliberately failing to emphasize or allude to it. ~*n.* **soft pedal. 3.** a foot-operated lever on a piano, the left one of two, that either moves the whole action closer to the strings so that the hammers strike with less force or causes fewer of the strings to sound.

soft sell *n. Chiefly U.S.* a method of selling based on indirect suggestion or inducement.

soft soap *n.* **1.** *Med.* Also called: **green soap.** a soft or liquid alkaline soap used in treating certain skin disorders. **2.** *Inf.* flattering, persuasive, or cajoling talk. ~*vb.* **soft-soap. 3.** to use such talk on (a person).

soft-spoken *adj.* **1.** speaking or said with a soft gentle voice. **2.** able to persuade or impress by glibness of tongue.

soft spot *n.* a sentimental fondness (esp. in **have a soft spot for**).

soft touch *n. Inf.* a person easily persuaded or imposed on, esp. to lend money.

software ('sɒft‚wɛə) *n. Computers.* the programs that can be used with a particular computer system, esp. those supplied by the manufacturers. Cf. **hardware** (sense 2).

softwood ('sɒft‚wʊd) *n.* **1.** the open-grained wood of any of numerous coniferous trees, such as pine and cedar. **2.** any tree yielding this wood.

softy *or* **softie** ('sɒftɪ) *n., pl.* **softies.** *Inf.* a person who is sentimental, weakly foolish, or lacking in physical endurance.

SOGAT ('səʊgæt) *n.* (in Britain) *acronym for* Society of Graphical and Allied Trades.

soggy ('sɒgɪ) *adj.* **-gier, -giest. 1.** soaked with liquid. **2.** (of bread, pastry, etc.) moist and heavy. **3.** *Inf.* lacking in spirit or positiveness. —'**soggily** *adv.* —'**sogginess** *n.*

soh *or* **so** (səʊ) *n. Music.* (in tonic sol-fa) the name used for the fifth note or dominant of any scale.

soigné *or* (*fem.*) **soignée** ('swɑːnjeɪ) *adj.* well-groomed; elegant.

soil[1] (sɔɪl) *n.* **1.** the top layer of the land surface of the earth that is composed of disintegrated rock particles, humus, water, and air. **2.** a type of this material having specific characteristics: *loamy soil.* **3.** land, country, or region: *one's native soil.* **4. the soil.** life and work on a farm; land: *he belonged to the soil.* **5.** any place or thing encouraging growth or development.

soil[2] (sɔɪl) *vb.* **1.** to make or become dirty or stained. **2.** (*tr.*) to pollute with sin or disgrace; sully; defile. ~*n.* **3.** the state or result of soiling. **4.** refuse, manure, or excrement.

soil pipe *n.* a pipe that conveys sewage or waste water from a toilet, etc., to a soil drain or sewer.

soiree ('swɑːreɪ) *n.* an evening party or gathering, usually at a private house, esp. where guests listen to, play, or dance to music.

sojourn ('sɒdʒɜːn, 'sʌdʒ-) *n.* **1.** a temporary stay. ~*vb.*

2. (*intr.*) to stay or reside temporarily. —'**sojourner** *n.*

sol[1] (sɒl) *n. Music.* another name for **soh.**

sol[2] (sɒl) *n.* a colloid that has a continuous liquid phase, esp. one in which a solid is suspended in a liquid.

sola *Latin.* ('səʊlə) *adj.* the feminine form of **solus.**

solace ('sɒlɪs) *n.* **1.** comfort in misery, disappointment, etc. **2.** something that gives comfort or consolation. ~*vb.* (*tr.*) **3.** to give comfort or cheer to (a person) in time of sorrow, distress, etc. **4.** to alleviate (sorrow, misery, etc.). —'**solacer** *n.*

solan *or* **solan goose** ('səʊlən) *n.* an archaic name for the gannet.

solar ('səʊlə) *adj.* **1.** of or relating to the sun. **2.** operating by or utilizing the energy of the sun: *solar cell.* **3.** *Astron.* determined from the motion of the earth relative to the sun: *solar year.* **4.** *Astrol.* subject to the influence of the sun.

solarium (səʊ'lɛərɪəm) *n., pl.* **-laria** (-'lɛərɪə) *or* **-lariums. 1.** a room built largely of glass to afford exposure to the sun. **2.** a bed equipped with ultraviolet lights used for acquiring an artificial suntan. **3.** an establishment offering such facilities.

solar plexus *n.* **1.** *Anat.* the network of nerves situated behind the stomach that supply the abdominal organs. **2.** (*not in technical usage*) the part of the stomach beneath the diaphragm; pit of the stomach.

solar system *n.* the system containing the sun and the bodies held in its gravitational field, including the planets (Mercury, Venus, earth, Mars, Jupiter, Saturn, Uranus, Neptune, Pluto), the asteroids, and comets.

sold (səʊld) *vb.* **1.** the past tense or past participle of **sell.** ~*adj.* **2. sold on.** *Sl.* uncritically attached to or enthusiastic about.

solder ('sɒldə; *U.S.* 'sɒdər) *n.* **1.** an alloy for joining two metal surfaces by melting the alloy so that it forms a thin layer between the surfaces. **2.** something that joins things together firmly; a bond. ~*vb.* **3.** to join or mend or be joined or mended with or as if with solder. —'**solderable** *adj.* —'**solderer** *n.*

soldering iron *n.* a hand tool consisting of a handle fixed to an iron or copper tip that is heated and used to melt and apply solder.

soldier ('səʊldʒə) *n.* **1. a.** a person who serves in an army. **b.** Also called: **common soldier.** a noncommissioned member of an army as opposed to a commissioned officer. **2.** a man with military skill or experience, but no longer serving in an army: *an old soldier.* **3.** a person who works diligently for a cause. **4.** *Zool.* an individual in a colony of social insects, esp. ants, that has powerful jaws adapted for defending the colony, crushing food, etc. ~*vb.* (*intr.*) **5.** to serve as a soldier. **6.** to malinger or shirk. —'**soldierly** *adj.*

soldier of fortune *n.* a man who seeks money or adventure as a soldier; mercenary.

soldier on *vb.* (*intr., adv.*) to persist in one's efforts in spite of difficulties, pressure, etc.

sole[1] (səʊl) *adj.* **1.** (*prenominal*) being the only one; only. **2.** (*prenominal*) of or relating to one individual or group and no other: *sole rights.* **3.** *Law.* having no wife or husband. **4.** an archaic word for **solitary.** —'**soleness** *n.*

sole[2] (səʊl) *n.* **1.** the underside of the foot. **2.** the underside of a shoe. **3. a.** the bottom of a furrow. **b.** the bottom of a plough. **4.** the underside of a golf club head. ~*vb.* (*tr.*) **5.** to provide (a shoe) with a sole.

sole[3] (səʊl) *n., pl.* **sole** *or* **soles.** any of various tongue-shaped flatfishes, esp. the **European sole:** most common in warm seas and highly valued as food fishes.

solecism ('sɒlɪ‚sɪzəm) *n.* **1. a.** the nonstandard use of a grammatical construction. **b.** any mistake, incongruity, or absurdity. **2.** a violation of good manners. —'**solecist** *n.* —‚**sole'cistic** *adj.* —‚**sole'cistically** *adv.*

THESAURUS

soften abate, allay, alleviate, appease, assuage, calm, cushion, diminish, ease, lessen, lighten, lower, melt, mitigate, moderate, modify, mollify, muffle, palliate, quell, relax, soothe, still, subdue, temper, tone down, turn down

soften up conciliate, disarm, melt, softsoap (*Inf.*), weaken, win over, work on

softhearted charitable, compassionate, generous, indulgent, kind, sentimental, sympathetic, tender, tenderhearted, warmhearted

soil[1] *n.* **1.** clay, dirt, dust, earth, ground, loam **2.** country, land, region, terra firma

soil[2] *v.* bedraggle, befoul, begrime, besmirch, defile, dirty, foul, maculate (*Literary*), muddy, pollute, smear, spatter, spot, stain, sully, tarnish

sojourn 1. *n.* rest, stay, stop, stopover, visit **2.** *v.* abide, dwell, lodge, reside, rest, stay, stop, tarry

solace 1. *n.* alleviation, assuagement, comfort, consolation, relief **2.** *v.* allay, alleviate, comfort, console, mitigate, soften, soothe

soldier enlisted man (*U.S.*), fighter, GI (*U.S. inf.*), man-at-arms, military man, redcoat, serviceman, squaddy (*Brit. inf.*), Tommy (*Brit.*), trooper, warrior

sole alone, exclusive, individual, one, one

solely (ˈsəʊllɪ) adv. 1. only; completely. 2. without others; singly; alone. 3. for one thing only.

solemn (ˈsɒləm) adj. 1. characterized or marked by seriousness or sincerity: a solemn vow. 2. characterized by pomp, ceremony, or formality. 3. serious, glum, or pompous. 4. inspiring awe: a solemn occasion. 5. performed with religious ceremony. 6. gloomy or sombre: solemn colours. —**solemnify** (səˈlɛmnɪˌfaɪ) vb. —**solemnly** adv. —**solemnness** or **solemness** n.

solemnity (səˈlɛmnɪtɪ) n., pl. -**ties**. 1. the state or quality of being solemn. 2. (often pl.) solemn ceremony, observance, etc. 3. Law. a formality necessary to validate a deed, contract, etc.

solemnize or -**ise** (ˈsɒləmˌnaɪz) vb. (tr.) 1. to celebrate or observe with rites or formal ceremonies, as a religious occasion. 2. to celebrate or perform the ceremony of (marriage). 3. to make solemn or serious. 4. to perform or hold (ceremonies, etc.) in due manner. —ˌsolemniˈzation or -iˈsation n. —ˈsolemˌnizer or -iser n.

solenoid (ˈsəʊlɪˌnɔɪd) n. 1. a coil of wire, usually cylindrical, in which a magnetic field is set up by passing a current through it. 2. a coil of wire, partially surrounding an iron core, that is made to move inside the coil by the magnetic field set up by a current: used to convert electrical to mechanical energy, as in the operation of a switch. —ˌsoleˈnoidal adj.

sol-fa (ˈsɒlˈfɑː) n. 1. short for **tonic sol-fa**. ~vb. -**faing**, -**faed**. 2. U.S. to use tonic sol-fa syllables in singing (a tune).

solicit (səˈlɪsɪt) vb. 1. (when intr., foll. by for) to make a request, application, or entreaty to (a person for business, support, etc.). 2. to accost (a person) with an offer of sexual relations in return for money. 3. to provoke or incite (a person) to do something wrong or illegal. —soˌliciˈtation n.

solicitor (səˈlɪsɪtə) n. 1. (in Britain) a lawyer who advises clients on matters of law, draws up legal documents, prepares cases for barristers, etc. 2. (in the U.S.) an officer responsible for the legal affairs of a town, city, etc. 3. a person who solicits. —soˈlicitorˌship n.

Solicitor General n., pl. **Solicitors General.** (in Britain) the law officer of the Crown ranking next to the Attorney General (in Scotland to the Lord Advocate) and acting as his assistant.

solicitous (səˈlɪsɪtəs) adj. 1. showing consideration, concern, attention, etc. 2. keenly anxious or willing; eager. —soˈlicitousness n.

solicitude (səˈlɪsɪˌtjuːd) n. 1. the state or quality of being solicitous. 2. (often pl.) something that causes anxiety or concern. 3. anxiety or concern.

solid (ˈsɒlɪd) adj. 1. of, concerned with, or being a substance in a physical state in which the force of attraction between its molecules or atoms is large enough to hold them in fixed positions and cause the substance to resist changes in size and shape. 2. consisting of matter all through. 3. of the same substance all through: solid rock. 4. sound; proved or provable: solid facts. 5. reliable or sensible; upstanding: a solid citizen. 6. firm, strong, compact, or substantial: a solid table; solid ground. 7. (of a meal or food) substantial. 8. (often postpositive) without interruption or respite: solid bombardment. 9. financially sound or solvent: a solid institution. 10. strongly linked or consolidated: a solid relation-

ship. 11. Geom. having three dimensions. 12. (of a word composed of two or more elements) written or printed as a single word without a hyphen. 13. Geom. of or relating to three-dimensional bodies or objects. 14. Printing. with no space or leads between lines of type. 15. **solid for.** unanimously in favour of. 16. (of a writer, work, etc.) adequate; sensible. 17. of or having a single uniform colour or tone. 18. Austral. sl. excessively severe or unreasonable. ~n. 19. Geom. **a.** a closed surface in three-dimensional space. **b.** such a surface together with the volume enclosed by it. 20. a solid substance, such as wood, iron, or diamond. —**solidity** (səˈlɪdɪtɪ) n. —**solidly** adv. —**solidness** n.

solidarity (ˌsɒlɪˈdærɪtɪ) n., pl. -**ties**. unity of interests, sympathies, etc., as among members of the same class.

solid geometry n. the branch of geometry concerned with solid geometric figures.

solidify (səˈlɪdɪˌfaɪ) vb. -**fying**, -**fied**. 1. to make or become solid or hard. 2. to make or become strong, united, determined, etc. —soˌlidifiˈcation n. —soˈlidiˌfier n.

solid-state n. 1. (modifier) (of an electronic component or device) consisting chiefly or exclusively of semiconductor materials or components and operating or controlled by means of their electrical properties. 2. (modifier) of, concerned with, characteristic of, or consisting of solid matter.

solidus (ˈsɒlɪdəs) n., pl. -**di** (-ˌdaɪ). 1. Also called: **diagonal, separatrix, shilling mark, slash, stroke, virgule**. a short oblique stroke used in text to separate items of information, such as days, months, and years in dates (18/7/80), alternative words (and/or), numerator from denominator in fractions (55/103), etc. 2. a gold coin of the Byzantine empire.

soliloquy (səˈlɪləkwɪ) n., pl. -**quies**. 1. the act of speaking alone or to oneself, esp. as a theatrical device. 2. a speech in a play that is spoken in soliloquy.

solipsism (ˈsɒlɪpˌsɪzəm) n. Philosophy. the theory that the self is the only thing that can be known to exist. —ˈsolipsist n., adj. —ˌsolipˈsistic adj.

solitaire (ˈsɒlɪˌtɛə, ˌsɒlɪˈtɛə) n. 1. Also called: **pegboard**. a game played by one person, esp. one involving moving and taking pegs in a pegboard with the object of being left with only one. 2. the U.S. name for **patience** (the card game). 3. a gem, esp. a diamond, set alone in a ring. 4. any of several extinct birds related to the dodo. 5. any of several dull grey North American songbirds.

solitary (ˈsɒlɪtərɪ, -trɪ) adj. 1. following or enjoying a life of solitude: a solitary disposition. 2. experienced or performed alone: a solitary walk. 3. (of a place) unfrequented. 4. (prenominal) single; sole: a solitary cloud. 5. having few companions; lonely. 6. (of animals) not living in organized colonies or large groups: solitary bees. 7. (of flowers) growing singly. ~n., pl. -**taries**. 8. a person who lives in seclusion; hermit. 9. Inf. short for **solitary confinement.** —ˈsolitarily adv. —ˈsolitariness n.

solitary confinement n. isolation imposed on a prisoner, as by confinement in a special cell.

solitude (ˈsɒlɪˌtjuːd) n. 1. the state of being solitary or secluded. 2. Poetic. a solitary place. —ˌsoliˈtudinous adj.

THESAURUS

and only, only, single, singular, solitary

solecism blunder, boo-boo (Inf.), breach of etiquette, cacology, faux pas, gaffe, gaucherie, impropriety, incongruity, indecorum, lapse, mistake

solely alone, completely, entirely, exclusively, merely, only, single-handedly, singly

solemn 1. earnest, glum, grave, portentous, sedate, serious, sober, staid, thoughtful 2. august, awe-inspiring, ceremonial, ceremonious, dignified, formal, grand, grave, imposing, impressive, majestic, momentous, stately 3. devotional, hallowed, holy, religious, reverential, ritual, sacred, sanctified, venerable

solemnity 1. earnestness, grandeur, gravity, impressiveness, momentousness, portentousness, sacredness, sanctity, seriousness 2. Often plural celebration, ceremonial,

ceremony, formalities, observance, proceedings, rite, ritual

solemnize celebrate, commemorate, honour, keep, observe

solicit ask, beg, beseech, canvass, crave, entreat, implore, importune, petition, plead for, pray, seek, supplicate

solicitous anxious, apprehensive, attentive, careful, caring, concerned, eager, earnest, troubled, uneasy, worried, zealous

solicitude anxiety, attentiveness, care, concern, considerateness, consideration, regard, worry

solid adj. 1. compact, concrete, dense, firm, hard, massed, stable, strong, sturdy, substantial, unshakable 2. genuine, good, pure, real, reliable, sound 3. agreed, complete, continuous, unalloyed, unanimous, unbroken, undivided, uninterrupted, united, unmixed 4. con-

stant, decent, dependable, estimable, law-abiding, level-headed, reliable, sensible, serious, sober, trusty, upright, upstanding, worthy

solidarity accord, camaraderie, cohesion, community of interest, concordance, esprit de corps, harmony, like-mindedness, singleness of purpose, soundness, stability, team spirit, unanimity, unification, unity

solidify cake, coagulate, cohere, congeal, harden, jell, set

solitary adj. 1. desolate, hidden, isolated, lonely, out-of-the-way, remote, retired, secluded, sequestered, unfrequented, unvisited 2. alone, lone, single, sole 3. cloistered, companionless, friendless, hermitical, lonely, lonesome, reclusive, unsociable, unsocial ~n. 4. hermit, introvert, loner (Inf.), lone wolf, recluse

solo ('səυləυ) n., pl. **-los. 1.** (pl. **-los** or **-li** (-liː)). a musical composition for one performer with or without accompaniment. **2.** any of various card games in which each person plays on his own, such as solo whist. **3.** a flight in which an aircraft pilot is unaccompanied. **4. a.** any performance carried out by an individual without assistance. **b.** (as modifier): a solo attempt. ~adj. **5.** Music. unaccompanied: a sonata for cello solo. ~adv. **6.** by oneself; alone: to fly solo. ~vb. **7.** (intr.) to operate an aircraft alone. —**soloist** ('səυləυɪst) n.

Solomon ('sɒləmən) n. a 10th-century B.C. king of Israel, credited with great wisdom. —**Solomonic** (ˌsɒlə'mɒnɪk) adj.

Solomon's seal n. **1.** another name for **Star of David. 2.** any of several plants of N temperate regions, having greenish or yellow paired flowers, long narrow waxy leaves, and prominent leaf scars.

so long sentence substitute **1.** Inf. farewell; goodbye. ~adv. **2.** S. African sl. for the time being; meanwhile.

solstice ('sɒlstɪs) n. **1.** either the shortest day of the year (**winter solstice**), or the longest day of the year (**summer solstice**). **2.** either of the two points on the ecliptic at which the sun is overhead at the tropic of Cancer or Capricorn at the summer and winter solstices. —**solstitial** (sɒl'stɪʃəl) adj.

soluble ('sɒljυb°l) adj. **1.** (of a substance) capable of being dissolved, esp. easily dissolved. **2.** capable of being solved or answered. —ˌsolu'bility n. —'solubly adv.

solus Latin. ('səυlυs) or (fem.) **sola** adj. alone; by oneself (formerly used in stage directions).

solute (sɒ'ljuːt) n. **1.** the substance in a solution that is dissolved. ~adj. **2.** Bot. loose or unattached; free.

solution (sə'luːʃən) n. **1.** a homogeneous mixture of two or more substances in which the molecules or atoms of the substances are completely dispersed. **2.** the act or process of forming a solution. **3.** the state of being dissolved (esp. in **in solution**). **4.** a mixture of substances in which one or more components are present as small particles with statement when substituted for the variables in an equation.

solve (sɒlv) vb. (tr.) **1.** to find the explanation for or solution to (a mystery, problem, etc.). **2.** Maths. **a.** to work out the answer to (a problem). **b.** to obtain the roots of (an equation). —'**solvable** adj.

solvent ('sɒlvənt) adj. **1.** capable of meeting financial obligations. **2.** (of a substance, esp. a liquid) capable of dissolving another substance. ~n. **3.** a liquid capable of dissolving another substance. **4.** something that solves. —'**solvency** n.

Som. abbrev. for Somerset.

somatic (səυ'mætɪk) adj. **1.** of or relating to the soma: somatic cells. **2.** of or relating to an animal body or body wall as distinct from the viscera, limbs, and head. **3.** of or relating to the human body as distinct from the mind: a somatic disease. —**so'matically** adv.

somato- or before a vowel **somat-** combining form. body: somatotype.

sombre or U.S. **somber** ('sɒmbə) adj. **1.** dismal; melancholy: a sombre mood. **2.** dim, gloomy, or shadowy. **3.** (of colour, clothes, etc.) sober, dull, or dark. —'**sombrely** or U.S. '**somberly** adv. —'**sombreness** or U.S. '**somberness** n. —**sombrous** ('sɒmbrəs) adj.

sombrero (sɒm'brɛərəυ) n., pl. **-ros.** a hat with a wide brim, as worn in Mexico.

some (sʌm; unstressed səm) determiner. **1. a.** (a) certain unknown or unspecified: some people never learn. **b.** (as pronoun; functioning as sing. or pl.): some can teach and others can't. **2. a.** an unknown or unspecified quantity or amount of: there's some rice on the table; he owns some horses. **b.** (as pronoun; functioning as sing.

or pl.): we'll buy some. **3. a.** a considerable number or amount of: he lived some years afterwards. **b.** a little: show him some respect. **4.** (usually stressed) Inf. an impressive or remarkable: that was some game! **5.** about; approximately: some thirty pounds. ~adv. **6.** a certain amount (more) (in **some more** and **and then some**). **7.** U.S., not standard. to a certain degree or extent: I like him some.

-some[1] suffix forming adjectives. characterized by; tending to: awesome; tiresome.

-some[2] suffix forming nouns. indicating a group of a specified number of members: threesome.

-some[3] (səυm) n. combining form. a body: chromosome.

somebody ('sʌmbədɪ) pron. **1.** some person; someone. ~n., pl. -**bodies. 2.** a person of great importance: he is somebody in this town.
▷ **Usage.** See at **everyone.**

someday ('sʌmˌdeɪ) adv. at some unspecified time in the (distant) future.

somehow ('sʌmˌhaυ) adv. **1.** in some unspecified way. **2.** Also: **somehow or other.** by any means that are necessary.

someone ('sʌmˌwʌn, -wən) pron. some person; somebody.
▷ **Usage.** See at **everyone.**

someplace ('sʌmˌpleɪs) adv. U.S. inf. in, at, or to some unspecified place or region.

somersault or **summersault** ('sʌməˌsɔːlt) n. **1. a.** a forward roll in which the head is placed on the ground and the trunk and legs are turned over it. **b.** a similar roll in a backward direction. **2.** an acrobatic feat in which either of these rolls is performed in midair, as in diving or gymnastics. **3.** a complete reversal of opinion, policy, etc. ~vb. **4.** (intr.) to perform a somersault.

something ('sʌmˌθɪŋ) pron. **1.** an unspecified or unknown thing; some thing: take something warm with you. **2. something or other.** one unspecified thing or an alternative thing. **3.** an unspecified or unknown amount: something less than a hundred. **4.** an impressive or important person, thing, or event: isn't that something? ~adv. **5.** to some degree; a little; somewhat: to look something like me. **6.** (foll. by an adj.) Inf. (intensifier): it hurts something awful. **7. something else.** Sl., chiefly U.S. a remarkable person or thing.

sometime ('sʌmˌtaɪm) adv. **1.** at some unspecified point of time. ~adj. **2.** (prenominal) having been at one time; former: the sometime President.

sometimes ('sʌmˌtaɪmz) adv. **1.** now and then; from time to time. **2.** Obs. formerly; sometime.

someway ('sʌmˌweɪ) adv. in some unspecified manner.

somewhat ('sʌmˌwɒt) adv. (not used with a negative) rather; a bit: she found it somewhat odd.

somewhere ('sʌmˌwɛə) adv. **1.** in, to, or at some unknown or unspecified place or point: somewhere in England; somewhere between 3 and 4 o'clock. **2. get somewhere.** Inf. to make progress.

somnambulate (sɒm'næmbjυˌleɪt) vb. (intr.) to walk while asleep. —**som'nambulance** n. —**som'nambulant** adj., n. —**somˌnambu'lation** n. —**som'nambuˌlator** n.

somnambulism (sɒm'næmbjυˌlɪzəm) n. a condition characterized by walking while asleep or in a hypnotic trance. Also called: **noctambulism.** —**som'nambulist** n.

somnolent ('sɒmnələnt) adj. **1.** drowsy; sleepy. **2.** causing drowsiness. —'**somnolence** or '**somnolency** n. —'**somnolently** adv.

son (sʌn) n. **1.** a male offspring; a boy or man in relation to his parents. **2.** a male descendant. **3.** (often cap.) a familiar term of address for a boy or man. **4.** a male

---

THESAURUS

solitude 1. isolation, loneliness, privacy, reclusiveness, retirement, seclusion **2.** Poetic desert, emptiness, waste, wasteland, wilderness

solution 1. answer, clarification, elucidation, explanation, explication, key, resolution, result, solving, unfolding, unravelling **2.** blend, compound, emulsion, mix, mixture, solvent, suspension (Chem.) **3.** disconnection, dissolution, liquefaction, melting

solve answer, clarify, clear up, crack, decipher, disentangle, elucidate, explain, expound, get to the bottom of, interpret, re-

solve, unfold, unravel, work out

sombre dark, dim, dismal, doleful, drab, dull, dusky, funereal, gloomy, grave, joyless, lugubrious, melancholy, mournful, obscure, sad, sepulchral, shadowy, shady, sober

somebody n. big noise (Brit. sl.), big shot (Sl.), big wheel (Sl.), bigwig (Sl.), celebrity, dignitary, heavyweight (Inf.), household name, luminary, name, notable, personage, person of note, public figure, star, superstar, V.I.P.

someday eventually, one day, one of these (fine) days, sooner or later, ultimately

somehow by fair means or foul, by hook or (by) crook, by some means or other, come hell or high water (Inf.), come what may, one way or another

sometimes at times, every now and then, every so often, from time to time, now and again, now and then, occasionally, off and on, once in a while, on occasion

somnolent comatose, dozy, drowsy, halfawake, heavy-eyed, nodding off (Inf.), sleepy, soporific, torpid

from a certain country, environment, etc.: *a son of the circus.* Related adj.: **filial.** —**'sonless** *adj.*

Son (sʌn) *n. Christianity.* the second person of the Trinity, Jesus Christ.

sonar ('səʊnɑː) *n.* another name for an **echo sounder.**

sonata (sə'nɑːtə) *n.* **1.** an instrumental composition, usually in three or more movements, for piano alone (**piano sonata**) or for any other instrument with or without piano accompaniment (**violin sonata, cello sonata,** etc.). **2.** a one-movement keyboard composition of the baroque period.

son et lumière ('sɒn eɪ 'luːmɪˌɛə) *n.* an entertainment staged at night at a famous building, historical site, etc., whereby the history of the location is presented by means of lighting effects, sound effects, and narration.

song (sɒŋ) *n.* **1. a.** a piece of music, usually employing a verbal text, composed for the voice, esp. one intended for performance by a soloist. **b.** the whole repertory of such pieces. **c.** (*as modifier*): *a song book.* **2.** poetical composition; poetry. **3.** the characteristic tuneful call or sound made by certain birds or insects. **4.** the act or process of singing: *they raised their voices in song.* **5. for a song.** at a bargain price. **6. on song.** *Brit. inf.* performing at peak efficiency or ability.

songbird ('sɒŋˌbɜːd) *n.* **1.** any of a suborder of passerine birds having highly developed vocal organs and, in most, a musical call. **2.** any bird having a musical call.

songster ('sɒŋstə) *n.* **1.** a singer or poet. **2.** a singing bird; songbird. —**'songstress** *fem. n.*

song thrush *n.* a common Old World thrush with a spotted breast, noted for its song.

sonic ('sɒnɪk) *adj.* **1.** of, involving, or producing sound. **2.** having a speed about equal to that of sound in air.

sonic barrier *n.* another name for **sound barrier.**

sonic boom *n.* a loud explosive sound caused by the shock wave of an aircraft, etc., travelling at supersonic speed.

son-in-law *n., pl.* **sons-in-law.** the husband of one's daughter.

sonnet ('sɒnɪt) *Prosody.* ~*n.* **1.** a verse form consisting of 14 lines in iambic pentameter with a fixed rhyme scheme, usually divided into octave and sestet or, in the English form, into three quatrains and a couplet. ~*vb.* **2.** (*intr.*) to compose sonnets. **3.** (*tr.*) to celebrate in a sonnet.

sonny ('sʌnɪ) *n., pl.* **-nies.** *Often patronizing.* a familiar term of address to a boy or man.

sonorous (sə'nɔːrəs, 'sɒnərəs) *adj.* **1.** producing or capable of producing sound. **2.** (of language, sound, etc.) deep or resonant. **3.** (esp. of speech) high-flown; grandiloquent. —**sonority** (sə'nɒrɪtɪ) *n.* —**so'norously** *adv.* —**so'norousness** *n.*

sonsy *or* **sonsie** ('sɒnsɪ) *adj.* **-sier, -siest.** *Irish, Scot., & English dialect.* **1.** plump; buxom. **2.** cheerful.

soon (suːn) *adv.* **1.** in or after a short time; in a little while; before long. **2. as soon as.** at the very moment that: *as soon as she saw him.* **3. as soon...as.** used to indicate that the second alternative is not preferable to the first: *I'd just as soon go by train as drive.*

sooner ('suːnə) *adv.* **1.** the comparative of **soon:** *he came sooner than I thought.* **2.** rather; in preference: *I'd sooner die than give up.* **3. no sooner...than.** immediately after or when: *no sooner had he got home than the rain stopped.* **4. sooner or later.** eventually; inevitably.

soot (sʊt) *n.* **1.** finely divided carbon deposited from flames during the incomplete combustion of organic substances such as coal. ~*vb.* **2.** (*tr.*) to cover with soot. —**'sooty** *adj.*

sooth (suːθ) *Arch. or poetic.* ~*n.* **1.** truth or reality (esp. in **in sooth**). ~*adj.* **2.** true or real.

soothe (suːð) *vb.* **1.** (*tr.*) to make calm or tranquil. **2.** (*tr.*) to relieve or assuage (pain, longing, etc.). **3.** (*intr.*) to bring tranquillity or relief. —**'soother** *n.* —**'soothingly** *adv.* —**'soothingness** *n.*

soothsayer ('suːθˌseɪə) *n.* a seer or prophet.

sop (sɒp) *n.* **1.** (*often pl.*) food soaked in a liquid before being eaten. **2.** a concession, bribe, etc., given to placate or mollify: *a sop to one's feelings.* **3.** *Inf.* a stupid or weak person. ~*vb.* **sopping, sopped. 4.** (*tr.*) to dip or soak (food) in liquid. **5.** (when *intr.*, often foll. by *in*) to soak or be soaked. **6.** (*tr., adv.*) to mop or absorb (liquid) as with a sponge.

sop. *abbrev. for* soprano.

sophism ('sɒfɪzəm) *n.* an argument that is invalid, specious, or misleading.

sophist ('sɒfɪst) *n.* **1.** (*often cap.*) **a.** any of a group of pre-Socratic professional philosophers. **b.** any of a group of later philosophers who made an art of effective but misleading argument. **2.** a person who uses clever or quibbling but unsound arguments.

sophisticate *vb.* (sə'fɪstɪˌkeɪt) **1.** (*tr.*) to make (someone) less natural or innocent, as by education. **2.** to pervert or corrupt (an argument, etc.) by sophistry. **3.** (*tr.*) to make more complex or refined. **4.** *Rare.* to falsify (a text, etc.) by alterations. ~*n.* (sə'fɪstɪˌkeɪt, -kɪt). **5.** a sophisticated person. —**so,phisti'cation** *n.* —**so'phisti,cator** *n.*

sophisticated (sə'fɪstɪˌkeɪtɪd) *adj.* **1.** having refined or cultured tastes and habits. **2.** appealing to sophisticates: *a sophisticated restaurant.* **3.** unduly refined or cultured. **4.** pretentiously or superficially wise. **5.** (of machines, methods, etc.) complex and refined.

sophistry ('sɒfɪstrɪ) *n., pl.* **-ries. 1. a.** a method of argument that is seemingly plausible though actually invalid and misleading. **b.** the art of using such arguments. **2.** subtle but unsound or fallacious reasoning. **3.** an instance of this.

sophomore ('sɒfəˌmɔː) *n. Chiefly U.S.* a second-year student.

-sophy *n. combining form.* indicating knowledge or an intellectual system: *philosophy.* —**-sophic** *or* **-sophical** *adj. combining form.*

soporific (ˌsɒpə'rɪfɪk) *adj. also* ˌsopor'iferous. **1.** inducing sleep. **2.** drowsy; sleepy. ~*n.* **3.** a drug or other agent that induces sleep.

sopping ('sɒpɪŋ) *adj.* completely soaked; wet through. Also: **sopping wet.**

soppy ('sɒpɪ) *adj.* **-pier, -piest. 1.** wet or soggy. **2.** *Brit. inf.* silly or sentimental. **3. soppy on.** *Brit. inf.* foolishly charmed or affected by. —**'soppily** *adv.* —**'soppiness** *n.*

soprano (sə'prɑːnəʊ) *n., pl.* **-pranos** *or* **-prani** (-'prɑːniː). **1.** the highest adult female voice. **2.** the voice of a young boy before puberty. **3.** a singer with such a voice. **4.** the highest part of a piece of harmony. **5. a.** the highest or second highest instrument in a family of instruments. **b.** (*as modifier*): *a soprano saxophone.* ~See also **treble.**

sorbet ('sɔːbɪt, -beɪ) *n.* **1.** a water ice made from fruit juice, egg whites, milk, etc. **2.** a U.S. word for **sherbet** (sense 1).

sorcerer ('sɔːsərə) *or* (*fem.*) **sorceress** ('sɔːsərɪs) *n.* a person who seeks to control and use magic powers; a wizard or magician.

sorcery ('sɔːsərɪ) *n., pl.* **-ceries.** the art, practices, or spells of magic, esp. black magic.

THESAURUS

song air, anthem, ballad, canticle, canzonet, carol, chant, chorus, ditty, hymn, lay, lyric, melody, number, pop song, psalm, shanty, strain, tune

song and dance ado, commotion, flap (*Inf.*), fuss, hoo-ha, kerfuffle (*Inf.*), performance (*Inf.*), pother, shindig (*Sl.*), shindy (*Sl.*), stir, to-do

soon anon (*Archaic*), any minute now, before long, betimes (*Archaic*), in a little while, in a minute, in a short time, in the near future, shortly

soothe allay, alleviate, appease, assuage, calm, calm down, compose, ease, hush, lull,

mitigate, mollify, pacify, quiet, relieve, settle, smooth down, soften, still, tranquillize

soothing balsamic, calming, demulcent, easeful, emollient, lenitive, palliative, relaxing, restful

soothsayer augur, diviner, foreteller, prophet, seer, sibyl

sophisticated 1. blasé, citified, cosmopolitan, cultivated, cultured, jet-set, refined, seasoned, urbane, worldly, worldly-wise, world-weary **2.** advanced, complex, complicated, delicate, elaborate, highly-developed, intricate, multifaceted, refined, subtle

sophistication finesse, poise, savoir-

faire, *savoir-vivre*, urbanity, worldliness, worldly wisdom

sophistry casuistry, fallacy, quibble, sophism

soporific 1. *adj.* hypnotic, sedative, sleep-inducing, sleepy, somniferous (*Rare*), somnolent, tranquillizing **2.** *n.* anaesthetic, hypnotic, narcotic, opiate, sedative, tranquillizer

soppy corny (*Inf.*), daft (*Inf.*), drippy (*Inf.*), gushy (*Inf.*), lovey-dovey, mawkish, overemotional, schmaltzy (*Sl.*), sentimental, silly, slushy (*Inf.*), soft (*Inf.*), weepy (*Inf.*)

sorcerer enchanter, mage (*Archaic*), magician, magus, necromancer, sorceress,

sordid ('sɔːdɪd) adj. **1.** dirty, foul, or squalid. **2.** degraded; vile; base. **3.** selfish and grasping: sordid avarice. —'**sordidly** adv. —'**sordidness** n.

sore (sɔː) adj. **1.** (esp. of a wound, injury, etc.) painfully sensitive; tender. **2.** causing annoyance: a sore point. **3.** urgent; pressing: in sore need. **4.** (postpositive) grieved; distressed. **5.** causing grief or sorrow. ~n. **6.** a painful or sensitive wound, injury, etc. **7.** any cause of distress or vexation. ~adv. **8.** Arch. direly; sorely (now only in such phrases as **sore pressed, sore afraid**). —'**soreness** n.

sorely ('sɔːlɪ) adv. **1.** painfully or grievously: sorely wounded. **2.** pressingly or greatly: to be sorely taxed.

sorghum ('sɔːgəm) n. any grass of the Old World genus Sorghum, having glossy seeds: cultivated for grain, hay, and as a source of syrup.

soroptimist (sə'rɒptɪmɪst) n. a member of Soroptimist International, an organization of clubs for professional and executive businesswomen.

sorority (sə'rɒrɪtɪ) n., pl. -**ties.** Chiefly U.S. a social club or society for university women.

sorrel[1] ('sɒrəl) n. **1. a.** a light brown to brownish-orange colour. **b.** (as adj.): a sorrel carpet. **2.** a horse of this colour.

sorrel[2] ('sɒrəl) n. **1.** any of several plants of Eurasia and North America, having acid-tasting leaves used in salads and sauces. **2.** short for **wood sorrel.**

sorrow ('sɒrəʊ) n. **1.** the feeling of sadness, grief, or regret associated with loss, bereavement, sympathy for another's suffering, etc. **2.** a particular cause or source of this. **3.** Also called: **sorrowing.** the outward expression of grief or sadness. ~vb. **4.** (intr.) to mourn or grieve. —'**sorrowful** adj. —'**sorrowfully** adv. —'**sorrowfulness** n.

sorry ('sɒrɪ) adj. -**rier, -riest. 1.** (usually postpositive; often foll. by for) feeling or expressing pity, sympathy, grief, or regret: I feel sorry for him. **2.** pitiful, wretched, or deplorable: a sorry sight. **3.** poor; paltry: a sorry excuse. **4.** affected by sorrow; sad. **5.** causing sorrow or sadness. ~interj. **6.** an exclamation expressing apology. —'**sorrily** adv. —'**sorriness** n.

sort (sɔːt) n. **1.** a class, group, kind, etc., as distinguished by some common quality or characteristic. **2.** a type of character, nature, etc.: he's a good sort. **3.** Austral. sl. a person, esp. a girl. **4.** a more or less definable or adequate example (of): it's a sort of review. **5.** (often pl.) Printing. any of the individual characters making up a fount of type. **6.** Arch. manner; way: in this sort we struggled home. **7. after a sort.** to some extent. **8. of sorts** or **of a sort. a.** of an inferior kind. **b.** of an indefinite kind. **9. out of sorts.** not in normal good health, temper, etc. **10. sort of.** in some way or other; as it were; rather. ~vb. **11.** (tr.) to arrange according to class, type, etc. **12.** (tr.) Sl., chiefly Brit. to put (a car, etc.) into working order. **13.** (intr.) Arch. to agree; accord. —'**sortable** adj. —'**sorter** n.

sortie ('sɔːtɪ) n. **1. a.** (of troops, etc.) the act of emerging from a contained or besieged position. **b.** the troops doing this. **2.** an operational flight made by one aircraft. ~vb. -**tieing, -tied. 3.** (intr.) to make a sortie.

sort out vb. (tr., adv.) **1.** to take or separate, as from a larger group: to sort out the likely ones. **2.** Inf. to find a solution to (a problem, etc.), esp. to make clear or tidy: to sort out the mess. **3.** Inf. to organize into an orderly and disciplined group. **4.** Inf. to beat or punish.

SOS n. **1.** an internationally recognized distress signal in which the letters SOS are repeatedly spelt out, as by radio telegraphy: used esp. by ships and aircraft. **2.** Inf. a call for help.

sosatie ('sɔ,sɑːtɪ) n. S. African. curried meat on skewers.

so-so Inf. ~adj. **1.** (postpositive) neither good nor bad. ~adv. **2.** in an average or indifferent manner.

sostenuto (,sɒstə'nuːtəʊ) adj., adv. Music. to be performed in a smooth sustained manner.

sot (sɒt) n. **1.** a habitual or chronic drunkard. **2.** a person stupefied by or as if by drink. —'**sottish** adj.

sotto voce ('sɒtəʊ 'vəʊtʃɪ) adv. in an undertone.

sou (suː) n. **1.** a former French coin of low denomination. **2.** a very small amount of money: I haven't a sou.

soubrette (suː'brɛt) n. **1.** a minor female role in comedy, often that of a pert lady's maid. **2.** any pert or flirtatious girl.

soubriquet ('suːbrɪ,keɪ) n. a variant spelling of **sobriquet.**

soufflé ('suːfleɪ) n. **1.** a light fluffy dish made with beaten egg whites combined with cheese, fish, etc. **2.** a similar sweet or savoury cold dish, set with gelatine. ~adj. also **souffléed. 3.** made light and puffy, as by beating and cooking.

sough (saʊ) vb. **1.** (intr.) (esp. of the wind) to make a sighing sound. ~n. **2.** a soft continuous murmuring sound.

sought (sɔːt) vb. the past tense or past participle of **seek.**

souk (suːk) n. an open-air marketplace in Muslim countries, esp. North Africa and the Middle East.

soul (səʊl) n. **1.** the spirit or immaterial part of man, the seat of human personality, intellect, will, and emotions: regarded as an entity that survives the body after death. **2.** Christianity. the spiritual part of a person, capable of redemption from sin through divine grace. **3.** the essential part or fundamental nature of anything. **4.** a person's feelings or moral nature. **5. a.** Also called: **soul music.** a type of Black music resulting from the addition of jazz, gospel, and pop elements to the urban blues style. **b.** (as modifier): a soul singer. **6.** nobility of spirit or temperament: a man of great soul. **7.** an inspiring or leading figure, as of a movement. **8. the life and soul.** Inf. a person regarded as the main source of gaiety, merriment, etc.: the life and soul of the party. **9.** a person regarded as typifying some characteristic or quality: the soul of discretion. **10.** a person; individual: an honest soul. **11. upon my soul!** an exclamation of surprise.

THESAURUS

warlock, witch, wizard

sorcery black art, black magic, charm, divination, enchantment, incantation, magic, necromancy, spell, witchcraft, witchery, wizardry

sordid 1. dirty, filthy, foul, mean, seamy, seedy, sleazy, slovenly, slummy, squalid, unclean, wretched **2.** backstreet, base, debauched, degenerate, degraded, despicable, disreputable, low, shabby, shameful, vicious, vile **3.** avaricious, corrupt, covetous, grasping, mercenary, miserly, niggardly, selfish, self-seeking, ungenerous, venal

sore adj. **1.** angry, burning, chafed, inflamed, irritated, painful, raw, reddened, sensitive, smarting, tender **2.** annoying, distressing, grievous, harrowing, severe, sharp, troublesome **3.** acute, critical, desperate, dire, extreme, pressing, urgent **4.** afflicted, aggrieved, angry, annoyed, grieved, hurt, irked, irritated, pained, peeved (Inf.), resentful, stung, upset, vexed ~n. **5.** abscess, boil, chafe, gathering, inflammation, ulcer

sorrow n. **1.** affliction, anguish, distress, grief, heartache, heartbreak, misery, mourning, regret, sadness, unhappiness, woe **2.** affliction, blow, hardship, misfortune, trial, tribulation, trouble, woe, worry ~v. **3.** agonize, bemoan, be sad, bewail, grieve, lament, moan, mourn, weep

sorrowful affecting, afflicted, dejected, depressed, disconsolate, distressing, doleful, grievous, heartbroken, heart-rending, heavy-hearted, lamentable, lugubrious, melancholy, miserable, mournful, painful, piteous, rueful, sad, sick at heart, sorry, tearful, unhappy, woebegone, woeful, wretched

sorry 1. apologetic, conscience-stricken, contrite, guilt-ridden, in sackcloth and ashes, penitent, regretful, remorseful, repentant, self-reproachful, shamefaced **2.** disconsolate, distressed, grieved, melancholy, mournful, sad, sorrowful, unhappy **3.** commiserative, compassionate, full of pity, moved, pitying, sympathetic **4.** abject, base, deplorable, dismal, distressing, mean, miserable, paltry, pathetic, piteous, pitiable, pitiful, poor, sad, shabby, vile, wretched

sort n. **1.** brand, breed, category, character, class, denomination, description, family, genus, group, ilk, kind, make, nature, order, quality, race, species, stamp, style, type, variety **2. out of sorts** crotchety, down in the dumps (Inf.), down in the mouth (Inf.), grouchy (Inf.), in low spirits, mopy, not up to par, not up to snuff (Inf.), off colour, poorly (Inf.), under the weather (Inf.) **3. sort of** as it were, in part, moderately, rather, reasonably, slightly, somewhat, to some extent ~v. **4.** arrange, assort, catalogue, categorize, choose, class, classify, distribute, divide file, grade, group, order, put in order, rank, select, separate, systematize

sort out 1. clarify, clear up, organize, put or get straight, resolve, tidy up **2.** pick out, put on one side, segregate, select, separate, sift

soul 1. animating principle, essence, intellect, life, mind, psyche, reason, spirit, vital force **2.** being, body, creature, individual, man, mortal, person, woman **3.** embodiment, essence, incarnation, personification, quintessence, type **4.** animation, ardour, courage, energy, feeling, fervour, force, inspiration, nobility, vitality, vivacity

soul-destroying *adj.* (of an occupation, situation, etc.) unremittingly monotonous.

soul food *n. Inf.* food, such as chitterlings, yams, etc., traditionally eaten by U.S. Negroes.

soulful ('soʊlfʊl) *adj.* expressing profound thoughts or feelings. —'**soulfully** *adv.* —'**soulfulness** *n.*

soulless ('soʊllɪs) *adj.* 1. lacking humanizing qualities or influences; mechanical: *soulless work.* 2. (of a person) lacking in sensitivity or nobility. —'**soullessness** *n.*

soul mate *n.* a person for whom one has a deep affinity, esp. a lover, wife, husband, etc.

soul-searching *n.* 1. deep or critical examination of one's motives, actions, beliefs, etc. ~*adj.* 2. displaying the characteristics of this.

sound[1] (saʊnd) *n.* 1. **a.** a periodic disturbance in the pressure or density of a fluid or in the elastic strain of a solid, produced by a vibrating object. It travels as longitudinal waves. **b.** (*as modifier*): *a sound wave.* 2. the sensation produced by such a periodic disturbance in the organs of hearing. 3. anything that can be heard. 4. (*modifier*): of or relating to radio as distinguished from television: *sound broadcasting.* 5. a particular instance or type of sound: *the sound of running water.* 6. volume or quality of sound: *a radio with poor sound.* 7. the area or distance over which something can be heard: *within the sound of Big Ben.* 8. impression or implication: *I don't like the sound of that.* 9. (*often pl.*) *Sl.* music, esp. rock, jazz, or pop. ~*vb.* 10. to cause (an instrument, etc.) to make a sound or (of an instrument, etc.) to emit a sound. 11. to announce or be announced by a sound: *to sound the alarm.* 12. (*intr.*) (of a sound) to be heard. 13. (*intr.*) to resonate with a certain quality or intensity: *to sound loud.* 14. (*copula*) to give the impression of being as specified: *to sound reasonable.* 15. (*tr.*) to pronounce distinctly or audibly: *to sound one's consonants.* —'**soundable** *adj.* —'**soundless** *adj.*

sound[2] (saʊnd) *adj.* 1. free from damage, injury, decay, etc. 2. firm; substantial: *a sound basis.* 3. financially safe or stable: *a sound investment.* 4. showing good judgment or reasoning; wise: *sound advice.* 5. valid, logical, or justifiable: *a sound argument.* 6. *Now rare.* ethically correct; honest. 7. (of sleep) deep; peaceful; unbroken. 8. thorough: *a sound examination.* ~*adv.* 9. soundly; deeply: now archaic except when applied to sleep. —'**soundly** *adv.* —'**soundness** *n.*

sound[3] (saʊnd) *vb.* 1. to measure the depth of (a well, the sea, etc.) by plumb line, sonar, etc. 2. to seek to discover (someone's views, etc.), as by questioning. 3. (*intr.*) (of a whale, etc.) to dive downwards swiftly and deeply. 4. *Med.* **a.** to probe or explore (a bodily cavity or passage) by means of a sound. **b.** to examine (a patient) by means of percussion and auscultation. ~*n.* 5. *Med.* an instrument for insertion into a bodily cavity or passage to dilate strictures, dislodge foreign material, etc. ~See also **sound out.** —'**sounder** *n.*

sound[4] (saʊnd) *n.* 1. a relatively narrow channel between two larger areas of sea or between an island and the mainland. 2. an inlet or deep bay of the sea. 3. the air bladder of a fish.

sound barrier *n.* (*not in technical usage*) a hypothetical barrier to flight at or above the speed of sound, when a sudden large increase in drag occurs. Also called: **sonic barrier.**

sounding ('saʊndɪŋ) *n.* 1. (*sometimes pl.*) the act or process of measuring depth of water or examining the bottom of a river, lake, etc., as with a sounding line. 2. an observation or measurement of atmospheric conditions, as made using a sonde. 3. (*often pl.*) measurements taken by sounding. 4. (*pl.*) a place where a sound-

ing line will reach the bottom, esp. less than 100 fathoms in depth.

sounding board *n.* 1. Also called: **soundboard.** a thin wooden board in a violin, piano, etc., serving to amplify the vibrations produced by the strings passing across it. 2. Also called: **soundboard.** a thin screen suspended over a pulpit, stage, etc., to reflect sound towards an audience. 3. a person, group, experiment, etc., used to test a new idea, policy, etc.

sound out *vb.* (*tr., adv.*) to question (someone) in order to discover (opinions, facts, etc.).

soundproof ('saʊnd,pruːf) *adj.* 1. not penetrable by sound. ~*vb.* 2. (*tr.*) to render soundproof.

soundtrack ('saʊnd,træk) *n.* 1. the recorded sound accompaniment to a film. 2. a narrow strip along the side of a spool of film, which carries the sound accompaniment.

sound wave *n.* a wave that propagates sound.

soup (suːp) *n.* 1. a liquid food made by boiling or simmering meat, fish, vegetables, etc. 2. *Inf.* a photographic developer. 3. *Inf.* anything resembling soup, esp. thick fog. 4. a slang name for **nitroglycerin.** 5. **in the soup.** *Sl.* in trouble or difficulties. —'**soupy** *adj.*

soupçon *French.* (sup'sɔ̃) *n.* a slight amount; dash.

soup kitchen *n.* 1. a place or mobile stall where food and drink, esp. soup, is served to destitute people. 2. *Mil.* a mobile kitchen.

soup up *vb.* (*tr., adv.*) *Sl.* to modify (a car or motorcycle engine) in order to increase its power. Also: **hot up** or (*esp. U.S.*) **hop up.**

sour (saʊə) *adj.* 1. having or denoting a sharp biting taste like that of lemon juice or vinegar. 2. made acid or bad, as in the case of milk, by the action of microorganisms. 3. having a rancid or unwholesome smell. 4. (of a person's temperament) sullen, morose, or disagreeable. 5. (esp. of the weather) harsh and unpleasant. 6. disagreeable; distasteful: *a sour experience.* 7. (of land, etc.) lacking in fertility, esp. due to excessive acidity. 8. (of petrol) containing a relatively large amount of sulphur compounds. 9. **go** *or* **turn sour.** to become unfavourable or inharmonious: *his marriage went sour.* ~*n.* 10. something sour. 11. *Chiefly U.S.* an iced drink usually made with spirits, lemon juice, and ice: *a whiskey sour.* 12. an acid used in bleaching clothes or in curing skins. ~*vb.* 13. to make or become sour. —'**sourish** *adj.* —'**sourly** *adv.* —'**sourness** *n.*

source (sɔːs) *n.* 1. the point or place from which something originates. 2. **a.** a spring that forms the starting point of a stream. **b.** the area where the headwaters of a river rise. 3. a person, group, etc., that creates, issues, or originates something: *the source of a complaint.* 4. **a.** any person, book, organization, etc., from which information, evidence, etc., is obtained. **b.** (*as modifier*): *source material.* 5. anything, such as a story or work of art, that provides a model or inspiration for a later work. 6. **at source.** at the point of origin.

sourdough ('saʊə,dəʊ) *Western U.S., Canada, & Alaska.* ~*adj.* 1. (of bread) made with fermented dough used as leaven. ~*n.* 2. an old-time prospector or pioneer.

sour grapes *n.* the attitude of despising something because one cannot have it oneself.

sourpuss ('saʊə,pʊs) *n. Inf.* a person who is habitually gloomy or sullen.

sourveld ('saʊə,fɛlt) *n.* (in South Africa) a particular type of grazing.

souse (saʊs) *vb.* 1. to plunge (something) into water or other liquid. 2. to drench or be drenched. 3. (*tr.*) to pour or dash (liquid) over (a person or thing). 4. to steep or cook (food) in a marinade. 5. *Sl.* to make or be-

---

THESAURUS

sound[1] *n.* 1. din, noise, report, resonance, reverberation, tone, voice 2. drift, idea, implication(s), impression, look, tenor 3. earshot, hearing, range ~*v.* 4. echo, resonate, resound, reverberate 5. appear, give the impression of, look, seem, strike one as being 6. announce, articulate, declare, enunciate, express, pronounce, signal, utter

sound[2] *adj.* 1. complete, entire, firm, fit, hale, hale and hearty, healthy, intact, perfect, robust, solid, sturdy, substantial, undamaged, unhurt, unimpaired, uninjured, vigorous, well-constructed, whole 2. correct, fair, just, level-headed, logical, orthodox, proper,

prudent, rational, reasonable, reliable, responsible, right, right-thinking, sensible, true, trustworthy, valid, well-founded, well-grounded, wise 3. established, orthodox, proven, recognized, reliable, reputable, safe, secure, solid, solvent, stable, tried-and-true 4. deep, peaceful, unbroken, undisturbed, untroubled

sound[3] *v.* 1. fathom, plumb, probe 2. examine, inspect, investigate, test

sound out canvass, examine, probe, pump, question, see how the land lies

sour *adj.* 1. acetic, acid, acidulated, bitter, pungent, sharp, tart, unpleasant 2. bad, cur-

dled, fermented, gone off, rancid, turned, unsavoury, unwholesome 3. acrid, acrimonious, churlish, crabbed, cynical, disagreeable, discontented, embittered, grouchy (*Inf.*), grudging, ill-natured, ill-tempered, jaundiced, peevish, tart, ungenerous, waspish ~*v.* 4. alienate, disenchant, embitter, envenom, exacerbate, exasperate, turn off (*Inf.*)

source 1. author, begetter, beginning, cause, commencement, derivation, fountainhead, origin, originator, rise, spring, wellspring 2. authority, informant

come drunk. ~n. 6. the liquid used in pickling. 7. the act or process of sousing. 8. Sl. a drunkard.

soutane (su:'tæn) n. R.C. Church. a priest's cassock.

south (sauθ) n. 1. one of the four cardinal points of the compass, at 180° from north and 90° clockwise from east and anticlockwise from west. 2. the direction along a meridian towards the South Pole. 3. **the south.** (often cap.) any area lying in or towards the south. ~adj. 4. in, towards, or facing the south. 5. (esp. of the wind) from the south. ~adv. 6. in, to, towards, or (esp. of the wind) from the south.

South (sauθ) n. **the.** 1. the southern part of England, generally regarded as lying to the south of an imaginary line between the Wash and the Severn. 2. (in the U.S.) **a.** the states south of the Mason-Dixon Line that formed the Confederacy during the Civil War. **b.** the Confederacy itself. ~adj. 3. of or denoting the southern part of a specified country, area, etc.

southeast (,sauθ'i:st; Naut. ,sau'i:st) n. 1. the point of the compass or the direction midway between south and east. ~adj. also **,south'eastern.** 2. (sometimes cap.) of or denoting the southeastern part of a specified country, area, etc. 3. in, towards, or facing the southeast. 4. (esp. of the wind) from the southeast. ~adv. 5. in, to, towards, or (esp. of the wind) from the southeast — **,south'easterly** adj., adv., n. — **,south'easternmost** adj. — **,south'eastward** adj.

Southeast (,sauθ'i:st) n. (usually preceded by the) the southeastern part of Britain, esp. the London area.

southeaster (,sauθ'i:stə; Naut. ,sau'i:stə) n. a strong wind or storm from the southeast.

southerly ('sʌðəli) adj. 1. of or situated in the south. ~adv., adj. 2. towards the south. 3. from the south. ~n., pl. -lies. 4. a wind from the south. — **'southerliness** n.

southern ('sʌðən) adj. 1. in or towards the south. 2. (of a wind, etc.) coming from the south. 3. native to or inhabiting the south. — **'southern,most** adj.

Southern ('sʌðən) adj. of, relating to, or characteristic of the south of a particular region or country.

Southern Cross n. a small constellation in the S hemisphere whose four brightest stars form a cross. It is represented on the national flags of Australia and New Zealand.

Southerner ('sʌðənə) n. (sometimes not cap.) a native or inhabitant of the south of any specified region, esp. the South of England or the Southern states of the U.S.

southern hemisphere n. (often caps.) that half of the earth lying south of the equator.

southern lights n. another name for **aurora australis.**

southpaw ('sauθ,pɔ:) Inf. ~n. 1. a left-handed boxer. 2. any left-handed person. ~adj. 3. of or relating to a southpaw.

South Pole n. 1. the southernmost point on the earth's axis, at the latitude of 90°S. 2. Astron. the point of intersection of the earth's extended axis and the southern half of the celestial sphere.

South Seas pl. n. the seas south of the equator.

south-southeast n. 1. the point on the compass or the direction midway between southeast and south. ~adj., adv. 2. in, from, or towards this direction.

south-southwest n. 1. the point on the compass or the direction midway between south and southwest. ~adj., adv. 2. in, from, or towards this direction.

southward ('sauθwəd; Naut. 'sʌðəd) adj. 1. situated, directed, or moving towards the south. ~n. 2. the southward part, direction, etc. ~adv. 3. Also: **southwards.** towards the south.

southwest (,sauθ'wɛst; Naut. ,sau'wɛst) n. 1. the point of the compass or the direction midway between west and south. ~adj. also **,south'western.** 2. (sometimes cap.) of or denoting the southwestern part of a specified country, area, etc.: southwest Italy. 3. in or towards the

southwest. 4. (esp. of the wind) from the southwest. ~adv. 5. in, to, towards, or (esp. of the wind) from the southwest — **,south'westerly** adj., adv., n. — **,south-'westernmost** adj. — **,south'westward** adj.

Southwest (,sauθ'wɛst) n. (usually preceded by the) the southwestern part of Britain, esp. Cornwall, Devon, and Somerset.

southwester (,sauθ'wɛstə; Naut. ,sau'wɛstə) n. a strong wind or storm from the southwest.

souvenir (,su:və'nɪə, 'su:və,nɪə) n. 1. an object that recalls a certain place, occasion, or person; memento. 2. Rare. a thing recalled. ~vb. 3. (tr.) Austral. & N.Z., sl. to steal or keep for one's own use; purloin.

sou'wester (,sau'wɛstə) n. a waterproof hat having a very broad rim behind, worn esp. by seamen.

sovereign ('sɒvrɪn) n. 1. a person exercising supreme authority, esp. a monarch. 2. a former British gold coin worth one pound sterling. ~adj. 3. supreme in rank or authority: a sovereign lord. 4. excellent or outstanding: a sovereign remedy. 5. of or relating to a sovereign. 6. independent of outside authority: a sovereign state. — **'sovereignly** adv.

sovereignty ('sɒvrəntɪ) n., pl. -ties. 1. supreme and unrestricted power, as of a state. 2. the position, dominion, or authority of a sovereign. 3. an independent state.

soviet ('səʊvɪət, 'sɒv-) n. 1. (in the Soviet Union) an elected government council at the local, regional, and national levels, culminating in the Supreme Soviet. ~adj. 2. of or relating to a soviet. — **'sovie,tism** n.

Soviet ('səʊvɪət, 'sɒv-) adj. of or relating to the Soviet Union, its people, or its government.

sow[1] (səʊ) vb. **sowing, sowed; sown** or **sowed.** 1. to scatter or place (seed, a crop, etc.) in or on (a piece of ground, field, etc.) so that it may grow: to sow wheat; to sow a strip of land. 2. (tr.) to implant or introduce: to sow a doubt in someone's mind. — **'sower** n.

sow[2] (sau) n. 1. a female adult pig. 2. the female of certain other animals, such as the mink. 3. Metallurgy. **a.** the channels for leading molten metal to the moulds in casting pig iron. **b.** iron that has solidified in these channels.

soya bean ('sɔɪə) or U.S. **soybean** ('sɔɪ,bi:n) n. 1. an Asian bean plant cultivated for its nutritious seeds, for forage, and to improve the soil. 2. the seed, used as food, forage, and as the source of an oil.

soy sauce (sɔɪ) n. a salty dark brown sauce made from fermented soya beans, used esp. in Chinese cookery. Also called: **soya sauce.**

sozzled ('sɒzəld) adj. an informal word for **drunk.**

sp. abbrev. for: 1. special. 2. (pl. **spp.**) species. 3. specific. 4. specimen. 5. spelling.

Sp. abbrev. for: 1. Spain. 2. Spaniard. 3. Spanish.

spa (spɑ:) n. a mineral spring or a place or resort where such a spring is found.

space (speɪs) n. 1. the unlimited three-dimensional expanse in which all material objects are located. Related adj.: **spatial.** 2. an interval of distance or time between two points, objects, or events. 3. a blank portion or area. 4. **a.** unoccupied area or room: there is no space for a table. **b.** (in combination): space-saving. Related adj.: **spacious.** 5. **a.** the region beyond the earth's atmosphere containing other planets, stars, galaxies, etc.; universe. **b.** (as modifier): a space probe. 6. a seat or place, as on a train, aircraft, etc. 7. Printing. a piece of metal, less than type-high, used to separate letters or words. 8. Music. any of the gaps between the lines that make up the staff. 9. Also called: **spacing.** Telegraphy. the period of time that separates characters in Morse code. ~vb. (tr.) 10. to place or arrange at intervals or with spaces between. 11. to divide into or by spaces: to space one's time evenly. 12. Printing. to separate (letters, words, or lines) by the insertion of spaces. — **'spacer** n.

space age n. 1. the period in which the exploration of space has become possible. ~adj. **space-age.** 2. (usual-

---

THESAURUS

souse drench, dunk, immerse, marinate (Cookery), pickle, soak, steep

souvenir keepsake, memento, relic, remembrancer (Archaic), reminder, token

sovereign n. 1. chief, emperor, empress, king, monarch, potentate, prince, queen, ruler, shah, supreme ruler, tsar ~adj. 2. absolute, chief, dominant, imperial, kingly, mo-

narchal, paramount, predominant, principal, queenly, regal, royal, ruling, supreme, unlimited 3. effectual, efficacious, efficient, excellent

sovereignty ascendancy, domination, kingship, primacy, supremacy, supreme power, suzerainty, sway

sow broadcast, disseminate, implant, in-

seminate, lodge, plant, scatter, seed

space 1. amplitude, capacity, elbowroom, expanse, extension, extent, leeway, margin, play, room, scope, spaciousness, volume 2. blank, distance, gap, interval, lacuna, omission 3. duration, interval, period, span, time, while 4. accommodation, berth, place, seat

ly prenominal) futuristic or ultramodern.

space-bar *n.* a horizontal bar on a typewriter that is depressed in order to leave a space between words, letters, etc.

space capsule *n.* a vehicle, sometimes carrying men or animals, designed to obtain scientific information from space, planets, etc., and be recovered on returning to earth.

spacecraft ('speɪsˌkrɑːft) *n.* a manned or unmanned vehicle designed to orbit the earth or travel to celestial objects.

spaceman ('speɪsˌmæn) *or* (*fem.*) **spacewoman** *n.,* *pl.* **-men** *or* (*fem.*) **-women.** a person who travels in outer space.

space probe *n.* a vehicle, such as a satellite, equipped to obtain scientific information, normally transmitted back to earth by radio, about a planet, conditions in space, etc.

spaceship ('speɪsˌʃɪp) *n.* a manned spacecraft.

space shuttle *n.* a vehicle designed to be used for at least 100 space flights, carrying men and materials to space stations or bases on the moon, etc.

space station *n.* any large manned artificial satellite designed to orbit the earth during a long period of time thus providing a base for scientific research in space and a construction site, launching pad, and docking arrangements for spacecraft.

spacesuit ('speɪsˌsuːt, -ˌsjuːt) *n.* a sealed and pressurized suit worn by astronauts providing an artificial atmosphere, acceptable temperature, radio-communication link, and protection from radiation.

space-time *or* **space-time continuum** *n. Physics.* the four-dimensional continuum having three spatial coordinates and one time coordinate that together completely specify the location of a particle or an event.

spacious ('speɪʃəs) *adj.* having a large capacity or area. —'**spaciously** *adv.* —'**spaciousness** *n.*

spade[1] (speɪd) *n.* **1.** a tool for digging, typically consisting of a flat rectangular steel blade attached to a long wooden handle. **2.** something resembling a spade. **3.** a cutting tool for stripping the blubber from a whale or skin from a carcass. **4. call a spade a spade.** to speak plainly and frankly. ~*vb.* **5.** (*tr.*) to use a spade on. —'**spader** *n.*

spade[2] (speɪd) *n.* **1. a.** the black symbol on a playing card resembling a heart-shaped leaf with a stem. **b.** a card with one or more of these symbols or (*when pl.*) the suit of cards so marked, usually the highest ranking of the four. **2.** a derogatory word for a Negro. **3. in spades.** *U.S. inf.* in an extreme or emphatic way.

spadework ('speɪdˌwɜːk) *n.* dull or routine preparatory work.

spadix ('speɪdɪks) *n., pl.* **spadices** (speɪ'daɪsiːz). a spike of small flowers on a fleshy stem, the whole being enclosed in a spathe.

spaghetti (spə'gɛtɪ) *n.* pasta in the form of long strings.

spaghetti junction *n.* a junction, usually between motorways, in which there are a large number of intersecting roads used by a large volume of high-speed traffic.

spaghetti western *n.* a cowboy film made by an Italian director in Europe.

spake (speɪk) *vb. Arch.* a past tense of **speak.**

Spam (spæm) *n. Trademark.* a kind of tinned luncheon meat, made largely from pork.

span[1] (spæn) *n.* **1.** the interval, space, or distance between two points, such as the ends of a bridge or arch. **2.** the complete duration or extent: *the span of his life.* **3.** short for **wingspan. 4.** a unit of length based on the width of an expanded hand, usually taken as nine inches. ~*vb.* **spanning, spanned.** (*tr.*) **5.** to stretch or extend across, over, or around. **6.** to provide with something that spans: *to span a river with a bridge.* **7.** to measure or cover, esp. with the extended hand.

span[2] (spæn) *n.* a team of horses or oxen, esp. two matched animals.

span[3] (spæn) *vb. Arch. or dialect.* a past tense of **spin.**

Span. *abbrev. for* Spanish.

spandrel *or* **spandril** ('spændrəl) *n. Archit.* **1.** an approximately triangular surface bounded by the outer curve of an arch and the adjacent wall. **2.** the surface area between two adjacent arches and the horizontal cornice above them.

spangle ('spæŋgəl) *n.* **1.** a small thin piece of metal or other shiny material used as a decoration, esp. on clothes; sequin. **2.** any glittering or shiny spot or object. ~*vb.* **3.** (*intr.*) to glitter or shine with or like spangles. **4.** (*tr.*) to cover with spangles. —'**spangly** *adj.*

Spaniard ('spænjəd) *n.* a native or inhabitant of Spain.

spaniel ('spænjəl) *n.* **1.** a breed of gundog with long frilled ears and a silky coat. **2.** an obsequiously devoted person.

Spanish ('spænɪʃ) *n.* **1.** the official language of Spain, Mexico, and most countries of South and Central America except Brazil. Spanish is an Indo-European language belonging to the Romance group. **2. the Spanish.** (*functioning as pl.*) Spaniards collectively. ~*adj.* **3.** of or relating to the Spanish language or its speakers. **4.** of or relating to Spain or Spaniards.

Spanish fly *n.* **1.** a European blister beetle, the dried bodies of which yield cantharides. **2.** another name for **cantharides.**

Spanish Main *n.* **1.** the mainland of Spanish America, esp. the N coast of South America. **2.** the Caribbean Sea, the S part of which in colonial times was the haunt of pirates.

spank[1] (spæŋk) *vb.* **1.** (*tr.*) to slap with the open hand, esp. on the buttocks. ~*n.* **2.** one or a series of these slaps.

spank[2] (spæŋk) *vb.* (*intr.*) to go at a quick and lively pace.

spanking[1] ('spæŋkɪŋ) *n.* a series of spanks, usually as a punishment for children.

spanking[2] ('spæŋkɪŋ) *adj.* (*prenominal*) **1.** *Inf.* outstandingly fine, smart, large, etc. **2.** quick and energetic. **3.** (*esp. of a breeze*) fresh and brisk.

spanner ('spænə) *n.* **1.** a steel hand tool with jaws or a hole, designed to grip a nut or bolt head. **2. spanner in the works.** *Brit. inf.* an impediment or annoyance.

span roof *n.* a roof consisting of two equal sloping sides.

spanspek ('spænˌspɛk) *n. S. African.* the sweet melon.

spar[1] (spɑː) *n.* **1.** any piece of nautical gear resembling a pole and used as a mast, boom, gaff, etc. **2.** a principal supporting structural member of an aerofoil that runs from tip to tip or root to tip.

spar[2] (spɑː) *vb.* **sparring, sparred.** (*intr.*) **1.** *Boxing.* to box using light blows, as in training. **2.** to dispute or argue. **3.** (*of gamecocks, etc.*) to fight with the feet or spurs. ~*n.* **4.** an unaggressive fight.

spar[3] (spɑː) *n.* any of various minerals, such as feldspar, that are light-coloured, crystalline, and easily cleavable.

spare (spɛə) *vb.* **1.** (*tr.*) to refrain from killing, punishing, or injuring. **2.** (*tr.*) to release or relieve, as from pain, suffering, etc. **3.** (*tr.*) to refrain from using: *spare the rod, spoil the child.* **4.** (*tr.*) to be able to afford or give: *I can't spare the time.* **5.** (*usually passive*) (esp. of Providence) to allow to survive: *I'll see you next year if we are spared.* **6.** (*intr.*) *Now rare.* to act or live frugally. **7. not spare oneself.** to exert oneself to the full. **8. to spare.** more than is required: *two minutes to spare.* ~*adj.* **9.** (*often immediately postpositive*) in excess of what is needed; additional. **10.** able to be used when needed: *a spare part.* **11.** (of a person) thin and lean. **12.** scanty or meagre. **13.** (*postpositive*) *Brit. sl.* upset, angry, or distracted (esp. in **go spare**). ~*n.* **14.** a duplicate kept as a replacement in case of damage or loss. **15.** a spare tyre. **16.** *Tenpin bowling.* **a.** the act of knocking down all the pins with the two bowls of a single frame. **b.** the score thus made. —'**sparely** *adv.* —'**spareness** *n.* —'**sparer** *n.*

THESAURUS

spaceman *or* **spacewoman** astronaut, cosmonaut

spacious ample, broad, capacious, comfortable, commodious, expansive, extensive, huge, large, roomy, sizable, uncrowded, vast

spadework donkey-work, groundwork,

labour, preparation

span *n.* **1.** amount, distance, extent, length, reach, spread, stretch **2.** duration, period, spell, term ~*v.* **3.** arch across, bridge, cross, extend across, link, range over, traverse, vault

spank *v.* belt (*Sl.*), cuff, give (someone) a hiding (*Inf.*), put (someone) over one's knee, slap, slipper (*Inf.*), smack, tan (*Sl.*), wallop (*Inf.*)

spar *v.* argue, bicker, dispute, exchange blows, fall out (*Inf.*), have a tiff, lead a cat-

sparerib ('spεə,rɪb) n. a cut of pork ribs with most of the meat trimmed off.

spare tyre n. 1. an additional tyre carried by a motor vehicle in case of puncture. 2. Brit. sl. a deposit of fat just above the waist.

sparing ('spεərɪŋ) adj. 1. (sometimes foll. by of) economical or frugal (with). 2. scanty; meagre. 3. merciful or lenient. —'**sparingly** adv. —'**sparingness** n.

spark[1] (spɑːk) n. 1. a fiery particle thrown out or left by burning material or caused by the friction of two hard surfaces. 2. a. a momentary flash of light accompanied by a sharp crackling noise, produced by a sudden electrical discharge through the air or some other insulating medium between two points. b. the electrical discharge itself. c. (as modifier): a spark gap. 3. anything that serves to animate or kindle. 4. a trace or hint: a spark of interest. 5. vivacity, enthusiasm, or humour. 6. a small piece of diamond, as used in cutting glass. ~vb. 7. (intr.) to give off sparks. 8. (of the sparking plug or ignition system of an internal-combustion engine) to produce a spark. 9. (tr.; often foll. by off) to kindle or animate.

spark[2] (spɑːk) Rare (except for sense 2). ~n. 1. a fashionable or gallant young man. 2. **bright spark**. Brit., usually ironic. a person who appears clever or witty. ~vb. 3. to woo (a person). —'**sparkish** adj.

sparking plug n. a device screwed into the cylinder head of an internal-combustion engine to ignite the explosive mixture by means of an electric spark. Also called: **spark plug**.

sparkle ('spɑːkəl) vb. 1. to issue or reflect or cause to issue or reflect bright points of light. 2. (intr.) (of wine, mineral water, etc.) to effervesce. 3. (intr.) to be vivacious or witty. ~n. 4. a point of light, spark, or gleam.

sparkler ('spɑːklə) n. 1. a type of firework that throws out sparks. 2. Inf. a sparkling gem.

sparring partner ('spɑːrɪŋ) n. a person who practises with a boxer during training.

sparrow ('spærəu) n. 1. any of various weaverbirds, esp. the house sparrow, having a brown or grey plumage and feeding on seeds or insects. 2. U.S. any of various North American finches, such as the chipping sparrow, that have a dullish streaked plumage.

sparrowhawk ('spærəu,hɔːk) n. any of several small hawks of Eurasia and N Africa that prey on smaller birds.

sparse (spɑːs) adj. scattered or scanty; not dense. —'**sparsely** adv. —'**sparseness** or '**sparsity** n.

Spartan ('spɑːtən) adj. 1. of or relating to the ancient Greek city of Sparta or its citizens. 2. (sometimes not cap.) very strict or austere: a Spartan upbringing. 3. (sometimes not cap.) possessing courage and resolve. ~n. 4. a citizen of Sparta. 5. (sometimes not cap.) a disciplined or brave person.

spasm ('spæzəm) n. 1. an involuntary muscular contraction, esp. one resulting in cramp or convulsion. 2. a sudden burst of activity, emotion, etc.

spasmodic (spæz'mɒdɪk) or **spasmodical** adj. 1. taking place in sudden brief spells. 2. of or characterized by spasms. —**spas'modically** adv.

spastic ('spæstɪk) adj. 1. affected by or resembling spasms. 2. Derog. sl. clumsy, incapable or incompetent. ~n. 3. a person who has cerebral palsy. 4. Derog. sl. a clumsy, incapable, or incompetent person. —'**spastically** adv.

spat[1] (spæt) n. 1. Now rare. a slap or smack. 2. a slight quarrel. ~vb. **spatting, spatted**. 3. Rare. to slap (someone). 4. (intr.) U.S. to have a slight quarrel.

spat[2] (spæt) vb. a past tense or past participle of **spit**[1].

spat[3] (spæt) n. another name for **gaiter** (sense 2).

spat[4] (spæt) n. 1. a larval oyster or similar bivalve mollusc. 2. such oysters or other molluscs collectively.

spate (speɪt) n. 1. a fast flow, rush, or outpouring: a spate of words. 2. Chiefly Brit. a sudden flood: the rivers were in spate. 3. Chiefly Brit. a sudden heavy downpour.

spathe (speɪð) n. a large bract that encloses the inflorescence of several members of the lily family. —**spathaceous** (spə'θeɪʃəs) adj.

spatial or **spacial** ('speɪʃəl) adj. 1. of or relating to space. 2. existing or happening in space. —**spatiality** (,speɪʃɪ'ælɪtɪ) n. —'**spatially** adv.

spatter ('spætə) vb. 1. to scatter or splash (a substance, esp. a liquid) or (of a substance) to splash (something) in scattered drops: to spatter mud on the car; mud spattered in her face. 2. (tr.) to sprinkle, cover, or spot (with a liquid). 3. (tr.) to slander or defame. 4. (intr.) to shower or rain down: bullets spattered around them. ~n. 5. the sound of spattering. 6. something spattered, such as a spot or splash. 7. the act or an instance of spattering.

spatula ('spætjʊlə) n. a utensil with a broad flat blade, used for lifting, spreading, or stirring foods, etc. —'**spatular** adj.

spavin ('spævɪn) n. enlargement of the hock of a horse by a bony growth (**bony spavin**) or distension of the ligament (**bog spavin**), often resulting in lameness. —'**spavined** adj.

spawn (spɔːn) n. 1. the mass of eggs deposited by fish, amphibians, or molluscs. 2. Often derog. offspring, product, or yield. 3. Bot. the nontechnical name for **mycelium**. ~vb. 4. (of fish, amphibians, etc.) to produce or deposit (eggs). 5. Often derog. (of people) to produce (offspring). 6. to produce or engender. —'**spawner** n.

spay (speɪ) vb. (tr.) to remove the ovaries from (a female animal).

speak (spiːk) vb. **speaking, spoke, spoken**. 1. to make (verbal utterances); utter (words). 2. to communicate or express (something) in or as if in words. 3. (intr.) to deliver a speech, discourse, etc. 4. (tr.) to know how to talk in (a language or dialect): he does not speak German. 5. (intr.) to make a characteristic sound: the clock spoke. 6. (intr.) (of hounds used in hunting) to give tongue; bark. 7. (tr.) Naut. to hail and communicate with (another vessel) at sea. 8. (intr.) (of a musical instrument) to produce a sound. 9. (intr.; foll. by for) to be representative or advocate (of). 10. **on speaking terms**. on good terms; friendly. 11. **so to speak**. in a manner of speaking; as it were. 12. **speak one's mind**. to express one's opinions frankly and plainly. 13. **to speak of**. of a significant or worthwhile nature: no support to speak of. ~See also **speak for, speak out, speak up**. —'**speakable** adj.

THESAURUS

and-dog life, scrap (Inf.), skirmish, spat (U.S.), squabble, wrangle, wrestle

spare adj. 1. additional, emergency, extra, free, going begging (Inf.), in excess, in reserve, leftover, odd, over, superfluous, supernumerary, surplus, unoccupied, unused, unwanted 2. gaunt, lank, lean, meagre, slender, slight, slim, wiry 3. economical, frugal, meagre, modest, scanty, sparing 4. **go spare** Brit. sl. become angry (distracted, distraught, enraged, mad (Inf.), upset), blow one's top (Inf.), do one's nut (Brit. sl.), go up the wall (Sl.), have or throw a fit (Inf.) ~v. 5. afford, allow, bestow, dispense with, do without, give, grant, let (someone) have, manage without, part with, relinquish 6. be merciful to, deal leniently with, go easy on (Inf.), have mercy on, leave, let off (Inf.), pardon, refrain from, release, relieve from, save from

spare time free time, leisure, odd moments, time on one's hands, time to kill

sparing careful, chary, cost-conscious,

economical, frugal, money-conscious, prudent, saving, thrifty

spark n. 1. flare, flash, flicker, gleam, glint, scintillation, spit 2. atom, hint, jot, scintilla, scrap, trace, vestige ~v. 3. Often with **off** animate, excite, inspire, kindle, precipitate, provoke, set in motion, set off, start, stimulate, stir, touch off, trigger (off)

sparkle v. 1. beam, coruscate, dance, flash, gleam, glint, glisten, glister (Archaic), glitter, glow, scintillate, shimmer, shine, spark, twinkle, wink 2. bubble, effervesce, fizz, fizzle ~n. 3. brilliance, coruscation, dazzle, flash, flicker, gleam, glint, radiance, spark, twinkle 4. animation, dash, élan, gaiety, life, panache, spirit, vim (Sl.), vitality, vivacity, zip (Inf.)

sparse few and far between, meagre, scanty, scarce, scattered

spartan 1. abstemious, ascetic, austere, bleak, disciplined, extreme, frugal, plain, rigorous, self-denying, severe, stern, strict,

stringent 2. bold, brave, courageous, daring, dauntless, doughty, fearless, hardy, heroic, intrepid, resolute, unflinching, valorous

spasm 1. contraction, convulsion, paroxysm, throe (Rare), twitch 2. access, burst, eruption, fit, frenzy, outburst, seizure

spasmodic convulsive, erratic, fitful, intermittent, irregular, jerky, sporadic

spate deluge, flood, flow, outpouring, rush, torrent

speak 1. articulate, communicate, converse, discourse, enunciate, express, make known, pronounce, say, state, talk, tell, utter, voice 2. address, argue, declaim, deliver an address, descant, discourse, harangue, hold forth, lecture, plead, speechify, spiel (Inf.) 3. With **of** advert to, allude to, comment on, deal with, discuss, make reference to, mention, refer to

speakeasy ('spiːkˌiːzɪ) *n., pl.* **-easies.** *U.S.* a place where alcoholic drink was sold illicitly during Prohibition.

speaker ('spiːkə) *n.* **1.** a person who speaks, esp. at a formal occasion. **2.** See **loudspeaker.** —'**speakerˌship** *n.*

Speaker ('spiːkə) *n.* the presiding officer in any of numerous legislative bodies, including the House of Commons in Britain and Canada and the House of Representatives in the U.S., Australia, and New Zealand.

speak for *vb.* (*intr., prep.*) **1.** to speak as a representative of (other people). **2. speak for itself.** to be so evident that no further comment is necessary. **3. speak for yourself.** *Inf.* (used as an imperative) do not presume that other people agree with you.

speaking ('spiːkɪŋ) *adj.* **1.** (*prenominal*) eloquent, impressive, or striking. **2. a.** able to speak. **b.** (*in combination*) able to speak a particular language: *French-speaking.*

speaking clock *n. Brit.* a telephone service that gives a verbal statement of the time.

speak out *vb.* (*intr., adv.*) **1.** to state one's beliefs, objections, etc., bravely and firmly. **2.** to speak more loudly and clearly.

speak up *vb.* (*intr., adv.*) **1.** to speak more loudly. **2.** to state one's beliefs, objections, etc., bravely and firmly.

spear[1] (spɪə) *n.* **1.** a weapon consisting of a long shaft with a sharp pointed end of metal, stone, or wood that may be thrown or thrust. **2.** a similar implement used to catch fish. ~*vb.* **3.** to pierce (something) with or as if with a spear.

spear[2] (spɪə) *n.* a shoot, stalk, or blade, as of grass.

spearhead ('spɪəˌhɛd) *n.* **1.** the pointed head of a spear. **2.** the leading force in a military attack. **3.** any person or thing that leads or initiates an attack, campaign, etc. ~*vb.* **4.** (*tr.*) to lead or initiate (an attack, campaign, etc.).

spearmint ('spɪəˌmɪnt) *n.* a purple-flowered mint plant of Europe, having leaves that yield an oil used for flavouring.

spec (spɛk) *n.* **1. on spec.** *Inf.* as a speculation or gamble: *all the tickets were sold so I went to the theatre on spec.* ~*adj.* **2.** (*prenominal*) *Austral. & N.Z. inf.* speculative: *a spec developer.*

spec. *abbrev. for:* **1.** special. **2.** specification. **3.** speculation.

special ('spɛʃəl) *adj.* **1.** distinguished from, set apart from, or excelling others of its kind. **2.** (*prenominal*) designed or reserved for a particular purpose. **3.** not usual or commonplace. **4.** (*prenominal*) particular or primary: *his special interest was music.* **5.** of or relating to the education of handicapped children: *a special school.* ~*n.* **6.** a special person or thing, such as an extra edition of a newspaper or a train reserved for a particular purpose. **7.** a dish or meal given prominence, esp. at a low price, in a café, etc. **8.** short for **special constable.** —'**specially** *adv.* —'**specialness** *n.*

▷ **Usage.** See at **especial.**

Special Branch *n.* (in Britain) the department of the police force that is concerned with political security.

special constable *n.* a person recruited for temporary or occasional police duties, esp. in time of emergency.

special delivery *n.* the delivery of a piece of mail outside the time of a scheduled delivery.

specialist ('spɛʃəlɪst) *n.* a person who specializes in a particular area of activity, field of research, etc. —'**specialˌism** *n.* —ˌspecial'**istic** *adj.*

speciality (ˌspɛʃɪ'ælɪtɪ) *or* **specialty** ('spɛʃəltɪ) *n., pl.* **-ties.** **1.** a special interest or skill. **2. a.** a service or product specialized in, as at a restaurant. **b.** (*as modifier*): *a speciality dish.* **3.** a special feature or characteristic.

specialize *or* **-ise** ('spɛʃəˌlaɪz) *vb.* **1.** (*intr.*) to train in or devote oneself to a particular area of study, occupation, or activity. **2.** (*usually passive*) to cause (organisms or parts) to develop in a way most suited to a particular environment or way of life or (of organisms, etc.) to develop in this way. **3.** (*tr.*) to modify for a special use or purpose. —ˌspeciali'**zation** *or* **-i'sation** *n.*

special licence *n. Brit.* a licence permitting a marriage to take place by dispensing with the usual legal conditions.

specialty ('spɛʃəltɪ) *n., pl.* **-ties.** **1.** *Law.* a formal contract or obligation expressed in a deed. **2.** the usual U.S. spelling of **speciality.**

specie ('spiːʃiː) *n.* **1.** coin money, as distinguished from bullion or paper money. **2. in specie. a.** (of money) in coin. **b.** in kind.

species ('spiːʃiːz; *Latin* 'spiːʃɪˌiːz) *n., pl.* **-cies.** **1.** *Biol.* **a.** any of the taxonomic groups into which a genus is divided, the members of which are capable of interbreeding. **b.** the animals of such a group. **c.** any group of related animals or plants not necessarily of this taxonomic rank. **2.** *Logic.* a group of objects or individuals, all sharing common attributes, that forms a subdivision of a genus. **3.** a kind, sort, or variety: *a species of treachery.* **4.** *Chiefly R.C. Church.* the outward form of the bread and wine in the Eucharist. **5.** *Obs.* an outward appearance or form.

specif. *abbrev. for* specifically.

specific (spɪ'sɪfɪk) *adj.* **1.** explicit, particular, or definite. **2.** relating to a specified or particular thing: *a specific treatment for arthritis.* **3.** of or relating to a biological species. **4.** (of a disease) caused by a particular pathogenic agent. **5.** *Physics.* **a.** characteristic of a property of a substance, esp. in relation to the same property of a standard reference substance: *specific gravity.* **b.** characteristic of a property of a substance per unit mass, length, area, volume, etc.: *specific heat.* **c.** (of an extensive physical quantity) divided by mass: *specific volume.* **6.** denoting a tariff levied at a fixed sum per unit of weight, quantity, volume, etc., irrespective of value. ~*n.* **7.** (*sometimes pl.*) a designated quality, thing, etc. **8.** *Med.* any drug used to treat a particular disease. —spe'**cifically** *adv.* —**specificity** (ˌspɛsɪ-'fɪsɪtɪ) *n.*

specification (ˌspɛsɪfɪ'keɪʃən) *n.* **1.** the act or an instance of specifying. **2.** (in patent law) a written statement accompanying an application for a patent that describes the nature of an invention. **3.** (*usually pl.*) a detailed description of the criteria for the constituents, construction, appearance, performance, etc., of a material, apparatus, etc., or of the standard of workmanship required in its manufacture. **4.** an item, detail, etc., specified.

specific gravity *n.* the ratio of the density of a substance to that of water.

specify ('spɛsɪˌfaɪ) *vb.* **-fying, -fied.** (*tr.; may take a clause as object*) **1.** to refer to or state specifically. **2.** to state as a condition. **3.** to state or include in the specification of. —'**speciˌfiable** *adj.* —**specificative**

═══ THESAURUS ═══

speaker lecturer, mouthpiece, orator, public speaker, spieler (*Inf.*), spokesman, spokesperson, spokeswoman, word-spinner

speak for act for *or* on behalf of, appear for, hold a brief for, hold a mandate for, represent

speaking *adj.* eloquent, expressive, moving, noticeable, striking

speak out *or* **up** 1. make oneself heard, say it loud and clear, speak loudly 2. have one's say, make one's position plain, sound off, speak one's mind, stand up and be counted

speak to 1. accost, address, apostrophize, direct one's words at, talk to 2. admonish, bring to book, dress down (*Inf.*), lecture, rebuke, reprimand, scold, tell off (*Inf.*), tick off (*Inf.*), warn

spearhead *v.* be in the van, blaze the trail, head, initiate, launch, lay the first stone, lead, lead the way, pioneer, set in motion, set off

special 1. distinguished, especial, exceptional, extraordinary, festive, gala, important, memorable, momentous, out of the ordinary, red-letter, significant, uncommon, unique, unusual 2. appropriate, certain, characteristic, distinctive, especial, individual, particular, peculiar, precise, specialized, specific 3. chief, main, major, particular, primary

specialist *n.* authority, connoisseur, consultant, expert, master, professional

speciality claim to fame, distinctive *or* distinguishing feature, forte, *pièce de résistance*, special, specialty

species breed, category, class, collection, description, group, kind, sort, type, variety

specific *adj.* 1. clear-cut, definite, exact, explicit, express, limited, particular, precise, unambiguous, unequivocal 2. characteristic, distinguishing, especial, peculiar, special

specification condition, detail, item, particular, qualification, requirement, stipulation

specify be specific about, cite, define, designate, detail, enumerate, indicate, individualize, itemize, mention, name, particularize, spell out, stipulate

('spɛsɪfɪˌkeɪtɪv) *adj.*

specimen ('spɛsɪmɪn) *n.* **1. a.** an individual, object, or part regarded as typical of its group or class. **b.** (*as modifier*): *a specimen page.* **2.** *Med.* a sample of tissue, blood, urine, etc., taken for diagnostic examination or evaluation. **3.** the whole or a part of an organism, plant, rock, etc., collected and preserved as an example of its class, species, etc. **4.** *Inf., often derog.* a person.

specious ('spiːʃəs) *adj.* **1.** apparently correct or true, but actually wrong or false. **2.** deceptively attractive in appearance. —**'speciously** *adv.* —**speciosity** (ˌspiːʃɪ-'ɒsɪtɪ) *or* **'speciousness** *n.*

speck (spɛk) *n.* **1.** a very small mark or spot. **2.** a small or tiny piece of something. ~*vb.* **3.** (*tr.*) to mark with specks or spots.

speckle ('spɛkəl) *n.* **1.** a small mark usually of a contrasting colour, as on the skin, a bird's plumage, or eggs. ~*vb.* **2.** (*tr.*) to mark with or as if with speckles.

specs (spɛks) *pl. n. Inf.* **1.** short for **spectacles**. **2.** short for **specifications** (see sense 3)).

spectacle ('spɛktəkəl) *n.* **1.** a public display or performance, esp. a showy or ceremonial one. **2.** a thing or person seen, esp. an unusual or ridiculous one: *he makes a spectacle of himself.* **3.** a strange or interesting object or phenomenon.

spectacles ('spɛktəkəlz) *pl. n.* **1.** a pair of glasses for correcting defective vision. Often (*informal*) shortened to **specs**. **2. pair of spectacles.** *Cricket.* a score of 0 in each innings of a match. —**'spectacled** *adj.*

spectacular (spɛk'tækjʊlə) *adj.* **1.** of or resembling a spectacle; impressive, grand, or dramatic. **2.** unusually marked or great: *a spectacular increase.* ~*n.* **3.** a lavishly produced performance. —**spec'tacularly** *adv.*

spectator (spɛk'teɪtə) *n.* a person viewing anything; onlooker; observer.

spectra ('spɛktrə) *n.* the plural of **spectrum**.

spectral ('spɛktrəl) *adj.* **1.** of or like a spectre. **2.** of or relating to a spectrum. —**spectrality** (spɛk'trælɪtɪ) *n.* —**'spectrally** *adv.*

spectre *or U.S.* **specter** ('spɛktə) *n.* **1.** a ghost; phantom; apparition. **2.** an unpleasant or menacing mental image: *the spectre of redundancy.*

spectro- *combining form.* indicating a spectrum: *spectrogram.*

spectroscope ('spɛktrəˌskəʊp) *n.* any of a number of instruments for dispersing electromagnetic radiation and thus forming or recording a spectrum. —**spectroscopic** (ˌspɛktrə'skɒpɪk) *or* **ˌspectro'scopical** *adj.*

spectroscopy (spɛk'trɒskəpɪ) *n.* the science and practice of using spectrometers and spectroscopes and of analysing spectra. —**spec'troscopist** *n.*

spectrum ('spɛktrəm) *n., pl* **-tra** (-trə). **1.** the distribution of colours produced when white light is dispersed by a prism or diffraction grating. There is a continuous change in wavelength from red, the longest wavelength, to violet, the shortest. Seven colours are usually distinguished: violet, indigo, blue, green, yellow, orange, and

red. **2.** the whole range of electromagnetic radiation with respect to its wavelength or frequency. **3.** any particular distribution of electromagnetic radiation often showing lines or bands characteristic of the substance emitting the radiation or absorbing it. **4.** any similar distribution or record of the energies, velocities, masses, etc., of atoms, ions, electrons, etc.: *a mass spectrum.* **5.** any range or scale, as of capabilities, emotions, or moods.

speculate ('spɛkjʊˌleɪt) *vb.* **1.** (when *tr., takes a clause as object*) to conjecture without knowing the complete facts. **2.** (*intr.*) to buy or sell securities, property, etc., in the hope of deriving capital gains. **3.** (*intr.*) to risk loss for the possibility of considerable gain. **4.** (*intr.*) *N.Z.* in rugby football, to make an emergency undirected kick at the ball. —ˌ**specu'lation** *n.* —**'specuˌlator** *n.*

sped (spɛd) *vb.* a past tense or past participle of **speed**.

speech (spiːtʃ) *n.* **1. a.** the act or faculty of speaking. **b.** (*as modifier*): *speech therapy.* **2.** that which is spoken; utterance. **3.** a talk or address delivered to an audience. **4.** a person's characteristic manner of speaking. **5.** a national or regional language or dialect. **6.** *Linguistics.* another word for **parole** (sense 3).

speech day *n. Brit.* (in schools) an annual day on which prizes are presented, speeches are made by guest speakers, etc.

speechify ('spiːtʃɪˌfaɪ) *vb.* **-fying, -fied.** (*intr.*) **1.** to make a speech or speeches. **2.** to talk pompously and boringly. —**'speechiˌfier** *n.*

speechless ('spiːtʃlɪs) *adj.* **1.** not able to speak. **2.** temporarily deprived of speech. **3.** not expressed or able to be expressed in words: *speechless fear.* —**'speechlessly** *adv.* —**'speechlessness** *n.*

speed (spiːd) *n.* **1.** the act or quality of acting or moving fast; rapidity. **2.** the rate at which something moves, is done, or acts. **3.** *Physics.* **a.** a scalar measure of the rate of movement of a body expressed either as the distance travelled divided by the time taken (**average speed**) or the rate of change of position with respect to time at a particular point (**instantaneous speed**). **b.** another word for **velocity** (sense 2). **4.** a rate of rotation, usually expressed in revolutions per unit time. **5. a.** a gear ratio in a motor vehicle, bicycle, etc. **b.** (*in combination*): *a three-speed gear.* **6.** *Photog.* a numerical expression of the sensitivity to light of a particular type of film, paper, or plate. **7.** *Photog.* a measure of the ability of a lens to pass light from an object to the image position. **8.** a slang word for **amphetamine**. **9.** *Arch.* prosperity or success. ~*vb.* **speeding; sped** *or* **speeded. 10.** to move or go or cause to move or go quickly. **11.** (*intr.*) to drive (a motor vehicle) at a high speed, esp. above legal limits. **12.** (*tr.*) to help further the success or completion of. **13.** (*intr.*) *Sl.* to take or be under the influence of amphetamines. **14.** (*intr.*) to operate or run at a high speed. **15.** *Arch.* **a.** (*intr.*) to prosper or succeed. **b.** (*tr.*) to wish success to. —**'speeder** *n.*

speedboat ('spiːdˌbəʊt) *n.* a high-speed motorboat.

speed limit *n.* the maximum permitted speed at

THESAURUS

specimen copy, embodiment, example, exemplar, exemplification, exhibit, individual, instance, model, pattern, proof, representative, sample, type

specious casuistic, deceptive, fallacious, misleading, plausible, sophistic, sophistical, unsound

speck 1. blemish, blot, defect, dot, fault, flaw, fleck, mark, mote, speckle, spot, stain 2. atom, bit, dot, grain, iota, jot, mite, modicum, particle, shred, tittle, whit

speckled brindled, dappled, dotted, flecked, freckled, mottled, speckledy, spotted, spotty, sprinkled, stippled

spectacle 1. display, event, exhibition, extravaganza, pageant, parade, performance, show, sight 2. curiosity, laughing stock, marvel, phenomenon, scene, sight, wonder

spectacular 1. *adj.* breathtaking, daring, dazzling, dramatic, eye-catching, fantastic (*Inf.*), grand, impressive, magnificent, marked, remarkable, sensational, splendid, staggering, striking, stunning (*Inf.*) 2. *n.* display, extravaganza, show, spectacle

spectator beholder, bystander, eyewitness, looker-on, observer, onlooker, viewer, watcher, witness

spectre apparition, ghost, phantom, presence, shade (*Literary*), shadow, spirit, vision, wraith

speculate 1. cogitate, conjecture, consider, contemplate, deliberate, hypothesize, meditate, muse, scheme, suppose, surmise, theorize, wonder 2. gamble, have a flutter (*Inf.*), hazard, play the market, risk, take a chance with, venture

speculation 1. conjecture, consideration, contemplation, deliberation, guess, guesswork, hypothesis, opinion, supposition, surmise, theory 2. gamble, gambling, hazard, risk

speculative 1. abstract, academic, conjectural, hypothetical, notional, suppositional, tentative, theoretical 2. chancy (*Inf.*), dicey (*Sl.*), hazardous, risky, uncertain, unpredictable

speech 1. communication, conversation, dialogue, discussion, intercourse, talk 2. address, discourse, disquisition, harangue,

homily, lecture, oration, spiel (*Inf.*) 3. articulation, dialect, diction, enunciation, idiom, jargon, language, lingo (*Inf.*), parlance, tongue, utterance, voice

speechless 1. dumb, inarticulate, mum, mute, silent, tongue-tied, unable to get a word out (*Inf.*), wordless 2. *Fig.* aghast, amazed, astounded, dazed, dumbfounded, dumbstruck, shocked, thunderstruck

speed *n.* 1. acceleration, celerity, expedition, fleetness, haste, hurry, momentum, pace, precipitation, quickness, rapidity, rush, swiftness, velocity ~*v.* 2. belt (along) (*Sl.*), bomb (along), bowl along, career, dispatch, exceed the speed limit, expedite, flash, gallop, get a move on (*Inf.*), go hell for leather (*Inf.*), go like a bat out of hell (*Inf.*), go like the wind, hasten, hurry, lose no time, make haste, press on, put one's foot down (*Inf.*), quicken, race, rush, sprint, step on it (*Inf.*), tear, urge, zoom 3. advance, aid, assist, boost, expedite, facilitate, further, help, impel, promote

which a vehicle may travel on certain roads.

speedo ('spi:dəʊ) n., pl. **-os.** an informal name for **speedometer.**

speedometer (spɪ'dɒmɪtə) n. a device fitted to a vehicle to measure and display the speed of travel. See also **mileometer.**

speed up vb. (adv.) **1.** to increase or cause to increase in speed or rate; accelerate. ~n. **speed-up. 2.** an instance of this; acceleration.

speedway ('spi:d,weɪ) n. **1.** the sport of racing on light powerful motorcycles round cinder tracks. **2.** the track or stadium where such races are held. **3.** U.S. **a.** a race-track for cars. **b.** a road on which fast driving is allowed.

speedwell ('spi:d,wɛl) n. any of various temperate plants, such as the **common speedwell** and the **germander speedwell,** having small blue or pinkish-white flowers.

speedy ('spi:dɪ) adj. **-ier, -iest. 1.** characterized by speed. **2.** done or decided without delay. —'**speedily** adv. —'**speediness** n.

spek (spɛk) n. S. African. bacon.

speleology or **spelaeology** (ˌspi:lɪ'ɒlədʒɪ) n. **1.** the scientific study of caves. **2.** the sport or pastime of exploring caves. —**speleological** or **spelaeological** (ˌspi:lɪə-'lɒdʒɪkəl) adj. —ˌspele'ologist or ˌspelae'ologist n.

spell¹ (spɛl) vb. **spelling; spelt** or **spelled. 1.** to write or name in correct order the letters that comprise the conventionally accepted form of (a word). **2.** (tr.) (of letters) to go to make up the conventionally established form of (a word) when arranged correctly: d-o-g spells dog. **3.** (tr.) to indicate or signify: such actions spell disaster. ~See also **spell out.** —'**spellable** adj.

spell² (spɛl) n. **1.** a verbal formula considered as having magical force. **2.** any influence that can control the mind or character; fascination. **3.** a state induced as by the pronouncing of a spell; trance: to break the spell. **4. under a spell.** held in or as if in a spell.

spell³ (spɛl) n. **1.** an indeterminate, usually short, period of time: a spell of cold weather. **2.** a period or tour of duty after which one person or group relieves another. **3.** Austral. a period or interval of rest. ~vb. **4.** (tr.) to take over from (a person) for an interval of time; relieve temporarily.

spellbind ('spɛl,baɪnd) vb. **-binding, -bound.** to cause to be spellbound; entrance or enthral. —'**spell-,binder** n.

spell out vb. (tr., adv.) **1.** to make clear, distinct, or explicit; clarify in detail: let me spell out the implications. **2.** to read laboriously or with difficulty, working out each word letter by letter. **3.** to discern by study; puzzle out.

spelt¹ (spɛlt) vb. a past tense or past participle of **spell¹.**

spelt² (spɛlt) n. a species of wheat that was formerly much cultivated and was used to develop present-day cultivated wheats.

spelunker (spɪ'lʌŋkə) n. a person whose hobby is the exploration of caves. —**spe'lunking** n.

spend (spɛnd) vb. **spending, spent. 1.** to pay out (money, wealth, etc.). **2.** (tr.) to concentrate (time, effort, etc.) upon an object, activity, etc. **3.** (tr.) to pass (time) in a specific way, place, etc. **4.** (tr.) to use up completely: the hurricane spent its force. **5.** (tr.) to give up (one's

blood, life, etc.) in a cause. **6.** (intr.) Obs. to be used up or exhausted. **7. spend a penny.** Brit. inf. to urinate. —'**spendable** adj. —'**spender** n.

spendthrift ('spɛnd,θrɪft) n. **1.** a person who spends money in an extravagant manner. ~adj. **2.** (usually prenominal) of or like a spendthrift.

spent (spɛnt) vb. **1.** the past tense or past participle of **spend.** ~adj. **2.** used up or exhausted; consumed.

sperm (spɜːm) n. **1.** another name for **semen. 2.** a male reproductive cell; male gamete.

spermaceti (ˌspɜːmə'sɛtɪ, -'si:tɪ) n. a white waxy substance obtained from oil from the head of the sperm whale.

spermato-, spermo- or before a vowel **spermat-, sperm-** combining form. **1.** indicating sperm: spermatogenesis. **2.** indicating seed: spermatophyte.

spermatozoon (ˌspɜːmətəʊ'zəʊɒn) n., pl. **-zoa** (-'zəʊə). any of the male reproductive cells released in the semen during ejaculation. Also called: **sperm, zoosperm.** —ˌspermato'zoal, ˌspermato'zoan, or ˌspermato'zoic adj.

spermicide ('spɜːmɪ,saɪd) n. any agent that kills spermatozoa. —ˌspermi'cidal adj.

sperm oil n. an oil obtained from the head of the sperm whale, used as a lubricant.

sperm whale n. a large toothed whale, having a square-shaped head and hunted for sperm oil, spermaceti, and ambergris. Also called: **cachalot.**

spew (spju:) vb. **1.** to eject (the contents of the stomach) involuntarily through the mouth; vomit. **2.** to spit (spittle, phlegm, etc.) out of the mouth. **3.** (usually foll. by out) to send or be sent out in a stream: flames spewed out. ~n. **4.** something ejected from the mouth. ~Also (archaic): **spue.** —'**spewer** n.

sp. gr. abbrev. for specific gravity.

sphagnum ('sfægnəm) n. any moss of the genus Sphagnum, of temperate bogs: layers of these mosses decay to form peat. Also called: **peat moss, bog moss.** —'**sphagnous** adj.

sphere (sfɪə) n. **1.** Maths. **a.** a three-dimensional closed surface such that every point on the surface is equidistant from a given point, the centre. **b.** the solid figure bounded by this surface or the space enclosed by it. **2.** any object having approximately this shape; a globe. **3.** the night sky considered as a vaulted roof; firmament. **4.** any heavenly object such as a planet, natural satellite, or star. **5.** (in the Ptolemaic or Copernican systems of astronomy) one of a series of revolving hollow globes, arranged concentrically, on whose transparent surfaces the sun, the moon, the planets, and fixed stars were thought to be set. **6.** a particular field of activity; environment. **7.** a social class or stratum of society. ~vb. (tr.) Chiefly poetic. **8.** to surround or encircle. **9.** to place aloft or in the heavens. —'**spheral** adj.

spherical ('sfɛrɪkəl) or **spheric** adj. **1.** shaped like a sphere. **2.** of or relating to a sphere: spherical geometry. **3.** Geom. formed on the surface of or inside a sphere: a spherical triangle. **4. a.** of or relating to heavenly bodies. **b.** of or relating to the spheres of the Ptolemaic or the Copernican system. —'**spherically** adv. —'**sphericalness** n.

spheroid ('sfɪərɔɪd) n. **1.** Also called: **ellipsoid of revolution.** a geometric surface produced by rotating an el-

---

THESAURUS

speed up accelerate, gather momentum, get moving, get under way, increase, increase the tempo, open up the throttle, put one's foot down (Inf.), put on speed

speedy expeditious, express, fast, fleet, fleet of foot, hasty, headlong, hurried, immediate, nimble, precipitate, prompt, quick, rapid, summary, swift, winged

spell¹ n. bout, course, interval, patch, period, season, stint, stretch, term, time, tour of duty, turn

spell² n. **1.** abracadabra, charm, conjuration, exorcism, incantation, sorcery, witchery **2.** allure, bewitchment, enchantment, fascination, glamour, magic, trance

spell³ v. amount to, augur, herald, imply, indicate, mean, point to, portend, presage, promise, signify, suggest

spellbound bemused, bewitched, capti-

vated, charmed, enthralled, entranced, fascinated, gripped, hooked (Inf.), mesmerized, possessed, rapt, transfixed, transported, under a spell

spelling orthography

spell out 1. clarify, elucidate, make clear or plain, make explicit, specify **2.** discern, make out, puzzle out

spend 1. disburse, expend, fork out (Sl.), lay out, pay out, shell out (Inf.), splash out (Brit. inf.) **2.** blow (Sl.), consume, deplete, dispense, dissipate, drain, empty, exhaust, fritter away, run through, squander, use up, waste **3.** apply, bestow, concentrate, devote, employ, invest, lavish, put in, use **4.** fill, occupy, pass, while away

spendthrift 1. n. big spender, prodigal, profligate, spender, squanderer, waster, wastrel **2.** adj. extravagant, improvident,

prodigal, profligate, wasteful

spent adj. **1.** all in (Sl.), burnt out, bushed (U.S. inf.), dead beat (Inf.), debilitated, dog-tired (Inf.), done in or up (Inf.), drained, exhausted, fagged (out) (Inf.), knackered (Sl.), played out (Inf.), prostrate, ready to drop (Inf.), shattered (Inf.), tired out, weakened, wearied, weary, whacked (Brit. inf.), worn out **2.** consumed, expended, finished, gone, used up

sphere 1. ball, circle, globe, globule, orb **2.** capacity, compass, department, domain, employment, field, function, pale, province, range, rank, realm, scope, station, stratum, territory, walk of life

spherical globe-shaped, globular, orbicular, rotund, round

lipse about one of its two axes and having circular plane sections perpendicular to the axis of revolution. ~*adj.* **2.** shaped like but not exactly a sphere. —**spher'oidal** *adj.* —,**spheroid'icity** *n.*

sphincter ('sfɪŋktə) *n. Anat.* a ring of muscle surrounding the opening of a hollow organ or body and contracting to close it. —'**sphincteral** *adj.*

sphinx (sfɪŋks) *n., pl.* **sphinxes** *or* **sphinges** ('sfɪndʒiːz). **1.** any of a number of huge stone statues built by the ancient Egyptians, having the body of a lion and the head of a man. **2.** an inscrutable person.

Sphinx (sfɪŋks) *n.* **the. 1.** *Greek myth.* a monster with a woman's head and a lion's body. She lay outside Thebes, asking travellers a riddle and killing them when they failed to answer it. Oedipus answered the riddle and the Sphinx then killed herself. **2.** the huge statue of a sphinx near the pyramids at Gisa in Egypt.

spice (spaɪs) *n.* **1. a.** any of a variety of aromatic vegetable substances, such as ginger, cinnamon, or nutmeg, used as flavourings. **b.** these substances collectively. **2.** something that represents or introduces zest, charm, or gusto. **3.** *Rare.* a small amount. ~*vb.* (*tr.*) **4.** to prepare or flavour (food) with spices. **5.** to introduce charm or zest into.

spick-and-span *or* **spic-and-span** ('spɪkən'spæn) *adj.* **1.** extremely neat and clean. **2.** new and fresh.

spicy ('spaɪsɪ) *adj.* **-ier, -iest. 1.** seasoned with or containing spice. **2.** highly flavoured; pungent. **3.** *Inf.* suggestive of scandal or sensation. —'**spicily** *adv.* —'**spiciness** *n.*

spider ('spaɪdə) *n.* **1.** any of various predatory silk-producing arachnids, having four pairs of legs and a rounded unsegmented body. **2.** any of various similar or related arachnids. **3.** any implement or tool having the shape of a spider. **4.** any part of a machine having a number of radiating spokes, tines, or arms. **5.** Also called: **octopus.** *Brit.* a cluster of elastic straps fastened at a central point and used to hold a load on a car rack, motorcycle, etc. **6.** *Snooker, etc.* a rest having long legs, used to raise the cue above the level of the height of the ball. —'**spidery** *adj.*

spider monkey *n.* **1.** any of several arboreal New World monkeys of Central and South America, having very long legs, a long prehensile tail, and a small head. **2. woolly spider monkey.** a rare related monkey of SE Brazil.

spiel (ʃpiːl) *Sl., chiefly U.S.* ~*n.* **1.** glib plausible talk, associated esp. with salesmen. ~*vb.* **2.** (*intr.*) to deliver a prepared spiel. **3.** (*tr.;* usually foll. by *off*) to recite (a prepared oration). —'**spieler** *n.*

spigot ('spɪgət) *n.* **1.** a stopper for the vent hole of a cask. **2.** a tap, usually of wood, fitted to a cask. **3.** a U.S. name for **tap²** (sense 1). **4.** a short projection on one component designed to fit into a hole on another, esp. the male part of a joint between two pipes.

spike¹ (spaɪk) *n.* **1.** a sharp point. **2.** any sharp-pointed object, esp. one made of metal. **3.** a long metal nail. **4.** (*pl.*) shoes with metal projections on the sole and heel for greater traction, as used by athletes. ~*vb.* (*tr.*) **5.** to secure or supply with or as with spikes. **6.** to render ineffective or block the intentions of; thwart. **7.** to impale on a spike. **8.** to add (alcohol) to a drink. **9.** *Volleyball.* to hit (a ball) sharply downwards with an overarm motion from the front of one's own court into the opposing court. **10.** (formerly) to render (a cannon) ineffective by blocking its vent with a spike. **11. spike someone's guns.** to thwart someone's purpose. —'**spiky** *adj.*

spike² (spaɪk) *n. Bot.* **1.** an inflorescence consisting of a raceme of sessile flowers. **2.** an ear of wheat, barley, etc.

spikelet ('spaɪklɪt) *n. Bot.* a small spike, esp. the inflorescence of most grasses and sedges.

spikenard ('spaɪknɑːd, 'spaɪkə,nɑːd) *n.* **1.** an aromatic Indian plant, having rose-purple flowers. **2.** an aromatic ointment obtained from this plant. **3.** any of various

similar or related plants. **4.** a North American plant having small green flowers and an aromatic root. ~Also called (for senses 1, 2): **nard.**

spill¹ (spɪl) *vb.* **spilling; spilt** *or* **spilled.** (*mainly tr.*) **1.** (when *intr.*, usually foll. by *from, out of,* etc.) to fall or cause to fall from or as from a container, esp. unintentionally. **2.** to disgorge (contents, occupants, etc.) or (of contents, occupants, etc.) to be disgorged. **3.** to shed (blood). **4.** Also: **spill the beans.** *Inf.* to reveal (a secret). **5.** *Naut.* to let (wind) escape from a sail or (of the wind) to escape from a sail. ~*n.* **6.** *Inf.* a fall or tumble. **7.** short for **spillway. 8.** a spilling of liquid, etc., or the amount spilt. **9.** *Austral.* the declaring of several political jobs vacant when one higher up becomes so. —'**spillage** *n.* —'**spiller** *n.*

spill² (spɪl) *n.* a splinter of wood or strip of twisted paper with which pipes, fires, etc., are lit.

spillikin, spilikin ('spɪlɪkɪn), *or* **spellican** ('spɛlɪkən) *n.* a thin strip of wood, cardboard, or plastic, esp. one used in spillikins.

spill over *vb.* **1.** (*intr., adv.*) to overflow or be forced out of an area, container, etc. ~*n.* **spillover. 2.** *Chiefly U.S.* the act of spilling over. **3.** *Chiefly U.S.* the excess part of something.

spillway ('spɪl,weɪ) *n.* a channel that carries away surplus water, as from a dam.

spin (spɪn) *vb.* **spinning, spun. 1.** to rotate or cause to rotate rapidly, as on an axis. **2. a.** to draw out and twist (natural fibres, as of silk or cotton) into a long continuous thread. **b.** to make such a thread or filament from (synthetic resins, etc.), usually by forcing through a nozzle. **3.** (of spiders, silkworms, etc.) to form (webs, cocoons, etc.) from a silky fibre exuded from the body. **4.** (*tr.*) to shape (metal) into a rounded form on a lathe. **5.** (*tr.*) *Inf.* to tell (a tale, story, etc.) by drawing it out at great length (esp. in **spin a yarn**). **6.** to bowl, pitch, hit, or kick (a ball) so that it rotates in the air and changes direction or speed on bouncing, or (of a ball) to be projected in this way. **7.** (*intr.*) (of wheels) to revolve rapidly without causing propulsion. **8.** to cause (an aircraft) to dive in a spiral descent or (of an aircraft) to dive in a spiral descent. **9.** (*intr.;* foll. by *along*) to drive or travel swiftly. **10.** (*tr.*) Also: **spin-dry.** to rotate (clothes) in a washing machine in order to extract surplus water. **11.** (*intr.*) to reel or grow dizzy, as from turning around: *my head is spinning.* **12.** (*intr.*) to fish by drawing a revolving lure through the water. ~*n.* **13.** a swift rotating motion; instance of spinning. **14.** *Physics.* **a.** the intrinsic angular momentum of an elementary particle or atomic nucleus. **b.** a quantum number determining values of this angular momentum. **15.** a condition of loss of control of an aircraft or an intentional flight manoeuvre in which the aircraft performs a continuous spiral descent. **16.** a spinning motion imparted to a ball, etc. **17.** *Inf.* a short or fast drive, ride, etc., esp. in a car, for pleasure. **18.** *Inf., chiefly Brit.* a state of agitation or confusion. **19.** *Austral. & N.Z. inf.* a period of a specified kind of fortune: *a bad spin.* ~See also **spin out.**

spina bifida ('spaɪnə 'bɪfɪdə) *n.* a congenital condition in which the meninges of the spinal cord protrude through a gap in the backbone, sometimes causing enlargement of the skull and paralysis.

spinach ('spɪnɪdʒ, -ɪtʃ) *n.* **1.** an annual plant cultivated for its dark green edible leaves. **2.** the leaves, eaten boiled as a vegetable.

spinal ('spaɪn°l) *adj.* of or relating to the spine or the spinal cord. —'**spinally** *adv.*

spinal column *n.* a series of contiguous or interconnecting bony or cartilaginous segments that surround and protect the spinal cord. Also called: **spine, vertebral column.** Nontechnical name: **backbone.**

spinal cord *n.* the thick cord of nerve tissue within the spinal canal, which together with the brain forms the central nervous system.

spin bowler *n. Cricket.* a bowler who specializes in

THESAURUS

spice *n.* **1.** relish, savour, seasoning **2.** colour, excitement, gusto, kick (*Inf.*), pep, piquancy, tang, zap (*Sl.*), zest, zip (*Inf.*)

spike *n.* **1.** barb, point, prong, spine ~*v.* **2.** impale, spear, spit, stick **3.** block, foil, frustrate, render ineffective, thwart

spill *v.* **1.** discharge, disgorge, overflow, overturn, scatter, shed, slop over, spill or run

over, throw off, upset **2. spill the beans** *Inf.* betray a secret, blab, blow the gaff (*Brit. sl.*), give the game away, inform, let the cat out of the bag, split (*Sl.*), squeal (*Sl.*), talk out of turn, tattle ~*n.* **3.** *Inf.* accident, cropper (*Inf.*), fall, tumble

spin *v.* **1.** gyrate, pirouette, reel, revolve, rotate, turn, twirl, twist, wheel, whirl **2.** con-

coct, develop, invent, narrate, recount, relate, tell, unfold **3.** be giddy, be in a whirl, grow dizzy, reel, swim, whirl ~*n.* **4.** gyration, revolution, roll, twist, whirl **5.** (flat) spin *Inf.* agitation, commotion, flap (*Inf.*), panic, state (*Inf.*), tiz-woz (*Inf.*), tizzy (*Inf.*) **6.** *Inf.* drive, hurl (*Scot.*), joy ride (*Inf.*), ride, turn, whirl

bowling balls with a spinning motion.

spindle ('spɪndəl) *n.* **1.** a rod or stick that has a notch in the top, used to draw out natural fibres for spinning into thread, and a long narrow body around which the thread is wound when spun. **2.** one of the thin rods or pins bearing bobbins upon which spun thread is wound in a spinning machine. **3.** any of various parts in the form of a rod, esp. a rotating rod that acts as an axle, etc. **4.** a piece of wood that has been turned, such as a table leg. **5.** a small square metal shaft that passes through the lock of a door and to which the door knobs or handles are fixed. **6.** *Biol.* a spindle-shaped bundle of nuclear fibres that is formed in a cell during mitosis and meiosis and along which chromosomes migrate to opposite ends of the cell. **7.** a device consisting of a sharp upright spike on a pedestal on which bills, order forms, etc., are impaled. ~*vb.* **8.** (*tr.*) to form into a spindle or equip with spindles. **9.** (*intr.*) *Rare.* (of a plant, stem, shoot, etc.) to grow rapidly and become elongated and thin.

spindlelegs ('spɪndəl,lɛgz) *or* **spindleshanks** *pl. n.* **1.** long thin legs. **2.** (*functioning as sing.*) a person who has such legs.

spindly ('spɪndlɪ) *adj.* **-dlier, -dliest.** tall, slender, and frail; attenuated.

spindrift ('spɪn,drɪft) *or* **spoondrift** *n.* spray blown up from the sea.

spin-dry *vb.* **-drying, -dried.** (*tr.*) to dry (clothes, etc.) in a spin-dryer.

spin-dryer *n.* a device that extracts water from clothes, etc., by spinning them in a perforated drum.

spine (spaɪn) *n.* **1.** the spinal column. **2.** the sharply pointed tip or outgrowth of a leaf, stem, etc. **3.** *Zool.* a hard pointed process or structure, such as the quill of a porcupine. **4.** Also called: **backbone.** a bound edge or back of a book. **5.** a ridge, esp. of a hill. **6.** strength of endurance, will, etc. **7.** anything resembling the spinal column in function or importance; main support or feature. —**spined** *adj.*

spineless ('spaɪnlɪs) *adj.* **1.** lacking a backbone. **2.** having no spiny processes: *spineless stems.* **3.** lacking character, resolution, or courage. —'**spinelessly** *adv.* —'**spinelessness** *n.*

spinet (spɪ'nɛt, 'spɪnɪt) *n.* a small type of harpsichord having one manual.

spinnaker ('spɪnəkə; *Naut.* 'spæŋkə) *n.* a large light triangular racing sail set from the foremast of a yacht.

spinner ('spɪnə) *n.* **1.** a person or thing that spins. **2.** *Cricket.* **a.** a ball that is bowled with a spinning motion. **b.** a bowler who specializes in bowling such balls. **3.** a streamlined fairing that fits over the hub of an aircraft propeller. **4.** a fishing lure with a fin or wing that revolves.

spinneret ('spɪnə,rɛt) *n.* **1.** any of several organs in spiders and certain insects through which silk threads are exuded. **2.** a finely perforated dispenser through which a liquid is extruded in the production of synthetic fibres.

spinney ('spɪnɪ) *n. Chiefly Brit.* a small wood or copse.

spinning ('spɪnɪŋ) *n.* **1.** the act or process of spinning. **2.** the act or technique of casting and drawing a revolving lure through the water so as to imitate a live fish, etc.

spinning jenny *n.* an early type of spinning frame with several spindles, invented in 1764.

spinning wheel *n.* a wheel-like machine for spinning at home, having one hand- or foot-operated spindle.

spin-off *n.* any product or development derived incidentally from the application of existing knowledge or enterprise.

spin out *vb.* (*tr., adv.*) **1.** to extend or protract (a story, etc.) by including superfluous detail. **2.** to spend or pass (time). **3.** to contrive to cause (money, etc.) to last as long as possible.

spinster ('spɪnstə) *n.* **1.** an unmarried woman regarded as being beyond the age of marriage. **2.** (formerly) a woman who spins thread for her living. —'**spinster-,hood** *n.* —'**spinsterish** *adj.*

spiny ('spaɪnɪ) *adj.* **-ier, -iest.** **1.** (of animals) having or covered with quills or spines. **2.** (of plants) covered with spines; thorny. **3.** troublesome; puzzling. —'**spininess** *n.*

spiracle ('spaɪərəkəl, 'spaɪrə-) *n.* **1.** any of several paired apertures in the cuticle of an insect, by which air enters and leaves the trachea. **2.** a small paired rudimentary gill slit in skates, rays, and related fishes. **3.** any similar respiratory aperture, such as the blowhole in whales. —**spiracular** (spɪ'rækjulə) *adj.* —**spi'raculate** *adj.*

spiraea *or esp. U.S.* **spirea** (spaɪ'rɪə) *n.* any of various rosaceous plants, having sprays of small white or pink flowers. See also **meadowsweet** (sense 2).

spiral ('spaɪərəl) *n.* **1.** *Geom.* one of several plane curves formed by a point winding about a fixed point at an ever-increasing distance from it. **2.** a curve that lies on a cylinder or cone, at a constant angle to the line segments making up the surface; helix. **3.** something that pursues a winding, usually upward, course or that displays a twisting form or shape. **4.** a flight manoeuvre in which an aircraft descends describing a helix of comparatively large radius with the angle of attack within the normal flight range. **5.** *Econ.* a continuous upward or downward movement in economic activity or prices, caused by interaction between prices, wages, demand, and production. ~*adj.* **6.** having the shape of a spiral. ~*vb.* **-ralling, -ralled** *or U.S.* **-raling, -raled.** **7.** to assume or cause to assume a spiral course or shape. **8.** (*intr.*) to increase or decrease with steady acceleration: *prices continue to spiral.* —'**spirally** *adv.*

spirant ('spaɪərənt) *adj.* **1.** *Phonetics.* another word for **fricative.** ~*n.* **2.** a fricative consonant.

spire (spaɪə) *n.* **1.** Also called: **steeple.** a tall structure that tapers upwards to a point, esp. one on a tower or roof or one that forms the upper part of a steeple. **2.** a slender tapering shoot or stem, such as a blade of grass. **3.** the apical part of any tapering formation; summit. ~*vb.* **4.** (*intr.*) to assume the shape of a spire; point up. **5.** (*tr.*) to furnish with a spire or spires. —'**spiry** *adj.*

spirit[1] ('spɪrɪt) *n.* **1.** the force or principle of life that animates the body of living things. **2.** temperament or disposition: *truculent in spirit.* **3.** liveliness; mettle: *they set to it with spirit.* **4.** the fundamental, emotional, and activating principle of a person; will: *the experience broke his spirit.* **5.** a sense of loyalty or dedication: *team spirit.* **6.** the prevailing element; feeling: *a spirit of joy pervaded the atmosphere.* **7.** state of mind or mood; attitude: *he did it in the wrong spirit.* **8.** (*pl.*) an emotional state, esp. with regard to exaltation or dejection: *in high spirits.* **9.** a person characterized by some activity, quality, or disposition: *a leading spirit of the movement.* **10.** the deeper more significant meaning as opposed to a pedantic interpretation: *the spirit of the law.* **11.** that which constitutes a person's intangible being as contrasted with his physical presence: *I shall be with you in spirit.* **12. a.** an incorporeal being, esp. the soul of a dead person. **b.** (*as modifier*): *spirit world.* ~*vb.* (*tr.*) **13.** (usually foll. by *away* or *off*) to carry off mysteriously or secretly. **14.** (often foll. by *up*) to impart animation or determination to. —'**spiritless** *adj.*

spirit[2] ('spɪrɪt) *n.* **1.** (*often pl.*) any distilled alcoholic liquor such as whisky or gin. **2.** *Chem.* **a.** an aqueous solution of ethanol, esp. one obtained by distillation. **b.** the active principle or essence of a substance, extracted as a liquid, esp. by distillation. **3.** *Pharmacol.* a solution of a volatile substance, esp. a volatile oil, in alcohol. **4.** *Alchemy.* any of the four substances sulphur, mercury, sal ammoniac, or arsenic.

THESAURUS

spine **1.** backbone, spinal column, vertebrae, vertebral column **2.** barb, needle, quill, rachis, ray, spike, spur

spine-chilling bloodcurdling, eerie, frightening, hair-raising, horrifying, scary (*Inf.*), spooky (*Inf.*), terrifying

spineless cowardly, faint-hearted, feeble, gutless (*Inf.*), inadequate, ineffective, irresolute, lily-livered, soft, spiritless, squeamish, submissive, vacillating, weak, weak-kneed (*Inf.*), weak-willed, without a will of one's own, yellow (*Inf.*)

spin out amplify, delay, drag out, draw out, extend, lengthen, pad out, prolong, prolongate, protract

spiral **1.** *adj.* circular, cochlear, cochleate (*Biol.*), coiled, corkscrew, helical, scrolled, voluted, whorled, winding **2.** *n.* coil, cork-screw, curlicue, gyre (*Literary*), helix, screw, volute, whorl

spirit *n.* **1.** air, breath, life, life force, psyche, soul, vital spark **2.** attitude, character, complexion, disposition, essence, humour, outlook, quality, temper, temperament **3.** animation, ardour, backbone, courage, dauntlessness, earnestness, energy, enterprise, enthusiasm, fire, force, gameness, grit, guts (*Inf.*), life, liveliness, mettle, resolution,

Spirit ('spirit) *n.* **the. a.** another name for the **Holy Ghost. b.** God, esp. when regarded as transcending material limitations.
spirited ('spiritid) *adj.* **1.** displaying animation, vigour, or liveliness. **2.** (*in combination*) characterized by mood, temper, or disposition as specified: *high-spirited; public-spirited.* —'**spiritedly** *adv.* —'**spiritedness** *n.*
spirit gum *n.* a glue made from gum dissolved in ether used to affix a false beard, etc.
spirit lamp *n.* a lamp that burns methylated or other spirits instead of oil.
spirit level *n.* a device for setting horizontal surfaces, consisting of a block of material in which a sealed tube partially filled with liquid is set so that the air bubble rests between two marks on the tube when the block is horizontal.
spiritual ('spiritʃuəl) *adj.* **1.** relating to the spirit or soul and not to physical nature or matter; intangible. **2.** of or relating to sacred things, the Church, religion, etc. **3.** standing in a relationship based on communication between souls or minds: *a spiritual father.* **4.** having a mind or emotions of a high and delicately refined quality. ~*n.* **5.** Also called: **Negro spiritual.** a type of religious song originating among Negro slaves in the American South. **6.** (*often pl.*) the sphere of religious, spiritual, or ecclesiastical matters, or such matters in themselves. —,**spiritu'ality** *n.* —'**spiritually** *adv.*
spiritualism ('spiritʃuə,lizəm) *n.* **1.** the belief that the disembodied spirits of the dead, surviving in another world, can communicate with the living in this world, esp. through mediums. **2.** the doctrines and practices associated with this belief. **3.** *Philosophy.* the belief that because reality is to some extent immaterial it is therefore spiritual. **4.** any doctrine that prefers the spiritual to the material. —'**spiritualist** *n.*
spirituous ('spiritʃuəs) *adj.* **1.** characterized by or containing alcohol. **2.** (of a drink) being a spirit. —**spirituosity** (,spiritʃu'ositi) *or* '**spirituousness** *n.*
spirt (spɜːt) *n.* a variant spelling of **spurt.**
spit[1] (spit) *vb.* **spitting, spat** *or* **spit. 1.** (*intr.*) to expel saliva from the mouth; expectorate. **2.** (*intr.*) *Inf.* to show disdain or hatred by spitting. **3.** (of a fire, hot fat, etc.) to eject (sparks, etc.) violently and with an explosive sound. **4.** (*intr.*) to rain very lightly. **5.** (*tr.;* often foll. by *out*) to eject or discharge (something) from the mouth: *he spat the food out.* **6.** (*tr.;* often foll. by *out*) to utter (short sharp words or syllables), esp. in a violent manner. **7. spit it out!** *Brit. sl.* a command given to someone that he should speak forthwith. ~*n.* **8.** another name for **spittle** (sense 1). **9.** a light or brief fall of rain, snow, etc. **10.** the act or an instance of spitting. **.11.** *Inf.,* chiefly *Brit.* another word for **spitting image.** —'**spitter** *n.*
spit[2] (spit) *n.* **1.** a pointed rod on which meat is skewered and roasted before or over an open fire. **2.** Also called: **rotisserie, rotating spit.** a similar device fitted onto a cooker. **3.** an elongated often hooked strip of sand or shingle projecting from a shore. ~*vb.* **spitting, spitted. 4.** (*tr.*) to impale on or transfix with or as if with a spit.
spit and polish *n. Inf.* punctilious attention to neatness, discipline, etc., esp. in the armed forces.
spite (spait) *n.* **1.** maliciousness; venomous ill will. **2.**

an instance of such malice; grudge. **3. in spite of.** (*prep.*) in defiance of; regardless of; notwithstanding. ~*vb.* (*tr.*) **4.** to annoy in order to vent spite. —'**spiteful** *adj.*
spitfire ('spit,faiə) *n.* a person given to outbursts of spiteful temper, esp. a woman or girl.
spitting image *n. Inf.* a person who bears a strong physical resemblance to another. Also called: **spit, spit and image.**
spittle ('spitəl) *n.* **1.** the fluid secreted in the mouth; saliva. **2.** Also called: **cuckoo spit, frog spit.** the frothy substance secreted on plants by the larvae of certain froghoppers.
spittoon (spi'tuːn) *n.* a receptacle for spit, usually in a public place.
spiv (spiv) *n. Brit. sl.* a person who makes a living by underhand dealings or swindling; black-marketeer. —'**spivvy** *adj.*
splake (spleik) *n.* a type of hybrid trout bred by Canadian zoologists.
splash (splæʃ) *vb.* **1.** to scatter (liquid) about in blobs; spatter. **2.** to descend or cause to descend upon in scattered blobs: *he splashed his jacket; rain splashed against the window.* **3.** to make (one's way) by or as if by splashing: *he splashed through the puddle.* **4.** (*tr.*) to print (a story or photograph) prominently in a newspaper. ~*n.* **5.** an instance or sound of splashing. **6.** an amount splashed. **7.** a mark or patch created by or as if by splashing. **8.** *Inf.* an extravagant display, usually for effect (esp. in **make a splash**). **9.** a small amount of soda water, etc., added to an alcoholic drink. —'**splashy** *adj.*
splashdown ('splæʃ,daun) *n.* **1.** the controlled landing of a spacecraft on water at the end of a space flight. **2.** the time scheduled for this event. ~*vb.* **splash down. 3.** (*intr., adv.*) (of a spacecraft) to make a splashdown.
splatter ('splætə) *vb.* **1.** to splash with small blobs. ~*n.* **2.** a splash of liquid, mud, etc.
splay (splei) *adj.* **1.** spread out; broad and flat. **2.** turned outwards in an awkward manner. ~*vb.* **3.** to spread out; turn out or expand. ~*n.* **4.** a surface of a wall that forms an oblique angle to the main flat surfaces, esp. at a doorway or window opening.
splayfoot ('splei,fut) *n., pl.* -**feet.** *Pathol.* another word for **flatfoot.** —'**splay,footed** *adj.*
spleen (spliːn) *n.* **1.** a spongy highly vascular organ situated near the stomach in mammals. It forms lymphocytes, produces antibodies, and filters bacteria and foreign particles from the blood. **2.** the corresponding organ in other animals. **3.** spitefulness or ill humour: *to vent one's spleen.* **4.** *Arch.* the organ in the human body considered to be the seat of the emotions. **5.** *Arch.* another word for **melancholy.** —'**spleenish** *or* '**spleeny** *adj.*
spleenwort ('spliːn,wɜːt) *n.* any of various ferns that often grow on walls.
splendid ('splendid) *adj.* **1.** brilliant or fine, esp. in appearance. **2.** characterized by magnificence. **3.** glorious or illustrious: *a splendid reputation.* **4.** brightly gleaming; radiant: *splendid colours.* **5.** very good or satisfactory: *a splendid time.* —'**splendidly** *adv.* —'**splendidness** *n.*

THESAURUS

sparkle, spunk (*Inf.*), stoutheartedness, vigour, warmth, zest **4.** motivation, resolution, resolve, will, willpower **5.** atmosphere, feeling, gist, humour, tenor, tone **6.** essence, intent, intention, meaning, purport, purpose, sense, substance **7.** *Plural* feelings, frame of mind, humour, mood, morale **8.** apparition, ghost, phantom, shade (*Literary*), shadow, spectre, spook (*Inf.*), sprite, vision ~*v.* **9.** *With away or off* abduct, abstract, carry, convey, make away with, purloin, remove, seize, snaffle (*Brit. inf.*), steal, whisk

spirited active, animated, ardent, bold, courageous, energetic, game, high-spirited, lively, mettlesome, plucky, sparkling, sprightly, spunky (*Inf.*), vigorous, vivacious

spirits alcohol, firewater, liquor, strong liquor, the hard stuff (*Inf.*)

spiritual ·devotional, divine, ethereal, ghostly, holy, immaterial, incorporeal, non-

material, otherworldly, pure, religious, sacred

spit 1. *v.* discharge, eject, expectorate, hiss, spew, splutter, sputter, throw out **2.** *n.* dribble, drool, saliva, slaver, spittle, sputum

spite *n.* **1.** animosity, bitchiness (*Sl.*), gall, grudge, hate, hatred, ill will, malevolence, malice, malignity, pique, rancour, spitefulness, spleen, venom **2. in spite of** despite, in defiance of, notwithstanding, regardless of ~*v.* **3.** annoy, discomfit, gall, harm, hurt, injure, needle (*Inf.*), nettle, offend, pique, provoke, put out, put (someone's) nose out of joint (*Inf.*), vex

spiteful barbed, bitchy (*Inf.*), catty (*Inf.*), cruel, ill-disposed, ill-natured, malevolent, malicious, malignant, rancorous, snide, splenetic, venomous, vindictive

splash *v.* **1.** bespatter, shower, slop, slosh (*Inf.*), spatter, splodge, spray, spread, sprin-

kle, squirt, strew, wet **2.** bathe, dabble, paddle, plunge, wade, wallow **3.** batter, break, buffet, dash, plash, plop, smack, strike, surge, wash **4.** blazon, broadcast, flaunt, headline, plaster, publicize, tout, trumpet ~*n.* **5.** burst, dash, patch, spattering, splodge, touch **6.** *Inf.* display, effect, impact, sensation, splurge, stir **7. make a splash** be ostentatious, cause a stir, cut a dash, go overboard (*Inf.*), go to town (*Inf.*), splurge

splash out be extravagant, lash out (*Inf.*), push the boat out (*Brit. inf.*), spare no expense, spend, splurge

spleen acrimony, anger, animosity, animus, bad temper, bile, bitterness, gall, hatred, hostility, ill humour, ill will, malevolence, malice, malignity, peevishness, pique, rancour, resentment, spite, spitefulness, venom, vindictiveness, wrath

splendid 1. admirable, brilliant, excep-

splendiferous (splɛnˈdɪfərəs) *adj. Facetious.* grand; splendid: *a really splendiferous meal.*

splendour *or U.S.* **splendor** (ˈsplɛndə) *n.* **1.** the state or quality of being splendid. **2. sun in splendour.** *Heraldry.* a representation of the sun with rays and a human face.

splenetic (splɪˈnɛtɪk) *adj. also* **spleˈnetical. 1.** of or relating to the spleen. **2.** spiteful or irritable; peevish. ~*n.* **3.** a spiteful or irritable person. —**spleˈnetically** *adv.*

splenic (ˈsplɛnɪk, ˈspliː-) *adj.* **1.** of, relating to, or in the spleen. **2.** having a disease or disorder of the spleen.

splice (splaɪs) *vb.* (*tr.*) **1.** to join (two ropes) by intertwining the strands. **2.** to join up the trimmed ends of (two pieces of wire, film, etc.) with solder or an adhesive material. **3.** to join (timbers) by overlapping and binding or bolting the ends together. **4.** (*usually passive*) *Inf.* to enter into marriage: *the couple got spliced.* **5. splice the mainbrace.** *Naut.* to issue and partake of alcoholic spirits. ~*n.* **6.** a join made by splicing. **7.** the place where such a join occurs. **8.** the wedge-shaped end of a cricket-bat handle that fits into the blade. —ˈ**splicer** *n.*

splint (splɪnt) *n.* **1.** a rigid support for restricting movement of an injured part, esp. a broken bone. **2.** a thin sliver of wood, esp. one used to light cigars, a fire, etc. **3.** a thin strip of wood woven with others to form a chair seat, basket, etc. **4.** *Vet. science.* a bony enlargement of the cannon bone of a horse. ~*vb.* **5.** to apply a splint to (a broken arm, etc.).

splinter (ˈsplɪntə) *n.* **1.** a small thin sharp piece of wood, glass, metal, etc., broken off from a whole. **2.** a metal fragment from a shell, bomb, etc., thrown out during an explosion; piece of shrapnel. ~*vb.* **3.** to reduce or be reduced to sharp fragments. **4.** to break or be broken off in small sharp fragments. —ˈ**splintery** *adj.*

splinter group *n.* a number of members of an organization, political party, etc., who split from the main body and form an independent association of their own.

split (splɪt) *vb.* **splitting, split. 1.** to break or cause to break, esp. forcibly, by cleaving into separate pieces, often into two roughly equal pieces. **2.** to separate or be separated from a whole: *he split a piece of wood from the block.* **3.** to separate or be separated into factions, usually through discord. **4.** (often foll. by *up*) to separate or cause to separate through a disagreement. **5.** (often *tr.,* often foll. by *up*) to divide or be divided among two or more persons: *split up the pie among us.* **6.** *Sl.* to depart; leave: *let's split.* **7.** (*tr.*) to separate (something) into its components by interposing something else: *to split a word with hyphens.* **8.** (*intr.;* usually foll. by *on*) *Sl.* to betray; inform: *he split on me to the cops.* **9.** (*tr.*) *U.S. politics.* to mark (a ballot, etc.) so as to vote for the candidates of more than one party: *he split the ticket.* **10. split hairs.** to make a fine but needless distinction. **11. split one's sides.** to laugh very heartily. **12. split the difference.** to settle a dispute by compromise. ~*n.* **13.** the act or process of splitting. **14.** a gap or rift caused by a piece removed by the process of splitting. **15.** a breach or schism in a group or the faction resulting from such a breach. **16.** a dessert of sliced fruit and ice cream, covered with whipped cream, nuts, etc.: *banana split.* **17.** *Tenpin bowling.* a formation of the pins after the first bowl in which there is a large gap between two pins or groups of pins. **18.** *Inf.* an arrangement or process of dividing up loot or money. See also **split up.** —ˈ**splitter** *n.*

split infinitive *n.* (in English grammar) an infinitive used with another word between *to* and the verb itself, as in *to really finish it.*

▷ **Usage.** The traditional rule against placing an adverb between *to* and its verb is gradually disappearing. Although it is true that a split infinitive may result in a clumsy sentence, this is not enough to justify the absolute condemnation that this practice has attracted. Indeed, very often the most natural position of the adverb is between *to* and the verb (*he decided to really try*) and to change it would result in an artificial and awkward construction (*he really decided to try*). The current view is therefore that the split infinitive is not a grammatical error. Nevertheless, many writers prefer to avoid splitting infinitives in formal English, since readers with a more traditional point of view are likely to interpret this as incorrect.

split-level *adj.* (of a house, room, etc.) having the floor level of one part about half a storey above the floor level of an adjoining part.

split pea *n.* a pea dried and split and used in soups, pease pudding, or as a vegetable.

split personality *n.* **1.** the tendency to change rapidly in mood or temperament. **2.** a nontechnical term for **multiple personality** or **schizophrenia.**

splits (splɪts) *n.* (in gymnastics, etc.) the act of sinking to the floor to achieve a sitting position in which both legs are straight, pointing in opposite directions, and at right angles to the body.

split second *n.* **1.** an infinitely small period of time; instant. ~*adj.* **split-second.** (*prenominal*) **2.** made or arrived at in an infinitely short time: *a split-second decision.* **3.** depending upon minute precision: *split-second timing.*

splitting (ˈsplɪtɪŋ) *adj.* **1.** (of a headache) intolerably painful; acute. **2.** (of the head) assailed by an overpowering unbearable pain.

split up *vb.* (*adv.*) **1.** (*tr.*) to separate out into parts; divide. **2.** (*intr.*) to become parted through disagreement: *they split up after years of marriage.* **3.** to break down or be capable of being broken down into constituent parts. ~*n.* **split-up. 4.** an act or the instance of separating.

splodge (splɒdʒ) *n.* **1.** a large irregular spot or blot. ~*vb.* **2.** (*tr.*) to mark (something) with such a blot or blots. —ˈ**splodgy** *adj.*

splotch (splɒtʃ) *n., vb.* the usual U.S. word for **splodge.** —ˈ**splotchy** *adj.*

splurge (splɜːdʒ) *n.* **1.** an ostentatious display, esp. of wealth. **2.** a bout of unrestrained extravagance. ~*vb.* **3.** (often foll. by *on*) to spend (money) extravagantly.

splutter (ˈsplʌtə) *vb.* **1.** to spit out (saliva, food particles, etc.) from the mouth in an explosive manner, as through choking or laughing. **2.** to utter (words) with spitting sounds, as through rage or choking. **3.** to eject or be ejected in an explosive manner: *sparks spluttered from the fire.* **4.** (*tr.*) to bespatter (a person) with tiny particles explosively ejected. ~*n.* **5.** the process or noise of spluttering. **6.** spluttering incoherent speech. **7.** anything ejected through spluttering. —ˈ**splutterer** *n.*

spode (spəʊd) *n.* (*sometimes cap.*) china or porcelain manufactured by Josiah Spode, English potter (1754–1827), or his company.

spoil (spɔɪl) *vb.* **spoiling, spoilt** *or* **spoiled. 1.** (*tr.*) to cause damage to (something), in regard to its value, beauty, usefulness, etc. **2.** (*tr.*) to weaken the character of (a child) by complying unrestrainedly with its desires. **3.** (*intr.*) (of perishable substances) to become unfit for consumption or use. **4.** (*intr.*) *Sport.* to disrupt the play

---

THESAURUS

tional, glorious, grand, heroic, illustrious, magnificent, outstanding, rare, remarkable, renowned, sterling, sublime, superb, supreme **2.** costly, dazzling, gorgeous, imposing, impressive, lavish, luxurious, magnificent, ornate, resplendent, rich, sumptuous, superb **3.** excellent, fantastic (*Inf.*), fine, first-class, glorious, great (*Inf.*), marvellous, wonderful **4.** beaming, bright, brilliant, glittering, glowing, lustrous, radiant, refulgent

splendour brightness, brilliance, ceremony, dazzle, display, effulgence, glory, gorgeousness, grandeur, lustre, magnificence, majesty, pomp, radiance, refulgence, renown, resplendence, richness, show, so-

lemnity, spectacle, stateliness, sumptuousness

splice *v.* braid, entwine, graft, interlace, intertwine, intertwist, interweave, join, knit, marry, mesh, plait, unite, wed, yoke

splinter 1. *n.* chip, flake, fragment, needle, paring, shaving, sliver **2.** *v.* break into smithereens, disintegrate, fracture, shatter, shiver, split

split *v.* **1.** bifurcate, branch, break, break up, burst, cleave, come apart, come undone, crack, disband, disunite, diverge, fork, gape, give way, go separate ways, open, part, pull apart, rend, rip, separate, slash, slit, snap, splinter **2.** allocate, allot, apportion, carve

up, distribute, divide, divvy up (*Inf.*), dole out, halve, parcel out, partition, share out, slice up **3.** *With on Sl.* betray, give away, grass (*Brit. sl.*), inform on, peach (*Sl.*), squeal (*Sl.*). ~*n.* **4.** breach, crack, damage, division, fissure, gap, rent, rip, separation, slash, slit, tear **5.** breach, break, break-up, difference, discord, disruption, dissension, disunion, divergence, division, estrangement, partition, rift, rupture, schism ~*adj.* **6.** ambivalent, bisected, broken, cleft, cracked, divided, dual, fractured, ruptured, twofold

split up break up, disband, divorce, go separate ways, part, part company, separate

or style of an opponent, as to prevent him from settling into a rhythm. **5.** *Arch.* to strip (a person or place) of (property) by force. **6. be spoiling for.** to have an aggressive desire for (a fight, etc.). ~*n.* **7.** waste material thrown up by an excavation. **8.** any treasure accumulated by a person. **9.** *Obs.* the act of plundering.

spoilage ('spɔɪlɪdʒ) *n.* **1.** the act or an instance of spoiling or the state or condition of being spoilt. **2.** an amount of material that has been wasted by being spoilt: *considerable spoilage.*

spoiler ('spɔɪlə) *n.* **1.** plunderer or robber. **2.** a person or thing that causes spoilage or corruption. **3.** a device fitted to an aircraft wing to increase drag and reduce lift. **4.** a similar device fitted to a car. **5.** *Sport.* a competitor who adopts spoiling tactics.

spoils (spɔɪlz) *pl. n.* **1.** (*sometimes sing.*) valuables seized by violence, esp. in war. **2.** *Chiefly U.S.* the rewards and benefits of public office regarded as plunder for the winning party or candidate. See also **spoils system.**

spoilsport ('spɔɪlˌspɔːt) *n. Inf.* a person who spoils the pleasure of other people.

spoils system *n. Chiefly U.S.* the practice of filling appointive public offices with friends and supporters of the ruling political party.

spoke[1] (spəʊk) *vb.* **1.** the past tense of **speak. 2.** *Arch. or dialect.* a past participle of **speak.**

spoke[2] (spəʊk) *n.* **1.** a radial member of a wheel, joining the hub to the rim. **2.** a radial projection from the rim of a wheel, as in a ship's wheel. **3.** a rung of a ladder. **4. put a spoke in someone's wheel.** *Brit.* to thwart the plans of a person. ~*vb.* **5.** (*tr.*) to equip with or as if with spokes.

spoken ('spəʊkən) *vb.* **1.** the past participle of **speak.** ~*adj.* **2.** uttered in speech. **3.** (*in combination*) having speech as specified: *soft-spoken.* **4. spoken for.** engaged or reserved.

spokeshave ('spəʊkˌʃeɪv) *n.* a small plane with two handles, one on each side of its blade, used for shaping or smoothing cylindrical wooden surfaces, such as spokes.

spokesman ('spəʊksmən) *n., pl.* **-men.** a person authorized to speak on behalf of another person or group. —'**spokes,woman** *fem. n.*

spoliation (ˌspəʊlɪ'eɪʃən) *n.* **1.** the act or an instance of despoiling or plundering. **2.** the authorized plundering of neutral vessels on the seas by a belligerent state in time of war. **3.** *Law.* the material alteration of a document so as to render it invalid. **4.** *English ecclesiastical law.* the taking of the fruits of a benefice by a person not entitled to them. —'**spoliatory** *adj.*

spondee ('spɒndiː) *n. Prosody.* a metrical foot consisting of two long syllables (ˉ ˉ). —**spondaic** (spɒn'deɪɪk) *adj.*

sponge (spʌndʒ) *n.* **1.** any of various multicellular typically marine animals, usually occurring in complex sessile colonies in which the porous body is supported by a fibrous, calcareous, or siliceous skeletal framework. **2.** a piece of the light porous highly absorbent elastic skeleton of certain sponges, used in bathing, cleaning, etc. **3.** any of a number of materials resembling a sponge. **4.** another word for **sponger. 5.** *Inf.* a person who indulges in heavy drinking. **6.** leavened dough, esp. before kneading. **7.** See **sponge cake. 8.** Also called: **sponge pudding.** *Brit.* a light steamed or baked spongy pudding. **9.** porous metal capable of absorbing large quantities of gas: *platinum sponge.* **10.** a rub with a sponge. **11. throw in** (*or* **up**) **the sponge** (*or* **towel**). **a.** (in boxing) to concede defeat by the throwing of a sponge or towel into the ring by a second. **b.** to give up after considerable effort. ~*vb.* **12.** (*tr.; often foll. by off or down*) to clean

(something) by wiping or rubbing with a damp or wet sponge. **13.** (*tr.; usually foll. by off, away, out,* etc.) to remove (marks, etc.) by rubbing with a damp or wet sponge or cloth. **14.** (when *tr.,* often foll. by *up*) to absorb (liquids, esp. when spilt) in the manner of a sponge. **15.** (*intr.*) to go collecting sponges. **16. a.** (foll. by *off*) to get something from (someone) by presuming on his generosity: *to sponge a meal off someone.* **b.** (foll. by *off* or *on*) to obtain one's subsistence, etc., unjustifiably from: *he sponges off his friends.* —'**spongy** *adj.*

sponge bag *n.* a small bag made of plastic or sponge rubber that holds toilet articles, used esp. when travelling.

sponge cake *n.* a light porous cake, made of eggs, sugar, flour, and flavourings without any fat.

sponger ('spʌndʒə) *n.* **1.** *Inf.* a person who lives off other people by continually taking advantage of their generosity; parasite or scrounger. **2.** a person or ship employed in collecting sponges.

sponsor ('spɒnsə) *n.* **1.** a person or group that promotes either another person or group in an activity or the activity itself, either for profit or charity. **2.** *Chiefly U.S.* a person or business firm that pays the costs of a radio or television programme in return for advertising time. **3.** a legislator who presents and supports a bill, motion, etc. **4.** Also called: **godparent. a.** an authorized witness who makes the required promises on behalf of a person to be baptized and thereafter assumes responsibility for his Christian upbringing. **b.** a person who presents a candidate for confirmation. ~*vb.* **5.** (*tr.*) to act as a sponsor for. —**sponsorial** (spɒn'sɔːrɪəl) *adj.* —'**sponsor,ship** *n.*

spontaneity (ˌspɒntə'niːɪtɪ, -'neɪ-) *n., pl.* **-ties. 1.** the state or quality of being spontaneous. **2.** (*often pl.*) the exhibiting of spontaneous actions, impulses, or behaviour.

spontaneous (spɒn'teɪnɪəs) *adj.* **1.** occurring, produced, or performed through natural processes without external influence. **2.** arising from an unforced personal impulse; voluntary; unpremeditated. **3.** (of plants) growing naturally; indigenous. —**spon'taneously** *adv.* —**spon'taneousness** *n.*

spontaneous combustion *n.* the ignition of a substance or body as a result of internal oxidation processes, without the application of an external source of heat.

spoof (spuːf) *Inf.* ~*n.* **1.** a mildly satirical mockery or parody; lampoon. **2.** a good-humoured deception or trick. ~*vb.* **3.** to indulge in a spoof of (a person or thing). —'**spoofer** *n.*

spook (spuːk) *Inf.* ~*n.* **1.** a ghost or a person suggestive of this. **2.** *U.S. sl.* a spy. ~*vb.* (*tr.*) **3.** *U.S.* to frighten: *to spook horses; to spook a person.* **4.** *U.S.* (of a ghost) to haunt. —'**spooky** *adj.*

spool (spuːl) *n.* **1.** a device around which magnetic tape, film, cotton, etc., can be wound, with plates at top and bottom to prevent it from slipping off. **2.** anything round which other materials, esp. thread, are wound. ~*vb.* **3.** (sometimes foll. by *up*) to wind or be wound onto a spool.

spoon (spuːn) *n.* **1.** a utensil having a shallow concave part, usually elliptical in shape, attached to a handle, used in eating or serving food, stirring, etc. **2.** Also called: **spoonbait.** an angling lure consisting of a bright piece of metal which swivels on a trace to which are attached a hook or hooks. **3.** a golf club with a shorter shaft and shallower face than a brassie. **4. be born with a silver spoon in one's mouth.** to inherit wealth or social standing. **5. wooden spoon.** *Brit.* another name for **booby prize. 6.** *Rowing.* a type of oar blade that is curved at the edges and tip. ~*vb.* **7.** (*tr.*) to scoop up or transfer

---

THESAURUS

spoil *v.* **1.** blemish, damage, debase, deface, destroy, disfigure, harm, impair, injure, mar, mess up, ruin, upset, wreck **2.** baby, cocker (*Rare*), coddle, cosset, indulge, kill with kindness, mollycoddle, overindulge, pamper, spoon-feed **3.** addle, become tainted, curdle, decay, decompose, go bad, go off (*Brit. inf.*), mildew, putrefy, rot, turn **4. spoiling for** bent upon, desirous of, eager for, enthusiastic about, keen to, looking for, out to get (*Inf.*), raring to

spoils boodle (*Sl., chiefly U.S.*), booty, gain, loot, pickings, pillage, plunder, prey, prizes,

rapine, swag (*Sl.*)

spoilsport damper, dog in the manger, kill-joy, misery (*Brit. inf.*), party-pooper (*U.S. sl.*), wet blanket (*Inf.*)

spoken expressed, oral, phonetic, put into words, said, told, unwritten, uttered, verbal, viva voce, voiced, by word of mouth

spongy absorbent, cushioned, cushiony, elastic, light, porous, springy

sponsor 1. *n.* angel (*Inf.*), backer, godparent, guarantor, patron, promoter **2.** *v.* back, finance, fund, guarantee, lend one's

name to, patronize, promote, put up the money for, subsidize

spontaneous extempore, free, impromptu, impulsive, instinctive, natural, unbidden, uncompelled, unconstrained, unforced, unpremeditated, unprompted, voluntary, willing

spontaneously extempore, freely, impromptu, impulsively, instinctively, off one's own bat, off the cuff (*Inf.*), of one's own accord, on impulse, quite unprompted, voluntarily

(food, liquid, etc.) from one container to another with or as if with a spoon. **8.** (*intr.*) *Old-fashioned sl.* to kiss and cuddle. **9.** *Sport.* to hit (a ball) with a weak lifting motion, as in golf, cricket, etc. —'**spoon,ful** *n.*

spoonbill ('spuːn,bɪl) *n.* any of several wading birds of warm regions, having a long horizontally flattened bill.

spoonerism ('spuːnə,rɪzəm) *n.* the transposition of the initial consonants or consonant clusters of a pair of words, often resulting in an amusing ambiguity, such as *hush my brat* for *brush my hat.*

spoon-feed *vb.* **-feeding, -fed.** (*tr.*) **1.** to feed with a spoon. **2.** to overindulge or spoil. **3.** to provide (a person) with ready-made opinions, judgments, etc.

spoor (spuə, spɔː) *n.* **1.** the trail of an animal or person, esp. as discernible to the eye. ~*vb.* **2.** to track (an animal) by following its trail.

sporadic (spə'rædɪk) *or* **sporadical** *adj.* **1.** occurring at irregular points in time; intermittent: *sporadic firing.* **2.** scattered; isolated: *a sporadic disease.* —**spo'radical-ly** *adv.*

sporangium (spə'rændʒɪəm) *n., pl.* **-gia** (-dʒɪə). any organ, esp. in fungi, in which asexual spores are produced. —**spo'rangial** *adj.*

spore (spɔː) *n.* **1.** a reproductive body, produced by some protozoans and many plants, that develops into a new individual. A **sexual spore** is formed after the fusion of gametes and an **asexual spore** is the result of asexual reproduction. **2.** a germ cell, seed, dormant bacterium, or similar body. ~*vb.* **3.** (*intr.*) to produce, carry, or release spores.

spore case *n.* the nontechnical name for **sporangium.**

sporran ('spɒrən) *n.* a large pouch, usually of fur, worn hanging from a belt in front of the kilt in Scottish Highland dress.

sport (spɔːt) *n.* **1.** an individual or group activity pursued for exercise or pleasure, often taking a competitive form. **2.** such activities considered collectively. **3.** any pastime indulged in for pleasure. **4.** the pleasure derived from a pastime, esp. hunting, shooting, or fishing. **5.** playful or good-humoured joking: *to say a thing in sport.* **6.** derisive mockery or the object of such mockery: *to make sport of someone.* **7.** someone or something that is controlled by external influences: *the sport of fate.* **8.** *Inf.* (sometimes qualified by *good, bad,* etc.) a person who reacts cheerfully in the face of adversity, esp. a good loser. **9.** *Inf.* a person noted for being scrupulously fair and abiding by the rules of a game. **10.** *Inf.* a person who leads a merry existence, esp. a gambler: *he's a bit of a sport.* **11.** *Austral. & N.Z. inf.* a form of address used esp. between males. **12.** *Biol.* **a.** an animal or plant that differs conspicuously from other organisms of the same species, usually because of a mutation. **b.** an anomalous characteristic of such an organism. ~*vb.* **13.** (*tr.*) *Inf.* to wear or display in an ostentatious or proud manner: *she was sporting a new hat.* **14.** (*intr.*) to skip about or frolic happily. **15.** to amuse (oneself), esp. in outdoor physical recreation. **16.** (*intr.; often foll. by with*) *Arch.* to make fun (of). **17.** (*intr.*) *Biol.* to produce or undergo a mutation. —'**sporter** *n.* —'**sportful** *adj.* —'**sportfully** *adv.* —'**sportfulness** *n.*

sporting ('spɔːtɪŋ) *adj.* **1.** (*prenominal*) of, relating to, or used or engaged in a sport or sports. **2.** relating or conforming to sportsmanship; fair. **3.** of or relating to gambling. **4.** willing to take a risk. —'**sportingly** *adv.*

sportive ('spɔːtɪv) *adj.* **1.** playful or joyous. **2.** done in jest rather than seriously. —'**sportively** *adv.* —'**sportiveness** *n.*

sports (spɔːts) *n.* **1.** (*modifier*) relating to, concerned

with, or used in sports: *sports equipment.* **2.** Also called: **sports day.** *Brit.* a meeting held at a school or college for competitions in various athletic events.

sports car *n.* a production car designed for speed and manoeuvrability, having a low body and usually seating only two persons.

sportscast ('spɔːts,kɑːst) *n. U.S.* a radio or television broadcast consisting of sports news. —'**sports,caster** *n.*

sports jacket *n.* a man's informal jacket, made esp. of tweed.

sportsman ('spɔːtsmən) *n., pl.* **-men.** **1.** a man who takes part in sports, esp. of the outdoor type. **2.** a person who exhibits fairness, generosity, observance of the rules, and good humour when losing. —'**sportsman-,like** *or* '**sportsmanly** *adj.* —'**sportsman-,ship** *n.*

sportswear ('spɔːts,wɛə) *n.* clothes worn for sport or outdoor leisure wear.

sportswoman ('spɔːts,wumən) *n., pl.* **women.** a woman who takes part in sports, esp. of the outdoor type.

sporty ('spɔːtɪ) *adj.* **-ier, -iest.** **1.** vulgarly ostentatious; stylish, loud, or gay. **2.** relating to or appropriate to a sportsman or sportswoman. **3.** (of women) amorous or wanton; lusty. —'**sportily** *adv.* —'**sportiness** *n.*

spot (spɒt) *n.* **1.** a small mark on a surface, such as a circular patch or stain, differing in colour or texture from its surroundings. **2.** a location: *this is the exact spot.* **3.** a blemish of the skin, esp. a pimple or one occurring through some disease. **4.** a blemish on the character of a person; moral flaw. **5.** *Inf.* a place of entertainment: *a night spot.* **6.** *Inf., chiefly Brit.* a small quantity or amount: *a spot of lunch.* **7.** *Inf.* an awkward situation: *that puts me in a spot.* **8.** a short period between regular television or radio programmes that is used for advertising. **9.** a position or length of time in a show assigned to a specific performer. **10.** short for **spotlight.** **11.** (in billiards) **a.** Also called: **spot ball.** the white ball that is distinguished from the plain by a mark or spot. **b.** the player using this ball. **12.** (*modifier*) **a.** to be paid or delivered immediately: *spot cash.* **b.** involving immediate cash payment: *spot sales.* **13. change one's spots.** (*used mainly in negative constructions*) to reform one's character. **14. high spot.** an outstanding event: *the high spot of the holiday.* **15. knock spots off.** to outstrip or outdo with ease. **16. on the spot. a.** immediately. **b.** at the place in question. **c.** in the best position to deal with a situation. **d.** in an awkward predicament. **e.** (*as modifier*): *our on-the-spot reporter.* **17. soft spot.** a special sympathetic affection or weakness for a person or thing. **18. tight spot.** a serious, difficult, or dangerous situation. **19. weak spot. a.** some aspect of a character or situation that is susceptible to criticism. **b.** a flaw in a person's knowledge. ~*vb.* **spotting, spotted.** **20.** (*tr.*) to observe or perceive suddenly; discern. **21.** to put stains or spots upon (something). **22.** (*intr.*) (of some fabrics) to be susceptible to spotting by or as if by water: *silk spots easily.* **23.** (*tr.*) to place here and there: *they spotted observers along the border.* **24.** (*tr.*) *Billiards.* to place (a ball) on one of the table spots. **25.** to look out for and note (trains, talent, etc.). **26.** (*intr.*) to rain slightly; spit. —'**spotless** *adj.*

spot check *n.* **1.** a quick random examination. ~*vb.* **spot-check.** **2.** (*tr.*) to perform a spot check on.

spotlight ('spɒt,laɪt) *n.* **1.** a powerful light focused so as to illuminate a small area. **2. the.** the focus of attention. ~*vb.* **-lighting, -lit** *or* **-lighted.** (*tr.*) **3.** to direct a spotlight on. **4.** to focus attention on.

THESAURUS

sporadic infrequent, intermittent, irregular, isolated, occasional, on and off, random, scattered, spasmodic

sport *n.* **1.** amusement, diversion, entertainment, exercise, game, pastime, physical activity, play, recreation **2.** badinage, banter, frolic, fun, jest, joking, kidding (*Inf.*), merriment, mirth, raillery, teasing **3.** buffoon, butt, derision, fair game, game, laughing stock, mockery, plaything, ridicule ~*v.* **4.** With amuse oneself, dally, flirt, play, take advantage of, toy, treat lightly *or* cavalierly, trifle **5.** *Inf.* display, exhibit, show off, wear **6.** caper, disport, frolic, gambol, play, romp

sporting fair, game (*Inf.*), gentlemanly, sportsman-like

sportive coltish, frisky, frolicsome, full of beans (*Inf.*), full of fun, gamesome, gay, joyous, kittenish, lively, merry, playful, prankish, rollicking, skittish, sprightly

spot *n.* **1.** blemish, blot, blotch, daub, discoloration, flaw, mark, pimple, plook (*Scot.*), pustule, smudge, speck, stain, taint **2.** locality, location, place, point, position, scene, site, situation **3.** *Inf.* bit, little, morsel, splash **4.** *Inf.* difficulty, mess, plight, predicament, quandary, trouble ~*v.* **5.** catch sight of, descry, detect, discern, espy, identify, make out, observe, pick out, recognize, see, sight **6.**

besmirch, blot, dirty, dot, fleck, mark, mottle, soil, spatter, speckle, splodge, splotch, stain, sully, taint, tarnish

spotless above reproach, blameless, chaste, faultless, flawless, gleaming, immaculate, innocent, irreproachable, pure, shining, snowy, unblemished, unimpeachable, unstained, unsullied, untarnished, virgin, virginal, white

spotlight *Fig.* **1.** *v.* accentuate, draw attention to, feature, focus attention on, give prominence to, highlight, illuminate, point up, throw into relief **2.** *n.* attention, fame, interest, limelight, notoriety, public attention, public eye

spot-on *adj. Brit. inf.* absolutely correct; very accurate.

spotted ('spɒtɪd) *adj.* **1.** characterized by spots or marks, esp. in having a pattern of spots. **2.** stained or blemished; soiled or bespattered.

spotted dick *or* **dog** *n. Brit.* a steamed or boiled suet pudding containing dried fruit and shaped into a roll.

spotter ('spɒtə) *n.* **1. a.** a person or thing that watches or observes. **b.** (*as modifier*): *a spotter plane.* **2.** a person who makes a hobby of watching for and noting numbers or types of trains, buses, etc.: *a train spotter.* **3.** *Mil.* a person who advises adjustment of fire on a target by observations. **4.** a person, esp. one engaged in civil defence, who watches for enemy aircraft.

spotty ('spɒtɪ) *adj.* **-tier, -tiest. 1.** abounding in or characterized by spots or marks, esp. on the skin. **2.** not consistent or uniform; irregular or uneven. —'**spottily** *adv.* —'**spottiness** *n.*

spouse *n.* (spaʊs, spaʊz). **1.** a person's partner in marriage. Related adj.: **spousal.** ~*vb.* (spaʊz, spaʊs). **2.** (*tr.*) *Obs.* to marry.

spout (spaʊt) *vb.* **1.** to discharge (a liquid) in a continuous jet or in spurts, esp. through a narrow gap or under pressure, or (of a liquid) to gush thus. **2.** (of a whale, etc.) to discharge air through the blowhole in a spray at the surface of the water. **3.** *Inf.* to utter (a stream of words) on a subject. ~*n.* **4.** a tube, pipe, chute, etc., allowing the passage or pouring of liquids, grain, etc. **5.** a continuous stream or jet of liquid. **6.** short for **waterspout. 7. up the spout.** *Sl.* **a.** ruined or lost: *any hope of rescue is right up the spout.* **b.** pregnant. —'**spouter** *n.*

sprain (spreɪn) *vb.* **1.** (*tr.*) to injure (a joint) by a sudden twisting or wrenching of its ligaments. ~*n.* **2.** the injury, characterized by swelling and temporary disability.

sprang (spræŋ) *vb.* the past tense of **spring.**

sprat (spræt) *n.* **1.** Also called: **brisling.** a small marine food fish of the herring family. **2.** any of various small or young herrings.

sprawl (sprɔːl) *vb.* **1.** (*intr.*) to sit or lie in an ungainly manner with one's limbs spread out. **2.** to fall down or knock down with the limbs spread out in an ungainly way. **3.** to spread out or cause to spread out in a straggling fashion: *his handwriting sprawled all over the paper.* ~*n.* **4.** the act or an instance of sprawling. **5.** a sprawling posture or arrangement of items. —'**sprawly** *adj.*

spray[1] (spreɪ) *n.* **1.** fine particles of a liquid. **2. a.** a liquid, such as perfume, paint, etc., designed to be discharged from an aerosol or atomizer: *hair spray.* **b.** the aerosol or atomizer itself. **3.** a quantity of small objects flying through the air: *a spray of bullets.* ~*vb.* **4.** to scatter (liquid) in the form of fine particles. **5.** to discharge (a liquid) from an aerosol or atomizer. **6.** (*tr.*) to treat or bombard with a spray: *to spray the lawn.* —'**sprayer** *n.*

spray[2] (spreɪ) *n.* a single slender shoot, twig, or branch that bears buds, leaves, flowers, or berries, either growing on or detached from a plant.

spray gun *n.* a device that sprays a fluid in a finely divided form by atomizing it in an air jet.

spread (sprɛd) *vb.* **spreading, spread. 1.** to extend or unfold or be extended or unfolded to the fullest width: *she spread the map.* **2.** to extend or cause to extend over a larger expanse: *the milk spread all over the floor; the economic unrest spread over several years.* **3.** to apply or be applied in a coating: *butter does not spread very well when cold.* **4.** to distribute or be distributed over an area or region. **5.** to display or be displayed in its fullest extent: *the landscape spread before us.* **6.** (*tr.*) to prepare (a table) for a meal. **7.** (*tr.*) to lay out (a meal) on a table. **8.** to send or be sent out in all directions; disseminate or be disseminated: *someone was spreading rumours; the disease spread quickly.* **9.** (of rails, wires, etc.) to force or be forced apart. **10.** to increase the breadth of (a part), esp. to flatten the head of a rivet by pressing, hammering, or forging. **11.** (*tr.*) *Agriculture.* **a.** to lay out (hay) in a relatively thin layer to dry. **b.** to scatter (seed, manure, etc.) over an area. **12.** (*tr.*; often foll. by *around*) *Inf.* to make (oneself) agreeable to a large number of people. ~*n.* **13.** the act or process of spreading; diffusion, dispersion, expansion, etc. **14.** *Inf.* the wingspan of an aircraft. **15.** an extent of space or time; stretch: *a spread of 50 years.* **16.** *Inf., chiefly U.S.* a ranch or large tract of land. **17.** the limit of something fully extended: *the spread of a bird's wings.* **18.** a covering for a table or bed. **19.** *Inf.* a large meal or feast, esp. when it is laid out on a table. **20.** a food which can be spread on bread, etc.: *salmon spread.* **21.** two facing pages in a book or other publication. **22.** a widening of the hips and waist: *middle-age spread.* ~*adj.* **23.** extended or stretched out, esp. to the fullest extent. —'**spreadable** *adj.* —'**spreader** *n.*

spread-eagle *adj. also* **spread-eagled. 1.** lying or standing with arms and legs outstretched. ~*vb.* **2.** to assume or cause to assume the shape of a spread eagle.

spree (spriː) *n.* **1.** a session of considerable overindulgence, esp. in drinking, squandering money, etc. **2.** a romp.

sprig (sprɪg) *n.* **1.** a shoot, twig, or sprout of a tree, shrub, etc.; spray. **2.** an ornamental device resembling a spray of leaves or flowers. **3.** Also called: **dowel pin.** a small wire nail without a head. **4.** *Inf., rare.* a youth. **5.** *Inf., rare.* a person considered as the descendant of an established family, social class, etc. ~*vb.* **sprigging, sprigged.** (*tr.*) **6.** to fasten or secure with sprigs. **7.** to ornament (fabric, etc.) with a design of sprigs. —'**sprigger** *n.* —'**spriggy** *adj.*

sprightly ('spraɪtlɪ) *adj.* **-lier, -liest. 1.** full of vitality; lively and gay. ~*adv.* **2.** *Obs.* in a gay or lively manner. —'**sprightliness** *n.*

spring (sprɪŋ) *vb.* **springing, sprang** *or* **sprung; sprung. 1.** to move or cause to move suddenly upwards or forwards in a single motion. **2.** to release or be released from a forced position by elastic force: *the bolt sprang back.* **3.** (*tr.*) to leap or jump over. **4.** (*intr.*) to come or arise suddenly. **5.** (*intr.*) (of a part of a mechanism, etc.) to jump out of place. **6.** to make (wood, etc.) warped or split or (of wood, etc.) to become warped or split. **7.** to happen or cause to happen unexpectedly: *to spring a surprise.* **8.** (*intr.*; usually foll. by *from*) to originate; be descended: *the idea sprang from a chance meeting; he sprang from peasant stock.* **9.** (*intr.*; often foll. by *up*) to come into being or appear suddenly: *factories springing up.* **10.** (*intr.*) (of game or quarry) to start or rise suddenly from cover. **11.** to explode (a mine) or (of a mine) to explode. **12.** (*tr.*) to provide with a spring or springs. **13.** (*tr.*) *Inf.* to arrange the escape of (someone) from prison. **14.** (*intr.*) *Arch. or poetic.* (of daylight or dawn) to begin to appear. ~*n.* **15.** the act or an instance of springing. **16.** a leap, jump, or bound. **17. a.** the quality of resilience; elasticity. **b.** (*as modifier*): *spring steel.* **18.** the act or an instance of moving rapidly back from a position of tension. **19. a.** a natural outflow of ground water, as forming the source of a stream. **b.** (*as modifier*): *spring water.* **20. a.** a device, such as a coil or strip

spotted dappled, dotted, flecked, mottled, pied, poĺka-dot, specked, speckled

spouse better half (*Inf.*), companion, consort, helpmate, husband, mate, partner, wife

spout *v.* **1.** discharge, emit, erupt, gush, jet, shoot, spray, spurt, squirt, stream, surge **2.** *Inf.* declaim, expatiate, go on (*Inf.*), hold forth, orate, pontificate, rabbit on (*Brit. sl.*), ramble (on), rant, speechify, spiel (*Inf.*), talk

sprawl *v.* flop, loll, lounge, ramble, slouch, slump, spread, straggle, trail

spray[1] *v.* **1.** atomize, diffuse, scatter, shower, sprinkle ~*n.* **2.** drizzle, droplets, fine mist, moisture, spindrift, spoondrift **3.** aerosol, atomizer, sprinkler

spray[2] *n.* bough, branch, corsage, floral arrangement, shoot, sprig

spread *v.* **1.** be displayed, bloat, broaden, dilate, expand, extend, fan out, open, open out, sprawl, stretch, swell, unfold, unfurl, unroll, widen **2.** escalate, multiply, mushroom, proliferate **3.** advertise, blazon, broadcast, bruit, cast, circulate, cover, diffuse, disseminate, distribute, make known, make public, proclaim, promulgate, propagate, publicize, publish, radiate, scatter, shed, strew, transmit **4.** arrange, array, cover, furnish, lay, prepare, set ~*n.* **5.** advance, advancement, development, diffusion, dispersion, dissemination, escalation, expansion, increase, prolif-

eration, spreading, suffusion, transmission **6.** compass, extent, period, reach, span, stretch, sweep, term **7.** *Inf.* array, banquet, blowout (*Sl.*), feast, repast

spree bacchanalia, bender (*Inf.*), binge (*Inf.*), carouse, debauch, fling, jag (*Sl.*), junketing, orgy, revel, splurge

sprightly active, agile, airy, alert, animated, blithe, brisk, cheerful, energetic, frolicsome, gay, jaunty, joyous, lively, nimble, perky, playful, spirited, sportive, spry, vivacious

of steel, that stores potential energy when it is compressed, stretched, or bent and releases it when the restraining force is removed. **b.** (*as modifier*): *a spring mattress.* **21.** a structural defect such as a warp or bend. **22. a.** (*sometimes cap.*) the season of the year between winter and summer, astronomically from the March equinox to the June solstice in the N hemisphere and from the September equinox to the December solstice in the S hemisphere. **b.** (*as modifier*): *spring showers.* Related adj.: **vernal.** **23.** the earliest or freshest time of something. **24.** a source or origin. **25.** Also called: **spring line.** *Naut.* a mooring line, usually one of a pair that cross amidships. —**'springless** *adj.* —**'spring,like** *adj.*

spring balance *or esp. U.S.* **spring scale** *n.* a device in which an object to be weighed is attached to the end of a helical spring, the extension of which indicates the weight of the object on a calibrated scale.

springboard ('sprɪŋ,bɔːd) *n.* **1.** a flexible board, usually projecting low over the water, used for diving. **2.** a similar board used for gaining height or momentum in gymnastics. **3.** *Austral.* a board inserted into the trunk of a tree at some height above the ground on which a lumberjack stands to chop down the tree. **4.** anything that serves as a point of departure or initiation.

springbok *or* **springbuck** ('sprɪŋ,bʌk) *n., pl.* **-bok, -boks** *or* **-buck, -bucks.** an antelope of semidesert regions of southern Africa, which moves in leaps.

Springbok ('sprɪŋ,bʌk, -,bɒk) *n.* an amateur athlete who has represented South Africa in international competitions, esp. in cricket or rugby.

spring chicken *n.* **1.** *Chiefly U.S.* a young chicken, tender for cooking, esp. one from two to ten months old. **2.** *Inf.* a young, inexperienced, or unsophisticated person.

spring-clean *vb.* **1.** to clean (a house) thoroughly: traditionally at the end of the winter. ~*n.* **2.** an instance of this. —**,spring-'cleaning** *n.*

springer ('sprɪŋə) *n.* **1.** a person or thing that springs. **2.** short for **springer spaniel.** **3.** *Archit.* **a.** the first and lowest stone of an arch. **b.** the impost of an arch.

springer spaniel *n.* a breed of spaniel with a silky coat, usually black or liver and white.

spring onion *n.* an immature form of the onion, widely cultivated for its tiny bulb and long green leaves which are eaten in salads, etc. Also called: **scallion.**

spring tide *n.* **1.** either of the two tides that occur at or just after new moon and full moon: the greatest rise in tidal level. Cf. **neap tide.** **2.** any great rush or flood.

springtime ('sprɪŋ,taɪm) *n.* **1.** Also called: **springtide** ('sprɪŋ,taɪd). the season of spring. **2.** the earliest, usually the most attractive, period of the existence of something.

springy ('sprɪŋɪ) *adj.* **-ier, -iest.** **1.** possessing or characterized by resilience or bounce. **2.** (of a place) having many springs of water. —**'springily** *adv.* —**'springiness** *n.*

sprinkle ('sprɪŋkəl) *vb.* **1.** to scatter (liquid, powder, etc.) in tiny particles or droplets over (something). **2.** (*tr.*) to distribute over (something): *the field was sprinkled with flowers.* **3.** (*intr.*) to drizzle slightly. ~*n.* **4.** the act or an instance of sprinkling or a quantity that is sprinkled. **5.** a slight drizzle. —**'sprinkler** *n.*

sprinkling ('sprɪŋklɪŋ) *n.* a small quantity or amount: *a sprinkling of common sense.*

sprint (sprɪnt) *n.* **1.** *Athletics.* **a.** a short race run at top speed. **b.** a fast finishing run at the end of a longer race. **2.** any quick run. ~*vb.* **3.** (*intr.*) to go at top speed, as in running, cycling, etc. —**'sprinter** *n.*

sprit (sprɪt) *n. Naut.* a light spar pivoted at the mast and crossing a fore-and-aft quadrilateral sail diagonally to the peak.

sprite (spraɪt) *n.* **1.** (in folklore) a nimble elflike creature, esp. one associated with water. **2.** a small dainty person.

spritsail ('sprɪt,seɪl; *Naut.* 'sprɪtsəl) *n. Naut.* a sail extended by a sprit.

sprocket ('sprɒkɪt) *n.* **1.** Also called: **sprocket wheel.** a relatively thin wheel having teeth projecting radially from the rim, esp. one that drives or is driven by a chain. **2.** an individual tooth on such a wheel. **3.** a cylindrical wheel with teeth on one or both rims for pulling film through a camera or projector.

sprout (spraʊt) *vb.* **1.** (of a plant, seed, etc.) to produce (new leaves, shoots, etc.). **2.** (*intr.; often foll. by up*) to begin to grow or develop. ~*n.* **3.** a newly grown shoot or bud. **4.** something that grows like a sprout. **5.** See **Brussels sprout.**

spruce[1] (spruːs) *n.* **1.** any coniferous tree of a N temperate genus, cultivated for timber and for ornament. They grow in a pyramidal shape and have needle-like leaves and light-coloured wood. **2.** the wood of any of these trees.

spruce[2] (spruːs) *adj.* neat, smart, and trim. —**'sprucely** *adv.* —**'spruceness** *n.*

spruce up *vb.* (*adv.*) to make (oneself, a person, or thing) smart and neat.

sprung (sprʌŋ) *vb.* the past participle or a past tense of **spring.**

spry (spraɪ) *adj.* **spryer, spryest** *or* **sprier, spriest.** active and brisk; nimble. —**'spryly** *adv.* —**'spryness** *n.*

spud (spʌd) *n.* **1.** an informal word for **potato.** **2.** a narrow-bladed spade for cutting roots, digging up weeds, etc. ~*vb.* **3.** (*tr.*) to eradicate (weeds) with a spud. **4.** (*intr.*) to drill the first foot of an oil well.

spue (spjuː) *vb.* **spuing, spued.** an archaic spelling of **spew.** —**'spuer** *n.*

spume (spjuːm) *n.* **1.** foam or surf, esp. on the sea; froth. ~*vb.* **2.** (*intr.*) to foam or froth. —**'spumous** *or* **'spumy** *adj.*

spun (spʌn) *vb.* **1.** the past tense or past participle of **spin.** ~*adj.* **2.** formed or manufactured by spinning: *spun gold; spun glass.*

spunk (spʌŋk) *n.* **1.** *Inf.* courage or spirit. **2.** touchwood or tinder. —**'spunky** *adj.* —**'spunkily** *adv.*

spur (spɜː) *n.* **1.** a pointed device or sharp spiked wheel fixed to the heel of a rider's boot to enable him to urge his horse on. **2.** anything serving to urge or encourage. **3.** a sharp horny projection from the leg in male birds, such as the domestic cock. **4.** a pointed process in any of various animals. **5.** a tubular extension at the base of the corolla in flowers such as larkspur. **6.** a short or stunted branch of a tree. **7.** a ridge projecting laterally from a mountain or mountain range. **8.** another name for **groyne.** **9.** Also called: **spur track.** a railway branch line or siding. **10.** a sharp cutting instrument attached to the leg of a gamecock. **11. on the spur of the moment.** on impulse. **12. win one's spurs. a.** *History.* to earn knighthood. **b.** to prove one's ability; gain distinction. ~*vb.* **spurring, spurred.** **13.** (*tr.*) to goad or urge with or as if with spurs. **14.** (*intr.*) to go or ride quickly; press on. **15.** (*tr.*) to provide with a spur or spurs.

spurge (spɜːdʒ) *n.* any of various plants that have milky sap and small flowers typically surrounded by conspicuous bracts.

spurious ('spjʊərɪəs) *adj.* **1.** not genuine or real. **2.** (of

---

THESAURUS

spring *v.* **1.** bounce, bound, hop, jump, leap, rebound, recoil, vault **2.** *Often with* **from** arise, be derived, be descended, come, derive, descend, emanate, emerge, grow, issue, originate, proceed, start, stem **3.** *With* **up** appear, burgeon, come into existence *or* being, develop, mushroom, shoot up ~*n.* **4.** bound, buck, hop, jump, leap, saltation, vault **5.** bounce, bounciness, buoyancy, elasticity, flexibility, give (*Inf.*), recoil, resilience, springiness **6.** beginning, cause, fountainhead, origin, root, source, well, wellspring ~*adj.* **7.** *Of the season* springlike, vernal

sprinkle *v.* dredge, dust, pepper, powder, scatter, shower, spray, strew

sprinkling admixture, dash, dusting, few, handful, scatter, scattering, smattering, sprinkle

sprint *v.* dart, dash, go at top speed, hare (*Brit. inf.*), hotfoot, put on a burst of speed, race, scamper, shoot, tear, whiz (*Inf.*)

sprite apparition, brownie, dryad, elf, fairy, goblin, imp, leprechaun, naiad, nymph, pixie, spirit, sylph

sprout *v.* bud, develop, germinate, grow, push, shoot, spring, vegetate

spruce as if one had just stepped out of a bandbox, dainty, dapper, elegant, natty (*Inf.*),

neat, smart, trig (*Archaic*), trim, well-groomed, well turned out

spry active, agile, alert, brisk, nimble, nippy (*Brit. inf.*), quick, ready, sprightly, supple

spur *v.* **1.** animate, drive, goad, impel, incite, press, prick, prod, prompt, stimulate, urge ~*n.* **2.** goad, prick, rowel **3.** impetus, incentive, incitement, inducement, motive, stimulus **4. on the spur of the moment** impetuously, impromptu, impulsively, on impulse, on the spot, unpremeditatedly, unthinkingly, without planning, without thinking

a plant part or organ) resembling another part in appearance only; false: *a spurious fruit*. **3.** *Rare.* illegitimate. —'**spuriously** *adv*. —'**spuriousness** *n*.

spurn (sp3ːn) *vb*. **1.** to reject (a person or thing) with contempt. **2.** (when *intr.*, often foll. by *against*) *Arch*. to kick (at). ~*n*. **3.** an instance of spurning. **4.** *Arch*. a kick or thrust. —'**spurner** *n*.

spurt *or* **spirt** (sp3ːt) *vb*. **1.** to gush or cause to gush forth in a sudden stream or jet. **2.** to make a sudden effort. ~*n*. **3.** a sudden stream or jet. **4.** a short burst of activity, speed, or energy.

sputnik ('sputnɪk, 'spʌt-) *n*. any of a series of Soviet artificial satellites, **Sputnik 1** (launched in 1957) being the first man-made satellite to orbit the earth.

sputter ('spʌtə) *vb*. **1.** another word for **splutter** (senses 1-3). **2.** *Physics*. **a.** to undergo or cause to undergo a process in which atoms of a solid are removed from its surface by the impact of high-energy ions. **b.** to coat (a metal) onto (a solid surface) by this process. ~*n*. **3.** the process or noise of sputtering. **4.** incoherent stammering speech. **5.** something ejected while sputtering. —'**sputterer** *n*.

sputum ('spjuːtəm) *n*., *pl*. **-ta** (-tə). saliva ejected from the mouth, esp. mixed with mucus.

spy (spaɪ) *n*., *pl*. **spies**. **1.** a person employed by a state or institution to obtain secret information from rival countries, organizations, companies, etc. **2.** a person who keeps secret watch on others. **3.** *Obs*. a close view. ~*vb*. **spying, spied**. **4.** (*intr.*; usually foll. by *on*) to keep a secret or furtive watch (on). **5.** (*intr.*) to engage in espionage. **6.** (*tr.*) to catch sight of; descry.

spyglass ('spaɪˌglɑːs) *n*. a small telescope.

spy out *vb*. (*tr.*, *adv.*) **1.** to discover by careful observation. **2.** to make a close scrutiny of.

sq. *abbrev. for*: **1.** sequence. **2.** square. **3.** (*pl.* **sqq.**) the following one.

Sq. *abbrev. for*: **1.** Squadron. **2.** Square.

squab (skwɒb) *n*., *pl*. **squabs** *or* **squab**. **1.** a young unfledged bird, esp. a pigeon. **2.** a short fat person. **3. a.** a well-stuffed bolster or cushion. **b.** a sofa. ~*adj*. **4.** (of birds) unfledged. **5.** short and fat. —'**squabby** *adj*.

squabble ('skwɒbəl) *vb*. **1.** (*intr.*) to quarrel over a small matter. ~*n*. **2.** a petty quarrel. —'**squabbler** *n*.

squad (skwɒd) *n*. **1.** the smallest military formation, typically a dozen soldiers, esp. a drill formation. **2.** any small group of people engaged in a common pursuit. **3.** *Sport*. a number of players from which a team is to be selected.

squadron ('skwɒdrən) *n*. **1.** a subdivision of a naval fleet detached for a particular task. **2.** a cavalry unit comprising two or more troops. **3.** the basic tactical and administrative air force unit comprising two or more flights.

squadron leader *n*. an officer holding commissioned rank, between flight lieutenant and wing commander in the air forces of Britain and certain other countries.

squalid ('skwɒlɪd) *adj*. **1.** dirty and repulsive, esp. as a result of neglect or poverty. **2.** sordid. —**squalidity** (skwɒ'lɪdɪtɪ) *or* '**squalidness** *n*. —'**squalidly** *adv*.

squall[1] (skwɔːl) *n*. **1.** a sudden strong wind or brief turbulent storm. **2.** any sudden commotion. ~*vb*. **3.** (*intr.*) to blow in a squall. —'**squally** *adj*.

squall[2] (skwɔːl) *vb*. **1.** (*intr.*) to cry noisily; yell. ~*n*. **2.** a shrill or noisy yell or howl. —'**squaller** *n*.

squalor ('skwɒlə) *n*. the condition or quality of being squalid; disgusting filth.

squander ('skwɒndə) *vb*. (*tr.*) to spend wastefully or extravagantly; dissipate. —'**squanderer** *n*. —'**squanderingly** *adv*.

square (skwɛə) *n*. **1.** a plane geometric figure having four equal sides and four right angles. **2.** any object, part, or arrangement having this or a similar shape. **3.** an open area in a town, sometimes including the surrounding buildings, which may form a square. **4.** *Maths*. the product of two equal factors; the second power: *the square of 2 is written* 2^2. **5.** an instrument having two strips of wood, metal, etc., set in the shape of a T or L, used for constructing or testing right angles. **6.** *Inf*. a person who is old-fashioned in views, customs, appearance, etc. **7.** *Obs*. a standard, pattern, or rule. **8. back to square one**. indicating a return to the starting point because of failure, lack of progress, etc. **9. on the square. a.** at right angles. **b.** *Inf*. honestly and openly. **10. out of square. a.** not at right angles or not having a right angle. **b.** not in order or agreement. ~*adj*. **11.** being a square in shape or section. **12.** having or forming one or more right angles or being at right angles to something. **13. a.** (*prenominal*) denoting a measure of area of any shape: *a circle of four square feet*. **b.** (*immediately postpositive*) denoting a square having a specified length on each side: *a board four feet square*. **14.** fair and honest (esp. in a *square deal*). **15.** straight, even, or level: *a square surface*. **16.** *Cricket*. at right angles to the wicket: *square leg*. **17.** *Soccer, hockey, etc.* in a straight line across the pitch: *a square pass*. **18.** *Naut*. (of the sails of a square-rigged ship) set at right angles to the keel. **19.** *Inf*. old-fashioned. **20.** stocky or sturdy: *square shoulders*. **21.** (*postpositive*) having no remaining debts or accounts to be settled. **22.** (*prenominal*) unequivocal or straightforward: *a square contradiction*. **23.** (*postpositive*) neat and tidy. **24. all square**. on equal terms; even in score. **25. square meal**. a meal consisting of enough food to satisfy. **26. square peg** (**in a round hole**). a person or thing that is a misfit. ~*vb*. (*mainly tr.*) **27.** to make into a square or similar shape. **28.** *Maths*. to raise (a number or quantity) to the second power. **29.** to test or adjust for deviation with respect to a right angle, plane surface, etc. **30.** (sometimes foll. by *off*) to divide into squares. **31.** to position so as to be rectangular, straight, or level: *to square the shoulders*. **32.** (sometimes foll. by *up*) to settle (debts, accounts, etc.). **33.** to level (the score) in a game, etc. **34.** (*also intr.*; often foll. by *with*) to agree or cause to agree: *your ideas don't square with mine*. **35.** to arrange (something) or come to an arrangement with (someone) as by bribery: *he squared the speeding summons*. **36. square the circle**. to attempt the impossible (in reference to the insoluble problem of constructing a square having exactly the same area as a given circle). ~*adv*. **37.** in order to be square. **38.** at right angles. **39.** *Soccer, hockey, etc.* in a straight line across the pitch: *to pass the ball square*. **40.** *Inf*. squarely. ~See also **square off, square up**. —'**squareness** *n*. —'**squarer** *n*.

square-bashing *n*. *Brit. mil. sl*. drill on a barrack square.

square bracket *n*. **1.** either of a pair of characters, [ ],

---

spurious artificial, bogus, contrived, counterfeit, deceitful, fake, false, feigned, forged, imitation, mock, phoney (*Sl.*), pretended, pseudo (*Inf.*), sham, simulated, specious, unauthentic

spurn cold-shoulder, contemn, despise, disdain, disregard, rebuff, reject, repulse, scorn, slight, snub, turn one's nose up at (*Inf.*)

spurt 1. *v.* burst, erupt, gush, jet, shoot, spew, squirt, surge 2. *n.* access, burst, fit, rush, spate, surge

spy *n.* 1. double agent, fifth columnist, foreign agent, mole, secret agent, secret service agent, undercover agent ~*v.* 2. *Usually with* **on** follow, keep under surveillance, keep watch on, shadow, tail (*Inf.*), trail, watch 3. catch sight of, descry, espy, glimpse, notice, observe, set eyes on, spot

spying *n.* espionage, secret service

squabble 1. *v.* argue, bicker, brawl, clash, dispute, fall out (*Inf.*), fight, have words, quarrel, row, scrap (*Inf.*), wrangle 2. *n.* argument, barney (*Inf.*), difference of opinion, disagreement, dispute, fight, row, scrap (*Inf.*), set-to (*Inf.*), spat, tiff

squad band, company, crew, force, gang, group, team, troop

squalid broken-down, decayed, dirty, disgusting, fetid, filthy, foul, low, nasty, poverty-stricken, repulsive, run-down, seedy, sleazy, slovenly, slummy, sordid, unclean

squalor decay, filth, foulness, meanness, sleaziness, slumminess, squalidness, wretchedness

squander be prodigal with, blow (*Sl.*), consume, dissipate, expend, fritter away, frivol away, lavish, misspend, misuse, run through, scatter, spend, spend like water, throw away, waste

square *Fig. v.* 1. *Often with* **with** accord, agree, conform, correspond, fit, harmonize, match, reconcile, tally 2. *Sometimes with* **up** balance, clear (up), discharge, liquidate, make even, pay off, quit, satisfy, settle 3. accommodate, adapt, adjust, align, even up, level, regulate, suit, tailor, true (up) 4. *Sl.* bribe, buy off, corrupt, fix (*Inf.*), rig, suborn ~*adj.* 5. aboveboard, decent, equitable, ethical, fair, fair and square, genuine, honest, just, on the level (*Inf.*), straight, straightforward, upright 6. *Inf.* behind the times (*Inf.*), bourgeois, conservative, conventional, old-fashioned, out of date, straight (*Sl.*), strait-laced, stuffy ~*n.* 7. *Inf.* antediluvian, back number (*Inf.*), conservative, die-hard, fuddy-duddy (*Inf.*), old buffer (*Brit. inf.*), (old) fogy, stick-in-the-mud (*Inf.*), traditionalist

used to enclose a section of writing or printing to separate it from the main text. **2.** Also called: **bracket.** either of these characters used as a sign of aggregation in mathematical or logical expressions.

square dance *n.* **1.** any of various formation dances in which the couples form squares. ~*vb.* **square-dance. 2.** (*intr.*) to perform such a dance. —'**square-**'**dancer** *n.*

square leg *n. Cricket.* **1.** a fielding position on the on side approximately at right angles to the batsman. **2.** a person who fields in this position.

squarely ('skwɛəlɪ) *adv.* **1.** in a direct way; straight: *he hit me squarely on the nose.* **2.** in an honest, frank, and just manner. **3.** at right angles.

square measure *n.* a unit or system of units for measuring areas.

square off *vb.* (*intr., adv.*) to assume a posture of offence or defence, as in boxing.

square-rigged *adj. Naut.* rigged with square sails.

square root *n.* a number or quantity that when multiplied by itself gives a given number or quantity: *2 is the square root of 4.*

square up *vb.* (*adv.*) **1.** to pay or settle (bills, debts, etc.). **2.** *Inf.* to arrange or be arranged satisfactorily. **3.** (*intr.; foll. by to*) to prepare to be confronted (with), esp. courageously.

squash[1] ('skwɒʃ) *vb.* **1.** to press or squeeze or be pressed or squeezed in or down so as to crush, distort, or pulp. **2.** (*tr.*) to suppress or overcome. **3.** (*tr.*) to humiliate or crush (a person), esp. with a disconcerting retort. **4.** (*intr.*) to make a sucking, splashing, or squelching sound. **5.** (often foll. by *in* or *into*) to enter or insert in a confined space. ~*n.* **6.** *Brit.* a still drink made from fruit juice or fruit syrup diluted with water. **7.** a crush, esp. of people in a confined space. **8.** something squashed. **9.** the act or sound of squashing or the state of being squashed. **10.** Also called: **squash rackets.** a game for two or four players played in an enclosed court with a small rubber ball and light long-handled rackets. **11.** Also called: **squash tennis.** a similar game played with larger rackets and a larger pneumatic ball. —'**squasher** *n.*

squash[2] ('skwɒʃ) *n., pl.* **squashes** or **squash. 1.** *U.S.* any of various marrow-like plants, the fruits of which have a hard rind surrounding edible flesh. **2.** the fruit, eaten as a vegetable.

squashy ('skwɒʃɪ) *adj.* **-ier, -iest. 1.** easily squashed; pulpy: *a squashy peach.* **2.** soft and wet; marshy. —'**squashily** *adv.* —'**squashiness** *n.*

squat (skwɒt) *vb.* **squatting, squatted.** (*intr.*) **1.** to rest in a crouching position with the knees bent and the weight on the feet. **2.** to crouch down, esp. in order to hide. **3.** *Law.* to occupy land to which the occupant has no legal title. ~*adj.* **4.** Also: **squatty** ('skwɒtɪ). short and broad. ~*n.* **5.** a squatting position. **6.** a house occupied by squatters. —'**squatly** *adv.* —'**squatness** *n.*

squatter ('skwɒtə) *n.* **1.** (in Britain) a person who occupies land wrongfully. **2.** (in Australia) **a.** a grazier with extensive holdings. **b.** *History.* a person occupying land as tenant of the Crown.

squaw (skwɔː) *n.* **1.** a North American Indian woman. **2.** *Sl., usually facetious.* a woman or wife.

squawk (skwɔːk) *n.* **1.** a loud raucous cry; screech. **2.** *Inf.* a loud complaint. ~*vb.* **3.** to utter (with) a squawk. **4.** (*intr.*) *Inf.* to complain loudly. —'**squawker** *n.*

squeak (skwiːk) *n.* **1.** a short shrill cry or high-pitched sound. **2.** *Inf.* an escape (esp. in **narrow squeak, near squeak**). ~*vb.* **3.** to make or cause to make a squeak. **4.** *U.S.* to pass with only a narrow margin: *to squeak through an examination.* **5.** (*intr.*) *Inf.* to confess information about oneself or another. **6.** (*tr.*) to utter with a

squeak. —'**squeaker** *n.* —'**squeaky** *adj.*

squeal (skwiːl) *n.* **1.** a high shrill yelp, as of pain. **2.** a screaming sound. ~*vb.* **3.** to utter (with) a squeal. **4.** (*intr.*) *Sl.* to confess information about another. **5.** (*intr.*) *Inf., chiefly Brit.* to complain loudly. —'**squealer** *n.*

squeamish ('skwiːmɪʃ) *adj.* **1.** easily sickened or nauseated. **2.** easily shocked; prudish. **3.** easily frightened: *squeamish about spiders.* —'**squeamishly** *adv.* —'**squeamishness** *n.*

squeegee ('skwiːdʒiː) *or* **squilgee** *n.* **1.** an implement with a rubber blade used for wiping away surplus water from a surface, such as a windowpane. **2.** any of various similar devices used in photography for pressing water out of wet prints or negatives or for squeezing prints onto a glazing surface. ~*vb.* **-geeing, -geed. 3.** to remove (liquid) from (something) by use of a squeegee.

squeeze (skwiːz) *vb.* (*mainly tr.*) **1.** to grip or press firmly, esp. so as to crush or distort. **2.** to crush or press (something) so as to extract (a liquid): *to squeeze juice from an orange; to squeeze an orange.* **3.** to apply gentle pressure to, as in affection or reassurance: *he squeezed her hand.* **4.** to push or force in a confined space: *to squeeze six lettuces into one box; to squeeze through a crowd.* **5.** to hug closely. **6.** to oppress with exacting demands, such as excessive taxes. **7.** to exert pressure on (someone) in order to extort (something): *to squeeze money out of a victim by blackmail.* **8.** (*tr.*) *Bridge, whist.* to lead a card that forces (opponents) to discard potentially winning cards. ~*n.* **9.** the act or an instance of squeezing or of being squeezed. **10.** a hug or handclasp. **11.** a crush of people in a confined space. **12.** *Chiefly Brit.* a condition of restricted credit imposed by a government to counteract price inflation. **13.** an amount extracted by squeezing: *a squeeze of lemon juice.* **14.** *Inf.* pressure brought to bear in order to extort something (esp. in **put the squeeze on**). **15.** Also called: **squeeze play.** *Bridge, whist.* a manoeuvre that forces opponents to discard potentially winning cards. —'**squeezable** *adj.* —'**squeezer** *n.*

squelch (skwɛltʃ) *vb.* **1.** (*intr.*) to walk laboriously through soft wet material or with wet shoes, making a sucking noise. **2.** (*intr.*) to make such a noise. **3.** (*tr.*) to crush completely; squash. **4.** (*tr.*) *Inf.* to silence, as by a crushing retort. ~*n.* **5.** a squelching sound. **6.** something that has been squelched. **7.** *Inf.* a crushing remark. —'**squelcher** *n.*

squib (skwɪb) *n.* **1.** a firework that burns with a hissing noise and culminates in a small explosion. **2.** a short witty attack; lampoon. **3. damp squib.** something intended but failing to impress. ~*vb.* **squibbing, squibbed. 4.** (*intr.*) to sound, move, or explode like a squib. **5.** to let off or shoot a squib. **6.** to write a squib against (someone).

squid (skwɪd) *n., pl.* **squid** or **squids.** any of various ten-limbed pelagic cephalopod molluscs of most seas, having a torpedo-shaped body ranging from about 10 centimetres to 16.5 metres long. See also **cuttlefish.**

squiffy ('skwɪfɪ) *adj.* **-fier, -fiest.** *Brit. inf.* slightly drunk.

squiggle ('skwɪgəl) *n.* **1.** a mark or movement in the form of a wavy line; curlicue. **2.** an illegible scrawl. ~*vb.* **3.** (*intr.*) to wriggle. **4.** (*intr.*) to form or draw squiggles. **5.** (*tr.*) to make into squiggles. —'**squiggler** *n.* —'**squiggly** *adj.*

squill (skwɪl) *n.* **1.** Also called: **sea squill.** a Mediterranean plant of the lily family. **2.** any of various related Old World plants. **3.** the bulb of the sea squill, which is sliced, dried, and used medicinally, as an expectorant.

squint (skwɪnt) *vb.* **1.** (*usually intr.*) to cross or partly close (the eyes). **2.** (*intr.*) to have a squint. **3.** (*intr.*) to

---

THESAURUS

squash *v.* **1.** compress, crush, distort, flatten, mash, pound, press, pulp, smash, stamp on, trample down **2.** annihilate, crush, humiliate, put down (*Sl.*), put (someone) in his (*or* her) place, quash, quell, silence, sit on (*Inf.*), suppress

squashy mushy, pappy, pulpy, soft, spongy, yielding

squawk *v.* **1.** cackle, crow, cry, hoot, screech, yelp **2.** *Inf.* complain, kick up a fuss (*Inf.*), protest, raise Cain (*Sl.*), squeal (*Inf.*)

squeak *v.* peep, pipe, shrill, squeal, whine, yelp

squeal *n.* **1.** scream, screech, shriek, wail, yell, yelp, yowl ~*v.* **2.** scream, screech, shout, shriek, shrill, wail, yelp **3.** *Sl.* betray, blab, grass (*Brit. sl.*), inform on, peach (*Sl.*), rat on, sell (someone) down the river (*Inf.*), sing (*Sl.*), snitch (*Sl.*) **4.** *Inf.* complain, kick up a fuss (*Inf.*), moan, protest, squawk (*Inf.*)

squeamish 1. delicate, fastidious, finicky, nice (*Rare*), particular, prissy (*Inf.*), prudish, punctilious, scrupulous, strait-laced **2.** nauseous, qualmish, queasy, queer, sick, sickish

squeeze *v.* **1.** clutch, compress, crush,

grip, nip, pinch, press, squash, wring **2.** cram, crowd, force, jam, jostle, pack, press, ram, stuff, thrust, wedge **3.** clasp, cuddle, embrace, enfold, hold tight, hug **4.** bleed (*Inf.*), bring pressure to bear on, extort, lean on (*Inf.*), milk, oppress, pressurize, put the screws on (*Inf.*), put the squeeze on (*Inf.*), wrest ~*n.* **5.** clasp, embrace, handclasp, hold, hug **6.** congestion, crowd, crush, jam, press, squash

look or glance sideways or askance. ~*n.* **4.** the non-technical name for **strabismus**. **5.** the act or an instance of squinting; glimpse. **6.** a narrow oblique opening in a wall or pillar of a church to permit a view of the main altar from a side aisle or transept. ~*adj.* **7.** having a squint. —'**squinter** *n.* —'**squinty** *adj.*

squire (skwaɪə) *n.* **1.** a country gentleman in England, esp. the main landowner in a rural community. **2.** *Feudal history.* a young man of noble birth, who attended upon a knight. **3.** *Rare.* a man who courts or escorts a woman. **4.** *Inf.,* chiefly *Brit.* a term of address used by one man to another. ~*vb.* **5.** (*tr.*) (of a man) to escort a woman.

squirearchy or **squirarchy** ('skwaɪə,rɑːkɪ) *n., pl.* -**chies.** **1.** government by squires. **2.** squires collectively, esp. as a political or social force. —**squire'archal, squir'archal** or **squire'archical, squir'archical** *adj.*

squirm (skwɜːm) *vb.* (*intr.*) **1.** to move with a wriggling motion; writhe. **2.** to feel deep mental discomfort, guilt, embarrassment, etc. ~*n.* **3.** a squirming movement. —'**squirmer** *n.* —'**squirmy** *adj.*

squirrel ('skwɪrəl) *n., pl.* -**rels** or -**rel.** **1.** any of various arboreal rodents having a bushy tail and feeding on nuts, seeds, etc. **2.** any of various related rodents, such as a ground squirrel or a marmot. **3.** the fur of such an animal. **4.** *Inf.* a person who hoards things.

squirt (skwɜːt) *vb.* **1.** to force (a liquid) or (of a liquid) to be forced out of a narrow opening. **2.** to cover or spatter with liquid so ejected. ~*n.* **3.** a jet or amount of liquid so ejected. **4.** the act or an instance of squirting. **5.** an instrument used for squirting. **6.** *Inf.* **a.** a person regarded as insignificant or contemptible. **b.** a short person. —'**squirter** *n.*

squish (skwɪʃ) *vb.* **1.** (*tr.*) to crush, esp. so as to make a soft splashing noise. **2.** (*intr.*) (of mud, etc.) to make a splashing noise. ~*n.* **3.** a soft squashing sound. —'**squishy** *adj.*

Sr *the chemical symbol for* strontium.

Sr. or **Sr** *abbrev. for:* **1.** (after a name) senior. **2.** Señor. **3.** Sir. **4.** Sister (religious).

S.R.C. (in Britain) *abbrev. for* Science Research Council.

Sri Lankan (srɪ 'læŋkən) *adj.* **1.** of Sri Lanka, a republic in S Asia, or its inhabitants. ~*n.* **2.** an inhabitant of Sri Lanka.

S.R.N. (in Britain) *abbrev. for* State Registered Nurse.

SS *abbrev. for:* **1.** Saints. **2.** a paramilitary organization within the Nazi party that provided Hitler's bodyguard, security forces, concentration camp guards, etc. **3.** steamship.

S.S. *abbrev. for* steamship.

SSE *abbrev. for* south-southeast.

SSR *abbrev. for* Soviet Socialist Republic.

S.S.R.C. (in Britain) *abbrev. for* Social Science Research Council.

SSW *abbrev. for* south-southwest.

st. *abbrev. for:* **1.** stanza. **2.** statute. **3.** *Cricket.* stumped by. **4.** stone.

St. or **St** *abbrev. for:* **1.** Saint (all entries that are usually preceded by *St.* are in this dictionary listed alphabetically under **Saint**). **2.** statute. **3.** Strait. **4.** Street.

-st *suffix.* a variant of **-est.**

stab (stæb) *vb.* **stabbing, stabbed.** **1.** (*tr.*) to pierce or injure with a sharp pointed instrument. **2.** (*tr.*) (of a sharp pointed instrument) to pierce or wound. **3.** (when *intr.,* often foll. by *at*) to make a thrust; jab. **4.** (*tr.*) to inflict with a sharp pain. **5. stab in the back. a.** (*vb.*) to damage (the reputation, etc., of a person, esp. a friend) in a surreptitious way. **b.** (*n.*) a treacherous action or remark that causes the downfall of or injury to a person. ~*n.* **6.** the act or an instance of stabbing. **7.** an injury or rift made by stabbing. **8.** a sudden sensation, esp. an unpleasant one: *a stab of pity.* **9.** an attempt (esp. in **make a stab at**). —'**stabber** *n.*

stabile ('steɪbaɪl) *n.* **1.** *Arts.* a stationary abstract construction, usually of wire, metal, wood, etc. ~*adj.* **2.** fixed; stable. **3.** resistant to chemical change.

stability (stə'bɪlɪtɪ) *n., pl.* -**ties.** **1.** the quality of being stable. **2.** the ability of an aircraft to resume its original flight path after inadvertent displacement.

stabilize or **-ise** ('steɪbɪ,laɪz) *vb.* **1.** to make or become stable or more stable. **2.** to keep or be kept stable. **3.** (*tr.*) to put or keep (an aircraft, vessel, etc.) in equilibrium by one or more special devices, or (of an aircraft, etc.) to become stable. —,**stabili'zation** or -**i'sation** *n.*

stabilizer or **-iser** ('steɪbɪ,laɪzə) *n.* **1.** any device for stabilizing an aircraft. **2.** a substance added to something to maintain it in a stable or unchanging state. **3.** *Naut.* **a.** a system of pairs of fins projecting from the hull of a ship and controllable to counteract roll. **b.** See **gyro-stabilizer**. **4.** a person or thing that stabilizes.

stable[1] ('steɪbəl) *n.* **1.** a building, usually consisting of stalls, for the lodging of horses or other livestock. **2.** the animals lodged in such a building, collectively. **3. a.** the racehorses belonging to a particular establishment or owner. **b.** the establishment itself. **c.** (*as modifier*): *stable companion.* **4.** *Inf.* a source of training, such as a school, theatre, etc.: *the two athletes were out of the same stable.* **5.** a number of people considered as a source of a particular talent: *a stable of writers.* **6.** (*modifier*) relating to, or suitable for a stable: *stable door.* ~*vb.* **7.** to put, keep, or be kept in a stable.

stable[2] ('steɪbəl) *adj.* **1.** steady in position or balance; firm. **2.** lasting: *a stable relationship.* **3.** steadfast or firm of purpose. **4.** (of an elementary particle, etc.) not undergoing decay; not radioactive. **5.** (of a chemical compound) not readily partaking in a chemical change. —'**stableness** *n.* —'**stably** *adv.*

staccato (stə'kɑːtəʊ) *adj.* **1.** *Music.* (of notes) short, clipped, and separate. **2.** characterized by short abrupt sounds, as in speech: *a staccato command.* ~*adv.* **3.** (esp. used as a musical direction) in a staccato manner.

stack (stæk) *n.* **1.** an ordered pile or heap. **2.** a large orderly pile of hay, straw, etc., for storage in the open air. **3.** (*often pl.*) compactly spaced bookshelves, used to house collections of books in an area usually prohibited to library users. **4.** a number of aircraft circling an airport at different altitudes, awaiting their signal to land. **5.** a large amount. **6.** *Mil.* a pile of rifles or muskets in the shape of a cone. **7.** *Brit.* a measure of coal or wood equal to 108 cubic feet. **8. a.** In full **chimney stack**. the part of a chimney that rises above the roof of a building. **b.** short for **smokestack**. **9.** a vertical pipe, such as the funnel of a ship or the soil pipe attached to the side of a building. **10.** a high column of rock, esp. one isolated from the mainland by the erosive action of the sea. **11.** an area in a computer memory for temporary storage. ~*vb.* (*tr.*) **12.** to place in a stack; pile. **13.** to load or fill up with piles of something: *to stack a lorry with bricks.* **14.** to control a number of aircraft waiting to land at an airport so that each flies at a different altitude. **15. stack the cards.** to prearrange the order of a pack of cards secretly so as to cheat. —'**stacker** *n.*

stadium ('steɪdɪəm) *n., pl.* -**diums** or -**dia** (-dɪə). **1.** a sports arena with tiered seats for spectators. **2.** (in ancient Greece) a course for races, usually located between two hills providing slopes for tiers of seats. **3.** an ancient Greek measure of length equivalent to about 607 feet or 184 metres.

staff (stɑːf) *n., pl.* **staffs** *for senses 1–3;* **staffs** or **staves** (steɪvz) *for senses 4–9.* **1.** '**a.** a group of people employed by a company, individual, etc., for executive, clerical, sales work, etc. **b.** (*as modifier*): *a staff doctor.* **2.** the body of teachers or lecturers of an educational institution. **3.** *Mil.* the officers appointed to assist a command-

---

THESAURUS

squire *v.* accompany, attend, companion, escort

squirm agonize, fidget, flounder, shift, twist, wiggle, wriggle, writhe

stab *v.* **1.** bayonet, cut, gore, injure, jab, knife, pierce, puncture, run through, spear, stick, thrust, transfix, wound **2. stab in the back** betray, break faith with, deceive, do the dirty on (*Brit. sl.*), double-cross (*Inf.*), give the Judas kiss to, inform on, let down,

play false, sell, sell out (*Inf.*), slander ~*n.* **3.** gash, incision, jab, puncture, rent, thrust, wound **4.** ache, pang, prick, twinge **5. make a stab at** attempt, endeavour, essay, have a go (crack, shot) (*Inf.*), try, try one's hand at, venture

stability constancy, durability, firmness, permanence, solidity, soundness, steadfastness, steadiness, strength

stable abiding, constant, deep-rooted, du-

rable, enduring, established, fast, firm, fixed, immutable, invariable, lasting, permanent, reliable, secure, sound, steadfast, steady, strong, sturdy, sure, unalterable, unchangeable, unwavering, well-founded

stack 1. *n.* clamp (*Brit. agriculture*), cock, heap, hoard, load, mass, mound, mountain, pile **2.** *v.* accumulate, amass, assemble, bank up, heap up, load, pile, stockpile

er, service, or central headquarters organization. **4.** a stick with some special use, such as a walking stick or an emblem of authority. **5.** something that sustains or supports: *bread is the staff of life.* **6.** a pole on which a flag is hung. **7.** a pole used as a handle. **8.** *Chiefly Brit.* a graduated rod used in surveying, esp. for sighting to with a levelling instrument. **9.** Also called: **stave.** *Music.* **a.** the system of horizontal lines grouped into sets of five (four in plainsong) upon which music is written. The spaces between them are employed in conjunction with a clef in order to give a graphic indication of pitch. **b.** any set of five lines in this system together with its clef: *the treble staff.* ~*vb.* **10.** (*tr.*) to employ or provide with a staff.

staff nurse *n.* a qualified nurse ranking immediately below a sister.

staff officer *n.* a commissioned officer serving on the staff of a commander, service, or central headquarters.

Staffs. (stæfs) *abbrev. for* Staffordshire.

staff sergeant *n. Mil.* **1.** *Brit.* a noncommissioned officer holding sergeant's rank and carrying out certain special duties. **2.** *U.S.* a noncommissioned officer who ranks: **a.** (in the Army) above sergeant and below sergeant first class. **b.** (in the Air Force) above airman first class and below technical sergeant. **c.** (in the Marine Corps) above sergeant and below gunnery sergeant.

stag (stæg) *n.* **1.** the adult male of a deer. **2.** a man unaccompanied by a woman at a social gathering. **3.** *Stock exchange, Brit.* a speculator who buys heavily on a new share issue in anticipation of a rise in its price and thus an opportunity for quick profit on resale. **4.** (*modifier*) (of a social gathering) attended by men only. ~*adv.* **5.** without a female escort.

stag beetle *n.* any of various beetles, the males of which have large branched mandibles.

stage (steɪdʒ) *n.* **1.** a distinct step or period of development, growth, or progress. **2.** a raised area or platform. **3.** the platform in a theatre where actors perform. **4. the.** the theatre as a profession. **5.** any scene regarded as a setting for an event or action. **6.** a portion of a journey or a stopping-place after such a portion. **7.** short for **stagecoach. 8.** *Brit.* a division of a bus route for which there is a fixed fare. **9.** one of the separate propulsion units of a rocket that can be jettisoned when it has burnt out. **10.** a small stratigraphical unit; a subdivision of a rock series or system. **11.** the platform on a microscope on which the specimen is mounted for examination. **12.** *Electronics.* a part of a complex circuit, esp. a transistor with the associated elements required to amplify a signal in an amplifier. **13. by** *or* **in easy stages.** not hurriedly: *he learnt French by easy stages.* ~*vb.* **14.** (*tr.*) to perform (a play), esp. on a stage: *to stage "Hamlet".* **15.** (*tr.*) to set the action of a play in a particular time or place. **16.** (*tr.*) to plan, organize, and carry out (an event).

stagecoach (ˈsteɪdʒˌkəʊtʃ) *n.* a large four-wheeled horse-drawn vehicle formerly used to carry passengers, mail, etc., on a regular route.

stage direction *n.* an instruction to an actor or director, written into the script of a play.

stage door *n.* a door at a theatre leading backstage.

stage fright *n.* nervousness or panic that may beset a person about to appear in front of an audience.

stagehand (ˈsteɪdʒˌhænd) *n.* a person who sets the stage, moves props, etc., in a theatrical production.

stage-manage *vb.* **1.** to work as stage manager (for a play, etc.). **2.** (*tr.*) to arrange, present, or supervise from behind the scenes.

stage manager *n.* a person who supervises the stage arrangements of a theatrical production.

stage-struck *adj.* infatuated with the glamour of the-

atrical life, esp. with the desire to act.

stage whisper *n.* **1.** a loud whisper from one actor to another onstage intended to be heard by the audience. **2.** any loud whisper that is intended to be overheard.

stagflation (stægˈfleɪʃən) *n.* an inflationary economic situation characterized by a decline in industrial output.

stagger (ˈstægə) *vb.* **1.** (*usually intr.*) to walk or cause to walk unsteadily as if about to fall. **2.** (*tr.*) to astound or overwhelm, as with shock: *I am staggered by his ruthlessness.* **3.** (*tr.*) to place or arrange in alternating or overlapping positions or time periods to prevent confusion or congestion: *a staggered junction; to stagger holidays.* **4.** (*intr.*) to falter or hesitate: *his courage staggered in the face of the battle.* ~*n.* **5.** the act or an instance of staggering. —ˈstaggerer *n.* —ˈstaggering *adj.* —ˈstaggeringly *adv.*

staggers (ˈstægəz) *n.* **1.** a form of vertigo associated with decompression sickness. **2.** Also called: **blind staggers.** a disease of horses and some other domestic animals characterized by a swaying unsteady gait, caused by infection or lesions of the central nervous system.

staging (ˈsteɪdʒɪŋ) *n.* any temporary structure used in the process of building, esp. the horizontal platforms supported by scaffolding.

stagnant (ˈstægnənt) *adj.* **1.** (of water, etc.) standing still; without flow or current. **2.** brackish and foul from standing still. **3.** stale, sluggish, or dull from inaction. **4.** not growing or developing; static. —ˈstagnancy *n.*

stagnate (stægˈneɪt) *vb.* (*intr.*) to be or become stagnant. —stagˈnation *n.*

stag party *n.* a party for men only, esp. one held for a man just before he is married.

stagy *or U.S.* **stagey** (ˈsteɪdʒɪ) *adj.* **stagier, stagiest.** theatrical or dramatic. —ˈstagily *adv.* —ˈstaginess *n.*

staid (steɪd) *adj.* of a settled, sedate, and steady character. —ˈstaidly *adv.* —ˈstaidness *n.*

stain (steɪn) *vb.* (*mainly tr.*) **1.** to mark or discolour with patches of something that dirties. **2.** to dye with a penetrating dyestuff or pigment. **3.** to bring disgrace or shame on: *to stain one's honour.* **4.** to colour (specimens) for microscopic study by treatment with a dye or similar reagent. **5.** (*intr.*) to produce indelible marks or discoloration: *does ink stain?* ~*n.* **6.** a spot, mark, or discoloration. **7.** a moral taint; blemish or slur. **8.** a dye or similar reagent, used to colour specimens for microscopic study. **9.** a solution or liquid used to penetrate the surface of a material, esp. wood, and impart a rich colour without covering up the surface or grain. **10.** any dye used to colour textiles and hides. —ˈstainable *adj.* —ˌstainaˈbility *n.* —ˈstainer *n.*

stained glass *n.* **a.** glass that has been coloured, as by fusing with a film of metallic oxide or burning pigment into the surface. **b.** (*as modifier*): *a stained-glass window.*

stainless (ˈsteɪnlɪs) *adj.* **1.** resistant to discoloration, esp. that resulting from corrosion; rust-resistant: *stainless steel.* **2.** having no blemish: *stainless reputation.* —ˈstainlessly *adv.*

stainless steel *n.* **a.** a type of steel resistant to corrosion as a result of the presence of large amounts of chromium. **b.** (*as modifier*): *stainless-steel cutlery.*

stair (stɛə) *n.* **1.** one of a flight of stairs. **2.** a series of steps: *a narrow stair.*

staircase (ˈstɛəˌkeɪs) *n.* a flight of stairs, its supporting framework, and, usually, a handrail or banisters.

stairs (stɛəz) *pl. n.* **1.** a flight of steps leading from one storey or level to another, esp. indoors. **2. below stairs.** *Brit.* in the servants' quarters.

stairway (ˈstɛəˌweɪ) *n.* a means of access consisting of stairs; staircase or flight of steps.

THESAURUS

staff *n.* **1.** employees, lecturers, officers, organization, personnel, teachers, team, workers, work force **2.** cane, pole, prop, rod, stave, wand

stage **1.** *n.* division, juncture, lap, leg, length, level, period, phase, point, step **2.** *v.* arrange, do, engineer, give, lay on, mount, orchestrate, organize, perform, play, present, produce, put on

stagger *v.* **1.** falter, hesitate, lurch, reel, sway, teeter, totter, vacillate, waver, wobble **2.** amaze, astonish, astound, bowl over (*Inf.*),

confound, dumbfound, flabbergast, give (someone) a shock, nonplus, overwhelm, shake, shock, strike (someone) dumb (*Inf.*), stun, stupefy, surprise, take (someone) aback, take (someone's) breath away, throw off balance **3.** alternate, overlap, step, zigzag

stagnant brackish, motionless, quiet, sluggish, stale, standing, still

stagnate decay, decline, deteriorate, fester, go to seed, idle, languish, lie fallow, rot, rust, stand still, vegetate

staid calm, composed, decorous, demure,

grave, quiet, sedate, self-restrained, serious, sober, solemn, steady

stain *v.* **1.** blemish, blot, colour, dirty, discolour, dye, mark, soil, spot, tarnish, tinge **2.** besmirch, blacken, contaminate, corrupt, defile, deprave, disgrace, drag through the mud, sully, taint ~*n.* **3.** blemish, blot, discoloration, dye, spot, tint **4.** blemish, blot on the escutcheon, disgrace, dishonour, infamy, reproach, shame, slur, stigma

stairwell ('stɛə,wɛl) *n.* a vertical shaft or opening that contains a staircase.

stake¹ (steɪk) *n.* **1.** a stick or metal bar driven into the ground as a marker, part of a fence, support for a plant, etc. **2.** one of a number of vertical posts that fit into sockets around a flat truck or railway wagon to hold the load in place. **3.** a method or the practice of executing a person by binding him to a stake in the centre of a pile of wood that is then set on fire. **4. pull up stakes.** to leave one's home or resting-place and move on. ~*vb.* (*tr.*) **5.** to tie, fasten, or tether with or to a stake. **6.** (often foll. by *out* or *off*) to fence or surround with stakes. **7.** (often foll. by *out*) to lay (a claim) to land, rights, etc. **8.** to support with a stake.

stake² (steɪk) *n.* **1.** the money or valuables that a player must hazard in order to buy into a gambling game or make a bet. **2.** an interest, often financial, held in something: *a stake in the company's future.* **3.** (often *pl.*) the money that a player has available for gambling. **4.** (often *pl.*) a prize in a race, etc., esp. one made up of contributions from contestants or owners. **5.** (*pl.*) a horse race in which all owners of competing horses contribute to the prize. **6. at stake.** at risk: *lives are at stake.* ~*vb.* (*tr.*) **7.** to hazard (money, etc.) on a result. **8.** to invest in or support with money, etc.: *to stake a business.*

stakeout ('steɪkaut) *U.S. sl.* ~*n.* **1.** a police surveillance. **2.** an area or house kept under such surveillance. ~*vb.* **stake out. 3.** (*tr., adv.*) to keep under surveillance.

Stakhanovism (stæ'kænə,vɪzəm) *n.* (in the Soviet Union) a system designed to raise production by offering incentives to efficient workers. —**Sta'khanov,ite** *n.*

stalactite ('stælək,taɪt) *n.* a cylindrical mass of calcium carbonate hanging from the roof of a limestone cave: formed by precipitation from continually dripping water. Cf. **stalagmite.** —**stalactiform** (stə'læktɪ,fɔːm) *adj.* —**stalactitic** (,stælək'tɪtɪk) *or* ,**stalac'titical** *adj.*

stalagmite ('stæləg,maɪt) *n.* a cylindrical mass of calcium carbonate projecting upwards from the floor of a limestone cave: formed by precipitation from continually dripping water. Cf. **stalactite.** —**stalagmitic** (,stæləg-'mɪtɪk) *or* ,**stalag'mitical** *adj.*

stale (steɪl) *adj.* **1.** (esp. of food) hard, musty, or dry from being kept too long. **2.** (of beer, etc.) flat and tasteless from being kept open too long. **3.** (of air) stagnant; foul. **4.** uninteresting from overuse: *stale clichés.* **5.** no longer new: *stale news.* **6.** lacking in energy or ideas through overwork or lack of variety. **7.** *Law.* (of a claim, etc.) having lost its effectiveness or force, as by failure to act or by the lapse of time. ~*vb.* **8.** to make or become stale. —**staleness** *n.*

stalemate ('steɪl,meɪt) *n.* **1.** a chess position in which any of a player's possible moves would place his king in check: in this position the game ends in a draw. **2.** a situation in which two opposing forces find that further action is impossible or futile; deadlock. ~*vb.* **3.** (*tr.*) to subject to a stalemate.

Stalinism ('stɑːlɪ,nɪzəm) *n.* the theory and form of government associated with Joseph *Stalin* (1879–1953), general secretary of the Communist Party of the Soviet Union 1922–53: a variant of Marxism-Leninism characterized by totalitarianism, rigid bureaucracy, and loyalty to the Soviet state. —**'Stalinist** *n., adj.*

stalk¹ (stɔːk) *n.* **1.** the main stem of a herbaceous plant. **2.** any of various subsidiary plant stems, such as a leafstalk or flower stalk. **3.** a slender supporting structure in animals such as crinoids and barnacles. **4.** any long slender supporting shaft or column. —**stalked** *adj.* —**'stalk,like** *adj.*

stalk² (stɔːk) *vb.* **1.** to follow or approach (game, prey, etc.) stealthily and quietly. **2.** to spread over (a place) in a menacing or grim manner: *fever stalked the camp.* **3.** (*intr.*) to walk in a haughty, stiff, or threatening way. **4.** to search (a piece of land) for prey. ~*n.* **5.** the act of stalking. **6.** a stiff or threatening stride. —**'stalker** *n.*

stalking-horse *n.* **1.** a horse or an imitation one used by a hunter to hide behind while stalking. **2.** something serving as a means of concealing plans; pretext. **3.** *Chiefly U.S.* a candidate put forward to divide the opposition or mask the candidacy of another person for whom the stalking-horse would then withdraw.

stall¹ (stɔːl) *n.* **1. a.** a compartment in a stable or shed for a single animal. **b.** another name for **stable¹. 2.** a small often temporary stand or booth for the sale of goods. **3.** (in a church) **a.** one of a row of seats usually divided by armrests or a small screen, for the choir or clergy. **b.** a pen. **4.** an instance of an engine stalling. **5.** a condition of an aircraft in flight in which a reduction in speed or an increase in the aircraft's angle of attack causes a sudden loss of lift resulting in a downward plunge. **6.** any small room or compartment. **7.** *Brit.* **a.** a seat in a theatre or cinema, usually fixed to the floor. **b.** (*pl.*) the area of seats on the ground floor of a theatre or cinema nearest to the orchestra pit or screen. **8.** a tubelike covering for a finger, as in a glove. **9.** (*pl.*) In full **starting stalls.** *Brit.* a line of stalls in which horses are enclosed at the start of a race and from which they are released by simultaneous springing open of retaining barriers at the front of each stall. ~*vb.* **10.** to cause (a motor vehicle or its engine) to stop, usually by incorrect use of the clutch or incorrect adjustment of the fuel mixture, or, (of an engine or motor vehicle) to stop, usually for these reasons. **11.** to cause (an aircraft) to go into a stall or (of an aircraft) to go into a stall. **12.** to stick or cause to stick fast, as in mud or snow. **13.** (*tr.*) to confine (an animal) in a stall.

stall² (stɔːl) *vb.* **1.** to employ delaying tactics towards (someone); be evasive. ~*n.* **2.** an evasive move; pretext.

stallion ('stæljən) *n.* an uncastrated male horse, esp. one used for breeding.

stalwart ('stɔːlwət) *adj.* **1.** strong and sturdy; robust. **2.** solid, dependable, and courageous. **3.** resolute and firm. ~*n.* **4.** a stalwart person, esp. a supporter. —**'stalwartly** *adv.* —**'stalwartness** *n.*

stamen ('steɪmɛn) *n., pl.* **stamens** *or* **stamina** ('stæmɪnə). the male reproductive organ of a flower, consisting of a stalk (filament) bearing an anther in which pollen is produced. —**staminiferous** (,stæmɪ-'nɪfərəs) *adj.*

stamina¹ ('stæmɪnə) *n.* enduring energy, strength, and resilience.

stamina² ('stæmɪnə) *n.* a plural of **stamen.**

stammer ('stæmə) *vb.* **1.** to speak or say (something) in a hesitant way, esp. as a result of a speech disorder or through fear, stress, etc. ~*n.* **2.** a speech disorder characterized by involuntary repetitions and hesitations. —**'stammerer** *n.* —**'stammeringly** *adv.*

stamp (stæmp) *vb.* **1.** (when *intr.,* often foll. by *on*) to bring (the foot) down heavily (on the ground, etc.). **2.** (*intr.*) to walk with heavy or noisy footsteps. **3.** (*intr.;* foll. by *on*) to repress or extinguish: *he stamped on criticism.* **4.** (*tr.*) to impress or mark (a device or sign) on (something). **5.** to mark (something) with an official seal or device: *to stamp a passport.* **6.** (*tr.*) to fix or impress permanently: *the date was stamped on her memory.* **7.** (*tr.*) to affix a postage stamp to. **8.** (*tr.*) to distinguish or reveal: *that behaviour stamps him as a cheat.* **9.** to pound or crush (ores, etc.). ~*n.* **10.** the act or an instance of stamping. **11. a.** See **postage stamp. b.** a mark applied to postage stamps for cancellation. **12.** a

---

THESAURUS

stake¹ *n.* **1.** pale, paling, picket, pole, post, spike, stave, stick ~*v.* **2.** brace, prop, secure, support, tether, tie up **3.** *Often with* **out** define, delimit, demarcate, lay claim to, mark out, outline, reserve

stake² *n.* **1.** ante, bet, chance, hazard, peril, pledge, risk, venture, wager **2.** claim, concern, interest, investment, involvement, share ~*v.* **3.** bet, chance, gamble, hazard, imperil, jeopardize, pledge, put on, risk, venture, wager

stale 1. decayed, dry, faded, fetid, flat, fusty, hard, insipid, musty, old, sour, stagnant,

tasteless **2.** antiquated, banal, cliché-ridden, common, commonplace, drab, effete, flat, hackneyed, insipid, old hat, overused, platitudinous, repetitious, stereotyped, threadbare, trite, unoriginal, worn-out

stalk *v.* **1.** creep up on, follow, haunt, hunt, pursue, shadow, tail (*Inf.*), track **2.** flounce, march, pace, stride, strut

stall *v.* beat about the bush (*Inf.*), equivocate, hedge, play for time, prevaricate, stonewall, temporize

stalwart athletic, beefy (*Inf.*), brawny, daring, dependable, hefty (*Inf.*), husky (*Inf.*),

indomitable, intrepid, lusty, manly, muscular, redoubtable, robust, rugged, sinewy, staunch, stout, strapping, strong, sturdy, valiant, vigorous

stamina energy, force, grit (*Inf.*), indefatigability, lustiness, power, power of endurance, resilience, resistance, staying power, strength, vigour

stammer *v.* falter, hem and haw, hesitate, pause, splutter, stumble, stutter

similar piece of gummed paper used for commercial or trading purposes. **13.** a block, die, etc., used for imprinting a design or device. **14.** a design, device, or mark that has been stamped. **15.** a characteristic feature or trait; hallmark: *the stamp of authenticity.* **16.** a piece of gummed paper or other mark applied to official documents to indicate payment, validity, ownership, etc. **17.** *Brit. inf.* a national insurance contribution, formerly recorded by means of a stamp on an official card. **18.** type or class: *men of his stamp.* **19.** an instrument or machine for crushing or pounding ores, etc., or the pestle in such a device. —'**stamper** *n.*

stampede (stæm'pi:d) *n.* **1.** an impulsive headlong rush of startled cattle or horses. **2.** headlong rush of a crowd. **3.** any sudden large-scale action, such as a rush of people to support a candidate. **4.** *Canad.* a rodeo. ~*vb.* **5.** to run away or cause to run away in a stampede. —**stam'peder** *n.*

stamping ground *n.* a habitual or favourite meeting or gathering place.

stamp out *vb.* (*tr., adv.*) **1.** to put out or extinguish by stamping: *to stamp out a fire.* **2.** to suppress by force: *to stamp out a rebellion.*

stance (stæns, stɑ:ns) *n.* **1.** the manner and position in which a person or animal stands. **2.** *Sport.* the posture assumed when about to play the ball, as in golf, cricket, etc. **3.** emotional or intellectual attitude: *a leftist stance.* **4.** *Chiefly Scot.* a place where a vehicle waits: *taxi stance.*

stanch (stɑ:ntʃ) *or* **staunch** (stɔ:ntʃ) *vb.* **1.** to stem the flow of (a liquid, esp. blood) or (of a liquid) to stop flowing. **2.** to prevent the flow of a liquid, esp. blood, from (a hole, wound, etc.). —'**stanchable** *or* '**staunchable** *adj.* —'**stancher** *or* '**stauncher** *n.*

stanchion ('stɑ:nʃən) *n.* **1.** any vertical pole, beam, rod, etc., used as a support. ~*vb.* **2.** (*tr.*) to provide or support with a stanchion or stanchions.

stand (stænd) *vb.* **standing, stood.** (*mainly intr.*) **1.** (*also tr.*) to be or cause to be in an erect or upright position. **2.** to rise to, assume, or maintain an upright position. **3.** (*copula*) to have a specified height when standing: *to stand six feet.* **4.** to be situated or located: *the house stands in the square.* **5.** to be in a specified state or condition: *to stand in awe of someone.* **6.** to adopt or remain in a resolute position or attitude. **7.** (*may take an infinitive*) to be in a specified position: *I stand to lose money in this venture.* **8.** to remain in force or continue in effect: *my orders stand.* **9.** to come to a stop or halt, esp. temporarily. **10.** (of water, etc.) to collect and remain without flowing. **11.** (often foll. by *at*) (of a score, account, etc.) to indicate the specified position: *the score stands at 20 to 1.* **12.** (*also tr.; when intr.,* foll. by *for*) tolerate or bear: *I won't stand for your nonsense; I can't stand spiders.* **13.** (*tr.*) to resist; survive: *to stand the test of time.* **14.** (*tr.*) to submit to: *to stand trial.* **15.** (often foll. by *for*) *Chiefly Brit.* to be or become a candidate: *stand for Parliament.* **16.** to navigate in a specified direction: *we were standing for Madeira.* **17.** (of a gun dog) to point at game. **18.** to halt, esp. to give action, repel attack, or disrupt an enemy advance when retreating. **19.** (*tr.*) *Inf.* to bear the cost of; pay for: *to stand someone a drink.* **20. stand a chance.** to have a hope or likelihood of winning, succeeding, etc. **21. stand fast.** to maintain one's position firmly. **22. stand one's ground.** to maintain a stance or position in the face of opposition. **23. stand still. a.** to remain motionless. **b.** (foll. by *for*)

U.S. to tolerate: *I won't stand still for your threats.* ~*n.* **24.** the act or an instance of standing. **25.** an opinion, esp. a resolutely held one: *he took a stand on capital punishment.* **26.** a halt or standstill. **27.** a place where a person or thing stands. **28.** *Austral.* **a.** a position on the floor of a shearing shed allocated to one shearer. **b.** the shearer's equipment. **29.** a structure on which people can sit or stand. **30.** a frame or rack on which such articles as coats and hats may be hung. **31.** a small table or piece of furniture where articles may be placed or stored: *a music stand.* **32.** a supporting framework, esp. for a tool or instrument. **33.** a stall, booth, or counter from which goods may be sold. **34.** a halt to give action, etc., esp. during a retreat and having some duration or success. **35.** *Cricket.* an extended period at the wicket by two batsmen. **36.** a growth of plants in a particular area, esp. trees in a forest or a crop in a field. **37.** a stop made by a touring theatrical company, pop group, etc., to give a performance (esp. in **one-night stand**). **38.** (of a gun dog) the act of pointing at game. ~See also **stand by, stand down,** etc. —'**stander** *n.*

standard ('stændəd) *n.* **1.** an accepted or approved example of something against which others are judged or measured. **2.** (*often pl.*) a principle of propriety, honesty, and integrity. **3.** a level of excellence or quality. **4.** any distinctive flag or device etc., as of a nation, sovereign, or special cause, etc., or the colours of a cavalry regiment. **5.** a flag or emblem formerly used to show the central or rallying point of an army in battle. **6.** the commodity or commodities in which is stated the value of a basic monetary unit: *the gold standard; the silver standard.* **7.** an authorized model of a unit of measure or weight. **8.** a unit of board measure equal to 1980 board feet. **9.** (in coinage) the prescribed proportion by weight of precious metal and base metal that each coin must contain. **10.** an upright pole or beam, esp. one used as a support. **11. a.** a piece of furniture consisting of an upright pole or beam on a base or support. **b.** (*as modifier*): *a standard lamp.* **12. a.** a plant, esp. a fruit tree, that is trained so that it has an upright stem free of branches. **b.** (*as modifier*): *a standard cherry.* **13.** a song or piece of music that has remained popular for many years. **14.** *S. African.* a form or grade in school. ~*adj.* **15.** of the usual, regularized, medium, or accepted kind: *a standard size.* **16.** of recognized authority, competence, or excellence: *the standard work on Greece.* **17.** denoting or characterized by idiom, vocabulary, etc., that is regarded as correct and acceptable by educated native speakers. **18.** *Brit.* (formerly) (of eggs) of a size that is smaller than *large* and larger than *medium.*

standard-bearer *n.* **1.** a man who carries a standard. **2.** a leader of a cause or party.

standard gauge *n.* **1.** a railway track with a distance of 56½ inches between the lines; used on most railways. ~*adj.* **standard-gauge** *or* **standard-gauged. 2.** of, relating to, or denoting a railway with a standard gauge.

standardize *or* **-ise** ('stændə,daɪz) *vb.* **1.** to make or become standard. **2.** (*tr.*) to test by or make a comparison with a standard. —,**standardi'zation** *or* **-i'sation** *n.* —'**standard,izer** *or* **-,iser** *n.*

standard of living *n.* a level of subsistence or material welfare of a community, class, or person.

standard time *n.* the official local time of a region or country determined by the distance from Greenwich of a line of longitude passing through the area.

stand by *vb.* **1.** (*intr., adv.*) to be available and ready

stamp *v.* **1.** beat, crush, trample **2.** engrave, fix, impress, imprint, inscribe, mark, mould, print **3.** betray, brand, categorize, exhibit, identify, label, mark, pronounce, reveal, show to be, typecast ~*n.* **4.** brand, cast, earmark, hallmark, imprint, mark, mould, signature **5.** breed, cast, character, cut, description, fashion, form, kind, sort, type

stamp collecting philately

stampede *n.* charge, flight, rout, rush, scattering

stamp out crush, destroy, eliminate, eradicate, extinguish, extirpate, put down, put out, quell, quench, scotch, suppress

stance **1.** bearing, carriage, deportment, posture **2.** attitude, position, stand, standpoint, viewpoint

stand *v.* **1.** be upright, be vertical, erect, mount, place, position, put, rank, rise, set **2.** be in force, belong, be situated *or* located, be valid, continue, exist, halt, hold, obtain, pause, prevail, remain, rest, stay, stop **3.** abide, allow, bear, brook, cope with, countenance, endure, experience, handle, put up with (*Inf.*), stomach, submit to, suffer, support, sustain, take, thole (*Dialect*), tolerate, undergo, wear (*Brit. sl.*), weather, withstand ~*n.* **4.** halt, rest, standstill, stay, stop, stopover **5.** attitude, determination, firm stand, opinion, position, stance, standpoint **6.** base, booth, bracket, dais, frame, grandstand, place, platform, rack, rank, stage, staging, stall, stance (*Chiefly Scot.*), support, table

standard[1] *n.* **1.** average, benchmark, can-

on, criterion, example, gauge, grade, guide, guideline, measure, model, norm, pattern, principle, requirement, rule, sample, specification, touchstone, type, yardstick **2.** *Often plural* code of honour, ethics, ideals, moral principles, morals, principles ~*adj.* **3.** accepted, average, basic, customary, normal, orthodox, popular, prevailing, regular, set, staple, stock, typical, usual **4.** approved, authoritative, classic, definitive, established, official, recognized

standard[2] *n.* banner, colours, ensign, flag, pennant, pennon, streamer

standardize assimilate, bring into line, institutionalize, mass-produce, regiment, stereotype

to act if needed. **2.** (*intr., adv.*) to be present as an on-looker or without taking any action: *he stood by at the accident.* **3.** (*intr., prep.*) to be faithful to: *to stand by one's principles.* ~*n.* **stand-by. 4. a.** a person or thing that is ready for use or can be relied on in an emergency. **b.** (*as modifier*): *stand-by provisions.*

stand down *vb.* (*adv.*) **1.** (*intr.*) to resign or with-draw, esp. in favour of another. **2.** (*intr.*) to leave the witness box in a court of law after giving evidence. **3.** *Chiefly Brit.* to go or be taken off duty.

stand for *vb.* (*intr., prep.*) **1.** to represent or mean. **2.** *Chiefly Brit.* to be or become a candidate for. **3.** to support or recommend. **4.** *Inf.* to tolerate or bear: *he won't stand for it.*

stand in *vb.* **1.** (*intr., adv.*; usually foll. by *for*) to act as a substitute. **2. stand (someone) in good stead.** to be of benefit or advantage to. ~*n.* **stand-in. 3. a.** a person or thing that serves as a substitute. **b.** (*as modifier*): *a stand-in teacher.* **4.** a person who substitutes for an ac-tor during intervals of waiting or in dangerous stunts.

standing ('stændɪŋ) *n.* **1.** social or financial position, status, or reputation: *a man of some standing.* **2.** length of existence, experience, etc. **3.** (*modifier*) used to stand in or on: *standing room.* ~*adj.* **4.** *Athletics.* **a.** (of the start of a race) begun from a standing position. **b.** (of a jump, leap, etc.) performed from a stationary position without a run-up. **5.** (*prenominal*) permanent, fixed, or lasting. **6.** (*prenominal*) still or stagnant: *a standing pond.* **7.** *Printing.* (of type) set and stored for future use.

standing order *n.* **1.** Also called: **banker's order.** an instruction to a bank by a depositor to pay a stated sum at regular intervals. **2.** a rule or order governing the procedure, conduct, etc., of a legislative body. **3.** *Mil.* one of a number of orders which have long-term validity.

standoff ('stænd,ɒf) *n.* **1.** *U.S.* the act or an instance of standing off or apart. **2.** a deadlock or stalemate. ~*vb.* **stand off** (*adv.*). **3.** (*intr.*) to navigate a vessel so as to avoid the shore, an obstruction, etc. **4.** (*tr.*) to keep or cause to keep at a distance. **5.** (*intr.*) to reach a dead-lock or stalemate. **6.** (*tr.*) to dismiss (workers), esp. tem-porarily.

standoffish (,stænd'ɒfɪʃ) *adj.* reserved, haughty, or aloof.

stand out *vb.* (*intr., adv.*) **1.** to be distinctive or con-spicuous. **2.** to refuse to agree or comply: *they stood out for a better price.* **3.** to protrude or project. **4.** to navi-gate a vessel away from a port, harbour, etc. ~*n.* **stand-out. 5.** *U.S. inf.* a person or thing that is distinctive or outstanding.

standpipe ('stænd,paɪp) *n.* a vertical pipe, open at the upper end, attached to a pipeline or tank serving to limit the pressure head to that of the height of the pipe.

standpoint ('stænd,pɔɪnt) *n.* a physical or mental posi-tion from which things are viewed.

standstill ('stænd,stɪl) *n.* a complete cessation of move-ment; halt: *come to a standstill.*

stand to *vb.* **1.** (*adv.*) *Mil.* to assume positions or cause to assume positions to resist a possible attack. **2. stand to reason.** to conform with the dictates of reason: *it stands to reason.*

stand up *vb.* (*adv.*) **1.** (*intr.*) to rise to the feet. **2.** (*intr.*) to resist or withstand wear, criticism, etc. **3.** (*tr.*) *Inf.* to fail to keep an appointment with, esp. intentional-ly. **4. stand up for.** to support, side with, or defend. **5. stand up to. a.** to confront or resist courageously. **b.** to withstand or endure (wear, criticism, etc.). ~*adj.* **stand-up.** (*prenominal*) **6.** having or being in an erect position: *a stand-up collar.* **7.** done, taken, etc., while standing: *a stand-up meal.* **8.** (of a comedian) performing solo.

stank (stæŋk) *vb.* a past tense of **stink.**

stannary ('stænərɪ) *n., pl.* **-ries.** a place or region where tin is mined or worked.

stanza ('stænzə) *n. Prosody.* a fixed number of verse lines arranged in a definite metrical pattern, forming a unit of a poem. —**'stanzaed** *adj.* —**stanzaic** (stæn-'zeɪɪk) *adj.*

staphylo- *combining form.* **1.** uvula: *staphyloplasty.* **2.** resembling a bunch of grapes: *staphylococcus.*

staphylococcus (,stæfɪləʊ'kɒkəs) *n., pl.* **-cocci** (-'kɒksaɪ). any spherical Gram-positive bacterium of the genus *Staphylococcus,* typically occurring in clusters and causing boils, infection in wounds, and septicaemia. Often shortened to **staph.** —**staphylococcal** (,stæfɪləʊ-'kɒkəl) *adj.*

staple¹ ('steɪpəl) *n.* **1.** a short length of thin wire bent into a square U-shape, used to fasten papers, cloth, etc. **2.** a short length of stiff wire formed into a U-shape with pointed ends, used for holding a hasp to a post, securing electric cables, etc. ~*vb.* **3.** (*tr.*) to secure (papers, wire, etc.) with staples. —**'stapler** *n.*

staple² ('steɪpəl) *adj.* **1.** of prime importance; principal: *staple foods.* **2.** (of a commodity) forming a predomi-nant element in the product, consumption, or trade of a nation, region, etc. ~*n.* **3.** a staple commodity. **4.** a main constituent; integral part. **5.** *Chiefly U.S.* a princi-pal raw material produced or grown in a region. **6.** the fibre of wool, cotton, etc., graded as to length and degree of fineness. ~*vb.* **7.** (*tr.*) to arrange or sort (wool, cot-ton, etc.) according to length and fineness.

star (stɑː) *n.* **1.** any of a vast number of celestial objects visible in the clear night sky as points of light. **2. a.** a hot gaseous mass, such as the sun, that radiates energy, esp. as heat and light, and in some cases as radio waves and x-rays. **b.** (*as modifier*): *a star catalogue.* Related adjs.: **astral, sidereal, stellar.** **3.** *Astrol.* **a.** a celestial body, esp. a planet, supposed to influence events, personalities, etc. **b.** (*pl.*) another word for **horoscope** (sense 1). **4.** an emblem shaped like a conventionalized star, often used as a symbol of rank, an award, etc. **5.** a small white blaze on the forehead of an animal, esp. a horse. **6. a.** a distinguished or glamorous celebrity, often from the en-tertainment world. **b.** (*as modifier*): *star quality.* **7.** an-other word for **asterisk. 8. see stars.** to see or seem to see bright moving pinpoints of light, as from a blow on the head, increased blood pressure, etc. ~*vb.* **starring, starred. 9.** (*tr.*) to mark or decorate with a star or stars. **10.** to feature or be featured as a star: *"Greed" starred Erich von Stroheim; Olivier starred in "Hamlet".* —**'starless** *adj.* —**'star,like** *adj.*

starboard ('stɑːbəd, -,bɔːd) *n.* **1.** the right side of an aeroplane or vessel when facing the nose or bow. Cf. **port². ~*adj.* 2.** relating to or on the starboard. ~*vb.* **3.** to turn or be turned towards the starboard.

starch (stɑːtʃ) *n.* **1.** a polysaccharide composed of glu-cose units that occurs widely in plant tissues in the form of storage granules. **2.** a starch obtained from potatoes and some grain: it is fine white powder that, in solution with water, is used to stiffen fabric. **3.** any food contain-ing a large amount of starch, such as rice and potatoes. **4.** stiff or pompous formality. ~*vb.* **5.** (*tr.*) to stiffen with or soak in starch. —**'starcher** *n.*

starchy ('stɑːtʃɪ) *adj.* **-ier, -iest. 1.** of or containing starch. **2.** *Inf.* extremely formal, stiff, or conventional: *a starchy manner.* **3.** stiffened with starch. —**'starchily** *adv.* —**'starchiness** *n.*

star-crossed *adj.* dogged by ill luck; destined to mis-fortune.

stardom ('stɑːdəm) *n.* **1.** the fame and prestige of be-ing a star in films, sport, etc. **2.** the world of celebrities.

stare (stɛə) *vb.* (*intr.*) **1.** (often foll. by *at*) to look or

---

THESAURUS

stand by 1. back, befriend, be loyal to, champion, defend, stick up for (*Inf.*), support, take (someone's) part, uphold 2. be pre-pared, wait, wait in the wings

stand for 1. betoken, denote, exemplify, indicate, mean, represent, signify, symbolize 2. *Inf.* bear, brook, endure, lie down under (*Inf.*), put up with, suffer, tolerate, wear (*Brit. inf.*)

stand in for cover for, deputize for, do duty for, hold the fort, replace, take the place of, understudy

standing *n.* 1. condition, credit, emi-nence, estimation, footing, position, rank, reputation, repute, station, status 2. continu-ance, duration, existence, experience ~*adj.* 3. fixed, lasting, permanent, perpetual, regu-lar, repeated 4. erect, perpendicular, ram-pant (*Heraldry*), upended, upright, vertical

stand out attract attention, be highlight-ed, be prominent (conspicuous, distinct, striking), be thrown into relief, bulk large, catch the eye, leap to the eye, project, stare one in the face (*Inf.*), stick out a mile (*Inf.*)

standpoint angle, point of view, posi-tion, post, stance, station, vantage point, viewpoint

stand up for champion, come to the de-fence of, defend, side with, stick up for (*Inf.*), support, uphold

stand up to brave, confront, defy, en-dure, oppose, resist, withstand

star 1. *n.* celebrity, draw (*Inf.*), idol, lead, leading man *or* lady, luminary, main attrac-tion, name 2. *adj.* brilliant, celebrated, illus-trious, leading, major, paramount, principal, prominent, talented, well-known

gaze fixedly, often with hostility or rudeness. **2.** to stand out as obvious; glare. **3. stare one in the face.** to be glaringly obvious or imminent. ~*n.* **4.** the act or an instance of staring. —'**starer** *n.*

starfish ('stɑː,fɪʃ) *n., pl.* -**fish** *or* -**fishes.** any of various echinoderms, typically having a flattened body covered with a flexible test and five arms radiating from a central disc.

stargaze ('stɑː,geɪz) *vb.* (*intr.*) **1.** to observe the stars. **2.** to daydream. —'**star,gazer** *n.* —'**star,gazing** *n., adj.*

stark (stɑːk) *adj.* **1.** (*usually prenominal*) devoid of any elaboration; blunt: *the stark facts.* **2.** grim; desolate: *a stark landscape.* **3.** (*usually prenominal*) utter; absolute: *stark folly.* **4.** *Arch.* severe; violent. **5.** *Arch. or poetic.* rigid, as in death (esp. in **stiff and stark, stark dead**). **6.** short for **stark-naked.** ~*adv.* **7.** completely: *stark mad.* **8.** *Rare.* starkly. —'**starkly** *adv.* —'**starkness** *n.*

stark-naked *adj.* completely naked. Informal word (*postpositive*): **starkers** ('stɑːkəz).

starlet ('stɑːlɪt) *n.* **1.** a young actress who is projected as a potential star. **2.** a small star.

starlight ('stɑː,laɪt) *n.* **1.** the light emanating from the stars. ~*adj. also* **starlighted.** **2.** of or like starlight. **3.** Also: **starlit** ('stɑːlɪt). illuminated by starlight.

starling ('stɑːlɪŋ) *n.* any gregarious passerine songbird of an Old World family, esp. the **common starling,** which has a blackish iridescent plumage and a short tail.

Star of David ('deɪvɪd) *n.* an emblem symbolizing Judaism and consisting of a six-pointed star formed by superimposing one equilateral triangle upon another of equal size.

starry ('stɑːrɪ) *adj.* -**rier,** -**riest.** **1.** filled, covered with, or illuminated by stars. **2.** of, like, or relating to a star or stars. —'**starriness** *n.*

starry-eyed *adj.* given to naive wishes, judgments, etc.; full of unsophisticated optimism.

Stars and Stripes *n.* **the.** the national flag of the United States of America, consisting of 50 white stars representing the present states on a blue field and seven red and six white horizontal stripes representing the original states. Also called: the **Star-Spangled Banner.**

Star-Spangled Banner *n.* **the.** **1.** the national anthem of the United States of America. **2.** another term for the **Stars and Stripes.**

star-studded *adj.* featuring a large proportion of well-known performers: *a star-studded cast.*

start (stɑːt) *vb.* **1.** to begin or cause to begin (something or to do something); come or cause to come into being, operation, etc.: *he started a quarrel; they started to work.* **2.** (when *intr.,* sometimes foll. by *on*) to make or cause to make a beginning of (a process, series of actions, etc.): *they started on the project.* **3.** (sometimes foll. by *up*) to set or be set in motion: *he started up the machine.* **4.** (*intr.*) to make a sudden involuntary movement, as from fright; jump. **5.** (*intr.;* sometimes foll. by *up, away,* etc.) to spring or jump suddenly from a position or place. **6.** to establish or be established; set up: *to start a business.* **7.** (*tr.*) to support (someone) in the first part of a venture, career, etc. **8.** to work or cause to work loose. **9.** to enter or be entered in a race. **10.** (*intr.*) to flow violently from a source: *wine started from a hole in the cask.* **11.** (*tr.*) to rouse (game) from a hiding place, lair, etc. **12.** (*intr.*) *Brit. inf.* to commence quarrelling or causing a disturbance. **13. to start with.** in the first place. ~*n.* **14.** the first or first part of a series of actions, a journey, etc. **15.** the place or time of

starting, as of a race or performance. **16.** a signal to proceed, as in a race. **17.** a lead or advantage, either in time or distance, in a competitive activity: *he had an hour's start on me.* **18.** a slight involuntary movement, as through fright, surprise, etc.: *she gave a start as I entered.* **19.** an opportunity to enter a career, undertake a project, etc. **20.** *Inf.* a surprising incident. **21. by fits and starts.** spasmodically; without concerted effort. **22. for a start.** in the first place. ~See also **start off, start on,** etc.

starter ('stɑːtə) *n.* **1.** Also called: **self-starter.** a device for starting an internal-combustion engine, usually consisting of a powerful electric motor that engages with the flywheel. **2.** a person who supervises and signals the start of a race. **3.** a competitor who starts in a race or contest. **4.** *Austral. inf.* an acceptable or practicable proposition, plan, idea, etc. **5.** *Chiefly Brit.* the first course of a meal. **6. for starters.** *Sl.* in the first place.

startle ('stɑːtəl) *vb.* to be or cause to be surprised or frightened, esp. so as to start involuntarily. —'**startler** *n.* —'**startling** *adj.*

start off *vb.* (*adv.*) **1.** (*intr.*) to set out on a journey. **2.** to be or make the first step in an activity; initiate: *he started the show off with a lively song.* **3.** (*tr.*) to cause (a person) to act or do something, such as to laugh, to tell stories, etc.

start on *vb.* (*intr., prep.*) *Brit. inf.* to pick a quarrel with; upbraid.

start out *vb.* (*intr., adv.*) **1.** to set out on a journey. **2.** to take the first steps, as in life, one's career, etc.: *he started out as a salesman.* **3.** to take the first actions in an activity in a particular way or with a specified aim: *they started out wanting a house, but eventually bought a flat.*

start up *vb.* (*adv.*) **1.** to come or cause to come into being for the first time; originate. **2.** (*intr.*) to spring or jump suddenly. **3.** to set in motion, activity, etc.: *he started up the engine.*

starve (stɑːv) *vb.* **1.** to die or cause to die from lack of food. **2.** to deprive (a person or animal) or (of a person, etc.) to be deprived of food. **3.** (*intr.*) *Inf.* to be very hungry. **4.** (foll. by *of* or *for*) to deprive or be deprived (of something), esp. so as to cause suffering or malfunctioning: *the engine was starved of fuel.* **5.** (*tr.;* foll. by *into*) to bring (to) a specified condition by starving: *to starve someone into submission.* **6.** *Arch.* or *dialect.* to be or cause to be extremely cold. —**star'vation** *n.*

starveling ('stɑːvlɪŋ) *Arch.* ~*n.* **1. a.** a starving or poorly fed person, animal, etc. **b.** (*as modifier*): *a starveling child.* ~*adj.* **2.** insufficient; meagre; scant.

stash (stæʃ) *Inf.* ~*vb.* **1.** (*tr.;* often foll. by *away*) to put or store (money, valuables, etc.) in a secret place, as for safekeeping. ~*n.* **2.** *Chiefly U.S.* a secret store or the place where this is hidden.

stasis ('steɪsɪs) *n.* **1.** *Pathol.* a stagnation in the normal flow of bodily fluids, such as the blood or urine. **2.** a state or condition in which there is no action or progress.

-**stat** *n. combining form.* indicating a device that causes something to remain stationary or constant: *thermostat.*

state (steɪt) *n.* **1.** the condition of a person, thing, etc., with regard to main attributes. **2.** the structure or form of something: *a solid state.* **3.** any mode of existence. **4.** position in life or society; estate. **5.** ceremonious style, as befitting wealth or dignity: *to live in state.* **6.** a sovereign political power or community. **7.** the territory oc-

---

THESAURUS

stare *v.* gape, gawk, gawp (*Brit. sl.*), gaze, goggle, look, rubberneck (*Sl.*), watch

stark *adj.* **1.** absolute, arrant, bald, bare, blunt, consummate, downright, entire, flagrant, out-and-out, palpable, patent, pure, sheer, simple, unalloyed, unmitigated, utter **2.** austere, bare, barren, bleak, cold, depressing, desolate, drear (*Literary*), dreary, forsaken, grim, harsh, plain, severe, solitary, unadorned ~*adv.* **3.** absolutely, altogether, clean, completely, entirely, quite, utterly, wholly

stark-naked in a state of nature, in one's birthday suit (*Inf.*), in the altogether (*Inf.*), in the buff (*Inf.*), in the raw (*Inf.*), naked, nude, stark, starkers (*Inf.*), stripped, unclad, undressed, without a stitch on (*Inf.*)

start *v.* **1.** appear, arise, begin, come into being, come into existence, commence, depart, first see the light of day, get on the road, get under way, go ahead (*Inf.*), hit the road (*Inf.*), issue, leave, originate, pitch in (*Inf.*), sally forth, set off, set out **2.** activate, embark upon, engender, enter upon, get going, initiate, instigate, kick off (*Inf.*), make a beginning, open, originate, put one's hand to the plough (*Inf.*), set about, set in motion, start the ball rolling, take the first step, take the plunge (*Inf.*), turn on **3.** begin, create, establish, father, found, inaugurate, initiate, institute, introduce, launch, lay the foundations of, pioneer, set up **4.** blench, flinch, jerk, jump, recoil, shy, twitch ~*n.* **5.** beginning, birth, commencement, dawn, first step(s),

foundation, inauguration, inception, initiation, kickoff (*Inf.*), onset, opening, outset **6.** advantage, edge, head start, lead **7.** backing, break (*Inf.*), chance, helping hand, introduction, opening, opportunity, sponsorship **8.** convulsion, jar, jump, spasm, twitch

startle agitate, alarm, amaze, astonish, astound, frighten, give (someone) a turn (*Inf.*), make (someone) jump, scare, shock, surprise, take (someone) aback

startling alarming, astonishing, astounding, extraordinary, shocking, staggering, sudden, surprising, unexpected, unforeseen

starving faint from lack of food, famished, hungering, hungry, ravenous, ready to eat a horse (*Inf.*), sharp-set, starved

cupied by such a community. **8.** the sphere of power in such a community: *affairs of state.* **9.** (*often cap.*) one of a number of areas or communities having their own governments and forming a federation under a sovereign government, as in the U.S. **10.** (*often cap.*) the body politic of a particular sovereign power, esp. as contrasted with a rival authority such as the Church. **11.** *Obs.* a class or order; estate. **12.** *Inf.* a nervous, upset, or excited condition (esp. in **in a state**). **13. lie in state.** (of a body) to be placed on public view before burial. **14. state of affairs.** a situation; circumstances or condition. ~*modifier.* **15.** controlled or financed by a state: *state university.* **16.** of, relating to, or concerning the State: *State trial.* **17.** involving ceremony or concerned with a ceremonious occasion: *state visit.* ~*vb.* (*tr.; may take a clause as object*) **18.** to articulate in words; utter. **19.** to declare formally or publicly. —**'statable** *or* **'stateable** *adj.* —**'statehood** *n.*

stateless ('steɪtlɪs) *adj.* **1.** without nationality: *stateless persons.* **2.** without a state or states. —**'statelessness** *n.*

stately ('steɪtlɪ) *adj.* **-lier, -liest. 1.** characterized by a graceful, dignified, and imposing appearance or manner. ~*adv.* **2.** in a stately manner. —**'stateliness** *n.*

stately home *n. Brit.* a large mansion, esp. one open to the public.

statement ('steɪtmənt) *n.* **1.** the act of stating. **2.** something that is stated, esp. a formal prepared announcement or reply. **3.** *Law.* a declaration of matters of fact. **4.** an account containing a summary of bills or invoices and displaying the total amount due. **5.** an account prepared by a bank for a client, usually at regular intervals, to show all credits and debits and the balance at the end of the period. **6.** a computer instruction written in a source language, such as FORTRAN, which is converted into one or more machine code instructions by a compiler.

state-of-the-art *adj.* (*prenominal*) (of hi-fi equipment, recordings, etc.) the most recent and therefore considered the best; up-to-the-minute: *a state-of-the-art amplifier.*

State Registered Nurse *n.* a nurse who has had extensive training and passed examinations enabling her to perform all nursing services.

stateroom ('steɪt,ru:m, -,rʊm) *n.* **1.** a private cabin or room on a ship, train, etc. **2.** *Chiefly Brit.* a large room in a palace or other building for use on state occasions.

state school *n.* any school maintained by the state, in which education is free.

statesman ('steɪtsmən) *n., pl.* **-men. 1.** a political leader whose wisdom, integrity, etc., win great respect. **2.** a person active and influential in the formulation of high government policy. —**'statesman-,like** *or* **'statesmanly** *adj.* —**'statesmanship** *n.* —**'states,woman** *fem. n.*

static ('stætɪk) *adj. also* **statical. 1.** not active or moving; stationary. **2.** (of a weight, force, or pressure) acting but causing no movement. **3.** of or concerned with forces that do not produce movement. **4.** relating to or causing stationary electric charges; electrostatic. **5.** of or relating to interference in the reception of radio or television transmissions. **6.** of or concerned with statics. **7.** *Computers.* (of a memory) not needing its contents refreshed periodically. ~*n.* **8.** random hissing or crackling or a speckled picture caused by interference in the reception of radio or television transmissions. **9.** electric sparks or crackling produced by friction. —**'statically** *adv.*

static electricity *n.* electricity that is not dynamic or flowing as a current.

statics ('stætɪks) *n.* (*functioning as sing.*) the branch of mechanics concerned with the forces that produce a state of equilibrium in a system.

station ('steɪʃən) *n.* **1.** the place or position at which a thing or person stands. **2. a.** a place along a route or line at which a bus, train, etc., stops for fuel or to pick up or let off passengers or goods, esp. one with ancillary buildings and services. **b.** (*as modifier*): *a station buffet.* **3. a.** the headquarters or local offices of an organization such as the police or fire services. **b.** (*as modifier*): *a station sergeant.* See **police station, fire station. 4.** a building, depot, etc., with special equipment for some particular purpose: *power station; petrol station.* **5.** *Mil.* a place of duty: *an action station.* **6.** *Navy.* **a.** a location to which a ship or fleet is assigned for duty. **b.** an assigned location for a member of a ship's crew. **7.** *Inf.* a television or radio channel. **8.** a position or standing, as in a particular society or organization. **9.** the type of one's occupation; calling. **10.** (in British India) a place where the British district officials or garrison officers resided. **11.** *Biol.* the habitat occupied by a particular animal or plant. **12.** *Austral. & N.Z.* a large sheep or cattle farm. **13.** (*sometimes cap.*) *R.C. Church.* **a.** one of the stations of the Cross. **b.** any of the churches (**station churches**) in Rome used as points of assembly for religious processions and ceremonies on particular days (**station days**). ~*vb.* **14.** (*tr.*) to place in or assign to a station.

stationary ('steɪʃənrɪ) *adj.* **1.** not moving; standing still. **2.** not able to be moved. **3.** showing no change: *the doctors said his condition was stationary.* **4.** tending to remain in one place.

stationer ('steɪʃənə) *n.* a person who sells stationery or a shop where stationery is sold.

stationery ('steɪʃənrɪ) *n.* any writing materials, such as paper, envelopes, pens, ink, rulers, etc.

stationmaster ('steɪʃən,mɑ:stə) *n.* the senior official in charge of a railway station.

station wagon *n.* another name for **estate car.**

statism ('steɪtɪzəm) *n.* the theory or practice of concentrating economic and political power in the state. —**'statist** *n.*

statistic (stə'tɪstɪk) *n.* a datum capable of exact numerical representation, such as the correlation coefficient of two series or the standard deviation of a sample. —**sta'tistical** *adj.* —**sta'tistically** *adv.* —**statistician** (,stætɪ'stɪʃən) *n.*

statistics (stə'tɪstɪks) *n.* **1.** (*functioning as sing.*) a science concerned with the collection, classification, and interpretation of quantitative data and with the application of probability theory to the analysis and estimation of population parameters. **2.** the quantitative data themselves.

statuary ('stætjʊərɪ) *n., pl.* **-aries. 1.** statues collectively. **2.** the art of making statues. ~*adj.* **3.** of or for statues.

statue ('stætju:) *n.* a wooden, stone, metal, plaster, or other sculpture of a human or animal figure, usually life-size or larger.

statuesque (,stætjʊ'ɛsk) *adj.* like a statue, esp. in possessing great formal beauty or dignity. —**,statu'esquely** *adv.* —**,statu'esqueness** *n.*

statuette (,stætjʊ'ɛt) *n.* a small statue.

stature ('stætʃə) *n.* **1.** height, esp. of a person or animal when standing. **2.** the degree of development of a person: *the stature of a champion.* **3.** intellectual or moral greatness: *a man of stature.*

status ('steɪtəs) *n., pl.* **-tuses. 1.** a social or professional position, condition, or standing. **2.** the relative position or standing of a person or thing. **3.** a high position or standing: *he has acquired a new status in that job.* **4.** the legal standing or condition of a person. **5.** a state of affairs.

THESAURUS

state[1] *v.* **1.** affirm, articulate, assert, asseverate, aver, declare, enumerate, explain, expound, express, present, propound, put, report, say, specify, voice ~*n.* **2.** case, category, circumstances, condition, mode, pass, plight, position, predicament, shape, situation, state of affairs **3.** attitude, frame of mind, humour, mood, spirits **4.** ceremony, dignity, display, glory, grandeur, majesty, pomp, splendour, style **5.** *Inf.* bother, flap (*Inf.*), panic, pother, tiz-woz (*Inf.*), tizzy (*Inf.*) **6. in a state** *Inf.* agitated, all steamed up

(*Sl.*), anxious, distressed, disturbed, flustered, het up, panic-stricken, ruffled, upset

state[2] *n.* body politic, commonwealth, country, federation, government, kingdom, land, nation, republic, territory

stately august, ceremonious, deliberate, dignified, elegant, grand, imperial, imposing, impressive, lofty, majestic, measured, noble, pompous, regal, royal, solemn

statement account, announcement, communication, communiqué, declaration, explanation, proclamation, recital, relation,

report, testimony, utterance

static changeless, constant, fixed, immobile, inert, motionless, stagnant, stationary, still, unmoving, unvarying

station *n.* **1.** base, depot, headquarters, location, place, position, post, seat, situation **2.** appointment, business, calling, employment, grade, occupation, position, post, rank, situation, sphere, standing, status ~*v.* **3.** assign, establish, fix, garrison, install, locate, post, set

stationary at a standstill, fixed, inert,

status quo (kwəʊ) *n.* (usually preceded by *the*) the existing state of affairs.

status symbol *n.* a possession which is regarded as proof of the owner's social position, wealth, prestige, etc.

statute ('stætjuːt) *n.* **1. a.** an enactment of a legislative body expressed in a formal document. **b.** this document. **2.** a permanent rule made by a body or institution.

statute law *n.* **1.** a law enacted by a legislative body. **2.** a particular example of this. ~Cf. **common law, equity.**

statutory ('stætjʊtərɪ, -trɪ) *adj.* **1.** of, relating to, or having the nature of a statute. **2.** prescribed or authorized by statute. **3.** (of an offence, etc.) **a.** recognized by statute. **b.** subject to a punishment or penalty prescribed by statute. —'**statutorily** *adv.*

staunch[1] (stɔːntʃ) *adj.* **1.** loyal, firm, and dependable: *a staunch supporter.* **2.** solid or substantial in construction. **3.** *Rare.* (of a ship, etc.) watertight; seaworthy. —'**staunchly** *adv.* —'**staunchness** *n.*

staunch[2] (stɔːntʃ) *vb., n.* a variant of **stanch.**

stave (steɪv) *n.* **1.** any one of a number of long strips of wood joined together to form a barrel, bucket, boat hull, etc. **2.** any of various bars, slats, or rods, usually of wood, such as a rung of a ladder. **3.** any stick, staff, etc. **4.** a stanza or verse of a poem. **5.** *Music.* **a.** *Brit.* an individual group of five lines and four spaces used in staff notation. **b.** another word for **staff**[1] (sense 9). ~*vb.* **staving, staved** *or* **stove. 6.** (often foll. by *in*) to break or crush (the staves of a boat, barrel, etc.) or (of the staves of a boat) to be broken or crushed. **7.** (*tr.;* usually foll. by *in*) to burst or force (a hole in something). **8.** (*tr.*) to provide (a ladder, chair, etc.) with staves.

stave off *vb.* (*tr., adv.*) to avert or hold off, esp. temporarily: *to stave off hunger.*

staves (steɪvz) *n.* the plural of **staff**[1] or **stave.**

stay[1] (steɪ) *vb.* **1.** (*intr.*) to continue or remain in a certain place, position, etc.: *to stay outside.* **2.** (*copula*) to continue to be; remain: *to stay awake.* **3.** (*intr.;* often foll. by *at*) to reside temporarily: *to stay at a hotel.* **4.** (*tr.*) to remain for a specified period: *to stay the weekend.* **5.** (*intr.*) *Central Scot. dialect.* to reside permanently or habitually: *she stays on a housing scheme.* **6.** to stop or cause to stop. **7.** (*intr.*) to wait, pause, or tarry. **8.** (*tr.*) to delay or hinder. **9.** (*tr.*) **a.** to discontinue or suspend (a judicial proceeding). **b.** to hold in abeyance or restrain from enforcing (an order, decree, etc.). **10.** to endure (something testing or difficult, such as a race): *stay the course.* **11.** (*tr.*) to hold back or restrain: *to stay one's anger.* **12.** (*tr.*) to satisfy or appease (an appetite, etc.) temporarily. **13. stay put.** See **put** (sense 18). ~*n.* **14.** the act of staying or sojourning in a place or the period during which one stays. **15.** the act of stopping or restraining or state of being stopped, etc. **16.** the suspension of a judicial proceeding, etc.: *stay of execution.* —'**stayer** *n.*

stay[2] (steɪ) *n.* **1.** anything that supports or steadies, such as a prop or buttress. **2.** a thin strip of metal, plastic, bone, etc., used to stiffen corsets, etc. ~*vb.* (*tr.*) *Arch.* **3.** (often foll. by *up*) to prop or hold. **4.** (often foll. by *up*) to comfort or sustain. **5.** (foll. by *on* or *upon*) to cause to rely or depend.

stay[3] (steɪ) *n.* a rope, cable, or chain, usually one of a set, used for bracing uprights, such as masts, funnels, flagpoles, chimneys, etc.; guy.

stay-at-home *adj.* **1.** (of a person) enjoying a quiet, settled, and unadventurous use of leisure. ~*n.* **2.** a stay-at-home person.

staying power *n.* endurance; stamina.

staysail ('steɪˌseɪl; *Naut.* 'steɪsəl) *n.* an auxiliary sail, often triangular, set on a stay.

S.T.D. *abbrev. for* Doctor of Sacred Theology.

STD code *n. Brit.* a code of two or more digits, other than those comprising a subscriber's local telephone number, that determines the routing of a call.

stead (stɛd) *n.* **1.** (preceded by *in*) *Rare.* the place, function, or position that should be taken by another: *to come in someone's stead.* **2. stand (someone) in good stead.** to be useful or of good service to (someone). ~*vb.* **3.** (*tr.*) *Arch.* to help or benefit.

steadfast *or* **stedfast** ('stɛdfəst, -ˌfɑːst) *adj.* **1.** (esp. of a person's gaze) fixed in intensity or direction; steady. **2.** unwavering or determined in purpose, loyalty, etc.: *steadfast resolve.* —'**steadfastly** *or* '**stedfastly** *adv.* —'**steadfastness** *or* '**stedfastness** *n.*

steady ('stɛdɪ) *adj.* **-ier, -iest. 1.** not able to be moved or disturbed easily; stable. **2.** free from fluctuation. **3.** not easily excited; imperturbable. **4.** staid; sober. **5.** regular; habitual: *a steady drinker.* **6.** continuous: *a steady flow.* **7.** *Naut.* (of a vessel) keeping upright, as in heavy seas. ~*vb.* **steadying, steadied. 8.** to make or become steady. ~*adv.* **9.** in a steady manner. **10. go steady.** *Inf.* to date one person regularly. ~*n., pl.* **steadies. 11.** *Inf.* one's regular boyfriend or girlfriend. ~*interj.* **12.** *Naut.* an order to the helmsman to stay on a steady course. **13.** a warning to keep calm, be careful, etc. **14.** *Brit.* a command to get set to start, as in a race: *ready, steady, go!* —'**steadily** *adv.* —'**steadiness** *n.*

steady state *n. Physics.* the condition of a system when some or all of the quantities describing it are independent of time but not necessarily in thermodynamic or chemical equilibrium.

steak (steɪk) *n.* **1.** In full: **beefsteak.** a lean piece of beef that can be grilled, fried, etc. **2.** any of various cuts of beef, for braising, stewing, etc. **3.** a thick slice of pork, veal, cod, salmon, etc. **4.** minced meat prepared in the same way as steak: *hamburger steak.*

steakhouse ('steɪkˌhaʊs) *n.* a restaurant that has steaks as its speciality.

steak tartare *or* **tartar** *n.* raw minced steak, mixed with onion, seasonings, and raw egg. Also called: **tartare steak, tartar steak.**

steal (stiːl) *vb.* **stealing, stole, stolen. 1.** to take (something) from (someone, etc.) without permission or unlawfully, esp. in a secret manner. **2.** (*tr.*) to obtain surreptitiously. **3.** (*tr.*) to appropriate (ideas, etc.) without acknowledgment, as in plagiarism. **4.** to move or convey stealthily: *they stole along the corridor.* **5.** (*intr.*) to pass unnoticed: *the hours stole by.* **6.** (*tr.*) to win or gain by strategy or luck, as in various sports: *to steal a few yards.* **7. steal a march on.** to obtain an advantage over, esp. by a trick. **8. steal someone's thunder.** to detract from the attention due to another. **9. steal the show.** to be looked upon as the most interesting, popular, etc., esp. unexpectedly. ~*n.* **10.** *Inf.* the act of stealing. **11.** *U.S. inf.* something stolen or acquired easily or at little cost. —'**stealer** *n.*

stealth (stɛlθ) *n.* **1.** the act or characteristic of moving with extreme care and quietness, esp. so as to avoid detection. **2.** cunning or underhand procedure or dealing. —'**stealthy** *adj.*

---

moored, motionless, parked, standing, static, stock-still, unmoving

status condition, consequence, degree, distinction, eminence, grade, position, prestige, rank, standing

stay *v.* 1. abide, continue, delay, establish oneself, halt, hang around (*Inf.*), hover, linger, loiter, pause, put down roots, remain, reside, settle, sojourn, stand, stay put, stop, tarry, wait 2. *Often with* **at** be accommodated at, lodge, put up at, sojourn, visit 3. adjourn, defer, discontinue, hold in abeyance, hold over, prorogue, put off, suspend 4. *Archaic* arrest, check, curb, delay, detain, hinder, hold, impede, obstruct, prevent ~*n.* 5. holiday, sojourn, stop, stopover, visit 6. deferment, delay, halt, pause, postponement, re-

mission, reprieve, stopping, suspension

staying power endurance, stamina, strength, toughness

steadfast constant, dedicated, dependable, established, faithful, fast, firm, fixed, intent, loyal, persevering, reliable, resolute, single-minded, stable, staunch, steady, unfaltering, unflinching, unswerving, unwavering

steady *adj.* 1. firm, fixed, immovable, safe, stable, substantial, unchangeable, uniform 2. balanced, calm, dependable, equable, having both feet on the ground, imperturbable, level-headed, reliable, sedate, sensible, serene, serious-minded, settled, sober, staid, steadfast 3. ceaseless, confirmed, consistent, constant, continuous, even, faithful, habitual, incessant, nonstop, persistent, regular, rhyth-

mic, unbroken, unfaltering, unfluctuating, uninterrupted, unremitting, unvarying, unwavering ~*v.* 4. balance, brace, secure, stabilize, support 5. compose *or* calm oneself, cool down, sober (up), get a grip on oneself (*Inf.*)

steal 1. appropriate, be light-fingered, embezzle, filch, half-inch (*Inf.*), heist (*U.S. sl.*), lift (*Inf.*), misappropriate, nick (*Sl.*), peculate, pilfer, pinch (*Inf.*), pirate, plagiarize, poach, prig (*Brit. sl.*), purloin, shoplift, snitch (*Sl.*), swipe (*Sl.*), take, thieve, walk *or* make off with 2. creep, flit, insinuate oneself, slink, slip, sneak, tiptoe

stealing embezzlement, larceny, misappropriation, pilferage, pilfering, plagiarism, robbery, shoplifting, theft, thievery, thieving

steam (sti:m) *n.* **1.** the gas or vapour into which water is changed when boiled. **2.** the mist formed when such gas or vapour condenses in the atmosphere. **3.** any vaporous exhalation. **4.** *Inf.* power, energy, or speed. **5. get up steam. a.** (of a ship, etc.) to work up a sufficient head of steam in a boiler to drive an engine. **b.** *Inf.* to go quickly. **6. let** (*or* **blow**) **off steam.** *Inf.* to release pent-up energy, feelings, etc., esp. when angry. **7. under one's own steam.** without the assistance of others. **8.** (*modifier*) driven, operated, heated, powered, etc., by steam: *a steam radiator.* **9.** (*modifier*) treated by steam: *steam ironed.* ~*vb.* **10.** to emit or be emitted as steam. **11.** (*intr.*) to generate steam, as a boiler, etc. **12.** (*intr.*) to move or travel by steam power, as a ship, etc. **13.** (*intr.*) *Inf.* to proceed quickly and sometimes forcefully. **14.** to cook or be cooked in steam. **15.** (*tr.*) to treat with steam or apply steam to, as in cleaning, pressing clothes, etc. ~See also **steam up.**

steam-engine *n.* an engine that uses steam to produce mechanical work, esp. one in which steam from a boiler is expanded in a cylinder to drive a reciprocating piston.

steamer ('sti:mə) *n.* **1.** a boat or ship driven by steam engines. **2.** a vessel used to cook food by steam.

steam iron *n.* an electric iron that emits steam from channels in the iron face to facilitate pressing and ironing, the steam being produced from water contained within the iron.

steam radio *n. Inf.* radio considered as different from and (sometimes) more old-fashioned than television.

steamroller ('sti:m,rəʊlə) *n.* **1.** a steam-powered vehicle with heavy rollers used for compressing road surfaces during road-making. **2. a.** an overpowering force or person that overcomes all opposition. **b.** (*as modifier*): *steamroller tactics.* ~*vb.* **3.** (*tr.*) to crush (opposition, etc.) by overpowering force.

steamship ('sti:m,ʃɪp) *n.* a ship powered by one or more steam engines.

steam up *vb.* (*adv.*) **1.** to cover (windows, etc.) or (of windows, etc.) to become covered with a film of condensed steam. **2.** (*tr.; usually passive*) *Sl.* to excite or make angry: *he's all steamed up about the delay.*

steamy ('sti:mɪ) *adj.* **-ier, -iest. 1.** of, resembling, full of, or covered with steam. **2.** *Inf.* lustful or erotic: *steamy nightlife.* —'**steaminess** *n.*

stearic (stɪ'ærɪk) *adj.* **1.** of or relating to suet or fat. **2.** of, consisting of, containing, or derived from stearic acid.

stearic acid *n.* a colourless odourless insoluble waxy carboxylic acid used for making candles and suppositories.

stearin *or* **stearine** ('stɪərɪn) *n.* **1.** Also called: **tristearin.** a colourless crystalline ester of glycerol and stearic acid, present in fats and used in soap and candles. **2.** fat in its solid form.

steatite ('stɪə,taɪt) *n.* another name for **soapstone.** —**steatitic** (,stɪə'tɪtɪk) *adj.*

steed (sti:d) *n. Arch. or literary.* a horse, esp. one that is spirited or swift.

steel (sti:l) *n.* **1. a.** any of various alloys based on iron containing carbon and often small quantities of other elements such as phosphorus, sulphur, manganese, chromium, and nickel. Steels exhibit a variety of properties, such as strength, machinability, malleability, etc., depending on their composition and the way they have been treated. **b.** (*as modifier*): *steel girders.* See also **stainless steel. 2.** something that is made of steel. **3.** a steel stiffener in a corset, etc. **4.** a ridged steel rod used for sharpening knives. **5.** the quality of hardness, esp. with regard to a person's character or attitudes. **6.** *Canad.* a railway track or line. **7. cold steel.** bladed weapons. ~*vb.* (*tr.*) **8.** to fit, plate, edge, or point with steel. **9.** to make hard and unfeeling: *he steeled his heart against her sorrow; he steeled himself for the blow.* —'**steely** *adj.* —'**steeliness** *n.*

steel band *n. Music.* a type of band, popular in the Caribbean Islands, consisting mainly of percussion instruments made from oildrums, hammered or embossed to obtain different notes.

steel blue *n., adj.* **a.** a dark bluish-grey colour. **b.** (*as adj.*): *steel-blue eyes.*

steel wool *n.* a tangled or woven mass of fine steel fibres, used for cleaning or polishing.

steelworks ('sti:l,wɜːks) *n.* a plant in which steel is made from iron ore and rolled or forged into bars, sheets, etc. —'**steel,worker** *n.*

steelyard ('sti:l,jɑːd) *n.* a portable balance consisting of a pivoted bar with two unequal arms. The load is suspended from the shorter one and the bar is returned to the horizontal by adding weights to the longer one.

steep[1] (sti:p) *adj.* **1. a.** having or being a slope or gradient approaching the perpendicular. **b.** (*as n.*): *the steep.* **2.** *Inf.* (of a fee, price, demand, etc.) unduly high; unreasonable (esp. in **that's a bit steep**). **3.** *Inf.* excessively demanding or ambitious: *a steep task.* **4.** *Brit. inf.* (of a statement) extreme or far-fetched. —'**steeply** *adv.* —'**steepness** *n.*

steep[2] (sti:p) *vb.* **1.** to soak or be soaked in a liquid in order to soften, cleanse, extract an element, etc. **2.** (*tr.; usually passive*) to saturate; imbue: *steeped in ideology.* ~*n.* **3.** an instance or the process of steeping or the condition of being steeped. **4.** a liquid or solution used for the purpose of steeping something. —'**steeper** *n.*

steepen ('sti:pən) *vb.* to become or cause to become steep or steeper.

steeple ('sti:pəl) *n.* **1.** a tall ornamental tower that forms the superstructure of a church, temple, etc. **2.** such a tower with the spire above it. **3.** any spire or pointed structure. —'**steepled** *adj.*

steeplechase ('sti:pəl,tʃeɪs) *n.* **1.** a horse race over a course equipped with obstacles to be jumped. **2.** a track race in which the runners have to leap hurdles, a water jump, etc. **3.** *Arch.* **a.** a horse race across a stretch of open countryside including obstacles to be jumped. **b.** a rare word for **point-to-point.** ~*vb.* **4.** (*intr.*) to take part in a steeplechase. —'**steeple,chasing** *n.* —'**steeple,chaser** *n.*

steeplejack ('sti:pəl,dʒæk) *n.* a person trained and skilled in the construction and repair of steeples, chimneys, etc.

steer[1] (stɪə) *vb.* **1.** to direct the course of (a vehicle or vessel) with a steering wheel, rudder, etc. **2.** (*tr.*) to guide with tuition: *his teachers steered him through his exams.* **3.** (*tr.*) to direct the movements or course of (a person, conversation, etc.). **4.** to pursue (a specified course). **5.** (*intr.*) (of a vessel, vehicle, etc.) to admit of being guided in a specified fashion: *this boat does not steer properly.* **6. steer clear of.** to keep away from; shun. —'**steerable** *adj.* —'**steerer** *n.*

steer[2] (stɪə) *n.* a castrated male ox or bull; bullock.

steerage ('stɪərɪdʒ) *n.* **1.** the cheapest accommodation on a passenger ship, originally the compartments containing steering apparatus. **2.** an instance or the practice of steering and its effect on a vessel or vehicle.

steering committee *n.* a committee set up to prepare and arrange topics to be discussed, the order of business, etc., for a legislative assembly or other body.

steering wheel *n.* a wheel turned by the driver of a motor vehicle, ship, etc., when he wishes to change direction.

steersman ('stɪəzmən) *n., pl.* **-men.** the helmsman of a vessel.

stein (staɪn) *n.* an earthenware beer mug, esp. of a German design.

steinbok ('staɪn,bɒk) *or* **steenbok** *n., pl.* **-boks** *or* **-bok. 1.** a small antelope of central and southern Africa, having a reddish-brown coat and straight horns. **2.** another name for **ibex.**

stele ('sti:lɪ, sti:l) *n., pl.* **stelae** ('sti:li:) *or* **steles** ('sti:lɪz, sti:lz). **1.** an upright stone slab or column decorated with figures or inscriptions, common in prehistoric times. **2.** a prepared vertical surface that has a com-

---

THESAURUS

stealth furtiveness, secrecy, slyness, sneakiness, stealthiness, surreptitiousness, unobtrusiveness

stealthy clandestine, covert, furtive, secret, secretive, skulking, sly, sneaking, sneaky, surreptitious, underhand

steel *v.* brace, fortify, grit one's teeth, harden, make up one's mind

steep[1] *adj.* **1.** abrupt, headlong, precipitous, sheer **2.** *Inf.* excessive, exorbitant, extortionate, extreme, high, overpriced, stiff, uncalled-for, unreasonable

steep[2] *v.* **1.** damp, drench, imbrue (*Rare*), immerse, macerate, marinate (*Cookery*), moisten, soak, souse, submerge **2.** fill, imbue, infuse, permeate, pervade, saturate, suffuse

steer 1. be in the driver's seat, conduct, control, direct, govern, guide, pilot **2. steer clear of** avoid, circumvent, eschew, evade, give a wide berth to, sheer off, shun

memorative inscription or design, esp. one on the face of a building. **3.** the conducting tissue of the stems and roots of plants, which is in the form of a cylinder. ~Also called (for senses 1, 2): **stela** ('sti:lə). —**stelar** ('sti:lə) *adj.*

stellar ('stɛlə) *adj.* **1.** of, relating to, or resembling a star or stars. **2.** of or relating to star entertainers.

stem[1] (stɛm) *n.* **1.** the main axis of a plant, which bears the leaves, axillary buds, and flowers and contains a hollow cylinder of vascular tissue. **2.** any similar subsidiary structure in such plants that bears a flower, fruit, or leaf. **3.** a corresponding structure in algae and fungi. **4.** any long slender part, such as the hollow part of a tobacco pipe between the bit and the bowl. **5.** the main line of descent or branch of a family. **6.** any shank or cylindrical pin or rod, such as the pin that carries the winding knob on a watch. **7.** *Linguistics.* the form of a word that remains after removal of all inflectional affixes. **8.** the main, usually vertical, stroke of a letter or of a musical note such as a minim. **9. a.** the main upright timber or structure at the bow of a vessel. **b.** the very forward end of a vessel (esp. in **from stem to stern**). ~*vb.* **stemming, stemmed. 10.** (*intr.*; usually foll. by *from*) to be derived; originate. **11.** (*tr.*) to make headway against (a tide, wind, etc.). **12.** (*tr.*) to remove or disengage the stem or stems from. —**'stem,like** *adj.*

stem[2] (stɛm) *vb.* **stemming, stemmed. 1.** (*tr.*) to restrain or stop (the flow of something) by or as if by damming up. **2.** (*tr.*) to pack tightly or stop up. **3.** *Skiing.* to manoeuvre (a ski or skis), as in performing a stem. ~*n.* **4.** Also called: **stem turn.** *Skiing.* a technique in which the heel of one ski or both skis is forced outwards from the direction of movement in order to slow down or turn.

stemmed (stɛmd) *adj.* **1. a.** having a stem. **b.** (*in combination*): *a long-stemmed glass.* **2.** having had the stem or stems removed.

stench (stɛntʃ) *n.* a strong and extremely˙ offensive odour; stink.

stencil ('stɛnsəl) *n.* **1.** a device for applying a design, characters, etc., to a surface, consisting of a thin sheet of plastic, metal, etc. in which the design or characters have been cut so that ink or paint can be applied through the incisions onto the surface. **2.** a design or characters produced in this way. ~*vb.* **-cilling, -cilled** or *U.S.* **-ciling, -ciled.** (*tr.*) **3.** to mark (a surface) with a stencil. **4.** to produce (characters or a design) with a stencil.

Sten gun (stɛn) *n.* a light sub-machine-gun formerly used in the British Army.

steno- *or before a vowel* **sten-** *combining form.* indicating narrowness or contraction: *stenography; stenosis.*

stenographer (stə'nɒgrəfə) *n.* the U.S. name for **shorthand typist.**

stenography (stə'nɒgrəfɪ) *n.* **1.** the act or process of writing in shorthand by hand or machine. **2.** matter written in shorthand. —**stenographic** (,stɛnə'græfɪk) *adj.*

stentorian (stɛn'tɔːrɪən) *adj.* (of the voice, etc.) uncommonly loud: *stentorian tones.*

step (stɛp) *n.* **1.** the act of raising the foot and setting it down again in coordination with the transference of the weight of the body. **2.** the distance or space covered by such a motion. **3.** the sound made by such a movement. **4.** the impression made by such movement of the foot; footprint. **5.** the manner of walking or moving the feet; gait: *a proud step.* **6.** a sequence of foot movements that make up a particular dance or part of a dance: *the steps of the waltz.* **7.** any of several paces or rhythmic movements in marching, dancing, etc.: *the goose step.* **8.** (*pl.*) a course followed by a person in walking or as walking: *they followed in their leader's steps.* **9.** one of a sequence of separate consecutive stages in the progression

towards some goal. **10.** a rank or grade in a series or scale. **11.** an object or device that offers support for the foot when ascending or descending. **12.** (*pl.*) a flight of stairs, esp. out of doors. **13.** (*pl.*) another name for **stepladder. 14.** a very short easily travelled distance: *it is only a step.* **15.** *Music.* a melodic interval of a second. **16.** an offset or change in the level of a surface similar to the step of a stair. **17.** a strong block or frame bolted on the keel of a vessel and fitted to receive the base of a mast. **18.** a ledge cut in mining or quarrying excavations. **19. break step.** to cease to march in step. **20. keep step.** to remain walking, marching, dancing, etc., in unison or in a specified rhythm. **21. in step. a.** marching, dancing, etc., in conformity with a specified pace or moving in unison with others. **b.** *Inf.* in agreement or harmony. **22. out of step. a.** not moving in conformity with a specified pace or in accordance with others. **b.** *Inf.* not in agreement; out of harmony. **23. step by step.** with care and deliberation; gradually. **24. take steps.** to undertake measures (to do something). **25. watch one's step. a.** *Inf.* to conduct oneself with caution and good behaviour. **b.** to walk or move carefully. ~*vb.* **stepping, stepped. 26.** (*intr.*) to move by raising the foot and then setting it down in a different position, transferring the weight of the body to this foot and repeating the process with the other foot. **27.** (*intr.*; often foll. by *in, out,* etc.) to move or go on foot, esp. for a short distance: *step this way.* **28.** (*intr.*) *Inf.,* chiefly *U.S.* to move, often in an attractive graceful manner, as in dancing: *he can really step around.* **29.** (*intr.*; usually foll. by *on* or *upon*) to place or press the foot; tread: *to step on the accelerator.* **30.** (*intr.*; usually foll. by *into*) to enter (into a situation) apparently with ease: *she stepped into a life of luxury.* **31.** (*tr.*) to walk or take (a number of paces, etc.): *to step ten paces.* **32.** (*tr.*) to perform the steps of: *they step the tango well.* **33.** (*tr.*) to set or place (the foot). **34.** (*tr.*; usually foll. by *off* or *out*) to measure (some distance of ground) by stepping. **35.** (*tr.*) to arrange in or supply with a series of steps so as to avoid coincidence or symmetry. **36.** (*tr.*) to raise (a mast) and fit it into its step. ~See also **step down, step in,** etc. —**'step,like** *adj.*

step- *combining form.* indicating relationship through the previous marriage of a spouse or parent: *stepson; stepfather.*

stepbrother ('stɛp,brʌðə) *n.* a son of one's˙stepmother or stepfather by a union with someone other than one's father or mother.

stepchild ('stɛp,tʃaɪld) *n., pl.* **-children.** a stepson or stepdaughter.

stepdaughter ('stɛp,dɔːtə) *n.* a daughter of one's husband or wife by a former union.

step down *vb.* (*adv.*) **1.** (*tr.*) to reduce gradually. **2.** (*intr.*) *Inf.* to resign or abdicate (from a position). **3.** (*intr.*) *Inf.* to assume an inferior or less senior position. ~*adj.* **step-down.** (*prenominal*) **4.** (of a transformer) reducing a high voltage to a lower voltage. Cf. **step-up** (sense 3). ~*n.* **step-down. 5.** *Inf.* a decrease in quantity or size.

stepfather ('stɛp,fɑːðə) *n.* a man who has married one's mother after the death or divorce of one's father.

stephanotis (,stɛfə'nəʊtɪs) *n.* any of various climbing shrubs of Madagascar and Malaya, cultivated for their fragrant white waxy flowers.

step in *vb.* **1.** (*intr., adv.*) *Inf.* to intervene or involve oneself. ~*adj.* **step-in. 2.** (*prenominal*) (of garments, etc.) put on by being stepped into; without fastenings. **3.** (of a ski binding) engaging automatically when the boot is positioned on the ski. ~*n.* **step-in. 4.** (*often pl.*) a step-in garment, esp. underwear.

stepladder ('stɛp,lædə) *n.* a folding portable ladder that is made of broad flat steps fixed to a supporting

---

THESAURUS

stem[1] **1.** *n.* axis, branch, peduncle, shoot, stalk, stock, trunk **2.** *v. Usually with* **from** arise, be caused (bred, brought about, generated) by, derive, develop, emanate, flow, issue, originate

stem[2] *v.* bring to a standstill, check, contain, curb, dam, hold back, oppose, resist, restrain, stanch, stay (*Archaic*), stop, withstand

stench foul odour, mephitis, noisomeness, pong (*Brit. inf.*), reek, stink

step *n.* **1.** footfall, footprint, footstep, gait,

impression, pace, print, stride, trace, track, walk **2.** act, action, deed, expedient, manoeuvre, means, measure, move, procedure, proceeding **3. take steps** act, intervene, move in, prepare, take action, take measures, take the initiative **4.** advance, advancement, move, phase, point, process, progression, stage **5.** degree, level, rank, remove **6.** doorstep, round, rung, stair, tread **7. in step** coinciding, conforming, in harmony (agreement, conformity, unison), in line **8. out of step** erratic, incongruous, in disagreement, out of

harmony, out of line, out of phase, pulling different ways **9. watch one's step** be discreet (canny, careful, cautious), be on one's guard, have one's wits about one, look out, mind how one goes, mind one's p's and q's, take care, take heed, tread carefully ~*v.* **10.** move, pace, tread, walk

step in become involved, chip in (*Inf.*), intercede, intervene, take action, take a hand

frame hinged at the top to another supporting frame.

stepmother ('stɛp,mʌðə) *n.* a woman who has married one's father after the death or divorce of one's mother.

step on *vb. (intr., prep.)* **1.** to place or press the foot on. **2.** *Inf.* to behave harshly or contemptuously towards. **3. step on it.** *Inf.* to go more quickly; hurry up.

step out *vb. (intr., adv.)* **1.** to go outside or leave a room, etc., esp. briefly. **2.** to begin to walk more quickly and take longer strides. **3.** *U.S. inf.* to withdraw from involvement.

step-parent ('stɛp,pɛərənt) *n.* a stepfather or stepmother.

steppe (stɛp) *n. (often pl.)* an extensive grassy plain usually without trees.

stepping stone *n.* **1.** one of a series of stones acting as footrests for crossing streams, marshes, etc. **2.** a circumstance that assists progress towards some goal.

stepsister ('stɛp,sɪstə) *n.* a daughter of one's stepmother or stepfather by a union with someone other than one's father or mother.

stepson ('stɛp,sʌn) *n.* a son of one's husband or wife by a former union.

step up *vb. (adv.) Inf.* **1.** *(tr.)* to increase or raise by stages; accelerate. **2.** *(intr.)* to make progress or effect an advancement; be promoted. *~adj.* **step-up.** *(prenominal)* **3.** (of a transformer) increasing a low voltage to a higher voltage. Cf. **step-down** (sense 4). *~n.* **step-up. 4.** *Inf.* an increment in quantity, size, etc.

-ster *suffix forming nouns.* **1.** indicating a person who is engaged in a certain activity: *prankster; songster.* **2.** indicating a person associated with or being something specified: *mobster; youngster.*

stere (stɪə) *n.* a unit used to measure volumes of stacked timber equal to one cubic metre (35.315 cubic feet).

stereo ('stɛrɪəu, 'stɪər-) *adj.* **1.** stereophonic. **2.** stereoscopic. *~n., pl.* **stereos. 3.** stereophonic sound: *to broadcast in stereo.* **4.** *Inf.* a stereophonic gramophone, tape recorder, etc. **5.** *Photog.* **a.** a stereoscopic photography. **b.** a stereoscopic photograph. **6.** *Printing.* short for **stereotype.**

stereo- or sometimes before a vowel **stere-** *combining form.* indicating three-dimensional quality or solidity: *stereoscope.*

stereophonic (,stɛrɪə'fɒnɪk, ,stɪər-) *adj.* (of a system for recording, reproducing, or broadcasting sound) using two or more separate microphones to feed two or more loudspeakers through separate channels in order to give a spatial effect to the sound. Sometimes shortened to **stereo.** —,**stereo'phonically** *adv.* —**stereophony** (,stɛrɪ-'ɒfənɪ, ,stɪər-) *n.*

stereoscope ('stɛrɪə,skəup, 'stɪər-) *n.* an optical instrument for viewing two-dimensional pictures, giving an illusion of depth and relief. It has a binocular eyepiece through which two slightly different pictures of an object are viewed, one with each eye. —**stereoscopic** (,stɛrɪə-'skɒpɪk, ,stɪər-) *adj.*

stereotype ('stɛrɪə,taɪp, 'stɪər-) *n.* **1. a.** a method of producing cast-metal printing plates from a mould made from a forme of type. **b.** the plate so made. **2.** an idea, convention, etc., that has grown stale through fixed usage. **3.** a standardized image or conception of a type of person, etc. *~vb. (tr.)* **4. a.** to make a stereotype of. **b.** to print from a stereotype. **5.** to impart a fixed usage or convention to. —**stereo,typer** or **'stereo,typist** *n.*

stereotyped ('stɛrɪə,taɪpt, 'stɪər-) *adj.* **1.** lacking originality or individuality; conventional; trite. **2.** reproduced from or on a stereotype printing plate.

sterile ('stɛraɪl) *adj.* **1.** unable to produce offspring; infertile. **2.** free from living, esp. pathogenic, microorganisms. **3.** (of plants or their parts) not producing or bearing seeds, fruit, spores, stamens, or pistils. **4.** lacking inspiration or vitality; fruitless. —**'sterilely** *adv.* —**sterility** (stɛ'rɪlɪtɪ) *n.*

sterilize or **-ise** ('stɛrɪ,laɪz) *vb. (tr.)* to render sterile; make infertile or barren. —,**sterili'zation** or **-i'sation**

n. —'steri,lizer or **-iser** *n.*

sterling ('stɜːlɪŋ) *n.* **1. a.** British money: *pound sterling.* **b.** *(as modifier):* sterling reserves. **2.** the official standard of fineness of British coins: for gold 0.91666 and for silver 0.925. **3. a.** short for **sterling silver. b.** *(as modifier): a sterling bracelet.* **4.** an article or articles manufactured from sterling silver. *~adj.* **5.** *(prenominal)* of excellent quality; first-class: *sterling bravery.*

sterling area *n.* a group of countries that use sterling as a medium of international payments. Also called: **scheduled territories.**

sterling silver *n.* **1.** an alloy containing not less than 92.5 per cent of silver. **2.** sterling-silver articles collectively.

stern¹ (stɜːn) *adj.* **1.** showing uncompromising or inflexible resolve; firm or authoritarian. **2.** lacking leniency or clemency. **3.** relentless; unyielding: *the stern demands of parenthood.* **4.** having an austere or forbidding appearance or nature. —**'sternly** *adv.* —**'sternness** *n.*

stern² (stɜːn) *n.* **1.** the rear or after part of a vessel, opposite the bow or stem. **2.** the rear part of any object. *~adj.* **3.** relating to or located at the stern.

sternum ('stɜːnəm) *n., pl.* **-na** (-nə) or **-nums. 1.** (in man) a long flat vertical bone in front of the thorax, to which are attached the collarbone and the first seven pairs of ribs. Nontechnical name: **breastbone. 2.** the corresponding part in many other vertebrates. —**'sternal** *adj.*

steroid ('stɛrɔɪd) *n. Biochem.* any of a large group of organic compounds containing a characteristic chemical ring system, including sterols, bile acids, many hormones, and the D vitamins. —**ste'roidal** *adj.*

sterol ('stɛrɒl) *n. Biochem.* any of a group of natural steroid alcohols, such as cholesterol, that are waxy insoluble substances.

stertorous ('stɜːtərəs) *adj.* **1.** marked by heavy snoring. **2.** breathing in this way. —**'stertorously** *adv.* —**'stertorousness** *n.*

stet (stɛt) *n.* **1.** a word or mark indicating that certain deleted typeset or written matter is to be retained. *~vb.* **stetting, stetted. 2.** *(tr.)* to mark (matter) thus.

stethoscope ('stɛθə,skəup) *n. Med.* an instrument for listening to the sounds made within the body, typically consisting of a hollow disc that transmits the sound through hollow tubes to earpieces. —**stethoscopic** (,stɛθə'skɒpɪk) *adj.* —**stethoscopy** (stɛ'θɒskəpɪ) *n.*

stetson ('stɛtsən) *n.* a man's felt slouch hat with a broad brim and high crown.

stevedore ('stiːvɪ,dɔː) *n.* **1.** a person employed to load or unload ships. *~vb.* **2.** to load or unload (a ship, ship's cargo, etc.).

stew (stjuː) *n.* **1. a.** a dish of meat, fish, or other food, cooked by stewing. **b.** *(as modifier):* stew pot. **2.** *Inf.* a difficult or worrying situation or a troubled state (esp. in **in a stew**). **3.** a heterogeneous mixture: *a stew of people of every race.* **4.** *(usually pl.) Arch.* a brothel. *~vb.* **5.** to cook or cause to cook by long slow simmering. **6.** *(intr.) Inf.* to be troubled or agitated. **7.** *(intr.) Inf.* to be oppressed with heat or crowding. **8.** to cause (tea) to become bitter or (of tea) to become bitter through infusing for too long. **9. stew in one's own juice.** to suffer unaided the consequences of one's actions.

steward ('stjuːəd) *n.* **1.** a person who administers the property, house, finances, etc., of another. **2.** a person who manages the eating arrangements, staff, or service at a club, hotel, etc. **3.** a waiter on a ship or aircraft. **4.** a mess attendant in a naval mess. **5.** a person who helps to supervise some event or proceedings in an official capacity. **6.** short for **shop steward.** *~vb.* **7.** to act or serve as a steward (of something). —**'steward,ship** *n.*

stewardess ('stjuːədɪs, ,stjuːə'dɛs) *n.* a woman steward on an aircraft or ship.

stewed (stjuːd) *adj.* **1.** (of meat, fish, etc.) cooked by stewing. **2.** *Brit.* (of tea) bitter through having been left to infuse for too long. **3.** a slang word for **drunk.**

step up accelerate, augment, boost, escalate, increase, intensify, raise, speed up, up

stereotype 1. *n.* formula, mould, pattern, received idea 2. *v.* categorize, conventionalize, dub, pigeonhole, standardize, take to be, typecast

sterile 1. abortive, bare, barren, dry, emp-

ty, fruitless, infecund, unfruitful, unproductive, unprofitable, unprolific 2. antiseptic, aseptic, disinfected, germ-free, sterilized

sterilize autoclave, disinfect, fumigate, purify

sterling authentic, excellent, first-class, genuine, pure, real, sound, standard, substan-

tial, superlative, true

stern austere, authoritarian, bitter, cruel, flinty, forbidding, frowning, grim, hard, harsh, inflexible, relentless, rigid, rigorous, serious, severe, steely, strict, unrelenting, unsparing, unyielding

stick[1] (stɪk) *n.* **1.** a small thin branch of a tree. **2. a.** any long thin piece of wood. **b.** such a piece of wood having a characteristic shape for a special purpose: *a walking stick; a hockey stick.* **c.** a baton, wand, staff, or rod. **3.** an object or piece shaped like a stick: *a stick of celery.* **4.** in full: **control stick.** the lever by which a pilot controls the movements of an aircraft. **5.** *Inf.* the lever used to change gear in a motor vehicle. **6.** *Naut.* a mast or yard. **7. a.** a group of bombs arranged to fall at intervals across a target. **b.** a number of paratroops jumping in sequence. **8.** (*usually pl.*) a piece of furniture: *these few sticks are all I have.* **9.** (*pl.*) *Inf.* a rural area considered remote or backward (esp. in **in the sticks**). **10.** (*pl.*) *Hockey.* a declaration made by the umpire if a player's stick is above the shoulders. **11.** *Inf.* a dull boring person. **12.** (usually preceded by *old*) *Inf.* a familiar name for a person: *not a bad old stick.* **13.** punishment; beating. **14. in a cleft stick.** in a difficult position. **15. wrong end of the stick.** a complete misunderstanding of a situation, explanation, etc. ~*vb.* **sticking, sticked. 16.** to support (a plant) with sticks; stake.

stick[2] (stɪk) *vb.* **sticking, stuck. 1.** (*tr.*) to pierce or stab with or as if with something pointed. **2.** to thrust or push (a sharp or pointed object) or (of a sharp or pointed object) to be pushed into or through another object. **3.** (*tr.*) to fasten in position by pushing or forcing a point into something: *to stick a peg in a hole.* **4.** (*tr.*) to fasten in position by or as if by pins, nails, etc.: *to stick a picture on the wall.* **5.** (*tr.*) to transfix or impale on a pointed object. **6.** (*tr.*) to cover with objects piercing or set in the surface. **7.** (when *intr.*, foll. by *out, up, through,* etc.) to put forward or be put forward; protrude or cause to protrude: *to stick one's head out.* **8.** (*tr.*) *Inf.* to place or put in a specified position: *stick your coat on this chair.* **9.** to fasten or be fastened by or as if by an adhesive substance: *stick the pages together; they won't stick.* **10.** (*tr.*) *Inf.* to cause to become sticky. **11.** (when *tr.*, usually *passive*) to come or cause to come to a standstill: *stuck in a traffic jam; the wheels stuck.* **12.** (*intr.*) to remain for a long time: *the memory sticks in my mind.* **13.** *Sl., chiefly Brit.* to tolerate; abide: *I can't stick that man.* **14.** (*intr.*) to be reluctant. **15.** (*tr.; usually passive*) *Inf.* to cause to be at a loss; baffle or puzzle: *I was totally stuck for an answer.* **16.** (*tr.*) *Sl.* to force or impose something unpleasant on: *they stuck me with the bill.* **17.** (*tr.*) to kill by piercing or stabbing. **18. stick in one's throat.** *Inf.* to be difficult or impossible for one to accept. **19. stick to the ribs.** *Inf.* (of food) to be hearty and satisfying. ~*n.* **20.** the state or condition of adhering. **21.** *Inf.* a substance causing adhesion. **22.** *Obs.* something that causes delay or stoppage. ~See also **stick around, stick by,** etc.

stick around *or* **about** *vb.* (*intr., adv.*) *Inf.* to remain in a place, esp. awaiting something.

stick by *vb.* (*intr., prep.*) to remain faithful to; adhere to.

sticker ('stɪkə) *n.* **1.** an adhesive label, poster, or paper. **2.** a person or thing that sticks. **3.** a persevering or industrious person. **4.** something prickly, such as a thorn, that clings to one's clothing, etc. **5.** *Inf.* something that perplexes. **6.** *Inf.* a knife used for stabbing or piercing.

sticking plaster *n.* a thin cloth with an adhesive substance on one side, used for covering slight or superficial wounds.

stick insect *n.* any of various mostly tropical insects that have an elongated cylindrical body and long legs and resemble twigs.

stick-in-the-mud *n. Inf.* a conservative person who lacks initiative or imagination.

stickleback ('stɪkəl,bæk) *n.* any of various small fishes that have a series of spines along the back and occur in cold and temperate northern regions.

stickler ('stɪklə) *n.* **1.** (usually foll. by *for*) a person who makes insistent demands: *a stickler for accuracy.* **2.** a problem or puzzle.

stick out *vb.* (*adv.*) **1.** to project or cause to project. **2.** (*tr.*) *Inf.* to endure (something disagreeable) (esp. in **stick it out**). **3. stick out a mile** *or* **like a sore thumb.** *Inf.* to be extremely obvious. **4. stick out for.** (*intr.*) to insist on (a demand), refusing to yield until it is met.

stick to *vb.* (*prep., mainly intr.*) **1.** (*also tr.*) to adhere or cause to adhere. **2.** to continue constantly at. **3.** remain faithful to. **4.** not to move or digress from: *the speaker stuck closely to his subject.* **5. stick to someone's fingers.** *Inf.* to be stolen by someone.

stick-up *n.* **1.** *Sl., chiefly U.S.* a robbery at gunpoint; hold-up. ~*vb.* **stick up.** (*adv.*) **2.** (*tr.*) *Sl., chiefly U.S.* to rob, esp. at gunpoint. **3. stick up for.** (*intr.*) *Inf.* to support or defend: *stick up for oneself.*

sticky ('stɪkɪ) *adj.* **-ier, -iest. 1.** covered or daubed with an adhesive or viscous substance: *sticky fingers.* **2.** having the property of sticking to a surface. **3.** (of weather or atmosphere) warm and humid; muggy. **4.** *Inf.* difficult, awkward, or painful: *a sticky business.* ~*vb.* **5.** (*tr.*) *Inf.* to make sticky. —'**stickily** *adv.* —'**stickiness** *n.*

sticky wicket *n.* **1.** a cricket pitch that is rapidly being dried by the sun after rain and is particularly conducive to spin. **2.** *Inf.* a difficult or awkward situation.

stiff (stɪf) *adj.* **1.** not easily bent; rigid; inflexible. **2.** not working or moving easily or smoothly: *a stiff handle.* **3.** difficult to accept in its severity or harshness: *a stiff punishment.* **4.** moving with pain or difficulty; not supple: *a stiff neck.* **5.** difficult; arduous: *a stiff climb.* **6.** unrelaxed or awkward; formal. **7.** firmer than liquid in consistency; thick or viscous. **8.** powerful; strong: *a stiff breeze; a stiff drink.* **9.** excessively high: *a stiff price.* **10.** lacking grace or attractiveness. **11.** stubborn or stubbornly maintained: *a stiff fight.* **12.** *Obs.* tightly stretched; taut. **13.** *Sl.* intoxicated. **14. stiff upper lip.** See **lip** (sense 7). **15. stiff with.** *Inf.* amply provided with. ~*n.* **16.** *Sl.* a corpse. ~*adv.* **17.** completely or utterly: *bored stiff; frozen stiff.* —'**stiffish** *adj.* —'**stiffly** *adv.* —'**stiffness** *n.*

stiffen ('stɪfən) *vb.* **1.** to make or become stiff or stiffer. **2.** (*intr.*) to become suddenly tense or unyielding. —'**stiffener** *n.*

stiff-necked *adj.* haughtily stubborn or obstinate.

stifle ('staɪfəl) *vb.* **1.** (*tr.*) to smother or suppress: *stifle a cough.* **2.** to feel or cause to feel discomfort and difficulty in breathing. **3.** to prevent or be prevented from breathing so as to cause death. **4.** (*tr.*) to crush or stamp out.

stigma ('stɪgmə) *n., pl.* **stigmas** *or* **stigmata** ('stɪgmətə,

---

THESAURUS

stick[1] *v.* **1.** adhere, affix, attach, bind, bond, cement, cleave, cling, fasten, fix, fuse, glue, hold, hold on, join, paste, weld **2.** dig, gore, insert, jab, penetrate, pierce, pin, poke, prod, puncture, spear, stab, thrust, transfix **3.** *With out, up* etc. bulge, extend, jut, obtrude, poke, project, protrude, show **4.** *Inf.* deposit, drop, fix, install, lay, place, plant, plonk, position, put, set, store, stuff **5.** be bogged down, become immobilized, be embedded, catch, clog, come to a standstill, jam, lodge, snag, stop **6.** linger, persist, remain, stay **7.** *Sl.* abide, bear up under, endure, get on with, stand, stomach, take, tolerate **8. stick it out** *Inf.* bear, endure, grin and bear it (*Inf.*), last out, put up with (*Inf.*), see it through, see through to the bitter end, soldier on, take it (*Inf.*), weather **9. stick up for** *Inf.* champion, defend, stand up for, support, take the part *or* side of, uphold

stick[2] *n.* **1.** baton, birch, cane, pole, rod,

staff, stake, switch, twig, wand **2.** *Inf.* fuddy-duddy (*Inf.*), (old) fogy, pain (*Inf.*), prig, stick-in-the-mud (*Inf.*) **3.** *Brit. sl.* abuse, blame, criticism, flak (*Inf.*), hostility, punishment

stick to adhere to, cleave to, continue in, honour, keep, persevere in, remain loyal (faithful, true), stick at

sticky 1. adhesive, claggy (*Dialect*), clinging, gluey, glutinous, gooey (*Inf.*), gummy, syrupy, tacky, tenacious, viscid, viscous **2.** *Inf.* awkward, delicate, difficult, discomforting, embarrassing, hairy (*Sl.*), nasty, painful, thorny, tricky, unpleasant **3.** clammy, close, humid, muggy, oppressive, sultry, sweltering

stiff 1. brittle, firm, hard, hardened, inelastic, inflexible, rigid, solid, solidified, taut, tense, tight, unbending, unyielding **2.** artificial, austere, ceremonious, chilly, cold, constrained, forced, formal, laboured, mannered, pompous, priggish, prim, punctilious,

standoffish, starchy (*Inf.*), stilted, uneasy, unnatural, unrelaxed, wooden **3.** arthritic, awkward, clumsy, creaky (*Inf.*), crude, graceless, inelegant, jerky, rheumaticky (*Inf.*), ungainly, ungraceful, unsupple **4.** arduous, difficult, exacting, fatiguing, formidable, hard, laborious, tough, trying, uphill **5.** austere, cruel, drastic, extreme, great, hard, harsh, heavy, inexorable, oppressive, pitiless, rigorous, severe, sharp, strict, stringent **6.** brisk, fresh, powerful, strong, vigorous

stiffen brace, coagulate, congeal, crystallize, harden, jell, reinforce, set, solidify, starch, tauten, tense, thicken

stifle 1. asphyxiate, choke, smother, strangle, suffocate **2.** check, choke back, cover up, curb, extinguish, hush, muffle, prevent, repress, restrain, silence, smother, stop, suppress

stɪgˈmɑːtə). **1.** a distinguishing mark of social disgrace: *the stigma of having been in prison.* **2.** a small scar or mark such as a birthmark. **3.** *Pathol.* any mark on the skin, such as one characteristic of a specific disease. **4.** *Bot.* the terminal part of the ovary, at the end of the style, where deposited pollen enters the gynoecium. **5.** *Zool.* **a.** a pigmented eyespot in some invertebrates. **b.** the spiracle of an insect. **6.** *Arch.* a mark branded on the skin. **7.** (*pl.*) *Christianity.* marks resembling the wounds of the crucified Christ, believed to appear on the bodies of certain individuals.

stigmatize *or* **-ise** (ˈstɪgməˌtaɪz) *vb.* (*tr.*) **1.** to mark out or describe as bad. **2.** to mark with a stigma or stigmata. —ˌstigmatiˈzation *or* **-iˈsation** *n.* —ˈstigmaˌtizer *or* **-iser** *n.*

stile (staɪl) *n.* **1.** a set of steps or rungs in a wall or fence to allow people, but not animals, to pass over. **2.** short for **turnstile.**

stiletto (stɪˈlɛtəʊ) *n., pl.* **-tos. 1.** a small dagger with a slender tapered blade. **2.** a sharply pointed tool used to make holes in leather, cloth, etc. **3.** Also called: **spike heel, stiletto heel.** a very high heel on a woman's shoe, tapering to a very narrow tip. ~*vb.* **-toeing, -toed. 4.** (*tr.*) to stab with a stiletto.

still¹ (stɪl) *adj.* **1.** (*usually predicative*) motionless; stationary. **2.** undisturbed or tranquil; silent and calm. **3.** not sparkling or effervescent. **4.** gentle or quiet; subdued. **5.** *Obs.* (of a child) dead at birth. ~*adv.* **6.** continuing now or in the future as in the past: *do you still love me?* **7.** up to this or that time; yet: *I still don't know your name.* **8.** (often used with a comparative) even or yet: *still more insults.* **9.** quiet or without movement: *sit still.* **10.** *Poetic & dialect.* always. ~*n.* **11.** *Poetic.* silence or tranquillity: *the still of the night.* **12. a.** a still photograph, esp. of a scene from a film. **b.** (*as modifier*): *a still camera.* ~*vb.* **13.** to make or become still, quiet, or calm. **14.** (*tr.*) to allay or relieve: *her fears were stilled.* ~*sentence connector.* **15.** even then; nevertheless: *the child has some new toys and still cries.* —ˈstillness *n.*

still² (stɪl) *n.* an apparatus for carrying out distillation, used esp. in the manufacture of spirits.

stillborn (ˈstɪlˌbɔːn) *adj.* **1.** (of a foetus) dead at birth. **2.** (of an idea, plan, etc.) fruitless; abortive; unsuccessful. —ˈstillˌbirth *n.*

still life *n., pl.* **still lifes. 1. a.** a painting or drawing of inanimate objects, such as fruit, flowers, etc. **b.** (*as modifier*): *a still-life painting.* **2.** the genre of such paintings.

still room *n. Brit.* **1.** a room in which distilling is carried out. **2.** a pantry or storeroom, as in a large house.

stilt (stɪlt) *n.* **1.** either of a pair of two long poles with footrests on which a person stands and walks, as used by circus clowns. **2.** a long post or column that is used with others to support a building above ground level. **3.** any of several shore birds similar to the avocets but having a straight bill. ~*vb.* **4.** (*tr.*) to raise or place on or as if on stilts.

stilted (ˈstɪltɪd) *adj.* **1.** (of speech, writing, etc.) formal, pompous, or bombastic. **2.** not flowing continuously or naturally: *stilted conversation.* **3.** *Archit.* (of an arch) having vertical piers between the impost and the springing. —ˈstiltedly *adv.* —ˈstiltedness *n.*

Stilton (ˈstɪltən) *n.* either of two rich cheeses, blue-veined (**blue Stilton**) or white (**white Stilton**), both very strong in flavour.

stimulant (ˈstɪmjʊlənt) *n.* **1.** a drug or similar substance that increases physiological activity, esp. of a particular organ. **2.** any stimulating agent or thing. ~*adj.* **3.** stimulating.

stimulate (ˈstɪmjʊˌleɪt) *vb.* **1.** (*tr.*) to arouse or quicken the activity or senses of. **2.** (*tr.*) *Physiol.* to excite (a nerve, organ, etc.) with a stimulus. **3.** (*intr.*) to act as a stimulant or stimulus. —ˌstimuˈlation *n.* —ˈstimulative *adj., n.* —ˈstimuˌlator *or* ˈstimuˌlater *n.*

stimulus (ˈstɪmjʊləs) *n., pl.* **-li** (-ˌlaɪ, -ˌliː). **1.** something that stimulates or acts as an incentive. **2.** any drug, agent, electrical impulse, or other factor able to cause a response in an organism.

sting (stɪŋ) *vb.* **stinging, stung. 1.** (of certain animals and plants) to inflict a wound on (an organism) by the injection of poison. **2.** to feel or cause to feel a sharp mental or physical pain. **3.** (*tr.*) to goad or incite (esp. in **sting into action**). **4.** (*tr.*) *Inf.* to cheat, esp. by overcharging. ~*n.* **5.** a skin wound caused by the poison injected by certain insects or plants. **6.** pain caused by or as if by the sting of a plant or animal. **7.** a mental pain or pang: *a sting of conscience.* **8.** a sharp pointed organ, such as the ovipositor of a wasp, by which poison can be injected. **9.** the ability to sting: *a sharp sting in his criticism.* **10.** something as painful or swift of action as a sting: *the sting of death.* **11.** a sharp stimulus or incitement. —ˈstinger *n.* —ˈstingingness *n.*

stinging nettle *n.* See **nettle** (sense 1).

stingray (ˈstɪŋˌreɪ) *n.* any of various rays having a whiplike tail bearing a serrated venomous spine capable of inflicting painful weals.

stingy (ˈstɪndʒɪ) *adj.* **-gier, -giest. 1.** unwilling to spend or give. **2.** insufficient or scanty. —ˈstingily *adv.* —ˈstinginess *n.*

stink (stɪŋk) *n.* **1.** a strong foul smell; stench. **2.** *Sl.* a great deal of trouble (esp. in **to make** *or* **raise a stink**). **3.** **like stink.** intensely; furiously. ~*vb.* **stinking, stank** *or* **stunk; stunk.** (*mainly intr.*) **4.** to emit a foul smell. **5.** *Sl.* to be thoroughly bad or abhorrent: *this town stinks.* **6.** *Inf.* to have a very bad reputation: *his name stinks.* **7.** to be of poor quality. **8.** (foll. by *of* or *with*) *Sl.* to have or appear to have an excessive amount (of money). **9.** (*tr.*; usually foll. by *up*) *Inf.* to cause to stink. ~See also **stink out.**

stink bomb *n.* a small bomb, used by practical jokers, containing a liquid with an offensive smell.

stinker (ˈstɪŋkə) *n.* **1.** a person or thing that stinks. **2.** *Sl.* a difficult or very unpleasant person or thing. **3.** *Sl.* something of very poor quality. **4.** *Inf.* any of several fulmars or related birds that feed on carrion.

stinking (ˈstɪŋkɪŋ) *adj.* **1.** having a foul smell. **2.** *Inf.* unpleasant or disgusting. **3.** (*postpositive*) *Sl.* very drunk. **4. cry stinking fish.** to decry something, esp. one's own products. ~*adv.* **5.** *Inf.* (intensifier, expressing contempt): *stinking rich.* —ˈstinkingly *adv.* —ˈstinkingness *n.*

stink out *vb.* (*tr., adv.*) **1.** to drive out or away by a foul smell. **2.** *Brit.* to cause to stink: *the smell of orange peel stinks out the room.*

stinkwood (ˈstɪŋkˌwʊd) *n.* **1.** any of various trees having offensive-smelling wood, esp. a southern African lauraceous tree yielding a hard wood used for furniture. **2.** the heavy durable wood of any of these trees.

stint (stɪnt) *vb.* **1.** to be frugal or miserly towards (someone) with (something). **2.** *Arch.* to stop or check (something). ~*n.* **3.** an allotted or fixed amount of work. **4.** a limitation or check. —ˈstinter *n.*

stipend (ˈstaɪpɛnd) *n.* a fixed or regular amount of money paid as a salary or allowance, as to a clergyman.

stipendiary (staɪˈpɛndɪərɪ) *adj.* **1.** receiving or working for regular pay: *a stipendiary magistrate.* **2.** paid for

---

still 1. *adj.* at rest, calm, hushed, inert, lifeless, motionless, noiseless, pacific, peaceful, placid, quiet, restful, serene, silent, smooth, stationary, stilly (*Poetic*), tranquil, undisturbed, unruffled, unstirring **2.** *v.* allay, alleviate, appease, calm, hush, lull, pacify, quiet, quieten, settle, silence, smooth, smooth over, soothe, subdue, tranquillize **3.** *conj.* but, for all that, however, nevertheless, notwithstanding, yet **4.** *n.* *Poetic* hush, peace, quiet, silence, stillness, tranquillity

stilted artificial, bombastic, constrained, forced, grandiloquent, high-flown, high-sounding, inflated, laboured, pedantic, pompous, pretentious, stiff, unnatural, wooden

stimulant analeptic, bracer (*Inf.*), energizer, excitant, pep pill (*Inf.*), pick-me-up (*Inf.*), restorative, reviver, tonic, upper (*Sl.*)

stimulate animate, arouse, encourage, fan, fire, foment, goad, impel, incite, inflame, instigate, prompt, provoke, quicken, rouse, spur, turn on (*Inf.*), urge, whet

stimulating exciting, exhilarating, galvanic, inspiring, intriguing, provocative, provoking, rousing, stirring, thought-provoking

stimulus encouragement, fillip, goad, incentive, incitement, inducement, provocation, shot in the arm (*Inf.*), spur

sting *v.* **1.** burn, hurt, pain, smart, tingle, wound **2.** anger, gall, incense, inflame, infuriate, nettle, pique, provoke, rile **3.** *Inf.* cheat, defraud, do (*Sl.*), fleece, overcharge, rip off (*Sl.*), swindle, take for a ride (*Inf.*)

stint 1. *n.* assignment, bit, period, quota, share, shift, spell, stretch, term, time, tour, turn **2.** *v.* begrudge, be sparing (frugal, mingy (*Brit. inf.*), parsimonious), economize, hold back, save, scrimp, skimp on, spoil the ship for a ha'porth of tar, withhold

by a stipend. ~*n., pl.* **-aries. 3.** a person who receives regular payment.

stipple ('stɪpəl) *vb.* **1.** (*tr.*) to draw, engrave, or paint using dots or flecks. ~*n.* also **stippling. 2.** the technique of stippling or a picture produced by or using stippling. —'**stippler** *n.*

stipulate ('stɪpjʊˌleɪt) *vb.* **1.** (*tr.; may take a clause as object*) to specify, often as a condition of an agreement. **2.** (*intr.;* foll. by *for*) to insist (on) as a term of an agreement. **3.** (*tr.; may take a clause as object*) to guarantee or promise. —ˌstipu'lation *n.* —'stipuˌlator *n.*

stipule ('stɪpjuːl) *n.* a small paired usually leaflike outgrowth occurring at the base of a leaf or its stalk. —**stipular** ('stɪpjʊlə) *adj.*

stir[1] (stɜː) *vb.* **stirring, stirred. 1.** to move an implement such as a spoon around in (a liquid) so as to mix up the constituents. **2.** to change or cause to change position; disturb or be disturbed. **3.** (*intr.;* often foll. by *from*) to venture or depart (from one's usual or preferred place). **4.** (*intr.*) to be active after a rest; be up and about. **5.** (*tr.*) to excite or stimulate, esp. emotionally. **6.** to move (oneself) briskly or vigorously; exert (oneself). **7.** (*tr.*) to rouse or awaken: *to stir someone from sleep; to stir memories.* **8.** (when *tr.,* foll. by *up*) to cause or incite others to cause (trouble, arguments, etc.). **9. stir one's stumps.** to move or become active. ~*n.* **10.** the act or an instance of stirring or the state of being stirred. **11.** a strong reaction, esp. of excitement: *his publication caused a stir.* **12.** a slight movement. ~See also **stir up.** —'**stirrer** *n.*

stir[2] (stɜː) *n.* **1.** a slang word for **prison:** *in stir.* **2.** *N.Z. sl.* a noisy party. **3. stir-crazy.** *U.S. sl.* mentally disturbed as a result of being in prison.

stirk (stɜːk) *n.* **1.** a heifer of 6 to 12 months old. **2.** a yearling heifer or bullock.

stirring ('stɜːrɪŋ) *adj.* **1.** exciting the emotions; stimulating. **2.** active, lively, or busy. —'**stirringly** *adv.*

stirrup ('stɪrəp) *n.* **1.** Also called: **stirrup iron.** either of two metal loops on a riding saddle, with a flat footpiece through which a rider puts his foot for support. They are attached to the saddle by **stirrup leathers. 2.** a U-shaped support or clamp. **3.** *Naut.* one of a set of ropes fastened to a yard at one end and having a thimble at the other through which a footrope is rove for support.

stirrup cup *n.* a cup containing an alcoholic drink offered to a horseman ready to ride away.

stirrup pump *n.* a hand-operated pump, the base of the cylinder of which is placed in a bucket of water: used in fighting fires.

stir up *vb.* (*adv.*) to set or be set in motion; instigate or be instigated: *he stirred up trouble.*

stitch (stɪtʃ) *n.* **1.** a link made by drawing a thread through material by means of a needle. **2.** a loop of yarn formed around an implement used in knitting, crocheting, etc. **3.** a particular method of stitching or shape of stitch. **4.** a sharp spasmodic pain in the side resulting from running or exercising. **5.** (*usually used with a negative*) *Inf.* the least fragment of clothing: *he wasn't wearing a stitch.* **6.** *Agriculture.* the ridge between two furrows. **7. in stitches.** laughing uncontrollably. **8. drop a stitch.** to allow a loop of wool to fall off a knitting needle accidentally while knitting. ~*vb.* **9.** (*tr.*) to sew, fasten, etc., with stitches. **10.** (*intr.*) to be engaged in sewing. **11.** (*tr.*) to bind together (the leaves of a book, pamphlet, etc.) with wire staples or thread. ~*n., vb.* **12.** an

informal word for **suture** (senses 1b., 5). —'**stitcher** *n.*

stoat (stəʊt) *n.* a small Eurasian mammal, closely related to the weasels, having a brown coat and a black-tipped tail: in the northern parts of its range it has a white winter coat and is then known as an ermine.

stock (stɒk) *n.* **1. a.** (*sometimes pl.*) the total goods or raw material kept on the premises of a shop or business. **b.** (*as modifier): a stock book.* **2.** a supply of something stored for future use. **3.** *Finance.* **a.** the capital raised by a company through the issue and subscription of shares entitling their holders to dividends, partial ownership, and usually voting rights. **b.** the proportion of such capital held by an individual shareholder. **c.** the shares of a specified company or industry. **4.** standing or status. **5. a.** farm animals, such as cattle and sheep, bred and kept for their meat, skins, etc. **b.** (*as modifier): stock farming.* **6.** the trunk or main stem of a tree or other plant. **7.** *Horticulture.* **a.** a rooted plant into which a scion is inserted during grafting. **b.** a plant or stem from which cuttings are taken. **8.** the original type from which a particular race, family, group, etc., is derived. **9.** a race, breed, or variety of animals or plants. **10.** (*often pl.*) a small pen in which a single animal can be confined. **11.** a line of descent. **12.** any of the major subdivisions of the human species; race or ethnic group. **13. a.** the handle of a handgun. **b.** the part of a machine gun that connects the slide to the shoulder piece. **14.** the handle of something, such as a whip or fishing rod. **15.** the main body of a tool, such as the block of a plane. **16.** short for **gunstock** or **rolling stock. 17.** (formerly) the part of a plough to which the irons and handles were attached. **18.** the main upright part of a supporting structure. **19.** a liquid or broth in which meat, fish, bones, or vegetables have been simmered for a long time. **20.** film material before exposure and processing. **21.** Also called: **gillyflower.** any of several cruciferous plants such as **evening** or **night-scented stock,** of the Mediterranean region: cultivated for their brightly coloured flowers. **22. Virginian stock.** a similar and related North American plant. **23.** a long usually white neckcloth wrapped around the neck, worn in the 18th century and as part of modern riding dress. **24. a.** the repertoire of plays available to a repertory company. **b.** (*as modifier): a stock play.* **25.** a log or block of wood. **26.** See **laughing stock. 27. in stock. a.** stored on the premises or available for sale or use. **b.** supplied with goods of a specified kind. **28. out of stock. a.** not immediately available for sale or use. **b.** not having goods of a specified kind immediately available. **29. take stock. a.** to make an inventory. **b.** to make a general appraisal, esp. of prospects, resources, etc. **30. take stock in.** to attach importance to. **31. lock, stock, and barrel.** See **lock**[1] (sense 7). ~*adj.* **32.** staple; standard: *stock sizes in clothes.* **33.** (*prenominal*) being a cliché; hackneyed: *a stock phrase.* ~*vb.* **34.** (*tr.*) to keep (goods) for sale. **35.** (*intr.;* usually foll. by *up* or *up on*) to obtain a store of (something) for future use or sale: *to stock up on beer.* **36.** (*tr.*) to supply with live animals, fish, etc.: *to stock a farm.* **37.** (*tr.*) to fasten or supply with a stock. **38.** (*intr.*) (of a plant) to put forth new shoots. **39.** (*tr.*) *Obs.* to punish by putting in the stocks. —'**stocker** *n.*

stockade (stɒ'keɪd) *n.* **1.** an enclosure or barrier of stakes and timbers. ~*vb.* **2.** (*tr.*) to surround with a stockade.

stockbreeder ('stɒkˌbriːdə) *n.* a person who breeds or rears livestock as an occupation. —'**stockˌbreeding** *n.*

THESAURUS

stipulate agree, contract, covenant, engage, guarantee, insist upon, lay down, lay down *or* impose conditions, make a point of, pledge, postulate, promise, require, settle, specify

stipulation agreement, clause, condition, contract, engagement, precondition, prerequisite, provision, proviso, qualification, requirement, restriction, settlement, *sine qua non,* specification, term

stir *v.* **1.** agitate, beat, disturb, flutter, mix, move, quiver, rustle, shake, tremble **2.** *Often with* **up** animate, arouse, awaken, excite, incite, inflame, instigate, kindle, prompt, provoke, quicken, raise, spur, stimulate, urge **3.** affect, electrify, excite, fire, inspire, move, thrill, touch **4.** bestir, be up and about (*Inf.*), budge, exert oneself, get a move on (*Inf.*),

get moving (*Inf.*), hasten, look lively (*Inf.*), make an effort, mill about, move, shake a leg (*Inf.*) ~*n.* **5.** activity, ado, agitation, bustle, commotion, disorder, disturbance, excitement, ferment, flurry, fuss, movement, to-do, tumult, uproar

stirring animating, dramatic, emotive, exciting, exhilarating, heady, impassioned, inspiring, intoxicating, lively, moving, rousing, spirited, stimulating, thrilling

stock *n.* **1.** array, assets, assortment, cache, choice, commodities, fund, goods, hoard, inventory, merchandise, range, reserve, reservoir, selection, stockpile, store, supply, variety, wares **2.** *Animals* beasts, cattle, domestic animals, flocks, herds, horses, livestock, sheep **3.** ancestry, background, breed, descent, extraction, family, forebears,

house, line, lineage, line of descent, parentage, pedigree, race, strain, type, variety **4.** *Money* capital, funds, investment, property **5. take stock** appraise, estimate, review the situation, see how the land lies, size up (*Inf.*), weigh up ~*adj.* **6.** banal, basic, commonplace, conventional, customary, formal, hackneyed, ordinary, overused, regular, routine, run-of-the-mill, set, standard, staple, stereotyped, traditional, trite, usual, worn-out ~*v.* **7.** deal in, handle, keep, sell, supply, trade in **8.** *With* **up** accumulate, amass, buy up, gather, hoard, lay in, put away, replenish, save, store (up), supply **9.** equip, fill, fit out, furnish, kit out, provide with, provision, supply

stockbroker ('stɒk‚brəʊkə) *n.* a person who buys and sells securities on a commission basis for customers. Cf. **stockjobber.** —**stockbrokerage** ('stɒk‚brəʊkərɪdʒ) *or* '**stock‚broking** *n.*

stock car *n.* **1.** a car, usually a production saloon, strengthened and modified for a form of racing in which the cars often collide. **2.** *U.S.* a railway wagon for carrying livestock.

stock exchange *n.* **1.** Also called: **stock market. a.** a highly organized market facilitating the purchase and sale of securities and operated by professional stockbrokers and stockjobbers according to fixed rules. **b.** a place where securities are regularly traded. **c.** (*as modifier*): *a stock-exchange operator; stock-exchange prices.* **2.** the prices or trading activity of a stock exchange: *the stock exchange fell heavily today.*

stockholder ('stɒk‚həʊldə) *n.* **1.** an owner of corporate capital stock. **2.** *Austral.* a person who keeps livestock. —'**stock‚holding** *n.*

stockinet (‚stɒkɪ'nɛt) *n.* a machine-knitted elastic fabric used, esp. formerly, for stockings, undergarments, etc.

stocking ('stɒkɪŋ) *n.* **1.** one of a pair of close-fitting garments made of knitted yarn to cover the foot and part or all of the leg. **2.** something resembling this in position, function, appearance, etc. **3. in (one's) stocking feet.** wearing stockings or socks but no shoes.

stock in trade *n.* **1.** goods in stock necessary for carrying on a business. **2.** anything constantly used by someone as a part of his profession, occupation, or trade: *friendliness is the salesman's stock in trade.*

stockist ('stɒkɪst) *n. Commerce, Brit.* a dealer who undertakes to maintain stocks of a specified product at or above a certain minimum in return for favourable buying terms granted by the manufacturer of the product.

stockjobber ('stɒk‚dʒɒbə) *n.* **1.** *Brit.* a wholesale dealer on a stock exchange who operates as an intermediary between brokers without transacting directly with the public and derives his income from the spread between the bid and offered prices. Cf. **stockbroker. 2.** *U.S., disparaging.* a stockbroker, esp. one dealing in worthless securities. —'**stock‚jobbery** *or* '**stock‚jobbing** *n.*

stock market *n.* another name for **stock exchange.**

stockpile ('stɒk‚paɪl) *vb.* **1.** to acquire and store a large quantity of (something). ~*n.* **2.** a large store or supply accumulated for future use. —'**stock‚piler** *n.*

stockpot ('stɒk‚pɒt) *n. Chiefly Brit.* a pot in which stock for soup, etc., is made.

stockroom ('stɒk‚ruːm, -‚rʊm) *n.* a room in which a stock of goods is kept, as in a shop or factory.

stocks (stɒks) *pl.n.* **1.** *History.* an instrument of punishment consisting of a heavy wooden frame with holes in which the feet, hands, or head of an offender were locked. **2.** a frame used to support a boat while under construction. **3. on the stocks.** in preparation or under construction.

stock-still *adv.* absolutely still; motionless.

stocktaking ('stɒk‚teɪkɪŋ) *n.* **1.** the examination, counting, and valuing of goods on hand in a shop, etc. **2.** a reassessment of one's current situation, progress, prospects, etc.

stocky ('stɒkɪ) *adj.* **-ier, -iest.** (usually of a person) thickset; sturdy. —'**stockily** *adv.* —'**stockiness** *n.*

stockyard ('stɒk‚jɑːd) *n.* a large yard with pens or covered buildings where farm animals are assembled, sold, etc.

stodge (stɒdʒ) *Inf.* ~*n.* **1.** heavy filling starchy food. **2.** a dull person or subject. ~*vb.* **3.** to stuff (oneself or another) with food.

stodgy ('stɒdʒɪ) *adj.* **-ier, -iest.** **1.** (of food) heavy or uninteresting. **2.** excessively formal and conventional. —'**stodgily** *adv.* —'**stodginess** *n.*

stoep (stuːp) *n.* (in South Africa) a verandah.

stoic ('stəʊɪk) *n.* **1.** a person who maintains stoical qualities. ~*adj.* **2.** a variant of **stoical.**

Stoic ('stəʊɪk) *n.* **1.** a member of the ancient Greek school of philosophy founded by Zeno of Citium (?336–?264 B.C.), holding that virtue and happiness can be attained only by submission to destiny and the natural law. ~*adj.* **2.** of or relating to the doctrines of the Stoics.

stoical ('stəʊɪkəl) *adj.* characterized by impassivity or resignation. —'**stoically** *adv.*

stoicism ('stəʊɪ‚sɪzəm) *n.* **1.** indifference to pleasure and pain. **2.** (*cap.*) the philosophy of the Stoics.

stoke (stəʊk) *vb.* **1.** to feed, stir, and tend (a fire, furnace, etc.). **2.** (*tr.*) to tend the furnace of; act as a stoker for.

stokehold ('stəʊk‚həʊld) *n. Naut.* **1.** a coal bunker for a ship's furnace. **2.** the hold for a ship's boilers; fire room.

stokehole ('stəʊk‚həʊl) *n.* **1.** another word for **stokehold. 2.** a hole in a furnace through which it is stoked.

stoker ('stəʊkə) *n.* a person employed to tend a furnace, as on a steamship.

stoke up *vb.* (*adv.*) **1.** to feed and tend (a fire, etc.) with fuel. **2.** (*intr.*) to fill oneself with food.

stole[1] (stəʊl) *vb.* the past tense of **steal.**

stole[2] (stəʊl) *n.* **1.** a long scarf or shawl, worn by women. **2.** a long narrow scarf worn by various officiating clergymen.

stolen ('stəʊlən) *vb.* the past participle of **steal.**

stolid ('stɒlɪd) *adj.* showing little or no emotion or interest. —**stolidity** (stɒ'lɪdɪtɪ) *or* '**stolidness** *n.* —'**stolidly** *adv.*

stoma ('stəʊmə) *n., pl.* **stomata** ('stəʊmətə, 'stɒm-, stəʊ'mɑːtə). **1.** *Bot.* an epidermal pore in plant leaves, that controls the passage of gases into and out of a plant. **2.** *Zool., anat.* a mouth or mouthlike part.

stomach ('stʌmək) *n.* **1.** (in vertebrates) the enlarged muscular saclike part of the alimentary canal in which food is stored until it has been partially digested. Related *adj.:* **gastric. 2.** the corresponding organ in invertebrates. **3.** the abdominal region. **4.** desire, appetite, or inclination: *I have no stomach for arguments.* ~*vb.* (*tr.; used mainly in negative constructions*) **5.** to tolerate; bear: *I can't stomach his bragging.* **6.** to eat or digest: *he cannot stomach oysters.*

stomachache ('stʌmək‚eɪk) *n.* pain in the stomach, as from acute indigestion. Also called: **stomach upset, upset stomach.**

stomacher ('stʌməkə) *n.* a decorative V-shaped panel of stiff material worn over the chest and stomach by men and women in the 16th century, later only by women.

stomach pump *n. Med.* a suction device for removing stomach contents via an orally-inserted tube.

-stome *n. combining form.* indicating a mouth or opening resembling a mouth: *peristome.*

-stomous *adj. combining form.* having a specified type of mouth.

stomp (stɒmp) *vb.* **1.** (*intr.*) to tread or stamp heavily. ~*n.* **2.** a rhythmical stamping jazz dance. —'**stomper** *n.*

-stomy *n. combining form.* indicating a surgical operation performed to make an artificial opening into or for a specified part: *cytostomy.*

stone (stəʊn) *n.* **1.** the hard compact nonmetallic material of which rocks are made. **2.** a small lump of rock; pebble. **3.** In full: **gemstone.** a precious or semiprecious stone esp. one cut and polished. **4. a.** a piece of rock designed or shaped for some particular purpose. **b.** (*in combination*): *gravestone; millstone.* **5. a.** something that resembles a stone. **b.** (*in combination*): *hailstone.* **6.** the woody central part of such fruits as the peach and plum, that contains the seed; endocarp. **7.** any similar

---

THESAURUS

stocky chunky, dumpy, mesomorphic, solid, stubby, stumpy, sturdy, thickset

stodgy 1. filling, heavy, leaden, starchy, substantial 2. boring, dull, dull as ditchwater, formal, fuddy-duddy (*Inf.*), heavy going, laboured, staid, stuffy, tedious, turgid, unexciting, unimaginative, uninspired

stoical calm, cool, dispassionate, impassive, imperturbable, indifferent, long-suffering, philosophic, phlegmatic, resigned, stoic, stolid

stoicism acceptance, calmness, dispassion, fatalism, forbearance, fortitude, impassivity, imperturbability, indifference, long-suffering, patience, resignation, stolidity

stolid apathetic, bovine, doltish, dull, heavy, lumpish, obtuse, slow, stupid, unemotional, wooden

stomach *n.* 1. abdomen, belly, breadbasket (*Sl.*), gut (*Inf.*), inside(s) (*Inf.*), paunch, pot, potbelly, spare tyre (*Inf.*), tummy (*Inf.*) 2. appetite, desire, inclination, mind, relish, taste ~*v.* 3. abide, bear, endure, put up with (*Inf.*), reconcile *or* resign oneself to, submit to, suffer, swallow, take, tolerate

hard part of a fruit, such as the stony seed of a date. **8.**
(*pl.* **stone**) *Brit.* a unit of weight, used esp. to express human body weight, equal to 14 pounds or 6.350 kilograms.
9. Also called: **granite.** the rounded heavy mass of granite or iron used in the game of curling. **10.** *Pathol.* a nontechnical name for **calculus.** **11.** *Printing.* a table with a very flat iron or stone surface upon which pages are composed. **12.** (*modifier*) relating to or made of stone: *a stone house.* **13.** (*modifier*) made of stoneware: *a stone jar.* **14. cast a stone** (**at**). cast aspersions (upon). **15. heart of stone.** an obdurate or unemotional nature. **16. leave no stone unturned.** to do everything possible to achieve an end. ~*adv.* **17.** (intensifier): *stone cold; stone deaf.* ~*vb.* (*tr.*) **18.** to throw stones at, esp. to kill. **19.** to remove the stones from. **20.** to furnish or provide with stones. **21. stone the crows.** *Brit. inf.* an expression of surprise or dismay. — '**stoner** *n.*

Stone Age *n.* a period in human culture identified by the use of stone implements.

stonechat ('stəʊn,tʃæt) *n.* an Old World songbird having a black plumage with a reddish-brown breast.

stone-cold *adj.* **1.** completely cold. **2. stone-cold sober.** completely sober.

stonecrop ('stəʊn,krɒp) *n.* any of various N temperate plants having fleshy leaves and typically red, yellow, or white flowers.

stonecutter ('stəʊn,kʌtə) *n.* **1.** a person who is skilled in cutting and carving stone. **2.** a machine used to dress stone. — '**stone,cutting** *n.*

stoned (stəʊnd) *adj. Sl.* in a state of intoxication, stupor, or euphoria induced by drugs or alcohol.

stone fruit *n.* the nontechnical name for **drupe.**

stonemason ('stəʊn,meɪsən) *n.* a person who is skilled in preparing stone for building. — '**stone,masonry** *n.*

stone's throw *n.* a short distance.

stonewall (,stəʊn'wɔːl) *vb.* **1.** (*intr.*) *Cricket.* (of a batsman) to play defensively. **2.** to obstruct or hinder (parliamentary business). — ,**stone'waller** *n.*

stoneware ('stəʊn,wɛə) *n.* **1.** a hard opaque pottery, fired at a very high temperature. ~*adj.* **2.** made of stoneware.

stonework ('stəʊn,wɜːk) *n.* **1.** any construction made of stone. **2.** the process of dressing or setting stones. — '**stone,worker** *n.*

stony *or* **stoney** ('stəʊnɪ) *adj.* **-ier, -iest.** **1.** of or resembling stone. **2.** abounding in stone or stones. **3.** unfeeling or obdurate. **4.** short for **stony-broke.** — '**stonily** *adv.* — '**stoniness** *n.*

stony-broke *adj. Brit. sl.* completely without money; penniless.

stood (stʊd) *vb.* the past tense or past participle of **stand.**

stooge (stuːdʒ) *n.* **1.** an actor who feeds lines to a comedian or acts as his butt. **2.** *Sl.* someone who is taken advantage of by another. ~*vb.* **3.** (*intr.*) *Sl.* to act as a stooge.

stool (stuːl) *n.* **1.** a simple seat or footrest consisting of a small flat piece of wood, etc., resting on three or four legs, a pedestal, etc. **2.** a rootstock or base of a plant from which shoots, etc., are produced. **3.** a cluster of shoots growing from such a base. **4.** *Chiefly U.S.* a decoy used in hunting. **5.** waste matter evacuated from the bowels. **6.** a lavatory seat. **7.** (in W Africa, esp. Ghana) a chief's throne. **8. fall between two stools.** to fail through vacillation between two alternatives. ~*vb.* (*intr.*) **9.** (of a plant) to send up shoots from the base of the stem, rootstock, etc. **10.** to lure wildfowl with a decoy.

stool ball *n.* a game resembling cricket, still played by

girls and women in Sussex, England.

stool pigeon *n.* **1.** a living or dummy pigeon used to decoy others. **2.** an informer for the police. **3.** *U.S. sl.* a person acting as a decoy.

stoop[1] (stuːp) *vb.* (*mainly intr.*) **1.** (*also tr.*) to bend (the body) forward and downward. **2.** to carry oneself with head and shoulders habitually bent forward. **3.** (often foll. by *to*) to abase or degrade oneself. **4.** (often foll. by *to*) to condescend; deign. **5.** (of a bird of prey) to swoop down. ~*n.* **6.** the act, position, or characteristic of stooping. **7.** a lowering from a position of dignity or superiority. **8.** a downward swoop, esp. of a bird of prey.

stoop[2] (stuːp) *n. U.S.* an open porch or small platform with steps leading up to it at the entrance to a building.

stop (stɒp) *vb.* **stopping, stopped.** **1.** to cease from doing or being (something); discontinue. **2.** to cause (something moving) to halt or (of something moving) to come to a halt. **3.** (*tr.*) to prevent the continuance or completion of. **4.** (*tr.*; often foll. by *from*) to prevent or restrain: *to stop George from fighting.* **5.** (*tr.*) to keep back: *to stop supplies.* **6.** (*tr.*) to intercept or hinder in transit: *to stop a letter.* **7.** (*tr.*; often foll. by *up*) to block or plug, esp. so as to close: *to stop up a pipe.* **8.** (*tr.*; often foll. by *up*) to fill a hole or opening in: *to stop up a wall.* **9.** (*tr.*) to staunch or stem: *to stop a wound.* **10.** (*tr.*) to instruct a bank not to honour (a cheque). **11.** (*tr.*) to deduct (money) from pay. **12.** (*tr.*) *Brit.* to provide with punctuation. **13.** (*tr.*) *Boxing.* to beat (an opponent) by a knockout. **14.** (*tr.*) *Inf.* to receive (a blow, hit, etc.). **15.** (*intr.*) to stay or rest: *we stopped at the Robinsons'.* **16.** (*tr.*) *Rare.* to defeat, beat, or kill. **17.** (*tr.*) *Music.* **a.** to alter the vibrating length of (a string on a violin, guitar, etc.) by pressing down on it at some point with the finger. **b.** to alter the vibrating length of an air column in a wind instrument by closing (a finger hole, etc.). **c.** to produce (a note) in this manner. **18.** *Bridge.* to have a protecting card or winner in (a suit in which one's opponents are strong). **19. stop at nothing.** to allow no doubts or scruples to hinder one. ~*n.* **20.** an arrest of movement or progress. **21.** the act of stopping or the state of being stopped. **22.** a place where something halts or pauses: *a bus stop.* **23.** a stay in or as if in the course of a journey. **24.** the act or an instance of blocking or obstructing. **25.** a plug or stopper. **26.** a block, screw, etc. that prevents, limits, or terminates the motion of a mechanism or moving part. **27.** *Brit.* a punctuation mark, esp. a full stop. **28.** *Music.* **a.** the act of stopping the string, finger hole, etc., of an instrument. **b.** a set of organ pipes or harpsichord strings that may be allowed to sound as a group by muffling or silencing all other such sets. **c.** a knob, lever, or handle on an organ, etc., that is operated to allow sets of pipes to sound. **d.** an analogous device on a harpsichord or other instrument with variable registers, such as an electrophonic instrument. **29. pull out all the stops.** to play at full volume. **b.** to spare no effort. **30.** Also called: **stop consonant.** *Phonetics.* any of a class of consonants articulated by first making a complete closure at some point of the vocal tract and then releasing it abruptly with audible plosion. **31.** Also called: **f-stop.** *Photog.* **a.** a setting of the aperture of a camera lens, calibrated to the corresponding f-number. **b.** another name for **diaphragm** (sense 4). **32.** Also called: **stopper.** *Bridge.* a protecting card or winner in a suit in which one's opponents are strong. ~See also **stop off, stopover.** — '**stoppable** *adj.*

stopcock ('stɒp,kɒk) *n.* a valve to control or stop the flow of a fluid in a pipe.

stopgap ('stɒp,gæp) *n.* **a.** a temporary substitute. **b.** (*as modifier*): *a stopgap programme.*

THESAURUS

stony *Fig.* adamant, blank, callous, chilly, expressionless, frigid, hard, heartless, hostile, icy, indifferent, inexorable, merciless, obdurate, pitiless, unfeeling, unforgiving, unresponsive

stoop v. **1.** be bowed *or* round-shouldered, bend, bow, crouch, descend, duck, hunch, incline, kneel, lean, squat **2.** *Often with* **to** condescend, deign, demean oneself, descend, lower oneself, resort, sink, vouchsafe ~*n.* **3.** bad posture, droop, round-shoulderedness, sag, slouch, slump

stop v. **1.** be over, break off, bring *or* come

to a halt, bring *or* come to a standstill, call it a day (*Inf.*), cease, come to an end, conclude, cut out (*Inf.*), cut short, desist, discontinue, draw up, end, finish, halt, leave off, pack in (*Brit. inf.*), pause, peter out, pull up, put an end to, quit, refrain, run down, run its course, shut down, stall, terminate **2.** arrest, bar, block, break, check, close, forestall, frustrate, hinder, hold back, impede, intercept, interrupt, obstruct, plug, prevent, rein in, repress, restrain, seal, silence, staunch, stem, suspend **3.** break one's journey, lodge, put up, rest, sojourn, stay, tarry ~*n.* **4.** cessation,

conclusion, discontinuation, end, finish, halt, standstill **5.** break, rest, sojourn, stay, stopover, visit **6.** bar, block, break, check, control, hindrance, impediment, plug, stoppage **7.** depot, destination, halt, stage, station, termination, terminus

stopgap 1. *n.* improvisation, makeshift, resort, shift, substitute, temporary expedient **2.** *adj.* emergency, impromptu, improvised, makeshift, provisional, rough-and-ready, temporary

stop off, **stop in**, *or esp. U.S.* **stop by** *vb.* (*intr., adv.; often foll. by at*) to halt and call somewhere, as on a visit or errand, esp. en route to another place.

stopover ('stɒp,əʊvə) *n.* **1.** a stopping place on a journey. ~*vb.* **stop over**. **2.** (*intr., adv.*) to make a stopover.

stoppage ('stɒpɪdʒ) *n.* **1.** the act of stopping or the state of being stopped. **2.** something that stops or blocks. **3.** a deduction of money, as from pay. **4.** an organized cessation of work, as during a strike.

stopper ('stɒpə) *n.* **1.** Also called: **stopple**. a plug or bung for closing a bottle, pipe, duct, etc. **2.** a person or thing that stops or puts an end to something. **3.** *Bridge*. another name for **stop** (sense 32). ~*vb.* **4.** (*tr.*) Also: **stopple**. to close or fit with a stopper.

stop press *n. Brit.* **1.** news items inserted into a newspaper after the printing has been started. **2.** the space regularly left blank for this.

stopwatch ('stɒp,wɒtʃ) *n.* a type of watch used for timing sporting events, etc., accurately, having a device for stopping the hands instantly.

storage ('stɔːrɪdʒ) *n.* **1.** the act of storing or the state of being stored. **2.** space or area reserved for storing. **3.** a charge made for storing. **4.** *Computers.* **a.** the act or process of storing information in a computer memory or on magnetic tape, etc. **b.** (*as modifier*): *storage capacity*.

storage battery *n.* another name (esp. U.S.) for **accumulator** (sense 1).

storage device *n.* a piece of computer equipment, such as a magnetic tape, disk, drum, etc., in or on which information can be stored.

storage heater *n.* an electric device capable of accumulating and radiating heat generated by off-peak electricity.

store (stɔː) *vb.* **1.** (*tr.*) to keep, set aside, or accumulate for future use. **2.** (*tr.*) to place in a warehouse, depository, etc., for safekeeping. **3.** (*tr.*) to supply, provide, or stock. **4.** (*intr.*) to be put into storage. **5.** *Computers.* to enter or retain (information) in a storage device. ~*n.* **6. a.** an establishment for the retail sale of goods and services. **b.** (*in combination*): *storefront*. **7. a** large supply or stock kept for future use. **8.** short for **department store**. **9. a.** a storage place such as a warehouse or depository. **b.** (*in combination*): *storeman*. **10.** the state of being stored (esp. **in store**). **11.** a large amount or quantity. **12.** *Computers, chiefly Brit.* another name for **memory** (sense 7). **13. in store**. forthcoming or imminent. **14. lay, put,** *or* **set store by**. to value or reckon as important. ~*adj.* **15.** (of cattle, sheep, etc.) bought lean to be fattened up for market. —'**storable** *adj.*

storehouse ('stɔː,haʊs) *n.* a place where things are stored.

storeroom ('stɔː,ruːm, -,rʊm) *n.* **1.** a room in which things are stored. **2.** room for storing.

stores (stɔːz) *pl. n.* supply or stock of something, esp. essentials, for a specific purpose.

storey *or U.S.* **story** ('stɔːrɪ) *n., pl.* **-reys** *or* **-ries**. **1.** a floor or level of a building. **2.** a set of rooms on one level.

storied ('stɔːrɪd) *adj.* **1.** recorded in history or in a story. **2.** decorated with narrative scenes.

stork (stɔːk) *n.* any of a family of large wading birds, chiefly of warm regions of the Old World, having very long legs and a long stout pointed bill, and typically having a white-and-black plumage.

storm (stɔːm) *n.* **1. a.** a violent weather condition of strong winds, rain, hail, thunder, lightning, blowing sand, snow, etc. **b.** (*as modifier*): *storm cloud.* **c.** (*in combination*): *stormproof.* **2.** *Meteorol.* a wind of force 10 on the Beaufort scale, reaching speeds of 55 to 63 m.p.h. **3.** a violent disturbance or quarrel. **4.** a direct assault on a stronghold. **5.** a heavy discharge or rain, as of bullets or missiles. **6. storm in a teacup.** *Brit.* a violent fuss or disturbance over a trivial matter. **7. take by storm. a.** to capture or overrun by a violent assault. **b.** to overwhelm and enthral. ~*vb.* **8.** to attack or assault (something) suddenly and violently. **9.** (*intr.*) to be vociferously angry. **10.** (*intr.*) to move or rush violently or angrily. **11.** (*intr.; with it* as subject) to rain, hail, or snow hard and be very windy, often with thunder and lightning.

storm centre *n.* **1.** the centre of a cyclonic storm, etc., where pressure is lowest. **2.** the centre of any disturbance or trouble.

storm door *n.* an additional door outside an ordinary door, providing extra insulation against wind, cold, rain, etc.

storm-trooper *n.* **1.** a member of the Nazi S.A. **2.** a member of a force of shock troops.

stormy ('stɔːmɪ) *adj.* **-ier, -iest. 1.** characterized by storms. **2.** involving or characterized by violent disturbance or emotional outburst. —'**stormily** *adv.* —'**storminess** *n.*

stormy petrel *n.* **1.** Also called: **storm petrel.** any of various small petrels typically having dark plumage and paler underparts. **2.** a person who brings or portends trouble.

story[1] ('stɔːrɪ) *n., pl.* **-ries. 1.** a narration of a chain of events told or written in prose or verse. **2.** Also called: **short story.** a piece of fiction, briefer and usually less detailed than a novel. **3.** Also called: **story line.** the plot of a book, film, etc. **4.** an event that could be the subject of a narrative. **5.** a report or statement on a matter or event. **6.** the event or material for such a report. **7.** *Inf.* a lie, fib, or untruth. **8. cut** (*or* **make**) **a long story short.** to leave out details in a narration. **9. the same old story.** the familiar or regular course of events. **10. the story goes.** it is commonly said or believed. ~*vb.* **-rying, -ried.** (*tr.*) **11.** to decorate (a pot, wall, etc.) with scenes from history or legends.

story[2] ('stɔːrɪ) *n., pl.* **-ries.** another spelling (esp. U.S.) of **storey.**

storybook ('stɔːrɪ,bʊk) *n.* **1.** a book containing stories, esp. for children. ~*adj.* **2.** unreal or fantastic: *a storybook world.*

stoup *or* **stoop** (stuːp) *n.* **1.** a small basin for holy water. **2.** *Brit. dialect.* a bucket or cup.

stout (staʊt) *adj.* **1.** solidly built or corpulent. **2.** (*prenominal*) resolute or valiant: *stout fellow.* **3.** strong, substantial, and robust. **4.** a **stout heart.** courage; resolution. ~*n.* **5.** strong porter highly flavoured with malt. —'**stoutly** *adv.* —'**stoutness** *n.*

stouthearted (,staʊt'hɑːtɪd) *adj.* valiant; brave. —,**stout'heartedly** *adv.* —,**stout'heartedness** *n.*

stove[1] (stəʊv) *n.* **1.** another word for **cooker** (sense 1). **2.** any heating apparatus, such as a kiln.

stove[2] (stəʊv) *vb.* a past tense or past participle of **stave.**

stovepipe ('stəʊv,paɪp) *n.* **1.** a pipe that serves as a

THESAURUS

stoppage 1. abeyance, arrest, close, closure, cutoff, deduction, discontinuance, halt, hindrance, lay-off, shutdown, standstill, stopping **2.** blockage, check, curtailment, interruption, obstruction, occlusion, stopping up

store *v.* **1.** accumulate, deposit, garner, hoard, husband, keep, keep in reserve, lay by *or* in, lock away, put aside, put aside for a rainy day, put by, put in storage, reserve, salt away, save, stash (*Inf.*), stock, stockpile ~*n.* **2.** abundance, accumulation, cache, fund, hoard, lot, mine, plenty, plethora, provision, quantity, reserve, reservoir, stock, stockpile, supply, wealth **3.** chain store, department store, emporium, market, mart, outlet, shop, supermarket **4.** depository, repository, storehouse, storeroom, warehouse **5. set store by** appreciate, esteem, hold in high regard, prize, think highly of, value

storm *n.* **1.** blast, blizzard, cyclone, gale, gust, hurricane, squall, tempest, tornado, whirlwind **2.** *Fig.* agitation, anger, clamour, commotion, disturbance, furore, hubbub, outbreak, outburst, outcry, passion, roar, row, rumpus, stir, strife, tumult, turmoil, violence ~*v.* **3.** assail, assault, beset, charge, rush, take by storm ~*n.* **4.** assault, attack, blitz, blitzkrieg, offensive, onset, onslaught, rush ~*v.* **5.** bluster, complain, fly off the handle (*Inf.*), fume, rage, rant, rave, scold, thunder **6.** flounce, fly, rush, stalk, stamp, stomp (*Inf.*)

stormy blustering, blustery, boisterous, dirty, foul, gusty, raging, rough, squally, tempestuous, turbulent, wild, windy

story 1. account, anecdote, chronicle, fictional account, history, legend, narration, narrative, novel, recital, record, relation, romance, tale, version, yarn **2.** *Inf.* falsehood, fib, fiction, lie, untruth, white lie **3.** article, feature, news, news item, report, scoop

stout 1. big, bulky, burly, corpulent, fat, fleshy, heavy, obese, on the large *or* heavy side, overweight, plump, portly, rotund, substantial, tubby **2.** able-bodied, athletic, beefy (*Inf.*), brawny, hardy, hulking, husky (*Inf.*), lusty, muscular, robust, stalwart, strapping, strong, sturdy, substantial, tough, vigorous **3.** bold, brave, courageous, dauntless, doughty, fearless, gallant, intrepid, lion-hearted, manly, plucky, resolute, valiant, valorous

stouthearted bold, brave, courageous, dauntless, doughty, fearless, great-hearted, gutsy (*Sl.*), heroic, indomitable, intrepid, lion-hearted, plucky, spirited, stalwart, valiant, valorous

flue to a stove. **2.** Also called: **stovepipe hat.** a man's tall silk hat.

stow (stəʊ) *vb.* (*tr.*) **1.** (often foll. by *away*) to pack or store. **2.** to fill by packing. **3.** *Naut.* to pack or put away (cargo, sails, etc.). **4.** to have enough room for. **5.** (*usually imperative*) *Brit. sl.* to cease from: *stow your noise!*

stowage ('stəʊɪdʒ) *n.* **1.** space, room, or a charge for stowing goods. **2.** the act or an instance of stowing or the state of being stowed. **3.** something that is stowed.

stowaway ('stəʊəˌweɪ) *n.* **1.** a person who hides aboard a vehicle, ship, or aircraft in order to gain free passage. ~*vb.* **stow away. 2.** (*intr., adv.*) to travel in such a way.

S.T.P. *abbrev. for:* **1.** *Trademark.* scientifically treated petroleum: an oil substitute promising renewed power for an internal-combustion engine. **2.** standard temperature and pressure. **3.** Professor of Sacred Theology. ~*n.* **4.** a synthetic hallucinogenic drug related to mescaline.

strabismus (strə'bɪzməs) *n.* abnormal parallel alignment of one or both eyes, characterized by a turning inwards or outwards from the nose: caused by paralysis of an eye muscle, etc. Also called: **squint.** —**stra'bismal, stra'bismic,** *or* **stra'bismical** *adj.*

straddle ('strædəl) *vb.* **1.** (*tr.*) to have one leg, part, or support on each side of. **2.** (*tr.*) *U.S. inf.* to be in favour of both sides of (something). **3.** (*intr.*) to stand, walk, or sit with the legs apart. **4.** (*tr.*) to spread (the legs) apart. **5.** *Gunnery.* to fire a number of shots slightly beyond and slightly short of (a target) to determine the correct range. **6.** (*intr.*) (in poker, of the second player after the dealer) to double the ante before looking at one's cards. ~*n.* **7.** the act or position of straddling. **8.** a noncommittal attitude or stand. **9.** *Stock Exchange.* a contract or option permitting its purchaser either to sell securities to or buy securities from the maker of the contract within a specified period of time. **10.** *Athletics.* a high-jumping technique in which the body is parallel with the bar and the legs straddle it at the highest point of the jump. **11.** (in poker) the stake put up after the ante in poker by the second player after the dealer. —**'straddler** *n.*

Stradivarius (ˌstrædɪ'vɛərɪəs) *n.* any of a number of violins manufactured in Italy by Antonio Stradivari (?1644–1737), or his family. Often shortened to (informal) **Strad.**

strafe (streɪf, strɑːf) *vb.* (*tr.*) **1.** to bombard (troops, etc.) from the air. **2.** *Sl.* to punish harshly. ~*n.* **3.** an act or instance of strafing. —**'strafer** *n.*

straggle ('strægəl) *vb.* (*intr.*) **1.** to go, come, or spread in a rambling or irregular way. **2.** to linger behind or wander from a main line or part. —**'straggler** *n.* —**'straggly** *adj.*

straight (streɪt) *adj.* **1.** not curved or crooked; continuing in the same direction without deviating. **2.** straightforward, outright, or candid: *a straight rejection.* **3.** even, level, or upright. **4.** in keeping with the facts; accurate. **5.** honest, respectable, or reliable. **6.** accurate or logical: *straight reasoning.* **7.** continuous; uninterrupted. **8.** (esp. of an alcoholic drink) undiluted; neat. **9.** not crisp, kinked, or curly: *straight hair.* **10.** correctly arranged; orderly. **11.** (of a play, acting style, etc.) straightforward or serious. **12.** *Boxing.* (of a blow, etc.) delivered with an unbent arm: *a straight left.* **13.** (of the cylinders of an internal-combustion engine) in line, rather than in a V-formation or in some other arrangement: *a straight eight.* **14.** a slang word for **heterosexual. 15.** *Inf.* no longer owing or being owed something: *if*

you buy the next round we'll be straight. **16.** *Sl.* conventional in views, customs, appearance, etc. ~*adv.* **17.** in a straight line or direct course. **18.** immediately; at once: *he came straight back.* **19.** in an even, level, or upright position. **20.** without cheating, lying, or unreliability: *tell it to me straight.* **21.** continuously; uninterruptedly. **22.** (often foll. by *out*) frankly; candidly: *he told me straight out.* **23. go straight.** *Inf.* to reform after having been dishonest or a criminal. ~*n.* **24.** the state of being straight. **25.** a straight line, form, part, or position. **26.** *Brit.* a straight part of a racetrack. **27.** *Poker.* **a.** five cards that are in sequence irrespective of suit. **b.** a hand containing such a sequence. **c.** (*as modifier*): *a straight flush.* **28.** *Sl.* a conventional person. **29.** *Sl.* a cigarette containing only tobacco, without drugs. —**'straightly** *adv.* —**'straightness** *n.*

straightaway (ˌstreɪtə'weɪ) *adv. also* **straight away. 1.** at once. ~*n.* **2.** the U.S. word for **straight** (sense 26).

straightedge ('streɪtˌɛdʒ) *n.* a stiff strip of wood or metal with one edge straight, used for ruling straight lines. —**'straightˌedged** *adj.*

straighten ('streɪtən) *vb.* (sometimes foll. by *up* or *out*) **1.** to make or become straight. **2.** to make neat or tidy. —**'straightener** *n.*

straighten out *vb.* (*adv.*) **1.** to make or become less complicated or confused. **2.** *U.S.* to reform or become reformed.

straight face *n.* a serious facial expression, esp. one that conceals the impulse to laugh. —**'straight-'faced** *adj.*

straight fight *n.* a contest between two candidates only.

straightforward (ˌstreɪt'fɔːwəd) *adj.* **1.** (of a person) honest, frank, or simple. **2.** *Chiefly Brit.* (of a task, etc.) simple; easy. ~*adv., adj.* **3.** in a straight course. —**ˌstraight'forwardly** *adv.* —**ˌstraight'forwardness** *n.*

straightjacket ('streɪtˌdʒækɪt) *n.* a less common spelling of **straitjacket.**

straight man *n.* a subsidiary actor who acts as stooge to a comedian.

straight-out *adj. U.S. inf.* **1.** complete; thoroughgoing. **2.** frank or honest.

straightway ('streɪtˌweɪ) *adv. Arch.* at once.

strain¹ (streɪn) *vb.* **1.** to draw or be drawn taut; stretch tight. **2.** to exert, tax, or use (resources) to the utmost extent. **3.** to injure or damage or be injured or damaged by overexertion: *he strained himself.* **4.** to deform or be deformed as a result of a stress. **5.** (*intr.*) to make intense or violent efforts; strive. **6.** to subject or be subjected to mental tension or stress. **7.** to pour or pass (a substance) or (of a substance) to be poured or passed through a sieve, filter, or strainer. **8.** (*tr.*) to draw off or remove (one part of a substance or mixture from another) by or as if by filtering. **9.** (*tr.*) to clasp tightly; hug. **10.** (*intr.*; foll. by *at*) to push, pull, or work with violent exertion (upon). ~*n.* **11.** the act or an instance of straining. **12.** the damage resulting from excessive exertion. **13.** an intense physical or mental effort. **14.** *Music.* (*often pl.*) a theme, melody, or tune. **15.** a great demand on the emotions, resources, etc. **16.** a way of speaking; tone of voice: *don't go on in that strain.* **17.** *Physics.* the change in dimension of a body under load expressed as the ratio of the total deflection or change in dimension to the original unloaded dimension.

strain² (streɪn) *n.* **1.** the main body of descendants from one ancestor. **2.** a group of organisms within a species or variety, distinguished by one or more minor charac-

---

THESAURUS

stow bundle, cram, deposit, jam, load, pack, put away, secrete, stash (*Inf.*), store, stuff, tuck

straggle drift, lag, loiter, ramble, range, roam, rove, spread, stray, string out, trail, wander

straight *adj.* **1.** direct, near, short, undeviating, unswerving **2.** aligned, erect, even, horizontal, in line, level, perpendicular, plumb, right, smooth, square, true, upright, vertical **3.** blunt, candid, forthright, frank, honest, outright, plain, point-blank, straightforward, unqualified **4.** above board, accurate, authentic, decent, equitable, fair, fair and square, honest, honourable, just, law-abiding, reliable, respectable, trustworthy,

upright **5.** arranged, in order, neat, orderly, organized, put to rights, shipshape, sorted out, tidy **6.** consecutive, continuous, nonstop, running, solid, successive, sustained, through, uninterrupted, unrelieved **7.** *Sl.* bourgeois, conservative, conventional, orthodox, square (*Inf.*), traditional **8.** neat, pure, unadulterated, undiluted, unmixed ~*adj.* **9.** as the crow flies, at once, directly, immediately, instantly **10.** candidly, frankly, honestly, in plain English, point-blank, pulling no punches (*Inf.*), with no holds barred

straightaway at once, directly, immediately, instantly, now, on the spot, right away, straightway (*Archaic*), there and then,

this minute, without any delay, without more ado

straighten arrange, neaten, order, put in order, set or put to rights, smarten up, spruce up, tidy (up)

straighten out become clear, clear up, correct, disentangle, put right, rectify, regularize, resolve, settle, sort out, unsnarl, work out

straightforward 1. above board, candid, direct, forthright, genuine, guileless, honest, open, sincere, truthful **2.** clear-cut, easy, elementary, routine, simple, uncomplicated, undemanding

teristics. **3.** a variety of bacterium or fungus, esp. one used for a culture. **4.** a streak; trace. **5.** *Arch.* a kind, type, or sort.

strained ('streind) *adj.* **1.** (of an action, performance, etc.) not natural or spontaneous. **2.** (of an atmosphere, relationship, etc.) not relaxed; tense. —'**strainedness** *n.*

strainer ('streinə) *n.* **1.** a sieve used for straining sauces, vegetables, tea, etc. **2.** a gauze or simple filter used to strain liquids.

strait (streit) *n.* **1.** (*often pl.*) a narrow channel of the sea linking two larger areas of sea. **2.** (*often pl.*) a position of acute difficulty (often in **in dire** or **desperate straits**). **3.** *Arch.* a narrow place or passage. *~adj.* **4.** *Arch.* (of spaces, etc.) affording little room. —'**straitly** *adv.* —'**straitness** *n.*

straiten ('streit°n) *vb.* **1.** (*tr.; usually passive*) to embarrass or distress, esp. financially. **2.** (*tr.*) to limit, confine, or restrict. **3.** *Arch.* to make or become narrow.

straitjacket or **straightjacket** ('streit,dʒækit) *n.* a jacket made of strong canvas material with long sleeves for binding the arms of violent prisoners or mental patients.

strait-laced or **straight-laced** *adj.* prudish or puritanical.

strand¹ (strænd) *vb.* **1.** to leave or drive (ships, fish, etc.) aground or ashore or (of ships etc.) to be left or driven ashore. **2.** (*tr.; usually passive*) to leave helpless, as without transport or money, etc. *~n. Chiefly poetic.* **3.** a shore or beach.

strand² (strænd) *n.* **1.** a set of or one of the individual fibres or threads of string, wire, etc., that form a rope, cable, etc. **2.** a single length of string, hair, wool, wire, etc. **3.** a string of pearls or beads. **4.** a constituent element of something. *~vb.* **5.** (*tr.*) to form (a rope, cable, etc.) by winding strands together.

strange (streindʒ) *adj.* **1.** odd, unusual, or extraordinary; peculiar. **2.** not known, seen, or experienced before; unfamiliar. **3.** not easily explained. **4.** (usually foll. by *to*) inexperienced (in) or unaccustomed (to): *strange to a task.* **5.** not of one's own kind, locality, etc.; alien; foreign. **6.** shy; distant; reserved. **7. strange to say.** it is unusual or surprising that. *~adv.* **8.** *Not standard.* in a strange manner. —'**strangely** *adv.*

stranger ('streindʒə) *n.* **1.** any person whom one does not know. **2.** a person who is new to a particular locality, from another region, town, etc. **3.** a guest or visitor. **4.** (foll. by *to*) a person who is unfamiliar (with) or new (to) something: *he is no stranger to computers.*

strangle ('stræŋg°l) *vb.* **1.** (*tr.*) to kill by compressing the windpipe; throttle. **2.** (*tr.*) to prevent or inhibit the growth or development of: *to strangle originality.* **3.** (*tr.*) to suppress (an utterance) by or as if by swallowing suddenly: *to strangle a cry.* —'**strangler** *n.*

stranglehold ('stræŋg°l,hould) *n.* **1.** a wrestling hold in which a wrestler's arms are pressed against his opponent's windpipe. **2.** complete power or control over a person or situation.

strangulate ('stræŋgjʊ,leit) *vb.* (*tr.*) **1.** to constrict (a hollow organ, vessel, etc.) so as to stop the flow of air,

blood, etc., through it. **2.** another word for **strangle**. —,**strangu'lation** *n.*

strap (stræp) *n.* **1.** a long strip of leather or similar material, for binding trunks, baggage, etc. **2.** a strip of leather or similar material used for carrying, lifting, or holding. **3.** a loop of leather, rubber, etc., suspended from the roof in a bus or train for standing passengers to hold on to. **4.** a razor strop. **5. the strap.** a beating with a strap as a punishment. **6.** short for **shoulder strap**. *~vb.* **strapping, strapped.** (*tr.*) **7.** to tie or bind with a strap. **8.** to beat with a strap. **9.** to sharpen with a strap or strop.

straphanger ('stræp,hæŋə) *n. Inf.* a passenger in a bus, train, etc., who has to travel standing, esp. holding on to a strap. —'**strap,hanging** *n.*

strapping ('stræpiŋ) *adj.* (*prenominal*) tall and sturdy.

strata ('stra:tə) *n.* the plural of **stratum**.

▷ **Usage.** In careful usage, *strata* is the standard plural of *stratum* and is not treated as singular.

stratagem ('strætidʒəm) *n.* a plan or trick, esp. to deceive an enemy.

strategic (strə'ti:dʒik) or **strategical** *adj.* **1.** of or characteristic of strategy. **2.** important to strategy. **3.** (of weapons, esp. missiles) directed against an enemy's homeland rather than used on a battlefield. Cf. **tactical**. —**stra'tegically** *adv.*

strategics (strə'ti:dʒiks) *n.* strategy, esp. in a military sense.

strategy ('strætidʒi) *n., pl.* **-gies. 1.** the art or science of the planning and conduct of a war. **2.** the practice or art of using stratagems, as in politics, business, etc. **3.** a plan or stratagem. —'**strategist** *n.*

strath (stræθ) *n. Scot.* a broad valley or glen.

strathspey (,stræθ'spei) *n.* a slow Scottish reel with gliding steps.

strati- *combining form.* indicating stratum or strata: *stratigraphy.*

stratify ('stræti,fai) *vb.* **-fying, -fied. 1.** to form or be formed in layers or strata. **2.** *Sociol.* to divide (a society) into status groups or (of a society) to develop such groups. —,**stratifi'cation** *n.*

stratocumulus (,strætəʊ'kju:mjʊləs) *n., pl.* **-li** (-,lai). *Meteorol.* a uniform stretch of cloud containing dark grey globular masses.

stratosphere ('strætə,sfiə) *n.* the atmospheric layer lying between the troposphere and the mesosphere, in which temperature generally increases with height. —**stratospheric** (,strætə'sfɛrik) or ,**strato'spherical** *adj.*

stratum ('stra:təm) *n., pl.* **-ta** (-tə) or **-tums. 1.** (*usually pl.*) any of the distinct layers into which sedimentary rocks are divided. **2.** *Biol.* a single layer of tissue or cells. **3.** a layer of any material, esp. one of several parallel layers. **4.** a layer of ocean or atmosphere either naturally or arbitrarily demarcated. **5.** a level of a social hierarchy. —'**stratal** *adj.*

stratus ('streitəs) *n., pl.* **-ti** (-tai). a grey layer cloud.

straw (strɔ:) *n.* **1. a.** stalks of threshed grain, esp. of wheat, rye, oats, or barley, used in plaiting hats, baskets,

---

THESAURUS

strain¹ *v.* 1. distend, draw tight, extend, stretch, tauten, tighten 2. drive, exert, fatigue, injure, overexert, overtax, overwork, pull, push to the limit, sprain, tax, tear, tire, twist, weaken, wrench 3. endeavour, go all out for (*Inf.*), labour, make a supreme effort, strive, struggle 4. filter, percolate, purify, riddle, screen, seep, separate, sieve, sift *~n.* 5. effort, exertion, force, injury, pull, sprain, struggle, tautness, tension, tensity (*Rare*), wrench 6. anxiety, burden, pressure, stress, tension 7. *Often plural* air, lay, measure (*Poetic*), melody, song, theme, tune

strain² *n.* 1. ancestry, blood, descent, extraction, family, lineage, pedigree, race, stock 2. streak, suggestion, suspicion, tendency, trace, trait 3. humour, manner, spirit, style, temper, tone, vein, way

strained artificial, awkward, constrained, difficult, embarrassed, false, forced, laboured, put on, self-conscious, stiff, tense, uncomfortable, uneasy, unnatural, unrelaxed

strait-laced moralistic, narrow, narrow-minded, of the old school, old-

maidish (*Inf.*), overscrupulous, prim, proper, prudish, puritanical, strict, Victorian

straits *n. Sometimes singular* 1. crisis, difficulty, dilemma, distress, embarrassment, emergency, extremity, hardship, hole (*Sl.*), mess, pass, perplexity, plight, predicament, pretty or fine kettle of fish (*Inf.*) 2. channel, narrows, sound

strand *n.* fibre, filament, length, lock, rope, string, thread, tress, twist

stranded 1. aground, ashore, beached, cast away, grounded, marooned, wrecked 2. *Fig.* abandoned, helpless, high and dry, homeless, left in the lurch, penniless

strange 1. abnormal, astonishing, bizarre, curious, eccentric, exceptional, extraordinary, fantastic, funny, irregular, marvellous, mystifying, odd, out-of-the-way, peculiar, perplexing, queer, rare, remarkable, singular, unaccountable, uncanny, uncommon, unheard of, weird, wonderful 2. alien, exotic, foreign, new, novel, outside one's experience, remote, unexplored, unfamiliar, unknown, untried 3. *Often with* **to** a stranger to,

ignorant of, inexperienced, new to, unaccustomed, unpractised, unseasoned, unused, unversed in 4. awkward, bewildered, disoriented, ill at ease, lost, out of place, uncomfortable

stranger alien, foreigner, guest, incomer, new arrival, newcomer, outlander, unknown, visitor

strangle 1. asphyxiate, choke, garrotte, smother, strangulate, suffocate, throttle 2. gag (*Inf.*), inhibit, repress, stifle, suppress

strap *n.* 1. belt, leash, thong, tie *~v.* 2. bind, buckle, fasten, lash, secure, tie, truss 3. beat, belt, flog, lash, scourge, whip

stratagem artifice, device, dodge, feint, intrigue, manoeuvre, plan, plot, ploy, ruse, scheme, subterfuge, trick, wile

strategic 1. cardinal, critical, crucial, decisive, key, vital 2. calculated, deliberate, diplomatic, planned, politic

strategy approach, grand design, manoeuvring, plan, planning, policy, procedure, programme, scheme

etc., or as fodder. **b.** (*as modifier*): *a straw hat.* **2.** a single dry or ripened stalk, esp. of a grass. **3.** a long thin hollow paper or plastic tube, used for sucking up liquids into the mouth. **4.** (*usually used with a negative*) anything of little value or importance: *I wouldn't give a straw for our chances.* **5.** a measure or remedy that one turns to in desperation (esp. in **clutch** or **grasp at a straw** or **straws**). **6. a.** a pale yellow colour. **b.** (*as adj.*): *straw hair.* **7. the last straw.** a final blow or calamity. **8. straw in the wind.** a hint or indication. —**'strawy** *adj.*

strawberry ('strɔːbərɪ, -brɪ) *n.*, *pl.* **-ries.** **1.** any of various low-growing rosaceous plants which have red edible fruits and spread by runners. **2. a.** the fruit of any of these plants, consisting of a sweet fleshy receptacle bearing small seedlike parts (the true fruits). **b.** (*as modifier*): *strawberry ice cream.* **3. a.** a purplish-red colour. **b.** (*as adj.*): *strawberry shoes.*

strawberry blonde *adj.* **1.** (of hair) reddish blonde. ~*n.* **2.** a woman with such hair.

strawberry mark *n.* a soft vascular red birthmark. Also called: **strawberry.**

strawflower ('strɔːˌflaʊə) *n.* an Australian plant in which the coloured bracts retain their colour when the plant is dried.

straw vote or **poll** *n. Chiefly U.S.* an unofficial poll or vote taken to determine the opinion of a group or the public on some issue.

stray (streɪ) *vb.* (*intr.*) **1.** to wander away, as from the correct path or from a given area. **2.** to wander haphazardly. **3.** to digress from the point, lose concentration, etc. **4.** to deviate from certain moral standards. ~*n.* **5. a.** a domestic animal, fowl, etc., that has wandered away from its place of keeping and is lost. **b.** (*as modifier*): *stray dogs.* **6.** a lost or homeless person, esp. a child: *waifs and strays.* **7.** an occurrence, specimen, etc., that is out of place or outside the usual pattern. ~*adj.* **8.** scattered, random, or haphazard. —**'strayer** *n.*

streak (striːk) *n.* **1.** a long thin mark, stripe, or trace of some contrasting colour. **2.** (of lightning) a sudden flash. **3.** an element or trace, as of some quality or characteristic. **4.** a strip, vein, or layer. **5.** a short stretch or run, esp. of good or bad luck. **6.** *Inf.* an act or the practice of running naked through a public place. ~*vb.* **7.** (*tr.*) to mark or daub with a streak or streaks. **8.** (*intr.*) to form streaks or become streaked. **9.** (*intr.*) to move rapidly in a straight line. **10.** (*intr.*) *Inf.* to run naked through a public place in order to shock or amuse. —**streaked** *adj.* —**'streaker** *n.* —**'streak,like** *adj.* —**'streaky** *adj.*

stream (striːm) *n.* **1.** a small river; brook. **2.** any steady flow of water or other fluid. **3.** something that resembles a stream in moving continuously in a line or particular direction. **4.** a rapid or unbroken flow of speech, etc.: *a stream of abuse.* **5.** *Brit.* any of several parallel classes of schoolchildren, or divisions of children within a class, grouped together because of similar ability. **6. go** (or **drift**) **with the stream.** to conform to the accepted standards. ~*vb.* **7.** to emit or be emitted in a continuous flow: *his nose streamed blood.* **8.** (*intr.*) to move in unbroken succession, as a crowd of people, vehicles, etc. **9.** (*intr.*) to float freely or with a waving motion: *bunting streamed in the wind.* **10.** (*tr.*) to unfurl (a flag, etc.). **11.** *Brit. education.* to group or divide (children) in streams.

streamer ('striːmə) *n.* **1.** a long narrow flag or part of a flag. **2.** a long narrow coiled ribbon of coloured paper that becomes unrolled when tossed. **3.** a stream of light, esp. one appearing in some forms of the aurora. **4.** *Journalism.* a large heavy headline printed across the width of a page.

streamline ('striːmˌlaɪn) *n.* **1.** a contour on a body that offers the minimum resistance to a gas or liquid flowing around it. ~*vb.* **2.** (*tr.*) to make streamlined.

streamlined ('striːmˌlaɪnd) *adj.* **1.** offering or designed to offer the minimum resistance to the flow of a gas or liquid. **2.** made more efficient, esp. by simplifying.

stream of consciousness *n.* **1.** *Psychol.* the continuous flow of ideas, thoughts, and feelings forming the content of an individual's consciousness. **2.** a literary technique that reveals the flow of thoughts and feelings of characters through long passages of soliloquy.

street (striːt) *n.* **1. a.** a public road that is usually lined with buildings, esp. in a town: *Oxford Street.* **b.** (*as modifier*): *a street directory.* **2.** the buildings lining a street. **3.** the part of the road between the pavements, used by vehicles. **4.** the people living, working, etc., in a particular street. **5. man in the street.** an ordinary or average citizen. **6. on the streets.** earning a living as a prostitute. **7.** (**right**) **up one's street.** (just) what one knows or likes best. **8. streets ahead of.** superior to, more advanced than, etc. **9. streets apart.** markedly different.

street Arab *n.* a homeless child, esp. one who survives by begging and stealing; urchin.

streetcar ('striːtˌkɑː) *n.* the usual U.S. name for **tram** (sense 1).

streetwalker ('striːtˌwɔːkə) *n.* a prostitute who solicits on the streets. —**'street,walking** *n.*, *adj.*

strength (strɛŋθ) *n.* **1.** the state or quality of being physically or mentally strong. **2.** the ability to withstand or exert great force, stress, or pressure. **3.** something regarded as beneficial or a source of power: *their chief strength is technology.* **4.** potency, as of a drink, drug, etc. **5.** power to convince; cogency: *the strength of an argument.* **6.** degree of intensity or concentration of colour, light, sound, flavour, etc. **7.** (of an army, group, etc.) having part of the full complement as specified: *at full strength; below strength.* **8. from strength to strength.** with ever-increasing success. **9. in strength.** in large numbers. **10. on the strength of.** on the basis of or relying upon. **11. the strength of.** *Austral. inf.* the essential facts about.

strengthen ('strɛŋθən) *vb.* to make or become stronger. —**'strengthener** *n.*

strenuous ('strɛnjʊəs) *adj.* **1.** requiring or involving the use of great energy or effort. **2.** characterized by great activity, effort, or endeavour. —**'strenuousness** *n.* —**'strenuously** *adv.*

strepto- *combining form.* **1.** indicating a shape resembling a twisted chain: *streptococcus.* **2.** indicating streptococcus.

streptococcus (ˌstrɛptəʊ'kɒkəs) *n.*, *pl.* **-cocci** (-'kɒksaɪ). any spherical bacterium of the genus *Streptococcus,* typically occurring in chains and including many pathogenic species. Often shortened to **strep.** —**streptococcal** (ˌstrɛptəʊ'kɒkəl) or **streptococcic** (ˌstrɛptəʊ'kɒksɪk) *adj.*

THESAURUS

stray v. 1. deviate, digress, diverge, get off the point, get sidetracked, go off at a tangent, ramble 2. be abandoned *or* lost, drift, err, go astray, lose one's way, meander, range, roam, rove, straggle, wander ~*adj.* 3. abandoned, homeless, lost, roaming, vagrant 4. accidental, chance, erratic, freak, odd, random, scattered

streak n. 1. band, layer, line, slash, smear, strip, stripe, stroke, vein 2. dash, element, strain, touch, trace, vein ~ v. 3. band, daub, fleck, slash, smear, striate, stripe 4. dart, flash, fly, hurtle, move like greased lightning (*Inf.*), speed, sprint, sweep, tear, whistle, whiz (*Inf.*), zoom

stream 1. n. beck, brook, burn, course, creek (*U.S.*), current, drift, flow, freshet, outpouring, rill, river, rivulet, run, rush, surge, tide, torrent, tributary 2. v. cascade, course,

emit, flood, flow, glide, gush, issue, pour, run, shed, spill, spout

streamer banner, colours, ensign, flag, gonfalon, pennant, pennon, ribbon, standard

streamlined efficient, modernized, organized, rationalized, sleek, slick, smooth, smooth-running, time-saving, well-run

street 1. avenue, boulevard, lane, road, roadway, row, terrace, thoroughfare 2. (**right**) **up one's street** acceptable, compatible, congenial, familiar, one's cup of tea (*Inf.*), pleasing, suitable, to one's liking, to one's taste

strength 1. backbone, brawn, brawniness, courage, firmness, fortitude, health, lustiness, might, muscle, robustness, sinew, stamina, stoutness, sturdiness, toughness 2. cogency, concentration, effectiveness, efficacy, energy, force, intensity, potency, pow-

er, resolution, spirit, vehemence, vigour, virtue (*Archaic*) 3. advantage, anchor, asset, mainstay, security, strong point, succour, tower of strength

strengthen 1. animate, brace up, consolidate, encourage, fortify, give new energy to, harden, hearten, invigorate, nerve, nourish, rejuvenate, restore, stiffen, toughen 2. bolster, brace, build up, buttress, confirm, corroborate, enhance, establish, give a boost to, harden, heighten, increase, intensify, justify, reinforce, steel, substantiate, support

strenuous 1. arduous, demanding, exhausting, hard, Herculean, laborious, taxing, toilsome, tough, tough going, unrelaxing, uphill 2. active, bold, determined, eager, earnest, energetic, persistent, resolute, spirited, strong, tireless, vigorous, zealous

streptomycin (ˌstrɛptəʊˈmaɪsɪn) *n.* an antibiotic obtained from the bacterium *Streptomyces griseus:* used in the treatment of tuberculosis and other bacterial infections.

stress (strɛs) *n.* **1.** special emphasis or significance. **2.** emphasis placed upon a syllable by pronouncing it more loudly than those that surround it. **3.** such emphasis as part of a rhythm in music or poetry. **4.** a syllable so emphasized. **5.** *Physics.* **a.** force or a system of forces producing deformation or strain. **b.** the force acting per unit area. **6.** mental, emotional, or physical strain or tension. ~*vb.* (*tr.*) **7.** to give emphasis or prominence to. **8.** to pronounce (a word or syllable) more loudly than those that surround it. **9.** to subject to stress. —ˈ**stressful** *adj.*

stretch (strɛtʃ) *vb.* **1.** to draw out or extend or be drawn out or extended in length, area, etc. **2.** to extend or be extended to an undue degree, esp. so as to distort or lengthen permanently. **3.** to extend (the limbs, body, etc.). **4.** (*tr.*) to reach or suspend (a rope, etc.) from one place to another. **5.** (*tr.*) to draw tight; tighten. **6.** (often foll. by *out, forward,* etc.) to reach or hold (out); extend. **7.** (*intr.;* usually foll. by *over*) to extend in time: *the course stretched over three months.* **8.** (*intr.;* foll. by *for, over,* etc.) (of a region, etc.) to extend in length or area. **9.** (*intr.*) (esp. of a garment) to be capable of expanding, as to a larger size: *socks that will stretch.* **10.** (*tr.*) to put a great strain upon or extend to the limit. **11.** to injure (a muscle, tendon, etc.) by means of a strain or sprain. **12.** (*tr.;* often foll. by *out*) to make do with (limited resources): *to stretch one's budget.* **13.** (*tr.*) *Inf.* to expand or elaborate (a story, etc.) beyond what is credible or acceptable. **14.** (*tr.; often passive*) to extend, as to the limit of one's abilities or talents. **15.** *Arch. or sl.* to hang or be hanged by the neck. **16. stretch a point. a.** to make a concession or exception not usually made. **b.** to exaggerate. **17. stretch one's legs.** to take a walk, esp. after a period of inactivity. ~*n.* **18.** the act of stretching or state of being stretched. **19.** a large or continuous expanse or distance: *a stretch of water.* **20.** extent in time, length, area, etc. **21. a.** capacity for being stretched, as in some garments. **b.** (*as modifier*): *stretch pants.* **22.** the section or sections of a racecourse that are straight, esp. the final section leading to the finishing line. **23.** *Sl.* a term of imprisonment. **24. at a stretch.** Chiefly *Brit.* **a.** with some difficulty; by making a special effort. **b.** if really necessary or in extreme circumstances. **c.** at one time: *he sometimes read for hours at a stretch.* —ˈ**stretchable** *adj.* —ˌ**stretcha·bil·ity** *n.* —ˈ**stretchy** *adj.*

stretcher (ˈstrɛtʃə) *n.* **1.** a device for transporting the ill, wounded, or dead, consisting of a sheet of canvas stretched between two poles. **2.** a strengthening often decorative member joining the legs of a chair, table, etc. **3.** the wooden frame on which canvas is stretched and fixed for oil painting. **4.** a tie beam or brace used in a structural framework. **5.** a brick or stone laid horizontally with its length parallel to the length of a wall. **6.** *Rowing.* a fixed board across a boat on which an oarsman braces his feet. **7.** *Austral.* a camp bed.

stretcher-bearer *n.* an attendant who helps to carry a stretcher or litter, esp. in wartime.

strew (struː) *vb.* **strewing, strewed; strewn** or **strewed.** to spread or scatter or be spread or scattered, as over a surface or area. —ˈ**strewer** *n.*

strewth (struːθ) *interj.* an expression of surprise or dismay.

stria (ˈstraɪə) *n.,* *pl.* **striae** (ˈstraɪiː). (*often pl.*) **1.** Also called: **striation.** *Geol.* any of the parallel scratches or grooves on the surface of a rock over which a glacier has flowed or on the surface of a crystal. **2.** *Biol., anat.* a narrow band of colour or a ridge, groove, or similar lin-

ear mark. **3.** *Archit.* a narrow channel, such as a flute on the shaft of a column.

striation (straɪˈeɪʃən) *n.* **1.** an arrangement or pattern of striae. **2.** the condition of being striate. **3.** another word for **stria** (sense 1).

stricken (ˈstrɪkən) *adj.* **1.** laid low, as by disease or sickness. **2.** deeply affected, as by grief, love, etc. **3.** *Arch.* wounded or injured. **4. stricken in years.** made feeble by age. —ˈ**strickenly** *adv.*

strict (strɪkt) *adj.* **1.** adhering closely to specified rules, ordinances, etc. **2.** complied with or enforced stringently; rigorous: *a strict code of conduct.* **3.** severely correct in attention to conduct or morality: *a strict teacher.* **4.** (of a punishment, etc.) harsh; severe. **5.** (*prenominal*) complete; absolute: *strict secrecy.* —ˈ**strictly** *adv.* —ˈ**strictness** *n.*

stricture (ˈstrɪktʃə) *n.* **1.** a severe criticism; censure. **2.** *Pathol.* an abnormal constriction of a tubular organ or part. —ˈ**strictured** *adj.*

stride (straɪd) *n.* **1.** a long step or pace. **2.** the space measured by such a step. **3.** a striding gait. **4.** an act of forward movement by a horse, etc. **5.** progress or development (esp. in **make rapid strides**). **6.** a regular pace or rate of progress: *to get into one's stride; to be put off one's stride.* **7.** (*pl.*) *Austral. inf.* men's trousers. **8. take (something) in one's stride.** to do (something) without difficulty or effort. ~*vb.* **striding, strode, stridden.** **9.** (*intr.*) to walk with long regular or measured paces, as in haste, etc. **10.** (*tr.*) to cover or traverse by striding: *he strode thirty miles.* **11.** (often foll. by *over, across,* etc.) to cross (over a space, obstacle, etc.) with a stride. **12.** *Arch. or poetic.* to straddle or bestride. —ˈ**strider** *n.*

strident (ˈstraɪdənt) *adj.* **1.** (of a shout, voice, etc.) loud or harsh. **2.** urgent, clamorous, or vociferous: *strident demands.* —ˈ**stridence** or ˈ**stridency** *n.* —ˈ**stridently** *adv.*

strife (straɪf) *n.* **1.** angry or violent struggle; conflict. **2.** rivalry or contention, esp. of a bitter kind. **3.** *Austral. & N.Z. inf.* trouble or discord of any kind. **4.** *Arch.* striving.

strike (straɪk) *vb.* **striking, struck.** **1.** to deliver (a blow or stroke) to (a person). **2.** to come or cause to come into sudden or violent contact (with). **3.** (*tr.*) to make an attack on. **4.** to produce (fire, sparks, etc.) or (of fire, sparks, etc.) to be produced by ignition. **5.** to cause (a match) to light by friction or (of a match) to be lighted. **6.** to press (the key of a piano, organ, etc.) or to sound (a specific note) in this or a similar way. **7.** to indicate (a specific time) by the sound of a hammer striking a bell or by any other percussive sound. **8.** (of a venomous snake) to cause injury by biting. **9.** (*tr.*) to affect or cause to affect deeply, suddenly, or radically: *her appearance struck him as strange.* **10.** (*past participle* **struck** or **stricken**) (*tr.; passive;* usually foll. by *with*) to render incapable or nearly so: *stricken with grief.* **11.** (*tr.*) to enter the mind of: *it struck me that he had become very quiet.* **12.** (*past participle* **struck** or **stricken**) to render: *struck dumb.* **13.** (*tr.*) to be perceived by; catch: *the glint of metal struck his eye.* **14.** to arrive at or come upon (something), esp. suddenly or unexpectedly: *to strike the path for home; to strike upon a solution.* **15.** (*intr.;* sometimes foll. by *out*) to set (out) or proceed, esp. upon a new course: *to strike out for the coast.* **16.** (*tr.; usually passive*) to afflict with a disease, esp. unexpectedly: *he was struck with polio.* **17.** (*tr.*) to discover or come upon a source of (ore, petroleum, etc.). **18.** (*tr.*) (of a plant) to produce or send down (a root or roots). **19.** (*tr.*) to take apart or pack up; break (esp. in **strike camp**). **20.** (*tr.*) to take down or dismantle (a stage set). **21.** (*tr.*) *Naut.* **a.** to lower or remove (a specified piece of gear). **b.** to haul down or dip (a flag, sail, etc.) in salute or in surrender. **22.** to attack (an objective). **23.** to im-

stress *n.* **1.** emphasis, force, importance, significance, urgency, weight **2.** anxiety, burden, hassle (*Inf.*), nervous tension, oppression, pressure, strain, tautness, tension, trauma, worry **3.** accent, accentuation, beat, emphasis ~*v.* **4.** accentuate, belabour, dwell on, emphasize, harp on, lay emphasis upon, point up, repeat, rub in, underline, underscore

stretch *v.* **1.** cover, extend, put forth, reach, spread, unfold, unroll **2.** distend, draw out, elongate, expand, inflate, lengthen, pull, pull out of shape, rack, strain, swell, tighten ~*n.* **3.** area, distance, expanse, extent, spread, sweep, tract **4.** bit, period, run, space, spell, stint, term, time

strict 1. austere, authoritarian, firm, harsh, no-nonsense, rigid, rigorous, severe, stern, stringent **2.** accurate, close, exact, faithful, meticulous, particular, precise, religious, scrupulous, true **3.** absolute, complete, perfect, total, utter

strident clamorous, clashing, discordant, grating, harsh, jangling, jarring, rasping, raucous, screeching, shrill, stridulant, stridulous, unmusical, vociferous

strife animosity, battle, bickering, clash, clashes, combat, conflict, contention, contest, controversy, discord, dissension, friction, quarrel, rivalry, row, squabbling, struggle, warfare, wrangling

pale the hook in the mouth of (a fish) by suddenly tightening or jerking the line after the bait has been taken. **24.** (*tr.*) to form or impress (a coin, metal, etc.) by or as if by stamping. **25.** to level (a surface) by use of a flat board. **26.** (*tr.*) to assume or take up (an attitude, posture, etc.). **27.** (*intr.*) (of workers in a factory, etc.) to cease work collectively as a protest against working conditions, low pay, etc. **28.** (*tr.*) to reach by agreement: *to strike a bargain.* **29.** (*tr.*) to form (a jury, esp. a special jury) by cancelling certain names among those nominated for jury service until only the requisite number remains. **30. strike home. a.** to deliver an effective blow. **b.** to achieve the intended effect. **31. strike it rich.** *Inf.* **a.** to discover an extensive deposit of a mineral, petroleum, etc. **b.** to have an unexpected financial success. ~*n.* **32.** an act or instance of striking. **33.** a cessation of work, as a protest against working conditions or low pay: *on strike.* **34.** a military attack, esp. an air attack on a surface target: *air strike.* **35.** *Baseball.* a pitched ball judged good but missed or not swung at, three of which cause a batter to be out. **36.** Also called: **ten-strike.** *Tenpin bowling.* **a.** the act or an instance of knocking down all the pins with the first bowl of a single frame. **b.** the score thus made. **37.** a sound made by striking. **38.** the mechanism that makes a clock strike. **39.** the discovery of a source of ore, petroleum, etc. **40.** the horizontal direction of a fault, rock stratum, etc. **41.** *Angling.* the act or an instance of striking. **42.** *Inf.* an unexpected or complete success, esp. one that brings financial gain. **43. take strike.** *Cricket.* (of a batsman) to prepare to play a ball delivered by the bowler. ~See also **strike off, strike out,** etc.

strikebreaker ('straɪkˌbreɪkə) *n.* a person who tries to make a strike ineffectual by working or by taking the place of those on strike. —'**strike,breaking** *n., adj.*

strike off *vb.* (*tr.*) **1.** to remove or erase from (a list, record, etc.) by or as if by a stroke of the pen. **2.** (*adv.*) to cut off or separate by or as if by a blow: *she was struck off from the inheritance.*

strike out *vb.* (*adv.*) **1.** (*tr.*) to remove or erase. **2.** (*intr.*) to start out or begin: *to strike out on one's own.* **3.** *Baseball.* to put out or be put out on strikes. **4.** (*intr.*) *U.S. inf.* to fail utterly.

strike pay *n.* money paid to strikers from the funds of a trade union.

striker ('straɪkə) *n.* **1.** a person who is on strike. **2.** the hammer in a timepiece that rings a bell or alarm. **3.** any part in a mechanical device that strikes something, such as the firing pin of a gun. **4.** *Soccer, inf.* an attacking player, esp. one who generally positions himself near his opponent's goal in the hope of scoring. **5.** *Cricket.* the batsman who is about to play a ball.

strike up *vb.* (*adv.*) **1.** (of a band, orchestra, etc.) to begin to play or sing. **2.** (*tr.*) to bring about; cause to begin: *to strike up a friendship.*

striking ('straɪkɪŋ) *adj.* **1.** attracting attention; fine; impressive: *a striking beauty.* **2.** conspicuous; noticeable: *a striking difference.* —'**strikingly** *adv.* —'**strikingness** *n.*

Strine (straɪn) *n.* a humorous transliteration of Australian pronunciation, as in *Gloria Soame* for *glorious home.*

string (strɪŋ) *n.* **1.** a thin length of cord, twine, fibre, or similar material used for tying, hanging, binding, etc. **2.** a group of objects threaded on a single strand: *a string of beads.* **3.** a series or succession of things, events, etc.: *a string of oaths.* **4.** a number, chain, or group of similar things, animals, etc., owned by or associated with one person or body: *a string of girlfriends.* **5.** a tough fibre or cord in a plant. **6.** *Music.* a tightly stretched wire, cord, etc., found on stringed instruments, such as the violin, guitar, and piano. **7.** short for **bowstring. 8.** *Archit.* short for **string course** or **stringer** (sense 1). **9.** (*pl.;*

usually preceded by *the*) **a.** violins, violas, cellos, and double basses collectively. **b.** the section of a symphony orchestra constituted by such instruments. **10.** (*pl.*) complications or conditions (esp. in **strings attached**). **11.** (*modifier*) composed of string-like strands woven in a large mesh: *a string bag; string vest.* **12. first** (**second,** etc.) **string.** a person or thing regarded as a primary (secondary, etc.) source of strength. **13. keep on a string.** to have control or a hold over (a person), esp. emotionally. **14. pull strings.** *Inf.* to exert power or influence, esp. secretly or unofficially. **15. pull the strings.** to have real or ultimate control of something. ~*vb.* **stringing, strung. 16.** (*tr.*) to provide with a string or strings. **17.** (*tr.*) to suspend or stretch from one point to another. **18.** (*tr.*) to thread on a string. **19.** (*tr.*) to form or extend in a line or series. **20.** (foll. by *out*) to space or spread out at intervals. **21.** (*tr.*; usually foll. by *up*) *Inf.* to kill (a person) by hanging. **22.** (*tr.*) to remove the stringy parts from (vegetables, esp. beans). **23.** (*intr.*) (esp. of viscous liquids) to become stringy or ropy. **24.** (*tr.;* often foll. by *up*) to cause to be tense or nervous. —'**string,like** *adj.*

string along *vb.* (*adv.*) *Inf.* **1.** (*intr.*: often foll. by *with*) to agree or appear to be in agreement (with). **2.** (*intr.*: often foll. by *with*) to accompany. **3.** to deceive or hoax, esp. in order to gain time.

stringboard ('strɪŋˌbɔːd) *n.* a skirting that covers the ends of the steps in a staircase. Also called: **stringer.**

string course *n. Archit.* an ornamental projecting band or continuous moulding along a wall. Also called: **cordon.**

stringed (strɪŋd) *adj.* (of musical instruments) having or provided with strings.

stringent ('strɪndʒənt) *adj.* **1.** requiring strict attention to rules, procedure, detail, etc. **2.** *Finance.* characterized by or causing a shortage of credit, loan capital, etc. —'**stringency** *n.* —'**stringently** *adv.*

stringer ('strɪŋə) *n.* **1.** *Archit.* **a.** a long horizontal timber beam that is used for structural purposes. **b.** another name for **stringboard. 2.** *Naut.* a longitudinal structural brace for strengthening the hull of a vessel. **3.** a journalist retained by a newspaper or news service on a part-time basis to cover a particular town or area.

string quartet *n. Music.* **1.** an instrumental ensemble consisting of two violins, one viola, and one cello. **2.** a piece of music for such a group.

stringy ('strɪŋɪ) *adj.* **-ier, -iest. 1.** made of strings or resembling strings. **2.** (of meat, etc.) fibrous. **3.** (of a person's build) wiry; sinewy. **4.** (of liquids) forming in strings. —'**stringily** *adv.* —'**stringiness** *n.*

strip¹ (strɪp) *vb.* **stripping, stripped. 1.** to take or pull (the covering, clothes, etc.) off (oneself, another person, or thing). **2.** (*intr.*) **a.** to remove all one's clothes. **b.** to perform a striptease. **3.** (*tr.*) to denude or empty completely. **4.** (*tr.*) to deprive of: *he was stripped of his pride.* **5.** (*tr.*) to rob or plunder. **6. a.** to remove the leaves from the stalks of (tobacco, etc.). **b.** to separate the leaves from the stems of (tobacco, etc.). **7.** (*tr.*) *Agriculture.* to draw the last milk from (a cow). **8.** to dismantle (an engine, mechanism, etc.). **9.** to tear off or break (the thread) from (a screw, bolt, etc.) or (the teeth) from (a gear). **10.** (often foll. by *down*) to remove the accessories from (a motor vehicle): *his car was stripped down.* ~*n.* **11.** the act or an instance of undressing or of performing a striptease.

strip² (strɪp) *n.* **1.** a relatively long, flat, narrow piece of something. **2.** short for **airstrip. 3.** *Inf.* the clothes worn by the members of a team, esp. a football team. **4. tear (someone) off a strip.** to rebuke (someone) angrily. ~*vb.* **stripping, stripped. 5.** to cut or divide into strips.

THESAURUS

strike *v.* 1. bang, beat, box, buffet, chastise, clobber (*Sl.*), clout (*Inf.*), clump (*Sl.*), cuff, hammer, hit, knock, lay a finger on (*Inf.*), pound, punish, slap, smack, smite, sock (*Sl.*), thump, wallop (*Inf.*) 2. be in collision with, bump into, clash, collide with, come into contact with, dash, hit, knock into, run into, smash into, touch 3. drive, force, hit, impel, thrust 4. affect, come to, come to the mind of, dawn on or upon, hit, impress, make an impact on, occur to, reach, register (*Inf.*),

seem 5. *Sometimes with* **upon** come upon *or* across, discover, encounter, find, happen *or* chance upon, hit upon, light upon, reach, stumble upon *or* across, turn up, uncover, unearth 6. affect, assail, assault, attack, deal a blow to, devastate, fall upon, hit, invade, set upon, smite 7. achieve, arrange, arrive at, attain, effect, reach 8. down tools, mutiny, revolt, walk out

striking astonishing, conspicuous, dazzling, extraordinary, forcible, impressive,

memorable, noticeable, out of the ordinary, outstanding, stunning (*Inf.*), wonderful

string *n.* 1. cord, fibre, twine 2. chain, file, line, procession, queue, row, sequence, series, strand, succession ~*v.* 3. festoon, hang, link, loop, sling, stretch, suspend, thread 4. *With* **out** disperse, extend, fan out, lengthen, protract, space out, spread out, straggle

stringent binding, demanding, exacting, inflexible, rigid, rigorous, severe, strict, tight, tough

strip cartoon n. a sequence of drawings in a newspaper, magazine, etc., relating a humorous story or an adventure. Also called: **comic strip.**

strip club n. a small club in which striptease performances take place.

stripe[1] (straɪp) n. **1.** a relatively long band of colour or texture that differs from the surrounding material or background. **2.** a fabric having such bands. **3.** a strip, band, or chevron worn on a military uniform, etc., esp. to indicate rank. **4.** *Chiefly U.S.* kind; type: *a man of a certain stripe.* ~vb. **5.** (tr.) to mark with stripes. —**striped** adj.

stripe[2] (straɪp) n. a stroke from a whip, rod, cane, etc.

strip lighting n. electric lighting by means of long glass tubes that are fluorescent lamps or that contain long filaments.

stripling ('strɪplɪŋ) n. a lad.

stripper ('strɪpə) n. **1.** a striptease artist. **2.** a person or thing that strips. **3.** a device or substance for removing paint, varnish, etc.

striptease ('strɪp,tiːz) n. **a.** a form of erotic entertainment in which a person gradually undresses to music. **b.** (as modifier): *a striptease club.* —**'strip,teaser** n.

stripy ('straɪpɪ) adj. **stripier, stripiest.** marked by or with stripes; striped.

strive (straɪv) vb. **striving, strove, striven. 1.** (may take a clause as object or an infinitive) to make a great and tenacious effort. **2.** (intr.) to fight; contend. —**'striver** n.

strobe (strəʊb) n. short for **strobe lighting** or **stroboscope.**

strobe lighting n. **1.** a high-intensity flashing beam of light produced by rapid electrical discharges in a tube or by a perforated disc rotating in front of an intense light source. **2.** the use of or the apparatus for producing such light. Sometimes shortened to **strobe.**

stroboscope ('strəʊbə,skəʊp) n. **1.** an instrument producing an intense flashing light, the frequency of which can be synchronized with some multiple of the frequency of rotation, vibration, or operation of an object, etc., making it appear stationary. Sometimes shortened to **strobe. 2.** a similar device synchronized with the shutter of a camera so that a series of still photographs can be taken of a moving object. —**stroboscopic** (,strəʊbə-'skɒpɪk) or **,strobo'scopical** adj. —**,strobo'scopically** adv.

strode (strəʊd) vb. the past tense of **stride.**

stroganoff ('strɒgə,nɒf) n. a dish of sliced beef cooked with onions and mushrooms, served in a sour-cream sauce. Also called: **beef stroganoff.**

stroke (strəʊk) n. **1.** the act or an instance of striking; a blow, knock, or hit. **2.** a sudden action, movement, or occurrence: *a stroke of luck.* **3.** a brilliant or inspired act or feat: *a stroke of genius.* **4.** *Pathol.* apoplexy; rupture of a blood vessel in the brain resulting in loss of consciousness, often followed by paralysis, or embolism or thrombosis affecting a cerebral vessel. **5. a.** the striking of a clock. **b.** the hour registered by this: *on the stroke of three.* **6.** a mark made by a writing implement. **7.** another name for **solidus,** used esp. when dictating or reading aloud. **8.** a light touch or caress, as with the fingers. **9.** a pulsation, esp. of the heart. **10.** a single complete movement or one of a series of complete movements. **11.** *Sport.* the act or manner of striking the ball with a racket, club, bat, etc. **12.** any one of the repeated movements used by a swimmer. **13.** a manner of swimming, esp. one of several named styles such as the crawl. **14. a.** any one of a series of linear movements of a reciprocating part, such as a piston. **b.** the distance travelled by such a part from one end of its movement to the other. **15.** a single pull on an oar or oars in rowing. **16.** manner or style of rowing. **17.** the oarsman who sits nearest the stern of a shell, facing the cox, and sets the rate of rowing. **18. a stroke (of work).** (usually used with a negative) a small amount of work. **19. off one's stroke.** performing or working less well than usual. **20. on the stroke.** punctually. **21. at a stroke.** with one action. ~vb. **22.** (tr.) to touch, brush, or caress lightly or gently. **23.** (tr.) to mark a line or a stroke on or through. **24.** to act as the stroke of (a racing shell). **25.** (tr.) *Sport.* to strike (a ball) with a smooth swinging blow.

stroll (strəʊl) vb. **1.** to walk about in a leisurely manner. **2.** (intr.) to wander about. ~n. **3.** a leisurely walk.

strong (strɒŋ) adj. **stronger** ('strɒŋgə), **strongest** ('strɒŋgɪst). **1.** involving or possessing strength. **2.** solid or robust; not easily broken or injured. **3.** resolute or morally firm. **4.** intense in quality; not faint or feeble: *a strong voice; a strong smell.* **5.** easily defensible; incontestable or formidable. **6.** concentrated; not weak or diluted. **7. a.** (postpositive) containing or having a specified number: *a navy 40 000 strong.* **b.** (in combination): *a 40 000-strong navy.* **8.** having an unpleasantly powerful taste or smell. **9.** having an extreme or drastic effect: *strong discipline.* **10.** emphatic or immoderate: *strong language.* **11.** convincing, effective, or cogent. **12.** (of a colour) having a high degree of saturation or purity; produced by a concentrated quantity of colouring agent. **13.** *Grammar.* **a.** of or denoting a class of verbs, in certain languages including the Germanic languages, whose conjugation shows vowel gradation, as *sing, sang, sung.* **b.** belonging to any part-of-speech class, in various languages, whose inflections follow the less regular of two possible patterns. Cf. **weak** (sense 9). **14.** (of a wind, current, etc.) moving fast. **15.** (of a syllable) accented or stressed. **16.** (of an industry, market, etc.) firm in price or characterized by firm or increasing prices. **17.** (of certain acids and bases) producing high concentrations of hydrogen or hydroxide ions in aqueous solution. **18. have a strong stomach.** not to be prone to nausea. ~adv. **19.** *Inf.* in a strong way; effectively: *going strong.* **20. come on strong.** to speak or act forcefully or persuasively. —**'strongly** adv. —**'strongness** n.

strong-arm *Inf.* ~n. **1.** (modifier) of or involving physical force or violence: *strong-arm tactics.* ~vb. **2.** (tr.) to show violence towards.

strongbox ('strɒŋ,bɒks) n. a box or safe in which valuables are locked for safety.

strong drink n. alcoholic drink.

stronghold ('strɒŋ,həʊld) n. **1.** a defensible place; fortress. **2.** a major centre or area of predominance.

strong-minded adj. having strength of mind; resolute and determined. —**,strong-'mindedly** adv. —**,strong-'mindedness** n.

THESAURUS

strings *Fig.* catches (*Inf.*), complications, conditions, obligations, prerequisites, provisos, qualifications, requirements, stipulations

strip[1] v. **1.** bare, denude, deprive, despoil, dismantle, divest, empty, gut, lay bare, loot, peel, pillage, plunder, ransack, rob, sack, skin, spoil **2.** disrobe, unclothe, uncover, undress

strip[2] n. band, belt, bit, fillet, piece, ribbon, shred, slip, swathe, tongue

striped banded, barred, striated, stripy

stripling adolescent, boy, fledgling, hobbledehoy (*Archaic*), lad, shaver (*Inf.*), young fellow, youngster, youth

strive attempt, compete, contend, do all one can, do one's best, do one's utmost, endeavour, exert oneself, fight, go all out (*Inf.*), labour, leave no stone unturned, make every effort, strain, struggle, toil, try, try hard

stroke n. **1.** accomplishment, achievement, blow, feat, flourish, hit, knock, move, movement, pat, rap, thump **2.** apoplexy, attack, collapse, fit, seizure, shock ~v. **3.** caress, fondle, pat, pet, rub

stroll 1. v. amble, make one's way, mooch (*Inf.*), mosey (*Inf.*), promenade, ramble, saunter, stooge (*Inf.*), stretch one's legs, take a turn, toddle, wander **2.** n. airing, breath of air, constitutional, excursion, promenade, ramble, turn, walk

strong 1. athletic, beefy (*Inf.*), brawny, burly, capable, hale, hardy, healthy, Herculean, lusty, muscular, powerful, robust, sinewy, sound, stalwart, stout, strapping, sturdy, tough, virile **2.** aggressive, brave, courageous, determined, firm in spirit, forceful, hard as nails, hard-nosed (*Inf.*), high-powered, plucky, resilient, resolute, resourceful, self-assertive, steadfast, stouthearted, tenacious, tough, unyielding **3.** acute, dedicated, deep, deep-rooted, eager, fervent, fervid, fierce, firm, intense, keen, severe, staunch, vehement, violent, zealous **4.** clear, clear-cut, cogent, compelling, convincing, distinct, effective, formidable, great, marked, overpowering, persuasive, potent, redoubtable, sound, telling, trenchant, unmistakable, urgent, weighty, well-established, well-founded **5.** Draconian, drastic, extreme, forceful, severe **6.** durable, hard-wearing, heavy-duty, on a firm foundation, reinforced, sturdy, substantial, well-armed, well-built, well-protected **7.** bold, bright, brilliant, dazzling, glaring, loud, stark **8.** biting, concentrated, heady, highly-flavoured, highly-seasoned, hot, intoxicating, piquant, pungent, pure, sharp, spicy, undiluted

stronghold bastion, bulwark, castle, citadel, fastness, fort, fortress, keep, refuge

strong-minded determined, firm, independent, iron-willed, resolute, strong-willed, unbending, uncompromising

strongroom ('strɒŋˌruːm, -ˌrʊm) *n.* a specially designed room in which valuables are locked for safety.

strontium ('strɒntɪəm) *n.* a soft silvery-white element of the alkaline earth group of metals. The radioisotope **strontium-90**, with a half-life of 28.1 years, is used in nuclear power sources and is a hazardous nuclear fall-out product. Symbol: Sr; atomic no.: 38; atomic wt.: 87.62.

strop (strɒp) *n.* 1. a leather strap or an abrasive strip for sharpening razors. 2. a rope or metal band around a block or deadeye for support. ~*vb.* **stropping, stropped.** 3. (*tr.*) to sharpen (a razor, etc.) on a strop.

stroppy ('strɒpɪ) *adj.* **-pier, -piest.** *Brit. sl.* angry or awkward.

strove (strəʊv) *vb.* the past tense of **strive.**

struck (strʌk) *vb.* 1. the past tense or past participle of **strike.** ~*adj.* 2. *Chiefly U.S.* (of an industry, factory, etc.) shut down or otherwise affected by a labour strike.

structural ('strʌktʃərəl) *adj.* 1. of, relating to, or having structure or a structure. 2. of or relating to the structure of the earth's crust. 3. of or relating to the structure of organisms. 4. *Chem.* of or involving the arrangement of atoms in molecules. —'**structurally** *adv.*

structuralism ('strʌktʃərəˌlɪzəm) *n.* 1. an approach to social sciences and to literature in terms of oppositions, contrasts, and hierarchical structures, esp. as they might reflect universal mental characteristics or organizing principles. 2. an approach to linguistics that analyses and describes the structure of language, as distinguished from its comparative and historical aspects. —'**structuralist** *n., adj.*

structure ('strʌktʃə) *n.* 1. a complex construction or entity. 2. the arrangement and interrelationship of parts in a construction. 3. the manner of construction or organization. 4. *Chem.* the arrangement of atoms in a molecule of a chemical compound. 5. *Geol.* the way in which a mineral, rock, etc., is made up of its component parts. ~*vb.* 6. to impart a structure to.

strudel ('struːdəl) *n.* a thin sheet of filled dough rolled up and baked: *apple strudel.*

struggle ('strʌɡəl) *vb.* 1. (*intr.; usually foll. by for or against; may take an infinitive*) to exert strength, energy, and force; work or strive. 2. (*intr.*) to move about strenuously so as to escape from something confining. 3. (*intr.*) to contend, battle, or fight. 4. (*intr.*) to go or progress with difficulty. ~*n.* 5. a laboured or strenuous exertion or effort. 6. a fight or battle. 7. the act of struggling. —'**struggler** *n.*

strum (strʌm) *vb.* **strumming, strummed.** 1. to sound (the strings of a guitar, etc.) with a downward or upward sweep of the thumb or of a plectrum. 2. to play (chords, a tune, etc.) in this way. —'**strummer** *n.*

strumpet ('strʌmpɪt) *n.* a prostitute or promiscuous woman.

strung (strʌŋ) *vb.* 1. a past tense and past participle of **string.** ~*adj.* 2. a. (of a piano, etc.) provided with strings. b. (*in combination*): *gut-strung.* 3. **highly strung.** very nervous or volatile in character.

strung up *adj.* (*postpositive*) *Inf.* tense or nervous.

strut (strʌt) *vb.* **strutting, strutted.** 1. (*intr.*) to walk in a pompous manner; swagger. 2. (*tr.*) to support or provide with struts. ~*n.* 3. a structural member, esp. as part of a framework. 4. an affected, proud, or stiff walk. —'**strutter** *n.* —'**struttingly** *adv.*

strychnine ('strɪkniːn) *n.* a white crystalline very poisonous alkaloid, obtained from the plant nux vomica:

used in small quantities as a stimulant.

stub (stʌb) *n.* 1. a short piece remaining after something has been cut, removed, etc.: *a cigar stub.* 2. the residual piece or section of a receipt, ticket, cheque, etc. 3. the usual U.S. word for **counterfoil.** 4. any short projection or blunted end. 5. the stump of a tree or plant. ~*vb.* **stubbing, stubbed.** (*tr.*) 6. to strike (one's toe, foot, etc.) painfully against a hard surface. 7. (usually foll. by *out*) to put (out a cigarette or cigar) by pressing the end against a surface. 8. to clear (land) of stubs. 9. to dig up (the roots) of (a tree or bush).

stubble ('stʌbəl) *n.* 1. **a.** the stubs of stalks left in a field where a crop has been harvested. **b.** (*as modifier*): *a stubble field.* 2. any bristly growth. —'**stubbled** or '**stubbly** *adj.*

stubborn ('stʌbən) *adj.* 1. refusing to comply, agree, or give in. 2. difficult to handle, treat, or overcome. 3. persistent and dogged. —'**stubbornly** *adv.* —'**stubbornness** *n.*

stubby ('stʌbɪ) *adj.* **-bier, -biest.** 1. short and broad; stumpy or thickset. 2. bristling and stiff. ~*n. Austral. sl.* 3. a small bottle of beer. —'**stubbily** *adv.* —'**stubbiness** *n.*

stucco ('stʌkəʊ) *n., pl.* **-coes** or **-cos.** 1. a weather-resistant mixture of dehydrated lime, powdered marble, and glue, used in decorative mouldings on buildings. 2. any of various types of cement or plaster used for coating outside walls. 3. Also called: **stuccowork.** decorative work moulded in stucco. ~*vb.* **-coing, -coed.** 4. (*tr.*) to apply stucco to.

stuck (stʌk) *vb.* 1. the past tense or past participle of **stick².** ~*adj.* 2. *Inf.* baffled or nonplussed. 3. (foll. by *on*) *Sl.* keen (on) or infatuated (with). 4. **get stuck in** or **into.** *Inf.* **a.** to perform (a task) with determination. **b.** to attack (a person).

stuck-up *adj. Inf.* conceited, arrogant, or snobbish. —'**stuck-'upness** *n.*

stud¹ (stʌd) *n.* 1. a large-headed nail or other projection protruding from a surface, usually as decoration. 2. a type of fastener consisting of two discs at either end of a short shank, used to fasten shirtfronts, collars, etc. 3. a vertical member used with others to construct the framework of a wall. 4. the cross bar in the centre of a link of a heavy chain. 5. one of a number of rounded projections on the sole of a boot or shoe to give better grip, as on a football boot. ~*vb.* **studding, studded.** (*tr.*) 6. to provide, ornament, or make with studs. 7. to dot or cover with: *the park was studded with daisies.* 8. to provide or support (a wall, partition, etc.) with studs.

stud² (stʌd) *n.* 1. a group of pedigree animals, esp. horses, kept for breeding purposes. 2. any male animal kept principally for breeding purposes, esp. a stallion. 3. a farm or stable where a stud is kept. 4. the state or condition of being kept for breeding purposes: *at stud; put to stud.* 5. (*modifier*) of or relating to such animals or the place where they are kept: *a stud farm; a stud horse.* 6. *Sl.* a virile or sexually active man.

studbook ('stʌdˌbʊk) *n.* a written record of the pedigree of a purebred stock, esp. of racehorses.

student ('stjuːdənt) *n.* 1. a person following a course of study, as in a school, college, university, etc. 2. a person who makes a thorough study of a subject.

studied ('stʌdɪd) *adj.* carefully practised, designed, or premeditated: *a studied reply.* —'**studiedly** *adv.* —'**studiedness** *n.*

studio ('stjuːdɪəʊ) *n., pl.* **-dios.** 1. a room in which an art-

---

THESAURUS

structure *n.* 1. arrangement, configuration, conformation, construction, design, fabric, form, formation, interrelation of parts, make, make-up, organization 2. building, construction, edifice, erection, pile ~*v.* 3. arrange, assemble, build up, design, organize, put together, shape

struggle *v.* 1. exert oneself, go all out (*Inf.*), labour, make every effort, strain, strive, toil, work, work like a Trojan ~*n.* 2. effort, exertion, grind (*Inf.*), labour, long haul, pains, scramble, toil, work ~*v.* 3. battle, compete, contend, fight, grapple, lock horns, scuffle, wrestle ~*n.* 4. battle, brush, clash, combat, conflict, contest, encounter, hostilities, skirmish, strife, tussle

strut *v.* parade, peacock, prance, stalk, swagger

stub *n.* butt, counterfoil, dog-end (*Inf.*), end, fag end (*Inf.*), remnant, stump, tail, tail end

stubborn bull-headed, contumacious, cross-grained, dogged, dour, fixed, headstrong, inflexible, intractable, mulish, obdurate, obstinate, opinionated, persistent, pig-headed, recalcitrant, refractory, self-willed, stiff-necked, tenacious, unbending, unmanageable, unshakable, unyielding, wilful

stuck 1. cemented, fast, fastened, firm, fixed, glued, joined 2. *Inf.* at a loss, at a standstill, at one's wits' end, baffled, beaten, bereft of ideas, nonplussed, stumped, up against a brick wall (*Inf.*) 3. *Sl. With* **on** enthusiastic about, hung up on (*Sl.*), infatuated, keen,

mad, obsessed with, wild about (*Inf.*) 4. **get stuck into** *Inf.* get down to, make a start on, set about, tackle

stuck-up arrogant, big-headed (*Inf.*), conceited, condescending, haughty, high and mighty (*Inf.*), hoity-toity (*Inf.*), patronizing, proud, snobbish, snooty (*Inf.*), swollen-headed, toffee-nosed (*Sl.*), uppish (*Brit. inf.*), uppity (*Inf.*)

stud *v.* bejewel, bespangle, dot, fleck, ornament, spangle, speckle, spot, sprinkle

student apprentice, disciple, learner, observer, pupil, scholar, undergraduate

studied calculated, conscious, deliberate, intentional, planned, premeditated, purposeful, well-considered, wilful

ist, photographer, or musician works. **2.** a room used to record television or radio programmes, make films, etc. **3.** (*pl.*) the premises of a radio, television, or film company.

studio couch *n.* an upholstered couch, usually backless, convertible into a double bed.

studious (ˈstjuːdɪəs) *adj.* **1.** given to study. **2.** of a serious, thoughtful, and hard-working character. **3.** showing deliberation, care, or precision. —ˈ**studiously** *adv.* —ˈ**studiousness** *n.*

study (ˈstʌdɪ) *vb.* **studying, studied.** **1.** to apply the mind to the learning or understanding of (a subject), esp. by reading. **2.** (*tr.*) to investigate or examine, as by observation, research, etc. **3.** (*tr.*) to look at minutely; scrutinize. **4.** (*tr.*) to give much careful or critical thought to. **5.** to take a course in (a subject), as at a college. **6.** (*tr.*) to try to memorize: *to study a part for a play.* **7.** (*intr.*) to meditate or contemplate; reflect. ~*n.*, *pl.* **studies.** **8. a.** the act or process of studying. **b.** (*as modifier*): *study group.* **9.** a room used for studying, reading, writing, etc. **10.** (*often pl.*) work relating to a particular discipline: *environmental studies.* **11.** a product of studying, such as a written paper or book. **12.** a drawing, sculpture, etc., executed for practice or in preparation for another work. **13.** a musical composition intended to develop one aspect of performing technique. **14. in a brown study.** in a reverie or daydream.

stuff (stʌf) *vb.* (*mainly tr.*) **1.** to pack or fill completely; cram. **2.** (*intr.*) to eat large quantities. **3.** to force, shove, or squeeze: *to stuff money into a pocket.* **4.** to fill (food such as poultry or tomatoes) with a stuffing. **5.** to fill (an animal's skin) with material so as to restore the shape of the live animal. **6.** *Taboo sl.* to have sexual intercourse with (a woman). **7.** *U.S.* to fill (a ballot box) with fraudulent votes. ~*n.* **8.** the raw material or fabric of something. **9.** woollen cloth or fabric. **10.** any general or unspecified substance or accumulation of objects. **11.** stupid or worthless actions, speech, etc. **12.** a slang word for **money.** **13.** *Sl.* a drug, esp. cannabis. **14.** *Inf.* **do one's stuff.** to do what is expected of one. **15. that's the stuff.** that is what is needed. **16.** *Taboo sl. offensive.* a girl or woman considered sexually (esp. in **bit of stuff**). —ˈ**stuffer** *n.*

stuffed shirt *n. Inf.* a pompous person.

stuffing (ˈstʌfɪŋ) *n.* **1.** the material with which something is stuffed. **2.** a mixture of ingredients with which poultry, meat, etc., is stuffed before cooking. **3. knock the stuffing out of (someone).** to defeat (someone) utterly.

stuffy (ˈstʌfɪ) *adj.* **-ier, -iest.** **1.** lacking fresh air. **2.** excessively dull, staid, or conventional. **3.** (of the nasal passages) blocked with mucus. —ˈ**stuffily** *adv.* —ˈ**stuffiness** *n.*

stultify (ˈstʌltɪˌfaɪ) *vb.* **-fying, -fied.** (*tr.*) **1.** to make useless, futile, or ineffectual, esp. by routine. **2.** to cause to appear absurd or inconsistent. —ˌ**stultifiˈcation** *n.* —ˈ**stultiˌfier** *n.*

stumble (ˈstʌmbᵊl) *vb.* (*intr.*) **1.** to trip or fall while walking or running. **2.** to walk in an awkward, unsteady, or unsure way. **3.** to make mistakes or hesitate in speech or actions. **4.** (foll. by *across* or *upon*) to come (across) by accident. ~*n.* **5.** a false step, trip, or blunder. **6.** the act of stumbling. —ˈ**stumbler** *n.* —ˈ**stumblingly** *adv.*

stumbling block *n.* any impediment or obstacle.

stump (stʌmp) *n.* **1.** the base of a tree trunk left standing after the tree has been felled or has fallen. **2.** the part of something, such as a tooth, limb, or blade, that remains after a larger part has been removed. **3.** (*often pl.*) *Inf.* a leg (esp. in **stir one's stumps**). **4.** *Cricket.* any of three upright wooden sticks that, with two bails laid across them, form a wicket (the **stumps**). **5.** Also called: **tortillon.** a short sharply-pointed stick of cork or rolled paper or leather, used in drawing and shading. **6.** a heavy tread or the sound of heavy footsteps. **7.** a platform used by an orator when addressing a meeting. ~*vb.* **8.** (*tr.*) to stop, confuse, or puzzle. **9.** (*intr.*) to plod or trudge heavily. **10.** (*tr.*) *Cricket.* to dismiss (a batsman) by breaking his wicket with the ball or with the ball in the hand while he is out of his crease. **11.** *Chiefly U.S.* to campaign or canvass (an area), esp. by political speech-making. —ˈ**stumper** *n.*

stump up *vb.* (*adv.*) *Brit. inf.* to give (the money required).

stumpy (ˈstʌmpɪ) *adj.* **-ier, -iest.** **1.** like a stump. **2.** full of stumps. —ˈ**stumpiness** *n.*

stun (stʌn) *vb.* **stunning, stunned.** (*tr.*) **1.** to render unconscious, as by a heavy blow or fall. **2.** to shock or overwhelm. **3.** to surprise or astound. ~*n.* **4.** the state or effect of being stunned.

stung (stʌŋ) *vb.* the past tense or past participle of **sting.**

stunk (stʌŋk) *vb.* a past tense or past participle of **stink.**

stunner (ˈstʌnə) *n. Inf.* a person or thing of great beauty, quality, size, etc.

stunning (ˈstʌnɪŋ) *adj. Inf.* very attractive, impressive, astonishing, etc. —ˈ**stunningly** *adv.*

stunt[1] (stʌnt) *vb.* **1.** (*tr.*) to prevent or impede (the growth or development) of (a plant, animal, etc.). ~*n.* **2.** the act or an instance of stunting. **3.** a person, animal, or plant that has been stunted. —ˈ**stunted** *adj.* —ˈ**stuntedness** *n.*

stunt[2] (stʌnt) *n.* **1. a.** a feat of daring or skill. **b.** (*as modifier*): *a stunt man.* **2.** anything spectacular or unusual done for attention. ~*vb.* **3.** (*intr.*) to perform a stunt or stunts.

stupefacient (ˌstjuːpɪˈfeɪʃɪənt) *or* **stupefactive**

THESAURUS

studio atelier, workshop

studious academic, assiduous, attentive, bookish, careful, diligent, eager, earnest, hard-working, intellectual, meditative, reflective, scholarly, sedulous, serious, thoughtful

study *v.* 1. apply oneself (to), bone up (on) (*Inf.*), burn the midnight oil, cogitate, con (*Archaic*), consider, contemplate, cram (*Inf.*), examine, go into, hammer away at, learn, lucubrate (*Rare*), meditate, mug up (*Brit. sl.*), ponder, pore over, read, read up, swot (up) (*Brit. inf.*) 2. analyse, deliberate, examine, investigate, look into, peruse, research, scrutinize, survey ~*n.* 3. academic work, application, book work, cramming (*Inf.*), learning, lessons, reading, research, school work, swotting (*Brit. inf.*), thought 4. analysis, attention, cogitation, consideration, contemplation, examination, inquiry, inspection, investigation, review, scrutiny, survey

stuff *v.* 1. compress, cram, crowd, fill, force, jam, load, pack, pad, push, ram, shove, squeeze, stow, wedge 2. gobble, gorge, gormandize, guzzle, make a pig of oneself (*Inf.*), overindulge, sate, satiate ~*n.* 3. belongings, bits and pieces, clobber (*Brit. sl.*), effects, equipment, gear, goods and chattels, impedimenta, junk, kit, luggage, materials, objects, paraphernalia, possessions, tackle, things, trappings 4. cloth, fabric, material, raw material, textile 5. essence, matter, pith, quintessence, staple, substance 6. balderdash, baloney (*Inf.*), bosh (*Inf.*), bunk (*Inf.*), bunkum, claptrap (*Inf.*), foolishness, humbug, nonsense, poppycock (*Inf.*), rot, rubbish, stuff and nonsense, tommyrot, tripe (*Inf.*), twaddle, verbiage

stuffing 1. filler, kapok, packing, quilting, wadding 2. farce, farcemeat, forcemeat

stuffy 1. airless, close, fetid, frowsty, fuggy, heavy, muggy, oppressive, stale, stifling, suffocating, sultry, unventilated 2. conventional, deadly, dreary, dull, fusty, humourless, musty, old-fashioned, old-fogyish, pompous, priggish, prim, prim and proper, staid, stilted, stodgy, strait-laced, uninteresting

stumble 1. blunder about, come a cropper (*Inf.*), fall, falter, flounder, hesitate, lose one's balance, lurch, reel, slip, stagger, trip 2. *With* **on** *or* **upon** blunder upon, chance upon, come across, discover, encounter, find, happen upon, light upon, run across, turn up 3. falter, fluff (*Inf.*), stammer, stutter

stump *v.* 1. baffle, bewilder, bring (someone) up short, confound, confuse, dumbfound, flummox, foil, mystify, outwit, perplex, puzzle, stop, stymie 2. clomp, clump, lumber, plod, stamp, stomp (*Inf.*), trudge

stump up chip in (*Inf.*), come across with (*Inf.*), contribute, cough up (*Inf.*), donate, fork out (*Sl.*), hand over, pay, shell out (*Inf.*)

stun *Fig.* amaze, astonish, astound, bewilder, confound, confuse, daze, dumbfound, flabbergast (*Inf.*), hit (someone) like a ton of bricks (*Inf.*), knock out, knock (someone) for six (*Inf.*), overcome, overpower, shock, stagger, strike (someone) dumb (*Inf.*), stupefy, take (someone's) breath away

stung angered, exasperated, goaded, hurt, incensed, nettled, piqued, resentful, roused, wounded

stunned *Fig.* astounded, at a loss for words, bowled over (*Inf.*), dazed, devastated, dumbfounded, flabbergasted (*Inf.*), numb, shocked, staggered, struck dumb (*Inf.*)

stunning beautiful, brilliant, dazzling, devastating (*Inf.*), gorgeous, great (*Inf.*), heavenly, impressive, lovely, marvellous, out of this world (*Inf.*), ravishing, remarkable, sensational, smashing (*Inf.*), spectacular, striking, wonderful

stunt *n.* act, deed, exploit, feat, feature, gest (*Archaic*), *tour de force*, trick

stunted diminutive, dwarfed, dwarfish, little, small, tiny, undersized

(ˌstjuːpɪˈfæktɪv) n. 1. a drug that causes stupor. ~adj. 2. of, relating to, or designating this type of drug.

stupefaction (ˌstjuːpɪˈfækʃən) n. 1. astonishment. 2. the act of stupefying or the state of being stupefied.

stupefy (ˈstjuːpɪˌfaɪ) vb. -fying, -fied. (tr.) 1. to render insensitive or lethargic. 2. to confuse or astound. —ˈstupeˌfier n.

stupendous (stjuːˈpɛndəs) adj. astounding, wonderful, huge, etc. —stuˈpendously adv. —stuˈpendousness n.

stupid (ˈstjuːpɪd) adj. 1. lacking in common sense, perception, or intelligence. 2. (usually postpositive) dazed or stupefied: stupid from lack of sleep. 3. slow-witted. 4. trivial, silly, or frivolous. —stuˈpidity or ˈstupidness n.

stupor (ˈstjuːpə) n. 1. a state of unconsciousness. 2. mental dullness; torpor. —ˈstuporous adj.

sturdy (ˈstɜːdɪ) adj. -dier, -diest. 1. healthy, strong, and vigorous. 2. strongly built; stalwart. —ˈsturdily adv. —ˈsturdiness n.

sturgeon (ˈstɜːdʒən) n. any of various primitive bony fishes of temperate waters of the N hemisphere, having an elongated snout and rows of spines along the body.

stutter (ˈstʌtə) vb. 1. to speak (a word, phrase, etc.) with recurring repetition of consonants, esp. initial ones. 2. to make (an abrupt sound) repeatedly: the gun stuttered. ~n. 3. the act or habit of stuttering. 4. a stuttering sound. —ˈstutterer n. —ˈstuttering n., adj. —ˈstutteringly adv.

sty[1] (staɪ) n., pl. sties. 1. a pen in which pigs are housed. 2. any filthy or corrupt place. ~vb. stying, stied. 3. to enclose or be enclosed in a sty.

sty[2] or **stye** (staɪ) n., pl. sties or styes. inflammation of a sebaceous gland of the eyelid.

Stygian (ˈstɪdʒɪən) adj. 1. of or relating to the Styx, a river in Hades. 2. Chiefly literary. dark, gloomy, or hellish.

style (staɪl) n. 1. a form of appearance, design, or production; type or make. 2. the way in which something is done: good style. 3. the manner in which something is expressed or performed, considered as separate from its intrinsic content, meaning, etc. 4. a distinctive, formal, or characteristic manner of expression in words, music, painting, etc. 5. elegance or refinement of manners, dress, etc. 6. prevailing fashion in dress, looks, etc. 7. a fashionable or ostentatious mode of existence: to live in style. 8. the particular mode of orthography, punctuation, design, etc., followed in a book, journal, etc., or in a printing or publishing house. 9. Chiefly Brit. the distinguishing title or form of address of a person or firm. 10. Bot. the long slender extension of the ovary, bearing the stigma. 11. a method of expressing or calculating dates. 12. another word for stylus (sense 1). 13. the arm of a sundial. ~vb. (mainly tr.) 14. to design, shape, or tailor: to style hair. 15. to adapt or make suitable for. 16. to make consistent or correct according to a printing or publishing style. 17. to name or call; designate: to style a man a fool. —ˈstylar adj. —ˈstyler n.

stylish (ˈstaɪlɪʃ) adj. having style; smart; fashionable. —ˈstylishly adv. —ˈstylishness n.

stylist (ˈstaɪlɪst) n. 1. a person who performs, writes, or acts with attention to style. 2. a designer of clothes, décor, etc. 3. a hairdresser who styles hair.

stylistic (staɪˈlɪstɪk) adj. of or relating to style, esp. artistic or literary style. —ˈstylistically adv.

stylize or **-ise** (ˈstaɪlaɪz) vb. (tr.) to give a conventional or established stylistic form to. —ˌstyliˈzation or -iˈsation n.

stylo- or before a vowel **styl-** combining form. 1. (in biology) a style. 2. indicating a column or point: stylobate; stylograph.

stylus (ˈstaɪləs) n., pl. -li (-laɪ) or -luses. 1. Also called: style. a pointed instrument for engraving, drawing or writing. 2. a tool used in ancient times for writing on wax tablets, which was pointed at one end and blunt at the other for erasing. 3. a device attached to the cartridge in the pickup arm of a gramophone that rests in the groove in the record, transmitting the vibrations to the sensing device in the cartridge.

stymie or **stymy** (ˈstaɪmɪ) vb. -mieing, -mied or -mying, -mied. (tr.; often passive) 1. to hinder or thwart. 2. Golf. to impede with a stymie. ~n., pl. -mies. 3. Golf. a situation in which an opponent's ball is blocking the line between the hole and the ball about to be played. 4. a situation of obstruction.

styptic (ˈstɪptɪk) adj. also **styptical**. 1. contracting the blood vessels or tissues. ~n. 2. a styptic drug.

styrene (ˈstaɪriːn) n. a colourless oily volatile flammable liquid made from ethylene and benzene. It readily polymerizes and is used in making synthetic plastics and rubbers.

suasion (ˈsweɪʒən) n. a rare word for **persuasion**. —ˈsuasive adj.

suave (swɑːv) adj. (esp. of a man) displaying smoothness and sophistication in manner; urbane. —ˈsuavely adv. —**suavity** (ˈswɑːvɪtɪ) or **suaveness** n.

sub (sʌb) n. 1. short for several words beginning with sub-, such as **subeditor, submarine, subordinate, subscription**, and **substitute**. 2. Brit. inf. an advance payment of wages or salary. ~vb. **subbing, subbed**. 3. (intr.) to serve as a substitute. 4. Brit. inf. to grant or receive (an advance payment of wages or salary).

sub- prefix. 1. situated under or beneath: subterranean. 2. secondary in rank; subordinate: subeditor. 3. falling short of; less than or imperfectly: subarctic; subhuman. 4. forming a subdivision or subordinate part: subcommittee. 5. (in chemistry) a. indicating that a compound contains a relatively small proportion of a specified element: suboxide. b. indicating that a salt is basic salt: subacetate.

subaltern (ˈsʌbəltən) n. 1. a commissioned officer below the rank of captain in certain armies, esp. the British. ~adj. 2. of inferior position or rank. 3. Logic. (of a proposition) particular, esp. in relation to a universal of the same quality.

THESAURUS

stupefaction amazement, astonishment, awe, wonder, wonderment

stupefy amaze, astound, bewilder, confound, daze, dumbfound, knock senseless, numb, shock, stagger, stun

stupendous amazing, astounding, breathtaking, colossal, enormous, fabulous (Inf.), fantastic (Inf.), gigantic, huge, marvellous, mind-blowing (Sl.), mind-boggling (Inf.), out of this world (Inf.), overwhelming, phenomenal, prodigious, staggering, stunning (Inf.), superb, surpassing belief, surprising, tremendous (Inf.), vast, wonderful

stupid 1. Boeotian, brainless, cretinous, deficient, dense, dim, doltish, dopey (Sl.), dozy (Brit. inf.), dull, dumb (Inf., chiefly U.S.), foolish, gullible, half-witted, moronic, naive, obtuse, simple, simple-minded, slow, slow on the uptake (Inf.), slow-witted, sluggish, stolid, thick, thickheaded, unintelligent, witless, woodenheaded (Inf.) 2. crackbrained, futile, half-baked (Inf.), idiotic, ill-advised, imbecilic, inane, indiscreet, irrelevant, irresponsible, laughable, ludicrous, meaningless, mindless, nonsensical, pointless, puerile, rash, senseless, short-sighted, trivial, unintel-

ligent, unthinking 3. dazed, groggy, in a daze, insensate, punch-drunk, semiconscious, senseless, stunned, stupefied

stupidity 1. asininity, brainlessness, denseness, dimness, dopiness (Sl.), doziness (Brit. inf.), dullness, dumbness (Inf., chiefly U.S.), feeble-mindedness, imbecility, lack of brain, lack of intelligence, naivety, obtuseness, puerility, simplicity, slowness, thickheadedness, thickness 2. absurdity, fatuity, fatuousness, folly, foolhardiness, foolishness, futility, idiocy, impracticality, inanity, indiscretion, ineptitude, irresponsibility, ludicrousness, lunacy, madness, pointlessness, rashness, senselessness, silliness

sturdy athletic, brawny, built to last, determined, durable, firm, flourishing, hardy, hearty, lusty, muscular, powerful, resolute, robust, secure, solid, stalwart, staunch, steadfast, stouthearted, substantial, vigorous, well-built, well-made

stutter v. falter, hesitate, speak haltingly, splutter, stammer, stumble

style n. 1. cut, design, form, hand, manner, technique 2. fashion, mode, rage, trend, vogue 3. approach, custom, manner, method,

mode, way 4. bon ton, chic, cosmopolitanism, dash, dressiness (Inf.), élan, elegance, fashionableness, flair, grace, panache, polish, refinement, savoir-faire, smartness, sophistication, stylishness, taste, urbanity 5. affluence, comfort, ease, elegance, gracious living, grandeur, luxury 6. appearance, category, characteristic, genre, kind, pattern, sort, spirit, strain, tenor, tone, type, variety 7. diction, expression, mode of expression, phraseology, phrasing, treatment, turn of phrase, vein, wording ~v. 8. adapt, arrange, cut, design, dress, fashion, shape, tailor 9. address, call, christen, denominate, designate, dub, entitle, label, name, term

stylish à la mode, chic, classy (Sl.), dapper, dressy (Inf.), fashionable, in fashion, in vogue, modish, natty (Inf.), polished, smart, snappy, snazzy (Inf.), trendy (Brit. inf.), urbane, voguish, well turned-out

suave affable, agreeable, bland, charming, civilized, courteous, diplomatic, gracious, obliging, pleasing, polite, smooth, smooth-tongued, sophisticated, svelte, urbane, worldly

subaqua (ˌsʌbˈækwə) *adj.* of or relating to underwater sport: *subaqua swimming*.

subaqueous (sʌbˈeɪkwɪəs, -ˈækwɪ-) *adj.* occurring, formed, or used under water.

subconscious (sʌbˈkɒnʃəs) *adj.* 1. acting or existing without one's awareness. ~*n.* 2. *Psychol.* that part of the mind considered to be outside or only partly within one's conscious awareness. —**sub'consciously** *adv.* —**sub'consciousness** *n.*

subcontinent (sʌbˈkɒntɪnənt) *n.* a large land mass that is a distinct part of a continent, such as India is of Asia. —**subcontinental** (ˌsʌbkɒntɪˈnɛntəl) *adj.*

subcontract *n.* (sʌbˈkɒntrækt). 1. a subordinate contract under which the supply of materials, services, or labour is let out to someone other than a party to the main contract. ~*vb.* (ˌsʌbkənˈtrækt). 2. (*intr.;* often foll. by *for*) to enter into or make a subcontract. 3. (*tr.*) to let out (work) on a subcontract. —**ˌsubcon'tractor** *n.*

subculture (ˈsʌbˌkʌltʃə) *n.* a subdivision of a national culture or an enclave within it with a distinct integrated network of behaviour, beliefs, and attitudes. —**sub'cultural** *adj.*

subcutaneous (ˌsʌbkjuːˈteɪnɪəs) *adj. Med.* situated, used, or introduced beneath the skin. —**ˌsubcu'taneously** *adv.*

subdivide (ˌsʌbdɪˈvaɪd, ˈsʌbdɪˌvaɪd) *vb.* to divide (something) resulting from an earlier division. —**ˈsubdi,vision** *n.*

subdominant (sʌbˈdɒmɪnənt) *Music.* ~*n.* 1. the fourth degree of a major or minor scale. 2. a key or chord based on this. ~*adj.* 3. of or relating to the subdominant.

subdue (səbˈdjuː) *vb.* **-duing, -dued.** (*tr.*) 1. to establish ascendancy over by force. 2. to overcome and bring under control, as by intimidation or persuasion. 3. to hold in check or repress (feelings, etc.). 4. to render less intense or less conspicuous. —**sub'duable** *adj.* —**sub'dual** *n.*

subeditor (sʌbˈɛdɪtə) *n.* a person who checks and edits copy, esp. on a newspaper.

subfusc (ˈsʌbfʌsk) *adj.* 1. devoid of brightness or appeal; drab, dull, or dark. ~*n.* 2. (at Oxford University) formal academic dress.

subhuman (sʌbˈhjuːmən) *adj.* 1. of or designating animals below man (*Homo sapiens*) in evolutionary development. 2. less than human.

subj. *abbrev. for:* 1. subject. 2. subjective(ly). 3. subjunctive.

subjacent (sʌbˈdʒeɪsənt) *adj.* 1. forming a foundation; underlying. 2. lower than. —**sub'jacency** *n.* —**sub'jacently** *adv.*

subject *n.* (ˈsʌbdʒɪkt). 1. the predominant theme or topic, as of a book, discussion, etc. 2. any branch of learning considered as a course of study. 3. *Grammar.* a word or phrase about which something is predicated or stated in a sentence; for example, *the cat* in the sentence *The cat catches mice*. 4. a person or thing that undergoes experiment, treatment, etc. 5. a person under the rule of a monarch, government, etc. 6. an object, figure, scene, etc., as portrayed by an artist or photographer. 7. *Philosophy.* **a.** that which thinks or feels as opposed to

the object of thinking and feeling; the self or the mind. **b.** the essential nature or substance of something as opposed to its attributes. 8. Also called: **theme.** *Music.* the principal motif of a fugue, the basis from which the musical material is derived in a sonata-form movement, or the recurrent figure in a rondo. 9. *Logic.* the term of a proposition about which something is asserted. 10. an originating motive. 11. **change the subject.** to select a new topic of conversation. ~*adj.* (ˈsʌbdʒɪkt). (*usually postpositive* and foll. by *to*) 12. being under the power or sovereignty of a ruler, government, etc.: *subject peoples.* 13. showing a tendency (towards): *a child subject to indiscipline.* 14. exposed or vulnerable: *subject to ribaldry.* 15. conditional upon: *the results are subject to correction.* ~*adv.* (ˈsʌbdʒɪkt). 16. **subject to.** (*prep.*) under the condition that: *we accept, subject to her agreement.* ~*vb.* (səbˈdʒɛkt). (*tr.*) 17. (foll. by *to*) to cause to undergo: *they subjected him to torture.* 18. (*often passive;* foll. by *to*) to expose or render vulnerable or liable (to some experience): *he was subjected to great danger.* 19. (foll. by *to*) to bring under the control or authority (of): *to subject a soldier to discipline.* 20. *Rare.* to present for consideration; submit. —**sub'jectable** *adj.* —**sub'jection** *n.*

subjective (səbˈdʒɛktɪv) *adj.* 1. of, proceeding from, or relating to the mind of the thinking subject and not the nature of the object being considered. 2. of, relating to, or emanating from a person's emotions, prejudices, etc. 3. relating to the inherent nature of a person or thing; essential. 4. existing only as perceived and not as a thing in itself. 5. *Med.* (of a symptom, condition, etc.) experienced only by the patient and incapable of being recognized or studied by anyone else. 6. *Grammar.* denoting a case of nouns and pronouns, esp. in languages having only two cases, that identifies the subject of a finite verb and (in formal use in English) is selected for predicate complements, as in *It is I.* ~*n.* 7. *Grammar.* **a.** the subjective case. **b.** a subjective word or speech element. Cf. **objective.** —**sub'jectively** *adv.* —**ˌsubjec'tivity** or **sub'jectiveness** *n.*

subjoin (sʌbˈdʒɔɪn) *vb.* (*tr.*) to add or attach at the end of something spoken, written, etc. —**sub'joinder** *n.*

sub judice (ˈdʒuːdɪsɪ) *adj.* (*usually postpositive*) before a court of law or a judge; under judicial consideration.

subjugate (ˈsʌbdʒʊˌgeɪt) *vb.* (*tr.*) 1. to bring into subjection. 2. to make subservient or submissive. —**subjugable** (ˈsʌbdʒəgəbəl) *adj.* —**ˌsubju'gation** *n.* —**ˈsubjuˌgator** *n.*

subjunctive (səbˈdʒʌŋktɪv) *adj.* 1. *Grammar.* denoting a mood of verbs used when the content of the clause is being doubted, supposed, feared true, etc., rather than being asserted. In the following sentence, *were* is in the subjunctive: *I'd think very seriously about that if I were you.* Cf. **indicative.** ~*n.* 2. *Grammar.* **a.** the subjunctive mood. **b.** a verb in this mood. —**sub'junctively** *adv.*

sublease *n.* (ˈsʌbˌliːs). 1. a lease of property made by a lessee or tenant of that property. ~*vb.* (sʌbˈliːs). 2. to grant a sublease of (property); sublet. 3. (*tr.*) to obtain or hold by sublease. —**sublessee** (ˌsʌblɛˈsiː) *n.* —**sublessor** (ˌsʌblɛˈsɔː) *n.*

sublet (sʌbˈlɛt) *vb.* **-letting, -let.** 1. to grant a sublease

subaquatic *adj.*	subclause *n.*
subaverage *adj.*	subcommittee *n.*
subbranch *n.*	subcranial *adj.*
subcategory *n.*	subdepot *n.*
subchapter *n.*	subentry *n.*

subforeman *n.*	subregion *n.*
subfreezing *adj.*	subsection *n.*
subfunction *n.*	subseries *n.*
subgroup *n.*	subsystem *n.*
subparagraph *n.*	subzero *adj.*

⬛ T H E S A U R U S ⬛

subconscious *adj.* hidden, inner, innermost, intuitive, latent, repressed, subliminal, suppressed

subdue 1. beat down, break, conquer, control, crush, defeat, discipline, gain ascendancy over, get the better of, get the upper hand over, get under control, humble, master, overcome, overpower, overrun, put down, quell, tame, trample, triumph over, vanquish 2. check, control, mellow, moderate, quieten down, repress, soften, suppress, tone down

subdued 1. chastened, crestfallen, dejected, downcast, down in the mouth, grave, out of spirits, quiet, repentant, repressed, re-

strained, sad, sadder and wiser, serious, sobered, solemn 2. dim, hushed, low-key, muted, quiet, shaded, sober, soft, subtle, toned down, unobtrusive

subject *n.* 1. affair, business, field of enquiry *or* reference, issue, matter, object, point, question, subject matter, substance, theme, topic 2. case, client, guinea pig (*Inf.*), participant, patient, victim 3. citizen, dependant, liegeman, national, subordinate, vassal ~*adj.* 4. at the mercy of, disposed, exposed, in danger of, liable, open, prone, susceptible, vulnerable 5. conditional, contingent, dependent 6. answerable, bound by, captive, dependent, enslaved, inferior, obedi-

ent, satellite, subjugated, submissive, subordinate, subservient ~*v.* 7. expose, lay open, make liable, put through, submit, treat

subjective biased, emotional, idiosyncratic, instinctive, intuitive, nonobjective, personal, prejudiced

subjugate bring (someone) to his knees, bring to heel, bring under the yoke, conquer, crush, defeat, enslave, hold sway over, master, overcome, overpower, overthrow, put down, quell, reduce, rule over, subdue, suppress, tame, vanquish

of (property). **2.** to let out (work, etc.) under a subcontract.

sublieutenant (ˌsʌbləˈtɛnənt) n. the most junior commissioned officer in the Royal Navy and certain other navies. —ˌsublieuˈtenancy n.

sublimate (ˈsʌblɪˌmeɪt) vb. **1.** Psychol. to direct the energy of (a primitive impulse) into activities that are considered to be socially more acceptable. **2.** (tr.) to make purer; refine. **3.** Chem. a less common word for **sublime** (senses 8, 9). ~n. **4.** Chem. the material obtained when a substance is sublimed. —ˌsubliˈmation n.

sublime (səˈblaɪm) adj. **1.** of high moral, intellectual, or spiritual value; noble; exalted. **2.** inspiring deep veneration or awe: sublime beauty. **3.** Poetic. of proud bearing or aspect. **4.** Arch. raised up. ~n. **the sublime. 5.** something that is sublime. **6.** the ultimate degree or perfect example: the sublime of folly. ~vb. **7.** (tr.) to make higher or purer. **8.** to change or cause to change directly from a solid to a vapour or gas without first melting. **9.** to undergo or cause to undergo this process followed by a reverse change directly from a vapour to a solid: to sublime iodine onto glass. —subˈlimely adv. —sublimity (səˈblɪmɪtɪ) n.

subliminal (sʌbˈlɪmɪnəl) adj. **1.** resulting from processes of which the individual is not aware. **2.** (of stimuli) less than the minimum intensity or duration required to elicit a response. —subˈliminally adv.

sub-machine-gun n. a portable automatic or semi-automatic gun with a short barrel, designed to be fired from the hip or shoulder.

submarine (ˈsʌbməˌriːn, ˌsʌbməˈriːn) n. **1.** a vessel, esp. a warship, capable of operating below the surface of the sea. **2.** (modifier) **a.** of or relating to a submarine: a submarine captain. **b.** below the surface of the sea: a submarine cable. —submariner (sʌbˈmærɪnə) n.

submerge (səbˈmɜːdʒ) or **submerse** (səbˈmɜːs) vb. **1.** to plunge, sink, or dive or cause to plunge, sink, or dive below the surface of water, etc. **2.** (tr.) to cover with water or other liquid. **3.** (tr.) to hide; suppress. **4.** (tr.) to overwhelm, as with work, etc. —subˈmergence or submersion (səbˈmɜːʃən) n.

submersible (səbˈmɜːsɪbəl) or **submergible** (səbˈmɜːdʒɪbəl) adj. **1.** able to be submerged. **2.** capable of operating under water, etc. ~n. **3.** a warship designed to operate under water for short periods. —subˌmersiˈbility or subˌmergiˈbility n.

submission (səbˈmɪʃən) n. **1.** an act or instance of submitting. **2.** something submitted; a proposal, etc. **3.** the quality or condition of being submissive. **4.** the act of referring a document, etc., for the consideration of someone else.

submissive (səbˈmɪsɪv) adj. of, tending towards, or indicating submission, humility, or servility. —subˈmissively adv. —subˈmissiveness n.

submit (səbˈmɪt) vb. **-mitting, -mitted. 1.** (often foll. by to) to yield (oneself), as to the will of another person, a superior force, etc. **2.** (foll. by to) to subject or be voluntarily subjected (to analysis, treatment, etc.). **3.** (tr.; often foll. by to) to refer (something to someone) for judgment or consideration. **4.** (tr.; may take a clause as object) to state, contend, or propose deferentially. **5.** (intr.; often foll. by to) to defer or accede (to the decision, etc., of another). —subˈmittable or subˈmissible adj. —subˈmittal n. —subˈmitter n. —subˈmittingly adv.

subnormal (sʌbˈnɔːməl) adj. **1.** less than the normal. **2.** having a low intelligence. ~n. **3.** a subnormal person. —subnormality (ˌsʌbnɔːˈmælɪtɪ) n.

subordinate adj. (səˈbɔːdɪnɪt). **1.** of lesser order or importance. **2.** under the authority or control of another: a subordinate functionary. ~n. (səˈbɔːdɪnɪt). **3.** a person or thing that is subordinate. ~vb. (səˈbɔːdɪˌneɪt). (tr.; usually foll. by to) **4.** to put in a lower rank or position (than). **5.** to make subservient: to subordinate mind to heart. —subˈordinately adv. —subordiˈnation n. —subˈordinative adj.

subordinate clause n. Grammar. a clause with an adjectival, adverbial, or nominal function, rather than one that functions as a separate sentence in its own right.

suborn (səˈbɔːn) vb. (tr.) **1.** to bribe, incite, or instigate (a person) to commit a wrongful act. **2.** Law. to induce (a witness) to commit perjury. —subornation (ˌsʌbɔːˈneɪʃən) n. —subornative (sʌˈbɔːnətɪv) adj. —subˈorner n.

subplot (ˈsʌbˌplɒt) n. a subordinate or auxiliary plot in a novel, play, film, etc.

subpoena (səbˈpiːnə) n. **1.** a writ issued by a court of justice requiring a person to appear before the court at a specified time. ~vb. **-naing, -naed. 2.** (tr.) to serve with a subpoena.

sub rosa (ˈrəʊzə) adv. in secret.

subroutine (ˈsʌbruːˌtiːn) n. a section of a computer program that is stored only once but can be used at several different points in the program. Also called: **procedure.**

subscribe (səbˈskraɪb) vb. **1.** (usually foll. by to) to pay or promise to pay (money) as a contribution (to a fund, for a magazine, etc.), esp. at regular intervals. **2.** to sign (one's name, etc.) at the end of a document. **3.** (intr.; foll. by to) to give support or approval: to subscribe to the theory of transubstantiation. —subˈscriber n.

subscriber trunk dialling n. Brit. a service by which telephone subscribers can obtain trunk calls by dialling direct without the aid of an operator. Abbrev.: **STD**

subscript (ˈsʌbskrɪpt) adj. **1.** Printing. (of a character) written or printed below the base line. Cf. **superscript.** ~n. **2.** Also called: **subindex.** a subscript character.

subscription (səbˈskrɪpʃən) n. **1.** a payment or promise of payment for consecutive issues of a magazine, newspaper, book, etc., over a specified period of time. **2.** money paid or promised, as to a charity, or the fund raised in this way. **3.** an offer to buy shares or bonds issued by a company. **4.** the act of signing one's name to a document, etc. **5.** a signature or other appendage attached to the bottom of a document, etc. **6.** agreement or acceptance expressed by or as if by signing one's name. **7.** a signed document, statement, etc. **8.** Chiefly Brit. the membership dues or fees paid to a society or club. **9.** an advance order for a new product. **10. a.** the sale of books, etc., prior to publishing. **b.** (as modifier): a subscription edition. —subˈscriptive adj. —subˈscriptively adv.

subsequent (ˈsʌbsɪkwənt) adj. occurring after; succeeding. —ˈsubsequence or ˈsubsequentness n. —ˈsubsequently adv.

subservient (səbˈsɜːvɪənt) adj. **1.** obsequious. **2.** serving as a means to an end. **3.** a less common word for

---

THESAURUS

sublime elevated, eminent, exalted, glorious, grand, great, high, imposing, lofty, magnificent, majestic, noble, transcendent

submerge deluge, dip, drown, duck, dunk, engulf, flood, immerse, inundate, overflow, overwhelm, plunge, sink, swamp

submerged drowned, immersed, subaquatic, subaqueous, submarine, submersed, sunk, sunken, undersea, underwater

submission 1. acquiescence, assent, capitulation, giving in, surrender, yielding 2. compliance, deference, docility, meekness, obedience, passivity, resignation, submissiveness, tractability, unassertiveness 3. argument, contention, proposal 4. entry, handing in, presentation, submitting, tendering

submissive abject, accommodating, acquiescent, amenable, biddable, bootlicking (Inf.), compliant, deferential, docile, dutiful,

humble, ingratiating, lowly, malleable, meek, obedient, obeisant, obsequious, passive, patient, pliant, resigned, subdued, tractable, uncomplaining, unresisting, yielding

submit 1. accede, acquiesce, agree, bend, bow, capitulate, comply, defer, endure, give in, hoist the white flag, knuckle under, lay down arms, put up with (Inf.), resign oneself, stoop, succumb, surrender, throw in the sponge, toe the line, tolerate, yield 2. commit, hand in, present, proffer, put forward, refer, table, tender 3. advance, argue, assert, claim, contend, move, propose, propound, put, state, suggest, volunteer

subordinate adj. 1. dependent, inferior, junior, lesser, lower, minor, secondary, subject, subservient 2. ancillary, auxiliary, subsidiary, supplementary ~n. 3. aide, assistant, attendant, dependant, inferior, junior, sec-

ond, subaltern, underling

subordination inferior or secondary status, inferiority, servitude, subjection, submission

subscribe 1. chip in (Inf.), contribute, donate, give, offer, pledge, promise 2. acquiesce, advocate, agree, consent, countenance, endorse, support

subscription annual payment, contribution, donation, dues, gift, membership fee, offering

subsequent after, consequent, consequential, ensuing, following, later, succeeding, successive

subsequently afterwards, at a later date, consequently, in the aftermath (of), in the end, later

subordinate (sense 2). —**sub'serviently** *adv.* —**sub'servience** *or* **sub'serviency** *n.*
subset ('sʌb,sɛt) *n.* a mathematical set contained within a larger set.
subside (səb'saɪd) *vb. (intr.)* **1.** to become less loud, excited, violent, etc.; abate. **2.** to sink or fall to a lower level. **3.** (of the surface of the earth, etc.) to cave in; collapse. **4.** (of sediment, etc.) to sink or descend to the bottom; settle. —**sub'sidence** *n.* —**sub'sider** *n.*
subsidiary (səb'sɪdɪərɪ) *adj.* **1.** serving to aid or supplement; auxiliary. **2.** of lesser importance; subordinate. ~*n., pl.* **-aries. 3.** a subsidiary person or thing. **4.** Also called: **subsidiary company.** a company with at least half of its capital stock owned by another company. —**sub'sidiarily** *adv.* —**sub'sidiariness** *n.*
subsidize *or* **-ise** ('sʌbsɪ,daɪz) *vb. (tr.)* **1.** to aid or support with a subsidy. **2.** to obtain the aid of by means of a subsidy. —**,subsidi'zation** *or* **-i'sation** *n.* —**'subsi,dizer** *or* **-i,diser** *n.*
subsidy ('sʌbsɪdɪ) *n., pl.* **-dies. 1.** a financial aid supplied by a government, as to industry, for public welfare, the balance of payments, etc. **2.** *English history.* a financial grant made originally for special purposes by Parliament to the Crown. **3.** any monetary aid, grant, or contribution.
subsist (səb'sɪst) *vb. (mainly intr.)* **1.** (often foll. by *on*) to be sustained; manage to live: *to subsist on milk.* **2.** to continue in existence. **3.** (foll. by *in*) to lie or reside by virtue (of); consist. **4.** *(tr.) Obs.* to provide with support. —**sub'sistent** *adj.*
subsistence (səb'sɪstəns) *n.* **1.** the means by which one maintains life. **2.** the act or condition of subsisting.
subsistence farming *n.* a type of farming in which most of the produce is consumed by the farmer and his family.
subsoil ('sʌb,sɔɪl) *n.* **1.** Also called: **undersoil.** the layer of soil beneath the surface soil and overlying the bedrock. ~*vb.* **2.** *(tr.)* to plough (land) to a depth so as to break up the subsoil.
subsonic (sʌb'sɒnɪk) *adj.* being, having, or travelling at a velocity below that of sound.
substance ('sʌbstəns) *n.* **1.** the tangible basic matter of which a thing consists. **2.** a specific type of matter, esp. a homogeneous material with definite or fairly definite chemical composition. **3.** the essence, meaning, etc., of a discourse, thought, or written article. **4.** solid or meaningful quality: *an education of substance.* **5.** material density or body: *a vacuum has no substance.* **6.** material possessions or wealth: *a man of substance.* **7. in substance.** with regard to the salient points.
substandard (sʌb'stændəd) *adj.* below an established or required standard.
substantial (səb'stænʃəl) *adj.* **1.** of a considerable size or value: *substantial funds.* **2.** worthwhile; important; telling: *a substantial reform.* **3.** having wealth or importance: *a substantial member of the community.* **4.** (of food or a meal) sufficient and nourishing. **5.** solid or strong: *a substantial door.* **6.** real; actual; true: *substan-*

tial evidence. **7.** of or relating to the basic or fundamental substance or aspects of a thing. ~*n.* **8.** *(often pl.) Rare.* an essential or important element. —**substantiality** (səb,stænʃɪ'ælɪtɪ) *or* **sub'stantialness** *n.* —**sub'stantially** *adv.*
substantiate (səb'stænʃɪ,eɪt) *vb. (tr.)* **1.** to establish as valid or genuine. **2.** to give form or real existence to. —**sub,stanti'ation** *n.*
substantive ('sʌbstəntɪv) *n.* **1.** *Grammar.* a noun or pronoun used in place of a noun. ~*adj.* **2.** of, relating to, containing, or being the essential element of a thing. **3.** having independent function, resources, or existence. **4.** of substantial quantity. **5.** solid in foundation or basis. **6.** *Grammar.* denoting, relating to, or standing in place of a noun. **7.** (of a dye or colour) staining the material directly without use of a mordant. —**substantival** (,sʌbstən'taɪvəl) *adj.* —**,substan'tivally** *adv.* —**'substantively** *adv.*
substitute ('sʌbstɪ,tjuːt) *vb.* **1.** (often foll. by *for*) to serve or cause to serve in place of another person or thing. **2.** *Chem.* to replace (an atom or group in a molecule) with (another atom or group). ~*n.* **3. a.** a person or thing that serves in place of another, such as a player in a game who takes the place of an injured colleague. **b.** *(as modifier): a substitute goalkeeper.* —**,substi'tutable** *adj.* —**,substi'tution** *n.* —**'substi,tutive** *adj.*
subsume (səb'sjuːm) *vb. (tr.)* **1.** to incorporate (an idea, case, etc.) under a comprehensive or inclusive classification. **2.** to consider (an instance of something) as part of a general rule. —**sub'sumable** *adj.* —**sub'sumption** (səb'sʌmpʃən) *n.*
subtenant (sʌb'tɛnənt) *n.* a person who rents or leases property from a tenant. —**sub'tenancy** *n.*
subtend (səb'tɛnd) *vb. (tr.)* **1.** *Geom.* to be opposite to and delimit (an angle or side). **2.** (of a bract, stem, etc.) to have (a bud or similar part) growing in its axil.
subterfuge ('sʌbtə,fjuːdʒ) *n.* a stratagem employed to conceal something, evade an argument, etc.
subterranean (,sʌbtə'reɪnɪən) *adj.* **1.** Also: **subterrestrial.** situated, living, or operating below the surface of the earth. **2.** existing or operating in concealment. —**,subter'raneanly** *or* **,subter'raneously** *adv.*
subtitle ('sʌb,taɪtəl) *n.* **1.** an additional subordinate title given to a literary or other work. **2.** *(often pl.)* Also called: **caption.** *Films.* **a.** a written translation superimposed on a film that has foreign dialogue. **b.** explanatory text on a silent film. ~*vb.* **3.** *(tr.; usually passive)* to provide a subtitle for.
subtle ('sʌtəl) *adj.* **1.** not immediately obvious or comprehensible. **2.** difficult to detect or analyse, often through being delicate or highly refined: *a subtle scent.* **3.** showing or making or capable of showing or making fine distinctions of meaning. **4.** marked by or requiring mental acuteness or ingenuity; discriminating. **5.** delicate or faint: *a subtle shade.* **6.** cunning or wily: *a subtle rogue.* **7.** operating or executed in secret: *a subtle intrigue.* —**'subtleness** *n.* —**'subtly** *adv.*

◼️ THESAURUS ◼️

subservient **1.** abject, bootlicking *(Inf.),* deferential, inferior, obsequious, servile, slavish, subject, submissive, sycophantic, truckling **2.** accessory, ancillary, auxiliary, conducive, helpful, instrumental, serviceable, subordinate, subsidiary, useful

subside **1.** abate, decrease, de-escalate, diminish, dwindle, ease, ebb, lessen, let up, level off, melt away, moderate, peter out, quieten, recede, slacken, wane **2.** cave in, collapse, decline, descend, drop, ebb, lower, settle, sink

subsidence 1. decline, descent, ebb, settlement, settling, sinking **2.** abatement, decrease, de-escalation, diminution, easing off, lessening, slackening

subsidiary aiding, ancillary, assistant, auxiliary, contributory, cooperative, helpful, lesser, minor, secondary, serviceable, subordinate, subservient, supplemental, supplementary, useful

subsidize finance, fund, promote, put up the money for, sponsor, support, underwrite

subsidy aid, allowance, assistance, contri-

bution, financial aid, grant, help, subvention, support

subsist be, continue, eke out an existence, endure, exist, keep going, last, live, make ends meet, remain, stay alive, survive, sustain oneself

subsistence aliment, existence, food, keep, livelihood, living, maintenance, provision, rations, support, survival, sustenance, upkeep, victuals

substance 1. body, element, fabric, material, stuff, texture **2.** burden, essence, gist, gravamen *(Law),* import, main point, matter, meaning, pith, significance, subject, sum and substance, theme **3.** actuality, concreteness, entity, force, reality **4.** affluence, assets, estate, means, property, resources, wealth

substantial 1. ample, big, considerable, generous, goodly, important, large, significant, sizable, tidy *(Inf.),* worthwhile **2.** bulky, durable, firm, hefty, massive, solid, sound, stout, strong, sturdy, well-built **3.** actual, existent, material, positive, real, true, valid, weighty

substantially essentially, in essence, in

essentials, in substance, in the main, largely, materially, to a large extent

substantiate affirm, attest to, authenticate, bear out, confirm, corroborate, establish, prove, support, validate, verify

substitute *v.* **1.** change, commute, exchange, interchange, replace, swap *(Inf.),* switch **2.** *With* **for** act for, be in place of, cover for, deputize, double for, fill in for, hold the fort for, relieve, stand in for, take over ~*n.* **3.** agent, depute *(Chiefly Scot.),* deputy, equivalent, expedient, locum, locum tenens, makeshift, proxy, relief, replacement, representative, reserve, stand-by, stopgap, sub, supply, surrogate, temp *(Inf.),* temporary ~*adj.* **4.** acting, additional, alternative, proxy, replacement, reserve, second, surrogate, temporary

substitution change, exchange, interchange, replacement, swap *(Inf.),* switch

subterfuge artifice, deception, deviousness, dodge, duplicity, evasion, excuse, machination, manoeuvre, ploy, pretence, pretext, quibble, ruse, shift, stall, stratagem, trick

subtlety ('sʌtəltı) n., pl. **-ties.** **1.** the state or quality of being subtle; delicacy. **2.** a fine distinction. **3.** something subtle.

subtonic (sʌb'tɒnɪk) n. *Music.* the seventh degree of a major or minor scale.

subtract (səb'trækt) vb. **1.** to calculate the difference between (two numbers or quantities) by subtraction. **2.** to remove (a part of a thing, quantity, etc.) from the whole. —**sub'tractive** adj. —**sub'tracter** n.

subtraction (səb'trækʃən) n. **1.** the act or process of subtracting. **2.** a mathematical operation in which the difference between two numbers or quantities is calculated.

suburb ('sʌbɜːb) n. a residential district situated on the outskirts of a city or town.

suburban (sə'bɜːbən) adj. **1.** of, in, or inhabiting a suburb or the suburbs. **2.** characteristic of a suburb or the suburbs. **3.** *Mildly derog.* narrow or unadventurous in outlook. ~n. **4.** Also called: **suburbanite.** a person who lives in a suburb. —**su'burba₁nize** or **-ise** vb.

suburbia (sə'bɜːbıə) n. **1.** suburbs or the people living in them considered as an identifiable community or class in society. **2.** the life, customs, etc., of suburbanites.

subvention (səb'vɛnʃən) n. a grant, aid, or subsidy, as from a government.

subversion (səb'vɜːʃən) n. **1.** the act or an instance of subverting a legally constituted government, institution, etc. **2.** the state of being subverted; destruction or ruin.

subversive (səb'vɜːsɪv) adj. **1.** liable to subvert or overthrow a government, legally constituted institution, etc. ~n. **2.** a person engaged in subversive activities, etc. —**sub'versively** adv. —**sub'versiveness** n.

subvert (səb'vɜːt) vb. (tr.) **1.** to bring about the complete downfall or ruin of (something existing by a system of law, etc.). **2.** to undermine the moral principles of (a person, etc.). —**sub'verter** n.

subway ('sʌb₁weı) n. **1.** *Brit.* an underground tunnel enabling pedestrians to cross a road, railway, etc. **2.** an underground tunnel for traffic, power supplies, etc. **3.** an underground railway.

succeed (sək'siːd) vb. **1.** (intr.) to accomplish an aim, esp. in the manner desired. **2.** (intr.) to happen in the manner desired: *the plan succeeded.* **3.** (intr.) to acquit oneself satisfactorily or do well, as in a specified field. **4.** (when intr., often foll. by to) to come next in order (after someone or something). **5.** (when intr., often foll. by to) to take over an office, post, etc. (from a person). **6.** (intr.; usually foll. by to) to come into possession (of property, etc.); inherit. **7.** (intr.) to have a result according to a specified manner: *the plan succeeded badly.* —**suc'ceeder** n. —**suc'ceedingly** adv.

success (sək'sɛs) n. **1.** the favourable outcome of something attempted. **2.** the attainment of wealth, fame, etc. **3.** an action, performance, etc., that is characterized by success. **4.** a person or thing that is successful.

successful (sək'sɛsfʊl) adj. **1.** having succeeded in one's endeavours. **2.** marked by a favourable outcome. **3.** having obtained fame, wealth, etc. —**suc'cessfully** adv. —**suc'cessfulness** n.

succession (sək'sɛʃən) n. **1.** the act or an instance of one person or thing following another. **2.** a number of people or things following one another in order. **3.** the act, process, or right by which one person succeeds to the office, etc., of another. **4.** the order that determines how one person or thing follows another. **5.** a line of descent to a title, etc. **6. in succession.** in a manner such that one thing is followed uninterruptedly by another. —**suc'cessional** adj.

successive (sək'sɛsɪv) adj. **1.** following another without interruption. **2.** of or involving succession: *a successive process.* —**suc'cessively** adv. —**suc'cessiveness** n.

successor (sək'sɛsə) n. a person or thing that follows, esp. a person who succeeds another.

succinct (sək'sıŋkt) adj. marked by brevity and clarity; concise. —**suc'cinctly** adv. —**suc'cinctness** n.

succour or *U.S.* **succor** ('sʌkə) n. **1.** help or assistance, esp. in time of difficulty. **2.** a person or thing that provides help. ~vb. **3.** (tr.) to give aid to.

succubus ('sʌkjʊbəs) n., pl. **-bi** (-₁baı). **1.** Also called: **succuba.** a female demon fabled to have sexual intercourse with sleeping men. Cf. **incubus.** **2.** any evil demon.

succulent ('sʌkjʊlənt) adj. **1.** juicy. **2.** (of plants) having thick fleshy leaves or stems. ~n. **3.** a plant that can exist in arid conditions by using water stored in its fleshy tissues. —**'succulence** or **'succulency** n. —**'succulently** adv.

succumb (sə'kʌm) vb. (intr.; often foll. by to) **1.** to give way to the force (of) or desire (for). **2.** to be fatally overwhelmed by disease, etc.); die (of).

such (sʌtʃ) (often foll. by a corresponding subordinate clause introduced by *that* or *as*) ~determiner. **1. a.** of the sort specified or understood: *such books.* **b.** (as pronoun): *such is life; robbers, rapists, and such.* **2.** so great; so much: *such a help.* **3. a. as such.** in the capacity previously specified or understood: *a judge as such hasn't so much power.* **b.** in itself or themselves: *intelligence as such can't guarantee success.* **4. such and such.** specific, but not known or named: *at such and such a time.* **5. such as. a.** for example: *animals, such as tigers.* **b.** of a similar kind as; like: *people such as your friend.* **c.** of the (usually small) amount, etc.: *the food, such as there was, was excellent.* **6. such that.** so that: used to express purpose or result: *power such that it was effortless.* ~adv. **7.** (intensifier): *such nice people; such a nice person.*

THESAURUS

subtle 1. deep, delicate, discriminating, ingenious, nice, penetrating, profound, refined, sophisticated **2.** delicate, faint, implied, indirect, insinuated, slight, understated **3.** artful, astute, crafty, cunning, designing, devious, intriguing, keen, Machiavellian, scheming, shrewd, sly, wily

subtlety 1. acumen, acuteness, cleverness, delicacy, discernment, fine point, intricacy, nicety, refinement, sagacity, skill, sophistication **2.** discernment, discrimination, finesse, penetration **3.** artfulness, astuteness, craftiness, cunning, deviousness, guile, slyness, wiliness

subtract deduct, detract, diminish, remove, take away, take from, take off, withdraw

suburbs dormitory area (*Brit.*), environs, faubourgs, neighbourhood, outskirts, precincts, purlieus, residential areas, suburbia

subversive 1. adj. destructive, incendiary, inflammatory, insurrectionary, overthrowing, perversive, riotous, seditious, treasonous, underground, undermining **2.** n. deviationist, dissident, fifth columnist, insurrectionary, quisling, saboteur, seditionary, seditionist, terrorist, traitor

subvert 1. demolish, destroy, invalidate, overturn, raze, ruin, sabotage, undermine, upset, wreck **2.** confound, contaminate, corrupt, debase, demoralize, deprave, pervert, poison, vitiate

succeed 1. arrive (*Inf.*), be successful, come off (*Inf.*), do all right for oneself (*Inf.*), do the trick (*Inf.*), flourish, gain one's end, get to the top (*Inf.*), make good, make it (*Inf.*), prosper, thrive, triumph, turn out well, work **2.** be subsequent, come next, ensue, follow, result, supervene **3.** *Usually with* to accede, assume the office of, come into, come into possession of, enter upon, inherit, replace, take over

succeeding ensuing, following, next, subsequent, successive

success 1. ascendancy, eminence, fame, favourable outcome, fortune, happiness, hit (*Inf.*), luck, prosperity, triumph **2.** best seller, big name, celebrity, hit (*Inf.*), market leader, sensation, smash hit (*Inf.*), somebody, star, V.I.P., winner

successful acknowledged, at the top of the tree, best-selling, booming, efficacious, favourable, flourishing, fortunate, fruitful, lucky, lucrative, moneymaking, out in front (*Inf.*), paying, profitable, prosperous, rewarding, thriving, top, unbeaten, victorious, wealthy

successfully famously (*Inf.*), favour-ably, in triumph, swimmingly, victoriously, well, with flying colours

succession 1. chain, continuation, course, cycle, flow, order, procession, progression, run, sequence, series, train **2. in succession** consecutively, one after the other, one behind the other, on the trot (*Inf.*), running, successively **3.** accession, assumption, elevation, entering upon, inheritance, taking over **4.** descendants, descent, line, lineage, race

successive consecutive, following, in a row, in succession, sequent, succeeding

succinct brief, compact, compendious, concise, condensed, gnomic, in a few well-chosen words, laconic, pithy, summary, terse, to the point

succour 1. v. aid, assist, befriend, comfort, encourage, foster, give aid and encouragement to, help, minister to, nurse, relieve, render assistance to, support **2.** n. aid, assistance, comfort, help, relief, support

succulent juicy, luscious, lush, mellow, moist, mouthwatering, rich

succumb capitulate, die, fall, fall victim to, give in, give way, go under, knuckle under, submit, surrender, yield

suck (sʌk) vb. **1.** to draw (a liquid or other substance) into the mouth by creating a partial vacuum in the mouth. **2.** to draw in (fluid, etc.) by or as if by a similar action: *plants suck moisture from the soil.* **3.** to drink milk from (a mother's breast); suckle. **4.** (tr.) to extract fluid content from (a solid food): *to suck a lemon.* **5.** (tr.) to take into the mouth and moisten, dissolve, or roll around with the tongue: *to suck one's thumb.* **6.** (tr.; often foll. by *down, in,* etc.) to draw by using irresistible force. **7.** (intr.) (of a pump) to draw in air because of a low supply level or leaking valves, etc. **8.** (tr.) to assimilate or acquire (knowledge, comfort, etc.). ~n. **9.** the act or an instance of sucking. **10.** something that is sucked, esp. milk from the mother's breast. **11. give suck to.** to give (a baby or young animal) milk from the breast or udder. **12.** an attracting or sucking force. **13.** a sound caused by sucking. ~See also **suck in, suck up to.**

sucker ('sʌkə) n. **1.** a person or thing that sucks. **2.** Sl. a person who is easily deceived or swindled. **3.** Sl. a person who cannot resist the attractions of a particular type of person or thing: *he's a sucker for blondes.* **4.** a young animal that is not yet weaned. **5.** Zool. an organ specialized for sucking or adhering. **6.** a cup-shaped device, generally made of rubber, that may be attached to articles allowing them to adhere to a surface by suction. **7.** Bot. **a.** a strong shoot that arises in a mature plant from a root, rhizome, or the base of the main stem. **b.** a short branch of a parasitic plant that absorbs nutrients from the host. **8.** a pipe or tube through which a fluid is drawn by suction. **9.** any of various small mainly North American cyprinoid fishes having a large sucking mouth. **10.** any of certain fishes that have sucking discs, esp. the sea snail. **11.** a piston in a suction pump or the valve in such a piston. ~vb. **12.** (tr.) to strip the suckers from (a plant). **13.** (intr.) (of a plant) to produce suckers.

suck in vb. (adv.) **1.** (tr.) to attract by using an inexorable force, inducement, etc. **2.** to draw in (one's breath) sharply.

suckle ('sʌkəl) vb. **1.** to give (a baby or young animal) milk from the breast or (of a baby, etc.) to suck milk from the breast. **2.** (tr.) to bring up; nurture. —'**suckler** n.

suckling ('sʌklɪŋ) n. **1.** an infant or young animal that is still taking milk from the mother. **2.** a very young child.

sucks (sʌks) interj. Sl. **1.** an expression of disappointment. **2.** an exclamation of defiance or derision (esp. in **yah boo sucks to you**).

suck up to vb. (intr., adv. + prep.) Inf. to flatter for one's own profit; toady.

sucrose ('sju:krəʊz, -krəʊs) n. the technical name for **sugar** (sense 1).

suction ('sʌkʃən) n. **1.** the act or process of sucking. **2.** the force produced by a pressure difference, as the force holding a suction cap onto a surface. **3.** the act or process of producing such a force. —'**suctional** adj.

Sudanese (ˌsu:də'ni:z) adj. **1.** of or relating to the Sudan, in NE Africa. ~n. **2.** a native or inhabitant of the Sudan.

sudatory ('sju:dətərɪ, -trɪ) adj. **1.** relating to or producing sweating. ~n., pl. **-ries. 2.** a sudatory agent.

sudden ('sʌdən) adj. **1.** occurring or performed quickly and without warning. **2.** marked by haste; abrupt. **3.** Rare. rash; precipitate. ~n. **4.** Arch. an abrupt occurrence (in **on a sudden**). **5. all of a sudden.** without warning; unexpectedly. —'**suddenly** adv. —'**suddenness** n.

sudden infant death syndrome n. a technical name for **cot death.**

sudorific (ˌsju:də'rɪfɪk) adj. **1.** producing or causing sweating. ~n. **2.** a sudorific agent.

suds (sʌdz) pl. n. **1.** the bubbles on the surface of water in which soap, detergents, etc., have been dissolved; lather. **2.** soapy water. —'**sudsy** adj.

sue (sju:, su:) vb. **suing, sued. 1.** to institute legal proceedings (against). **2.** to make suppliant requests of (someone for something). —'**suer** n.

suede (sweɪd) n. **a.** a leather with a fine velvet-like nap on the flesh side, produced by abrasive action. **b.** (as modifier): *a suede coat.*

suet ('su:ɪt, 'sju:ɪt) n. a hard waxy fat around the kidneys and loins in sheep, cattle, etc., used in cooking and making tallow. —'**suety** adj.

suet pudding n. Brit. any of a variety of puddings made with suet and steamed or boiled.

suffer ('sʌfə) vb. **1.** to undergo or be subjected to (pain, punishment, etc.). **2.** (tr.) to undergo or experience (anything): *to suffer a change of management.* **3.** (intr.) to be set at a disadvantage: *this author suffers in translation.* **4.** (tr.) Arch. to tolerate; permit (someone to do something): *suffer the little children to come unto me.* **5. suffer from. a.** to be ill with, esp. recurrently. **b.** to be given to: *he suffers from a tendency to exaggerate.* —'**sufferer** n. —'**suffering** n.

sufferance ('sʌfərəns, 'sʌfrəns) n. **1.** tolerance arising from failure to prohibit; tacit permission. **2.** capacity to endure pain, injury, etc. **3.** the state or condition of suffering. **4. on sufferance.** tolerated with reluctance.

suffice (sə'faɪs) vb. **1.** to be adequate or satisfactory for (something). **2. suffice it to say that.** (takes a clause as object) let us say no more than that; I shall just say that.

sufficiency (sə'fɪʃənsɪ) n., pl. **-cies. 1.** the quality or condition of being sufficient. **2.** an adequate amount. **3.** Arch. efficiency.

sufficient (sə'fɪʃənt) adj. **1.** enough to meet a need or purpose; adequate. **2.** Logic. (of a condition) assuring the truth of a statement, fact, etc., logically following from the condition once that condition has been fulfilled. Cf. **necessary** (sense 3b). **3.** Arch. competent; capable. ~n. **4.** a sufficient quantity. —**suf'ficiently** adv.

suffix n. ('sʌfɪks). **1.** Grammar. an affix that follows the stem to which it is attached, as for example -s and -ness in dogs and softness. Cf. **prefix** (sense 1). **2.** anything added at the end of something else. ~vb. ('sʌfɪks, sə'fɪks). **3.** (tr.) Grammar. to add (a morpheme) as a suffix to a word.

suffocate ('sʌfəˌkeɪt) vb. **1.** to kill or be killed by the deprivation of oxygen, as by obstruction of the air passage or inhalation of noxious gases. **2.** to block the air passages or have the air passages blocked. **3.** to feel or cause to feel discomfort from heat and lack of air. —ˌsuffo'cation n.

suffragan ('sʌfrəgən) adj. **1. a.** (of any bishop of a diocese) subordinate to and assisting his superior archbishop or metropolitan. **b.** (of any assistant bishop) assisting the bishop of his diocese but having no ordinary jurisdiction in that diocese. ~n. **2.** a suffragan bishop. —'**suffraganˌship** n.

suffrage ('sʌfrɪdʒ) n. **1.** the right to vote, esp. in public elections; franchise. **2.** the exercise of such a right; casting a vote. **3.** a short intercessory prayer.

suffragette (ˌsʌfrə'dʒɛt) n. a female advocate of the extension of the franchise to women, esp. a militant one, as in Britain at the beginning of the 20th century.

suffuse (sə'fju:z) vb. (tr.; usually passive) to spread or flood through or over (something). —**suffusion** (sə-

---

sucker butt, cat's paw, dupe, easy game or mark (Inf.), fool, mug (Sl.), pushover (Sl.), sap (Sl.), sitting duck (Inf.), victim

sudden abrupt, hasty, hurried, impulsive, quick, rapid, rash, swift, unexpected, unforeseen, unusual

suddenly abruptly, all at once, all of a sudden, on the spur of the moment, out of the blue (Inf.), unexpectedly, without warning

sue 1. Law bring an action against (someone), charge, have the law on (someone) (Inf.), indict, institute legal proceedings against (someone), prefer charges against (someone), prosecute, summon, take (someone) to court 2. appeal for, beg, beseech, entreat, petition, plead, solicit, supplicate

suffer 1. ache, agonize, be affected, be in pain, be racked, feel wretched, go through a lot (Inf.), grieve, have a thin or bad time, hurt 2. bear, endure, experience, feel, go through, put up with (Inf.), support, sustain, tolerate, undergo 3. appear in a poor light, be handicapped, be impaired, deteriorate, fall off, show to disadvantage 4. Archaic allow, let, permit

suffering n. affliction, agony, anguish, discomfort, distress, hardship, martyrdom, misery, ordeal, pain, torment, torture

suffice answer, be sufficient (adequate, enough), content, do, fill the bill (Inf.), meet requirements, satisfy, serve

sufficient adequate, competent, enough, enow (Archaic), satisfactory

suffocate asphyxiate, choke, smother, stifle, strangle

suffuse bathe, cover, flood, imbue, infuse, mantle, overspread, permeate, pervade, spread over, steep, transfuse

ˈfjuːʒən) *n.* —**sufˈfusive** *adj.*

sugar (ˈʃʊgə) *n.* **1.** Also called: **sucrose, saccharose.** a white crystalline sweet carbohydrate, a disaccharide, found in many plants: used esp. as a sweetening agent in food and drinks. Related adj.: **saccharine. 2.** any of a class of simple water-soluble carbohydrates, such as sucrose, lactose, and fructose. **3.** *Inf., chiefly U.S.* a term of affection, esp. for one's sweetheart. ~*vb.* **4.** (*tr.*) to add sugar to; make sweet. **5.** (*tr.*) to cover or sprinkle with sugar. **6.** (*intr.*) to produce sugar. **7. sugar the pill** *or* **medicine.** to make something unpleasant more agreeable by adding something pleasant. —ˈ**sugared** *adj.*

sugar beet *n.* a variety of beet cultivated for its white roots from which sugar is obtained.

sugar cane *n.* a coarse perennial grass of Old World tropical regions, having tall stout canes that yield sugar: cultivated chiefly in the West Indies and the southern U.S.

sugaring off *n. Canad.* the boiling down of maple sap to produce sugar, traditionally a social event in early spring.

sugar loaf *n.* **1.** a large conical mass of hard refined sugar. **2.** something resembling this.

sugar maple *n.* a North American maple tree, grown as a source of sugar, which is extracted from the sap, and for its hard wood.

sugary (ˈʃʊgərɪ) *adj.* **1.** of, like, or containing sugar. **2.** excessively sweet. **3.** deceptively pleasant; insincere. —ˈ**sugariness** *n.*

suggest (səˈdʒɛst) *vb.* (*tr.; may take a clause as object*) **1.** to put forward (a plan, idea, etc.) for consideration: *I suggest Smith for the post; a plan suggested itself.* **2.** to evoke (a person, thing, etc.) in the mind by the association of ideas: *that painting suggests home to me.* **3.** to give an indirect or vague hint of: *his face always suggests his peace of mind.* —**sugˈgester** *n.*

suggestible (səˈdʒɛstɪbəl) *adj.* **1.** easily influenced by ideas provided by other persons. **2.** characteristic of something that can be suggested. —**sugˌgestiˈbility** *n.*

suggestion (səˈdʒɛstʃən) *n.* **1.** something that is suggested. **2.** a hint or indication: *a suggestion of the odour of violets.* **3.** *Psychol.* the process whereby the mere presentation of an idea to a receptive individual leads to the acceptance of that idea. See also **autosuggestion.**

suggestive (səˈdʒɛstɪv) *adj.* **1.** (*postpositive;* foll. by *of*) conveying a hint (of something). **2.** tending to suggest something improper or indecent. —**sugˈgestively** *adv.* —**sugˈgestiveness** *n.*

suicidal (ˌsuːɪˈsaɪdəl, ˌsjuː-) *adj.* **1.** involving, indicating, or tending towards suicide. **2.** liable to result in suicide: *a suicidal attempt.* **3.** liable to destroy one's own interests or prospects; dangerously rash. —ˌ**suiˈcidally** *adv.*

suicide (ˈsuːɪˌsaɪd, ˈsjuː-) *n.* **1.** the act or an instance of killing oneself intentionally. **2.** the self-inflicted ruin of one's own prospects or interests: *a merger would be financial suicide.* **3.** a person who kills himself intentionally. **4.** (*modifier*) reckless; extremely dangerous: *a suicide mission.*

suit (suːt, sjuːt) *n.* **1.** any set of clothes of the same or similar material designed to be worn together, now usually (for men) a jacket with matching trousers or (for women) a jacket with matching or contrasting skirt or trousers. **2.** (*in combination*) any outfit worn for a specific purpose: *a spacesuit.* **3.** any set of items, such as

parts of personal armour. **4.** any of the four sets of 13 cards in a pack of playing cards, being spades, hearts, diamonds, and clubs. **5.** a civil proceeding; lawsuit. **6.** the act or process of suing in a court of law. **7.** a petition or appeal made to a person of superior rank or status or the act of making such a petition. **8.** a man's courting of a woman. **9. follow suit. a.** to play a card of the same suit as the card played immediately before it. **b.** to act in the same way as someone else. **10. strong** *or* **strongest suit.** something that one excels in. ~*vb.* **11.** to make or be fit or appropriate for: *that dress suits your figure.* **12.** to meet the requirements or standards (of). **13.** to be agreeable or acceptable to (someone). **14. suit oneself.** to pursue one's own intentions without reference to others.

suitable (ˈsuːtəbəl, ˈsjuːt-) *adj.* appropriate; proper; fit. —ˌ**suitaˈbility** *or* **ˈsuitableness** *n.* —**ˈsuitably** *adv.*

suitcase (ˈsuːtˌkeɪs, ˈsjuːt-) *n.* a portable rectangular travelling case for clothing, etc.

suite (swiːt) *n.* **1.** a series of items intended to be used together; set. **2.** a set of connected rooms in a hotel. **3.** a matching set of furniture, esp. of two armchairs and a settee. **4.** a number of attendants or followers. **5.** *Music.* **a.** an instrumental composition consisting of several movements in the same key based on or derived from dance rhythms, esp. in the baroque period. **b.** an instrumental composition in several movements less closely connected than a sonata.

suitor (ˈsuːtə, ˈsjuːt-) *n.* **1.** a man who courts a woman; wooer. **2.** *Law.* a person who brings a suit in a court of law; plaintiff.

sulk (sʌlk) *vb.* **1.** (*intr.*) to be silent and resentful because of a wrong done to one; brood sullenly: *the child sulked after being slapped.* ~*n.* **2.** (*often pl.*) a state or mood of feeling resentful or sullen: *he's in a sulk; he's got the sulks.* **3.** Also called: **sulker.** a person who sulks.

sulky¹ (ˈsʌlkɪ) *adj.* **-ier, -iest. 1.** sullen, withdrawn, or moody, through or as if through resentment. **2.** dull or dismal: *sulky weather.* —ˈ**sulkily** *adv.* —**ˈsulkiness** *n.*

sulky² (ˈsʌlkɪ) *n., pl.* **sulkies.** a light two-wheeled vehicle for one person, usually drawn by one horse.

sullen (ˈsʌlən) *adj.* **1.** unwilling to talk or be sociable; sulky; morose. **2.** sombre; gloomy: *a sullen day.* ~*n.* **3.** (*pl.*) *Arch.* a sullen mood. —ˈ**sullenly** *adv.* —**ˈsullenness** *n.*

sully (ˈsʌlɪ) *vb.* **-lying, -lied.** (*tr.*) to stain or tarnish (a reputation, etc.) or (of a reputation) to become stained or tarnished.

sulph- *or U.S.* **sulf-** *combining form.* containing sulphur: *sulphate.*

sulpha drug (ˈsʌlfə) *n.* any of a group of sulphonamides that inhibit the activity of bacteria and are used to treat bacterial infections.

sulphate (ˈsʌlfeɪt) *n.* **1.** any salt or ester of sulphuric acid. ~*vb.* **2.** (*tr.*) to treat with a sulphate or convert into a sulphate. **3.** to undergo or cause to undergo the formation of a layer of lead sulphate on the plates of an accumulator. —**sulˈphation** *n.*

sulphide (ˈsʌlfaɪd) *n.* a compound of sulphur with a more electropositive element.

sulphite (ˈsʌlfaɪt) *n.* any salt or ester of sulphurous acid. —**sulphitic** (sʌlˈfɪtɪk) *adj.*

sulphonamide (sʌlˈfɒnəˌmaɪd) *n.* any of a class of organic compounds containing the group -SO_2NH_2 or a

---

THESAURUS

suggest 1. advise, advocate, move, offer a suggestion, propose, put forward, recommend 2. bring to mind, connote, evoke, put one in mind of 3. hint, imply, indicate, insinuate, intimate, lead one to believe

suggestion 1. motion, plan, proposal, proposition, recommendation 2. breath, hint, indication, insinuation, intimation, suspicion, trace, whisper

suggestive 1. *With* of evocative, expressive, indicative, redolent, reminiscent 2. bawdy, blue, immodest, improper, indecent, indelicate, off colour, provocative, prurient, racy, ribald, risqué, rude, smutty, spicy (*Inf.*), titillating, unseemly

suit *v.* 1. agree, agree with, answer, be acceptable to, become, befit, be seemly, conform to, correspond, do, go with, gratify, harmonize, match, please, satisfy, tally 2. ac-

commodate, adapt, adjust, fashion, fit, modify, proportion, tailor ~*n.* 3. addresses, appeal, attentions, courtship, entreaty, invocation, petition, prayer, request 4. *Law* action, case, cause, lawsuit, proceeding, prosecution, trial 5. clothing, costume, dress, ensemble, habit, outfit 6. **follow suit** accord with, copy, emulate, run with the herd, take one's cue from

suitability appropriateness, aptness, fitness, opportuneness, rightness, timeliness

suitable acceptable, applicable, apposite, appropriate, apt, becoming, befitting, convenient, cut out for, due, fit, fitting, in character, in keeping, opportune, pertinent, proper, relevant, right, satisfactory, seemly, suited

suite 1. apartment, collection, furniture, rooms, series, set 2. attendants, entourage, escort, followers, retainers, retinue, train

suitor admirer, beau, follower (*Obsolete*), swain (*Archaic*), wooer

sulk be in a huff, be put out, brood, have the hump (*Brit. inf.*), look sullen, pout

sulky aloof, churlish, cross, disgruntled, ill-humoured, in the sulks, moody, morose, perverse, petulant, put out, querulous, resentful, sullen, vexed

sullen brooding, cheerless, cross, dismal, dull, gloomy, glowering, heavy, moody, morose, obstinate, out of humour, perverse, silent, sombre, sour, stubborn, surly, unsociable

sullenness glumness, heaviness, ill humour, moodiness, moroseness, sourness, sulkiness, sulks

group derived from this. An important class of sulphonamides is the sulpha drugs.

sulphur *or U.S.* **sulfur** ('sʌlfə) *n.* **a.** an allotropic nonmetallic element, occurring free in volcanic regions and in combined state in gypsum, pyrite, and galena. It is used in the production of sulphuric acid, in the vulcanization of rubber, and in fungicides. Symbol: S; atomic no.: 16; atomic wt.: 32.064. **b.** (*as modifier*): *sulphur springs.* —**sulphuric** *or U.S.* **sulfuric** (sʌl'fjuərɪk) *adj.*

sulphureous (sʌl'fjuərɪəs) *n.* **1.** another word for **sulphurous** (sense 1). ~*adj.* **2.** of the yellow colour of sulphur.

sulphuric acid *n.* a colourless dense oily corrosive liquid used in accumulators and in the manufacture of fertilizers, dyes, and explosives. Formula: H_2SO_4.

sulphurize *or* **-ise** ('sʌlfju,raɪz) *vb.* (*tr.*) to combine or treat with sulphur or a sulphur compound. —**sulphurization** *or* **-i'sation** *n.*

sulphurous ('sʌlfərəs) *adj.* **1.** Also: **sulphureous**. of, relating to, or resembling sulphur: *a sulphurous colour.* **2.** of or containing sulphur in the divalent state: *sulphurous acid.* **3.** of or relating to hellfire. **4.** hot-tempered. —**'sulphurously** *adv.* —**'sulphurousness** *n.*

sultan ('sʌltən) *n.* **1.** the sovereign of a Muslim country, esp. of the former Ottoman Empire. **2.** a small domestic fowl with a white crest and heavily feathered legs and feet: originated in Turkey.

sultana (sʌl'tɑːnə) *n.* **1. a.** the dried fruit of a small white seedless grape, originally produced in SW Asia; seedless raisin. **b.** the grape itself. **2.** Also called: **sultaness.** a wife, concubine, or female relative of a sultan. **3.** a mistress; concubine.

sultanate ('sʌltə,neɪt) *n.* **1.** the territory or a country ruled by a sultan. **2.** the office, rank, or jurisdiction of a sultan.

sultry ('sʌltrɪ) *adj.* **-trier, -triest. 1.** (of weather or climate) oppressively hot and humid. **2.** characterized by or emitting oppressive heat. **3.** displaying or suggesting passion; sensual: *sultry eyes.* —**'sultrily** *adv.* —**'sultriness** *n.*

sum (sʌm) *n.* **1.** the result of the addition of numbers, quantities, objects, etc. **2.** one or more columns or rows of numbers to be added, subtracted, multiplied, or divided. **3.** *Maths.* the limit of the first *n* terms of a converging infinite series as *n* tends to infinity. **4.** a quantity, esp. of money: *he borrows enormous sums.* **5.** the essence or gist of a matter (esp. in **in sum, in sum and substance**). **6.** a less common word for **summary. 7.** (*modifier*) complete or final (esp. in **sum total**). ~*vb.* **summing, summed. 8.** (often foll. by *up*) to add or form a total of (something). **9.** (*tr.*) to calculate the sum of (the terms in a sequence). ~See also **sum up.**

Sumerian (suː'mɪərɪən, -'mɛər-) *n.* **1.** a member of a people who established a civilization in Sumer, in SW Asia, during the 4th millennium B.C. **2.** the extinct language of this people. ~*adj.* **3.** of or relating to ancient Sumer, its inhabitants, or their language or civilization.

summarize *or* **-ise** ('sʌmə,raɪz) *vb.* (*tr.*) to make or be a summary of; express concisely. —**,summari'zation** *or* **-i'sation** *n.* —**'summa,rizer, -iser,** *or* **'summarist** *n.*

summary ('sʌmərɪ) *n., pl.* **-maries. 1.** a brief account giving the main points of something. ~*adj.* (*usually prenominal*). **2.** performed arbitrarily and quickly, without formality: *a summary execution.* **3.** (of legal proceedings) short and free from the complexities and delays of a full trial. **4. summary jurisdiction.** the right a court has to adjudicate immediately upon some matter. **5.** giving the gist or essence. —**'summarily** *adv.* —**'summariness** *n.*

summation (sʌ'meɪʃən) *n.* **1.** the act or process of determining a sum. **2.** the result of such an act or process. **3.** *U.S. law.* the concluding statements made by opposing counsel in a case before a court. —**sum'mational** *adj.*

summer ('sʌmə) *n.* **1.** (*sometimes cap.*) **a.** the warmest season of the year, between spring and autumn, astronomically from the June solstice to the September equinox in the N hemisphere and at the opposite time of year in the S hemisphere. **b.** (*as modifier*): *summer flowers.* Related adj.: **aestival. 2.** the period of hot weather associated with the summer. **3.** a time of blossoming, greatest happiness, etc. **4.** *Chiefly poetic.* a year represented by this season: *a child of nine summers.* ~*vb.* **5.** (*intr.*) to spend the summer (at a place). **6.** (*tr.*) to keep or feed (farm animals) during the summer: *they summered their cattle on the mountain slopes.* —**'summery** *adj.*

summerhouse ('sʌmə,haus) *n.* a small building in a garden or park, used for shade or recreation in the summer.

summersault ('sʌmə,sɔːlt) *n., vb.* a variant spelling of **somersault.**

summer school *n.* a school, academic course, etc., held during the summer.

summer solstice *n.* **1.** the time at which the sun is at its northernmost point in the sky (southernmost point in the S hemisphere). It occurs about June 21 (December 22 in the S hemisphere). **2.** *Astron.* the point on the celestial sphere, opposite the **winter solstice,** at which the ecliptic is furthest north from the celestial equator.

summertime ('sʌmə,taɪm) *n.* **1.** the period or season of summer. **2.** *Brit.* any daylight-saving time, esp. British Summer Time.

summing-up *n.* **1.** a review or summary of the main points of an argument, speech, etc. **2.** concluding statements made by a judge to the jury before they retire to consider their verdict.

summit ('sʌmɪt) *n.* **1.** the highest point or part, esp. of a mountain; top. **2.** the highest possible degree or state; peak or climax: *the summit of ambition.* **3.** the highest level, importance, or rank: *a meeting at the summit.* **4. a.** a meeting of chiefs of governments or other high officials. **b.** (*as modifier*): *a summit conference.*

summon ('sʌmən) *vb.* (*tr.*) **1.** to order to come; send for, esp. to attend court, by issuing a summons. **2.** to order or instruct (to do something) or call (to something): *the bell summoned them to their work.* **3.** to call upon to meet or convene. **4.** (often foll. by *up*) to muster or gather (one's strength, courage, etc.). **5.** *Arch.* to call upon to surrender.

summons ('sʌmənz) *n., pl.* **-monses. 1.** a call, signal, or order to do something, esp. to attend at a specified place or time. **2. a.** an official order requiring a person to attend court, either to answer a charge or to give evidence. **b.** the writ making such an order. **3.** a call or command given to the members of an assembly to convene a meeting. ~*vb.* **4.** to take out a summons against (a person).

sumptuary ('sʌmptjuərɪ) *adj.* relating to or controlling expenditure or extravagance.

sumptuous ('sʌmptjuəs) *adj.* **1.** expensive or extravagant: *sumptuous costumes.* **2.** magnificent; splendid: *a sumptuous scene.* —**'sumptuously** *adv.* —**'sumptuousness** *n.*

sum up *vb.* (*adv.*) **1.** to summarize (the main points of an argument, etc.). **2.** (*tr.*) to form a quick opinion of: *I summed him up in five minutes.*

sun (sʌn) *n.* **1.** the star that is the source of heat and light for the planets in the solar system. Related adj.: **solar. 2.** any star around which a planetary system re-

---

THESAURUS

sultry 1. close, hot, humid, muggy, oppressive, sticky, stifling, stuffy, sweltering **2.** come-hither (*Inf.*), erotic, passionate, provocative, seductive, sensual, sexy (*Inf.*), voluptuous

sum aggregate, amount, entirety, quantity, reckoning, score, sum total, tally, total, totality, whole

summarily arbitrarily, at short notice, expeditiously, forthwith, immediately, on the spot, peremptorily, promptly, speedily, swiftly, without delay, without wasting words

summarize abridge, condense, encapsulate, epitomize, give a rundown of, give the

main points of, outline, précis, put in a nutshell, review, sum up

summary 1. *n.* abridgment, abstract, compendium, digest, epitome, essence, extract, outline, précis, recapitulation, résumé, review, rundown, summing-up, synopsis **2.** *adj.* arbitrary, brief, compact, compendious, concise, condensed, cursory, hasty, laconic, perfunctory, pithy, succinct

summit acme, apex, crown, crowning point, culmination, head, height, peak, pinnacle, top, zenith

summon 1. arouse, assemble, bid, call, call together, cite, convene, convoke, invite,

rally, rouse, send for **2.** *Often with* **up** call into action, draw on, gather, invoke, mobilize, muster

sumptuous costly, dear, de luxe, expensive, extravagant, gorgeous, grand, lavish, luxurious, magnificent, opulent, plush (*Inf.*), posh (*Inf.*), rich, ritzy (*Sl.*), splendid, superb

sum up 1. close, conclude, put in a nutshell, recapitulate, review, summarize **2.** estimate, form an opinion of, get the measure of, size up (*Inf.*)

volves. **3.** the sun as it appears at a particular time or place: *the winter sun*. **4.** the radiant energy, esp. heat and light, received from the sun; sunshine. **5.** a person or thing considered as a source of radiant warmth, glory, etc. **6.** a pictorial representation of the sun, often depicted with a human face. **7.** *Poetic*. a year or a day. **8.** *Poetic*. a climate. **9.** *Arch*. sunrise or sunset (esp. in **from sun to sun**). **10. catch the sun.** to become slightly sunburnt. **11. place in the sun.** a prominent or favourable position. **12. take** *or* **shoot the sun.** *Naut*. to measure the altitude of the sun in order to determine latitude. **13. touch of the sun.** slight sunstroke. **14. under** *or* **beneath the sun.** on earth; at all: *nobody under the sun eats more than you do*. ~*vb*. **sunning, sunned. 15.** to expose (oneself) to the sunshine. **16.** (*tr*.) to expose to the sunshine in order to warm, tan, etc.

Sun. *abbrev. for* Sunday.

sun bath *n*. the exposure of the body to the rays of the sun or a sun lamp, esp. in order to get a suntan.

sunbathe ('sʌn,beɪð) *vb*. (*intr*.) to bask in the sunshine, esp. in order to get a suntan. —'**sun,bather** *n*.

sunbeam ('sʌn,biːm) *n*. a beam, ray, or stream of sunlight.

sunburn ('sʌn,bɜːn) *n*. **1.** inflammation of the skin caused by overexposure to the sun. **2.** another word for **suntan.** —'**sun,burnt** *or* '**sun,burned** *adj*.

sunburst ('sʌn,bɜːst) *n*. **1.** a burst of sunshine, as through a break in the clouds. **2.** a pattern or design resembling that of the sun. **3.** a jewelled brooch with this pattern.

sundae ('sʌndɪ, -deɪ) *n*. ice cream topped with a sweet sauce, nuts, whipped cream, etc.

Sunday ('sʌndɪ) *n*. the first day of the week and the Christian day of worship.

Sunday best *n*. one's best clothes, esp. regarded as those most suitable for churchgoing.

Sunday school *n*. **1. a.** a school for the religious instruction of children on Sundays, usually held in a church. **b.** (*as modifier*): *a Sunday-school outing*. **2.** the members of such a school.

sunder ('sʌndə) *Arch. or literary*. ~*vb*. **1.** to break or cause to break apart or in pieces. ~*n*. **2. in sunder.** into pieces; apart.

sundial ('sʌn,daɪəl) *n*. a device indicating the time during the hours of sunlight by means of a stationary arm (the **gnomon**) that casts a shadow onto a plate or surface marked in hours.

sundown ('sʌn,daʊn) *n*. another name for **sunset**.

sundowner ('sʌn,daʊnə) *n*. **1.** *Austral. sl.* a tramp, esp. one who seeks food and lodging at sundown when it is too late to work. **2.** *Inf., chiefly Brit.* an alcoholic drink taken at sunset.

sundry ('sʌndrɪ) *determiner*. **1.** several or various; miscellaneous. ~*pron*. **2. all and sundry.** everybody. ~*n*., *pl.* **-dries. 3.** (*pl.*) miscellaneous unspecified items. **4.** *Austral*. (in cricket) an extra; a bye, leg bye, wide, or no ball.

sunfish ('sʌn,fɪʃ) *n*., *pl.* **-fish** *or* **-fishes. 1.** any of various large fishes of temperate and tropical seas, esp. one which has a large rounded compressed body, long pointed dorsal and anal fins, and a fringelike tail fin. **2.** any of various small predatory North American freshwater percoid fishes, typically having a compressed brightly coloured body.

sunflower ('sʌn,flaʊə) *n*. **1.** any of several American plants having very tall thick stems, large flower heads with yellow rays, and seeds used as food, esp. for poultry. See also **Jerusalem artichoke. 2. sunflower seed oil.** the oil extracted from sunflower seeds, used as a salad oil, in margarine, etc.

sung (sʌŋ) *vb*. **1.** the past participle of **sing**. ~*adj*. **2.** produced by singing: *a sung syllable*.

▷ **Usage.** See at **ring²**.

sunglasses ('sʌn,glɑːsɪz) *pl. n.* glasses with darkened or polarizing lenses that protect the eyes from the sun's glare.

sun-god *n*. **1.** the sun considered as a personal deity. **2.** a deity associated with the sun or controlling its movements.

sunk (sʌŋk) *vb*. **1.** a past tense or past participle of **sink**. ~*adj*. **2.** *Inf.* with all hopes dashed; ruined.

sunken ('sʌŋkən) *vb*. **1.** a past participle of **sink**. ~*adj*. **2.** unhealthily hollow: *sunken cheeks*. **3.** situated at a lower level than the surrounding or usual one: *a sunken bath*. **4.** situated under water; submerged. **5.** depressed; low: *sunken spirits*.

sunk fence *n*. a ditch, one side of which is made into a retaining wall so as to enclose an area of land while remaining hidden in the total landscape. Also called: **ha-ha.**

sun lamp *n*. **1.** a lamp that generates ultraviolet rays, used for obtaining an artificial suntan, for muscular therapy, etc. **2.** a lamp used in film studios, etc., to give an intense beam of light by means of parabolic mirrors.

sunless ('sʌnlɪs) *adj*. **1.** without sun or sunshine. **2.** gloomy; depressing. —'**sunlessly** *adv*.

sunlight ('sʌnlaɪt) *n*. **1.** the light emanating from the sun. **2.** an area or the time characterized by sunshine. —'**sunlit** *adj*.

sun lounge *or U.S.* **sun parlor** *n.* a room with large windows positioned to receive as much sunlight as possible.

sunny ('sʌnɪ) *adj*. **-nier, -niest. 1.** full of or exposed to sunlight. **2.** radiating good humour. **3.** of or resembling the sun. —'**sunnily** *adv*. —'**sunniness** *n*.

sunrise ('sʌn,raɪz) *n*. **1.** the daily appearance of the sun above the horizon. **2.** the atmospheric phenomena accompanying this appearance. **3.** Also called (esp. U.S.): **sunup.** the time at which the sun rises at a particular locality.

sunset ('sʌn,sɛt) *n*. **1.** the daily disappearance of the sun below the horizon. **2.** the atmospheric phenomena accompanying this disappearance. **3.** Also called: **sundown.** the time at which the sun sets at a particular locality. **4.** the final stage or closing period, as of a person's life.

sunshade ('sʌn,ʃeɪd) *n*. a device, esp. a parasol or awning, serving to shade from the sun.

sunshine ('sʌn,ʃaɪn) *n*. **1.** the light received directly from the sun. **2.** the warmth from the sun. **3.** a sunny area. **4.** a light-hearted term of affection. —'**sunshiny** *adj*.

sunshine roof *or* **sunroof** ('sʌn,ruːf) *n*. a panel in the roof of a car that may be opened by sliding it back.

sunspot ('sʌn,spɒt) *n*. **1.** any of the dark cool patches that appear on the surface of the sun and last about a week. **2.** *Inf.* a sunny holiday resort. **3.** *Austral*. a small cancerous spot produced by overexposure to the sun.

sunstroke ('sʌn,strəʊk) *n*. heatstroke caused by prolonged exposure to intensely hot sunlight.

suntan ('sʌn,tæn) *n*. **a.** a brownish colouring of the skin caused by the formation of the pigment melanin within the skin on exposure to the ultraviolet rays of the sun or a sunlamp. Often shortened to **tan. b.** (*as modifier*): *suntan oil*. —'**sun,tanned** *adj*.

sup¹ (sʌp) *vb*. **supping, supped.** (*intr*.) *Arch*. to have supper.

sup² (sʌp) *vb*. **supping, supped. 1.** to partake of (liquid) by swallowing a little at a time. **2.** *N. English dialect*. to drink. ~*n*. **3.** a sip.

sup. *abbrev. for*: **1.** above. **2.** superior. **3.** *Grammar*.

THESAURUS

sun 1. *n*. daystar (*Poetic*), eye of heaven, Helios (*Greek myth*), Phoebus (*Greek myth*), Phoebus Apollo (*Greek myth*), Sol (*Roman myth*) **2.** *v*. bake, bask, sunbathe, tan

sunburnt bronzed, brown, brown as a berry, burnt, like a lobster, peeling, red, ruddy, scarlet, tanned

sundry assorted, different, divers (*Archaic*), miscellaneous, several, some, varied, various

sunk all washed up (*Inf.*), done for (*Inf.*), finished, lost, on the rocks, ruined

sunken 1. concave, drawn, haggard, hollow, hollowed **2.** at a lower level, below ground, buried, depressed, immersed, lower, recessed, submerged

sunless bleak, cheerless, cloudy, dark, depressing, gloomy, grey, hazy, overcast, sombre

sunny 1. bright, brilliant, clear, fine, luminous, radiant, summery, sunlit, sunshiny, unclouded, without a cloud in the sky **2.** *Fig.*

beaming, blithe, buoyant, cheerful, cheery, genial, happy, joyful, light-hearted, optimistic, pleasant, smiling

sunrise aurora (*Poetic*), break of day, cockcrow, dawn, daybreak, daylight, dayspring (*Poetic*), sunup

sunset close of (the) day, dusk, eventide, gloaming, nightfall, sundown

superlative. **4.** supplement. **5.** supplementary. **6.** supply.

super ('suːpə, 'sjuːpə) *adj.* **1.** *Inf.* **a.** outstanding; superfine; superb. **b.** (*in combination*): *superstar.* ~*n.* **2. a.** a product of superior quality, size, etc. **b.** such quality, etc. ~*interj.* **3.** *Chiefly Brit.* good! excellent!

super- *prefix.* **1.** placed above or over: *superscript.* **2.** of greater size, extent, quality, etc.: *supermarket.* **3.** beyond a standard or norm: *supersonic.* **4.** indicating that a chemical compound contains a specified element in a higher proportion than usual: *superphosphate.*

superable ('suːpərəb^əl, 'sjuː-) *adj.* able to be surmounted or overcome. —**supera'bility** *or* **'superableness** *n.* —**'superably** *adv.*

superannuate (ˌsuːpər'ænjuˌeɪt, ˌsjuː-) *vb.* (*tr.*) **1.** to pension off. **2.** to discard as obsolete or old-fashioned.

superannuated (ˌsuːpər'ænjuˌeɪtɪd, ˌsjuː-) *adj.* **1.** discharged, esp. with a pension, owing to age or illness. **2.** too old to serve usefully. **3.** obsolete.

superannuation (ˌsuːpərˌænjuˈeɪʃən, ˌsjuː-) *n.* **a.** the amount deducted regularly from employees' incomes in a contributory pension scheme. **b.** the pension finally paid. **2.** the act or process of superannuating or the condition of being superannuated.

superb (suːˈpɜːb, sjuː-) *adj.* **1.** surpassingly good; excellent. **2.** majestic or imposing. **3.** magnificently rich; luxurious. —**su'perbly** *adv.* —**su'perbness** *n.*

supercargo (ˌsuːpəˈkɑːgəʊ, ˌsjuː-) *n., pl.* **-goes.** an officer on a merchant ship who supervises commercial matters and is in charge of the cargo.

supercharge ('suːpəˌtʃɑːdʒ, 'sjuː-) *vb.* (*tr.*) **1.** to increase the intake pressure of (an internal-combustion engine) with a supercharger; boost. **2.** to charge (the atmosphere, a remark, etc.) with an excess amount of (tension, emotion, etc.). **3.** to apply pressure to (a fluid); pressurize.

supercharger ('suːpəˌtʃɑːdʒə, 'sjuː-) *n.* a device that increases the mass of air drawn into an internal-combustion engine by raising the intake pressure. Also called: **blower, booster.**

supercilious (ˌsuːpəˈsɪlɪəs, ˌsjuː-) *adj.* displaying arrogant pride, scorn, or indifference. —**super'ciliously** *adv.* —**super'ciliousness** *n.*

superconductivity (ˌsuːpəˌkɒndʌkˈtɪvɪtɪ, ˌsjuː-) *n.* *Physics.* the property of certain substances that have almost no electrical resistance at temperatures close to absolute zero. —**superconduction** (ˌsuːpəkənˈdʌkʃən, ˌsjuː-) *n.* —**supercon'ductive** *or* **supercon'ducting** *adj.* —**supercon'ductor** *n.*

supercool (ˌsuːpəˈkuːl, ˌsjuː-) *vb.* *Chem.* to cool or be cooled without freezing or crystallization to a temperature below that at which freezing or crystallization should occur.

superego (ˌsuːpərˈiːgəʊ, -ˈɛgəʊ, ˌsjuː-) *n., pl.* **-gos.** *Psychoanal.* that part of the unconscious mind that acts as a conscience for the ego.

supererogation (ˌsuːpərˌɛrəˈgeɪʃən, ˌsjuː-) *n.* **1.** the performance of work in excess of that required or expected. **2.** *R.C. Church.* supererogatory prayers, devotions, etc.

superficial (ˌsuːpəˈfɪʃəl, ˌsjuː-) *adj.* **1.** of, near, or forming the surface: *superficial bruising.* **2.** displaying a lack of thoroughness or care: *a superficial inspection.* **3.** only outwardly apparent rather than genuine or actual: *the similarity was merely superficial.* **4.** of little substance or significance; trivial: *superficial differences.* **5.** lacking profundity: *the film's plot was quite superficial.* **6.** (of measurements) involving only the surface area. —**superficiality** (ˌsuːpəˌfɪʃɪˈælɪtɪ) *n.* —**super'ficially** *adv.*

superfine (ˌsuːpəˈfaɪn, ˌsjuː-) *adj.* **1.** of exceptional fineness or quality. **2.** excessively refined. —**super'fineness** *n.*

superfluous (suːˈpɜːfluəs, sjuː-) *adj.* **1.** exceeding what is sufficient or required. **2.** not necessary or relevant; uncalled for. —**super'fluity** *or* **su'perfluousness** *n.* —**su'perfluously** *adv.*

superheat (ˌsuːpəˈhiːt, ˌsjuː-) *vb.* (*tr.*) **1.** to heat (a vapour, esp. steam) to a temperature above its saturation point for a given pressure. **2.** to heat (a liquid) to a temperature above its boiling point without boiling occurring. **3.** to heat excessively; overheat. —**super'heater** *n.*

superhuman (ˌsuːpəˈhjuːmən, ˌsjuː-) *adj.* **1.** having powers above and beyond those of mankind. **2.** exceeding normal human ability or experience. —**super'humanly** *adv.*

superimpose (ˌsuːpərɪmˈpəʊz, ˌsjuː-) *vb.* (*tr.*) **1.** to set or place on or over something else. **2.** (usually foll. by *on* or *upon*) to add (to). —**super,impo'sition** *n.*

superinduce (ˌsuːpərɪnˈdjuːs, ˌsjuː-) *vb.* (*tr.*) to introduce as an additional feature, factor, etc. —**superinduction** (ˌsuːpərɪnˈdʌkʃən, ˌsjuː-) *n.*

superintend (ˌsuːpərɪnˈtɛnd, ˌsjuː-) *vb.* to undertake the direction or supervision (of); manage. —**superin'tendence** *n.*

superintendent (ˌsuːpərɪnˈtɛndənt, ˌsjuː-) *n.* **1.** a person who directs and manages an organization, office, etc. **2.** (in Britain) a senior police officer higher in rank than an inspector but lower than a chief superintendent. **3.** (in the U.S.) the head of a police department. **4.** *Chiefly U.S.* a caretaker. ~*adj.* **5.** of or relating to supervision; superintending. —**superin'tendency** *n.*

superior (suːˈpɪərɪə, sjuː-) *adj.* **1.** greater in quality, quantity, etc. **2.** of high or extraordinary worth, merit, etc. **3.** higher in rank or status. **4.** displaying a conscious sense of being above or better than others; supercilious. **5.** (*often postpositive;* foll. by *to*) not susceptible (to) or influenced (by). **6.** placed higher up; further from the base. **7.** *Astron.* (of a planet) having an orbit further from the sun than the orbit of the earth. **8.** (of a plant ovary) situated above the calyx and other floral parts. **9.** *Printing.* (of a character) written or printed above the line; superscript. ~*n.* **10.** a person or thing of greater rank or quality. **11.** *Printing.* a character set in a superior position. **12.** (*often cap.*) the head of a community in a religious order. —**su'perioress** *fem. n.* —**superiority** (suːˌpɪərɪˈɒrɪtɪ, sjuː-) *n.*

superlative (suːˈpɜːlətɪv, sjuː-) *adj. pl.* **1.** of outstanding quality, degree, etc.; supreme. **2.** *Grammar.* denoting the form of an adjective or adverb that expresses the highest or a very high degree of quality. In English this is usually marked by the suffix *-est* or the word *most,* as

---

THESAURUS

superb admirable, breathtaking, choice, excellent, exquisite, fine, first-rate, gorgeous, grand, magnificent, marvellous, of the first water, splendid, superior, unrivalled

supercilious arrogant, condescending, contemptuous, disdainful, haughty, high and mighty (*Inf.*), hoity-toity (*Inf.*), imperious, insolent, lofty, lordly, overbearing, patronizing, proud, scornful, snooty (*Inf.*), stuck-up (*Inf.*), toffee-nosed (*Sl.*), uppish (*Brit. inf.*), vainglorious

superficial **1.** exterior, external, on the surface, peripheral, shallow, skin-deep, slight, surface **2.** casual, cosmetic, cursory, desultory, hasty, hurried, inattentive, nodding, passing, perfunctory, sketchy, slapdash **3.** empty, empty-headed, frivolous, lightweight, shallow, silly, trivial **4.** apparent, evident, ostensible, outward, seeming

superficiality emptiness, lack of depth, lack of substance, shallowness, triviality

superficially apparently, at first glance, externally, on the surface, ostensibly, to the casual eye

superfluous excess, excessive, extra, in excess, left over, needless, on one's hands, pleonastic (*Rhetoric*), redundant, remaining, residuary, spare, superabundant, supererogatory, supernumerary, surplus, surplus to requirements, uncalled-for, unnecessary, unneeded, unrequired

superhuman **1.** herculean, heroic, phenomenal, prodigious, stupendous, valiant **2.** divine, paranormal, preternatural, supernatural

superintend administer, control, direct, inspect, look after, manage, overlook, oversee, run, supervise

superintendence care, charge, control, direction, government, guidance, inspection, management, supervision, surveillance

superintendent administrator, chief, conductor, controller, director, governor, inspector, manager, overseer, supervisor

superior *adj.* **1.** better, grander, greater, higher, more advanced (expert, extensive, skilful), paramount, predominant, preferred, prevailing, surpassing, unrivalled **2.** a cut above (*Inf.*), admirable, choice, de luxe, distinguished, excellent, exceptional, exclusive, fine, first-class, first-rate, good, good quality, high calibre, high-class, of the first order **3.** airy, condescending, disdainful, haughty, lofty, lordly, patronizing, pretentious, snobbish, stuck-up (*Inf.*), supercilious ~*n.* **4.** boss (*Inf.*), chief, director, manager, principal, senior, supervisor

superiority advantage, ascendancy, excellence, lead, predominance, pre-eminence, preponderance, prevalence, supremacy

in *loudest* or *most loudly*. **3.** (of language or style) excessive; exaggerated. ~*n.* **4.** a thing that excels all others or is of the highest quality. **5.** *Grammar.* the superlative form of an adjective. **6.** the highest degree; peak. —**su'perlatively** *adv.* —**su'perlativeness** *n.*

superman ('su:pə,mæn, 'sju:-) *n., pl.* **-men.** **1.** (in the philosophy of Nietzsche) an ideal man who would rise above good and evil and who represents the goal of human evolution. **2.** any man of apparently superhuman powers.

supermarket ('su:pə,mɑːkɪt, 'sju:-) *n.* a large self-service store retailing food and household supplies.

supernal (su:'pɜːnəl, sju:-) *adj. Literary.* **1.** divine; celestial. **2.** of, from above, or from the sky. —**su'pernally** *adv.*

supernatural (,su:pə'nætʃərəl, ,sju:-) *adj.* **1.** of or relating to things that cannot be explained according to natural laws. **2.** of or caused as if by a god; miraculous. **3.** of or involving occult beings. **4.** exceeding the ordinary; abnormal. ~*n.* **5. the.** supernatural forces, occurrences, and beings collectively. —,**super'naturally** *adv.* —,**super'naturalness** *n.*

supernova (,su:pə'nəʊvə, ,sju:-) *n., pl.* **-vae** (-viː) *or* **-vas.** a star that explodes owing to instabilities following the exhaustion of its nuclear fuel, becoming for a few days up to one hundred million times brighter than the sun. Cf. **nova.**

supernumerary (,su:pə'njuːmərərɪ, ,sju:-) *adj.* **1.** exceeding a regular or proper number; extra. **2.** functioning as a substitute or assistant with regard to a regular body or staff. ~*n., pl.* **-aries.** **3.** a person or thing that exceeds the required or regular number. **4.** a substitute or assistant. **5.** an actor who has no lines, esp. a nonprofessional one.

superphosphate (,su:pə'fɒsfeɪt, ,sju:-) *n.* **1.** a mixture of the diacid calcium salt of orthophosphoric acid with calcium sulphate and small quantities of other phosphates: used as a fertilizer. **2.** a salt of phosphoric acid formed by incompletely replacing its acidic hydrogen atoms.

superpose (,su:pə'pəʊz, ,sju:-) *vb.* (*tr.*) *Geom.* to place (one figure) upon another so that their perimeters coincide.

superpower ('su:pə,paʊə, 'sju:-) *n.* **1.** an extremely powerful state, such as the U.S. **2.** extremely high power, esp. electrical or mechanical. —'**super,powered** *adj.*

superscribe (,su:pə'skraɪb, ,sju:-) *vb.* (*tr.*) to write (an inscription, name, etc.) above, on top of, or outside. —**superscription** (,su:pə'skrɪpʃən, ,sju:-) *n.*

superscript ('su:pə,skrɪpt, 'sju:-) *adj.* **1.** *Printing.* (of a character) written or printed above the line; superior. Cf. **subscript.** ~*n.* **2.** a superscript or superior character.

supersede (,su:pə'siːd, ,sju:-) *vb.* (*tr.*) **1.** to take the place of (something old-fashioned or less appropriate); supplant. **2.** to replace in function, office, etc.; succeed. **3.** to discard or set aside or cause to be set aside as obsolete or inferior. —,**super'sedence** *n.* —**supersedure** (,su:pə'siːdʒə, ,sju:-) *n.* —**supersession** (,su:pə'sɛʃən, ,sju:-) *n.*

supersonic (,su:pə'sɒnɪk, ,sju:-) *adj.* being, having, or capable of a velocity in excess of the velocity of sound. —,**super'sonically** *adv.*

supersonics (,su:pə'sɒnɪks, ,sju:-) *n.* (*functioning as sing.*) **1.** the study of supersonic motion. **2.** a less common name for **ultrasonics.**

superstition (,su:pə'stɪʃən, ,sju:-) *n.* **1.** irrational belief usually founded on ignorance or fear and characterized by obsessive reverence for omens, charms, etc. **2.** a notion, act or ritual that derives from such belief. **3.** any irrational belief, esp. with regard to the unknown. —,**super'stitious** *adj.*

superstore ('su:pə,stɔː) *n.* a large supermarket.

superstructure ('su:pə,strʌktʃə, 'sju:-) *n.* **1.** the part of a building above its foundation. **2.** any structure or concept erected on something else. **3.** *Naut.* any structure above the main deck of a ship with sides flush with the sides of the hull. **4.** the part of a bridge supported by the piers and abutments. —'**super,structural** *adj.*

supertanker ('su:pə,tæŋkə, 'sju:-) *n.* a large fast tanker of more than 275 000 tons capacity.

supertax ('su:pə,tæks, 'sju:-) *n.* a tax levied in addition to the basic or normal tax, esp. a surtax on incomes above a certain level.

supervene (,su:pə'viːn, ,sju:-) *vb.* (*intr.*) **1.** to follow closely; ensue. **2.** to occur as an unexpected or extraneous development. —,**super'venience** *or* **supervention** (,su:pə'vɛnʃən, ,sju:-) *n.* —,**super'venient** *adj.*

supervise ('su:pə,vaɪz, 'sju:-) *vb.* (*tr.*) **1.** to direct or oversee the performance or operation of. **2.** to watch over so as to maintain order, etc. —**supervision** (,su:pə'vɪʒən, ,sju:-) *n.* —'**super,visor** *n.*

supine *adj.* (su:'paɪn, sju:-; 'su:paɪn, 'sju:-). **1.** lying or resting on the back with the face, palm, etc., upwards. **2.** displaying no interest or animation; lethargic. ~*n.* ('su:paɪn, 'sju:-). **3.** *Grammar.* a noun form derived from a verb in Latin, often used to express purpose with verbs of motion. —**su'pinely** *adv.* —**su'pineness** *n.*

supper ('sʌpə) *n.* **1.** an evening meal, esp. a light one. **2.** an evening social event featuring a supper. **3. sing for one's supper.** to obtain something by performing a service. —'**supperless** *adj.*

supplant (sə'plɑːnt) *vb.* (*tr.*) to take the place of, often by trickery or force. —**sup'planter** *n.*

supple ('sʌpəl) *adj.* **1.** bending easily without damage. **2.** capable of or showing easy or graceful movement; lithe. **3.** mentally flexible; responding readily. **4.** disposed to agree, sometimes to the point of servility. ~*vb.* **5.** *Rare.* to make or become supple. —'**suppleness** *n.*

supplement *n.* ('sʌplɪmənt). **1.** an addition designed to complete, make up for a deficiency, etc. **2.** a section appended to a publication to supply further information, correct errors, etc. **3.** a magazine or section inserted into a newspaper or periodical, such as one issued every week. **4.** *Geom.* **a.** either of a pair of angles whose sum is 180°. **b.** an arc of a circle that when added to another arc forms a semicircle. ~*vb.* ('sʌplɪ,mɛnt). **5.** (*tr.*) to provide a supplement to, esp. in order to remedy a deficiency. —,**supple'mentary** *adj.* —,**supplemen'tation** *n.*

supplementary angle *n.* either of two angles whose sum is 180°.

supplementary benefit *n.* (in Britain) a weekly allowance paid to various groups of people by the state to bring their incomes up to minimum levels established by law.

suppliant ('sʌplɪənt) *adj.* **1.** expressing entreaty or supplication. ~*n., adj.* **2.** another word for **supplicant.** —'**suppliantly** *adv.*

supplicant ('sʌplɪkənt) *or* **suppliant** *n.* **1.** a person who supplicates. ~*adj.* **2.** entreating humbly; supplicating.

THESAURUS

superlative *adj.* consummate, crack (*Sl.*), excellent, greatest, highest, magnificent, matchless, of the first water, of the highest order, outstanding, peerless, supreme, surpassing, transcendent, unparalleled, unrivalled, unsurpassed

supernatural abnormal, dark, ghostly, hidden, miraculous, mysterious, mystic, occult, paranormal, phantom, preternatural, psychic, spectral, supranatural, uncanny, unearthly, unnatural

supersede annul, displace, oust, overrule, remove, replace, set aside, supplant, supplement, suspend, take over, take the place of, usurp

supervise administer, be on duty at, be

responsible for, conduct, control, direct, handle, have *or* be in charge of, inspect, keep an eye on, look after, manage, oversee, preside over, run, superintend

supervision administration, auspices, care, charge, control, direction, guidance, instruction, management, oversight, stewardship, superintendence, surveillance

supervisor administrator, boss (*Inf.*), chief, foreman, inspector, manager, overseer, steward, superintendent

supervisory administrative, executive, managerial, overseeing, superintendent

supplant displace, oust, overthrow, remove, replace, supersede, take over, take the place of, undermine, unseat

supple bending, elastic, flexible, limber, lithe, plastic, pliable, pliant

supplement 1. *n.* added feature, addendum, addition, appendix, codicil, complement, extra, insert, postscript, pull-out, sequel 2. *v.* add, augment, complement, extend, fill out, reinforce, supply, top up

supplementary accompanying, additional, ancillary, auxiliary, complementary, extra, secondary, supplemental

suppliant 1. *adj.* begging, beseeching, craving, entreating, imploring, importunate, on bended knee 2. *n.* applicant, petitioner, suitor, supplicant

supplicate (ˈsʌplɪˌkeɪt) vb. **1.** to make a humble request to (someone); plead. **2.** (tr.) to ask for or seek humbly. —ˌsuppliˈcation n. —ˈsuppliˌcatory adj.

supply¹ (səˈplaɪ) vb. **-plying, -plied. 1.** (tr.; often foll. by *with*) to furnish with something required. **2.** (tr.; often foll. by *to* or *for*) to make available or provide (something desired or lacking): *to supply books to the library.* **3.** (tr.) to provide for adequately; satisfy: *who will supply their needs?* **4.** to serve as a substitute, usually temporary, in (another's position, etc.): *there are no clergymen to supply the pulpit.* **5.** (tr.) Brit. to fill (a vacancy, position, etc.). ~n., pl. **-plies. 6. a.** the act of providing or something provided. **b.** (as modifier): *a supply dump.* **7.** (often pl.) an amount available for use; stock. **8.** (pl.) food, equipment, etc., needed for a campaign or trip. **9.** Econ. **a.** willingness and ability to offer goods and services for sale. **b.** the amount of a commodity that producers are willing and able to offer for sale at a specified price. Cf. **demand** (sense 9). **10.** Mil. **a.** the management and disposal of food and equipment. **b.** (as modifier): *supply routes.* **11.** (often pl.) a grant of money voted by a legislature for government expenses. **12.** (in Parliament and similar legislatures) the money voted annually for the expenses of the civil service and armed forces. **13. a.** a person who acts as a temporary substitute, esp. a clergyman. **b.** (as modifier): *a supply teacher.* **14.** a source of electrical energy, gas, etc. —**supˈpliable** adj. —**supˈplier** n.

supply² (ˈsʌplɪ) or **supplely** (ˈsʌplɪ) adv. in a supple manner.

support (səˈpɔːt) vb. (tr.) **1.** to carry the weight of. **2.** to bear (pressure, weight, etc.). **3.** to provide the necessities of life for (a family, person, etc.). **4.** to tend to establish (a theory, statement, etc.) by providing new facts. **5.** to speak in favour of (a motion). **6.** to give aid or courage to. **7.** to give approval to (a cause, principle, etc.); subscribe to. **8.** to endure with forbearance: *I will no longer support bad behaviour.* **9.** to give strength to; maintain: *to support a business.* **10.** Films, theatre. **a.** to play a subordinate role to. **b.** to accompany (the feature) in a film programme. **11.** to act or perform (a role or character). ~n. **12.** the act of supporting or the condition of being supported. **13.** a thing that bears the weight or part of the weight of a construction. **14.** a person who or thing that furnishes aid. **15.** the means of maintenance of a family, person, etc. **16.** (often preceded by *the*) an actor or group of actors playing subordinate roles. **17.** Med. an appliance worn to ease the strain on an injured bodily structure or part. **18.** Also: **athletic support.** a more formal term for **jockstrap.** —**supˈportable** adj. —**supˈportive** adj.

supporter (səˈpɔːtə) n. **1.** a person who or thing that acts as a support. **2.** a person who backs a sports team, politician, etc. **3.** a garment or device worn to ease the strain on or restrict the movement of a bodily structure or part. **4.** Heraldry. a figure or beast in a coat of arms depicted as holding up the shield.

suppose (səˈpəʊz) vb. (tr.; may take a clause as object) **1.** to presume (something) to be true without certain knowledge: *I suppose he meant to kill her.* **2.** to consider as a possible suggestion for the sake of discussion, etc.: *suppose that he wins.* **3.** (of theories, propositions, etc.) to imply the inference or assumption (of): *your policy supposes full employment.* —**supˈposable** adj. —**supˈposer** n.

supposed (səˈpəʊzd, -ˈpəʊzɪd) adj. **1.** (prenominal) presumed to be true without certain knowledge. **2.** (prenominal) believed to be true on slight grounds; highly doubtful. **3.** (səˈpəʊzd) (postpositive; foll. by *to*) expected or obliged (to): *I'm supposed to be there.* **4.** (postpositive; used in negative; foll. by *to*) expected or obliged not (to): *you're not supposed to walk on the grass.* —**supposedly** (səˈpəʊzɪdlɪ) adv.

supposition (ˌsʌpəˈzɪʃən) n. **1.** the act of supposing. **2.** a fact, theory, etc., that is supposed. —ˌsuppoˈsitional adj. —ˌsuppoˈsitionally adv.

suppositious (ˌsʌpəˈzɪʃəs) or **supposititious** (səˌpɒzɪˈtɪʃəs) adj. **1.** deduced from supposition; hypothetical. **2.** substituted with intent to mislead or deceive. —ˌsuppoˈsitiously or supˌposiˈtitiously adv. —ˌsuppoˈsitiousness or supˌposiˈtitiousness n.

suppository (səˈpɒzɪtərɪ, -trɪ) n., pl. **-ries.** Med. a solid medication for insertion into the vagina, rectum, or urethra, where it melts and releases the active substance.

suppress (səˈprɛs) vb. (tr.) **1.** to put an end to; prohibit. **2.** to hold in check; restrain: *I was obliged to suppress a smile.* **3.** to withhold from circulation or publication: *to suppress seditious pamphlets.* **4.** to stop the activities of; crush: *to suppress a rebellion.* **5.** Electronics. **a.** to reduce or eliminate (unwanted oscillations) in a circuit. **b.** to eliminate (a particular frequency or frequencies) in a signal. **6.** Psychiatry. to resist consciously an idea or a desire entering one's mind. —**supˈpressible** adj. —**supˈpression** n. —**supˈpressive** adj. —**supˈpressor** or **supˈpresser** n.

suppurate (ˈsʌpjʊˌreɪt) vb. (intr.) Pathol. (of a wound, sore, etc.) to discharge pus; fester. —ˌsuppuˈration n. —ˈsuppurative adj.

supra- prefix. over, above, beyond, or greater than: *supranational.*

supranational (ˌsuːprəˈnæʃnəl, ˌsjuː-) adj. involving or relating to more than one nation. —ˌsupraˈnationalism n.

supremacy (sʊˈprɛməsɪ, sjʊ-) n. **1.** supreme power; authority. **2.** the quality or condition of being supreme.

supreme (sʊˈpriːm, sjʊ-) adj. **1.** of highest status or power. **2.** (usually prenominal) of highest quality, im-

THESAURUS

supplication appeal, entreaty, invocation, petition, plea, pleading, prayer, request, solicitation, suit

supply v. **1.** afford, cater to or for, come up with, contribute, endow, fill, furnish, give, grant, minister, outfit, produce, provide, purvey, replenish, satisfy, stock, store, victual, yield ~n. **2.** cache, fund, hoard, quantity, reserve, reservoir, source, stock, stockpile, store **3.** *Usually plural* equipment, food, foodstuff, items, materials, necessities, provender, provisions, rations, stores

support v. **1.** bear, bolster, brace, buttress, carry, hold, hold up, prop, reinforce, shore up, sustain, underpin, uphold **2.** be a source of strength to, buoy up, cherish, finance, foster, fund, keep, look after, maintain, nourish, provide for, strengthen, subsidize, succour, sustain, take care of, underwrite **3.** advocate, aid, assist, back, boost (someone's) morale, champion, defend, forward, go along with, help, promote, second, side with, stand behind, stand up for, stick up for (*Inf.*), take (someone's) part, take up the cudgels for, uphold **4.** attest to, authenticate, bear out, confirm, corroborate, document, endorse, lend credence to, substantiate, verify **5.** bear, brook, countenance, endure, put up with (*Inf.*), stand (for), stomach, submit,

suffer, thole (*Dialect*), tolerate, undergo ~n. **6.** abutment, back, brace, foundation, lining, pillar, post, prop, shore, stanchion, stay, stiffener, underpinning **7.** aid, approval, assistance, backing, blessing, championship, comfort, encouragement, friendship, furtherance, help, loyalty, moral support, patronage, protection, relief, succour, sustenance **8.** keep, livelihood, maintenance, subsistence, sustenance, upkeep **9.** backbone, backer, comforter, mainstay, prop, second, stay, supporter, tower of strength

supporter adherent, advocate, ally, apologist, champion, co-worker, defender, fan, follower, friend, helper, patron, sponsor, upholder, well-wisher

supportive caring, encouraging, helpful, reassuring, sympathetic, understanding

suppose **1.** assume, calculate (*U.S. dialect*), conjecture, dare say, expect, guess (*Inf.*), imagine, infer, judge, opine, presume, presuppose, surmise, take as read, take for granted, think **2.** believe, conceive, conclude, conjecture, consider, fancy, hypothesize, imagine, postulate, pretend

supposed **1.** accepted, alleged, assumed, hypothetical, presumed, presupposed, professed, putative, reputed, rumoured **2.** *With to* expected, meant, obliged, ought, required

supposedly allegedly, at a guess, avowedly, by all accounts, hypothetically, ostensibly, presumably, professedly, purportedly, theoretically

supposition conjecture, doubt, guess, guesswork, hypothesis, idea, notion, postulate, presumption, speculation, surmise, theory

suppress **1.** beat down, check, clamp down on, conquer, crack down on, crush, drive underground, extinguish, overpower, overthrow, put an end to, quash, quell, quench, snuff out, stamp out, stop, subdue, trample on **2.** censor, conceal, contain, cover up, curb, hold in or back, hold in check, keep secret, muffle, muzzle, repress, restrain, silence, smother, stifle, withhold

suppression check, clampdown, crackdown, crushing, dissolution, elimination, extinction, inhibition, prohibition, quashing, smothering, termination

supremacy absolute rule, ascendancy, dominance, domination, dominion, lordship, mastery, paramountcy, predominance, pre-eminence, primacy, sovereignty, supreme authority, sway

portance, etc. **3.** greatest in degree; extreme: *supreme folly.* **4.** (*prenominal*) final or last, ultimate: *the supreme judgment.* —**su'premely** *adv.* —**su'premeness** *n.*

Supreme Being *n.* God.

supremo (suˈpriːməʊ, sjʊ-) *n., pl.* **-mos.** *Brit. inf.* a person in overall authority.

Supt. *or* **supt.** *abbrev. for* superintendent.

sur-¹ *prefix.* over; above; beyond: *surcharge; surrealism.* Cf. **super-**.

sur-² *prefix.* variant of **sub-** before *r: surrogate.*

surcease (sɜːˈsiːs) *Arch.* ~*n.* **1.** cessation or intermission. ~*vb.* **2.** to desist from (some action). **3.** to cease or cause to cease.

surcharge *n.* (ˈsɜːˌtʃɑːdʒ). **1.** a charge in addition to the usual payment, tax, etc. **2.** an excessive sum charged, esp. when unlawful. **3.** an extra and usually excessive burden or supply. **4.** an overprint that alters the face value of a postage stamp. ~*vb.* (sɜːˈtʃɑːdʒ, ˈsɜːˌtʃɑːdʒ). *(tr.)* **5.** to charge an additional sum, tax, etc. **6.** to overcharge (a person) for something. **7.** to put an extra physical burden upon; overload. **8.** to fill to excess; overwhelm. **9.** *Law.* to insert credits that have been omitted in (an account). **10.** to overprint a surcharge on (a stamp).

surcoat (ˈsɜːˌkəʊt) *n.* **1.** a tunic, often embroidered with heraldic arms, worn by a knight over his armour during the Middle Ages. **2.** an outer coat or other garment.

surd (sɜːd) *n.* **1.** *Maths.* a number containing an irrational root, such as $2\sqrt{3} + 3\sqrt{2} + 6$. **2.** *Phonetics.* a voiceless consonant, such as (t). ~*adj.* **3.** of or relating to a surd.

sure (ʃʊə, ʃɔː) *adj.* **1.** (sometimes foll. by *of*) free from hesitancy or uncertainty (with regard to a belief, conviction, etc.): *we are sure of the accuracy of the data; I am sure that he is lying.* **2.** (foll. by *of*) having no doubt, as of the occurrence of a future state or event: *sure of success.* **3.** always effective; unfailing: *a sure remedy.* **4.** reliable in indication or accuracy: *a sure criterion.* **5.** (of persons) worthy of trust or confidence: *a sure friend.* **6.** not open to doubt: *sure proof.* **7.** admitting of no vacillation or doubt: *he is sure in his beliefs.* **8.** bound to be or occur; inevitable: *victory is sure.* **9.** (*postpositive*) bound inevitably (to be or do something); certain: *she is sure to be there.* **10.** physically secure or dependable: *a sure footing.* **11. be sure.** (*usually imperative or dependent imperative; takes a clause as object or an infinitive, sometimes with* to *replaced by* and) to be careful or certain: *be sure and shut the door; be sure to shut the door.* **12. for sure.** without a doubt; surely. **13. make sure. a.** (*takes a clause as object*) to make certain; ensure. **b.** (foll. by *of*) to establish or confirm power or possession (over). **14. sure enough.** *Inf.* as might have been confidently expected; definitely: *often used as a sentence substitute.* **15. to be sure. a.** without doubt; certainly. **b.** it has to be acknowledged; admittedly. ~*adv.* **16.** (*sentence modifier*) *U.S. inf.* without question; certainly. **17.** (*sentence substitute*) *U.S. inf.* willingly; yes. —**'sureness** *n.*

sure-fire *adj.* (*usually prenominal*) *Inf.* certain to succeed or meet expectations; assured.

sure-footed *adj.* **1.** unlikely to fall, slip, or stumble. **2.** not likely to err or fall. —ˌsure-**'footedly** *adv.* —ˌsure-**'footedness** *n.*

surely (ˈʃʊəlɪ, ˈʃɔː-) *adv.* **1.** without doubt; assuredly. **2.** without fail; inexorably (esp. in **slowly but surely**). **3.** (*sentence modifier*) am I not right in thinking that?; I am sure that: *surely you don't mean it?* **4.** *Rare.* in a sure

manner. **5.** *Arch.* safely; securely. **6.** (*sentence substitute*) *Chiefly U.S.* willingly; yes.

surety (ˈʃʊətɪ, ˈʃʊərɪtɪ) *n., pl.* **-ties. 1.** a person who assumes legal responsibility for the fulfilment of another's debt or obligation and himself becomes liable if the other defaults. **2.** security given against loss or damage or as a guarantee that an obligation will be met. **3.** *Obs.* the quality or condition of being sure. **4. stand surety.** to act as a surety. —ˈsurety,ship *n.*

surf (sɜːf) *n.* **1.** waves breaking on the shore or on a reef. **2.** foam caused by the breaking of waves. ~*vb.* **3.** (*intr.*) to take part in surfing. —**'surfy** *adj.*

surface (ˈsɜːfɪs) *n.* **1. a.** the exterior face of an object or one such face. **b.** (*as modifier*): *surface gloss.* **2.** the area or size of such a face. **3.** material resembling such a face, with length and width but without depth. **4. a.** the superficial appearance as opposed to the real nature. **b.** (*as modifier*): *a surface resemblance.* **5.** *Geom.* **a.** the complete boundary of a solid figure. **b.** a continuous two-dimensional configuration. **6. a.** the uppermost level of the land or sea. **b.** (*as modifier*): *surface transportation.* **7. come to the surface.** to emerge; become apparent. **8. on the surface.** to all appearances. ~*vb.* **9.** to rise or cause to rise to or as if to the surface (of water, etc.). **10.** (*tr.*) to treat the surface of, as by polishing, smoothing, etc. **11.** (*tr.*) to furnish with a surface. **12.** (*intr.*) to become apparent; emerge. —**'surfacer** *n.*

surface tension *n.* **1.** a property of liquids caused by intermolecular forces near the surface leading to the apparent presence of a surface film and to capillarity, etc. **2.** a measure of this.

surfboard (ˈsɜːfˌbɔːd) *n.* a long narrow board used in surfing.

surfeit (ˈsɜːfɪt) *n.* **1.** (usually foll. by *of*) an excessive amount. **2.** overindulgence, esp. in eating or drinking. **3.** disgust, nausea, etc., caused by such overindulgence. ~*vb.* **4.** (*tr.*) to supply or feed excessively; satiate. **5.** (*intr.*) *Arch.* to eat, drink, or be supplied to excess.

surfing (ˈsɜːfɪŋ) *n.* the sport of riding towards shore on the crest of a wave by standing or lying on a surfboard. —**'surfer** *or* **'surf,rider** *n.*

surg. *abbrev. for:* **1.** surgeon. **2.** surgery. **3.** surgical.

surge (sɜːdʒ) *n.* **1.** a strong rush or sweep; sudden increase: *a surge of anger.* **2.** the rolling swell of the sea. **3.** a heavy rolling motion or sound: *the surge of the trumpets.* **4.** an undulating rolling surface, as of hills. **5.** a billowing cloud or volume. **6.** *Naut.* a temporary release or slackening of a rope or cable. **7.** a large momentary increase in the voltage or current in an electric circuit. **8.** an instability or unevenness in the power output of an engine. ~*vb.* **9.** (*intr.*) (of waves, the sea, etc.) to rise or roll with a heavy swelling motion. **10.** (*intr.*) to move like a heavy sea. **11.** *Naut.* to slacken or temporarily release (a rope or cable) from a capstan or (of a rope, etc.) to be slackened or released and slip back. **12.** (*intr.*) (of an electric current or voltage) to undergo a large momentary increase. **13.** (*tr.*) *Rare.* to cause to move in or as if in a wave or waves. —**'surger** *n.*

surgeon (ˈsɜːdʒən) *n.* **1.** a medical practitioner who specializes in surgery. **2.** a medical officer in the Royal Navy.

surgery (ˈsɜːdʒərɪ) *n., pl.* **-geries. 1.** the branch of medicine concerned with manual or operative procedures, esp. incision into the body. **2.** the performance of such procedures by a surgeon. **3.** *Brit.* a place where a doctor, dentist, etc., can be consulted. **4.** *U.S.* an operating theatre.

surgical (ˈsɜːdʒɪkəl) *adj.* of, relating to, involving, or used in surgery. —**'surgically** *adv.*

THESAURUS

supreme cardinal, chief, crowning, culminating, extreme, final, first, foremost, greatest, head, highest, incomparable, leading, matchless, paramount, peerless, predominant, pre-eminent, prevailing, prime, principal, sovereign, superlative, surpassing, top, ultimate, unsurpassed, utmost

sure 1. assured, certain, clear, confident, convinced, decided, definite, free from doubt, persuaded, positive, satisfied **2.** accurate, dependable, effective, foolproof, honest, indisputable, infallible, never-failing, precise, reliable, sure-fire (*Inf.*), tried and true, trustworthy, trusty, undeniable, undoubted, unerr-

ing, unfailing, unmistakable, well-proven **3.** assured, bound, guaranteed, ineluctable, inescapable, inevitable, irrevocable **4.** fast, firm, fixed, safe, secure, solid, stable, steady

surely assuredly, beyond the shadow of a doubt, certainly, come what may, definitely, doubtlessly, for certain, indubitably, inevitably, inexorably, undoubtedly, unquestionably, without doubt, without fail

surface *n.* **1.** covering, exterior, façade, face, facet, outside, plane, side, skin, superficies (*Rare*), top, veneer **2. on the surface** apparently, at first glance, ostensibly, outwardly, superficially, to all appearances, to the

casual eye ~*adj.* **3.** apparent, exterior, external, outward, superficial ~*v.* **4.** appear, come to light, come up, crop up (*Inf.*), emerge, materialize, rise, transpire

surfeit 1. *n.* excess, glut, overindulgence, plethora, satiety, superabundance, superfluity **2.** *v.* cram, fill, glut, gorge, overfeed, overfill, satiate, stuff

surge 1. *v.* billow, eddy, gush, heave, rise, roll, rush, swell, swirl, tower, undulate, well forth **2.** *n.* billow, breaker, efflux, flood, flow, gush, intensification, outpouring, roller, rush, swell, uprush, upsurge, wave

surgical boot *n.* a specially designed boot or shoe that compensates for deformities of the foot or leg.

surgical spirit *n.* methylated spirit used medically for sterilizing.

surly ('sɜːlɪ) *adj.* **-lier, -liest.** **1.** sullenly ill-tempered or rude. **2.** (of an animal) ill-tempered or refractory. —'**surlily** *adv.* —'**surliness** *n.*

surmise *vb.* (sɜː'maɪz). **1.** (when *tr., may take a clause as object*) to infer (something) from incomplete or uncertain evidence. ~*n.* (sɜː'maɪz, 'sɜːmaɪz). **2.** an idea inferred from inconclusive evidence. —**surmisedly** (sɜː'maɪzɪdlɪ) *adv.*

surmount (sɜː'maʊnt) *vb.* (*tr.*) **1.** to prevail over; overcome. **2.** to ascend and cross to the opposite side of. **3.** to lie on top of or rise above. **4.** to put something on top of or above. —**sur'mountable** *adj.*

surname ('sɜːˌneɪm) *n.* **1.** a family name as opposed to a Christian name. **2.** (formerly) a descriptive epithet attached to a person's name to denote a personal characteristic, profession, etc.; nickname. ~*vb.* **3.** (*tr.*) to furnish with or call by a surname. —'**surˌnamer** *n.*

surpass (sɜː'pɑːs) *vb.* (*tr.*) **1.** to be greater than in degree, extent, etc. **2.** to be superior to in achievement or excellence. **3.** to overstep the limit or range of: *the theory surpasses my comprehension.* —**sur'passable** *adj.*

surplice ('sɜːplɪs) *n.* a loose wide-sleeved liturgical vestment of linen, reaching to the knees, worn over the cassock by clergymen, choristers, and acolytes.

surplus ('sɜːpləs) *n., pl.* **-pluses.** **1.** a quantity or amount in excess of what is required. **2.** *Accounting.* **a.** an excess of total assets over total liabilities. **b.** an excess of actual net assets over the nominal value of capital stock. **c.** an excess of revenues over expenditures. **3.** *Econ.* **a.** an excess of government revenues over expenditures. **b.** an excess of receipts over payments on the balance of payments. ~*adj.* **4.** being in excess; extra.

surprise (sə'praɪz) *vb.* (*tr.*) **1.** to cause to feel amazement or wonder. **2.** to encounter or discover unexpectedly or suddenly. **3.** to capture or assault suddenly and without warning. **4.** to present with something unexpected, such as a gift. **5.** (foll. by *into*) to provoke (someone) to unintended action by a trick, etc. **6.** (often foll. by *from*) to elicit by unexpected behaviour or by a trick: *to surprise information from a prisoner.* ~*n.* **7.** the act or an instance of surprising; the act of taking unawares. **8.** a sudden or unexpected event, gift, etc. **9.** the feeling or condition of being surprised; astonishment. **10.** (*modifier*) causing, characterized by, or relying upon surprise: *a surprise move.* **11. take by surprise. a.** to come upon suddenly and without warning. **b.** to capture unexpectedly or catch unprepared. **c.** to astonish; amaze. —**sur'prising** *adj.*

surrealism (sə'rɪəˌlɪzəm) *n.* (*sometimes cap.*) a movement in art and literature in the 1920s, which developed esp. from dada, characterized by the evocative juxtaposition of incongruous images in order to include uncon-

scious and dream elements. —**su'rreal** *adj.* —**sur're-alist** *n., adj.* —**surˌreal'istic** *adj.*

surrender (sə'rɛndə) *vb.* **1.** (*tr.*) to relinquish to another under duress or on demand: *to surrender a city.* **2.** (*tr.*) to relinquish or forego (an office, position, etc.), esp. as a voluntary concession to another: *he surrendered his place to a lady.* **3.** to give (oneself) up physically, as to an enemy. **4.** to allow (oneself) to yield, as to a temptation, influence, etc. **5.** (*tr.*) to give up (hope, etc.) **6.** (*tr.*) *Law.* to give up or restore (an estate), esp. to give up a lease before expiration of the term. **7. surrender to bail.** to present oneself at court at the appointed time after having been on bail. ~*n.* **8.** the act or instance of surrendering. **9.** *Insurance.* the voluntary discontinuation of a life policy by its holder in return for a consideration (the **surrender value**). **10.** *Law.* **a.** the yielding up or restoring of an estate, esp. the giving up of a lease before its term has expired. **b.** the giving up to the appropriate authority of a fugitive from justice. **c.** the act of surrendering or being surrendered to bail. **d.** the deed by which a legal surrender is effected.

surreptitious (ˌsʌrəp'tɪʃəs) *adj.* **1.** done, acquired, etc., in secret or by improper means. **2.** operating by stealth. —ˌ**surrep'titiously** *adv.* —ˌ**surrep'titiousness** *n.*

surrogate *n.* ('sʌrəgɪt). **1.** a person or thing acting as a substitute. **2.** *Chiefly Brit.* a deputy, such as a clergyman appointed to deputize for a bishop in granting marriage licences. **3.** (in some U.S. states) a judge with jurisdiction over the probate of wills, etc. **4.** (*modifier*) of, relating to, or acting as a surrogate: *a surrogate pleasure.* ~*vb.* ('sʌrəˌgeɪt). (*tr.*) **5.** to put in another's position as a deputy, substitute, etc. —**surrogateˌship** *n.* —ˌ**surro-'gation** *n.*

surround (sə'raʊnd) *vb.* (*tr.*) **1.** to encircle or enclose or cause to be encircled or enclosed. **2.** to deploy forces on all sides of (a place or military formation), so preventing access or retreat. **3.** to exist around: *the people who surround her.* ~*n.* **4.** *Chiefly Brit.* a border, esp. the area of uncovered floor between the walls of a room and the carpet or around an opening or panel. **5.** *Chiefly U.S.* **a.** a method of capturing wild beasts by encircling the area in which they are believed to be. **b.** the area so encircled. —**sur'rounding** *adj.*

surroundings (sə'raʊndɪŋz) *pl. n.* the conditions, scenery, etc., around a person, place, or thing; environment.

surtax ('sɜːˌtæks) *n.* **1.** a tax, usually highly progressive, levied on the amount by which a person's income exceeds a specific level. **2.** an additional tax on something that has already been taxed. ~*vb.* **3.** (*tr.*) to assess for liability to surtax; charge with an extra tax.

surtout ('sɜːtuː) *n.* a man's overcoat resembling a frock coat, popular in the late 19th century.

surveillance (sɜː'veɪləns) *n.* close observation or supervision over a person, group, etc., esp. one in custody or under suspicion. —**sur'veillant** *adj., n.*

survey *vb.* (sɜː'veɪ, 'sɜːveɪ). **1.** (*tr.*) to view or consider in a comprehensive or general way. **2.** (*tr.*) to examine carefully, as or as if to appraise value. **3.** to plot a de-

---

THESAURUS

surly bearish, brusque, churlish, crabbed, cross, crusty, curmudgeonly, grouchy (*Inf.*), gruff, ill-natured, morose, perverse, sulky, sullen, testy, uncivil, ungracious

surmise 1. *v.* come to the conclusion, conclude, conjecture, consider, deduce, fancy, guess, hazard a guess, imagine, infer, opine, presume, speculate, suppose, suspect **2.** *n.* assumption, conclusion, conjecture, deduction, guess, hypothesis, idea, inference, notion, possibility, presumption, speculation, supposition, suspicion, thought

surmount conquer, exceed, master, overcome, overpower, overtop, pass, prevail over, surpass, triumph over, vanquish

surpass beat, best, eclipse, exceed, excel, go one better than (*Inf.*), outdo, outshine, outstrip, override, overshadow, top, tower above, transcend

surpassing exceptional, extraordinary, incomparable, matchless, outstanding, phenomenal, rare, supreme, transcendent, unrivalled

surplus 1. *n.* balance, excess, remainder, residue, superabundance, superfluity, surfeit **2.** *adj.* excess, extra, in excess, left over, odd, remaining, spare, superfluous, unused

surprise *v.* **1.** amaze, astonish, astound, bewilder, bowl over (*Inf.*), confuse, disconcert, flabbergast (*Inf.*), leave open-mouthed, nonplus, stagger, stun, take aback **2.** burst in on, catch in the act *or* red-handed, catch napping, catch unawares *or* off-guard, come down on like a bolt from the blue, discover, spring upon, startle ~*n.* **3.** amazement, astonishment, bewilderment, incredulity, stupefaction, wonder **4.** bolt from the blue, bombshell, eye-opener (*Inf.*), jolt, revelation, shock, start (*Inf.*)

surprised amazed, astonished, at a loss, caught on the hop (*Brit. inf.*), caught on the wrong foot (*Inf.*), disconcerted, incredulous, nonplussed, open-mouthed, speechless, startled, taken aback, taken by surprise, thunderstruck, unable to believe one's eyes

surprising amazing, astonishing, astounding, extraordinary, incredible, marvellous, remarkable, staggering, startling, unexpected, unlooked-for, unusual, wonderful

surrender *v.* **1.** abandon, cede, concede, deliver up, forego, give up, part with, relinquish, renounce, resign, waive, yield **2.** capitulate, give in, give oneself up, give way, lay down arms, quit, show the white flag, submit, succumb, throw in the towel, yield ~*n.* **3.** capitulation, delivery, relinquishment, renunciation, resignation, submission, yielding

surreptitious clandestine, covert, fraudulent, furtive, secret, sly, sneaking, stealthy, unauthorized, underhand, veiled

surround 1. close in on, encircle, enclose, encompass, envelop, environ, fence in, girdle, hem in, ring **2.** *Military* besiege, invest (*Rare*), lay siege to

surrounding nearby, neighbouring

surroundings background, environment, environs, location, milieu, neighbourhood, setting

surveillance care, control, direction, inspection, observation, scrutiny, superintendence, supervision, vigilance, watch

tailed map of (an area of land) by measuring or calculating distances and height. **4.** *Brit.* to inspect a building to determine its condition and value. **5.** to examine a vessel thoroughly in order to determine its seaworthiness. **6.** (*tr.*) to run a statistical survey on (incomes, opinions, etc.). ~*n.* ('sɜːveɪ). **7.** a comprehensive or general view. **8.** a critical, detailed, and formal inspection. **9.** *Brit.* an inspection of a building to determine its condition and value. **10.** a report incorporating the results of such an inspection. **11. a.** a body of surveyors. **b.** an area surveyed.
surveying (sɜː'veɪɪŋ) *n.* **1.** the study or practice of making surveys of land. **2.** the setting out on the ground of the positions of proposed construction or engineering works.
surveyor (sɜː'veɪə) *n.* **1.** a person whose occupation is to survey land or buildings. See also **quantity surveyor.** **2.** *Chiefly Brit.* a person concerned with the official inspection of something for purposes of measurement and valuation. **3.** a person who carries out surveys, esp. of ships (**marine surveyor**) to determine seaworthiness, etc. **4.** a customs official. **5.** *Arch.* a supervisor. —**sur'veyor,ship** *n.*
survival (sə'vaɪvəl) *n.* **1.** a person or thing that survives, such as a custom. **2. a.** the act or fact of surviving or condition of having survived. **b.** (*as modifier*): *survival kit.*
survive (sə'vaɪv) *vb.* **1.** (*tr.*) to live after the death of (another). **2.** to continue in existence or use after (a passage of time, adversity, etc.). **3.** *Inf.* to endure (something): *I don't know how I survive such an awful job.* —**sur'vivor** *n.*
sus (sʌs) *Brit. sl.* ~*n.* **1.** short for **suspicion,** with reference to police powers (**sus laws**) of detaining for questioning, searching, etc. any person suspected of criminal intent: *he was picked up on sus.* ~*vb.* **2.** a variant spelling of **suss.**
susceptibility (sə,septə'bɪlɪtɪ) *n., pl.* -**ties.** **1.** the quality or condition of being susceptible. **2.** the ability or tendency to be impressed by emotional feelings. **3.** (*pl.*) emotional sensibilities; feelings. **4.** *Physics.* **a.** Also called: **electric susceptibility.** (of a dielectric) the amount by which the relative permittivity differs from unity. **b.** Also called: **magnetic susceptibility.** (of a magnetic medium) the amount by which the relative permeability differs from unity.
susceptible (sə'septəbəl) *adj.* **1.** (*postpositive;* foll. by *of* or *to*) yielding readily (to); capable (of): *hypotheses susceptible of refutation; susceptible to control.* **2.** (*postpositive;* foll. by *to*) liable to be afflicted (by): *susceptible to colds.* **3.** easily impressed emotionally. —**sus'ceptibly** *adv.*
suspect *vb.* (sə'spɛkt). **1.** (*tr.*) to believe guilty of a specified offence without proof. **2.** (*tr.*) to think false, questionable, etc.: *she suspected his sincerity.* **3.** (*tr.; may take a clause as object*) to surmise to be the case; think probable: *to suspect fraud.* **4.** (*intr.*) to have suspicion. ~*n.* ('sʌspɛkt). **5.** a person under suspicion. ~*adj.* ('sʌspɛkt). **6.** causing or open to suspicion.
suspend (sə'spɛnd) *vb.* **1.** (*tr.*) to hang from above. **2.** (*tr.; passive*) to cause to remain floating or hanging: *a cloud of smoke was suspended over the town.* **3.** (*tr.*) to render inoperative or cause to cease, esp. temporarily. **4.** (*tr.*) to hold in abeyance; postpone action on. **5.** (*tr.*)

to debar temporarily from privilege, office, etc., as a punishment. **6.** (*tr.*) *Chem.* to cause (particles) to be held in suspension in a fluid. **7.** (*tr.*) *Music.* to continue (a note) until the next chord is sounded, with which it usually forms a dissonance. See **suspension** (sense 11). **8.** (*intr.*) to cease payment, as from incapacity to meet financial obligations. —**sus,pendi'bility** *n.*
suspended animation *n.* a temporary cessation of the vital functions, as by freezing an organism.
suspended sentence *n.* a sentence of imprisonment that is not served by an offender unless he commits a further offence during its currency.
suspender (sə'spɛndə) *n.* **1.** (*often pl.*) *Brit.* **a.** an elastic strap attached to a belt or corset having a fastener at the end, for holding up women's stockings. **b.** a similar fastener attached to a garter worn by men in order to support socks. **2.** (*pl.*) the U.S. name for **braces. 3.** a person or thing that suspends, such as one of the vertical cables in a suspension bridge.
suspender belt *n.* a belt with suspenders hanging from it to hold up women's stockings.
suspense (sə'spɛns) *n.* **1.** the condition of being insecure or uncertain. **2.** mental uncertainty; anxiety: *their father's illness kept them in a state of suspense.* **3.** excitement felt at the approach of the climax: *a play of terrifying suspense.* **4.** the condition of being suspended. —**sus'penseful** *adj.*
suspension (sə'spɛnʃən) *n.* **1.** an interruption or temporary revocation: *the suspension of a law.* **2.** a temporary debarment, as from position, privilege, etc. **3.** a deferment, esp. of a decision, judgment, etc. **4.** *Law.* a postponement of execution of a sentence or the deferring of a judgment, etc. **5.** cessation of payment of business debts, esp. as a result of insolvency. **6.** the act of suspending or the state of being suspended. **7.** a system of springs, shock absorbers, etc., that supports the body of a wheeled vehicle and insulates it from shocks transmitted by the wheels. **8.** a device or structure, usually a wire or spring, that serves to suspend or support something, such as the pendulum of a clock. **9.** *Chem.* a dispersion of fine solid or liquid particles in a fluid, the particles being supported by buoyancy. See also **colloid. 10.** the process by which eroded particles of rock are transported in a river. **11.** *Music.* one or more notes of a chord that are prolonged until a subsequent chord is sounded, usually to form a dissonance.
suspension bridge *n.* a bridge suspended from cables or chains that hang between two towers and are anchored at both ends.
suspicion (sə'spɪʃən) *n.* **1.** the act or an instance of suspecting; belief without sure proof, esp. that something is wrong. **2.** the feeling of mistrust of a person who suspects. **3.** the state of being suspected: *to be shielded from suspicion.* **4.** a slight trace. **5. above suspicion.** in such a position that no guilt may be thought or implied, esp. through having an unblemished reputation. **6. on suspicion.** as a suspect. **7. under suspicion.** regarded with distrust. —**sus'picional** *adj.*
suspicious (sə'spɪʃəs) *adj.* **1.** exciting or liable to excite suspicion; questionable. **2.** disposed to suspect something wrong. **3.** indicative or expressive of suspicion. —**sus'piciously** *adv.* —**sus'piciousness** *n.*

THESAURUS

survey *v.* **1.** contemplate, examine, inspect, look over, observe, reconnoitre, research, review, scan, scrutinize, study, supervise, view **2.** appraise, assess, estimate, measure, plan, plot, prospect, size up, take stock of, triangulate ~*n.* **3.** examination, inquiry, inspection, overview, perusal, random sample, review, scrutiny, study
survive be extant, endure, exist, hold out, keep body and soul together (*Inf.*), last, live, live on, outlast, outlive, pull through, remain alive, subsist
susceptibility liability, predisposition, proneness, propensity, responsiveness, sensitivity, suggestibility, vulnerability, weakness
susceptible 1. *Usually with* to disposed, given, inclined, liable, open, predisposed, prone, subject, vulnerable **2.** alive to, easily moved, impressionable, receptive, respon-

sive, sensitive, suggestible, tender
suspect *v.* **1.** distrust, doubt, harbour suspicions about, have one's doubts about, mistrust, smell a rat (*Inf.*) **2.** believe, conclude, conjecture, consider, fancy, feel, guess, have a sneaking suspicion, hazard a guess, speculate, suppose, surmise, think probable ~*adj.* **3.** doubtful, dubious, fishy (*Inf.*), open to suspicion, questionable
suspend 1. append, attach, dangle, hang, swing **2.** adjourn, arrest, cease, cut short, debar, defer, delay, discontinue, hold off, interrupt, lay aside, pigeonhole, postpone, put off, shelve, stay, withhold
suspense 1. anticipation, anxiety, apprehension, doubt, expectancy, expectation, indecision, insecurity, irresolution, tension, uncertainty, wavering **2. in suspense** anxious,

in an agony of doubt, keyed up, on edge, on tenterhooks
suspension abeyance, adjournment, break, breaking off, deferment, delay, disbarment, discontinuation, interruption, moratorium, postponement, remission, respite, stay
suspicion 1. bad vibes (*Inf.*), chariness, distrust, doubt, funny feeling (*Inf.*), jealousy, lack of confidence, misgiving, mistrust, qualm, scepticism, wariness **2. above suspicion** above reproach, blameless, honourable, like Caesar's wife, pure, sinless, unimpeachable, virtuous **3.** conjecture, guess, gut feeling (*Inf.*), hunch, idea, impression, notion, supposition, surmise **4.** glimmer, hint, shade, shadow, *soupçon,* strain, streak, suggestion, tinge, touch, trace
suspicious 1. apprehensive, distrustful,

suss (sʌs) vb. (tr.) Brit. sl. 1. (often foll. by out) to attempt to work out (a situation, person's character, etc.), esp. using one's intuition. 2. to become aware of; suspect (esp. in suss it).

sustain (sə'steɪn) vb. (tr.) 1. to hold up under; withstand: to sustain great provocation. 2. to undergo (an injury, loss, etc.); suffer: to sustain a broken arm. 3. to maintain or prolong: to sustain a discussion. 4. to support physically from below. 5. to provide for or give support to, esp. by supplying necessities: to sustain one's family. 6. to keep up the vitality or courage of. 7. to uphold or affirm the justice or validity of: to sustain a decision. 8. to establish the truth of; confirm. —**sus'tainable** adj. —**sustainedly** (sə'steɪnɪdlɪ) adv. —**sus'tainer** n. —**sus'tainment** n.

sustenance ('sʌstənəns) n. 1. means of sustaining health or life; nourishment. 2. means of maintenance; livelihood. 3. Also: **sustention** (sə'stɛnʃən). the act or process of sustaining or the quality of being sustained.

susurrate ('sjuːsə,reɪt) vb. (intr.) Literary. to make a soft rustling sound; whisper; murmur. —,susur'ration or 'susurrus n.

sutler ('sʌtlə) n. (formerly) a merchant who accompanied an army in order to sell provisions to the soldiers.

suttee (sʌ'tiː, 'sʌtiː) n. 1. the former Hindu custom whereby a widow burnt herself to death on her husband's funeral pyre. 2. a widow performing this. —**sut'teeism** n.

suture ('suːtʃə) n. 1. Surgery. a. catgut, silk thread, or wire used to stitch together two bodily surfaces. b. the surgical seam formed after stitching. 2. Anat. a type of immovable joint, esp. between the bones of the skull (**cranial suture**). 3. a seam or joining, as in sewing. 4. Zool. a line of junction in a mollusc shell. ~vb. 5. (tr.) Surgery. to join (the edges of a wound, etc.) by means of sutures. —**'sutural** adj.

suzerain ('suːzə,reɪn) n. 1. a. a state or sovereign exercising some degree of dominion over a dependent state, usually controlling its foreign affairs. b. (as modifier): a suzerain power. 2. a. a feudal overlord. b. (as modifier): suzerain lord. —**'suze,rainty** n.

svelte (svɛlt, sfɛlt) adj. attractively or gracefully slim; slender.

SW abbrev. for southwest(ern).

Sw. abbrev. for: 1. Sweden. 2. Swedish.

swab (swɒb) n. 1. Med. a. a small piece of cotton, gauze, etc., for use in applying medication, cleansing a wound, or obtaining a specimen of a secretion, etc. b. the specimen so obtained. 2. a mop for cleaning floors, decks, etc. 3. a brush used to clean a firearm's bore. 4. Sl. an uncouth or worthless fellow. ~vb. swabbing, swabbed. 5. (tr.) to clean or medicate with or as if with a swab. 6. (tr.; foll. by up) to take up with a swab. —**'swabber** n.

swaddle ('swɒdəl) vb. (tr.) 1. to wind a bandage round. 2. to wrap (a baby) in swaddling clothes. 3. to restrain as if by wrapping with bandages; smother. ~n. 4. Chiefly U.S. swaddling clothes.

swag (swæg) n. 1. Sl. property obtained by theft or other illicit means. 2. Sl. goods; valuables. 3. an ornamental festoon of fruit, flowers, or drapery or a representation of this. 4. a swaying movement; lurch. 5. Austral. inf. a swagman's pack containing personal belongings, etc. ~vb. swagging, swagged. 6. Chiefly Brit. to lurch or sag or cause to lurch or sag. 7. (tr.) to adorn or arrange with swags.

swagger ('swægə) vb. 1. (intr.) to walk or behave in an arrogant manner. 2. (intr.; often foll. by about) to brag loudly. ~n. 3. arrogant gait or manner. ~adj. 4. Brit. inf., rare. elegantly fashionable. —**'swaggerer** n. —**'swaggeringly** adv.

swagger stick or esp. Brit. **swagger cane** n. a short cane or stick carried on occasion mainly by army officers.

swagman ('swæg,mæn, -mən) n., pl. **-men.** Austral. inf. & N.Z. obs. a tramp or vagrant worker who carries his possessions on his back. Also called: **swaggie**.

Swahili (swɑː'hiːlɪ) n. 1. a language of E Africa that is an official language of Kenya and Tanzania and is widely used as a lingua franca throughout E and central Africa. 2. (pl. **-lis** or **-li**) a member of a people speaking this language, living chiefly in Zanzibar. —**Swa'hilian** adj.

swain (sweɪn) n. Arch. or poetic. 1. a male lover or admirer. 2. a country youth.

swallow[1] ('swɒləʊ) vb. (mainly tr.) 1. to pass (food, drink, etc.) through the mouth to the stomach by means of the muscular action of the oesophagus. 2. (often foll. by up) to engulf or destroy as if by ingestion. 3. Inf. to believe gullibly: he will never swallow such an excuse. 4. to refrain from uttering or manifesting: to swallow one's disappointment. 5. to endure without retaliation. 6. to enunciate (words, etc.) indistinctly; mutter. 7. (often foll. by down) to eat or drink reluctantly. 8. (intr.) to perform or simulate the act of swallowing, as in gulping. 9. **swallow one's words**. to retract a statement, argument, etc., often in humiliating circumstances. ~n. 10. the act of swallowing. 11. the amount swallowed at any single time; mouthful. 12. Rare. another word for **throat** or **gullet**. —**'swallowable** adj. —**'swallower** n.

swallow[2] ('swɒləʊ) n. any of various passerine songbirds having long pointed wings, a forked tail, short legs, and a rapid flight.

swallow dive n. a type of dive in which the diver arches back while in the air, keeping his legs straight and together and his arms outstretched, finally entering the water headfirst. U.S. equivalent: **swan dive**.

swallowtail ('swɒləʊ,teɪl) n. 1. any of various butterflies of Europe, having a tail-like extension of each hind wing. 2. the forked tail of a swallow or similar bird. —**'swallow-,tailed** adj.

swam (swæm) vb. the past tense of **swim**.

swami ('swɑːmɪ) n., pl. **-mies** or **-mis**. (in India) a title of respect for a Hindu saint or religious teacher.

swamp (swɒmp) n. 1. permanently waterlogged ground that is usually overgrown and sometimes partly forested. Cf. **marsh**. ~vb. 2. to drench or submerge or be drenched or submerged. 3. Naut. to cause (a boat) to sink or fill with water or (of a boat) to sink or fill with water. 4. to overburden or overwhelm or be overburdened or overwhelmed, as by excess work or great numbers. 5. (tr.) to render helpless. Related adj.: **paludal**. —**'swampy** adj.

swan (swɒn) n. 1. any of various large aquatic birds having a long neck and usually a white plumage. 2. Rare, literary. a poet. b. (cap. when part of a title or epithet): the Swan of Avon (Shakespeare). ~vb. **swanning, swanned**. 3. (intr.; usually foll. by around or about) Inf. to wander idly. —**'swan,like** adj.

swank (swæŋk) Inf. ~vb. 1. (intr.) to show off or swagger. ~n. 2. Also called: **swankpot**. Brit. a swaggering or conceited person. 3. Chiefly U.S. showy elegance or style. 4. swagger; ostentation. —**'swanky** adj.

swan's-down n. 1. the fine soft down feathers of a swan, used to trim powder puffs, clothes, etc. 2. a thick soft fabric of wool with silk, cotton, or rayon, used for in-

---

THESAURUS

doubtful, jealous, mistrustful, sceptical, suspecting, unbelieving, wary 2. doubtful, dubious, fishy (Inf.), funny, irregular, of doubtful honesty, open to doubt or misconstruction, queer, questionable, shady (Inf.), suspect

sustain 1. bear, carry, keep from falling, keep up, support, uphold 2. bear, bear up under, endure, experience, feel, suffer, undergo, withstand 3. aid, assist, comfort, foster, help, keep alive, nourish, nurture, provide for, relieve 4. approve, confirm, continue, keep alive, keep going, keep up, maintain, prolong, protract, ratify 5. endorse, uphold, validate, verify

sustained constant, continuous, nonstop, perpetual, prolonged, steady, unremitting

sustenance 1. aliment, comestibles, daily bread, eatables, edibles, food, nourishment, provender, provisions, rations, refection, refreshments, victuals 2. livelihood, maintenance, subsistence, support

swagger 1. v. bluster, boast, brag, bully, gasconade (Rare), hector, parade, prance, show off (Inf.), strut, swank (Inf.) 2. n. arrogance, bluster, braggadocio, display, gasconade (Rare), ostentation, pomposity, show, showing off (Inf.), swank (Inf.), swashbuckling

swallow v. 1. absorb, consume, devour, down (Inf.), drink, eat, gulp, ingest, swig (Inf.), swill, wash down 2. Often with up absorb, assimilate, consume, engulf, envelop,

overrun, overwhelm, use up, waste 3. choke back, hold in, repress 4. Inf. accept, believe, buy (Inf.), fall for

swamp n. 1. bog, everglade(s) (U.S.), fen, marsh, mire, morass, moss (Scot., & northern English dialect), quagmire, slough ~v. 2. capsize, drench, engulf, flood, inundate, overwhelm, sink, submerge, swallow up, upset, wash over, waterlog 3. beset, besiege, deluge, flood, inundate, overload, overwhelm, snow under

swampy boggy, fenny, marish (Obsolete), marshy, miry, quaggy, waterlogged, wet

fants' clothing, etc. **3.** a cotton fabric with a heavy nap.

swan song *n.* **1.** the last act, publication, etc. of a person before retirement or death. **2.** the song that a dying swan is said to sing.

swan-upping *n. Brit.* **1.** the practice or action of marking nicks in swans' beaks as a sign of ownership. **2.** the annual swan-upping of royal cygnets on the River Thames.

swap *or* **swop** (swɒp) *Inf.* ~*vb.* **swapping, swapped** *or* **swopping, swopped. 1.** to trade or exchange (something or someone) for another. ~*n.* **2.** an exchange. **3.** something that is exchanged. —**'swapper** *or* **'swopper** *n.*

sward (swɔːd) *or* **swarth** (swɔːθ) *n.* **1.** turf or grass or a stretch of turf or grass. ~*vb.* **2.** to cover or become covered with grass.

swarm[1] (swɔːm) *n.* **1.** a group of bees, led by a queen, that has left the parent hive to start a new colony. **2.** a large mass of small animals, esp. insects. **3.** a throng or mass, esp. when moving or in turmoil. ~*vb.* **4.** *(intr.)* (of small animals, esp. bees) to move in or form a swarm. **5.** *(intr.)* to congregate, move about or proceed in large numbers. **6.** (when *intr.*, often foll. by *with*) to overrun or be overrun (with): *the house swarmed with rats.* **7.** *(tr.)* to cause to swarm.

swarm[2] (swɔːm) *vb.* (when *intr.*, usually foll. by *up*) to climb (a ladder, etc.) by gripping with the hands and feet: *the boys swarmed up the rigging.*

swarthy ('swɔːðɪ) *adj.* **-ier, -iest.** dark-hued or dark-complexioned. —**'swarthily** *adv.* —**'swarthiness** *n.*

swash (swɒʃ) *vb.* **1.** *(intr.)* (esp. of water or things in water) to wash or move with noisy splashing. **2.** *(tr.)* to dash (a liquid, esp. water) against or upon. **3.** *(intr.) Arch.* to swagger. ~*n.* **4.** Also called: **send.** the dashing movement or sound of water, as of waves on a beach. **5.** Also called: **swash channel.** a channel of moving water cutting through or running behind a sandbank. **6.** *Arch.* swagger or bluster.

swashbuckler ('swɒʃˌbʌklə) *n.* a swaggering or daredevil adventurer or bully.

swastika ('swɒstɪkə) *n.* **1.** a primitive religious symbol or ornament in the shape of a Greek cross, usually having the ends of the arms bent at right angles. **2.** this symbol with clockwise arms, the emblem of Nazi Germany.

swat (swɒt) *vb.* **swatting, swatted.** *(tr.)* **1.** to strike or hit sharply: *to swat a fly.* ~*n.* **2.** a sharp or violent blow. —**'swatter** *n.*

swatch (swɒtʃ) *n.* **1.** a sample of cloth or other material. **2.** a number of such samples, usually fastened together in book form.

swath (swɔːθ) *or* **swathe** (sweɪð) *n., pl.* **swaths** (swɔːðz) *or* **swathes. 1.** the width of one sweep of a scythe or of the blade of a mowing machine. **2.** the strip cut by these in one course. **3.** the quantity of cut grass, hay, etc. left in one such course. **4.** a long narrow strip or belt.

swathe (sweɪð) *vb.* *(tr.)* **1.** to bandage (a wound, limb, etc.), esp. completely. **2.** to wrap a band, garment, etc., around, esp. so as to cover completely; swaddle. **3.** to envelop. ~*n.* **4.** a bandage or wrapping. **5.** a variant spelling of **swath.**

sway (sweɪ) *vb.* **1.** (usually *intr.*) to swing or cause to swing to and fro: *the door swayed in the wind.* **2.** (usually *intr.*) to lean or incline or cause to lean or incline to one side or in different directions in turn. **3.** (usually

intr.) to vacillate or cause to vacillate between two or more opinions. **4.** to be influenced or swerve or influence or cause to swerve to or from a purpose or opinion. **5.** *Arch. or poetic.* to rule or wield power (over). ~*n.* **6.** control; power. **7.** a swinging or leaning movement. **8.** *Arch.* dominion; governing authority. **9. hold sway.** to be master; reign.

swear (sweə) *vb.* **swearing, swore, sworn. 1.** to declare or affirm (a statement) as true, esp. by invoking a deity, etc., as witness. **2.** (foll. by *by*) **a.** to invoke (a deity, etc.) by name as a witness or guarantee to an oath. **b.** to trust implicitly; have complete confidence (in). **3.** *(intr.;* often foll. by *at)* to curse, blaspheme, or use swearwords. **4.** (when *tr., may take a clause as object or an infinitive*) to promise solemnly on oath; vow. **5.** *(tr.)* to assert or affirm with great emphasis or earnestness. **6.** *(intr.)* to give evidence or make any statement or solemn declaration on oath. **7.** to take an oath in order to add force or solemnity to (a statement or declaration). ~*n.* **8.** a period of swearing. —**'swearer** *n.*

swear in *vb.* *(tr., adv.)* to administer an oath to (a person) on his assuming office, entering the witness box to give evidence, etc.

swear off *vb.* *(intr., prep.)* to promise to abstain from something: *to swear off drink.*

swearword ('sweəˌwɜːd) *n.* a socially taboo word of a profane, obscene, or insulting character.

sweat (swɛt) *n.* **1.** the secretion from the sweat glands, esp. when profuse and visible, as during strenuous activity, from excessive heat, etc.; perspiration. **2.** the act or process of secreting this fluid. **3.** the act of inducing the exudation of moisture. **4.** drops of moisture given forth or gathered on the surface of something. **5.** *Inf.* a state or condition of worry or eagerness (esp. in **in a sweat**). **6.** *Inf.* drudgery or hard labour: *mowing lawns is a real sweat!* **7. no sweat!** *(interj.) Sl.* an expression conveying consent or assurance. ~*vb.* **sweats, sweating; sweat** *or* **sweated. 8.** to secrete (sweat) through the pores of the skin, esp. profusely; perspire. **9.** *(tr.)* to make wet or stain with perspiration. **10.** to give forth or cause to give forth (moisture) in droplets: *the maple sweats sap.* **11.** *(intr.)* to collect and condense moisture on an outer surface: *a glass of beer sweating.* **12.** *(intr.)* (of a liquid) to pass through a porous surface in droplets. **13.** (of tobacco leaves, hay, etc.) to exude moisture and, sometimes, begin to ferment or to cause (tobacco leaves, etc.) to exude moisture. **14.** *(tr.)* to heat (food, esp. vegetables) slowly in butter in a tightly closed saucepan. **15.** *(tr.)* to join (pieces of metal) by pressing together and heating. **16.** *(tr.)* to heat (solder) until it melts. **17.** *(tr.)* to heat (partially fused metal) to extract an easily fusible constituent. **18.** *Inf.* to suffer anxiety, impatience, or distress. **19.** *Inf.* to overwork or be overworked. **20.** *(tr.) Inf.* to employ at very low wages and under bad conditions. **21.** *(tr.) Inf.* to extort, esp. by torture: *to sweat information out of a captive.* **22.** *(intr.) Inf.* to suffer punishment: *you'll sweat for this!* **23. sweat blood.** *Sl.* **a.** to work very hard. **b.** to be filled with anxiety or impatience. —**'sweaty** *adj.*

sweatband ('swɛtˌbænd) *n.* **1.** a band of material set in a hat or cap to protect it from sweat. **2.** a piece of cloth tied around the forehead to keep sweat out of the eyes or around the wrist to keep the hands dry, as in sports.

sweated ('swɛtɪd) *adj.* **1.** made by exploited labour: *sweated goods.* **2.** (of workers, etc.) forced to work in poor conditions for low pay.

THESAURUS

swap, swop *v.* bandy, barter, exchange, interchange, switch, trade, traffic

swarm *n.* **1.** army, bevy, concourse, crowd, drove, flock, herd, horde, host, mass, multitude, myriad, shoal, throng ~*v.* **2.** congregate, crowd, flock, mass, stream, throng **3.** *With* abound, be alive (infested, overrun), bristle, crawl, teem

swarthy black, brown, dark, dark-complexioned, dark-skinned, dusky, swart (*Archaic*), tawny

swashbuckling bold, daredevil, dashing, flamboyant, gallant, mettlesome, roisterous, spirited, swaggering

swastika fylfot

swathe bandage, bind, bundle up, cloak, drape, envelop, enwrap, fold, furl, lap, muffle

up, sheathe, shroud, swaddle, wrap

sway *v.* **1.** bend, fluctuate, incline, lean, lurch, oscillate, rock, roll, swing, wave **2.** affect, control, direct, dominate, govern, guide, induce, influence, persuade, prevail on, win over ~*n.* **3.** ascendency, authority, clout (*Inf.*), command, control, dominion, government, influence, jurisdiction, power, predominance, rule, sovereignty **4. hold sway** predominate, prevail, reign, rule, run

swear 1. affirm, assert, attest, avow, declare, depose, give one's word, pledge oneself, promise, state under oath, take an oath, testify, vow, warrant **2.** be foul-mouthed, blaspheme, curse, cuss (*Inf.*), imprecate, take the Lord's name in vain, turn the air blue, utter profanities **3.** *With* by depend on,

have confidence in, rely on, trust

swearing bad language, blasphemy, cursing, cussing (*Inf.*), foul language, imprecations, malediction, profanity

sweat *n.* **1.** diaphoresis (*Medical*), exudation, perspiration, sudor (*Medical*) **2.** *Inf.* agitation, anxiety, distress, flap (*Inf.*), panic, strain, worry **3.** *Inf.* backbreaking task, chore, drudgery, effort, labour ~*v.* **4.** break out in a sweat, exude moisture, glow, perspire **5.** *Inf.* agonize, be on pins and needles (*Inf.*), be on tenterhooks, chafe, fret, lose sleep over, suffer, torture oneself, worry **6. sweat it out** *Inf.* endure, see (something) through, stay the course, stick it out (*Inf.*)

sweater ('swɛtə) n. 1. a garment made of knitted or crocheted material covering the upper part of the body, esp. a heavy one worn for warmth. 2. a person or thing that sweats. 3. an employer who overworks and underpays his employees.

sweat off or **away** vb. (tr., adv.) Inf. to get rid of (weight) by strenuous exercise or sweating.

sweat out vb. (tr., adv.) 1. to cure or lessen the effects of (a cold, respiratory infection, etc.) by sweating. 2. Inf. to endure (hardships) for a time (often in **sweat it out**). 3. **sweat one's guts out**. Inf. to work extremely hard.

sweat shirt n. a long-sleeved knitted cotton sweater worn by athletes, etc.

sweatshop ('swɛt,ʃɒp) n. a workshop where employees work long hours under bad conditions for low wages.

sweat suit n. a suit worn by athletes for training comprising knitted cotton trousers and a light cotton sweater.

swede (swi:d) n. 1. a Eurasian plant cultivated for its bulbous edible root, which is used as a vegetable and as cattle fodder. 2. the root. ~Also called: **Swedish turnip.**

Swede (swi:d) n. a native, citizen, or inhabitant of Sweden, a kingdom in E Scandinavia.

Swedish ('swi:dɪʃ) adj. 1. of, relating to, or characteristic of Sweden, its people, or their language. ~n. 2. the official language of Sweden.

sweep (swi:p) vb. **sweeping, swept.** 1. to clean or clear (a space, chimney, etc.) with a brush, broom, etc. 2. (often foll. by up) to remove or collect (dirt, rubbish, etc.) with a brush, broom, etc. 3. to move in a smooth or continuous manner, esp. quickly or forcibly: cars swept along the road. 4. to move in a proud or dignified fashion: she swept past. 5. (tr.) to spread or pass rapidly across, through, or along (a region, area, etc.): the news swept through the town. 6. (tr.) to direct (the gaze, line of fire, etc.) over; survey. 7. (tr.; foll. by away or off) to overwhelm emotionally: she was swept away by his charm. 8. (tr.) to brush or lightly touch (a surface, etc.): the dress swept along the ground. 9. (tr.; often foll. by away) to convey, clear, or abolish, esp. with strong or continuous movements: the sea swept the sandcastle away; secondary modern schools were swept away. 10. (intr.) to extend gracefully or majestically, esp. in a wide circle: the plains sweep down to the sea. 11. to search (a body of water) for mines, etc., by dragging. 12. (tr.) to win overwhelmingly, esp. in an election: Labour swept the country. 13. (tr.) to propel (a boat) with sweeps. 14. **sweep the board. a.** (in gambling) to win all the cards or money. **b.** to achieve a triumphant success. 15. **sweep (something) under the carpet.** to conceal (something, esp. a problem) in the hope that it will be overlooked by others. ~n. 16. the act or an instance of sweeping; removal by or as if by a brush or broom. 17. a swift or steady movement, esp. in an arc. 18. the distance, arc, etc., through which something, such as a pendulum, moves. 19. a wide expanse or scope: the sweep of the plains. 20. any curving line or contour. 21. short for **sweepstake.** 22. **a.** a long oar used on an open boat. **b.** Austral. a person steering a surf boat with such an oar at the stern. 23. any of the sails of a windmill. 24. Electronics. a steady horizontal or circular movement of an electron beam across or around the fluorescent screen of a cathode-ray tube. 25. a curving driveway. 26. Chiefly Brit. See **chimney sweep.** 27. another name for **swipe** (sense 4). 28. **clean sweep. a.** an overwhelming victory or success. **b.** a complete change; purge: to make a clean sweep. —'**sweepy** adj.

sweeper ('swi:pə) n. 1. a person employed to sweep, such as a roadsweeper. 2. any device for sweeping: a carpet sweeper. 3. Inf., soccer. a player who supports the main defenders, as by intercepting loose balls, etc.

sweeping ('swi:pɪŋ) adj. 1. comprehensive and wide-ranging: sweeping reforms. 2. indiscriminate or without reservations: sweeping statements. 3. decisive or overwhelming: a sweeping victory. 4. taking in a wide area: a sweeping glance. 5. driving steadily onwards, esp. over a large area: a sweeping attack. —'**sweepingly** adv. —'**sweepingness** n.

sweepstake ('swi:p,steɪk) or esp. U.S. **sweepstakes** n. 1. **a.** a lottery in which the stakes of the participants constitute the prize. **b.** the prize itself. 2. any event involving such a lottery, esp. a horse race. ~Often shortened to **sweep.**

sweet (swi:t) adj. 1. having or denoting a pleasant taste like that of sugar. 2. agreeable to the senses or the mind: sweet music. 3. having pleasant manners; gentle: a sweet child. 4. (of wine, etc.) having a relatively high sugar content; not dry. 5. (of foods) not decaying or rancid: sweet milk. 6. not salty: sweet water. 7. free from unpleasant odours: sweet air. 8. containing no corrosive substances: sweet soil. 9. (of petrol) containing no sulphur compounds. 10. sentimental or unrealistic. 11. Jazz. performed with a regular beat, with the emphasis on clearly outlined melody and little improvisation. 12. Arch. respected; dear (used in polite forms of address): sweet sir. 13. effortlessly done: a sweet shot. 14. **sweet on.** fond of or infatuated with. 15. **at one's own sweet will.** as it suits oneself alone. 16. **keep (someone) sweet.** to ingratiate oneself in order to ensure cooperation. ~adv. 17. Inf. in a sweet manner. ~n. 18. a sweet taste or smell; sweetness in general. 19. (often pl.) Brit. any of numerous kinds of confectionery consisting wholly or partly of sugar, esp. of sugar boiled and crystallized (**boiled sweets**). 20. Brit. any sweet dish served as a dessert. 21. dear; sweetheart (used as a form of address). 22. anything that is sweet. 23. (often pl.) a pleasurable experience, state, etc.: the sweets of success. —'**sweetish** adj. —'**sweetly** adv. —'**sweetness** n.

sweet-and-sour adj. (of food) cooked in a sauce made from sugar and vinegar and other ingredients.

sweetbread ('swi:t,brɛd) n. the pancreas or the thymus gland of an animal, used for food.

sweetbrier ('swi:t,braɪə) n. a Eurasian rose having a tall bristly stem, fragrant leaves, and single pink flowers. Also called: **eglantine.**

sweet corn n. 1. a variety of maize whose kernels are rich in sugar and eaten as a vegetable when young. 2. the unripe ears of maize, esp. the sweet kernels removed from the cob, cooked as a vegetable.

sweeten ('swi:tən) vb. (mainly tr.) 1. (also intr.) to make or become sweet or sweeter. 2. to mollify or soften (a person). 3. to make more agreeable. 4. (also intr.) Chem. to free or be freed from unpleasant odours, acidic or corrosive substances, or the like.

sweetener ('swi:tənə) n. 1. a sweetening agent, esp. one that does not contain sugar. 2. a slang word for **bribe.**

sweetheart ('swi:t,hɑ:t) n. 1. a person loved by another. 2. Inf. a lovable, generous, or obliging person. 3. a term of endearment.

sweetie ('swi:tɪ) n. Inf. 1. sweetheart; darling: used as a term of endearment. 2. Brit. a child's word for **sweet**

THESAURUS

sweaty clammy, drenched (bathed, soaked) in perspiration, glowing, perspiring, sticky, sweating

sweep v. 1. brush, clean, clear, remove 2. career, flounce, fly, glance, glide, hurtle, pass, sail, scud, skim, tear, zoom ~n. 3. arc, bend, curve, gesture, move, movement, stroke, swing 4. compass, extent, range, scope, span, stretch, vista

sweeping 1. all-embracing, all-inclusive, bird's-eye, broad, comprehensive, extensive, global, radical, thoroughgoing, wide, wide-ranging 2. across-the-board, blanket, exaggerated, indiscriminate, overdrawn, overstated, unqualified, wholesale

sweet adj. 1. cloying, honeyed, luscious, melting, saccharine, sugary, sweetened, syrupy, toothsome 2. affectionate, agreeable, amiable, appealing, attractive, beautiful, charming, delightful, engaging, fair, gentle, kind, lovable, sweet-tempered, taking, tender, unselfish, winning, winsome 3. beloved, cherished, darling, dear, dearest, pet, precious, treasured 4. aromatic, balmy, clean, fragrant, fresh, new, perfumed, pure, redolent, sweet-smelling, wholesome 5. dulcet, euphonic, euphonious, harmonious, mellow, melodious, musical, silver-toned, silvery, soft, sweet-sounding, tuneful 6. **sweet on** enamoured of, gone on (Sl.), head over heels in love with, infatuated by, in love with, keen on, obsessed or bewitched by, taken with,

wild or mad about (Inf.) ~n. 7. afters (Brit. inf.), dessert, pudding, sweet course 8. Usually plural bonbon, candy (U.S.), confectionery, sweetie, sweetmeats

sweeten 1. honey, sugar, sugar-coat 2. alleviate, appease, mollify, pacify, soften up, soothe, sugar the pill

sweetheart admirer, beau, beloved, boyfriend, darling, dear, flame (Inf.), follower (Obsolete), girlfriend, inamorata, inamorato, love, lover, steady (Inf.), suitor, swain (Archaic), sweetie (Inf.), truelove, valentine

sweet-scented ambrosial, aromatic, fragrant, perfumed, sweet-smelling

(sense 19). **3.** *Chiefly Brit.* an endearing person.

sweetmeat ('swi:t,mi:t) *n.* a sweetened delicacy, such as a preserve, sweet, or, formerly, a cake or pastry.

sweet pea *n.* a climbing plant of S Europe, widely cultivated for its butterfly-shaped fragrant flowers of delicate pastel colours.

sweet pepper *n.* **1.** a pepper plant with large bell-shaped fruits that are eaten unripe (**green pepper**) or ripe (**red pepper**). **2.** the fruit.

sweet potato *n.* **1.** a twining plant of tropical America, cultivated in the tropics for its edible fleshy yellow root. **2.** the root.

sweet-talk *U.S. inf.* ~*vb.* **1.** to coax, flatter, or cajole (someone). ~*n.* **sweet talk.** **2.** cajolery; coaxing.

sweet tooth *n.* a strong liking for sweet foods.

sweetveld ('swi:t,fɛlt) *n.* (in South Africa) a particular type of grazing.

sweet william ('wɪljəm) *n.* a widely cultivated Eurasian plant with flat clusters of white, pink, red, or purple flowers.

swell (swɛl) *vb.* **swelling, swelled; swollen** *or* **swelled.** **1.** to grow or cause to grow in size, esp. as a result of internal pressure. **2.** to expand or cause to expand at a particular point or above the surrounding level; protrude. **3.** to grow or cause to grow in size, amount, intensity, or degree: *the party is swelling with new recruits.* **4.** to puff or be puffed up with pride or another emotion. **5.** (*intr.*) (of seas or lakes) to rise in waves. **6.** (*intr.*) to well up or overflow. **7.** (*tr.*) to make (a musical phrase) increase gradually in volume and then diminish. ~*n.* **8. a.** the undulating movement of the surface of the open sea. **b.** a succession of waves or a single large wave. **9.** a swelling or being swollen; expansion. **10.** an increase in quantity or degree; inflation. **11.** a bulge; protuberance. **12.** a gentle hill. **13.** *Inf.* a person very fashionably dressed. **14.** *Inf.* a man of high social or political standing. **15.** *Music.* a crescendo followed by an immediate diminuendo. **16.** Also called: **swell organ.** *Music.* **a.** a set of pipes on an organ housed in a box (**swell box**) fitted with a shutter operated by a pedal, which can be opened or closed to control the volume. **b.** the manual on an organ controlling this. ~*adj.* **17.** *Inf.* stylish or grand. **18.** *Sl.* excellent; first-class.

swelled head *or* **swollen head** *n. Inf.* an inflated view of one's own worth, often caused by sudden success.

swelling ('swɛlɪŋ) *n.* **1.** the act of expansion or inflation. **2.** the state of being or becoming swollen. **3.** a swollen or inflated part or area. **4.** an abnormal enlargement of a bodily structure or part, esp. as the result of injury. Related adj.: **tumescent.**

swelter ('swɛltə) *vb.* **1.** (*intr.*) to suffer under oppressive heat, esp. to perspire and feel faint. **2.** (*tr.*) *Rare.* to cause to suffer under oppressive heat. ~*n.* **3.** a sweltering condition (esp. in **in a swelter**). **4.** oppressive humid heat.

sweltering ('swɛltərɪŋ) *adj.* oppressively hot and humid: *a sweltering day.* —**'swelteringly** *adv.*

swept (swɛpt) *vb.* the past tense of **sweep.**

sweptwing ('swɛpt,wɪŋ) *adj.* (of an aircraft, missile, etc.) having wings swept backwards.

swerve (swɜːv) *vb.* **1.** to turn or cause to turn aside, usually sharply or suddenly, from a course. ~*n.* **2.** the act, instance, or degree of swerving. —**'swervable** *adj.* —**'swerver** *n.* —**'swervingly** *adv.*

swift (swɪft) *adj.* **1.** moving or able to move quickly; fast. **2.** occurring or performed quickly or suddenly; instant. **3.** (*postpositive;* foll. by *to*) prompt to act or respond: *swift to take revenge.* ~*adv.* **4. a.** swiftly or quickly. **b.** (*in combination*): *swift-moving.* ~*n.* **5.** any of various insectivorous birds of the Old World. They have long narrow wings and spend most of the time on the wing. **6.** any of certain North American lizards of the iguana family that can run very rapidly. **7.** the main cylinder in a carding machine. **8.** an expanding reel used to hold skeins of silk. —**'swiftly** *adv.* —**'swiftness** *n.*

swig (swɪg) *Inf.* ~*n.* **1.** a large swallow or deep drink, esp. from a bottle. ~*vb.* **swigging, swigged.** **2.** to drink (some liquid) deeply, esp. from a bottle. —**'swigger** *n.*

swill (swɪl) *vb.* **1.** to drink large quantities of (liquid, esp. alcoholic drink); guzzle. **2.** (*tr.;* often foll. by *out*) *Chiefly Brit.* to drench or rinse in large amounts of water. **3.** (*tr.*) to feed swill to (pigs, etc.). ~*n.* **4.** wet feed, esp. for pigs, consisting of kitchen waste, skim milk, etc. **5.** refuse, esp. from a kitchen. **6.** a deep drink, esp. beer. **7.** any liquid mess. **8.** the act of swilling. —**'swiller** *n.*

swim (swɪm) *vb.* **swimming, swam, swum.** **1.** (*intr.*) to move along in water, etc., by means of movements of the body, esp. the arms and legs, or (in the case of fish) tail and fins. **2.** (*tr.*) to cover (a distance or stretch of water) in this way. **3.** (*tr.*) to compete in (a race) in this way. **4.** (*intr.*) to be supported by and on a liquid; float. **5.** (*tr.*) to use (a particular stroke) in swimming. **6.** (*intr.*) to move smoothly, usually through air or over a surface. **7.** (*intr.*) to reel or seem to reel: *my head swam; the room swam around me.* **8.** (*intr.;* often foll. by *in* or *with*) to be covered or flooded with water or other liquid. **9.** (*intr.;* often foll. by *in*) to be liberally supplied (with): *he's swimming in money.* **10.** (*tr.*) to cause to float or swim. **11. swim with** (*or* **against**) **the stream** *or* **tide.** to conform to (or resist) prevailing opinion. ~*n.* **12.** the act, an instance, or period of swimming. **13.** any graceful gliding motion. **14.** a condition of dizziness; swoon. **15.** a pool in a river good for fishing. **16. in the swim.** *Inf.* fashionable or active in social or political activities. —**'swimmable** *adj.* —**'swimmer** *n.* —**'swimming** *n., adj.*

swim bladder *n. Ichthyol.* another name for **air bladder** (sense 1).

swimming bath *n.* (often *pl.*) an indoor swimming pool.

swimming costume *or* **bathing costume** *n. Chiefly Brit.* any garment worn for swimming or sunbathing, such as a woman's one-piece garment covering most of the torso but not the limbs. Usual U.S. term **bathing suit.**

swimmingly ('swɪmɪŋlɪ) *adv.* successfully, effortlessly, or well (esp. in **go swimmingly**).

swimming pool *n.* an artificial pool for swimming.

swimsuit ('swɪm,suːt, -,sjuːt) *n.* a woman's one-piece swimming garment that leaves the arms and legs bare.

swindle ('swɪndəl) *vb.* **1.** to cheat (someone) of money, etc.; defraud. **2.** (*tr.*) to obtain (money, etc.) by fraud.

THESAURUS

swell *v.* 1. balloon, become bloated *or* distended, become larger, be inflated, belly, billow, bloat, bulge, dilate, distend, enlarge, expand, extend, fatten, grow, increase, protrude, puff up, rise, round out, tumefy, well up 2. add to, aggravate, augment, enhance, heighten, intensify, mount, surge ~*n.* 3. billow, rise, surge, undulation, wave 4. *Inf.* beau, blade (*Archaic*), cockscomb (*Inf.*), dandy, fashion plate, fop, nob (*Sl.*), toff (*Brit. sl.*) ~*adj.* 5. *Inf.* de luxe, exclusive, fashionable, grand, plush *or* plushy (*Inf.*), posh (*Inf.*), ritzy (*Sl.*), smart, stylish

swelling *n.* blister, bruise, bulge, bump, dilation, distension, enlargement, inflammation, lump, protuberance, puffiness, tumescence

swerve *v.* bend, deflect, depart from, deviate, diverge, incline, sheer off, shift, skew, stray, swing, turn, turn aside, veer, wander, wind

swift abrupt, expeditious, express, fast, fleet, fleet-footed, flying, hurried, nimble, nippy (*Brit. inf.*), prompt, quick, rapid, ready, short, short-lived, spanking, speedy, sudden, winged

swiftly as fast as one's legs can carry one, (at) full tilt, double-quick, fast, hotfoot, hurriedly, in less than no time, nippily (*Brit. inf.*), posthaste, promptly, rapidly, speedily, without losing time

swiftness alacrity, celerity, dispatch, expedition, fleetness, promptness, quickness, rapidity, speed, speediness, velocity

swill *v.* 1. consume, drain, drink (down), gulp, guzzle, imbibe, pour down one's gullet, quaff, swallow, swig (*Inf.*), toss off 2. *Often with* **out** drench, flush, rinse, sluice, wash down, wash out ~*n.* 3. hogwash, mash, mush, pigswill, scourings, slops, waste

swimmingly as planned, cosily, effortlessly, like a dream, like clockwork, smooth-ly, successfully, very well, with no trouble, without a hitch

swindle 1. *v.* bamboozle (*Inf.*), bilk (of), cheat, con (*Sl.*), deceive, defraud, diddle (*Inf.*), do (*Sl.*), dupe, fleece, hornswoggle (*Sl.*), overcharge, pull a fast one (on someone) (*Inf.*), put one over on (someone) (*Inf.*), rip (someone) off (*Sl.*), rook (*Sl.*), take (someone) for a ride (*Inf.*), take to the cleaners (*Inf.*), trick 2. *n.* con trick (*Inf.*), deceit, deception, double-dealing, fiddle (*Brit. inf.*), fraud, imposition, knavery, racket, rip-off (*Sl.*), roguery, sharp practice, swizz (*Brit. inf.*), swizzle (*Brit. inf.*), trickery

swindler charlatan, cheat, confidence man, con man (*Sl.*), fraud, impostor, knave (*Archaic*), mountebank, rascal, rogue, rook (*Sl.*), shark, sharper, trickster

~*n.* **3.** a fraudulent scheme or transaction. —**'swindler** *n.*

swine (swaɪn) *n., pl.* **swine. 1.** a coarse or contemptible person. **2.** another name for a **pig.** —**'swinish** *adj.* —**'swinishly** *adv.* —**'swinishness** *n.*

swine fever *n.* an infectious viral disease of pigs, characterized by fever and diarrhoea.

swineherd ('swaɪn,hɜːd) *n.* a person who looks after pigs.

swing (swɪŋ) *vb.* **swinging, swung. 1.** to move or cause to move rhythmically to and fro, as a free-hanging object; sway. **2.** (*intr.*) to move, walk, etc., with a relaxed and swaying motion. **3.** to pivot or cause to pivot, as on a hinge. **4.** to move or cause to move in a curve: *the car swung around the bend.* **5.** to move or cause to move by suspending or being suspended. **6.** to hang or be hung so as to be able to turn freely. **7.** (*intr.*) *Sl.* to be hanged: *he'll swing for it.* **8.** to alter or cause to alter habits, a course, etc. **9.** (*tr.*) *Inf.* to influence ȯr manipulate successfully: *I hope he can swing the deal.* **10.** (*tr.*; foll. by *up*) to raise or hoist, esp. in a sweeping motion. **11.** (*intr.*; often foll. by *at*) to hit out or strike (at), esp. with a sweeping motion. **12.** (*tr.*) to wave (a weapon, etc.) in a sweeping motion; flourish. **13.** to arrange or play (music) with the rhythmically flexible and compulsive quality associated with jazz. **14.** (*intr.*) (of popular music, esp. jazz, or of the musicians who play it) to have this quality. **15.** *Sl.* to be lively and modern. **16.** (*intr.*) *Cricket.* to bowl (a ball) with swing or (of a ball) to move with a swing. **17. swing the lead.** to malinger or make up excuses. ~*n.* **18.** the act or manner of swinging or the distance covered while swinging: *a wide swing.* **19.** a sweeping stroke or blow. **20.** *Boxing.* a wide punch from the side similar to but longer than a hook. **21.** *Cricket.* the lateral movement of a bowled ball through the air. **22.** any free swaying motion. **23.** any curving movement; sweep. **24.** something that swings or is swung, esp. a suspended seat on which a person may swing back and forth. **25.** a kind of popular dance music influenced by jazz, usually played by big bands and originating in the 1930s. **26.** *Prosody.* a steady distinct rhythm or cadence in prose or verse. **27.** *Inf.* the normal round or pace: *the swing of things.* **28.** a fluctuation, as in some business activity, voting pattern, etc. **29.** *Canad.* in the North, a train of freight sleighs or canoes. **30.** *Chiefly U.S.* a circular tour. **31. in full swing.** operating with full vigour.

swingboat ('swɪŋ,bəʊt) *n.* a piece of fairground equipment consisting of a boat-shaped carriage for swinging in.

swingeing ('swɪndʒɪŋ) *adj. Chiefly Brit.* punishing; severe.

swingle ('swɪŋɡəl) *n.* **1.** a flat-bladed wooden instrument used for beating and scraping flax or hemp to remove coarse matter from it. ~*vb.* **2.** to use a swingle on.

swingletree ('swɪŋɡəl,triː) *n.* a crossbar in a horse's harness to which the ends of the traces are attached.

swipe (swaɪp) *vb.* **1.** (when *intr.*, usually foll. by *at*) to hit hard with a sweeping motion. **2.** (*tr.*) *Sl.* to steal. ~*n.* **3.** *Inf.* a hard blow. **4.** Also called: **sweep.** a type of lever for raising and lowering a weight, such as a bucket in a well.

swirl (swɜːl) *vb.* **1.** to turn or cause to turn in a twisting spinning fashion. **2.** (*intr.*) to be dizzy; swim: *my head was swirling.* ~*n.* **3.** a whirling or spinning motion, esp. in water. **4.** a whorl; curl. **5.** the act of swirling or stirring. **6.** dizzy confusion or disorder. —**'swirling** *adj.* —**'swirly** *adj.*

swish (swɪʃ) *vb.* **1.** to move with or make or cause to move with or make a whistling or hissing sound. **2.** (*intr.*) (esp. of fabrics) to rustle. **3.** (*tr.*) *Sl., now rare.* to whip; flog. **4.** (*tr.*; foll. by *off*) to cut with a swishing blow. ~*n.* **5.** a hissing or rustling sound or movement.

6. a rod for flogging or a blow from this. ~*adj.* **7.** *Inf., chiefly Brit.* fashionable; smart. —**'swishy** *adj.*

Swiss (swɪs) *adj.* **1.** of, relating to, or characteristic of Switzerland, a republic in W central Europe, its inhabitants, or their dialects of German, French, and Italian. ~*n.* **2.** a native or inhabitant of Switzerland.

swiss roll *n.* a sponge cake spread with jam, cream, or some other filling, and rolled up.

switch (swɪtʃ) *n.* **1.** a mechanical, electrical, or electronic device for opening or closing a circuit or for diverting a current from one part of a circuit to another. **2.** a swift and usually sudden shift or change. **3.** an exchange or swap. **4.** a flexible rod or twig, used esp. for punishment. **5.** the sharp movement or blow of such an instrument. **6.** a tress of false hair used to give added length or bulk to a woman's own hair style. **7.** the tassel-like tip of the tail of cattle and certain other animals. **8.** any of various card games in which the suit is changed during play. **9.** *U.S.* a railway siding. **10.** *U.S.* a railway point. **11.** *Austral. inf.* short for **switchboard** (sense 1). ~*vb.* **12.** to shift, change, turn aside, or change the direction of (something). **13.** to exchange (places); replace (something by something else). **14.** *Chiefly U.S.* to transfer or be transferred from one railway track to another. **15.** (*tr.*) to cause (an electric current) to start or stop flowing or to change its path by operating a switch. **16.** (*tr.*) to lash or whip with or as if with a switch. —**'switcher** *n.*

switchback ('swɪtʃ,bæk) *n.* **1.** a steep mountain road, railway, or track with hairpin bends or a hairpin bend on such a road, etc. **2.** another word (esp. Brit.) for **roller coaster.**

switchboard ('swɪtʃ,bɔːd) *n.* **1.** an installation in a telephone exchange, office, etc., at which the interconnection of telephone lines is manually controlled. **2.** a similar installation by which certain electrical equipment is operated.

switch off *vb.* (*adv.*) **1.** to cause (a device) to stop operating as by moving a switch, knob, or lever. **2.** *Inf.* to cease to interest or be interested; make or become bored, alienated, etc.

switch on *vb.* (*adv.*) **1.** to cause (a device) to operate as by moving a switch, knob, or lever. **2.** (*tr.*) *Inf.* to produce (charm, tears, etc.) suddenly or automatically. **3.** (*tr.*) *Inf.* (now dated) to make up-to-date, esp. outlook, dress, etc. **4.** (*tr.*) *Sl.* to arouse emotionally or sexually. **5.** (*intr.*) *Sl.* to take or become intoxicated by drugs. **6.** (*tr.*) *Sl.* to introduce (someone) to drugs.

swither ('swɪðə) *Scot. dialect. vb.* (*intr.*) **1.** to hesitate; be perplexed. ~*n.* **2.** hesitation; perplexity; agitation.

swivel ('swɪvəl) *n.* **1.** a coupling device which allows an attached object to turn freely. **2.** such a device made of two parts which turn independently, such as a compound link of a chain. **3. a.** a pivot on which is mounted a gun that may be swung horizontally from side to side. **b.** Also called: **swivel gun.** the gun itself. ~*vb.* **-elling, -elled** or *U.S.* **-eling, -eled. 4.** to turn or swing on or as if on a pivot. **5.** (*tr.*) to provide with, secure by, or support with a swivel.

swivel chair *n.* a chair, the seat of which is joined to the legs by a swivel and which thus may be spun round.

swizz or **swiz** (swɪz) *n. Inf.* a swindle; fraud.

swizzle ('swɪzəl) *n.* **1.** an alcoholic drink containing gin or rum. **2.** Also called: **swizz.** *Brit. inf.* a swindle or disappointment. ~*vb.* **3.** (*tr.*) to stir a swizzle stick in (a drink).

swizzle stick *n.* a small rod used to agitate an effervescent drink to facilitate the escape of carbon dioxide.

swob (swɒb) *n., vb.,* **swobbing, swobbed.** a less common spelling of **swab.**

swollen ('swəʊlən) *vb.* **1.** the past participle of **swell.** ~*adj.* **2.** tumid or enlarged as by swelling. **3.** turgid or bombastic. —**'swollenness** *n.*

swoon (swuːn) *vb.* (*intr.*) **1.** a literary word for **faint. 2.**

---

swing *v.* **1.** be pendent, be suspended, dangle, hang, move back and forth, suspend **2.** fluctuate, oscillate, rock, sway, vary, veer, vibrate, wave **3.** *Usually with* **round** curve, pivot, rotate, swivel, turn, turn on one's heel, wheel ~*n.* **4.** fluctuation, oscillation, stroke, sway, swaying, vibration **5. in full swing** animated, at its height, lively, on the go (*Inf.*), under way

swinging dynamic, fashionable, full of go or pep (*Inf.*), groovy (*Sl.*), hip (*Sl.*), in the swim (*Inf.*), lively, trendy (*Brit. inf.*), up-to-date, up to the minute, with it (*Inf.*)

swirl *v.* agitate, boil, churn, eddy, spin, surge, twirl, twist, whirl

switch *v.* **1.** change, change course, deflect, deviate, divert, exchange, interchange, rearrange, replace by, shift, substitute, swap

(*Inf.*), trade, turn aside ~*n.* **2.** about-turn, alteration, change, change of direction, exchange, reversal, shift, substitution, swap (*Inf.*) ~*v.* **3.** lash, swish, twitch, wave, whip

swollen bloated, distended, dropsical, enlarged, inflamed, puffed up, puffy, tumescent, tumid

to become ecstatic. ~*n.* **3.** an instance of fainting. ~Also (archaic or dialect): **swound** (swaʊnd).

swoop (swuːp) *vb.* **1.** (*intr.;* usually foll. by *down, on,* or *upon*) to sweep or pounce suddenly. **2.** (*tr.;* often foll. by *up, away,* or *off*) to seize or scoop suddenly. ~*n.* **3.** the act of swooping. **4.** a swift descent.

swoosh (swuʃ) *vb.* **1.** to make or cause to make a rustling or swirling sound, esp. when moving or pouring out. ~*n.* **2.** a swirling or rustling sound or movement.

swop (swɒp) *n., vb.,* **swopping, swopped.** a variant spelling of **swap.**

sword (sɔːd) *n.* **1.** a thrusting, striking, or cutting weapon with a long blade having one or two cutting edges, a hilt, and usually a crosspiece or guard. **2.** such a weapon worn on ceremonial occasions as a symbol of authority. **3.** something resembling a sword, such as the snout of a swordfish. **4. cross swords.** to argue or fight. **5. the sword. a.** violence or power, esp. military power. **b.** death; destruction: *to put to the sword.*

swordbearer *n.* an official who carries a ceremonial sword.

sword dance *n.* a dance in which the performers dance nimbly over swords on the ground or brandish them in the air. —**sword dancer** *n.* —**sword dancing** *n.*

swordfish (ˈsɔːd‚fɪʃ) *n., pl.* **-fish** *or* **-fishes.** a large fish with a very long upper jaw: valued as a food and game fish.

Sword of Damocles (ˈdæmə‚kliːz) *n.* a closely impending disaster.

swordplay (ˈsɔːd‚pleɪ) *n.* **1.** the action or art of fighting with a sword. **2.** verbal sparring.

swordsman (ˈsɔːdzmən) *n., pl.* **-men.** one who uses or is skilled in the use of a sword. —**'swordsman‚ship** *n.*

swordstick (ˈsɔːd‚stɪk) *n.* a hollow walking stick containing a short sword or dagger.

swore (swɔː) *vb.* the past tense of **swear.**

sworn (swɔːn) *vb.* **1.** the past participle of **swear.** ~*adj.* **2.** bound, pledged, or made inveterate, by or as if by an oath: *a sworn statement; he was sworn to God.*

swot[1] (swɒt) *Brit. inf.* ~*vb.* **swotting, swotted. 1.** (often foll. by *up*) to study (a subject) intensively, as for an examination; cram. ~*n.* **2.** Also called: **swotter** (ˈswɒtə). a person who works or studies hard. **3.** hard work or grind.

swot[2] (swɒt) *vb.* **swotting, swotted,** *n.* a variant of **swat.**

swum (swʌm) *vb.* the past participle of **swim.**

swung (swʌŋ) *vb.* the past tense or past participle of **swing.**

sybarite (ˈsɪbə‚raɪt) *n.* **1.** (*sometimes cap.*) a devotee of luxury and the sensual vices. ~*adj.* **2.** luxurious; sensuous. —**sybaritic** (‚sɪbəˈrɪtɪk) *adj.* —‚**syba'ritically** *adv.* —**'sybaritism** *n.*

sycamore (ˈsɪkə‚mɔː) *n.* **1.** a Eurasian maple tree, naturalized in Britain and North America, having five-lobed leaves and two-winged fruits. **2.** *U.S.* an American plane tree. **3.** a tree of N Africa and W Asia, having an edible figlike fruit.

sycophant (ˈsɪkəfənt) *n.* a person who uses flattery to win favour from individuals wielding influence; toady. —**'sycophancy** *n.* —**sycophantic** (‚sɪkəˈfæntɪk) *or* ‚**syco'phantish** *adj.* —‚**syco'phantically** *or* ‚**syco'phantishly** *adv.*

syllabic (sɪˈlæbɪk) *adj.* **1.** of or relating to syllables or the division of a word into syllables. **2.** denoting a kind of verse line based on a specific number of syllables rather than being regulated by stresses or quantities. **3.** (of a consonant) constituting a syllable. ~*n.* **4.** a syllabic consonant. —**syl'labically** *adv.*

syllabify (sɪˈlæbɪ‚faɪ) *or* **syllabicate** *vb.* **-fying, -fied** *or* **-cating, -cated.** (*tr.*) to divide (a word) into its constituent syllables. —**syl‚labifi'cation** *or* **syl‚labi'cation** *n.*

syllable (ˈsɪləbəl) *n.* **1.** a combination or set of one or more units of sound in a language that must consist of a

sonorous element (a sonant or vowel) and may or may not contain less sonorous elements (consonants or semivowels) flanking it on either or both sides: for example "paper" has two syllables. **2.** (in the writing systems of certain languages, esp. ancient ones) a symbol or set of symbols standing for a syllable. **3.** the least mention: *don't breathe a syllable of it.* **4. in words of one syllable.** simply; bluntly. ~*vb.* **5.** to pronounce syllables of (a text); articulate. **6.** (*tr.*) to write down in syllables.

syllabub *or* **sillabub** (ˈsɪlə‚bʌb) *n.* **1.** a spiced drink made of milk with rum, port, brandy, or wine, often hot. **2.** *Brit.* a cold dessert made from milk or cream beaten with sugar, wine, and lemon juice.

syllabus (ˈsɪləbəs) *n., pl.* **-buses** *or* **-bi** (-‚baɪ). **1.** an outline of a course of studies, text, etc. **2.** *Brit.* **a.** the subjects studied for a particular course. **b.** a list of these subjects.

syllogism (ˈsɪlə‚dʒɪzəm) *n.* **1.** a deductive inference by which a conclusion is derived from two propositions, the **major premiss** and the **minor premiss.** The subject of the conclusion, the **minor term** (H), appears in the minor premiss, the predicate of the conclusion, the **major term** (G), appears in the major premiss, and the **middle term** (F), appears in both premisses, but not in the conclusion. The most common type of syllogism consists of categorical statements, such as *all F are G, all H are F, therefore all H are G.* **2.** a piece of deductive reasoning from the general to the particular. —‚**syllo'gistic** *adj.* —**'syllo‚gize** *or* **-ise** *vb.*

sylph (sɪlf) *n.* **1.** a slender graceful girl or young woman. **2.** any of a class of imaginary beings assumed to inhabit the air. —**'sylph‚like** *adj.*

sylvan *or* **silvan** (ˈsɪlvən) *Chiefly poetic.* ~*adj.* **1.** of or consisting of woods or forests. **2.** in woods or forests. **3.** idyllically rural or rustic. ~*n.* **4.** an inhabitant of the woods, esp. a spirit.

sym- *prefix.* variant of **syn-** before *b, p,* and *m.*

symbiosis (‚sɪmbɪˈəʊsɪs) *n.* **1.** a close association of two interdependent animal or plant species. **2.** a similar relationship between persons or groups. —‚**symbi'otic** *adj.*

symbol (ˈsɪmbəl) *n.* **1.** something that represents or stands for something else, usually by convention or association, esp. a material object used to represent something abstract. **2.** an object, person, idea, etc., used in a literary work, film, etc., to stand for or suggest something else with which it is associated. **3.** a letter, figure, or sign used in mathematics, science, music, etc. to represent a quantity, phenomenon, operation, function, etc. ~*vb.* **-bolling, -bolled** *or U.S.* **-boling, -boled. 4.** (*tr.*) another word for **symbolize.**

symbolic (sɪmˈbɒlɪk) *or* **symbolical** *adj.* **1.** of or relating to a symbol or symbols. **2.** serving as a symbol. **3.** characterized by the use of symbols or symbolism. —**sym'bolically** *adv.*

symbolism (ˈsɪmbə‚lɪzəm) *n.* **1.** the representation of something in symbolic form or the attribution of symbolic character to something. **2.** a system of symbols or symbolic representation. **3.** symbolic significance or quality. **4.** (*often cap.*) a late 19th-century movement in art that sought to express mystical or abstract ideas through the symbolic use of images. —**'symbolist** *n., adj.*

symbolize *or* **-ise** (ˈsɪmbə‚laɪz) *vb.* **1.** (*tr.*) to serve as or be a symbol of. **2.** (*tr.;* usually foll. by *by*) to represent by a symbol or symbols. **3.** (*intr.*) to use symbols. **4.** (*tr.*) to treat or regard as symbolic. —‚**symboli'zation** *or* **-i'sation** *n.*

symmetry (ˈsɪmɪtrɪ) *n., pl.* **-tries. 1.** similarity, correspondence, or balance among systems or parts of a system. **2.** *Maths.* an exact correspondence in position or form about a given point, line, or plane. **3.** beauty or harmony of form based on a proportionate arrangement of parts. —**sym'metrical** *adj.*

sympathetic (‚sɪmpəˈθɛtɪk) *or* **sympathetical** *adj.* **1.** characterized by, feeling, or showing sympathy;

THESAURUS

swoop 1. *v.* descend, dive, pounce, rush, stoop, sweep 2. *n.* descent, drop, lunge, plunge, pounce, rush, stoop, sweep

sword 1. blade, brand (*Archaic*), trusty steel 2. **cross swords** argue, come to blows, dispute, fight, spar, wrangle 3. **the sword** aggression, arms, butchery, death, massacre,

military might, murder, slaying, violence, war

syllabus course of study, curriculum

symbol badge, emblem, figure, image, logo, mark, representation, sign, token, type

symbolic, symbolical allegorical, emblematic, figurative, representative, significant, token, typical

symbolize betoken, body forth, connote, denote, exemplify, mean, personify, represent, signify, stand for, typify

symmetrical balanced, in proportion, proportional, regular, well-proportioned

symmetry agreement, balance, correspondence, evenness, form, harmony, order, proportion, regularity

understanding. **2.** in accord with the subject's personality or mood; congenial: *a sympathetic atmosphere*. **3.** (when *postpositive*, often foll. by *to* or *towards*) showing agreement (with) or favour (towards). **4.** *Anat., physiol.* of or relating to the division of the autonomic nervous system that acts in opposition to the parasympathetic system accelerating the heartbeat, dilating the bronchi, inhibiting the smooth muscles of the digestive tract, etc. **5.** relating to vibrations occurring as a result of similar vibrations in a neighbouring body: *sympathetic strings on a sitar*. —**sympa'thetically** *adv.*

sympathetic magic *n.* a type of magic in which it is sought to produce a large-scale effect, often at a distance, by performing some small-scale ceremony resembling it, such as the pouring of water on an altar to induce rainfall.

sympathize or **-ise** ('sɪmpə,θaɪz) *vb.* (*intr.*; often foll. by *with*) **1.** to feel or express compassion or sympathy (for); commiserate: *he sympathized with my troubles*. **2.** to share or understand the sentiments or ideas (of); be in sympathy (with). —**sympa,thizer** or **-iser** *n.* —**sympa,thizingly** or **-isingly** *adv.*

sympathy ('sɪmpəθɪ) *n., pl.* **-thies. 1.** the sharing of another's emotions, esp. of sorrow or anguish; compassion. **2.** affinity or harmony, usually of feelings or interests, between persons or things: *to be in sympathy with someone*. **3.** mutual affection or understanding arising from such a relationship. **4.** the condition of a physical system or body when its behaviour is similar or corresponds to that of a different system that influences it, such as the vibration of sympathetic strings. **5.** (*sometimes pl.*) a feeling of loyalty, support, or accord, as for an idea, cause, etc. **6.** *Physiol.* the relationship between two organs or parts whereby a change in one affects the other.

symphonic poem *n. Music.* an extended orchestral composition, originated by Liszt, based on nonmusical material, such as a work of literature or folk tale. Also called: **tone poem.**

symphony ('sɪmfənɪ) *n., pl.* **-nies. 1.** an extended large-scale orchestral composition, usually with several movements, at least one of which is in sonata form. **2.** a piece of instrumental music in up to three very short movements, used as an overture to or interlude in a baroque opera. **3.** any purely orchestral movement in a vocal work, such as a cantata or oratorio. **4.** short for **symphony orchestra. 5.** anything distinguished by a harmonious composition: *the picture was a symphony of green.* **6.** *Arch.* harmony in general; concord. —**symphonic** (sɪm'fɒnɪk) *adj.* —**sym'phonically** *adv.*

symphony orchestra *n. Music.* an orchestra capable of performing symphonies, esp. a large orchestra comprising strings, brass, woodwind, harp and percussion.

symposium (sɪm'pəʊzɪəm) *n., pl.* **-siums** or **-sia** (-zɪə). **1.** a conference or meeting for the discussion of some subject, esp. an academic topic or social problem. **2.** a collection of scholarly contributions on a given subject. **3.** (in classical Greece) a drinking party with intellectual conversation, music, etc.

symptom ('sɪmptəm) *n.* **1.** *Med.* any sensation or change in bodily function experienced by a patient that is associated with a particular disease. **2.** any phenomenon or circumstance accompanying something and regarded as evidence of its existence; indication. —**sympto'matic** *adj.*

syn. *abbrev. for* synonym(ous).

syn- *prefix.* **1.** with or together: *synecology.* **2.** fusion: *syngamy.*

synagogue ('sɪnə,gɒg) *n.* **1. a.** a building for Jewish religious services and religious instruction. **b.** (*as modifi-*

er): *synagogue services.* **2.** a congregation of Jews who assemble for worship or religious study. **3.** the religion of Judaism as organized in such congregations. —**synagogical** (,sɪnə'gɒdʒɪkəl) or **synagogal** ('sɪnə,gɒgəl) *adj.*

sync (sɪŋk) *Films, television, computers. Inf.* ~*vb.* **1.** to synchronize. ~*n.* **2.** synchronization.

synchro- *combining form.* indicating synchronization: *synchromesh.*

synchromesh ('sɪŋkrəʊ,mɛʃ) *adj.* **1.** (of a gearbox, etc.) having a system of clutches that synchronizes the speeds of the driving and driven members before engagement to avoid shock in gear changing and to reduce noise and wear. ~*n.* **2.** a gear system having these features.

synchronism ('sɪŋkrə,nɪzəm) *n.* **1.** the quality or condition of being synchronous. **2.** a chronological list of historical persons and events, arranged to show parallel or synchronous occurrence. **3.** the representation in a work of art of one or more incidents that occurred at separate times. —**synchro'nistic** or **,synchro'nistical** *adj.* —**,synchro'nistically** *adv.*

synchronize or **-ise** ('sɪŋkrə,naɪz) *vb.* **1.** (when *intr.*, usually foll. by *with*) to occur or recur or cause to occur or recur at the same time or in unison. **2.** to indicate or cause to indicate the same time: *synchronize your watches.* **3.** (*tr.*) *Films.* to establish (the picture and soundtrack records) in their correct relative position. **4.** (*tr.*) to designate events as simultaneous. —**,synchroni'zation** or **-i'sation** *n.* —**synchro,nizer** or **-iser** *n.*

synchronous ('sɪŋkrənəs) *adj.* **1.** occurring at the same time. **2.** *Physics.* (of periodic phenomena, such as voltages) having the same frequency and phase. **3.** occurring or recurring exactly together and at the same rate. —**synchronously** *adv.* —**synchronousness** *n.* —**synchrony** *n.*

syncline ('sɪŋklaɪn) *n.* a downward fold of stratified rock in which the strata slope towards a vertical axis. —**syn'clinal** *adj.*

syncopate ('sɪŋkə,peɪt) *vb.* (*tr.*) **1.** *Music.* to modify or treat (a beat, rhythm, note, etc.) by syncopation. **2.** to shorten (a word) by omitting sounds or letters from the middle. —**,synco'pation** *n.* —**'synco,pator** *n.*

syncope ('sɪŋkəpɪ) *n.* **1.** a technical word for a **faint. 2.** the omission of sounds or letters from the middle of a word. —**syncopic** (sɪŋ'kɒpɪk) or **'syncopal** *adj.*

syncretize or **-ise** ('sɪŋkrɪ,taɪz) *vb.* to attempt to combine the characteristic teachings, beliefs, or practices of (differing systems of religion or philosophy). —**,syncreti'zation** or **-i'sation** *n.*

syndic ('sɪndɪk) *n.* **1.** *Brit.* a business agent of some universities or other bodies. **2.** (in several countries) a government administrator or magistrate with varying powers. —**'syndical** *adj.*

syndicalism ('sɪndɪkə,lɪzəm) *n.* **1.** a revolutionary movement and theory advocating seizure of the means of production and distribution by syndicates of workers, esp. by a general strike. **2.** an economic system resulting from such action. —**'syndical** *adj.* —**'syndicalist** *adj., n.* —**,syndical'istic** *adj.*

syndicate *n.* ('sɪndɪkɪt). **1.** an association of business enterprises or individuals organized to undertake a joint project. **2.** a news agency that sells articles, photographs, etc., to a number of newspapers for simultaneous publication. **3.** any association formed to carry out an enterprise of common interest to its members. **4.** a board of syndics or the office of syndic. ~*vb.* ('sɪndɪ,keɪt). **5.** (*tr.*) to sell (articles, photographs, etc.) to several newspapers for simultaneous publication. **6.** to form a syndicate of (people). —**,syndi'cation** *n.*

syndrome ('sɪndrəʊm) *n.* **1.** *Med.* any combination·of signs and symptoms that are indicative of a particular

sympathetic 1. affectionate, caring, commiserating, compassionate, concerned, condoling, feeling, interested, kind, kindly, pitying, responsive, supportive, tender, understanding, warm, warm-hearted **2.** *Often with* **to** agreeable, approving, encouraging, favourably disposed, friendly, in sympathy with, pro, well-disposed **3.** agreeable, appreciative, companionable, compatible, congenial, friendly, like-minded, responsive, well-intentioned

sympathetically appreciatively, feelingly, kindly, perceptively, responsively, sensitively, understandingly, warm-heartedly, warmly, with compassion, with feeling, with interest

sympathize 1. bleed for, commiserate, condole, empathize, feel for, feel one's heart go out to, grieve with, have compassion, offer consolation, pity, share another's sorrow **2.** agree, be in accord, be in sympathy, go along with, identify with, side with, understand

sympathizer condoler, fellow traveller,

partisan, supporter, well-wisher

sympathy 1. commiseration, compassion, condolence(s), empathy, pity, tenderness, thoughtfulness, understanding **2.** affinity, agreement, congeniality, correspondence, fellow feeling, harmony, rapport, union, warmth

symptom expression, indication, mark, note, sign, syndrome, token, warning

symptomatic characteristic, indicative, suggestive

disease or disorder. **2.** a symptom, characteristic, or set of symptoms or characteristics indicating the existence of a condition, problem, etc. —**syndromic** (sɪn'drɒmɪk) adj.

synecdoche (sɪn'ɛkdəkɪ) n. a figure of speech in which a part is substituted for a whole or a whole for a part, as in *50 head of cattle* for *50 cows*, or *the army* for *a soldier*. —**synecdochic** (ˌsɪnɛk'dɒkɪk) or ˌsynec'dochical adj.

synod ('sɪnəd, 'sɪnɒd) n. **1.** a local or special ecclesiastical council, esp. of a diocese, formally convened to discuss ecclesiastical affairs. **2.** *Rare.* any council, esp. for discussion. —'**synodal** or **syn'odical** adj.

synonym ('sɪnənɪm) n. **1.** a word that means the same or nearly the same as another word, such as *bucket* and *pail*. **2.** a word or phrase used as another name for something, such as *Hellene* for a *Greek*. —ˌsyno'nymic or ˌsyno'nymical adj. —ˌsyno'nymity n.

synonymous (sɪ'nɒnɪməs) adj. **1.** (often foll. by *with*) being a synonym (of). **2.** (*postpositive; foll. by with*) closely associated (with) or suggestive (of): *his name was synonymous with greed.* —**syn'onymously** adv. —**syn'onymousness** n.

synopsis (sɪ'nɒpsɪs) n., pl. -**ses** (-siːz). a brief review of a subject; summary.

synoptic (sɪ'nɒptɪk) adj. **1.** of or relating to a synopsis. **2.** (often cap.) *Bible.* **a.** (of the Gospels of Matthew, Mark, and Luke) presenting the narrative of Christ's life, ministry, etc. from a point of view held in common by all three, and with close similarities in content, order, etc. **b.** of or relating to these three Gospels. **3.** *Meteorol.* concerned with the distribution of meteorological conditions over a wide area at a given time: *a synoptic chart.* ~n. **4.** (often cap.) *Bible.* **a.** any of the three synoptic Gospels. **b.** any of the authors of these. —**syn'optically** adv. —**syn'optist** n.

synovia (saɪ'nəʊvɪə, sɪ-) n. a transparent viscid lubricating fluid, secreted by the membrane lining joints, tendon sheaths, etc. —**syn'ovial** adj.

syntax ('sɪntæks) n. **1.** the branch of linguistics that deals with the grammatical arrangement of words and morphemes in sentences. **2.** the totality of facts about the grammatical arrangement of words in a language. **3.** a systematic statement of the rules governing the grammatical arrangement of words and morphemes in a language. **4.** a systematic statement of the rules governing the properly formed formulas of a logical system. —**syn'tactic** or **syn'tactical** adj. —**syn'tactically** adv.

synthesis ('sɪnθɪsɪs) n., pl. -**ses** (-ˌsiːz). **1.** the process of combining objects or ideas into a complex whole. **2.** the combination or whole produced by such a process. **3.** the process of producing a compound by a chemical reaction or series of reactions, usually from simpler starting materials. **4.** *Linguistics.* the use of inflections rather than word order and function words to express the syntactic relations in a language. **5.** deductive reasoning from the general to the particular or from cause to effect. —**'synthesist** n.

synthesize ('sɪnθɪˌsaɪz), **synthetize** or -**sise**, -**tise** vb. **1.** to combine or cause to combine into a whole. **2.** (tr.) to produce by synthesis. —ˌsynthesi'zation, ˌsyntheti'zation or -si'sation, -ti'sation n.

synthesizer ('sɪnθɪˌsaɪzə) n. **1.** short for **Moog synthesizer**. **2.** a person or thing that synthesizes.

synthetic (sɪn'θɛtɪk) adj. also **synthetical**. **1.** (of a substance or material) made artificially by chemical reaction. **2.** not genuine; insincere: *synthetic compassion.* **3.** denoting languages, such as Latin, whose morphology is characterized by synthesis. **4.** *Philosophy.* (of a proposition) having a truth value that is not determined solely by virtue of the meanings of the words, as in *all men are arrogant.* ~n. **5.** a synthetic substance or material. —**syn'thetically** adv.

syphilis ('sɪfɪlɪs) n. a venereal disease caused by infection with the microorganism *Treponema pallidum:* characterized by an ulcerating chancre, usually on the exter-

nal genitals and progressing through the lymphatic system to nearly all tissues of the body, producing serious clinical manifestations. —**syphilitic** (ˌsɪfɪ'lɪtɪk) adj. —'**syphiˌloid** adj.

syphon ('saɪfən) n. a variant spelling of **siphon**.

Syriac ('sɪrɪˌæk) n. a dialect of Aramaic spoken in Syria until about the 13th century A.D.

Syrian ('sɪrɪən) adj. **1.** of or relating to Syria, a republic in W Asia, its people, or their dialect of Arabic. ~n. **2.** a native or inhabitant of Syria.

syringa (sɪ'rɪŋgə) n. another name for **mock orange** and **lilac** (sense 1).

syringe ('sɪrɪndʒ, sɪ'rɪndʒ) n. **1.** *Med.* a hypodermic syringe or a rubber ball with a slender nozzle, for use in withdrawing or injecting fluids, cleaning wounds, etc. **2.** any similar device for injecting, spraying, or extracting liquids by means of pressure or suction. ~vb. **3.** (tr.) to cleanse, inject, or spray with a syringe.

syrup ('sɪrəp) n. **1.** a solution of sugar dissolved in water and often flavoured with fruit juice: used for sweetening fruit, etc. **2.** any of various thick sweet liquids prepared for cooking or table use from molasses, sugars, etc. **3.** *Inf.* cloying sentimentality. **4.** a liquid medicine containing a sugar solution for flavouring or preservation. ~Also: **sirup**. —'**syrupy** adj.

system ('sɪstəm) n. **1.** a group or combination of interrelated, interdependent, or interacting elements forming a collective entity; a methodical or coordinated assemblage of parts, facts, concepts, etc. **2.** any scheme of classification or arrangement. **3.** a network of communications, transportation, or distribution. **4.** a method or complex of methods: *he has a perfect system at roulette.* **5.** orderliness; an ordered manner. **6. the system.** (often cap.) society seen as an environment exploiting, restricting, and repressing individuals. **7.** an organism considered as a functioning entity. **8.** any of various bodily parts or structures that are anatomically or physiologically related: *the digestive system.* **9.** one's physiological or psychological constitution: *get it out of your system.* **10.** any assembly of electronic, electrical, or mechanical components with interdependent functions, usually forming a self-contained unit: *a brake system.* **11.** a group of celestial bodies that are associated as a result of natural laws, esp. gravitational attraction: *the solar system.* **12.** a point of view or doctrine used to interpret a branch of knowledge. **13.** *Mineralogy.* one of a group of divisions into which crystals may be placed on the basis of the lengths and inclinations of their axes. **14.** *Geol.* a stratigraphical unit for the rock strata formed during a period of geological time.

systematic (ˌsɪstɪ'mætɪk) adj. **1.** characterized by the use of order and planning; methodical: *a systematic administrator.* **2.** comprising or resembling a system: *systematic theology.* **3.** Also: **systematical**. *Biol.* of or relating to taxonomic classification. —ˌsystem'atically adv. —'systemaˌtism n. —'systematist n.

systematize ('sɪstɪməˌtaɪz), **systemize** or -**tise**, -**mise** vb. (tr.) to arrange in a system. —ˌsystemati'zation, -i'sation or ˌsystemi'zation, -i'sation n. —'systemaˌtizer, -iser or 'systemˌizer, -ˌiser n.

systemic (sɪ'stɛmɪk, -'stiː-) adj. **1.** another word for **systematic** (senses 1, 2). **2.** *Physiol.* (of a poison, disease, etc.) affecting the entire body. **3.** (of an insecticide, fungicide, etc.) designed to be absorbed by a plant into its tissues. ~n. **4.** a systemic insecticide, fungicide, etc. —sys'temically adv.

systems analysis n. the analysis of the methods involved in scientific and industrial operations, usually with a computer so that an improved system can be designed.

systole ('sɪstəlɪ) n. contraction of the heàrt, during which blood is pumped into the aorta and the arteries. —**systolic** (sɪ'stɒlɪk) adj.

THESAURUS

synthesis 1. amalgamation, coalescence, combination, integration, unification, welding 2. amalgam, blend, combination, composite, compound, fusion, union

synthetic artificial, ersatz, fake, manmade, manufactured, mock

system 1. arrangement, classification, combination, coordination, organization, scheme, setup (Sl.), structure 2. fixed order, frame of reference, method, methodology, modus operandi, practice, procedure, routine, technique, theory, usage 3. definite plan, logical process, method, methodicalness, orderliness, regularity, systematization

systematic businesslike, efficient, methodical, orderly, organized, precise, standardized, systematized, well-ordered

T

t *or* **T** (ti:) *n., pl.* **t's, T's,** *or* **Ts.** **1.** the 20th letter of the English alphabet. **2.** a speech sound represented by this letter. **3.** something shaped like a T. **4. to a T.** in every detail; perfectly.

t *symbol for:* **1.** ton(s). **2.** tonne(s). **3.** troy (weight). **4.** *Statistics.* distribution.

T *symbol for:* **1.** absolute temperature. **2.** tera-. **3.** *Chem.* tritium. **4.** tesla. **5.** surface tension.

t. *abbrev. for:* **1.** *Commerce.* tare. **2.** teaspoon(ful). **3.** temperature. **4.** *Music.* tempo. **5.** *Music.* Also **T.** tenor. **6.** *Grammar.* tense. **7.** transitive.

ta (tɑː) *interj. Brit. inf.* thank you.

Ta *the chemical symbol for* tantalum.

TA (in Britain) *abbrev. for* Territorial Army (now superseded by **TAVR**).

tab[1] (tæb) *n.* **1.** a small flap of material, esp. one on a garment for decoration or for fastening to a button. **2.** any similar flap, such as a piece of paper attached to a file for identification. **3.** *Brit. mil.* the insignia on the collar of a staff officer. **4.** *U.S.* a bill, esp. for a meal or drinks. **5. keep tabs on.** *Inf.* to keep a watchful eye on. ~*vb.* **tabbing, tabbed.** **6.** (*tr.*) to supply with a tab or tabs.

tab[2] (tæb) *n.* short for **tabulator** or **tablet.**

tabard ('tæbəd) *n.* a sleeveless or short-sleeved jacket, esp. one worn by a herald, bearing a coat of arms, or by a knight over his armour.

Tabasco (tə'bæskəʊ) *n. Trademark.* a very hot red sauce made from matured capsicums.

tabby ('tæbɪ) *adj.* **1.** (esp. of cats) brindled with dark stripes or wavy markings on a lighter background. **2.** having a wavy or striped pattern, particularly in colours of grey and brown. ~*n., pl.* **-bies.** **3.** a tabby cat. **4.** any female domestic cat. **5.** a fabric with a watered pattern, esp. silk or taffeta.

tabernacle ('tæbə,nækəl) *n.* **1.** (*often cap.*) *Old Testament.* **a.** the portable sanctuary in which the ancient Israelites carried the Ark of the Covenant. **b.** the Jewish Temple. **2.** any place of worship that is not called a church. **3.** *R.C. Church.* a receptacle in which the Blessed Sacrament is kept. **4.** *Chiefly R.C. Church.* a canopied niche. **5.** *Naut.* a strong framework for holding the foot of a mast, allowing it to be swung down to pass under low bridges, etc. —**taber'nacular** *adj.*

table ('teɪbəl) *n.* **1.** a flat horizontal slab or board supported by one or more legs. **2. a.** such a slab or board on which food is served. **b.** (*as modifier*): *table linen.* **3.** food as served in a particular household, etc.: *a good table.* **4.** such a piece of furniture specially designed for any of various purposes: *a bird table.* **5. a.** a company of persons assembled for a meal, game, etc. **b.** (*as modifier*): *table talk.* **6.** any flat or level area, such as a plateau. **7.** a rectangular panel set below or above the face of a wall. **8.** *Archit.* another name for **string course.** **9.** any of various flat surfaces, as an upper horizontal facet of a cut gem. **10.** *Music.* the sounding board of a violin, guitar, etc. **11. a.** an arrangement of words, numbers, or signs, usually in parallel columns. **b.** See **multiplication table.** **12.** a tablet on which laws were inscribed by the ancient Romans, the Hebrews, etc. **13. turn the tables.** to cause a complete reversal of circumstances. ~*vb.* (*tr.*) **14.** to place on a table. **15.** to submit (a bill, etc.) for consideration by a legislative body. **16.** to suspend discussion of (a bill, etc.) indefinitely. **17.** to enter or form into a list.

tableau ('tæbləʊ) *n., pl.* **-leaux** (-ləʊ, -ləʊz) *or* **-leaus.** **1.** a pause on stage when all the performers briefly freeze in position. **2.** any dramatic group or scene.

tablecloth ('teɪbəl,klɒθ) *n.* a cloth for covering the top of a table, esp. during meals.

table d'hôte ('tɑːbəl 'dəʊt) *adj.* **1.** (of a meal) consisting of a set number of courses with limited choice of dishes offered at a fixed price. Cf. **à la carte.** ~*n., pl.* **tables d'hôte** ('tɑːbəlz 'dəʊt). **2.** a table d'hôte meal or menu.

tableland ('teɪbəl,lænd) *n.* flat elevated land.

table licence *n.* a licence authorizing the sale of alcoholic drinks with meals only.

tablespoon ('teɪbəl,spuːn) *n.* **1.** a spoon, larger than a dessertspoon, used for serving food, etc. **2.** Also called: **tablespoonful.** the amount contained in such a spoon. **3.** a unit of capacity used in cooking, medicine, etc., equal to half a fluid ounce.

tablet ('tæblɪt) *n.* **1.** a pill made of a compressed medicinal substance. **2.** a flattish cake of some substance, such as soap. **3.** a slab of stone, wood, etc., esp. one used for inscriptions. **4. a.** a rigid sheet, as of bark, etc., used for similar purposes. **b.** (*often pl.*) a set of these fastened together. **5.** a pad of writing paper. **6.** *Scot.* a sweet made from butter, sugar, and condensed milk, usually shaped into flat oblong cakes.

table tennis *n.* a miniature form of tennis played on a table with bats and a hollow ball.

tabloid ('tæblɔɪd) *n.* a newspaper with pages about 30 cm (12 inches) by 40 cm (16 inches), usually with many photographs and a concise and often sensational style.

taboo *or* **tabu** (tə'buː) *adj.* **1.** forbidden or disapproved of: *taboo words.* **2.** (in Polynesia) marked off as sacred and forbidden. ~*n., pl.* **-boos** *or* **-bus.** **3.** any prohibition resulting from social or other conventions. **4.** ritual restriction or prohibition, esp. of something that is considered holy or unclean. ~*vb.* **5.** (*tr.*) to place under a taboo.

tabor *or* **tabour** ('teɪbə) *n.* a small drum used esp. in the Middle Ages, struck with one hand while the other held a pipe.

tabular ('tæbjʊlə) *adj.* **1.** arranged in systematic or table form. **2.** calculated from or by means of a table. **3.** like a table in form; flat. —**'tabularly** *adv.*

tabulate *vb.* ('tæbjʊ,leɪt). (*tr.*) **1.** to set out, arrange, or write in tabular form. **2.** to form or cut with a flat surface. ~*adj.* ('tæbjʊlɪt, -,leɪt). **3.** having a flat surface. —**'tabulable** *adj.* —**,tabu'lation** *n.*

tabulator ('tæbjʊ,leɪtə) *n.* **1.** a device for setting the stops that locate the column margins on a typewriter. **2.** *Computers.* a machine that reads data from one medium, such as punched cards, producing lists, tabulations, or totals.

tachograph ('tækə,grɑːf) *n.* a tachometer that produces a record (**tachogram**) of its readings, esp. a device for recording the speed of and distance covered by a vehicle.

tachometer (tæ'kɒmɪtə) *n.* any device for measuring speed, esp. the rate of revolution of a shaft. Tachometers are often fitted to cars to indicate the number of revolutions per minute of the engine. —**ta'chometry** *n.*

tacit ('tæsɪt) *adj.* **1.** implied without direct expression; understood: *a tacit agreement.* **2.** silent. —**'tacitly** *adv.*

taciturn ('tæsɪ,tɜːn) *adj.* habitually silent, reserved, or uncommunicative. —**,taci'turnity** *n.* —**'taci,turnly** *adv.*

THESAURUS

table *n.* **1.** bench, board, counter, slab, stand **2.** board, diet, fare, food, spread (*Inf.*), victuals **3.** flat, flatland, plain, plateau, tableland **4.** agenda, catalogue, chart, diagram, digest, graph, index, inventory, list, plan, record, register, roll, schedule, synopsis, tabulation ~*v.* **5.** enter, move, propose, put forward, submit, suggest

tableau picture, representation, scene, spectacle

taboo **1.** *adj.* anathema, banned, beyond the pale, disapproved of, forbidden, frowned on, not allowed, not permitted, outlawed, prohibited, proscribed, ruled out, unacceptable, unmentionable, unthinkable **2.** *n.* anathema, ban, disapproval, interdict, prohibition, proscription, restriction

tabulate arrange, catalogue, categorize, chart, classify, codify, index, list, order, range, systematize, tabularize

tacit implicit, implied, inferred, silent, taken for granted, undeclared, understood, unexpressed, unspoken, unstated, wordless

taciturn aloof, antisocial, close-lipped, cold, distant, dumb, mute, quiet, reserved, reticent, silent, tight-lipped, uncommunicative, unforthcoming, withdrawn

TU V

tack[1] (tæk) n. 1. a short sharp-pointed nail, with a large flat head. 2. *Brit.* a long loose temporary stitch used in dressmaking, etc. 3. a temporary fastening. 4. stickiness. 5. *Naut.* the heading of a vessel sailing to windward, stated in terms of the side of the sail against which the wind is pressing. 6. *Naut.* a. a course sailed with the wind blowing from forward of the beam. b. one such course or a zigzag pattern of such courses. 7. *Naut.* a. a sheet for controlling the weather clew of a course. b. the weather clew itself. 8. *Naut.* the forward lower clew of a fore-and-aft sail. 9. a course of action or policy. 10. **on the wrong tack.** under a false impression. ~vb. 11. to secure by a tack or tacks. 12. *Brit.* to sew (something) with long loose temporary stitches. 13. (*tr.*) to attach or append. 14. *Naut.* to change the heading of (a sailing vessel) to the opposite tack. 15. *Naut.* to steer (a sailing vessel) on alternate tacks. 16. (*intr.*) *Naut.* (of a sailing vessel) to proceed on a different tack or to alternate tacks. 17. (*intr.*) to follow a zigzag route; keep changing one's course of action. —'**tacker** n.

tack[2] (tæk) n. riding harness for horses, such as saddles, bridles, etc.

tackle ('tækəl) n. 1. an arrangement of ropes and pulleys designed to lift heavy weights. 2. the equipment required for a particular occupation, etc. 3. *Naut.* the halyards and other running rigging aboard a vessel. 4. *Sport.* a physical challenge to an opponent, as to prevent his progress with the ball. ~vb. 5. (*tr.*) to undertake (a task, etc.). 6. (*tr.*) to confront (esp. an opponent) with a difficult proposition. 7. *Sport.* to challenge (an opponent) with a tackle. —'**tackler** n.

tacky[1] ('tækɪ) adj. **tackier, tackiest.** slightly sticky or adhesive. —'**tackiness** n.

tacky[2] ('tækɪ) adj. **tackier, tackiest.** *U.S. inf.* 1. shabby or shoddy. 2. ostentatious and vulgar. 3. (of a person) eccentric; crazy. —'**tackiness** n.

tact (tækt) n. 1. a sense of what is fitting and considerate in dealing with others, so as to avoid giving offence. 2. skill in handling difficult situations; diplomacy. —'**tactful** adj. —'**tactfulness** n. —'**tactless** adj. —'**tactlessness** n.

tactic ('tæktɪk) n. a piece of tactics; tactical move.

tactical ('tæktɪkəl) adj. 1. of, relating to, or employing tactics: *a tactical error.* 2. (of missiles, bombing, etc.) for use in or supporting limited military operations; short-range. 3. skilful, adroit, or diplomatic. —'**tactically** adv.

tactics ('tæktɪks) pl. n. 1. (*functioning as sing.*) *Mil.* the art and science of the detailed direction and control of movement or manoeuvre to achieve an aim or task. 2. the manoeuvres used to achieve an aim or task. 3. plans followed in order to achieve a certain aim. —tac'**tician** n.

tactile ('tæktaɪl) adj. 1. of, relating to, affecting, or having a sense of touch. 2. *Now rare.* capable of being touched; tangible. —**tactility** (tæk'tɪlɪtɪ) n.

tadpole ('tæd,pəʊl) n. the aquatic larva of frogs, toads, etc., which develops from a limbless tailed form with external gills into a form with internal gills, limbs, and a reduced tail.

taffeta ('tæfɪtə) n. a thin crisp lustrous plain-weave fabric of silk, rayon, etc., used esp. for women's clothes.

taffrail ('tæf,reɪl) n. *Naut.* a rail at the stern of a vessel.

Taffy ('tæfɪ) n., pl. **-fies.** a slang word or nickname for a Welshman.

tag[1] (tæg) n. 1. a piece of paper, leather, etc., for attaching to something as a mark or label: *a price tag.* 2. a small piece of material hanging from a part or piece. 3. a point of metal, etc. at the end of a cord or lace. 4. an epithet or verbal appendage, the refrain of a song, the moral of a fable, etc. 5. a brief quotation. 6. an ornamental flourish. 7. the tip of an animal's tail. 8. a matted lock of wool or hair. ~vb. **tagging, tagged.** (*mainly tr.*) 9. to mark with a tag. 10. to add or append as a tag. 11. to supply prose or blank verse with rhymes. 12. (*intr.*; usually foll. by *on* or *along*) to trail (behind). 13. to name or call (someone something). 14. to cut the tags of wool or hair from (an animal).

tag[2] (tæg) n. 1. a children's game in which one player chases the others in an attempt to catch one of them who will then become the chaser. 2. the act of tagging one's partner in tag wrestling. 3. (*modifier*) denoting a wrestling contest between two teams of two wrestlers, in which only one from each team may be in the ring at one time. The contestant outside the ring may change places with his team-mate inside the ring after touching his hand. ~vb. **tagging, tagged.** (*tr.*) 4. to catch (another child) in the game of tag. 5. (in tag wrestling) to touch the hand of (one's partner).

Tagalog (tə'gɑːlɒg) n., pl. **-logs** or **-log.** 1. a member of a people of the Philippines. 2. the language of this people. ~adj. 3. of or relating to this people or their language.

tag end n. 1. *Chiefly U.S.* the last part of something. 2. a loose end of cloth, thread, etc.

tagetes (tæ'dʒiːtiːz) n. any of a genus of plants with yellow or orange flowers, including the French and African marigolds.

tagliatelle (,tæljə'tɛlɪ) n. a form of pasta made in narrow strips.

tail[1] (teɪl) n. 1. the rear part of the vertebrate body that contains an elongation of the vertebral column, esp. forming a flexible appendage. 2. anything resembling such an appendage; the bottom, lowest, or rear part. 3. the last part or parts: *the tail of the storm.* 4. the rear part of an aircraft including the fin, tailplane, and control surfaces. 5. *Astron.* the luminous stream of gas and dust particles driven from the head of a comet when close to the sun. 6. the rear portion of a bomb, rocket, missile, etc., usually fitted with guiding or stabilizing vanes. 7. a line of people or things. 8. a long braid or tress of hair: *a pigtail.* 9. a final short line in a stanza. 10. *Inf.* a person employed to follow and spy upon another. 11. an informal word for **buttocks.** 12. *Taboo sl., chiefly U.S.* a. the female genitals. b. a woman considered sexually (esp. in **piece of tail, bit of tail**). 13. the foot of a page. 14. the lower end of a pool or part of a stream. 15. *Inf.* the course or track of a fleeing person or animal. 16. (*modifier*) coming from or situated in the rear: *a tail wind.* 17. **turn tail.** to run away; escape. 18. **with one's tail between one's legs.** in a state of utter defeat or confusion. ~vb. 19. to form or cause to form the tail. 20. to remove the tail of (an animal). 21. (*tr.*) to remove the stalk of. 22. (*tr.*) to connect (objects, ideas, etc.) together by or as if by the tail. 23. (*tr.*) *Inf.* to follow stealthily. 24. (*intr.*) (of a vessel) to assume a specified position, as when at a mooring. 25. (*tr.*) to build the end of (a brick, joist, etc.) into a wall or (of a brick, etc.) to have one end built into a wall. ~See also **tail off.** —'**tailless** adj.

tail[2] (teɪl) *Law.* ~n. 1. the limitation of an estate or interest to a person and the heirs of his body. ~adj. 2. (*immediately postpositive*) limited in this way. —'**tailless** adj.

---

tack n. 1. drawing pin, nail, pin, staple, thumbtack (*U.S.*), tintack 2. approach, bearing, course, direction, heading, line, method, path, plan, procedure, tactic, way ~v. 3. affix, attach, fasten, fix, nail, pin, staple 4. baste, stitch 5. add, annex, append, attach, tag

tackle n. 1. accoutrements, apparatus, equipment, gear, implements, outfit, paraphernalia, rig, rigging, tools, trappings 2. block, challenge, stop ~v. 3. apply oneself to, attempt, begin, come *or* get to grips with, deal with, embark upon, engage in, essay, get stuck into (*Inf.*), have a go at (*Inf.*), set about, take on, try, turn one's hand to, undertake 4. block, bring down, challenge, clutch,

confront, grab, grasp, halt, intercept, seize, stop, take hold of, throw

tact address, adroitness, consideration, delicacy, diplomacy, discretion, finesse, judgment, perception, savoir-faire, sensitivity, skill, thoughtfulness, understanding

tactful careful, considerate, delicate, diplomatic, discreet, judicious, perceptive, polished, polite, politic, prudent, sensitive, subtle, thoughtful, understanding

tactic 1. approach, course, device, line, manoeuvre, means, method, move, ploy, policy, scheme, stratagem, tack, trick, way 2. *Plural* campaign, generalship, manoeuvres, plans, strategy

tactical adroit, artful, clever, cunning,

diplomatic, politic, shrewd, skilful, smart, strategic

tactician brain (*Inf.*), campaigner, coordinator, director, general, mastermind, planner, strategist

tactless blundering, boorish, careless, clumsy, discourteous, gauche, harsh, impolite, impolitic, imprudent, inconsiderate, indelicate, indiscreet, inept, injudicious, insensitive, maladroit, rough, rude, sharp, thoughtless, uncivil, undiplomatic, unfeeling, unkind, unsubtle

tail n. 1. appendage, conclusion, empennage, end, extremity, rear end, tailpiece, train 2. file, line, queue, tailback, train 3. *Of hair* braid, pigtail, plait, ponytail, tress 4. *Inf.*

tailback ('teɪlˌbæk) *n.* a queue of traffic stretching back from an obstruction.

tailboard ('teɪlˌbɔːd) *n.* a board at the rear of a lorry, etc., that can be removed or let down.

tail coat *n.* **1.** a man's black coat having a horizontal cut over the hips and a tapering tail with a vertical slit up to the waist. **2.** a cutaway frock coat, part of morning dress.

tail gate *n.* a gate that is used to control the flow of water at the lower end of a lock.

tailgate ('teɪlˌgeɪt) *n.* **1.** another name (esp. U.S.) for **tailboard.** ~*vb.* **2.** *U.S.* to drive very close behind (a vehicle).

taillight ('teɪlˌlaɪt) *or* **taillamp** *n.* the U.S. names for **rear light.**

tail off *or* **away** *vb.* (*adv., usually intr.*) to decrease or cause to decrease in quantity, degree, etc., esp. gradually.

tailor ('teɪlə) *n.* **1.** a person who makes, repairs, or alters outer garments, esp. men's wear. Related adj.: **sartorial. 2.** *Chiefly Austral.* a voracious and active marine food fish. ~*vb.* **3.** to cut or style (material, etc.) to satisfy certain requirements. **4.** (*tr.*) to adapt so as to make suitable. **5.** (*intr.*) to work as a tailor. —'**tailored** *adj.*

tailorbird ('teɪləˌbɜːd) *n.* any of several tropical Asian warblers that build nests by sewing together large leaves using plant fibres.

tailor-made *adj.* **1.** made by a tailor to fit exactly. **2.** perfectly meeting a particular purpose. ~*n.* **3.** a tailor-made garment. **4.** *Inf.* a factory-made cigarette.

tailpiece ('teɪlˌpiːs) *n.* **1.** an extension or appendage that lengthens or completes something. **2.** a decorative design at the foot of a page or end of a chapter. **3.** *Music.* a piece of wood to which the strings of a violin, etc., are attached at their lower end. **4.** a short beam or rafter that has one end embedded in a wall.

tailpipe ('teɪlˌpaɪp) *n.* a pipe from which exhaust gases are discharged, esp. the terminal pipe of the exhaust system of a motor vehicle.

tailplane ('teɪlˌpleɪn) *n.* a horizontal aerofoil at the tail of an aircraft to provide longitudinal stability. Also called (chiefly U.S.): **horizontal stabilizer.**

tails (teɪlz) *pl. n.* **1.** an informal name for **tail coat.** ~*interj., adv.* **2.** with the reverse side of a coin uppermost.

tailspin ('teɪlˌspɪn) *n.* **1.** *Aeronautics.* another name for **spin** (sense 15). **2.** *Inf.* a state of confusion or panic.

tailwind ('teɪlˌwɪnd) *n.* a wind blowing in the same direction as the course of an aircraft or ship.

taint (teɪnt) *vb.* **1.** to affect or be affected by pollution or contamination. **2.** to tarnish (someone's reputation, etc.). ~*n.* **3.** a defect or flaw. **4.** a trace of contamination or infection. —'**taintless** *adj.*

take (teɪk) *vb.* **taking, took, taken.** (*mainly tr.*) **1.** (*also intr.*) to gain possession of (something) by force or effort. **2.** to appropriate or steal. **3.** to receive or accept into a relationship with oneself: *to take a wife.* **4.** to pay for or buy. **5.** to rent or lease. **6.** to obtain by regular payment. **7.** to win. **8.** to obtain or derive from a source. **9.** to assume the obligations of: *to take office.* **10.** to endure, esp. with fortitude: *to take punishment.* **11.** to adopt as a symbol of duty, etc.: *to take the veil.* **12.** to receive in a specified way: *she took the news very well.* **13.** to adopt as one's own· *to take someone's part in a quarrel.* **14.** to receive and make use of: *to take advice.* **15.** to receive into the body, as by eating, inhaling, etc. **16.** to eat, drink, etc., esp. habitually. **17.** to have or be engaged in for one's benefit or use: *to take a rest.* **18.** to work at or study: *to take economics at college.* **19.** to make, do, or perform (an action). **20.** to make use of: *to take an opportunity.* **21.** to put into effect: *to take measures.* **22.** (*also intr.*) to make a photograph of or admit of being photographed. **23.** to act or perform. **24.** to write down or copy: *to take notes.* **25.** to experience or feel: *to take offence.* **26.** to consider or regard: *I take him to be honest.* **27.** to accept as valid: *I take your point.* **28.** to hold or maintain in the mind: *his father took a dim view of his career.* **29.** to deal or contend with. **30.** to use as a particular case: *take hotels for example.* **31.** (*intr.; often foll. by from*) to diminish or detract: *the actor's bad performance took from the effect of the play.* **32.** to confront successfully: *the horse took the jump at the third attempt.* **33.** (*intr.*) to have or produce the intended effect: *her vaccination took.* **34.** (*intr.*) (of plants, etc.) to start growing successfully. **35.** to aim or direct: *he took a swipe at his opponent.* **36.** to deal a blow to in a specified place. **37.** *Arch.* to have sexual intercourse with. **38.** to remove from a place. **39.** to carry along or have in one's possession. **40.** to convey or transport. **41.** to use as a means of transport: *I shall take the bus.* **42.** to conduct or lead. **43.** to escort or accompany. **44.** to bring or deliver to a state, position, etc.: *his ability took him to the forefront.* **45.** to seek: *to take cover.* **46.** to ascertain by measuring, etc.: *to take a pulse.* **47.** (*intr.*) (of a mechanism) to catch or engage (a part). **48.** to put an end to: *she took her own life.* **49.** to come upon unexpectedly. **50.** to contract: *he took a chill.* **51.** to affect or attack: *the fever took him one night.* **52.** (*copula*) to become suddenly or be rendered (ill): *he was taken sick.* **53.** (*also intr.*) to absorb or become absorbed by something: *to take a polish.* **54.** (*usually passive*) to charm: *she was very taken with the puppy.* **55.** (*intr.*) to be or become popular; win favour. **56.** to require: *that task will take all your time.* **57.** to subtract or deduct. **58.** to hold: *the suitcase won't take all your clothes.* **59.** to quote or copy. **60.** to proceed to occupy: *to take a seat.* **61.** (often foll. by *to*) to use or employ: *to take steps to ascertain the answer.* **62.** to win or capture (a trick, piece, etc.). **63.** *Sl.* to cheat, deceive, or victimize. **64. take amiss.** to be annoyed or offended by. **65. take at one's word.** to believe to be true or truthful. **66. take five** (*or* **ten**). *Inf., chiefly U.S.* to take a break of five (or ten) minutes. **67. take heart.** to be encouraged. **68. take it.** *Inf.* to stand up to or endure criticism, harsh treatment, etc. **69. take one's time.** to use as much time as is needed. **70. take place.** to happen or occur. **71. take (someone's) name in vain. a.** to use a name, esp. of God, disrespectfully or irreverently. **b.** *Jocular.* to say a person's name. **72. take upon oneself.** to assume the right to do or responsibility for something. ~*n.* **73.** the act of taking. **74.** the number of quarry killed or captured. **75.** *Inf., chiefly U.S.* the amount of anything taken, esp. money. **76.** *Films.* **a.** one of a series of recordings from which the best will be selected. **b.** the process of taking one such recording. **c.** a scene photographed without interruption. ~See also **take after, take back, take down, etc.** —'**takable** *or* '**takeable** *adj.* —'**taker** *n.*

THESAURUS

backside (*Inf.*), behind (*Inf.*), bottom, buttocks, croup, posterior, rear (*Inf.*), rear end, rump **5. turn tail** cut and run, escape, flee, make off, retreat, run away, run for it (*Inf.*), run off, scarper (*Brit. sl.*), show a clean pair of heels, skedaddle (*Inf.*), take off (*Inf.*), take to one's heels ~*v.* **6.** *Inf.* dog the footsteps of, follow, keep an eye on, shadow, stalk, track, trail

tail off *or* **away** decrease, die out, drop, dwindle, fade, fall away, peter out, wane

tailor 1. *n.* clothier, costumier, couturier, dressmaker, garment maker, outfitter, seamstress **2.** *v.* accommodate, adapt, adjust, alter, convert, cut, fashion, fit, modify, mould, shape, style, suit

taint *v.* **1.** adulterate, blight, contaminate, corrupt, dirty, foul, infect, poison, pollute, soil, spoil **2.** besmirch, blacken, blemish, blot,

brand, damage, defile, disgrace, dishonour, muddy, ruin, shame, smear, stain, stigmatize, sully, tarnish, vitiate ~*n.* **3.** black mark, blemish, blot, blot on one's escutcheon, defect, disgrace, dishonour, fault, flaw, shame, smear, spot, stain, stigma **4.** contagion, contamination, infection, pollution

take *v.* **1.** abduct, acquire, arrest, capture, carry off, catch, clutch, ensnare, entrap, gain possession of, get, get hold of, grasp, grip, have, help oneself to, lay hold of, obtain, receive, secure, seize, win **2.** abstract, appropriate, carry off, filch, misappropriate, nick (*Brit. sl.*), pinch (*Inf.*), pocket, purloin, run off with, steal, swipe (*Sl.*), walk off with **3.** book, buy, engage, hire, lease, pay for, pick, purchase, rent, reserve, select **4.** abide, bear, brave, brook, endure, go through, pocket, put up with (*Inf.*), stand, stomach, submit to, suffer, swallow, thole (*Scot.*), tolerate, undergo,

weather, withstand **5.** consume, drink, eat, imbibe, ingest, inhale, swallow **6.** accept, adopt, assume, enter upon, undertake **7.** do, effect, execute, have, make, perform **8.** assume, believe, consider, deem, hold, interpret as, perceive, presume, receive, regard, see as, think of as, understand **9.** be efficacious, do the trick (*Inf.*), have effect, operate, succeed, work **10.** bear, bring, carry, cart, convey, ferry, fetch, haul, tote (*Inf.*), transport **11.** accompany, bring, conduct, convoy, escort, guide, lead, usher **12.** attract, become popular, captivate, charm, delight, enchant, fascinate, please, win favour **13.** call for, demand, necessitate, need, require **14.** deduct, eliminate, remove, subtract **15.** accept, accommodate, contain, have room for, hold **16.** *Sl.* bilk, cheat, con (*Inf.*), deceive, defraud, do (*Sl.*), dupe, fiddle (*Inf.*), gull (*Archaic*), pull a fast one on (*Inf.*), swindle ~*n.* **17.** catch,

take after vb. (intr., prep.) to resemble in appearance, character, behaviour, etc.

take apart vb. (tr., adv.) **1.** to separate (something) into component parts. **2.** to criticize severely.

takeaway ('teɪkəˌweɪ) Brit., Austral. & N.Z. ~adj. **1.** sold for consumption away from the premises: a takeaway meal. **2.** selling food for consumption away from the premises: a takeaway Indian restaurant. ~n. **3.** a shop or restaurant that sells such food. ~U.S. word: **takeout.**

take back vb. (adv., mainly tr.) **1.** to retract or withdraw (something said, written, promised, etc.). **2.** to regain possession of. **3.** to return for exchange. **4.** (also intr.) Printing. to move (copy) to the previous line.

take down vb. (tr., adv.) **1.** to record in writing. **2.** to dismantle or tear down. **3.** to lower or reduce in power, arrogance, etc. (esp. in **to take down a peg**). ~adj. **take-down. 4.** made or intended to be disassembled.

take for vb. **1.** (tr., prep.) Inf. to consider or suppose to be, esp. mistakenly: the fake coins were taken for genuine; who do you take me for? **2. take for granted. a.** to accept or assume without question. **b.** to fail to appreciate the value, merit, etc., of.

take-home pay n. the remainder of one's pay after all income tax and other compulsory deductions have been made.

take in vb. (tr., adv.) **1.** to understand. **2.** to include. **3.** to receive into one's house in exchange for payment: to take in washing; take in lodgers. **4.** to make (clothing, etc.) smaller by altering seams. **5.** Inf. to cheat or deceive.

taken ('teɪkən) vb. **1.** the past participle of **take.** ~adj. **2.** (postpositive foll. by with) enthusiastically impressed (by); infatuated (with).

take off vb. (adv.) **1.** (tr.) to remove (a garment). **2.** (intr.) (of an aircraft) to become airborne. **3.** Inf. to set out or cause to set out on a journey: they took off for Spain. **4.** (tr.) (of a disease) to kill. **5.** (tr.) Inf. to mimic. ~n. **takeoff. 6.** the act or process of making an aircraft airborne. **7.** the stage of a country's economic development when rapid and sustained economic growth is first achieved. **8.** Inf. an act of mimicry.

take on vb. (adv., mainly tr.) **1.** to employ or hire. **2.** to assume or acquire: his voice took on a plaintive note. **3.** to agree to do; undertake. **4.** to compete against; fight. **5.** (intr.) Inf. to exhibit great emotion, esp. of grief.

take out vb. (tr., adv.) **1.** to extract or remove. **2.** to obtain or secure (a licence, patent, etc.). **3.** to go out with; escort. **4.** Bridge. to bid a different suit from (one's partner) in order to rescue him from a difficult contract. **5.** Austral. inf. to win, esp. in sport. **6. take it** or **a lot out of.** Inf. to sap the energy or vitality of. **7. take out on.** Inf. to vent (anger, etc.) on. **8. take someone out of himself.** Inf. to make a person forget his anxieties, problems, etc. ~adj. **takeout. 9.** Bridge. of or designating a conventional informatory bid, asking one's partner to bid an-

other suit. ~adj., n. **10.** an informal word (chiefly U.S.) for takeaway.

take over vb. (adv.) **1.** to assume the control or management of. **2.** Printing. to move (copy) to the next line. ~n. **takeover. 3.** the act of seizing or assuming power, control, etc.

take to vb. (intr., prep.) **1.** to make for; flee to: to take to the hills. **2.** to have a liking for. **3.** to have recourse to: to take to the bottle. **4. take to heart.** to regard seriously.

take up vb. (adv., mainly tr.) **1.** to adopt the study, practice, or activity of: to take up gardening. **2.** N.Z. to occupy and break in (uncultivated land): he took up some hundreds of acres in the back country. **3.** to shorten (a garment). **4.** to pay off (a note, mortgage, etc.). **5.** to agree to or accept (an invitation, etc.). **6.** to pursue further or resume (something): he took up French where he left off. **7.** to absorb (a liquid). **8.** to act as a patron to. **9.** to occupy or fill (space or time). **10.** to interrupt, esp. in order to contradict or criticize. **11. take up on. a.** to argue with (someone): can I take you up on two points in your talk? **b.** to accept what is offered by (someone): let me take you up on your invitation. **12. take up with. a.** to discuss with (someone); refer to. **b.** (intr.) to begin to keep company or associate with.

taking ('teɪkɪŋ) adj. **1.** charming, fascinating, or intriguing. **2.** Inf. infectious; catching. ~n. **3.** something taken. **4.** (pl.) receipts; earnings. —'**takingly** adv. —'**takingness** n.

talc (tælk) n. also **talcum. 1.** See **talcum powder. 2.** a soft mineral, consisting of magnesium silicate, used in the manufacture of ceramics and paints and as a filler in talcum powder, etc. ~vb. **talcking, talcked** or **talcing, talced. 3.** (tr.) to apply talc to. —'**talcose** or '**talcous** adj.

talcum powder ('tælkəm) n. a powder made of purified talc, usually scented, used for perfuming the body and for absorbing excess moisture.

tale (teɪl) n. **1.** a report, narrative, or story. **2.** one of a group of short stories. **3. a.** a malicious or meddlesome rumour or piece of gossip. **b.** (in combination): talebearer; taleteller. **4.** a fictitious or false statement. **5. tell tales. a.** to tell fanciful lies. **b.** to report malicious stories, trivial complaints, etc., esp. to someone in authority. **6. tell a tale.** to reveal something important. **7. tell its own tale.** to be self-evident. **8.** Arch. a number; amount.

talent ('tælənt) n. **1.** innate ability, aptitude, or faculty; above average ability: a talent for cooking; a child with talent. **2.** a person or persons possessing such ability. **3.** any of various ancient units of weight and money. **4.** Inf. girls collectively: the local talent. —'**talented** adj.

talent scout n. a person whose occupation is the search for talented sportsmen, performers, etc., for engagements as professionals.

talisman ('tælɪzmən) n., pl. **-mans. 1.** a stone or other

THESAURUS

gate, haul, proceeds, profits, receipts, return, revenue, takings, yield

take back 1. disavow, disclaim, recant, renounce, retract, unsay, withdraw **2.** get back, recapture, reclaim, reconquer, regain, repossess, retake **3.** accept back, exchange, give one a refund for

take down 1. make a note of, minute, note, put on record, record, set down, transcribe, write down **2.** depress, drop, haul down, let down, lower, pull down, remove, take off **3.** demolish, disassemble, dismantle, level, raze, take apart, take to pieces, tear down **4.** deflate, humble, humiliate, mortify, put down (Sl.)

take in 1. absorb, assimilate, comprehend, digest, grasp, understand **2.** comprise, contain, cover, embrace, encompass, include **3.** accommodate, admit, let in, receive **4.** Inf. bilk, cheat, con (Inf.), deceive, do (Sl.), dupe, fool, gull (Archaic), hoodwink, mislead, pull the wool over (someone's) eyes (Inf.), swindle, trick

takeoff 1. departure, launch, liftoff **2.** Inf. caricature, imitation, lampoon, mocking, parody, satire, send-up (Brit. inf.), spoof (Inf.), travesty

take off 1. discard, divest oneself of, doff, drop, peel off, remove, strip off **2.** become airborne, leave the ground, lift off, take to the air **3.** Inf. beat it (Sl.), decamp, depart, disappear, go, hit the road (Sl.), leave, set out, split (Sl.), strike out **4.** Inf. caricature, hit off, imitate, lampoon, mimic, mock, parody, satirize, send up (Brit. inf.), spoof (Inf.), travesty

take on 1. employ, engage, enlist, enrol, hire, retain **2.** acquire, assume, come to have **3.** accept, address oneself to, agree to do, have a go at (Inf.), tackle, undertake **4.** compete against, contend with, enter the lists against, face, fight, match oneself against, oppose, pit oneself against, vie with **5.** Inf. break down, get excited, get upset (Inf.), give way, make a fuss

take over assume control of, become leader of, come to power, gain control of, succeed to, take command of

take to 1. flee to, head for, make for, man, run for **2.** become friendly, be pleased by, be taken with, conceive an affection for, get on with, like, warm to **3.** have recourse to, make a habit of, resort to

take up 1. adopt, assume, become in-

volved in, engage in, start **2.** begin again, carry on, continue, follow on, go on, pick up, proceed, recommence, restart, resume **3.** absorb, consume, cover, extend over, fill, occupy, use up

taking adj. **1.** attractive, beguiling, captivating, charming, compelling, delightful, enchanting, engaging, fascinating, fetching (Inf.), intriguing, pleasing, prepossessing, winning **2.** Inf. catching, contagious, infectious ~n. **3.** Plural earnings, gain, gate, income, pickings, proceeds, profits, receipts, returns, revenue, take, yield

tale 1. account, anecdote, conte, fable, fiction, legend, narration, narrative, novel, relation, report, romance, saga, short story, story, yarn (Inf.) **2.** cock-and-bull story (Inf.), fabrication, falsehood, fib, lie, rigmarole, rumour, spiel (Inf.), tall story (Inf.), untruth

talent ability, aptitude, bent, capacity, endowment, faculty, flair, forte, genius, gift, knack, parts, power

talented able, artistic, brilliant, gifted, well-endowed

small object, usually inscribed or carved, believed to protect the wearer from evil influences. **2.** anything thought to have magical or protective powers. —**talismanic** (ˌtælɪzˈmænɪk) adj.

talk (tɔːk) vb. **1.** (intr.; often foll. by to or with) to express one's thoughts, feelings, or desires by means of words (to). **2.** (intr.) to communicate by other means: lovers talk with their eyes. **3.** (intr.; usually foll. by about) to exchange ideas or opinions (about). **4.** (intr.) to articulate words. **5.** (tr.) to give voice to; utter: to talk rubbish. **6.** (tr.) to discuss: to talk business. **7.** (intr.) to reveal information. **8.** (tr.) to know how to communicate in (a language or idiom): he talks English. **9.** (intr.) to spread rumours or gossip. **10.** (intr.) to make sounds suggestive of talking. **11.** (intr.) to be effective or persuasive: money talks. **12. now you're talking.** Inf. at last you're saying something agreeable. **13. talk big.** to boast. **14. talk shop.** to speak about one's work, esp. when meeting socially. **15. you can talk.** Inf. you don't have to worry about doing a particular thing yourself. **16. you can** or **can't talk.** Inf. you yourself are guilty of offending in the very matter you are upholding or decrying. ~n. **17.** a speech or lecture. **18.** an exchange of ideas or thoughts. **19.** idle chatter, gossip, or rumour. **20.** a subject of conversation; theme. **21.** (often pl.) a conference, discussion, or negotiation. **22.** a specific manner of speaking: children's talk. ~See also **talk back, talk down,** etc. —**'talker** n.

talkative ('tɔːkətɪv) adj. given to talking a great deal. —**'talkatively** adv. —**'talkativeness** n.

talk back vb. **1.** (intr., adv.) to answer boldly or impudently. ~n. **talkback. 2.** Television, radio. a system of telephone links enabling spoken directions to be given during the production of a programme.

talk down vb. (adv.) **1.** (intr.; often foll. by to) to behave (towards) in a superior manner. **2.** (tr.) to override (a person) by continuous or loud talking. **3.** (tr.) to give instructions to (an aircraft) by radio to enable it to land.

talkie ('tɔːkɪ) n. U.S. inf. an early film with a soundtrack. Full name: **talking picture.**

talking book n. a recording of a book, designed to be used by the blind.

talking-to n. Inf. a session of criticism, as of a subordinate by a person in authority.

talk into vb. (tr., prep.) to persuade to by talking: I talked him into buying the house.

talk out vb. (adv.) **1.** (tr.) to resolve or eliminate by talking. **2.** (tr.) Brit. to block (a bill, etc.) in a legislative body by lengthy discussion. **3. talk out of.** (tr.) to dissuade from by talking.

talk round vb. **1.** (tr., adv.) Also: **talk over.** to persuade to one's opinion. **2.** (intr., prep.) to discuss (a subject), esp. without coming to a conclusion.

tall (tɔːl) adj. **1.** of more than average height. **2.** (postpositive) having a specified height: five feet tall. **3.** Inf. exaggerated or incredible: a tall story. **4.** Inf. difficult to accomplish: a tall order. —**'tallness** n.

tallboy ('tɔːlˌbɔɪ) n. a high chest of drawers made in two sections and placed one on top of the other.

tallow ('tæləʊ) n. **1.** a fatty substance extracted chiefly from the suet of sheep and cattle: used for making soap,

candles, food, etc. ~vb. **2.** (tr.) to cover or smear with tallow. —**'tallowy** adj.

tally ('tælɪ) vb. **-lying, -lied. 1.** (intr.) to correspond one with the other: the two stories don't tally. **2.** (tr.) to supply with an identifying tag. **3.** (intr.) to keep score. **4.** (tr.) Obs. to record or mark. ~n., pl. **-lies. 5.** any record of debit, credit, the score in a game, etc. **6.** Austral. & N.Z. the number of sheep shorn in a specified period. **7.** an identifying label or mark. **8.** a counterpart or duplicate of something. **9.** a stick used (esp. formerly) as a record of the amount of a debt according to the notches cut in it. **10.** a notch or mark made on such a stick. **11.** a mark used to represent a certain number in counting.

tally-ho (ˌtælɪˈhəʊ) interj. **1.** the cry of a participant at a hunt when the quarry is sighted. ~n., pl. **-hos. 2.** an instance of crying tally-ho. **3.** another name for a **four-in-hand** (sense 1). ~vb. **-hoing, -hoed** or **-ho'd. 4.** (intr.) to make the cry of tally-ho.

Talmud ('tælmʊd) n. Judaism. the compilation of ancient Jewish law and tradition comprising the Mishnah and the Gemara. —**Tal'mudic** or **Tal'mudical** adj. —**'Talmudism** n. —**'Talmudist** n.

talon ('tælən) n. **1.** a sharply hooked claw, esp. of a bird of prey. **2.** anything resembling this. **3.** the part of a lock that the key presses on when it is turned. **4.** Piquet, etc. the pile of cards left after the deal. **5.** Archit. another name for **ogee.** —**'taloned** adj.

tam (tæm) n. short for **tam-o'-shanter.**

tamarind ('tæmərɪnd) n. **1.** a tropical evergreen tree having yellow flowers and brown pods. **2.** the fruit of this tree, used as a food and to make beverages and medicines. **3.** the wood of this tree.

tamarisk ('tæmərɪsk) n. any of a genus of trees and shrubs of the Mediterranean region and S and SE Asia, having scalelike leaves, slender branches, and feathery flower clusters.

tambour ('tæmbʊə) n. **1.** Real tennis. the sloping buttress on one side of the receiver's end of the court. **2.** a small embroidery frame, consisting of two hoops over which the fabric is stretched while being worked. **3.** embroidered work done on such a frame. **4.** a sliding door on desks, cabinets, etc., made of thin strips of wood glued onto a canvas backing. **5.** Archit. a wall that is circular in plan, esp. one that supports a dome or one that is surrounded by a colonnade. **6.** a drum. ~vb. **7.** to embroider on a tambour.

tambourine (ˌtæmbəˈriːn) n. Music. a percussion instrument consisting of a single drumhead of skin stretched over a circular wooden frame hung with pairs of metal discs that jingle when it is struck or shaken. —**ˌtambou'rinist** n.

tame (teɪm) adj. **1.** changed by man from a wild state into a domesticated or cultivated condition. **2.** (of animals) not fearful of human contact. **3.** meek or submissive. **4.** flat, insipid, or uninspiring. ~vb. (tr.) **5.** to make tame; domesticate. **6.** to break the spirit of, subdue, or curb. **7.** to tone down, soften, or mitigate. —**'tamable** or **'tameable** adj. —**'tamely** adv. —**'tameness** n. —**'tamer** n.

Tamil ('tæmɪl) n., pl. **-ils** or **-il. 1.** a member of a mixed Dravidian and Caucasoid people of S India and Sri Lanka.

THESAURUS

talk v. **1.** articulate, chat, chatter, communicate, converse, crack (Scot.), express oneself, gab (Inf.), give voice to, gossip, natter, prate, prattle, rap (Sl.), say, speak, utter, verbalize, witter (Inf.) **2.** chew the rag (Inf.), confabulate, confer, have a confab (Inf.), hold discussions, negotiate, palaver, parley **3.** blab, crack, give the game away, grass (Sl.), inform, reveal information, sing (Inf.), spill the beans (Inf.), squeak (Inf.), squeal (Sl.) ~n. **4.** address, discourse, disquisition, dissertation, harangue, lecture, oration, sermon, speech **5.** blather, blether, chat, chatter, chit-chat, conversation, crack (Scot.), gab (Inf.), gossip, hearsay, jaw (Sl.), natter, rap (Sl.), rumour, tittle-tattle **6.** colloquy, conclave, confab (Inf.), confabulation, conference, consultation, dialogue, discussion, meeting, negotiation, palaver, parley, seminar, symposium **7.** argot, dialect, jargon, language, lingo (Inf.), patois, slang, speech, words

talkative big-mouthed (Sl.), chatty, effu-

sive, gabby (Inf.), garrulous, gossipy, long-winded, loquacious, mouthy, prolix, verbose, voluble, wordy

talker conversationalist, lecturer, orator, speaker, speechmaker

talking-to criticism, dressing-down (Inf.), lecture, rap on the knuckles (Inf.), rebuke, reprimand, reproach, reproof, row, scolding, slating (Inf.), telling-off (Inf.), ticking-off (Inf.), wigging (Brit. sl.)

tall 1. big, elevated, giant, high, lanky, lofty, soaring, towering **2.** Inf. absurd, embellished, exaggerated, far-fetched, implausible, incredible, overblown, preposterous, steep (Brit. inf.), unbelievable **3.** Inf. demanding, difficult, exorbitant, hard, unreasonable, well-nigh impossible

tally v. **1.** accord, agree, coincide, concur, conform, correspond, fit, harmonize, jibe (Inf.), match, parallel, square, suit **2.** compute, count up, keep score, mark, reckon, record, register, total ~n. **3.** count, mark,

reckoning, record, running total, score, total **4.** counterfoil, counterpart, duplicate, match, mate, stub

tame adj. **1.** amenable, broken, cultivated, disciplined, docile, domesticated, gentle, obedient, tractable **2.** fearless, unafraid, used to human contact **3.** compliant, docile, manageable, meek, obedient, spiritless, subdued, submissive, unresisting **4.** bland, boring, dull, flat, humdrum, insipid, lifeless, prosaic, tedious, unexciting, uninspiring, uninteresting, vapid, wearisome ~v. **5.** break in, domesticate, gentle, house-train, make tame, pacify, train **6.** break the spirit of, bridle, bring to heel, conquer, curb, discipline, enslave, humble, master, repress, subdue, subjugate, suppress **7.** mitigate, mute, soften, soft-pedal (Inf.), subdue, temper, tone down, water down

2. the language of this people. ~*adj.* **3.** of or relating to this people or their language.

tam-o'-shanter (ˌtæməˈʃæntə) *n.* a Scottish brimless wool or cloth cap with a bobble in the centre.

tamp (tæmp) *vb.* (*tr.*) **1.** to force or pack down firmly by repeated blows. **2.** to pack sand, earth, etc. into (a drill hole) over an explosive.

tamper[1] (ˈtæmpə) *vb.* (*intr.*) **1.** (usually foll. by *with*) to interfere or meddle. **2.** to use bribery or blackmail. **3.** (usually foll. by *with*) to attempt to influence, esp. by bribery. —ˈtamperer *n.*

tamper[2] (ˈtæmpə) *n.* **1.** a person or thing that tamps, esp. an instrument for packing down tobacco in a pipe. **2.** a casing around the core of a nuclear weapon to increase its efficiency by reflecting neutrons and delaying the expansion.

tampon (ˈtæmpɒn) *n.* **1.** a plug of lint, cotton wool, etc., inserted into a wound or body cavity to stop the flow of blood, absorb secretions, etc. ~*vb.* **2.** (*tr.*) to plug (a wound, etc.) with a tampon. —ˈtamponage *n.*

tan[1] (tæn) *n.* **1.** the brown colour produced by the skin after exposure to ultraviolet rays, esp. those of the sun. **2.** a yellowish-brown colour. ~*vb.* **tanning, tanned. 3.** to go brown or cause to go brown after exposure to ultraviolet rays. **4.** to convert (a skin or hide) into leather by treating it with a tanning agent. **5.** (*tr.*) *Sl.* to beat or flog. ~*adj.* **tanner, tannest. 6.** of the colour tan. —ˈtannable *adj.* —ˈtannish *adj.*

tan[2] (tæn) *n.* abbrev. for tangent (sense 2).

tandem (ˈtændəm) *n.* **1.** a bicycle with two sets of pedals and two saddles, arranged one behind the other for two riders. **2.** a two-wheeled carriage drawn by two horses harnessed one behind the other. **3.** a team of two horses so harnessed. **4.** any arrangement of two things in which one is placed behind the other. ~*adj.* **5.** *Brit.* used as, used in, or routed through an intermediate automatic telephone exchange. ~*adv.* **6.** one behind the other.

Tandoori (ˌtænˈdʊəri) *n.* an Indian method of cooking meat or vegetables on a spit in a clay oven.

tang (tæŋ) *n.* **1.** a strong taste or flavour. **2.** a pungent or characteristic smell. **3.** a trace, touch, or hint of something. **4.** the pointed end of a tool, such as a chisel, file, knife, etc., which is fitted into a handle, shaft, or stock.

tangent (ˈtændʒənt) *n.* **1.** a geometric line, curve, plane, or curved surface that touches another curve or surface at one point but does not intersect it. **2.** (of an angle) a trigonometric function that in a right-angled triangle is the ratio of the length of the opposite side to that of the adjacent side; the ratio of sine to cosine. Abbrev.: **tan. 3.** *Music.* a small piece of metal that strikes the string of a clavichord. **4. on** or **at a tangent.** on a completely different or divergent course, esp. of thought. ~*adj.* **5. a.** of or involving a tangent. **b.** touching at a single point. **6.** touching. —ˈtangency *n.*

tangential (tænˈdʒɛnʃəl) *adj.* **1.** of, being, or in the direction of a tangent. **2.** *Astron.* (of velocity) in a direction perpendicular to the line of sight of a celestial object. **3.** of superficial relevance only; digressive. —tanˌgentiˈality *n.* —tanˈgentially *adv.*

tangerine (ˌtændʒəˈriːn) *n.* **1.** an Asian citrus tree cultivated for its small orange-like fruits. **2.** the fruit of this tree, having sweet spicy flesh. **3.** a reddish-orange colour.

tangible (ˈtændʒəbəl) *adj.* **1.** capable of being touched or felt. **2.** capable of being clearly grasped by the mind. **3.** having a physical existence: *tangible property.* —ˌtangiˈbility or ˈtangibleness *n.* —ˈtangibly *adv.*

tangle (ˈtæŋgəl) *n.* **1.** a confused or complicated mass of

hairs, lines, fibres, etc., knotted or coiled together. **2.** a complicated problem, condition, or situation. ~*vb.* **3.** to become or cause to become twisted together in a confused mass. **4.** (*intr.*; often foll. by *with*) to come into conflict; contend. **5.** (*tr.*) to involve in matters which hinder or confuse. **6.** (*tr.*) to ensnare or trap, as in a net. —ˈtangly *adj.*

tango (ˈtæŋgəʊ) *n., pl.* **-gos. 1.** a Latin-American dance characterized by long gliding steps and sudden pauses. **2.** a piece of music composed for or in the rhythm of this dance. ~*vb.* **-going, -goed. 3.** (*intr.*) to perform this dance.

tank (tæŋk) *n.* **1.** a large container or reservoir for liquids or gases. **2.** an armoured combat vehicle moving on tracks and armed with guns, etc. **3.** *Brit. or U.S. dialect.* a reservoir, lake, or pond. **4.** *Austral.* a reservoir formed by excavation and damming. **5.** *Sl.*, chiefly *U.S.* a jail. **6.** Also called: **tankful.** the quantity contained in a tank. ~*vb.* **7.** (*tr.*) to put or keep in a tank. ~See also **tank up.**

tankard (ˈtæŋkəd) *n.* a large one-handled drinking vessel sometimes fitted with a hinged lid.

tanker (ˈtæŋkə) *n.* a ship, lorry, or aeroplane designed to carry liquid in bulk, such as oil.

tank farming *n.* another name for **hydroponics.** —**tank farmer** *n.*

tank up *vb.* (*adv.*) *Chiefly Brit.* **1.** to fill the tank of (a vehicle) with petrol. **2.** *Sl.* to imbibe a large quantity of alcoholic drink.

tanner[1] (ˈtænə) *n.* a person who tans skins and hides.

tanner[2] (ˈtænə) *n. Brit.* an informal word for **sixpence.**

tannery (ˈtænəri) *n., pl.* **-neries.** a place or building where skins and hides are tanned.

tannic (ˈtænɪk) *adj.* of, relating to, containing, or produced from tan, tannin, or tannic acid.

tannin (ˈtænɪn) *n.* any of a class of yellowish compounds found in many plants and used as tanning agents, mordants, medical astringents, etc. Also called: **tannic acid.**

Tannoy (ˈtænɔɪ) *n. Trademark.* a type of public address system.

tansy (ˈtænzi) *n., pl.* **-sies.** any of numerous plants having yellow flowers in flat-topped clusters and formerly used in medicine and for seasoning.

tantalize or **-ise** (ˈtæntəˌlaɪz) *vb.* (*tr.*) to tease or make frustrated, as by tormenting with the sight of something desired but inaccessible. —ˈtantaˌlizer or **-iser** *n.* —ˈtantaˌlizingly or **-isingly** *adv.*

tantalum (ˈtæntələm) *n.* a hard greyish-white metallic element: used in electrolytic rectifiers and in alloys to increase hardness and chemical resistance, esp. in surgical instruments. Symbol: Ta; atomic no.: 73; atomic wt.: 180.95.

tantalus (ˈtæntələs) *n. Brit.* a case in which bottles may be locked with their contents tantalizingly visible.

tantamount (ˈtæntəˌmaʊnt) *adj.* (*postpositive;* foll. by *to*) as good (as); equivalent in effect (to).

tantrum (ˈtæntrəm) *n.* (*often pl.*) a childish fit of rage; outburst of bad temper.

Taoism (ˈtɑːəʊˌɪzəm) *n.* a system of religion and philosophy based on the teachings of Lao-tze, 6th-century B.C. Chinese philosopher, and advocating a simple honest life and noninterference with the course of natural events. —ˈTaoist *n., adj.* —ˌTaoˈistic *adj.*

tap[1] (tæp) *vb.* **tapping, tapped. 1.** to strike (something) lightly and usually repeatedly. **2.** to produce by striking in this way: *to tap a rhythm.* **3.** (*tr.*) to strike lightly with (something): *to tap one's finger on the desk.* **4.** (*intr.*) to walk with a tapping sound. **5.** (*tr.*) to attach reinforcing pieces to (the toe or heel of a shoe). ~*n.* **6.** a light blow

---

THESAURUS

tamper 1. alter, damage, fiddle (*Inf.*), fool about (*Inf.*), interfere, intrude, meddle, mess about, monkey around, muck about (*Brit. sl.*), poke one's nose into (*Inf.*), tinker **2.** bribe, corrupt, fix (*Inf.*), get at, influence, manipulate, rig
tangible actual, concrete, corporeal, definite, discernible, evident, manifest, material, objective, palpable, perceptible, physical, positive, real, solid, substantial, tactile, touchable
tangle *n.* **1.** coil, confusion, entanglement, jam, jungle, knot, mass, mat, mesh, snarl,

twist, web **2.** complication, entanglement, fix (*Inf.*), imbroglio, labyrinth, maze, mess, mix-up ~*v.* **3.** coil, confuse, entangle, interlace, interlock, intertwist, interweave, jam, kink, knot, mat, mesh, snarl, twist **4.** *Often with* **with** come into conflict, come up against, contend, contest, cross swords, dispute, lock horns **5.** catch, drag into, embroil, enmesh, ensnare, entangle, entrap, implicate, involve

tangled 1. entangled, jumbled, knotted, knotty, matted, messy, scrambled, snarled, tousled, twisted **2.** complex, complicated,

confused, convoluted, involved, knotty, messy, mixed-up
tantalize baffle, balk, disappoint, entice, frustrate, keep (someone) hanging on, lead on, make (someone's) mouth water, provoke, taunt, tease, thwart, titillate, torment, torture
tantamount as good as, commensurate, equal, equivalent, synonymous, the same as
tantrum fit, flare-up, hysterics, ill humour, outburst, paddy (*Brit. inf.*), storm, temper, wax (*Inf.*)

or knock, or the sound made by it. **7.** the metal piece attached to the toe or heel of a shoe used for tap dancing. **8.** short for **tap-dancing.**

tap² ('tæp) n. **1.** a valve by which a fluid flow from a pipe can be controlled. U.S. names: **faucet, spigot. 2.** a stopper to plug a cask or barrel. **3.** a particular quality of alcoholic drink, esp. when contained in casks: *an excellent tap.* **4.** *Brit.* short for **taproom. 5.** the withdrawal of fluid from a bodily cavity. **6.** a tool for cutting female screw threads. **7.** *Electronics, chiefly U.S.* a connection made at some point between the end terminals of an inductor, resistor, etc. Usual *Brit.* name: **tapping. 8.** a concealed listening or recording device connected to a telephone or telegraph wire. **9. on tap. a.** *Inf.* ready for use. **b.** (of drinks) on draught. ~*vb.* **tapping, tapped.** (*tr.*) **10.** to furnish with a tap. **11.** to draw off with or as if with a tap. **12.** *Brit. sl.* **a.** to ask (someone) for money: *he tapped me for a fiver.* **b.** to obtain (money) from someone. **13.** to connect a tap to (a telephone or telegraph wire). **14.** to make a connection to (a pipe, drain, etc.). **15.** to cut a female screw thread in (an object or material) by use of a tap. —'**tapper** n.

tap dance n. **1.** a step dance in which the performer wears shoes equipped with taps that make a rhythmic sound on the stage as he dances. ~*vb.* (*intr.*) **tap-dance. 2.** to perform a tap dance. —'**tap-,dancer** n. —'**tap-,dancing** n.

tape (teɪp) n. **1.** a long thin strip of cotton, linen, etc., used for binding, fastening, etc. **2.** a long narrow strip of paper, metal, etc. **3.** a string stretched across the track at the end of a race course. **4.** See **magnetic tape, ticker tape, tape recording.** ~*vb.* (*mainly tr.*) **5.** to furnish with tapes. **6.** to bind, measure, secure, or wrap with tape. **7.** (*usually passive*) *Brit. inf.* to take stock of (a person or situation). **8.** (*also intr.*) Also: **tape-record.** to record (speech, music, etc.). —'**tape,like** *adj.* —'**taper** n.

tape deck n. the platform supporting the spools, cassettes, or cartridges of a tape recorder, incorporating the motor and the playback, recording, and erasing heads.

tape machine n. a telegraphic device that records current stock quotations electronically or on ticker tape. U.S. equivalent: **ticker.**

tape measure n. a tape or length of metal marked off in inches, centimetres, etc., used for measuring. Also called (esp. U.S.): **tapeline.**

taper ('teɪpə) *vb.* **1.** to become or cause to become narrower towards one end. **2.** to become or cause to become smaller or less significant. ~n. **3.** a thin candle. **4.** a thin wooden or waxed strip for transferring a flame; spill. **5.** a narrowing. **6.** any feeble light. —'**taperer** n. —'**taperingly** *adv.*

tape recorder n. an electrical device used for recording sounds on magnetic tape and usually also for reproducing them.

tape recording n. **1.** the act of recording on magnetic tape. **2.** the magnetized tape used for this. **3.** the speech, music, etc., so recorded.

tapestry ('tæpɪstrɪ) n., pl. **-tries. 1.** a heavy woven fabric, often in the form of a picture, used for wall hangings, furnishings, etc. **2.** another word for **needlepoint.** —'**tapestried** *adj.*

tapeworm ('teɪp,wɜːm) n. any of a class of parasitic ribbon-like flatworms. The adults inhabit the intestines of vertebrates.

tapioca (,tæpɪ'əʊkə) n. a beadlike starch obtained from cassava root, used in cooking as a thickening agent, esp. in puddings.

tapir ('teɪpə) n., pl. **-pirs** or **-pir.** any of various mammals of South and central America and SE Asia, having an elongated snout, three-toed hind legs, and four-toed forelegs.

tappet ('tæpɪt) n. a mechanical part that reciprocates to receive or transmit intermittent motion.

taproom ('tæp,ruːm, -,rʊm) n. a bar, as in a hotel or pub.

taproot ('tæp,ruːt) n. the main root of plants such as the dandelion, which grows vertically downwards and bears smaller lateral roots.

taps (tæps) n. **1.** (in army camps, etc.) a signal given on a bugle, drum, etc., indicating that lights are to be put out. **2.** any similar signal, as at a military funeral.

tapster ('tæpstə) n. **1.** *Rare.* a barman. **2.** (in W Africa) a man who taps palm trees.

tar¹ (tɑː) n. **1.** any of various dark viscid substances obtained by the destructive distillation of organic matter such as coal, wood, or peat. **2.** another name for **coal tar.** ~*vb.* **tarring, tarred.** (*tr.*) **3.** to coat with tar. **4. tar and feather.** to punish by smearing tar and feathers over (someone). **5. tarred with the same brush.** having the same faults. —'**tarry** *adj.* —'**tarriness** n.

tar² (tɑː) n. an informal word for **seaman.**

taramasalata (,tærəməsə'lɑːtə) n. a creamy pale pink paté, made from the roe of grey mullet or smoked cod and served as an hors d'oeuvre.

tarantella (,tærən'telə) n. **1.** a peasant dance from S Italy. **2.** a piece of music composed for or in the rhythm of this dance.

tarantula (tə'ræntjʊlə) n., pl. **-las** or **-lae** (-,liː). **1.** any of various large hairy spiders of tropical America. **2.** a large hairy spider of S Europe.

tarboosh (tɑː'buːʃ) n. a felt or cloth brimless cap, usually red and often with a silk tassel, worn by Muslim men.

tardy ('tɑːdɪ) *adj.* **-dier, -diest. 1.** occurring later than expected. **2.** slow in progress, growth, etc. —'**tardily** *adv.* —'**tardiness** n.

tare¹ (tɛə) n. **1.** any of various vetch plants of Eurasia and N Africa. **2.** the seed of any of these plants. **3.** *Bible.* a weed, thought to be the darnel.

tare² (tɛə) n. **1.** the weight of the wrapping or container in which goods are packed. **2.** a deduction from gross weight to compensate for this. **3.** the weight of an unladen vehicle. ~*vb.* **4.** (*tr.*) to weigh (a package, etc.) in order to calculate the amount of tare.

target ('tɑːgɪt) n. **1. a.** an object or area at which an archer or marksman aims, usually a round flat surface marked with concentric rings. **b.** (*as modifier*): *target practice.* **2. a.** any point or area aimed at. **b.** (*as modifier*): *target area.* **3.** a fixed goal or objective. **4.** a person or thing at which an action or remark is directed or the object of a person's feelings. **5.** a joint of lamb consisting of the breast and neck. **6.** (*formerly*) a small round shield. **7.** *Physics, electronics.* **a.** a substance subjected to bombardment by electrons or other particles, or to irradiation. **b.** an electrode in a television camera tube whose surface is scanned by the electron beam. **8.** *Electronics.* an object detected by the reflection of a radar or sonar signal, etc. ~*vb.* **9.** (*tr.*) to make a target of.

tariff ('tærɪf) n. **1. a.** a tax levied by a government on imports or occasionally exports. **b.** a system or list of such taxes. **2.** any schedule of prices, fees, fares, etc. **3.** *Chiefly Brit.* **a.** a method of charging for the supply of services such as gas and electricity. **b.** a schedule of such charges. **4.** *Chiefly Brit.* a bill of fare with prices listed; menu. ~*vb.* **5.** to set a tariff on. **6.** to price according to a schedule of tariffs.

tarlatan ('tɑːlətən) n. an open-weave cotton fabric, used for stiffening garments.

Tarmac ('tɑːmæk) n. *Tradename.* (*often not cap.*) a paving material that consists of crushed stone rolled and bound with a mixture of tar and bitumen, esp. as used for a road, airport runway, etc. Full name: **Tarmacadam** (,tɑːmə'kædəm). See also **macadam.**

tarn (tɑːn) n. a small mountain lake or pool.

tarnish ('tɑːnɪʃ) *vb.* **1.** to lose or cause to lose the shine, esp. by exposure to air or moisture resulting in surface

---

▌THESAURUS▐

tap¹ 1. *v.* beat, drum, knock, pat, rap, strike, touch **2.** *n.* beat, knock, light blow, pat, rap, touch

tap² n. 1. faucet (*U.S.*), spigot, spout, stopcock, valve **2.** bung, plug, spile, stopper **3.** bug (*Inf.*), listening device **4. on tap a.** *Inf.* at hand, available, in reserve, on hand, ready **b.** on draught ~*v.* **5.** bleed, broach, drain, draw off, open, pierce, siphon off, unplug **6.** draw on, exploit, make use of, milk, mine, put to use, turn to account, use, utilize **7.** bug (*Inf.*), eavesdrop on, listen in on

tape *n.* **1.** band, ribbon, strip ~*v.* **2.** bind, seal, secure, stick, wrap **3.** record, tape-record, video

taper 1. come to a point, narrow, thin **2.** *With* **off** decrease, die away, die out, dwindle, fade, lessen, reduce, subside, thin out, wane, weaken, wind down

target 1. aim, ambition, bull's-eye, end, goal, intention, mark, object, objective **2.** butt, quarry, scapegoat, victim

tariff 1. assessment, duty, excise, impost, levy, rate, tax, toll **2.** bill of fare, charges, menu, price list, schedule

oxidation; discolour. **2.** to stain or become stained; taint. ~*n.* **3.** a tarnished condition, surface, or film. —**'tarnishable** *adj.*

taro ('tɑːrəʊ) *n., pl.* **-ros. 1.** an Asian plant, cultivated in the tropics for its large edible rootstock. **2.** the rootstock of this plant.

tarot ('tærəʊ) *n.* **1.** one of a special pack of cards, now used mainly for fortune-telling. **2.** a card in a tarot pack with distinctive symbolic design. ~*adj.* **3.** relating to tarot cards.

tarpaulin (tɑː'pɔːlɪn) *n.* **1.** a heavy waterproof fabric made of canvas or similar material coated with tar, wax, or paint. **2.** a sheet of this fabric. **3.** a hat made of or covered with this fabric, esp. a sailor's hat. **4.** a rare word for seaman.

tarragon ('tærəgən) *n.* **1.** an aromatic plant of the Old World, having leaves which are used as seasoning. **2.** the leaves of this plant.

tarry ('tærɪ) *vb.* **-rying, -ried. 1.** (*intr.*) to delay; linger. **2.** (*intr.*) to remain temporarily or briefly. **3.** (*intr.*) to wait or stay. **4.** (*tr.*) *Arch. or poetic.* to await. —**'tarrier** *n.*

tarsal ('tɑːsəl) *adj.* **1.** of the tarsus or tarsi. ~*n.* **2.** a tarsal bone.

tarsus ('tɑːsəs) *n., pl.* **-si** (-saɪ). **1.** the bones of the ankle and heel, collectively. **2.** the corresponding part in other mammals and in amphibians and reptiles. **3.** the connective tissue supporting the free edge of each eyelid. **4.** the part of an insect's leg that lies distal to the tibia.

tart[1] (tɑːt) *n.* **1.** *Chiefly Brit.* a pastry case often having no top crust, with a filling of fruit, jam, custard, etc. **2.** *Chiefly U.S.* a small open pie with a fruit filling. **3.** *Inf.* a promiscuous woman, esp. a prostitute. ~*vb.* **4.** See **tart up.**

tart[2] (tɑːt) *adj.* **1.** (of a flavour, etc.) sour; acid. **2.** cutting; sharp: *a tart remark.* —**'tartly** *adv.* —**'tartness** *n.*

tartan ('tɑːtən) *n.* **1. a.** a design of straight lines, crossing at right angles to give a chequered appearance, esp. the distinctive design or designs associated with each Scottish clan. **b.** (*as modifier*): *a tartan kilt.* **2.** a fabric or garment with this design.

tartar[1] ('tɑːtə) *n.* **1.** a hard deposit on the teeth, consisting of food, cellular debris, and mineral salts. **2.** a brownish-red substance consisting mainly of potassium hydrogen tartrate, deposited during the fermentation of wine.

tartar[2] ('tɑːtə) *n.* (*sometimes cap.*) a fearsome or vindictive person, esp. a woman.

Tartar ('tɑːtə) *n., adj.* a variant spelling of **Tatar.**

tartaric (tɑː'tærɪk) *adj.* of, containing, or derived from tartar or tartaric acid.

tartaric acid *n.* a colourless crystalline acid which is found in many fruits: used in soft drinks, confectionery, and baking powders and in tanning and photography.

tartar sauce *n.* a mayonnaise sauce mixed with hard-boiled egg yolks, chopped herbs, capers, etc.

tart up *vb.* (*adv.*) *Brit. sl.* **1.** to dress and make (oneself) up in a provocative or promiscuous way. **2.** (*tr.*) to

reissue or decorate in a cheap and flashy way: *to tart up a bar.*

Tarzan ('tɑːzən) *n.* (*sometimes not cap.*) *Inf., often ironical.* a man with great physical strength, agility, and virility.

task (tɑːsk) *n.* **1.** a specific piece of work required to be done. **2.** an unpleasant or difficult job or duty. **3.** any piece of work. **4. take to task.** to criticize or reprove. ~*vb.* (*tr.*) **5.** to assign a task to. **6.** to subject to severe strain; tax.

task force *n.* **1.** a military unit formed to undertake a specific mission. **2.** any organization set up to carry out a continuing task.

taskmaster ('tɑːsk,mɑːstə) *n.* a person, discipline, etc., that enforces work, esp. hard or continuous work. —**'task,mistress** *fem. n.*

Tasmanian devil (tæz'meɪnɪən) *n.* a small ferocious carnivorous marsupial of Tasmania.

tass (tæs) *or* **tassie** ('tæsɪ) *n. Northern Brit. dialect.* **1.** a cup or glass. **2.** its contents.

Tass (tæs) *n.* the principal news agency of the Soviet Union.

tassel ('tæsəl) *n.* **1.** a tuft of loose threads secured by a knot or knob, used to decorate soft furnishings, clothes, etc. **2.** anything resembling this, esp. the tuft of stamens at the tip of a maize inflorescence. ~*vb.***-selling, -selled** *or U.S.***-seling, -seled. 3.** (*tr.*) to adorn with tassels. **4.** (*intr.*) (of maize) to produce stamens in a tuft.

taste (teɪst) *n.* **1.** the sense by which the qualities and flavour of a substance are distinguished by the taste buds. **2.** the sensation experienced by means of the taste buds. **3.** the act of tasting. **4.** a small amount eaten, drunk, or tried on the tongue. **5.** a brief experience of something: *a taste of the whip.* **6.** a preference or liking for something. **7.** the ability to make discerning judgments about aesthetic, artistic, and intellectual matters. **8.** judgment of aesthetic or social matters according to a generally accepted standard: *bad taste.* **9.** discretion; delicacy: *that remark lacks taste.* ~*vb.* **10.** to distinguish the taste of (a substance) by means of the taste buds. **11.** (*usually tr.*) to take a small amount of (a food, liquid, etc.) into the mouth, esp. in order to test the quality. **12.** (often foll. by *of*) to have a specific flavour or taste. **13.** (when *intr.*, usually foll. by *of*) to have an experience of (something): *to taste success.* **14.** (*tr.*) an archaic word for **enjoy.** —**'tastable** *adj.*

taste bud *n.* any of the elevated sensory organs on the surface of the tongue, by means of which the sensation of taste is experienced.

tasteful ('teɪstfʊl) *adj.* indicating good taste: *a tasteful design.* —**'tastefully** *adv.* —**'tastefulness** *n.*

tasteless ('teɪstlɪs) *adj.* **1.** lacking in flavour; insipid. **2.** lacking social or aesthetic taste. —**'tastelessly** *adv.* —**'tastelessness** *n.*

taster ('teɪstə) *n.* **1.** a person who samples food or drink for quality. **2.** any device used in tasting or sampling. **3.** a person employed, esp. formerly, to taste food and drink prepared for a king, etc., to test for poison.

tasty ('teɪstɪ) *adj.* **tastier, tastiest. 1.** having a pleasant flavour. **2.** *Rare.* showing good taste. —**'tastily** *adv.*

THESAURUS

tarnish 1. *v.* befoul, blacken, blemish, blot, darken, dim, discolour, drag through the mud, dull, lose lustre *or* shine, rust, soil, spot, stain, sully, taint 2. *n.* blackening, black mark, blemish, blot, discoloration, rust, spot, stain, taint

tarry abide, bide, dally, dawdle, delay, dwell, hang around (*Inf.*), linger, lodge, loiter, lose time, pause, remain, rest, sojourn, stay, take one's time, wait

tart[1] 1. pastry, pie, tartlet 2. call girl, fallen woman, *fille de joie*, floozy (*Sl.*), harlot, hooker (*U.S. sl.*), loose woman, prostitute, slut, streetwalker, strumpet, trollop, whore, woman of easy virtue

tart[2] 1. acid, acidulous, astringent, bitter, piquant, pungent, sharp, sour, tangy, vinegary 2. acrimonious, astringent, barbed, biting, caustic, crusty, cutting, harsh, nasty, scathing, sharp, short, snappish, testy, trenchant, wounding

task *n.* 1. assignment, business, charge, chore, duty, employment, enterprise, exer-

cise, job, labour, mission, occupation, toil, undertaking, work 2. **take to task** blame, censure, criticize, lecture, reprimand, reproach, reprove, scold, tell off (*Inf.*), upbraid ~*v.* 3. assign to, charge, entrust 4. burden, exhaust, load, lumber (*Brit. inf.*), oppress, overload, push, saddle, strain, tax, test, weary

taste *n.* 1. flavour, relish, savour, smack, tang 2. bit, bite, dash, drop, morsel, mouthful, nip, sample, sip, *soupçon*, spoonful, swallow, titbit, touch 3. appetite, bent, desire, fancy, fondness, inclination, leaning, liking, palate, partiality, penchant, predilection, preference, relish 4. appreciation, cultivation, culture, discernment, discrimination, elegance, grace, judgment, perception, polish, refinement, style 5. correctness, decorum, delicacy, discretion, nicety, politeness, propriety, restraint, tact, tactfulness ~*v.* 6. differentiate, discern, distinguish, perceive 7. assay, nibble, relish, sample, savour, sip, test, try 8. have a flavour of, savour of, smack of 9. come

up against, encounter, experience, feel, have knowledge of, know, meet with, partake of, undergo

tasteful aesthetically pleasing, artistic, beautiful, charming, cultivated, cultured, delicate, discriminating, elegant, exquisite, fastidious, graceful, handsome, harmonious, in good taste, polished, refined, restrained, smart, stylish

tasteless 1. bland, boring, dull, flat, flavourless, insipid, mild, stale, tame, thin, uninspired, uninteresting, vapid, watered-down, weak 2. cheap, coarse, crass, crude, flashy, garish, gaudy, graceless, gross, impolite, improper, indecorous, indelicate, indiscreet, inelegant, low, rude, tactless, tawdry, uncouth, unseemly, vulgar

tasty appetizing, delectable, delicious, flavourful, flavoursome, full-flavoured, good-tasting, luscious, palatable, sapid, savoury, scrumptious (*Inf.*), toothsome, yummy (*Sl.*)

—'**tastiness** n.

tat[1] (tæt) vb. **tatting, tatted.** to make (something) by tatting.

tat[2] (tæt) n. **1.** tatty articles or a tatty condition. **2.** a tangled mass.

tat[3] (tæt) n. See **tit for tat.**

ta-ta (tæ'tɑː) sentence substitute. Brit. inf. goodbye; farewell.

Tatar or **Tartar** ('tɑːtə) n. **1. a.** a member of a Mongoloid people who established a powerful state in central Asia in the 13th century. **b.** a descendant of this people, now scattered throughout the Soviet Union. **2.** the Turkic language or dialects spoken by this people. ~adj. **3.** of or relating to the Tatars. —**Tatarian** (tɑː'tɛərɪən), **Tar'tarian** or **Tataric** (tɑː'tærɪk), **Tar'taric** adj.

tater ('teɪtə) n. a dialect word for potato.

tatter ('tætə) vb. **1.** to make or become ragged or worn to shreds. ~n. **2.** a torn or ragged piece, esp. of material.

tatting ('tætɪŋ) n. **1.** an intricate type of lace made by looping a thread of cotton or linen by means of a hand shuttle. **2.** the act or work of producing this.

tattle ('tætl) vb. **1.** (intr.) to gossip about another's personal matters. **2.** (tr.) to reveal by gossiping. **3.** (intr.) to talk idly; chat. ~n. **4.** the act or an instance of tattling. **5.** a scandalmonger or gossip. —'**tattler** n.

tattletale ('tætl,teɪl) Chiefly U.S. ~n. **1.** a scandalmonger or gossip. ~adj. **2.** telltale.

tattoo[1] (tæ'tuː) n., pl. **-toos. 1.** (formerly) a signal by drum or bugle ordering the military to return to their quarters. **2.** a military display or pageant. **3.** any similar beating on a drum, etc.

tattoo[2] (tæ'tuː) vb. **-tooing, -tooed. 1.** to make (pictures or designs) on (the skin) by pricking and staining with indelible colours. ~n., pl. **-toos. 2.** a design made by this process. **3.** the practice of tattooing. —**tat'tooer** or **tat'tooist** n.

tatty ('tætɪ) adj. **-tier, -tiest.** Chiefly Brit. worn out, shabby, or unkempt. —'**tattiness** n.

tau (tɔː, taʊ) n. the 19th letter in the Greek alphabet (T or τ).

taught (tɔːt) vb. the past tense or past participle of **teach.**

taunt (tɔːnt) vb. (tr.) **1.** to provoke or deride with mockery, contempt, or criticism. **2.** to tease; tantalize. ~n. **3.** a jeering remark. —'**taunter** n. —'**tauntingly** adv.

taupe (təʊp) n. **a.** a brownish-grey colour. **b.** (as modifier): a taupe coat.

Taurus ('tɔːrəs) n. **1.** Astron. a constellation in the N hemisphere. **2.** Astrol. Also called: the **Bull.** the second sign of the zodiac. The sun is in this sign between about April 20 and May 20.

taut (tɔːt) adj. **1.** tightly stretched; tense. **2.** showing nervous strain; stressed. **3.** Chiefly naut. in good order; neat. —'**tautly** adv. —'**tautness** n.

tauten ('tɔːtən) vb. to make or become taut.

tautology (tɔː'tɒlədʒɪ) n., pl. **-gies. 1.** the use of words that merely repeat elements of the meaning already conveyed, as in Will these supplies be adequate enough? in place of Will these supplies be adequate? **2.** Logic. a proposition that is always true, as in either the sun is out or the sun is not out. —**tautological** (,tɔːtə'lɒdʒɪkəl), ,tauto'logic, or tau'tologous adj.

tavern ('tævən) n. **1.** a less common word for **pub. 2.** U.S. & N.Z. a place licensed for the sale and consumption of alcoholic drink.

tawdry ('tɔːdrɪ) adj. **-drier, -driest.** cheap, showy, and of poor quality: tawdry jewellery. —'**tawdrily** adv. —'**tawdriness** n.

tawny ('tɔːnɪ) n. **a.** a light brown to brownish-orange colour. **b.** (as adj.): tawny port. —'**tawniness** n.

tawny owl n. a European owl having a reddish-brown plumage and a round head.

tawse or **taws** (tɔːz) n. Scot. a leather strap having one end cut into thongs, formerly used as an instrument of punishment by a schoolmaster.

tax (tæks) n. **1.** a compulsory financial contribution imposed by a government to raise revenue, levied on income or property, on the prices of goods and services, etc. **2.** a heavy demand on something; strain. ~vb. (tr.) **3.** to levy a tax on (persons, companies, etc.). **4.** to make heavy demands on; strain. **5.** to accuse or blame. **6.** Law. to determine (the amount legally chargeable or allowable to a party to a legal action): to tax costs. —'**taxable** adj. —'**taxer** n.

taxation (tæk'seɪʃən) n. **1.** the act or principle of levying taxes or the condition of being taxed. **2. a.** an amount assessed as tax. **b.** a tax rate. **3.** revenue from taxes. —**tax'ational** adj.

tax avoidance n. reduction or minimization of tax liability by lawful methods.

tax-deductible adj. legally deductible from income or wealth before tax assessment.

tax evasion n. reduction or minimization of tax liability by illegal methods.

tax haven n. a country or state having a lower rate of taxation than elsewhere.

taxi ('tæksɪ) n., pl. **taxis** or **taxies. 1.** Also called: **cab, taxicab.** a car, usually fitted with a taximeter, that may be hired to carry passengers to any specified destination. ~vb. **taxiing** or **taxying, taxied. 2.** to cause (an aircraft) to move along the ground, esp. before takeoff and after landing, or (of an aircraft) to move along the ground in this way. **3.** (intr.) to travel in a taxi.

taxidermy ('tæksɪ,dɜːmɪ) n. the art or process of preparing, stuffing, and mounting animal skins so that they have a lifelike appearance. —,**taxi'dermal** or ,**taxi'dermic** adj. —'**taxi,dermist** n.

taximeter ('tæksɪ,miːtə) n. a meter fitted to a taxi to register the fare, based on the length of the journey.

taxi rank n. a place where taxis wait to be hired.

taxonomy (tæk'sɒnəmɪ) n. **1.** the branch of biology concerned with the classification of organisms into groups based on similarities of structure, origin, etc. **2.** the science or practice of classification. —**taxonomic** (,tæksə'nɒmɪk) or ,**taxo'nomical** adj. —,**taxo'nomically** adv. —**tax'onomist** n.

taxpayer ('tæks,peɪə) n. a person or organization that pays taxes.

tax return n. a declaration of personal income used as a basis for assessing an individual's liability for taxation.

Tb the chemical symbol for terbium.

T.B. or **t.b.** abbrev. for: **1.** tuberculosis. **2.** torpedo-boat.

T-bone steak n. a large choice steak cut from the sirloin of beef, containing a T-shaped bone.

tbs. or **tbsp.** abbrev. for tablespoon(ful).

Tc the chemical symbol for technetium.

te or **ti** (tiː) n. Music. (in tonic sol-fa) the syllable used for the seventh note or subtonic of any scale.

Te the chemical symbol for tellurium.

tea (tiː) n. **1.** an evergreen shrub of tropical and subtropical Asia, having white fragrant flowers: family Theaceae. **2. a.** the dried leaves of this shrub, used to make a beverage by infusion in boiling water. **b.** such a beverage, served hot or iced. **3. a.** any of various similar plants or any plants that are used to make a tealike beverage. **b.** any such beverage. **4.** Also called: **afternoon tea.** Chiefly Brit. a light meal eaten in midafternoon, usu-

---

THESAURUS

taunt 1. v. deride, flout, gibe, guy (Inf.), insult, jeer, mock, provoke, reproach, revile, ridicule, sneer, tease, torment, twit, upbraid **2.** n. barb, censure, cut, derision, dig, gibe, insult, jeer, provocation, reproach, ridicule, sarcasm, teasing

taut 1. flexed, rigid, strained, stressed, stretched, tense, tight **2.** Nautical in good order, neat, orderly, shipshape, spruce, tidy, tight, trim, well-ordered, well-regulated

tavern alehouse (Archaic), bar, boozer (Brit. inf.), hostelry, inn, pub (Brit. inf.), public house

tawdry brummagem, cheap, cheap-jack (Inf.), flashy, gaudy, gimcrack, glittering, meretricious, plastic (Sl.), raffish, showy, tacky, tasteless, tatty, tinsel, tinselly, vulgar

tax n. **1.** assessment, charge, contribution, customs, duty, excise, imposition, impost, levy, rate, tariff, tithe, toll, tribute **2.** burden, demand, drain, load, pressure, strain, weight ~v. **3.** assess, charge, demand, exact, extract, impose, levy a tax on, rate, tithe **4.** burden, drain, enervate, exhaust, load, make heavy demands on, overburden, push, put pressure on, sap, strain, stretch, task, try, weaken, wear out, weary, weigh heavily on **5.** accuse, arraign, blame, charge, impeach, impugn, incriminate, lay at one's door

taxing burdensome, demanding, enervating, exacting, heavy, onerous, punishing, sapping, stressful, tiring, tough, trying, wearing, wearisome

ally consisting of tea and cakes, etc. **5.** See **high tea. 6.** *U.S.* a slang word for **marijuana.**

tea bag *n.* a small bag containing tea leaves, infused in boiling water to make tea.

tea ball *n. Chiefly U.S.* a perforated metal ball filled with tea leaves and used to make tea.

teacake ('tiː,keɪk) *n. Brit.* a flat bun, usually eaten toasted and buttered.

teach (tiːtʃ) *vb.* **teaching, taught. 1.** (*tr.; may take a clause as object or an infinitive;* often foll. by *how*) to help to learn; tell or show (how). **2.** to give instruction or lessons in (a subject) to (a person or animal). **3.** (*tr.; may take a clause as object or an infinitive*) to cause to learn or understand: *experience taught him that he could not be a journalist.* —'**teachable** *adj.*

teacher ('tiːtʃə) *n.* a person whose occupation is teaching others, esp. children.

tea chest *n.* a large foil-lined plywood box used for shipping tea and frequently subsequently as a container for other items.

teaching ('tiːtʃɪŋ) *n.* **1.** the art or profession of a teacher. **2.** something taught; precept.

tea cosy *n.* a covering for a teapot to keep the contents hot.

teacup ('tiː,kʌp) *n.* **1.** a cup out of which tea may be drunk. **2.** Also called: **teacupful.** the amount a teacup will hold, about four fluid ounces.

teahouse ('tiː,haʊs) *n.* a restaurant, esp. in Japan or China, where tea and light refreshments are served.

teak (tiːk) *n.* **1.** a large tree of the East Indies. **2.** the hard resinous yellowish-brown wood of this tree, used for furniture making, etc.

teal (tiːl) *n., pl.* **teals** or **teal. 1.** any of various small freshwater ducks that are related to the mallard. **2.** a greenish-blue colour.

team (tiːm) *n.* (*sometimes functioning as pl.*) **1.** a group of people organized to work together. **2.** a group of players forming one of the sides in a sporting contest. **3.** two or more animals working together, as to pull a vehicle. **4.** such animals and the vehicle. ~*vb.* **5.** (when *intr.*, often foll. by *up*) to make or cause to make a team. **6.** (*tr.*) *U.S.* to drag or transport in or by a vehicle. **7.** (*intr.*) *U.S.* to drive a team.

team-mate *n.* a fellow member of a team.

team spirit *n.* willingness to cooperate as part of a team.

teamster ('tiːmstə) *n.* **1.** a driver of a team of horses. **2.** *U.S.* the driver of a lorry.

teamwork ('tiːm,wɜːk) *n.* **1.** the cooperative work done by a team. **2.** the ability to work efficiently as a team.

teapot ('tiː,pɒt) *n.* a container with a lid, spout, and handle, in which tea is made and from which it is served.

tear[1] (tɪə) *n.* **1.** a drop of the secretion of the lacrimal glands. See **tears. 2.** something shaped like a falling drop: *a tear of amber.* ~Also called: **teardrop.** —'**tearless** *adj.*

tear[2] (tɛə) *vb.* **tearing, tore, torn. 1.** to cause to come apart or to come apart; rip. **2.** (*tr.*) to make (a hole or split) in (something). **3.** (*intr.;* often foll. by *along*) to hurry or rush. **4.** (*tr.;* usually foll. by *away* or *from*) to remove or take by force. **5.** (when *intr.*, often foll. by *at*) to cause pain, distress, or anguish (to). **6. tear one's hair.** *Inf.* to be angry, frustrated, very worried, etc. ~*n.* **7.** a hole, cut, or split. **8.** the act of tearing. ~See also **tear away, tear down,** etc. —'**tearable** *adj.* —'**tearer** *n.*

tear away (tɛə) *vb.* **1.** (*tr., adv.*) to persuade (oneself

or someone else) to leave. ~*n.* **tearaway. 2.** *Brit.* a reckless impetuous person.

tear down (tɛə) *vb.* (*tr., adv.*) to destroy or demolish: *to tear down an argument.*

tear duct (tɪə) *n.* a short tube in the inner corner of the eyelid through which tears drain into the nose. Technical name: **lacrimal duct.**

tearful ('tɪəfʊl) *adj.* **1.** crying or about to cry. **2.** tending to produce tears; sad. —'**tearfully** *adv.* —'**tearfulness** *n.*

tear gas (tɪə) *n.* a gas that makes the eyes smart and water, causing temporary blindness; used in warfare and to control riots.

tearing ('tɛərɪŋ) *adj.* violent or furious (esp. in **tearing hurry** or **rush**). —'**tearingly** *adv.*

tear into (tɛə) *vb.* (*intr., prep.*) *Inf.* to attack vigorously and damagingly.

tear-jerker ('tɪə,dʒɜːkə) *n. Inf.* an excessively sentimental film, play, book, etc.

tearoom ('tiː,ruːm, -,rʊm) *n. Brit.* a restaurant where tea and light refreshments are served. Also called: **teashop.**

tears (tɪəz) *pl. n.* **1.** the clear salty solution secreted by the lacrimal glands that lubricates and cleanses the surface of the eyeball. **2.** a state of intense frustration (esp. in **bored to tears**). **3. in tears.** weeping.

tease (tiːz) *vb.* **1.** to annoy (someone) by deliberately offering something with the intention of delaying or withdrawing the offer. **2.** to vex (someone) maliciously or playfully. **3.** (*tr.*) to separate the fibres of; comb; card. **4.** (*tr.*) to raise the nap of (a fabric) with a teasel. **5.** another word (esp. U.S.) for **backcomb. 6.** (*tr.*) to loosen or pull apart (biological tissues, etc.). ~*n.* **7.** a person or thing that teases. **8.** the act of teasing. —'**teaser** *n.* —'**teasingly** *adv.*

teasel, teazel, or **teazle** ('tiːzəl) *n.* **1.** any of various plants (esp. the **fuller's teasel**) of Eurasia and N Africa, having prickly leaves and prickly heads of yellow or purple flowers. **2. a.** the dried flower head of the fuller's teasel, used for teasing. **b.** any implement used for the same purpose. ~*vb.* **-selling, -selled** or *U.S.* **-seling, -seled. 3.** (*tr.*) to tease (a fabric). —'**teaseller** *n.*

teaspoon ('tiː,spuːn) *n.* **1.** a small spoon used for stirring tea, etc. **2.** Also called: **teaspoonful.** the amount contained in such a spoon. **3.** a unit of capacity used in cooking, medicine, etc., equal to about one fluid dram.

teat (tiːt) *n.* **1. a.** the nipple of a mammary gland. **b.** (in cows, etc.) any of the projections from the udder. **2.** something resembling a teat such as the rubber mouthpiece of a feeding bottle.

tea towel or **cloth** *n.* a towel for drying dishes, etc. *U.S.* name: **dishtowel.**

tech. *abbrev. for:* **1.** technical. **2.** technology. **3.** *Inf.* technical college.

technetium (tɛk'niːʃɪəm) *n.* a silvery-grey metallic element, artificially produced by bombardment of molybdenum by deuterons. The radioisotope **technetium-99m** is used in radiotherapy. Symbol: Tc; atomic no.: 43; half-life of most stable isotope, [97]Tc: 2.6×10^6 years.

technic (tɛk'niːk) *n. another word for* **technique.**

technical ('tɛknɪkəl) *adj.* **1.** of or specializing in industrial, practical, or mechanical arts and applied sciences: *a technical institute.* **2.** skilled in practical arts rather than abstract thinking. **3.** relating to a particular field of activity: *the technical jargon of linguistics.* **4.** existing by virtue of a strict application of the rules or a strict interpretation of the wording: *a technical loophole in the law.* **5.** of or showing technique: *technical brilliance.*

THESAURUS

teach advise, coach, demonstrate, direct, discipline, drill, edify, educate, enlighten, give lessons in, guide, impart, implant, inculcate, inform, instil, instruct, school, show, train, tutor

teacher coach, dominie (*Scot.*), don, educator, guide, guru, instructor, lecturer, master, mentor, mistress, pedagogue, professor, schoolmaster, schoolmistress, schoolteacher, trainer, tutor

team *n.* **1.** band, body, bunch, company, crew, gang, group, line-up, set, side, squad, troupe **2.** pair, span, yoke ~*v.* **3.** *Often with* **up** band together, cooperate, couple, get to-

gether, join, link, unite, work together, yoke

tear *v.* **1.** claw, divide, lacerate, mangle, mutilate, pull apart, rend, rip, rive, run, rupture, scratch, sever, shred, split, sunder **2.** belt (*Sl.*), bolt, career, charge, dart, dash, fly, gallop, hurry, race, run, rush, shoot, speed, sprint, zoom **3.** grab, pluck, pull, rip, seize, snatch, wrench, wrest, yank ~*n.* **4.** hole, laceration, mutilation, rent, rip, run, rupture, scratch, split

tearful 1. blubbering, crying, in tears, lachrymose, sobbing, weeping, weepy (*Inf.*), whimpering **2.** distressing, dolorous, lamentable, mournful, pathetic, pitiable, pitiful,

poignant, sad, sorrowful, upsetting, woeful

tears 1. blubbering, crying, distress, lamentation, mourning, pain, regret, sadness, sobbing, sorrow, wailing, weeping, whimpering, woe **2. in tears** blubbering, crying, distressed, sobbing, visibly moved, weeping, whimpering

tease aggravate (*Inf.*), annoy, badger, bait, bedevil, chaff, gibe, goad, guy (*Inf.*), lead on, mock, needle, pester, plague (*Inf.*), provoke, rag, rib (*Inf.*), ridicule, tantalize, taunt, torment, twit, vex, worry

—**'technically** *adv.* —**'technicalness** *n.*

technicality (ˌtɛknɪ'kælɪtɪ) *n., pl.* **-ties. 1.** a petty formal point arising from a strict interpretation of rules, etc. **2.** the state or quality of being technical. **3.** technical methods and vocabulary.

technical knockout *n. Boxing.* a judgment of a knockout given when a boxer is in the referee's opinion too badly beaten to continue without risk of serious injury.

technician (tɛk'nɪʃən) *n.* **1.** a person skilled in mechanical or industrial techniques or in a particular technical field. **2.** a person employed in a laboratory, etc., to do mechanical and practical work. **3.** a person having specific artistic or mechanical skill, esp. if lacking flair.

Technicolor ('tɛknɪˌkʌlə) *n. Trademark.* the process of producing colour film by means of superimposing synchronized films of the same scene, each of which has a different colour filter.

technique (tɛk'niːk) *n.* **1.** a practical method, skill, or art applied to a particular task. **2.** proficiency in a practical or mechanical skill. **3.** special facility; knack.

techno- *combining form.* **1.** craft or art: *technology; technography.* **2.** technological or technical: *technocracy.*

technocracy (tɛk'nɒkrəsɪ) *n., pl.* **-cies.** government by scientists, engineers, and other such experts. —**technocrat** ('tɛknəˌkræt) *n.* —ˌtechno'cratic *adj.*

technology (tɛk'nɒlədʒɪ) *n., pl.* **-gies. 1.** the application of practical or mechanical sciences to industry or commerce. **2.** the methods, theory, and practices governing such application. **3.** the total knowledge and skills available to any human society. —**technological** (ˌtɛknə'lɒdʒɪkəl) *adj.* —**tech'nologist** *n.*

tectonics (tɛk'tɒnɪks) *n. (functioning as sing.)* **1.** the art and science of construction or building. **2.** the study of the processes by which the earth's surface has attained its present structure.

ted[1] (tɛd) *vb.* **tedding, tedded.** to shake out (hay), so as to dry it.

ted[2] (tɛd) *n. Inf.* short for **teddy boy.**

tedder ('tɛdə) *n.* **1.** a machine equipped with a series of small rotating forks for tedding hay. **2.** a person who teds.

teddy bear ('tɛdɪ) *n.* a stuffed toy bear. Often shortened to **teddy.**

teddy boy *n.* **1.** (in Britain, esp. in the mid-1950s) one of a cult of youths who wore mock Edwardian fashions. **2.** any tough or delinquent youth.

Te Deum (ˌtiː 'diːəm) *n.* **1.** an ancient Latin hymn in rhythmic prose. **2.** a musical setting of this hymn. **3.** a service of thanksgiving in which the recital of this hymn forms a central part.

tedious ('tiːdɪəs) *adj.* causing fatigue or tedium; monotonous. —**'tediousness** *n.*

tedium ('tiːdɪəm) *n.* the state of being bored or the quality of being boring; monotony.

tee[1] (tiː) *n.* **1.** a pipe fitting in the form of a letter *T*, used to join three pipes. **2.** a metal section with a cross section in the form of a letter *T*.

tee[2] (tiː) *Golf.* ~*n.* **1.** an area from which the first stroke of a hole is made. **2.** a support for a golf ball, usually a small wooden or plastic peg, used when teeing off or in long grass, etc. ~*vb.* **teeing, teed. 3.** (when *intr.*, often foll. by *up*) to position (the ball) ready for striking, on or as if on a tee. ~See also **tee off.**

tee[3] (tiː) *n.* **1.** a mark used as a target in certain games such as curling and quoits. **2. to a tee.** perfectly or exactly.

tee-hee ('tiː'hiː) *interj., n., vb.* a variant spelling of **te-hee.**

teem[1] (tiːm) *vb. (intr.;* usually foll. by *with)* to be prolific or abundant (in).

teem[2] (tiːm) *vb.* **1.** *(intr.;* often foll. by *down* or *with rain)* to pour in torrents. **2.** *(tr.)* to pour or empty out.

teen (tiːn) *adj. Inf.* another word for **teenage.**

teenage ('tiːnˌeɪdʒ) *adj. also* **teenaged.** *(prenominal)* of or relating to the time in a person's life between the ages of 13 and 19.

teenager ('tiːnˌeɪdʒə) *n.* a person between the ages of 13 and 19 inclusive.

teens (tiːnz) *pl. n.* **1.** the years of a person's life between the ages of 13 and 19 inclusive. **2.** all the numbers that end in *-teen.*

teeny ('tiːnɪ) *adj.* **-nier, -niest.** extremely small; tiny. Also: **teeny-weeny** ('tiːnɪ'wiːnɪ) *or* **teensy-weensy** ('tiːnzɪ 'wiːnzɪ).

teenybopper ('tiːnɪˌbɒpə) *n. Sl.* a young teenager, usually a girl, who avidly follows fashions in clothes and pop music.

tee off *vb. (adv.)* **1.** *Golf.* to strike (the ball) from a tee. **2.** *Inf.* to begin; start.

teepee ('tiːpiː) *n.* a variant spelling of **tepee.**

tee-shirt *n.* a variant of **T-shirt.**

teeter ('tiːtə) *vb.* **1.** to move or cause to move unsteadily; wobble. ~*n., vb.* **2.** another word for **seesaw.**

teeth (tiːθ) *n.* **1.** the plural of **tooth. 2.** the most violent part: *the teeth of the gale.* **3.** the power to produce a desired effect: *that law has no teeth.* **4. by the skin of one's teeth.** See **skin. 5. get one's teeth into.** to become engrossed in. **6. in the teeth of.** in direct opposition to; against. **7. to the teeth.** to the greatest possible degree: *armed to the teeth.* **8. show one's teeth.** to threaten.

teethe (tiːð) *vb. (intr.)* to cut one's baby (deciduous) teeth.

teething ring *n.* a hard ring on which babies may bite while teething.

teething troubles *pl. n.* the problems that arise during the initial stages of a project, etc.

teetotal (tiː'təʊtəl) *adj.* **1.** of or practising abstinence from alcoholic drink. **2.** *Inf.* complete. —**tee'totaller** *n.* —**tee'totalism** *n.*

te-hee (tiː'hiː) *interj.* **1.** an exclamation of laughter, esp. when mocking. ~*n.* **2.** a chuckle. ~*vb.* **-heeing, -heed. 3.** *(intr.)* to snigger or laugh, esp. derisively.

tel. *abbrev. for:* **1.** telegram. **2.** telegraph(ic). **3.** telephone.

tel- *combining form.* a variant of **tele-** before a vowel.

tele- *combining form.* **1.** at or over a distance; distant: *telescope; telekinesis.* **2.** television: *telecast.*

telecast ('tɛləˌkɑːst) *vb.* **-casting, -cast** *or* **-casted. 1.** to broadcast by television. ~*n.* **2.** a television broadcast. —**'tele,caster** *n.*

telecommunications (ˌtɛlɪkəˌmjuːnɪ'keɪʃənz) *n. (functioning as sing.)* the science and technology of communications by telephony, radio, television, etc.

telegram ('tɛlɪˌgræm) *n.* a communication transmitted by telegraph.

telegraph ('tɛlɪˌgrɑːf) *n.* **1. a.** a device, system, or process by which information can be transmitted over a distance, esp. using radio signals or coded electrical signals sent along a transmission line. **b.** *(as modifier):* *telegraph pole.* ~*vb.* **2.** to send a telegram to (a person or place); wire. **3.** *(tr.)* to transmit or send by telegraph. **4.** *(tr.)* to give advance notice of (anything), esp. unintentionally. **5.** *(tr.) Canad. inf.* to cast (votes) illegally by impersonating registered voters. —**telegrapher** (tə'lɛgrəfə) *or* **te'legraphist** *n.* —ˌtele'graphic *adj.*

THESAURUS

technique 1. approach, course, fashion, manner, means, method, mode, modus operandi, procedure, style, system, way **2.** address, adroitness, art, artistry, craft, craftsmanship, delivery, execution, facility, knack, know-how *(Inf.)*, performance, proficiency, skill, touch
tedious annoying, banal, boring, deadly dull, drab, dreary, dull, fatiguing, humdrum, irksome, laborious, lifeless, long-drawn-out, monotonous, prosaic, prosy, soporific, tiring, unexciting, uninteresting, vapid, wearisome
tedium banality, boredom, deadness,

drabness, dreariness, dullness, ennui, lifelessness, monotony, routine, sameness, tediousness, the doldrums

teem abound, be abundant, bear, be crawling with, be full of, be prolific, brim, bristle, burst at the seams, overflow, produce, pullulate, swarm

teeming abundant, alive, brimful, brimming, bristling, bursting, chock-a-block, chock-full, crawling, fruitful, full, numerous, overflowing, packed, replete, swarming, thick

teenage adolescent, immature, juvenile, youthful
teenager adolescent, boy, girl, juvenile, minor, youth
teetotaller abstainer, nondrinker, Rechabite
telegram cable, radiogram, telegraph, telex, wire *(Inf.)*
telegraph *n.* **1.** tape machine *(Stock Exchange),* teleprinter, telex **2.** cable, radiogram, telegram, telex, wire *(Inf.)* ~*v.* **3.** cable, send, telex, transmit, wire *(Inf.)*

telegraphy (tɪ'lɛgrəfɪ) *n.* **1.** a system of telecommunications involving any process providing reproduction at a distance of written, printed, or pictorial matter. **2.** the skill or process of operating a telegraph.

telekinesis (ˌtɛlɪkaɪ'niːsɪs) *n.* **1.** the movement of a body caused by thought or willpower without the application of a physical force. **2.** the ability to cause such movement. —**telekinetic** (ˌtɛlɪkɪ'nɛtɪk) *adj.*

telemeter (tɪ'lɛmɪtə) *n.* **1.** any device for recording or measuring a distant event and transmitting the data to a receiver. **2.** any device used to measure a distance without directly comparing it with a measuring rod, etc. ~*vb.* **3.** (*tr.*) to obtain and transmit (data) from a distant source. —**telemetric** (ˌtɛlɪ'mɛtrɪk) *adj.*

teleology (ˌtɛlɪ'ɒlədʒɪ, ˌtiːlɪ-) *n.* **1.** *Philosophy.* **a.** the study of the evidence of design or purpose in nature. **b.** the ultimate purpose of things, esp. natural processes. **c.** the belief that final causes exist. **2.** *Biol.* the belief that natural phenomena have a predetermined purpose and are not determined by mechanical laws. —**teleological** (ˌtɛlɪə'lɒdʒɪkəl, ˌtiːlɪ-) *adj.* —**tele'ologist** *n.*

telepathy (tɪ'lɛpəθɪ) *n.* the communication between people of thoughts, feelings, etc., involving mechanisms that cannot be understood in terms of known scientific laws. —**telepathic** (ˌtɛlɪ'pæθɪk) *adj.* —**te'lepathist** *n.* —**te'lepa,thize** *or* **-ise** *vb.* (*intr.*).

telephone ('tɛlɪˌfəʊn) *n.* **1.** an electrical device for transmitting speech, consisting of a microphone and receiver mounted on a handset. **2. a.** a worldwide system of communications using telephones. The microphone in one telephone converts sound waves into electrical oscillations that are transmitted along a telephone wire or by radio to one or more distant sets. **b.** (*as modifier*): *a telephone exchange.* ~*vb.* **3.** to call or talk to (a person) by telephone. **4.** to transmit (a message, etc.) by telephone. —**'tele,phoner** *n.*

telephone box *n.* a soundproof enclosure from which a paid telephone call can be made. Also called: **telephone kiosk, telephone booth.**

telephone directory *n.* a book listing the names, addresses, and telephone numbers of subscribers in a particular area.

telephonist (tɪ'lɛfənɪst) *n. Brit.* a person who operates a telephone switchboard. Also called (esp. U.S.): **telephone operator.**

telephony (tɪ'lɛfənɪ) *n.* a system of telecommunications for the transmission of speech or other sounds.

telephotography (ˌtɛlɪfə'tɒgrəfɪ) *n.* the process or technique of photographing distant objects using a telephoto lens.

telephoto lens ('tɛlɪˌfəʊtəʊ) *n.* a lens system that can be attached to a camera to increase the effective focal length of the camera lens and thus produce a magnified image of a distant object.

teleprinter ('tɛlɪˌprɪntə) *n.* **1.** a telegraph apparatus consisting of a keyboard transmitter, which converts a typed message into coded pulses for transmission along a wire or cable, and a printing receiver, which converts incoming signals and prints out the message. U.S. name: **teletypewriter. 2.** a network of such devices. **3.** a similar device used for direct input/output of data into a computer at a distant location.

Teleprompter ('tɛlɪˌprɒmptə) *n. Trademark.* a device for displaying a television script so that the speaker can read it while appearing to look at the camera.

telescope ('tɛlɪˌskəʊp) *n.* **1.** an optical instrument for making distant objects appear closer by use of a combination of lenses (**refracting telescope**) or lenses and curved mirrors (**reflecting telescope**). **2.** any instrument, such as a radio telescope, for collecting, focusing, and detecting electromagnetic radiation from space. ~*vb.* **3.** to crush together or be crushed together, as in a collision. **4.** to fit together like a set of cylinders that slide into one another, thus allowing extension and shortening. **5.** to make or become smaller or shorter. —**tele'scopic** *adj.*

teletext ('tɛlɪˌtɛkst) *n.* a videotext service in which the consumer is not able to interact with the computer. Cf. **viewdata.**

Teletype ('tɛlɪˌtaɪp) *n.* **1.** *Trademark.* a type of teleprinter. **2.** (*sometimes not cap.*) a network of such devices. ~*vb.* **3.** (*sometimes not cap.*) to transmit (a message) by Teletype.

televise ('tɛlɪˌvaɪz) *vb.* **1.** to put on television. **2.** (*tr.*) to transmit by television.

television ('tɛlɪˌvɪʒən) *n.* **1.** the system or process of producing on a distant screen a series of transient visible images, usually with an accompanying sound signal. Electrical signals, converted from optical images by a camera tube, are transmitted by radio waves or by cable and reconverted into optical images by means of a television tube inside a television set. **2.** Also called: **television set.** a device designed to receive and convert incoming electrical signals into a series of visible images on a screen together with accompanying sound. **3.** the content, etc., of television programmes. **4.** the occupation or profession concerned with any aspect of the broadcasting of television programmes. **5.** (*modifier*) of, relating to, or used in the transmission or reception of video and audio UHF or VHF radio signals: *a television transmitter.* ~Abbrev.: **TV**

telex ('tɛlɛks) *n.* **1.** an international telegraph service in which teleprinters are rented out to subscribers. **2.** a teleprinter used in such a service. **3.** a message transmitted or received by telex. ~*vb.* **4.** to transmit (a message) to (a person, etc.) by telex.

tell (tɛl) *vb.* **telling, told. 1.** (when *tr.*, *may take a clause as object*) to let know or notify. **2.** (*tr.*) to order or instruct. **3.** (when *intr.*, usually foll. by *of*) to give an account or narration of. **4.** (*tr.*) to communicate by words; utter: *to tell the truth.* **5.** (*tr.*) to make known: *to tell fortunes.* **6.** (*intr.*; often foll. by *of*) to serve as an indication: *her blush told of her embarrassment.* **7.** (*tr.*; used with *can*, etc.; *may take a clause as object*) to discover or discern: *I can tell what is wrong.* **8.** (*tr.*; used with *can*, etc.) to distinguish or discriminate: *he couldn't tell chalk from cheese.* **9.** (*intr.*) to have or produce an impact, effect, or strain: *every step told on his bruised feet.* **10.** (*intr.*; sometimes foll. by *on*) *Inf.* to reveal secrets or gossip (about). **11.** (*tr.*) to assure: *I tell you, I've had enough!* **12.** (*tr.*) to count (votes). **13. tell the time.** to read the time from a clock. **14. you're telling me.** *Sl.* I know that very well. —**'tellable** *adj.*

tell apart *vb.* (*tr.*, *adv.*) to distinguish between.

teller ('tɛlə) *n.* **1.** *Chiefly U.S.* a bank clerk. **2.** a person appointed to count votes. **3.** a person who tells; narrator.

telling ('tɛlɪŋ) *adj.* **1.** having a marked effect or impact. **2.** revealing. —**'tellingly** *adv.*

tell off *vb.* (*tr.*, *adv.*) **1.** *Inf.* to reprimand; scold. **2.** to count and select for duty.

telltale ('tɛlˌteɪl) *n.* **1.** a person who tells tales about others. **2. a.** an outward indication of something concealed. **b.** (*as modifier*): *a telltale paw mark.* **3.** a device used to monitor a process, machine, etc.

tellurian (tɛ'lʊərɪən) *adj.* **1.** of the earth. ~*n.* **2.** (*esp.* in science fiction) an inhabitant of the earth.

tellurium (tɛ'lʊərɪəm) *n.* a brittle silvery-white nonmetallic element. Symbol: Te; atomic no.: 52; atomic wt.: 127.60.

THESAURUS

telepathy mind-reading, sixth sense, thought transference

telephone 1. *n.* blower (*Inf.*), handset, line, phone 2. *v.* buzz (*Inf.*), call, call up, dial, get on the blower (*Inf.*), give (someone) a buzz (*Inf.*), give (someone) a call, give (someone) a ring (*Brit.*), give someone a tinkle (*Brit. inf.*), phone, put a call through to, ring (*Brit.*)

telescope *n.* 1. glass, spyglass ~*v.* 2. concertina, crush, squash 3. abbreviate, abridge, compress, condense, consolidate, contract, curtail, cut, shorten, shrink, trim, truncate

television gogglebox (*Brit. sl.*), idiot box (*Sl.*), receiver, small screen (*Inf.*), telly (*Brit. inf.*), the box (*Brit. inf.*), the tube (*Sl.*), TV, TV set

tell *v.* 1. acquaint, announce, apprise, communicate, confess, disclose, divulge, express, impart, inform, let know, make known, mention, notify, proclaim, reveal, say, speak, state, utter 2. authorize, bid, call upon, command, direct, enjoin, instruct, order, require, summon 3. chronicle, depict, describe, give an account of, narrate, portray, recount, rehearse, relate, report 4. comprehend, discern, discover, make out, see, understand 5. differentiate, discern, discriminate, distinguish, identify 6. carry weight, count, have *or* take effect, have force, make its presence felt, register, take its toll, weigh 7. calculate, compute, count, enumerate, number, reckon, tally

telling considerable, decisive, effective, effectual, forceful, forcible, impressive, influential, marked, potent, powerful, significant, solid, striking, trenchant, weighty

telly ('tɛlɪ) n., pl. **-lies.** Inf., chiefly Brit. short for television.

temerity (tɪ'mɛrɪtɪ) n. rashness or boldness. —**temerarious** (ˌtɛmə'rɛərɪəs) adj.

temp (tɛmp) Inf. ~n. **1.** a person, esp. a typist or other office worker, employed on a temporary basis. ~vb. (intr.) **2.** to work as a temp.

temp. abbrev. for: **1.** temperature. **2.** temporary. **3.** tempore.

temper ('tɛmpə) n. **1.** a frame of mind; mood or humour. **2.** a sudden outburst of anger. **3.** a tendency to exhibit anger; irritability. **4.** a mental condition of moderation and calm (esp. in **keep one's temper** or **lose one's temper**). **5.** the degree of hardness, elasticity, etc. of a metal. ~vb. (tr.) **6.** to make more acceptable or suitable by adding something else; moderate: he tempered his criticism with sympathy. **7.** to strengthen or toughen (a metal), as by heating and quenching. **8.** Music. **a.** to adjust the frequency differences between the notes of a scale on (a keyboard instrument). **b.** to make such an adjustment to the pitches of notes in (a scale). —**'temperable** adj. —**'temperer** n.

tempera ('tɛmpərə) n. **1.** a painting medium for powdered pigments, consisting usually of egg yolk and water. **2. a.** any emulsion used as a painting medium, with casein, glue, wax, etc., as a base. **b.** the paint made from this. **3.** the technique of painting with tempera.

temperament ('tɛmpərəmənt) n. **1.** a person's character, disposition, and tendencies. **2.** excitability, moodiness, or anger. **3.** the characteristic way an individual behaves, esp. towards other people. **4. a.** an adjustment made to the frequency differences between notes on a keyboard instrument to allow modulation to other keys. **b.** any of several systems of such adjustment, esp. **equal temperament,** a system giving a scale based on an octave divided into twelve exactly equal semitones. **5.** Obs. the characteristic way an individual behaves, viewed as the result of the influence of the four humours.

temperamental (ˌtɛmpərə'mɛntəl) adj. **1.** easily upset or irritated; excitable. **2.** of or caused by temperament. **3.** Inf. working erratically and inconsistently; unreliable. —ˌtempera'mentally adv.

temperance ('tɛmpərəns) n. **1.** restraint or moderation, esp. in yielding to one's appetites or desires. **2.** abstinence from alcoholic drink.

temperate ('tɛmpərɪt) adj. **1.** having a climate intermediate between tropical and polar; moderate or mild in temperature. **2.** mild in quality or character; exhibiting temperance. —**'temperately** adv. —**'temperateness** n.

Temperate Zone n. those parts of the earth's surface lying between the Arctic Circle and the tropic of Cancer and between the Antarctic Circle and the tropic of Capricorn.

temperature ('tɛmprɪtʃə) n. **1.** the degree of hotness of a body, substance, or medium, esp. as measured on a scale that has one or more fixed reference points. **2.** Inf. a body temperature in excess of the normal.

tempered ('tɛmpəd) adj. **1.** Music. adjusted in accordance with a system of temperament. **2.** (in combina-

tion) having a temper or temperament as specified: ill-tempered.

tempest ('tɛmpɪst) n. **1.** Chiefly literary. a violent wind or storm. **2.** a violent commotion, uproar, or disturbance.

tempestuous (tɛm'pɛstjʊəs) adj. **1.** of or relating to a tempest. **2.** violent or stormy. —**tem'pestuously** adv. —**tem'pestuousness** n.

template or **templet** ('tɛmplɪt) n. **1.** a gauge or pattern, cut out in wood or metal, used in woodwork, etc., to help shape something accurately. **2.** a pattern cut out in card or plastic, used to reproduce shapes. **3.** a short beam that is used to spread a load, as over a doorway. **4.** Biochem. the molecular structure of a compound that serves as a pattern for the production of another compound.

temple¹ ('tɛmpəl) n. **1.** a building or place dedicated to the worship of a deity or deities. **2.** a Mormon church. **3.** U.S. another name for a synagogue. **4.** a Christian church. **5.** Theol. any place or object regarded as a shrine where God makes himself present. **6.** a building regarded as the focus of an activity, interest, or practice: a temple of the arts.

temple² ('tɛmpəl) n. the region on each side of the head in front of the ear and above the cheek bone.

temple³ ('tɛmpəl) n. the part of a loom that keeps the cloth being woven stretched to the correct width.

Temple ('tɛmpəl) n. **1.** a building in London that belonged to the Templars: it now houses two law societies. **2.** any of three buildings erected by the Jews in ancient Jerusalem for the worship of Jehovah.

tempo ('tɛmpəʊ) n., pl. **-pos** or **-pi** (-piː). **1.** the speed at which a piece of music is meant to be played. **2.** rate or pace.

temporal¹ ('tɛmpərəl) adj. **1.** of or relating to time. **2.** of secular as opposed to spiritual or religious affairs. **3.** lasting for a relatively short time. **4.** Grammar. of or relating to tense or the linguistic expression of time. —ˌtempo'rality n. —**'temporally** adv.

temporal² ('tɛmpərəl) adj. Anat. of or near the temple or temples.

temporal bone n. either of two compound bones forming the sides of the skull.

temporary ('tɛmpərərɪ) adj. **1.** not permanent; provisional. **2.** lasting only a short time. ~n. **3.** a person employed on a temporary basis. —**'temporarily** adv. —**'temporariness** n.

temporize or **-ise** ('tɛmpəˌraɪz) vb. (intr.) **1.** to delay, act evasively, or protract a negotiation, etc., esp. in order to gain time or effect a compromise. **2.** to adapt oneself to the circumstances, as by temporary or apparent agreement. —ˌtempori'zation or **-i'sation** n. —**'tempoˌrizer** or **-iser** n.

tempt (tɛmpt) vb. (tr.) **1.** to entice to do something, esp. something morally wrong or unwise. **2.** to allure or attract. **3.** to give rise to a desire in (someone) to do something; dispose. **4.** to risk provoking (esp. in **tempt fate**). —**'temptable** adj. —**'tempter** n. —**'temptress** fem. n.

temptation (tɛmp'teɪʃən) n. **1.** the act of tempting or

temper n. **1.** attitude, character, constitution, disposition, frame of mind, humour, mind, mood, nature, temperament, tenor, vein **2.** bad mood, fit of pique, fury, paddy (Brit. inf.), passion, rage, tantrum, wax (Inf.) **3.** anger, annoyance, heat, hot-headedness, ill humour, irascibility, irritability, irritation, passion, peevishness, petulance, resentment, surliness **4.** calm, calmness, composure, cool (Sl.), coolness, equanimity, good humour, moderation, self-control, tranquillity ~v. **5.** abate, admix, allay, assuage, calm, lessen, mitigate, moderate, mollify, palliate, restrain, soften, soft-pedal (Inf.), soothe, tone down **6.** anneal, harden, strengthen, toughen

temperament **1.** bent, cast of mind, character, complexion, constitution, disposition, frame of mind, humour, make-up, mettle, nature, outlook, personality, quality, soul, spirit, stamp, temper, tendencies, tendency **2.** anger, excitability, explosiveness, hot-headedness, impatience, mercurialness, moodiness, moods, petulance, volatility

temperamental **1.** capricious, easily

upset, emotional, erratic, excitable, explosive, fiery, highly strung, hot-headed, hypersensitive, impatient, irritable, mercurial, moody, neurotic, passionate, petulant, sensitive, touchy, volatile **2.** congenital, constitutional, inborn, ingrained, inherent, innate, natural **3.** erratic, inconsistent, undependable, unpredictable, unreliable

temperance **1.** continence, discretion, forbearance, moderation, restraint, self-control, self-discipline, self-restraint **2.** abstemiousness, abstinence, prohibition, sobriety, teetotalism

temperate **1.** agreeable, balmy, calm, clement, cool, fair, gentle, mild, moderate, pleasant, soft **2.** calm, composed, dispassionate, equable, even-tempered, mild, moderate, reasonable, self-controlled, self-restrained, sensible, stable **3.** abstemious, abstinent, continent, moderate, sober

tempest **1.** cyclone, gale, hurricane, squall, storm, tornado, typhoon **2.** commotion, disturbance, ferment, furore, storm, tumult, upheaval, uproar

tempestuous **1.** agitated, blustery, boisterous, breezy, gusty, raging, squally, stormy, turbulent, windy **2.** agitated, boisterous, emotional, excited, feverish, furious, heated, hysterical, impassioned, intense, passionate, stormy, turbulent, uncontrolled, violent, wild

temple church, holy place, place of worship, sanctuary, shrine

temporarily briefly, fleetingly, for a little while, for a moment, for a short time, for a short while, for the moment, for the time being, momentarily, pro tem

temporary brief, ephemeral, evanescent, fleeting, fugacious, fugitive, here today and gone tomorrow, impermanent, interim, momentary, passing, pro tem, pro tempore, provisional, short-lived, transient, transitory

tempt **1.** allure, appeal to, attract, coax, decoy, draw, entice, inveigle, invite, lead on, lure, make one's mouth water, seduce, tantalize, whet the appetite of, woo **2.** bait, dare, fly in the face of, provoke, risk, test, try

the state of being tempted. **2.** a person or thing that tempts.

tempting ('tɛmptɪŋ) *adj.* attractive or inviting: *a tempting meal.* —**'temptingly** *adv.*

tempus fugit *Latin.* ('tɛmpəs 'fjuːdʒɪt) time flies.

ten (tɛn) *n.* **1.** the cardinal number that is the sum of nine and one. It is the base of the decimal number system and the base of the common logarithm. **2.** a numeral in, X, etc., representing this number. **3.** something representing or consisting of ten units. **4.** Also called: **ten o'clock.** ten hours after noon or midnight. ~*determiner.* **5.** amounting to ten. ~Related adj.: **decimal.** —**tenth** *adj.*

ten. *Music. abbrev. for:* **1.** tenor. **2.** tenuto.

tenable ('tɛnəb°l) *adj.* able to be upheld, believed, maintained, or defended. —**,tena'bility** *or* **'tenableness** *n.* —**'tenably** *adv.*

tenacious (tɪ'neɪʃəs) *adj.* **1.** holding firmly: *a tenacious grip.* **2.** retentive: *a tenacious memory.* **3.** stubborn or persistent. **4.** holding together firmly; cohesive. **5.** tending to stick or adhere. —**te'naciously** *adv.* —**te'naciousness** *or* **tenacity** (tɪ'næsɪtɪ) *n.*

tenancy ('tɛnənsɪ) *n., pl.* **-cies.** **1.** the temporary possession or holding by a tenant of lands or property owned by another. **2.** the period of holding or occupying such property. **3.** the period of holding office, a position, etc.

tenant ('tɛnənt) *n.* **1.** a person who holds, occupies, or possesses land or property, esp. from a landlord. **2.** a person who has the use of a house, etc., subject to the payment of rent. **3.** any holder or occupant. ~*vb.* **4.** (*tr.*) to hold as a tenant. —**'tenantable** *adj.* —**'tenantless** *adj.*

tenant farmer *n.* a person who farms land rented from another, the rent usually taking the form of crops or livestock.

tenantry ('tɛnəntrɪ) *n.* **1.** tenants collectively. **2.** the status or condition of being a tenant.

tench (tɛntʃ) *n.* a European freshwater game fish of the carp family.

Ten Commandments *pl. n.* **the.** *Old Testament.* the commandments summarizing the basic obligations of man towards God and his fellow-men, delivered to Moses on Mount Sinai engraved on two tables of stone (Exodus 20:1–17).

tend¹ (tɛnd) *vb.* (when *intr.*, usually foll. by *to* or *towards*) **1.** (when *tr.*, *takes an infinitive*) to have a general disposition (to do something); be inclined: *children tend to prefer sweets to meat.* **2.** (*intr.*) to have or be an influence (towards a specific result). **3.** (*intr.*) to go or move (in a particular direction): *to tend to the south.*

tend² (tɛnd) *vb.* **1.** (*tr.*) to care for. **2.** (when *intr.*, often

foll. by *on* or *to*) to attend (to). **3.** (*tr.*) to handle or control. **4.** (*intr.*; often foll. by *to*) *Inf.*, chiefly *U.S.* to pay attention.

tendency ('tɛndənsɪ) *n., pl.* **-cies.** **1.** (often foll. by *to*) an inclination, predisposition, propensity, or leaning. **2.** the general course, purport, or drift of something, esp. a written work.

tendentious *or* **tendencious** (tɛn'dɛnʃəs) *adj.* having or showing an intentional tendency or bias, esp. a controversial one. —**ten'dentiously** *or* **ten'denciously** *adv.* —**ten'dentiousness** *or* **ten'denciousness** *n.*

tender¹ ('tɛndə) *adj.* **1.** easily broken, cut, or crushed; soft. **2.** easily damaged; vulnerable or sensitive: *at a tender age.* **3.** having or expressing warm feelings. **4.** kind or sympathetic: *a tender heart.* **5.** arousing warm feelings; touching. **6.** gentle and delicate: *a tender breeze.* **7.** requiring care in handling: *a tender question.* **8.** painful or sore. **9.** sensitive to moral or spiritual feelings. **10.** (*postpositive;* foll. by *of*) protective: *tender of one's emotions.* —**'tenderly** *adv.* —**'tenderness** *n.*

tender² ('tɛndə) *vb.* (*tr.*) **1.** to give, present, or offer: *to tender a bid.* **2.** *Law.* to offer (money or goods) in settlement of a debt or claim. ~*n.* **3.** the act or an instance of tendering; offer. **4.** a formal offer to supply specified goods or services at a stated cost or rate. **5.** something, esp. money, used as an official medium of payment: *legal tender.* —**'tenderer** *n.*

tender³ ('tɛndə) *n.* **1.** a small boat towed or carried by a ship. **2.** a vehicle drawn behind a steam locomotive to carry the fuel and water. **3.** a person who tends.

tenderfoot ('tɛndə,fʊt) *n., pl.* **-foots** *or* **-feet.** **1.** a newcomer, esp. to the mines or ranches of the southwestern U.S. **2.** (formerly) a beginner in the Scouts.

tenderize *or* **-ise** ('tɛndə,raɪz) *vb.* (*tr.*) to make (meat) tender, as by pounding it or adding a substance to break down the fibres. —**'tender,izer** *or* **-,iser** *n.*

tenderloin ('tɛndə,lɔɪn) *n.* a tender cut of pork or other meat from between the sirloin and ribs.

tendon ('tɛndən) *n.* a cord or band of tough tissue that attaches a muscle to a bone or some other part; sinew.

tendril ('tɛndrɪl) *n.* a threadlike leaf or stem that attaches climbing plants to a support by twining or adhering.

tenebrous ('tɛnəbrəs) *or* **tenebrious** (tə'nɛbrɪəs) *adj.* gloomy, shadowy, or dark.

tenement ('tɛnəmənt) *n.* **1.** Also called: **tenement building.** a large building divided into rooms or flats. **2.** a dwelling place or residence. **3.** *Chiefly Brit.* a room or flat for rent. **4.** *Property law.* any form of permanent property, such as land, dwellings, offices, etc. —**tenemental** (,tɛnə'mɛnt°l) *adj.*

tenet ('tɛnɪt, 'tiːnɪt) *n.* a belief, opinion, or dogma.

tenfold ('tɛn,fəʊld) *adj.* **1.** equal to or having 10 times

THESAURUS

temptation allurement, appeal, attraction, attractiveness, bait, blandishments, coaxing, come-on (*Inf.*), decoy, draw, enticement, inducement, invitation, lure, pull, seduction, snare, tantalization

tempting alluring, appetizing, attractive, enticing, inviting, mouthwatering, seductive, tantalizing

tenable arguable, believable, defendable, defensible, justifiable, maintainable, plausible, rational, reasonable, sound, viable

tenacious 1. clinging, fast, firm, forceful, iron, strong, tight, unshakable 2. retentive, unforgetful 3. adamant, determined, dogged, firm, inflexible, intransigent, obdurate, obstinate, persistent, pertinacious, resolute, staunch, steadfast, strong-willed, stubborn, sure, unswerving, unyielding 4. coherent, cohesive, solid, strong, tough 5. adhesive, clinging, gluey, glutinous, mucilaginous, sticky

tenacity 1. fastness, firmness, force, forcefulness, power, strength 2. firm grasp, retention, retentiveness 3. application, determination, diligence, doggedness, firmness, inflexibility, intransigence, obduracy, obstinacy, perseverance, persistence, pertinacity, resoluteness, resolution, resolve, staunchness, steadfastness, strength of purpose, strength of will, stubbornness 4. coherence, cohesiveness, solidity, solidness, strength,

toughness 5. adhesiveness, clinginess, stickiness

tenancy 1. holding, lease, occupancy, occupation, possession, renting, residence 2. incumbency, period of office, tenure, time in office

tenant holder, inhabitant, leaseholder, lessee, occupant, occupier, renter, resident

tend¹ 1. be apt, be biased, be disposed, be inclined, be liable, be likely, gravitate, have a leaning, have an inclination, have a tendency, incline, lean, trend 2. aim, bear, be conducive, conduce, contribute, go, head, influence, lead, make for, move, point

tend² attend, care for, cater to, control, cultivate, feed, guard, handle, keep, keep an eye on, look after, maintain, manage, minister to, nurse, nurture, protect, see to, serve, take care of, wait on, watch, watch over

tendency 1. bent, disposition, inclination, leaning, liability, partiality, penchant, predilection, predisposition, proclivity, proneness, propensity, readiness, susceptibility 2. bearing, bias, course, direction, drift, drive, heading, movement, purport, tenor, trend, turning

tender¹ 1. breakable, delicate, feeble, fragile, frail, soft, weak 2. callow, green, immature, impressionable, inexperienced, new, raw, sensitive, unripe, vulnerable, wet behind the ears (*Inf.*), young, youthful 3. affec-

tionate, amorous, benevolent, caring, compassionate, considerate, fond, gentle, humane, kind, loving, merciful, pitiful, sentimental, softhearted, sympathetic, tenderhearted, warm, warm-hearted 4. emotional, evocative, moving, poignant, romantic, touching 5. complicated, dangerous, difficult, risky, sensitive, ticklish, touchy, tricky 6. aching, acute, bruised, inflamed, irritated, painful, raw, sensitive, smarting, sore

tender² v. 1. extend, give, hand in, offer, present, proffer, propose, put forward, submit, suggest, volunteer ~n. 2. bid, estimate, offer, proffer, proposal, submission, suggestion 3. currency, medium, money, payment, specie

tenderness 1. delicateness, feebleness, fragility, frailness, sensitiveness, sensitivity, softness, vulnerability, weakness 2. callowness, greenness, immaturity, impressionableness, inexperience, newness, rawness, sensitivity, vulnerability, youth, youthfulness 3. affection, amorousness, attachment, benevolence, care, compassion, consideration, devotion, fondness, gentleness, humaneness, humanity, kindness, liking, love, mercy, pity, sentimentality, softheartedness, sympathy, tenderheartedness, warm-heartedness, warmth 4. ache, aching, bruising, inflammation, irritation, pain, painfulness, rawness, sensitiveness, sensitivity, smart, soreness

as many or as much. **2.** composed of 10 parts. ~*adv.*
3. by or up to 10 times as many or as much.

ten-gallon hat *n.* (in the U.S.) a cowboy's broad-brimmed felt hat with a very high crown.

tenner ('tɛnə) *n. Inf.* **1.** *Brit.* **a.** a ten-pound note. **b.** the sum of ten pounds. **2.** *U.S.* a ten-dollar bill.

tennis ('tɛnɪs) *n.* **a.** a racket game played between two players or pairs of players who hit a ball to and fro over a net on a rectangular court of grass, asphalt, clay, etc. See also **lawn tennis, real tennis, table tennis. b.** (*as modifier*): *tennis court; tennis racket.*

tennis elbow *n.* inflammation of the elbow caused by exertion in playing tennis, etc.

tenon ('tɛnən) *n.* **1.** the projecting end of a piece of wood formed to fit into a corresponding mortise in another piece. ~*vb.* (*tr.*) **2.** to form a tenon on (a piece of wood). **3.** to join with a tenon and mortise. —'**tenoner** *n.*

tenon saw *n.* a small fine-toothed saw with a strong back, used esp. for cutting tenons.

tenor ('tɛnə) *n.* **1.** *Music.* **a.** the male voice intermediate between alto and baritone. **b.** a singer with such a voice. **c.** a saxophone, horn, etc., intermediate between the alto and baritone or bass. **2.** general drift of thought; purpose. **3.** a settled course of progress. **4.** *Arch.* general tendency. **5.** *Law.* **a.** the exact words of a deed, etc. **b.** an exact copy.

tenpin bowling ('tɛn,pɪn) *n.* a bowling game in which bowls are rolled down a lane to knock over the ten target pins. Also called (esp. U.S.): **tenpins.**

tense[1] (tɛns) *adj.* **1.** stretched or stressed tightly; taut or rigid. **2.** under mental or emotional strain. **3.** producing mental or emotional strain: *a tense day.* **4.** *Phonetics.* pronounced with considerable muscular effort, as the vowel (i:) in "beam". ~*vb.* (often foll. by *up*) **5.** to make or become tense. —'**tensely** *adv.* —'**tenseness** *n.*

tense[2] (tɛns) *n. Grammar.* a category of the verb or verbal inflections, such as present, past, and future, that expresses the temporal relations between what is reported in a sentence and the time of its utterance. —'**tenseless** *adj.*

tensile ('tɛnsaɪl) *adj.* **1.** of or relating to tension. **2.** sufficiently ductile to be stretched or drawn out. —**tensility** (tɛn'sɪlɪtɪ) *or* '**tensileness** *n.*

tensile strength *n.* a measure of the ability of a material to withstand a longitudinal stress, expressed as the greatest stress that the material can stand without breaking.

tension ('tɛnʃən) *n.* **1.** the act of stretching or the state or degree of being stretched. **2.** mental or emotional strain; stress. **3.** a situation or condition of hostility, suspense, or uneasiness. **4.** *Physics.* a force that tends to produce an elongation of a body or structure. **5.** *Physics.* voltage, electromotive force, or potential difference. **6.** a device for regulating the tension in a part, string, thread, etc., as in a sewing machine. —'**tensional** *adj.* —'**tensionless** *adj.*

tent (tɛnt) *n.* **1.** a portable shelter of canvas, plastic, etc. supported on poles and fastened to the ground by pegs and ropes. **2.** something resembling this in function or shape. ~*vb.* **3.** (*intr.*) to camp in a tent. **4.** (*tr.*) to cover with or as if with a tent or tents. **5.** (*tr.*) to provide with a tent as shelter. —'**tented** *adj.* —'**tentage** *n.*

tentacle ('tɛntəkəl) *n.* **1.** any of various elongated flexible organs that occur near the mouth in many invertebrates and are used for feeding, grasping, etc. **2.** any of the hairs on the leaf of an insectivorous plant that are used to capture prey. —'**tentacled** *adj.* —**tentacular** (tɛn'tækjʊlə) *adj.*

tentative ('tɛntətɪv) *adj.* **1.** provisional or experimental. **2.** hesitant, uncertain, or cautious. —'**tentatively**

adv. —'**tentativeness** *n.*

tenter ('tɛntə) *n.* **1.** a frame on which cloth is stretched in order that it may retain its shape while drying. **2.** a person who stretches cloth on a tenter. ~*vb.* **3.** (*tr.*) to stretch (cloth) on a tenter.

tenterhook ('tɛntə,hʊk) *n.* **1.** one of a series of hooks used to hold cloth on a tenter. **2. on tenterhooks.** in a state of tension or suspense.

tent stitch *n.* another term for **petit point.**

tenuous ('tɛnjʊəs) *adj.* **1.** insignificant or flimsy: *a tenuous argument.* **2.** slim, fine, or delicate: *a tenuous thread.* **3.** diluted or rarefied in consistency or density: *a tenuous fluid.* —**tenuity** (tɛ'njuɪtɪ) *n.* —'**tenuously** *adv.* —'**tenuousness** *n.*

tenure ('tɛnjʊə, 'tɛnjə) *n.* **1.** the possession or holding of an office or position. **2.** the length of time an office, position, etc., lasts. **3.** *U.S.* the improved security status of a person after having been in the employ of the same company or institution for a specified period. **4. a.** the holding of property, esp. realty, in return for services rendered, etc. **b.** the duration of such holding. —**ten'urial** *adj.*

tenuto (tɪ'njuːtəʊ) *adj., adv. Music.* (of a note) to be held for or beyond its full time value.

tepee *or* **teepee** ('tiːpiː) *n.* a cone-shaped tent of animal skins used by American Indians.

tepid ('tɛpɪd) *adj.* **1.** slightly warm; lukewarm. **2.** relatively unenthusiastic or apathetic. —**tepidity** (tɛ'pɪdɪtɪ) *or* '**tepidness** *n.* —'**tepidly** *adv.*

tequila (tɪ'kiːlə) *n.* **1.** a spirit that is distilled in Mexico from an agave plant and forms the basis of many mixed drinks. **2.** the plant from which this drink is made.

ter. *abbrev. for:* **1.** terrace. **2.** territory.

ter- *combining form.* three, third, or three times.

terbium ('tɜːbɪəm) *n.* a soft malleable silvery-grey element of the lanthanide series of metals. Symbol: Tb; atomic no.: 65; atomic wt.: 158.925. —'**terbic** *adj.*

tercel ('tɜːsəl) *or* **tiercel** *n.* a male falcon or hawk, esp. as used in falconry.

tercentenary (,tɜːsɛn'tiːnərɪ) *or* **tercentennial** *adj.* **1.** of a period of 300 years. **2.** of a 300th anniversary. ~*n.,* **-tenaries** *or* **-tennials. 3.** an anniversary of 300 years.

tercet ('tɜːsɪt, tɜː'sɛt) *n.* a group of three lines of verse that rhyme together or are connected by rhyme with adjacent groups of three lines.

teredo (tɛ'riːdəʊ) *n., pl.* **-dos** *or* **-dines** (-dɪ,niːz). any of a genus of marine bivalve molluscs.

tergiversate ('tɜːdʒɪvə,seɪt) *vb.* (*intr.*) **1.** to change sides or loyalties. **2.** to be evasive or ambiguous. —,**tergiver'sation** *n.* —'**tergiver,sator** *n.*

term (tɜːm) *n.* **1.** a name, expression, or word used for some particular thing, esp. in a specialized field of knowledge: *a medical term.* **2.** any word or expression. **3.** a limited period of time: *a prison term.* **4.** any of the divisions of the academic year during which a school, college, etc., is in session. **5.** a point in time determined for an event or for the end of a period. **6.** the period at which childbirth is imminent. **7.** *Law.* **a.** an estate or interest in land limited to run for a specified period. **b.** the duration of an estate, etc. **c.** a period of time during which sessions of courts of law are held. **d.** time allowed to a debtor to settle. **8.** *Maths.* any distinct quantity making up a fraction or proportion, or contained in a polynomial, sequence, series, etc. **9.** *Logic.* **a.** the word or phrase that forms either the subject or predicate of a proposition. **b.** any of the three subjects or predicates occurring in a syllogism. **10.** *Archit.* a sculptured post, esp. one in the form of an armless bust or an animal on the top of a square pillar. ~*vb.* **11.** (*tr.*) to designate;

THESAURUS

tense *adj.* **1.** rigid, strained, stretched, taut, tight **2.** anxious, apprehensive, edgy, fidgety, jittery (*Inf.*), jumpy, keyed up, nervous, on edge, overwrought, restless, strained, strung up (*Inf.*), under pressure, uptight (*Sl.*), wound up (*Inf.*), wrought up **3.** exciting, moving, nerve-racking, stressful, worrying ~*v.* **4.** brace, flex, strain, stretch, tauten, tighten

tension 1. pressure, rigidity, stiffness, straining, stress, stretching, tautness, tightness **2.** anxiety, apprehension, edginess, hostility, ill feeling, nervousness, pressure, rest-

lessness, strain, stress, suspense, the jitters (*Inf.*), unease

tentative 1. conjectural, experimental, indefinite, provisional, speculative, unconfirmed, unsettled **2.** backward, cautious, diffident, doubtful, faltering, hesitant, timid, uncertain, undecided, unsure

tenuous 1. doubtful, dubious, flimsy, insignificant, insubstantial, nebulous, questionable, shaky, sketchy, slight, weak **2.** attenuated, delicate, fine, gossamer, slim

tepid 1. lukewarm, slightly warm, warmish

2. apathetic, cool, half-hearted, indifferent, lukewarm, unenthusiastic

term *n.* **1.** appellation, denomination, designation, expression, locution, name, phrase, title, word **2.** duration, interval, period, season, space, span, spell, time, while **3.** course, session **4.** bound, boundary, close, conclusion, confine, culmination, end, finish, fruition, limit, terminus ~*v.* **5.** call, denominate, designate, dub, entitle, label, name, style

call: *he was termed a thief.* —**'termly** *adj., adv.*

termagant (ˈtɜːməgənt) *n. Rare.* a shrewish woman; scold.

terminable (ˈtɜːmɪnəbəl) *adj.* 1. able to be terminated. 2. terminating after a specific period or event. —ˌtermina'bility *or* 'terminableness *n.* —'terminably *adv.*

terminal (ˈtɜːmɪnəl) *adj.* 1. of, being, or situated at an end, terminus, or boundary. 2. of or occurring after or in a term: *terminal examinations.* 3. (of a disease) terminating in death. 4. of or relating to the storage or delivery of freight at a warehouse. ~*n.* 5. a terminating point, part, or place. 6. **a.** a point at which current enters or leaves an electrical device, such as a battery or a circuit. **b.** a conductor by which current enters or leaves at such a point. 7. *Computers.* a device having input/output links with a computer. 8. *Archit.* **a.** an ornamental carving at the end of a structure. **b.** another name for **term** (sense 10). 9. **a.** a point or station at the end of the line of a railway or at an airport, serving as an important access point for passengers or freight. **b.** a less common name for **terminus** (sense 2). —'terminally *adv.*

terminal velocity *n.* 1. the constant maximum velocity reached by a body falling under gravity through a fluid, esp. the atmosphere. 2. the velocity of a missile or projectile when it reaches its target. 3. the maximum velocity attained by a rocket, missile, or shell flying in a parabolic flight path. 4. the maximum velocity that an aircraft can attain.

terminate (ˈtɜːmɪˌneɪt) *vb.* (when *intr.* often foll. by *in* or *with*) to form, be, or put an end to; conclude. —'terminative *adj.* —'termiˌnator *n.*

termination (ˌtɜːmɪ'neɪʃən) *n.* 1. the act of terminating or the state of being terminated. 2. something that terminates. 3. a final result. —ˌtermi'national *adj.*

terminology (ˌtɜːmɪ'nɒlədʒɪ) *n., pl.* -gies. 1. the body of specialized words relating to a particular subject. 2. the study of terms. —**terminological** (ˌtɜːmɪnə'lɒdʒɪkəl) *adj.* —ˌtermi'nologist *n.*

terminus (ˈtɜːmɪnəs) *n., pl.* -ni (-naɪ) *or* -nuses. 1. the last or final part or point. 2. either end of a railway, bus route, etc., or a station or town at such a point. 3. a goal aimed for. 4. a boundary or boundary marker. 5. *Archit.* another name for **term** (sense 10).

termite (ˈtɜːmaɪt) *n.* any of an order of whitish ant-like social insects of warm and tropical regions. Some species feed on wood, causing damage to buildings, trees, etc. —**termitic** (tɜː'mɪtɪk) *adj.*

terms (tɜːmz) *pl. n.* 1. (usually specified prenominally) the actual language or mode of presentation used: *he described the project in loose terms.* 2. conditions of an agreement. 3. a sum of money paid for a service. 4. (usually preceded by *on*) mutual relationship or standing: *they are on affectionate terms.* 5. **bring to terms.** to cause to agree or submit. 6. **in terms of.** as expressed by; regarding: *in terms of money he was no better off.* 7. **come to terms.** to reach acceptance or agreement.

tern (tɜːn) *n.* any of several aquatic birds related to the gulls, having a forked tail, long narrow wings, and a typi-

cally black-and-white plumage.

ternary (ˈtɜːnərɪ) *adj.* 1. consisting of three or groups of three. 2. *Maths.* (of a number system) to the base three.

Terpsichore (tɜːp'sɪkərɪ) *n.* the Muse of the dance and of choral song.

Terpsichorean (ˌtɜːpsɪkə'rɪən, -'kɔːrɪən) *Often used facetiously.* ~*adj. also* **Terpsichoreal.** 1. of or relating to dancing. ~*n.* 2. a dancer.

terrace (ˈtɛrəs) *n.* 1. a horizontal flat area of ground, often one of a series in a slope. 2. **a.** a row of houses, usually identical and having common dividing walls, or the street onto which they face. **b.** (*cap. when part of a street name*): *Grosvenor Terrace.* 3. a paved area alongside a building, serving partly as a garden. 4. a balcony or patio. 5. the flat roof of a house built in a Spanish or Oriental style. 6. a flat area bounded by a short steep slope formed by the down-cutting of a river or by erosion. 7. (*usually pl.*) unroofed tiers around a football pitch on which the spectators stand. ~*vb.* (*tr.*) 8. to make into or provide with a terrace or terraces.

terraced house *n. Brit.* a house that is part of a terrace. U.S. name: **row house.**

terra cotta (ˈtɛrə 'kɒtə) *n.* 1. a hard unglazed brownish-red earthenware, or the clay from which it is made. 2. something made of terra cotta, such as a sculpture. 3. a strong reddish-brown to brownish-orange colour. —'terra-'cotta *adj.*

terra firma (ˈfɜːmə) *n.* the solid earth; firm ground.

terrain (ˈtɛreɪn) *n.* a piece of ground, esp. with reference to its physical character or military potential: *a rocky terrain.*

terra incognita *Latin.* (ˈtɛrə ɪn'kɒgnɪtə) *n.* an unexplored or unknown land, region, or area.

terrapin (ˈtɛrəpɪn) *n.* any of various web-footed reptiles that live on land and in fresh water and feed on small aquatic animals. Also called: **water tortoise.**

terrarium (tɛ'rɛərɪəm) *n., pl.* -rariums *or* -raria (-'rɛərɪə). a closed container in which small terrestrial animals or plants are kept.

terrazzo (tɛ'rætsəʊ) *n.* a floor made by setting marble chips into a layer of mortar and polishing the surface.

terrestrial (tə'rɛstrɪəl) *adj.* 1. of the earth. 2. of the land as opposed to the sea or air. 3. (of animals and plants) living or growing on the land. 4. earthly, worldly, or mundane. ~*n.* 5. an inhabitant of the earth. —ter'restrially *adv.*

terrible (ˈtɛrəbəl) *adj.* 1. very serious or extreme. 2. *Inf.* of poor quality; unpleasant or bad. 3. causing terror. 4. causing awe. —'terribleness *n.* —'terribly *adv.*

terrier (ˈtɛrɪə) *n.* any of several usually small, active, and short-bodied breeds of dog, originally trained to hunt animals living underground.

terrific (tə'rɪfɪk) *adj.* 1. very great or intense. 2. *Inf.* very good; excellent. 3. very frightening. —ter'rifically *adv.*

terrify (ˈtɛrɪˌfaɪ) *vb.* -fying, -fied. (*tr.*) to inspire fear or dread in; frighten greatly. —'terriˌfier *n.* —'terriˌfyingly *adv.*

THESAURUS

terminal *adj.* 1. bounding, concluding, extreme, final, last, limiting, ultimate, utmost 2. deadly, fatal, incurable, killing, lethal, mortal ~*n.* 3. boundary, end, extremity, limit, termination, terminus 4. depot, end of the line, station, terminus

terminate abort, bring *or* come to an end, cease, close, complete, conclude, cut off, discontinue, end, expire, finish, issue, lapse, put an end to, result, run out, stop, wind up

termination abortion, cessation, close, completion, conclusion, consequence, cut-off point, discontinuation, effect, end, ending, expiry, finale, finis, finish, issue, result, wind-up (*Inf.*)

terminology argot, cant, jargon, language, lingo (*Inf.*), nomenclature, patois, phraseology, terms, vocabulary

terminus 1. boundary, close, end, extremity, final point, goal, limit, target, termination 2. depot, end of the line, garage, last stop, station

terms 1. language, manner of speaking,

phraseology, terminology 2. conditions, particulars, premises (*Law*), provisions, provisos, qualifications, specifications, stipulations 3. charges, fee, payment, price, rates 4. footing, position, relations, relationship, standing, status 5. **come to terms** be reconciled, come to an agreement, come to an understanding, conclude agreement, learn to live with, reach acceptance, reach agreement

terrible 1. bad, dangerous, desperate, extreme, serious, severe 2. *Inf.* abhorrent, awful, bad, beastly (*Inf.*), dire, dreadful, duff (*Brit. sl.*), foul, frightful, hateful, hideous, loathsome, obnoxious, odious, offensive, poor, repulsive, revolting, rotten (*Inf.*), unpleasant, vile 3. appalling, awful, dread, dreaded, dreadful, fearful, frightful, gruesome, harrowing, horrendous, horrible, horrid, horrifying, monstrous, shocking

terribly awfully (*Inf.*), decidedly, desperately, exceedingly, extremely, gravely, greatly, much, seriously, thoroughly, very

terrific 1. awesome, awful, dreadful, enor-

mous, excessive, extreme, fearful, fierce, gigantic, great, harsh, horrific, huge, intense, monstrous, severe, terrible, tremendous 2. *Inf.* ace (*Inf.*), amazing, breathtaking, excellent, fabulous (*Inf.*), fantastic (*Inf.*), fine, great (*Inf.*), magnificent, marvellous, outstanding, sensational (*Inf.*), smashing (*Inf.*), stupendous, super (*Inf.*), superb, very good, wonderful

terrified alarmed, appalled, awed, dismayed, frightened, frightened out of one's wits, horrified, horror-struck, intimidated, panic-stricken, petrified, scared, scared stiff, scared to death, shocked, terror-stricken

terrify alarm, appal, awe, dismay, fill with terror, frighten, frighten out of one's wits, horrify, intimidate, make one's blood run cold, make one's flesh creep, make one's hair stand on end, petrify, put the fear of God into, scare, scare to death, shock, terrorize

terrine (tɛˈriːn) n. 1. an oval earthenware cooking dish with a tightly fitting lid used for patés, etc. 2. the food cooked or served in such a dish, esp. paté.

territorial (ˌtɛrɪˈtɔːrɪəl) adj. 1. of or relating to a territory or territories. 2. restricted to or owned by a particular territory. 3. local or regional. 4. Zool. establishing and defending a territory. 5. pertaining to a territorial army, providing a reserve of trained men for use in emergency. —ˌterriˈtoriˈality n. —ˌterriˈtorially adv.

Territorial (ˌtɛrɪˈtɔːrɪəl) n. a member of a territorial army.

Territorial Army n. (in Britain) a standing reserve army originally organized between 1907 and 1908. Full name: **Territorial and Volunteer Reserve.**

territorial waters pl. n. the waters over which a nation exercises jurisdiction and control.

territory (ˈtɛrɪtərɪ) n., pl. -ries. 1. any tract of land; district. 2. the geographical domain under the jurisdiction of a political unit, esp. of a sovereign state. 3. the district for which an agent, etc., is responsible. 4. an area inhabited and defended by an animal or a pair of animals. 5. an area of knowledge. 6. (in football, hockey, etc.) the area defended by a team. 7. (often cap.) a region of a country, esp. of a federal state, that enjoys less autonomy and a lower status than most constituent parts of the state. 8. (often cap.) a protectorate or other dependency of a country.

terror (ˈtɛrə) n. 1. great fear, panic, or dread. 2. a person or thing that inspires great dread. 3. Inf. a troublesome person or thing, esp. a child. 4. terrorism. —ˈterrorful adj. —ˈterrorless adj.

terrorism (ˈtɛrəˌrɪzəm) n. 1. the act of terrorizing. 2. the systematic use of violence and intimidation to achieve some goal. 3. the state of being terrorized. 4. government or opposition to government by means of terror. —ˈterrorist n., adj.

terrorize or **-ise** (ˈtɛrəˌraɪz) vb. (tr.) 1. to coerce or control by violence, fear, threats, etc. 2. to inspire with dread; terrify. —ˌterroriˈzation or -iˈsation n. —ˈterrorˌizer or -ˌiser n.

terry (ˈtɛrɪ) n., pl. -ries. 1. an uncut loop in the pile of towelling or a similar fabric. 2. a fabric with such a pile.

terse (tɜːs) adj. 1. neatly brief and concise. 2. curt; abrupt. —ˈtersely adv. —ˈterseness n.

tertiary (ˈtɜːʃərɪ) adj. 1. third in degree, order, etc. 2. (of an industry) involving services as opposed to extraction or manufacture, such as transport, finance, etc. 3. R.C. Church. of or relating to a Third Order. 4. Chem. a. (of an organic compound) having a functional group attached to a carbon atom that is attached to three other groups. b. (of an amine) having three organic groups attached to a nitrogen atom. c. (of a salt) derived from a tribasic acid by replacement of all its acidic hydrogen atoms with metal atoms or electropositive groups. 5. Ornithol., rare. of or designating any of the small flight feathers attached to the part of the humerus nearest to the body. ~n., pl. -tiaries. 6. Ornithol., rare. any of the tertiary feathers. 7. R.C. Church. a member of a Third Order.

Tertiary (ˈtɜːʃərɪ) adj. 1. of, denoting, or formed in the first period of the Cenozoic era. ~n. 2. the. the Tertiary period or rock system.

Terylene (ˈtɛrəˌliːn) n. Trademark. a synthetic polyester fibre or fabric. U.S. name (trademark): **Dacron.**

tessellate (ˈtɛsɪˌleɪt) vb. 1. (tr.) to construct, pave, or inlay with a mosaic of small tiles. 2. (intr.) (of identical shapes) to fit together exactly.

tessera (ˈtɛsərə) n., pl. -serae (-səˌriː). 1. a small square tile of stone, glass, etc., used in mosaics. 2. a die, tally, etc., used in classical times, made of bone or wood. —ˈtesseral adj.

test¹ (tɛst) vb. 1. to ascertain (the worth, capability, or endurance) of (a person or thing) by subjection to certain examinations, etc.; try. 2. (often foll. by for) to carry out an examination on (a substance, material, or system) to indicate the presence of a substance or the possession of a property: to test food for arsenic. ~n. 3. a method, practice, or examination designed to test a person or thing. 4. a series of questions or problems designed to test a specific skill or knowledge. 5. a standard of judgment; criterion. 6. a. a chemical reaction or physical procedure for testing a substance, material, etc. b. a chemical reagent used in such a procedure. c. the result of the procedure or the evidence gained from it. 7. Sport. See test match. 8. Arch. a declaration of trust, loyalty, etc. 9. (modifier) performed as a test: test drive. —ˈtestable adj. —ˈtester n.

test² (tɛst) n. the hard outer covering of certain invertebrates and tunicates.

testa (ˈtɛstə) n., pl. -tae (-tiː). the hard outer layer of a seed.

testaceous (tɛˈsteɪʃəs) adj. Biol. 1. of or possessing a test or testa. 2. of the reddish-brown colour of terra cotta.

testament (ˈtɛstəmənt) n. 1. Law. a will (esp. in last will and testament). 2. a proof, attestation, or tribute. 3. a. a covenant instituted between God and man. b. a copy of either the Old or the New Testament, or of the complete Bible. —ˌtestaˈmental adj. —ˌtestaˈmentary adj.

Testament (ˈtɛstəmənt) n. 1. either of the two main parts of the Bible; the Old Testament or the New Testament. 2. the New Testament as distinct from the Old.

testate (ˈtɛsteɪt, ˈtɛstɪt) adj. 1. having left a legally valid will at death. ~n. 2. a person who dies testate. —**testacy** (ˈtɛstəsɪ) n.

testator (tɛˈsteɪtə) or (fem.) **testatrix** (tɛˈsteɪtrɪks) n. a person who makes a will, esp. one who dies testate.

test case n. a legal action that serves as a precedent in deciding similar succeeding cases.

testicle (ˈtɛstɪkəl) n. either of the two male reproductive glands, in most mammals enclosed within the scrotum, that produce spermatozoa. —**testicular** (tɛˈstɪkjʊlə) adj.

testify (ˈtɛstɪˌfaɪ) vb. -fying, -fied. 1. (when tr., may take a clause as object) to state (something) formally as a declaration of fact. 2. Law. to declare or give (evidence) under oath, esp. in court. 3. (when intr., often foll. by to) to be evidence (of); serve as witness (to). 4. (tr.) to declare or acknowledge openly. —ˌtestifiˈcation n. —ˈtestiˌfier n.

testimonial (ˌtɛstɪˈməʊnɪəl) n. 1. a recommendation of the character, ability, etc., of a person or of the quality of a product or service. 2. a formal statement of truth or fact. 3. a tribute given for services or achievements. ~adj. 4. of or relating to a testimony or testimonial.

testimony (ˈtɛstɪmənɪ) n., pl. -nies. 1. a declaration of truth or fact. 2. Law. evidence given by a witness, esp. in court under oath. 3. evidence testifying to something: her success was a testimony to her good luck. 4. Old Testament. the Ten Commandments.

testis (ˈtɛstɪs) n., pl. -tes (-tiːz). another word for **testicle.**

test match n. (in various sports, esp. cricket) any of a

THESAURUS

territory area, bailiwick, country, district, domain, land, province, region, sector, state, terrain, tract, zone

terror 1. alarm, anxiety, awe, consternation, dismay, dread, fear, fear and trembling, fright, horror, intimidation, panic, shock 2. bogeyman, bugbear, devil, fiend, monster, scourge

terrorize 1. browbeat, bully, coerce, intimidate, menace, oppress, strong-arm (Inf.), threaten 2. alarm, appal, awe, dismay, fill with terror, frighten, frighten out of one's wits, horrify, inspire panic in, intimidate, make one's blood run cold, make one's flesh creep, make one's hair stand on end, petrify, put the fear of God into, scare, scare to

death, shock, strike terror into, terrify

terse 1. aphoristic, brief, clipped, compact, concise, condensed, crisp, elliptical, epigrammatic, gnomic, incisive, laconic, neat, pithy, sententious, short, succinct, summary, to the point 2. abrupt, brusque, curt, short, snappy

test 1. v. analyse, assay, assess, check, examine, experiment, investigate, prove, put to the proof, put to the test, try, try out, verify 2. n. analysis, assessment, attempt, catechism, check, evaluation, examination, investigation, ordeal, probation, proof, trial

testament 1. last wishes, will 2. attestation, demonstration, earnest, evidence, ex-

emplification, proof, testimony, tribute, witness

testify affirm, assert, attest, bear witness, certify, corroborate, declare, depone (Scots Law), depose (Law), evince, give testimony, show, state, swear, vouch, witness

testimonial certificate, character, commendation, credential, endorsement, recommendation, reference, tribute

testimony 1. affidavit, affirmation, attestation, avowal, confirmation, corroboration, declaration, deposition, evidence, information, profession, statement, submission, witness 2. corroboration, demonstration, evidence, indication, manifestation, proof, support, verification

series of international matches.

testosterone (tɛ'stɒstə,rəʊn) n. a potent steroid hormone secreted mainly by the testes.

test paper n. 1. *Chem.* paper impregnated with an indicator for use in chemical tests. 2. a. the question sheet of a test. b. the paper completed by a test candidate.

test pilot n. a pilot who flies aircraft of new design to test their performance in the air.

test tube n. 1. a cylindrical round-bottomed glass tube open at one end: used in scientific experiments. 2. (*modifier*) made synthetically in, or as if in, a test tube: *a test-tube product.*

test-tube baby n. 1. a foetus that has developed from an ovum fertilized in an artificial womb. 2. a baby conceived by artificial insemination.

testy ('tɛstɪ) adj. -tier, -tiest. irritable or touchy. —'testily adv. —'testiness n.

tetanus ('tɛtənəs) n. 1. Also called: lockjaw. an acute infectious disease in which sustained muscular spasm, contraction, and convulsion are caused by the release of toxins from a bacterium. 2. *Physiol.* any tense contraction of a muscle. —'tetanal adj. —'teta,noid adj.

tetchy ('tɛtʃɪ) adj. tetchier, tetchiest. being or inclined to be cross, irritable, or touchy. —'tetchily adv. —'tetchiness n.

tête-à-tête (,teɪtɑ:'teɪt) n., pl. -têtes or -tête. 1. a. a private conversation between two people. b. (*as modifier*): *a tête-à-tête conversation.* 2. a small sofa for two people, esp. one that is S-shaped in plan so that the sitters are almost face to face. ~adv. 3. intimately; in private.

tether ('tɛðə) n. 1. a rope, chain, etc., by which an animal is tied to a particular spot. 2. the range of one's endurance, etc. 3. at the end of one's tether. distressed or exasperated to the limit of one's endurance. ~vb. 4. (*tr.*) to tie with or as if with a tether.

tetra- or before a vowel **tetr-** combining form. four: *tetrameter.*

tetrad ('tɛtræd) n. a group or series of four.

tetraethyl lead (,tɛtrə'i:θaɪl lɛd) n. a colourless oily insoluble liquid used in petrol to prevent knocking.

tetragon ('tɛtrə,gɒn) n. a less common name for quadrilateral.

tetrahedron (,tɛtrə'hi:drən) n., pl. -drons or -dra (-drə). a solid figure having four plane faces. A regular tetrahedron has faces that are equilateral triangles. —,tetra'hedral adj.

tetralogy (tɛ'trælədʒɪ) n., pl. -gies. a series of four related works, as in drama or opera.

tetrameter (tɛ'træmɪtə) n. *Prosody.* 1. a line of verse consisting of four metrical feet. 2. a verse composed of such lines.

Teut. abbrev. for Teuton(ic).

Teuton ('tju:tən) n. 1. a member of an ancient Germanic people from Jutland who migrated to S Gaul in the 2nd century B.C. 2. a member of any people speaking a Germanic language, esp. a German. ~adj. 3. Teutonic.

Teutonic (tju:'tɒnɪk) adj. 1. characteristic of or relating to the German people. 2. of the ancient Teutons. 3. (not used in linguistics) of or relating to the Germanic languages.

text (tɛkst) n. 1. the main body of a printed or written work as distinct from commentary, notes, illustrations, etc. 2. the words of something printed or written. 3. the original exact wording of a work as distinct from a revision or translation. 4. a short passage of the Bible used as a starting point for a sermon. 5. the topic or subject of a discussion or work. 6. short for textbook. 7. any novel, play, etc. prescribed as part of a course of study.

textbook ('tɛkst,bʊk) n. a book used as a standard source of information on a particular subject. —'text,bookish adj.

textile ('tɛkstaɪl) n. 1. any fabric or cloth, esp. woven. 2. raw material suitable to be made into cloth. ~adj. 3. of or relating to fabrics.

textual ('tɛkstjʊəl) adj. 1. of or relating to a text or texts. 2. based on a text. —'textually adv.

textualism ('tɛkstjʊə,lɪzəm) n. 1. doctrinaire adherence to a text, esp. of the Bible. 2. textual criticism, esp. of the Bible. —'textualist n., adj.

texture ('tɛkstʃə) n. 1. the surface of a material, esp. as perceived by the sense of touch. 2. the structure, appearance, and feel of a woven fabric. 3. the general structure and disposition of the constituent parts of something: *the texture of a cake.* 4. the distinctive character or quality of something: *the texture of life in America.* ~vb. 5. (*tr.*) to give a distinctive texture to. —'textural adj. —'texturally adv.

T.G.W.U. (in Britain) abbrev. for Transport and General Workers' Union.

Th the chemical symbol for thorium.

Th. abbrev. for Thursday.

Thai (taɪ) adj. 1. of Thailand, its people, or their language. ~n. 2. (*pl.* Thais or Thai) a native or inhabitant of Thailand. 3. the language of Thailand, sometimes classified as belonging to the Sino-Tibetan family.

thalidomide (θə'lɪdə,maɪd) n. a. a drug formerly used as a sedative and hypnotic but withdrawn from use when found to cause abnormalities in developing foetuses. b. (*as modifier*): *a thalidomide baby.*

thallium ('θælɪəm) n. a soft malleable highly toxic white metallic element. Symbol: Tl; atomic no.: 81; atomic wt.: 204.37.

than (ðæn; unstressed ðən) conj. (*coordinating*), prep. 1. used to introduce the second element of a comparison, the first element of which expresses difference: *shorter than you.* 2. used after adverbs such as *rather* or *sooner* to introduce a rejected alternative in an expression of preference: *rather than be imprisoned, I shall die.* 3. other than. besides; in addition to.

▷ **Usage.** In sentences such as *he does it far better than I,* *than* is usually regarded in careful usage as a conjunction governing an unexpressed verb: *he does it far better than I (do it).* The case of any pronoun therefore depends on whether it is the subject or the object of that unexpressed verb: *she likes him more than I (like him); she likes him more than (she likes) me.* However, in informal usage *than* is often treated as a preposition and any pronoun is therefore used in its objective form, so that *she likes him more than me* is ambiguous.

thane or **thegn** (θeɪn) n. 1. (in Anglo-Saxon England) a member of an aristocratic class who held land from the king or from another nobleman in return for certain services. 2. (in medieval Scotland) a person of rank holding land from the king. —**thanage** ('θeɪnɪdʒ) n.

thank (θæŋk) vb. (*tr.*) 1. to convey feelings of gratitude to. 2. to hold responsible: *he has his creditors to thank for his bankruptcy.*

thankful ('θæŋkfʊl) adj. grateful and appreciative. —'thankfully adv. —'thankfulness n.

thankless ('θæŋklɪs) adj. 1. receiving no thanks or appreciation. 2. ungrateful. —'thanklessly adv. —'thanklessness n.

thanks (θæŋks) pl. n. 1. an expression of appreciation or gratitude. 2. thanks to. because of: *thanks to him we lost the match.* ~interj. 3. *Inf.* an exclamation expressing gratitude or appreciation.

thanksgiving ('θæŋks,gɪvɪŋ) n. 1. the act of giving thanks. 2. a formal public expression of thanks to God.

that (ðæt; unstressed ðət) determiner. (*used before a sing.* n.) 1. a. used preceding a noun that has been mentioned or is understood: *that idea of yours.* b. (*as pronoun*): *don't eat that.* 2. a. used preceding a noun that denotes something more remote or removed: *that building over there is for sale.* b. (*as pronoun*): *that is John and this is his wife.* 3. used to refer to something that is familiar: *that old chap from across the street.* 4. and (all) that. *Inf.* everything connected with the subject mentioned: *he knows a lot about building and that.* 5. at that. (*completive-intensive*) additionally, all things con-

---

THESAURUS

text 1. body, contents, main body, matter 2. wording, words 3. *Bible* paragraph, passage, sentence, verse 4. argument, matter, motif, subject, theme, topic 5. reader, reference book, source, textbook

texture character, composition, consistency, constitution, fabric, feel, grain, make, quality, structure, surface, tissue, weave

thank express gratitude, say thank you, show gratitude, show one's appreciation

thankful appreciative, beholden, grateful, indebted, obliged, pleased, relieved

thankless 1. fruitless, unappreciated, unprofitable, unrequited, unrewarding, useless 2. inconsiderate, unappreciative, ungracious, ungrateful, unmindful, unthankful

thanks 1. acknowledgment, appreciation, credit, gratefulness, gratitude, recognition, thanksgiving 2. **thanks to** as a result of, because of, by reason of, due to, owing to, through

sidered, or nevertheless: *I might decide to go at that.* **6.** **like that. a.** effortlessly: *he gave me the answer just like that.* **b.** of such a nature, character, etc.: *he paid for all our tickets—he's like that.* **7. that is. a.** to be precise. **b.** in other words. **c.** for example. **8. that's that.** there is no more to be done, discussed, etc. **9. with** (*or* **at**) **that.** thereupon. *~conj.* (*subordinating*) **10.** used to introduce a noun clause: *I believe that you'll come.* **11.** used to introduce: **a.** a clause of purpose: *they fought that others might have peace.* **b.** a clause of result: *he laughed so hard that he cried.* **c.** a clause after an understood sentence expressing desire, indignation, or amazement: *oh, that I had never lived! ~adv.* **12.** used to reinforce the specification of a precise degree already mentioned: *go just that fast and you should be safe.* **13.** Also: **all that.** (*usually used with a negative*) *Inf.* (intensifier): *he wasn't that upset at the news.* **14.** *Brit. dialect.* (intensifier): *the cat was that weak after the fight.* *~pron.* **15.** used to introduce a restrictive relative clause: *the book that we want.* **16.** used to introduce a clause with the verb *to be* to emphasize the extent to which the preceding noun is applicable: *genius that she is, she outwitted the computer.*
▷ **Usage.** Precise stylists maintain a distinction between *that* and *which: that* is used as a relative pronoun in restrictive clauses and *which* in nonrestrictive clauses. In *the book that is on the table is mine,* the clause *that is on the table* is used to distinguish one particular book (the one on the table) from another or others (which may be anywhere, but not on the table). In *the book, which is on the table, is mine,* the *which* clause is merely descriptive or incidental. The more formal the level of language, the more important it is to preserve the distinction between the two relative pronouns; but in informal or colloquial usage, the words are often used interchangeably.

thatch (θætʃ) *n.* **1. a.** Also called: **thatching.** a roofing material that consists of straw, reed, etc. **b.** a roof made of such a material. **2.** anything resembling this, such as the hair of the head. **3.** Also called: **thatch palm.** any of various palms with leaves suitable for thatching. *~vb.* **4.** to cover with thatch. —**'thatcher** *n.*

thaw (θɔː) *vb.* **1.** to melt or cause to melt: *the snow thawed.* **2.** to become or cause to become unfrozen; defrost. **3.** to be the case that the ice or snow is melting: *it's thawing fast.* **4.** (*intr.*) to become more relaxed or friendly. *~n.* **5.** the act or process of thawing. **6.** a spell of relatively warm weather, causing snow or ice to melt. **7.** an increase in relaxation or friendliness.

Th.D. *abbrev. for* Doctor of Theology.

the[1] (*stressed or emphatic* ðiː; *unstressed before a consonant* ðə; *unstressed before a vowel* ðɪ) *determiner.* (*article*) **1.** used preceding a noun that has been previously specified: *the pain should disappear soon.* Cf. **a**[1]. **2.** used to indicate a particular person, object, etc.: *ask the man standing outside.* Cf. **a**[1]. **3.** used preceding certain nouns associated with one's culture, society, or community: *to go to the doctor; to listen to the news.* **4.** used preceding present participles and adjectives when they function as nouns: *the singing is awful.* **5.** used preceding titles and certain uniquely specific or proper nouns: *the United States; the Chairman.* **6.** used preceding a qualifying adjective or noun in certain names or titles: *Edward the First.* **7.** used preceding a noun to make it refer to its class generically: *the white seal is hunted for its fur.* **8.** used instead of *my, your, her,* etc., with parts of the body: *take me by the hand.* **9.** (*usually stressed*) the best, only, or most remarkable: *Harry's is the club in this town.* **10.** used with proper nouns when qualified: *written by the young Hardy.* **11.** another word for **per:** *fifty pence the pound.* **12.** Often facetious or derog. **my:** our: *the wife goes out on Thursdays.* **13.** used preceding a unit of time in phrases or titles indicating an outstanding person, event, etc.: *housewife of the year.*
the[2] (ðə, ðɪ) *adv.* **1.** (*often foll. by for*) used before comparative adjectives or adverbs for emphasis: *she looks the happier for her trip.* **2.** used correlatively before each of two comparative adjectives or adverbs to indi-

cate equality: *the sooner you come, the better; the more I see you, the more I love you.*

theatre *or* U.S. **theater** ('θɪətə) *n.* **1.** a building designed for the performance of plays, operas, etc. **2.** a large room or hall, usually with a raised platform and tiered seats for an audience. **3.** a room in a hospital equipped for surgical operations. **4.** plays regarded collectively as a form of art. **5. the theatre.** the world of actors, theatrical companies, etc. **6.** a setting for dramatic or important events. **7.** writing that is suitable for dramatic presentation: *a good piece of theatre.* **8.** *Austral. & N.Z.* the usual word for cinema. **9.** a major area of military activity. **10.** a circular or semicircular open-air building with tiers of seats.

theatrical (θɪ'ætrɪkəl) *adj.* **1.** of or relating to the theatre or dramatic performances. **2.** exaggerated and affected in manner or behaviour; histrionic. —**the,atri'cality** *or* **the'atricalness** *n.* —**the'atrically** *adv.*

theatricals (θɪ'ætrɪkəlz) *pl. n.* dramatic performances, esp. as given by amateurs.

thee (ðiː) *pron.* **1.** the objective form of **thou. 2.** (*subjective*) *Rare.* refers to the person addressed: used mainly by members of the Society of Friends.

theft (θɛft) *n.* **1.** the dishonest taking of property belonging to another person with the intention of depriving the owner permanently of its possession. **2.** *Rare.* something stolen.

their (ðɛə) *determiner.* **1.** of or associated in some way with them: *their own clothes; she tried to combat their mocking her.* **2.** belonging to or associated with people in general: *in many countries they wash their clothes in the river.* **3.** *Not standard.* belonging to or associated with an indefinite antecedent such as *one, whoever,* or *anybody: everyone should bring their own lunch.*

theirs (ðɛəz) *pron.* **1.** something or someone belonging to or associated with them: *theirs is difficult.* **2.** *Not standard.* something or someone belonging to or associated with an indefinite antecedent such as *one, whoever,* or *anybody: everyone thinks theirs is best.* **3. of theirs.** belonging to or associated with them.

theism ('θiːɪzəm) *n.* **1.** the belief in one God as the creator and ruler of the universe. **2.** the belief in the existence of a God or gods. —**'theist** *n., adj.* —**the'istic** *or* **the'istical** *adj.*

them (ðɛm; *unstressed* ðəm) *pron.* **1.** (*objective*) refers to things or people other than the speaker or people addressed: *I'll kill them; what happened to them? ~determiner.* **2.** a nonstandard word for those: *three of them oranges.*
▷ **Usage.** See at **me.**

theme (θiːm) *n.* **1.** an idea or topic expanded in a discourse, discussion, etc. **2.** (in literature, music, art, etc.) a unifying idea, image, or motif, repeated or developed throughout a work. **3.** *Music.* **a.** a group of notes forming a recognizable melodic unit, often used as the basis of the musical material in a composition. **b.** a short essay, esp. one set as an exercise for a student. **5.** *Grammar.* another word for **root**[1] *or* **stem**[1] (sense 7). —**thematic** (θɪ'mætɪk) *adj.*

themselves (ðəm'sɛlvz) *pron.* **1. a.** the reflexive form of *they* or *them.* **b.** (*intensifier*): *the team themselves voted on it.* **2.** (*preceded by a copula*) their normal or usual selves: *they don't seem themselves any more.* **3.** Also **themself.** *Not standard.* a reflexive form of an indefinite antecedent such as *one, whoever,* or *anybody: everyone has to look after themselves.*
▷ **Usage.** See at **myself.**

then (ðɛn) *adv.* **1.** at that time; over that period of time. **2.** (*sentence modifier*) in that case; that being so: *then why don't you ask her? go on then, take it.* *~* **3.** *sentence connector.* after that; with that: *then John left the room.* *~n.* **4.** that time: *from then on.* *~adj.* **5.** (*prenominal*) existing, functioning, etc., at that time: *the then prime minister.*

thence (ðɛns) *adv.* **1.** from that place. **2.** Also: **thenceforth** ('ðɛns'fɔːθ). from that time or event; thereafter. **3.** therefore.

THESAURUS

thaw defrost, dissolve, liquefy, melt, soften, unfreeze, warm

theatrical **1.** dramatic, dramaturgic, melodramatic, scenic, Thespian **2.** affected, artificial, ceremonious, dramatic, exaggerated, hammy (*Inf.*), histrionic, mannered, os-

tentatious, overdone, pompous, showy, stagy, stilted, unreal

theft embezzlement, fraud, larceny, pilfering, purloining, rip-off (*Sl.*), robbery, stealing, swindling, thievery, thieving

theme **1.** argument, burden, idea, keynote,

matter, subject, subject matter, text, thesis, topic **2.** leitmotiv, motif, recurrent image, unifying idea **3.** composition, dissertation, essay, exercise, paper

theocracy (θɪ'ɒkrəsɪ) *n., pl.* **-cies. 1.** government by a deity or by a priesthood. **2.** a community under such government. —'**theo,crat** *n.* —,**theo'cratic** *adj.*

theodolite (θɪ'ɒdə,laɪt) *n.* a surveying instrument for measuring horizontal and vertical angles, consisting of a small tripod-mounted telescope. Also called (in the U.S.): **transit.** —**theodolitic** (θɪ,ɒdə'lɪtɪk) *adj.*

theol. *abbrev. for:* **1.** theologian. **2.** theological. **3.** theology.

theologian (,θɪə'ləʊdʒɪən) *n.* a person versed in or engaged in the study of theology.

theology (θɪ'ɒlədʒɪ) *n., pl.* **-gies. 1.** the systematic study of the existence and nature of the divine and its relationship to other beings. **2.** the systematic study of Christian revelation concerning God's nature and purpose. **3.** a specific system, form, or branch of this study. —,**theo-**'**logical** *adj.* —**the**'**ologist** *n.*

theorem ('θɪərəm) *n.* a proposition or formula, esp. one that can be deduced from axioms or previously proved propositions. —**theorematic** (,θɪərə'mætɪk) *or* **theoremic** (,θɪə'rɛmɪk) *adj.*

theoretical (,θɪə'rɛtɪkəl) *or* **theoretic** *adj.* **1.** of or based on theory. **2.** lacking practical application or actual existence; hypothetical. **3.** using or dealing in theory; impractical. —,**theo'retically** *adv.*

theoretician (,θɪərɪ'tɪʃən) *n.* a student or user of the theory rather than the practical aspects of a subject.

theorize *or* **-ise** ('θɪə,raɪz) *vb.* (*intr.*) to produce or use theories; speculate. —'**theorist** *n.* —'**theo,rizer** *or* **-iser** *n.*

theory ('θɪərɪ) *n., pl.* **-ries. 1.** a plan formulated in the mind only. **2.** a system of rules, procedures, and assumptions used to produce a result. **3.** abstract knowledge or reasoning. **4.** a set of hypotheses related by logical or mathematical arguments to explain a wide variety of connected phenomena in general terms: *the theory of relativity.* **5.** a nontechnical name for hypothesis.

theosophy (θɪ'ɒsəfɪ) *n.* **1.** any of various religious or philosophical systems claiming to be based on or to express an intuitive insight into the divine nature. **2.** the system of beliefs of the Theosophical Society founded in 1875, claiming to be derived from the sacred writings of Brahmanism and Buddhism. —**theosophic** (,θɪə'sɒfɪk) *or* ,**theo'sophical** *adj.* —**the'osophist** *n.*

therapeutic (,θɛrə'pjuːtɪk) *adj.* **1.** of or relating to the treatment of disease; curative. **2.** serving or performed to maintain health: *therapeutic abortion.* —,**thera'peutically** *adv.*

therapeutics (,θɛrə'pjuːtɪks) *n.* (*functioning as sing.*) the branch of medicine concerned with the treatment of disease.

therapy ('θɛrəpɪ) *n., pl.* **-pies. a.** the treatment of disorders or disease. **b.** (*in combination*): *physiotherapy.* —'**therapist** *n.*

there (ðɛə) *adv.* **1.** in, at, or to that place, point, case, or respect: *we never go there; I agree with you there.* ~*pron.* **2.** used as a grammatical subject with some verbs, esp. *be*, when the true subject follows the verb: *there is a girl in that office.* ~*adj.* **3.** (*postpositive*) who or which is in that place or position: *that boy there did it.* **4. all there.** (*predicative*) of normal intelligence. **5. so there.** an exclamation that usually follows a declaration of refusal or defiance. **6. there you are. a.** an expression used when handing a person something requested or desired. **b.** an exclamation of triumph. ~*n.* **7.** that place: *near there.* ~*interj.* **8.** an expression of sympathy, as in consoling a child.

▷ **Usage.** Careful writers and speakers ensure that the verb agrees with the number of the subject in such constructions as *there is a man waiting* and *there are several people waiting.* However, where the subject is compound even careful speakers frequently use the singular as in *there is a pen and a book on the table.*

thereabouts ('ðɛərə,baʊts) *or* **thereabout** *adv.*

near that place, time, amount, etc.

thereafter (,ðɛər'ɑːftə) *adv.* from that time on or after that time.

thereby (,ðɛə'baɪ, 'ðɛə,baɪ) *adv.* **1.** by that means; because of that. **2.** *Arch.* thereabouts.

therefore ('ðɛə,fɔː) *sentence connector.* **1.** thus; hence: *those people have their umbrellas up; therefore, it must be raining.* **2.** consequently; as a result.

therefrom (,ðɛə'frɒm) *adv. Arch.* from that or there: *the roads that lead therefrom.*

therein (,ðɛər'ɪn) *adv. Formal or law.* in or into that place, thing, etc.

thereof (,ðɛər'ɒv) *adv. Formal or law.* **1.** of or concerning that or it. **2.** from or because of that.

thereon (,ðɛər'ɒn) *adv. Arch.* thereupon.

thereto (,ðɛə'tuː) *adv.* **1.** *Formal or law.* to that or it. **2.** *Obs.* in addition to that.

thereunder (,ðɛər'ʌndə) *adv. Formal or law.* **1.** (in documents, etc.) below that or it; subsequently in that; thereafter. **2.** under the terms or authority of that.

thereupon (,ðɛərə'pɒn) *adv.* **1.** immediately after that; at that point. **2.** *Formal or law.* upon that thing, point, subject, etc.

therm (θɜːm) *n. Brit.* a unit of heat equal to 100 000 British thermal units. One therm is equal to $1.055\ 056 \times 10^8$ joules.

thermal ('θɜːməl) *adj.* **1.** Also: **thermic.** of, caused by, or generating heat. **2.** hot or warm: *thermal baths.* **3.** (of garments) specially made so as to have exceptional heat-retaining qualities: *thermal underwear.* ~*n.* **4.** a column of rising air caused by local unequal heating of the land surface, and used by gliders and birds to gain height. —'**thermally** *adv.*

thermionic (,θɜːmɪ'ɒnɪk) *adj.* of, relating to, or operated by electrons emitted from materials at high temperatures: *a thermionic valve.*

thermionic valve *or esp. U.S.* **tube** *n.* an electronic valve in which electrons are emitted from a heated rather than a cold cathode.

thermo- *or before a vowel* **therm-** *combining form.* related to, caused by, or measuring heat: *thermodynamics; thermophile.*

thermocouple ('θɜːməʊ,kʌpəl) *n.* **1.** a device for measuring temperature consisting of a pair of wires of different metals joined at both ends. One junction is at the temperature to be measured, the second at a lower fixed temperature. The current generated in the circuit is proportional to the temperature difference. **2.** a similar device with only one junction between two dissimilar metals.

thermodynamics (,θɜːməʊdaɪ'næmɪks) *n.* (*functioning as sing.*) the branch of physical science concerned with the interrelationship and interconversion of different forms of energy. —,**thermody'namic** *adj.*

thermoelectric (,θɜːməʊɪ'lɛktrɪk) *or* **thermoelectrical** *adj.* **1.** of, relating to, used in, or operated by the conversion of heat energy to electrical energy. **2.** of, relating to, used in, or operated by the conversion of electrical energy.

thermometer (θə'mɒmɪtə) *n.* an instrument used to measure temperature, esp. one in which a thin column of liquid, such as mercury, expands and contracts within a graduated sealed tube. —**ther'mometry** *n.*

thermonuclear (,θɜːməʊ'njuːklɪə) *adj.* **1.** involving nuclear fusion. **2.** involving thermonuclear weapons.

thermoplastic (,θɜːməʊ'plæstɪk) *adj.* **1.** (of a material, esp. a synthetic plastic) becoming soft when heated and rehardening on cooling without appreciable change of properties. ~*n.* **2.** a synthetic plastic or resin, such as polystyrene, with these properties.

Thermos *or* **Thermos flask** ('θɜːməs) *n. Trademark.* a type of stoppered vacuum flask, esp. one used to keep beverages or soup hot.

THESAURUS

theological divine, doctrinal, ecclesiastical, religious

theorem deduction, dictum, formula, hypothesis, principle, proposition, rule, statement

theoretical abstract, academic, conjectural, hypothetical, ideal, impractical, pure, speculative

theorize conjecture, formulate, guess, hypothesize, project, propound, speculate, suppose

theory 1. assumption, conjecture, guess, hypothesis, presumption, speculation, supposition, surmise, thesis 2. philosophy, plan, proposal, scheme, system

therapeutic ameliorative, analeptic, beneficial, corrective, curative, good, healing, remedial, restorative, salubrious, salutary, sanative

therapy cure, healing, remedial treatment, remedy, treatment

therefore accordingly, as a result, consequently, ergo, for that reason, hence, so, then, thence, thus, whence

thermosetting (ˌθɜːməʊˈsɛtɪŋ) *adj.* (of a material, esp. a synthetic plastic) hardening permanently after one application of heat and pressure.

thermostat (ˈθɜːməˌstæt) *n.* **1.** a device that maintains a system at a constant temperature. **2.** a device that sets off a sprinkler, etc. at a certain temperature. —ˌthermoˈstatic *adj.* —ˌthermoˈstatically *adv.*

thesaurus (θɪˈsɔːrəs) *n., pl.* **-ri** (-raɪ) *or* **-ruses. 1.** a book containing systematized lists of synonyms and related words. **2.** a dictionary of selected words or topics. **3.** *Rare.* a treasury.

these (ðiːz) *determiner.* **a.** the form of **this** used before a plural noun: *these men.* **b.** (*as pronoun*): *I don't much care for these.*

thesis (ˈθiːsɪs) *n., pl.* **-ses** (-siːz). **1.** a dissertation resulting from original research, esp. when submitted for a degree or diploma. **2.** a theory maintained in argument. **3.** a subject for a discussion or essay. **4.** an unproved statement put forward as a premiss in an argument.

Thespian (ˈθɛspɪən) *adj.* **1.** of or relating to Thespis, 6th-century B.C. Greek poet. **2.** of or relating to drama and the theatre; dramatic. ~*n.* **3.** *Often facetious.* an actor or actress.

Thess. *Bible. abbrev. for* Thessalonians.

theta (ˈθiːtə) *n.* the eighth letter of the Greek alphabet (Θ, θ).

they (ðeɪ) *pron.* (*subjective*) **1.** refers to people or things other than the speaker or people addressed: *they fight among themselves.* **2.** refers to people in general: *in Australia they have Christmas in the summer.* **3.** *Not standard.* refers to an indefinite antecedent such as one, whoever, or anybody: *if anyone objects, they can go.*

they'd (ðeɪd) *contraction of* they would *or* they had.

they'll (ðeɪl) *contraction of* they will *or* they shall.

they're (ðɛə, ˈðeɪə) *contraction of* they are.

they've (ðeɪv) *contraction of* they have.

thiamine (ˈθaɪəˌmiːn, -mɪn) *or* **thiamin** (ˈθaɪəmɪn) *n.* a white crystalline vitamin that occurs in the outer coat of rice and other grains. It forms part of the vitamin B complex: deficiency leads to nervous disorders and to the disease beriberi. Also called: **vitamin B₁, aneurin.**

thick (θɪk) *adj.* **1.** of relatively great extent from one surface to the other: *a thick slice of bread.* **2. a.** (*postpositive*) of specific fatness: *ten centimetres thick.* **b.** (*in combination*): *a six-inch-thick wall.* **3.** having a dense consistency: *thick soup.* **4.** abundantly covered or filled: *a piano thick with dust.* **5.** impenetrable; dense: *a thick fog.* **6.** stupid, slow, or insensitive. **7.** throaty or badly articulated: *a voice thick with emotion.* **8.** (of accents, etc.) pronounced. **9.** *Inf.* very friendly (esp. in **thick as thieves**). **10.** a bit thick. *Brit.* unfair or excessive. **11. a thick ear.** *Inf.* a blow on the ear. ~*adv.* **12.** in order to produce something thick: *to slice bread thick.* **13.** profusely; in quick succession (esp. in **thick and fast**). **14. lay it on thick.** *Inf.* **a.** to exaggerate a story, etc. **b.** to flatter excessively. ~*n.* **15.** a thick piece or part. **16. the thick.** the most intense or active part. **17. through thick and thin.** in good times and bad. —ˈthickish *adj.* —ˈthickly *adv.*

thicken (ˈθɪkən) *vb.* **1.** to make or become thick or thicker. **2.** (*intr.*) to become more involved: *the plot thickened.* —ˈthickener *n.*

thickening (ˈθɪkənɪŋ) *n.* **1.** something added to a liquid to thicken it. **2.** a thickened part or piece.

thicket (ˈθɪkɪt) *n.* a dense growth of small trees, shrubs, and similar plants.

thickhead (ˈθɪkˌhɛd) *n.* **1.** a stupid or ignorant person; fool. **2.** any of a family of Australian and SE Asian songbirds. —ˌthickˈheaded *adj.* —ˌthickˈheadedness *n.*

thickness (ˈθɪknɪs) *n.* **1.** the state or quality of being thick. **2.** the dimension through an object, as opposed to length or width. **3.** a layer.

thickset (ˌθɪkˈsɛt) *adj.* **1.** stocky in build; sturdy. **2.** densely planted or placed. ~*n.* **3.** a rare word for thicket.

thick-skinned *adj.* insensitive to criticism or hints; not easily upset or affected.

thick-witted *or* **thick-skulled** *adj.* stupid, dull, or slow to learn. —ˌthickˈwittedly *adv.* —ˌthickˈwittedness *n.*

thief (θiːf) *n., pl.* **thieves** (θiːvz). a person who steals something from another. —ˈthievish *adj.*

thieve (θiːv) *vb.* to steal (someone's possessions). —ˈthievery *n.* —ˈthievingly *adv.*

thigh (θaɪ) *n.* **1.** the part of the leg between the hip and the knee in man. **2.** the corresponding part in other vertebrates and insects. Related adj.: **femoral.**

thighbone (ˈθaɪˌbəʊn) *n.* a nontechnical name for the femur.

thimble (ˈθɪmbəl) *n.* **1.** a cap of metal, plastic, etc., used to protect the end of the finger when sewing. **2.** any small metal cap resembling this. **3.** *Naut.* a loop of metal having a groove at its outer edge for a rope or cable.

thimblerig (ˈθɪmbəlˌrɪg) *n.* a game in which the operator rapidly moves about three inverted thimbles, one of which conceals a token, the other player betting on which thimble the token is under. —ˈthimbleˌrigger *n.*

thin (θɪn) *adj.* **thinner, thinnest. 1.** of relatively small extent from one side or surface to the other. **2.** slim or lean. **3.** sparsely placed; meagre: *thin hair.* **4.** of low density: *a thin liquid.* **5.** weak; poor: *a thin disguise.* **6. thin on the ground.** few in number; scarce. ~*adv.* **7.** in order to produce something thin: *to cut bread thin.* ~*vb.* **thinning, thinned. 8.** to make or become thin or sparse. —ˈthinly *adv.* —ˈthinness *n.*

thine (ðaɪn) *determiner. Arch.* **a.** (*preceding a vowel*) of or associated with you (thou): *thine eyes.* **b.** (*as pronoun*): *thine is the greatest burden.*

thing (θɪŋ) *n.* **1.** an object, fact, affair, circumstance, or concept considered as being a separate entity. **2.** any inanimate object. **3.** an object or entity that cannot or need not be precisely named. **4.** *Inf.* a person or animal: *you poor thing.* **5.** an event or act. **6.** a thought or statement. **7.** *Law.* property. **8.** a device, means, or instrument. **9.** (*often pl.*) a possession, article of clothing, etc. **10.** *Inf.* a preoccupation or obsession (esp. in **have a thing about**). **11.** an activity or mode of behaviour satisfying to one's personality (esp. in **do one's (own) thing**).

THESAURUS

thesis 1. composition, disquisition, dissertation, essay, monograph, paper, treatise **2.** contention, hypothesis, idea, line of argument, opinion, proposal, proposition, theory, view **3.** area, subject, theme, topic **4.** assumption, postulate, premiss, proposition, statement, supposition, surmise

thick *adj.* **1.** broad, bulky, deep, fat, solid, substantial, wide **2.** close, clotted, coagulated, compact, concentrated, condensed, crowded, deep, dense, heavy, impenetrable, opaque **3.** abundant, brimming, bristling, bursting, chock-a-block, chock-full, covered, crawling, frequent, full, numerous, packed, replete, swarming, teeming **4.** blockheaded, brainless, dense, dim-witted (*Inf.*), dopey (*Sl.*), dull, insensitive, moronic, obtuse, slow, slow-witted, stupid, thickheaded **5.** dense, heavy, impenetrable, soupy **6.** distorted, guttural, hoarse, husky, inarticulate, indistinct, throaty **7.** broad, decided, distinct, marked, pronounced, rich, strong **8.** *Inf.* chummy (*Inf.*), close, confidential, devoted, familiar, friendly, hand in glove, inseparable, intimate, matey (*Brit. inf.*), on good terms, pally (*Inf.*), well in (*Inf.*) **9. a bit thick** excessive, over the score (*Inf.*), too much, unfair, unjust, unreasonable ~*n.* **10.** centre, heart, middle, midst

thicken cake, clot, coagulate, condense, congeal, deepen, gel, inspissate (*Archaic*), jell, set

thickset 1. beefy (*Inf.*), brawny, bulky, burly, heavy, muscular, powerfully built, stocky, strong, stubby, sturdy, well-built **2.** closely packed, dense, densely planted, solid, thick

thick-skinned callous, case-hardened, hard-boiled (*Inf.*), hardened, impervious, insensitive, stolid, tough, unfeeling, unsusceptible

thief bandit, burglar, cheat, cracksman (*Sl.*), crook (*Inf.*), embezzler, housebreaker, larcenist, mugger (*Inf.*), pickpocket, pilferer, plunderer, purloiner, robber, shoplifter, stealer, swindler

thieve cheat, embezzle, filch, half-inch (*Inf.*), knock off (*Sl.*), lift (*Inf.*), misappropriate, nick (*Brit. sl.*), peculate, pilfer, pinch (*Inf.*), plunder, poach, purloin, rip off (*Sl.*), rob, run off with, snitch (*Sl.*), steal, swindle, swipe (*Sl.*)

thin *adj.* **1.** attenuate, attenuated, fine, narrow, threadlike **2.** delicate, diaphanous, filmy, fine, flimsy, gossamer, seethrough, sheer, translucent, transparent, unsubstantial **3.** bony, emaciated, lank, lanky, lean, light, meagre, scraggy, scrawny, skeletal, skinny, slender, slight, slim, spare, spindly, thin as a rake, undernourished, underweight **4.** deficient, meagre, scanty, scarce, scattered, skimpy, sparse, wispy **5.** dilute, diluted, rarefied, runny, watery, weak, wishy-washy (*Inf.*) **6.** feeble, flimsy, inadequate, insufficient, lame, poor, scant, scanty, shallow, slight, superficial, unconvincing, unsubstantial, weak ~*v.* **7.** attenuate, cut back, dilute, diminish, emaciate, prune, rarefy, reduce, refine, trim, water down, weaken, weed out

12. the thing. the latest fashion. **13. make a thing of.** exaggerate the importance of.

thingumabob or **thingamabob** ('θɪŋəmə,bɒb) n. Inf. a person or thing the name of which is unknown, temporarily forgotten, or deliberately overlooked. Also: **thingumajig, thingamajig,** or **thingummy.**

think (θɪŋk) vb. **thinking, thought.** **1.** (tr.; may take a clause as object) to consider, judge, or believe: he thinks my ideas impractical. **2.** (intr.; often foll. by about) to exercise the mind as in order to make a decision; ponder. **3.** (intr.) to be capable of conscious thought: man is the only animal that thinks. **4.** to remember; recollect. **5.** (intr.; foll. by of) to make the mental choice (of): think of a number. **6.** (may take a clause as object or an infinitive) **a.** to expect; suppose. **b.** to be considerate enough (to do something): he did not think to thank them. **7.** (intr.) to focus the attention on being: think big. **8. think better of. a.** to change one's mind about (a course of action, decision, etc.). **b.** to have a more favourable opinion of (a person). **9. think nothing of. a.** to regard as routine or natural. **b.** to have no compunction or hesitation about. **10. think twice.** to consider carefully before deciding. ~n. **11.** Inf. a careful, open-minded assessment. **12.** (modifier) Inf. characterized by or involving thinkers, thinking, or thought. —'**thinkable** adj. —'**thinker** n.

thinking ('θɪŋkɪŋ) n. **1.** opinion or judgment. **2.** the process of thought. ~adj. **3.** (prenominal) using or capable of using intelligent thought: thinking people. **4. put on one's thinking cap.** to ponder a matter or problem.

think over vb. (tr., adv.) to ponder or consider.

think-tank n. Inf. a group of specialists commissioned to undertake intensive study and research into specified problems.

think up vb. (tr., adv.) to invent or devise.

thinner ('θɪnə) n. a solvent, such as turpentine, added to paint or varnish to dilute it, reduce its opacity or viscosity, or increase its penetration.

thin-skinned adj. sensitive to criticism or hints; easily upset or affected.

third (θɜːd) adj. (usually prenominal) **1. a.** coming after the second in numbering, position, etc.; being the ordinal number of three: often written 3rd. **b.** (as n.): the third got a prize. **2.** rated, graded, or ranked below the second level. **3.** denoting the third from lowest forward ratio of a gearbox in a motor vehicle. ~n. **4. a.** one of three equal parts of an object, quantity, etc. **b.** (as modifier): a third part. **5.** the fraction equal to one divided by three (1/3). **6.** the forward ratio above second of a gearbox in a motor vehicle. **7. a.** the interval between one note and another three notes away from it counting inclusively along the diatonic scale. **b.** one of two notes constituting such an interval in relation to the other. **8.** Brit. an honours degree of the third and usually the lowest class. Full term: **third class honours degree.** ~adv. **9.** Also: **thirdly.** in the third place. —'**thirdly** adv.

third class n. **1.** the class or grade next in value, quality, etc., to the second. ~adj. (**third-class** when prenominal). **2.** of the class or grade next in value, quality, etc., to the second. ~adv. **3.** by third-class transport, etc.

third degree n. Inf. torture or bullying, esp. used to extort confessions or information.

third-degree burn n. Pathol. the most severe type of burn, involving the destruction of both epidermis and dermis.

third dimension n. the dimension of depth by which a solid object may be distinguished from a two-dimensional drawing or picture of it.

third man n. Cricket. a fielding position on the off side near the boundary behind the batsman's wicket.

third party n. **1.** a person who is involved by chance or only incidentally in a legal proceeding, agreement, or other transaction. ~adj. **2.** Insurance. providing protection against liability caused by accidental injury or death of other persons.

third person n. a grammatical category of pronouns and verbs used when referring to objects or individuals other than the speaker or his addressee or addressees.

third-rate adj. mediocre or inferior.

Third World n. the countries of Africa, Asia, and Latin America collectively, esp. when viewed as underdeveloped.

thirst (θɜːst) n. **1.** a craving to drink, accompanied by a feeling of dryness in the mouth and throat. **2.** an eager longing, craving, or yearning. ~vb. (intr.) **3.** to feel a thirst.

thirsty ('θɜːstɪ) adj. **thirstier, thirstiest. 1.** feeling a desire to drink. **2.** dry; arid. **3.** (foll. by for) feeling an eager desire. **4.** causing thirst. —'**thirstily** adv. —'**thirstiness** n.

thirteen ('θɜː'tiːn) n. **1.** the cardinal number that is the sum of ten and three and is a prime number. **2.** a numeral 13, XIII, etc., representing this number. **3.** something representing or consisting of 13 units. ~determiner. **4. a.** amounting to thirteen. **b.** (as pronoun): thirteen of them fell. —'**thir'teenth** adj.

thirty ('θɜːtɪ) n., pl. -ties. **1.** the cardinal number that is the product of ten and three. **2.** a numeral 30, XXX, etc., representing this number. **3.** (pl.) the numbers 30-39, esp. the 30th to the 39th year of a person's life or of a century. **4.** the amount or quantity that is three times as big as ten. **5.** something representing or consisting of 30 units. ~determiner. **6. a.** amounting to thirty. **b.** (as pronoun): thirty are broken. —'**thirtieth** adj.

Thirty-nine Articles pl. n. a set of formulas defining the doctrinal position of the Church of England, drawn up in the 16th century.

this (ðɪs) determiner. (used before a sing. n.) **1. a.** used preceding a noun referring to something or someone that is closer: look at this picture. **b.** (as pronoun): take this. **2. a.** used preceding a noun that has just been mentioned or is understood: this plan of yours won't work. **b.** (as pronoun): I first saw this on Sunday. **3. a.** used to re-

---

THESAURUS

thing 1. affair, article, being, body, circumstance, concept, entity, fact, matter, object, part, portion, something, substance **2.** act, deed, event, eventuality, feat, happening, incident, occurrence, phenomenon, proceeding **3.** apparatus, contrivance, device, gadget, implement, instrument, machine, means, mechanism, tool **4.** aspect, detail, facet, factor, feature, item, particular, point, statement, thought **5.** Plural baggage, belongings, bits and pieces, clobber (Brit. sl.), clothes, effects, equipment, gear (Inf.), goods, impedimenta, luggage, odds and ends, paraphernalia, possessions, stuff **6.** Inf. attitude, bee in one's bonnet, fetish, fixation, hang-up (Inf.), idée fixe, mania, obsession, phobia, preoccupation, quirk

think v. **1.** believe, conceive, conclude, consider, deem, determine, esteem, estimate, hold, imagine, judge, reckon, regard, suppose, surmise **2.** brood, cerebrate, chew over (Inf.), cogitate, consider, contemplate, deliberate, have in mind, meditate, mull over, muse, ponder, reason, reflect, revolve, ruminate, turn over in one's mind, weigh up **3.**

call to mind, recall, recollect, remember **4.** anticipate, envisage, expect, foresee, imagine, plan for, presume, suppose **5. think better of** change one's mind about, decide against, go back on, have second thoughts about, reconsider, repent, think again, think twice about **6. think much of** admire, attach importance to, esteem, have a high opinion of, hold in high regard, rate (Sl.), respect, set store by, think highly of, value **7. think nothing of** consider unimportant, have no compunction about, have no hesitation about, regard as routine, set no store by, take in one's stride ~n. **8.** assessment, consideration, contemplation, deliberation, look, reflection

thinkable conceivable, feasible, imaginable, likely, possible, reasonable, within the bounds of possibility

thinker brain (Inf.), intellect (Inf.), mastermind, philosopher, sage, theorist, wise man

thinking 1. n. assessment, conclusions, conjecture, idea, judgment, opinion, outlook, philosophy, position, reasoning, theory, thoughts, view **2.** adj. contemplative, cul-

tured, intelligent, meditative, philosophical, ratiocinative, rational, reasoning, reflective, sophisticated, thoughtful

think over chew over (Inf.), consider, consider the pros and cons of, contemplate, give thought to, mull over, ponder, reflect upon, turn over in one's mind, weigh up

think up come up with, concoct, contrive, create, devise, dream up, imagine, improvise, invent, visualize

thin-skinned easily hurt, hypersensitive, quick to take offence, sensitive, soft, susceptible, tender, touchy, vulnerable

third-rate bad, duff (Brit. sl.), indifferent, inferior, low-grade, mediocre, poor, poor-quality, ropy (Brit. inf.), shoddy

thirst n. **1.** craving to drink, drought, dryness, thirstiness **2.** appetite, craving, desire, eagerness, hankering, hunger, keenness, longing, lust, passion, yearning, yen (Inf.)

thirsty 1. arid, dehydrated, dry, parched **2.** athirst, avid, burning, craving, desirous, dying, eager, greedy, hankering, hungry, itching, longing, lusting, thirsting, yearning

fer to something about to be said, read, etc.: *consider this argument.* **b.** (*as pronoun*): *listen to this.* **4. a.** the present or immediate: *this time you'll know better.* **b.** (*as pronoun*): *before this, I was mistaken.* **5.** *Inf.* an emphatic form of **a** or **the**[1]: *I saw this big brown bear.* **6. this and that.** various unspecified and trivial actions, matters, objects, etc. **7. with** (*or* **at**) **this.** after this; thereupon. ~*adv.* **8.** used with adjectives and adverbs to specify a precise degree that is about to be mentioned: *go just this fast and you'll be safe.*

thistle ('θɪs²l) *n.* **1.** any of a genus of plants of the composite family, having prickly-edged leaves, dense flower heads, and feathery hairs on the seeds. **2.** any of various similar or related plants. —'**thistly** *adj.*

thistledown ('θɪs²l,daʊn) *n.* the mass of feathery plumed seeds produced by a thistle.

thither ('ðɪðə) *or* **thitherward** *adv. Obs.* to or towards that place; in that direction.

tho *or* **tho'** (ðəʊ) *U.S. or poetic.* a variant spelling of **though.**

thole[1] (θəʊl) *or* **tholepin** ('θəʊl,pɪn) *n.* a wooden pin or one of a pair, set upright in the gunwales of a rowing boat to serve as a fulcrum in rowing.

thole[2] (θəʊl) *vb.* **1.** (*tr.*) *N Brit. dialect.* to put up with; bear. **2.** an archaic word for **suffer.**

Thompson sub-machine-gun ('tɒmsən) *n. Trademark.* a .45 calibre sub-machine-gun.

thong (θɒŋ) *n.* **1.** a thin strip of leather or other material. **2.** a whip or whiplash, esp. one made of leather. **3.** *Chiefly U.S., Austral. & N.Z.* the usual name for **flip-flop** (sense 5).

thoracic (θɔː'ræsɪk) *or* **thoracal** ('θɔːrək²l) *adj.* of, near, or relating to the thorax.

thorax ('θɔːræks) *n., pl.* **thoraxes** *or* **thoraces** ('θɔːrə,siːz, θɔː'reɪsiːz). **1.** the part of the human body enclosed by the ribs. **2.** the corresponding part in other vertebrates. **3.** the part of an insect's body between the head and abdomen.

thorium ('θɔːrɪəm) *n.* a silvery-white radioactive metallic element. It is used in electronic equipment and as a nuclear power source. Symbol: Th; atomic no.: 90; atomic wt.: 232.04. —'**thoric** *adj.*

thorn (θɔːn) *n.* **1.** a sharp pointed woody extension of a stem or leaf. Cf. **prickle** (sense 1). **2.** any of various trees or shrubs having thorns, esp. the hawthorn. **3.** a Germanic character of runic origin (þ) used in Icelandic to represent the sound of *th*, as in *thin, bath.* **4.** this same character as used in Old and Middle English as an alternative to *edh.* **5.** a source of irritation (esp. in **a thorn in one's side** *or* flesh). —'**thornless** *adj.*

thorny ('θɔːnɪ) *adj.* **thornier, thorniest. 1.** bearing or covered with thorns. **2.** difficult or unpleasant. **3.** sharp. —'**thornily** *adv.* —'**thorniness** *n.*

thorough ('θʌrə) *adj.* **1.** carried out completely and carefully. **2.** (*prenominal*) utter: *a thorough bore.* **3.** painstakingly careful. —'**thoroughly** *adv.* —'**thoroughness** *n.*

thoroughbred ('θʌrə,brɛd) *adj.* **1.** purebred. ~*n.* **2.** a

pedigree animal; purebred. **3.** a person regarded as being of good breeding.

Thoroughbred ('θʌrə,brɛd) *n.* a British breed of horse the ancestry of which can be traced to English mares and Arab sires.

thoroughfare ('θʌrə,fɛə) *n.* **1.** a road from one place to another, esp. a main road. **2.** way through, access, or passage: *no thoroughfare.*

thoroughgoing ('θʌrə,gəʊɪŋ) *adj.* **1.** extremely thorough. **2.** (*usually prenominal*) absolute; complete: *thoroughgoing incompetence.*

those (ðəʊz) *determiner.* the form of **that** used before a plural noun.

thou[1] (ðaʊ) *pron.* (*subjective*) **1.** *Arch. or Brit. dialect.* refers to the person addressed: used mainly in familiar address. **2.** (*usually cap.*) refers to God when addressed in prayer, etc.

▷ **Usage.** Although *thou* has now disappeared from general use in English and is restricted to certain dialects, it was part of standard English until the 18th century. *Thou* was a form of address reserved for God, friends, family, and those inferior in age and status and was therefore similar in meaning and use to the modern French *tu.* *You* was the more formal mode of address until the disappearance of *thou.*

thou[2] (θaʊ) *n., pl.* **thous** *or* **thou. 1.** one thousandth of an inch. **2.** *Inf.* short for thousand.

though (ðəʊ) *conj.* (*subordinating*) **1.** (sometimes preceded by *even*) despite the fact that: *though he tries hard, he always fails.* **2. as though.** as if: *he looked as though he'd seen a ghost.* ~*adv.* **3.** nevertheless; however: *he can't dance; he sings well, though.*

thought (θɔːt) *vb.* **1.** the past tense or past participle of **think.** ~*n.* **2.** the act or process of thinking. **3.** a concept, opinion, or idea. **4.** ideas typical of a particular time or place: *German thought in the 19th century.* **5.** application of mental attention; consideration. **6.** purpose or intention: *I have no thought of giving up.* **7.** expectation: *no thought of reward.* **8.** a small amount; trifle: *you could be a thought more enthusiastic.* **9.** kindness or regard.

thoughtful ('θɔːtful) *adj.* **1.** considerate in the treatment of other people. **2.** showing careful thought. **3.** pensive; reflective. —'**thoughtfully** *adv.* —'**thoughtfulness** *n.*

thoughtless ('θɔːtlɪs) *adj.* **1.** inconsiderate. **2.** having or showing lack of thought. —'**thoughtlessly** *adv.* —'**thoughtlessness** *n.*

thousand ('θaʊzənd) *n.* **1.** the cardinal number that is the product of 10 and 100. **2.** a numeral 1000, 10³, M, etc., representing this number. **3.** (*often pl.*) a very large but unspecified number, amount, or quantity. **4.** something representing or consisting of 1000 units. ~*determiner.* **5. a.** amounting to a thousand. **b.** (*as pronoun*): *a thousand is hardly enough.* ~Related adj.: **millenary.** —'**thousandth** *adj.*

thrall (θrɔːl) *n.* **1.** Also: **thraldom** *or* **thralldom** ('θrɔːldəm). the state or condition of being in the power

---

T H E S A U R U S

thorn 1. barb, prickle, spike, spine **2.** affliction, annoyance, bane, bother, curse, irritant, irritation, nuisance, pest, plague, scourge, torment, torture, trouble

thorny 1. barbed, bristling with thorns, bristly, pointed, prickly, sharp, spiky, spinous, spiny **2.** awkward, difficult, harassing, hard, irksome, problematic, sticky (*Inf.*), ticklish, tough, troublesome, trying, unpleasant, upsetting, vexatious, worrying

thorough *or* **thoroughgoing 1.** all-embracing, all-inclusive, assiduous, careful, complete, comprehensive, conscientious, efficient, exhaustive, full, in-depth, intensive, leaving no stone unturned, meticulous, painstaking, scrupulous, sweeping **2.** absolute, arrant, complete, downright, entire, out-and-out, perfect, pure, sheer, total, unmitigated, unqualified, utter

thoroughbred blood, full-blooded, of unmixed stock, pedigree, pure-blooded, purebred

thoroughfare access, avenue, highway, passage, passageway, road, roadway, street, way

thoroughly 1. assiduously, carefully, completely, comprehensively, conscientiously, efficiently, exhaustively, from top to bottom, fully, inside out, intensively, leaving no stone unturned, meticulously, painstakingly, scrupulously, sweepingly, through and through, throughout **2.** absolutely, completely, downright, entirely, perfectly, quite, totally, to the full, utterly, without reservation

though 1. *conj.* albeit, allowing, although, despite the fact that, even if, even supposing, granted, notwithstanding, while **2.** *adv.* all the same, for all that, however, nevertheless, nonetheless, notwithstanding, still, yet

thought 1. brainwork, cerebration, cogitation, consideration, contemplation, deliberation, introspection, meditation, musing, reflection, regard, rumination, thinking **2.** assessment, belief, concept, conception, conclusion, conjecture, conviction, estimation, idea, judgment, notion, opinion, thinking, view **3.** attention, consideration, heed, regard, scrutiny, study **4.** aim, design, idea, intention, notion, object, plan, purpose **5.** anticipation, aspiration, dream, expectation,

hope, prospect **6.** dash, jot, little, small amount, *soupçon*, touch, trifle, whisker (*Inf.*) **7.** anxiety, attentiveness, care, compassion, concern, kindness, regard, solicitude, sympathy, thoughtfulness

thoughtful 1. attentive, caring, considerate, helpful, kind, kindly, solicitous, unselfish **2.** astute, canny, careful, cautious, circumspect, deliberate, discreet, heedful, mindful, prudent, wary, well thought-out **3.** contemplative, deliberative, in a brown study, introspective, lost in thought, meditative, musing, pensive, rapt, reflective, ruminative, serious, studious, thinking, wistful

thoughtless 1. impolite, inconsiderate, indiscreet, insensitive, rude, selfish, tactless, uncaring, undiplomatic, unkind **2.** absent-minded, careless, foolish, heedless, ill-considered, imprudent, inadvertent, inattentive, injudicious, mindless, neglectful, negligent, rash, reckless, regardless, remiss, silly, stupid, unmindful, unobservant, unthinking

of another person. **2.** a person who is in such a state. **3.** a person totally subject to some need, desire, appetite, etc. ~*vb.* **4.** (*tr.*) to enslave or dominate.

thrash (θræʃ) *vb.* **1.** (*tr.*) to beat soundly, as with a whip or stick. **2.** (*tr.*) to defeat totally; overwhelm. **3.** (*intr.*) to beat or plunge about in a wild manner. **4.** to sail (a boat) against the wind or tide or (of a boat) to sail in this way. **5.** another word for **thresh.** ~*n.* **6.** the act of thrashing; blow; beating.

thrashing ('θræʃɪŋ) *n.* a physical assault; flogging.

thrash out *vb.* (*tr., adv.*) to discuss fully or vehemently, esp. in order to come to an agreement.

thread (θrɛd) *n.* **1.** a fine strand, filament or fibre of some material. **2.** a fine cord of twisted filaments, esp. of cotton, used in sewing, etc. **3.** any of the filaments of which a spider's web is made. **4.** any fine line, stream, mark, or piece. **5.** the helical ridge on a screw, bolt, nut, etc. **6.** a very thin seam of coal or vein of ore. **7.** something acting as the continuous link or theme of a whole: *the thread of the story.* **8.** the course of an individual's life believed in Greek mythology to be spun, measured, and cut by the Fates. ~*vb.* **9.** (*tr.*) to pass (thread, film, tape, etc.) through (something). **10.** (*tr.*) to string on a thread: *she threaded the beads.* **11.** to make (one's way) through or over (something). **12.** (*tr.*) to produce a screw thread. **13.** (*tr.*) to pervade: *hysteria threaded his account.* **14.** (of boiling syrup) to form a fine thread when poured from a spoon. —'**threader** *n.* —'**thread,like** *adj.*

threadbare ('θrɛd,bɛə) *adj.* **1.** (of cloth, clothing, etc.) having the nap worn off so that the threads are exposed; worn out. **2.** meagre or poor. **3.** hackneyed: *a threadbare argument.* **4.** wearing threadbare clothes; shabby.

threadworm ('θrɛd,wɜːm) *n.* any of various nematodes, esp. the pinworm.

threat (θrɛt) *n.* **1.** a declaration of the intention to inflict harm, pain, or misery. **2.** an indication of imminent harm, danger, or pain. **3.** a person or thing that is regarded as dangerous or likely to inflict pain or misery.

threaten ('θrɛt°n) *vb.* **1.** (*tr.*) to be a threat to. **2.** to be a menacing indication of (something); portend. **3.** (when *tr., may take a clause as object*) to express a threat to (a person or people). —'**threatener** *n.* —'**threateningly** *adv.*

three (θriː) *n.* **1.** the cardinal number that is the sum of two and one and is a prime number. **2.** a numeral 3, III, (iii), representing this number. **3.** something representing or consisting of three units. **4.** Also called: **three o'clock.** three hours after noon or midnight. ~*determiner.* **5. a.** amounting to three. **b.** (*as pronoun*): *three were killed.* ~Related adjs.: **ternary, tertiary, treble, triple.**

three-decker *n.* **1. a.** anything having three levels or layers. **b.** (*as modifier*): *a three-decker sandwich.* **2.** a warship with guns on three decks.

three-dimensional *adj.* **1.** of, having, or relating to three dimensions. **2.** simulating the effect of depth. **3.** having volume. **4.** lifelike.

threefold ('θriː,fəʊld) *adj.* **1.** equal to or having three times as many or as much; triple. **2.** composed of three parts. ~*adv.* **3.** by or up to three times as many or as much.

three-legged race *n.* a race in which pairs of competitors run with their adjacent legs tied together.

threepenny bit *or* **thrupenny bit** ('θrʌpnɪ, -ənɪ, 'θrɛp-) *n.* a twelve-sided British coin valued at three old pence, obsolete since 1971.

three-ply *adj.* **1.** having three layers or thicknesses. **2.** (of wool, etc.) three-stranded.

three-point turn *n.* a complete turn of a motor vehicle using forward and reverse gears.

three-quarter *adj.* **1.** being three quarters of something. **2.** being of three quarters the normal length. ~*n.* **3.** *Rugby.* any of the players between the full back and the forwards.

threescore ('θriː'skɔː) *determiner.* an archaic word for **sixty.**

threesome ('θriːsəm) *n.* **1.** a group of three. **2.** *Golf.* a match in which a single player playing his own ball competes against two others playing on the same ball. **3.** any game, etc., for three people. **4.** (*modifier*) performed by three.

threnody ('θrɛnədɪ, 'θriː-) *or* **threnode** ('θriːnəʊd, 'θrɛn-) *n., pl.* **threnodies** *or* **threnodes.** an ode, song, or speech of lamentation, esp. for the dead. —**threnodic** (θrɪ'nɒdɪk) *adj.* —**threnodist** ('θrɛnədɪst, 'θriː-) *n.*

thresh (θrɛʃ) *vb.* **1.** to beat or rub stalks of ripe corn, etc. either with a hand implement or a machine to separate the grain from the husks and straw. **2.** (*tr.*) to beat or strike. **3.** (*intr.;* often foll. by *about*) to toss and turn; thrash.

thresher ('θrɛʃə) *n.* **1.** a person or thing that threshes, esp. a machine for threshing crops. **2.** any of a genus of large sharks occurring in tropical and temperate seas. They have a very long whiplike tail.

threshold ('θrɛʃəʊld, 'θrɛʃ,həʊld) *n.* **1.** a sill, esp. one made of stone or hardwood, placed at a doorway. **2.** any doorway or entrance. **3.** the starting point of an experience, event, or venture. **4.** *Psychol.* the strength at which a stimulus is just perceived: *the threshold of pain.* **5.** the minimum intensity or value of a signal, etc., that will produce a response or specified effect. **6.** (*modifier*) of a pay agreement, clause, etc., that raises wages to compensate for increases in the cost of living. ~Related adj.: **liminal.**

threw (θruː) *vb.* the past tense of **throw.**

thrice (θraɪs) *adv.* **1.** three times. **2.** threefold. **3.** *Arch.* greatly.

thrift (θrɪft) *n.* **1.** wisdom and caution in the management of money. **2.** Also called: **sea pink.** any of a genus of perennial low-growing plants of Europe, W Asia, and North America, having narrow leaves and round heads of pink or white flowers. —'**thriftless** *adj.* —'**thriftlessly** *adv.*

thrifty ('θrɪftɪ) *adj.* **thriftier, thriftiest. 1.** showing thrift; economical or frugal. **2.** *Rare.* thriving or prospering. —'**thriftily** *adv.* —'**thriftiness** *n.*

thrill (θrɪl) *n.* **1.** a sudden sensation of excitement and pleasure. **2.** a situation producing such a sensation. **3.** a trembling sensation caused by fear or emotional shock. **4.** *Pathol.* an abnormal slight tremor. ~*vb.* **5.** to feel or cause to feel a thrill. **6.** to tremble or cause to tremble; vibrate or quiver. —'**thrilling** *adj.*

THESAURUS

thrash 1. beat, belt, birch, cane, chastise, drub, flagellate, flog, give (someone) a (good) hiding (*Inf.*), hide (*Inf.*), horsewhip, lambaste, leather, paste (*Sl.*), punish, scourge, spank, take a stick to, tan (*Sl.*), whip 2. beat, beat (someone) hollow (*Brit. inf.*), clobber (*Brit. sl.*), crush, defeat, drub, hammer (*Inf.*), maul, overwhelm, paste (*Sl.*), rout, slaughter (*Inf.*), trounce, wipe the floor with (*Inf.*) 3. flail, heave, jerk, plunge, squirm, thresh, toss, toss and turn, writhe

thrashing 1. beating, belting, caning, chastisement, drubbing, flogging, hiding (*Inf.*), lashing, pasting (*Sl.*), punishment, tanning (*Sl.*), whipping 2. beating, defeat, drubbing, hammering (*Inf.*), hiding (*Inf.*), mauling, pasting (*Sl.*), rout, trouncing

thrash out argue out, debate, discuss, have out, resolve, settle, solve, talk over

thread *n.* 1. cotton, fibre, filament, line, strand, string, yarn 2. course, direction, drift,

motif, plot, story line, strain, tenor, theme, train of thought ~*v.* 3. ease, inch, loop, meander, pass, pick (one's way), squeeze through, string, wind

threadbare 1. down at heel, frayed, old, ragged, scruffy, shabby, tattered, tatty, used, worn, worn-out 2. clichéd, cliché-ridden, common, commonplace, conventional, corny (*Inf.*), familiar, hackneyed, overused, stale, stereotyped, stock, tired, trite, well-worn

threat 1. commination, intimidatory remark, menace, threatening remark, warning 2. foreboding, foreshadowing, omen, portent, presage, warning, writing on the wall 3. danger, hazard, menace, peril, risk

threaten 1. endanger, imperil, jeopardize, put at risk, put in jeopardy 2. be imminent, be in the air, be in the offing, forebode, foreshadow, hang over, impend, loom over, portend, presage, warn 3. browbeat, bully, cow, intimidate, lean on (*Sl.*), make threats

to, menace, pressurize, terrorize, warn

threatening 1. bullying, cautionary, comminatory, intimidatory, menacing, minatory, terrorizing, warning 2. baleful, grim, inauspicious, ominous, sinister

threesome triad, trilogy, trine, trinity, trio, triple, triplet, triplex, triptych, triumvirate, triune, troika

threshold 1. door, doorsill, doorstep, doorway, entrance, sill 2. beginning, brink, dawn, inception, opening, outset, start, starting point, verge 3. lower limit, minimum

thrift carefulness, economy, frugality, good husbandry, parsimony, prudence, saving, thriftiness

thriftless extravagant, improvident, imprudent, lavish, prodigal, profligate, spendthrift, unthrifty, wasteful

thrifty careful, economical, frugal, parsimonious, provident, prudent, saving, sparing

thrill *n.* 1. adventure, buzz (*Sl.*), charge

thriller ('θrɪlə) n. a book, film, play, etc., depicting crime, mystery, or espionage in an atmosphere of excitement and suspense.

thrips (θrɪps) n., pl. **thrips.** any of various small slender-bodied insects typically having piercing mouthparts and feeding on plant sap.

thrive (θraɪv) vb. **thriving; thrived** or **throve; thrived** or **thriven** ('θrɪvən). (intr.) 1. to grow strongly and vigorously. 2. to do well; prosper.

thro' or **thro** (θruː) prep., adv. Poetic. variant spellings of **through.**

throat (θrəʊt) n. 1. a. that part of the alimentary and respiratory tracts extending from the back of the mouth to just below the larynx. b. the front part of the neck. 2. something resembling a throat, esp. in shape or function: the throat of a chimney. 3. **cut one's (own) throat.** to bring about one's own ruin. 4. **jump down someone's throat.** to be quick to criticize someone. 5. **ram** or **force (something) down someone's throat.** to insist that someone listen to or accept (something). 6. **stick in one's throat.** to be difficult for one to utter or believe, esp. because of reluctance or dislike. ~Related adjs.: **guttural, laryngeal.**

throaty ('θrəʊtɪ) adj. **throatier, throatiest.** 1. indicating a sore throat; hoarse: a throaty cough. 2. of or produced in the throat. 3. deep, husky, or guttural. —'**throatily** adv.

throb (θrɒb) vb. **throbbing, throbbed.** (intr.) 1. to pulsate or beat repeatedly, esp. with increased force. 2. (of engines, drums, etc.) to have a strong rhythmic vibration or beat. ~n. 3. a throbbing, esp. a rapid pulsation as of the heart: a throb of pleasure.

throes (θrəʊz) pl. n. 1. a condition of violent pangs, pain, or convulsions: death throes. 2. **in the throes of.** struggling with great effort with.

thrombosis (θrɒm'bəʊsɪs) n., pl. **-boses** (-bəʊsiːz). 1. the formation or presence of a thrombus. 2. Inf. short for **coronary thrombosis.** —**thrombotic** (θrɒm'bɒtɪk) adj.

throne (θrəʊn) n. 1. the ceremonial seat occupied by a monarch, bishop, etc. on occasions of state. 2. the power or rank ascribed to a royal person. 3. a person holding royal rank. 4. (pl.; often cap.) the third of the nine orders into which the angels are divided in medieval angelology. ~vb. 5. to place or be placed on a throne.

throng (θrɒŋ) n. 1. a great number of people or things crowded together. ~vb. 2. to gather in or fill (a place) in large numbers; crowd. 3. (tr.) to hem in (a person); jostle.

throstle ('θrɒsəl) n. 1. a poetic name for the song thrush. 2. a spinning machine for wool or cotton in which the fibres are twisted and wound continuously.

throttle ('θrɒtəl) n. 1. Also called: **throttle valve.** any device that controls the quantity of fuel or fuel and air mixture entering an engine. 2. an informal or dialect word for throat. ~vb. (tr.) 3. to kill or injure by squeezing the throat. 4. to suppress. 5. to control or restrict (a flow of fluid) by means of a throttle valve. —'**throttler** n.

through (θruː) prep. 1. going in at one side and coming out at the other side of: a path through the wood. 2. occupying or visiting several points scattered around in (an area). 3. as a result of; by means of. 4. Chiefly U.S. up to and including: Monday through Friday. 5. during: through the night. 6. at the end of; having completed. 7. **through with.** having finished with (esp. when dissatisfied with). ~adj. 8. (postpositive) having successfully completed some specified activity. 9. (on a telephone line) connected. 10. (postpositive) no longer able to function successfully in some specified capacity: as a journalist, you're through. 11. (prenominal) (of a route, journey, etc.) continuous or unbroken: a through train. ~adv. 12. through some specified thing, place, or period of time. 13. **through and through.** thoroughly; completely.

throughout (θruː'aʊt) prep. 1. right through; through the whole of (a place or a period of time): throughout the day. ~adv. 2. throughout some specified period or area.

throughput ('θruːˌpʊt) n. the quantity of raw material processed in a given period, esp. by a computer.

throve (θrəʊv) vb. a past tense of **thrive.**

throw (θrəʊ) vb. **throwing, threw, thrown.** (mainly tr.) 1. (also intr.) to project (something) through the air, esp. with a rapid motion of the arm. 2. (foll. by in, on, onto, etc.) to put or move suddenly, carelessly, or violently. 3. to bring to or cause to be in a specified state or condition, esp. suddenly: the news threw them into a panic. 4. to direct or cast (a shadow, light, etc.). 5. to project (the voice) so as to make it appear to come from other than its source. 6. to give or hold (a party). 7. to cause to fall or be upset: the horse threw his rider. 8. a. to tip (dice) out onto a flat surface. b. to obtain (a specified number) in this way. 9. to shape on a potter's wheel. 10. to move (a switch or lever) to engage or disengage a mechanism. 11. to be subjected to (a fit). 12. to turn (wood, etc.) on a lathe. 13. Inf. to baffle or astonish; confuse: the question threw me. 14. Boxing. to deliver (a punch). 15. Wrestling. to hurl (an opponent) to the ground. 16. Inf. to lose (a contest, etc.) deliberately. 17. a. to play (a card). b. to discard (a card). 18. (of an animal) to give birth to (young). 19. to twist or spin (filaments) into thread. 20. Austral. inf. (often foll. by at) to mock or poke fun. 21. **throw cold water on.** Inf. to discourage or disparage. 22. **throw oneself at.** to strive actively to attract the attention or affection of. 23. **throw oneself into.** to involve oneself enthusiastically in. 24. **throw oneself on.** to rely entirely upon. ~n. 25. the act or an instance of throwing. 26. the distance over which anything may be thrown: a stone's throw. 27. Inf. a chance or try. 28. an act or result of throwing dice. 29. a. the eccentricity of a cam. b. the radial distance between the central axis of a crankshaft and the axis of a crankpin forming part of the shaft. 30. U.S. a decorative blanket or cover. 31. Geol. the vertical displacement of rock strata at a fault. 32. Physics. the deflection of a measuring instrument as a result of a fluctuation. ~See also **throwaway, throwback, throw in,** etc. —'**thrower** n.

throwaway ('θrəʊəˌweɪ) adj. 1. (prenominal) Chiefly Brit. said or done incidentally, esp. for rhetorical effect; casual: a throwaway remark. ~n. 2. a. anything that can be thrown away or discarded. b. (as modifier): a

(Sl.), flush of excitement, glow, kick (Inf.), pleasure, sensation, stimulation, tingle, titillation 2. flutter, fluttering, quiver, shudder, throb, tremble, tremor, vibration ~v. 3. arouse, electrify, excite, flush, get a charge (Sl.), get a kick (Inf.), glow, move, send (Sl.), stimulate, stir, tingle, titillate 4. flutter, quake, quiver, shake, shudder, throb, tremble, vibrate

thrilling 1. electrifying, exciting, gripping, hair-raising, rip-roaring (Inf.), riveting, rousing, sensational, stimulating, stirring 2. quaking, shaking, shivering, shuddering, trembling, vibrating

thrive advance, bloom, boom, burgeon, develop, do well, flourish, get on, grow, grow rich, increase, prosper, succeed, wax

thriving blooming, booming, burgeoning, developing, doing well, flourishing, going strong (Inf.), growing, healthy, prosperous, successful, wealthy, well

throb 1. v. beat, palpitate, pound, pulsate,

pulse, thump, vibrate 2. n. beat, palpitation, pounding, pulsating, pulse, thump, thumping, vibration

throng 1. n. assemblage, concourse, congregation, crowd, crush, horde, host, jam, mass, mob, multitude, pack, press, swarm 2. v. bunch, congregate, converge, cram, crowd, fill, flock, hem in, herd, jam, mill around, pack, press, swarm around, troop

throttle v. 1. choke, garrotte, strangle, strangulate 2. control, gag (Inf.), inhibit, silence, stifle, suppress

through prep. 1. between, by, from end to end of, from one side to the other of, in and out of, past 2. as a consequence or result of, because of, by means of, by virtue of, by way of, using, via, with the help of 3. during, in, in the middle of, throughout 4. With at the end of, done, finished, having completed, having had enough of ~adj. 5. completed, done, ended, finished, terminated, washed up (Inf.) ~adv. 6. **through and through** alto-

gether, completely, entirely, fully, thoroughly, totally, to the core, unreservedly, utterly, wholly

throughout all over, all the time, all through, during the whole of, everywhere, for the duration of, from beginning to end, from end to end, from start to finish, from the start, over the length and breadth of, right through, the whole time, through the whole of

throw v. 1. cast, chuck (Inf.), fling, heave, hurl, launch, lob (Inf.), pitch, project, propel, put, send, shy, sling, toss 2. Inf. astonish, baffle, confound, confuse, disconcert, dumbfound, put one off one's stroke, throw off, throw one off one's stride, throw out 3. bring down, dislodge, fell, floor, hurl to the ground, overturn, unseat, upset ~n. 4. cast, fling, heave, lob (Inf.), pitch, projection, put, shy, sling, toss 5. Inf. attempt, chance, essay, gamble, hazard, try, venture, wager

throwaway carton. **3.** *Chiefly U.S.* a handbill. ~*vb.*
throw away. (*tr., adv.*) **4.** to get rid of; discard. **5.** to fail to make good use of; waste.

throwback ('θrəʊˌbæk) *n.* **1. a.** a person, animal, or plant that has the characteristics of an earlier or more primitive type. **b.** a reversion to such an organism. ~*vb.* **throw back.** (*adv.*) **2.** (*intr.*) to revert to an earlier or more primitive type. **3.** (*tr.;* foll. by *on*) to force to depend (on): *the crisis threw her back on her faith in God.*

throw in *vb.* (*tr., adv.*) **1.** to add at no additional cost. **2.** to contribute or interpose (a remark, argument, etc.). **3. throw in the towel** (*or* **sponge**). to give in; accept defeat. ~*n.* **throw-in. 4.** *Soccer.* the method of putting the ball into play after it has gone into touch by throwing it to a teammate.

throw off *vb.* (*tr., adv.*) **1.** to free oneself of; discard. **2.** to produce or utter in a casual manner. **3.** to escape from or elude. **4.** to confuse or disconcert. **5.** (often foll. by *at*) *Austral. inf.* to deride or ridicule.

throw out *vb.* (*tr., adv.*) **1.** to discard or reject. **2.** to expel or dismiss, esp. forcibly. **3.** to construct (something projecting or prominent). **4.** to put forward or offer. **5.** to utter in a casual or indirect manner. **6.** to confuse or disconcert. **7.** to give off or emit. **8.** *Cricket.* (of a fielder) to put (the batsman) out by throwing the ball to hit the wicket. **9.** *Baseball.* to make a throw to a teammate who in turn puts out (a base runner).

throw over *vb.* (*tr., adv.*) **1.** to forsake or abandon; jilt.

throw together *vb.* (*tr., adv.*) **1.** to assemble hurriedly. **2.** to cause to become casually acquainted.

throw up *vb.* (*adv., mainly tr.*) **1.** to give up; abandon. **2.** to construct hastily. **3.** to reveal; produce. **4.** (*also intr.*) *Inf.* to vomit.

thru (θruː) *prep., adv., adj. U.S. not standard.* a variant spelling of **through.**

thrum¹ (θrʌm) *vb.* **thrumming, thrummed. 1.** to strum rhythmically but without expression on (a musical instrument). **2.** (*intr.*) to drum incessantly: *rain thrummed on the roof.* ~*n.* **3.** a repetitive strumming.

thrum² (θrʌm) *n.* **1. a.** any of the unwoven ends of warp thread remaining on the loom when the web has been removed. **b.** such ends of thread collectively. **2.** a fringe or tassel of short unwoven threads. ~*vb.* **thrumming, thrummed. 3.** (*tr.*) to trim with thrums.

thrush¹ (θrʌʃ) *n.* any of a subfamily of songbirds esp. those having a brown plumage with a spotted breast, such as the mistle thrush and song thrush.

thrush² (θrʌʃ) *n.* **1.** a fungal disease, esp. of infants, characterized by the formation of whitish spots. **2.** a vaginal infection caused by the same fungus. **3.** a softening of the frog of a horse's hoof characterized by inflammation and a thick foul discharge.

thrust (θrʌst) *vb.* **1.** to put with force into (something); push through or against. **2.** to force (oneself or another) into some condition or situation. **3.** to make a stab or lunge at. ~*n.* **4.** a forceful drive, push, stab, or lunge. **5.** a force, esp. one that produces motion. **6. a.** a propulsive force produced by the fluid pressure or the change of momentum of the fluid in a jet engine, rocket engine, etc. **b.** a similar force produced by a propeller. **7.** a

continuous pressure exerted by one part of an object, structure, etc., against another. **8.** force, impetus, or drive.

thruster ('θrʌstə) *n.* **1.** a person or thing that thrusts. **2.** a small rocket engine, esp. one used to correct the altitude or course of a spacecraft.

thud (θʌd) *n.* **1.** a dull heavy sound. **2.** a blow or fall that causes such a sound. ~*vb.* **thudding, thudded. 3.** to make or cause to make such a sound.

thug (θʌg) *n.* **1.** a tough and violent man, esp. a criminal. **2.** (*sometimes cap.*) (formerly) a member of an organization of robbers and assassins in India. —'**thuggery** *n.* —'**thuggish** *adj.*

thulium ('θjuːlɪəm) *n.* a malleable ductile silvery-grey element. The radioisotope **thulium-170** is used as an electron source in portable x-ray units. Symbol: Tm; atomic no.: 69; atomic wt.: 168.93.

thumb (θʌm) *n.* **1.** the first and usually shortest and thickest of the digits of the hand. **2.** the corresponding digit in other vertebrates. **3.** the part of a glove shaped to fit the thumb. **4. all thumbs.** clumsy. **5. thumbs down.** an indication of refusal or disapproval. **6. thumbs up.** an indication of encouragement or approval. **7. under someone's thumb.** at someone's mercy or command. ~*vb.* **8.** (*tr.*) to touch, mark, or move with the thumb. **9.** to attempt to obtain (a lift or ride) by signalling with the thumb. **10.** (when *intr.,* often foll. by *through*) to flip the pages of (a book, etc.) in order to glance at the contents. **11. thumb one's nose at.** to deride or mock, esp. by placing the thumb on the nose with fingers extended.

thumb index *n.* **1.** a series of indentations cut into the fore-edge of a book to facilitate quick reference. ~*vb.* **thumb-index. 2.** (*tr.*) to furnish with a thumb index.

thumbnail ('θʌmˌneɪl) *n.* **1.** the nail of the thumb. **2.** (*modifier*) concise and brief: *a thumbnail sketch.*

thumbscrew ('θʌmˌskruː) *n.* **1.** an instrument of torture that pinches or crushes the thumbs. **2.** a screw with projections on its head enabling it to be turned by the thumb and forefinger.

thump (θʌmp) *n.* **1.** the sound of a heavy solid body hitting a comparatively soft surface. **2.** a heavy blow with the hand. ~*vb.* **3.** (*tr.*) to strike or beat heavily; pound. **4.** (*intr.*) to throb, beat, or pound violently. —'**thumper** *n.*

thumping ('θʌmpɪŋ) *adj.* (*prenominal*) *Sl.* huge or excessive: *a thumping loss.*

thunder ('θʌndə) *n.* **1.** a loud cracking or deep rumbling noise caused by the rapid expansion of atmospheric gases which are suddenly heated by lightning. **2.** any loud booming sound. **3.** *Rare.* a violent threat or denunciation. **4. steal someone's thunder.** to lessen the effect of someone's idea or action by anticipating it. ~*vb.* **5.** to make (a loud sound) or utter (words) in a manner suggesting thunder. **6.** (*intr.;* with *it* as subject) to be the case that thunder is being heard. **7.** (*intr.*) to move fast and heavily: *the bus thundered downhill.* **8.** (*intr.*) to utter vehement threats or denunciation; rail. —'**thundery** *adj.* —'**thunderer** *n.*

THESAURUS

throw away 1. cast off, discard, dispense with, dispose of, ditch (*Sl.*), dump (*Inf.*), get rid of, jettison, reject, scrap, throw out **2.** blow (*Sl.*), fail to exploit, fritter away, lose, make poor use of, squander, waste

throw off 1. abandon, cast off, discard, drop, free oneself of, rid oneself of, shake off **2.** elude, escape from, evade, get away from, give (someone) the slip, leave behind, lose, outdistance, outrun, shake off, show a clean pair of heels to **3.** confuse, disconcert, disturb, put one off one's stroke, throw (*Inf.*), throw one off one's stride, unsettle, upset

throw out 1. cast off, discard, dismiss, dispense with, ditch (*Sl.*), dump (*Inf.*), eject, evict, expel, get rid of, jettison, kick out (*Inf.*), reject, scrap, show the door to, throw away, turf out (*Brit. inf.*), turn down **2.** confuse, disconcert, disturb, put one off one's stroke, throw (*Inf.*), throw one off one's stride, unsettle, upset **3.** diffuse, disseminate, emit, give off, put forth, radiate

thrust *v.* **1.** butt, drive, elbow *or* shoulder

one's way, force, impel, jam, plunge, poke, press, prod, propel, push, ram, shove, urge **2.** jab, lunge, pierce, stab, stick ~*n.* **3.** drive, lunge, poke, prod, push, shove, stab **4.** impetus, momentum, motive force, motive power, propulsive force

thud *n./v.* clump, clunk, crash, knock, smack, thump, wallop (*Inf.*)

thug assassin, bandit, bruiser (*Inf.*), bully boy, cutthroat, gangster, hooligan, killer, mugger (*Inf.*), murderer, robber, ruffian, tough

thumb *n.* **1.** pollex **2. all thumbs** butter-fingered (*Inf.*), cack-handed (*Inf.*), clumsy, ham-fisted (*Inf.*), inept, maladroit **3. thumbs down** disapproval, negation, no, rebuff, refusal, rejection **4. thumbs up** acceptance, affirmation, approval, encouragement, go-ahead (*Inf.*), green light, O.K. (*Inf.*), yes ~*v.* **5.** hitch (*Inf.*), hitchhike **6.** *Often with* **through** browse through, flick through, flip through, glance at, leaf through, riffle through, run one's eye over, scan the pages of, skim

through, turn over **7.** dog-ear, finger, handle, mark **8. thumb one's nose at** be contemptuous of, cock a snook at, deride, flout, jeer at, laugh at, laugh in the face of, mock, ridicule, show contempt for, show disrespect to

thumbnail *adj.* brief, compact, concise, pithy, quick, short, succinct

thump 1. *n.* bang, blow, clout (*Inf.*), clunk, crash, knock, rap, smack, thud, thwack, wallop (*Inf.*), whack **2.** *v.* bang, batter, beat, belabour, clout (*Inf.*), crash, hit, knock, lambaste (*Sl.*), pound, rap, smack, strike, thrash, throb, thud, thwack, wallop (*Inf.*), whack

thumping colossal, enormous, excessive, exorbitant, gargantuan, gigantic, great, huge, impressive, mammoth, massive, monumental, terrific, thundering (*Sl.*), titanic, tremendous, whopping (*Inf.*)

thunder *n.* **1.** boom, booming, cracking, crash, crashing, detonation, explosion, pealing, rumble, rumbling ~*v.* **2.** blast, boom, clap, crack, crash, detonate, explode, peal, resound, reverberate, roar, rumble **3.** bark,

thunderbolt (ˈθʌndəˌbəʊlt) *n.* **1.** a flash of lightning accompanying thunder. **2.** the imagined agency of destruction produced by a flash of lightning. **3.** (in mythology) the destructive weapon wielded by several gods, esp. the Greek god Zeus. **4.** something very startling.

thunderclap (ˈθʌndəˌklæp) *n.* **1.** a loud outburst of thunder. **2.** something as violent or unexpected as a clap of thunder.

thundercloud (ˈθʌndəˌklaʊd) *n.* a towering electrically charged cumulonimbus cloud associated with thunderstorms.

thundering (ˈθʌndərɪŋ) *adj.* (*prenominal*) *Sl.* very great or excessive: *a thundering idiot.*

thunderous (ˈθʌndərəs) *adj.* **1.** producing thunder. **2.** resembling thunder, esp. in loudness. —**ˈthunderously** *adv.*

thunderstorm (ˈθʌndəˌstɔːm) *n.* a storm with thunder and lightning and usually heavy rain or hail.

thunderstruck (ˈθʌndəˌstrʌk) *or* **thunderstricken** (ˈθʌndəˌstrɪkən) *adj.* **1.** completely taken aback; amazed or shocked. **2.** *Rare.* struck by lightning.

thurible (ˈθjʊərɪbəl) *n.* another word for **censer.**

Thurs. *abbrev. for* Thursday.

Thursday (ˈθɜːzdɪ) *n.* the fifth day of the week; fourth day of the working week.

thus (ðʌs) *adv.* **1.** Also: **thusly.** in this manner: *do it thus.* **2.** to such a degree: *thus far and no further.* ~ **3.** sentence connector. therefore: *We have failed. Thus we have to take the consequences.*

thwack (θwæk) *vb.* **1.** to beat, esp. with something flat. ~*n.* **2. a.** a blow with something flat. **b.** the sound made by it.

thwart (θwɔːt) *vb.* **1.** to oppose successfully or prevent; frustrate. **2.** *Obs.* to be or move across. ~*n.* **3.** an oarsman's seat lying across a boat. ~*adj.* **4.** passing or being situated across. ~*prep., adv.* **5.** *Obs.* across.

thy (ðaɪ) *determiner.* (*usually preceding a consonant*) *Arch.* or *Brit. dialect.* belonging to or associated in some way with you (thou): *thy goodness and mercy.*

thyme (taɪm) *n.* any of various small shrubs having a strong odour, small leaves, and white, pink, or red flowers. —**ˈthymic** *adj.* —**ˈthymy** *adj.*

thymol (ˈθaɪmɒl) *n.* a white crystalline substance obtained from thyme and used as a fungicide, antiseptic, in perfumery, etc.

thymus (ˈθaɪməs) *n., pl.* **-muses** *or* **-mi** (-maɪ). a glandular organ of vertebrates, consisting in man of two lobes situated below the thyroid. It atrophies with age and is almost nonexistent in the adult.

thyroid (ˈθaɪrɔɪd) *adj.* **1.** of or relating to the thyroid gland. **2.** of or relating to the largest cartilage of the larynx. ~*n.* **3.** see **thyroid gland. 4.** a preparation of the thyroid gland of certain animals, used to treat hypothyroidism.

thyroid gland *n.* an endocrine gland of vertebrates, consisting in man of two lobes near the base of the neck. It secretes hormones that control metabolism and body growth.

thyself (ðaɪˈsɛlf) *pron. Arch.* **1. a.** the reflexive form of *thou* or *thee.* **b.** (intensifier): *thou, thyself, wouldst know.* **2.** (*preceded by a copula*) your (thy) normal or usual self.

ti (tiː) *n. Music.* a variant spelling of **te.**

Ti *the chemical symbol for* titanium.

tiara (tɪˈɑːrə) *n.* **1.** a woman's semicircular jewelled headdress for formal occasions. **2.** a high headdress worn by Persian kings in ancient times. **3.** a headdress worn by the pope, consisting of a beehive-shaped diadem surrounded by three coronets. —**tiˈaraed** *adj.*

tibia (ˈtɪbɪə) *n., pl.* **tibiae** (ˈtɪbɪˌiː) *or* **tibias. 1.** the inner and thicker of the two bones of the human leg below the knee; shinbone. **2.** the corresponding bone in other vertebrates. **3.** the fourth segment of an insect's leg. —**ˈtibial** *adj.*

tic (tɪk) *n.* spasmodic twitching of a particular group of muscles.

tick¹ (tɪk) *n.* **1.** a recurrent metallic tapping or clicking sound, such as that made by a clock. **2.** *Brit. inf.* a moment or instant. **3.** a mark (√) used to check off or indicate the correctness of something. ~*vb.* **4.** to produce or indicate by a recurrent tapping sound: *the clock ticked the minutes away.* **5.** (when *tr.*, often foll. by *off*) to mark or check with a tick. **6. what makes someone tick.** the basic drive or motivation of a person. ~See also **tick off, tick over.**

tick² (tɪk) *n.* any of a large group of small parasitic arachnids typically living on the skin of warm-blooded animals and feeding on the blood and tissues of their hosts.

tick³ (tɪk) *n.* **1.** the strong covering of a pillow, mattress, etc. **2.** *Inf.* short for **ticking.**

tick⁴ (tɪk) *n. Brit. inf.* account or credit (esp. in **on tick**).

ticker (ˈtɪkə) *n.* **1.** *Sl.* **a.** the heart. **b.** a watch. **2.** a person or thing that ticks. **3.** the U.S. word for **tape machine.**

ticker tape *n.* a continuous paper ribbon on which a tape machine prints current stock quotations.

ticket (ˈtɪkɪt) *n.* **1. a.** a piece of paper, cardboard, etc., showing that the holder is entitled to certain rights, such as travel on a train or bus, entry to a place of public entertainment, etc. **b.** (*modifier*) concerned with the issue, sale, or checking of tickets: *a ticket collector.* **2.** a piece of card, cloth, etc., attached to an article showing information such as its price, size, etc. **3.** a summons served for a parking or traffic offence. **4.** *Inf.* the certificate of competence issued to a ship's captain or an aircraft pilot. **5.** *U.S.* the group of candidates nominated by one party in an election; slate. **6.** *Chiefly U.S.* the declared policy of a political party at an election. **7.** *Brit. inf.* a certificate of discharge from the armed forces. **8.** *Inf.* the right or appropriate thing: *that's the ticket.* **9. have (got) tickets on oneself.** *Austral. inf.* to be conceited. ~*vb.* (*tr.*) **10.** to issue or attach a ticket or tickets to.

ticking (ˈtɪkɪŋ) *n.* a strong cotton fabric, often striped, used esp. for mattress and pillow covers.

tickle (ˈtɪkəl) *vb.* **1.** to touch or stroke, so as to produce pleasure, laughter, or a twitching sensation. **2.** (*tr.*) to excite pleasurably; gratify. **3.** (*tr.*) to delight or entertain (often in **tickle one's fancy**). **4.** (*intr.*) to itch or tingle. **5.** (*tr.*) to catch (a fish, esp. a trout) with the hands. **6. tickle pink** *or* **to death.** to please greatly. ~*n.* **7.** a sensation of light stroking or itching. **8.** the act of tickling. **9.** *Canad.* in the Atlantic Provinces, a narrow strait.

tickler (ˈtɪklə) *n.* **1.** Also called: **tickler file.** *U.S.* a memorandum book. **2.** *U.S.* a single-entry business journal. **3.** a person or thing that tickles. **4.** *Inf., chiefly Brit.* a difficult problem.

ticklish (ˈtɪklɪʃ) *adj.* **1.** sensitive to being tickled. **2.** delicate or difficult. **3.** easily upset or offended. —**ˈticklishly** *adv.* —**ˈticklishness** *n.*

THESAURUS

bellow, declaim, roar, shout, yell **4.** curse, denounce, fulminate, rail, threaten, utter threats

thundering decided, enormous, excessive, great, monumental, remarkable, unmitigated, utter

thunderous booming, deafening, earsplitting, loud, noisy, resounding, roaring, tumultuous

thunderstruck aghast, amazed, astonished, astounded, bowled over (*Inf.*), dazed, dumbfounded, flabbergasted (*Inf.*), floored (*Inf.*), knocked for six (*Inf.*), left speechless, nonplussed, open-mouthed, paralysed, petrified, rooted to the spot, shocked, staggered, struck dumb, stunned, taken aback

thus 1. as follows, in this fashion (manner, way), like so, like this, so, to such a degree **2.** accordingly, consequently, ergo, for this reason, hence, on that account, so, then, therefore

thwart baffle, balk, check, defeat, foil, frustrate, hinder, impede, obstruct, oppose, outwit, prevent, stop, stymie

tick¹ *n.* **1.** clack, click, clicking, tap, tapping, ticktock **2.** *Brit. inf.* flash, half a mo (*Brit. inf.*), instant, jiffy (*Inf.*), minute, moment, sec (*Inf.*), second, shake (*Inf.*), split second, trice, twinkling, two shakes of a lamb's tail (*Inf.*) **3.** dash, mark, stroke ~*v.* **4.** clack, click, tap, ticktock **5.** check off, choose, indicate, mark, mark off, select **6. what makes someone tick** drive, motivation, motive, *raison d'être*

tick² account, credit, deferred payment, the slate (*Brit. inf.*)

ticket 1. card, certificate, coupon, pass, slip, token, voucher **2.** card, docket, label, marker, slip, sticker, tab, tag

tickle *Fig.* amuse, delight, divert, entertain, excite, gratify, please, thrill, titillate

ticklish awkward, critical, delicate, difficult, nice, risky, sensitive, thorny, touchy, tricky, uncertain, unstable, unsteady

tick off 1. check off, mark off, put a tick at **2.** *Inf.* berate, censure, chide, haul over the coals (*Inf.*), lecture, rebuke, reprimand, reproach, reprove, scold, take to task, tear off a strip (*Inf.*), tell off (*Inf.*), upbraid

tick off *vb.* (*tr., adv.*) **1.** to mark with a tick. **2.** *Inf., chiefly Brit.* to scold; reprimand.

tick over *vb.* (*intr., adv.*) **1.** Also: **idle.** *Brit.* (of an engine) to run at low speed with the throttle control closed and the transmission disengaged. **2.** to run smoothly without any major changes.

ticktack ('tɪk,tæk) *n.* **1.** *Brit.* a system of sign language, mainly using the hands, by which bookmakers transmit their odds to each other at race courses. **2.** *U.S.* a ticking sound.

ticktock ('tɪk,tɒk) *n.* **1.** a ticking sound as made by a clock. ~*vb.* **2.** (*intr.*) to make a ticking sound.

tidal ('taɪd²l) *adj.* **1.** relating to, characterized by, or affected by tides. **2.** dependent on the tide: *a tidal ferry.* —'**tidally** *adv.*

tidal wave *n.* **1.** a nontechnical name for **tsunami. 2.** an unusually large incoming wave, often caused by high winds and spring tides. **3.** a forceful and widespread movement in public opinion, action, etc.

tiddler ('tɪdlə) *n. Brit. inf.* **1.** a very small fish, esp. a stickleback. **2.** a small child.

tiddly[1] ('tɪdlɪ) *adj. Brit.* small; tiny.

tiddly[2] ('tɪdlɪ) *adj. Sl., chiefly Brit.* slightly drunk.

tiddlywinks ('tɪdlɪ,wɪŋks) *n.* a game in which players try to flick discs of plastic into a cup by pressing them with other larger discs.

tide (taɪd) *n.* **1.** the cyclic rise and fall of sea level caused by the gravitational pull of the sun and moon. There are usually two high tides and two low tides in each lunar day. **2.** the current, ebb, or flow of water at a specified place resulting from these changes in level. **3.** See **ebb** (sense 3) and **flood** (sense 3). **4.** a widespread tendency or movement. **5.** a critical point in time; turning point. **6.** *Arch. except in combination.* a season or time: *Christmastide.* **7.** *Arch.* a favourable opportunity. ~*vb.* **8.** to carry or be carried with or as if with the tide. **9.** (*intr.*) to ebb and flow like the tide. —'**tideless** *adj.*

tidemark ('taɪd,mɑːk) *n.* **1.** a mark left by the highest or lowest point of a tide. **2.** *Chiefly Brit.* a mark showing a level reached by a liquid: *a tidemark on the bath.* **3.** *Inf., chiefly Brit.* a dirty mark on the skin, indicating the extent to which someone has washed.

tide over *vb.* (*tr.*) to help to get through (a period of difficulty, distress, etc.).

tidings ('taɪdɪŋz) *pl. n.* information or news.

tidy ('taɪdɪ) *adj.* **-dier, -diest. 1.** characterized by or indicating neatness and order. **2.** *Inf.* considerable: *a tidy sum of money.* ~*vb.* **-dying, -died. 3.** (when *intr.*, usually foll. by *up*) to put (things) in order; neaten. ~*n., pl.* **-dies. 4. a.** a small container for odds and ends. **b. sink tidy.** a container to retain rubbish that might clog the plug hole. **5.** *Chiefly U.S.* an ornamental protective covering for the back or arms of a chair. —'**tidily** *adv.* —'**tidiness** *n.*

tie (taɪ) *vb.* **tying, tied. 1.** (when *tr.*, often foll. by *up*) to fasten or be fastened with string, thread, etc. **2.** to make (a knot or bow) in (something). **3.** (*tr.*) to restrict or secure. **4.** to equal (the score) of (a competitor, etc.). **5.** (*tr.*) *Inf.* to unite in marriage. **6.** *Music.* **a.** to execute (two successive notes) as though they formed one note. **b.** to connect (two printed notes) with a tie. ~*n.* **7.** a bond, link, or fastening. **8.** a restriction or restraint. **9.** a string, wire, etc., with which something is tied. **10.** a long narrow piece of material worn, esp. by men, under the collar of a shirt, tied in a knot close to the throat with the ends hanging down the front. *U.S. name:* **necktie. 11. a.** an equality in score, attainment, etc., in a contest. **b.** the match or competition in which such a result is attained. **12.** a structural member such as a tie beam or tie rod. **13.** *Sport, Brit.* a match or game in an eliminating competition: *a cup tie.* **14.** (*usually pl.*) a shoe fastened by means of laces. **15.** the U.S. name for **sleeper** (on a railway track). **16.** *Music.* a slur connecting two notes of the same pitch indicating that the sound is to be prolonged for their joint time value. ~See also **tie in, tie up.**

tie beam *n.* a horizontal beam that serves to prevent two other structural members from separating, esp. one that connects two corresponding rafters in a roof or roof truss.

tied (taɪd) *adj. Brit.* **1.** (of a public house, etc.) obliged to sell only the beer, etc., of a particular brewery. **2.** (of a house) rented out to the tenant for as long as he is employed by the owner.

tie-dyeing, tie-dye *or* **tie and dye** *n.* a method of dyeing textiles to produce patterns by tying sections of the cloth together so that they will not absorb the dye. —'**tie-,dyed** *adj.*

tie in *vb.* (*adv.*) **1.** to come or bring into a certain relationship; coordinate. ~*n.* **tie-in. 2.** a link, relationship, or coordination. **3.** publicity material, a book, etc., linked to a film, etc. **4.** *U.S.* **a.** a sale or advertisement offering products of which a purchaser must buy one or more in addition to his purchase. **b.** an item sold or advertised in this way. **c.** (*as modifier*): *a tie-in sale.*

tiepin ('taɪ,pɪn) *n.* an ornamental pin of various shapes used to pin the two ends of a tie to a shirt.

tier[1] (tɪə) *n.* **1.** one of a set of rows placed one above and behind the other, such as theatre seats. **2. a.** a layer or level. **b.** (*in combination*): *a three-tier cake.* ~*vb.* **3.** to be or arrange in tiers.

tier[2] ('taɪə) *n.* a person or thing that ties.

tiercel ('tɪəs²l) *n.* a variant of **tercel.**

tie up *vb.* (*adv.*) **1.** (*tr.*) to bind securely with or as if with string, rope, etc. **2.** to moor (a vessel). **3.** (*tr.; often passive*) to engage the attentions of. **4.** (*tr.; often passive*) to conclude (the organization of something). **5.** to come or bring to a complete standstill. **6.** (*tr.*) to commit (funds, etc.) and so make unavailable for other uses. **7.** (*tr.*) to subject (property) to conditions that prevent sale, alienation, etc. ~*n.* **tie-up. 8.** a link or connection. **9.** *Chiefly U.S.* a standstill. **10.** *Chiefly U.S.* an informal term for **traffic jam.**

tiff (tɪf) *n.* **1.** a petty quarrel. **2.** a fit of ill humour. ~*vb.* **3.** (*intr.*) to have or be in a tiff.

tiffin ('tɪfɪn) *n.* (in India) a light meal, esp. at midday.

tiger ('taɪgə) *n.* **1.** a large feline mammal of forests in most of Asia, having a tawny yellow coat with black stripes. **2.** a dynamic, forceful, or cruel person. —'**tigerish** *or* '**tigrish** *adj.*

tiger lily *n.* a lily plant of China and Japan cultivated for its flowers, which have black-spotted orange petals.

tiger moth *n.* any of various moths having wings that are conspicuously marked with stripes and spots.

tiger's-eye ('taɪgəz,aɪ) *or* **tigereye** *n.* a semi-precious golden-brown stone.

tight (taɪt) *adj.* **1.** stretched or drawn so as not to be loose; taut. **2.** fitting in a close manner. **3.** held, made, fixed, or closed firmly and securely: *a tight knot.* **4. a.** of close and compact construction or organization, esp. so as to be impervious to water, air, etc. **b.** (*in combination*): *airtight.* **5.** unyielding or stringent. **6.** cramped or constricted: *a tight fit.* **7.** mean or miserly. **8.** difficult and problematic: *a tight situation.* **9.** hardly profitable: *a tight bargain.* **10.** *Econ.* **a.** (of a commodity) difficult to obtain. **b.** (of funds, money, etc.) difficult and expensive

---

THESAURUS

tide 1. course, current, ebb, flow, stream **2.** course, current, direction, drift, movement, tendency, trend

tide over aid, assist, bridge the gap, help, keep one going, keep one's head above water, keep the wolf from the door, see one through

tidings advice, bulletin, communication, greetings, information, intelligence, message, news, report, word

tidy *adj.* **1.** businesslike, clean, cleanly, methodical, neat, ordered, orderly, shipshape, spick-and-span, spruce, systematic, trim, well-groomed, well-kept, well-ordered **2.** *Inf.* ample, considerable, fair, generous, good,

goodly, handsome, healthy, large, largish, respectable, sizable, substantial ~*v.* **3.** clean, groom, neaten, order, put in order, put in trim, put to rights, spruce up, straighten

tie *v.* **1.** attach, bind, connect, fasten, interlace, join, knot, lash, link, make fast, moor, rope, secure, tether, truss, unite **2.** bind, confine, hamper, hinder, hold, limit, restrain, restrict **3.** be even, be neck and neck, draw, equal, match ~*n.* **4.** band, bond, connection, cord, fastening, fetter, joint, knot, ligature, link, rope, string **5.** affiliation, allegiance, bond, commitment, connection, duty, kinship, liaison, obligation, relationship **6.** encumbrance, hindrance, limitation, restraint,

restriction **7.** dead heat, deadlock, draw, stalemate **8.** *Brit.* contest, fixture, game, match

tier bank, echelon, file, layer, level, line, order, rank, row, series, storey, stratum

tie-up association, connection, coordination, hook-up, liaison, link, linkup, relation, relationship, tie-in

tie up 1. attach, bind, pinion, restrain, tether, truss **2.** lash, make fast, moor, rope, secure **3.** engage, engross, keep busy, occupy **4.** bring to a close, conclude, end, finish off, settle, terminate, wind up, wrap up (*Inf.*)

to borrow. **c.** (of markets) characterized by excess demand or scarcity. **11.** (of a match or game) very close or even. **12.** *Inf.* drunk. **13.** *Inf.* (of a person) showing tension. **14. sit tight.** to maintain one's position, stand, or opinion firmly. ~*adv.* **15.** in a close, firm, or secure way. —**'tightly** *adv.* —**'tightness** *n.*

tighten ('taitªn) *vb.* **1.** to make or become tight or tighter. **2. tighten one's belt.** to economize.

tightfisted (,tait'fistid) *adj.* mean; miserly.

tightknit (,tait'nit) *adj.* **1.** closely integrated: *a tight-knit community.* **2.** organized carefully.

tight-lipped *adj.* **1.** secretive or taciturn. **2.** with the lips pressed tightly together, as through anger.

tightrope ('tait,rəup) *n.* a rope stretched taut on which acrobats walk or perform balancing feats. —**tightrope walker** *n.*

tights (taits) *pl. n.* **1.** Also called (esp. U.S. and Austral.): **pantihose.** a one-piece clinging garment covering the body from the waist to the feet, worn by women and also by acrobats, dancers, etc. **2.** a similar garment formerly worn by men, as in the 16th century with a doublet.

tigress ('taigris) *n.* **1.** a female tiger. **2.** a fierce, cruel, or wildly passionate woman.

tike (taik) *n.* a variant spelling of **tyke.**

tilde ('tildə) *n.* the diacritical mark (˜) placed over a letter to indicate a nasal sound, as in Spanish *señor.*

tile (tail) *n.* **1.** a flat thin slab of fired clay, rubber, linoleum, etc. used with others to cover a roof, floor, wall, etc. **2.** a short pipe made of earthenware, plastic, etc., used with others to form a drain. **3.** tiles collectively. **4.** a rectangular block used as a playing piece in mahjong and other games. **5. on the tiles.** *Inf.* on a spree, esp. of drinking or debauchery. ~*vb.* **6.** (*tr.*) to cover with tiles. —**'tiler** *n.*

tiling ('tailiŋ) *n.* **1.** tiles collectively. **2.** something made of or surfaced with tiles.

till[1] (til) *conj., prep.* short for **until.** Also (not standard): **'til.**

▷ **Usage.** *Till* is a variant of *until* that is acceptable at all levels of language. *Until* is, however, often preferred at the beginning of a sentence in formal writing.

till[2] (til) *vb.* **1.** to cultivate and work (land) for the raising of crops. **2.** (*tr.*) to plough. —**'tillable** *adj.* —**'tiller** *n.*

till[3] (til) *n.* **1.** a box, case, or drawer in which money is kept, esp. in a shop. **2.** another term for **cash register.**

tillage ('tilidʒ) *n.* **1.** the act, process, or art of tilling. **2.** tilled land.

tiller ('tilə) *n. Naut.* a handle fixed to the top of a rudderpost to serve as a lever in steering it. —**'tillerless** *adj.*

tilt (tilt) *vb.* **1.** to incline or cause to incline at an angle. **2.** (*usually intr.*) to attack or overthrow (a person) in a tilt or joust. **3.** (when *intr.*, often foll. by *at*) to aim or thrust: *to tilt a lance.* **4.** (*tr.*) to forge with a tilt hammer. ~*n.* **5.** a slope or angle: *at a tilt.* **6.** the act of tilting. **7.** (esp. in medieval Europe) **a.** a jousting contest. **b.** a thrust with a lance or pole delivered during a tournament. **8.** any dispute or contest. **9.** (at) **full tilt.** at full speed or force. —**'tilter** *n.*

tilth (tilθ) *n.* **1.** the act or process of tilling land. **2.** the condition of soil or land that has been tilled.

Tim. *Bible. abbrev. for* Timothy.

timber ('timbə) *n.* **1. a.** wood, esp. when regarded as a construction material. **b.** (*as modifier*): *a timber cottage.* Usual U.S. word: **lumber. 2. a.** trees collectively. **b.** *Chiefly U.S.* woodland. **3.** a piece of wood used in a structure. **4.** *Naut.* a frame in a wooden vessel. ~*vb.* **5.** (*tr.*) to provide with timbers. ~*interj.* **6.** a lumberjack's

shouted warning when a tree is about to fall. —**'timbered** *adj.* —**'timbering** *n.*

timber line *n.* the altitudinal or latitudinal limit of tree growth. Also called: **tree line.**

timbre ('timbə, 'tæmbə) *n.* **1.** *Phonetics.* the distinctive tone quality differentiating one vowel or sonant from another. **2.** *Music.* tone colour or quality of sound.

timbrel ('timbrəl) *n. Chiefly biblical.* a tambourine.

Timbuktu (,timbʌk'tuː) *n.* **1.** a town in central Mali: terminus of a trans-Saharan caravan route. **2.** any distant or outlandish place: *from here to Timbuktu.*

time (taim) *n.* **1.** the continuous passage of existence in which events pass from a state of potentiality in the future, through the present, to a state of finality in the past. Related adj.: **temporal. 2.** *Physics.* a quantity measuring duration, usually with reference to a periodic process such as the rotation of the earth or the vibration of electromagnetic radiation emitted from certain atoms. Time is considered as a fourth dimension required to specify an event. **3.** a specific point on this continuum expressed in hours and minutes: *the time is four o'clock.* **4.** a system of reckoning for expressing time: *Greenwich mean time.* **5. a.** a definite and measurable portion of this continuum. **b.** (*as modifier*): *time limit.* **6. a.** an accepted period such as a day, season, etc. **b.** (*in combination*): *springtime.* **7.** an unspecified interval; a while. **8.** (*often pl.*) a period or point marked by specific attributes or events: *the Victorian times.* **9.** a sufficient interval or period: *have you got time to help me?* **10.** an instance or occasion: *I called you three times.* **11.** an occasion or period of specified quality: *have a good time.* **12.** the duration of human existence. **13.** the heyday of human life: *in her time she was a great star.* **14.** a suitable moment: *it's time I told you.* **15.** the expected interval in which something is done. **16.** a particularly important moment, esp. childbirth or death: *her time had come.* **17.** (*pl.*) indicating a degree or amount calculated by multiplication with the number specified: *ten times three is thirty.* **18.** (*often pl.*) the fashions, thought, etc., of the present age (esp. in **ahead of one's time, behind the times**). **19.** *Brit.* Also: **closing time.** the time at which bars, pubs, etc. are legally obliged to stop selling alcoholic drinks. **20.** *Inf.* a term in jail (esp. in **do time**). **21. a.** a customary or full period of work. **b.** the rate of pay for this period. **22.** Also (esp. U.S.): **metre. a.** the system of combining beats or pulses in music into successive groupings by which the rhythm of the music is established. **b.** a specific system having a specific number of beats in each grouping or bar: *duple time.* **23.** *Music.* short for **time value. 24. against time.** in an effort to complete something in a limited period. **25. ahead of time.** before the deadline. **26. at one time. a.** once; formerly. **b.** simultaneously. **27. at the same time. a.** simultaneously. **b.** nevertheless; however. **28. at times.** sometimes. **29. beat time.** to indicate the tempo of a piece of music by waving a baton or a hand, etc. **30. for the time being.** for the moment; temporarily. **31. from time to time.** at intervals; occasionally. **32. have no time for.** to have no patience with; not tolerate. **33. in good time. a.** early. **b.** quickly. **34. in no time.** very quickly. **35. in one's own time. a.** outside paid working hours. **b.** at one's own rate. **36. in time. a.** early or at the appointed time. **b.** *Music.* at a correct metrical or rhythmical pulse. **37. keep time.** to observe correctly the accent or rhythmical pulse of a piece of music in relation to tempo. **38. make time (with).** *U.S. inf.* to succeed in seducing. **39. in the nick of time.** at the last possible moment. **40. on time. a.** at the expected or scheduled time. **b.** *U.S.* payable in instalments. **41. pass the time of day.** to exchange casual greetings (with an ac-

---

THESAURUS

tight 1. close, close-fitting, compact, constricted, cramped, fast, firm, fixed, narrow, rigid, secure, snug, stiff, stretched, taut, tense 2. hermetic, impervious, proof, sealed, sound, watertight 3. harsh, inflexible, rigid, rigorous, severe, stern, strict, stringent, tough, uncompromising, unyielding 4. close, grasping, mean, miserly, niggardly, parsimonious, penurious, sparing, stingy, tightfisted 5. dangerous, difficult, hazardous, perilous, precarious, problematic, sticky (*Inf.*), ticklish, tough, tricky, troublesome, worrisome 6. close, even, evenly-balanced, near, well-matched 7.

Inf. drunk, half cut (*Brit. sl.*), half seas over (*Brit. inf.*), inebriated, in one's cups, intoxicated, pickled (*Inf.*), pie-eyed (*Sl.*), plastered (*Sl.*), smashed (*Sl.*), sozzled (*Inf.*), stewed (*Sl.*), stoned (*Sl.*), three sheets in the wind (*Sl.*), tiddly (*Brit. sl.*), tipsy, under the influence (*Inf.*)

tighten close, constrict, cramp, fasten, fix, narrow, rigidify, screw, secure, squeeze, stiffen, stretch, tauten, tense

till[1] cultivate, dig, plough, turn over, work

till[2] cash box, cash drawer, cash register

tilt *v.* 1. cant, incline, lean, list, slant, slope,

tip 2. attack, break a lance, clash, contend, cross swords, duel, encounter, fight, joust, overthrow, spar ~*n.* 3. angle, cant, inclination, incline, list, pitch, slant, slope 4. *Medieval history* clash, combat, duel, encounter, fight, joust, lists, set-to (*Inf.*), tournament, tourney 5. (at) **full tilt** for dear life, full force, full speed, headlong, like a bat out of hell (*Inf.*), like the clappers (*Brit. inf.*)

timber beams, boards, forest, logs, planks, trees, wood

quaintance). **42. time and again.** frequently. **43. time off.** a period when one is absent from work for a holiday, through sickness, etc. **44. time out of mind.** from time immemorial. **45. time of one's life.** a very enjoyable or memorable period of time. **46.** (*modifier*) operating automatically at or for a set time: *time lock; time switch.* ~*vb.* (*tr.*) **47.** to ascertain the duration or speed of. **48.** to set a time for. **49.** to adjust to keep accurate time. **50.** to pick a suitable time for. **51.** *Sport.* to control the execution or speed of (an action). ~*interj.* **52.** the word called out by a publican signalling that it is closing time.

time and a half *n.* the rate of pay equalling one and a half times the normal rate, often offered for overtime work.

time and motion study *n.* the analysis of industrial or work procedures to determine the most efficient methods of operation. Also: **time and motion, time study, motion study.**

time bomb *n.* a bomb containing a timing mechanism that determines the time at which it will detonate.

time capsule *n.* a container holding articles, documents, etc., representative of the current age, buried for discovery in the future.

time clock *n.* a clock which records, by punching or stamping **timecards** inserted into it, the time of arrival or departure of people, such as employees in a factory.

time exposure *n.* **1.** an exposure of a photographic film for a relatively long period, usually a few seconds. **2.** a photograph produced by such an exposure.

time-honoured *adj.* having been observed for a long time and sanctioned by custom.

timekeeper ('taɪmˌkiːpə) *n.* **1.** a person or thing that keeps or records time. **2.** an employee who maintains a record of the hours worked by the other employees. **3.** an employee whose record of punctuality is of a specified nature: *a bad timekeeper.* —**'time**ˌkeeping *n.*

timeless ('taɪmlɪs) *adj.* **1.** unaffected or unchanged by time; ageless. **2.** eternal. —**'timelessly** *adv.* —**'timelessness** *n.*

timely ('taɪmlɪ) *adj.* **-lier, -liest,** *adv.* at the right or an opportune or appropriate time.

time-out *n. Chiefly U.S.* **1.** *Sport.* an interruption in play during which players rest, discuss tactics, etc. **2.** a period of rest; break.

timepiece ('taɪmˌpiːs) *n.* any of various devices, such as a clock, watch, or chronometer, which measure and indicate time.

timer ('taɪmə) *n.* **1.** a device for measuring, recording, or indicating time. **2.** a switch or regulator that causes a mechanism to operate at a specific time. **3.** a person or thing that times.

timeserver ('taɪmˌsɜːvə) *n.* a person who compromises and changes his opinions, way of life, etc., to suit the current fashions.

time sharing *n.* **1.** a system by which users at different terminals of a computer can, because of its high speed, apparently communicate with it at the same time. **2.** a system of part-ownership of a property, such as a flat or villa, for use as a holiday home, whereby each partici-

pant owns the property for a particular period every year.

time signature *n. Music.* a sign usually consisting of two figures, one above the other, the upper figure representing the number of beats per bar and the lower one the time value of each beat: it is placed after the key signature.

timetable ('taɪmˌteɪbəl) *n.* a list or table of events arranged according to the time when they take place; schedule.

timeworn ('taɪmˌwɔːn) *adj.* **1.** showing the adverse effects of overlong use or of old age. **2.** hackneyed; trite.

time zone *n.* a region throughout which the same standard time is used. There are 24 time zones in the world, demarcated approximately by meridians at 15° intervals, an hour apart.

timid ('tɪmɪd) *adj.* **1.** easily frightened or upset, esp. by human contact; shy. **2.** indicating shyness or fear. —**ti'midity** *or* **'timidness** *n.* —**'timidly** *adv.*

timing ('taɪmɪŋ) *n.* the regulation of actions or remarks in relation to others to produce the best effect, as in music, the theatre, etc.

timorous ('tɪmərəs) *adj.* **1.** fearful or timid. **2.** indicating fear or timidity. —**'timorously** *adv.* —**'timorousness** *n.*

timpani *or* **tympani** ('tɪmpənɪ) *pl. n.* (*sometimes functioning as sing.*) a set of kettledrums. —**'timpanist** *or* **'tympanist** *n.*

tin (tɪn) *n.* **1.** a malleable silvery-white metallic element, used extensively in alloys, esp. bronze and pewter, and as a noncorroding coating for steel. Symbol: Sn; atomic no.: 50; atomic wt.: 118.69. **2.** Also called (esp. U.S.): **can.** an airtight sealed container of thin sheet metal coated with tin, used for preserving and storing food or drink. **3.** any container made of metallic tin. **4.** Also called: **tinful.** the contents of a tin. **5.** *N.Z. & Austral.* galvanized iron: *a tin roof.* **6.** any metal regarded as cheap or flimsy. **7.** *Brit.* a loaf of bread with a rectangular shape. **8.** *N.Z.* a receptacle for home-baked biscuits, etc. (esp. in **to fill her tins** to bake a supply of biscuits, etc.). ~*vb.* **tinning, tinned.** (*tr.*) **9.** to put (food, etc.) into a tin or tins; preserve in a tin. **10.** to plate or coat with tin. **11.** to prepare (a metal) for soldering or brazing by applying a thin layer of solder to the surface. ~Related adjs.: **stannic, stannous.**

tin can *n.* a metal food container, esp. when empty.

tincture ('tɪŋktʃə) *n.* **1.** a medicinal extract in a solution of alcohol. **2.** a tint, colour, or tinge. **3.** a slight flavour, aroma, or trace. **4.** a colour or metal used on heraldic arms. **5.** *Obs.* a dye. ~*vb.* **6.** (*tr.*) to give a tint or colour to.

tinder ('tɪndə) *n.* **1.** dry wood or other easily combustible material used for lighting a fire. **2.** anything inflammatory or dangerous. —**'tindery** *adj.*

tinderbox ('tɪndəˌbɒks) *n.* **1.** a box used formerly for holding tinder, esp. one fitted with a flint and steel. **2.** a person or thing that is particularly touchy or explosive.

tine (taɪn) *n.* **1.** a slender prong, esp. of a fork. **2.** any of the sharp terminal branches of a deer's antler. —**tined** *adj.*

tinfoil ('tɪnˌfɔɪl) *n.* **1.** thin foil made of tin or an alloy of

---

THESAURUS

time *n.* **1.** age, chronology, date, duration, epoch, era, generation, hour, interval, period, season, space, span, spell, stretch, term, while **2.** instance, juncture, occasion, point, stage **3.** allotted span, day, duration, life, life span, lifetime, season **4.** heyday, hour, peak **5.** *Mus.* beat, measure, metre, rhythm, tempo **6. all the time** always, at all times, constantly, continually, continuously, ever, for the duration, perpetually, throughout **7. at one time a.** for a while, formerly, hitherto, once, once upon a time, previously **b.** all at once, at the same time, simultaneously, together **8. at times** every now and then, every so often, from time to time, now and then, occasionally, once in a while, on occasion, sometimes **9. behind the times** antiquated, dated, obsolete, old-fashioned, old hat, outdated, outmoded, out of date, out of fashion, out of style, passé, square (*Inf.*) **10. for the time being** for now, for the moment, for the present, in the meantime, meantime, meanwhile, pro tem,

temporarily **11. from time to time** at times, every now and then, every so often, now and then, occasionally, once in a while, on occasion, sometimes **12. in good time a.** early, on time, with time to spare **b.** quickly, rapidly, speedily, swiftly, with dispatch **13. in no time** before one knows it, before you can say Jack Robinson, in an instant, in a trice (flash, jiffy, moment), in two shakes of a lamb's tail (*Inf.*), quickly, rapidly, speedily, swiftly **14. in time a.** at the appointed time, early, in good time, on schedule, on time, with time to spare **b.** by and by, eventually, one day, someday, sooner or later, ultimately **15. on time** in good time, on the dot, punctually **16. time and again** frequently, many times, often, on many occasions, over and over again, repeatedly, time after time ~*v.* **17.** clock, control, count, judge, measure, regulate, schedule, set

timeless abiding, ageless, ceaseless, changeless, deathless, endless, enduring,

eternal, everlasting, immortal, immutable, imperishable, indestructible, lasting, permanent, persistent, undying

timely appropriate, at the right time, convenient, judicious, opportune, prompt, propitious, punctual, seasonable, suitable, well-timed

timetable agenda, calendar, curriculum, diary, list, order of the day, programme, schedule

timid afraid, apprehensive, bashful, cowardly, coy, diffident, faint-hearted, fearful, irresolute, modest, mousy, nervous, pusillanimous, retiring, shrinking, shy, timorous

timorous afraid, apprehensive, bashful, cowardly, coy, diffident, faint-hearted, fearful, frightened, irresolute, mousy, nervous, pusillanimous, retiring, shrinking, shy, timid, trembling

tin and lead. **2.** thin foil made of aluminium; used for wrapping foodstuffs.

ting (tɪŋ) n. **1.** a high metallic sound such as that made by a small bell. ~vb. **2.** to make or cause to make such a sound.

ting-a-ling ('tɪŋə'lɪŋ) n. the sound of a small bell.

tinge (tɪndʒ) n. **1.** a slight tint or colouring. **2.** any slight addition. ~vb. **tingeing** or **tinging, tinged.** (tr.) **3.** to colour or tint faintly. **4.** to impart a slight trace to: *her thoughts were tinged with nostalgia.*

tingle ('tɪŋɡəl) vb. **1.** (usually intr.) to feel or cause to feel a prickling, itching, or stinging sensation of the flesh, as from a cold plunge. ~n. **2.** a sensation of tingling. —'**tingler** n. —'**tingly** adj.

tin god n. **1.** a self-important person. **2.** a person erroneously regarded as holy or venerable.

tinker ('tɪŋkə) n. **1.** (esp. formerly) a travelling mender of pots and pans. **2.** a clumsy worker. **3.** a person who enjoys playing with mechanical things. ~vb. **4.** (intr.; foll. by with) to play, fiddle, or meddle (with machinery, etc.), esp. while undertaking repairs. **5.** to mend (pots and pans) as a tinker. —'**tinkerer** n.

tinker's damn or **cuss** n. Sl. the slightest heed (esp. in **not give a tinker's damn** or **cuss**).

tinkle ('tɪŋkəl) vb. **1.** to ring with a high tinny sound like a small bell. **2.** (tr.) to announce or summon by such a ringing. **3.** (intr.) Brit. inf. to urinate. ~n. **4.** a high clear ringing sound. **5.** the act of tinkling. **6.** Brit. inf. a telephone call. —'**tinkly** adj.

tin lizzie ('lɪzɪ) n. Inf. an old or decrepit car.

tinny ('tɪnɪ) adj. **-nier, -niest. 1.** of or resembling tin. **2.** cheap or shoddy. **3.** (of a sound) high, thin, and metallic. **4.** (of food or drink) flavoured with metal, as from a container. **5.** Austral. inf. lucky. ~n. **6.** Austral. sl. a can of beer. —'**tinnily** adv. —'**tinniness** n.

tin-opener n. a small tool for opening tins.

tin plate n. **1.** thin steel sheet coated with a layer of tin that protects the steel from corrosion. ~vb. **tin-plate. 2.** (tr.) to coat with a layer of tin.

tinpot ('tɪn,pɒt) adj. (prenominal) Brit. inf. inferior, cheap, or worthless.

tinsel ('tɪnsəl) n. **1.** a decoration consisting of a piece of string with thin strips of metal foil attached along its length. **2.** a yarn or fabric interwoven with strands of glittering thread. **3.** anything cheap, showy, and gaudy. ~vb. **-selling, -selled** or U.S. **-seling, -seled.** (tr.) **4.** to decorate with or as if with tinsel: *snow tinsels the trees.* **5.** to give a gaudy appearance to.

tinsmith ('tɪn,smɪθ) n. a person who works with tin or tin plate.

tint (tɪnt) n. **1.** a shade of a colour, esp. a pale one. **2.** a colour that is softened by the addition of white. **3.** a tinge. **4.** a dye for the hair. **5.** a trace or hint. **6.** Engraving. uniform shading, produced esp. by hatching. ~vb. **7.** (tr.) to colour or tinge. **8.** (intr.) to acquire a tint. —'**tinter** n.

tintinnabulation (,tɪntɪ,næbju'leɪʃən) n. the act or an instance of the ringing or pealing of bells.

tiny ('taɪnɪ) adj. **-nier, -niest.** very small. —'**tinily** adv. —'**tininess** n.

tip[1] (tɪp) n. **1.** a narrow or pointed end of something. **2.** the top or summit. **3.** a small piece forming an end: *a metal tip on a cane.* ~vb. **tipping, tipped.** (tr.) **4.** to adorn or mark the tip of. **5.** to form or cause to form a tip. —'**tipless** adj.

tip[2] (tɪp) vb. **tipping, tipped. 1.** to tilt or cause to tilt. **2.** (tr.; usually foll. by over or up) to tilt or cause to tilt, so as to overturn or fall. **3.** Brit. to dump (rubbish, etc.). **4.** **tip one's hat:** to raise one's hat in salutation. ~n. **5.** a tipping or being tipped. **6.** Brit. a dump for refuse, etc. —'**tipper** n.

tip[3] (tɪp) n. **1.** a payment given for services in excess of the standard charge; gratuity. **2.** a helpful hint or warning. **3.** a piece of inside information, esp. in betting or investing. ~vb. **tipping, tipped. 4.** to give a tip to. —'**tipper** n.

tip[4] (tɪp) vb. **tipping, tipped.** (tr.) **1.** to hit or strike lightly. ~n. **2.** a light blow.

tip-off n. **1.** a warning or hint, esp. given confidentially and based on inside information. **2.** Basketball. the act or an instance of putting the ball in play by the referee throwing it high between two opposing players. ~vb. **tip off. 3.** (tr., adv.) to give a hint or warning to.

tippet ('tɪpɪt) n. **1.** a woman's fur cape for the shoulders. **2.** the long stole of Anglican clergy worn during a service. **3.** a long streamer-like part to a sleeve, hood, etc., esp. in the 16th century.

tipple ('tɪpəl) vb. **1.** to make a habit of taking (alcoholic drink), esp. in small quantities. ~n. **2.** alcoholic drink. —'**tippler** n.

tipstaff ('tɪp,stɑːf) n. **1.** a court official. **2.** a metal-tipped staff formerly used as a symbol of office.

tipster ('tɪpstə) n. a person who sells tips on horse racing, the stock market, etc.

tipsy ('tɪpsɪ) adj. **-sier, -siest. 1.** slightly drunk. **2.** slightly tilted or tipped; askew. —'**tipsily** adv. —'**tipsiness** n.

tiptoe ('tɪp,təʊ) vb. **toeing, toed.** (intr.) **1.** to walk with the heels off the ground. **2.** to walk silently or stealthily. ~n. **3. on tiptoe. a.** on the tips of the toes or on the ball of the foot and the toes. **b.** eagerly anticipating something. **c.** stealthily or silently. ~adv. **4.** on tiptoe. ~adj. **5.** walking or standing on tiptoe.

tiptop (,tɪp'tɒp) adj., adv. **1.** at the highest point of health, excellence, etc. **2.** at the topmost point. ~n. **3.** the best in quality. **4.** the topmost point.

tip-up adj. (prenominal) able to be turned upwards around a hinge or pivot: *a tip-up seat.*

TIR abbrev. for Transports Internationaux Routiers.

tirade (taɪ'reɪd) n. a long angry speech or denunciation.

tire[1] (taɪə) vb. **1.** (tr.) to reduce the energy of, esp. by exertion; weary. **2.** (tr.; often passive) to reduce the tolerance of; bore or irritate: *I'm tired of the children's chatter.* **3.** (intr.) to become wearied or bored; flag.

tire[2] (taɪə) n., vb. the U.S. spelling of **tyre.**

tired (taɪəd) adj. **1.** weary; fatigued. **2.** no longer fresh; hackneyed.

tireless ('taɪəlɪs) adj. unable to be tired. —'**tirelessly** adv. —'**tirelessness** n.

THESAURUS

tinge n. **1.** cast, colour, dye, shade, stain, tincture, tint, wash **2.** bit, dash, drop, pinch, smack, smattering, soupçon, sprinkling, suggestion, touch, trace ~v. **3.** colour, dye, imbue, shade, stain, suffuse, tinge, tint

tingle 1. v. have goose pimples, itch, prickle, sting, tickle **2.** n. goose pimples, itch, itching, pins and needles (Inf.), prickling, quiver, shiver, stinging, thrill, tickle, tickling

tinker v. dabble, fiddle (Inf.), meddle, mess about, monkey, muck about (Brit. sl.), play, potter, toy

tinsel adj. brummagem, cheap, flashy, gaudy, meretricious, ostentatious, pinchbeck, plastic (Sl.), sham, showy, specious, superficial, tawdry, trashy

tint n. **1.** cast, colour, hue, shade, tone **2.** dye, rinse, stain, tincture, tinge, wash **3.** hint, shade, suggestion, tinge, touch, trace ~v. **4.** colour, dye, rinse, stain, tincture, tinge **5.** affect, colour, influence, taint, tinge

tiny diminutive, dwarfish, infinitesimal, in-

significant, Lilliputian, little, microscopic, mini, miniature, minute, negligible, petite, pint-sized (Inf.), puny, pygmy, slight, small, trifling, wee

tip[1] **1.** n. apex, cap, crown, end, extremity, head, peak, point, summit, top **2.** v. cap, crown, finish, surmount, top

tip[2] v. **1.** cant, capsize, incline, lean, list, overturn, slant, spill, tilt, topple over, upend, upset **2.** Brit. ditch (Sl.), dump, empty, pour out, unload ~n. **3.** Brit. dump, midden (Dialect), refuse heap, rubbish heap

tip[3] n. **1.** baksheesh, gift, gratuity, perquisite, pourboire **2.** Also **tip-off** clue, forecast, gen (Brit. inf.), hint, information, inside information, pointer, suggestion, warning, word, word of advice ~v. **3.** remunerate, reward **4.** Also **tip off** advise, caution, forewarn, give a clue, give a hint, suggest, tip (someone) the wink (Brit. inf.), warn

tipple 1. v. bend the elbow (Inf.), drink, imbibe, indulge (Inf.), quaff, swig, take a drink,

tope **2.** n. alcohol, booze (Inf.), drink, John Barleycorn, liquor, poison (Inf.)

tippler bibber, boozer (Inf.), drinker, drunk, drunkard, inebriate, soak (Sl.), sot, sponge (Inf.), toper

tirade abuse, denunciation, diatribe, fulmination, harangue, invective, lecture, outburst, philippic

tire 1. drain, droop, enervate, exhaust, fag (Inf.), fail, fatigue, flag, jade, knacker (Sl.), sink, take it out of (Inf.), wear down, wear out, weary, whack (Brit. inf.) **2.** annoy, bore, exasperate, harass, irk, irritate, weary

tired 1. all in (Sl.), asleep or dead on one's feet, dead beat (Inf.), dog-tired (Inf.), done in (Inf.), drained, drooping, drowsy, enervated, exhausted, fagged (Inf.), fatigued, flagging, jaded, knackered (Sl.), ready to drop, sleepy, spent, weary, whacked (Brit. inf.), worn out **2.** With **of** annoyed with, bored with, exasperated by, fed up with, irked by, irritated by, sick of, weary of **3.** clichéd, conventional,

tiresome ('taɪəsəm) *adj.* boring and irritating. —'**tiresomely** *adv.* —'**tiresomeness** *n.*

tiro ('taɪrəʊ) *n., pl.* **ros.** a variant spelling of **tyro.**

tissue ('tɪsjuː, 'tɪʃuː) *n.* **1.** a part of an organism consisting of a large number of cells having a similar structure and function: nerve tissue. **2.** a thin piece of soft absorbent paper used as a disposable handkerchief, towel, etc. **3.** See **tissue paper. 4.** an interwoven series: *a tissue of lies.* **5.** a woven cloth, esp. of a light gauzy nature. ~*vb.* (*tr.*) **6.** to decorate or clothe with tissue or tissue paper.

tissue paper *n.* very thin soft delicate paper used to wrap breakable goods, as decoration, etc.

tit¹ (tɪt) *n.* any of numerous small active Old World songbirds, esp. the bluetit, great tit, etc. They have a short bill and feed on insects and seeds.

tit² (tɪt) *n.* **1.** *Sl.* a female breast. **2.** a teat or nipple. **3.** *Derog.* a young woman. **4.** *Taboo sl.* a despicable or unpleasant person.

Tit. *Bible. abbrev. for* Titus.

titan ('taɪtən) *n.* a person of great strength or size.

titanic (taɪ'tænɪk) *adj.* huge.

titanium (taɪ'teɪnɪəm) *n.* a strong malleable white metallic element, which is very corrosion-resistant. It is used in the manufacture of strong lightweight alloys, esp. aircraft parts. Symbol: Ti; atomic no.: 22; atomic wt.: 47.90.

titbit ('tɪt,bɪt) *or esp. U.S.* **tidbit** *n.* **1.** a tasty small piece of food; dainty. **2.** a pleasing scrap of anything, such as scandal.

titfer ('tɪtfə) *n. Cockney rhyming sl.* a hat.

tit for tat *n.* an equivalent given in return or retaliation; blow for blow.

tithe (taɪð) *n.* **1.** (*often pl.*) a tenth part of produce, income, or profits, contributed for the support of the church or clergy. **2.** any levy, esp. of one tenth. **3.** a tenth or very small part of anything. ~*vb.* **4.** (*tr.*) **a.** to exact or demand a tithe from. **b.** to levy a tithe upon. **5.** (*intr.*) to pay a tithe or tithes. —'**tithable** *adj.*

tithe barn *n.* a large barn where, formerly, the agricultural tithe of a parish was stored.

titillate ('tɪtɪ,leɪt) *vb.* (*tr.*) **1.** to arouse or excite pleasurably. **2.** to cause a tickling or tingling sensation in, esp. by touching. —'**titil,latingly** *adv.* —,**titil'lation** *n.*

titivate *or* **tittivate** ('tɪtɪ,veɪt) *vb.* to smarten up; spruce up. —,**titi'vation** *or* ,**titti'vation** *n.*

title ('taɪtəl) *n.* **1.** the distinctive name of a work of art, musical or literary composition, etc. **2.** a descriptive name or heading of a section of a book, speech, etc. **3.** See **title page. 4.** a name or epithet signifying rank, office, or function. **5.** a formal designation, such as *Mr.* **6.** an appellation designating nobility. **7.** *Films.* **a.** short for **subtitle. b.** written material giving credits in a film or television programme. **8.** *Sport.* a championship. **9.** *Law.* **a.** the legal right to possession of property, esp. real property. **b.** the basis of such right. **c.** the documentary evidence of such right: *title deeds.* **10. a.** any customary or established right. **b.** a claim based on such a right. **11.** a definite spiritual charge or office in the church as a prerequisite for ordination. **12.** *R.C. Church.* a titular church. ~*vb.* **13.** (*tr.*) to give a title to.

title deed *n.* a document evidencing a person's legal right or title to property, esp. real property.

titleholder ('taɪtəl,həʊldə) *n.* a person who holds a title, esp. a sporting championship.

title page *n.* the page in a book that gives the title, author, publisher, etc.

title role *n.* the role of the character after whom a play, etc., is named.

titmouse ('tɪt,maʊs) *n., pl.* **-mice.** another name for **tit¹.**

titrate ('taɪtreɪt) *vb.* (*tr.*) to measure the volume or concentration of (a solution) by titration. —**ti'tratable** *adj.*

titration (taɪ'treɪʃən) *n.* an operation in which a measured amount of one solution is added to a known quantity of another solution until the reaction between the two is complete. If the concentration of one solution is known, that of the other can be calculated.

titter ('tɪtə) *vb.* (*intr.*) **1.** to snigger, esp. derisively or in a suppressed way. ~*n.* **2.** a suppressed laugh, chuckle, or snigger. —'**titterer** *n.* —'**titteringly** *adv.*

tittle ('tɪtəl) *n.* **1.** a small mark in printing or writing, esp. a diacritic. **2.** a jot; particle.

tittle-tattle *n.* **1.** idle chat or gossip. ~*vb.* **2.** (*intr.*) to chatter or gossip. —'**tittle-,tattler** *n.*

tittup ('tɪtəp) *vb.*-**tupping,-tupped** *or U.S.* -**tuping, -tuped. 1.** (*intr.*) to prance or frolic. ~*n.* **2.** a caper.

titular ('tɪtjʊlə) *adj.* **1.** of, relating to, or of the nature of a title. **2.** in name only. **3.** bearing a title. **4.** *R.C. Church.* designating any of certain churches in Rome to whom cardinals or bishops are attached as their nominal incumbents. ~*n., pl.* -**lars** *or* -**laries. 5.** the bearer of a title. **6.** the bearer of a nominal office.

tizzy ('tɪzɪ) *n., pl.* -**zies.** a state of confusion or excitement. Also called: **tiz-woz.**

T-junction *n.* a road junction in which one road joins another at right-angles but does not cross it.

Tl *the chemical symbol for* thallium.

Tm *the chemical symbol for* thulium.

T. M. *abbrev. for* transcendental meditation.

TNT *n.* 2,4,6-trinitrotoluene; a yellow solid: used chiefly as a high explosive.

to (tuː; *unstressed* tʊ, tə) *prep.* **1.** used to indicate the destination of the subject or object of an action: *he climbed to the top.* **2.** used to mark the indirect object of a verb: *telling stories to children.* **3.** used to mark the infinitive of a verb: *he wanted to go.* **4.** as far as; until: *working from Monday to Friday.* **5.** used to indicate equality: *16 ounces to the pound.* **6.** against; upon; onto: *put your ear to the wall.* **7.** before the hour of: *five to four.* **8.** accompanied by: *dancing to loud music.* **9.** as compared with, as against: *the score was eight to three.* **10.** used to indicate a resulting condition: *they starved to death.* ~*adv.* **11.** towards a fixed position, esp. (of a door) closed.

▷ **Usage.** In formal usage, *to* is always used with an infinitive and never omitted as in *come see the show.* The use of *and* instead of *to* (*try and come*) is very common in informal speech but is avoided by careful writers.

toad (təʊd) *n.* **1.** any of a group of amphibians similar to frogs but more terrestrial, having a drier warty skin. **2.** a loathsome person. —'**toadish** *adj.*

toadflax ('təʊd,flæks) *n.* a perennial plant having narrow leaves and spurred two-lipped yellow-orange flowers. Also called: **butter-and-eggs.**

toad-in-the-hole *n. Brit.* a dish made of sausages baked in a batter.

toadstool ('təʊd,stuːl) *n.* (*not in technical use*) any basidiomycetous fungus with a capped spore-producing body that is poisonous. Cf. **mushroom.**

toady ('təʊdɪ) *n., pl.* **toadies. 1.** Also **toadeater.** a person who flatters and ingratiates himself in a servile way; sycophant. ~*vb.* **2.** to fawn on and flatter (someone). —'**toadyish** *adj.* —'**toadyism** *n.*

THESAURUS

corny (*Inf.*), familiar, hackneyed, old, outworn, stale, stock, threadbare, trite, well-worn

tireless determined, energetic, indefatigable, industrious, resolute, unflagging, untiring, unwearied, vigorous

tiresome annoying, boring, dull, exasperating, flat, irksome, irritating, laborious, monotonous, tedious, trying, uninteresting, vexatious, wearing, wearisome

tiring arduous, demanding, enervative, exacting, exhausting, fatiguing, laborious, strenuous, tough, wearing, wearying

tissue 1. fabric, gauze, mesh, structure, stuff, texture, web 2. paper, paper handkerchief, wrapping paper 3. accumulation,

chain, collection, combination, concatenation, conglomeration, fabrication, mass, network, pack, series, web

titbit bonne bouche, choice item, dainty, delicacy, goody (*Inf.*), juicy bit, morsel, scrap, snack, treat

titillate arouse, excite, interest, provoke, stimulate, tantalize, tease, thrill, tickle, turn on (*Sl.*)

titillating arousing, exciting, interesting, lewd, lurid, provocative, sensational, stimulating, suggestive, teasing, thrilling

titivate doll up (*Sl.*), do up (*Inf.*), make up, prank, preen, primp, prink, refurbish, smarten up, tart up (*Brit. sl.*), touch up

title n. 1. caption, heading, inscription, la-

bel, legend, name, style 2. appellation, denomination, designation, epithet, handle (*Sl.*), moniker (*Inf.*), name, nickname, nom de plume, pseudonym, sobriquet, term 3. championship, crown, laurels 4. claim, entitlement, ownership, prerogative, privilege, right ~*v.* 5. call, designate, label, name, style, term

titter chortle (*Inf.*), chuckle, giggle, laugh, snigger, te-hee

titular honorary, in name only, nominal, puppet, putative, so-called, theoretical, token

toady 1. *n.* apple polisher (*U.S. sl.*), bootlicker (*Inf.*), crawler (*Sl.*), creep (*Sl.*), fawner, flatterer, flunkey, groveller, hanger-on,

to and fro *adj.*, **to-and-fro** *adv.* **1.** back and forth. **2.** here and there. —**toing and froing** *n.*

toast[1] ('təʊst) *n.* **1. a.** sliced bread browned by exposure to heat. **b.** (*as modifier*): *a toast rack.* ~*vb.* **2.** (*tr.*) to brown under a grill or over a fire: *to toast cheese.* **3.** to warm or be warmed: *to toast one's hands by the fire.*

toast[2] ('təʊst) *n.* **1.** a tribute or proposal of health, success, etc., given to a person or thing and marked by people raising glasses and drinking together. **2.** a person or thing honoured by such a tribute or proposal. **3.** (*esp.* formerly) an attractive woman to whom such tributes are frequently made. ~*vb.* **4.** to propose or drink a toast to (a person or thing).

toaster ('təʊstə) *n.* a person or thing that toasts, esp. an electrical device for toasting bread.

toastmaster ('təʊst,mɑːstə) *n.* a person who introduces speakers, proposes toasts, etc., at public dinners. —'**toast,mistress** *fem. n.*

tobacco (tə'bækəʊ) *n., pl.* **-cos** *or* **-coes.** **1.** any of a genus of plants having mildly narcotic properties, one species of which is cultivated as the chief source of commercial tobacco. **2.** the leaves of certain of these plants dried and prepared for snuff, chewing, or smoking.

tobacconist (tə'bækənɪst) *n. Chiefly Brit.* a person or shop that sells tobacco, cigarettes, pipes, etc.

-to-be *adj.* (*in combination*) about to be; future: *a mother-to-be; the president-to-be.*

toboggan (tə'bɒgən) *n.* **1.** a light wooden frame on runners used for sliding over snow and ice. **2.** a long narrow sledge made of a thin board curved upwards at the front. ~*vb.* (*intr.*) **3.** to ride on a toboggan. —to'**bogganer** *or* to'**bogganist** *n.*

toby jug ('təʊbɪ) *n.* a beer mug or jug in the form of a stout seated man wearing a three-cornered hat and smoking a pipe. Also called: **toby.**

toccata (tə'kɑːtə) *n.* a rapid keyboard composition for organ, harpsichord, etc., usually in a rhythmically free style.

Toc H ('tɒk 'eɪtʃ) *n.* a society formed after World War I to encourage Christian comradeship.

tocsin ('tɒksɪn) *n.* **1.** an alarm or warning signal, esp. one sounded on a bell. **2.** an alarm bell.

tod (tɒd) *n.* **on one's tod.** *Brit. sl.* on one's own.

today (tə'deɪ) *n.* **1.** this day, as distinct from yesterday or tomorrow. **2.** the present age. ~*adv.* **3.** during or on this day. **4.** nowadays.

toddle ('tɒdəl) *vb.* (*intr.*) **1.** to walk with short unsteady steps, as a child. **2.** (foll. by *off*) *Jocular.* to depart. **3.** (foll. by *round*, *over*, etc.) *Jocular.* to stroll. ~*n.* **4.** the act or an instance of toddling.

toddler ('tɒdlə) *n.* a young child, usually between the ages of one and two and a half.

toddy ('tɒdɪ) *n., pl.* **-dies.** **1.** any hot sweet drink made with whisky. **2.** the sap of various palm trees used as a beverage.

to-do *n., pl.* **-dos.** a commotion, fuss, or quarrel.

toe (təʊ) *n.* **1.** any one of the digits of the foot. **2.** the corresponding part in other vertebrates. **3.** the part of a shoe, etc., covering the toes. **4.** anything resembling a toe in shape or position. **5. on one's toes.** alert. **6. tread on someone's toes.** to offend a person, esp. by trespassing on his field of responsibility. ~*vb.* **toeing, toed.** **7.** (*tr.*) to touch, kick, or mark with the toe. **8.** (*tr.*) to drive (a nail, etc.) obliquely. **9.** (*intr.*) to walk with the toes pointing in a specified direction: *to toe inwards.* **10. toe the line** *or* **mark.** to conform strictly to rules.

toecap ('təʊ,kæp) *n.* a reinforced covering for the toe of a boot or shoe.

toed (təʊd) *adj.* **1.** having a part resembling a toe. **2.** fixed by nails driven in at the foot. **3.** (*in combination*) having a toe or toes as specified: *five-toed; thick-toed.*

toehold ('təʊ,həʊld) *n.* **1.** a small foothold to facilitate climbing. **2.** any means of gaining access, support, etc. **3.** a wrestling hold in which the opponent's toe is held and his leg twisted.

toenail ('təʊ,neɪl) *n.* **1.** a thin horny translucent plate covering part of the surface of the end joint of each toe. **2.** *Carpentry.* a nail driven obliquely. ~*vb.* **3.** (*tr.*) *Carpentry.* to join (beams) by driving nails obliquely.

toff (tɒf) *n. Brit. sl.* a well-dressed or upper-class person, esp. a man.

toffee *or* **toffy** ('tɒfɪ) *n., pl.* **-fees** *or* **-fies.** **1.** a sweet made from sugar or treacle boiled with butter, nuts, etc. **2. for toffee.** (preceded by *can't*) *Inf.* to be incompetent at: *he can't sing for toffee.*

toffee-apple *n.* an apple fixed on a stick and coated with a thin layer of toffee.

toffee-nosed *adj. Sl.,* chiefly *Brit.* pretentious or supercilious; used esp. of snobbish people.

tog (tɒg) *n.* **1.** (*usually pl.*) a garment, esp. for sport or swimming. ~*vb.* **togging, togged.** **2.** (often foll. by *up* or *out*) to dress, esp. in smart clothes.

toga ('təʊgə) *n.* **1.** a garment worn by citizens of ancient Rome, consisting of a piece of cloth draped around the body. **2.** a robe of office. —**togaed** ('təʊgəd) *adj.*

together (tə'gɛðə) *adv.* **1.** with cooperation and interchange between constituent elements, members, etc.: *we worked together.* **2.** in or into contact with each other: *to stick papers together.* **3.** in or into one place; with each other: *the people are gathered together.* **4.** at the same time. **5.** considered collectively: *all our wages put together couldn't buy that car.* **6.** continuously: *working for eight hours together.* **7.** closely or compactly united or held: *water will hold the dough together.* **8.** mutually or reciprocally: *to multiply seven and eight together.* **9.** *Inf.* organized: *to get things together.* ~*adj.* **10.** *Sl.,* chiefly *U.S.* (of a person) calm and collected; organized. **11. together with.** in addition to.
▷ **Usage.** See at **plus.**

togetherness (tə'gɛðənɪs) *n.* a feeling of closeness or affection from being united with other people.

toggle ('tɒgəl) *n.* **1.** a peg or rod at the end of a rope, chain, or cable, for fastening by insertion through an eye in another rope, chain, etc. **2.** a bar-shaped button inserted through a loop for fastening. **3.** a toggle joint or a device having such a joint. ~*vb.* **4.** (*tr.*) to supply or fasten with a toggle.

toggle joint *n.* a device consisting of two arms pivoted at a common joint and at their outer ends and used to apply pressure by straightening the angle between the two arms.

toggle switch *n.* an electric switch having a projecting lever that is manipulated in a particular way to open or close a circuit.

toil (tɔɪl) *n.* **1.** hard or exhausting work. ~*vb.* (*intr.*) **2.** to labour. **3.** to progress with slow painful movements. —'**toiler** *n.*

toilet ('tɔɪlɪt) *n.* **1.** another word for **lavatory.** **2.** the act of dressing and preparing oneself. **3.** a dressing table. **4.** *Rare.* costume. **5.** the cleansing of a wound, etc., after an operation or childbirth.

toilet paper *or* **tissue** *n.* thin absorbent paper, often wound in a roll round a cardboard cylinder (**toilet roll**), used for cleaning oneself after defecation or urination.

toiletry ('tɔɪlɪtrɪ) *n., pl.* **-ries.** an object or cosmetic used in making up, dressing, etc.

THESAURUS

jackal, lackey, lickspittle, minion, parasite, spaniel, sycophant, truckler, yes man **2.** *v.* be obsequious to, bow and scrape, butter up, crawl, creep, cringe, curry favour with, fawn on, flatter, grovel, kiss the feet of, kowtow to, lick the boots of (*Inf.*), suck up to (*Inf.*)

toast[1] *v.* brown, grill, heat, roast, warm

toast[2] *n.* **1.** compliment, drink, health, pledge, salutation, salute, tribute **2.** darling, favourite, heroine ~*v.* **3.** drink to, drink (to) the health of, pledge, salute

together *adv.* **1.** as a group, as one, cheek by jowl, closely, collectively, hand in glove, hand in hand, in a body, in concert, in co-

operation, in unison, jointly, mutually, shoulder to shoulder, side by side **2.** all at once, as one, at one fell swoop, at the same time, concurrently, contemporaneously, en masse, in unison, simultaneously, with one accord **3.** consecutively, continuously, in a row, in succession, one after the other, on end, successively, without a break, without interruption **4.** *Inf.* arranged, fixed, ordered, organized, settled, sorted out, straight, to rights ~*adj.* **5.** *Sl.* calm, composed, cool, stable, well-adjusted, well-balanced, well-organized

toil 1. *n.* application, donkey-work, drudgery, effort, elbow grease (*Inf.*), exertion,

graft (*Inf.*), hard work, industry, labour, pains, slog, sweat, travail **2.** *v.* drag oneself, drudge, graft (*Inf.*), grind (*Inf.*), grub, knock oneself out, labour, push oneself, slave, slog, strive, struggle, sweat (*Inf.*), work, work like a dog, work like a Trojan, work one's fingers to the bone

toilet 1. ablutions (*Military inf.*), bathroom, bog (*Brit. sl.*), closet, convenience, gents (*Brit. inf.*), ladies' room, latrine, lavatory, loo (*Brit. inf.*), outhouse, powder room, privy, urinal, washroom, water closet, W.C. **2.** ablutions, bathing, dressing, grooming, toilette

toilette (twɑːˈlɛt) *n.* another word for **toilet** (sense 2).

toilet training *n.* the training of an infant to use toilet facilities properly.

toilet water *n.* a form of liquid perfume lighter than cologne.

toilsome (ˈtɔɪlsəm) *or* **toilful** *adj.* laborious. —ˈtoilsomely *adv.* —ˈtoilsomeness *n.*

Tokay (təʊˈkeɪ) *n.* **1.** a sweet wine made near Tokaj, Hungary. **2.** a variety of grape used to make this. **3.** a similar wine made elsewhere.

token (ˈtəʊkən) *n.* **1.** an indication, warning, or sign of something. **2.** a symbol or visible representation of something. **3.** something that indicates authority, proof, etc. **4.** a metal or plastic disc, such as a substitute for currency for use in slot machines. **5.** a memento. **6.** a gift voucher that can be used as payment for goods of a specified value. **7.** (*modifier*) as a matter of form only; nominal: *a token increase in salary.* ~*vb.* **8.** (*tr.*) to act or serve as a warning or symbol of; betoken.

tokenism (ˈtəʊkəˌnɪzəm) *n.* the practice of making only a token effort or doing no more than the minimum, esp. in order to comply with a law.

token strike *n.* a brief strike intended to convey strength of feeling on a disputed issue.

told (təʊld) *vb.* **1.** the past tense or past participle of **tell.** ~*adj.* **2. all told.** in all: *there were seven all told.*

tolerable (ˈtɒlərəbəl) *adj.* **1.** able to be tolerated; endurable. **2.** permissible. **3.** *Inf.* fairly good. —ˌtolera'bility *n.* —ˈtolerably *adv.*

tolerance (ˈtɒlərəns) *n.* **1.** the state or quality of being tolerant. **2.** capacity to endure something, esp. pain or hardship. **3.** the permitted variation in some characteristic of an object or workpiece. **4.** the capacity to endure the effects of a poison or other substance, esp. when taken over a prolonged period.

tolerant (ˈtɒlərənt) *adj.* **1.** able to tolerate the beliefs, actions, etc., of others. **2.** permissive. **3.** able to withstand extremes. **4.** exhibiting tolerance to a drug. —ˈtolerantly *adv.*

tolerate (ˈtɒləˌreɪt) *vb.* (*tr.*) **1.** to treat with indulgence or forbearance. **2.** to permit. **3.** to be able to bear; put up with. **4.** to have tolerance for (a drug, etc.). —ˈtolerˌator *n.*

toleration (ˌtɒləˈreɪʃən) *n.* **1.** the act or practice of tolerating. **2.** freedom to hold religious opinions that differ from the established religion of a country. —ˌtolerˈationist *n.*

toll¹ (təʊl) *vb.* **1.** to ring slowly and recurrently. **2.** (*tr.*) to summon or announce by tolling. **3.** *U.S.* to decoy (game, esp. ducks). ~*n.* **4.** the act or sound of tolling.

toll² (təʊl, tol) *n.* **1. a.** an amount of money levied, esp. for the use of certain roads, bridges, etc. **b.** (*as modifier*): *toll road; toll bridge.* **2.** loss or damage incurred through a disaster, etc.: *the war took its toll of the inhabitants.* **3.** (*formerly*) the right to levy a toll.

tollgate (ˈtəʊlˌgeɪt, ˈtɒl-) *n.* a gate across a toll road or bridge at which travellers must pay.

tolu (tɒˈluː) *n.* an aromatic balsam obtained from a South American tree.

toluene (ˈtɒljuˌiːn) *n.* a colourless volatile flammable liquid obtained from petroleum and coal tar and used as a solvent and in the manufacture of many organic chemicals.

tom (tom) *n.* **a.** the male of various animals, esp. the cat. **b.** (*as modifier*): *a tom turkey.* **c.** (*in combination*): *tomcat.*

tomahawk (ˈtɒməˌhɔːk) *n.* a fighting axe with a stone or iron head, used by the North American Indians.

tomato (təˈmɑːtəʊ) *n., pl.* -**toes.** **1.** a South American plant widely cultivated for its red fleshy many-seeded fruits. **2.** the fruit of this plant, eaten in salads, as a vegetable, etc.

tomb (tuːm) *n.* **1.** a place, esp. a vault beneath the ground, for the burial of a corpse. **2.** a monument to the dead. **3. the tomb.** a poetic term for death.

tombola (tɒmˈbəʊlə) *n. Brit.* a type of lottery, esp. at a fête, in which tickets are drawn from a revolving drum.

tomboy (ˈtɒmˌbɔɪ) *n.* a girl who acts or dresses in a boyish way, liking rough outdoor activities. —ˈtomˌboyish *adj.* —ˈtomˌboyishly *adv.*

tombstone (ˈtuːmˌstəʊn) *n.* another word for **gravestone.**

tome (təʊm) *n.* **1.** a large weighty book. **2.** one of several volumes of a work.

tomfool (ˌtɒmˈfuːl) *n.* **a.** a fool. **b.** (*as modifier*): *tomfool ideas.* —ˌtomˈfoolishness *n.*

tomfoolery (ˌtɒmˈfuːlərɪ) *n., pl.* -**eries.** **1.** foolish behaviour. **2.** utter nonsense; rubbish.

tommy (ˈtɒmɪ) *n., pl.* -**mies.** (*often cap.*) *Brit. inf.* a private in the British Army.

Tommy gun *n.* an informal name for **Thompson submachine-gun.**

tommyrot (ˈtɒmɪˌrɒt) *n.* utter nonsense.

tomorrow (təˈmɒrəʊ) *n.* **1.** the day after today. **2.** the future. ~*adv.* **3.** on the day after today. **4.** at some time in the future.

Tom Thumb *n.* a dwarf; midget.

tomtit (ˌtɒmˈtɪt) *n. Brit.* any of various tits, esp. the blue-tit.

tom-tom *or* **tam-tam** *n.* a drum usually beaten with the hands as a signalling instrument.

-tomy *n. combining form.* indicating a surgical cutting of a specified part or tissue: *lobotomy.*

ton¹ (tʌn) *n.* **1.** Also called: **long ton.** *Brit.* a unit of weight equal to 2240 pounds or 1016.046 909 kilograms. **2.** Also called: **short ton, net ton.** *U.S. & Canad.* a unit of weight equal to 2000 pounds or 907.184 kilograms. **3.** See **metric ton, tonne.** a unit of weight equal to 1000 kilograms. **4.** Also called: **freight ton, measurement ton.** a unit of volume or weight used for charging or measuring freight in shipping. It is usually equal to 40 cubic feet, 1 cubic metre, or 1000 kilograms. **5.** Also called: **displacement ton.** a unit used for measuring the displacement of a ship, equal to 35 cubic feet of sea water or 2240 pounds. **6.** Also called: **register ton.** a unit of internal capacity of ships equal to 100 cubic feet. ~*adv.* **7. tons.** (*intensifier*): *the new flat is tons better than the old one.*

ton² (tʌn) *n. Sl., chiefly Brit.* a score or achievement of a hundred, esp. a hundred miles per hour, as on a motorcycle.

tonal (ˈtəʊnəl) *adj.* **1.** of or relating to tone. **2.** of or utilizing the diatonic system; having an established key. **3.**

THESAURUS

token *n.* **1.** badge, clue, demonstration, earnest, evidence, expression, index, indication, manifestation, mark, note, proof, representation, sign, symbol, warning **2.** keepsake, memento, memorial, remembrance, reminder, souvenir ~*adj.* **3.** hollow, minimal, nominal, perfunctory, superficial, symbolic

tolerable 1. acceptable, allowable, bearable, endurable, sufferable, supportable **2.** acceptable, adequate, all right, average, fair, fairly good, fair to middling, good enough, indifferent, mediocre, middling, not bad (*Inf.*), O.K. (*Inf.*), ordinary, passable, run-of-the-mill, so-so (*Inf.*), unexceptional

tolerance 1. broad-mindedness, charity, forbearance, indulgence, lenity, magnanimity, open-mindedness, patience, permissiveness, sufferance, sympathy **2.** endurance, fortitude, hardiness, hardness, resilience, resistance, stamina, staying power, toughness **3.** fluctuation, play, swing, variation

tolerant 1. broad-minded, catholic, charitable, fair, forbearing, latitudinarian, liberal, long-suffering, magnanimous, open-minded, patient, sympathetic, unbigoted, understanding, unprejudiced **2.** complaisant, easy-going, free and easy, indulgent, kind-hearted, lax, lenient, permissive, soft

tolerate abide, accept, admit, allow, bear, brook, condone, countenance, endure, indulge, permit, pocket, put up with (*Inf.*), receive, sanction, stand, stomach, submit to, suffer, swallow, take, thole (*Scot.*), turn a blind eye to, undergo, wink at

toleration 1. acceptance, allowance, condonation, endurance, indulgence, permissiveness, sanction, sufferance **2.** freedom of conscience, freedom of worship, religious freedom

toll¹ *v.* **1.** chime, clang, knell, peal, ring, sound, strike **2.** announce, call, signal, summon, warn ~*n.* **3.** chime, clang, knell, peal, ring, ringing, tolling

toll² 1. assessment, charge, customs, demand, duty, fee, impost, levy, payment, rate, tariff, tax, tribute **2.** cost, damage, inroad, loss, penalty

tomb burial chamber, catacomb, crypt, grave, mausoleum, sepulchre, vault

tombstone gravestone, headstone, marker, memorial, monument

tome book, volume, work

tomfoolery 1. buffoonery, childishness, clowning, fooling around (*Inf.*), foolishness, horseplay, idiocy, larks (*Inf.*), messing around (*Inf.*), shenanigans (*Inf.*), silliness, skylarking (*Inf.*), stupidity **2.** balderdash, baloney (*Inf.*), bilge (*Inf.*), bosh (*Inf.*), bunk (*Inf.*), bunkum, claptrap (*Inf.*), hogwash, hooey (*Sl.*), inanity, nonsense, poppycock (*Inf.*), rot, rubbish, stuff and nonsense, tommyrot, tosh, trash, twaddle

(of an answer in a fugue) not having the same melodic intervals as the subject, so as to remain in the original key. —'**tonally** adv.

tonality (təʊ'nælɪtɪ) n., pl. -ties. 1. Music. a. the presence of a musical key in a composition. b. the system of major and minor keys prevalent in Western music. 2. the overall scheme of colours and tones in a painting.

tone (təʊn) n. 1. sound with reference to quality, pitch, or volume. 2. U.S. another word for **note** (sense 10). 3. an interval of a major second; whole tone. 4. Also called: **Gregorian tone.** any of several plainsong melodies or other chants used in the singing of psalms. 5. Linguistics. any of the pitch levels or pitch contours at which a syllable may be pronounced, such as high tone, falling tone, etc. 6. the quality or character of a sound: a nervous tone of voice. 7. general aspect, quality, or style. 8. high quality or style: to lower the tone of a place. 9. the quality of a given colour; shade; tint. 10. Physiol. a. the normal tension of a muscle at rest. b. the natural firmness of the tissues and normal functioning of bodily organs in health. 11. the overall effect of the colour values and gradations of light and dark in a picture. 12. Photog. a colour of a particular area on a negative or positive that can be distinguished from surrounding areas. ~vb. 13. (intr.; often foll. by with) to be of a matching or similar tone (to). 14. (tr.) to give a tone to or correct the tone of. 15. (tr.) Photog. to soften or change the colour of the tones of (a photographic image). ~See also **tone down, tone up.** —'**toneless** adj. —'**tonelessly** adv. —'**toner** n.

tone-deaf adj. unable to distinguish subtle differences in musical pitch. —**tone deafness** n.

tone down vb. (adv.) to moderate or become moderated in tone: to tone down an argument.

tone poem n. another term for **symphonic poem.**

tone up vb. (adv.) to make or become more vigorous, healthy, etc.

tong (tɒŋ) n. (formerly) a secret society of Chinese Americans.

tongs (tɒŋz) pl. n. an instrument for grasping or lifting, consisting of a hinged, sprung, or pivoted pair of arms or levers, joined at one end. Also called: **pair of tongs.**

tongue (tʌŋ) n. 1. a movable mass of muscular tissue attached to the floor of the mouth in most vertebrates. It is used in tasting, eating, and (in man) speaking. Related adj.: **lingual.** 2. an analogous organ in invertebrates. 3. the tongue of certain animals used as food. 4. a language, dialect, or idiom: the English tongue. 5. the ability to speak: to lose one's tongue. 6. a manner of speaking: a glib tongue. 7. utterance or voice (esp. in **give tongue**). 8. anything which resembles a tongue in shape or function. 9. a promontory or spit of land. 10. a flap of leather on a shoe. 11. Music. the reed of an oboe or similar instrument. 12. the clapper of a bell. 13. the harnessing pole of a horse-drawn vehicle. 14. a projection on a machine part that serves as a guide for assembly, etc. 15. a projecting strip along an edge of a board that is made to fit a groove in another board. 16. **hold one's tongue.** to keep quiet. 17. **on the tip of one's tongue.** about to come to mind. 18. **with (one's) tongue in (one's) cheek.** Also: **tongue in cheek.** with insincere or ironical intent. ~vb. **tonguing, tongued.** 19. to articulate (notes on a wind instrument) by tonguing. 20. (tr.) to lick, feel, or touch with the tongue. 21. (tr.) to provide (a board) with a tongue. 22. (intr.) (of a piece of land) to project into a body of water. —'**tongueless** adj. —'**tongue,like** adj.

tongue-tie n. a congenital condition in which the tongue has restricted mobility as the result of an abnormally short fraenum.

tongue-tied adj. 1. speechless, esp. with embarrassment or shyness. 2. having a condition of tongue-tie.

tongue twister n. a sentence or phrase that is difficult to articulate clearly and quickly, such as Peter Piper picked a peck of pickled pepper.

tonguing ('tʌŋɪŋ) n. a technique of playing (any nonlegato passage) on a wind instrument by obstructing and uncovering the air passage through the lips with the tongue.

tonic ('tɒnɪk) n. 1. a medicinal preparation that improves the functioning of the body or increases the feeling of well-being. 2. anything that enlivens or strengthens. 3. Also called: **tonic water.** a mineral water, usually carbonated and containing quinine and often mixed with gin or other alcoholic drinks. 4. Music. a. the first degree of a major or minor scale and the tonal centre of a piece composed in a particular key. b. a key or chord based on this. ~adj. 5. serving to enliven and invigorate: a tonic wine. 6. of or relating to a tone or tones. 7. Music. of the first degree of a major or minor scale. 8. of or denoting the general effect of colour and light and shade in a picture. 9. Physiol. of or affecting normal muscular or bodily tone: a tonic spasm. —'**tonically** adv.

tonic sol-fa n. a method of teaching music, by which syllables are used as names for the notes of the major scale in any key.

tonight (tə'naɪt) n. 1. the night or evening of this present day. ~adv. 2. in or during the night or evening of this day. 3. Obs. last night.

tonnage or **tunnage** ('tʌnɪdʒ) n. 1. the capacity of a merchant ship expressed in tons. 2. the weight of the cargo of a merchant ship. 3. the total amount of shipping of a port or nation. 4. a duty on ships based either on their capacity or their register tonnage.

tonne (tʌn) n. another name for **metric ton.**

tonsil ('tɒnsəl) n. either of two small masses of lymphatic tissue situated one on each side of the back of the mouth. —'**tonsillar** adj.

tonsillectomy (,tɒnsɪ'lektəmɪ) n., pl. -mies. surgical removal of the tonsils.

tonsillitis (,tɒnsɪ'laɪtɪs) n. inflammation of the tonsils. —**tonsillitic** (,tɒnsɪ'lɪtɪk) adj.

tonsorial (tɒn'sɔːrɪəl) adj. Often facetious. of barbering or hairdressing.

tonsure ('tɒnʃə) n. 1. (in certain religions and monastic orders) a. the shaving of the head or the crown of the head only. b. the part of the head left bare by shaving. ~vb. 2. (tr.) to shave the head of. —'**tonsured** adj.

ton-up Brit. inf. ~adj. (prenominal) 1. (esp. of a motorcycle) capable of speeds of a hundred miles per hour or more. 2. liking to travel at such speeds: a ton-up boy. ~n. 3. a person who habitually rides at such speeds.

too (tuː) adv. 1. as well; in addition; also: can I come too? 2. in or to an excessive degree: I have too many things to do. 3. extremely: you're too kind. 4. U.S. inf. indeed: used to reinforce a command: you will too do it! ▷ **Usage.** See at **very.**

took (tʊk) vb. the past tense of **take.**

tool (tuːl) n. 1. a. an implement, such as a hammer, saw, or spade, that is used by hand. b. a power-driven instrument; machine tool. c. (in combination): a toolkit. 2. the cutting part of such an instrument. 3. any of the instruments used by a bookbinder to impress a design on a book cover. 4. anything used as a means of achieving an end. 5. a person used to perform dishonourable or unpleasant tasks for another. 6. a necessary medium or adjunct to one's profession: numbers are the tools of the mathematician's trade. ~vb. 7. to work, cut, or form (something) with a tool. 8. (tr.) to decorate a book cover with a bookbinder's tool. 9. (tr.) to furnish with tools. —'**tooler** n.

THESAURUS

tone n. 1. accent, emphasis, force, inflection, intonation, modulation, pitch, strength, stress, timbre, tonality, volume 2. air, approach, aspect, attitude, character, drift, effect, feel, frame, grain, manner, mood, note, quality, spirit, style, temper, tenor, vein 3. cast, colour, hue, shade, tinge, tint ~v. 4. blend, go well with, harmonize, match, suit

tone down dampen, dim, mitigate, moderate, modulate, play down, reduce, restrain,

soften, soft-pedal (Inf.), subdue, temper

tongue 1. argot, dialect, idiom, language, lingo (Inf.), parlance, patois, speech, talk, vernacular 2. articulation, speech, utterance, verbal expression, voice

tongue-tied at a loss for words, dumb, dumbstruck, inarticulate, mute, speechless, struck dumb

tonic analeptic, boost, bracer (Inf.), cordial, fillip, livener, pick-me-up (Inf.), refresh-

er, restorative, roborant, shot in the arm (Inf.), stimulant

too 1. also, as well, besides, further, in addition, into the bargain, likewise, moreover, to boot 2. excessively, exorbitantly, extremely, immoderately, inordinately, over-, overly, unduly, unreasonably, very

tool n. 1. apparatus, appliance, contraption, contrivance, device, gadget, implement, instrument, machine, utensil 2. agency, agent,

tool-maker ('tu:l₁meɪkə) n. a person who specializes in the production or reconditioning of precision tools, cutters, etc. —'**tool-₁making** n.

toot (tu:t) vb. **1.** to give or cause to give (a short blast, hoot, or whistle). ~n. **2.** the sound made by or as if by a horn, whistle, etc. **3.** U.S. sl. a drinking spree. **4.** Austral. sl. a lavatory. —'**tooter** n.

tooth (tu:θ) n., pl. **teeth** (ti:θ). **1.** any of various bonelike structures set in the jaws of most vertebrates and used for biting, tearing, or chewing. Related adj.: **dental**. **2.** any of various similar structures in invertebrates. **3.** anything resembling a tooth in shape, prominence, or function: *the tooth of a comb.* **4.** any of the indentations on the margin of a leaf, petal, etc. **5.** any of the projections on a gear, sprocket, rack, etc. **6.** taste or appetite (esp. in **sweet tooth**). **7. long in the tooth.** old or ageing. **8. tooth and nail.** with ferocity and force. ~vb. (tu:ð, tu:θ). **9.** (tr.) to provide with a tooth or teeth. **10.** (intr.) (of two gearwheels) to engage. —'**toothless** adj. —'**tooth₁like** adj.

toothache ('tu:θ₁eɪk) n. a pain in or about a tooth. Technical name: **odontalgia.**

toothbrush ('tu:θ₁brʌʃ) n. a small brush, usually with a long handle, for cleaning the teeth.

toothpaste ('tu:θ₁peɪst) n. a paste used for cleaning the teeth, applied with a toothbrush.

toothpick ('tu:θ₁pɪk) n. a small sharp sliver of wood, plastic, etc., used for extracting pieces of food from between the teeth.

tooth powder n. a powder used for cleaning the teeth, applied with a toothbrush.

toothsome ('tu:θsəm) adj. of delicious or appetizing appearance, flavour, or smell.

toothy ('tu:θɪ) adj. **toothier, toothiest.** having or showing numerous, large, or projecting teeth: *a toothy grin.* —'**toothily** adv. —'**toothiness** n.

tootle ('tu:t∘l) vb. **1.** to toot or hoot softly or repeatedly. ~n. **2.** a soft hoot or series of hoots. —'**tootler** n.

top¹ (top) n. **1.** the highest or uppermost part of anything: *the top of a hill.* **2.** the most important or successful position. *the top of the class.* **3.** the part of a plant that is above ground: *carrot tops.* **4.** a thing that forms or covers the uppermost part of anything, esp. a lid or cap. **5.** the highest degree or point: *at the top of his career.* **6.** the most important person. **7.** the best part of anything. **8.** the loudest or highest pitch (esp. in **top of one's voice**). **9.** another name for **top gear. 10.** Cards. the highest card of a suit in a player's hand. **11.** Sport. a stroke that hits the ball above its centre. **12.** a platform around the head of a lower mast of a sailing vessel. **13.** a garment, esp. for a woman, that extends from the shoulders to the waist or hips. **14. blow one's top.** to lose one's temper. **15. on top of. a.** in addition to. **b.** Inf. in complete control of (a difficult situation, etc.). **16. off the top of one's head.** with no previous preparation; extempore. **17. over the top. a.** over the parapet or leading edge of a trench. **b.** over the limit. **18. the top of the morning.** a conventional Irish morning greeting. ~adj. **19.** of, relating to, serving as, or situated on the top. ~vb. **topping, topped.** (mainly tr.) **20.** to form a top on (something): *to top a cake with cream.* **21.** to remove the top of or from. **22.** to reach or pass the top of. **23.** to be at the top of: *he tops the team.* **24.** to exceed or surpass. **25.** (also intr.) Sport. **a.** to hit (a ball) above the centre. **b.** to make (a stroke) by hitting the ball in this way. ~See also **top out, tops, top up.**

top² (top) n. **1.** a toy that is spun on its pointed base. **2. sleep like a top.** to sleep very soundly.

topaz ('təʊpæz) n. **1.** a hard glassy mineral consisting of a silicate of aluminium and fluorine in crystalline form.

It is yellow, pink, or colourless, and is a valuable gemstone. **2. oriental topaz.** a yellowish-brown variety of sapphire. **3.** either of two South American hummingbirds.

topcoat ('top₁kəʊt) n. an outdoor coat worn over a suit, etc.

top dog n. Inf. the leader or chief of a group.

top-drawer adj. of the highest standing, esp. socially.

top dressing n. a surface application of some material, such as fertilizer. —'**top-₁dress** vb. (tr.)

tope¹ (təʊp) vb. to consume (alcoholic drink) as a regular habit, usually in large quantities. —'**toper** n.

tope² (təʊp) n. a small grey shark of European coastal waters.

topee or **topi** ('təʊpiː, -pɪ) n., pl. **-pees** or **-pis.** another name for **pith helmet.**

top-flight adj. of superior or excellent quality.

topgallant (₁top'gælənt; Naut. tə'gælənt) n. **1.** a mast on a square-rigger above a topmast or an extension of a topmast. **2.** a sail set on a yard of a topgallant mast. **3.** (modifier) of or relating to a topgallant.

top gear n. **1.** Also called: **top.** the highest forward ratio of a gearbox in a motor vehicle. **2.** the highest speed, greatest energy or state of preparedness, etc.

top hat n. a man's hat with a tall cylindrical crown and narrow brim, often made of silk, now worn for some formal occasions.

top-heavy adj. **1.** unstable through being overloaded at the top. **2.** Finance. characterized by too much debt capital in relation to revenue or profit; overcapitalized.

top-hole interj., adj. Brit. inf. excellent; splendid.

topi n., pl. **-pis. 1.** ('təʊpiː). an African antelope. **2.** ('təʊpiː, -pɪ). another name for **pith helmet.**

topiary ('təʊpɪərɪ) adj. **1.** of, relating to, or characterized by the trimming or training of trees or bushes into artificial decorative shapes. ~n., pl. **-aries. 2.** topiary work. **3.** a topiary garden. —'**topiarist** n.

topic ('topɪk) n. **1.** a subject or theme of a speech, book, etc. **2.** a subject of conversation.

topical ('topɪk∘l) adj. **1.** of, relating to, or constituting current affairs. **2.** relating to a particular place; local. **3.** of or relating to a topic or topics. **4.** (of a drug, ointment, etc.) for application to the body surface; local. —**topicality** (₁topɪ'kælɪtɪ) n. —'**topically** adv.

topknot ('top₁not) n. **1.** a crest, tuft, decorative bow, chignon, etc., on the top of the head. **2.** any of several European flatfishes.

topless ('toplɪs) adj. **1.** having no top. **2. a.** denoting a costume which has no covering for the breasts. **b.** wearing such a costume.

top-level n. (modifier) of, involving, or by those on the highest level of influence or authority: *top-level talks.*

topmast ('top₁mɑːst; Naut. 'topməst) n. the mast next above a lower mast on a sailing vessel.

topmost ('top₁məʊst) adj. at or nearest the top.

topnotch ('top'notʃ) adj. Inf. excellent; superb. —'**top-'notcher** n.

topo- or before a vowel **top-** combining form. indicating place or region: *topography; topology.*

topography (tə'pogrəfɪ) n., pl. **-phies. 1.** the study or detailed description of the surface features of a region. **2.** the detailed mapping of the configuration of a region. **3.** the land forms or surface configuration of a region. **4.** the surveying of a region's surface features. **5.** the study or description of the configuration of any object. —**to-'pographer** n. —**topographic** (₁topə'græfɪk) or ₁topo-'**graphical** adj.

topology (tə'polədʒɪ) n. **1.** the branch of mathematics concerned with generalization of the concepts of conti-

---

THESAURUS

intermediary, means, medium, vehicle, wherewithal **3.** cat's-paw, creature, dupe, flunkey, hireling, jackal, lackey, minion, pawn, puppet, stooge (Sl.) ~v. **4.** chase, cut, decorate, ornament, shape, work

top n. **1.** acme, apex, apogee, crest, crown, culmination, head, height, high point, meridian, peak, pinnacle, summit, vertex, zenith **2.** cap, cork, cover, lid, stopper **3.** first place, head, highest rank, lead **4. blow one's top** blow up (Inf.), do one's nut (Brit. sl.), explode, fly into a temper, fly off the handle (Inf.), go spare (Brit. sl.), have a fit (Inf.),

lose one's temper, see red (Inf.), throw a tantrum **5. over the top** a bit much (Inf.), excessive, going too far, immoderate, inordinate, over the limit, too much, uncalled-for ~adj. **6.** best, chief, crack (Inf.), crowning, culminating, dominant, elite, finest, first, foremost, greatest, head, highest, lead, leading, pre-eminent, prime, principal, ruling, sovereign, superior, topmost, upper, uppermost ~v. **7.** cap, cover, crown, finish, garnish, roof, tip **8.** ascend, climb, crest, reach the top of, scale, surmount **9.** be first, be in charge of, command, head, lead, rule **10.** beat, best, better,

eclipse, exceed, excel, go beyond, outdo, outshine, outstrip, surpass, transcend

topic issue, matter, point, question, subject, subject matter, text, theme, thesis

topical 1. contemporary, current, newsworthy, popular, up-to-date, up-to-the-minute **2.** local, parochial, regional, restricted

topmost dominant, foremost, highest, leading, loftiest, paramount, principal, supreme, top, upper, uppermost

nuity, limit, etc. **2.** a branch of geometry describing the properties of a figure that are unaffected by continuous distortion. **3.** *Maths.* a family of subsets of a given set *S*, such that *S* is a topological space. **4.** the study of the topography of a given place. **5.** the anatomy of any specific bodily area, structure, or part. —**topologic** (ˌtɒpə-ˈlɒdʒɪk) *or* **topo'logical** *adj.* —ˌtopo'logically *adv.* —to-'pologist *n.*

top out *vb.* (*adv.*) to place the highest part of a building in position.

topper ('tɒpə) *n.* **1.** an informal name for **top hat.** **2.** a person or thing that tops or excels.

topping ('tɒpɪŋ) *n.* **1.** something that tops something else, esp. a sauce or garnish for food. ~*adj.* **2.** high or superior in rank, degree, etc. **3.** *Brit. sl.* excellent; splendid.

topple ('tɒpəl) *vb.* **1.** to tip over or cause to tip over, esp. from a height. **2.** (*intr.*) to lean precariously or totter.

tops (tɒps) *n. Sl.* **1. the tops.** a person or thing of top quality. ~*adj.* **2.** (*postpositive*) excellent.

topsail ('tɒpˌseɪl; *Naut.* 'tɒpsəl) *n.* a square sail carried on a yard set on a topmast.

top-secret *adj.* classified as needing the highest level of secrecy and security.

topside ('tɒpˌsaɪd) *n.* **1.** the uppermost side of anything. **2.** *Brit.* a lean cut of beef from the thigh containing no bone. **3.** (*often pl.*) **a.** the part of a ship's sides above the waterline. **b.** the parts of a ship above decks.

topsoil ('tɒpˌsɔɪl) *n.* the surface layer of soil.

topsy-turvy ('tɒpsɪ'tɜːvɪ) *adj.* **1.** upside down. **2.** in a state of confusion. ~*adv.* **3.** in a topsy-turvy manner. ~*n.* **4.** a topsy-turvy state.

top up *vb.* (*tr., adv.*) *Brit.* to raise the level of (a liquid, powder, etc.) in (a container), usually bringing it to the brim of the container.

toque (təʊk) *n.* **1.** a woman's small round brimless hat. **2.** *Canad.* a knitted cap with a round tassel on top. **3.** a small plumed hat popular in the 16th century.

tor (tɔː) *n.* a high hill, esp. a bare rocky one.

Torah ('tɔːrə) *n.* **1. a.** the Pentateuch. **b.** the scroll on which this is written. **2.** the whole body of the Jewish sacred writings and tradition including oral expositions of the Law.

torch (tɔːtʃ) *n.* **1.** a small portable electric lamp powered by batteries. U.S. word: **flashlight. 2.** a wooden or tow shaft dipped in wax or tallow and set alight. **3.** anything regarded as a source of enlightenment, guidance, etc. **4.** any apparatus with a hot flame for welding, brazing, etc. **5. carry a torch for.** to be in love with, esp. unrequitedly.

torchbearer ('tɔːtʃˌbɛərə) *n.* **1.** a person or thing that carries a torch. **2.** a person who leads or inspires.

tore (tɔː) *vb.* the past tense of **tear²**.

toreador ('tɒrɪəˌdɔː) *n.* a bullfighter.

torero (tɒˈrɛərəʊ) *n., pl.* **-ros.** a bullfighter, esp. one who fights on foot.

torment *vb.* (tɔːˈmɛnt). (*tr.*) **1.** to afflict with great pain, suffering, or anguish; torture. **2.** to tease or pester in an annoying way. ~*n.* ('tɔːmɛnt). **3.** physical or mental pain. **4.** a source of pain, worry, annoyance, etc. —**tor'mentor** *n.* —**tor'mentedly** *adv.*

tormentil ('tɔːməntɪl) *n.* a perennial plant of Europe and W Asia, having yellow flowers, and an astringent root used in medicine, tanning, and dyeing.

torn (tɔːn) *vb.* **1.** the past participle of **tear²**. **2. that's torn it.** *Brit. sl.* an unexpected event or circumstance has upset one's plans. ~*adj.* **3.** split or cut. **4.** divided

or undecided, as in preference: *torn between staying and leaving.*

tornado (tɔːˈneɪdəʊ) *n., pl.* **-does** *or* **-dos. 1.** a violent storm with winds whirling around a small area of extremely low pressure, usually characterized by a dark funnel-shaped cloud causing damage along its path. **2.** a small but violent squall or whirlwind. **3.** any violently active or destructive person or thing. —**tornadic** (tɔː-ˈnædɪk) *adj.*

torpedo (tɔːˈpiːdəʊ) *n., pl.* **-does. 1.** a cylindrical self-propelled weapon carrying explosives that is launched from aircraft, ships, or submarines and follows an underwater path to hit its target. **2.** a submarine mine. **3.** U.S. a firework with a percussion cap. **4.** an electric ray. ~*vb.* **5.** (*tr.*) to attack or hit (a ship, etc.) with one or a number of torpedoes. —**tor'pedo-ˌlike** *adj.*

torpedo boat *n.* a small high-speed warship designed to carry out torpedo attacks.

torpid ('tɔːpɪd) *adj.* **1.** apathetic; sluggish. **2.** (of a hibernating animal) dormant. **3.** unable to move or feel. —**tor'pidity** *or* '**torpidness** *n.* —'**torpidly** *adv.*

torpor ('tɔːpə) *n.* a state of torpidity.

torque (tɔːk) *n.* **1.** a necklace or armband made of twisted metal. **2.** any force that causes rotation.

torr (tɔː) *n.* a unit of pressure equal to one millimetre of mercury (133.322 newtons per square metre).

torrent ('tɒrənt) *n.* **1.** a fast or violent stream, esp. of water. **2.** an overwhelming flow of thoughts, words, sound, etc. —**torrential** (tɒˈrɛnʃəl) *adj.*

torrid ('tɒrɪd) *adj.* **1.** so hot and dry as to parch or scorch. **2.** arid or parched. **3.** highly charged emotionally: *a torrid love scene.* —**tor'ridity** *or* '**torridness** *n.* —'**torridly** *adv.*

Torrid Zone *n. Rare.* that part of the earth's surface lying between the tropics of Cancer and Capricorn.

torsion ('tɔːʃən) *n.* **1. a.** the twisting of a part by application of equal and opposite torques. **b.** the internal torque so produced. **2.** a twisting or being twisted. —'**torsional** *adj.* —'**torsionally** *adv.*

torso ('tɔːsəʊ) *n., pl.* **-sos** *or* **-si** (-sɪ). **1.** the trunk of the human body. **2.** a statue of a nude human trunk, esp. without the head or limbs.

tort (tɔːt) *n. Law.* a civil wrong or injury arising out of an act or failure to act, independently of any contract, for which an action for damages may be brought.

tortilla (tɔːˈtiːə) *n. Mexican cookery.* a kind of thin pancake made from corn meal.

tortoise ('tɔːtəs) *n.* **1.** any of a family of herbivorous reptiles having a heavy dome-shaped shell and clawed limbs. **2.** a slow-moving person.

tortoiseshell ('tɔːtəsˌʃɛl) *n.* **1.** the horny yellow-and-brown mottled shell of the hawksbill turtle: used for making ornaments, jewellery, etc. **2.** a small synthetic substance. **3.** a breed of domestic cat having black, cream, and brownish markings. **4.** any of several butterflies having orange-brown wings with black markings. **5. a.** a yellowish-brown mottled colour. **b.** (*as adj.*): *a tortoiseshell décor.* **6.** (*modifier*) made of tortoiseshell.

tortuous ('tɔːtjʊəs) *adj.* **1.** twisted or winding. **2.** devious or cunning. **3.** intricate. —'**tortuously** *adv.* —'**tortuousness** *n.* —**tortuosity** (ˌtɔːtjʊˈɒsɪtɪ) *n.*

torture ('tɔːtʃə) *vb.* (*tr.*) **1.** to cause extreme physical pain to, esp. to extract information, etc.: *to torture prisoners.* **2.** to give mental anguish to. **3.** to twist into a grotesque form. ~*n.* **4.** physical or mental anguish. **5.** the practice of torturing a person. **6.** a cause of mental agony. —'**torturer** *n.* —'**torturous** *adj.* —'**torturously** *adv.*

THESAURUS

topple 1. capsize, collapse, fall, fall headlong, fall over, keel over, knock down, knock over, overbalance, overturn, tip over, totter, tumble, upset **2.** bring down, bring low, oust, overthrow, overturn, unseat

topsy-turvy chaotic, confused, disarranged, disorderly, disorganized, inside-out, jumbled, messy, mixed-up, untidy, upside-down

torment *v.* **1.** afflict, agonize, crucify, distress, excruciate, harrow, pain, rack, torture **2.** annoy, bedevil, bother, chivvy, devil (*Inf.*), harass, harry, hound, irritate, nag, persecute, pester, plague, provoke, tease, trouble, vex,

worry ~*n.* **3.** agony, anguish, distress, hell, misery, pain, suffering, torture **4.** affliction, annoyance, bane, bother, harassment, irritation, nag, nagging, nuisance, pain in the neck (*Inf.*), persecution, pest, plague, provocation, scourge, thorn in one's flesh, trouble, vexation, worry

torn *adj.* **1.** cut, lacerated, ragged, rent, ripped, slit, split **2.** divided, in two minds (*Inf.*), irresolute, split, uncertain, undecided, unsure, vacillating, wavering

tornado cyclone, gale, hurricane, squall, storm, tempest, twister (*U.S. inf.*), typhoon, whirlwind, windstorm

torpor accidie, acedia, apathy, dormancy, drowsiness, dullness, inactivity, inanition, indolence, inertia, inertness, languor, laziness, lethargy, listlessness, numbness, passivity, sloth, sluggishness, somnolence, stagnancy, stupor, torpidity

torrent cascade, deluge, downpour, effusion, flood, flow, gush, outburst, rush, spate, stream, tide

tortuous 1. bent, circuitous, convoluted, crooked, curved, indirect, mazy, meandering, serpentine, sinuous, twisted, twisting, winding, zigzag **2.** ambiguous, complicated, convoluted, cunning, deceptive, devious, in-

Tory ('tɔːrɪ) n., pl. **-ries**. **1.** a member of the Conservative Party in Great Britain or Canada. **2.** a member of the English political party that opposed the exclusion of James, Duke of York from the royal succession (1679–80). Tory remained the label for conservative interests until they gave birth to the Conservative Party in the 1830s. **3.** an American supporter of the British cause; loyalist. Cf. **Whig**. **4.** (sometimes not cap.) an ultraconservative or reactionary. ~adj. **5.** of, characteristic of, or relating to Tories. **6.** (sometimes not cap.) ultraconservative or reactionary. —**'Toryism** n.

toss (tɒs) vb. **1.** (tr.) to throw lightly, esp. with the palm of the hand upwards. **2.** to fling or be flung about, esp. in an agitated or violent way: a ship tosses in a storm. **3.** to discuss or put forward for discussion in an informal way. **4.** (tr.) (of a horse, etc.) to throw (its rider). **5.** (tr.) (of an animal) to butt with the head or the horns and throw into the air. **6.** (tr.) to shake or disturb. **7.** to toss up a coin with (someone) in order to decide something. **8.** (intr.) to move away angrily or impatiently. ~n. **9.** an abrupt movement. **10.** a rolling or pitching motion. **11.** the act or an instance of tossing. **12.** the act of tossing up a coin. See **toss-up**. **13.** a fall from a horse. —**'tosser** n.

toss off vb. (adv.) **1.** (tr.) to perform, write, etc., quickly and easily. **2.** (tr.) to drink at one draught. **3.** Brit. taboo. to masturbate.

toss up vb. (adv.) **1.** to spin (a coin) in the air in order to decide between alternatives by guessing which side will fall uppermost. ~n. **toss-up**. **2.** an instance of tossing up a coin. **3.** Inf. an even chance or risk.

tot¹ (tɒt) n. **1.** a young child; toddler. **2.** Chiefly Brit. a small amount of anything. **3.** a small measure of spirits.

tot² (tɒt) vb. **totting, totted**. (usually foll. by up) Chiefly Brit. to total; add.

total ('təʊtəl) n. **1.** the whole, esp. regarded as the complete sum of a number of parts. ~adj. **2.** complete; absolute. **3.** (prenominal) being or related to a total. ~vb. **-talling, -talled** or U.S. **-taling, -taled. 4.** (when intr., sometimes foll. by to) to amount: to total six pounds. **5.** (tr.) to add up. —**'totally** adv.

totalitarian (təʊ,tælɪ'tɛərɪən) adj. of, denoting, relating to, or characteristic of a dictatorial one-party state that regulates every realm of life. —**to,tali'tarianism** n.

totality (təʊ'tælɪtɪ) n., pl. **-ties**. **1.** the whole amount. **2.** the state of being total.

totalizator ('təʊtəlaɪ,zeɪtə), **totalizer** or **totalisator, totaliser** n. **1.** a system of betting on horse races in which the aggregate stake, less tax, etc., is paid out to winners in proportion to their stake. **2.** the machine that records bets in this system and works out odds, pays out winnings, etc. ~U.S. term **pari-mutuel**.

tote¹ (təʊt) Inf. ~vb. **1.** (tr.) to carry, convey, or drag. ~n. **2.** the act of or an instance of toting. **3.** something toted. —**'toter** n.

tote² (təʊt) n. (usually preceded by the) Inf. short for **totalizator**.

tote bag n. a large handbag or shopping bag.

totem ('təʊtəm) n. **1.** (in some societies, esp. among North American Indians) an object, animal, plant, etc., symbolizing a clan, family, etc., often having ritual associations. **2.** a representation of such an object. —**totemic** (təʊ'tɛmɪk) adj. —**'totem,ism** n.

totem pole n. a pole carved or painted with totemic figures set up by certain North American Indians as a tribal symbol, etc.

tother or **t'other** ('tʌðə) Arch. or dialect. the other.

totter ('tɒtə) vb. (intr.) **1.** to move in an unsteady manner. **2.** to sway or shake as if about to fall. **3.** to be failing, unstable, or precarious. ~n. **4.** the act or an instance of tottering. —**'totterer** n. —**'tottery** adj.

toucan ('tuːkən) n. any of a family of tropical American fruit-eating birds having a large brightly coloured bill and a bright plumage.

touch (tʌtʃ) n. **1.** the sense by which the texture and other qualities of objects can be experienced when they come in contact with a part of the body surface, esp. the tips of the fingers. Related adj.: **tactile**. **2.** the quality of an object as perceived by this sense; feel; feeling. **3.** the act or an instance of something coming into contact with the body. **4.** a gentle push, tap, or caress. **5.** a small amount; hint: a touch of sarcasm. **6.** a noticeable effect; influence: the house needed a woman's touch. **7.** any slight stroke or mark. **8.** characteristic manner or style. **9.** a detail of some work: she added a few finishing touches to the book. **10.** a slight attack, as of a disease. **11.** a specific ability or facility. **12.** the state of being aware of a situation or in contact with someone. **13.** the state of being in physical contact. **14.** a trial or test (esp. in **put to the touch**). **15.** Rugby, soccer, etc. the area outside the touchlines, beyond which the ball is out of play (esp. in **in touch**). **16.** a scoring hit in fencing. **17.** an estimate of the amount of gold in an alloy as obtained by use of a touchstone. **18.** the technique of fingering a keyboard instrument. **19.** the quality of the action of a keyboard instrument with regard to the ease with which the keys may be depressed. **20.** Sl. **a.** the act of asking for money, often by devious means. **b.** the money received. **c.** a person asked for money in this way. ~vb. **21.** (tr.) to cause or permit a part of the body to come into contact with. **22.** (tr.) to tap, feel, or strike. **23.** to come or cause to come into contact with. **24.** (intr.) to be in contact. **25.** (tr.; usually used with a negative) to take hold of (a person or thing), esp. in violence. **26.** to be adjacent to (each other). **27.** (tr.) to move or disturb by handling. **28.** (tr.) to have an effect on. **29.** (tr.) to produce an emotional response in. **30.** (tr.; usually used with a negative) to partake of, eat, or drink. **31.** (tr.; usually used with a negative) to handle or deal with: I wouldn't touch that business. **32.** (when intr., often foll. by on) to allude (to) briefly or in passing. **33.** (tr.) to tinge or tint slightly: brown hair touched with gold. **34.** (tr.) to spoil slightly: blackfly touched the flowers. **35.** (tr.) to mark, as with a brush or pen. **36.** (tr.) to compare in quality or attainment. **37.** (tr.) to reach or attain: he touched the high point in his career. **38.** (intr.) to dock or stop briefly: the ship touches at Tenerife. **39.** (tr.) Sl. to ask for a loan or gift of money from. ~See also **touchdown, touch off, touch up**. —**'touchable** adj. —**'toucher** n.

THESAURUS

direct, involved, mazy, misleading, roundabout, tricky

torture 1. v. afflict, agonize, crucify, distress, excruciate, harrow, lacerate, martyr, pain, persecute, put on the rack, rack, torment **2.** n. affliction, agony, anguish, distress, hell, laceration, martyrdom, misery, pain, pang(s), persecution, rack, suffering, torment

toss v. **1.** cast, chuck (Inf.), fling, flip, hurl, launch, lob (Inf.), pitch, project, propel, shy, sling, throw **2.** agitate, disturb, jiggle, joggle, jolt, rock, roll, shake, thrash, tumble, wriggle, writhe **3.** heave, labour, lurch, pitch, roll, wallow ~n. **4.** cast, fling, lob (Inf.), pitch, shy, throw

tot¹ n. **1.** baby, child, infant, little one, mite, toddler, wean (Scot.) **2.** dram, finger, measure, nip, shot (Inf.), slug, snifter (Inf.), toothful

tot² v. add up, calculate, count up, reckon, sum (up), tally, total

total 1. n. aggregate, all, amount, entirety,

full amount, mass, sum, totality, whole **2.** adj. absolute, all-out, complete, comprehensive, consummate, downright, entire, full, gross, integral, out-and-out, outright, perfect, sheer, sweeping, thorough, thoroughgoing, unconditional, undisputed, undivided, unmitigated, unqualified, utter, whole **3.** v. add up, amount to, come to, mount up to, reach, reckon, sum up, tot up

totalitarian authoritarian, despotic, dictatorial, monolithic, one-party, oppressive, tyrannous, undemocratic

totality 1. aggregate, all, entirety, everything, sum, total, whole **2.** completeness, entireness, fullness, wholeness

totally absolutely, completely, comprehensively, consummately, entirely, fully, perfectly, quite, thoroughly, unconditionally, unmitigatedly, utterly, wholeheartedly, wholly

totter falter, lurch, quiver, reel, rock, shake, stagger, stumble, sway, teeter, tremble, walk unsteadily, waver

touch n. **1.** feel, feeling, handling, palpa-

tion, physical contact, tactility **2.** blow, brush, caress, contact, fondling, hit, pat, push, stroke, tap **3.** bit, dash, detail, drop, hint, intimation, jot, pinch, smack, small amount, smattering, soupçon, speck, spot, suggestion, suspicion, taste, tincture, tinge, trace, whiff **4.** direction, effect, hand, influence **5.** approach, characteristic, handiwork, manner, method, style, technique, trademark, way **6.** ability, adroitness, art, artistry, command, deftness, facility, flair, knack, mastery, skill, virtuosity **7.** acquaintance, awareness, communication, contact, correspondence, familiarity, understanding ~v. **8.** brush, caress, contact, feel, finger, fondle, graze, handle, hit, lay a finger on, palpate, pat, push, strike, stroke, tap **9.** abut, adjoin, be in contact, border, brush, come together, contact, converge, graze, impinge upon, meet **10.** affect, disturb, get through to, get to (Inf.), have an effect on, impress, influence, inspire, make an impression on, mark, melt, move, soften, stir, strike, upset **11.** be a party to, concern

touch and go *adj.* (**touch-and-go** *when prenominal*). risky or critical.

touchdown ('tʌtʃ,daʊn) *n.* 1. the moment at which a landing aircraft or spacecraft comes into contact with the landing surface. 2. *Rugby.* the act of placing or touching the ball on the ground behind the goal line, as in scoring a try. 3. *American football.* a scoring play for six points achieved by being in possession of the ball in the opponents' end zone. Abbrev.: **TD.** ~*vb.* **touch down.** (*intr., adv.*) 4. (of an aircraft, etc.) to land. 5. *Rugby.* to place the ball behind the goal line, as when scoring a try.

touché (tuː'ʃeɪ) *interj.* 1. an acknowledgment of a scoring hit in fencing. 2. an acknowledgment of the striking home of a remark, witty reply, etc.

touched (tʌtʃt) *adj.* (*postpositive*) 1. moved to sympathy or emotion. 2. showing slight insanity.

touching ('tʌtʃɪŋ) *adj.* 1. evoking or eliciting tender feelings. ~*prep.* 2. on the subject of; relating to. —'**touchingly** *adv.*

touch judge *n.* one of the two linesmen in rugby.

touchline ('tʌtʃ,laɪn) *n.* either of the lines marking the side of the playing area in certain games, such as rugby.

touch off *vb.* (*tr., adv.*) 1. to cause to explode, as by touching with a match. 2. to cause (a disturbance, violence, etc.) to begin.

touchpaper ('tʌtʃ,peɪpə) *n.* paper soaked in saltpetre for firing gunpowder.

touchstone ('tʌtʃ,stəʊn) *n.* 1. a criterion or standard. 2. a hard dark stone that is used to test gold and silver from the streak they produce on it.

touch-type *vb.* (*intr.*) to type without looking at the keyboard. —'**touch-,typist** *n.*

touch up *vb.* (*tr., adv.*) 1. to put extra or finishing touches to. 2. to enhance, renovate, or falsify by putting extra touches to. 3. *Brit. sl.* to touch or caress (someone).

touchwood ('tʌtʃ,wʊd) *n.* something, esp. dry wood or fungus material, used as tinder.

touchy ('tʌtʃɪ) *adj.* **touchier, touchiest.** 1. easily upset or irritated. 2. extremely risky. 3. easily ignited. —'**touchily** *adv.* —'**touchiness** *n.*

tough (tʌf) *adj.* 1. strong or resilient; durable. 2. not tender. 3. hardy and fit. 4. rough or pugnacious. 5. resolute or intractable. 6. difficult or troublesome to do or deal with: *a tough problem.* 7. *Inf.* unfortunate or unlucky: *it's tough on him.* ~*n.* 8. a rough, vicious, or pugnacious person. ~*adv.* 9. *Inf.* violently, aggressively, or intractably: *to treat someone tough.* —'**toughly** *adv.* —'**toughness** *n.*

toughen ('tʌfən) *vb.* to make or become tough or tougher. —'**toughener** *n.*

tough-minded *adj.* practical, unsentimental, or intractable. —,**tough-'mindedness** *n.*

toupee ('tuːpeɪ) *n.* a hairpiece worn by men to cover a bald place.

tour (tʊə) *n.* 1. an extended journey visiting places of interest along the route. 2. *Mil.* a period of service, esp. in one place of duty. 3. a short trip, as for inspection. 4. a trip made by a theatre company, orchestra, etc., to perform in several different places. ~*vb.* 5. to make a tour of (a place).

tour de force *French.* (tur də 'fɔrs) *n., pl.* **tours de force** (tur). a masterly or brilliant stroke, creation, effect, or accomplishment.

tourism ('tʊərɪzəm) *n.* tourist travel, esp. when regarded as an industry.

tourist ('tʊərɪst) *n.* 1. a. a person who travels for pleasure, usually sightseeing and staying in hotels. b. (*as modifier*): *tourist attractions.* 2. a person on an excursion or sightseeing tour. 3. Also called: **tourist class.** the lowest class of accommodation on a passenger ship. ~*adj.* 4. of or relating to tourist accommodation. —**tour'istic** *adj.*

touristy ('tʊərɪstɪ) *adj. Inf., often derog.* abounding in or designed for tourists.

tourmaline ('tʊəmə,liːn) *n.* any of a group of hard glassy minerals of variable colour consisting of a complex silicate of boron and aluminium in crystalline form: used in jewellery and optical and electrical equipment.

tournament ('tʊənəmənt) *n.* 1. a sporting competition in which contestants play a series of games to determine an overall winner. 2. a meeting for athletic or other sporting contestants: *an archery tournament.* 3. *Medieval history.* a martial sport or contest in which mounted combatants fought for a prize.

tournedos ('tʊənə,dəʊ) *n., pl.* **-dos** (-,dəʊz). a thick round steak of beef.

tourniquet ('tʊənɪ,keɪ) *n. Med.* any device for constricting an artery of the arm or leg to control bleeding.

tousle ('taʊzəl) *vb.* (*tr.*) 1. to tangle, ruffle, or disarrange. 2. to treat roughly. ~*n.* 3. a disorderly, tangled, or rumpled state. 4. a dishevelled or disordered mass, esp. of hair.

tout (taʊt) *vb.* 1. *Inf.* to solicit (business, customers, etc.), esp. in a brazen way. 2. (*intr.*) a. to spy on racehorses being trained in order to obtain information for betting purposes. b. to sell such information or to take bets, esp. in public places. ~*n.* 3. a person who touts. —'**touter** *n.*

tow¹ (təʊ) *vb.* 1. (*tr.*) to pull or drag (a vehicle, boat, etc.), esp. by means of a rope or cable. ~*n.* 2. the act or an instance of towing. 3. the state of being towed (esp. in **in tow, under tow, on tow**). 4. something towed. 5. something used for towing. 6. **in tow.** in one's charge or under one's influence. —'**towable** *adj.* —'**towage** *n.*

tow² (təʊ) *n.* the coarse and broken fibres of hemp, flax, jute, etc., preparatory to spinning. —'**towy** *adj.*

toward *adj.* ('təʊəd). 1. *Now rare.* in progress; afoot. 2. *Obs.* about to happen; imminent. 3. *Obs.* promising or favourable. ~*prep.* (tə'wɔːd, tɔːd). 4. a variant of **towards.**

towards (tə'wɔːdz, tɔːdz) *prep.* 1. in the direction or vicinity of: *towards London.* 2. with regard to: *her feelings towards me.* 3. as a contribution or help to: *money*

THESAURUS

oneself with, consume, deal with, drink, eat, get involved in, handle, have to do with, partake of, use, utilize 12. *With* on allude to, bring in, cover, deal with, mention, refer to, speak of 13. bear upon, concern, have to do with, interest, pertain to, regard 14. be a match for, be in the same league as, be on a par with, come near, come up to, compare with, equal, hold a candle to (*Inf.*), match, parallel, rival 15. arrive at, attain, come to, reach

touchiness bad temper, crabbedness, fretfulness, grouchiness, irascibility, irritability, peevishness, pettishness, petulance, surliness, testiness, tetchiness, ticklishness

touching affecting, emotive, heartbreaking, melting, moving, pathetic, piteous, pitiable, pitiful, poignant, sad, stirring, tender

touchstone criterion, guage, measure, norm, standard, yardstick

touch up 1. finish off, perfect, put the finishing touches to, round off 2. brush up, enhance, fake (up), falsify, give a face-lift to, gloss over, improve, patch up, polish up,

renovate, retouch, revamp, titivate, whitewash (*Inf.*)

touchy bad-tempered, captious, crabbed, cross, easily offended, grouchy, grumpy, irascible, irritable, oversensitive, peevish, pettish, petulant, querulous, quick-tempered, splenetic, surly, testy, tetchy, thin-skinned, ticklish

tough *adj.* 1. cohesive, durable, firm, hard, inflexible, leathery, resilient, resistant, rigid, rugged, solid, stiff, strong, sturdy, tenacious 2. brawny, fit, hard as nails, hardened, hardy, resilient, seasoned, stalwart, stout, strapping, strong, sturdy, vigorous 3. hard-bitten, pugnacious, rough, ruffianly, ruthless, vicious, violent 4. adamant, callous, exacting, firm, hard, hard-boiled (*Inf.*), hard-nosed (*Sl.*), inflexible, intractable, merciless, obdurate, obstinate, refractory, resolute, severe, stern, strict, stubborn, unbending, unforgiving, unyielding 5. arduous, baffling, difficult, exacting, exhausting, hard, intractable, irksome, knotty, laborious, perplexing, puzzling, strenuous, thorny, troublesome, uphill 6. *Inf.* bad, hard cheese (*Brit. sl.*), hard lines (*Brit. inf.*), hard

luck, lamentable, regrettable, too bad (*Inf.*), unfortunate, unlucky ~*n.* 7. bravo, bruiser (*Inf.*), brute, bully, bully boy, hooligan, rough (*Inf.*), roughneck (*Sl.*), rowdy, ruffian, thug

tour *n.* 1. excursion, expedition, jaunt, journey, outing, peregrination, progress, trip 2. circuit, course, round ~*v.* 3. explore, go on the road, go round, holiday in, journey, sightsee, travel round, travel through, visit

tourist excursionist, globetrotter, holidaymaker, journeyer, sightseer, traveller, tripper, voyager

tournament 1. competition, contest, event, match, meeting, series 2. *Medieval* joust, the lists, tourney

tow *v.* drag, draw, haul, lug, pull, trail, trawl, tug

towards 1. en route for, for, in the direction of, in the vicinity of, on the road to, on the way to, to 2. about, concerning, for, regarding, with regard to, with respect to 3. almost, close to, coming up to, getting on for, just before, nearing, nearly, not quite, shortly before

towards a new car. **4.** just before: *towards noon.*
~Also: **toward.**

towbar ('təʊˌbɑː) *n.* a rigid metal bar or frame used for towing vehicles.

towel ('taʊəl) *n.* **1.** a piece of absorbent cloth or paper used for drying things. **2. throw in the towel.** to give up completely.~*vb.*-**elling, -elled** *or U.S.* -**eling, -eled. 3.** (*tr.*) to dry or wipe with a towel. **4.** (*tr.;* often foll. by *up*) *Austral. sl.* to assault or beat (a person).

towelling ('taʊəlɪŋ) *n.* an absorbent fabric used for making towels, bathrobes, etc.

tower ('taʊə) *n.* **1.** a tall, usually square or circular structure, sometimes part of a larger building and usually built for a specific purpose. **2.** a place of defence or retreat. **3. tower of strength.** a person who gives support, comfort, etc. ~*vb.* **4.** (*intr.*) to be or rise like a tower; loom.

towering ('taʊərɪŋ) *adj.* **1.** very tall; lofty. **2.** outstanding, as in importance or stature. **3.** (*prenominal*) very intense: *a towering rage.*

towhead ('təʊˌhɛd) *n. Often disparaging.* **1.** a person with blond or yellowish hair. **2.** a head of such hair. —**'tow,headed** *adj.*

towline ('təʊˌlaɪn) *n.* another name for **towrope.**

town (taʊn) *n.* **1.** a densely populated urban area, typically smaller than a city and larger than a village. **2.** a city, borough, or other urban area. **3.** (in the U.S.) a territorial unit of local government that is smaller than a county; township. **4.** the nearest town or commercial district. **5.** London or the chief city of an area. **6.** the inhabitants of a town. **7. go to town. a.** to make a great or unrestricted effort. **b.** *Austral. & N.Z. inf.* to lose one's temper. **8. on the town.** seeking out entertainments and amusements. —**'townish** *adj.*

town clerk *n.* **1.** (in Britain until 1974) the secretary and chief administrative officer of a town or city. **2.** (in the U.S.) the official who keeps the records of a town.

town crier *n.* (formerly) a person employed to make public announcements in the streets.

townee (taʊ'niː) *or U.S.* **townie** *or* **towny** ('taʊnɪ) *n. Inf., often disparaging.* a permanent resident in a town, esp. as distinct from country dwellers or students.

town gas *n.* coal gas manufactured for domestic and industrial use.

town hall *n.* the chief building in which municipal business is transacted, often with a hall for public meetings.

town house *n.* **1.** a house in an urban area, esp. a fashionable one. **2.** a person's town residence as distinct from his country residence.

town planning *n.* the comprehensive planning of the physical and social development of a town. *U.S. term:* **city planning.**

township ('taʊnʃɪp) *n.* **1.** a small town. **2.** (in the U.S. and Canada) a territorial area, esp. a subdivision of a county: often organized as a unit of local government. **3.** (in Canada) a land-survey area, usually 36 square miles (93 square kilometres). **4.** (in South Africa) a planned urban settlement of Black Africans or Coloureds. **5.** *English history.* **a.** any of the local districts of a large parish. **b.** the parish itself.

townsman ('taʊnzmən) *n., pl.* -**men. 1.** an inhabitant of a town. **2.** a person from the same town as oneself. —**'towns,woman** *fem. n.*

townspeople ('taʊnzˌpiːpəl) *or* **townsfolk** ('taʊnzˌfəʊk) *pl. n.* the inhabitants of a town; citizens.

towpath ('təʊˌpɑːθ) *n.* a path beside a canal or river, used by people or animals towing boats. Also called: **towing path.**

towrope ('təʊˌrəʊp) *n.* a rope or cable used for towing a vehicle or vessel. Also called: **towline.**

tox-, toxic- *or before a consonant* **toxo-, toxico-** *combining form.* indicating poison: *toxaemia.*

toxaemia *or U.S.* **toxemia** (tɒk'siːmɪə) *n.* **1.** a condition characterized by the presence of bacterial toxins in the blood. **2.** the condition in pregnancy of pre-eclampsia or eclampsia. —**tox'aemic** *or U.S.* **tox'emic** *adj.*

toxic ('tɒksɪk) *adj.* **1.** of or caused by a toxin or poison. **2.** harmful or deadly. —**'toxically** *adv.* —**toxicity** (tɒk'sɪsɪtɪ) *n.*

toxicant ('tɒksɪkənt) *n.* **1.** a toxic substance; poison. ~*adj.* **2.** poisonous; toxic.

toxicology (ˌtɒksɪ'kɒlədʒɪ) *n.* the branch of science concerned with poisons, their effects, antidotes, etc. —**toxicological** (ˌtɒksɪkə'lɒdʒɪkəl) *or* **toxico'logic** *adj.* —**toxi'cologist** *n.*

toxin ('tɒksɪn) *n.* **1.** any of various poisonous substances produced by microorganisms that stimulate the production of neutralizing substances (antitoxins) in the body. **2.** any other poisonous substance of plant or animal origin.

toy (tɔɪ) *n.* **1.** an object designed to be played with. **2. a.** something that is a nonfunctioning replica of something else, esp. a miniature one. **b.** (*as modifier*): *a toy guitar.* **3.** any small thing of little value; trifle. **4. a.** something small or miniature. **b.** (*as modifier*): *a toy poodle.* ~*vb.* **5.** (*intr.;* usually foll. by *with*) to play, fiddle, or flirt.

trace[1] (treɪs) *n.* **1.** a mark or other sign that something has been in a place. **2.** a scarcely detectable amount or characteristic. **3.** a footprint or other indication of the passage of an animal or person. **4.** any line drawn by a recording instrument or a record consisting of a number of such lines. **5.** something drawn, such as a tracing. **6.** *Chiefly U.S.* a beaten track or path. ~*vb.* **7.** (*tr.*) to follow, discover, or ascertain the course or development of something. **8.** (*tr.*) to track down and find, as by following a trail. **9.** to copy (a design, map, etc.) by drawing over the lines visible through a superimposed sheet of transparent paper. **10.** (*tr.;* often foll. by *out*) **a.** to draw or delineate (a plan or diagram) of. **b.** to outline or sketch (an idea, etc.). **11.** (*tr.*) to decorate with tracery. **12.** (usually foll. by *back*) to follow or be followed to source; date back: *his ancestors trace back to the 16th century.* —**'traceable** *adj.* —**,tracea'bility** *or* **'traceableness** *n.* —**'traceably** *adv.*

trace[2] (treɪs) *n.* **1.** either of the two side straps that connect a horse's harness to the whiffletree. **2.** *Angling.* a short piece of gut or nylon attaching a hook or fly to a line. **3. kick over the traces.** to escape or defy control.

trace element *n.* any of various chemical elements that occur in very small amounts in organisms and are essential for many physiological and biochemical processes.

tracer ('treɪsə) *n.* **1.** a person or thing that traces. **2.** ammunition that can be observed when in flight by the burning of chemical substances in the base of the projectile. **3.** *Med.* any radioactive isotope introduced into the body to study metabolic processes, etc., by following its progress with a Geiger counter or other detector. **4.** an investigation to trace missing cargo, mail, etc.

tracer bullet *n.* a round of small arms ammunition containing a tracer.

tracery ('treɪsərɪ) *n., pl.* -**eries. 1.** a pattern of interlacing ribs, esp. as used in the upper part of a Gothic window, etc. **2.** any fine pattern resembling this. —**'traceried** *adj.*

trachea (trə'kiːə) *n., pl.* -**cheae** (-'kiːiː). **1.** *Anat., zool.* the tube that conveys inhaled air from the larynx to the bronchi. **2.** any of the tubes in insects and related animals that convey air from the spiracles to the tissues. —**tra'cheal** *or* **tra'cheate** *adj.*

tracheitis (ˌtreɪkɪ'aɪtɪs) *n.* inflammation of the trachea.

tracheotomy (ˌtrækɪ'ɒtəmɪ) *n., pl.* -**mies.** surgical incision into the trachea, as performed when the air passage has been blocked.

trachoma (trə'kəʊmə) *n.* a chronic contagious viral dis-

THESAURUS

tower *n.* **1.** belfry, column, obelisk, pillar, skyscraper, steeple, turret **2.** castle, citadel, fort, fortification, fortress, keep, refuge, stronghold ~*v.* **3.** ascend, be head and shoulders above, dominate, exceed, loom, mount, overlook, overtop, rear, rise, soar, surpass, top, transcend

toxic baneful (*Archaic*), deadly, harmful,

lethal, noxious, pernicious, pestilential, poisonous, septic

toy *n.* **1.** doll, game, plaything **2.** bauble, gewgaw, knick-knack, trifle, trinket ~*v.* **3.** amuse oneself, dally, fiddle (*Inf.*), flirt, play, sport, trifle, wanton

trace *n.* **1.** evidence, indication, mark, record, relic, remains, remnant, sign, survival, token, vestige **2.** bit, dash, drop, hint, iota, jot,

shadow, *soupçon*, suggestion, suspicion, tincture, tinge, touch, trifle, whiff **3.** footmark, footprint, footstep, path, slot, spoor, track, trail ~*v.* **4.** ascertain, detect, determine, discover, ferret out, find, follow, hunt down, pursue, search for, seek, shadow, stalk, track, trail, unearth **5.** chart, copy, delineate, depict, draw, map, mark out, outline, record, show, sketch

ease of the eye characterized by inflammation of the conjunctiva and cornea and the formation of scar tissue. —**trachomatous** (trə'kɒmətəs) *adj.*

tracing ('treɪsɪŋ) *n.* 1. a copy made by tracing. 2. the act of making a trace. 3. a record made by an instrument.

track (træk) *n.* 1. the mark or trail left by something that has passed by. 2. any road or path, esp. a rough one. 3. a rail or pair of parallel rails on which a vehicle, such as a locomotive, runs. 4. a course of action, thought, etc.: *don't start on that track again!* 5. a line of motion or travel, such as flight. 6. an endless band on the wheels of a tank, tractor, etc., to enable it to move across rough ground. 7. **a.** a course for running or racing. **b.** (*as modifier*): *track events.* 8. *U.S.* **a.** sports performed on a track. **b.** track and field events as a whole. 9. a path on a magnetic recording medium, esp. magnetic tape, on which music or speech is recorded. 10. Also called: **band.** any of a number of separate sections in the recording on either side of a gramophone record. 11. the distance between the points of contact with the ground of a pair of wheels, as of a motor vehicle. 12. **keep** (*or* **lose**) **track of.** to follow (or fail to follow) the passage, course, or progress of. 13. **off the beaten track.** isolated; secluded. 14. **off the track.** away from what is correct or true. 15. **on the track of.** on the scent or trail of; pursuing. ~*vb.* 16. to follow the trail of (a person, animal, etc.). 17. to follow the flight path of (a satellite, etc.) by picking up signals transmitted or reflected by it. 18. *U.S. railways.* **a.** to provide with a track. **b.** to run on a track of (a certain width). 19. (of a camera or cameraoperator) to follow (a moving object) while operating. 20. to follow a track through (a place): *to track the jungles.* 21. (*intr.*) (of the pick-up, stylus, etc., of a gramophone) to follow the groove of a record. —**'tracker** *n.*

track down *vb.* (*tr., adv.*) to find by tracking or pursuing.

track record *n. Inf.* the past record of the accomplishments and failures of a person, business, etc.

tracks (træks) *pl. n.* 1. (*sometimes sing.*) marks, such as footprints, etc., left by someone or something that has passed. 2. **in one's tracks.** on the very spot where one is standing. 3. **make tracks.** to leave or depart. 4. **make tracks for.** to go or head towards.

track shoe *n.* either of a pair of light running shoes fitted with steel spikes for better grip.

tracksuit ('træk,su:t) *n.* a warm suit worn by athletes, esp. during training.

tract[1] (trækt) *n.* 1. an extended area, as of land. 2. *Anat.* a system of organs, glands, etc., that has a particular function: *the digestive tract.* 3. *Arch.* an extended period of time.

tract[2] (trækt) *n.* a treatise or pamphlet, esp. a religious or moralistic one.

tractable ('træktəbəl) *adj.* 1. easily controlled or persuaded. 2. readily worked; malleable. —,**tracta'bility** *or* '**tractableness** *n.* —'**tractably** *adv.*

traction ('trækʃən) *n.* 1. the act of drawing or pulling, esp. by motive power. 2. the state of being drawn or pulled. 3. *Med.* the application of a steady pull on a limb, etc., using a system of weights and pulleys or splints. 4. adhesive friction, as between a wheel of a motor vehicle and the road. —'**tractional** *adj.* —**tractive** ('træktɪv) *adj.*

traction engine *n.* a steam-powered locomotive used, esp. formerly, for drawing heavy loads along roads or over rough ground.

tractor ('træktə) *n.* 1. a motor vehicle with large rear wheels or endless belt treads, used to pull heavy loads, esp. farm machinery. 2. a short vehicle with a driver's cab, used to pull a trailer, as in an articulated lorry.

trad (træd) *n.* 1. *Chiefly Brit.* traditional jazz. ~*adj.* 2. short for **traditional.**

trade (treɪd) *n.* 1. the act or an instance of buying and selling goods and services. 2. a personal occupation, esp. a craft requiring skill. 3. the people and practices of an industry, craft, or business. 4. exchange of one thing for something else. 5. the regular clientele of a firm or industry. 6. amount of custom or commercial dealings; business. 7. a specified market or business: *the tailoring trade.* 8. an occupation in commerce, as opposed to a profession. ~*vb.* 9. (*tr.*) to buy and sell (merchandise). 10. to exchange (one thing) for another. 11. (*intr.*) to engage in trade. 12. (*intr.*) to deal or do business (with). ~See also **trade-in, trade on.** —'**tradable** *or* '**tradeable** *adj.*

trade-in *n.* 1. **a.** a used article given in part payment for the purchase of a new article. **b.** a transaction involving such part payment. **c.** the valuation put on the article traded in. ~*vb.* **trade in.** 2. (*tr., adv.*) to give (a used article) as part payment for a new article.

trademark ('treɪd,mɑːk) *n.* 1.**a.** the name or other symbol used by a manufacturer or dealer to distinguish his products from those of competitors. **b. registered trademark.** one that is officially registered and legally protected. 2. any distinctive sign or mark of the presence of a person or animal. ~*vb.* (*tr.*) 3. to label with a trademark. 4. to register as a trademark.

trade name *n.* 1. the name used by a trade to refer to a commodity, service, etc. 2. the name under which a commercial enterprise operates in business.

trade-off *n.* an exchange, esp. as a compromise.

trade on *vb.* (*intr., prep.*) to exploit or take advantage of: *he traded on her endless patience.*

trader ('treɪdə) *n.* 1. a person who engages in trade. 2. a vessel regularly employed in trade. 3. *Stock Exchange, U.S.* a member who operates mainly on his own account.

tradescantia (,trædɪs'kænʃɪə) *n.* any of a genus of plants widely cultivated for their striped variegated leaves.

trade secret *n.* a secret formula, technique, process, etc., known and used to advantage by only one manufacturer.

tradesman ('treɪdzmən) *n., pl.* -**men.** 1. a man engaged in trade, esp. a retail dealer. 2. a skilled worker. —'**trades,woman** *fem. n.*

Trades Union Congress *n.* the major association of British trade unions, which includes all the larger unions. Abbrev.: **T.U.C.**

trade union *or* **trades union** *n.* an association of employees formed to improve their incomes and working conditions by collective bargaining. —**trade unionism** *or* **trades unionism** *n.* —**trade unionist** *or* **trades unionist** *n.*

trade wind (wɪnd) *n.* a wind blowing obliquely towards the equator either from the northeast in the N hemisphere or the southeast in the S hemisphere, between

---

THESAURUS

track *n.* 1. footmark, footprint, footstep, mark, path, scent, slot, spoor, trace, trail, wake 2. course, flight path, line, orbit, path, pathway, road, track, trajectory, way 3. line, permanent way, rail, rails 4. **keep track of** follow, keep an eye on, keep in sight, keep in touch with, keep up to date with, keep up with, monitor, oversee, watch 5. **lose track of** lose, lose sight of, misplace ~*v.* 6. chase, dog, follow, follow the trail of, hunt down, pursue, shadow, stalk, tail (*Inf.*), trace, trail

track down apprehend, bring to light, capture, catch, dig up, discover, expose, ferret out, find, hunt down, run to earth, sniff out, trace, unearth

tracks 1. footprints, impressions, imprints, tyremarks, tyreprints, wheelmarks 2. **make tracks** beat it (*Sl.*), depart, disappear, get going, get moving, go, head off, hit the road

(*Sl.*), leave, set out, split (*Sl.*), take off (*Inf.*) 3. **stop in one's tracks** bring to a standstill, freeze, immobilize, petrify, rivet to the spot, stop dead, transfix

tract[1] area, district, estate, expanse, extent, lot, plot, quarter, region, stretch, territory, zone

tract[2] booklet, brochure, disquisition, dissertation, essay, homily, leaflet, monograph, pamphlet, tractate, treatise

tractable 1. amenable, biddable, compliant, controllable, docile, governable, manageable, obedient, persuadable, submissive, tame, willing, yielding 2. ductile, fictile, malleable, plastic, pliable, pliant, tractile, workable

traction adhesion, drag, draught, drawing, friction, grip, haulage, pull, pulling, purchase, resistance

trade *n.* 1. barter, business, buying and selling, commerce, dealing, exchange, traffic, transactions, truck 2. avocation, business, calling, craft, employment, job, line, line of work, métier, occupation, profession, pursuit, skill 3. deal, exchange, interchange, swap 4. clientele, custom, customers, market, patrons, public ~*v.* 5. bargain, barter, buy and sell, deal, do business, exchange, have dealings, peddle, traffic, transact, truck 6. barter, exchange, swap, switch

trader broker, buyer, dealer, marketer, merchandiser, merchant, seller

tradesman 1. dealer, merchant, retailer, seller, shopkeeper, vendor 2. artisan, craftsman, journeyman, skilled worker, workman

latitudes 30° N and S.

trading estate n. Chiefly Brit. a large area in which a number of commercial or industrial firms are situated.

trading stamp n. a stamp of stated value given by some retail organizations to customers, redeemable for merchandise or cash.

tradition (trə'dɪʃən) n. 1. the handing down from generation to generation of customs, beliefs, etc. 2. the body of customs, thought, etc., belonging to a particular country, people, family, or institution over a long period. 3. a specific custom or practice of long standing. 4. Christianity. a doctrine regarded as having been established by Christ or the apostles though not contained in Scripture. 5. (often cap.) Judaism. a body of laws regarded as having been handed down from Moses orally. 6. the beliefs and customs of Islam supplementing the Koran. 7. Law, chiefly Roman & Scot. the act of formally transferring ownership of movable property. —**tra-'ditionless** adj.

traditional (trə'dɪʃənəl) adj. 1. of, relating to, or being a tradition. 2. of the style of jazz originating in New Orleans, characterized by collective improvisation by a front line of trumpet, trombone, and clarinet. —**tra'di-tionalist** n. —**tra'ditionally** adv.

traduce (trə'djuːs) vb. (tr.) to speak badly or maliciously of. —**tra'ducement** n. —**tra'ducer** n.

traffic ('træfɪk) n. 1. a. the vehicles coming and going in a street, town, etc. b. (as modifier): traffic lights. 2. the movement of vehicles, people, etc., in a particular place or for a particular purpose: sea traffic. 3. (usually foll. by with) dealings or business. 4. trade, esp. of an illicit or improper kind: drug traffic. 5. the aggregate volume of messages transmitted through a communications system in a given period. 6. Chiefly U.S. the number of customers patronizing a commercial establishment in a given time period. ~vb. -**ficking, -ficked.** (intr.) 7. (often foll. by in) to carry on trade or business, esp. of an illicit kind. 8. (usually foll. by with) to have dealings. —**'trafficker** n.

trafficator ('træfɪˌkeɪtə) n. (formerly) an illuminated arm on a motor vehicle that was raised to indicate a left or right turn.

traffic island n. another name for **island** (sense 2).

traffic light or **signal** n. one of a set of coloured lights placed at crossroads, junctions, etc., to control the flow of traffic.

traffic warden n. a person who is appointed to supervise road traffic and report traffic offences.

tragedian (trə'dʒiːdɪən) or (fem.) **tragedienne** (trə-ˌdʒiːdɪ'ɛn) n. 1. an actor who specializes in tragic roles. 2. a writer of tragedy.

tragedy ('trædʒɪdɪ) n., pl. **-dies.** 1. a play in which the protagonist falls to disaster through the combination of a personal failing and circumstances with which he cannot deal. 2. any dramatic or literary composition dealing with serious or sombre themes and ending with disaster. 3. the branch of drama dealing with such themes. 4. the unfortunate aspect of something. 5. a shocking or sad event; disaster.

tragic ('trædʒɪk) or **tragical** adj. 1. of, relating to, or characteristic of tragedy. 2. mournful or pitiable. —**'tragically** adv.

tragicomedy (ˌtrædʒɪ'kɒmɪdɪ) n., pl. **-dies.** 1. a drama in which aspects of both tragedy and comedy are found.

2. an event or incident having both comic and tragic aspects. —ˌtragi'comic or ˌtragi'comical adj.

trail (treɪl) vb. 1. to drag, stream, or permit to drag or stream along a surface, esp. the ground. 2. to make (a track) through (a place). 3. to follow or hunt (an animal or person) by following marks or tracks. 4. (when intr., often foll. by behind) to lag or linger behind (a person or thing). 5. (intr.) (esp. of plants) to extend or droop over or along a surface. 6. (tr.) to tow (a caravan, etc.) behind a motor vehicle. 7. (tr.) to carry (a rifle) at the full length of the right arm in a horizontal position, with the muzzle to the fore. 8. (intr.) to move wearily or slowly. ~n. 9. a print, mark, or scent made by a person, animal, or object. 10. the act or an instance of trailing. 11. a path, track, or road, esp. one roughly blazed. 12. something that trails behind or trails in loops or strands. 13. the part of a towed gun carriage and limber that connects the two when in movement and rests on the ground as a partial support when unlimbered.

trailblazer ('treɪlˌbleɪzə) n. 1. a leader or pioneer in a particular field. 2. a person who blazes a trail. —'**trail-ˌblazing** adj., n.

trailer ('treɪlə) n. 1. a road vehicle, usually two-wheeled, towed by a motor vehicle: used for transporting boats, etc. 2. the rear section of an articulated lorry. 3. a series of short extracts from a film, used to advertise it in a cinema or on television. 4. a person or thing that trails. 5. the U.S. name for **caravan** (sense 1).

trailing arbutus n. a creeping evergreen ericaceous plant of E North America, having clusters of fragrant pink or white flowers.

train (treɪn) vb. 1. (tr.) to guide or teach (to do something), as by subjecting to various exercises or experiences. 2. (tr.) to control or guide towards a specific goal: to train a plant up a wall. 3. (intr.) to do exercises and prepare for a specific purpose. 4. (tr.) to improve or curb by subjecting to discipline: to train the mind. 5. (tr.) to focus or bring to bear (on something): to train a telescope on the moon. ~n. 6. a line of coaches or wagons coupled together and drawn by a railway locomotive. 7. a sequence or series: a train of disasters. 8. a procession of people, vehicles, etc., travelling together, such as one carrying equipment in support of a military operation. 9. a series of interacting parts through which motion is transmitted: a train of gears. 10. a fuse or line of gunpowder to an explosive charge, etc. 11. something drawn along, such as the long back section of a dress that trails along the floor. 12. a retinue or suite. —'**trainable** adj.

trainbearer ('treɪnˌbɛərə) n. an attendant who holds up the train of a dignitary's robe.

trainee (treɪ'niː) n. a. a person undergoing training. b. (as modifier): a trainee journalist.

trainer ('treɪnə) n. 1. a person who trains athletes. 2. a piece of equipment employed in training, such as a simulated aircraft cockpit. 3. a person who schools racehorses.

training ('treɪnɪŋ) n. 1. a. the process of bringing a person, etc., to an agreed standard of proficiency, etc., by practice and instruction. b. (as modifier): training college. 2. **in training. a.** undergoing physical training. b. physically fit. 3. **out of training.** physically unfit.

train spotter n. a person who collects the numbers of railway locomotives.

THESAURUS

tradition convention, custom, customs, established practice, folklore, habit, institution, lore, praxis, ritual, unwritten law, usage

traditional accustomed, ancestral, conventional, customary, established, fixed, folk, historic, long-established, old, oral, time-honoured, transmitted, unwritten, usual

traffic n. 1. coming and going, freight, movement, passengers, transport, transportation, vehicles 2. barter, business, buying and selling, commerce, communication, dealing, dealings, doings, exchange, intercourse, peddling, relations, trade, truck ~v. 3. bargain, barter, buy and sell, deal, do business, exchange, have dealings, have transactions, market, peddle, trade, truck

tragedy adversity, affliction, calamity, catastrophe, disaster, grievous blow, misfortune

tragic anguished, appalling, awful, calamitous, catastrophic, deadly, dire, disastrous, doleful, dreadful, fatal, grievous, heartbreaking, heart-rending, ill-fated, ill-starred, lamentable, miserable, mournful, pathetic, pitiable, ruinous, sad, shocking, sorrowful, unfortunate, woeful, wretched

trail v. 1. dangle, drag, draw, hang down, haul, pull, stream, tow 2. chase, follow, hunt, pursue, shadow, stalk, tail (Inf.), trace, track 3. bring up the rear, dawdle, drag oneself, fall behind, follow, hang back, lag, linger, loiter, straggle, traipse (Inf.) 4. dangle, droop, extend, hang, straggle ~n. 5. footprints, footsteps, mark, marks, path, scent, spoor, trace, track, wake 6. beaten track, footpath, path, road, route, track, way 7. appendage, stream, tail, train

train v. 1. coach, discipline, drill, educate,

guide, improve, instruct, prepare, rear, rehearse, school, teach, tutor 2. exercise, improve, prepare, work out 3. aim, bring to bear, direct, focus, level, line up, point ~n. 4. chain, concatenation, course, order, progression, sequence, series, set, string, succession 5. caravan, column, convoy, file, procession 6. appendage, tail, trail 7. attendants, cortege, court, entourage, followers, following, household, retinue, staff, suite

trainer coach

training 1. coaching, discipline, education, grounding, guidance, instruction, schooling, teaching, tuition, tutelage, upbringing 2. body building, exercise, practice, preparation, working-out

traipse *or* **trapes** (treɪps) *Inf.* ~*vb.* **1.** (*intr.*) to walk heavily or tiredly. ~*n.* **2.** a long or tiring walk; trudge.

trait (treɪt, treɪ) *n.* **1.** a characteristic feature or quality distinguishing a particular person or thing. **2.** *Rare.* a touch or stroke.

traitor ('treɪtə) *n.* a person who is guilty of treason or treachery, in betraying friends, country, a cause, etc. —'**traitorous** *adj.* —'**traitress** *fem. n.*

trajectory (trə'dʒɛktərɪ) *n., pl.* -**ries. 1.** the path described by an object moving in air or space, esp. the curved path of a projectile. **2.** *Geom.* a curve that cuts a family of curves or surfaces at a constant angle.

tram (træm) *n.* **1.** Also called: **tramcar.** an electrically driven public transport vehicle that runs on rails let into the surface of the road. U.S. names: **streetcar, trolley car. 2.** a small vehicle on rails for carrying loads in a mine; tub. —'**tramless** *adj.*

tramline ('træm,laɪn) *n.* **1.** (*often pl.*) Also called: **tramway.** the tracks on which a tram runs. **2.** the route taken by a tram. **3.** (*often pl.*) the outer markings along the sides of a tennis or badminton court.

trammel ('træməl) *n.* **1.** (*often pl.*) a hindrance to free action or movement. **2.** Also called: **trammel net.** a fishing net in three sections, the two outer nets having a large mesh and the middle one a fine mesh. **3.** *Rare.* a fowling net. **4.** *U.S.* a shackle for a horse. **5.** a device for drawing ellipses consisting of a flat sheet having a cruciform slot in which run two pegs attached to a beam. **6.** (*sometimes pl.*) a beam compass. **7.** a device set in a fireplace to support cooking pots. ~*vb.* -**elling, -elled** *or U.S.* -**eling, -eled.** (*tr.*) **8.** to hinder or restrain. **9.** to catch or ensnare.

tramp (træmp) *vb.* **1.** (*intr.*) to walk long and far; hike. **2.** to walk heavily or firmly across or through (a place). **3.** (*intr.*) to wander about as a vagabond or tramp. **4.** (*intr.*) to tread or trample. ~*n.* **5.** a person who travels about on foot, living by begging or doing casual work. **6.** a long hard walk; hike. **7.** a heavy or rhythmic tread. **8.** the sound of heavy treading. **9.** a merchant ship that does not run on a regular schedule but carries cargo wherever the shippers desire. **10.** *Sl., chiefly U.S.* a prostitute or promiscuous girl or woman. —'**trampish** *adj.*

trample ('træmpəl) *vb.* (when *intr.*, usually foll. by *on, upon,* or *over*) **1.** to stamp or walk roughly (on). **2.** to encroach (upon) so as to violate or hurt. ~*n.* **3.** the action or sound of trampling. —'**trampler** *n.*

trampoline ('træmpəlɪn, -,liːn) *n.* **1.** a tough canvas sheet suspended by springs or cords from a frame, used by acrobats, gymnasts, etc. ~*vb.* **2.** (*intr.*) to exercise on a trampoline. —'**trampoliner** *or* '**trampolinist** *n.*

trance (trɑːns) *n.* **1.** a hypnotic state resembling sleep. **2.** any mental state in which a person is unaware of the environment, characterized by loss of voluntary movement, rigidity, and lack of sensitivity to external stimuli. **3.** a dazed or stunned state. **4.** a state of ecstasy or mystic absorption so intense as to cause a temporary loss of consciousness at the earthly level. **5.** *Spiritualism.* a state in which a medium can supposedly be controlled by an intelligence from without as a means of communication with the dead. ~*vb.* **6.** (*tr.*) to put into or as into a trance. —'**trance,like** *adj.*

trannie *or* **tranny** ('trænɪ) *n. Inf., chiefly Brit.* a transistor radio.

tranquil ('trænkwɪl) *adj.* calm, peaceful, or quiet. —'**tranquilly** *adv.*

tranquillity *or U.S.* (*sometimes*) **tranquility** (træŋ-'kwɪlɪtɪ) *n.* a state of calm or quietude.

tranquillize, -ise, *or U.S.* **tranquilize** ('træŋkwɪ-,laɪz) *vb.* to make or become calm or calmer. —,**tranquilli'zation** *or* -**i'sation** *n.*

tranquillizer *or* -**iser** ('træŋkwɪ,laɪzə) *n.* **1.** a drug that calms a person. **2.** anything that tranquillizes.

trans. *abbrev. for:* **1.** transaction. **2.** transferred. **3.** transitive. **4.** translated. **5.** translator. **6.** transport(ation). **7.** transverse.

trans- *prefix.* **1.** across, beyond, crossing, on the other side: *transatlantic.* **2.** changing thoroughly: *transliterate.* **3.** transcending: *transubstantiation.* **4.** transversely: *transect.* **5.** (*often in italics*) indicating that a chemical compound has a molecular structure in which two identical groups or atoms are on opposite sides of a double bond: *trans*-butadiene.

transact (træn'zækt) *vb.* to do, conduct, or negotiate (business, a deal, etc.). —**trans'actor** *n.*

transaction (træn'zækʃən) *n.* **1.** something that is transacted, esp. a business deal. **2.** a transacting or being transacted. **3.** (*pl.*) the records of the proceedings of a society, etc. —**trans'actional** *adj.*

transalpine (trænz'ælpaɪn) *adj.* (*prenominal*) **1.** situated in or relating to places beyond the Alps, esp. from Italy. **2.** passing over the Alps.

transatlantic (,trænzət'læntɪk) *adj.* **1.** on or from the other side of the Atlantic. **2.** crossing the Atlantic.

transceiver (træn'siːvə) *n.* a combined radio transmitter and receiver which does not allow simultaneous transmission and reception.

transcend (træn'sɛnd) *vb.* **1.** to go above or beyond (a limit, expectation, etc.), as in degree or excellence. **2.** (*tr.*) to be superior to.

transcendent (træn'sɛndənt) *adj.* **1.** exceeding or surpassing in degree or excellence. **2.** (in the philosophy of Kant) beyond or before experience. **3.** *Theol.* (of God) having existence outside the created world. **4.** free from the limitations inherent in matter. ~*n.* **5.** *Philosophy.* a transcendent thing. —**tran'scendence** *or* **tran'scendency** *n.* —**tran'scendently** *adv.*

transcendental (,trænsɛn'dɛntəl) *adj.* **1.** transcendent, superior, or surpassing. **2.** (in the philosophy of Kant) **a.** (of a judgment or logical deduction) being both synthetic and a priori. **b.** of or relating to knowledge of the presuppositions of thought. **3.** *Philosophy.* beyond our experience of phenomena, although not beyond potential experience. **4.** *Philosophy.* of or relating to those

---

THESAURUS

trait attribute, characteristic, feature, idiosyncrasy, lineament, mannerism, peculiarity, quality, quirk

traitor apostate, back-stabber, betrayer, deceiver, defector, deserter, double-crosser (*Inf.*), fifth columnist, informer, Judas, miscreant, quisling, rebel, renegade, snake in the grass (*Inf.*), turncoat

traitorous apostate, disloyal, double-crossing (*Inf.*), double-dealing, faithless, false, perfidious, renegade, seditious, treacherous, treasonable, unfaithful, untrue

trajectory course, flight, flight path, line, path, route, track

trammel **1.** *n.* bar, block, bond, chain, check, clog, curb, fetter, handicap, hindrance, impediment, obstacle, rein, shackle, stumbling block **2.** *v.* bar, block, capture, catch, check, clog, curb, enmesh, ensnare, entrap, fetter, hamper, handicap, hinder, impede, net, restrain, restrict, snag, tie

tramp *v.* **1.** footslog, hike, march, ramble, range, roam, rove, slog, trek, walk, yomp **2.** march, plod, stamp, stump, toil, traipse (*Inf.*), trudge, walk heavily **3.** crush, stamp, stomp (*Inf.*), trample, tread, walk over ~*n.* **4.** derelict, dosser (*Brit. sl.*), down-and-out, drifter, hobo (*Chiefly U.S.*), vagabond, vagrant **5.** hike, march, ramble, slog, trek **6.** footfall, footstep, stamp, tread

trample **1.** crush, flatten, run over, squash, stamp, tread, walk over **2.** do violence to, encroach upon, hurt, infringe, ride roughshod over, show no consideration for, violate

trance abstraction, daze, dream, ecstasy, hypnotic state, muse, rapture, reverie, spell, stupor, unconsciousness

tranquil at peace, calm, composed, cool, pacific, peaceful, placid, quiet, restful, sedate, serene, still, undisturbed, unexcited, unperturbed, unruffled, untroubled

tranquillity ataraxia, calm, calmness, composure, coolness, equanimity, hush, imperturbability, peace, peacefulness, placidity, quiet, quietness, quietude, repose, rest, restfulness, sedateness, serenity, stillness

tranquillize calm, compose, lull, pacify, quell, quiet, relax, sedate, settle one's nerves, soothe

tranquillizer barbiturate, bromide, downer (*Sl.*), opiate, red (*Sl.*), sedative

transact accomplish, carry on, carry out, conclude, conduct, discharge, do, enact, execute, handle, manage, negotiate, perform, prosecute, see to, settle, take care of

transaction **1.** action, affair, bargain, business, coup, deal, deed, enterprise, event, matter, negotiation, occurrence, proceeding, undertaking **2.** *Plural* affairs, annals, doings, goings-on (*Inf.*), minutes, proceedings, record

transcend eclipse, exceed, excel, go above, go beyond, leave behind, leave in the shade (*Inf.*), outdo, outrival, outshine, outstrip, outvie, overstep, rise above, surpass

transcendence, transcendency ascendancy, excellence, greatness, incomparability, matchlessness, paramountcy, pre-eminence, sublimity, superiority, supremacy

transcendent consummate, exceeding, extraordinary, incomparable, matchless, peerless, pre-eminent, second to none, sublime, superior, transcendental, unequalled, unique, unparalleled, unrivalled

theories that explain knowledge with reference to the process of knowing. **5.** *Theol.* supernatural or mystical. **6.** *Maths.* **a.** (of a number or quantity) not being a root of any polynomial with rational coefficients. **b.** (of a function) not capable of expression in terms of a finite number of arithmetical operations. —**,transcen'dentally** *adv.*

transcendentalism (,trænsɛn'dɛntə,lɪzəm) *n.* **1. a.** any system of philosophy, esp. that of Kant, holding that the key to reality lies in the critical examination of reason. **b.** any system of philosophy, esp. that of Emerson, that emphasizes intuition as a means to knowledge or the importance of the search for the divine. **2.** vague philosophical speculation. **3.** the state of being transcendental. **4.** something, such as thought or language, that is transcendental. —**,transcen'dentalist** *n., adj.*

transcendental meditation *n.* a technique, based on Hindu traditions, for relaxing and refreshing the mind and body through the silent repetition of a mantra.

transcribe (træn'skraɪb) *vb.* (*tr.*) **1.** to write, type, or print out fully from speech, notes, etc. **2.** to transliterate or translate. **3.** to make an electrical recording of (a programme or speech) for a later broadcast. **4.** *Music.* to rewrite (a piece of music) for an instrument or medium other than that originally intended; arrange. **5.** *Computers.* **a.** to transfer (information) from one storage device to another. **b.** to transfer (information) from a computer to an external storage device. —**tran'scribable** *adj.* —**tran'scriber** *n.*

transcript ('trænskrɪpt) *n.* **1.** a written, typed, or printed copy or manuscript made by transcribing. **2.** *Chiefly U.S.* an official record of a student's school progress. **3.** any reproduction or copy.

transcription (træn'skrɪpʃən) *n.* **1.** the act or an instance of transcribing or the state of being transcribed. **2.** something transcribed. **3.** a representation in writing of the actual pronunciation of a speech sound, word, etc., using phonetic symbols. —**tran'scriptional** *or* **tran'scriptive** *adj.*

transducer (trænz'djuːsə) *n.* any device, such as a microphone or electric motor, that converts one form of energy into another.

transept ('trænsɛpt) *n.* either of the two wings of a cruciform church at right angles to the nave. —**tran'septal** *adj.*

transfer *vb.* (træns'fɜː), **-ferring, -ferred. 1.** to change or go or cause to change or go from one thing, person, or point to another. **2.** to change (buses, trains, etc.). **3.** *Law.* to make over (property, etc.) to another; convey. **4.** to displace (a drawing, design, etc.) from one surface to another. **5.** (of a football player) to change clubs or (of a club, manager, etc.) to sell or release (a player) to another club. **6.** to leave one school, college, etc., and enrol at another. **7.** to change (the meaning of a word, etc.), esp. by metaphorical extension. ~*n.* ('trænsfɜː). **8.** the act, process, or system of transferring, or the state of being transferred. **9.** a person or thing that transfers or is transferred. **10.** a design or drawing that is transferred from one surface to another. **11.** *Law.* the passing of title to property or other right from one person to another; conveyance. **12.** any document or form effecting or regulating a transfer. **13.** *Chiefly U.S.* a ticket that allows a passenger to change routes. —**trans'ferable** *or* **trans'ferrable** *adj.* —**'transference** ('trænsfərəns) *n.*

transfiguration (,trænsfɪgjʊ'reɪʃən) *n.* a transfiguring

or being transfigured.

Transfiguration (,trænsfɪgjʊ'reɪʃən) *n.* **1.** *New Testament.* the change in the appearance of Christ that took place before three disciples (Matthew 17:1–9). **2.** the Church festival held in commemoration of this on Aug. 6.

transfigure (træns'fɪgə) *vb.* (*usually tr.*) **1.** to change or cause to change in appearance. **2.** to become or cause to become more exalted. —**trans'figurement** *n.*

transfix (træns'fɪks) *vb.* **-fixing, -fixed** *or* **-fixt.** (*tr.*) **1.** to render motionless, esp. with horror or shock. **2.** to impale or fix with a sharp weapon or other device. —**transfixion** (træns'fɪkʃən) *n.*

transform *vb.* (træns'fɔːm). **1.** to alter or be altered in form, function, etc. **2.** (*tr.*) to convert (one form of energy) to another form. **3.** (*tr.*) *Maths.* to change the form of (an equation, etc.) by a mathematical transformation. **4.** (*tr.*) to change (an alternating current or voltage) using a transformer. ~*n.* ('træns,fɔːm). **5.** *Maths.* the result of a mathematical transformation. —**trans'formable** *adj.* —**trans'formative** *adj.*

transformation (,trænsfə'meɪʃən) *n.* **1.** a change or alteration, esp. a radical one. **2.** a transforming or being transformed. **3.** *Maths.* **a.** a change in position or direction of the reference axes in a coordinate system without an alteration in their relative angle. **b.** a change in an expression or equation resulting from the substitution of one set of variables by another. **4.** *Physics.* a change in an atomic nucleus to a different nuclide as the result of the emission of either an alpha-particle or a beta-particle. **5.** an apparently miraculous change in the appearance of a stage set. —**,transfor'mational** *adj.*

transformer (træns'fɔːmə) *n.* **1.** a device that transfers an alternating current from one circuit to one or more other circuits, usually with a change of voltage. **2.** a person or thing that transforms.

transfuse (træns'fjuːz) *vb.* (*tr.*) **1.** to permeate or infuse. **2. a.** to inject (blood, etc.) into a blood vessel. **b.** to give a transfusion to (a patient). —**trans'fuser** *n.* —**trans'fusible** *or* **trans'fusable** *adj.* —**trans'fusive** *adj.*

transfusion (træns'fjuːʒən) *n.* **1.** a transfusing. **2.** the injection of blood, blood plasma, etc., into the blood vessels of a patient.

transgress (trænz'grɛs) *vb.* **1.** to break (a law, etc.). **2.** to go beyond or overstep (a limit). —**trans'gressive** *adj.* —**trans'gression** *n.* —**trans'gressor** *n.*

transient ('trænzɪənt) *adj.* **1.** for a short time only; temporary or transitory. ~*n.* **2.** a transient person or thing. —**'transiently** *adv.* —**'transience, 'transiency,** *or* **'transientness** *n.*

transistor (træn'zɪstə) *n.* **1.** a semiconductor device, having three or more terminals attached to electrode regions, in which current flowing between two electrodes is controlled by a voltage or current applied to one or more specified electrodes. The device has replaced the valve in most circuits since it is much smaller and works at a much lower voltage. **2.** *Inf.* a transistor radio.

transistorize *or* **-ise** (træn'zɪstə,raɪz) *vb.* **1.** to convert to the use or manufacture of transistors and other solid-state components. **2.** (*tr.*) to equip with transistors and other solid-state components.

transit ('trænsɪt, 'trænz-) *n.* **1. a.** the passage or conveyance of goods or people. **b.** (*as modifier*): *a transit visa.* **2.** a change or transition. **3.** a route. **4.** *Astron.* **a.** the passage of a celestial body or satellite across the face of a larger body as seen from the earth. **b.** the apparent

---

THESAURUS

transcribe 1. copy out, engross, note, reproduce, rewrite, set out, take down, transfer, write out 2. interpret, render, translate, transliterate 3. record, tape, tape-record

transcript carbon, carbon copy, copy, duplicate, manuscript, note, notes, record, reproduction, transcription, translation, transliteration, version

transfer 1. v. carry, change, consign, convey, displace, hand over, make over, move, pass on, relocate, remove, shift, translate, transmit, transplant, transport, transpose, turn over 2. n. change, displacement, handover, move, relocation, removal, shift, transference, translation, transmission, transposition

transfix 1. engross, fascinate, halt or stop

in one's tracks, hold, hypnotize, mesmerize, paralyse, petrify, rivet the attention of, root to the spot, spellbind, stop dead, stun 2. fix, impale, pierce, puncture, run through, skewer, spear, spit, transpierce

transform alter, change, convert, make over, metamorphose, reconstruct, remodel, renew, revolutionize, transfigure, translate, transmogrify (*Jocular*), transmute

transformation alteration, change, conversion, metamorphosis, radical change, renewal, revolution, revolutionary change, sea change, transfiguration, transmogrification (*Jocular*), transmutation

transgress break, break the law, contravene, defy, disobey, do *or* go wrong, encroach, err, exceed, fall from grace, go

astray, go beyond, infringe, lapse, misbehave, offend, overstep, sin, trespass, violate

transgression breach, contravention, crime, encroachment, error, fault, infraction, infringement, iniquity, lapse, misbehaviour, misdeed, misdemeanour, offence, sin, trespass, violation, wrong, wrongdoing

transgressor criminal, culprit, delinquent, evildoer, felon, lawbreaker, malefactor, miscreant, offender, sinner, trespasser, villain, wrongdoer

transient brief, ephemeral, evanescent, fleeting, flying, fugacious, fugitive, here today and gone tomorrow, impermanent, momentary, passing, short, short-lived, short-term, temporary, transitory

passage of a celestial body across the meridian. **5. in transit.** while being conveyed; during passage. ~*vb.* **6.** to make a transit through or over (something).

transit camp *n.* a camp in which refugees, soldiers, etc., live temporarily.

transition (trænˈzɪʃən) *n.* **1.** change or passage from one state or stage to another. **2.** the period of time during which something changes. **3.** *Music.* **a.** a movement from one key to another; modulation. **b.** a linking passage between two divisions in a composition; bridge. **4.** a style of architecture in the late 11th and early 12th centuries, characterized by late Romanesque forms combined with early Gothic details. **5.** *Physics.* a change in the configuration of an atomic nucleus, involving either a change in energy level or a transformation to another element or isotope. **6.** a sentence, passage, etc., that links sections of a written work. —**tranˈsitional** *adj.* —**tranˈsitionally** *adv.*

transitive (ˈtrænsɪtɪv) *adj.* **1.** *Grammar.* **a.** denoting an occurrence of a verb when it requires a direct object or denoting a verb that customarily requires a direct object. **b.** (*as n.*): *these verbs are transitives.* **2.** *Logic.* having the property that if one object bears a relationship to a second object that also bears the same relationship to a third object, then the first object bears this relationship to the third object: *if x = y and y = z then x = z.* ~Cf. **intransitive.** —**ˈtransitively** *adv.* —**ˈtransitiveness** *or* ˌtransiˈtivity *n.*

transitory (ˈtrænsɪtərɪ, -trɪ) *adj.* of short duration; transient or ephemeral. —**ˈtransitoriness** *n.*

translate (trænsˈleɪt, trænz-) *vb.* **1.** to express or be capable of being expressed in another language. **2.** (*intr.*) to act as translator. **3.** (*tr.*) to express or explain in simple or less technical language. **4.** (*tr.*) to interpret or infer the significance of (gestures, symbols, etc.). **5.** (*tr.*) to transform or convert: *to translate hope into reality.* **6.** to transfer from one place or position to another. **7.** (*tr.*) *Theol.* to transfer (a person) from one place or plane of existence to another, as from earth to heaven. **8.** *Physics.* to cause (a body) to move laterally in space without rotation or angular displacement. —**ˈtransˈlatable** *adj.* —**ˈtransˈlator** *n.*

translation (trænsˈleɪʃən, trænz-) *n.* **1.** something that is or has been translated. **2.** a translating or being translated. **3.** *Maths.* a transformation in which the origin of a coordinate system is moved to another position so that each axis retains the same direction. —**ˈtransˈlational** *adj.*

transliterate (trænzˈlɪtəˌreɪt) *vb.* (*tr.*) to transcribe (a word, etc.) into corresponding letters of another alphabet. —ˌtransˈliterˈation *n.* —**ˈtransˈliterˌator** *n.*

translucent (trænzˈluːsənt) *adj.* allowing light to pass through partially or diffusely; semitransparent. —**ˈtransˈlucence** *or* **transˈlucency** *n.* —**ˈtransˈlucently** *adv.*

transmigrate (ˌtrænzmaɪˈgreɪt) *vb.* (*intr.*) **1.** to move from one place, state, or stage to another. **2.** *Theol.* (of souls) to pass from one body into another at death. —ˌtransmiˈgration *n.* —**ˈtransˈmigratory** *adj.*

transmission (trænzˈmɪʃən) *n.* **1.** the act or process of transmitting. **2.** something that is transmitted. **3.** the extent to which a body or medium transmits light, sound, etc. **4.** the transference of motive force or power. **5.** a system of shafts, gears, etc., that transmits power, esp. the arrangement of such parts that transmits the power of the engine to the driving wheels of a motor vehicle. **6.** the act or process of sending a message, picture, or other information by means of radio waves, electrical signals, light signals, etc. **7.** a radio or television broadcast. —**ˈtransˈmissible** *adj.* —**ˈtransˈmissive** *adj.*

transmit (trænzˈmɪt) *vb.* **-mitting, -mitted.** **1.** (*tr.*) to pass or cause to go from one place or person to another; transfer. **2.** (*tr.*) to pass on or impart (a disease, etc.). **3.** (*tr.*) to hand down to posterity. **4.** (*tr.; usually passive*) to pass (an inheritable characteristic) from parent to offspring. **5.** to allow the passage of (particles, energy, etc.): *radio waves are transmitted through the atmosphere.* **6. a.** to send out (signals) by means of radio waves or along a transmission line. **b.** to broadcast (a radio or television programme). **7.** (*tr.*) to transfer (a force, motion, etc.) from one part of a mechanical system to another. —**ˈtransˈmittable** *or* **transˈmittible** *adj.* —**ˈtransˈmittal** *n.*

transmitter (trænzˈmɪtə) *n.* **1.** a person or thing that transmits. **2.** the equipment used for generating and amplifying a radio-frequency carrier, modulating the carrier with information, and feeding it to an aerial for transmission. **3.** the microphone in a telephone that converts sound waves into audio-frequency electrical signals. **4.** a device that converts mechanical movements into coded electrical signals transmitted along a telegraph circuit.

transmogrify (trænzˈmɒgrɪˌfaɪ) *vb.* **-fying, -fied.** (*tr.*) *Jocular.* to change or transform into a different shape, esp. a grotesque or bizarre one. —**ˈtransˌmogrifiˈcation** *n.*

transmute (trænzˈmjuːt) *vb.* (*tr.*) **1.** to change the form, character, or substance of. **2.** to alter (an element, metal, etc.) by alchemy. —**ˈtransˌmutaˈbility** *n.* —**ˈtransˈmutable** *adj.* —ˌtransmuˈtation *n.*

transom (ˈtrænsəm) *n.* **1.** a horizontal member across a window. **2.** a horizontal member that separates a door from a window over it. **3.** the usual U.S. name for **fanlight.** **4.** *Naut.* **a.** a surface forming the stern of a vessel. **b.** any of several transverse beams used for strengthening the stern of a vessel. —**ˈtransomed** *adj.*

transparency (trænsˈpærənsɪ) *n., pl.* **-cies.** **1.** Also called: **transparence.** the state of being transparent. **2.** Also called: **slide.** a positive photograph on a transparent base, usually mounted in a frame or between glass plates. It can be viewed by means of a slide projector.

transparent (trænsˈpærənt) *adj.* **1.** permitting the uninterrupted passage of light; clear. **2.** easy to see through, understand, or recognize; obvious. **3.** permitting the free passage of electromagnetic radiation. **4.** candid, open, or frank. —**ˈtransˈparently** *adv.* —**ˈtransˈparentness** *n.*

THESAURUS

transit *n.* **1.** carriage, conveyance, crossing, motion, movement, passage, portage, shipment, transfer, transport, transportation, travel, traverse **2.** alteration, change, changeover, conversion, shift, transition **3. in transit** during passage, en route, on the journey, on the move, on the road, on the way, while travelling ~*v.* **4.** cross, journey, move, pass, travel, traverse

transition alteration, change, changeover, conversion, development, evolution, flux, metamorphosis, metastasis, passage, passing, progression, shift, transit, transmutation, upheaval

transitional changing, developmental, fluid, intermediate, passing, provisional, temporary, transitionary, unsettled

transitory brief, ephemeral, evanescent, fleeting, flying, fugacious, here today and gone tomorrow, impermanent, momentary, passing, short, short-lived, short-term, temporary, transient

translate **1.** construe, convert, decipher, decode, interpret, paraphrase, render, transcribe, transliterate **2.** elucidate, explain, make clear, paraphrase, put in plain English, simplify, spell out, state in layman's language **3.** alter, change, convert, metamorphose, transfigure, transform, transmute, turn **4.** carry, convey, move, remove, send, transfer, transplant, transport, transpose

translation **1.** construction, decoding, gloss, interpretation, paraphrase, rendering, rendition, transcription, transliteration, version **2.** elucidation, explanation, paraphrase, rephrasing, rewording, simplification **3.** alteration, change, conversion, metamorphosis, transfiguration, transformation, transmutation **4.** conveyance, move, removal, transference, transposition

translator interpreter, linguist, metaphrast, paraphrast

transmission **1.** carriage, communication, conveyance, diffusion, dispatch, dissemination, remission, sending, shipment, spread, transfer, transference, transport **2.** broadcasting, dissemination, putting out, relaying, sending, showing **3.** broadcast, programme, show

transmit **1.** bear, carry, communicate, convey, diffuse, dispatch, disseminate, forward, hand down, hand on, impart, pass on, remit, send, spread, take, transfer, transport **2.** broadcast, disseminate, put on the air, radio, relay, send, send out

transparency **1.** clarity, clearness, diaphaneity, diaphanousness, filminess, gauziness, limpidity, limpidness, pellucidity, pellucidness, sheerness, translucence, translucency, transparence **2.** apparentness, distinctness, explicitness, obviousness, patentness, perspicuousness, plainness, unambiguousness, visibility **3.** candidness, directness, forthrightness, frankness, openness, straightforwardness **4.** photograph, slide

transparent **1.** clear, crystal clear, crystalline, diaphanous, filmy, gauzy, limpid, lucent, lucid, pellucid, seethrough, sheer, translucent, transpicuous **2.** apparent, as plain as the nose on one's face (*Inf.*), distinct, easy, evident, explicit, manifest, obvious, pa-

transpire (træn'spaɪə) vb. 1. (intr.) Inf. to happen or occur. 2. (intr.) to come to light; be known. 3. Physiol. to give off or exhale (water or vapour) through the skin, a mucous membrane, etc. 4. (of plants) to lose (water), esp. through the stomata of the leaves. —**transpiration** (ˌtrænspə'reɪʃən) n. —**tran'spiratory** adj.

▷ **Usage.** It is often maintained that transpire should not be used to mean happen or occur, as in the event tran-spired late in the evening, and that the word is properly used to mean become known, as in it transpired later that the thief had been caught. The word is, however, widely used in the first sense, esp. in spoken English.

transplant vb. (træns'plɑːnt). 1. (tr.) to remove or transfer (esp. a plant) from one place to another. 2. (intr.) to be capable of being transplanted. 3. Surgery. to transfer (an organ or tissue) from one part of the body or from one person to another. ~n. ('træns.plɑːnt). 4. Surgery. a. the procedure involved in such a transfer. b. the organ or tissue transplanted. —**trans'plantable** adj. —ˌtransplan'tation n.

transponder (træn'spɒndə) n. a type of radio or radar transmitter-receiver that transmits signals automatical-ly when it receives predetermined signals.

transport vb. (træns'pɔːt). (tr.) 1. to carry or cause to go from one place to another, esp. over some distance. 2. to deport or exile to a penal colony. 3. (usually pas-sive) to have a strong emotional effect on. ~n. ('træns.pɔːt). 4. a. the business or system of transporting goods or people. b. (as modifier): a modernized transport sys-tem. 5. Brit. freight vehicles generally. 6. a. a vehicle used to transport goods or people, esp. troops. b. (as modifier): a transport plane. 7. a transporting or being transported. 8. ecstasy, rapture, or any powerful emo-tion. 9. a convict sentenced to be transported. —**trans-'portable** adj. —**trans'porter** n.

transportation (ˌtrænspɔː'teɪʃən) n. 1. a means or sys-tem of transporting. 2. the act of transporting or the state of being transported. 3. (esp. formerly) deporta-tion to a penal colony.

transport café ('træns.pɔːt) n. Brit. an inexpensive eating place on a main route, used mainly by long-distance lorry drivers.

transpose (træns'pəuz) vb. 1. (tr.) to alter the positions of; interchange, as words in a sentence. 2. Music. to play (notes, music, etc.) in a different key from that originally intended. 3. (tr.) Maths. to move (a term) from one side of an equation to the other with a corre-sponding reversal in sign. —**trans'posable** adj. —**trans-'posal** n. —**trans'poser** n. —**transposition** (ˌtrænspə-'zɪʃən) n.

transsexual (trænz'sɛksjʊəl) n. 1. a person who is completely identified with the opposite sex. 2. a person who has undergone medical procedures to alter sexual characteristics to those of the opposite sex.

transship (træns'ʃɪp) or **tranship** vb. -**shipping**, -**shipped**. to transfer or be transferred from one vessel to another. —**trans'shipment** or **tran'shipment** n.

transubstantiation (ˌtrænsəbˌstænʃɪ'eɪʃən) n. 1. (esp. in Roman Catholic theology) a. the doctrine that the whole substance of the bread and wine changes into the substance of the body and blood of Christ when conse-crated in the Eucharist. b. the mystical process by which this is believed to take place during consecration. Cf. **consubstantiation.** 2. a substantial change; transmu-tation. —ˌtransubˌstanti'ationalist n.

transuranic (ˌtrænzjʊ'rænɪk), **transuranian** (ˌtrænzjʊ'reɪnɪən), or **transuranium** adj. 1. (of an el-ement) having an atomic number greater than that of uranium. 2. of or having the behaviour of transuranic elements.

transverse (trænz'vɜːs) adj. 1. crossing from side to side; athwart; crossways. ~n. 2. a transverse piece or object. —**trans'versely** adv.

transvestite (trænz'vɛstaɪt) n. a person who seeks sex-ual pleasure from wearing clothes of the opposite sex. —**trans'vestism** or **trans'vestitism** n.

trap[1] (træp) n. 1. a mechanical device or enclosed place or pit in which something, esp. an animal, is caught or penned. 2. any device or plan for tricking a person or thing into being caught unawares. 3. anything resem-bling a trap or prison. 4. a fitting for a pipe in the form of a U-shaped or S-shaped bend that contains standing water to prevent the passage of gases. 5. any similar de-vice. 6. a device that hurls clay pigeons into the air to be fired at by trapshooters. 7. Greyhound racing. any one of a line of boxlike stalls in which greyhounds are enclosed before the start of a race. 8. See **trap door.** 9. a light two-wheeled carriage. 10. a slang word for mouth. 11. Golf. an obstacle or hazard, esp. a sand trap. 12. (pl.) Jazz sl. percussion instruments. ~vb. **trapping, trapped.** 13. to catch, take, or pen in a trap. 14. (tr.) to ensnare by trickery; trick. 15. (tr.) to provide (a pipe) with a trap. 16. to set traps in (a place), esp. for animals. —'trap.like adj.

trap[2] (træp) vb. **trapping, trapped.** (tr.; often foll. by out) to dress or adorn.

trap[3] (træp) or **traprock** ('træp.rɒk) n. 1. any fine-grained often columnar dark igneous rock, esp. basalt. 2. any rock in which oil or gas has accumulated.

trap door n. a door or flap flush with and covering an opening, esp. in a ceiling.

trapeze (trə'piːz) n. a free-swinging bar attached to two ropes, used by circus acrobats, etc.

trapezium (trə'piːzɪəm) n., pl. -**ziums** or -**zia** (-zɪə). 1. Chiefly Brit. a quadrilateral having two parallel sides of unequal length. Usual U.S. name: **trapezoid.** 2. Chiefly U.S. a quadrilateral having neither pair of sides parallel. —**tra'pezial** adj.

trapezoid ('træpɪˌzɔɪd) n. 1. a quadrilateral having nei-ther pair of sides parallel. 2. the usual U.S. name for **trapezium.**

trapper ('træpə) n. a person who traps animals, esp. for their furs or skins.

trappings ('træpɪŋz) pl. n. 1. superficial additions or adornments: the trappings of vanity. 2. ceremonial har-ness for a horse or other animal.

Trappist ('træpɪst) n. a. a member of a branch of the Cistercian order of Christian monks, which originated at La Trappe in France in 1664. They are noted for their rule of silence. b. (as modifier): a Trappist monk.

trash (træʃ) n. 1. foolish ideas or talk; nonsense. 2. Chiefly U.S. useless or unwanted matter or objects. 3. a literary or artistic production of poor quality. 4. Chiefly U.S. a poor or worthless person or a group of such peo-ple. 5. bits that are broken or lopped off, esp. the trim-mings from trees or plants. 6. the dry remains of sugar cane after the juice has been extracted. ~vb. 7. to re-move the outer leaves and branches from (growing

---

THESAURUS

tent, perspicuous, plain, recognizable, unam-biguous, understandable, undisguised, visible 3. candid, direct, forthright, frank, open, plain-spoken, straight, straightforward, un-ambiguous, unequivocal

transpire 1. Inf. arise, befall, chance, come about, come to pass (Archaic), happen, occur, take place, turn up 2. become known, be disclosed, be discovered, be made public, come out, come to light, emerge

transplant displace, relocate, remove, resettle, shift, transfer, uproot

transport v. 1. bear, bring, carry, con-vey, fetch, haul, move, remove, run, ship, take, transfer 2. banish, deport, exile, sen-tence to transportation 3. captivate, carry away, delight, electrify, enchant, enrapture, entrance, move, ravish, spellbind ~n. 4. con-veyance, transportation, vehicle 5. carriage,

conveyance, removal, shipment, shipping, transference, transportation 6. cloud nine (Inf.), enchantment, euphoria, heaven, rap-ture, seventh heaven 7. bliss, delight, ecstasy, happiness, ravishment

transpose alter, change, exchange, interchange, move, rearrange, relocate, re-order, shift, substitute, swap (Inf.), switch, transfer

transverse athwart, crossways, cross-wise, diagonal, oblique

trap n. 1. ambush, gin, net, noose, pitfall, snare, springe, toils 2. ambush, artifice, de-ception, device, ruse, stratagem, subterfuge, trick, wile ~v. 3. catch, corner, enmesh, en-snare, entrap, snare, take 4. ambush, beguile, deceive, dupe, ensnare, inveigle, trick

trapped ambushed, at bay, beguiled, caught, cornered, cut off, deceived, duped,

ensnared, in a tight corner, in a tight spot, in-veigled, netted, snared, stuck (Inf.), sur-rounded, tricked, with one's back to the wall

trappings accoutrements, adornments, decorations, dress, equipment, finery, fit-tings, fixtures, fripperies, furnishings, gear, livery, ornaments, panoply, paraphernalia, raiment (Archaic), things, trimmings

trash 1. balderdash, drivel, foolish talk, hogwash, inanity, nonsense, rot, rubbish, tripe (Inf.), trumpery, twaddle 2. dregs, dross, garbage, junk, litter, offscourings, ref-use, rubbish, sweepings, waste

trashy brummagem, catchpenny, cheap, cheap-jack (Inf.), flimsy, inferior, meretri-cious, rubbishy, shabby, shoddy, tawdry, thrown together, tinsel, worthless

plants, esp. sugar cane). —'**trashy** *adj.*
trattoria (ˌtrætə'rɪə) *n.* an Italian restaurant.
trauma ('trɔːmə) *n., pl.* **-mata** (-mətə) *or* **-mas.** 1. *Psychol.* a powerful shock that may have long-lasting effects. 2. *Pathol.* any bodily injury or wound. —**traumatic** (trɔː'mætɪk) *adj.* —**trau'matically** *adv.* —'**trauma,tize** *or* **-ise** *vb.*
travail ('træveɪl) *n. Literary.* 1. painful or excessive labour or exertion. 2. the pangs of childbirth; labour. ~*vb.* 3. (*intr.*) to suffer or labour painfully, esp. in childbirth.
travel ('trævəl) *vb.* **-elling, -elled** *or U.S.* **-eling, -eled.** (*mainly intr.*) 1. to go, move, or journey from one place to another. 2. (*tr.*) to go, move, or journey through or across (an area, region, etc.). 3. to go, move, or cover a distance. 4. to go from place to place as a salesman. 5. (esp. of perishable goods) to withstand a journey. 6. (of light, sound, etc.) to be transmitted or move. 7. to progress or advance. 8. *Basketball.* to take an excessive number of steps while holding the ball. 9. (of part of a mechanism) to move in a fixed path. 10. *Inf.* to move rapidly. ~*n.* 11. **a.** the act of travelling. **b.** (*as modifier*): *a travel brochure.* Related adj.: **itinerant.** 12. (*usually pl.*) a tour or journey. 13. the distance moved by a mechanical part, such as the stroke of a piston. 14. movement or passage.
travel agency *or* **bureau** *n.* an agency that arranges and negotiates flights, holidays, etc., for travellers. —**travel agent** *n.*
traveller ('trævələ, 'trævlə) *n.* 1. a person who travels, esp. habitually. 2. See **travelling salesman.** 3. a part of a mechanism that moves in a fixed course.
traveller's cheque *n.* a cheque sold by a bank, etc., to the bearer, who signs it on purchase and can cash it abroad by signing it again.
travelling salesman *n.* a salesman who travels within an assigned territory in order to sell merchandise or to solicit orders for the commercial enterprise he represents by direct personal contact with customers and potential customers.
travelogue *or U.S. (sometimes)* **travelog** ('trævəlɒg) *n.* a film, lecture, or brochure on travels and travelling.
traverse ('trævɜːs) *vb.* 1. to pass or go over or back and forth over (something); cross. 2. (*tr.*) to go against; oppose. 3. to move sideways or crossways. 4. (*tr.*) to extend or reach across. 5. to turn (an artillery gun) laterally or (of an artillery gun) to turn laterally. 6. (*tr.*) to examine carefully. 7. (*tr.*) *Law.* to deny (an allegation). 8. *Mountaineering.* to move across (a face) horizontally. ~*n.* 9. something being or lying across, such as a transom. 10. a gallery or loft inside a building that crosses it. 11. an obstruction. 12. a protective bank or other barrier across a trench or rampart. 13. a railing, screen, or curtain. 14. the act or an instance of traversing or crossing. 15. *Mountaineering.* the act or an instance of moving horizontally across a face. 16. a path or road across. 17. *Naut.* the zigzag course of a vessel tacking frequently. 18. *Law.* the formal denial of a fact alleged in the opposite party's pleading. 19. *Surveying.* a survey consisting of a series of straight lines, the length of each and the angle between them being measured. ~*adj.* 20. being or lying across; transverse. —'**traversable** *adj.* —**tra** -

'**versal** *n.* —'**traverser** *n.*
travesty ('trævɪstɪ) *n., pl.* **-ties.** 1. a farcical or grotesque imitation; mockery; parody. ~*vb.* **-tying, -tied.** (*tr.*) 2. to make or be a travesty of.
travois (trə'vɔɪ) *n., pl.* **-vois** (-'vɔɪz). 1. *History.* a sled formerly used by the Plains Indians of North America, consisting of two poles joined by a frame and pulled by an animal. 2. *Canad.* a similar sled used for dragging logs.
trawl (trɔːl) *n.* 1. Also called: **trawl net.** a large net, usually in the shape of a sock or bag, drawn at deep levels behind special boats (trawlers). 2. Also called: **trawl line.** a long line to which numerous shorter hooked lines are attached, suspended between buoys. 3. the act of trawling. ~*vb.* 4. to catch (fish) with a trawl net or trawl line.
trawler ('trɔːlə) *n.* 1. a vessel used for trawling. 2. a person who trawls.
tray (treɪ) *n.* 1. a thin flat board or plate of metal, plastic, etc., usually with a raised edge, on which things can be carried. 2. a shallow receptacle for papers, etc., sometimes forming a drawer in a cabinet or box.
treacherous ('tretʃərəs) *adj.* 1. betraying or likely to betray faith or confidence. 2. unstable, unreliable, or dangerous. —'**treacherously** *adv.* —'**treacherousness** *n.*
treachery ('tretʃərɪ) *n., pl.* **-eries.** 1. the act or an instance of wilful betrayal. 2. the disposition to betray.
treacle ('triːkəl) *n.* 1. Also called: **black treacle.** *Brit.* a dark viscous syrup obtained during the refining of sugar. 2. *Brit.* another name for **golden syrup.** 3. anything sweet and cloying. —'**treacly** *adj.*
tread (trɛd) *vb.* **treading, trod, trodden** *or* **trod.** 1. to walk or trample in, on, over, or across (something). 2. (when *intr.*, foll. by *on*) to crush or squash by or as if by treading. 3. (*intr.*; sometimes foll. by *on*) to subdue or repress. 4. (*tr.*) to do by walking or dancing: *to tread a measure.* 5. (*tr.*) (of a male bird) to copulate with (a female bird). 6. **tread lightly.** to proceed with delicacy or tact. 7. **tread on someone's toes.** to infringe on someone's sphere of action, feelings, etc. 8. **tread water.** to stay afloat in an upright position by moving the legs in a walking motion. ~*n.* 9. a manner or style of walking, dancing, etc.: *a light tread.* 10. the act of treading. 11. the top surface of a step in a staircase. 12. the outer part of a tyre or wheel that makes contact with the road, esp. the grooved surface of a pneumatic tyre. 13. the part of a rail that wheels touch. 14. the part of a shoe that is generally in contact with the ground. —'**treader** *n.*
treadle ('trɛdəl) *n.* 1. a lever operated by the foot to drive a machine. ~*vb.* 2. to work (a machine) with a treadle.
treadmill ('trɛdˌmɪl) *n.* 1. Also called: **treadwheel.** (formerly) an apparatus turned by the weight of men or animals climbing steps on the periphery of a cylinder or wheel. 2. a dreary round or routine.
treason ('triːzən) *n.* 1. betrayal of one's sovereign or country, esp. by attempting to overthrow the government. 2. any treachery or betrayal. —'**treasonable** *or* '**treasonous** *adj.* —'**treasonably** *adv.*

THESAURUS

traumatic agonizing, damaging, disturbing, hurtful, injurious, painful, scarring, shocking, upsetting, wounding

travel *v.* 1. cross, go, journey, make a journey, make one's way, move, proceed, progress, ramble, roam, rove, take a trip, tour, traverse, trek, voyage, walk, wander, wend 2. be transmitted, carry, get through, move ~*n.* 3. *Usually plural* excursion, expedition, globetrotting, journey, movement, passage, peregrination, ramble, tour, touring, trip, voyage, walk, wandering

traveller 1. excursionist, explorer, globetrotter, gypsy, hiker, holiday-maker, journeyer, migrant, nomad, passenger, tourist, tripper, voyager, wanderer, wayfarer 2. agent, commercial traveller, rep, representative, salesman, travelling salesman

travelling *adj.* itinerant, migrant, migratory, mobile, moving, nomadic, peripatetic, restless, roaming, roving, touring, unsettled,

wandering, wayfaring

traverse 1. bridge, cover, cross, cut across, go across, go over, make one's way across, negotiate, pass over, ply, range, roam, span, travel over, wander 2. balk, contravene, counter, counteract, deny, frustrate, go against, hinder, impede, obstruct, oppose, thwart 3. check, consider, examine, eye, inspect, investigate, look into, look over, pore over, range over, review, scan, scrutinize, study

travesty 1. *n.* burlesque, caricature, distortion, lampoon, mockery, parody, perversion, send-up (*Brit. inf.*), sham, spoof (*Inf.*), takeoff (*Inf.*) 2. *v.* burlesque, caricature, deride, distort, lampoon, make a mockery of, make fun of, mock, parody, pervert, ridicule, send up (*Brit. inf.*), sham, spoof (*Inf.*), take off (*Inf.*)

treacherous 1. deceitful, disloyal, double-crossing (*Inf.*), double-dealing, duplic-

itous, faithless, false, perfidious, recreant (*Archaic*), traitorous, treasonable, unfaithful, unreliable, untrue, untrustworthy 2. dangerous, deceptive, hazardous, icy, perilous, precarious, risky, slippery, slippy (*Inf.*), tricky, unreliable, unsafe, unstable

treachery betrayal, disloyalty, double-cross (*Inf.*), double-dealing, duplicity, faithlessness, infidelity, perfidiousness, perfidy, stab in the back, treason

tread *v.* 1. hike, march, pace, plod, stamp, step, stride, tramp, trudge, walk 2. crush underfoot, squash, trample 3. bear down, crush, oppress, quell, repress, ride roughshod over, subdue, subjugate, suppress 4. **tread on someone's toes** affront, annoy, bruise, disgruntle, get someone's back up (*Sl.*), hurt, hurt someone's feelings, infringe, injure, irk, offend, vex ~*n.* 5. footfall, footstep, gait, pace, step, stride, walk

treason disaffection, disloyalty, duplicity,

treasure ('trɛʒə) n. 1. wealth and riches, usually hoarded, esp. in the form of money, precious metals, or gems. 2. a thing or person that is highly prized or valued. ~vb. (tr.) 3. to prize highly as valuable, rare, or costly. 4. to store up and save; hoard.

treasure hunt n. a game in which players act upon successive clues to find a hidden prize.

treasurer ('trɛʒərə) n. a person appointed to look after the funds of a society, company, city, or other governing body. —'**treasurer,ship** n.

treasure-trove n. 1. Law. any articles, such as coins, etc., found hidden and of unknown ownership. 2. any valuable discovery.

treasury ('trɛʒərɪ) n., pl. -uries. 1. a storage place for treasure. 2. the revenues or funds of a government, private organization, or individual. 3. a place where funds are kept and disbursed. 4. a person or thing regarded as a valuable source of information. 5. a collection of highly valued poems, etc.; anthology.

Treasury ('trɛʒərɪ) n. (in various countries) the government department in charge of finance.

Treasury Bench n. (in Britain) the front bench to the right of the Speaker in the House of Commons, traditionally reserved for members of the Government.

treat (tri:t) n. 1. a celebration, entertainment, gift, or feast given for or to someone and paid for by another. 2. any delightful surprise or specially pleasant occasion. 3. the act of treating. ~vb. 4. (tr.) to deal with or regard in a certain manner: she treats school as a joke. 5. (tr.) to apply treatment to. 6. (tr.) to subject to a process or to the application of a substance. 7. (often foll. by to) to provide (someone) (with) as a treat. 8. (intr.; usually foll. by of) to deal (with), as in writing or speaking. 9. (intr.) to discuss settlement. —'**treatable** adj. —'**treater** n.

treatise ('tri:tɪz) n. a formal work on a subject, esp. one that deals systematically with its principles and conclusions.

treatment ('tri:tmənt) n. 1. the application of medicines, surgery, etc., to a patient. 2. the manner of handling a person or thing, as in a literary or artistic work. 3. the act, practice, or manner of treating. 4. **the treatment**. Sl. the usual manner of dealing with a particular type of person (esp. in **give someone the (full) treatment**).

treaty ('tri:tɪ) n., pl. -ties. 1. a. a formal agreement between two or more states, such as an alliance or trade arrangement. b. the document in which such a contract is written. 2. any pact or agreement. 3. an agreement between two parties concerning the purchase of property at a price privately agreed between them.

treble ('trɛbəl) adj. 1. threefold; triple. 2. of or denoting a soprano voice or part or a high-pitched instrument. ~n. 3. treble the amount, size, etc. 4. a soprano voice or part or a high-pitched instrument. 5. the highest register of a musical instrument. 6. the high-frequency gain of an audio amplifier, esp. in a record player or tape recorder. 7. a. the narrow inner ring on a dartboard. b. a hit on this ring. ~vb. 8. to make or become three times

as much. —'**trebly** adv.

treble chance n. a method of betting in football pools in which the chances of winning are related to the number of draws and the number of home and away wins forecast by the competitor.

treble clef n. Music. the clef that establishes G a fifth above middle C as being on the second line of the staff. Symbol: 𝄞

tree (tri:) n. 1. any large woody perennial plant with a distinct trunk giving rise to branches. Related adj.: **arboreal**. 2. any plant that resembles this. 3. a wooden post, bar, etc. 4. See **family tree, shoetree, saddletree**. 5. Chem. a treelike crystal growth. 6. a branching diagrammatic representation of something. 7. **at the top of the tree**. in the highest position of a profession, etc. 8. **up a tree**. U.S. inf. in a difficult situation; trapped or stumped. ~vb. (tr.) 9. to drive or force up a tree. 10. U.S. inf. to force into a difficult situation. 11. to stretch on a shoetree. —'**treeless** adj. —'**treelessness** n. —'**tree,like** adj.

tree creeper n. any of a family of small songbirds of the N hemisphere, having a slender downward-curving bill. They creep up trees to feed on insects.

tree line n. another name for **timber line**.

tree surgery n. the treatment of damaged trees by filling cavities, applying braces, etc. —**tree surgeon** n.

trefoil ('trɛfɔɪl) n. 1. any of a genus of leguminous plants having leaves divided into three leaflets. 2. any of various related plants having similar leaves. 3. a flower or leaf having three lobes. 4. Archit. an ornament in the form of three arcs arranged in a circle. —'**trefoiled** adj.

trek (trɛk) n. 1. a long and often difficult journey. 2. S. African. a journey or stage of a journey, esp. a migration by ox wagon. ~vb. **trekking, trekked.** 3. (intr.) to make a trek. —'**trekker** n.

trellis ('trɛlɪs) n. 1. a structure of latticework, esp. one used to support climbing plants. ~vb. (tr.) 2. to interweave (strips of wood, etc.) to make a trellis. 3. to provide or support with a trellis. —'**trellis,work** n.

tremble ('trɛmbəl) vb. (intr.) 1. to vibrate with short slight movements; quiver. 2. to shake involuntarily, as with cold or fear; shiver. 3. to experience fear or anxiety. ~n. 4. the act or an instance of trembling. —'**trembler** n. —'**tremblingly** adv. —'**trembly** adj.

tremendous (trɪ'mɛndəs) adj. 1. vast; huge. 2. Inf. very exciting or unusual. 3. Inf. (intensifier): a tremendous help. 4. Arch. terrible or dreadful. —tre'**mendously** adv. —tre'**mendousness** n.

tremolo ('trɛmə,ləʊ) n., pl. -los. Music. 1. (in playing the violin, cello, etc.) the rapid reiteration of a note or notes to produce a trembling effect. 2. (in singing) a fluctuation in pitch. 3. a device, as on an organ, that produces a tremolo effect.

tremor ('trɛmə) n. 1. an involuntary shudder or vibration. 2. any trembling movement. 3. a vibrating or trembling effect, as of sound or light. 4. a minor earthquake. ~vb. 5. (intr.) to tremble. —'**tremorous** adj.

tremulous ('trɛmjʊləs) adj. 1. vibrating slightly; qua-

THESAURUS

lese-majesty, mutiny, perfidy, sedition, subversion, traitorousness, treachery

treasonable disloyal, false, mutinous, perfidious, seditious, subversive, traitorous, treacherous, treasonous

treasure n. 1. cash, fortune, funds, gold, jewels, money, riches, valuables, wealth 2. apple of one's eye, darling, gem, jewel, nonpareil, paragon, pearl, precious, pride and joy, prize ~v. 3. adore, cherish, dote upon, esteem, hold dear, idolize, love, prize, revere, value, venerate, worship 4. accumulate, cache, collect, garner, hoard, husband, lay up, salt away, save, stash (away) (Inf.), store up

treasury 1. bank, cache, hoard, repository, store, storehouse, vault 2. assets, capital, coffers, exchequer, finances, funds, money, resources, revenues

treat n. 1. banquet, celebration, entertainment, feast, gift, party, refreshment 2. delight, enjoyment, fun, gratification, joy, pleasure, satisfaction, surprise, thrill ~v. 3. act towards, behave towards, consider, deal

with, handle, look upon, manage, regard, use 4. apply treatment to, attend to, care for, doctor, medicate, nurse 5. buy for, entertain, feast, foot or pay the bill, give, lay on, pay for, provide, regale, stand (Inf.), take out, wine and dine 6. be concerned with, contain, deal with, discourse upon, discuss, go into, touch upon 7. bargain, come to terms, confer, have talks, make terms, negotiate, parley

treatise disquisition, dissertation, essay, exposition, monograph, pamphlet, paper, study, thesis, tract, work, writing

treatment 1. care, cure, healing, medication, medicine, remedy, surgery, therapy 2. action towards, behaviour towards, conduct, dealing, handling, management, manipulation, reception, usage

treaty agreement, alliance, bargain, bond, compact, concordat, contract, convention, covenant, entente, pact

trek 1. n. expedition, footslog, hike, journey, long haul, march, odyssey, slog, tramp 2. v. footslog, hike, journey, march, plod, range,

roam, rove, slog, traipse (Inf.), tramp, trudge, yomp

tremble 1. v. oscillate, quake, quiver, rock, shake, shake in one's shoes, shiver, shudder, teeter, totter, vibrate, wobble 2. n. oscillation, quake, quiver, shake, shiver, shudder, tremor, vibration, wobble

tremendous 1. appalling, awesome, awful, colossal, deafening, dreadful, enormous, fearful, formidable, frightful, gargantuan, gigantic, great, huge, immense, mammoth, monstrous, prodigious, stupendous, terrible, terrific, titanic, towering, vast, whopping (Inf.) 2. Inf. ace (Inf.), amazing, excellent, exceptional, extraordinary, fabulous (Inf.), fantastic (Inf.), great, incredible, marvellous, super (Inf.), terrific (Inf.), wonderful

tremor 1. agitation, quaking, quaver, quiver, quivering, shake, shaking, shiver, tremble, trembling, trepidation, vibration, wobble 2. earthquake, quake (Inf.), shock

vering; trembling. **2.** showing or characterized by fear, anxiety, excitement, etc. —'**tremulously** adv. —'**tremulousness** n.

trench (trɛntʃ) n. **1.** a deep ditch. **2.** a ditch dug as a fortification, having a parapet of earth. ~vb. **3.** to make a trench in (a place). **4.** (tr.) to fortify with a trench. **5.** to slash or be slashed. **6.** (intr.; foll. by on or upon) to encroach or verge.

trenchant ('trɛntʃənt) adj. **1.** keen or incisive: trenchant criticism. **2.** vigorous and effective: a trenchant foreign policy. **3.** distinctly defined. **4.** Arch. or poetic. sharp. —'**trenchancy** n. —'**trenchantly** adv.

trench coat n. a belted waterproof coat resembling a military officer's coat.

trencher ('trɛntʃə) n. **1.** (esp. formerly) a wooden board on which food was served or cut. **2.** Also called: **trencher cap.** a mortarboard.

trencherman ('trɛntʃəmən) n., pl. **-men.** a person who enjoys food; hearty eater.

trench warfare n. a type of warfare in which opposing armies face each other in entrenched positions.

trend (trɛnd) n. **1.** general tendency or direction. **2.** fashion; mode. ~vb. **3.** (intr.) to take a certain trend.

trendsetter ('trɛnd,sɛtə) n. a person or thing that creates, or may create, a new fashion. —'**trend,setting** adj.

trendy ('trɛndɪ) Brit. inf. ~adj. **trendier, trendiest. 1.** consciously fashionable. ~n. **2.** a trendy person. —'**trendily** adv. —'**trendiness** n.

trepidation (,trɛpɪ'deɪʃən) n. **1.** a state of fear or anxiety. **2.** a condition of quaking or palpitation, esp. one caused by anxiety.

trespass ('trɛspəs) vb. (intr.) **1.** (often foll. by on or upon) to go or intrude (on the property, privacy, or preserves of another) with no right or permission. **2.** Law. to commit trespass. **3.** Arch. (often foll. by against) to sin or transgress. ~n. **4.** Law. a. any unlawful act committed with force, which causes injury to another person, his property or rights. **b.** a wrongful entry upon another's land. **5.** an intrusion on another's privacy or preserves. **6.** a sin or offence. —'**trespasser** n.

tress (trɛs) n. **1.** (often pl.) a lock of hair, esp. a long lock of woman's hair. **2.** a plait or braid of hair. ~vb. (tr.) **3.** to arrange in tresses. —'**tressy** adj.

trestle ('trɛsəl) n. **1.** a framework in the form of a horizontal member supported at each end by a pair of splayed legs, used to carry scaffold boards, a table top, etc. **2. a.** a framework of timber, metal, or reinforced concrete that is used to support a bridge or ropeway. **b.** a bridge constructed of such frameworks.

trews (tru:z) pl. n. Chiefly Brit. close-fitting trousers, now usually for women, originally of tartan cloth and worn by certain Scottish soldiers.

T.R.H. abbrev. for Their Royal Highnesses.

tri- prefix. **1.** three or thrice: triaxial; trigon; trisect. **2.** occurring every three: trimonthly.

triad ('traɪæd) n. **1.** a group of three; trio. **2.** Chem. an atom, element, group, or ion that has a valency of three. **3.** Music. a three-note chord consisting of a note and the third and fifth above it. **4.** an aphoristic literary form used in medieval Welsh and Irish literature. —**tri'adic** adj. —'**triadism** n.

Triad ('traɪæd) n. any of various Chinese secret criminal societies, involved in drug trafficking.

trial ('traɪəl, traɪl) n. **1. a.** the act or an instance of trying or proving; test or experiment. **b.** (as modifier): a trial run. **2.** Law. **a.** the judicial examination and determination of the' issues in a civil or criminal cause by a competent tribunal. **b.** the determination of an accused person's guilt or innocence after hearing evidence and the judicial examination of the issues involved. **c.** (as modifier): trial proceedings. **3.** an effort or attempt to do something. **4.** trouble or grief. **5.** an annoying or frustrating person or thing. **6.** (often pl.) a competition for individuals: sheepdog trials. **7. on trial. a.** undergoing trial, esp. before a court of law. **b.** being tested, as before a commitment to purchase.

trial and error n. a method of discovery, solving problems, etc., based on practical experiment and experience rather than on theory: he learnt to cook by trial and error.

trial balance n. Book-keeping. a statement of all the debit and credit balances in the ledger of a double-entry system, drawn up to test their equality.

triangle ('traɪ,æŋgəl) n. **1.** Geom. a three-sided polygon that can be classified by angle, as in an acute triangle, or by side, as in an equilateral triangle. **2.** any object shaped like a triangle. **3.** any situation involving three parties or points of view. **4.** Music. a percussion instrument consisting of a sonorous metal bar bent into a triangular shape, beaten with a metal stick. **5.** a group of three. —**triangular** (traɪ'æŋgjulə) adj.

triangulate vb. (traɪ'æŋgju,leɪt) (tr.) **1. a.** to survey by the method of triangulation. **b.** to calculate trigonometrically. **2.** to divide into triangles. **3.** to make triangular. ~adj. (traɪ'æŋgjulɪt, -,leɪt). **4.** marked with or composed of triangles. —**tri'angulately** adv.

triangulation (traɪ,æŋgju'leɪʃən) n. a method of surveying in which an area is divided into triangles, one side (the base line) and all angles of which are measured and the lengths of the other lines calculated trigonometrically.

Triassic (traɪ'æsɪk) adj. **1.** of or formed in the first period of the Mesozoic era. ~n. **2. the.** Also called: **Trias.** the Triassic period or rock system.

tribe (traɪb) n. **1.** a social division of a people, esp. of a preliterate people, defined in terms of common descent, territory, culture, etc. **2.** an ethnic or ancestral division of ancient cultures, esp.: **a.** one of the political divisions of the Roman people. **b.** any of the 12 divisions of ancient Israel, each of which was believed to be descended from one of the 12 patriarchs. **3.** Inf. **a.** a large number of persons, animals, etc. **b.** a specific class or group of persons. **c.** a family, esp. a large one. **4.** Biol. a taxonomic group that is a subdivision of a subfamily. —'**tribal** adj.

tribesman ('traɪbzmən) n., pl. **-men.** a member of a tribe.

tribulation (,trɪbju'leɪʃən) n. **1.** a cause of distress. **2.**

THESAURUS

trench channel, cut, ditch, drain, earthwork, entrenchment, excavation, fosse, furrow, gutter, pit, trough, waterway

trenchant 1. acerbic, acid, acidulous, acute, astringent, biting, caustic, cutting, hurtful, incisive, keen, mordant, penetrating, piquant, pointed, pungent, sarcastic, scathing, severe, sharp, tart 2. driving, effective, effectual, emphatic, energetic, forceful, potent, powerful, strong, vigorous 3. clear, clear-cut, crisp, distinct, distinctly defined, explicit, salient, unequivocal, well-defined

trend n. 1. bias, course, current, direction, drift, flow, inclination, leaning, tendency 2. craze, fad (Inf.), fashion, look, mode, rage, style, thing, vogue ~v. 3. bend, flow, head, incline, lean, run, stretch, swing, tend, turn, veer

trepidation agitation, alarm, anxiety, apprehension, blue funk (Inf.), butterflies (Inf.), cold feet (Inf.), cold sweat (Inf.), consternation, dismay, disquiet, disturbance, dread, emotion, excitement, fear, fright, jit-

ters (Inf.), nervousness, palpitation, perturbation, quivering, shaking, the heebie-jeebies (Sl.), trembling, tremor, uneasiness, worry

trespass v. 1. encroach, infringe, intrude, invade, obtrude, poach 2. Archaic offend, sin, transgress, violate, wrong ~n. 3. encroachment, infringement, intrusion, invasion, poaching, unlawful entry, wrongful entry 4. breach, crime, delinquency, error, evildoing, fault, infraction, iniquity, injury, misbehaviour, misconduct, misdeed, misdemeanour, offence, sin, transgression, wrongdoing

trespasser 1. infringer, interloper, intruder, invader, poacher, unwelcome visitor 2. Archaic criminal, delinquent, evildoer, malefactor, offender, sinner, transgressor, wrongdoer

tress braid, curl, lock, plait, ringlet

triad threesome, trilogy, trine, trinity, trio, triple, triplet, triptych, triumvirate, triune

trial n. 1. assay, audition, check, dry run (Inf.), examination, experience, experiment, probation, proof, test, testing, test-run 2. con-

test, hearing, judicial examination, litigation, tribunal 3. attempt, crack (Inf.), effort, endeavour, go, shot (Inf.), stab, try, venture, whack (Inf.) 4. adversity, affliction, burden, cross to bear, distress, grief, hardship, hard times, load, misery, ordeal, pain, suffering, tribulation, trouble, unhappiness, vexation, woe, wretchedness 5. bane, bother, hassle (Inf.), irritation, nuisance, pain in the neck (Inf.), pest, plague (Inf.), thorn in one's flesh, vexation ~adj. 6. experimental, exploratory, pilot, probationary, provisional, testing

tribe blood, caste, clan, class, division, dynasty, ethnic group, family, gens, house, people, race, seed, sept, stock

tribulation adversity, affliction, bad luck, blow, burden, care, cross to bear, curse, distress, grief, heartache, ill fortune, misery, misfortune, ordeal, pain, reverse, sorrow, suffering, trial, trouble, unhappiness, vexation, woe, worry, wretchedness

a state of suffering or distress.

tribunal (traɪˈbjuːnəl, trɪ-) *n.* **1.** a court of justice. **2.** (in England) a special court, convened by the government to inquire into a specific matter. **3.** a raised platform containing the seat of a judge.

tribune¹ (ˈtrɪbjuːn) *n.* **1.** (in ancient Rome) **a.** an officer elected by the plebs to protect their interests. **b.** a senior military officer. **2.** a person who upholds public rights. —**tribunate** (ˈtrɪbjʊnɪt) *or* **ˈtribune₁ship** *n.*

tribune² (ˈtrɪbjuːn) *n.* **1. a.** the apse of a Christian basilica that contains the bishop's throne. **b.** the throne itself. **2.** a gallery or raised area in a church. **3.** *Rare.* a raised platform; dais.

tributary (ˈtrɪbjʊtərɪ) *n., pl.* **-taries. 1.** a stream, river, or glacier that feeds another larger one. **2.** a person, nation, or people that pays tribute. ~*adj.* **3.** (of a stream, etc.) feeding a larger stream. **4.** given or owed as a tribute. **5.** paying tribute. —**ˈtributarily** *adv.*

tribute (ˈtrɪbjuːt) *n.* **1.** a gift or statement made in acknowledgment, gratitude, or admiration. **2.** a payment by one ruler or state to another, usually as an acknowledgment of submission. **3.** the obligation to pay tribute.

trice (traɪs) *n.* a moment; instant (esp. in **in a trice**).

triceps (ˈtraɪsɛps) *n., pl.* **-cepses** (-sɛpsɪz) *or* **-ceps.** any muscle having three heads, esp. the one that extends the forearm.

tricho- *or before a vowel* **trich-** *combining form.* indicating hair or a part resembling hair: *trichocyst.*

trichromatic (ˌtraɪkrəʊˈmætɪk) *or* **trichromic** (traɪˈkrəʊmɪk) *adj.* **1.** involving the combination of three primary colours. **2.** of or having normal colour vision. **3.** having or involving three colours. —**triˈchromaˌtism** *n.*

trick (trɪk) *n.* **1.** a deceitful or cunning action or plan. **2. a.** a mischievous, malicious, or humorous action or plan; joke. **b.** (*as modifier*): *a trick spider.* **3.** an illusory or magical feat. **4.** a simple feat learned by an animal or person. **5.** an adroit or ingenious device; knack: *a trick of the trade.* **6.** a habit or mannerism. **7.** a turn of duty. **8.** *Cards.* a batch of cards containing one from each player, usually played in turn and won by the player or side that plays the card with the highest value. **9. do the trick.** *Inf.* to produce the desired result. **10. how's tricks?** *Sl.* how are you? ~*vb.* **11.** (*tr.*) to defraud, deceive, or cheat (someone). —**ˈtrickery** *n.*

trickle (ˈtrɪkəl) *vb.* **1.** to run or cause to run in thin or slow streams. **2.** (*intr.*) to move gradually: *the crowd trickled away.* ~*n.* **3.** a thin, irregular, or slow flow of something. **4.** the act of trickling.

trick out *or* **up** *vb.* (*tr., adv.*) to dress up; deck out: *tricked out in frilly dresses.*

trickster (ˈtrɪkstə) *n.* a person who deceives or plays tricks.

tricky (ˈtrɪkɪ) *adj.* **-kier, -kiest. 1.** involving snags or difficulties. **2.** needing careful handling. **3.** sly; wily: *a tricky dealer.* —**ˈtrickily** *adv.* —**ˈtrickiness** *n.*

tricolour *or U.S.* **tricolor** (ˈtrɪkələ, ˈtraɪˌkʌlə) *adj. also* **tricoloured** *or U.S.* **tricolored** (ˈtraɪˌkʌləd). **1.** having or involving three colours. ~*n.* **2.** (*often cap.*) the French flag, having three stripes in blue, white, and red. **3.** any flag, badge, etc., with three colours.

tricot (ˈtrɪkəʊ, ˈtriː-) *n.* **1.** a thin rayon or nylon fabric knitted or resembling knitting, used for dresses, etc. **2.** a type of ribbed dress fabric.

tricycle (ˈtraɪsɪkəl) *n.* a three-wheeled cycle, esp. one driven by pedals. —**ˈtricyclist** *n.*

trident (ˈtraɪdənt) *n.* a three-pronged spear.

Tridentine (traɪˈdɛntaɪn) *adj.* **1. a.** *History.* of the Council of Trent in the 16th century. **b.** in accord with Tridentine doctrine: *Tridentine mass.* ~*n.* **2.** an orthodox Roman Catholic.

tried (traɪd) *vb.* the past tense or past participle of **try.**

triennial (traɪˈɛnɪəl) *adj.* **1.** relating to, lasting for, or occurring every three years. ~*n.* **2.** a third anniversary. **3.** a triennial period, thing, or occurrence. —**triˈennially** *adv.*

trier (ˈtraɪə) *n.* a person or thing that tries.

trifle (ˈtraɪfəl) *n.* **1.** a thing of little or no value or significance. **2.** a small amount; bit: *a trifle more enthusiasm.* **3.** *Brit.* a cold dessert made with sponge cake spread with jam or fruit, soaked in wine or sherry, covered with custard and cream. ~*vb.* **4.** (*intr.; usually foll. by with*) to deal (with) as if worthless; dally: *to trifle with a person's affections.* **5.** to waste (time) frivolously. —**ˈtrifler** *n.*

trifling (ˈtraɪflɪŋ) *adj.* **1.** insignificant or petty. **2.** frivolous or idle. —**ˈtriflingly** *adv.*

triforium (traɪˈfɔːrɪəm) *n., pl.* **-ria** (-rɪə). an arcade above the arches of the nave, choir, or transept of a church.

trig (trɪg) *Arch. or dialect.* ~*adj.* **1.** neat or spruce. ~*vb.* **trigging, trigged. 2.** to make or become trim or spruce. —**ˈtrigly** *adv.* —**ˈtrigness** *n.*

trig. *abbrev. for:* **1.** trigonometry. **2.** trigonometrical.

trigger (ˈtrɪgə) *n.* **1.** a small lever that activates the firing mechanism of a firearm. **2.** a device that releases a spring-loaded mechanism. **3.** any event that sets a course of action in motion. ~*vb.* (*tr.*) **4.** (*usually foll. by off*) to give rise (to); set (off). **5.** to fire or set in motion by or as by pulling a trigger.

trigger-happy *adj. Inf.* **1.** tending to resort to the use of firearms or violence irresponsibly. **2.** tending to act rashly.

trigonometry (ˌtrɪgəˈnɒmɪtrɪ) *n.* the branch of mathematics concerned with the properties of trigonometric functions and their application to the determination of the angles and sides of triangles: used in surveying, navigation, etc. —**trigonometric** (ˌtrɪgənəˈmɛtrɪk) *or* **ˌtrigonoˈmetrical** *adj.*

trig point *n. Inf.* a point on a hilltop, etc., used for triangulation by a surveyor. Also called: **trig station.**

trike (traɪk) *n.* short for **tricycle.**

trilby (ˈtrɪlbɪ) *n., pl.* **-bies.** a man's soft felt hat with an indented crown.

trill (trɪl) *n.* **1.** *Music.* a rapid alternation between a principal note and the note above it. **2.** a shrill warbling sound, esp. as made by some birds. **3.** the articulation of an (r) sound produced by the rapid vibration of the tongue or the uvula. ~*vb.* **4.** to sound, sing, or play (a trill or with a trill). **5.** (*tr.*) to pronounce (an r sound) by the production of a trill.

trillion (ˈtrɪljən) *n.* **1.** (in Britain and Germany) the number represented as one followed by eighteen zeros (10^{18}); a million million million. U.S. word: **quintillion. 2.** (in the U.S. and France) the number represented as one followed by twelve zeros (10^{12}); a million million.

THESAURUS

tribunal bar, bench, court, hearing, judgment seat, judicial examination, trial

tribute 1. accolade, acknowledgment, applause, commendation, compliment, encomium, esteem, eulogy, gift, gratitude, honour, laudation, panegyric, praise, recognition, respect, testimonial **2.** charge, contribution, customs, duty, excise, homage, impost, offering, payment, ransom, subsidy, tax, toll

trick *n.* **1.** artifice, con (*Sl.*), deceit, deception, device, dodge, feint, fraud, gimmick, hoax, imposition, imposture, manoeuvre, ploy, ruse, stratagem, subterfuge, swindle, trap, wile **2.** antic, cantrip (*Scot.*), caper, device, feat, frolic, gag (*Sl.*), gambol, jape, joke, juggle, legerdemain, leg-pull (*Brit. inf.*), practical joke, prank, put-on (*Sl.*), sleight of hand, stunt **3.** art, command, craft, device, expertise, gift, hang (*Inf.*), knack, know-how (*Inf.*), secret, skill, technique **4.** characteristic,

crotchet, foible, habit, idiosyncrasy, mannerism, peculiarity, practice, quirk, trait **5. do the trick** *Inf.* be effective *or* effectual, have effect, produce the desired result, work ~*v.* **6.** bamboozle (*Inf.*), cheat, con (*Sl.*), deceive, defraud, delude, dupe, fool, gull (*Archaic*), have (someone) on, hoax, hoodwink, impose upon, mislead, pull the wool over (someone's) eyes, put one over on (someone) (*Inf.*), swindle, take in (*Inf.*), trap

trickery cheating, chicanery, con (*Sl.*), deceit, deception, dishonesty, double-dealing, fraud, funny business, guile, hanky-panky (*Inf.*), hoax, imposture, jiggery-pokery (*Inf.*), monkey business (*Inf.*), pretence, skulduggery (*Inf.*), swindling

trickle 1. *v.* crawl, creep, dribble, drip, drop, exude, ooze, percolate, run, seep, stream **2.** *n.* dribble, drip, seepage

tricky 1. complicated, delicate, difficult,

knotty, problematic, risky, sticky (*Inf.*), thorny, ticklish, touch-and-go **2.** artful, crafty, cunning, deceitful, deceptive, devious, foxy, scheming, slippery, sly, subtle, wily

trifle *n.* **1.** bagatelle, bauble, child's play, gewgaw, knick-knack, nothing, plaything, toy, triviality **2.** bit, dash, drop, jot, little, pinch, spot, touch, trace ~*v.* **3.** amuse oneself, coquet, dally, dawdle, flirt, fritter, idle, mess about, palter, play, toy, wanton, waste, waste time

trifling empty, frivolous, idle, inconsiderable, insignificant, minuscule, negligible, paltry, petty, piddling (*Inf.*), puny, shallow, silly, slight, small, tiny, trivial, unimportant, valueless, worthless

trigger *v.* activate, bring about, cause, elicit, generate, give rise to, produce, prompt, provoke, set in motion, set off, spark off, start

Brit. word: **billion.** ~*determiner.* **3.** (preceded by *a* or a numeral) amounting to a trillion. —'**trillionth** *n., adj.*

trillium ('trɪljəm) *n.* any of a genus of herbaceous plants of Asia and North America, having a whorl of three leaves at the top of the stem with a single white, pink, or purple three-petalled flower.

trilobite ('traɪlə,baɪt) *n.* any of various extinct marine arthropods abundant in Palaeozoic times, having a segmented exoskeleton divided into three parts. —**trilobitic** (,traɪlə'bɪtɪk) *adj.*

trilogy ('trɪlədʒɪ) *n., pl.* -**gies. 1.** a series of three related works, esp. in literature, etc. **2.** (in ancient Greece) a series of three tragedies performed together.

trim (trɪm) *adj.* **trimmer, trimmest. 1.** neat and spruce in appearance. **2.** slim; slender. **3.** in good condition. ~*vb.* **trimming, trimmed.** (*mainly tr.*) **4.** to put in good order, esp. by cutting or pruning. **5.** to shape and finish (timber). **6.** to adorn or decorate. **7.** (sometimes foll. by *off* or *away*) to cut so as to remove: *to trim off a branch.* **8.** to cut down to the desired size or shape. **9.** *Naut.* **a.** (*also intr.*) to adjust the balance of (a vessel) or (of a vessel) to maintain an even balance, by distribution of ballast, cargo, etc. **b.** (*also intr.*) to adjust (a vessel's sails) to take advantage of the wind. **10.** to balance (an aircraft) before flight by adjusting the position of the load or in flight by the use of trim tabs, fuel transfer, etc. **11.** (*also intr.*) to modify (one's opinions, etc.) for expediency. **12.** *Inf.* to thrash or beat. **13.** *Inf.* to rebuke. ~*n.* **14.** a decoration or adornment. **15.** decorative metalwork on a motor car. **16.** proper order or fitness; good shape. **17.** a haircut that neatens but does not alter the existing hairstyle. **18.** *Naut.* **a.** the general set and appearance of a vessel. **b.** the difference between the draught of a vessel at the bow and at the stern. **c.** the fitness of a vessel. **d.** the position of a vessel's sails relative to the wind. **19.** dress or equipment. **20.** *U.S.* window-dressing. **21.** the attitude of an aircraft in flight when the pilot allows the main control surfaces to take up their own positions. **22.** material that is trimmed off. **23.** decorative mouldings, such as architraves, picture rails, etc. —'**trimly** *adv.* —'**trimness** *n.*

trimaran ('traɪmə,ræn) *n.* a vessel, usually of shallow draught, with two hulls flanking the main hull.

trimming ('trɪmɪŋ) *n.* **1.** an extra piece used to decorate or complete. **2.** (*pl.*) additional ornaments or accompaniments: *roast turkey with all the trimmings.* **3.** (*pl.*) parts that are cut off.

Trinitarian (,trɪnɪ'tɛərɪən) *n.* **1.** a person who believes in the doctrine of the Trinity. ~*adj.* **2.** of or relating to the doctrine of the Trinity or those who uphold it. —,**Trini'tarian,ism** *n.*

trinitroglycerin (traɪ,naɪtrəʊ'glɪsərɪn) *n.* the full name for **nitroglycerin.**

trinitrotoluene (traɪ,naɪtrəʊ'tɒljʊ,iːn) *or* **trinitrotoluol** (traɪ,naɪtrəʊ'tɒljʊ,ɒl) *n.* the full name for TNT.

trinity ('trɪnɪtɪ) *n., pl.* -**ties. 1.** a group of three. **2.** the state of being threefold.

Trinity ('trɪnɪtɪ) *n. Christian theol.* the union of three persons, the Father, Son, and Holy Ghost, in one Godhead.

Trinity Sunday *n.* the Sunday after Whit Sunday.

trinket ('trɪŋkɪt) *n.* **1.** a small or worthless ornament or piece of jewellery. **2.** a trivial object; trifle.

trio ('triːəʊ) *n., pl.* **trios. 1.** a group of three. **2.** *Music.* **a.** a group of three singers or instrumentalists or a piece of music composed for such a group. **b.** a subordinate section in a scherzo, minuet, etc.

trip (trɪp) *n.* **1.** an outward and return journey, often for a specific purpose. **2.** any journey. **3.** a false step; stumble. **4.** any slip or blunder. **5.** a light step or tread. **6.** a manoeuvre or device to cause someone to trip. **7.** Also called: **tripper.** any catch on a mechanism that acts as a switch. **8.** *Inf.* a hallucinogenic drug experience. ~*vb.* **tripping, tripped. 9.** (often foll. by *up,* or when *intr.,* by *on* or *over*) to stumble or cause to stumble. **10.** to make or cause to make a mistake. **11.** (*tr.;* often foll. by *up*) to trap or catch in a mistake. **12.** (*intr.*) to go on a short journey. **13.** (*intr.*) to move or tread lightly. **14.** *Inf.* to experience the effects of a hallucinogenic drug. **15.** to activate a mechanical trip.

tripartite (traɪ'pɑːtaɪt) *adj.* **1.** divided into or composed of three parts. **2.** involving three participants. **3.** (esp. of leaves) consisting of three parts formed by divisions extending almost to the base. —**tri'partitely** *adv.*

tripe (traɪp) *n.* **1.** the stomach lining of an ox, cow, etc., prepared for cooking. **2.** *Inf.* something silly; rubbish.

triple ('trɪpəl) *adj.* **1.** consisting of three parts; threefold. **2.** (of musical time or rhythm) having three beats in each bar. **3.** three times as great or as much. ~*n.* **4.** a threefold amount. **5.** a group of three. ~*vb.* **6.** to increase threefold; treble. —'**triply** *adv.*

triple jump *n.* an athletic event in which the competitor has to perform successively a hop, a step, and a jump in continuous movement.

triple point *n. Chem.* the temperature and pressure at which the three phases of a substance are in equilibrium.

triplet ('trɪplɪt) *n.* **1.** a group or set of three similar things. **2.** one of three offspring born at one birth. **3.** *Music.* a group of three notes played in a time value of two, four, etc.

triplicate *adj.* ('trɪplɪkɪt). **1.** triple. ~*vb.* ('trɪplɪ,keɪt). **2.** to multiply or be multiplied by three. ~*n.* ('trɪplɪkɪt). **3. a.** a group of three things. **b.** one of such a group. **4. in triplicate.** written out with three copies. —,**tripli'cation** *n.*

tripod ('traɪpɒd) *n.* **1.** a three-legged stand to which a camera, etc., can be attached to hold it steady. **2.** a stand or table having three legs. —**tripodal** ('trɪpədəl) *adj.*

tripos ('traɪpɒs) *n. Brit.* the final honours degree examinations at Cambridge University.

tripper ('trɪpə) *n.* **1.** *Chiefly Brit.* a tourist. **2.** another word for **trip** (sense 7). **3.** any device that causes a trip to operate.

triptych ('trɪptɪk) *n.* **1.** a set of three pictures or panels, usually hinged so that the two wing panels fold over the larger central one: often used as an altarpiece. **2.** a set of three hinged writing tablets.

trireme ('traɪriːm) *n.* an ancient Greek galley with three banks of oars on each side.

trisect (traɪ'sɛkt) *vb.* (*tr.*) to divide into three parts, esp.

THESAURUS

trim 1. compact, dapper, natty (*Inf.*), neat, nice, orderly, shipshape, smart, soigné, soignée, spick-and-span, spruce, tidy, well-groomed, well-ordered, well turned-out **2.** fit, shapely, sleek, slender, slim, streamlined, svelte, willowy ~*v.* **3.** barber, clip, crop, curtail, cut, cut back, dock, even up, lop, pare, prune, shave, shear, tidy **4.** adorn, array, beautify, bedeck, deck out, decorate, dress, embellish, embroider, garnish, ornament, trick out **5.** adjust, arrange, balance, distribute, order, prepare, settle ~*n.* **6.** adornment, border, decoration, edging, embellishment, frill, fringe, garnish, ornamentation, piping, trimming **7.** condition, fettle, fitness, form, health, order, repair, shape (*Inf.*), situation, state **8.** clipping, crop, cut, pruning, shave, shearing, tidying up, trimming **9.** array, attire, dress, equipment, gear, trappings

trimming 1. adornment, border, braid, decoration, edging, embellishment, frill, fringe, garnish, ornamentation, piping **2.** Plu-

ral accessories, accompaniments, appurtenances, extras, frills, garnish, ornaments, paraphernalia, trappings **3.** *Plural* brash, clippings, cuttings, ends, parings, shavings

trinity threesome, triad, trilogy, trine, trio, triple, triplet, triptych, triumvirate, triune

trinket bagatelle, bauble, bibelot, gewgaw, gimcrack, kickshaw, knick-knack, nothing, ornament, piece of bric-a-brac, toy, trifle

trio threesome, triad, trilogy, trine, trinity, triple, triplet, triptych, triumvirate, triune

trip *n.* **1.** errand, excursion, expedition, foray, jaunt, journey, outing, ramble, run, tour, travel, voyage **2.** blunder, boob (*Brit. sl.*), error, fall, false move, false step, faux pas, indiscretion, lapse, misstep, slip, stumble ~*v.* **3.** blunder, boob (*Brit. sl.*), err, fall, go wrong, lapse, lose one's balance, miss, miscalculate, misstep, slip, slip up (*Inf.*), stumble, tumble **4.** catch out, confuse, disconcert, put off one's stride, throw off, trap, unsettle **5.** go,

ramble, tour, travel, voyage **6.** caper, dance, flit, frisk, gambol, hop, skip, spring, tread lightly **7.** *Inf.* get high (*Inf.*), get stoned (*Sl.*), take drugs, turn on (*Sl.*) **8.** activate, engage, flip, pull, release, set off, switch on, throw, turn on

tripe balderdash, bunkum, claptrap (*Inf.*), drivel, foolish talk, garbage, guff (*Sl.*), hogwash, inanity, nonsense, poppycock (*Inf.*), rot, rubbish, trash, trumpery, twaddle

triple 1. *adj.* threefold, three times as much, three-way, tripartite **2.** *n.* threesome, triad, trilogy, trine, trinity, trio, triplet, triumvirate, triune **3.** *v.* increase threefold, treble, triplicate

triplet threesome, triad, trilogy, trine, trinity, trio, triple, triumvirate, triune

tripper excursionist, holiday-maker, journeyer, sightseer, tourist, voyager

three equal parts. —**trisection** (traɪˈsɛkʃən) n.

triste (triːst) adj. an archaic word for **sad**.

trite (traɪt) adj. hackneyed; dull: a trite comment. —ˈ**tritely** adv. —ˈ**triteness** n.

trismus (ˈtrɪzməs) n. Pathol. the state of being unable to open the mouth because of sustained contractions of the jaw muscles, caused by tetanus. Nontechnical name: **lockjaw**.

tritium (ˈtrɪtɪəm) n. a radioactive isotope of hydrogen. Symbol: T or ^{3}H; half-life: 12.5 years.

Triton (ˈtraɪtən) n. Greek myth. a sea god depicted as having the upper parts of a man with a fishtail.

triumph (ˈtraɪəmf) n. 1. the feeling of exultation and happiness derived from a victory or major achievement. 2. the act or condition of being victorious; victory. 3. (in ancient Rome) a procession held in honour of a victorious general. ~vb. (intr.) 4. (often foll. by over) to win a victory or control: to triumph over one's weaknesses. 5. to rejoice over a victory. 6. to celebrate a Roman triumph. —**triumphal** (traɪˈʌmfəl) adj.

triumphant (traɪˈʌmfənt) adj. 1. experiencing or displaying triumph. 2. exultant through triumph. —**triˈumphantly** adv.

triumvir (traɪˈʌmvə) n., pl. **-virs** or **-viri** (-vɪˌriː). (esp. in ancient Rome) a member of a triumvirate. —**triˈumviral** adj.

triumvirate (traɪˈʌmvɪrɪt) n. 1. (in ancient Rome) a board of three officials jointly responsible for some task. 2. joint rule by three men. 3. any group of three men associated in some way. 4. the office of a triumvir.

trivalent (traɪˈveɪlənt, ˈtrɪvələnt) adj. Chem. 1. having a valency of three. 2. having three valencies. ~Also: **tervalent**. —**triˈvalency** n.

trivet (ˈtrɪvɪt) n. 1. a stand, usually three-legged and metal, on which cooking vessels are placed over a fire. 2. a short metal stand on which hot dishes are placed on a table. 3. **as right as a trivet**. in perfect health.

trivia (ˈtrɪvɪə) pl. n. petty details or considerations; trifles; trivialities.

trivial (ˈtrɪvɪəl) adj. 1. of little importance; petty or frivolous: trivial complaints. 2. ordinary or commonplace; trite: trivial conversation. 3. Biol. **a.** denoting the common name of an organism. **b.** denoting the specific name of an organism in binomial nomenclature. —ˌtriviˈality n. —ˈtriviaˌlize or **-ise** vb. —ˈtrivially adv. —ˈtrivialness n.

trochee (ˈtrəʊkiː) n. a metrical foot of two syllables, the first long and the second short. —**trochaic** (trəʊˈkeɪɪk) adj.

trod (trɒd) vb. the past tense or a past participle of **tread**.

trodden (ˈtrɒdən) vb. a past participle of **tread**.

trode (trəʊd) vb. Arch. a past tense of **tread**.

troglodyte (ˈtrɒɡləˌdaɪt) n. 1. a cave dweller, esp. of prehistoric times. 2. Inf. a person who lives alone and appears eccentric. —**troglodytic** (ˌtrɒɡləˈdɪtɪk) adj.

troika (ˈtrɔɪkə) n. 1. a Russian vehicle drawn by three horses abreast. 2. three horses harnessed abreast. 3. a triumvirate.

Trojan (ˈtrəʊdʒən) n. 1. a native or inhabitant of ancient Troy. 2. a person who is hard-working and determined. ~adj. 3. of or relating to ancient Troy or its inhabitants.

Trojan Horse n. 1. Greek myth. the huge wooden hollow figure of a horse left outside Troy by the Greeks and dragged inside by the Trojans. The men concealed inside it opened the city to the final Greek assault. 2. a trap intended to undermine an enemy.

troll[1] (trəʊl) vb. 1. Angling. **a.** to draw (a baited line, etc.) through the water. **b.** to fish (a stretch of water) by trolling. **c.** to fish (for) by trolling. 2. to roll or cause to roll. 3. Arch. to sing (a refrain, chorus, etc.) in a loud hearty voice. 4. (intr.) Brit. inf. to walk or stroll. ~n. 5. a trolling. 6. Angling. a bait or lure used in trolling. —ˈ**troller** n.

troll[2] (trəʊl) n. (in Scandinavian folklore) one of a class of supernatural creatures that dwell in caves or mountains and are depicted either as dwarfs or as giants.

trolley (ˈtrɒlɪ) n. 1. Brit. a small table on castors used for conveying food, etc. 2. Brit. a four-wheeled cart for transporting luggage at a station, etc., or for carrying shopping. 3. Brit. See **trolley bus**. 4. U.S. See **trolley car**. 5. a device that collects the current from an overhead wire, third rail, etc., to drive the motor of an electric vehicle. 6. a pulley or truck that travels along an overhead wire in order to support a suspended load. 7. Chiefly Brit. a low truck running on rails, used in factories, mines, etc. 8. a truck, cage, or basket suspended from an overhead track or cable for carrying loads in a mine, etc.

trolley bus n. an electrically driven public-transport vehicle that does not run on rails but takes its power from an overhead wire.

trolley car n. a U.S. name for **tram**[1] (sense 1).

trollop (ˈtrɒləp) n. 1. a promiscuous woman, esp. a prostitute. 2. an untidy woman; slattern.

trombone (trɒmˈbəʊn) n. a brass instrument, a low-pitched counterpart of the trumpet, consisting of a tube the effective length of which is varied by means of a U-shaped slide. —**tromˈbonist** n.

trompe l'oeil (French trɔ̃p ˈlœj) n., pl. **trompe l'oeils** (trɔ̃p ˈlœj). 1. a painting, etc., giving a convincing illusion of reality. 2. an effect of this kind.

troop (truːp) n. 1. a large group or assembly. 2. a subdivision of a cavalry regiment of about company size. 3. (pl.) armed forces; soldiers. 4. a large group of Scouts comprising several patrols. ~vb. 5. (intr.) to gather, move, or march in or as if in a crowd. 6. (tr.) Mil., chiefly Brit. to parade (the colour or flag) ceremonially.

trooper (ˈtruːpə) n. 1. a soldier in a cavalry regiment. 2. U.S., Austral. a mounted policeman. 3. U.S. a state policeman. 4. a cavalry horse. 5. Inf., chiefly Brit. a troopship.

troopship (ˈtruːpˌʃɪp) n. a ship used to transport military personnel.

trope (trəʊp) n. a word or expression used in a figurative sense.

trophy (ˈtrəʊfɪ) n., pl. **-phies**. 1. an object such as a silver cup that is symbolic of victory in a contest, esp. a sporting contest; prize. 2. a memento of success, esp. one taken in war or hunting. 3. (in ancient Greece and Rome) a memorial to a victory, usually consisting of captured arms raised on the battlefield or in a public place. 4. an ornamental carving that represents a group of weapons, etc.

tropic (ˈtrɒpɪk) n. 1. (sometimes cap.) either of the parallel lines of latitude at about 23½°N (**tropic of Cancer**) and 23½°S (**tropic of Capricorn**) of the equator. 2. the tropics. (often cap.) that part of the earth's surface between the tropics of Cancer and Capricorn. 3. Astron. either of the two parallel circles on the celestial sphere

---

THESAURUS

trite banal, bromidic, clichéd, common, commonplace, corny (Sl.), dull, hack, hackneyed, ordinary, pedestrian, routine, run-of-the-mill, stale, stereotyped, stock, threadbare, tired, uninspired, unoriginal, worn

triumph n. 1. elation, exultation, happiness, joy, jubilation, pride, rejoicing 2. accomplishment, achievement, ascendancy, attainment, conquest, coup, feat, hit (Inf.), mastery, sensation, smash (Inf.), smash-hit (Inf.), success, tour de force, victory, walk-over (Inf.) ~v. 3. Often with over best, carry the day, come out on top (Inf.), dominate, flourish, get the better of, overcome, overwhelm, prevail, prosper, subdue, succeed, take the honours, thrive, vanquish, win 4. celebrate, crow, exult, gloat, glory, jubilate, re-

joice, revel, swagger

triumphant boastful, celebratory, cock-a-hoop, conquering, dominant, elated, exultant, glorious, jubilant, proud, rejoicing, successful, swaggering, triumphal, undefeated, victorious, winning

trivia details, minutiae, petty details, trifles, trivialities

trivial commonplace, everyday, frivolous, incidental, inconsequential, inconsiderable, insignificant, little, meaningless, minor, negligible, paltry, petty, puny, slight, small, trifling, trite, unimportant, valueless, worthless

triviality 1. frivolity, inconsequentiality, insignificance, littleness, meaninglessness, negligibility, paltriness, pettiness, slightness, smallness, triteness, unimportance, value-

lessness, worthlessness 2. detail, no big thing, no great matter, nothing, petty detail, technicality, trifle

troop n. 1. assemblage, band, body, bunch (Inf.), company, contingent, crew (Inf.), crowd, drove, flock, gang, gathering, group, herd, horde, multitude, pack, squad, swarm, team, throng, unit 2. Plural armed forces, army, fighting men, men, military, servicemen, soldiers, soldiery ~v. 3. crowd, flock, march, parade, stream, swarm, throng, traipse (Inf.)

trophy award, bays, booty, cup, laurels, memento, prize, souvenir, spoils

having the same latitudes and names as the lines on the earth. ~*adj.* **4.** tropical.

tropical ('trɒpɪkl) *adj.* **1.** situated in, used in, characteristic of, or relating to the tropics. **2.** (of weather) very hot, esp. when humid. **3.** of a trope. —,tropi'cal-ity *n.* —'tropically *adv.*

tropism ('trəʊpɪzəm) *n.* the response of an organism, esp. a plant, to an external stimulus by growth in a direction determined by the stimulus. —,tropis'matic *adj.*

tropo- *combining form.* indicating change or a turning: *tropophyte.*

troposphere ('trɒpə,sfɪə) *n.* the lowest atmospheric layer, about 18 kilometres (11 miles) thick at the equator to about 6 km (4 miles) at the Poles, in which air temperature decreases normally with height at about 6.5°C per km.

trot (trɒt) *vb.* **trotting, trotted.** **1.** to move or cause to move at a trot. ~*n.* **2.** a gait of a horse in which diagonally opposite legs come down together. **3.** a steady brisk pace. **4.** (in harness racing) a race for horses that have been trained to trot fast. **5.** *Chiefly Brit.* a small child. **6.** *U.S. sl.* a student's crib. **7. on the trot.** *Inf.* **a.** one after the other: *to read two books on the trot.* **b.** busy, esp. on one's feet. **8. the trots.** *Inf.* diarrhoea.

Trot (trɒt) *n. Inf.* a follower of Trotsky; Trotskyite.

troth (trəʊθ) *n. Arch.* **1.** a pledge of fidelity, esp. a betrothal. **2.** truth (esp. in **in troth**). **3.** loyalty; fidelity.

trot out *vb.* (*tr., adv.*) *Inf.* to bring forward, as for approbation or admiration, esp. repeatedly.

Trotskyism ('trɒtskɪ,ɪzəm) *n.* the theory of communism of Leon Trotsky (1879–1940), Russian revolutionary and writer, in which he called for immediate worldwide revolution by the proletariat. —'Trotskyite *or* 'Trotskyist *n., adj.*

trotter ('trɒtə) *n.* **1.** a horse that is specially trained to trot fast. **2.** (*usually pl.*) the foot of certain animals, esp. of pigs.

troubadour ('truːbə,dʊə) *n.* any of a class of lyric poets who flourished principally in Provence and N Italy from the 11th to the 13th centuries, writing chiefly on courtly love.

trouble ('trʌbəl) *n.* **1.** a state of mental distress or anxiety. **2.** a state of disorder or unrest: *industrial trouble.* **3.** a condition of disease, pain, or malfunctioning: *liver trouble.* **4.** a cause of distress, disturbance, or pain. **5.** effort or exertion taken to do something. **6.** liability to suffer punishment or misfortune (esp. in **be in trouble**): *he's in trouble with the police.* **7.** the condition of an unmarried girl who becomes pregnant (esp. in **in trouble**). ~*vb.* **8.** (*tr.*) to cause trouble to. **9.** (*intr.*; usually with a negative and foll. by *about*) to put oneself to inconvenience; be concerned: *don't trouble about me.* **10.** (*intr.*; usually with a negative) to take pains; exert oneself. **11.** (*tr.*) to cause inconvenience or discomfort to. **12.** (*tr.*; usually passive) to agitate or make rough: *the seas were troubled.* **13.** (*tr.*) *Caribbean.* to interfere with. —'troubler *n.*

troublemaker ('trʌbəl,meɪkə) *n.* a person who makes

trouble, esp. between people. —'trouble,making *adj., n.*

troubleshooter ('trʌbəl,ʃuːtə) *n.* a person who locates the cause of trouble and removes or treats it, as in the running of a machine. —'trouble,shooting *n., adj.*

troublesome ('trʌbəlsəm) *adj.* **1.** causing trouble. **2.** characterized by violence; turbulent. —'troublesome-ness *n.*

troublous ('trʌbləs) *adj. Arch. or literary.* unsettled; agitated. —'troublously *adv.*

trough (trɒf) *n.* **1.** a narrow open container, esp. one in which food or water for animals is put. **2.** a narrow channel, gutter, or gulley. **3.** a narrow depression, as between two waves. **4.** *Meteorol.* an elongated area of low pressure. **5.** a single or temporary low point; depression. **6.** *Physics.* the portion of a wave in which the amplitude lies below its average value. **7.** *Econ.* the lowest point of the trade cycle. —'trough,like *adj.*

trounce (traʊns) *vb.* (*tr.*) to beat or defeat utterly; thrash.

troupe (truːp) *n.* **1.** a company of actors or other performers, esp. one that travels. ~*vb.* **2.** (*intr.*) (esp. of actors) to move or travel in a group.

trouser ('traʊzə) *n.* (*modifier*) of or relating to trousers: *trouser buttons.*

trousers ('traʊzəz) *pl. n.* a garment shaped to cover the body from the waist to the ankles or knees with separate tube-shaped sections for both legs.

trousseau ('truːsəʊ) *n., pl.* **-seaux** *or* **-seaus** (-səʊz). the clothes, linen, etc., collected by a bride for her marriage.

trout (traʊt) *n., pl.* **trout** *or* **trouts.** any of various game fishes, mostly of fresh water in northern regions. They are related to the salmon but are smaller and spotted.

trove (trəʊv) *n.* See **treasure-trove.**

trow (trəʊ) *vb. Arch.* to think, believe, or trust.

trowel ('traʊəl) *n.* **1.** any of various small hand tools having a flat metal blade attached to a handle, used for scooping or spreading plaster or similar materials. **2.** a similar tool with a curved blade used by gardeners for lifting plants, etc. ~*vb.* **-elling, -elled** *or U.S.* **-eling, -eled.** **3.** (*tr.*) to use a trowel on.

troy weight *or* **troy** (trɔɪ) *n.* a system of weights used for precious metals and gemstones, based on the grain. 24 grains = 1 pennyweight; 20 pennyweights = 1 (troy) ounce; 12 ounces = 1 (troy) pound.

truant ('truːənt) *n.* **1.** a person who is absent without leave, esp. from school. ~*adj.* **2.** being or relating to a truant. ~*vb.* **3.** (*intr.*) to play truant. —'truancy *n.*

truce (truːs) *n.* **1.** an agreement to stop fighting, esp. temporarily. **2.** temporary cessation of something unpleasant.

truck¹ (trʌk) *n.* **1.** *Brit.* a vehicle for carrying freight on a railway; wagon. **2.** another name (esp. U.S.) for **lorry.** **3.** Also called: **truckload.** the amount carried by a truck. **4.** a frame carrying two or more pairs of wheels attached under an end of a railway coach, etc. **5.** the frame carrying the wheels below a skateboard. **6.** *Naut.* a disc-shaped block fixed to the head of a mast having

---

THESAURUS

tropical hot, humid, lush, steamy, stifling, sultry, sweltering, torrid

trot *v.* **1.** canter, go briskly, jog, lope, run, scamper ~*n.* **2.** brisk pace, canter, jog, lope, run **3. on the trot** *Inf.* consecutively, in a row, in succession, one after the other, without break, without interruption

trot out bring forward, bring up, come out with, drag up, exhibit, recite, rehearse, reiterate, relate, repeat

trouble *n.* **1.** agitation, annoyance, anxiety, disquiet, distress, grief, heartache, irritation, misfortune, pain, sorrow, suffering, torment, tribulation, vexation, woe, worry **2.** agitation, bother (*Inf.*), commotion, discontent, discord, disorder, dissatisfaction, disturbance, row, strife, tumult, unrest **3.** ailment, complaint, defect, disability, disease, disorder, failure, illness, malfunction, upset **4.** bother, concern, danger, difficulty, dilemma, dire straits, hot water (*Inf.*), mess, nuisance, pest, pickle (*Inf.*), predicament, problem, scrape (*Inf.*), spot (*Inf.*) **5.** attention, bother, care, effort, exertion, inconvenience, labour, pains, struggle, thought, work ~*v.* **6.**

afflict, agitate, annoy, bother, discompose, disconcert, disquiet, distress, disturb, fret, grieve, harass, inconvenience, pain, perplex, perturb, pester, plague, sadden, torment, upset, vex, worry **7.** be concerned, bother, burden, discomfort, discommode, disturb, impose upon, incommode, inconvenience, put out **8.** exert oneself, go to the effort of, make an effort, take pains, take the time

troublemaker *agent provocateur*, agitator, firebrand, incendiary, instigator, meddler, mischief-maker, rabble-rouser, stormy petrel

troublesome **1.** annoying, arduous, bothersome, burdensome, demanding, difficult, harassing, hard, importunate, inconvenient, irksome, irritating, laborious, oppressive, pestilential, plaguy (*Inf.*), taxing, tiresome, tricky, trying, upsetting, vexatious, wearisome, worrisome, worrying **2.** disorderly, insubordinate, rebellious, recalcitrant, refractory, rowdy, turbulent, uncooperative, undisciplined, unruly, violent

trough **1.** crib, manger, water trough **2.** canal, channel, depression, ditch, duct, flume,

furrow, gully, gutter, trench, watercourse

trounce beat, clobber (*Brit. sl.*), crush, defeat heavily *or* utterly, drub, give a hiding (*Inf.*), give a pasting (*Sl.*), hammer (*Inf.*), lick (*Inf.*), make mincemeat of, overwhelm, paste (*Sl.*), rout, slaughter (*Inf.*), thrash, walk over (*Inf.*), wipe the floor with (*Inf.*)

troupe band, cast, company

trouper actor, artiste, entertainer, performer, player, theatrical, thespian

truancy absence, absence without leave, malingering, shirking, skiving (*Brit. sl.*)

truant *n.* **1.** absentee, delinquent, deserter, dodger, malingerer, runaway, shirker, skiver (*Brit. sl.*), straggler **2.** *adj.* absent, absent without leave, A.W.O.L., missing, skiving (*Brit. sl.*) ~*v.* **3.** absent oneself, desert, dodge, go missing, malinger, play truant, run away, shirk, skive (*Brit. sl.*), twag (*Dialect*)

truce armistice, break, ceasefire, cessation, cessation of hostilities, intermission, interval, let-up (*Inf.*), lull, moratorium, peace, respite, rest, stay, treaty

holes for receiving halyards. **7.** any wheeled vehicle used to move goods. ~*vb.* **8.** to convey (goods) in a truck. **9.** (*intr.*) *Chiefly U.S.* to drive a truck.

truck² (trʌk) *n.* **1.** commercial goods. **2.** dealings (esp. in **have no truck with**). **3.** commercial exchange. **4.** payment of wages in kind. **5.** miscellaneous articles. **6.** *Inf.* rubbish. **7.** *U.S.* vegetables grown for market. ~*vb.* **8.** to exchange (goods); barter. **9.** (*intr.*) to traffic or negotiate.

trucking ('trʌkɪŋ) *n. U.S.* the transportation of goods by lorry.

truckle ('trʌkəl) *vb.* (*intr.*; usually foll. by *to*) to yield weakly; give in. —'**truckler** *n.*

truculent ('trʌkjʊlənt) *adj.* **1.** defiantly aggressive, sullen, or obstreperous. **2.** *Arch.* savage, fierce, or harsh. —'**truculence** *or* '**truculency** *n.* —'**truculently** *adv.*

trudge (trʌdʒ) *vb.* **1.** (*intr.*) to walk or plod heavily or wearily. **2.** (*tr.*) to pass through or over by trudging. ~*n.* **3.** a long tiring walk. —'**trudger** *n.*

true (truː) *adj.* **truer, truest.** **1.** not false, fictional, or illusory; factual; conforming with reality. **2.** (*prenominal*) real; not synthetic. **3. a.** faithful and loyal. **b.** (*as n.*): *the loyal and the true.* **4.** conforming to a required standard, law, or pattern: *a true aim.* **5.** exactly in tune. **6.** (of a compass bearing) according to the earth's geographical rather than magnetic poles: *true north.* **7.** *Biol.* conforming to the typical structure of a designated type. **8.** *Physics.* not apparent or relative. ~*n.* **9.** correct alignment (esp. in **in true, out of true**). ~*adv.* **10.** truthfully; rightly. **11.** precisely or unswervingly. ~*vb.* **truing, trued.** **12.** (*tr.*) to adjust so as to make true. —'**trueness** *n.*

true-blue *adj.* **1.** unwaveringly or staunchly loyal. ~*n.* **true blue. 2.** *Chiefly Brit.* a staunch royalist or conservative.

true-life *adj.* directly comparable to reality: *a true-life story.*

truelove ('truːˌlʌv) *n.* someone truly loved; sweetheart.

truffle ('trʌfəl) *n.* **1.** any of various edible subterranean European fungi. They have a tuberous appearance and are regarded as a delicacy. **2.** Also called: **rum truffle.** *Chiefly Brit.* a sweet resembling this fungus in shape, flavoured with chocolate or rum.

trug (trʌg) *n.* a long shallow basket for carrying flowers, fruit, etc.

truism ('truːɪzəm) *n.* an obvious truth; platitude. —**tru-**
'**istic** *or* **tru**'**istical** *adj.*

truly ('truːlɪ) *adv.* **1.** in a true, just, or faithful manner. **2.** (intensifier): *a truly great man.* **3.** indeed; really.

trump¹ (trʌmp) *n.* **1.** Also called: **trump card. a.** any card from the suit chosen as trumps. **b.** this suit itself; trumps. **2.** a decisive or advantageous move, resource, action, etc. **3.** *Inf.* a fine or reliable person. ~*vb.* **4.** to play a trump card on a plain suit. **5.** (*tr.*) to outdo or surpass. ~See also **trumps, trump up.**

trump² (trʌmp) *n. Arch. or literary.* **1.** a trumpet or the

sound produced by one. **2. the last trump.** the final trumpet call on the Day of Judgment.

trumpery ('trʌmpərɪ) *n., pl.* **-eries. 1.** foolish talk or actions. **2.** a useless or worthless article; trinket. ~*adj.* **3.** useless or worthless.

trumpet ('trʌmpɪt) *n.* **1.** a valved brass instrument of brilliant tone consisting of a narrow tube ending in a flared bell. **2.** any similar instrument, esp. a straight instrument used for fanfares, signals, etc. **3.** a loud sound such as that of a trumpet, esp. when made by an animal. **4.** an eight-foot reed stop on an organ. **5.** something resembling a trumpet in shape. **6.** short for **ear trumpet. 7.** *Brit.* **blow one's own trumpet.** to boast about oneself; brag. ~*vb.* **8.** to proclaim or sound loudly. —'**trumpeter** *n.*

trumps (trʌmps) *pl. n.* **1.** *Cards.* any one of the four suits that outranks all the other suits for the duration of a deal or game. **2. turn up trumps.** (of a person) to bring about a happy or successful conclusion, esp. unexpectedly.

trump up *vb.* (*tr., adv.*) to invent (a charge, accusation, etc.) so as to deceive.

truncate *vb.* (trʌŋ'keɪt, 'trʌŋkeɪt). **1.** (*tr.*) to shorten by cutting. ~*adj.* ('trʌŋkeɪt). **2.** cut short; truncated. **3.** *Biol.* having a blunt end. —**trun'cation** *n.*

truncated ('trʌŋkeɪtɪd) *adj.* **1.** (of a cone, prism, etc.) having an apex or end removed by a plane intersection. **2.** shortened by or as if by cutting off; truncate.

truncheon ('trʌntʃən) *n.* **1.** *Chiefly Brit.* a short thick club or cudgel carried by a policeman. **2.** a baton of office.

trundle ('trʌndəl) *vb.* **1.** to move heavily on or as if on wheels: *the bus trundled by.* ~*n.* **2.** a trundling. **3.** a small wheel or roller.

trunk (trʌŋk) *n.* **1.** the main stem of a tree. **2.** a large strong case or box used to contain clothes, etc., when travelling and for storage. **3.** the body excluding the head, neck, and limbs; torso. **4.** the elongated nasal part of an elephant. **5.** the U.S. name for **boot¹** (sense 2). **6.** the main stem of a nerve, blood vessel, etc. **7.** *Naut.* a watertight boxlike cover within a vessel, such as one used to enclose a centreboard. **8.** an enclosed duct or passageway for ventilation, etc. **9.** (*modifier*) of a main road, railway, etc., in a network: *a trunk line.*

trunk call *n. Chiefly Brit.* a long-distance telephone call.

trunk line *n.* **1.** a direct link between two telephone exchanges or switchboards that are a considerable distance apart. **2.** the main route or routes on a railway.

trunk road *n. Brit.* a main road, esp. one that is suitable for heavy vehicles.

trunks (trʌŋks) *pl. n.* **1.** a man's garment worn for swimming, extending from the waist to the thigh. **2.** shorts worn for some sports. **3.** *Chiefly Brit.* men's underpants with legs that reach midthigh.

trunnion ('trʌnjən) *n.* one of a pair of coaxial projec-

THESAURUS

truck *n.* **1.** commercial goods, commodities, goods, merchandise, stock, stuff, wares **2.** barter, business, buying and selling, commerce, communication, connection, contact, dealings, exchange, relations, trade, traffic ~*v.* **3.** bargain, barter, buy and sell, deal, do business, exchange, have dealings, negotiate, swap, trade, traffic, transact business

truculent aggressive, antagonistic, bad-tempered, bellicose, belligerent, combative, contentious, cross, defiant, fierce, hostile, ill-tempered, itching *or* spoiling for a fight (*Inf.*), obstreperous, pugnacious, scrappy (*Inf.*), sullen, violent

trudge 1. *v.* clump, drag oneself, footslog, hike, lumber, march, plod, slog, stump, traipse (*Inf.*), tramp, trek, walk heavily, yomp **2.** *n.* footslog, haul, hike, march, slog, traipse (*Inf.*), tramp, trek, yomp

true *adj.* **1.** accurate, actual, authentic, bona fide, correct, exact, factual, genuine, legitimate, natural, precise, pure, real, right, truthful, valid, veracious, veritable **2.** confirmed, constant, dedicated, devoted, dutiful, faithful, fast, firm, honest, honourable, loyal, pure, sincere, staunch, steady, true-blue, trustworthy, trusty, unswerving, upright **3.**

accurate, correct, exact, on target, perfect, precise, proper, spot-on (*Brit. inf.*), unerring ~*adv.* **4.** honestly, rightly, truthfully, veraciously, veritably **5.** accurately, correctly, on target, perfectly, precisely, properly, unerringly **6. come true** become reality, be granted, be realized, come to pass, happen, occur

truism axiom, bromide, cliché, commonplace, platitude, stock phrase, trite saying

truly 1. accurately, authentically, beyond doubt, beyond question, correctly, exactly, factually, genuinely, in actuality, in fact, in reality, in truth, legitimately, precisely, really, rightly, truthfully, veraciously, veritably, without a doubt **2.** confirmedly, constantly, devotedly, dutifully, faithfully, firmly, honestly, honourably, loyally, sincerely, staunchly, steadily, with all one's heart, with dedication, with devotion **3.** exceptionally, extremely, greatly, indeed, of course, really, to be sure, verily, very

trumped-up concocted, contrived, cooked-up (*Inf.*), fabricated, fake, false, falsified, invented, made-up, phoney (*Sl.*), untrue

trumpery *n.* **1.** balderdash, bilge (*Inf.*), bunkum, claptrap (*Inf.*), drivel, foolishness, foolish talk, garbage, guff (*Sl.*), hogwash,

idiocy, inanity, nonsense, poppycock (*Inf.*), rot, rubbish, stuff, trash, tripe (*Inf.*), twaddle **2.** bagatelle, bauble, gewgaw, kickshaw, knick-knack, toy, trifle, trinket ~*adj.* **3.** brummagem, cheap, flashy, meretricious, nasty, rubbishy, shabby, shoddy, tawdry, trashy, trifling, useless, valueless, worthless

trumpet *n.* **1.** bugle, clarion, horn **2.** bay, bellow, call, cry, roar **3. blow one's own trumpet** boast, brag, crow, sing one's own praises, vaunt ~*v.* **4.** advertise, announce, broadcast, extol, noise abroad, proclaim, publish, shout from the rooftops, sound loudly, tout (*Inf.*)

trump up concoct, contrive, cook up (*Inf.*), create, fabricate, fake, invent, make up

truncate abbreviate, clip, crop, curtail, cut, cut short, lop, pare, prune, shorten, trim

truncheon baton, club, cudgel, staff

trunk 1. bole, stalk, stem, stock **2.** body, torso **3.** proboscis, snout **4.** bin, box, case, chest, coffer, crate, kist (*Scot.*), locker, portmanteau

tions attached to opposite sides of a container, cannon, etc., to provide a support about which it can turn.

truss (trʌs) vb. (tr.) **1.** (sometimes foll. by up) to tie, bind, or bundle. **2.** to bind the wings and legs of (a fowl) before cooking. **3.** to support or stiffen (a roof, bridge, etc.) with structural members. **4.** Med. to supply or support with a truss. ~n. **5.** a structural framework of wood or metal used to support a roof, bridge, etc. **6.** Med. a device for holding a hernia in place, typically consisting of a pad held in position by a belt. **7.** a cluster of flowers or fruit growing at the end of a single stalk. **8.** Naut. a metal fitting fixed to a yard at its centre for holding it to a mast. **9.** another name for **corbel**. **10.** a bundle or pack. **11.** Chiefly Brit. a bundle of hay or straw, esp. one having a fixed weight of 36, 56, or 60 pounds. —'**trussing** n.

trust (trʌst) n. **1.** reliance on and confidence in the truth, worth, reliability, etc., of a person or thing; faith. Related adj.: **fiducial**. **2.** a group of commercial enterprises combined to control the market for any commodity. **3.** the obligation of someone in a responsible position. **4.** custody, charge, or care. **5.** a person or thing in which confidence or faith is placed. **6.** commercial credit. **7. a.** an arrangement whereby a person to whom the legal title to property is conveyed (the trustee) holds such property for the benefit of those entitled to the beneficial interest. **b.** property that is the subject of such an arrangement. Related adj.: **fiduciary**. **8.** (modifier) of or relating to a trust or trusts. ~vb. **9.** (tr.; may take a clause as object) to expect, hope, or suppose. **10.** (when tr., may take an infinitive; when intr., often foll. by in or to) to place confidence in (someone to do something); rely (upon). **11i.** (tr.) to consign for care. **12.** (tr.) to allow (someone to do something) with confidence in his or her good sense or honesty. **13.** (tr.) to extend business credit to. —'**trustable** adj. —'**truster** n.

trustee (trʌˈstiː) n. **1.** a person to whom the legal title to property is entrusted. **2.** a member of a board that manages the affairs of an institution or organization. —**truˈsteeship** n.

trustful ('trʌstfʊl) or **trusting** adj. characterized by a tendency or readiness to trust others. —'**trustfully** or '**trustingly** adv.

trust fund n. money, securities, etc., held in trust.

trustworthy ('trʌst,wɜːðɪ) adj. worthy of being trusted; honest, reliable, or dependable. —'**trust,worthily** adv. —'**trust,worthiness** n.

trusty ('trʌstɪ) adj. **trustier, trustiest**. **1.** faithful or reliable. ~n., pl. **trusties**. **2.** a trustworthy convict to whom special privileges are granted. —'**trustily** adv. —'**trustiness** n.

truth (truːθ) n. **1.** the quality of being true, genuine, actual, or factual. **2.** something that is true as opposed to false. **3.** a proven or verified fact, principle, etc.: the truths of astronomy. **4.** a concept or system of concepts, regarded as accurately representing some aspect of the world, the universe, etc.: the truths of ancient religions. **5.** fidelity to a standard or law. **6.** faithful reproduction

or portrayal. **7.** honesty. **8.** accuracy, as in the setting of a mechanical instrument. **9.** loyalty. ~Related adjs.: **veritable, veracious**. —'**truthless** adj.

truthful ('truːθfʊl) adj. **1.** telling the truth; honest. **2.** realistic: a truthful portrayal of the king. —'**truthfully** adv. —'**truthfulness** n.

try (traɪ) vb. **trying, tried**. **1.** (when tr., may take an infinitive, sometimes with to replaced by and) to make an effort or attempt. **2.** (tr.; often foll. by out) to sample, test, or give experimental use to (something). **3.** (tr.) to put strain or stress on: he tries my patience. **4.** (tr.; often passive) to give pain, affliction, or vexation to. **5. a.** to examine and determine the issues involved in (a cause) in a court of law. **b.** to hear evidence in order to determine the guilt or innocence of (an accused). **6.** (tr.) to melt (fat, lard, etc.) in order to separate out impurities. ~n., pl. **tries**. **7.** an experiment or trial. **8.** an attempt or effort. **9.** Rugby. the act of an attacking player touching the ball down behind the opposing team's goal line. **10.** American football. an attempt made after a touchdown to score an extra point, as by kicking a goal.

trying ('traɪɪŋ) adj. upsetting, difficult, or annoying. —'**tryingly** adv.

try on vb. (tr., adv.) **1.** to put on (a garment) to find out whether it fits, etc. **2.** Inf. to attempt to deceive or fool (esp. in **try it on**). ~n. **try-on**. **3.** Brit. inf. something done to test out a person's tolerance, etc.

try out vb. (adv.) **1.** (tr.) to test or put to experimental use. **2.** (when intr., usually foll. by for) U.S. (of an athlete, actor, etc.) to undergo a test or to submit (an athlete, actor, etc.) to a test to determine suitability for a place in a team, an acting role, etc. ~n. '**tryout** n.

trysail ('traɪ,seɪl; Naut. 'traɪsəl) n. a small fore-and-aft sail set on a sailing vessel in foul weather to help keep her head to the wind.

tryst (trɪst, traɪst) n. Arch. or literary. **1.** an appointment to meet, esp. secretly. **2.** the place of such a meeting or the meeting itself. —'**tryster** n.

tsar or **czar** (zɑː) n. **1.** (until 1917) the emperor of Russia. **2.** a tyrant; autocrat. **3.** Inf. a person in authority. —'**tsardom** or '**czardom** n.

tsarevitch or **czarevitch** ('zɑːrəvɪtʃ) n. a son of a Russian tsar, esp. the eldest son.

tsarina, czarina (zɑːˈriːnə) or **tsaritsa, czaritza** (zɑːˈrɪtsə) n. the wife of a Russian tsar; Russian empress.

tsetse fly or **tzetze fly** ('tsetsɪ) n. any of various bloodsucking African dipterous flies which transmit various diseases, esp. sleeping sickness.

T-shirt or **tee-shirt** n. a pullover cotton shirt usually having short sleeves and no collar.

tsp. abbrev. for teaspoon.

T-square n. a T-shaped ruler used for drawing horizontal lines and to support set squares when drawing vertical and inclined lines.

tsunami (tsʊˈnɑːmɪ) n. a huge destructive wave, esp. one caused by an earthquake. Also called: **tidal wave**.

TT or **T.T.** abbrev. for: **1.** teetotal. **2.** teetotaller. **3.** Tourist Trophy. **4.** tuberculin tested.

THESAURUS

truss v. **1.** bind, bundle, fasten, make fast, pack, pinion, secure, strap, tether, tie ~n. **2.** beam, brace, buttress, joist, prop, shore, stanchion, stay, strut, support **3.** Medical bandage, support **4.** bale, bundle, package, packet

trust n. **1.** assurance, belief, certainty, certitude, confidence, conviction, credence, credit, expectation, faith, hope, reliance **2.** duty, obligation, responsibility **3.** care, charge, custody, guard, guardianship, protection, safekeeping, trusteeship ~v. **4.** assume, believe, expect, hope, presume, suppose, surmise, think likely **5.** bank on, believe, count on, depend on, have faith in, lean on, pin one's faith on, place confidence in, place one's trust in, place reliance on, rely upon, swear by, take at face value **6.** assign, command, commit, confide, consign, delegate, entrust, give, put into the hands of, sign over, turn over

trustful, trusting confiding, credulous, gullible, innocent, naive, optimistic, simple, unguarded, unsuspecting, unsuspicious, unwary

trustworthy dependable, ethical, honest, honourable, level-headed, mature, principled, reliable, responsible, righteous, sensible, steadfast, to be trusted, true, trusty, truthful, upright

trusty dependable, faithful, firm, honest, reliable, responsible, solid, staunch, steady, straightforward, strong, true, trustworthy, upright

truth **1.** accuracy, actuality, exactness, fact, factuality, factualness, genuineness, legitimacy, precision, reality, truthfulness, validity, veracity, verity **2.** candour, constancy, dedication, devotion, dutifulness, faith, faithfulness, fidelity, frankness, honesty, integrity, loyalty, naturalism, realism, uprightness **3.** axiom, certainty, fact, law, maxim, proven principle, reality, truism, verity

truthful accurate, candid, correct, exact, faithful, forthright, frank, honest, literal, naturalistic, plain-spoken, precise, realistic, reliable, sincere, straight, straightforward, true, trustworthy, veracious, veritable

try v. **1.** aim, attempt, do one's best, do one's damnedest (Inf.), endeavour, essay, exert oneself, have a go (crack, shot, stab, whack),

make an attempt, make an effort, seek, strive, struggle, undertake **2.** appraise, check out, evaluate, examine, experiment, inspect, investigate, prove, put to the test, sample, taste, test **3.** afflict, annoy, inconvenience, irk, irritate, pain, plague, strain, stress, tax, tire, trouble, upset, vex, weary **4.** adjudge, adjudicate, examine, hear ~n. **5.** attempt, crack (Inf.), effort, endeavour, essay, go, shot (Inf.), stab, whack (Inf.) **6.** appraisal, evaluation, experiment, inspection, sample, taste, test, trial

trying aggravating (Inf.), annoying, arduous, bothersome, difficult, exasperating, fatiguing, hard, irksome, irritating, stressful, taxing, tiresome, tough, troublesome, upsetting, vexing, wearisome

try out appraise, check out, evaluate, experiment with, inspect, put into practice, put to the test, sample, taste, test

tsar, czar autocrat, despot, emperor, head, leader, overlord, ruler, sovereign, tyrant

TU or **T.U.** *abbrev. for* trade union.

Tu. *abbrev. for* Tuesday.

tub (tʌb) *n.* **1.** a large open flat-bottomed container of metal or wood, used for washing, storage, etc. **2.** a small plastic or cardboard container of similar shape for ice cream, margarine, etc. **3.** another word (esp. U.S.) for **bath**¹ (sense 1). **4.** Also called: **tubful.** the amount a tub will hold. **5.** a clumsy slow boat or ship. **6. a.** a small vehicle on rails for carrying loads in a mine. **b.** a container for lifting coal or ore up a mine shaft. ~*vb.* **tubbing, tubbed. 7.** *Brit. inf.* to wash (oneself) in a tub. **8.** (*tr.*) to keep or put in a tub. —'**tubbable** *adj.* —'**tubber** *n.*

tuba ('tju:bə) *n., pl.* **-bas** or **-bae** (-bi:). **1.** a valved brass instrument of bass pitch, in which the bell points upwards and the mouthpiece projects at right angles. **2.** a powerful reed stop on an organ.

tubby ('tʌbɪ) *adj.* **-bier, -biest. 1.** plump. **2.** shaped like a tub. —'**tubbiness** *n.*

tube (tju:b) *n.* **1.** a long hollow cylindrical object, used for the passage of fluids or as a container. **2.** a collapsible cylindrical container of soft metal or plastic closed with a cap, used to hold viscous liquids or pastes. **3.** *Anat.* short for **Eustachian tube** or **Fallopian tube. 4.** any hollow structure. **5.** (*sometimes cap.*) *Brit.* **a. the tube.** an underground railway system, esp. that in London. U.S. equivalent: **subway. b.** the tunnels through which the railway runs. **6.** *Electronics.* **a.** another name for **valve** (sense 3). **b.** See **electron tube, cathode-ray tube. 7.** *Sl., chiefly U.S.* a television set. **8.** *Austral. sl.* a bottle or can of beer. ~*vb.* (*tr.*) **9.** to supply with a tube. **10.** to convey in a tube. **11.** to shape like a tube. —'**tubeless** *adj.*

tuber ('tju:bə) *n.* **1.** a fleshy underground stem or root. **2.** *Anat.* a raised area; swelling.

tubercle ('tju:bəkəl) *n.* **1.** any small rounded nodule or elevation, esp. on the skin, on a bone, or on a plant. **2.** any small rounded pathological lesion, esp. one characteristic of tuberculosis.

tubercular (tju'bɜːkjulə) *adj. also* **tuberculous. 1.** of or symptomatic of tuberculosis. **2.** of or relating to a tubercle. **3.** characterized by the presence of tubercles. ~*n.* **4.** a person with tuberculosis.

tuberculin (tju'bɜːkjulɪn) *n.* a sterile liquid prepared from cultures of attenuated tubercle bacillus and used in the diagnosis of tuberculosis.

tuberculin tested *adj.* (of milk) produced by cows that have been certified as free of tuberculosis.

tuberculosis (tjuˌbɜːkjuˈləʊsɪs) *n.* a communicable disease caused by infection with the tubercle bacillus, most frequently affecting the lungs.

tuberous ('tju:bərəs) or **tuberose** ('tju:bəˌrəʊs) *adj.* **1.** (of plants) forming, bearing, or resembling a tuber or tubers. **2.** *Anat.* of or having warty protuberances or tubers.

tubing ('tju:bɪŋ) *n.* **1.** tubes collectively. **2.** a length of tube. **3.** a system of tubes. **4.** fabric in the form of a tube.

tub-thumper *n.* a noisy, violent, or ranting public speaker. —'**tub-ˌthumping** *adj., n.*

tubular ('tju:bjulə) *adj.* **1.** Also: **tubiform** ('tju:bɪˌfɔːm). having the form of a tube or tubes. **2.** of or relating to a tube or tubing.

tubule ('tju:bju:l) *n.* any small tubular structure.

T.U.C. (in Britain) *abbrev. for* Trades Union Congress.

tuck (tʌk) *vb.* **1.** (*tr.*) to push or fold into a small confined space or concealed place or between two surfaces. **2.** (*tr.*) to thrust the loose ends or sides of (something) into a confining space, so as to make neat and secure. **3.** to make a tuck or tucks in (a garment). **4.** (*usually tr.*) to draw together, contract, or pucker. ~*n.* **5.** a tucked object or part. **6.** a pleat or fold in a part of a garment, usually stitched down. **7.** the part of a vessel where the planks meet at the sternpost. **8.** *Brit. inf.* **a.** food, esp. cakes and sweets. **b.** (*as modifier*): *a tuck box.* **9.** the

action of drawing the knees up to the chest in certain dives. ~See also **tuck away, tuck in.**

tuck away *vb.* (*tr., adv.*) *Inf.* **1.** to eat (a large amount of food). **2.** to store, esp. in a place difficult to find.

tucker¹ ('tʌkə) *n.* **1.** a person or thing that tucks. **2.** a detachable yoke of lace, linen, etc., often white, worn over the breast, as of a low-cut dress. **3.** *Austral. & N.Z.* an informal word for food.

tucker² ('tʌkə) *vb.* (*tr.; often passive;* usually foll. by *out*) *Inf., chiefly U.S.* to weary or tire.

tuck in *vb.* (*adv.*) **1.** (*tr.*) Also: **tuck into.** to put to bed and make snug. **2.** (*tr.*) to thrust the loose ends or sides of (something) into a confining space: *tuck the blankets in.* **3.** (*intr.*) Also: **tuck into.** *Inf.* to eat, esp. heartily. ~*n.* **tuck-in. 4.** *Brit. inf.* a meal, esp. a large one.

tuck shop *n. Chiefly Brit.* a shop, esp. one near a school, where cakes and sweets are sold.

Tudor ('tju:də) *n.* **1.** an English royal house ruling from 1485 to 1603. ~*adj.* **2.** denoting a style of architecture characterized by half-timbered houses.

Tues. *abbrev. for* Tuesday.

Tuesday ('tju:zdɪ) *n.* the third day of the week, second day of the working week.

tufa ('tju:fə) *n.* a porous rock formed of calcium carbonate deposited from springs. —**tufaceous** (tju:ˈfeɪʃəs) *adj.*

tuff (tʌf) *n.* a hard volcanic rock consisting of consolidated fragments of lava. —**tuffaceous** (tʌˈfeɪʃəs) *adj.*

tuffet ('tʌfɪt) *n.* a small mound or low seat.

tuft (tʌft) *n.* **1.** a bunch of feathers, grass, hair, etc., held together at the base. **2.** a cluster of threads drawn tightly through upholstery, a quilt, etc., to secure the padding. **3.** a small clump of trees or bushes. **4.** (formerly) a gold tassel on the cap worn by titled undergraduates at English universities. ~*vb.* **5.** (*tr.*) to provide or decorate with a tuft or tufts. **6.** to form or be formed into tufts. **7.** to secure with tufts. —'**tufted** *adj.* —'**tufty** *adj.*

tug (tʌg) *vb.* **tugging, tugged. 1.** (when *intr.,* sometimes foll. by *at*) to pull or drag with sharp or powerful movements. **2.** (*tr.*) to tow (a vessel) by means of a tug. ~*n.* **3.** a strong pull or jerk. **4.** Also called: **tugboat.** a boat with a powerful engine, used for towing barges, ships, etc. **5.** a hard struggle or fight. —'**tugger** *n.*

tug of war *n.* **1.** a contest in which two people or teams pull opposite ends of a rope in an attempt to drag the opposition over a central line. **2.** any hard struggle between two factions.

tuition (tjuːˈɪʃən) *n.* **1.** instruction, esp. that received individually or in a small group. **2.** the payment for instruction, esp. in colleges or universities. —**tuˈitional** or **tuˈitionary** *adj.*

tulip ('tju:lɪp) *n.* **1.** any of various spring-blooming bulb plants having long broad pointed leaves and single showy bell-shaped flowers. **2.** the flower or bulb.

tulip tree *n.* **1.** Also called: **tulip poplar.** a North American tree having tulip-shaped greenish-yellow flowers and long conelike fruits. **2.** any of various other trees with tulip-shaped flowers, such as the magnolia.

tulle (tju:l) *n.* a fine net fabric of silk, rayon, etc.

tumble ('tʌmbəl) *vb.* **1.** to fall or cause to fall, esp. awkwardly, precipitately, or violently. **2.** (*intr.;* usually foll. by *about*) to roll or twist, esp. in playing. **3.** (*intr.*) to perform leaps, somersaults, etc. **4.** to move in a heedless or hasty way. **5.** (*tr.*) to polish (gemstones) in a tumbler. **6.** (*tr.*) to disturb, rumple, or toss around. ~*n.* **7.** a tumbling. **8.** a fall or toss. **9.** an acrobatic feat, esp. a somersault. **10.** a state of confusion. **11.** a confused heap or pile.

tumble-down *adj.* falling to pieces; dilapidated; crumbling.

tumbler ('tʌmblə) *n.* **1. a.** a flat-bottomed drinking glass with no handle or stem. **b.** Also called: **tumblerful.** its contents. **2.** a person who performs somersaults and other acrobatic feats. **3.** Also called: **tumble drier, tumbler drier.** a machine that dries clothes by tumbling

tuck *v.* **1.** fold, gather, insert, push ~*n.* **2.** fold, gather, pinch, pleat **3.** *Inf.* comestibles, eats (*Sl.*), food, grub (*Sl.*), nosh (*Sl.*), scoff (*Sl.*), victuals

tuck in 1. bed down, enfold, fold under, make snug, put to bed, swaddle, wrap up **2.** eat heartily, get stuck in (*Sl.*).

tug 1. *v.* drag, draw, haul, heave, jerk, lug,

pull, tow, wrench, yank **2.** *n.* drag, haul, heave, jerk, pull, tow, traction, wrench, yank

tuition education, instruction, lessons, schooling, teaching, training, tutelage, tutoring

tumble 1. *v.* drop, fall, fall end over end, fall headlong, fall head over heels, flop, lose one's footing, pitch, plummet, roll, stumble,

topple, toss, trip up **2.** *n.* collapse, drop, fall, flop, headlong fall, plunge, roll, spill, stumble, toss, trip

tumble-down crumbling, decrepit, dilapidated, disintegrating, falling to pieces, ramshackle, rickety, ruined, shaky, tottering

them in warmed air. **4.** a box or drum rotated so that the contents (usually gemstones) become smooth and polished. **5.** the part of a lock that retains or releases the bolt and is moved by the action of a key. **6.** a lever in a gunlock that receives the action of the mainspring when the trigger is pressed and thus forces the hammer forwards. **7.** a part that moves a gear in a train of gears into and out of engagement.

tumbrel or **tumbril** ('tʌmbrəl) n. **1.** a farm cart, esp. one that tilts backwards to deposit its load. A cart of this type was used to take condemned prisoners to the guillotine during the French Revolution. **2.** (formerly) a covered cart used to carry ammunition, tools, etc.

tumid ('tju:mɪd) adj. **1.** enlarged or swollen. **2.** bulging. **3.** pompous or fulsome in style. —**tu'midity** or **'tumidness** n. —**'tumidly** adv.

tummy ('tʌmɪ) n., pl. **-mies.** Also called: **tum.** an informal or childish word for **stomach.**

tumour or U.S. **tumor** ('tju:mə) n. Pathol. **a.** any abnormal swelling. **b.** a mass of tissue formed by a new growth of cells. —**'tumorous** adj.

tumult ('tju:mʌlt) n. **1.** a loud confused noise, as of a crowd; commotion. **2.** violent agitation or disturbance. **3.** great emotional agitation.

tumultuous (tju:'mʌltjʊəs) adj. **1.** uproarious, riotous, or turbulent. **2.** greatly agitated, confused, or disturbed. **3.** making a loud or unruly disturbance. —**tu'multuously** adv. —**tu'multuousness** n.

tumulus ('tju:mjʊləs) n. Archaeol. (no longer in technical usage) another word for **barrow²**.

tun (tʌn) n. **1.** a large beer cask. **2.** a measure of capacity, usually equal to 252 wine gallons. ~vb. **tunning, tunned.** **3.** (tr.) to put into or keep in tuns.

tuna¹ ('tju:nə) n., pl. **-na** or **-nas.** another name for **tunny.**

tuna² ('tju:nə) n. any of various tropical American prickly pear cacti.

tundra ('tʌndrə) n. a vast treeless zone lying between the ice cap and the timber line of North America and Eurasia and having a permanently frozen subsoil.

tune (tju:n) n. **1.** a melody, esp. one for which harmony is not essential. **2.** the condition of producing accurately pitched notes, intervals, etc. (esp. in **in tune, out of tune**). **3.** accurate correspondence of pitch and intonation between instruments (esp. in **in tune, out of tune**). **4.** the correct adjustment of a radio, television, etc., with respect to the required frequency. **5.** a frame of mind; mood. **6. call the tune.** to be in control of the proceedings. **7. change one's tune.** to change one's mind or opinion. **8. to the tune of.** Inf. to the amount or extent of. ~vb. **9.** to adjust (a musical instrument) to a certain pitch. **10.** to adjust (a note, etc.) so as to bring it into harmony or concord. **11.** (tr.) to adapt or adjust (oneself); attune. **12.** (tr.; often foll. by up) to make fine adjustments to (an engine, machine, etc.) to obtain optimum performance. **13.** Electronics. to adjust (one or more circuits) for resonance at a desired frequency. ~See also **tune in, tune up.** —**'tuneless** adj. —**'tuner** n.

tuneful ('tju:nfʊl) adj. **1.** having a pleasant tune; melodious. **2.** producing a melody or music. —**'tunefully** adv. —**'tunefulness** n.

tune in vb. (adv.; often foll. by to) **1.** to adjust (a radio or television) to receive (a station or programme). **2.** Sl. to make or become more aware, knowledgeable, etc., (about).

tune up vb. (adv.) **1.** to adjust (a musical instrument) to a particular pitch. **2.** to tune (instruments) to a common pitch. **3.** (tr.) to adjust (an engine) in (a car, etc.) to improve performance. ~n. **tune-up.** **4.** adjustments

made to an engine to improve its performance.

tungsten ('tʌŋstən) n. a hard malleable ductile greyish-white element. It is used in lamp filaments, electrical contact points, x-ray targets, and, alloyed with steel, in high-speed cutting tools. Symbol: W; atomic no.: 74; atomic wt.: 183.85.

tunic ('tju:nɪk) n. **1.** any of various hip-length or knee-length garments, such as the loose sleeveless garb worn in ancient Greece or Rome, the jacket of some soldiers, or a woman's hip-length garment, worn with a skirt or trousers. **2.** a covering, lining, or enveloping membrane of an organ or part. **3.** Also called: **tunicle.** a short vestment worn by a bishop or subdeacon.

tuning fork n. a two-pronged metal fork that when struck produces a pure note of constant specified pitch. It is used to tune musical instruments and in acoustics.

tunnel ('tʌnəl) n. **1.** an underground passageway, esp. one for trains or cars. **2.** any passage or channel through or under something. ~vb. **-nelling, -nelled** or U.S. **-neling, -neled.** **3.** (tr.) to make or force (a way) through or under (something). **4.** (intr.; foll. by through, under, etc.) to make or force a way (through or under something). —**'tunneller** n.

tunnel vision n. **1.** a condition in which lateral vision is greatly restricted. **2.** narrowness of viewpoint resulting from concentration on a single idea, opinion, etc.

tunny ('tʌnɪ) n., pl. **-nies** or **-ny.** **1.** Also called: **tuna.** any of a genus of large marine spiny-finned fishes, chiefly of warm waters. They are important food fishes. **2.** any of various similar and related fishes.

tup (tʌp) n. **1.** Chiefly Brit. a male sheep; ram. **2.** the head of a pile-driver or steam hammer. ~vb. **tupping, tupped.** **3.** (tr.) (of a ram) to mate with (a ewe).

tuppence ('tʌpəns) n. Brit. a variant spelling of **twopence.** —**'tuppenny** adj.

turban ('tɜ:bən) n. **1.** a man's headdress, worn esp. by Muslims, Hindus, and Sikhs, made by swathing a length of linen, silk, etc., around the head or around a caplike base. **2.** a woman's brimless hat resembling this. **3.** any headdress resembling this. —**'turbaned** adj.

turbid ('tɜ:bɪd) adj. **1.** muddy or opaque, as a liquid clouded with a suspension of particles. **2.** dense, thick, or cloudy: turbid fog. **3.** in turmoil or confusion. —**turbidity** or **'turbidness** n. —**'turbidly** adv.

turbine ('tɜ:bɪn, -baɪn) n. any of various types of machine in which the kinetic energy of a moving fluid, as water, steam, air, etc., is converted into mechanical energy by causing a bladed rotor to rotate.

turbo- combining form. of, relating to, or driven by a turbine: turbofan.

turbofan (,tɜ:bəʊ'fæn) n. **1.** a type of bypass engine in which a large fan driven by a turbine forces air rearwards around the exhaust gases in order to increase the propulsive thrust. **2.** an aircraft driven by turbofans. **3.** the fan in such an engine.

turbojet (,tɜ:bəʊ'dʒɛt) n. **1.** a turbojet engine. **2.** an aircraft powered by turbojet engines.

turbojet engine n. a gas turbine in which the exhaust gases provide the propulsive thrust to drive an aircraft.

turboprop (,tɜ:bəʊ'prɒp) n. **1.** a gas turbine for driving an aircraft propeller. **2.** an aircraft powered by turboprops.

turbot ('tɜ:bət) n., pl. **-bot** or **-bots.** **1.** a European flatfish having a speckled scaleless body covered with tubercles. It is highly valued as a food fish. **2.** any of various similar or related fishes.

turbulence ('tɜ:bjʊləns) n **1.** a state or condition of confusion, movement, or agitation. **2.** Meteorol. instabil-

---

▬▬▬▬▬▬▬ THESAURUS ▬▬▬▬▬▬

tumour cancer, carcinoma (Medical), growth, lump, neoplasm (Medical), sarcoma (Medical), swelling

tumult ado, affray (Law), agitation, altercation, bedlam, brawl, brouhaha, clamour, commotion, din, disorder, disturbance, excitement, fracas, hubbub, hullabaloo, outbreak, pandemonium, quarrel, racket, riot, row, ruction (Inf.), stir, strife, turmoil, unrest, upheaval, uproar

tumultuous agitated, boisterous, clamorous, confused, disorderly, disturbed, excited, fierce, hectic, irregular, lawless, noisy, obstreperous, passionate, raging, restless, ri-

otous, rowdy, rumbustious, stormy, turbulent, unrestrained, unruly, uproarious, violent, vociferous, wild

tune n. **1.** air, melody, melody line, motif, song, strain, theme **2.** agreement, concert, concord, consonance, euphony, harmony, pitch, sympathy, unison **3.** attitude, demeanour, disposition, frame of mind, mood **4. call the tune** be in charge (command, control), call the shots (Sl.), command, dictate, govern, lead, rule, rule the roost **5. change one's tune** change one's mind, do an about-face, have a change of heart, reconsider, take a different tack, think again ~v. **6.** adapt, ad-

just, attune, bring into harmony, harmonize, pitch, regulate

tuneful catchy, consonant (Music), easy on the ear (Inf.), euphonious, harmonious, mellifluous, melodic, melodious, musical, pleasant, symphonic

tuneless atonal, cacophonous, clashing, discordant, dissonant, harsh, unmelodic, unmelodious, unmusical

tunnel **1.** n. burrow, channel, hole, passage, passageway, shaft, subway, underpass **2.** v. burrow, dig, dig one's way, excavate, mine, penetrate, scoop out, undermine

ity in the atmosphere causing gusty air currents and cumulonimbus clouds.

turbulent ('tɜːbjʊlənt) *adj.* **1.** being in a state of turbulence. **2.** wild or insubordinate; unruly. —'**turbulently** *adv.*

turd (tɜːd) *n. Taboo.* **1.** a piece of excrement. **2.** *Sl.* a contemptible person or thing.

tureen (tə'riːn) *n.* a large deep usually rounded dish with a cover, used for serving soups, stews, etc.

turf (tɜːf) *n., pl.* **turfs** *or* **turves.** **1.** the surface layer of fields and pastures, consisting of earth containing a dense growth of grasses with their roots; sod. **2.** a piece cut from this layer. **3. the turf. a.** a track where horse races are run. **b.** horse racing as a sport or industry. **4.** (in Ireland) another word for **peat.** ~*vb.* **5.** (*tr.*) to cover with pieces of turf.

turf accountant *n. Brit.* a formal name for a **bookmaker.**

turf out *vb.* (*tr., adv.*) *Brit. inf.* to throw out or dismiss; eject.

turgescent (tɜː'dʒɛsᵊnt) *adj.* becoming or being swollen; inflated; tumid. —**tur'gescence** *n.*

turgid ('tɜːdʒɪd) *adj.* **1.** swollen and distended. **2.** (of language) pompous; bombastic. —**tur'gidity** *or* '**turgidness** *n.* —'**turgidly** *adv.*

Turk (tɜːk) *n.* **1.** a native, inhabitant, or citizen of Turkey. **2.** a native speaker of any Turkic language. **3.** a brutal or domineering person.

Turk. *abbrev. for:* **1.** Turkey. **2.** Turkish.

turkey ('tɜːkɪ) *n., pl.* **-keys** *or* **-key.** **1.** a large bird of North America, having a bare wattled head and neck and a brownish plumage. The male has a fan-shaped tail. It is widely domesticated for its flesh. **2.** *U.S. inf.* a dramatic production that fails; flop. **3. cold turkey.** *Slang.* a method of curing drug addiction by abrupt withdrawal of all drugs. **4. talk turkey.** *Inf., chiefly U.S.* to discuss frankly and practically.

turkey cock *n.* **1.** a male turkey. **2.** an arrogant person.

Turkish ('tɜːkɪʃ) *adj.* **1.** of Turkey, its people, or their language. ~*n.* **2.** the official language of Turkey, belonging to the Turkic branch of the Altaic family.

Turkish bath *n.* **1.** a type of bath in which the bather sweats freely in a steam room, is then´washed, often massaged, and has a cold plunge or shower. **2.** (sometimes *pl.*) an establishment where such a bath is obtainable.

Turkish coffee *n.* very strong black coffee.

Turkish delight *n.* a jelly-like sweet flavoured with flower essences, usually cut into cubes and covered in icing sugar.

Turkish towel *n.* a rough loose-piled towel.

turmeric ('tɜːmərɪk) *n.* **1.** a tropical Asian plant, *Curcuma longa,* having yellow flowers and an aromatic underground stem. **2.** the powdered stem of this plant, used as a condiment and as a yellow dye.

turmoil ('tɜːmɔɪl) *n.* violent or confused movement; agitation; tumult.

turn (tɜːn) *vb.* **1.** to move around an axis: *to turn a knob.* **2.** (sometimes foll. by *round*) to change or cause

to change positions by moving through an arc of a circle: *he turned the chair to face the light.* **3.** to change or cause to change in course, direction, etc. **4.** to go or pass to the other side of (a corner, etc.). **5.** to assume or cause to assume a rounded, curved, or folded form: *the road turns here.* **6.** to reverse or cause to reverse position. **7.** (*tr.*) to perform or do by a rotating movement: *to turn a somersault.* **8.** (*tr.*) to shape or cut a thread in (a workpiece) by rotating it on a lathe against a cutting tool. **9.** (when *intr.,* foll. by *into* or *to*) to change or convert or be changed or converted. **10.** (foll. by *into*) to change or cause to change in nature, character, etc.: *the frog turned into a prince.* **11.** (*copula*) to change so as to become: *he turned nasty.* **12.** to cause (foliage, etc.) to change colour or (of foliage, etc.) to change colour. **13.** to cause (milk, etc.) to become rancid or sour or (of milk, etc.) to become rancid or sour. **14.** to change or cause to change in subject, trend, etc.: *the conversation turned to fishing.* **15.** to direct or apply or be directed or applied: *he turned his attention to the problem.* **16.** (*intr.;* usually foll. by *to*) to appeal or apply (to) for help, advice, etc. **17.** to reach, pass, or progress beyond in age, time, etc.: *she has just turned twenty.* **18.** (*tr.*) to cause or allow to go: *to turn an animal loose.* **19.** to affect or be affected with nausea. **20.** to affect or be affected with giddiness: *my head is turning.* **21.** (*tr.*) to affect the mental or emotional stability of (esp. in **turn** (someone's) **head**). **22.** (*tr.*) to release from a container. **23.** (*tr.*) to render into another language. **24.** (usually foll. by *against* or *from*) to transfer or reverse (one's loyalties, affections, etc.). **25.** (*tr.*) to bring (soil) from lower layers to the surface. **26.** to blunt (an edge) or (of an edge) to become blunted. **27.** (*tr.*) to give a graceful form to: *to turn a compliment.* **28.** (*tr.*) to reverse (a cuff, collar, etc.). **29.** (*intr.*) *U.S.* to be merchandised as specified: *shirts are turning well this week.* **30.** *Cricket.* to spin (the ball) or (of the ball) to spin. **31. turn one's hand to.** to undertake (something practical). **32. turn tail.** *Inf.* to run away; flee. ~*n.* **33.** a turning or being turned. **34.** a movement of complete or partial rotation. **35.** a change of direction or position. **36.** direction or drift: *his thoughts took a new turn.* **37.** a deviation from a course or tendency. **38.** the place, point, or time at which a deviation or change occurs. **39.** another word for **turning** (sense 1). **40.** the right or opportunity to do something in an agreed order or succession: *now it's George's turn.* **41.** a change in nature, condition, etc.: *his illness took a turn for the worse.* **42.** a period of action, work, etc. **43.** a short walk, ride, or excursion. **44.** natural inclination: *a speculative turn of mind.* **45.** distinctive form or style: *a neat turn of phrase.* **46.** requirement, need, or advantage: *to serve someone's turn.* **47.** a deed that helps or hinders someone. **48.** a twist, bend, or distortion in shape. **49.** *Music.* a melodic ornament consisting of two auxiliary notes above and below a principal note, all four notes being rapidly executed. **50.** a short theatrical act. **51.** *Stock exchange. Brit.* the difference between a stockjobber's bid and offer prices, representing the jobber's income. **52.** *Inf.* a shock or surprise. **53. by turns.** one after another; alternately. **54. turn and turn about.** one after another; alternately. **55. to a**

THESAURUS

turbulence agitation, boiling, commotion, confusion, disorder, instability, pandemonium, roughness, storm, tumult, turmoil, unrest, upheaval

turbulent 1. agitated, blustery, boiling, choppy, confused, disordered, foaming, furious, raging, rough, tempestuous, tumultuous, unsettled, unstable **2.** agitated, anarchic, boisterous, disorderly, insubordinate, lawless, mutinous, obstreperous, rebellious, refractory, riotous, rowdy, seditious, tumultuous, unbridled, undisciplined, ungovernable, unruly, uproarious, violent, wild

turf 1. clod, divot, grass, green, sod, sward **2. the turf** horse-racing, racecourse, racetrack, racing, the flat

turmoil agitation, bedlam, brouhaha, bustle, chaos, commotion, confusion, disorder, disturbance, ferment, flurry, hubbub, noise, pandemonium, row, stir, strife, trouble, tumult, turbulence, uproar, violence

turn *v.* **1.** circle, go round, gyrate, move in a

circle, pivot, revolve, roll, rotate, spin, swivel, twirl, twist, wheel, whirl **2.** change course, change position, go back, move, return, reverse, shift, swerve, switch, veer, wheel **3.** arc, come round, corner, go round, negotiate, pass, pass around, take a bend **4.** adapt, alter, become, change, convert, divert, fashion, fit, form, metamorphose, mould, mutate, remodel, shape, transfigure, transform, transmute **5.** become rancid, curdle, go bad, go off (*Brit. inf.*), go sour, make rancid, sour, spoil, taint **6.** appeal, apply, approach, go, have recourse, look, resort **7.** nauseate, sicken, upset **8.** apostatize, bring round (*Inf.*), change one's mind, change sides, defect, desert, go over, influence, persuade, prejudice, prevail upon, renege, retract, talk into **9.** construct, deliver, execute, fashion, frame, make, mould, perform, shape, write **10. turn tail** beat a hasty retreat, bolt, cut and run (*Inf.*), flee, run away, run off, show a clean pair of heels, take off (*Inf.*), take to one's heels ~*n.* **11.** bend, change, circle, curve, cy-

cle, gyration, pivot, reversal, revolution, rotation, spin, swing, turning, twist, whirl **12.** bias, direction, drift, heading, tendency, trend **13.** bend, change of course, change of direction, curve, departure, deviation, shift **14.** chance, crack (*Inf.*), fling, go, opportunity, period, round, shift, shot (*Inf.*), spell, stint, succession, time, try, whack (*Inf.*) **15.** airing, circuit, constitutional, drive, excursion, jaunt, outing, promenade, ride, saunter, spin (*Inf.*), stroll, walk **16.** affinity, aptitude, bent, bias, flair, gift, inclination, knack, leaning, propensity, talent **17.** cast, fashion, form, format, guise, make-up, manner, mode, mould, shape, style, way **18.** act, action, deed, favour, gesture, service **19.** bend, distortion, twist, warp **20.** *Inf.* fright, scare, shock, start, surprise **21. by turns** alternately, in succession, one after another, reciprocally, turn and turn about **22. to a turn** correctly, exactly, just right, perfectly, precisely

turn. to the proper amount; perfectly. ~See also **turn down, turn in, turn off,** etc. —'**turner** n.

turnabout ('tɜːnə,baut) n. 1. the act of turning so as to face a different direction. 2. a change or reversal of opinion, attitude, etc.

turnaround ('tɜːnə,raund) n. 1. a. the act or process in which a ship, aircraft, etc., unloads at the end of a trip and reloads for the next trip. b. the time taken for this. 2. the total time taken by a vehicle in a round trip. 3. another word for **turnabout.**

turnbuckle ('tɜːn,bʌkəl) n. an open mechanical sleeve usually having a swivel at one end and a thread at the other to enable a threaded wire or rope to be tightened.

turncoat ('tɜːn,kəut) n. a person who deserts one cause or party for the opposite faction.

turn down vb. (tr., adv.) 1. to reduce (the volume or brightness) of (something). 2. to reject or refuse. 3. to fold down (a collar, sheets, etc.). ~adj. **turndown.** 4. (prenominal) designed to be folded down.

turn in vb. (adv.) Inf. 1. (intr.) to go to bed for the night. 2. (tr.) to hand in; deliver. 3. to give up or conclude (something). 4. (tr.) to record (a score, etc.). 5. **turn in on oneself.** to become preoccupied with one's own problems.

turning ('tɜːnɪŋ) n. 1. a road, river, or path that turns off the main way. 2. the point where such a way turns off. 3. a bend in a straight course. 4. an object made on a lathe. 5. the process or skill of turning objects on a lathe. 6. (pl.) the waste produced in turning on a lathe.

turning circle n. the smallest circle in which a vehicle can turn.

turning point n. 1. a moment when the course of events is changed. 2. a point at which there is a change in direction or motion.

turnip ('tɜːnɪp) n. 1. a widely cultivated plant of the cabbage family with a large yellow or white edible root. 2. the root of this plant, which is eaten as a vegetable.

turnkey ('tɜːn,kiː) n. Arch. a keeper of the keys, esp. in a prison; warder or jailer.

turn off vb. 1. (intr.) to leave (a road, etc.). 2. (intr.) (of a road, etc.) to deviate from (another road, etc.). 3. (tr., adv.) to cause (something) to cease operating by turning a knob, pushing a button, etc. 4. (tr.) Inf. to cause (a person, etc.) to feel dislike or distaste for (something): *this music turns me off.* 5. (tr., adv.) Brit. inf. to dismiss from employment. ~n. **turn-off.** 6. a road or other way branching off from the main thoroughfare. 7. something or someone that turns one off (see sense 4).

turn on vb. 1. (tr., adv.) to cause (something) to operate by turning a knob, etc. 2. (intr., prep.) to depend or hinge on: *the success of the party turns on you.* 3. (prep.) to become hostile or to retaliate: *the dog turned on the children.* 4. (tr., adv.) Inf. to produce (charm, tears, etc.) suddenly or automatically. 5. (tr., adv.) Sl. to arouse emotionally or sexually. 6. (intr., adv.) Sl. to take or become intoxicated by drugs. 7. (tr., adv.) Sl. to introduce (someone) to drugs. ~n. **turn-on.** 8. something or someone that turns one on (see sense 5).

turn out vb. (adv.) 1. (tr.) to cause (something, esp. a

light) to cease operating by or as if by turning a knob, etc. 2. (tr.) to produce by an effort or process. 3. (tr.) to dismiss, discharge, or expel. 4. (tr.) to clear or clean the contents of. 5. (copula) to prove to be as specified. 6. (tr.) to fit as with clothes: *that woman turns her children out well.* 7. (intr.) to assemble or gather. 8. (of a soldier) to parade or call (a soldier) to parade. 9. (intr.) Inf. to get out of bed. ~n. **turnout.** 10. the body of people appearing together at a gathering. 11. the quantity or amount produced. 12. an array of clothing or equipment.

turn over vb. (adv.) 1. to change or cause to change position, esp. so as to reverse top and bottom. 2. to start (an engine), esp. with a starting handle, or (of an engine) to start or function correctly. 3. to shift or cause to shift position, as by rolling from side to side. 4. (tr.) to deliver; transfer. 5. (tr.) to consider carefully. 6. (tr.) a. to sell and replenish (stock in trade). b. to transact business and so generate gross revenue of (a specified sum). 7. (tr.) to invest and recover (capital). 8. (tr.) Sl. to rob. ~n. **turnover.** 9. a. the amount of business transacted during a specified period. b. the rate at which stock in trade is sold and replenished. 10. a change or reversal of position. 11. a small pastry case filled with fruit or jam, etc. 12. a. the number of workers employed by a firm in a given period to replace those who have left. b. the ratio between this number and the average number of employees during the same period. 13. Banking. the amount of capital funds loaned on call during a specified period. ~adj. **turnover.** 14. (prenominal) designed to be turned over.

turnpike ('tɜːn,paik) n. 1. History. a. a barrier set across a road to prevent passage until a toll had been paid. b. a road on which a turnpike was operated. 2. an obsolete word for **turnstile.** 3. U.S. a motorway for use of which a toll is charged.

turnstile ('tɜːn,stail) n. a mechanical barrier with metal arms that are turned to admit one person at a time.

turntable ('tɜːn,teibəl) n. 1. the circular platform that rotates a gramophone record while it is being played. 2. a circular platform used for turning locomotives and cars. 3. the revolvable platform on a microscope on which specimens are examined.

turn to vb. (intr., adv.) to set about a task.

turn up vb. (adv.) 1. (intr.) to arrive or appear. 2. to find or be found, esp. by accident. 3. (tr.) to increase the flow, volume, etc., of. ~n. **turn-up.** 4. (often pl.) Brit. the turned-up fold at the bottom of some trouser legs. U.S. name: **cuff.** 5. Inf. an unexpected or chance occurrence.

turpentine ('tɜːpən,tain) n. 1. Also called: **gum turpentine.** any of various oleoresins obtained from various coniferous trees and used as the main source of commercial turpentine. 2. a sticky oleoresin that exudes from the terebinth tree. 3. Also called: **oil of turpentine, spirits of turpentine.** a colourless volatile oil distilled from turpentine oleoresin. It is used as a solvent for paints and in medicine. 4. Also called: **turpentine substitute, white spirit.** (not in technical usage) any one of

THESAURUS

turn down 1. diminish, lessen, lower, muffle, mute, quieten, reduce the volume of, soften 2. decline, rebuff, refuse, reject, repudiate, say no to, spurn, throw out

turn in 1. go to bed, go to sleep, hit the sack (Sl.), retire for the night 2. deliver, give back, give up, hand in, hand over, return, submit, surrender, tender

turning bend, crossroads, curve, junction, side road, turn, turn-off

turning point change, climacteric, crisis, critical moment, crossroads, crux, decisive moment, moment of decision, moment of truth

turn off 1. branch off, change direction, depart from, deviate, leave, quit, take another road, take a side road 2. cut out, kill, put out, shut down, stop, switch off, turn out, unplug 3. Inf. alienate, bore, disenchant, disgust, displease, irritate, lose one's interest, nauseate, offend, put off, repel, sicken

turn on 1. activate, energize, ignite, put on, set in motion, start, start up, switch on 2. balance, be contingent on, be decided by, de-

pend, hang, hinge, pivot, rest 3. assail, assault, attack, fall on, lose one's temper with, round on 4. Sl. arouse, arouse one's desire, attract, excite, please, stimulate, thrill, titillate, work up 5. Sl. get high (Inf.), get stoned (Sl.), take drugs, trip (Inf.) 6. Sl. expose, get one started with, inform, initiate, introduce, show

turnout 1. assemblage, assembly, attendance, audience, congregation, crowd, gate, number, throng 2. amount produced, output, outturn (Rare), production, production quota, productivity, turnover, volume, yield 3. array, attire, costume, dress, equipage, equipment, gear, get-up (Inf.), outfit, rigout (Inf.)

turn out 1. put out, switch off, turn off, unplug 2. bring out, fabricate, finish, make, manufacture, process, produce, put out 3. axe (Inf.), banish, cashier, cast out, deport, discharge, dismiss, dispossess, drive out, drum out, evict, expel, fire (Inf.), give one the sack (Inf.), kick out (Inf.), oust, put out, sack (Inf.), throw out, turf out (Brit. inf.), unseat 4. clean out, clear, discharge, empty,

take out the contents of 5. become, come about, come to be, come to light, crop up (Inf.), develop, emerge, end up, eventuate, evolve, happen, prove to be, result, transpire (Inf.), work out 6. accoutre, apparel (Archaic), attire, clothe, dress, fit, outfit, rig out 7. appear, assemble, attend, be present, come, gather, go, put in an appearance, show up (Inf.), turn up

turnover 1. business, flow, output, outturn (Rare), production, productivity, volume, yield 2. change, coming and going, movement, replacement

turn up 1. appear, arrive, attend, come, put in an appearance, show (Sl.), show one's face, show up (Inf.) 2. appear, become known, be found, bring to light, come to light, come to pass, come up with, crop up (Inf.), dig up, disclose, discover, expose, find, pop up, reveal, transpire, unearth 3. amplify, boost, enhance, increase, increase the volume of, intensify, make louder, raise

a number of thinners for paints and varnishes, consisting of fractions of petroleum. Related adj.: **terebinthine.** ~*vb.* (*tr.*) **5.** to treat or saturate with turpentine.

turpitude ('tɜːpɪˌtjuːd) *n.* base character or action; depravity.

turps (tɜːps) *n. Brit.* short for **turpentine** (sense 3).

turquoise ('tɜːkwɔɪz, -kwɑːz) *n.* **1.** a greenish-blue fine-grained mineral consisting of hydrated copper aluminium phosphate. It is used as a gemstone. **2. a.** the colour of turquoise. **b.** (*as adj.*): *a turquoise dress.*

turret ('tʌrɪt) *n.* **1.** a small tower that projects from the wall of a building, esp. a castle. **2. a.** a self-contained structure, capable of rotation, in which weapons are mounted, esp. in tanks and warships. **b.** a similar structure on an aircraft. **3.** a lathe part that has a number of tools projecting radially from it that, as it turns, are presented to the workpiece in succession. —**'turreted** adj.

turtle ('tɜːt°l) *n.* **1.** any of various aquatic reptiles, esp. those having a flattened shell enclosing the body and flipper-like limbs adapted for swimming. **2. turn turtle.** to capsize.

turtledove ('tɜːt°lˌdʌv) *n.* **1.** any of several Old World doves having a brown plumage with speckled wings and a long dark tail. **2.** a gentle or loving person.

turtleneck ('tɜːt°lˌnɛk) *n.* a round high close-fitting neck on a sweater or the sweater itself.

tusk (tʌsk) *n.* **1.** a pointed elongated usually paired tooth in the elephant, walrus, and certain other mammals. **2.** a tusklike tooth or part. **3.** a sharp pointed projection. ~*vb.* **4.** to stab, tear, or gore with the tusks. —**tusked** adj.

tussle ('tʌs°l) *vb.* **1.** (*intr.*) to fight or wrestle in a vigorous way. ~*n.* **2.** a vigorous fight; scuffle; struggle.

tussock ('tʌsək) *n.* a dense tuft of vegetation, esp. of grass. —**'tussocky** adj.

tut (tʌt) *or* **tut-tut** *interj.* **1.** an exclamation of mild reprimand, disapproval, or surprise ~*vb.* **tutting, tutted.** (*intr.*) **2.** to express disapproval by the exclamation of "tut" or "tut-tut". ~*n.* **3.** the act of tutting or tut-tutting.

tutelage ('tjuːtɪlɪdʒ) *n.* **1.** the act or office of a guardian or tutor. **2.** instruction or guidance, esp. by a tutor. **3.** the condition of being under the supervision of a guardian or tutor.

tutor ('tjuːtə) *n.* **1.** a teacher, usually instructing individual pupils. **2.** (at universities, colleges, etc.) a member of staff responsible for the teaching and supervision of a certain number of students. ~*vb.* **3.** to act as a tutor to (someone). **4.** (*tr.*) to act as guardian to. —**'tutorage** or **'tutor,ship** *n.*

tutorial (tjuːˈtɔːrɪəl) *n.* **1.** a period of intensive tuition given by a tutor to an individual student or to a small group of students. ~*adj.* **2.** of or relating to a tutor.

tutti ('tʊtɪ) *adj., adv. Music.* to be performed by the whole orchestra, choir, etc.

tutti-frutti ('tuːtɪ'fruːtɪ) *n.* **1.** an ice cream or a confection containing small pieces of candied or fresh fruits. **2.** a preserve of chopped mixed fruits. **3.** a flavour like that of many fruits combined.

tutu ('tuːtuː) *n.* a very short skirt worn by ballerinas, made of projecting layers of stiffened material.

tu-whit tu-whoo (tə'wɪt tə'wuː) *interj.* an imitation of the sound made by an owl.

tuxedo (tʌk'siːdəʊ) *n., pl.* **-dos.** the usual U.S. name for **dinner jacket.**

TV *abbrev. for* television.

twaddle ('twɒd°l) *n.* **1.** silly, trivial, or pretentious talk or writing. ~*vb.* **2.** (*intr.*) to talk or write in a silly or pretentious way. —**'twaddler** n.

twain (tweɪn) *determiner, n.* an archaic word for **two.**

twang (twæŋ) *n.* **1.** a sharp ringing sound produced by or as if by the plucking of a taut string. **2.** the act of

plucking a string to produce such a sound. **3.** a strongly nasal quality in a person's speech. ~*vb.* **4.** to make or cause to make a twang. **5.** to strum (music, a tune, etc.). **6.** to speak with a nasal voice. **7.** (*intr.*) to be released or move with a twang: *the arrow twanged away.* —**'twangy** adj.

twat (twæt, twɒt) *n. Taboo sl.* **1.** the female genitals. **2.** a foolish person.

tweak (twiːk) *vb.* **1.** (*tr.*) to twist or pinch with a sharp or sudden movement. ~*n.* **2.** a tweaking.

twee (twiː) *adj. Brit. inf.* excessively sentimental, sweet, or pretty.

tweed (twiːd) *n.* **1.** a thick woollen cloth produced originally in Scotland. **2.** (*pl.*) clothes made of this.

tweedy ('twiːdɪ) *adj.* **tweedier, tweediest.** **1.** of, made of, or resembling tweed. **2.** showing a fondness for a hearty outdoor life, usually associated with wearers of tweeds.

tweet (twiːt) *interj.* **1.** an imitation of the thin chirping sound made by small birds. ~*vb.* **2.** (*intr.*) to make this sound.

tweeter ('twiːtə) *n.* a loudspeaker used in high-fidelity systems for the reproduction of high audio frequencies. It is usually employed in conjunction with a woofer.

tweezers ('twiːzəz) *pl. n.* a small pincer-like instrument for handling small objects, plucking out hairs, etc. Also called: **pair of tweezers, tweezer** (esp. U.S.).

Twelfth Day *n.* Jan. 6, the twelfth day after Christmas and the feast of the Epiphany.

twelfth man *n.* a reserve player in a cricket team.

twelve (twɛlv) *n.* **1.** the cardinal number that is the sum of ten and two. **2.** a numeral, 12, XII, etc., representing this number. **3.** something representing or consisting of 12 units. **4.** Also called: **twelve o'clock.** noon or midnight. ~*determiner.* **5. a.** amounting to twelve. **b.** (*as pronoun*): *twelve have arrived.* ~Related adj.: **duodecimal.** —**twelfth** adj.

twelvemonth ('twɛlvˌmʌnθ) *n. Chiefly Brit.* an archaic or dialect word for a **year.**

twelve-tone *adj.* of or denoting the type of serial music which uses as musical material the 12 semitones of the chromatic scale.

twenty ('twɛntɪ) *n., pl.* **-ties.** **1.** the cardinal number that is the product of ten and two. **2.** a numeral, 20, XX, etc., representing this number. **3.** something representing or consisting of 20 units. ~*determiner.* **4. a.** amounting to twenty: *twenty questions.* **b.** (*as pronoun*): *to order twenty.* —**'twentieth** adj.

twerp *or* **twirp** (twɜːp) *n. Inf.* a silly, weak-minded, or contemptible person.

twice (twaɪs) *adv.* **1.** two times; on two occasions or in two cases. **2.** double in degree or quantity: *twice as long.*

twiddle ('twɪd°l) *vb.* **1.** (when *intr.*, often foll. by *with*) to twirl or fiddle (with), often in an idle way. **2. twiddle one's thumbs.** to do nothing; be unoccupied. **3.** (*intr.*) to turn, twirl, or rotate. **4.** (*intr.*) *Rare.* to be occupied with trifles. ~*n.* **5.** an act or instance of twiddling. —**'twiddler** n.

twig¹ (twɪg) *n.* **1.** any small branch or shoot of a tree. **2.** something resembling this, esp. a minute branch of a blood vessel. —**'twiggy** adj.

twig² (twɪg) *vb.* **twigging, twigged.** *Brit. inf.* **1.** to understand (something). **2.** to find out or suddenly comprehend (something): *he hasn't twigged yet.*

twilight ('twaɪˌlaɪt) *n.* **1.** the soft diffused light occurring when the sun is just below the horizon, esp. following sunset. **2.** the period in which this light occurs. **3.** any faint light. **4.** a period in which strength, importance, etc., are waning. **5.** (*modifier*) of or relating to twilight; dim. —**twilit** ('twaɪˌlɪt) adj.

THESAURUS

tussle 1. *v.* battle, brawl, contend, fight, grapple, scrap (*Inf.*), scuffle, struggle, vie, wrestle **2.** *n.* battle, bout, brawl, competition, conflict, contention, contest, fight, fracas, fray, punch-up (*Inf.*), scrap (*Inf.*), scuffle, set-to (*Inf.*), struggle

tutor 1. *n.* coach, educator, governor, guardian, guide, guru, instructor, lecturer, master, mentor, preceptor, schoolmaster, teacher **2.** *v.* coach, direct, discipline, drill,

edify, educate, guide, instruct, lecture, school, teach, train

tutorial 1. *n.* individual instruction, lesson, seminar **2.** *adj.* coaching, guiding, instructional, teaching

TV gogglebox (*Brit. sl.*), idiot box (*Sl.*), receiver, small screen (*Inf.*), television, television set, telly (*Brit. inf.*), the box (*Brit. inf.*), the tube (*Sl.*), TV set

twaddle 1. *n.* balderdash, blather, bun-

kum, chatter, claptrap (*Inf.*), drivel, foolish talk, gabble, garbage, gobbledegook (*Inf.*), gossip, guff (*Sl.*), hogwash, hot air (*Inf.*), inanity, nonsense, piffle (*Inf.*), poppycock (*Inf.*), rigmarole, rot, rubbish, tattle, trash, trumpery, verbiage, waffle (*Inf.*) **2.** *v.* blather, chatter, gabble, gossip, prattle, rattle on, talk nonsense, talk through one's hat, tattle, waffle (*Inf.*)

twilight zone n. 1. an inner-city area where houses have become dilapidated. 2. any indefinite or transitional condition or area.

twill (twɪl) adj. 1. (in textiles) of a weave in which the yarns are worked to produce an effect of parallel diagonal lines or ribs. ~n. 2. any fabric so woven. ~vb. 3. (tr.) to weave in this fashion.

twin (twɪn) n. 1. a. either of two persons or animals conceived at the same time. b. (as modifier): a twin brother. See also **identical** (sense 3), **fraternal** (sense 3). 2. a. either of two persons or things that are identical or very similar. b. (as modifier): twin carburettors. 3. Also called: **macle**. a crystal consisting of two parts each of which has a definite orientation to the other. ~vb. **twinning, twinned.** 4. to pair or be paired together; couple. 5. (intr.) to bear twins. 6. (intr.) (of a crystal) to form into a twin.

twin bed n. one of a pair of matching single beds.

twine (twaɪn) n. 1. string made by twisting together fibres of hemp, cotton, etc. 2. a twining. 3. something produced or characterized by twining. 4. a twist, coil, or convolution. 5. a knot, tangle, or snarl. ~vb. 6. (tr.) to twist together; interweave. 7. (tr.) to form by or as if by twining. 8. (when intr., often foll. by around) to wind or cause to wind, esp. in spirals. —'**twiner** n.

twin-engined adj. (of an aeroplane) having two engines.

twinge (twɪndʒ) n. 1. a sudden brief darting or stabbing pain. 2. a sharp emotional pang. ~vb. 3. to have or cause to have a twinge.

twinkle ('twɪŋkəl) vb. (mainly intr.) 1. to emit or reflect light in a flickering manner; shine brightly and intermittently; sparkle. 2. (of the eyes) to sparkle, esp. with amusement or delight. 3. Rare. to move about quickly. ~n. 4. a flickering brightness; sparkle. 5. an instant. 6. a rare word for wink. —'**twinkler** n.

twinkling ('twɪŋklɪŋ) or **twink** (twɪŋk) n. a very short time; instant; moment. Also called: **twinkling of an eye.**

twin-set n. Brit. a matching jumper and cardigan.

twirl (twɜːl) vb. 1. to move around rapidly and repeatedly in a circle. 2. (tr.) to twist, wind, or twiddle, often idly: she twirled her hair around her finger. 3. (intr.; often foll. by around or about) to turn suddenly to face another way. ~n. 4. a rotating or being rotated; whirl or twist. 5. something wound around or twirled; coil. 6. a written flourish. —'**twirler** n.

twist (twɪst) vb. 1. to cause (one end or part) to turn or (of one end or part) to turn in the opposite direction from another; coil or spin. 2. to distort or be distorted. 3. to wind or twine. 4. to force or be forced out of the natural form or position. 5. to change for the worse in character, meaning, etc.; pervert: she twisted the statement. 6. to revolve; rotate. 7. (tr.) to wrench with a turning action. 8. (intr.) to follow a winding course. 9.

(intr.) to squirm, as with pain. 10. (intr.) to dance the twist. 11. **twist someone's arm.** to persuade or coerce someone. ~n. 12. a twisting. 13. something formed by or as if by twisting. 14. a decisive change of direction, aim, meaning, or character. 15. (in a novel, play, etc.) an unexpected event, revelation, etc. 16. a bend: a twist in the road. 17. a distortion of the original shape or form. 18. a jerky pull, wrench, or turn. 19. a strange personal characteristic, esp. a bad one. 20. a confused tangle made by twisting. 21. a twisted thread used in sewing where extra strength is needed. 22. **the twist.** a dance popular in the 1960s, in which dancers vigorously twist the hips. 23. a loaf or roll made of pieces of twisted dough. 24. a thin sliver of peel from a lemon, lime, etc., twisted and added to a drink. 25. a. a cigar made by twisting three cigars around one another. b. chewing tobacco made in the form of a roll by twisting the leaves together. 26. Physics. torsional deformation or shear stress or strain. 27. Sport, chiefly U.S. spin given to a ball in various games. 28. **round the twist.** Brit. sl. mad; eccentric.

twister ('twɪstə) n. 1. Brit. a swindling or dishonest person. 2. a person or thing that twists. 3. U.S. an informal name for tornado. 4. a ball moving with a twisting motion.

twit[1] (twɪt) vb. **twitting, twitted.** 1. (tr.) to tease, taunt, or reproach, often in jest. ~n. 2. U.S. inf. a nervous or excitable state. 3. Rare. a reproach; taunt.

twit[2] (twɪt) n. Inf., chiefly Brit. a foolish or stupid person; idiot.

twitch (twɪtʃ) vb. 1. to move in a jerky spasmodic way. 2. to pull (something) with a quick jerky movement. 3. (intr.) to hurt with a sharp spasmodic pain. ~n. 4. a sharp jerking movement. 5. a mental or physical twinge. 6. a sudden muscular spasm, esp. one caused by a nervous condition. 7. a loop of cord used to control a horse by drawing it tight about its upper lip.

twitter ('twɪtə) vb. 1. (intr.) (esp. of a bird) to utter a succession of chirping sounds. 2. (intr.) to talk or move rapidly and tremulously. 3. (intr.) to giggle. 4. (tr.) to utter in a chirping way. ~n. 5. a twittering sound. 6. the act of twittering. 7. a state of nervous excitement (esp. in **in a twitter**). —'**twitterer** n. —'**twittery** adj.

two (tuː) n. 1. the cardinal number that is the sum of one and one. 2. a numeral, 2, II, (ii), etc., representing this number. 3. something representing or consisting of two units. 4. Also called: **two o'clock.** two hours after noon or midnight. 5. **in two.** in or into two parts. 6. **put two and two together.** to make an inference from available evidence, esp. an obvious inference. 7. **that makes two of us.** the same applies to me. ~determiner. 8. a. amounting to two: two nails. b. (as pronoun): he bought two. ~Related adjs.: **binary, double, dual.**

two-edged adj. 1. having two cutting edges. 2. (esp.

THESAURUS

tweak v./n. jerk, nip, pinch, pull, squeeze, twist, twitch

twig branch, offshoot, shoot, spray, sprig, stick, withe

twilight n. 1. dimness, dusk, evening, gloaming (Scot.), half-light, sundown, sunset 2. decline, ebb, last phase ~adj. 3. crepuscular, darkening, dim, evening 4. declining, dying, ebbing, final, last

twin 1. n. clone, corollary, counterpart, double, duplicate, fellow, likeness, lookalike, match, mate, ringer (Sl.) 2. adj. corresponding, double, dual, duplicate, geminate, identical, matched, matching, paired, parallel, twofold 3. v. couple, join, link, match, pair, yoke

twine n. 1. cord, string, yarn 2. coil, convolution, interlacing, twist, whorl 3. knot, snarl, tangle ~v. 4. braid, entwine, interlace, interweave, knit, plait, splice, twist, twist together, weave 5. bend, coil, curl, encircle, loop, meander, spiral, surround, twist, wind, wrap, wreathe

twinge bite, gripe, pain, pang, pinch, prick, sharp pain, spasm, stab, stitch, throb, throe (Rare), tic, tweak, twist, twitch

twinkle v. 1. blink, coruscate, flash, flicker, gleam, glint, glisten, glitter, scintillate, shimmer, shine, sparkle, wink ~n. 2. blink,

coruscation, flash, flicker, gleam, glimmer, glistening, glittering, light, scintillation, shimmer, shine, spark, sparkle, wink 3. flash, instant, jiffy (Inf.), moment, second, shake (Inf.), split second, tick (Inf.), trice, twinkling, two shakes of a lamb's tail (Inf.)

twinkling 1. blink, coruscation, flash, flashing, flicker, gleam, glimmer, glistening, glittering, scintillation, shimmer, shining, sparkle, twinkle, wink 2. flash, instant, jiffy (Inf.), moment, second, shake (Inf.), split second, tick (Inf.), trice, twinkle, two shakes of a lamb's tail (Inf.)

twirl v. 1. gyrate, pirouette, pivot, revolve, rotate, spin, turn, turn on one's heel, twiddle, twist, wheel, whirl, wind ~n. 2. gyration, pirouette, revolution, rotation, spin, turn, twist, wheel, whirl 3. coil, spiral, twist

twist v. 1. coil, corkscrew, curl, encircle, entwine, intertwine, screw, spin, swivel, twine, weave, wind, wrap, wreathe, wring 2. contort, distort, screw up 3. kink, sprain, turn, wrench 4. alter, change, distort, falsify, garble, misquote, misrepresent, pervert, warp 5. squirm, wriggle, writhe 6. **twist someone's arm** bully, coerce, force, persuade, pressurize, talk into ~n. 7. coil, curl, curl, spin, swivel, twine, wind 8. braid, coil, curl, hank, plug, quid, roll 9. change, development, revelation,

slant, surprise, turn, variation 10. arc, bend, convolution, curve, meander, turn, undulation, zigzag 11. defect, deformation, distortion, flaw, imperfection, kink, warp 12. jerk, pull, sprain, turn, wrench 13. aberration, bent, characteristic, crotchet, eccentricity, fault, foible, idiosyncrasy, oddity, peculiarity, proclivity, quirk, trait 14. confusion, entanglement, kink, knot, mess, mix-up, snarl, tangle 15. **round the twist** barmy (Sl.), batty (Sl.), bonkers (Brit. sl.), crazy, cuckoo (Inf.), daft (Inf.), insane, mad, not all there, not right in the head, nuts (Sl.), nutty (Sl.), nutty as a fruitcake (Sl.), off one's rocker (Sl.)

twister cheat, con man (Inf.), crook (Inf.), deceiver, fraud, rogue, swindler, trickster

twit[1] v. banter, berate, blame, censure, deride, jeer, make fun of, scorn, taunt, tease, upbraid

twit[2] ass, blockhead, chump (Inf.), clown, dope (Sl.), fool, halfwit, idiot, juggins (Brit. inf.), nincompoop, ninny, nitwit, silly-billy (Inf.), simpleton, twerp (Inf.)

twitch 1. v. blink, flutter, jerk, jump, pluck, pull, snatch, squirm, tug, yank 2. n. blink, flutter, jerk, jump, pull, spasm, tic, tremor, twinge

of a remark) having two interpretations, such as *she looks nice when she smiles.*

two-faced *adj.* deceitful; hypocritical.

twofold ('tu:ˌfəʊld) *adj.* **1.** equal to twice as many or twice as much. **2.** composed of two parts. ~*adv.* **3.** doubly.

two-handed *adj.* **1.** requiring the use of both hands. **2.** ambidextrous. **3.** requiring the participation or co-operation of two people.

twopence *or* **tuppence** ('tʌpəns) *n. Brit.* **1.** the sum of two pennies. **2.** (*used with a negative*) something of little value (in **not care** *or* **give twopence**). **3.** a former British silver coin.

twopenny *or* **tuppenny** ('tʌpənɪ) *adj. Chiefly Brit.* **1.** Also: **twopenny-halfpenny.** cheap or tawdry. **2.** (*intensifier*): *a twopenny damn.* **3.** worth two pence.

two-piece *adj.* **1.** consisting of two separate parts, usually matching, as of a garment. ~*n.* **2.** such an outfit.

two-ply *adj.* **1.** made of two thicknesses, layers, or strands. ~*n., pl.* **-plies. 2.** a two-ply wood, knitting yarn, etc.

two-sided *adj.* **1.** having two sides or aspects. **2.** controversial; debatable.

twosome ('tu:səm) *n.* **1.** two together, esp. two people. **2.** a match between two people.

two-step *n.* **1.** a ballroom dance in duple time. **2.** a piece of music for or in the rhythm of such a dance.

two-stroke *adj.* of an internal-combustion engine whose piston makes two strokes for every explosion. U.S. word: **two-cycle.**

two-time *vb. Inf.* to deceive (someone, esp. a lover) by carrying on a relationship with another. —'**two-ˌtimer** *n.*

two-way *adj.* **1.** moving, permitting movement, or operating in either of two opposite directions. **2.** involving two participants. **3.** involving reciprocal obligation or mutual action. **4.** (of a radio, telephone, etc.) allowing communications in two directions using both transmitting and receiving equipment.

tycoon (taɪˈkuːn) *n.* a businessman of great wealth and power.

tyee salmon *n.* another name for **Chinook salmon.**

tyke *or* **tike** (taɪk) *n.* **1.** *Inf.* a small or cheeky child. **2.** *N Brit. dialect.* a dog, esp. a mongrel. **3.** *N Brit. dialect.* a rough ill-mannered person. **4.** *Brit. sl., often offens.* a person from Yorkshire. **5.** *Austral. sl. offens.* a Roman Catholic.

tympani ('tɪmpənɪ) *pl. n.* a variant spelling of **timpani.**

tympanic membrane *n.* the thin membrane separating the external ear from the middle ear. It transmits vibrations, produced by sound waves, to the cochlea. Nontechnical name: **eardrum.**

tympanum ('tɪmpənəm) *n., pl.* **-nums** *or* **-na** (-nə). **1. a.** the cavity of the middle ear. **b.** another name for **tympanic membrane. 2.** any diaphragm resembling that in the middle ear in function. **3.** *Archit.* **a.** the recessed space bounded by the cornices of a pediment, esp. one that is triangular in shape. **b.** the recessed space bounded by an arch and the lintel of a doorway or window below it. **4.** *Music.* a tympan or drum. **5.** a scoop wheel for raising water. —**tympanic** (tɪmˈpænɪk) *adj.*

Tynwald ('tɪnwəld, 'taɪn-) *n.* **the.** the Parliament of the Isle of Man.

type (taɪp) *n.* **1.** a kind, class, or category, the constituents of which share similar characteristics. **2.** a subdivision of a particular class; sort: *what type of shampoo do you use?* **3.** the general form, plan, or design distinguishing a particular group. **4.** *Inf.* a person who typifies a particular quality: *he's the administrative type.* **5.** *Inf.* a

person, esp. of a specified kind: *he's a strange type.* **6. a.** a small block of metal or more rarely wood bearing a letter or character in relief for use in printing. **b.** such pieces collectively. **7.** characters printed from type; print. **8.** *Biol.* **a.** the taxonomic group the characteristics of which are used for defining the next highest group. **b.** (*as modifier*): *a type genus.* **9.** the characteristic device on a coin. **10.** *Chiefly theol.* a figure, episode, or symbolic factor resembling some future reality in such a way as to foreshadow or prefigure it. ~*vb.* **11.** to write (copy) on a typewriter. **12.** (*tr.*) to be a symbol of; typify. **13.** (*tr.*) to decide the type of. **14.** (*tr.*) *Med.* to determine the blood group of (a blood sample). **15.** (*tr.*) *Chiefly theol.* to foreshadow or serve as a symbol of (some future reality).

typecast ('taɪpˌkɑːst) *vb.* **-casting, -cast.** (*tr.*) to cast (an actor) in the same kind of role continually, esp. because of his physical appearance or previous success in such roles.

typeface ('taɪpˌfeɪs) *n.* another name for **face** (sense 14).

typescript ('taɪpˌskrɪpt) *n.* **1.** a typed copy of a document, etc. **2.** any typewritten material.

typeset ('taɪpˌsɛt) *vb.* **-setting, -set.** *Printing.* to set (textual matter) in type.

typesetter ('taɪpˌsɛtə) *n.* **1.** a person who sets type; compositor. **2.** a typesetting machine.

typewrite ('taɪpˌraɪt) *vb.* **-writing, -wrote, -written.** to write by means of a typewriter; type. —'**type,writing** *n.*

typewriter ('taɪpˌraɪtə) *n.* a keyboard machine for writing mechanically in characters resembling print.

typhoid ('taɪfɔɪd) *Pathol.* ~*adj. also* **typhoidal. 1.** resembling typhus. ~*n.* **2.** short for **typhoid fever.**

typhoid fever *n.* an acute infectious disease characterized by high fever, spots, abdominal pain, etc. It is caused by a bacillus ingested with food or water.

typhoon (taɪˈfuːn) *n.* a violent tropical storm or cyclone, esp. in the China Seas and W Pacific. —**typhonic** (taɪ-ˈfɒnɪk) *adj.*

typhus ('taɪfəs) *n.* any one of a group of acute infectious rickettsial diseases characterized by high fever, skin rash, and severe headache. Also called: **typhus fever.** —'**typhous** *adj.*

typical ('tɪpɪk³l) *or* **typic** *adj.* **1.** being or serving as a representative example of a particular type; characteristic. **2.** considered to be an example of some undesirable trait: *that is typical of you!* **3.** of or relating to a representative specimen or type. **4.** conforming to a type. **5.** *Biol.* having most of the characteristics of a particular taxonomic group. —'**typically** *adv.* —'**typicalness** *or* ˌ**typiˈcality** *n.*

typify ('tɪpɪˌfaɪ) *vb.* **-fying, -fied.** (*tr.*) **1.** to be typical of; characterize. **2.** to symbolize or represent completely, by or as if by a type. —ˌ**typifiˈcation** *n.*

typist ('taɪpɪst) *n.* a person who types, esp. for a living.

typo ('taɪpəʊ) *n., pl.* **-pos.** *Inf.* a typographical error. Also called (*Brit.*): **literal.**

typography (taɪˈpɒgrəfɪ) *n.* **1.** the art, craft, or process of composing type and printing from it. **2.** the planning, selection, and setting of type for a printed work. —ty-'**pographer** *n.* —**typographical** (ˌtaɪpəˈgræfɪk³l) *or* ˌ**typo-** '**graphic** *adj.* —ˌ**typo**'**graphically** *adv.*

tyrannical (tɪˈrænɪk³l) *or* **tyrannic** *adj.* characteristic of or relating to a tyrant or to tyranny; oppressive. —ty'**rannically** *adv.*

tyrannize *or* **-ise** ('tɪrəˌnaɪz) *vb.* (when *intr.*, often foll. by *over*) to rule or exercise power over (people) in a cruel or oppressive manner. —'**tyran,nizer** *or* **-iser** *n.*

tyrannosaur (tɪˈrænəˌsɔː) *or* **tyrannosaurus**

THESAURUS

two-edged ambiguous, ambivalent, backhanded, double-edged, equivocal

two-faced deceitful, deceiving, dissembling, double-dealing, duplicitous, false, hypocritical, insincere, Janus-faced, perfidious, treacherous, untrustworthy

tycoon baron, big cheese (*Sl.*), big noise (*Sl.*), capitalist, captain of industry, fat cat (*Sl.*), financier, industrialist, magnate, merchant prince, mogul, plutocrat, potentate, wealthy businessman

type 1. breed, category, class, classifica-

tion, form, genre, group, ilk, kidney, kind, order, sort, species, strain, subdivision, variety **2.** case, characters, face, fount, print, printing **3.** archetype, epitome, essence, example, exemplar, model, original, paradigm, pattern, personification, prototype, quintessence, specimen, standard

typhoon cyclone, squall, storm, tempest, tornado, tropical storm

typical archetypal, average, characteristic, classic, conventional, essential, illustrative, in character, indicative, in keeping,

model, normal, orthodox, representative, standard, stock, true to type, usual

typify characterize, embody, epitomize, exemplify, illustrate, incarnate, personify, represent, sum up, symbolize

tyrannical absolute, arbitrary, authoritarian, autocratic, coercive, cruel, despotic, dictatorial, domineering, high-handed, imperious, inhuman, magisterial, oppressive, overbearing, overweening, peremptory, severe, tyrannous, unjust, unreasonable

(tɪˌrænəˈsɔːrəs) *n.* any of various large carnivorous two-footed dinosaurs common in North America in Upper Jurassic and Cretaceous times.

tyranny (ˈtɪrənɪ) *n., pl.* **-nies. 1. a.** government by a tyrant; despotism. **b.** oppressive and unjust government by more than one person. **2.** arbitrary, unreasonable, or despotic behaviour or use of authority. **3.** a tyrannical act. —**ˈtyrannous** *adj.*

tyrant (ˈtaɪrənt) *n.* **1.** a person who governs oppressively, unjustly, and arbitrarily; despot. **2.** any person who exercises authority in a tyrannical manner.

tyre *or U.S.* **tire** (taɪə) *n.* **1.** a rubber ring placed over the rim of a wheel of a road vehicle to provide traction and reduce road shocks, esp. a hollow inflated ring

(**pneumatic tyre**) consisting of a reinforced outer casing enclosing an inner tube. **2.** a metal band or hoop attached to the rim of a wooden cartwheel.

Tyrian (ˈtɪrɪən) *n.* **1.** a native or inhabitant of ancient Tyre, a port in S Lebanon and centre of ancient Phoenician culture. ~*adj.* **2.** of or relating to ancient Tyre.

Tyrian purple *n.* **1.** a deep purple dye obtained from certain molluscs and highly prized in antiquity. **2.** a vivid purplish-red colour.

tyro *or* **tiro** (ˈtaɪrəʊ) *n., pl.* **-ros.** a novice or beginner.

tzar (zɑː) *n.* a variant spelling of **tsar.**

tzetze fly (ˈtsɛtsɪ) *n.* a variant spelling of **tsetse fly.**

THESAURUS

tyranny absolutism, authoritarianism, autocracy, coercion, cruelty, despotism, dictatorship, harsh discipline, high-handedness, imperiousness, oppression, peremptoriness, reign of terror, unreasonableness

tyrant absolutist, authoritarian, autocrat, bully, despot, dictator, Hitler, martinet, oppressor, slave-driver

tyro apprentice, beginner, catechumen, greenhorn (*Inf.*), initiate, learner, neophyte, novice, novitiate, pupil, student, trainee

u *or* **U** (juː) *n., pl.* **u's, U's,** *or* **Us.** **1.** the 21st letter and fifth vowel of the English alphabet. **2.** any of several speech sounds represented by this letter, as in *mute, cut,* or *minus.* **3. a.** something shaped like a U. **b.** (*in combination*): *a U-bolt.*

U *symbol for:* **1.** united. **2.** unionist. **3.** university. **4.** (in Britain) **a.** universal (used to describe a category of film certified as suitable for viewing by anyone). **b.** (*as modifier*): *a U certificate film.* **5.** *Chem.* uranium. *~adj.* **6.** *Brit. inf.* (esp. of language habits) characteristic of or appropriate to the upper class.

ubiquitous (juːˈbɪkwɪtəs) *adj.* having or seeming to have the ability to be everywhere at once. —u'biquitously *adv.* —u'biquity *n.*

U-boat *n.* a German submarine, esp. in World Wars I and II.

u.c. *Printing. abbrev. for* upper case.

UCCA (ˈʌkə) *n.* (in Britain) *acronym for* Universities Central Council on Admissions.

udder (ˈʌdə) *n.* the large baglike mammary gland of cows, sheep, etc., having two or more teats.

UDI *abbrev. for* Unilateral Declaration of Independence.

UEFA (juːˈeɪfə, ˈjuːfə) *n. acronym for* Union of European Football Associations.

UFO (*sometimes* ˈjuːfəʊ) *abbrev. for* unidentified flying object.

ugh (ʊx, ʊh, ʌh) *interj.* an exclamation of disgust, annoyance, or dislike.

ugli (ˈʌglɪ) *n., pl.* **-lis** *or* **-lies.** a large juicy yellow-skinned citrus fruit of the West Indies: a cross between a tangerine, grapefruit, and orange. Also called: **ugli fruit.**

ugly (ˈʌglɪ) *adj.* **-lier, -liest.** **1.** of unpleasant or unsightly appearance. **2.** repulsive or displeasing in any way: *war is ugly.* **3.** ominous or menacing: *an ugly situation.* **4.** bad-tempered or sullen: *an ugly mood.* —'uglily *adv.* —'ugliness *n.*

ugly duckling *n.* a person or thing, initially ugly and unpromising, that changes into something beautiful or admirable.

UHF *Radio. abbrev. for* ultrahigh frequency.

uh-huh *sentence substitute. Inf.* a less emphatic variant of **yes.**

UHT *abbrev. for* ultra-heat-treated (milk or cream).

U.K. *abbrev. for* United Kingdom.

ukase (juːˈkeɪz) *n.* **1.** (in imperial Russia) an edict of the tsar. **2.** a rare word for **edict.**

Ukrainian (juːˈkreɪnɪən) *adj.* **1.** of or relating to the Ukraine, its people, or their language. *~n.* **2.** the official language of the Ukrainian SSR: an East Slavonic language closely related to Russian. **3.** a native or inhabitant of the Ukraine.

ukulele *or* **ukelele** (ˌjuːkəˈleɪlɪ) *n.* a small four-stringed guitar, esp. of Hawaii.

ulcer (ˈʌlsə) *n.* **1.** a disintegration of the surface of the skin or a mucous membrane resulting in an open sore that heals very slowly. **2.** a source or element of corruption or evil.

ulcerate (ˈʌlsəˌreɪt) *vb.* to make or become ulcerous. —ˌulce'ration *n.* —'ulce,rative *adj.*

ulcerous (ˈʌlsərəs) *adj.* **1.** relating to or characterized by an ulcer or ulcers. **2.** being or having a corrupting influence. —'ulcerously *adv.*

ullage (ˈʌlɪdʒ) *n.* **1.** the volume by which a liquid container falls short of being full. **2. a.** the quantity of liquid lost from a container due to leakage or evaporation. **b.** (in customs terminology) the amount of liquid remaining in a container after such loss.

ulna (ˈʌlnə) *n., pl.* **-nae** (-niː) *or* **-nas.** **1.** the inner and longer of the two bones of the human forearm. **2.** the corresponding bone in other vertebrates. —'ulnar *adj.*

ulster (ˈʌlstə) *n.* a man's heavy double-breasted overcoat with a belt or half-belt at the back.

Ulsterman (ˈʌlstəmən) *n., pl.* **-men.** a native or inhabitant of Ulster. —'Ulster,woman *fem. n.*

ult. *abbrev. for:* **1.** ultimate(ly). **2.** ultimo.

ulterior (ʌlˈtɪərɪə) *adj.* **1.** lying beneath or beyond what is revealed or supposed: *ulterior motives.* **2.** succeeding, subsequent, or later. **3.** lying beyond a certain line or point. —ul'teriorly *adv.*

ultimate (ˈʌltɪmɪt) *adj.* **1.** conclusive in a series or process; final: *an ultimate question.* **2.** the highest or most significant: *the ultimate goal.* **3.** elemental, fundamental, or essential. *~n.* **4.** the most significant, highest, or greatest thing. —'ultimately *adv.* —'ultimateness *n.*

ultimatum (ˌʌltɪˈmeɪtəm) *n., pl.* **-tums** *or* **-ta** (-tə). **1.** a final communication by a party setting forth conditions on which it insists, as during negotiations on some topic. **2.** any final or peremptory demand or proposal.

ultimo (ˈʌltɪˌməʊ) *adv. Now rare except when abbreviated in formal correspondence.* in or during the previous month: *a letter of the 7th ultimo.* Abbrev.: **ult.**

ultra (ˈʌltrə) *adj.* **1.** extreme or immoderate, esp. in beliefs or opinions. *~n.* **2.** an extremist.

ultra- *prefix.* **1.** beyond or surpassing a specified extent, range, or limit: *ultramicroscopic.* **2.** extreme or extremely: *ultramodern.*

ultraconservative (ˌʌltrəkənˈsɜːvətɪv) *adj.* **1.** highly reactionary. *~n.* **2.** a reactionary person.

ultrahigh frequency (ˈʌltrəˌhaɪ) *n.* a radio-frequency band or radio frequency lying between 3000 and 300 megahertz. Abbrev.: **UHF**

ultramarine (ˌʌltrəməˈriːn) *n.* **1.** a blue pigment obtained by powdering natural lapis lazuli or made synthetically: used in paints, printing ink, plastics, etc. **2.** a vivid blue colour. *~adj.* **3.** of the colour ultramarine. **4.** from across the seas.

ultramontane (ˌʌltrəmɒnˈteɪn) *adj.* **1.** on the other side of the mountains, esp. the Alps, from the speaker or writer. **2.** of or relating to a movement in the Roman Catholic Church which favours the centralized authority and influence of the pope as opposed to local independence. *~n.* **3.** a resident or native from beyond the mountains, esp. the Alps. **4.** a member of the ultramontane party of the Roman Catholic Church.

ultrasonic (ˌʌltrəˈsɒnɪk) *adj.* of, concerned with, or producing waves with the same nature as sound waves but frequencies above audio frequencies. —ˌultra'sonically *adv.*

ultrasonics (ˌʌltrəˈsɒnɪks) *n.* (*functioning as sing.*) the branch of physics concerned with ultrasonic waves. Also called: **supersonics.**

ultrasound (ˌʌltrəˈsaʊnd) *n.* ultrasonic waves of the same nature as sound, used in cleaning metallic parts,

echo sounding, medical diagnosis and therapy, etc.
ultraviolet (ˌʌltrəˈvaɪəlɪt) n. 1. the part of the electromagnetic spectrum with wavelengths shorter than light but longer than x-rays; in the range 0.4×10^{-5} and 5×10^{-9} metres. ~adj. 2. of, relating to, or consisting of radiation lying in the ultraviolet: *ultraviolet radiation*.
ululate (ˈjuːljʊˌleɪt) vb. (intr.) to howl or wail, as with grief. —**ˈululant** adj. —**ˌuluˈlation** n.
umbel (ˈʌmbəl) n. a racemose inflorescence, characteristic of umbelliferous plants, in which the flowers arise from the same point in the main stem and have stalks of the same length, to give a cluster with the youngest flowers at the centre. —**umbellate** (ˈʌmbɪlɪt, -ˌleɪt) or **umbellar** (ʌmˈbɛlə) adj. —**umbellule** (ʌmˈbɛljuːl) n.
umbelliferous (ˌʌmbɪˈlɪfərəs) adj. of or belonging to a family of herbaceous plants and shrubs, typically having hollow stems, divided or compound leaves, and flowers in umbels: includes fennel, parsley, carrot, and parsnip. —**umˈbellifer** n.
umber (ˈʌmbə) n. 1. any of various natural brown earths containing ferric oxide together with lime and oxides of aluminium, manganese, and silicon. 2. any of the dark brown to greenish-brown colours produced by this pigment. 3. Obs. shade or shadow. ~adj. 4. of, relating to, or stained with umber.
umbilical (ʌmˈbɪlɪkəl, ˌʌmbɪˈlaɪkəl) adj. 1. of, relating to, or resembling the umbilicus or the umbilical cord. 2. in the region of the umbilicus: *an umbilical hernia*.
umbilical cord n. 1. the long flexible tubelike structure connecting a foetus with the placenta. 2. any flexible cord, tube, or cable, as between an astronaut walking in space and his spacecraft.
umbilicus (ʌmˈbɪlɪkəs, ˌʌmbɪˈlaɪkəs) n., pl. **-bilici** (-ˈbɪlɪˌsaɪ, -bəˈlaɪsaɪ). 1. Biol. a hollow or navel-like structure, such as the cavity at the base of a gastropod shell. 2. Anat. a technical name for the **navel**.
umbra (ˈʌmbrə) n., pl. **-brae** (-briː) or **-bras**. 1. a region of complete shadow resulting from the obstruction of light by an opaque object, esp. the shadow cast by the moon onto the earth during a solar eclipse. 2. the darker inner region of a sunspot. —**umbral** adj.
umbrage (ˈʌmbrɪdʒ) n. 1. displeasure or resentment; offence (in **give** or **take umbrage**). 2. the foliage of trees, considered as providing shade. 3. Rare. shadow or shade.
umbrella (ʌmˈbrɛlə) n. 1. a portable device used for protection against rain, snow, etc., and consisting of a light canopy supported on a collapsible metal frame

mounted on a central rod. 2. the flattened cone-shaped body of a jellyfish. 3. a protective shield or screen, esp. of aircraft or gunfire. 4. anything that has the effect of a protective screen, general cover, or organizing agency. —**umˈbrella-ˌlike** adj.
umbrella tree n. a North American magnolia having long leaves clustered into an umbrella formation at the ends of the branches and having unpleasant-smelling white flowers.
umiak or **oomiak** (ˈuːmɪˌæk) n. a large open boat made of stretched skins, used by Eskimos.
umlaut (ˈumlaut) n. 1. the mark (¨) placed over a vowel in some languages, such as German, indicating modification in the quality of the vowel. 2. (esp. in Germanic languages) the change of a vowel within a word brought about by the assimilating influence of a vowel or semivowel in a preceding or following syllable.
umpire (ˈʌmpaɪə) n. 1. an official who rules on the playing of a game, as in cricket. 2. a person who rules on or judges disputes between contesting parties. ~vb. 3. to act as umpire in (a game, dispute, or controversy).
umpteen (ˌʌmpˈtiːn) determiner. Inf. a. very many: *umpteen things to do*. b. (as pronoun): *umpteen of them came*. —**ˌumpˈteenth** n., adj.
UN or **U.N.** abbrev. for United Nations.
un-¹ prefix. (freely used with adjectives, participles, and their derivative adverbs and nouns: less frequently used with certain other nouns) not; contrary to; opposite of: *uncertain; untidiness; unbelief; untruth*.
un-² prefix forming verbs. 1. denoting reversal of an action or state: *uncover; untangle*. 2. denoting removal from, release, or deprivation: *unharness; unthrone*. 3. (intensifier): *unloose*.
unable (ʌnˈeɪbəl) adj. (postpositive; foll. by to) lacking the necessary power, ability, or authority (to do something); not able.
unaccountable (ˌʌnəˈkauntəbəl) adj. 1. allowing of no explanation; inexplicable. 2. extraordinary: *an unaccountable fear of heights*. 3. not accountable or answerable to. —**ˌunacˌcountaˈbility** n. —**ˌunacˈcountably** adv.
unaccustomed (ˌʌnəˈkʌstəmd) adj. 1. (foll. by to) not used (to): *unaccustomed to pain*. 2. not familiar. —**ˌunacˈcustomedness** n.
unadopted (ˌʌnəˈdɒptɪd) adj. 1. (of a child) not adopt-

unabashed adj.	**unaided** adj.	**unarguable** adj.	**unblinking** adj.
unabated adj.	**unaligned** adj.	**unartistic** adj.	**unblock** vb.
unabbreviated adj.	**unalleviated** adj.	**unashamed** adj.	**unbreakable** adj.
unabridged adj.	**unallied** adj.	**unasked** adj.	**unbuckle** vb.
unacceptable adj.	**unallowable** adj.	**unassisted** adj.	**unburied** adj.
unaccompanied adj.	**unalterable** adj.	**unassorted** adj.	**uncaged** adj.
unaccomplished adj.	**unambigious** adj.	**unattainable** adj.	**uncashed** adj.
unacknowledged adj.	**unamiable** adj.	**unattended** adj.	**uncaught** adj.
unacquainted adj.	**unamused** adj.	**unattractive** adj.	**unceasing** adj.
unaddressed adj.	**unannounced** adj.	**unauthentic** adj.	**uncensored** adj.
unadorned adj.	**unanswerable** adj.	**unauthorized** adj.	**uncensured** adj.
unadulterated adj.	**unanswered** adj.	**unavailable** adj.	**unchain** vb.
unadventurous adj.	**unappealing** adj.	**unbiased** or	**unchallenged** adj.
unadvertised adj.	**unappetizing** adj.	**unbiassed** adj.	**uncharacteristic** adj.
unaffiliated adj.	**unappreciated** adj.	**unbleached** adj.	**uncharged** adj.
unafraid adj.	**unapproved** adj.	**unblemished** adj.	**unchecked** adj.

THESAURUS

umbrage anger, chagrin, displeasure, grudge, high dudgeon, huff, indignation, offence, pique, resentment, sense of injury
umbrella 1. brolly (*Brit. inf.*), gamp (*Brit. inf.*) 2. aegis, agency, cover, patronage, protection
umpire 1. n. adjudicator, arbiter, arbitrator, judge, moderator, ref (*Inf.*), referee 2. v. adjudicate, arbitrate, call (*Sport*), judge, moderate, referee
umpteen a good many, a thousand and one, considerable, countless, ever so many, millions, n, numerous, very many
unabashed blatant, bold, brazen, confident, unawed, unblushing, unconcerned, undaunted, undismayed, unembarrassed
unable impotent, inadequate, incapable,

ineffectual, no good, not able, not equal to, not up to, powerless, unfit, unfitted, unqualified
unabridged complete, full-length, uncondensed, uncut, unexpurgated, unshortened, whole
unacceptable disagreeable, displeasing, distasteful, improper, inadmissible, insupportable, objectionable, offensive, undesirable, unpleasant, unsatisfactory, unwelcome
unaccompanied a cappella (*Music*), alone, by oneself, lone, on one's own, solo, unescorted
unaccomplished 1. incomplete, unachieved, uncompleted, undone, unfinished, unperformed 2. inexpert, lacking finesse, un-

cultivated, unskilful, unskilled
unaccountable 1. baffling, incomprehensible, inexplicable, inscrutable, mysterious, odd, peculiar, puzzling, strange, unexplainable, unfathomable, unintelligible 2. astonishing, extraordinary, uncommon, unheard-of, unusual, unwonted 3. clear, exempt, free, not answerable, not responsible, unliable
unaccustomed 1. *With* to a newcomer to, a novice at, green, inexperienced, not given to, not used to, unfamiliar with, unpractised, unused to, unversed in 2. new, out of the ordinary, remarkable, special, strange, surprising, uncommon, unexpected, unfamiliar, unprecedented, unusual, unwonted

ed. **2.** *Brit.* (of a road, etc.) not maintained by a local authority.

unadvised (ˌʌnədˈvaɪzd) *adj.* **1.** rash or unwise. **2.** not having received advice. **—unadvisedly** (ˌʌnədˈvaɪzɪdlɪ) *adv.* **—unadˈvisedness** *n.*

unaffected¹ (ˌʌnəˈfɛktɪd) *adj.* unpretentious, natural, or sincere. **—unafˈfectedly** *adv.* **—unafˈfectedness** *n.*

unaffected² (ˌʌnəˈfɛktɪd) *adj.* not affected.

unalienable (ʌnˈeɪljənəbəl) *adj. Law.* a variant of **inalienable.**

un-American *adj.* **1.** not in accordance with the aims, ideals, customs, etc., of the U.S. **2.** against the interests of the U.S. **—ˌun-Aˈmericanism** *n.*

unanimous (juːˈnænɪməs) *adj.* **1.** in complete agreement. **2.** characterized by complete agreement: *a unanimous decision.* **—uˈnanimously** *adv.* **—unanimity** (ˌjuːnəˈnɪmɪtɪ) *n.*

unapproachable (ˌʌnəˈprəʊtʃəbəl) *adj.* **1.** discouraging intimacy, friendliness, etc.; aloof. **2.** inaccessible. **—ˌunapˈproachableness** *n.* **—ˌunapˈproachably** *adv.*

unarmed (ʌnˈɑːmd) *adj.* **1.** without weapons. **2.** (of animals and plants) having no claws, prickles, spines, thorns, or similar structures.

unassailable (ˌʌnəˈseɪləbəl) *adj.* **1.** able to withstand attack. **2.** undeniable or irrefutable. **—ˌunasˈsailableness** *n.* **—ˌunasˈsailably** *adv.*

unassuming (ˌʌnəˈsjuːmɪŋ) *adj.* modest or unpretentious. **—ˌunasˈsumingly** *adv.* **—ˌunasˈsumingness** *n.*

unattached (ˌʌnəˈtætʃt) *adj.* **1.** not connected with any specific thing, body, group, etc. **2.** not engaged or married. **3.** (of property) not seized or held as security.

unavailing (ˌʌnəˈveɪlɪŋ) *adj.* useless or futile. **—ˌunaˈvailingly** *adv.*

unaware (ˌʌnəˈwɛə) *adj.* **1.** (*postpositive*) not aware or conscious (of): *unaware of the danger he ran across the road.* ~*adv.* **2.** a variant of **unawares. —ˌunaˈwareness** *n.*

▷ **Usage.** Careful users of English distinguish between the adjective *unaware* (to be ignorant of) and the adverb *unawares* (by surprise): *they were unaware of the danger; the danger caught them unawares.*

unawares (ˌʌnəˈwɛəz) *adv.* **1.** without prior warning or plan: *she caught him unawares.* **2.** without knowing: *he lost it unawares.*

▷ **Usage.** See at **unaware.**

unbalanced (ʌnˈbælənst) *adj.* **1.** lacking balance. **2.** irrational or unsound; erratic. **3.** mentally disordered or deranged. **4.** (in double-entry book-keeping) not having total debit balances equal to total credit balances.

unbearable (ʌnˈbɛərəbəl) *adj.* not able to be borne or endured. **—unˈbearably** *adv.*

unclaimed *adj.*	unconcluded *adj.*	uncorroborated *adj.*	undemonstrative *adj.*
unclassified *adj.*	unconfined *adj.*	uncritical *adj.*	undependable *adj.*
unclear *adj.*	unconfirmed *adj.*	uncrowned *adj.*	undeserved *adj.*
unclog *vb.*	unconnected *adj.*	uncultivated *adj.*	undeserving *adj.*
unclouded *adj.*	unconquered *adj.*	uncultured *adj.*	undetected *adj.*
uncluttered *adj.*	unconsidered *adj.*	uncured *adj.*	undeterred *adj.*
uncoloured *adj.*	unconsummated *adj.*	uncurl *vb.*	undeveloped *adj.*
uncombed *adj.*	uncontaminated *adj.*	undamaged *adj.*	undiagnosed *adj.*
uncommercial *adj.*	uncontested *adj.*	undated *adj.*	undignified *adj.*
uncompetitive *adj.*	uncontrollable *adj.*	undeclared *adj.*	undiluted *adj.*
uncomplaining *adj.*	uncontrolled *adj.*	undecorated *adj.*	undiminished *adj.*
uncompleted *adj.*	uncontroversial *adj.*	undefeated *adj.*	undiplomatic *adj.*
uncomplicated *adj.*	unconverted *adj.*	undefended *adj.*	undisciplined *adj.*
uncomplimentary *adj.*	unconvincing *adj.*	undefiled *adj.*	undiscovered *adj.*
uncomprehending *adj.*	uncooperative *adj.*	undemanding *adj.*	undiscriminating *adj.*
unconcealed *adj.*	uncoordinated *adj.*	undemocratic *adj.*	undismayed *adj.*

THESAURUS

unaffected¹ artless, genuine, honest, ingenuous, naive, natural, plain, simple, sincere, straightforward, unassuming, unpretentious, unsophisticated, unspoilt, unstudied, without airs

unaffected² aloof, impervious, not influenced, proof, unaltered, unchanged, unimpressed, unmoved, unresponsive, unstirred, untouched

unafraid confident, daring, dauntless, fearless, intrepid, unfearing, unshakable

unalterable fixed, fixed as the laws of the Medes and the Persians, immutable, invariable, permanent, steadfast, unchangeable, unchanging

unanimity accord, agreement, chorus, concert, concord, concurrence, consensus, harmony, like-mindedness, one mind, unison, unity

unanimous agreed, agreeing, at one, common, concerted, concordant, harmonious, in agreement, in complete accord, like-minded, of one mind, united

unanimously by common consent, nem. con., unitedly, unopposed, with one accord, without exception, without opposition

unanswerable **1.** absolute, conclusive, incontestable, incontrovertible, indisputable, irrefutable, unarguable, undeniable **2.** insoluble, insolvable, unascertainable, unexplainable, unresolvable

unanswered disputed, ignored, in doubt, open, undecided, undenied, unnoticed, unrefuted, unresolved, unsettled, up in the air, vexed

unappetizing distasteful, insipid, offputting (*Brit. inf.*), tasteless, unappealing, unattractive, uninteresting, uninviting, unpalatable, unpleasant, unsavoury, vapid

unapproachable **1.** aloof, chilly, cool,

distant, frigid, offish (*Inf.*), remote, reserved, standoffish, unfriendly, unsociable, withdrawn **2.** inaccessible, out of reach, out-of-the-way, remote, un-get-at-able (*Inf.*), unreachable

unarmed assailable, defenceless, exposed, helpless, open, open to attack, unarmoured, unprotected, weak, weaponless, without arms

unasked **1.** gratuitous, spontaneous, unbidden, undemanded, undesired, uninvited, unprompted, unrequested, unsought, unwanted **2.** off one's own bat, of one's own accord, voluntarily, without prompting

unassailable **1.** impregnable, invincible, invulnerable, secure, well-defended **2.** absolute, conclusive, incontestable, incontrovertible, indisputable, irrefutable, positive, proven, sound, undeniable

unassertive backward, bashful, diffident, meek, mousy, retiring, self-effacing, timid, timorous, unassuming

unassuming diffident, humble, meek, modest, quiet, reserved, retiring, self-effacing, simple, unassertive, unobtrusive, unostentatious, unpretentious

unattached **1.** autonomous, free, independent, nonaligned, unaffiliated, uncommitted **2.** a free agent, available, by oneself, footloose and fancy-free, not spoken for, on one's own, single, unengaged, unmarried

unattended **1.** abandoned, disregarded, ignored, left alone, not cared for, unguarded, unwatched **2.** alone, on one's own, unaccompanied, unescorted

unauthorized illegal, unapproved, unconstitutional, unlawful, unofficial, unsanctioned, unwarranted

unavailing abortive, bootless, fruitless, futile, idle, ineffective, ineffectual, of no

avail, pointless, to no purpose, unproductive, unsuccessful, useless, vain

unavoidable bound to happen, certain, compulsory, fated, ineluctable, inescapable, inevitable, inexorable, necessary, obligatory, sure

unaware heedless, ignorant, incognizant, oblivious, unconscious, unenlightened, uninformed, unknowing, unmindful, unsuspecting

unawares **1.** aback, abruptly, by surprise, off guard, on the hop (*Brit. inf.*), suddenly, unexpectedly, unprepared, without warning **2.** accidentally, by accident, by mistake, inadvertently, mistakenly, unconsciously, unintentionally, unknowingly, unwittingly

unbalanced **1.** asymmetrical, irregular, lopsided, not balanced, shaky, unequal, uneven, unstable, unsymmetrical, wobbly **2.** crazy, demented, deranged, disturbed, eccentric, erratic, insane, irrational, lunatic, mad, *non compos mentis*, not all there, touched, unhinged, unsound, unstable **3.** biased, inequitable, one-sided, partial, partisan, prejudiced, unfair, unjust

unbearable insufferable, insupportable, intolerable, oppressive, too much (*Inf.*), unacceptable, unendurable

unbeatable indomitable, invincible, more than a match for, unconquerable, unstoppable, unsurpassable

unbeaten **1.** triumphant, unbowed, undefeated, unsubdued, unsurpassed, unvanquished, victorious, winning **2.** new, untouched, untried, untrodden, virgin

unbecoming **1.** ill-suited, inappropriate, incongruous, unattractive, unbefitting, unfit, unflattering, unsightly, unsuitable, unsuited **2.** discreditable, improper, indecorous, indeli-

unbeknown (ˌʌnbɪˈnəʊn) adv. (sentence modifier; foll. by to) without the knowledge (of a person): unbeknown to him she had left the country. Also (esp. Brit.): **unbeknownst**.

unbelievable (ˌʌnbɪˈliːvəbəl) adj. unable to be believed; incredible. —ˌunbeˌlievaˈbility n. —ˌunbeˈlievably adv.

unbeliever (ˌʌnbɪˈliːvə) n. a person who does not believe, esp. in religious matters.

unbend (ʌnˈbɛnd) vb. -bending, -bent. 1. to release or be released from the restraints of formality and ceremony. 2. Inf. to relax (the mind) or (of the mind) to become relaxed. 3. to become or be made straightened out from an originally bent shape. 4. (tr.) Naut. a. to remove (a sail) from a stay, mast, etc. b. to untie (a rope, etc.) or cast (a cable) loose.

unbending (ʌnˈbɛndɪŋ) adj. 1. rigid or inflexible. 2. characterized by sternness or severity: an unbending rule. —unˈbendingly adv. —unˈbendingness n.

unbidden (ʌnˈbɪdən) adj. 1. not ordered or commanded; voluntary or spontaneous. 2. not invited or asked.

unbind (ʌnˈbaɪnd) vb. -binding, -bound. (tr.) 1. to set free from restraining bonds or chains. 2. to unfasten or make loose (a bond, etc.).

unblushing (ʌnˈblʌʃɪŋ) adj. immodest or shameless. —unˈblushingly adv.

unbolt (ʌnˈbəʊlt) vb. (tr.) 1. to unfasten a bolt of (a door). 2. to undo (the nut) on a bolt.

unborn (ʌnˈbɔːn) adj. 1. not yet born or brought to birth. 2. still to come in the future: the unborn world.

unbosom (ʌnˈbʊzəm) vb. (tr.) to relieve (oneself) of (secrets, etc.) by telling someone.

unbounded (ʌnˈbaʊndɪd) adj. having no boundaries or limits. —unˈboundedly adv. —unˈboundedness n.

unbowed (ʌnˈbaʊd) adj. 1. not bowed or bent. 2. free or unconquered.

unbridled (ʌnˈbraɪdəld) adj. 1. with all restraints removed. 2. (of a horse, etc.) wearing no bridle. —unˈbridledly adv. —unˈbridledness n.

unbroken (ʌnˈbrəʊkən) adj. 1. complete or whole. 2. continuous or incessant. 3. undaunted in spirit. 4. (of animals, esp. horses) not tamed; wild. 5. not disturbed or upset: the unbroken quiet of the afternoon. 6. (of a record, esp. at sport) not improved upon. —unˈbrokenly adv. —unˈbrokenness n.

unburden (ʌnˈbɜːdən) vb. (tr.) 1. to remove a load or burden from. 2. to relieve or make free (one's mind, oneself, etc.) of a worry, trouble, etc., by revelation or confession.

uncalled-for adj. unnecessary or unwarranted.

uncanny (ʌnˈkænɪ) adj. 1. characterized by apparently supernatural wonder, horror, etc. 2. beyond what is normal: uncanny accuracy. —unˈcannily adv. —unˈcanniness n.

uncared-for adj. not cared for; neglected.

unceremonious (ˌʌnsɛrɪˈməʊnɪəs) adj. without ceremony; informal, abrupt, rude, or undignified. —ˌuncereˈmoniously adv. —ˌuncereˈmoniousness n.

uncertain (ʌnˈsɜːtən) adj. 1. not able to be accurately known or predicted: the issue is uncertain. 2. (when postpositive, often foll. by of) not sure or confident (about): he was uncertain of the date. 3. not precisely determined or decided: uncertain plans. 4. not to be depended upon: an uncertain vote. 5. liable to variation; changeable: the weather is uncertain. 6. in no uncertain terms. a. unambiguously. b. forcefully. —unˈcertainly adv. —unˈcertainty n.

undisputed adj.	**unengaged** adj.	**unfetter** vb.	**unfurnished** adj.
undistinguishable adj.	**unenlightened** adj.	**unfettered** adj.	**ungenerous** adj.
undistinguished adj.	**unenterprising** adj.	**unflattering** adj.	**ungracious** adj.
undisturbed adj.	**unenthusiastic** adj.	**unforced** adj.	**ungrammatical** adj.
undivided adj.	**unenviable** adj.	**unforeseeable** adj.	**ungrateful** adj.
undrinkable adj.	**unescorted** adj.	**unforeseen** adj.	**unhampered** adj.
uneaten adj.	**unethical** adj.	**unforgettable** adj.	**unharmed** adj.
unedited adj.	**unexaggerated** adj.	**unforgivable** adj.	**unheated** adj.
uneducable adj.	**unexpired** adj.	**unforgiven** adj.	**unheeded** adj.
uneducated adj.	**unexplained** adj.	**unforgiving** adj.	**unheeding** adj.
unemancipated adj.	**unexploited** adj.	**unforgotten** adj.	**unhelpful** adj.
unemotional adj.	**unexplored** adj.	**unformed** adj.	**unheralded** adj.
unencumbered adj.	**unexpressed** adj.	**unforthcoming** adj.	**unheroic** adj.
unending adj.	**unexpurgated** adj.	**unfortified** adj.	**unhesitating** adj.
unendowed adj.	**unfashionable** adj.	**unfrequented** adj.	**unhindered** adj.
unendurable adj.	**unfeigned** adj.	**unfulfilled** adj.	**unhuman** adj.

THESAURUS

unbelief atheism, disbelief, distrust, doubt, incredulity, scepticism

unbelievable astonishing, beyond belief, far-fetched, implausible, impossible, improbable, inconceivable, incredible, outlandish, preposterous, questionable, staggering, unconvincing, unimaginable, unthinkable

unbeliever agnostic, atheist, disbeliever, doubting Thomas, infidel, sceptic

unbelieving disbelieving, distrustful, doubtful, doubting, dubious, incredulous, sceptical, suspicious, unconvinced

unbend 1. be informal, calm down, cool it (Sl.), ease up, let it all hang out (Sl.), let oneself go, let up, loosen up, relax, slacken, slow down, take it easy (Inf.), unbutton (Inf.), unwind 2. put straight, straighten, uncoil, uncurl

unbending 1. aloof, distant, formal, inflexible, reserved, rigid, stiff, uptight (Sl.) 2. firm, hard-line, intractable, resolute, severe, strict, stubborn, tough, uncompromising, unyielding

unbiased disinterested, dispassionate, equitable, even-handed, fair, impartial, just, neutral, objective, open-minded, unprejudiced

unbidden 1. free, spontaneous, unforced, unprompted, voluntary, willing 2. unasked, uninvited, unwanted, unwelcome

unbind free, loosen, release, set free, un-

chain, undo, unfasten, unfetter, unloose, unshackle, untie, unyoke

unblemished flawless, immaculate, perfect, pure, spotless, unflawed, unspotted, unstained, unsullied, untarnished

unborn 1. awaited, embryonic, expected, in utero 2. coming, future, hereafter, latter, subsequent, to come

unbosom admit, confess, confide, disburden, disclose, divulge, get (something) off one's chest (Inf.), get (something) out of one's system, lay bare, let out, reveal, tell, unburden

unbounded absolute, boundless, endless, immeasurable, infinite, limitless, unbridled, unchecked, unconstrained, uncontrolled, unlimited, unrestrained, vast

unbreakable armoured, durable, indestructible, infrangible, lasting, nonbreakable, resistant, rugged, shatterproof, solid, strong, toughened

unbridled excessive, intemperate, licentious, rampant, riotous, unchecked, unconstrained, uncontrolled, uncurbed, ungovernable, ungoverned, unrestrained, unruly, violent, wanton

unbroken 1. complete, entire, intact, solid, total, unimpaired, whole 2. ceaseless, constant, continuous, endless, incessant, progressive, serried, successive, uninterrupted, unremitting 3. deep, fast, profound, sound, undisturbed, unruffled, untroubled 4. un-

bowed, unsubdued, untamed

unburden 1. disburden, discharge, disencumber, ease the load, empty, lighten, relieve, unload 2. come clean (Inf.), confess, confide, disclose, get (something) off one's chest (Inf.), lay bare, make a clean breast of, reveal, tell all, unbosom

uncalled-for gratuitous, inappropriate, needless, undeserved, unjust, unjustified, unnecessary, unprovoked, unwarranted, unwelcome

uncanny 1. creepy (Inf.), eerie, eldritch (Poetic), mysterious, preternatural, queer, spooky (Inf.), strange, supernatural, unearthly, unnatural, weird 2. astonishing, astounding, exceptional, extraordinary, fantastic, incredible, inspired, miraculous, prodigious, remarkable, singular, unheard-of, unusual

unceasing ceaseless, constant, continual, continuing, continuous, endless, incessant, never-ending, nonstop, perpetual, persistent, unending, unfailing, unremitting

uncertain 1. ambiguous, chancy, conjectural, doubtful, incalculable, indefinite, indeterminate, indistinct, questionable, risky, speculative, undetermined, unforeseeable, unpredictable 2. ambivalent, doubtful, dubious, hazy, in two minds, irresolute, unclear, unconfirmed, undecided, undetermined, unfixed, unresolved, unsettled, unsure, up in the

unchristian (ʌnˈkrɪstʃən) *adj.* **1.** not in accordance with the principles or ethics of Christianity. **2.** non-Christian or pagan. —**un'christianly** *adv.*

uncial ('ʌnsɪəl) *adj.* **1.** of, relating to, or written in majuscule letters, as used in Greek and Latin manuscripts of the third to ninth centuries, that resemble modern capitals, but are characterized by much greater curvature. ~*n.* **2.** an uncial letter or manuscript. —'**uncially** *adv.*

uncircumcised (ʌnˈsɜːkəmˌsaɪzd) *adj.* **1.** not circumcised. **2.** not Jewish; gentile. **3.** *Theol.* not purified. —ˌ**uncircum'cision** *n.*

uncivil (ʌnˈsɪvəl) *adj.* **1.** lacking civility or good manners. **2.** an obsolete word for **uncivilized.** —**uncivility** (ˌʌnsɪˈvɪlɪtɪ) *n.* —**un'civilly** *adv.*

uncivilized *or* **-ised** (ʌnˈsɪvɪˌlaɪzd) *adj.* **1.** (of a tribe or people) not yet civilized, esp. preliterate. **2.** lacking culture or sophistication. —**un'civi,lizedness** *or* **-isedness** *n.*

unclasp (ʌnˈklɑːsp) *vb.* **1.** (*tr.*) to unfasten the clasp of (something). **2.** to release one's grip (upon an object).

uncle ('ʌŋkəl) *n.* **1.** a brother of one's father or mother. **2.** the husband of one's aunt. **3.** a term of address sometimes used by children for a male friend of their parents. **4.** *Sl.* a pawnbroker. ~Related adj.: **avuncular.**

unclean (ʌnˈkliːn) *adj.* lacking moral, spiritual, or physical cleanliness. —**un'cleanness** *n.*

Uncle Sam (sæm) *n.* a personification of the government of the United States.

Uncle Tom (tɒm) *n.* *U.S. inf., derog.* a Negro whose behaviour towards white people is regarded as servile.

unclose (ʌnˈkləʊz) *vb.* **1.** to open or cause to open. **2.** to come or bring to light.

unclothe (ʌnˈkləʊð) *vb.* **-clothing, -clothed** *or* **-clad.** (*tr.*) **1.** to take off garments from; strip. **2.** to uncover or lay bare.

uncoil (ʌnˈkɔɪl) *vb.* to unwind or become unwound; untwist.

uncomfortable (ʌnˈkʌmftəbəl) *adj.* **1.** not comfortable. **2.** feeling or causing discomfort or unease; disquieting. —**un'comfortableness** *n.* —**un'comfortably** *adv.*

uncommitted (ˌʌnkəˈmɪtɪd) *adj.* not bound or pledged to a specific opinion, course of action, or cause.

uncommon (ʌnˈkɒmən) *adj.* **1.** outside or beyond normal experience, etc. **2.** in excess of what is normal: *an uncommon liking for honey.* ~*adv.* **3.** an archaic word for **uncommonly** (sense 2). —**un'commonness** *n.*

uncommonly (ʌnˈkɒmənlɪ) *adv.* **1.** in an uncommon or unusual manner or degree; rarely. **2.** (intensifier): *you're uncommonly friendly.*

uncommunicative (ˌʌnkəˈmjuːnɪkətɪv) *adj.* disinclined to talk or give information or opinions. —ˌ**uncom'municatively** *adv.* —ˌ**uncom'municativeness** *n.*

uncompromising (ʌnˈkɒmprəˌmaɪzɪŋ) *adj.* not prepared to give ground or to compromise. —**un'compro,misingly** *adv.*

unconcern (ˌʌnkənˈsɜːn) *n.* apathy or indifference.

unconcerned (ˌʌnkənˈsɜːnd) *adj.* **1.** lacking in concern or involvement. **2.** untroubled. —**unconcernedly** (ˌʌnkənˈsɜːnɪdlɪ) *adv.*

unconditional (ˌʌnkənˈdɪʃənəl) *adj.* without conditions or limitations; total: *unconditional surrender.* —ˌ**uncon'ditionally** *adv.*

unhurried *adj.*	**uninjured** *adj.*	**unlit** *adj.*	**unobserved** *adj.*
unhurt *adj.*	**uninspired** *adj.*	**unmanageable** *adj.*	**unobtainable** *adj.*
unhygienic *adj.*	**uninspiring** *adj.*	**unmarked** *adj.*	**unobtained** *adj.*
unidentified *adj.*	**unintelligent** *adj.*	**unmarried** *adj.*	**unobtrusive** *adj.*
unillustrated *adj.*	**unintelligible** *adj.*	**unmatched** *adj.*	**unopened** *adj.*
unimaginable *adj.*	**unintended** *adj.*	**unmemorable** *adj.*	**unopposed** *adj.*
unimaginative *adj.*	**unintentional** *adj.*	**unmerchantable** *adj.*	**unoriginal** *adj.*
unimpeded *adj.*	**uninteresting** *adj.*	**unmoved** *adj.*	**unorthodox** *adj.*
unimportant *adj.*	**uninterrupted** *adj.*	**unmusical** *adj.*	**unostentatious** *adj.*
unimpressed *adj.*	**uninvited** *adj.*	**unnamed** *adj.*	**unpaid** *adj.*
uninformative *adj.*	**uninviting** *adj.*	**unnavigable** *adj.*	**unpalatable** *adj.*
uninformed *adj.*	**unjustified** *adj.*	**unnegotiable** *adj.*	**unpardonable** *adj.*
uninhabitable *adj.*	**unladylike** *adj.*	**unneighbourly** *adj.*	**unpasteurized** *adj.*
uninhabited *adj.*	**unlawful** *adj.*	**unnoticed** *adj.*	**unpatriotic** *adj.*
uninhibited *adj.*	**unlicensed** *adj.*	**unobjectionable** *adj.*	**unperceptive** *adj.*
uninitiated *adj.*	**unlined** *adj.*	**unobliging** *adj.*	**unperfected** *adj.*

THESAURUS

air, vacillating, vague **3.** changeable, erratic, fitful, hesitant, inconstant, insecure, irregular, precarious, unpredictable, unreliable, vacillating, variable, wavering

uncertainty ambiguity, bewilderment, confusion, dilemma, doubt, hesitancy, hesitation, inconclusiveness, indecision, irresolution, lack of confidence, misgiving, mystification, perplexity, puzzlement, qualm, quandary, scepticism, state of suspense, unpredictability, vagueness

unchangeable changeless, constant, fixed, immutable, inevitable, invariable, irreversible, permanent, stable, steadfast, strong, unalterable

unchanging abiding, changeless, constant, continuing, enduring, eternal, immutable, imperishable, lasting, permanent, perpetual, unchanged, unfading, unvarying

uncharitable cruel, hardhearted, insensitive, mean, merciless, stingy, unchristian, unfeeling, unforgiving, unfriendly, ungenerous, unkind, unsympathetic

uncharted not mapped, strange, undiscovered, unexplored, unfamiliar, unknown, unplumbed, virgin

unchaste depraved, dissolute, fallen, immodest, immoral, impure, lewd, loose, promiscuous, unvirtuous, wanton

uncivil bad-mannered, bearish, boorish, brusque, churlish, discourteous, disrespectful, gruff, ill-bred, ill-mannered, impolite, rude, surly, uncouth, unmannerly

uncivilized **1.** barbarian, barbaric, barbarous, illiterate, primitive, savage, wild **2.** beyond the pale, boorish, brutish, churlish, coarse, gross, philistine, uncouth, uncultivated, uncultured, uneducated, unmannered, unpolished, unsophisticated, vulgar

unclean contaminated, corrupt, defiled, dirty, evil, filthy, foul, impure, nasty, polluted, soiled, spotted, stained, sullied, tainted

uncomfortable **1.** awkward, causing discomfort, cramped, disagreeable, hard, ill-fitting, incommodious, irritating, painful, rough, troublesome **2.** awkward, confused, discomfited, disquieted, distressed, disturbed, embarrassed, ill at ease, out of place, self-conscious, troubled, uneasy

uncommitted floating, free, free-floating, neutral, nonaligned, nonpartisan, not involved, (sitting) on the fence, unattached, uninvolved

uncommon **1.** bizarre, curious, few and far between, infrequent, novel, odd, out of the ordinary, peculiar, queer, rare, scarce, singular, strange, unfamiliar, unusual **2.** distinctive, exceptional, extraordinary, incomparable, inimitable, notable, noteworthy, outstanding, rare, remarkable, singular, special, superior, unparalleled, unprecedented

uncommonly **1.** hardly ever, infrequently, not often, occasionally, only now and then, rarely, scarcely ever, seldom **2.** exceptionally, extremely, particularly, peculiarly, remarkably, strangely, unusually, very

uncommunicative close, curt, guarded, reserved, reticent, retiring, secretive, short, shy, silent, taciturn, tight-lipped, unforthcoming, unresponsive, unsociable, withdrawn

uncompromising decided, firm, hard-line, inexorable, inflexible, intransigent, obdurate, obstinate, rigid, steadfast, strict, stubborn, tough, unbending, unyielding

unconcern aloofness, apathy, detachment, indifference, insouciance, lack of interest, nonchalance, remoteness, uninterest, uninterestedness

unconcerned **1.** aloof, apathetic, cool, detached, dispassionate, distant, incurious, indifferent, oblivious, uninterested, uninvolved, unmoved, unsympathetic **2.** blithe, carefree, careless, easy, insouciant, nonchalant, not bothered, relaxed, serene, unperturbed, unruffled, untroubled, unworried

unconditional absolute, categorical, complete, downright, entire, explicit, full, out-and-out, outright, plenary, positive, thoroughgoing, total, unlimited, unqualified, unreserved, unrestricted, utter

uncongenial antagonistic, antipathetic, disagreeable, discordant, displeasing, distasteful, incompatible, not one's cup of tea (*Inf.*), unharmonious, uninviting, unpleasant, unsuited, unsympathetic

unconnected **1.** detached, disconnected, divided, independent, separate **3.** disconnected, disjointed, illogical, incoherent, irrel-

unconscionable (ʌnˈkɒnʃənəbəl) *adj.* **1.** unscrupulous or unprincipled: *an unconscionable liar.* **2.** immoderate or excessive: *unconscionable demands.* —**unˈconscionably** *adv.*

unconscious (ʌnˈkɒnʃəs) *adj.* **1.** lacking normal sensory awareness of the environment; insensible. **2.** not aware of one's actions, behaviour, etc.: *unconscious of his bad manners.* **3.** characterized by lack of awareness or intention: *an unconscious blunder.* **4.** coming from or produced by the unconscious: *unconscious resentment.* ∼*n.* **5.** *Psychoanal.* the part of the mind containing instincts, impulses, images, and ideas that are not available for direct examination. —**unˈconsciously** *adv.* —**unˈconsciousness** *n.*

unconstitutional (ˌʌnkɒnstɪˈtjuːʃənəl) *adj.* at variance with or not permitted by a constitution. —ˌunconstiˌtutionˈality *n.*

unconventional (ˌʌnkənˈvɛnʃənəl) *adj.* not conforming to accepted rules or standards. —ˌunconˈventionˈality *n.* —ˌunconˈventionally *adv.*

uncork (ʌnˈkɔːk) *vb.* (*tr.*) **1.** to draw the cork from (a bottle, etc.). **2.** to release or unleash (emotions, etc.).

uncouple (ʌnˈkʌpəl) *vb.* **1.** to disconnect or unfasten or become disconnected or unfastened. **2.** (*tr.*) to set loose; release.

uncouth (ʌnˈkuːθ) *adj.* lacking in good manners, refinement, or grace. —**unˈcouthly** *adv.* —**unˈcouthness** *n.*

uncover (ʌnˈkʌvə) *vb.* **1.** (*tr.*) to remove the cover, cap, top, etc., from. **2.** (*tr.*) to reveal or disclose: *to uncover a*

plot. **3.** to take off (one's head covering), esp. as a mark of respect.

unction (ˈʌŋkʃən) *n.* **1.** *Chiefly R.C. & Eastern Churches.* the act of anointing with oil in sacramental ceremonies, in the conferring of holy orders. **2.** excessive suavity or affected charm. **3.** an ointment or unguent. **4.** anything soothing. —**ˈunctionless** *adj.*

unctuous (ˈʌŋktjʊəs) *adj.* **1.** slippery or greasy. **2.** affecting an oily charm. —**unctuosity** (ˌʌŋktjuˈɒsɪtɪ) *or* **ˈunctuousness** *n.* —**ˈunctuously** *adv.*

undaunted (ʌnˈdɔːntɪd) *adj.* not put off, discouraged, or beaten. —**unˈdauntedly** *adv.* —**unˈdauntedness** *n.*

undeceive (ˌʌndɪˈsiːv) *vb.* (*tr.*) to reveal the truth to (someone previously misled or deceived). —ˌundeˈceivable *adj.* —ˌundeˈceiver *n.*

undecided (ˌʌndɪˈsaɪdɪd) *adj.* **1.** not having made up one's mind. **2.** (of an issue, problem, etc.) not agreed or decided upon. —ˌundeˈcidedly *adv.* —ˌundeˈcidedness *n.*

undeniable (ˌʌndɪˈnaɪəbəl) *adj.* **1.** unquestionably or obviously true. **2.** of unquestionable excellence: *a man of undeniable character.* **3.** unable to be resisted or denied. —ˌundeˈniableness *n.* —ˌundeˈniably *adv.*

under (ˈʌndə) *prep.* **1.** directly below; on, to, or beneath the underside or base of: *under one's feet.* **2.** less than: *under forty years.* **3.** lower in rank than: *under a corporal.* **4.** subject to the supervision, jurisdiction, control, or influence of. **5.** subject to (conditions); in (certain circumstances). **6.** within a classification of: *a book under*

unperturbable *adj.*	**unproclaimed** *adj.*	**unrecognizable** *adj.*	**unresolved** *adj.*
unperturbed *adj.*	**unproductive** *adj.*	**unrecognized** *adj.*	**unrestrained** *adj.*
unplanned *adj.*	**unprofitable** *adj.*	**unreconciled** *adj.*	**unrestricted** *adj.*
unplayable *adj.*	**unpromising** *adj.*	**unrecorded** *adj.*	**unromantic** *adj.*
unpleasing *adj.*	**unprompted** *adj.*	**unrefined** *adj.*	**unsafe** *adj.*
unplug *vb.*	**unpronounceable** *adj.*	**unregistered** *adj.*	**unsatisfactory** *adj.*
unpolished *adj.*	**unpropitious** *adj.*	**unregulated** *adj.*	**unsatisfied** *adj.*
unpolluted *adj.*	**unprotected** *adj.*	**unrehearsed** *adj.*	**unsatisfying** *adj.*
unpopulated *adj.*	**unprotesting** *adj.*	**unrelated** *adj.*	**unscheduled** *adj.*
unpredictable *adj.*	**unproved** *adj.*	**unreliable** *adj.*	**unscientific** *adj.*
unprepared *adj.*	**unproven** *adj.*	**unrepeatable** *adj.*	**unseasoned** *adj.*
unprepossessing *adj.*	**unprovoked** *adj.*	**unrepentant** *adj.*	**unseaworthy** *adj.*
unpresentable *adj.*	**unpublished** *adj.*	**unreported** *adj.*	**unsegregated** *adj.*
unpressed *adj.*	**unpunished** *adj.*	**unrepresentative** *adj.*	**unselective** *adj.*
unpretentious *adj.*	**unquestioning** *adj.*	**unrepresented** *adj.*	**unselfconscious** *adj.*
unpriced *adj.*	**unrealistic** *adj.*	**unrequited** *adj.*	**unsentimental** *adj.*

THESAURUS

evant, meaningless, nonsensical, not related, unrelated

unconquerable **1.** indomitable, invincible, unbeatable, undefeatable, unyielding **2.** enduring, ingrained, innate, insurmountable, inveterate, irrepressible, irresistible, overpowering

unconscionable **1.** amoral, criminal, unethical, unfair, unjust, unprincipled, unscrupulous **2.** excessive, exorbitant, extravagant, extreme, immoderate, inordinate, outrageous, preposterous, unreasonable

unconscious **1.** blacked out (*Inf.*), comatose, dead to the world, insensible, knocked out, numb, out, out cold, senseless, stunned **2.** blind to, deaf to, heedless, ignorant, in ignorance, lost to, oblivious, unaware, unknowing, unmindful, unsuspecting **3.** accidental, inadvertent, unintended, unintentional, unpremeditated, unwitting **4.** automatic, gut (*Inf.*), inherent, innate, instinctive, involuntary, latent, reflex, repressed, subconscious, subliminal, suppressed, unrealized

uncontrollable beside oneself, carried away, frantic, furious, irrepressible, irresistible, like one possessed, mad, strong, ungovernable, unmanageable, unruly, violent, wild

uncontrolled boisterous, furious, lacking self-control, out of control, out of hand, rampant, riotous, running wild, unbridled, unchecked, uncurbed, undisciplined, ungoverned, unrestrained, unruly, unsubmissive, untrammelled, violent

unconventional atypical, bizarre, bohemian, different, eccentric, far-out (*Sl.*), freakish (*Inf.*), idiosyncratic, individual, indi-

vidualistic, informal, irregular, nonconformist, odd, offbeat, original, out of the ordinary, uncustomary, unorthodox, unusual, way-out (*Inf.*)

unconvincing dubious, feeble, fishy (*Inf.*), flimsy, hard to believe, implausible, improbable, inconclusive, lame, questionable, specious, suspect, thin, unlikely, unpersuasive, weak

uncoordinated all thumbs, awkward, bumbling, bungling, butterfingered (*Inf.*), clodhopping (*Inf.*), clumsy, graceless, heavy-footed, inept, lumbering, maladroit, ungainly, ungraceful

uncounted countless, infinite, innumerable, legion, multitudinous, myriad, numberless, unnumbered, untold

uncouth awkward, barbaric, boorish, clownish, clumsy, coarse, crude, gawky, graceless, gross, ill-mannered, loutish, loberly, oafish, rough, rude, rustic, uncivilized, uncultivated, ungainly, unrefined, unseemly, vulgar

uncover **1.** bare, lay open, lift the lid, open, show, strip, take the wraps off, unwrap **2.** bring to light, disclose, discover, divulge, expose, lay bare, make known, reveal, unearth, unmask

uncritical easily pleased, indiscriminate, undiscerning, undiscriminating, unexacting, unfussy, unperceptive, unselective, unthinking

undeceive be honest with, correct, disabuse, disillusion, enlighten, open (someone's) eyes (to), put (someone) right, set

(someone) straight, shatter (someone's) illusions

undecided **1.** ambivalent, dithering, doubtful, dubious, hesitant, in two minds, irresolute, swithering (*Scot.*), torn, uncertain, uncommitted, unsure, wavering **2.** debatable, indefinite, in the balance, moot, open, pending, tentative, unconcluded, undetermined, unsettled, up in the air, vague

undecipherable crabbed, cryptic, hieroglyphic, illegible, impenetrable, incomprehensible, indecipherable, indistinct, undistinguishable, unreadable, unrecognizable

undefended defenceless, exposed, naked, open to attack, unarmed, unfortified, unguarded, unprotected, vulnerable, wide open

undefiled chaste, clean, clear, flawless, immaculate, pure, sinless, spotless, unblemished, unsoiled, unspotted, unstained, unsullied, virginal

undefined **1.** formless, hazy, indefinite, indistinct, shadowy, tenuous, vague **2.** imprecise, indeterminate, inexact, unclear, unexplained, unspecified

undemonstrative aloof, cold, contained, distant, formal, impassive, reserved, restrained, reticent, stiff, stolid, unaffectionate, uncommunicative, unemotional, unresponsive, withdrawn

undeniable beyond (a) doubt, beyond question, certain, clear, evident, incontestable, incontrovertible, indisputable, indubitable, irrefutable, manifest, obvious, patent, proven, sound, sure, unassailable, undoubted, unquestionable

theology. **7.** known by: *under an assumed name.* **8.** planted with: *a field under corn.* **9.** powered by: *under sail.* **10.** *Astrol.* during the period that the sun is in (a sign of the zodiac): *born under Aries.* ~*adv.* **11.** below; to a position underneath something. **12. one degree under.** *Inf.* off colour; ill.

under- *prefix.* **1.** below or beneath: *underarm; underground.* **2.** of lesser importance or lower rank: *undersecretary.* **3.** insufficient or insufficiently: *underemployed.* **4.** indicating secrecy or deception: *underhand.*

underachieve (ˌʌndərəˈtʃiːv) *vb.* (*intr.*) to fail to achieve an expected result. —**underaˈchiever** *n.* —ˌunderaˈchievement *n.*

underarm (ˈʌndərˌɑːm) *adj.* **1.** (of a measurement) extending along the arm from wrist to armpit. **2.** *Cricket, tennis, etc.* of or denoting a style of throwing, bowling, or serving in which the hand is swung below shoulder level. **3.** below the arm. ~*adv.* **4.** in an underarm style.

underbid (ˌʌndəˈbɪd) *vb.* **-bidding, -bid.** **1.** to submit a bid lower than that of (others): *Irena underbid the other dealers.* **2.** to submit an excessively low bid for. **3.** *Bridge.* to make a bid that will win fewer tricks than expected: *he underbid his hand.* —**underˈbidder** *n.*

undercarriage (ˈʌndəˌkærɪdʒ) *n.* **1.** Also called: **landing gear.** the assembly of wheels, shock absorbers, struts, etc., that supports an aircraft on the ground and enables it to take off and land. **2.** the framework that supports the body of a vehicle, carriage, etc.

undercharge (ˌʌndəˈtʃɑːdʒ) *vb.* **1.** to charge too little for. **2.** (*tr.*) to load (a gun, cannon, etc.) with an inadequate charge.

underclothes (ˈʌndəˌkləʊðz) *pl. n.* a variant of **underwear.** Also called: **underclothing.**

undercoat (ˈʌndəˌkəʊt) *n.* **1.** a coat of paint or other substance applied before the top coat. **2.** a coat worn under an overcoat. ~*vb.* **3.** (*tr.*) to apply an undercoat to (a surface).

undercover (ˌʌndəˈkʌvə) *adj.* done or acting in secret: *undercover operations.*

undercurrent (ˈʌndəˌkʌrənt) *n.* **1.** a current that is not apparent at the surface or lies beneath another current. **2.** an opinion, emotion, etc., lying beneath apparent feeling or meaning. ~Also called: **underflow.**

undercut *vb.* (ˌʌndəˈkʌt), **-cutting, -cut.** **1.** to charge less than (a competitor) in order to obtain trade. **2.** to cut away the under part of (something). **3.** *Golf, tennis, etc.* to hit (a ball) in such a way as to impart backspin. ~*n.* (ˈʌndəˌkʌt). **4.** the act of cutting underneath. **5.** a part that is cut away underneath. **6.** a tenderloin of beef. **7.** *Forestry, chiefly U.S.* a notch cut in a tree trunk, to en-

sure a clean break in felling. **8.** *Tennis, golf, etc.* a stroke that imparts backspin to the ball.

underdeveloped (ˌʌndədɪˈvɛləpt) *adj.* **1.** immature or undersized. **2.** relating to societies in which both the surplus capital and the social organization necessary to advance are lacking. **3.** *Photog.* (of a film, etc.) processed in developer for less than the required time.

underdog (ˈʌndəˌdɒg) *n.* **1.** the losing competitor in a fight or contest. **2.** a person in adversity or a position of inferiority.

underdone (ˌʌndəˈdʌn) *adj.* insufficiently or lightly cooked.

underemployed (ˌʌndərɪmˈplɔɪd) *adj.* not fully or adequately employed.

underestimate *vb.* (ˌʌndərˈɛstɪˌmeɪt). (*tr.*) **1.** to make too low an estimate of: *he underestimated the cost.* **2.** to think insufficiently highly of: *to underestimate a person.* ~*n.* (ˌʌndərˈɛstɪmɪt). **3.** too low an estimate. —ˌunderˌestiˈmation *n.*

underexpose (ˌʌndərɪkˈspəʊz) *vb.* (*tr.*) **1.** *Photog.* to expose (a film, plate, or paper) for too short a period or with insufficient light so as not to produce the required effect. **2.** (*often passive*) to fail to subject to appropriate or expected publicity. —ˌunderexˈposure *n.*

underfelt (ˈʌndəˌfɛlt) *n.* thick felt laid between floorboards and carpet to increase insulation.

underfoot (ˌʌndəˈfʊt) *adv.* **1.** underneath the feet; on the ground. **2.** in a position of subjugation.

undergarment (ˈʌndəˌgɑːmənt) *n.* any garment worn under the visible outer clothes, usually next to the skin.

undergo (ˌʌndəˈgəʊ) *vb.* **-going, -went, -gone.** (*tr.*) to experience, endure, or sustain: *to undergo a change of feelings.* —ˌunderˈgoer *n.*

undergraduate (ˌʌndəˈgrædjʊɪt) *n.* a person studying in a university for a first degree. Sometimes shortened to **undergrad.**

underground *adj.* (ˈʌndəˌgraʊnd), *adv.* (ˌʌndəˈgraʊnd). **1.** occurring, situated, used, or going below ground level: *an underground explosion.* **2.** secret; hidden: *underground activities.* ~*n.* (ˈʌndəˌgraʊnd). **3.** a space or region below ground level. **4. a.** a movement dedicated to overthrowing a government or occupation forces, as in the European countries occupied by the German army in World War II. **b.** (*as modifier*): *an underground group.* **5.** (*often preceded by the*) an electric passenger railway operated in underground tunnels. U.S. equivalent: **subway.** **6.** (*usually preceded by the*) **a.** any avant-garde, experimental, or subversive movement in popular art, films, etc. **b.** (*as modifier*): *the underground press.*

unshaved *adj.*	unsubstantiated *adj.*	untested *adj.*	unversed *adj.*
unshaven *adj.*	unsuccessful *adj.*	unthoughtful *adj.*	unwanted *adj.*
unshrinkable *adj.*	unsuitable *adj.*	unthought-of *adj.*	unwarned *adj.*
unsigned *adj.*	unsuited *adj.*	untiring *adj.*	unwarned *adj.*
unsinkable *adj.*	unsullied *adj.*	untouched *adj.*	unwashed *adj.*
unsmiling *adj.*	unsupervised *adj.*	untrained *adj.*	unwavering *adj.*
unsold *adj.*	unsupported *adj.*	untreated *adj.*	unwearying *adj.*
unsolicited *adj.*	unsure *adj.*	untried *adj.*	unwedded or unwed *adj.*
unsolved *adj.*	unsurpassed *adj.*	untroubled *adj.*	unwelcome *adj.*
unsought *adj.*	unsuspecting *adj.*	untrustworthy *adj.*	unwinking *adj.*
unspectacular *adj.*	unsweetened *adj.*	unusable *adj.*	unworkable *adj.*
unspoiled *adj.*	unsympathetic *adj.*	unvanquished *adj.*	unworkmanlike *adj.*
unspoken *adj.*	untainted *adj.*	unvaried *adj.*	unworn *adj.*
unsporting *adj.*	untamed *adj.*	unvarnished *adj.*	unworried *adj.*
unstinted *adj.*	untasted *adj.*	unvarying *adj.*	unwounded *adj.*
unsubdued *adj.*	untaxed *adj.*	unverified *adj.*	unyielding *adj.*

THESAURUS

under *prep.* **1.** below, beneath, on the bottom of, underneath **2.** directed by, governed by, inferior to, junior to, reporting to, secondary to, subject to, subordinate to, subservient to **3.** belonging to, comprised in, included in, subsumed under ~*adv.* **4.** below, beneath, down, downward, lower, to the bottom

underclothes lingerie, smalls (*Inf.*), underclothing, undergarments, underlinen, underthings (*Inf.*), underwear, undies (*Inf.*)

undercover clandestine, concealed, confidential, covert, hidden, hush-hush (*Inf.*), intelligence, private, secret, spy, surreptitious, underground

undercurrent **1.** crosscurrent, rip, rip

current, riptide, underflow, undertow **2.** atmosphere, aura, drift, feeling, flavour, hidden feeling, hint, murmur, overtone, sense, suggestion, tendency, tenor, tinge, trend, undertone, vibes (*Inf.*), vibrations

undercut **1.** sacrifice, sell at a loss, sell cheaply, undercharge, underprice, undersell **2.** cut away, cut out, excavate, gouge out, hollow out, mine, undermine

underdog fall guy (*Inf.*), little fellow (*Inf.*), loser, victim, weaker party

underestimate belittle, hold cheap, minimize, miscalculate, misprize, not do justice to, rate too low, sell short (*Inf.*), set no

store by, think too little of, underrate, undervalue

undergo bear, be subjected to, endure, experience, go through, stand, submit to, suffer, sustain, weather, withstand

underground *adj.* **1.** below ground, below the surface, buried, covered, subterranean **2.** clandestine, concealed, covert, hidden, secret, surreptitious, undercover **3.** alternative, avant-garde, experimental, radical, revolutionary, subversive ~*n.* **4.** the **underground** **4.** the metro, the subway, the tube (*Brit.*) **5.** the Maquis, partisans, the Resistance

undergrowth ('ʌndə,grəʊθ) *n.* small trees, bushes, ferns, etc., growing beneath taller trees in a wood or forest.

underhand ('ʌndə,hænd) *adj. also* **underhanded. 1.** clandestine, deceptive, or secretive. **2.** *Sport.* another word for **underarm** (sense 2). ~*adv.* **3.** in an underhand manner or style.

underlay *vb.* (,ʌndə'leɪ), **-laying, -laid.** (*tr.*) **1.** to place (something) under or beneath. **2.** to support by something laid beneath. **3.** to achieve the correct printing pressure all over (a forme block) or to bring (a block) up to type height by adding material, such as paper, beneath it. ~*n.* (,ʌndə,leɪ). **4.** a lining, support, etc., laid underneath something else. **5.** *Printing.* material, such as paper, used to underlay a forme or block. **6.** felt, rubber, etc., laid beneath a carpet to increase insulation and resilience.

underlie (,ʌndə'laɪ) *vb.* **-lying, -lay, -lain.** (*tr.*) **1.** to lie or be placed under or beneath. **2.** to be the foundation, cause, or basis of: *careful planning underlies all our decisions.* **3.** to be the root or stem from which (a word) is derived: *"happy" underlies "happiest".* —,**under'lier** *n.*

underline (,ʌndə'laɪn) *vb.* (*tr.*) **1.** to put a line under. **2.** to state forcibly; emphasize.

underling ('ʌndəlɪŋ) *n.* a subordinate or lackey.

underlying (,ʌndə'laɪɪŋ) *adj.* **1.** concealed but detectable: *underlying guilt.* **2.** fundamental; basic. **3.** lying under. **4.** *Finance.* (of a claim, liability, etc.) taking precedence; prior.

undermentioned ('ʌndə,menʃənd) *adj.* mentioned below or subsequently.

undermine (,ʌndə'maɪn) *vb.* (*tr.*) **1.** (of the sea, wind, etc.) to wear away the bottom or base of (land, cliffs, etc.). **2.** to weaken gradually or insidiously: *insults undermined her confidence.* **3.** to tunnel or dig beneath. —,**under'miner** *n.* —,**under'miningly** *adv.*

underneath (,ʌndə'niːθ) *prep., adv.* **1.** under; beneath. ~*adj.* **2.** lower. ~*n.* **3.** a lower part, surface, etc.

undernourish (,ʌndə'nʌrɪʃ) *vb.* (*tr.*) to deprive of or fail to provide nutrients essential for health and growth. —,**under'nourishment** *n.*

underpants ('ʌndə,pænts) *pl. n.* a man's undergarment covering the body from the waist or hips to the top of the thighs or knees. Often shortened to **pants.**

underpass ('ʌndə,pɑːs) *n.* **1.** a section of a road that passes under another road, railway line, etc. **2.** another word for **subway** (sense 1).

underpay (,ʌndə'peɪ) *vb.* **-paying, -paid.** to pay (someone) insufficiently. —,**under'payment** *n.*

underpin (,ʌndə'pɪn) *vb.* **-pinning, -pinned.** (*tr.*) **1.** to support from beneath, esp. by a prop: *to underpin a wall.* **2.** to give corroboration, strength, or support to.

underplay (,ʌndə'pleɪ) *vb.* **1.** to play (a role) with restraint or subtlety. **2.** to underact (an effect) by deliberate lack of emphasis. **3.** (*intr.*) *Cards.* to lead or follow suit with a lower card when holding a higher one.

underprivileged (,ʌndə'prɪvɪlɪdʒd) *adj.* lacking the rights and advantages of other members of society; deprived.

underproduction (,ʌndəprə'dʌkʃən) *n. Commerce.* production below full capacity or below demand.

underrate (,ʌndə'reɪt) *vb.* (*tr.*) to underestimate.

undersea ('ʌndə,siː) *adj., adv. also* **underseas** (,ʌndə'siːz). below the surface of the sea.

undersecretary (,ʌndə'sɛkrətrɪ) *n., pl.* **-taries. 1.** (in Britain) **a.** any of various senior civil servants in certain government departments. **b.** short for **undersecretary of state:** any of various high officials subordinate only to the minister in charge of a department. **2.** (in the U.S.) a high government official subordinate only to the secretary in charge of a department.

undersell (,ʌndə'sɛl) *vb.* **-selling, -sold. 1.** to sell for less than the usual price. **2.** (*tr.*) to sell at a price lower than that of (another seller). **3.** (*tr.*) to advertise (merchandise) with moderation or restraint. —,**under'seller** *n.*

undersexed (,ʌndə'sɛkst) *adj.* having weaker sex urges or responses than is considered normal.

undershirt ('ʌndə,ʃɜːt) *n. Chiefly U.S.* an undergarment worn under a blouse or shirt. Brit. name: **vest.**

undershoot (,ʌndə'ʃuːt) *vb.* **-shooting, -shot. 1.** (of a pilot) to cause (an aircraft) to land short of (a runway) or (of an aircraft) to land in this way. **2.** to shoot a projectile so that it falls short of (a target).

underside ('ʌndə,saɪd) *n.* the bottom or lower surface.

undersigned ('ʌndə,saɪnd) *n.* **1. the.** the person or persons who have signed at the foot of a document, statement, etc. ~*adj.* **2.** having signed one's name at the foot of a document, statement, etc.

undersized (,ʌndə'saɪzd) *adj.* of less than usual size.

underskirt ('ʌndə,skɜːt) *n.* any skirtlike garment worn under a skirt or dress; petticoat.

understand (,ʌndə'stænd) *vb.* **-standing, -stood. 1.** (*may take a clause as object*) to know and comprehend the nature or meaning of: *I understand you.* **2.** (*may take a clause as object*) to realize or grasp (something): *he understands your position.* **3.** (*tr.; may take a clause as object*) to assume, infer, or believe: *I understand you are thinking of marrying.* **4.** (*tr.*) to know how to translate or read: *can you understand Spanish?* **5.** (*tr.; may take a clause as object; often passive*) to accept as a condition or proviso: *it is understood that children must be kept quiet.* **6.** (*tr.*) to be sympathetic to or compatible with: *we understand each other.* —,**under'standable** *adj.* —,**under'standably** *adv.*

understanding (,ʌndə'stændɪŋ) *n.* **1.** the ability to learn, judge, make decisions, etc. **2.** personal opinion or interpretation of a subject: *my understanding of your predicament.* **3.** a mutual agreement or compact, esp. an informal or private one. **4.** *Chiefly Brit.* an unofficial engagement to be married. **5. on the understanding that.** providing. ~*adj.* **6.** sympathetic, tolerant, or wise towards people. **7.** possessing judgment and intelligence. —,**under'standingly** *adv.*

understate (,ʌndə'steɪt) *vb.* **1.** to state (something) in restrained terms, often to obtain an ironic effect. **2.** to state that (something, such as a number) is less than it is. —,**under'statement** *n.*

understood (,ʌndə'stʊd) *vb.* **1.** the past tense or past participle of **understand.** ~*adj.* **2.** implied or inferred. **3.** taken for granted.

understudy ('ʌndə,stʌdɪ) *vb.* **-studying, -studied. 1.**

◤ THESAURUS ◢

undergrowth bracken, brambles, briars, brush, brushwood, scrub, underbrush, underbush, underwood

underhand clandestine, crafty, crooked (*Inf.*), deceitful, deceptive, devious, dishonest, dishonourable, fraudulent, furtive, secret, secretive, sly, sneaky, stealthy, surreptitious, treacherous, underhanded, unethical, unscrupulous

underline 1. italicize, mark, rule a line under, underscore **2.** accentuate, bring home, call *or* draw attention to, emphasize, give emphasis to, highlight, point up, stress

underling flunky, hireling, inferior, lackey, menial, minion, nonentity, retainer, servant, slave, subordinate, understrapper

underlying 1. concealed, hidden, latent, lurking, veiled **2.** basal, basic, elementary, essential, fundamental, intrinsic, primary, prime, root

undermine 1. dig out, eat away at,

erode, excavate, mine, tunnel, undercut, wear away **2.** debilitate, disable, impair, sabotage, sap, subvert, threaten, weaken

underprivileged badly off, deprived, destitute, disadvantaged, impoverished, in need, in want, needy, poor

underrate belittle, discount, disparage, fail to appreciate, misprize, not do justice to, set (too) little store by, underestimate, undervalue

undersized atrophied, dwarfish, miniature, pygmy, runtish, runty, small, squat, stunted, tiny, underdeveloped, underweight

understand 1. appreciate, apprehend, be aware, catch on (*Inf.*), comprehend, conceive, cotton on (*Inf.*), discern, fathom, follow, get, get the hang of (*Inf.*), get to the bottom of, grasp, know, make head *or* tail of (*Inf.*), make out, penetrate, perceive, realize, recognize, savvy (*Sl.*), see, take in, tumble to (*Inf.*), twig (*Brit. inf.*) **2.** assume, be informed,

believe, conclude, gather, hear, learn, presume, suppose, take it, think **3.** accept, appreciate, be able to see, commiserate, show compassion for, sympathize with, tolerate

understanding *n.* **1.** appreciation, awareness, comprehension, discernment, grasp, insight, intelligence, judgment, knowledge, penetration, perception, sense **2.** belief, conclusion, estimation, idea, interpretation, judgment, notion, opinion, perception, view, viewpoint **3.** accord, agreement, common view, gentlemen's agreement, meeting of minds, pact ~*adj.* **4.** accepting, compassionate, considerate, discerning, forbearing, forgiving, kind, kindly, patient, perceptive, responsive, sensitive, sympathetic, tolerant

understood 1. implicit, implied, inferred, tacit, unspoken, unstated **2.** accepted, assumed, axiomatic, presumed, taken for granted

(*tr.*) to study (a role or part) so as to be able to replace the usual actor or actress if necessary. **2.** to act as understudy to (an actor or actress). ~*n.*, *pl.* **-studies.** **3.** an actor or actress who studies a part so as to be able to replace the usual actor or actress if necessary. **4.** anyone who is trained to take the place of another in case of need.

undertake (ˌʌndə'teɪk) *vb.* **-taking, -took, -taken.** **1.** (*tr.*) to contract to or commit oneself to (something) or (to do something): *to undertake a job.* **2.** (*tr.*) to attempt to; agree to start. **3.** (*tr.*) to take (someone) in charge. **4.** (*tr.*) to promise.

undertaker ('ʌndəˌteɪkə) *n.* a person whose profession is the preparation of the dead for burial or cremation and the management of funerals; funeral director.

undertaking ('ʌndəˌteɪkɪŋ) *n.* **1.** a task, venture, or enterprise. **2.** an agreement to do something. **3.** the business of an undertaker.

under-the-counter *adj.* (**under the counter** when postpositive). done or sold illicitly and secretly.

underthrust ('ʌndəˌθrʌst) *n.* *Geol.* a reverse fault in which the rocks on the lower surface of a fault plane have moved under the relatively static rocks on the upper surface.

undertone ('ʌndəˌtəʊn) *n.* **1.** a quiet or hushed tone of voice. **2.** an underlying suggestion in words or actions: *his offer has undertones of dishonesty.*

undertow ('ʌndəˌtəʊ) *n.* **1.** the seaward undercurrent following the breaking of a wave on the beach. **2.** any strong undercurrent flowing in a different direction from the surface current.

undervalue (ˌʌndə'væljuː) *vb.* **-valuing, -valued.** (*tr.*) to value at too low a level or price. —ˌunder'valu'ation *n.* —ˌunder'valuer *n.*

underwater ('ʌndə'wɔːtə) *adj.* **1.** being, occurring, or going under the surface of the water, esp. the sea: *underwater exploration.* **2.** *Naut.* below the water line of a vessel. ~*adv.* **3.** beneath the surface of the water.

under way *adj.* (*postpositive*) **1.** in progress; in operation: *the show was under way.* **2.** *Naut.* in motion in the direction headed.

underwear ('ʌndəˌweə) *n.* clothing worn under the out-er garments, usually next to the skin.

underweight (ˌʌndə'weɪt) *adj.* weighing less than is average, expected, or healthy.

underwent (ˌʌndə'wɛnt) *vb.* the past tense of **undergo**.

underwood ('ʌndəˌwʊd) *n.* a less common word for **undergrowth**.

underworld ('ʌndəˌwɜːld) *n.* **1. a.** criminals and their associates. **b.** (*as modifier*): *underworld connections.* **2.** *Greek & Roman myth.* the regions below the earth's surface regarded as the abode of the dead. **3.** the antipodes.

underwrite ('ʌndəˌraɪt, ˌʌndə'raɪt) *vb.* **-writing, -wrote, -written.** (*tr.*) **1.** *Finance.* to undertake to purchase at an agreed price any unsold portion of (a public issue of shares, etc.). **2.** to accept financial responsibility for (a commercial project or enterprise). **3.** *Insurance.* **a.** to sign and issue (an insurance policy) thus accepting liability. **b.** to insure (a property or risk). **c.** to accept liability up to (a specified amount) in an insurance policy. **4.** to write (words, a signature, etc.) beneath (other written matter). **5.** to support. —'underˌwriter *n.*

undesirable (ˌʌndɪ'zaɪərəbəl) *adj.* not desirable or pleasant; objectionable. —ˌundeˌsira'bility or ˌunde'sirableness *n.* —ˌunde'sirably *adv.*

undies ('ʌndɪz) *pl. n. Inf.* women's underwear.

undine ('ʌndiːn) *n.* any of various female water spirits.

undo (ʌn'duː) *vb.* **-doing, -did, -done.** (*mainly tr.*) **1.** (*also intr.*) to untie, unwrap, or open or become untied, unwrapped, etc. **2.** to reverse the effects of. **3.** to cause the downfall of.

undoing (ʌn'duːɪŋ) *n.* **1.** ruin; downfall. **2.** the cause of downfall: *drink was his undoing.*

undone[1] (ʌn'dʌn) *adj.* not done or completed; unfinished.

undone[2] (ʌn'dʌn) *adj.* **1.** ruined; destroyed. **2.** unfastened; untied.

undoubted (ʌn'daʊtɪd) *adj.* beyond doubt; certain or indisputable. —**un'doubtedly** *adv.*

undreamed (ʌn'driːmd) *adj.* also **undreamt** (ʌn'drɛmt) (often foll. by *of*) not thought of, conceived, or imagined.

undress (ʌn'drɛs) *vb.* **1.** to take off clothes from (oneself or another). **2.** (*tr.*) to strip of ornamentation. **3.**

THESAURUS

understudy *n.* double, fill-in, replacement, reserve, stand-in, sub, substitute

undertake 1. agree, bargain, commit oneself, contract, covenant, engage, guarantee, pledge, promise, stipulate, take upon oneself **2.** attempt, begin, commence, embark on, endeavour, enter upon, set about, tackle, take on, try

undertaker funeral director, mortician (U.S.)

undertaking 1. affair, attempt, business, effort, endeavour, enterprise, game, operation, project, task, venture **2.** assurance, commitment, pledge, promise, solemn word, vow, word, word of honour

undertone 1. low tone, murmur, subdued voice, whisper **2.** atmosphere, feeling, flavour, hint, suggestion, tinge, touch, trace, undercurrent

undervalue depreciate, hold cheap, look down on, make light of, minimize, misjudge, misprize, set no store by, underestimate, underrate

underwater submarine, submerged, sunken, undersea

under way afoot, begun, going on, in motion, in operation, in progress, started

underwear lingerie, smalls (*Inf.*), underclothes, underclothing, undergarments, underlinen, undies (*Inf.*), unmentionables

underweight half-starved, puny, skin and bone, skinny, undernourished, undersized

underworld 1. criminal element, criminals, gangland (*Inf.*), gangsters, organized crime **2.** abode of the dead, Hades, hell, infernal region, nether regions, nether world, the inferno

underwrite 1. back, finance, fund, guarantee, insure, provide security, sponsor, sub-sidize **2.** countersign, endorse, initial, sign, subscribe **3.** agree to, approve, consent, okay (*Inf.*), sanction

undesirable disagreeable, disliked, distasteful, dreaded, objectionable, obnoxious, offensive, out of place, repugnant, (to be) avoided, unacceptable, unattractive, unpleasing, unpopular, unsavoury, unsuitable, unwanted, unwelcome, unwished-for

undeveloped embryonic, immature, inchoate, in embryo, latent, potential, primordial (*Biol.*)

undignified beneath one, beneath one's dignity, improper, inappropriate, indecorous, inelegant, infra dig (*Inf.*), lacking dignity, unbecoming, ungentlemanly, unladylike, unrefined, unseemly, unsuitable

undisciplined disobedient, erratic, fitful, obstreperous, uncontrolled, unpredictable, unreliable, unrestrained, unruly, unschooled, unsteady, unsystematic, untrained, wayward, wild, wilful

undisguised complete, evident, explicit, genuine, manifest, obvious, open, out-and-out, overt, patent, thoroughgoing, transparent, unconcealed, unfeigned, unmistakable, utter, wholehearted

undisputed accepted, acknowledged, beyond question, certain, conclusive, freely admitted, incontestable, incontrovertible, indisputable, irrefutable, not disputed, recognized, sure, unchallenged, uncontested, undeniable, undoubted, unquestioned

undistinguished commonplace, everyday, indifferent, mediocre, no great shakes (*Inf.*), nothing to write home about (*Inf.*), ordinary, pedestrian, prosaic, run-of-the-mill, so-so (*Inf.*), unexceptional, unexciting, unimpressive, unremarkable

undisturbed 1. not moved, quiet, unin-terrupted, untouched, without interruption **2.** calm, collected, composed, equable, even, motionless, placid, serene, tranquil, unagitated, unbothered, unperturbed, unruffled, untroubled

undivided combined, complete, concentrated, concerted, entire, exclusive, full, solid, thorough, unanimous, undistracted, united, whole, wholehearted

undo 1. disengage, disentangle, loose, loosen, open, unbutton, unfasten, unlock, untie, unwrap **2.** annul, cancel, invalidate, neutralize, nullify, offset, reverse, wipe out **3.** bring to naught, defeat, destroy, impoverish, invalidate, mar, overturn, quash, ruin, shatter, subvert, undermine, upset, wreck

undoing 1. collapse, defeat, destruction, disgrace, downfall, humiliation, overthrow, overturn, reversal, ruin, ruination, shame **2.** affliction, blight, curse, fatal flaw, misfortune, the last straw, trial, trouble, weakness

undone incomplete, left, neglected, not completed, not done, omitted, outstanding, passed over, unattended to, unfinished, unfulfilled, unperformed

undoubted acknowledged, certain, definite, evident, incontrovertible, indisputable, indubitable, obvious, sure, undisputed, unquestionable, unquestioned

undoubtedly assuredly, beyond a shadow of (a) doubt, beyond question, certainly, definitely, doubtless, of course, surely, undeniably, unmistakably, unquestionably, without doubt

undreamed of astonishing, inconceivable, incredible, miraculous, undreamt, unexpected, unforeseen, unheard-of, unimagined, unsuspected, unthought-of

(*tr.*) to remove the dressing from (a wound). ~*n.* 4. partial or complete nakedness. 5. informal or normal working clothes or uniform.

undue (ʌnˈdjuː) *adj.* 1. excessive or unwarranted. 2. unjust, improper, or illegal. 3. (of a debt, bond, etc.) not yet payable.

undulant ('ʌndjʊlənt) *adj. Rare.* resembling waves; undulating. —'**undulance** *n.*

undulate *vb.* ('ʌndjʊˌleɪt). 1. to move or cause to move in waves or as if in waves. 2. to have or provide with a wavy form or appearance. ~*adj.* ('ʌndjʊlɪt, -ˌleɪt). 3. having a wavy or rippled appearance, margin, or form: *an undulate leaf.* —'**undu,lator** *n.* —'**undulatory** *adj.*

undulation (ˌʌndjʊˈleɪʃən) *n.* 1. the act or an instance of undulating. 2. any wave or wavelike form, line, etc.

unduly (ʌnˈdjuːlɪ) *adv.* immoderately; excessively.

undying (ʌnˈdaɪɪŋ) *adj.* unending; eternal. —**un'dyingly** *adv.*

unearned (ʌnˈɜːnd) *adj.* 1. not deserved. 2. not yet earned.

unearned income *n.* income from property, investment, etc., comprising rent, interest, and dividends.

unearth (ʌnˈɜːθ) *vb.* (*tr.*) 1. to dig up out of the earth. 2. to reveal or discover, esp. by exhaustive searching.

unearthly (ʌnˈɜːθlɪ) *adj.* 1. ghostly; eerie: *unearthly screams.* 2. heavenly; sublime: *unearthly music.* 3. ridiculous or unreasonable (esp. in **unearthly hour**). —**un'earthliness** *n.*

uneasy (ʌnˈiːzɪ) *adj.* 1. (of a person) anxious; apprehensive. 2. (of a condition) precarious: *an uneasy truce.* 3. (of a thought, etc.) disquieting. —**un'easily** *adv.* —**un'easiness** *n.*

uneatable (ʌnˈiːtəbəl) *adj.* (of food) not fit or suitable for eating, esp. because it is rotten or unattractive.
▷ **Usage.** See at **inedible.**

uneconomic (ˌʌniːkəˈnɒmɪk, ʌnˌɛkə-) *adj.* not economic; not profitable.

unemployed (ˌʌnɪmˈplɔɪd) *adj.* 1. **a.** without remunerative employment; out of work. **b.** (*as collective n.* preceded by *the*): *the unemployed.* 2. not being used; idle.

unemployment (ˌʌnɪmˈplɔɪmənt) *n.* 1. the condition of being unemployed. 2. the number of unemployed workers, often as a percentage of the total labour force.

unemployment benefit *n.* (in the British National Insurance scheme) a regular payment to a person who is out of work and has usually paid a fixed number of insurance contributions. Informal term: **dole.**

unequal (ʌnˈiːkwəl) *adj.* 1. not equal in quantity, size, rank, value, etc. 2. (foll. by *to*) inadequate; insufficient. 3. not evenly balanced. 4. (of character, quality, etc.) irregular; inconsistent. 5. (of a contest, etc.) having competitors of different ability.

unequalled *or U.S.* **unequaled** (ʌnˈiːkwəld) *adj.* not equalled; unrivalled; supreme.

unequivocal (ˌʌnɪˈkwɪvəkəl) *adj.* not ambiguous; plain. —ˌ**une'quivocally** *adv.* —ˌ**une'quivocalness** *n.*

unerring (ʌnˈɜːrɪŋ) *adj.* 1. not missing the mark or target. 2. consistently accurate; certain. —**un'erringly** *adv.* —**un'erringness** *n.*

UNESCO (juːˈnɛskəʊ) *n. acronym for* United Nations Educational, Scientific, and Cultural Organization.

uneven (ʌnˈiːvən) *adj.* 1. (of a surface, etc.) not level or flat. 2. spasmodic or variable. 3. not parallel, straight, or horizontal. 4. not fairly matched: *an uneven race.* 5. *Arch.* not equal. —**un'evenly** *adv.* —**un'evenness** *n.*

uneventful (ˌʌnɪˈvɛntfʊl) *adj.* ordinary, routine, or quiet. —ˌ**une'ventfully** *adv.* —ˌ**une'ventfulness** *n.*

unexampled (ˌʌnɪgˈzɑːmpəld) *adj.* without precedent or parallel.

unexceptionable (ˌʌnɪkˈsɛpʃənəbəl) *adj.* beyond criticism or objection. —ˌ**unex'ceptionably** *adv.*

unexceptional (ˌʌnɪkˈsɛpʃənəl) *adj.* 1. usual, ordinary, or normal. 2. subject to or allowing no exceptions. —ˌ**unex'ceptionally** *adv.*

unexpected (ˌʌnɪkˈspɛktɪd) *adj.* surprising or unforeseen. —ˌ**unex'pectedly** *adv.* —ˌ**unex'pectedness** *n.*

unfailing (ʌnˈfeɪlɪŋ) *adj.* 1. not failing; unflagging. 2. continuous. 3. sure; certain. —**un'failingly** *adv.* —**un'failingness** *n.*

unfair (ʌnˈfɛə) *adj.* 1. characterized by inequality or injustice. 2. dishonest or unethical. —**un'fairly** *adv.* —**un'fairness** *n.*

THESAURUS

undress 1. *v.* disrobe, divest oneself of, peel off (*Sl.*), shed, strip, take off one's clothes 2. *n.* disarray, dishabille, nakedness, nudity

undue disproportionate, excessive, extravagant, extreme, immoderate, improper, inordinate, intemperate, needless, overmuch, too great, too much, uncalled-for, undeserved, unnecessary, unseemly, unwarranted

unduly disproportionately, excessively, extravagantly, immoderately, improperly, inordinately, out of all proportion, overly, overmuch, unjustifiably, unnecessarily, unreasonably

undying constant, continuing, deathless, eternal, everlasting, immortal, imperishable, indestructible, inextinguishable, infinite, perennial, permanent, perpetual, sempiternal (*Literary*), undiminished, unending, unfading

unearth 1. dig up, disinter, dredge up, excavate, exhume 2. bring to light, discover, expose, ferret out, find, reveal, root up, turn up, uncover

unearthly 1. eerie, eldritch (*Poetic*), ghostly, haunted, nightmarish, phantom, spectral, spooky (*Inf.*), strange, uncanny, weird 2. ethereal, heavenly, not of this world, preternatural, sublime, supernatural 3. abnormal, absurd, extraordinary, ridiculous, strange, ungodly (*Inf.*), unholy (*Inf.*), unreasonable

uneasiness agitation, alarm, anxiety, apprehension, apprehensiveness, disquiet, doubt, misgiving, nervousness, perturbation, qualms, suspicion, worry

uneasy 1. agitated, anxious, apprehensive, discomposed, disturbed, edgy, ill at ease, impatient, jittery (*Inf.*), nervous, on edge, perturbed, restive, restless, troubled, uncomfortable, unsettled, upset, worried 2. awkward, constrained, insecure, precarious, shaky, strained, tense, uncomfortable, unstable 3. bothering, dismaying, disquieting, disturbing, troubling, upsetting, worrying

uneconomic loss-making, nonpaying, non-profit-making, nonviable, unprofitable

uneducated 1. ignorant, illiterate, unlettered, unread, unschooled, untaught 2. benighted, lowbrow, uncultivated, uncultured

unemotional apathetic, cold, cool, impassive, indifferent, listless, passionless, phlegmatic, reserved, undemonstrative, unexcitable, unfeeling, unimpressionable, unresponsive

unemployed idle, jobless, laid off, on the dole (*Brit. inf.*), out of a job, out of work, redundant, resting (*of an actor*), workless

unending ceaseless, constant, continual, endless, eternal, everlasting, incessant, interminable, never-ending, perpetual, unceasing, unremitting

unendurable insufferable, insupportable, intolerable, more than flesh and blood can stand, unbearable

unenthusiastic apathetic, blasé, bored, half-hearted, indifferent, lukewarm, neutral, nonchalant, unimpressed, uninterested, unmoved, unresponsive

unenviable disagreeable, painful, thankless, uncomfortable, undesirable, unpleasant

unequal 1. different, differing, disparate, dissimilar, not uniform, unlike, unmatched, variable, varying 2. *With* to found wanting, inadequate, insufficient, not up to 3. asymmetrical, disproportionate, ill-matched, irregular, unbalanced, uneven

unequalled beyond compare, incomparable, inimitable, matchless, nonpareil, para-
mount, peerless, pre-eminent, second to none, supreme, transcendent, unmatched, unparalleled, unrivalled, unsurpassed, without equal

unequivocal absolute, certain, clear, clear-cut, decisive, definite, direct, evident, explicit, incontrovertible, indubitable, manifest, plain, positive, straight, unambiguous, uncontestable, unmistakable

unethical dirty, dishonest, dishonourable, disreputable, illegal, immoral, improper, shady (*Inf.*), underhand, unfair, unprincipled, unprofessional, unscrupulous, wrong

uneven 1. bumpy, not flat, not level, not smooth, rough 2. broken, changeable, fitful, fluctuating, intermittent, irregular, jerky, patchy, spasmodic, unsteady, variable 3. asymmetrical, lopsided, not parallel, odd, out of true, unbalanced 4. disparate, ill-matched, one-sided, unequal, unfair

uneventful boring, commonplace, dull, humdrum, monotonous, ordinary, quiet, routine, tedious, unexceptional, unexciting, uninteresting, unmemorable, unremarkable, unvaried

unexceptional common or garden (*Inf.*), commonplace, conventional, insignificant, mediocre, normal, ordinary, pedestrian, run-of-the-mill, undistinguished, unimpressive, unremarkable, usual

unexpected abrupt, accidental, astonishing, chance, fortuitous, not bargained for, out of the blue, startling, sudden, surprising, unanticipated, unforeseen, unlooked-for, unpredictable

unfailing 1. bottomless, boundless, ceaseless, continual, continuous, endless, inexhaustible, never-failing, persistent, unflagging, unlimited 2. certain, constant, dependable, faithful, infallible, loyal, reliable,

unfaithful (ʌnˈfeɪθfʊl) *adj.* **1.** not true to a promise, vow, etc. **2.** not true to a wife, husband, lover, etc., esp. in having sexual intercourse with someone else. **3.** inaccurate; untrustworthy: *unfaithful copy.* **4.** *Obs.* not having religious faith. —un'**faithfully** *adv.* —un'**faithfulness** *n.*

unfamiliar (ˌʌnfəˈmɪljə) *adj.* **1.** not known or experienced; strange. **2.** (*postpositive;* foll. by *with*) not familiar. —**unfamiliarity** (ˌʌnfəˌmɪlɪˈærɪtɪ) *n.* —ˌunfaˈmiliarly *adv.*

unfasten (ʌnˈfɑːsən) *vb.* to undo, untie, or open or become undone, untied, or opened.

unfathomable (ʌnˈfæðəməbəl) *adj.* **1.** incapable of being fathomed; immeasurable. **2.** incomprehensible. —un'**fathomableness** *n.* —un'**fathomably** *adv.*

unfavourable *or U.S.* **unfavorable** (ʌnˈfeɪvərəbəl) *adj.* not favourable; adverse or inauspicious. —un'**favourably** *or U.S.* un'**favorably** *adv.*

unfeeling (ʌnˈfiːlɪŋ) *adj.* **1.** without sympathy; callous. **2.** without physical feeling or sensation. —un'**feelingly** *adv.* —un'**feelingness** *n.*

unfinished (ʌnˈfɪnɪʃt) *adj.* **1.** incomplete or imperfect. **2.** (of paint, polish, varnish, etc.) without an applied finish; rough. **3.** (of fabric) unbleached or not processed.

unfit (ʌnˈfɪt) *adj.* **1.** (*postpositive;* often foll. by *for*) unqualified, incapable, or incompetent: *unfit for military service.* **2.** (*postpositive;* often foll. by *for*) unsuitable or inappropriate: *the ground was unfit for football.* **3.** in poor physical condition. ~*vb.* **-fitting, -fitted. 4.** (*tr.*) *Rare.* to render unfit. —un'**fitly** *adv.* —un'**fitness** *n.*

unfix (ʌnˈfɪks) *vb.* (*tr.*) **1.** to unfasten, detach, or loosen. **2.** to unsettle or disturb.

unflappable (ʌnˈflæpəbəl) *adj. Inf.* hard to upset; calm; composed. —un,flappa'**bility** *n.* —un'**flappably** *adv.*

unfledged (ʌnˈflɛdʒd) *adj.* **1.** (of a young bird) not having developed adult feathers. **2.** immature and undeveloped.

unflinching (ʌnˈflɪntʃɪŋ) *adj.* not shrinking from danger, difficulty, etc. —un'**flinchingly** *adv.*

unfold (ʌnˈfəʊld) *vb.* **1.** to open or spread out or be opened or spread out from a folded state. **2.** to reveal or be revealed: *the truth unfolds.* **3.** to develop or expand or be developed or expanded. —un'**folder** *n.*

unfortunate (ʌnˈfɔːtʃənɪt) *adj.* **1.** causing or attended by misfortune. **2.** unlucky or unhappy: *an unfortunate character.* **3.** regrettable or unsuitable: *an unfortunate speech.* ~*n.* **4.** an unlucky person. —un'**fortunately** *adv.*

unfounded (ʌnˈfaʊndɪd) *adj.* **1.** (of ideas, allegations, etc.) baseless; groundless. **2.** not yet founded or established. —un'**foundedly** *adv.* —un'**foundedness** *n.*

unfreeze (ʌnˈfriːz) *vb.* **-freezing, -froze, -frozen. 1.** to thaw or cause to thaw. **2.** (*tr.*) to relax governmental restrictions on (wages, prices, credit, etc.) or on the manufacture or sale of (goods, etc.).

unfriendly (ʌnˈfrɛndlɪ) *adj.* **-lier, -liest. 1.** not friendly; hostile. **2.** unfavourable or disagreeable. ~*adv.* **3.** *Rare.* in an unfriendly manner. —un'**friendliness** *n.*

unfrock (ʌnˈfrɒk) *vb.* (*tr.*) to deprive (a person in holy orders) of ecclesiastical status.

unfurl (ʌnˈfɜːl) *vb.* to unroll, unfold, or spread out or be unrolled, unfolded, or spread out from a furled state.

ungainly (ʌnˈɡeɪnlɪ) *adj.* **-lier, -liest. 1.** lacking grace when moving. **2.** difficult to move or use; unwieldy. —un'**gainliness** *n.*

ungodly (ʌnˈɡɒdlɪ) *adj.* **-lier, -liest. 1. a.** wicked, sinful. **b.** (*as collective n.* preceded by *the*): *the ungodly.* **2.** *Inf.* unseemly; outrageous (esp. in **an ungodly hour**). —un'**godliness** *n.*

ungovernable (ʌnˈɡʌvənəbəl) *adj.* not able to be disci-

THESAURUS

staunch, steadfast, sure, tried and true, true

unfair **1.** arbitrary, biased, bigoted, discriminatory, inequitable, one-sided, partial, partisan, prejudiced, unjust **2.** crooked (*Inf.*), dishonest, dishonourable, uncalled-for, unethical, unprincipled, unscrupulous, unsporting, unwarranted, wrongful

unfaithful **1.** deceitful, disloyal, faithless, false, false-hearted, perfidious, recreant (*Archaic*), traitorous, treacherous, treasonable, unreliable, untrustworthy **2.** adulterous, faithless, fickle, inconstant, two-timing (*Inf.*), unchaste, untrue **3.** distorted, erroneous, imperfect, imprecise, inaccurate, inexact, unreliable, untrustworthy

unfamiliar **1.** alien, curious, different, little known, new, novel, out-of-the-way, strange, unaccustomed, uncommon, unknown, unusual **2.** *With* **with** a stranger to, inexperienced in, unaccustomed to, unacquainted, unconversant, uninformed about, uninitiated in, unpractised in, unskilled at, unversed in

unfashionable antiquated, behind the times, dated, obsolete, old-fashioned, old hat, out, outmoded, out of date, out of fashion, passé, unpopular

unfasten detach, disconnect, let go, loosen, open, separate, uncouple, undo, unlace, unlock, untie

unfathomable **1.** bottomless, immeasurable, unmeasured, unplumbed, unsounded **2.** abstruse, baffling, deep, esoteric, impenetrable, incomprehensible, indecipherable, inexplicable, profound, unknowable

unfavourable **1.** adverse, bad, contrary, disadvantageous, hostile, ill-suited, infelicitous, inimical, low, negative, poor, unfortunate, unfriendly, unsuited **2.** inauspicious, inopportune, ominous, threatening, unlucky, unpromising, unpropitious, unseasonable, untimely, untoward

unfeeling **1.** apathetic, callous, cold, cruel, hardened, hardhearted, heartless, inhuman, insensitive, pitiless, stony, uncaring, unsympathetic **2.** insensate, insensible, numb, sensationless

unfinished **1.** deficient, half-done, imperfect, incomplete, in the making, lacking, unaccomplished, uncompleted, undone, unfulfilled, wanting **2.** bare, crude, natural, raw, rough, sketchy, unpolished, unrefined, unvarnished

unfit **1.** ill-equipped, inadequate, incapable, incompetent, ineligible, no good, not cut out for, not equal to, not up to, unprepared, unqualified, untrained, useless **2.** ill-adapted, inadequate, inappropriate, ineffective, not designed, not fit, unsuitable, unsuited, useless **3.** debilitated, decrepit, feeble, flabby, in poor condition, out of kelter, out of shape, out of trim, unhealthy

unflappable calm, collected, composed, cool, impassive, imperturbable, level-headed, not given to worry, self-possessed, unruffled

unflattering **1.** blunt, candid, critical, honest, uncomplimentary, warts and all **2.** not shown in the best light, not shown to advantage, plain, unattractive, unbecoming, unprepossessing

unflinching bold, constant, determined, firm, resolute, stalwart, staunch, steadfast, steady, unfaltering, unshaken, unshrinking, unswerving, unwavering

unfold **1.** disentangle, expand, flatten, open, spread out, straighten, stretch out, undo, unfurl, unravel, unroll, unwrap **2.** *Fig.* clarify, describe, disclose, divulge, explain, illustrate, make known, present, reveal, show, uncover **3.** bear fruit, develop, evolve, expand, grow, mature

unforeseen abrupt, accidental, out of the blue, startling, sudden, surprise, surprising, unanticipated, unexpected, unlooked-for, unpredicted

unforgettable exceptional, extraordinary, fixed in the mind, impressive, memorable, never to be forgotten, notable

unforgivable deplorable, disgraceful, indefensible, inexcusable, shameful, unjustifiable, unpardonable, unwarrantable

unfortunate **1.** adverse, calamitous, disastrous, ill-fated, ill-starred, inopportune, ruinous, unfavourable, untoward **2.** cursed, doomed, hapless, hopeless, luckless, out of luck, poor, star-crossed, unhappy, unlucky, unprosperous, unsuccessful, wretched **3.** deplorable, ill-advised, inappropriate, infelicitous, lamentable, regrettable, unbecoming, unsuitable

unfounded baseless, fabricated, false, groundless, idle, spurious, trumped up, unjustified, unproven, unsubstantiated, vain, without basis, without foundation

unfrequented deserted, godforsaken, isolated, lone, lonely, off the beaten track, remote, sequestered, solitary, uninhabited, unvisited

unfriendly **1.** aloof, antagonistic, chilly, cold, disagreeable, distant, hostile, ill-disposed, inhospitable, not on speaking terms, quarrelsome, sour, surly, uncongenial, unneighbourly, unsociable **2.** alien, hostile, inauspicious, inhospitable, inimical, unfavourable, unpropitious

unfruitful barren, fruitless, infecund, infertile, sterile, unproductive, unprofitable, unprolific, unrewarding

ungainly awkward, clumsy, gangling, gawky, inelegant, loutish, lubberly, lumbering, slouching, uncoordinated, uncouth, ungraceful

ungodly **1.** blasphemous, corrupt, depraved, godless, immoral, impious, irreligious, profane, sinful, vile, wicked **2.** *Inf.* dreadful, horrendous, intolerable, outrageous, unearthly, unholy (*Inf.*), unreasonable, unseemly

ungovernable rebellious, refractory, uncontrollable, unmanageable, unrestrainable, unruly, wild

ungracious bad-mannered, churlish, discourteous, ill-bred, impolite, offhand, rude, uncivil, unmannerly

ungrateful heedless, ingrate (*Archaic*), selfish, thankless, unappreciative, unmindful, unthankful

plined, restrained, etc.: *an ungovernable temper.* —**un-
'governableness** *n.* —**un'governably** *adv.*
unguarded (ʌn'gɑːdɪd) *adj.* **1.** unprotected; vulnerable.
2. open; frank. **3.** incautious. —**un'guardedly** *adv.*
—**un'guardedness** *n.*
unguent ('ʌŋgwənt) *n.* a less common name for an
ointment.
ungulate ('ʌŋgjʊlɪt, -ˌleɪt) *n.* any of a large group of
mammals all of which have hooves: divided into odd-
toed ungulates (**perissodactyls**) and even-toed ungulates
(**artiodactyls**).
unhallowed (ʌn'hæləʊd) *adj.* **1.** not consecrated or
holy: *unhallowed ground.* **2.** sinful.
unhand (ʌn'hænd) *vb.* (*tr.*) *Arch. or literary.* to release
from the grasp.
unhappy (ʌn'hæpɪ) *adj.* **-pier, -piest. 1.** not joyful; sad
or depressed. **2.** unfortunate or wretched: *an unhappy
fellow.* **3.** tactless or inappropriate: *an unhappy remark.*
—**un'happily** *adv.* —**un'happiness** *n.*
unhealthy (ʌn'hɛlθɪ) *adj.* **-healthier, -healthiest. 1.** characterized by ill-health; sick. **2.** characteristic of, conducive to, or resulting from ill-health: *an unhealthy complexion.* **3.** morbid or unwholesome. **4.** *Inf.* dangerous;
risky. —**un'healthily** *adv.* —**un'healthiness** *n.*
unheard-of *adj.* **1.** previously unknown: *an unheard-
of actress.* **2.** without precedent: *an unheard-of treatment.* **3.** highly offensive: *unheard-of behaviour.*
unhinge (ʌn'hɪndʒ) *vb.* (*tr.*) **1.** to remove (a door, etc.)
from its hinges. **2.** to derange or unbalance (a person,
his mind, etc.). **3.** to disrupt or unsettle (a process or
state of affairs).
unholy (ʌn'həʊlɪ) *adj.* **-lier, -liest. 1.** not holy or sacred.
2. immoral or depraved. **3.** *Inf.* outrageous or unnatural:
an unholy alliance. —**un'holiness** *n.*
unhook (ʌn'hʊk) *vb.* **1.** (*tr.*) to remove (something)
from a hook. **2.** (*tr.*) to unfasten the hook of (a dress,
etc.). **3.** (*intr.*) to become unfastened or be capable of
unfastening: *the dress wouldn't unhook.*
unhorse (ʌn'hɔːs) *vb.* (*tr.*) **1.** (*usually passive*) to knock
or throw from a horse. **2.** to overthrow or dislodge, as
from a powerful position.
uni ('juːnɪ) *n. Austral. & Scot. inf.* short for **university.**
uni- *combining form.* consisting of, relating to, or hav-

ing only one: *unilateral.*
unicameral (ˌjuːnɪ'kæmərəl) *adj.* of or characterized
by a single legislative chamber. —**uni'cameralism** *n.*
—**uni'cameralist** *n.* —**uni'camerally** *adv.*
UNICEF ('juːnɪˌsɛf) *n. acronym for* United Nations
Children's Fund (formerly, United Nations International
Children's Emergency Fund).
unicellular (ˌjuːnɪ'sɛljʊlə) *adj.* (of organisms, such as
protozoans and certain algae) consisting of a single cell.
—**uni,cellu'larity** *n.*
unicorn ('juːnɪˌkɔːn) *n.* **1.** an imaginary creature usually depicted as a white horse with one long spiralled horn
growing from its forehead. **2.** *Old Testament.* a two-
horned animal: mistranslation in the Authorized Version
of the original Hebrew.
unicycle ('juːnɪˌsaɪkəl) *n.* a one-wheeled vehicle driven
by pedals, esp. one used in a circus, etc. Also called:
monocycle. —**'uni,cyclist** *n.*
unidirectional (ˌjuːnɪdɪ'rɛkʃənəl) *adj.* having, moving
in, or operating in only one direction.
UNIDO (juː'niːdəʊ) *n. acronym for* United Nations Industrial Development Organization.
uniform ('juːnɪˌfɔːm) *n.* **1.** a prescribed identifying set
of clothes for the members of an organization, such as
soldiers or schoolchildren. **2.** a single set of such
clothes. **3.** a characteristic feature of some class or
group. ~*adj.* **4.** unchanging in form, quality, etc.: *a uniform surface.* **5.** alike or like: *a line of uniform toys.*
~*vb.* (*tr.*) **6.** to fit out (a body of soldiers, etc.) with uniforms. **7.** to make uniform. —**'uni'formity** *n.* —**'uni-
,formly** *adv.* —**'uni,formness** *n.*
unify ('juːnɪˌfaɪ) *vb.* **-fying, -fied.** to make or become
one; unite. —**'uni,fiable** *adj.* —**,unifi'cation** *n.* —**'uni-
,fier** *n.*
unilateral (ˌjuːnɪ'lætərəl) *adj.* **1.** of, having, affecting,
or occurring on only one side. **2.** involving or performed
by only one party of several: *unilateral disarmament.* **3.**
Law. (of contracts, obligations, etc.) made by, affecting,
or binding one party only. **4.** *Bot.* having or designating
parts situated or turned to one side of an axis. —**,uni-
'lateralism** *n.* —**,uni'laterally** *adv.*
unimpeachable (ˌʌnɪm'piːtʃəbəl) *adj.* unquestionable
as to honesty, truth, etc. —**,unim'peachably** *adv.*

THESAURUS

unguarded 1. careless, foolhardy, heedless, ill-considered, impolitic, imprudent, incautious, indiscreet, rash, thoughtless, uncircumspect, undiplomatic, unthinking, unwary
2. defenceless, open to attack, undefended,
unpatrolled, unprotected, vulnerable 3. artless, candid, direct, frank, guileless, open,
straightforward

unhappy 1. blue, crestfallen, dejected, depressed, despondent, disconsolate, dispirited,
down, downcast, gloomy, long-faced, melancholy, miserable, mournful, sad, sorrowful 2.
cursed, hapless, ill-fated, ill-omened, luckless,
unfortunate, unlucky, wretched 3. awkward,
clumsy, gauche, ill-advised, ill-timed, inappropriate, inept, infelicitous, injudicious,
malapropos, tactless, unsuitable, untactful

unharmed in one piece (*Inf.*), intact,
safe, safe and sound, sound, undamaged, unhurt, uninjured, unscarred, unscathed, untouched, whole, without a scratch

unhealthy 1. ailing, delicate, feeble,
frail, infirm, in poor health, invalid, poorly
(*Inf.*), sick, sickly, unsound, unwell, weak 2.
deleterious, detrimental, harmful, insalubrious, insanitary, noisome, noxious, unwholesome 3. bad, baneful (*Archaic*), corrupt, corrupting, degrading, demoralizing, morbid,
negative, undesirable

unheard-of 1. little known, obscure, undiscovered, unfamiliar, unknown, unregard-
ed, unremarked, unsung 2. inconceivable,
never before encountered, new, novel, singular, unbelievable, undreamed of, unexampled, unique, unprecedented, unusual 3. disgraceful, extreme, offensive, outlandish, outrageous, preposterous, shocking, unacceptable, unthinkable

unheeded disobeyed, disregarded, forgotten, ignored, neglected, overlooked, unfol-

lowed, unnoticed, unobserved, untaken

unhesitating 1. implicit, resolute,
steadfast, unfaltering, unquestioning, unreserved, unswerving, unwavering, wholehearted 2. immediate, instant, instantaneous,
prompt, ready, without delay

unhinge 1. confound, confuse, craze, derange, disorder, distemper (*Archaic*), drive
out of one's mind, madden, unbalance, unsettle 2. detach, disconnect, disjoint, dislodge,
remove

unholy 1. base, corrupt, depraved, dishonest, evil, heinous, immoral, iniquitous, irreligious, profane, sinful, ungodly, vile, wicked 2.
Inf. appalling, awful, dreadful, horrendous,
outrageous, shocking, unearthly, ungodly
(*Inf.*), unnatural, unreasonable

unhoped-for beyond one's wildest
dreams, incredible, like a dream come true,
out of the blue, surprising, unanticipated, unbelievable, undreamed of, unexpected, unimaginable, unlooked-for

unhurried calm, deliberate, easy, easy-
going, leisurely, sedate, slow, slow and
steady, slow-paced

unidentified anonymous, mysterious,
nameless, unclassified, unfamiliar, unknown,
unmarked, unnamed, unrecognized, unrevealed

unification alliance, amalgamation,
coalescence, coalition, combination, confederation, federation, fusion, merger, union,
uniting

uniform *n.* 1. costume, dress, garb, habit,
livery, outfit, regalia, regimentals, suit ~*adj.*
2. consistent, constant, equable, even, regular, smooth, unbroken, unchanging, undeviating, unvarying 3. alike, equal, identical, like,
same, selfsame, similar

uniformity 1. constancy, evenness,
homogeneity, invariability, regularity, sameness, similarity 2. drabness, dullness, flatness, lack of diversity, monotony, sameness,
tedium

unify amalgamate, bind, bring together,
combine, confederate, consolidate, federate,
fuse, join, merge, unite

unimaginable beyond one's wildest
dreams, fantastic, impossible, inconceivable,
incredible, indescribable, ineffable, mind-
boggling (*Inf.*), unbelievable, unheard-of, unthinkable

unimaginative barren, commonplace,
derivative, dry, dull, hackneyed, lifeless,
matter-of-fact, ordinary, pedestrian, predictable, prosaic, routine, tame, uncreative, uninspired, unoriginal, unromantic, usual

unimpassioned calm, collected, composed, controlled, cool, dispassionate, impassive, moderate, rational, sedate, temperate,
tranquil, undemonstrative, unemotional, unmoved

unimpeachable above reproach, beyond criticism, beyond question, blameless,
faultless, impeccable, irreproachable, perfect, unassailable, unblemished, unchallenge-
able, unexceptionable, unquestionable

unimpeded free, open, unblocked, unchecked, unconstrained, unhampered, unhindered, unrestrained, untrammelled

unimportant immaterial, inconsequential, insignificant, irrelevant, low-ranking,
minor, not worth mentioning, nugatory, of no
account, of no consequence, of no moment,
paltry, petty, slight, trifling, trivial, worthless

uninhabited abandoned, barren, desert,
deserted, desolate, empty, unoccupied, un-

uninterested (ʌn'ıntrıstıd) *adj.* 1. indifferent. 2. having no personal interest. —**un'interestedly** *adv.* —**un'interestedness** *n.*

▷ **Usage.** See at **disinterested.**

union ('juːnjən) *n.* 1. the condition of being united, the act of uniting, or a conjunction formed by such an act. 2. an association, alliance, or confederation of individuals or groups for a common purpose, esp. political. 3. agreement or harmony. 4. short for **trade union.** 5. the act or state of marriage or sexual intercourse. 6. a device on a flag representing union, such as another flag depicted in the top left corner. 7. a device for coupling pipes. 8. (*often cap.*) **a.** an association of students at a university or college formed to look after the students' interests. **b.** the building or buildings housing the facilities of such an organization. 9. *Maths.* a set containing all members of two given sets. Symbol: ∪ 10. (in 19th-century England) a number of parishes united for the administration of poor relief. 11. *Textiles.* a piece of cloth or fabric consisting of two different kinds of yarn. 12. (*modifier*) of or related to a union, esp. a trade union. —**'union₁ism** *n.*

union catalogue *n.* a catalogue listing every publication held at cooperating libraries.

Unionist ('juːnjənıst) *n.* 1. a member or supporter of the Unionist Party. 2. a supporter of the U.S. federal Union, esp. during the Civil War. ~*adj.* 3. of, resembling, or relating to Unionists. —**'Union₁ism** *n.*

unionize *or* **-nise** ('juːnjə₁naız) *vb.* 1. to organize (workers) into a trade union. 2. to join or cause to join a trade union. 3. (*tr.*) to subject to the rules or codes of a trade union. —**₁unioni'zation** *or* **-i'sation** *n.*

Union Jack *n.* the national flag of Great Britain, being a composite design composed of St. George's Cross (England), Saint Andrew's Cross (Scotland), and Saint Patrick's Cross (Ireland). Also called: **Union flag.**

union shop *n.* an establishment whose employment policy is governed by a contract between employer and a trade union permitting the employment of nonunion labour only on the condition that such labour joins the union within a specified time period.

unique (juː'niːk) *adj.* 1. being the only one of a particular type. 2. without equal or like. 3. *Inf.* very remarkable. 4. *Maths.* leading to only one result: *the sum of two integers is unique.* —**u'niquely** *adv.* —**u'niqueness** *n.*

▷ **Usage.** Certain words in English, such as *unique, perfect,* and *simultaneous,* describe absolute states, that is to say, states that cannot be qualified; something is either *unique* or it is *not unique,* but it cannot be, for example, *rather unique.* Careful users of English therefore avoid the use of comparatives or intensifiers where absolute states are concerned: *that is very exceptional* (not *very unique*); *this one comes nearer to perfection* (not *is more perfect*).

unisex ('juːnı₁sɛks) *adj.* of or relating to clothing, a hair style, hairdressers, etc., that can be worn or used by either sex.

unisexual (₁juːnı'sɛksjʊəl) *adj.* 1. of one sex only. 2. (of some organisms) having either male or female reproductive organs but not both. —**₁uni₁sexu'ality** *n.* —**₁uni'sexually** *adv.*

unison ('juːnısən) *n.* 1. *Music.* **a.** the interval between two notes of identical pitch. **b.** (*modifier*) played or sung at the same pitch: *unison singing.* 2. complete agreement (esp. in **in unison**). —**u'nisonous, u'nisonal,** *or* **u'nisonant** *adj.*

unit ('juːnıt) *n.* 1. a single undivided entity or whole. 2. any group or individual, esp. when regarded as a basic element of a larger whole. 3. a mechanical part or assembly of parts that performs a subsidiary function: *a filter unit.* 4. a complete system or establishment that performs a specific function: *a production unit.* 5. a subdivision of a larger military formation. 6. a standard amount of a physical quantity, such as length, mass, energy, etc., specified multiples of which are used to express magnitudes of that physical quantity: *the second is a unit of time.* 7. the amount of a drug, vaccine, etc., needed to produce a particular effect. 8. the digit or position immediately to the left of the decimal point. 9. (*modifier*) having or relating to a value of one: *a unit vector.* 10. *N.Z.* a self-propelled railcar. 11. *Austral. & N.Z.* a small self-contained dwelling, such as a flat, in a complex of such dwellings.

Unitarian (₁juːnı'tɛərıən) *n.* 1. *Theol.* a person who believes that God is one being and rejects the doctrine of the Trinity. 2. a member of the Church (**Unitarian Church**) that embodies this system of belief. ~*adj.* 3. of or relating to Unitarians or Unitarianism. —**₁Uni'taria₁nism** *n.*

unitary ('juːnıtərı, -trı) *adj.* 1. of a unit or units. 2. based on or characterized by unity. 3. individual; whole.

unit cost *n.* the actual cost of producing one article.

unite (juː'naıt) *vb.* 1. to make or become an integrated whole or a unity. 2. to join, unify or be unified in purpose, action, beliefs, etc. 3. to enter or cause to enter into an association or alliance. 4. to adhere or cause to adhere; fuse. 5. (*tr.*) to possess (qualities) in combination or at the same time: *he united charm with severity.*

united (juː'naıtıd) *adj.* 1. produced by two or more persons or things in combination or from their union or amalgamation: *a united effort.* 2. in agreement. 3. in association or alliance. —**u'nitedly** *adv.* —**u'nitedness** *n.*

United Kingdom *n.* a kingdom of NW Europe, consisting chiefly of the island of Great Britain together with Northern Ireland. It became the **United Kingdom of Great Britain and Northern Ireland** in 1922, after the rest of Ireland became autonomous.

United Nations *n.* an international organization of independent states, with its headquarters in New York City, that was formed in 1945 to promote peace and international cooperation and security. Abbrev.: **UN**

unit price *n.* a price for foodstuffs, etc., stated or shown as the cost per unit, as per pound, per kilogram, per dozen, etc.

unit trust *n. Brit.* an investment trust that issues units

THESAURUS

populated, unsettled, untenanted, vacant, waste

uninhibited 1. candid, frank, free, free and easy, informal, instinctive, liberated, natural, open, relaxed, spontaneous, unrepressed, unreserved, unselfconscious 2. free, unbridled, unchecked, unconstrained, uncontrolled, uncurbed, unrestrained, unrestricted

uninspired commonplace, dull, humdrum, indifferent, ordinary, prosaic, stale, stock, unexciting, unimaginative, uninspiring, uninteresting, unoriginal

unintelligent brainless, dense, dull, empty-headed, foolish, gormless (*Brit. inf.*), obtuse, slow, stupid, thick, unreasoning, unthinking

unintelligible double Dutch (*Brit. inf.*), illegible, inarticulate, incoherent, incomprehensible, indecipherable, indistinct, jumbled, meaningless, muddled, unfathomable

unintentional accidental, casual, fortuitous, inadvertent, involuntary, unconscious, undesigned, unintended, unpremeditated, unthinking, unwitting

uninterested apathetic, blasé, bored,

distant, impassive, incurious, indifferent, listless, unconcerned, uninvolved, unresponsive

uninteresting boring, commonplace, drab, dreary, dry, dull, flat, humdrum, monotonous, tedious, tiresome, unenjoyable, uneventful, unexciting, uninspiring, wearisome

uninterrupted constant, continual, continuous, nonstop, peaceful, steady, sustained, unbroken, undisturbed, unending

uninvited not asked, not invited, unasked, unbidden, unwanted, unwelcome

uninviting disagreeable, offensive, offputting (*Brit. inf.*), repellent, repulsive, unappealing, unappetizing, unattractive, undesirable, unpleasant, untempting, unwelcoming

union 1. amalgam, amalgamation, blend, combination, conjunction, fusion, junction, mixture, synthesis, uniting 2. alliance, association, Bund, coalition, confederacy, confederation, federation, league 3. accord, agreement, concord, concurrence, harmony, unanimity, unison, unity 4. coition, coitus, copulation, coupling, intercourse, marriage, matrimony, wedlock

unique 1. lone, one and only, only, single,

solitary, sui generis 2. incomparable, inimitable, matchless, nonpareil, peerless, unequalled, unexampled, unmatched, unparalleled, unrivalled, without equal

unison accord, accordance, agreement, concert, concord, cooperation, harmony, unanimity, unity

unit 1. assembly, detachment, entity, group, section, system, whole 2. component, constituent, element, item, member, module, part, piece, portion, section, segment 3. measure, measurement, module, quantity

unite 1. amalgamate, blend, coalesce, combine, confederate, consolidate, couple, fuse, incorporate, join, link, marry, merge, unify, wed 2. ally, associate, band, close ranks, club together, cooperate, join forces, join together, league, pool, pull together

united 1. affiliated, allied, banded together, collective, combined, concerted, in partnership, leagued, pooled, unified 2. agreed, in accord, in agreement, like-minded, of like mind, of one mind, of the same opinion, one, unanimous

for public sale, the holders of which are creditors and not shareholders with their interests represented by a trust company independent of the issuing agency.

unity ('ju:nɪtɪ) *n., pl.* **-ties. 1.** the state or quality of being one; oneness. **2.** the act, state, or quality of forming a whole from separate parts. **3.** something whole or complete that is composed of separate parts. **4.** mutual agreement; harmony or concord: *the participants were no longer in unity.* **5.** uniformity or constancy: *unity of purpose.* **6.** *Maths.* **a.** the number or numeral one. **b.** a quantity assuming the value of one: *the area of the triangle was regarded as unity.* **c.** the element of a set producing no change in a number following multiplication. **7.** any one of the three principles of dramatic structure by which the action of a play should be limited to a single plot (unity of action), a single location (unity of place), and a single day (unity of time).

Univ. *abbrev. for* University.

univalent (ju:nɪ'veɪlənt, ju:'nɪvələnt) *adj.* **1.** (of a chromosome during meiosis) not paired with its homologue. **2.** *Chem.* another word for **monovalent.** —ˌuni'valency *n.*

universal (ˌju:nɪ'vɜ:səl) *adj.* **1.** of or typical of the whole of mankind or of nature. **2.** common to or proceeding from all in a particular group. **3.** applicable to or affecting many individuals, conditions, or cases. **4.** existing or prevailing everywhere. **5.** applicable or occurring throughout or relating to the universe: *a universal constant.* **6.** (esp. of a language) capable of being used and understood by all. **7.** embracing or versed in many fields of knowledge, activity, interest, etc. **8.** *Machinery.* designed or adapted for a range of sizes, fittings, or uses. **9.** *Logic.* (of a proposition) affirming or denying something about every member of a class of objects, as in *all men are wicked.* Cf. **particular** (sense 6). **10.** *Arch.* entire; whole. ~*n.* **11.** *Philosophy.* a general term or concept or the type such a term signifies; a Platonic idea or Aristotelian form. **12.** *Logic.* a universal proposition. **13.** a characteristic common to every member of a particular culture or to every human being.

universality (ˌju:nɪvɜ:'sælɪtɪ) *n., pl.* **-ties.** the state or quality of being universal.

universal joint *or* **coupling** *n.* a form of coupling between two rotating shafts allowing freedom of movement in all directions.

universally (ˌju:nɪ'vɜ:səlɪ) *adv.* everywhere or in every case: *this principle applies universally.*

universe ('ju:nɪˌvɜ:s) *n.* **1.** *Astron.* the aggregate of all existing matter, energy, and space. **2.** human beings collectively. **3.** a province or sphere of thought or activity.

university (ˌju:nɪ'vɜ:sɪtɪ) *n., pl.* **-ties. 1.** an institution of higher education having authority to award bachelors' and higher degrees, usually having research facilities. **2.** the buildings, members, staff, or campus of a university.

unjust (ʌn'dʒʌst) *adj.* not in accordance with accepted standards of fairness or justice; unfair. —**un'justly** *adv.* —**un'justness** *n.*

unkempt (ʌn'kɛmpt) *adj.* **1.** (of the hair) uncombed; di-

shevelled. **2.** ungroomed; slovenly: *unkempt appearance.* —**un'kemptly** *adv.* —**un'kemptness** *n.*

unkind (ʌn'kaɪnd) *adj.* lacking kindness; unsympathetic or cruel. —**un'kindly** *adv.* —**un'kindness** *n.*

unknown (ʌn'nəʊn) *adj.* **1.** not known, understood, or recognized. **2.** not established, identified, or discovered: *an unknown island.* **3.** not famous: *some unknown artist.* ~*n.* **4.** an unknown person, quantity, or thing. **5.** *Maths.* a variable whose values are solutions of a conditional equation. **6. unknown quantity.** a person or thing whose action, effect, etc., is unknown or unpredictable. —**un'knownness** *n.*

unlace (ʌn'leɪs) *vb.* (*tr.*) **1.** to loosen or undo the lacing of (shoes, etc.). **2.** to unfasten or remove garments, etc., of (oneself or another) by or as if by undoing lacing.

unlearn (ʌn'lɜ:n) *vb.* **-learning, -learnt** *or* **-learned** (-'lɜ:nd). to try to forget (something learnt) or to discard (accumulated knowledge).

unlearned (ʌn'lɜ:nɪd) *adj.* ignorant or untaught. —**un'learnedly** *adv.*

unlearnt (ʌn'lɜ:nt) *or* **unlearned** (ʌn'lɜ:nd) *adj.* **1.** known without being consciously learnt. **2.** not learnt or taken notice of: *unlearnt lessons.*

unleash (ʌn'li:ʃ) *vb.* (*tr.*) **1.** to release from or as if from a leash. **2.** to free from restraint.

unleavened (ʌn'lɛvənd) *adj.* (of bread, etc.) made from a dough containing no yeast or leavening.

unless (ʌn'lɛs) *conj.* (*subordinating*) except under the circumstances that; except on the condition that: *they'll sell it unless he hears otherwise.*

▷ **Usage.** Careful writers of English who wish to keep their style clear and concise avoid the use of the expressions *unless and until* and *unless or until.* The difference in meaning of these two words is, in this context, not sufficient to make mentioning them both worthwhile; either would be adequate alone: *Unless* (or *until*, but not *unless and until*) *a candidate is nominated, the election cannot take place.*

unlettered (ʌn'lɛtəd) *adj.* uneducated; illiterate.

unlike (ʌn'laɪk) *adj.* **1.** not alike; dissimilar or unequal; different. ~*prep.* **2.** not like; not typical of: *unlike his father he lacks intelligence.* —**un'likeness** *n.*

unlikely (ʌn'laɪklɪ) *adj.* not likely; improbable. —**un'likeliness** *or* **un'likelihood** *n.*

unlimited (ʌn'lɪmɪtɪd) *adj.* **1.** without limits or bounds: *unlimited knowledge.* **2.** not restricted, limited, or qualified: *unlimited power.* —**un'limitedly** *adv.* —**un'limitedness** *n.*

unlisted (ʌn'lɪstɪd) *adj.* **1.** not entered on a list. **2.** (of securities) not quoted on a stock exchange.

unload (ʌn'ləʊd) *vb.* **1.** to remove a load or cargo from (a ship, lorry, etc.). **2.** to discharge (cargo, freight, etc.). **3.** (*tr.*) to relieve of a burden or troubles. **4.** (*tr.*) to give vent to (anxiety, troubles, etc.). **5.** (*tr.*) to get rid of or dispose of, esp. surplus goods. **6.** (*tr.*) to remove the charge of ammunition from (a firearm). —**un'loader** *n.*

unlock (ʌn'lɒk) *vb.* **1.** (*tr.*) to unfasten (a lock, door, etc.). **2.** (*tr.*) to release or let loose. **3.** (*tr.*) to provide

---

THESAURUS

unity 1. entity, integrity, oneness, singleness, undividedness, unification, union, wholeness **2.** accord, agreement, concord, concurrence, consensus, harmony, peace, solidarity, unanimity

universal all-embracing, catholic, common, ecumenical, entire, general, omnipresent, total, unlimited, whole, widespread, worldwide

universality all-inclusiveness, completeness, comprehensiveness, entirety, generality, generalization, totality, ubiquity

universally always, everywhere, in all cases, in every instance, invariably, uniformly, without exception

universe cosmos, creation, everything, macrocosm, nature, the natural world

unjust biased, inequitable, one-sided, partial, partisan, prejudiced, undeserved, unfair, unjustified, unmerited, wrong, wrongful

unjustifiable indefensible, inexcusable, outrageous, unacceptable, unforgivable, unjust, unpardonable, unwarrantable, wrong

unkempt bedraggled, blowzy, disar-

ranged, dishevelled, disordered, frowzy, messy, rumpled, scruffy, shabby, shaggy, slatternly, sloppy (*Inf.*), slovenly, sluttish, tousled, uncombed, ungroomed, untidy

unkind cruel, hardhearted, harsh, inconsiderate, inhuman, insensitive, malicious, mean, nasty, spiteful, thoughtless, uncaring, uncharitable, unchristian, unfeeling, unfriendly, unsympathetic

unknown 1. alien, concealed, dark, hidden, mysterious, new, secret, strange, unrecognized, unrevealed, untold **2.** anonymous, nameless, uncharted, undiscovered, unexplored, unidentified, unnamed **3.** humble, little known, obscure, undistinguished, unfamiliar, unheard-of, unrenowned, unsung

unladylike coarse, ill-bred, impolite, indelicate, rude, uncivil, ungracious, unmannerly, unrefined

unlamented unbemoaned, unbewailed, undeplored, unmissed, unmourned, unregretted, unwept

unlawful actionable, against the law, banned, criminal, forbidden, illegal, illegiti-

mate, illicit, outlawed, prohibited, unauthorized, unlicensed

unlettered ignorant, illiterate, uneducated, unlearned, unschooled, untaught, untutored

unlike contrasted, different, dissimilar, distinct, divergent, diverse, ill-matched, incompatible, not alike, opposite, unequal, unrelated

unlikely 1. doubtful, faint, improbable, not likely, remote, slight, unimaginable **2.** implausible, incredible, questionable, unbelievable, unconvincing

unlimited 1. boundless, countless, endless, extensive, great, illimitable, immeasurable, immense, incalculable, infinite, limitless, unbounded, vast **2.** absolute, all-encompassing, complete, full, total, unconditional, unconstrained, unfettered, unqualified, unrestricted

unload disburden, discharge, dump, empty, off-load, relieve, unburden, unlade, unpack

the key to: *unlock a puzzle.* **4.** (*intr.*) to become un-locked. **—un'lockable** *adj.*

unlooked-for *adj.* unexpected; unforeseen.

unloose (ʌnˈluːs) *or* **unloosen** *vb.* (*tr.*) **1.** to set free; release. **2.** to loosen or relax (a hold, grip, etc.). **3.** to unfasten or untie.

unlovely (ʌnˈlʌvlɪ) *adj.* **1.** unpleasant in appearance. **2.** unpleasant in character. **—un'loveliness** *n.*

unlucky (ʌnˈlʌkɪ) *adj.* **1.** characterized by misfortune or failure: *an unlucky chance.* **2.** ill-omened; inauspicious: *an unlucky date.* **3.** regrettable; disappointing. **—un'luckily** *adv.* **—un'luckiness** *n.*

unmake (ʌnˈmeɪk) *vb.* **-making, -made.** (*tr.*) **1.** to undo or destroy. **2.** to depose from office or authority. **3.** to alter the nature of.

unman (ʌnˈmæn) *vb.* **-manning, -manned.** (*tr.*) **1.** to cause to lose courage or nerve. **2.** to make effeminate. **3.** to remove the men from.

unmanly (ʌnˈmænlɪ) *adj.* **1.** not masculine or virile. **2.** ignoble, cowardly, or dishonourable. **~adv. 3.** *Arch.* in an unmanly manner. **—un'manliness** *n.*

unmanned (ʌnˈmænd) *adj.* **1.** lacking personnel or crew: *an unmanned ship.* **2.** (of aircraft, spacecraft, etc.) operated by automatic or remote control. **3.** uninhabited.

unmannerly (ʌnˈmænəlɪ) *adj.* **1.** lacking manners; discourteous. **~adv. 2.** *Arch.* rudely; discourteously. **—un'mannerliness** *n.*

unmask (ʌnˈmɑːsk) *vb.* **1.** to remove (the mask or disguise) from (someone or oneself). **2.** to appear or cause to appear in true character. **—un'masker** *n.*

unmeaning (ʌnˈmiːnɪŋ) *adj.* **1.** having no meaning. **2.** showing no intelligence; vacant: *an unmeaning face.* **—un'meaningly** *adv.* **—un'meaningness** *n.*

unmentionable (ʌnˈmɛnʃənəbəl) *adj.* **a.** unsuitable or forbidden as a topic of conversation. **b.** (*as n.*): *the unmentionable.* **—un'mentionableness** *n.* **—un'mentionably** *adv.*

unmerciful (ʌnˈmɜːsɪful) *adj.* **1.** showing no mercy; relentless. **2.** extreme or excessive. **—un'mercifully** *adv.*

—un'mercifulness *n.*

unmistakable *or* **unmistakeable** (ˌʌnmɪsˈteɪkəbəl) *adj.* not mistakable; clear, obvious, or unambiguous. **—ˌunmis'takably** *or* **ˌunmis'takeably** *adv.*

unmitigated (ʌnˈmɪtɪˌgeɪtɪd) *adj.* **1.** not diminished in intensity, severity, etc. **2.** (*prenominal*) (intensifier): *an unmitigated disaster.* **—un'miti₁gatedly** *adv.*

unmoral (ʌnˈmɒrəl) *adj.* outside morality; amoral. **—unmorality** (ˌʌnməˈrælɪtɪ) *n.* **—un'morally** *adv.*

unmuzzle (ʌnˈmʌzəl) *vb.* (*tr.*) **1.** to take the muzzle off (a dog, etc.). **2.** to free from control or censorship.

unnatural (ʌnˈnætʃərəl) *adj.* **1.** contrary to nature; abnormal. **2.** not in accordance with accepted standards of behaviour or right and wrong: *unnatural love.* **3.** uncanny; supernatural: *unnatural phenomena.* **4.** affected or forced: *an unnatural manner.* **5.** inhuman or monstrous: *an unnatural crime.* **—un'naturally** *adv.* **—un'naturalness** *n.*

unnecessary (ʌnˈnɛsɪsərɪ) *adj.* not necessary. **—un'necessarily** *adv.* **—un'necessariness** *n.*

unnerve (ʌnˈnɜːv) *vb.* (*tr.*) to cause to lose courage, strength, confidence, self-control, etc.

unnumbered (ʌnˈnʌmbəd) *adj.* **1.** countless; innumerable. **2.** not counted or assigned a number.

U.N.O. *abbrev. for* United Nations Organization.

unoccupied (ʌnˈɒkjuˌpaɪd) *adj.* **1.** (of a building) without occupants. **2.** unemployed or idle. **3.** (of an area or country) not overrun by foreign troops.

unorganized *or* **-nised** (ʌnˈɔːgəˌnaɪzd) *adj.* **1.** not arranged into an organized system, structure, or unity. **2.** (of workers) not unionized. **3.** nonliving; inorganic.

unpack (ʌnˈpæk) *vb.* **1.** to remove the packed contents of (a case, trunk, etc.). **2.** (*tr.*) to take (something) out of a packed container. **3.** (*tr.*) to unload: *to unpack a mule.* **—un'packer** *n.*

unparalleled (ʌnˈpærəˌlɛld) *adj.* unmatched; unequalled.

unparliamentary (ˌʌnpɑːləˈmɛntərɪ) *adj.* not consistent with parliamentary procedure or practice. **—ˌunparlia'mentarily** *adv.* **—ˌunparlia'mentariness** *n.*

THESAURUS

unlock free, let loose, open, release, unbar, unbolt, undo, unfasten, unlatch

unlooked-for chance, fortuitous, out of the blue, surprise, surprising, unanticipated, undreamed of, unexpected, unforeseen, unhoped-for, unpredicted, unthought-of

unloved disliked, forsaken, loveless, neglected, rejected, spurned, uncared-for, uncherished, unpopular, unwanted

unlucky 1. cursed, disastrous, hapless, luckless, miserable, unfortunate, unhappy, unsuccessful, wretched **2.** doomed, ill-fated, ill-omened, ill-starred, inauspicious, ominous, unfavourable, untimely

unmanageable 1. awkward, bulky, cumbersome, difficult to handle, inconvenient, unhandy, unwieldy **2.** difficult, fractious, intractable, obstreperous, out of hand, refractory, stroppy (*Brit. sl.*), uncontrollable, unruly, wild

unmannerly badly behaved, bad-mannered, discourteous, disrespectful, ill-bred, ill-mannered, impolite, misbehaved, rude, uncivil, uncouth

unmarried bachelor, celibate, maiden, single, unattached, unwed, unwedded, virgin

unmask bare, bring to light, disclose, discover, expose, lay bare, reveal, show up, uncloak, uncover, unveil

unmatched beyond compare, consummate, incomparable, matchless, paramount, peerless, second to none, supreme, unequalled, unparalleled, unrivalled, unsurpassed

unmentionable disgraceful, disreputable, forbidden, frowned on, immodest, indecent, scandalous, shameful, shocking, taboo, unspeakable, unutterable

unmerciful brutal, cruel, hard, heartless, implacable, merciless, pitiless, relentless, remorseless, ruthless, uncaring, unfeeling, unsparing

unmindful careless, forgetful, heedless, inattentive, indifferent, lax, neglectful, negligent, oblivious, remiss, slack, unheeding

unmistakable certain, clear, conspicuous, decided, distinct, evident, glaring, indisputable, manifest, obvious, palpable, patent, plain, positive, pronounced, sure, unambiguous, unequivocal

unmitigated 1. grim, harsh, intense, oppressive, persistent, relentless, unabated, unalleviated, unbroken, undiminished, unmodified, unqualified, unredeemed, unrelieved **2.** absolute, arrant, complete, consummate, downright, out-and-out, outright, perfect, rank, sheer, thorough, thoroughgoing, utter

unmoved 1. fast, firm, in place, in position, steady, unchanged, untouched **2.** cold, dry-eyed, impassive, indifferent, unaffected, unfeeling, unimpressed, unresponsive, unstirred, untouched **3.** determined, firm, inflexible, resolute, resolved, steadfast, undeviating, unshaken, unwavering

unnatural 1. aberrant, abnormal, anomalous, irregular, odd, perverse, perverted, unusual **2.** bizarre, extraordinary, freakish, outlandish, queer, strange, supernatural, unaccountable, uncanny **3.** affected, artificial, assumed, contrived, factitious, false, feigned, forced, insincere, laboured, mannered, phoney (*Sl.*), self-conscious, stagy, stiff, stilted, strained, studied, theatrical **4.** brutal, callous, cold-blooded, evil, fiendish, heartless, inhuman, monstrous, ruthless, savage, unfeeling, wicked

unnecessary dispensable, expendable, inessential, needless, nonessential, redundant, supererogatory, superfluous, surplus to requirements, uncalled-for, unneeded, unrequired, useless

unnerve confound, daunt, demoralize, disarm, disconcert, discourage, dishearten, dismay, dispirit, fluster, frighten, intimidate,

rattle (*Inf.*), shake, throw off balance, unhinge, unman, upset

unnoticed disregarded, ignored, neglected, overlooked, undiscovered, unheeded, unobserved, unperceived, unrecognized, unremarked, unseen

unobtrusive humble, inconspicuous, keeping a low profile, low-key, meek, modest, quiet, restrained, retiring, self-effacing, subdued, unassuming, unnoticeable, unostentatious, unpretentious

unoccupied 1. empty, tenantless, uninhabited, untenanted, vacant **2.** at leisure, disengaged, idle, inactive, unemployed

unofficial informal, personal, private, unauthorized, unconfirmed, wildcat

unorthodox abnormal, heterodox, irregular, unconventional, uncustomary, unusual, unwonted

unpaid 1. due, not discharged, outstanding, overdue, owing, payable, unsettled **2.** honorary, unsalaried, voluntary

unpalatable bitter, disagreeable, displeasing, distasteful, offensive, repugnant, unappetizing, unattractive, uneatable, unpleasant, unsavoury

unparalleled beyond compare, consummate, exceptional, incomparable, matchless, peerless, rare, singular, superlative, unequalled, unique, unmatched, unprecedented, unrivalled, unsurpassed, without equal

unpardonable deplorable, disgraceful, indefensible, inexcusable, outrageous, scandalous, shameful, unforgivable, unjustifiable

unperturbed calm, collected, composed, cool, placid, poised, self-possessed, tranquil, undismayed, unflustered, unruffled, untroubled, unworried

unperson ('ʌnpɜːsˀn) *n.* a person whose existence is officially denied or ignored.

unpick (ʌn'pɪk) *vb.* (*tr.*) 1. to undo (the stitches) of (a piece of sewing). 2. to unravel or undo (a garment, etc.).

unpin (ʌn'pɪn) *vb.* **-pinning, -pinned.** (*tr.*) 1. to remove a pin or pins from. 2. to unfasten by removing pins.

unpleasant (ʌn'plɛzˀnt) *adj.* not pleasant or agreeable. **—un'pleasantly** *adv.* **—un'pleasantness** *n.*

unplumbed (ʌn'plʌmd) *adj.* 1. unfathomed; unsounded. 2. not understood in depth. 3. (of a building) having no plumbing.

unpopular (ʌn'pɒpjʊlə) *adj.* not popular with an individual or group of people. **—unpopularity** (ʌnˌpɒpjʊ'lærɪtɪ) *n.* **—un'popularly** *adv.*

unpractised *or U.S.* **unpracticed** (ʌn'præktɪst) *adj.* 1. without skill, training, or experience. 2. not used or done often or repeatedly. 3. not yet tested.

unprecedented (ʌn'prɛsɪˌdɛntɪd) *adj.* having no precedent; unparalleled. **—un'prece,dentedly** *adv.*

unprincipled (ʌn'prɪnsɪpˀld) *adj.* lacking moral principles; unscrupulous. **—un'principledness** *n.*

unprintable (ʌn'prɪntəbˀl) *adj.* unsuitable for printing for reasons of obscenity, libel, etc. **—un'printableness** *n.* **—un'printably** *adv.*

unprofessional (ˌʌnprə'fɛʃənˀl) *adj.* 1. contrary to the accepted code of conduct of a profession. 2. amateur. 3. not belonging to or having the required qualifications for a profession. **—unpro'fessionally** *adv.*

unqualified (ʌn'kwɒlɪˌfaɪd) *adj.* 1. lacking the necessary qualifications. 2. not restricted or modified: *an unqualified criticism.* 3. (*usually prenominal*) (intensifier): *an unqualified success.* **—un'quali,fiable** *adj.*

unquestionable (ʌn'kwɛstʃənəbˀl) *adj.* 1. indubitable or indisputable. 2. not admitting of exception: *an unquestionable ruling.* **—un,questiona'bility** *n.* **—un'questionably** *adv.*

unquiet (ʌn'kwaɪət) *Chiefly literary.* ~*adj.* 1. characterized by disorder or tumult: *unquiet times.* 2. anxious;

uneasy. ~*n.* 3. a state of unrest. **—un'quietly** *adv.* **—un'quietness** *n.*

unquote (ʌn'kwəʊt) *interj.* 1. an expression used parenthetically to indicate that the preceding quotation is finished. ~*vb.* 2. to close (a quotation), esp. in printing.

unravel (ʌn'rævˀl) *vb.* **-elling, -elled** *or U.S.* **-eling, -eled.** 1. (*tr.*) to reduce (something knitted or woven) to separate strands. 2. (*tr.*) to explain or solve: *the mystery was unravelled.* 3. (*intr.*) to become unravelled.

unread (ʌn'rɛd) *adj.* 1. (of a book, etc.) not yet read. 2. (of a person) having read little.

unreadable (ʌn'riːdəbˀl) *adj.* 1. illegible; undecipherable. 2. difficult or tedious to read. **—un,reada'bility** *or* **un'readableness** *n.*

unready (ʌn'rɛdɪ) *adj.* 1. not ready or prepared. 2. slow or hesitant to see or act. **—un'readily** *adv.* **—un'readiness** *n.*

unreal (ʌn'rɪəl) *adj.* 1. imaginary or fanciful or seemingly so: *an unreal situation.* 2. having no actual existence or substance. 3. insincere or artificial. **—unreality** (ˌʌnrɪ'ælɪtɪ) *n.* **—un'really** *adv.*

unreasonable (ʌn'riːznəbˀl) *adj.* 1. immoderate: *unreasonable demands.* 2. refusing to listen to reason. 3. lacking judgment. **—un'reasonableness** *n.* **—un'reasonably** *adv.*

unreasoning (ʌn'riːzənɪŋ) *adj.* not controlled by reason; irrational. **—un'reasoningly** *adv.*

unregenerate (ˌʌnrɪ'dʒɛnərɪt) *adj. also* **unregenerated.** 1. unrepentant; unreformed. 2. obstinately adhering to one's own views. ~*n.* 3. an unregenerate person. **—,unre'generacy** *n.* **—,unre'generately** *adv.*

unrelenting (ˌʌnrɪ'lɛntɪŋ) *adj.* 1. refusing to relent or take pity. 2. not diminishing in determination, speed, effort, force, etc. **—,unre'lentingly** *adv.* **—,unre'lentingness** *n.*

unremitting (ˌʌnrɪ'mɪtɪŋ) *adj.* never slackening or stopping; unceasing; constant. **—,unre'mittingly** *adv.* **—,unre'mittingness** *n.*

unreserved (ˌʌnrɪ'zɜːvd) *adj.* 1. without reserve; hav-

THESAURUS

unpleasant abhorrent, bad, disagreeable, displeasing, distasteful, ill-natured, irksome, nasty, objectionable, obnoxious, repulsive, troublesome, unattractive, unlikable, unlovely, unpalatable

unpopular avoided, detested, disliked, not sought out, out in the cold, out of favour, rejected, shunned, unattractive, undesirable, unloved, unwanted, unwelcome

unprecedented abnormal, exceptional, extraordinary, freakish, new, novel, original, remarkable, singular, unexampled, unheard-of, unparalleled, unrivalled, unusual

unpredictable chance, changeable, doubtful, erratic, fickle, fluky (*Inf.*), iffy, inconstant, random, unforeseeable, unreliable, unstable, variable

unprejudiced balanced, even-handed, fair, fair-minded, impartial, just, nonpartisan, objective, open-minded, unbiased, uninfluenced

unpremeditated extempore, impromptu, impulsive, offhand, off the cuff (*Inf.*), spontaneous, spur-of-the-moment, unplanned, unprepared

unprepared 1. half-baked (*Inf.*), illconsidered, incomplete, not thought out, unfinished, unplanned 2. caught napping, caught on the hop (*Brit. inf.*), surprised, taken aback, taken off guard, unaware, unready, unsuspecting 3. ad-lib, extemporaneous, improvised, off the cuff (*Inf.*), spontaneous

unpretentious homely, honest, humble, modest, plain, simple, straightforward, unaffected, unassuming, unimposing, unobtrusive, unostentatious, unspoiled

unprincipled amoral, corrupt, crooked, deceitful, devious, dishonest, immoral, tricky, unconscionable, underhand, unethical, unprofessional, unscrupulous

unproductive 1. bootless, fruitless, futile, idle, ineffective, inefficacious, otiose, un-

availing, unprofitable, unremunerative, unrewarding, useless, vain, valueless, worthless 2. barren, dry, fruitless, sterile, unprolific

unprofessional 1. improper, lax, negligent, unethical, unfitting, unprincipled, unseemly, unworthy 2. amateur, amateurish, incompetent, inefficient, inexperienced, inexpert, untrained

unpromising adverse, discouraging, doubtful, gloomy, inauspicious, infelicitous, ominous, unfavourable, unpropitious

unprotected defenceless, exposed, helpless, naked, open, open to attack, pregnable, unarmed, undefended, unguarded, unsheltered, unshielded, vulnerable

unqualified 1. ill-equipped, incapable, incompetent, ineligible, not equal to, not up to, unfit, unprepared 2. categorical, downright, outright, unconditional, unmitigated, unreserved, unrestricted, without reservation 3. absolute, complete, consummate, downright, out-and-out, thorough, thoroughgoing, total, utter

unquestionable absolute, beyond a shadow of doubt, certain, clear, conclusive, definite, faultless, flawless, incontestable, incontrovertible, indisputable, indubitable, irrefutable, manifest, patent, perfect, selfevident, sure, undeniable, unequivocal, unmistakable

unreadable 1. crabbed, illegible, undecipherable 2. badly written, dry as dust, heavy going, turgid

unreal 1. chimerical, dreamlike, fabulous, fanciful, fictitious, illusory, imaginary, makebelieve, phantasmagoric, storybook, visionary 2. hypothetical, immaterial, impalpable,

insubstantial, intangible, mythical, nebulous 3. artificial, fake, false, insincere, mock, ostensible, pretended, seeming, sham

unrealistic 1. half-baked (*Inf.*), impracticable, impractical, improbable, quixotic, romantic, starry-eyed, theoretical, unworkable 2. non-naturalistic, unauthentic, unlifelike, unreal

unreasonable 1. excessive, exorbitant, extortionate, extravagant, immoderate, steep (*Brit. inf.*), too great, uncalled-for, undue, unfair, unjust, unwarranted 2. arbitrary, biased, blinkered, capricious, erratic, headstrong, inconsistent, opinionated, quirky 3. absurd, far-fetched, foolish, illogical, irrational, mad, nonsensical, preposterous, senseless, silly, stupid

unrefined 1. crude, raw, unfinished, unpolished, unpurified, untreated 2. boorish, coarse, inelegant, rude, uncultured, unsophisticated, vulgar

unregenerate 1. godless, impious, profane, sinful, unconverted, unreformed, unrepentant, wicked 2. hardened, intractable, obdurate, obstinate, recalcitrant, refractory, self-willed, stubborn

unrelated 1. different, dissimilar, not kin, not kindred, not related, unconnected, unlike 2. beside the point, extraneous, inapplicable, inappropriate, irrelevant, not germane, unassociated, unconnected

unreliable 1. disreputable, irresponsible, not conscientious, treacherous, undependable, unstable, untrustworthy 2. deceptive, delusive, erroneous, fake, fallible, false, implausible, inaccurate, mistaken, specious, uncertain, unconvincing, unsound

unrepentant abandoned, callous, hardened, impenitent, incorrigible, not contrite, obdurate, shameless, unregenerate, unremorseful, unrepenting

ing an open manner. **2.** without reservation. **3.** not booked or bookable. —**unreservedly** (ˌʌnrɪˈzɜːvɪdlɪ) adv. —ˌunreˈservedness n.

unrest (ʌnˈrɛst) n. **1.** a troubled or rebellious state of discontent. **2.** an uneasy or troubled state.

unrighteous (ʌnˈraɪtʃəs) adj. **1. a.** sinful; wicked. **b.** (as n.): the unrighteous. **2.** not fair or right; unjust. —**unˈrighteously** adv. —**unˈrighteousness** n.

unripe (ʌnˈraɪp) or **unripened** adj. **1.** not fully matured. **2.** not fully prepared or developed; not ready. —**unˈripeness** n.

unrivalled (ʌnˈraɪvəld) adj. having no equal; matchless.

unroll (ʌnˈrəʊl) vb. **1.** to open out or unwind (something rolled, folded, or coiled) or (of something rolled, etc.) to become opened out or unwound. **2.** to make or become visible or apparent, esp. gradually; unfold.

unruffled (ʌnˈrʌfəld) adj. **1.** unmoved; calm. **2.** still: the unruffled seas. —**unˈruffledness** n.

unruly (ʌnˈruːlɪ) adj. **-lier, -liest.** disposed to disobedience or indiscipline. —**unˈruliness** n.

unsaddle (ʌnˈsædəl) vb. **1.** to remove the saddle from (a horse, mule, etc.). **2.** (tr.) to unhorse.

unsaid (ʌnˈsɛd) adj. not said or expressed; unspoken.

unsaturated (ʌnˈsætʃəˌreɪtɪd) adj. **1.** not saturated. **2.** (of a chemical compound, esp. an organic compound) containing one or more double or triple bonds and thus capable of undergoing addition reactions. —ˌunsatuˈration n.

unsavoury or U.S. **unsavory** (ʌnˈseɪvərɪ) adj. **1.** objectionable or distasteful: an unsavoury character. **2.** disagreeable in odour or taste. —**unˈsavourily** or U.S. **unˈsavorily** adv. —**unˈsavouriness** or U.S. **unˈsavoriness** n.

unsay (ʌnˈseɪ) vb. **-saying, -said.** (tr.) to retract or withdraw (something said or written).

unscathed (ʌnˈskeɪðd) adj. not harmed or injured.

unscramble (ʌnˈskræmbəl) vb. (tr.) **1.** Inf. to resolve from confusion or disorderliness. **2.** to restore (a scrambled message) to an intelligible form. —**unˈscrambler** n.

unscrew (ʌnˈskruː) vb. **1.** (tr.) to remove a screw from (an object). **2.** (tr.) to loosen (a screw, lid, etc.) by rotating, usually in an anticlockwise direction. **3.** (intr.) (esp. of an engaged threaded part) to become loosened or separated.

unscrupulous (ʌnˈskruːpjʊləs) adj. without scruples; unprincipled. —**unˈscrupulously** adv. —**unˈscrupulousness** n.

unseasonable (ʌnˈsiːzənəbəl) adj. **1.** (esp. of the weather) inappropriate for the season. **2.** untimely; inopportune. —**unˈseasonableness** n. —**unˈseasonably** adv.

unseat (ʌnˈsiːt) vb. (tr.) **1.** to throw or displace from a seat, saddle, etc. **2.** to depose from office or position.

unseeded (ʌnˈsiːdɪd) adj. (of players in various sports) not assigned to a preferential position in the preliminary rounds of a tournament.

unseemly (ʌnˈsiːmlɪ) adj. **1.** not in good style or taste. **2.** Obs. unattractive. ~adv. **3.** Rare. in an unseemly manner. —**unˈseemliness** n.

unselfish (ʌnˈsɛlfɪʃ) adj. not selfish; generous. —**unˈselfishly** adv. —**unˈselfishness** n.

unsettle (ʌnˈsɛtəl) vb. **1.** (usually tr.) to change or become changed from a fixed or settled condition. **2.** (tr.) to confuse or agitate (emotions, the mind, etc.). —**unˈsettlement** n.

unsettled (ʌnˈsɛtəld) adj. **1.** lacking order or stability: an unsettled era. **2.** unpredictable: an unsettled climate. **3.** constantly changing or moving from place to place: an unsettled life. **4.** (of controversy, etc.) not brought to an agreed conclusion. **5.** (of debts, law cases, etc.) not disposed of. —**unˈsettledness** n.

unsheathe (ʌnˈʃiːð) vb. (tr.) to draw or pull out (something, esp. a weapon) from a sheath.

unsightly (ʌnˈsaɪtlɪ) adj. unpleasant or unattractive to look at; ugly. —**unˈsightliness** n.

unskilful or U.S. **unskillful** (ʌnˈskɪlful) adj. lacking dexterity or proficiency. —**unˈskilfully** or U.S. **unˈskillfully** adv. —**unˈskilfulness** or U.S. **unˈskillfulness** n.

unskilled (ʌnˈskɪld) adj. **1.** not having or requiring any special skill or training: an unskilled job. **2.** having no skill; inexpert.

unsociable (ˌʌnˈsəʊʃəl) adj. **1.** (of a person) disinclined to associate or fraternize with others. **2.** unconducive to social intercourse: an unsociable neighbourhood. —ˌunˌsociaˈbility or unˈsociableness n.

unsocial (ˌʌnˈsəʊʃəl) adj. **1.** not social; antisocial. **2.** (of the hours of work of certain jobs) falling outside the normal working day.

THESAURUS

unreserved 1. demonstrative, extrovert, forthright, frank, free, open, openhearted, outgoing, outspoken, uninhibited, unrestrained, unreticent 2. absolute, complete, entire, full, total, unconditional, unlimited, unqualified, wholehearted, without reservation

unresolved doubtful, moot, open to question, pending, problematical, unanswered, undecided, undetermined, unsettled, unsolved, up in the air, vague, yet to be decided

unrest 1. agitation, disaffection, discontent, discord, dissatisfaction, dissension, protest, rebellion, sedition, strife, tumult, turmoil 2. agitation, anxiety, disquiet, distress, perturbation, restlessness, uneasiness, worry

unrestrained abandoned, boisterous, free, immoderate, inordinate, intemperate, natural, unbounded, unbridled, unchecked, unconstrained, uncontrolled, unhindered, uninhibited, unrepressed

unrestricted 1. absolute, free, free-for-all (Inf.), freewheeling (Inf.), open, unbounded, uncircumscribed, unhindered, unlimited, unregulated 2. clear, open, public, unobstructed, unopposed

unrivalled beyond compare, incomparable, matchless, nonpareil, peerless, supreme, unequalled, unexcelled, unmatched, unparalleled, unsurpassed, without equal

unruly disobedient, disorderly, fractious, headstrong, insubordinate, intractable, lawless, mutinous, obstreperous, rebellious, refractory, riotous, rowdy, turbulent, uncontrollable, ungovernable, unmanageable, wayward, wild, wilful

unsafe dangerous, hazardous, insecure, perilous, precarious, risky, threatening, treacherous, uncertain, unreliable, unsound, unstable

unsaid left to the imagination, tacit, undeclared, unexpressed, unspoken, unstated, unuttered, unvoiced

unsatisfactory deficient, disappointing, displeasing, inadequate, insufficient, mediocre, not good enough, not up to par, not up to scratch (Inf.), poor, unacceptable, unsuitable, unworthy, weak

unsavoury 1. distasteful, nasty, objectionable, obnoxious, offensive, repellent, repugnant, repulsive, revolting, unpleasant 2. disagreeable, distasteful, nauseating, sickening, unappetizing, unpalatable

unscrupulous conscienceless, corrupt, crooked (Inf.), dishonest, dishonourable, exploitative, immoral, improper, knavish, roguish, ruthless, unconscientious, unconscionable, unethical, unprincipled

unseasonable ill-timed, inappropriate, inopportune, mistimed, out of keeping, unsuitable, untimely

unseat 1. throw, unhorse, unsaddle 2. depose, dethrone, discharge, dismiss, displace, oust, overthrow, remove

unseemly discreditable, disreputable, improper, inappropriate, indecorous, indelicate, in poor taste, out of keeping, out of place, unbecoming, unbefitting, undignified, unrefined, unsuitable

unseen concealed, hidden, invisible, lurking, obscure, undetected, unnoticed, unobserved, unobtrusive, unperceived, veiled

unselfish altruistic, charitable, devoted,

disinterested, generous, humanitarian, kind, liberal, magnanimous, noble, self-denying, selfless, self-sacrificing

unsettle agitate, bother, confuse, discompose, disconcert, disorder, disturb, fluster, perturb, rattle (Inf.), ruffle, throw (Inf.), throw into confusion (disorder, uproar), throw off balance, trouble, unbalance, upset

unsettled 1. disorderly, insecure, shaky, unstable, unsteady 2. changeable, changing, inconstant, uncertain, unpredictable, variable 3. agitated, anxious, confused, disturbed, flustered, on edge, perturbed, restive, restless, shaken, tense, troubled, uneasy, unnerved 4. debatable, doubtful, moot, open, undecided, undetermined, unresolved 5. due, in arrears, outstanding, owing, payable, pending 6. uninhabited, unoccupied, unpeopled, unpopulated

unshakable absolute, constant, firm, fixed, resolute, staunch, steadfast, sure, unassailable, unswerving, unwavering, well-founded

unshaken calm, collected, composed, impassive, unaffected, unalarmed, undaunted, undismayed, undisturbed, unmoved, unperturbed, unruffled

unsheltered exposed, open, out in the open, unprotected, unscreened, unshielded

unsightly disagreeable, hideous, horrid, repulsive, revolting (Inf.), ugly, unattractive, unpleasant, unprepossessing

unskilled amateurish, inexperienced, uneducated, unprofessional, unqualified, untalented, untrained

unsociable chilly, cold, distant, hostile, inhospitable, introverted, reclusive, retiring,

unsophisticated (ˌʌnsəˈfɪstɪˌkeɪtɪd) *adj.* **1.** lacking experience or worldly wisdom. **2.** marked by a lack of refinement or complexity: *an unsophisticated machine.* **3.** unadulterated or genuine. —ˌunsoˈphistiˌcatedly *adv.* —ˌunsoˈphistiˌcatedness *or* ˌunsoˌphistiˈcation *n.*

unsound (ʌnˈsaund) *adj.* **1.** diseased, weak, or unstable: *of unsound mind.* **2.** unreliable or fallacious: *unsound advice.* **3.** lacking strength or firmness: *unsound foundations.* **4.** of doubtful financial or commercial viability: *an unsound enterprise.* —**unˈsoundly** *adv.* —**unˈsoundness** *n.*

unsparing (ʌnˈspɛərɪŋ) *adj.* **1.** not sparing or frugal; lavish. **2.** showing harshness or severity. —**unˈsparingly** *adv.* —**unˈsparingness** *n.*

unspeakable (ʌnˈspiːkəbəl) *adj.* **1.** incapable of expression in words: *unspeakable ecstasy.* **2.** indescribably bad or evil. **3.** not to be uttered: *unspeakable thoughts.* —**unˈspeakableness** *n.* —**unˈspeakably** *adv.*

unstable (ʌnˈsteɪbəl) *adj.* **1.** lacking stability, fixity, or firmness. **2.** disposed to temperamental or psychological variability. **3.** (of a chemical compound) readily decomposing. **4.** *Physics.* **a.** (of an elementary particle) having a very short lifetime. **b.** spontaneously decomposing by nuclear decay: *an unstable nuclide.* —**unˈstableness** *n.* —**unˈstably** *adv.*

unsteady (ʌnˈstɛdɪ) *adj.* **1.** not securely fixed: *an unsteady foothold.* **2.** (of behaviour, etc.) erratic. **3.** without regularity. **4.** (of a manner of walking, etc.) precarious or staggering, as from intoxication. —**unˈsteadily** *adv.* —**unˈsteadiness** *n.*

unstring (ʌnˈstrɪŋ) *vb.* **-stringing, -strung.** (*tr.*) **1.** to remove the strings of. **2.** (of beads, etc.) to remove from a string. **3.** to weaken emotionally (a person or his nerves).

unstructured (ʌnˈstrʌktʃəd) *adj.* without formal structure or systematic organization.

unstrung (ʌnˈstrʌŋ) *adj.* **1.** emotionally distressed; unnerved. **2.** (of a stringed instrument) with the strings detached.

unstuck (ʌnˈstʌk) *adj.* **1.** freed from being stuck, glued, fastened, etc. **2. come unstuck.** to suffer failure or disaster.

unstudied (ʌnˈstʌdɪd) *adj.* **1.** natural. **2.** (foll. by *in*) without knowledge or training.

unsubstantial (ˌʌnsəbˈstænʃəl) *adj.* **1.** lacking weight or firmness. **2.** (of an argument) of doubtful validity. **3.** of no material existence. —ˌunsubˌstantiˈality *n.* —ˌunsubˈstantially *adv.*

unsung (ʌnˈsʌŋ) *adj.* **1.** not acclaimed or honoured: *unsung deeds.* **2.** not yet sung.

unsuspected (ˌʌnsəˈspɛktɪd) *adj.* **1.** not under suspicion. **2.** not known to exist. —ˌunsusˈpectedly *adv.* —ˌunsusˈpectedness *n.*

unswerving (ʌnˈswɜːvɪŋ) *adj.* not turning aside; constant.

untangle (ʌnˈtæŋgəl) *vb.* (*tr.*) **1.** to free from a tangled condition. **2.** to free from confusion.

untaught (ʌnˈtɔːt) *adj.* **1.** without training or education. **2.** attained or achieved without instruction.

unthinkable (ʌnˈθɪŋkəbəl) *adj.* **1.** not to be contemplated; out of the question. **2.** unimaginable; inconceivable. **3.** unreasonable; improbable. —**unˈthinkably** *adv.*

unthinking (ʌnˈθɪŋkɪŋ) *adj.* **1.** lacking thoughtfulness; inconsiderate. **2.** heedless; inadvertent. **3.** not thinking or able to think. —**unˈthinkingly** *adv.* —**unˈthinkingness** *n.*

unthrone (ʌnˈθrəʊn) *vb.* (*tr.*) a less common word for **dethrone.**

untidy (ʌnˈtaɪdɪ) *adj.* **-dier, -diest. 1.** not neat; slovenly. ~*vb.* **-dying, -died. 2.** (*tr.*) to make untidy. —**unˈtidily** *adv.* —**unˈtidiness** *n.*

untie (ʌnˈtaɪ) *vb.* **-tying, -tied. 1.** to unfasten or free (a knot or something that is tied) or (of a knot, etc.) to be-

---

THESAURUS

standoffish, uncongenial, unforthcoming, unfriendly, unneighbourly, unsocial, withdrawn

unsolicited free-will, gratuitous, spontaneous, unasked for, uncalled-for, unforced, uninvited, unrequested, unsought, unwelcome, voluntary, volunteered

unsophisticated 1. artless, childlike, guileless, inexperienced, ingenuous, innocent, naive, natural, unaffected, untutored, unworldly **2.** plain, simple, straightforward, uncomplex, uncomplicated, uninvolved, unrefined, unspecialized **3.** genuine, not artificial, pure, unadulterated

unsound 1. ailing, defective, delicate, deranged, diseased, frail, ill, in poor health, unbalanced, unhealthy, unhinged, unstable, unwell, weak **2.** defective, erroneous, fallacious, false, faulty, flawed, ill-founded, illogical, invalid, shaky, specious, unreliable, weak **3.** flimsy, insecure, not solid, rickety, shaky, tottering, unreliable, unsafe, unstable, unsteady, wobbly

unspeakable 1. beyond description, beyond words, inconceivable, indescribable, ineffable, inexpressible, overwhelming, unbelievable, unimaginable, unutterable, wonderful **2.** abominable, appalling, awful, bad, dreadful, evil, execrable, frightful, heinous, horrible, loathsome, monstrous, odious, repellent, shocking, too horrible for words

unspoiled, unspoilt 1. intact, perfect, preserved, unaffected, unblemished, unchanged, undamaged, unharmed, unimpaired, untouched **2.** artless, innocent, natural, unaffected, unassuming, unstudied, wholesome

unspoken 1. assumed, implicit, implied, left to the imagination, not put into words, not spelt out, tacit, taken for granted, undeclared, understood, unexpressed, unspoken, unstated **2.** mute, silent, unsaid, unuttered, voiceless, wordless

unstable 1. insecure, not fixed, precarious, rickety, risky, shaky, tottering, unsettled, unsteady, wobbly **2.** capricious, change-

able, erratic, fitful, fluctuating, inconsistent, inconstant, irrational, unpredictable, unsteady, untrustworthy, vacillating, variable, volatile

unsteady 1. infirm, insecure, precarious, reeling, rickety, shaky, tottering, treacherous, unsafe, unstable, wobbly **2.** changeable, erratic, flickering, flighty, fluctuating, inconstant, irregular, unreliable, unsettled, vacillating, variable, volatile, wavering

unsubstantial 1. airy, flimsy, fragile, frail, inadequate, light, slight, thin **2.** erroneous, full of holes, ill-founded, superficial, tenuous, unsound, unsupported, weak **3.** dreamlike, fanciful, illusory, imaginary, immaterial, impalpable, visionary

unsubstantiated open to question, unattested, unconfirmed, uncorroborated, unestablished, unproven, unsupported

unsuccessful 1. abortive, bootless, failed, fruitless, futile, ineffective, unavailing, unproductive, useless, vain **2.** balked, defeated, foiled, frustrated, hapless, ill-starred, losing, luckless, unfortunate, unlucky

unsuitable improper, inapposite, inappropriate, inapt, incompatible, incongruous, ineligible, infelicitous, out of character, out of keeping, out of place, unacceptable, unbecoming, unbefitting, unfitting, unseasonable, unseemly, unsuited

unsung anonymous, disregarded, neglected, unacclaimed, unacknowledged, uncelebrated, unhailed, unhonoured, unknown, unnamed, unrecognized

unsure 1. insecure, lacking in confidence, unassured, unconfident **2.** distrustful, doubtful, dubious, hesitant, in a quandary, irresolute, mistrustful, sceptical, suspicious, unconvinced, undecided

unsurpassed consummate, exceptional, incomparable, matchless, nonpareil, paramount, peerless, second to none, superlative, supreme, transcendent, unequalled, unexcelled, unparalleled, unrivalled, without an equal

unsuspecting confiding, credulous, gullible, inexperienced, ingenuous, innocent, naive, off guard, trustful, trusting, unconscious, unsuspicious, unwarned, unwary

unswerving constant, dedicated, devoted, direct, firm, resolute, single-minded, staunch, steadfast, steady, true, undeviating, unfaltering, unflagging, untiring, unwavering

unsympathetic apathetic, callous, cold, compassionless (*Rare*), cruel, hard, harsh, heartless, indifferent, insensitive, soulless, stony-hearted, uncompassionate, unconcerned, unfeeling, unkind, unmoved, unpitying, unresponsive

untamed barbarous, feral, fierce, not broken in, savage, unbroken, uncontrollable, undomesticated, untameable, wild

untangle clear up, disentangle, explain, extricate, solve, straighten out, unravel, unsnarl

untenable fallacious, flawed, groundless, illogical, indefensible, insupportable, shaky, unreasonable, unsound, unsustainable, weak

unthinkable 1. absurd, illogical, impossible, improbable, not on (*Inf.*), out of the question, preposterous, unlikely, unreasonable **2.** beyond belief, beyond the bounds of possibility, implausible, inconceivable, incredible, insupportable, unbelievable, unimaginable

unthinking 1. blundering, inconsiderate, insensitive, rude, selfish, tactless, thoughtless, undiplomatic **2.** careless, heedless, impulsive, inadvertent, instinctive, mechanical, negligent, oblivious, rash, senseless, unconscious, unmindful, vacant, witless

untidy bedraggled, chaotic, cluttered, disorderly, higgledy-piggledy (*Inf.*), jumbled, littered, messy, muddled, muddly, mussy (*U.S. inf.*), rumpled, slatternly, slipshod, sloppy (*Inf.*), slovenly, topsy-turvy, unkempt

untie free, loosen, release, unbind, undo, unfasten, unknot, unlace

come unfastened. **2.** (*tr.*) to free from constraint or re-striction.

until (ʌn'tɪl) *conj.* (*subordinating*) **1.** up to (a time) that: *he laughed until he cried.* **2.** (used with a negative) before (a time or event): *until you change, you can't go out.* ~*prep.* **3.** (often preceded by *up*) in or throughout the period before: *he waited until six.* **4.** (used with a negative) earlier than; before: *he won't come until tomorrow.*
▷ **Usage.** See at till¹ and **unless.**

untimely (ʌn'taɪmlɪ) *adj.* **1.** occurring before the expected, normal, or proper time: *an untimely death.* **2.** inappropriate to the occasion, time, or season: *his joking at the funeral was most untimely.* ~*adv.* **3.** prematurely or inopportunely. —**un'timeliness** *n.*

unto ('ʌntuː) *prep.* an archaic word for **to.**

untold (ʌn'təʊld) *adj.* **1.** incapable of description: *untold suffering.* **2.** incalculably great in number or quantity: *untold thousands.* **3.** not told.

untouchable (ʌn'tʌtʃəbəl) *adj.* **1.** lying beyond reach. **2.** above reproach, suspicion, or impeachment. **3.** unable to be touched. ~*n.* **4.** a member of the lowest class in India, whom those of the four main castes were formerly forbidden to touch. —**un,toucha'bility** *n.*

untoward (,ʌntə'wɔːd) *adj.* **1.** characterized by misfortune or annoyance. **2.** not auspicious; unfavourable. **3.** unseemly. **4.** *Arch.* perverse. **5.** *Obs.* awkward. —,**unto'wardly** *adv.* —,**unto'wardness** *n.*

untrue (ʌn'truː) *adj.* **1.** incorrect or false. **2.** disloyal. **3.** diverging from a rule, standard, or measure; inaccurate. —**un'truly** *adv.*

untruthful (ʌn'truːθful) *adj.* **1.** (of a person) given to lying. **2.** diverging from the truth. —**un'truthfully** *adv.* —**un'truthfulness** *n.*

untutored (ʌn'tjuːtəd) *adj.* **1.** without formal education. **2.** lacking sophistication or refinement.

unused *adj.* **1.** (ʌn'juːzd). not being or never having been made use of. **2.** (ʌn'juːst). (*postpositive; foll. by to*) not accustomed or used (to something).

unusual (ʌn'juːʒʊəl) *adj.* uncommon; extraordinary: *an unusual design.* —**un'usually** *adv.*

unutterable (ʌn'ʌtərəbəl) *adj.* incapable of being ex-pressed in words. —**un'utterableness** *n.* —**un'utterably** *adv.*

unvarnished (ʌn'vɑːnɪʃt) *adj.* plain, simple.

unveil (ʌn'veɪl) *vb.* **1.** (*tr.*) to remove the cover from, esp. in the ceremonial unveiling of a monument, etc. **2.** to remove the veil from (one's own or another person's face). **3.** (*tr.*) to make (something concealed) known or public.

unveiling (ʌn'veɪlɪŋ) *n.* **1.** a ceremony involving the removal of a veil covering a statue, etc., for the first time. **2.** the presentation of something, esp. for the first time.

unvoiced (ʌn'vɔɪst) *adj.* **1.** not expressed or spoken. **2.** articulated without vibration of the vocal cords; voiceless.

unwary (ʌn'wɛərɪ) *adj.* lacking caution or prudence. —**un'warily** *adv.* —**un'wariness** *n.*

unwell (ʌn'wɛl) *adj.* (*postpositive*) not well; ill.

unwept (ʌn'wɛpt) *adj.* **1.** not wept for or lamented. **2.** *Rare.* (of tears) not shed.

unwholesome (ʌn'həʊlsəm) *adj.* **1.** detrimental to physical or mental health: *an unwholesome climate.* **2.** morally harmful: *unwholesome practices.* **3.** indicative of illness, esp. in appearance. **4.** (esp. of food) of inferior quality. —**un'wholesomeness** *n.*

unwieldy (ʌn'wiːldɪ) *adj.* **1.** too heavy, large, or awkwardly shaped to be easily handled. **2.** ungainly; clumsy. —**un'wieldily** *adv.* —**un'wieldiness** *n.*

unwilling (ʌn'wɪlɪŋ) *adj.* **1.** reluctant. **2.** performed or said with reluctance. —**un'willingly** *adv.* —**un'willingness** *n.*

unwind (ʌn'waɪnd) *vb.* **-winding, -wound. 1.** to slacken, undo, or unravel or cause to slacken, undo, or unravel. **2.** (*tr.*) to disentangle. **3.** to make or become relaxed: *he finds it hard to unwind.* —**un'windable** *adj.*

unwise (ʌn'waɪz) *adj.* lacking wisdom or prudence. —**un'wisely** *adv.* —**un'wiseness** *n.*

unwitting (ʌn'wɪtɪŋ) *adj.* (*usually prenominal*) **1.** not knowing or conscious. **2.** not intentional; inadvertent. —**un'wittingly** *adv.* —**un'wittingness** *n.*

THESAURUS

untimely awkward, badly timed, early, ill-timed, inappropriate, inauspicious, inconvenient, inopportune, mistimed, premature, unfortunate, unseasonable, unsuitable

untiring constant, dedicated, determined, devoted, dogged, incessant, indefatigable, patient, persevering, persistent, staunch, steady, tireless, unfaltering, unflagging, unremitting, unwearied

untold 1. indescribable, inexpressible, undreamed of, unimaginable, unspeakable, unthinkable, unutterable 2. countless, incalculable, innumerable, measureless, myriad, numberless, uncountable, uncounted, unnumbered 3. hidden, private, secret, undisclosed, unknown, unpublished, unrecounted, unrelated, unrevealed

untouched 1. intact, safe and sound, undamaged, unharmed, unhurt, uninjured, unscathed, without a scratch 2. dry-eyed, indifferent, unaffected, unconcerned, unimpressed, unmoved, unstirred

untoward 1. annoying, awkward, disastrous, ill-timed, inconvenient, inimical, irritating, troublesome, unfortunate, vexatious 2. adverse, contrary, inauspicious, inopportune, unfavourable, unlucky, untimely 3. improper, inappropriate, indecorous, out of place, unbecoming, unfitting, unseemly, unsuitable

untrained amateur, green, inexperienced, raw, uneducated, unpractised, unqualified, unschooled, unskilled, untaught, untutored

untroubled calm, composed, cool, peaceful, placid, serene, steady, tranquil, unagitated, unconcerned, undisturbed, unflappable (*Inf.*), unflustered, unperturbed, unruffled, unstirred, unworried

untrue 1. deceptive, dishonest, erroneous, fallacious, false, inaccurate, incorrect, lying, misleading, mistaken, sham, spurious, un-

truthful, wrong 2. deceitful, disloyal, faithless, false, forsworn, inconstant, perfidious, traitorous, treacherous, two-faced, unfaithful, untrustworthy 3. deviant, distorted, inaccurate, off, out of line, out of true, wide

untrustworthy capricious, deceitful, devious, dishonest, disloyal, fair-weather, faithless, false, fickle, fly-by-night (*Inf.*), not to be depended on, slippery, treacherous, tricky, two-faced, undependable, unfaithful, unreliable, untrue, untrusty

untruth 1. deceitfulness, duplicity, falsity, inveracity (*Rare*), lying, mendacity, perjury, truthlessness, untruthfulness 2. deceit, fabrication, falsehood, falsification, fib, fiction, lie, prevarication, story, tale, trick, whopper (*Inf.*)

untruthful crooked (*Inf.*), deceitful, deceptive, dishonest, dissembling, false, fibbing, hypocritical, lying, mendacious

unusual abnormal, atypical, bizarre, curious, different, exceptional, extraordinary, odd, out of the ordinary, phenomenal, queer, rare, remarkable, singular, strange, surprising, uncommon, unconventional, unexpected, unfamiliar, unwonted

unutterable beyond words, extreme, indescribable, ineffable, overwhelming, unimaginable, unspeakable

unvarnished bare, candid, frank, honest, naked, plain, pure, pure and simple, simple, sincere, stark, straightforward, unadorned, unembellished

unveil bare, bring to light, disclose, divulge, expose, lay bare, lay open, make known, make public, reveal, uncover

unwanted de trop, going begging, outcast, rejected, superfluous, surplus to requirements, unasked, undesired, uninvited, unneeded, unsolicited, unwelcome, useless

unwarranted gratuitous, groundless,

indefensible, inexcusable, uncalled-for, unjust, unjustified, unprovoked, unreasonable, wrong

unwary careless, hasty, heedless, imprudent, incautious, indiscreet, rash, reckless, thoughtless, uncircumspect, unguarded, unwatchful

unwavering consistent, dedicated, determined, resolute, single-minded, staunch, steadfast, steady, undeviating, unfaltering, unflagging, unshakable, unshaken, unswerving, untiring

unwelcome 1. excluded, rejected, unacceptable, undesirable, uninvited, unpopular, unwanted, unwished for 2. disagreeable, displeasing, distasteful, thankless, undesirable, unpleasant

unwell ailing, ill, indisposed, in poor health, off colour, out of sorts, poorly (*Inf.*), sick, sickly, under the weather (*Inf.*), unhealthy

unwholesome 1. deleterious, harmful, insalubrious, junk (*Inf.*), noxious, poisonous, tainted, unhealthy, unnourishing 2. bad, corrupting, degrading, demoralizing, depraving, evil, immoral, perverting, wicked 3. anaemic, pale, pallid, pasty, sickly, wan

unwieldy 1. awkward, burdensome, cumbersome, inconvenient, unhandy, unmanageable 2. bulky, clumsy, hefty, massive, ponderous, ungainly, weighty

unwilling averse, demurring, disinclined, grudging, indisposed, laggard (*Rare*), loath, not in the mood, opposed, reluctant, resistant, unenthusiastic

unwind 1. disentangle, slacken, uncoil, undo, unravel, unreel, unroll, untwine, untwist 2. calm down, let oneself go, loosen up, quieten down, relax, sit back, slow down, take a break, take it easy (*Inf.*), wind down

unwise foolhardy, foolish, ill-advised, ill-

unwonted (ʌnˈwəʊntɪd) adj. **1.** out of the ordinary; unusual. **2.** (usually foll. by to) Arch. unaccustomed; unused. —**unˈwontedly** adv.

unworldly (ʌnˈwɜːldlɪ) adj. **1.** not concerned with material values or pursuits. **2.** lacking sophistication; naive. **3.** not of this earth or world. —**unˈworldliness** n.

unworthy (ʌnˈwɜːðɪ) adj. **1.** (often foll. by of) not deserving or worthy. **2.** (often foll. by of) beneath the level considered befitting (to): that remark is unworthy of you. **3.** lacking merit or value. **4.** (of treatment) not warranted. —**unˈworthily** adv. —**unˈworthiness** n.

unwrap (ʌnˈræp) vb. -**wrapping**, -**wrapped**. to remove the covering or wrapping from (something) or (of something wrapped) to have the covering come off.

unwritten (ʌnˈrɪtən) adj. **1.** not printed or in writing. **2.** effective only through custom.

unzip (ʌnˈzɪp) vb. -**zipping**, -**zipped**. to unfasten the zip of (a garment, etc.) or (of a zip or garment with a zip) to become unfastened: her skirt unzipped as she sat down.

up (ʌp) prep. **1.** indicating movement from a lower to a higher position: climbing up a mountain. **2.** at a higher or further level or position in or on: a shop up the road. ~adv. **3.** (often particle) to an upward, higher, or erect position, esp. indicating readiness for an activity: up and doing something. **4.** (particle) indicating intensity or completion of an action: he tore up the cheque. **5.** to the place referred to or where the speaker is: the man came up and asked the way. **6. a.** to a more important place: up to London. **b.** to a more northerly place: up to Scotland. **c.** (of a member of some British universities) to or at university. **d.** in a particular part of the country: up north. **7.** above the horizon: the sun is up. **8.** to appear for trial: up before the magistrate. **9.** having gained: ten pounds up on the deal. **10.** higher in price: coffee is up again. **11.** raised (for discussion, etc.): the plan was up for consideration. **12.** taught: well up in physics. **13.** (functioning as imperative) get, stand, etc., up: up with you! **14. up with.** (functioning as imperative) wanting the beginning or continuation of: up with the monarchy! **15. something's up.** Inf. something strange is happening. **16. up against. a.** touching. **b.** having to cope with: look what we're up against now. **17. up for.** as a candidate or applicant for: he's up for re-election again. **18. up to. a.** devising or scheming: she's up to no good. **b.** dependent or incumbent upon: the decision is up to you. **c.** equal to (a challenge, etc.) or capable of (doing, etc.): are you up to playing in the final? **d.** as far as: up to his waist in mud. **e.** as many as: up to two years' waiting time. **f.** comparable with: not up to your normal standard. **19. up top.** Inf. in the head or mind. **20. what's up?** Inf. what is the matter? ~adj. **21.** (predicative) of a high or higher position. **22.** (predicative) out of bed: the children aren't up yet. **23.** (prenominal) of or relating to a train or trains to a more important place or one regarded as higher: the up platform. ~vb. **upping, upped. 24.** (tr.) to increase or raise. **25.** (intr.; foll. by and with a verb) Inf. to do (something) suddenly, etc.: she upped and married someone else. ~n. **26.** a high point (esp. in **ups and downs**). **27.** Sl. another word for **upper** (sense 8). **28. on the up and up. a.** trustworthy or honest. **b.** Brit. on the upward trend or movement: our firm's on the up and up.

up-and-coming adj. promising continued or future success; enterprising.

upbeat (ˈʌpˌbiːt) n. **1.** Music. **a.** an unaccented beat, esp. the last bar. **b.** the upward gesture of a conductor's baton indicating this. ~adj. **2.** Inf. marked by cheerfulness or optimism.

upbraid (ʌpˈbreɪd) vb. (tr.) **1.** to reprove or reproach angrily. **2.** to find fault with. —**upˈbraider** n. —**upˈbraiding** n.

upbringing (ˈʌpˌbrɪŋɪŋ) n. the education of a person during his formative years.

upcast (ˈʌpˌkɑːst) n. **1.** material cast or thrown up. **2.** a ventilation shaft through which air leaves a mine. **3.** Geol. (in a fault) the section of strata that has been displaced upwards. ~adj. **4.** directed or thrown upwards. ~vb. -**casting**, -**cast**. **5.** (tr.) to throw or cast up.

upcountry (ʌpˈkʌntrɪ) adj. **1.** of or coming from the interior of a country or region. ~n. **2.** the interior part of a region or country. ~adv. **3.** towards, in, or into the interior part of a country or region.

update vb. (ʌpˈdeɪt). (tr.) **1.** to bring up to date. **2.** Computers. to modify (a computer instruction) so that the address number is increased each time an instruction is carried out. ~n. (ˈʌpˌdeɪt). **3.** the act of updating or something that is updated. —**upˈdater** n.

upend (ʌpˈɛnd) vb. **1.** to turn or set or become turned or set on end. **2.** (tr.) to affect or upset drastically.

upgrade vb. (ʌpˈgreɪd). (tr.) **1.** to assign or promote (a person or job) to a higher professional rank or position. **2.** to raise in value, importance, esteem, etc. **3.** to improve (a breed of livestock) by crossing with a better strain. ~n. (ˈʌpˌgreɪd). **4.** U.S. an upward slope. **5. on the upgrade.** improving or progressing, as in importance, status, health, etc. —**upˈgrader** n.

upheaval (ʌpˈhiːvəl) n. **1.** a strong, sudden, or violent disturbance, as in politics. **2.** Geol. another word for **uplift** (sense 7).

uphill (ˈʌpˈhɪl) adj. **1.** inclining, sloping, or leading upwards. **2.** requiring protracted effort: an uphill task. ~adv. **3.** up an incline or slope. **4.** against difficulties. ~n. **5.** a rising incline.

uphold (ʌpˈhəʊld) vb. -**holding**, -**held**. (tr.) **1.** to maintain or defend against opposition. **2.** to give moral support to. **3.** Rare. to support physically. **4.** to lift up. —**upˈholder** n.

upholster (ʌpˈhəʊlstə) vb. (tr.) to fit (chairs, sofas, etc.) with padding, springs, webbing, and covering. —**upˈholsterer** n. —**upˈholstery** n.

upkeep (ˈʌpˌkiːp) n. **1.** the act or process of keeping something in good repair, esp. over a long period; maintenance. **2.** the cost of maintenance.

upland (ˈʌplənd) n. **1.** an area of high or relatively high ground. ~adj. **2.** relating to or situated in an upland.

uplift vb. (ʌpˈlɪft). (tr.) **1.** to raise; lift up. **2.** to raise morally, spiritually, etc. **3.** Scot. & N.Z. to collect; pick up (goods, documents, etc.). ~n. (ˈʌpˌlɪft). **4.** the act, process, or result of lifting up. **5.** the act or process of bettering moral, social, or cultural conditions, etc. **6.** (as modifier) designating a brassiere for lifting and supporting the breasts: an uplift bra. **7.** the process or result of land being raised to a higher level, as during a period of

---

THESAURUS

considered, ill-judged, impolitic, improvident, imprudent, inadvisable, indiscreet, injudicious, irresponsible, rash, reckless, senseless, short-sighted, silly, stupid

unwitting 1. ignorant, innocent, unaware, unconscious, unknowing, unsuspecting **2.** accidental, chance, inadvertent, involuntary, undesigned, unintended, unintentional, unmeant, unplanned

unworldly 1. abstract, celestial, metaphysical, nonmaterialistic, religious, spiritual, transcendental **2.** green, idealistic, inexperienced, innocent, naive, raw, trusting, unsophisticated **3.** ethereal, extraterrestrial, otherworldly, unearthly

unworthy 1. With of beneath the dignity of, improper, inappropriate, out of character, out of place, unbecoming, unbefitting, unfitting, unseemly, unsuitable **2.** base, contemptible, degrading, discreditable, disgraceful, dishonourable, disreputable, igno-

ble, shameful **3.** ineligible, not deserving of, not fit for, not good enough, not worth, undeserving

unwritten 1. oral, unrecorded, vocal, word-of-mouth **2.** accepted, conventional, customary, tacit, traditional, understood, unformulated

unyielding adamant, determined, firm, hardline, immovable, inexorable, inflexible, intractable, obdurate, obstinate, relentless, resolute, rigid, staunch, steadfast, stubborn, tough, unbending, uncompromising, unwavering

upbringing breeding, bringing-up, care, cultivation, education, nurture, raising, rearing, tending, training

upgrade advance, ameliorate, better, elevate, enhance, improve, promote, raise

upheaval cataclysm, disorder, disruption, disturbance, eruption, overthrow, revolution, turmoil, violent change

uphill adj. **1.** ascending, climbing, mounting, rising **2.** arduous, difficult, exhausting, gruelling, hard, laborious, punishing, Sisyphean, strenuous, taxing, tough, wearisome

uphold advocate, aid, back, champion, defend, encourage, endorse, hold to, justify, maintain, promote, stand by, support, sustain, vindicate

upkeep 1. conservation, keep, maintenance, preservation, repair, running, subsistence, support, sustenance **2.** expenditure, expenses, oncosts (Brit.), operating costs, outlay, overheads, running costs

uplift v. **1.** elevate, heave, hoist, lift up, raise **2.** advance, ameliorate, better, civilize, cultivate, edify, improve, inspire, raise, refine, upgrade ~n. **3.** advancement, betterment, cultivation, edification, enhancement, enlightenment, enrichment, improvement, refinement

mountain building. —**up'lifter** n.

upmost ('ʌp‚məʊst) adj. another word for **uppermost** (sense 1).

upon (ə'pɒn) prep. 1. another word for **on**. 2. indicating a position reached by going up: *climb upon my knee.* 3. imminent for: *the weekend was upon us again.*

upper ('ʌpə) adj. 1. higher or highest in relation to physical position, wealth, rank, status, etc. 2. (*cap. when part of a name*) lying farther upstream, inland, or farther north: *the upper valley of the Loire.* 3. (*cap. when part of a name*) Geol., archaeol. denoting the late part or division of a period, system, etc.: *Upper Palaeolithic.* 4. Maths. (of a limit or bound) greater than or equal to one or more numbers or variables. ~n. 5. the higher of two objects, people, etc. 6. the part of a shoe above the sole, covering the upper surface of the foot. 7. **on one's uppers.** destitute. 8. Sl. any of various drugs having a stimulant effect.

upper case Printing. ~n. 1. the top half of a compositor's type case in which capital letters, reference marks, and accents are kept. ~adj. (**upper-case** when prenominal). 2. of or relating to capital letters kept in this case and used in the setting or production of printed or typed matter.

upper class n. 1. the class occupying the highest position in the social hierarchy, esp. the aristocracy. ~adj. (**upper-class** when prenominal). 2. of or relating to the upper class.

upper crust n. Inf. the upper class.

uppercut ('ʌpə‚kʌt) n. 1. a short swinging upward blow with the fist delivered at an opponent's chin. ~vb. -**cutting, -cut.** 2. to hit (an opponent) with an uppercut.

upper hand n. **the.** the position of control (esp. in **have** or **get the upper hand**).

upper house n. (often cap.) one of the two houses of a bicameral legislature.

uppermost ('ʌpə‚məʊst) adj. also **upmost**. 1. highest in position, power, importance, etc. ~adv. 2. in or into the highest position, etc.

uppish ('ʌpɪʃ) adj. Brit. inf. snobbish, arrogant, or presumptuous. —'**uppishly** adv. —'**uppishness** n.

uppity ('ʌpɪtɪ) adj. Inf. 1. not yielding easily to persuasion or control. 2. another word for **uppish**.

upright ('ʌp‚raɪt) adj. 1. vertical or erect. 2. honest or just. ~adv. 3. vertically. ~n. 4. a vertical support, such as a stake or post. 5. short for **upright piano**. 6. the state of being vertical. —'**up‚rightly** adv. —'**up‚rightness** n.

upright piano n. a piano which has a rectangular vertical case.

uprising ('ʌp‚raɪzɪŋ, ʌp'raɪzɪŋ) n. 1. a revolt or rebellion. 2. Arch. an ascent.

uproar ('ʌp‚rɔ:) n. a commotion or disturbance characterized by loud noise and confusion.

uproarious (ʌp'rɔːrɪəs) adj. 1. causing or character-

ized by an uproar. 2. extremely funny. 3. (of laughter, etc.) loud and boisterous. —**up'roariously** adv. —**up'roariousness** n.

uproot (ʌp'ruːt) vb. (tr.) 1. to pull up by or as if by the roots. 2. to displace (a person or persons) from native or habitual surroundings. 3. to remove or destroy utterly. —**up'rooter** n.

upset vb. (ʌp'sɛt), -**setting, -set.** (mainly tr.) 1. (also intr.) to tip or be tipped over; overturn or spill. 2. to disturb the normal state or stability of: *to upset the balance of nature.* 3. to disturb mentally or emotionally. 4. to defeat or overthrow, usually unexpectedly. 5. to make physically ill: *seafood always upsets my stomach.* 6. to thicken or spread (the end of a bar, etc.) by hammering. ~n. ('ʌp‚sɛt). 7. an unexpected defeat or reversal, as in a contest or plans. 8. a disturbance or disorder of the emotions, body, etc. ~adj. (ʌp'sɛt). 9. overturned or capsized. 10. emotionally or physically disturbed or distressed. 11. disordered; confused. 12. defeated or overthrown. —**up'setter** n. —**up'settingly** adv.

upset price n. the lowest price acceptable for something that is for sale, esp. a house. Cf. **reserve price**.

upshot ('ʌp‚ʃɒt) n. 1. the final result; conclusion; outcome. 2. Archery. the final shot in a match.

upside down ('ʌp‚saɪd) adj. 1. (usually postpositive) turned over completely; inverted. 2. (**upside-down** when prenominal): *an upside-down world.* ~adv. 3. in an inverted fashion. 4. in a chaotic manner.

upsides ('ʌp‚saɪdz) adv. Inf., chiefly Brit. (foll. by with) equal or level (with), as through revenge or retaliation.

upsilon ('ʌpsɪ‚lɒn) n. 1. the 20th letter in the Greek alphabet (Υ or υ), a vowel transliterated as y or u. 2. a heavy short-lived subatomic particle produced by bombarding beryllium nuclei with high-energy protons.

upstage ('ʌp'steɪdʒ) adv. 1. on, at, or to the rear of the stage. ~adj. 2. of or relating to the back half of the stage. 3. Inf. haughty. ~vb. (tr.) 4. to move upstage of (another actor), thus forcing him to turn away from the audience. 5. Inf. to draw attention to oneself from (someone else). 6. Inf. to treat haughtily.

upstairs ('ʌp'stɛəz) adv. 1. up the stairs; to or on an upper floor or level. 2. Inf. to or into a higher rank or office. 3. **kick upstairs.** Inf. to promote to a higher position, esp. one that carries less power. ~n. 4. **a.** an upper floor or level. **b.** (as modifier): *an upstairs room.* 5. Brit. inf. the masters of a household collectively, esp. of a large house.

upstanding (ʌp'stændɪŋ) adj. 1. of good character. 2. upright and vigorous in build. 3. **be upstanding.** (in a court of law) a direction to all persons present to rise to their feet before the judge enters or leaves the court.

upstart ('ʌp‚stɑːt) n. 1. **a.** a person, group, etc., that has risen suddenly to a position of power or wealth. **b.** (as modifier): *an upstart family.* 2. **a.** an arrogant person. **b.** (as modifier): *his upstart ambition.*

THESAURUS

upper 1. high, higher, loftier, top, topmost 2. elevated, eminent, greater, important, superior

upper-class aristocratic, blue-blooded, highborn, high-class, noble, patrician, top-drawer, well-bred

upper hand advantage, ascendancy, control, dominion, edge, mastery, superiority, supremacy, sway, whip hand

uppermost 1. highest, loftiest, most elevated, top, topmost, upmost 2. chief, dominant, foremost, greatest, leading, main, paramount, predominant, pre-eminent, primary, principal, supreme

uppish affected, arrogant, conceited, high and mighty (Inf.), hoity-toity (Inf.), overweening, presumptuous, putting on airs, self-important, snobbish, stuck-up (Inf.), supercilious, toffee-nosed (Inf.), uppity (Inf.)

upright 1. erect, on end, perpendicular, straight, vertical 2. Fig. above board, conscientious, ethical, faithful, good, high-minded, honest, honourable, incorruptible, just, principled, righteous, straightforward, true, trustworthy, unimpeachable, virtuous

uprising disturbance, insurgence, insurrection, mutiny, outbreak, putsch, rebellion,

revolt, revolution, rising, upheaval

uproar brawl, brouhaha, clamour, commotion, confusion, din, furore, hubbub, hullabaloo, hurly-burly, mayhem, noise, outcry, pandemonium, racket, riot, ruckus (Inf.), ruction (Inf.), rumpus, turbulence, turmoil

uproarious 1. clamorous, confused, disorderly, loud, noisy, riotous, rowdy, tempestuous, tumultuous, turbulent, wild 2. convulsive (Inf.), hilarious, hysterical, killing (Inf.), rib-tickling, rip-roaring (Inf.), screamingly funny, side-splitting, very funny 3. boisterous, gleeful, loud, rollicking, unrestrained

upset v. 1. capsize, knock over, overturn, spill, tip over, topple over 2. change, disorder, disorganize, disturb, mess up, mix up, put out of order, spoil, turn topsy-turvy 3. agitate, bother, discompose, disconcert, dismay, disquiet, distress, disturb, fluster, grieve, perturb, ruffle, throw (someone) off balance, trouble 4. be victorious over, conquer, defeat, get the better of, overcome, overthrow, triumph over, win against the odds ~n. 5. defeat, reverse, shake-up (Inf.), sudden change, surprise 6. bug (Inf.), complaint, disorder, disturbance, illness, indisposition, malady, queasiness, sickness 7. agitation, bother, discomposure, disquiet, distress, disturbance,

shock, trouble, worry ~adj. 8. capsized, overturned, spilled, tipped over, toppled, tumbled, upside down 9. disordered, disturbed, gippy (Sl.), ill, poorly (Inf.), queasy, sick 10. agitated, bothered, confused, disconcerted, dismayed, disquieted, distressed, disturbed, frantic, grieved, hurt, overwrought, put out, ruffled, troubled, worried 11. at sixes and sevens, chaotic, confused, disordered, in disarray or disorder, messed up, muddled, topsy-turvy 12. beaten, conquered, defeated, overcome, overthrown, vanquished

upshot conclusion, consequence, culmination, end, end result, event, finale, issue, outcome, payoff (Inf.), result

upside down 1. bottom up, inverted, on its head, overturned, upturned, wrong side up 2. Inf. chaotic, confused, disordered, higgledy-piggledy (Inf.), in confusion (chaos, disarray, disorder), jumbled, muddled, topsy-turvy

upstanding 1. ethical, good, honest, honourable, incorruptible, moral, principled, true, trustworthy, upright 2. firm, hale and hearty, hardy, healthy, robust, stalwart, strong, sturdy, upright, vigorous

upstart arriviste, nobody, nouveau riche,

upstream ('ʌp'striːm) *adv., adj.* in or towards the higher part of a stream; against the current.

upsurge *vb.* (ʌp'sɜːdʒ). **1.** (*intr.*) *Chiefly literary.* to surge up. ~*n.* ('ʌp,sɜːdʒ). **2.** a rapid rise or swell.

upswing ('ʌp,swɪŋ) *n.* **1.** *Econ.* a recovery period in the trade cycle. **2.** an upward swing or movement or any increase or improvement.

upsy-daisy ('ʌpsɪ'deɪzɪ) *or* **upsadaisy** *interj.* an expression, usually of reassurance, uttered as when someone, esp. a child, stumbles or is being lifted up.

uptake ('ʌp,teɪk) *n.* **1.** a pipe, shaft, etc., that is used to convey smoke or gases, esp. one that connects a furnace to a chimney. **2.** lifting up. **3. quick** (*or* **slow**) **on the uptake.** *Inf.* quick (or slow) to understand or learn.

upthrust ('ʌp,θrʌst) *n.* **1.** an upward push or thrust. **2.** *Geol.* a violent upheaval of the earth's surface.

uptight (ʌp'taɪt) *adj. Sl.* **1.** displaying tense repressed nervousness, irritability, or anger. **2.** unable to give expression to one's feelings.

up-to-date *adj.* **a.** modern or fashionable: *an up-to-date magazine.* **b.** (*predicative*): *the magazine is up to date.* —'**up-to-'dateness** *n.*

upturn *vb.* (ʌp'tɜːn). **1.** to turn or cause to turn over or upside down. **2.** (*tr.*) to create disorder. **3.** (*tr.*) to direct upwards. ~*n.* ('ʌp,tɜːn). **4.** an upward trend or improvement. **5.** an upheaval.

upward ('ʌpwəd) *adj.* **1.** directed or moving towards a higher point or level. ~*adv.* **2.** in an upward direction. —'**upwardly** *adv.* —'**upwardness** *n.*

upward mobility *n.* movement from a lower to a higher economic and social status.

upwind ('ʌp'wɪnd) *adv.* **1.** into or against the wind. **2.** towards or on the side where the wind is blowing; windward. ~*adj.* **3.** going against the wind: *the upwind leg of the course.* **4.** on the windward side.

uraemia *or U.S.* **uremia** (juˈriːmɪə) *n. Pathol.* the accumulation of waste products, normally excreted in the urine, in the blood. —u'**raemic** *or U.S.* u'**remic** *adj.*

uranium (juˈreɪnɪəm) *n.* a radioactive silvery-white metallic element of the actinide series. It occurs in several minerals including pitchblende, carnotite, and autunite and is used chiefly as a source of nuclear energy by fission of the radioisotope **uranium-235.** Symbol: U; atomic no.: 92; atomic wt.: 238.03; half-life of most stable isotope, ^{238}U: 4.51×10^9 years.

Uranus[1] (juˈreɪnəs) *n. Greek myth.* the personification of the sky, who, as a god, ruled the universe and fathered the Titans and Cyclopes. He was overthrown by his son Cronus.

Uranus[2] (juˈreɪnəs) *n.* the seventh planet from the sun, sometimes visible to the naked eye.

urban ('ɜːbən) *adj.* **1.** of, relating to, or constituting a city or town. **2.** living in a city or town. —Cf. **rural.**

urban district *n.* **1.** (in England and Wales from 1888 to 1974 and Northern Ireland from 1898 to 1973) an urban division of an administrative county with an elected council in charge of housing and environmental services. **2.** (in the Republic of Ireland) any of 49 medium-sized towns with their own elected councils.

urbane (ɜː'beɪn) *adj.* characterized by elegance or sophistication. —ur'**banely** *adv.* —ur'**baneness** *n.*

urban guerrilla *n.* a guerrilla who operates in a town or city, engaging in terrorism, kidnapping, etc.

urbanity (ɜː'bænɪtɪ) *n., pl.* **-ties. 1.** the quality of being urbane. **2.** (*usually pl.*) civilities or courtesies.

urbanize *or* **-nise** ('ɜːbə,naɪz) *vb.* (*tr.*) (*usually passive*) **a.** to make (esp. a predominantly rural area or country) more industrialized and urban. **b.** to cause the migra-

tion of an increasing proportion of (rural dwellers) into cities. —,**urbani'zation** *or* **-ni'sation** *n.*

urban renewal *n.* the process of redeveloping dilapidated or no longer functional urban areas.

urchin ('ɜːtʃɪn) *n.* **1.** a mischievous roguish child, esp. one who is young, small, or raggedly dressed. **2.** See **sea urchin. 3.** an archaic or dialect name for a **hedgehog. 4.** *Obs.* an elf or sprite.

Urdu ('ʊədu:, 'ɜː-) *n.* an official language of Pakistan, also spoken in India. It belongs to the Indic branch of the Indo-European family of languages, being closely related to Hindi.

urea ('jʊərɪə) *n.* a white water-soluble crystalline compound, produced by protein metabolism and excreted in urine. A synthetic form is used as a fertilizer and animal feed. Formula: $CO(NH_2)_2$. —u'**real** *or* u'**reic** *adj.*

ureter (ju'riːtə) *n.* the tube that conveys urine from the kidney to the urinary bladder or cloaca. —u'**reteral** *or* **ureteric** (,jʊərɪ'tɛrɪk) *adj.*

urethra (ju'riːθrə) *n., pl.* **-thrae** (-θriː) *or* **-thras.** the canal that in most mammals conveys urine from the bladder out of the body. In human males it also conveys semen. —u'**rethral** *adj.*

urethritis (,jʊərɪ'θraɪtɪs) *n.* inflammation of the urethra. —**urethritic** (,jʊərɪ'θrɪtɪk) *adj.*

urge (ɜːdʒ) *vb.* **1.** (*tr.*) to plead, press, or move (someone to do something): *we urged him to surrender.* **2.** (*tr.; may take a clause as object*) to advocate or recommend earnestly and persistently: *to urge the need for safety.* **3.** (*tr.*) to impel, drive, or hasten onwards: *he urged the horses on.* ~*n.* **4.** a strong impulse, inner drive, or yearning. —'**urgingly** *adv.*

urgent ('ɜːdʒənt) *adj.* **1.** requiring or compelling speedy action or attention: *the matter is urgent.* **2.** earnest and persistent. —**urgency** ('ɜːdʒənsɪ) *n.* —'**urgently** *adv.*

uric ('jʊərɪk) *adj.* of, concerning, or derived from urine.

uric acid *n.* a white odourless tasteless crystalline product of protein metabolism, present in the blood and urine. Formula: $C_5H_4N_4O_3$.

urinal (ju'raɪnəl, 'jʊərɪ-) *n.* **1.** a sanitary fitting, esp. one fixed to a wall, used by men for urination. **2.** a room containing urinals. **3.** any vessel for holding urine prior to its disposal.

urinary ('jʊərɪnərɪ) *adj.* **1.** *Anat.* of or relating to urine or to the organs and structures that secrete and pass urine. ~*n., pl.* **-naries. 2.** a reservoir for urine.

urinate ('jʊərɪ,neɪt) *vb.* (*intr.*) to excrete or void urine. —,**uri'nation** *n.* —'**urinative** *adj.*

urine ('jʊərɪn) *n.* the pale yellow slightly acid fluid excreted by the kidneys, containing waste products removed from the blood. It is stored in the urinary bladder and discharged through the urethra.

urinogenital (,jʊərɪnəʊ'dʒɛnɪtəl) *adj.* another word for **urogenital.**

urn (ɜːn) *n.* **1.** a vaselike receptacle or vessel, esp. a large bulbous one with a foot. **2.** a vase used as a receptacle for the ashes of the dead. **3.** a large vessel, usually of metal, with a tap, used for making and holding tea, coffee, etc. —'**urn,like** *adj.*

urogenital (,jʊərəʊ'dʒɛnɪtəl) *or* **urinogenital** *adj.* of or relating to the urinary and genital organs and their functions. Also: **genitourinary.**

urology (ju'rɒlədʒɪ) *n.* the branch of medicine concerned with the study and treatment of diseases of the urogenital tract. —**urologic** (,jʊərə'lɒdʒɪk) *adj.* —u'**rologist** *n.*

Ursa Major ('ɜːsə 'meɪdʒə) *n., Latin genitive* **Ursae**

THESAURUS

parvenu, social climber, status seeker

up-to-date all the rage, current, fashionable, in, in vogue, modern, newest, now (*Inf.*), stylish, trendy (*Brit. inf.*), up-to-the-minute, with it (*Inf.*)

urban city, civic, inner-city, metropolitan, municipal, oppidan (*Rare*), town

urbane civil, civilized, cosmopolitan, courteous, cultivated, cultured, debonair, elegant, mannerly, polished, refined, smooth, sophisticated, suave, well-bred, well-mannered

urbanity charm, civility, courtesy, culture, elegance, grace, mannerliness, polish,

refinement, sophistication, suavity, worldliness

urchin brat, gamin, guttersnipe, mudlark (*Sl.*), ragamuffin, street Arab, waif, young rogue

urge v. **1.** appeal to, beg, beseech, entreat, exhort, implore, plead, press, solicit **2.** advise, advocate, champion, counsel, insist on, push for, recommend, support **3.** compel, constrain, drive, egg on, encourage, force, goad, hasten, impel, incite, induce, instigate, press, propel, push, spur, stimulate ~n. **4.** compulsion, desire, drive, fancy, impulse, itch, longing, wish, yearning, yen (*Inf.*)

urgency exigency, extremity, gravity, hurry, imperativeness, importance, importunity, necessity, need, pressure, seriousness, stress

urgent 1. compelling, critical, crucial, immediate, imperative, important, instant, not to be delayed, pressing, top-priority **2.** clamorous, earnest, importunate, insistent, intense, persistent, persuasive

urinate leak (*Sl.*), make water, micturate, pass water, pee (*Sl.*), spend a penny (*Brit. inf.*), tinkle (*Brit. inf.*), wee (*Inf.*), wee-wee (*Inf.*)

Majoris ('ɜːsɪ: mə'dʒɔːrɪs). an extensive conspicuous constellation in the N hemisphere. The seven brightest stars form the **Plough**. Also called: the **Great Bear,** the **Bear.**

Ursa Minor ('ɜːsə 'maɪnə) n., Latin genitive **Ursae Minoris** ('ɜːsiː mɪ'nɔːrɪs). a small faint constellation, the brightest star of which is the Pole Star. Also called: the **Little Bear,** the **Bear.**

ursine ('ɜːsaɪn) adj. of, relating to, or resembling a bear or bears.

Ursuline ('ɜːsjʊˌlaɪn) n. a member of one of an order of nuns devoted to teaching in the Roman Catholic Church: founded in 1537 at Brescia.

us (ʌs) pron. (objective) **1.** refers to the speaker or writer and another person or other people: to decide among us. **2.** refers to all people or people in general: this table shows us the tides. **3.** an informal word for **me**: give us a kiss! **4.** a formal word for **me** used by editors, monarchs, etc.

▷ **Usage.** See at **me.**

U.S. abbrev. for United States.

U.S.A. abbrev. for: **1.** United States Army. **2.** United States of America.

usable or **useable** ('juːzəbᵊl) adj. able to be used. —ˌusaˈbility or ˌuseaˈbility n.

usage ('juːsɪdʒ, -zɪdʒ) n. **1.** the act or a manner of using; use; employment. **2.** constant use, custom, or habit. **3.** something permitted or established by custom or practice. **4.** what is actually said in a language, esp. as contrasted with what is prescribed.

use vb. (juːz). (tr.) **1.** to put into service or action; employ for a given purpose: to use a spoon to stir with. **2.** to make a practice or habit of employing; exercise: he uses his brain. **3.** to behave towards in a particular way, esp. for one's own ends: he uses people. **4.** to consume, expend, or exhaust: the engine uses very little oil. **5.** Chiefly U.S. to partake of (alcoholic drink, drugs, etc.) or smoke (tobacco, marijuana, etc.). ~n. (juːs). **6.** the act of using or the state of being used: the carpet wore out through constant use. **7.** the ability or permission to use. **8.** the occasion to use: I have no use for this paper. **9.** an instance or manner of using. **10.** usefulness; advantage: it is of no use to complain. **11.** custom; habit: long use has inured him to it. **12.** the purpose for which something is used; end. **13.** Christianity. a distinctive form of liturgical or ritual observance, esp. one that is traditional. **14.** the enjoyment of property, land, etc., by occupation or by deriving revenue from it. **15.** Law. the beneficial enjoyment of property the legal title to which is held by another person as trustee. **16. have no use for. a.** to have no need of. **b.** to have a contemptuous dislike for. **17. make use of.** to employ; use. —**'user** n.

used (juːzd) adj. bought or sold second-hand: used cars.

used to (juːst) adj. **1.** accustomed to: I am used to hitchhiking. ~vb. (tr.) **2.** (takes an infinitive or implied infinitive) used as an auxiliary to express habitual or accustomed actions, states, etc., taking place in the past but not continuing into the present: I don't drink these days, but I used to.

useful ('juːsfʊl) adj. **1.** able to be used advantageously, beneficially, or for several purposes. **2.** Inf. commendable or capable: a useful term's work. —**'usefully** adv. —**'usefulness** n.

useless ('juːslɪs) adj. **1.** having no practical use or advantage. **2.** Inf. ineffectual, weak, or stupid: he's useless at history. —**'uselessly** adv. —**'uselessness** n.

usher ('ʌʃə) n. **1.** an official who shows people to their seats, as in a church or theatre. **2.** a person who acts as doorkeeper, esp. in a court of law. **3.** (in England) a minor official charged with maintaining order in a court of law. **4.** an officer responsible for preceding persons of rank in a procession. **5.** Brit., obs. a teacher. ~vb. (tr.) **6.** to conduct or escort, esp. in a courteous or obsequious way. **7.** (usually foll. by in) to be a precursor or herald (of).

usherette (ˌʌʃəˈrɛt) n. a woman assistant in a cinema, etc., who shows people to their seats.

U.S.S.R. abbrev. for Union of Soviet Socialist Republics.

usual ('juːʒʊəl) adj. **1.** of the most normal, frequent, or regular type: that's the usual sort of application to send. ~n. **2.** ordinary or commonplace events (esp. in **out of the usual**). **3. the usual.** Inf. the habitual or usual drink, etc. —**'usually** adv. —**'usualness** n.

usurp (juːˈzɜːp) vb. to seize or appropriate (land, a throne, etc.) without authority. —ˌusurˈpation n. —uˈsurper n. —uˈsurpingly adv.

usury ('juːʒərɪ) n., pl. **-ries. 1.** the practice of loaning money at an exorbitant rate of interest. **2.** an unlawfully high rate of interest. **3.** Obs. moneylending. —**usurious** (juːˈʒʊərɪəs) adj.

utensil (juːˈtɛnsəl) n. an implement, tool, or container for practical use: writing utensils.

uterine ('juːtəˌraɪn) adj. **1.** of, relating to, or affecting the uterus. **2.** (of offspring) born of the same mother but not the same father.

uterus ('juːtərəs) n., pl. **uteri** ('juːtəˌraɪ). **1.** Anat. a hollow muscular organ lying within the pelvic cavity of female mammals. It houses the developing foetus. Nontechnical name: **womb. 2.** the corresponding organ in other animals.

utilitarian (juːˌtɪlɪˈtɛərɪən) adj. **1.** of or relating to utilitarianism. **2.** designed for use rather than beauty. ~n. **3.** a person who believes in utilitarianism.

utilitarianism (juːˌtɪlɪˈtɛərɪəˌnɪzəm) n. Ethics. **1.** the theory that the highest good lies in the greatest good of the greatest numbers. **2.** the theory that the criterion of virtue is utility.

utility (juːˈtɪlɪtɪ) n., pl. **-ties. 1. a.** the quality of practical use; usefulness. **b.** (as modifier): a utility fabric. **2.** something useful. **3. a.** a public service, such as the bus system. **b.** (as modifier): utility vehicle. **4.** Econ. the ability of a commodity to satisfy human wants.

utility room n. a room, esp. in a private house, used for storage, laundry, etc.

utilize or **-lise** ('juːtɪˌlaɪz) vb. (tr.) to make practical or worthwhile use of. —**'utiˌlizable** or **-ˌlisable** adj.

THESAURUS

usable at one's disposal, available, current, fit for use, functional, in running order, practical, ready for use, serviceable, utilizable, valid, working

usage 1. control, employment, handling, management, operation, regulation, running, treatment, use **2.** convention, custom, form, habit, matter of course, method, mode, practice, procedure, regime, routine, rule, tradition, wont

use v. **1.** apply, avail oneself of, bring into play, employ, exercise, find a use for, make use of, operate, ply, practise, profit by, put to use, turn to account, utilize, wield, work **2.** act towards, behave towards, deal with, exploit, handle, manipulate, misuse, take advantage of, treat **3.** consume, exhaust, expend, run through, spend, waste ~n. **4.** application, employment, exercise, handling, operation, practice, service, treatment, usage, wear and tear **5.** advantage, application, avail, benefit, good, help, mileage (Inf.), point, profit, service, usefulness, utility, value, worth **6.** custom, habit, practice, usage,

way, wont **7.** call, cause, end, necessity, need, object, occasion, point, purpose, reason

used cast-off, hand-me-down (Inf.), nearly new, not new, reach-me-down (Inf.), second-hand, shopsoiled, worn

used to accustomed to, at home in, attuned to, familiar with, given to, habituated to, hardened to, in the habit of, inured to, tolerant of, wont to

useful advantageous, all-purpose, beneficial, effective, fruitful, general-purpose, helpful, of help, of service, of use, practical, profitable, salutary, serviceable, valuable, worthwhile

useless 1. bootless, disadvantageous, fruitless, futile, hopeless, idle, impractical, ineffective, ineffectual, of no use, pointless, profitless, unavailing, unproductive, unworkable, vain, valueless, worthless **2.** Inf. hopeless, incompetent, ineffectual, inept, no good, stupid, weak

use up absorb, burn up, consume, deplete, devour, drain, exhaust, finish, fritter away, run through, squander, swallow up, waste

usher n. **1.** attendant, doorkeeper, escort, guide, usherette ~v. **2.** conduct, direct, escort, guide, lead, pilot, show in or out, steer **3.** Usually with **in** bring in, herald, inaugurate, initiate, introduce, launch, open the door to, pave the way for, precede, ring in

usual accustomed, common, constant, customary, everyday, expected, familiar, fixed, general, habitual, normal, ordinary, regular, routine, standard, stock, typical, wonted

usually as a rule, as is the custom, as is usual, by and large, commonly, for the most part, generally, habitually, in the main, mainly, mostly, most often, normally, on the whole, ordinarily, regularly, routinely

utility advantageousness, avail, benefit, convenience, efficacy, fitness, point, practicality, profit, service, serviceableness, use, usefulness

utilize appropriate, avail oneself of, employ, have recourse to, make the most of, make use of, profit by, put to use, resort to, take advantage of, turn to account, use

—,utili'zation *or* -li'sation *n.* —'uti,lizer *or* ,liser *n.*

utmost ('ʌt,məʊst) *or* **uttermost** *adj.* (*prenominal*) **1.** of the greatest possible degree or amount: *the utmost degree.* **2.** at the furthest limit: *the utmost town on the peninsula.* ~*n.* **3.** the greatest possible degree, extent, or amount: *he tried his utmost.*

Utopia (juːˈtəʊpɪə) *n.* (*sometimes not cap.*) any real or imaginary society, place, state, etc., considered to be perfect or ideal. —**U'topian** *adj.*

utricle ('juːtrɪkəl) *n., pl.* **utricles. 1.** *Anat.* the larger of the two parts of the membranous labyrinth of the internal ear. **2.** *Bot.* the bladder-like one-seeded indehiscent fruit of certain plants. —**u'tricular** *adj.*

utter[1] ('ʌtə) *vb.* **1.** to give audible expression to (something): *to utter a growl.* **2.** *Criminal law.* to put into circulation (counterfeit coin, forged banknotes, etc.). **3.** (*tr.*) to make publicly known; publish: *to utter slander.* —'**utterable** *adj.* —'**utterableness** *n.* —'**utterer** *n.*

utter[2] ('ʌtə) *adj.* (*prenominal*) (intensifier): *an utter fool; the utter limit.* —'**utterly** *adv.*

utterance ('ʌtərəns) *n.* **1.** something uttered, such as a statement. **2.** the act or power of uttering or the ability to utter.

uttermost ('ʌtə,məʊst) *adj., n.* a variant of **utmost.**

U-turn *n.* **1.** a turn made by a vehicle in the shape of a U, resulting in a reversal of direction. **2.** a complete change in direction of political policy, etc.

U.V. *abbrev. for* ultraviolet.

uvula ('juːvjʊlə) *n., pl.* **-las** *or* **-lae** (-,liː). a small fleshy finger-like flap of tissue that hangs in the back of the throat and is an extension of the soft palate.

uxorious (ʌkˈsɔːrɪəs) *adj.* excessively attached to or dependent on one's wife. —**ux'oriously** *adv.* —**ux'oriousness** *n.*

THESAURUS

utmost *adj.* **1.** chief, extreme, greatest, highest, maximum, paramount, pre-eminent, supreme **2.** extreme, farthest, final, last, most distant, outermost, remotest, uttermost ~*n.* **3.** best, greatest, hardest, highest, most

Utopia bliss, Eden, Erewhon, Garden of Eden, heaven, ideal life, paradise, perfect place, seventh heaven, Shangri-la

Utopian 1. *adj.* airy, chimerical, dream, fanciful, fantasy, ideal, idealistic, illusory, imaginary, impractical, perfect, romantic, visionary **2.** *n.* Don Quixote, dreamer, idealist, romanticist, visionary

utter[1] *v.* **1.** articulate, enunciate, express, pronounce, put into words, say, speak, verbalize, vocalize, voice **2.** declare, divulge, give expression to, make known, proclaim, promulgate, publish, reveal, state

utter[2] *adj.* absolute, arrant, complete, consummate, downright, entire, out-and-out, perfect, sheer, stark, thorough, thoroughgoing, total, unmitigated, unqualified

utterly absolutely, completely, entirely, extremely, fully, perfectly, thoroughly, totally, to the core, wholly

V

v or **V** (viː) n., pl. **v's**, **V's**, or **Vs**. **1.** the 22nd letter of the English alphabet. **2.** a speech sound represented by this letter, usually a voiced fricative, as in *vote*. **3. a.** something shaped like a V. **b.** (*in combination*): *a V neck*.

v symbol. for: **1.** Physics. velocity. **2.** volt.

V symbol. for: **1.** Physics. velocity. **2.** (in transformational grammar) verb. **3.** volume (capacity). **4.** volt. **5.** Chem. vanadium. **6.** victory. ~**7.** the Roman numeral for five.

v. abbrev. for: **1.** ventral. **2.** verb. **3.** verse. **4.** verso. **5.** (usually italic) versus. **6.** very. **7.** vide: see. **8.** volume.

V. abbrev. for: **1.** Venerable. **2.** (in titles) Very. **3.** (in titles) Vice. **4.** Viscount.

V.A. abbrev. for: **1.** Vicar Apostolic. **2.** (Order of) Victoria and Albert.

vac (væk) n. Brit. inf. short for **vacation**.

vacancy ('veɪkənsɪ) n., pl. **-cies**. **1.** the state or condition of being vacant or unoccupied; emptiness. **2.** an unoccupied post or office: *we have a vacancy in the accounts department*. **3.** lack of thought or intelligent awareness. **4.** Obs. idleness or a period spent in idleness.

vacant ('veɪkənt) adj. **1.** without any contents; empty. **2.** (postpositive; foll. by *of*) devoid of (something specified). **3.** having no incumbent: *a vacant post*. **4.** having no tenant or occupant: *a vacant house*. **5.** characterized by or resulting from lack of thought or intelligent awareness. **6.** (of time, etc.) not allocated to any activity: *a vacant hour in one's day*. **7.** spent in idleness or inactivity: *a vacant life*. —**'vacantly** adv.

vacate (vəˈkeɪt) vb. (mainly tr.) **1.** to cause (something) to be empty, esp. by departing from or abandoning it: *to vacate a room*. **2.** (also intr.) to give up the tenure, possession, or occupancy of (a place, post, etc.). **3.** Law. **a.** to cancel. **b.** to annul. —**va'catable** adj.

vacation (vəˈkeɪʃən) n. **1.** Chiefly Brit. a period of the year when the law courts or universities are closed. **2.** U.S. a holiday. **3.** the act of departing from or abandoning property, etc. ~vb. **4.** (intr.) U.S. to take a holiday. —**va'cationer** or **va'cationist** n.

vaccinate ('væksɪˌneɪt) vb. to inoculate (a person) with vaccine so as to produce immunity against a specific disease. —**ˌvacci'nation** n. —**'vacci,nator** n.

vaccine ('væksiːn) n. Med. **1.** a suspension of dead, attenuated, or otherwise modified microorganisms for inoculation to produce immunity to a disease by stimulating the production of antibodies. **2.** a preparation of the virus of cowpox inoculated in humans to produce immunity to smallpox. **3.** (modifier) of or relating to vaccination or vaccinia. —**'vaccinal** adj.

vacillate ('væsɪˌleɪt) vb. (intr.) **1.** to fluctuate in one's opinions. **2.** to sway from side to side physically. —**ˌvacil'lation** n. —**'vacil,lator** n.

vacuity (væˈkjuːɪtɪ) n., pl. **-ties**. **1.** the state or quality of being vacuous. **2.** an empty space or void. **3.** a lack or absence of something specified: *a vacuity of wind*. **4.** lack of normal intelligence or awareness. **5.** a statement, saying, etc., that is inane or pointless.

vacuous ('vækjʊəs) adj. **1.** empty. **2.** bereft of ideas or intelligence. **3.** characterized by or resulting from va-

cancy of mind: *a vacuous gaze*. **4.** indulging in no useful mental or physical activity. —**'vacuously** adv.

vacuum ('vækjʊəm) n., pl. **vacuums** or **vacua** ('vækjʊə). **1.** a region containing no free matter; in technical contexts now often called: **free space**. **2.** a region in which gas is present at a low pressure. **3.** the degree of exhaustion of gas within an enclosed space: *a perfect vacuum*. **4.** a feeling of emptiness: *his death left a vacuum in her life*. **5.** short for **vacuum cleaner**. **6.** (modifier) of, containing, producing, or operated by a low gas pressure: *a vacuum brake*. ~vb. **7.** to clean (something) with a vacuum cleaner.

vacuum cleaner n. an electrical household appliance used for cleaning floors, carpets, etc., by suction. —**vacuum cleaning** n.

vacuum flask n. an insulating flask that has double walls, usually of silvered glass, with an evacuated space between them. It is used for maintaining substances at high or low temperatures. Also called: **Thermos**.

vacuum-packed adj. packed in an airtight container or packet under low pressure in order to maintain freshness, prevent corrosion, etc.

vacuum pump n. a pump for producing a low gas pressure.

vacuum tube or **valve** n. another name for **valve** (sense 3).

V.A.D. abbrev. for Voluntary Aid Detachment.

vade mecum ('vɑːdɪ 'meɪkʊm) n. a handbook or other aid carried on the person for immediate use when needed.

vagabond ('vægəˌbɒnd) n. **1.** a person with no fixed home. **2.** an idle wandering beggar or thief. **3.** (modifier) of or like a vagabond. —**'vaga,bondage** n.

vagary ('veɪgərɪ, vəˈgɛərɪ) n., pl. **-garies**. an erratic notion or action.

vagina (vəˈdʒaɪnə) n., pl. **-nas** or **-nae** (-niː). **1.** the canal in most female mammals that extends from the cervix of the uterus to an external opening between the labia minora. **2.** Anat., biol. any sheath or sheathlike structure. —**vag'inal** adj.

vaginismus (ˌvædʒɪˈnɪzməs) n. painful spasm of the vagina.

vaginitis (ˌvædʒɪˈnaɪtɪs) n. inflammation of the vagina.

vagrant ('veɪgrənt) n. **1.** a person of no settled abode, income, or job; tramp. ~adj. **2.** wandering about. **3.** of or characteristic of a vagrant or vagabond. **4.** moving in an erratic fashion; wayward. **5.** (of plants) showing straggling growth. —**'vagrantly** adv.

vague (veɪg) adj. **1.** (of statements, meaning, etc.) imprecise: *vague promises*. **2.** not clearly perceptible or discernible: *a vague idea*. **3.** not clearly or definitely established or known: *a vague rumour*. **4.** (of a person or his expression) absent-minded. —**'vaguely** adv. —**'vagueness** n.

vain (veɪn) adj. **1.** inordinately proud of one's appearance, possessions, or achievements. **2.** given to ostentatious display. **3.** worthless. **4.** senseless or futile. ~n. **5. in vain.** fruitlessly. **6. take someone's name in vain.** to use the name of someone without due respect. —**'vainly** adv. —**'vainness** n.

THESAURUS

vacancy 1. job, opening, opportunity, position, post, room, situation **2.** absent-mindedness, abstraction, blankness, inanity, inattentiveness, incomprehension, incuriousness, lack of interest, vacuousness **3.** emptiness, gap, space, vacuum, void

vacant 1. available, disengaged, empty, free, idle, not in use, to let, unemployed, unengaged, unfilled, unoccupied, untenanted, void **2.** absent-minded, abstracted, blank, dreaming, dreamy, expressionless, idle, inane, incurious, thoughtless, unthinking, vacuous

vacuum emptiness, free space, gap, nothingness, space, vacuity, void

vagabond 1. n. beggar, bum (U.S. inf.), down-and-out, hobo (U.S.), itinerant, knight of the road, migrant, nomad, outcast, rascal, rover, tramp, vagrant, wanderer, wayfarer **2.** adj. destitute, down and out, drifting, fly-by-night (Inf.), footloose, homeless, idle, itinerant, journeying, nomadic, rootless, roving, shiftless, vagrant, wandering

vagary caprice, crotchet, fancy, humour, megrim (Archaic), notion, whim, whimsy

vagrant 1. n. beggar, bird of passage, bum (U.S. inf.), hobo (U.S.), itinerant, person of no fixed address, rolling stone, tramp, wanderer **2.** adj. itinerant, nomadic, roaming, rootless, roving, unsettled, vagabond

vague amorphous, blurred, dim, doubtful, fuzzy, generalized, hazy, ill-defined, imprecise, indefinite, indeterminate, indistinct, lax, loose, nebulous, obscure, shadowy, uncertain, unclear, unknown, unspecified, woolly

vaguely absent-mindedly, dimly, evasively, imprecisely, in a general way, obscurely, slightly, through a glass darkly, vacantly

vagueness ambiguity, impreciseness, inexactitude, lack of preciseness, looseness, obscurity

vain 1. arrogant, bigheaded (Inf.), cocky, conceited, egotistical, inflated, narcissistic, ostentatious, overweening, peacockish,

vainglory ('veɪnˌglɔːrɪ) n. 1. boastfulness or vanity. 2. ostentation. —**vain'glorious** adj.

valance ('væləns) n. a short piece of drapery hung along a shelf or bed to hide structural detail. —**'valanced** adj.

vale (veɪl) n. a literary word for **valley.**

valediction (ˌvælɪ'dɪkʃən) n. 1. the act or an instance of saying goodbye. 2. any valedictory statement, speech, etc. —ˌ**vale'dictory** adj., n.

valence ('veɪləns) n. Chem. 1. another name (esp. U.S.) for **valency. 2.** the phenomenon of forming chemical bonds.

valency ('veɪlənsɪ) or esp. U.S. **valence** n., pl. **-cies.** Chem. a property of atoms or groups equal to the number of atoms of hydrogen that the atom or group could combine with or displace in forming compounds.

valentine ('væhənˌtaɪn) n. 1. a card or gift expressing love or affection, sent, often anonymously, on Saint Valentine's Day. 2. a sweetheart selected for such a greeting.

valerian (və'lɪərɪən) n. 1. Also called: **allheal.** a Eurasian plant having small white or pinkish flowers and a medicinal root. 2. a sedative drug made from the dried roots of this plant.

valet ('vælɪt, 'væleɪ) n. 1. a manservant who acts as personal attendant to his employer, looking after his clothing, serving his meals, etc. 2. a manservant who attends to the requirements of patrons in a hotel, etc.; steward.

valetudinarian (ˌvælɪˌtjuːdɪ'nɛərɪən) or **valetudinary** (ˌvælɪ'tjuːdɪnərɪ) n., pl. **-narians** or **-naries.** 1. a person who is chronically sick. 2. a hypochondriac. 3. an old person who is in good health. ~adj. 4. relating to or resulting from poor health. 5. being a valetudinarian. —ˌ**vale,tudi'narianism** n.

Valhalla (væl'hælə) n. Norse myth. the great hall of Odin where warriors who die as heroes in battle dwell eternally.

valiant ('væljənt) adj. 1. courageous or intrepid. 2. marked by bravery or courage: a valiant deed. —**'valiantly** adv.

valid ('vælɪd) adj. 1. having some foundation; based on truth. 2. legally acceptable: a valid licence. 3. a. having legal force. b. having legal authority. 4. having some force or cogency: a valid point in a debate. 5. Logic. (of an inference) having premisses and a conclusion so related that if the premisses are true, the conclusion must be true. —**'validly** adv. —**validity** (və'lɪdɪtɪ) n.

validate ('vælɪˌdeɪt) vb. (tr.) 1. to confirm or corroborate. 2. to give legal force or official confirmation to. —ˌ**vali'dation** n.

valise (və'liːz) n. a small overnight travelling case.

Valkyrie (væl'kɪərɪ, 'vælkɪərɪ) n. Norse myth. any of the beautiful maidens who serve Odin and ride over battlefields to claim the dead heroes and take them to Valhalla.

valley ('vælɪ) n. 1. a long depression in the land surface, usually containing a river, formed by erosion or by movements in the earth's crust. 2. the broad area drained by a single river system: the Thames valley. 3. any elongated depression resembling a valley.

valour or U.S. **valor** ('vælə) n. courage or bravery, esp. in battle. —**'valorous** adj.

valuable ('væljuəb²l) adj. 1. having considerable monetary worth. 2. of considerable importance or quality: valuable information. 3. able to be valued. ~n. 4. (usually pl.) a valuable article of personal property, esp. jewellery. —**'valuably** adv.

valuation (ˌvæljuˈeɪʃən) n. 1. the act of valuing, esp. a formal assessment of the worth of property, jewellery, etc. 2. the price arrived at by the process of valuing: I set a high valuation on technical ability. —ˌ**valu'ational** adj.

value ('væljuː) n. 1. the desirability of a thing, often in respect of some property such as usefulness or exchangeability. 2. an amount, esp. a material or monetary one, considered to be a fair exchange in return for a thing: the value of the picture is £10 000. 3. satisfaction: value for money. 4. precise meaning or significance. 5. (pl.) the moral principles or accepted standards of a person or group. 6. Maths. a particular magnitude, number, or amount: the value of the variable was 7. 7. Music. the duration of a note. 8. (in painting, drawing, etc.) a. a gradation of tone from light to dark. b. the relation of one of these elements to another or to the whole picture. 9. Phonetics. the quality of the speech sound associated with a written character representing it: "g" has the value (dʒ) in English "gem". ~vb. **-uing, -ued.** (tr.) 10. to assess or estimate the worth, merit, or desirability of. 11. to have a high regard for, esp. in respect of worth, usefulness, merit, etc. 12. (foll. by at) to fix the financial or material worth of (a unit of currency, work of art etc.). —**'valued** adj. —**'valueless** adj. —**'valuer** n.

value-added tax n. Brit. the full name for **VAT**

value judgment n. a subjective assessment based on one's own values or those of one's class.

valve (vælv) n. 1. any device that shuts off, starts, regulates, or controls the flow of a fluid. 2. Anat. a flaplike structure in a hollow organ, such as the heart, that controls the one-way passage of fluid through that organ. 3. Also called: **tube.** an evacuated electron tube containing a cathode, anode, and, usually, one or more additional control electrodes. When a positive potential is applied to the anode, it produces a one-way flow of current. 4. Zool. any of the separable pieces that make up the shell of a mollusc. 5. Music. a device on some brass instruments by which the effective length of the tube may be varied to enable a chromatic scale to be produced. 6. Bot. any of the several parts that make up a dry dehiscent fruit, esp. a capsule. —**'valveless** adj. —**'valve,like** adj.

valvular ('vælvjulə) adj. 1. of, relating to, operated by, or having a valve or valves. 2. having the shape or function of a valve.

vamoose (və'muːs) vb. (intr.) U.S. sl. to leave a place hurriedly; decamp.

vamp¹ (væmp) Inf. ~n. 1. a seductive woman who exploits men by use of her sexual charms. ~vb. 2. to exploit (a man) in the fashion of a vamp.

vamp² (væmp) n. 1. something patched up to make it look new. 2. the reworking of a story, etc. 3. an improvised accompaniment. 4. the front part of the upper of a shoe. ~vb. 5. (tr.; often foll. by up) to make a renova-

---

THESAURUS

pleased with oneself, proud, self-important, stuck-up (Inf.), swaggering, swanky (Inf.), swollen-headed (Inf.), vainglorious 2. abortive, empty, fruitless, futile, hollow, idle, nugatory, pointless, senseless, time-wasting, trifling, trivial, unavailing, unimportant, unproductive, unprofitable, useless, worthless 3. **be vain** have a high opinion of oneself, have a swelled head (Inf.), have one's head turned, think a lot of oneself, think oneself it (Inf.), think oneself the cat's whiskers or pyjamas (Sl.) 4. **in vain** bootless, fruitless(ly), ineffectual(ly), to no avail, to no purpose, unsuccessful(ly), useless(ly), vain(ly), wasted, without success

valedictory adj. farewell, final, parting

valiant bold, brave, courageous, dauntless, doughty, fearless, gallant, heroic, indomitable, intrepid, lion-hearted, plucky, redoubtable, stouthearted, valorous, worthy

valid 1. binding, cogent, conclusive, convincing, efficacious, efficient, good, just, logical, powerful, sound, substantial, telling, weighty, well-founded, well-grounded 2. authentic, bona fide, genuine, in force, lawful, legal, legally binding, legitimate, official

validity 1. cogency, force, foundation, grounds, point, power, soundness, strength, substance, weight 2. authority, lawfulness, legality, legitimacy, right

valley coomb, cwm (Welsh), dale, dell, depression, dingle, glen, hollow, strath (Scot.), vale

valour boldness, bravery, courage, derring-do (Archaic), doughtiness, fearlessness, gallantry, heroism, intrepidity, lion-heartedness, spirit

valuable adj. 1. costly, dear, expensive, high-priced, precious 2. beneficial, cherished, esteemed, estimable, held dear, helpful, important, prized, profitable, serviceable, treasured, useful, valued, worthwhile,

worthy ~n. 3. Usually plural heirloom, treasure(s)

value n. 1. cost, equivalent, market price, monetary worth, rate 2. advantage, benefit, desirability, help, importance, merit, profit, serviceableness, significance, use, usefulness, utility, worth 3. Plural code of behaviour, ethics, (moral) standards, principles ~v. 4. account, appraise, assess, compute, estimate, evaluate, price, put a price on, rate, set at, survey 5. appreciate, cherish, esteem, hold dear, hold in high regard or esteem, prize, regard highly, respect, set store by, treasure

valued cherished, dear, esteemed, highly regarded, loved, prized, treasured

valueless miserable, no good, of no earthly use, of no value, unsaleable, useless, worthless

tion (of). **6.** to improvise (an accompaniment) to (a tune).

vampire ('væmpaɪə) *n.* **1.** (in European folklore) a corpse that rises nightly from its grave to drink the blood of the living. **2.** See **vampire bat. 3.** a person who preys mercilessly upon others. —**vampiric** (væm'pɪrɪk) *adj.* —**'vampirism** *n.*

vampire bat *n.* a bat of tropical regions of Central and South America, having sharp incisor and canine teeth and feeding on the blood of birds and mammals.

van[1] (væn) *n.* **1.** short for **caravan** (sense 1). **2.** a motor vehicle for transporting goods, etc., by road. **3.** *Brit.* a closed railway wagon in which the guard travels, for transporting goods, etc.

van[2] (væn) *n.* short for **vanguard.**

vanadium (və'neɪdɪəm) *n.* a toxic silvery-white metallic element used in steel alloys and as a catalyst. Symbol: V; atomic no.: 23; atomic wt.: 50.94.

Van Allen belt (væn 'ælən) *n.* either of two regions of charged particles above the earth, the inner one extending from 2400 to 5600 kilometres above the earth and the outer one from 13 000 to 19 000 kilometres.

vandal ('vændəl) *n.* a person who deliberately causes damage to personal or public property. —**'vandal,ism** *n.*

vandalize *or* **-lise** ('vændə,laɪz) *vb.* (*tr.*) to destroy or damage (something) by an act of vandalism.

Vandyke beard ('vændaɪk) *n.* a short pointed beard. Often shortened to **Vandyke.**

vane (veɪn) *n.* **1.** Also called: **weather vane.** a flat plate or blade of metal mounted on a vertical axis in an exposed position to indicate wind direction. **2.** any one of the flat blades or sails forming part of the wheel of a windmill. **3.** any flat or shaped plate used to direct fluid flow, esp. in a turbine, etc. **4.** a fin or plate fitted to a projectile or missile to provide stabilization or guidance. **5.** *Ornithol.* the flat part of a feather. **6.** *Surveying.* **a.** a sight on a quadrant or compass. **b.** the movable marker on a levelling staff. —**vaned** *adj.*

vanguard ('væn,gɑːd) *n.* **1.** the leading division or units of an army. **2.** the leading position in any movement or field, or the people who occupy such a position.

vanilla (və'nɪlə) *n.* **1.** any of a genus of tropical climbing orchids having spikes of large fragrant flowers and long fleshy pods containing the seeds (beans). **2.** the pod or bean of certain of these plants, used to flavour food, etc. **3.** a flavouring extract prepared from vanilla beans and used in cooking. —**va'nillic** *adj.*

vanish ('vænɪʃ) *vb.* (*intr.*) **1.** to disappear, esp. suddenly or mysteriously. **2.** to cease to exist. **3.** *Maths.* to become zero. —**'vanisher** *n.* —**'vanishment** *n.*

vanishing cream *n.* a cosmetic cream that is colourless once applied, used as a foundation for powder or as a cleansing cream.

vanishing point *n.* **1.** the point to which parallel lines appear to converge in the rendering of perspective, usually on the horizon. **2.** a point at which something disappears.

vanity ('vænɪtɪ) *n., pl.* **-ties. 1.** the state or quality of being vain. **2.** ostentation occasioned by ambition or pride. **3.** an instance of being vain or something about which one is vain. **4.** the state or quality of being valueless or futile.

vanity case *or* **box** *n.* a woman's small hand case used to carry cosmetics, etc.

vanity unit *n.* a hand basin built into a wooden Formica-covered or tiled top, usually with a built-in cup-

board below it. Also called (trademark): **Vanitory unit.**

vanquish ('væŋkwɪʃ) *vb.* (*tr.*) **1.** to defeat or overcome in a battle, contest, etc. **2.** to defeat in argument or debate. **3.** to conquer (an emotion). —**'vanquishable** *adj.* —**'vanquisher** *n.*

vantage ('vɑːntɪdʒ) *n.* **1.** a state, position, or opportunity affording superiority or advantage. **2.** superiority or benefit accruing from such a position, etc. **3.** *Tennis.* short for **advantage.**

vapid ('væpɪd) *adj.* **1.** bereft of strength, sharpness, flavour, etc. **2.** boring or dull: *vapid talk.* —**va'pidity** *n.* —**'vapidly** *adv.*

vapor ('veɪpə) *n., vb.* the U.S. spelling of **vapour.**

vaporize *or* **-rise** ('veɪpə,raɪz) *vb.* **1.** to change or cause to change into vapour or into the gaseous state. **2.** to evaporate or disappear or cause to evaporate or disappear, esp. suddenly. —,vapori'zation *or* -ri'sation *n.* —,vapo'rizer *or* -'riser *n.*

vaporous ('veɪpərəs) *adj.* **1.** resembling or full of vapour. **2.** lacking permanence or substance. **3.** given to foolish imaginings. —**'vaporously** *adv.* —**vaporosity** (,veɪpə'rɒsɪtɪ) *n.*

vapour *or U.S.* **vapor** ('veɪpə) *n.* **1.** particles of moisture or other substance suspended in air and visible as clouds, smoke, etc. **2.** a gaseous substance at a temperature below its critical temperature. **3.** a substance that is in a gaseous state at a temperature below its boiling point. **4. the vapours.** *Arch.* a depressed mental condition believed originally to be the result of vaporous exhalations from the stomach. —*vb.* **5.** to evaporate or cause to evaporate. **6.** (*intr.*) to make vain empty boasts. —**'vapourer** *or U.S.* **'vaporer** *n.* —**'vapourish** *or U.S.* **'vaporish** *adj.* —**'vapour-,like** *or U.S.* **'vapor-,like** *adj.* —**'vapoury** *or U.S.* **'vapory** *adj.*

vapour lock *n.* a stoppage in a pipe carrying a liquid caused by a bubble of gas, esp. in the pipe feeding the carburettor of an internal-combustion engine.

var. *abbrev. for:* **1.** variable. **2.** variant. **3.** variation. **4.** variety. **5.** various.

variable ('vɛərɪəbəl) *adj.* **1.** liable to or capable of change: *variable weather.* **2.** (of behaviour, emotions, etc.) lacking constancy. **3.** *Maths.* having a range of possible values. **4.** (of a species, etc.) liable to deviate from the established type. **5.** (of a wind) varying in direction and intensity. **6.** (of an electrical component or device) designed so that a characteristic property, such as resistance, can be varied. —*n.* **7.** something that is subject to variation. **8.** *Maths.* **a.** a quantity or function that can assume any of a set of specified values. **b.** a symbol, esp. *x, y,* or *z,* representing any unspecified number, quantity, etc., belonging to a set. **9.** *Logic.* a symbol, esp. *x, y,* or *z,* representing any member of a class of entities. **10.** a variable wind. **11.** (*pl.*) a region where variable winds occur. —,varia'bility *or* 'variableness *n.* —'variably *adv.*

variance ('vɛərɪəns) *n.* **1.** the act of varying or the quality, state, or degree of being divergent. **2.** an instance of diverging; dissension. **3. at variance. a.** (often foll. by *with*) (of facts, etc.) not in accord. **b.** (of persons) in a state of dissension. **4.** *Statistics.* a measure of dispersion; the square of the standard deviations. **5.** a difference or discrepancy between two steps in a legal proceeding, esp. between a statement and the evidence given to support it. **6.** *Chem.* the number of degrees of freedom of a system, used in the phase rule.

variant ('vɛərɪənt) *adj.* **1.** liable to or displaying variation. **2.** deviating from a norm, standard, or type: *variant spelling.* —*n.* **3.** something that deviates or

---

▮ THESAURUS ▮

vanguard advance guard, forefront, forerunners, front, front line, front rank, leaders, spearhead, trailblazers, trendsetters, van

vanish become invisible, be lost to sight, die out, disappear, disappear from sight or from the face of the earth, dissolve, evanesce, evaporate, exit, fade (away), melt (away)

vanity 1. affected ways, airs, arrogance, bigheadedness (*Inf.*), conceit, conceitedness, egotism, narcissism, ostentation, pretension, pride, self-admiration, self-love, showing off (*Inf.*), swollen-headedness (*Inf.*), vainglory 2. emptiness, frivolity, fruitlessness, futility,

hollowness, inanity, pointlessness, profitlessness, triviality, unproductiveness, unreality, unsubstantiality, uselessness, worthlessness

vanquish beat, conquer, crush, defeat, get the upper hand over, master, overcome, overpower, overwhelm, put down, put to flight, put to rout, quell, reduce, repress, rout, subdue, subjugate, triumph over

vapour breath, dampness, exhalation, fog, fumes, haze, miasma, mist, smoke, steam

variable capricious, chameleonic, changeable, fickle, fitful, flexible, fluctuating, inconstant, mercurial, mutable, protean, shifting, temperamental, unstable, unsteady, vacillating, wavering

variance 1. difference, difference of opinion, disagreement, discord, discrepancy, dissension, dissent, divergence, inconsistency, lack of harmony, strife, variation 2. at variance at loggerheads, at odds, at sixes and sevens (*Inf.*), conflicting, in disagreement, in opposition, out of harmony, out of line

variant 1. *adj.* alternative, derived, different, divergent, exceptional, modified 2. *n.* alternative, derived form, development, modification, sport (*Biol.*), variation

varies from a norm, standard, or type.

variation (ˌvɛərɪˈeɪʃən) n. 1. the act, process, condition, or result of changing or varying. 2. an instance of varying or the amount, rate, or degree of such change. 3. something that deviates from a standard, convention, or norm. 4. *Music.* a repetition of a musical theme in which the rhythm, harmony, or melody is altered or embellished. 5. *Biol.* a marked deviation from the typical form or function. 6. *Astron.* any change in or deviation from the mean motion or orbit of a planet, satellite, etc. 7. *Ballet.* a solo dance. —ˌvariˈational *adj.*

varicoloured or U.S. **varicolored** (ˈvɛərɪˌkʌləd) *adj.* having many colours.

varicose (ˈværɪˌkəʊs) *adj.* of or resulting from varicose veins: *a varicose ulcer.*

varicose veins *n.* a condition in which the superficial veins, esp. of the legs, become tortuous, knotted, and swollen.

varied (ˈvɛərɪd) *adj.* 1. displaying or characterized by variety; diverse. 2. modified or altered: *the amount may be varied without notice.* 3. varicoloured; variegated. —ˈvariedly *adv.*

variegated (ˈvɛərɪˌgeɪtɪd) *adj.* 1. displaying differently coloured spots, streaks, etc. 2. (of foliage) having pale patches.

variety (vəˈraɪɪtɪ) n., pl. **-ties.** 1. the quality or condition of being diversified or various. 2. a collection of unlike things, esp. of the same general group. 3. a different form or kind within a general category: *varieties of behaviour.* 4. a type of animal or plant produced by artificial breeding. 5. a. entertainment consisting of a series of short unrelated acts, such as comedy turns, songs, etc. b. (*as modifier*): *a variety show.*

variorum (ˌvɛərɪˈɔːrəm) *adj.* 1. containing notes by various scholars or various versions of the text. ~n. 2. an edition or text of this kind.

various (ˈvɛərɪəs) *determiner.* 1. several different: *he is an authority on various subjects.* ~adj. 2. of different kinds, though often within the same general category: *his disguises are many and various.* 3. (*prenominal*) relating to a collection of separate persons or things: *the various members of the club.* 4. displaying variety; many-sided: *his various achievements.* —ˈvariously *adv.* —ˈvariousness *n.*

▷ *Usage. Various of,* as in *he wrote to various of his friends,* is not current in good usage. Careful writers prefer *various* or *several of* to *various of: he wrote to various friends; he wrote to several of his friends.*

varix (ˈvɛərɪks) n., pl. **varices** (ˈværɪˌsiːz). *Pathol.* a. a tortuous dilated vein. b. a similar condition affecting an artery or lymphatic vessel.

varlet (ˈvɑːlɪt) n. *Arch.* 1. a menial servant. 2. a knight's page. 3. a rascal. —ˈvarletry n.

varmint (ˈvɑːmɪnt) n. *Inf.* an irritating or obnoxious person or animal.

varnish (ˈvɑːnɪʃ) n. 1. a preparation consisting of a solvent, a drying oil, and usually resin, rubber, etc., for application to a surface where it yields a hard glossy, usually transparent, coating. 2. a similar preparation consisting of a substance, such as shellac, dissolved in a volatile solvent, such as alcohol. It hardens to a film on evaporation of the solvent. 3. the sap of certain trees used to produce such a coating. 4. a smooth surface, coated with or as with varnish. 5. an artificial, superficial, or deceptively pleasing manner, covering, etc. 6. *Chiefly Brit.* another word for **nail polish.** ~vb. (tr.) 7. to cover with varnish. 8. to give a smooth surface to, as if by painting with varnish. 9. to impart a more attractive appearance to. —ˈvarnisher n.

varsity (ˈvɑːsɪtɪ) n., pl. **-ties.** *Brit. inf.* short for **university.**

varve (vɑːv) n. *Geol.* a band of sediment deposited in glacial lakes, consisting of a light layer and a dark layer deposited at different seasons.

vary (ˈvɛərɪ) vb. **varying, varied.** 1. to cause or undergo change or modification in appearance, character, form, etc. 2. to be different or cause to be different; be subject to change. 3. (tr.) to give variety to. 4. (intr.; foll. by *from*) to deviate, as from a convention, standard, etc. 5. (intr.) to change in accordance with another variable: *her mood varies with the weather.* —ˈvaryingly *adv.*

vas (væs) n., pl. **vasa** (ˈveɪsə). *Anat., zool.* a vessel or tube that carries a fluid.

vascular (ˈvæskjʊlə) *adj. Biol., anat.* of, relating to, or having vessels that conduct and circulate fluids: *a vascular bundle.* —**vascularity** (ˌvæskjʊˈlærɪtɪ) n. —ˈvascularly *adv.*

vas deferens (ˈvæs ˈdɛfəˌrɛnz) n., pl. **vasa deferentia** (ˈveɪsə ˌdɛfəˈrɛnʃɪə). *Anat.* the duct within each testis that conveys spermatozoa to the ejaculatory duct.

vase (vɑːz) n. a vessel used as an ornament or for holding cut flowers.

vasectomy (væˈsɛktəmɪ) n., pl. **-mies.** surgical removal of all or part of the vas deferens, esp. as a method of contraception.

Vaseline (ˈvæsɪˌliːn) n. a trademark for **petrolatum.**

vassal (ˈvæsəl) n. 1. (in feudal society) a man who entered into a relationship with a lord to whom he paid homage and fealty in return for protection and often a fief. 2. a. a person, nation, etc., in a subordinate or dependent position relative to another. b. (*as modifier*): *vassal status.* ~adj. 3. of or relating to a vassal. —ˈvassalage n.

vast (vɑːst) *adj.* 1. unusually large in size, degree, or number. 2. (*prenominal*) (intensifier): *in vast haste.* ~n. 3. **the vast.** *Chiefly poetic.* immense or boundless space. —ˈvastly *adv.* —ˈvastness n.

vat (væt) n. 1. a large container for holding or storing liquids. 2. *Chem.* a preparation of reduced vat dye. ~vb. **vatting, vatted.** 3. (tr.) to place, store, or treat in a vat.

VAT (*sometimes* væt) *Brit. abbrev. for* value-added tax; a tax levied on the difference between the cost of materials and the selling price of the commodity.

Vatican (ˈvætɪkən) n. 1. a. the palace of the popes in Rome, which includes administrative offices and is attached to the basilica of St. Peter's. b. (*as modifier*): *the Vatican Council.* 2. a. the authority of the Pope and the papal curia. b. (*as modifier*): *a Vatican edict.*

vaudeville (ˈvəʊdəvɪl, ˈvɔː-) n. 1. *Chiefly U.S.* variety entertainment consisting of short acts such as acrobatic turns, song-and-dance routines etc. 2. a light or comic theatrical piece interspersed with songs and dances. —ˌvaudeˈvillian n., *adj.*

vault[1] (vɔːlt) n. 1. an arched structure that forms a roof or ceiling. 2. a room, esp. a cellar, having an arched roof down to floor level. 3. a burial chamber, esp. when underground. 4. a strongroom for the storage of valuables. 5. an underground room used for the storage of wine, food, etc. 6. *Anat.* any arched or domed bodily cavity or space: *the cranial vault.* 7. something suggestive of an arched structure, as the sky. ~vb. 8. (tr.) to furnish with or as if with an arched roof. 9. (tr.) to construct in the shape of a vault. 10. (intr.) to curve in the shape of a vault.

vault[2] (vɔːlt) vb. 1. to spring over (an object), esp. with the aid of a long pole or with the hands resting on the object. 2. (intr.) to do, achieve, or attain something as if by a leap: *he vaulted to fame.* ~n. 3. the act of vaulting. —ˈvaulter n.

THESAURUS

variation alteration, break in routine, change, departure, departure from the norm, deviation, difference, discrepancy, diversification, diversity, innovation, modification, novelty, variety

varied assorted, different, diverse, heterogeneous, miscellaneous, mixed, motley, sundry, various

variety 1. change, difference, discrepancy, diversification, diversity, many-sidedness, multifariousness, variation 2. array, assortment, collection, cross section, intermixture, medley, miscellany, mixture, multiplicity, range 3. brand, breed, category, class, kind, make, order, sort, species, strain, type

various assorted, different, differing, disparate, distinct, divers (*Archaic*), diverse, diversified, heterogeneous, many, many-sided, miscellaneous, several, sundry, varied, variegated

varnish v. adorn, decorate, embellish, gild, glaze, gloss, japan, lacquer, polish, shellac

vary alter, alternate, be unlike, change, depart, differ, disagree, diverge, diversify, fluctuate, intermix, modify, permutate, reorder, transform

varying changing, different, distinct, distinguishable, diverse, fluctuating, inconsistent

vast astronomical, boundless, colossal, enormous, extensive, gigantic, great, huge, illimitable, immeasurable, immense, limitless, mammoth, massive, measureless, monstrous, monumental, never-ending, prodi-

vaulting¹ ('vɔːltɪŋ) n. one or more vaults in a building or such structures considered collectively.

vaulting² ('vɔːltɪŋ) adj. **1.** (prenominal) excessively confident: vaulting arrogance. **2.** (prenominal) used to vault: a vaulting pole.

vaunt (vɔːnt) vb. **1.** (tr.) to describe, praise, or display (one's success, possessions, etc.) boastfully. **2.** (intr.) Rare or literary. to brag. ~n. **3.** a boast. —'vaunter n. —'vauntingly adv.

vb. abbrev. for verb.

V.C. abbrev. for: **1.** Vice Chairman. **2.** Vice Chancellor. **3.** Vice Consul. **4.** Victoria Cross.

VD abbrev. for venereal disease.

VDU Computers. abbrev. for visual display unit.

veal (viːl) n. the flesh of the calf used as food.

vector ('vɛktə) n. **1.** Maths. a variable quantity, such as force, that has magnitude and direction and can be resolved into components. **2.** Also called: carrier. Pathol. an organism, esp. an insect, that carries a disease-producing microorganism from one host to another. **3.** the course or compass direction of an aircraft. ~vb. **4.** (tr.) to direct or guide (a pilot, aircraft, etc.) by directions transmitted by radio. —vectorial (vɛk'tɔːrɪəl) adj.

Veda ('veɪdə) n. any or all of the most ancient sacred writings of Hinduism, esp. the Rig-Veda, Yajur-Veda, Sama-Veda, and Atharva-Veda.

vedette (vɪ'dɛt) n. **1.** Naval. a small patrol vessel. **2.** Mil. a mounted sentry posted forward of a formation's position.

veer (vɪə) vb. **1.** to alter direction. **2.** (intr.) to change from one position, opinion, etc., to another. **3.** (intr.) (of the wind) to change direction clockwise in the northern hemisphere and anticlockwise in the southern. ~n. **4.** a change of course or direction. —'veeringly adv.

veg (vɛdʒ) n. Inf. a vegetable or vegetables.

Vega ('viːgə) n. the brightest star in the constellation Lyra and one of the most conspicuous in the N hemisphere.

vegan ('viːgən) n. a vegetarian who eats no animal products.

vegetable ('vɛdʒtəbəl) n. **1.** any of various herbaceous plants having parts that are used as food, such as peas, potatoes, cauliflower, and onions. **2.** Inf. a person who has lost control of his mental faculties, limbs, etc., as from an injury, mental disease, etc. **3.** a dull inactive person. **4.** (modifier) consisting of or made from edible vegetables: a vegetable diet. **5.** (modifier) of, characteristic of, derived from, or consisting of plants or plant material: the vegetable kingdom. **6.** Rare. any member of the plant kingdom.

vegetable marrow n. **1.** a plant, probably native to America but widely cultivated for its oblong green striped fruit which is eaten as a vegetable. **2.** the fruit of this plant. Often shortened to **marrow.**

vegetable oil n. any of a group of oils that are obtained from plants.

vegetal ('vɛdʒɪtəl) adj. **1.** of or characteristic of vegetables or plant life. **2.** vegetative.

vegetarian (ˌvɛdʒɪ'tɛərɪən) n. **1.** a person who advocates or practises the exclusion of meat and fish, and sometimes egg, milk, and cheese from the diet. ~adj. **2.** Cookery. strictly, consisting of vegetables and fruit only, but often including milk, cheese, eggs, etc. —ˌvege'tarianism n.

vegetate ('vɛdʒɪˌteɪt) vb. (intr.) **1.** to grow like a plant. **2.** to lead a life characterized by monotony, passivity, or mental inactivity.

vegetation (ˌvɛdʒɪ'teɪʃən) n. **1.** plant life as a whole, esp. the plant life of a particular region. **2.** the process of vegetating. —ˌvege'tational adj.

vegetative ('vɛdʒɪtətɪv) adj. **1.** of or concerned with plant life or plant growth. **2.** (of reproduction) characterized by asexual processes. **3.** of or relating to functions such as digestion and circulation rather than sexual reproduction. **4.** (of a style of living, etc.) unthinking or passive. —'vegetatively adv.

vehement ('viːɪmənt) adj. **1.** marked by intensity of feeling or conviction. **2.** (of actions, gestures, etc.) characterized by great energy, vigour, or force. —'vehemence n. —'vehemently adv.

vehicle ('viːɪkəl) n. **1.** any conveyance in or by which people or objects are transported, esp. one fitted with wheels. **2.** a medium for the expression or communication of ideas, power, etc. **3.** Pharmacol. a therapeutically inactive substance mixed with the active ingredient to give bulk to a medicine. **4.** Also called: base. a painting medium, such as oil, in which pigments are suspended. **5.** (in the performing arts) a play, etc., that enables a particular performer to display his talents. —vehicular (vɪ'hɪkjulə) adj.

veil (veɪl) n. **1.** a piece of more or less transparent material, usually attached to a hat or headdress, used to conceal or protect a woman's face and head. **2.** part of a nun's headdress falling round the face onto the shoulders. **3.** something that covers, conceals, or separates: a veil of reticence. **4.** the veil. the life of a nun in a religious order. **5.** take the veil. to become a nun. **6.** Also called: velum. Bot. a membranous structure, esp. the thin layer of cells covering a young mushroom. ~vb. **7.** (tr.) to cover, conceal, or separate with or as if with a veil. **8.** (intr.) to wear or put on a veil. —'veiler n. —'veil-ˌlike adj.

veiled (veɪld) adj. **1.** disguised: a veiled insult. **2.** (of sound, tone, the voice, etc.) not distinct. —veiledly ('veɪldlɪ) adv.

vein (veɪn) n. **1.** any of the tubular vessels that convey oxygen-depleted blood to the heart. Cf. artery. **2.** any of the hollow branching tubes that form the supporting framework of an insect's wing. **3.** any of the vascular bundles of a leaf. **4.** a clearly defined mass of ore, mineral, etc. **5.** an irregular streak of colour or alien substance in marble, wood, or other material. **6.** a distinctive trait or quality in speech, writing, character, etc.: a vein of humour. **7.** a temporary attitude or temper: the debate entered a frivolous vein. ~vb. (tr.) **8.** to diffuse over or cause to diffuse over in streaked patterns. **9.** to fill, furnish, or mark with or as if with veins. —'veinless adj. —'vein-ˌlike adj. —'veiny adj.

velar ('viːlə) adj. **1.** of or attached to a velum: velar tentacles. **2.** Phonetics. articulated with the soft palate and the back of the tongue, as in (k) or (ŋ).

Velcro ('vɛlkrəʊ) n. Trademark. a fastening consisting of two strips of nylon fabric, one having tiny hooked threads and the other a coarse surface, that form a strong bond when pressed together.

veld or **veldt** (fɛlt, vɛlt) n. elevated open grassland in Southern Africa.

veleta or **valeta** (və'liːtə) n. a ballroom dance in triple time.

vellum ('vɛləm) n. **1.** a fine parchment prepared from the skin of a calf, kid, or lamb. **2.** a work printed or written on vellum. **3.** a creamy coloured heavy paper re-

---

THESAURUS

gious, sweeping, tremendous, unbounded, unlimited, vasty (Archaic), voluminous, wide

vault¹ v. bound, clear, hurdle, jump, leap, spring

vault² n. **1.** arch, ceiling, roof, span **2.** catacomb, cellar, crypt, mausoleum, tomb, undercroft **3.** depository, repository, strongroom ~v. **4.** arch, bend, bow, curve, overarch, span

vaulted arched, cavernous, domed, hemispheric

vaunt boast about, brag about, crow about, exult in, flaunt, give oneself airs about, make a display of, make much of, parade, prate about, show off, talk big about (Inf.)

veer be deflected, change, change course,

change direction, sheer, shift, swerve, tack, turn

vegetate 1. be inert, deteriorate, exist, go to seed, idle, languish, loaf, moulder, stagnate **2.** burgeon, germinate, grow, shoot, spring, sprout, swell

vehemence ardour, eagerness, earnestness, emphasis, energy, enthusiasm, fervency, fervour, fire, force, forcefulness, heat, impetuosity, intensity, keenness, passion, verve, vigour, violence, warmth, zeal

vehement ardent, eager, earnest, emphatic, enthusiastic, fervent, fervid, fierce, forceful, forcible, impassioned, impetuous, intense, passionate, powerful, strong, violent, zealous

vehicle Fig. apparatus, channel, means, means of expression, mechanism, medium, organ

veil 1. v. cloak, conceal, cover, dim, disguise, hide, mantle, mask, obscure, screen, shield **2.** n. blind, cloak, cover, curtain, disguise, film, mask, screen, shade, shroud

veiled concealed, covert, disguised, hinted at, implied, masked, suppressed

vein 1. blood vessel, course, current, lode, seam, stratum, streak, stripe **2.** dash, hint, strain, streak, thread, trait **3.** attitude, bent, character, faculty, humour, mode, mood, note, style, temper, tenor, tone, turn

sembling vellum. ~*adj.* **4.** made of or resembling vellum.

velocipede (vɪˈlɒsɪˌpiːd) *n.* an early form of bicycle, esp. one propelled by pushing along the ground with the feet. —**veˈlociˌpedist** *n.*

velocity (vɪˈlɒsɪtɪ) *n., pl.* **-ties. 1.** speed of motion or operation; swiftness. **2.** *Physics.* **a.** a measure of the rate of motion of a body expressed as the rate of change of its position in a particular direction with time. **b.** (*not in technical usage*) another word for **speed** (sense 3).

velours *or* **velour** (vɛˈlʊə) *n.* any of various fabrics with a velvet-like finish, used for upholstery, clothing, etc.

velouté (vəˈluːteɪ) *n.* a rich white sauce or soup made from stock, egg yolks, and cream.

velvet (ˈvɛlvɪt) *n.* **1. a.** a fabric of silk, cotton, nylon, etc., with a thick close soft pile. **b.** (*as modifier*): *velvet curtains.* **2.** anything with a smooth soft surface. **3. a.** smoothness. **b.** (*as modifier*): *a velvet night.* **4.** the furry covering of the newly formed antlers of a deer. **5.** *Sl. chiefly U.S.* **a.** gambling winnings. **b.** a gain. **6. on velvet.** *Sl.* in a condition of ease, advantage, or wealth. **7. velvet glove.** gentleness, often concealing strength or determination (esp. in **an iron hand in a velvet glove**). —ˈvelvet-ˌlike *adj.* —ˈvelvety *adj.*

velveteen (ˌvɛlvɪˈtiːn) *n.* **1.** a cotton fabric resembling velvet with a short thick pile, used for clothing, etc. **2.** (*pl.*) trousers made of velveteen.

Ven. *abbrev. for* Venerable.

vena cava (ˈviːnə ˈkeɪvə) *n., pl.* **venae cavae** (ˈviːniː ˈkeɪviː). either one of two large veins that convey oxygen-depleted blood to the heart.

venal (ˈviːnəl) *adj.* **1.** easily bribed or corrupted: *a venal magistrate.* **2.** characterized by corruption or bribery. —veˈnality *n.* —ˈvenally *adv.*

venation (viːˈneɪʃən) *n.* **1.** the arrangement of the veins in a leaf or in the wing of an insect. **2.** such veins collectively. —veˈnational *adj.*

vend (vɛnd) *vb.* **1.** to sell or be sold. **2.** to sell (goods) for a living.

vendetta (vɛnˈdɛtə) *n.* **1.** a private feud, originally between Corsican or Sicilian families, in which the relatives of a murdered person seek vengeance by killing the murderer or some member of his family. **2.** any prolonged feud. —venˈdettist *n.*

vendible (ˈvɛndəbəl) *adj.* **1.** saleable or marketable. ~*n.* **2.** (*usually pl.*) *Rare.* a saleable object. —ˌvendiˈbility *n.*

vending machine *n.* a machine that automatically dispenses consumer goods such as cigarettes or food, when money is inserted.

vendor (ˈvɛndɔː) *or* **vender** (ˈvɛndə) *n. Chiefly law.* **1.** a person who sells something, esp. real property. **2.** another name for **vending machine.**

veneer (vɪˈnɪə) *n.* **1.** a thin layer of wood, plastic, etc., with a decorative or fine finish that is bonded to the surface of a less expensive material, usually wood. **2.** a superficial appearance: *a veneer of gentility.* **3.** any facing material that is applied to a different backing material. ~*vb.* (*tr.*) **4.** to cover (a surface) with a veneer. **5.** to conceal (something) under a superficially pleasant surface. —veˈneerer *n.*

venerable (ˈvɛnərəbəl) *adj.* **1.** (esp. of a person) worthy of reverence on account of great age, religious associations, character, etc. **2.** (of inanimate objects) hallowed on account of age or historical or religious association. **3.** *R.C. Church.* a title bestowed on a deceased person

when the first stage of his canonization has been accomplished. **4.** *Church of England.* a title given to an archdeacon. —ˌveneraˈbility *or* ˈvenerableness *n.* —ˈvenerably *adv.*

venerate (ˈvɛnəˌreɪt) *vb.* (*tr.*) **1.** to hold in deep respect. **2.** to honour in recognition of qualities of holiness, excellence, etc. —ˈvenerˌator *n.*

veneration (ˌvɛnəˈreɪʃən) *n.* **1.** a feeling or expression of awe or reverence. **2.** the act of venerating or the state of being venerated.

venereal (vɪˈnɪərɪəl) *adj.* **1.** of or infected with venereal disease. **2.** (of a disease) transmitted by sexual intercourse. **3.** of or involving the genitals. **4.** of or relating to sexual intercourse or erotic desire.

venereal disease *n.* any of various diseases, such as syphilis or gonorrhoea, transmitted by sexual intercourse. Abbrev.: **VD**

Venetian (vɪˈniːʃən) *adj.* **1.** of, relating to, or characteristic of Venice, a port in NE Italy or its inhabitants. ~*n.* **2.** a native or inhabitant of Venice. **3.** See **Venetian blind.**

Venetian blind *n.* a window blind consisting of a number of horizontal slats whose angle may be altered to let in more or less light.

vengeance (ˈvɛndʒəns) *n.* **1.** the act of or desire for taking revenge. **2. with a vengeance.** (intensifier): *he's a coward with a vengeance.*

vengeful (ˈvɛndʒful) *adj.* **1.** desiring revenge. **2.** characterized by or indicating a desire for revenge. **3.** inflicting or taking revenge: *with vengeful blows.* —ˈvengefully *adv.*

venial (ˈviːnɪəl) *adj.* easily excused or forgiven: *a venial error.* —ˌveniˈality *n.* —ˈvenially *adv.*

venial sin *n. Christian theol.* a sin regarded as involving only a partial loss of grace.

venison (ˈvɛnɪzən, -sən) *n.* the flesh of a deer, used as food.

Venn diagram (vɛn) *n. Maths., logic.* a diagram in which mathematical sets or terms of a categorical statement are represented by circles whose relative positions give the relationships between the sets or terms.

venom (ˈvɛnəm) *n.* **1.** a poisonous fluid secreted by such animals as certain snakes and scorpions and usually transmitted by a bite or sting. **2.** malice; spite. —ˈvenomous *adj.* —ˈvenomously *adv.* —ˈvenomousness *n.*

venous (ˈviːnəs) *adj.* **1.** *Physiol.* of or relating to the blood circulating in the veins. **2.** of or relating to the veins.

vent[1] (vɛnt) *n.* **1.** a small opening for the escape of fumes, liquids, etc. **2.** the shaft of a volcano through which lava and gases erupt. **3.** the external opening of the urinary or genital systems of lower vertebrates. **4.** a small aperture at the breech of old guns through which the charge was ignited. **5. give vent to.** to release (an emotion, idea, etc.) in an outburst. ~*vb.* (*mainly tr.*) **6.** to release or give expression or utterance to (an emotion, etc.): *he vents his anger on his wife.* **7.** to provide a vent for or make vents in. **8.** to let out (steam, etc.) through a vent.

vent[2] (vɛnt) *n.* **1.** a vertical slit at the back or both sides of a jacket. ~*vb.* **2.** (*tr.*) to make a vent or vents in (a jacket).

ventilate (ˈvɛntɪˌleɪt) *vb.* (*tr.*) **1.** to drive foul air out of (an enclosed area). **2.** to provide with a means of airing. **3.** to expose (a question, grievance, etc.) to public discussion. **4.** *Physiol.* to oxygenate (the blood). —ˈventilable

---

THESAURUS

venal bent (*Sl.*), corrupt, corruptible, crooked (*Inf.*), dishonourable, grafting, mercenary, prostituted, purchasable, rapacious, simoniacal, sordid, unprincipled

vendetta bad blood, blood feud, feud, quarrel

veneer *n. Fig.* appearance, façade, false front, finish, front, gloss, guise, mask, pretence, semblance, show

venerable august, esteemed, grave, honoured, respected, revered, reverenced, sage, sedate, wise, worshipped

venerate adore, esteem, hold in awe, honour, look up to, respect, revere, reverence, worship

veneration adoration, awe, deference, esteem, respect, reverence, worship

vengeance 1. an eye for an eye, avenging, lex talionis, reprisal, requital, retaliation, retribution, revenge, settling of scores 2. **with a vengeance a.** forcefully, furiously, vehemently, violently **b.** and no mistake, extremely, greatly, to the full, to the utmost, with no holds barred

venial allowable, excusable, forgivable, insignificant, minor, pardonable, slight, trivial

venom 1. bane, poison, toxin 2. acidity, acrimony, bitterness, gall, grudge, hate, ill will, malevolence, malice, maliciousness, malig-

nity, rancour, spite, spitefulness, spleen, virulence

venomous 1. baneful (*Archaic*), envenomed, mephitic, noxious, poison, poisonous, toxic, virulent 2. baleful, hostile, malicious, malignant, rancorous, savage, spiteful, vicious, vindictive, virulent

vent 1. *n.* aperture, duct, hole, opening, orifice, outlet, split 2. *v.* air, come out with, discharge, emit, empty, express, give expression to, give vent to, pour out, release, utter, voice

ventilate *Fig.* air, bring out into the open, broadcast, debate, discuss, examine, make known, scrutinize, sift, talk about

adj. —ˌventiˈlation *n.*

ventilator ('vɛntɪˌleɪtə) *n.* an opening or device, such as a fan, used to ventilate a room, building, etc.

ventral ('vɛntrəl) *adj.* **1.** relating to the front part of the body. **2.** of or situated on the upper or inner side of a plant organ, esp. a leaf, that is facing the axis. —'ventrally *adv.*

ventricle ('vɛntrɪkəl) *n. Anat.* **1.** a chamber of the heart that receives blood from the atrium and pumps it to the arteries. **2.** any one of the four main cavities of the vertebrate brain. **3.** any of various other small cavities in the body. —ven'tricular *adj.*

ventriloquism (vɛn'trɪləˌkwɪzəm) *or* **ventriloquy** *n.* the art of producing vocal sounds that appear to come from another source. —**ventriloquial** (ˌvɛntrɪ'loʊkwɪəl) *adj.* —ˌventri'loquially *adv.* —ven'triloquist *n.* —ven'trilo,quize *or* ,quise *vb.*

venture ('vɛntʃə) *vb.* **1.** (*tr.*) to expose to danger: *he ventured his life.* **2.** (*tr.*) to brave the dangers of (something): *I'll venture the seas.* **3.** (*tr.*) to dare (to do something): *does he venture to object?* **4.** (*tr.; may take a clause as object*) to express in spite of possible criticism: *I venture that he is not that honest.* **5.** (*intr.*; often foll. by *out, forth,* etc.) to embark on a possibly hazardous journey, etc.: *to venture forth upon the high seas.* ~*n.* **6.** an undertaking that is risky or of uncertain outcome. **7.** a commercial undertaking characterized by risk of loss as well as opportunity for profit. **8.** something hazarded or risked in an adventure. **9. at a venture.** at random. —'venturer *n.*

Venture Scout *or* **Venturer** *n. Brit.* a member of the senior branch of the Scouts.

venturesome ('vɛntʃəsəm) *or* **venturous** ('vɛntʃərəs) *adj.* **1.** willing to take risks; daring. **2.** hazardous.

venue ('vɛnjuː) *n.* **1.** *Law.* **a.** the place in which a cause of action arises. **b.** the place fixed for the trial of a cause. **c.** the locality from which the jurors must be summoned. **2.** a meeting place. **3.** the scene of an action, such as a football match or concert.

Venus[1] ('viːnəs) *n.* the Roman goddess of love. Greek counterpart: **Aphrodite.**

Venus[2] ('viːnəs) *n.* one of the inferior planets and the second nearest to the sun, visible as a bright morning or evening star. —**Venusian** (vɪ'njuːzɪən) *n., adj.*

Venus's-flytrap *or* **Venus flytrap** *n.* an insectivorous plant having hinged two-lobed leaves that snap closed when the sensitive hairs on the surface are touched.

veracious (vɛ'reɪʃəs) *adj.* **1.** habitually truthful or honest. **2.** accurate. —ve'raciously *adv.* —ve'raciousness *n.*

veracity (vɛ'ræsɪtɪ) *n., pl.* **-ties.** **1.** truthfulness or honesty, esp. when consistent or habitual. **2.** accuracy. **3.** a truth.

veranda *or* **verandah** (və'rændə) *n.* **1.** a porch or portico, sometimes partly enclosed, along the outside of a building. **2.** *N.Z.* a continuous overhead canopy that gives shelter to pedestrians.

verb (vɜːb) *n.* **1.** (in traditional grammar) any of a large class of words that serve to indicate the occurrence or performance of an action, the existence of a state, etc. Such words as *run, make, do,* etc., are verbs. **2.** (in modern descriptive linguistic analysis) **a.** a word or group of words that functions as the predicate of a sentence or introduces the predicate. **b.** (*as modifier*): *a verb phrase.* Abbrev.: **vb.** *or* **v.**

verbal ('vɜːbəl) *adj.* **1.** of, relating to, or using words: *merely verbal concessions.* **2.** oral rather than written: *a verbal agreement.* **3.** verbatim; literal: *an almost verbal copy.* **4.** *Grammar.* of or relating to verbs or a verb.

—'verbally *adv.*

verbalism ('vɜːbəˌlɪzəm) *n.* **1.** a verbal expression; phrase or word. **2.** an exaggerated emphasis on the importance of words. **3.** a statement lacking real content.

verbalize *or* **-lise** ('vɜːbəˌlaɪz) *vb.* **1.** to express (an idea, etc.) in words. **2.** to change (any word) into a verb or derive a verb from (any word). **3.** (*intr.*) to be verbose. —ˌverbali'zation *or* li'sation *n.*

verbal noun *n.* a noun derived from a verb, such as *smoking* in the sentence *smoking is bad for you.*

verbatim (vɜː'beɪtɪm) *adv., adj.* using exactly the same words; word for word.

verbena (vɜː'biːnə) *n.* **1.** any of a genus of plants of tropical and temperate America, having red, white, or purple fragrant flowers: much cultivated as garden plants. **2.** any of various similar plants, esp. the lemon verbena.

verbiage ('vɜːbɪɪdʒ) *n.* the excessive and often meaningless use of words.

verbose (vɜː'bəʊs) *adj.* using or containing an excess of words, so as to be pedantic or boring. —ver'bosely *adv.* —verbosity (vɜː'bɒsɪtɪ) *n.*

verdant ('vɜːdənt) *adj.* **1.** covered with green vegetation. **2.** (of plants, etc.) green in colour. **3.** unsophisticated; green. —'verdancy *n.* —'verdantly *adv.*

verdict ('vɜːdɪkt) *n.* **1.** the findings of a jury on the issues of fact submitted to it for examination and trial. **2.** any decision or conclusion.

verdigris ('vɜːdɪgrɪs) *n.* **1.** a green or bluish patina formed on copper, brass, or bronze. **2.** a green or blue crystalline substance obtained by the action of acetic acid on copper and used as a fungicide and pigment.

verdure ('vɜːdʒə) *n.* **1.** flourishing green vegetation or its colour. **2.** a condition of freshness or healthy growth. —'verdured *adj.*

verge[1] (vɜːdʒ) *n.* **1.** an edge or rim; margin. **2.** a limit beyond which something occurs: *on the verge of ecstasy.* **3.** *Brit.* a grass border along a road. **4.** *Archit.* the edge of the roof tiles projecting over a gable. **5.** *English legal history.* **a.** the area encompassing the royal court that is subject to the jurisdiction of the Lord High Steward. **b.** a rod or wand carried as a symbol of office or emblem of authority, as in the Church. ~*vb.* **6.** (*intr.*; foll. by *on*) to be near (to): *to verge on chaos.* **7.** (when *intr.*, sometimes foll. by *on*) to serve as the edge of (something): *this narrow strip verges the road.*

verge[2] (vɜːdʒ) *vb.* (*intr.*; foll. by *to* or *towards*) to move or incline in a certain direction.

verger ('vɜːdʒə) *n. Chiefly Church of England.* **1.** a church official who acts as caretaker and attendant. **2.** an official who carries the verge or rod of office before a bishop or dean in ceremonies and processions.

veriest ('vɛrɪɪst) *adj. Arch.* (intensifier): *the veriest coward.*

verify ('vɛrɪˌfaɪ) *vb.* **-fying, -fied.** (*tr.*) **1.** to prove to be true; confirm. **2.** to check or determine the correctness or truth of by investigation, etc. **3.** *Law.* to substantiate or confirm (an oath). —'veriˌfiable *adj.* —'veriˌfiably *adv.* —ˌverifi'cation *n.* —'veriˌfier *n.*

verily ('vɛrɪlɪ) *adv.* (sentence modifier) *Arch.* in truth; truly: *verily, thou art a man of God.*

verisimilar (ˌvɛrɪ'sɪmɪlə) *adj.* probable; likely.

verisimilitude (ˌvɛrɪsɪ'mɪlɪˌtjuːd) *n.* **1.** the appearance or semblance of truth or reality. **2.** something that merely seems to be true or real, such as a doubtful statement.

veritable ('vɛrɪtəbəl) *adj.* (prenominal) (intensifier; usually qualifying a word used metaphorically): *he's a veritable swine!* —'veritableness *n.* —'veritably *adv.*

verity ('vɛrɪtɪ) *n., pl.* **-ties.** **1.** the quality or state of be-

---

THESAURUS

venture *v.* **1.** chance, endanger, hazard, imperil, jeopardize, put in jeopardy, risk, speculate, stake, wager **2.** advance, dare, dare say, hazard, make bold, presume, stick one's neck out (*Inf.*), take the liberty, volunteer **3.** *With* **out, forth,** *etc.* embark on, go, plunge into, set out ~*n.* **4.** adventure, chance, endeavour, enterprise, fling, gamble, hazard, jeopardy, project, risk, speculation, undertaking

verbal literal, oral, spoken, unwritten, verbatim, word-of-mouth

verbally by word of mouth, orally

verbatim exactly, precisely, to the letter, word for word

verbose circumlocutory, diffuse, garrulous, long-winded, periphrastic, pleonastic, prolix, tautological, windy, wordy

verbosity garrulity, logorrhoea, long-windedness, loquaciousness, prolixity, rambling, verbiage, verboseness, windiness, wordiness

verdict adjudication, conclusion, decision, finding, judgment, opinion, sentence

verge **1.** *n.* border, boundary, brim, brink, edge, extreme, limit, lip, margin, roadside, threshold **2.** *v.* approach, border, come near

verification authentication, confirmation, corroboration, proof, substantiation, validation

verify attest, attest to, authenticate, bear out, check, confirm, corroborate, prove, substantiate, support, validate

ing true, real, or correct. **2.** a true statement, idea, etc.

vermicelli (ˌvɜːmɪˈsɛlɪ, -ˈtʃɛlɪ) n. **1.** very fine strands of pasta, used in soups. **2.** tiny chocolate strands used to coat cakes, etc.

vermicide (ˈvɜːmɪˌsaɪd) n. any substance used to kill worms. —ˌvermiˈcidal adj.

vermicular (vɜːˈmɪkjʊlə) adj. **1.** resembling the form, motion, or tracks of worms. **2.** of worms or wormlike animals. —verˈmiculate adj. —verˌmicuˈlation n.

vermiform (ˈvɜːmɪˌfɔːm) adj. resembling a worm.

vermiform appendix n. a wormlike pouch extending from the lower end of the caecum in some mammals. Also called: **appendix.**

vermilion (vəˈmɪljən) n. **1. a.** a bright red to reddish-orange colour. **b.** (as adj.): a vermilion car. **2.** mercuric sulphide, esp. when used as a bright red pigment; cinnabar.

vermin (ˈvɜːmɪn) n. **1.** (functioning as pl.) small animals collectively, esp. insects and rodents, that are troublesome to man, domestic animals, etc. **2.** pl. **-min.** an unpleasant person. —ˈverminous adj.

vermouth (ˈvɜːməθ) n. any of several wines containing aromatic herbs.

vernacular (vəˈnækjʊlə) n. **1. the.** the commonly spoken language or dialect of a particular people or place. **2.** jargon relating to a particular trade, occupation, etc. **3.** a vernacular term. ~adj. **4.** relating to or in the vernacular. **5.** native to a particular place. **6.** designating or relating to the common name of an animal or plant. —verˈnacularly adv.

vernal (ˈvɜːnəl) adj. **1.** of or occurring in spring. **2.** Poetic. of or characteristic of youth. —ˈvernally adv.

vernier (ˈvɜːnɪə) n. **1.** a small movable scale running parallel to the main graduated scale in certain measuring instruments, such as theodolites, used to obtain a fractional reading of one of the divisions on the main scale. **2.** (modifier) relating to or fitted with a vernier: a vernier scale.

Veronal (ˈvɛrənəl) n. a trademark for a barbiturate sedative drug.

veronica (vəˈrɒnɪkə) n. any plant of a genus, including the speedwells, of temperate and cold regions, having small blue, pink, or white flowers and flattened notched fruits.

verruca (vɛˈruːkə) n., pl. **-cae** (-siː) or **-cas. 1.** Pathol. a wart, esp. one growing on the hand or foot. **2.** Biol. a wartlike outgrowth.

versatile (ˈvɜːsəˌtaɪl) adj. **1.** capable of or adapted for many different uses, skills, etc. **2.** variable. **3.** Bot. (of an anther) attached to the filament by a small area so that it moves freely in the wind. **4.** Zool. able to turn forwards and backwards. —ˈversaˌtilely adv. —versatility (ˌvɜːsəˈtɪlɪtɪ) n.

verse (vɜːs) n. **1.** (not in technical usage) a stanza of a poem. **2.** poetry as distinct from prose. **3. a.** a series of metrical feet forming a rhythmical unit of one line. **b.** (as modifier): verse line. **4.** a specified type of metre or metrical structure: iambic verse. **5.** one of the series of short subsections into which most of the writings in the Bible are divided. **6.** a poem. ~vb. **7.** a rare word for **versify.**

versed (vɜːst) adj. (postpositive; foll. by in) thoroughly knowledgeable (about), acquainted (with), or skilled (in).

versification (ˌvɜːsɪfɪˈkeɪʃən) n. **1.** the technique or art of versifying. **2.** the form or metrical composition of a poem. **3.** a metrical version of a prose text.

versify (ˈvɜːsɪˌfaɪ) vb. **-fying, -fied.** to render (something) into verse. —ˈversiˌfier n.

version (ˈvɜːʃən) n. **1.** an account of a matter from a

certain point of view, as contrasted with others: his version of the accident is different from the policeman's. **2.** a translation, esp. of the Bible, from one language into another. **3.** a variant form of something. **4.** an adaptation, as of a book or play into a film. **5.** Med. manual turning of a foetus to correct an irregular position within the uterus. —ˈversional adj.

verso (ˈvɜːsəʊ) n., pl. **-sos. 1. a.** the back of a sheet of printed paper. **b.** the left-hand pages of a book, bearing the even numbers. **2.** the side of a coin opposite to the obverse.

versus (ˈvɜːsəs) prep. **1.** (esp. in a competition or lawsuit) against. Abbrev.: **v.** or (esp. U.S.) **vs. 2.** in contrast with.

vertebra (ˈvɜːtɪbrə) n., pl. **-brae** (-briː) or **-bras.** one of the bony segments of the spinal column. —ˈvertebral adj. —ˈvertebrally adv.

vertebrate (ˈvɜːtɪˌbreɪt, -brɪt) n. **1.** any animal of a subphylum characterized by a bony skeleton and a well-developed brain: the group contains fishes, amphibians, reptiles, birds, and mammals. ~adj. **2.** of or belonging to this subphylum.

vertex (ˈvɜːtɛks) n., pl. **-texes** or **-tices** (-tɪˌsiːz). **1.** the highest point. **2.** Maths. **a.** the point opposite the base of a figure. **b.** the point of intersection of two sides of a plane figure or angle. **c.** the point of intersection of a pencil of lines or three or more planes of a solid figure. **3.** Anat. the crown of the head.

vertical (ˈvɜːtɪkəl) adj. **1.** at right angles to the horizon; upright: a vertical wall. **2.** extending in a perpendicular direction. **3.** directly overhead. **4.** Econ. of or relating to associated or consecutive, though not identical, stages of industrial activity: vertical integration. **5.** of or relating to the vertex. **6.** Anat. of or situated at the top of the head (vertex). ~n. **7.** a vertical plane, position, or line. **8.** a vertical post, pillar, etc. —ˌvertiˈcality n. —ˈvertically adv.

vertiginous (vɜːˈtɪdʒɪnəs) adj. **1.** of, relating to, or having vertigo. **2.** producing dizziness. **3.** whirling. **4.** changeable; unstable. —verˈtiginously adv.

vertigo (ˈvɜːtɪgəʊ) n., pl. **vertigoes** or **vertigines** (vɜːˈtɪdʒɪˌniːz). Pathol. a sensation of dizziness resulting from a disorder of the sense of balance.

vertu (vɜːˈtuː) n. a variant spelling of **virtu.**

vervain (ˈvɜːveɪn) n. any of several plants of the genus Verbena, having square stems and long slender spikes of purple, blue, or white flowers.

verve (vɜːv) n. great vitality and liveliness.

very (ˈvɛrɪ) adv. **1.** (intensifier) used to add emphasis to adjectives that are able to be graded: very good; very tall. ~adj. (prenominal) **2.** (intensifier) used with nouns preceded by a definite article or possessive determiner, in order to give emphasis to the significance or relevance of a noun in a particular context, or to give exaggerated intensity to certain nouns: the very man I want to see; the very back of the room. **3.** (intensifier) used in metaphors to emphasize the applicability of the image to the situation described: he was a very lion in the fight. **4.** Arch. genuine: the very living God.

▷ **Usage.** In strict usage adverbs of degree such as very, too, quite, really, and extremely are used only to qualify adjectives: he is very happy; she is too sad. By this rule, these words should not be used to qualify past participles that follow the verb to be, since they would then be technically qualifying verbs. With the exception of certain participles, such as tired or disappointed, that have come to be regarded as adjectives, all other past participles are qualified by adverbs such as much, greatly, seriously, or excessively: he has been much (not very) inconvenienced.

THESAURUS

vernacular 1. adj. colloquial, common, indigenous, informal, local, mother, native, popular, vulgar **2.** n. argot, cant, dialect, idiom, jargon, native language, parlance, patois, speech, vulgar tongue

versatile adaptable, adjustable, all-purpose, all-round, flexible, functional, handy, many-sided, multifaceted, protean, resourceful, variable

versed accomplished, acquainted, competent, conversant, experienced, familiar, knowledgeable, practised, proficient, quali-

fied, seasoned, skilled, well informed, well up in (Inf.)

version 1. account, adaptation, exercise, interpretation, portrayal, reading, rendering, side, translation **2.** design, form, kind, model, style, type, variant

vertical erect, on end, perpendicular, upright

vertigo dizziness, giddiness, light-headedness, loss of equilibrium, swimming of the head

verve animation, brio, dash, élan, energy, enthusiasm, force, get-up-and-go (Inf.), gusto,

life, liveliness, punch (Inf.), sparkle, spirit, vigour, vim (Sl.), vitality, vivacity, zeal, zip (Inf.)

very adv. **1.** absolutely, acutely, awfully (Inf.), decidedly, deeply, eminently, exceedingly, excessively, extremely, greatly, highly, jolly (Brit.), noticeably, particularly, profoundly, really, remarkably, superlatively, surpassingly, terribly, truly, uncommonly, unusually, wonderfully ~adj. **2.** actual, appropriate, exact, express, identical, perfect, precise, real, same, selfsame, unqualified **3.** bare, mere, plain, pure, sheer, simple

very high frequency *n.* a single radio frequency or band lying between 300 and 30 megahertz. Abbrev.: **VHF**

Very light (ˈvɛrɪ) *n.* a coloured flare fired from a special pistol (**Very pistol**) for signalling at night, esp. at sea.

very low frequency *n.* a radio frequency band or radio frequency lying between 30 and 3 kilohertz. Abbrev.: **VLF**

vesicle (ˈvɛsɪkəl) *n.* **1.** *Pathol.* **a.** any small sac or cavity, esp. one containing serous fluid. **b.** a blister. **2.** *Geol.* a rounded cavity within a rock. **3.** *Bot.* a small bladder-like cavity occurring in certain seaweeds. **4.** any small cavity or cell. —**vesicular** (vɛˈsɪkjʊlə) *adj.*

vesper (ˈvɛspə) *n.* **1.** an evening prayer, service, or hymn. **2.** an archaic word for **evening**. **3.** (*modifier*) of or relating to vespers.

vespers (ˈvɛspəz) *n.* **1.** *Chiefly R.C. Church.* the sixth of the seven canonical hours of the divine office. **2.** another word for **evensong**.

vessel (ˈvɛsəl) *n.* **1.** any object used as a container, esp. for a liquid. **2.** a passenger or freight-carrying ship, boat, etc. **3.** *Anat.* a tubular structure that transports such body fluids as blood and lymph. **4.** *Bot.* a tubular element of xylem tissue transporting water. **5.** *Rare.* a person regarded as a vehicle for some purpose or quality.

vest (vɛst) *n.* **1.** an undergarment covering the body from the shoulders to the hips, made of cotton, nylon, etc. **2.** the usual U.S. and Austral. word for **waistcoat**. **3.** *Obs.* any form of dress. ~*vb.* **4.** (*tr.;* foll. by *in*) to place or settle (power, rights, etc., in): *power was vested in the committee.* **5.** (*tr.;* foll. by *with*) to bestow or confer (on): *the company was vested with authority.* **6.** (usually foll. by *in*) to confer (a right, title, etc., upon) or (of a right, title, etc.) to pass to or devolve (upon). **7.** to clothe. **8.** (*intr.*) to put on clothes, ecclesiastical vestments, etc.

vestal (ˈvɛstəl) *adj.* **1.** chaste or pure. **2.** of or relating to the Roman goddess Vesta. ~*n.* **3.** a chaste woman, esp. a nun.

vestal virgin *n.* (in ancient Rome) one of the virgin priestesses whose lives were dedicated to Vesta and to maintaining the sacred fire in her temple.

vested (ˈvɛstɪd) *adj. Property law.* having a present right to the immediate or future possession and enjoyment of property.

vested interest *n.* **1.** *Property law.* an existing right to the immediate or future possession and enjoyment of property. **2.** a strong personal concern in a state of affairs, etc. **3.** a person or group that has such an interest.

vestibule (ˈvɛstɪˌbjuːl) *n.* **1.** a small entrance hall or anteroom. **2.** any small bodily cavity at the entrance to a passage or canal.

vestige (ˈvɛstɪdʒ) *n.* **1.** a small trace; hint: *a vestige of truth.* **2.** *Biol.* an organ or part of an organism that is a small nonfunctioning remnant of a functional organ in an ancestor. —**ves'tigial** *adj.*

vestment (ˈvɛstmənt) *n.* **1.** a garment or robe, esp. one denoting office, authority, or rank. **2.** any of various ceremonial garments worn by the clergy at religious serv-

ices, etc. —**vestmental** (vɛstˈmɛntəl) *adj.*

vestry (ˈvɛstrɪ) *n., pl.* **-tries. 1.** a room in or attached to a church in which vestments, sacred vessels, etc., are kept. **2.** a room in or attached to some churches, used for Sunday school, etc. **3. a.** *Church of England.* a meeting of all the members of a parish or their representatives, to transact the official and administrative business of the parish. **b.** the parish council. —**'vestral** *adj.*

vesture (ˈvɛstʃə) *Arch.* ~ *n.* **1.** a garment or something that seems like a garment: *a vesture of cloud.* ~*vb.* **2.** (*tr.*) to clothe. —**'vestural** *adj.*

vet[1] (vɛt) *n.* **1.** short for **veterinary surgeon.** ~*vb.* **vetting, vetted. 2.** (*tr.*) *Chiefly Brit.* to examine and appraise: *the candidates were well vetted.* **3.** to examine, treat, or cure (an animal).

vet[2] (vɛt) *n. U.S.* short for **veteran** (senses 2, 3).

vet. *abbrev. for:* **1.** veteran. **2.** veterinarian. **3.** veterinary. ~ Also (for senses 2, 3): **veter.**

vetch (vɛtʃ) *n.* **1.** any of various climbing plants having pinnate leaves, typically blue or purple flowers, and tendrils on the stems. **2.** any of various similar and related plants, such as the kidney vetch. **3.** the beanlike fruit of any of these plants.

veteran (ˈvɛtərən) *n.* **1. a.** a person or thing that has given long service in some capacity. **b.** (*as modifier*): *veteran firemen.* **2.** a soldier who has seen considerable active service. **3.** *U.S.* a person who has served in the military forces.

veteran car *n. Brit.* a car constructed before 1919, esp. one constructed before 1905.

veterinary (ˈvɛtərɪnərɪ) *adj.* of or relating to veterinary science.

veterinary science *or* **medicine** *n.* the branch of medicine concerned with the health of animals and the treatment of injuries or diseases that affect them.

veterinary surgeon *n. Brit.* a person qualified to practise veterinary medicine. U.S. term: **veterinarian.**

veto (ˈviːtəʊ) *n., pl.* **-toes. 1.** the power to prevent legislation or action proposed by others: *the presidential veto.* **2.** the exercise of this power. ~*vb.* **-toing, -toed.** (*tr.*) **3.** to refuse consent to (a proposal, esp. a government bill). **4.** to prohibit, ban, or forbid: *her parents vetoed her trip.* —**'vetoer** *n.*

vex (vɛks) *vb.* (*tr.*) **1.** to anger or annoy. **2.** to confuse; worry. **3.** *Arch.* to agitate. —**'vexer** *n.* —**'vexingly** *adv.*

vexation (vɛkˈseɪʃən) *n.* **1.** the act of vexing or the state of being vexed. **2.** something that vexes.

vexatious (vɛkˈseɪʃəs) *adj.* **1.** vexing or tending to vex. **2.** vexed. **3.** *Law.* (of a legal action or proceeding) instituted without sufficient grounds, esp. so as to cause annoyance to the defendant. —**vex'atiously** *adv.*

VHF *or* **vhf** *Radio. abbrev. for* very high frequency.

via (ˈvaɪə) *prep.* by way of; by means of; through: *to London via Paris.*

viable (ˈvaɪəbəl) *adj.* **1.** capable of becoming actual, etc.: *a viable proposition.* **2.** (of seeds, eggs, etc.) capable of normal growth and development. **3.** (of a foetus) having reached a stage of development at which further development can occur independently of the

---

THESAURUS

vessel 1. barque (*Poetic*), boat, craft, ship **2.** container, pot, receptacle, utensil

vest *v.* **1.** *With* in *or* with authorize, be devolved upon, bestow, confer, consign, empower, endow, entrust, furnish, invest, lodge, place, put in the hands of, settle **2.** apparel, bedeck, clothe, cover, dress, envelop, garb, robe

vestibule anteroom, entrance hall, foyer, hall, lobby, porch, portico

vestige evidence, glimmer, hint, indication, relic, remainder, remains, remnant, residue, scrap, sign, suspicion, token, trace, track

vestigial imperfect, incomplete, nonfunctional, rudimentary, surviving, undeveloped

vet *v.* appraise, check, check out, examine, give (someone *or* something) the once-over (*Inf.*), investigate, look over, pass under review, review, scan, scrutinize, size up (*Inf.*)

veteran 1. *n.* master, old hand, old stager, old-timer, past master, past mistress, pro (*Inf.*), trouper, warhorse (*Inf.*) **2.** *adj.* adept, battle-scarred, expert, long-serving, old, proficient, seasoned

veto 1. *v.* ban, disallow, forbid, give the thumbs down to, interdict, kill (*Inf.*), negative, prohibit, put the kibosh on (*Sl.*), refuse permission, reject, rule out, turn down **2.** *n.* ban, embargo, interdict, nonconsent, prohibition

vex afflict, aggravate (*Inf.*), agitate, annoy, bother, bug (*Inf.*), displease, distress, disturb, exasperate, fret, gall, grate on, harass, irritate, molest, needle (*Inf.*), nettle, offend, peeve (*Inf.*), perplex, pester, pique, plague, provoke, put out, rile, tease, torment, trouble, upset, worry

vexation 1. aggravation (*Inf.*), annoyance, displeasure, dissatisfaction, exasperation, frustration, irritation, pique **2.** bother, difficulty, headache (*Inf.*), irritant, misfor-

tune, nuisance, problem, thorn in one's flesh, trouble, upset, worry

vexatious afflicting, aggravating (*Inf.*), annoying, bothersome, burdensome, disagreeable, disappointing, distressing, exasperating, harassing, irksome, irritating, nagging, plaguy (*Archaic*), provoking, teasing, tormenting, troublesome, trying, unpleasant, upsetting, worrisome, worrying

vexed 1. afflicted, aggravated (*Inf.*), agitated, annoyed, bothered, confused, displeased, distressed, disturbed, exasperated, fed up, harassed, irritated, miffed (*Inf.*), nettled, out of countenance, peeved (*Inf.*), perplexed, provoked, put out, riled, ruffled, tormented, troubled, upset, worried **2.** contested, controversial, disputed, moot, much debated

viable applicable, feasible, operable, practicable, usable, within the bounds of possibility, workable

mother. —**via'bility** n.

viaduct ('vaɪə,dʌkt) n. a bridge, esp. for carrying a road or railway across a valley, etc.

vial ('vaɪəl) n. a less common variant of **phial.**

viand ('vi:ənd) n. **1.** a type of food, esp. a delicacy. **2.** (pl.) provisions.

viaticum (vaɪ'ætɪkəm) n., pl. **-ca** (-kə) or **-cums. 1.** Holy Communion as administered to a person dying or in danger of death. **2.** Rare. provisions or a travel allowance for a journey.

vibes (vaɪbz) pl. n. Inf. **1.** short for **vibraphone. 2.** qualities in a person, thing, etc. which produce an emotional response. **3.** a characteristic atmosphere felt to be emanating from a place, object, etc.

vibrant ('vaɪbrənt) adj. **1.** characterized by or exhibiting vibration. **2.** giving an impression of vigour and activity. **3.** caused by vibration; resonant. —**'vibrancy** n. —**'vibrantly** adv.

vibraphone ('vaɪbrə,fəʊn) n. a percussion instrument consisting of a set of metal bars placed over tubular metal resonators, which are made to vibrate electronically. —**'vibra,phonist** n.

vibrate (vaɪ'breɪt) vb. **1.** to move or cause to move back and forth rapidly. **2.** to oscillate. **3.** to resonate or cause to resonate. **4.** (intr.) to waver. **5.** Physics. to produce or undergo an oscillatory process, as of an alternating current. **6.** (intr.) Rare. to respond emotionally; thrill. —**vibratile** ('vaɪbrə,taɪl) adj. —**vi'brative** or **vibratory** ('vaɪbrətərɪ) adj.

vibration (vaɪ'breɪʃən) n. **1.** the act or an instance of vibrating. **2.** Physics. **a.** a periodic motion about an equilibrium position, such as in the propagation of sound. **b.** a single cycle of such a motion. **3.** the process or state of vibrating or being vibrated. —**vi'brational** adj.

vibrato (vɪ'brɑ:təʊ) n., pl. **-tos.** Music. **1.** a slight, rapid, and regular fluctuation in the pitch of a note produced on a stringed instrument by a shaking movement of the hand stopping the strings. **2.** an oscillatory effect produced in singing by fluctuation in breath pressure or pitch.

vibrator (vaɪ'breɪtə) n. **a.** a device for producing a vibratory motion, such as one used in massage. **b.** such a device with a vibrating part or tip, used as a dildo.

vicar ('vɪkə) n. **1.** Church of England. **a.** (in Britain) a clergyman appointed to act as priest of a parish. **b.** a clergyman who acts as assistant to or substitute for the rector of a parish at Communion. **2.** R.C. Church. a bishop or priest representing the pope and exercising a limited jurisdiction. **3.** Also called: **lay vicar, vicar choral.** Church of England. a member of a cathedral choir appointed to sing certain parts of the services. —**vicarial** (vɪ'keərɪəl) adj. —**vicarly** adj.

vicarage ('vɪkərɪdʒ) n. the residence or benefice of a vicar.

vicar apostolic n. R.C. Church. a titular bishop having jurisdiction in missionary countries.

vicar general n., pl. **vicars general.** an official, usually a layman, appointed to assist the bishop of a diocese in discharging his administrative or judicial duties.

vicarious (vɪ'keərɪəs, vaɪ-) adj. **1.** undergone at second hand through sympathetic participation in another's experiences. **2.** undergone or done as the substitute for another: vicarious punishment. **3.** delegated: vicarious authority. **4.** taking the place of another. —**vi'cariously** adv. —**vi'cariousness** n.

Vicar of Christ n. R.C. Church. the pope when regarded as Christ's earthly representative.

vice¹ (vaɪs) n. **1.** an immoral, wicked, or evil habit, action, or trait. **2.** frequent indulgence in immoral or degrading practices. **3.** a specific form of pernicious conduct, esp. prostitution or sexual perversion. **4.** an imperfection in character, conduct, etc.: smoking is his only vice. **5.** a bad trick or disposition, as of horses, dogs, etc.

vice² or U.S. (often) **vise** (vaɪs) n. **1.** an appliance for holding an object while work is done on it, usually having a pair of jaws. ~vb. **2.** (tr.) to grip (something) with or as if with a vice.

vice³ (vaɪs) adj. **1. a.** (prenominal) serving in the place of. **b.** (in combination): viceroy. ~n. **2.** Inf. a person who serves as a deputy to another.

vice⁴ ('vaɪsɪ) prep. instead of; as a substitute for.

vice admiral n. a commissioned officer of flag rank in certain navies, junior to an admiral and senior to a rear admiral.

vice chancellor n. **1.** the chief executive or administrator at some British universities. **2.** (in the U.S.) a judge in courts of equity subordinate to the chancellor. **3.** (formerly in England) a senior judge of the court of chancery who acted as assistant to the Lord Chancellor. **4.** a person serving as the deputy of a chancellor. —**vice-'chancellor,ship** n.

vicegerent (,vaɪs'dʒɛrənt) n. **1.** a person appointed to exercise all or some of the authority of another. **2.** R.C. Church. the pope or any other representative of God or Christ on earth, such as a bishop. ~adj. **3.** invested with or characterized by delegated authority. —**vice'gerency** n.

vice president n. an officer ranking immediately below a president and serving as his deputy. A vice president takes the president's place during his absence or incapacity, after his death, and in certain other circumstances. Abbrev.: **V.P.** —**vice-'presidency** n.

viceroy ('vaɪsrɔɪ) n. a governor of a colony, country, or province who acts for and rules in the name of his sovereign or government. Related adj.: **viceregal.** —**vice-roy,ship** or **vice'royalty** n.

vice squad n. a police division to which is assigned the enforcement of gaming and prostitution laws.

vice versa ('vaɪsɪ 'vɜːsə) adv. the other way around.

vichy water ('vɪʃɪ) n. **1.** (sometimes cap.) a natural mineral water from springs at Vichy in France, reputed to be beneficial to the health. **2.** any sparkling mineral water resembling this.

vicinity (vɪ'sɪnɪtɪ) n., pl. **-ties. 1.** a surrounding area; neighbourhood. **2.** the fact or condition of being close in space or relationship.

vicious ('vɪʃəs) adj. **1.** wicked or cruel: a vicious thug. **2.** characterized by violence or ferocity: a vicious blow. **3.** Inf. unpleasantly severe; harsh: a vicious wind. **4.** characterized by malice: vicious lies. **5.** (esp. of dogs, horses, etc.) ferocious or hostile. **6.** characterized by or leading to vice. **7.** invalidated by defects; unsound: a vicious inference. —**'viciously** adv. —**'viciousness** n.

vicious circle n. **1.** a situation in which an attempt to resolve one problem creates new problems that lead back to the original situation. **2.** Logic. **a.** an invalid form of reasoning in which a conclusion is derived from a premiss originally deduced from that same conclusion. **b.** a circular definition.

vicissitude (vɪ'sɪsɪ,tjuːd) n. **1.** variation or mutability in nature or life, esp. successive alternation from one condition or thing to another. **2.** a variation in circumstance, fortune, etc. —**vi,cissi'tudinous** adj.

victim ('vɪktɪm) n. **1.** a person or thing that suffers harm, death, etc.: victims of tyranny. **2.** a person who is tricked or swindled. **3.** a living person or animal sacrificed in a religious rite.

THESAURUS

vibrant 1. aquiver, oscillating, palpitating, pulsating, quivering, trembling **2.** alive, animated, colourful, dynamic, electrifying, full of pep (Inf.), responsive, sensitive, sparkling, spirited, vivacious, vivid

vibrate fluctuate, judder (Inf.), oscillate, pulsate, pulse, quiver, resonate, reverberate, shake, shiver, sway, swing, throb, tremble, undulate

vibration juddering (Inf.), oscillation, pulsation, pulse, quiver, resonance, reverberation, shaking, throb, throbbing, trembling, tremor

vice 1. corruption, degeneracy, depravity, evil, evildoing, immorality, iniquity, profligacy, sin, venality, wickedness **2.** blemish, defect, failing, fault, imperfection, shortcoming, weakness

vicinity area, district, environs, locality, neck of the woods (Inf.), neighbourhood, precincts, propinquity, proximity, purlieus

vicious 1. abandoned, abhorrent, atrocious, bad, barbarous, corrupt, cruel, dangerous, debased, degenerate, degraded, depraved, diabolical, ferocious, fiendish, foul, heinous, immoral, infamous, monstrous, profligate, savage, sinful, unprincipled, vile, violent, wicked, worthless, wrong **2.** backbiting, bitchy (Sl.), cruel, defamatory, malicious, mean, rancorous, slanderous, spiteful, venomous, vindictive

viciousness 1. badness, corruption, cruelty, depravity, ferocity, immorality, profligacy, savagery, wickedness **2.** bitchiness (Sl.), malice, rancour, spite, spitefulness, venom

victim 1. casualty, fatality, injured party, martyr, sacrifice, scapegoat, sufferer **2.** dupe, easy prey, fall guy (Inf.), gull (Archaic), innocent, sitting target, sucker (Sl.)

victimize or **-mise** ('vɪktɪˌmaɪz) vb. (tr.) **1.** to punish or discriminate against selectively or unfairly. **2.** to make a victim of. —ˌvictimiˈzation or -miˈsation n. —ˈvictimˌizer or -ˌiser n.

victor ('vɪktə) n. **1. a.** a person, nation, etc., that has defeated an adversary in war, etc. **b.** (as modifier): the victor army. **2.** the winner of any contest, conflict, or struggle.

victoria (vɪkˈtɔːrɪə) n. **1.** a light four-wheeled horse-drawn carriage with a folding hood, two passenger seats, and a seat in front for the driver. **2.** Also called: **victoria plum.** Brit. a large sweet variety of plum, red and yellow in colour.

Victoria Cross n. the highest decoration for gallantry in the face of the enemy awarded to the British and Commonwealth armed forces: instituted in 1856 by Queen Victoria.

Victorian (vɪkˈtɔːrɪən) adj. **1.** of or characteristic of Victoria (1819-1901), queen of Great Britian and Northern Ireland, or of the period of her reign (1837-1901). **2.** exhibiting the characteristics popularly attributed to the Victorians, esp. prudery or hypocrisy. ~n. **3.** a person who lived during the reign of Queen Victoria.

Victoriana (vɪkˌtɔːrɪˈɑːnə) n. objects, ornaments, etc., of the Victorian period.

victorious (vɪkˈtɔːrɪəs) adj. **1.** having defeated an adversary: the victorious nations. **2.** of, indicative of, or characterized by victory: a victorious conclusion. —**vicˈtoriously** adv.

victory ('vɪktərɪ) n., pl. **-ries. 1.** final and complete superiority in a war. **2.** a successful military engagement. **3.** a success attained in a contest or struggle or over an opponent, obstacle, or problem. **4.** the act of triumphing or state of having triumphed.

victual ('vɪtəl) vb. **-ualling, -ualled** or U.S. **-ualing, -ualed.** to supply with or obtain victuals. —**'victualless** adj.

victuals ('vɪtəlz) pl. n. (sometimes sing.) food or provisions.

vide ('vaɪdɪ) (used to direct a reader to a specified place in a text, another book, etc.) refer to, see (often in **vide ante** (see before), **vide infra** (see below), **vide supra** (see above), etc.). Abbrev.: **v., vid.**

videlicet (vɪˈdiːlɪˌsɛt) adv. namely: used to specify items, etc. Abbrev.: **viz.**

video ('vɪdɪˌəʊ) adj. **1.** relating to or employed in the transmission or reception of a televised image. **2.** of, concerned with, or operating at video frequencies. ~n., pl. **-os. 3.** the visual elements of a television broadcast. **4.** U.S. an informal name for **television. 5.** short for **video cassette recorder. 6.** the facility of or apparatus for recording video-frequency signals: have you got video yet?

video cassette recorder n. a machine for recording television programmes on video tape cassettes.

video frequency n. the frequency of a signal conveying the image and synchronizing pulses in a television broadcasting system. It lies in the range from about 50 hertz to 5 megahertz.

videophone ('vɪdɪəˌfəʊn) n. a telephonic device in which there is both verbal and visual communication between parties.

video tape n. **1.** magnetic tape used mainly for recording the video-frequency signals of a television programme or film for subsequent transmission. ~vb.

video-tape. 2. to record (a programme, etc.) on video tape.

vie (vaɪ) vb. **vying, vied.** (intr.; foll. by with or for) to contend for superiority or victory (with) or strive in competition (for). —**'vier** n. —**'vying** adj., n.

Vietnamese (ˌvjɛtnəˈmiːz) adj. **1.** of or characteristic of Vietnam, in SE Asia, its people, or their language. ~n., pl. **-ese. 2.** a native or inhabitant of Vietnam. **3.** the language of Vietnam.

view (vjuː) n. **1.** the act of seeing or observing. **2.** vision or sight, esp. range of vision: the church is out of view. **3.** a scene, esp. of a fine tract of countryside: the view from the top was superb. **4.** a pictorial representation of a scene, such as a photograph. **5.** (sometimes pl.) opinion: my own view on the matter differs from yours. **6.** (foll. by to) a desired end or intention: he has a view to securing further qualifications. **7.** a general survey of a topic, subject, etc. **8.** visual aspect or appearance: they look the same in outward view. **9.** a sight of a hunted animal before or during the chase. **10. in view of.** taking into consideration. **11. on view.** exhibited to the public gaze. **12. take a dim** or **poor view of.** to regard (something) with disfavour. **13. with a view to. a.** with the intention of. **b.** in anticipation or hope of. ~vb. **14.** (tr.) to look at. **15.** (tr.) to consider in a specified manner: they view the growth of Communism with horror. **16.** to examine or inspect carefully: to view the accounts. **17.** (tr.) to contemplate: to view the difficulties. **18.** to watch (television). **19.** (tr.) to sight (a hunted animal) before or during the chase. —**'viewable** adj. —**'viewing** n. —**'viewless** adj.

viewdata ('vjuːˌdeɪtə) n. a videotext service in which the consumer is linked to a computer by telephone and is thus able to select the information required. Cf. **teletext.**

viewer ('vjuːə) n. **1.** a person who views something, esp. television. **2.** any optical device by means of which something is viewed, esp. one used for viewing photographic transparencies.

viewfinder ('vjuːˌfaɪndə) n. a device on a camera, consisting of a lens system, enabling the user to see what will be included in his photograph.

viewpoint ('vjuːˌpɔɪnt) n. **1.** the mental attitude that determines a person's judgments. **2.** a place from which something can be viewed.

vigil ('vɪdʒɪl) n. **1.** a purposeful watch maintained, esp. at night, to guard, observe, pray, etc. **2.** the period of such a watch. **3.** R.C. Church, Church of England. the eve of certain major festivals, formerly observed as a night spent in prayer.

vigilance ('vɪdʒɪləns) n. **1.** the fact, quality, or condition of being vigilant. **2.** the abnormal state or condition of being unable to sleep.

vigilance committee n. (in the U.S.) a self-appointed body of citizens organized to maintain order, etc., where an efficient system of courts does not exist.

vigilant ('vɪdʒɪlənt) adj. keenly alert to or heedful of trouble or danger. —**'vigilantly** adv.

vigilante (ˌvɪdʒɪˈlæntɪ) n. **1.** a member of a vigilance committee. **2.** a self-appointed protector of public order.

vignette (vɪˈnjɛt) n. **1.** a small illustration placed at the beginning or end of a book or chapter. **2.** a short graceful literary essay or sketch. **3.** a photograph, drawing, etc., with edges that are shaded off. **4.** any small endearing scene, view, etc. ~vb. (tr.) **5.** to finish (a photograph, etc.) with a fading border in the form of a vi-

---

THESAURUS

victimize 1. discriminate against, have a down on (someone) (Inf.), have it in for (someone) (Inf.), have one's knife into (someone), persecute, pick on **2.** cheat, deceive, defraud, dupe, exploit, fool, gull (Archaic), hoodwink, prey on, swindle, take advantage of, use

victor champ (Inf.), champion, conquering hero, conqueror, first, prizewinner, top dog (Inf.), vanquisher, winner

victorious champion, conquering, first, prizewinning, successful, triumphant, vanquishing, winning

victory conquest, laurels, mastery, success, superiority, the palm, the prize, triumph, win

victuals bread, comestibles, eatables,

eats (Sl.), edibles, food, grub (Sl.), meat, nosh (Sl.), provisions, rations, stores, supplies, viands, vittles (Obsolete)

view n. **1.** aspect, landscape, outlook, panorama, perspective, picture, prospect, scene, spectacle, vista **2.** range or field of vision, sight, vision **3.** Sometimes plural attitude, belief, conviction, feeling, impression, judgment, notion, opinion, point of view, sentiment, thought, way of thinking **4.** contemplation, display, examination, inspection, look, scan, scrutiny, sight, survey, viewing **5. with a view to** in order to, in the hope of, so as to, with the aim or intention of ~v. **6.** behold, contemplate, examine, explore, eye, gaze at, inspect, look at, observe, regard, scan, spectate, stare at, survey, watch, witness **7.** con-

sider, deem, judge, look on, regard, think about

viewer observer, one of an audience, onlooker, spectator, TV watcher, watcher

viewpoint angle, frame of reference, perspective, point of view, position, slant, stance, standpoint, vantage point, way of thinking

vigilant alert, Argus-eyed, attentive, careful, cautious, circumspect, keeping one's eyes peeled or skinned (Inf.), on one's guard, on one's toes, on the alert, on the lookout, on the qui vive, on the watch, sleepless, unsleeping, wakeful, watchful, wide awake

gnette. **6.** to portray in or as in a vignette. —**vi'gnettist** n.

vigorous ('vɪgərəs) adj. **1.** endowed with bodily or mental strength or vitality. **2.** displaying, characterized by, or performed with vigour: *vigorous growth.* —**'vigorously** adv.

vigour or U.S. **vigor** ('vɪgə) n. **1.** exuberant and resilient strength of body or mind. **2.** substantial effective energy or force: *the vigour of the tempest.* **3.** forcefulness: *I was surprised by the vigour of her complaints.* **4.** the capacity for survival or strong healthy growth in a plant or animal. **5.** the most active period or stage of life, manhood, etc.

Viking ('vaɪkɪŋ) n. (*sometimes not cap.*) **1.** Also called: **Norseman, Northman.** any of the Danes, Norwegians, and Swedes who raided by sea most of N and W Europe from the 8th to the 11th centuries. **2.** (*modifier*) of, relating to, or characteristic of a Viking or Vikings: *a Viking ship.*

vile (vaɪl) adj. **1.** abominably wicked; shameful or evil. **2.** morally despicable; ignoble: *vile accusations.* **3.** disgusting to the senses or emotions; foul: *a vile smell.* **4.** tending to humiliate or degrade: *only slaves would perform such vile tasks.* **5.** unpleasant or bad: *vile weather.* —**'vilely** adv. —**'vileness** n.

vilify ('vɪlɪ‚faɪ) vb. **-fying, -fied.** (*tr.*) to revile with abusive language; malign. —**vilification** (‚vɪlɪfɪ'keɪʃən) n. —**'vili‚fier** n.

villa ('vɪlə) n. **1.** (in ancient Rome) a country house, usually consisting of farm buildings and residential quarters around a courtyard. **2.** a large country residence. **3.** Brit. a detached or semidetached suburban house.

village ('vɪlɪdʒ) n. **1.** a small group of houses in a country area, larger than a hamlet. **2.** the inhabitants of such a community collectively. **3.** an incorporated municipality smaller than a town in various parts of the U.S. and Canada. **4.** (*modifier*) of or characteristic of a village: *a village green.* —**'villager** n.

villain ('vɪlən) n. **1.** a wicked or malevolent person. **2.** (in a novel, play, etc.) the main evil character and antagonist to the hero. **3.** Often jocular. a rogue. **4.** Obs. an uncouth person; boor. —**'villainess** fem. n.

villainous ('vɪlənəs) adj. **1.** of, like, or appropriate to a villain. **2.** very bad or disagreeable: *villainous climate.* —**'villainously** adv. —**'villainousness** n.

villainy ('vɪlənɪ) n., pl. **-lainies. 1.** vicious behaviour or action. **2.** an evil or criminal act or deed. **3.** the fact or condition of being villainous.

villein ('vɪlən) n. (in medieval Europe) a peasant personally bound to his lord, to whom he paid dues and services in return for his land. —**'villeinage** n.

vim (vɪm) n. Sl. exuberant vigour and energy.

vinaigrette (‚vɪnɪ'grɛt) n. **1.** Also called: **vinegarette.** a small decorative bottle or box with a perforated top, used for holding smelling salts, etc. **2.** Also called: **vinaigrette sauce.** a French dressing used esp. with salads.

vinculum ('vɪŋkjuləm) n., pl. **-la** (-lə). **1.** a horizontal line drawn above a group of mathematical terms, used as a sign of aggregation in mathematical expressions, as in $\overline{x + y}$. **2.** Anat. any bandlike structure, esp. one uniting two or more parts.

vindicable ('vɪndɪkəbəl) adj. capable of being vindicated; justifiable. —**‚vindica'bility** n.

vindicate ('vɪndɪ‚keɪt) vb. (*tr.*) **1.** to clear from guilt, blame, etc., as by evidence or argument. **2.** to provide justification for: *his promotion vindicated his unconventional attitude.* **3.** to uphold or defend (a cause, etc.): *to vindicate a claim.* —**'vindi‚cator** n. —**'vindi‚catory** adj.

vindication (‚vɪndɪ'keɪʃən) n. **1.** the act of vindicating or the condition of being vindicated. **2.** a fact, evidence, etc., that serves to vindicate a claim.

vindictive (vɪn'dɪktɪv) adj. **1.** disposed to seek vengeance. **2.** characterized by spite or rancour. **3.** English law. (of damages) in excess of the compensation due to the plaintiff and imposed in punishment of the defendant. —**vin'dictively** adv. —**vin'dictiveness** n.

vine (vaɪn) n. **1.** any of various plants, esp. the grapevine, having long flexible stems that creep along the ground or climb by clinging to a support by means of tendrils, leafstalks, etc. **2.** the stem of such a plant. —**'viny** adj.

vinegar ('vɪnɪgə) n. **1.** a sour-tasting liquid consisting of impure dilute acetic acid, made by fermentation of beer, wine, or cider. It is used as a condiment or preservative. **2.** sourness or peevishness of temper, speech, etc. —**'vinegarish** adj. —**'vinegary** adj.

vinery ('vaɪnərɪ) n., pl. **-eries. 1.** a hothouse for growing grapes. **2.** another name for a **vineyard. 3.** vines collectively.

vineyard ('vɪnjəd) n. a plantation of grapevines, esp. where wine grapes are produced.

vingt-et-un French. (vɛ̃te'œ̃) n. another name for **pontoon²**.

viniculture ('vɪnɪ‚kʌltʃə) n. the process or business of growing grapes and making wine. —**‚vini'cultural** adj. —**‚vini'culturist** n.

vinous ('vaɪnəs) adj. **1.** of or characteristic of wine. **2.** indulging in or indicative of indulgence in wine.

vintage ('vɪntɪdʒ) n. **1.** the wine obtained from a harvest of grapes, esp. in an outstandingly good year. **2.** the harvest from which such a wine is obtained. **3. a.** the harvesting of wine grapes. **b.** the season of harvesting these grapes or for making wine. **4.** a time of origin: *a car of Edwardian vintage.* ~adj. **5.** (of wine) of an outstandingly good year. **6.** representative of the best and most typical: *vintage Shakespeare.* **7.** old-fashioned; dated.

vintage car n. Chiefly Brit. an old car, esp. one constructed between 1919 and 1930.

vintner ('vɪntnə) n. a wine merchant.

vinyl ('vaɪnɪl) n. **1.** (*modifier*) of or containing the monovalent group of atoms CH_2CH-: *vinyl chloride.* **2.** (*modifier*) of or made of a vinyl resin: *a vinyl raincoat.* **3.** any vinyl resin or plastic, esp. PVC.

viol ('vaɪəl) n. any of a family of stringed musical instruments that preceded the violin family, consisting of a fretted fingerboard, a body rather like that of a violin but having a flat back and six strings, played with a curved bow.

THESAURUS

vigorous active, brisk, dynamic, effective, efficient, energetic, enterprising, flourishing, forceful, forcible, full of energy, hale, hale and hearty, hardy, healthy, intense, lively, lusty, powerful, red-blooded, robust, sound, spanking, spirited, strenuous, strong, virile, vital, zippy (*Inf.*)

vigorously all out, eagerly, energetically, forcefully, hammer and tongs, hard, like mad (*Sl.*), lustily, strenuously, strongly, with a vengeance, with might and main

vigour activity, animation, dash, dynamism, energy, force, forcefulness, gusto, health, liveliness, might, oomph (*Inf.*), pep, power, punch (*Inf.*), robustness, snap (*Inf.*), soundness, spirit, strength, verve, vim (*Sl.*), virility, vitality, zip (*Inf.*)

vile 1. abandoned, abject, appalling, bad, base, coarse, contemptible, corrupt, debased, degenerate, degrading, depraved, despicable, disgraceful, evil, humiliating, ignoble, impure, loathsome, low, mean, miserable, nefarious, perverted, shocking, sinful, ugly, vicious, vulgar, wicked, worthless, wretched **2.** disgusting, foul, horrid, loathsome, nasty, nauseating, noxious, offensive, repellent, repugnant, repulsive, revolting, sickening

vilify abuse, asperse, bad-mouth (*U.S. sl.*), berate, calumniate, debase, decry, defame, denigrate, disparage, malign, pull to pieces (*Inf.*), revile, run down, slander, smear, speak ill of, traduce, vilipend (*Rare*), vituperate

villain 1. blackguard, caitiff (*Archaic*), criminal, evildoer, knave (*Archaic*), libertine, malefactor, miscreant, profligate, rapscallion, reprobate, rogue, scoundrel, wretch **2.** antihero, baddy (*Inf.*) **3.** devil, monkey, rascal, rogue, scallywag (*Inf.*), scamp

villainous atrocious, bad, base, blackguardly, criminal, cruel, debased, degenerate, depraved, detestable, diabolical, evil, fiendish, hateful, heinous, ignoble, infamous, inhuman, mean, nefarious, outrageous, ruffianly, scoundrelly, sinful, terrible, thievish, vicious, vile, wicked

villainy atrocity, baseness, crime, criminality, delinquency, depravity, devilry, iniquity, knavery, rascality, sin, turpitude, vice, wickedness

vindicate 1. absolve, acquit, clear, defend, do justice to, exculpate, excuse, exonerate, free from blame, justify, rehabilitate **2.** advocate, assert, establish, maintain, support, uphold

vindication apology, assertion, defence, exculpating, exculpation, excuse, exoneration, justification, maintenance, plea, rehabilitation, substantiation, support

vindictive full of spleen, implacable, malicious, malignant, rancorous, relentless, resentful, revengeful, spiteful, unforgiving, unrelenting, vengeful, venomous

vintage 1. n. collection, crop, epoch, era, generation, harvest, origin, year **2.** adj. best, choice, classic, mature, prime, rare, ripe, select, superior, venerable

viola[1] (vɪˈəʊlə) *n.* **1.** a bowed stringed instrument, the alto of the violin family; held beneath the chin when played. **2.** any of various instruments of the viol family, such as the viola da gamba.

viola[2] (ˈvaɪələ, vaɪˈəʊ-) *n.* any of various temperate perennial herbaceous plants, the flowers of which have showy irregular petals, white, yellow, blue, or mauve in colour.

viola da gamba (vɪˈəʊlə də ˈgæmbə) *n.* the second largest and lowest member of the viol family.

violate (ˈvaɪəˌleɪt) *vb.* (*tr.*) **1.** to break, disregard, or infringe on (a law, agreement, etc.). **2.** to rape or otherwise sexually assault. **3.** to disturb rudely or improperly. **4.** to treat irreverently or disrespectfully: *he violated a sanctuary.* —**ˈviolable** *adj.* —ˌvioˈlation *n.* —ˈvioˌlator *or* ˈvioˌlater *n.*

violence (ˈvaɪələns) *n.* **1.** the exercise or an instance of physical force, usually effecting or intended to effect injuries, destruction, etc. **2.** powerful, untamed, or devastating force: *the violence of the sea.* **3.** great strength of feeling, as in language, etc. **4.** an unjust, unwarranted, or unlawful display of force. **5. do violence to. a.** to inflict harm upon: *they did violence to the prisoners.* **b.** to distort the sense or intention of: *the reporters did violence to my speech.*

violent (ˈvaɪələnt) *adj.* **1.** marked or caused by great physical force or violence: *a violent stab.* **2.** (of a person) tending to the use of violence, esp. in order to injure or intimidate others. **3.** marked by intensity of any kind: *a violent clash of colours.* **4.** characterized by an undue use of force. **5.** caused by or displaying strong or undue mental or emotional force. —**ˈviolently** *adv.*

violet (ˈvaɪəlɪt) *n.* **1.** any of various temperate perennial herbaceous plants of the genus *Viola,* such as the **sweet** (or **garden**) **violet,** having mauve or bluish flowers with irregular showy petals. **2.** any other plant of the genus *Viola,* such as the wild pansy. **3.** any of various similar but unrelated plants, such as the African violet. **4. a.** any of a group of colours that have a purplish-blue hue. They lie at one end of the visible spectrum. **b.** (*as adj.*): *a violet dress.* **5.** a dye or pigment of or producing these colours. **6.** violet clothing: *dressed in violet.* **7. shrinking violet.** *Inf.* a shy person.

violin (ˌvaɪəˈlɪn) *n.* a bowed stringed instrument, the highest member of the violin family, consisting of a fingerboard, a hollow wooden body with waisted sides, and a sounding board connected to the back by means of a soundpost that also supports the bridge. It has two f-shaped sound holes cut in the belly.

violinist (ˌvaɪəˈlɪnɪst) *n.* a person who plays the violin.

violist (ˈvaɪəlɪst) *n.* a person who plays the viol.

violoncello (ˌvaɪələnˈtʃɛləʊ) *n., pl.* **-los.** the full name for **cello.** —ˌviolonˈcellist *n.*

V.I.P. *Inf. abbrev. for* very important person.

viper (ˈvaɪpə) *n.* **1.** any of a family of venomous Old World snakes having hollow fangs in the upper jaw that are used to inject venom. **2.** any of various other snakes, such as the horned viper. **3.** a malicious or treacherous person.

virago (vɪˈrɑːgəʊ) *n., pl.* **-goes** *or* **-gos. 1.** a loud, violent, and ill-tempered woman. **2.** *Arch.* a strong or warlike woman. —**viˈragoˌlike** *adj.*

viral (ˈvaɪrəl) *adj.* of or caused by a virus.

virgin (ˈvɜːdʒɪn) *n.* **1.** a person, esp. a woman, who has never had sexual intercourse. **2.** an unmarried woman who has taken a religious vow of chastity. **3.** any female animal that has never mated. **4.** a female insect that produces offspring by parthenogenesis. ~*adj.* (*usually prenominal*) **5.** of, suitable for, or characteristic of a virgin or virgins. **6.** pure and natural, uncorrupted or untouched: *virgin purity.* **7.** not yet cultivated, explored, exploited, etc., by man: *the virgin forests.* **8.** being the first or happening for the first time. **9.** (of a metal) made from an ore rather than from scrap. **10.** occurring naturally in a pure and uncombined form: *virgin silver.*

Virgin[1] (ˈvɜːdʒɪn) *n.* **1. the.** See **Virgin Mary. 2.** a statue or other artistic representation of the Virgin Mary.

Virgin[2] (ˈvɜːdʒɪn) *n.* **the.** the constellation Virgo, the sixth sign of the zodiac.

virginal[1] (ˈvɜːdʒɪnəl) *adj.* **1.** of, characterized by, or maintaining a state of virginity; chaste. **2.** extremely pure or fresh. —**ˈvirginally** *adv.*

virginal[2] (ˈvɜːdʒɪnəl) *n.* (*often pl.*) a smaller version of the harpsichord, but oblong in shape, having one manual and no pedals. —**ˈvirginalist** *n.*

Virgin Birth *n.* the doctrine that Jesus Christ was conceived solely by the direct intervention of the Holy Spirit so that Mary remained miraculously a virgin during and after his birth.

Virginia creeper (vəˈdʒɪnɪə) *n.* a woody vine of North America, having tendrils with adhesive tips, bluish-black berry-like fruits, and compound leaves that turn red in autumn: widely planted for ornament.

virginity (vəˈdʒɪnɪtɪ) *n.* **1.** the condition or fact of being a virgin. **2.** the condition of being untouched, unsullied, etc.

Virgin Mary *n.* Mary, the mother of Christ. Also called: the **Virgin.**

Virgo (ˈvɜːgəʊ) *n., Latin genitive* **Virginis** (ˈvɜːdʒɪnɪs). **1.** *Astron.* a large constellation on the celestial equator. **2.** *Astrol.* the sixth sign of the zodiac. The sun is in this sign between about Aug. 23 and Sept. 22.

virgule (ˈvɜːgjuːl) *n. Printing.* another name for **solidus.**

virile (ˈvɪraɪl) *adj.* **1.** of or having the characteristics of an adult male. **2.** of or capable of copulation or procreation. **3.** strong, forceful, or vigorous. —**virility** (vɪˈrɪlɪtɪ) *n.*

virology (vaɪˈrɒlədʒɪ) *n.* the branch of medicine concerned with the study of viruses. —**virological** (ˌvaɪrəˈlɒdʒɪkəl) *adj.*

virtu *or* **vertu** (vɜːˈtuː) *n.* **1.** a taste or love for curios or works of fine art. **2.** such objects collectively. **3.** the quality of being appealing to a connoisseur (esp. in **articles of virtu; objects of virtu**).

virtual (ˈvɜːtʃʊəl) *adj.* having the essence or effect but not the appearance or form of: *a virtual revolution.* —ˌvirtuˈality *n.*

virtually (ˈvɜːtʃʊəlɪ) *adv.* in effect though not in fact; practically; nearly.

virtue (ˈvɜːtjuː) *n.* **1.** the quality or practice of moral excellence or righteousness. **2.** a particular moral excellence: *the virtue of tolerance.* **3.** any of the cardinal virtues (prudence, justice, fortitude, and temperance) or theological virtues (faith, hope, and charity). **4.** any admirable quality or trait. **5.** an effective, active, or inherent power. **6.** chastity, esp. in women. **7. by** *or* **in virtue of.** by reason of. **8. make a virtue of necessity.** to acquiesce in doing something unpleasant with a show of grace because one must do it in any case.

THESAURUS

violate 1. break, contravene, disobey, disregard, encroach upon, infract, infringe, transgress **2.** abuse, assault, befoul, debauch, defile, desecrate, dishonour, invade, outrage, pollute, profane, rape, ravish

violation 1. abuse, breach, contravention, encroachment, infraction, infringement, transgression, trespass **2.** defilement, desecration, profanation, sacrilege, spoliation

violence 1. bestiality, bloodshed, bloodthirstiness, brutality, brute force, cruelty, destructiveness, ferocity, fierceness, fighting, force, frenzy, fury, murderousness, passion, rough handling, savagery, strong-arm tactics (*Inf.*), terrorism, thuggery, vehemence, wildness **2.** boisterousness, power, raging, roughness, storminess, tumult, turbulence, wildness **3.** abandon, acuteness, fervour, force, harshness, intensity, severity, sharpness, vehemence

violent 1. berserk, bloodthirsty, brutal, cruel, destructive, fiery, forcible, furious, headstrong, homicidal, hot-headed, impetuous, intemperate, maddened, maniacal, murderous, passionate, powerful, raging, riotous, rough, savage, strong, uncontrollable, ungovernable, unrestrained, vehement, vicious, wild **2.** blustery, boisterous, devastating, full of force, gale force, powerful, raging, ruinous, strong, tempestuous, tumultuous, turbulent, wild **3.** acute, agonizing, biting, excruciating, extreme, harsh, inordinate, intense, outrageous, painful, severe, sharp

virgin 1. *n.* damsel (*Archaic*), girl, maid (*Archaic*), maiden (*Archaic*), vestal, virgo intacta **2.** *adj.* chaste, fresh, immaculate, maidenly, modest, new, pristine, pure, snowy, uncorrupted, undefiled, unsullied, untouched, unused, vestal, virginal

virile forceful, lusty, macho, male, manlike, manly, masculine, potent, red-blooded, robust, strong, vigorous

virility machismo, manhood, masculinity, potency, vigour

virtual essential, implicit, implied, in all but name, indirect, potential, practical, tacit, unacknowledged

virtually as good as, effectually, for all practical purposes, in all but name, in effect, in essence, nearly, practically, to all intents and purposes

virtue 1. ethicalness, excellence, goodness, high-mindedness, incorruptibility, in-

virtuoso (ˌvɜ:tjʊˈəʊzəʊ) n., pl. **-sos** or **-si** (-si:). **1.** a consummate master of musical technique and artistry. **2.** a person who has a masterly or dazzling skill or technique in any field of activity. **3.** a connoisseur or collector of art objects. **4.** (modifier) showing masterly skill or brilliance: a virtuoso performance. —**virtuosic** (ˌvɜ:tjʊˈɒsɪk) adj. —ˌvirtuˈosity n.

virtuous (ˈvɜ:tʃʊəs) adj. **1.** characterized by or possessing virtue or moral excellence. **2.** (of women) chaste or virginal. —ˈvirtuously adv.

virulent (ˈvɪrʊlənt) adj. **1. a.** (of a microorganism) extremely infective. **b.** (of a disease) having a violent effect. **2.** extremely poisonous, injurious, etc. **3.** extremely bitter, hostile, etc. —ˈvirulence n. —ˈvirulently adv.

virus (ˈvaɪrəs) n., pl. **-ruses. 1.** any of a group of submicroscopic entities consisting of a single nucleic acid surrounded by a protein coat and capable of replication only within the cells of animals and plants. **2.** Inf. a disease caused by a virus. **3.** any corrupting or infecting influence.

visa (ˈvi:zə) n., pl. **-sas. 1.** an endorsement in a passport or similar document, signifying that the document is in order and permitting its bearer to travel into or through the country of the government issuing it. ～vb. **-saing, -saed. 2.** (tr.) to enter a visa into (a passport).

visage (ˈvɪzɪdʒ) n. Chiefly literary. **1.** face or countenance. **2.** appearance.

vis-à-vis (ˌvi:zɑ:ˈvi:) prep. **1.** in relation to. **2.** face to face with. ～adv., adj. **3.** face to face; opposite. ～n., pl. **vis-à-vis. 4.** a person or thing that is situated opposite to another. **5.** a person who corresponds to another in office, capacity, etc.

viscera (ˈvɪsərə) pl. n., sing. **viscus** (ˈvɪskəs). **1.** Anat. the large internal organs of the body collectively, esp. those in the abdominal cavity. **2.** (less formally) the intestines; guts.

visceral (ˈvɪsərəl) adj. **1.** of or affecting the viscera. **2.** characterized by instinct rather than intellect. —ˈviscerally adv.

viscid (ˈvɪsɪd) adj. **1.** cohesive and sticky. **2.** (esp. of a leaf) covered with a sticky substance. —visˈcidity n.

viscose (ˈvɪskəʊs) n. **1. a.** a viscous orange-brown solution obtained by dissolving cellulose in sodium hydroxide and carbon disulphide. It can be converted back to cellulose by an acid, as in the manufacture of rayon and cellophane. **b.** (as modifier): viscose rayon. **2.** rayon made from this material.

viscosity (vɪsˈkɒsɪtɪ) n., pl. **-ties. 1.** the state or property of being viscous. **2.** Physics. **a.** the extent to which a fluid resists a tendency to flow. **b.** Also called: **absolute viscosity.** a measure of this resistance, measured in newton seconds per metre squared. Symbol: η

viscount (ˈvaɪkaʊnt) n. **1.** (in the British Isles) a nobleman ranking below an earl and above a baron. **2.** (in various countries) a son or younger brother of a count. **3.** (in medieval Europe) the deputy of a count. —ˈviscountcy or ˈviscounty n. —ˈviscountess fem. n.

viscous (ˈvɪskəs) adj. **1.** (of liquids) thick and sticky. **2.** having or involving viscosity. —ˈviscously adv.

vise (vaɪs) n., vb. U.S. a variant spelling of **vice²**.

visibility (ˌvɪzɪˈbɪlɪtɪ) n. **1.** the condition or fact of being visible. **2.** clarity of vision or relative possibility of seeing. **3.** the range of vision: visibility is 500 yards.

visible (ˈvɪzɪbəl) adj. **1.** capable of being perceived by the eye. **2.** capable of being perceived by the mind: no visible dangers. **3.** available: the visible resources. **4.** of or relating to the balance of trade: visible transactions. —ˈvisibly adv.

vision (ˈvɪʒən) n. **1.** the act, faculty, or manner of perceiving with the eye; sight. **2.** the ability or an instance of great perception, esp. of future developments: a man of vision. **3.** mystical or religious experience of seeing some supernatural event, person, etc.: the vision of St. John of the Cross. **4.** that which is seen, esp. in such a mystical experience. **5.** (sometimes pl.) a vivid mental image produced by the imagination: he had visions of becoming famous. **6.** a person or thing of extraordinary beauty.

visionary (ˈvɪʒənərɪ) adj. **1.** marked by vision or foresight: a visionary leader. **2.** incapable of being realized or effected. **3.** (of people) characterized by idealistic or radical ideas, esp. impractical ones. **4.** given to having visions. **5.** of, of the nature of, or seen in visions. ～n., pl.-aries. **6.** a visionary person.

visit (ˈvɪzɪt) vb. **1.** to go or come to see (a person, place, etc.). **2.** to stay with (someone) as a guest. **3.** to go or come to (an institution, place, etc.) for the purpose of inspecting or examining. **4.** (tr.) (of a disease, disaster, etc.) to afflict. **5.** (tr.; foll. by upon or on) to inflict (punishment, etc.). **6.** (often foll. by with) U.S. inf. to chat (with someone). ～n. **7.** the act or an instance of visiting. **8.** a stay as a guest. **9.** a professional or official call. **10.** a formal call for the purpose of inspection or examination. **11.** International law. the right of an officer of a belligerent state to stop and search neutral ships in war to verify their nationality and ascertain whether they carry contraband. **12.** U.S. inf. a chat. —ˈvisitable adj.

visitant (ˈvɪzɪtənt) n. **1.** a ghost; apparition. **2.** a visitor or guest, usually from far away. **3.** Also called: **visitor.** a migratory bird that is present in a particular region only at certain times: a summer visitant.

visitation (ˌvɪzɪˈteɪʃən) n. **1.** an official call or visit for the purpose of inspecting or examining an institution. **2.** a visiting of punishment or reward from heaven. **3.** any disaster or catastrophe: a visitation of the plague. **4.** an appearance or arrival of a supernatural being. **5.** Inf. an unduly prolonged social call.

Visitation (ˌvɪzɪˈteɪʃən) n. **1. a.** the visit made by the Virgin Mary to her cousin Elizabeth (Luke 1:39-56). **b.** the Church festival commemorating this, held on July 2. **2.** a religious order of nuns, the **Order of the Visitation,** founded in 1610 and dedicated to contemplation.

visitor (ˈvɪzɪtə) n. **1.** a person who pays a visit. **2.** another name for **visitant** (sense 3).

visor or **vizor** (ˈvaɪzə) n. **1.** a piece of armour fixed or hinged to the helmet to protect the face and furnished with slits for the eyes. **2.** another name for **peak** (on a cap). **3.** a small movable screen used as protection against glare from the sun, esp. one attached above the

---

THESAURUS

tegrity, justice, morality, probity, quality, rectitude, righteousness, uprightness, worth, worthiness **2.** advantage, asset, attribute, credit, good point, good quality, merit, plus (Inf.), strength **3.** chastity, honour, innocence, morality, purity, virginity **4. by virtue of** as a result of, by dint of, by reason of, in view of, on account of, owing to, thanks to

virtuosity n. brilliance, éclat, expertise, finish, flair, mastery, panache, polish, skill

virtuoso 1. n. artist, genius, maestro, magician, master, master hand **2.** adj. bravura (Music), brilliant, dazzling, masterly

virtuous 1. blameless, ethical, excellent, exemplary, good, high-principled, honest, honourable, incorruptible, moral, praiseworthy, pure, righteous, upright, worthy **2.** celibate, chaste, clean-living, innocent, pure, spotless, virginal

virulent 1. baneful (Archaic), deadly, infective, injurious, lethal, malignant, pernicious, poisonous, septic, toxic, venomous **2.** acrimonious, bitter, envenomed, hostile, ma-

levolent, malicious, rancorous, resentful, spiteful, splenetic, venomous, vicious, vindictive

visible anywhere to be seen, apparent, clear, conspicuous, detectable, discernible, discoverable, distinguishable, evident, in sight, in view, manifest, not hidden, noticeable, observable, obvious, palpable, patent, perceivable, perceptible, plain, to be seen, unconcealed, unmistakable

vision 1. eyes, eyesight, perception, seeing, sight, view **2.** breadth of view, discernment, farsightedness, foresight, imagination, insight, intuition, penetration, prescience **3.** castle in the air, concept, conception, daydream, dream, fantasy, idea, ideal, image, mental picture, pipe dream **4.** apparition, chimera, delusion, ghost, hallucination, illusion, mirage, phantasm, phantom, revelation, spectre, wraith **5.** dream, feast for the eyes, perfect picture, picture, sight, sight for sore eyes, spectacle

visionary adj. **1.** dreaming, dreamy,

idealistic, quixotic, romantic, starry-eyed, with one's head in the clouds **2.** chimerical, delusory, fanciful, fantastic, ideal, idealized, illusory, imaginary, impractical, prophetic, speculative, unreal, unrealistic, unworkable, utopian ～n. **3.** daydreamer, Don Quixote, dreamer, enthusiast (Archaic), idealist, mystic, prophet, romantic, seer, theorist, utopian, zealot

visit v. **1.** be the guest of, call in, call on, drop in on (Inf.), go to see, inspect, look (someone) up, pay a call on, pop in (Inf.), stay at, stay with, stop by, take in (Inf.) **2.** afflict, assail, attack, befall, descend upon, haunt, smite, trouble **3.** With **on** or **upon** bring down upon, execute, impose, inflict, wreak ～n. **4.** call, sojourn, stay, stop

visitation 1. examination, inspection, visit **2.** bane, blight, calamity, cataclysm, catastrophe, disaster, infliction, ordeal, punishment, scourge, trial

visitor caller, company, guest, visitant

windscreen of a motor vehicle. **4.** *Arch. or literary.* a mask or any other means of disguise. —'**visored** *or* '**vizored** *adj.*

vista ('vɪstə) *n.* **1.** a view, esp. through a long narrow avenue of trees, buildings, etc., or such a passage or avenue itself. **2.** a comprehensive mental view of a distant time or a lengthy series of events. —'**vistaed** *adj.*

visual ('vɪʒʊəl, -zjʊ-) *adj.* **1.** of, done by, or used in seeing: *visual powers.* **2.** another word for **optical. 3.** capable of being seen; visible. **4.** of, occurring as, or induced by a mental image. —'**visually** *adv.*

visual aids *pl. n.* devices, such as films, slides, models, and blackboards, that display in visual form material to be understood or remembered.

visual display unit *n. Computers.* a device that displays characters or line drawings representing data in a computer memory. It usually has a keyboard for the input of information or inquiries. Abbrev.: **VDU**

visualize *or* **-lise** ('vɪʒʊə,laɪz) *vb.* to form a mental image of (something incapable of being viewed or not at that moment visible). —,**visuali'zation** *or* **-li'sation** *n.*

vital ('vaɪtəl) *adj.* **1.** essential to maintain life: *the lungs perform a vital function.* **2.** forceful, energetic, or lively: *a vital person.* **3.** of, having, or displaying life: *a vital organism.* **4.** indispensable or essential: *books vital to this study.* **5.** of great importance: *a vital game.* ~*n.* **6.** (*pl.*) the bodily organs, such as the brain, liver, heart, lungs, etc., that are necessary to maintain life. **7.** (*pl.*) the essential elements of anything. —'**vitally** *adv.*

vitality (vaɪ'tælɪtɪ) *n., pl.* **-ties. 1.** physical or mental vigour, energy, etc. **2.** the power or ability to continue in existence, live, or grow: *the vitality of a movement.*

vitalize *or* **-lise** ('vaɪtə,laɪz) *vb.* (*tr.*) to make vital, living, or alive. —,**vitali'zation** *or* **-li'sation** *n.*

vital statistics *pl. n.* **1.** quantitative data concerning human life or the conditions affecting it, such as the death rate. **2.** *Inf.* the measurements of a woman's bust, waist, and hips.

vitamin ('vɪtəmɪn, 'vaɪ-) *n.* any of a group of substances that are essential, in small quantities, for the normal functioning of metabolism in the body. They cannot usually be synthesized in the body but they occur naturally in certain foods. —,**vita'minic** *adj.*

vitamin A *n.* **1.** Also called: **vitamin A₁, retinol.** a fat-soluble yellow unsaturated alcohol occurring in green and yellow vegetables, butter, egg yolk, and fish-liver oil. It is essential for the prevention of night blindness and the protection of epithelial tissue. **2.** Also called: **vitamin A₂,** a vitamin that occurs in the tissues of freshwater fish and has a function similar to that of vitamin A₁.

vitamin B *n., pl.* **B vitamins.** any of the vitamins in the vitamin B complex.

vitamin B complex *n.* a large group of water-soluble vitamins occurring esp. in liver and yeast: includes thiamine (**vitamin B₁**), riboflavin (**vitamin B₂**), nicotinic acid, pyridoxine (**vitamin B₆**), pantothenic acid, biotin, choline, folic acid, and cyanocobalamin (**vitamin B₁₂**). Sometimes shortened to **B complex.**

vitamin C *n.* another name for **ascorbic acid.**

vitamin D *n., pl.* **D vitamins.** any of the fat-soluble vitamins, including calciferol (**vitamin D₂**) and cholecalciferol (**vitamin D₃**), occurring in fish-liver oils, milk, butter, and eggs: used in the treatment of rickets.

vitamin D₁ *n.* the first isolated form of vitamin D, consisting of calciferol and its precursor, lumisterol.

vitamin E *n.* any of a group of fat-soluble alcohols that occur in lettuce, egg yoke, etc.; necessary for fertility in some animals.

vitamin K *n., pl.* **K vitamins.** any of the fat-soluble vitamins, including phylloquinone (**vitamin K₁**) and the menaquinones (**vitamin K₂**), which are essential for the normal clotting of blood.

vitamin P *n., pl.* **P vitamins.** any of a group of water-soluble crystalline substances occurring mainly in citrus fruits, blackcurrants, and rose hips: they regulate the permeability of the blood capillaries. Also called: **citrin, bioflavonoid.**

vitiate ('vɪʃɪ,eɪt) *vb.* (*tr.*) **1.** to make faulty or imperfect. **2.** to debase or corrupt. **3.** to destroy the force or legal effect of (a deed, etc.). —,**viti'ation** *n.* —'**viti,ator** *n.*

viticulture ('vɪtɪ,kʌltʃə) *n.* **1.** the science, art, or process of cultivating grapevines. **2.** the study of grapes and the growing of grapes. —,**viti'culturist** *n.*

vitreous ('vɪtrɪəs) *adj.* **1.** of or resembling glass. **2.** made of or containing glass. **3.** of or relating to the vitreous humour or vitreous body. —'**vitreously** *adv.* —'**vitreousness** *n.*

vitreous humour *or* **body** *n.* a transparent gelatinous substance that fills the interior of the eyeball between the lens and the retina.

vitrify ('vɪtrɪ,faɪ) *vb.* **-fying, -fied.** to convert or be converted into glass or a glassy substance. —'**vitri,fiable** *adj.* —**vitrification** (,vɪtrɪfɪ'keɪʃən) *n.*

vitriol ('vɪtrɪ,ɒl) *n.* **1.** another name for **sulphuric acid. 2.** any one of a number of sulphate salts, such as ferrous sulphate (**green vitriol**) or copper sulphate (**blue vitriol**). **3.** speech, writing, etc., displaying vituperation or bitterness.

vitriolic (,vɪtrɪ'ɒlɪk) *adj.* **1.** (of a strong acid) highly corrosive. **2.** severely bitter or caustic.

vituperate (vɪ'tjuːpə,reɪt) *vb.* to berate or rail against abusively; revile. —**vi,tuper'ation** *n.* —**vi'tuper,ator** *n.*

viva¹ ('viːvə) *interj.* long live; up with (a specified person or thing).

viva² ('vaɪvə) *Brit.* ~*n.* **1.** an oral examination. ~*vb.* **-vaing, -vaed.** (*tr.*) **2.** to examine orally.

vivace (vɪ'vɑːtʃɪ) *adj., adv. Music.* to be performed in a brisk lively manner.

vivacious (vɪ'veɪʃəs) *adj.* full of high spirits and animation. —**vi'vaciously** *adv.* —**vi'vaciousness** *n.*

vivacity (vɪ'væsɪtɪ) *n., pl.* **-ties.** the quality or condition of being vivacious.

vivarium (vaɪ'vɛərɪəm) *n., pl.* **-iums** *or* **-ia** (-ɪə). a place where live animals are kept under natural conditions for study, etc.

viva voce ('vaɪvə 'vəʊtʃɪ) *adv., adj.* **1.** by word of mouth. ~*n., vb.* **2.** the full form of **viva².**

vivid ('vɪvɪd) *adj.* **1.** (of a colour) very bright; intense. **2.** brilliantly coloured: *vivid plumage.* **3.** conveying to the mind striking realism, freshness, or trueness to life: *a vivid account.* **4.** (of a memory, etc.) remaining distinct in the mind. **5.** (of the imagination, etc.) prolific in the formation of lifelike images. **6.** uttered, operating, or acting with vigour: *vivid expostulations.* **7.** full of life or vitality: *a vivid personality.* —'**vividly** *adv.* —'**vividness** *n.*

vivify ('vɪvɪ,faɪ) *vb.* **-fying, -fied.** (*tr.*) **1.** to bring to life; animate. **2.** to make more vivid or striking. —,**vivifi'cation** *n.*

viviparous (vɪ'vɪpərəs) *adj.* **1.** (of most mammals) giv-

THESAURUS

visual 1. ocular, optic, optical 2. discernible, observable, perceptible, visible

visualize conceive of, conjure up a mental picture of, envisage, imagine, picture, see in the mind's eye

vital 1. basic, cardinal, essential, fundamental, imperative, indispensable, necessary, requisite 2. critical, crucial, decisive, important, key, life-or-death, significant, urgent 3. animated, dynamic, energetic, forceful, full of the joy of living, lively, spirited, vibrant, vigorous, vivacious, zestful 4. alive, animate, generative, invigorative, life-giving, live, living, quickening

vitality animation, energy, exuberance, go (*Inf.*), life, liveliness, lustiness, pep, robustness, sparkle, stamina, strength, vigour,

vim (*Sl.*), vivaciousness, vivacity

vitriolic *Fig.* acerbic, acid, bitchy (*Sl.*), bitter, caustic, destructive, dripping with malice, envenomed, sardonic, scathing, venomous, virulent, withering

vituperation abuse, billingsgate, blame, castigation, censure, fault-finding, flak (*Inf.*), invective, obloquy, rebuke, reprimand, reproach, scurrility, tongue-lashing, vilification

vituperative abusive, belittling, calumniatory, censorious, defamatory, denunciatory, derogatory, harsh, insulting, malign, opprobrious, sardonic, scurrilous, withering

vivacious animated, bubbling, cheerful, ebullient, effervescent, frolicsome, full of life, gay, high-spirited, jolly, light-hearted,

lively, merry, scintillating, sparkling, spirited, sportive, sprightly, vital

vivacity animation, ebullience, effervescence, energy, gaiety, high spirits, life, liveliness, pep, quickness, sparkle, spirit, sprightliness

vivid 1. bright, brilliant, clear, colourful, glowing, intense, rich 2. distinct, dramatic, graphic, highly-coloured, lifelike, memorable, powerful, realistic, sharp, sharply-etched, stirring, strong, telling, true to life 3. active, animated, dynamic, energetic, expressive, flamboyant, lively, quick, spirited, striking, strong, vigorous

ing birth to living offspring that develop within the uterus of the mother. **2.** (of seeds) germinating before separating from the parent plant. **3.** (of plants) producing bulbils or young plants instead of flowers. —**viviparity** (ˌvɪvɪˈpærɪtɪ) *or* **viˈviparousness** *n.* —**viˈviparously** *adv.*

vivisect (ˈvɪvɪˌsɛkt, ˌvɪvɪˈsɛkt) *vb.* to subject (an animal) to vivisection. —**ˈviviˌsector** *n.*

vivisection (ˌvɪvɪˈsɛkʃən) *n.* the act or practice of performing experiments on living animals, involving cutting into or dissecting the body. —ˌviviˈsectional *adj.* —ˌviviˈsectionist *n.*

vixen (ˈvɪksən) *n.* **1.** a female fox. **2.** a quarrelsome or spiteful woman. —**ˈvixenish** *adj.* —**ˈvixenly** *adv., adj.*

viz. *abbrev. for* videlicet.

vizier (vɪˈzɪə) *n.* a high official in certain Muslim countries, esp. in the former Ottoman Empire. —**viˈzierate** *n.* —**viˈzierial** *adj.* —**viˈziership** *n.*

vizor (ˈvaɪzə) *n.* a variant spelling of **visor.**

V-J Day *n.* the day marking the Allied victory over Japan in World War II (Aug. 15, 1945).

V.L. *abbrev. for* Vulgar Latin.

VLF *or* **vlf** *Radio. abbrev. for* very low frequency.

V neck *n.* a neck on a garment that comes down to a point, resembling the shape of the letter 'V'. —**ˈV-ˌneck** *or* **ˈV-ˌnecked** *adj.*

voc. *or* **vocat.** *abbrev. for* vocative.

vocab (ˈvəʊkæb) *n.* short for **vocabulary.**

vocable (ˈvəʊkəbˀl) *n.* any word, either written or spoken, regarded simply as a sequence of letters or spoken sounds. —**ˈvocably** *adv.*

vocabulary (vəˈkæbjʊlərɪ) *n., pl.* **-laries. 1.** a listing, either selective or exhaustive, containing the words and phrases of a language, with meanings or translations into another language. **2.** the aggregate of words in the use or comprehension of a specified person, class, etc. **3.** all the words contained in a language. **4.** a range or system of symbols or techniques constituting a means of communication or expression, as any of the arts or crafts: *a wide vocabulary of textures and colours.*

vocal (ˈvəʊkəl) *adj.* **1.** of or designed for the voice: *vocal music.* **2.** produced or delivered by the voice: *vocal noises.* **3.** connected with the production of the voice: *vocal organs.* **4.** frequently disposed to outspoken speech, criticism, etc.: *a vocal minority.* **5.** full of sound or voices: *a vocal assembly.* **6.** endowed with a voice. **7.** *Phonetics.* **a.** of or relating to a speech sound. **b.** of or relating to a voiced speech sound, esp. a vowel. —*n.* **8.** a piece of jazz or pop music that is sung. **9.** a performance of such a piece of music. —**vocality** (vəʊˈkælɪtɪ) *n.* —**ˈvocally** *adv.*

vocal cords *pl. n.* either of two pairs of membranous folds in the larynx. The upper pair (**false vocal cords**) are not concerned with vocal production; the lower pair (**true vocal cords**) can be made to vibrate and produce sound when air from the lungs is forced over them.

vocalist (ˈvəʊkəlɪst) *n.* a singer, esp. one who regularly appears with a jazz band or pop group.

vocalize *or* **-ise** (ˈvəʊkəˌlaɪz) *vb.* **1.** to express with or use the voice. **2.** (*tr.*) to make vocal or articulate. **3.** (*tr.*) *Phonetics.* to articulate (a speech sound) with voice. **4.** (*intr.*) to sing a melody on a vowel, etc. —**ˌvocaliˈzation** *or* **iˈsation** *n.* —**ˈvocalˌizer** *or* **ˌiser** *n.*

vocation (vəʊˈkeɪʃən) *n.* **1.** a specified profession or trade. **2. a.** a special urge or predisposition to a particular calling or career, esp. a religious one. **b.** such a calling or career.

vocational guidance *n.* a guidance service based on psychological tests and interviews to find out what career may best suit a person.

vocative (ˈvɒkətɪv) *adj.* **1.** *Grammar.* denoting a case of nouns, in some inflected languages, used when the referent of the noun is being addressed. —*n.* **2.** *Grammar.* **a.** the vocative case. **b.** a vocative noun or speech element.

vociferate (vəʊˈsɪfəˌreɪt) *vb.* to exclaim or cry out about (something) clamorously or insistently. —**voˌciferˈation** *n.*

vociferous (vəʊˈsɪfərəs) *adj.* **1.** characterized by vehemence or noisiness: *vociferous protests.* **2.** making an outcry: *a vociferous mob.* —**voˈciferously** *adv.* —**voˈciferousness** *n.*

vodka (ˈvɒdkə) *n.* an alcoholic drink originating in Russia, made from grain, potatoes, etc., usually consisting only of rectified spirit and water.

vogue (vəʊɡ) *n.* **1.** the popular style at a specified time (esp. in **in vogue**). **2.** a period of general or popular usage or favour: *the vogue for such dances is now over.* —*adj.* **3.** (*usually prenominal*) fashionable: *a vogue word.* —**ˈvoguish** *adj.*

voice (vɔɪs) *n.* **1.** the sound made by the vibration of the vocal cords, esp. when modified by the tongue and mouth. **2.** the natural and distinctive tone of the speech sounds characteristic of a particular person. **3.** the condition, quality, or tone of such sounds: *a hysterical voice.* **4.** the musical sound of a singing voice, with respect to its quality or tone: *she has a lovely voice.* **5.** the ability to speak, sing, etc.: *he has lost his voice.* **6.** a sound resembling or suggestive of vocal utterance: *the voice of hard experience.* **7.** written or spoken expression, as of feeling, opinion, etc. (esp. in **give voice to**). **8.** a stated choice, wish, or opinion: *to give someone a voice in a decision.* **9.** an agency through which is communicated another's purpose, etc.: *such groups are the voice of our enemies.* **10.** *Music.* **a.** musical notes produced by vibrations of the vocal chords at various frequencies and in certain registers: *a tenor voice.* **b.** (in harmony) an independent melodic line or part: *a fugue in five voices.* **11.** *Phonetics.* the sound characterizing the articulation of several speech sounds, including all vowels or sonants, that is produced when the vocal cords are set in vibration by the breath. **12.** *Grammar.* a category of the verb that expresses whether the relation between the subject and the verb is that of agent and action, action and recipient, or some other relation. **13.** **in voice.** in a condition to sing or speak well. **14. with one voice.** unanimously. —*vb.* (*tr.*) **15.** to give expression to: *to voice a complaint.* **16.** to articulate (a speech sound) with voice. **17.** *Music.* to adjust (a wind instrument or organ pipe) so that it conforms to the correct standards of tone colour, pitch, etc. —**ˈvoicer** *n.*

voiced (vɔɪst) *adj.* **1.** declared or expressed by the voice. **2.** (*in combination*) having a voice as specified: *loud-voiced.* **3.** *Phonetics.* articulated with accompanying vibration of the vocal cords: *in English* (b) *is a voiced consonant.*

voiceless (ˈvɔɪslɪs) *adj.* **1.** without a voice. **2.** not articulated: *voiceless misery.* **3.** silent. **4.** *Phonetics.* articulated without accompanying vibration of the vocal cords: *In English* (p) *is a voiceless consonant.* —**ˈvoicelessly** *adv.*

voice-over *n.* the voice of an unseen commentator heard during a film, etc.

voiceprint (ˈvɔɪsˌprɪnt) *n.* a graphic representation of a person's voice recorded electronically, usually having time plotted along the horizontal axis and the frequency of the speech on the vertical axis.

void (vɔɪd) *adj.* **1.** without contents. **2.** not legally binding: *null and void.* **3.** (of an office, house, etc.) unoccupied. **4.** (*postpositive;* foll. by *of*) destitute or devoid:

THESAURUS

vixen *Fig.* fury, harpy, harridan, hellcat, scold, shrew, spitfire, termagant (*Rare*), virago, Xanthippe

vocabulary dictionary, glossary, language, lexicon, wordbook, word hoard, words, word stock

vocal *adj.* **1.** articulate, articulated, oral, put into words, said, spoken, uttered, voiced **2.** articulate, blunt, clamorous, eloquent, expressive, forthright, frank, free-spoken, noisy, outspoken, plain-spoken, strident, vociferous

vocation business, calling, career, employment, job, life's work, life work, métier, mission, office, post, profession, pursuit, role, trade

vociferous clamant, clamorous, loud, loudmouthed (*Inf.*), noisy, obstreperous, ranting, shouting, strident, uproarious, vehement

vogue *n.* **1.** craze, custom, *dernier cri*, fashion, last word, mode, style, the latest, the rage, the thing (*Inf.*), trend, way **2.** acceptance, currency, fashionableness, favour, popularity, prevalence, usage, use ~*adj.* **3.** fashionable, in, modish, now (*Inf.*), popular, prevalent, trendy (*Brit. inf.*), up-to-the-minute, voguish, with it (*Inf.*)

voice *n.* **1.** articulation, language, power of speech, sound, tone, utterance, words **2.** decision, expression, part, say, view, vote, will, wish **3.** agency, instrument, medium, mouthpiece, organ, spokesman, spokesperson, spokeswoman, vehicle ~*v.* **4.** air, articulate, assert, come out with (*Inf.*), declare, divulge, enunciate, express, give expression *or* utterance to, put into words, say, utter, ventilate

void of resources. **5.** useless: *all his efforts were rendered void.* **6.** (of a card suit or player) having no cards in a particular suit: *his spades were void.* ~*n.* **7.** an empty space or area: *the huge desert voids of Asia.* **8.** a feeling or condition of loneliness or deprivation. **9.** a lack of any cards in one suit: *to have a void in spades.* ~*vb.* (mainly *tr.*) **10.** to make ineffective or invalid. **11.** to empty (contents, etc.) or make empty of contents. **12.** (*also intr.*) to discharge the contents of (the bowels or urinary bladder). —**'voidable** *adj.* —**'voider** *n.*

voile (vɔɪl) *n.* a light semitransparent fabric of silk, rayon, cotton, etc., used for dresses, scarves, shirts, etc.

vol. *abbrev. for:* **1.** volcano. **2.** volume. **3.** volunteer.

volatile ('vɒlə,taɪl) *adj.* **1.** (of a substance) capable of readily changing from a solid or liquid form to a vapour. **2.** (of persons) disposed to caprice or inconstancy. **3.** (of circumstances) liable to sudden change. **4.** lasting only a short time: *volatile business interests.* **5.** *Computers.* (of a memory) not retaining stored information when the power supply is cut off. ~*n.* **6.** a volatile substance. —**'volatileness** *or* **volatility** (,vɒlə'tɪlɪtɪ) *n.*

volatilize *or* **-lise** (vɒ'lætɪ,laɪz) *vb.* to change or cause to change from a solid or liquid to a vapour. —**vo'lati,lizable** *or* **-,lisable** *adj.* —**vo,latili'zation** *or* **-li'sation** *n.*

vol-au-vent (French vɔlo'vɑ̃) *n.* a very light puff pastry case filled with a savoury mixture in a sauce.

volcanic (vɒl'kænɪk) *adj.* **1.** of, produced by, or characterized by the presence of volcanoes: *a volcanic region.* **2.** suggestive of or resembling an erupting volcano: *a volcanic era.* —**vol'canically** *adv.* —**volcanicity** (,vɒlkə-'nɪsɪtɪ) *n.*

volcano (vɒl'keɪnəʊ) *n., pl.* **-noes** *or* **-nos.** **1.** an opening in the earth's crust from which molten lava, rock fragments, ashes, dust, and gases are ejected from below the earth's surface. **2.** a mountain formed from volcanic material ejected from a vent in a central crater.

vole (vəʊl) *n.* any of various small rodents, mostly of Eurasia and North America, having a stocky body, short tail, and inconspicuous ears.

volition (və'lɪʃən) *n.* **1.** the act of exercising the will: *of one's own volition.* **2.** the faculty of conscious choice, decision, and intention. **3.** the resulting choice or resolution. —**vo'litional** *adj.*

volitive ('vɒlɪtɪv) *adj.* of, relating to, or emanating from the will.

volley ('vɒlɪ) *n.* **1.** the simultaneous discharge of several weapons, esp. firearms. **2.** the projectiles or missiles so discharged. **3.** a burst of oaths, protests, etc., occurring simultaneously or in rapid succession. **4.** *Sport.* a stroke, shot, or kick at a moving ball before it hits the ground. **5.** *Cricket.* the flight of such a ball or the ball itself. ~*vb.* **6.** to discharge (weapons, etc.) in or as if in a volley or (of weapons, etc.) to be discharged. **7.** (*tr.*) to utter vehemently. **8.** (*tr.*) *Sport.* to strike or kick (a moving ball) before it hits the ground. —**'volleyer** *n.*

volleyball ('vɒlɪ,bɔːl) *n.* **1.** a game in which two teams hit a large ball back and forth over a high net with their hands. **2.** the ball used in this game.

vols. *abbrev. for* volumes.

volt[1] (vəʊlt) *n.* the derived SI unit of electric potential; the potential difference between two points on a conductor carrying a current of 1 ampere, when the power dissipated between these points is 1 watt. Symbol: V

volt[2] *or* **volte** (vɒlt) *n.* **1.** a small circle executed in dressage. **2.** a leap made in fencing to avoid an opponent's thrust.

voltage ('vəʊltɪdʒ) *n.* an electromotive force or potential difference expressed in volts.

voltaic (vɒl'teɪɪk) *adj.* another word for **galvanic** (sense 1).

volte-face ('vɒlt'fɑːs) *n., pl.* **volte-face.** **1.** a reversal, as in opinion. **2.** a change of position so as to look, lie, etc., in the opposite direction.

voltmeter ('vəʊlt,miːtə) *n.* an instrument for measuring potential difference or electromotive force.

voluble ('vɒljʊbəl) *adj.* **1.** talking easily and at length. **2.** *Arch.* easily turning or rotating. **3.** *Rare.* (of a plant) twining or twisting. —**,volu'bility** *or* **'volubleness** *n.* —**'volubly** *adv.*

volume ('vɒljuːm) *n.* **1.** the magnitude of the three-dimensional space enclosed within or occupied by an object, geometric solid, etc. **2.** a large mass or quantity: *the volume of protest.* **3.** an amount or total: *the volume of exports.* **4.** fullness of sound. **5.** the control on a radio, etc., for adjusting the intensity of sound. **6.** a bound collection of printed or written pages; book. **7.** any of several books either bound in an identical format or part of a series. **8.** the complete set of issues of a periodical over a specified period, esp. one year. **9.** *History.* a roll of parchment, etc. **10. speak volumes.** to convey much significant information.

volumetric (,vɒlju'metrɪk) *adj.* of, concerning, or using measurement by volume: *volumetric analysis.* —**,volu-'metrically** *adv.*

voluminous (və'luːmɪnəs) *adj.* **1.** of great size, quantity, or extent. **2.** (of writing) consisting of or sufficient to fill volumes. —**voluminosity** (və,luːmɪ'nɒsɪtɪ) *n.* —**vo'luminously** *adv.*

voluntary ('vɒləntərɪ) *adj.* **1.** performed, undertaken, or brought about by free choice or willingly: *a voluntary donation.* **2.** (of persons) serving or acting in a specified function without compulsion or promise of remuneration: *a voluntary social worker.* **3.** done by, composed of, or functioning with the aid of volunteers: *a voluntary association.* **4.** exercising or having the faculty of willing: *a voluntary agent.* **5.** spontaneous: *voluntary laughter.* **6.** *Law.* **a.** acting or done without legal obligation, compulsion, or persuasion. **b.** made without payment or recompense: *a voluntary conveyance.* **7.** (of the muscles of the limbs, neck, etc.) having their action controlled by the will. **8.** maintained by the voluntary actions or contributions of individuals and not by the state: *voluntary schools.* ~*n., pl.* **-taries.** **9.** *Music.* a composition or improvisation, usually for organ, played at the beginning or end of a church service. —**'voluntarily** *adv.*

volunteer (,vɒlən'tɪə) *n.* **1. a.** a person who performs or offers to perform voluntary service. **b.** (*as modifier*): *a volunteer system.* **2.** a person who freely undertakes military service. **3. a.** a plant that grows from seed that has not been deliberately sown. **b.** (*as modifier*): *a volunteer plant.* ~*vb.* **4.** to offer (oneself or one's services) for an undertaking by choice and without request or obligation. **5.** (*tr.*) to perform, give, or communicate voluntarily: *to volunteer help.* **6.** (*intr.*) to enlist voluntarily for military service.

voluptuary (və'lʌptjʊərɪ) *n., pl.* **-aries.** **1.** a person devoted to luxury and sensual pleasures. ~*adj.* **2.** of or furthering sensual gratification or luxury.

voluptuous (və'lʌptjʊəs) *adj.* **1.** relating to, characterized by, or consisting of pleasures of the body or senses. **2.** devoted or addicted to sensual indulgence or luxurious pleasures. **3.** sexually alluring, esp. through shapeliness or fullness: *a voluptuous woman.* —**vo'luptuously** *adv.* —**vo'luptuousness** *n.*

THESAURUS

void *adj.* **1.** bare, clear, drained, emptied, empty, free, tenantless, unfilled, unoccupied, vacant **2.** *With of* destitute, devoid, lacking, without **3.** dead, ineffective, ineffectual, inoperative, invalid, nonviable, nugatory, null and void, unenforceable, useless, vain, worthless ~*n.* **4.** blank, blankness, emptiness, gap, lack, opening, space, vacuity, vacuum, want ~*v.* **5.** discharge, drain, eject, eliminate (*Physiol.*), emit, empty, evacuate **6.** abnegate, cancel, invalidate, nullify, rescind

volatile airy, changeable, erratic, explosive, fickle, flighty, gay, giddy, inconstant, lively, mercurial, sprightly, unsettled, unsta-

ble, unsteady, up and down (*Inf.*), variable, whimsical

volition choice, choosing, determination, discretion, election, free will, option, preference, purpose, resolution, will

volley *n.* barrage, blast, bombardment, burst, cannonade, discharge, explosion, fusillade, hail, salvo, shower

volubility fluency, garrulity, gift of the gab (*Inf.*), glibness, loquaciousness, loquacity

voluble articulate, blessed with the gift of the gab (*Inf.*), fluent, forthcoming, glib, loquacious, talkative

volume 1. aggregate, amount, body, bulk, capacity, compass, cubic content, dimen-

sions, mass, quantity, total **2.** book, publication, tome, treatise

voluminous ample, big, billowing, bulky, capacious, cavernous, copious, full, large, massive, prolific, roomy, vast

voluntarily by choice, freely, of one's own accord, of one's own free will, on one's own initiative, willingly, without being asked, without prompting

voluntary discretional, free, gratuitous, honorary, intended, intentional, optional, spontaneous, uncompelled, unconstrained, unforced, unpaid, volunteer, willing

volunteer *v.* advance, let oneself in for (*Inf.*), need no invitation, offer, offer one's services, present, proffer, propose, put for-

volute ('vɒljuːt, vəˈluːt) n. 1. a spiral or twisting turn, form, or object. 2. Also called: **helix.** a carved ornament, esp. as used on an Ionic capital, that has the form of a spiral scroll. 3. any of the whorls of the spirally coiled shell of a snail or similar gastropod mollusc. 4. any of a family of tropical marine gastropod molluscs having a spiral shell with beautiful markings. ~adj. also **voluted** (vəˈluːtɪd). 5. having the form of a volute; spiral. —**voˈlution** n.

vomit ('vɒmɪt) vb. 1. to eject (the contents of the stomach) through the mouth as the result of involuntary muscular spasms of the stomach and oesophagus. 2. to eject or be ejected forcefully. ~n. 3. the matter ejected in vomiting. 4. the act of vomiting. 5. an emetic. —'**vomiter** n.

voodoo ('vuːduː) n., pl. -doos. 1. Also called: **voodooism.** a religious cult involving witchcraft, common among Negroes in Haiti and other Caribbean islands. 2. a person who practises voodoo. 3. a charm, spell, or fetish involved in voodoo worship. ~adj. 4. relating to or associated with voodoo. ~vb. -dooing, -dooed. 5. (tr.) to affect by or as if by the power of voodoo. —'**voodooist** n.

voracious (vɒˈreɪʃəs) adj. 1. devouring or craving food in great quantities. 2. very eager or unremitting in some activity: voracious reading. —**voracity** (vɒˈræsɪtɪ) or **voˈraciousness** n.

vortex ('vɔːteks) n., pl. -texes or -tices (-tɪˌsiːz). 1. a whirling mass or motion of liquid, gas, flame, etc., such as the spiralling movement of water around a whirlpool. 2. any activity or way of life regarded as irresistibly engulfing. —**vortical** ('vɔːtɪkəl) adj.

votary ('vəʊtərɪ) n., pl. -ries, also **votarist.** 1. R.C. Church, Eastern Churches. a person, such as a monk or nun, who has dedicated himself or herself to religion by taking vows. 2. a devoted adherent of a religion, cause, etc. ~adj. 3. ardently devoted to the services or worship of God or a saint. —'**votaress** fem. n.

vote (vəʊt) n. 1. an indication of choice, opinion, or will on a question, such as the choosing of a candidate: 10 votes for Jones. 2. the opinion of a group of persons as determined by voting: it was put to the vote. 3. a body of votes or voters collectively: the Jewish vote. 4. the total number of votes cast. 5. the ticket, ballot, etc., by which a vote is expressed. 6. a. the right to vote; franchise. b. a person regarded as the embodiment of this right. 7. a means of voting, such as a ballot. 8. Chiefly Brit. a grant or other proposition to be voted upon. ~vb. 9. (when tr., takes a clause as object or an infinitive) to express or signify (one's preference or will) (for or against some question, etc.): to vote by ballot. 10. (intr.) to declare oneself as being (something or in favour of something) by exercising one's vote: to vote socialist. 11. (tr.; foll. by into or out of, etc.) to appoint or elect (a person to or from a particular post): he was voted out of office. 12. to determine the condition of in a specified way by voting: the court voted itself out of existence. 13. to authorize or allow by voting: vote us a rise. 14. Inf. to declare by common opinion: the party was voted a failure. —'**votable** or '**voteable** adj.

vote down vb. (tr., adv.) to decide against or defeat in a vote: the bill was voted down.

voter ('vəʊtə) n. a person who can or does vote.

votive ('vəʊtɪv) adj. 1. given, undertaken, or dedicated in fulfilment of or in accordance with a vow. 2. R.C. Church. having the nature of a voluntary offering: a votive Mass.

vouch (vaʊtʃ) vb. 1. (intr.; usually foll. by for) to give personal assurance: I'll vouch for his safety. 2. (when tr., usually takes a clause as object; when intr., usually foll. by for) to furnish supporting evidence (for) or func-

tion as proof (of). 3. (tr.) Arch. to cite (authors, principles, etc.) in support of something.

voucher ('vaʊtʃə) n. 1. a document serving as evidence for some claimed transaction, as the receipt or expenditure of money. 2. Brit. a ticket or card serving as a substitute for cash: a gift voucher. 3. a person or thing that vouches for the truth of some statement, etc.

vouchsafe (ˌvaʊtʃˈseɪf) vb. (tr.) 1. to give or grant or condescend to give or grant: she vouchsafed no reply. 2. (may take a clause as object or an infinitive) to agree, promise, or permit, often graciously or condescendingly: he vouchsafed to come yesterday.

vow (vaʊ) n. 1. a solemn or earnest pledge or promise binding the person making it to perform a specified act or behave in a certain way. 2. a solemn promise made to a deity or saint, by which the promiser pledges himself to some future act or way of life. 3. **take vows.** to enter a religious order and commit oneself to its rule of life by the vows of poverty, chastity, and obedience. ~vb. 4. (tr.; may take a clause as object or an infinitive) to pledge, promise, or undertake solemnly: he vowed to return. 5. (tr.) to dedicate or consecrate to God or a saint. 6. (tr.; usually takes a clause as object) to assert or swear emphatically. 7. (intr.) Arch. to declare solemnly. —'**vower** n.

vowel ('vaʊəl) n. 1. Phonetics. a voiced speech sound whose articulation is characterized by the absence of obstruction in the vocal tract, allowing the breath stream free passage. The timbre of a vowel is chiefly determined by the position of the tongue and the lips. 2. a letter or character representing a vowel. —'**vowel-**,**like** adj.

vox (vɒks) n., pl. **voces** ('vəʊsiːz). a voice or sound.

vox populi ('pɒpjʊˌlaɪ) n. the voice of the people; popular or public opinion.

voyage ('vɔɪdʒ) n. 1. a journey, travel, or passage, esp. one to a distant land or by sea or air. ~vb. 2. to travel over or traverse (something): we will voyage to Africa. —'**voyager** n.

voyeur (vwaɪˈɜː) n. a person who obtains sexual pleasure from the observation of people undressing, having intercourse, etc. —**voˈyeurism** n. —,**voyeur'istic** adj.

V. Rev. abbrev. for Very Reverend.

vs. abbrev. for versus.

V.S. abbrev. for Veterinary Surgeon.

V-sign n. 1. (in Britain) an offensive gesture made by sticking up the index and middle fingers with the palm of the hand inwards. 2. a similar gesture with the palm outwards meaning victory or peace.

V.S.O. abbrev. for: 1. very superior old: used to indicate that a brandy, port, etc., is between 12 and 17 years old. 2. (in Britain) Voluntary Service Overseas: an organization that sends young volunteers to use and teach their skills in developing countries.

V.S.O.P. abbrev. for very special old pale: used to indicate that a brandy, port, etc., is between 20 and 25 years old.

VTOL ('viːtɒl) n. vertical takeoff and landing; a system in which an aircraft can take off and land vertically.

VTR abbrev. for video tape recorder.

vulcanite ('vʌlkəˌnaɪt) n. a hard usually black rubber produced by vulcanizing natural rubber with sulphur. It is used for electrical insulators, etc. Also called: **ebonite.**

vulcanize or **-nise** ('vʌlkəˌnaɪz) vb. (tr.) 1. to treat (rubber) with sulphur under heat and pressure to improve elasticity and strength or to produce a hard substance such as vulcanite. 2. to treat (substances other than rubber) by a similar process in order to improve

---

THESAURUS

ward, put oneself at (someone's) disposal, step forward, suggest, tender
voluptuous 1. epicurean, hedonistic, licentious, luxurious, pleasure-loving, self-indulgent, sensual, sybaritic 2. ample, buxom, curvaceous (Inf.), enticing, erotic, full-bosomed, provocative, seductive, shapely, well-stacked (Brit. sl.)
voluptuousness carnality, curvaceousness (Inf.), licentiousness, opulence, seductiveness, sensuality, shapeliness
vomit v. belch forth, be sick, bring up, disgorge, eject, emit, heave, puke (Sl.), regurgi-

tate, retch, sick up (Inf.), spew out or up, throw up (Inf.)
voracious avid, devouring, gluttonous, greedy, hungry, insatiable, omnivorous, prodigious, rapacious, ravening, ravenous, uncontrolled, unquenchable
vote n. 1. ballot, franchise, plebiscite, poll, referendum, right to vote, show of hands, suffrage ~v. 2. ballot, cast one's vote, elect, go to the polls, opt, return 3. Inf. declare, judge, pronounce, propose, recommend, suggest
vouch Usually with **for** affirm, answer for, assert, asseverate, attest to, back, certify,

confirm, give assurance of, go bail for, guarantee, stand witness, support, swear to, uphold
vouchsafe accord, cede, condescend to give, confer, deign, favour (someone) with, grant, yield
vow 1. v. affirm, consecrate, dedicate, devote, pledge, promise, swear, undertake solemnly 2. n. oath, pledge, promise, troth (Archaic)
voyage n. crossing, cruise, journey, passage, travels, trip

their properties. —ˌvulcani'zation or -ni'sation n.

Vulg. abbrev. for Vulgate.

vulgar ('vʌlgə) adj. **1.** marked by lack of taste, culture, delicacy, manners, etc.: vulgar language. **2.** (often cap.; usually prenominal) denoting a form of a language, esp. of Latin, current among common people, esp. at a period when the formal language is archaic. **3.** Arch. of or current among the great mass of common people. —'vulgarly adv.

vulgar fraction n. another name for **simple fraction.**

vulgarian (vʌl'gɛərɪən) n. a vulgar person, esp. one who is rich or has pretensions to good taste.

vulgarism ('vʌlgəˌrɪzəm) n. **1.** a coarse, crude, or obscene expression. **2.** a word or phrase found only in the vulgar form of a language.

vulgarity (vʌl'gærɪtɪ) n., pl. -ties. **1.** the condition of being vulgar; lack of good manners. **2.** a vulgar action, phrase, etc.

vulgarize or **-rise** ('vʌlgəˌraɪz) vb. (tr.) **1.** to make (something little known or difficult to understand) widely known or popular among the public. **2.** to make commonplace or vulgar. —ˌvulgari'zation or -ri'sation n.

Vulgar Latin n. any of the dialects of Latin spoken in the Roman Empire other than classical Latin.

Vulgate ('vʌlgeɪt, -gɪt) n. **a.** (from the 13th century onwards) the fourth-century Latin version of the Bible produced by Jerome. **b.** (as modifier): the Vulgate version.

vulnerable ('vʌlnərəbəl) adj. **1.** capable of being physically or emotionally wounded or hurt. **2.** open to temptation, censure, etc. **3.** Mil. exposed to attack. **4.** Bridge. (of a side who have won one game towards rubber) subject to increased bonuses or penalties. —ˌvulnera'bility n. —'vulnerably adv.

vulpine ('vʌlpaɪn) adj. **1.** of, relating to, or resembling a fox. **2.** crafty, clever, etc.

vulture ('vʌltʃə) n. **1.** any of various very large diurnal birds of prey of Africa, Asia, and warm parts of Europe, typically having broad wings and soaring flight and feeding on carrion. **2.** any similar bird of North, Central, and South America. **3.** a person or thing that preys greedily and ruthlessly on others, esp. the helpless. —**vulturine** ('vʌltʃəˌraɪn) or **'vulturous** adj.

vulva ('vʌlvə) n., pl. -vae (-viː) or -vas. the external genitals of human females, including the labia, mons pubis, clitoris, and the vaginal orifice. —'vulvar adj. —**vulvitis** (vʌl'vaɪtɪs) n.

v.v. abbrev. for vice versa.

THESAURUS

vulgar 1. blue, boorish, cheap and nasty, coarse, common, crude, dirty, flashy, gaudy, gross, ill-bred, impolite, improper, indecent, indecorous, indelicate, low, nasty, naughty, off colour, ribald, risqué, rude, suggestive, tasteless, tawdry, uncouth, unmannerly, unrefined 2. general, native, ordinary, unrefined, vernacular

vulgarity bad taste, coarseness, crudeness, crudity, gaudiness, grossness, indecorum, indelicacy, lack of refinement, ribaldry, rudeness, suggestiveness, tastelessness, tawdriness

vulnerable accessible, assailable, defenceless, exposed, open to attack, sensitive, susceptible, tender, thin-skinned, unprotected, weak, wide open

W

w or **W** ('dʌbəl,juː) n., pl. **w's, W's,** or **Ws. 1.** the 23rd letter of the English alphabet. **2.** a speech sound represented by this letter, usually a bilabial semivowel, as in *web.*

W symbol for: **1.** watt. **2.** West. **3.** Physics. work. **4.** Chem. tungsten. **5.** women's (size).

w. abbrev. for: **1.** week. **2.** weight. **3.** width. **4.** wife. **5.** with. **6.** Cricket. **a.** wide. **b.** wicket.

W. abbrev. for: **1.** Wales. **2.** Welsh.

W.A. abbrev. for Western Australia.

WAAC (wæk) n. **1.** acronym for Women's Army Auxiliary Corps. **2.** Also called: **waac.** a member of this corps.

wacky ('wækɪ) adj. **wackier, wackiest.** Sl. eccentric or unpredictable. —**'wackily** adv. —**'wackiness** n.

wad (wɒd) n. **1.** a small mass or ball of fibrous or soft material, such as cotton wool, used esp. for packing or stuffing. **2. a.** a plug of paper, cloth, leather, etc., pressed against a charge to hold it in place in a muzzle-loading cannon. **b.** a disc of paper, felt, etc., used to hold in place the powder and shot in a shotgun cartridge. **3.** a roll or bundle of something, esp. of banknotes. ~vb. **wadding, wadded. 4.** to form (something) into a wad. **5.** (tr.) to roll into a wad or bundle. **6.** (tr.) **a.** to hold (a charge) in place with a wad. **b.** to insert a wad into (a gun). **7.** (tr.) to pack or stuff with wadding.

wadding ('wɒdɪŋ) n. **1. a.** any fibrous or soft substance used as padding, stuffing, etc. **b.** a piece of this. **2.** material for wads used in cartridges or guns.

waddle ('wɒdəl) vb. (intr.) **1.** to walk with short steps, rocking slightly from side to side. ~n. **2.** a swaying gait or motion. —**'waddler** n.

wade (weɪd) vb. **1.** to walk with the feet immersed in (water, a stream, etc.). **2.** (intr.; often foll. by through) to proceed with difficulty: to wade through a book. **3.** (intr.; foll. by in or into) to attack energetically. ~n. **4.** the act or an instance of wading. —**'wadable** or **'wadeable** adj.

wader ('weɪdə) n. **1.** a person or thing that wades. **2.** Also called: **wading bird.** any of various long-legged birds, esp. herons, storks, etc., that live near water and feed on fish, etc.

waders ('weɪdəz) pl. n. long waterproof boots, sometimes extending to the chest like trousers, worn by anglers.

wadi or **wady** ('wɒdɪ) n., pl. **-dies.** a watercourse in N Africa and Arabia, dry except in the rainy season.

wafer ('weɪfə) n. **1.** a thin crisp sweetened biscuit, served with ice cream, etc. **2.** Christianity. a thin disc of unleavened bread used in the Eucharist. **3.** Pharmacol. an envelope of rice paper enclosing a medicament. **4.** Electronics. a small thin slice of semiconductor material, such as silicon, that is separated into numerous individual components or circuits. **5.** a small thin disc of adhesive material used to seal letters, etc. ~vb. **6.** (tr.) to seal or fasten with a wafer. —**'wafery** adj.

waffle¹ ('wɒfəl) n. Chiefly U.S. **a.** a crisp golden-brown pancake, with deep indentations on both sides. **b.** (as modifier): waffle iron.

waffle² ('wɒfəl) Inf., chiefly Brit. ~vb. **1.** (intr.; often foll. by on) to speak or write in a vague and wordy manner. ~n. **2.** vague and wordy speech or writing.

waft (wɑːft, wɒft) vb. **1.** to carry or be carried gently on or as if on the air or water. ~n. **2.** the act or an instance of wafting. **3.** something, such as a scent, carried on the air. **4.** Naut. (formerly) a signal flag hoisted furled to signify various messages depending on where it was flown.

wag¹ (wæg) vb. **wagging, wagged. 1.** to move or cause to move rapidly and repeatedly from side to side or up and down. **2.** to move (the tongue) or (of the tongue) to be moved rapidly in talking, esp. in gossip. **3.** to move (the finger) or (of the finger) to be moved from side to side, in or as in admonition. ~n. **4.** the act or an instance of wagging.

wag² (wæg) n. a humorous or jocular person; wit. —**'waggish** adj.

wage (weɪdʒ) n. **1.** (often pl.) payment in return for work or services, esp. that made to workmen on a daily, hourly, weekly, or piecework basis. Cf. **salary. 2.** (pl.) Econ. the portion of the national income accruing to labour as earned income, as contrasted with the unearned income accruing to capital in the form of rent, interest, and dividends. **3.** (often pl.) recompense, return, or yield. ~vb. (tr.) **4.** to engage in. —**'wageless** adj.

wager ('weɪdʒə) n. **1.** an agreement to pay an amount of money as a result of the outcome of an unsettled matter. **2.** an amount staked on the outcome of such an event. **3. wager of battle.** (in medieval Britain) a pledge to do battle to decide guilt or innocence by single combat. **4. wager of law.** English legal history. a form of trial in which the accused offered to make oath of his innocence, supported by the oaths of 11 of his neighbours declaring their belief in his statements. ~vb. **5.** (when tr., may take a clause as object) to risk or bet (something) on the outcome of an unsettled matter. —**'wagerer** n.

waggle ('wægəl) vb. **1.** to move or cause to move with a rapid shaking or wobbling motion. ~n. **2.** a rapid shaking or wobbling motion. —**'waggly** adj.

Wagnerian (vɑːgˈnɪərɪən) adj. **1.** of or suggestive of the dramatic musical compositions of Richard Wagner (1813–83), German composer, their massive scale, dramatic and emotional intensity, etc. ~n. also **Wagnerite. 2.** a follower or disciple of the music or theories of Richard Wagner.

wagon or **waggon** ('wægən) n. **1.** any of various types of wheeled vehicles, ranging from carts to lorries, esp. a vehicle with four wheels drawn by a horse, tractor, etc., and used for carrying heavy loads. **2.** Brit. a railway freight truck, esp. an open one. **3.** an obsolete word for chariot. **4. on** (or **off**) **the wagon.** Inf. abstaining (or no longer abstaining) from alcoholic drinks. —**'wagonless** or **'waggonless** adj.

wagonette or **waggonette** (ˌwægəˈnɛt) n. a light four-wheeled horse-drawn vehicle with two lengthwise seats facing each other behind a crosswise driver's seat.

wagtail ('wæg,teɪl) n. any of various passerine songbirds of Eurasia and Africa, having a very long tail that wags when the bird walks.

waif (weɪf) n. **1.** a person, esp. a child, who is homeless, friendless, or neglected. **2.** anything found and not claimed, the owner being unknown.

THESAURUS

wad ball, block, bundle, chunk, hunk, lump, mass, plug, roll

wadding filler, lining, packing, padding, stuffing

waddle rock, shuffle, sway, toddle, totter, wobble

wade 1. ford, paddle, splash, walk through 2. With **through** drudge, labour, peg away, plough through, toil, work one's way 3. With **in** or **into** assail, attack, get stuck in (Sl.), go for, launch oneself at, light into (Inf.), set about, tackle, tear into (Inf.)

waffle 1. v. blather, jabber, prate, prattle, rabbit on (Brit. sl.), verbalize, witter on (Inf.) 2. n. blather, jabber, padding, prating, prattle, prolixity, verbiage, verbosity, wordiness

waft 1. v. bear, be carried, carry, convey, drift, float, ride, transmit, transport 2. n. breath, breeze, current, draught, puff, whiff

wag 1. v. bob, flutter, nod, oscillate, quiver, rock, shake, stir, vibrate, waggle, wave, wiggle 2. n. bob, flutter, nod, oscillation, quiver, shake, toss, vibration, waggle, wave, wiggle

wage 1. n. Also **wages** allowance, compensation, earnings, emolument, fee, hire, pay, payment, recompense, remuneration, reward, stipend 2. v. carry on, conduct, engage in, practise, proceed with, prosecute, pursue, undertake

wager 1. n. bet, flutter (Brit. inf.), gamble, pledge, punt, stake, venture 2. v. bet, chance, gamble, hazard, lay, pledge, punt, put on, risk, speculate, stake, venture

waggle 1. v. flutter, oscillate, shake, wag, wave, wiggle, wobble 2. n. flutter, oscillation, shake, wag, wave, wiggle, wobble

waif foundling, orphan, stray

wail (weɪl) vb. 1. (intr.) to utter a prolonged high-pitched cry, as of grief or misery. 2. (intr.) to make a sound resembling such a cry: the wind wailed in the trees. 3. (tr.) to lament, esp. with mournful sounds. ~n. 4. a prolonged high-pitched mournful cry or sound. —'wailer n. —'wailingly adv.

wain (weɪn) n. Chiefly poetic. a farm wagon or cart.

wainscot ('weɪnskət) n. 1. Also called: **wainscoting** or **wainscotting.** a lining applied to the walls of a room, esp. one of wood panelling. 2. the lower part of the walls of a room, esp. when finished in a material different from the upper part. 3. fine quality oak used as wainscot. ~vb. 4. (tr.) to line (a wall of a room) with a wainscot.

waist (weɪst) n. 1. Anat. the constricted part of the trunk between the ribs and hips. 2. the part of a garment covering the waist. 3. the middle part of an object that resembles the waist in narrowness or position. 4. the middle part of a ship. 5. the middle section of an aircraft fuselage. 6. the constriction between the thorax and abdomen in wasps and similar insects. —'waistless adj.

waistband ('weɪst,bænd) n. an encircling band of material to finish and strengthen a skirt or trousers at the waist.

waistcoat ('weɪs,kəʊt) n. 1. a man's sleeveless waistlength garment worn under a suit jacket, usually buttoning up the front. 2. a similar garment worn by women. ~U.S. name: **vest.** —'waist,coated adj.

waistline ('weɪst,laɪn) n. 1. a line around the body at the narrowest part of the waist. 2. the intersection of the bodice and the skirt of a dress, etc., or the level of this.

wait (weɪt) vb. 1. (when intr., often foll. by for, until, or to) to stay in one place or remain inactive in expectation (of something). 2. to delay temporarily or be temporarily delayed: that work can wait. 3. (when intr., usually foll. by for) (of things) to be ready or at hand; be in store (for a person): supper was waiting for them when they got home. 4. (intr.) to act as a waiter or waitress. ~n. 5. the act or an instance of waiting. 6. a period of waiting. 7. (pl.) Rare. a band of musicians who go around the streets, esp. at Christmas, singing and playing carols. 8. **lie in wait.** to prepare an ambush (for someone).

waiter ('weɪtə) n. 1. a man whose occupation is to serve at table, as in a restaurant. 2. a person who waits. 3. a tray or salver.

waiting game n. the postponement of action or decision in order to gain the advantage.

waiting list n. a list of people waiting to obtain some object, treatment, status, etc.

waiting room n. a room in which people may wait, as at a railway station, doctor's or dentist's surgery, etc.

wait on or **upon** vb. (intr., prep.) 1. to serve at the table of. 2. to act as an attendant to.

waitress ('weɪtrɪs) n. a woman who serves at table, as in a restaurant.

wait up vb. (intr., adv.) to delay going to bed in order to await some event.

waive (weɪv) vb. (tr.) 1. to set aside or relinquish: to waive one's right to something. 2. to refrain from enforcing or applying (a law, penalty, etc.). 3. to defer.

waiver ('weɪvə) n. 1. the voluntary relinquishment, expressly or by implication, of some claim or right. 2. the act or an instance of relinquishing a claim or right. 3. a formal statement in writing of such relinquishment.

wake¹ (weɪk) vb. **waking, woke, woken.** 1. (often foll. by up) to rouse or become roused from sleep. 2. (often foll. by up) to rouse or become roused from inactivity. 3. (intr.; often foll. by to or up to) to become conscious or aware: at last he woke up to the situation. 4. (intr.) to be or remain awake. ~n. 5. a watch or vigil held over the body of a dead person during the night before burial. 6. (in Ireland) the festivities held at a funeral. 7. the patronal or dedication festival of English parish churches. 8. a solemn or ceremonial vigil. 9. (usually pl.) an annual holiday in any of various towns in northern England, when the local factory or factories close. —'waker n.

▷ **Usage.** Where there is an object and the sense is the literal one wake (up) and waken are the commonest forms: I wakened him; I woke him (up). Both verbs are also commonly used without an object: I woke up. Awake and awaken are preferred to other forms of wake where the sense is a figurative one: he awoke to the danger.

wake² (weɪk) n. 1. the waves or track left by a vessel or other object moving through water. 2. the track or path left by anything that has passed: wrecked houses in the wake of the hurricane.

wakeful ('weɪkfʊl) adj. 1. unable or unwilling to sleep. 2. sleepless. 3. alert. —'wakefully adv. —'wakefulness n.

waken ('weɪkən) vb. to rouse or be roused from sleep or some other inactive state.

▷ **Usage.** See at wake¹.

wale (weɪl) n. 1. the raised mark left on the skin after the stroke of a rod or whip. 2. the weave or texture of a fabric, such as the ribs in corduroy. 3. Naut. a ridge of planking along the rail of a ship. ~vb. 4. to raise a wale or wales on by striking. 5. to weave with a wale.

walk (wɔːk) vb. 1. (intr.) to move along or travel on foot at a moderate rate; advance in such a manner that at least one foot is always on the ground. 2. (tr.) to pass through, on, or over on foot, esp. habitually. 3. (tr.) to cause, assist, or force to move along at a moderate rate: to walk a dog. 4. (tr.) to escort or conduct by walking: to walk someone home. 5. (intr.) (of ghosts, spirits, etc.) to appear or move about in visible form. 6. (intr.) to follow a certain course or way of life: to walk in misery. 7. (tr.) to bring into a certain condition by walking: I walked my shoes to shreds. 8. **walk the plank.** See plank (sense 4). 9. **walk on air.** to be delighted or exhilarated. 10. **walk tall.** U.S. inf. to have self-respect or pride. 11. **walk the streets.** to be a prostitute. ~n. 12. the act or an instance of walking. 13. the distance or extent walked. 14. a manner of walking; gait. 15. a place set aside for walking; promenade. 16. a chosen profession or sphere of activity (esp. in **walk of life**). 17. a. an arrangement of trees or shrubs in widely separated rows. b. the space between such rows. 18. an enclosed ground for the exercise or feeding of domestic animals, esp. horses. 19. Chiefly Brit. the route covered in the course of work, as by a tradesman or postman. 20. Obs. the section of a forest controlled by a keeper. ~See also walk out, etc. —'walkable adj.

walkabout ('wɔːkə,baʊt) n. 1. a periodic nomadic excursion into the Australian bush made by an Aborigine.

THESAURUS

wail 1. v. bemoan, bewail, cry, deplore, grieve, howl, keen, lament, ululate, weep, yowl 2. n. complaint, cry, grief, howl, keen, lament, lamentation, moan, ululation, weeping, yowl

wait 1. v. abide, bide one's time, cool one's heels, dally, delay, hang fire, hold back, hold on (Inf.), linger, mark time, pause, remain, rest, stand by, stay, tarry 2. n. delay, halt, hold-up, interval, pause, rest, stay

waiter, waitress attendant, server, steward, stewardess

wait on or **upon** attend, minister to, serve, tend

waive abandon, defer, dispense with, forgo, give up, postpone, put off, refrain from, relinquish, remit, renounce, resign, set aside, surrender

waiver abandonment, abdication, disclaimer, giving up, relinquishment, remission, renunciation, resignation, setting aside, surrender

wake¹ v. 1. arise, awake, awaken, bestir, come to, get up, rouse, rouse from sleep, stir 2. activate, animate, arouse, awaken, enliven, excite, fire, galvanize, kindle, provoke, quicken, stimulate, stir up ~n. 3. deathwatch, funeral, vigil, watch

wake² aftermath, backwash, path, track, trail, train, wash, waves

wakeful 1. insomniac, restless, sleepless, unsleeping 2. alert, alive, attentive, heedful, observant, on guard, on the alert, on the lookout, on the qui vive, unsleeping, vigilant, wary, watchful

waken activate, animate, arouse, awake, awaken, be roused, come awake, come to,

enliven, fire, galvanize, get up, kindle, quicken, rouse, stimulate, stir

walk v. 1. advance, amble, foot it, go, go by shanks's pony (Inf.), go on foot, hike, hoof it (Sl.), march, move, pace, perambulate, promenade, saunter, step, stride, stroll, traipse (Inf.), tramp, travel on foot, trek, trudge 2. accompany, convoy, escort, take ~n. 3. constitutional, hike, march, perambulation, promenade, ramble, saunter, stroll, traipse (Inf.), tramp, trek, trudge, turn 4. carriage, gait, manner of walking, pace, step, stride 5. aisle, alley, avenue, esplanade, footpath, lane, path, pathway, pavement, promenade, sidewalk, trail 6. area, arena, calling, career, course, field, line, métier, profession, sphere, trade, vocation

2. an occasion when celebrities, royalty, etc., walk among and meet the public.

walker ('wɔːkə) n. **1.** a person who walks. **2.** Also called: **baby walker.** a tubular frame on wheels or casters to support a baby learning to walk. **3.** a similar support for walking, often with rubber feet, for use by the disabled or convalescents.

walkie-talkie or **walky-talky** (ˌwɔːkɪ'tɔːkɪ) n., pl. -**talkies.** a small combined radio transmitter and receiver that can be carried around by one person: widely used by the police, medical services, etc.

walk-in adj. (of a cupboard, etc.) large enough to allow a person to enter and move about in.

walking stick n. **1.** a stick or cane carried in the hand to assist walking. **2.** the usual U.S. name for **stick insect.**

walk-on n. **a.** a small part in a play or theatrical entertainment, esp. one without any lines. **b.** (as modifier): a walk-on part.

walk out vb. (intr., adv.) **1.** to leave without explanation, esp. in anger. **2.** to go on strike. **3. walk out on.** Inf. to abandon or desert. **4. walk out with.** Brit., obs. or dialect. to court or be courted by. ~n. **walkout.** **5.** a strike by workers. **6.** the act of leaving a meeting, conference, etc., as a protest.

walkover ('wɔːkˌəʊvə) n. **1.** Inf. an easy or unopposed victory. **2.** Horse racing. **a.** the running or walking over the course by the only contestant entered in a race at the time of starting. **b.** a race won in this way. ~vb. **walk over.** (intr., mainly prep.) **3.** (also adv.) to win a race by a walkover. **4.** Inf. to beat (an opponent) conclusively or easily.

walkway ('wɔːkˌweɪ) n. a passage or path for pedestrians, esp. one that is sheltered.

wall (wɔːl) n. **1. a.** a vertical construction made of stone, brick, wood, etc., with a length and height much greater than its thickness, used to enclose, divide, or support. **b.** (as modifier): wall hangings. Related adj.: **mural.** **2.** (often pl.) a structure or rampart built to protect and surround a position or place for defensive purposes. **3.** Anat. any lining, membrane, or investing part that encloses or bounds a bodily cavity or structure: abdominal wall. Technical name: **paries.** Related adj.: **parietal.** **4.** anything that suggests a wall in function or effect: a wall of fire. **5. bang one's head against a brick wall.** to try to achieve something impossible. **6. drive** (or **push**) **to the wall.** to force into an awkward situation. **7. go to the wall.** Inf. to be ruined. **8. go** (or **send**) **up the wall.** Sl. to become (or cause to become) crazy or furious. **9. have one's back to the wall.** to be in a very difficult situation. ~vb. (tr.) **10.** to protect, provide, or confine with or as if with a wall. **11.** (often foll. by up) to block (an opening) with a wall. **12.** (often foll. by in or up) to seal by or within a wall or walls. —**walled** adj. —**'wall-less** adj.

wallaby ('wɒləbɪ) n., pl. -**bies** or -**by.** any of various herbivorous marsupials of Australia and New Guinea, similar to but smaller than kangaroos.

Wallaby ('wɒləbɪ) n., pl. -**bies.** a member of the international rugby union football team of Australia.

wallah or **walla** ('wɒlə) n. (usually in combination) Inf. a person involved with or in charge of (a specified thing): the book wallah.

wall bars pl. n. a series of horizontal bars attached to a wall and used in gymnastics.

wallboard ('wɔːlˌbɔːd) n. a thin board made of materials, such as compressed wood fibres or gypsum plaster, between stiff paper, and used to cover walls, partitions, etc.

wallet ('wɒlɪt) n. **1.** a small folding case, usually of leather, for holding paper money, documents, etc. **2.** Arch., chiefly Brit. a rucksack or knapsack.

walleye ('wɔːlˌaɪ) n., pl. -**eyes** or -**eye.** **1.** a divergent squint. **2.** opacity of the cornea. **3.** an eye having a white or light-coloured iris. **4.** Also called: **walleyed pike.** a North American pikeperch valued as a food and game fish. —'**wall,eyed** adj.

wallflower ('wɔːlˌflaʊə) n. **1.** Also called: **gillyflower.** a cruciferous plant of S Europe, grown for its clusters of yellow, orange, brown, red, or purple fragrant flowers and naturalized on old walls, cliffs, etc. **2.** Inf. a person who stays on the fringes of a dance or party on account of lacking a partner or being shy.

Walloon (wɒ'luːn) n. **1.** a member of a French-speaking people living chiefly in S Belgium and adjacent parts of France. **2.** the French dialect of Belgium. ~adj. **3.** of or characteristic of the Walloons or their dialect.

wallop ('wɒləp) vb. **1.** (tr.) Inf. to beat soundly; strike hard. **2.** (tr.) Inf. to defeat utterly. **3.** (intr.) (of liquids) to boil violently. ~n. **4.** Inf. a hard blow. **5.** Inf. the ability to hit powerfully, as of a boxer. **6.** Inf. a forceful impression. **7.** Brit. sl. beer.

walloping ('wɒləpɪŋ) Inf. ~n. **1.** a thrashing. ~adj. **2.** (intensifier): a walloping drop in sales.

wallow ('wɒləʊ) vb. (intr.) **1.** (esp. of certain animals) to roll about in mud, water, etc., for pleasure. **2.** to move about with difficulty. **3.** to indulge oneself in possessions, emotion, etc.: to wallow in self-pity. ~n. **4.** the act or an instance of wallowing. **5.** a muddy place where animals wallow. —'**wallower** n.

wallpaper ('wɔːlˌpeɪpə) n. **1.** paper usually printed or embossed with designs for pasting onto walls and ceilings. ~vb. **2.** to cover (a surface) with wallpaper.

Wall Street n. a street in lower Manhattan, New York, where the Stock Exchange and major banks are situated, regarded as the embodiment of American finance.

wall-to-wall adj. (esp. of carpeting) completely covering a floor.

walnut ('wɔːlˌnʌt) n. **1.** any of a genus of deciduous trees of America, SE Europe, and Asia. They have aromatic leaves and flowers in catkins and are grown for their edible nuts and for their wood. **2.** the nut of any of these trees, having a wrinkled two-lobed seed and a hard wrinkled shell. **3.** the wood of any of these trees, used in making furniture, etc. **4.** a light yellowish-brown colour. ~adj. **5.** made from the wood of a walnut tree: a walnut table. **6.** of the colour walnut.

walrus ('wɔːlrəs, 'wɒl-) n., pl. -**ruses** or -**rus.** a mammal of northern seas, having a tough thick skin, upper canine teeth enlarged as tusks, and coarse whiskers and feeding mainly on shellfish.

waltz (wɔːls) n. **1.** a ballroom dance in triple time in which couples spin around as they progress round the room. **2.** a piece of music composed for or in the rhythm of this dance. ~vb. **3.** to dance or lead (someone) in or as in a waltz. —'**waltzer** n.

wampum ('wɒmpəm) n. (formerly) money used by North American Indians, made of cylindrical shells strung or woven together. Also called: **peag, peage.**

wan (wɒn) adj. **wanner, wannest. 1.** unnaturally pale, esp. from sickness, grief, etc. **2.** suggestive of ill health, unhappiness, etc. **3.** (of light, stars, etc.) faint or dim. —'**wanly** adv. —'**wanness** n.

wand (wɒnd) n. **1.** a slender supple stick or twig. **2.** a thin rod carried as a symbol of authority. **3.** a rod used by a magician, etc. **4.** Inf. a conductor's baton. **5.** Archery. a marker used to show the distance at which the archer stands from the target.

THESAURUS

walker footslogger, hiker, pedestrian, rambler, wayfarer

walkout industrial action, protest, stoppage, strike

walk out 1. flounce out, get up and go, leave suddenly, storm out, take off (Inf.) **2.** down tools, go on strike, stop work, strike, take industrial action, withdraw one's labour **3. With on** abandon, chuck (Inf.), desert, forsake, jilt, leave, leave in the lurch, pack in (Inf.), run away from, throw over

walkover child's play (Inf.), doddle (Brit. sl.), easy victory, picnic (Inf.), piece of cake

(Inf.), pushover (Sl.), snap (Inf.)

wall 1. divider, enclosure, panel, partition, screen **2.** barricade, breastwork, bulwark, embankment, fortification, palisade, parapet, rampart, stockade **3.** barrier, block, fence, hedge, impediment, obstacle, obstruction **4. go to the wall** Inf. be ruined, collapse, fail, fall, go bust (Inf.), go under **5. drive up the wall** Sl. annoy, dement, derange, drive crazy, drive insane, exasperate, infuriate, irritate, madden, send off one's head (Sl.), try

wallet case, holder, notecase, pocketbook, pouch, purse

wallow 1. lie, roll about, splash around, tumble, welter **2.** flounder, lurch, stagger, stumble, wade **3.** bask, delight, glory, indulge oneself, luxuriate, relish, revel, take pleasure

wan 1. anaemic, ashen, bloodless, cadaverous, colourless, discoloured, ghastly, livid, pale, pallid, pasty, sickly, washed out, waxen, wheyfaced, white **2.** dim, faint, feeble, pale, weak

wand baton, rod, sprig, stick, twig, withe, withy

wander ('wɒndə) vb. (mainly intr.) **1.** (also tr.) to move or travel about, in, or through (a place) without any definite purpose or destination. **2.** to proceed in an irregular course. **3.** to go astray, as from a path or course. **4.** (of thoughts, etc.) to lose concentration. **5.** to think or speak incoherently or illogically. ~n. **6.** the act or an instance of wandering. —'**wanderer** n. —'**wandering** adj., n.

wandering Jew n. any of several related creeping or trailing plants of tropical America, such as tradescantia.

Wandering Jew n. (in medieval legend) a character condemned to roam the world eternally because he mocked Christ on the day of the Crucifixion.

wanderlust ('wɒndə,lʌst) n. a great desire to travel and rove about.

wane (weɪn) vb. (intr.) **1.** (of the moon) to show a gradually decreasing portion of illuminated surface, between full moon and new moon. **2.** to decrease gradually in size, strength, power, etc. **3.** to draw to a close. ~n. **4.** a decrease, as in size, strength, power, etc. **5.** the period during which the moon wanes. **6.** a drawing to a close. **7.** a rounded surface or defective edge of a plank, where the bark was. **8. on the wane.** in a state of decline. —'**waney** or '**wany** adj.

wangle ('wæŋgəl) Inf. ~vb. **1.** (tr.) to use devious methods to get or achieve (something) for (oneself or another): he wangled himself a salary increase. **2.** to manipulate or falsify (a situation, etc.). ~n. **3.** the act or an instance of wangling. —'**wangler** n.

wank (wæŋk) Taboo sl. ~vb. **1.** (intr.) to masturbate. ~n. **2.** an instance of wanking.

wankel engine ('wæŋkəl) n. a type of rotary four-stroke internal-combustion engine without reciprocating parts. It consists of one or more elliptical combustion chambers within which a curved triangular-shaped piston rotates, the explosion of compressed gas, dividing the combustion chamber into three gastight sections.

want (wɒnt) vb. **1.** (tr.) to feel a need or longing for: I want a new hat. **2.** (when tr., may take a clause as object or an infinitive) to wish, need, or desire (something or to do something): he wants to go home. **3.** (intr.; usually used with a negative and often foll. by for) to be lacking or deficient (in something necessary or desirable): the child wants for nothing. **4.** (tr.) to feel the absence of: lying on the ground makes me want my bed. **5.** (tr.) to fall short by (a specified amount). **6.** (tr.) Chiefly Brit. to have need of or require (doing or being something): your shoes want cleaning. **7.** (intr.) to be destitute. **8.** (tr.; often passive) to seek or request the presence of: you're wanted upstairs. **9.** (tr.; takes an infinitive) Inf. should or ought (to do something): you don't want to go out so late. ~n. **10.** the act or an instance of wanting. **11.** anything that is needed, desired, or lacked: to supply someone's wants. **12.** a lack, shortage, or ab-

sence: for want of common sense. **13.** the state of being in need: the state should help those in want. **14.** a sense of lack; craving. —'**wanter** n.

wanting ('wɒntɪŋ) adj. (postpositive) **1.** lacking or absent. **2.** not meeting requirements or expectations: you have been found wanting.

wanton ('wɒntən) adj. **1.** dissolute, licentious, or immoral. **2.** without motive, provocation, or justification: wanton destruction. **3.** maliciously and unnecessarily cruel. **4.** unrestrained: wanton spending. **5.** Arch. or poetic. playful or capricious. **6.** Arch. (of vegetation, etc.) luxuriant. ~n. **7.** a licentious person, esp. a woman. ~vb. **8.** (intr.) to behave in a wanton manner. —'**wantonly** adv. —'**wantonness** n.

wapiti ('wɒpɪtɪ) n., pl. -tis. a large North American deer with large much-branched antlers.

war (wɔː) n. **1.** open armed conflict between two or more parties, nations, or states. Related adj.: **belligerent** (see sense 2). **2.** a particular armed conflict: the 1973 war in the Middle East. **3.** the techniques of armed conflict as a study, science, or profession. **4.** any conflict or contest: the war against crime. **5.** (modifier) of, resulting from, or characteristic of war: war damage; a war story. **6. in the wars.** Inf. (esp. of a child) hurt or knocked about, esp. as a result of quarrelling and fighting. ~vb. **warring, warred. 7.** (intr.) to conduct a war.

War. abbrev. for Warwickshire.

warble ('wɔːbəl) vb. **1.** to sing (words, songs, etc.) with trills, runs, and other embellishments. **2.** (tr.) to utter in a song. ~n. **3.** the act or an instance of warbling.

warbler ('wɔːblə) n. **1.** a person or thing that warbles. **2.** a small active passerine songbird of the Old World having a cryptic plumage and slender bill, that is an arboreal insectivore. **3.** a small bird of an American family, similar to the Old World songbird but often brightly coloured.

war crime n. a crime committed in wartime in violation of the accepted customs, such as ill-treatment of prisoners of war, etc. —**war criminal** n.

war cry n. **1.** a rallying cry used by combatants in battle. **2.** a cry, slogan, etc., used to rally support for a cause.

ward (wɔːd) n. **1.** (in many countries) one of the districts into which a city, town, parish, or other area is divided for administration, election of representatives, etc. **2. a.** a room in a hospital, esp. one for patients requiring similar kinds of care: a maternity ward. **b.** (as modifier): ward maid. **3.** one of the divisions of a prison. **4.** an open space enclosed within the walls of a castle. **5.** Law. Also called: **ward of court.** a person, esp. a minor or one legally incapable of managing his own affairs, placed under the control or protection of a guardian or of a court. **6.** the state of being under guard or in custody. **7.** a means of protection. **8. a.** an internal ridge or bar in a

---

THESAURUS

wander v. **1.** cruise, drift, knock about, knock around, meander, mooch around (Sl.), peregrinate, ramble, range, roam, rove, straggle, stravaig (Scot.), stray, stroll, traipse (Inf.) **2.** depart, deviate, digress, divagate (Rare), diverge, err, get lost, go astray, go off at a tangent, go off course, lapse, lose concentration, lose one's train of thought, lose one's way, swerve, veer **3.** babble, be delirious, be incoherent, ramble, rave, speak incoherently, talk nonsense ~n. **4.** cruise, excursion, meander, peregrination, ramble, traipse (Inf.)

wanderer bird of passage, drifter, gypsy, itinerant, nomad, rambler, ranger, rolling stone, rover, stroller, traveller, vagabond, vagrant, voyager

wandering drifting, homeless, itinerant, migratory, nomadic, peripatetic, rambling, rootless, roving, strolling, travelling, vagabond, vagrant, voyaging, wayfaring

wane v. **1.** abate, atrophy, decline, decrease, die out, dim, diminish, draw to a close, drop, dwindle, ebb, fade, fade away, fail, lessen, sink, subside, taper off, weaken, wind down, wither ~n. **2.** abatement, atrophy, decay, declension, decrease, diminution, drop, dwindling, ebb, fading, failure, fall, falling off, lessening, sinking, subsidence, taper-

ing off, withering **3. on the wane** at its lowest ebb, declining, dropping, dwindling, dying out, ebbing, fading, lessening, obsolescent, on its last legs, on the decline, on the way out, subsiding, tapering off, weakening, withering

want v. **1.** covet, crave, desire, feel a need for, hanker after, have a fancy for, have a yen for (Inf.), hunger for, long for, need, pine for, require, thirst for, wish, yearn for **2.** be able to do with, be deficient in, be short of, be without, call for, demand, fall short in, have need of, lack, miss, need, require, stand in need of ~n. **3.** appetite, craving, demand, desire, fancy, hankering, hunger, longing, necessity, need, requirement, thirst, wish, yearning, yen (Inf.) **4.** absence, dearth, default, deficiency, famine, insufficiency, lack, paucity, scantiness, scarcity, shortage **5.** destitution, indigence, need, neediness, pauperism, penury, poverty, privation

wanting 1. absent, incomplete, lacking, less, missing, short, shy **2.** defective, deficient, disappointing, faulty, imperfect, inadequate, inferior, leaving much to be desired, not good enough, not up to expectations, not up to par, patchy, poor, sketchy, substandard, unsound

wanton adj. **1.** abandoned, dissipated, dissolute, fast, immoral, lecherous, lewd, liber-

tine, libidinous, licentious, loose, lustful, of easy virtue, promiscuous, rakish, shameless, unchaste **2.** arbitrary, cruel, evil, gratuitous, groundless, malevolent, malicious, motiveless, needless, senseless, spiteful, uncalled-for, unjustifiable, unjustified, unprovoked, vicious, wicked, wilful **3.** careless, devil-may-care, extravagant, heedless, immoderate, intemperate, lavish, outrageous, rash, reckless, unrestrained, wild ~n. **4.** Casanova, debauchee, Don Juan, harlot, lecher, libertine, loose woman, profligate, prostitute, rake, roué, slut, strumpet, tart (Inf.), trollop, voluptuary, whore, woman of easy virtue ~v. **5.** debauch, dissipate, revel, riot, sleep around (Inf.), wench (Archaic), whore **6.** fritter away, misspend, squander, throw away, waste

war 1. n. armed conflict, battle, bloodshed, combat, conflict, contention, contest, enmity, fighting, hostilities, hostility, strife, struggle, warfare **2.** v. battle, campaign against, carry on hostilities, clash, combat, conduct a war, contend, contest, fight, make war, strive, struggle, take up arms, wage war

war cry battle cry, rallying cry, slogan, war whoop

lock that prevents an incorrectly cut key from turning. **b.** a corresponding groove cut in a key. ~*vb.* **9.** (*tr.*) *Arch.* to guard or protect. —**'wardless** *adj.*

-ward *suffix.* **1.** (*forming adjectives*) indicating direction towards: *a backward step.* **2.** (*forming adverbs*) a variant and the usual U.S. form of **-wards.**

warden ('wɔːdⁿn) *n.* **1.** a person who has the charge or care of something, esp. a building, or someone. **2.** a public official, esp. one responsible for the enforcement of certain regulations: *traffic warden.* **3.** a person employed to patrol a national park or a safari park. **4.** *Chiefly U.S.* the chief officer in charge of a prison. **5.** *Brit.* the principal of any of various universities or colleges. **6.** See **churchwarden** (sense 1).

warder ('wɔːdə) *or* (*fem.*) **wardress** *n.* **1.** *Chiefly Brit.* an officer in charge of prisoners in a jail. **2.** a person who guards or has charge of something.

wardrobe ('wɔːdrəʊb) *n.* **1.** a tall closet or cupboard, with a rail or hooks on which to hang clothes. **2.** the total collection of articles of clothing belonging to one person. **3. a.** the collection of costumes belonging to a theatre or theatrical company. **b.** (*as modifier*): *wardrobe mistress.*

wardrobe mistress *n.* the person in charge of the costumes in a theatrical company.

wardroom ('wɔːd,ruːm, -,rum) *n.* **1.** the quarters assigned to the officers (except the captain) of a warship. **2.** the officers of a warship collectively, excepting the captain.

-wards *or* **-ward** *suffix forming adverbs.* indicating direction towards: *a step backwards.* Cf. **-ward.**

wardship ('wɔːdʃɪp) *n.* the state of being a ward.

ware (wɛə) *n.* (*often in combination*) **1.** (*functioning as sing.*) articles of the same kind or material: *silverware.* **2.** porcelain or pottery of a specified type: *jasper ware.* ~See also **wares.**

warehouse *n.* ('wɛə,haʊs). **1.** a place where goods are stored prior to their use, distribution, or sale. **2.** *Chiefly Brit.* a large commercial, esp. wholesale, establishment. ~*vb.* ('wɛə,haʊz, -,haʊs). **3.** (*tr.*) to store or place in a warehouse. ~See also **'ware,houseman** *n.*

wares (wɛəz) *pl. n.* **1.** articles of manufacture considered as being for sale. **2.** any talent or asset regarded as a saleable commodity.

warfare ('wɔː,fɛə) *n.* **1.** the act, process, or an instance of waging war. **2.** conflict or strife.

war game *n.* **1.** a notional tactical exercise for training military commanders, in which no military units are actually deployed. **2.** a game in which model soldiers are used to create battles, esp. past battles, in order to study tactics.

warhead ('wɔː,hɛd) *n.* the part of the fore end of a missile or projectile that contains explosives.

warhorse ('wɔː,hɔːs) *n.* **1.** a horse used in battle. **2.** *Inf.* a veteran soldier or politician.

warlike ('wɔː,laɪk) *adj.* **1.** of, relating to, or used in war. **2.** hostile or belligerent. **3.** fit or ready for war.

warlock ('wɔː,lɒk) *n.* a man who practises black magic.

warm (wɔːm) *adj.* **1.** characterized by or having a moderate degree of heat. **2.** maintaining or imparting heat: *a warm coat.* **3.** having or showing ready affection, kindliness, etc.: *a warm personality.* **4.** lively or passionate: *a warm debate.* **5.** cordial or enthusiastic: *warm support.* **6.** quickly or easily aroused: *a warm temper.* **7.** (of colours) predominantly red or yellow in tone. **8.** (of a scent, trail, etc.) recently made. **9.** near to finding a hidden object or guessing facts, as in children's games. **10.** *Inf.* uncomfortable or disagreeable, esp. because of the proximity of danger. ~*vb.* **11.** (sometimes foll. by *up*) to make or become warm or warmer. **12.** (when *intr.*, often foll. by *to*) to make or become excited, enthusiastic, etc. (about): *he warmed to the idea of buying a new car.* **13.** (*intr.*, often foll. by *to*) to feel affection, kindness, etc. (for someone): *I warmed to her mother from the start.* ~*n.* **14.** *Inf.* a warm place or area: *come into the warm.* **15.** *Inf.* the act or an instance of warming or being warmed. ~See also **warm up.** —**'warmer** *n.* —**'warmish** *adj.* —**'warmly** *adv.* —**'warmness** *n.*

warm-blooded *adj.* **1.** ardent, impetuous, or passionate. **2.** *Zool.* Also: **homoiothermic.** having a constant body temperature, usually higher than that of the surroundings. —**,warm-'bloodedness** *n.*

war memorial *n.* a monument, usually an obelisk or cross, to those who die in a war, esp. those from a particular locality.

warm front *n.* *Meteorol.* the boundary between a warm air mass and the cold air above.

warm-hearted *adj.* kindly, generous, or readily sympathetic. —**,warm-'heartedly** *adv.* —**,warm-'heartedness** *n.*

warming pan *n.* a pan, often of copper and having a long handle, filled with hot coals and formerly drawn over the sheets to warm a bed.

warmonger ('wɔː,mʌŋgə) *n.* a person who fosters warlike ideas or advocates war. —**'war,mongering** *n.*

warmth (wɔːmθ) *n.* **1.** the state, quality, or sensation of being warm. **2.** intensity of emotion: *he denied the accusation with some warmth.* **3.** affection or cordiality.

warm up *vb.* (*adv.*) **1.** to make or become warm or warmer. **2.** (*intr.*) to exercise immediately before a game or contest. **3.** to run (an engine, etc.) until the working temperature is attained, or (of an engine, etc.) to undergo this process. **4.** to make or become more animated: *the party warmed up when Tom came.* **5.** to reheat (already cooked food) or (of such food) to be reheated. ~*n.* **warm-up. 6.** the act or an instance of warming up.

warn (wɔːn) *vb.* **1.** to notify or make (someone) aware of danger, harm, etc. **2.** (*tr.; often takes a negative and an infinitive*) to advise or admonish (someone) as to ac-

---

THESAURUS

ward **1.** area, district, division, precinct, quarter, zone **2.** apartment, cubicle, room **3.** charge, dependant, minor, protégé, pupil **4.** care, charge, custody, guardianship, keeping, protection, safekeeping

warden administrator, caretaker, curator, custodian, guardian, janitor, keeper, ranger, steward, superintendent, warder, watchman

warder, wardress custodian, gaoler, guard, jailer, keeper, prison officer, screw (*Sl.*), turnkey (*Archaic*)

ward off avert, avoid, beat off, block, deflect, fend off, forestall, keep at arm's length, keep at bay, parry, repel, stave off, thwart, turn aside, turn away

wardrobe **1.** closet, clothes cupboard, clothes-press **2.** apparel, attire, clothes, collection of clothes, outfit

warehouse depository, depot, stockroom, store, storehouse

wares commodities, goods, lines, manufactures, merchandise, produce, products, stock, stuff

warfare armed conflict, armed struggle, arms, battle, blows, campaigning, clash of arms, combat, conflict, contest, discord,

fighting, hostilities, passage of arms, strategy, strife, struggle, war

warily cagily (*Inf.*), carefully, cautiously, charily, circumspectly, distrustfully, gingerly, guardedly, suspiciously, vigilantly, watchfully, with care

wariness alertness, attention, caginess (*Inf.*), care, carefulness, caution, circumspection, discretion, distrust, foresight, heedfulness, mindfulness, prudence, suspicion, vigilance, watchfulness

warlike aggressive, bellicose, belligerent, bloodthirsty, combative, hawkish, hostile, inimical, jingoistic, martial, militaristic, military, pugnacious, sabre-rattling, unfriendly, warmongering

warm *adj.* **1.** balmy, heated, lukewarm, moderately hot, pleasant, sunny, tepid, thermal **2.** affable, affectionate, amiable, amorous, cheerful, cordial, friendly, genial, happy, hearty, hospitable, kindly, loving, pleasant, tender **3.** animated, ardent, cordial, earnest, effusive, emotional, enthusiastic, excited, fervent, glowing, heated, intense, keen, lively, passionate, spirited, stormy, vehement, vigorous, violent, zealous **4.** irascible, irritable, passionate, quick, sensitive, short,

touchy **5.** *Inf.* dangerous, disagreeable, hazardous, perilous, tricky, uncomfortable, unpleasant ~*v.* **6.** heat, heat up, melt, thaw, warm up **7.** animate, awaken, excite, get going (*Inf.*), interest, make enthusiastic, put some life into, rouse, stimulate, stir, turn on (*Sl.*)

warm-blooded ardent, earnest, emotional, enthusiastic, excitable, fervent, impetuous, lively, passionate, rash, spirited, vivacious

warm-hearted affectionate, compassionate, cordial, generous, kind-hearted, kindly, loving, sympathetic, tender, tenderhearted

warmonger belligerent, hawk, jingo, militarist, sabre-rattler

warmth **1.** heat, hotness, warmness **2.** animation, ardour, eagerness, earnestness, effusiveness, enthusiasm, excitement, fervency, fervour, fire, heat, intensity, passion, spirit, transport, vehemence, vigour, violence, zeal, zest **3.** affability, affection, amorousness, cheerfulness, cordiality, happiness, heartiness, hospitableness, kindliness, love, tenderness

tion, conduct, etc.: *I warn you not to do that again.* **3.** (*takes a clause as object or an infinitive*) to inform (someone) in advance: *he warned them that he would arrive late.* **4.** (*tr.; usually foll. by* away, off, *etc.*) to give notice to go away, be off, etc. —'**warner** *n.*

warning ('wɔːnɪŋ) *n.* **1.** a hint, intimation, threat, etc., of harm or danger. **2.** advice to beware or desist. **3.** an archaic word for **notice** (sense 6). ~*adj.* **4.** (*prenominal*) intended or serving to warn: *a warning look.* —'**warningly** *adv.*

warp (wɔːp) *vb.* **1.** to twist or cause to twist out of shape, as from heat, damp, etc. **2.** to turn or cause to turn from a true, correct, or proper course. **3.** *Naut.* to move (a vessel) by hauling on a rope fixed to a stationary object ashore or (of a vessel) to be moved thus. **4.** (*tr.*) to flood (land) with water from which alluvial matter is deposited. ~*n.* **5.** the state or condition of being twisted out of shape. **6.** a twist, distortion, or bias. **7.** a mental or moral deviation. **8.** the yarns arranged lengthways on a loom, forming the threads through which the weft yarns are woven. **9.** *Naut.* a rope used for warping a vessel. **10.** alluvial sediment deposited by water. —'**warpage** *n.* —'**warper** *n.*

war paint *n.* **1.** painted decoration of the face and body applied by certain North American Indians before battle. **2.** *Inf.* finery or regalia. **3.** *Inf.* cosmetics.

warpath ('wɔː,pɑːθ) *n.* **1.** the route taken by North American Indians on a warlike expedition. **2. on the warpath. a.** preparing to engage in battle. **b.** *Inf.* in a state of anger.

warrant ('wɒrənt) *n.* **1.** anything that gives authority for an action or decision; authorization. **2.** a document that certifies or guarantees, such as a receipt, licence, or commission. **3.** *Law.* an authorization issued by a magistrate allowing a constable or other officer to search or seize property, arrest a person, or perform some other specified act. **4.** (in certain armed services) the official authority for the appointment of warrant officers. ~*vb.* (*tr.*) **5.** to guarantee the quality, condition, etc., of (something). **6.** to give authority or power to. **7.** to attest to the character, worthiness, etc., of. **8.** to guarantee (a purchaser of merchandise) against loss of, damage to, or misrepresentation concerning the merchandise. **9.** *Law.* to guarantee (the title to an estate or other property). **10.** to declare confidently. —'**warrantable** *adj.* —,**warranta'bility** *n.* —'**warrantably** *adv.* —'**warranter** *n.*

warrant officer *n.* an officer in certain armed services who holds a rank between those of commissioned and noncommissioned officers. In the British army the rank has two classes: regimental sergeant major and company sergeant major.

warrantor ('wɒrən,tɔː) *n.* an individual or company that provides a warranty.

warranty ('wɒrəntɪ) *n., pl.* **-ties. 1.** *Property law.* a covenant, express or implied, by which the vendor of real property vouches for the security of the title conveyed. **2.** *Contract law.* an express or implied term in a contract collateral to the main purpose, such as an undertaking that goods contracted to be sold shall meet specified requirements as to quality, etc. **3.** *Insurance law.* an undertaking by the party insured that the facts given regarding the risk are as stated.

warren ('wɒrən) *n.* **1.** a series of interconnected underground tunnels in which rabbits live. **2.** a colony of rabbits. **3.** an overcrowded area or dwelling. **4.** *Chiefly Brit.* an enclosed place where small game animals or

birds are kept, esp. for breeding.

warrior ('wɒrɪə) *n.* **a.** a person engaged in, experienced in, or devoted to war. **b.** (*as modifier*): *a warrior nation.*

warship ('wɔː,ʃɪp) *n.* a vessel armed, armoured, and otherwise equipped for naval warfare.

wart (wɔːt) *n.* **1.** *Pathol.* any firm abnormal elevation of the skin caused by a virus. **2.** *Bot.* a small rounded outgrowth. —'**warty** *adj.*

wart hog *n.* a wild pig of S and E Africa, having heavy tusks, wart-like protuberances on the face, and a mane of coarse hair.

wartime ('wɔː,taɪm) *n.* **a.** a period or time of war. **b.** (*as modifier*): *wartime conditions.*

wary ('wɛərɪ) *adj.* **warier, wariest. 1.** watchful, cautious, or alert. **2.** characterized by caution or watchfulness. —'**warily** *adv.* —'**wariness** *n.*

was (wɒz; *unstressed* wəz) *vb.* (used with *I, he, she, it,* and with singular nouns) **1.** the past tense (indicative mood) of **be. 2.** *Not standard.* a form of the subjunctive mood used in place of *were,* esp. in conditional sentences: *if the film was to be with you, would you be able to process it?*

wash (wɒʃ) *vb.* **1.** to apply water or other liquid, usually with soap, to (oneself, clothes, etc.) in order to cleanse. **2.** (*tr.; often foll. by* away, from, off, *etc.*) to remove by the application of water or other liquid and usually soap: *she washed the dirt from her clothes.* **3.** (*intr.*) to be capable of being washed without damage or loss of colour. **4.** (of an animal such as a cat) to cleanse (itself or another animal) by licking. **5.** (*tr.*) to cleanse from pollution or defilement. **6.** (*tr.*) to make wet or moist. **7.** (often foll. by away, *etc.*) to move or be moved by water: *the flood washed away the bridge.* **8.** (esp. of waves) to flow or sweep against or over (a surface or object), often with a lapping sound. **9.** to form by erosion or be eroded: *the stream washed a ravine in the hill.* **10.** (*tr.*) to apply a thin coating of paint, metal, etc., to. **11.** (*tr.*) to separate (ore, etc.) from (gravel, etc.) by immersion in water. **12.** (*intr.; usually used with a negative*) *Inf., chiefly Brit.* to admit of testing or proof: *your excuses won't wash.* **13. wash one's hands. a.** *Euphemistic.* to go to the lavatory. **b.** (usually foll. by *of*) to refuse to accept responsibility (for). ~*n.* **14.** the act or process of washing. **15.** a quantity of articles washed together. **16.** a preparation or thin liquid used as a coating or in washing: *a thin wash of paint.* **17.** *Med.* **a.** any medicinal lotion for application to a part of the body. **b.** (*in combination*): *an eyewash.* **18. a.** the technique of making wash drawings. **b.** See **wash drawing. 19.** the erosion of soil by the action of flowing water. **20.** a mass of alluvial material transported and deposited by flowing water. **21.** land that is habitually washed by tidal or river waters. **22.** the disturbance in the air or water produced at the rear of an aircraft, boat, or other moving object. **23.** gravel, earth, etc., from which valuable minerals may be washed. **24.** waste liquid matter or liquid refuse, esp. as fed to pigs. **25.** an alcoholic liquid resembling strong beer, resulting from the fermentation of wort in the production of whisky. **26. come out in the wash.** *Inf.* to become known or apparent in the course of time. ~See also **wash down, wash out, wash up.**

washable ('wɒʃəbəl) *adj.* (esp. of fabrics or clothes) capable of being washed without deteriorating. —,**washa'bility** *n.*

wash-and-wear *adj.* (of fabrics, garments, etc.) requiring only light washing, short drying time, and little or no ironing.

THESAURUS

warn admonish, advise, alert, apprise, caution, forewarn, give fair warning, give notice, inform, make (someone) aware, notify, put one on one's guard, summon, tip off

warning **1.** *n.* admonition, advice, alarm, alert, augury, caution, caveat, foretoken, hint, notice, notification, omen, premonition, presage, sign, signal, threat, tip, tip-off, token, word, word to the wise **2.** *adj.* admonitory, cautionary, monitory, ominous, premonitory, threatening

warrant *n.* **1.** assurance, authority, authorization, carte blanche, commission, guarantee, licence, permission, permit, pledge, sanction, security, warranty ~*v.* **2.** affirm, answer for, assure, attest, avouch,

certify, declare, guarantee, pledge, secure, stand behind, underwrite, uphold, vouch for **3.** approve, authorize, call for, commission, demand, empower, entitle, excuse, give ground for, justify, license, necessitate, permit, require, sanction

warrantable accountable, allowable, defensible, justifiable, lawful, necessary, permissible, proper, reasonable, right

warrior champion, combatant, fighter, fighting man, man-at-arms, soldier

wary alert, attentive, cagey (*Inf.*), careful, cautious, chary, circumspect, distrustful, guarded, heedful, leery (*Sl.*), on one's guard, on the lookout, on the qui vive, prudent, suspicious, vigilant, watchful, wide-awake

wash *v.* **1.** bath, bathe, clean, cleanse, launder, moisten, rinse, scrub, shampoo, shower, wet **2.** *With* **away** bear away, carry off, erode, move, sweep away, wash off **3.** *Inf.* bear scrutiny, be convincing, be plausible, carry weight, hold up, hold water, stand up, stick **4. wash one's hands of** abandon, accept no responsibility for, give up on, have nothing to do with, leave to one's own devices ~*n.* **5.** ablution, bath, bathe, cleaning, cleansing, laundering, rinse, scrub, shampoo, shower, washing **6.** ebb and flow, flow, roll, surge, sweep, swell, wave **7.** coat, coating, film, layer, overlay, screen, stain, suffusion

washbasin ('wɒʃˌbeɪsən) n. a basin or bowl for washing the face and hands. Also called: **washbowl**.

washboard ('wɒʃˌbɔːd) n. **1.** a board having a surface, usually of corrugated metal, on which, esp. formerly, clothes were scrubbed. **2.** such a board used as a rhythm instrument played with the fingers in skiffle, country-and-western music, etc. **3.** Naut. a vertical planklike shield fastened to the gunwales of a boat to prevent water from splashing over the side.

wash down vb. (tr., adv.) **1.** to wash completely, esp. from top to bottom. **2.** to take drink with or after (food or another drink).

wash drawing n. a pen-and-ink drawing that has been lightly brushed over with water to soften the lines.

washed out adj. (**washed-out** when prenominal). **1.** faded or colourless. **2.** exhausted, esp. when being pale in appearance.

washed up adj. (**washed-up** when prenominal). Inf., chiefly U.S. no longer hopeful, etc.: our hopes for the new deal are all washed up.

washer ('wɒʃə) n. **1.** a person or thing that washes. **2.** a flat ring or drilled disc of metal used under the head of a bolt or nut. **3.** any flat ring of rubber, felt, metal, etc., used to provide a seal under a nut or in a tap or valve seat. **4.** See **washing machine**. **5.** Austral. a face cloth; flannel.

washerwoman ('wɒʃəˌwumən) or (masc.) **washer-man**, n., pl. **-women** or **-men**. a person who washes clothes for a living.

washing ('wɒʃɪŋ) n. **1.** articles that have been or are to be washed together on a single occasion. **2.** something, such as gold dust, that has been obtained by washing. **3.** a thin coat of something applied in liquid form.

washing machine n. a mechanical apparatus, usually powered by electricity, for washing clothing, linens, etc.

washing soda n. crystalline sodium carbonate, esp. when used as a cleansing agent.

washing-up n. Brit. **1.** the washing of dishes, cutlery, etc., after a meal. **2.** dishes and cutlery waiting to be washed up. **3.** (as modifier): a washing-up machine.

wash out vb. (adv.) **1.** (tr.) to wash (the inside of something) so as to remove (dirt). **2.** Also: **wash off.** to remove or be removed by washing: grass stains don't wash out easily. ~n. **washout**. **3.** Geol. **a.** erosion of the earth's surface by the action of running water. **b.** a narrow channel produced by this. **4.** Inf. **a.** a total failure or disaster. **b.** an incompetent person.

washroom ('wɒʃˌruːm, -ˌrum) n. U.S. a euphemism for **lavatory**.

washstand ('wɒʃˌstænd) n. a piece of furniture designed to hold a basin, etc., for washing the face and hands.

wash up vb. (adv.) **1.** Chiefly Brit. to wash (dishes, cutlery, etc.) after a meal. **2.** (intr.) U.S. to wash one's face and hands.

washy ('wɒʃɪ) adj. **washier**, **washiest**. **1.** over-diluted, watery, or weak. **2.** lacking intensity or strength. —'**washiness** n.

wasp (wɒsp) n. **1.** a social hymenopterous insect, such as the **common wasp**, having a black-and-yellow body and an ovipositor specialized for stinging. **2.** any of various solitary hymenopterans, such as the digger wasp and gall wasp. —'**wasp**,**like** adj. —'**waspy** adj. —'**waspily** adv. —'**waspiness** n.

Wasp or **WASP** (wɒsp) n. U.S., usually derog. a person descended from N European, usually Protestant, stock, forming a group often considered the most dominant, privileged, and influential in American society.

waspish ('wɒspɪʃ) adj. **1.** relating to or suggestive of a wasp. **2.** easily annoyed or angered. —'**waspishly** adv.

wasp waist n. a very slender waist, esp. one that is tightly corseted. —'**wasp-**,**waisted** adj.

wassail ('wɒseɪl) n. **1.** (formerly) a toast or salutation made to a person at festivities. **2.** a festivity when much drinking takes place. **3.** alcoholic drink drunk at such a festivity, esp. spiced beer or mulled wine. ~vb. **4.** to drink the health of (a person) at a wassail. **5.** (intr.) to go from house to house singing carols at Christmas. —'**wassailer** n.

wastage ('weɪstɪdʒ) n. **1.** anything lost by wear or waste. **2.** the process of wasting. **3.** reduction in size of a work force by retirement, etc. (esp. in **natural wastage**).

waste (weɪst) vb. **1.** (tr.) to use, consume, or expend thoughtlessly, carelessly, or to no avail. **2.** (tr.) to fail to take advantage of: to waste an opportunity. **3.** (when intr., often foll. by away) to lose or cause to lose bodily strength, health, etc. **4.** to exhaust or become exhausted. **5.** (tr.) to ravage. ~n. **6.** the act of wasting or state of being wasted. **7.** a failure to take advantage of something. **8.** anything unused or not used to full advantage. **9.** anything or anyone rejected as useless, worthless, or in excess of what is required. **10.** garbage, rubbish, or trash. **11.** a land or region that is devastated or ruined. **12.** a land or region that is wild or uncultivated. **13.** Physiol. **a.** the useless products of metabolism. **b.** indigestible food residue. **14.** Law. reduction in the value of an estate caused by act or neglect, esp. by a life tenant. ~adj. **15.** rejected as useless, unwanted, or worthless. **16.** produced in excess of what is required. **17.** not cultivated, inhabited, or productive: waste land. **18. a.** of or denoting the useless products of metabolism. **b.** of or denoting indigestible food residue. **19.** destroyed, devastated, or ruined. **20. lay waste.** to devastate or destroy. —'**waster** n.

wasteful ('weɪstful) adj. **1.** tending to waste or squander. **2.** causing waste or devastation. —'**wastefully** adv. —'**wastefulness** n.

wasteland ('weɪstˌlænd) n. **1.** a barren or desolate area of land. **2.** a region, period in history, etc., that is considered spiritually, intellectually, or aesthetically barren or desolate.

wastepaper ('weɪstˌpeɪpə) n. paper discarded after use.

wasting ('weɪstɪŋ) adj. (prenominal) reducing the vitality, strength, or robustness of the body: a wasting disease. —'**wastingly** adv.

wastrel ('weɪstrəl) n. **1.** a wasteful person; spendthrift; prodigal. **2.** an idler or vagabond.

watch (wɒtʃ) vb. **1.** to look at or observe closely or attentively. **2.** (intr., foll. by for) to wait attentively. **3.** to guard or tend (something) closely or carefully. **4.** (intr.) to keep vigil. **5.** (tr.) to maintain an interest in: to watch the progress of a child at school. **6. watch it!** be careful! ~n. **7. a.** a small portable timepiece, usually worn strapped to the wrist (a **wristwatch**) or in a waistcoat pocket. **b.** (as modifier): a watch spring. **8.** a watching. **9.** a period of vigil, esp. during the night. **10.** (formerly) one of a set of periods into which the night was divided. **11.** Naut. **a.** any of the periods, usually of four hours, dur-

---

THESAURUS

washed out 1. blanched, bleached, colourless, etiolated, faded, flat, lacklustre, mat, pale **2.** all in (Sl.), dead on one's feet, dog-tired (Inf.), done in (Inf.), drained, drawn, exhausted, fatigued, haggard, knackered (Sl.), pale, spent, tired-out, wan, weary, worn-out

washout 1. disappointment, disaster, dud (Inf.), failure, fiasco, flop (Inf.), mess **2.** failure, incompetent, loser

waspish bad-tempered, cantankerous, captious, crabbed, crabby, cross, crotchety (Inf.), fretful, grumpy, ill-tempered, irascible, irritable, peevish, peppery, pettish, petulant, snappish, splenetic, testy, touchy, waxy (Brit. sl.)

waste v. **1.** blow (Sl.), dissipate, fritter away, frivol away (Inf.), lavish, misuse, run through, squander, throw away **2.** atrophy, consume, corrode, crumble, debilitate, decay, decline, deplete, disable, drain, dwindle, eat away, ebb, emaciate, enfeeble, exhaust, fade, gnaw, perish, sap the strength of, sink, undermine, wane, wear out, wither **3.** despoil, destroy, devastate, lay waste, pillage, rape, ravage, raze, ruin, sack, spoil, wreak havoc upon ~n. **4.** dissipation, expenditure, extravagance, frittering away, loss, lost opportunity, misapplication, misuse, prodigality, squandering, unthriftiness, wastefulness **5.** desolation, destruction, devastation, havoc, ravage, ruin **6.** debris, dregs, dross, garbage, leavings, leftovers, litter, offal, offscourings, refuse, rubbish, scrap, sweepings, trash **7.** desert, solitude, void, wasteland, wild, wilder-ness ~adj. **8.** leftover, superfluous, supernumerary, unused, useless, worthless **9.** bare, barren, desolate, devastated, dismal, dreary, empty, uncultivated, uninhabited, unproductive, wild **10.** lay waste depredate (Rare), despoil, destroy, devastate, pillage, rape, ravage, raze, ruin, sack, spoil, wreak havoc upon

wasteful extravagant, improvident, lavish, prodigal, profligate, ruinous, spendthrift, thriftless, uneconomical, unthrifty

wastrel 1. prodigal, profligate, spendthrift, squanderer **2.** drone, good-for-nothing, idler, layabout, loafer, loser, malingerer, ne'er-do-well, shirker, waster

ing which part of a ship's crew are on duty. **b.** those officers and crew on duty during a specified watch. **12.** the period during which a guard is on duty. **13.** (formerly) a watchman or band of watchmen. **14. on the watch.** on the lookout. ~See also **watch out.** —'watcher n.

watchdog ('wɒtʃ,dɒg) n. **1.** a dog trained to guard property. **2. a.** a person or group that acts as a protector against inefficiency, etc. **b.** (as modifier): a watchdog committee.

watch fire n. a fire kept burning at night as a signal or for warmth and light by a person keeping watch.

watchful ('wɒtʃful) adj. **1.** vigilant or alert. **2.** Arch. not sleeping. —'watchfully adv. —'watchfulness n.

watchmaker ('wɒtʃ,meɪkə) n. a person who makes or mends watches. —'watch,making n.

watchman ('wɒtʃmən) n., pl. -men. **1.** a person employed to guard buildings or property. **2.** (formerly) a man employed to patrol or guard the streets at night.

watch night n. **1.** (in Protestant churches) the night of December 31, during which a service is held to mark the passing of the old year. **2.** the service held on this night.

watch out vb. (intr., adv.) to be careful or on one's guard.

watchstrap ('wɒtʃ,stræp) n. a strap of leather, cloth, etc., attached to a watch for fastening it around the wrist. Also called (U.S.): **watchband.**

watchtower ('wɒtʃ,tauə) n. a tower on which a sentry keeps watch.

watchword ('wɒtʃ,wɜːd) n. **1.** another word for **password.** **2.** a rallying cry or slogan.

water ('wɔːtə) n. **1.** a clear colourless tasteless odourless liquid that is essential for plant and animal life and constitutes, in impure form, rain, oceans, rivers, lakes, etc. Formula: H_2O. Related adj.: **aqueous.** **2. a.** any body or area of this liquid, such as a sea, lake, river, etc. **b.** (as modifier): water sports; a water plant. Related adj.: **aquatic.** **3.** the surface of such a body or area: fish swam below the water. **4.** any form or variety of this liquid, such as rain. **5.** any of various solutions of chemical substances in water: ammonia water. **6.** Physiol. **a.** any fluid secreted from the body, such as sweat, urine, or tears. **b.** the amniotic fluid surrounding a foetus in the womb. **7.** a wavy lustrous finish on some fabrics, esp. silk. **8.** Arch. the degree of brilliance in a diamond. **9.** excellence, quality, or degree (in **of the first water**). **10.** Finance. capital stock issued without a corresponding increase in paid-up capital. **11.** (modifier) Astrol. of or relating to the three signs of the zodiac Cancer, Scorpio, and Pisces. **12. above the water.** Inf. out of trouble or difficulty, esp. financial trouble. **13. hold water.** to prove credible, logical, or consistent: the alibi did not hold water. **14. in deep water.** in trouble or difficulty. **15. make water. a.** to urinate. **b.** (of a boat, etc.) to let in water. **16. throw** (or **pour**) **cold water on.** Inf. to discourage. **17. water under the bridge.** events that are past and done with. ~vb. **18.** (tr.) to sprinkle, moisten, or soak with water. **19.** (tr.; often foll. by down) to weaken by the addition of water. **20.** (intr.) (of the eyes) to fill with tears. **21.** (intr.) (of the mouth) to salivate, esp. in anticipation of food (esp. in **make one's mouth water**). **22.** (tr.) to irrigate or provide with water: to water the land. **23.** (intr.) to drink water. **24.** (intr.) (of a ship, etc.) to take

in a supply of water. **25.** (tr.) Finance. to raise the par value of (issued capital stock) without a corresponding increase in the real value of assets. **26.** (tr.) to produce a wavy lustrous finish on (fabrics, esp. silk). ~See also **water down.** —'waterer n. —'waterless adj.

water bed n. a waterproof mattress filled with water.

water biscuit n. a thin crisp plain biscuit, usually served with butter or cheese.

water buffalo or **ox** n. a member of the cattle tribe of swampy regions of S Asia, having widely spreading back-curving horns. Domesticated forms are used as draught animals.

water butt n. a barrel for collecting rainwater, esp. from a drainpipe.

water cannon n. an apparatus for pumping water through a nozzle at high pressure, used in quelling riots.

water chestnut n. **1.** a floating aquatic plant of Asia, having four-pronged edible nutlike fruits. **2. Chinese water chestnut.** a Chinese plant with an edible succulent corm. **3.** the corm of the Chinese water chestnut, used in Oriental cookery.

water clock or **glass** n. any of various devices for measuring time that use the escape of water as the motive force.

water closet n. **1.** a lavatory flushed by water. **2.** a small room that has a lavatory.

watercolour or U.S. **watercolor** ('wɔːtə,kʌlə) n. **1.** water-soluble pigment, applied in transparent washes and without the admixture of white pigment in the lighter tones. **2. a.** a painting done in watercolours. **b.** (as modifier): a watercolour masterpiece. **3.** the art or technique of painting with such pigments. —'water,colourist or U.S. 'water,colorist n.

water-cool vb. (tr.) to cool (an engine, etc.) by a flow of water circulating in an enclosed jacket. —'water-,cooled adj.

watercourse ('wɔːtə,kɔːs) n. **1.** a stream, river, or canal. **2.** the channel, bed, or route along which this flows.

watercress ('wɔːtə,krɛs) n. an Old World cruciferous plant of clear ponds and streams, having pungent leaves that are used in salads and as a garnish.

water diviner n. Brit. a person able to locate the presence of water, esp. underground, with a divining rod.

water down vb. (tr., adv.) **1.** to dilute or weaken with water. **2.** to modify, esp. so as to omit anything unpleasant or offensive: to water down the truth. —,watered-'down adj.

waterfall ('wɔːtə,fɔːl) n. a cascade of falling water where there is a vertical or almost vertical step in a river.

waterfowl ('wɔːtə,faul) n. **1.** any aquatic freshwater bird, esp. any species of the family Anatidae (ducks, geese, and swans). **2.** such birds collectively.

waterfront ('wɔːtə,frʌnt) n. the area of a town or city alongside a body of water, such as a harbour or dockyard.

water gate n. **1.** a gate in a canal, etc., that can be opened or closed to control the flow of water. **2.** a gate through which access may be gained to a body of water.

Watergate ('wɔːtə,geɪt) n. an incident during the 1972 U.S. presidential campaign, when agents employed by the re-election organization of President Richard Nixon

THESAURUS

watch v. **1.** contemplate, eye, gaze at, look, look at, look on, mark, note, observe, pay attention, peer at, regard, see, stare at, view **2.** attend, be on the alert, be on the lookout, be wary, be watchful, keep an eye open (Inf.), look out, take heed, wait **3.** guard, keep, look after, mind, protect, superintend, take care of, tend ~n. **4.** chronometer, clock, pocket watch, timepiece, wristwatch **5.** alertness, attention, eye, heed, inspection, lookout, notice, observation, supervision, surveillance, vigil, vigilance, watchfulness

watchdog **1.** guard dog **2.** custodian, guardian, inspector, monitor, protector, scrutineer

watcher looker-on, lookout, observer, onlooker, spectator, spy, viewer, witness

watchful alert, attentive, circumspect, guarded, heedful, observant, on one's guard, on the lookout, on the qui vive, on the watch,

suspicious, vigilant, wary, wide awake

watchfulness alertness, attention, attentiveness, caution, cautiousness, circumspection, heedfulness, vigilance, wariness

watchman caretaker, custodian, guard, security guard, security man

watch out be alert, be careful, be on one's guard, be on the alert, be on (the) watch, be vigilant, be watchful, have a care, keep a sharp lookout, keep a weather eye open, keep one's eyes open, keep one's eyes peeled or skinned (Inf.), look out, mind out, watch oneself

watch over defend, guard, keep safe, look after, preserve, protect, shelter, shield, stand guard over

watchword **1.** countersign, magic word, password, shibboleth **2.** battle cry, byword, catch phrase, catchword, maxim, motto, rallying cry, slogan

water n. **1.** Adam's ale or wine, aqua, H2O **2. hold water** bear examination or scrutiny, be credible (logical, sound), make sense, pass the test, ring true, work **3. of the first water** excellent, of the best, of the best quality, of the finest quality, of the highest degree, of the highest grade ~v. **4.** damp, dampen, douse, drench, flood, hose, irrigate, moisten, soak, souse, spray, sprinkle **5.** add water to, adulterate, dilute, put water in, thin, water down, weaken

water down **1.** add water to, adulterate, dilute, put water in, thin, water, weaken **2.** adulterate, mitigate, qualify, soften, tone down, weaken

waterfall cascade, cataract, chute, fall, force (Northern Brit.), linn (Scot.)

were caught breaking into the Democratic Party headquarters in the Watergate building, Washington, D.C. The political scandal was exacerbated by attempts to conceal the fact that White House officials had approved the burglary.

water gauge *n.* an instrument that indicates the presence or the quantity of water in a tank, reservoir, or boiler feed. Also called: **water glass.**

water glass *n.* **1.** a viscous syrupy solution of sodium silicate in water: used as a protective coating for cement and a preservative, esp. for eggs. **2.** another name for **water gauge.**

water hole *n.* **1.** a depression, such as a pond or pool, containing water, esp. one used by animals as a drinking place. **2.** a source of drinking water in a desert.

water ice *n.* an ice cream made from a frozen sugar syrup flavoured with fruit juice or purée.

watering can *n.* a container with a handle and a spout with a perforated nozzle used to sprinkle water over plants.

watering place *n.* **1.** a place where drinking water for people or animals may be obtained. **2.** *Brit.* a spa. **3.** *Brit.* a seaside resort.

water jump *n.* a ditch or brook over which athletes or horses must jump in a steeplechase or similar contest.

water level *n.* **1.** the level reached by the surface of a body of water. **2.** the water line of a boat or ship.

water lily *n.* any of various aquatic plants of temperate and tropical regions, having large leaves and showy flowers that float on the surface of the water.

water line *n.* **1.** a line marked at the level around a vessel's hull to which the vessel will be immersed when afloat. **2.** a line marking the level reached by a body of water.

waterlogged ('wɔːtəˌlɒgd) *adj.* **1.** saturated with water. **2.** (of a vessel still afloat) having taken in so much water as to be unmanageable.

Waterloo (ˌwɔːtəˈluː) *n.* **1.** a small town in Belgium south of Brussels: battle (1815) fought nearby in which British and Prussian forces under the Duke of Wellington and Blücher routed the French under Napoleon. **2.** a total or crushing defeat (esp. in **meet one's Waterloo**).

water main *n.* a principal supply pipe in an arrangement of pipes for distributing water.

waterman ('wɔːtəmən) *n.*, *pl.* **-men.** a skilled boatman. —'**waterman**ˌship *n.*

watermark ('wɔːtəˌmɑːk) *n.* **1.** a mark impressed on paper during manufacture, visible when the paper is held up to the light. **2.** another word for **water line.** ~*vb.* (*tr.*) **3.** to mark (paper) with a watermark.

water meadow *n.* a meadow that remains fertile by being periodically flooded by a stream.

watermelon ('wɔːtəˌmɛlən) *n.* **1.** an African melon widely cultivated for its large edible fruit. **2.** the fruit of this plant, which has a hard green rind and sweet watery reddish flesh.

water nymph *n.* any fabled nymph of the water, such as the Naiad, Nereid, or Oceanid of Greek mythology.

water pipe *n.* **1.** a pipe for water. **2.** another name for **hookah.**

water pistol *n.* a toy pistol that squirts a stream of water or other liquid.

water polo *n.* a game played in water by two teams of seven swimmers in which each side tries to throw or propel an inflated ball into the opponents' goal.

water power *n.* **1.** the power latent in a dynamic or static head of water as used to drive machinery, esp. for generating electricity. **2.** a source of such power, such as a drop in the level of a river, etc.

waterproof ('wɔːtəˌpruːf) *adj.* **1.** not penetrable by water. Cf. **water-repellent.** ~*n.* **2.** *Chiefly Brit.* a waterproof garment, esp. a raincoat. ~*vb.* (*tr.*) **3.** to make (a fabric, etc.) waterproof.

water rat *n.* **1.** any of several small amphibious rodents, esp. the water vole or the muskrat. **2.** any of various amphibious rats of New Guinea, the Philippines, and Australia.

water rate *n.* a charge made for the public supply of water.

water-repellent *adj.* (of fabrics or garments, etc.) having a finish that resists the absorption of water.

watershed ('wɔːtəˌʃɛd) *n.* **1.** the dividing line between two adjacent river systems, such as a ridge. **2.** an important period or factor that serves as a dividing line.

waterside ('wɔːtəˌsaɪd) *n.* **a.** the area of land beside a body of water. **b.** (*as modifier*): *waterside houses.*

water-ski *n.* **1.** a type of ski used for planing or gliding over water. ~*vb.* **-skiing, -skied** *or* **-ski'd. 2.** (*intr.*) to ride over water on water-skis while holding a rope towed by a speedboat. —'**water-**ˌskier *n.* —'**water-**ˌskiing *n.*

water snake *n.* any of various snakes that live in or near water, esp. any of a genus of harmless North American snakes.

water softener *n.* **1.** any substance that lessens the hardness of water, usually by precipitating calcium and magnesium ions. **2.** an apparatus that is used to remove chemicals that cause hardness.

waterspout ('wɔːtəˌspaʊt) *n.* **1.** *Meteorol.* **a.** a tornado occurring over water, that forms a column of water and mist. **b.** a sudden downpour of heavy rain. **2.** a pipe or channel through which water is discharged.

water table *n.* **1.** the level below which the ground is saturated with water. **2.** a stringcourse that has a moulding designed to throw rainwater clear of the wall below.

watertight ('wɔːtəˌtaɪt) *adj.* **1.** not permitting the passage of water either in or out: *a watertight boat.* **2.** without loopholes: *a watertight argument.* **3.** kept separate from other subjects or influences.

water tower ('taʊə) *n.* a reservoir or storage tank mounted on a tower-like structure so that water can be distributed at a uniform pressure.

water vapour *n.* water in the gaseous state, esp. when due to evaporation at a temperature below the boiling point.

waterway ('wɔːtəˌweɪ) *n.* a river, canal, or other navigable channel used as a means of travel or transport.

water wheel *n.* **1.** a simple water-driven turbine consisting of a wheel having vanes set axially across its rim, used to drive machinery. **2.** a wheel with buckets attached to its rim for raising water from a stream, pond, etc.

water wings *pl. n.* an inflatable rubber device shaped like a pair of wings, which is placed under the arms of a person learning to swim.

waterworks ('wɔːtəˌwɜːks) *n.* **1.** (*functioning as sing.*) an establishment for storing, purifying, and distributing water for community supply. **2.** (*functioning as pl.*) a display of water in movement, as in fountains. **3.** (*functioning as pl.*) *Brit. inf.* the urinary system. **4.** (*functioning as pl.*) *Sl.* crying; tears.

watery ('wɔːtərɪ) *adj.* **1.** relating to, containing, or resembling water. **2.** discharging or secreting water or a water-like fluid. **3.** tearful; weepy. **4.** insipid, thin, or weak.

watt (wɒt) *n.* the derived SI unit of power, equal to 1 joule per second; the power dissipated by a current of 1 ampere flowing across a potential difference of 1 volt. Symbol: W

wattage ('wɒtɪdʒ) *n.* **1.** power, esp. electric power, measured in watts. **2.** the power rating, measured in watts, of an electrical appliance.

wattle ('wɒtəl) *n.* **1.** a frame of rods or stakes interwoven with twigs, branches, etc., esp. when used to make fences. **2.** the material used in such a construction. **3.** a loose fold of skin, often brightly coloured, hanging from the neck or throat of certain birds, lizards, etc. **4.** any of various chiefly Australian acacia trees having spikes of small brightly coloured flowers and flexible branches. ~*vb.* (*tr.*) **5.** to construct from wattle. **6.** to bind or frame with wattle. **7.** to weave or twist (branches, twigs, etc.) into a frame. ~*adj.* **8.** made of, formed by, or covered with wattle. —'**wattled** *adj.*

wattle and daub *n.* a form of wall construction con-

■ THESAURUS ■

watertight 1. sound, waterproof **2.** airtight, firm, flawless, foolproof, impregnable, incontrovertible, sound, unassailable

watery 1. aqueous, damp, fluid, humid, liquid, marshy, moist, soggy, squelchy, wet **2.** rheumy, tear-filled, tearful, weepy **3.** adulterated, dilute, diluted, flavourless, insipid, runny, tasteless, thin, washy, watered-down, waterish, weak, wishy-washy (*Inf.*)

sisting of interwoven twigs plastered with a mixture of clay, water, and sometimes chopped straw.

waul *or* **wawl** ('wɔːl) *vb.* (*intr.*) to cry or wail plaintively like a cat.

wave (weɪv) *vb.* **1.** to move or cause to move freely to and fro: *the banner waved in the wind.* **2.** (*intr.*) to move the hand to and fro as a greeting. **3.** to signal or signify by or as if by waving something. **4.** (*tr.*) to direct to move by or as if by waving something: *he waved me on.* **5.** to form or be formed into curves, undulations, etc. **6.** (*tr.*) to set waves in (the hair). ~*n.* **7.** one of a sequence of ridges or undulations that moves across the surface of a body of a liquid, esp. the sea. **8.** any undulation on or at the edge of a surface reminiscent of such a wave: *a wave across the field of corn.* **9. the waves.** the sea. **10.** anything that suggests the movement of a wave, as by a sudden rise: *a crime wave.* **11.** a widespread movement that advances in a body: *a wave of settlers.* **12.** the act or an instance of waving. **13.** *Physics.* an energy-carrying disturbance propagated through a medium or space by a progressive local displacement of the medium or a change in its physical properties, but without any overall movement of matter. **14.** *Physics.* a graphical representation of a wave obtained by plotting the magnitude of the disturbance against time at a particular point in the medium or space. **15.** a prolonged spell of some particular type of weather: *a heat wave.* **16.** an undulating curve or series of curves or loose curls in the hair. —'**waveless** *adj.* —'**wave,like** *adj.*

waveband ('weɪv,bænd) *n.* a range of wavelengths or frequencies used for a particular type of radio transmission.

wave down *vb.* (*tr., adv.*) to signal with a wave to (a driver or vehicle) to stop.

wavelength ('weɪv,lɛŋθ) *n.* **1.** the distance, measured in the direction of propagation, between two points of the same phase in consecutive cycles of a wave. Symbol: λ **2.** the wavelength of the carrier wave used by a particular broadcasting station. **3. on someone's** (*or* **the same**) **wavelength.** *Inf.* having similar views, feelings, or thoughts (as someone else).

wavelet ('weɪvlɪt) *n.* a small wave.

waver ('weɪvə) *vb.* (*intr.*) **1.** to be irresolute; hesitate between two possibilities. **2.** to become unsteady. **3.** to fluctuate. **4.** to move back and forth or one way and another. **5.** (of light) to flicker or flash. ~*n.* **6.** the act or an instance of wavering. —'**waverer** *n.* —'**waveringly** *adv.*

wavy ('weɪvɪ) *adj.* **wavier, waviest. 1.** abounding in or full of waves. **2.** moving or proceeding in waves. **3.** (of hair) set in or having waves. —'**wavily** *adv.* —'**waviness** *n.*

wax¹ (wæks) *n.* **1.** any of various viscous or solid materials of natural origin: characteristically lustrous, insoluble in water, and sensitive to heat, they consist largely of esters of fatty acids. **2.** any of various similar substances, such as paraffin wax, that have a mineral origin and consist largely of hydrocarbons. **3.** short for **beeswax** *or* **sealing wax. 4.** a resinous preparation used by shoemakers to rub on thread. **5.** any substance or object that is pliable or easily moulded: *he was wax in their hands.* **6.** (*modifier*) made of or resembling wax: *a wax figure.* **7. put on wax.** to make a gramophone record of. ~*vb.* **8.** (*tr.*) to coat, polish, etc., with wax. **9.** (*tr.*) *Inf.* to make a gramophone record of. —'**waxer** *n.*

wax² (wæks) *vb.* (*intr.*) **1.** to become larger, more powerful, etc. **2.** (of the moon) to show a gradually increasing portion of illuminated surface, between new moon and full moon. **3.** to become: *to wax eloquent.*

wax³ (wæks) *n. Inf., chiefly Brit.* a fit of rage or temper:

he's in a wax today.

waxen ('wæksən) *adj.* **1.** made of, treated with, or covered with wax. **2.** resembling wax in colour or texture.

wax light *n.* a candle or taper of wax.

wax paper *n.* paper treated or coated with wax or paraffin to make it waterproof.

waxwing ('wæks,wɪŋ) *n.* any of a genus of gregarious passerine songbirds having red waxy wing tips and crested heads.

waxwork ('wæks,wɜːk) *n.* **1.** an object reproduced in wax, esp. as an ornament. **2.** a life-size lifelike figure, esp. of a famous person, reproduced in wax. **3.** (*pl.; functioning as sing. or pl.*) a museum or exhibition of wax figures.

waxy ('wæksɪ) *adj.* **waxier, waxiest. 1.** resembling wax in colour, appearance, or texture. **2.** made of, covered with, or abounding in wax. —'**waxily** *adv.* —'**waxiness** *n.*

way (weɪ) *n.* **1.** a manner, method, or means: *a way of life.* **2.** a route or direction: *the way home.* **3. a.** a means or line of passage, such as a path or track. **b.** (*in combination*): *waterway.* **4.** space or room for movement or activity (esp. in **make way, in the way, out of the way**). **5.** distance, usually distance in general: *you've come a long way.* **6.** a passage or journey: *on the way.* **7.** characteristic style or manner: *I did it my way.* **8.** (*often pl.*) habits: *he has some offensive ways.* **9.** an aspect of something; particular: *in many ways he was right.* **10. a.** a street in or leading out of a town. **b.** (*cap.* when part of a street name): *Icknield Way.* **11.** something that one wants in a determined manner (esp. in **get** *or* **have one's** (**own**) **way**). **12.** the experience or sphere in which one comes into contact with things (esp. in **come one's way**). **13.** *Inf.* a state or condition, usually financial or concerning health (esp. in **in a good** (*or* **bad**) **way**). **14.** *Inf.* the area or direction of one's home: *drop in if you're ever over my way.* **15.** movement of a ship or other vessel. **16.** a guide along which something can be moved, such as the surface of a lathe along which the tailstock slides. **17.** (*pl.*) the wooden or metal tracks down which a ship slides to be launched. **18.** a course of life including experiences, conduct, etc.: *the way of sin.* **19. by the way.** (*sentence modifier*) incidentally. **20. by way of. a.** via. **b.** serving as: *by way of introduction.* **c.** in the state or condition of: *by way of being an artist.* **21. each way.** (of a bet) laid on a horse, dog, etc., to win or gain a place. **22. give way. a.** to collapse or break down. **b.** to yield. **23. give way to. a.** to step aside for or stop for. **b.** to give full rein to (emotions, etc.). **24. go out of one's way.** to take considerable trouble or inconvenience oneself. **25. have a way with.** to have such a manner or skill as to handle successfully. **26. have it both ways.** to enjoy two things that would normally be mutually exclusive. **27. in a way.** in some respects. **28. in no way.** not at all. **29. lead the way. a.** to go first. **b.** to set an example. **30. make one's way. a.** to proceed or advance. **b.** to achieve success in life. **31. on the way out.** *Inf.* **a.** becoming unfashionable, etc. **b.** dying. **32. out of the way. a.** removed or dealt with so as to be no longer a hindrance. **b.** remote. **c.** unusual and sometimes improper. **33. see one's way** (**clear**). to find it possible and be willing (to do something). **34. under way.** having started moving or making progress. ~*adv.* **35.** *Inf.* **a.** at a considerable distance or extent: *way over yonder.* **b.** very far: *they're way up the mountain.*

▷ **Usage.** The use of *the way* for *as* in sentences such as *he does not write the way his father did* is well established in the U.S. and is common in British informal usage. Careful writers, however, prefer *as* in formal contexts.

THESAURUS

wave *v.* **1.** brandish, flap, flourish, flutter, move to and fro, oscillate, quiver, ripple, shake, stir, sway, swing, undulate, wag, waver, wield **2.** beckon, direct, gesticulate, gesture, indicate, sign, signal ~*n.* **3.** billow, breaker, comber, ridge, ripple, roller, sea surf, swell, undulation, unevenness **4.** current, drift, flood, ground swell, movement, outbreak, rash, rush, stream, surge, sweep, tendency, trend, upsurge

waver **1.** be indecisive, be irresolute, be unable to decide, be unable to make up one's mind, blow hot and cold (*Inf.*), dither, falter,

fluctuate, hesitate, hum and haw, seesaw, shillyshally (*Inf.*), swither (*Scot.*), vacillate **2.** flicker, fluctuate, quiver, reel, shake, sway, totter, tremble, undulate, vary, wave, weave, wobble

wax *v.* become fuller, become larger, develop, dilate, enlarge, expand, fill out, get bigger, grow, increase, magnify, mount, rise, swell

way **1.** approach, course of action, fashion, manner, means, method, mode, practice, procedure, process, scheme, system, technique **2.** access, avenue, channel, course,

direction, highway, lane, path, pathway, road, route, street, thoroughfare, track, trail **3.** elbowroom, opening, room, space **4.** distance, journey, length, stretch, trail **5.** advance, approach, journey, march, passage, progress **6.** characteristic, conduct, custom, habit, idiosyncrasy, manner, nature, personality, practice, style, trait, usage, wont **7.** aspect, detail, feature, particular, point, respect, sense **8.** aim, ambition, choice, demand, desire, goal, pleasure, will, wish **9.** *Inf.* circumstance, condition, fettle, shape (*Inf.*), situation, state, status **10.** forward motion,

waybill ('weɪ,bɪl) *n.* a document attached to goods in transit specifying their nature, point of origin, and destination as well as the route to be taken and the rate to be charged.

wayfarer ('weɪ,fɛərə) *n.* a person who goes on a journey. —'way,faring *n., adj.*

waylay (weɪ'leɪ) *vb.* **-laying, -laid.** (*tr.*) **1.** to lie in wait for and attack. **2.** to await and intercept unexpectedly. —way'layer *n.*

wayleave ('weɪ,liːv) *n.* access to property granted by a landowner for payment, for example to allow a contractor access to a building site.

way-out *adj. Inf.* **1.** extremely unconventional or experimental. **2.** excellent or amazing.

ways and means *pl. n.* **1.** the revenues and methods of raising the revenues needed for the functioning of a state or other political unit. **2.** the methods and resources for accomplishing some purpose.

wayside ('weɪ,saɪd) *n.* **1. a.** the side or edge of a road. **b.** (*modifier*) situated by the wayside: *a wayside inn.* **2. fall by the wayside.** to cease or fail to continue doing something: *of the nine starters, three fell by the wayside.*

wayward ('weɪwəd) *adj.* **1.** wanting to have one's own way regardless of others. **2.** capricious, erratic, or unpredictable. —'waywardly *adv.* —'waywardness *n.*

Wb *Physics. abbrev. for* weber.

w.b. *abbrev. for:* **1.** water ballast. **2.** Also: **W/B, W.B.** waybill. **3.** westbound.

w.c. *abbrev. for* water closet.

W.C. *or* **WC** *abbrev. for:* **1.** water closet. **2.** (in London postal code) West Central.

we (wiː) *pron.* (*subjective*) **1.** refers to the speaker or writer and another person or other people: *we should go now.* **2.** refers to all people or people in general: *the planet on which we live.* **3.** a formal word for **I** used by editors or other writers, and formerly by monarchs. **4.** *Inf.* used instead of *you* with a tone of condescension or sarcasm: *how are we today?*

W.E.A. (in Britain) *abbrev. for* Workers' Educational Association.

weak (wiːk) *adj.* **1.** lacking in physical or mental strength or force. **2.** liable to yield, break, or give way: *a weak link in a chain.* **3.** lacking in resolution or firmness of character. **4.** lacking strength, power, or intensity: *a weak voice.* **5.** lacking strength in a particular part: *a team weak in defence.* **6. a.** not functioning as well as is normal: *weak eyes.* **b.** easily upset: *a weak stomach.* **7.** lacking in conviction, persuasiveness, etc.: *a weak argument.* **8.** lacking in political or strategic strength: *a weak state.* **9.** lacking the usual, full, or desirable strength of flavour: *weak tea.* **10.** *Grammar.* **a.** denoting or belonging to a class of verbs, in Germanic languages, whose conjugation relies on inflectional endings rather than internal vowel gradation, as *look, looks, looking, looked.* **b.** belonging to any part-of-speech class, in any of various languages, whose inflections follow the more regular of two possible patterns. **11.** (of a syllable) not accented or stressed. **12.** (of an industry, market, securities, etc.) falling in price or characterized by falling prices. —'weakish *adj.*

weaken ('wiːkən) *vb.* to become or cause to become weak or weaker. —'weakener *n.*

weak-kneed *adj. Inf.* yielding readily to force, intimidation, etc. —,weak-'kneedly *adv.*

weakling ('wiːklɪŋ) *n.* a person or animal that is lacking in strength or weak in constitution or character.

weakly ('wiːklɪ) *adj.* **-lier, -liest.** **1.** sickly; feeble. ~*adv.* **2.** in a weak or feeble manner.

weak-minded *adj.* **1.** lacking in stability of mind or character. **2.** another word for feeble-minded. —,weak-'mindedly *adv.* —,weak-'mindedness *n.*

weakness ('wiːknɪs) *n.* **1.** a being weak. **2.** a failing, as in a person's character. **3.** a self-indulgent liking: *a weakness for chocolates.*

weal[1] (wiːl) *n.* a raised mark on the skin produced by a blow.

weal[2] (wiːl) *n. Arch.* prosperity or wellbeing (now esp. in **the public weal, the common weal**).

weald (wiːld) *n. Brit. arch.* open or forested country.

wealth (wɛlθ) *n.* **1.** a large amount of money and valuable material possessions. **2.** the state of being rich. **3.** a great profusion: *a wealth of gifts.* **4.** *Econ.* all goods and services with monetary or productive value.

wealth tax *n.* a tax on personal property.

wealthy ('wɛlθɪ) *adj.* **wealthier, wealthiest.** **1.** possessing wealth; rich. **2.** of or relating to wealth. **3.** abounding: *wealthy in friends.* —'wealthily *adv.* —'wealthiness *n.*

wean[1] (wiːn) *vb.* (*tr.*) **1.** to cause (a child or young mammal) to replace mother's milk by other nourishment. **2.** (usually foll. by *from*) to cause to desert former habits, pursuits, etc.

wean[2] (weɪn) *n. Scot. & northern Brit. dialect.* a child.

weapon ('wɛpən) *n.* **1.** an object or instrument used in fighting. **2.** anything that serves to get the better of an opponent: *his power of speech was his best weapon.* **3.** any part of an animal that is used to defend itself, to attack prey, etc., such as claws or a sting. —'weaponed *adj.* —'weaponless *adj.*

weaponry ('wɛpənrɪ) *n.* weapons regarded collectively.

wear (wɛə) *vb.* **wearing, wore, worn.** **1.** (*tr.*) to carry or have (a garment, etc.) on one's person as clothing, ornament, etc. **2.** (*tr.*) to carry or have on one's person habitually: *she wears a lot of red.* **3.** (*tr.*) to have in one's aspect: *to wear a smile.* **4.** (*tr.*) to display, show, or fly: *a ship wears its colours.* **5.** to deteriorate or cause to deteriorate by constant use or action. **6.** to produce or be produced by constant rubbing, scraping, etc.: *to wear a hole in one's trousers.* **7.** to bring or be brought to a specified condition by constant use or action: *to wear a tyre to shreds.* **8.** (*intr.*) to submit to constant use or ac-

---

THESAURUS

headway, movement, passage, progress **11. by the way** by the by, en passant, incidentally, in parenthesis, in passing **12. give way a.** break down, cave in, collapse, crack, crumple, fall, fall to pieces, give, go to pieces, subside **b.** accede, acknowledge defeat, acquiesce, back down, concede, make concessions, withdraw, yield **13. under way** afoot, begun, going, in motion, in progress, moving, on the go (*Inf.*), on the move, started

wayfarer bird of passage, globetrotter, Gypsy, itinerant, journeyer, nomad, rover, traveller, trekker, voyager, walker, wanderer

wayfaring *adj.* drifting, itinerant, journeying, nomadic, peripatetic, rambling, roving, travelling, voyaging, walking, wandering

waylay accost, ambush, attack, catch, hold up, intercept, lie in wait for, pounce on, set upon, surprise, swoop down on

wayward capricious, changeable, contrary, contumacious, cross-grained, disobedient, erratic, fickle, flighty, froward, headstrong, inconstant, incorrigible, insubordinate, intractable, mulish, obdurate, obstinate, perverse, rebellious, refractory, self-willed, stubborn, undependable, ungovern-

able, unmanageable, unpredictable, unruly, wilful

weak 1. anaemic, debilitated, decrepit, delicate, effete, enervated, exhausted, faint, feeble, fragile, frail, infirm, languid, puny, shaky, sickly, spent, tender, unsound, unsteady, wasted, weakly **2.** cowardly, impotent, indecisive, ineffectual, infirm, irresolute, namby-pamby, powerless, soft, spineless, timorous, weak-kneed (*Inf.*) **3.** distant, dull, faint, imperceptible, low, muffled, poor, quiet, slight, small, soft **4.** deficient, faulty, inadequate, lacking, poor, substandard, understrength, wanting **5.** feeble, flimsy, hollow, inconclusive, invalid, lame, pathetic, shallow, slight, unconvincing, unsatisfactory **6.** defenceless, exposed, helpless, unguarded, unprotected, unsafe, untenable, vulnerable, wide open **7.** diluted, insipid, milk-and-water, runny, tasteless, thin, under-strength, waterish, watery, wishy-washy (*Inf.*)

weaken 1. abate, debilitate, depress, diminish, droop, dwindle, ease up, enervate, fade, fail, flag, give way, impair, invalidate, lessen, lower, mitigate, moderate, reduce, sap, sap the strength of, soften up, temper, tire, undermine, wane **2.** adulterate, cut, de-

base, dilute, thin, thin out, water down

weakling coward, doormat (*Sl.*), drip (*Inf.*), jellyfish (*Inf.*), milksop, mouse, sissy, wet (*Brit. inf.*), wimp (*Inf.*)

weakness 1. debility, decrepitude, enervation, faintness, feebleness, fragility, frailty, impotence, infirmity, irresolution, powerlessness, vulnerability **2.** Achilles heel, blemish, chink in one's armour, defect, deficiency, failing, fault, flaw, imperfection, lack, shortcoming **3.** fondness, inclination, liking, passion, penchant, predilection, proclivity, proneness, soft spot

wealth 1. affluence, assets, capital, cash, estate, fortune, funds, goods, lucre, means, money, opulence, pelf, possessions, property, prosperity, resources, riches, substance **2.** abundance, bounty, copiousness, cornucopia, fullness, plenitude, plenty, profusion, richness, store

wealthy affluent, comfortable, filthy rich (*Sl.*), flush (*Inf.*), in the money (*Inf.*), loaded (*Sl.*), made of money (*Inf.*), moneyed, on easy street (*Sl.*), opulent, prosperous, quids in (*Sl.*), rich, rolling in it (*Sl.*), stinking rich (*Sl.*), well-heeled (*Sl.*), well-off, well-to-do

tion in a specified way: *his suit wears well.* **9.** (*tr.*) to harass or weaken. **10.** (when *intr.*, often foll. by *on*) (of time) to pass or be passed slowly. **11.** (*tr.*) *Brit. inf.* to accept: *Larry won't wear that argument.* ~*n.* **12.** the act of wearing or state of being worn. **13. a.** anything designed to be worn: *leisure wear.* **b.** (*in combination*): *nightwear.* **14.** deterioration from constant or normal use. **15.** the quality of resisting the effects of constant use. ~See also **wear down, wear off, wear out.** —'**wearer** *n.*

wear and tear *n.* damage, depreciation, or loss resulting from ordinary use.

wear down *vb.* (*adv.*) **1.** to consume or be consumed by long or constant wearing, rubbing, etc. **2.** to overcome or be overcome gradually by persistent effort.

wearing ('wɛərɪŋ) *adj.* causing fatigue or exhaustion; tiring. —'**wearingly** *adv.*

wearisome ('wɪərɪsəm) *adj.* causing fatigue or annoyance; tedious. —'**wearisomely** *adv.*

wear off *vb.* (*adv.*) **1.** to decrease in intensity gradually: *the pain will wear off in an hour.* **2.** to disappear or cause to disappear gradually through exposure, use, etc.

wear out *vb.* (*adv.*) **1.** to make or become unfit or useless through wear. **2.** (*tr.*) to exhaust or tire.

weary ('wɪərɪ) *adj.* **-rier, -riest. 1.** tired or exhausted. **2.** causing fatigue or exhaustion. **3.** caused by or suggestive of weariness: *a weary laugh.* **4.** (*postpositive*, often foll. by *of* or *with*) discontented or bored. ~*vb.* **-rying, -ried. 5.** to make or become weary. **6.** to make or become discontented or impatient. —'**weariless** *adj.* —'**wearily** *adv.* —'**weariness** *n.* —'**wearyingly** *adv.*

weasel ('wiːzəl) *n., pl.* **-sel** or **-sels. 1.** any of various small predatory mammals, such as the **European weasel,** having reddish-brown fur, an elongated body and neck, and short legs. **2.** *Inf.* a sly or treacherous person. —'**weaselly** *adv.*

weather ('wɛðə) *n.* **1. a.** the day-to-day meteorological conditions, esp. temperature, cloudiness, and rainfall, affecting a specific place. **b.** (*modifier*): relating to the forecasting of weather: *a weather ship.* **2. make heavy weather. a.** (of a vessel) to roll and pitch in heavy seas. **b.** (foll. by *of*) that to carry out with great effort or labour. **3. under the weather.** *Inf.* not in good health. ~*adj.* **4.** (*prenominal*) on or at the side or part towards the wind: *the weather anchor.* Cf. **lee** (sense 2). ~*vb.* **5.** to expose or be exposed to the action of the weather. **6.** to undergo or cause to undergo changes, such as discoloration, due to the action of the weather. **7.** (*intr.*) to withstand the action of the weather. **8.** (when *intr.*, foll. by *through*) to endure (a crisis, danger, etc.). **9.** (*tr.*) to slope (a surface, such as a roof) so as to throw rainwater clear. **10.** (*tr.*) to sail to the windward of: *to weather a point.* —'**weatherer** *n.*

weather-beaten *adj.* **1.** showing signs of exposure to the weather. **2.** tanned or hardened by exposure to the weather.

weatherboard ('wɛðə,bɔːd) *n.* a timber board, with a rabbet along the front of its top edge and along the back of its lower edge, that is fixed horizontally with others to form an exterior cladding on a wall or roof. —'**weather-,boarding** *n.*

weather-bound *adj.* (of a vessel, aircraft, etc.) delayed by bad weather.

weathercock ('wɛðə,kɒk) *n.* **1.** a weather vane in the form of a cock. **2.** a person who is fickle or changeable.

weather eye *n.* **1.** the vision of a person trained to observe changes in the weather. **2.** *Inf.* an alert or observant gaze. **3. keep one's weather eye open.** to stay on the alert.

weather house *n.* a model house, usually with two human figures, one that enters to foretell bad weather and one that enters to foretell good weather.

weathering ('wɛðərɪŋ) *n.* the mechanical and chemical breakdown of rocks by the action of rain, snow, cold, etc.

weatherman ('wɛðə,mæn) *n., pl.* **-men.** *Inf.* a person who forecasts the weather, esp. one who works in a meteorological office.

weatherproof ('wɛðə,pruːf) *adj.* **1.** designed or able to withstand exposure to weather without deterioration. ~*vb.* **2.** (*tr.*) to render (something) weatherproof.

weather strip *n.* a thin strip of compressible material, such as spring metal, felt, etc., that is fitted between the frame of a door or window and the opening part to exclude wind and rain. Also called: **weatherstripping.**

weather vane *n.* a vane designed to indicate the direction in which the wind is blowing.

weather-wise *adj.* **1.** skilful in predicting weather conditions. **2.** skilful in predicting trends in opinion, reactions, etc.

weatherworn ('wɛðə,wɔːn) *adj.* another word for **weather-beaten.**

weave (wiːv) *vb.* **weaving, wove** or **weaved; woven** or **weaved. 1.** to form (a fabric) by interlacing (yarn, etc.), esp. on a loom. **2.** (*tr.*) to make or construct by such a process: *to weave a shawl.* **3.** (of a spider) to make (a web). **4.** to construct by interlacing (twigs, etc.). **5.** (*tr.*) to construct by combining separate elements into a whole. **6.** (*tr.*; often foll. by *in, into, through,* etc.) to introduce: *to weave factual details into a fiction.* **7.** to create (a way, etc.) by moving from side to side: *to weave through a crowd.* **8. get weaving.** *Inf.* to hurry. ~*n.* **9.** the method or pattern of weaving or the structure of a woven fabric: *an open weave.* —'**weaver** *n.*

weaverbird ('wiːvə,bɜːd) or **weaver** *n.* any of a family of small Old World passerine songbirds, having a short thick bill and a dull plumage and building covered

---

THESAURUS

wear *v.* **1.** bear, be clothed in, be dressed in, carry, clothe oneself, don, dress in, have on, put on, sport **2.** display, exhibit, fly, show **3.** abrade, consume, corrode, deteriorate, erode, fray, grind, impair, rub, use, wash away, waste **4.** bear up, be durable, endure, hold up, last, stand up **5.** annoy, drain, enervate, exasperate, fatigue, harass, irk, pester, tax, undermine, vex, weaken, weary **6.** *Brit. sl.* accept, allow, brook, countenance, fall for, permit, put up with (*Inf.*), stand for, stomach, swallow (*Inf.*), take ~*n.* **7.** employment, mileage (*Inf.*), service, use, usefulness, utility **8.** apparel, attire, clothes, costume, dress, garb, garments, gear, habit, outfit, things **9.** abrasion, attrition, corrosion, damage, depreciation, deterioration, erosion, friction, use, wear and tear

wear down 1. abrade, be consumed, consume, corrode, erode, grind down, rub away **2.** chip away at (*Inf.*), fight a war of attrition against, overcome gradually, reduce, undermine

weariness drowsiness, enervation, exhaustion, fatigue, languor, lassitude, lethargy, listlessness, prostration, tiredness

wearing exasperating, exhausting, fatiguing, irksome, oppressive, taxing, tiresome, tiring, trying, wearisome

wearisome annoying, boring, bothersome, burdensome, dull, exasperating, exhausting, fatiguing, humdrum, irksome, monotonous, oppressive, pestilential, prosaic, tedious, troublesome, trying, uninteresting, vexatious, wearing

wear off 1. abate, decrease, diminish, disappear, dwindle, ebb, fade, lose effect, lose strength, peter out, subside, wane, weaken **2.** abrade, disappear, efface, fade, rub away

wear out 1. become useless, become worn, consume, deteriorate, erode, fray, impair, use up, wear through **2.** enervate, exhaust, fag out (*Inf.*), fatigue, frazzle (*Inf.*), knacker (*Brit. sl.*), prostrate, sap, tire, weary

weary *adj.* **1.** all in (*Sl.*), asleep or dead on one's feet (*Inf.*), dead beat (*Inf.*), dog-tired (*Inf.*), done in (*Inf.*), drained, drooping, drowsy, enervated, exhausted, fagged (*Inf.*), fatigued, flagging, jaded, knackered (*Sl.*), ready to drop, sleepy, spent, tired, wearied, whacked (*Brit. inf.*), worn out **2.** arduous, enervative, irksome, laborious, taxing, tiresome, tiring, wearing, wearisome **3.** bored, browned-off (*Inf.*), discontented, fed up, impatient, indifferent, jaded, sick (*Inf.*), sick and tired (*Inf.*) ~*v.* **4.** burden, debilitate, drain, droop, enervate, fade, fag (*Inf.*), fail, fatigue, grow tired, sap, take it out of (*Inf.*),

tax, tire, tire out, wear out **5.** annoy, become bored, bore, exasperate, have had enough, irk, jade, make discontented, plague, sicken, try the patience of, vex

weather *n.* **1.** climate, conditions **2. under the weather a.** ailing, below par, ill, indisposed, nauseous, not well, off-colour, out of sorts, poorly (*Inf.*), seedy (*Inf.*), sick **b.** crapulent, crapulous, drunk, groggy (*Inf.*), hung over (*Inf.*), inebriated, intoxicated, one over the eight (*Sl.*), the worse for drink, three sheets in the wind (*Inf.*), under the influence (*Inf.*) ~*v.* **3.** expose, harden, season, toughen **4.** bear up against, brave, come through, endure, get through, live through, make it (*Inf.*), overcome, pull through, resist, ride out, rise above, stand, stick it out (*Inf.*), suffer, surmount, survive, withstand

weave 1. blend, braid, entwine, fuse, incorporate, interlace, intermingle, intertwine, introduce, knit, mat, merge, plait, twist, unite **2.** build, construct, contrive, create, fabricate, make, make up, put together, spin **3.** crisscross, move in and out, weave one's way, wind, zigzag **4. get weaving** *Inf.* get a move on, get going, get one's finger out (*Brit. inf.*), get under way, hurry, make a start, shake a leg (*Sl.*), start

nests: includes the house sparrow.

web (wɛb) *n.* **1.** any structure, fabric, etc., formed by or as if by weaving or interweaving. **2.** a mesh of fine tough threads built by a spider from a liquid secreted from its spinnerets and used to trap insects. **3.** a similar network of threads spun by certain insect larvae, such as the silkworm. **4.** a fabric, esp. one in the process of being woven. **5.** a membrane connecting the toes of some aquatic birds or the digits of such aquatic mammals as the otter. **6.** the vane of a bird's feather. **7.** a thin piece of metal, esp. one connecting two thicker parts as in an H-beam or an I-beam. **8. a.** a continuous strip of paper as formed on a paper machine or fed from a reel into some printing presses. **b.** (*as modifier*): *web offset.* **9.** any structure, construction, etc., that is intricately formed or complex: *a web of intrigue.* ~*vb.* **webbing, webbed. 10.** (*tr.*) to cover with or as if with a web. **11.** (*tr.*) to entangle or ensnare. **12.** (*intr.*) to construct a web. —'**webless** *adj.*

webbed (wɛbd) *adj.* **1.** (of the feet of certain animals) having the digits connected by a thin fold of skin. **2.** having or resembling a web.

webbing ('wɛbɪŋ) *n.* **1.** a strong fabric of hemp, cotton, jute, etc., woven in strips and used under springs in upholstery or for straps, etc. **2.** the skin that unites the digits of a webbed foot.

weber ('veɪbə) *n.* the derived SI unit of magnetic flux; the flux that, when linking a circuit of one turn, produces in it an emf of 1 volt as it is reduced to zero at a uniform rate in one second. Symbol: Wb

webfoot ('wɛb‚fʊt) *n.* **1.** *Zool.* a foot having the toes connected by folds of skin. **2.** *Anat.* a foot having an abnormal membrane connecting adjacent toes.

wed (wɛd) *vb.* **wedding, wedded** *or* **wed. 1.** to take (a person of the opposite sex) as a husband or wife; marry. **2.** (*tr.*) to join (two people) in matrimony. **3.** (*tr.*) to unite closely. —'**wedded** *adj.*

we'd (wi:d; *unstressed* wɪd) *contraction of* we had *or* we would.

Wed. *abbrev. for* Wednesday.

wedding ('wɛdɪŋ) *n.* **1. a.** the act of marrying or the celebration of a marriage. **b.** (*as modifier*): *wedding day.* **2.** the anniversary of a marriage (in such combinations as **silver wedding** or **diamond wedding**).

wedding breakfast *n.* the meal usually served after a wedding ceremony or just before the bride and bridegroom leave for their honeymoon.

wedding cake *n.* a rich fruit cake, with one, two, or more tiers, covered with almond paste and decorated with royal icing, which is served at a wedding reception.

wedding ring *n.* a band ring with parallel sides, typically of precious metal, worn to indicate married status.

wedge (wɛdʒ) *n.* **1.** a block of solid material, esp. wood or metal, that is shaped like a narrow V in cross section and can be pushed or driven between two objects or parts of an object in order to split or secure them. **2.** any formation, structure, or substance in the shape of a wedge: *a wedge of cheese.* **3.** something such as an idea, action, etc., that tends to cause division. **4.** *Golf.* a club, a No. 10 iron with a face angle of more than 50°, used for bunker or pitch shots. **5.** (*formerly*) a body of troops formed in a V-shape. **6. thin end of the wedge.** anything unimportant in itself that implies the start of something much larger. ~*vb.* **7.** (*tr.*) to secure with or as if with a wedge. **8.** to squeeze or be squeezed like a wedge into a narrow space. **9.** (*tr.*) to force apart or divide with or as if with a wedge. —'**wedge‚like** *adj.* —'**wedgy** *adj.*

Wedgwood ('wɛdʒwʊd) *Trademark.* ~*n.* **1. a.** pottery produced at the Wedgwood factory, near Stoke-on-Trent. **b.** such pottery having applied decoration in white on a coloured ground. ~*adj.* **2. a.** relating to pottery made at the Wedgwood factory. **b.** characteristic of such pottery: *Wedgwood blue.*

wedlock ('wɛdlɒk) *n.* **1.** the state of being married. **2. born** *or* **conceived out of wedlock.** born or conceived when one's parents are not legally married.

Wednesday ('wɛnzdɪ) *n.* the fourth day of the week; third day of the working week.

wee[1] (wi:) *adj.* very small; tiny; minute.

wee[2] (wi:) *Inf., chiefly Brit.* ~*n.* **1. a.** the act or an instance of urinating. **b.** urine. ~*vb.* **2.** (*intr.*) to urinate. ~Also: **wee-wee.**

weed (wi:d) *n.* **1.** any plant that grows wild and profusely, esp. one that grows among cultivated plants, depriving them of space, food, etc. **2.** *Sl.* **a. the weed.** tobacco. **b.** a cigarette, often one containing marijuana. **c.** marijuana. **3.** *Inf.* a thin or unprepossessing person. **4.** an inferior horse, esp. one showing signs of weakness. ~*vb.* **5.** to remove (useless or troublesome plants) from (a garden, etc.). —'**weeder** *n.* —'**weedless** *adj.*

weedkiller ('wi:d‚kɪlə) *n.* a substance, usually a chemical or hormone, used for killing weeds.

weed out *vb.* (*tr., adv.*) to separate out, remove, or eliminate (anything unwanted): *to weed out troublesome students.*

weeds (wi:dz) *pl. n.* a widow's black mourning clothes. Also called: **widow's weeds.**

weedy ('wi:dɪ) *adj.* **weedier, weediest. 1.** full of or containing weeds: *weedy land.* **2.** (of a plant) resembling a weed in straggling growth. **3.** *Inf.* thin or weakly in appearance.

week (wi:k) *n.* **1.** a period of seven consecutive days, esp. one beginning with Sunday. Related adj.: **hebdomadal. 2.** a period of seven consecutive days beginning from or including a specified day: *a week from Wednesday.* **3.** the period of time within a week devoted to work. ~*adv.* **4.** *Chiefly Brit.* seven days before or after a specified day: *I'll visit you Wednesday week.*

weekday ('wi:k‚deɪ) *n.* any day of the week other than Sunday and, often, Saturday.

weekend *n.* (‚wi:k'ɛnd). **1. a.** the end of the week, esp. the period from Friday night until the end of Sunday. **b.** (*as modifier*): *a weekend party.* ~*vb.* ('wi:k‚ɛnd). **2.** (*intr.*) *Inf.* to spend or pass a weekend.

weekends (‚wi:k'ɛndz) *adv. Inf.* at the weekend, esp. regularly or during every weekend.

weekly ('wi:klɪ) *adj.* **1.** happening or taking place once a week or every week. **2.** determined or calculated by the week. ~*adv.* **3.** once a week or every week. ~*n., pl.* **lies. 4.** a newspaper or magazine issued every week.

weeny ('wi:nɪ) *adj.* **-nier, -niest.** *Inf.* very small; tiny.

weep (wi:p) *vb.* **weeping, wept. 1.** to shed (tears). **2.** (*tr.; foll. by out*) to utter, shedding tears. **3.** (when *intr.,* foll. by *for*) to lament (for something). **4.** to exude (drops of liquid). **5.** (*intr.*) (of a wound, etc.) to exude a watery fluid. ~*n.* **6.** a spell of weeping.

weeping ('wi:pɪŋ) *adj.* (of plants) having slender hanging branches. —'**weepingly** *adv.*

weepy ('wi:pɪ) *Inf.* ~*adj.* **weepier, weepiest. 1.** liable or tending to weep. ~*n., pl.* **weepies. 2.** a sentimental film or book. —'**weepiness** *n.*

weevil ('wi:vɪl) *n.* any of numerous beetles, many having elongated snouts, that are pests, feeding on plants and plant products. —'**weevily** *adj.*

wee-wee *n., vb.* a variant of **wee**[2].

weft (wɛft) *n.* the yarn woven across the width of the fabric through the lengthwise warp yarn. Also called: **filling, woof.**

weigh[1] (weɪ) *vb.* **1.** (*tr.*) to measure the weight of. **2.** (*intr.*) to have weight: *she weighs more than her sister.* **3.** (*tr.; often foll. by out*) to apportion according to weight. **4.** (*tr.*) to consider carefully: *to weigh the facts of a case.* **5.** (*intr.*) to be influential: *his words weighed little with the jury.* **6.** (*intr.; often foll. by on*) to be oppressive (to). **7. weigh anchor.** to raise a vessel's an-

---

THESAURUS

web 1. cobweb, spider's web 2. interlacing, lattice, mesh, net, netting, network, screen, tangle, toils, weave, webbing

wed 1. become man and wife, be married to, espouse, get hitched (*Inf.*), get married, join, make one, marry, splice (*Inf.*), take as one's husband, take as one's wife, take to wife, tie the knot (*Inf.*), unite 2. ally, blend, coalesce, combine, commingle, dedicate,

fuse, interweave, join, link, marry, merge, unify, unite, yoke

wedding espousals, marriage, marriage ceremony, nuptial rite, nuptials, wedlock

wedge 1. *n.* block, chock, chunk, lump, wodge (*Brit. inf.*) 2. *v.* block, cram, crowd, force, jam, lodge, pack, ram, split, squeeze, stuff, thrust

wedlock marriage, matrimony

weed out dispense with, eliminate, eradi-

cate, extirpate, get rid of, remove, root out, separate out, shed, uproot

weekly by the week, every week, hebdomadal, hebdomadally, hebdomadary, once a week

weep bemoan, bewail, blub (*Sl.*), blubber, boohoo, complain, cry, greet (*Dialect*), keen, lament, moan, mourn, shed tears, snivel, sob, ululate, whimper, whinge (*Inf.*)

chor or (of a vessel) to have its anchor raised preparatory to departure. —'**weighable** adj. —'**weigher** n.

weigh² (wei) n. **under weigh.** a variant spelling of **under way.**

weighbridge ('wei,bridʒ) n. a machine for weighing vehicles, etc., by means of a metal plate set into a road.

weigh down vb. (adv.) to press (a person, etc.) down by or as if by weight: *his troubles weighed him down.*

weigh in vb. (intr., adv.) **1. a.** (of a boxer or wrestler) to be weighed before a bout. **b.** (of a jockey) to be weighed after, or sometimes before, a race. **2.** Inf. to contribute, as in a discussion, etc.: *he weighed in with a few sharp comments.* ~n. **weigh-in. 3.** the act of checking a competitor's weight, as in boxing, racing, etc.

weight (weit) n. **1.** a measure of the heaviness of an object; the amount anything weighs. **2.** Physics. the vertical force experienced by a mass as a result of gravitation. **3.** a system of units used to express weight: *troy weight.* **4.** a unit used to measure weight: *the kilogram is the weight used in SI units.* **5.** any mass or heavy object used to exert pressure or weigh down. **6.** an oppressive force: *the weight of cares.* **7.** any heavy load: *the bag was such a weight.* **8.** the main force; preponderance: *the weight of evidence.* **9.** importance; influence: *his opinion carries weight.* **10.** Statistics. one of a set of coefficients assigned to items of a frequency distribution that are analysed in order to represent the relative importance of the different items. **11.** Printing. the apparent blackness of a printed typeface. **12. pull one's weight.** Inf. to take one's share of responsibility. **13. throw one's weight around.** Inf. to act in an overauthoritarian manner. ~vb. (tr.) **14.** to add weight to. **15.** to burden or oppress. **16.** Statistics. to attach a weight or weights to. —'**weighter** n.

weighting ('weitiŋ) n. an additional allowance, esp. one paid to compensate for higher living costs: *a London weighting.*

weightlifting ('weit,liftiŋ) n. the sport of lifting barbells of specified weights in a prescribed manner. —'**weight,lifter** n.

weighty ('weiti) adj. **weightier, weightiest. 1.** having great weight. **2.** important. **3.** causing worry. —'**weightily** adv. —'**weightiness** n.

weir (wiə) n. **1.** a low dam that is built across a river to raise the water level, divert the water, or control its flow. **2.** a series of traps or enclosures placed in a stream to catch fish.

weird (wiəd) adj. **1.** suggestive of or relating to the supernatural; eerie. **2.** strange or bizarre. **3.** Arch. of or relating to fate or the Fates. ~n. **4.** Arch., chiefly Scot. **a.** fate or destiny. **b.** one of the Fates. —'**weirdly** adv. —'**weirdness** n.

weirdo ('wiədəʊ) or **weirdie** ('wiədi) n., pl.-**dos** or -**dies.** Inf. a person who behaves in a bizarre or eccentric manner.

welch (welʃ) vb. a variant spelling of **welsh.**

welcome ('welkəm) adj. **1.** gladly and cordially received or admitted: *a welcome guest.* **2.** bringing pleasure: *a welcome gift.* **3.** freely permitted or invited: *you are welcome to call.* **4.** under no obligation (only in such phrases as **you're welcome,** as conventional responses to thanks). ~sentence substitute. **5.** an expression of cordial greeting. ~n. **6.** the act of greeting or receiving a person or thing; reception: *the new theory had a cool welcome.* **7. wear out** or **overstay one's welcome.** to come more often or stay longer than is pleasing. ~vb. (tr.) **8.** to greet the arrival of (guests, etc.) cordially. **9.** to receive or accept, esp. gladly. —'**welcomely** adv. —'**welcomer** n.

weld (weld) vb. **1.** (tr.) to unite (pieces of metal or plastic), as by softening with heat and hammering or by fusion. **2.** to bring or admit of being brought into close union. ~n. **3.** a joint formed by welding. —'**weldable** adj. —,**welda'bility** n. —'**welder** or '**weldor** n.

welfare ('wel,feə) n. **1.** health, happiness, prosperity, and wellbeing in general. **2. a.** financial and other assistance given to people in need. **b.** (as modifier): *welfare services.* **3.** Also called: **welfare work.** plans or work to better the social or economic conditions of various underprivileged groups. **4. on welfare.** Chiefly U.S. in receipt of financial aid from a government agency or other source.

welfare state n. a system in which the government undertakes the chief responsibility for providing for the social and economic security of its population, usually through unemployment insurance, old age pensions, and other social-security measures.

well¹ (wel) adv. **better, best. 1.** (often used in combination) in a satisfactory manner: *the party went very well.* **2.** (often used in combination) in a skilful manner: *she plays the violin well.* **3.** in a correct or careful manner: *listen well to my words.* **4.** in a prosperous manner: *to live well.* **5.** (usually used with auxiliaries) suitably; fittingly: *you can't very well say that.* **6.** intimately: *I knew him well.* **7.** in a kind or favourable manner: *she speaks well of you.* **8.** fully: *to be well informed.* **9.** by a considerable margin: *let me know well in advance.* **10.** (preceded by could, might, or may) indeed: *you may well*

well-acquainted adj.	well-constructed adj.	well-equipped adj.	well-matched adj.
well-adjusted adj.	well-contented adj.	well-established adj.	well-merited adj.
well-advertised adj.	well-controlled adj.	well-fed adj.	well-paid adj.
well-aired adj.	well-cooked adj.	well-finished adj.	well-placed adj.
well-attended adj.	well-covered adj.	well-furnished adj.	well-prepared adj.
well-aware adj.	well-defended adj.	well-hidden adj.	well-provided adj.
well-behaved adj.	well-deserved adj.	well-housed adj.	well-qualified adj.
well-beloved adj. n.	well-developed adj.	well-illustrated adj.	well-received adj.
well-built adj.	well-documented adj.	well-judged adj.	well-satisfied adj.
well-clothed adj.	well-dressed adj.	well-kept adj.	well-spent adj.
well-concealed adj.	well-earned adj.	well-liked adj.	well-timed adj.
well-conducted adj.	well-educated adj.	well-loved adj.	well-trained adj.
well-considered adj.	well-endowed adj.	well-made adj.	well-used adj.

THESAURUS

weigh 1. have a weight of, measure the weight of, put on the scales, tip the scales at (Inf.) **2.** apportion, deal out, dole out, measure **3.** consider, contemplate, deliberate upon, evaluate, examine, give thought to, meditate upon, mull over, ponder, reflect upon, study, think over **4.** be influential, carry weight, count, cut any ice (Inf.), have influence, impress, matter, tell **5.** bear down, burden, oppress, prey

weigh down bear down, burden, depress, get down, oppress, overburden, overload, press down, trouble, weigh upon, worry

weight n. **1.** avoirdupois, burden, gravity, heaviness, heft (Inf.), load, mass, poundage, pressure, tonnage **2.** ballast, heavy object, load, mass **3.** burden, load, millstone, oppression, pressure, strain **4.** greatest force, main force, onus, preponderance **5.** authority,

clout (Inf.), consequence, consideration, efficacy, emphasis, impact, import, importance, influence, moment, persuasiveness, power, significance, substance, value ~v. **6.** add weight to, ballast, charge, freight, increase the load on, increase the weight of, load, make heavier **7.** burden, encumber, handicap, impede, oppress, overburden, weigh down **8.** bias, load, unbalance

weighty 1. burdensome, cumbersome, dense, heavy, hefty (Inf.), massive, ponderous **2.** consequential, considerable, critical, crucial, forcible, grave, important, momentous, portentous, serious, significant, solemn, substantial **3.** backbreaking, burdensome, crushing, demanding, difficult, exacting, onerous, oppressive, taxing, worrisome, worrying

weird bizarre, creepy (Inf.), eerie, eldritch

(Poetic), far-out (Sl.), freakish, ghostly, grotesque, mysterious, odd, outlandish, queer, spooky (Inf.), strange, supernatural, uncanny, unearthly, unnatural

welcome adj. **1.** acceptable, accepted, agreeable, appreciated, delightful, desirable, gladly received, gratifying, pleasant, pleasing, pleasurable, refreshing, wanted **2.** at home, free, invited, under no obligation ~n. **3.** acceptance, entertainment, greeting, hospitality, reception, salutation ~v. **4.** accept gladly, bid welcome, embrace, greet, hail, meet, offer hospitality to, receive, receive with open arms, roll out the red carpet for, usher in

welfare advantage, benefit, good, happiness, health, interest, profit, prosperity, success, wellbeing

have to do it yourself. **11. all very well.** used ironically to express discontent, dissent, etc. **12. as well. a.** in addition; too. **b.** (preceded by *may* or *might*) with equal effect: *you might as well come.* **13. as well as.** in addition to. **14. (just) as well.** preferable or advisable: *it would be just as well if you paid me now.* **15. leave well (enough) alone.** to refrain from interfering with something that is satisfactory. **16. well and good.** used to indicate calm acceptance, as of a decision. ~*adj.* (*usually postpositive*) **17.** (*when prenominal, usually used with a negative*) in good health: *I'm very well, thank you; he's not a well man.* **18.** satisfactory or pleasing. **19.** prudent; advisable: *it would be well to make no comment.* **20.** prosperous or comfortable. **21.** fortunate: *it is well that you agreed to go.* ~*interj.* **22. a.** an expression of surprise, indignation, or reproof. **b.** an expression of anticipation in waiting for an answer or remark. ~*sentence connector.* **23.** an expression used to preface a remark, gain time, etc.: *well, I don't think I will come.*

well² (wɛl) *n.* **1.** a hole or shaft bored into the earth to tap a supply of water, oil, gas, etc. **2.** a natural pool where ground water comes to the surface. **3. a.** a cavity, space, or vessel used to contain a liquid. **b.** (*in combination*): *an inkwell.* **4.** an open shaft through the floors of a building, such as one used for a staircase. **5.** a deep enclosed space in a building or between buildings that is open to the sky. **6.** a bulkheaded compartment built around a ship's pumps for protection and ease of access. **7.** (in England) the open space in the centre of a law court. **8.** an abundant source: *he is a well of knowledge.* ~*vb.* **9.** to flow or cause to flow upwards or outwards: *tears welled from her eyes.*

we'll (wiːl) *contraction of* we will *or* we shall.

well-appointed *adj.* (**well appointed** *when postpositive*). well equipped or furnished.

well-balanced *adj.* (**well balanced** *when postpositive*). **1.** having good balance or proportions. **2.** sane or sensible.

wellbeing ('wɛl'biːɪŋ) *n.* the condition of being contented, healthy, or successful; welfare.

well-bred *adj.* (**well bred** *when postpositive*). **1.** Also: **well-born.** of respected or noble lineage. **2.** indicating good breeding: *well-bred manners.* **3.** of good thoroughbred stock: *a well-bred spaniel.*

well-connected *adj.* (**well connected** *when postpositive*). having influential or important relatives or friends.

well-disposed *adj.* (**well disposed** *when postpositive*). inclined to be sympathetic, kindly, or friendly.

well-done *adj.* (**well done** *when postpositive*). **1.** (of food, esp. meat) cooked thoroughly. **2.** made or accomplished satisfactorily.

well-groomed *adj.* (**well groomed** *when postpositive*). having a tidy pleasing appearance.

well-grounded *adj.* (**well grounded** *when postpositive*). **1.** well instructed in the basic elements of a subject. **2.** based on good reasons.

wellhead ('wɛl,hɛd) *n.* **1.** the source of a well or stream. **2.** a source, fountainhead, or origin.

well-heeled *adj.* (**well heeled** *when postpositive*). *Sl.*

rich; prosperous; wealthy.

wellies ('wɛlɪz) *pl. n. Brit. inf.* Wellington boots.

well-informed *adj.* (**well informed** *when postpositive*). **1.** having knowledge about a great variety of subjects: *he seems to be a well-informed person.* **2.** possessing reliable information on a particular subject.

Wellington boots ('wɛlɪŋtən) *pl. n.* **1.** *Brit.* another name for **gumboots.** Often shortened to **wellingtons, wellies. 2.** military leather boots covering the front of the knee but cut away at the back to allow easier bending of the knee.

well-intentioned *adj.* (**well intentioned** *when postpositive*). having benevolent intentions, usually with unfortunate results.

well-known *adj.* (**well known** *when postpositive*). **1.** widely known; famous; celebrated. **2.** known fully or clearly.

well-meaning *adj.* (**well meaning** *when postpositive*). having or indicating good intentions, usually with unfortunate results.

well-nigh *adv. Arch. or poetic.* nearly; almost: *it's well-nigh three o'clock.*

▷ **Usage.** In strict usage, *well-nigh* is an adverb meaning *nearly* or *almost* and not a preposition meaning *near: he well-nigh cried; he was near* (not *well-nigh*) *death.*

well-off *adj.* (**well off** *when postpositive*). **1.** in a comfortable or favourable position or state. **2.** financially well provided for; moderately rich.

well-preserved *adj.* (**well preserved** *when postpositive*). **1.** kept in a good condition. **2.** continuing to appear youthful: *she was a well-preserved old lady.*

well-read ('wɛl'rɛd) *adj.* (**well read** *when postpositive*). having read widely and intelligently; erudite.

well-rounded *adj.* (**well rounded** *when postpositive*). **1.** rounded in shape ● ●●● developed: *a well-rounded figure.* **2.** full, varied ●●●●●●fying: *a well-rounded life.*

well-spoken *adj.* (●●● **spoken** *when postpositive*). **1.** having a clear, articulate, and socially acceptable accent and way of speaking. **2.** spoken satisfactorily or pleasingly.

wellspring ('wɛlsprɪŋ) *n.* **1.** the source of a spring or stream. **2.** a source of abundant supply.

well-thought-of *adj.* respected.

well-to-do *adj.* moderately wealthy.

well-wisher *n.* a person who shows benevolence or sympathy towards a person, cause, etc. —'**well-** ,**wishing** *adj., n.*

well-worn *adj.* (**well worn** *when postpositive*). **1.** so much used as to be affected by wear: *a well-worn coat.* **2.** hackneyed: *a well-worn phrase.*

welsh *or* **welch** (wɛlʃ) *vb.* (*intr.*; often foll. by *on*) **1.** to fail to pay a gambling debt. **2.** to fail to fulfil an obligation. —'**welsher** *or* '**welcher** *n.*

Welsh (wɛlʃ) *adj.* **1.** of, relating to, or characteristic of Wales, its people, their language, or their dialect of English. ~*n.* **2.** a language of Wales, belonging to the S Celtic branch of the Indo-European family. **3. the Welsh.** (*functioning as pl.*) the natives or inhabitants of Wales.

THESAURUS

well¹ *adv.* **1.** agreeably, capitally, famously (*Inf.*), happily, in a satisfactory manner, nicely, pleasantly, satisfactorily, smoothly, splendidly, successfully **2.** ably, adeptly, adequately, admirably, conscientiously, correctly, effectively, efficiently, expertly, proficiently, properly, skilfully, with skill **3.** accurately, attentively, carefully, closely **4.** comfortably, flourishingly, prosperously **5.** correctly, easily, fairly, fittingly, in all fairness, justly, properly, readily, rightly, suitably **6.** closely, completely, deeply, fully, intimately, personally, profoundly, thoroughly **7.** approvingly, favourably, glowingly, graciously, highly, kindly, warmly **8.** abundantly, amply, completely, considerably, fully, greatly, heartily, highly, substantially, sufficiently, thoroughly, very much **9. as well** also, besides, in addition, into the bargain, to boot, too **10. as well as** along with, at the same time as, in addition to, including, over and above ~*adj.* **11.** able-bodied, fit, hale, healthy, hearty, in fine fettle, in good health,

robust, sound, strong, up to par **12.** advisable, agreeable, bright, fine, fitting, flourishing, fortunate, good, happy, lucky, pleasing, profitable, proper, prudent, right, satisfactory, thriving, useful

well² *n.* **1.** fountain, pool, source, spring, waterhole **2.** bore, hole, pit, shaft **3.** fount, mine, repository, source, wellspring ~*v.* **4.** flow, gush, jet, ooze, pour, rise, run, seep, spout, spring, spurt, stream, surge, trickle

well-balanced 1. graceful, harmonious, proportional, symmetrical, well-proportioned **2.** judicious, level-headed, rational, reasonable, sane, sensible, sober, sound, together (*Sl.*), well-adjusted

well-bred 1. aristocratic, blue-blooded, gentle, highborn, noble, patrician, well-born **2.** civil, courteous, courtly, cultivated, cultured, gallant, genteel, gentlemanly, ladylike, mannerly, polished, polite, refined, urbane, well-brought-up, well-mannered

well-fed 1. healthy, in good condition, well-nourished **2.** chubby, fat, fleshy, plump,

podgy, portly, rotund, rounded, stout

well-groomed dapper, neat, smart, spruce, tidy, trim, well-dressed, well turned out

well-known celebrated, familiar, famous, illustrious, notable, noted, popular, renowned, widely known

well-nigh all but, almost, just about, more or less, nearly, next to, practically, virtually

well-off 1. comfortable, flourishing, fortunate, lucky, successful, thriving **2.** affluent, comfortable, flush (*Inf.*), loaded (*Sl.*), moneyed, prosperous, rich, wealthy, well-heeled (*Sl.*), well-to-do

well-thought-of admired, esteemed, highly regarded, of good repute, reputable, respected, revered, venerated

well-to-do affluent, comfortable, flush (*Inf.*), loaded (*Sl.*), moneyed, prosperous, rich, wealthy, well-heeled (*Sl.*), well-off

Welsh dresser *n.* a sideboard with drawers and cupboards below and open shelves above.

Welsh rabbit *n.* a savoury dish consisting of melted cheese sometimes mixed with milk, seasonings, etc., on hot buttered toast. Also called: **Welsh rarebit, rarebit.**

welt (wɛlt) *n.* **1.** a raised or strengthened seam in a garment. **2.** another word for **weal**[1]. **3.** (in shoemaking) a strip of leather, etc., put in between the outer sole and the inner sole and upper. ~*vb.* (*tr.*) **4.** to put a welt in (a garment, etc.). **5.** to beat soundly.

welter ('wɛltə) *vb.* (*intr.*) **1.** to roll about, writhe, or wallow. **2.** (esp. of the sea) to surge, heave, or toss. **3.** to lie drenched in a liquid, esp. blood. ~*n.* **4.** a confused mass; jumble.

welterweight ('wɛltə,weit) *n.* **1. a.** a professional boxer weighing 140–147 pounds (63.5–66.5 kg). **b.** an amateur boxer weighing 63.5–67 kg (140–148 pounds). **2.** a wrestler in a similar weight category (usually 154–172 pounds (70–78 kg)).

wen (wɛn) *n. Pathol.* a sebaceous cyst, esp. one occurring on the scalp.

wench (wɛntʃ) *n.* **1.** a girl or young woman: now used facetiously. **2.** *Arch.* a female servant. **3.** *Arch.* a prostitute. ~*vb.* (*intr.*) **4.** *Arch.* to frequent the company of prostitutes. —'**wencher** *n.*

wend (wɛnd) *vb.* to direct (one's course or way); travel.

wensleydale ('wɛnzlɪ,deɪl) *n.* **1.** a type of white cheese with a flaky texture. **2.** a breed of sheep with long woolly fleece.

went (wɛnt) *vb.* the past tense of **go.**

wept (wɛpt) *vb.* the past tense or past participle of **weep.**

were (wɜː; *unstressed* wə) *vb.* the plural form of the past tense (indicative mood) of **be** and the singular form used with *you*. It is also used as a subjunctive, esp. in conditional sentences.

▷ **Usage.** *Were,* as a remnant of the past subjunctive in English, is used in formal contexts in clauses expressing hypotheses (*if he were to die, she would inherit everything*), suppositions contrary to fact (*if I were you, I would be careful*), and desire (*I wish he were there now*). In informal speech, however, *was* is often used instead.

we're (wɪə) *contraction of* we are.

weren't (wɜːnt) *contraction of* were not.

werewolf ('wɪə,wʊlf, 'wɛə-) *n., pl.* **-wolves.** a person fabled in folklore and superstition to have been changed into a wolf by being bewitched or said to be able to assume wolf form at will.

wert (wɜːt; *unstressed* wət) *vb. Arch. or dialect.* (used with the pronoun *thou* or its relative equivalent) a singular form of the past tense (indicative mood) of **be.**

Wesleyan ('wɛzlɪən) *adj.* **1.** of or deriving from John Wesley (1703–91), English preacher who founded Methodism. **2.** of or characterizing Methodism, esp. in its original form. ~*n.* **3.** a follower of John Wesley. **4.** a member of the Methodist Church. —'**Wesleyanism** *n.*

west (wɛst) *n.* **1.** the direction along a parallel towards the sunset, at 270° clockwise from north. **2. the west.** (*often cap.*) any area lying in or towards the west. Related adjs.: **Hesperian, Occidental.** ~*adj.* **3.** situated in, moving towards, or facing the west. **4.** (esp. of the wind) from the west. ~*adv.* **5.** in, to, towards, or (esp. of the wind) from the west. **6. go west.** *Inf.* **a.** to be lost or destroyed. **b.** to die.

West (wɛst) *n.* **the. 1.** the western part of the world contrasted historically and culturally with the East or Orient. **2.** the non-Communist countries of Europe and America contrasted with the Communist states of the East. **3.** (in the U.S.) that part of the U.S. lying approximately to the west of the Mississippi. **4.** (in the ancient and medieval world) the Western Roman Empire and, later, the Holy Roman Empire. ~*adj.* **5.** of or denoting the western part of a specified country, area, etc.

westbound ('wɛst,baʊnd) *adj.* going or leading towards the west.

West Country *n.* **the.** the southwest of England, esp. Cornwall, Devon, and Somerset.

West End *n.* **the.** a part of W central London containing the main shopping and entertainment areas.

westerly ('wɛstəlɪ) *adj.* **1.** of, relating to, or situated in the west. ~*adv., adj.* **2.** towards or in the direction of the west. **3.** (esp. of the wind) from the west. ~*n., pl.* **-lies.** **4.** a wind blowing from the west. —'**westerliness** *n.*

western ('wɛstən) *adj.* **1.** situated in or facing the west. **2.** going or directed to or towards the west. **3.** (of a wind, etc.) coming from the west. **4.** native to the west. **5.** *Music.* See **country-and-western.** —'**western,most** *adj.*

Western ('wɛstən) *adj.* **1.** of or characteristic of the Americas and the parts of Europe not under Communist rule. **2.** of or characteristic of the West as opposed to the Orient. **3.** of or characteristic of the western states of the U.S. ~*n.* (*often not cap.*) **4.** a film, book, etc., concerned with life in the western states of the U.S., esp. during the era of exploration.

westerner ('wɛstənə) *n.* (*sometimes cap.*) a native or inhabitant of the west or of any specific region.

western hemisphere *n.* (*often caps.*) **1.** that half of the globe containing the Americas, lying to the west of the Greenwich or another meridian. **2.** the lands contained in this, esp. the Americas.

westernize *or* **-ise** ('wɛstə,naɪz) *vb.* (*tr.*) to influence or make familiar with the customs, practices, etc., of the West. —,**westerni'zation** *or* **-i'sation** *n.*

Westminster ('wɛst,mɪnstə) *n.* **1.** Also called: **City of Westminster.** a borough of Greater London, on the River Thames. **2.** the Houses of Parliament at Westminster.

west-northwest *n.* **1.** the point on the compass or the direction midway between west and northwest, 292° 30′ clockwise from north. ~*adj., adv.* **2.** in, from, or towards this direction.

west-southwest *n.* **1.** the point on the compass or the direction midway between southwest and west, 247° 30′ clockwise from north. ~*adj., adv.* **2.** in, from, or towards this direction.

westward ('wɛstwəd) *adj.* **1.** moving, facing, or situated in the west. ~*adv.* **2.** Also: **westwards.** towards the west. ~*n.* **3.** the westward part, direction, etc. —'**westwardly** *adj., adv.*

wet (wɛt) *adj.* **wetter, wettest. 1.** moistened, covered, saturated, etc., with water or some other liquid. **2.** not yet dry or solid: *wet varnish.* **3.** rainy: *wet weather.* **4.** employing a liquid, usually water: *a wet method of chemical analysis.* **5.** *Chiefly U.S.* permitting the free sale of alcoholic beverages: *a wet state.* **6.** *Brit. inf.* feeble or foolish. **7. wet behind the ears.** *Inf.* immature or inexperienced. ~*n.* **8.** wetness or moisture. **9.** rainy weather. **10.** *Chiefly U.S.* a person who advocates free sale of alcoholic beverages. **11.** *Brit. inf.* a feeble or foolish person. **12.** (*often cap.*) *Brit. inf.* a Conservative politician who is not a hardliner. **13. the wet.** *Austral.* (in northern and central Australia) the rainy season. ~*vb.* **wetting, wet** *or* **wetted. 14.** to make or become wet. **15.** to urinate on (something). **16. wet one's whistle.** *Inf.* to take a drink. —'**wetly** *adv.* —'**wetness** *n.* —'**wettable** *adj.* —'**wetter** *n.* —'**wettish** *adj.*

wet blanket *n. Inf.* a person whose low spirits or lack of enthusiasm have a depressing effect on others.

wet dream *n.* an erotic dream accompanied by an emission of semen.

wether ('wɛðə) *n.* a male sheep, esp. a castrated one.

wet nurse *n.* **1.** a woman hired to suckle the child of another. ~*vb.* **wet-nurse.** (*tr.*) **2.** to act as a wet nurse to (a child). **3.** *Inf.* to attend with great devotion.

wet suit *n.* a close-fitting rubber suit used by skindivers, yachtsmen, etc., to retain body heat.

we've (wiːv) *contraction of* we have.

whack (wæk) *vb.* (*tr.*) **1.** to strike with a sharp resound-

---

THESAURUS

wet *adj.* **1.** aqueous, damp, dank, drenched, dripping, humid, moist, moistened, saturated, soaked, soaking, sodden, soggy, sopping, waterlogged, watery, wringing wet **2.** clammy, dank, drizzling, humid, misty, pouring, raining, rainy, showery, teeming **3.** *Brit. inf.* effete, feeble, foolish, ineffectual, irresolute, namby-pamby, silly, soft, spineless, timorous, weak, weedy (*Inf.*) **4. wet behind the ears** *Inf.* born yesterday, callow, green, immature, inexperienced, innocent, naive, new, raw ~*n.* **5.** clamminess, condensation, damp, dampness, humidity, liquid, moisture, water, wetness **6.** damp weather, drizzle, rain, rains, rainy season, rainy weather **7.** *Brit. inf.* drip (*Inf.*), milksop, weakling, weed (*Inf.*), wimp (*Inf.*) ~*v.* **8.** damp, dampen, dip, douse, drench, humidify, irrigate, moisten, saturate, soak, splash, spray, sprinkle, steep, water

ing blow. **2.** (*usually passive*) *Brit. inf.* to exhaust completely. ~*n.* **3.** a sharp resounding blow or the noise made by such a blow. **4.** *Inf.* a share or portion. **5.** *Inf.* a try or attempt (esp. in **have a whack at**). —'**whacker** *n.*

whacking ('wækɪŋ) *Inf., chiefly Brit.* ~*adj.* **1.** enormous. ~*adv.* **2.** (intensifier): *a whacking big lie.*

whale (weɪl) *n., pl.* **whales** *or* **whale. 1.** any of the larger cetacean mammals, excluding dolphins, porpoises, and narwhals. They have flippers, a streamlined body, and a horizontally flattened tail and breathe through a blowhole on the top of the head. **2. a whale of a.** *Inf.* an exceptionally large, fine, etc., example of a (person or thing).

whaleboat ('weɪl,bəʊt) *n.* a narrow boat from 20 to 30 feet long having a sharp prow and stern, formerly used in whaling. Also called: **whaler.**

whalebone ('weɪl,bəʊn) *n.* **1.** Also called: **baleen.** a horny elastic material forming numerous thin plates that hang from the upper jaw in the toothless (whalebone) whales and strain plankton from water entering the mouth. **2.** a thin strip of this substance, used in stiffening corsets, bodices, etc.

whalebone whale *n.* any whale belonging to a cetacean suborder having a double blowhole and strips of whalebone between the jaws instead of teeth: includes the rorquals, right whales, and the blue whale.

whaler ('weɪlə) *n.* **1.** Also called (U.S.): **whaleman.** a person employed in whaling. **2.** a vessel engaged in whaling. **3.** *Austral. obs. sl.* a tramp or sundowner. **4.** an aggressive shark of Australian coastal waters.

whaling ('weɪlɪŋ) *n.* the work or industry of hunting and processing whales for food, oil, etc.

wham (wæm) *n.* **1.** a forceful blow or impact or the sound produced by it. ~*vb.* **whamming, whammed. 2.** to strike or cause to strike with great force.

wharf (wɔːf) *n., pl.* **wharves** (wɔːvz) *or* **wharfs. 1.** a platform at a harbour or navigable river for the docking, loading, and unloading of ships. ~*vb.* (*tr.*) **2.** to moor or dock at a wharf. **3.** to store or unload on a wharf.

wharfage ('wɔːfɪdʒ) *n.* **1.** accommodation for ships at wharves. **2.** a charge for use of a wharf. **3.** wharves collectively.

wharfinger ('wɔːfɪndʒə) *n.* an owner or manager of a wharf.

what (wɒt; *unstressed* wət) *determiner.* **1. a.** used with a noun in requesting further information about the identity or categorization of something: *what job does he do?* **b.** (*as pronoun*): *what is her address?* **c.** (*used in indirect questions*): *tell me what he said.* **2. a.** the (person, thing, persons, or things) that: *we photographed what animals we could see.* **b.** (*as pronoun*): *bring me what you've written.* **3.** (intensifier; used in exclamations): *what a good hook!* ~*adv.* **4.** in what respect? to what degree?: *what do you care?* **5. what about.** what do you think, know, etc., concerning? **6. what for.** for what purpose? why? **7. what have you.** someone or something unknown or unspecified: *cars, motorcycles, or what have you.* **8. what if. a.** what would happen if? **b.** what difference would it make if? **9. what matter.** what does it matter? **10. what's what.** *Inf.* the true state of affairs.
▷ **Usage.** In good usage, *what* is never used for *which*, as in *he gave me the letter what he had written. What* is used, however, for the things which and that or those which: *he saw what* (that which) *he had done.*

whatever (wɒt'ɛvə, wət-) *pron.* **1.** everything or anything that: *do whatever he asks you to.* **2.** no matter what: *whatever he does, he is forgiven.* **3.** *Inf.* an unknown or unspecified thing or things: *take a hammer, chisel, or whatever.* **4.** an intensive form of *what*, used in questions: *whatever can he have said to upset her so much?* ~*determiner.* **5.** an intensive form of *what*: use *whatever tools you can get hold of.* ~*adj.* **6.** (postpositive) absolutely; whatsoever: *I saw no point whatever in continuing.*

whatnot ('wɒt,nɒt) *n.* **1.** Also called: **what-d'you-call-it.** *Inf.* a person or thing the name of which is unknown or forgotten. **2.** *Inf.* unspecified assorted material. **3.** a

portable stand with shelves for displaying ornaments, etc.

whatsoever (,wɒtsəʊ'ɛvə) *adj.* **1.** (*postpositive*) at all: used as an intensifier with indefinite pronouns and determiners such as *none, anybody*, etc. ~*pron.* **2.** an archaic word for **whatever.**

wheat (wiːt) *n.* **1.** any of a genus of grasses, native to the Mediterranean region and W Asia but widely cultivated, having erect flower spikes and light brown grains. **2.** the grain of any of these grasses, used in making flour, pasta, etc.

wheatear ('wiːt,ɪə) *n.* a small northern songbird having a pale grey back, black wings and tail, white rump, and pale brown underparts.

wheaten ('wiːtən) *adj.* **1.** made of the grain or flour of wheat. **2.** of a pale yellow colour.

wheat germ *n.* the vitamin-rich embryo of the wheat kernel.

wheatmeal ('wiːt,miːl) *n.* **a.** a brown flour intermediate between white flour and wholemeal flour. **b.** (*as modifier*): *a wheatmeal loaf.*

wheedle ('wiːdəl) *vb.* **1.** to persuade or try to persuade (someone) by coaxing words, flattery, etc. **2.** (*tr.*) to obtain thus: *she wheedled some money out of her father.* —'**wheedler** *n.* —'**wheedlingly** *adv.*

wheel (wiːl) *n.* **1.** a solid disc, or a circular rim joined to a hub by spokes, that is mounted on a shaft about which it can turn, as in vehicles. **2.** anything like a wheel in shape or function. **3.** a device consisting of or resembling a wheel: *a steering wheel; a water wheel.* **4.** (usually preceded by *the*) a medieval torture consisting of a wheel to which the victim was tied and then had his limbs struck and broken by an iron bar. **5.** short for **potter's wheel. 6.** the act of turning. **7.** a pivoting movement of troops, ships, etc. **8.** a type of firework coiled to make it rotate when let off. **9.** a set of short rhyming lines forming the concluding part of a stanza. **10.** *U.S.* an informal word for **bicycle. 11.** *Inf., chiefly U.S.* a person of great influence (esp. in **big wheel**). **12. at the wheel. a.** driving or steering a vehicle or vessel. **b.** in charge. ~*vb.* **13.** to turn or cause to turn on or as if on an axis. **14.** to move or cause to move on or as if on wheels; roll. **15.** (*tr.*) to perform with or in a circular movement. **16.** (*tr.*) to provide with a wheel or wheels. **17.** (*intr.*; often foll. by *about*) to change direction. **18. wheel and deal.** *Inf., chiefly U.S.* to operate free of restraint, esp. to advance one's own interests.

wheelbarrow ('wiːl,bærəʊ) *n.* a simple vehicle for carrying small loads, typically being an open container supported by a wheel at the front and two legs behind.

wheelbase ('wiːl,beɪs) *n.* the distance between the front and back axles of a motor vehicle.

wheelchair ('wiːl,tʃɛə) *n.* a special chair on large wheels, for use by invalids or others for whom walking is impossible or inadvisable.

wheeler ('wiːlə) *n.* **1.** Also called: **wheel horse.** a horse or other draught animal nearest the wheel. **2.** (*in combination*) something equipped with a specified sort or number of wheels: *a three-wheeler.* **3.** a person or thing that wheels.

wheeler-dealer *n. Inf., chiefly U.S.* a person who wheels and deals.

wheelhouse ('wiːl,haʊs) *n.* another term for **pilot house.**

wheels (wiːlz) *pl. n.* **1.** the main directing force behind an organization, movement, etc.: *the wheels of government.* **2.** an informal word for **car. 3. wheels within wheels.** a series of intricately connected events, plots, etc.

wheelwright ('wiːl,raɪt) *n.* a person who makes or mends wheels as a trade.

wheeze (wiːz) *vb.* **1.** to breathe or utter (something) with a rasping or whistling sound. **2.** to make or move with a noise suggestive of wheezy breathing. ~*n.* **3.** a husky, rasping, or whistling sound or breathing. **4.** *Brit. sl.* a trick, idea, or plan. **5.** *Inf.* a hackneyed joke or anecdote. —'**wheezer** *n.* —'**wheezingly** *adv.* —'**wheezy** *adj.* —'**wheezily** *adv.* —'**wheeziness** *n.*

THESAURUS

wharf dock, jetty, landing stage, pier, quay
wheedle butter up, cajole, charm, coax, court, draw, entice, flatter, inveigle, persuade, talk into, worm
wheel *n.* **1.** circle, gyration, pivot, revolu-

tion, roll, rotation, spin, turn, twirl, whirl **2. at the wheel** at the helm, driving, in charge, in command, in control, in the driving seat, steering ~*v.* **3.** circle, gyrate, orbit, pirouette, revolve, roll, rotate, spin, swing, swivel,

turn, twirl, whirl

wheeze *v.* **1.** breathe roughly, catch one's breath, cough, gasp, hiss, rasp, whistle ~*n.* **2.** cough, gasp, hiss, rasp, whistle **3.** *Brit. sl.* ex-

whelk (wɛlk) *n.* a marine gastropod mollusc of coastal waters and intertidal regions, having a strong snail-like shell.

whelp (wɛlp) *n.* 1. a young offspring of certain animals, esp. of a wolf or dog. 2. *Disparaging.* a youth. 3. *Jocular.* a young child. 4. *Naut.* any of the ridges, parallel to the axis, on the drum of a capstan to keep a rope, cable, or chain from slipping. ~*vb.* 5. (of an animal or, disparagingly, a woman) to give birth to (young).

when (wɛn) *adv.* 1. **a.** at what time? over what period?: *when is he due?* **b.** (*used in indirect questions*): *ask him when he's due.* 2. **say when.** to state when an action is to be stopped or begun, as when someone is pouring a drink. ~*conj.* 3. (*subordinating*) at a time at which; just as; after: *I found it easily when I started to look seriously.* 4. although: *he drives when he might walk.* 5. considering the fact that: *how did you pass the exam when you'd not worked for it?* ~*pron.* 6. at which (time); over which (period): *an age when men were men.* ~*n.* 7. a question as to the time of some occurrence.

▷ **Usage.** Care should be taken so that *when* and *where* refer explicitly to time or place, and are not used loosely to substitute for *in which* after the verb *to be*: *paralysis is a condition in which* (not *when* or *where*) *parts of the body cannot be moved.*

whence (wɛns) *Arch. or formal.* ~*adv.* 1. from what place, cause, or origin? ~*pron.* 2. (*subordinating*) from what place, cause, or origin.

▷ **Usage.** Careful users of English avoid the expression *from whence,* since *whence* already means from which place: *the tradition whence* (not *from whence*) *such ideas flow.*

whencesoever (ˌwɛnssəʊˈɛvə) *conj.* (*subordinating*), *adv. Arch.* from whatever place, cause, or origin.

whenever (wɛnˈɛvə) *conj.* 1. (*subordinating*) at every or any time that; when: *I laugh whenever I see that.* ~*adv. also* **when ever.** 2. no matter when: *it'll be here, whenever you decide to come for it.* 3. *Inf.* at an unknown or unspecified time: *I'll take it if it comes today, tomorrow, or whenever.* 4. an intensive form of *when,* used in questions: *whenever did he escape?*

whensoever (ˌwɛnsəʊˈɛvə) *conj., adv. Rare.* an intensive form of **whenever.**

where (wɛə) *adv.* 1. **a.** in, at, or to what place, point, or position?: *where are you going?* **b.** (*used in indirect questions*): *I don't know where they are.* ~*pron.* 2. in, at, or to which (place): *the hotel where we spent our honeymoon.* ~*conj.* 3. (*subordinating*) in the place at which: *where we live it's always raining.* ~*n.* 4. a question as to the position, direction, or destination of something.

▷ **Usage.** See at **when.**

whereabouts (ˈwɛərəˌbaʊts) *adv.* 1. at what approximate place; where: *whereabouts are you?* ~*n.* 2. (*functioning as sing.*) the place, esp. the approximate place, where a person or thing is.

whereas (wɛərˈæz) *conj.* 1. (*coordinating*) but on the other hand: *I like to go swimming whereas Sheila likes to sail.* ~*sentence connector.* 2. (in formal documents) it being the case that; since.

whereat (wɛərˈæt) *Arch.* ~*adv.* 1. at or to which place. ~*sentence connector.* 2. upon which occasion.

whereby (wɛəˈbaɪ) *pron.* by or because of which: *the means whereby he took his life.*

wherefore (ˈwɛəˌfɔː) *n.* 1. (*usually pl.*) an explanation or reason (esp. in the **whys and wherefores**). ~*adv.* 2. *Arch.* why? ~*sentence connector.* 3. *Arch. or formal.* for which reason: used in legal preambles.

wherein (wɛərˈɪn) *Arch. or formal.* ~*adv.* 1. in what place or respect? ~*pron.* 2. in which place, thing, etc.

whereof (wɛərˈɒv) *Arch. or formal.* ~*adv.* 1. of what or which person or thing? ~*pron.* 2. of which (person or thing): *the man whereof I speak is no longer alive.*

whereon (wɛərˈɒn) *Arch.* ~*adv.* 1. on what thing or place? ~*pron.* 2. on which thing, place, etc.

wheresoever (ˌwɛəsəʊˈɛvə) *conj.* (*subordinating*), *adv.,*

pron. Rare. an intensive form of **wherever.**

whereupon (ˌwɛərəˈpɒn) *sentence connector.* at which; at which point; upon which.

wherever (wɛərˈɛvə) *pron.* 1. at, in, or to every place or point which; where: *wherever she went, he would be there.* ~*conj.* 2. (*subordinating*) in, to, or at whatever place: *wherever we go the weather is always bad.* ~*adv. also* **where ever.** 3. no matter where: *I'll find you, wherever you are.* 4. at, in, or to an unknown or unspecified place: *I'll go anywhere to escape: London, Paris, or wherever.* 5. an intensive form of *where,* used in questions: *wherever can they be?*

wherewithal (ˈwɛəwɪˌðɔːl) *n.* **the wherewithal.** necessary funds, resources, or equipment: *these people lack the wherewithal for a decent existence.*

wherry (ˈwɛrɪ) *n., pl.* **-ries.** 1. any of certain kinds of half-decked commercial boats. 2. a light rowing boat. —ˈwherryman *n.*

whet (wɛt) *vb.* **whetting, whetted.** (*tr.*) 1. to sharpen, as by grinding or friction. 2. to increase (the appetite, desire, etc.); stimulate. ~*n.* 3. the act of whetting. 4. a person or thing that whets. —ˈwhetter *n.*

whether (ˈwɛðə) *conj.* 1. (*subordinating*) used to introduce an indirect question or a clause after a verb expressing or implying doubt or choice: *he doesn't know whether she's in Britain or whether she's gone to France.* 2. (*coordinating*) either: *any man, whether liberal or conservative, would agree with me.* 3. **whether or no.** in any case: *he will be here tomorrow, whether or no.* 4. **whether...or** (**whether**). if on the one hand...or even if on the other hand: *you'll eat that, whether you like it or not.*

whetstone (ˈwɛtˌstəʊn) *n.* 1. a stone used for sharpening edged tools, knives, etc. 2. something that sharpens.

whew (hwjuː) *interj.* an exclamation or sharply exhaled breath expressing relief, delight, etc.

whey (weɪ) *n.* the watery liquid that separates from the curd when the milk is clotted, as in making cheese.

wheyface (ˈweɪˌfeɪs) *n.* 1. a pale bloodless face. 2. a person with such a face. —ˈwheyˌfaced *adj.*

which (wɪtʃ) *determiner.* 1. **a.** used with a noun in requesting that its referent be further specified, identified, or distinguished: *which house did you want to buy?* **b.** (*as pronoun*): *which did you find?* **c.** (*used in indirect questions*): *I wondered which apples were cheaper.* 2. **a.** whatever of a class; whichever: *bring which car you want.* **b.** (*as pronoun*): *choose which of the cars suits you.* ~*pron.* 3. used in relative clauses with inanimate antecedents: *the house, which is old, is in poor repair.* 4. as; and that: used in relative clauses with verb phrases or sentences as their antecedents: *he died of cancer, which is what I predicted.* 5. **the which.** an archaic form of **which** often used as a sentence connector.

▷ **Usage.** See at **that.**

whichever (wɪtʃˈɛvə) *determiner.* 1. **a.** any (one, two, etc., out of several): *take whichever car you like.* **b.** (*as pronoun*): *choose whichever appeals to you.* 2. **a.** no matter which (one or ones): *whichever card you pick you'll still be making a mistake.* **b.** (*as pronoun*): *it won't make any difference, whichever comes first.*

whiff (wɪf) *n.* 1. a passing odour. 2. a brief gentle gust of air. 3. a single inhalation or exhalation from the mouth or nose. ~*vb.* 4. to puff or waft. 5. (*tr.*) to sniff or smell. 6. (*intr.*) *Brit. sl.* to stink.

whiffle (ˈwɪfəl) *vb.* 1. (*intr.*) to think or behave in an erratic or unpredictable way. 2. to blow or be blown fitfully or in gusts. 3. (*intr.*) to whistle softly.

Whig (wɪg) *n.* 1. a member of the English political party that opposed the succession to the throne of James, Duke of York (1679–80), on the grounds that he was a Catholic. Standing for a limited monarchy, the Whigs later represented the desires of industrialists and Dissenters for political and social reform, and provided the core of the Liberal Party. 2. (in the U.S.) a supporter of the War of American Independence. Cf. **Tory.** 3. a member of the American political party that opposed

---

THESAURUS

pedient, idea, plan, ploy, ruse, scheme, stunt, trick, wrinkle (*Inf.*) 4. *Inf.* anecdote, chestnut (*Inf.*), crack (*Sl.*), gag (*Sl.*), joke, old joke, one-liner (*Sl.*), story

whereabouts location, position, site, situation

wherewithal capital, equipment, es-

sentials, funds, means, money, ready (*Inf.*), ready money, resources, supplies

whet 1. edge, file, grind, hone, sharpen, strop 2. animate, arouse, awaken, enhance, excite, incite, increase, kindle, pique, provoke, quicken, rouse, stimulate, stir

whiff *n.* 1. aroma, blast, breath, draught,

gust, hint, odour, puff, scent, smell, sniff ~*v.* 2. breathe, inhale, puff, smell, smoke, sniff, waft 3. *Brit. sl.* hum (*Sl.*), pong (*Brit. inf.*), reek, stink

the Democrats from about 1834 to 1855 and represented propertied and professional interests. **4.** *History.* a Scottish Presbyterian, esp. one in rebellion against the Crown. ~*adj.* **5.** of, characteristic of, or relating to Whigs. —'**Whiggery** *or* '**Whiggism** *n.* —'**Whiggish** *adj.*

while (waɪl) *conj. also* **whilst** (waɪlst). **1.** (*subordinating*) at the same time that: *please light the fire while I'm cooking.* **2.** (*subordinating*) all the time that: *I stay inside while it's raining.* **3.** (*subordinating*) in spite of the fact that: *while I agree about his brilliance I still think he's rude.* **4.** (*coordinating*) whereas; and in contrast: *houses are expensive, while flats are cheap.* ~*prep., conj.* **5.** *N English dialect.* another word for **until:** *you'll have to wait while Monday.* ~*n.* **6.** (*usually used in adverbial phrases*) a period or interval of time: *once in a long while.* **7.** trouble or time (esp. in **worth one's while**): *it's hardly worth your while to begin work today.*

▷ **Usage.** The main sense of *while* is *during the time that.* However, many careful users of English would now accept as established the use of *while* to mean *although: while he disliked working, he was obliged to do so.* In careful usage, *while* is not used to mean *whereas* or *and: he thought that they were in Paris, whereas* (not *while*) *they had gone on to Rome; his friends went to Paris for their holiday, his brother to Rome, and* (not *while*) *his parents went to Berlin.* Careful writers try to avoid any ambiguity that may result from the possibility of two interpretations of *while* in context: *while* (*although* or *during the time that*) *his brother worked in the park, he refused to do any gardening at home.*

while away *vb.* (*tr., adv.*) to pass (time) idly and usually pleasantly.

whilst (waɪlst) *conj. Chiefly Brit.* another word for **while** (senses 1–4).

whim (wɪm) *n.* **1.** a sudden, passing, and often fanciful idea; impulsive or irrational thought. **2.** a horse-drawn winch formerly used in mining to lift ore or water.

whimper ('wɪmpə) *vb.* **1.** (*intr.*) to cry, sob, or whine softly or intermittently. **2.** to complain or say (something) in a whining plaintive way. ~*n.* **3.** a soft plaintive whine. —'**whimperer** *n.* —'**whimpering** *n., adj.* —'**whimperingly** *adv.*

whimsical ('wɪmzɪk²l) *adj.* **1.** spontaneously fanciful or playful. **2.** given to whims; capricious. **3.** quaint, unusual, or fantastic. —**whimsicality** (,wɪmzɪ'kælɪtɪ) *n.* —'**whimsically** *adv.*

whimsy *or* **whimsey** ('wɪmzɪ) *n., pl.* **-sies** *or* **-seys.** **1.** a capricious idea or notion. **2.** light or fanciful humour. **3.** something quaint or unusual. ~*adj.* **-sier, -siest.** **4.** quaint, comical, or unusual, often in a tasteless way.

whin¹ (wɪn) *n.* another name for **gorse.**

whin² (wɪn) *n.* any dark hard fine-grained rock, such as basalt. Also called: **whinstone.**

whinchat ('wɪn,tʃæt) *n.* an Old World songbird having a mottled brown-and-white plumage with pale cream underparts.

whine (waɪn) *n.* **1.** a long high-pitched plaintive cry or moan. **2.** a continuous high-pitched sound. **3.** a peevish complaint, esp. one repeated. ~*vb.* **4.** to make a whine or utter in a whine. —'**whiner** *n.* —'**whiningly** *adv.* —'**whiny** *adj.*

whinny ('wɪnɪ) *vb.* **-nying, -nied.** (*intr.*) **1.** (of a horse) to neigh softly or gently. **2.** to make a sound resembling a neigh, such as a laugh. ~*n., pl.* **-nies.** **3.** a gentle or low-pitched neigh.

whip (wɪp) *vb.* **whipping, whipped.** **1.** to strike (a person or thing) with several strokes of a strap, rod, etc. **2.** (*tr.*) to punish by striking in this manner. **3.** (*tr.; foll. by out, away,* etc.) to pull, remove, etc., with sudden rapid

motion: *to whip out a gun.* **4.** (*intr.; foll. by down, into, out of,* etc.) *Inf.* to come, go, etc., in a rapid sudden manner: *they whipped into the bar for a drink.* **5.** to strike or be struck as if by whipping: *the tempest whipped the surface of the sea.* **6.** (*tr.*) to bring, train, etc., forcefully into a desired condition. **7.** (*tr.*) *Inf.* to overcome or outdo. **8.** (*tr.; often foll. by on, out,* or *off*) to drive, urge, compel, etc., by or as if by whipping. **9.** (*tr.*) *Inf.* to steal. **10.** (*tr.*) to wrap or wind (a cord, thread, etc.) around (a rope, cable, etc.) to prevent chafing or fraying. **11.** (*tr.*) (in fly-fishing) to cast the fly repeatedly onto (the water) in a whipping motion. **12.** (*tr.*) (in sewing) to join, finish, or gather with whipstitch. **13.** to beat (eggs, cream, etc.) with a whisk or similar utensil to incorporate air. **14.** (*tr.*) to spin (a top). ~*n.* **15.** a device consisting of a lash or flexible rod attached at one end to a stiff handle and used for driving animals, inflicting corporal punishment, etc. **16.** a whipping stroke or motion. **17.** a person adept at handling a whip, as a coachman, etc. **18.** (in a legislative body) **a.** a member of a party chosen to organize and discipline the members of his faction. **b.** a call issued to members of a party, insisting with varying degrees of urgency upon their presence or loyal voting behaviour. **c.** (in the Brit. Parliament) a schedule of business sent to members of a party, indicating for which items their attendance is most important. **19.** an apparatus for hoisting, consisting of a rope, pulley, and snatch block. **20.** any of a variety of desserts made from egg whites or cream beaten stiff. **21.** See **whipper-in.** **22.** flexibility, as in the shaft of a golf club, etc. **23. a fair crack of the whip.** *Inf.* a fair chance or opportunity. ~See also **whip-round, whip up.** —'**whip,like** *adj.* —'**whipper** *n.*

whipcord ('wɪp,kɔːd) *n.* **1.** a strong worsted or cotton fabric with a diagonally ribbed surface. **2.** a closely twisted hard cord used for the lashes of whips, etc.

whip hand *n.* (usually preceded by *the*) **1.** (in driving horses, etc.) the hand holding the whip. **2.** advantage or dominating position.

whiplash ('wɪp,læʃ) *n.* a quick lash or stroke of a whip or like that of a whip.

whiplash injury *n. Med. inf.* any injury to the neck resulting from a sudden thrusting forwards and snapping back of the unsupported head. Technical name: **hyperextension-hyperflexion injury.**

whipper-in *n., pl.* **whippers-in.** a person employed to assist the huntsman managing the hounds.

whippersnapper ('wɪpə,snæpə) *n.* an insignificant but pretentious or cheeky person, often a young one. Also called: **whipster.**

whippet ('wɪpɪt) *n.* a small slender breed of dog similar to a greyhound.

whipping ('wɪpɪŋ) *n.* **1.** a thrashing or beating with a whip or similar implement. **2.** cord or twine used for binding or lashing. **3.** the binding formed by wrapping a rope, etc. with cord or twine.

whipping boy *n.* a person of little importance who is blamed for the errors, incompetence, etc., of others, esp. his superiors; scapegoat.

whippoorwill ('wɪpu,wɪl) *n.* a nightjar of North and Central America, having a dark plumage with white patches on the tail.

whip-round *Inf., chiefly Brit.* ~*n.* **1.** an impromptu collection of money. ~*vb.* **whip round.** **2.** (*intr., adv.*) to make such a collection.

whipstock ('wɪp,stɒk) *n.* a whip handle.

whip up *vb.* (*tr., adv.*) **1.** to excite; arouse: *to whip up a mob; to whip up discontent.* **2.** *Inf.* to prepare quickly: *to whip up a meal.*

THESAURUS

whim caprice, conceit, craze, crotchet, fad (*Inf.*), fancy, freak, humour, impulse, notion, passing thought, quirk, sport, sudden notion, urge, vagary, whimsy

whimper **1.** *v.* blub (*Sl.*), blubber, cry, grizzle (*Inf.*), mewl, moan, pule, snivel, sob, weep, whine, whinge (*Inf.*) **2.** *n.* moan, snivel, sob, whine

whimsical capricious, chimerical, crotchety, curious, droll, eccentric, fanciful, fantastic, fantastical, freakish, funny, mischievous, odd, peculiar, playful, quaint, queer, singular, unusual, waggish, weird

whine *n.* **1.** cry, moan, plaintive cry, sob,

wail, whimper **2.** beef (*Sl.*), complaint, gripe (*Inf.*), grouse, grumble, moan ~*v.* **3.** beef (*Sl.*), bellyache (*Sl.*), carp, complain, cry, gripe (*Inf.*), grizzle (*Inf.*), grouse, grumble, moan, sob, wail, whimper, whinge (*Inf.*)

whip *v.* **1.** beat, birch, cane, castigate, flagellate, flog, give a hiding (*Inf.*), lash, leather, punish, scourge, spank, strap, switch, tan (*Sl.*), thrash **2.** exhibit, flash, jerk, produce, pull, remove, seize, show, snatch, whisk **3.** *Inf.* dart, dash, dive, flit, flounce, fly, rush, shoot, tear, whisk **4.** *Inf.* beat, best, clobber (*Sl.*), conquer, defeat, drub, hammer (*Inf.*), lick (*Inf.*), outdo, overcome, overpower,

overwhelm, rout, take apart (*Sl.*), thrash, trounce, wipe the floor with (*Inf.*), worst **5.** agitate, compel, drive, foment, goad, hound, incite, instigate, prick, prod, provoke, push, spur, stir, urge, work up **6.** beat, whisk ~*n.* **7.** birch, bullwhip, cane, cat-o'-nine-tails, crop, horsewhip, knout, lash, rawhide, riding crop, scourge, switch, thong

whipping beating, birching, caning, castigation, flagellation, flogging, hiding (*Inf.*), lashing, leathering, punishment, spanking, tanning (*Sl.*), the strap, thrashing

whir *or* **whirr** (wɜː) *n.* **1.** a prolonged soft swish or buzz, as of a motor working or wings flapping. **2.** a bustle or rush. ~*vb.* **whirring, whirred.** **3.** to make or cause to make a whir.

whirl (wɜːl) *vb.* **1.** to spin, turn, or revolve or cause to spin, turn, or revolve. **2.** (*intr.*) to turn around or away rapidly. **3.** (*intr.*) to have a spinning sensation, as from dizziness, etc. **4.** to move or drive or be moved or driven at high speed. ~*n.* **5.** the act or an instance of whirling; swift rotation or a rapid whirling movement. **6.** a condition of confusion or giddiness: *her accident left me in a whirl.* **7.** a swift round, as of events, meetings, etc. **8.** a tumult; stir. **9.** *Inf.* a brief trip, dance, etc. **10.** **give (something) a whirl.** *Inf.* to attempt or give a trial to (something). —'**whirler** *n.* —'**whirlingly** *adv.*

whirligig ('wɜːlɪˌɡɪɡ) *n.* **1.** any spinning toy, such as a top. **2.** another name for **merry-go-round.** **3.** anything that whirls about, spins, or moves in a circular or giddy way: *the whirligig of social life.*

whirlpool ('wɜːlˌpuːl) *n.* **1.** a powerful circular current or vortex of water. **2.** something resembling a whirlpool in motion or the power to attract into its vortex.

whirlwind ('wɜːlˌwɪnd) *n.* **1.** a column of air whirling around and towards a more or less vertical axis of low pressure, which moves along the land or ocean surface. **2. a.** a motion or course resembling this, esp. in rapidity. **b.** (*as modifier*): *a whirlwind romance.* **3.** an impetuously active person.

whirlybird ('wɜːlɪˌbɜːd) *n.* an informal word for **helicopter.**

whisk (wɪsk) *vb.* **1.** (*tr.*; often foll. by *away* or *off*) to brush, sweep, or wipe off lightly. **2.** (*tr.*) to move, carry, etc., with a light or rapid sweeping motion: *the taxi whisked us to the airport.* **3.** (*intr.*) to move, go, etc., quickly and nimbly: *to whisk downstairs for a drink.* **4.** (*tr.*) to whip (eggs, etc.) to a froth. ~*n.* **5.** the act of whisking. **6.** a light rapid sweeping movement. **7.** a utensil for whipping eggs, etc. **8.** a small brush or broom. **9.** a small bunch or bundle, as of grass, straw, etc.

whisker ('wɪskə) *n.* **1.** any of the stiff sensory hairs growing on the face of a cat, rat, or other mammal. Technical name: **vibrissa.** **2.** any of the hairs growing on a man's face, esp. on the cheeks or chin. **3.** (*pl.*) a beard or that part of it growing on the sides of the face. **4.** (*pl.*) *Inf.* a moustache. **5.** *Chem.* a very fine filamentary crystal having greater strength than the bulk material. **6.** a person or thing that whisks. **7.** a narrow margin or small distance: *he escaped death by a whisker.* —'**whiskered** *or* '**whiskery** *adj.*

whiskey ('wɪskɪ) *n.* whisky made in the U.S. or Ireland.

whiskey sour *n.* *U.S.* a mixed drink of whisky and lime or lemon juice, sometimes sweetened.

whisky ('wɪskɪ) *n., pl.* **-kies.** a spirit made by distilling fermented cereals, which is matured and often blended.

whisky mac *n.* *Brit.* a drink consisting of whisky and ginger wine.

whisper ('wɪspə) *vb.* **1.** to speak or utter (something) in a soft hushed tone, esp. without vibration of the vocal cords. **2.** (*intr.*) to speak secretly or furtively, as in promoting intrigue, gossip, etc. **3.** (*intr.*) (of leaves, trees, etc.) to make a low soft rustling sound. **4.** (*tr.*) to utter or suggest secretly or privately: *to whisper treason.* ~*n.* **5.** a low soft voice: *to speak in a whisper.* **6.** something uttered in such a voice. **7.** a low soft rustling sound. **8.** a trace or suspicion. **9.** *Inf.* a rumour. —'**whisperer** *n.*

whist[1] (wɪst) *n.* a card game for four in which the two sides try to win the balance of the 13 tricks: forerunner of bridge.

whist[2] (wɪst) *or* **whisht** (wɪʃt) *Arch. or dialect, esp. Scot.* ~*interj.* **1.** hush! be quiet! ~*adj.* **2.** silent or still.

whistle ('wɪsəl) *vb.* **1.** to produce (shrill or flutelike sounds), as by passing breath through a narrow constriction most easily formed by the pursed lips. **2.** (*tr.*) to signal or command by whistling or blowing a whistle: *the referee whistled the end of the game.* **3.** (of a kettle, train, etc.) to produce (a shrill sound) caused by the emission of steam through a small aperture. **4.** (*intr.*) to move with a whistling sound caused by rapid passage through the air. **5.** (of animals, esp. birds) to emit (a shrill sound) resembling human whistling. ~*n.* **6.** a device for making a shrill high-pitched sound by means of air or steam under pressure. **7.** a shrill sound effected by whistling or blowing a whistle. **8.** a whistling sound, as of a bird, bullet, the wind, etc. **9.** a signal, etc., transmitted by or as if by a whistle. **10.** the act of whistling. **11.** an instrument, usually made of metal, that is blown down its end to produce a tune, signal etc. **12. clean as a whistle.** perfectly clean or clear. **13. wet one's whistle.** *Inf.* to take a drink. **14. blow the whistle.** (usually foll. by *on*) *U.S. inf.* **a.** to inform (on). **b.** to bring a stop (to). **15. whistle in the dark.** to behave so as to maintain one's courage or spirits during a time of danger or difficulty.

whistle for *vb.* (*intr., prep.*) *Inf.* to seek or expect in vain.

whistle stop *n.* **1.** *U.S.* **a.** a minor railway station where trains stop only on signal. **b.** a small town having such a station. **2. a.** a brief appearance in a town, esp. by a political candidate. **b.** (*as modifier*): *a whistle-stop tour.*

whistle up *vb.* (*tr., adv.*) to call or summon (a person or animal) by whistling.

whit (wɪt) *n.* (*usually used with a negative*) the smallest particle; iota; jot: *he has changed not a whit.*

Whit (wɪt) *n.* **1.** See **Whitsuntide.** ~*adj.* **2.** of or relating to Whitsuntide.

white (waɪt) *adj.* **1.** having no hue, owing to the reflection of all or almost all incident light. **2.** (of light, such as sunlight) consisting of all the colours of the spectrum or produced by certain mixtures of primary colours, as red, green, and blue. **3.** comparatively white or whitish-grey or having parts of this colour: *white clover.* **4.** (of an animal) having pale-coloured or white skin, fur, or feathers. **5.** bloodless or pale, as from pain, emotion, etc. **6.** (of hair, etc.) grey, usually from age. **7.** benevolent or without malicious intent: *white magic.* **8.** colourless or transparent: *white glass.* **9.** capped with or accompanied by snow: *a white Christmas.* **10.** blank, as an unprinted area of a page. **11.** (of wine) made from pale grapes or from black grapes separated from their skins. **12.** (of coffee or tea) with milk or cream. **13.** denoting flour, or bread made from flour, that has had part of the grain removed. **14.** *Physics.* having or characterized by a continuous distribution of energy, wavelength, or frequency: *white noise.* **15.** *Inf.* honourable or generous. **16.** *Poetic or arch.* having a fair complexion; blond. **17. bleed white.** to deprive slowly of resources. ~*n.* **18.** a white colour. **19.** the condition of being white; whiteness. **20.** the white or lightly coloured part of something. **21.** (usually preceded by *the*) the viscous fluid that surrounds the yolk of a bird's egg, esp. a hen's egg; albumen. **22.** *Anat.* the white part (sclera) of the eyeball. **23.** any of various butterflies having white wings with scanty black markings. **24.** *Chess, draughts.* **a.** a white or light-coloured piece or square. **b.** the player playing with such pieces. **25.** anything that has or is characterized by a white colour, such as a white paint or white clothing. **26.** *Archery.* the outer ring of the target, having the lowest score. ~*vb.* **27.** *Obs.* to make or become white. ~ See also **white out, whites.** —'**whitely** *adv.* —'**whitish** *adj.* —'**whiteness** *n.*

THESAURUS

whirl *v.* **1.** circle, gyrate, pirouette, pivot, reel, revolve, roll, rotate, spin, swirl, turn, twirl, twist, wheel **2.** feel dizzy, reel, spin ~*n.* **3.** birl (*Scot.*), circle, gyration, pirouette, reel, revolution, roll, rotation, spin, swirl, turn, twirl, twist, wheel **4.** confusion, daze, dither, flurry, giddiness, spin **5.** flurry, merry-go-round, round, series, succession **6.** agitation, bustle, commotion, confusion, flurry, hurly-burly, stir, tumult, uproar **7. give (something) a whirl** *Inf.* attempt, have a bash (crack, go, shot, stab, whack) (*Inf.*), try

whirlwind **1.** *n.* dust devil, tornado, waterspout **2.** *adj.* hasty, headlong, impetuous, impulsive, lightning, quick, rapid, rash, short, speedy, swift

whisk *v.* **1.** brush, flick, sweep, whip, wipe **2.** dart, dash, fly, hasten, hurry, race, rush, shoot, speed, sweep, tear **3.** beat, fluff up, whip ~*n.* **4.** brush, flick, sweep, whip, wipe **5.** beater

whisky barley-bree (*Scot.*), bourbon, John Barleycorn, malt, rye, Scotch, usquebaugh

whisper *v.* **1.** breathe, murmur, say softly,

speak in hushed tones, utter under the breath **2.** gossip, hint, insinuate, intimate, murmur, spread rumours **3.** hiss, murmur, rustle, sigh, sough, susurrate (*Literary*), swish ~*n.* **4.** hushed tone, low voice, murmur, soft voice, undertone **5.** hiss, murmur, rustle, sigh, sighing, soughing, susurration *or* susurrus (*Literary*), swish **6.** breath, fraction, hint, shadow, suggestion, suspicion, tinge, trace, whiff **7.** *Inf.* buzz, gossip, innuendo, insinuation, report, rumour, word

white **1.** ashen, bloodless, ghastly, grey,

White (waɪt) n. **1.** a member of the Caucasoid race. **2.** a person of European ancestry. ~adj. **3.** denoting or relating to a White or Whites.

white ant n. another name for **termite**.

whitebait ('waɪt,beɪt) n. **1.** the edible young of herrings, sprats, etc., cooked and eaten whole as a delicacy. **2.** any of various small silvery fishes.

white blood cell n. a nontechnical name for **leucocyte**.

whitecap ('waɪt,kæp) n. a wave with a white broken crest.

white-collar adj. of or designating nonmanual and usually salaried workers employed in professional and clerical occupations.

white dwarf n. one of a large class of small faint stars of enormous density, thought to mark the final stage in a star's evolution.

white elephant n. **1.** a rare albino variety of the Indian elephant, regarded as sacred in parts of S Asia. **2.** a possession that is unwanted by its owner. **3.** a rare or valuable possession the upkeep of which is very expensive.

white feather n. **1.** a symbol or mark of cowardice. **2. show the white feather.** to act in a cowardly manner.

whitefish ('waɪt,fɪʃ) n., pl. **-fish** or **-fishes**. **1.** a food fish typically of deep cold lakes of the N hemisphere, having large silvery scales and a small head. **2.** (in the Brit. fishing industry) any edible marine fish or invertebrate excluding herrings but including trout, salmon, and all shellfish.

white flag n. a white flag or a piece of white cloth hoisted to signify surrender or request a truce.

whitefly ('waɪt,flaɪ) n., pl. **-flies.** any of a family of insects typically having a body covered with powdery wax. Many are pests of greenhouse crops.

white friar n. a Carmelite friar, so called because of the white cloak that forms part of the habit of this order.

white gold n. any of various white lustrous hardwearing alloys containing gold together with platinum and palladium and sometimes smaller amounts of silver, nickel, or copper.

white goods pl. n. **1.** household linen such as sheets, towels, tablecloths, etc. **2.** large household appliances, such as refrigerators or cookers.

Whitehall (,waɪt'hɔːl) n. **1.** a street in London stretching from Trafalgar Square to the Houses of Parliament: site of the main government offices. **2.** the British Government.

white heat n. **1.** intense heat characterized by emission of white light. **2.** Inf. a state of intense excitement or activity.

white hope n. Inf. a person who is expected to bring honour or glory to his group, team, etc.

white horse n. **1.** the outline of a horse carved into the side of a chalk hill, usually dating to the Neolithic, Bronze, or Iron Ages. **2.** a wave with a white broken crest.

white-hot adj. **1.** at such a high temperature that white light is emitted. **2.** Inf. in a state of intense emotion.

White House n. **the. 1.** the official Washington residence of the president of the U.S. **2.** the U.S. presidency.

white lead (lɛd) n. **1.** a white solid usually regarded as a mixture of lead carbonate and lead hydroxide; basic lead carbonate: used in paint and in making putty and ointments for the treatment of burns. **2.** either of two similar white pigments based on lead sulphate or lead silicate.

white lie n. a minor or unimportant lie, esp. one uttered in the interests of tact or politeness.

white light n. light that contains all the wavelengths of visible light at approximately equal intensities, as in sunlight.

White man's burden n. the supposed duty of the White race to bring education and Western culture to the non-White inhabitants of their colonies.

white matter n. the whitish tissue of the brain and spinal cord, consisting mainly of nerve fibres covered with a protective white fatlike substance.

white meat n. any meat that is light in colour, such as veal or the breast of turkey.

whiten ('waɪtᵊn) vb. to make or become white or whiter; bleach. —'**whitener** n. —'**whitening** n.

white noise n. sound or electrical noise that has a relatively wide continuous range of frequencies of uniform intensity.

white out vb. (adv.) **1.** (intr.) to lose or lack daylight visibility owing to snow or fog. **2.** (tr.) to create or leave white spaces in (printed or other matter). ~n. **whiteout. 3.** a polar atmospheric condition consisting of lack of visibility and sense of distance and direction due to a uniform whiteness of a heavy cloud cover and snow-covered ground, which reflects almost all the light it receives.

white paper n. (often caps.) an official government report in any of a number of countries, including Britain, Australia, New Zealand, and Canada, which sets out the government's policy on a matter that is or will come before Parliament.

white pepper n. a condiment, less pungent than black pepper, made from the husked dried beans of the pepper plant.

whites (waɪts) pl. n. **1.** household linen or cotton goods, such as sheets. **2.** white or off-white clothing, such as that worn for playing cricket.

white sale n. a sale of household linens at reduced prices.

white sauce n. a thick sauce made from flour, butter, seasonings, and milk or stock.

white slave n. a girl or woman forced or soldinto prostitution. —**white slavery** n. —,**white-'slaver** n.

white spirit n. a colourless liquid obtained from petroleum and used as a substitute for turpentine.

white tie n. **1.** a white bow tie worn as part of a man's formal evening dress. **2. a.** formal evening dress for men. **b.** (as modifier): a white-tie occasion.

whitewash ('waɪt,wɒʃ) n. **1.** a substance used for whitening walls and other surfaces, consisting of a suspension of lime or whiting in water. **2.** Inf. deceptive or specious words or actions intended to conceal defects, gloss over failings, etc. **3.** Inf. a game in which the loser fails to score. ~vb. (tr.) **4.** to cover with whitewash. **5.** Inf. to conceal, gloss over, or suppress. **6.** Inf. to defeat (someone) in a game by preventing him from scoring. —'**white,washer** n.

white whale n. a small white toothed whale of northern waters. Also called: **beluga.**

whitewood ('waɪt,wud) n. **1.** any of various trees with light-coloured wood, such as the tulip tree, basswood, and cottonwood. **2.** the wood of any of these trees.

whitey or **whity** ('waɪtɪ) n. Chiefly U.S. (used contemptuously by Negroes) a White man or White men collectively.

whither ('wɪðə) Arch. or poetic. ~adv. **1.** to what place? **2.** to what end or purpose? ~conj. **3.** to whatever place, purpose, etc.

whithersoever (,wɪðəsəʊ'ɛvə) adv., conj. Arch. or poetic. to whichever place.

whiting¹ ('waɪtɪŋ) n. **1.** an important gadoid food fish of European seas, having a dark back with silvery sides and underparts. **2.** any of various similar fishes.

whiting² ('waɪtɪŋ) n. white chalk that has been ground and washed, used in making whitewash, metal polish, etc. Also called: **whitening.**

whitlow ('wɪtləʊ) n. any pussy inflammation of the end of a finger or toe.

Whitsun ('wɪtsᵊn) n. **1.** short for **Whitsuntide.** ~adj. **2.** of or relating to Whit Sunday or Whitsuntide.

Whit Sunday n. the seventh Sunday after Easter, observed as a feast in commemoration of the descent of the Holy Spirit on the apostles. In Scotland, it is one of the four quarter days. Also called: **Pentecost.**

Whitsuntide ('wɪtsᵊn,taɪd) n. the week that begins with Whit Sunday, esp. the first three days.

THESAURUS

pale, pallid, pasty, wan, waxen, wheyfaced **2.** grey, grizzled, hoary, silver, snowy **3.** clean, immaculate, innocent, pure, spotless, stainless, unblemished, unsullied
white-collar clerical, executive, non-

manual, office, professional, salaried
whiten blanch, bleach, blench, etiolate, fade, go white, pale, turn pale
whitewash 1. n. camouflage, concealment, cover-up, deception, extenuation **2.** v.

camouflage, conceal, cover up, extenuate, gloss over, make light of, suppress

whittle ('wɪtᵊl) vb. 1. to cut or shave strips or pieces from (wood, a stick, etc.), esp. with a knife. 2. (tr.) to make or shape by paring or shaving. 3. (tr.; often foll. by away, down, off, etc.) to reduce, destroy, or wear away gradually.

whiz or **whizz** (wɪz) vb. whizzing, whizzed. 1. to make or cause to make a loud humming or buzzing sound. 2. to move or cause to move with such a sound. 3. (intr.) Inf. to move or go rapidly. ~n. 4. a loud humming or buzzing sound. 5. Inf. a person who is extremely skilful at some activity.

whiz kid, whizz kid, or **wiz kid** n. Inf. a person who is pushing, enthusiastic, and outstandingly successful for his or her age.

who (huː) pron. 1. which person? what person? used in direct and indirect questions: he can't remember who did it; who met you? 2. used to introduce relative clauses with antecedents referring to human beings: the people who lived here have left. 3. the one or ones who; whoever: bring who you want. 4. who's who. a. the identity of individual, esp. important, people: to know who's who. b. a book or list containing the names and short biographies of prominent persons.
▷ Usage. See at whom.

W.H.O. abbrev. for World Health Organization.

whoa (wəʊ) interj. a command used esp. to horses to stop or slow down.

whodunit or **whodunnit** (huːˈdʌnɪt) n. Inf. a novel, play, etc., concerned with a crime, usually murder.

whoever (huːˈɛvə) pron. 1. any person who: whoever wants it can have it. 2. no matter who: I'll come round tomorrow, whoever may be here. 3. an intensive form of who, used in questions: whoever could have thought that? 4. Inf. an unspecified person: give those to Cathy or whoever.

whole (həʊl) adj. 1. containing all the component parts necessary to form a total; complete: a whole apple. 2. constituting the full quantity, extent, etc. 3. uninjured or undamaged. 4. healthy. 5. having no fractional or decimal part; integral: a whole number. 6. designating a relationship by descent from the same parents; full: whole brothers. 7. out of whole cloth. U.S. inf. entirely without a factual basis. ~adv. 8. in an undivided or unbroken piece: to swallow a plum whole. ~n. 9. all the parts, elements, etc., of a thing. 10. an assemblage of parts viewed together as a unit. 11. a thing complete in itself. 12. as a whole. considered altogether; completely. 13. on the whole. a. taking all things into consideration. b. in general. —'wholeness n.

wholefood ('həʊl,fuːd) n. (sometimes pl.) a. food that has been refined or processed as little as possible and is eaten in its natural state, such as brown rice, wholemeal flour, etc. b. (as modifier): a wholefood restaurant.

wholehearted (,həʊl'hɑːtɪd) adj. done, acted, given, etc., with total sincerity, enthusiasm, or commitment. —,whole'heartedly adv.

wholemeal ('həʊl,miːl) adj. Brit. (of flour, bread, etc.) made from the entire wheat kernel. Also called (esp. U.S.): whole-wheat.

whole note n. the usual U.S. name for semibreve.

whole number n. 1. an integer. 2. a natural number.

wholesale ('həʊl,seɪl) n. 1. the business of selling goods to retailers in larger quantities than they are sold to final consumers but in smaller quantities than they are purchased from manufacturers. Cf. retail (sense 1). ~adj. 2. of or engaged in such business. 3. made, done, etc., on a large scale or without discrimination. ~adv. 4. on a large scale or without discrimination. ~vb. 5. to sell (goods) at wholesale. —'whole,saler n.

wholesome ('həʊlsəm) adj. 1. conducive to health or physical wellbeing. 2. conducive to moral wellbeing. 3. characteristic or suggestive of health or wellbeing, esp. in appearance. —'wholesomely adv. —'wholesomeness n.

whole-wheat adj. another term (esp. U.S.) for wholemeal.

wholism ('həʊlɪzəm) n. a variant of holism. —who'listic adj.

who'll (huːl) contraction of who will or who shall.

wholly ('həʊlɪ) adv. 1. completely, totally, or entirely. 2. without exception; exclusively.

whom (huːm) pron. the objective form of who, used when who is not the subject of its own clause: whom did you say you had seen? he can't remember whom he saw.
▷ Usage. In formal English, careful writers always use whom when the objective form of who is required. In informal contexts, however, many careful speakers consider whom to be unnatural, esp. at the beginning of a sentence: who were you looking for? Careful speakers usually prefer whom where it closely follows a preposition: to whom did you give it? as contrasted with who did you give it to?

whomever (huːmˈɛvə) pron. the objective form of whoever: I'll hire whomever I can find.

whoop (wuːp) vb. 1. to utter (speech) with loud cries, as of excitement. 2. (huːp) Med. to cough convulsively with a crowing sound. 3. (of certain birds) to utter (a hooting cry). 4. (tr.) to urge on or call with or as if with whoops. 5. (wʊp, wuːp). whoop it up. Inf. a. to indulge in a noisy celebration. b. Chiefly U.S. to arouse enthusiasm. ~n. 6. a loud cry, esp. one expressing excitement. 7. (huːp) Med. the convulsive crowing sound made during whooping cough.

whoopee Inf. ~interj. (wʊ'piː). 1. an exclamation of joy, excitement, etc. ~n. ('wʊpiː). 2. make whoopee. a. to engage in noisy merrymaking. b. to make love.

whooping cough ('huːpɪŋ) n. an acute infectious disease characterized by coughing spasms that end with a shrill crowing sound on inspiration. Technical name: pertussis.

whoops (wʊps) interj. an exclamation of surprise or of apology.

whop (wɒp) Inf. ~vb. whopping, whopped. 1. (tr.) to strike, beat, or thrash. 2. (tr.) to defeat utterly. 3. (intr.) to drop or fall. ~n. 4. a heavy blow or the sound made by such a blow.

whopper ('wɒpə) n. Inf. 1. anything uncommonly large of its kind. 2. a big lie.

whopping ('wɒpɪŋ) adj. Inf. uncommonly large.

whore (hɔː) n. 1. a prostitute or promiscuous woman: often a term of abuse. ~vb. (intr.) 2. to be or act as a prostitute. 3. (of a man) to have promiscuous sexual relations, esp. with prostitutes. 4. (often foll. by after) to

---

THESAURUS

whittle 1. carve, cut, hew, pare, shape, shave, trim 2. consume, destroy, eat away, erode, reduce, undermine, wear away

whole adj. 1. complete, entire, full, in one piece, integral, total, unabridged, uncut, undivided 2. faultless, flawless, good, in one piece, intact, inviolate, mint, perfect, sound, unbroken, undamaged, unharmed, unhurt, unimpaired, uninjured, unmutilated, unscathed, untouched 3. able-bodied, better, cured, fit, hale, healed, healthy, in fine fettle, in good health, recovered, robust, sound, strong, well ~adv. 4. in one, in one piece ~n. 5. aggregate, all, everything, lot, sum total, the entire amount, total 6. ensemble, entirety, entity, fullness, piece, totality, unit, unity 7. on the whole a. all in all, all things considered, by and large, taking everything into consideration b. as a rule, for the most part, generally, in the main, in general, mostly, predominantly

wholehearted committed, complete, dedicated, determined, devoted, earnest, emphatic, enthusiastic, genuine, heartfelt, hearty, real, sincere, true, unfeigned, unqualified, unreserved, unstinting, warm, zealous

wholesale 1. adj. all-inclusive, broad, comprehensive, extensive, far-reaching, indiscriminate, mass, sweeping, wide-ranging 2. adv. all at once, comprehensively, extensively, indiscriminately, on a large scale, without exception

wholesome 1. beneficial, good, healthful, health-giving, healthy, helpful, hygienic, invigorating, nourishing, nutritious, salubrious, salutary, sanitary, strengthening 2. clean, decent, edifying, ethical, exemplary, honourable, improving, innocent, moral, nice, pure, respectable, righteous, uplifting, virtuous, worthy

wholly 1. all, altogether, completely, comprehensively, entirely, fully, heart and soul, in every respect, one hundred per cent (Inf.), perfectly, thoroughly, totally, utterly 2. exclusively, only, solely, without exception

whoop cheer, cry, halloo, holler (Inf.), hoot, hurrah, scream, shout, shriek, yell

whore n. 1. brass (Sl.), call girl, cocotte, courtesan, demimondaine, demirep (Rare), fallen woman, fille de joie, harlot, hooker (U.S. sl.), hustler (U.S. sl.), lady of the night, loose woman, prostitute, streetwalker, strumpet, tart (Inf.), trollop, woman of easy virtue, woman of ill repute ~v. 2. be on the game (Sl.), hustle (U.S. sl.), prostitute oneself, sell one's body, sell oneself, solicit, walk the streets 3. fornicate, lech (Inf.), sleep around (Inf.), wanton, wench (Archaic), womanize seek that which is immoral, idolatrous, etc. —'**whorish** adj. —'**whoredom** n.

whorehouse ('hɔː,haʊs) n. another word for **brothel**.

whorl (wɜːl) n. 1. Bot. a radial arrangement of petals, stamens, leaves, etc., around a stem. 2. Zool. a single turn in a spiral shell. 3. one of the basic patterns of the human fingerprint, formed by several complete circular ridges one inside another. 4. anything shaped like a coil. —**whorled** adj.

whortleberry ('wɜːtˀl,bɛrɪ) n., pl. -ries. 1. Also called: **bilberry, huckleberry**, and (Brit.) **blaeberry**. a small Eurasian ericaceous shrub with greenish-pink flowers and edible sweet blackish berries. 2. the fruit of this shrub. 3. **bog whortleberry**. a related plant of mountain regions, having pink flowers and black fruits.

who's (huːz) contraction of who is or who has.

whose (huːz) determiner 1. a. of who? belonging to who? used in direct and indirect questions: I told him whose fault it was; whose car is this? b. (as pronoun): whose is that? 2. of who; of which: used as a relative pronoun: a house whose windows are broken; a man whose reputation has suffered.
▷ Usage. Since whose is the possessive of both who and which, it is quite acceptable to use whose of things as well as of people in careful usage: these are the houses whose foundations are unsteady; this is the man whose leg was broken.

whosoever (,huːsəʊ'ɛvə) pron. an archaic or formal word for **whoever**.

why (waɪ) adv. 1. a. for what reason?: why are you here? b. (used in indirect questions): tell me why you're here. ~pron. 2. for or because of which: there is no reason why he shouldn't come. ~n., pl. **whys**. 3. (usually pl.) a question as to the cause of something (esp. in the **whys and wherefores**). ~interj. 4. an introductory expression of surprise, indignation, etc.: why, don't be silly!

W.I. abbrev. for: 1. West Indian. 2. West Indies. 3. (in Britain) Women's Institute.

wick[1] (wɪk) n. 1. a cord or band of loosely twisted or woven fibres, as in a candle, that supplies fuel to a flame by capillary action. 2. **get on (someone's) wick**. Brit. sl. to cause irritation to (a person).

wick[2] (wɪk) n. Arch. a village or hamlet.

wicked (wɪkɪd) adj. 1. a. morally bad. b. (as collective n. preceded by the): the wicked. 2. mischievous or roguish, esp. in a playful way: a wicked grin. 3. causing injury or harm. 4. troublesome, unpleasant, or offensive. —'**wickedly** adv. —'**wickedness** n.

wicker ('wɪkə) n. 1. a slender flexible twig or shoot, esp. of willow. 2. short for **wickerwork**. ~adj. 3. made, consisting of, or constructed from wicker.

wickerwork ('wɪkə,wɜːk) n. a. a material consisting of wicker. b. (as modifier): a wickerwork chair.

wicket ('wɪkɪt) n. 1. a small door or gate, esp. one that is near to or part of a larger one. 2. Chiefly U.S. a small window or opening in a door, esp. one fitted with a grating or glass pane. 3. a small sluicegate. 4. a. Cricket. either of two constructions, 22 yards apart, consisting of three stumps stuck in the ground with two wooden bails resting on top, at which the batsman stands. b. the strip of ground between these. c. a batsman's turn at batting or the period during which two batsmen bat: a third-wicket partnership. d. the act or instance of a batsman being got out: the bowler took six wickets. 5. **keep wicket**. to act as a wicketkeeper. 6. **on a good, sticky, etc.**,

wicket. Inf. in an advantageous, awkward, etc., situation.

wicketkeeper ('wɪkɪt,kiːpə) n. Cricket. the player on the fielding side positioned directly behind the wicket.

widdershins ('wɪdə,ʃɪnz) adv. Chiefly Scot. a variant spelling of **withershins**.

wide (waɪd) adj. 1. having a great extent from side to side. 2. spacious or extensive. 3. a. (postpositive) having a specified extent, esp. from side to side: two yards wide. b. (in combination): extending throughout: nationwide. 4. remote from the desired point, mark, etc.: your guess is wide of the mark. 5. (of eyes) opened fully. 6. loose, full, or roomy: wide trousers. 7. exhibiting a considerable spread: a wide variation. 8. Phonetics. another word for **lax** (sense 4) or **open** (sense 32). 9. Brit. sl. unscrupulous and astute: a wide boy. ~adv. 10. over an extensive area: to travel far and wide. 11. to the full extent: he opened the door wide. 12. far from the desired point, mark, etc. ~n. 13. (in cricket) a bowled ball that is outside the batsman's reach and scores a run for the batting side. —'**widely** adv. —'**wideness** n. —'**widish** adj.

wide-angle lens n. a lens system on a camera that can cover an angle of view of 60° or more and therefore has a small focal length.

wide-awake adj. (wide awake when postpositive). 1. fully awake. 2. keen, alert, or observant. ~n. 3. Also called: **wide-awake hat**. a hat with a low crown and very wide brim.

wide-eyed adj. innocent or credulous.

widen ('waɪdᵊn) vb. to make or become wide or wider. —'**widener** n.

wide-open adj. (wide open when postpositive). 1. open to the full extent. 2. (postpositive) exposed to attack; vulnerable. 3. uncertain as to outcome. 4. U.S. inf. (of a town or city) lax in the enforcement of certain laws, esp. those relating to the sale of alcohol, gambling, etc.

widespread ('waɪd,sprɛd) adj. 1. extending over a wide area. 2. accepted by or occurring among many people.

widgeon ('wɪdʒən) n. a variant spelling of **wigeon**.

widow ('wɪdəʊ) n. 1. a woman whose husband has died, esp. one who has not remarried. 2. (with a modifier) Inf. a woman whose husband frequently leaves her alone, in order to indulge in a sport, etc.: a golf widow. 3. Printing. a short line at the end of a paragraph, esp. one that occurs as the top line of a page or column. 4. (in some card games) an additional hand or set of cards exposed on the table. ~vb. (tr.; usually passive) 5. to cause to become a widow. 6. to deprive of something valued. —'**widowhood** n.

widower ('wɪdəʊə) n. a man whose wife has died and who has not remarried.

widow's peak n. a V-shaped point in the hairline in the middle of the forehead.

width (wɪdθ) n. 1. the linear extent or measurement of something from side to side. 2. the state or fact of being wide. 3. a piece or section of something at its full extent from side to side: a width of cloth. 4. the distance across a rectangular swimming bath, as opposed to its length.

wield (wiːld) vb. (tr.) 1. to handle or use (a weapon, tool, etc.). 2. to exert or maintain (power or authority). —'**wieldable** adj. —'**wielder** n.

THESAURUS

wicked 1. abandoned, abominable, amoral, atrocious, bad, black-hearted, corrupt, debased, depraved, devilish, dissolute, egregious, evil, fiendish, flagitious, foul, guilty, heinous, immoral, impious, iniquitous, irreligious, nefarious, scandalous, shameful, sinful, unprincipled, unrighteous, vicious, vile, villainous, worthless 2. arch, impish, incorrigible, mischievous, naughty, rascally, roguish 3. acute, agonizing, awful, crashing, destructive, dreadful, fearful, fierce, harmful, injurious, intense, mighty, painful, severe, terrible 4. bothersome, difficult, distressing, galling, offensive, troublesome, trying, unpleasant 5. Sl. adept, adroit, deft, expert, masterly, mighty, outstanding, powerful, skilful, strong

wide adj. 1. ample, broad, catholic, comprehensive, distended, encyclopedic, expanded, expansive, extensive, far-reaching, general, immense, inclusive, large, sweeping, vast 2. away, distant, off, off course, off target, remote 3. dilated, distended, expanded, fully open, outspread, outstretched 4. ample, baggy, capacious, commodious, full, loose, roomy, spacious ~adv. 5. as far as possible, completely, fully, right out, to the furthest extent 6. astray, nowhere near, off course, off target, off the mark, out

wide-awake 1. conscious, fully awake, roused, wakened 2. alert, aware, heedful, keen, observant, on one's toes, on the alert, on the ball (Inf.), on the qui vive, vigilant, wary, watchful

wide-eyed credulous, green, impressionable, ingenuous, innocent, naive, simple,

trusting, unsophisticated, unsuspicious, wet behind the ears (Inf.)

widen broaden, dilate, enlarge, expand, extend, open out or up, open wide, spread, stretch

wide-open 1. fully extended, fully open, gaping, outspread, outstretched, splayed, spread 2. at risk, defenceless, exposed, in danger, in peril, open, susceptible, unprotected, vulnerable 3. anybody's guess (Inf.), indeterminate, uncertain, unpredictable, unsettled, up for grabs (Inf.)

widespread broad, common, epidemic, extensive, far-flung, far-reaching, general, pervasive, popular, prevalent, rife, sweeping, universal, wholesale

width breadth, compass, diameter, extent, girth, measure, range, reach, scope, span,

wife (waɪf) n., pl. **wives** (waɪvz). **1.** a man's partner in marriage; a married woman. Related adj.: **uxorial. 2.** an archaic or dialect word for **woman. 3. take to wife.** to marry (a woman). —'**wifehood** n. —'**wifeliness** n. —'**wifely** adj.

wig (wɪg) n. **1.** an artificial head of hair, either human or synthetic, worn to disguise baldness, as part of a theatrical or ceremonial dress, as a disguise, or for adornment. ~vb. **wigging, wigged.** (tr.) **2.** Brit. sl. to berate severely. —**wigged** adj. —'**wigless** adj.

wigeon or **widgeon** ('wɪdʒən) n. **1.** a Eurasian duck of marshes, swamps, etc., the male of which has a reddish-brown head and chest and grey-and-white back and wings. **2. American wigeon.** Also called: **baldpate.** a similar bird of North America, the male of which has a white crown.

wigging ('wɪgɪŋ) n. Brit. sl. a reprimand.

wiggle ('wɪgəl) vb. **1.** to move or cause to move with jerky movements, esp. from side to side. ~n. **2.** the act of wiggling. —'**wiggler** n. —'**wiggly** adj.

wight (waɪt) n. Arch. a human being.

wigwam ('wɪgˌwæm) n. **1.** any dwelling of the North American Indians, esp. one made of bark, rushes, or skins spread over a set of arched poles lashed together. **2.** a similar structure for children.

wilco ('wɪlkəʊ) interj. an expression in signalling, telecommunications, etc., indicating that a message just received will be complied with.

wild (waɪld) adj. **1.** (of animals) living independently of man; not domesticated or tame. **2.** (of plants) growing in a natural state; not cultivated. **3.** uninhabited; desolate: a wild stretch of land. **4.** living in a savage or uncivilized way: wild tribes. **5.** lacking restraint or control: wild merriment. **6.** of great violence: a wild storm. **7.** disorderly or chaotic: wild talk. **8.** dishevelled; untidy: wild hair. **9.** in a state of extreme emotional intensity: wild with anger. **10.** reckless: wild speculations. **11.** random: a wild guess. **12.** (postpositive; foll. by about) Inf. intensely enthusiastic: I'm wild about my new boyfriend. **13.** (of a card, such as a joker in some games) able to be given any value the holder pleases. ~adv. **14.** in a wild manner. **15. run wild. a.** to grow without cultivation or care: the garden has run wild. **b.** to behave without restraint: he has let his children run wild. ~n. **16.** (often pl.) a desolate or uninhabited region. **17. the wild. a.** a free natural state of living. **b.** the wilderness. —'**wildish** adj. —'**wildly** adv. —'**wildness** n.

wild carrot n. an umbelliferous plant of temperate regions, having clusters of white flowers and hooked fruits. Also called: **Queen Anne's lace.**

wildcat ('waɪldˌkæt) n., pl. -**cats** or -**cat. 1.** a wild European cat that resembles the domestic tabby but is larger and has a bushy tail. **2.** any of various other felines, such as the lynx and the caracal. **3.** U.S. another name for **bobcat. 4.** Inf. a savage or aggressive person. **5.** an exploratory drilling for petroleum or natural gas. **6.** (modifier) Chiefly U.S. involving risk, esp. financially or commercially unsound: a wildcat project. ~vb. **catting, catted. 7.** (intr.) to drill for petroleum or natural gas in an area having no known reserves. —'**wild,catter** n.

—'**wild,catting** n., adj.

wildcat strike n. a strike begun by workers spontaneously or without union approval.

wildebeest ('wɪldɪˌbiːst, 'vɪl-) n., pl. -**beests** or -**beest.** another name for **gnu.**

wilderness ('wɪldənɪs) n. **1.** a wild uninhabited uncultivated region. **2.** any desolate area. **3.** a confused mass or collection. **4. a voice (crying) in the wilderness.** a person, group, etc., making a suggestion or plea that is ignored.

wildfire ('waɪldˌfaɪə) n. **1.** a highly flammable material, such as Greek fire, formerly used in warfare. **2. a.** a raging and uncontrollable fire. **b.** anything that is disseminated quickly (esp. in **spread like wildfire). 3.** another name for **will-o'-the-wisp.**

wild flower n. **1.** any flowering plant that grows in an uncultivated state. **2.** the flower of such a plant.

wildfowl ('waɪldˌfaʊl) n. **1.** any bird that is hunted by man, esp. any duck or similar aquatic bird. **2.** such birds collectively. —'**wild,fowler** n. —'**wild,fowling** adj., n.

wild-goose chase n. an absurd or hopeless pursuit, as of something unattainable.

wildlife ('waɪldˌlaɪf) n. wild animals and plants collectively: a term used esp. of fauna.

wild oats pl. n. Sl. the indiscretions of youth, esp. dissoluteness before settling down (esp. in **sow one's wild oats).**

wild rice n. an aquatic North American grass with dark-coloured edible grain.

wild silk n. **1.** silk produced by wild silkworms. **2.** a fabric made from this, or from short fibres of silk designed to imitate it.

Wild West n. the western U.S. during its settlement, esp. with reference to its frontier lawlessness.

wile (waɪl) n. **1.** trickery, cunning, or craftiness. **2.** (usually pl.) an artful or seductive trick or ploy. ~vb. **3.** (tr.) to lure, beguile, or entice.

wilful or U.S. **willful** ('wɪlfʊl) adj. **1.** intent on having one's own way; headstrong or obstinate. **2.** intentional: wilful murder. —'**wilfully** or U.S. '**willfully** adv. —'**wilfulness** or U.S. '**willfulness** n.

will[1] (wɪl) vb. past **would.** (takes an infinitive without to or an implied infinitive) used as an auxiliary. **1.** (esp. with you, he, she, it, they, or a noun as subject) to make the future tense. Cf. **shall** (sense 1). **2.** to express resolution on the part of the speaker: I will buy that radio if it's the last thing I do. **3.** to indicate willingness or desire: will you help me with this problem? **4.** to express commands: you will report your findings to me tomorrow. **5.** to express ability: this rope will support a load. **6.** to express probability or expectation: that will be Jim telephoning. **7.** to express customary practice or inevitability: boys will be boys. **8.** (with the infinitive always implied) to express desire: usually in polite requests: stay if you will. **9. what you will.** whatever you like.
▷ **Usage.** See at **shall.**

will[2] (wɪl) n. **1.** the faculty of conscious and deliberate choice of action. Related adj.: **voluntary. 2.** the act or an instance of asserting a choice. **3. a.** the declaration of a person's wishes regarding the disposal of his property after his death. **b.** a document in which such wishes

---

THESAURUS

thickness, wideness

wield 1. brandish, employ, flourish, handle, manage, manipulate, ply, swing, use **2.** apply, be possessed of, command, control, exercise, exert, have, have at one's disposal, hold, maintain, make use of, manage, possess, put to use, utilize

wife better half (Humorous), bride, helpmate, helpmeet, little woman (Inf.), mate, old lady (Inf.), old woman (Inf.), partner, spouse, (the) missis or missus (Inf.), woman (Inf.)

wild adj. **1.** feral, ferocious, fierce, savage, unbroken, undomesticated, untamed **2.** free, indigenous, native, natural, uncultivated **3.** desert, deserted, desolate, empty, godforsaken, trackless, uncivilized, uncultivated, uninhabited, unpopulated, virgin **4.** barbaric, barbarous, brutish, ferocious, fierce, primitive, rude, savage, uncivilized **5.** boisterous, chaotic, disorderly, impetuous, lawless, noisy, riotous, rough, rowdy, self-willed, tur-

bulent, unbridled, uncontrolled, undisciplined, unfettered, ungovernable, unmanageable, unrestrained, unruly, uproarious, violent, wayward **6.** blustery, choppy, furious, howling, intense, raging, rough, tempestuous, violent **7.** dishevelled, disordered, straggly, tousled, unkempt, untidy, windblown **8.** at one's wits' end, berserk, beside oneself, crazed, crazy, delirious, demented, excited, frantic, frenzied, hysterical, irrational, mad, maniacal, rabid, raving **9.** extravagant, fantastic, flighty, foolhardy, foolish, giddy, ill-considered, impracticable, imprudent, madcap, outrageous, preposterous, rash, reckless **10.** Inf. agog, avid, crazy (Inf.), daft (Inf.), eager, enthusiastic, excited, mad (Inf.), nuts (Sl.), potty (Inf.) ~adv. **11. run wild a.** grow unchecked, ramble, spread, straggle **b.** abandon all restraint, cut loose, go on the rampage, kick over the traces, rampage, run free, run riot, stray ~n. **12.** Often plural back of beyond (Inf.), desert, middle of nowhere

(Inf.), uninhabited area, wasteland, wilderness

wilderness 1. desert, jungle, waste, wasteland, wild **2.** clutter, confused mass, confusion, congeries, jumble, maze, muddle, tangle, welter

wildlife flora and fauna

wile 1. artfulness, artifice, cheating, chicanery, craft, craftiness, cunning, fraud, guile, slyness, trickery **2.** Usually plural artifice, contrivance, device, dodge, imposition, lure, manoeuvre, ploy, ruse, stratagem, subterfuge, trick

wilful 1. adamant, bull-headed, determined, dogged, froward, headstrong, inflexible, intractable, intransigent, mulish, obdurate, obstinate, persistent, perverse, pigheaded, refractory, self-willed, stubborn, uncompromising, unyielding **2.** conscious, deliberate, intended, intentional, purposeful, volitional, voluntary, willed

are expressed. **4.** desire; wish. **5.** determined intention: *where there's a will there's a way.* **6.** disposition towards others: *he bears you no ill will.* **7. at will.** at one's own desire or choice. **8. with the best will in the world.** even with the best of intentions. ~*vb. (mainly tr.; often takes a clause as object or an infinitive)* **9.** *(also intr.)* to exercise the faculty of volition in an attempt to accomplish (something): *he willed his wife's recovery from her illness.* **10.** to give (property) by will to a person, society, etc.: *he willed his art collection to the nation.* **11.** *(also intr.)* to order or decree: *the king wills that you shall die.* **12.** to choose or prefer: *wander where you will.* —'**willer** *n.*

willies ('wɪlɪz) *pl. n.* **the.** *Sl.* nervousness, jitters, or fright (esp. in **give** (*or* **get**) **the willies**).

willing ('wɪlɪŋ) *adj.* **1.** favourably disposed or inclined; ready. **2.** cheerfully compliant. **3.** done, given, accepted, etc., freely or voluntarily. —'**willingly** *adv.* —'**willingness** *n.*

will-o'-the-wisp (ˌwɪləðə'wɪsp) *n.* **1.** Also called: **friar's lantern, ignis fatuus, jack-o'-lantern.** a pale flame or phosphorescence sometimes seen over marshy ground at night. It is believed to be due to the spontaneous combustion of methane originating from decomposing organic matter. **2.** a person or thing that is elusive or allures and misleads.

willow ('wɪləʊ) *n.* **1.** any of a large genus of trees and shrubs, such as the weeping willow and osiers of N temperate regions, which have graceful flexible branches and flowers in catkins. **2.** the whitish wood of certain of these trees. **3.** something made of willow wood, such as a cricket bat.

willowherb ('wɪləʊˌhɜːb) *n.* any of various temperate and arctic plants having narrow leaves and terminal clusters of pink, purplish, or white flowers.

willow pattern *n.* **a.** a pattern incorporating a willow tree, river, bridge, and figures, typically in blue on a white ground, used on pottery and porcelain. **b.** *(as modifier): a willow-pattern plate.*

willowy ('wɪləʊɪ) *adj.* **1.** slender and graceful. **2.** flexible or pliant. **3.** covered or shaded with willows.

willpower ('wɪlˌpaʊə) *n.* **1.** the ability to control oneself and determine one's actions. **2.** firmness of will.

willy-nilly ('wɪlɪ'nɪlɪ) *adv.* **1.** whether desired or not. ~*adj.* **2.** occurring or taking place whether desired or not.

wilt¹ (wɪlt) *vb.* **1.** to become or cause to become limp or drooping: *insufficient water makes plants wilt.* **2.** to lose or cause to lose courage, strength, etc. ~*n.* **3.** the act of wilting or state of becoming wilted. **4.** any of various plant diseases characterized by permanent wilting.

wilt² (wɪlt) *vb. Arch. or dialect.* (used with the pronoun *thou* or its relative equivalent) a singular form of the present tense (indicative mood) of **will¹**.

Wilton ('wɪltən) *n.* a kind of carpet with a close velvet pile of cut loops.

Wilts. (wɪlts) *abbrev. for* Wiltshire.

wily ('waɪlɪ) *adj.* **wilier, wiliest.** sly or crafty. —'**wiliness** *n.*

wimble ('wɪmbəl) *n.* **1.** any of a number of hand tools used for boring holes. ~*vb.* **2.** to bore (a hole) with a wimble.

wimple ('wɪmpəl) *n.* **1.** a piece of cloth draped around the head to frame the face, worn by women in the Middle Ages and still a part of the habit of some nuns. ~*vb.* **2.** *(tr.) Arch.* to cover with or put a wimple on. **3.** *Arch.* (esp. of a veil) to lie or cause to lie in folds or pleats.

Wimpy ('wɪmpɪ) *n. Trademark.* a hamburger served in a soft bread roll.

win (wɪn) *vb.* **winning, won.** **1.** *(intr.)* to achieve first place in a competition. **2.** *(tr.)* to gain (a prize, first place, etc.) in a competition. **3.** *(tr.)* to succeed in or gain (something) with an effort: *we won recognition.* **4. win one's spurs. a.** to achieve recognition in some field of endeavour. **b.** *History.* to be knighted. **5.** to gain victory or triumph in (a battle, argument, etc.). **6.** *(tr.)* to earn (a living, etc.) by work. **7.** *(tr.)* to capture: *the Germans never won Leningrad.* **8.** (when intr., foll. by *out, through,* etc.) to reach with difficulty (a desired position) or become free, loose, etc., with effort: *the boat won the shore.* **9.** *(tr.; often foll. by over)* to gain the support or consent of (someone): *only I can win him over!* **10.** *(tr.)* to gain (the sympathy, loyalty, etc.) of someone. **11.** *(tr.)* to persuade (a woman, etc.) to marry one. **12.** *(tr.)* to extract (ore, coal, etc.) from a mine or (metal or other minerals) from ore. **13. you can't win.** *Inf.* an expression of resignation after an unsuccessful attempt to overcome difficulties. ~*n.* **14.** *Inf.* a success, victory, or triumph. **15.** *poetry:* winnings. —'**winnable** *adj.*
> **Usage.** *Win* has become common in informal English as a noun meaning gain or victory. It is, however, regarded by careful users of English as inappropriate in formal contexts.

wince (wɪns) *vb.* **1.** *(intr.)* to start slightly, as with sudden pain; flinch. ~*n.* **2.** the act of wincing. —'**wincer** *n.* —'**wincingly** *adv.*

winceyette (ˌwɪnsɪ'ɛt) *n. Brit.* a plain-weave cotton fabric with slightly raised two-sided nap.

winch (wɪntʃ) *n.* **1.** a windlass driven by a hand- or power-operated crank. **2.** a hand- or power-operated crank by which a machine is driven. ~*vb.* **3.** *(tr.; often foll. by up or in)* to pull or lift using a winch.

Winchester disk ('wɪntʃɪstə) *n. Computers.* an inflexible disk in a sealed container with more storage capacity than a floppy disk. Also called: **hard disk, rigid disk.**

Winchester rifle *n. Trademark.* a breech-loading slide-action repeating rifle. Often shortened to **Winchester.**

wind¹ (wɪnd) *n.* **1.** a current of air, sometimes of considerable force, moving generally horizontally from areas of high pressure to areas of low pressure. **2.** *Chiefly poetic.* the direction from which a wind blows, usually a cardinal point of the compass. **3.** air artificially moved, as by a fan, pump, etc. **4.** a trend, tendency, or force: *the winds of revolution.* **5.** *Inf.* a hint; suggestion: *we got wind that you were coming.* **6.** something deemed insubstantial: *his talk was all wind.* **7.** breath, as used in respiration or talk: *you're just wasting wind.* **8.** (often used in sports) the power to breathe normally: *his wind is weak.* **9.** *Music.* **a.** a wind instrument or wind instruments considered collectively. **b.** *(often pl.)* the musicians who play wind instruments in an orchestra. **c.** *(modifier)* of or composed of wind instruments: *a wind ensemble.* **10.** gas generated in the alimentary canal.

THESAURUS

will *n.* **1.** choice, decision, determination, discretion, option, prerogative, volition **2.** declaration, last wishes, testament **3.** choice, decision, decree, desire, fancy, inclination, mind, pleasure, preference, wish **4.** aim, determination, intention, purpose, resolution, resolve, willpower **5.** attitude, disposition, feeling **6. at will** as one pleases, as one thinks fit, as one wishes, at one's desire (discretion, inclination, pleasure, whim, wish) ~*v.* **7.** bid, bring about, cause, command, decree, determine, direct, effect, ordain, order, resolve **8.** choose, desire, elect, opt, prefer, see fit, want, wish **9.** bequeath, confer, give, leave, pass on, transfer

willing agreeable, amenable, compliant, consenting, content, desirous, disposed, eager, enthusiastic, favourable, game (*Inf.*), happy, inclined, in favour, in the mood, nothing loath, pleased, prepared, ready, so-minded

willingly by choice, cheerfully, eagerly, freely, gladly, happily, of one's own accord, of one's own free will, readily, voluntarily, with all one's heart, without hesitation, with pleasure

willingness agreeableness, agreement, consent, desire, disposition, enthusiasm, favour, good will, inclination, volition, will, wish

willpower determination, drive, firmness of purpose *or* will, fixity of purpose, force *or* strength of will, grit, resolution, resolve, self-control, self-discipline, single-mindedness

wilt 1. become limp *or* flaccid, droop, sag, shrivel, wither **2.** diminish, dwindle, ebb, fade, fail, flag, languish, lose courage, melt away, sag, sink, wane, weaken, wither

wily arch, artful, astute, cagey (*Inf.*), crafty, crooked, cunning, deceitful, deceptive, designing, fly (*Sl.*), foxy, guileful, intriguing, scheming, sharp, shifty, shrewd, sly, tricky, underhand

win *v.* **1.** achieve first place, achieve mastery, be victorious, carry all before one, carry the day, come first, conquer, finish first, gain victory, overcome, prevail, succeed, take the prize, triumph **2.** accomplish, achieve, acquire, attain, bag (*Inf.*), catch, collect, come away with, earn, gain, get, net, obtain, pick up, procure, receive, secure **3. Often with over** allure, attract, bring *or* talk round, carry, charm, convert, convince, disarm, induce, influence, persuade, prevail upon, sway ~*n.* **4.** *Inf.* conquest, success, triumph, victory

wince 1. *v.* blench, cower, cringe, draw back, flinch, quail, recoil, shrink, start **2.** *n.* cringe, flinch, start

11. the air on which the scent of an animal is carried to hounds or on which the scent of a hunter is carried to his quarry. **12. between wind and water. a.** the part of a vessel's hull below the water line that is exposed by rolling or by wave action. **b.** any particularly susceptible point. **13. break wind.** to release intestinal gas through the anus. **14. get** *or* **have the wind up.** *Inf.* to become frightened. **15. how** *or* **which way the wind blows** *or* **lies.** what appears probable. **16. in the wind.** about to happen. **17. in the teeth** (*or* **eye**) **of the wind.** directly into the wind. **18. into the wind.** against the wind or upwind. **19. off the wind.** *Naut.* away from the direction from which the wind is blowing. **20. on the wind.** *Naut.* as near as possible to the direction from which the wind is blowing. **21. put the wind up.** *Inf.* to frighten or alarm. **22. raise the wind.** *Brit. inf.* to obtain the necessary funds. **23. sail close** *or* **near to the wind.** to come near the limits of danger or indecency. **24. take the wind out of someone's sails.** to disconcert or deflate someone. ~*vb.* (*tr.*) **25.** to cause (someone) to be short of breath: *the blow winded him.* **26. a.** to detect the scent of. **b.** to pursue (quarry) by following its scent. **27.** to expose to air, as in drying, etc. —'**windless** *adj.*

wind² (waɪnd) *vb.* **winding, wound.** **1.** (often foll. by *around, about,* or *upon*) to turn or coil (string, cotton, etc.) around some object or point or (of string, etc.) to be turned, etc., around some object or point: *he wound a scarf around his head.* **2.** (*tr.*) to cover or wreathe by or as if by coiling, wrapping, etc.: *we wound the body in a shroud.* **3.** (*tr.;* often foll. by *up*) to tighten the spring of (a clockwork mechanism). **4.** (*tr.;* foll. by *off*) to remove by uncoiling or unwinding. **5.** (*usually intr.*) to move or cause to move in a sinuous, spiral, or circular course: *the river winds through the hills.* **6.** (*tr.*) to introduce indirectly or deviously: *he is winding his own opinions into the report.* **7.** (*tr.*) to cause to twist or revolve: *he wound the handle.* **8.** (*tr.;* usually foll. by *up* or *down*) to move by cranking: *please wind up the window.* ~*n.* **9.** the act of winding or state of being wound. **10.** a single turn, bend, etc.: *a wind in the river.* ~See also **wind down, wind up.** —'**windable** *adj.* —'**winder** *n.*

windbag ('wɪnd,bæg) *n.* **1.** *Sl.* a voluble person who has little of interest to communicate. **2.** the bag in a set of bagpipes, which provides a continuous flow of air to the pipes.

windblown ('wɪnd,bləʊn) *adj.* **1.** blown by the wind. **2.** (of trees, shrubs, etc.) growing in a shape determined by the prevailing winds.

wind-borne *adj.* (esp. of plant seeds or pollen) transported by wind.

windbreak ('wɪnd,breɪk) *n.* a fence, line of trees, etc., serving as a protection from the wind by breaking its force.

windcheater ('wɪnd,tʃiːtə) *n.* a warm jacket, usually with a close-fitting knitted neck, cuffs, and waistband.

wind cone (wɪnd) *n.* another name for **windsock.**

wind down (waɪnd) *vb.* (*adv.*) **1.** (*tr.*) to lower or move down by cranking. **2.** (*intr.*) (of a clock spring) to become slack. **3.** (*intr.*) to diminish gradually in force or power; relax.

winded ('wɪndɪd) *adj.* **1.** out of breath, as from strenuous exercise. **2.** (*in combination*) having breath or wind as specified: *broken-winded; short-winded.*

windfall ('wɪnd,fɔːl) *n.* **1.** a piece of unexpected good fortune, esp. financial gain. **2.** something blown down by the wind, esp. a piece of fruit.

windflower ('wɪnd,flaʊə) *n.* any of various anemone plants, such as the wood anemone.

wind gauge (wɪnd) *n.* **1.** another name for **anemometer.** **2.** a scale on a gun sight indicating the amount of deflection necessary to allow for windage. **3.** *Music.* a

device for measuring the wind pressure in the bellows of an organ.

winding ('waɪndɪŋ) *n.* **1.** a curving or sinuous course or movement. **2.** anything that has been wound or wrapped around something. **3.** a particular manner or style in which something has been wound. **4.** a curve, bend, or complete turn in wound material, a road, etc. **5.** (*often pl.*) devious thoughts or behaviour: *the tortuous windings of political argumentation.* **6.** one or more turns of wire forming a continuous coil through which an electric current can pass, as used in transformers, generators, etc. —'**windingly** *adv.*

winding sheet *n.* a sheet in which a corpse is wrapped for burial; shroud.

wind instrument (wɪnd) *n.* any musical instrument sounded by the breath, such as the woodwinds and brass instruments of an orchestra.

windjammer ('wɪnd,dʒæmə) *n.* a large merchant sailing ship.

windlass ('wɪndləs) *n.* **1.** a machine for raising weights by winding a rope or chain upon a barrel or drum driven by a crank, motor, etc. ~*vb.* **2.** (*tr.*) to raise or haul (a weight, etc.) by means of a windlass.

windmill ('wɪnd,mɪl, 'wɪn,mɪl) *n.* **1.** a machine for grinding or pumping driven by a set of adjustable vanes or sails that are caused to turn by the force of the wind. **2.** the set of vanes or sails that drives such a mill. **3.** Also called: **whirligig.** *Brit.* a toy consisting of plastic or paper vanes attached to a stick in such a manner that they revolve like the sails of a windmill. **4.** an imaginary opponent or evil (esp. in **tilt at** *or* **fight windmills**). ~*vb.* **5.** to move or cause to move like the arms of a windmill.

window ('wɪndəʊ) *n.* **1.** a light framework, made of timber, metal, or plastic, that contains glass or glazed opening frames and is placed in a wall or roof to let in light or air or to see through. Related adj.: **fenestral.** **2.** an opening in the wall or roof of a building that is provided to let in light or air or to see through. **3.** Short for **windowpane.** **4.** the area behind a glass window in a shop used for display. **5.** any opening or structure resembling a window in function or appearance, such as the transparent area of an envelope revealing an address within. **6.** *Astronautics.* Also called: **launch window.** the limited period during which a spacecraft can be launched on a particular mission. **7.** *Physics.* a region of the spectrum in which a medium transmits electromagnetic radiation. **8.** (*modifier*) of or relating to a window or windows: *a window ledge.* ~*vb.* **9.** (*tr.*) to furnish with or as if with windows.

window box *n.* a long narrow box, placed on or outside a windowsill, in which plants are grown.

window-dressing *n.* **1.** the ornamentation of shop windows, designed to attract customers. **2.** the pleasant aspect of an idea, etc., which is stressed to conceal the real nature. —'**window-,dresser** *n.*

windowpane ('wɪndəʊ,peɪn) *n.* a sheet of glass in a window.

window seat *n.* **1.** a seat below a window, esp. in a bay window. **2.** a seat beside a window in a bus, train, etc.

window-shop *vb.* **-shopping, -shopped.** (*intr.*) to look at goods in shop windows without buying them. —'**window-,shopper** *n.* —'**window-,shopping** *n.*

windowsill ('wɪndəʊ,sɪl) *n.* a sill below a window.

windpipe ('wɪnd,paɪp) *n.* a nontechnical name for **trachea** (sense 1).

windscreen ('wɪnd,skriːn) *n.* *Brit.* the sheet of flat or curved glass that forms a window of a motor vehicle, esp. the front window. U.S. name: **windshield.**

windscreen wiper *n.* *Brit.* an electrically operated blade with a rubber edge that wipes a windscreen clear

---

THESAURUS

wind¹ **1.** *n.* air, air-current, blast, breath, breeze, current of air, draught, gust, zephyr **2.** *Inf.* clue, hint, inkling, intimation, notice, report, rumour, suggestion, tidings, warning, whisper **3.** babble, blather, bluster, boasting, empty talk, gab (*Inf.*), hot air, humbug, idle talk, talk, verbalizing **4.** breath, puff, respiration **5.** *Inf.* flatulence, flatus, gas **6. get** *or* **have the wind up** *Inf.* be afraid (alarmed, frightened, scared), fear, take fright **7. in the wind** about to happen, approaching, close at hand, coming, imminent, impending, in the

offing, near, on the cards (*Inf.*), on the way **8. put the wind up** *Inf.* alarm, discourage, frighten, frighten off, scare, scare off

wind² *v.* **1.** coil, curl, encircle, furl, loop, reel, roll, spiral, turn around, twine, twist, wreathe **2.** bend, curve, deviate, meander, ramble, snake, turn, twist, zigzag ~*n.* **3.** bend, curve, meander, turn, twist, zigzag

wind down cool off, decline, diminish, dwindle, lessen, reduce, relax, slacken, subside, taper off, unwind

winded breathless, gasping for breath, out

of breath, out of puff, panting, puffed, puffed out

windfall bonanza, find, godsend, jackpot, manna from heaven, stroke of luck

winding **1.** *n.* bend, convolution, curve, meander, turn, twist, undulation **2.** *adj.* anfractuous, bending, circuitous, convoluted, crooked, curving, flexuous, indirect, meandering, roundabout, serpentine, sinuous, spiral, tortuous, turning, twisting

of rain, snow, etc. U.S. name: **windshield wiper.**

windshield (ˈwɪndˌʃiːld) n. the U.S. name for **windscreen.**

windsock (ˈwɪndˌsɒk) n. a truncated cone of textile mounted on a mast so that it is free to rotate about a vertical axis: used, esp. at airports, to indicate the local wind direction. Also called: **air sock, drogue, wind sleeve, wind cone.**

Windsor chair (ˈwɪnzə) n. a simple wooden chair, popular in England and America from the 18th century, usually having a shaped seat, splayed legs, and a back of many spindles.

Windsor knot n. a wide triangular knot, produced by making extra turns in tying a tie.

windsurfing (ˈwɪndˌsɜːfɪŋ) n. the sport of riding on water using a surfboard steered and propelled by an attached sail.

windswept (ˈwɪndˌswɛpt) adj. open to or swept by the wind.

wind tunnel (wɪnd) n. a chamber for testing the aerodynamic properties of aircraft, aerofoils, etc., in which a current of air can be maintained at a constant velocity.

wind up (waɪnd) vb. (adv.) **1.** to bring to or reach a conclusion: he wound up the proceedings. **2.** (tr.) to tighten the spring of (a clockwork mechanism). **3.** (tr.; usually passive) Inf. to make nervous, tense, etc.: he was all wound up before the big fight. **4.** (tr.) to roll (thread, etc.) into a ball. **5.** an informal word for **liquidate** (sense 2). **6.** (intr.) Inf. to end up (in a specified state): you'll wind up without any teeth. ~n. **wind-up.** Inf., chiefly U.S. **7.** the act of concluding. **8.** the end.

windward (ˈwɪndwəd) Chiefly naut. ~adj. **1.** of, in, or moving to the quarter from which the wind blows. ~n. **2.** the windward point. **3.** the side towards the wind. ~adv. **4.** towards the wind. ~Cf. **leeward.**

windy (ˈwɪndɪ) adj. **windier, windiest. 1.** of, resembling, or relating to wind; stormy. **2.** swept by or open to powerful winds. **3.** marked by or given to prolonged and often boastful speech: windy orations. **4.** void of substance. **5.** an informal word for **flatulent. 6.** Sl. frightened. —ˈwindily adv. —ˈwindiness n.

wine (waɪn) n. **1. a.** an alcoholic drink produced by the fermenting of grapes with water and sugar. **b.** (as modifier): the wine harvest. **c.** an alcoholic drink produced in this way from other fruits, flowers, etc.: elderberry wine. **2. a.** a dark red colour, sometimes with a purplish tinge. **b.** (as adj.): wine-coloured. **3.** anything resembling wine in its intoxicating or invigorating effect. **4. new wine in old bottles.** something new added to or imposed upon an old or established order. ~vb. **5.** (intr.) to drink wine. **6. wine and dine.** to entertain or be entertained with wine and fine food. —ˈwineless adj.

winebibber (ˈwaɪnˌbɪbə) n. a person who drinks a great deal of wine. —ˈwineˌbibbing n.

wine cellar n. **1.** a place, such as a dark cool cellar, where wine is stored. **2.** the stock of wines stored there.

wineglass (ˈwaɪnˌɡlɑːs) n. **1.** a glass drinking vessel, typically having a small bowl on a stem, with a flared foot. **2.** Also called: **wineglassful.** the amount that such a glass will hold.

winepress (ˈwaɪnˌprɛs) n. any equipment used for squeezing the juice from grapes in order to make wine.

wineskin (ˈwaɪnˌskɪn) n. the skin of a sheep or goat sewn up and used as a holder for wine.

wing (wɪŋ) n. **1.** either of the modified forelimbs of a bird that are covered with large feathers and specialized for flight in most species. **2.** one of the organs of flight of an insect, consisting of a membranous outgrowth from the thorax containing a network of veins. **3.** either of the organs of flight in certain other animals, esp. the forelimb of a bat. **4. a.** a half of the main supporting aerofoil on an aircraft, confined to one side of it. **b.** the full span of the main supporting aerofoil on both sides of an aircraft. **5.** an organ, structure, or apparatus resembling a wing. **6.** anything suggesting a wing in form, function, or position, such as a sail of a windmill or a ship. **7.** Bot. **a.** either of the lateral petals of a sweetpea or related flower. **b.** any of various outgrowths of a plant part, esp. the process on a wind-dispersed fruit or seed. **8.** a means or cause of flight or rapid motion; flight: fear gave wings to his feet. **9.** Brit. the part of a car body that surrounds the wheels. U.S. name: **fender. 10.** Soccer, hockey, etc. **a.** either of the two sides of the pitch near the touchline. **b.** a player stationed in such a position; winger. **11.** a faction or group within a political party or other organization. See also **left wing, right wing. 12.** a part of a building that is subordinate to the main part. **13.** the space offstage to the right or left of the acting area in a theatre. **14. in** or **on the wings.** ready to step in when needed. **15.** either of the two pieces that project forwards from the sides of some chairbacks. **16.** (pl.) an insignia in the form of stylized wings worn by a qualified aircraft pilot. **17.** an air force unit, esp. an RAF unit larger than a squadron. **18.** any of various flattened organs or extensions in lower animals, esp. when used in locomotion. **19. on the wing. a.** flying. **b.** travelling. **20. take wing. a.** to lift off or fly away. **b.** to depart in haste. **c.** to become joyful. **21. under one's wing.** in one's care. **22. clip (someone's) wings.** to restrict (someone's) freedom. **23. on wings.** flying or as if flying. **24. spread** or **stretch one's wings.** to make full use of one's abilities. ~vb. (mainly tr.) **25.** (also intr.) to make (one's) way swiftly on or as if on wings. **26.** to shoot or wound (a bird, person, etc.) superficially, in the wing or arm, etc. **27.** to cause to fly or move swiftly: to wing an arrow. **28.** to provide with wings. —ˈwingless adj. —ˈwing,like adj.

wing chair n. an easy chair having wings on each side of the back.

wing commander n. an officer holding commissioned rank in certain air forces, such as the Royal Air Force: junior to a group captain and senior to a squadron leader.

wing nut n. a threaded nut tightened by hand by means of two flat lugs or wings projecting from the central body. Also called: **butterfly nut.**

wingspan (ˈwɪŋˌspæn) or **wingspread** (ˈwɪŋˌsprɛd) n. the distance between the wing tips of an aircraft, bird, etc.

wink (wɪŋk) vb. **1.** (intr.) to close and open one eye quickly, deliberately, or in an exaggerated fashion to convey friendliness, etc. **2.** to close and open (an eye or the eyes) momentarily. **3.** (tr.; foll. by away, back, etc.) to force away (tears, etc.) by winking. **4.** (tr.) to signal with a wink. **5.** (intr.) (of a light) to gleam or flash intermittently. ~n. **6.** a winking movement, esp. one conveying a signal, etc., or such a signal. **7.** an interrupted flashing of light. **8.** a brief moment of time. **9.** Inf. the smallest amount, esp. of sleep. **10. tip the wink.** Brit. inf. to give a hint.

wink at vb. (intr., prep.) to connive at; disregard: the authorities winked at corruption.

winker (ˈwɪŋkə) n. **1.** a person or thing that winks. **2.** Northern Brit. dialect. an eye. **3.** another name for **blinker**[1] (sense 1).

winkle (ˈwɪŋkəl) n. **1.** See **periwinkle**[1]. ~vb. **2.** (tr.; usually foll. by out, out of, etc.) Inf., chiefly Brit. to extract or prise out.

winner (ˈwɪnə) n. **1.** a person or thing that wins. **2.** Sl. a person or thing that seems sure to win or succeed.

THESAURUS

wind up 1. bring to a close, close, close down, conclude, end, finalize, finish, liquidate, settle, terminate, tie up the loose ends (Inf.), wrap up **2.** Inf. excite, make nervous, make tense, put on edge, work up **3.** Inf. be left, end one's days, end up, find oneself, finish up

windy 1. blowy, blustering, blustery, boisterous, breezy, gusty, squally, stormy, tempestuous, wild, windswept **2.** boastful, bombastic, diffuse, empty, garrulous, long-winded, loquacious, meandering, pompous, prolix, rambling, turgid, verbose, wordy **3.** Sl. afraid, chicken (Sl.), cowardly, fearful, frightened, nervous, scared, timid

wing n. **1.** organ of flight, pennon (Poetic), pinion (Poetic) **2.** arm, branch, circle, clique, coterie, faction, group, grouping, section, segment, set, side **3.** adjunct, annexe, ell, extension ~v. **4.** fly, glide, soar **5.** fleet, fly, hasten, hurry, race, speed, zoom **6.** clip, hit, nick, wound

wink v. **1.** bat, blink, flutter, nictate, nictitate **2.** flash, gleam, glimmer, sparkle, twinkle ~n. **3.** blink, flutter, nictation **4.** flash, gleam, glimmering, sparkle, twinkle **5.** instant, jiffy (Inf.), moment, second, split second, twinkling

wink at allow, blink at, condone, connive at, disregard, ignore, overlook, pretend not to notice, put up with (Inf.), shut one's eyes to, tolerate, turn a blind eye to

winkle out dig out, dislodge, draw out, extract, extricate, force out, prise out, smoke out, worm out

winner champ (Inf.), champion, conquering hero, conqueror, first, master, vanquisher, victor

winning ('wɪnɪŋ) *adj.* 1. (of a person, character, etc.) charming, engaging, or attractive. ~*n.* 2. a shaft or seam of coal. 3. (*pl.*) money, prizes, or valuables won, esp. in gambling. —'**winningly** *adv.* —'**winningness** *n.*

Winnipeg couch ('wɪnɪˌpɛg) *n. Canad.* a couch with no arms or back, opening out into a double bed.

winnow ('wɪnəʊ) *vb.* 1. to separate (grain) from (chaff) by means of a wind or current of air. 2. (*tr.*) to examine in order to select the desirable elements. 3. (*tr.*) *Rare.* to blow upon; fan. ~*n.* 4. **a.** a device for winnowing. **b.** the act or process of winnowing. —'**winnower** *n.*

wino ('waɪnəʊ) *n., pl.* -**os.** *Chiefly U.S.* a person who habitually drinks wine as a means of getting drunk.

winsome ('wɪnsəm) *adj.* charming; winning; engaging: *a winsome smile.* —'**winsomely** *adv.*

winter ('wɪntə) *n.* 1. **a.** (*sometimes cap.*) the coldest season of the year, between autumn and spring, astronomically from the December solstice to the March equinox in the N hemisphere and at the opposite time of year in the S hemisphere. **b.** (*as modifier*): *winter pasture.* 2. the period of cold weather associated with the winter. 3. a time of decline, decay, etc. 4. *Chiefly poetic.* a year represented by this season: *a man of 72 winters.* ~Related adj.: **hibernal.** ~*vb.* 5. (*intr.*) to spend the winter in a specified place. 6. to keep or feed (farm animals, etc.) during the winter or (of farm animals) to be kept or fed during the winter. —'**winterer** *n.* —'**winterless** *adj.*

wintergreen ('wɪntəˌgriːn) *n.* 1. any of a genus of evergreen ericaceous shrubs, esp. a subshrub of E North America, which has white bell-shaped flowers and edible red berries. 2. **oil of wintergreen.** an aromatic compound, formerly made from this and various other plants but now synthesized: used medicinally and for flavouring. 3. any of a genus of plants, such as **common wintergreen,** of temperate and arctic regions, having rounded leaves and small pink globose flowers. 4. **chickweed wintergreen.** a plant of N Europe and N Asia belonging to the primrose family, having white flowers and leaves arranged in a whorl.

winter solstice *n.* the time at which the sun is at its southernmost point in the sky (northernmost point in the S hemisphere) appearing at noon at its lowest altitude above the horizon. It occurs about December 22 (June 21 in the S hemisphere).

winter sports *pl. n.* sports held in the open air on snow or ice, esp. skiing.

wintertime ('wɪntəˌtaɪm) *n.* the winter season. Also (archaic): **wintertide** ('wɪntəˌtaɪd).

wintry ('wɪntrɪ) *or* **wintery** ('wɪntərɪ) *adj.* -**trier,** -**triest.** 1. (esp. of weather) of or characteristic of winter. 2. lacking cheer or warmth; bleak. —'**wintrily** *adv.* —'**wintriness** *or* '**winteriness** *n.*

winy ('waɪnɪ) *adj.* **winier, winiest.** having the taste or qualities of wine; heady.

wipe (waɪp) *vb.* (*tr.*) 1. to rub (a surface or object) lightly, esp. with (a cloth, hand, etc.), as in removing dust, water, etc. 2. (usually foll. by *off, away, from, up,* etc.) to remove by or as if by rubbing lightly: *he wiped the dirt from his hands.* 3. to eradicate or cancel (a thought, memory, etc.). 4. *Austral. inf.* to abandon or reject (a person). 5. to apply (oil, etc.) by wiping. 6. **wipe the floor with (someone).** *Inf.* to defeat decisively. ~*n.* 7. the act or an instance of wiping. 8. *Dialect.* a sweeping blow.

wipe out *vb.* (*adv.*) 1. (*tr.*) to destroy completely. 2. (*tr.*) *Inf.* to kill. 3. (*intr.*) to fall off a surfboard. ~*n.* **wipeout.** 4. an act or instance of wiping out. 5. the interference of one radio signal by another so that reception is impossible.

wiper ('waɪpə) *n.* 1. any piece of cloth, such as a hand-

kerchief, etc., used for wiping. 2. a cam rotated to allow a part to fall under its own weight, as used in stamping machines, etc. 3. See **windscreen wiper.** 4. *Electrical engineering.* a movable conducting arm that makes contact with a row or ring of contacts.

wire (waɪə) *n.* 1. a slender flexible strand or rod of metal. 2. a cable consisting of several metal strands twisted together. 3. a flexible metallic conductor, esp. one made of copper, usually insulated, and used to carry electric current in a circuit. 4. (*modifier*) of, relating to, or made of wire: *a wire fence.* 5. anything made of wire, such as wire netting. 6. a long continuous wire or cable connecting points in a telephone or telegraph system. 7. *Old-fashioned.* an informal name for **telegram** or **telegraph.** 8. *U.S. horse racing.* the finishing line on a racecourse. 9. a snare made of wire for rabbits and similar animals. 10. **get in under the wire.** *Inf., chiefly U.S.* to accomplish something with little time to spare. 11. **get one's wires crossed.** *Inf.* to misunderstand. 12. **pull wires.** *Chiefly U.S.* to exert influence behind the scenes; pull strings. ~*vb.* (*mainly tr.*) 13. (*also intr.*) to send a telegram to (a person or place). 14. to send (news, a message, etc.) by telegraph. 15. to equip (an electrical system, circuit, or component) with wires. 16. to fasten or furnish with wire. 17. to snare with wire. —'**wire,like** *adj.*

wire-gauge *n.* 1. a flat plate with slots in which standard wire sizes can be measured. 2. a standard system of sizes for measuring the diameters of wires.

wire-haired *adj.* (of an animal) having a rough wiry coat.

wireless ('waɪəlɪs) *n., Chiefly Brit., old-fashioned.* another word for **radio.**

wireless telegraphy *n.* another name for **radio-telegraphy.**

wire netting *n.* a net made of wire, often galvanized, that is used for fencing, etc.

wirepuller ('waɪəˌpʊlə) *n. Chiefly U.S.* a person who uses private or secret influence for his own ends. —'**wire,pulling** *n.*

wire service *n. Chiefly U.S.* an agency supplying news, etc., to newspapers, radio, and television stations, etc.

wiretap ('waɪəˌtæp) *vb.* -**tapping, -tapped.** to make a connection to a telegraph or telephone wire in order to obtain information secretly. —'**wire,tapper** *n.*

wire wool *n.* a mass of fine wire, used esp. to clean kitchen articles.

wireworm ('waɪəˌwɜːm) *n.* the wormlike larva of various beetles, which feeds on the roots of many plants and is a serious pest.

wiring ('waɪərɪŋ) *n.* 1. the network of wires used in an electrical system, device, or circuit. ~*adj.* 2. used in wiring.

wiry ('waɪərɪ) *adj.* **wirier, wiriest.** 1. (of people or animals) slender but strong in constitution. 2. made of or resembling wire, esp. in stiffness: *wiry hair.* 3. (of a sound) produced by or as if by a vibrating wire. —'**wirily** *adv.* —'**wiriness** *n.*

wisdom ('wɪzdəm) *n.* 1. the ability or result of an ability to think and act utilizing knowledge, experience, understanding, common sense, and insight. 2. accumulated knowledge or enlightenment. 3. *Arch.* a wise saying or wise sayings. ~Related adj.: **sagacious.**

wisdom tooth *n.* 1. any of the four molar teeth, one at the back of each side of the jaw, that are the last of the permanent teeth to erupt. Technical name: **third molar.** 2. **cut one's wisdom teeth.** to arrive at the age of discretion.

wise[1] (waɪz) *adj.* 1. possessing, showing, or prompted by wisdom or discernment. 2. prudent; sensible. 3.

THESAURUS

winning 1. alluring, amiable, attractive, bewitching, captivating, charming, delectable, delightful, disarming, enchanting, endearing, engaging, fascinating, fetching, lovely, pleasing, prepossessing, sweet, taking, winsome 2. conquering, successful, triumphant, victorious

winnings booty, gains, prize(s), proceeds, profits, spoils, takings

winnow comb, cull, divide, fan, part, screen, select, separate, separate the wheat from the chaff, sift, sort out

wintry 1. brumal, chilly, cold, freezing, frosty, frozen, harsh, hibernal, hiemal, icy, snowy 2. bleak, cheerless, cold, desolate, dismal

wipe v. 1. brush, clean, dry, dust, mop, rub, sponge, swab 2. clean off, erase, get rid of, remove, rub off, take away, take off ~n. 3. brush, lick, rub, swab

wipe out annihilate, blot out, destroy, efface, eradicate, erase, expunge, exterminate, extirpate, kill to the last man, massacre, obliterate

wiry 1. lean, sinewy, strong, tough 2. bristly, kinky, stiff

wisdom astuteness, circumspection, comprehension, discernment, enlightenment, erudition, foresight, insight, intelligence, judgment, judiciousness, knowledge, learning, penetration, prudence, reason, sagacity, sapience, sense, sound judgment, understanding

shrewd; crafty: *a wise plan.* **4.** well-informed; erudite. **5.** informed or knowing (esp. in **none the wiser**). **6.** *Sl.* (*postpositive;* often foll. by *to*) in the know, esp. possessing inside information (about). **7.** *Arch.* possessing powers of magic. **8. be** *or* **get wise.** (often foll. by *to*) *Inf.* to be or become aware or informed (of something). **9. put wise.** (often foll. by *to*) *Sl.* to inform or warn (of). ~*vb.* **10.** See **wise up.** —'**wisely** *adv.* —'**wiseness** *n.*

wise² (waɪz) *n. Arch.* way, manner, fashion, or respect (esp. in **any wise, in no wise**).

-wise *adv. combining form.* **1.** indicating direction or manner: *clockwise; likewise.* **2.** with reference to: *businesswise.*

▷ **Usage.** The addition of *-wise* to a noun as a replacement for a lengthier phrase (such as *as far as...is concerned*) is considered unacceptable by most careful speakers and writers: *talentwise, he's a little weak* (he's a little weak as regards talent); *the company is thriving profitwise* (as far as profits are concerned, the company is thriving).

wiseacre ('waɪzˌeɪkə) *n.* **1.** a person who wishes to seem wise. **2.** a wise person: often used facetiously or contemptuously.

wisecrack ('waɪzˌkræk) *Inf.* ~*n.* **1.** a flippant jibe or sardonic remark. ~*vb.* (*intr.*) **2.** to make a wisecrack. —'**wise,cracker** *n.*

wise guy *n. Sl.* a person who is given to making conceited, sardonic, or insolent comments.

wise up *vb.* (*adv.*) *Sl.,* chiefly *U.S.* (often foll. by *to*) to become or cause to become aware or informed (of).

wish (wɪʃ) *vb.* **1.** (when *tr.,* takes a clause as object or an infinitive; when *intr.,* often foll. by *for*) to want or desire (something, often that which cannot be or is not the case): *I wish I lived in Italy.* **2.** (*tr.*) to feel or express a desire or hope concerning the future or fortune of: *I wish you well.* **3.** (*tr.*) to desire or prefer to be as specified. **4.** (*tr.*) to greet as specified: *he wished us good afternoon.* ~*n.* **5.** the expression of some desire or mental inclination: *to make a wish.* **6.** something desired or wished for: *he got his wish.* **7.** (*usually pl.*) expressed hopes or desire, esp. for someone's welfare, health, etc. **8.** (*often pl.*) *Formal.* a polite order or request. —'**wisher** *n.*

wishbone ('wɪʃˌbəʊn) *n.* the V-shaped bone above the breastbone in most birds consisting of the fused clavicles.

wishful ('wɪʃfʊl) *adj.* having wishes or characterized by wishing. —'**wishfully** *adv.* —'**wishfulness** *n.*

wishful thinking *n.* the erroneous belief that one's wishes are in accordance with reality. —**wishful thinker** *n.*

wish on *vb.* (*tr., prep.*) to hope that (someone or something) should be imposed (on someone); foist: *I wouldn't wish my wife on anyone.*

wishy-washy ('wɪʃɪˌwɒʃɪ) *adj. Inf.* **1.** lacking in substance, force, colour, etc. **2.** watery; thin.

wisp (wɪsp) *n.* **1.** a thin, light, delicate, or fibrous piece or strand, such as a streak of smoke or a lock of hair. **2.** a small bundle, as of hay or straw. **3.** anything slender and delicate: *a wisp of a girl.* **4.** a mere suggestion or hint. **5.** a flock of birds, esp. snipe. —'**wisp,like** *adj.* —'**wispy** *adj.*

wist (wɪst) *vb. Arch.* the past tense or past participle of **wit²**.

wisteria (wɪ'stɪərɪə) *n.* any twining woody vine of the genus *Wisteria,* of E Asia and North America, having blue, purple, or white flowers in large drooping clusters.

wistful ('wɪstfʊl) *adj.* sadly pensive, esp. about something yearned for. —'**wistfully** *adv.* —'**wistfulness** *n.*

wit¹ (wɪt) *n.* **1.** the talent or quality of using unexpected associations between contrasting or disparate words or ideas to make a clever humorous effect. **2.** speech or writing showing this quality. **3.** a person possessing, showing, or noted for such an ability. **4.** practical intelligence (esp. in **have the wit to**). **5.** *Arch.* mental capacity or a person possessing it.

wit² (wɪt) *vb.* **1.** *Arch.* to be or become aware of (something). ~*adv.* **2. to wit.** that is to say; namely (used to introduce statements, as in legal documents).

witblitz ('vɪtˌblɪts) *n. S. African.* alcoholic drink illegally distilled.

witch (wɪtʃ) *n.* **1.** a person, usually female, who practises or professes to practise magic or sorcery, esp. black magic, or is believed to have dealings with the devil. **2.** an ugly or wicked old woman. **3.** a fascinating or enchanting woman. ~*vb.* (*tr.*) **4.** a less common word for **bewitch.** —'**witch,like** *adj.*

witchcraft ('wɪtʃˌkrɑːft) *n.* **1.** the art or power of bringing magical or preternatural power to bear or the act or practice of attempting to do so. **2.** the influence of magic or sorcery. **3.** fascinating or bewitching influence or charm.

witch doctor *n.* a man in certain societies, esp. preliterate ones, who appears to possess magical powers, used esp. to cure sickness but also to harm people. Also called: **shaman, medicine man.**

witch-elm *n.* a variant spelling of **wych-elm.**

witchery ('wɪtʃərɪ) *n., pl.* **-eries.** **1.** the practice of witchcraft. **2.** magical or bewitching influence or charm.

witches' Sabbath *n.* another name for **Sabbath** (sense 4).

witch hazel *or* **wych-hazel** *n.* **1.** any of a genus of trees and shrubs of North America, having ornamental yellow flowers and medicinal properties. **2.** an astringent medicinal solution containing an extract of the bark and leaves of one of these shrubs, applied to treat bruises, inflammation, etc.

witch-hunt *n.* a rigorous campaign to expose dissenters on the pretext of safeguarding the public welfare. —'**witch-,hunting** *n., adj.*

with (wɪð, wɪθ) *prep.* **1.** using; by means of: *he killed her with an axe.* **2.** accompanying; in the company of: *the lady you were with.* **3.** possessing; having: *a man with a red moustache.* **4.** concerning or regarding: *be patient with her.* **5.** in spite of: *with all his talents, he was still humble.* **6.** used to indicate a time or distance by which something is away from something else: *with three miles to go, he collapsed.* **7.** in a manner characterized by: *writing with abandon.* **8.** caused or prompted by: *shaking with rage.* **9.** often used with a verb indicating a reciprocal action or relation between the subject and the preposition's object: *agreeing with me.* **10. with it.** *Inf.* **a.** fashionable; in style. **b.** comprehending what is happening or being said. **11. with that.** after that.

withal (wɪ'ðɔːl) *adv.* **1.** *Literary.* as well. **2.** *Arch.* therewith. ~*prep.* **3.** (*postpositive*) an archaic word for **with.**

withdraw (wɪð'drɔː) *vb.* **-drawing, -drew, -drawn.** **1.** (*tr.*) to take or draw back or away; remove. **2.** (*tr.*) to remove from deposit or investment in a bank, etc. **3.** (*tr.*) to retract or recall (a promise, etc.). **4.** (*intr.*) to retire or retreat: *the troops withdrew.* **5.** (*intr.;* often foll. by *from*) to depart (from): *he withdrew from public life.* **6.** (*intr.*) to detach oneself socially, emotionally, or mentally. —**with'drawer** *n.*

THESAURUS

wise 1. aware, clever, discerning, enlightened, erudite, informed, intelligent, judicious, knowing, perceptive, politic, prudent, rational, reasonable, sagacious, sage, sapient, sensible, shrewd, sound, understanding, well-advised, well-informed **2. put wise** *Sl.* alert, apprise, clue in *or* up, inform, let (someone) into the secret, notify, tell, tip off, warn

wisecrack 1. *n.* barb, funny (*Inf.*), gag (*Sl.*), jest, jibe, joke, pithy remark, quip, sardonic remark, smart remark, witticism **2.** *v.* be facetious, jest, jibe, joke, quip, tell jokes

wish *v.* **1.** aspire, covet, crave, desiderate, desire, hanker, hope, hunger, long, need, set one's heart on, sigh for, thirst, want, yearn **2.**

bid, greet with **3.** ask, bid, command, desire, direct, instruct, order, require ~*n.* **4.** aspiration, desire, hankering, hope, hunger, inclination, intention, liking, longing, thirst, urge, want, whim, will, yearning **5.** bidding, command, desire, order, request, will

wistful contemplative, disconsolate, dreaming, dreamy, forlorn, longing, meditative, melancholy, mournful, musing, pensive, reflective, sad, thoughtful, yearning

wit 1. badinage, banter, drollery, facetiousness, fun, humour, jocularity, levity, pleasantry, raillery, repartee, wordplay **2.** card (*Inf.*), comedian, epigrammatist, *farceur,* humorist, joker, punster, wag **3.** acumen, brains, cleverness, common sense, compre-

hension, discernment, ingenuity, insight, intellect, judgment, mind, nous (*Brit. sl.*), perception, practical intelligence, reason, sense, understanding, wisdom

witch enchantress, magician, necromancer, occultist, sorceress

witchcraft enchantment, incantation, magic, necromancy, occultism, sorcery, sortilege, spell, the black art, the occult, voodoo, witchery, witching, wizardry

withdraw 1. draw back, draw out, extract, pull out, remove, take away, take off **2.** abjure, disavow, disclaim, recall, recant, rescind, retract, revoke, take back, unsay **3.** absent oneself, back out, depart, detach oneself, disengage, drop out, fall back, go, leave,

withdrawal (wıð'drɔːəl) *n.* **1.** an act or process of withdrawing. **2.** the period a drug addict goes through following abrupt termination in the use of narcotics, usually characterized by physical and mental symptoms (**withdrawal symptoms**).

withdrawn (wıð'drɔːn) *vb.* **1.** the past participle of **withdraw.** ~*adj.* **2.** unusually reserved or shy. **3.** secluded or remote.

withe (wıθ, wıð, waıð) *n.* **1.** a strong flexible twig, esp. of willow, suitable for binding things together; withy. **2.** a band or rope of twisted twigs or stems. ~*vb.* **3.** (*tr.*) to bind with withes.

wither ('wıðə) *vb.* **1.** (*intr.*) (esp. of a plant) to droop, wilt, or shrivel up. **2.** (*intr.; often foll. by away*) to fade or waste: *all hope withered away.* **3.** (*intr.*) to decay or disintegrate. **4.** (*tr.*) to cause to wilt or lose vitality. **5.** (*tr.*) to abash, esp. with a scornful look. —'**witherer** *n.* —'**witheringly** *adv.*

withers ('wıðəz) *pl. n.* the highest part of the back of a horse, behind the neck between the shoulders.

withershins ('wıðə,ʃınz) *or* **widdershins** *adv. Chiefly Scot.* in the direction contrary to the apparent course of the sun; anticlockwise.

withhold (wıð'həuld) *vb.* -**holding**, -**held**. **1.** (*tr.*) to keep back: *he withheld his permission.* **2.** (*tr.*) to hold back; restrain. **3.** (*intr.; usually foll. by from*) to refrain or forbear. —**with'holder** *n.*

within (wı'ðın) *prep.* **1.** in; inside; enclosed or encased by. **2.** before (a period of time) has elapsed: *within a week.* **3.** not differing by more than (a specified amount) from: *live within your means.* ~*adv.* **4.** *Formal.* inside; internally.

without (wı'ðaut) *prep.* **1.** not having: *a traveller without much money.* **2.** not accompanied by: *he came without his wife.* **3.** not making use of: *it is not easy to undo screws without a screwdriver.* **4.** (*foll. by a present participle*) not, while not, or after not: *she can sing for two minutes without drawing breath.* **5.** *Arch.* on the outside of: *without the city walls.* ~*adv.* **6.** *Formal.* outside.

withstand (wıð'stænd) *vb.* -**standing**, -**stood**. **1.** (*tr.*) to resist. **2.** (*intr.*) to remain firm in endurance or opposition. —**with'stander** *n.*

withy ('wıðı) *n., pl.* **withies.** a variant spelling of **withe** (senses 1, 2).

witless ('wıtlıs) *adj.* lacking wit, intelligence, or sense. —'**witlessly** *adv.* —'**witlessness** *n.*

witness ('wıtnıs) *n.* **1.** a person who has seen or can give first-hand evidence of some event. **2.** a person or thing giving or serving as evidence. **3.** a person who testifies, esp. in a court of law, to events or facts within his own knowledge. **4.** a person who attests to the genuineness of a document, signature, etc., by adding his own signature. **5. bear witness. a.** to give written or oral testimony. **b.** to be evidence or proof of. ~*Related adj.:* **testimonial.** ~*vb.* **6.** (*tr.*) to see, be present at, or know at first hand. **7.** to give as evidence (of). **8.** (*tr.*) to be the scene or setting of: *this field has witnessed a battle.* **9.** (*intr.*) to testify, esp. in a court of law, to events within a person's own knowledge. **10.** (*tr.*) to attest to the genuineness of (a document, etc.) by adding one's own signature. —'**witnesser** *n.*

witness box *or esp. U.S.* **witness stand** *n.* the place in a court of law in which witnesses stand to give evidence.

wits (wıts) *pl. n.* **1.** (*sometimes sing.*) the ability to reason and act, esp. quickly (esp. in **have one's wits about one**). **2.** (*sometimes sing.*) right mind, sanity (esp. in **out of one's wits**). **3. at one's wits' end.** at a loss to know how to proceed. **4. live by one's wits.** to gain a livelihood by craftiness rather than by hard work.

-**witted** *adj.* (*in combination*) having wits or intelligence as specified: *slow-witted; dim-witted.*

witter ('wıtə) *vb.* (*intr.*) *Inf.* (often foll. by *on*) to chatter or babble pointlessly or at unnecessary length.

witticism ('wıtı,sızəm) *n.* a clever or witty remark.

witting ('wıtıŋ) *adj. Rare.* **1.** deliberate; intentional. **2.** aware. —'**wittingly** *adv.*

witty ('wıtı) *adj.* -**tier**, -**tiest.** **1.** characterized by clever humour or wit. **2.** *Arch. or Brit. dialect.* intelligent. —'**wittily** *adv.* —'**wittiness** *n.*

wives (waıvz) *n.* **1.** the plural of **wife. 2. old wives' tale.** a superstitious tradition, occasionally one that contains an element of truth.

wizard ('wızəd) *n.* **1.** a male witch or a man who practises or professes to practise magic or sorcery. **2.** a person who is outstandingly clever in some specified field. ~*adj.* **3.** *Inf., chiefly Brit.* superb; outstanding. **4.** of or relating to a wizard or wizardry. —'**wizardly** *adj.*

wizardry ('wızədrı) *n.* the art, skills, and practices of a wizard, sorcerer, or magician.

wizen ('wızᵊn) *vb.* to make or become shrivelled. —'**wizened** *adj.*

wk. *abbrev. for:* **1.** (*pl.* **wks.**) week. **2.** work.

WNW *abbrev. for* west-northwest.

W.O. *abbrev. for:* **1.** War Office. **2.** Warrant Officer. **3.** wireless operator.

woad (wəud) *n.* **1.** a European cruciferous plant, formerly cultivated for its leaves, which yield a blue dye. **2.** the dye obtained from this plant, used esp. by the ancient Britons, as a body dye.

wobble ('wɒbᵊl) *vb.* **1.** (*intr.*) to move or sway unsteadily. **2.** (*intr.*) to shake: *her voice wobbled with emotion.* **3.** (*intr.*) to vacillate with indecision. **4.** (*tr.*) to cause to wobble. ~*n.* **5.** a wobbling movement or sound. —'**wobbler** *n.* —'**wobbly** *adj.* —'**wobbliness** *n.*

wodge (wɒdʒ) *n. Brit. inf.* a thick lump or chunk cut or broken off something.

woe (wəu) *n.* **1.** *Literary.* intense grief. **2.** (*often pl.*) affliction or misfortune. **3. woe betide** (**someone**). misfor-

make oneself scarce (*Inf.*), pull back, pull out, retire, retreat, secede

withdrawal 1. extraction, removal **2.** abjuration, disavowal, disclaimer, recall, recantation, repudiation, rescission, retraction, revocation **3.** departure, disengagement, exit, exodus, retirement, retreat, secession

withdrawn 1. aloof, detached, distant, introverted, quiet, reserved, retiring, shrinking, shy, silent, taciturn, timorous, uncommunicative, unforthcoming **2.** hidden, isolated, out-of-the-way, private, remote, secluded, solitary

wither 1. blast, blight, decay, decline, desiccate, disintegrate, droop, dry, fade, languish, perish, shrink, shrivel, wane, waste, wilt **2.** abash, blast, humiliate, mortify, put down (*Sl.*), shame, snub

withering 1. blasting, blighting, devastating, humiliating, hurtful, mortifying, scornful, snubbing **2.** deadly, death-dealing, destructive, devastating, killing, murderous, slaughterous

withhold 1. check, conceal, deduct, hide, hold back, keep, keep back, keep secret, refuse, repress, reserve, resist, restrain, retain, sit on (*Inf.*), suppress **2.** *With* **from** forbear, keep oneself, refrain, stop oneself

withstand 1. bear, brave, combat, confront, cope with, defy, endure, face, grapple with, hold off, hold out against, oppose, put up with (*Inf.*), resist, stand up to, suffer, take, take on, thwart, tolerate, weather **2.** endure, hold *or* stand one's ground, hold out, remain firm, stand, stand fast, stand firm

witness *n.* **1.** beholder, bystander, eyewitness, looker-on, observer, onlooker, spectator, viewer, watcher **2.** attestant, corroborator, deponent, testifier **3. bear witness a.** depone, depose, give evidence, give testimony, testify **b.** attest, bear out, be evidence of, be proof of, betoken, confirm, constitute proof of, corroborate, demonstrate, evince, prove, show, testify to, vouch for ~*v.* **4.** attend, be present at, look on, mark, note, notice, observe, perceive, see, view, watch **5.** attest, authenticate, bear out, bear witness, confirm, corroborate, depone, depose, give evidence, give testimony, testify **6.** countersign, endorse, sign

wits 1. acumen, astuteness, brains (*Inf.*), cleverness, comprehension, faculties, ingenuity, intelligence, judgment, nous (*Brit. sl.*), reason, sense, understanding **2. at one's wits' end** at a loss, at the end of one's tether,

baffled, bewildered, in despair, lost, stuck (*Inf.*), stumped

witticism bon mot, clever remark, epigram, one-liner (*Sl.*), play on words, pleasantry, pun, quip, repartee, riposte, sally, witty remark

witty amusing, brilliant, clever, droll, epigrammatic, facetious, fanciful, funny, gay, humorous, ingenious, jocular, lively, original, piquant, sparkling, waggish, whimsical

wizard 1. conjurer, enchanter, mage (*Archaic*), magician, magus, necromancer, occultist, shaman, sorcerer, thaumaturge (*Rare*), warlock, witch **2.** ace (*Inf.*), adept, expert, genius, hotshot (*Inf.*), maestro, master, prodigy, star, virtuoso, whiz (*Inf.*), whizz kid (*Inf.*), wiz (*Inf.*)

wizened dried up, gnarled, lined, sere (*Archaic*), shrivelled, shrunken, withered, worn, wrinkled

wobble *v.* **1.** quake, rock, seesaw, shake, sway, teeter, totter, tremble, vibrate, waver **2.** be unable to make up one's mind, be undecided, dither, fluctuate, hesitate, shillyshally (*Inf.*), swither (*Scot.*), vacillate, waver ~*n.* **3.** quaking, shake, tremble, tremor, unsteadiness, vibration tune will befall (someone): *woe betide you if you arrive late.* ~*interj.* **4.** Also: **woe is me.** *Arch.* an exclamation of sorrow or distress.

woebegone ('wəʊbɪˌgɒn) *adj.* sorrowful or sad in appearance.

woeful ('wəʊfʊl) *adj.* **1.** expressing or characterized by sorrow. **2.** bringing or causing woe. **3.** pitiful; miserable: *a woeful standard of work.* —'**woefully** *adv.* —'**woefulness** *n.*

wog (wɒg) *n. Brit. sl., derog.* a foreigner, esp. one who is not White.

wok (wɒk) *n.* a large metal Chinese cooking pot having a curved base like a bowl and traditionally with a wooden handle.

woke (wəʊk) *vb.* a past tense of **wake**[1].

woken ('wəʊkən) *vb.* a past participle of **wake**[1].

wold (wəʊld) *n. Chiefly literary.* a tract of open rolling country, esp. upland.

wolf (wʊlf) *n., pl.* **wolves. 1.** a predatory canine mammal which hunts in packs and was formerly widespread in North America and Eurasia but is now less common. Related adj.: **lupine. 2.** any of several similar and related canines, such as the red wolf and the coyote (**prairie wolf). 3.** the fur of any such animal. **4.** a voracious or fiercely cruel person or thing. **5.** *Inf.* a man who habitually tries to seduce women. **6.** Also called: **wolf note.** *Music.* **a.** an unpleasant sound produced in some notes played on the violin, etc., owing to resonant vibrations of the belly. **b.** an out-of-tune effect produced on keyboard instruments accommodated esp. to the system of mean-tone temperament. **7. cry wolf.** to give a false alarm. **8. have** *or* **hold a wolf by the ears.** to be in a desperate situation. **9. keep the wolf from the door.** to ward off starvation or privation. **10. lone wolf.** a person or animal who prefers to be alone. **11. wolf in sheep's clothing.** a malicious person in a harmless or benevolent disguise. ~*vb.* **12.** (*tr.*; often foll. by *down*) to gulp (down). **13.** (*intr.*) to hunt wolves. —'**wolfish** *adj.* —'**wolf**ˌ**like** *adj.*

Wolf Cub *n. Brit.* the former name for **Cub Scout.**

wolfhound ('wʊlfˌhaʊnd) *n.* the largest breed of dog, used formerly to hunt wolves.

wolfram ('wʊlfrəm) *n.* another name for **tungsten.**

wolframite ('wʊlfrəˌmaɪt) *n.* a black to reddish-brown mineral, a compound of tungsten, iron, and manganese: it is the chief ore of tungsten.

wolfsbane ('wʊlfsˌbeɪn) *or* **wolf's bane** *n.* any of several poisonous N temperate plants of the ranunculaceous genus *Aconitum* having hoodlike flowers.

wolf whistle *n.* **1.** a whistle made by a man to express admiration of a woman's appearance. ~*vb.* **wolf-whistle. 2.** (when *intr.*, sometimes foll. by *at*) to make such a whistle (at someone).

wolverine ('wʊlvəˌriːn) *n.* a large musteline mammal of northern forests of Eurasia and North America having dark very thick water-resistant fur. Also called: **glutton.**

wolves (wʊlvz) *n.* the plural of **wolf.**

woman ('wʊmən) *n., pl.* **women. 1.** an adult female human being. **2.** (*modifier*) female or feminine: *a woman politician.* **3.** women collectively. **4.** (usually preceded by *the*) feminine nature or feelings: *babies bring out the woman in him.* **5.** a female servant or domestic help. **6.** a man considered as having female characteristics, such as meekness. **7.** *Inf.* a wife or girlfriend. **8. the little woman.** *Inf.* one's wife. **9. woman of the streets.** a prostitute. ~*vb.* (*tr.*) **10.** *Obs.* to make effeminate. —'**womanless** *adj.* —'**woman-**ˌ**like** *adj.*

womanhood ('wʊmənˌhʊd) *n.* **1.** the state or quality of being a woman or being womanly. **2.** women collectively.

womanish ('wʊmənɪʃ) *adj.* **1.** having qualities regarded as unsuitable to a man. **2.** characteristic of or suitable for a woman. —'**womanishly** *adv.* —'**womanishness** *n.*

womanize *or* **-nise** ('wʊməˌnaɪz) *vb.* **1.** (*intr.*) *Inf.* (of a man) to indulge in casual affairs with women. **2.** (*tr.*) to make effeminate. —'**woman**ˌ**izer** *or* **-**ˌ**iser** *n.*

womanly ('wʊmənlɪ) *adj.* **1.** possessing qualities, such as warmth, attractiveness, etc., generally regarded as typical of a woman. **2.** characteristic of or belonging to a woman.

womb (wuːm) *n.* **1.** the nontechnical name for **uterus. 2.** a hollow space enclosing something. **3.** a place where something is conceived: *the Near East is the womb of western civilization.* **4.** *Obs.* the belly. —**wombed** *adj.* —'**womb**ˌ**like** *adj.*

wombat ('wɒmbæt) *n.* a burrowing herbivorous Australian marsupial having short limbs, a heavy body, and coarse dense fur.

women ('wɪmɪn) *n.* the plural of **woman.**

womenfolk ('wɪmɪnˌfəʊk) *pl. n.* **1.** women collectively. **2.** a group of women, esp. the female members of one's family.

Women's Institute *n.* (in Commonwealth countries) a society for women interested in engaging in craft and cultural activities.

Women's Liberation *n.* a movement directed towards the removal of attitudes and practices that preserve inequalities based upon the assumption that men are superior to women. Also called: **women's lib.**

won (wʌn) *vb.* the past tense and past participle of **win.**

wonder ('wʌndə) *n.* **1.** the feeling excited by something strange; a mixture of surprise, curiosity, and sometimes awe. **2.** something that causes such a feeling, such as a miracle. **3.** (*modifier*) exciting wonder by virtue of spectacular results achieved, feats performed, etc.: *a wonder drug.* **4. do** *or* **work wonders.** to achieve spectacularly fine results. **5. nine days' wonder.** a subject that arouses general surprise or public interest for a short time. **6. no wonder.** (*sentence connector*) (I am) not surprised at all (that): *no wonder he couldn't come.* **7. small wonder.** (*sentence connector*) (I am) hardly surprised (that): *small wonder he couldn't make it tonight.* ~*vb.* (when *tr.*, may take a clause as object) **8.** (when *intr.*, often foll. by *about*) to indulge in speculative inquiry: *I wondered about what she said.* **9.** (when *intr.*, often foll. by *at*) to be amazed (at something): *I wonder at your impudence.* —'**wonderer** *n.* —'**wonderment** *n.*

wonderful ('wʌndəfʊl) *adj.* **1.** exciting a feeling of wonder. **2.** extremely fine; excellent. —'**wonderfully** *adv.*

wonderland ('wʌndəˌlænd) *n.* **1.** an imaginary land of

THESAURUS

woe adversity, affliction, agony, anguish, burden, curse, dejection, depression, disaster, distress, gloom, grief, hardship, heartache, heartbreak, melancholy, misery, misfortune, pain, sadness, sorrow, suffering, trial, tribulation, trouble, unhappiness, wretchedness

woeful 1. afflicted, agonized, anguished, calamitous, catastrophic, cruel, deplorable, disastrous, disconsolate, distressing, doleful, dreadful, gloomy, grieving, grievous, heartbreaking, heart-rending, lamentable, miserable, mournful, pathetic, piteous, pitiable, pitiful, plaintive, sad, sorrowful, tragic, unhappy, wretched **2.** appalling, awful, bad, deplorable, disappointing, disgraceful, dreadful, duff (*Brit. Sl.*), feeble, hopeless, inadequate, lousy (*Inf.*), mean, miserable, paltry, pathetic, pitiable, pitiful, poor, rotten (*Inf.*), shocking, sorry, terrible, wretched

wolf *n.* **1.** *Fig.* devil, fiend, killer, mercenary, pirate, predator, robber, savage, shark

2. *Inf.* Casanova, Don Juan, lady-killer, lecher, Lothario, philanderer, seducer, womanizer ~*v.* **3.** *With* **down** bolt, cram, devour, gobble, gollop, gorge, gulp, pack away (*Inf.*), scoff (*Sl.*), stuff

woman 1. bird (*Sl.*), chick (*Sl.*), dame (*Sl.*), female, girl, lady, lass, lassie, maid (*Archaic*), maiden (*Archaic*), miss, she **2.** chambermaid, char (*Inf.*), charwoman, domestic, female servant, handmaiden, housekeeper, lady-in-waiting, maid, maidservant **3.** *Inf.* bride, girl, girlfriend, ladylove, mate, mistress, old lady (*Inf.*), partner, spouse, sweetheart, wife

womanizer Casanova, Don Juan, lady-killer, lecher, Lothario, philanderer, seducer, wolf (*Inf.*)

womanly female, feminine, ladylike, matronly, motherly, tender, warm

wonder *n.* **1.** admiration, amazement, astonishment, awe, bewilderment, curiosity, fascination, stupefaction, surprise, wonder-

ment **2.** curiosity, marvel, miracle, nonpareil, phenomenon, portent, prodigy, rarity, sight, spectacle, wonderment ~*v.* **3.** ask oneself, be curious, be inquisitive, conjecture, cudgel one's brains (*Inf.*), doubt, inquire, meditate, ponder, puzzle, query, question, speculate, think **4.** be amazed (astonished, awed, dumbstruck), be flabbergasted (*Inf.*), boggle, gape, gawk, marvel, stand amazed, stare

wonderful 1. amazing, astonishing, astounding, awe-inspiring, awesome, extraordinary, fantastic, incredible, marvellous, miraculous, odd, peculiar, phenomenal, remarkable, staggering, startling, strange, surprising, unheard-of, wondrous **2.** ace (*Inf.*), admirable, brilliant, excellent, fabulous (*Inf.*), fantastic (*Inf.*), great (*Inf.*), magnificent, marvellous, outstanding, sensational, smashing (*Inf.*), stupendous, super (*Inf.*), superb, terrific, tiptop, tremendous

marvels or wonders. **2.** an actual place or scene of great or strange beauty or wonder.

wondrous ('wʌndrəs) *Arch. or literary.* ~*adj.* **1.** exciting wonder; marvellous. ~*adv.* **2.** (intensifier): *it is wondrous cold.* —'**wondrously** *adv.* —'**wondrousness** *n.*

wonky ('wɒŋkɪ) *adj.* **-kier, -kiest.** *Brit. sl.* **1.** unsteady. **2.** askew. **3.** liable to break down.

wont (wəʊnt) *adj.* **1.** (*postpositive*) accustomed (to doing something): *he was wont to come early.* ~*n.* **2.** a manner or action habitually employed by or associated with someone (often in **as is my wont, as is his wont,** etc.). ~*vb.* **3.** (when *tr., usually passive*) to become or cause to become accustomed.

won't (wəʊnt) *contraction of* will not.

wonted ('wəʊntɪd) *adj.* **1.** (*postpositive*) accustomed (to doing something). **2.** (*prenominal*) usual: *she is in her wonted place.*

woo (wuː) *vb.* **wooing, wooed. 1.** to seek the affection, favour, or love of (a woman) with a view to marriage. **2.** (*tr.*) to seek after zealously: *to woo fame.* **3.** (*tr.*) to beg or importune (someone). —'**wooer** *n.* —'**wooingly** *adv.*

wood (wʊd) *n.* **1.** the hard fibrous substance consisting of xylem tissue that occurs beneath the bark in trees, shrubs, and similar plants. **2.** the trunks of trees that have been cut and prepared for use as a building material. **3.** a collection of trees, shrubs, grasses, etc., usually dominated by one or a few species of tree: usually smaller than a forest: *an oak wood.* Related adj.: **sylvan. 4.** fuel; firewood. **5.** *Golf.* **a.** a long-shafted club with a wooden head, used for driving. **b.** (*as modifier*): *a wood shot.* **6.** *Tennis, etc.* the frame of a racket: *he hit a winning shot off the wood.* **7.** one of the biased wooden bowls used in the game of bowls. **8.** *Music.* short for **woodwind. 9. from the wood.** (of a beverage) from a wooden container rather than a metal or glass one. **10. out of the wood** *or* **woods.** clear of or safe from dangers or doubts: *we're not out of the woods yet.* **11. see the wood for the trees.** (*used with a negative*) to obtain a general view of a situation without allowing details to cloud one's analysis: *he can't see the wood for the trees.* **12.** (*modifier*) made of, employing, or handling wood: *a wood fire.* **13.** (*modifier*) dwelling in or situated in a wood: *a wood nymph.* ~*vb.* **14.** (*tr.*) to plant a wood upon. **15.** to supply or be supplied with firewood.

wood alcohol *n.* another name for **methanol.**

wood anemone *n.* any of several woodland anemone plants having finely divided leaves and solitary white flowers. Also called: **windflower.**

woodbine ('wʊd,baɪn) *n.* **1.** a honeysuckle of Europe, SW Asia, and N Africa, having fragrant yellow flowers. **2.** *U.S.* another name for **Virginia creeper. 3.** *Austral. sl.* an Englishman.

woodcarving ('wʊd,kɑːvɪŋ) *n.* **1.** the act of carving wood. **2.** a work of art produced by carving wood. —'**wood,carver** *n.*

woodchuck ('wʊd,tʃʌk) *n.* a North American marmot having coarse reddish-brown fur. Also called: **ground hog.**

woodcock ('wʊd,kɒk) *n.* an Old World game bird resembling the snipe but larger and having shorter legs and neck.

woodcraft ('wʊd,krɑːft) *n. Chiefly U.S.* **1.** ability and experience in matters concerned with living in a wood or forest. **2.** ability or skill at woodwork, carving, etc.

woodcut ('wʊd,kʌt) *n.* **1.** a block of wood with a design, illustration, etc., from which prints are made. **2.** a print from a woodcut.

woodcutter ('wʊd,kʌtə) *n.* **1.** a person who fells trees or chops wood. **2.** a person who makes woodcuts. —'**wood,cutting** *n.*

wooded ('wʊdɪd) *adj.* **a.** covered with or abounding in

woods or trees. **b.** (*in combination*): *a soft-wooded tree.*

wooden ('wʊdən) *adj.* **1.** made from or consisting of wood. **2.** awkward or clumsy. **3.** bereft of spirit or animation: *a wooden expression.* **4.** obstinately unyielding: *a wooden attitude.* **5.** mentally slow or dull. **6.** not highly resonant: *a wooden thud.* —'**woodenly** *adv.*

wood engraving *n.* **1.** the art of engraving pictures or designs on wood for printing by cutting across the grain. **2.** a block of wood so engraved or a print taken from it. —**wood engraver** *n.*

wooden spoon *n.* a booby prize, esp. in sporting contests.

woodland ('wʊdlənd) *n.* **a.** land that is mostly covered with woods or dense growths of trees and shrubs. **b.** (*as modifier*): *woodland fauna.* —'**woodlander** *n.*

woodlouse ('wʊd,laʊs) *n., pl.* **-lice** (-,laɪs). any of various small terrestrial isopod crustaceans having a flattened segmented body and occurring in damp habitats.

woodpecker ('wʊd,pɛkə) *n.* a climbing bird, such as the **green woodpecker,** having a brightly coloured plumage and strong chisel-like bill with which it bores into trees for insects.

wood pigeon *n.* a large Eurasian pigeon having white patches on the wings and neck. Also called: **ringdove, cushat.**

woodpile ('wʊd,paɪl) *n.* **1.** a pile or heap of firewood. **2. nigger in the woodpile.** See **nigger** (sense 3).

wood pulp *n.* **1.** wood that has been ground to a fine pulp for use in making newsprint and other cheap forms of paper. **2.** finely pulped wood that has been digested by a chemical, such as caustic soda: used in making paper.

woodruff ('wʊdrʌf) *n.* any of several plants, esp. the sweet woodruff of Eurasia, which has small sweet-scented white flowers and whorls of narrow fragrant leaves used to flavour wine and liqueurs and in perfumery.

woods (wʊdz) *pl. n.* **1.** closely packed trees forming a forest or wood, esp. a specific one. **2.** another word for **backwoods** (sense 2). **3.** the woodwind instruments in an orchestra. **4. this** (**that, our,** *etc.*) **neck of the woods.** this particular area or piece of territory.

woodshed ('wʊd,ʃɛd) *n.* a small outbuilding where firewood, garden tools, etc., are stored.

wood sorrel *n.* a Eurasian plant having trifoliate leaves, an underground creeping stem, and white purple-veined flowers.

woodwind ('wʊd,wɪnd) *Music.* ~*adj.* **1.** of, relating to, or denoting a type of wind instrument, formerly made of wood but now often made of metal, such as the flute. ~*n.* **2.** (*functioning as pl.*) woodwind instruments collectively.

woodwork ('wʊd,wɜːk) *n.* **1.** the art or craft of making things in wood. **2.** components made of wood, such as doors, staircases, etc.

woodworking ('wʊd,wɜːkɪŋ) *n.* **1.** the process of working wood. ~*adj.* **2.** of, relating to, or used in woodworking. —'**wood,worker** *n.*

woodworm ('wʊd,wɜːm) *n.* **1.** any of various insect larvae that bore into wooden furniture, etc., esp. the larvae of the furniture beetle and the deathwatch beetle. **2.** the condition caused in wood by any of these larvae.

woody ('wʊdɪ) *adj.* **woodier, woodiest. 1.** abounding in or covered with forest or woods. **2.** connected with, belonging to, or situated in a wood. **3.** consisting of or containing wood or lignin: *woody tissue; woody stems.* **4.** resembling wood in hardness or texture. —'**woodiness** *n.*

woody nightshade *n.* a scrambling woody Eurasian plant, having purple flowers and producing poisonous red berry-like fruits. Also called: **bittersweet.**

woof[1] (wuːf) *n.* **1.** the crosswise yarns that fill the warp

---

THESAURUS

wont 1. *adj.* accustomed, given, in the habit of, used **2.** *n.* custom, habit, practice, rule, use, way

wonted 1. accustomed, given, habituated, in the habit of, used **2.** accustomed, common, conventional, customary, familiar, frequent, habitual, normal, regular, usual

woo chase, court, cultivate, importune, pay court to, pay one's addresses to, pay suit to, press one's suit with, pursue, seek after, seek the hand of, seek to win, solicit the good will of, spark (*Rare*)

wood 1. *Also* **woods** coppice, copse, forest, grove, thicket, trees, woodland **2. out of the wood(s)** clear, home and dry (*Brit. sl.*), in the clear, out of danger, safe, safe and sound, secure **3.** planks, timber

wooded forested, sylvan (*Poetic*), timbered, tree-clad, tree-covered, woody

wooden 1. ligneous, made of wood, of wood, timber, woody **2.** awkward, clumsy,

gauche, gawky, graceless, inelegant, maladroit, rigid, stiff, ungainly **3.** blank, colourless, deadpan, dull, emotionless, empty, expressionless, glassy, lifeless, spiritless, unemotional, unresponsive, vacant **4.** inflexible, obstinate, rigid, stiff, unbending, unyielding **5.** dense, dim, dim-witted (*Inf.*), dull, dull-witted, obtuse, slow, stupid, thick, witless, woodenheaded (*Inf.*) **6.** dull, muffled

yarns in weaving; weft. **2.** a woven fabric or its texture.

woof² (wuf) *interj.* **1.** an imitation of the bark or growl of a dog. ~*vb.* **2.** (*intr.*) (of dogs) to bark.

woofer ('wu:fə) *n.* a loudspeaker used in high-fidelity systems for the reproduction of low audio frequencies.

wool (wul) *n.* **1.** the outer coat of sheep, yaks, etc., which consists of short curly hairs. **2.** yarn spun from the coat of sheep, etc., used in weaving, knitting, etc. **3. a.** cloth or a garment made from this yarn. **b.** (*as modifier*): *a wool dress.* **4.** any of certain fibrous materials: *glass wool; steel wool.* **5.** *Inf.* short thick curly hair. **6.** a tangled mass of soft fine hairs that occurs in certain plants. **7.** **dyed in the wool.** confirmed in one's beliefs or opinions. **8. lose** (*or* **keep**) **one's wool.** *Brit. inf.* to lose (or keep) one's temper. **9. pull the wool over someone's eyes.** to deceive or delude someone. —'**wool-**｜**like** *adj.*

wool fat *or* **grease** *n.* another name for **lanolin.**

woolgathering ('wul｜gæðərɪŋ) *n.* idle or absent-minded daydreaming.

woolgrower ('wul｜grəuə) *n.* a person who keeps sheep for their wool. —'**wool**｜**growing** *n.*

woollen *or* U.S. **woolen** ('wulən) *adj.* **1.** relating to or consisting partly or wholly of wool. ~*n.* **2.** (*often pl.*) a garment or piece of cloth made wholly or partly of wool, esp. a knitted one.

woolly *or* U.S. (*often*) **wooly** ('wulɪ) *adj.* **woollier, woolliest. 1.** consisting of, resembling, or having the nature of wool. **2.** covered or clothed in wool or something resembling it. **3.** lacking clarity or substance: *woolly thinking.* **4.** *Bot.* covered with long soft whitish hairs: *woolly stems.* ~*n., pl.* **-lies. 5.** (*often pl.*) a garment, such as a sweater, made of wool or something similar. —'**woollily** *adv.* —'**woolliness** *n.*

woolpack ('wul｜pæk) *n.* **1.** the cloth wrapping used to pack a bale of wool. **2.** a bale of wool.

woolsack ('wul｜sæk) *n.* **1.** a sack containing or intended to contain wool. **2.** (in Britain) the seat of the Lord Chancellor in the House of Lords, formerly made of a large square sack of wool.

woozy ('wu:zɪ) *adj.* **woozier, wooziest.** *Inf.* **1.** dazed or confused. **2.** experiencing dizziness, nausea, etc., as a result of drink. —'**woozily** *adv.* —'**wooziness** *n.*

wop (wɒp) *n. Sl., derog.* a member of a Latin people, esp. an Italian.

Worcester sauce ('wustə) *n.* a commercially prepared piquant sauce, made from a basis of soy sauce, with vinegar, spices, etc.

word (wɜːd) *n.* **1.** one of the units of speech or writing that is the smallest isolable meaningful element of the language, although linguists would analyse these further into morphemes. **2.** an instance of vocal intercourse; chat, talk, or discussion: *to have a word with someone.* **3.** an utterance or expression, esp. a brief one: *a word of greeting.* **4.** news or information: *he sent word that he would be late.* **5.** a verbal signal for action; command: *when I give the word, fire!* **6.** an undertaking or promise: *he kept his word.* **7.** an autocratic decree; order: *his word must be obeyed.* **8.** a watchword or slogan, as of a political party: *the word now is "freedom".* **9.** *Computers.* a set of bits used to store, transmit, or operate upon an item of information in a computer. **10. as good as one's word.** doing what one has undertaken to do. **11. at a word.** at once. **12. by word of mouth.** through the medium of human speech. **13. in a word.** briefly or in short. **14. my word! a.** an exclamation of surprise, annoyance,

etc. **b.** *Austral.* an exclamation of agreement. **15. of one's word.** given to or noted for keeping one's promises: *I am a man of my word.* **16. put in a word** *or* **good word for.** to make favourable mention of (someone); recommend. **17. take someone at his** *or* **her word.** to assume that someone means, or will do, what he or she says: *when he told her to go, she took him at his word and left.* **18. take someone's word for it.** to accept or believe what someone says. **19. the last word. a.** the closing remark of a conversation or argument, esp. a remark that supposedly settles an issue. **b.** the latest or most fashionable design, make, or model: *the last word in bikinis.* **c.** the finest example (of some quality, condition, etc.): *the last word in luxury.* **20. the word.** the proper or most fitting expression: *cold is not the word for it, it's freezing!* **21. upon** *or* **on my word! a.** *Arch.* on my honour. **b.** an exclamation of surprise, annoyance, etc. **22. word for word.** (of a report, etc.) using exactly the same words as those employed in the situation being reported; verbatim. **23. word of honour.** a promise; oath. **24.** (*modifier*) of, relating to, or consisting of words: *a word list.* ~*vb.* **25.** (*tr.*) to state in words, usually specially selected ones; phrase. ~See also **words.** —'**wordless** *adj.* —'**wordlessly** *adv.*

Word (wɜːd) *n.* **the. 1.** *Christianity.* the 2nd person of the Trinity. **2.** Scripture, the Bible, or the Gospels as embodying or representing divine revelation. Often called: **the Word of God.**

word blindness *n.* the nontechnical name for **alexia** and **dyslexia.** —'**word-**｜**blind** *adj.*

word game *n.* any game involving the formation, discovery, or alteration of a word or words.

wording ('wɜːdɪŋ) *n.* **1.** the way in which words are used to express a statement, report, etc., esp. a written one. **2.** the words themselves.

word order *n.* the arrangement of words in a phrase, clause, or sentence.

word-perfect *or* U.S. **letter-perfect** *adj.* **1.** correct in every detail. **2.** (of a speaker, actor, etc.) knowing one's speech, role, etc., perfectly.

word processing *n.* the storage and organization of language by electronic means, esp. for business purposes.

word processor *n.* an installation for word processing, typically consisting of a keyboard and a VDU incorporating a microprocessor with storage and processing capabilities.

words (wɜːdz) *pl. n.* **1.** the text of a part of an actor, etc. **2.** the text of a song, as opposed to the music. **3.** angry speech (esp. in **have words with someone**). **4. eat one's words.** to retract a statement. **5. for words.** (preceded by *too* and an adj. or adv.) indescribably; extremely: *the play was too funny for words.* **6. have no words for.** to be incapable of describing. **7. in other words.** expressing the same idea but differently. **8. in so many words.** explicitly or precisely. **9. of many** (*or* **few**) **words.** (not) talkative. **10. put into words.** to express in speech or writing. **11. say a few words.** to give a brief speech. **12. take the words out of one's** (*or* **someone's**) **mouth.** to say exactly what someone else was about to say. **13. words fail me.** I am too happy, sad, amazed, etc., to express my thoughts.

wordy ('wɜːdɪ) *adj.* **wordier, wordiest.** using or containing an excess of words: *a wordy document.* —'**wordily** *adv.* —'**wordiness** *n.*

wore (wɔː) *vb.* the past tense of **wear.**

THESAURUS

wool 1. fleece, hair, yarn **2. dyed in the wool** confirmed, diehard, fixed, hardened, inflexible, inveterate, settled, unchangeable, uncompromising, unshakable **3. pull the wool over someone's eyes** bamboozle (*Inf.*), con (*Sl.*), deceive, delude, dupe, fool, hoodwink, lead (someone) up the garden path (*Inf.*), pull a fast one (on someone) (*Inf.*), put one over on (*Sl.*), take in (*Inf.*), trick

woolgathering absent-mindedness, abstraction, building castles in the air, daydreaming, dreaming, inattention, musing, preoccupation, reverie

woolly *adj.* **1.** fleecy, flocculent, hairy, made of wool, shaggy, woollen **2.** blurred, clouded, confused, foggy, fuzzy, hazy, ill-defined, indefinite, indistinct, muddled, nebu-

lous, unclear, vague

word *n.* **1.** brief conversation, chat, chit-chat, colloquy, confab (*Inf.*), confabulation, consultation, discussion, talk, tête-à-tête **2.** brief statement, comment, declaration, expression, remark, utterance **3.** expression, locution, name, term, vocable **4.** account, advice, bulletin, communication, communiqué, dispatch, gen (*Brit. inf.*), information, intelligence, intimation, message, news, notice, report, tidings **5.** command, go-ahead (*Inf.*), green light, order, signal **6.** affirmation, assertion, assurance, guarantee, oath, parole, pledge, promise, solemn oath, solemn word, undertaking, vow, word of honour **7.** bidding, command, commandment, decree, edict, mandate, order, ukase (*Rare*), will **8.**

countersign, password, slogan, watchword **9. in a word** briefly, concisely, in a nutshell, in short, succinctly, to put it briefly, to sum up ~*v.* **10.** couch, express, phrase, put, say, state, utter

wordplay punning, puns, repartee, wit, witticisms

words 1. lyrics, text **2.** altercation, angry exchange, angry speech, argument, barney (*Inf.*), bickering, disagreement, dispute, falling-out (*Inf.*), quarrel, row, run-in (*Inf.*), set-to (*Inf.*), squabble

wordy diffuse, discursive, garrulous, long-winded, loquacious, pleonastic, prolix, rambling, verbose, windy

work (wɜːk) *n.* **1.** physical or mental effort directed towards doing or making something. **2.** paid employment at a job or a trade, occupation, or profession. **3.** a duty, task, or undertaking. **4.** something done, made, etc., as a result of effort or exertion: *a work of art.* **5.** another word for **workmanship** (sense 3). **6.** the place, office, etc., where a person is employed. **7. a.** decoration, esp. of a specified kind. **b.** (in combination): *wirework.* **8.** an engineering structure such as a bridge, building, etc. **9.** *Physics.* the transfer of energy expressed as the product of a force and the distance through which its point of application moves in the direction of the force. **10.** a structure, wall, etc., built or used as part of a fortification system. **11. at work. a.** at one's job or place of employment. **b.** in action; operating. **12. make short work of.** *Inf.* to dispose of very quickly. **13.** (*modifier*) of, relating to, or used for work: *work clothes; a work permit; a work song.* ~*vb.* **14.** (*intr.*) to exert effort in order to do, make, or perform something. **15.** (*intr.*) to be employed. **16.** (*tr.*) to carry on operations, activity, etc., in (a place or area): *that salesman works the southern region.* **17.** (*tr.*) to cause to labour or toil: *he works his men hard.* **18.** to operate or cause to operate, esp. properly or effectively: *to work a lathe; that clock doesn't work.* **19.** (*tr.*) to till or cultivate (land). **20.** to handle or manipulate or be handled or manipulated: *to work dough.* **21.** to shape or process or be shaped or processed: *to work copper.* **22.** to reach or cause to reach a specific condition, esp. gradually: *the rope worked loose.* **23.** (*intr.*) to move in agitation: *his face worked with anger.* **24.** (*tr.*; often foll. by *up*) to provoke or arouse: *to work someone into a frenzy.* **25.** (*tr.*) to effect or accomplish: *to work one's revenge.* **26.** to make (one's way) with effort: *he worked his way through the crowd.* **27.** (*tr.*) to make or decorate by hand in embroidery, tapestry, etc.: *she was working a sampler.* **28.** (*intr.*) (of liquids) to ferment, as in brewing. **29.** (*tr.*) *Inf.* to manipulate or exploit to one's own advantage. ~See also **work in, work off,** etc. —**ʹworkless** *adj.*

workable (ʹwɜːkəbəl) *adj.* **1.** practicable or feasible. **2.** able to be worked. —**ˌworkaʹbility** *or* **ʹworkableness** *n.*

workaday (ʹwɜːkəˌdeɪ) *adj.* (*usually prenominal*) **1.** being a part of general human experience; ordinary. **2.** suitable for working days; everyday or practical.

workaholic (ˌwɜːkəʹhɒlɪk) *n.* a person obsessively addicted to work.

workbench (ʹwɜːkˌbɛntʃ) *n.* a heavy table at which work is done by a carpenter, mechanic, toolmaker, etc.

worker (ʹwɜːkə) *n.* **1.** a person or thing that works, usually at a specific job: *a research worker.* **2.** an employee, as opposed to an employer or manager. **3.** a manual labourer working in a manufacturing industry. **4.** any other member of the working class. **5.** a sterile female member of a colony of bees, ants, or wasps that forages for food, cares for the larvae, etc.

work force *n.* **1.** the total number of workers employed by a company on a specific job, project, etc. **2.** the total number of people who could be employed: *the country's work force is growing.*

workhouse (ʹwɜːkˌhaʊs) *n.* **1.** (formerly in England) an institution maintained at public expense where able-bodied paupers did unpaid work in return for food and accommodation. **2.** (in the U.S.) a prison for petty of-

fenders serving short sentences at manual labour.

work in *vb.* (*adv.*) **1.** to insert or become inserted: *she worked the patch in carefully.* **2.** (*tr.*) to find space for: *I'll work this job in during the day.* ~*n.* **work-in. 3.** a form of industrial action in which a factory that is to be closed down is occupied and run by its workers.

working (ʹwɜːkɪŋ) *n.* **1.** the operation or mode of operation of something. **2.** the act or process of moulding something pliable. **3.** a convulsive or jerking motion, as from excitement. **4.** (*often pl.*) a part of a mine or quarry that is being or has been worked. ~*adj.* (*prenominal*) **5.** relating to or concerned with a person or thing that works: *a working man.* **6.** concerned with, used in, or suitable for work: *working clothes.* **7.** (of a meal or occasion) during which business discussions are carried on: *a working lunch.* **8.** capable of being operated or used: *a working model; in working order.* **9.** adequate for normal purposes: *a working majority; a working knowledge of German.* **10.** (of a theory, etc.) providing a basis, usually a temporary one, on which operations or procedures may be carried out. **11. are you working?** *N.Z.* a question used to mean "are you still using this telephone line?"

working class *n.* **1.** Also called: **proletariat.** the social stratum, usually of low status, that consists of those who earn wages, esp. as manual workers. ~*adj.* **working-class. 2.** of, relating to, or characteristic of the working class.

working day *or esp. U.S.* **workday** *n.* **1.** a day on which work is done, esp. for an agreed or stipulated number of hours in return for a salary or wage. **2.** the part of the day allocated to work.

working party *n.* **1.** a committee established to investigate a problem, question, etc. **2.** a group of soldiers or prisoners assigned to perform some manual task or duty.

workload (ʹwɜːkˌləʊd) *n.* the amount of work to be done, esp. in a specified period.

workmanlike (ʹwɜːkmənˌlaɪk) *or* **workmanly** (ʹwɜːkmənlɪ) *adj.* appropriate to or befitting a good workman.

workmanship (ʹwɜːkmənˌʃɪp) *n.* **1.** the art or skill of a workman. **2.** the art or skill with which something is made or executed. **3.** the degree of art or skill exhibited in the finished product. **4.** the piece of work so produced.

workmate (ʹwɜːkˌmeɪt) *n.* a person who works with another; fellow worker.

work of art *n.* **1.** a piece of fine art, such as a painting or sculpture. **2.** something that may be likened to a piece of fine art, esp. in beauty, intricacy, etc.

work off *vb.* (*tr.*, *adv.*) **1.** to get rid of or dissipate, as by effort: *he worked off some of his energy by digging the garden.* **2.** to discharge (a debt) by labour rather than payment.

work on *vb.* (*intr.*, *prep.*) to persuade or influence or attempt to persuade or influence.

work out *vb.* (*adv.*) **1.** (*tr.*) to achieve or accomplish by effort. **2.** (*tr.*) to solve or find out by reasoning or calculation: *to work out an answer; to work out a sum.* **3.** (*tr.*) to devise or formulate: *to work out a plan.* **4.** (*intr.*) to prove satisfactory: *did your plan work out?* **5.** (*intr.*) to happen as specified: *it all worked out well.* **6.** (*intr.*)

THESAURUS

work *n.* **1.** drudgery, effort, elbow grease (*Inf.*), exertion, grind (*Inf.*), industry, labour, slog, sweat, toil, travail (*Literary*) **2.** business, calling, craft, duty, employment, job, line, livelihood, métier, occupation, office, profession, pursuit, trade **3.** assignment, chore, commission, duty, job, stint, task, undertaking **4.** achievement, composition, creation, handiwork, *oeuvre,* opus, performance, piece, production **5.** art, craft, skill, workmanship **6. out of work** idle, jobless, on the dole (*Brit. inf.*), on the street, out of a job, unemployed ~*v.* **7.** drudge, exert oneself, labour, peg away, slave, slog (away), sweat, toil **8.** be employed, be in work, do business, earn a living, have a job **9.** act, control, direct, drive, handle, manage, manipulate, move, operate, ply, use, wield **10.** function, go, operate, perform, run **11.** cultivate, dig, farm, till **12.** fashion, form, handle, knead,

make, manipulate, mould, process, shape **13.** be agitated, convulse, move, twitch, writhe **14. Often with up** arouse, excite, move, prompt, provoke, rouse, stir **15.** accomplish, achieve, bring about, carry out, cause, contrive, create, effect, encompass, execute, implement **16.** force, make one's way, manoeuvre, move, progress **17.** *Inf.* arrange, bring off, contrive, exploit, fiddle (*Inf.*), fix (*Inf.*), handle, manipulate, pull off, swing (*Inf.*)

workable doable, feasible, possible, practicable, practical, viable

workaday common, commonplace, everyday, familiar, humdrum, mundane, ordinary, practical, prosaic, routine

worker artisan, craftsman, employee, hand, labourer, proletarian, tradesman, wage earner, working man, working woman, workman

working *n.* **1.** action, functioning, man-

ner, method, mode of operation, operation, running **2.** *Plural* diggings, excavations, mine, pit, quarry, shaft ~*adj.* **3.** active, employed, in a job, in work, labouring **4.** functioning, going, operative, running **5.** effective, practical, useful, viable

workman artificer, artisan, craftsman, employee, hand, journeyman, labourer, mechanic, operative, tradesman, worker

workmanlike, workmanly adept, careful, efficient, expert, masterly, painstaking, professional, proficient, satisfactory, skilful, skilled, thorough

workmanship art, artistry, craft, craftsmanship, execution, expertise, handicraft, handiwork, manufacture, skill, technique, work

to take part in physical exercise, as in training. **7.** (*tr.*) to remove all the mineral in (a mine, etc.) that can be profitably exploited. **8.** (*intr.; often foll. by to or at*) to reach a total: *your bill works out at a pound.* ~*n.* **workout.** **9.** a session of physical exercise, esp. for training or practice.

workroom ('wɜːkˌruːm, -ˌrum) *n.* **1.** a room in which work, usually manual labour, is done. **2.** a room in a house set aside for a hobby.

works (wɜːks) *pl. n.* **1.** (*often functioning as sing.*) a place where a number of people are employed, such as a factory. **2.** the sum total of a writer's or artist's achievements, esp. when considered together: *the works of Shakespeare.* **3.** the deeds of a person, esp. virtuous or moral deeds: *works of charity.* **4.** the interior parts of the mechanism of a machine, etc.: *the works of a clock.* **5. the works.** *Sl.* **a.** full or extreme treatment. **b.** a very violent physical beating: *to give someone the works.*

workshop ('wɜːkˌʃɒp) *n.* **1.** a room or building in which manufacturing or other forms of manual work are carried on. **2.** a room in a private dwelling, school, etc., set aside for crafts. **3.** a group of people engaged in study or work on a creative project or subject: *a music workshop.*

workshy ('wɜːkˌʃaɪ) *adj.* not inclined to work.

worktable ('wɜːkˌteɪbªl) *n.* **a.** any table at which writing, sewing, or other work may be done. **b.** (in English cabinetwork) a small elegant table fitted with sewing accessories.

work-to-rule *n.* **1.** a form of industrial action in which employees adhere strictly to all the working rules laid down by their employers, with the deliberate intention of reducing the rate of working. ~*vb.* **work to rule.** **2.** (*intr.*) to decrease the rate of working by this means.

work up *vb.* (*tr., mainly adv.*) **1.** to arouse the feelings of; excite. **2.** to cause to grow or develop: *to work up a hunger.* **3.** (*also prep.*) to move or cause to move gradually upwards. **4.** to manipulate or mix into a specified object or shape. **5.** to gain skill at (a subject).

world (wɜːld) *n.* **1.** the earth as a planet, esp. including its inhabitants. **2.** mankind; the human race. **3.** people generally; the public: *in the eyes of the world.* **4.** social or public life: *to go out into the world.* **5.** the universe or cosmos; everything in existence. **6.** a complex united whole regarded as resembling the universe. **7.** any star or planet, esp. one that might be inhabited. **8.** (*often cap.*) a division or section of the earth, its history, or its inhabitants: *the Ancient World; the Third World.* **9.** an area, sphere, or realm considered as a complete environment: *the animal world.* **10.** any field of human activity or way of life or those involved in it: *the world of television.* **11.** a period or state of existence: *the next world.* **12.** the total circumstances and experience of an individual that make up his life: *you have shattered my world.* **13.** a large amount, number, or distance: *worlds apart.* **14.** worldly or secular life, ways, or people. **15. bring into the world. a.** (of a midwife, doctor, etc.) to deliver (a baby). **b.** to give birth to. **16. come into the world.** to be born. **17. dead to the world.** *Inf.* unaware of one's surroundings, esp. fast asleep or very drunk. **18. for the world.** (*used with a negative*) for any inducement, however great. **19. for all the world.** in every way; exactly. **20. in the world.** (intensifier; *usually used with a negative*): *no-one in the world can change things.* **21. the best of both worlds.** the benefits from two differ-

ent ways of life, philosophies, etc. **22. man** (*or woman*) **of the world.** a man (or woman) experienced in social or public life. **23. on top of the world.** *Inf.* elated or very happy. **24. out of this world.** *Inf.* wonderful; excellent. **25. set the world on fire.** to be exceptionally or sensationally successful. **26. think the world of.** to be extremely fond of or hold in very high esteem. **27. world of one's own.** a state of mental detachment from other people. **28. world without end.** for ever. **29.** (*modifier*) of or concerning most or all countries; worldwide: *world politics; a world record.* **30.** (*in combination*) throughout the world: *world-famous.*

World Bank *n.* an international cooperative organization established in 1945 to assist economic development, esp. of backward nations, by the advance of loans guaranteed by member governments. Officially called: **International Bank for Reconstruction and Development.**

world-beater *n.* a person or thing that surpasses all others in its category; champion.

World Cup *n.* an international association football championship competition held every four years between national teams selected through preliminary tournaments.

worldly ('wɜːldlɪ) *adj.* **-lier, -liest. 1.** not spiritual; mundane or temporal. **2.** Also: **worldly-minded.** absorbed in or concerned with material things. **3.** Also: **worldly-wise.** versed in the ways of the world; sophisticated. —'**worldliness** *n.*

world-shaking *adj.* of enormous significance; momentous.

World War I *n.* the war (1914–18), fought mainly in Europe and the Middle East, in which the Allies (principally France, Russia, Britain, Italy after 1915, and the U.S. after 1917) defeated the Central Powers (principally Germany, Austria-Hungary, and Turkey). Also called: **First World War, Great War.**

World War II *n.* the war (1939–45) in which the Allies (Britain and France) declared war on Germany (Sept. 3, 1939) as a result of the German invasion of Poland (Sept. 1, 1939). Italy entered the war on the side of Germany (forming the Axis) on June 10, 1940. On June 22, 1941 the Axis powers attacked the Soviet Union and on Dec. 7, 1941 the Japanese attacked the U.S. at Pearl Harbor. On Sept. 8, 1943 Italy surrendered, the war in Europe ending on May 7, 1945 with the unconditional surrender of the Germans. The Japanese capitulated on Aug. 14, 1945. Also called: **Second World War.**

world-weary *adj.* no longer finding pleasure in living. —'**world-ˌweariness** *n.*

worldwide ('wɜːld'waɪd) *adj.* applying or extending throughout the world; universal.

worm (wɜːm) *n.* **1.** any of various invertebrates, esp. the annelids (earthworms, etc.), nematodes (roundworms), and flatworms, having a slender elongated body. **2.** any of various insect larvae having an elongated body, such as the silkworm and wireworm. **3.** any of various unrelated animals that resemble annelids, nematodes, etc., such as the glow-worm and shipworm. **4.** a gnawing or insinuating force or agent that torments or slowly eats away. **5.** a wretched or spineless person. **6.** anything that resembles a worm in appearance or movement. **7.** a shaft on which a helical groove has been cut, as in a gear arrangement in which such a shaft meshes

---

THESAURUS

work out 1. accomplish, achieve, attain, win **2.** calculate, clear up, figure out, find out, puzzle out, resolve, solve **3.** arrange, construct, contrive, develop, devise, elaborate, evolve, form, formulate, plan, put together **4.** be effective, flourish, go as planned, go well, prosper, prove satisfactory, succeed **5.** come out, develop, evolve, go, happen, pan out (*Inf.*), result, turn out **6.** do exercises, drill, exercise, practise, train, warm up **7.** add up to, amount to, come to, reach, reach a total of

works 1. factory, mill, plant, shop, workshop **2.** canon, *oeuvre*, output, productions, writings **3.** actions, acts, deeds, doings **4.** action, guts (*Sl.*), innards (*Inf.*), insides (*Inf.*), machinery, mechanism, movement, moving parts, parts, workings

workshop 1. atelier, factory, mill, plant,

shop, studio, workroom, works **2.** class, discussion group, seminar, study group

work up agitate, animate, arouse, enkindle, excite, foment, generate, get (someone) all steamed up (*Sl.*), incite, inflame, instigate, move, rouse, spur, stir up, wind up (*Inf.*)

world 1. earth, earthly sphere, globe **2.** everybody, everyone, humanity, humankind, human race, man, mankind, men, the public, the race of man **3.** cosmos, creation, existence, life, nature, universe **4.** heavenly body, planet, star **5.** area, domain, environment, field, kingdom, province, realm, sphere, system **6.** age, days, epoch, era, period, times **7. for all the world** exactly, in every respect, in every way, just as if, just like, precisely, to all intents and purposes **8. on top of the world** *Inf.* beside oneself with joy, ecstatic, elated, exultant, happy, in raptures, on cloud

nine (*Inf.*), overjoyed, over the moon (*Inf.*) **9. out of this world** *Inf.* excellent, fabulous (*Inf.*), fantastic (*Inf.*), great (*Inf.*), incredible, indescribable, marvellous, superb, unbelievable, wonderful

worldly 1. carnal, earthly, fleshly, lay, mundane, physical, profane, secular, sublunary, temporal, terrestrial **2.** avaricious, covetous, grasping, greedy, materialistic, selfish, worldly-minded **3.** blasé, cosmopolitan, experienced, knowing, politic, sophisticated, urbane, well versed in the ways of the world, worldly-wise

worldwide general, global, international, omnipresent, pandemic, ubiquitous, universal

with a toothed wheel. **8.** a spiral pipe cooled by air or flowing water, used as a condenser in a still. ~*vb.* **9.** to move, act, or cause to move or act with the slow sinuous movement of a worm. **10.** (foll. by *in, into, out of*, etc.) to make (one's way) slowly and stealthily; insinuate (oneself). **11.** (*tr.; often foll. by out of or from*) to extract (information, a secret, etc.) from by persistent questioning. **12.** (*tr.*) to free from or purge of worms. —'**wormer** *n*. —'**worm,like** *adj.*

wormcast ('wɜːm,kɑːst) *n.* a coil of earth or sand that has been excreted by a burrowing earthworm or lugworm.

worm-eaten *adj.* **1.** eaten into by worms: *a worm-eaten table.* **2.** decayed; rotten. **3.** old-fashioned; antiquated.

worm gear *n.* **1.** a device consisting of a threaded shaft (**worm**) that mates with a gear wheel (**worm wheel**) so that rotary motion can be transferred between two shafts at right angles to each other. **2.** Also called: **worm wheel.** a gear wheel driven by a threaded shaft or worm.

wormhole ('wɜːm,həʊl) *n.* a hole made by a worm in timber, plants, etc. —'**worm,holed** *adj.*

worms (wɜːmz) *n.* any disease or disorder, usually of the intestine, characterized by infestation with parasitic worms.

wormwood ('wɜːm,wʊd) *n.* **1.** Also called: **absinthe.** any of various plants of a chiefly N temperate genus, esp. a European plant yielding a bitter extract used in making absinthe. **2.** something that embitters, such as a painful experience.

wormy ('wɜːmɪ) *adj.* **wormier, wormiest. 1.** worm-infested or worm-eaten. **2.** resembling a worm in appearance, ways, or condition. **3.** (of wood) having irregular small tunnels bored into it and tracked over its surface, made by worms. **4.** low or grovelling. —'**worminess** *n*.

worn (wɔːn) *vb.* **1.** the past participle of **wear.** ~*adj.* **2.** affected, esp. adversely, by long use or action: *a worn suit.* **3.** haggard; drawn. **4.** exhausted; spent. —'**worn-ness** *n*.

worn-out *adj.* (**worn out** when postpositive). **1.** worn or used until threadbare, valueless, or useless. **2.** exhausted; very weary.

worrisome ('wʌrɪsəm) *adj.* **1.** causing worry; vexing. **2.** tending to worry. —'**worrisomely** *adv.*

worry ('wʌrɪ) *vb.* **-rying, -ried. 1.** to be or cause to be anxious or uneasy, esp. about something uncertain or potentially dangerous. **2.** (*tr.*) to disturb the peace of mind of; bother: *don't worry me with trivialities.* **3.** (*intr.; often foll. by along or through*) to proceed despite difficulties. **4.** (*intr.; often foll. by away*) to struggle or work: *to worry away at a problem.* **5.** (*tr.*) (of a dog, wolf, etc.) to lacerate or kill by biting, shaking, etc. **6.** (when *intr.,* foll. by *at*) to bite, tear, or gnaw (at) with the teeth: *a dog worrying a bone.* **7.** (*tr.*) to touch or poke repeatedly and idly. **8. not to worry.** *Inf.* you need not worry. ~*n., pl.* **-ries. 9.** a state or feeling of anxiety. **10.** a person or thing that causes anxiety. **11.** an act of worrying.

worry beads *pl. n.* a string of beads that when fingered or played with supposedly relieves nervous tension.

worse (wɜːs) *adj.* **1.** the comparative of **bad. 2. none the worse for.** not harmed by (adverse events or circumstances). **3. the worse for wear. a.** shabby or worn. **b.** a slang term for **drunk. 4. worse luck!** *Inf.* unhappily; un-

fortunately. **5.** (*postpositive*) **worse off.** in a worse, esp. a worse financial, condition. ~*n.* **6.** something that is worse. **7. for the worse.** into a less desirable or inferior state or condition: *a change for the worse.* **8. go from bad to worse.** to deteriorate even more. ~*adv.* **9.** in a more severe or unpleasant manner. **10.** in a less effective or successful manner.

worsen ('wɜːsən) *vb.* to grow or cause to grow worse.

worship ('wɜːʃɪp) *vb.* **-shipping, -shipped** or *U.S.* **-shiping, -shiped. 1.** (*tr.*) to show profound religious devotion and respect to; adore or venerate (God or any person or thing considered divine). **2.** (*tr.*) to be devoted to and full of admiration for. **3.** (*intr.*) to have or express feelings of profound adoration. **4.** (*intr.*) to attend services for worship. ~*n.* **5.** religious adoration or devotion. **6.** the formal expression of religious adoration; rites, prayers, etc. **7.** admiring love or devotion. —'**worshipper** *n*.

Worship ('wɜːʃɪp) *n. Chiefly Brit.* (preceded by *Your, His,* or *Her*) a title used to address or refer to a mayor or magistrate.

worshipful ('wɜːʃɪpfʊl) *adj.* **1.** feeling or showing reverence or adoration. **2.** (*often cap.*) *Chiefly Brit.* a title used to address or refer to various people or bodies of distinguished rank. —'**worshipfully** *adv.* —'**worshipfulness** *n*.

worst (wɜːst) *adj.* **1.** the superlative of **bad.** ~*adv.* **2.** in the most extreme or bad manner or degree. **3.** least well, suitably, or acceptably. **4.** (*in combination*) in or to the smallest degree or extent; least: *worst-loved.* ~*n.* **5. the worst.** the least good or most inferior person, thing, or part in a group, narrative, etc. **6.** (often preceded by *at*) the most poor, unpleasant, or unskilled quality or condition: *television is at its worst these days.* **7.** the greatest amount of damage or wickedness of which a person or group is capable: *the invaders came and did their worst.* **8.** the weakest effort or poorest achievement that a person or group is capable of making: *the applicant did his worst at the test because he did not want the job.* **9. at worst. a.** in the least favourable interpretation or view. **b.** under the least favourable conditions. **10. if the worst comes to the worst.** if all the more desirable alternatives become impossible or if the worst possible thing happens. **11. come off worst** or **get the worst of it.** to enjoy the least benefit from an issue or be defeated in it. ~*vb.* **12.** (*tr.*) to get the advantage over; defeat or beat.

worsted ('wʊstɪd) *n.* **1.** a closely twisted yarn or thread made from combed long-staple wool. **2.** a fabric made from this, with a hard smooth close-textured surface and no nap. **3.** (*modifier*) made of this yarn or fabric: *a worsted suit.*

wort (wɜːt) *n.* **1.** (*in combination*) any of various unrelated plants, esp. ones formerly used to cure diseases: *liverwort.* **2.** the sweet liquid from the soaked mixture of warm water and ground malt, used to make a malt liquor.

worth (wɜːθ) *adj.* (governing a noun with prepositional force) **1.** worthy of; meriting or justifying: *it's not worth discussing.* **2.** having a value of: *the book is worth £30.* **3. for all one is worth.** to the utmost. **4. worth one's weight in gold.** extremely helpful, kind, etc. ~*n.* **5.** high quality; excellence. **6.** value; price. **7.** the amount of something of a specified value: *five pounds' worth of petrol.*

THESAURUS

worn 1. frayed, ragged, shabby, shiny, tattered, tatty, the worse for wear, threadbare **2.** careworn, drawn, haggard, lined, pinched, wizened **3.** exhausted, fatigued, jaded, played-out (*Inf.*), spent, tired, tired out, wearied, weary, worn-out

worn-out 1. broken-down, clapped-out (*Brit. inf.*), decrepit, done, frayed, on its last legs, ragged, run-down, shabby, tattered, tatty, threadbare, used, used-up, useless, worn **2.** all in (*Sl.*), dead *or* out on one's feet (*Inf.*), dog-tired (*Inf.*), done in (*Inf.*), exhausted, fatigued, fit to drop, jiggered (*Dialect*), knackered (*Brit. sl.*), played-out, prostrate, spent, tired, tired out, weary

worried afraid, anxious, apprehensive, bothered, concerned, distracted, distraught, distressed, disturbed, fearful, fretful, fright-

ened, ill at ease, nervous, on edge, overwrought, perturbed, tense, tormented, troubled, uneasy, unquiet, upset

worry *v.* **1.** agonize, annoy, badger, be anxious, bother, brood, disquiet, distress, disturb, feel uneasy, fret, harass, harry, hassle (*Inf.*), hector, importune, irritate, make anxious, perturb, pester, plague, tantalize, tease, torment, trouble, unsettle, upset, vex **2.** attack, bite, gnaw at, go for, harass, harry, kill, lacerate, savage, tear ~*n.* **3.** annoyance, care, irritation, pest, plague, problem, torment, trial, trouble, vexation **4.** annoyance, anxiety, apprehension, care, concern, disturbance, fear, irritation, misery, misgiving, perplexity, torment, trouble, unease, vexation, woe

worsen aggravate, damage, decay, decline, degenerate, deteriorate, exacerbate,

get worse, go downhill (*Inf.*), go from bad to worse, retrogress, sink, take a turn for the worse

worship 1. *v.* adore, adulate, deify, exalt, glorify, honour, idolize, laud, love, praise, pray to, put on a pedestal, respect, revere, reverence, venerate **2.** *n.* adoration, adulation, deification, devotion, exaltation, glorification, glory, homage, honour, laudation, love, praise, prayer(s), regard, respect, reverence

worst *v.* beat, best, conquer, crush, defeat, gain the advantage over, get the better of, master, overcome, overpower, overthrow, subdue, subjugate, vanquish

worth 1. aid, assistance, avail, benefit, credit, desert(s), estimation, excellence, goodness, help, importance, merit, quality,

worthless ('wɜːθlɪs) *adj.* **1.** without value or usefulness. **2.** without merit; good-for-nothing. —'**worthlessly** *adv.* —'**worthlessness** *n.*

worthwhile ('wɜːθ'waɪl) *adj.* sufficiently important, rewarding, or valuable to justify time or effort spent.

worthy ('wɜːðɪ) *adj.* **-thier, -thiest. 1.** (*postpositive;* often foll. by *of* or an infinitive) having sufficient merit or value (for something or someone specified); deserving. **2.** having worth, value, or merit. ~*n., pl.* **-thies. 3.** *Often facetious.* a person of merit or importance. —'**worthily** *adv.* —'**worthiness** *n.*

would (wʊd; *unstressed* wəd) *vb.* (takes an infinitive without *to* or an implied infinitive) used as an auxiliary: **1.** to form the past tense or subjunctive mood of **will**[1]. **2.** (with *you, he, she, it, they*, or a noun as subject) to indicate willingness or desire in a polite manner: *would you help me, please?* **3.** to describe a past action as being accustomed or habitual: *every day we would go for walks.* **4.** I wish: *would that he were here.*
▷ *Usage.* See at **should.**

would-be *adj.* (*prenominal*) **1.** *Usually derog.* wanting or professing to be: *a would-be politician.* **2.** intended to be: *would-be generosity.*

wound[1] (wuːnd) *n.* **1.** any break in the skin or an organ or part as the result of violence or a surgical incision. **2.** any injury or slight to the feelings or reputation. ~*vb.* **3.** to inflict a wound or wounds upon (someone or something). —'**woundingly** *adv.*

wound[2] (waʊnd) *vb.* the past tense or past participle of **wind**[2].

wove (wəʊv) *vb.* a past tense of **weave.**

woven ('wəʊvən) *vb.* a past participle of **weave.**

wow (waʊ) *interj.* **1.** an exclamation of admiration, amazement, etc. ~*n.* **2.** *Sl., chiefly U.S.* a person or thing that is amazingly successful, attractive, etc. ~*vb.* **3.** (*tr.*) *Sl., chiefly U.S.* to arouse great enthusiasm in.

w.p.m. *abbrev.* for words per minute.

W.R.A.C. (in Britain) *abbrev.* for Women's Royal Army Corps.

wrack[1] or **rack** (ræk) *n.* **1.** collapse or destruction (esp. in **wrack and ruin**). **2.** something destroyed or a remnant of such.

wrack[2] (ræk) *n.* **1.** seaweed or other marine vegetation that is floating in the sea or has been cast ashore. **2.** any of various seaweeds, such as serrated wrack.

W.R.A.F. (in Britain) *abbrev.* for Women's Royal Air Force.

wraith (reɪθ) *n.* **1.** the apparition of a person living or thought to be alive, supposed to appear around the time of his death. **2.** a ghost or any apparition. —'**wraith-,like** *adj.*

wrangle ('ræŋgəl) *vb.* **1.** (*intr.*) to argue, esp. noisily or angrily. **2.** (*tr.*) to encourage, persuade, or obtain by argument. **3.** (*tr.*) *Western U.S. & Canad.* to herd (cattle or horses). ~*n.* **4.** a noisy or angry argument.

wrap (ræp) *vb.* **wrapping, wrapped.** (*mainly tr.*) **1.** to fold or wind (paper, cloth, etc.) around (a person or thing) so as to cover. **2.** (often foll. by *up*) to fold paper, etc., around to fasten securely. **3.** to surround or conceal by surrounding. **4.** to enclose, immerse, or absorb: *wrapped in sorrow.* **5.** to fold, wind, or roll up. **6.** (*intr.;* often foll. by *about, around,* etc.) to be or become wound or extended. **7.** (often foll. by *up*) Also: **rap.** *Austral. inf.* to praise (someone). ~*n.* **8.** a garment worn wrapped around the body, esp. the shoulders, such as a shawl or cloak. **9.** *Chiefly U.S.* wrapping or a wrapper. **10.** Also called: **rap.** *Austral. inf.* a commendation. **11. keep under wraps.** to keep secret. **12. take the wraps off.** to reveal.

wrapper ('ræpə) *n.* **1.** the cover, usually of paper or cellophane, in which something is wrapped. **2.** the ripe firm tobacco leaf forming the outermost portion of a cigar. **3.** a dust jacket of a book. **4.** a loose negligee or dressing gown.

wrapping ('ræpɪŋ) *n.* the material used to wrap something.

wrapround ('ræp,raʊnd) *adj.* **1.** made so as to be wrapped round something: *a wrapround skirt.* **2.** surrounding, curving round, or overlapping. ~*n.* **3.** *Printing.* a flexible plate of plastic, metal, or rubber that is made flat but used wrapped round the plate cylinder of a rotary press.

wrap up *vb.* (*adv.*) **1.** (*tr.*) to fold paper around. **2.** to put warm clothes on. **3.** (*usually imperative*) *Sl.* to be silent. **4.** (*tr.*) *Inf.* **a.** to settle the final details of. **b.** to make a summary of.

wrasse (ræs) *n.* a marine fish of tropical and temperate seas, having thick lips, strong teeth, and usually a bright coloration: many are used as food fishes.

wrath (rɒθ) *n.* **1.** angry, violent, or stern indignation. **2.** divine vengeance or retribution. **3.** *Arch.* a fit of anger or an act resulting from anger. —'**wrathful** *adj.*

wreak (riːk) *vb.* (*tr.*) **1.** to inflict (vengeance, etc.) or to cause (chaos, etc.): *to wreak havoc on the enemy.* **2.** to express, or gratify (anger, hatred, etc.). **3.** *Arch.* to take vengeance for. —'**wreaker** *n.*

wreath (riːθ) *n., pl.* **wreaths** (riːðz, riːθs). **1.** a band of flowers or foliage intertwined into a ring, usually placed on a grave as a memorial or worn on the head as a garland or a mark of honour. **2.** any circular or spiral band or formation. **3.** loosely, any floral design placed on a grave as a memorial. —'**wreath,like** *adj.*

wreathe (riːð) *vb.* **1.** to form into or take the form of a wreath by intertwining or twisting together. **2.** (*tr.*) to decorate, crown, or encircle with wreaths. **3.** to move or cause to move in a twisting way: *smoke wreathed up to the ceiling.*

wreck (rɛk) *vb.* **1.** to involve in or suffer disaster or destruction. **2.** (*tr.*) to cause the wreck of (a ship). ~*n.* **3. a.** the accidental destruction of a ship at sea. **b.** the ship so destroyed. **4.** *Maritime law.* goods cast ashore from a wrecked vessel. **5.** a person or thing that has suffered ruin or dilapidation. **6.** Also called: **wreckage** ('rɛkɪdʒ). the remains of something that has been destroyed. **7.** Also called: **wreckage.** the act of wrecking or the state of being wrecked.

THESAURUS

usefulness, utility, value, virtue, worthiness **2.** cost, price, rate, valuation, value

worthless 1. futile, ineffectual, insignificant, inutile, meaningless, miserable, no use, nugatory, paltry, pointless, poor, rubbishy, trashy, trifling, trivial, unavailing, unimportant, unusable, useless, valueless, wretched **2.** abandoned, abject, base, contemptible, depraved, despicable, good-for-nothing, ignoble, useless, vile

worthwhile beneficial, constructive, gainful, good, helpful, justifiable, productive, profitable, useful, valuable, worthy

worthy 1. *adj.* admirable, commendable, creditable, decent, dependable, deserving, estimable, excellent, good, honest, honourable, laudable, meritorious, praiseworthy, reliable, reputable, respectable, righteous, upright, valuable, virtuous, worthwhile **2.** *n.* big shot (*Sl.*), bigwig (*Sl.*), dignitary, luminary, notable, personage

wound *n.* **1.** cut, damage, gash, harm, hurt, injury, laceration, lesion, slash **2.** anguish, distress, grief, heartbreak, injury, insult, of-

fence, pain, pang, sense of loss, shock, slight, torment, torture, trauma ~*v.* **3.** cut, damage, gash, harm, hit, hurt, injure, irritate, lacerate, pierce, slash, wing **4.** annoy, cut (someone) to the quick, distress, grieve, hurt, hurt the feelings of, mortify, offend, pain, shock, sting, traumatize

wrangle 1. *v.* altercate, argue, bicker, brawl, contend, disagree, dispute, fall out (*Inf.*), fight, have words, quarrel, row, scrap, squabble **2.** *n.* altercation, angry exchange, argy-bargy (*Brit. inf.*), barney (*Inf.*), bickering, brawl, clash, contest, controversy, dispute, falling-out (*Inf.*), quarrel, row, set-to (*Inf.*), slanging match (*Brit.*), squabble, tiff

wrap 1. *v.* absorb, bind, bundle up, cloak, cover, encase, enclose, enfold, envelop, fold, immerse, muffle, pack, package, roll up, sheathe, shroud, surround, swathe, wind **2.** *n.* cape, cloak, mantle, shawl, stole

wrapper case, cover, envelope, jacket, packaging, paper, sheath, sleeve, wrapping

wrap up 1. bundle up, enclose, enwrap, giftwrap, pack, package **2.** dress warmly,

muffle up, put warm clothes on, wear something warm **3.** *Sl.* be quiet, be silent, hold one's tongue, put a sock in it (*Brit. sl.*), shut one's face (*Brit. sl.*), shut one's mouth (*Sl.*), shut one's trap (*Sl.*), shut up **4.** *Inf.* bring to a close, conclude, end, finish off, polish off, round off, terminate, tidy up, wind up

wrath anger, choler, displeasure, exasperation, fury, indignation, ire, irritation, passion, rage, resentment, temper

wrathful angry, beside oneself with rage, displeased, enraged, furious, incensed, indignant, infuriated, irate, on the warpath (*Inf.*), raging, wroth (*Archaic*)

wreath band, chaplet, coronet, crown, festoon, garland, loop, ring

wreathe adorn, coil, crown, encircle, enfold, entwine, envelop, enwrap, festoon, intertwine, interweave, surround, twine, twist, wind, wrap, writhe

wreck *v.* **1.** break, dash to pieces, demolish, destroy, devastate, mar, play havoc with, ravage, ruin, shatter, smash, spoil **2.** founder, go *or* run aground, run onto the rocks, ship-

wrecker ('rɛkə) n. **1.** a person or thing that ruins or destroys. **2.** *Chiefly U.S.* a person whose job is to demolish buildings or dismantle cars. **3.** (formerly) a person who lures ships to destruction to plunder the wreckage. —'**wrecking** n., adj.

wren (rɛn) n. **1.** any small brown passerine songbird of a chiefly American family (in Britain **wren,** in the U.S. **winter wren**). They have a slender bill and feed on insects. **2.** any of various similar birds, such as the Australian warblers, New Zealand wrens, etc.

Wren (rɛn) n. *Inf.* (in Britain and certain other nations) a member of the Women's Royal Naval Service.

wrench (rɛntʃ) vb. **1.** to give (something) a sudden or violent twist or pull, esp. so as to remove (something) from that to which it is attached: *to wrench a door off its hinges.* **2.** (tr.) to twist suddenly so as to sprain (a limb): *to wrench one's ankle.* **3.** (tr.) to give pain to. **4.** (tr.) to twist from the original meaning or purpose. **5.** (intr.) to make a sudden twisting motion. ~n. **6.** a forceful twist or pull. **7.** an injury to a limb, caused by twisting. **8.** sudden pain caused esp. by parting. **9.** a parting that is difficult or painful to make. **10.** a distorting of the original meaning or purpose. **11.** a spanner, esp. one with adjustable jaws.

wrest (rɛst) vb. (tr.) **1.** to take or force away by violent pulling or twisting. **2.** to seize forcibly by violent or unlawful means. **3.** to obtain by laborious effort. **4.** to distort in meaning, purpose, etc. ~n. **5.** the act or an instance of wresting. **6.** *Arch.* a small key used to tune a piano or harp. —'**wrester** n.

wrestle ('rɛsəl) vb. **1.** to fight (another person) by holding, throwing, etc., without punching with the closed fist. **2.** (intr.) to participate in wrestling. **3.** (when intr., foll. by *with* or *against*) to fight with (a person, problem, or thing): *wrestle with one's conscience.* **4.** (tr.) to move laboriously, as with wrestling movements. ~n. **5.** the act of wrestling. **6.** a struggle or tussle. —'**wrestler** n.

wrestling ('rɛslɪŋ) n. any of certain sports in which the contestants fight each other according to various rules governing holds and usually forbidding blows with the closed fist. The principal object is to overcome the opponent either by throwing or pinning him to the ground or by causing him to submit.

wretch (rɛtʃ) n. **1.** a despicable person. **2.** a person pitied for his misfortune.

wretched ('rɛtʃɪd) adj. **1.** in poor or pitiful circumstances. **2.** characterized by or causing misery. **3.** despicable; base. **4.** poor, inferior, or paltry. **5.** (prenominal) (intensifier qualifying something undesirable): *a wretched nuisance.* —'**wretchedly** adv. —'**wretchedness** n.

wrick (rɪk) n. **1.** a sprain or strain. ~vb. **2.** (tr.) to sprain or strain.

wriggle ('rɪgəl) vb. **1.** to make or cause to make twisting movements. **2.** (intr.) to progress by twisting and turning. **3.** (tr.; foll. by *into* or *out of*) to manoeuvre oneself by clever or devious means: *wriggle out of an embarrassing situation.* ~n. **4.** a wriggling movement or action. **5.** a sinuous marking or course. —'**wriggler** n. —'**wriggly** adj.

wright (raɪt) n. (now chiefly in combination) a person who creates, builds, or repairs something specified: *a playwright; a shipwright.*

wring (rɪŋ) vb. **wringing, wrung. 1.** (often foll. by *out*) to twist and compress to squeeze (a liquid) from (cloth, etc.). **2.** (tr.) to twist forcibly: *wring its neck.* **3.** (tr.) to clasp and twist (one's hands), esp. in anguish. **4.** (tr.) to distress: *wring one's heart.* **5.** (tr.) to grip (someone's hand) vigorously in greeting. **6.** (tr.) to obtain as by forceful means: *wring information out of.* **7. wringing wet.** soaking; drenched. ~n. **8.** an act or the process of wringing.

wringer ('rɪŋə) n. a machine for drying clothes, textiles, etc., often consisting of two rollers between which the cloth is squeezed. Also called (Brit.): **mangle.**

wrinkle[1] ('rɪŋkəl) n. **1.** a slight ridge in the smoothness of a surface, such as a crease in the skin as a result of age. ~vb. **2.** to make or become wrinkled, as by crumpling, creasing, or puckering. —'**wrinkly** adj.

wrinkle[2] ('rɪŋkəl) n. *Inf.* a clever or novel trick, hint, or device.

wrist (rɪst) n. **1.** *Anat.* the joint between the forearm and the hand. Technical name: **carpus. 2.** the part of a sleeve or glove that covers the wrist.

wristwatch ('rɪst,wɒtʃ) n. a watch worn strapped around the wrist.

writ (rɪt) n. **1.** a document under seal, issued in the name of the Crown or a court, commanding the person to whom it is addressed to do or refrain from doing some specified act. **2.** *Arch.* a piece or body of writing: *Holy Writ.*

write (raɪt) vb. **writing, wrote, written. 1.** to draw or mark (symbols, words, etc.) on a surface, usually paper, with a pen, pencil, or other instrument. **2.** to describe or record (ideas, experiences, etc.) in writing. **3.** to compose (a letter) to or correspond regularly with (a person, organization, etc.). **4.** (tr.; may take a clause as object) to say or communicate by letter: *he wrote that he was on his way.* **5.** (tr.) *Inf., chiefly U.S.* to send a letter to (a person, etc.). **6.** to write (words) in cursive as opposed to printed style. **7.** (tr.) to be sufficiently familiar with (a specified style, language, etc.) to use it in writing. **8.** to be the author or composer of (books, music, etc.). **9.** (tr.) to fill in the details for (a document, form, etc.). **10.** (tr.) to draw up or draft. **11.** (tr.) to produce by writing: *he wrote ten pages.* **12.** (tr.) to show clearly: *envy was written all over his face.* **13.** (tr.) to spell, inscribe, or entitle. **14.** (tr.) to ordain or prophesy: *it is written.* **15.** (intr.) to produce writing as specified. **16.** *Computers.* to record (data) in a location in a storage device, such as a drum. **17.** (tr.) See **underwrite** (sense 3a). ~See also **write down, write in,** etc. —'**writable** adj.

▷ **Usage.** Careful writers and speakers avoid the omission of *to* after the verb *write* in clauses without a direct object: *I'll write to you* (not *I'll write you*). This omission of *to* is very common in informal English in the U.S., but is nevertheless not accepted as good formal usage.

write down vb. (adv.) **1.** (tr.) to set down in writing. **2.** (tr.) to harm or belittle by writing about (a person) in derogatory terms. **3.** (intr.; foll. by *to* or *for*) to write in a simplified way (to a supposedly less cultured readership). **4.** (tr.) *Accounting.* to decrease the book value of (an asset). ~n. **write-down. 5.** *Accounting.* a reduction made in the book value of an asset.

write in vb. **1.** (tr.) to insert in (a document, form, etc.) in writing. **2.** (tr., adv.) to write a letter to a compa-

---

THESAURUS

wreck, strand ~n. **3.** derelict, hulk, shipwreck, sunken vessel **4.** desolation, destruction, devastation, disruption, mess, overthrow, ruin, undoing

wreckage debris, fragments, hulk, pieces, remains, rubble, ruin, wrack

wrench v. **1.** force, jerk, pull, rip, tear, tug, twist, wrest, wring, yank **2.** distort, rick, sprain, strain ~n. **3.** jerk, pull, rip, tug, twist, yank **4.** sprain, strain, twist **5.** ache, blow, pain, pang, shock, upheaval, uprooting **6.** adjustable spanner, shifting spanner, spanner

wrestle battle, combat, contend, fight, grapple, scuffle, strive, struggle, tussle

wretch 1. blackguard, cur, good-for-nothing, miscreant, outcast, profligate, rascal, rat (Inf.), rogue, rotter (Sl.), ruffian, scoundrel, swine, vagabond, villain, worm **2.** poor thing, unfortunate

wretched 1. abject, brokenhearted,

cheerless, comfortless, crestfallen, dejected, deplorable, depressed, disconsolate, distressed, doleful, downcast, forlorn, gloomy, hapless, hopeless, melancholy, miserable, pathetic, pitiable, pitiful, poor, sorry, unfortunate, unhappy, woebegone, woeful, worthless **2.** calamitous, deplorable, inferior, miserable, paltry, pathetic, poor, sorry, worthless **3.** base, contemptible, despicable, low, lowdown (Inf.), mean, paltry, scurvy, shabby, shameful, vile

wriggle v. **1.** jerk, jiggle, squirm, turn, twist, wag, waggle, wiggle, writhe **2.** crawl, slink, snake, twist and turn, worm, zigzag **3.** crawl, dodge, extricate oneself, manoeuvre, sneak, talk one's way out, worm ~n. **4.** jerk, jiggle, squirm, turn, twist, wag, waggle, wiggle

wring 1. coerce, extort, extract, force, screw, squeeze, twist, wrench, wrest **2.** dis-

tress, hurt, lacerate, pain, pierce, rack, rend, stab, tear at, wound

wrinkle[1] **1.** n. corrugation, crease, crinkle, crow's-foot, crumple, fold, furrow, gather, line, pucker, rumple **2.** v. corrugate, crease, crinkle, crumple, fold, furrow, gather, line, pucker, ruck, rumple

wrinkle[2] device, dodge, gimmick, idea, plan, ploy, ruse, scheme, stunt, tip, trick, wheeze (Brit. sl.)

writ court order, decree, document, summons

write author (Nonstandard), commit to paper, compose, copy, correspond, create, draft, draw up, indite, inscribe, jot down, pen, put down in black and white, put in writing, record, scribble, set down, take down, tell, transcribe

ny, institution, etc. **3.** (*tr., adv.*) *U.S.* to vote for (a person not on a ballot) by inserting name.

write off *vb.* (*tr., adv.*) **1.** *Accounting.* **a.** to cancel (a bad debt or obsolete asset) from the accounts. **b.** to consider (a transaction, etc.) as a loss or set off (a loss) against revenues. **c.** to depreciate (an asset) by periodic charges. **d.** to charge (a specified amount) against gross profits as depreciation of an asset. **2.** to cause or acknowledge the complete loss of. **3.** to dismiss from consideration. ~*n.* **write-off.** **4.** *Accounting.* **a.** the act of cancelling a bad debt or obsolete asset from the accounts. **b.** the bad debt or obsolete asset cancelled. **c.** the amount cancelled against gross profits, corresponding to the book value of the bad debt or obsolete asset. **5.** *Inf.* something damaged beyond repair, esp. a car.

write out *vb.* (*tr., adv.*) **1.** to put into writing or reproduce in full form in writing. **2.** to exhaust (oneself or one's creativity) by excessive writing. **3.** to remove (a character) from a television or radio series.

writer ('raɪtə) *n.* **1.** a person who writes books, articles, etc., esp. as an occupation. **2.** the person who has written something specified. **3.** a person who is able to write or write well. **4.** a scribe or clerk. **5.** a composer of music. **6. Writer to the Signet.** (in Scotland) a member of an ancient society of solicitors, now having the exclusive privilege of preparing crown writs.

write up *vb.* (*tr., adv.*) **1.** to describe fully, complete, or bring up to date in writing: *write up a diary.* **2.** to praise or bring to public notice in writing. **3.** *Accounting.* **a.** to place an excessively high value on (an asset). **b.** to increase the book value of (an asset) in order to reflect more accurately its current worth in the market. ~*n.* **write-up.** **4.** a published account of something, such as a review in a newspaper or magazine.

writhe (raɪð) *vb.* **1.** to twist or squirm in or as if in pain. **2.** (*intr.*) to move with such motions. **3.** (*intr.*) to suffer acutely from embarrassment, revulsion, etc. ~*n.* **4.** the act or an instance of writhing. —'**writher** *n.*

writing ('raɪtɪŋ) *n.* **1.** a group of letters or symbols written or marked on a surface as a means of communicating. **2.** short for **handwriting. 3.** anything expressed in letters, esp. a literary composition. **4.** the work of a writer. **5.** literary style, art, or practice. **6.** written form: *give it to me in writing.* **7.** (*modifier*) related to or used in writing: *writing ink.* **8. writing on the wall.** a sign or signs of approaching disaster.

writing desk *n.* a piece of furniture with a writing surface and drawers and compartments for papers, etc.

writing paper *n.* paper sized to take writing ink and used for letters and other manuscripts.

written ('rɪtən) *vb.* **1.** the past participle of **write.** ~*adj.* **2.** taken down in writing; transcribed: *written evidence; the written word.*

W.R.N.S. *abbrev. for* Women's Royal Naval Service. See also **Wren.**

wrong (rɒŋ) *adj.* **1.** not correct or truthful: *the wrong answer.* **2.** acting or judging in error: *you are wrong to think that.* **3.** (*postpositive*) immoral; bad: *it is wrong to cheat.* **4.** deviating from or unacceptable to correct or conventional laws, usage, etc. **5.** not intended or wanted: *the wrong road.* **6.** (*postpositive*) not working prop-

erly; amiss: *something is wrong with the engine.* **7.** (of a side, esp. of a fabric) intended to face the inside so as not to be seen. **8. get on the wrong side of.** *Inf.* to come into disfavour with. **9. go down the wrong way.** (of food) to pass into the windpipe instead of the gullet. ~*adv.* **10.** in the wrong direction or manner. **11. go wrong. a.** to turn out other than intended. **b.** to make a mistake. **c.** (of a machine, etc.) to cease to function properly. **d.** to go astray morally. **12. get wrong. a.** to fail to understand properly. **b.** to fail to provide the correct answer to. ~*n.* **13.** a bad, immoral, or unjust thing or action. **14.** *Law.* **a.** an infringement of another person's rights, rendering the offender liable to a civil action: *a private wrong.* **b.** a violation of public rights and duties, affecting the community as a whole and actionable at the instance of the Crown: *a public wrong.* **15. in the wrong.** mistaken or guilty. ~*vb.* (*tr.*) **16.** to treat unjustly. **17.** to discredit, malign, or misrepresent. —'**wronger** *n.* —'**wrongly** *adv.* —'**wrongness** *n.*

wrongdoer ('rɒŋ,duːə) *n.* a person who acts immorally or illegally. —'**wrong,doing** *n.*

wrongful ('rɒŋfʊl) *adj.* unjust or illegal. —'**wrongfully** *adv.* —'**wrongfulness** *n.*

wrong-headed *adj.* **1.** constantly wrong in judgment. **2.** foolishly stubborn. —,**wrong-'headedly** *adv.* —,**wrong-'headedness** *n.*

wrote (rəʊt) *vb.* the past tense of **write.**

wroth (rəʊθ, rɒθ) *adj. Arch. or literary.* angry; irate.

wrought (rɔːt) *vb.* **1.** *Arch.* a past tense or past participle of **work.** ~*adj.* **2.** *Metallurgy.* shaped by hammering or beating. **3.** (*often in combination*) formed, fashioned, or worked as specified: *well-wrought.* **4.** decorated or made with delicate care.

wrought iron *n.* **a.** a pure form of iron having a low carbon content and often used for decorative work. **b.** (*as modifier*): *wrought-iron gates.*

wrought-up *or* **worked-up** *adj.* excited or agitated.

wrung (rʌŋ) *vb.* the past tense or past participle of **wring.**

W.R.V.S. *abbrev. for* Women's Royal Voluntary Service.

wry (raɪ) *adj.* **wrier, wriest** *or* **wryer, wryest. 1.** twisted, contorted, or askew. **2.** (of a facial expression) produced or characterized by contorting of the features. **3.** dryly humorous; sardonic. **4.** warped, misdirected, or perverse. ~*vb.* **wrying, wried. 5.** (*tr.*) to twist or contort. —'**wryly** *adv.* —'**wryness** *n.*

wryneck ('raɪ,nɛk) *n.* **1.** either of two cryptically coloured Old World woodpeckers, which do not drum on trees. **2.** *Pathol.* an abnormal position of the head, usually with the neck twisted to one side. **3.** *Inf.* a person who has a twisted neck.

WSW *abbrev. for* west-southwest.

wt. *abbrev. for* weight.

wych-elm *or* **witch-elm** ('wɪtʃ,ɛlm) *n.* **1.** a Eurasian elm tree, having a rounded shape, longish pointed leaves, clusters of small flowers, and winged fruits. **2.** the wood of this tree.

wynd (waɪnd) *n. Scot.* a narrow lane or alley.

THESAURUS

write off 1. cancel, cross out, disregard, forget about, give up for lost, score out, shelve **2.** *Inf.* crash, damage beyond repair, destroy, smash up, total (*U.S. sl.*), wreck

writer author, columnist, essayist, hack, littérateur, man of letters, novelist, penman, penny-a-liner (*Rare*), penpusher, scribbler, scribe, wordsmith

writhe contort, distort, jerk, squirm, struggle, thrash, thresh, toss, twist, wiggle, wriggle

writing 1. calligraphy, chirography, hand, handwriting, penmanship, print, scrawl, scribble, script **2.** book, composition, document, letter, opus, publication, work **3.** belles-lettres, letters, literature

wrong *adj.* **1.** erroneous, fallacious, false, faulty, inaccurate, incorrect, in error, mistaken, off beam (*Inf.*), off target, out, unsound, untrue, wide of the mark **2.** bad, blameworthy, criminal, crooked, dishonest, dishonourable, evil, felonious, illegal, illicit,

immoral, iniquitous, reprehensible, sinful, unethical, unfair, unjust, unlawful, wicked, wrongful **3.** funny, improper, inappropriate, inapt, incongruous, incorrect, indecorous, infelicitous, malapropos, not done, unacceptable, unbecoming, unconventional, undesirable, unfitting, unhappy, unseemly, unsuitable **4.** amiss, askew, awry, defective, faulty, not working, out of commission, out of order **5.** inside, inverse, opposite, reverse ~*adv.* **6.** amiss, askew, astray, awry, badly, erroneously, inaccurately, incorrectly, mistakenly, wrongly **7. go wrong a.** come to grief (*Inf.*), come to nothing, fail, fall through, flop (*Inf.*), miscarry, misfire **b.** boob (*Brit. sl.*), err, go astray, make a mistake, slip up (*Inf.*) **c.** break down, cease to function, conk out (*Inf.*), fail, go kaput (*Inf.*), go on the blink (*Sl.*), go phut (*Inf.*), malfunction, misfire **d.** err, fall from grace, go astray, go off the straight and narrow (*Inf.*), go to the bad, lapse, sin ~*n.* **8.** abuse, bad *or* evil deed,

crime, error, grievance, immorality, inequity, infraction, infringement, iniquity, injury, injustice, misdeed, offence, sin, sinfulness, transgression, trespass, unfairness, wickedness **9. in the wrong** at fault, blameworthy, guilty, in error, mistaken, off beam (*Inf.*), off course, off target, to be blamed ~*v.* **10.** abuse, cheat, discredit, dishonour, harm, hurt, ill-treat, ill-use, impose upon, injure, malign, maltreat, misrepresent, mistreat, oppress, take advantage of

wrongdoer criminal, culprit, delinquent, evildoer, lawbreaker, malefactor, miscreant, offender, sinner, transgressor, trespasser (*Archaic*)

wrongful blameworthy, criminal, dishonest, dishonourable, evil, felonious, illegal, illegitimate, illicit, immoral, improper, reprehensible, unethical, unfair, unjust, unlawful, wicked

wry 1. askew, aslant, awry, contorted, crooked, deformed, distorted, off the level,

x *or* **X** (ɛks) *n., pl.* **x's, X's,** *or* **Xs.** **1.** the 24th letter of the English alphabet. **2.** a speech sound sequence represented by this letter, pronounced as *ks* or *gz* or, in initial position, *z,* as in *xylophone.*

x *symbol for:* **1.** *Commerce, finance, etc. ex.* **2.** *Maths.* the *x*-axis or a coordinate measured along the *x*-axis in a Cartesian coordinate system. **3.** *Maths.* an algebraic variable. **4.** multiplication.

X *symbol for:* **1.** denoting any unknown, unspecified, or variable factor, number, person, or thing. **2.** (on letters, cards, etc.) denoting a kiss. **3.** (on ballot papers, etc.) indicating choice. **4.** (on examination papers, etc.) indicating error. **5.** for Christ; Christian. **∼6.** *the Roman numeral for* ten. See **Roman numerals.**

xanthein ('zænθɪɪn) *n.* the soluble part of the yellow pigment that is found in the cell sap of some flowers.

xanthine ('zænθiːn, -θaɪn) *n.* **1.** a crystalline compound found in urine, blood, certain plants, and certain animal tissues. Formula: $C_5H_4N_4O_2$. **2.** any of three substituted derivatives of xanthine, which act as stimulants and diuretics.

Xanthippe (zæn'θɪpɪ) *or* **Xantippe** (zæn'tɪpɪ) *n.* **1.** the wife of Socrates, proverbial as a scolding and quarrelsome woman. **2.** any nagging, peevish, or irritable woman.

xantho- *or before a vowel* **xanth-** *combining form.* indicating yellow: *xanthophyll.*

x-axis *n.* a reference axis, usually horizontal, of a graph or two- or three-dimensional Cartesian coordinate system along which the *x*-coordinate is measured.

X-chromosome *n.* the sex chromosome that occurs in pairs in the diploid cells of the females of many animals, including humans, and as one of a pair with the Y-chromosome in those of males. Cf. **Y-chromosome.**

Xe *the chemical symbol for* xenon.

xebec, zebec, *or* **zebeck** ('ziːbɛk) *n.* a small three-masted Mediterranean vessel with both square and lateen sails, formerly used by Algerian pirates and later used for commerce.

xeno- *or before a vowel* **xen-** *combining form.* indicating something strange, different, or foreign: *xenogamy.*

xenon ('zɛnɒn) *n.* a colourless odourless gaseous element occurring in trace amounts in air; formerly considered inert, it is now known to form compounds and is used in radio valves, stroboscopic and bactericidal lamps, and bubble chambers. Symbol: Xe; atomic no.: 54; atomic wt.: 131.30.

xenophobia (,zɛnə'fəʊbɪə) *n.* hatred or fear of foreigners or strangers or of their politics or culture. **—'xeno-phobe** *n.* **—,xeno'phobic** *adj.*

xero- *or before a vowel* **xer-** *combining form.* indi-

cating dryness: *xeroderma.*

xerography (zɪ'rɒgrəfɪ) *n.* a photocopying process in which an electrostatic image is formed on a selenium plate or cylinder. The plate or cylinder is dusted with a resinous powder, which adheres to the charged regions, and the image is then transferred to a sheet of paper on which it is fixed by heating. **—xe'rographer** *n.* **—xero-graphic** (,zɪərə'græfɪk) *adj.* **—,xero'graphically** *adv.*

Xerox ('zɪərɒks) *n.* **1.** *Trademark.* **a.** a xerographic copying process. **b.** a machine employing this process. **c.** a copy produced by this process. **∼vb. 2.** to produce a copy of (a document, illustration, etc.) by this process.

Xhosa ('kɔːsə) *n.* **1.** (*pl.* **-sa** *or* **-sas**) a member of a cattle-rearing Negroid people of southern Africa, living chiefly in Cape Province of the Republic of South Africa. **2.** the language of this people, belonging to the Bantu group and characterized by several clicks in its sound system. **—'Xhosan** *adj.*

xi (zaɪ, saɪ, ksaɪ, ksiː) *n., pl.* **xis.** the 14th letter in the Greek alphabet (Ξ, ξ).

Xmas ('ɛksməs, 'krɪsməs) *n. Inf.* short for **Christmas.**

x-ray *or* **X-ray** *n.* **1. a.** electromagnetic radiation with wavelengths (100–0.4 nanometres) between that of ultraviolet radiation and gamma radiation. They are emitted when atoms, esp. heavy atoms, are bombarded with fast electrons. **b.** (*as modifier*): *x-ray astronomy.* **2.** a picture produced by exposing photographic film to x-rays: used in medicine as a diagnostic aid as parts of the body, such as bones, absorb x-rays and so appear as opaque areas on the picture. **∼vb.** (*tr.*) **3.** to photograph (part of the body, etc.) using x-rays. **4.** to treat or examine by means of x-rays.

xylem ('zaɪləm, -lɛm) *n.* a plant tissue that conducts water and mineral salts from the roots to all other parts, provides mechanical support, and forms the wood of trees and shrubs.

xylene ('zaɪliːn) *n.* an aromatic hydrocarbon existing in three isomeric forms, all three being colourless flammable volatile liquids used as solvents and in the manufacture of synthetic resins, dyes, and insecticides; dimethylbenzene.

xylo- *or before a vowel* **xyl-** *combining form.* **1.** indicating wood: *xylophone.* **2.** indicating xylene: *xylidine.*

xylophone ('zaɪlə,fəʊn) *n. Music.* a percussion instrument consisting of a set of wooden bars of graduated length. It is played with hard-headed hammers. **—xy-lophonic** (,zaɪlə'fɒnɪk) *adj.* **—xylophonist** (zaɪ'lɒfə-nɪst) *n.*

xylose ('zaɪləʊz, -ləʊs) *n.* a white crystalline sugar found in wood and straw. It is extracted by hydrolysis with acids and used in dyeing, tanning, and in foods for diabetics.

THESAURUS

Xmas Christmas, Christmastide, festive season, Noel, Yule (*Archaic*), Yuletide (*Archaic*)

X-rays Röntgen rays (*Old name*)

Y

y or **Y** (waɪ) n., pl. **y's**, **Y's**, or **Ys**. 1. the 25th letter of the English alphabet. 2. a speech sound represented by this letter, usually a semivowel, as in *yawn*, or a vowel, as in *symbol* or *shy*. 3. something shaped like a Y.

y *Maths. symbol for:* 1. the *y*-axis or a coordinate measured along the *y*-axis in a Cartesian coordinate system. 2. an algebraic variable.

Y *symbol for:* 1. any unknown or variable factor, number, or thing. 2. *Chem.* yttrium.

y. *abbrev. for:* 1. yard. 2. year. 3. yen.

-y¹ or **-ey** *suffix forming adjectives.* 1. *(from nouns)* characterized by; consisting of; filled with; resembling: *sunny; sandy; smoky; classy.* 2. *(from verbs)* tending to; acting or existing as specified: *leaky; shiny.*

-y², **-ie**, or **-ey** *suffix of nouns. Inf.* 1. denoting smallness and expressing affection and familiarity: *a doggy; Jamie.* 2. a person or thing concerned with or characterized by being: *a groupie; a goalie; a fatty.*

-y³ *suffix forming nouns.* 1. *(from verbs)* indicating the act of doing what is indicated by the verbal element: *inquiry.* 2. *(esp. with combining forms of Greek, Latin, or French origin)* indicating state, condition, or quality: *geography; jealousy.*

yacht (jɒt) n. 1. a vessel propelled by sail or power, used esp. for pleasure cruising, racing, etc. ~vb. 2. *(intr.)* to sail or cruise in a yacht. —'**yachting** n., adj.

yachtsman ('jɒtsmən) or *(fem.)* **yachtswoman** n., pl. **-men** or **-women**. a person who sails a yacht or yachts. —'**yachtsman,ship** n.

yack (jæk) n., vb. a variant spelling of **yak²**.

yah (jɑ:, jɛə) *sentence substitute.* 1. an informal word for yes. ~interj. 2. an exclamation of derision or disgust.

yahoo (jə'hu:) n., pl. **-hoos**. a crude, brutish, or obscenely coarse person. —**ya'hooism** n.

Yahweh ('jɑːweɪ) or **Yahveh** ('jɑːveɪ) n. *Old Testament.* the personal covenant name of God.

yak¹ (jæk) n. an ox of Tibet having long shaggy hair.

yak² (jæk) *Sl.* ~n. 1. noisy, continuous, and trivial talk. ~vb. **yakking, yakked.** 2. *(intr.)* to chatter or talk in this way.

Yale lock (jeɪl) n. *Trademark.* a type of cylinder lock using a flat serrated key.

yam (jæm) n. 1. any of various twining plants of tropical and subtropical regions, cultivated for their edible tubers. 2. the starchy tuber of any of these plants, eaten as a vegetable. 3. *Southern U.S.* the sweet potato.

yammer ('jæmə) *Inf.* ~vb. 1. to utter or whine in a complaining manner. 2. to make (a complaint) loudly or persistently. ~n. 3. a yammering sound. 4. nonsense; jabber. —'**yammerer** n.

Yang (jæŋ) n. See **Yin and Yang.**

yank (jæŋk) vb. 1. to pull with a sharp movement; tug. ~n. 2. a jerk.

Yank (jæŋk) n. 1. a slang word for an American. 2. *U.S. inf.* short for **Yankee**.

Yankee ('jæŋkɪ) or *(inf.)* **Yank** n. 1. *Often disparaging.* a native or inhabitant of the U.S.; American. 2. a native or inhabitant of New England. 3. a native or inhabitant of the Northern U.S., esp. a Northern soldier in the Civil War. ~adj. 4. of, relating to, or characteristic of Yankees.

yap (jæp) vb. **yapping, yapped.** *(intr.)* 1. (of a dog) to bark in quick sharp bursts; yelp. 2. *Inf.* to talk at length in an annoying or stupid way; jabber. ~n. 3. a high-pitched or sharp bark; yelp. 4. *Sl.* annoying or stupid speech; jabber. 5. *Sl., chiefly U.S.* a derogatory word for mouth. —'**yapper** n. —'**yappingly** adv.

yarborough ('jɑːbərə, -brə) n. *Bridge, whist.* a hand of 13 cards in which no card is higher than nine.

yard¹ (jɑːd) n. 1. a unit of length equal to 3 feet and defined in 1963 as exactly 0.9144 metre. 2. a cylindrical wooden or hollow metal spar, slung from a mast of a vessel, and used for suspending a sail.

yard² (jɑːd) n. 1. a piece of enclosed ground, often adjoining or surrounded by a building or buildings. 2. **a.** an enclosed or open area used for some commercial activity, for storage, etc.: *a builder's yard.* **b.** *(in combination): a shipyard.* 3. a U.S. word for **garden** (sense 1). 4. an area having a network of railway tracks and sidings, used for storing rolling stock, making up trains, etc. 5. *U.S. & Canad.* the winter pasture of deer, moose, and similar animals.

Yard (jɑːd) n. **the.** *Brit. inf.* short for **Scotland Yard.**

yardage ('jɑːdɪdʒ) n. a length measured in yards.

yardarm ('jɑːd,ɑːm) n. *Naut.* the outer end of a yard, outside the sheave holes.

yardstick ('jɑːd,stɪk) n. 1. a measure or standard used for comparison. 2. a graduated stick, one yard long, used for measurement.

yarmulke ('jɑːməlkə) n. *Judaism.* a man's skullcap worn at prayer, and by strongly religious Jews at all times.

yarn (jɑːn) n. 1. a continuous twisted strand of natural or synthetic fibres, used in weaving, knitting, etc. 2. *Inf.* a long and often involved story, usually of incredible or fantastic events. 3. **spin a yarn.** *Inf.* **a.** to tell such a story. **b.** to make up a series of excuses. ~vb. 4. *(intr.)* to tell such a story or stories.

yarrow ('jærəʊ) n. any of several plants of the composite family of Eurasia, having finely dissected leaves and flat clusters of white flower heads. Also called: **milfoil.**

yashmak or **yashmac** ('jæʃmæk) n. the face veil worn by Muslim women when in public.

yatter ('jætə) *Slang.* ~vb. *(intr.)* 1. to chatter. ~n. 2. idle chat.

yaw (jɔː) vb. 1. *(intr.)* (of an aircraft, etc.) to turn about its vertical axis. 2. *(intr.)* (of a ship, etc.) to deviate temporarily from a straight course. 3. *(tr.)* to cause (an aircraft, ship, etc.) to yaw. ~n. 4. the movement of an aircraft, etc., about its vertical axis. 5. the deviation of a vessel from a straight course.

yawl (jɔːl) n. 1. a two-masted sailing vessel with a small mizzenmast aft of the rudderpost. 2. a ship's small boat, usually rowed by four or six oars.

yawn (jɔːn) vb. 1. *(intr.)* to open the mouth wide and take in air deeply, often as in involuntary reaction to sleepiness or boredom. 2. *(tr.)* to express or utter while yawning. 3. *(intr.)* to be open wide as if threatening to engulf (someone or something): *the mine shaft yawned below.* ~n. 4. the act or an instance of yawning. —'**yawner** n. —'**yawningly** adv.

yaws (jɔːz) pl. n. an infectious disease of tropical climates characterized by red skin eruptions.

y-axis n. a reference axis of a graph or two- or three-dimensional Cartesian coordinate system along which the *y*-coordinate is measured.

Yb *the chemical symbol for* ytterbium.

Y-chromosome n. the sex chromosome that occurs as one of a pair with the X-chromosome in the diploid cells of the males of many animals, including humans. Cf. **X-chromosome.**

yclept (ɪ'klɛpt) ~adj. *Obs.* having the name of; called.

yd or **yd.** *abbrev. for* yard (measure).

Y.D.T. (in Canada) *abbrev. for* Yukon Daylight Time.

ye¹ (jiː, *unstressed* jɪ) pron. 1. *Arch.* refers to more than one person including the person addressed. 2. Also: **ee** (iː). *Dialect.* refers to one person addressed: *I tell ye.*

ye² (ðiː, *spelling pron.* jiː) determiner. a form of **the¹**, used as a supposed archaism: *ye olde oake.*

▮THESAURUS▮

yank v./n. hitch, jerk, pull, snatch, tug, wrench

yardstick benchmark, criterion, gauge, measure, standard, touchstone

yarn n. 1. fibre, thread 2. *Inf.* anecdote, cock-and-bull story *(Inf.)*, fable, story, tale, tall story

yawning cavernous, chasmal, gaping, vast, wide, wide-open

yea (jeɪ) *sentence substitute.* **1.** a less common word for **aye** (yes). ~*adv.* **2.** (*sentence modifier*) *Arch.* or *literary.* indeed; truly: *yea, though they spurn me, I shall prevail.*

year (jɪə) *n.* **1.** the period of time, the **calendar year,** containing 365 days or in a **leap year** 366 days. It is divided into 12 calendar months, and reckoned from January 1 to December 31. **2.** a period of twelve months from any specified date. **3.** a specific period of time, usually occupying a definite part or parts of a twelve-month period, used for some particular activity: *a school year.* **4.** Also called: **astronomical year, tropical year, equinoctial year.** the period of time, the **solar year,** during which the earth makes one revolution around the sun, measured between two successive vernal equinoxes: equal to 365.242 19 days. **5.** the period of time, the **sidereal year,** during which the earth makes one revolution around the sun, measured between two successive conjunctions of a particular star: equal to 365.256 36 days. **6.** the period of time, the **lunar year,** containing 12 lunar months and equal to 354.3671 days. **7.** the period of time taken by a specified planet to complete one revolution around the sun. **8.** (*pl.*) age, esp. old age: *a man of his years should be more careful.* **9.** (*pl.*) time: *in years to come.* **10.** a group of pupils or students, who are taught or study together. **11. the year dot.** *Inf.* as long ago as can be remembered. **12. year in, year out.** regularly or monotonously, over a long period. ~Related adj.: **annual.**

▷ **Usage.** In writing spans of years, it is important to choose a style that avoids ambiguity. The practice adopted in this dictionary is, in four-figure dates, to specify the last two digits of the second date if it falls within the same century as the first: *1801–08; 1850–51; 1899–1901.* In writing three-figure B.C. dates, it is advisable to give both dates in full: *159–156* B.C., not *159–56* B.C. unless of course the span referred to consists of 103 years rather than three years. It is also advisable to specify B.C. or A.D. in years under 1000 unless the context makes this self-evident.

yearbook (ˈjɪəˌbʊk) *n.* an almanac or other reference book published annually and containing details of events of the previous year.

yearling (ˈjɪəlɪŋ) *n.* **1.** the young of any of various animals, including the antelope and buffalo, between one and two years of age. **2.** a thoroughbred racehorse counted as being one year old until the second January 1 following its birth. **3. a.** a bond that is intended to mature after one year. **b.** (*as modifier*): *yearling bonds.* ~*adj.* **4.** being a year old.

yearlong (ˈjɪəˈlɒŋ) *adj.* throughout a whole year.

yearly (ˈjɪəlɪ) *adj.* **1.** occurring, done, appearing, etc., once a year or every year; annual. **2.** lasting or valid for a year; annual: *a yearly subscription.* ~*adv.* **3.** once a year; annually.

yearn (jɜːn) *vb.* (*intr.*) **1.** (usually foll. by *for* or *after* or an infinitive) to have an intense desire or longing (for). **2.** to feel tenderness or affection. —ˈyearner *n.* —ˈyearning *n., adj.* —ˈyearningly *adv.*

yeast (jiːst) *n.* **1.** any of various single-celled fungi which reproduce by budding and are able to ferment sugars: a rich source of vitamins of the B complex. **2.** a commercial preparation containing yeast cells and inert material such as meal, that is used in raising dough for bread and for fermenting beer, whisky, etc. **3.** a preparation containing yeast cells, used to treat diseases caused by vitamin B deficiency. **4.** froth or foam, esp. on beer. ~*vb.* **5.** (*intr.*) to froth or foam. —ˈyeastless *adj.* —ˈyeast,like *adj.*

yeasty (ˈjiːstɪ) *adj.* **yeastier, yeastiest. 1.** of, resembling, or containing yeast. **2.** fermenting or causing fermentation. **3.** tasting of or like yeast. **4.** insubstantial or frivolous. **5.** restless, agitated, or unsettled. **6.** covered with or containing froth or foam. —ˈyeastily *adv.* —ˈyeastiness *n.*

yell (jɛl) *vb.* **1.** to shout, scream, cheer, or utter in a loud or piercing way. ~*n.* **2.** a loud piercing inarticulate cry, as of pain, anger, or fear. **3.** *U.S.* a rhythmic cry,

used in cheering in unison. —ˈyeller *n.*

yellow (ˈjɛləʊ) *n.* **1.** any of a group of colours such as that of a lemon or of gold, that vary in saturation but have the same hue. Yellow is the complementary colour of blue. Related adj.: **xanthous. 2.** a pigment or dye of or producing these colours. **3.** yellow cloth or clothing: *dressed in yellow.* **4.** the yolk of an egg. **5.** a yellow ball in snooker, etc. ~*adj.* **6.** of the colour yellow. **7.** yellowish in colour or having parts or marks that are yellowish. **8.** having a yellowish skin; Mongoloid. **9.** *Inf.* cowardly or afraid. **10.** offensively sensational, as a cheap newspaper (esp. in **yellow press**). ~*vb.* **11.** to make or become yellow. —ˈyellowish *adj.* —ˈyellowness *n.* —ˈyellowy *adj.*

yellow-belly *n., pl.* **-lies.** a slang word for **coward.** —ˈyellow-ˌbellied *adj.*

yellow card *n. Soccer.* a card of a yellow colour raised by a referee in international competitions to warn a player who has violated a rule.

yellow fever *n.* an acute infectious disease of tropical and subtropical climates, characterized by fever, haemorrhages, vomiting, and jaundice: caused by a virus transmitted by the bite of a certain mosquito. Also called: **yellow jack.**

yellow flag *n.* a yellow flag flown to show that a vessel is in quarantine.

yellowhammer (ˈjɛləʊˌhæmə) *n.* a European bunting, having a yellowish head and body and brown-streaked wings and tail.

yellow pages *pl. n.* a classified telephone directory or section of a directory that lists subscribers by the business or service provided.

yellow streak *n.* a cowardly or weak trait.

yellowwood (ˈjɛləʊˌwʊd) *n.* **1.** any of several leguminous trees of the southeastern U.S., having clusters of white flowers and yellow wood yielding a yellow dye. **2.** Also called: **West Indian satinwood.** a rutaceous tree of the West Indies, with smooth hard wood. **3.** any of several other trees with yellow wood, esp. a conifer of southern Africa the wood of which is used for furniture and building. **4.** the wood of any of these trees.

yelp (jɛlp) *vb.* **1.** (esp. of a dog) to utter a sharp or high-pitched cry or bark, often indicating pain. ~*n.* **2.** a sharp or high-pitched cry or bark. —ˈyelper *n.*

yen[1] (jɛn) *n., pl.* **yen.** the standard monetary unit of Japan.

yen[2] (jɛn) *Inf.* ~*n.* **1.** a longing or desire. ~*vb.* **yenning, yenned. 2.** (*intr.*) to yearn.

yeoman (ˈjəʊmən) *n., pl.* **-men. 1.** *History.* **a.** a member of a class of small freeholders who cultivated their own land. **b.** an attendant or lesser official in a royal or noble household. **2.** (in Britain) another name for **yeoman of the guard. 3.** (*modifier*) characteristic of or relating to a yeoman. —ˈyeomanly *adj.*

yeoman of the guard *n.* a member of the ceremonial bodyguard (**Yeomen of the Guard**) of the English monarch.

yeomanry (ˈjəʊmənrɪ) *n.* **1.** yeomen collectively. **2.** (in Britain) a volunteer cavalry force, organized in 1761 for home defence: merged into the Territorial Army in 1907.

yep (jɛp) *sentence substitute.* an informal word for **yes.**

yes (jɛs) *sentence substitute.* **1.** used to express affirmation, consent, agreement, or approval or to answer when one is addressed. **2.** used to signal someone to speak or keep speaking, enter a room, or do something. ~*adv.* **3.** (*sentence modifier*) used to emphasize a positive statement, esp. when disagreeing: *yes I can.* ~*n.* **4.** an answer or vote of *yes.* **5.** (*often pl.*) a person who votes in the affirmative.

yes man *n.* a servile, submissive, or acquiescent subordinate, assistant, or associate.

yester- *prefix.* indicating a period of time before the present one: *yesteryear.*

yesterday (ˈjɛstədɪ, -ˌdeɪ) *n.* **1.** the day immediately preceding today. **2.** (*often pl.*) the recent past. ~*adv.*

THESAURUS

yearly annual, annually, every year, once a year, per annum
yearn ache, covet, crave, desire, hanker, have a yen for (*Inf.*), hunger, itch, languish, long, lust, pant, pine, set one's heart upon

yell 1. *v.* bawl, holler (*Inf.*), howl, scream, screech, shout, shriek, squeal **2.** *n.* cry, howl, scream, screech, shriek, whoop
yelp cry, yammer (*Inf.*), yap, yip (*Chiefly U.S.*), yowl

yes man bootlicker (*Inf.*), bosses' lackey, company man, crawler (*Sl.*), creature, minion, sycophant, timeserver, toady

3. on or during the day before today. **4.** in the recent past.

yesteryear (ˈjɛstəˌjɪə) *Formal or literary.* ~*n.* **1.** last year or the past in general. ~*adv.* **2.** during last year or the past in general.

yet (jɛt) **1.** *sentence connector.* nevertheless; still; in spite of that: *I want to and yet I haven't the courage.* ~*adv.* **2.** (*usually used with a negative or interrogative*) so far; up until then or now: *they're not home yet; is it teatime yet?* **3.** (*often preceded by just; usually used with a negative*) now (as contrasted with later): *we can't stop yet.* **4.** (*often used with a comparative*) even; still: *yet more potatoes for sale.* **5.** eventually in spite of everything: *we'll convince him yet.* **6. as yet.** so far; up until then or now.

yeti (ˈjɛti) *n.* another term for **abominable snowman.**

yew (juː) *n.* **1.** any coniferous tree of the Old World and North America having flattened needle-like leaves, fine-grained elastic wood, and cuplike red waxy cones resembling berries. **2.** the wood of any of these trees, used to make bows for archery. **3.** *Archery.* a bow made of yew.

Y-fronts *pl. n.* boys' or men's underpants having a front opening within an inverted Y shape.

Y.H.A. (in Britain) *abbrev. for* Youth Hostels Association.

yid (jɪd) *n. Sl.* a derogatory word for a Jew.

Yiddish (ˈjɪdɪʃ) *n.* a language spoken as a vernacular by Jews in Europe and elsewhere by Jewish emigrants, usually written in the Hebrew alphabet. It is a dialect of High German with an admixture of words of Hebrew, Romance, and Slavonic origin.

yield (jiːld) *vb.* **1.** to give forth or supply (a product, result, etc.), esp. by cultivation, labour, etc.; produce or bear. **2.** (*tr.*) to furnish as a return: *the shares yielded three per cent.* **3.** (*tr.; often foll. by up*) to surrender or relinquish, esp. as a result of force, persuasion, etc. **4.** (*intr.; sometimes foll. by to*) to give way, submit, or surrender, as through force or persuasion: *she yielded to his superior knowledge.* **5.** (*intr.; often foll. by to*) to agree; comply; assent: *he eventually yielded to their request for money.* **6.** (*tr.*) to grant or allow; concede: *to yield right of way.* ~*n.* **7.** the result, product, or amount yielded. **8.** the profit or return, as from an investment or tax. **9.** the annual income provided by an investment. **10.** the energy released by the explosion of a nuclear weapon. **11.** *Chem.* the quantity of a specified product obtained in a reaction or series of reactions. —ˈyieldable *adj.* —ˈyielder *n.*

yielding (ˈjiːldɪŋ) *adj.* **1.** compliant, submissive, or flexible. **2.** pliable or soft: *a yielding material.*

Yin and Yang (jɪn) *n.* two complementary principles of Chinese philosophy: Yin is negative, dark, and feminine, Yang is positive, bright, and masculine.

yippee (jɪˈpiː) *interj.* an exclamation of joy, pleasure, anticipation, etc.

-yl *suffix of nouns.* (in chemistry) indicating a group or radical: *methyl.*

Y.M.C.A. *abbrev. for* Young Men's Christian Association.

-yne *suffix forming nouns.* denoting an organic chemical containing a triple bond: *alkyne.*

yob (jɒb) *or* **yobbo** (ˈjɒbəʊ) *n., pl.* **yobs** *or* **yobbos.** *Brit. sl.* an aggressive and surly youth, esp. a teenager.

yodel (ˈjəʊdəl) *n.* **1.** an effect produced in singing by an abrupt change of register from the chest voice to falsetto, esp. in folk songs of the Swiss Alps. ~*vb.* -**delling,** -**delled** *or U.S.* -**deling,** -**deled. 2.** to sing (a song) in which a yodel is used. —ˈyodeller *n.*

yoga (ˈjəʊgə) *n.* (*often cap.*) **1.** a Hindu system of philosophy aiming at the mystical union of the self with the Supreme Being in a state of complete awareness and tranquillity through certain physical and mental exercises. **2.** any method by which such awareness and tranquillity are attained, esp. a course of related exercises and postures. —**yogic** (ˈjəʊgɪk) *adj.* —ˈyogism *n.*

yoghurt *or* **yogurt** (ˈjɒgət) *n.* a thick custard-like food prepared from milk curdled by bacteria, often sweetened and flavoured with fruit.

yogi (ˈjəʊgɪ) *n., pl.* -**gis** *or* -**gin** (-gɪn). a person who is a master of yoga.

yo-heave-ho (ˌjəʊhiːvˈhəʊ) *interj.* a cry formerly used by sailors while pulling or lifting together in rhythm.

yoicks (haɪk; *spelling pron.* jɔɪks) *interj.* a cry used by fox-hunters to urge on the hounds.

yoke (jəʊk) *n., pl.* **yokes** *or* **yoke. 1.** a wooden frame, usually consisting of a bar with an oxbow at either end, for attaching to the necks of a pair of draught animals, esp. oxen, so that they can be worked as a team. **2.** something resembling a yoke in form or function, such as a frame fitting over a person's shoulders for carrying buckets. **3.** an oppressive force or burden: *under the yoke of a tyrant.* **4.** a pair of oxen or other draught animals joined by a yoke. **5.** a part that secures two or more components so that they move together. **6.** a fitted part of a garment, esp. around the neck, shoulders, and chest or around the hips, to which a gathered, pleated, flared, or unfitted part is attached. **7.** (in the ancient world) a symbolic yoke, consisting of two upright spears with a third lashed across them, under which conquered enemies were compelled to march, esp. in Rome. **8.** a mark, token, or symbol of slavery, subjection, or suffering. **9.** *Now rare.* a link, tie, or bond: *the yoke of love.* ~*vb.* **10.** (*tr.*) to secure or harness (a draught animal) to (a plough, vehicle, etc.) by means of a yoke. **11.** to join or be joined by means of a yoke; couple, unite, or link.

yokel (ˈjəʊkəl) *n. Disparaging.* (used chiefly by townspeople) a person who lives in the country, esp. one who is simple and old-fashioned.

yolk (jəʊk) *n.* **1.** the substance in an animal ovum that nourishes the developing embryo. **2.** a greasy substance in the fleece of sheep. —ˈyolky *adj.*

Yom Kippur (jɒm ˈkɪpə; *Hebrew* jɔm kiˈpur) *n.* an annual Jewish holiday celebrated as a day of fasting, on which prayers of penitence are recited in the synagogue. Also called: **Day of Atonement.**

yon (jɒn) *determiner.* **1.** *Chiefly N Brit.* **a.** an archaic or dialect word for **that:** *yon man.* **b.** (*as pronoun*): *yon's a fool.* ~ **2.** a variant of **yonder.**

yonder (ˈjɒndə) *adv.* **1.** at, in, or to that relatively distant place; over there. ~*determiner.* **2.** being at a distance, either within view or as if within view: *yonder valleys.*

yoo-hoo (ˈjuːˌhuː) *interj.* a call to attract a person's attention.

yore (jɔː) *n.* **1.** time long past (now only **of yore**). ~*adv.* **2.** *Obs.* in the past; long ago.

york (jɔːk) *vb.* (*tr.*) *Cricket.* to bowl (a batsman) by pitching the ball under or just beyond the bat.

yorker (ˈjɔːkə) *n. Cricket.* a ball bowled so as to pitch just under or just beyond the bat.

Yorkist (ˈjɔːkɪst) *English history.* ~*n.* **1.** a member or adherent of the royal House of York, esp. during the wars of the Roses. ~*adj.* **2.** of, belonging to, or relating to the supporters or members of the House of York.

Yorks. (jɔːks) *abbrev. for* Yorkshire.

Yorkshire pudding (ˈjɔːkʃɪə) *n. Chiefly Brit.* a light puffy baked pudding made from a batter of flour, eggs, and milk, traditionally served with roast beef.

Yorkshire terrier *n.* a very small breed of terrier with a long straight glossy coat.

you (juː; *unstressed* jʊ) *pron.* (*subjective or objective*) **1.**

THESAURUS

yet 1. as yet, so far, thus far, until now, up to now **2.** however, nevertheless, notwithstanding, still **3.** additionally, as well, besides, further, in addition, into the bargain, moreover, over and above, still, to boot **4.** already, just now, now, right now, so soon

yield *v.* **1.** afford, bear, bring forth, bring in, earn, furnish, generate, give, net, pay, produce, provide, return, supply ~*n.* **2.** crop, earnings, harvest, income, output, produce, profit, return, revenue, takings ~*v.* **3.** abandon, abdicate, admit defeat, bow, capitulate, cave in (*Inf.*), cede, cry quits, give in, give up the struggle, give way, knuckle under, lay down one's arms, part with, raise the white flag, relinquish, resign, resign oneself, submit, succumb, surrender, throw in the towel **4.** accede, agree, allow, bow, comply, concede, consent, go along with, grant, permit

yielding 1. accommodating, acquiescent, biddable, compliant, docile, easy, flexible, obedient, pliant, submissive, tractable **2.** elastic, pliable, quaggy, resilient, soft, spongy, springy, supple, unresisting

yoke *n.* **1.** bond, chain, coupling, ligament, link, tie **2.** bondage, burden, enslavement, helotry, oppression, serfdom, service, servility, servitude, slavery, thraldom, vassalage ~*v.* **3.** bracket, connect, couple, harness, hitch, join, link, tie, unite

yokel boor, bucolic, clodhopper (*Inf.*), (country) bumpkin, country cousin, countryman, hick (*Inf., chiefly U.S.*), hillbilly, hind (*Obsolete*), peasant (*Inf.*), rustic

refers to the person addressed or to more than one person including the person or persons addressed: *you know better; the culprit is among you*. **2.** refers to an unspecified person or people in general: *you can't tell the boys from the girls.* ~*n.* **3.** *Inf.* the personality of the person being addressed: *that hat isn't really you.* **4. you know what** *or* **who.** a thing or person that the speaker does not want to specify.
▷ **Usage.** See at **me.**

you'd (juːd; *unstressed* jʊd) *contraction of* you had *or* you would.

you'll (juːl; *unstressed* jʊl) *contraction of* you will *or* you shall.

young (jʌŋ) *adj.* **younger** (ˈjʌŋɡə), **youngest** (ˈjʌŋɡɪst). **1. a.** having lived, existed, or been made or known for a relatively short time: *a young man; a young movement; a young country.* **b.** (*as collective n.; preceded by the*): *the young.* **2.** youthful or having qualities associated with youth; vigorous or lively. **3.** of or relating to youth: *in my young days.* **4.** having been established or introduced for a relatively short time: *a young member.* **5.** in an early stage of progress or development; not far advanced: *the day was young.* **6.** (*often cap.*) of or relating to a rejuvenated group or movement or one claiming to represent the younger members of the population: *Young Socialists.* ~*n.* **7.** (*functioning as pl.*) offspring, esp. young animals: *a rabbit with her young.* **8. with young.** (of animals) pregnant. —ˈ**youngish** *adj.*

youngster (ˈjʌŋstə) *n.* **1.** a young person; child or youth. **2.** a young animal, esp. a horse.

your (jɔː, jʊə; *unstressed* jə) *determiner.* **1.** of, belonging to, or associated with you: *your nose; your house.* **2.** belonging to or associated with an unspecified person or people in general: *the path is on your left heading north.* **3.** *Inf.* used to indicate all things or people of a certain type: *your part-time worker is a problem.*

you're (jɔː; *unstressed* jə) *contraction of* you are.

yours (jɔːz, jʊəz) *pron.* **1.** something or someone belonging to or associated with you. **2.** your family: *greetings to you and yours.* **3.** used in conventional closing phrases at the end of a letter: *yours sincerely; yours faithfully.* **4. of yours.** belonging to or associated with you.

yourself (jɔːˈsɛlf, jʊə-) *pron., pl.* **-selves. 1. a.** the reflexive form of *you.* **b.** (intensifier): *you yourself control your destiny.* **2.** (*preceded by a copula*) your usual self: *you're not yourself.*
▷ **Usage.** See at **myself.**

yours truly *pron.* an informal term for *I* or *me.*

youth (juːθ) *n., pl.* **youths** (juːðz). **1.** the quality or condition of being young, immature, or inexperienced: *his youth told against him in the contest.* **2.** the period between childhood and maturity. **3.** the freshness, vigour, or vitality characteristic of young people. **4.** any period

of early development. **5.** a young person, esp. a young man or boy. **6.** young people collectively: *youth everywhere is rising in revolt.*

youthful (ˈjuːθfʊl) *adj.* **1.** of, relating to, possessing, or characteristic of youth. **2.** fresh, vigorous, or active: *he's surprisingly youthful for his age.* **3.** in an early stage of development: *a youthful culture.* **4.** Also: **young.** (of a river, valley, or land surface) in the early stage of the cycle of erosion, characterized by steep slopes, lack of flood plains, and V-shaped valleys. —ˈ**youthfully** *adv.* —ˈ**youthfulness** *n.*

youth hostel *n.* one of an organization of inexpensive lodging places for young people travelling cheaply. Often shortened to **hostel.**

you've (juːv; *unstressed* jʊv) *contraction of* you have.

yowl (jaʊl) *vb.* **1.** to express with or produce a loud mournful wail or cry; howl. ~*n.* **2.** a wail or howl. —ˈ**yowler** *n.*

yo-yo (ˈjəʊjəʊ) *n., pl.* **-yos.** a toy consisting of a spool attached to a string, the end of which is held while it is repeatedly spun out and reeled in.

yr. *abbrev. for:* **1.** (*pl.* **yrs.**) year. **2.** younger. **3.** your.

yrs. *abbrev. for:* **1.** years. **2.** yours.

Y.S.T. (in Canada) *abbrev. for* Yukon Standard Time.

Y.T. *abbrev. for* Yukon Territory.

ytterbium (ɪˈtɜːbɪəm) *n.* a soft malleable silvery element of the lanthanide series of metals that is used to improve the mechanical properties of steel. Symbol: Yb; atomic no.: 70; atomic wt.: 173.04.

yttrium (ˈɪtrɪəm) *n.* a silvery metallic element used in various alloys, in lasers, and as a catalyst. Symbol: Y; atomic no.: 39; atomic wt.: 88.90.

yuan (ˈjuːˈæn) *n., pl.* **-an.** the standard monetary unit of the People's Republic of China.

yucca (ˈjʌkə) *n.* any of a genus of liliaceous plants of tropical and subtropical America, having stiff lancelike leaves and spikes of white flowers.

Yugoslav *or* **Jugoslav** (ˈjuːɡəʊˌslɑːv) *n.* **1.** a native or inhabitant of Yugoslavia, a federal republic in SE Europe, on the Adriatic. **2.** (not in technical use) another name for **Serbo-Croatian** (the language). ~*adj.* **3.** of, relating to, or characteristic of Yugoslavia or its people.

yuk (jʌk) *interj. Sl.* an exclamation indicating contempt, dislike, or disgust. —ˈ**yukky** *adj.*

yule (juːl) *n.* (*sometimes cap.*) *Literary, arch., or dialect.* **a.** Christmas or the Christmas season. **b.** (*in combination*): *yuletide.*

yummy (ˈjʌmɪ) *Sl.* ~*interj.* **1.** Also: **yum-yum.** an exclamation indicating pleasure or delight, as in anticipation of delicious food. ~*adj.* **-mier, -miest. 2.** delicious, delightful, or attractive.

Y.W.C.A. *abbrev. for* Young Women's Christian Association.

THESAURUS

young *adj.* **1.** adolescent, callow, green, growing, immature, infant, in the springtime of life, junior, juvenile, little, unfledged, youthful **2.** at an early stage, early, fledgling, new, newish, not far advanced, recent, undeveloped ~*n.* **3.** babies, brood, family, issue, litter, little ones, offspring, progeny

youngster boy, cub, girl, juvenile, kid (*Inf.*), lad, lass, pup (*Inf.*), teenager, teeny-

bopper (*Sl.*), urchin, young adult, young hopeful, young person, young shaver (*Inf.*), young 'un (*Inf.*), youth

youth 1. adolescence, boyhood, early life, girlhood, immaturity, juvenescence, salad days, young days **2.** adolescent, boy, kid (*Inf.*), lad, shaveling (*Archaic*), stripling, teenager, young man, young shaver (*Inf.*), youngster **3.** teenagers, the rising genera-

tion, the young, younger generation, young people

youthful 1. boyish, childish, girlish, immature, inexperienced, juvenile, pubescent, puerile, young **2.** active, fresh, spry, vigorous, young at heart, young looking

Z

z or **Z** (zɛd; *U.S.* ziː) *n.*, *pl.* **z's**, **Z's**, or **Zs**. **1.** the 26th and last letter of the English alphabet. **2.** a speech sound represented by this letter. **3. a.** something shaped like a Z. **b.** (*in combination*): *a Z-bend in a road.*

z *Maths. symbol for:* **1.** the z-axis or a coordinate measured along the z-axis in a Cartesian or cylindrical coordinate system. **2.** an algebraic variable.

Z *symbol for:* **1.** any unknown, variable, or unspecified factor, number, person, or thing. **2.** *Chem.* atomic number. **3.** *Physics.* impedance. **4.** zone.

zabaglione (ˌzæbəˈljəʊnɪ) *n.* a light foamy dessert made of egg yolks, sugar, and marsala, whipped together and served hot in a glass.

zany (ˈzeɪnɪ) *adj.* **-nier, -niest. 1.** comical in an endearing way; imaginatively funny or comical, esp. in behaviour. *~n.*, *pl.* **-nies. 1.** a clown or buffoon, esp. one in old comedies who imitated other performers with ludicrous effect. **2.** a ludicrous or foolish person. —**ˈzanily** *adv.* —**ˈzaniness** *n.*

zap (zæp) *Sl.* *~vb.* **zapping, zapped. 1.** (*tr.*) to attack, kill, or destroy, as with a sudden bombardment. **2.** (*intr.*) to move quickly. *~n.* **3.** energy, vigour, or pep. *~interj.* **4.** an exclamation used to express sudden or swift action.

z-axis *n.* a reference axis of a three-dimensional Cartesian coordinate system along which the z-coordinate is measured.

zeal (ziːl) *n.* fervent or enthusiastic devotion, often extreme or fanatical in nature, as to a religious movement, political cause, ideal, or aspiration.

zealot (ˈzɛlət) *n.* an immoderate, fanatical, or extremely zealous adherent to a cause, esp. a religious one. —**ˈzealotry** *n.*

zealous (ˈzɛləs) *adj.* filled with or inspired by intense enthusiasm or zeal; ardent; fervent. —**ˈzealously** *adv.* —**ˈzealousness** *n.*

zebra (ˈzɛbrə, ˈziːbrə) *n.*, *pl.* **-ras** or **-ra.** any of several mammals of the horse family, such as the common zebra of southern and eastern Africa, having distinctive black-and-white striped hides. —**zebrine** (ˈziːbraɪn, ˈzɛb-) *or* **ˈzebroid** *adj.*

zebra crossing *n. Brit.* a pedestrian crossing marked on a road by broad alternate black and white stripes. Once on the crossing the pedestrian has right of way.

zebu (ˈziːbuː) *n.* a domesticated ox having a humped back, long horns, and a large dewlap: used in India and E Asia as a draught animal.

zed (zɛd) *n.* the British spoken form of the letter z.

zee (ziː) *n.* the U.S. word for zed (letter z).

Zeitgeist *German.* (ˈtsaɪtˌɡaɪst) *n.* the spirit, attitude, or general outlook of a specific time or period, esp. as it is reflected in literature, philosophy, etc.

Zen (zɛn) *Buddhism.* *~n.* **1.** a Japanese school, of 12th-century Chinese origin, teaching that contemplation of one's essential nature to the exclusion of all else is the only way of achieving pure enlightenment. **2.** (*modifier*) of or relating to this school: *Zen Buddhism.* —**ˈZenic** *adj.* —**ˈZenist** *n.*

zenana (zɛˈnɑːnə) *n.* (in the East, esp. in Muslim and Hindu homes) part of a house reserved for the women and girls of a household.

Zend-Avesta (ˌzɛndəˈvɛstə) *n.* the Avesta together with the traditional interpretive commentary known as the Zend, esp. as preserved in the Avestan language among the Parsees.

zenith (ˈzɛnɪθ) *n.* **1.** *Astron.* the point on the celestial sphere vertically above an observer. **2.** the highest point; peak; acme: *the zenith of someone's achievements.* —**ˈzenithal** *adj.*

zephyr (ˈzɛfə) *n.* **1.** a soft or gentle breeze. **2.** any of several delicate soft yarns, fabrics, or garments, usually of wool.

zeppelin (ˈzɛpəlɪn) *n.* (*sometimes cap.*) a large cylindrical rigid airship designed to carry passengers, bombs, etc.

zero (ˈzɪərəʊ) *n.*, *pl.* **-ros** or **-roes. 1.** the symbol 0, indicating an absence of quantity or magnitude; nought. Former name: **cipher. 2.** the integer denoted by the symbol 0; nought. **3.** the ordinal number between +1 and −1. **4.** nothing; nil. **5.** a person or thing of no significance; nonentity. **6.** the lowest point or degree: *his prospects were put at zero.* **7.** the line or point on a scale of measurement from which the graduations commence. **8. a.** the temperature, pressure, etc., that registers a reading of zero on a scale. **b.** the value of a variable, such as temperature, obtained under specified conditions. **9.** *Maths.* **a.** the cardinal number of a set with no members. **b.** the identity element of addition. *~adj.* **10.** having no measurable quantity, magnitude, etc. **11.** *Meteorol.* **a.** (of a cloud ceiling) limiting visibility to 15 metres (50 feet) or less. **b.** (of horizontal visibility) limited to 50 metres (165 feet) or less. *~vb.* **-roing, -roed. 12.** (*tr.*) to adjust (an instrument, apparatus, etc.) so as to read zero or a position taken as zero. *~determiner.* **13.** *Inf.*, *chiefly U.S.* no (thing) at all: *this job has zero interest.*

zero gravity *n.* the state or condition of weightlessness.

zero hour *n.* **1.** *Mil.* the time set for the start of an attack or the initial stage of an operation. **2.** *Inf.* a critical time, esp. at the commencement of an action.

zero-rated *adj.* denoting goods on which the buyer pays no value-added tax although the seller can claim back any tax he has paid.

zest (zɛst) *n.* **1.** invigorating or keen excitement or enjoyment: *a zest for living.* **2.** added interest, flavour, or charm; piquancy: *her presence gave zest to the occasion.* **3.** something added to give flavour or relish. **4.** the peel or skin of an orange or lemon, used as flavouring in drinks, etc. *~vb.* **5.** (*tr.*) to give flavour, interest, or piquancy to. —**ˈzestful** *adj.* —**ˈzestfully** *adv.* —**ˈzestfulness** *n.* —**ˈzesty** *adj.*

zeta (ˈziːtə) *n.* the sixth letter in the Greek alphabet (Z, ζ).

zeugma (ˈzjuːɡmə) *n.* a figure of speech in which a word is used to modify or govern two or more words although appropriate to only one of them or making a different sense with each, as in *Mr. Pickwick took his hat and his leave* (Charles Dickens). —**zeugmatic** (zjuːɡˈmætɪk) *adj.*

ziggurat (ˈzɪɡʊˌræt) *n.* a type of rectangular temple tower or tiered mound erected by the Sumerians, Akkadians, and Babylonians in Mesopotamia.

zigzag (ˈzɪɡˌzæɡ) *n.* **1.** a line or course characterized by sharp turns in alternating directions. **2.** one of the series of such turns. **3.** something having the form of a zigzag. *~adj.* **4.** (*usually prenominal*) formed in or proceeding in a zigzag. **5.** (of a sewing machine) capable of producing stitches in a zigzag. *~vb.* **-zagging, -zagged. 6.** to

---

THESAURUS

zeal ardour, devotion, eagerness, earnestness, enthusiasm, fanaticism, fervency, fervour, fire, gusto, keenness, militancy, passion, spirit, verve, warmth, zest

zealot bigot, enthusiast, extremist, fanatic, fiend (*Inf.*), maniac, militant

zealous afire, ardent, burning, devoted, eager, earnest, enthusiastic, fanatical, fervent, fervid, impassioned, keen, militant, passionate, rabid, spirited

zenith acme, apex, apogee, climax, height, high noon, high point, meridian, peak, pinnacle, summit, top, vertex

zero 1. cipher, naught, nil, nothing, nought **2.** bottom, lowest point *or* ebb, nadir, nothing, rock bottom

zero hour appointed hour, crisis, moment of decision, moment of truth, turning point, vital moment

zest 1. appetite, delectation, enjoyment, gusto, keenness, relish, zeal, zing (*Inf.*) **2.** charm, flavour, interest, kick (*Inf.*), piquancy, pungency, relish, savour, smack, spice, tang, taste

proceed or cause to proceed in a zigzag. **7.** (*tr.*) to form into a zigzag.

zillion ('zɪljən) *Inf.* ~*n., pl.* **-lions** *or* **-lion. 1.** (*often pl.*) an extremely large but unspecified number, quantity, or amount: *zillions of flies in this camp.* ~*determiner.* **2.** amounting to a zillion: *a zillion different problems.*

zimmer ('zɪmə) *n.* Also: **zimmer aid.** another name for **walker** (sense 3).

zinc (zɪŋk) *n.* **1.** a brittle bluish-white metallic element that is a constituent of several alloys, esp. brass and nickel-silver, and is used in die-casting, galvanizing metals, and in battery electrodes. Symbol: Zn; atomic no.: 30; atomic wt.: 65.37. **2.** *Inf.* corrugated galvanized iron. —'**zincic** *adj.* —'**zincky, 'zincy,** *or* '**zinky** *adj.*

zincography (zɪŋ'kɒgrəfɪ) *n.* the art or process of engraving zinc to form a printing plate. —**zin'cographer** *n.* —**zincograph** ('zɪŋkə,grɑːf) *n.*

zinc ointment *n.* a medicinal ointment consisting of zinc oxide, petrolatum, and paraffin.

zinc oxide *n.* a white insoluble powder used as a pigment in paints (**zinc white** or **Chinese white**), cosmetics, glass, and printing inks. It is an antiseptic and astringent and is used in making zinc ointment. Formula: ZnO. Also called: **flowers of zinc.**

zing (zɪŋ) *n. Inf.* **1.** a short high-pitched buzzing sound, as of a bullet or vibrating string. **2.** vitality; zest. ~*vb.* **3.** (*intr.*) to make or move with or as if with a high-pitched buzzing sound. —'**zingy** *adj.*

zinnia ('zɪnɪə) *n.* any of a genus of annual or perennial plants of the composite family, of tropical and subtropical America, having solitary heads of brightly coloured flowers.

Zion ('zaɪən) *or* **Sion** *n.* **1.** the hill on which the city of Jerusalem stands. **2.** *Judaism.* **a.** the ancient Israelites of the Bible. **b.** the modern Jewish nation. **c.** Israel as the national home of the Jewish people. **3.** *Christianity.* heaven regarded as the city of God and the final abode of his elect.

Zionism ('zaɪə,nɪzəm) *n.* **1.** a political movement for the establishment and support of a national homeland for Jews in Palestine, now concerned chiefly with the development of the modern state of Israel. **2.** a policy or movement for Jews to return to Palestine from the Diaspora. —'**Zionist** *n., adj.* —**Zion'istic** *adj.*

zip (zɪp) *n.* **1. a.** Also called: **zip fastener.** a fastening device operating by means of two parallel rows of metal or plastic teeth on either side of a closure that are interlocked by a sliding tab. U.S. term: **zipper. b.** (*modifier*) having such a device: *a zip bag.* **2.** a short sharp whizzing sound, as of a passing bullet. **3.** *Inf.* energy; vigour; vitality. ~*vb.* **zipping, zipped. 4.** (*tr.*; often foll. by *up*) to fasten (clothing, etc.) with a zip. **5.** (*intr.*) to move with a zip: *the bullet zipped past.* **6.** (*intr.*; often foll. by *along, through*, etc.) to hurry; rush.

zip code *n.* the U.S. equivalent of **postcode.**

zippy ('zɪpɪ) *adj.* **-pier, -piest.** *Inf.* full of energy; lively.

zircon ('zɜːkɒn) *n.* a reddish-brown, grey, green, blue, or colourless hard mineral consisting of zirconium silicate: it is used as a gemstone and a refractory.

zirconium (zɜː'kəʊnɪəm) *n.* a greyish-white metallic element, occurring chiefly in zircon, that is exceptionally corrosion-resistant and has low neutron absorption. It is used as a coating in nuclear and chemical plants, as a deoxidizer in steel, and alloyed with niobium in superconductive magnets. Symbol: Zr; atomic no.: 40; atomic wt.: 91.22. —**zirconic** (zɜː'kɒnɪk) *adj.*

zither ('zɪðə) *n.* a plucked musical instrument consisting of numerous strings stretched over a resonating box, a few of which may be stopped on a fretted fingerboard. —'**zitherist** *n.*

zloty ('zlɒtɪ) *n., pl.* **-tys** *or* **-ty.** the standard monetary unit of Poland.

Zn *the chemical symbol for* zinc.

zo- *combining form.* variant of **zoo-** before a vowel.

-zoa *suffix forming plural proper nouns.* indicating groups of animal organisms: *Protozoa.*

zodiac ('zəʊdɪ,æk) *n.* **1.** an imaginary belt extending 8° either side of the ecliptic, which contains the 12 **zodiacal constellations** and within which the moon and planets appear to move. It is divided into 12 equal areas, called

signs of the zodiac, each named after the constellation which once lay in it. **2.** *Astrol.* a diagram, usually circular, representing this belt and showing the symbols, illustrations, etc., associated with each of the 12 signs of the zodiac, used to predict the future. —**zodiacal** (zəʊ-'daɪəkəl) *adj.*

zombie *or* **zombi** ('zɒmbɪ) *n., pl.* **-bies** *or* **-bis. 1.** a person who is or appears to be lifeless, apathetic, or totally lacking in independent judgment; automaton. **2.** a supernatural spirit that reanimates a dead body. **3.** a corpse brought to life in this manner.

zone (zəʊn) *n.* **1.** a region, area, or section characterized by some distinctive feature or quality. **2.** an area subject to a particular political, military, or government function, use, or jurisdiction: *a demilitarized zone.* **3.** (*often cap.*) *Geog.* one of the divisions of the earth's surface, esp. divided into latitudinal belts according to temperature. See **Torrid Zone, Frigid Zone, Temperate Zone. 4.** *Geol.* a distinctive layer or region of rock, characterized by particular fossils, etc. **5.** *Ecology.* an area, esp. a belt of land, having a particular flora and fauna determined by the prevailing environmental conditions. **6.** *Maths.* a portion of a sphere between two parallel planes intersecting the sphere. **7.** *Arch. or literary.* a girdle or belt. ~*vb.* (*tr.*) **8.** to divide into zones, as for different use, jurisdiction, activities, etc. **9.** to designate as a zone. **10.** to mark with or divide into zones. —'**zonal** *adj.* —'**zonated** *adj.* —'**zoning** *n.*

zoo (zuː) *n., pl.* **zoos.** a place where live animals are kept, studied, bred, and exhibited to the public. Formal term: **zoological garden.**

zoo- *or before a vowel* **zo-** *combining form.* indicating animals: *zooplankton.*

zooid ('zəʊɔɪd) *n.* **1.** any independent animal body, such as an individual of a coelenterate colony. **2.** a motile cell or body, such as a gamete, produced by an organism.

zool. *abbrev. for:* **1.** zoological. **2.** zoology.

zoological garden *n.* the formal term for **zoo.**

zoology (zəʊ'ɒlədʒɪ, zu:-) *n., pl.* **-gies. 1.** the study of animals, including their classification, structure, physiology, and history. **2.** the biological characteristics of a particular animal or animal group. **3.** the fauna characteristic of a particular region. —**zoological** (,zəʊə'lɒdʒɪkəl, ,zu:ə-) *adj.* —**zo'ologist** *n.*

zoom (zuːm) *vb.* **1.** to make or cause to make a continuous buzzing or humming sound. **2.** to move or cause to move with such a sound. **3.** (*intr.*) to move very rapidly; rush: *we zoomed through town.* **4.** to cause (an aircraft) to climb briefly at an unusually steep angle, or (of an aircraft) to climb in this way. **5.** (*intr.*) (of prices) to rise rapidly. ~*n.* **6.** the sound or act of zooming. **7.** See **zoom lens.**

zoom in *or* **out** *vb.* (*intr., adv.*) *Photog., films, television.* to increase or decrease rapidly the magnification of the image of a distant object by means of a zoom lens.

zoom lens *n.* a lens system that allows the focal length of a camera lens to be varied continuously without altering the sharpness of the image.

-zoon *n. combining form.* indicating an individual animal or an independently moving entity derived from an animal: *spermatozoon.*

zoophyte ('zəʊə,faɪt) *n.* any animal resembling a plant, such as a sea anemone. —**zoophytic** (,zəʊə'fɪtɪk) *or* ,**zoo'phytical** *adj.*

Zoroastrianism (,zɒrəʊ'æstrɪən,ɪzəm) *or* **Zoroastrism** *n.* the dualistic religion founded by the Persian prophet Zoroaster in the late 7th or early 6th centuries B.C. and set forth in the sacred writings of the Zend-Avesta. It is based on the concept of a continuous struggle between Ormazd (or Ahura Mazda), the god of creation, light, and goodness, and his arch enemy, Ahriman, the spirit of evil and darkness.

zoster ('zɒstə) *n. Pathol.* short for **herpes zoster.**

Zouave (zu:'ɑːv, zwɑːv) *n.* **1.** (formerly) a member of a body of French infantry composed of Algerian recruits noted for their dash, hardiness, and colourful uniforms. **2.** a member of any body of soldiers wearing a similar uniform, esp. a volunteer in such a unit of the Union Army in the American Civil War.

zounds (zaʊndz) *or* **swounds** (zwaʊndz, zaʊndz) *interj. Arch.* a mild oath indicating surprise, indignation, etc.

▬▬▬▬▬ THESAURUS ▬▬▬▬▬

zone area, belt, district, region, section, sector, sphere

Zr *the chemical symbol for* zirconium.

zucchetto (tsuːˈkɛtəʊ, suː-, zuː-) *n., pl.* **-tos.** *R.C. Church.* a small round skullcap worn by certain ecclesiastics and varying in colour according to the rank of the wearer, the Pope wearing white, cardinals red, bishops violet, and others black.

zucchini (tsuːˈkiːnɪ, zuː-) *n., pl.* **-ni** *or* **-nis.** another name for **courgette.**

Zulu (ˈzuːlʊ, -luː) *n.* **1.** (*pl.* **-lus** *or* **-lu**) a member of a tall Negroid people of SE Africa, living chiefly in N Natal, who became dominant during the 19th century due to a warrior-clan system organized by the powerful leader, Tchaka. **2.** the language of this people.

zygo- *or before a vowel* **zyg-** *combining form.* indicating a pair or a union: *zygodactyl; zygospore.*

zygote (ˈzaɪgəʊt, ˈzɪg-) *n.* **1.** the cell resulting from the union of an ovum and a spermatozoon. **2.** the organism that develops from such a cell. **—zygotic** (zaɪˈgɒtɪk, zɪ-) *adj.* **—zyˈgotically** *adv.*

zymo- *or before a vowel* **zym-** *combining form.* indicating fermentation: *zymology.*

zymotic (zaɪˈmɒtɪk) *adj.* **1.** of, relating to, or causing fermentation. **2.** relating to or caused by infection; denoting or relating to an infectious disease. **—zyˈmotically** *adv.*

zymurgy (ˈzaɪmɜːdʒɪ) *n.* the branch of chemistry concerned with fermentation processes in brewing, etc.